C000058837

ISBN 978-0-260-00820-6
PIBN 10921844

National Civic Federation

MONTHLY REVIEW

Vol. I. No. 1 NEW YORK, APRIL, 1903 Ten Cents

SHOULD UNIONS INCORPORATE?

[illegible]M BY REPRESENTATIVES OF EMPLOYERS, WAGE EARNERS AND THE GENERAL PUBLIC—OPINIONS OF MEMBERS OF THE BAR

In view of the many recent proceedings against trade unions by way of injunctions and suits for damages, the National Civic Federation addressed inquiries to a number of representative men asking for a statement of opinion regarding the proper course for trade unions to take in the matter of incorporation. Attention was called to the Taff Vale decision in Great Britain and to several cases in the United States where members of unincorporated unions have been held personally liable for damages and costs of prosecution. The question was asked whether, in defending such suits, the unions would be placed in a better or in a worse position if they were incorporated than they are at present when unincorporated. Inquiry was also made as to whether a special law should be enacted for the incorporation of unions, one differing from the law for business corporations, and if so, what should be its terms.

In preparing this symposium for the press we have been compelled to omit much interesting matter from the various contributions, being limited as to space.

EMPLOYERS

Don C. Seitz, Member of the American Newspaper Publishers' Association and Business Manager of the New York "World":

When an employer recognizes a labor union, he ceases to recognize the individual. The latter has no place in the economy of his establishment. He must deal with the concrete idea represented by unionism and forsake the theory that he can handle the individual as such. This we have done, and the results, I think, are satisfactory, so far as anything that interferes with liberty of action and freedom of purpose can be satisfactory. When, however, we do get ourselves into this attitude we certainly increase the responsibility of the union, and expect this responsibility to be met.

Coercive as most unions are, they naturally cannot learn to respect the rights of the employer or men who will not affiliate with them. I think there is now less tyranny in the printing trade than formerly, and we have the insurance of our admirable arbitration agreement. Certainly, too, there are more intelligence and a greater appreciation of what is right among most of our employes than in any other grade of labor, and the proposition I am about to present is not specific to our own interests. I believe that we shall have constant and more menacing troubles unless the newspapers, whose duty it is to arouse public sentiment and bring issues home to the minds of the people, shall insist that labor unions be made legally responsible bodies by incorporation. This done, a vast deal of trouble would disappear. It would, no doubt, be difficult to organize unions, because of the responsibilities involved by such legislation, as men would stop and do some thinking before assuming a legal liability, but in the end the unions that were brave enough and honest enough to comply with the conditions would benefit largely by the result. In short, legislation should be had to provide for the incorporation of the trade unions just as we have it for forming other corporations or trusts, and self-constituted bodies founded to coerce employers would have no status under the law and would become conspiracies, where they failed to comply with the requirement to incorporate.

You cannot properly establish the Merry Toughs' Social Club without incorporating it. You cannot join with a few friends to promote the simplest business enterprise without incorporating it. You cannot even establish a church without going through a legal process. But it is perfectly possible to get together a body of workingmen, who, without regard to your contracts or their obligations, take you by the throat with intimidation and boycott, without any serious fear of interference by law or any collection of damages from the courts.

Large sums of money are raised by the unions from individual assessments, but not one cent of this is reachable to recompense the industry that bears the brunt of the conflict. When the suggestion is made to the average labor leader that such incorporation ought to be enforced, we at once meet with the answer that it would be fatal to their methods, which is an open confession that their methods are illegal and wrong. Business men incur millions of responsibility in obedience to the law, while labor, much more closely knit, is immune.

It is only recently in overburdened England that the court of last resort ordered the Amalgamated Society of Railroad Servants to pay the Taff Vale Railroad £28,000 damages for a strike and boycott. The appellate court held that, incorporated or not, an organized body could not keep itself outside the law, and that it must be held pecuniarily responsible for its acts. This decision of vast importance to all concerned swept away the pleasant fiction that lawlessness and boycott are always to be condoned where the "workingman" is trying to "elevate" himself. In short, in England the worm has turned, and hereafter the unions will be forced to meet the responsibility they incur, just as the railroad does when it wrecks a train and kills or injures its passengers. The playful incendiaries, the murderous boycotters, and the delightful dynamiters may escape as individuals, but the union which precipitated the conflict which brought this all about must settle. This is what we must come to here, if there is to be any human right or human liberty left in the land.

The argument in favor of incorporating is a simple one. A certain number of carpenters desire to get together for the betterment of their condition. They must raise a fund, elect officers. They must have a concrete existence, if they would incorporate as a business body. This would be the situation: When an employer called upon the guild, as it would best be named, the condition of employment could be made plain; the responsibility of taking the work would be incurred and the duty of performing it would be enforced. Can there be any honest objection to this practice? We have now in this city the most chaotic conditions. Men drop out every day at will in the building trades, and great losses are incurred by the contractor and owner, and the situation is fast becoming intolerable.

Judge Parker, in a recent decision, holds that the laborer has the right to do as he pleases about working or not working. This is incontestably true, yet I should say that when the laborer had agreed to perform a certain task for a certain price, there should be some method of making him keep his agreement. The employer is responsible for wages, and if he has agreed to hire a man for a year and uses him only one day, the law makes him pay for the whole period. But the plasterer can throw down his trowel and quit in the middle of his employment because he dislikes the expression on his foreman's face. If, however, we had an incorporated union of plasterers instead of a guerrilla one, the union would have to come forward and complete the task.

James A. Miller, Chairman Legal Committee of Building Contractors' Council, Chicago, Ill.:

Without being a lawyer, and without having consulted one on the subject, I should say that a law might pass the scrutiny of the courts that would make criminal certain acts done by a combination (unincorporated) that would not be so if done by a corporation having capital stock, or, perhaps, having bonds on file with the Secretary of State that could be reached for damages. In this way the unions might decide it to be to their advantage to incorporate.

The advisability of such a law is another question. As I understand it, the Taff Vale decision does not have much bearing upon the question under discussion. Its great importance is to the registered unions of Great Britain, who thought that by the law that provided for their registration, etc., they could not be sued. Acting on this theory, most of those unions have large funds, really intended for insurance benefits, etc. There is no doubt that those unions would not have had on hand such large funds to be seized for damages if they had not been firmly of the opinion that those funds could not be reached. Nor would they have committed so openly (that is, in such a way as to easily fasten the responsibility upon them) the acts that made them liable.

I should say that if the responsibility of trade unions can be increased by requiring them to incorporate, without at the same time increasing their power, it might be well to advocate such a plan. If, on the other hand, they can only be required to incorporate by granting additional power to those that do incorporate, I am afraid the result would be productive of more harm than good. Before any plan for requiring incorporation is indorsed, it should be decided what form of incorporation is to be advocated, whether a capital stock is to be required or whether it is to be such as can be had in this State "not for profit"—with no or a nominal capital stock. If there is to be no capital stock, I do not see what is to be gained by incorporating. If there is capital stock or a fund that can be reached for damages, then it must be considered what acts and whose acts will make the union and its fund liable.

Will it simply be the breaking of a contract entered into by the union, or will it be any unlawful act done by the union causing damage? Will the union be liable only for what it does as a union, or will it be liable for the acts of its officers and of its individual members? If liable for the acts of its officers and members, must it be shown that those acts were authorized by the union? This would often be difficult, if not impossible. I can understand how a union might make a contract to furnish men of a certain standard of skill and at a certain rate of wages up to a certain number of men under a penalty of damages if it failed, which would make the union a contractor for labor.

Aside from such arrangement as that, I think the responsibility of the union for breaking of contracts entered into by it would not be worth much, as it could avoid that liability by secretly advising or permitting its members to do individually what the union would be liable for if done by the union. Whether any of these devices for increasing the responsibility of the unions to the employers, where that end is to be attained by increasing the power of the unions over the workman by enabling these organizations to farm out labor, as do the Chinese companies, will tend to improve the character of the working man, may well be questioned.

Again, as I understand it, what society and employers want is not damages from unions for injuries unlawfully inflicted, but they want the unions restrained from committing these unlawful acts. The courts have a way to do this when their aid can be invoked—by injunction.

The law in this State as to the liability of the members of a union for damages to an employer is that if an officer or member of a union in the course of any unlawful strike does damage to such employer then every member of the union is liable for such damage. He is liable in tort, which enables the employer, judgment having been obtained and unpaid, to send him to jail and keep him there as long as the debt is unpaid and the employer pays his board.

In my opinion, that is all the law the employer needs. What society needs is not more or different laws, but an honest and courageous enforcement of the laws as they are. If the laws that we now have can not be enforced because the judges fear the union vote, or because the whole machinery of justice in our State courts is paralyzed for that same reason, what is the use of bothering about more laws?

Marcus A. Hanna, of M. A. Hanna & Co.:

I do not believe under the present condition of things in incorporation of trade unions. I heard the argument that it was an absolute necessity that such incorporation must be had, because a contract with workingmen was worthless. The test has come, for, when in their dire extremity, the anthracite miners of Pennsylvania appealed to their fellows in the bituminous fields in the West to come out and strike in sympathy, in order that conditions might be forced upon this country which would enforce a settlement of the trouble, it is known to many others that the bituminous coal miners thus appealed to were under contract for a year, known as the Interstate Contract, between the producers and the operators of those sections of the country. Under the constitution of the United Mine Workers it became the duty of their president to call together a delegates' convention to act upon that question. Those of us who had followed this trouble from the beginning with interest and anxiety felt that it was an important moment in the history of the labor question as to how that would be settled. For my part I had confidence as to the outcome. The convention met at Indianapolis, represented by persons or proxies of 1,000 delegates, and the appeal was made coming from the striking miners of the anthracite region to their fellow workmen under most distressing circumstances and conditions, under influences which are so potent among that class—brotherhood sympathy. That convention appointed a committee of twenty-three to consider the application. They spent nearly a whole night considering it; they were confronted with the fact that they had made a contract with their employers, which for the fourth time had been made, to work for a scale agreed upon, to be in operation for one year, upon which the sales of coal were made and contracts binding upon the operators were made. After full consideration, allowing sentiment to play its part upon the minds and hearts of those men, with calm, cool judgment and loyalty to their agreement, that committee reported unanimously against a sympathetic strike. That report was made to that convention the day following, and was adopted unanimously by 1,000 votes. They agreed to stand by the word they had given in making that contract.

Now, that case came up at a time when all the conditions surrounding it were as aggravating and forcible as could be brought into play. Therefore I say that the test has come and the men have won the confidence of the whole people of this country, and as far as I am concerned, satisfied me that we want no incorporation of labor organizations.

Wm. Green, Chairman Executive Committee, New York Typothetae:

We think that the incorporation of labor unions would undoubtedly add to their responsibility. The bone and sinew of any labor organization lies in its ability to support its members when out of work, whether they be out of work on account of sickness, stagnation of business or strikes. To accomplish this, it is necessary for the organization to have a well-filled treasury. In the case of an incorporated union, we think that its treasurer and other officers could be held to stricter account in law than if the organization were not incorporated. As for suing of individual members, that, we think, would be unprofitable and fruitless. A union that is an incorporated body certainly has more dignity in the eyes of employers than an unincorporated one; particularly so when its members in the latter case frankly acknowledge that in order to evade responsibility they decline to incorporate.

S. R. Callaway, President American Locomotive Company, New York:

I do not see any great advantage to be derived from the incorporation of labor unions. It is more important, in my opinion, to have reasonably fair-minded men at the head of the organizations, who will give some consideration to the other fellow's side of the case. This remark might also be made applicable to employers of labor.

H. B. Parsons, Vice-President Wells Fargo & Co., New York:

It is desirable, from my point of view, that labor unions should incorporate, and it will be an added advantage if, in doing so, they embody beneficial, financial features, such as sick funds, insurance, and, possibly, pensions. Unions generally, as now constituted, have little or no financial responsibility. In cases where, as has been done, employers secure damages, they will be reluctant to attempt to recover from individuals, and if they did, the courts would be likely to deal with all possible lenience as respects the employes, since there might seem to be an element of persecution in attempting to hold one person responsible for the misdeeds of many. It would also seem to be reasonable to expect that unions, when once incorporated, and being subject to legal responsibility, would exercise more care and restraint in adopting the suggestions of its members, and in acting upon impulse.

Ottò M. Eidlitz, Secretary United Building Trades, New York:

In my opinion the incorporation of unions would add to their responsibility in that in case of difficulty the trade, as an organization, would have to answer for its vote in meeting. And if a union felt that its treasury and standing might be jeopardized, it would tend to make it more conservative and to see that its actions were strictly within the law. The assessing of damages on individuals for the act of the union seems to me unfair, and would only tend to increase our list of martyrs. Furthermore, the very act of incorporation would make the body subject more or less to State supervision and the regulations of the law, and through this very fact tend to bring home to the officers and Executive Committee the fact that they are not free lances.

J. Kruttschnitt, General Manager and Fourth Vice-President Southern Pacific Company:

In my opinion, many of the illegal acts committed by officers of labor unions and by the members individually are prompted by a lack of sense of responsibility, and anything that will bring home to the members and officers of such organizations the fact that no damage or injury can be inflicted without incurring responsibility, for reparation thereof, is not only very much to be desired, but is, in my opinion, imperatively necessary to check the spirit of lawlessness that now at once develops on the inauguration of a strike. [illegible] frequently found in dealing with subo[illegible] quickest way to make them abando[illegible] considered policy is to give them fre[illegible] carry it out, with the distinct understanding that the responsibility for success or failure will rest on their shoulders: the responsibility for failure, of course, being followed by loss of official position, and we have never failed in such cases to secure much more conservative action on the part of the officer involved. Conservatism must necessarily follow responsibility, and however this can be brought about, whether by incorporation of the unions or by decisions of the courts against members, I am firmly of the belief that establishing the principle that a party inflicting an injury must pay the resulting damages will confine the efforts of labor leaders to their legitimate functions and will discourage the present practice of declaring actual war on persons and property as soon as any contention arises on any industrial question.

Oscar C. Davis, Second Vice-President Georg[illegible] Keith Company, Campello, Mass.:

We heartily indorse any measures which [illegible] sult in the incorporation of unions and in [illegible] to their responsibility. They are almost [illegible]n as they are managed to-day, in that they emp[illegible]cers, pay salaries and make contracts, and we see no reason why, if the employers are incorporated and can give perfectly good financial security for all their contracts, the labor unions should not do likewise, and become corporate bodies. We think this would hasten the day when we would have fewer strikes and greater prosperity. In a recent article by the president of the Boot and Shoe Workers' Union, the writer noticed that about the only argument against incorporation was, firstly, we don't need to; secondly, we might lose our money; but from the standpoint of the employers we see no reason why, if the unions are acting in good faith, they should not furnish as good security as they now demand of the employer. When we have contracts the breaking of which will result in the loss of dollars to the unions as well as to the employers, we will have a distinct step in advance of the present method of absolute security on one side and insecurity on the other.

Henry R. Towne, President Yale & Towne Manufacturing Company, New York:

I have for some time urged that both the unions and the employers' associations should be incorporated, and that the latter can well afford to set an example in this respect to the former. The functions of these bodies have become of great importance to their constituents and to the public, equally so at times with the function of the courts so far as practical effects are concerned. With the power which this implies there exists, and must be recognized, the resulting responsibility. The Taff Vale decision recognizes this fact.

Employers are increasingly discovering that the law affords remedies for many of the injuries heretofore inflicted by organized labor. It is earnestly to be hoped that the law will be appealed to increasingly in such cases, and if so I believe the result will be to establish the responsibility in damages of any organization which has the power to inflict injury and exercises that power in ways not authorized by law. When this point is reached it will be immaterial, so far as responsibility in damages is concerned, whether the unions are or are not incorporated, and as incorporation will give them protection and strength in other directions it seems reasonable to anticipate that it will be availed of. It is certainly desirable and should be encouraged.

E. F. Du Brul, Commissioner National Metal Trades Association, Cincinnati, Ohio:

I do not see that incorporation would increase the responsibility of the unions in any particular. You cannot compel them to incorporate, and if they did they would have no more property as a union than they have now. The incorporation of the union would probably relieve the members of personal liability, which, in view of the Taff Vale decision and the Dayton and Indianapolis Drop Forging Company cases, would be a hardship on the employer who suffers damages.

Walter L. Pierce, General Manager Lidgerwood Manufacturing Company, New York:

I can see one advantage in its favor from the standpoint of manufacturers, and that is that if a union wants an agreement with any body of manufacturers they are certainly more likely to get favorable consideration if incorporated. As I am on record as being in favor of such agreements, and as the first objection of those not in favor is the "irresponsibility of the unions," it seems to me such incorporation will be of distinct advantage in procuring agreements now impossible to obtain, and, in view of the Taff Vale decision, I see no objection to it.

W. H. Pfahler, of Philadelphia, National Founders' Association:

I have no doubt whatever that the laws which we have in this country could hold a labor union as a body, and no doubt its members individually, liable for damages which may occur during a strike; but it is my sincere hope that the settlement between employer and employe may never reach the necessity of an appeal to the civil courts. The advance that is being made along the line of personal interest on the part of manufacturers in the relation which they bear to their employes is daily establishing the fact that the whole problem is one of bargain and sale. The only question involved in labor disputes is the question of wages; no matter what demands are made by the manufacturers, it invariably resolves itself into a question of earnings of mechanical labor. This being the case, the only plain rule is to negotiate with the labor element collectively, or through their recognized union, or its representatives. To bring this about, the greatest work is to reduce the employer from a position of sentimental opposition to trade unions to one of recognition of the force which they exert in the problem. When this occurs, the buyer and seller meet upon the same level that the parties to any other commercial transaction do, and negotiate for the one simple matter of wages. I think the extent to which the National Civic Federation can aid the accomplishment of this condition, and to that extent only, can it hope to be successful.

WAGE EARNERS

Samuel Gompers, President American Federation of Labor:

Some years ago the Federal Congress passed a law for the incorporation of our trade unions. Beyond question, the advocates of that bill really believed they were doing the organized workers a real service; but at the time, and since, we have repeatedly warned our fellow-unionists to refrain from seeking the so-called protection of that law, which, in the cases referred to, justified the suspicion and conclusion that the courts would in time have declared our unions liable to be mulcted in damages and their funds confiscated—a repetition of the history of the robbery of the guilds a few centuries ago. It is the same species of legislation as the enactment of the law to regulate interstate commerce and the so-called anti-trust law, both of which were ostensibly enacted for the protection of the interests of the people, when, as a matter of fact the only uses to which they have been put have been to furnish some pretense or excuse for the issuance of injunctions against organized workers engaged in disputes with their employers, and for the indictment and the possible imprisonment of men for the exercise of their natural and lawful rights.

Recently the unfounded charge against organized labor has been repeated to the effect that trade unions violate agreements entered into with employers; and the uninformed, and particularly those antagonistic employers to organized labor, urge as a remedy for this imagined evil the compulsory incorporation of the trade unions, so that, as those referred to urge, "the trade unions may be held legally responsible" for the faithful carrying out of agreements, and to be liable in damages in the event of their violation. On the surface this proposition seems fair; but when we bear in mind the fact that often judges have deep-seated prejudice against organizations of labor, that the far-fetched interpretation in the Taff Vale case, where an organization of labor in Great Britain was mulcted in damages for the actions of an individual member, under the law passed by the British Parliament as a "concession to labor," and that the enunciation of judicial principles is mutually interpreted and held by the judiciary of all English-speaking countries, it is not difficult to divine the purpose that the advocates of compulsory incorporation of trade unions have in view. They would mulct or outlaw our unions, the organizations which are the factors in our modern life to work for human progress by natural, rational, peaceable and evolutionary means.

E. E. Clark, Grand Chief Conductor Order of Railway Conductors:

I have never understood or heard that corporations were formed for the purpose of taking on added responsibility; on the contrary, I have understood that they were formed for the purpose of escaping personal responsibility. The existing laws permit of the formation of corporations for pecuniary profit or for charitable purposes, and in each instance the exemptions and liabilities of the corporations and their stockholders or members are clearly defined. It seems to me very inconsistent for any one to demand that labor organizations shall incorporate under existing laws. If incorporation of labor unions is desired it is, to my mind, incumbent upon the State Legislatures to enact healthy laws under which the members of labor unions are given exemption from corporate responsibilities, in substance just as stockholders of corporations for pecuniary profit are given exemption from liability for corporate debts or acts, and under which the incorporated trade union shall have the same exemption from responsibility for personal acts of members in violation of law which a corporation for pecuniary profit has from liability for individual acts of its stockholders. While I have never been disposed to take an arbitrary or positive stand against incorporation of trade unions under any and all conditions, I feel that I should be obliged to oppose any effort to force them to incorporate until the proper foundation has been laid as above suggested.

Herman Grossman, President International Ladies' Garment Workers' Union, New York:

It is my opinion that incorporation can under no circumstances be injurious to trade unions. The United Brotherhood of Cloakmakers, the most important local of the International Ladies' Garment Workers' Union, which is an organization incorporated under the membership corporation law of the State of New York, has found it much easier to defeat claims of employers for damages caused by members of the organization than those trade unions which are voluntary associations. In 1901, several applications were made for injunctions against the brotherhood. Numerous affidavits alleging acts of violence on the part of persons who were claimed to be members of the brotherhood were presented in support of the application. The court refused, however, to grant the injunction, on the ground that there was no proof that the acts complained of were authorized by the organization.

Since no corporation can be held liable for individual acts of its members, acts not authorized by the corporation, incorporated trade unions have no reason to fear a lawsuit against them for wrongful acts of their members.

Our organization has had very few lawsuits against manufacturers. I don't remember a single case which came to trial. We had about half a dozen cases in the Supreme Court several years ago; they were all settled or compromised. In almost all of the said cases the question of the legality of our contract with the employers was raised, and uniformly decided in our favor. The points raised against the contract were that it was unconscionable, in restraint of trade and against public policy. As I said before, these points were overruled.

The only serious disadvantage the trade unions are working under now is the complete absence in the statutes of various States of laws defining the rights, powers, duties and limitations of trade unions. For example, in the State of New York there is really no law under which a trade union can be incorporated properly.

Those trade unions which have incorporated under the New York laws have incorporated under an elastic section, (section 30 of the membership corporation law) which limits the organization under that section of corporations which cannot be incorporated under any other laws. The trade union is by no means the favorite of the law. What is needed is a systematization of the laws relating to trade unions and to labor generally. The laws should permit trade unions to incorporate on the same basis as co-operative societies, and the right should be given to the organization to declare the stock of an offending member forfeited for a violation of the rules of the organization. They should also have the privilege of organizing sick and death benefits. This would give the trade union a certain degree of control over its members, and contracts entered into between the organizations and employers could be enforced by either side without resorting to the courts.

James M. Lynch, President International Typographical Union:

Those well versed in the idea of incorporation and the methods of lawyers and courts well know the menace contained in the suggestion. It would take a trade union antagonist with money at his command but a short time to wreck a labor organization through judicial procedure. . . . Regardless of the innocence of an incorporated trade union of charges preferred by an antagonist, it would take much money to establish that innocence. It may be said that trade unionists should be willing to contribute liberally for their defense, but it must be remembered that where the toiler is able to contribute one cent the corporation can without strain put up a dollar. We must continue to depend upon public sympathy and public support, and not on courts, the course of which in the past displays corporation and capitalistic sympathy, if not dictation. We should have no hesitancy in upholding our present methods, and instead of excusing we should justify them. If we are opposed to trade union incorporation we should not be afraid to assert that opposition boldly, confident in the belief that our cause is just and that it should not be retarded by legal trickery and judicial subservience. The International Typographical Union has had some rather unpleasant and costly legal experience.

Charles O. Sherman, General Secretary United Metal Workers' International Union, Chicago:

I do not hesitate to emphatically state that I am opposed to the incorporating of any trade union, for I consider that incorporation proceedings would be only a step nearer the danger line which would put the trade organizations at the mercy of the courts, and it is unnecessary for me to apprise you of what this means. Under the system in which we live it is not a case of justice in court; it is a case of law, and the law is so framed by those who are cunning that it is in the shape of a drag net which is so contrived that the minnows are all captured while the whales escape. I mean by this that it is seldom that labor unions can go into court and expect justice, but they always expect plenty of law; for that reason, I am opposed. I believe that great danger confronts all trade unions in the United States, and if they do not adopt a different policy at an early date the organizations will be completely at the mercy of the courts, which are owned and controlled by the money powers in most instances, and the only policy I could recommend under this system would be to vote for no man for public office, no matter be it for judge down to common constable, unless he be a thorough trade unionist, one who is in good standing and in good repute with the movement. When I say a trade unionist I do not mean a lawyer who claims to be in sympathy with the union, because in most cases they are not, but conduct themselves in a way that will bring to them the greater remuneration.

W. O. Powell. President Shirt, Waist and Laundry Workers, Troy, N. Y.:

I cannot see where the incorporation of a union would benefit the union, since the greater number of laws on our statute books are not only favorable to the element represented by capital, but their dispensation is also in the hands of the same power. This fact is recognized by the manufacturer and consumer alike, and I think is so recognized by the Civic Federation. Either with or without incorporation, the danger to the trade union will be remedied, since all unions are founded on the principle of arbitration, through trade agreement, and there would be no chance for loss on the part of the employer, as a strike would thus be avoided. No strike has taken place where a trade agreement has been in force. Strikes only take place where there are no trade agreements, or when trade agreements have willfully been broken by the employer. No labor union fears a loss from this source. Unions are not money making institutions; they are schools for teaching certain principles. They neither have nor hold shares of stock or bonds of gold. Their stock in trade is their inherent right to work or not and when at work to receive a wage that they have set on their labor as a value for that labor.

The American laborers of to-day fear nothing. Should the framers of laws compel them to incorporate, let those framers look to it well that the laws are not misconstrued to the disadvantage of the incorporated laborers.

John McNeil, President Boiler Makers and Iron Ship Builders of America, Kansas City, Kansas:

Under the present conditions I am not in favor of the incorporation of labor organizations in this country. There is not discipline enough among the men, and the employers do not in any way assist the national officers to establish same; while in the old country, of which I am a native, the employers did everything in their power to assist the national officers to establish discipline among the members by helping them to enforce fines upon the members who violated the law. My opinion is that the Taff Vale decision in Great Britain in no way affects the labor organizations in this country.

Edward A. Moffett, Editor "The Bricklayer and Mason," New York:

I am not aware that in this country unincorporated trade unions can be mulcted for damages the same as in partnerships. True, there have been one or two such decisions made here and there; but these decisions have not been followed by other courts. If these decisions had been generally accepted there would not be the present agitation to have trade unions incorporated. This agitation is predicated upon the irresponsibility of trade unions in the courts. Some half-dozen of our subordinate unions are incorporated. Philadelphia (bricklayers) Union No. 7, New York City, Boston (bricklayers), and perhaps two or three others. But I believe the feeling of our membership generally is strongly against incorporation.

A. S. Hughes, President National Brotherhood of Operative Potters, East Liverpool, Ohio:

Our organization was incorporated under the laws of Ohio in 1895. We allowed our charter to lapse some eighteen months ago, as we had been threatened with damage suits by several manufacturers where some of our members had disputes and were about to strike had they not succeeded in settling the matters at issue.

J. H. Patterson, Secretary Paving Cutters' Union of America, Lithonia, Ga.:

I am opposed to the incorporation of trade unions, because it would mean the destruction of our unions, from the fact that the employers would keep us in court all the time. It would not be a question as to the right or wrong of it, but simply a question of the longest purse. Whether we gained or lost the decision would have no bearing on the results whatever, as litigation would never cease, and the never-ending legal proceedings could have but one ending, and that would be death and despair to labor organizations, and the birth of anarchy in their stead. I believe that the present conditions do not call for new laws on the subject, as the laws now in force are able to afford ample protection to the employer, if he really has a bona fide case.

John Tobin, Editor "Shoe Workers' Journal":

Objections to incorporated trade unions rest, first, upon the needlessness of such a move, and, second, upon the danger of bankrupting the treasuries of trade unions by and through litigation if they should become incorporated. It is not necessary to incorporate a trade union to insure the inviolability of contracts that may be entered into between trade unions and employers. During the four years that the Boot and Shoe Workers' Union has been in existence we have made contracts with employers from all parts of the country. Our contracts, as all contracts that are worthy of the name, involve mutual obligations and mutual advantages. In our agreement with shoe manufacturers we surrender the right to strike. Our employers surrender their arbitrary right to enforce conditions to their liking by such arbitrary methods as the lockout. . . . Leaving out of consideration all questions of honor, it appears that our own best interests will prompt us to live religiously up to our agreements. . . . It is not on record that we have in any single instance given our employers occasion to regret that we were not incorporated so that we might be compelled to do that which we otherwise would not do. . . . The danger of such a move to trade unions is clearly indicated in the investigation which took place before President Roosevelt's arbitration commission. A glance at the dizzy array of legal talent at the command of the coal operators gives us a forecast of what trade unions will be called upon to do in order to protect their interests in a court of law. Coal operators count their resources by the million and hundreds of millions. Trade unions are not so well fixed. Their treasuries are not so abnormally large as that of the designing employer who may find it to his interest to first bankrupt the trade union by legal procedure and then when it is impoverished proceed against it in the industrial field by lockout or otherwise.

Geo. W. Perkins, President International Cigarmakers' Union:

Organized labor has nothing to fear from any of its acts, but it will not consent to become incorporated and placed in a position where it will be unable to transact its lawful business and discharge its full duties to its members. We object to being placed in a position where we cannot do business that is strictly lawful without the consent of the judiciary. We object to being placed in a position where we would have to wait the result of cumbersome law proceedings before we can do things that are perfectly lawful. We object to spending large sums of money to fight for the right to do things that are now conceded to be right and lawful. We protest against being compelled to again fight over the ground that it has taken years of ceaseless agitation and great sacrifice to achieve. We have by the force of right and justice battered down the laws of repression and oppression. We have overcome deep-seated prejudice that was nursed by the privileged few, and used against every honest effort of labor to better its condition. We protest with all the vigor at our command against being compelled to battle all over again against legal fogyism and prejudice. We will never incorporate until our legal status is well established and laws enacted that fully protect the rights we have secured as the result of years of trade union activity. If we were incorporated a board of directors would have a legal right to transact all of our business between conventions. We are too jealous of our liberties, our rights, and the initiative and referendum to surrender them to a board of directors, even if it was composed of angels. Not that we would dispute the honesty of the board of directors, but because we are opposed to surrendering the life of joint self-government, such as now prevails in the international unions.

Daniel J. Keefe, President International Longshoremen:

The intellectual faculties rule in labor organizations to-day and are guided by a moral obligation in our relations with each other and with our employers. This moral obligation enters into all our contracts and agreements. True, the contracts are expected to be such as will stand in law, but rarely has either party resorted to the courts to compel a performance of a contract. In our organization I feel free to state that none of the employers who sign annual contracts with us as an organization would feel any more secure, or that the obligation was any less binding on us because they were dealing with a labor organization not incorporated by law. It therefore is not the legal obligation, it is the integrity, the sense of fairness, the spirit of justice, the faithful performance of our former obligations that is the sole and only guarantee of our employers, who regard our word as good as our bond. In a word, it is the intelligent application of strict business principles and a recognition of our honor in every contract or agreement. No business man does business without first ascertaining and satisfying himself as to the financial standing and rating of a firm or corporation. The fact that a company can be sued and a judgment recovered does not warrant a desire for trade, in the absence of other important considerations. The reputation of a company for fair dealing, how they respect an obligation, etc., and whether they are safe people to do business with, are the considerations. The commercial world does not move solely because of law courts and court officers, and the acts of men are guided, after all, more from a sense of moral obligation than in violation of the same.

No, I do not recognize any crying need of labor organizations becoming incorporated, nor have I found any demand for the same on the part of the corporations and employers doing business with our organization. I do not wish to be understood as opposing such action by those believing it essential to the well being of all concerned. Only, I fail to recognize any solution of the labor problem by any statute or legal enactment. I certainly maintain that more ample redress is obtainable to-day for damages where liability of labor organizations can be proved than can be hoped to be obtained by labor organizations where corporations have violated the law.

Henry White, General Secretary United Garment Workers of America:

Incorporation would afford no advantage to labor unions for the chief reason that they have no standing in court as a contracting party, and their legal status would not be improved by it. The object, therefore, of incorporating would be lost, while on the other hand, the funds of the unions could be more readily attached either by workmen having a grievance against the union, or by employers subject to loss on account of the union's action. I have yet to learn of an instance where a union has succeeded in recovering damages for violation of an agreement on the part of an employer, and in the very nature of things, as I will attempt to explain, it will be impossible. Our own national union, for example, has hundreds of agreements with manufacturers in which bonds were given to insure their faithful performance, and in every case where the union sued for the forfeiture of the bonds it failed, although the violation of the contract was not questioned. It was held by the courts that the agreement was not valid because obtained under duress, that the employer was not free to refuse to sign the contract presented, as it would be impossible for him to continue in business otherwise. "Duress" could always be alleged because the trade unions represent an aggressive movement. The working class, on account of its former dependent state and the ground it has still to cover, has got to force its way. The pressure of society is normally against the wage worker, the point of least resistance, and this pressure can only be neutralized by counter-resistance, which implies a struggle.

We would not have gone into court to obtain redress for violation of contract were it not for the bonds referred to, as there is no disposition on the part of the unions to hold an employer to the terms of an agreement by legal procedure. The observance of a contract between an employer and a union must necessarily depend upon the honor of either side. The remedy for breach of contract lies in an appeal to public opinion, the intercession of a third party, or the offensive or resisting power of each, acting, of course, within legal bounds.

Even if such contracts were enforcible in law, there could be no basis for estimating the amount of the damage either side would be entitled to, because of the indefinite quantities involved and the problematical nature of the disputes. An agreement between an individual workman and an employer is something definite and tangible, but in the case of associated workmen treating with associated employers new problems of equity arise, so that legal rules, based upon precedent and the previous experience of society, could hardly apply. Hence the subject is beyond the province of courts of law to deal with, and that also explains why compulsory arbitration is untenable.

An additional reason why unions cannot have the same standing in court with the other side is because the union itself is not an entity to sue or be sued civilly, as it does not agree to perform any service in consideration of the conditions of labor stipulated in an agreement. The union simply acts as an intermediary for the individual workman. The only guarantee the union gives is that the workman will not, during the term of the agreement, make any further demands, that it will intercede in the event of any difference arising in the interest of peace, and enforce the same terms upon competitors wherever possible.

J. W. Sullivan, Typographical Union, New York:

A union has ways of its own in conducting the affairs that relate mainly to itself and its membership. It is a big self-governing family. In periods of strike the prescribed order of written constitution or by-law sometimes proves less desirable than the short cut obvious as a war measure. The members then become aware that in drawing up their laws they were unable to foresee the situation confronting them, and they may, for example, unconstitutionally confide absolute power temporarily in an officer or a committee. In times of peace a union often reaches conclusions and interpretations dictated by the common sense of a meeting rather than by the statutes as written, leaving the majority either satisfied or in a mood to accept the judgment for better or worse. Such proceedings may relate to trials of members, to executive session work, to appropriation of funds, to informalities or irregularities in elections or referendum votes, to the opening or closing of books for inspection, to the reading or the silencing of reports, to appointing or dismissing committees, to maintaining discipline, to accepting or rejecting candidates for membership, to suspending or expelling or reinstating members, to passing judgment on aggressions of employers tending to end in strike, to investigating the conduct of members prejudicial to the organization, and to settling questions in which rule or precedent or necessity of the local union conflicts with international union law. In all such proceedings two principles usually govern—self-preservation of the union and good fellowship. A popular employer, in general fair, who in a fit of temper has wilfully violated a clause in a contract or the union scale, will be adjudged innocent. A sound and active union man who has misappropriated a small sum will be found not guilty and given time to refund. In these matters an unincorporated union is in the main a law unto itself. It is free. It may make many changes in its internal methods and in administration without lessening its responsibility as a contracting party.

But an incorporated union would in all these steps be subject to much revision and correction through the agencies of the law. Work, here, for judges, lawyers and enemies. The incorporated body, as a creature of the State, must be kept in health by the State. Disturbers, instigated by influences inimical to a union, might kindly aid the State. In incorporating, a union would have admitted non-kinsfolk as masters at the family table—the judge, of another blood, come to set things right; the sheriff, with keys to a jail and a money-sack for fines; the policeman, with a club and handcuffs.

These officials occasionally regulate family affairs now in the unions, but the courts, only acting when called upon, refuse to interfere if the union's proceedings are in accordance with its own rules, which are subject to change at the will of the majority. But if these rules depended for regularity upon the terms of incorporation, and if informers were sent into the unions to report infractions, the sins of unions would be multiplied and the lawsuits ensuing would work pleasure to scabs. The knowing are fully conscious of what they are saying when they express a desire for an increase of the authority of the law over trade unions. They would wreck them from within.

THE PUBLIC

Charles W. Eliot, President Harvard University:

Incorporation with a limited liability has always seemed to me to be a measure of protection for the individual stockholder. As a rule incorporation does not expose the shareholders to new and larger risks, but on the contrary diminishes or restricts his liability. The unions, however, do not take this view of the matter, and will not, until the courts hold unincorporated unions, or the members thereof, liable for the damages which they inflict, or for the damages inflicted in their interests. If the courts in considerable number pursue this policy, and succeed in collecting damages, the unions will wish to be incorporated in order to limit the legal responsibility of their members. I am not in favor of compulsory incorporation for unions, or for anybody else, because incorporation is to my mind a privilege and not a duty to which the people should be forced.

Warren A. Reed, Chairman Massachusetts Board of Mediation and Arbitration:

I understand the law in this country to be that the members of an unincorporated trade union can be sued as well as the union itself could be in its own name if incorporated, but under proceedings somewhat more complicated than would be used if the corporation were sued.

The law in relation to proceedings against unincorporated societies or voluntary associations is well stated by Lord Lindley in the Taff Vale Railway case. He says:

My Lords, the problem how to adapt legal proceedings to unincorporated societies consisting of many members is by no means new. The rules as to parties to common law actions were too rigid for practical purposes when those rules had to be applied to such societies. But the rules as to parties to suits in equity were not the same as those which governed courts of common law, and were long since adapted to meet the difficulties presented by a multiplicity of persons interested in the subject matter of litigation. Some of such persons were allowed to sue and be sued on behalf of themselves and all others having the same interest. This was done avowedly to prevent a failure of justice.

. . . I have myself no doubt whatever that if the trade union could not be sued in this case in its registered name, some of its members (namely its executive committee) could be sued on behalf of themselves and the other members of the society and an injunction and judgment for damages could be obtained in a proper case in an action so framed. Further, it is in my opinion equally plain that if the trustees in whom the property of the society is legally vested were added as parties, an order could be made in the same action for the payment by them out of the funds of the society of all damages and costs for which the plaintiff might obtain judgment against the trade union.

In a suit against the members of a union, I suppose that both the property of the union and the property of its members could be reached. If the union were incorporated, only the property of the corporation could be reached. It appears to me that from a purely legal standpoint the responsibility would not be increased, for the reason that, when incorporated, only the property of the corporation can be reached, but when not incorporated, the property of the association, held by trustees or otherwise, and also the property of the private individuals can be reached.

While I do not think that incorporation would add to the legal responsibility of the unions, still, for some reason, probably because it is somewhat more difficult to reach the funds of a union when it is not incorporated, there have been comparatively few suits against them. There seems, therefore, to be a practical immunity from liability to suit which, at present at least, serves the purpose of actual freedom from liability. As long as this continues it may fairly be claimed that incorporation would practically increase the liability of the unions.

John M. Gray, Professor, Northwestern University, Evanston, Illinois:

While it is a perfectly recognized fact that in applying either the principles of common law or of interpretation to statutes the courts always attempt to resolve the genuine doubts in favor of what they consider the practicably desirable thing. I am not a lawyer and make no pretense of being able to unravel the finer distinctions of judicial reasoning. As it appears to my lay mind, the decision in the case referred to has gone considerably further than has ever been done before in applying the principles of incorporation to the unincorporated, voluntary associations of laborers known as unions. Personally I question if our courts would at present care to go so far. As I understand that decision, it treats the labor union exactly as if it were incorporated. Although the question of incorporation in this country is one in which there is considerable difference of opinion, personally I do not believe that incorporation would be either in the interests of the laborers themselves or of society as a whole. It follows from this necessarily that I should not like to see the Taff Vale decision applied to our own labor unions, nor would I like to see the unions compelled by law to take out formal acts of incorporation. I believe that much educational work will be necessary before actual incorporation is desirable. I do not believe that this education will be acquired without considerable friction and many hardships.

Henry W. Farnam, Professor, Yale University, New Haven:

I have had no experience which would justify me in stating whether or not incorporation would add to the responsibility of trade unions. If the statement which I have seen frequently made is true, according to which they can be sued even without incorporation, then it would perhaps not add to their legal responsibility in case of a lawsuit. But I believe that it would add to the feeling of responsibility which the leaders would be governed by, and that is, after all, the main point. My own opinion is that if we emphasized collective responsibility, the result would be somewhat like the principle of limited liability applied to a corporation. The trade union as a whole would be under bonds, but it would not be possible to enjoin, as has been done in some cases, individual members of the union. You understand, however, that I am not a lawyer and do not speak ex cathedra on a legal question.

Henry Demarest Lloyd, author of "Wealth Against Commonwealth," "A Country Without Strikes," "Labor Co-partnership," etc.:

Incorporation has never, so far as I know, been forced upon any class of the community. It is, on the contrary, a privilege granted by the law to those who comply with certain provisions for the purpose of gaining the benefit conferred. The suggestion, so freely made by some of our divines and other eminent peace-makers, that the workingmen should be compelled to incorporate, is merely the crack of the slave master's whip heard again.

The trade unions of New Zealand and Australia have incorporated almost universally, because by doing so they have been given valuable privileges, such as the power to hold real estate, sue members for dues, punish officers—most of all, to secure arbitration in case of dispute with employers. If the leaders of the American world desire our trade unions to incorporate, let them offer them inducements which will make it worth their while to do so.

Wm. Stainsby, Chief, Bureau of Statistics, New Jersey:

There have been no cases in this State that illustrate the point, but I am of the opinion that damages can be recovered in a court of equity or by an action in tort in a court of law from individual members of unions that are not incorporated. There is nothing in the statutes authorizing the formation of labor unions which shields individuals comprising these organizations from responsibility under the common or statute laws for injuries inflicted upon others. It does not seem to me that anything of value as a remedy can be added to existing law by the incorporation of unions. Only a comparatively few of them have funds, and these are, generally speaking, the most conservative in the matter of undertaking trade movements which would be likely to furnish a basis for legal action against them. A large number of unions are organized that pass out of existence in less than one year. These are to a large extent the outgrowth of incidents that have caused temporary friction between employers and workmen. When these are settled, the organizations which grew out of them pass away as a general thing. This bureau made an inquiry in 1901 to ascertain the membership, age, benefit features and some other information of trade unions in New Jersey. Out of the one hundred and ten blanks sent out, only sixty-three were returned. From the data which these reports contained it was shown that twenty-three of the organizations making them were organized less than one year, and eleven others between one and four years. The total membership of the sixty-three unions at the time their reports were made was 13,380, and the total aggregate amount of money in their treasuries was found to be $13,339.06, or less than one dollar for each member. Solicitude for this trifling sum of money would add little, if at all, to the responsibility of the unions. In my opinion, there is nothing to be gained by compulsory incorporation, as it would not increase to any appreciable extent the civil remedies for abuses by trade unions which I believe are available under the law as it stands at present.

A. F. Weber, Chief Statistician, Department of Labor, Albany, New York:

The compulsory incorporation of trade unions does not seem advisable to me at the present time. The principal argument in favor of that policy is the impossibility of holding unincorporated unions to their contracts. No one familiar with industrial operations is disposed to deny that local unions have been wont to keep or break agreements at their own convenience. But the remedy for this lack of control may be found in the organization of employers, without resorting to experimental legislation which might introduce greater evils than the existing ones. The contracts so frequently broken by unions are almost always contracts with individual employers. Just as rapidly as the employers have come together for concerted action and replaced these individual agreements with one general agreement between the association of employers and the union of workingmen, they have been able to hold the unions strictly to the terms of their agreement. It is in this way that the mason builders in New York and Boston have for some fifteen years preserved industrial peace with the journeymen bricklayers and masons. In those cities the single annual agreement entered into by reprsentatives of the two bodies of employers and employes has been kept inviolate, while in cities where agreements have been signed by individual employers there have been frequent strikes, lockouts and violations of contract.

The experience in the coal mining industry has been the same. In the anthracite district, agreements, so far as they have been entered into at all, have been signed by individual operators and have not proved satisfactory to either side. But in Illinios and other central States, the agreement is between an employers' association and the international union of miners. All the testimony available goes to show that during the five years' duration of this arrangement industrial relations have been more stable and satisfactory in every way than they ever were before 1898, or than they are at the present time in regions where such an arrangement is wanting. Considering the fact that a large proportion of the workmen in the mining industry are unskilled and uneducated, that experience seems to afford a complete answer to the affirmation that responsibility can be secured among such workingmen only through the incorporation of their unions. Other tests of loyalty to the joint agreement are familiar—such as that of the longshoremen's union when the International President sent non-union men to work in the place of members who had gone on strike contrary to the agreement—while the history of railroad transportation in this country shows that stability has been achieved in the degree that the principle of collective bargaining and the joint agreement have been recognized. Contracts would not be treated with greater respect by incorporated unions of the engineers, conductors, etc., than they are now by the unincorporated organizations.

On the other hand, compulsory incorporation might discourage the movement toward organization, which we all recognize as the basis of the economic independence of wage workers. Such would be the effect if that policy promoted litigation, which it would probably do; for it would be difficult to frame a law that would make the union responsible for the acts of its officers or committees and not hold it responsible for unauthorized acts of its individual members. In the affairs of the ordinary business corporation, the unauthorized acts of an individual stockholder cannot embarrass the corporation because all power is lodged in the hands of the directors. But authority in a trade union cannot be so readily concentrated in a board of directors, since an agreement with employers necessarily calls for the co-operation of every individual member; and if the courts should entertain suits against the union for unauthorized acts of individual members, the field for intrigues between designing employers and avaricious members would be very large. The unions might find it impossible to maintain any funds whatsoever and that would of course spell the death of unionism and collective bargaining.

Any such movement to injure or destroy trade unionism would be disastrous to the best interests of the people, because collective bargaining through the organization of labor is an indisputable necessity in modern industry. If a frank, open policy of organization is prevented or seriously embarrassed by legal restrictions, there will probably come into existence secret and unlawful combinations such as agitated England before the repeal of the combination laws. And if the trade unions' educational work among the emigrants—an educational work that ranks second only to the work of the public schools in American life—should be stopped or seriously hampered, we should soon witness a revolution in our politics only dimly foreshadowed in the Socialism engendered by the recent coal strike. The effect of the Taff Vale decision in England has been a markedly increased participation in politics by the organized workers, as a class.

David Ross, Secretary, Bureau of Labor Statistics, Illinois:

The present opposition of labor men to the incorporation of labor unions is based on the fact, first, that the membership is necessarily of a heterogeneous character, and second, the financial liability resulting to the union from the possible indiscretion of individual action. If the courts of this country, however, hold that the fact that they are not incorporated does not exempt them from the liability of money damages growing out of the act of individual members, then they should avail themselves of the legal advantages which incorporation insures.

J. G. Schonfarber, Maryland Bureau of Statistics:

I cannot see how the incorporation of unions will increase the responsibility of the individuals composing the unions. In the State of Maryland, when they are not incorporated, the members of the organization are individually responsible as co-partners before the law. When incorporated, the individual is relieved to some extent of the responsibility, and the incorporated unions are responsible as an organization. I think that there is much to be said in favor of the incorporation of unions for the reason last noted.

E. Dana Durand, Former Secretary Industrial Commission:

In my judgment, based on considerable study of the cases in which labor organizations have been sued as such, the incorporation of labor unions would tend to make them more readily subject to legal responsibility than they are at present. It is possible to sue them, in some States, at present, but owing to the lack of definite legal organization it is rather more common to sue individual officers or members than the body as such, while doubtless in other instances employers and others aggrieved refrain altogether from bringing suit for fear of the difficulty of enforcing judgment. I doubt very much, however, whether it would be to the interests of the working class to insist on the incorporation of trade unions, except in conjunction with other provisions of law, defining the acts which unions may lawfully do, in a more liberal manner than the courts have been accustomed, in many cases, to define them. If unions are to be sued for engaging in a strike, as appears possible in view of recent injunctions, or for peaceful picketing, it seems desirable that the suits should encounter as much difficulty as possible, rather than that the way for them should be made easier. At the same time, I believe that in the long run, with proper safeguarding of their rights, unions will gain by accepting additional responsibility, especially in regard to their agreements with employers.

Hamilton Holt, Office Editor "Independent":

My own impression is that unless we have compulsory arbitration (which I personally favor), it would not be wise to incorporate trade unions, but if we have compulsory arbitration, the union should be incorporated in much the same way as in New Zealand.

Rev. Thomas R. Slicer, Pastor All Souls, New York:

In my judgment, the only way to remove all doubt and conflict of authority in the matter of the responsibility of labor unions, is that the national organization shall direct that each union be incorporated in the State in which it has been formed, just as though it were free from all sentimental considerations. That would define by terms of incorporation, their responsibility, and require the issue to them of charters, which would fix their status before the law. If the unions wish fair treatment, and are willing to make their contribution to a responsible business arrangement, this seems to me the only path for them to pursue; and I say this as profoundly interested in their well-being. It would tend to conservatism in their action, would assist in making contracts that should be binding, and leave each union free to control the character of its membership. I have also an impression that any irresponsibility in the individual union would be linked in this way to the national organization, so that it might be controlled.

Thomas F. Woodlock, Editor "Wall Street Journal":

It is clear that by incorporation a labor union becomes a legal entity with full power of making contracts and with full responsibility for obligations thus entered into. Other things being equal and in view of the uncertainty of the law with respect to the responsibility and liability of unions not incorporated, I can see no valid reason against the principle of incorporation for labor unions. The objections urged by the labor leaders are not objections in principle but arise out of circumstances which the leaders believe exist in the relations between capital and labor. The description given in your letter of the uncertainty surrounding the question of liability of unincorporated unions seems to me itself the best argument for incorporation.

F. A. Halsey, Associate Editor "American Machinist," New York:

It seems to me the discussion is of academic interest only. I can see no value in the discussion of the incorporation of labor unions so long as the unions themselves are determined they will not incorporate. From their standpoint, it seems to me clear that the incorporation would be against their own interests, and hence their attitude is perfectly understandable.

John Graham Brooks, Author of "The Social Unrest":

I am absolutely certain that in the trade union, into which come the foreign classes (and in the anthracite regions there are some nineteen of such classes), the larger part of which are afraid of the judge, the policeman and the law—let it once be known that they are incorporated and instantly the large class that is now making the strength of the unions will refuse to join them.

To weaken the trade union is in my opinion as grave an affront as we could put upon any form of our social development at present. . . . I do not believe that anything that weakens the trade union is socially safe, because on the whole, the stronger a trade union, the more socially responsible it becomes. Remember the lawlessness of the locomotive engineers twenty years ago. With more strength, they have learned conduct. I could mention scores of unions, which when their strength became sufficient to keep their best men in the front showed good behavior, on the whole, in proportion to their increase of strength. That process should go on. I can prove that if we can get responsibility persuasively or voluntarily instead of by legal enforcement, the result will be educational, and we shall get a higher kind. To weaken the unions leads precisely to the status of things throughout the United Mine Workers; it was at the weakest point of the anthracite workers that the ratio of strikes was highest; and where the leaders had real power lawlessness was less frequent and strikes fewest.

If you go among the bituminous miners you will find that just in proportion as a joint agreement is reached among the men strikes disappear, and that friendliness toward the joint agreement grows in proportion as the union grows in strength. You will find that after the joint agreement—and this is my substitute for incorporation—is established between the bituminous operators and the men, the representatives of the employers and the employed come together systematically, and that strikes are stopped until an understanding is arrived at. . . . More than seventy per cent. of the awards of decisions under the Bituminous Coal Fields Arbitration Board—representing the miners on one side and the operators on the other—have been against the miners. They have accepted these with frankness and have gone on with their work. . . . If I wanted to do just as much harm as I could to trade unions, I should incorporate them to-morrow; but it would harm the social state as well. I do not dare to discuss it here, but, in my opinion, it would drive trade unionism, because it would weaken it, straight toward a crude form of political Socialism. From the conservative point of view, from the point of view of those that want incorporation, that must be reckoned with. Just as fast as any force cripples any trade union, we get the appearance of the Socialist Mayor. I have told a good many, "You may take your choice." Ultimately, therefore, on the basis of the principle of "power with responsibility" we may expect, when we have trained trade unions, as the English spinners have been trained, that they will say: "Well, we are willing to do it if you want; we are doing what incorporation will do." It seems to me that the educational influence of this solution is so precious that to preclude it by legal incorporation is simply a mistake.

MEMBERS OF THE BAR

Charles J. Bonaparte, Attorney-at-Law, Baltimore:

There is certainly nothing new in the doctrine that the members of labor unions can be sued individually for any illegal interference with the business either of their employers or any other persons. As long ago as in the time of the Year Books it was held that: "Where a violent or malicious act is done to a man's occupation, profession, or way of getting a livelihood, there an action lies in all cases." And Lord Holt (Keeble vs. Hickeringill, 11 East, 576, Note) says: "If a man should lie in wait and fright the boys from going to school, that schoolmaster might have an action for the loss of his scholars."

The principles, therefore, on which actions against members of labor unions for any form of violence or intimidation or for conspiracy have been sustained by the courts is as old as the common law. The responsibility of individual members of such unions depends upon the question whether they can be shown to have participated in or authorized the illegal acts. If, for example, these acts were authorized at a meeting of the union, those members present and voting for the resolution authorizing them would be responsible; those members who were absent, or, if present, voted against the resolution, would not be responsible, unless they afterward participated personally in the illegal acts. The mere fact of a man's belonging to a union or to any other association formed for a lawful purpose would not of itself make him personally responsible for the illegal acts of the association. If the union is incorporated, it will be responsible to the extent of its corporate property for illegal acts done under its corporate sanction; this, however, will not relieve the individual members of the corporation from responsibility likewise. Indirectly, in such a case, even innocent members of the union would, of course, be held responsible to the extent of their interest in the corporate property. It must be remembered in this connection that, for any one to be responsible, he must be shown to have committed an illegal act. I do not think it is to the well considered interest of any member of the community to be allowed to violate the law with impunity, and for this reason it seems to me that the more readily and satisfactorily those guilty of violations of law can be made to respond in damages, the less danger there will be of innocent persons suffering or of persons of good intentions being led into illegal acts through ignorance, bad advice or lack of reasonable self-control. I do not think, therefore, that the possibility of evasion of legal responsibility for acts which, *ex hypothesi*, must be illegal, otherwise no responsibility for them would accrue to any one at all, is a legitimate argument either for or against the incorporation of trade unions.

It is a general principle of the law of torts that there is no right to contribution among wrong-doers, therefore each individual against whom a judgment is recovered under such an action is responsible for its full amount without regard to the number of his co-defendants; although, of course, the plaintiff can have but one satisfaction. It is, however, inaccurate to describe this responsibility as "the same as in a partnership."

Levy Mayer, General Counsel Illinois Manufacturers' Association:

A corporation exists as such only by virtue of a grant from the State, and the acceptance of such grant by the persons composing the corporation. No one can be compelled to accept such a grant, nor be compelled to become a member of the corporation against his will. To compel labor unions to incorporate is to compel individuals composing the union to become members of a corporation, and to assume the burdens and responsibilities of that relation without their consent, or to prohibit such members from voluntarily associating themselves together for a lawful purpose. It is not within the province of the Legislature to say to a person: "You cannot join a union unless that union is incorporated." That would be equivalent to saying that a person desiring to become a member of a labor union has to become a member of the corporation, or cease to be a "union" laborer. Such persons would thus be prevented from pursuing a lawful purpose, and would be deprived of a right to assemble together for a purpose not in violation of law. The proposed law would interfere with the liberty of the citizen, the right of lawful assembly, and the freedom of contract. This view is supported by authorities. Chancellor Kent, in his Commentaries (Vol. 2, p. 277), says:

"It requires the acceptance of a charter to create a corporate body; for the government cannot compel persons to become an incorporated body without their consent, or the consent of at least a major part of them."

In Mason vs. Finch, 28 Mich., 282, the Supreme Court of Michigan laid down the law as follows:

"It would not be competent for the legislature . . . to compel any person or society to become incorporated without its consent."

In Hampshire vs. Franklin, 16 Mass., 76, 87, the Supreme Court of Massachusetts said:

"No man can be compelled by the legislature to become a member of a corporation without his consent."

See also Angell & Ames on Corporations (11th Ed.), Secs. 31, 81, 86.

Again, the proposed law, if applicable only to "labor unions" and not to all other unincorporated associations similarly situated, would probably violate the constitutional inhibition against "class legislation." There is nothing in the nature of a "labor union" which requires special regulation, which does not equally apply to other unincorporated associations. The members of a labor union are joined together in furtherance of a common enterprise, in which the public at large is not directly interested or concerned. If the public is affected, it is only indirectly. Such union, therefore, is not a public association in the same sense that it is subject to public regulation and control.

I have heretofore, on April 12, 1902, given an opinion to the association that the members of a labor union are legally responsible for damages caused by an illegal boycott. The compulsory incorporation of a labor union would not make the members of the association any more responsible than they are at present, except in so far as the corporation might possess property. The creation of a corporation not for pecuniary profit does not and would not ordinarily create any more financial responsibility than now exists on the part of individuals who would constitute the corporation.

For the reasons above stated, I am of the opinion that the proposed law, if enacted, would be unconstitutional. Even if the law were constitutional, I do not believe it would accomplish the purpose for which it would be designed. If a law could be devised to compel the formation of such corporations, it would soon be discovered that such corporations could readily avoid accumulating or possessing any property.

Fred. H. Cooke, Attorney-at-Law, New York, Author "Trade and Labor Combinations":

The importance of the decision of the House of Lords in Taff Vale Railway Company vs. Amalgamated Society of Railway Servants, L. R. App. Cas. 426 (1901) resulting in the recovery for a large amount of damages against the defendant trade union, has, in my opinion, been much exaggerated. That an association of this character should be mulcted in so large an amount is, to say the least, unusual, and may be a sociological fact of interest and importance. But from a strictly legal standpoint the decision is comparatively insignificant. The doctrines applied are trite, and it was simply a narrow question of statutory construction that was really involved.

The effect of the decision was that the defendant trade union was liable in an action for damages, that is, in tort, for unlawful acts of its agents in the course of the management of a strike.

Before considering the precise ground of such decision, let us consider the general principles applicable in determining the liability of a trade union or its officers, members or agents for such acts.

In the absence of statutory provision a trade union is nothing but a number of persons associated for a particular purpose. As in the case of such association generally, (frequently termed voluntary associations) the law ignores the circumstance of association in determining liability for unlawful acts of members of the association. That is to say, if the members of a trade union, whether acting singly or in combination, assault a person or trespass upon his property, or otherwise injure him, it is merely as individuals that they can be held liable. For instances of members being thus held liable, injunctions being allowed, see Hopkins vs. Oxley Stove Company, 83 Fed. 913; 49 U. S. App. 709 (8th Cir. 1897); Cumberland Glass Manufacturing Company vs. Glass Bottle Blowers' Association, 59 N. J. Eq. 49; Atl. 208 (1899); Reinecke Coal Mining Company vs. Wood, 112 Fed. 477 (Cir. Ct. Ky. 1901); Sherry vs. Perkins, 147 Mass. 212; 17 N. E. 307 (1888); Murdock vs. Walker, 152 Pa. St. 595; 25 Atl. 492 (1893); Wick China Company vs. Brown, 164 Pa. St. 449; 30 Atl. 261 (1894). So in action for damages; Temperton vs. Russell, 1 L. R. Q. B. (1893) 715; Quinn vs. Leathern, L. R. App. Cas. (1901) 495. See also Thomas vs. Cin-

(Continued on Page 18.)

THE CHICAGO BOARD OF ARBITRATION

A unique and probably the most successful and scientific voluntary body of arbitrators in this country to-day is the Chicago Board of Arbitration, composed of the heads of seven employers' associations and the heads of the seven corresponding labor organizations.

It is unique in that while there are seven labor organizations and the corresponding associations of employers, they are all connected with one industry, teaming.

It is successful in that it settles nearly every trouble that arises in Chicago in any line and in a manner satisfactory to both sides.

It is scientific in that it recognizes the full value of joint trade agreements between associations of employers and organizations of employes, each side seeing the justice and necessity of the other being completely organized.

The membership of this organization is as follows:

Harry G. Selfridge, Manager of Marshall Field & Co., representing the Dry Goods Stores.

John S. Field, President of the Knickerbocker Ice Company, representing the Ice, Stone, Lime and Cement Interests.

Henry B. Steele, President of Steele-Wedeles Company, representing the Wholesale Grocers and kindred lines.

Arthur Dixon, President of the Arthur Dixon Transfer Company, representing the Transfer Companies.

S. T. Edwards, President of S. W. Edwards & Sons, representing the Board of Trade and the Hay, Grain and Feed Dealers.

Frank H. Hebard, President of Hebard's Express & Van Company, representing Express and General Delivery Owners.

F. G. Hartwell, President of the F. G. Hartwell Coal Company, representing the Coal Team Owners.

The Teamsters are:

Albert Young, President of the Teamsters' National Union of America.

James B. Barry, Secretary of the Teamsters' Joint Council.

Frank H. Ray, Business Agent of the Commission Teamsters' Union.

Thomas L. Hughes, Business Agent Stone, Lime and Cement Teamsters.

Milton Booth, Secretary and Treasurer Coal Teamsters' Union.

William McNabb, Vice-President Hack, Cab and Coupe Drivers' Union.

Charles G. Sagerstrom, Secretary of Local No. 2, Teamsters' National Union of America.

CHICAGO BOARD OF ARBITRATION

F. G. HARTWELL WM. McNABB F. H. RAY C. G. SAGERSTROM THOS. L. HUGHES JOHN S. FIELD

ARTHUR DIXON ALBERT YOUNG F. H. HEBARD HARRY G. SELFRIDGE MILTON BOOTH S. T. EDWARDS J. B. BARRY H. B. STEELE

The Board elected Harry G. Selfridge Chairman, and James B. Barry, Secretary.

Just how a board made up of teamsters on one side and team owners on the other could become involved in a strike of the Garment Workers, or of the Bakers' Union, or the Rubber Workers' Union, is highly interesting, but not at all surprising when one considers that there are few industries in this country that do not employ teamsters. The common mode of procedure is as follows: A strike may occur in the plants of a manufacturing company. At once the strikers throw out picket lines. Soon a teamster approaches with a load of coal or flour, or a drayman starts away with a load of the manufacturer's product. The picket immediately stops him and intercedes in behalf of his brethren on strike, asking the driver not to deliver anything to or for the manufacturer. The teamster telephones to his local president and the manufacturer telephones to the team-owner, who in turn notifies the president of the association for the subdivision of teaming concerned. Officers of both sides then go to the seat of trouble and try to bring about either a settlement or the submission of the matter to their Board of Arbitration. This is a common weekly occurrence. If the conciliatory efforts of this joint committee do not prevail and the strike continues, the teamsters, honoring their contract with the team owners, decline to be interfered with by the pickets, and in some instances have even attacked them when they persisted in their interference.

The genius who is responsible for the organization of this board is John C. Driscoll, the General Secretary of the Associated Teaming Interests of Chicago. He first organized the Coal Team Owners and was made their secretary. He then allied himself with Albert Young, President of the Teamsters' National Union of America, and they worked out a joint trade agreement for the industry of coal teaming. As the work developed Mr. Driscoll saw the necessity of organizing all the branches of employers engaged in teaming and of aiding Mr. Young in organizing the various subdivisions of teamsters. He is the conciliator of the arbitration board and is continually preventing strikes by his great tact, indomitable energy and enthusiastic faith in his work.

The moral power which is the outgrowth of independent investigation and awards made by the Chicago Board of Arbitration has proved of great value in settling strikes and lockouts by mediation. In many instances the board has gone out of its way to secure concessions from both sides before calling employer and employe to a joint meeting. The board, as one of its first duties, if possible brings about a conference between the two contending factions, and in these efforts, supported by the influence of its members and the standing it has attained in the eyes of the Chicago public, it is generally successful. It has found in a majority of cases that the chief requisite is a frank conference between employers and representatives of employes. In general there are points of misunderstanding which can be cleared up in no other way. At these conferences the members of the board, with their extensive experience, are usually able to make suggestions of value in promoting a settlement.

The three strikes first adjusted—those of the department store delivery drivers, the packing house teamsters, and the freight handlers—attracted widespread attention because their effect was felt by the public directly and very seriously.

For the purpose of carrying out its projected work and broadening it to cover every dispute between labor and capital in Chicago—which in every instance excepting the messenger boys' strike has affected the teamsters directly or indirectly—the Chicago Board of Arbitration was made a permanent body. It is doing its good work well, as the following summary of cases it has disposed of shows:

The formation of the board was completed in detail about June 23, 1902. The first case to come before it was that of the Parmelee Transfer Company, on July 7, and the Teamsters' Union. The company requested arbitration when threatened by a strike, the result being an amicable adjustment and an agreement for one year.

The great freight handlers' strike came next. On July 7 the Freight Handlers' Union called a general strike on all the railroads in Chicago. Suspension of work continued for several days, the teamsters of the city becoming more and more involved. On July 10, when the commerce of Chicago was practically at a standstill, arbitration was sought by the freight handlers at the hands of the Board of Arbitration. The matter was taken up and brought to the attention of the railroads, and though not finally disposed of by the board, yet through the efforts of Albert Young, President of the Teamsters' National Union, who insisted and demanded that the teamsters keep inviolate the agreement they had made just previous with the team owners, in connection with the efforts of the Secretary of the Associated Teaming Interests and of the individual members of the Board of Arbitration, a vast quantity of freight was moved on July 16, and the strike ended.

Since that time the board has prevented and arbitrated strikes and difficulties as follows:

Van Teamsters' Organization vs. the Furniture Movers and Expressmen's Association.

Arthur Bassett vs. W. G. Livingston, President of the Van Team Owners' Association. Settlement made before the board on September 9.

Lumbermen's Association vs. Local Union No. 19, of the Teamsters. Threatened strike of Lumber Teamsters against the Lumbermen's Association. The question of a wage scale for one year was brought before the board and settled December 22.

Newspaper Delivery Drivers' Union vs. Western News Company, Joseph Russell vs. Western News Company. Settled in the board December 27.

Lincoln Park Commissioners vs. Park Teamsters. Case of John Meyer vs. Lincoln Park Commissioners. Strike called and lasted three days. Park Board requested arbitration from the board. Settled January 8, 1903.

Building Managers' Association vs. Office Building, Janitors and Window Washers' Union and the Chicago Elevator Conductors and Starters' Union. Strike called and lasted eight days. Board requested to arbitrate and the case was settled on February 13.

Chicago City Railway Company vs. Street Car Employes' Union. Arbitration requested of the board by the street car company and refused by the union. When the teamsters backed up the request of the company for arbitration the street car employes receded from their position. February 16.

The board holds employers and employes to a strict observance of contracts. It contends that compacts must be kept, with honorable action on both sides. It regards a working agreement or contract as a covenant in which the integrity of all concerned is at stake.

In the contests thus far settled by the board neither side in controversy has been dissatisfied. Both have usually concluded that they received justice and fair treatment. The agreements reached through the good offices of the board are remarkable, in that they cover a large number of workers and greater business interests than have been similarly dealt with in the other industrial centers of the country.

It would be difficult to arrive at an estimate of the aggregate saving effected by the board's adjustment of strikes. Three distinct interests are considered in every case—the employers, the employes and the general public. The loss to the public occasioned by a strike or lockout is often immense as compared with that which falls upon either the employers or the workmen. This was notably true in the freight handlers' strike, which, according to estimates generally accepted, was conducted at an aggregate cost of $1,000,000 a day. Considering the loss suffered throughout the vast territory tributary to Chicago through the suspension of traffic into and out of the city, it is safe to say that the value of the board's work in hastening the end of that strike cannot be computed.

The Chicago Board of Arbitration has thus performed timely and important services to employers and employes and to the general public. Merely as an educator, encouraging and promoting the ideas of consultation, conciliation and arbitration, its existence has been of great value. With the increasing attention paid arbitration by both employers and employes, and with the steady growth of public sentiment in that direction, and of recognition by the public of the usefulness of arbitration tribunals, the future of the Chicago Board of Arbitration as an agency for industrial peace would appear to possess great possibilities.

JOHN C. DRISCOLL
Mediator, Chicago Board of Arbitration

Mr. Driscoll, as Secretary of the Board, has acted as mediator in settling many disputes without calling a meeting of the board. The following are to be mentioned:

Van and Express Teamsters of Chicago vs. Employers, April 10. Threatened strike on account of wage scale. Satisfactory agreement for one year entered into April 18, 1902.

Truck Teamsters' Local vs. J. C. Pennoyer Company's barns, May 1. Strike lasted two days, adjusted and agreement made for one year on May 3.

Stromberg-Carlson strike May 31. Strike had lasted for three months. Mr. Driscoll's services requested on May 30. Satisfactory settlement made next day with five labor organizations for one year.

Master Boiler Makers and Employes, Thursday, August 7. Call for sympathetic strike of teamsters. Prevented by Secretary and strike called off.

Kellogg-Switchboard Company, strike, August 9. Strike lasted fifteen days; settlement made after three days' conference.

Keith Lumber Company, August 26. Teamsters strike for two days. Settled in four hours by Secretary.

Montgomery Ward & Co. vs. Shipping Room Employes. Sympathetic action of teamsters called for; prevented by the Secretary and arbitration suggested and satisfactory settlement made September 18.

Strike of Stablemen's Union vs. Department Stores, September 1. Strike lasted three weeks. Attempted sympathetic strike of teamsters prevented by Secretary. Strike adjusted by committee in office of the board.

Retail Furniture Dealers' Association and Drivers and Helpers' Union. Strike declared by teamsters and helpers. Secretary brought it to a stop and helped to bring about a satisfactory agreement for one year. September 25.

Schmidt Bakery (National Biscuit Company) vs. Drivers. Question of wages and threatened strike. Matter adjusted in three hours by Secretary on September 27.

Rubber Workers' Union vs. Morgan & Wright (first settlement). Original strike lasted one day. Agreement brought about; broken four days later; strike declared and lasted six weeks. Endeavors of Secretary forced settlement and strike ended January 3, 1903.

South Chicago Team Owners vs. Teamsters. Strike of Coal Teamsters. Lasted ten days, settled by Secretary November 3.

Newspaper Local No. 6 of Newspaper Delivery Drivers. Question of wages. Difficulty adjusted and agreement signed about November 10.

Wholesale Shoe Manufacturers and Employes. Strike on for four weeks. Satisfactory adjustment made by Secretary on November 11.

Piano Team Owners' Association formed November 12, and an agreement until April 1, between employers and employes drawn up by Mr. Driscoll.

Auditorium Hotel, December 19. Strike of engineers and firemen prevented and a satisfactory scale and agreement for that plant brought about.

Strike of elevator men at The Fair; lasted ten hours. Sympathetic strike of teamsters and firemen prevented by Secretary and satisfactory settlement made December 20.

Strike at Bremner Bakery (National Biscuit Company). Strike called; lasted seven days; adjusted satisfactorily by Secretary on January 20.

Sibley Warehouse vs. Freight Handlers. Threatened strike of freight handlers; trouble prevented by Secretary and satisfactorily settled January 22.

Kennedy Biscuit Company (National Biscuit Company). Strike lasted three days. Teamsters refused sympathetic action and strike settled January 30.

Globe Iron and Wire Works vs. United Metal Workers. Question of wages and hours. Strike lasted three days. Satisfactory settlement and agreement made in Secretary's office on January 31.

"Special Order" clothing makers' strike, February 4. Strike lasted four weeks. Various conferences held. Agreement broken and efforts of Secretary, with national officials of the American Federation of Labor, at last settled the trouble.

Truck Team Owners' Association and Truck Teamsters' agreement. New agreement for one year, made in Secretary's office, December 27.

Dernberg Manufacturing Company, strike of cloak makers to enforce wage scale, settled and agreement signed for one year, March 7.

Settlements between individual team owners and teamsters are daily occurring. From three to seven cases or disputes are handled on an average in Mr. Driscoll's rooms day in and day out.

In the earlier days of the teamsters' organization the actions of the members promised little good for the peace of Chicago. Other unions that struck on any pretense whatever counted on the teamsters' assistance, which was given without much hesitation. The climax in the aggressions of the coal teamsters was reached when they made the extraordinary demand that unless the managers of the large office buildings agree to give up the use of fuel gas during the summer they would not deliver coal at any time. But in the course of time the teamsters themselves felt seriously the burden thrown on them by unions unable to win their own battles. Hence a teamster on approaching the scene of a strike came to change his attitude. Instead of joining in the strike with little ceremony, he would wait until his union instituted some inquiry into its merits and the methods by which it had been authorized. This deepening wisdom at length crystallized into a law which has been growing in favor with all the teamsters of the city.

(Concluded on Page 15.)

MONTHLY REVIEW
OF THE
National Civic Federation

Published on the Fifteenth of Each Month

Offices: 281 Fourth Avenue, New York
Telephone, 4220 18th
RALPH M. EASLEY, Editor

Vol. I. New York, April, 1903 No. 1
Ten Cents per Copy: One Dollar per Year

The National Civic Federation

281 Fourth Avenue, New York City

Marcus A. Hanna, Chairman.
Samuel Gompers, First Vice-Chairman.
Oscar S. Straus, Second Vice-Chairman.
Cornelius N. Bliss Treasurer.
Ralph M. Easley, General Secretary.

EXECUTIVE COMMITTEE.

ON THE PART OF THE PUBLIC.

Grover Cleveland, ex-President of the United States, Princeton, N. J.

Cornelius N. Bliss, ex-Secretary of the Interior, New York City.

David R. Francis, President Louisiana Purchase Exposition, St. Louis.

August Belmont, banker, New York.

Oscar S. Straus, member of the Court of Arbitration at The Hague, New York City.

Charles Francis Adams, former President of Union Pacific Railroad, Boston.

Archbishop John Ireland, of the Roman Catholic Church, St. Paul.

Bishop Henry C. Potter, of the Protestant Episcopal Church, New York City.

Spencer Trask, banker, New York.

Charles W. Eliot, President Harvard University, Cambridge, Mass.

Franklin MacVeagh, merchant, Chicago.

James H. Eckels, former Comptroller of Currency of the United States, Chicago.

John J. McCook, lawyer, New York City.

John G. Milburn, lawyer, Buffalo.

Charles J. Bonaparte, lawyer, Baltimore.

Ralph M. Easley, General Secretary of the National Civic Federation, New York City.

ON THE PART OF EMPLOYERS.

Marcus A. Hanna, coal mines, iron, shipping and street railways, Cleveland.

Charles M. Schwab, President United States Steel Corporation, New York City.

William L. Elkins, director Pennsylvania Railroad, Philadelphia.

John B. McDonald, contractor Rapid Transit Subway Construction, New York.

Frederick D. Underwood, President Erie Railroad, New York.

S. R. Callaway, President American Locomotive Works, New York City.

Charles A. Moore, President The Shaw Electric Crane Company, New York City.

Edward P. Ripley, President Atchison, Topeka & Santa Fe Railway System, Chicago.

J. Kruttschnitt, Vice-President Southern Pacific Company, San Francisco.

H. H. Vreeland, President National Street Railway Association, New York City.

Lewis Nixon, President United States Shipbuilding Company, New York City.

Samuel Mather, Picands, Mather & Co., Cleveland, O.

Charles H. Taylor, Jr., President American Publishers' Association, Boston.

Marcus M. Marks, President National Association of Clothing Manufacturers, New York City.

James A. Chambers, President American Window Glass Company, Pittsburgh.

William H. Pfahler, former President National Founders' Association, Philadelphia.

ON THE PART OF WAGE EARNERS.

Samuel Gompers, President American Federation of Labor, Washington.

John Mitchell, President United Mine Workers of America, Indianapolis.

Edgar E. Clark, Grand Chief Conductor, Order of Railway Conductors, Cedar Rapids, Iowa.

Theodore J. Shaffer, President Amalgamated Association of Iron, Steel and Tin Workers, Pittsburgh.

James Duncan, General Secretary Granite Cutters' National Union, Washington.

Daniel J. Keefe, President International Longshoremen's Association, Detroit.

James O'Connell, President International Association of Machinists, Washington.

Martin Fox, President Iron Molders' Union of North America, Cincinnati.

James M. Lynch, President International Typographical Union, Indianapolis.

J. J. Hannahan, Grand Master Brotherhood of Locomotive Firemen, Peoria, Ill.

Henry White, General Secretary United Garment Workers of America, New York.

William D. Mahon, President Amalgamated Association of Street Railway Employes of America, Detroit.

Denis A. Hayes, President Glass Bottle Blowers' Association of United States and Canada, Philadelphia.

William Huber, President United Brotherhood of Carpenters and Joiners of America, Indianapolis.

John Tobin, General President Boot and Shoe Workers' Union, Boston.

THE LABOR OUTLOOK.

While there has been the usual "spring crop" of petty strikes throughout the country, mostly in the building trades, the industrial situation is particularly free at this time of any national strikes. The textile strike at Lowell is local, and with the settlement of the Wabash and the New Haven and Hartford difficulties there passed away any danger of serious trouble among the railroad workers. The renewal of the agreement between the operators and the miners in the bituminous fields and the three years' award in the anthracite field furnish a stable situation in that universal necessity. The convention of the Amalgamated Iron, Steel and Tin Workers now in session is not expected to develop any unreasonable demands. With the coal and iron industries and the railroads free from troubles the manufacturing world has the assurance of a favorable labor outlook.

THE CONCILIATION COMMITTEE'S POWERS.

There is more or less misunderstanding as to the mode of procedure adopted by the Conciliation Committee of the Civic Federation in case of a strike, and surprise has several times been expressed because the committtee did not rush in at every strike that occurred. The confusion arises somewhat from the fact that in the case of State Boards it is made the duty by law to investigate, and in Massachusetts, New York, and several other States the power is given to subpœna witnesses and to compel the production of books. A voluntary board, however, has no power, and unless it proceeds with caution will be rebuffed by one side or the other, or by both sides, certainly by the side that thinks it can win if let alone. The method pursued by the committee is laid down in the by-laws, from which the following quotation is made:

The Committee of Conciliation shall upon notice from the Chairman of threatened strike or lockout of more than local magnitude use its good offices in restoring harmonious relations, reporting its action to the Executive Committee.

Should the efforts of the Conciliation Committee prove ineffective, and should both parties to the dispute desire the services of the Executive Committee of this Department, they may be invited to select two employers and two wage earners from said Executive Committee, to serve as an Arbitration Board. Should the four find it necessary to appoint an umpire to finally decide the dispute, they may select a fifth member from the group representing the public. Nothing in this Article shall be construed to prevent the Conciliation Committee from securing, when desirable, arbitrators outside or the Executive Committee.

MACHINISTS' ANNUAL CONVENTION.

The International Association of Machinists will hold its annual convention at Milwaukee May 4, and its official organ urges the selection of delegates with "cool and clear judgment" to handle the questions of great importance which are to come up. Among these are the piece work and premium systems, the shorter work day in the railway service, and the organization of the less skilled men in machine departments.

Piece work is strongly opposed by the Machinists' Union, and the constitution contains a clause to the effect that any member accepting piece work in any shop where it does not exist shall be subject to expulsion. The subject has been debated at every convention of the organization and is prominent in many of its disagreements with employers. At the recent conference of the National Civic Federation both sides of the question were forcibly presented by labor representatives, while the secretary of the machinists' organization in Great Britain, the Amalgamated Society of Engineers, advocated what he called the "safeguarded premium system," lately adopted by his society. In commenting on the attitude of the coming convention of the machinists toward piece and premium systems, the editor of their official journal says:

The way it will be settled means much for our organization. The *Journal* has always advocated its recognition and control as being the better way to settle the question. This has been demonstrated over and over again by the leading and most successful labor organizations of our time. If the organization acts wisely and conservatively it will adopt this policy with good grace. We must face the inevitable sooner or later.

A BUREAU OF INFORMATION.

In answering many requests for information regarding arbitration, trade agreements, organizations of employers and workmen, addresses of officers of such organizations, and similar subjects a bureau of information has gradually been established, which it is intended to enlarge in order to be made as widely useful as possible.

The MONTHLY REVIEW will contain answers to many of these inquiries, and a pamphlet is in preparation containing copies of the principal arbitration and trade agreement contracts. This will be furnished free when published, and will be followed by similar publications.

THE INDUSTRIAL DEPARTMENT, NATIONAL CIVIC FEDERATION.

The Industrial Department of the National Civic Federation was organized at a national conference held in Chicago under the auspices of that organization in December, 1900, and to a committee of twelve, styled the "Conciliation Committee of the National Civic Federation," was committed the work of promoting the movement. This provisional conciliation committee, however, after an experience gained in dealing with the threatened coal strike in March, 1901, in aiding in the settlement of the Albany street car strike in June of that year, and in the course of its efforts in the United States Steel strike which soon followed, discovered that it could be of permanent value only in so far as it was able to go below the surface and reach the causes of strikes and lockouts. Then it was that the more comprehensive title, the "Industrial Department," was adopted, the membership increased to three hundred and an Executive Committee of Thirty-Six chosen at the annual meeting December, 1901. At this meeting, in conformity with the larger view then taken, a broader programme, mainly educational, was laid out. It included—

First—Joint national conferences, where representative employers, labor leaders and men representing the general public would discuss face to face the various questions involved in the industrial disturbances so frequently arising.

Second—The publication and wide distribution of an industrial journal treating broadly of the same questions and promoting conciliation, arbitration, collective bargaining and a general spirit of broadness and fairness.

Third—The organization of local affiliated bodies in all large industrial centres, to be composed of the more conservative representatives of capital, labor and the public, which should not only act in case of local disturbances but serve as a medium through which the National Committee might reach a larger constituency.

Fourth—The organization of permanent boards of conciliation to use their good offices where possible before strikes should be declared and to endeavor to settle strikes under way.

It was conceded that if the United States is to maintain its commercial supremacy it must not be handicapped by industrial disturbances at home, but rather must "capital" and "labor" recognize that in the largest sense their interests are mutual, and that if American institutions and popular government are to have successful development they require as a first consideration a peaceable understanding between employers and workmen.

EDUCATIONAL WORK.

It was agreed that the large and in many respects more fundamental work of the committee would be that of inquiry and education regarding the causes of industrial disturbances. "Mutuality of interests" is the goal, but it must be worked out through solving such concrete questions as "fair wages," "shorter hours," "restriction of output," "minimum wage," "apprenticeship," "employment of non-unionists," "jurisdictional quarrels between unions," "sympathetic strikes," "boycotts," "piece work and premium systems of payment," "government by injunction," "the incorporation of unions," and similar practical questions.

Many of these questions arise in every dispute and every agreement between employers and employes. For instance, the Union Pacific Railroad has been confronted for several months by a general strike of machinists over the question of "piece work," and it is a "burning issue" in thousands of factories to-day, yet so little is it understood by the general public that in several letters received from prominent men referring to the programme of the annual meeting the word was spelled "peace" work. This question is so complicated that some unions differ diametrically from others upon it, and so do the employers. The question of "restricting output" is one of such vital importance to American industry that a thorough investigation is being made to determine just how much and what kind of restriction is imposed and what, if any, are the justifications. There can be no denial of the charge that some unions impose restrictions for no other apparent purpose than to make places for more men, while there are some restrictions that employers concede can be justified upon humanitarian principles. To solve such practical questions is to build a solid foundation for stable industrial conditions, and in no other way can it be done.

The Civic Federation, in line with this programme, has taken up these intricate human problems in its national conferences, as may be seen in the "Report" of the one held in New York, December, 1902. The widespread demand for this report, from labor leaders, superintendents, foremen and employers throughout the country is a proof of the serious attention now being given by practical men to such economic issues. This aroused interest has paved the way for the second part of the programme, the publication and distribution of this REVIEW, through which these problems may be further discussed in detail by those who are directly concerned therein.

That educational work with both employers and employes is the highest need of the hour is manifest to any one who has had experience in dealing with industrial troubles, and is well explained by the following utterances of representatives on each side:

A large employer who tried to perfect an organization of the firms of his industry whose purpose should be to deal with labor said to the writer after the first meeting of some sixty employers:

"I never saw such a narrow, selfish, ignorant set of men on labor matters as the ones we got together. They could not agree to any one proposition; each was suspicious of the other and was ready to go out of the room and knife every other member if he could gain some advantage thereby. Talk about 'fair' and 'intelligent' dealing with labor, they had not the first idea of it. Only one of them had ever heard of a joint trade agreement, and he was against it because he said he did not believe in discussing the matter of wages and hours with his employes, that being the province only of the directors of the corporation."

The need of this education for the workmen is well stated by Mr. Clarence S. Darrow, late counsel of the United Mine Workers before the Anthracite Coal Strike Commission, in a recent article in *Boyce's Weekly*. He says:

"Trade unionism was never in a more critical condition than it is to-day. The phenomenal growth of labor organizations within the last few months has brought into its ranks a large number of men who are utterly unfamiliar with the principles of trade unionism, and with the discipline that must go with organized labor. It has also brought into its ranks a large number of men who have no positive views in reference to trade unionism, and no sympathy with its principles; but who have joined the movement for the purpose of 'buying peace,' as many men join the church who are not positive believers in the Christian religion. Then, too, the power of trade unionism has caused many of its members and organizations to be arrogant and overbearing: to make unreasonable demands and to indulge in all sorts of trouble between themselves, and petty annoyances to employers and the public. This could not possibly be avoided, as labor organizations have grown so rapidly that the leaders have not been able to properly take care of the members and place them upon a substantial working basis. It will take a considerable time for this great mass of new recruits to be properly disciplined and thoroughly organized and made to understand the principles of trade unionism so that they may work in harmony with each other and for the interests of the general public.

"This condition has brought much adverse criticism to the trade union movement. Many kindly disposed people who wished to be favorable to trade unions have been subjected to petty annoyances, and have formed opinions hostile to labor unions, because they have not considered the difficulty encountered by labor leaders in bringing all these raw recruits into the labor organizations."

LOCAL ORGANIZATIONS.

The organization of the local branches provided for in the original programme was not begun until this spring, when the first one, the New York Council, was organized (in March, 1903). St. Louis, Chicago, Buffalo, Cleveland, Pittsburg, Philadelphia, Boston and Baltimore will be organized during the summer. These local councils promise to be important organs of the movement, for they come close to the rank and file of workers and employers on whom depend the execution of all plans for conciliation and education. They include the business agents and prominent members of local unions, as well as employers, "commissioners" of employers' associations, and representatives of "the public," and the work already done by the New York Civic Federation in dealing with a half-dozen strikes and threatened strikes is conclusive of the large field for usefulness of similar bodies in other industrial centres. Through these local committees it is possible to reach the men actually at work in factories, shops and mines, as well as their employers, and to bring to both sides the experience and assistance of those who have been longer in the work of conciliation and collective bargaining. It is expected that the REVIEW will furnish the needed means of communication between local Civic Federations throughout the country.

CONCILIATION COMMITTEE.

The Conciliation Committee, to deal with strikes and lockouts, was appointed in March, 1902. As disturbances of that character are always conspicuous the efforts of this committee became correspondingly conspicuous, and the public unfortunately, but naturally, gained the idea that the "Committee of Thirty-Six," so-called, was the entire organization and had been created only for arbitration purposes, it being frequently spoken of as a "Hague Commission," "Board of Arbitration," etc. But it was not contemplated that the Executive Committee, as a whole, should arbitrate anything; if so, it would have been organized on a different basis. The declaration of principles has only one reference to arbitration—namely, where all means of conciliation fail and both sides wish to avail themselves of the good offices of individual members of the committee. When a controversy reaches the arbitration stage there is generally no trouble in finding arbitrators. Only once in more than one hundred cases has the committee been asked to arbitrate a question. It is through conciliation and mediation that the committee has been able to do its best work, and it is a kind of work the purpose of which would be entirely defeated if given publicity. For instance, one of the "labor chiefs" notified the Federation officers that he was fearful a strike was imminent in his organization which would involve 12,000 men, unless he could get a conference with the representatives of the employers. He said he had written to the President asking for such an interview but had received no reply. A member of the Conciliation Committtee found a friend who was a director in this particular corporation, and as there was a meeting of the directors the next day he saw to it that this matter reached the board. The President was not averse to meeting the man on the score of principle, but he had not realized that it was important. The day after, the "labor chief" received a courteous reply to his request and an appointment for a conference. This occurred in due time, and the strike did not take place.

One day recently there were three conferences going on at the Civic Federation headquarters at the same time, one relative to an important controversy in San Francisco, another to one in New Orleans, and a third concerning New York. Two of these proved very successful and the third has been continued. In each case the parties in interest would have resented publicity of the questions in dispute, regarding them as of a character not yet passing beyond the limits of private business. Most of the work done by the Conciliation Committee is of this character.

Probably the committee's most valuable work, from a public standpoint, and yet the public knows little if anything about it, occurred in connection with the threatened sympathetic strikes during the steel strike of 1901 and the coal strike of 1902. Had either of these occurred all industries would undoubtedly have been tied up, with effects far more disastrous to the country than those that actually followed the original strikes. After the steel workers went out the coal miners and railroad men seriously threatened to follow. The Conciliation Committee at this juncture, through conferences in New York, Atlantic City, Pittsburg, Buffalo and Cleveland, succeeded not only in checking this movement but in enlisting national labor leaders in the work of bringing about a settlement. When the recent anthracite strike had aroused among the mine-workers such an enthusiastic sentiment toward sympathetic action in the bituminous field, the labor members of the Conciliation Committee, through conferences and field work in several States, joined in turning the current that led to that unanimous and notable declaration of the Indianapolis convention to stand by its contracts at all hazards.

All the educational work referred to is essential to another important function of the department, the promoting of what are known as "joint trade agreements" between associations of employers and associations of employes.

Such agreements now exist between twenty-five or more joint associations, and so successful have they proved that those best acquainted with their operations believe that it is along this line that "the way out" will eventually be found, and that as long as both organized capital and organized labor are permanent social factors the sooner they can be brought to recognize and deal with each other the better for all interests.

The work of the Conciliation Committee is unquestionably of great value and will increase in importance as its auxiliary committees are appointed in the large industrial centres to deal with local disturbances; yet the promotion of the "joint trade agreement" system, based upon the educational work outlined above, is probably the fundamental and most lasting work which can be done by the Industrial Department.

THE CONTENDING FORCES

The growing strength of labor organizations in the United States is something that employers and the public have come to recognize. Beginning as local unions in different cities, all of the different crafts, to the number of 120 or more, have effected national or international organizations, and 105 of these bodies have united in the American Federation of Labor. Local unions of the various trades of a single industry have also federated in local councils, such as those of the building trades, metal trades, marine trades, teamsters and clothing workers. There are also State federations and city central labor unions, composed of delegates from all crafts within their jurisdiction, and subordinate to the American Federation of Labor.

With this centralized organization of labor it becomes possible to put organizers in the field, in order to increase membership and multiply the number of local unions. The American Federation publishes a list of more than 1,000 salaried and unsalaried organizers throughout the country. It reports 1,608 local and "Federal" labor unions organized as feeders for existing and future national unions. The labor press has also had a remarkable growth, the national organizations usually having their official organs, supplemented by local papers, the entire number being nearly three hundred. Here is a well developed and powerful machine for agitation and co-operation, with increasing discipline over individuals and locals, all working to one purpose, "the increase of wages, the shortening of hours and the betterment of conditions."

The fact that membership in these labor organizations is variously estimated at only 10 to 15 per cent. of the total number of wage earners in the country should not be used to blind the observer to their influence. The great majority of unorganized wage earners are scattered in agriculture, in small towns and in domestic and personal service, but in several large concentrated industries, like the building trades and the textile mills, an organization often includes nearly all the workers, and in other industries, such as railroads, it includes nearly all the skilled workers, on whom the unskilled depend for employment. It is also frequently the case that non-unionists are in full sympathy and act with the union, as when the 8,000 organized anthracite mine workers in 1900 took out on strike nearly 140,000 men.

It is natural, and, indeed, inevitable, that the rise of such an organized power in American industry should lead employers also to organize in order to meet it. The Stove Founders' National Defense Association and the American Newspaper Publishers' Association, for example, are bodies of employers who deal respectively with the international unions of molders and the international union of compositors. Where the competitive field is narrower, as in the building trades, we have local associations, such as the Master Carpenters', Master Plumbers' and Master Painters' associations, to deal with the district councils of the Carpenters', Plumbers' and Painters' unions, and so on.

While these unions of employers are organized to negotiate with labor unions, by no means are they non-resistant and submissive associations. They are also equipped both to withstand and to attack the unions. They prepare themselves for strikes and lockouts; they accumulate a treasury and enforce discipline and strive to enlist every employer in their line of business. They prepare to meet force with equal force. But before going to these extremes they resort to negotiation and bargaining with the representatives of the unions, making trade agreements for one or more years, with provisions for settling disputes by conference or arbitration.

This policy is very different from that of another class of employers' associations which deal with labor problems and have sprung up in the last few years for the purpose of defending themselves against the "tyrannical and unjust demands of unions." The largest employers' organization of this class is that of the National Association of Manufacturers, which until a year ago was largely devoted to matters of commerce. It became interested in the labor situation through its vigorous and successful opposition to the "eight hour" and "anti-injunction" bills in the last session of Congress. Its hostile attitude is clearly shown in the annual address of its President at New Orleans, in indorsing the statement that organized labor is "a system which seems to be hopelessly and irredeemably bad, a bar to all true progress, a danger to the state and a menace to civilization." He follows this by saying:

> To my mind, this is not the proper time to talk conciliation. . . . Conciliation implies a yielding attitude and a recognition of the validity of destructive demands made by the opposing side. Since the principles and demands of organized labor are absolutely untenable to those believing in the individualistic social order, an attitude of conciliation would mean an attitude of compromise with regard to fundamental convictions. . . . Neither is it the time to talk arbitration or "joint agreements." To arbitrate questions of wages and hours is to introduce artificial methods of determining what they shall be, and an equitable arrangement as to either cannot be effected artificially. . . . The truth is that arbitration to employers means a surrender to the demands of labor as surely as yielding to them direct. Will the employers of this country allow the apparent peace, bought at the price of arbitration, lull them into a feeling of security? If they do, they will awaken some day to find their rights have been stolen while they slept. Arbitration is only putting off the day of reckoning. It means that more arbitrations are to follow, that the peace purchased in the first instance must be repurchased over and over again, and that the price paid will be higher each time. Does it not point to inevitable disaster? And is it not the course of wisdom to check an evil in its inception?

The Employers' Association of Dayton was organized for the specific purpose of "smashing the unions," and its President says: "The only way to settle a controversy with organized labor is to have absolutely no dealings with it." This organization has twenty or more branches, principally, if not entirely, in towns under 50,000 inhabitants, and claims to be rapidly growing.

The National Metal Trades Association is composed of several hundred employers. It formerly had a national agreement with the International Association of Machinists, but this was broken, and was followed by what is known as the Machinists' strike of 1901. The association deals with the machinists' organization in many localities, but, as a national organization, is more or less hostile to organized labor. The breaking of the contract in 1901 was deplored by the conservative element on both sides, and it is hoped by many that it will eventually be renewed, but the National Metal Trades Association cannot now fairly be classed with either the National Founders' Association or the National Association of Manufacturers.

A national anti-boycott association of employers was organized in New York last November. It is a secret organization, having for its purpose the defense of any member who is boycotted. The original idea was to have a fund of $500,000 ready to fight for any one of its members.

Numerous employers' associations are springing up in different localities, which, while they do not openly declare against organized labor, are largely in the control of employers who are more or less unfriendly.

Co-incident with this movement of employers is an organization styled the "National League of Independent Workmen of America," with headquarters at Elmira, N. Y., and locals in several places. This league is an organization of non-union men. It has recently been indorsed by the National Metal Trades Association.

Two of the above mentioned employers' associations, the National Association of Manufacturers and the National Metal Trades Association, publish periodicals, ably edited and largely devoted to attacks on organized labor. The Dayton organization has also announced the publication at an early date of an official organ.

The attitude of this extreme class of employers and employers' associations is quite similar to that of the extreme wing of the labor movement—the Socialists. Socialists denounce the unions and the leaders of the unions for entering into agreements with employers, just as extremists among employers denounce all movements looking toward dealing with unions. The Socialists affirm that the class struggle is irrepressible, and that the workingmen must fight their employers to the bitter end and make no compromise. There are also a number of labor organizations controlled by the Socialists which take similar ground respecting employers. The community of sentiment between the Socialists and this class of employers' associations appears plainly in an editorial in the Socialist *Daily People* (New York, April 7, 1903), commenting upon the foregoing extract from the annual address of the President of the National Manufacturers' Association. The Socialist editor says that the president is correct in holding that an "equitable arrangement" cannot be effected by the "artificial" method of conciliation or arbitration. An "equitable arrangement," he says, "can only be effected by allowing the class struggle full scope; and as a means to this end nothing is so much to be welcomed as the straight-out tactics" of that association. "Socialism," the editor concludes, "will triumph as a result."

If these two extreme wings of irreconcilables have their way the outcome will be either arbitrary control by labor or arbitrary control by capital. If all employers stood for intolerance and bigotry, or if all unions stood for tyrannical and unreasonable methods, the end would necessarily be a revolution. But the American people, as a whole, are not willing to enter upon such a permanent warfare of "capital" and "labor." They have enough practical sense to recognize conditions as they exist, and they have the courage and patience to deal with them. That there is a common ground where both employer and employe can meet with honor and satisfaction to each is amply proved by the success of existing national trade agreements as well as numerous local agreements. One of the national employers' associations now a party to a trade agreement was organized for the purpose of destroying the union, much like the new associations just mentioned, but after three or four years' experience it decided in favor of the greater advantages of a treaty with the union. Another employers' association was organized at the request of the union itself. Whatever their origin they all now recognize the right of organization on both sides and the advantages of "collective bargaining."

JOINT TRADE AGREEMENTS

At three national conferences on conciliation and arbitration held under the auspices of the National Civic Federation resolutions were adopted recommending the system of "joint trade agreements" as the most satisfactory method of securing industrial peace. The conference of December, 1900, issued an address containing the following:

> To the end that tranquillity in the industrial world may prevail, this Conference on Conciliation and Arbitration would make the following recommendations to the American people:
>
> First—That employers and wage-earners should enter into annual or semi-annual agreements or contracts.
>
> Second—That all industries in the United States should establish boards of conciliation within the several and varied interests, to which boards of conciliation all differences and disputes arising between employer and employe, if not readily adjusted between the immediate interests concerned, may be referred for settlement.

The National Committee appointed at the convention of 1900, in a statement of purpose, scope and method for the prevention of industrial disturbances, expressed this opinion:

> Trade agreements between employers and workmen where established for a definite term of years have so fully demonstrated their value in maintaining industrial peace that they should be generally adopted.

The Committee of Thirty-Six appointed at the conference of December, 1901, also adopted a "statement of purpose," which declared—

> That mutual agreements as to conditions under which labor shall be performed should be encouraged, and that when agreements are made, the terms thereof should be faithfully adhered to, both in letter and spirit, by both parties.

"Industrial peace," "harmony of capital and labor," "arbitration," "conciliation," all somewhat vague and indefinite terms, indicate in general a hope that strikes and lockouts may be avoided, but a "trade agreement" has come to indicate a definite and specific method, which, above all others, leads to the realization of this hope. The resolutions and policy of the National Civic Federation in this regard are not based merely on theoretical grounds, but are the result of experience in various industries through a period long enough to bring conviction to those who have participated in the work. It is not asserted that by means of trade agreements all the problems of employe and employer may be solved, nor even that a trade agreement can readily be framed and faithfully observed in any and every industry. Chauncey H. Castle, President of the Stove Founders' National Defense Association, speaking of twelve years' practical working under agreements with the Iron Molders' Union, said a year ago: "The results have been satisfactory beyond all former expectation of possibilities, and it is my impression, gathered from such experience, that a strong organization of workmen which is of age sufficient to have participated in many strikes and lockouts, which is officered by skillful and earnest men, who have at heart the best interests of their constituents, can and will hold out and maintain agreements made with employers or with organizations of employers." Unfortunately, several of the existing trade agreements were entered on only after prolonged strikes and lockouts as a means of preventing such disasters in the future. But there are indications that the lesson of these experiences is being observed in other industries, and that in the future there may be expected an increasing number of trade agreements without the preliminary test of a general strike or lockout.

A successful trade agreement system presupposes organization on both sides—a union of workmen and a union of employers. The agreement is made by the representatives of each side, and there can be no representation without organization. This does not necessarily mean that the two organizations shall be incorporated in order that their agreements may be enforced by the courts. Hitherto incorporation has been effected by very few, if any, of the associations, either of employers or workmen, that have successfully carried out trade agreements. More important than incorporation is strong organization on each side. There always will be found individual employers and individual workmen or unions that will break an agreement if they can. These may be held in check whenever they belong to an organization which covers a large part of the industry. An agreement between an organization of employers and an organization of workmen is backed by the machinery and the power to enforce observance. In the thirteen years of the Iron Molders' and Stove

Founders' agreements there has not been a contract violation nor a strike or lockout, except occasionally in a single shop, soon settled by the national officers of the two organizations. The bituminous coal operators testify to the integrity and even sternness of the district and national officers of the United Mine Workers in compelling local unions to live up to the annual interstate and district agreements. These officers, as in all labor unions, have power to fine and expel members and to revoke the charters of local bodies that interfere with the enforcement of trade contracts.

The longshoremen's organization in their contracts with the dock managers on the Great Lakes have occasionally been called upon to discipline their members for violations, and in the case of the Buffalo strike in 1900 the International President, after revoking the charter of the local union and supplying the places of a majority of the strikers with union men from other locals, filled the remaining places with non-union men. Mr. Samuel Mather, of the Dock Managers' Association, which includes such firms as the Standard Oil Company, the United States Steel Company, M. A. Hanna & Co., says regarding their agreements with the Longshoremen's Union:

I am very happy to be able to testify that since that continuous arrangement was inaugurated, about three years ago, our business has been conducted with very great advantage compared with what prevailed before. . . . If any occasion of dispute arises, it has not caused the work to terminate, but it has been first locally settled, if possible, and if occasion necessitated has gone up to the chief council. That has worked satisfactorily, as I say, for three years, and is a great improvement over the arrangement, or rather lack of arrangement, that existed before. I can testify a little as to the improvement, for before that, as I said at first, each dock claimed different wages, frequently different terms, and it had to be fought out individually.

Every successful trade agreement contains an arbitration or adjustment clause which provides that where there is an alleged violation the representatives of the two parties shall be called in to decide and interpret the agreement. An essential part of this clause is the requirement that there shall be no strike nor lockout pending investigation and appeal. The officers of the union and the commissioner of the employers' association, who together investigate local troubles, are usually able to reach a decision without calling in a third party, and this unanimity goes far toward bringing united action of both associations in dealing with the offending member.

One of the permanent advantages of the trade agreement system is the influence which organized employers can have in improving the organization of the workmen. As long as employers are hostile, or as long as an association of employers exists solely to fight the union, the latter is forced to put forward its fighting men. But when employers organize for conference and agreement, and are able to remove the long standing suspicions of the workmen, a change comes in union leadership. The officers become negotiators and bargainers—business men, like their employers. The Anthracite Coal Strike Commission, after five months' investigation of labor conditions in the coal regions, reached this conclusion on that point:

Experience shows that the more full the recognition given to a trade union the more business-like and responsible it becomes. Through dealing with business men in business matters its more intelligent, conservative and responsible members come to the front and gain general control and direction of its affairs. If the energy of the employer is directed to discouragement and repression of the union he need not be surprised if the more radically inclined members are the ones most frequently heard.

This conclusion of the strike commission is nowhere more vividly emphasized than in the attitude of labor leaders regarding the coal strike itself. When large numbers of the rank and file had demanded a sympathetic strike of the bituminous miners, who were working under agreements with their employers, Mr. Henry White, secretary of the United Garment Workers of America, in addressing the miners' representatives, wrote:

The desperate expedient of a general strike every one would regard as sheer madness, because it would only intensify the distress, impose great suffering upon non-combatants without rendering any direct aid to those now involved. It would shake confidence in organized labor and create a feeling that it cannot be trusted with power; that the good it may do will be more than offset by the harm. Besides, the violation of agreements, which such an act implies, would be a blow at the integrity of the labor movement, from which it could not hope to recover. If the unions are to ignore agreements whenever it is to their advantage, the other side would be justified in doing likewise, and consequently they would have no binding force, and there would be no method by which understandings could be carried out and peace insured for stated periods. As agreements are the means by which employers are held to the terms conceded to the workers, the vitiating of the principle of agreements would be far more detrimental to the workers than to the employers.

Mr. John Mitchell, President of the Mine Workers' organization, in addressing the convention called to consider the petition for a sympathetic strike, took the same ground, and his advice prevailed. He said:

I have during all my life in the labor movement declared that contracts mutually made should during their life be kept inviolate, and while at times it may appear to the superficial observer or to those immediately concerned that advantage could be gained by setting agreements aside, such advantage, if gained, would in the very nature of things be temporary, and would ultimately result in disaster, because a disregard of contracts strikes at the very vitals of organized labor. The effect of such action would be to destroy confidence, to array in open hostility to our cause all forces of society, and to crystallize public sentiment in opposition to our movement.

The elevating effects of the agreement system upon the intelligence and character of the union leaders is clearly shown in a communication received from Mr. Francis L. Robbins, President of the Pittsburg Coal Company, in writing of the sixth annual joint convention of operators and mine workers of the interstate bituminous field, held at Indianapolis in February, 1903. He says:

Looking back over the recent convention, and comparing it with the conventions held at the inception of the movement, one is struck by the change in the personnel of the miners' delegates. Instead of seeing flannel shirts, hob-nail shoes, no vests and often no coats, you meet a body of men as well dressed as any body of men gathered from the middle class in any Eastern city. There has been a corresponding change in the intelligence, as shown in the faces of the delegates, and particularly perceptible to those who have argued scale questions before these meetings for the past fifteen years. It is a critical audience of practical workmen, who are quick to detect sophistry or misleading statements. It used to be that the discussion of questions before the convention was quite general, but it is now confined to a few leaders on both the operators' and miners' sides. The discussion is for the purpose of molding opinion, but the result is reached in the scale committee, which is composed of an equal number of operators and miners, subject, however, to the indorsement of the joint convention, which under the rules requires the unanimous indorsement of the operators and miners of each State represented. That these agreements are to be considered sacred and inviolate was settled in the miners' convention of last July, when by unanimous vote the miners declared against any sympathetic strike and in favor of a strict observance of contract agreements.

The heads of nearly every association of employers who have had experience in trade agreements will say of the union officers as Colonel Frederick Driscoll, Commissioner of the American Newspaper Publishers' Association, says of the typographical and pressmen's officers: "I have always found the International Presidents ever ready to co-operate with me in adjusting differences and settling trouble when it first arises. By means of this policy of mutual conciliation, it is gratifying to be able to state that since the establishment of our industrial bureau there has not been a single strike in any one of the offices of our members, covering a period of two years and eight months;" or as Mr. H. W. Hoyt, ex-President of the National Founders' Association, says of the iron molders: "The consequence has been that a more experienced, intelligent and tolerant body of men have been called into action, and that the rank and file of union men are rapidly becoming educated to the new method of dealing with their affairs individually and collectively, while the manufacturers have been educated to a more liberal and just consideration of the employes' interests." Mr. Hoyt also says, speaking to fellow employers:

As long as the wage-earner believes, or is taught to assume, that society is in league to rob him, as an individual, of some of the purchasing power of his services, so long must society reckon with him in his collective capacity. The employer who elects to ignore this fact is often as much of a menace to the industrial peace as is the agitator who plays upon the prejudices and inflames the passions of the men he falsely serves. But the conditions are improving on both sides. The progressive manufacturer has learned that a union is not an altogether reprehensible evil in social economics, and readily admits that when organized wage-earners are dominated by strong, conservative men they will meet the employer half-way in arbitration.

When the two organizations have reached the point of mutual confidence they are prepared to take up the alleged abuses of labor unions and to deal with them effectively. The National Founders and the Iron Molders, in addition to their regular joint conferences, have recently instituted other conferences on questions of apprentices, restriction of output, limitation of a man's earning capacity, the flat minimum wage and other issues of a similar nature. While these conferences have not always led to practical results, yet, as stated by the president of the association, Mr. Frederick T. Towne, "they have been educational to both parties, and, as such, have been of great value. Progress has been slow, but none the less sure, and the disposition evidenced by both sides to give full consideration to the claims of the other and the openly expressed desire to reach a settlement on the many points of difference which will be mutually acceptable is the best assurance that the day is not far distant when many of these issues will be adjusted to the satisfaction of both organizations."

As an evidence of the solicitude shown by national officers of unions for the proper education of their members in the enforcement of agreements, the practice of the International Longshoremen's Union is significant. In order that every one of the 70,000 members of the association may be fully informed as to the terms of the joint agreement under which he is working, each is furnished with a copy of the agreement in book form, printed in his own language, and the rules of the organization require that he must have a copy with him at all times while at work, so that if a question arises he can consult his book of agreement and see what is expected of him.

The practical operations of the trade agreement systems disprove the criticism that they mean a surrender to unjust or uneconomic demands of labor. This criticism is based on a confusion of the term "arbitration" with that of "joint trade agreement." In the case of arbitration a third party, believed to be disinterested, is called in, and he is often tempted to "split the difference" without reference to the merits of the case, but as an easy way out of it. But joint trade agreements are almost never determined in this way. It is usually only where the public is forced to take a hand, as in the anthracite coal strike, or where the terms of the agreement are to be interpreted in case of its alleged violation that a third party is sometimes, but not often, called in. It is exactly because the third party inclines to compromise that the two parties to the agreement provide their own committees for investigation when a dispute arises, with the object of making a finding on its merits. In the case of the stove manufacturers their findings have frequently resulted in a decrease of wages instead of the increase demanded by the workmen, and on this account the employes have learned to be careful in repeating such demands.

The different trade agreement systems in the United States are, of course, not all identical in detail, though in essential points, such as provision for arbitration, all are alike. Some differences arise from the nature of the industry or the conditions of the unions. The Amalgamated Association of Iron and Steel Workers, the first organization to secure a national system, beginning in 1865, made its agreements with different associations of iron and steel manufacturers. When these were all incorporated in the Republic Iron and Steel Company and the United States Steel Corporation the Amalgamated Association continued to make separate agreements with the two great consolidated bodies.

The trade agreement is not new. As early as 1874 coal miners' unions and coal operators made agreements, which with the disruption of the unions were discontinued, but they were revived on a much larger scale in 1898, when the United Mine Workers secured its first agreement with the bituminous coal operators in the four States, Ohio, Indiana, Illinois and Pennsylvania. The Iron Molders' Union entered into its first agreement with the Stove Founders' National Defense Association in 1891 and with the National Founders' Association in 1898. The longshoremen on the great lakes secured their first agreement with the dock managers in 1898.

Agreements are more widespread than is commonly known. The Lithographers' International Association has agreements with associations of employes, and the Glass Bottle Blowers' Association of the United States and the Flint Glass Workers' Union have for many years had agreements with associations of manufacturers. The great railroad brotherhoods have many agreements with individual railway systems.

Another class of agreements is that made by local unions guaranteed by the international union. This is the characteristic of the two agreements between the International Typographical Union and the Pressmen's Union on the one side and the National Publishers' Association on the other. The national agreement stipulates the terms on which the local agreements shall be made, and the two associations guarantee their enforcement. Similar to these are the agreements made by the United Garment Workers of America, the Boot and Shoe Workers' Union, the United Hatters of North America, the United Brewery Workers, and the International Cigar Makers' Union, in all of which, in return usually for the privilege of using the label, and for the obligation on the part of the union to keep the employer fully supplied with all the help required, it is provided that only union members shall be employed. The United Garment Workers in January, 1903, for the first time, made a written agreement with an association of employers, the National Wholesale Tailors' Association. The Garment Workers have also a system of conferences and verbal agreements with the National Clothiers' Association. The Amalgamated Association of Street Railway Employes is guarantor to agreements with companies entered upon by local unions, but recently in instances the National Association itself has made agreements directly. The International Association of Machinists enforces some 2,000 local agreements.

There are a large number of local agreements in the building trades in various cities, twenty-four unions in New York City having agreements with associations, as is the case with a large proportion of the unions in San Francisco, Chicago and other cities.

These are the leading agreement systems at present in operation in the United States, and the testimony of both employers and workmen indicates that in dealing with the problem of organized labor they have been remarkably successful, often far beyond the expectations of those who first entered upon them.

It is the conviction of members of the National Civic Federation that in placing trade agreements foremost in the plans for industrial peace and in basing these trade agreements on the educational work outlined in a preceding article, its programme is in the highest degree constructive rather than destructive. Instead of retarding the advance of organized capital and labor, this association joins with those who would reach a higher state of industrial civilization through a system of agreements which recognize the power and the rights of these great contending forces. Its members are not averse to criticising whatever is false and mistaken in the methods of each, but have the larger purpose of making both really responsible and worthy of mutual confidence.

THE SYMPOSIUM ON INCORPORATION OF LABOR UNIONS.

With the apparently increasing power of trade unions it is to be expected that a demand should arise for their proportionate responsibility. The grounds of this demand vary, but they usually turn on different meanings of the word responsibility, as will be seen in our symposium on the incorporation of unions. Some of our contributors advocate incorporation in order to hold the unions responsible for violation of contracts; others do so with the intention of fixing responsibility on them for unlawful acts—known legally as "torts." The latter group is again to be sub-divided accordingly as the members have in mind the acts of different parties in varying conditions—some contemplating the acts of officers and members authorized by the union; others the acts of members unauthorized by the union; and still others the acts of sympathizers not members and not authorized by the union.

Certain of the legal contributors to the symposium hold that for illegal acts—"torts"—such as trespass, intimidation, boycott, violence, etc., authorized by the union or its officers, the unions can already, even though not incorporated, be held legally responsible to the extent of their treasuries, and also that each member of the union can be held legally responsible to the extent of his private estate. They also hold that the incorporation of the union would not relieve the individual member of legal responsibility for illegal acts. Incorporation "would not in the least protect individual leaders and members from being 'joined' as defendants in suits for damages for conspiracies and other 'torts.'" (Adams.) Incorporation "will not relieve the individual members of the corporation from responsibility likewise." (Bonaparte.) According to these views incorporation of a union would not increase its responsibility for illegal acts of its members.

One of the employers (Seitz), however, seems to hold that by incorporation the union could be held for illegal acts done by sympathizers in the prosecution of a strike. Other contributors hold exactly the opposite view, that incorporation would relieve the union of liability for damages inflicted in its interests (Eliot), and the only answer received from an incorporated union cites this as the main advantage gained by incorporation. (Grossman.) Extending responsibility of a corporation to cover the unauthorized acts either of members or non-members does not seem to be advocated by the legal writers, and they hold that an unincorporated union would not be held in damages for the unlawful acts of members or non-members committed in sympathy with the union's cause, but without authorization from the union or its officers. This does not apply to the acts of officers themselves, since their acts are held to be those of the union. One employer (Miller) holds that what society and employers want is not damages from unions for injuries unlawfully inflicted, but restraint from committing these unlawful acts, and this, he says, can be had through the injunction.

The other kind of responsibility is for violation of contracts. Those who desire it hold that employers cannot enter on contracts with unions on fair terms, because, while the employer is financially and legally responsible, the union is only morally responsible. Here, again, two very different kinds of responsibility are in view. The one responsibility is for individual members, the other for joint action of all the members. One contributor (Seitz) seems to maintain that the union should be held financially liable for a violation of contract by a member who, for example, leaves his work without consent of his employer. This would seem to be a kind of responsibility which very few unions would care to assume, and it is a misapprehension of the whole nature of a union agreement with employers. By such an agreement the union would become a contractor to farm out labor. Certain unions, such as the Garment Workers and the Longshoremen, agree to furnish what labor is required by the employer, but they relieve themselves of the usual responsibility of a contractor by a proviso that the employer may hire non-members if the union cannot supply the force required. But this class of union contracts is exceptional. Union agreements are not contracts to furnish labor; each laborer makes his own labor contract directly with his employer. The union agreement is simply an understanding by which the parties represented agree to make similar contracts respecting hours, wages and work. The employer enforces his side of the agreement through his right to discharge the workman, and the union enforces its side by its right to strike. One employer (Miller) fears that should the unions thus become contractors to farm out labor, as do the Chinese companies, their greatly increased power would be productive of more harm than good, and would not tend to improve the character of the working man; and, on the other hand, if they should not become contractors for labor their responsibility could be easily evaded, even though they were incorporated.

Other contributors hold the customary view that the union should be held responsible only for the joint action of its members, such as a stoppage of work by a strike, or the support of a member who violates his agreement. Here the question arises, Would incorporation of unions lessen the number of strikes in violation of agreements not to strike? Answering this in the affirmative, several writers refer to the probable added feeling of responsibility on the part of leaders and members which would come through incorporation. Others, replying in the negative, point out the very small funds in the union treasuries. (Stainsby.) But more generally it is held that incorporation is not necessary in order to promote the observance of contracts. Several union representatives assert that unions do not violate their agreements and that only employers do. Others do not go so far. One employer, a prominent member of the National Founders and the Stove Founders' Association (Pfahler) argues that where employers free themselves of sentimental opposition to trade unions and then deal with their agents on a business basis, the unions are in a better position to be held accountable. Other contributors (Hanna, Brooks) strongly urge that the trade agreement is the proper substitute for incorporation. A statistician (Weber) asserts that nearly all violations occur in the field of agreements with individual employers, and that there have been very few violations of trade agreements made between associations of employers and associations of workmen. Certain union representatives admit the lack of discipline within some unions, but hold that all are gradually being educated to higher standards and that this education will be the more rapid as employers show a greater willingness to make and observe agreements.

Supposing it is not necessary to have incorporation in order to compel unions to abide by their contracts, the converse proposition is presented by a union representative (White), who contends that unions, even if incorporated, cannot secure damages from employers who violate their contracts with the unions. Referring to the experience of the Garment Workers, who have brought suits on bonds given by employers, he argues that the employer can raise in defense the plea of duress, since he was compelled, in view of the alternative of seeing his business ruined, to agree to the terms laid down by the unions. On the other hand, a representative of another branch of the clothing industry (Grossman), whose union is incorporated, states that the legality of their contracts has been sustained in the courts; but a former counsel of this union (Hourwich) thinks the union would have fared better if it had given up its corporate organization.

The objections raised to incorporation by the unions are, of course, first of all, the liability of exposing their treasuries to attack. But if the trend of legal answers is correct, as stated, these treasuries are already liable for unlawful acts even without incorporation, and there is even an intimation (Adams) that they are also liable for violations of contract.

If this be true the danger which the unions may meet through incorporation must be found elsewhere. Several writers (Frankenheimer, Sullivan, Williams, Weber) contend that the real danger lies in the internal affairs of the union. The union must have almost arbitrary control over its members in the way of discipline, and were it incorporated its constitution and by-laws would be subject to judicial inquiry, and it would be continually in court on suits brought by dissatisfied or expelled members, oftentimes instigated by employers. It is pointed out (Frankenheimer) that the New York Stock Exchange, under advice of the ablest legal talent, avoids incorporation in order that it may enforce complete discipline upon its members without interference by the courts.

Some of the writers (Perkins, Williams) fear also that judicial interference would operate against the democratic character of union management, would do away with the initiative and referendum and would make the directors and officers powerful and oligarchic. This result would stand in the way of growth in membership, which would be unfortunate both to the unions and to society. To incorporate the unions would drive them into politics and a crude form of Socialism. (Brooks.)

There is a curious contrast in the opinions regarding the attitude of the courts. The union spokesmen in general speak of the hostility of the courts to unions and their bias toward the employers, mentioning the interstate commerce and anti-trust laws as having been perverted from their original object to the injury of unions. Yet some of the employers speak of the whole machinery of justice in our State courts as paralyzed by fear of the union vote. Not more law is needed, they say, but more honest and courageous enforcement of the laws as they are (Miller), and incorporation would not add responsibility, since prosecuting attorneys, judges and juries would, through their sympathies with the unions, temper the laws even more than now.

Other contributors, while not emphasizing the attitude of the courts toward either side, believe that their tedious processes place the unions at a disadvantage. At present there is a disparity between the treasuries of unions and corporations, the latter having an unlimited call on high-priced legal counsel.

Of those who answer the question as to the need of a special law for the incorporation of unions, the legal writers all agree that such a law is necessary, but there is only one writer (Hourwich) who offers suggestions as to its necessary provisions. One union officer (Clark) would have the benefit funds separated from the other funds, and would have the union exempt from responsibility for the personal acts of members in violation of law. It is pointed out (Cooke) that the federal law providing for the incorporation of unions exempts members as well as the corporation itself from liability for "the acts of members or others in violation of law." Other contributors think it would be difficult and even impossible to frame a special law making the union responsible for authorized acts and not responsible for unauthorized acts.

Compulsory incorporation is rejected by all who refer to it, one legal writer (Mayer) pointing out that it would be equivalent to prohibiting workmen from enjoying the liberty of the citizen, the freedom of contract, and the right of free assembly.

Finally, several union representatives dismiss the whole subject by boldly asserting that, whatever the arguments presented, the unions *will not* incorporate. This assertion is hardly vital, since it is conceivable that a special law could be so framed that the unions would choose incorporation as an alternative to increasingly drastic decisions against them when not incorporated. One writer (Lloyd) suggests that under a compulsory arbitration law, like those of New Zealand and Australia, the unions would find a decided advantage in incorporation.

The symposium as a whole seems to indicate that the customary arguments for and against incorporation of unions are invalid, since they turn on the responsibility of unions for unlawful acts. Incorporation would not increase or decrease their responsibility in this respect. Both the treasury of the union and the property of the members are liable in damages on account of such acts whether the union is incorporated or unincorporated. In this respect the symposium is a valuable contribution on the subject.

As regards the enforcement of contracts, the opinions in the symposium are at wide variance, both from the standpoint of the union in enforcing the agreement upon employers and from the standpoint of employers in enforcing the agreement upon the workmen. That existing laws governing corporations are not adapted to the needs of labor unions is generally admitted in the suggestion that special laws should be enacted for the purpose. These suggestions and propositions will be submitted to the meeting of the Executive Committee of the National Civic Federation in May for such action as may be decided upon in the way of further investigation and reports by a special committee on labor legislation.

THE ANTHRACITE COAL STRIKE AWARD.

BY JOHN R. COMMONS.

The report and award of the Anthracite Coal Strike Commission is generally recognized as the most important document ever issued on the modern labor question. It is such, not because it grants an advance in wages or a reduction in hours, but because it frames a constitution for the government of a great industry.

A distinction must be made between the "report" of the Commission and its "award." The report includes a general discussion of the rights and duties of unions and employers, but the award deals with the situation at hand. They are in contrast at three or four points. The report states that the evidence does not show that wages are lower than those in the bituminous field or in other occupations requiring equal skill and training, yet the award grants an increase of 10 to 20 per cent. in wages. The report argues against recognition of the existing union, but the award grants it actual recognition. The report declines to recommend a trade agreement, but the award is itself a trade agreement. The report rejects compulsory arbitration, but the award is the result of practically compulsory arbitration. On one large issue—the rights of the non-union workmen—the report and award coincide.

Although the commission stated in its report that the question of recognition of the United Mine Workers of America was not within its jurisdiction, yet it was confronted by a definite situation. It was required to provide a settlement that would prevent strikes for three years, but its own existence would terminate at once. It had no authority to create a permanent government commission to interpret the award whenever disputed; neither could it leave the enforcement of the award to the employer through the ordinary process of dismissing the workman who disobeys, because the union had already taken from the employer his unlimited right to dismiss. Here was a new self-governing power in the anthracite industry, and this power had to be enlisted to hold its members to the award. The United Mine Workers of America had divided the anthracite field into three districts. With these divisions in view the award says:

> If there shall be a division of the whole region into three districts, in each of which there shall exist an organization representing a majority of the mine workers of such districts, one of said board of conciliation shall be appointed by each of said organizations, and three other persons shall be appointed by the operators, the operators in each of said districts appointing one person.

This is a common-sense recognition of conditions as they exist. The board of conciliation, thus constituted with equal representation of the mine workers' union and the operators, is the permanent court to which all disagreements respecting the award, and all disagreements not covered by the award, must be appealed. This board is similar to those already created in the voluntary systems of trade agreements, and is such as would necessarily have been created in the anthracite field had the operators recognized the union of their own accord. Should the board be unable to decide an appeal, it must be referred to an umpire, appointed, at the request of the board, by the Federal Judge designated in the award. Meanwhile there must be no lockout or strike. These are the usual provisions in the voluntary systems, with the single exception that the choice of umpire is prescribed in advance. It is evidently expected that when this board of conciliation gets into working order very few, if any, points will need to be referred to the umpire.

In the section of the award relating to the non-union workmen the commission deals with the most difficult problem of the whole situation. It says:

> No person shall be refused employment, or in any way discriminated against on account of membership or non-membership in any labor organization; and there shall be no discrimination against or interference with any employe who is not a member of any labor organization by members of such organization.

By the award the non-unionists get the advance in pay granted to the unionists, many of them without the expense and suffering of the strike, and without contributing to support the union. This, as recognized by the Commission, provokes hostility toward them. But by the award the non-unionists can look only to the employer for protection, since he has no representative on the board of conciliation. The employer can protect him only while at work, and only the law, as the Commission recognizes when condemning the boycott, can protect him outside the colliery. On the other hand, the employer is forbidden to discriminate in his favor as against the unionist. On the whole, the entire award in no way diminishes the strength of the union, and if the union adopts certain recommendations of the report the award will serve to strengthen it.

These recommendations are for a diminished voice of boys in the affairs of the locals, a two-thirds vote instead of a majority, and vote by ballot instead of show of hands in ordering a strike. If the award is faithfully obeyed and the parties thereby learn to deal with each other through the board of conciliation, and if the above recommendations are adopted by the union, the hope of the Commission will be well grounded that a voluntary trade agreement will in due time commend itself to both sides.

A Business Conference.

The Stove Manufacturers' Association and the Iron Molders of North America met in their sixteenth joint annual session last month and after a week's conference unanimously readopted the scale of the previous year. The Molders demanded a 10 per cent. increase, but, as is their practice, the two organizations took up the matter and settled it in a business manner.

Iron Workers' Referendum.

At the Toronto Convention of the Iron Molders' Union of Northern America last September a resolution was adopted instructing the incoming officers to refuse to allow their names to be used in connection with the National Civic Federation.

This resolution has been submitted to a referendum vote initiated by the Iron Molders' Conference Board of New York and Vicinity.

The vote has not yet been received from all the local unions, but it is learned that the returns at hand indicate that the Toronto resolution will be rescinded by a very large majority.

THE CHICAGO BOARD OF ARBITRATION.

(Concluded from Page 9.)

By resolutions passed by the Teamsters' Joint Council March 27 this law was thenceforth to be rigidly observed. It is that no local union shall go on a sympathetic strike unless with the approval of two-thirds of the local unions in the vicinity of the point at which the strike is in progress, or of two-thirds of a joint council where one is organized. An individual member violating this law is to have charges preferred against him, and a local union is to be subjected to discipline by the National Executive Board. President Young declared: "We shall show no mercy to any teamster or any local that dares to go on a sympathetic strike which we have not indorsed. This constant striking has got to cease." Four unions the same night asked the council for aid in strikes, but were all refused. They were offered the services of the teamsters to procure arbitration, which they were constrained to accept. When one of the four cases came up, President Young asked the committee if the union would arbitrate. The reply was: "We have nothing to arbitrate." A teamster called out: "Then we have nothing to do with you." The committee thereupon changed front and expressed a desire to meet the employers through President Young, who consented to act for them. The Council had determined that the teamsters' unions were not to be used to win strikes unless all honorable means to bring about a settlement had been exhausted.

Albert Young, president of the Teamsters' National Union of America, the recognized leader of the workers' representative on the board, is at the head of nearly 35,000 organized teamsters in Chicago. He is cool, calm and shrewd. Himself a coal team driver in Chicago for years, he was active in forming a union of coal teamsters about three years ago. The move proved speedily successful. To-day in Chicago every teamster, from the garbage man to the undertaker's driver is in a union. As a worker and organizer Mr. Young is tireless.

The seven business men members of the Chicago Board of Arbitration are of stable reputation in the commercial world. Among the more prominent is Harry G. Selfridge, the chairman. For many years he has been manager of the retail house of Marshall Field & Co. Mr. Selfridge is popular with both the millionaire and the workingman, and through his personality and wide acquaintance has been instrumental in bringing the right men together, man fashion, to promote peace. The fact that busy men will give their time to the patient adjudication of labor contests is fresh proof of the love of fair play and the readiness to strive for the public good always characteristic of notable elements in American Society.

Chicago feels the better for the existence of the board. The ideas on which it is founded, the steps by which it proceeds in bringing about peace, are attracting attention in every city in the United States. The labors of the board have served to prove that the judicial quality is to be found among men in every walk of life. The board in its various branches, of which, as has been said, there are at present seven, is capable of quickly taking hold of any form of the work for which it was organized. That is to say, Chicago is responding with heart and brain to the most recent demand for a public duty.

OFFICERS OF THE NATIONAL CIVIC FEDERATION

CORNELIUS N. BLISS
Treasurer

SAMUEL GOMPERS
First Vice-Chairman

MARCUS A. HANNA
Chairman

OSCAR S. STRAUS
Second Vice-Chairman

RALPH M. EASLEY
General Secretary

JURISDICTIONAL ARBITRATION IN THE NEW YORK UNITED BOARD OF BUILDING TRADES.

Among the obstacles that block the road to an understanding between employers and employed few are more vexatious to either side than "jurisdictional quarrels" between unions. The employer may wish to give work to union workmen, and union workmen may want his work, but that is not enough. Another question yet arises: To which union shall the work be allotted? The various subdivisions of an industry being each organized separately, the dividing line is in many cases not easy to draw. In this matter there has been difficulty in probably every city in this country. How the problem is being worked out in practice is shown in one notable instance by the experience of the New York United Board of Building Trades.

For six years prior to March 11, 1902, the unions of the New York building trades were divided into two unfriendly consolidated bodies. The one sent representatives to the Board of Delegates, the other to the Building Trades Council. United in the Board were the trades engaged mostly in outside work—the housesmiths, brownstone cutters, granite cutters, derrickmen, sheet metal workers, bricklayers and their laborers, cement layers and their laborers, and the encaustic tile layers; in the Council were mostly inside trades—painters and decorators, carpenters and joiners, electrical workers, marble mosaic workers, plasterers, steam and hot water fitters.

The employing builder suffered acutely from this division. In the morning he might arrange as to wages and workday with the business agents of the outside men only to have the agents of the inside men make conflicting demands in the afternoon. The unions claimed overlapping jurisdictions, each agent energetically seeking work for his own members. The employer who had decided to give work only to union men not infrequently failed to hire them, as two unions, each claiming a part of his work, would strike against each other. As a consequence, the Board might bar the Council's men or the Council declare war on the Board. Cessations of work by large forces of workmen through these causes were of almost weekly occurrence. Construction on some of the largest of New York's great modern buildings came to a standstill, not because of lockouts, low wages, employment of non-union men, not even on a question of unionism, but through the counter-claims of clashing unions.

Attempts to merge Council and Board in one central body failed time and again. But the point was finally reached at which the unions having the largest interests saw that more was to be gained in combination than by wrenching work from the other unions through striking. The members in general wanted regular work. All the unions were therefore brought to unite in a new central body, the United Board of Building Trades.

The new Board, whose delegates had settled into earnestness through experience, adopted a strictly practical constitution. This accords two votes to each union, which may be represented by five business agents, no credentials being received for less than three months, and a two-thirds vote being required to admit a union to membership. By its rules the Board excludes alleged unions not formed in good faith or lacking financial means—the strays or petty schemers of the political or industrial field.

Discipline in routine matters is exacting. Delegates directed to serve as committeemen failing to report at an appointed place thirty minutes after the stated time are fined $3; delegates must be present at every meeting of the Board or be fined $1; at Board sessions indecorum brings a fine of $1 and disobedience of the Chair $3. Fines must be paid within eight days. Delegates refusing to comply with the procedure prescribed in the constitution for grievances are suspended for six months.

The unions may independently arrange their differences with employers, but when a grievance is brought before the Board by a delegate it becomes the affair of the Board. A controversy is investigated by a committee of all the delegates from the unions having men on the work concerned, and a two-thirds vote is required to call a strike. If the committee fails to agree, the union aggrieved may bring the subject before the Board, where a majority of the delegates having men on the work may bring the question to an issue. If these delegates refuse to do so, the aggrieved delegate may select as a committeeman a delegate having men on the work, a delegate refusing to strike may select another, and with the president of the Board as a third member the committee reinvestigates the complaint, its decision being final. No grievance is received from unions not associated with the Board, nor can they be tendered any assistance. By these various means the causes of many strikes in years past are avoided.

The Board refuses indiscriminate support to unions asking for advances in wages or for a shorter workday. To acquire the right of assistance in such cases a union must submit to the Board its demands in writing a month previous to the proposed change. A committee of five deliberates on the question and makes its recommendations to the Board, which then considers it at a special meeting. For the coming 1st of May the steam fitters, marble cutters and iron shipbuilders are asking an increase of fifty cents a day, and the plasterers a scale of $5.50 a day. Last year the bricklayers' helpers made demands which the Board refused to indorse until the increase asked for was cut down one-half.

But the highly important labors of the Board are an outcome of the conditions which gave it life. It requires unions in controversy to submit their disputes to Board arbitration. Each party in a difference appoints three Board members as arbitrators, a seventh being selected as umpire by the six, or, they failing, by the Board itself. A union disregarding the decision of an arbitration committee is suspended, to be reinstated only on payment of not less than $100 and abiding by the decision. Pending an arbitration the other allied unions remain neutral, thus protecting alike the interests of the builders, the owners of buildings under construction and the public.

The first result of this arbitration law was largely to prevent disputes between unions, the delegates ceasing their aggressions on one another's jurisdictions. Differences that arose despite individual delegate diplomacy passed, not under the might of the stronger, but under the law of careful investigation and impartial judgment supervised by the entire body. In all, fifteen cases have been adjusted in the year since the formation of the Board.

Only one case went to the length of requiring the Board of Delegates itself to elect the umpire. In a dispute between the steam fitters and the plumbers over the work of pneumatic tubing the two committees of three were unable to agree on the seventh member. The Board chose a hoisting engineer. His opinion was that pneumatic tubing was not essentially either steam fitting or plumbing, but by reason of priority of action in unionizing the work and of effective action in obtaining higher wages he awarded labor of this character to the steam fitters.

Of the other cases, the following serve to show the victories of the system of arbitration as well as the intricacies that on occasions nearly baffle the arbitrators:

April 9, 1902—Mosaic and Encaustic Tile Layers (300 members) vs. Marble and Enamel Mosaic Workers (200 members). The question was as to which union should lay a certain ceramic tile. The Marble and Enamel Mosaic Workers claimed it, as the piece measureu less than a square inch. But the committee unanimously awarded it to their opponents. The defeated union refused to abide by the decision. It was suspended. It issued a protest to the Board and a printed appeal to all associations in the building trades. Not until January 14, 1903, was this union readmitted to membership. It re-entered on paying its fine of $100 and on accepting the restrictions imposed by the Board, such as working only with union helpers recognized by the Mosiac Helpers.

April 18—Laborers' Protective Union (12,000 members) vs. Cement and Asphalt Laborers (700 members). Disputed jurisdiction. Decision: All rough concreting on brick arches and cellars to be done by the first named union; all rough concreting on patent arches to be done by the last named. A feature of this contested case is that the Laborers' Protective Union is composed of laborers for the bricklayers, whose union is not connected with the United Board.

May 2—Electrical Workers (2,000 members) vs. Gas and Electrical Fixtures Union (300 members). Infringement. The latter claimed as their work the

OFFICERS OF THE CIVIC FEDERATION OF NEW YORK CITY

CORNELIUS N. BLISS
Treasurer

WILLIAM H. FARLEY
First Vice-Chairman

LEWIS NIXON
Chairman

COL. JOHN J. McCOOK
Second Vice-Chairman

SAMUEL B. DONNELLY
Secretary

electric wires running through gas fixtures. The umpire decided in favor of the electric workers. As a consequence the defeated union decided to give up its separate organization, and it was merged in that of the electric workers.

May 16—Portable Hoisting Engineers (250 members) vs. Safety Association of Steam Engineers (700 members). By the award in this case the first named union was granted the exclusive right to the hoisting of all brick, mortar, iron and other material not already controlled by the United Derrickmen. To the Safety Association was given the right to all engineering work in connection with excavations.

July 28—Electrical Workers vs. Elevator Constructors (1,000 members). Question of electric wiring in elevators. The Elevator Constructors, refusing to arbitrate, were suspended. The Otis Company being interested, the question was submitted to one of its representatives as unofficial umpire. He awarded the wiring to the electricians, whereupon the Elevator Constructors sought and obtained re-admission to the Board.

August 6—Plain and Ornamental Plasterers (3,000 members) vs. Cement Masons (600 members). Decision: All cement base run for sanitary purposes that do not exceed six inches over the floor is to go to the cement masons; all run after the floor is laid, to the plasterers.

September 19—Electrical Workers vs. Portable Hoisting Engineers. Decision: The installation and running of electric pumps awarded to electrical workers. By this verdict the board recognized the introduction of improved machinery and ranged itself against the restriction of output through the employment of unnecessary workmen on machines of inferior efficiency. One electrician may tend three or even four electric pumps that displace steam pumps each managed by an engineer.

October 1—Salamander Association of Boiler and Pipe Coverers (500 members) vs. Housesmiths and Bridgemen's union (4,000 members). The decision in this case was so complicated and heavily weighted with technicalities that the Board recommended that the Salamander Association become a branch of the Housesmiths and Bridgemen's Union, with the right to labor at any branch of the trade. The Metallic Lathers were placed in the same relationship.

January 14—Amalgamated Sheet Metal Workers (3,000 members) vs. Housesmiths and Bridgemen's Union. Question: Which union shall handle ten-gauge iron, in metal furnishings? This inquiry is still pending, requiring much investigation.

January 16—Plain and Ornamental Plasterers vs. Salamander Association. Decision: The disputed work belonged to the plasterers, but if they were unable to supply workmen the Salamander Association might take it.

January 23—Plumbers and Gasfitters (4,000 members) vs. Steam and Hot Water Fitters. Question: Which union should run the pipes for the ice making machinery used in hotels and apartment houses? The committees failed to agree. The Board awarded the work to the steamfitters. There was menace of a large strike over this question, and suspension on large buildings actually occurred, but the plumbers yielded in the end.

Two cases are in the hands of arbitrators at present, in the one the machinists and housesmiths being involved, and in the other the elevator constructors and the portable engineers. Meantime, all the workmen concerned are at their employment, the parties to the dispute maintaining a status quo and the other unions remaining neutral. March 23 a constitutional amendment was adopted by which arbitration decisions must be reached within two weeks.

Questions other than those relating to arbitration or to the routine of the agents' work are constantly arising. One of the most important in the Board's first year has been the old rivalry between the two general organizations of carpenters. Previous to the formation of the Board a large construction company had decided to employ only members of the National Brotherhood of Carpenters. This body as well as the Amalgamated Society of Carpenters and Joiners came into the new United Board of Building Trades. A committee which essayed to settle the differences between the two unions failed. The Board decided to remain neutral. The Brotherhood, dissatisfied, withdrew from the Board in July. The Board, seeking peace with the employers, permits Brotherhood carpenters to work with the allied unions, but in case the Brotherhood attempts to discriminate against Amalgamated men the Board shuts out Brotherhood members. This is the only jurisdictional fight now on. The American Federation of Labor is attempting to arrange the long-standing differences between the two carpenters' unions, having at the New Orleans convention in November last arranged for their arbitration. The vital cause of continued separation, it is said, lies in the benefit features of the two bodies. The Amalgamated Society, associated with the great English Society, possesses proportionately a large treasury and pays high benefits.

On April 7 the Brotherhood began in New York a general strike against the Amalgamated Society.

While the Brotherhood of Carpenters was represented in the Board it asked indorsement of a demand for an increase in wages from $4 to $4.50 a day, to take effect July 1, 1902. The Board deemed the notice to the employers insufficient. The Brotherhood, accepting the decision, changed the date to September 1. This period was approved by the Board, and the increase took place.

A constitutional question arose in the Board on the interpretation of the phrase "other buildings" as applied to the East River bridges. The Board decided that the work might go to the organization first on the spot to obtain it. Here much depends on the activity of the various business agents, who thus become employment mediaries.

Smaller matters are brought before the Board. A housesmith complained that an electrician was punching a hole in an iron beam that belonged to him. Before the business agent reached the scene of action the hole was punched.

The Board makes no agreements with employing builders. It favors agreements between each union and its own employers. There is no general employers' association in the building trades. Each branch, however, has its association. The Board advocates arbitration in each branch between association and union.

Inasmuch as the United Board meets three times a week, with an obligatory attendance of members, and the interests of each trade are jealously guarded by its own agents, the possibilities of trade quarrels, of interruptions in work, of irresponsible action by individual agents, of oppressions of employers are reduced to a minimum. The delegates of to-day declare that they are animated by a desire for peace with employers and for a mutual confidence productive of a high standard of honor on the part of all interests engaged in the building trades.

The REVIEW is under obligations to Secretary William H. Farley of the United Board for the data herewith produced.

The unions at present represented in the Board are:

Amalgamated Painters and Decorators.
Amalgamated Society of Carpenters and Joiners.
Amalgamated Sheet Metal Workers.
Building Material Drivers.
Brotherhood of Painters and Decorators.
Brick and Building Material Handlers.
Boilermakers and Iron Ship Builders.
Cement Masons' Union, No. 1.
Cement and Asphalt Laborers.
Dock Builders.
Electrical Workers, No. 3.
Elevator Constructors.
Granite Cutters' Union.
Housesmiths and Bridgemen's Union.
House Shorers and Movers' Union.
International Association of Machinists.
Journeyman Stone Cutters' Association.
Laborers' Protective Union.
Marble Cutters.
Marble Polishers and Rubbers' Union.
Marble Cutters' Helpers.
Metallic Lathers' Union.
Marble and Enamel Mosaic Workers.
Mosaic Helpers.
Mosaic and Encaustic Tile Layers' Union.
Plain and Ornamental Plasterers.
Plasterers' Laborers.
Plumbers and Gas Fitters' Local No. 2.
Portable Hoisting Engineers.
Slate, Tile and Metal Roofers.
Safety Association of Steam Engineers.
Steam and Hot Water Fitters.
Steam and Hot Water Fitters' Helpers.
Salamander Association of Boiler and Pipe Coverers.
Second-hand Building Material Handlers.
Tar, Felt and Waterproof Workers.
Tile Layers' Helpers.
United Derrickmen, Riggers and Pointers' Union.
Wood Lathers' Union.
Blue Stone Cutters.

SHOULD TRADE UNIONS INCORPORATE?

(Continued from Page 7.)

cinnati, N. O. & T. P. Ry Co. 62 Fed. 803 (Cir. Ct. Ohio, 1894); Brace vs. Evans, 3 Ry. & Corp. L. J. 560 (1888); Carew vs. Rutherford, 106 Mass. 1 (1870). That, however, the trade union itself is not liable in such a case, see American Steel and Wire Company vs. Wire Drawers' Union, 90 Fed. 598 (Cir. Ct. Ohio, 1898); Plant vs. Woods, 176 Mass. 492,504; 57 N. E. 1011 (1900); 22 Encyclopædia of Pleading and Practice, p. 242.

In some instances, indeed, an unincorporated trade union seems to have been assumed to be liable in the absence of statutory provision, but this assumption doubtless resulted from inadvertence. See, for instance, Consolidated Steel and Wire Company vs. Murray, 80 Fed. 811 (Cir. Ct. Ohio, 1897). And the following are instances of trade unions being held liable, in some of which, at least, such unions were, so far as appears, unincorporated: Thus, in allowing injunctions, Coeur D'Alene Consolidated and Mining Company vs. Miners' Union, 51 Fed. 260 (Cir. Ct. Idaho, 1892); American Steel and Wire Company vs. Wire Drawers' Union, 90 Fed. 608 (Cir. Ct. Ohio, 1898); Otis Steel Company vs. Local Union No. 218, 110 Fed. 698 (Cir. Ct. Ohio, 1901); Southern Railway Company vs. Machinists' Local Union, 111 Fed. 49 (Cir. Ct. Tenn., 1901); Allis Chalmers Company vs. Reliable Lodge, 111 Fed. 264 (Cir. Ct. Ill., 1901); Vegelahn vs. Guntner, 167 Mass. 92; 44 N. E. 1077 (1896). So in an action for damages, Old Dominion Steamship Company vs. McKenna, 30 Fed. 48 (Cir. Ct. N. Y., 1887).

But the liability of the union in such a case is sometimes created by statute. Thus, in the State of New York, by provisions substantially in force since 1851, "an unincorporated association, consisting of seven or more persons," may be sued in the name of its president or treasurer, and a judgment against it binds its property. Code. Civ. Pro., Sections 1919 and 1921. The action, though in form against such officer, is in substance and reality against the association. Mason vs. Holmes, 30 Misc. 719; 64 N. Y. Suppl. 596 (1900). These provisions unquestionably apply to a trade union. Indeed, by virtue thereof, in Curran vs. Galen, 152 N. Y. 33; 46 N. E. 297 (1897); affirming 2 Misc. 553; 22 N. Y. Suppl. 826 (1893), an action for damages was held to lie against an unincorporated trade union for acts resulting in taking away the plaintiff's means of earning a livelihood, and preventing him from obtaining employment. Why, then, attach so much importance to the decision in the Taff Vale Railway Company case, when we have a decision at home that covers the ground thereof? For other instances of unincorporated trade unions held liable by virtue of such provisions see Connell vs. Stalker, 20 Misc. 423; 45 N. Y. Suppl. 1048; 21 Misc. 609; 48 N. Y. Suppl. 77 (1897); Coons vs. Christie, 24 Miscl. 296; 53 N. Y. Suppl. 668 (1898); Matthews vs. Shankland, 25 Misc. 604; 56 N. Y. Suppl. 123 (1898); Beattie vs. Callanan, 67 N. Y. App. D. 14; 73 N. Y. Suppl. 518 (1901). See also Van Aernam vs. Bleistein, 102 N. Y. 355 (1886); Rourke vs. Elk Drug Co. 75 N. Y. App. D. 145; 77 N. Y. Suppl. 373 (1902); Hanke vs. Cigarmakers' International Union, 27 Misc. 529; 58 N. Y. Suppl. 412 (1899).

Similar statutory provisions exist in other States; thus Connecticut (General Statutes, Sec. 588); Michigan (3 Compiled Laws, Sec. 10,025); New Jersey (2 General Statutes, Sec. 2,588). See Beck vs. Railway Teamsters' Protective Union, 118 Mich. 497; 77 N. W. 24 (1898); Mayer vs. Stonecutters' Association 47 N. J. Eq. 519; 20 Atl. 492 (1890); Barr vs. Essex Trades Council, 53 N. J. Eq. 101; 30 Atl. 881 (1894).

I have already said that in the Taff Vale Railway Company case it was simply a narrow question of statutory construction that was involved. That is to say, an unincorporated trade union was held liable in an action for damages, notwithstanding the absence of any statutory provision expressly making it thus liable, such liability being, however, regarded as inferentially created by other provisions, particularly those enabling it to hold property and act by agents. The liability there regarded as inferentially created is, as we have just seen, expressly created by statutes in New York and other States. I repeat, then, that, from a strictly legal standpoint, the decision is comparatively insignificant.

By act of Congress of June, 1886, C. 567, as well as by statutes in a number of States, provision is made for the incorporation of trade unions. The following provisions applicable to a trade union created by act of Congress are typical of provisions applicable to corporations generally. It has the right "to sue and be sued, to implead and be impleaded, to grant and receive in its corporate or technical name property, real, personal and mixed, and to use said property and the proceeds and income thereof for the objects of said corporation.' It may be added that its liability to be sued involves subjection of its property to a judgment obtained against it. Such a union would also be subject to various statutory provisions, differing in detail according to the locality. By way of illustration merely is here stated the following provision of the act of Congress of June, 1898, C. 370, applicable to unions incorporated under the act of 1886: "A member shall cease to be such by participation in or by instigating force or violence against persons or property during strikes, lockouts, or boycotts, or by seeking to prevent others from working, through violence, threats or intimidations. Members of such incorporations shall not be personally liable for the acts, debts or obligations of the corporations, nor shall such corporations be liable for the acts of members or others in violation of law." Under such a provision it would hardly be held, as in the Taff Vale Railway Company case, that a trade union is liable for the unlawful acts of its agents. But for instances of incorporated trade unions held liable for the unlawful acts of their agents see Moores vs. Bricklayers' Union, 7 Ry. and Corp. L. J. 108 (1889); Casey vs. Cincinnati Typographical Union, 45 Fed. 135 (Cir. Ct. Ohio, 1891); Lucke vs. Clothing Cutters', etc., Assembly, 77 Md. 396; 26 Atl. 505 (1893).

In view of what we have seen, incorporation of a trade union, ordinarily at least, creates a responsibility not existing independently of statute, though the extent of such responsibility may widely vary, according to local statutory provisions. But it is clear that incorporation is not necessary for the purpose of creating such responsibility wherever there exist provisions of the character already considered, making even an unincorporated trade union liable to be sued.

I do not dwell here upon the economic or sociological effects of such creation of responsibility, though here is involved a broad and interesting field of inquiry, including such questions as whether the existence of such responsibility will tend to discourage the creation of such unions or their active intervention in strikes or boycotts instituted in the interest of their members.

F. J. Stimson, Counsellor-at-Law, Boston, Author of "Government by Injunction," "Handbook to the Labor Laws of the United States," etc.:

Answering your question so far as I am able to at present, I agree with your American authorities that the Taff Vale decision lays down no new principle of law. There was some shadow of holding in England under the trade unions act that there might be a *tertium quid* between a band of individuals and a corporation, but there is nothing of the sort in this country. I think trade unions must, therefore, take one of two courses, either frankly accept the situation, and incorporate, thereby accepting a full-grown man's responsibility for his acts, or else they must carefully divide their combative functions from their charitable functions, and see to it that all their funds are put in the hands of trustees, to be used only for charitable purposes. The dangers (of incorporating) are certainly no greater than at present. The danger they apprehend, of vexatious litigation by the employer, is as yet, at least, unproved. No cases of incorporation of trade unions have yet come under my personal observation. To the question whether a special law should be enacted for the incorporation of unions different from that for business corporations, I should reply—most certainly.

Charles Frederick Adams, Counsellor-at-Law, New York:

My impression is that, while incorporation might easily make the unionists more vulnerable in respect of their collectively-owned assets, it would not in the least protect individual leaders and members from being "joined" as defendants in suits for damages for "conspiracies" and other torts. The fact that an incorporated union had officially participated in the wrong would be no defense for any individuals who should be charged with having personally aided and abetted. Were the cause of this action a breach of a contract made by the corporation as such, and to which the members were not parties as individuals, then, of course, only the corporation and its assets would be responsible. But in tort I believe incorporation would only provide an additional defendant. Had I to advise a union without further study and investigation, I would feel bound to advise against incorporation (though I am not at all dogmatic on that side of the question).

The existing general statutes do not seem to me to provide suitably for the incorporation of trade unions. My impression is that, professedly at least, the Taff Vale decision proceeds upon an express statutory prohibition of "watching and besetting," which the defendants were held to have disregarded. Strictly speaking, therefore, it is a precedent only for cases of some analogous breach of law, and not in and of itself a making illegal picketing, etc., in jurisdictions in which these would else have been legal. Our Court of Appeals would have to stultify itself to hold—in the absence of any change in the law of New York since its recent decision—that picketing, etc., without violence or threats of illegal acts, would give the offended employers a right to damages.

John Brooks Leavitt, Counsellor-at-Law, New York:

I have long been of opinion that the trade unions would consult their best interests if they were to incorporate. My reason is that I think incorporation would tend to have a steadying influence upon them, and bring their most conservative and cool-headed men to the front. They would then realize, as they do not now in full measure, the danger of jeopardizing their funds by ill-advised action. The objection which they usually make to incorporation, that it would subject them to suits, is without foundation, because they can be sued now. The Taff Vale decision announced nothing new on principle. It simply applied to labor organizations the same law which has for many years been applied to other unincorporated bodies. It has been the law of this State for fifty odd years that any unincorporated association can be sued in the name of its president or treasurer. Most of the States have similar statutes. The idea that men may do things in association and by remaining unincorporated evade responsibility for such actions finds no countenance in the law. Moreover, it seems to me that such an objection to incorporation is a counsel of fear and unworthy of the attention of any body of earnest and right-minded men. Why should an association of men seek to evade the consequences of its own acts? This is a counsel of weakness, not of strength. Moreover, such an objection is bound to alienate the sympathies of the public, because it contains the implication that the trade unions propose a line of conduct which is illegal. If any other body of men were to suggest such a thing, there would be universal condemnation. Trade unions are good things and should be encouraged, but lawless unions should be condemned as unsparingly as we would denounce any lawless organization of capitalists. The scales of justice must be held evenly, and disobedience of the law must not be countenanced in trade unions any more than in financial combinations.

Geo. Fred Williams, Counsellor-at-Law, Boston:

With respect to the incorporation of the labor union, I am most decidedly against such a movement. The law applicable to the labor union in England is not applicable to our own unions for the reason that while the unions in England are not in a sense corporations they are none the less recognized as entities by law, and are registered under the labor union act. This makes them practically corporations. I see no reason why the labor men should organize to throw themselves into the clutches of the capitalist courts and make it easy for them to wreck the organizations. When one sees the scandalous way in which the anti-trust act has been turned against labor when it was clearly aimed at trade monopolies one realizes how far the law can be stretched by prejudiced courts to oppress the weaker party. But, apart from this consideration, it seems to me that the incorporation of trade unions would be fatal, because it would take away the democratic character of the organization. A corporation is not democratic in any sense; it is distinctly a representative form of control, and in the manner in which the corporate powers can be manipulated the representative control can very easily be made despotic. Any lawyer who has had to do with corporations knows what a helpless creature the minority stockholder is. As it is now, trade unions are democratic bodies depending upon the immediate and ready willingness of their members to act in union, but requiring constant appeals to the constituency for authority. This democratic form should be preserved, and I believe that incorporation would speedily be followed either by the disintegration of the unions or by a form of despotic management or both. Labor unions will get just the recognition that the power of their numbers and their co-operation commands. I see absolutely no gain and a very plain loss from incorporation.

John De Witt Warner, Counsellor at Law, New York:

My own impression is that the Taff Vale decision scarcely goes beyond principles of law already followed in the United States; also that this and similar cases have so largely turned upon the special circumstances of each that their value as precedents is slight. They are, however, among such "straws" as late uses of injunction, serious as indicating how forgetful are growing the courts of how limited is the scope within which, after all, they can beneficently or effectively deal with wage, labor, and other social-economic questions. Late judicial decisions do not seem to me of importance either for or against incorporation by trade unions—the principles of law involved being, I believe, equally applicable (though with somewhat of difference in method) to both incorporated and unincorporated associations. For other reasons, however, I believe trade unions should not incorporate, except in cases where there may be special reason therefor. In my opinion, any special law for incorporation of trade unions would be apt to hurt their efficiency rather than improve it.

I. A. Hourwich, formerly counsel to the Ladies' Garment Workers' International Union:

I have never doubted the authority of the courts to render a judgment for damages against an unincorporated trade union. I expressed this view in my testimony before the Industrial Commission prior to the Taff Vale decision. I think, however, that an important distinction must be drawn between the liability of a trade union for the acts of its officers or authorized agents and the attempt to fasten upon a union the responsibility for unauthorized acts of individual members. I doubt very much whether a shareholder of an unincorporated mining company could be made legally liable for every brawl that might occur between any one of its members and a stranger in a mining camp. The cases are exactly alike. Assuming that every member of an unincorporated trade union is subject to an unlimited liability for torts committed by the union or any of its officers, agents, or members, I should certainly regard incorporation as the lesser evil. To be sure, an incorporated trade union would find it difficult, if not impossible, under the present corporation law to enforce in court its agreements with employers of labor; still, even an unincorporated union is practically without a remedy for breach of contract by an employer. Thus the injury from incorporation would be purely theoretical, while, on the other hand, the property of the individual member of the union would be protected from judgments against the union.

I believe that neither the business corporation law nor the membership corporation law of New York, or analogous acts in other States, nor the national trade union law, is suited to the needs of a trade union. A special law is needed, which should recognize a trade union as a form of association distinct from a business corporation, on the one hand, and from a social club, on the other. Collective bargaining should be expressly enumerated among the objects of a trade union. The law should also expressly declare that contracts of employment between a trade union and an employer could be abrogated or modified only with the consent of the union or its duly authorized agents. There should be a further provision that a trade union may sue upon such agreements, as a "trustee of an express trust" (using the terminology of the New York Code of Civil Procedure), for the benefit of its members. Lastly, trade unions should be relieved from the rigid technical rules governing the conduct of business by stock corporations.

The only incorporated trade union that has come under my close personal observation was the United Brotherhood of Cloakmakers of New York. It did not give up its corporate organization, but I believe it would have fared better if it had. The strict forms prescribed by law for the conduct of corporate business could not be observed by workingmen; as a result, the business transacted by the union would not appear in all particulars from its records, and the union would suffer in consequence when it sued or was sued in court.

The legal status of trade unions in England is determined by the Trade Union Acts of 1871 and 1876. Those two statutes were enacted for a specific purpose, viz.: to remove the disabilities imposed upon trade unions by the common law, which regarded them as combinations in restraint of trade, within the definition of criminal conspiracy. Being an illegal combination, a trade union could neither hold property nor seek redress in the courts for embezzlement of its funds by its officers.

As a statutory exception from the common law, the trade union acts are restricted to the objects for which they were enacted; and Section 4 of the Act of 1871 expressly declares that "nothing in this act shall enable any court to entertain any legal proceeding instituted with the object of directly enforcing or recovering damages for the breach" of any of the agreements made by a trade union in the prosecution of its purposes, viz.: "regulating the relations between workmen and masters, or between workmen and workmen" (Amendment Act, 1876, Sec. 16). The law no longer holds such purposes unlawful, but it refuses to interfere in their behalf, as it would refuse to enforce a contract for services rendered by a matrimonial bureau.

Furthermore, Section 32 of the Act of 1871 prohibits in a quite comprehensive manner any act which may come under the definition of picketing.

Judicial interpretation has done little, if anything, toward the development of the new legal principles embodied in the acts of 1871 and 1876. In the case of Rigby vs. Connol ([1880] 14 Ch. D. 489) the court merely reiterated the provisions of the statute. In the now famous case of the Taff Vale Railway Company vs. Amalgamated Society of Railway Servants ([1901] A. C., 426), the point directly decided by the House of Lords related merely to the technical form in which an action could be brought against a trade union. The appellant (the railway company) contended that a registered trade union may be sued in its registered name, which counsel for the union denied on technical grounds (pp. 434-435). Had this view been sustained by the Lords, the complaint would have been dismissed, but it would not have benefited the trade union, because the plaintiff could still have brought an action against the officers of the trade union in their representative capacity (Opinion by Lord Lindley).

The decision on the main point can have no application in the United States, the legal status of trade unions here being essentially different from that created by the English Trade Union Acts. In England a registered trade union is not deemed a corporation, whereas in this country an incorporated trade union is treated as a corporation, it may accordingly be sued in its corporate name and is subject to liability for the acts of its officers upon the same principles as any other corporation. An unincorporated trade union may in all States be sued in a representative action brought against its officers (N. Y. Code of Civil Procedure, Sec. 448, reproduced in other Codes; Story, Equity Pleading, Sec. 107).

The National Trade Union Act, as well as the laws of all industrial States, expressly declare that workmen may lawfully combine for the purpose of obtaining an advance of wages or maintaining the existing rate. Among the lawful purposes of a trade union, within the definition of Section 1 of the national law, are include "such other object or objects for which working people may lawfully combine, having in view their mutual protection or benefit." The language of this section is broad enough to embrace agreements between a trade union and an employer for "the regulation of wages, hours, and conditions of labor;" it must be noted that Section 1 applies to all trade unions, whether incorporated or not. A trade agreement between a labor union and an employer will, therefore, be enforced in the Federal and State courts.

Whether, in the United States, an unincorporated trade union could be held liable in damages for tortious acts of its officers, is a question upon which there is room for difference of legal opinion. The dictum of the court in the Taff Vale case will carry weight as an authority in this country as well as in England, inasmuch as the view expressed by the Lords is in this respect not based upon the English registration act, but upon the general law governing the liability of a principal for the torts committed by his agent.

John Frankenheimer, Counsellor-at-Law, New York:

The question Should trade unions be incorporated? will be found, in its final analysis, to be predicated upon the question Do you believe in trade unions? For those who believe in trade unions will answer your question quite differently from those who oppose this established form of labor organization. As a believer in trade unionism, I shall answer your question from the trade union standpoint. There is no blinking the fact that the struggle between capital and labor has many of the features of an internecine warfare. The forces on each side are becoming daily more disciplined and consolidated; the trust on one side, the federated trade unions on the other. In a struggle of this kind discipline will count. Whatever will weaken the disciplinary control of a trade union over its members will necessarily weaken the trade union in its contest with organized capital. It is because incorporation of a trade union will deprive it of much of the power it now possesses over its members and the management of its internal affairs that the chief legal objection to incorporation seems to lie from the trade union standpoint. It is well settled that a voluntary unincorporated association—such as a trade union, club or stock exchange—has a much greater power not only over [illegible] but also over the expulsion of [illegible] incorporated association. Membe[illegible] ation is a statutory right in the m[illegible], which can neither be withheld not [illegible] away by the act of the corporation unless the power to do so be given by the charter. On the other hand membership in a voluntary association is derived exclusively from the body that bestows it, and may be conferred or withheld at its pleasure. A person acquires by his admission to membership in a voluntary association only such rights as the constitution and by-laws of the association give him. He may be suspended or expelled according to the rules of the association, and if the proceedings are regular and the investigation a fair one the decision of the association cannot be reviewed on the merits by the courts. As was said recently in a stock exchange suit, voluntary associations are themselves the exclusive judges of their mode and manner of proceeding in the suspension or expulsion of a member.

It has repeatedly been said by the courts that [illegible] power over voluntary associations was not as [illegible] as it is over corporations; that the constitution of [illegible]untary associations is the contract between the pa[illegible] and that if its provisions are not illegal, immor[illegible] contrary to public policy, it must be upheld wh[illegible] reasonable or not, and that this is one of the mai[illegible]tinctions between a voluntary association and a [illegible]ration.

It is undoubtedly because of this greater disci[illegible] power of a voluntary association over its m[illegible] that the most successful trade union in this co[illegible] the New York Stock Exchange—has refused [illegible] incorporated. Members of this association will admit that the maintenance of the standard rate of commissions and of the established rules of the trade are due to the untrammeled power of suspension and expulsion vested in the Governing Committee of the Exchange. Members have been suspended or expelled for "splitting" commissions, "bucketing" orders, "fraudulent" sales and other acts deemed detrimental to the best trade interests of the association, and although frequent appeals have been made to the courts in such cases the invariable answer has been that the court cannot interfere if the proceedings are regular. It stands to reason that a powerful and wealthy trade organization—such as the Stock Exchange—which commands the best legal talent, would not persist in remaining an unincorporated association unless it derived great advantage therefrom.

The fundamental advantage of an unincorporated association over a corporation is the greater power the former possesses over its members and over the management of its internal affairs, and its greater freedom from interference by the courts in these matters.

I take it that from the trade union standpoint the object desired is untrammeled disciplinary power over its members and freedom from interference in its internal affairs by the courts. This can undoubtedly be attained more completely in the form of a voluntary association than in that of a corporation, and for this reason, if for no other, trade unions should oppose incorporation.

Were a trade union to be incorporated, every member who may have been disciplined, suspended or expelled would appeal to the courts for redress, and the organization would be constantly embroiled in litigation of this kind. Moreover sinister influences might be brought to bear upon a sufficiently strong minority to justify interference by the courts in the internal affairs of the association, if incorporated, which would not be justified, however strong the minority, if the association were a voluntary one.

As to the legal liability of a trade union for the authorized acts of its members or officers, there is no difference, under the laws of the State of New York, in this respect between a voluntary association and a corporation. The former can sue and be sued as well as the latter.

In my opinion, considering the whole question from the standpoint of the labor unions—and this is the only practical point of view to take of the question—incorporation of trade unions is inexpedient. It will weaken the power of the association over its members and over its management of its internal affairs, and will increase greatly the power of the courts over the association in all its affairs. Let the trade unions follow the example of the New York Stock Enchange—which is essentially a trade union and a very successful one—and persist in maintaining their present voluntary and unincorporated organization.

(New York Times, March 4.)

THE CIVIC FEDERATION OF NEW YORK CITY.

Lewis Nixon Elected Chairman of the Newly Organized Body.

List of Members in the Three Sections Representing the Public, The Employers, and the Workmen.

The Civic Federation of New York City was organized yesterday afternoon in the rooms of the New York Board of Trade and Transportation, 203 Broadway. This is the local committee of the National Civic Federation, organized in the pursuance of the policy of establishing local federations which was adopted at the last meeting of the National body.

Oscar S. Straus, Vice-President of the National Civic Federation and President New York Board of Trade and Transportation, called the meeting to order and spoke briefly of the aims of the Civic Federation and of the benefits to be derived from the arbitration of questions arising out of the competition and strife between capital and labor.

"The stronger each side grows," he said, "and the stronger the leaders they have, the fewer will be the occasions for conflict."

Ralph M. Easley, Secretary of the National Civic Federation, then read the names of those composing the three sections of the committee. "Each of the persons named," he said, "had given his word to assist in the work."

The following is a portion of the list of acceptants:

ON THE PART OF EMPLOYERS.

John B. McDonald, contractor Rapid Transit Subway.
S. P. McConnell, President the George A. Fuller Company.
Frederick D. Underwood, President Erie Railroad.
Lewis Nixon, President United States Shipbuilding Company.
Charles T. Wills, builder.
W. C. Brown, Vice President New York Central Railroad.
William H. Baldwin, Jr., President Long Island Railroad.
S. R. Callaway, President American Locomotive Works.
Otto M. Eidlitz, President Master Mason Builders.
Robert C. Ogden, John Wanamaker & Co.
John H. Starin, President Starin Transportation Line.
William Brewster, Brewster Carriage Manufacturing Company.
Peter Doelger, Jr., Peter Doelger Brewing Company.
Louis B. Schram, India Wharf Brewing Company.
Hosmer B. Parsons, Vice President Wells, Fargo & Co.
R. W. Nelson, President American Type Founders' Company.
J. W. Dunn, President International Steam Pump Company.
William D. Baldwin, President Otis Elevator Company.
Charles A. Moore, Manning, Maxwell & Moore.
Edward R. Ladew, Fayerweather & Ladew.
Marcus M. Marks, President National Clothiers' Association.
Edward Payson Call, President New York Publishers' Association.
J. Alexander Hayden, Chairman Association of Interior Decorators and Cabinetmakers.
William H. Parsons, Parsons Paper Company.
Charles Wilhelms, President United States Lithographers' Association.
Walter L. Pierce, Lidgerwood Manufacturing Company.
Frank B. Chambers, Manager Rogers, Peet & Co.
J. W. Williams, Williams Drop Forgings Company, Brooklyn.
William Green, Chairman New York Typothetæ.
Warner Leeds, Vice President American Tin Plate Company.
A. Beverly Smith, Secretary United States Lithographers' Association, East.

ON THE PART OF THE PUBLIC.

Cornelius N. Bliss, Bliss, Fabyan & Co.
August Belmont, banker.
The Right Rev. Henry C. Potter, Bishop Protestant Episcopal Church.
The Right Rev. John M. Farley, Archbishop Roman Catholic Church.
Oscar Straus, President New York Board of Trade and Transportation.
Spencer Trask, banker.
James Speyer, banker.
Emerson McMillin, banker.
John J. McCook, lawyer.
Albert Shaw, editor Review of Reviews.
The Rev. Dr. William S. Rainsford, rector St. George's Church.
Nicholas Murray Butler, President Columbia University.
V. Everit Macy, capitalist.
The Rev. Dr. Thomas R. Slicer, pastor All Souls' Church.
R. Watson Gilder, editor Century Magazine.
The Rev. John P. Peters, rector St. Michael's Church.
Felix Adler, professor, Columbia University.
Hamilton Holt, editor Independent.
John R. Commons, statistician.
Walter H. Page, editor World's Work.
Lyman Abbott, editor Outlook.
George Gunton, President Institute of Social Economics.
H. H. Cammann, real estate.
T. F. Woodlock, editor Wall Street Journal.
H. C. Watson, editor Dun's Review.
John B. Clark, professor, Columbia University.
Charles Sprague Smith, director People's Institute.

ON THE PART OF WAGE EARNERS.

William H. Farley, Mosaic and Encaustic Tile Layers.
Edward Kelly, Electrical Workers.
M. A. McConville, Engineers' Subway Conference Board.
M. J. Ford, Machinists.
R. Pattison, Sheet Metal Workers.
Henry White, Garment Workers.
William Davis, Brotherhood of Locomotive Engineers.
Samuel B. Donnelly, Typographical Union.
J. J. Pallas, Patternmakers, Subway Conference Board.
W. A. Perrine, Molders.
John J. Donovan, Plasterers.
G. H. Warner, Machinists.
Marsden G. Scott, President Typographical Union No. 6.
George E. Pepper, President Amalgamated Association Street Railway Employes, New York Division.
James Daly, Dock Builders.
Edward A. Moffett, editor Bricklayer and Mason.
James P. Archibald, Brotherhood Painters and Decorators.
Robert Thompson, Brotherhood of Carpenters.
William Fyfe, Amalgamated Carpenters.
W. Long, Lithographers.
John Phillips, Hatters.
A. J. Boulton, Stereotypers.
Francis J. McKay, Boilermakers and Iron Shipbuilders.
Herman Robinson, Retail Clerks.
J. B. Wilson, Machinists.
James Roach, Steam and Hot Water Fitters.
Robert E. Neidig, Housesmiths.
James P. Holland, Stationary Firemen.
Charles Delaney, Granite Cutters.
J. W. Sullivan, Typographical Union.

Nearly all of those named were present. When the names of the committee had been read the following permanent officers were elected:

Chairman—Lewis Nixon.
First Vice-Chairman—William H. Farley.
Second Vice-Chairman—Col. John J. McCook.
Treasurer—Cornelius N. Bliss.
Secretary—Samuel B. Donnelly.

In taking the chair Mr. Nixon said in part:

"The acceptance of a place on this committee means to each of you an obligation the demands of which cannot be ignored, and under which active service cannot be shirked. The meeting a few weeks ago of a parent Federation brought to the public a realization of the possibilities of its work. The active participation here to-day of leaders in all lines of human endeavor is an earnest of the sincerity of the movement and an evidence that they will use every effort to extend its sphere of usefulness. The make-up of this committee can be taken to mean that no misuse of the committee can or will be permitted for selfish advancement of the claims of either side."

Mr. White offered resolutions, which were adopted, authorizing the chairman to appoint an executive committee of fifteen, five representing each group, who with the officers of the Council, and the resident members of the National Executive Committee, ex-officio, shall direct the general affairs of the Civic Federation of New York City; also to appoint a committee composed of three members from each group to draw up by-laws.

(New York Herald, March 15, 1903.)

SHIPYARD STRIKE ENDS.

First Triumph of the New York Civic Federation.

One Union Had Decided to Fine Any of Its Strikers for Disorder About the Affected Yards.

The threatened general strike in all the yards, which would have tied up the entire shipbuilding trade in New York and vicinity and have driven a great part of the shipbuilding trade permanently from the metropolitan district, was averted yesterday. After a conference lasting for over four hours between representatives of the New York Metal Trades Association, the New York Civic Federation, and the Marine Trades Council, an agreement was reached by which all sympathetic strikes of all the trades in the Townsend-Downey yard and the sympathetic strike of boilermakers in the other shipbuilding yards are to be declared off, pending negotiations for a settlement of the original strike of the boilermakers in the Townsend-Downey yards, which started all the trouble.

The Marine Trades Council will hold a special meeting to-morrow night, and is expected to ratify this agreement and declare the sympathetic strikes off. A joint committee of employers and employes will meet probably about Wednesday, when it is expected the entire trouble will be ended and the original strike, which was to force the discharge of two non-union men, declared off.

The New York Civic Federation, which has only recently been organized, has been working for several days in trying to bring about the result that was reached yesterday. This is considered a signal victory for the Federation, as it is the first local labor trouble it has had anything to do with.

It looked for a while yesterday forenoon as if all negotiations for a settlement were off. The same committee which met the Executive Committee of the Metal Trades' Association Friday called on the Executive Committee early in the day, and found it apparently against meeting the representatives of the strikers. The committee finally agreed to meet the representatives of the men. The latter, however, objected, and it looked again as if no conference could take place. The conference was finally arranged, and began at 2:30 P. M., in the office of the Civic Federation, 281 Fourth Avenue.

The following attended the conference:

For the Metal Trades Association: Charles H. Smith, President; H. N. Covell, Vice-President; Wallace Downey, W. H. Atkinson and M. K. Bowman.

For the employers' department of the Civic Federation: Lewis Nixon, Marcus M. Marks, Emerson McMillin and A. B. Smith.

For the employes' department of the Civic Federation: Henry White, Garment Workers; W. H. Farley, Secretary Board of Building Trades, and Edward Kelly, Electrical Workers; Edward A. Moffett, editor "Bricklayer and Mason," and J. W. Sullivan, Typographical Union No. 6.

For the Marine Trades Council: Francis J. McKay, Brotherhood of Boilermakers and Iron Shipbuilders; Richard Pattison, Amalgamated Sheet Metal Workers; Samuel B. Donnelly, Secretary New York Civic Federation, and John R. Commons, Assistant Secretary National Civic Federation.

The conference was secret and the telephone was kept busy while it was going on. The labor delegates, it was said, had to communicate with the representatives of the respective unions involved. At about 6:30 P. M. the meeting broke up and everybody looked happy.

"It's nearly all settled," said one of the labor men as he went out. An hour later a statement was given out by Ralph M. Easley, of the National Civic Federation, in which he said, after stating the names of those who attended the conference:

"After a session of four hours an agreement was reached whereby the sympathetic strike of all the boilermakers and helpers in all the shops of members of the New York Metal Trades' Association and of the carpenters, joiners, painters, machinists, blacksmiths, and patternmakers who went out of the yards of the Townsend-Downey Shipbuilding Company in sympathy on March 10, is to be declared off on or before March 18. It was agreed that a joint conference between committees of the New York Metal Trades Association and the Marine Trades Council is to be held for the purpose of discussing the original strike of the boilermakers and shipbuilders at the Townsend-Downey yards and to consider other matters relating to trade conditions.

"The original misunderstanding was caused by the misinterpretation of the meaning of letters which passed between the two organizations. When this misunderstanding was cleared away during the conference, better relations were at once established, which led up to the settlement as stated. Mr. McKay of the Marine Trades Council and the committee of the Metal Trades Association, who had up to that time been unwilling to meet for the discussion of the differences, were congratulated by the members of the Civic Federation on the spirit of conservatism they had shown and their willingness to reach an honorable settlement."

National Civic Federation

MONTHLY REVIEW

VOL. I. No. 2 NEW YORK, JUNE, 1903 TEN CENTS

THE MOSELY INDUSTRIAL COMMISSION

ITS REPORT AN EXTRAORDINARY COLLECTION OF TESTIMONY RELATIVE TO THE SUPREMACY OF THE UNITED STATES

The reports of the Mosely Commission, issued in London a month ago, have not by far obtained the attention they deserve in this country. They form in fact a highly important contribution to the works of the day that treat of America's working people and its resources and industrial accomplishments. The writers of the reports know their several subjects intimately, they have made their comparisons at first hand from actual observation, and their verdict leaves no room for doubt as to their intention to give the truth as they see it.

As is known, the members made their trip in the United States as guests of Mr. Mosely, an English capitalist. On their arrival here the Civic Federation undertook the task of planning their itinerary, of appointing a committee to attend them in their travels, and of seeing to it that they should be introduced in the various cities under favorable auspices. While some of the members also made independent trips, the entire party visited Niagara, Buffalo, Cleveland, Chicago, Dayton, Pittsburg, Philadelphia, Washington and New York. In this city they attended the Civic Federation's conference of last December, contributing to its success by their impromptu discussions, fortified as they were by fresh facts from their experience at home and in this country.

The members arrived from England in small parties at the ports of Philadelphia, New York, Boston, and Quebec, on or about Nov. 8, and, assembling at Niagara Falls, Nov. 12, for the most part journeyed afterward in a body. As they sailed for England Dec. 19-25, their general observations were necessarily hurried.

(Photographed at Niagara Falls Power Plant.)

Upper Row (from left to right)—Messrs. Lapping, Dyson, Wilkie, Hornidge, MacDonald.
In Front—Mr. Samuel B. Donnelly (Typographical Union), New York.

Second Row—Messrs. Coffey, Cummings, Powerman, Taylor, Deller, Holmshaw, Steadman, Wilkinson, Sutherland (Central News Agency), Flynn.

Third Row—Messrs. Walls, Crawford, Ham, Ashton, Marks (President National Association of Clothiers, United States), Mosely, Jones, Kelly, Cox, Barnes.

The members of the commission were:

Thos. Ashton, Amalgamated Association of Operative Cotton Spinners;
G. N. Barnes, Amalgamated Society of Engineers;
C. W. Bowerman, London Society of Compositors;
W. Coffey, London Consolidated Society of Journeymen Bookbinders;
Jas. Cox, Associated Iron and Steel Workers of Great Britain;
H. Crawford, General Union of Operative Carpenters and Joiners;
D. C. Cummings, United Society of Boiler Makers and Iron Shipbuilders;
M. Deller, National Association of Operative Plasterers;
Wm. Dyson, Amalgamated Society of Paper Makers;
T. A. Flynn, Amalgamated Society of Tailors;
Harry Ham, National Amalgamated Furnishing Trades Association;
R. Holmshaw, Sheffield Cutlery Council;
W. B. Hornidge, National Union of Boot and Shoe Operatives;
Thos. Jones, representing the Midland Counties Trades Federation;
G. D. Kelley, Amalgamated Society of Lithographic Printers of Great Britain and Ireland;
G. J. Lapping, Amalgamated Society of Leather Workers;
Jas. MacDonald, London Trades Council;
J. Maddison, Friendly Society of Ironfounders of Great Britain and Ireland;
W. C. Steadman, Trades Union Parliamentary Committee;
H. R. Taylor, Operative Bricklayers' Society;
P. Walls, National Federation of Blastfurnacemen;
Alex. Wilkie, Associated Shipwrights' Society;
W. H. Wilkinson, Northern Counties Amalgamated Associations of Weavers.

All the members (with one exception) sent in reports, each writing after his own plan, especially of matters relating to his occupation, but at the close of his report giving replies to a schedule of forty-one questions, some of them subdivided, relating to labor and other economic conditions in the United States as compared with those of England.

Taking up first the questions of immediate interest to the wage-earners, we have the following:

WAGES IN AMERICA FAR HIGHER.

"How does the value of the American wage in your trade compare with that of the English, cost of living being taken into account?"

To this, the main question among wage-workers, all the members of the commission give a verdict for America. The carpenter says money wages are "very much higher," but as to the value, "everything averages about equal, except rent and clothes." But he also says the thrifty man can certainly save more in America than in England; he "found there was plenty of employment and generally much better paid." He compares in a table the wages and expenses of an unmarried joiner or carpenter in New York with those of one in London. His result is: "The American can save nearly double, though he works four hours less per week." Other members are all more unqualifiedly of the opinion that, in their respective trades, the American working man is the better paid. The blast furnace man says: "The American is fully 25 per cent. better off." The iron founder: "Undoubtedly the American has a great deal the best of the English worker." The machinist: "About 15 or 20 per cent. higher on the base line and proportionately more on the maximum." The boilermaker: "Average wages of time-workers are 75 to 100 per cent. higher in our trade than at home, and I am inclined to the opinion that, notwithstanding the greater cost of outer clothing, housing accommodation, and fuel, a careful, sober, steady man could, whilst keeping himself efficiently provided for, save more in America than in England, foodstuffs being certainly cheaper." The cutlery worker: "Wages are generally about 100 per cent. higher;" . . . "it will cost the American wage-earner 50 per cent. more to live than the English worker." The cotton spinner thinks the advantage of the American over the English spinner in wages is 40 per cent. The weaver, speaking for his trade, says 10 to 15 per cent.; the tailor, 50 per cent.; the bricklayer, 50 per cent.; the plasterer, 25 per cent.; the lithographer, 60 per cent.; the bookbinder, 20 per cent. Mr. Steadman, representing the Parliamentary Committee of the Trade Union Congress, says "50 per cent. better off."

LITTLE DIFFERENCE IN HOURS.

"What are the hours of work in your trade in America, and how do they compare with the hours in England?"

The replies to this question will bring some surprise to those Americans who have accepted the prevalent idea that English trade unionists have a uniform eight hour day. In the building trades ten hours seems to be the rule in England, while in this country, in the larger cities at least, it is eight. When the greater proportion of the union men in the building trades here is remembered, the comparison becomes the more favorable to America. The plasterer of the commission reports: "The hours worked in America are some two hours per day less than those worked in England." The replies of the bricklayer and carpenter refer to the eight-hour day in American cities without stating the length of their own work-day. The bookbinder says: "The hours worked in our trade are generally slightly in excess of the usual practice here. There are, however, some important exceptions, where the eight-hour day is established." The steel worker reports of wages and hours: "There are all the elements of a fair comparison in the sheet trade, tinplate trade, and puddling. In both countries there are standard tonnage rates governing this class of work, and a comparison works out at practically two, two-and-a-half, and three times respectively in favor of the American workman. Very elaborate wages lists and scales are annually agreed to between the employers' and the workmen's associations, copies of which I have. Sheet and tin-bar mills work eight-hour shifts, with a limited output, and at some places puddlers also work eight-hour shifts; in most other departments the double shift is worked similar to this country." Elsewhere he notes that in the tin plate mills the workers "can often get their limited turns work out in seven hours." The leather worker reports: "The hours worked in the States leather industries are for the most part 60 per week; in a few cases, 59 hours. In one firm, where over 75 per cent. of the employes were on piecework, I believe the hours were 54, but this was an exception. In this country the hours vary from 54 to 57 per week, and in some cases they work 58½." The tailor reports for his trade that hours in America and England are "very similar." "Counting the Saturday half holiday our hours are shorter." The compositor reports: "The hours are somewhat longer than those prevailing in this country." He gives no figures for comparison. The printer in America would have derived more satisfaction from his report had he done so, keeping in mind the fact of the far greater relative number of compositors in the daily newspaper branch here, in which perhaps 1,000 have a seven-hour day and fully 10,000 eight hours, while in the book and job branch the eight-hour day has been attained in several cities, while in all the rest the nine-hour day is uniform. The lithographer reports the workday "the same practically." Of the other trades, the blast furnace man reports the ratio as twelve in America to eight and ten in England; the iron founder, nine and a half to nine; the machinist nine and a half to eight and a half; the boilermaker and the shipwright, ten to eight and the cutler, the tube worker, the spinner, the weaver, the boot and shoe worker, and the furniture worker ten to nine. To make the comparison of the national workdays complete one must observe that the Mosely Commission did not represent the cigar makers, of whom 33,000 in this country have the eight-hour day; nor the coal miners, whose union, with more than 250,000 men, has of recent years shortened the workday here to eight hours; nor silver or copper miners, whose thousands in America work eight hours or less; nor the railroad men, who in general have shorter hours than in England and outnumber the English railway servants as ten to one.

THE SAME SPEED.

"Does the American workman do more, or less in an hour, on average, than the English workman?"

To this the steel worker replies: "Much has been made of the statement that men are so rushed in American works that only the young and strong can stand the strain, and that only for a short time. No statement could be wider of the actual truth." He also reports "greater productiveness with less physical exertion, consequent upon greater adaptability of machinery and labor-saving appliances." The blast furnace man says: "We failed to find ocular evidence of the American workman running at high pressure." The boilermaker writes: "As for working hard, it was generally admitted that it was impossible for men to work harder than the piecework shipyard worker does in Great Britain." "As to whether more work is done in an hour than in England, I unhesitatingly say no." The shipwright: "By those from whom we made inquiries, many of whom have worked both in this country and America, we are assured that they worked no harder in the American shipyards than they do in the British yards." The cutlery worker: "The American does not actually work harder than the English workman in an hour." The cotton spinner: "Very little difference between them when they are employed under similar conditions." "Generally speaking, American workmen attend to a larger number of machines than is the case in England, but taking quantity and quality of work into consideration I don't think they work any harder than the English workman." The weaver: "I do not think there is much difference." But he says further: "The output in the American cotton mills is less per loom per week than in the English mills, though shorter hours are worked in the English mills." The tailor: "In the best New York and Chicago firms a journeyman tailor earns £6 in less time and in a more easy and leisurely manner than a London tailor earns £3." "The labor performed by the American is less than in England, as a consequence of improved and selected machinery. The machine is the recognized working man of America." The plasterer: "Plasterers complain that the rushing, at least in New York, is done chiefly by 'new chums' from this country, Scotsmen being the greatest delinquents in this respect. I failed to observe the great rush at work that I expected to see. Upon inquiring at one job the time taken to complete the work and comparing same with a similar amount in this country, I found that in many cases which came under my personal observation—when at work at the trade—we did equally as much." The carpenter: "I thought now was my opportunity to ask from a man who had worked on both sides of the Atlantic whether the men worked harder in America than in the old country? His answer was emphatic: 'The machinery does the work here; I never worked so hard in all my life as I did in London.'" And he says further: "In every shop I went into the great majority of the men had worked in the old country, and their opinion was that they did not work so hard in America as in England." The furniture worker remarks of a billiard table factory: "The men in this shop, although they kept moving, did not in any way appear to distress themselves." The paper maker reports: "The working at high pressure and the everlasting hustle ascribed to American workshops is a myth and exists in imagination only." The compositor: "In the offices I visited the men appeared to be working comfortably, and there was a distinct absence of the 'hustle' which one had expected to find without having to hunt for it." Of a daily newspaper office he writes: "I failed to find any trace of the feverish 'bustle' which unconsciously I had been led to expect—in fact, I have seen men at home working at much higher pressure upon a precisely similar class of work." And further: "American printers compared with English, as a general rule do not appear to work harder, if as hard." The bookbinder: "I failed to find any grounds, so far as our trade is concerned, for the assertion that the men work so much harder. Everywhere men were working fairly, with little show of that feverish haste that one would expect to find after reading some statements that have been spread abroad. I am quite sure that the average rate of work in London is quite as rapid as that prevailing in New York."

The bricklayer throws light on charges made by the London "Times" against the British bricklayers: "In attempting to make comparisons as to output, it must be borne in mind that this cannot be done equitably without taking into consideration the whole of the factors which govern the amount of work produced, the chief of them being the class of materials used, the conditions under which the work is performed, and the class and stability of the work produced. In other words, if the average number of bricks laid per day by the workman in America is compared with the average number of bricks laid per day by the workman in this country, the conditions not being equal, the comparison would be an unfair one, as the class of work produced in the two countries is not at all comparable—because, as I pointed out before, the proportion of faced work in America is infinitesimal compared with that produced in this country; and I am quite certain that if the American workman was called on to produce the same class of work under the same conditions as regards the number of angles, the bond, perpends, flushing and grouting up, selection of material and clean finish, he would not be able to produce more than the British workman, if as much. That the average output (in bulk) of the bricklayer in America is greater than the average output here is in my opinion correct, but to compare two such entirely different classes of work would be obviously unfair and misleading. . . . After considering the whole of the facts and circumstances relative to the question, I am convinced that the bricklayer here gives better value for the low wage he receives than the bricklayer in America gives for a much higher wage. The one gives a smaller quantity but better quality for a low wage; the other gives a larger quantity of lower quality for a much higher wage."

AMERICAN SANITARY CONDITIONS SUPERIOR.

"Are the needs of the workers in the matter of sanitation, ventilation, and general comfort in the factory better met in America than in England?"

On this question there is some difference of opinion, but on the whole the balance is much in favor of America. The machinist reports: "The needs of the works in the matters mentioned are no better provided for in America than in England; in fact, I should say that, excepting the workshops which have been mentioned as being well found, the American workshops, so far as I could see, are dirtier, more insanitary, and more congested than the ordinary English workshop. But it should be said for the American workshops that they are generally well heated by hot-air blasts or piping in winter time, and cooled by fan or other arrangement in summer. This is a matter almost entirely ignored in this country." The spinner says: "From what I saw, I should say they are not." And the weaver: "Not so good in America as in cotton mills in England." The boot and shoe worker: "In some instances the condition in relation to baths, etc., are superior to anything I have seen in England; otherwise there are factories and conditions that would not be tolerated in any industrial centre in England." The leather worker replies: "Not as a general rule." The plasterer reports: "Undoubtedly the building operatives in both America and Canada work under conditions much inferior to those at home or even the rest of the American workmen." The foregoing constitutes the body of opinion unfavorable to America in this respect. Nearly all the other delegates are more or less strongly of the opinion that workshop conditions are better in America than in England. Several of them simply answer the question by "yes." The blast furnace man says: "Generally." The iron founder: "So far as my experience goes, they are better cared for in America." The steel worker: "Yes, on the whole." The boilermaker: "Sanitary comfort, ventilation, and general comfort are to a great many employers something worthy of attention, and wherever possible work is inclosed in shops sufficiently heated to permit of the men working in their shirt sleeves in comfort in midwinter." The cutlery worker says: "In the cutlery trade the workshops, as a rule, are better fitted up than the generality of Sheffield workshops." "Speaking generally the comfort of the worker is more considered there than here." The tailor reports: "We have nothing in England to equal in ventilation, sanitation, light and general comfort the best which obtains in America. Ironmolder and clerk leave the works spick and span. A grimy workman is a strange spectacle in American cities." The carpenter's statement is: "The workshops generally are kept much cleaner, and the appliances for warming the shops in the winter make it much better for the workman and the work than in England." The bookbinder remarks: "The shops in the States were noticeable for the frequency with which they were swept and the precaution taken to prevent accumulation of dust and litter." The compositor reports: "In the case of the larger, and what may be termed special, factories—such as at Dayton—the sanitation, ventilation, and general comfort of the workers were far ahead of anything I have seen in this country; and in the majority of the offices I visited the general conditions were decidedly good, the method and style of building throughout the States assisting greatly so far as light and air are concerned—two most important and essential features so far as the worker in the printing trade is concerned." . . . "I was greatly struck with the cleanliness of the printing offices I visited, as well as with their light and lofty appearance."

AMERICAN OPPORTUNITIES INCOMPARABLY THE BEST.

"Speaking generally, are there greater opportunities for the working man to rise in America than in England?"

Every one of the members of the commission answers this question in the affirmative, several of them with emphasis and replying at length.

"Do you consider the general conditions of life of the workman better in America than in Englan :

A. MOSELY.

The majority, considering mainly the economic situation, reply yes; several, however, apparently on patriotic grounds, or from a more general view of society, reply no.

Thus, on the whole, in matters of which the members may be taken as best qualified to judge—matters of prime importance to the wage-earner,—wages, the workday, the rate of speed exacted, workshop conditions, opportunities, and general social conditions,—the Mosely Commission tells the American workingmen they are much better off than the English workingmen, and consequently than those of any other nation.

ADVANTAGES OF AMERICAN CAPITAL.

A Land of Great Resources, the Latest and Best Machinery, and Almost Perfect Methods.

The delegates saw wonders in American natural resources, and to some extent in American machinery and administrative methods. But of the quality of the product they have occasionally criticism.

The blast furnace man writes: The Americans "have immense mineral resources, unparalleled waterways, and railway communication." The steel worker: "To give some idea of the American natural resources I may state a fact in connection with this work. The coal mine—a drift mine—is in close proximity to the works. The seam is about five feet thick, and the coal is conveyed to the works by electric traction, and also round the works, being emptied into the various furnace coal bins from these overhead trucks. The total cost of mining, royalty, conveying coal from mine to furnace, including everything, is 75 cents per ton, and I was assured that within a few months they would be producing a ton of finished tin plates with one ton of coal consumed. I would like, in concluding, to indicate three general features of American industry to which I largely attribute their success. 1. The enormous mineral deposits, waterways, and cheap transit. 2. The control or ownership by the manufacturer (through combination or direct purchase) of the raw materials—ore, lime, coal and coke. 3. The marvelous engineering ingenuity and initiative, remarkable through every phase of manufacture in its reduction of manual labor, combined with great productiveness."

The machinist says: "Americans have, of course, natural and other advantages over us. They have great resources of raw material and a protected home market for manufactures. But, on the other hand, we have social advantages over Americans in the form of good roads, trained hands, and all the accumulated accessories of civilization which are relatively lacking in newer communities."

The cutler's report contains this passage: "The natural advantages of America and the uses made of them play no small part in developing the industrial life of the country. Natural oil and gas, which are gotten so easily and cheaply from the earth, must of necessity give a great impetus to certain industries. At the Homestead steel works all the heating of the ingots for the rolling mills is done by the aid of natural gas, not one ounce of coal being used for this purpose. The usual sidings full of coal wagons that one is so familiar with at works of this description are absent. The saving of labor in stoking alone must be enormous. The splendid waterways are of great use and provide a cheap and ready means of conveyance both inland and to the ocean. Thus the iron ore is brought from Lake Superior by the great lake steamers, which on their return take back a cargo of coal. At Buffalo this use of the waterways is illustrated by the way the corn is brought down and coal taken back from lake to lake."

The delegate from the Midland Counties Trades Federation offers as an opinion: "As to how America is able to pay higher wages and yet successfully compete with us in the markets of the world, I believe it is due to the vast natural resources she has in mines and minerals, improved methods of mining, the utilization of her vast waterways, and the superior railways she possesses."

The leather worker observes: "We cannot compete with any certainty of success with the States for the markets of the world, as with their great natural advantages they can undersell us."

The compositor speaks of the "huge natural resources at the command" of Americans.

The bookbinder mentions America's "enormous natural resources." "For instance, the iron ore is found in immense quantities, cropping up on the surface, and is obtainable by the simplest outlay for labor, no mining being necessary. Again, splendid waterways are ready to the hand of the enterprising promotors of the industry for which they can be best utilized. These and many other advantages, provided by the bountiful hand of nature, enable the American manufacturer to produce cheaply and in large quantities at lower rates than is possible in countries where heavy cost of mining, construction of roads and canals, add so materially to the charges upon output."

The lithographer thus expresses his views on this point: "The prosperity of the United States is attributed to various causes. Those which, in my opinion, operate most strongly in effecting it, are, in the first place, the splendid natural resources of the country, rich in mineral and natural productiveness; in the second place, the superior education given to the American youth, which better fits him for the industrial contest into which he must enter; and in the third place, the advantage of better machinery of the newest and most approved type. The number of labor-saving appliances in use for almost everything is perfectly astounding."

Of the machinery in use in America, the machinist's report naturally has most to say. Following are passages: "Here lies the distinctive feature of American industry, viz., the hankering after the latest machinery and best methods of working, which pervade American industrialism. In some respects American workshops are better equipped than English. They are equipped with a greater variety of special tools made for special work of repetition character, and on the other hand there is less range in regard to the size of tools in the workshops, and, therefore, because of that I think greater production. . . . American engineers have been able to do things wholesale; in fact, they have been pressed to do so, and this has led to the adoption of plans for the manipulation of parts in a wholesale way by operating upon a number at a time, and by all sorts of little contrivances for securing uniformity and dispatch. The American manager is more enterprising and more ready to introduce the latest and best of everything. . . . The spirit of enterprise is more general in America, and, as I have previously stated, there is an all-round readiness to accept new ideas, and a general hankering for machinery and appliances."

The steel worker, after remarking that the best equipped works for manufacturing plates, rails, sheets, wire rods, etc., "are far ahead of us in the outlay of their plants and their productiveness," says: "There is no doubt that the leading mills of American manufacture are far ahead of our own best mills in their arrangement and outputs. I have seen nothing like it in this country—either in the matter of output or labor-saving appliances. To the average British iron and steel workers the output of these mills will be incredible. . . . Another important item in successful mill work is the facilities of 'feeding' the mills. Such a thing as waiting for the furnace is unknown, and the charging and drawing appliances are perfect. . . . It is almost impossible to overstate the arrangements of these mills, the perfect dispatch with which everything is done, and the incredibly small amount of manual labor required in comparison with our own mills. Everything is straight and continuous. Not only are the mills well fed, but such is the space and equipment that there is no hitch or block through to the finish. From leaving the furnace there is no handling of material until the rail is slipped on the straightener's block."

The shipwright says the greater output of the American "is due to the organization of the works, the class of work, and the superior tools and machinery placed at his disposal."

The spinner writes on this point: "Comparing American factories with English factories and their equipment for production, I can only say, so far as the cotton spinning industry is concerned, that the only advantage that I found to obtain in the American mills is that a much better material is used than is the case for the same counts of yarn in the English mills. I don't think the American cotton mills are better managed than the English mills." And the weaver: "The keen appreciation which Americans have for up-to-date machinery, and the readiness with which they adopt labor-saving machinery of any kind, is remarkable." And the tailor: "No money is spared in the equipment of American factories; the best only is good enough. Production is correspondingly increased and insured." The carpenter and joiner found "machines doing what we entirely do by hand labor at home." "Employers in America vie with each other to get the latest up-to-date machines."

The furniture worker ventures this opinion: "If employers having the means would speculate in laying down as perfect plants as those I saw in Grand Rapids I am sure we should hear less about American competition."

The paper maker has this: "When we leave the natural resources and go in the mill, there is no doubt we are also lagging behind, the mechanical equipment of the American mills being superior to the great majority of the mills in this country, not only in the machinery actually necessary for paper manufacture, but for labor-saving also. The idea of the American is, from the time the raw material enters the mill, to get as much of it made into the finished article in the shortest possible time, everything necessary in its manufacture being regulated by this desire."

The lithographer reports: "Assuming that our employers will provide machinery and other necessary means of production equal to those in use in America, this country need have no cause for alarm with respect to a transference of trade to the United States, so far as applies to lithography."

On the general question as to whether factories in America are better equipped for production than in England, all the replies were in the affirmative, except four, two being "no" and two "perhaps."

AMERICAN PRODUCTS NOT SUPERIOR.

As to quality of American product, while there is praise, especially for the output of some of the metal trades, considerable fault is found. Following are extracts from the reports:

The machinist: 'From the point of view of quality I feel quite sure that British goods have nothing to fear, providing that British designers are encouraged." "The factories certainly do not turn out better work. Qualitatively the work is inferior to British work. This is marked in industries other than engineering, notably in cutlery and newspapers. It is also true to some extent as applied to the engineering industry, not so far as fitting parts are concerned, these being largely standardized, but in the dispensing with all polish and finish not absolutely necessary, and in skimpiness of material, which is also softer and less durable than that used in Great Britain."

The boiler maker: "The life of an American locomotive is not to be compared with the life of a British one. . . . Summing the whole matter up, American locomotives compared with our own are extremely ugly, and of inferior work and finish, and although it may be argued that they serve their purpose, yet I should be sorry to see such an age of utility in our country that would sacrifice all beauty and finish, believing, as I do, that if anything is worth doing at all it is worth doing well."

The shipwright: "So far as could be ascertained from interviews with representative workmen and others of reliable authority, the work carried on is not so substantial as with us, and there does not appear to be the same regard for completeness as there is in the yards of this country. The vital distinction between the yards of this country and America appears to be that the work in the British shipyards not only has a better finish but is of a much more stable and enduring character."

The spinner: "The system of working in the spinning and carding departments of the American mills is much different from what obtains in the English mills, and my opinion is that the advantage is on the side of the English system, both in respect to the cost and the quality of production—all other things b. equal."

The boot and shoe worker: "Machinery in the boot trade is run at a greater speed with advantage in relation to quantity, but loss of quality in production." The leather worker: "I am of the opinion that taking the goods all round we produce a better article than they do in the States."

The plasterer found many faults in American methods in building. In Washington, even in the room in which the President received the delegates, "the plastered walls were very poorly finished, although it is only fair to say that some decent work was to be found in the Congress House and Library." In New York: "The work was both good and bad; the latter could not be worse, but here let it be said that the good was on a par with our best. I rejoiced to find at least some real plastering, it being the first seen during my stay, either in Canada or the States."

The furniture worker reports: "I spent an hour or two in inspecting the furniture department of stores, but found (with one exception) nothing half so perfect in design or workmanship as is to be found in a second-class shop in Tottenham Court Road, London."

The paper maker: "In many cases the quality and finish of the manufactured article is inferior to English make."

SOCIOLOGICAL QUERIES.

The common school education of the youth of America elicited general admiration from the delegates. The tailor thus begins his report: "It is a humiliating fact that the children of our industrial population receive an education very much inferior to that given to the children of the United States of America. Not only is education in that country free, but it is continued up to the age of eighteen, and in some States even university education is free. So far as American law is concerned, every boy and girl starts life with at least a high school education." . . . "With us the poverty of parents means compulsory ignorance of the children."

One of the forty-one set questions was: "Does gambling or horse racing, etc., enter as largely into the life of the American as of the English working man?" To this three of the delegates gave no answer, sixteen say, some of them emphatically, it does not, while three say it does. The cutler avows: "It is undoubtedly true that there is less drinking among American workmen than we find among our own." "There is a remarkable absence of bad language in the streets." The Midland Counties delegate says: "There is not so much horse racing as here, and, so far as one could see, but little gambling, except at some clubs one could read about at times."

Several delegates are of the opinion that whereas in England the introduction of machinery moves the employer to reduce wages, in America it brings an increase. None of them found evidence that increased output through efficiency at piecework was a forerunner of wage reduction. Most of them believe the American employer is ready to increase wages with increased output. They also heard that suggestions for improvements are welcomed and rewarded, while American employers are in general more accessible than are the English. The building trades delegates and those of the cotton mills think the worker is thrown out of work before he grows old in their occupations, but the other representatives saw no evidences of the fact in their trades.

MR. MOSELY'S VIEWS.

The preface to the volume is written by Mr. Mosely. Following are noteworthy passages: "My personal conclusion is that the true born American is a better educated, better housed, better fed, better clothed, and more energetic man than his British brother, and infinitely more sober; as a natural consequence, he is more capable of using his brains as well as his hands. Many of the men, however, holding leading positions are either English or Scotch, and the American himself is justly proud of his British descent."

"One of the principal reasons why the American workman is better than the Britisher is that he has received a sounder and better education, whereby he has been more thoroughly fitted for the struggles of after life; and I believe all my delegates were themselves immensely impressed with the generally high standard of education in the United States—a standard it would be well for our own nation to copy as far as practicable." "Labor saving machinery is widely used everywhere and is encouraged by the unions and welcomed by the men, because experience has shown them that in reality machinery is their best friend."

"My own observations lead me to believe that the average American manufacturer runs his machinery at a much higher speed than is the usual practice in England—in other words, for 'all it is worth,' and the men ably second the employers' efforts in this direction. In England it has been the rule for generations past that as soon as a man earns beyond a certain amount of wages the price for his work is cut down; and he, finding that working harder or running his machine quicker (naturally a greater strain) brings in the long run no larger reward, slackens his efforts accordingly." "In many trades, a joint committee of employers and employes meet periodically to settle rates for piecework, by mutual consent, and if such an arrangement were adopted all round I am sure it would be found beneficial; and this is what is practically done in all American industries."

"Of course the true solution of the whole problem is profit-sharing in some shape or form, and it is towards this goal that I feel both masters and men alike should turn their eyes."

"The United States is advancing by leaps and bounds. She is beginning to feel the beneficial effects of the education of her masses, and an enormous territory teeming with natural resources as yet but meagerly developed." "At the present time the home market of the United States is so fully occupied with its own developments that the export trade has as yet been comparatively little thought of; but as time goes on and the numerous factories that are being erected all over the country come into full bearing America is bound to become the keenest of competitors in the markets of the world." "That already she has her eye on the export trade is plain to every one except the wilfully blind; but at present she is only getting ready. When America wishes to export goods she intends to dictate freights, which she could not do if she had no mercantile marine of her own."

"That the American workman earns higher wages is beyond question. As a consequence, the average married man owns the house he lives in, which not only gives him a stake in the country but saves payment of rent, enabling him either to increase his savings or to purchase further comforts."

"Food is as cheap (if not cheaper) in the United States as in England, whilst general necessaries may, I think, be put on the same level. Rent, clothes made to order, and a variety of things, including all luxuries, are considerably dearer. Luxuries, however, do not enter much into the every day consumption of the average working man in this country, and if in the United States he can get them at all (even though he have to pay a high price for them) that is surely an advantage by comparison."

"The American workman drinks but little, and his house is usually well furnished and fitted with luxuries in the way of bathrooms, laundries, hot water and heating systems, and other items mostly unknown to the British workman."

"One of the points the delegates were invited to investigate was whether or not the workman in the United States wears out faster than the Englishman. Personally, I think so. It is generally admitted that the American workman, in consequence of labor saving machines and the excellence of the factory organization, does not need to put forth any greater effort in his work than is the case here, if as much. He is infinitely better paid, therefore better housed, fed, clothed, and moreover is much more sober. Under such conditions he must naturally be more healthy, a proposition that I think cannot be denied. In American factories, speaking generally, great attention is paid to the necessities and comfort of the workers. Separate lockers (of which the workman has the key) are provided for working clothing; consequently the man can arrive at and leave his work well clad, changing at the factory. The shops are usually very well ventilated, although it is customary to keep them at a temperature many degrees above the average in this country; but this is liked or would not be done, and is in fact a national characteristic; and there is after all a good deal to be said in favor of being able to walk into a factory which is well warmed and where the tools do not freeze the hands as soon as touched. Excellent lavatories with shower baths, etc., and many other comforts for the employes, are the rule rather than the exception in the large factories; and in fact the American manufacturer has realized that if he wishes the best results from the hands he employs he must provide for their comfort and cleanliness. It is not a question of philanthropy, but of practical business."

"One point that has struck me with enormous force, as I believe it has all the delegates, is the close touch and sympathy between master and man, which is carried a step further in the enlistment of the men's good offices to improve factory methods."

"Fuel and raw materials are much the same price in the United States as in Europe, and it therefore cannot be claimed that she has very much advantage on this score; but facilities for transport, both by rail and water, are undoubtedly both better and cheaper, and I think one of the points absolutely necessary to the success of British industry is a close examination and revision of our railway rates as against those of our competitors."

"In conclusion, I can only say that if we are to hold our own in the commerce of the world, both masters and men must be up and doing. Old methods must be dropped, old machinery abandoned. Practical education of the masses must be instituted and carried out upon a logical basis and with efficiency."

THE CIVIC FEDERATION.

The delegates who were present in New York at the time of the meeting of the Civic Federation signed the following document expressing their desire to see some similar organization established in England:

"In the course of our travels and investigations in the United States the excellent results achieved by the National Civic Federation of America have been brought to our notice, the Federation having been successful, among other things, in bringing capital and labor into closer touch, thus providing a practical solution of many of the difficulties and vexed questions that arise between the two.

"One of the most important features of the Federation is the section whose duty it is to get information of the first sign of impending trouble, and in the earliest stages of dispute to step in for the purpose of bringing the contending parties together at a round-table conference before any breach has actually taken place and before either side has assumed a position from which it can recede only with difficulty, and, in our opinion, it would be of benefit to both workers and employers were some similar organization brought into being in Great Britain.

"In expressing this view we do not desire in any way to interfere with the bodies which already exist for mediation and conciliation in the Board of Trade, Chambers of Commerce, Trade Conciliation Boards, etc., or agreements between employers' associations and workmen's organizations, but, if possible, to establish a further means, not so much for the adjustment of troubles after they have arisen as for their prevention.

"As representatives of our respective trade unions, it will be our duty on our return to our own country to place before our members the objects of this branch of the work of the Civic Federation, and we also hope to have the co-operation of other trade organizations, large and small, throughout the United Kingdom."

Delegate Walls writes of the Civic Federation: "I was much impressed with the good work done in America by the Civic Federation, more particularly when I had an opportunity of attending its meetings at the Board of Trade Hall, New York. When the Civic Federation was first spoken of to the members of the commission, several seemed to have an idea that it was a kind of Board of Arbitration. If I thought that such a body would attempt to assume the role of arbitration, or in any way interfere in the technicalities of a dispute, I would have nothing to do with it; but its sole function is to use every means possible to bring contending parties together, particularly before the real rupture takes place, or before it becomes too great to be easily healed. I have no hesitation in saying that, had there been a similar institution in this country, it would have saved many thousands of pounds to both capital and labor and many a bitter tear. We have yet the more or less isolated employer, who has not been accustomed to a union. and dreads the thought of it. He has read of the agent as the paid agitator and has a kind of holy horror of him. On the other hand, we have the workman to whom a union is new and who has no more idea how to handle it than a three-year-old boy has to manage a toy locomotive. The existence of such conditions form a sort of industrial powder magazine, where the smallest spark is certain to create an explosion. When it takes place both parties stand on their dignity, and every hour the gulf grows wider. The function of a similar body to the Civic Federation would be to bring the contending parties face to face. Such a body could not fail to do good in this country."

Delegate Barnes: "Of course, I had full opportunities, so far as three days' attendance at its annual convention could give them, of getting to know the men at the head of it. These are the representatives of American organized labor, of American employers, organized and unorganized, and of the best elements in American public opinion. I saw and conversed with many of them, and had every reason to respect their ability and sincerity. . . . An organization of the character suggested in this country might at all events bring in the best elements of public opinion, and thus tend to bring parties together and help to breach over the chasm between man and man which so far has been a condition of modern industry brought about by larger corporations and workshops."

Delegate Cummings: "I heartily approve of the formation of such bodies as the Civic Federation, and would at all times lend my assistance to the formation of any similar body at home having for its object the obtaining of industrial peace by reason and common sense aided by intelligent public opinion. . . . The Civic Federation of America, or rather its industrial department, certainly sets out in a direction new to us. . . . Although willing to act as a conciliation committee and also to arbitrate, if desired by both sides, yet that is not their principal function; the chief object is to step in before an actual strike or lockout takes place and try to bring the contending parties together with the object of securing a reasonable settlement. The formation in Great Britain of a body similar to the Civic Federation is well worthy of a trial."

Delegate Wilkie: "I am in entire sympathy with its aims and objects.

Delegate Ashton: "I quite approve of its aims in trying to avoid strikes and lockouts by conciliation and other methods which employers and workpeople may be agreeable to adopt."

Delegate Wilkinson: "I fully approve of the working of the Civic Federation. I see no reason why such an organization, if one is not already in existence, should not be introduced in England on the same lines as the American organization. I am in favor of taking steps to establish such an organization."

Delegate Flynn: "To my mind it appears that work of the description carried on by the Civic Federation confers lasting benefits upon all sections of the community. Run on such lines, there is a boundless field of operations before the Civic Federation. The confidence of the working classes is neither easily given nor easily withdrawn, and while the wage-earner must in the main hammer out the metal of his own life, it is pleasant and cheering to know that outside industrial strife there is a weight of public opinion which may be used to bring about and maintain just and honorable settlements of what would otherwise become bitter and disastrous disputes. The Civic Federation has my vote."

Delegate Deller: "I approve of any method of preventing strikes or lockouts that does not interfere with the collective bargaining of the worker."

Delegate Crawford: "Any independent body of gentlemen who would form themselves into an association, so as to bring the two contending parties together to discuss their grievances in an amicable way, as the Civic Federation of America did in the case of the coal strike, would have my approval in principle."

Delegate Bowerman: "With respect to the question as to whether I approve of the working of the Civic Federation, and if any organization on the same or somewhat modified lines could be introduced into England, I should welcome any movement having for its object the bringing together of employers and employed for the purpose of settling terms and conditions of employment or of amicably arranging disputed points."

Delegate Coffey: "In England we have for many years been familiar with the work accomplished by boards of arbitration and conciliation. It was with very favorable disposition, therefore, that we gave attention to the work of the Civic Federation of America. This Federation has for its object the prevention of trade disputes by means of influencing the contending parties to confer in friendly discussion upon their points of difference. It seems, upon reflection, that there is room for such a body as the Civic Federation, and that its establishment would be likely to result in much benefit to trade and commercial interests generally. In a general way the public takes but a cursory and superficial interest in labor questions, regarding them as matters to be settled by experts. The Civic Federation aims at introducing this third element, or, at least, of inducing it to assist in bringing about the peaceful solution of labor problems. This would not be by taking sides but by friendly persuasion, inducing the contending parties to meet and discuss their difficulties in each other's presence and so arrive at a friendly settlement. This organization would, therefore, embrace not only the experts, not alone the keen man of business intent on securing at all costs the terms that he requires, not only the workmen's representative, anxious and even eager to stand out for the full concession of the demands of his organization, but also the statesman, the churchman, the professional man; in fact, the representatives of the great class that is usually seriously affected by the disturbance of the ordinary course of business on the occurrence of trade troubles. For this reason alone, I am completely and decidedly in favor of moving for the formation of a body on similar lines to the Civic Federation."

Delegate Cox: "There was a time in our own trade union movement when the jingo spirit was dominant. Saner methods now prevail, and a strike over a wage question is the exception rather than the rule. Whether the Civic Federation will succeed in educating American opinion up to the same level, I cannot say. An organization of that character should be purely educational; there are times when both workmen and employers resent any outside interference. When both parties are educated up to the ideal that strikes and lockouts are both futile and criminal, that justice to both can be secured by other methods, there will be no difficulty in arriving at satisfactory mutual arrangements."

FOR INDUSTRIAL PEACE

REPRESENTATIVES OF EMPLOYERS, WAGE EARNERS AND THE PUBLIC SPEAK IN FAVOR OF CONFERENCE AND CONCILIATION

A remarkable gathering was that at the dinner given on Wednesday evening, May 13, by the Executive and Conciliation Committees of the New York

SENATOR MARCUS A. HANNA.

Civic Federation to the members of the Executive Committee, National Civic Federation, in attendance at their semi-annual meeting in New York.

The following list of the men who sat together at the tables in itself speaks volumes for the work already accomplished by the organization and of its possibilities for the future:

Lewis Nixon, Chairman.
Senator Marcus A. Hanna.
Archbishop John Ireland.
President John Mitchell, of the United Mine Workers.
Spencer Trask, of Spencer Trask & Co., bankers.
Wm. H. Farley, Secretary United Board of Building Trades, New York.
Frederick D. Underwood, President Erie Railroad.
Emerson McMillin, banker.
Otto Eidlitz, Secretary United Building Trades.
Marcus M. Marks, President National Clothiers' Association.
Franklin MacVeagh, of Franklin MacVeagh & Co., wholesale grocers, Chicago.
W. W. Miller, Manager of New Orleans Street Railway Company.
H. H. Vreeland, President National Street Railway Association.
M. M. Garland, ex-President Amalgamated Association of Iron, Steel and Tin Workers.
Daniel J. Keefe, President International Longshoremen's Association.
W. D. Mahon, President Amalgamated Association of Street Railway Employes of America.
Col. John J. McCook.
H. C. Watson, Editor "Dun's Review."
Edward A. Moffett, Editor "Bricklayer and Mason."
Louis B. Schram, President Associated Brewers.
T. H. Smith, President New York Metal Trades Association.
George Gunton, President Institute of Social Economics.
Walter H. Page, Editor "World's Work."
Henry White, General Secretary United Garment Workers.
H. C. Hunter, Commissioner New York Metal Trades Association.
Patrick Calhoun, street railway director.
Phil. G. Brady, Vice-President, and Francis J. McKay, local business agent, Brotherhood of Boilermakers and Iron Shipbuilders of America.
Ralph M. Easley, General Secretary National Civic Federation.
John Philips, Secretary United Hatters of America.
Charles Delaney, Granite Cutters.
R. E. Neidig, Housesmiths.
R. W. Nelson, President American Typefounders' Company.
J. B. Wilson, Machinists.
T. F. Woodlock, Editor "Wall Street Journal."
James P. Archibald, Brotherhood of Painters and Paper Hangers.
Wm. Fyfe, Amalgamated Society of Carpenters and Joiners.
Joseph Mulaney, Salamander Boiler and Pipe Coverers.
A. J. Boulton, Stereotypers.
John R. Commons, Secretary Conciliation Committee, New York Civic Federation.
Henry L. Cargill.
Samuel B. Donnelly and J. W. Sullivan, Typographical Union.

Chairman Nixon, in calling the guests to order after the dinner, tersely referred to the organization of the Civic Federation, its work thus far, and its opportunities for the future. His remarks carried the assemblage to a high plane of thought and sentiment, which was uninterruptedly maintained the entire evening. In introducing Senator Hanna as the first speaker, Mr. Nixon said: "I am going to ask him to say to you to-night something about his experience and give you the benefit of some of his wisdom."

SENATOR HANNA'S SPEECH.

Mr. Hanna spoke as follows:

Mr. Chairman and Gentlemen: It is certainly a great pleasure to me to be able to attend this meeting, composed as it is, in large part, of the members of the newly chosen committee of New York which has undertaken this great task. I do not know that you fully appreciate, gentlemen, all that you have undertaken, but, in the light of the experience of the national organization I feel at liberty to hold out to you every encouragement for the future. When I joined the national organization two years ago, I must confess that I myself had some doubts with reference to the practicability and efficiency of such an organization. I had been in touch with labor all my life. I had witnessed the many vicissitudes, and many times the troubles, that crept into industrial life, but I learned my lesson thirty years ago when after a disastrously long strike in the coal regions of Ohio I was impressed with the idea that there ought to be a better way to settle disputes between employer and employe than by strikes and lockouts. This idea was an inspiration to me, because as I went on and became connected with different industrial interests that brought me in touch with all classes of labor and made a trial of my theory I found how easy it was when men could be brought face to face to find a middle ground upon which all could agree. It is with some pride that I often make the statement to the public that, having learned that lesson and having put into practice what I have learned and preached, I have never had a strike since. [Applause.] It was because of the faith established by that experience that I entered into this work, and I was encouraged when I found that the men engaged in it were experienced, that they viewed the question with good common sense and were imbued with the same spirit that filled me, and that we could rely upon their efforts and loyalty to the principles of the federation.

I stated in the meeting to-day that there are no real discouragements as to the future, although under present conditions we seem confronted with almost insurmountable difficulties. There has not been a failure, with one exception, and that not entirely a failure, in the efforts of this organization. We are not yet perfect in our organization, because we have not reached a point where the people interested fully appreciate and understand all there is in this great question. We are approaching better things rapidly and successfully, and I may speak of this organization as a success now, surrounded as I am by the men in New York who have undertaken the auxiliary work in this city. When I see around me men representing all classes, equally interested, a class of men that do things, and when they undertake a mission will accomplish it, I feel justified in making such a claim. Multiplying such organizations as yours, establishing them in all the centres of the country, step by step all these difficulties which seem to beset our path to-day will fade away, and each man who is a pioneer now in this work will live to see the time when he will be called blessed by his fellowmen. We shall need solid common sense, practical business methods, pure motives, and a spirit to settle questions, not for the advantage of one side, but to the mutual advantage of both. I feel hopeful as to the success of these efforts. Much depends upon the success of this auxiliary in New York City. You are the first in the field, and it is a field ripe for your labors. You confront conditions calling for serious consideration, and I emphasize that reflection in the

JOHN MITCHELL.

presence of trade unionists. What brings up almost a crisis, gentlemen, in this question, is the recognition of organized labor. I have been connected and dealt with organized labor for thirty years. I have seen it grow in strength just in proportion as it has proceeded along the lines of good judgment and common sense. Its position to-day is very much stronger than ever before in our industrial history, but it will require the soundest judgment, the greatest amount of forbearance, and the strictest loyalty to the principles which are the foundation of the work of the National Civic Federation to meet this crisis. I wish to make an appeal to-night to you gentlemen who have undertaken the work in this city to stand firmly upon the principles which this federation has put forth. I mean by that a recognition of the rights of both classes and a determination by those who represent either class in the organization to stand firmly for those principles and insist upon their observance. No army ever succeeded without discipline, not only discipline in the ranks but in the leadership, and that discipline must come from experience. No general

ARCHBISHOP JOHN IRELAND.

can command an army without experience as a soldier as well as a leader, and on the representatives of labor and capital will devolve the greatest responsibility in times like this. To-day I have learned through various sources of the situation in New York. I am not surprised that there are disagreements. I am not surprised that there should be conditions which should lead to serious difficulties, with feeling on both sides, but, in view of the experience of our organization I should say there is not anything before you insurmountable, any more than there has been before the national organization; and my advice is, be conservative and, above all things, be patient. It is just as important to organized labor that its modes of government and methods of operation should be on sound business principles as that it should succeed in its efforts temporarily. We are building a structure not for to-day. Success is not for to-day. It is for the future, and the success of a movement like this, contributing to the advantage of all classes, has a higher motive and better objects than the mere gaining of a point or points to a controversy. Looking into the future, this movement means the elevation of the laboring class to a higher plane. It means better citizenship, better government; a feeling of humanity underlies this movement, and those of us who are missionaries in the field are aware of a growing interest as we meet with success in grappling with difficulties that are hard to overcome. I beg leave to suggest to those representing employers and employes that under these conditions in New York, for the moment and for the immediate future everything else in your business, in your everyday life, should be made subsidiary to the important task which lies before you. Don't say you have not time; don't feel that you have not the inclination; take hold of this question, because, believe me, my friends, the results will be successful if the efforts are loyal to principle, and in the end you will be more than repaid a thousand fold for the time that you may give and the effort you may expend.

It is all wrong to suppose that the laboring element of this country is not ready and willing to join in this movement. I speak from experience. In all the cases that have come to me, many of them entirely outside of the national committee work here, I have found the labor organizations ready and willing to go more than half way. I have found some difficulty in overcoming the prejudices that have been growing up for years in the minds of men who have not appreciated and not fully understood the importance of this work for mutual benefit. Our progress is a work of education. We cannot expect that all classes of men, coming from all the nations of the world, even from countries where from their earliest days men are led to believe that they are little better than slaves, shall be able in a day to free themselves from their earlier influences, which have been all against the employer, while their associations have been simply the basis for the creation of a prejudice. They have come to this country, known to be a land of liberty and equality, and they do not immediately fully appreciate and understand America's free institutions or our American government, and it is only fair for those of us who pride ourselves upon our American citizenship, upon nativity in this great country, and upon a higher plane of education and enlightenment, that, when we come to study these questions of mutual interest, we shall study them from the standpoint of the "other fellow," and take into consideration his conditions in early life and have a care before attributing to him selfishness entirely. At the same time, that very spirit of our American institutions demands of all citizens a rigid adherence to our constitutional rights and the observance and execution of every law. The peace of our people depend on the enforcement of our laws, and the protection of life and property must be taken into account and fully observed. It becomes the duty of you who are at the head of labor organizations to spread this doctrine, and in the way of education insist that it shall be carried out, in order to break down the prejudices that have grown up against organized labor as the result of strikes, of cases of lawlessness, and of even destruction of life and property. It is the duty of those who have influence with organized labor and have to an extent in their hands the discipline over their organizations, first, to obey the laws of the land, and, secondly, to recognize equal rights among all people.

I tell the operators that it is their business, it is a part that belongs to them, to set the example in that direction. It is supposed that, from education and experience and higher conditions of citizenship and enlightenment, they should be better able to judge, better able to lead, in these things than many who follow in the ranks of organized labor. Wherever the greater proportion of intelligence and enlightenment lies belongs also the greater responsibility. It is the object lessons that we give to those in our employ, the examples we furnish to those whom we ask to join with us, that will bring success in obtaining their confidence.

My interest in all this work, gentlemen, has led me to believe that, if we can by any method establish a relation of mutual trust between the laborer and the employer, we shall lay the foundation stone of a structure that will endure for all time. Absolute confidence must be the foundation stone, because, unless the employer can establish such a relation between himself and his employes, when we come to consider a disagreement as to the wages or other conditions. men being naturally selfish, the employes will think of an employer's statement of facts, "Well, that's his side of the question, and he is arguing from a selfish standpoint." If I have been successful in dealing with labor unions for our organization, it has been because I have been successful in establishing the relation of mutual confidence. If I have been influential to-day in the share of the work that I am undertaking, it is because I have striven to obtain not only the confidence of the capitalists but also that of the wage earners. I would not have any heart in this work could I not be able to say conscientiously that the only object I have in undertaking it—and it is no small part of the work of my life—is to improve the condition of the classes who need help in this country, to elevate them in every way, to obtain for them a wider scope of education and welfare and through that to make them better citizens of a happier land. [Applause.]

I am glad to be able to say to-night that establishing this organization has had an immediate influence on other cities. St. Louis and Chicago have already fallen into line, and other cities which held back are now making arrangements to organize branch organizations. It is a source of great satisfaction to me to find that every man who originally enlisted in this work has grown more and more interested, has found it a work that brings a realization that he is doing good to his fellowmen, and this is now no small part of his inspiration. I have yet to know a man in labor or other circles who when results have proved beneficial has failed to realize the compensations. There is Christianity in the work, and the higher ambition of every true man will be stirred in the enjoyment of it.

Our national commercial supremacy is an object dear to every patriot, and, gentlemen, its continuance depends upon the solution of the labor problem. There is every reason why we should consider "self" as secondary in every conference. There is every reason why every man who represents a labor organization should put aside the feeling as to whether he individually is going to win or lose in a conference. And in my experience, in all the settlements of difficulties in which I have been concerned in thirty years I have found the highest appreciation of the benefits of industrial peace coming from the laboring class. That should be encouraging to you who have responsible positions in these labor organizations. In doing your missionary work among your fellows, you should incite in them the ambition to be better than they have been, to take a higher place in this city and in the industrial world. How true it is that all of our industries which have grown great through our natural resources and under our beneficent laws were first begun by the men who worked with their hands! The foundations of the great iron and steel industries of the United States were laid by men who came from England, practised and experienced in their art. Capital came to their aid, and that combination—of experience, of the hands of the working man, and of capital—has made us to-day the greatest industrial nation of the world. We have only entered upon a great world-wide commercial career. The future is all before us. With wisdom and patience, with the strict observance of economic laws and fidelity to American principles, there can be no other settlement of the social question than that there shall be a fair division of profits. To bring about that condition first of all—I repeat, soberly, emphatically—we must establish mutual confidence. For this we are laying the foundation by every single organization we make. There

LEWIS NIXON.

will be no failures if we enter upon our labors with the proper spirit. The golden rule is our motto, gentlemen. Stand by it, and we shall win. [Applause.]

Mr. John Mitchell was the second speaker. Mr. Nixon, in introducing him, said: "We have heard from a representative American employer, and now we want to hear from a representative American wage earner. It has not been so many months since one hearing of John Mitchell would expect to see 'a man with hoofs and horns,' and you see him a modest, unassuming American gentleman, unwearying in his demands for what he considers right, but willing and anxious to concede the rights of others."

Mr. Mitchell said, in part:

I have so recently recovered from the bruises of industrial war that it may seem somewhat satirical for me to say I am in favor of industrial peace. However, I believe that more strikes and more lockouts and more labor disturbances have grown out of the failure on the part of capitalists and labor men to meet in conference, to tell one another the truth, than from any other one thing. I believe there should be a greater bond of confidence between employers and employes. . . .

From my experience, I would say that trouble frequently occurs not because either side doesn't want to do what is right, but because we don't know one another. I have, I believe, as extensive an acquaintance with labor men as any one in this country, I know about as many employers as most men do, and my experience teaches me that the vast majority of both employers and employes and representative trade unionists want to do right. The trouble is that we don't understand what is right. We too often assume that we ourselves are infallible, but when we have a chance to sit down as we are to-night and talk things over, we are likely to make agreements.

Gentlemen, those who don't understand what we trade unionists stand for often misunderstand our movements and judge us by our faults alone. They are disposed to think that the trade union movement depends upon physical force for success. It is unfortunate that we are sometimes judged by our faults—and I am free to confess that we have them—God did not make perfect men. We have our faults and are sorry for them. We hope to grow better all the time, and we are growing better, but if I believed for one moment that the trade union movement depended upon physical force for its success I would leave it. If I believed that there were no other means of gaining success, or one thing un-American, in the trade union movement, I would not be a trade unionist. The trade union movement—ours—is an American movement. We do not in our country have the same principles of trade unionism that they have in some of the other countries. It is a rare thing in America to have an unreasonable restriction in the amount of work a man shall do. The American trade union believes in one restriction—the hours of labor—and that is the only restriction except in so far as it is necessary to protect the health of the operatives, and I think no manufacturer will object to restrictions of that kind.

In holding conferences, it is certainly necessary that the unions be represented by union committeemen. It must be apparent to every fair-minded man that a labor organization, like any and every other institution, must have trained men, specialists, indeed, to direct its affairs; and in these days of industrial concentration the organizations require and employ as officers the most skilled and best-informed persons they can find in their respective trades; and particularly it is essential that the unions be represented by men of wide experience and honest motives; men who are fearless in the prosecution of their duties; men who will insist upon labor receiving that portion of the profits of industry which properly belong to it; but who, at the same time, will recognize the right of the employers to receive that portion of the profits to which their investments entitle them.

The contracts made between the union representatives ought to be observed as sacredly and their provisions carried out as religiously as though it were a penal offense to violate them; and I am sure that experience has demonstrated that in those trades and industries where the employes are best organized and where the trade union is recognized and contracted with, strikes and labor disturbances have been least numerous.

It goes without saying that every strike and every lockout affects seriously others than those directly engaged in the strike or lockout. Great public interests are involved, and it is certainly a matter of no small concern to the public that some method be adopted through which strikes and lockouts may be entirely avoided, or at least reduced to the minimum. Experience has demonstrated that the most practical plan which the ingenuity of man has been able, up to this time, to devise is for employers to recognize the union; meet its representatives in conference; enter into trade agreements which define in detail the conditions of employment which shall obtain during the life of such agreements. The constitution and laws of nearly every labor organization make it an offense punishable by expulsion for any member to violate a trade agreement or even by subterfuge to evade any of its provisions. The officers of the trade organizations of the present day recognize the great responsibility resting upon them, and they are few, indeed, who dare, even if they were so inclined, ruthlessly to disregard the sacred obligations of a contract. I know of many instances where contracts which were in conflict with the constitution and laws of trade unions have been entered into with employers, and yet the officers and members of the trade organizations have insisted that the contracts superseded the constitution and laws and took precedence of them; in fact, I recall several specific cases where the members of a local union connected with a national organization went on strike for the purpose of enforcing a higher rate of wages than was provided for in the contract made between the national organization and an employers' association, in which the officers of the national union promptly filled the places of the strikers with other men in order that the union could not be charged with or convicted of breach of faith.

As the unions have grown in numerical strength, as their power and responsibility have increased, they have become correspondingly conservative in their administration. The labor unions are here; they are here to stay; they are a power which must be reckoned with; they were not formed from sentimental ideas; they do not advocate Utopian theories or impractical policies; they have not grown to their present vast magnitude without good cause. The time has passed when wages and conditions of employment can be fixed satisfactorily at the door of the factory or at the mouth of the mine; the workers insist—and justly, too—that their wages shall be agreed to in conference halls where reason and logic, conservatism and equity shall be the controlling influences; they insist upon being represented in these conferences by men qualified by education and experience to defend their interests in as able a manner as the interests of capital are defended and protected by its representatives.

I don't know that the joint conference is the solution of the labor problem, but it is the nearest that has been instituted among men. I believe that we will have strikes and lockouts as long as the world lasts. I don't look forward to the time when we shall all live in paradise. But I do believe it is the solemn duty of every good American citizen, be he workman or capitalist, to do his level best to bring about an honorable adjustment of this great question.

I believe the great question before the American people to-day is the labor question. It is the question that is brought home to every man and every woman. We ought to get our heads together and join in every effort to help solving. I believe the National Civic Federation is the best channel through which we can bring the apparently hostile forces of society together. It has men in it whose influence will reach throughout the country, if not the world.

I am glad to be with you to-night and pleased to know that the local branch in New York is doing so much good work. The Civic Federation is a good deal like some of the secret societies. People hear of their faults but often don't hear about the good things. The Civic Federation has averted many strikes through bringing men into conference with one another. Such events cannot usually be made public through the newspapers, but I know New York would not be doing business as it is to-day if the Civic Federation had not accomplished what it has. [Applause.]

In introducing Archbishop Ireland as the next speaker Mr. Nixon said: "There is a triple alliance, and we want to bring about a proper understanding among the three. It is natural we should want to hear from that other factor, the general public, and also naturally we turn to that first consideration with the general public, the church."

Archbishop Ireland said:

I assure you it is a great pleasure to be here this evening, and I came all the way from the Mississippi River in order to hear the wisdom spoken and mingle a voice with those words.

I am [referring to Mr. Nixon's introduction] here as a representative of the church, and I am glad to be here. I think that it is the place of the church to come forward in all such efforts as are being made to-day to bring together the different elements of society and to establish peace throughout the country. The church says, be just; give to every one his due; it says, love one another, rejoice in lifting up humanity; it says, give peace and happiness to all men; and those principles observed we will have peace and happiness, and whatever we are doing at present is really with the intention of applying those general precepts of the church. So I am at home as a minister of the church, when I find myself in conferences such as those of the Civic Federation. I am here as a lover of humanity and as a lover of my country. As a lover of humanity, I should wish, indeed, to see the sunlight of social peace beaming upon every countenance. I am not afraid of those labor movements which honored the latter part of the nineteenth century and which will honor the twentieth century. We need not go very far back in history to see the evidences of the need of some such movements. The conditions of the working classes of many countries of Europe, especially in the early part of the nineteenth century, were such as to stir up the heart of any one who loved his kind. So there has been work for the labor unions in bringing men together and saying, "Let us strive to lift up ourselves; let us strive to have justice and charity done to us." In all these things, why would not any one join who loves humanity? We wish to see no class oppressed. We wish to see no class unnecessarily impoverished. We wish to see the family life respected. We wish to have education brought to the homes of all our people, and this I am sure is the leading motive in the labor unions. This, I am sure, is what has been to a very large extent accomplished.

In the name of our country, I must do my best if I am a faithful American to contribute to the peace and harmony between the different classes. . . We are a great country, and as an industrial, commercial country, we lead the world. Why? Because we have the natural resources which no other country has, and then we have an intelligent people. We Americans can invade the markets of foreign countries with our products and sell cheaper than the manufacturers of those countries where labor is cheaper. Why? Because our workingmen are more intelligent, our employers, too, are more intelligent and display this intelligence by getting better machinery; and our men at the machinery can do more work in a given number of hours, far exceeding what men in other countries can do, and so we continue on these lines of commercial economic supremacy, and the world is assured to us. There is but one danger before us, and it is this, that, in the midst of our prosperity we should begin quarreling one with another. While traveling abroad I had once a very thoughtful man say to me: "You have labor troubles in America." I said: "Yes, I am sorry." He said: "I am not sorry; it will be to our benefit if they go on quarreling in America." And it is true. This demands that all classes should come together and say, we shall smother all our difficulties and maintain peace, otherwise we shall lose our economic industrial supremacy, and what a misfortune to the world if we do, and to ourselves. Think of the future opening to America. We invade the markets of every country, and now the Pacific ocean is preparing to bear American ships even in greater number than the Atlantic itself, sending our products throughout all Asia, so that the American workman and the American capitalist are really becoming the monarchs of the world. But for the accomplishment of that we must come together and live in peace and work together.

Now, as well as many others, I know the two classes that are constantly said to be in opposition—the laborers and capitalists. I know the laborers. My ministry largely is passed among them. My time largely is taken up in hearing their complaints and giving comfort to their wives and children. I know them well, and I know them all the more that I love them and that I listen with tender affection to all that they have to say. Surely it is the wish of my heart that the working people should be lifted to a higher plane and have their full part of all that is good and promising upon the land. At the same time, I am allowed from time to time to talk to my other friends —the employers and capitalists—and I hear their story, and sometimes I listen to the objections that they may, some of them, make to the laborers of the country, to their trade unions, and I have to repeat what has been said so well by Mr. Hanna and Mr. Mitchell, that generally the cause of difficulties comes from misunderstanding. . .

It is to the advantage of the capitalist and of the country to build up a happy, intelligent working class. was said, that however the world is to be fashioned, whatever may come, there will be the employer and employe. It is impossible that it should be otherwise; there will be those who have more than others. . . I believe far more, let me tell you, in justice than even I do in charity itself for the solution of this question.

There are two classes in the other countries, one that loves you and believes that American institutions are being tested, and their hearts will be broken if you make a mistake; and there are the others, envious of you, feeling that in equal battle they must be vanquished by you, and their hope is that you will break asunder the timbers of your continent. Their hope is that there will be industrial battles. I have heard them say, "Well, never mind, we can wait—you will have industrial wars, and then what then? Then you will have to have a strong hand and then the Republic will die." That is their hope. They are jealous of the republic; jealous of the immense advantages it gives its citizens and the hope they have is that the employers and employes cannot agree. They build their hopes with reference to industrial America upon quarrels. Well, then, let us come together and admit that we will not have these quarrels, for I admit myself that unless we come together God only knows what will happen, for we know that our prosperity comes from the fact that we have this great self-governing power.

Now let us say, bad as we are at times, there is no country in the world where employers and employes will come together as pleasantly, as lovingly, as they do here to-night. The spectacle which you see here this evening in this room is something that would amaze people in other countries. They would not believe me if I were to tell them face to face what I see. There is no other country where a man is a man, so much because he is a man, as here. There is no other country where there are opportunities for the laboring man, where he is industrious, as much as here in America. There is no other country where there are such rewards for capital invested, controlled and managed for the rights of, the justice of all. It is a country so great in promise that it dazzles you. We can only say God preserve it, and we, under God, each one of us, will do our share to protect it and guard it. [Applause.]

WM. H. FARLEY

OTTO M. EIDLITZ

EMERSON McMILLIN

COL. JOHN J. McCOOK

DANIEL J. KEEFE

On the other hand, I also say to them, that the labor unions have their great purpose to serve. At any rate, they are here. It is a condition, whether we like it or not, and it is folly to be knocking our heads against a stone wall dreaming of what we would like to have, instead of seeing what we have. Now, it is a fact with those great principles before us we ought to agree, and the way to agree is to come together.

I have learned immensely since I have become a member of the Civic Federation, and really one of the purposes in coming to the meetings is to go to school. I learn more in one of these meetings than I do in sitting in my rooms and reading volumes for hours and days. And I am becoming so well informed on these things that I can talk better to my hearers and with more satisfaction to myself. What I learn others will learn, representatives of labor will learn and vice versa. I am sure if I could pick out fifty or one hundred of the leading employers of the country and as many laborers of the country and keep them at school, through our good chairman, four or five times a year, we would come nearer to the solution than in any other manner. Mr. Mitchell said to-night that he would not encourage violence. Reproaches have been made that this was the tendency of labor unions, and, of course, if such were the tendency it would be all over. Both sides must remember that there is in America a supreme tribunal, public opinion. Sooner or later it comes right and public opinion in America aims at justice, aims at charity for all. Public opinion aims at the recognition of the right of all. It wants no class to be put down, however poor it is to-day, I say whatever its origin, whatever its color. Any movement to put down a class of people in America will ultimately fail, and consequently, you representatives of labor, of the poor and distressed may invoke public opinion; but, in order to make public opinion, be just and right yourself, make claims, but before making them be sure that you are right, and when you find that you are not right have the courage to recede. Remember that you are educating public opinion and that patience is one of the greatest virtues that you must have. I know the difficulties of leaders; it is very difficult to control crowds, because in the crowds there will be some unthinking radicals, but counsel patience and use your efforts to gain public opinion in your favor. Let public opinion realize that you condemn everything wrong or injurious to industry, and you will have it with you. And so it is with the employer. Let us give every one his due and let us above all aim at being right or at understanding, as it

BRIEF REMARKS BY OTHERS.

The remarks of the other speakers of the evening were of an informal character, hardly intended for publication. But, as the utterances of each in some manner illustrated the spirit of the occasion and expressed hopes common to all present, they are in part herewith given:

Mr. Spencer Trask, being introduced by Chairman Nixon as "a capitalist of the highest class," said in part: "I hardly feel equal to the task, the great responsibility of responding for capital. But I must say that if the capitalist were disposed to be very timid, I would feel more than ever that it was the time for capital to be very quiet. But I only want to add one word to that which has been said, and I hesitate to say anything that would dampen the enthusiasm and cause any of us to go away with the influence of this meeting in any way weakened. And yet I have heard recently from some of the leading representatives of capital that the great obstacle in regard to the immediate future, if not the far future, is this labor question. We hear a great deal about threatened tight money, the trusts, the tariff, etc., and yet underneath it all, underlying it all, is this question, What is to be the outcome of this labor problem? I must say that, after being present at this meeting the greater part of the day and to-night, personally I feel greatly relieved in regard to this very matter, and I could only wish that the words that have been said to-night could be heard throughout the length and breadth of the country. I know and believe that if there could be more opportunities given for contact between capital and labor many of these fancied difficulties would be dissipated entirely. When we first came in here the question happened to be mentioned in regard to calling each other 'Brother' among the various associations. I think it makes very little matter whether the term 'brother' is used, if the sentiment at the heart is there—if we feel that we are all a part of this brotherhood of man, of the federation of the world. When we once begin to feel that we are all striving for one great purpose, one great end, we shall not then question as to the outcome nor the means. It makes very little matter what side we are on, whether that of the capitalist or that of the laboring man, as long as we feel that we have but one life here, one duty before us, that God is overhead and that we are laboring for one another, and I know that those who come in contact with one another can but feel that. Those who have the right motives will feel it in time, and I want to reiterate that I have never felt so strongly the promised future welfare as I do to-night after listening to the words I have heard." [Applause.]

Of Mr. Farley, the next speaker, Mr. Nixon said: "He works for industrial peace every day of the year." Mr. Farley said: "Mr. Chairman and (I am going to use the word) 'Brothers,' since one of the speakers has referred to the use of the term 'brother.' In relation to the Civic Federation of the City of New York, I want to say that I watched it and was one of the first to join it, and I am proud to say I am a member of it, because knowing as I do the valuable work it has done, and the many strikes it has averted by bringing the parties together, I am sure it will do good in the future. . . . One of the biggest parts of the building trades troubles was settled to-day, and that settlement was brought about by a member of the Civic Federation, Mr. Hayden. Otherwise, good friends in the Federation are watching our movements and helping to keep us in the right path." [Applause.]

Mr. Nixon deemed it fitting that Mr. Otto Eidlitz should next be heard from. Mr. Eidlitz began his remarks by saying: "Mr. Chairman and Brothers"—laying stress on the word "brothers"—which brought out applause from all present. Mr. Eidlitz's short address was mainly directed toward clearing up points at issue in the New York building trades contests.

"There is one point," he said, "upon which Archbishop Ireland talked, that I desire to emphasize. He stated that the unions are here and are a factor to be dealt with. I feel that I can say to him frankly, after having studied the situation for about eighteen years, that the unions are here and should be here. Not only that it is right that they should be here, but it is a positive necessity for the right-minded employer that they should be here, and the only difficulty with the union is if it should not be properly run."

Col. McCook spoke as follows: "I have been a learner from the beginning, but I do wish to say that from what I have seen thus far of the operations of

(*Continued on page 15.*)

MONTHLY REVIEW
OF THE
National Civic Federation

Offices: 281 Fourth Avenue, New York
Telephone, 4220 18th
RALPH M. EASLEY, Editor

Vol. I. New York, June, 1903 No. 2.
Ten Cents per Copy: One Dollar per Year

The National Civic Federation

281 Fourth Avenue, New York City

Marcus A. Hanna, Chairman.
Samuel Gompers, First Vice-Chairman.
Oscar S. Straus, Second Vice-Chairman.
Cornelius N. Bliss, Treasurer.
Ralph M. Easley, General Secretary.

EXECUTIVE COMMITTEE

ON THE PART OF THE PUBLIC.

Grover Cleveland, ex-President of the United States, Princeton, N. J.
Cornelius N. Bliss, ex-Secretary of the Interior, New York City.
David R. Francis, President Louisiana Purchase Exposition, St. Louis.
August Belmont, banker, New York.
Oscar S. Straus, member of the Court of Arbitration at The Hague, New York City.
Charles Francis Adams, former President of Union Pacific Railroad, Boston.
Archbishop John Ireland, of the Roman Catholic Church, St. Paul.
Bishop Henry C. Potter, of the Protestant Episcopal Church, New York City.
Spencer Trask, banker, New York.
Charles W. Eliot, President Harvard University, Cambridge, Mass.
Franklin MacVeagh, merchant, Chicago.
James H. Eckels, former Comptroller of Currency of the United States, Chicago.
John J. McCook, lawyer, New York City.
John G. Milburn, lawyer, Buffalo.
Charles J. Bonaparte, lawyer, Baltimore.
Ralph M. Easley, General Secretary of the National Civic Federation, New York City.

ON THE PART OF EMPLOYERS.

Marcus A. Hanna, coal mines, iron, shipping and street railways, Cleveland.
Charles M. Schwab, President United States Steel Corporation, New York City.
William L. Elkins, director Pennsylvania Railroad, Philadelphia.
John B. McDonald, contractor Rapid Transit Subway Construction, New York.
Frederick D. Underwood, President Erie Railroad, New York.
S. R. Callaway, President American Locomotive Works, New York City.
Charles A. Moore, President The Shaw Electric Crane Company, New York City.
Edward P. Ripley, President Atchison, Topeka & Santa Fe Railway System, Chicago.
J. Kruttschnitt, Vice-President Southern Pacific Company, San Francisco.
H. H. Vreeland, President National Street Railway Association, New York City.
Lewis Nixon, President United States Shipbuilding Company, New York City.
Samuel Mather, Picands, Mather & Co., Cleveland, O.
Charles H. Taylor, Jr., President American Publishers' Association, Boston.
Marcus M. Marks, President National Association of Clothing Manufacturers, New York City.
James A. Chambers, President American Window Glass Company, Pittsburgh.
William H. Pfahler, former President National Founders' Association, Philadelphia.

ON THE PART OF WAGE EARNERS.

Samuel Gompers, President American Federation of Labor, Washington.
John Mitchell, President United Mine Workers of America, Indianapolis.
Edgar E. Clark, Grand Chief Conductor, Order of Railway Conductors, Cedar Rapids, Iowa.
Theodore J. Shaffer, President Amalgamated Association of Iron, Steel and Tin Workers, Pittsburgh.
James Duncan, General Secretary Granite Cutters' National Union, Washington.
Daniel J. Keefe, President International Longshoremen's Association, Detroit.
P. H. Morrissey, Grand Master Brotherhood Railroad Trainmen.
James O'Connell, President International Association of Machinists, Washington.
Martin Fox, President Iron Molders' Union of North America, Cincinnati.
James M. Lynch, President International Typographical Union, Indianapolis.
J. J. Hannahan, Grand Master Brotherhood of Locomotive Firemen, Peoria, Ill.
Henry White, General Secretary United Garment Workers of America, New York.
William D. Mahon, President Amalgamated Association of Street Railway Employes of America, Detroit.
Denis A. Hayes, President Glass Bottle Blowers' Association of United States and Canada, Philadelphia.
William Huber, President United Brotherhood of Carpenters and Joiners of America, Indianapolis.
John Tobin, General President Boot and Shoe Workers' Union, Boston.

THE FEVER FOR ORGANIZING.

Periods of industrial prosperity offer inducements to organizers both of new corporations and of new labor unions. During the first two years of the present "boom" the country was aroused, and even alarmed, by the rush of promoters to organize and reorganize industrial undertakings. A financial journal recently estimated the capitalization of these enterprises at $6,000,000,000. Now that several large speculations have collapsed and the public has learned the limits of others a lull has come and it is difficult to interest underwriters and investors in new ventures.

It was not until a year or two after the fever for capitalist organization had affected the financiers that the same kind of fever spread among labor organizations. Old unions expanded enormously, new unions sprang up everywhere. Unionism is now apparently nearing the top of this wave. Several notable successes, especially of the bituminous mine workers and the longshoremen, in 1897 and 1898, stimulated the less skilled and the unorganized labor over the country, and recruiting in this class of unions has since been remarkable. Older unions, especially in the building trades, have received unprecedented advances in wages.

Up to the present time the difficulty with capital has been mainly owing to the misgivings aroused by the losses of investors in several speculative securities floated a few years ago. But this distrust will have a new soil for growth in the anxiety as to labor demands. Employers in general are organizing, and while it was comparatively easy for the unions to get increases when speculation was active and promoters and underwriters wished to avoid unsettling confidence in their "undigested securities," it may be expected that future demands, if excessive, will be resisted, as the prospects for transferring the increase to the consumer and investor are diminished.

As the solid corporation built on substantial values may be expected to come out of the boom with well-equipped plants and good reserve funds, so those labor unions characterized by good discipline and fidelity to agreements will come out with recognition of their merits from the public and employers.

Fortunately, the danger of a panic from over-capitalized corporations seems to have passed, and the only present apprehensions in the business world are from "over-capitalized labor unions" of recent growth. The older and conservative unions have an obligation to the public and the new unions to guide and restrain the latter during their formation period. There are signs that the solid unions appreciate this responsibility. This is seen in the action of the Chicago Federation of Labor, which, though it rejected by a small majority the proposition to withhold from a union less than one year old any indorsement of a strike, yet unanimously decided to refuse support to any union on a strike if the Executive Committee of the Federation had not first been appealed to for its conciliatory offices. This action is strongly indorsed by labor representatives, and Mr. John Mitchell speaks of it as "an epoch in the advancement of labor." Apart from the greater sense of security on the part of the public, restraints of this kind should be encouraged on behalf of organized labor itself. Such restraints lessen the dangers ahead of new organizations, and strengthen the older ones in the confidence of employers and the public. They tend, above all, to remove the anxieties which in the past two months have materially checked industrial enterprise.

THE MOSELY COMMISSION.

To see ourselves as others see us has usually been prescribed as a cure for pride, but the reports of the Mosely Industrial Commission are calculated to exalt rather than to lower the pride of Americans in our industrial conditions. True, one who reads the reports can see proofs of the danger in generalizing for the whole country upon what the delegates happened to see in their three-weeks' trip. They visited the largest cities and the best establishments, but we must also believe that they corrected their impressions by conferring with their fellow craftsmen in this country. Each of the twenty-three members was not only an expert in his own line but a leading officer in his trade union, his business having been for many years to study labor and market conditions for the intensely practical purpose of improving the wages and shortening the hours of his fellow unionists. The opinions of such men in comparing conditions at home with those in America are worth far more than elaborate statistical tables.

They agree, as will be seen in our summary of their reports, that wages in America are 15 to 100 per cent. higher than in England, hours of labor about the same, and workshop sanitary conditions superior. Most interesting of all, and most authentic because contrary to their own preconceptions, they find that the American workman is not pressed and rushed while at work beyond the speed of English workmen. This certainly is also contrary to the general view in America. Undoubtedly each delegate felt that he had been brought to this country by Mr. Mosely for the purpose of taking back to the English unionists a warning against their alleged opposition to machinery and unrestricted production. They find, indeed, a greater output in America, but it is owing, they say, to the greater natural resources and the amazing eagerness of manufacturers for new ideas and the best machinery. Apparently, from their conclusions, it is the English manufacturers, rather than the English workmen, whom Mr. Mosely should have introduced to the superiorities of American industry.

Their observations in one respect are distinctly depreciative of American practices, namely the quality of the product. They state that not only is the quality inferior in beauty and finish but also in substantial and enduring character. This is one reason why in their view America's output is greater.

Above all is it a matter of satisfaction to hear, on almost unanimous testimony, that American workmen are much less given to gambling, horse-racing and drunkenness than British workmen.

The indorsement given by the delegates to the work of the National Civic Federation, and their desire to see a similar organization established in England, is all the more significant since English unions have advanced much further than American unions on the line of conciliation and trade agreements. The delegates strongly emphasize the non-arbitrative character of the Federation and base their indorsement on its promotion of conciliation and friendly discussion.

INEXCUSABLE MISSTATEMENTS.

The problems of employer and employe are by no means easy of solution, and their solution is not helped by inaccuracy in stating facts. Two or three recent announcements by prominent critics of the Civic Federation, whatever may be said of their line of argument, are open to serious objection on the score of carelessness in this elementary matter. From a recent address by the President of the National Manufacturers' Association we quote the following:

"There was one article in that Chicago newspaper to which I have referred that I have reserved to speak of last. This article is the one relating to the formation of a Civic Federation in Chicago. I do not desire to get into any controversy with any noted Senator or politician, but I could not do even partial justice to that newspaper without saying something about what this particular article contained. In this article a noted Senator is quoted as saying several things. In the first place he is made to say that he was glad to learn that the Chicago Federation of Labor had given birth to a central senate or strike committee. Immediately following the noted Senator on the platform came Mr. John Mitchell, whose union a few months ago voted solidly in favor of a general confiscation of wealth. Mr. Mitchell also spoke about this new strike institution. He said, to quote his words: 'It marked an epoch in the country for the best interests of organized labor.' There you have it, gentlemen: The editor, the politician and the strike leader, all standing together congratulating the city of Chicago on the acquisition of an institution which appears to have it in its power to say who shall have the right to labor and what wage scales employers must pay.

"Now, I do not know what this so-called labor senate will do for Chicago. Let us hope it will do nothing. But I can and you can well imagine what it is possible for it to do. As the editor hinted, it could tie up the industries of Chicago tighter than a drum. A central committee composed of men elected by labor unions is a dangerous depository of the power to rule or ruin the industries of a great city. What can the noted Senator of whom I spoke be thinking of when he makes haste to be among the first to doff his hat to this latest product of triumphant unionism?"

The action of the Chicago Federation of Labor which called forth this ridicule and denunciation was the adoption of this resolution:

"We, your Executive Board, recommend that the Chicago Federation of Labor take some action on the hasty calling of strikes at this time. We suggest that when there is any grievance existing the Executive Board should be notified before any strike is called, to try and settle the matter without a strike. We believe that many of the troubles arising at this time can be adjusted without strikes."

In advocating its passage, Barney Cohen, a member of the Executive Board of that body, said:

"I believe that many of the strikes now disturbing the city could be avoided if good judgment were used in the first place. By acting conservatively we can have the support of those who are now opposed to organized labor, and who think our main object is to stir up strife. On the contrary, the object of this Federation is to secure the best possible conditions for the workers, and to do so with as few strikes as possible."

When Senator Hanna and John Mitchell applauded the act as "epoch making in labor history," we believe they expressed no more than the sentiment of every intelligent observer of industrial progress in this country. It may well be hoped that every central labor body shall take similar action.

The statement as to "John Mitchell, whose union a few months ago voted solidly in favor of a general confiscation of wealth," is absurd. It doubtless has reference either to the vote of the miners' delegates at the New Orleans convention of the American Federation of Labor last November, or to the vote of the mine workers' convention at Indianapolis in February. There is not a scintilla of fact in the action of either body to justify the statement, as the official published records plainly show. At the annual meeting of the American Federation of Labor at New Orleans the following resolution was introduced by a Socialist:

"Resolved, That this twenty-second annual convention of the American Federation of Labor advises the working people to organize their economic and political power to secure for labor the full equivalent of its toil and the overthrowal of the wage system and the establishment of an industrial co-operative democracy."

After a discussion extending throughout one day the resolution was amended, on motion of the National Secretary of the Mine Workers, so as to strike out everything after the word "toil," leaving not a vestige of Socialism or "confiscation of wealth" in the resolution. But even in this amended form it was rejected by the convention, largely on the ground that it had been originally "introduced by a Socialist," and, as stated by one delegate, "might be construed by malicious enemies" against them.

The Indianapolis incident is as follows: At the Mine Workers' annual convention held February 19 last, certain Iowa delegates introduced the following:

"Resolved by the annual convention of the United Mine Workers of America that they go on record as favoring and indorsing international Socialism."

The Committee on Resolutions non-concurred in this resolution, and the convention sustained the committee by an overwhelming vote.

An officer of another association of employers, in his anxiety to discredit the National Civic Federation, quotes an Associated Press dispatch which placed a member of the Civic Federation in the attitude of having defied an injunction, and adds that "with this defiance on his lips he went to attend a session of the National Civic Federation." This alleged defiance occurred, according to the dispatch referred to, in May, 1900, just twelve months before the organization of the National Civic Federation.

COMMISSIONER DU BRUL'S OPEN LETTER.

Mr. Du Brul's declarations in another column as to the objects and spirit of the National Association of Manufacturers and the Dayton Employers' Association are quite positive; but it may be suggested that those organizations have energetic officials of their own, who can speak, if need be, with higher authority on their purposes.

In reference to the position of the National Metal Trades Association, of which Mr. Du Brul is the First Vice-President and Commissioner, the statement in the April REVIEW which has called forth the vigorous letter from Mr. Du Brul is as follows:

"The National Metal Trades Association is composed of several hundred employers. It formerly had a national agreement with the International Association of Machinists, but this was broken, and was followed by what is known as the machinists' strike of 1901. The association deals with the machinists' organization in many localities, but, as a national organization, is more or less hostile to organized labor. The breaking of the contract in 1901 was deplored by the conservative element on both sides, and it is hoped by many that it will eventually be renewed, but the National Metal Trades Association cannot now fairly be classed with either the National Founders' Association or the National Association of Manufacturers."

Of the five statements in the above paragraph four Mr. Du Brul undoubtedly will not question. This reduces his objection to a part of one of the statements, viz.: "but as a national organization is more or less hostile to organized labor."

The only other reference to the National Metal Trades Association in the article complained of is where the "Bulletin" of that association is referred to in connection with other periodicals as being "ably edited and largely devoted to attacks on organized labor."

Whatever evidence might be adduced to justify our statements, we accept at their full face value the official avowals as to the purpose and scope of the National Metal Trades Association. The REVIEW is only too glad to publish the assertion from Vice-President Du Brul that his organization is hostile only to the "illegal and unjust acts" of trade unions—a statement which it is safe to say would be indorsed by every right-minded citizen of this country.

THE LABOR OUTLOOK.

There has been a remarkable clearing of the industrial skies the past few weeks, whether viewed from a national or local viewpoint. A month ago there was great danger in what may be termed national industries, and local strikes were innumerable. In fact, compared with thirty days ago, it is safe to assert that there is an improvement of 75 per cent. There is not at this time any national strike on, nor is there one in view, and within the last week nearly all the important local troubles have been either settled or have progressed so far toward a settlement that they are no longer considered important factors in the industrial situation.

A month ago there was danger of a break coming between the Amalgamated Iron and Tin Workers and the United States Steel Corporation over the tinplate wage scale. The scale was signed up, however, last week, thus guaranteeing peace for another year in this basic industry. A satisfactory agreement was also reached between this same labor organization and the Republic Iron and Steel Company.

At the beginning of the month there were grave apprehensions in some quarters that another strike might occur in the anthracite coal region through the inability of the Anthracite Conciliation Board to organize, and although there are alarming headlines in the papers to-day an understanding will undoubtedly be reached.

The American Bridge Company's strike, affecting seven large cities, threatened at one time to involve the United States Steel Corporation in another conflict with organized labor. That has been satisfactorily settled within the month.

In the railroad world a month ago there was a serious strike in progress on the Union Pacific Railroad, and there were threatened strikes on the Southern Pacific Railroad, Northern Pacific and the Mobile and Ohio railroads, all of which have been settled or averted, and the ominous unrest of the brotherhood members on several of the large Western lines entering Chicago three weeks ago is no longer visible.

In what would be termed local difficulties, probably the most serious situation was the prospective tie-up of the entire building industry of New York and vicinity. The past week has seen advance made towards a satisfactory settlement. The New York Metal Trades Association and Marine Trades Council settled their strikes and lockouts on the first of the month. The threatened elevated railroad strike was averted and a contract signed for a year; while the subway strike has about "petered" out. The threatened strike of the clothing cutters, involving 30,000 employes, which for five weeks seemed inevitable, was finally averted by a joint trade agreement ratified June 1.

The Chicago situation, which presented so many ugly aspects the first of the month, practically cleared up the past few days. The International Harvester Company's plants, the great packing houses, the breweries, the laundries, the hotels and restaurants, the barbers, the metal trades and the railroads so far as their freight handlers are concerned, and a dozen other industries, were all involved in strikes during the month of May, and all were settled either through conciliation or arbitration.

In St. Louis, what gave promise of being a very bitter contest between the Mètal Trades Association and the machinists and blacksmiths was settled last week by an annual agreement; and what threatened to prove a serious strike of the teamsters and freight handlers has been settled the past forty-eight hours.

In Denver the situation, which portended all kinds of things at one time, has happily cleared up; and the troubles at Omaha are practically at an end.

The general tie-up of the street railways of San Francisco was averted by both sides referring the matter to their respective Presidents for arbitration.

The strike and lockout in the glove industry at Gloversville, N. Y., affecting 10,000 operatives, has just been settled by an agreement to arbitrate.

The Lowell cotton textile strike, while not settled, is expected by the mill agents to be soon brought to a close by the operatives returning to work.

Practically the only strike of any magnitude now on is that of the woolen textile industry at Philadelphia, and it is not believed it will be of long duration.

But there are other signs which are indicative of a better and more conservative tone in the industrial world. The action a few weeks ago of the Chicago Federation of Labor in regard to the indorsement of hasty and ill-considered strikes, wherein it declared that it would not indorse a strike unless the grievance had first been submitted to its Executive Committee and it given a chance to bring about a settlement, had the effect of making the Chicago Federation of Labor a conciliation committee, and it has proven one of the most potential factors in securing peace in Chicago.

The San Francisco Building Trades Council this week passed resolutions to the effect that no further demands for the increase of wages should be made without the entire body sanctioning it; that the indiscriminate demanding of the increase of wages would have the effect of scaring capital out of the building industry, and that a halt must be called.

At the meeting of the Brotherhood of Railway Trainmen in Denver this week Grand Master Morrissey declared that the time would soon come in the world of organized labor when the "contract breaker" would be as detestable as the "scab."

In the settlement of the wage scale with the American Tin Plate Company the Amalgamated Iron and Tin Plate Workers gave up a number of "time honored" restrictions that will increase the output 15 per cent.

In the settlement between the Wholesale Clothing Manufacturers' Association and the clothing cutters of New York City a shorter workday was granted in consideration of the union surrendering all arbitrary restrictions, the language of the contract being that "the men should do their best with due regard to their health, and be paid accordingly."

While these are among the incidents showing the growing conservatism and broadening of views of the wage workers, many incidents could also be given showing broadening in view of employers. Several organizations of employers, originally started for the purpose of "smashing the unions" have changed to the more rational policy of dealing and making joint trade agreements with them.

Conciliation and arbitration are surely rapidly gaining on the old-fashioned strike and lockout.

Trade Agreement in the New York Clothing Trade.

The Clothing Trade Association and the Clothing Cutters' Union of New York City on June 1st perfected the first written agreement between the two associations. Several conferences had been held during a period of six weeks, and until the last week it seemed impossible to avoid a costly strike or lockout, which would have thrown 30,000 people out of work. Finally, concessions were made on both sides. The union consented to forego payment for the eight legal holidays during the year, for which the members had hitherto been paid, and also to abolish restrictions on output. The manufacturers conceded a reduction of hours from 52 to 48 per week. A permanent joint committee was provided for to pass upon all complaints. Two members of the National Civic Federation held important positions in the negotiations, Mr. Marcus M. Marks being President of the Manufacturers' Association and Mr. Henry White Secretary of the United Garment Workers of America. It is stated that the tailors of New York will now endeavor to avert the usual annual strikes by the same method.

Glovemakers' Strike Ends.

Gloversville, N. Y., June 2.—The block cutters' strike, which was inaugurated March 18 and was followed May 8 by the manufacturers locking out the table cutters, thus affecting the 10,000 glove workers in Fulton County, was settled late this afternoon as a result of the intervention of Messrs. M. M. Marks and Samuel B. Donnelly, of New York, members of the Executive Committee of the National Civic Federation.

A conference this morning between these representatives and those of the Glove Manufacturing Association and the several unions interested resulted in the Table Cutters' Union rescinding resolutions previously passed and the Manufacturers' Association withdrawing the lockout resolution ordered by that body May 13.

It is further agreed that the difference between the block cutters and manufacturers, which has hung fire for a long time, will be arbitrated.

The settlement is thus made on mutual concessions and neither side claims a victory. The glove factories will resume operations full handed either to-morrow or Thursday.

Indorsement by Street Railway Employes.

The Amalgamated Association of Street Railway Employes of America passed the following resolutions at their convention at Pittsburg, May 4-9:

Whereas, The officers and members of the National Civic Federation during the past year have aided our international officers in securing conferences which have led to settlements that have been highly beneficial to our organization; therefore, be it

Resolved, That this Eighth Biennial Convention of the Amalgamated Association of Street Railway Employes of America, in session assembled, do hereby return a vote of thanks to the National Civic Federation for their advice and assistance; and further be it

Resolved, That we assure the members of our organization and our fellow workers in the different crafts throughout the country that we have confidence in the work of the Civic Federation and feel that they are doing a grand and noble work along the line of mediation and conciliation, not only for capital and labor, but for the welfare of our country as well.

An Open Letter.

To the Editor of the Review:

Dear Sir: In your issue, Volume 1, No. 1, of date April, 1903, you make several statements which are not correct, and which I trust you will correct by publishing this letter in your next issue.

In the first place, you state, regarding the National Association of Manufacturers, that the association indorsed statements made by its President at New Orleans. If you can find any indorsement of anybody's statements in the minutes of that convention, you will do more than the official reporter can do himself, and all of the acts of that convention are on record in the minutes.

Whatever may be Mr. Parry's personal opinions, and in whatever manner he may express them, the National Association of Manufacturers is on record with a declaration of principles and some resolutions, none of which is directed against the organization of labor as such. They are directed, and strongly so, against the vicious and lawless element in such organizations.

The National Association of Manufacturers is not an organization of employers as such, and, of itself, does not touch the labor question, excepting as it is affected by legislation. On the other hand, the association, by its acts, insists that the vicious and lawless element should not be considered the true representatives of the great body of organized labor, and in denouncing the vicious and lawless element it cannot be considered as an attack on the organization of labor. If you, sir, had investigated the matter more closely, you would surely not have made this mistake. Certainly you cannot believe that the vicious and lawless are an essential part of the organization of labor. Why, therefore, put yourself in the position of seeming to believe it by taking as gospel truth the garbled press reports of a convention representing two thousand patriotic manufacturers, who specifically went on record in these particulars?

E. F. DU BRUL.

Regarding the Employers' Association of Dayton and kindred organizations—here, again, whatever may be the personal opinions of the President of that organization, you are wrong in assuming that it was organized for the specific purpose of smashing unions. If you will take the slight trouble to read the constitution of that organization, you will see just why it was brought into being.

Now, regarding the National Metal Trades Association, of which I have the honor to be Commissioner, I beg to deny your statement that this organization is more or less hostile to the organization of labor. This organization is absolutely hostile to illegal acts, whether performed by workmen or by employers, organized or unorganized. Because we do not choose to make agreements with certain unions you seem to consider us hostile to their existence.

We had an experience that has made us chary of the present management of the Machinists' union. Perhaps we are wrong in our opinion in this regard, but in a number of cases of recent date, in attempting to deal with the Machinists' union, in various localities, we have found that it was impossible to do business with them. At this writing, in Rochester, New York, there is a strike on in a member's shop; a strike that seems to have been voted against the wishes of the employes of that shop, by the employes of other shops. The strike is an effort to compel the company to abolish the premium system, and so reduce the output and earnings of their men. The premium system has been in operation for two years, to the great satisfaction of not only the company, but also of its employes. In that case the official representatives of the Machinists' union of Rochester absolutely refused to submit the matters in dispute to a disinterested board of conciliation.

In Quincy, Ill., there is another case of the Machinists' union refusing to submit a demand to a board of conciliation. This demand was for the reinstatement of a man who personally has never asked to go back to work in the shop in which he formerly worked and which he left under circumstances that made it impossible for the employer to calculate as to how long the man would be absent.

In Elmira, N. Y., the machinists have demanded the abolition of the premium system in the Payne Engine Company's shop, and their representative, not reasoning at all, not arguing the question, not claiming any injustice, simply flatly stood on the proposition that the premium system would not be tolerated by that union.

In Milwaukee, Wis., there is a strike to compel the reinstatement of a foreman who was discharged for unsatisfactory service.

On the other hand, conferences are now going on in Pittsburg, St. Louis and Chicago, without strikes, which, it is hoped and believed, will result in amicable and equitable settlements.

All of the above strikes have been indorsed by the Grand Lodge of the Machinists' union, under misapprehension of the facts perhaps, but nevertheless they are indorsed.

These things, my dear Mr. Easley, are not theories, but they are facts, and the natural feeling among the members of the National Metal Trades Association is that, until we have evidence that the management of the Machinists' union shows itself, by its acts, to be such as the members of this association can place confidence in we had better not have another national agreement. On the other hand, this association is definitely on record as permitting agreements between its members and their employes, collectively, whenever the members feel that the collective management of their employes' affairs is businesslike and reasonable.

Now, referring to our periodical. It has been my aim and intention, in publishing our monthly "Bulletin" not to devote it to attacks on organized labor, but to devote it to denouncements of the evils that are now so prevalent with organized labor and which I firmly believe can be removed only by an awakening of public sentiment. If you had read our "Bulletin" as carefully as I shall read your publication, you would see, in every number, articles dealing with the problems of conciliation and arbitration. In the very first number, July, 1902, there was an exposition of the satisfactory settlement of machinist matters in St. Louis last year.

In the August number was reprinted an address delivered before the National Civic Federation at Chicago, in December, 1900, by Mr. Frederick P. Bagley, on the subject of the organization of employers as a prerequisite to conciliation and arbitration, and also a copy of a proposed agreement between the Stove Founders' Association and the Polishers' union; also a copy of the Pittsburg Machinists' agreement, and an account of arbitration in the Moran Shipyards, Seattle, Washington.

In the September number was a paper by one of our members, a discussion of arbitration with an odd arbitrator.

In the October number was a reprint of an article by Professor George Gunton on the foolishness of attempts at the suppression of trade unions, and a reprint of your own description of the National Civic Federation and its works. Also an account of the New York blacksmiths' strike of last August, in which the Civic Federation was of great assistance in bringing about a peaceable settlement by arbitration.

In the November number was a reprint of Mr. Herman Justi's address before the National Civic Federation at Chicago on Dec. 17, 1900, on the organization of employers as a prerequisite to conciliation and arbitration.

In the December number was a reprint of Mr. Justi's lecture on the organization of capital, delivered in Boston on Nov. 20, 1902, and a discussion of the acceptance of the premium plan in England by the Amalgamated Society of Engineers.

In the January number of this year appears Dr. Hillis' sermon, "Labor's War on Labor," an article from the "Union Chronicle" of Cincinnati, and an article from the "Nineteenth Century Review" on industrial troubles of America; also an article arguing for a better kind of organization of labor than some of the unions have at the present time.

In the February number we reprinted an address delivered by Mr. William H. Sayward, urging conciliation in the building trades, and also some commendatory editorials on "Organization of Employers," as suggested by Mr. Justi's Boston speech.

In the March number we reprinted more editorials along the above lines, and Mr. W. H. Pfahler's address before the American Association of Political and Social Science, on the "Co-operation of Labor and Capital."

In the April number we reprinted Mr. Pfahler's address before the American Economic Association on "Free Shops for Free Workmen," and also a letter of Mr. Goldwin Smith, one of the men to whom unions owe much in England for the repeal of the old combination laws.

Now, if the printing of articles of that sort, together with other articles which condemned the vicious practices of some unionists, are attacks on organized labor, I suppose that we are guilty.

I believe, with you, sir, that "there is a common ground where employer and employe can meet with satisfaction and honor to each," and wherever, in my work as Commissioner of this association, I find that a union involved with us is willing to deal fairly, I recommend as strongly as lies within my power that the employes be met more than halfway. In Cincinnati, prominent members of the National Metal Trades Association, imbued with the idea of fair dealing and conciliation, after having fought through a bitter strike two years ago, a strike which would never have occurred had the machinists' officials in this city and elsewhere not brought it about, have voluntarily and unasked consummated a reduction in the working time of the shops of the members here to fifty-five hours per week, with no reduction in pay.

In Cincinnati and in other places, the local secretaries act very largely in the capacity of joint "social secretaries" for members, listening to complaints of the workmen, hearing their grievances and seeing to it that abuses unsuspected by the employers are corrected.

I want to assure you, sir, that the membership of the National Metal Trades Association aims to deal fairly and justly by all of their employes, whether organized or unorganized. In this we may differ from others, but we take it that the Coal Strike Commission is, so far, the highest authority in these matters and we accept their good American dictum that "no discrimination shall be made against any employe because of his membership, or non-membership, in a labor organization," and we stand ready to enforce in our shops their further dictum that "no employe shall be discriminated against by the members of a labor organization because of his non-membership in such organization." If this is hostility to the organization of labor, then the Anthracite Coal Strike Commission is as hostile as we are. If the vigorous condemnation of lawless and vicious acts is hostility to organized labor, then this association is not as hostile to organized labor as that commission, for we can never use language as strong as that commission's report.

Even during the heat of the general machinists' strike of two years ago, when we adopted our present declaration of principles (every one of which has since been practically sustained in the coal strike report), this organization there went on record as favoring conciliation between employers and employes in the following words: "In cases of disagreement concerning matters not covered by the foregoing declaration, we advise our members to meet their employes either individually or collectively, and endeavor to adjust the difficulties on a fair and equitable basis. In case of inability to reach a satisfactory adjustment, we advise that they submit the question to arbitration by a board composed of six persons, three to be chosen by the employer and three to be chosen by the employe or employes. In order to receive the benefits of the arbitration, the employe, or employes, must continue in service and under the orders of the employer pending a decision. In case any member refuses to comply with this recommendation, he shall be denied the support of this association until it shall approve the action of said member." I wish to say further that in no case has a member received support in which he did not endeavor to adjust his difficulties as above.

In this connection, I beg to call your attention to the fact that Mr. W. H. Pfahler, one of the most earnest friends of organized labor and a member of your national board, is a valued and active honorary member of our Administrative Council; that Mr. Charles A. Moore, of New York City, a member of this association, is on your national committee and also on your New York committee; that Mr. Walter L. Pierce, a member of the New York Civic Federation, is a former President of this association and one of his associates in business, Mr. H. N. Covell, of the Lidgerwood Manufacturing Company, is now our First Vice-President. Furthermore, I beg you to remember that the New York Metal Trades Association, an offshoot of this body, by and with the consent, knowledge, approval and suggestion of this association, was eminently successful, in co-operation with you in several cases affecting our members in New York, in bringing about peaceable and equitable adjustments. In this particular see the item quoted on the last page of your very first "Review," headed: "Ship Yards Strike Ends."

Now, Mr. Easley, do you think it is fair to confound our hostility to illegal and unjust acts with hostility to the principle of organization, a principle which we ourselves are daily preaching to the employers?

I trust that this letter has not infringed too largely on your space, but I feel that the matter is of sufficient importance to demand full explanation, in order to put the National Metal Trades Association correctly before your readers.

We hardly dare hope to be understood by radical unionists, but we did not expect to have you misrepresent our aims in such an offhand, self-confident way, a way liable to stir up hard feelings rather than allay them.

I remain, sir, yours respectfully,

E. F. DU BRUL,
Commissioner National Metal Trades Association.
Cincinnati, O., May 1, 1903.

Hon. S. E. Morss an Early Advocate of Trade Agreements.

In reply to your inquiry I think the "Sentinel" was one of the first newspapers in the country, if not the very first, to enter into a time contract with the local Typographical Union. When I purchased an interest in this paper on Feb. 1, 1888, a strike of printers in the morning newspaper offices had recently taken place, and all the daily papers in the city were set up by non-union printers. One of the first things I did was to have a conference with the officers of the local typographical union. The "Sentinel" Company made a contract with the union which was, I believe, to run a certain length of time—three years, I think.

A few months later the other daily papers of the city made similar contracts with the union, and subsequently the newspapers of the city formed a Publishers' Association for the purpose of dealing with the labor unions, and contracts are now made from time to time between the Publishers' Association and the local Typographical Union. The results have been entirely satisfactory. While the unions have demanded and obtained very liberal concessions and I feel that the employes in the mechanical departments secure a disproportionate share of the product of the business, I will say that every contract made has been scrupulously fulfilled by the union and that there has been no friction of any kind after the contract has been executed. Similar arrangements have been in force in other cities for several years, and finally a contract was made last spring between the American Newspaper Publishers' Association on the one hand and the International Typographical Union and the International Printing Pressmen's Union on the other. This contract was ratified by a substantially unanimous vote of the Newspaper Publishers' Association. I think the general feeling is that these arrangements afford the best method available, under existing conditions, of regulations between newspaper publishers and the employes in their mechanical departments. Under these arrangements the liberty of action by proprietors is very largely restricted. They surrender a good many of the rights which the owners of the Pennsylvania coal mines claim to be inherent in proprietors. But on the other hand, they secure a high standard of service and efficiency and a large degree of stability, and when a three years' contract is made they know exactly what they can depend upon for that period.

While the unions are quite exacting and advance their claims at the termination of every contract, I personally believe in the right and duty of workingmen to organize and to use their organizations to secure such benefits as they can in the way of increased wages, shorter hours of labor, and improved conditions. If other large employers of labor would deal with their employes in the same spirit as the American newspaper publishers do there would not be many serious labor troubles. I must confess, however, that the publishers would have found it very difficult at any time for many years to ignore the Typographical and Pressmen's unions. These organizations are strong and are conducted with much intelligence and ability. Many publishers probably would prefer to deal with individual employes, but the newspaper proprietors are entitled to the credit, at least, of recognizing the cast-iron facts of the situation and conforming to them. They have met these organizations in a broad spirit, and the result is that for some years there have been very few strikes among the employes in the mechanical departments of newspapers.

S. E. MORSS,
President and Manager Indianapolis "Sentinel."

REMARKS BY CHAIRMAN FERD C. SCHWEDTMANN.

Made at the Organization of the St. Louis Branch of the National Civic Federation, May 1, 1903.

As an employer of labor, I have always taken the keenest interest in organizations formed for the purpose of better understanding between employers and wage earners. Many of the interests of the two are alike and neither can progress without the aid of the other.

FERD. C. SCHWEDTMANN.

An organization of employers to be successful in dealing with the labor problem must necessarily be built on two fundamental principles.

The first is meeting with workmen or their representatives for the purpose of determining conditions mutually satisfactory, under which workmen shall be employed.

The second is determination to have strikes and lockouts the very last recourse in all labor troubles and resort to them only after all other means, mediation, conciliation and voluntary arbitration, have failed. The St. Louis Metal Trades Association and the St. Louis Founders' Association, two organizations of employers of metal workers, are formed on these two basic principles. Of both these organizations I have the honor to be President.

Since the existence of these two organizations, St.

Louis has been comparatively free from labor troubles in our lines.

Ever since the inauguration of the National Civic Federation we have followed with interest the proceedings of this organization. The introduction of the third party, the public, in the prevention and settlement of labor difficulties appeals to the thinking mind as logic and a step much in advance of former methods.

The National Civic Federation decided a short time ago to establish local branches and soon afterward inaugurated the New York Civic Federation.

We felt that St. Louis must be the next place to have an organization to promote closer relations between employer and employe. After lengthy correspondence with the National Civic Federation the national officers have come to St. Louis to assist us in forming the St. Louis Civic Federation.

There is surely no city in the United States that will furnish a better field for co-operation of labor, employer and public than St. Louis. And of all the days of the year none is better fitted for which we celebrate the one hundredth anniversary of the Louisiana Purchase.

Combined efforts of the wage earner, the merchant, the learned man and the capitalist have changed the territory purchased one hundred years ago from a wilderness to a country equal in resources and culture to the oldest empire of the world. Without this co-operation between the classes it would again beco · the wilderness it was one hundred years ago.

To-day we have the opportunity to lay the corner stone of consideration and harmony between the classes. On this foundation we will build in commemoration of the St. Louis Exposition a monument a thousand times greater than the Eiffel Tower of the Paris Exposition and greater than the Field Museum of the Chicago Exposition. We will build the monument of Industrial Peace.

REMARKS BY JUDGE, MURRAY F. TULEY.

Made at the Organization of the Chicago Branch of the National Civic Federation, May 4, 1903.

I desire to say that I have kept close watch upon the proceedings of the National Civic Federation. I was invited to participate in its movements at its beginning. I did not do so, for the reason that I was somewhat suspicious that the movement was in the interest of capital and against labor. My reasons for entertaining such suspicion are unnecessary to state, but I am glad to be able to say that I am now satisfied that those suspicions were unfounded and that it is now and has been a genuinely disinterested movement in favor of conciliation and arbitration of labor difficulties.

As I understand it, it is not the intention in organizing this branch of the National Civic Federation to interfere in any manner with the local arbitration boards, but rather to tender assistance to such boards and to capital and labor in any difficulty arising between them.

The assistance of a branch of the national board might well be invoked in many labor difficulties, as many strikes and lockouts are national in their effects, particularly where they interfere with the due operation of interstate commerce.

I am also pleased to know that the chief effort of this national board, with its branches throughout the different States, has been and will be to educate the general public, the capitalists and the laboring men upon the great economic questions underlying their relations to each other.

Something has been said here about elevating the laboring man. He has secured by his own efforts a great elevation within the last twenty-five years, but he, as well as the capitalist, should be educated to a due recognition of the fact that a third party—the public—is interested to a larger extent than they themselves are, in the maintenance of peace and harmony in the carrying on of their joint operations.

The main difficulties arise between these two classes upon the question as to what proportion of the profits resulting from the joint operation of labor and capital shall be given to labor. A capitalist must recognize that the business carried on is not solely his business, and the employe must recognize that the work performed by him is not solely a matter of his own consideration, and both parties must deal with each other upon the idea that the business carried on is the joint business of employer and employe, and recognize the rights of each to an equitable share of the profits produced by such joint operation, and the question is, how peace and harmony between employer and employe can be best maintained to their joint advantage, and to the advantage of the general public.

So serious have become the troubles between capital and labor that we find ourselves tending toward one of two results, either that their difficulties—their strikes and lockouts—shall be prevented or settled by conciliation and arbitration or that they shall be settled by compulsory arbitration through the medium of the courts. If conciliation and arbitration shall prove to be a failure, the only other remedy would appear to be compulsory arbitration by law.

I have investigated the history of compulsory arbitration in the Australian colonies, France and other countries, and have come to the conclusion that compulsory arbitration is neither desirable nor advisable. The difficulty with it is that it destroys the individuality of both employer and employe, it degrades both of them; it deprives both of them of their constitutional rights and freedom of contract.

In England, in early times, justices of the peace were given power to fix rates of wages and hours of work, and history tells us that the justices of the peace became judicial despots within their jurisdiction.

Arbitration by the courts is not judicial work. The fixing of prices on articles, the fixing of wages and hours of labor, these things are business questions, not judicial questions, and the tendency of compulsory arbitration laws must inevitably be to create a judicial tyranny wherever they are carried into operation—a judicial tyranny resulting in the slavery both of employer and employe to the will of the judiciary.

I firmly believe that the remedy for our labor difficulties is voluntary conciliation and arbitration. Conciliation and arbitration do not mean the same thing. The first is a preventive of strikes, the latter is only resorted to from necessity.

My long experience on the chancery bench may be what has led me to the conviction that where both parties to a controversy are honest and desire nothing more than what is right, and are desirous of settling their controversy, such controversy can always be settled by ascertaining the right, the equity, underlying the controversy, and applying it to the matter in dispute.

Mr. Schilling has made reference to the fact that I was an umpire in the first great strike in the city of Chicago—what is called the bricklayers' strike, or the lockout of the bricklayers (as they contended) in 1887. That strike had continued nine or ten weeks; it was estimated there were 40,000 persons out of employment, as the strike of the bricklayers had tied up the work of all allied trades and building operations. A committee of five was chosen on each side, that is, five by the bricklayers and five by the Builders' Association, and to my surprise I was requested to act as umpire, as they said they could agree upon no other person, and I consented.

We met on Monday, the 4th day of July, 1887; the feeling was bitter and both sides were suspicious of the law as represented by myself, but we succeeded, by working twelve hours a day until Friday night of the same week, when we arrived at a settlement of the strike. It was settled then on a basis in nearly all respects similar to that which was followed in the settlement of the great coal strike.

The settlement provided for a board of arbitration, the members to be chosen from each side annually in the month of January. This board was to meet and fix a minimum rate of wages, pay for Sunday and overtime, and all other questions about which trouble could be anticipated. In case the arbitration committee could not settle any difficulty arising, the umpire was to be called upon. I was elected umpire for seven successive years, and never was once called upon to settle a difficulty between the parties.

I became so much in love with the theory of the settlement of controversies by conciliation and arbitration that I set to work to devise a law by which a controversy in a court of justice might be settled by conciliation and a judicial arbitration without expense and without delay, and without appeal or writ of error. That law was passed in 1889, and in substance it provided that any two persons having a controversy could appear in court with or without attorneys and ask the judge of a court of record to settle the controversy existing between them, and upon signing a certain stipulation provided by the law the court is required to hear the controversy without formal pleadings, without a jury, and to decide the same forthwith, or within a certain specific number of days fixed by the stipulation of the parties, and no record to be kept of the proceedings beyond the written stipulation of the parties and the judgment or decree of the court, which judgment or decree should recite what the controversy was that was submitted and should be conclusive.

This law worked well, parties have frequently availed themselves of the means provided, among others the well known case of Farwell vs. Sturgis, in which there was litigation enough to last for two or three generations, but which was promptly decided after a six weeks' hearing, and the validity of the finding in that case was afterward affirmed by the Supreme Court.

I am firmly convinced that the efforts to adjust labor difficulties by voluntary conciliation and arbitration will prove a complete success. There may be some evils to be suffered in arriving at it, but it is far better that they should be borne and the independence of the individual in his constitutional rights maintained than that he should be subject to compulsory arbitration by the courts.

JUDGE MURRAY F. TULEY.

By getting the employer and employe together, getting them to understand their relative rights in carrying on their joint operations, and that it is the duty of both parties to submit to what is right and equitable, in any difficulty that arises, a solution—not a solution, but a preventive—of labor difficulties will be obtained to a very large degree.

I am glad to be able to participate in this movement and I pledge you my hearty co-operation in any way that I can serve the cause.

THE DANGER IN GROUNDLESS STRIKES.

The strike is labor's last resource. Its use is a serious matter—so serious that the experienced labor organization will go out of its way to get a fair settlement by other means. So long as this weapon is held in reserve or used only when all other weapons fail its moral effect is great. When a union which has made itself known to the public as opposed to needless strikes finds itself so unjustly treated that a strike is unavoidable it has strong claims to public sympathy. The feeling will be widespread that such a body resorts to extreme measures only because all other methods of getting justice have failed. It is equally plain that the effect of frequent and groundless strikes must be to destroy public confidence in labor unions. Experienced labor leaders recognize this and are using their influence to prevent unnecessary and therefore unjustifiable strikes.—[Chicago News.

FOR INDUSTRIAL PEACE.

(*Concluded from page 9.*)

the National Civic Federation and the New York organization, I believe that no man, whether his connection be with the church, with great industrial affairs or with the leadership of some great trade union, can devote his time to a higher or better cause than the Civic Federation. I favor it on many grounds, but chiefly from the standpoint of the unions, because they make better men, better mechanics, better citizens, better Americans. I feel that on the side of capital the unions increase the responsibility of men who have often acquired their means and experience, beginning like the rest of us plain Americans, with hard effort. It has been my privilege of representing the public in this matter, not to do a great deal, but what little I have done has been with the greatest possible pleasure. I do feel that the New York Civic Federation will be an instrument, an auxiliary to the National Civic Federation, that will render unlimited service to all interests. I feel that as we are organized now, with our Conciliation Committee under Mr. McMillin subject to a telephone call and responding to any request coming within its province, with Mr. Marks, Mr. Easley, Mr. Farley and Mr. Nixon always ready, no matter what time of the day or night they are called upon (they make it a privilege as well as a duty to respond to that call, and we have seen in some instances where the call could not come too soon) it will be a very useful force. One instance of its good work came under my own observation recently, when I did not know that Mr. Mahon was in the city, when it was necessary for an interview to take place. A new organization had made demands which could not be acceded to by the directors, who were new to the situation, and who answered 'no.' There was a deadlock. The traffic of this great city was in imminent danger of being paralyzed at any moment. A telephone message from Mr. Easley's office announced that Mr. Mahon was here. That resulted in a talk with important officials of this corporation; that resulted in further conferences and better understanding, and in a very few hours the serious difficulty of the situation was removed. The service is going on uninterrupted and, so far as the public is concerned, nothing is known of the Federation's labors in its behalf. A service of that kind to a city like New York, with all its commercial interests, could not be measured. If that organization had not existed and Mr. Mahon had not been here, we cannot tell what would have happened. It is only one of I suppose thirty similar cases in which the members of the local Federation have had the opportunity of rendering service. We cannot give too much attention to this Federation. We cannot be too prompt in its service. It supports a great cause. It is a just cause and personally I shall do anything and everything within my power to advance the interests of the Federation and to bring men who apparently see things from different standpoints to see them right. Any man that does right himself and helps other men to do right is doing a great public service. This, gentlemen, I believe, is what we are all here to do. Our organization is a useful one, our cause great, and it will be blest, not only during our time, but in the future." [Applause.]

Mr. Underwood, being called on by the Chairman, replied: "I don't think I can say anything more that will throw light on this great work. I merely desire to say I am willing to learn and shall always feel it a privilege and duty to contribute as much of my time as possible toward bringing about the peaceable and honorable adjustments we are all seeking." [Applause.]

Mr. Nixon, in calling on the next speaker, Mr. Marks, said: "I want to pay a tribute to one always ready, no matter if it overtaxes his energies, one ready and willing to make sacrifices, both for his own side and the other whenever we have a difficulty, and that one is Mr. Marcus M. Marks." Mr. Marks was greeted heartily. He said: "Archbishop Ireland said we are here to learn. True, and we are also to be teachers. We come here to learn and go outside to teach. Unless the labor leaders go out and teach their people, unless the leaders of industries go out and impress the manufacturers, we fail in our purpose. Let us go outside and say to the manufacturers: 'Open your eyes; it is a condition, not a theory, that confronts us; be just! be patient!' and say to labor men: 'Don't be prejudiced because your employer is a so-called capitalist; be reasonable! respect the rights of others.' Gentlemen, I can say to-night it is the greatest blessing to us that the machinery of this Civic Federation has been given to us for the purpose of accomplishing good. It is a tremendous engine. It has the confidence of the community. Yes; let us spread the good influences of our conferences. We can thus make the Civic Federation a great power tending toward industrial peace." [Applause.]

Mr. Nixon, referring to Mr. McMillin, said he would like to hear from him, as another member of the New York branch engaged in active and effective work. Mr. McMillin declined to make a speech, saying: "I have really but one suggestion to make to-night and that is in the interest of the Committee on Conciliation. When the labor organizations send out their organizers to make new regiments they might instruct them to drill their men for ninety days in their own rules and laws before permitting them to rule themselves. We are having a great deal of trouble in the subway through a new organization becoming a little previous. If the organizers could drill such men up to self-government before letting them walk alone, it would relieve the Committee on Conciliation a great deal." [Laughter and applause.]

As the diners dispersed the comment was general that every one present might well say he had been present at an event certain to become historic. It had been plainly discernible to all that a new element was rapidly developing which would be destined to have a strong influence on the course of events in American industrial progress. The cause had already brought to the front eloquent and influential champions, all agreeing on the means to be pursued in pushing forward to the common end—peace and prosperity for all. As the evening had passed without a single untoward incident, it might be well hoped that the future course of the Federation would be helpful not only to New York but to the entire country.

THE EXCLUSION OF THE NON-UNION MAN.

BY MARCUS M. MARKS.

Questions of wages and of hours can usually be arranged if wage earners and their employers confer in the proper spirit and have sufficient patience and judgment.

The question of restriction of output—one of the most serious in connection with the labor problem—although generally understood by our national labor leaders, has not been brought home clearly to the rank and file of organized workmen. Unless union men realize the grave dangers underlying arbitrary restriction of output, the solution of the problem may ultimately force itself upon them when the advancement of the non-union man, who is free from restriction and thus able to push his way to the front, teaches in a striking way that the strength given to each individual should be developed and expressed in his work up to the extent permitted by security to health. The subject is one that needs considerable light, and it is only by frequent friendly conferences between employers and wage earners that we may hope to clear away the haze which in many cases still envelops the whole theory of restriction. The employer should never forget that he must insure full payment for extra service before the wage earner can be enthused into bringing out his best powers.

But there is one problem in connection with the labor movement regarding which there seems to be less hope for early understanding and agreement, and that is the status of the non-union man. Shall wage earners refuse to work with a man who cannot be persuaded by them to join their union? Shall the employer be urged to coerce this man into joining the union or else discharge him? These questions usually arouse considerable feeling on both sides, and employers as a rule refuse to confer on the matter, which they consider a question of principle and therefore not subject to arbitration. This disinclination to confer makes the question very serious, because, as already suggested, it is only by kindly discussion that misunderstanding between employers and wage earners can be removed.

In England, where the labor union movement is old established and twice as strong as in this country, union workmen do not object to non-union men being employed in the same shops. In this country a great many of the national labor leaders understand that the hope of the labor movement lies in evolution and not in revolution, and that workmen can best be brought into a union by convincing them that good is being accomplished by association. Our leading labor leaders realize that a man coerced into joining the union makes a poor union man and is apt to drop out when his affiliation is most needed; but many of the local leaders throughout the country do not yet fully appreciate this.

Only recently a conference between employes and employers was in danger of being seriously disturbed

MARCUS M. MARKS.

when the remark was made by one of the local representatives of the union that "he would rather work next to a man with the smallpox than next to a non-union man." Manufacturers present who happened to employ many non-union men of good character and ability were incensed at this statement, and it took coolness and patience to smooth over the situation. It was pointed out to this union man that as only ten to twenty per cent. of the workmen belong to unions, his remark was a gross insult to the vast majority of workmen in this country. Of course his statement was exaggerated and fortunately does not represent the feelings of union workmen as a class.

Most men now agree that great good can be accomplished, and is being accomplished, by unions of workmen as well as by associations of employers. But it must always be borne in mind that the best results are brought about by moving along the lines of least resistance. Persuasion and argument may be persistently used, but the line should be drawn at coercion. If a workman is convinced that it is not to his best interests to affiliate with the union, it is both unwise and wrong for his comrades to coerce him to join. If unionism is for the good of the wage earner, he is bound to find it out. Let the demonstration of the value of association be made clear and the union movement will win out in the end.

Many cases have presented themselves where serious strikes and lockouts were brought about because the unions insisted that the employer discharge non-union men, while, on the other hand, in some cases where this demand was not insisted upon, the men subsequently joined the union of their own volition.

The national labor leaders in the Civic Federation can do much to throw light on this dark place in the workings of local labor unions throughout the country, and it is to be hoped that these leaders will raise their voices fearlessly and frequently against coercive methods, which are against the spirit of the age and opposed to the best interests of true trade unionism.

Outside of its province to provide neutral ground

where contending parties may meet without loss of dignity or prestige to adjust matters of difference between capital and labor, the work of the Civic Federation is mainly educational. Leading men in many walks of life, coming together at its great conferences, exchange experiences resulting from broad, busy lives, and invariably leave one another the richer. However, were the good effect to end with the education of this Executive Committee the accomplishment would not be sufficient. Each man should become a center, radiating the good influences of the Civic Federation. The employers on this committee should pass on to their fellow employers the valuable ideas that have been absorbed at the meetings, and should counsel recognition of practical conditions as they exist in the labor world. They should advise and help to bring about frequent conferences between employer and employed, and impress on the employer the duty of great patience which his position in the community imposes upon him.

The labor leader has a corresponding duty. The atmosphere of the Civic Federation should be communicated as far as possible to his membership; his task in the future will be made easier and simpler if the rank and file of the organizations are impressed from time to time with the broad spirit of ideal unionism. If this policy of transmission is carried out thoroughly, the potent influence of the Civic Federation for good will be immeasurable. Then indeed will the members of the Federation, who are blest with the opportunity of using its powerful machinery, have ample cause to feel content with the results of their efforts.

THE WARFARE AGAINST UNIONISM. HOW SHALL IT BE MET?

BY HENRY WHITE.

General Secretary United Garment Workers of America.

The hostile declarations of a certain class of manufacturers against the unions, followed by the formation of business men's associations for the avowed purpose of fighting unionism, are evidence of the belief entertained by many employers that the vast power acquired by the unions is being used despotically and that the tendency is to become more so as their prestige increases.

HENRY WHITE.

So pronounced has this opposition become as to give rise to serious concern on the part of those most active in the labor movement. The welfare of the cause will not be served by making light of the accusations or belittling the antagonism engendered. Neither will it avail to reply in kind or to make extravagant claims for the unions. The better course is to consider the criticism calmly and to ascertain to what extent it is well founded, in order to remedy deficiencies.

The working class has all to gain by fair play. Until recent years helpless and disunited, it was long kept close to the life-line. The pressure of society bore heavily down upon it, and it could offer no counter-resistance. Through concerted action it has now gained a firm footing and has secured a measure of independence, a larger share in the product, and more recognition from society. There is nothing to interrupt its steady rise if its higher purposes are kept in view and it strives for the attainable. Should it depart from that course its steps will have to be retraced at a great cost. A few persons may levy tribute upon society or exact exorbitant pay for their services, but if the multitude attempts the same proceeding the harmony or balance of the social forces is upset, society being unable or unprepared to meet it. Any attempt also to apply to existing affairs the standards of justice based upon ideal conditions must meet with a like fate.

The necessity for labor organization is so apparent that the authorities in economic science are all agreed as to the indispensable services that the unions render. They are based upon principles that make them invulnerable when acting within the bounds of reason. That is why the unions need not fear to acknowledge their shortcomings. Just as consciousness of our faults is necessary to their correction, so will a frank admission of the defects of the union lead to their correction. Hence, if fear of the movement is largely inspired by the inability or unwillingness of its leaders to recognize its faults and limitations, an acknowledgment of them would do more to inspire confidence than the most vehement denial of the accusations. It cannot be held that a union, like a king, can do no wrong. No one can expect the labor movement to be the only perfect human institution; as the membership comprises the average persons, it is not to be supposed that on becoming members they will be transformed into saints. When actuated by a common grievance they appeal to the highest sentiment, but when they feel secure in their power they are likely, unless controlled by rare wisdom, to apply it as ruthlessly as the other side, and the latter, hard pressed in turn, are moved to make the same appeal to justice. That is human nature, and we might as well be candid about it. The unionist is liable to seize his opportunity, just as the employer has done, to exact all he can without regard to ultimate consequences, and when he feels safe becomes deaf to all entreaties. And when a union officer, who, because of his knowledge and experience, is enabled to look further ahead, counsels moderation, he is apt to be thrust aside, and the membership only brought to its senses after a contest in which it has lost the fruits of years of struggle.

Nearly all union officers and labor leaders of my acquaintance have often taken great risks in boldly standing out against excessive demands and unworthy methods of their membership. Although in their representative capacity they are placed in the position of supporting their unions against hostile attacks, yet they know, what they are loth to say to the members, that an occasional resistance by employers is necessary to keep the restless element within bounds. It is a question as to whether the checking process is to be done by the membership or by the employers after a wasteful fight.

An amazing change has come over the laborer. A generation ago he was submissive, stolid, and contented. He could be depended upon to support existing conditions, and he seemed devoid of any feeling of solidarity with his fellows. To-day he has pooled his interests with them, has bettered his condition substantially, and he even contends for some say in the conduct of business. The vital question now arises: "Will the unions show a consciousness of the responsibility that goes with power, develop the ability to restrain themselves, and keep on in the path of least resistance, or will they plunge ahead, driven on by the clamor of the unreflecting among the membership?" "Whither are they tending?" is the question sometimes anxiously asked by the most sincere friends of the working-class movement. Will the unions find their functions in society by serving as an agency for effecting a more equitable distribution of wealth, or will they clash with other social forces and precipitate a hurtful internal conflict?

There is little that is strange in the hostility of employers toward unions. Industrial improvement is not possible without some forcing. If the workmen had to wait until employers voluntarily offered to increase wages and shorten hours they would remain where they were. It is by asserting themselves that concessions are granted and recognition given. In time, as the employer realizes the futility of trying to destroy a union, he becomes reconciled to it as a factor to be dealt with in the conduct of his business, and his active opposition ceases, especially when he finds that he does not suffer as a competitor when wage conditions are made uniform. When, however, he becomes subject to harassing demands, his latent opposition is again aroused.

The present organized movement against unionism means something more than this normal opposition. It is due rather to the fear that industry is being menaced by an irresponsible and insatiable power. The unions can allay that fear only by the force of example—by demonstrating that it has no real basis.

ORGANIZATION AND CONCILIATION.

Hon. Oscar S. Straus, as President of the American Social Science Association, in an address on "Industrial Peace," at its session May 14, brought out these points:

OSCAR S. STRAUS.

The results accomplished by the National Civic Federation have not only justified its existence, but have also clearly shown that along the lines of its endeavors the best results toward adjusting labor disputes and securing industrial peace are attainable.

The "Conciliation Committee" has been applied to for its good offices within the past fifteen months in many important and large labor controversies. These applications have come sometimes from the one side, sometimes from the other side, and not infrequently from both sides. The committee has succeeded beyond its most sanguine expectations in bringing about or materially contributing toward an adjustment in nearly every instance, with the exception of the anthracite coal strike.

The plan of organization of the industrial department of the Civic Federation has been unfavorably criticised for not giving unorganized labor a representation, and as a consequence, unduly leaning toward, if not actively supporting, organized as against unorganized labor. This point of view did not escape the careful attention of the Executive Committee of the Federation, and for that reason its "statement of purpose" contains the following: "That at all times representatives of employers and workers, organized and unorganized, should confer for the adjustment of differences or disputes," etc.

Besides, these considerations presented themselves, that the third group, "on the part of the public," could certainly be relied upon to represent all the laboring elements irrespectively, just as they represented the welfare of the entire community. In what other way could it select representatives, for had the Civic Federation summoned unorganized labor to have a conference and select delegates or representatives for its committee, then it could have been charged that by that very act it had promoted the organization of unorganized labor.

As a member of the Conciliation Committee, I have had frequent conferences with many of the leading labor leaders in the country, and I am free to state my point of view has undergone a complete change in respect to the evolution of the labor question. I have grown more and more hopeful that, as this country was the first to organize religious and political equality, it will lead the way to a peaceful co-ordination of the economic forces by equalizing the opportunities for advancement, which is the nearest practical approach to economic equality. The maintenance of the open door of opportunity is a fundamental American doctrine as old as the Declaration of Independence.

Without organization, however, and with unrestrained competition, the well disposed employer is often prevented from granting his workmen more liberal terms which he regards as reasonable, so long as his less well disposed competitor holds out against making like reasonable concessions, and as a result strikes on the part of organized labor are brought about to correct evils growing out of a lack of harmony among unorganized employers.

Besides, strong organization among employers will have a far-reaching moral and disciplinary effect upon labor, and make it easier for the leaders to labor to control their followers and restrain them from making unreasonable demands. Just as among nations one sword keeps the other in its scabbard and makes for peace, so will equality of might conduce to equality of right, and strengthen the forces of wisdom and conservatism on both sides.

How much more intelligent and economical and useful a branch of the National Civic Federation in every city of importance in the Union than a national organization formed for the express purpose of pitting capital against labor, of fostering hatred and breeding strife!—[Chicago Post.

A CHECK ON RAW STRIKERS.

Hasty and ill-advised strikes were condemned by vote at a meeting of the Chicago Federation of Labor on May 4, and the Federation immediately proceeded to put its resolution into practice. A strike of the 6,000 employes at the Deering harvester plant and an attempt at calling out 7,000 at the McCormick plant were denounced on the floor of the Federation by Barney Cohen, a member of the Executive Board. The two plants are now a part of the International Harvester Company's property. Mr. Cohen said that from an investigation at the McCormick plant he thought there was no trouble there that could not be settled in half an hour by using good judgment. No demand had been made on the management by the employes. A number of these said that their only demand was the right to organize. "Superintendent Wood of the twine mills," said Committeeman Cohen, "told us that it would be the last thing he would think of to interfere with the personal liberty of his employes. The question of joining a union was one for themselves to decide. Superintendent Flather of the reaper works told us the same thing. No one had ever been discriminated against for being a member of the union. All of the blacksmiths and two-thirds of the machinists are union men. They have made no complaints of discrimination."

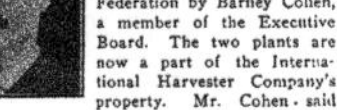

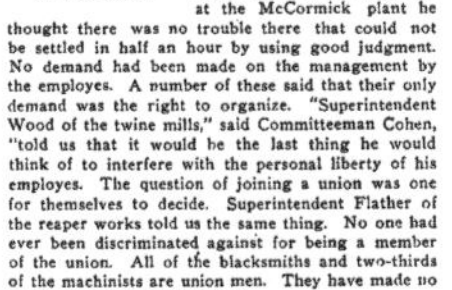

W. G. SCHARDT.

"I believe," continued Committeeman Cohen, "that many of the strikes now disturbing the city could be avoided if good judgment were used in the first place. By acting conservatively we can have the support of those who are now opposed to organized labor, and who think our main object is to stir up strife. On the contrary, the object of this federation is to secure the best possible conditions for the workers, and to do so with as few strikes as possible."

The recommendation of the Executive Board, as adopted by the Federation, was: "That the Federation take some action on the hasty calling of strikes at this time. We suggest that when there is any grievance existing the Executive Board should be notified before any strike is called to try and settle the matter without a strike. We believe that many of the troubles arising at this time can be adjusted without strikes."

The McCormick affair was quickly settled. The company invited an investigation of its works by representatives of the Chicago Federation of Labor. They found that the employes in general had no fault to find with their treatment by the company. President W. G. Schardt, of the Federation, on seeing the situation at the McCormick works, caused the union pickets to be withdrawn and interference with the company to be brought to an end. He and the Federation Executive Committee conducted negotiations for ten days with the officials of the International Harvester Company, at the end of which time the Deering strikers voted to return to work. Both sides made concessions and decided to submit their differences to arbitration by a joint committee representing the company and the Chicago Federation of Labor.

Complaints against the company in minor matters, especially by the girls and women, who were forced to work in unsatisfactory surroundings, were investigated by the company. As a result it will systematically set about improving the conditions.

The Secretary of the Chicago Federation estimates the union membership represented on its floor as 300,000, including thousands of youths under age and women. Many others are unskilled laborers, not naturalized citizens.

The Chicago Federation for two years has been actively engaged in the work of arbitration, of which its most active members are usually strong advocates. It is making a reputation in this regard as an agency for public order.

Mr. Schardt, the president, was a union carpenter in Spokane in 1896, the union's business agent in Seattle in 1891, and in a similar position in Chicago in 1894. From 1895 to 1902 he was financial secretary of Local No. 1 in Chicago. He is a skilled worker at his trade, and has established a reputation as an aggressive but moderate leader.

A DISTRICT AGREEMENT.

New York Metal Trades Association and the Brotherhood of Boilermakers and Iron Shipbuilders.

In the April number of the REVIEW an account was given of the conference between the New York Metal Trades Association and the Marine Trades Council which was brought about through the efforts of members of the New York Civic Federation. This conference agreed to call off the sympathetic strikes of the boilermakers in the shipbuilding yards of the members of the Metal Trades Association, and also the sympathetic strike of all the crafts in the Townsend-Downey Shipbuilding and Repair Company. After that agreement was made the boilermakers presented demands to all the employers in the New York district asking for an increase in wages, shorter hours, and exclusive employment of union members, to take effect May 1. Neither organization was at first willing again to enter into conference, both having determined that the only solution of their difficulties was to be found in a trial of strength. At this juncture, through the offices of Mr. Marcus M. Marks of the Civic Federation, the Metal Trades Association consented to hold a conference with the boilermakers, whose District Council also assented. Each side appointed five committeemen, who arranged a meeting for 11 o'clock on the last day of April. If the strike, which was to go into effect the next day, was to be avoided it was necessary that a prompt agreement be reached. The committees were in session continuously nineteen hours, from 11 o'clock on Thursday morning until 5 o'clock on the morning of May 1. They finally reached an agreement in which concessions were made on both sides.

While the union had demanded a nine-hour day on all shop work and a half-holiday during the summer months, it was agreed that the custom as to hours prevailing in the several plants should be continued. The agreement also provided:

"There shall be no restriction or discrimination on the part of workmen as to the handling of any materials entering into the construction of the work upon which they are employed.

"There shall be no limitation placed upon the work to be performed by any workman during working hours.

"There shall be no restriction as to use of machinery, or tools, or as to the number of men employed in the operation of the same.

"There shall be no restriction whatever as to the employment of foremen.

"There shall be no sympathetic strikes called on account of trades' disputes.

"No person other than authorized by the employer shall interfere with the workmen during working hours.

"The employer may employ or discharge, through his representative, any workmen, as he may see fit; but no workman is to be discriminated against on account of his connection with a labor organization.

"In cases where misunderstandings or disputes arise between the employer and workmen, the matter in question shall be submitted to arbitration without strikes, lockouts or stoppage of work pending the decision of the arbitration.

"Each member of the New York Metal Trades Association affected by this agreement shall be held individually responsible only for the performance of the same, and his, or its, violation of this agreement shall subject such member to expulsion from the association."

In return for the concessions of the boilermakers in the matter of discipline and management of the shops the employers conceded an advance of wages to $3 per day for boilermakers, riveters, chippers and caulkers, and an increase of 5 per cent. for others.

MR. GOMPERS GIVES SOUND ADVICE.

He Favors Employers' Unions and Rebukes a Reckless Organizer.

Two letters which President Gompers of the American Federation of Labor has recently written have been widely quoted by the press with approval.

Of the organization of employers he wrote:

SAMUEL GOMPERS.

"Employers will find it to their advantage to be organized, and not only this but to deal with organized labor. The movement to form unions among the business men will tend rather to prevent conflict than to promote trouble. The better the organization on both sides the better it will be for business. Organized employers will be better able to understand the demands of organized labor and to meet these demands without friction.

"There has been much hot talk about the increasing demands of labor. My experience has taught me not to be an alarmist, and I am not alarmed over this particular situation in general. So long as human nature is as it is there will be manifestations of discontent, both from laborers and from employers. But I believe that every day is making for better conditions. We hear more of labor troubles now than we did years ago, but we must not judge too hastily from this that laborers are any more widely discontented or that they are unreasonable. When an industrial dispute occurs in our time it involves so much that it must attract more attention. But every dispute is an influence toward a better condition of things in the future."

To an organizer of the Federation operating in San Antonio Mr. Gompers wrote:

"Through the courtesy of some fellow unionists, I am in receipt of copies of newspapers containing references to remarks alleged to have been made by you at a conference where the subject of unionizing the men employed in the Fire Department was under consideration, and that during this conference you made a statement substantially as follows: 'That being asked what the firemen, if organized into a union, would do in the event of a strike, you said you would be in favor of not letting an engine be touched, and that you would be willing to let the whole city burn.'

"I do not want to take it for granted that you did make the remarks referred to, and yet all the circumstances indicate it; but when I first saw the utterance it shocked me beyond expression. The American Federation of Labor is a standing protest against wanton destruction, injustice, brutality or inhumanity, and I would be recreant to that organization as well as to my entire make-up did I allow such a remark to go unrebuked, particularly when made by one holding a commission as organizer for the American Federation of Labor.

"You will please advise me promptly whether the remarks above stated have been made by you, or any remarks which are similar in substance. If you can give but an affirmative answer to this statement, you will please return the commission you hold as General Organizer for the American Federation of Labor."

NATIONAL ASSOCIATION OF MANUFACTURERS.

The Declaration of Principles Adopted at New Orleans, April 15, 1903.

1. Fair dealing is the fundamental and basic principle on which relations between employes and employers should rest.
2. The National Association of Manufacturers is not opposed to organizations of labor as such, but is unalterably opposed to boycotts, blacklists and other illegal acts of interference with the personal liberty of employer or employe.
3. No person should be refused employment or in any way discriminated against on account of membership or non-membership in any labor organization, and there should be no discriminating against or interference with any employe who is not a member of a labor organization by members of such organizations.
4. With due regard to contracts, it is the right of the employe to leave his employment whenever he sees fit, and it is the right of the employer to discharge any employe when he sees fit.
5. Employers must be free to employ their work people at wages mutually satisfactory, without interference or dictation on the part of individuals or organizations not directly parties to such contracts.
6. Employers must be unmolested and unhampered in the management of their business, in determining the amount and quality of their product, and in the use of any methods or systems of pay which are just and equitable.

7. In the interest of employes and employers of the country, no limitation should be placed upon the opportunities of any person to learn any trade to which he or she may be adapted.

8. The National Association of Manufacturers disapproves absolutely of strikes and lockouts, and favors an equitable adjustment of all differences between employers and employes by any amicable method that will preserve the rights of both parties.

9. The National Association of Manufacturers pledges itself to oppose any and all legislation not in accord with the foregoing declaration.

THE CIVIC FEDERATION INDORSED.

At the annual convention of the Amalgamated Association of Iron, Steel and Tin Workers, held at Columbus, O., in April, the following indorsement of the National Civic Federation by President T. J. Shaffer was unanimously approved by vote of the delegates, and it was resolved that the association adhere to its connection with the Civic Federation:

T. J. SHAFFER.

"The investor of capital has certain rights which we must grant, but at the same time he must recognize and grant to us conditions which belong to us, because without our co-operation he cannot succeed, and as a coadjutor we shall be without employment, if he be not with us.

"The time has come, and I believe it is propitious, when capital and labor in organized capacities, must unite to oppose and defeat the purposes of their common enemies. This union has been started, but has not attained the strength it must have to protect the interests of the employer and the employed. The union to which I refer is the Civic Federation, composed of statesmen, clergymen, philanthropists, educators, business men, and leaders of organized labor. They aim to procure industrial peace, equitable divisions of earnings, proper conditions, better citizenship and corrected government.

"When labor presents intelligently its claims to capital, educated by labor's reasoning, then shall capital and labor be partners and share equitably in common production and mutual investment. This desirable condition is sought by the Civic Federation, within whose ranks are men of thought, reason, soundness of judgment and pure tendency of heart and disposition."

Mr. Eidlitz on the Building Trades Unions.

Otto M. Eidlitz, Chairman of the Emergency Committee of the Building Trades Employers' Association, has made public this statement regarding the present employers' movement:

"It must be understood first, last and all the time that this is a movement that is making for industrial peace, that is our one and only aim. At the outset it may appear to some people that this is not the case. But in the end we will demonstrate that out one and only purpose has been to bring about peace and amity between employer and employe.

"There is an immense amount of work that we shall have to do before we can get down to a specific working plan. In the first place, we will have to find out the exact status of the relations between each of our associations and the labor unions with which it does business. In some instances men are out on strike and in others they are locked out, and in others they are prevented from working because of the rival claims of contending unions or because of the non-delivery of materials.

"In a matter of such great importance as this we must move very slowly. We cannot afford to make mistakes. The eyes of employers throughout the whole country are upon us. We are determined that this movement shall have a successful issue, and that the results we shall achieve will be beneficial to all of the interests involved.

"With great care we are working out our plan and scope, and until that has been completed it will be impossible for anybody to say pust what action we shall take in dealing with the different problems before us. In mapping out our plans we keep before us all the time the knowledge that unions of labor, instead of being a menace, are a help to us. We do not want to exterminate the labor unions or hamper them in any way. . We want the unions. They bring about competition, and competition is of the greatest value in every trade. We do not regard the unions as a necessary evil that we have got to meet. We welcome them.

"But we do think that there are some phases of unionism that are unfair. The foremost of these, in my opinion, is the discrimination of individual unions against individual employers. This, we believe, should be stopped."

High Commendation from Mr. Wallace Downey.

I desire to express my appreciation of the splendid services rendered by the New York Civic Federation in connection with the several difficulties that have existed during the past five months between the New York Metal Trades Association and the employes of the members of that association, particularly in the matter of the sympathetic strike called against the members of the New York Metal Trades Association last March. In this case after several conferences the interested parties had come to a deadlock, and there seemed no recourse except a continuation of the strike condition, until either one side or the other gave way. Then by an especially clever stroke the Civic Federation demonstrated its full value by creating an opportunity for the contending parties to meet under conditions which made for peace. Then as a result of most faithful and unbiased effort the merit of the matter was brought to the fore and an adjustment of the difficulty made, which was based absolutely on merit without concession to sentiment or prejudice. I take special pleasure in mentioning this matter since I am convinced that the Civic Federation will be a great power for good by standing firmly for the recognition of merit on either side of the many controversies that are bound to grow out of the present strained condition between capital and labor.

WALLACE DOWNEY.

Townsend-Downey Shipbuilding Company, 12 Broadway, New York, May 26, 1903.

TRADE AGREEMENT.

H. Coulby Praises the Longshoremen's Union.

I am asked, first, whether any improvement has taken place in the character of the longshoremen's organization and its observance of agreements; second, the effect upon the industry from the employers' standpoint which has followed the increase in wages during the past few years and the exclusive employment of union workmen coupled with the system of joint trade agreements.

In answer to your first question I will state that the dock managers of the great lakes are now entering upon their fourth year of dealing with the Longshoremen's Union by the contract system, and after giving it a fair trial I have no hesitation in saying it has been, on the whole, satisfactory to both the managers and the men. In fact the results have been such that the Lake Carriers' Association of the great lakes has this year, for the first time, made contracts with the Firemen, Water Tenders and Oilers' Union, the Seamen's Union and the Cooks' Union. The Great Lakes Towing Company has also just entered into contract with the Licensed Tugmen's Protective Association and Tug Firemen and Linemen's Organization for manning their tugs during the ensuing year. All of these contracts contain the usual arbitration clause and provide that the men shall continue to work pending such arbitration. In addition, it is provided that all men working under the contracts must be satisfactory to and under the direction and control of the management, which I regard as the most essential features of the contract, because it clearly defines the relation between employer and employe. The officers of the International Longshoremen, Marine and Transport Workers' Association were the pioneers in establishing the contract system on the lakes, and to them is largely due the success that has attended its adoption. They have always insisted that a contract once entered into must be lived up to conscientiously and faithfully. During the life of our first contract there naturally arose some misunderstandings and wrong constructions of its terms. At the following annual conference with the men these were largely cleared up and since that time I know of no serious instance where the contract has been violated.

In answer to your second question: I believe the increase of wages during the last few years is largely due to the inevitable law of supply and demand. We are enjoying an era of prosperity which has created a great demand for labor, and it is only natural to expect that it would result in a higher wage scale. The laborer is worthy of his hire and is entitled to his share of the results of the good times. I believe the supply of labor on the great lakes is nearly all included in the several unions. Just so long as labor leaders keep up their supply of labor to fill the trade agreements they enter into, insist upon the elimination of sympathetic strikes, and that all matters in dispute be submitted to arbitration, the men in the meantime continuing to work, and that they shall not encroach upon or interfere with the executive part of the work, I believe satisfactory results will be obtained for both sides through trade agreements. It is certainly a vast improvement over the old method which often resulted in strikes and interruptions two or three times a month.

The sociological problem of the ultimate outcome of the exclusive employment of union workmen, coupled with the system of trade agreements, must, in my judgment, remain for the present a tentative one. A student of the history of trade unions in England for the last century finds its pages filled with things that dwarf commercial development. To successfully apply this method of dealing between employer and employe entails responsibilities on both sides. The employer must recognize that while all men are not endowed with the same ability we are all human and entitled to fair treatment, and that the best results are always obtained from men who feel they are well treated. At the same time, he must jealously guard his right to run his own business in his own way, as there is a tendency in unions to encroach upon the executive part of the work. On the other hand the trade unions must recognize the right of every man living under our form of government to sell his labor in the best market he can find, to rely upon the power of moral suasion and example to recruit their ranks and eliminate from their creed the weapons of boycott, tyranny and oppression that seems in the past to have been part of their stock in trade.

H. COULBY.

Pickands, Mather & Co., Cleveland, O., May 4, 1903.

President Newman Warmly Commends the Longshoremen.

Prior to the year 1903 our company had no direct dealings with labor organizations; that is, while we employed mostly union men there were no formal contracts entered into. In consequence more or less trouble ensued, especially during the year 1902, when a general strike of our employes occurred lasting some five or six months. Our past trouble, in my opinion, was largely caused by a failure to meet the various organizations and arrive at proper bargains. The failure to do this I attribute to the organizations themselves, our company being desirous of such a meeting. But be that as it may, we have since that time met with the chief executive officers of the labor organizations, and after careful negotiations have completed bargains and written contracts for the employment of all men for the ensuing year, which agreements we have every reason to believe will be faithfully observed.

Our having met with the labor organizations and arrived at agreements indicates to me that the labor organizations are constantly improving in their general character and the personnel of their officers. And while the wage scale has in most every instance been increased over former years I can see advantages to the employer which should compensate for the increase in the wage scale. My opinion is that every employer of labor would do well to carefully negotiate with the officers of the various trade unions whose men they desire to employ, and undertake to arrive at satisfactory agreements before they decide that such agreements cannot be made or would not be carried out. Labor organizations as a rule, I believe, are desirous of observing the contracts they make, and with the good work the employer can accomplish at the time the bargains are made the importance of this to the trade unions will become more and more apparent and strikes and lockouts less frequent.

T. F. NEWMAN, President.

General Office The Great Lakes Towing Company. Cleveland, O.

(*Chicago Inter Ocean, May 5.*)

CAPITAL AND LABOR WELDED BY LEADERS.

Senator Hanna and John Mitchell Felicitate Chicago at Organization of Branch of National Civic Federation.

Distinguished Ohio Senator Refutes Anarchy Charges and Praises the Way Strikes Are Handled Here, but Is Mum on the Subject of Politics.

Capital and labor, figuratively speaking, put their feet under the same table at a love feast at the Auditorium Annex yesterday afternoon. The meeting marked the organization of a local branch of the National Civic Federation, with representatives from the money and working classes and from the general public to form an Executive Committee. In attendance and warmly championing the proposed movement were Senator M. A. Hanna, John Mitchell, William R. Harper, Bishop Fallows, the Rev. Emil G. Hirsch, George A. Schilling, Franklin MacVeagh, Lambert Tree, Judge Murray F. Tuley, John C. Driscoll, Albert Young, Daniel Keefe, Colonel John J. McCook of New York, and a large number of others. Senator Hanna and Mr. Mitchell assisted in the forming of a similar branch at St. Louis last Friday.

FRANKLIN MAC VEAGH.

R. M. Easley, secretary of the National Civic Federation, called the gathering to order a few minutes after 4 o'clock. Franklin MacVeagh was made chairman and John C. Harding secretary. In a few words of explanation the chairman stated the purposes of the session, and pointed out that the organization was not to be confounded with the local Civic Federation, although it had grown out of that body.

"The national movement was started in Chicago in 1900," said Mr. MacVeagh, "and, like many another good thing born here, moved to New York. It may be said that Chicago again assumes the leadership, for it is the only city in the country that has a Board of Arbitration, and the only city that has a Federation of Labor that is avowedly going about the work of conciliation.

REMEDIES AND PROBLEMS.

"It has been said that Chicago breeds the problems. It also breeds the remedies. The National Civic Federation, therefore, meets different conditions here from those existing in New York and St. Louis."

Mr. MacVeagh then introduced Senator Hanna.

"It is indeed a gratifying time to me," said Senator Hanna. "It is more than gratifying to see this representative assemblage of Chicago citizens from the world of capital, of labor, and of thought. I believe in organized labor, and have had to deal with it for thirty-five years. When I had an opportunity I became a member of this organization, because it represents principles in which I believe. When men with differences have met on a common ground, in a spirit of fairness, a peaceful settlement has been the result.

"The National Civic Federation is engaged in a work of education and the bringing of the differing forces together upon a middle ground where they can reach an agreement. There never was a time in the history of this country when the questions which we are organized to deal with have assumed such economic importance as at present.

PRAISES ORGANIZED LABOR.

"I am glad to learn since I came here of your splendid organization for arbitration. I am more than glad to learn that organized labor has taken the lead in such an important thing. We are not arbitrators. We have never been called upon to act in that capacity, but in our sphere and in our way we have brought the opposing forces together and settled disputes involving millions of dollars. In this work which you have undertaken to further, I say, gentlemen, God speed you."

John Mitchell, President of the United Mine Workers of America, said that he was glad to add his voice in the furthering of the work in hand.

"More strikes and more trouble," he said, "have resulted through the failure of representatives of labor and capital to get together than from any other cause. I desire to compliment the Chicago Federation of labor on its action of yesterday. It marks an epoch in the advancement of labor. The best thing, in my judgment, that trade unions can do is to adjust their difficulties without strikes.

NEED POWERFUL AUXILIARY.

"It will be a good thing for you all to form this branch of the National Civic Federation. You have a good Board of Arbitration, a good Federation of Labor, and you need this powerful auxiliary to aid both. In the language of Senator Hanna, I say, 'God speed you.'"

Judge Tuley, the Rev. Mr. Hirsch, Albert Young, President of the Teamsters' National Union of America; Daniel Keefe, President of the International Longshoremen's Association; Professor Laughlin, of the Chair of Political Economy in the University of Chicago, and Colonel John J. McCook, of New York, addressed the meeting in furtherance of the work and approbation of sentiments that had been expressed.

On motion of B. J. Rosenthal the chairman was instructed to form an executive committee of twenty-three members, seven representing capital, seven labor, and seven the public, and to include the chairman and secretary.

Mr. MacVeagh appointed the following:

Representing the public—Judge Tuley, W. J. Onahan, B. J. Rosenthal, Bishop Fallows, Prof. H. P. Judson, W. W. Tracey and George A. Schilling.

Representing employers—Charles R. Crane, T. K. Webster, John M. Clark, Charles H. Hulburd, G. Watson French, George C. Prussing and W. T. Brownridge.

Representing employes—William G. Schardt, Carpenters; J. Keppler, President district No. 8, International Machinists' union; Harry Horder, Locomotive Engineers; F. C. Bender, Teamsters; William Miller, Wood Workers; Charles A. McCarle, president L. T. P. Association of the Great Lakes, and J. J. Corcoran, Bricklayers and Stonemasons.

The committee of twenty-three at a meeting, May 8, placed sixty-six names on the rolls of the general committee. Of these twenty-two represented the employers, twenty-two the wage earners and a like number the public. Other members will be added from time to time.

George A. Schilling, John C. Harding and B. J. Rosenthal were appointed a committee on constitution and to perfect the organization.

The general committee are:

J. Keppler	A. C. Barlett	Judge Tuley
A. L. Young	H. G. Selfridge	W. J. Onahan
F. Buchanan	J. A. Poor	B. J. Rosenthal
J. Fitzpatrick	J. O. Armour	Samuel Fallows
Chas. Peterson	F. P. Bagley	H. P. Judson
G. Thompson	A. A. McCormick	H. W. Tracy
J. J. Corcoran	H. W. Hoyt	G. A. Schilling
Herman Lillien	H. F. Vories	F. MacVeagh
W. G. Schardt	J. H. Selz	J. H. Eckels
Charles Hanks	H. F. McCormick	E. J. James
J. C. Harding	R. A. Keyes	C. S. Darrow
Wm. Belloway	J. M. Roach	Lambert Tree
L. P. Stranlee	R. T. Lincoln	Adolf Kraus
W. Miller	J. C. Driscoll	T. C. MacMillan
A. W. Simpson	N. L. Brown	John S. Miller
F. A. Pouchot	E. P. Ripley	E. G. Hirsch
J. W. Morton	C. R. Crane	T. A. Moran
F. C. Bender	T. E. Webster	L. A. Seeberger
Matthew Carr	J. M. Clark	Rev. E. K. Kelley
H. W. Horder	C. H. Hulburd	Graham Taylor
Ralph Hahn	G. W. French	Rev. R. A. White
C. A. McCarle	G. C. Prussing	M. A. Ryerson
E. J. Conway	W. T. Brownridge	Judge Kavanagh

TRADE AGREEMENT OF MARBLE DEALERS AND MARBLE WORKERS.

The joint agreement adopted at Buffalo, N. Y., on March 18, 1903, by the executive committees of the National Association of Marble Dealers and the International Association of Marble Workers, the latest new trade agreement in the labor market, has several points of interest. It is an innovation in the agreement system of the building trades in that it is entered upon by national associations rather than by local associations. The agreement provides for conciliation committees, for a nine-hour work day, the abolition of piece work, the abolition of sympathetic strikes and sympathetic lockouts. It gives preference of employment to members of the Marble Workers' union, in so far as the union can supply a sufficient number of competent workmen, and stipulates that members of the union shall not work for firms or corporations which pay lower wages than those paid by members of the Employers' Association; nor shall they work upon material not finished by members of the organization on the basis of hours and wages stipulated in the agreement. All grievances or requests from the workmen are to be presented through the shop steward only.

The full text of the agreement is as follows:

Whereas, there has heretofore existed a sentiment that the members of the National Association of Marble Dealers and the members of the International Association of Marble Workers were necessarily enemies, and in consequence a mutual dislike and distrust of each other and of their respective organizations has arisen, provoking and stimulating strife and ill-will, resulting in severe pecuniary loss to both parties, now this conference is held for the purpose of cultivating a more intimate knowledge of each other and of their methods, aims and objects, believing that thereby friendly regard and respect may be engendered and such agreements reached as will dispel all inimical sentiments, prevent further strife and promote the material and moral interests of all parties concerned.

Resolved, That this meeting adopt the principle of conciliation in the settlement of any dispute between the members of the I. A. M. W. and the members of the N. A. M. D.

Resolved, That a Conciliation Committee be formed consisting of six members, three of whom shall be marble workers appointed by the International Association of Marble Workers and three persons appointed by the National Association of Marble Dealers. If a member of the Conciliation Committee is a party to the dispute, or a member of a local union whose member or members are involved, he cannot serve on the Conciliation Committee in the settlement of the case involved. The President of his National Organization shall appoint a member to take his place in the settlement of that particular dispute.

Resolved, Whenever there is a dispute between a member of the N. A. M. D. and the Marble Workers in his employ (when the latter are members of the I. A. M. W.) and it cannot be settled amicably between them, it shall be referred to the Presidents of the two associations before named, who shall themselves or by delegates give it due consideration. If they cannot decide it satisfactorily to themselves, they may, by mutual agreement, summon the Conciliation Committee, to whom the dispute shall be referred, and whose decision by a majority vote shall be final and binding upon each party for the term of twelve months; pending adjudication by the Presidents and the Conciliation Committee neither party to the dispute shall discontinue operations, but shall proceed with business in the ordinary manner. In case of a vacancy in the Committee of Conciliation, it shall be filed by the association originally nominating. No vote shall be taken except by a full committee, or by an even number of each party.

Resolved, That on or before the first of June, 1903, the N. A. M. D. will run the finishing departments of their factories nine hours per day. The men to receive for the nine hours the same amount of pay as they now receive for ten hours. Any change in wages that cannot be agreed upon between a member of the N. A. M. D. and his employes shall be settled in the manner provided for the settlement of other disputes.

Resolved, That on or before the first of June, 1903, the members of the N. A. M. D. will abolish piece work in their finishing departments, except for the polishing of plumbers' slabs, backs and aprons.

Resolved, That there shall be no sympathetic strikes or sympathetic lockouts in the shops.

Resolved, That the National Association of Marble Dealers recognize the International Association of Marble Workers on and after the first of June, 1903, and agrees to give preference of employment to members of the International Association of Marble Workers in so far as the I. A. M. W. can supply a sufficient number of competent workmen.

Resolved, That no member or members of the I. A. M. W. shall work for any person, firm or corporation (not a member of the N. A. M. D.) on the basis of over nine hours per day or for less wages than those being paid by members of the N. A. M. D. for similar services.

Resolved, That no member or members of the I. A. M. W. shall handle or set any marble that is not finished by members of the I. A. M. W. working on the basis of not more than a nine-hour day and receiving the same wages as are paid by members of the N. A. M. D. for similar services and under the same conditions.

Resolved, That any request emanating from and affecting the workmen in the shops (when they are members of the I. A. M. W.) in the employ of a member of the N. A. M. D. shall be presented through and handled by the shop steward only.

Resolved, That except where otherwise specified, these resolutions shall go into effect this eighteenth day of March, 1903.

National Association of Marble Dealers,
by
W. H. Evans, President,
Fredk. P. Bagley, Secretary,
Wm. Lautz,
Alex. Davidson,
Peter Gray,
Executive Committee.

International Association of Marble Workers,
by
Robt. W. DuBorg, Grand President,
John A. Carroll, Grand Vice-President,
Henry Roberts, Grand Secretary-Treasurer,
William J. Kelly, Secretary,
Thos. P. F. Reilly, Organizer,
A. J. Hambecker,
C. R. Bonter,
W. B. Wilson,
Grand Officers and Grand Executive Council.

(*St. Louis Republic, May 1.*)

"CIVIC FEDERATION IS SOLUTION OF LABOR AND CAPITAL PROBLEM."

Former President Grover Cleveland

United States Senator Hanna, John Mitchell, President of the United Mine Workers' Union, David R. Francis, President of the Louisiana Purchase Exposition, and Bishop D. S. Tuttle Address the National Civic Federation in the Interest of Peaceful Relations Between Employer and Employe.

MITCHELL URGES ORGANIZATIONS TO SUPPORT MOVEMENT.

Suggestions on Settlement of Labor and Capital Differences.

"It is necessary that neither capital nor labor should regard itself as infallible. In contentions which arise it is utterly impossible that both sides should be right. Both sides should concede that they may possibly be wrong."—Grover Cleveland.

"A proper understanding between labor and capital will be of great help to St. Louis, especially during the next year, when the responsibilities of St. Louis are so great. A delay of thirty days would mean that the Louisiana Purchase Exposition would not be completed when its gates are thrown open to the world."—David R. Francis.

"I have been before the public as one in favor of industrial war instead of industrial peace, but I want to tell you that never in my life did I urge a strike until all other means had been exhausted."—John Mitchell.

"If the employer and the employe will meet face to face; tell each other the truth and be honest with each other; strikes will be reduced to a minimum."—John Mitchell.

"I believe that strikes and lockouts have grown out of a failure of the employer and the employe to understand each other."—John Mitchell.

"The workingmen of St. Louis should give this movement their support."—John Mitchell.

"A united effort should be made to get these great factors, capital and labor, together. They must meet, and it seems to me the time to meet, to get together, is now."—Senator Hanna.

"In labor difficulties the public is the final arbiter."—Senator Hanna.

"In a labor controversy mutual confidence on both sides is the foundation that leads to good results."—Senator Hanna.

"Patience and common sense as against an appeal to force."—Bishop Tuttle.

A St. Louis branch of the National Civic Federation was established yesterday at a meeting held in the Administration Building at the World's Fair.

The purpose of the National Civic Federation is to promote a better feeling between capital and labor, to urge arbitration in difficulties which arise between the two great forces of capital and labor and to create means to avert strikes and lockouts and other troubles, serious alike to employer and employe.

The gathering in the Administration Building was a notable one. Among the speakers were former President Grover Cleveland, United States Senator Mark Hanna, John Mitchell, President of the United Mine Workers' Union and a labor leader of national reputation; Lewis Nixon, President of the New York Civic Federation, and best known as the designer of the battleship Oregon and as ex-leader of Tammany; Oscar S. Straus, member of The Hague Arbitration Court; David R. Francis, President of the Louisiana Purchase Exposition; Reverend Father D. S. Phelan, who was delegated to address the meeting by Archbishop Kain; the Right Reverend Daniel S. Tuttle; Bishop of the Episcopal Church; Festus J. Wade, President of the Mercantile Trust Company, and Albert Young, President of the National Teamsters' Union.

The chapel in the Administration Building was crowded and the utterances of every speaker were cheered. Former President Cleveland and Senator Hanna occupied seats near the chairman. They sat side by side and faced the audience. Directly in front of them sat John Mitchell, the resolute labor leader. The countenance of Mitchell bore a serious expression all during the proceedings. Senator Hanna smiled frequently, while Mr. Cleveland was quiet and attentative.

CLEVELAND AND HANNA APPLAUDED MITCHELL.

When John Mitchell arose to address the meeting Senator Hanna and Mr. Cleveland applauded vigorously, and Mr. Mitchell just as warmly applauded the words of Mr. Cleveland and Senator Hanna.

Festus J. Wade was made temporary chairman of the local federation, and J. A. Jackson of the Typographical Union was chosen secretary.

Former President Cleveland was the first speaker called upon. When Mr. Cleveland arose there was an outburst of applause that lasted several minutes. Mr. Cleveland is a member of the National Federation and he was one of the promoters of the organization.

"I came here this afternoon," said Mr. Cleveland, "not to speak, but to see in what spirit the Civic Federation of this city would be formed. I came here to gather new inspiration and hope from a movement in which I am deeply interested and one which has my hearty sympathy.

"I have always believed that those who labor with their hands and those who labor in other ways should be nearer together. There should be a balancing power, with the end that when differences arise peaceable adjustments could be made. It seems to me that when these differences arise, the first and best thing to do would be to see if the parties in antagonism cannot be reconciled.

POSSIBLE FOR EITHER SIDE TO BE WRONG.

'It is necessary that neither capital nor labor should regard itself as infallible. In contentions which arise it is utterly impossible that both sides should be right. Both sides should concede that they possibly may be wrong.

'If capital and labor can be brought to a realization of these things it is natural then to call in some one for the purpose of arbitration, and if the feeling of arbitration is stimulated and cultivated the day will come when we will have a tribunal that can settle these difficulties.

"A local organization of this character is absolutely necessary in the maintaining of peace between employer and employe. Most of the great labor troubles are the result of local differences. It is apparent, then, that expediency in the handling of these difficulties is necessary, and a local organization such as the Civic Federation is the solution of the grave problem of labor and capital.

"Upon the success of this movement here will depend the success of similar movements in other cities. This meeting is one of vast importance and St. Louis has the opportunity of setting a grand example for every city in the United States."

PRESIDENT FRANCIS LAUDS MOVEMENT.

President Francis, who followed Mr. Cleveland, said that he was in hearty accord with the movement.

"I trust," he said, "that this great celebration of the dedication of the Louisiana Purchase Exposition will be remembered as being the occasion of the birth of an organization destined to create a better understanding between the employers and the employes. A proper understanding between capital and labor will be of great help to St. Louis, especially during the next year, when the responsibilities of St. Louis are so great.

"The Civic Federation will be of great good to this community, and to all other communities, and I heartily approve of the objects of this meeting. As President of the Louisiana Purchase Exposition, and as a private citizen, I promise to lend a helping hand to this organization.

"On the World's Fair work there are now more than 5,000 men engaged, and differences between employers and employes during the present year in St. Louis would be most deplorable. A delay of thirty days would mean that the Louisiana Purchase Exposition would be incomplete when its gates are thrown open to the world."

John Mitchell, President of the United Mine Workers' Union, spoke briefly: "I am in favor of the organization of Civic Federations," said Mr. Mitchell, "and my advice to those under me is to support these movements. I favor local branches of the Civic Federation in all large cities and think they can work great good, both to employer and employe.

MITCHELL DECLARES IN FAVOR OF PEACE.

"I have been before the public as one in favor of industrial war instead of industrial peace, but I want to tell you that never in my life did I urge a strike until all other means had been exhausted.

"I believe that strikes and lockouts have grown out of the failure of the employer and the employe to understand each other. If they will meet face to face, tell each other the truth, and be honest with each other, strikes will be reduced to the minimum.

"A Civic Federation, I think, should make all possible effort to compel the rival forces—labor and capital—to meet together.

"I want to say to the workingmen of St. Louis that, in my judgment, labor organizations should give this movement their support. The Louisiana Purchase Exposition is a great project, and the workingmen of St. Louis should take a hearty interest in its building. It is necessary at this time that labor and the men who employ labor should have a thorough understanding, and the Civic Federation is the agency to perfect that understanding."

Senator Hanna is the President of the National Civic Federation, and much of his speech was along the line of work that had already been accomplished.

HANNA SAYS TIME TO GET TOGETHER IS NOW.

"It is fitting," said Senator Hanna, "that this meeting should be held following the great event of yesterday. There should be a united effort to bring these great industrial factors, labor and capital, together. They must meet, and it seems to me that the time to meet, to get together, is now."

Senator Hanna said that the work of the National Federation had met with universal success. He urged the business men to appreciate the importance of the local organization, and pointed out the work of the national organization as inspiration for renewed efforts on their part. He said that the public should take an interest in these great questions of labor and capital, for, after all, the public is the final arbiter, and mutual confidence on both sides of the controversy is the foundation that leads to good results.

Other speeches were made by Lewis Nixon, Albert Young, Reverend Father Phelan, Oscar Straus and Bishop Tuttle.

Father Phelan said that differences between labor and capital could no more be eliminated than wars between nations, but he expressed the opinion that many strikes are unnecessary and that they could be minimized as to extent and number.

Father Phelan made an argument in favor of a just wage for labor.

"It would be a crime," he said, "to raise the price of bread in time of famine," and at all times it is a crime to lower the price of labor."

BISHOP TUTTLE SAYS PATIENCE MUST BE EXERCISED.

Bishop Tuttle said the contending forces should exercise patience and good common sense as against an appeal to force. He said that patience would always win.

GROVER CLEVELAND,
Member Executive Committee, National Civic Federation.

Oscar Straus was the last speaker called upon, and in introducing him Chairman Wade said: "We always save the best for the last."

Mr. Straus was one of the founders of the Civic Federation in New York, and he outlined the plan of work that had been adopted in that city.

The gentlemen who will perfect the permanent organization of the St. Louis Civic Federation are:

Representing the public—Gov. D. R. Francis, President Louisiana Purchase Exposition; Festus J. Wade, President Mercantile Trust Company; Chas. H. Huttig, President Third National Bank; Thos S. McPheeters, President McPheeters Warehouse Company; Frederick N. Judson, lawyer; Dwight F. Davis, Security Building; Frederick M. Crunden, Public Librarian.

Representing employers—W. F. Niedringhouse, National Enameling and Stamping Company; Wm. S. McChesney, General Manager St. Louis Terminal Association; G. [illegible]lick, President St. Louis Building Contractors' Council; Frank N. Johnson, Simmons' Hardware Press Brick Company; Geo. F. Steedman, President Curtis & Co. Mfg. Company; F. C. Schwedtmann, President St. Louis [illegible] Trades Association.

Representing wage earners—J. A. Jackson, President Typographical Union No. 8; Harry A. Walters, Chairman Grievance Committee Locomotive Engineers of Terminal Railroad Association; L. W. Quick, National Secretary Order of Railway Telegraphers; Victor Kleiber, Business Agent Iron Molders' Union of North America; J. G. Hoppenjon, President Central Trades and Labor Union of St. Louis and Vicinity; R. DeBarry, Secretary Building Material Trades Council of St. Louis and Vicinity; W. W. Morrison, President Building Trades Council of St. Louis.

Festus J. Wade was elected chairman of the federation; W. F. Niedringhouse, first vice chairman; Richard DeBarry, second vice chairman; Charles H. Huttig, treasurer and Ferdinand C. Schwedtmann, secretary.

The Executive Committee is composed of the following: Representing the public—Frederick M. Crunden, Elias Michael, W. [illegible] Chaplin, Thos. S. McPheeters, F. N. Judson. Employes—W. A. Kenward, J. F. Wade, Thomas Kinsella, George C. Newman, H. A. Walters. Employers—George W. Brown, F. N. Johnson, George F. Steedman, H. G. [illegible]lick, Corwin H. Spencer.

The following were selected on the Conciliation Committee: Representing the public—Benjamin Schnurmacher, James W. [illegible], John F. Lee, Jas L. Blair, Dwight F. Davis. Employes—J. J. Morris, W. W. Morrison, M. J. Dwyer, R. S. [illegible]. Employers—F. A. Drew, Paul Brown, [illegible] Garrison, J. J. Collins, J. H. Conrades, [illegible]

National Civic Federation

MONTHLY REVIEW

VOL. I. NO. 3 — NEW YORK, OCTOBER, 1903 — TEN CENTS

[illegible] COMBINATIONS OF CAPITAL AND LABOR

DESTRUCTIVE COMPETITION THE EVIL TO BE MET—THE VARIOUS FORMS OF ORGANIZATION

T[illegible]xcessive competition is an evil is recognized by everyone when it occurs in his own business. It is recognized by capitalists, by farmers, by the professional classes and by wage-earners. The epithets used to describe it testify to the dislike of it. Excessive competition is "destructive," "unfair," and "cut-throat." The "price-cutter," "underseller" and "rebate giver" are as unprincipled in the eyes of the merchant and railroad manager as the "non-unionist" and "scab" in the eyes of the trade unionist. When excessive competition occurs in the field of capital it shows its havoc by depression of trade, long and risky credits, bankrup[illegible]and "demoralization." When it occurs in th[illegible]labor its consequences are the sweatin[illegible]rs, low wages, the "exploitation[illegible]ary and dangerous work places, [illegible]and other phases of poverty. And [illegible]s of results are usually found together, [illegible]ruin of the employer's business means the de[illegible]tion of employment, and the exploitation of labor means the survival of the unscrupulous employer.

Volumes might be filled with accounts of the efforts and methods both of capitalists and laborers to do away with destructive competition. And interesting enough is the fact that the methods of the two classes are similar. They all agree in the one policy of combining as many as possible of those who are competitors in an agreement not to compete with their fellows beyond a certain point and to deal effectively with those who will not enter into the agreement. The capitalists call themselves an "association," an "exchange," a "pool," a "trust," or even a "corporation," [illegible]he workmen commonly call themselves a "union." [illegible] capit[illegible]organizations, of course, differ widely in details, [illegible] the unions. A pool is more compact th[illegible]association, and a corporation or a trust than [illegible] so is a highly skilled union, like the glass [illegible]better disciplined than a miscellaneous uni[illegible]e cloak-makers. All originate in what th[illegible]r the absolute necessity of doing something to keep competitors from ruining one another, and al[illegible] are open to the temptation of overdoing a [illegible] and carrying their methods, which origi[illegible]-protection, over into monopoly and public [illegible] They have all been legislated against in vary[illegible]grees of penality. They have been haled before [illegible]courts, and the courts have handed down hope[illegible]essly contradictory decisions. They have been sustained in one State and overthrown in another, and the same courts have reversed themselves, leaving the ultimate policy of the country toward combinations unsettled. Whether they are criminal is not our present concern. We are exercised only with the economic fact that they have sprung into being to meet the real evil of mutual destruction through over-competition.

In the following columns we have collected brief accounts of various associations and unions, showing how similar are their methods in admitting and rejecting members, boycotting, posting spies and pickets, regulating output, setting up minimum wages and prices, and even entering offensive and defensive alliances.

BOYCOTT.

Boycotting in some of its forms is a natural and first-suggested means employed by both classes of associations in going beyond persuasion and putting pressure upon non-members to join in a common cause. Unions have developed large and systematic methods of boycotting, but their methods are much the same as those of the Publishers and Booksellers, the Wholesale Druggists, railroad associations which divert shipping from one line to another, and other capitalist associations.

The blacklist is a form of boycott, and similar in object to the boycott and blacklist, but the reverse in method, are the whitelist and the label, either of the Consumers' League or the union. The union label, in some trades like cigar making, clothing manufacturing, and breweries, has become a powerful instrument for directing consumers away from "unfair" establishments toward those which accept the union conditions of hours, wages, and employment. The Consumers' League, composed in part of wealthy society women, grants its label only to those manufacturers of women's wear who pass the standards of its inspectors, and their names are published in its "white-list."

These are organized methods for making effective a force recognized whenever men associate together for a common object. Even the Christian church, with its avowed love for all men, sometimes discriminates in favor of believers, for the Methodists in their "General Rules" expect church members "to evidence their desire of salvation by doing good, especially to them that are of the household of faith or groaning so to be; employing them preferably to others; buying one of another; helping each other in business; and so much the more because the world will love its own and them *only*."

MEMBERSHIP.

While combinations both of capital and labor strive to bring all competitors into their fold, they also agree in trying to limit the numbers of competitors. The unions have initiation fees, examination of candidates, and limits to the number of apprentices. The associations have initiation fees and sometimes limitations to membership. When union or association passes from mutual protection to mutual aggrandizement, the change is likely to appear in higher initiation fees or stricter limits on admission, as when the New York Stone Cutters or the New York Stock Exchange resolves to admit no more members.

MINIMUM WAGES AND PRICES.

Both classes of these combinations establish minimum rates, the one of prices and the other of wages, and these rates are based on the necessities of the weakest competitor, as may be seen in the case of pasenger fares on railroads. Professional associations, such as those of physicians, have a minimum scale of fees, sometimes unofficially promulgated as a part of code of ethics and sometimes drawn up and posted in the physician's office.

RESTRICTION OF OUTPUT.

When production is too great to support the minimum price,combinations sometimes place limits on the output, as when the whiskey pool limited production to twenty-eight per cent of each plant's capacity and the whiskey trust closed sixty-eight of its eighty distilleries, or as when a plumbers' union places a maximum on the amount of work a member shall perform and an assemblers' union on the amount of wages a member shall earn.

BUSINESS AGENTS.

Many organizations of both kinds have officers with duties designed to meet violations of the combination agreement. The walking delegate or business agent of the union who looks out for "scabs" and scale violators is similar to the inspectors of the Railway Classification Committee who examine shipments to discover whether shippers are cutting the freight rate scale by underbilling, and whether individual roads belonging to the association are conniving at the practice. Where, as in the hardware and iron and steel pools, there is a "commissioner," this officer is given the remarkable authority of apportioning the output to the several members, just as a walking delegate or a shop steward sometimes "calls down" a man who is working too fast.

PICKETS AND SPIES.

The Book Publishers' Association and the Wholesale Druggists have their spies and "pickets" for the purpose of watching a boycotted firm, to prevent it from obtaining a supply of books or proprietary drugs. These associations also, as well as many others, furnish their members and customers with lists of "fair" and "unfair" firms, carrying the "threat" open or implied, that those who deal with the unfair firms will themselves be cut off from supplies or customers.

JURISDICTION DISPUTES.

Many other points of resemblance, more or less refined, might be noted. Rival combinations and jurisdictional fights are as troublesome when occurring between railroads invading each other's territory, or between jobbers' associations and manufacturers' associations, as when occurring between the Carpenters' union and the Woodworkers' union, and both kinds of fights compel some sort of a working agreement to be brought about. Where both the union of labor and the union of capital are strong enough in the same industry they come to a "joint agreement," and these agreements are of all degrees, from unstable verbal agreements to those monopolistic, exclusive alliances by which non-members of both associations are shut out from business and work.

There are differences as well as resemblances. The nature of the trade, the number of competitors, the strength of the organization, and other circumstances produce infinite varieties in detail, and there are constantly occurring many fluctuations in strength, many amendments and revisions in by-laws and practices, but rules, methods and functionaries are all directed toward the main object of regulating or eliminating competition. When the capitalist association [illegible] the form of a trust it brings into play a me[illegible] of organization much superior to any possible [illegible] mere association or a trade union, since it is ba[illegible] common ownership. This object is aimed at in [illegible] degree in the "community of interest" so recently popularized in railroad alliances, after other forms of union had been tried unsuccessfully.

An examination of the brief accounts herewith given of combinations of capital and unions of labor will give an idea of how universal are these efforts to lessen the hardships of free competition. The list we give is by no means complete. There are 125 national and international trade unions, with about 2,400 Federal unions, and the Interstate Commerce Commission requires a volume of 295 pages in order to publish its list of commercial and agricultural and professional associations, a large number of which have as one of their objects the regulation of competition. Hence, if in the following article one association or union is mentioned rather than another, it cannot be regarded as in any way invidio[illegible]. The conclusion is almost inevitable that, no ma[illegible] how the courts and the legislatures treat [illegible] combinations, they are the product of necessity, a[illegible] such must be recognized. In some cases, such as [illegible] roads, they are recognized as necessary not only [illegible] protection to the members, but also for protection to the public, since rate-cutting is a discrimination between shippers which demoralizes the business of every industry that depends on transportation.

The problem regarding all of these combinations is not how to suppress them but how to preserve their benefits and prevent their excesses.

ASSOCIATED LABOR

The rules and methods of labor unions are the outgrowth of experience in dealing with the evils of competition. They might have been different if they had been drafted by philosophers. They differ widely among the unions in ways that can be accounted for only by the various competitive circumstances under which the unions are placed. Sometimes a natural strategic advantage, or a long experience, or a compact organization, leads one union to drop a practice which another considers essential. Yet all union rules and methods, whether governing membership, apprenticeship, working with non-unionists, minimum wage, piece work, machinery or output—all of which are described below—have come into vogue to protect the members at whatever points they feel competition to be destructive.

MEMBERSHIP.

From the standpoint of maintaining the position of the union the conditions of admission and the barriers raised against admission are first in importance. Nearly all unions in one form or another establish a term of probation or apprenticeship. In a few, such as the Amalgamated Iron and Steel Workers, where exceedingly high skill is necessary, there are no formal rules or conditions regarding apprentices. Notwithstanding that modern conditions of production have destroyed the old apprentice system in many trades, and that through the specialization of work and the splitting up of trades a workman can often learn his particular work in a few months, yet the majority of organizations require an apprenticeship of three or four years. A number, among them the pattern makers and watch-case engravers, require five years. The number of apprentices is also usually fixed at a definite ratio to the number of journeymen, the machinist ratio being one apprentice to five or ten journeymen. The iron moulders allow one apprentice to each shop and one to eight journeymen; the glass bottle blowers by agreement each year with the manufacturers limit the number of apprentices according to the state of the trade, the ratio of 1899 being one to fifteen, and in 1901 one to ten; but in some years they close their apprentice books entirely. The steam fitters' helpers in New York open their books twice a year and admit only a few applicants, according to the state of the trade, though the number of applicants is always large. The lithographers allow one apprentice to the first five journeymen or less, one additional apprentice for the next ten, another for the next fifteen and another for the next twenty-five. The stone-cutters forbid employing more than one in a shop which employs less than fifteen journeymen, more than two where there are less than one hundred journeymen, or more than four in any case whatever.

Local organizations of the various trades do not always adhere to the national rules, and the ratio may be larger or smaller than that provided in the national constitution, according to circumstances.

While the requirement of a period of apprenticeship is maintained as a means of providing an all-round training in the trade yet it is also certain that one of the motives is the desire to diminish the competition within the trade.

The initiation fee, imposed at admission either on a journeyman or an apprentice on completing his term, is usually placed at $3 to $5, but there are individual unions which have increased this fee to as high as $50 or $100. The fee of the architectural iron workers, the mosaic helpers, the electrical workers and others in New York is $100; of the longshoremen, $25; of the bituminous mine workers of Illinois, $50. The stone-cutters of New York at one time went so far as to close their books, not only against all outsiders, but against members of their own craft from other localities. The outcry against this exclusive policy was so great that it was revoked. In some cases the international organization has prohibited local unions from imposing high initiation fees, the United Garment Workers, for example, fixing the maximum at $5.

UNION AND NON-UNION WORKERS.

The exclusive employment of members of the union is maintained by the majority of unions wherever possible. They reason that in order to enforce the scale of wages and hours it is necessary that every workman be subject to discipline if he works below the scale, and that they cannot know whether he is actually working below the scale unless he is a member. If they can require his dismissal from employment for violating union rules they have the best possible means of holding him to fidelity to the union.

In this respect the railroad brotherhoods differ from other organizations, since they do not stipulate in any of their agreements that non-unionists shall not be employed. The longshoremen in their agreements with the dock managers, have a clause as follows:

Sec. 3. "All employes employed by the dock managers for the purpose of performing the work set forth in the schedules hereto attached shall be members of the local organization whenever such men can be had who can perform the work as is called for in the contract. When such men cannot be had the dock managers have the right to secure any other men who can perform the work in a satisfactory manner until such time as members of the International Longshoremen's Association can be procured."

In other unions, especially in the building trades, there is no provision for the employment of non-members, even when the number of members is not adequate for the work on hand. It is universally the case in those organizations that have the "union label" that establishments to which the label is granted shall agree to employ only members of the organization. In this case the label is a specific consideration given the employer in return for his promise to employ only union help. A reciprocal arrangement is also true of the arbitration agreement between the International Typographical Union and the American Publishers' Association, the international taking upon itself the obligation to furnish competent help in case the local union violates the agreement by a strike, and protecting the publisher against boycotts or "any other form of concerted interference with the peaceful operation of the department or departments of labor so contracted for by any union or unions with which he has contractual relations."

The object in the policy of exclusive employment is that which distinguishes the unions in general, namely, the prevention of destructive competition. By limiting employment to their own members, they prevent the introduction of workmen willing to work below the established scale of wages, [illegible] they protect such members as may offi[illegible] the organization.

RECIPROCAL EXCLUSIVE ARRANGEMENTS.

An extension of the principle of exclusi[illegible] ment is occasionally found in a reciprocal ar[illegible] to the effect that members of the union shall [illegible] for employers not members of the employe[illegible] association.

Arrangements of this kind, where both associations are strong, are apt to lead to excessive monopolies in that the employers use the unions to intrench themselves against competitors. It is alleged that in the building trades of Chicago at the present time there are serious abuses in combines between employers and employes. Recently a former member of the Sheet Metal Contractors' Association of that city brought suit against the association and the Sheet Metal Workers' Union, alleging that they had formed a pool by which he was prevented from getting [illegible]men on jobs obtained by bidding against the [illegible] the contractors' association.

The Chicago Tribune, August [illegible] the following:

"The Chicago Employing Plasterers' Asso[illegible] limited competition by a close agreement w[illegible] members of the plasterers' union. This is held to [illegible] the most perfect combination of its kind in the city, and through its ironclad rules has forced even the contractors doing subcontract work to pay tribute to the association.

"The agreement has rules covering the way work shall be done," said Attorney Charles D. Francis, "and these were not put into it to benefit the union, but to make the plans of the contractors possible."

These rules prohibit the completion of work by a firm that does not have the original contract. They prohibit the members of the union from working for firms that attempt to take work started by another firm. They do not even allow a plasterer to patch [illegible] the holes made by plumbers, steamfitters, or carpenters unless extra pay is obtained for the work.

The employing plasterers force the [illegible]rvance [illegible] this law in the following manner:

"Any person or persons who shall [illegible] or take contracts for any building or job in [illegible] of this rule shall be fined 5 per cent of the co[illegible]ce for the first offense, 10 per cent for the [illegible]ense, and for the third default he shall be s[illegible] such penalty as the joint arbitration board sha[illegible]

It is alleged that the plasterers have a p[illegible] buildings similar to that in the other trade[illegible] serted that this has increased prices be[illegible] 40 per cent and has given practically all the city into the hands of a few firms.

Other employers' associations in the bu[illegible] in Chicago alleged to have similar agreemen[illegible] derstandings with the unions are the Electrical [illegible] Association, the Master Steam Fitters' Associatio[illegible] the Master Roofers' Association, the Plumbers' Supplies Association, the steam heating and boiler an[illegible] fireproofing companies, and the sewer contractors.

The agreement of the coal team owners and co[illegible] team drivers of Chicago, adopted May 1, 1902, read[illegible] as follows:

"Party of the first part (the Coal Team Owners' Association) agrees to employ none but members of th[illegible] Coal Teamsters' Union, Local No. 4, in good stan[illegible] ing and carrying the regular working card of the organization.

"We (the Coal Teamsters' Union) further agree that we will not work for any firm that does not belong to the Coal Team Owners' Association."

In the agreements in the marble industry of New York it is provided:

"That the members of the Marble Industry Employers' Association agree to employ no cutters in New York City or vicinity (vicinity to be a radius of twenty-five miles from City Hall) excepting those being members of the Journeymen Marble Cutters' Association, or such others as will be recognized by them through application."

And also:

"The members of the Journeymen Marble Cutters' Association agree that they will not work for any person or persons doing business in New York City or vicinity not members of the Marble Industry Employers' Association in New York City and vicinity (vicinity to be a radius of twenty-five miles from City Hall)."

The arrangement in the stone cutting industry in New York, between the union and the employers' association is said to go so far as to provide for payment to the union treasury of a percentage on contracts in consideration of limiting their work to the members of the employers' association, and the employers thereby are enabled to do away with competition on contracts.

The agreement of July 1, 1902, between the Association of Master Plumbers and the Journeymen Plumbers and Gasfitters of New York contains the following section:

"Art. II. No master plumber shall employ any non-union man or men after receiving due notice from the Delegate or Chairman of the Joint Conference Board not to do so. A member violating this rule shall be fined twenty-five dollars and five dollars per day for each and every day he retains such man or men in his employ thereafter. Any journeyman plumber or gasfitter working for a non-union employer when notified not to do so by the Delegate or Chairman of the Joint Conference Board shall be fined four dollars and twenty-five cents for each and every day he continues so to do."

At a joint conference, held recently at Detroit, the Window Glass Workers of America and the American Window Glass Co. reached an agreement to withhold all the wage scales until the present available stock of glass in the country is depleted, and to keep all factories idle until a general resumption is ordered. An increase in wages was agreed upon and all current price-lists for glass were to be withdrawn in order that an advance of probably twenty per cent. to the public might be made. Owing to a split in the union this agreement has been hindered somewhat, and certain independent companies have begun work with the dissatisfied mechanics.

An interesting episode in this chapter of alliances between unions of employers and unions of workmen is found in the horseshoers' trade. The Master Horseshoers' Association is in most particulars similar in its objects and methods to the Journeymen Horseshoers' Union. The masters do not differ much from the journeymen in wealth or social standing. Owing to the very small amount of capital required to set up a blacksmith shop, journeymen often become employers and vice versa.

The organizations of the two sides in New York and several other American cities are at present engaged in a struggle over the question of label. The Masters' Association insists on putting exclusively its own label on horseshoes leaving the shops, while the journeymen demand that the label of their union also be included. As the patrons of the horseshoers are largely workmen, such as teamsters, coachmen and cab drivers, naturally in sympathy with the union journeymen, the employers regard the union label as too strong a weapon in the hands of the union in the case of a trade dispute. The constitution of the Masters' Association of New York provides penalties for members using the union label. On the other hand, in several cities the two labels are used side by side, with the effect of keeping down competition from newcomers.

The following provisions of the agreement between the Master Horseshoers' Association and Journeymen Horseshoers' Union of Pittsburg illustrate the trade situation in most of the large cities:

1. Members of Master Horseshoers shall not employ any journeyman unless he is a member of the Journeymen's Union, nor shall any journeyman work for any employer not a member of the Masters' Association.

2. Prior to a member of the Journeymen's Union starting a shop, he shall resign his membership in that body before joining the Masters' Association, and any Master quitting business shall resign from the Masters' Association before he can be admitted to membership in the Journeymen's Association.

3. No member of the Journeymen's Union shall work for so-called corporation shops that may hereafter be opened up, or for any corporation shop blacklisted by the Masters' Association.

6. The Journeyman shall observe that his employer lives strictly up to the rules of the Master Horseshoers' Protective Association.

The foregoing classes of agreements between employers and unions are well calculated to carry the principle of self-protection over into the policy of monopoly. There is another class of agreements, not open to the charge of monopoly, which simply provide that all employers in the same line shall be treated alike. For example, the agreement entered into March 18, 1903, between the National Association of Marble Dealers and the International Association of Marble Workers does not provide for exclusive employment on either side, but provides for preference of employment to members of the union and forbids the union to work for non-members of the employers' association for less wages than for members. Misunderstandings have arisen in the execution of this agreement, and a lockout has followed, but it illustrates the principle. Sections touching on this matter are as follows:

That the National Association of Marble Dealers recognize the International Association of Marble Workers on and after the first of June, 1903, and agrees to give preference of employment to members of the International Association of Marble Workers in so far as the I. A. M. W. can supply a sufficient number of competent workmen.

That no member or members of the I. A. M. W. shall work for any person, firm or corporation (not a member of the N. A. M. D.) on the basis of over nine hours per day or for less wages than those being paid by members of the N. A. M. D. for similar services.

That no member or members of the I. A. M. W. shall handle or set any marble that is not finished by members of the I. A. M. W. working on the basis of not more than a nine hour day and receiving the same wages as are paid members of the N. A. M. D. for similar services, and under the same conditions.

The following, similar in its aims, is the agreement between the Electrical Contractors' Association and Local No. 3 of the Brotherhood of Electrical Workers of New York City:

(3) That the members of the association shall employ only members of the union, as journeymen and helpers, to do electrical work in any building, bridge, ship, or pole work, and that in consideration of such exclusive employment the union agrees that it will not work for any electrical contractor not a member of the association who does not sign and conform to an agreement similar to this, the original of such agreement to be shown to the Secretary of the Association if requested.

WAGES AND HOURS.

Almost universally the union endeavors to establish the principle of a standard wage or a minimum wage, whether paid by the hour, day, or week, and a maximum number of hours per day or week. Employers argue that this wage is placed so high that they cannot afford to pay members more than the minimum, and the unions, with very few exceptions, refuse to grade workmen in classes with a different wage for each class. They hold that if the union assigns members to several classes there will be occasion for jealousy and favoritism, and if the employer assigns them to particular classes he will place as many as possible in the lowest class, which would be equivalent to cutting the scale of wages.

Unions do not generally prohibit members from receiving more than the minimum wage, but they establish the minimum on the basis of what they consider a fair wage for the bulk of their members. On this account those who in the opinion of the employer are not able to earn the minimum are discharged when business slackens and are the last to be employed when business expands. The unions enforce the minimum wage rule by fines and expulsion in case of its violation.

Occasionally unions modify the minimum wage rule by grading the workmen. The stonecutters of New York have three grades, the scale being $5 for the first grade, $4.50 for the second, and $4 for the third. Many unions issue special permits to old or sick or incapacitated men to work below the scale. This is usually done through a committee created for the purpose.

PIECE WORK.

Piece-work wages are opposed by a number of unions while by others they are favored.

The unions which object to piece work do so on the ground that it places them at a disadvantage in preventing the destructive competition which brings about the reduction in piece-work rates. Especially among the machinists, where there are great differences between job and job, piece-work rates practically do away with the union scale and reduce the remuneration of labor to a matter of individual bargain. The glass bottle blowers have elaborate printed price-lists containing more than 1,000 specifications. Where a union is not strongly organized the objection to piece-work is found in the fact that the employer frequently bases his pay on the output of the speedier men and cuts the prices so that the less capable are placed at a disadvantage and cannot earn the amount of wages which the union considers fair.

The following lists were prepared by the Industrial Commission:

Unions whose members work by the piece, at least in some department, without active opposition on the part of the organizations:

Boot and Shoe Workers.	Piano and Organ Workers.
Hatters.	Coopers.
Garment Workers.	Amalgamated Association of Iron, Steel and Tin Workers.
Tailors.	Stove Mounters.
Custom Clothing Makers.	Sheet Metal Workers.
Ladies Garment Workers.	Wire Weavers.
Lace Curtain Operatives.	Longshoremen.
Mule Spinners.	Cigarmakers.
Typographical Union.	Leather Workers on Horse Goods.
Steel and Copper Plate Printers	Stogie Makers.
Glass Bottle Blowers.	Upholsterers.
Flint Glass Blowers.	
Potters.	
United Mine Workers.	
Northern Mineral Mine Workers.	

Unions which either forbid piece-work or actively discourage it:

Bookbinders.	Machinists.
Bricklayers.	Amalgamated Society of Engineers.
Carpenters, Brotherhood.	Iron Moulders.
Painters (Paper-Hanging excepted).	Pattern Makers.
Plasterers.	Blacksmiths.
Plumbers.	Bakers.
Stonecutters.	Brickmakers.
Tile Layers.	Watch-Case Engravers.
Amalgamated Glass Workers.	Jewelry Workers.
Woodworkers.	Oil and Gas Well Workers.
Wood Carvers.	
Carriage Workers.	

OUTPUT.

In some instances where piece-work prevails the union has a rule prohibiting its members from earning more than a designated amount of wages and enforces this by fines and expulsion. Wherever this rule is imposed it is not done by the international, but by the local organizations, and therefore under the same international union a limit may be placed in one locality or one shop and not be found in other localities or other shops.

Even where unions are paid by the day or week, and not by the piece, they sometimes place limits on the amount of work, as when the clothing cutters limit the number of suits to fourteen a day. Similar limits are sometimes found among machinists, molders, polishers, tile layers, marble setters, plasterers, and others. One of the reasons given for limitation is the "unfair" competition of unusually swift workmen—"leaders," "pace-makers," "rushers," "rooters." This is seen in the following by-law of the Brotherhood of Carpenters of New York:

"Any member who does an unreasonable amount of work, or who acts as a leader for his employer for the purpose of getting all the work possible out of the men working in the same shop or job with him, shall be fined for the first offense ten dollars; for the second offense he shall be suspended or expelled."

The Amalgamated Iron and Steel Workers have for many years placed a limit on the output of the hot rolls in the sheet and tin plate mills. By agreement with their employers this limit has recently been modified in the case of tin plate, but it continues to be enforced in the sheet mills. In the window glass factories the union usually has secured a rest for the two hot months of July and August, and during the recent depression of trade this was increased to four or five months by agreement with the employers to prevent overproduction. The plumbers of Chicago in 1899 had the following rules regarding a day's work:

Rule 1. When working on lead work, eight wiped joints shall be considered a day's work.
Rule 2. When working on iron pipe, the measuring, cutting, threading, and placing in position of 15 threads of one inch, or under, shall be considered a day's work.
Rule 3. Ten threads on one and a quarter, one and a half, and two inch pipe shall be considered a day's work.
Rule 4. When running soil pipe in a vertical manner, the following shall be considered eight hours' work: 6 inch, 6 caulked joints; 5 inch, 6 caulked joints; 4 inch, 9 caulked joints; 3 inch, 10 caulked joints; 2 inch, 12 caulked joints.
Rule 5. When running soil pipe in a horizontal manner, the following shall be considered eight hours' work: 6 inch, 4 caulked joints; 5 inch, 4 caulked joints; 4 inch, 6 caulked joints; 3 inch, 6 caulked joints; 2 inch, 8 caulked joints.
Rule 6. When finishing on flats or apartments, hotel or office building, one fixture shall be considered an average day's work, except laundry tub, then each apartment shall constitute one fixture.
Rule 7. When working on Durham system, the running of 2½, 3, and 4 inch pipe, when working on stacks, three stories shall be considered a day's work. When working on 5, 6, and 8 inch pipe on stack, two stories shall be considered a day's work.
Rule 8. Pump pipe down spouts, and other straight stacks of pipe: 2½ and 3 inch, 50 feet shall be considered a day's work; 4 and 5 inch, 40 feet a day's work; 6 and 8 inch, 30 feet a day's work.
Rule 9. In cases where work is of a complicated nature, or workmen are delayed through no fault of theirs, the absolute performance of amounts as laid down in schedule shall not be considered as compulsory by this association.
Rule 11. Any member violating any of these rules shall be dealt with according to section 16 of working rules, which reads: 'A fine of one day's pay for first offense, and two days' pay for second offense, and if he persists in his violation, the association shall deal with him as it sees fit.'

The plasterers in New York have the following scale of work incorporated in their agreement with the employers' association, designed partly to prevent rush work on inferior and speculative buildings:

Section 1. In tenement houses where there are ten rooms and a lobby or hallway to each floor or flat, the time for scratch coating rooms and hallway on said flat or floor shall be two days, or one day each for two men.
Section 2. The time for browning in said tenement houses for ten rooms and hallway shall be six days, or three days each for two men.
Section 3. In browning where there are extra rooms or extra closets, there shall be extra proportionate time allowed.
Section 4. The time for hard finishing ten rooms and hallway in tenement houses shall be six days, or three days each for two men.
Section 5. For cornicing and finishing tops of rooms in tenement houses, the time for each room, with four angle and two break mitres, done with a common mould, about seven inches projection, shall be one day, or one-half day each for two men. When there is a square panel the time shall be one and one-half days, or three-quarters of a day each for two men.
Section 6. If the moulds are extra large, or extra members or quarter circles in panels, or extra panels on the ceiling, there must be extra proportionate time allowed.
Section 7. In the larger tenement houses, called apartment houses, where there are large front and back room of about 13x16, and the common cornice mould is about ten inches in projection, the time for cornicing such a room, with four angle and two break mitres in it, shall be three-quarters of a day each for two men, and when there is a square panel in each room the time shall be one day each for two men.
Section 8. In small rooms, where there are only four mitres where a common mould of six or seven inches is used, two men shall cornice three and finish ceilings and tops of walls of said rooms in one day. Coving in above class of buildings to come under the heading of cornicing.
Section 9. In private houses, known as speculation and such like, all cornicing and panelling shall be governed by the rules of large and small rooms in apartment houses, and if the parlors in said private houses are larger than the ordinary 13x16 feet parlors or apartment houses, or the moulds larger or more difficult to work, or more panelling on the ceiling, there must be extra proportionate time allowed.

The window glass cutters stipulate in their agreement with their employers that—

"No cutter shall be allowed to cut more than 3 pots or 360 boxes of double strength. The boss cutter shall be directed to see that cutters short in their quantity shall have spare cutting in preference to cutters who have their full quota."

While trade unions, generally recognizing that this is a mechanical age, are endeavoring to maintain wages while not opposing machinery, yet individual unions have placed obstacles in the way of machinery or its economical use. The pressmen's union, to protect its members, stipulates that on a double press one pressman and three press hands shall be employed, whereas in certain offices employers have contended that two press hands would be adequate; similarly on a quadruple press, the union requires four press hands, on a sextuple six, and on an octuple eight, being in each case two to three press hands more than some employers believe can be economically employed.

The International Association of Machinists has this rule:

"Any member running more than one machine in any shop where such is not now the practice, unless such introduction is upon the decision and advice of the local lodge and approved by the grand lodge, shall be expelled."

A statement by an officer of the union was issued in 1902 showing the gains made by the members of the International Association of Machinists during the previous two years as follows:

"We prevented the introduction of the two-machine system in 137 shops, employing 9,500 men. It is safe to say that if this system had been introduced the force of men would be reduced one-eighth; hence, in this we have saved the position of 1,188 men, whose daily wages would amount to $2,613.60 per day, or $818,056.80 per year.

"Thirty-seven lodges reported having prevented the introduction of the piece-work system in shops employing 4,500 men. This system, when in practical operation, reduces the force on a fair estimate one-fourth. Thus the positions of 1,125 men have been saved, which amounts to $2,475 per day, or $774,675 per year.

"From the above figures you will see that we have declared a dividend which has gone into the pockets of the machinists, through the efforts of the organization, amounting to a sum total of $2,181,278.22."

The Cigar-Makers' Union prohibits the use of the union label for cigars made in whole or in part by machinery, but does not forbid its members working on the cigar-making machine.

In the Report of the Industrial Commission the following statements are found:

"The stogie makers will refuse to admit machine workers to their organization, and both the coopers and the iron moulders maintained the same attitude up to 1899. It is only half a dozen years since the coopers appealed to the Federation of Labor to declare against ale and beer packages made by machinery. The Federation, however, did not approve the proposition. The stone cutters prevent the use of stone-planing machines wherever they can. When a new machine was invented two or three years ago for blowing lamp chimneys, the flint-glass workers proposed to the manufacturers that the machine be bought up and eliminated, and that the selling price of chimneys be advanced to pay the cost. The rules of the plumbers contain a long list of plumbing goods which were formerly made by hand as they were used, but which are now appearing in the market as products of machinery. The plumbers declare that this change is taking away the work of their trade, and that the use of these goods should be stopped. The plate-printers have always opposed the introduction of steam presses, and have succeeded in keeping them out of the largest plate printing office in America, that of the United States Bureau of Engraving and Printing. The reason given is that the work done on a hand-roller press is far better."

ASSOCIATED CAPITAL

PROPRIETARY DRUGS.

The Wholesale Druggists' Association, organized in 1882, represents 90 per cent of the wholesale jobbing trade of the United States. Of this trade 45 or 50 per cent is in the form of proprietary drugs, sold under trade-marks, copyrights or patents, which secure exclusive right of sale to the manufacturers. The manufacturers themselves, organized as the Proprietary Association of America, have an arrangement with the Wholesale Druggists' Association to control wholesale and retail prices. A number of retail associations have also been formed in the several States, with a National Association of Retail Druggists, which co-operates with the jobbers and the manufacturers' associations.

From its organization to the present time the Wholesale Druggists' Association has conducted a vigorous attack upon wholesale houses declining to become members of the association or to abide by its conditions with respect to sales. This contest has all the more significance for our present purpose because of the decision of the highest court of the State of New York sustaining the legality of the arrangements thus effected to regulate competition. This decision was rendered by the Court of Appeals April 28, 1903, in the case of John D. Park & Sons Company vs. The National Wholesale Druggists' Association. The facts, as agreed upon by both parties to the suit, were as follows:

The medicines are known as proprietary goods and their manufacture and sale are under the control of the manufacturer, who may fix his own price and adopt such plan for the sale as he in his judgment may determine. At one time the sale of these goods was largely made through travelling agents, who worked upon commission and supplied the goods to the customer or retailer. At the present time they are sold almost entirely to wholesalers and jobbers who are members or who abide by the rules of the Wholesale Druggists' Association.

Prior to the origin of this association the manufacturers sold goods to some of the wholesalers on more favorable terms than to others, thus permitting large dealers to make a profit while a great number of the smaller firms found the handling of proprietary goods unprofitable. The Druggists' Association devised a plan for the conduct of the business which was accepted by the Proprietary Association. It provided that the latter should establish a uniform jobbing price for fixed quantities, as well as a price to be charged by the wholesale druggists, which both were to agree to maintain, the wholesale druggists being allowed the difference between the jobbing and their selling prices as their profit.

In December, 1893, the so-called Detroit plan was adopted instructing a committee of the wholesalers' association to

Request the proprietors selling their preparations under the contract system to refuse supplies of their preparations to any party whom they may find on a full investigation to be wilfully, deliberately and systematically, even though secretly and indirectly, violating the contracts of any one party, until the subcommittee have become satisfied that such practice will be discontinued.
That our committee on Proprietary Goods be authorized to omit from future official lists of rebate articles the preparations of such proprietors as may continue supplying to parties found guilty of violating any contract under the foregoing resolution, and announce to our members that this committee will no longer regard such articles as really restricted.

This resolution is directed against such proprietary firms as refuse to enter into the agreement, and it was considered by the counsel for the plaintiff as equivalent to placing such manufacturers on a boycotted list. A further provision of the plan was:

That when complaints of violation are properly lodged with the committee in writing against any dealer the chairman, with the consent and advice of his associates, shall proceed to have thorough investigation of such charges made, and shall have full power to engage for this purpose any assistance he may deem proper to corroporate such charges.

Under this the committee employed spies, who tracked shipments to the Park Sons Company, and reported the names of the intermediaries through whom purchases had been made. These intermediaries were thereupon placed on the excluded list.

Another resolution establishes a whitelist and a blacklist:

That the committee on proprietary goods furnish rebate proprietors with a list of parties who advertise proprietary articles at cut rates at retail, also of parties who are purchasers for division, in violation of the letter and spirit of their contracts, and that we request that orders for such parties be not hereafter filled, except at long prices.

That in justice to those proprietors who have in the past and will now agree to act up to this measure of protection to retailers, the committee of proprietary goods note, in the official rebate list, the names of all manufacturers who will act in accordance with the spirit of that resolution.

That all proprietors selling goods on the contract plan are hereby requested to forward names of new firms or associations wishing to purchase goods to the sub-committee on rebate contract; said committee shall at once inquire as to the business methods and organizations of said firms or association, and report to the proprietors, in accordance with resolution No. 5, passed at the Indianapolis meeting of the N. W. D. A., if in their opinion said firm or association are entitled to purchase rebate goods. And all proprietors are requested to abide by said decision. On the adoption of this resolution by the association, a copy shall be forwarded to all parties selling goods on contract plan.

In conformity with these resolutions, joint committees of the Proprietary Association and the Druggists' Association were created, which proceeded to compile lists of the firms throughout the United States entitled to direct quantity sales at the rebate discount, and also to furnish to the proprietors lists of all firms refusing to abide by these rules or furnishing goods as intermediaries to other firms that so refused. The committees, through a system of spies, received daily reports of shipments to or from the firms on their blacklist and furnished these lists to all manufacturers of proprietary goods.

The Committee on Proprietary Goods at the session of the Wholesalers in 1902 affirmed that "the continuous advocacy of the rebate plan has involved no hardship upon any branch of the trade nor has it dulled the edge of competition. It has simply restrained it from taking an unreasonable and destructive form. The opportunities for those members which have ample capital and capable management are as great as ever and their operations have not been restrained with the practical working of the rebate plan."

The Committee of the Proprietary Association, at their session in 1902, reported:

"It is a pleasure to be able to say that all are coming to realize, as they have not heretofore, the immeasurable superiority of co-operation over the kind of competition that for forty years has tended to render the retail drug business more and more a life of profitless drudgery, while the profits of proprietors and jobbers have also seriously diminished.

"The great majority of the jobbers are living up to the terms established by the proprietors for the sale of their goods, but there are undoubtedly a number on the uniform list that need discipline of the kind they will certainly remember.

"The retail trade, or at least the members of the National Association, are with few exceptions carrying out conscientiously the stipulation made that, in exchange for an honest effort by proprietors and jobbers to secure them, the retailers, a reasonable profit on proprietaries, the various preparations of the proprietors shall be sold by them, when called for, *without argument.*"

The importance of the New York decision in the Park & Sons Company case make it worth while to give extracts showing the grounds of the decision. The court held that the wholesalers' contract system did not create a monopoly, since its terms were open to non-members as well as members of the association. Judge Haight, in the majority opinion, said:

"Under the plan adopted every dealer has the right to purchase goods from the manufacturers upon the same terms as the members of the association with the right to the same rebates or commissions upon complying with the requirements of the manufacturers with reference to following their price list in making sales of goods. . . . It is true it does away with the competition among the dealers as to prices, but it creates no restriction upon them as to the quantities they may be able to sell or the territory within which they may confine their transactions. . . . An active competition and rivalry in business is undoubtedly conducive to the public welfare, but we must not shut our eyes to the fact that competition may be carried to such an extent as to accomplish the financial ruin of those engaged therein and thus result in a derangement of business and inconvenience to consumers and in public harm. . . . It is true, many of the proprietors refuse to sell to the plaintiff proprietary goods except at long prices, which I understand to be the selling price. They have refused to allow plaintiff commissions or a rebate upon the goods purchased, but this refusal is based upon the ground that the plaintiff refused to sell at the price fixed by the proprietor. The plaintiff can at any time avail itself of the right to purchase upon the contract plan by complying with the requirements of the proprietors. The plaintiff could command large capital, and by reason of this they could purchase proprietary goods in larger quantities and more cheaply than the other wholesale and jobbing druggists, and that by reason of the contract plan the plaintiff was unable so to do. Under the contract plan the prices of these goods were made uniform for fixed quantities, and dealers possessing large capital and thereby enabled to purchase in large quantities could not purchase for a less sum than the ordinary wholesale and jobbing druggist, and not being able to purchase for a less sum could not handle the goods more cheaply. The situation is not new. It is one to which the attention of the public has been frequently drawn in recent years. The great merchants possessed of large capital will persuade manufacturers to sell to them more cheaply in consequence of their taking large quantities, and thus they are enabled to undersell and drive out of business the small merchants in their vicinity. I am not here to question the right of the big fish to eat up the little fish, the big storekeeper to undersell and drive out of business the little storekeeper, but I do believe that the little fellows have the right to protect their lives and their business, and if they can by force of argument and persuasion induce manufacturers to establish a uniform price for fixed quantities so that they can purchase as cheaply as the great merchants and thus compete with them in the retail trade, they have the right to do so, and that no court of equity ought to interfere and restrain them from the exercise of this privilege."

Since the decision of the New York court the arrangement is still maintained, works satisfactorily, and is earnestly defended by the association and those interested in its maintenance. A manufacturer signs a contract with the officers of the association agreeing that prices shall be maintained and that orders shall be refused from all dealers whose names appear upon a blacklist furnished the association from time to time. These conditions are being enforced, and since the Park suit the contract seems supreme. The jobber is permitted to cut the price on certain specified quantities, as, for instance, for orders for three dozen of Ayer's goods he may make a discount of 5 per cent at his discretion, and the same discount on orders amounting to $36 of Pierce's goods, etc., each proprietor electing the size of the quantity ordered that permits the discount. Retail druggists and wholesale druggists find it very difficult and always more expensive to buy these goods if they violate provisions of the contract.

There is in the drug line another scheme, known as the "Miles plan," inaugurated by the Miles Medicine Company. This company, which markets its goods through jobbers, prohibits a jobber from filling orders from any firm or person whose name is not found on the list furnished him by the Miles Company. To get on this list a retailer must contract to sell the Miles goods at full price. The retailer forwards his contract, if he is not already on the list, to his jobber. The jobber in turn forwards it to the proprietor, who, if accepting him as in good standing, adds the retailer's name to his general list. On receiving from a regular customer not on Miles's list an order containing an item calling for any of Miles' goods, the jobber fills the order less the Miles goods even if his customer is a valuable one to him. This causes much irritation to the retailer and considerable explanation from the wholesale druggist. The wholesalers, however, seem pleased with the plan, and are standing by it to a man.

BOOK PUBLISHERS AND BOOKSELLERS.

In the latter part of 1900, the American Publishers' Association was organized, with, it is supposed, about 95 per cent, both in number and extent of business, of the publishers of all kinds of books, magazines, and similar commodities throughout the United States. The association included such publishing houses as: McClure, Phillips & Co., D. Appleton & Co., Dodd, Mead & Co., Doubleday, Page & Co., The Funk & Wagnalls Company, Harper & Bros., Henry Holt & Co., Houghton, Mifflin & Co., The Macmillan Company, G. P. Putnam's Sons, The Baker & Taylor Company, Fleming H. Revell & Co., and others. Shortly thereafter the American Booksellers' Association was organized, composed of a large number of bookdealers at wholesale and retail, with about 90 per cent of all such dealers both in number and extent of business throughout the country.

The Publishers' Association adopted an agreement providing that all copyrighted books published by any of them after May 1, 1901, should be published and sold at retail net prices, that is, the published price, and not be subject to any discounts. It also provided that these books should be sold only to those booksellers who would maintain the retail net prices of such books for one year, and to those booksellers and jobbers only who would sell books at wholesale to no one known to them to cut or sell at a lower figure than such net retail prices, or whose name would be given to them by the association as one who had cut such net prices. An office was established for the purpose of carrying out this plan.

Soon afterward the American Booksellers' Association issued a statement announcing that the plan of the Publishers' Association would take effect May 1 and giving as reasons for this measure the demoralization of the book trade, both as regards publishers and retail dealers, in the cutting of prices by department stores, home library associations, and other mail order agencies which advertised books at "wholesale prices."

The Booksellers' Association stipulated that its members should co-operate with the American Publishers' Association in supporting the latter's agreement as to prices and conditions of sale. The Publishers' Association on its part refused to sell to the person violating his agreement any book published by any member of the Publishers' Association, whether copyrighted or not, until the association should be satisfied that such persons would co-operate with it and its members in maintaining the uniform net price system.

In carrying out the arrangement the American Booksellers' Association sent a circular letter to publishers who had not joined the Publishers' Association, containing the following statements:

"By special arrangement entered into with the Organization committee of the American Publishers' Association, the members of our association are bound not to buy, not to put in stock, nor to offer for sale the books of any publisher who shall finally decline to cooperate with us in the maintenance of the net price system by joining the American Publishers' Association and issuing books under the net price system. Inasmuch as the publishers have carried out their part of the agreement upon which our conduct was conditioned, it now becomes necessary for us to preserve our part of the agreement. We had sincerely hoped that you would be pleased to join the American Publishers' Association and co-operate with us through it in the maintenance of the net price system; and if you will take the matter into consideration at the present time, we are confident that you will now join the Publishers' Association and not compel us to take final action in this matter. We inclose a copy of the last issue of the Booksellers' Bulletin. By referring to page 6 of the Bulletin you will see that one publisher has already been cut off by the members of our association. We sincerely hope it will not be necessary to extend the list. Very truly yours,

"American Booksellers' Association."

The resolution on which the above notice was based is as follows, adopted by the American Booksellers' Association June 17, 1902.

Whereas, all publishers of trade books still remaining outside of the Publishers' Association have been repeatedly invited by us to join the organization and through it co-operate with us in the maintenance of the net price system, and,

Whereas, such publishers of general trade books as still remain outside of the Publishers' Association are continuing to sell their publications to the few persistent price-cutters, and thus encouraging them to continue their opposition to the net price system, therefore,

Be it Resolved that we, the American Booksellers' Association in convention assembled, do hereby instruct out secretary to give final notice to such publishers that it is our intention to apply Reform Resolution No. 1 unless they immediately join the American Publishers' Association and co-operation through it with us in the maintenance of the net price system, and therefore,

Be it Resolved that should any such publisher on receiving such notice decline to co-operate with us by failing to make application to the American Publishers' Association after receiving final notice, the secretary shall promptly issue notice to all members that Reform Resolution No. 1 is thereafter to be applied to such publisher, and all members shall discontinue handling the books of such publisher as provided by Reform Resolution No. 1 until further notice.

As a further illustration of the methods adopted and the success with which they were carried out the following extracts are given from a circular letter sent out by one of the publishers:

"Several things have already been demonstrated of interest to the entire trade in connection with the 'No Cut rate' movement.

"1. The substantial loyalty to the association of all dealers. In only one case (up to date of this letter) has there been any cutting of price,—one large department store in New York City.

"2. The vigor and promptness of the association to punish those who violate its regulations.. The association immediately took steps to assure itself that the cut in price was deliberate and intentional. The entire wholesale publishing trade was at once notified not to sell a *book of any kind* published by the members of the American Publishers' Association to the offending concern. There is every indication that this order will be loyally carried out by all publishers and wholesalers."

A number of department stores accepted the conditions imposed by the Publishers' Association, but the firm of R. H. Macy & Co., of New York, brought suit in December, 1902, in the New York Supreme Court for an injunction and for $100,000 damages against both the Publishers' Association and the Booksellers' Association. The petition cited that the two associations had entered into a combination to maintain prices and to prevent competition, and that they refused to sell any books to R. H. Macy & Co. It was also alleged by the plaintiff that the Publishers' Association had sent their spies into the store of Macy & Co. and had bribed their employes and followed them to their homes and elsewhere in order to discover the parties who were selling books to them in violation of their contract with the Publishers' Association not to do so; and that, in some cases, when these parties were discovered their supply of books was immediately cut off by all the publishers.

In reply, the President of the Publishers' Association contended that the object of the association was not to create a monopoly, since it admitted all reputable publishers that might wish to become members. Neither did the association attempt to fix the price of any one of the books. This was done by each publisher, and the effect of the rules was therefore not to stifle competition but rather to increase competition by providing settled methods of doing business. It was intended in no way to limit the sale of books, but to furnish them to all jobbers and dealers who would agree to prevent sales at less than the fixed retail price, and it was intended that such jobbers and dealers should be treated with justice and equality and without special concessions, rebates or discounts. It was held that the publishers' profits had not been increased by the association.

This suit was decided in a lower court in favor of the publishers and booksellers; in an intermediate court in favor of Macy & Co., and is now pending on appeal taken by the publishers to the Court of Appeals.

THE PLUMBING BUSINESS.

The National Association of Master Plumbers of the United States was organized in New York in 1883. In 1884 at Baltimore the organization adopted certain resolutions which have constituted a bone of contention ever since between the master plumbers and the manufacturers and jobbers of plumbers' materials, whose organization is the Confederated Supply Associations.

While the supply men seem to have been willing to confine their sales to people legitimately engaged in the plumbing trade, as originally called for in the Baltimore resolutions of the Master Plumbers' Association, they refused to go a step further and accede to the association's demand that they should sell only to its members. At a meeting at which the Central Supply Associations' organization was effected the following declaration of policy was adopted:

Whereas, Many members of this association have been requested by State and local master plumbers' associations to refrain from selling licensed master plumbers, regularly engaged in business, who are not members of said association; and

Whereas, We deem such discrimination inexpedient and unwise from a business point of view and contrary to the laws of the United States and the principles on which our government is formed; therefore, be it

Resolved, That we reserve the right to sell plumbing goods to any licensed master plumber, regularly engaged in business, in accordance with the definition of the Baltimore resolutions as made by the National Association of Master Plumbers, at its annual meeting in Washington in 1892.

The master plumbers adopted a policy of patronizing only those supply men who agreed to their demands, thus boycotting others. The struggle between the two associations went on with varying success, the supply men expressing their willingness to abide by the Baltimore resolutions of the plumbers and urging arbitration for grievances and disagreements between members of the two bodies. Finally a conference in New York of the executive committees of the two associations adopted an agreement embodied in seventeen resolutions, the more important of which read as follows:

Whereas, we believe it would be to the best interests of the manufacturers, jobbers and plumbers of the United States that the sale of plumbing goods be confined to master plumbers as herewith defined:

1. A master plumber is one who has an established place of business and represents the industry of plumbing, and who has qualified under State or local enactments regulating plumbing and plumbers where such exist; or, where no license is required, an individual or firm with an established place of business and representing the industry of plumbing;

2. Resolved, That we recommend the establishment of a Joint Standing Committee on Conciliation to which shall be referred all cases of dispute between the plumber and the dealer. This committee shall be constituted by the appointment of six members, three of whom shall be named by the President of the National Association of Master Plumbers, and three by the Chairman of the National Committee of the Confederated Supply Associations. In case they cannot agree they shall submit the question to three arbitrators, chosen in the usual way.

3. That plumbing goods shall not be sold to dealers who do not confine their sales to master plumbers.

8. Supply houses, doing a plumbing supply business and contracting for plumbing work, directly or indirectly, are considered unjust competitors.

9. Net prices or any discounts from list prices furnished to others than those allowed to buy under these resolutions are violations thereof.

11. The members of the National Association of Master Plumbers shall not sell plumbing material to consumers when they do not furnish the labor for putting the material in.

14. The penalty for violation of these resolutions shall be left to the discretion of the arbitrators and be commensurate with the violations and circumstances.

By these resolutions the master plumbers gave up their claim that plumbers' supplies were to be sold to members of their association only, while they succeeded in establishing a more strict definition of the master plumbers to whom the privileges of the trade were to be confined. The resolutions were adopted unanimously by both organizations.

But in spite of its acceptance by the convention of the master plumbers the agreement was repudiated by their National Executive Committee at a meeting held in Cleveland, October 8, 1901, where resolutions were unanimously passed which revived the old demand. As these "Cleveland resolutions" were "enthusiastically and resolutely approved" at the succeeding annual convention of the master plumbers held at Atlantic City, June 18, 1902, and as the master plumbers are still trying to enforce them, their most important provisions are quoted verbatim:

1. The members of the National Association of Master Plumbers are requested to confine their purchases of plumbing goods to manufacturers and jobbers who are willing to assist in improving the condition of the plumbing business, and who sell plumbing goods in localities where there are members of the National Association of Master Plumbers only to recognized master plumbers whose names appear in the national Directory of Master Plumbers, published under the supervision of the National Association of Master Plumbers. No plumbing goods shall be furnished to consumers under any condition.

2. It shall be the duty of the secretary of each State or local association affiliated with the National Association, to furnish a list of recognized master plumbers in his locality to the President of the National Association of Master Plumbers. All this must be submitted to the officers of the various State associations and approved by them before being sent to the National Association.

4. The names of manufacturers and jobbers who are considered in accord with these resolutions shall be printed in pamphlet form, under the supervision of the National Association of Master Plumbers, and distributed to those who are members of the N. A. of M. P., with the request that they bestow their patronage upon those whose names are upon the said list of manufacturers and jobbers. Supplements to this list shall be issued monthly, or more frequently if necessary.

5. Manufacturers and jobbers who sell or exchange plumbing goods with other manufacturers and jobbers who furnish plumbing goods to those not on said list of recognized master plumbers shall not be considered in accord with these resolutions.

6. In order to aid in honest dealing and the payment of just debts, manufacturers and jobbers are requested not to furnish plumbing goods to any one for a building, or addition to a building, where a manufacturer or a jobber in accord or a member of the N. A. of M. P. has not been paid in full what is justly due him for goods furnished for such building or for work performed upon such building. Manufacturers and jobbers furnishing plumbing goods contrary to this section shall not be considered in accord with these resolutions.

7. Master plumbers shall not finish work, or furnish plumbing goods for any building, or addition to any building, where a manufacturer or jobber in accord, or a member of the N. A. of M. P., has not been paid in full what is justly due him for goods furnished for such building, or for work performed upon such building. Master plumbers finishing work or furnishing goods for such buildings contrary to this section shall not be recognized as master plumbers.

10. It is a recognized rule in all lines of business that manufacturers and jobbers confine themselves to manufacturing and wholesaling. Manufacturers or jobbers who conduct a plumbing business directly or indirectly or who establish and maintain others in the plumbing business shall not be considered in accord with these resolutions.

11. Master plumbers selling plumbing goods that they do not install, or who install plumbing goods that they do not furnish, in localities where there are members of the N. A. of M. P., shall not be recognized as master plumbers.

12. Manufacturers, jobbers or their representatives in plumbing goods who give net prices or any discounts from list prices to those who are not recognized as master plumbers by the National Association shall not be considered in accord with these resolutions.

The Supply Associations refused to comply with the Cleveland resolutions, and at a meeting at Chicago, Nov. 12, 1902, the National Committee of the Confederated Supply Associations adopted what are known as the "Chicago trade resolutions," in which, reaffirming their belief in "the spirit of conciliation and arbitration," they laid down the following definition of a legitimate master plumber "to whom sales of supplies are to be confined:"

"A party who represents the industry of plumbing, who has an established place of business, doing a general merchant and contracting plumbing business with the public generally; who has qualified under the State and local enactments regulating plumbing and plumbers where such exist, or, where no license is required, who fulfils the other requirements, and represents the industry of plumbing in the locality."

Besides the legitimate master plumbers, section three provides that—

"The following are entitled to buy plumbing goods: Federal Government, State and county institutions. Also water works, railroads, steamship companies, ship building companies, car building companies, packing and stock yard companies, educational and charitable institutions, municipalities, manufacturing companies, for use only in the requirements of their business, providing they are regularly employing journeymen plumbers the year round to install same.

"No plumbing shall be sold to any of the aforementioned parties for use of any officers or private individuals connected with said excepted parties.

"No plumbing shall be sold to any of the aforemen- stores, mail order or catalogue houses, buildings, office buildings, or hotels, or retailers not doing a legitimate plumbing business."

The Chicago and Cleveland resolutions are at present still the subject of dispute. In the words of a prominent manufacturer of plumbers' supplies, as matters stand at present—

"The Cleveland resolutions are not strictly enforced. There is more or less elasticity about their enforcement, according to locality and custom. It is implied in them that legitimate plumbers, to whom the supply houses are required to limit their sales, are all in their directory. This is admittedly impossible. In many places only their association members are reported. We all sell to any legitimate plumber, regardless of his association membership, when he is otherwise in good repute."

The master plumbers, however, insist upon their demand that goods be sold to members of their association only, and resort to threats of boycott, as the following letter, recently sent by the secretary of a local association of the plumbers to a manufacturer of plumbers' supplies, shows:

Dear Sirs: On March 2, Mr. ——, Secretary of the — Local, wrote you that you had shipped tubs to —— people who were not members of the Northwestern Association, State or National. Yours of March 3 read as follows: That you had not done so, as far as you knew. You also say that Mr. ———'s letter to you of March 2 was indefinite. He, again, on March 7, wrote you in answer to yours that the tubs were shipped to ——— direct from your factory. Yours of March 11 says: 'The tubs were shipped on the order of a jobber." In connection with that I would say that we hold you accessory to this matter as much as if you had shipped them direct. If a horse is stolen, and you had helped to secrete him, the law says you are accessory to the crime, and the Northwestern will hold you to that point that you are a party to this wrong, and we will give you to March 23 to adjust this matter with the —— people to their satisfaction, and when it is settled they will report to me, and that will end the difficulty, but at the end of that time, if Mr. —— reports to me that this matter has not been settled satisfactorily, then the Northwestern will take this up against you in their usual custom. As this is the first offense against you, we hope you will be prompt in straightening this matter out, but you cannot be excused for selling to non-member on a jobber's order. Yours respectfully,

(Signed) ——.

The "usual custom" referred to is the placing of the manufacturer's name on the list of those "not in accord," which is equivalent to a boycott of his goods by the members of the association.

That these threats are being carried out in different parts of the country the following cases of recent date go to show:

The Spokane (Wash.) Chronicle of July 9, 1903, contained the following item of local news:

"In the case of Maxwell & Hollinberry vs. The Master Plumbers' Association, brought in the Superior Court for an injunction to stop the boycott which has been enforced against the plaintiffs, the final hearing of which was held July 2, Judge Kennan this morning granted a decree, perpetually restraining the defendants from intimidating Holly, Mason, Marks & Co., the Griffith Heating and Plumbing Supply Company, and all other dealers in plumbers' supplies and materials in the city of Spokane, either by use of threats, coercion, fine or otherwise, and from further interfering with the business of the plaintiffs or in any way injuring the trade of the plaintiffs by intimidation, threats or fine, either by agreement among said defendants, either express or implied, open or in secret."

The "Plumbers' Trade Journal" of August 1, 1903, contains the following:

"Suit was begun in the early part of last month at Birmingham, Ala., by J. E. Barnes against the Millner & Kettig Company and the Birmingham Pipe and Casting Company. The suit is brought under what is known as the Sherman anti-trust law, which forbids combinations.

"Barnes, who is a master plumber, claims that he cannot purchase plumbing material from either of these firms. The reason, he states, is owing to the fact that he is not a member of the National Association of Master Plumbers, and that both firms in question have conspired with said association and refuse to sell to them. The case will be watched with a good deal of interest."

In St. Louis the local association of master plumbers succeeded by threats and intimidation in compelling the manufacturers and jobbers to confine their sales to members of the plumbers' association only. A plumber by the name of Walsh found himself cut off effectually from all supplies, and applied to the court for relief. The "Plumbers' Trade Journal" of May 15, 1903 (page 479), contained the following account of the case:

"In the case of Walsh vs. Association of Master Plumbers of St. Louis et al., the St. Louis Court of Appeals held: 'Capitalists have the right to combine their capital in productive enterprises and by lawful competition drive the individual producer and the smaller one out of business. . . We think it is competent for the court to declare the agreement complained of as illegal and void, and to restrain the parties to the agreement from keeping its terms or demanding that they be kept, and thus have the respondent corporations and each of them free to deal or not to deal with the appellant (Walsh) as they may choose.'"

Barclay, J., concurring with the decision said:

"While any or all dealers in plumbing materials may *sponte sua* (of one's own accord) refuse to sell to appellant, they cannot combine and conspire to that end as the statute law now is."

An attempt was made in the early part of this year to bring the two warring organizations together. At a conference between the National Executive Committees of the two organizations held in February, 1903, the President of the Plumbers' Association proposed, as a basis for compromise, that in every locality where the plumbers' organization included two-thirds of the plumbers engaged in business and represented 75 per cent of the purchasing power, the dealers should confine their sales to members of the association. This was rejected by the supply people, and the conference was terminated. In the meantime, the over-aggressive policy of some of the local organizations resulting in adverse decisions from the courts, the National Association of Master Plumbers asked its local organizations not to take action in their controversies with the supply people except through the National Committee. Several of the local associations were displeased by this step, the dissatisfaction being especially great among the members of the Northwest Association of Pennsylvania, who seceded from the larger body.

HARDWARE.

Observers in close touch with the hardware trade differ as to the extent to which the hardware industry in the country is regulated by means of pools or "gentlemen's agreements." Varying estimates place the figures at from 60 to 95 per cent. of the output of the entire industry. Some of the most important lines, such as screws, shovels, axes, etc., are organized in pools. The general tendency is toward combination, since it is so often found that unrestrained competition is ruinous. Although many pools fail, yet almost invariably a new pool springs up to replace the old one, to profit by its mistakes and prove more stable. Moreover, after the prejudices and mutual suspicions of the members have been overcome, a pool that has attained success tends in the course of a few years to develop into a complete merging of the individual concerns into one company.

The avowed object of a pool is to maintain prices at a profitable level. The common means to that end is the apportionment of the market among the members in proportion to plant capacity. Ascertaining the capacity is confided to a special commissioner, who alone is thus made familiar with the facts regarding each plant, the members remaining in ignorance of the particulars of one another's business. The apportionment made, each member is told what his output is to be, and it becomes henceforth the commissioner's duty to audit the books of the constituent concerns at regular intervals, to see that all live up to the agreement. Members selling less than their share are compensated from the common fund, while those exceeding their allotment are required to pay into it the excess. Members detected in selling below the prices agreed on are subject to forfeiture of part or all of the money paid in by them as a guarantee of good faith. To insure more perfect control a central selling agency is sometimes established, often managed by the commissioner. In other cases the manufacturers composing the pool are left each to market his own product, the earnings being adjusted at stated intervals by the commisioner.

Not all the lines of hardware industry are organized in pools. Some are mere gentlemen's agreements, as in the case of the manufacturers of bolts and nuts. These agreements are sometimes in the nature of an informal understanding as to prices. More frequently they take the shape of a formal contract, signed by all the parties thereto, and providing for penalties in case of violation. All of these forms of agreement, however, have one feature distinguishing them from pools, which is that there is no attempt to regulate output or to allot it among the several manufacturers. The latter are free to compete for sales, so long as they do not attempt to undersell one another. Such agreements are known to exist among the manufacturers of hammers, tool-handles, cabinet backs and door-hangers, and other lines of builders' hardware.

The prices agreed upon by the manufacturers are those charged to jobbers. Between these two elements there is constant friction on account of direct sales by manufacturers to retailers, department stores and mail-order concerns. The jobbers have sought without success to become the agency for all the manufacturers' product, but the manufacturers will not even agree to sell to retailers at prices bearing a fixed percentage to the prices to the jobbers, and they vary the prices to the retailers with the size of orders, terms of payment, etc. In some cases, as in wood-screws and horseshoes, described more fully below, there are different scales of prices, according to the importance of the jobber.

In the skate and lawn-rake combinations each manufacturer has been assigned a number of jobbers, through whom he does business exclusively. The jobbers were not consulted in this assignment, but the experience of each mannfacturer as to what particular jobbers he did most business with was taken into account. The agreement, which is called "iron clad" in the trade, as it provides for severe penalties in case of violation, has been in force for several years and has worked very successfully. Jobbers are sometimes dissatisfied when unable to get the particular goods made by a manufacturer to whom they do not happen to be assigned, but they carry out the agreement faithfully, as they are bound in their turn to their respective manufacturers by contracts providing for a rebate on their prices at the end of the year, with loss of the rebates on any violation of the agreement. The pools and the agreements as a rule take in all the manufacturers in a given line. Competition sets in, if at all, at a later stage, when the high prices maintained by the combination make the field attractive to newcomers.

The mutual relations between the manufacturers and jobbers in the hardware trade are summed up in the following extract from a speech by E. B. Pike, of the Pike Manufacturing Company, New Hampshire, delivered before the annual convention of the Southern Hardware Jobbers' Association, in July, 1903:

"I believe it is the policy of the average manufacturer to depend upon the jobber to distribute his goods. Of course, some mistakes have occurred, some manufacturers have been foolish enough to sell their goods to retailers, some even to consumers, and some have been so absolutely bad that they have sold to catalogue houses. But I think most of them have sooner or later come to realize and repent of their sins.

"Of course every line of goods cannot be handled in the same way. Manufacturers of machinery must necessarily sell a large portion of their product direct to the user, while manufacturers of such articles as tacks and screws would be very foolish to do so."

At the same meeting, C. M. Fouche, of the Crucible Steel Company of America, Chattanooga, Tenn., made an address which contained the following statement:

"When it is thought that the manufacturer is making too much profit our jobbing friends will urge embryo manufacturers, with more money than brains, to go into the business, and we soon have over-production and the resultant seeking after markets by the manufacturer who cannot dispose of his goods through the regular channels."

The following are among the more important combinations in the hardware trade:

WOOD SCREWS POOL.—Has been in existence for about six months. It is organized as a regular pool on the lines above described. It has a commissioner who has charge of the pool funds and the matter of compensation and of charges for excess made to each manufacturer, according to his output. There is no common selling agency, but members are subject to forfeiture for selling below prices. There are three scales of prices: One for very large jobbers, another for the medium jobber, and a third for small jobbers or retailers. The effect of this pool has been to raise prices 40 per cent, but it is claimed that before the combination prices were unprofitable.

SHOVELS.—The association controls about two-thirds of the total output of the country. The manufacturers allow jobbers a rebate provided they refrain from purchasing from outside manufacturers.

AXES.—The pool controls practically the entire output of the industry. It has recently been formed and no changes in prices have yet been made, but an advance is expected. Among the concerns in the pool is the American Axe and Tool Company, a consolidation of about a dozen independent concerns, which control about one-half the entire output of axes in the country.

HORSESHOES.—Controlled by a pool organized on the lines described above. There is only one important concern, the Burden Iron Works, of Troy, N. Y., outside the pool. A new independent concern, the Standard Horseshoe Company, of South Waltham, Mass., has also come into the field recently, but it is not operating on a large scale at present. The prices of the pool are graded according to the importance of the jobber. A jobber ordering not less than one thousand kegs in six months is allowed a rebate of 7½ cents per keg, equivalent to 2½ per cent; those buying not less than two thousand kegs in the same period get a rebate of 15 cents per keg. The buyer in large quantities is thus deemed to be entitled to greater consideration and protection.

AGRICULTURAL HAND IMPLEMENTS.—Are controlled by a trust with only one serious competitor.

AMMUNITION.—Metallic ammunition, powder and shot. The association, controlling over 90 per cent of the total output, consists of three concerns: The Union Metallic Company, the Winchester Arms Company, and the United States Cartridge Company. The only outside concerns are the Robin Hood Powder Company, and the Peters Cartridge Company, of Cincinnati, O. This is said to be the most successful of all the pools and has been in existence for several years.

ICE CREAM FREEZERS.—There is a "gentlemen's agreement" as to prices on the part of the four concerns engaged in the manufacture of this article. It effectually keeps out competition.

IRON AND STEEL.

The following associations, pools or "gentlemen's agreements" are known to exist in the iron and steel industry:

The *Steel Rail Pool* includes all the leading concerns with two exceptions. The output of the pool, which is fully 90 per cent of the total output, is by agreement apportioned among the constituent concerns in proportion roughly corresponding to the capacity of their respective plants. The apportionment is a matter of bargaining, carried on every year at the renewal of the pool. There is no central selling agency, each company filling its own orders, but all the inquiries received by each company are compared daily at the office of the commissioner in New York to insure uniformity of prices and terms. The pool has been in existence several years.

The two outside concerns are the Colorado Fuel and Iron Company, which co-operates with the pool, and the Tennessee Coal, Iron and Railroad Company, which is a competitor.

STEEL BILLET ASSOCIATION.

The recent revival of this pool has been made possible through the decrease in the number of independent concerns as a result of consolidations. The pool includes now the United States Steel Corporation, the Jones & Laughlin Steel Company, the Wheeling Steel and Iron Company, the Cambria Steel Company, the Pennsylvania Steel Company, the Lackawanna Steel Company, and the Maryland Steel Company. Meetings are held in New York every day, at which inquiries and sales are regularly reported. The agreement refers exclusively to prices, which have been established for the principal points of consumption. Though popularly called a pool, the combination is merely a "gentlemen's agreement" and each firm is free to sell all it can.

The *Beam Association* is a regular pool organized in the form described under hardware. Owing to adverse court decisions the feature of compensation when falling short and payment for excess of allotments has been dropped. The output is still apportioned among the various concerns, and no one is permitted to exceed his share, the matter being regulated through a commissioner. A concern receiving orders in excess of its allotted share will turn them away, thus indirectly compelling the customer to apply to another member. The pool controls about 90 per cent of the total output.

The *Plate Association* includes all the principal manufacturers of plate, with the exception of the Lukens Iron and Steel Company, which, however, co-operates with the pool. Organized in the same manner as the Beam Association, this pool controls more than 90 per cent of the output.

The *Pig Iron Association* of the Mahoning and Shenango valleys maintains a common selling agency. It is a combination of outside furnaces which sell their output to the United States Steel Corporation. It has recently decided to shut down all of the furnaces for 30 days at some time prior to January, 1904, to prevent an accumulation of stock.

The *Association of Steel Bar Manufacturers*, west of the Alleghany Mountains, has been in existence for about two years. It is in the nature of a "gentlemen's agreement" to maintain prices.

There is an association of manufacturers of shaftings, which is not strong.

A meeting of representatives of blast furnaces located in eastern Pennsylvania and New Jersey was held Sept. 21 in New York, at which it was practically agreed to curtail production. One of the conferees is reported as giving out the following statement:

"No formal action was suggested or taken at the meeting. The question, however, came up as to whether it was advisable to undertake any restriction of output. It was decided that, first, no price agreement was worth talking about, and, second, that no formal restriction of output could be carried through. Informally, however, it was the sense of all present that we should limit production to consumption."

RAILROADS.

Probably in no other field of capital does destructive competition cause such waste as it does in the railroad business. It is no longer competition, it is "war." "No competition," says the Interstate Commerce Commission, "is so destructive as that between railways." If these wars are less frequent in recent years than they were in earlier stages of the business, it is because means have been found by combination or otherwise to prevent them. The fight is often as bitter to prevent a new road coming into the field as it is between existing roads, and the vigorous efforts of the Pennsylvania railroad interests to prevent the Gould lines from getting Atlantic Coast terminals are well known matters of recent history. Sometimes the contests between existing roads are carried to such extremes that they become actually ridiculous, as in the case of the passenger-rate war one year ago on lines between Chicago and Texas, as described in the following telegraphic item:

"Houston, Tex., Aug. 17.—Five hundred tickets were sold to Chicago yesterday at startling prices as the result of a war of ticket brokers, the outgrowth of the fight of the Missouri, Kansas & Texas, the International & Great Northern, the Cotton Belt and the Santa Fe for Northern passenger business.

"The lowest rate before yesterday was $18 for the round trip. One broker cut it to $8. Another broker at once cut it to $4. Yet another announced Houston to Chicago, 30 cents; Houston to St. Louis, 20 cents; Houston to Kansas City, 10 cents.

"Another met the cut and offered a $5 box of cigars with each ticket."

Railroad combinations differ from others in that railroads are public utilities, and railroad wars and discriminations inflict a public injury. On this account the Interstate Commerce Commission, representing the people, has recommended that poolings be legalized. For, says the Commission:

"If public transportation can be bought and sold like a commodity the largest purchaser will, some of the time if not all of the time, get the best terms. It is idle to expect that railroads will actually and all the while compete with each other as to every item of service or facility and at the same time expect that all their patrons, large and small, will be treated exactly alike. The policy now pursued cannot and will not prevent an outcome of vicious discrimination. And, what is most unfortunate of all, these discriminations favor the few and place the many at a disadvantage."

To place competition on a stable basis the railroads find it necessary to resort to two kinds of agreements, viz., uniform classification and uniform rate-fixing. For the purpose of classifying freight uniformly the different trunk lines of the country are associated through their representatives in what are known as Classification Committees. The entire United States is divided among three such committees, the Official, the Western, and the Southern.

The roads represented in the Official Classification Committee cover the territory lying north of the Ohio and Potomac Rivers and east of the Mississippi and the city of Chicago; those in the Western Committee the territory west of Chicago and the Mississippi River; and those in the Southern Committee the territory south of the Ohio and Potomac Rivers and east of the Mississippi.

The Classification Committees, composed as a rule of General Freight Agents or Traffic Managers, are voluntary associations of the railroads. Their object, as stated in the Articles of Association of the Southern Classification Committee, is to establish "uniform freight classification and the publicity of the same."

The membership of these committees ranges from fifteen in the Official Committee to forty-two in the Southern. In addition to the representatives of the roads each committee has a chairman, a paid officer, not representing any road. The Classification Committee, without attempting to fix the actual freight rates, confines itself to classifying commodities. Nevertheless, it is evident that by changing an article from one class to another, the classification committees are able in so far to fix rates. By making a sweeping change of this kind these committees in January, 1900, advanced freight rates 20 to 100 per cent.

The Official Classification Committee works hand in hand with the Trunk Lines Association, which includes the roads connecting the Atlantic Coast cities with Chicago. This association fixes the actual rates by classes and also the so-called "commodity rates," i. e., special rates on commodities not included in any of the regular classifications. There is no provision for penalties of any kind for violating the rates or the classifications, yet it is believed that the roads abide by both.

The way in which this observance of rates and classifications is brought about is one of the most interesting facts in the history of all the ingenious devices for escaping destructive competition. By the anti-trust laws as interpreted in the Trans-Missouri cases, the roads are prohibited from organizing pools or associations to agree on rates, and this decision has intensified their efforts toward the now famous method of "community of interest." A person or a corporation in the interest of a competing line secures enough of the stock of its competitor to influence the election of the board of directors. A Federal Court, in the Northern Securities decision, has interdicted this practice when managed by a holding company organized for the purpose, yet that other form of community of interest, where individuals hold stock in competing roads, is not checked and is an increasing influence as a means of preventing rate-cutting.

Each of the associations which co-operate with the classification committees maintains a staff of men who inspect shipments to prevent the practice, said to be common among shippers, of underbilling weights and misdescribing goods to get lower than the published and legal tariff rate. The practice, when successful amounts practically to a discrimination in freight rates, the unscrupulous and successful underbiller getting virtually a rebate on his freight bill. The inspectors are responsible directly to the associations, and not to the individual railroads, being constantly shifted about from one road to another. Though they are supposed to watch the shippers and not the railroads, the latter themselves are sometimes the instigators of underbilling as a means of secret discrimination, and it has been stated by a prominent representative in the Trunk Line Association that the practice is on the increase in the Official Territory.

The experience of the trunk lines in arranging differentials on the limited passenger fares between New York and Chicago is an interesting example of the principle of agreeing on a minimum compensation. When a passenger pays $8 more to ride between New York and Chicago on the Twentieth Century train than on the ordinary train this principle is recognized. The regular rate is based on the slowest line, which has $20 for a twenty-eight-hour run. To overcome in a measure the advantage of the quicker lines, the latter agree to charge the $8 excess. Were this not done all of the travel would be by the quicker lines, and the slower one might be forced into bankruptcy, to the ultimate disadvantage of all the lines.

The express companies and telegraph companies, like the railroads, have uniform rates for similar services.

LUMBER TRADE.

The National Wholesale Lumber Dealers' Association has for its object "the protection of its members against unbusinesslike methods of wholesale and retail lumber dealers and others. It shall give such security in the way of debarring 'scalpers,' the regulation of inspections and credits, the arbitration of disputed matters, as may be within the lawful power of such an association." (By-laws, Article I., Section 2).

Article XIX, referring to "relations with retail associations," provides that "whenever it shall be determined by the Board of Trustees . . . that any firm, person or corporation is not a legitimate customer for the wholesale trade according to the principles recognized by this association, as best conserving the interests of the lumber business, the members shall not thereafter sell to such person, firm or corporation."

Any member violating this provision "shall be notified to explain to the Committee on Arbitration, and should he fail to satisfactorily explain his conduct to said committee he shall be suspended or expelled by the Board of Directors as said Board may deem proper." (Article XV., Section 2.)

The local associations have their own rules for carrying out the spirit of these provisions. Thus the New York Lumber Trade Association has the following provisions regulating prices of lumber to members and to non-members of the association:

"First, the retail dealers hereby agree to purchase their stocks of spruce timber entirely from the wholesale commission houses who are members of the New York Lumber Trade Association in good and regulatar standing; second, the wholesale commission firms who are members of the New York Lumber Trade Association hereby agree to sell spruce timber in New York only to such persons, firms and corporations as shall be members of the New York Lumber Trade Association in good and regular standing.

"No member shall sell or deliver any lumber not mentioned in the above agreement in connection with or in consideration of the sale of lumber and timber mentioned in this agreement, at a less price than the wholesale price of such lumber in this market at the time of sale; members shall not sell to other members who are not in good standing with this association, except at the regular retail price."

Owing to the publicity recently given to these rules, the New York association has appointed a committee to revise them, and it is not yet announced whether changes have been made in the sections just quoted.

GROCERIES.

In the grocery business the increase in the number of "chain stores" and department stores is giving considerable concern to wholesalers and retailers, forcing them to organize more compactly for defensive purposes. Already one concern is operating 230 retail stores; another 114; and many from 5 to 50. The Retail Grocers' Association of Milwaukee has passed resolutions not to handle the products of manufacturers who place their goods in department stores, and the president of the association predicts that their action will be followed in every one of the States in which the National Retail Grocers' Association has branches. The National Association has recently passed resolutions asking manufacturers to maintain retail prices.

Wholesalers' and retailers' associations are working together in certain localities, as may be gathered from the following statement of the President of the Southern Wholesale Grocers' Association:

"About three years ago the retail grocers of Birmingham were in a bad way. There were dead beats coming into the town all the time, cutting and slashing prices and causing trouble to the retailers. What hurt the retailers hurt the wholesalers, and the wholesalers determined that the solution of the trouble was to organize the retailers so that they could protect themselves against irresponsible competitors. After the organization of the Birmingham retailers, the Minnesota wholesalers followed the lead, organizing the retailers of that State."

The "factor" or "equality" plan, which the wholesale grocers induced the sugar refiners to adopt in 1895, was designed to overcome the extreme competition which had wiped out the profits of the jobber. The plan provides for the payment of a rebate to the wholesalers by the refiners upon condition that they maintain the price fixed by the refiner. The refiners were to aid in the maintenance of the plan and to confine their business strictly to the jobbing interests, and on the other hand refiners not a party to it were not permitted to reach the market through the wholesale grocers, and no additions were to be made to the list of approved refiners. Thus importers and outside refiners were compelled to reach the retail trade direct or through outside jobbers. This arrangement was gradually broken into by the rise of new refiners and was definitely abandoned about a year ago. In its place has been substituted the "limited price" agreement between jobbers and refiners without the exclusive features. During the present year this also has been broken and prices have been cut, and for this the jobbers are blaming the refiners and the refiners the jobbers.

Similar price-fixing arrangements exist in many other lines of goods sold by the grocers.

Wholesale grocers' association in certain states and sections are beginning to show a tendency to take another step in eliminating competition, by organizing under the corporate form. Leading firms in Ohio have recently consolidated under a New Jersey charter, and are expecting to take in firms in other states.

THE CONFECTIONERY TRADE.

The collective regulation of the confectionery trade is divided between the organization of the jobbers and that of the manufacturers.

Among the objects of the National Jobbing Confectioners' Association, which are enumerated in Article II. of its Constitution, are "to establish a uniform price, to harmonize all conflicting interests, if possible, and protect all persons engaged in the business that are affiliated with this body."

In a resolution adopted in 1902, at the eighth annual convention of the jobbers' association in Philadelphia, the following passage occurs: "That we support those manufacturers who sell jobbers at jobbing prices and retailers at association prices." The National Association leaves its local organizations free to adopt any measures they think best calculated to attain their ends.

The Association of Confectionery Jobbers of New York City has recently assumed an aggressive policy in an attempt to regulate prices to the retail trade. It states, first, that owing to the small capital required to engage in the confectionery jobbing business there has been such an influx of dealers as to reduce prices to an unremunerative level, and, secondly, that unscrupulous members of the trade cut prices practically below cost to build up a trade quickly and secure a large credit, and then by failing in business recoup their losses. The association maintains that no jobber who intends to remain in business could adopt such methods, and therefore they are subjected to dishonest competition.

With a view to putting an end to this practice, injurious to the interests of manufacturer and jobber alike, the New York Confectionery Jobbers' Protective Association has adopted a system of fines terminating in expulsion directed against price cutters.

Section 8 of the association's by-laws reads:

"When a member is found guilty of selling below the price list of the association he shall be fined $10 and not above $50 for the first offense, $50 for the second offense, and may be expelled for any subsequent violation."

To make the punishment of expulsion effective the manufacturers were requested not to sell to jobbers who were not members of the association. It was also understood among the members of the jobbers' association that manufacturers refusing to comply with their demands were to be deprived of the jobbers' patronage.

The manufacturers on their part have taken a position which in many but not all respects is sympathetic with that of the jobbers. At the annual meeting of the manufacturers of the Eastern Confectioners' Association held at New York in April, 1902, the following were among the declarations adopted:

"Having this end in view, the manufacturers recognize that it is essential to the existence and well being of such associations that their membership should include, so far as may be practicable and possible, all jobbing confectionery houses doing business within the limits of the territory covered by the jobbers' associations, and the manufacturers are therefore in duty bound to lend their assistance in increasing and strengthening the membership of such jobbers' associations, so long as they are conducted on right and equitable principles. On the other hand, this association believes that no jobber should be constrained to become a member of any association in opposition to his own judgment and choice, much less should he be forced into membership by the use of threats or any form of intimidation.

"This association believes that manufacturers should refuse to sell their goods to any jobber of confectionery who bears the established reputation of being what is known as a 'cutter,' or who will deliberately and persistently undersell the schedule of prices adopted for his territory by a jobbers' association.

"This association, however, does not believe that jobbers' associations have any right to expect or demand that manufacturers shall refuse to furnish goods to a responsible and reputable jobber who will maintain association prices, whether said jobber belongs to said association or does not.

"The association further declares that it should be the unquestioned right of every manufacturer to sell to any jobber who maintains association prices without any discrimination on the part of the jobbers' association or any member thereof, against such manufacturer."

The latest expression of the attitude of the manufacturers is found in the following resolution adopted at a special meeting of the Eastern Confectioners' Association held at Gettysburg, July 8-9, 1903:

"The Eastern Confectioners' Association can not and will not blacklist any person or persons or take any action intended to injure any one's business or to drive him out of trade."

As stated by a prominent manufacturer against whom a boycott had been instituted by the jobbers' association, it has been his invariable practice to "cut off" every jobber, if after fair warning he did not cease cutting prices. But while he could do so of his own accord upon information received from the jobbers, without making himself liable to prosecution before the law, he could not discriminate against a non-member of the association at its request without exposing himself and the association to the danger of prosecution for conspiracy.

There is another noteworthy feature in the present disagreement between the manufacturers and the jobbers. The New York jobbers, believing that their field is overrun by unnecessary competitors, are exacting an initiation fee of $250. This keeps out of the association the candy jobber, who is practically a peddler and confines his sales to the small candy stores. The manufacturers, however, are disposed to welcome additions to the number of distributors so long as they sell at a reasonably profitable price. Hence one objection to the demand of the jobbers that the manufacturers confine sales to members of the jobbers' association.

The difference in attitude of the manufacturers and the jobbers is shown also in another point. The manufacturers contend that when a jobber is detected in cutting prices it should be the business only of the particular manufacturer who supplied the goods to discipline the jobber, and "cut him off" if necessary. The jobbers, on the contrary, insist that the jobber caught cutting prices of even one manufacturer should be "cut off" by all other manufacturers when notified to that effect by the jobbers' association.

THE JEWELRY TRADE.

Owing to the great variety of products no uniformity of trade methods prevails in this industry, conditions differing widely in the various lines of manufacture. Several lines have no regulations as to prices or methods of selling. The following trade organizations are believed to exist:

The watch case manufacturers have an understanding as to the distributors with whom they will deal. Each manufacturer has a list of jobbers whom he recognizes as his distributors, and will sell direct to no other individual or firm in the trade, whether jobber or retailer. The manufacturers deny the fact of this agreement, but the retailers find by a singular coincidence that the lists of distributors of the several manufacturers are identical. Prices to retailers have advanced, in some cases more than 50 per cent since this method of selling came into vogue. It is employed by all the leading manufacturers, such as the Elgin, the Waltham, the Crescent, the Keystone, the latter controlling several minor concerns, among them the Philadelphia, the Boss, etc.

The American Association of Wholesale Opticians has among its objects the doing away with excessive competition. Their members, however, aver that there is nothing beyond a gentlemen's agreement, remembering the anti-trust laws.

The cut glass manufacturers are similarly organized. The relations with jobbers are left to the discretion of the individual members, each being free to sell both to jobbers and retailers. The manufacturers fix the prices at which the jobbers are to sell to the retail trade, and keep them to strict account. A prominent manufacturer of cut glass states that they "cut off" one of the leading jobbing houses in the country as a punishment for selling to retailers at lower prices than the manufacturer himself. There is said also to be an informal understanding among the manufacturers as to prices.

The New England Manufacturing Jewelers' and Silversmiths' Association has a "gentlemen's agreement" as to prices.

ANTHRACITE COAL.

The production of anthracite coal is divided among the six "anthracite railroad lines" on the one hand and a number of private operators called "independents" on the other. The private coal operators ship their coal through one or other of the anthracite railroad companies or its subsidiary coal company. The railroad companies themselves have an understanding both as to rates and the apportionment of coal tonnage to each road. The tonnage is fixed in these proportions:

	Percentage of Total:
Lehigh Valley	22.88
Central of New Jersey	17.12
Delaware, Lackawanna and Western	19.52
Erie	5.84
New York, Susquehanna and Western	4.68
Philadelphia and Reading	29.96

The contract for buying the coal of the independent operators is made between each coal operator and the railroad company to which he sells his coal. But all the agreements, being the result of a joint deliberation by the representatives of the different roads and the independent operators, are identical.

The essential points in these agreements, as they exist at present, are that the operator agrees to deliver all of the anthracite coal mined or to be mined by him to the railroad coal company in question, to be marketed by the latter, the operator receiving 65 per cent of the tidewater price. The railway, however, does not undertake to buy all the coal that the operator produces. It only promises "to use its best efforts to find a market for the seller's coal, so as to enable the seller's collieries to be working as many days as practicable with due regard to the general market conditions." It also "agrees that it will not discriminate in favor of its own mines, or any persons, firms, or companies with which it has contracts to buy coal, but that the quantity to be ordered monthly shall be a just proportion of the entire quantity of coal agreed to be purchased by the buyer, measured by the colliery capacity of the respective sellers."

The colliery capacity is "determined as of the first of January, by the parties thereto, and on their failure to agree the President for the time being of the Guaranty Trust Company shall select a suitable expert for this purpose."

This anthracite railway pool has been successfully maintained since 1896, and when at one time it was threatened by the independent operators with a proposed railroad the roads affected took the heroic step of buying out the collieries of the largest independent coal company and thus breaking up the scheme. The deal was carried out on the joint account of the six anthracite companies. They took stock in a concern called the Temple Iron Company, in the proportion of their allotment of tonnage, and the Temple Iron Company was made the owner of the purchased collieries, with the Guaranty Trust Company of New York as trustee. The latter is intrusted with all the stock of the Temple Iron Company, together with the absolute right of voting it, and in turn it issues to the railroad companies their allotted certificates of beneficial interest in the stock.

INSURANCE.

Of the several classes of insurance companies, those in fire insurance have advanced furthest in regulating competition. The National Board of Fire Underwriters is a representative body of the largest companies, subordinate representative bodies being the State and rating associations and local boards of fire underwriters. The local boards, under direction from the head of each company, establish uniform rates for the different localities. They prescribe in the minutest detail the form of contract, the base rates, the additional rates for every specific kind of risk, such as the presence of gasoline, electric connections, etc., and the deductions to be allowed for safety devices diminishing fire risks. The boards, National, State and local, and the inspection bureaus, are conducted at an annual expense of $1,500,000, which is assessed on the several companies on the basis of their premium receipts.

The "giant" life insurance companies, viz., the Equitable, Mutual, and New York Life, in April, 1903, entered into a tripartite agreement to refrain from the use of "competitive literature" referring in any way directly or indirectly to any other American life company, and issued a list of the standard publications which agents are permitted to use as not coming under the head of that class of printed matter. They agreed to destroy within thirty days all printed matter of the character prescribed, the order to this effect being celebrated by their agents throughout the country by "competitive literature cremations." The life companies have no agreements as to benefits or premiums, and the life underwriters' associations throughout the country represent, not the companies, but individual agents.

The leading "industrial" companies have for some time had an agreement like that just effected between the life companies, by which "no agent is permitted to misrepresent the policy of his own or another company, must not abuse or malign a competitor, must not twist policy holders, while agents cannot be taken from one company to another, and should they leave voluntarily are not employed in the same city by another company until two years have elapsed. No company issues any literature attacking another company."

In liability insurance the companies establish "conference rates," though there are outside companies that refuse to be bound by them. The International Association of Accident Underwriters has not gone so far as to prescribe uniformity in benefits and premiums.

At least one State recognizes that insurance, like railroads, is a public business, and Illinois has enacted a law prohibiting agents from cutting premiums.

NEW YORK BANKS.

The objects of the New York Clearing House Association are the "effecting at one place of the daily exchanges between the several associated banks and the payment at the same place of the balances resulting from such exchanges" (Sec. 2). But in addition to this labor-saving mechanism the Clearing House Association has during the past three years provided a scale of commissions to be charged by the New York banks on out-of-town collections, with heavy penalties for violation. All banks, members or non-members, clearing through the association are required to charge a commission for collections on out-of-town checks at a rate varying from one-tenth of one per cent to one-quarter of one per cent of the amount collected, according to the distance from New York of the banks on which the checks are drawn. "No collecting bank shall, directly or indirectly, allow any abatement, rebate, or return for or on account of such charges or make in any form, whether of interest on balances or otherwise, any compensation therefor." A collecting bank found guilty of violating this rule must pay to the association the sum of $5,000, and in case of a second violation "any collecting bank may also in the discretion of the association be excluded from using its privileges directly or indirectly, and, if it is a member, expelled from the association." Expulsion from the association, by depriving it of the privileges of the Clearing House, is practically equivalent to driving a bank out of business. An estimate has been made that the foregoing rule of the Clearing House Association has saved the New York banks $3,000,000 yearly.

NEW YORK STOCK EXCHANGE.

Although the transactions by and through the Stock Exchange are of vital importance to the business world, yet, unlike financial exchanges in foreign countries, it is subject to no special laws or regulations of the State, and it is not incorporated, but is governed solely through rules laid down by its own membership.

The primary object of this voluntary organization is to protect the common interests of its members by maintaining a code of conduct and a standard of remuneration for the services which they render to their customers.

The number of members, limited at present to eleven hundred, cannot be increased "except by action of the Governing Committee," who prescribe "the number of increase and the terms of admission" subject to the approval of the members. "Members admitted by transfer shall pay to the exchange an initiation fee of $2,000," in addition to the amount they may have to pay to their predecessors who sell them their seats. Owing to the limited membership, there is a high money value on each seat, a recent sale being reported at more than $80,000.

Clearly defined rules stipulate the commissions to be charged by members. Every member is obliged to charge a commission "under all circumstances upon all purchases or sales of securities dealt in upon the exchange;" this commission must be "absolutely net and free from all or any rebatement, return, discount or allowance in any shape, or manner whatsoever, or by any method or arrangement, direct or indirect." Brokers are not allowed to divide commissions with brokers on rival exchanges. The minimum fees are fixed by the exchange at not less than one-eighth of one per cent on business for non-members, and not less than one-thirty-second of one per cent on business for members.

To insure due observance of this scale the exchange subjects the business of members to strict surveillance, requiring registry of partnerships, a limit to the number of partnerships, regulation of branch offices, salaries and not commissions for clerks and employes, submission of books and papers to investigating committees, and prohibiting partnership with suspended or expelled members or with members of a competing exchange, prohibiting transactions with non-members on the floor of the exchange, and prohibiting dealings upon any other exchange or in public outside the exchange. A member is also prohibited from establishing telephonic or telegraphic connection with non-members without the approval of the Committee of Arrangements. This provision is directed against furnishing stock quotations to non-members, especially to that class known as "bucket shops."

Penalties for violating these rules are suspension for the first offense, and expulsion for the second, on a majority vote of the Governing Committee.

ASSOCIATED PRESS.

Telegraphic news is essential to the business of a daily newspaper, and the Associated Press is a mutual association of such newspapers for the collection and distribution of news. It is conducted not for profit but for the mutual service of its members, and the expenses are shared according to a scale agreed upon. It is natural enough that, having perfected their organization for exchanging news and having made valuable connections with other agencies for collecting and distributing news, the members should not be inclined to admit competitors to the enjoyment of their facilities. In each locality the members of the Associated Press therefore have the right to admit or reject applications for membership and to set the fee for admission. The veto of one local member is enough to exclude an applicant.

The Associated Press makes a contract with each of its members setting forth the conditions under which news shall be furnished, and it was brought out in the suit for injunction on behalf of the Chicago Inter-Ocean Publishing Company against the Association that the members were forbidden to furnish any news report to any newspaper published in the territory described in the contract or to any other news agency;

and also to receive news from any other person or association "which shall have been declared by the Board of Directors or the stockholders to be antagonistic to the association." When the Inter-Ocean procured and published news received from another association, its fellow members in Chicago made complaint, and, according to the by-laws, gave notice to the Inter-Ocean that it would be suspended from membership. This was not carried out, however, because of the injunction obtained by the Inter-Ocean Company and sustained by the Supreme Court of Illinois on appeal. The court held that the Associated Press discharges a public duty, and that a public interest attaches thereto, and that it could not restrict competition by preventing its members from purchasing news from any other source than from itself. The restrictive clause of the contract was declared null and void.

On account of this hostile decision in Illinois the Associated Press gave up its Illinois charter and reincorporated in the State of New York. The Illinois decision does not require the Associated Press to admit an applicant to membership, and a case of that kind has never come up. Consequently, although the Associated Press is held to be a business affected with a public interest, yet the members in a locality continue to exclude outsiders and to protect themselves to that extent from excessive competition. For this reason the Associated Press franchise is undoubtedly the most valuable asset of a daily newspaper, since it is almost the sole protection which the business has against destructive competition.

FARMERS.

Efforts to prevent excessive competition among farmers are handicapped not only by the enormous number of the competitors in one country and in every country, all subject to the world's market prices, but by the isolation of the competitors, a large proportion of whom usually need ready cash. Where a crop is localized and the farmers can come together, it is not rare to find them resorting to the methods of other capitalists and the workingmen. The following news item is taken from a [illegible] of the "American [illegible]

[illegible] Hop Pool.

"[illegible] ...ary Winstanley of the Oregon [illegible] ...tion to A. Menke, a Sacramento [illegible]

[illegible] are so many missing hills in the Oregon hop [illegible] ...rds this year that it will be impossible for us to raise more than 50 to 75 per cent of last year's crop. We believe that this condition justifies us in asking you to co-operate with us in demanding better prices for our 1902 crop. Dealers are to-day offering to shade 20 cents, but there are no sellers, and we feel sure that hops will go to 30 cents if we unite in holding.'

"There follows a form of agreement which is being signed to pool the remaining portion of the 1902 crop and hold it until the selling price reaches 25 cents or more. The pool is not to be effective until 6,000 bales are secured under the agreement. If any grower signing is compelled to sell by emergency before the end is achieved he agrees to give five days' notice, and the managers of the pool are to have the option of purchase at the ruling prices."

Associations to some extent similar have existed, or been attempted, among fruit growers and dairymen. To control world-wide crops there have been popular movements like the Farmers' Alliance, which inaugurated a "hold-your-cotton" and "hold-your-wheat" agitation. The Cotton Growers' Protective Association, organized in 1899, makes an effort each year towards this end. It is reported that recently the Russian Minister of the Interior received an invitation from 30,000 American farmers to join in a movement to hold the present world's wheat crop for better prices.

Recently fifty representatives of agricultural associations in a dozen or more states met in Chicago and [illegible] a national body for the purpose of fixing [illegible] of all farm products, regulating the marketing [illegible] and constructing grain elevators and cold storage warehouses for the use of farmers.

One of the organizers said, in the course of an address:

"The farmer holds the destiny of the industrial world in his hand and he should [illegible] tion. We must form a nationa[l] [illegible] minimum price for our product an[d] [illegible] crops until we get our price. It is just a[s] [illegible] $1 for corn as it is to get 80 cents."

A despatch from Oklahoma Aug. 18 is along the same lines:

"The Farmers' Co-operative Union of America has organized under the laws of Oklahoma to secure and maintain better prices for farm products and specifically 'to force the price of this year's wheat to $1 a bushel on the Chicago market,' by storing and holding the supply in elevators owned by the union. The union is declared to be non-political."

Farmers often organize to do their own marketing, and thus protect the members from middle men, as illustrated in the milk trade of New York and vicinity.

The New York Milk Exchange is an association of city milk dealers which meets once a month, or more frequently if necessary, to fix the price to be paid for milk. This price rules throughout the entire territory tributary to the New York milk market. No dealer pays a higher price than that fixed by the exchange, but some dealers managed to pay a lower price to farmers who compete with one another. The farmers have long been dissatisfied with this arrangement, and the Five States Milk Producers' Exchange, at a meeting held at Binghamton, July 8, entered into an agreement to sell to the Pure Milk Company, a new corporation of dealers, "all of the milk produced from the cows owned or controlled by them severally, except milk used in their homes, for a term of five years, beginning October 1, 1903," at certain prices stipulated in the contract for each month of the year.

TRUSTS.

The foregoing examples of the many associations to regulate competition by agreement have the one great weakness that the parties to the arrangement cannot always be held to it strictly. Each competitor retains his business identity and the legal right to quit. This is because the courts are usually inimical to "combines" and refuse to enforce their contracts at law, to say nothing of actually enjoining and dissolving them. In France and Germany, where the courts sustain such agreements, they have been found satisfactory in controlling competition, and in those countries the so-called "syndicates" or associations like some of those just described, are the highest form of the movement away from competition and are found in nearly all industries under the sanction of law. But in the United States the hostility of legislatures and courts has had exactly the opposite effect from that intended. Instead of compelling the parties to revert to the former state of suicidal competition, it has forced them to take on the highest and most compact forms of anti-competitive organization to be found in any country, namely, the trust and the corporation. Under these the individual competitors actually give up their identity and the management of their business in order to make sure of escaping the ravages of competition. In the case of the trust in its original legal form, the several competitors handed over the shares of stock representing their properties to a board of trustees and received in return certificates of an interest in the profits. The trustees then elected the boards of directors of the formerly competitive companies. When the courts followed up their attack by dissolving the trusts, they simply changed their legal form from a "trust" to a "corporation" and continued the same as before so far as the matter of competition is concerned. This is the reason why the name "trust" sticks to them, and in this article we use the term in its popular sense. The identity of competitors, which is lost in the trust, is even more deeply buried in the corporation. The change is legal not economic. A corporation charter is taken out. Corporation shares are exchanged for the trust certificates. The trustees become directors. The officials of the trust are the officials of the corporation.

Thus the *trust* is the highest form and the culmination of the movement on the side of capital to do away with destructive competition. But it goes further than a mere corrective of evils, for it usually strives to eliminate competition itself, by consolidating all, or nearly [illegible] joint ownership of a single [illegible] ...s not always been successful in [illegible] ...ion, but there is no doubt that this [illegible] been the object. Says the National Biscuit Company to its stockholders:

"In the past the managers of large industrial corporations have thought it necessary to success to control or eliminate competition. So, when this company started, it was believed that we must control competition, and that to do this we must either fight competition or buy it. The first meant a ruinous war of prices; the second, constantly increasing competition. Experience soon proved to us that, instead of bringing success, either of these courses, if persevered in, must bring disaster. . . . It became the settled policy of this company to buy out no competitor."

But the Biscuit Company still continues to do all it can to escape from the pressure of destructive competition—it turns its energies, like hundreds of other companies in all lines of business, to specialties, trade marks and patents.

"On the package business we have practically no competition—not because the field is not open to all—not because we have had any special privileges, except such as were granted by the United States. These privileges lie in the patents we control and in our trade marks."

In a similar vein the president of the so-called whisky trust speaks of the monopolistic intentions of those who promoted the trusts. He says, in an official circular:

"Most of the recent consolidations of industrial enterprises have been based upon the theory of a practical monopoly for the purpose of regulating and maintaining prices. . . The constituent companies of the Distillers' Securities Corporation have gone all through this phase of the industrial problem, and since 1899 have conducted their business in open competition and free from all artificial combinations to control prices or markets."

It is now four years since trusts became epidemic. During these years, as estimated by the "Journal of Commerce," the capitalization of industrial consolidations amounted to $7,536,000,000, the largest flotations being in 1899 and 1901. The same journal mentions nearly 250 separate combinations in many lines of business, and it is no unusual thing to learn of a combination controlling 70, 80 or 90 per cent of the output in its particular line. The National Biscuit Company has 128 different plants in various cities. The Consolidated Tobacco Company makes 95 per cent of the cigarettes consumed in America, controls a majority of the plug and snuff concerns, has entered the cigar business, and has extended its business to England. To enumerate all of the trusts and to describe the extent to which they have gone in buying up competitors would be only to repeat familiar history. All sorts of competitive circumstances have played a part. In some cases, where the larger companies unite and only a few small and scattered companies are out, competition is controlled, and the little companies follow the prices set by the combine. In other cases, the smaller competitors combine, seeking to protect themselves from a large one, which thenceforth is perhaps induced to follow a less destructive policy towards the smaller ones. If not, the smaller ones must go a step further and buy off the big one.

The trusts furnish an impressive lesson to all organizations, both of capital and labor, of the limits beyond which organization cannot go in passing over from protection against excessive competition to attempted monopoly. Many of them have collapsed and the securities of nearly all have depreciated. A writer, recently speaking of the whole situation, states that "the actual market value of this prodigious product of the printing press to date is probably about 25 cents on the dollar."

It has also been found that new competitors could not be kept out, and the "Journal of Commerce" shows that, mainly in the past two years, new corporations, rivals to the consolidations, have come into the field with a capitalization of nearly $500,000,000.

This failure of so many trusts arouses the painful suspicion that the recognized arguments as to the "wastes of competition," "cost of advertising," "traveling salesmen," "savings in freight charges," "economy of administration," "control of the market," arguments sound enoug.. tive combinations, were sei.. tage of by mere promoters to .. projects.

.. because ..any of the trusts ..er and invited competition ..ed permanently by a condition of ..mpetition. In the very nature of the case such competition cannot continue. In fact, not all the trusts have failed. A goodly number have adopted a careful and far-sighted policy and have established their industries on an apparently stable basis.

SUMMARY

The foregoing recital shows that the efforts to escape destructive competition are almost universal. There is scarcely an industry that is free from combinations of capital or combination of labor in some form. The differences are found only in the extent to which the combination is successfully carried. There is an infinite variety in the methods of the various combinations, yet there is a general similarity in their efforts to regulate competition and to bring pressure to bear on persistent competitors, price-cutters, and non-unionists. What is true of the boycott, as stated by Carroll D. Wright, in his address before the National Asosciation of Manufacturers, is in general true of other methods of the two classes of combines. Mr. Wright said:

"Everybody boycotts somebody, and to a certain degree it is a legitimate weapon for the defense or protection of proper methods. Carried to the extreme it is a crime against the individual and prevents that development of private character which is essential to public virtue. It never does, therefore, for either the employer or the employe to accuse the other of resorting to methods common to both."

It may well be asked, in view of these universal efforts to regulate or eliminate competition, What is to be the outcome? and, What should be the policy of the general public toward combinations? We may ask, Shall all combinations be suppressed and all industries be compelled to submit to the unregulated competition of anarchism? Or, shall these combinations continue to grow and competition be entirely eliminated in the ideal state of socialism. If neither of these extremes should be followed, what shall be the middle ground where competition may continue without being destructive and where the public shall not be exploited by monopoly of capital or monopoly of labor?

This number of the "Review" will be sent to employers, workingmen, lawyers, economists, and in the next number will be published a symposium of the views of all classes of people upon the phase of the industrial situation above portrayed. This symposium ought to throw light on such practical questions as follows:

Shall these combinations be left to work out their purposes, or shall the courts and the legislatures [illegible] called upon to deal with them? Shall combinati[illegible] of capital be treated exactly the same as combinati[illegible] of labor, or shall the one be suppressed and the o[illegible] encouraged? Shall legislation regulate the terms [illegible] membership and compell the employers' association and the trades union to admit members on the qualifications and fees determined by law? If not by regulating membership, how can the rights of independent manufacturers, and dealers and workingmen be protected? How far shall publicity be carried, and [illegible] much can be accomplished by publicity?

These are a few of the many questions suggeste[illegible] the array of evidence which we have collected. [illegible] industrial problem is generally admitted to be the [illegible] ent problem of the day. It cannot be met by crimi[illegible] tion or recrimination, for all classes [illegible] more or [illegible] involved in similar practices. It c[illegible] candid and serious discussion bas[illegible] the facts, and to call forth such disc[illegible] to be gained in the foregoing review of combin[illegible] of capital and labor.

of members ... partnerships, a limit to the num ... regulation of branch offices, ... for clerks and employ ... to investigating ... hip with suspended or

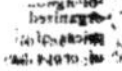

National Civic Federation
MONTHLY REVIEW

Vol. I. No. 4. NEW YORK, JUNE, 1904. TEN CENTS

THREATENED PARALYSIS OF THREE GREAT INDUSTRIES AVERTED.

TRADE AGREEMENTS, THROUGH FRANK CONFERENCES, PRODUCE PEACE IN THE BITUMINOUS COAL, THE TIN PLATE AND SHEET IRON AND THE LONGSHOREMEN'S INDUSTRIES.

FRANCIS L. ROBBINS,
President Pittsburg Coal Company.

INTERSTATE BITUMINOUS CONFERENCE.

A Trade Agreement That Prevented a Strike That Would Have Paralyzed Industries.

The last month has witnessed the most important agreement between labor and capital that has been reached in this country for many a year. This is the adjustment of the wage-scale for bituminous mining in the four States, Pennsylvania, Ohio, Indiana and Illinois, entering into the interstate joint agreement between miners and operators. The events culminating in this adjustment centered in the conference at Indianapolis between the representatives of the operators and the delegates of the United Mine Workers of America. This conference failed to reach a final agreement; for the miners' delegates, being restricted by instructions from local unions were not able, even had they wished, to follow the counsel of President John Mitchell of the United Mine Workers and of the officers of State organizations, to accept the compromise proposition advanced by President Francis M. Robbins of the Pittsburg Coal Company on behalf of the operators.

This proposition from the operators was rejected by the Indianapolis conference. But it was unanimously rejected, only after an understanding had been reached whereby the compromise offered should be referred to a vote of the miners' organizations in the four States. This was a practical method of overcoming the difficulty offered by the instructed delegates to the Indianapolis conference, who did not consider themselves at liberty to vote in that body to accept directly the offer of the operators. As was anticipated, in view of the openly expressed approval of President Mitchell and other leading representatives of the miners' organizations, this resort to referendum resulted in the acceptance of the new scale by the miners themselves, on March 15, of the compromise proposition.

A RED LETTER DAY.

Thus does that date, March 15, 1904, deserve recognition as a red-letter day in the calendar of the current history of the relations between labor and capital in the United States. Its decision meant the prevention of a strike whose possible consequences no man could foretell, and which have now happily been dismissed to the realm of hypothesis. It is plain enough, however, that the business interests of the country have escaped a disturbance potentially even more gravely disastrous than that which was actually caused by the anthracite coal strike of 1902. A bituminous strike in the four States might literally have stopped the commerce and paralyzed the industries of the country. More than this, and of a consequence more permanent, is the prevention of a disruption of the relations between organized labor and the employing coal operators in the four States concerned.

DANIEL J. KEEFE,
Longshoremen, Marine and Transport Workers' Asso.

The continuance of those relations is a conclusion of the greatest importance, not alone to the coal industry, but to producers and consumers affected by conditions in many other industries, especially in transportation and manufacture.

The most general and far-reaching significance is attached to the fact that organized labor has proved, in this instance, its willingness to adhere to a joint agreement as to wages, when that agreement involves a reduction in wages, based upon lower prices for the product

JOHN MITCHELL,
President United Mine Workers of America.

and other adverse conditions of trade. It has been alleged that the joint agreement, when put to the test, would prove to be an arrangement that would work only in one way—in the direction of a share always for the employe in larger profits of an industry, but never in the acceptance by the employe of his share of the privation caused by smaller profits. The interstate bituminous agreement involved precisely this proposition of the acceptance by the miners of a reduction in the scale of wages, in response to a reduction in the profits of the capital invested in the mining and marketing of coal. The action of the miners proves that organized labor can have the fairness to adhere to a joint agreement, when that agreement causes lower wages as well as when it causes higher. Their action furnishes a specific answer to the assertion of some employers that joint trade agreements are untrustworthy and ineffective.

A NOTEWORTHY BODY.

All these reasons lend vivid interest to the narrative of the proceedings of the Indianapolis conference and to the terms finally submitted to the referendum. The conference itself was an unusual body. Upon the side of the operators were men who, while standing firmly for what they maintained were the rights and the necessities of capital, asserted freely their hope that the interstate agreement might not be terminated, and avowed candidly their sympathy with organized labor. Upon the side of the miners were delegates whose appearance and manner bespoke the constant uplift of education, and whose words were sustained arguments, of course in support of their contention, but in large degree animated by a response to the friendly expressions of employers, and inspired by an apparent desire for co-operation. There were several critical passages in the debates. There were moments of dramatic earnestness, when none might tell how a passionate utterance, a misplaced word or a verbal collision might have widened the breach that it was the effort of the conservative leaders on both sides to bridge.

These debates reflected credit upon both the ingenuity and the prevailing sense of fairness of many of the speakers. The conference opened with the presentation by President Mitchell of the three demands of the miners. For these President Robbins offered as a substitute the first proposition of the operators. Upon that substitute the debate turned, with Messrs. Mitchell and Robbins as the leading champions of the two sides. But there were other doughty figures in the lists as well.

The three demands of the miners, as presented by Mr. Mitchell, were for payment upon a single, run-of-mine standard; for 7 cents a ton less for machine-mining; and for a uniform rate of wages for outside labor. The substitute offered by Mr. Robbins declared that "the conditions of the times and the reductions in the price of coal and the necessity of meeting competitive conditions, in districts where this interstate movement does not apply, demand and require a reduction of 15 per cent. from the present scale of wages."

PRESIDENT MITCHELL'S ARGUMENT.

Mr. Mitchell first stated his general argument. He uttered the broad proposition that the operators do not profit by paying low wages, and he enforced their position with this language:

"I am free to confess that it is to me a strange philosophy that a reduction of wages will relieve an industrial depression. I cannot understand how less wages will relieve over-production. To my mind the only way to relieve over-production is by making it possible for people to consume; and the workingman cannot purchase unless he has wages. A reduction in the price of mining means a reduction all around. If you reduce one industry it goes on and on, and finally the wages of all workers are reduced, for the purchasing power is cut off; and then you come back and start over and over again; it is an endless repetition. It means that when wages go down the consuming power of the purchasers is curtailed, and all the citizens of our country are compelled to suffer, whether they be workers or capitalists.

"I am, therefore, of the opinion that a reduction in wages will benefit no one; that it will not benefit the employer, who either secures it by agreement or is able to enforce it in the field of industrial conflict. Speaking specifically of our industry, my experience and my observation have been that whenever there was a reduction in the price of mining, that reduction has not benefited the operators. Instead of being benefited they were compelled to give, not only all of that reduction, but more, to the railroad companies who consumed a large portion of their product."

After discussing details of the industrial situation, Mr. Mitchell pointed out that lower wages and lower prices of coal would not bring about an increase in its consumption. Not one ton more of coal would be mined if coal were to sell for 10 cents a ton less. He then made this plea for harmony upon the then existing basis:

"The cost of living during the past six or seven years has increased in proportion to the increase in our wages, and, inasmuch as it is not within your power, even if you had the inclination, to offer us a reduction in the cost of our living, we cannot see our way clear to accept the proposition which you make. We are not living too well now. We are better than we have ever been before, but we are not going to return to the conditions that prevailed some years ago. The time will never come again, without consent at least, when the coal miners of this country will have to ask for charity when they are able to work, when they are willing to work, and when they are at work. We want these relations continued; we want you to be prosperous; we want to enjoy a reasonable degree of prosperity ourselves. We are free to say, we are glad to admit, that the conditions of our lives and of our labor were never better; but we also propose to say, and to insist, that they are not too good yet. We ask you, gentlemen, not to insist upon a reduction in wages where it can do you no good, and can do us incalculable injury. We ask you not to insist upon a part of our earnings in order to turn it over to the railroad companies. Let us go on as we are, making such modifications in our internal arrangements as seem necessary. Let us try and restore the good times, if we can."

Mr. Mitchell denied that the country had entered a period of industrial depression, that the demand for coal had in consequence decreased, and that the price of coal would necessarily fall. Mr. Mitchell supported these statements by a number of newspaper clippings, showing that mills that had been closed had resumed operation, in response to demand for their products that would continue during at least a year. He quoted from the last report of the Pittsburg Coal Company, and declared:

"I submit that, as a matter of fairness, it is not right for the operators to come into this convention and ask for a reduction in wages. If one company can increase

T. L. LEWIS.
Vice-President United Mine Workers.

its business and increase its receipts eighty-six per cent. in one year, I say they can well afford to stand a slight loss, a slight depression, without asking the miners to share it all for them. If I believed that the conditions of the coal trade were such as to warrant a reduction in wages, if I believed that industrial conditions generally warranted a decrease in wages, I would stand up here and advocate it. And I will say now that I wouldn't care if I were the only miner present that spoke for a reduction, I would do it if I believed it was warranted, and if I believed the future of this joint movement depended upon it. But I do not believe it."

Mr. Mitchell concluded his address with this plea for peace:

"I do earnestly hope that the operators present will see their way clear to withdraw their demand for a reduction in wages, and let this movement go on. They have enjoyed their full measure of prosperity during those last five or six years. We, too, have done very well. Our conditions of life and our conditions of labor are better than they ever were before; but, let me say to you, that in return for these better conditions of life and labor we have given you better service every year. The reports of our product show that for every day our people go down in the mines they give you a greater return. It shows you that we perform our labor better than we did during the old times when we were at war continuously. If it were possible for me to say anything that would perpetuate this movement, more than I have said, I should certainly not take my seat now. I hope that we will go on, and that we will continue to be, as we have been in the past six years, the leaders in the cause of industrial peace."

PRESIDENT ROBBINS' POSITION.

To this vigorous and eloquent appeal Mr. Robbins made cogent reply on behalf of the operators. He went at once to the basis of Mr. Mitchell's argument, the fact that iron and steel furnaces in the vicinity of Pittsburg had started up. Mr. Robbins admitted the fact, but he asked: "How have they started up? By a reduction for every man that works for them. Not a man but has stood a reduction in order to start them up. We have reduced our coal to start them up, also. That is why they are started. And it is why you will start, and why you will get more work if you will make a corresponding reduction in your wages."

Mr. Robbins then analyzed the report of the Pittsburg Coal Company, which Mr. Mitchell had cited as an evidence of the returns upon capital invested in the mining and selling of bituminous coal. Mr. Robbins pointed out that this statement covered the calendar year, from January 1, 1903, to January 1, 1904. It thus included three months, January, February and March, of the last scale year, when prices were abnormally high because of the anthracite strike and the scarcity of bituminous coal. In order to make its earning, the company had found it necessary to expend, in addition to the $32,000,000 original cash, $10,000,000 more. The earning had been six and three-quarter millions of dollars, upon an investment of $70,000,000, or less than 10 per cent. "That is a great thing to talk about, isn't it?" asked Mr. Robbins. "This company has gone into this investment of $70,000,000 in order to give you gentlemen employment, and it makes 10 per cent. on its investment."

In reply to a question by Mr. Mitchell, as to whether in addition to the $6,000,000 and more of profits the company had not been able to put $14,000,000 of its earnings into the purchase of property, Mr. Robbins admitted that this was approximately true, but that the investment covered a period of four years, not one year. Moreover, it had been made possible only by paying 7 per cent., reserving the rest of its profits for investment. An issue of $25,000,000 of bonds was about to be made for further investment. Then Mr. Robbins made this striking statement of the meaning to labor of this financing:

"Did you ever realize what an investment of a large operating company means? Do you realize that, to start with, it takes the coal in the ground, that is not worth five cents a ton, and everything from that on until it reaches the consumer is labor—labor for you, labor for the day men, labor for the railroad men, labor for the men where it goes into the vessel from the dock, labor for the vessel men that transport it over the lakes, labor for the men that take it from the vessel and put it on the dock, labor for the men that put it on the railroad, and for the railroad men that transport it, and for the laboring man that takes it out of the cars and deliver[illegible] the consumer? Did you ever realize that i[illegible] and that the people who have received this [illegible] per cent. are furnishing labor for the peop[illegible] country?"

PROFITS AND INVESTMENT.

Mr. Robbins asked the miners' delegates to divert their minds from the idea of the large earnings of the Pittsburg Coal Company. He reminded them that they should consider the aggregate of the capital invested. They would not think an earning of $20,000 or of $10,000 in a year so very much. Yet that would be only 10 per cent. on an investment of but $200,000, or of $100,000. He attributed to the fear by capital of trade-unionism the fact that the stock of the Pittsburg Company, which had sold at par, was quoted at 49 cents on the dollar, despite its earnings last year of 10 per cent.

From the report that Mr. Mitchell had quoted Mr. Robbins made this further quotation, as showing the disposition of the company toward its employes:

"In the last annual report attention was called to the operations of the Pittsburg Coal Company's Employes' Association, under which employes are enabled to purchase preferred stock of the company, to secure for themselves and their families benefits in cases of accident or death, and are assured pensions under prescribed conditions. The number of employes who are taking advantage of this opportunity to purchase stock has grown from 1,040 to 1,571 during the year just closed, and the number of shares of stock thus being acquired has increased from 7,723 to 11,315. There has been distributed in accident and death benefits during the year upward of $60,000, and the pension fund has grown to $23,601.07. Your officers' expectations of great mutual benefits through the working of the employes' association are being fully realized."

Mr. Mitchell announced that he gladly made acknowledgement of what the company was doing for its employes, but that he did not consider that pertinent to the questions under debate. Thereupon, Mr. Robbins turned his attention to the conditions in competitive fields. There, he asserted, reductions had been made which the miners in the joint agreement States had been unwilling to meet. Operators in other fields had the advantages of more hours of labor, lower wages, lower deadwork. These conditions had to be met. Mr. Robbins dramatically exclaimed:

"I shall never sign a scale except upon these conditions. It has come to the parting of the ways, so far as I am concerned, and so far as my companies are concerned. It has come to the point where, in justice to the people who have put their money in the company, whose report you have heard, that we shall stand for fairness and justice. It has come to the point that, when conditions of the country require a reduction, you should be men enough to meet the situation."

Mr. Robbins closed with the following expressions as to the pending crisis:

"I tell you, gentlemen, it is a most critical time for organized labor in this country. You will never in this world stand upon any such unfair proposition. If it means only one way, if it means that it is all an advance, and that you are never going to be like your fellow-workmen in other fields, that you will never accept a reduction, and accept it in order to supply them with coal at reduced prices as well as to supply railroads and steam producers of all kinds and descriptions, we should know it now. If you are to be a favored class that stands no reduction, but always onward for an advance, I am not with you.

"I have talked to you now as frankly and fairly as one man can talk to another. I have talked to you as honestly as any man ever spoke to another, with just as great a feeling in this heart of mine for you as you have for your fellow-men. I have been all through it. I started as a boy, and have done everything but dig coal, and I have done that on occasions. I have been through the whole thing, and I know it all, and it is perhaps because of that I have this feeling for you. It is, perhaps, because of that I interceded for you with the anthracite presidents before the strike occurred, and tried to get them to recognize you, and it is because of that I labored along with others in the Civic Federation. It is because of a feeling I have had that one man feels for another, but the base of it always was that when the time came when it would be necessary for you to do what was fair to meet fair conditions you would do it. If that feeling is not in your hearts, gentlemen, I am not with you."

Mr. Robbins announced his willingness for "an arbitration of what reduction you shall stand, based upon the reduced price of coal." Mr. Mitchell proposed instead to arbitrate what should be paid for machine mining as against pick mining. That proposition Mr. Robbins pronounced an absurdity, pointing out that only because of the introduction of machinery had the operators been able to advance wages in the past.

Mr. Tennant of Indiana reminded the conference that it was only a part of the American people. The people expected to pay less for coal. That was a concrete fact that could not be ignored.

Mr. Bogle, president of the Indiana operators, dwelt upon the fact that his was a State of individual operators. He protested, therefore, against basing the debate upon the operations of a large company.

VICE-PRESIDENT LEWIS SPEAKS.

Mr. T. L. Lewis, vice-president of the United Mine Workers, discussed the alleged reduction of wages in other industries and the shrinkage or values in this country. He said in part:

"We will not admit the statement that there is any shrinkage in values; and when we deny that statement some one will point out that all that is necessary to do is to pick up our daily papers and show where the stock of the United States Steel Trust has gone down from 90 to 50; that the common stock has gone down as low as 10 cents on the dollar; that the Pennsylvania Railroad Company has depreciated in value, and, in fact, that every other industrial and railroad stock in the country has been affected. Why? Is there any business man in this convention who will attempt to prove that the great railroad system owned by the Pennsylvania Railroad Company is of any less value now than it was one or two years ago? Is there any man in this convention who will attempt to prove that the mills, the railroads, the shipping interests, the docks, and, in fact, all the property of the United States Steel Company, so far as the real value of it is concerned, is any less in value now than it was one or two years ago? If there is, I want to hear that argument, and I want to have the argument borne out by facts. We know, and every one who has made a study of this question understands, that when the Steel Trust was organized the stock placed upon the market was fictitious in value, and not real. The men who promoted that great combination, and the men who promoted many other combinations, inflated the value for a purpose, and it is unnecessary for me to say why.

"It may be true that you are not receiving as much for your coal at this time as you were this time a year ago, but, according to your arguments at that time, you were receiving much higher rates per ton in the market than you expected to receive the year following the signing of that joint agreement.

T. J. SHAFFER,
President Amal. Asso. of Iron, Steel and Tin Workers.

"If this is true, why then should we be confronted with a proposition at this time for a reduction of our wages? One of the gentlemen on the other side stated this morning that the enemies of this movement said it was all right as long as wages were going up; that this movement was all right as long as we were making concessions and advancing the mining rate; but when the time came when it was necessary to stop, we might come to the parting of the ways.

"This year we have not asked for advance in the pick mining rate, but we have asked for a readjustment of the differential between pick and machine mining. Why do we ask that? Mr. Bogle said this morning that we have come into this convention time after time and demanded that we should have a fair share of the wealth we produced. That is the keynote of the whole thing. We are entitled to it. We do not deny to the operators that they shall have a legitimate profit on their investments in mining machinery; we do not deny to the operators that they shall get profits to offset certain risks they take in the industry; but we certainly do deny that the placing of the machines in the mines shall reap all the difference between pick mining at 90 cents and machine mining at 60 cents per ton in the Hocking district, and the same relative difference in other places."

In response to Mr. Lewis, Mr. Robbins went into a detailed explanation of contract prices, which may be summarized in his words:

"As far as the Pittsburg district is concerned, I want to reiterate that there is no trade, domestic, steam, railroad or any other trade in that district that has not met a very serious and a very large reduction, based upon meeting competition from outside fields that you are not in control of."

Discussion of prices was continued by Mr. Guthrie, Mr. Mullins and Mr. Chapman, Ohio operators, and by Mr. Patrick Dolan, president of the Western Pennsylvania miners.

The conference rejected the substitute offered by Mr. Robbins. The issues were then referred to the scale committee, which reported back to the conference, with the result already recorded.

This action was preceded by brief arguments. In support of his proposition, rejected by the conference but afterward approved by the referendum, Mr. Robbins said:

"This reduction is wholly inadequate to meet present conditions. We offer it only because of a desire to, if possible, reach a settlement and not to terminate this movement, and because of the two-year contract where we are willing to contribute our portion, yea, more than our portion, to the benefit that will arise from it to the labor of this country and the business interests of this country.

"We want to assure capital, which is timid in this country at this time, that this movement, which stands for so much, upon which is focused the eyes of the thinking people of this country, is a successful one. In arriving at this proposition we have been governed very largely by this feeling."

Mr. Mitchell addressed a circular letter to the miners, summarizing his reasons for advising their acceptance of the compromise proposition. His counsel and the influence of other influential leaders of organized labor had much weight in bringing about the approving vote.

SHEET AND TIN PLATE.

An Agreement Involving a Wage Reduction of 10 Per Cent for the Scale Year.

The April conference in Pittsburg between the sheet and tin plate manufacturers and a committee representing the Amalgamated Association resulted in an agreement for lower wages for the scale year. The workers felt themselves obliged to yield to the demand of the manufacturers for a reduction in wages. The manufacturers acquiesced in a reduction of 18 per cent. instead of their original demand of 20.

President Shaffer of the Amalgamated Association was chairman of the delegates' meeting, in which forty-three lodges were represented. Mr. James Campbell, of Youngstown, Ohio, was chairman of the manufacturers. The discussion was opened by President Shaffer, who was followed by W. T. Graham, president of the American Sheet and Tinplate Company. Thus the interests of the United States Steel Corporation and of the Amalgamated Association were brought, through their representatives, face to face. In order to get at the facts a committee was appointed, composed of an equal number of manufacturers and delegates, to go over the figures and ascertain what the result would be after the proposed reduction of 20 per cent. In this joint committee the following represented the delegates: Sheet Mill—R. R. Williams, Charles Hughes, Charles H. Brown and Moses Chivers. Tin Mill—William L. Hull, William G. Young, John Eynon and D. R. Rees.

Chairman Campbell appointed the following to represent the manufacturers: Sheet Mill—Messrs. Davis, Robinson, Beatty and Warner. Tin Mill—Messrs. Goldsmith, Phillips, Davey and Bennett.

After this committee had reported there was a general discussion, followed by an executive session. There it was decided to appoint a special committee of nine sheet and nine tin delegates, to confer further with the manufacturers. The sheet delegates chose as representatives: Charles Hughes, William Hilton, W. J. Penrce, Roland Layer, Otto Sellers, R. T. Lynch, Charles H. Brown, Thomas O'Hare and Andrew R. Black. The tin delegates chose Walter Larkin, Adolphus Edwards, John Kiddel, David J. Jenkins, William G. Young, John Eynon, David J. Davis, Harry Irvine and Frank Piggott. Walter Larkin was made chairman.

This committee labored assiduously with the manufacturers to secure better terms. Their conference lasted four days, so that, with the preceding conferences, eight days were consumed in reaching the settlement.

The *Amalgamated Journal*, the official organ of the

Amalgamated Association of Iron, Steel and Tinworkers, thinks that the reduction will be accepted with poor grace by a majority of the rank and file, but it asks for fair judgment for their representatives upon the conference committee, who bear the onus of accepting the reduction. The *Journal* declares that "it was only a realization that conditions were entirely against the workers that spurred them to shoulder the weight of such a burden." The *Journal* has this advice to offer to the workers' organization:

"Everything was done with an eye single to the future welfare of the sheet and tin trades and the general interests of the Amalgamated Association. The future alone will reveal the wisdom of the delegates in accepting the onerous conditions which they had to face, and much depends upon the way in which the membership will act in face of such adverse conditions. If the rank and file will heed the scores of admonitions that appeal to them from the past they will awake and realize that the time has come when they must organize more thoroughly. To sulk because reverses have come through circumstances over which the Association had no control, and which the delegates will fully explain to their sub-lodges, would be the height of foolishness. Let us profit by the mistakes of the past, improve the machinery of our organization, so that it will be able to cope with the modern conditions, which are entirely different from those that its founders had to deal with. Let us go forward, in spite of the obstacles that loom up in the way."

The *Labor World*, of Pittsburg, says of the agreement:

"Before any harsh criticism of the agreement has been entered into the condition that forced it must be fairly considered. If this is done it will readily be discovered that the agreement is absolutely one of expediency. It was effected solely to escape what were believed to be worse results. This, and this alone, was the reason for the delegates of the workmen conceding the reduction. After, to their own satisfaction, having fully grasped the situation in all of its ramifications, they were fully convinced that two evils confronted them. One of them was to refuse to grant any reduction, which meant a strike or lockout, and the other was to agree to work for reduced wages. These delegates arrived at the conclusion that the latter was the lesser of the two evils, and acted accordingly."

THE LONGSHOREMEN'S AGREEMENT.

Wages, Hours and Working Conditions at Lake Erie Ports for the Coming Year.

The agreement between the International Longshoremen, Marine and Transport Workers' Association and the dock managers at Lake Erie ports for the ensuing year was reached in April. This agreement is one of the most noteworthy of its class, as it has been found to operate effectively as a preventive of strikes or lockouts. The Longshoremen's Association, of which Mr. Daniel J Keefe is president, covers more territory than any other labor organization in the world. Its agreement is uniform, but covers thirty-nine divisions of trade. It is reached at an annual conference between representatives of the union and of the organized employers. The union delegates to this conference are vested with full power, without instructions, so that the agreement is not subject to ratification by a referendum. In the formation of the agreement, its subjects are referred to committees, and union men themselves present to these committees the employers' side of the case. By this method of procedure, the union conferees, when they meet the representatives of the employers, are able to discuss every article of the proposed contract, both from their own and the employers' point of view.

As a result, the annual conference is conducted with both dignity and harmony. Every demand made by the workers has been thoroughly threshed out in advance. The labor delegates are not likely to present a demand to the employers whose justice they have not been able to prove before a committee of their own fellow craftsmen. The conference this year was of the usual character. The Longshoremen's Union was organized by Mr. Keefe in 188[illegible]. The wage scale has been advanced an average of 60 per cent. since 1895. When the agreement is reached, its acceptance is made by unanimous vote, based upon the previous ascertainment of the will of a majority. The rule of the majority is thus made binding upon all. Any matter not covered by the agreement is subject to arbitration, as is any dispute as to the construction of the contract. The contract is printed, and a copy is furnished to every worker, so that he may at any moment refer to its exact language.

The joint conference adopted the following resolutions:

"That any and all contracts made between the local manager and the men directly involved shall be held in-

H. COULBY,
President of Dock Managers.

violate for all work not specifically covered in exhibits attached to and made part of this contract, and that any one trying to break such agreement, or in any way interfering with its performance, shall be barred as a representative, and shall not be permitted to work under this contract, and in all cases work shall not be interrupted on any account.

"That all grievances or suggested changes of form of contract shall be submitted in writing to the chairman of the dock managers and president of the I. L. M. and T. A. prior to the convening of the next convention, and that no statement of grievances shall be entertained unless so submitted.

"That in future conferences any new addition to be added to the present agreement must receive the two-thirds vote of the delegates of the conference."

The agreement is for the navigation season of 1904, and also covers winter work from December 1, 1904, un-

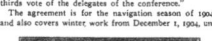

H. N. TAYLOR,
Illinois Coal Operators.

til May 1, 1905. Schedules of wages are attached as part of the agreement, marked "A," "B," "C" and "D." All employes are to be members of the local organizations, whenever such men can be had who can perform this work, as called for in the contract. When such men cannot be had, the dock managers have the right to secure any other men who can perform the work in a satisfactory manner, until members of the union can be secured. No man shall be discharged without just cause, and any man discharged shall be notified of the cause. The men may inspect bills of lading, to verify the tonnage. When unusual work arises in isolated cases not covered by this agreement, the men shall perform such labor. The compensation shall be adjusted between the representatives of the local organizations and the dock managers or owners. Any disagreement is to be arbitrated.

If any controversies and grievances cannot be settled by the local representatives of the union and employers, they shall be arbitrated by choosing a third disinterested man, the decision of any two to be final. "If the representative of the local organization and the representative of the employers cannot agree upon a third man, then each side shall choose a disinterested man—the two disinterested men thus chosen to choose a third disinterested man, and said three men shall constitute a board of arbitration, and the decision of a majority of said three shall be final, and all parties shall abide thereby." This board is to meet within ten days after the difference arises.

No beer, whiskey or other intoxicating liquors shall be brought upon the property of the dock managers. No man in an intoxicated condition or under the influence of liquor shall be permitted upon the premises of the dock managers. Employes are not permitted to leave the dock during working hours without permission. Pure and fresh drinking water, with oatmeal and ice, shall be provided on the dock.

CIVIC FEDERATION OF BOSTON.

The initial organization of the Civic Federation of Boston and vicinity was effected at a meeting at the Exchange Club, when addresses were made by Major Henry L. Higginson, who presided; Rt. Rev. William Lawrence, P. Daniel Driscoll, Lucius Tuttle, Henry Abrahams, Charles H. Taylor, Jr., and Ralph M. Easley. There was a large attendance of men prominent in business, labor, public life and the professions. The following committee of eighteen upon permanent organization and membership was appointed:

For the Employers: Arthur T. Lyman, Amory A. Lawrence, Lucius Tuttle, Frederick P. Fish and W. C. Winslow.

For the Unions: Dennis D. Driscoll, President of the Boston Central Labor Union; Jeremiah J. Donovan, President of the Boston Building Trades Council; R. H. Bradford, President of the Structural Building Trades' Alliance; Henry Abrahams, Secretary of the Central Labor and Cigarmakers' Unions, and Frank K. Foster, of the Typographical Union.

For the Public: Right Rev. William Lawrence, Charles Francis Adams, Charles S. Hamlin, John Mason Little and Louis D. Brandeis.

Major Henry L. Higginson, Charles H. Taylor, Jr., and James R. Crozier, President of the State Branch American Federation of Labor, were added as ex-officio members representing the public, employers and unions, respectively.

Unionism should mean competency and honesty of purpose. Earn your salary and earn something for the man who is paying it. There is nothing that adds as much to the cause of unionism as an honest, fair workingman, and no one thing detracts so much as a loafer. Therefore make an effort to be a credit to your union and yourself as well.—Baltimore Labor Herald.

Those flamboyant and cock-sure men who were so certain that the Civic Federation would cease its work upon the death of Senator Hanna are now explaining. The federation met last week and a record of its proceedings shows that it is full of life and vigor and will go forward in its noble work with increased ardor.—United Mine Workers' Journal.

The trade agreement, therefore, is the result of the matching of forces, and follows after both sides have demonstrated their ability to inflict damage upon the other. Under such conditions the best results are obtainable, and conciliation and arbitration become effective.—Weekly Bulletin of Clothing Trades.

A wage agreement affords every possible opportunity for employers and employed to settle their own disputes in their own practical way.—Labor World, Pittsburg.

SAMUEL GOMPERS, First Vice-President. OSCAR S. STRAUS, Second Vice-President. HENRY PHIPPS, Chairman Exec. Committee. AUGUST BELMONT, Chairman Finance Committee. CORNELIUS N. BLISS, Treasurer.

NEW OFFICERS OF THE NATIONAL CIVIC FEDERATION.

THE SUCCESSOR TO PRESIDENT HANNA TO BE CHOSEN BY A COMMITTEE—REPORT OF THE CHAIRMAN OF THE EXECUTIVE COUNCIL.

The Executive Committee of the National Civic Federation held its semi-annual meeting in the Fifth Avenue Hotel, New York City, on May 6. Wide interest was manifested in this gathering, both because of the general expectation that it would elect a successor to the late president of the Federation, Marcus A. Hanna, and because of the growing appreciation by the public of the purposes of the organization. The proceedings of the Executive Committee included, besides its regular business, a general interchange of views among its members, which disclosed a mutual determination to continue and extend the work of the Federation, and a spirit of confidence that its successful progress is assured. This feeling was strengthened by the reports presented, showing a record of notable accomplishment. All of the officers of the Federation were elected, except a new president, whose selection was referred to a Nominating Committee. A feature of the meeting was memorial addresses by members of the Executive Committee who had been closely associated with the late Mr. Hanna in his work.

The meeting was called to order by Samuel Gompers, first vice-president of the National Civic Federation and president of the American Federation of Labor. Those present were: Cornelius N. Bliss (ex-Secretary of the Interior), New York City; Oscar S. Straus (member of the Court of Arbitration at The Hague), New York City; Isaac N. Seligman (of J. & W. Seligman & Co.), New York City; Archbishop John Ireland (of the Roman Catholic Church), St. Paul, Minn.; Bishop Henry C. Potter (of the Protestant Episcopal Church), New York City; James Speyer (of Speyer & Co.), New York; V. Everit Macy (capitalist), New York City; Ralph M. Easley (chairman Executive Council), New York City; Henry Phipps (director United States Steel Corporation), New York City; August Belmont (president Interborough Rapid Transit Co.), New York City; Frederick P. Fish (president American Bell Telephone Co.), Boston; Francis L. Robbins (president Pittsburg Coal Company), Pittsburg; Samuel Mather (of Pickands, Mather & Co.), Cleveland; Dan R. Hanna (of M. A. Hanna & Co.), Cleveland; Charles A. Moore (Manning, Maxwell & Moore), New York City; Franklin MacVeagh (of Franklin MacVeagh & Co.), Chicago; H. H. Vreeland (president New York City Railway Company), New York City; Otto M. Eidlitz (chairman Board of Governors, Building Trades Employers' Association), New York City; Marcus M. Marks (president National Association of Clothing Manufacturers), New York City; Charles H. Taylor, Jr. (president American Newspaper Publishers' Association), Boston; Samuel Gompers (president American Federation of Labor), Washington; John Mitchell (president United Mine Workers of America), Indianapolis; Rezin Orr (treasurer Amalgamated Association Street Railway Employes of America), Detroit, proxy for E. E. Clark (grand chief conductor, Order of Railway Conductors), Cedar Rapids, Iowa; Frank Buchanan (president International Association Bridge and Structural Iron Workers), Chicago, proxy for James Duncan (general secretary Granite Cutters' National Union), Washington; Daniel J. Keefe (president International Longshoremen, Marine and Transportworkers' Association), Detroit, Mich.; P. H. Morrissey (grand master Brotherhood Railroad Trainmen), Cleveland; William H. Farley (secretary Mosaic and Encaustic Tile Workers' Association of New York City), proxy for James O'Connell (president International Association of Machinists), Washington; John Tobin (general president Boot and Shoe Workers' Union), Boston; Thomas B. Lavey (Iron Molders' Conference Board of New York City), proxy for Joseph F. Valentine (president Iron Molders' Union of North America), Cincinnati; James M. Lynch (president International Typographical Union), Indianapolis; J. J. Hannahan (grand master Brotherhood of Locomotive Firemen), Peoria, Ill.; Henry White (general secretary United Garment Workers of America), New York City; William Launer (general secretary Glass Bottle Blowers' Association, United States and Canada), Philadelphia, proxy for Denis A. Hayes (president of the same association); J. P. Archibald (secretary Brotherhood of Painters, Decorators and Paper Hangers of New York City), proxy for William Huber (president United Brotherhood of Carpenters and Joiners of America), Indianapolis.

VICE-PRESIDENT GOMPERS' ADDRESS.

In calling the body to order Mr. Gompers said:

"This is the first time since my connection with the National Civic Federation, and with its industrial branch—and my connection has been of quite a long duration—that I have had the honor of calling the meeting to order. I cannot say that it is a pleasure, except in a qualified sense, for I should have much preferred that we all would have had the pleasure and the honor of being called to order by the former president of the National Civic Federation, the gentleman who is no longer with us, and who a very few weeks ago passed from the midst of us and of those who knew and loved him to the Great Beyond. One of the things in which I am deficient is in readiness to pronounce an eulogium upon the dead. Notwithstanding my great admiration for the man, and his great qualities of heart and mind, I yet find myself in a position to express inadequately thoughts that press upon my mind. I might say that it was my pleasure to have known our dear dead friend, Marcus A. Hanna, for a number of years. Even during those dark days when calumnies were heaped upon his head, his stout heart and his great mind were able to withstand them, and he lived at least to the time when calumny had receded, and nearly every one, if not every one, had begun to realize the higher qualities of which he was possessed in so eminent a form. He was a friend to organized labor, because he was convinced that through its agencies it would be the means of accomplishing better conditions and be helpful in bringing about more rightful relations between employer and employe; because he believed and was convinced that, notwithstanding all the calumny that is heaped upon organized labor, he, having gone through that crucial test, knew to a very large extent what one would suffer, and what men always suffer, by being misrepresented and misunderstood; and he realized that in the labor movement there were men in whom he could have unbounded faith and confidence to do for their fellows the best that was to be done. He was not a friend and advocate of organized labor because of a fad or a mere sentiment or a whim. It had grown upon him as a deep-seated conviction. He had, perhaps, as good relations established between himself as an employer and his workmen as employes as obtained in any industry in our country. He was of those who were pioneers among the employers not only to recognize, but to come to agreements with labor in its organized capacity. He has done much for his fellow-men. He has done much, especially in the line of work that he had chosen for himself. He did much to help give tone and character and standing, and to contribute in a large measure, to all the successes of the National Civic Federation. I know I but express the views of all those who knew him, and certainly of those who are associated with us here to-day, when I say that it is a matter of deep regret, and it is with a sense of deep loss, that we regard the death of our honored chairman, Marcus A. Hanna.

"In calling this meeting to order, may I ask whether it would meet the approval of the gentlemen present if we devote a little time to some expressions from some of the men who are here with us, and who I know would like to express their sense of regret at the loss we have sustained; and I therefore suggest that we devote a little while to what may be termed a 'memorial service' in honor of the memory of the late Marcus A. Hanna, our chairman.

"If there be no objection, I think we can proceed on that line."

Mr. Oscar S. Straus then arose to offer resolutions

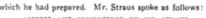

H. H. Vreeland, Chairman Welfare Department. Francis L. Robbins, Chairman Trade Agreement Com. John Mitchell, Chairman Trade Agreement Com. Ralph M. Easley, Chairman Executive Council. Samuel B. Donnelly, Secretary.

which he had prepared. Mr. Straus spoke as follows:

ADDRESS AND RESOLUTIONS BY MR. STRAUS.

"This occasion fills me with sadness, as it does all of you here who have been colleagues of our chairman in this work. Two and a half years ago, when we assembled in this city for the purpose of organizing the National Civic Federation, Senator Hanna was deeply engrossed in the work of national legislation; but he regarded this work which we were about to undertake of such transcendent importance, and his heart was so deeply interested, that he gave an expression of his views, briefly, to the press. I desire to recall to the memory and recollection of you, his colleagues in this work, the sentiments he expressed on that occasion:

"'I would rather have the credit of making successful the movement to bring labor and capital into closer relations of confidence and reliance than be President of the United States. If by resigning my seat in the United States Senate I could bring to fruition the plans that we are now fostering to make strikes, lockouts and great labor disputes impossible, I would gladly do so. I think it is the grandest thing that could be accomplished in this country. I would want no greater monument than to have the world remember that I did something to end wars between American labor and American capital.'

"It was my privilege on that occasion to introduce him, with these sentiments from his own lips, and I will extend my statement by reading from the opening of his speech on that occasion:

"'Gentlemen, these are my sentiments. They came from the heart, and they came after a long experience in the industrial world and almost daily contact with labor since I have been a man of business. . . . To say that I am interested is to put it very mildly, and although I did not intend that that sentiment should have the publicity that your president has given it—and, perhaps, it may have seemed a little egotistical to have mentioned it in that connection—I reaffirm the sentiment by the statement that I stand ready and willing and anxious to give the best that is in me while life remains to accomplish this purpose.'

"Mr. Chairman, I have the honor to introduce resolutions which but inadequately express the sentiments of my heart and the great loss that we have sustained:

"An all-wise Providence has called from the activities of this world Marcus A. Hanna, who was president of the National Civic Federation since December, 1901. His lamented death was a personal bereavement to us, his colleagues in this body, and the removal of a strong and earnest leader in its work; therefore, be it

"Resolved, That the National Civic Federation mourns the departure of a member who, as its official head, through his untiring energy, conspicuous ability and conscientious devotion, conveyed to the public mind the message of mutual confidence and respect, of equity and co-operation, in the relations between labor and capital; who had chosen the promotion of that purpose as the crowning work of his life, ranking it above all other ambitions, and with steadily increasing conviction regarding a share in its accomplishment as the most patriotic service he could render his country, and the most philanthropic legacy he could bequeath to humanity; whose training in business and whose knowledge of public affairs had endowed him with peculiar fitness to carry forward the work of this organization, through his intimate relations with both employer and employed; whose quality of sincerity conveyed the irresistible conviction of the profound and lofty motive that inspired his zealous devotion to the high purpose of the Federation;

"Resolved, That his associates and fellow workers here record their sincere appreciation of the far-seeing and kindly sagacity, the rare and discerning judgment and the brilliant and earnest leadership displayed by Mr. Hanna as the president of the National Civic Federation;

"Resolved, That we, in the knowledge of the consecration of head and heart by our late president to a work that implied incessant appeals to both reason and sympathy, hereby pledge our continued and loyal devotion to the great cause which his intelligent perception and humane personality were forceful in forwarding;

"Resolved, That these resolutions be spread upon the record of the Federation, and that an engrossed copy, signed by its officers, be sent to the family of Mr. Hanna."

REMARKS BY BISHOP POTTER.

The Rt. Rev. Henry C. Potter, of the diocese of New York, in seconding the resolutions, suggested a slight verbal change, which Mr. Straus accepted, so that the resolutions, as adopted, read as they appear above. Bishop Potter expanded his suggestion in these words:

"I wish to bring out the interesting development in his own mind, of a sense of the enormous importance and significance of the effort in which we are all concerned. I hope I shall not touch any of our political friends here; but there are two classes of gentlemen—one we call politicians, the other statesmen. Politicians are particularly interested in results. A statesman is a man who has the quality of vision; and that is the quality which we recognized in Mr. Gladstone, a distinct perception of great movements, great tendencies, and what they have meant, what they stood for. I cannot pretend that I was very enthusiastic when Mr. Hanna was elected chairman of this Federation. I had chiefly associated him with political processes, the friendships and intimacies which represented the former of the two classes I have just referred to. But what did impress me in his service as presiding officer of this body was not only his large equity, his sense of fairness, which was a very fine note of his nature, but there seemed to grow in his mind day by day a larger sense of the enormous value and gravity of the questions in which we are here concerned. They are questions which touch the whole foundations of human society, and the equities of which involve the relations of every man with every other man. And Mr. Hanna seemed to me to realize increasingly the great responsibility of his office and the enormous possibility of service and sacrifice that his calling as chairman of this Federation placed upon him. But he rose, step by step, to the possession of those finer qualities which so greatly endeared him to all of us. I learned to have a profound respect for his views and his rare sense of that which the movement really meant."

MR. MITCHELL SPEAKS FOR LABOR.

Mr. John Mitchell spoke as follows:

"I am sure I can but inadequately express the general sentiment of the laboring people of this country in saying that the loss of Senator Hanna brought to the working people a real sense of regret. My own personal relations with Senator Hanna were such that I knew him well. I knew his feelings well. I knew that he was sincere in this movement. I think no greater tribute could be paid to a man than the action of the coal miners in this country—400,000 of them—when on the day of his burial they stopped work and stayed away from the mines—laid aside their picks and shovels to do honor to the memory of him whom they believed to be their friend. I feel that his death is a distinct loss to this movement, a well nigh irreparable loss. He thought more of this movement than any other one thing in which he was engaged. I know that to be true. He has not only made the public statement to that effect, but he has told me on more than one occasion that he would rather be helpful in establishing rightful and proper relationships between capital and labor than be President of the United States. I don't know, Mr. Chairman, if there is anything further I can say. I feel that Senator Hanna has done his full share, not only in this movement, but in all his own relations with employes, to establish an ideal relationship between them."

CHARLES A. MOORE'S CHARACTERIZATION.

Charles A. Moore delivered the following tribute:

"I think the remarks made by Bishop Potter very clearly and nicely express the feeling that might be termed the general feeling throughout the country when our distinguished president and friend, Senator Hanna, was selected to preside over this important organization. Perhaps it is human nature to find fault; I don't call it criticism; but you found them saying that this selection was for political purposes. I know of no man who could have been selected for this very responsible and important position, who had to contend, personally and in the public mind, with greater obstacles to establish himself, as was necessary, in the confidence of all, than our recent president and departed friend. He was an aggressive man, a man of affairs, a man of great courage, who believed when he wanted to accomplish a purpose in the business of politics that he should go right to it, directly. He was essentially a direct man. I think that was one trait of character that he possessed to a degree that was remarkable and made him most successful. His diplomacy was what you might term a

'Hanna diplomacy.' It was not roundabout or subterranean—it was direct. He won the confidence of men. His manner was that of a man; and all the essential qualities we look for in the full grown, upright, forceful man he had to a wonderful degree. He had the wonderful gift of dealing with men in different walks of life from his own, with different ideas, and yet he could express his individual ideas frankly and directly and not offend those men. He had that quality to a marvellous degree. I think that, taking him as we see him now, under the present light of our organization, the results accomplished, it is doubtful if any man could have filled that place with all the qualities of mind and heart necessary to fill it to a successful termination as he did.

"Men believed in Marcus A. Hanna, and that was one great quality. He could make his fellow man believe he was honest; and unless he was honest he could not make him believe it. I do not know a man who ever made greater personal sacrifices. As he grew in this work I may plainly say that Senator Hanna grew to his job; and he did it because he consecrated himself to his work. I think that one of the most beautiful traits a man can develop is when, undertaking a work like this, he grows to fill it better than his best wishers expected him to do. Certainly, Senator Hanna filled this place even better than his most intimate friends thought him capable of doing. He has contributed much to the strength of this organization. He has helped to strip it of those ideas that are antagonistic to our work. He had to school himself, and he had to grow to his job; and he did it in a highly magnificent manner, that all are ready to recognize. Even those who differed with Mr. Hanna most positively learned to respect him for the evidences of his honesty and the sincerity of his work. I feel that we were all greatly favored in having known him—those who knew him in connection with this work and those who knew him in his lifework. He believed in good citizenship, integrity and honesty of purpose, and I never knew him in all his political work to suggest the doing of anything in an underhand, undignified manner. He went direct to the point. Confidence is a plant of slow growth, yet he had it almost entirely with the national leaders of labor. He had it with capital, and in a high degree with the public. As Bishop Potter has well expressed it, there were some who had their little doubts that there was some ulterior purpose in his taking the chairmanship of this organization, but he was able to dispel that, and get the confidence of the three groups; and without that his work would have been wasted. And he had that confidence to a marvellous degree. I am proud to have been a friend of and to have known Senator Hanna."

TRIBUTE OF CORNELIUS N. BLISS.

Cornelius N. Bliss, with evidence of emotion, uttered this personal appreciation:

"My relations with Senator Hanna have existed for many years. It was not here that I first met him. Perhaps it was owing to his influence, and because of his approval and desire, that I first became connected with this association, in which I am proud to have had this experience. My first acquaintance with Senator Hanna was many years ago, perhaps fifteen or more, and our relations have been exceedingly intimate. They were relations literally quite as intimate as any family relations. I not only admired him, but I had respect and affection for him, not only in his business relations, but in his relations here, and especially in his hospitable home and family relations. It is a matter of much regret to have been parted from him at this time, in the midst of his usefulness, and while he was rendering great service to the country. His services were appreciated by the great mass of the people throughout the country, as they were evident to us, his friends. Those who stood by his remains at the time of his funeral in Washington, and those who followed on to Cleveland, know the outpouring of sympathy and love that was expressed for him by those who surrounded him. I am grateful to him for having brought me into this work. Perhaps I have not done the work I might have done, but his example, influence and desire have led me to devote myself to it, so far as it is in my power to assist. I refer largely in my remarks to the personal, intimate, close relations to our departed friend."

D. J. KEEFE'S REMINISCENCE.

Mr. D. J. Keefe spoke as follows:

"Senator Hanna was what might be termed a 'big brother' to the longshoremen. Whenever there was a difference or misunderstanding between the employers and our association and we could not adjust it ourselves, we always called on him, and he never failed to bring about an amicable understanding. I can say without fear of contradiction that his attitude toward organized labor was friendly, for whenever it was possible for him to assist in any way he cheerfully did so.

"His death will be a great loss to humanity in general, and the loss to America cannot be calculated. He was a man whose efforts were untiring to make a better world, and in this he was a success, for he certainly accomplished much, as the future will demonstrate. Others will take up the work where he left off. His strength of character was ably demonstrated in his charity of speech and sentiment when speaking of the authors of the many vile cartoons in the past two Presidential campaigns.

"Lincoln emancipated the colored men, and had Senator Hanna lived he would have done relatively more for all the toilers—he would have accomplished the solution of the problem of capital and labor, and would have taught the employer and employe alike to do unto others as they would be done by. He certainly made the world better by his having lived in it, and his name will go down to posterity as an apostle of the common people.

"Organized labor has suffered a great loss, and from thousands of the wage workers' homes a fervent prayer will go up to God to have mercy upon their true friend and benefactor. He, like Lincoln, needs no marble pile to perpetuate his name—it will always be reverenced by the masses for his great deeds and untiring efforts."

The resolutions offered by Mr. Straus were adopted unanimously by a rising vote.

The minutes of the last meeting of the executive committee were approved. Mr. Easley read his report as chairman of the executive council, which, on motion of Mr. Macy, was approved and ordered published.

Mr. Easley's report follows:

THE FEDERATION AND ITS WORK.

"When the National Civic Federation was organized the scoffers at its undertaking were not altogether alone. Even some well-wishers of the movement had misgivings as to its practical value. They felt that as soon as the novelty should wear off it would be impossible to hold the interest of its members and of the public; and that the general proposition to try to bring about a better relation between capital and labor was a beautiful sentiment, but not practical. When, in answer to that, it was pointed out that the imposing array of names on the executive committee included those of large practical employers, public-spirited men and hard-headed labor leaders, it was said: 'Yes, but wait until you have tried your beautiful machine; wait until the labor leaders find out that they cannot win in every controversy that you have to deal with, and they will turn against you; wait until the employers find that they have to grant higher wages in settlement of disturbances that you have to deal with, and they will quit you.' Well, we have waited and gone through all that. We have had three and a half years of it. We have gone through the sentimental period, when everything was coming our way, so to speak; we have gone through the trying period of defeat, when everything was going the other way—the anthracite coal strike, for instance. We have, too, lost our great leader, the one who marshalled us night and day, under all circumstances, in time of defeat as well as victory, and yet we are to-day stronger as a movement than ever before. The early suspicions of organized labor have been allayed. The larger and more representative interests of capital have found that we are not a set of meddlers, but are seeking through conservative and educational methods to bring about more rightful relations between employers and employes; and that our movement is a practical effort to work out the great so-called 'labor problem' through evolutionary, rather than revolutionary, methods.

"These elements of difficulty or discouragement have been dissipated. They never were organized. But there have sprung up during the past year several employers' associations whose war cry is: 'Smash the unions,' 'Down with arbitration,' 'Beware of the National Civic Federation.'

"For example, we receive the following tribute from an officer of the Citizens' Industrial Association of America:

> A moment's consideration of the inestimable benefits resulting from organization in Chicago should convince the most skeptical. The Employers' Association of that labor plague spot of the world is fast redeeming the city and delivering its people from the bondage of organized labor; not by continuing the policy of organized labor's colleague, the National Civic Federation, which is the greatest menace to industrial peace now in existence, but by demanding a recognition of the constitutional rights of the citizen and then appealing to public sentiment through and by organization.

"Again, we have the deliberately chosen words of the president of the same association in plain opposition to both conciliation and arbitration:

> To my mind, this is not the proper time to talk conciliation. . . . Conciliation implies a yielding attitude and a recognition of the validity of destructive demands made by the opposing side. Since the principles and demands of organized labor are absolutely untenable to those believing in the individualistic social order, an attitude of conciliation would mean an attitude of compromise with regard to fundamental convictions. . . . Neither is it the time to talk arbitration or "joint agreements." To arbitrate questions of wages and hours is to introduce artificial methods of determining what they shall be, and an equitable arrangement as to either cannot be effected artificially.

"The first of these quotations is an overt effort to misrepresent the attitude of the Civic Federation by distorting its avowed friendship for organized labor as sympathy with the violence or disorder which, whenever and wherever they appear, are the most dangerous foes of the true interests of wage earners. The second quotation is a defiant and dogmatic rejection of methods of improving the relations between employer and employed that have been vindicated by their successful operation in practice.

"Socialism is another organized opponent to the work of peace and co-operation of the Civic Federation. It is to be noted that generally violence, in word or deed, when manifested in any labor union, is a symptom of the insidious invasion of the bacilli of socialism. To gain control and direction of organized labor the agents of socialism are putting forth every exertion. Socialists are opposed to the orderly and law-abiding elements that now direct, as a rule, the policy and control the action of labor organizations. Socialism recognizes in the National Civic Federation an ally of the self-respecting, self-restrained workingman. Therefore socialism foams at the mouth at the mention of the Federation. Thus, on May day in Chicago, Eugene V. Debs, its acknowledged national leader, flaunts this verbal red flag:

> Socialists in unions were rare exceptions a few years ago; to-day they have been multiplied by thousands. The time is not far when the socialists will be in the majority in the trades unions, and they will rescue the uinon movement from the withering hand of the leaders who dominate it, and from the blighting control of the Civic Federation, which has entered into an unholy alliance—the slaughterers of the laborer and those leaders in joint conspiracy against the union man.

"The methods of socialism are frequently masked. Sometimes the mask is torn off. This happened in the correspondence, made public in a report of the British Columbia Labor Commission, which includes written instructions from the president of the United Brotherhood of Railway Employes to his organizer, whose mission was to promote a strike by the employes of the Canadian Pacific Railway. One of these letters contains the following passage:

> In all your writings, carefully word your articles so as to develop a public sentiment for the U. B. R. E., the A. L. U. [the American Labor Union, a socialist labor organization, formed principally to fight the American Federation of Labor], and against the reactionary and capitalistic party now temporarily in control of the A. F. of L., but not against the masses of members comprising the A. F. of L. Continually separate the administration of the A. F. of L. from the A. F. of L. itself, and give all possible praise to the masses of the A. F. of L., but

Continued on Page 12.

MONTHLY REVIEW
OF THE
National Civic Federation

Offices: 281 Fourth Avenue, New York
Telephone, 389 Gramercy
RALPH M. EASLEY, Editor

Vol. I. New York, June, 1904 No. 4.
Ten Cents per Copy; One Dollar per Year.

The National Civic Federation

281 Fourth Avenue, New York City

EXECUTIVE COMMITTEE.

ON THE PART OF THE PUBLIC.

Grover Cleveland, ex-President of the United States, Princeton, N. J.

Andrew Carnegie, capitalist, New York.

Cornelius N. Bliss, ex-Secretary of the Interior, New York City.

Oscar S. Straus, member of the Court of Arbitration at The Hague, New York City.

Charles W. Eliot, President Harvard University, Cambridge, Mass.

Archbishop John Ireland, of the Roman Catholic Church, St. Paul, Minn.

Bishop Henry C. Potter, of the Protestant Episcopal Church, New York City.

David R. Francis, President Louisiana Purchase Exposition, St. Louis, Mo.

Isaac N. Seligman, of J. & W. Seligman & Co., New York City.

James Speyer, of Speyer & Co., New York.

Charles Francis Adams, Publicist, Boston.

John G. Milburn, lawyer, New York City.

V. Everit Macy, capitalist, New York City.

Charles J. Bonaparte, lawyer, Baltimore.

Ralph M. Easley, Chairman Executive Council, New York City.

ON THE PART OF EMPLOYERS.

Henry Phipps, director United States Steel Corporation, New York City.

August Belmont, President Interborough Rapid Transit Company, New York City.

Lucius Tuttle, President Boston & Maine Railroad, Boston.

Frederick P. Fish, President American Bell Telephone Company, Boston.

Francis L. Robbins, President Pittsburgh Coal Company, Pittsburgh.

H. H. Vreeland, President New York City Railway Company, New York City.

Samuel Mather, of Pickands, Mather & Co., Cleveland.

Charles A. Moore, Manning, Maxwell & Moore, New York City.

Franklin MacVeagh, of Franklin MacVeagh & Co., Chicago.

Charles H. Taylor, Jr., President American Newspaper Publishers' Association, Boston.

Dan R. Hanna, of M. A. Hanna & Co., Cleveland.

Marcus M. Marks, President National Association of Clothing Manufacturers, New York City.

Otto M. Eidlitz, Chairman Board of Governors, Building Trades Employers' Association, New York City.

Edward P. Ripley, President Atchison, Topeka & Santa Fe Railway System, Chicago.

William H. Pfahler, former President National Founders' Association, Philadelphia.

ON THE PART OF WAGE EARNERS.

Samuel Gompers, President American Federation of Labor, Washington.

John Mitchell, President United Mine Workers of America, Indianapolis.

E. E. Clark, Grand Chief Conductor, Order of Railway Conductors, Cedar Rapids, Iowa.

James Duncan, General Secretary Granite Cutters' National Union, Washington.

Daniel J. Keefe, President International Longshoremen, Marine and Transportworkers' Association, Detroit, Mich.

P. H. Morrissey, Grand Master, Brotherhood Railroad Trainmen, Cleveland.

Theodore J. Shaffer, President Amalgamated Association of Iron, Steel and Tin Workers, Pittsburgh.

J. J. Hannahan, Grand Master Brotherhood of Locomotive Firemen, Peoria, Ill.

James O'Connell, President International Association of Machinists, Washington.

John Tobin, General President Boot and Shoe Workers' Union, Boston.

Joseph F. Valentine, President Iron Moulders' Union of North America, Cincinnati.

James M. Lynch, President International Typographical Union, Indianapolis.

William D. Mahon, President Amalgamated Association of Street Railway Employes of America, Detroit, Mich.

Henry White, General Secretary United Garment Workers of America, New York City.

Denis A. Hayes, President Glass Bottle Blowers' Association of United States and Canada, Philadelphia.

William Huber, President United Brotherhood of Carpenters and Joiners of America, Indianapolis.

VICTORIES FOR TRADE AGREEMENTS.

A large part of this number of THE REVIEW is devoted to a presentation of recent impressive events in the actual operation of trade agreements. The space allotted to this subject is warranted by the magnitude and significance of these events. The three agreements that stand out most prominently in recent industrial history are those between the bituminous operators and the organized miners in four States; between the Amalgamated Association of Tin and Iron Workers and the employers, and between the Longshoremen's Union and the Dock Managers' Association of the Great Lakes. The conspicuous facts about these three agreements are that they have been continued after open and candid discussion in mutual conference, and that at least two of them have withstood the test of acceptance of reductions of wages by the workers' organizations. Especially gratifying and important to the business interests of the entire country has been the prevention of a bituminous coal strike, through the reaching of a thorough understanding of trade conditions, attained at the conference at Indianapolis between representatives of the miners and of the operators, some of whose most remarkable utterances we commend to the thoughtful appreciation of our readers.

This interstate bituminous conference with its outcome is the most momentous industrial event of the year. There was a period when a strike seemed inevitable. A general bituminous coal strike would mean literal paralysis of the manufacturing industries and carrying machinery of the continent. The country had suffered much from the anthracite strike. A bituminous strike would have been an immensely greater disaster. It was the lamented Marcus A. Hanna, then president of the National Civic Federation, who declared, realizing the enormous gravity of the situation, "Every possible effort must be put forth to prevent a strike." Every effort was made. All of them were concentrated in the Indianapolis conference, where Francis A. Robbins and John Mitchell were the leading champions of the two sides, although they were aided by strong and resourceful lieutenants. The discussion carried conviction to the leaders of the miners' cause that a reduction of wages was justly required by the market prices of coal. Simultaneously, it convinced the representatives of the operators of the fairness of certain propositions, including the cost of living, upon the side of the workers, which led them to recede from their original demand. Then was presented the remarkable spectacle of labor delegates to this conference, who had been bound by instructions to vote at Indianapolis against the compromise, appealing successfully to their constituents for its ratification.

These events gave active interest to the proceedings of a conference upon trade agreements, held in New York City on May 7, under the auspices of the National Civic Federation. The discussion at that conference was highly animated and instructive, and a verbatim report will appear in the next number of THE REVIEW.

Experience has proved the efficacy of the trade agreement as a way to avoid industrial strife. Discussion bids fair to promote its better understanding and its wider use.

The benefit of full and frank conference receives signal illustration in the renewal of the trade agreement for another year between the Molders' Union and the stove manufacturers. Their association demanded a reduction of 15 per cent in wages, upon the ground that market prices for their products had fallen, and would go lower. There was also a question at issue as to the ratio of apprentices. Both of these questions were discussed with the utmost freedom and candor in a conference at Chicago that lasted five days. The decision was to maintain the present rate of wages. This result was reached largely because the representatives of the molders were able to prove their contention that the cost of living had increased. As one of the manufacturers, Mr. Kahn, put it, "We are very much in the position of a married couple, and it is our business to get along in peace, for weal or woe." It is an interesting fact that several of the speakers at this conference attributed the higher prices of commodities for the household to the Russo-Japanese war. An amicable agreement as to apprentices, pronounced fair to both foundrymen and molders, was also reached. The *Iron Molders' Journal* attributes this outcome to the observance on both sides of "fair dealing as a cardinal principle," without "wrangling over petty technicalities," and predicts a continuance of the harmony that has prevailed in this trade during fourteen years.

AN EXHORTATION TO EMPLOYERS.

The day and the hour are here when the employer can display, to his own advantage and to the country's good, a spirit of reasonable liberality in his attitude toward the payment of the employed. The record of lower market prices, decreasing consumption of products, lighter transportation, reduced wages and economies in the number of workmen employed in improvements, enlargements or in new construction, testifies that the industries of the country, broadly speaking, have slackened in activity, and that commercial conditions are upon a lower level than they occupied during a time of some inflation, though not without the real substance of genuine prosperity. It is legitimate to hope that this condition will prove to be only a passing relaxation of the tense strain that commanded, in the stress of profitable production, the total sum of the combined energies of capital and labor. But the actual situation cannot be bettered by glossing the truth. It is both braver and more sensible to face the facts of the present as they are.

This industrial condition opens to employers an opportunity that should be seized for conservatism in their treatment of wages. It is a time when they may wisely refrain from taking undue advantage of a situation that may temporarily place it within their power to act selfishly and graspingly. When two jobs await every man able and willing to work, the condition invites demands for higher wages. When two men await every job, the reaction favors the enforcement of lower wages. The former case offers the opportunity for labor, whether organized or not, to refrain from excessive demands, with a sane eye to its future. The second case presents to employers, whether organized or individual, the opportunity to exercise discreet liberality and to call into play consideration and foresight that may avoid present resentment and forestall future reprisal. A prominent railway president recently uttered this economic truth: "The cost of maintaining an artificial market is greater than the profit." So, too, the profit of artificially depressing wages is less than the ultimate cost.

The time is peculiarly favorable for the exercise of self-restraint by employers in compelling wage reductions. Conservative leaders of the unions have shown upon their part a growing spirit of reasonableness and a wholesome inclination to fair dealing. The movement for conciliation, for harmonious relations, for industrial peace, has gained breadth and strength, because of this prevalent spirit of its leaders, throughout the ranks of organized labor. There is no doubt that the manifestation of this spirit has had its moderating effect upon the general attitude of public opinion toward the unions. These are influences that work for the common weal. They are impalpable, but nevertheless real assets in the total public welfare. They are elements that, properly encouraged and nourished, will become factors powerful among all the others that count for a return of the flood tide of industrial activity and commercial prosperity.

The employer who realizes this situation and

tempers his treatment of the employed with a measure of discretion in enforcing economies, and perhaps with an explanation of their necessity when they are imperative, will not only strengthen his individual position, but will contribute to the benefit, in the long run, of his entire industry and to the harmony that is essential to national health. It is a time to keep in mind the truth that the natural law of supply and demand should be modified in its operation between human beings by a due regard for the burdens that are made heavier by every decrease in the earnings of toil. This higher motive is re-enforced by the fact that reasonable altruism has one of its roots in selfishness. That is, broadly speaking, generosity, like honesty, is the best policy.

THE OPEN SHOP DEBATE.

There is an apparent tendency in the minds of some writers to regard the question of the "open" versus the "closed" shop as one of irreconcilable conflict. The issue has been depicted recently as one that will precipitate a series of battles that must culminate in a social revolution, whose outcome must be either anarchy or the extreme of paternalism, through governmental regulation of all trade agreements. Some alarmists depict the situation as beyond amelioration and as approaching rapidly a hostile alignment of forces whose clash must disturb and distress the national life, or even threaten its very existence.

The extremists upon either side, it is our judgment, are making too much clamor about imaginary perils that underlie the agitation of this question. No possible harm can be done by the freest and fullest debate of the open and closed shop. On the contrary, much good may be done by awakening public interest to an intelligent perception of the opposing arguments. But much harm may be done if alarmists, whether merely the victims of their own imaginary fears, or unduly impressed by a false estimate of the strength and arbitrary purpose of recently formed employers' associations, or moved by the socialistic and mischievous desire to stir up strife, are allowed to present unchallenged and uncorrected their distorted view of the case.

Those who profess to be able to see only fierce and relentless war in the growth of unions on the one side and of associated employers on the other, ignore the power of organized forces to establish stable conditions of peace based upon mutual responsibility, joined with mutual good faith in fulfilling obligations. The agitators dwell exclusively upon the "rights" of one side and of the other. They make a din of proclaiming "the legal and moral right" of the employer to discharge and to hire men without regard to the unions. They shout aloud that the non-unionist has "the legal and moral right" to sell his labor for whatever he can get, regardless of the union scale. They reach the crescendo of defiance in declaring that employers will never, never yield the "right to run their own business," and conversely they raise the battle-cry that the unions must resist to the death the open shop as an insidious menace to their existence.

It were well if there were less sound and fury about the "rights" of employer and employed, and more consideration of their equal capacity to realize their duty to each other and to the entire social fabric. Opposition of their interests, however highly organized upon both sides, does not necessarily mean combat without quarter. There is no occasion to fear the lining up of the two forces for a frank comparison of their positions. In such case the agitators will be left to do the fighting with words, while the calm common sense of both sides will discern the way to peace with both honor and profit. Actual experience has proved this to be true. "Defense" is a militant word. It implies hostility. It means forcible resistance to forcible aggression. Yet the Defense Association of Stove Manufacturers, formed for war, has in practice been converted into an association for the working out of pacific relations with the molders' unions and of stable trade conditions. That is only one example of how a warlike title has been compelled by the force of mutual interest to acquire a significance of actual friendliness. In this case, also, the open shop has proved not to mean, where it exists, the destruction of the union. Nor has the unionization of foundries made it impossible for the employers to continue to exercise their "right to run their own business."

There is a great deal of human nature in this particular question of open or closed shop. The personal equation is a highly important factor in the problem. The pessimists and those eager for fray would make it an intensely inflamed factor as well. When an employer demands an open shop as one of his "rights" and announces at the same time that with the open shop he will smash the union, it can hardly be expected that the union will tamely submit. When the closed shop means the control of a business by the union, leaving the employer only to pay the bills Saturday night, no one can blame the employer for determining to smash the union. Put either side in a position where it must fight for its life, and it will fight. But that extreme position is unnecessary. Exclusive contracts are practicable. Suppose a union agent to say: "Mr. Employer, we want a contract with you to do your work. You want your work well done. We don't object to working with non-union men, but an exclusive contract with us would make us able to discipline and control our men so that we can carry out our agreement and we can guarantee you better work." Is not that a proposal on a business basis? This is done every day without an outcry about abridged liberty in the building trades. Smith lets a contract for a house. The contractor hires all the men. Smith neither knows nor cares about their creed or their affiliations or lack of affiliations.

The truth is that no sensible person desires to destroy any of the "rights" of which we hear so much talk. Nor should any person desire to exercise individual rights without regard to the rights of others. The rights of indivduals and the rights of communities have been rubbing against each other throughout all the evolution of civilized society. Neither class of rights has been destroyed in that friction. Similarly, there may be an adjustment, through patience, tact and forbearance, of the right of the employer to make an exclusive contract with the union, and of the right of the non-union man to determine for himself whether he shall belong to a union or not, and to work without molestation wherever employed. Rights may be inalienable and yet reconcilable. The forces for their adjustment are mightier by far than are the forces that would create conflict and compel the inconceivable enthrallment of either labor or capital.

JOHN MITCHELL ON STRIKES AND LOCKOUTS.

Newspaper reports of an address delivered by Mr. John Mitchell at the conference upon trade agreements, held in New York City on May 6, under the auspices of the National Civic Federation, have misrepresented, unintentionally, of course, an attitude of the President of the United Mine Workers. The published reports made him appear as preferring strikes and lockouts to arbitration. In order to set right both Mr. Mitchell and newspaper comment, it is well to quote here an extract from a stenographic report of Mr. Mitchell's remarks:

"I say that neither side should surrender its right to strike or lock out. Failing in every other method to settle their differences, they [the workers] should always maintain the right to strike, or the employers the right to lock out their men. If they were to surrender absolutely those rights, then the chances are that the conditions of employment would be satisfactory neither to the men nor to the employers.

"My own judgment is that in preference to a strike we should resort to arbitration. There are questions I would not arbitrate at all. I would not arbitrate, under any conditions, my right to belong to a union. . . . You can't arbitrate fundamental principles. . . . As I said before, I favor settlement of it by agreement, and only arbitration in the event of failure to agree, and then in preference to strike."

This correct quotation places Mr. Mitchell in a position altogether different from favoring the strike and the lockout. He would rank them as last resorts. He would preserve the ultimate right to fight, because he regards that right as essential to the power to make treaties of peace. An alliance between two disarmed forces would be shorn of significance.

LABOR UNIONS AND GOVERNMENT.

A recent editorial in the New York Times contains several mis-statements of fact and wrong inferences, both in extracts from a speech delivered by Mr. Kirby, of the National Industrial Alliance, upon industrial conditions in Australia and New Zealand, and in comments upon his remarks. Mr. Kirby dwells at length upon the disastrous results of trade union legislation and compulsory arbitration in those colonies. Even from the standpoint of an organization that advocates the policy of "smashing" the unions, Mr. Kirby's inferences are erroneous; for the trade union control in Australia and New Zealand has been brought about, not through the union methods obtaining in the United States, but through partisan organization of the unions, which the American Federation of Labor earnestly opposes.

The unions in Australia and New Zealand were disastrously defeated in a general strike in 1891. To bring about that defeat the powers of the government were employed. As a consequence, the colonial unions abandoned the non-partisan tactics of trade unionism, which are maintained in this country, and directed their attention to organizing a political labor party. That party eventually gained control of the government in both these colonies. Whatever evil results may have followed have, therefore, come about, not through voluntary negotiation with employers, but through control of the legislatures and administrations by the labor vote. The policy of the "smashing" associations of employers, for whom Mr. Kirby speaks, if successful, would invite a similar change of policy on the part of the unions in the United States. Is that what the "smashing" employers' organizations desire? The unions in the United States have not organized a labor party to capture the State and Federal governments, but have operated along the lines of negotiation, conciliation and trade agreements, meeting the employers upon equal terms. Only when thoroughly convinced that employers will refuse to continue in these lines would the unions turn to partisan action here, in the manner forced upon the unions in Australia and New Zealand.

That the unions in Great Britain, because of the engineering strike and lockout in 1897, have met with overwhelming defeat, looking to the disintegration of the whole labor movement, is a most surprising mis-statement of the actual situation. The unions in the British shipbuilding industry, to which reference is particularly made, are to-day much stronger than ever before, and the principal union in that industry, the Boilermakers', took no part in the strike of

1897. The Amalgamated Society of Engineers, which was defeated in 1897, has entirely recovered its ground, and through a general arbitration and joint conference board is taking up subjects of dispute and reaching agreements with the federation of employers, through methods of conciliation.

The statement that "it has been declared illegal to strike against the employment of non-union men, or to demand the discharge of a man because he does not belong to a labor organization," is exactly the opposite to the fact in the English situation. The highest court in England, in the case of Allen vs. Flood, has held that a labor union not only has the right to strike, but the right to threaten to strike, against the employment of a non-union man. This decision in effect upholds the legality of the closed shop.

A REVIVED FALLACY QUASHED.

When a union demand for the closed shop in some industry is advanced, there is likely to reappear the familiar assertion that only 15 per cent. of the wage earners of the country are organized in trade unions. This statement is the premise of an argument that it would be monstrous tyranny for so small a proportion of workers to exclude from employment 85 per cent. of those who earn their livelihood by toil. Assuming, for the sake of discussion, that these figures are approximately correct, the argument is shattered in its application. It is only where a union has established a real ascendancy in a given trade that it can raise, with any hope of success, the issue of the closed shop. The alleged 85 per cent. of wage earners outside the unions are mainly in occupations in which there are no unions at all, or in which the unions are too weak to think of challenging a contest over the employment of workers outside their organizations.

The Chicago Tribune, in a recent editorial, states the case thus pithily:

"Suppose that the Plumbers' Union, controlling almost the entire plumbing trade, demands the exclusive employment of union plumbers. What species of argument is it to reply that the agricultural laborers are still wandering beyond the limits of the trade union fold? Suppose that the glass blowers, finding that here and there a non-union glass blower continues to escape the payment of union dues, refuse to allow the 'traitor' to work beside them. Will they be deterred by an enumeration of the washerwomen over whom trade unionism has not yet spread its shield?"

It seems to be necessary again and again to expose the fallacy of the much-quoted 85 per cent. of unorganized labor as a proof of union tyranny in the crafts where the movement for the closed shop is strongly supported. This is a singular example of the persistent fascination of a battered illusion.

The importance of maintaining a high standard of personnel in union representation and membership is emphasized by President Frank Buchanan, of the International Association of Bridge and Structural Iron Workers. We quote President Buchanan's official counsel, addressed to the local unions of New York: "Select men on their merits to represent you and see that the unions dictate to them instead of letting them dictate to the unions. Our associations should keep agreements inviolate. A fair agreement means a fair day's pay for a fair day's work. The men who are trying to use the unions to hold their jobs when they are unwilling to do a fair day's work in a workmanlike manner are enemies to the principles that trade unionism is founded upon, and an organization that will permit its strength to be used for such purposes will come to grief in the end."

There is a sermon in this message worth the attention of every union in the land.

There has been a noteworthy instance of the voluntary discipline in Chicago of a member of a union for "slugging" a non-union worker. The discipline, in the form of a fine of $20, was inflicted upon David Bergquist, a member of the Carriage and Wagonmakers' Union, for beating Harry T. Stevens, a fellow employe, for not joining the union, although that union has an open shop agreement with the Carriage and Wagon Makers' Association. Besides inflicting the fine, four members of the union testified before a magistrate against Bergquist, who was placed under $500 bonds to keep the peace. This is hailed as an indication of wholesome assertiveness by the conservative element in the local unions.

A STREET RAILWAY ARBITRATION.

The Finding of Oscar S. Straus as to the Differences Between the United Railroads of San Francisco and Their Employes.

The recent settlement of difficulties between the United Railroads of San Francisco and their employes lends renewed interest to the decision of the arbiter in the differences between that company and Division No. 205, Amalgamated Association of Street Railway Employes.

Oscar S. Straus,

All these differences, except the subject of employment and discharge, were referred on April 6, 1903, to W. D. Mahon, president of the Amalgamated Association, and Patrick Calhoun, representing the railroad company. They were authorized to appoint a third person to consider with them points upon which they were unable to agree, a majority vote to be decisive. Messrs. Calhoun and Mahon on June 15, 1903, telegraphed as follows to Mr. Oscar S. Straus, in New York:

"We have agreed upon you as third arbiter, to act with us in the settlement of certain differences between the United Railroad Companies of this city and the street car men's union. The evidence will be taken by a commissioner, and submitted to you in writing. This controversy is an important one, and we strongly urge you to accept."

To this Mr. Straus replied, on the same day: "In the line of the duty I have set before me to promote industrial peace, I accept, but regret this additional work coming upon me."

Subsequently the testimony was taken before a commissioner, covering nine closely typewritten volumes, besides many volumes of exhibits.

The first meeting of the commission was held on September 15, 1903, in the rooms of the New York Board of Trade and Transportation, 203 Broadway. Mr. Calhoun suggested that the commission should pass upon the question upon which the company had refused to give testimony, as to their ability to pay the wage demanded. It was unanimously decided by the commission that no testimony as to the ability or inability of the company to pay the wages that will be fixed by this commission would be received, as no question had arisen as to the company's lack of ability to pay its wage, or any wage this commission should decide. Further hearing of the commission was adjourned until October 12, 1903. Mr. A. A. Moore appeared as counsel for the railroads, and Hon. Edward J. Livernash appeared as counsel for the union.

The arguments on the part of counsel were heard on that day, and on the 20th, 21st and 22d of October following. Written briefs were subsequently handed in by the respective counsel.

The following decision, rendered by Mr. Straus, is here published for the first time:

It is the judgment of the undersigned there remain, of all the matter presented by the voluminous pleadings and correspondence framing the issues, but two questions for determination by this board, namely:

First—The question as to what is a fair wage rate.

Second—The question of hours of labor.

A FAIR WAGE RATE.

Of all questions that arise in industrial disputes none is more difficult to define and determine than what is a fair wage rate? Wishing to make my conclusions as brief and concise as possible, I will not enter into the economic speculations that this question gives rise to, as it can serve no purpose here. If arbitrations of this kind concerned the interpretation of a contract, or of laws or regulations, they would be free from many of the uncertainties, indefiniteness and difficulties that surround a decision. We are met at the outset with the absence of precedents to guide us. There are no terms of a contract to interpret, because the very fact that such an arbitration is agreed upon is because the parties have been unable to make a contract, and therefore appeal to the high sense of equity on the part of the persons selected as arbitrators to accord a fair wage for the services that are demanded. The earlier economists generally held to the ruling that wages, like any other commodity, are regulated by the demand and the supply. In our day, with the more humane consideration of this question, there has come about a decided departure from this rigid and often inhuman method of regulating wages. No doubt the organization of wage-earners on the one side and employers on the other, coupled with the more enlightened and humane views that characterize our age and civilization, have been responsible for the change. On the other hand, we must be mindful that nothing is so destructive of an industry as to yield to demands on the part of labor that may be uneconomic.

STANDARD OF WAGES.

By the testimony, it appears that the United Railroads of San Francisco are now paying a high rate of wage, and that there are only four street railway companies out of 345 of which statistics are given that pay a higher rate, and that these are located in Montana; and that these four pay an average rate ranging from 27.5 cents per hour to 29 cents, and that there are of this number only four companies that pay as high a rate as the company is now paying, namely, 25 cents. That these companies are located in Oakland, Cal., in San Francisco, and in Spokane, Wash., and also one in Chicago.

The standard of wages on the Pacific Coast, and especially in San Francisco, since 1849 has always been high, resulting from many causes. The migration from the East began in that year, impelled by the discoveries of gold, and by reason of the fact that the journey was a long and expensive one wages were much higher than in the middle or eastern part of the United States; and so, also, was the cost of living. As time has run on, and with the building of transcontinental lines, the disproportion has become less and less; but it still remains as a fact that, generally speaking, the rate of wages is somewhat higher in the city of San Francisco than in other cities of equal size throughout the United States. Doubtless it was for that reason, among others, that the United Railroads of San Francisco, after the strike in

April, 1902, settled by granting the men 25 cents per hour, with 30 cents for overtime, which, according to their own showing, was 10 to 15 per cent higher than paid by similar railroads in other cities, with the exception of those mentioned above.

COST OF LIVING.

The evidence shows, in comparing the cost of living in 1902 with that of 1903, that there has been an advance. It is claimed on behalf of the street railway employes, by a large mass of testimony they accumulated, that that advance has been from 20 to 30 per cent. On the other hand, it is claimed by the United Railroads, based upon Prof. Plehn's reports, that while there has been an advance, that advance does not exceed more than 3 per cent. The basis of the large mass of testimony offered by the street railway employes, derived from their own members, is lacking in definiteness, and in part in reliability. On the other hand, the basis of the exhaustive calculations made by Prof. Plehn are not entirely satisfactory or convincing. The testimony on both sides establishes, however, the fact that there has been for the periods mentioned a rise in the cost of living; that, on the average, the rent of rooms or apartments such as the employes live in has advanced about 10 per cent.

Referring to the increased cost of living, the Anthracite Coal Strike Commission (See Bulletin of the Department of Labor No. 146, May, 1903, page 472), say:

"This increase for the past few years, as ascertained for a forthcoming report, and taking into consideration the leading articles of consumption for food, amounts to 9.8 per cent. From this it is seen that, taking the average quantity of articles consumed per family, and assuming the price for 1901 to be 100, in 1898 they were 96.5; in 1899, 94.5; in 1900, 96.7; in 1902, 106.2."

Whether the increase of the cost of living in San Francisco for the first five months in 1903, as compared with the first five months in 1902, was abnormal or not, as compared with the rest of the United States, does not appear. It was claimed that part of the increase is due to the fact that labor is more generally organized in the different branches of industry in San Francisco than elsewhere, and that that has been one of the causes for a rise in the cost of living.

In view, therefore, of all the circumstances, I adjudge and award:

First—That the United Railroads of San Francisco pay to such of the members of Division No. 205, Amalgamated Association of Street Railway Employes of America, who are now and have been in their employ for a period under two years, prior to April 1, 1903, an increase of 5 per cent above 25 cents an hour, and to such of said employes who are now and have been prior to April 1, 1903, in their employ two years and over, an increase of 10 per cent above 25 cents an hour, and that for overtime the like percentages of increase above the present rate be paid.

Second—I adjudge and award that the United Railroads of San Francisco pay to such of its employes who are members of Division 205, Amalgamated Association of Street Railway Employes of America, who work by the day, and who are now and have been in their employ for a period of under two years prior to April 1, 1903, an increase of 5 per cent above the daily rate of wage they are now receiving, and to such of said employes who are now and have been prior to April 1, 1903, in their employ two years and over, an increase of 10 per cent above the rate of wage they are now receiving.

SCHEDULE OF HOURS.

It appears by the evidence that the average hours of actual labor by the body of regular men under the present schedule are 10 hours and 3 minutes, or thereabouts; that at the time when the strike was settled in April, 1902, the schedule which was agreed to by the company was 10 hours per day, to be completed within 14 hours, and that this schedule, upon the request of the union, was amended by extending the hours of labor to 11, to be completed within 15 hours. In comparing the hours of service on these railroads it does not appear that they are longer or more arduous than generally prevail in this line of service; nor does it appear that they are too long, considering the health and welfare of the men in this line of service, and in view of the fact that the climate of the Pacific Coast is exceptionally mild and free from that severity that obtains in the middle and eastern part of the United States.

Third—I adjudge and award that the same hours and schedules that now obtain be continued. It is always within the province of the railroad on the one side and the employes on the other to amend their schedules by mutual agreement. I therefore decline to disturb the present schedules.

Fourth—In accordance with the agreement under which this arbitration was entered upon the wage rate adjudged and awarded shall be deemed to go into effect as of the First of May, 1903, and continue until the First of May, 1904.

CONCLUSION.

In conclusion, I desire to add that in coming to the above decision I have endeavored to be just and equitable to both sides, and have been largely influenced by the desire and purpose to establish a permanent peace between the company and its employes, to encourage a spirit of mutual confidence, and to secure to the public what it has a right to demand, the best possible street railway service without friction, so as to avoid for many years to come conflict and disagreement between the corporation on the one side and the union on the other, although by this agreement the award, as aforesaid, is to be only binding for a period of one year.

I trust, and it is my expectation, that it will continue for a much longer period. The extensive preparation of this case, with its vast amount of testimony and the large cost and labor it has entailed upon both sides, has been so great that it is hoped that this will be an added reason for continuing the award for years to come beyond the period specified.

For the purpose of avoiding any dispute or disagreement regarding the meaning and interpretation of these awards, or regarding the persons to whom they shall apply, I suggest, in such event, the question be referred to arbitration, the arbitrators to be selected, one by the United Railroads, the other by the employes' union, and in case they disagree, a third arbitrator to be selected by these two, whose decision shall be final and conclusive.

OSCAR S. STRAUS.
W. D. MAHON.

Mr. Calhoun filed a dissenting opinion. Mr. Mahon also placed on record, in writing, his reasons for concurring in the decision of the third arbiter, Mr. Straus.

TRADE AGREEMENT CONFERENCE.

An Instructive Discussion Followed by the Appointment of a Standing Committee.

A meeting of the committee on trade agreements of the National Civic Federation was held at the Fifth Avenue Hotel on Saturday, May 7, 1904. Mr. Francis L. Robbins, president of the Pittsburg Coal Company, presided at the session until business called him away, when Mr. John Mitchell, president of the United Mine Workers of America, took the chair. A large number of representatives of both employer and employed were present. The time of the session was entirely consumed in an animated interchange of views concerning trade agreements and their operation. A noteworthy feature of the discussion was that not a single expression was heard against the trade agreement as a practical method of encouraging co-operation between employer and employed. A report of the discussion will appear in the next issue of THE REVIEW. The announcement was made that a standing joint committee on trade agreements would be appointed. This committee is composed of the following:

Francis L. Robbins, President Pittsburg Coal Company, Pittsburg, Pa.; Harry Coulby, Chairman Dock Managers' Association, Cleveland, Ohio; Isaac W. Frank, President National Founders' Association, Pittsburg, Pa.; Chauncey H. Castle, President Stove Manufacturers' National Defense Association, Quincy, Ill.; Otto M. Eidlitz, Chairman Board of Governors, New York Building Trades Association, New York City; Marcus M. Marks, President National Clothiers' Association, New York City; Charles H. Taylor, Jr., President American Newspaper Publishers' Association, Boston, Mass.; John Cooper, President Iron League, New York City; Louis B. Schram, Chairman Labor Committee, United States Brewers' Association, Brooklyn, N. Y.; John D. Hibbard, President Chicago Metal Trades Association, Chicago, Ill.; John Ralston, Chairman Glass Bottle and Vial Manufacturers' Association, Pittsburg, Pa.; W. C. Brown, Vice-President Lake Shore Railroad Company, Chicago, Ill.; Lucius Tuttle, President Boston and Maine Railroad Company, Boston, Mass.; Charles A. Moore, Member New York Metal Trades Association, New York City; Emerson McMillin, President American Light and Traction Company, New York City; William H. Pfahler, former President National Founders' Association, Philadelphia, Pa.; Walter L. Pierce, former President National Metal Trades Association, New York City; W. W. Miller, former Vice-President New Orleans City Railway Company, New York City; Grange Sard, of Rathborn, Sard & Co., Albany, N. Y.; John Mitchell, President United Mine Workers of America, Indianapolis, Ind.; Daniel J. Keefe, President International Longshoremen, Marine and Transportworkers' Association, Detroit, Mich.; James M. Lynch, President International Typographical Union, Indianapolis, Ind.; Theodore J. Shaffer, President Amalgamated Association Iron, Steel and Tin Workers, Pittsburg, Pa.; James O'Connell, President International Association of Machinists, Washington, D. C.; James Duncan, General Secretary Granite Cutters' National Union, Washington, D. C.; Frank Buchanan, President International Association Bridge and Structural Iron Workers, Chicago, Ill.; Henry White, General Secretary United Garment Workers of America, New York City; John Tobin, General President Boot and Shoe Workers' Union, Boston, Mass.; Denis A. Hayes, President Glass Bottle Blowers' Association, United States and Canada, Philadelphia, Pa.; John A. Moffatt, President National Hatters' Union, Orange, N. J.; M. Donnelly, President Meat Cutters and Butcher Workmen of North America, Chicago, Ill.; William H. Farley, Mosaic and Encaustic Tile Layers, New York City; John McNeil, President Boilermakers and Iron Shipbuilders of North America, Kansas City, Kan.; James Wilson, President Pattern Makers' League of North America, New York City; Edward J. Lynch, President International Assoc[illegible] Metal Polishers, Buffers and Brass Workers of No[illegible] New York City; W. D. Mahon, President A[illegible] Association Street Railway Employes of Ame[illegible] Mich.; James P. Archibald, Brotherhood [illegible] Decorators, New York City; Edgar E. Clark, Grand Chief Conductor, Order Railway Conductors, Cedar Rapids, Iowa; P. H. Morrissey, Grand Master Brotherhood Railroad Trainmen, Cleveland, Ohio; J. J. Hannahan, Grand Master Brotherhood Locomotive Firemen, Peoria, Ill.; Robert E. Neidig, Housesmiths, New York City; Edward A. Moffett, M. M. Garland, former President Iron, Steel and Tin Workers, Pittsburg, Pa.

CIVIC FEDERATION OF CLEVELAND.

The Civic Federation of Cleveland and vicinity completed its organization in March with the adoption of its by-laws. Its first formal action was the adoption of resolutions upon the death of Marcus A. Hanna, who was a personal friend as well as fellow-townsman of all

SAMUEL MATHER.

the members. He was a central figure at the initial meeting of the Cleveland Federation, to which he had declared his purpose of giving a great deal of attention.

The officers of the Cleveland Federation are: Chairman, Samuel Mather; secretary, James Reynolds; vice-

Continued on Page 16.

NEW FEDERATION OFFICERS.

Continued from Page 7.

without being personal or vindictive condemn the temporary capitalistic administration of the A. F. of L. in the strongest terms you can possibly empoy.

In this way you will constantly stimulate and augment a great public sentiment for the U. B. R. E.—for Industrial Unions, for the A. L. U. and for socialism (but don't use the word) and against capitalism and the Gompers faction, which is working in harmony with Marcus A. Hanna and the infamous Civic Federation to keep down

"Thus the Federation faces simultaneously the hatred of socialism and the opposition of the recently formed employers' associations. But these organizations, it is significant to observe, include none of the great employers of labor representing the basic industries, such as coal, iron and steel, building trades and railroads. They have enlisted chiefly small concerns, in country towns generally, whose combined capital and number of employes would not approach those interested in the single organization of the bituminous coal operators which has just so successfully worked out with the Mine Workers' Union the two years' joint trade agreement. While neither large nor influential to-day, they do constitute a warning to the more radical and arbitrary unions that there must be a modification of a policy that invites and encourages organized opposition of employers. Without such provocation a fighting organization, with nothing but a destructive programme, will never make much headway in this country.

RESULTS OF TRADE AGREEMENTS.

"Of far greater moment and of more wholesome interest are the trio of victories recently achieved for the policy of forming trade agreements, as advocated by the National Civic Federation. These were the settlement which resulted from the bituminous coal conference three weeks ago at Indianapolis; the more recent termination of the controversy between the organized longshoremen and the shipping interests of the Great Lakes, and the agreement upon a wage scale between the Amalgamated Iron, Steel and Tin Workers and the United States Steel Corporation and independent manufacturers at Pittsburg. These results were achieved by sane and rational methods, involving free and candid discussion of facts and conditions, as to prices of products, profits of capital and cost of living, between representatives of the parties interested, brought face to face. This method was the very one attacked by the president of an employers' association above quoted. In each of these three instances the leaders of the contending forces were members of the executive committee of the National Civic Federation. In the bituminous coal conference the country little realized how near it was to facing probably the greatest strike the world has ever seen. The anthracite coal strike last year would have paled into utter insignificance in comparison. Yet it was prevented by the vote of 150,000 miners to accept a reduction in wages, which is what the scoffers at the National Civic Federation said would never be done, predicting that when that strain came the theory of the trade agreement would not endure the test of practice.

"The three adjustments here recounted, together with the experience of our conciliation committees, have strongly emphasized the importance of the plan, determined at the meeting of the executive committee last December, to organize a special committee to promote the joint trade agreement idea throughout all industries that deal with organized labor. This committee, which is composed of the heads of the principal organizations now operating under such agreements, will hold its first meeting in this room to-morrow morning, the purpose being to compare experiences and discuss the merits and demerits of the various plans now in vogue. That there is great usefulness for such a committee was clearly shown in the settlement of the lithographers' troubles, which largely grew out of a confusion of ideas on both sides as to what subjects should properly be included in an agreement. At several stages of that controversy the associated employers and the men's organizations were found advocating propositions that, with older organizations, would have been exactly reversed. At this meeting to-morrow, in addition to the older organizations, there will be representatives of both sides of controversies in three different occupations where to-day no agreement exists; but we hope to be influential in promoting such agreements in these instances. Additional interest will attach to their presence because in one of these industries there exists an actual strike, while hostilities in the two others are threatened.

SECTIONS.

"Another proposition approved at the December meeting was the organization of various sections to deal with the especial problems that belong to a given industry. A great deal of study and effort has been devoted to this part of our work, with results that are quite gratifying. It has been necessary to make a special investigation of each field to ascertain just how far such sections would be practical and beneficial. As was pointed out at the December meeting, while there are some problems that are common to nearly all industries, there are so many especial problems that to treat them at all intelligently requires a special committee or section; for instance, the problems in the building trade are totally dissimilar from those in the metal trade, the textile industry, the street railway service, the railroad, mining and iron industries, and so on. This work cannot be rushed. It requires careful and patient effort. A detailed report of just what can be accomplished in each section would be rather more technical than interesting to a general committee such as this."

Mr. Easley's report at this point included an account of the organization of the Welfare Department. This portion of his report is incorporated in an article upon that department which appears upon another page of this issue of The Review. The report continued:

PUBLICATION DEPARTMENT.

"The Publication Department has been reorganized. Beginning with the 15th of May, The Review will be issued every month. Heretofore it has been published at irregular intervals. At present The Review is sent to 5,000 selected labor leaders, 5,000 large employers and 5,000 men who are professionally in touch with public opinion, such as preachers, editors and lawyers. But it is not the intention to limit the circulation of The Review to 15,000. That is only the basis of a vastly larger mailing list to be developed in the early future. It is expected that this periodical will be made self-supporting. With unrivalled facilities for obtaining facts and data as to the causes, the course and the treatment of industrial disturbances; with contributions to be secured from economic scholars, industrial experts and hard-headed men of practical affairs; with the sources at its command of all important industrial news, including judicial decisions and many events directly bearing upon the work of the Civic Federation, and with information freshly gathered as to industrial conditions in other countries, The Review may be made an educational force of great value.

"The evil that men or organizations do needs no vivifying stimulus. It is the good they do that can with advantage be brought into the light of publicity. That will be one purpose of our periodical. For example, when funerals were picketed in Chicago, the grewsome fact was heralded throughout the land. But when a little later in the same city a local union fined one of its members for assaulting a non-union workman and furnished the witnesses to secure his conviction in a criminal court, the incident received only passing local attention and elsewhere was ignored. Again, when a union at Schenectady that had fallen under socialistic influence expelled a member last year because he belonged to the militia, the widely published statement evoked severe and sweeping criticism of an attitude that was ascribed to unionism in general. But when, soon afterward, the annual convention of garment workers by a large majority declared its support of the militia, or when Mr. Gompers in a trenchant article defended the militia, daily journalism took no notice of the facts. The accusation that all labor organizations are opposed to the militia persists even until to-day in the editorial rooms of many journals. Upon the other hand, there are labor papers that convey to their readers the notion that there exist no fair employers, but that all are cruel taskmasters, exacting from downtrodden slaves the last ounce of agonized energy. Whenever a labor organization declares its firm and earnest disapproval of a wrong or opposition to an abuse it will be instructive and elevating for all other unions and for all employers to be informed of such action. Equally wholesome will it be for all employers and all unions to be informed of any action by individual or associations of employers tending to better conditions in any given industry.

"There is no publication to-day, except the National Civic Federation Review, that attempts to set forth the brighter, the humane and the uplifting aspects of affairs industrial. Nor will it fail to state the truth and to speak condemnation about actions or events that deserve such treatment.

"Moreover, no one can fail to recognize that there is a great and growing public interest in questions involved in the conduct of the great industries of the country, in problems of production and transportation. Trade terms so technical as once to be Greek to the general readers have become familiar and suggest topics about which there is an eager thirst for additional and accurate information. The public has become attentive to the questions suggested by such words and phrases as 'fair wages,' 'shorter hours,' 'industrial organization,' 'the open shop,' 'piece work,' 'blacklists,' 'boycotts,' 'restriction of output,' 'joint trade agreements,' 'minimum wage,' 'the sympathetic strike,' 'integrity of contracts,' 'conciliation and arbitration,' 'recognition of the union.' These are but a few of the topics that will be discussed as occasion arises. Thus it is hoped it will merit the attention and support of a large and growing constituency among the general public as well as among those whose investments or whose occupations create more direct concern in these subjects.

"The Publication Department, in addition to The Review, is planning to issue a weekly letter, to be furnished free of charge, to a large number of journals that desire to keep their readers informed about the very subjects with which the National Civic Federation is dealing."

Mr. Easley also presented the report of the sub-committee on conciliation on behalf of its chairman, Charles A. Moore. The report was approved.

Upon motion the chairman appointed the following committee to make nominations for officers of the organization for the ensuing year:

Employers—Franklin MacVeagh, Francis L. Robbins and Charles H. Taylor, Jr.

Labor—John Mitchell, Daniel J. Keefe and P. H. Morrissey.

Public—Right Rev. Henry C. Potter, Isaac N. Seligman and V. Everit Macy.

The meeting adjourned for luncheon at the Hoffman House, where its proceedings were continued. Informal and earnest addresses were delivered by Messrs. Fish, Belmont, MacVeagh, Phipps, Mitchell, Tobin and Morrissey. Mr. Moore acted as chairman, in his capacity as president of the New York Civic Federation, which tendered the luncheon. During these proceedings the nominating committee reported the following list of officers, who were unanimously elected for the ensuing year:

First Vice-President—Samuel Gompers.
Second Vice-President—Oscar S. Straus.
Treasurer—Cornelius N. Bliss.
Chairman Executive Committee—Henry Phipps.
Chairman Finance Committee—August Belmont.
Chairman Welfare Committee—H. H. Vreeland.
Chairman Conciliation Committee—Charles A. Moore.
Chairman Executive Council—Ralph M. Easley.
Secretary—S. B. Donnelly.

The committee on nominations was continued, with power to act upon the selection of a President.

The following is the text of a provision relating to wages upon government aided railway construction, contained in an act passed at the last session of the Dominion Parliament: "In every case in which the Parliament of Canada votes financial aid by way of subsidy or guarantee toward the cost of railway construction, all mechanics, laborers or other persons who perform labor in such construction shall be paid such wages as are generally accepted as current for competent workmen in the district in which the work is being performed, and if there is no current rate in the district, then a fair and reasonable rate, and in the event of a dispute arising as to what is the current or fair and reasonable rate, it shall be determined by the minister, whose decision shall be final."

HOW THE WELFARE DEPARTMENT WAS ORGANIZED.

STRIKING PICTURES PRESENTED AT ITS FIRST CONFERENCE OF THE ACTUAL OPERATION OF WELFARE WORK IN SEVERAL TYPICAL INDUSTRIES.

The Welfare Department of the National Civic Federation is in successful operation. The following account of its inauguration and its work is an extract from the report of the Chairman of the Executive Council, presented at the meeting of the Executive Committee on May 6:

"In accordance with the decision of the National Executive Committee that its efforts to better the relations between employers and employes would be materially aided by the promotion of what is called 'Welfare Work,' President Hanna appointed, January 6, a committee of prominent employers to organize the Welfare Department.

"The first meeting of the committee was held January 29 at the Waldorf, New York City, and was largely attended by these representative employers from the various sections of the country. Honorable Oscar S. Straus, on behalf of President Hanna, and Bishop Potter, on behalf of the Executive Committee, welcomed the members and congratulated the Civic Federation on having such a representative and influential committee to handle this important part of the work. Mr. H. H. Vreeland was requested to act as chairman. The last act of President Hanna in connection with the work of the National Civic Federation was the sending of the following telegram to us at this meeting:

Washington, D. C., January 29, 1904.

R. M. Easley, 281 Fourth Ave., New York City.

I should like to attend the Employes' Welfare Committee meeting this morning, but that, of course, is impossible. I appreciate the opportunity for good in that organization, and hope for beneficial results. Please express my best wishes to the members.

M. A. HANNA.

"It developed that it was the first time that employers who are especially interested in thus bettering the conditions of their employes had been brought together, and, instead of organizing or attempting to transact any business, the entire day, from 10:30 a. m. to 5 p. m., was spent in a general discussion of methods of installing and maintaining welfare work, and in a frank exchange of experiences. An adjournment was taken until February 24, a special committee being authorized to present a plan of work for consideration at that time.

"At the adjourned meeting a plan of work was adopted, which provides for:

1. Educating the public as to the real meaning and value of welfare work.
2. Interesting employers not giving such consideration to the welfare of their employes: and
3. The maintaining of a central bureau to provide inquiring employers with information as to especial successes and failures in welfare work and their causes.

"The plan also provides for a membership of both employers who are, and who are not, promoting welfare work, the idea being that the latter may become interested in undertaking such efforts, in this way. We have, therefore, extended an invitation to a number of employers to accept membership in this department, and have more than one hundred acceptances at the present time.

"Three different kinds of conferences have been provided for:

1. Conferences of employers for the discussion of the following and kindred subjects:
   - General policy to be pursued in installing and maintaining welfare work.
   - Housing of Labor (City and Country Mills).
   - Recreation.
   - Educational Efforts.
   - Sanitary Work Rooms.
   - Hospital Service.
   - Wash Rooms and Baths.
   - The Luncheon Room.
2. Public Conferences.
3. Conferences of Welfare Managers.

"The members of the Executive Committee determined that it would be important to hold a conference of welfare managers at an early time. Employers were requested to send to such a conference, which was held at the Waldorf, March 16, their representatives (who in a few instances have been called "Social Secretaries") engaged in any effort to better the conditions of their employes. As many employers personally accepted this invitation, it was not practicable to confine the meeting to the welfare managers. At this conference descriptive talks on the work in different industries, i. e., manufacturing, the retail store, and mining, were made at the morning session. The afternoon was devoted to short talks and a general discussion which was interesting and developed much valuable information. The proceedings will be issued shortly."

A clear idea of some of the specific things that have been done to better the condition of wage-earners may be gained from the following summarized extracts from addresses delivered at this conference. These extracts are descriptive of welfare work in a mill town, in a

H. H. Vreeland.

retail store, in a mining community, in the operation of a street railway, and in a small factory. The names of the speakers and of their establishments are not essential to an understanding of the condensed quotations:

IN A MILL TOWN.

It was our desire to improve the conditions of the employes, to teach them to help themselves, to direct them through a library to a higher education and to show them how to appreciate the higher ideals of life.

Naturally, the first place that we looked after was the mill where the employes spend most of their active hours. Ample light was provided so as to prevent dark corners and the depression of gloom. The best sanitary appliances were put in, all toilet rooms were finished with asphalt floors, the walls were lined with white enameled brick, all plumbing being exposed. One of the best things we ever did for our men was to provide baths. The only trouble is, we have not enough of them.

A modern system of ventilation was installed, insuring warm air in winter, cool air in summer, and fresh air at all times, and dissipating the dust and fumes incident to the industry. Special attention was given to the purity of the water supply. Seats were provided for women operatives which they could use when a little tired, or when the nature of the work permitted. Proper dressing rooms and lockers for the clothing were provided. The environment of the mill was made attractive; muddy roads were macadamized; lawns, shrubbery and vines were planted until all the surroundings became attractive to the eye. These improvements were immediately reflected in the homes of the employes, who were moved by the impulse of imitation to adorn their grounds.

The company adopted the plan of building houses to be leased to the men at a rental within their means. These houses are set back from the road so that in front there is room for lawns, flower beds and shrubbery. In the rear of the houses there are gardens and hen yards. Aside from such common service as the removal of ashes and garbage the company believes in simply helping the tenants to carry out their individual wishes so that each house and its surroundings express the character of its dwellers.

Upon a hill overlooking the mill and the houses is a reading room. That the library is appreciated and is a benefit is shown by the records of its circulation. It is in charge of a trained librarian and assistant. The success of the library is largely due to the fact that the men are provided with catalogues to take to their homes, where they may make selections at their leisure, and that they are also supplied with literature in their native tongues.

In an equally attractive situation is a building used for a dining hall and for social gatherings. The use of the dining room grew from merely furnishing hot coffee and tea, to providing substantial dinners costing from ten to twelve cents, with some simple luxuries obtainable for a few cents more. The patrons must wait upon themselves. There is a separate dining room for the women. This hall is used by the Women's Social Club, and for concerts, dances, lectures and other entertainments.

Near the mill is an industrial school building, in which there is a kindergarten, a room for manual training, a cooking school, and a place for teaching mechanical drawing.

A band was organized, the company furnishing rooms to practice in, and loaning money to buy instruments. This band plays at baseball games and at our Labor Day show, and gives concerts in the winter. There is an athletic field where our ball club has a game every Saturday afternoon with a visiting nine.

The location of our mill has made it possible for us to substitute a seashore bathing beach for the swimming pool provided by other manufacturers as an annex to their gymnasiums.

We make of Labor Day a fair of competitive exhibits and of athletic sports. The fair requires a large tent to shelter the exhibits of vegetables, fruit, fancy work, flowers, school work, cooking and poultry. The company offers prizes for these and also for the vegetable and flower gardens that are the best kept in summer.

We have a hospital for the care of those injured in the mill, or by outside accident. Trained nurses are in charge. Much of their time is given to visits to employes and in reporting to the company desirable sanitary improvements in the houses. These nurses are provided with a house for their own use. Their work has proved most important in improving health and arresting the spread of contagious diseases in epidemics, as well as bringing to the attention of the company any particular cases of need.

There are several voluntary benefit associations among the employes.

We have taken up welfare work by degrees, so that it has been a gradual development. Its success has been due largely to the fact that one person has given his entire time to the supervision of the work—a study of the needs of the especial type of employes, the solving of the problems and carrying out of the plans determined upon. A vital point frequently overlooked is that the officials in large concerns are too much engaged to give the time necessary to successfully manage welfare work without the assistance of such an agent. It is well in developing the problem to bring the people, through committees, as much as possible into the work; of course, how much depends entirely upon local conditions. As this can be done, it will gain their confidence and allay question of motives.

The problem that we have to deal with is that of the mill town. Naturally, when welfare work is introduced by the manufacturer in a city mill somewhat different lines must be pursued.

IN A DEPARTMENT STORE.

It was my first duty as welfare manager to acquire a thoroughly comprehensive idea of the store organization. In doing this I became acquainted with many employes and gained their confidence. After this I became the intermediary in complaints and grievances, and in questions of both promotion and discipline. The two purposes for which I was engaged were to insure just treatment and to improve the efficiency of employes.

Complaints have varied from unhygienic conditions to such fundamental things as wages and hours. My function is judicial. For its exercise it is essential that I have the privilege of entering into any queston that may arise in the house. I work with the superintendent, who is the one in power; but he has learned to hear facts presented to him from every proper source. Thus it has come to pass that his authority is not despotic, but intelligently informed in its exercise.

We have an association whose purposes are the improvement of unsatisfactory conditions in the store; the insurance against illness and death, and the arbitration of disagreements that have been appealed from initial decision. Members of the firm are members of the association, having the same voting power as any employe. The association may vote upon the store rules that affect the efficiency of the employes. A committee has power to award prizes for suggestions. There is an arbitration committee to which employes have the privilege of appeal from dismissal and for the adjustment of disputes. Members of this committee are elected by secret ballot from the employes on different floors. The firm has left this committee entirely alone and has accepted its judgments. A small majority of the decisions have been in favor of employes. The committee has proved able to adjust disputes as to discipline with less friction than has been developed by any other method that the firm has tried.

The clubhouse adjoining the store contains a luncheon room, social room, a library, and an emergency sickroom. Welfare work in a retail store also includes provision for visiting the sick, a savings bank, and classes for instruction in sales work and in preliminary branches for cash boys.

A STREET RAILWAY SYSTEM.

Labor organizations and secret beneficial associations reach only the individual. They do not get beyond into the home and family. Herein lies the peculiar opportunity for welfare work among street railway employes in a large city. Those under my direction number some fifteen thousand. Our first point is to make every man understand that no one can discharge him but himself. His continued employment is assured so long as he is progressive and faithful. Then we have a voluntary organization to provide insurance against sickness and death. This makes it certain that in case of death a man's family will be tided over its period of trouble. It is characteristic of the wife of the average laboring man that she will always land on her feet if given time.

Success in welfare work depends almost entirely upon the active interest taken in it by the men in control of the business. For instance, the president of a Western railroad told me that his attempts at welfare work had failed. I learned that he had never attended a meeting of the organization of his men since the first. I find it necessary to attend every meeting. I am always on the platform to speak to the men. All the officers of the company are interested in the work. In our clubroom you will find on one bench motormen, conductors and a vice-president; upon another bench engineers, machinists and a superintendent of transportation, or the head of the electrical department. In short, every one of our managers is in touch with the men.

We make the men understand that there is no charity connected with our organization. The company is pledged to supply rooms, light, heat and furniture; to pay the secretary and to assume generally all expense of operation, so that all money paid by employes will be returned to them in sick benefits, and death benefits, or will remain in the reserve fund. Every additional feature of the association's work has been provided by the men themselves. It elects its own officers, who control all of its affairs, the president of the company being ex-officio president of the association.

A large portion of the thousands of men live in boarding houses. They would have no place to go in the evening for warmth and companionship except the saloons or the pool rooms were it not for our club house. Our club rooms are filled every night in the week. They contain a library, pool tables and other games. The library is successful because of its use by the families of the men. The management caused it to be understood that catalogues should go into the house of every employe who had a family. We wished the wives and daughters and sons of our employes to use these books. As a result, the library is a family affair. It was turned over at least twenty-five times in its first winter. It is understood that if any man has a son or a daughter working for an education and special text books or books of reference are needed, it is only necessary for the employe to apply to the librarian and the books are bought and put in the library.

The company finds value in this welfare work, because it enlists in the company's business the personal interest of the individual employe and of his family as well.

Through the association any case of trouble or want in the families of the employes is promptly brought to my knowledge. It is the duty of every foreman to report every case of illness among the men under his charge or in their families. The company's physician reports periodically to me as to the condition of the families. If in any house there is insufficient food or fuel, the doctor has authority to relieve the difficulty. Through this association I know more of the men by name than the average railroad man who has only a thousand. I have never allowed an outsider to address our meetings, except upon a technical subject, unless I knew in advance every word he was going to say. The reason for this is that some one who didn't understand just what we were trying to accomplish might inadvertently work mischief. We have a school for the instruction of our new employes.

IN A MINING COMMUNITY.

Our welfare work is elementary. It is in the mining district of Lake Superior. Our miners are of all nationalities. The Cornishman will not mix with the Swede, nor the Frenchman with the Finlander; hence we have not attempted a clubhouse or social work. What we have done has been in the way of housing. Our employes are encouraged to buy their own houses. We do not lend them money, but we sell them land, allowing long time payments. We rent as few houses as we possibly can.

We offer prizes for well kept premises. The results are extremely satisfactory. The improvement of the town has been marked. Men will not only have vegetable gardens and plant vines and flowers, but the love of improvement thus stimulated leads them to paint their houses and fix their places up generally.

Our benefit fund is taken arbitrarily by the company from the wages of the men. The company, of course, contributes to this fund. It is used to maintain a hospital and corps of physicians. This arbitrary method is peculiar to us, and is warranted only by the reason that the employes are foreigners and accustomed to having things of this nature done for them by those in authority.

The work of our miners is dirty, and it is therefore impossible for them to wear their mining clothes on the street. Until recently very little attention had been given to comfort and cleanliness in the buildings provided for the miners to change their clothes. Our new "changing-house," as it is called, is a fireproof structure containing, among other things, shower baths, an adequate supply of wash troughs containing individual enamelled iron wash basins, with hot and cold water; drying racks for the mining clothes, lockers, an office for the shift bosses, an emergency hospital room, with all appliances, and a room in which the men may eat their luncheons.

A SMALL MANUFACTURER.

We have heard about welfare work in large establishments and communities. I would say a word about its operation in a smaller concern. We started on a small scale, and our welfare work grew with the business. In the beginning the main feature and, indeed, the successful foundation of our work lay in the meeting of the foremen with the men who actively manage the business. In this way we not only learned to work together harmoniously, which has been of vital importance to us, but the needs of the employes were brought to our attention; and these meetings led to the establishment of a luncheon room, better washrooms, a men's club, which is of great educational value; a library, a rest room for the women employes, an emergency sickroom, and other features.

The following are the officers of the Welfare Department:

Chairman, H. H. Vreeland; first vice-chairman, Cyrus H. McCormick; second vice-chairman, John H. Patterson; third vice-chairman, Edward A. Filene; treasurer, Cornelius N. Bliss.

Executive Committee.—George W. Brown (Treasurer United Shoe Machinery Company), Boston, Mass.; G. E Emmons (Manager Schenectady Works General Electric Co.), Schenectady, N. Y.; Edward A. Filene (Treasurer Wm. Filene's Sons Co.), Boston, Mass.; W. C. Fish (Manager Lynn Works General Electric Co.), West Lynn, Mass.; G. Watson French (President Bettendorf Metal Wheel Co.), Davenport, Iowa; Orrin S. Goan (Manager National Biscuit Co.), New York City; Wm. C. Greene (Treasurer Peace Dale Manufacturing Company), Peace Dale, R. I.; J. B. Greenhut (President Siegel-Cooper Co.), New York City; F. R. Hazard (President The Solvay Process Co.), Syracuse, N. Y.; H. J. Heinz (President H. J. Heinz Co.), Pittsburgh, Pa.; Edwin M Herr (Vice-President Westinghouse Air Brake Co.), Wilmerding, Pa.; Charles W. Hubbard (Treasurer Ludlow Manufacturing Associates), Boston, Mass.; Charles H. Hulburd (President Elgin National Watch Co.), Chicago, Ill.; John S. Huyler (President, Huyler's), New York City; M. E. Ingalls (President C., C., C. & St. L. Ry. Co.), Cincinnati, Ohio; John F. P. Lawton (Assistant Treasurer and Secretary Gorham Mfg. Co. of Rhode Island), Providence, R. I.; Warner M. Leeds (Vice-President American Sheet and Tin Plate Co.), Pittsburgh, Pa.; Arthur T. Lyman (Treasurer The Boston Manufacturing Co.), Boston, Mass.; W. G. Mather (President Cleveland Cliffs Iron Co.), Cleveland, Ohio; Cyrus H. McCormick (President International Harvester Co.), Chicago, Ill.; L. A. Osborne (Vice-President Westinghouse Electric and Manufacturing Co.), East Pittsburgh, Pa.; John H. Patterson (President National Cash Register Co.), Dayton, Ohio; H. D. Perky (President Natural Food Co.), Niagara Falls, N. Y.; A. J. Pitkin (Vice-President American Locomotive Co.), Schenectady, N. Y.; Ellison A. Smyth (President Pelzer Manufacturing Company), Pelzer, S. C.; Nathan Straus (R. H. Macy & Co.), New York City; H. H. Vreeland (President New York City Railway Co.), New York City; Ralph M. Easley (Chairman Executive Council, National Civic Federation), New York City.

On April 7 Chicago Stereotypers' Union No. 4 entered into agreements with the Chicago *Daily News*, *Record-Herald*, *Journal* and *Post*. A contract was signed in January with the *Tribune*. No. 4 now has agreements with all the Chicago daily newspapers published in English. Thus end the differences which have existed since 1898. Ex-President Colbert, of No. 16, acted as the representative of the International Typographical Union, and his work is highly commended. President Freel and Vice-President Straube represented the International Stereotypers' and Electrotypers' Union in the negotiations. The famous Chicago situation is now a thing of the past. Its conclusion demonstrates the wisdom of the policy of the International Typographical Union, and assures the stereotypers of an era of peace and prosperity in that locality.—*Typographical Journal*.

The Chicago Packing Trades Council, of which the Amalgamated Meat Cutters and Butcher Workmen is a part, has adopted these resolutions:

Whereas, Organized labor has been publicly criticised because some unions in times of difficulty with employers have been reported as resorting to violence; and

Whereas, The American labor movement can best protect and advance the interest of the workers by advocating and insisting upon a strict observance of the law by all its members; therefore, be it

Resolved, That the Packing Trades Council of Chicago and vicinity deprecates any methods of violence by any member or members of organized labor.

A NOTABLE CASE OF CONCILIATION THROUGH CONFERENCE.

INCIDENTS DRAMATIC, ENTERTAINING AND INSTRUCTIVE IN NEGOTIATIONS BETWEEN EMPLOYING LITHOGRAPHERS AND ALLIED UNIONS, UNDER THE AUSPICES OF THE CIVIC FEDERATION.

The history of the negotiations between the organizations of the employes and the employers in the Lithographers' Association affords an illustrative example of the methods of conciliation as employed by the Civic Federation. The organized unions and the employers' association contain 95 per cent of all the labor and capital employed and invested in this industry in the United States. The labor organizations involved in the dispute in this trade extended throughout the country. The employers are formed into a National Lithographers' Association, with divisions of the East, West and Pacific.

JAMES W. PARKER.

The negotiations between these two forces covered, altogether, a period lasting from October, 1903, to April, 1904. They secured one satisfactory adjustment in October, and another settlement in April. They involved the exercise of the utmost tact and patience; a gradual process of education, in which each side learned from the other; a constant avoidance of all appearance of interference from an outside source, coupled with a persistent effort to bring the contending parties face to face, and the necessity of creating a mutual confidence in the good faith of both parties. The several steps in these prolonged negotiations numbered nearly a score. Not only did they cover months, but they consumed the time and effort of disinterested persons, as well as of the representatives on both sides, to the extent that the sessions more than once were prolonged to the point of physical and mental exhaustion. The end of the long story may be told at the outset. It was the signing by both sides of a trade agreement, which included a provision for arbitration and a method for securing compliance with the final decision of that tribunal.

The peculiarity of this trade dispute lies in the fact that it originated with the desire of the organized employers to create a joint arbitration board for the settlement of all disputes and grievances, without strikes or lockouts. Upon their side, the organized employes declined to submit themselves to unrestricted arbitration, holding that to do so would be to surrender their right to strike, which was their chief weapon of self-defense, and that there were certain questions which in no event could they consent consistently to submit to arbitration. Instead of agreeing to the employers' proposition, the employes advanced several demands, including a half hour for meals at one and a half pay when on work overtime; a minimum wage, and a half holiday.

The two parties were thus apparently at a deadlock, when the conciliation committee of the New York Civic Federation was requested by an officer of the employers' association to use its good offices. Accordingly, the conciliation committee sent an invitation to the Lithographers' Association and to the Alliance of Unions to meet on Friday, October 23, 1903, to endeavor to reach a settlement "on matters at issue in the trade." This initial invitation was accepted by the Lithographers' Association, but was declined by the unions.

C. H. CANDLER.

A sub-committee, however, persuaded the committee of the unions to agree to a conference. This first meeting of the two sides lasted four hours, and adopted resolutions advising that the employers concede the half hour for a meal in overtime at the rate of one and a half pay; that there be no strike; that a joint committee be appointed of five members from each organization, with power to draw a complete agreement, to be reported to a joint conference committee.

The two committees met on October 27, but here arose a question that was to reappear many times during the subsequent negotiations. This was the authority of the committee representing the unions to act for their organizations. This point was discussed again and again. It reminded one of the care that is taken in the negotiations of international treaties, which must begin with the interchange of the credentials of envoys representing the governments concerned. In reality, these were pour parlers between the representatives of two contending bodies who had been induced to strive for peace rather than for war, and to work jointly for the formulation of a treaty. It was natural that each should demand that the other side demonstrate its authority to act for the organization, or organizations, that it claimed to represent.

Upon this very issue the first meeting of the joint committee resulted in failure. Again conciliation was

EMERSON McMILLIN.

brought into play, and after a conference with Mr. Marcus M. Marks, acting chairman of the conciliation committee, the employers' committee consented to another meeting with the committee of the unions on October 28. At this second meeting the question of authority was again raised, and it was agreed that the committee of the union should secure full power on the next evening from a special meeting of their organization.

This was done, and on October 30 the two committees, now with authority to act, met at the rooms of the Civic Federation.

This joint meeting, after six hours of discussion, agreed that there should be formed a joint commission empowered to settle all disputes, to be composed of an equal number of members, to be elected by the two bodies as each grievance should arise, its decisions to be subject to ratification by both associations; in case of disagreement by both sides, the question at issue to be decided by arbitration; the decisions of the arbiters to be final and binding. It was proposed that both associations should pledge themselves to "co-operate and use their entire joint influence and power to secure compliance with the decisions of this tribunal." The proposed agreement also included a pledge that there should be no strike or lockout during the period when the settlement of any question was pending.

In accordance with this agreement the two committees met in conference on the following day, took up the several demands and grievances presented by both sides and reached a settlement satisfactory to them all.

It will be observed that at this stage of the case there had been developed a device to insure the enforcement of any decision reached by arbitrators. This is implied in the pledge that both associations would "co-operate and use their entire joint influence and power" to sustain the decision. It is important to emphasize this point, because it reappears in the final agreement, perfected months afterward, and now in force in this industry. Thus ends the first chapter of this dispute.

Its second series of events was caused by the renewal of the desire of the Lithographers' Association for an arbitration agreement. This desire, before expressed as a request, was announced by the association on February 9, 1904, in the form of an ultimatum, that unless an arbitration agreement, to be binding for one year, should be signed by March 15 by the unions represented in the trade in the United States, the employers on that date would proceed to deal with their employes individually, and would no longer recognize the unions. The officers of the unions had refused to enter into such an agreement on the ground that it could not be brought before the national bodies before March 15, while the constitution of one of the largest of their national organizations forbade its local unions to enter into any arbitration agreement whatever. It was claimed that this prohibition could not be removed before the national convention of that organization in July. The union representatives offered to sign an agreement to secure stable conditions in the trade for one year, without reference to arbitration. The employers refused at this time to concede a moment's delay beyond March 15.

HENRY WHITE.

On February 13 tension was increased by the Lithographers' Association sending circulars to individual employes throughout the country notifying them of the ultimatum. The union officers claimed that this act was a breach of faith. The employing lithographers replied that their circular was only a statement of fact, which they feared the union leaders would not transmit to their membership. Thus an atmosphere of mutual distrust was created, which required much effort to dissipate.

At this juncture the conciliation committee of the Civic Federation was called into a number of conferences with each side. The employers demanded an agreement which should exclude no question whatever from arbitration. They alleged that the individual members of the unions throughout the country were eager to have this demand granted. On the labor side the several organizations involved were the Poster Artists' Association of America, the Lithographers' International Protection and Beneficial Association of the United States and Canada, the Lithographic Artists, Engravers and Designers' League of America, the International Protection Association of Lithographic Apprentices and Press Feeders of the United States and Canada, the Lithographic Stone and Plate Repairers' Association of the United States and Canada, and Local Union No. 19, Paper Cutters of New York and vicinity.

The officers of these organizations declared unalterable opposition to compulsory arbitration in the form of a self-perpetuating agreement, which they claimed was involved in the demand of the employers.

On March 4 the conciliation committee made some progress in a meeting at the rooms of the Civic Federation in urging upon union representatives the advantage of a fair arbitration agreement. On the following day the presidents of the national unions continued to insist to the conciliation committee that the questions of wages, hours and the closed shop must be excluded from arbitration; but a step had been gained in that the labor representatives no longer insisted that no arbitration agreement of any kind whatever could be reached before March 15, the date named in the employers' ultimatum. On March 12 further progress was made. The conciliation committee had a luncheon in the Fifth Avenue Hotel with the representatives of the employers, and succeeded in persuading them to admit that as the questions of wages and hours, as well as the closed shop, would not in any case be brought to arbitration for a year, these need not be included in their demand for an agreement. The employers finally authorized the conciliation committee to inform the labor side that they would give earnest consideration to an agreement of the kind they indicated, but that they would not promise to exclude the ratio of apprentices from arbitration until after the July convention. On the evening of the same day the labor members of the conciliation committee secured a promise from the presidents of the national organizations that they would propose an agreement of the kind outlined.

On Saturday at 4 p. m. the representatives of the two sides met, the conciliation committee being present. This conference lasted until 2 a. m., resulting in what was then assumed to be a settlement, pending ratification by the unions. Misunderstandings arose, which practically negatived what had been done. The lockout followed on March 15.

This was a condition of open hostility. It was a warfare perhaps secretly deplored by both parties, although both professed their ability to maintain their position indefinitely. Again there were preliminary conferences by members of the conciliation committee with representatives of both sides. Among those who represented the Civic Federation in these conferences, as they had throughout the previous stages of the difficulty, were Lewis B. Schram, Emerson McMillin, Marcus M. Marks, V. E. Macy, J. Alexander Hayden, Samuel B. Donnelly, James P. Archibald, Henry White and William H. Farley. It was finally arranged that conferences should be resumed on April 4. Mr. Emerson McMillin, of the conciliation committee, was chosen as chairman of these conferences, and Robert W. Hawthorne was made secretary. The representatives of the employers at these conferences were C. D. Gray, Charles Wilhelms, J. A. Davis, C. A. Candar, Charles A. Conradis and A. Beverly Smith. The representatives of the employes were J. W. Parker, William A. Coakley, Henry C. Ross, Michael J. Welch, James Pritchard, Matthew H. Smith and Mr. Pettigore. These meetings began at 10 a. m. on Monday, April 4, and from that hour until late on Monday afternoon the time was spent by Mr. McMillin and others in efforts to bring the representatives of the two sides formally into each other's presence. Each side naturally stood upon its dignity, and was reluctant even to seem to be making any overture. Much of this time was devoted to disclaiming a desire to debate various subjects that one side or the other did not wish to acknowledge a willingness to discuss at all. But at last a joint meeting was brought about. Its sessions continued until the following Monday. They usually began at 10 o'clock in the morning, and lasted until 6, 7, 8 or even 10 o'clock at night. Very often, after the formal sessions had adjourned, men on both sides would remain talking over details and moot points until very late at night.

By Friday evening of this week of intense effort all the questions of really essential importance but two had been threshed out and decided. But when Saturday came it was impossible to renew at once the joint sessions. The employes and the employers met in separate rooms. In fact, there were three rooms in use, for the employers were divided into two parties, that consulted separately. All of Saturday afternoon was devoted to persuading each side to agree to hold another joint session on Monday. There were men among both the employers and the employes who declared that the conference was a waste of time, that peace was impossible, and that the only outcome must be a fight to a finish. In reply to these assertions the argument was patiently and persistently advanced by Chairman McMillin that to break up the conference after a week of effort would be to abandon whatever result had been obtained by a vast amount of work; but would also leave in the air the very questions that must ultimately be brought to a ground of settlement, whether one month or three months hence.

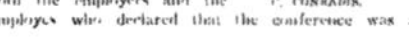

C. CONRADIS.

This argument finally prevailed, so that an agreement was reached to meet on Monday. But on Monday again there was required a strong effort to bring the two sides into a joint session. Up to 1 o'clock of that day the outcome was in doubt; but then at last both sides came together. The rest of the afternoon was devoted to a happy and mainly harmonious experience meeting, and the contract was signed at 5.30 p. m.

Throughout these meetings not only was it necessary to be tactful, but sometimes to disregard a strict enforcement of parliamentary rules. Two contracts had been drawn by the two sides as a basis of discussion. There was also a third proposed contract, prepared by a committee of the Civic Federation, many of whose provisions were acceptable to both sides. These three documents were discussed simultaneously. The one prepared on behalf of the Civic Federation and the one prepared on behalf of the employers had been written largely in similar form, and with like subdivision. Whenever a single paragraph was under discussion the meeting was permitted to discuss that paragraph simultaneously, as it appeared in each contract. This method, while perhaps not strictly in order, had the advantage of saving time and of causing each side to feel that its own paragraph had an equal status in the discussion. When the discussion of a single paragraph was concluded, that paragraph in either contract was adopted which had received the least amendment.

Scores of times a speaker of one party would declare, with heat, that if the other party took a certain position it would be useless to remain in the room any longer. The answer of the other side would invariably be that its position had been correctly stated, and that, an agreement being impossible, the meeting might as well come to an end. At such a juncture it became repeatedly the function of Chairman McMillin to say to the wranglers, in effect, "Gentlemen, you are here to agree, not to disagree." He would remind them that if they wanted to fight, the employers might be able to stand it for a certain period, and the employes might be able also to endure the cost of hostilities. But the Chair would also announce that the conference body would not adjourn until a contract had been worked out, ready for the signature of both parties. Then the joint session would resume business. In fact, the representatives of each side seemed glad to find themselves under the guidance of the National Civic Federation. They exhibited great respect for that organization, as well as unlimited confidence in its disinterestedness and its genuine desire to bring about a treaty of peace. It was this feeling that many times restrained some of the conferees from taking their hats and going away.

The intensity of the strain of these long sessions may be appreciated from the fact that on Saturday afternoon, at the end of that week, men were lying about on lounges and on the floor, in a state of physical and mental exhaustion.

Mr. McMillin, the chairman of the conference, says: upon both sides during the sessions of the conference. The representatives of the employes, upon questions of really vital consequence, showed a marked disposition to be fair.

J. A. DAVIS.

At the same time, they were very stubborn over little matters. This was more fortunate than may appear, for the decisions of the joint meeting as to disputed questions had to be voted upon by the two organizations. It was an advantage to the labor representatives to be able to show to their organization that the employers had made several concessions, where the employes had made one. Upon their side the employers showed also a willingness to be fair. Several of them displayed a special excellence in debate. They would concede the good points made by the other side, instead of combatting them needlessly. I recall one of the employes who could construct a sentence or build a paragraph in the most clear and forcible way, so as to cover the point in question, and yet to evade a phrase or a word that might have caused trouble. I believe that it would have been difficult for the employers to produce on their side a match for his ingenuity. Several of the employes were strong in debate, including one young man, who at times developed genuine eloquence. These representatives of labor showed themselves to be thoroughly posted upon every point, and were skilled in emphasizing the facts most telling in their favor.

"I recall two incidents that were decidedly amusing. In one paragraph of the contract drawn on behalf of the employes it was provided that the rate of wages should not be 'changed' during the life of the agreement. The employers' contract in the similar clause used the word 'reduced.' Of course, the employes would prefer that word to their own, and vice versa. Each side wanted the word of the other. The word 'reduced' was finally adopted.

"The other amusing incident related to apprentices. It has been the effort of employers to increase the ratio of apprentices. The employes were inclined to concede this, but not to stipulate it in the contract. Their contract embodied a clause permitting the retention by the employers of all with whom they had made written contracts during the lockout. Another provision was that the employers should take back all the union men who had been locked out, and also all who had gone out in sympathy. The employers declared that they would never take back the apprentices who had walked out. Instantly there was a hot fight on this subject. It was necessary for the chairman to point out to both sides that each was opposing a concession which it really desired. That is, the employers were fighting against a possible increase in apprentices, and the employes were fighting for what would result in such increase. In effect, each side was contending for what the other side desired."

CIVIC FEDERATION OF CLEVELAND.

Continued from Page 11.

chairman, William H. Hunt; treasurer, Harvey Coulby. The following is a list of its members:

On the part of Employers: Charles E. Adams, Vice-President and General Manager Cleveland Hardware Company; W. D. B. Alexander, President National Screw and Tack Company; C. O. Bassett, Secretary and Treasurer Forman-Bassett-Hatch Company, Printers and Publishers; Morris A. Black, H. Black & Co., Cloak Manufacturers; William H. Caniff, President New York Central and St. Louis Railroad Company; Henry Coulby, Pickands-Mather Company, also President Great Lakes Towing Company; K. F. Gill, John Gill & Sons, General Contractors; Dan R. Hanna; William H. Hunt, General Manager Cleveland Hydraulic Press Brick Company and President Cleveland Builders' Exchange; Samuel Mather, Pickands-Mather Company; Ernst Mueller, President Cleveland and Sandusky Brewing Company; P. C. O'Brien, President The P. C. O'Brien Company; W. K. Palmer, President Cleveland Window Glass Company; W. H. Teare, Potter, Teare & Co., Lumber; Lyman H. Treadway, Peck, Stowe & Wilcox Company.

On the part of the Wage Earners: A. W. Thompson, Typographical Union; Harry D. Thomas, United Trades and Labor Council; Frank Poplowsky, Plumbers' Union; W. J. Cannon, Cigarmakers' Union; A. B. Sheriff, Amalgamated Sheet Metal Workers; Frank Sullivan, Electrical Workers; H. D. McGregor, Stone Cutters' Union; Philip Hyde, Amalgamated Wood and Millworkers' Union; Albert Liebig, International Society Lathers' Union; John J. Patton, Longshoremen's Union; William Millison, Bricklayers' Union; Peter Curley, Metal Polishers and Brassworkers' Unions; Wesley Workman, United Brotherhood of Carpenters and Joiners; James Reynolds, Machinists' Union; Peter Hassenphlue, Painters' Union.

On the part of the Public: Right Rev. W. A. Leonard, D. D., Bishop Diocese of Ohio, Protestant Episcopal Church; Henry C. White, Judge Probate Court; Right Rev. Ignatius F. Horstmann, D. D., Bishop Diocese of Cleveland, Roman Catholic Church; Rev. Moses J. Gries, The Temple Congregation; Charles F. Brush; John C. Hutchins, Lawyer; J. J. Sullivan, President Central National Bank and President Chamber of Commerce; E. J. Blandin, Lawyer; Professor Edward L. Harris, Principal Central High School; Rev. John W. Malcolm, First Congregational Church; Elroy M. Avery; Dr. William H. Humiston; Rev. Charles F. Thwing, D. D., LL. D., President Western Reserve University.

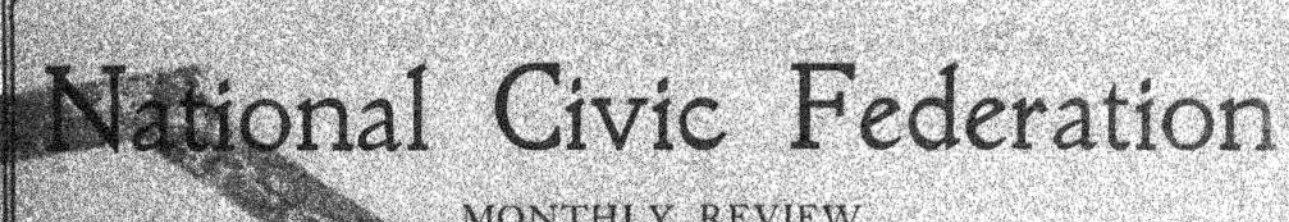

Vol. I. No. 5 NEW YORK, JULY, 1904 Ten Cents

IS THE CLOSED SHOP ILLEGAL AND CRIMINAL?

THE ILLINOIS DECISION BRINGS FORTH A VALUABLE SYMPOSIUM OF EXPERT OPINIONS CRITICIZING ITS REASONING AND ITS CONCLUSION.

FRANCIS ADAMS,
P. J., Illinois Appellate Court.

The decision of Judge Adams, of the Appellate Court of the First District of Illinois, rendered on June 6, is in effect that a contract for the exclusive employment of members of a union is in itself illegal and, in Illinois, criminal. If this decision is upheld by the Supreme Court of Illinois, as the expectation of counsel is that it will be, the Adams decision will hold a prominent place in the evolution of the legal status of the closed shop. The decision has attracted general attention among those interested in a question that ranks as a leading issue of the day.

The decision has been widely published in law journals and in the lay press. The portion of its text quoted below is limited as nearly as possible to the one general proposition, enunciated by the Appellate Court, that a contract for a closed shop is per se illegal. The decision discusses at length questions, involved or collateral, such as the exercise of duress, the freedom of contract, labor as property, discrimination between classes of citizens, conspiracy and monopoly.

The Monthly Review has obtained from a number of eminent lawyers and publicists opinions upon the validity and effect of the decisions, which are presented to its readers herewith. The effort was made to confine these opinions to the terms of the decision bearing directly upon the legality of a contract for a closed shop; but the other questions to which reference has been made are incidentally discussed by some of the writers.

The text of that portion of Judge Adams' decision which bears directly upon the question of the closed shop follows:

Judge Adams' Decision.

The purpose of the strike by complainant's employes and their prosecution of it, as described, was to compel the complainant to execute the agreements referred to and made a part of the bill. The drafts of agreements, three in number, purport to be with the different unions whose members were in complainant's employ. The draft of agreement with the Metal Polishers, Buffers, Platers, Brass Moulders, and Brass Workers' International Union of North America, International Union of Steam Engineers and International Brotherhood of Stationary Firemen contains the following:

Article 1. The party of the first part hereby agrees to employ none but members of the aforesaid organizations or those who carry the regular working card of the said organizations, provided the various crafts will furnish such competent help as may be required by the party of the first part within twenty-four hours after notification.

LOUIS D. BRANDEIS,
Lawyer and Publicist, Boston.

Art. VII. There shall be a steward for each craft in each factory appointed by the organization, whose duty it shall be to see that the men working in said factory belong to the organizations.

Art. VIII. It is hereby agreed by the party of tha first part that the business agent of the party of the second part shall have the privilege of interviewing any member of the party of the second part in the offices of the party of the first part during business hours.

FREDERICK H. COOKE,
Lawyer and Author, New York.

Art. X. A sympathetic strike to protect union principles shall not be considered a violation of this agreement.

Art. XI. All the apprentices shall belong to the union and carry the working card of the organization.

Art. XII. The member of apprentices not to exceed one for ten men or less of the different crafts.

That the purpose of the strike was to compel the execution of the drafts of agreement is clear. It is averred in the sworn bill and deposed to in the affidavits of De Wolf, complainant's president; Kellogg, its secretary and treasurer, and Edwards, its superintendent, that business agents of the different unions called on complainant and insisted on its executing the agreements and that, when complainant's president refused, on the ground that the proposed agreements were unreasonable, it was threatened by one of said business agents that unless complainant would sign the agreements a strike would be called and that said business agents called a strike, in response to which about 500 of complainant's employes quit its employ. Appellant's counsel admit in their brief the purpose of the strike is to "bring about the execution of the contracts," and at least three of the appellants so admit in their answers. It is unlawful to compel one to execute any contract. A contract executed under duress is voidable, and duress is present where a party "is constrained, under circumstances which deprive him of the exercise of free will, to agree or to perform the act sought to be avoided."

Duress exists when a person is induced to perform an act to avoid a threatened and impending calamity. Especially was the purpose to compel complainant to execute the agreements in question an unlawful purpose. Article I. of the agreement strikes at the right of contract and provides that complainant shall employ none but members of the several unions, thus discriminating in favor of one class of men and excluding all others. In Matthews vs. The People (202 Ill., 389), the court, discussing the constitutionality of the free employment agency act, says (page 401): "An employer whose workmen have left him and gone on a strike, especially when they have done so without any justifiable cause, is entitled to contract with other laborers or workmen to fill the places of those who have left him. Any workman seeking work has a right to make a contract with such employer to work for him in the place of any one of the men who have left him to go out upon a strike. Therefore the prohibition contained in section 8 strikes at right of contract, both on the part of the laborer and of the employer. It is now well settled that the privilege of contracting is both a liberty and a property right. Liberty includes the right to make and enforce contracts, because the right to make and enforce contracts is included in the right to acquire property. Labor is property. To deprive the laborer and the employer of this right to contract with one another is to violate section 2 of Article II. of the Constitution of Illinois, which provides that 'no person shall be deprived of life, liberty or property without due process of law.' It is equally a violation of the Fifth and Fourteenth Amendments of the Constitution of the United States. The provision embodied in section 8 'is a discrimination between different classes of citizens founded on no justifiable ground and an attempt to exercise legislative power in behalf of certain classes and against other classes, whether laborers seeking work or employers. In falls under the condemnation of the Constitution.'"

The agreements in question would, if executed, tend to create a monopoly in favor of the members of the different unions, to the exclusion of workmen not members of such unions, and are, in this respect unlawful. Contracts tending to create a monopoly are void.

The Legislature of the State cannot create a monopoly.

The purpose of the strikers is in violation of the criminal code, which provides as follows:

Section 158. If any two or more persons shall combine for the purpose of depriving the owner or possessor of property of its lawful use and management, or of preventing, by threats, suggestions of danger, or by any unlawful means, any person from being employed by or obtaining employment from any such owner or possessor of property, on such terms as the parties concerned may agree upon, such persons so offending shall be fined not exceeding $500 or confined in the county jail not exceeding six months.

Sec. 159. If any person shall, by threat, intimidation or unlawful interference, seek to prevent any other person from working or from obtaining work at any lawful business, on any terms that he may see fit, such person so offending may be fined not exceeding $200.

Not only was the purpose of the strike unlawful, but the means used to achieve the unlawful purpose were unlawful. The means used were the acts here before mentioned, and thereby injury to the complainant's business. The appellants and their associates intended to stop the business of the complainant so far as they possibly could, and the evidence shows that they did stop it in great part to complainant's injury. The following is contained in the brief of appellant's counsel, which we quote as illustrative of their view of the cause: "How do picketing, patrolling, persuading, or even slugging affect property rights, except in the most fantastic sense? Injury to business has no independent existence whatever, because business has no tangible existence to be injured in the true and unperverted sense."

In the case of the Union Pacific Railway Company vs. Rue, cited by counsel for appellants, the court says: "And that one's business is his or its property is likewise elementary and is conceded by all."

A man's business is his property. "The freedom of business action lies at the foundation of all commercial and industrial enterprises."

We know of no well considered case, or, indeed, of any case, holding that a combination of persons to injure the business of another is not unlawful. That the appellants, and others associated with them, acted in concert, in unlawfully endeavoring to injure, and, in fact, injuring complainant's business for an unlawful purpose, is fully sustained by the evidence. They conspired, breathed together, to effect the unlawful purpose, and by overt acts did all they possibly could to that end. It is not necessary to approve an express agreement between the appellants and those associated with them. It may be proved by circumstantial evidence.

Each conspirator is responsible for the acts and declarations of every other conspirator in furtherance of the common purpose. The conspiracy originated simultaneously with the calling of the strike and continued until the filing of the last petition, July 14, 1902. It was a single conspiracy. And the court, on the hearing of each of the second and third petitions, did not err in hearing the prior evidence. The evidence was competent as tracing and showing the character of the conspiracy. It is an indispensable condition of the enjoyment by each citizen of the liberty and rights guaranteed by the Constitution and laws that he shall respect and not unlawfully infringe upon the liberty or rights of any other citizen. This cannot be done with impunity.

LEVY MAYER,

Of Moran, Mayer & Meyer, Lawyers, Chicago:

The opinion of the Appellate Court is a thorough and rugged review, both upon principle and authority, of one of the most important questions that have ever confronted the employer. It is the first opinion rendered in this State upon the question of the legality of a contract by which the employer agrees not to employ non-union labor.

All other economic and legal questions aside, it now becomes in this State a complete answer to the demand of the closed shop that the law stamps such an arrangement as a criminal conspiracy. It is elementary that the crime of conspiracy consists of a combination of two or more persons to effect an illegal purpose. It has been asserted over and over again by those advocating the closed shop that an agreement to employ only union labor is perfectly legal and binding.

The courts have frequently heretofore held illegal an agreement among members of an association to withdraw their patronage from any one who sold to one who was not a member of the association or an agreement which permitted members of an association to make purchases only from such as sell exclusively to members of the association. I have never been able to appreciate the distinctions which some courts have endeavored to make between cases of the kind I have indicated, and cases where the right to employ non-union labor was involved. There is no doubt that persons may combine for legitimate purposes and that an individual may refuse to deal with any particular person or class of persons and base such refusal upon mere whim or caprice, but it has been my opinion, and I am more than gratified to find it sustained by the appellate court, that a number of persons can not combine with the object of compelling the adoption of a contract which prohibits the employer from employing non-union labor.

If such a contract is entered into it is illegal, and under the decision of the appellate court constitutes a criminal conspiracy, to which not only the union but the employer becomes a party and for which not only the employe but the employer is subject to fine or imprisonment in the penitentiary, or both, under our criminal statutes. There are a vast number of manufacturing concerns in this State that have written contracts with labor unions which prohibit the employment of non-union labor. Under this decision of the Appellate Court many hundreds, if not thousands [illegible] as well as many thousands of emplo[illegible] become parties to a ge[illegible] contracts furnish [illegible] proof. Where [illegible]ents exist the crime can not be [illegible] cancellation of the contracts, [illegible] recognition of the binding force [illegible]acts, in the light of the recent d[illegible] appellate court, may create trouble of [illegible]tle dreamed of by those who have permitt[illegible]emselves to be forced or lulled into them

The fact that laborers have the right to refuse to work for a man who does not employ union labor, or in order to better their condition or advance their wages, does not authorize the making of a contract under which the employer is compelled to employ only union labor and to discharge non-union labor. The rights of the employer and employe are, and should be, synonymous, but employes can not, by combination or union, without committing the crime of conspiracy, force employers to agree to employ only union labor. When employers do become parties to such an agreement they are equally guilty of conspiracy.

The opinio[illegible] appellate court should be studied at on[illegible] of labor in this State, and w[illegible] tion that he is a [illegible] floodgates will open and no[illegible] think, receive the protection that all of [illegible] tions and processes of the courts have heretofore been unable to give them.

LOUIS D. BRANDEIS,

Of Brandeis, Dunbar & Nutter, Lawyers, Boston:

The decision in the Kellogg Switchboard & Supply Co. case is merely an application of the well established and sound rule that picketing attended by intimidation and coercion is unlawful and will be enjoined. The opinion, however, contains an elaborate dictum which purports to lay down a rule that is both novel and unsound, namely, that a strike, though conducted in a lawful manner, is illegal if its purpose is to secure an agreement for the employment of union men exclusively. The reasoning of the court is not clear. The conclusions stated appear to rest upon the assumption that an effort to secure an agreement to employ exclusively one class of workmen is unlawful on four grounds:

First. As interfering with the employer's "right of contract."

Second. As unjustly discriminating in favor of one class and thereby interfering with the workman's "right to work."

Third. As tending to create a monopoly.

Fourth. As contravening the Illinois statute prohibiting combinations "for the purpose of depriving the owner or possessor of property of its lawful use and management."

None of these positions seems to me tenable.

As to the first ground: It does not interfere with the employer's right of contract to induce him to enter into a certain contract. Every contract which any person enters into interferes in some way with his future freedom of contract of other action. That is the very purpose of entering into a contract. The "right of contract" is the right to restrict one's freedom of action. This sacred right of contract is limited only by the requirements of public policy as expressed either in rules of the common law or of statutory prohibition.

The privilege for which employers have most strenuously contended in the past is the right to employ, that is to contract with, whom they please, —union or non-union men. The employer exercises this privilege when he elects from day to day to employ union men. No sufficient reason sug[illegible] itself why he should not be permitted to agr[illegible] advance for a limited time, or until further n[illegible] he will employ only union men.

If the effort of unions to secure from an employer

such an agreement should be held unlawful, it will not be because the employer's right of free contract is thereby interfered with, but because some paramount consideration of the public good requires that the right to free contract be in this respect abridged.

As to the second ground: It is not an unjust discrimination against certain workmen, or an interference with their right to work, for a private employer to employ only persons of a certain class. Nor does an agreement to make his selection on such lines, however capricious or unreasonable, interfere with any one's rights. A discrimination between two classes of workmen cannot be unjust unless there is a right not to be discriminated against, in other words, a right to equality of treatment. So far as relates to private employment, there is no such right. The right to work for a private employer is merely the right to be allowed to work if one can find a willing employer.

In the case of public employment the case is entirely different. The government must be run for the equal benefit of all. Every citizen has an equal right to the opportunity of being selected to serve the public in any capacity, and to receive such compensation as the public pays. Any discrimination in public employment in favor of one class of persons, for instance, union men, either by statute or ordinance or practice, is clearly illegal.

If the effort to secure an agreement to employ union men only is held to be unlawful, it will not be because any right to work now known to the law is thereby interfered with.

As to the third ground: An agreement to employ union men only undoubtedly tends in some degree to a monopoly, but the tendency ordinarily would be very slight and remote. It certainly is not the law that every contract which tends however slightly towards the creation of a monopoly is unlawful. If it were, no large manufacturer could contract to increase his plant, or contract for an exclusive right to a patent which would cheapen production, for such a course tends inevitably towards securing a larger share of the market, thereby driving out competition and to that extent tending towards a monopoly.

In the case of strikes employers usually assert with much vehemence that in the absence of intimidation, violence, or coercion, the places left vacant by union strikers could be readily filled by non-union men. It is conceivable that the union control in one or all branches of trade might become so great, or be exercised in such a manner as to present the evils attendant upon monopoly and call for intervention by laws. But if that time should come there would be no occasion for agreements to employ exclusively union men. At all events it seems clear that, at the present time, the mere attempt to secure for a particular concern with a $500,000 capital and employing five or six hundred hands an agreement that only union men be employed cannot be said to tend so strongly and immediately to monopoly as to be held unlawful on that ground.

As to the fourth ground: The effort to secure by a strike legally conducted an agreement to employ only union men does not deprive "the owner or possessor of property of its lawful use ant management." By making such an agreement, the owner or possessor of property of its lawful use and managemanagement." The effort to secure by a legally conducted strike the making of such an agreement cannot be said to deprive the property owner of its use and management unless

(a) the union should control substantially all the labor; in which event there would be no occasion for the agreement; or

(b) the right "to the use and management of property" should be held to include a right to compel people to work for the owner.

It certainly was not the purpose of the Illinois statute to inaugurate such a revolution of the social and industrial system.

The statutes of several of the States show that in the past it has been believed that the public welfare would be promoted by the development of trades unions. In Massachusetts, for instance, Revised Laws, Chap. 106, Section 12 provides:

"No person shall himself or by his agent, coerce or compel a person into a written or verbal agreement not to join or become a member of a labor organization as a condition of his securing employment or continuing in the employment of such person."

If in the future the public welfare should appear to require it, the legislature may further restrict the right of contract by prohibiting agreements for a closed shop, or further restrict the right of combination by prohibiting strikes for the purpose of securing such agreements; but it is believed that neither the common law nor the statutes contain at present such prohibitions, and it is extremely undesirable that judges should attempt to create them because of their individual views of "public policy." Let them rather bear in mind the words of that very wise and fearless judge, Sir George Jessel:

"It must not be forgotten that you are not to extend arbitrarily those rules which say that a given contract is void as being against public policy, because if there is one thing which more than another public policy requires, it is that men of full age and competent understanding shall have the utmost liberty of contracting, and that their contracts, when entered into freely and voluntarily, shall be held sacred and shall be enforced by courts of justice. Therefore, you have this paramount public policy to consider—that you are not lightly to interfere with this freedom of contract."

Experience—the natural law in the industrial world—will alone teach us the course best to be pursued, and I fancy that course, when laid out, will eventually follow the lines of liberty:—

In the first place, liberty on the part of the employer to agree with the union for a closed shop whenever the inducements offered are sufficient to lead him to voluntarily renounce for a time his absolute freedom to choose such workmen as he pleases. Then, a recognition by the unions that their interests will be best subserved by omitting all attempts to restrict the choice of the employes, and devoting their efforts to increasing the attractions of unionism for the workmen, and to removing the incidents of unionism most objectionable to the employer. The wisest labor leaders have already taken this position, and have among other things declared the policy that the union label must be regarded as a valuable privilege to be acquired through assent to the closed shop, but that where such assent and hence the union label are withheld, the union workman may still work side by side with his non-union brother.

FREDERICK H. COOKE,

Author of "The Law of Trade and Labor Combinations," New York City:

In Christensen v. People (Appellate Court Ill. 1st Dist., May 12, 1904), was rendered on a point of vital and far-reaching importance, a decision that to me seems obviously at variance with reason and with law. As, however, the court is not one of last resort, I take it that there remains the hope of correction.

In brief the point seems to be that a strike is unlawful for the purpose of inducing the employer to agree to employ none but members of labor unions. If this be sound law, efforts on behalf of the "closed shop" will encounter a serious if not insurmountable obstacle.

Now let us look for a moment at the reason of the matter, whatever may be technically the law. I suppose that no one in his senses has ever questioned the legal right of a housewife to employ in her kitchen Irish in preference to German servants, or vice versa. I suppose that it has never been seriously contended that such a course constitutes an illegal 'discrimination in favor of one class' (i. e., of Irish or German servants, as the case may be) or is illegal as "tending to create a monopoly in favor of the members of" the class of Irish, or German servants, as the case may be. (The language quoted was used in Christensen v. People). Take as another illustration the case of a railroad contractor employing Italians in preference to negroes, or vice versa.

I do not see that the action held illegal in Christenson v. People stands on any different basis. Until recently at least, I do not suppose that the right to employ union in preference to non-union men, or vice versa, was seriously questioned. How then can it be illegal to merely agree to do what one has a perfect right to do; or to merely request or induce one to agree to do what he has a perfect right to do? If this be illegal, we have surely departed widely from the ancient standards.

In what essential respect was the agreement declared illegal different from the every day agreement to serve another exclusively, or to deal with another exclusively? Time and time again have such agreements been sustained by the courts. I forbear to cite at length from the many decisions to this effect, but, for instances of agreements for exclusive service sustained, see Carnig v. Carr, 167 Mass. 544 (1897); Harrison v. Glucose Sugar Refining Co., 116 Fed. Rep. 304 (Circuit Court of Appeals, 7th Circuit, 1902); of agreements for exclusive dealing sustained, Brown v. Rounsavell, 78 Ill. 589 (1875); Ellerman v. Chicago Junction Railways, &c. Co. 49 N. J. Eq. 217, 252 (1891); Bald Eagle Valley R. R. Co. v. Nittany Valley R. R. Co., 171 Pa. 284, 299 (1895); Ferris v. American Brewing Co. 155 Ind. 539 (1900).

The fallacy underlying the decision in Christensen v. People is perhaps not hard to discover. Baldly stated (and such statement is sufficient to show the utter lack of reason therein) it seems to be that there rests upon any given employer a sort of obligation to employ all that are reasonably capable of performing the given work; that consequently it is an illegal "discrimination" to employ some in preference to others; at any rate, to employ members of a certain class in preference to those of another class, e. g. Germans in preference to Irish, Italians in preference to negroes, "non-union" in preference to "union" men.

Let us glance for a moment at the statement of the court in Christensen v. People that the agreement in question was illegal because "tending to create a monopoly in favor of the members of the different unions, to the exclusion of workmen not members of such unions." The point is in reality covered by what has just been said, but note what seems to be the underlying fallacy, that all "monopolies" are illegal. Now not even the most rabid anti-monopolist (unless perchance he be communist as well as anti-monopolist) really and sanely contends that all monopolies are illegal, though occasionally, even in judicial opinions, language may be used to that effect. Each instance of separate ownership of property, such as a house or watch, involves a monopoly, that is, of the right touse the house or the watch. And so of the instances of agreements for exclusive service or dealing, already referred to. Instances might be multiplied indefinitely. To me the contention that to employ only union men 'tends to create an (illegal) monopoly in favor of the members of the unions," seems about as rational as would the contention that the employment by the housewife in our illustration of German servants exclusively, "tends to create an illegal monopoly in favor of' German servants.

It is perhaps proper to add that the doctrine thus applied in Christensen v. People may find some encouragement in prior decisions of the Illinois court of last resort. See Adams v. Brenan, 177 Ill. 194 (1898); Fiske v. People, 188 Ill. 206 (1900), and compare Woodward v. Boston. 32 Am. Law Rev. 624 (Super. Ct. Mass. 1898). Perhaps too such doctrine finds encouragement in the much discussed decisions in People ex rel. Rodgers v. Coler, 166 N. Y. 1 (1901); People ex rel. Treat v. Coler, 166 N. Y. 144 (1901), where somewhat analogous situations were presented. These two decisions were by a divided court, however, and the dissenting opinions of Chief Justice Parker seem to me to furnish by far the better reason.

The decision in Christensen v. People may be opposed, in spirit at least, to that line of decisions holding a strike not illegal because of intent to procure the discharge of those not members of the union on whose behalf the strike is instituted. See in particular National Protective Assoc. v. Cumming, 170 N. Y. 315 (1902), in line with which seem to be Commonwealth v. Hunt, 4 Metc. (Mass.) 111 (1842); Clemmitt v. Watson, 14 Ind. App. 38 (1895). It must be confessed, however, that on this much debated point there are decisions seemingly not in harmony with those just cited: see Plant v. Woods, 176 Mass. 492 (1900); Quinn v. Leathem, App. Cas. 495 (English House of Lords, 1901).

It is perhaps scarcely necessary to add that in the preceding discussion I have taken no account of purely economic considerations. For the sake of the argument I am willing to admit that the movement on behalf of the closed shop is an unwise one; that it is unwise to attempt to procure the making and enforcement of an agreement such as the one now under consideration. But surely no one needs to be reminded that it is not the function of the law, at least not necessarily, to compel men to refrain from merely foolish action.

It should be noted that, whatever be the ultimate decision in Christensen v. People, it will not necessarily determine the legality of a strike to induce an employer to agree to employ none but members of labor unions. That is to say, while there is, in my view, nothing in the case presented to the court in Christensen v. People, to show that the particular strike under consideration was unlawful, it may well appear to be otherwise in the case of another strike for the same purpose. So far as appears in the report of the decision, there was nothing to show that efforts of the particular unions interested in the strike were prosecuted on so large a scale that if successful they were likely to give them a virtual monopoly of employment in their particular lines. If, for instance, it had appeared that such unions comprised within their membership, say half of the brass moulders, brass workers, etc., in Chicago and vicinity, and that their efforts were directed towards all or substantially all those employing non-union brass moulders, brass workers, etc., in such locality, there might have been plausibility in the contention that the case was within the so-called "trust" cases such as the Sugar Trust, Standard Oil cases and others, in that, as in those cases a monopoly of the supply of sugar or oil was sought to be created, so here a monopoly of labor of a particular kind. The trouble is, however, that here the court assumed without a basis of fact the existince of a tendency to create a monopoly in favor of the members of the unions.

In addition to his opinion upon the decision, Mr. Cooke prepared answers to a series of hypothetical questions as follows:

Q.—Suppose the manufacturer of a certain brand of baking powder makes a grocer a discount, provided the grocer agrees to sell that brand exclusively, —would such a contract be illegal or criminal?

A.—If the decision in Christensen v. People be sound, it seems to follow that such contract constitutes an illegal "discrimination in favor of one class" (i. e. those manufacturing such brand of powder) or is illegal as "tending to create a monopoly in favor of" such manufacturers. It seems, however, that the law is, or had been supposed to be, well settled to the contrary. It is interesting to note that the Supreme Court of Illinois (which has general power to review the decisions of the Appellate Court) has passed upon the legality of what is substantially the precise situation described in the above query. That court saw nothing illegal in a contract by which a wholesale dealer in Aetna sewing machines agreed to sell them to retail dealers agreeing to deal exclusively in Aetna machines and to purchase their supplies from such wholesale dealer; the latter, on the other hand, agreeing to furnish them the machines at a discount. The court said: "We see nothing in such a contract so in restraint of trade as to make in that respect against public policy, and require that it should be adjudged void. We know of no warrant of authority therefor." Brown v. Rounsavell, 78 Ill. 589 (1875). And there is a long succession of decisions to the same effect. In a standard legal text-book (Greenhood on Public Policy, p. 677) the author, after declaring the legality of contracts securing the exclusive custom of the party contracting, furnishes with others tom of the party contracting, furnishes with others the following illustrations of such contracts, sustained by the courts: "A publican in making settlement with his creditors agrees to buy all his beer of them." "A railroad company agrees that the cars of the covenantee should be the only cars employed in the transportation of locomotive engines and tenders over its road". "A. agrees to buy of B. all the groceries he may need, provided he will furnish them at as low prices as others." "A. covenants not to employ any other person than B. to make cordage for his friends." "A. covenants not to buy any meat for his trade for six months of any but the covenantee." The same author says (p. 680): "A contract binding the party making it to labor exclusively for it or to sell exclusively to one person, either for a limited period or for all time is not void."

JACKSON H. RALSTON,
Lawyer, Washington, D. C.

The following illustrations of contracts sustained by the courts are here furnished: "A binds himself not to write plays for any other than the H. theatre.' "A. covenants to work for no one except B. for seven years." "A. covenants to work for B. for life." And many other instances of such contracts sustained as legal might be cited.

Q.—Suppose a labor union, through its authorized agent, were to make a discount upon the prevalent wage, provided the employer agreed to employ only members of that union,—would such a contract be illegal or criminal?

Q.—Suppose a labor union, through its authorized agent, grants an employer the use of the union label, that label being an assurance of patronage by the ranks of organized labor, as a consideration for the employer's agreeing to employ only members of that union,—would such a contract be illegal or criminal?

Q.—Suppose a labor union, through its authorized agent, were to guarantee to an employer a constant supply of superior workmen, capable of turning out a product in quality or quantity exceeding the computed output of non-union workmen, as a consideration for the employer's agreeing to employ only members of the union under its terms as to wages hours and conditions of work (shop rules), —would such a contract be illegal or criminal?

A.—What has already been said seems applicable to these queries. The instance above given of a valid contract to purchase all of ones groceries from another, provided he will furnish them at as low prices as others, is particularly suggestive here. If a contract to deal on as favorable terms as others would be sustained, it would seem that a fortiori a contract to deal on more favorable terms would be.

Q.—Suppose an employer were to make it a condition of hiring a workman, or a number of workmen, that the workman or workmen should agree, in accepting the employer's terms as to wages, hours and conditions of work (shop rules), to abstain from belonging to any labor union,—would such a contract be illegal or criminal?

A.—The law seems settled to this extent at least, that a person may refuse to employ another because of membership in a labor union, and may even discharge him because of membership in such union. Indeed, such right of an employer is part of his constitutionally guaranteed liberty of contract. In about a third of the States there have been enacted in the supposed interest of the labor unions, statutes seeking to deprive the employer of such right, but in nearly every instance such legislation has been declared unconstitutional. Thus in Missouri, in State v. Julow, 129 Mo. 163 (1895); in Illinois, in Gillespie v. People, 188 Ill. 176 (1900); in Wisconsin, in State v. Kreutzberg, 114 Wis. 530 (1902). If now an employer has the right to refuse to employ, or to discharge, because of membership in a labor union, it would seem to me to follow that he may make nonmembership in a labor union a condition of employment, but it may remain for the courts to make this entirely clear.

Q.—Suppose a workman or a number of workmen, were to offer to work for lower wages or longer hours, or under shop conditions more economical to the employer, provided the employer would agree to employ no workmen belonging to a labor union,—would such a contract be illegal or criminal?

A.—If the decision in Christensen v. People be sound, there seems to be plausibility in the view that such contract constitutes an illegal discrimination against members of labor unions. Generally speaking, however, in accordance with what has been said above, it seems clear enough to me that there is nothing illegal in such a contract. It might make a difference however, should carrying out such a contract involve the discharge of union men already in the employ of such employer. Under certain conditions the action of the non-union might be held illegal as against such union men.

The questions quoted above were each answered negatively by Roger Fisher of New York and Louis D. Brandeis of Boston.

JACKSON H. RALSTON,

Of Ralston & Siddons, Attorneys and Counsellors at Law, Washington, D. C.:

The learned court ignores the fact that labor is property (so to speak) in the hands of the laborer, quite as much as a right to do business is property in the hands of the head of a mercantile establishment. The laborer may dispose of this property as he sees fit. He may allow it to go to waste by not working, and he may determine the price he will demand for it. And, similarly, if one man may determine these questions for himself, why may he not elect to join with one or more others and agree that he will labor or will not labor as they may, by a majority vote, determine? Is his labor any the less his own because he associates another man with himself in fixing the price or the circumstances under which he will dispose of it?

The appellate court apparently takes the position that however proper it may be for one man to determine that he will not work for another, yet the element of criminality is invoked when two or more men in the form of a union announce in advance that they will not work except in company with those whom they may select. But is not the right to take this position inseparable from their property right in their own labor, and having such property right, how can the law properly interfere with their actions? Suppose they unitedly determine not to labor in association with negroes, or under a red-haired foreman, or with men of another nationality?

Why may they not do so? In so doing, they simply dispose of their own property right as seems meet to them.

But it is said in effect by the opinion that if they so exercise their property right, they interfere with the property right of the employer in the conduct of his business. Not so. The two rights have their appropriate spheres of action, and do not interfere one with the other. The employer does not own the laborer, and not owning him, can not ask the courts to control the laborer's action by means of injunction. It is true that the laborer by his strike may injure the employer's business, but so in the laborer's judgment will the employer injure his property right in his own labor, if the employer, exercising that full liberty that belongs to him of right, employs those who are not members of the laborer's organization. In either event, injury may result, but would the application of a laborer to a court to enjoin the employer from employing whoever he may see fit, on the ground that such general employment affected injuriously the laborer's right to employment, be received with any favor? The proposition needs only to be stated, but it is the exact counterpart of the fallacious idea underlying Judge Adams' opinion.

Another fallacy may be referred to. It was said that the draft of an agreement with certain unions was sought to be inforced by threats; but so far as the principle we are now discussing is concerned, the so-called threats appear to have been merely that unless a certain agreement be accepted (the agreement not being, as we attempt to show, contrary to the law) the laborers in question would not work for the employer. As I have sought to indicate briefly, laborers, singly or jointly, have the right to refuse to labor for any reason or no reason. If this right exists, a threat to refuse their labor can not be unlawful. One or more of us may say to our grocer that if he does not attend our church we will not trade with him, because we prefer to trade with our own church members. As we have a right to place our trade wherever we see fit, such a threat can not be unlawful, and can not be the foundation of judicial action. Our right to determine our own employer rests upon the same right. The opinion appears to me to be deficient in not distinguishing properly between illegal threats and announcements that are essentially legal,—to which, in fact, the word threat is scarcely applicable.

The reference contained in the decision to the clause of the Criminal Code, denouncing those who combine to deprive the owner or possessor of property of its lawful use and management, or prevent by threats, suggestions of danger, or by any unlawful means, any person from being employed by or obtaining employment from any owner or possessor of property, does not seem a happy one, so far as the general theory sought to be sustained by the court is concerned. The court has largely inverted the meaning of this section. A combination under which working men refuse to be employed by the owner of property, unless certain conditions be granted, can not deprive the owner or possessor of property of its lawful use or of his property, unless he had a lawful right to the use of the labor of the men so united, and could enforce such use against their will. If he can not procure others to take their place, the employer may be injured in the sense that his property becomes less productive, but that is a consequence he has seen fit to accept for himself. In addition, as has been heretofore pointed out, a refusal by one or more persons to labor in association with another, can not of itself be illegal, unless the person aimed at has a moral right to compel the others to work with him, or unless the methods resorted to are illegal.

If the existence of the union made it more difficult for the employer to employ non-union men, and even if the element of criminality were involved, the employer could not resort to equity, unless he has a property right in the labor of the non-union men—something he could not demonstrate. Without this, reference to the criminal code becomes meaningless, since a court of equity can not enjoin a crime unless property or the right to property be involved.

Notwithstanding the strong opinion of the writer that the whole decision of the court is filled with logical errors, approaching almost to the point of absurdity, it does not follow that the judgment is erroneous. If illegal methods are employed to bring about even the doing of a lawful act, those guilty of their use may be subject to punishment, and it may have been in this case that there was such illegality connected with the particular acts charged against the defendants, involving contempt of court for violation of injunction against plain interference with what are really property rights as would justify their punishment.

The thing I criticise is the general theory enunciated by the court, and not the conclusion in this case.

WILLIAM VELPEAU ROOKER,
Lawyer, Indianapolis:

Judge Adams, it would seem, holds that a contract for a closed shop per se creates a monopoly and it is therefore void because monopolies are opposed to public policy. Judge Adams had not before him for his construction a particular contract for a closed shop (though he did have some proposals submitted

WILLIAM V. ROOKER,
Lawyer, Indianapolis.

by some unions, which proposals were not accepted and ought to have been resisted), and his opinion in respect to such contracts is therefore either obiter dictum or he bases his faith upon so broad an application of a familiar principle as to condemn all monopolies. It has long been suspected by some people that Chicago was lax in its standard of morals and integrity, and now Judge Adams makes it clear why his city may be as it is accused of being. The marriage relation creates a monopoly by the husband in the wife and vice versa, and that being contra bona mores, according to the Judge Adams rule, therefore we have Chicago rightfully revelling in free love. The powers of public officers are a monopoly, and therefore, if Judge Adams be right, we have great public trusts in Chicago correctly turned over to the grafters. Private ownership of property is a monopoly, and therefore, vide supra, the thieves and looters of Chicago are good people and all right. It is to be supposed that if some paper manufacturer were to agree that for a certain price, for a certain quality, upon certain installments of delivery, for certain installments of payments, he would for a certain time furnish the Chicago Tribune all its white paper, that contract, according to Judge Adams, would create a monopoly and be void. Or if that paper contract was lawful, then by what rule would the Tribune be denied the right to provide by like means any other of the staples it requires in its business, and whether its ink, its light, its fuel or its labor. To measure the constitutional validity of a contract by the degree of duress used in obtaining it, certainly brings into being a rule of construction new, alike to those who are familiar with the safeguard of the common law and those who are familiar with the usual limitations of the Constitution.

The purpose of a contract for a closed shop is only incidentally hostile to non-union labor. The object and intent is to give the union authority over the men employed to do certain work. The purpose is discipline. The object is to exact obedience to certain fixed scales of efficiency and decorum. The common law rule as to fellow servants makes employes responsible for the conduct of one another, to the extent of sacrificing limb and life. With so great a charge as this placed upon them, can it be said that there is or ought to be any moral or legal objection to employes exercising a voice in the selection of their fellow workmen—those for whose good conduct so great an indemnity in favor of the employer is by law exacted from the employe? To subordinate men and their individual interests so largely to the general welfare of the State, as Judge Adams appears inclined to do, would, it seems, bring us at once to the practical realization of socialism in its purest forms. Nor are the interests of the employes alone conserved by union contracts. There are times in factories and shops when the work is hard and when even the most faithful servant would rather be absent than present. It is on such occasions that the union must be able to compel obedience to its contract to furnish all the required labor and it to be of a specified quality for a specified price. If the employes were not under compulsion to obey, they could on such occasions leave the task and tell the master to do his own work. That is human nature. For such an offense the aggrieved master could not efficiently follow them elsewhere; there craft can. We must have the power to exact obedience; the same power Judge Adams exercised in his contempt proceedings. How would Judge Adams as a colonel of a regiment of even the bravest men like to engage to make a desperate assault without his men being enlisted or otherwise obligated to give him obedience in performing the task? How many men would be in their ranks when the point of assault was reached if his men in the first instance were not obligated to obedience? Even brave men avoid danger, and good soldiers go to all proper lengths to save their lives. So, good workmen have their preferences as to the labor they are called upon to perform, and as between themselves they require and prefer discipline.

Judge Adams seems to be suffering from judicial strabismus to the extent that he cannot see that the employer's constitutional right to contract would be destroyed rather than conserved by such a rule as the one stated by Judge Adams in the Christensen case. He ought to read dispassionately the constitution of some successful labor unions, then some contracts for closed shops, and then observe the current of authority as to contracts that are void not because they create monopolies, but because they create unlawful monopolies. If he had before him a statute prohibiting the exclusive employment of union men he would promptly declare that statute void because in derogation, not only of the constitutional right to contract, but also of the constitutional guarantees of the liberties of the citizen who has a right to be a member of any organization whose purposes are not within themselves unlawful.

JOHN E. PARSONS,
Lawyer, New York City:

In a leading English case it was held, the decision of the lower courts being affirmed by the English House of Lords, that it was the right of parties to make a combination with a view of keeping their trade in their own hands, and that parties who were excluded had no redress unless they could show that the object of the combination was to ruin their trade, or was the result of personal malice or ill-will. This, in my opinion, is the law of this country as

(Concluded on page 8.)

THE OPEN SHOP QUESTION IN GREAT BRITAIN.

ITS ADOPTION THERE GENERAL, ALTHOUGH NOT UNIVERSAL, WHILE UNION LABOR WINS THE PREFERENCE OF EMPLOYERS THROUGH ITS SUPERIORITY.

Much light is thrown upon the treatment of the question of the open shop by organized labor in the United Kingdom, through recent letters from several of its representative leaders, addressed to the National Civic Federation. These letters are responses to an inquiry addressed on behalf of that organization to the secretaries of leading British unions. This inquiry requested information as to the position taken by those unions as to the open shop, as to how it is treated in formal agreements with employers, as to the attitude of employers in general, and as to the comparative significance or importance of the question in Great Britain and the United States. All of the British union secretaries to whom this inquiry was addressed had visited the United States as members of Mr. Alfred Mosely's industrial commission, and had thus enjoyed the opportunity of comparing labor conditions in the two countries.

The replies here presented are from secretaries of unions that include the organized employes in nine great industries. These industries employ engineers, iron founders, iron and steel workers, tube trades, paper makers, weavers, cotton spinners, tailors and lithographic printers. The replies show that in all of them the open shop obtains either throughout the industry generally, or to a large extent, being greatly limited only in one industry. The lithographic printers have a union rule, of which all employers are notified, that no printer eligible to the union shall be employed, unless a member of the union. But there are exceptions to this rule in a few towns and cities, due to local or peculiar conditions, conceded by the unions. The iron founders secure a closed shop only where their organization is strong enough to enforce it. Elsewhere, they permit open shops, and they refrain from picketing in strikes. In the tube trades, there are cases where union men refuse to work with non-unionists. But this action has been taken without aid from the general union. In practice, the workers in some (the relative number is not specified) iron and steel works are all union men. But there is in that industry no distinct cleavage between union and non-union shops. Employers of tailors are said to prefer union shops, with a trade agreement including arbitration.

These five industries are those of the nine upon which reports are presented in which the open shop appears not to be universal. Of these five, the Lithographic printers constitute the only craft in which the open shop is a restricted, local concession, although the effect of the tailors' agreement is to cause employers to prefer union workers. The engineers have a general trade agreement with the employers which stipulates for the open shop. In this craft, only voluntary membership is regarded as valuable to a union. The cotton spinners have also a general agreement which ignores the subject of non-union employes. All mills are open, but 90 per cent of the English spinners belong to the organization, and it is stated that employers as a rule prefer union spinners, although refraining from expressing that preference. Many employers of iron founders will not permit members of the union to be foremen. The tube trades have no general agreement; but in rare cases, employers have refused to permit non-union men to share in a general advance of wages. The agreement of the iron and steel workers ignores non-union men, who must work under its provisions; but the policy of the open shop has prevailed in their industry for thirty years. The weavers' agreement does not mention non-union workers, who of course do not enjoy the benefit of the organization's funds in case of a strike. The paper makers work with non-union men when the latter receive the same rate of wages as do members of the society.

It will be noted that several of these unions attribute their strength to a high standard of membership that ensures superior workmanship, and to the accumulations of benefit funds. Some of the British union secretaries' comments upon trade union conditions in the United States are of interest.

Lithographic Printers.

George D. Kelley, General Secretary of The Amalgamated Society of Lithographic Printers of Great Britain and Ireland, writes from 63 Upper Brook Street, Manchester:

"In respect to the question of declining to work with non-union men, which you state is becoming a serious one in your country, I beg to say that here, so far as my own union is concerned, we do not experience much difficulty. I enclose the rule by which our members are governed. With every revision of rules a copy is forwarded to every employer, so that he has full opportunity of becoming acquainted with the rules in operation in the society. No serious objection has been taken by the employers to the rule in question, although some have taken exception, and occasionally as a consequence a little friction has arisen, which has generally been allayed and removed by an interview between the employer and myself, and the rule adhered to.

"In some few towns and cities in the United Kingdom the rule is not observed quite so closely as in others, but it is observed generally, and the few places referred to, where it is not operated quite so rigidly, are owing to some local cause or special influence which is respected and given way to. I may add that this society has very few disputes with employers. Should anything arise causing irritation or should we desire certain changes, an interview or interviews takes place between the employer and myself, and the matter is arranged between us, usually to the satisfaction of both, the whole question at issue having been by both discussed in a courteous and conciliatory manner. In fact, my experience, which is a wide one (being for twenty-five years a general secretary) has shown most clearly that better results can be obtained from a talk across the table, on a reasonable request, than by any other methods."

The rule enclosed by Mr. Kelley provides: "No member of this society shall work in any shop where there is also employed a non-union lithographic or collotype printer eligible for membership in this society." Other paragraphs of the rule provide for notification of the local branch of the union in case a non-union man should go to work in a shop, and provide for a committee of the union to "use the best means available to settle the difficulty." "No extreme measures shall be adopted except upon the decision of a special summoned meeting."

Amalgamated Engineers.

George H. Barnes, secretary of the Amalgamated Society of Engineers, established 1851, writes from its general office 110 Peckham Road, London, S. E.:

"You ask in what way the union of which I am secretary deals with the question of the non-union element. In our formal agreement with the employers it is stipulated that we work with the non-unionists. Such agreement has been in operation some seven years, but even before, when there was no agreement, the same practice obtained, that is to say, we relied upon moral suasion in regard to the non-unionists, so far as the attitude of the society as a whole was concerned. Of course, there have always been some members who have adopted a more militant attitude, but such has never received the formal endorsement of the Amalgamated Society of Engineers.

"I spoke in that sense during the proceedings of the Civic Federation meeting in December, 1902. I believe that forced men are no good to any organization which they may be compelled to join. You will note that I look at the matter from a practical point of view. Reams might be written in an abstract sense for and against coercion. Putting my position on it briefly, I should say that, even assuming the justice of force, it is no practical use; and the position of American labour unions, I think, is proof of the soundness of this view."

Amalgamated Tube Trades.

T. Jones is the General Secretary of the Amalgamated Tube Trade Society, which is affiliated with the Midland Counties Trades' Federation and is registered pursuant to Act of Parliament. The general office of the Society is in the London and North-western Hotel, Wednesbury. General Secretary Jones writes from 167 Dudley Road, Wolverhampton:

"I regret to say I can give you but little information on the subject. We have never been able to induce the employers to co-operate with us in the matter. What has been done is due to the action of the men in individual works. We have at some of the works had the men put down their tools and refuse to work with a man who was not paying his union money, with the result that they have had to borrow the money and pay up before they could start. In some cases, the manager has found the money for them. This action has taken place at several works, but I have had nothing to do with it. In one or two instances, the employers refuse to give any advance to those who were not in the society when there has been a general advance.

"The employers preferred non-union men when they could get them, because they could do as they pleased with them. There are but few trades in this locality who have not some of their workmen not in the society. No concerted action is taken, as a rule they use only moral suasion. They all recognize the evil effect of such methods. But the law is altogether in favour of the employers. This is emphasized by the Taft Vale decision."

Amalgamated Paper Makers.

William Dyson of the Amalgamated Society of Paper Makers writes from 7 Station Road, Woodley, Nr. Stockport:

"Our society does not object to our members working with 'non-unionists' providing the latter work under the same conditions and receive the same rate of wages as themselves. Consequently, it has not been necessary to make any agreement with the employers respecting the same. In justice to the employers, I may say the majority prefer unionists and when requiring them they apply to the society."

Society of Iron Founders.

J. Maddison, General Secretary of the Iron Founders' Society, established 1809, writes from its general office, 200 New Kent Road, London, S. E.:

"During my sojourn in America, the slight inquiries I found time to make into the conditions and methods of trade unions in your country elicited the fact that the contributions paid into the unions are much too low. Consequently, the unions have no backbone in them in the shape of benefits. As a result, members are indifferent as to allowing their membership to lapse, having nothing to lose, and re-enter any number of times. If they were liable to forfeiture of benefit with exclusion, they would be more careful about retaining their membership. Moreover, their financial position is very weak. When war is declared, their war chest is very far from being what it ought to be. According to wages received, they ought to pay at least 50 per cent higher contributions than we do in this country; whereas, they are something like 50 per cent below ours.

"The employers know full well that trade unionism means high rates of wages, which rightly or wrongly they regard as a deterrency to trade. At least their contention is in this strain, when arguing against advances or in favor of reductions in wages. Consequently, they encourage non-unionism as much as possible. A very large percentage of employers will not have a trade unionist in the position of foreman, if they know it. It is no uncommon occurrence for our branch secretaries to be victimised because they hold such positions. Of course, there are honorable exceptions to this rule.

"When a grievance arises that results in a strike or a lock-out, we generally refrain from picketing, leaving the employers to employ whom they choose. But I regret to say that the employers do not reciprocate this treatment by allowing us to go and work where we choose. No, they invariably blacklist our members, which means preventing them from working wherever they have the power to do so.

"Returning to the so-called 'scabs,' or free labour as they term themselves in this country, we leave them severely alone, believing that they do our cause more good inside a struck shop than outside; as from a workmanship point of view, 90 per cent are not worth their shop room. Indeed, the firm would not give them shop room, did peace prevail. Their very looks and get up betray their character, and the tenth man who may be a moderate workman is invariably a confirmed drunkard. So long as the strike may last, these free labor men are allowed to do anything they like.

"The authorities of the towns are largely made up of employers; consequently the law is administered very severely against the strike hands, who scarcely dare look at a 'scab,' lest they may be charged with assault. This is why we refrain from picketing. These 'scabs' are often very aggravating by openly boasting that they have broken so many strikes up, whereas their ability can command a job only where a strike exists. Thus they are always on the look-out for strikes, which are their only chance of obtaining work.

"For a time, these strikes have often appeared to go against us. . . . But by and by the shareholders' meeting takes place. The usual dividend has largely diminished, or disappeared altogether. It may be that the balance is on the wrong side of the ledger, which may be tolerated for a time. But the end must come. You cannot convince shareholders better than by reducing the dividend. The management are asked to give a reason for this falling off, when the truth has to be admitted—the molders' strike. It frequently happens after a strike has continued so long that we have regarded the shop as lost to us, the employers have caved in by clearing out the 'scabs' and sending for our men to return. . . .

"In reference to what you term open shop, I take that to mean open to all comers, regardless of whether they are trade unionists or not. This is what we term working mixed. We certainly do work mixed where we are not so well organized as we could wish; but where we are well organized, we refuse to work mixed.

"I am strongly of opinion that it is in the interests of the employers not to work mixed. Human nature is the same the world over. It is only reasonable to expect that considerable feeling exists between the non-union and union men, as the former are reaping the benefit of conditions brought about by and at the expense of the latter, and at no cost to themselves. Whilst this rankling feeling exists, it prevents men's minds being wholly concentrated in their work as it ought to be; hence they are not doing justice to their employer.

"Probably this feeling against non-unionists may be condemned by the employers and those representing the public in the Civic Federation. But I ask those gentlemen to imagine a case of a few men becoming residents of Chicago and refusing to pay rates, whilst they were enjoying the benefit of the sanitary arrangements and other privileges of the city, made at the cost of the ratepayers generally. I ask would such refusal be tolerated five minutes? Yet the one is just about as reasonable as the other.

"I sincerely hope that the praiseworthy efforts of the Civic Federation may be crowned with success."

Associated Iron and Steel Workers.

James Cox, General Secretary of the Associated Iron and Steel Workers of Great Britain writes from its head office, 6 Mount Pleasant, Darlington:

"I am in receipt of your enquiry concerning the action of our trades organization relative to the men who are not members, and the question of an 'open shop.' So far as our trades union is concerned, the policy we have adopted during these last thirty years has been that of an 'open shop.' It is perfectly true that at some works practically the whole of the men are members of our organization, while at other works it may be that not half or even a less number than that are not members.

"So far as non-union men are concerned, they are entirely ignored by us, and so far as general wages questions are concerned, while they have no voice in deciding upon those wages, they have to abide by the decisions of our organization and its agreements with the employers. Any non-union man who demurs to this would have the option given him by the employer immediately of either working under the terms agreed to by the employer and us, or leaving the works.

"We have some mills where employers go so far as to refuse to allow non-union men to work, while at other places non-union men are entirely ignored in all questions affecting either their wages or their work. So far as the iron and steel industry in this country is concerned, we have no shops defined as 'union' and 'non-union.' I do not believe there is a work in this country but what there are some union men and I have never yet met with an employer who has demurred to discuss wages questions with me, even if it affected only half a dozen men.

"Whether this policy of the 'open shop' commends itself to my fellow trades unionists in America I cannot say; but so far as our own industry is concerned in this country, I should be sorry to see any policy adopted which would bring about the distinct cleavage you have in your American mills of 'union' and 'non-union.'"

Amalgamated Weavers.

William H. Wilkinson is the representative of the Northern Counties Amalgamated Association of Weavers in the Joint Committee of Employers and Operators for North and Northeast Lancashire. He writes from the general office of the Weavers' Association, Ewbank Chambers, 17 St. James' Street, Accrington:

"So far as the weaving industry is concerned, we never make any agreements with the employers regarding the non-member element. All agreements made between our Amalgamation and the Employers' Amalgamation are made for members, the non-members not being mentioned, neither employer nor operative. I may add that in case of a strike none of the Operators' Amalgamation funds are paid to non-members."

Mr. Wilkinson enclosed the printed rules and regulations under which the joint committee of the employers and operators proceeds. The object of the joint committee is "To consider in their preliminary stages all trade disputes occurring in the weaving department, . . . and thereby endeavoring to preserve good feeling between employers and operators." The joint committee consists of twelve members, six representatives of the employers and six representatives of the weavers' associations. There are regular weekly meetings in Manchester and a special meeting must be held upon seven days' notice on either side. The business of the joint committee is "preliminary and consultative only." "It is not authorized to come to any final conclusion upon any of the matters brought under its notice." The general results of the various discussions must be reported to their constituents by the two sections of the committee. Its meetings are strictly confidential. The name of any member must not be quoted at any public meeting. Any dispute should first be brought before a local meeting of employers and operators. Failing settlement there, the dispute "should be brought before the joint committee prior to any notices for a strike being given by either employers or operators." These rules have been in force since July 3, 1896.

Society of Tailors.

Terence A. Flynn, General Secretary of the Amalgamated Society of Tailors, responded from the general office of that society, 415 Oxford Street, Manchester. Mr. Flynn wrote: "The question [of the closed shop] is not one which touches us to any extent. Some of the other industries are more hardly struck. I need not say that I wish your movement [the movement for better relations between employer and employed] success. If we had had some such body in past years, much trouble, misery and bitter feeling would have been averted. Still, I am pleased to say that a better feeling is asserting itself and the position is full of promise."

Mr. Flynn accompanied his letter with a paper which he had prepared for publication, upon some of his observations during his visit to the United States, from which the following are excerpts:

"Since Babel, I question if there has been gathered under a settled form of government such diversity of tongues and nationalities as obtains with you. Interwoven are inevitable racial differences, historical antipathies, preconceived and inherited methods of production and organization, all of which tend to entangle and obscure a problem which, even in this old Island, remains very much in a condition of nebulous expectancy. As a consequence, difficulties, which are natural with us, are with you very much involved, and the work of a trade union increased in severity of organization to a very considerable extent.

"Under such abnormal conditions it would appear that effective criticism becomes, in a manner, blunted, so much so, that it seems to me the practical question is, 'are there features in the British trade union movement which would repay consideration, if not adoption?'

"At the outset, I venture the opinion that your Federation of Labor exhibits an administrative capacity and brotherhood which entitles it to the good will of all interested in the welding of conflicting life into the solidarity of a nation. Human progress is seldom well ordered, but if discord is the accident, as I believe it is, in the affairs of the Federation, and steady, broad-based progress the ideal, then co-operation becomes an easy and a natural duty."

Mr. Flynn contrasts with this American body the individual unions of England, which, he says, are 'ready for immediate defense rather than federation, with its superior controlling, harmonizing and peace-making tendencies." He makes the interesting observation as to the influence of benefit funds against strikes:

"The adoption of friendly society benefits widened the scope of discussion, gave the man who could fight, but would rather give brain first chance, a front seat in council; increased the contribution and the amount in the total funds; and, in short, changed English trade unions from mere fighting machines into solidly established business firms.

"Following this came a close supervision of branches and the abolition (in most unions) of their right to declare a strike."

Mr. Flynn's paper continues:

"In my own union arbitration is compulsory. Every industrial centre has its properly consituted arbitration board, together with a court of appeal, formed of members of our employers' national council and the council of our union. The decisions of this board are final. We would not go back to the days of unlimited strike; our days may be tamer, but our lives are safer, and there is a mutual respect which counts for more in a tight corner than six months' warfare. That, at any rate, is our insular opinion.

"Our gain, however, does not stop at that. Arbitration tends to abolish strikes (of course, like yourselves, we retain the liberty to strike if needs must), it also tends in an even greater degree to abolish the blackleg, the scab, and the non-unionist. As a matter of fact, our employers prefer their shops to be union shops, as the union stops trouble with a heavy hand, our business being to see that all agreements are carried out faithfully and well, as much by our members as by the employers. Of course, these changes are not the work of a day nor of fifty years. Our union is the oldest trade union in England of which authentic records can be obtained. We can trace back through the centuries our victories and defeats. Sometimes compelling Parliament to abolish laws which especially pressed upon us (no mean task when Parliament was practically elected or returned by our feudal lords), at other times having special acts which aimed at wiping us out. Thus the hurly burly went on, now the top dog, but more often the bottom dog.

"Our last great and most disastrous struggle was in the early thirties of the last century, when we struck for an eight hours day, and although over sixty years have passed, the ill effects of that defeat can still be traced.

"Our present system is not the dream of a night, but the fruit of a hundred years of labored effort; of schemes and dreams and systems put forward and would best suit our purpose and circumstances; and dropped. From the dead hands of past generations of workers we have taken that which we thought to it we have added a system of arbitration, which we believe gives an intellect and a purpose to our movement that past efforts never had.

"If I may venture one further opinion, I would say the system and methods of organization adopted in America are very similar to ours of 25 and 50 years years ago. Perfected, I admit, nay, I am glad to admit the improvement, but in essential detail very similar; and it appears to me that when you come to consolidate the magnificent movement you are creating, like us, you will have to put more goods in your windows."

Operative Cotton Spinners.

Thomas Ashton, General Secretary of the Oldham Operative Cotton Spinners' Provincial Association, and President of the Amalgamated Spinners' Association, writes from the central office, Rock Street, Oldham:

"In reply to your inquiry as to the methods our association pursues with regard to non-unionist operative cotton spinners, I beg to say that the whole of the cotton mills are open for employment, both to union workmen and non-union workmen, and that no pressure is brought to bear upon the latter by the former beyond that of moral suasion, with a view of getting them to join the union.

"Of course, the union members are not supposed to assist non-union workmen in their employments, but union spinners assist one another in many ways, and in this way the non-union spinners are made to feel their position, as they are often placed in an awkward place in the carrying out of their duties. It is almost impossible for organized workers to have any sympathy with non-union workmen, as the latter receive the full advantage of the good work which the trade unions perform in the interests of their members; and yet they are too mean in principle to subscribe anything toward the expenses incurred in making their labour lives far more agreeable than they otherwise would be, were it not for the valuable work of the trade unions. Non-union cotton spinners are paid the same piece work rates and enjoy the same labour conditions, as do the trade union cotton spinners; but it is the latter and the organized employers who agree upon what these shall be. Non-union workmen have no voice in anything relating to work and wages, but they are content to accept of what trade union workmen can do for them, knowing full well that they will fare just the same as the trades unionist in everything pertaining to their labour. As a rule, employers don't bother their heads as to whether the spinners are union men, or non-unionists, but the bulk of them prefer the former class of workmen, as trade disputes are more easily adjusted by trade union efforts than it is possible when the workmen are not organized. I am pleased to say that upwards of 90 per cent of the operative cotton spinners are members of their trade union organization, and that the best of relations exist between them and their organized employers. From my long experience in the labour cause I am more than ever convinced that it is absolutely requisite for the welfare of the wage earning classes that they should be organized for trade union purposes, and I am surprised that any workman should be so dull in comprehension as to remain outside the ranks of organized labour. In any agreements we make with the organized employers the question of non-union workmen is never considered, but for all that, we have no love for such persons, as they act as a drag to the wheel of labour progress."

IS THE CLOSED SHOP ILLEGAL?

(Concluded from page 5.)

well. In the case referred to, it was a combination by owners of property. The principle equally applies to the case of owners of labor. Strikes are the remedy of workmen against attempted oppression by their employers. So long as workmen do not resort to intimidation or violence, I understand that in the absence of statutory provisions to the contrary their right to strike in larger or lesser numbers is absolute. They may do so without notice and under circumstances which are most favorable to the accomplishment of their wishes even if most injurious to employers, always provided that they do not resort to criminal means or to anything which is in the nature of intimidation or violence. And equally do I understand that in the absence of statutory legislation to the contrary it is the right of employers to employ or not employ whom they choose, and to make with their workmen any agreements which are for mutual interest, always provided that no criminal or illegal means are resorted to for the accomplishment of their end.

The converse is equally true. Strikes which involve intimidation or violence violate the law. And arrangements between employers and employed, the purpose of which is to prevent other workmen from obtaining employment, violate the law.

In my opinion the right, whether of the workman or of his employer, is a property right. It is protected or his employer, is a property right. It is protected by Federal and State constitutions, and no statute which endeavors to put a limitation upon it can stand.

The fundamental principle of our political system is the freedom of the individual and his right to be protected so long as he abstains from the perpetration of anything which is criminal or which violates the rights of others.

In expressing the above opinion I deal with the general situation. Corporations are creatures of statutes. Such statutes may within constitutional limitations subject their charters to reasonable restrictions. And I do not make any reference to arrangements which may be held to be in conflict with the law against monopoly or restraint of trade. They are foreign to the direct subject.

JOHN FRANKENHEIMER,

Of Kurzman & Frankenheimer, Lawyers, New York City:

The Illinois court holds that a contract proposed by trade unionists requiring their employer to hire only union labor is in violation of the employer's freedom of contract to hire any kind of labor that may suit him. But in its anxiety to preserve the sanctity of the doctrine of the freedom of contract, the Illinois court is blind to the fact that the freedom of contract implies as its correlative the freedom not to contract. If, as the Illinois court holds, the employer has the right to hire or to refuse to hire any kind of labor as his fancy may dictate, then the laborer has an equal right to work or refuse to work for any employer as to the laborer may seem best. If the employer can limit employment in his business to a specified kind of laborers, for instance, to white laborers or non-union laborers, and refuse to hire colored laborers or unionists, then the correlative right must exist in laborers—members of a trade union—to work only for an employer who will recognize their union and refuse to work for him unless he will limit employment in his business to members of their union. If the employer has the right to discriminate against unionists, the latter have an equal right to discriminate against an employer who will not support the union. If the employer in hiring a laborer can make it a condition of the employment that the laborer shall not be a member of a union, trade unionists in contracting with the employer have an equal right to make it a condition of their agreement to render service that the employer should hire only members of the union. If the employer can attach such a condition to his offer of employment, the trade unionists must possess an equal right to attach conditions to their offer of services. In homely phrase, what is sauce for the goose must be sauce for the gander. Unionists can say to their employer, "we will work only with unionists, we make a common sacrifice for a common benefit and we will help each other to get employment." There can be nothing illegal in the effort of unionists to make the shop in which they work a union shop, that is, to agree with the employer as a condition of rendering services to him that he will employ only members of the union. The employer is at liberty to refuse to limit employment to unionists, but if he does this the unionists must be at liberty to cease to work for him—that is, to strike! That is all the strikers did in the Illinois case in so far as they sought to induce their employer to make a contract with them. They had the right to strike for any reason deemed satisfactory to them. They had the right to endeavor by agreement with their employer to make the shop a union shop. They sought therefore by lawful means to attain a lawful end, and never before the decision in the Christensen case has this been declared to be an unlawful conspiracy.

It is to be regretted that the Illinois court went out of its way in the decision under discussion to render an unnecessary pronouncement against the principle of the union shop. Decisions of this kind serve only to undermine the confidence of workingmen in the absolute impartiality of our judicial tribunals, and tend to substantiate the charge that in the pending struggle between capital and labor judges are frequently influenced in their decisions by the natural bias which springs from environment.

Labor unions will receive additional protection against foes without from the Prince act, which has become a law in New York through the Governor's signature. This measure was passed by the legislature as a result of the indignation aroused by the disclosures made during the trial of Sam Parks on the charge of extortion. The new law makes the bribery of a walking delegate, business agent or any authorized representative of a labor union, a misdemeanor, punishable by fine and imprisonment. This does not create a new crime. It only specifies an offense that could before be reached only under the statute relating to extortion, which is thus extended to reach the briber. It is an act plainly intended for the benefit of organized labor as well as of employers. Its existence may exercise a deterrent influence upon those in a position of temptation.

The strike should be the last resort, after successive efforts at conciliation and arbitration have failed, and all chances for settlement abandoned.—"Cigar Makers' Official Journal."

LIBERTY, DEMOCRACY, PRODUCTIVITY AND THE CLOSED SHOP.

A REPLY TO THE ADDRESS OF MR. PARRY, CONVERTING AN ATTACK UPON THE CLOSED SHOP INTO AN ARGUMENT IN ITS FAVOR.

In his annual address as President of the National Association of Manufacturers, Mr. D. M. Parry remarks as an apparent cause of congratulation "that organized labor is learning a very valuable lesson in economics." Mr. Parry, himself, deserves congratulation for the rapidity with which he is learning from his own study of economic questions. He has discovered that low wages are not a benefit to society at large. In making this discovery, he has learned in a comparatively brief time a truth that has been attained by economists only after thought and discussion covering several decades. The old theory was that low wages caused low prices for products, and that their tendency was constantly beneficial to the entire community. That theory was long ago abandoned by economic students in favor of what is known as the doctrine of "the economy of high wages,"—the doctrine that in the modern age of machinery the highest wages are paid in those factories which turn out the cheapest products. Mr. Parry shows that he has graduated from the old notion when he announces his conviction that "high wages are a blessing, not a curse."

Opposition too Indiscriminate.

Mr. Parry has still to learn that his wholesale and indiscriminate opposition to the closed shop can not be sustained. He declares it to be his belief "that the day must come when no industry will be allowed to run on the closed shop plan;" and again, "that the closed shop is against public policy." With these propositions he couples the statement that the strides of this country in material welfare and in general intelligence are traceable to "the freedom of the individual," and declares that "all classes profit by the freedom of the individual to do as he pleases with his time, labor and property, so long as he does not infringe the equal freedom of another."

In my opinion, the application of the theory of the open shop to all industries is impracticable. This is a question upon which no sweeping decision can be reached, supported by sound reason, from the exclusive point of view of one side. Nor is it a question that can be answered by an indiscriminate conclusion of universal application. The question of open and closed shop must be considered in its application to different crafts.

The theory of trade unionism is that it tends to elevate the workingman of lowest earning capacity above a rate of payment which is less than the minimum wage necessary to sustain decent living. Its purpose and its actual tendency are to help in establishing an average minimum payment for labor that will be adjusted for the general good of all workingmen, and indirectly therefore of the whole community, since the workingmen form politically the mass of the voters, and economically the mass of the consumers. It must be conceded that this theory involves a certain sacrifice of that "liberty of the individual" which Mr. Parry regards as of supreme importance. This theory of unionism traverses, also, the general proposition with which President Eliot of Harvard University has approached this subject. If he has been quoted correctly in the daily press he regards the surrender of personal freedom to an association as "almost as great an obstacle to happiness as its loss to a despot or to a ruling class."

Sacrifices of Liberty.

Now liberty is indeed a precious thing. Liberty is in one aspect the fruit and flower of modern civilization. Yet there are some things even more valuable than the freedom of the individual. Liberty must be regarded as a means, rather than as an end in itself. Liberty implies equality, and in politics we have liberty because there exists political equality. But in the economic life, the equality in the parties to a contract is not always present. The liberty of the strong may become the license of the oppressor; the liberty of the weak may practically come to mean the subjection of the oppressed. It is, therefore, sometimes highly important to make a partial sacrifice of individual liberty in order to secure the maintenance of a greater equality, and thus the conditions for the restoration of an ultimate and enlarged liberty. This is what unionism seeks to do; this is its essential principle, and it is a principle that should command general public sympathy and approval.

Opened and Closed Shop.

Therefore, when Mr. Parry would make the rule of the open shop universal in all industries, on the ground that the closed shop is an infringement of individual liberty, he goes too far. In my opinion, the open shop would be beneficial in some industries

EDWIN R. A. SELIGMAN,
Professor in Columbia University.

and dangerous in others. The same statement may be made of the closed shop. For example, when the open shop would admit into an industry the cheap labor of indigent and ignorant immigrants, so as to create through the fierce competition of unorganized and necessitous labor a wage rate below the minimum essential for decent living, the open shop would obviously be a detriment. So long as this supply of crude labor from foreign countries continues, so long will such a domestic industry as garment-making, for example, need the protection afforded by the exclusive employment of members of a union, able to negotiate with employers a trade agreement that prescribes sanitary conditions of work and a wage which will permit living in accordance with the American standard. The closed shop here stands for the attainment of that equality between employer and employed, which is the surest guarantee of an ultimate liberty.

On the other hand, there are crafts in which the open shop might be beneficial, for the reason that the closed shop would tend to produce a monopoly. This danger of a monopoly of labor would become apparent in such a skilled calling as that of the glass blower. Any monopoly on the side of either capital or labor employed in ordinary industry is it is almost superfluous to state, in restraint of both production and trade, and is, therefore, a menace to prosperity. In the monopoly of labor in any craft lies the danger of unionism and the danger of the closed shop. A monopoly of skilled labor would tend to produce the same result as was reached by the guilds in the middle ages. The guilds were organized originally for the benefit both of the skilled workmen and of the consumers of their product. Ultimately they grew into craft monopolies, with resultant evils that are recounted in their history. Without doubt, the more advanced leaders of organized labor recognize this peril and do not hesitate to utter warnings against the danger of permitting the unions to create a monopoly of labor in any craft. It is doubtful, however, whether the rank and file of organized labor, are adequately instructed as to the reality of this peril.

Unionism and Democracy.

In some respects, the theory of the union is parallel to the political theory of democracy. The theory is based upon the proposition of human equality. In a certain and fundamentally important sense, the statement that one man is as good as another is true. The carrying out of that political idea has proved of the greatest benefit in our political system and has had its influence in making the average American citizen in many respects an admirable type. But in that very proposition lie the difficulties of democracy. For in another sense one man is not as good as another. Men are differentiated into classes by opportunity, by education and by efficiency. The real ideal of a democracy must be to level up, not to level down; and in this leveling up the true natural leaders must be given ample scope. But the end must be a democracy, not an aristocracy.

To transfer the illustration from politics to sociology, there underlies trade unionism a similar proposition on democracy. That is to say, unionism would not drag down the rewards of labor to the lowest earning capacity of the poorest workman. Rather would unionism tend to elevate the poorest workman so as to command a wage established on a minimum average higher than is essential to meet the bare necessities of existence.

The danger, however, in the practical operation of trade unionism lies in its working out toward the establishment of a fixed average payment for a day's work so as to put a check, or limit, upon the higher wages possible for superior individual merit. In that danger—the danger of the repression of individual excellence, and the limitation of its reward—is to be found the opportunity of opponents of organized labor for an attack upon it as a system. Therein, then, lies the necessity for intelligent leadership of organized labor to guard unionism against that attack.

Wages and Productivity.

Mr. Parry advances the general proposition that the rate of wages in any country is dependent upon the per capita production. It is doubtless true that the reward of labor, like the reward of capital, must be a certain portion of the sum of wealth produced in any industry, and varies in accordance with its effective contribution to the common output. Thus, productivity does bear a definite relation to the reward of labor. Moreover, capital and labor are intimately associated in this joint effort. If the productivity of capital can be increased through the use of fine machinery, not only will the return on capital be augmented, but the labor employed in using that machinery is certain to receive a higher reward than would labor employed in using inferior machinery, or no machinery at all. There are familiar illustrations of this truth to be seen on every side. The weaver, for example, using the best appliances in a New England mill will earn higher wages than can the hand loom weaver in the Southern hills.

But admitting Mr. Parry's proposition to be true, that the wage rate is dependent upon the per capita

(Concluded on page 16.)

MONTHLY REVIEW
OF THE
National Civic Federation

Offices: 281 Fourth Avenue, New York
Telephone, 389 Gramercy
RALPH M. EASLEY, Editor

The Editor alone is responsible for any unsigned article or unquoted statement published in THE MONTHLY REVIEW.

Ten Cents per Copy: One Dollar per Year.

LEGAL AND ECONOMIC ASPECTS OF THE CLOSED SHOP.

It is natural that the recent decision of the Appellate Court in Illinois that a contract between an employer and a union to employ union labor exclusively is illegal *per se* and in that State criminal should attract the attention throughout the country of both employers and wage-earners. That decision strikes at the very existence of the closed shop and of the union label. If its soundness were beyond question it would be a vital blow to an untold number of existing contracts and would place the ban of the law upon all efforts to extend the closed shop system. The open shop would of necessity prevail in all industries.

We believe that the decision is sound neither in law, nor in common sense, nor in policy. It declares that the specified agreement to employ only union workmen strikes at the right of contract. It appears to us that the decision itself strikes at that right. The decision appears also to strike by inference at trade customs that have been upheld in many courts and that are of common practice. If an employer may not agree to employ only a certain kind of labor, then a purchaser may not agree to buy only one brand of goods or to deal with one tradesman exclusively. Statutes to forbid employers to hire workmen upon the condition that they abstain from membership in a labor union have been declared unconstitutional wherever the test has been made. The same principle of freedom of contract underlying the closed shop agreement underlies the agreement to employ non-union labor exclusively. It is this principle that we wish to emphasize, without regard to the legality or illegality of the methods used to enforce a contract for the closed shop. Those methods are aside from the basic proposition. We invite attention to the opinions upon the Adams decision that have been contributed to THE REVIEW by several eminent members of the bar.

The discussion of the legal soundness of the Illinois decision leads to the more general economic question of the desirability of the closed shop. That is a question that may be solved through the practical processes of industrial life. Theory, based upon observation, may select trades or conditions wherein the closed shop would be in accordance with public policy, and may discover other trades or conditions wherein the open shop would be preferable. But it is highly desirable that the way to test theory by experience should not be closed by judicial dictum.

The group of letters also published in this issue of THE REVIEW, from officers of British unions in nine industries, illuminate the practice prevalent in the United Kingdom as to the open shop. It is to be observed that the open shop is there the general although not universal practice, and yet these letters show that the British trade unions occupy a strong position. Indeed, some of the letters, which are all written by men who have enjoyed an opportunity to observe labor conditions in the United States, dwell upon the financial strength of the British unions, due to the greater constancy of their membership and the higher ratio of dues to wages. These letters bring out also the importance to the union of being able to furnish superior workmen. That in several trades is cited as a reason for the preference manifested by employers for union labor, even though they may be opposed to the expressed recognition of an organization of wage-earners. The British unions, it is apparent, are thus encouraging a tendency in practice, if not in contract, toward the closed shop. That is a process of gradual evolution, to be carried forward by incessant striving toward excellence. The observation of that current process in Great Britain goes to sustain the contention of Henry White, that the danger of open shops to the continued life and progressive strength of unionism is likely to be exaggerated.

LAKE TRAFFIC RESUMED.

Because of the number and variety of the trades affected by the recent tie-up of transportation on the Great Lakes, it was difficult to make any accurate estimate of the loss to shippers and others. But the variety and complexity of these interests doubtless had their influence in causing the captains to return to work, thus enabling some three thousand vessels to be put into commission and permitting about 150,000 longshoremen and seamen to cease enforced idleness. The resumption of traffic is of especial importance to the coal, ore, grain and lumber interests.

The captains resumed work in accordance with the action of the Masters and Pilots' Association, which decided to "make the best of a bad situation," in the words of Captain Paul Howell, it being understood that the mates were to make an arrangement for themselves with the Lake Carriers' Association. The complication with federal laws made this strike peculiar. The successful operation of the agreement between the Lake Carriers and the Longshoremen should point the way to a permanent agreement between vessel owners and the captains, pilots and mates. The hearing of testimony as to the facts in the case by the Cleveland Civic Federation is set forth in an article upon another page.

A DEPARTMENT OF TRADE AGREEMENTS.

The proceedings of the Conference on Trade Agreements, held in New York City under the auspices of the National Civic Federation, possess more than sufficient interest and instruction to warrant the full report which we present in this number of THE REVIEW. A distinct disposition was shown among those who addressed the Conference, representative of both employers and employed, to extend the operation of trade agreements and to learn more of their forms and principles. In furtherance of this desire, a permanent Department of Trade Agreements of the National Civic Federation has been organized and will exercise its activities toward education and the encouragement of this method of securing industrial harmony based upon equitable terms and conditions.

An agreement has been signed at San Francisco between the Steam Schooner Managers' Association and the Sailors' Union of the Pacific, the Pacific Coast Marine Firemen's Union and the Marine Cooks' and Stewards' Association of the Pacific Coast. Generally speaking, the agreement continues for another year the existing conditions. The seamen are safeguarded against a reduction of pay, while the managers are assured of a stable wage rate. The working rules of the sailors' union are embodied in the agreement, which includes matters of overtime and meal hours, which have been regulated tacitly by custom, although more or less in dispute. Under the new agreement, the managers are to provide messrooms on board every vessel under their control, "where practicable." The "Coast Seamen's Journal" says of the agreement, that it "marks another step toward the permanent establishment of peaceful, business-like relations between the two essential factors in maritime commerce on the Pacific. The unions concerned do not pretend that the terms agreed upon are entirely satisfactory in every respect. With all its faults, however, the agreement is a fair and honorable compromise; if it doesn't mark much improvement upon previous conditions, it certainly marks no surrender of anything so far gained."

A NATIONAL CONFERENCE ON TRADE AGREEMENTS.

THEIR SUCCESSES AND FAILURES DISCUSSED BY REPRESENTATIVE EMPLOYERS AND WAGE-EARNERS—DEPARTMENT OF TRADE AGREEMENTS OF THE NATIONAL CIVIC FEDERATION.

The conference upon Trade Agreements, held in New York City on May 7, under the auspices of the National Civic Federation, was highly successful in attaining its purpose, which was the interchange of ideas and the comparison of experiences in forming these agreements, in making them binding, in their success and failure, in their inclusion of provisions for conciliation or arbitration, or both, and as to the subjects which should be specified or excluded. Those who took part in the conference included employers, individual or representing organizations in their industries, and employes, representing national or local bodies of organized labor. The discussion brought out a unanimous expression of belief in the desirability of trade agreements, and that they offer a practical method of attaining more harmonious relations between capital and labor in all the industries that were considered. In two trades, those of pattern-making and iron-molding, the movement for trade agreements national in scope received distinct impetus.

FRANCIS L. ROBBINS

The recital of experiences as well as the discussion of theories, by those who attended the conference was considered so valuable that the formation of a Department of Trade Agreements of the National Civic Federation was afterward effected.

Following is a detailed report of the conference. Direct quotations are from stenographic notes and condensed quotations are based upon them:

The conference was called to order on behalf of the National Civic Federation by Marcus M. Marks, president of the National Clothiers' Association, who stated that its purpose was to discuss trade agreements, with special reference to methods of arbitration or conference, and to the subjects that are proper for arbitration. He suggested that Francis L. Robbins, president of the Pittsburg Coal Company, who had recently participated in averting a threatened trouble in the soft coal industry, through the successful operation of a trade agreement, would be the most competent man present, at least on the part of employers, to lead the discussion. The suggestion was seconded by Isaac W. Frank, president of the National Founders' Association, and Mr. Robbins was unanimously chosen to preside.

Remarks of Chairman Robbins.

In taking the chair, Mr. Robbins said:

"There is nothing in my judgment that is so important for the future of this country as the joint trade agreement as a method of reaching harmonious relations between capital and labor. I think there is nothing that will solve the problem and avert difficulties, dangers and possibly disaster so well as the coming together of employers and employes to discuss the questions at issue between them and to arrive at what is known as the joint trade agreement.

"There is probably no trade wherein the difficulties are greater than in the coal mining industry, which presents a method of agreement that has been very successful. We do not claim for it that it is perfect by any manner of means, but we do claim that between the leaders of the operators and of the miners there has been that feeling of confidence of belief in each other, of fairness and of a sincere desire to reach an agreement, that has resulted in accomplishing the object.

"We leave nothing to arbitration. We do not believe in the principle, if you can get away from it. We believe that the people who know the conditions in their trade, both employers and employed, are better able to deal with these questions than any stranger. We believe that if you meet the issues with fairness and with conservatism, you can better come to an agreement that will be satisfactory than by leaving it to be arbitrated by some one else. Compulsion of any kind, either by legal authority or by the decision of some one to whom matters are referred, is never as satisfactory as a voluntary agreement between two interests. You always find that it will work out far better if you will make your own agreement amongst yourselves. Even if, in making that agreement, possibly one side or the other does not think that it is getting exactly what it is entitled to, better far a concession from either side in reaching a joint agreement than it is to leave it to some one else to decide for you. You know the conditions, and you will accept them and live up to them; and the people under you will be better satisfied.

"Mr. Mitchell, who has ably represented the mining industry in this country and who is thoroughly familiar with every particle, both theoretically and in practice, of the principles of joint trade agreements, and to whose conservative action and advice the joint trade agreement with the bituminous miners was reached recently, is here and can speak from the side of the employe. Mr. Keefe, who is here representing the Longshoremen's Union, stands in the same capacity as Mr. Mitchell—both conservative, fair-minded, competent men, representing interests that are hard to handle. I don't think in all the country there are any two interests harder to handle than those. These men can bear testimony to our methods of settling these questions, rather than by resorting to arbitration. I would be glad to hear from each of them."

GRANGE SARD

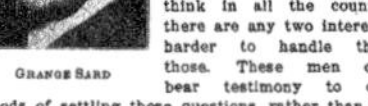

Mr. Mitchell's Address.

John Mitchell, president of the United Mine Workers of America, addressed the conference:

"The joint trade agreement is the most unmistakable recognition of the mutual dependence of capital and labor. It is the essence of trade-unionism. In the coal industry, where wages and conditions of employment are regulated by it, we have found that industry has thrived, that wages have been bettered, that conditions of employment have been more satisfactory than under any other method that has been tried in our trade. We have 350,000 coal miners who are working under agreement, whose wages and conditions of employment are determined by a joint conference.

"I do not know of any other industry that will show so marked a change as the coal industry. I remember only eight or nine years ago, when each employer fixed the conditions of employment at his own mines, when the workmen at those mines resorted to strikes or other means to change those conditions. The net result was that wages constantly fell, until the earnings of the miners were so low that they were unable to live and provide for themselves as we all believe American workmen should. And on the other hand, the profits of the operators had fallen so that many of them were in practical bankruptcy. One mine owner did not know what his neighbor was paying for labor. The man at one mine didn't know what the wages were at the neighboring mine. In the competition for business, there would be a cut here and a cut there, and so on all along the line; and with the desire to secure trade, the outcome was unsatisfactory to both sides.

Competition and Wages.

"In 1897 we held our first joint convention and fixed a uniform competitive wage scale. That is to say, in our trade the wages are not uniform, but they are fixed upon a competitive basis. The principal element entering into the wage scale in the mining industry is competitive opportunity of all interests represented. We have to make our mining scale so as to give, say, Mr. Robbins, in Pennsylvania, a wage scale that will enable him to compete with coal men in Ohio. It so happens that in this case the wages are the same, but if they could not enter into the same markets on the same competitive basis we would have to change the wage scale to enable them to do so.

"Of course, what is true of our trade would not necessarily be true of other trades. For instance, in the building trade there is no competition between men putting up a building in New York and men putting up a building in Chicago, but in the case of any commodity which is transported, such as coal, there is competition that has got to be taken into consideration in determining the wage scale. We adjust all our differences by agreement.

"The agreement provides not only for the wages but the hours of labor, and it determines in detail the conditions under which labor shall be performed. We provide in our agreements for every detail, We leave no question to arbitration.

Faults of Arbitration.

"I quite concur in the statement of Mr. Robbins that arbitration of wage questions should be avoided as far as is possible. Arbitration is provocable of strikes. That is, all my experience has been that where a trade agreement provides for a reference of questions to arbitration, it gives each side an opportunity—indeed, an invitation—to shirk responsibility. There is in every man's nature a certain fear of assuming responsibility. If he can shove it off upon somebody else he is often willing to do so. In our trade we take the position that we have got to settle these questions ourselves, and when we know we have got to settle them, we rise to the occasion and do it. So it seems to me that arbritration should be avoided in these joint agreements as far as possible.

JOHN MITCHELL

"In some of our districts, for instance in Indiana, when an agreement is made, if a dispute arises as to the meaning of it, it may be referred to a Board of Arbitration, in which a disinterested person acts as referee. But our experience there has been that many questions to both the operators and miners seem perfectly clear; but when a disinterested person was called in he could not understand them. He could not understand the technique of the mining code; he could not understand our technical terms. The result has been that decisions have been rendered which were not only unsatisfactory to us, but just as unsatisfactory to the employers. So I think that the best agreement and the best condition under which industry can be conducted is that where the arrangement is made direct between the representatives of the manufacturers and the representatives of the workmen.

The Process of Agreement.

"In the coal industry we have an arrangement

probably different from that existing in any other industry. It is impossible in our trade to put a condition of employment upon an operator, or for an operator to pass conditions upon a miner, that will be unsatisfactory to him. That is to say, in our conventions we cannot vote a condition of employment upon an operator or a miner without his consent. In our Inter-State conventions we make a representation based upon all the miners in Pennsylvania, Ohio, Indiana and Illinois, and we give to each of those districts four votes—that is, the miners have four votes from each district, and the operators have four votes from each district. Before a motion can be carried that fixes or affects our scale of wages, it must have the unanimous vote of all the miners and all the operators in that convention. If one miner or one operator vote in the negative, the vote will be lost. So you see the interests of all parties are protected, because it requires their consent before a motion can be carried; and we have found that to work out in mining matters entirely satisfactorily to us.

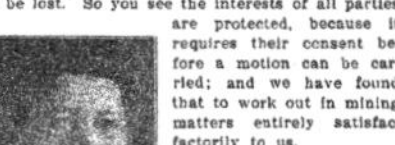
I. W. FRANK

Lower Wages Accepted.

"I might say that under this agreement wages have both advanced and declined. I have heard it said by employers many times that this trade agreement arrangement was all right as long as wages advanced, but as soon as the time came when workmen would be expected or compelled to take a reduction of wages, that then the joint agreement would go to pieces. We have disproved that in our trade. It is true we have received more advances than we have declines, but this year the miners represented in our organization and who took part in this joint convention voted to accept a reduction in wages; and I think their action has done more to strengthen and encourage this trade agreement than any other one thing that has happened in our industrial affairs.

Wages Relative to Profits.

"We try to fix our wages based on the selling price of coal. If the mine owners are securing large prices for coal, we expect at the end of our agreement to share in that prosperity. On the other hand, if prices of coal fall off—if there is a depression—we expect to take a reduction in our wages, and share adversity with our employers. Under our arrangement we have grown to know one another and have grown to know one another's business.

"We know just as well as employers what it costs them to produce coal. We know what their profits are, and we know what they pay for their freight rates. We know, in a general way, practically as much about their business as they themselves. And they are willing to let us know that. Indeed, I have on more than one occasion had coal operators ask me to come to their offices and go over their books; if I doubted at all the statements they made as to their profits they have asked me to go over their books and satisfy myself, and to go over their cost sheets so as to know exactly what the reports from their business were, and to know how the business was conducted. In that way we have established, not only very close, but the very closest business relations.

"Aside from that, we have established a very pleasant personal relation. And my experience in the labor movement has been that a close personal relation does very much at times to avoid strikes and turmoil. When we learn to understand that each side is earnestly and honestly striving to do what is right,—when we learn to know that—it does very much to stop these strikes and lock-outs.

Right to Strike and Lock Out.

"I want to express this one personal opinion as to the rights and the relations of each side; I personally favor strikes. That is to say, I would dislike to see the time come when men could not strike, or when employers could not close their shops, or mines, or railroads. I think behind all this lies our right to strike and the right of employers to lock us out. I think we must not surrender either of these rights. But a strike should in no instance be inaugurated, and there never should be a lock-out, until each side has exhausted every possible peaceful, conciliatory method at their command. I think they should try everything else. But when everything else has failed, and an adjustment cannot be reached, then I think the interest of industry—the interest of labor and the interest of capital—will be best conserved by retaining and maintaining the right to stop work

Conferences Prevent Strikes.

"We have been fortunate, and I believe we will continue to be fortunate in our trade, in averting strikes, whenever we have had conferences. As a matter of fact, we have never had a strike in the coal industry where we have first had a conference. The strikes in the coal industry have invariably taken place in those branches of our trade where employers or workmen have refused to confer. Wherever we have been able to meet in fair conference to consider a question upon its merits, we have reached an agreement. This spring we had some difficulty. It was the impression of many of our people that reduction in wages was not warranted. We adjourned our convention, and went home; but instead of going home and striking we went home and came back to our convention and tried it over again, and we kept at it. We threshed the thing out for weeks. But at the time we were arguing it—the time we were negotiating—everybody was at the mines and the men had work. And if we had stayed there from that time until now, I am sure that the interests of the country, the interests of both operators and miners, would have been better conserved than if we had been on strike.

Combinations of Capital and Labor.

"Now, gentlemen, it seems to me that where industry is carried on by agreement the most satisfactory conditions will prevail. This old idea of men conducting their affairs to suit themselves in doing business, without restraint, if permitted to go on, will lead to chaos and anarchy. It can do nothing else. Where we have these great combinations of employers and where we have great combinations of laborers, as we have and as we are bound to have, I believe firmly that the only possible condition of peace is where industry is carried on by mutual consent and by a trade agreement. It seems to me that that is the outcome, that that is the natural sequence, of these great combinations of employers on one side and the combinations of laborers on the other side; and there is no use of us even hoping that the conditions of industry will change and go back to what they were fifty years ago. We have got the combinations of capital and employers, and they are going to stay. We have got the combinations of labor and they are going to remain. We cannot change it if we would, and I don't think we would if we could. So it seems to me, gentlemen, that the sooner the employers of this country, the sooner the laborers of this country, agree to understand this mutual dependence, the better it will be for not only ourselves directly interested, but the better it will be for society as a whole."

Instructed Delegates.

In reply to a question by Isaac W. Frank as to why the bituminous agreement, involving a reduction of wages for the current year, had been submitted to a referendum, Mr. Mitchell explained that the reference was because delegates to this convention had been instructed. The instruction of delegates was not a rule of the organization. In a majority of cases, they were not instructed. Mr. Mitchell said that if the agreement reached at the conference had been rejected by the referendum, he supposed a strike would have followed. But the men would keep at work so long as negotiations continued. As to output, the only restriction was the eight hours working day. Practice had proved that miners produce more coal in eight hours than in ten. The agreement contained no restriction upon the quantity of coal to be produced by any miner in eight hours.

As to Union Labor.

Mr. Frank asked whether it was required that all miners employed must belong to the union. Mr. Mitchell replied:

"We do not require that a man who gets employment shall be a union man first, but on accepting employment he becomes a member of our union. In the anthracite region in Pennsylvania men are employed without discrimination. Also, there is no discrimination against a union man. In Central Pennsylvania and in the Pittsburg District, practically all the men belong to the union. There is nothing said in any of our contracts as to whether a man shall be a union or non-union man; not a single word."

FRANK BUCHANAN

"What is the effect?" asked Mr. Frank.

"The men join the union as a condition of employment," replied Mr. Mitchell.

Mr. Frank: "They do then require that men belong to the Union in order to be able to work in certain mines, whether the employer is desirous of employing whomsoever he pleases or not?"

Mr. Mitchell: "An employer has that right always to employ whoever he pleases. When a man secures employment, he becomes a member of our Union and works under our contract. The only way we can carry our contract out is by making him a party to it. The contract is between the operators and the union man who works, and the man who is not a member cannot be a party to that contract."

Mr. Mitchell further explained that not once in a thousand cases was it necessary to ask a man to join the union. The men joined voluntarily. The condition of a man not in the union would be no more onerous than that of any single man in a community where every other man believed in one practice. He had never known a strike for the specific purpose of preventing the employment of a minority of non-union men in a mine operated under the union agreement. Mr. Robbins added the explanation that he thought it unfair and unwise to send instructed delegates to a convention. Men should go to a conference free to listen to argument and to agree upon whatever was shown to be just.

Subjects Not Arbitrable.

Questions by Benjamin D. Traitel of the New York Building Trades Employers' Association and by A. Beverly Smith of the Lithographers' Association brought out this further statement as to his attitude toward strikes, lock-outs and arbitration, from Mr. Mitchell:

"Neither side should surrender its right to strike or lock-out. Failing in every other method to settle their differences, the men should always maintain the right to strike, or the employers the right to lock out their men. If they were to surrender absolutely those rights, then the chances are that the conditions of employment would be satisfactory neither to the men nor to the employers.

"My own judgment is that in preference to a strike we should resort to arbitration—I mean arbitration of the question of wages. There are questions I would not arbitrate at all. I would not arbitrate, under any condition, my right to belong to a union. And I would not arbitrate the hours of labor in our trade.

"If the question were raised in our trade as to whether or not we should abandon our eight hours a day, I would not submit that question to arbitration; and our employers would not ask us to, because it has been very satisfactory to both of us.

"There have been some failings, no doubt, which

have increased the cost of production in some instances; but on the whole the operators and the miners will both agree that eight hours is the most satisfactory for our trade. . . . The question of a man's right to belong to a union is particularly a question not to be arbitrated, because it is fundamental. You can't arbitrate fundamental principles. . . . I favor settlement by agreement, and only arbitration in the event of failing to agree, and then in preference to strike. I have advised miners in Kentucky to accept a reduction rather than arbitrate, in order to avoid the interference of outside interests."

Wm. O. Coakley of the Central Lithographic Council called Mr. Mitchell's attention to the statement that in the lithographic industry, after an agreement had been signed, some of the employers started to make individual contracts with workmen. Charles Wilhelms of the joint executive committee of the Lithographers' Association explained that a skilled artist, commanding a high wage, might cripple an employer's business by leaving him. Hence individual agreements with artists for longer periods than the year covered by the trade agreements were desirable. He maintained that his industry was one in which the strike and lock-out must be eliminated, any controversy to be settled finally by arbitration.

W. O. COAKLEY

The Longshoremen's Agreement.

At the request of Chairman Robbins, Daniel J. Keefe, president of the International Longshoremen, Marine and Transport Workers' Association, addressed the conference. He explained that his organization includes tug-boat captains, engineers, firemen, marine firemen, oilers, water tenders, divers, 'longshoremen, lumber inspectors, elevator employes, tally men, grain inspectors and others. Their wages ranged from $2 to $15 a day. The organization meets that of the employers once a year. It is one of the oldest organizations under a trade agreement. Each local body sends an accredited delegate to these joint meetings, instructed only to make the best possible agreement. There is no referendum, the delegates having full authority. In the same way the employers come to the meetings with full authority from their association, or the interest they represent, to make an agreement without referring it back. Mr. Keefe continued:

"Our agreements cover the wages and hours and general conditions. There is always a provision for arbitration on questions that are not understood, or in the event of any question arising as to the meaning of any part of the agreement. That, however, does not touch on the wage scale; nor the hours; nor the conditions specified. That is only usual on technical questions, and the arbitration board is only called in, or arbitration is only resorted to, after the employer and the men, or the representative of the men, have exhausted every means to adjust their differences. We have had only one case of arbitration in four years.

"The employers are just as anxious to continue this trade agreement as we are. There is no question of non-union men getting into the agreement, or controversy at all. They treat with the union for union men exclusively, so many as we can furnish them. When we can't furnish them, then they may employ any other men they desire until such time as union men put in an appearance. That is the desire of the employer as well as ourselves. We have no dispute relative to non-union men.

"The employer says to us, 'We want you to furnish all the men and be responsible for their acts during the life of this contract.' That we usually do. We do not have any strikes; we do not have any lock-outs. All the men in the different callings are part of the organization, and there is no opportunity of striking against non-union men. All the employers are party to a contract, through an association or as an individual, and there is no opportunity of misunderstanding on that side; and I am very much pleased to be able to say that the employers at no time have sought to take any advantage of changed conditions.

Necessity of Strike Removed.

"We, like the miners and some of the other organizations, were unable to present sufficient argument to continue the last year's wage, and so were obliged to take a reduction, but the reduction was taken by the delegates in that convention, who were clothed with power and with full authority to make the best possible arrangement. We have been working under this system for many years, and we have had no strike. We never talk strike. There is no necessity for it. We meet with the employers and discuss wage or conditions, and always arrive at an amicable understanding. It may not be just what we anticipated or think we ought to have, or the agreement may not be just as the employer would wish; it may not be wholly satisfactory to either of us, yet we agree to it and accept it and carry it out.

"We say to the employer, whether it is on a declining or an advancing market, that the very best service within us belongs to him in accordance with the contract. There are no disputes; and I can declare from the experience of one who has served on an arbitration board for years, that the results of arbitration are not satisfactory to either side at any time. Arbitrators, as a rule, cannot go into the thing fully. They are often incapable of understanding the entire matter in detail. They may view it from a law standpoint. One or the other side may be able to put up the abler and more forcible argument, yet it does not follow that the fellow with the most forcible argument is right.

"Many employers as well as workers want to arbitrate everything—to submit the whole agreement to arbitration. Now, that is impractical. It is impossible to have a satisfactory result through arbitration of that kind. Anything you agree to should not be submitted to arbitration—hours of labor, wages and general conditions; but if there is something where there is a question of doubt as to its meaning, and that can't be cleared up or agreed to by the parties directly interested, then it is only fair to submit it to arbitration. the men at all times continuing to work pending the decision.

The Majority Rules.

"I am able to say very little on the strike or lock-out, because we have no experience with them. If there is a violation of the agreement on the part of one or any of the employers, the men can't stop work. They must continue to work while we take the matter up and hear the employer who has violated the agreement or contract, and then we insist on the contract being complied with. But we cannot let the local organizations take it upon themselves to assume that responsibility. The employer, on the other hand, does not attempt to lay his boats up while any matter is in dispute between himself and his employes; he also continues to do business until a satisfactory adjustment is reached. But there is so little of that arises that I could not discuss it intelligently. We don't have any friction. Ninety-four per cent. of our men are working under those trade agreements, and we meet every year and renew them.

"Now, as to the form of the contract other than the wage scale and the hours, it cannot be changed except by a majority of both sides. The general contract must remain as it is, except by a majority vote of both sides, each side having the same voting power. Like the bituminous miners, we cut down the number of votes on each side. The employers may have forty or fifty representatives and we may have a hundred and fifty, but the voting power is identically the same—each side has five votes. They may be cast by individuals, or by one representative, as they may see fit. But the general contract cannot be changed, either by us or by the employers, nor any amendment made, except with the approval of a majority of both sides. That in itself prevents contention.

"Every member of our organization is furnished with a copy of the contract. He carries it in his coat or vest pocket, and at any time he can pull out his little book. We do that to prevent any confusion or misunderstanding or misinterpretation of the meaning of the contract. By furnishing every man with a copy of the contract he can see for himself just what it is, just what it means; and there is no danger of his making a mistake. The employers furnish their representatives, whether it be a captain, or a dock manager, or a warehouse man, with a similar copy, so that they, too, may know that the contract is being lived up to.

"But there is never any arbitration except on the matters that are not understood. We could not consistently submit anything to arbitration that is agreed to. If we agree that the number of hours to constitute a day's work is going to be eight, or ten, or fifteen, we have agreed to that and there is no question about that. If we agree that the wages will be $2 a day, or $15 a day, we cannot change those figures; we have agreed to them, and there can be no mistake as to them.

D. J. KEEFE

"The other principal parts of the contract are also thoroughly understood. If there is any part that is not understood and the representatives on both sides can't agree on its proper construction, it may be submitted to arbitration. There is nothing further that could be submitted to arbitration. I think that our system is as good as any established in this country, and as far reaching.

"Only recently at a meeting in Cleveland of a branch of the Civic Federation, Mr. Mather, who is one of the executive committee of the Civic Federation, made a statement that was rather flattering to the organization I represent. He said if the laundry workers, barbers and the restaurant employes and newspaper employes and shoe polishers had organizations conducted along the same lines as the 'longshoremen, he wouldn't let anybody else do any business for him. That is only one instance. During a misunderstanding with some of the Pickands-Mather interests, a statement was made that the 'longshoremen would strike. Mr. Mather said: 'Well, do you know I would be more surprised to have the 'longshoremen strike than if I went home and found Mrs. Mather and my family refusing to live with me any longer.'

"Those are the relations between the men we do business with and our organization, and perhaps we have made as much progress as any other branch of labor in this country; perhaps our wages have been increased as rapidly and our hours reduced as much as those of any other branch of labor. I feel confident that the same relations could and will exist if the other employers and the men will get together, setting their personalities aside, the employer removing the idea from his mind that he is going to run his own business just as he sees fit without any interference on the part of anybody, and the employe also agreeing that his local organization or his organization alone cannot make the wage and conditions under which he has got to work, but that the employer is a factor. If these get together and discuss their interests freely and fairly, there is no reason why an amicable understanding and trade agreement cannot be reached.

"The 'longshoremen when our union was formed were perhaps the most difficult class of men in the whole country to organize and to induce to respect a trade agreement. Since those days, however, the most artistic or scientific men working in connection with the water-front have made every possible effort to become a part of our association. The very highest paid men—men who a few years ago would not care even to have it known that they recognized a poor neighbor who worked as a 'longshoreman—are willing to become a part of the same organization, purely from a business standpoint, believing that the method pursued by the 'longshoremen is practical and that they have been able to gain the friendship and respect of the employers and the public through their fair and business-like policy."

A Broken Agreement.

Walter L. Pierce, formerly president of the National Metal Trades Association, spoke of the trade agreement with machinists, which had been formed by an arbitration committee, of which he was a member. After lasting about a year, that agreement "was broken by the machinists going on strike, although a part of the agreement was that no strikes or lock-outs should take place, and that any matters not covered by the agreement should be submitted to arbitration." Mr. Pierce said:

W. L. PIERCE

"The breaking of that agreement was a very severe blow to the agreement idea among the manufacturers. In that agreement there was a clause that no restriction should be placed upon labor or production. It was discovered after the agreement was made that the restriction of production and the freedom of employment were subject to the constitution of the union. In other words the employer did not have freedom of production because of the constitution of the union. Our manufacturers, having made an agreement as they supposed in good faith which permitted them freedom of employment, found that it did not permit them that freedom. Upon a number of other questions there was a difference of opinion. Our association notified the union that a committee on interpretation had been appointed and requesting a similar committee, but that was never acted on by the union, and a strike took place in violation of the agreement."

Mr. Pierce expressed the wish that other unions would adopt the principles that had been set forth by Mr. Mitchell and Mr. Keefe. He said that if any man had the right to belong to a union, the converse held true, that any man had the right not to join a union. He thought that if violence could be eliminated, it would affect favorably the attitude of public opinion toward unionism. He discountenanced picketing, as leading men into temptation. He urged the necessity of more uniform action by the unions. They "should establish certain broad principles as right for everybody," and he thought these principles had been enunciated by Mr. Mitchell and Mr. Keefe. If they could be applied to the metal trades, there would be no trouble about forming agreements.

The Chairman, Mr. Robbins, said by way of comment upon the broken machinists' agreement:

"As representing docks on the lakes, in which our company has over $10,000,000 invested, I shall endorse everything Mr. Keefe has said. We are perfectly willing that all our interests there shall be left in the hands of Mr. Keefe, representing the employes. Their fairness has been such that in one case at Sheboygan, where the local union refused to carry out its contract, they took away its charter from the organization, and there is no union in Sheboygan to-day because of it.

"It is only by conservative and fair action on both sides that agreements can be maintained. It is only by experience, by showing each side that an agreement is fair and that it is being applied to other trades, that a satisfactory conclusion can be reached."

Frank Buchanan, president of the International Association of Bridge and Structural Iron Workers, declared that "an agreement cannot be carried out to the interest of one party unless it is to the interest of the other." He pointed out that the miners and operators were not alone interested in the production of coal. That was of concern also to the steel industry and the railroads. Hence it was important to extend the principle of trade agreements to all interdependent industries. Justice was in his view essential to any agreement.

Necessity of Fair Play.

Mr. Buchanan added as an illustration: "Say that a labor organization is so powerful that it has the employer in a position where it could enforce an unjust condition on him. I maintain that it is not to the interest of the organization to do so; that it must consider the employer's interest, if that agreement is to be a success. If the employer is in a position where he is strong and the union is weak, if he forces an agreement on the union that is unjust and unsatisfactory, in my opinion it will reflect back upon the employer himself in time, to his injury."

Mr. Buchanan said: "I am a believer in a sympathetic movement, but I am not always a believer in a sympathetic strike. The abuse of the sympathetic movement is not proper, but it cannot be denied that the use of any sympathetic movement is proper. The steel worker is interested in the miner being at work, else the steel mills cannot get fuel. Agreements, Mr. Buchanan pointed out, had been violated by employers as well as by employes. But because a good law had been violated it did not follow that the law should be repealed. Rather, a way should be found to enforce that law. The influence of all should be exerted to enforce fair trade agreements. He held that if the structural iron workers were to take an arbitrary position, it would not only hamper their industry but would injure other trade organizations. It would then become the duty of those organizations to say to the structural iron workers that they must recede from their arbitrary position for the sake of the other industries of the country. "Peace is what we want. Disturbances cost everybody too much. Through such meetings as this, we may learn how to deal with this question of agreements for the best interests of all."

At this point Mr. Robbins was called away by a business engagement, and John Mitchell was unanimously chosen, on motion, to preside. Mr. Mitchell called upon John Flynn, of the Metal Polishers' Association. Mr. Flynn said that all the shop trades are in favor of agreements. He believed that if they were drawn up properly they could be kept by both sides. It was important to go over every question in preliminary conferences. Nothing should be left to arbitration. Yet, if it came to a dead-lock, the shop trades would favor calling in an arbitrator. He deprecated the idea of some employers that they could do business solely to suit themselves.

The Lithographic Industry.

Mr. Parker, representing the allied lithographers' unions, said that he recognized the right of employers to run their business to suit themselves, and also the right of employes to sell their labor as they pleased. But there is no reason, he insisted, why the two sides should not come together and reach an agreement satisfactory to both. An agreement should stipulate certain things that should not be arbitrated. This should be done when a trade is at peace, and when rational thought can be given to the subject. In the lithographers' industry, the employers wished to eliminate the open shop and the piece-work system. The employes were willing that the employers should put themselves on an equal basis with one another. Mr. Parker quoted a member of the Civic Federation as having said that where there was a piece-work system, the employes restricted the output. During a strike, the employers paid non-union men more for piece-work than they had been paying union men. This made it plain that the union itself had restricted output. Thereupon the price of piece-work was cut, until there was another strike. After that, an agreement was drawn by which the piece-work men were to produce all they could, while men paid by the day were to receive as much as they could make by the piece-work system. It was for the employers so to regulate the piece-work system that they would not be competing with one another. That would prevent cutting under the minimum wage; and at the same time no employe should be restricted in his output and the amount earned.

Mr. Parker argued for the closed shop, on the ground that the non-union man had no right to enjoy a rate of payment that had been gained by the efforts of the union. Nevertheless, any fair arbitrator would declare for the open shop, on the ground that any man has a right to accept employment anywhere. "Therefore," he said, "the unions work in a shop." A trade agreement should apply to all employes. There should be no individual agreements.

The Stove Manufacturers.

The Chairman called upon Grange Sard, of Rathborn, Sard & Co., representing the Stove Manufacturers' Association:

THOS. B. LAVEY

"I have been through the mill, so to speak. I have fought the union. I have thought it was to the interest of manufacturers to destroy the union. But I have been shown the error of my way, and I am prepared to say now and have thought for many years that it is the wise employer who encourages rather than discourages unionism.

"The Stove Manufacturers' Defense Association was organized in 1886 for the purpose of fighting the union, of resisting what we termed unjust demands. We had our fight with the union, and at the end we had both more respect for the power and fighting qualities of the other; so that in 1891 we had a conference committee appointed representing six employes and six employers. They drew up an agreement which should fix the rate of wages and the conditions in shops for the current year. Previous to that time, each manufacturer had settled his own difficulties, but they were settled after the blow was struck. A fundamental principle of each agreement was that if there was any grievance in any of the shops of members of our association, the manufacturer should not lock his men out, nor should the men strike, but that pending a conference to settle the difficulty, the men should all remain at work. Since 1891 we have had no strikes of any consequence.

"If any one thinks that these agreements are going to bring about the millennium, they are greatly mistaken. There is bound to be friction and trouble. But by means of these agreements the troubles are reduced to the minimum. There has been no serious interruption of our business, but we have progressed smoothly and satisfactorily—immensely satisfactorily to the workmen and to the employers as well.

What Agreements Should Embrace.

"We especially want to consider what these agreements shall embrace. No agreement can cover all questions as to the relation of capital and labor. Any attempt to make an agreement cover everything will simply result, in my judgment, in failure. The fewer important subjects it covers the better. You can't start off and have everything as right the first year as you will the second and the third. So do not try to make an agreement that shall provide for every possible contingency that may arise under any circumstances. Above all, don't attempt to put into the agreement matters of controversy which cannot possibly be settled by agreement. There are fundamental views which employer and employe hold, and they do not propose to give them up, and it is unwise to ask either side to renounce them in an agreement. So there are things which need not and ought not to be mentioned in an agreement, but an agreement may be made which I assure you by my personal experience may be the greatest means of settling disputes between labor and capital and that will remove the bitter feeling that does, but should not, exist between employer and employe.

"In order to make agreements effective you must recognize the union. Making your agreements with the union, you depend upon the union for carrying them out. If a man has a decided antipathy to unions he will not, naturally, participate in any such agreement; but the man who wants to fight it out on his own lines will have his troubles beyond expression. I want simply to impress you, from my experience, with the utmost value of agreements between employers and employes and the importance of having such agreements express certain essential things, such as wages and shop conditions, without any attempt to cover every possible contingency."

An Important Announcement.

James Wilson, president of the Pattern Makers' League of North America, being called upon, announced: "The pattern makers stand ready to meet at any time the representative of the National Metal Trades' Association for the purpose of consideration of an agreement international in its character, to cover the conditions of employment that shall exist in the pattern making industry of this country."

JOHN COOPER

Mr. Wilson said the Buffalo convention of employers about a year ago had declined to enter into an agreement with any organization of employes. He said that there had been one agreement that did not yield good results. But he believed in trying a gain. He believed in a minimum wage, but he knew of no labor organization that would restrict the earning capacity of any man. He added:

"If we have an agreement with any employer—whether organization or individual employer—and our members violate that agreement, we will not only take the charter away, but on strike we will furnish the employer with men to take their places. That should be the principle of the trades union. An employer should realize that with that agreement he is then assured that he is going to have no trouble; and I believe if the metal trades organization will overlook the difficulty that they have had with their first agreement and endeavor to profit by that experience and treat with the other metal trades or mental organizations, that agreements can be had with them that will settle trouble for the time being and lead to better understanding."

Founders and Molders.

The Chairman called upon Isaac W. Frank, of the National Founders' Association. He said:

"Our organization consists of molders. The father of our organization is the Stove Founders' Defense Association, which, as Mr. Sard stated, started for the purpose of annihilating the union. But our association did not start for that purpose; it started for the purpose of doing business with the union. We profited by the experience of the Stove Founders' Defense Association, who are dealing with the heads of the same organization as we deal with, and we endeavor by agreement to secure those harmonious relations between employer and employe that we all desire."

Mr. Frank read the text of the "New York Agreement." He pointed out that what this agreement termed a "committee of arbitration" was in fact a committee of conference, consisting of an equal number of representatives of the Founders' Association and the Iron Molders' Union, a majority to decide, and there to be no cessation of work pending adjudication. The agreement had been kept in the main, although there had been instances of its violation by both sides, in particular shops, or by local organizations. There existed differences as to fundamental principles. The Founders' Association had been endeavoring for four years to formulate a national agreement. It was represented in the negotiations by two logical and fair-minded men—Mr. Pessano of Detroit and Mr. Pfahler of Philadelphia. The stumbling-block was the demand of the union that it retain control of apprentices; that when a union was established in a shop, that must be a union shop, that piece-work existing would be permitted but could not be extended; and that the agreement must say nothing about improved appliances.

Mr. Frank urged that the unions unite with the employers in reaching an equitable agreement. He read, with comments, the formal declaration of policy by the National Founders' Association. This is the policy outlined in pursuance of resolutions passed at the 1903 convention and subsequent meetings of the administrative council.

An Association's Policy.

Attempts at arbitrary limitation of output, or at arbitrary demands for excessive output, by either molder or foundryman, will not receive the sanction of the association. Limitation of a man's earning capacity is not to be permitted, whether by the day, piece or premium system. The association will not permit fines and punishments to be inflicted upon members of unions for the purpose of handicapping them in their work. Prices for castings made by the piece, contract or premium system are to be such as to enable a competent molder to earn at least an equitable rate of wages, and are not to be reduced except by improved facilities, or agreement. The requirements of the employer solely are to determine the number of apprentices, helpers and handy-men. The foundryman may introduce machines and appliances to be operated by whomsoever he finds to his advantage.

It is the privilege of the employe to leave employment whenever he sees fit. It is the privilege of the employer to discharge any workman when he sees fit. There will be no arbitration with men on a strike. There will be no lockout on any arbitrable question unless arbitration fails. There will be no discrimination against membership in any organization. Every workman will be required to work peaceably and harmoniously with all fellow employes.

In case of disagreement, we advise conference, to be followed, if necessary, by arbitration under the New York Agreement, where it is applicable. In other cases, the question should be submitted to a board of six, three from each side, its decision to be final and binding. There must be no interruption of work pending a decision. Any member refusing to comply with this recommendation shall be denied the support of the association, unless it shall approve the member's action. Employers may pay wages mutually agreed upon, the rates to be governed by local or shop conditions. Mr. Frank concluded:

"Now, those, we believe, are broad principles. We believe that if the union will set aside some hidebound—if I may use the expression—conditions, that a restricted apprenticeship is necessary to their unionism, that a restricted shop is necessary to their unionism, that a restricted output is necessary—we can get together; but we cannot get together with those principles in force. I believe they are not in force in some of the unions. Let the progressive unions see the equity of the proposition that these things should be open and free to the employer, and then we can formulate an agreement that will be binding and lasting.

"But then comes the question of enforcing the agreement. I believe we can leave that to public sentiment to a great degree. I believe no man can go in the face of what the public declare to be right and just and hope to get public favor, and public favor on these propositions is everything."

The Molders' Side.

Thomas B. Lavey, proxy for Joseph F. Valentine, president of the Iron Molders' Union of North America, was called upon. He congratulated Mr. Sard upon the success of the agreement of his organization with the Molders' Union. In reply to Mr. Frank, Mr. Lavey said: "I am not entirely in harmony with Mr. Frank's views regarding our association. I want to say that in this district, comprising Greater New York and New Jersey, we control in our organization at least 157 shops covered mostly by agreements. We do not practice the abuses he speaks of; on the contrary, the agents here insist that the terms he specifically mentioned are carried out.

"We do not allow men to go out until the matter has been investigated. If they do go out, we order them back, and if they don't go back we insist on their charter being taken away from them. As a result, in this district we have harmony between employer and employe, resulting, so far as it concerns us locally, to the satisfaction of all.

"There is a difference of opinion regarding the New York Agreement read here. The terms of that agreement establish a condition that our organization followed until it was interpreted by some one wrongly. I have a copy of a letter showing how the previous president of the National Foundrymen's Association interpreted it. The late commissioner of the Foundrymen's Association interpreted it the same way. The present commissioner and the present president, I believe, interpret the agreement altogether differently. This is from the former president:

A. BEVERLY SMITH

Interpretation of the New York Agreement; how we understand it to be. In any case of difference between employers and employes, the men shall not strike nor the employer lock out their men until there has been arbitration. That either party in the event of dissatisfaction has the right to ask for arbitration, but pending such arbitration there shall be practically no change in the existing conditions in the foundry.

'That is the way we have interpreted that agreement. Within the past year it has been interpreted wrongly—that when either party makes a demand, or when foundry employes make a demand, that the men will work under the conditions demanded until such times as the matter is brought to the board of arbitration or brought to the investigating committee. Isn't that right?"

Mr. Frank said that Mr. Lavey's statement was correct. Mr. Lavey continued:

A Hope for National Agreement.

"So that is one more bone of contention before we are able to get on common ground, as we are with the Stove Foundrymen's Defense Association. I feel we must in the first place interpret any provision and have it fully understood.

"I am in hope, judging from the feeling of the men who expressed themselves here, that there is a prospect of agreement. I know there is. I feel that if at first you don't succeed, go at it again.

"Our hope is along the line of education. We have trouble with our local organization, the same as any national organization has trouble with theirs. We have local organizations that violate agreements. But our hope is in educating our men. We feel that it is necessary to work along the same lines as a good many organizations, and that is toward a successful national agreement. We feel that we will take care of the situation locally if we can get a national agreement. That is our only hope and prospect—a national agreement. But there are a great many differences of opinion that have got to be modified in order that harmony can prevail. The statement of Mr. Sard would verify the statement that I would make, that we are willing and anxious to do all we possibly can for the successful determination of the strike. Those little technicalities about men walking out of the shop because another man hasn't his card should not prevail. We are immediately notified, and we do not allow a man's business to be hampered until the case can be investigated. We generally provide for the eliminating of that man by mutual consent.

"On the whole, I think the only thing that leaves us very far apart at the present time towards national agreement is that we haven't really simmered all these questions down to a fine point. When we do, there is no question, I think, that we will reach a national agreement for the whole United States or at least the district that our organization claims to have jurisdiction over."

John Cooper, president of the New York Iron League, said that trade agreements depend for success greatly upon the men who handle them. If employers and employes are both reasonable and conservative, there is no trouble. Of the agreement with the iron-workers, he pointed out that its conditions are explicit, saying:

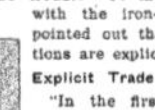
H. C. HUNTER

Explicit Trade Agreement.

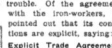

"In the first place the hours of labor are stipulated, the pay for overtime is stipulated, the holidays are stipulated, also that there shall be no discrimination against any of the material given a workman to use in the erection of a building, and no discrimination or curtailment in days' work. In the event of any complaint under this agreement—as we have on both sides radicals—it is provided that a Board of Solution, composed of three on one side and three on the other, meet and appoint an umpire to settle any point on which they cannot agree. But this Board of Solution only takes up questions that may arise from a misinterpretation or failure to carry out the agreement on the part of either side. We had a meeting of our board last week; three complaints were made and they were all settled without trouble. We haven't any plan of arbitration, because we thought the solution board meant a great deal more. Arbitration means compromise, and compromise means a bad taste in the mouth when you get through with it.

"Under our trade agreement, we propose to settle all matters between us and the iron workers if possible. When it comes to the relation of the iron workers to the other mechanics in the building, we are under another plan of arbitration which provides for no sympathetic strike and all questions of trade jurisdiction shall be settled without any strikes or lock-outs on either side.

Agreements Between Unions.

"Most of the strikes in New York City for the last eight or ten years have arisen over differences between workmen, one party claiming that he should do that or this part of the work. By this morning's mail I got a notice from the general board of arbitration stating a disputed point between iron workers and electrical apparatus workers,—simply a question of the drilling of holes in the building to provide for electric appliances; the iron worker claiming he should do it and the electrical man claiming it as part of his work. One case I remember, of two years ago, where two men both claimed the right to do the same work, and the superintendent, rather than have a strike, agreed to pay them both; so the iron man did the work and the electric light man drew his three days' pay for looking at him. Now an agreement is reached between the two unions as to what portion of the work each shall do, and no strike has taken place; the work goes on. The same condition may occur in another building and the arrangement now will settle the condition in that building also.

"I am thoroughly in favor of trade agreements. There should be no question about their containing all the clauses as to wages, hours and holidays and also avoiding sympathetic strikes; and a solution board. Get all those things down and get a reasonable number of men on both sides to discuss the matters, and there will be no trouble; but if not, there will be trouble.

Better Union Representation.

"I feel very much that the trend of unions to-day is for a better representation, that the men that we meet to-day are better than we met ten years ago. It is unfortunate that the men will not take as active part in the unions as they ought. They leave that to the men who have less to think of and who are not bound by family ties. They let them go to the meetings and run things to suit themselves. I think on the whole we have a very fair trade agreement, and we expect lasting peace and prosperity from it."

A. Beverly Smith of the joint executive committee of the Lithographers' Association said:

"We have heard to-day about various agreements for various trades. If we single out any one of these, we shall feel that one successful agreement should be applied to our industry, or that one unsuccessful agreement proves that trade agreements are a failure. Either opinion would be erroneous. In my judgment, the best agreement is the one that leaves as much as possible to be settled by joint action. Any agreement is a step out of chaos. It should contain no clause that has to be construed by courts or lawyers. Every clause should be fully understood by both sides. There should result from this meeting many more trade agreements. The violation of an agreement has become a moral crime.

"The first way to enforce an agreement is through thorough organization and united action on both sides. Every trade and all employers in each trade should be organized. Then say to any union that has entered into an agreement that it finds onerous, 'You must keep that agreement to its end and make a better one next time. If you break it, you will get no help from us; on the contrary, we will help the employers.' Equally, the association of employers must say to an employer who breaks an agreement, 'We will not associate with you.' I think that is the only way to enforce trade agreements. We have no courts in the industrial world. Our appeal should be to the public opinion that opposes the breaking, or even the bending, of an agreement during its life.

"There are two kinds of arbitration—before a trouble and after a trouble. To agree upon disputed questions in time of peace is preventive arbitration. Sometimes there are differences of opinion that cannot be justified. Are we then to say that there is nothing but the sword? Why not refer such a question to a disinterested person, before fighting, and abide by his decision for the time being? If his decision is wrong, a year or two will clear it away. It may work an injury to either employer or employe, but that very fact would cause the wrong to be righted by mutual action. I hold that employer and employe are equally interested in the way any business is conducted and in the conditions under which men labor. That interest is equal—not measured by the amount of capital invested or the amount of wages earned. If that is acknowledged, you have a line right down the center between labor and capital to which each must come and agree. In all trade, mutual action is necessary. Any trade agreement should contain a provision that the two parties can at any time agree to disregard the agreement, or to change its conditions, always by mutual act."

Mr. Mitchell, the chairman, said:

"This discussion has been very illuminating. No doubt this interchange of opinion will be productive of much good. I think we should keep in mind that in all our relations we ought to take into consideration human frailties and imperfections, and if we try to put ourselves occasionally in the other fellow's place we probably will be able better to appreciate his position and the feelings and conditions and environment that prompt him to do things that we believe may not be quite right. I think if we try to follow that rule in our business that it will establish a better relation.

"I am requested to announce that the National Civic Federation will appoint a permanent committee on trade agreements, through which we hope to have other meetings of this character and through which we hope to work out a satisfactory plan of trade agreement. In this meeting we seem all to have concurred in the opinion that trade agreements are the proper thing. We hold different views as to their form and what they should contain, but no doubt by getting together this committee will be better able to understand the detail of existing agreements and how to improve them."

Mr. Marks pointed out that the conference had been unanimous in agreeing that there should be agreement upon agreements. He requested that Wallace Downey, president of the New York Metal Trades Association, make a statement.

Mr. Downey announced that his association had voted almost unanimously that trade agreements are advisable. When it attempted to renew its contract with the boiler makers, they insisted that the contract should require the employment of only union men. Otherwise, they refused to renew the contract. The employers refused to contract with anybody to the exclusion of all individuals outside that body. He thought that trade agreements made in times of heated arguments sometimes contained provisions that were idiotic, from a conservative point of view. Contracts must be made honestly. He suggested that one way to enforce a contract would be for both parties to furnish a bond. That would open the way, in case of dispute, to appeal to the courts. In this way, the law of the land could be utilized. He did not believe in arbitration of rights. He did believe in labor unionism, as he did in the organization of employers. He hoped that organization of both sides would strip the situation of many technicalities.

WALLACE DOWNEY

The conference then adjourned.

LIBERTY, DEMOCRACY.

(Concluded from page 9.)

production, it is a proposition that can be made the premise of an argument in favor of the employment of union labor. The aim of the unions, as has been pointed out, should be, and when the unions are wisely led is coming more and more to be, not the limitation, but the development, of individual efficiency, and through it the attainment of superiority of workmanship for the group as a whole. The constant tendency of unionism under such conditions is to lift the lower grades of workmen toward higher capacity and excellence,—in short to raise their standard of life. This increased efficiency must result in greater productivity, both in quality and quantity, and granted a market of adequate purchasing and consuming capacity, the outcome must be a greater sum of wealth to be apportioned between capital and labor as the reward of their trained effort and intelligent co-operation.

EDWIN R. A. SELIGMAN.
Professor of Political Economy and Finance,
Columbia University, New York.

James E. Roderick, chief of the Department of Mines of Pennsylvania, in his report for 1903, issued in June, favors the enactment of a new mining law, for more effective prevention of accidents and other purposes. The mine inspectors and some of the operators are said also to desire new legislation. There has been a slight decrease in fatal accidents in mines, but compulsory employment of assistant firemen is advised by Mr. Roderick. He would advance the minimum age for employment outside the mines to 13 years, to conform with the school law of the State, and would require everybody employed to have a certificate from an inspector.

THE GREAT TEAMSTER TIE-UP AVERTED THROUGH CONFERENCE.

CONCILIATION, THROUGH THE NEW YORK CIVIC FEDERATION, SAVES THE CITY SERIOUS LOSS AND INCONVENIENCE AND EFFECTS A NEW TRADE AGREEMENT.

THOMAS F. McCARTHY,
President N. Y. Truck-Owners' Association.

A strike of organized teamsters, that would have brought to a standstill every truck in New York and, through sympathy, caused untold midsummer inconvenience and distress throughout the city, was recently averted by mutual conference, arranged through the efforts of the New York Civic Federation. Not only was the threatened strike averted, but out of an industrial controversy a satisfactory trade agreement, the first ever made between the organized New York truck-owners and teamsters, was evolved.

The settlement of any strike that causes loss and inconvenience to the community is always hailed with acclaim in the newspaper press and by the public. The averting of a strike, even though it would have caused ten-fold more expense and suffering than a strike that really occurred, usually attracts little public attention. In this case, however, there were attendant circumstances that gave some prominence to the adjustment of the difficulty. While the general public may not have realized fully the inconvenience and even suffering that it thus escaped, business interests were aware of their danger. Both truck-owners and teamsters have expressed their gratification at reaching a friendly settlement of their differences, without resort to costly hostilities. The adjustment illustrated again the practical value of conciliation and conference.

There had been increasing discontent among the local members of the International Brotherhood of Teamsters with both hours and wages. This discontent had grown in January into an open threat of a strike for shorter hours and higher pay, accompanied by a demand that the truck-owners employ only members of the Teamsters' Brotherhood. The New York Truck Owners' Association refused to consider the demand for the exclusive employment of union teamsters, or to recognize the union at all, and a strike seemed imminent.

The situation was made more acute by the existing trouble between the marine freight-handlers and the New York, New Haven & Hartford Railroad Company. The freight-handlers were looking to an alliance with the teamsters in their strike, and such an alliance would obviously have increased the difficulties of the railroad in handling its marine transportation. Even without this complication, a general strike of the teamsters would have meant a disaster to the entire city. It would have blocked all commerce by land and water by preventing the cartage of cases of merchandise. Through sympathy, it might have paralyzed local trade, by interfering with the delivery of all goods, wholesale and retail. Milk wagons, ice wagons and coal carts would not make their rounds. Household arrangements would have been thrown into confusion through the inability of dealers in all kinds of supplies to meet the regular, established requirements of their customers. The strike would have been felt in the kitchen and in the sick-room, as well as by the great shippers and transportation companies.

These were the circumstances that suggested an appeal to the good offices of the Civic Federation of New York. On Monday, May 23, Henry C. Hunter, secretary of the Truck Owners' Association, invited Marcus M. Marks, chairman of the Conciliation Committee of the Federation, to meet for a consultation the members of the Executive Committee of the Truck Owners. In accepting this invitation, Mr. Marks secured permission to bring with him John C. Eames, vice-president of the H. B. Claflin Company,

MARCUS M. MARKS,
Chairman N. Y. Conciliation Committee.

and J. C. Juhring, of Francis H. Leggett & Co. The entire situation was reviewed at a luncheon in the Astor House on that date. The Truck Owners present expressed strong objections to entering into any negotiations, fearing that they would involve a surrender of what they held to be an essential principle—the right to employ teamsters outside the unions. It was explained to them that a way could be devised to reach an agreement that, while recognizing the union, would not violate the abstract principle of the "open shop."

Accordingly, a conference was begun between the representatives of the Truck Owners' Association and a committee of the Teamsters' Brotherhood, in the office of Mr. Hunter, at No. 203 Broadway, Mr. Marks presiding on behalf of the Civic Federation.

Those present representing the Truck Owners' Association were: T. F. McCarthy, president; C. F. Coppins, vice-president; H. C. Hunter, secretary; Benjamin A. Jackson, Thomas Orr, J. M. Lowden, I. Goldberg, J. H. Wilks, Paul Vianne and W. Fox.

The representatives of the Brotherhood of Teamsters were: Edward Gould, general executive board; John Clark, William H. Ashton, joint executive council; Richard Condon, Dennis Crane, Philip Gould, Gustavus Becker, William Crawford, Valentine Hoffman, dry goods teamsters; George Prescott, Michael J. Rogan, building material teamsters.

This first conference was in continuous session until 7 p. m. The question of employing union labor exclusively was precipitated; and the conference was on the eve of breaking up without action of any kind,

EDWARD GOULD,
1st Vice-President Teamsters' International Brotherhood.

when Mr. Marks made a vigorous plea for another effort to reach an agreement, pointing out the critical nature of the situation and the importance of persisting in the negotiations. His argument, with the aid of some of the conservative men on each side, had the effect of securing an adjournment until 3 p. m. on Tuesday, May 24.

This second conference was occupied with fixing the hours for a day's work, including the time consumed in going to and from the stables; the rate of wages for the several classes of teamsters; the subject of overtime, about which there was much difficulty, its final adjustment being left to arbitration; and the question of the exclusive employment of union teamsters. Finally, the representatives of the teamsters, in view of the concessions that they had gained as to wages and hours, accepted the proposition that the truck-owners should agree not to discriminate against a driver because of his membership in the Brotherhood. The teamsters agreed to make no restriction or discrimination in the handling or trucking of any merchandise. The average increase of wages is about $1 a week, and the limit of ten hours for a day's work, excluding stabling, is a gain to the teamsters.

Although each of these subjects contained elements of acrimony, the representatives of both sides were remarkably self-controlled throughout the conference. The agreement was discussed line by line and section by section, in order to make certain the perfect mutual understanding of its terms. This process brought out occasional demonstrations of feeling, in some instances passionate in tone, but the spirit of patient consideration of the plan proposed for averting a grave danger was always resumed. The successful conclusion of the conference and the signing of the agreement were followed by a general interchange of congratulations and expressions of good-will, while Mr. Marks received from all present hearty assurances of appreciation for the manner in which he had guided the negotiations, as the chairman of the Conciliation Committee of the Civic Federation, to a satisfactory conclusion.

The agreement provides that there shall be no sympathetic strike during its term, which continues until April 30, 1905. The agreement is in the form of a contract. It is signed for the Truck Owners' Association by Thomas F. McCarthy, president, and for the International Brotherhood of Teamsters by Edward Gould, vice-president, and is witnessed by Marcus M. Marks of the Civic Federation.

A RAILROAD PRESIDENT TO RAILROAD UNIONISTS.

THE WISE COUNSEL OF CHARLES S. MELLEN TO ORGANIZED LABOR, WHOSE UNIONS HE BOTH CRITICISES AND ENCOURAGES.

Charles S. Mellen, president of the New York, New Haven and Hartford Railroad, delivered an address on April 28, before the West Side Workingmen's Club, in Hartford, upon the subject of trade unions. Mr. Mellen's expression of his opinions has elicited much comment. His address follows in part:

"The hope and future of this country lie in the common people, in the workingmen, in yourselves.

"This is the age of the workingman. Let him, with moderation, with conservatism, show his ability to assume responsibility, and there is no bound set to his attainments. Let him but exercise good judgment, and his ambitions will be attained in less time, with the good will of all, and be of more lasting benefit.

"The captains of industry of the future are among you struggling at day's wages for recognition. Men of affairs are looking earnestly for them, for there is a great dearth of men for the higher positions the modern industrial combinations are creating, and the duties of these positions are so exacting they wear out quickly those who fill them, causing constant changes.

"But they are not looking for firebrands, for trouble-breeders, for talkers, but rather for the quiet man who works while others do the talking—the one who is as much interested in his work as his wages, and such men, when found, need no help from any source to secure either recognition or increase of pay.

"To those of you who belong to unions I wish to say I believe they have accomplished much good; but they are, nevertheless, not an unmixed blessing to the laboring man. They tend to the discouragement of individual effort and reduce man to a part of a machine. They are a good thing for the drone, the inefficient man, for the walking delegate and the officers, but are unnecessary for the man who has the stuff and courage within himself to carve his own way in the world. There are many workingmen who can earn more than they do, whose employers would gladly pay them more, but that they have become classified, and an advance to them means an advance also to their inefficient associates of a similar class, making it often too formidable a matter for consideration. Therefore, when I say unions do much good, I mean they help the lame, the halt and the weary, at the expense of the really competent.

A Means of Averaging Wages.

"Divested of all claptrap, the union is simply a means of averaging wages, and an employer views it as such. It is a device for making those who are willing to work care for those who want to soldier. On the principle that every man must have a living somehow, in place of making the community contribute support openly, to which process there attaches some discredit, the really efficient workmen of a class receive less for their services, and thus help support those who are unable to earn as much, under normal conditions, through establishing a scale of averages.

"Now, having hurt the feelings of some of you by the foregoing, I am going to surprise you by saying that I regard the unions as a condition that has come to stay; that I have no prejudice whatever to properly-conducted ones, and express my wish that our men generally would join them, not that I would run a union plant as such, for I would not coerce my men nor consent to discriminations as between those who were and who were not members, but I would wish to have in the unions the conservative influence of many of the good men who are out, to counteract the floater, the anarchist, the man who has nothing at stake in the world, who works with his mouth more than his hands.

"The trouble with unionism is its intolerance.

"To succeed in this world, one must bear and forbear. The same spirit of intolerance that fills the union man toward the non-union is what history shows us to have prevailed ages ago in religion, in race prejudice, and in other ways. The cry of 'The Union or the Hospital!' has its counterpart in that of the older one of 'The Church or the Stake!' It is through the elimination of the feeling that physical force is necessary to the accomplishment of results that real progress is made. The time when brute strength shall rule is becoming a thing of the past. The advance has been slow, but looking back to the monuments history has left for our instruction, we can see most substantial progress has been made in this direction. You cannot force things your way, but you may direct them. You hurt immeasurably your cause when you descend to violence in language or action.

Seniority Rule a Bad Thing.

"The rule of seniority is a bad one. It is most discouraging to men of ability. It is repressive and oppressive, and puts many of little wit and less ability into positions they are unfitted for, and keeps out those who

CHARLES S. MELLEN,
President N. Y., N. H. & H. Railroad.

are more deserving and competent. It deteriorates the service. In the short time I have been in authority here I have been restricted from advancing those who had attracted my attention by their ability, through this rule. I fail to understand why young men assent to a rule that requires them to grow old in one line of employment before recognition becomes possible, no matter how well deserved. It is all wrong that a man should be held back by this rule from a position he is competent to fill, and see that position go to one his inferior in every respect, for no reason but he is higher up on the list of numbers of his class. The result makes for dissatisfaction, this makes for change, which in turn accounts for the large floating class in each grade of employment, with the responsible positions filled by old men.

"No one interest has done more to promote the trust or combination, the larger corporation, than organized labor. It has forced them into existence, for protection from exaction. And to what does it all tend? Given all your hotheads seek, and there will be no one to employ you, and public corporations must be run by the government. Capital will not seek investment where nothing but loss and controversy is to result. The rule of the radical will not prevail. The hothead must be retired, or in the contest in which he will involve you, you will go down in defeat. The contest will not be determined by numbers. Education and brains will outweigh numbers and brawn. The spectacled student is to be the general of future armies; captains of industry may not always be those who have worked with their hands. Give heed to whither you are drifting, for at the end there may be a rude awakening, from which those who believe in you, who are of you, would have you spared.

"My advice to you who have families, who have a stake in the world, is to join your unions, and make yourselves felt in them. Be always a force for conservatism. It seems to me as much in your interest to do this as that you shall attend the caucus and nominate good men for office and vote for them at the polls. Your apathy is the opportunity of the demagogue, the anarchist, the floater, who has nothing to lose.

"Whatever tends to better the condition of labor must command the earnest and honest consideration of every right-minded man. The brightest minds, the most practical, are studying the subject, and the great progress made by organized labor, to my mind, has been not by securing an increase of wages here and there, but by attracting the attention of such minds to a study of the conditions that have produced the present state of unrest. That force having been set in motion, it cannot be stayed, and its results can hardly fail to be of advantage to all.

Too Much Arbitrary Conduct.

"If I have criticised the unions, let me now say that I have seen much to deplore in the course of those in authority who have dealt with them. There has been too much of arbitrary and unreasonable conduct on that side, as well, and I desire to go on record here that arbitrary, unreasonable exercise of power by those temporarily in authority is as offensive to me as to any of you, and I am disposed to neither countenance nor condone it.

"You cannot get for a thing more than it is worth, except temporarily, and the cost of maintaining an artificial market is greater than the profit in it.

"Some gentlemen interested in high finance are only just beginning to realize this, and it is no wonder this fallacy has taken root elsewhere.

"With business falling off, day by day, here in New England, I find my political friends opposing an enlargement of our markets and preferring a phrase 'stand pat' to the substance which reciprocity with our neighbor, Canada, would give us; and when I feel they ought to know better, it is not in me to too severely criticise the employes of our company who feel they should have higher wages, when the conditions with which we are surrounded compel us to disagree with them.

"I would like to pay the men of our company better wages and allow them greater privileges than my neighbors, but if I do it some one else will take my place who will bring about an equitable comparison.

"If our employes could only know the struggle it has been the past few months to keep so many of them at work at all, they would feel our officials have had their interests in mind much more than they are willing to admit.

"I have never had so many bosses as I am working for at the present time. I never had to say 'no' so often when I wanted to say 'yes.' I am under more restraint than any of you, and yet I am pegging away all the time with all my strength to prevail, to keep my property strong for the benefit of the public, its stockholders, its employes, and with little advantage to myself.

"The foundation of everything good and desirable in the social or political system of the world is the home. The end for which we all should work is to make that home better, more attractive, more influential. We are permitted to live here not simply for our own gratification, but should so arrange our lives that others who follow us may not have the same old struggle to go through."

The men who emerge from great testings as heroes are the ones who have learned the habit of duty doing and of unselfishness through the quiet, unremembered days.—"Philadelphia Press."

THE CIVIC FEDERATION OF NEW YORK AND VICINITY.

[illegible]FICERS AND GENERAL BOARD—STRIKING TESTIMONY AS TO ITS SUCCESSFUL SERVICES FOR INDUSTRIAL PEACE.

The first annual meeting of the Civic Federation of New York and vicinity, in the rooms of the Board of Trade and Transportation, listened to addresses by Oscar Straus, who acted as chairman; Otto M. Eidlitz, Robert E. Neidig, Marcus M. Marks and others. Mr. Straus remarked that a seeming tendency to depreciate the work of the Civic Federation was because its work was not done with noise and clamor.

"I can announce," said Mr. Straus, "that in 95 per cent. of the cases in which we have tried to end labor troubles, we have succeeded." Mr. Straus also announced the progress in organizing other local branches of the Federation.

Otto M. Eidlitz, chairman of the Board of Governors of the Building Trades Employers' Association and president of the Mason Builders' Association, said:

"The building industry of New York City during the past four years has been in a deplorable condition. Chiefly owing to the efforts of the members of the Civic Federation it has at last emerged from that condition into what we believe to be the pure light. The most serious single phase of the situation was that in connection with the iron trade, and due largely to the efforts of members of the Civic Federation, this situation was cleared up in a proper way the past week."

Robert E. Neidig, who was active in the reorganization of the Housesmiths' Union, made this statement:

"The committee on our recent settlement and reorganization wish me to express gratitude and appreciation to the Civic Federation for its valuable services in arranging a meeting for us with our employers when it seemed as if such a meeting was impossible.

"We realize that it was entirely through the efforts of the Civic Féderation that the several meetings were arranged, and as a result of these meetings we were able to effect a settlement of the disastrous strike of the Housesmiths' and Bridgemen's Union, which had been on for eight months."

The meeting authorized a committee to elect officers and a General Board. That committee has performed its duty. The officers of the New York Civic Federation are: Chairman, Charles A. Moore; first vice-chairman, William H. Farley; second vice-chairman, V. Everit Macy; treasurer, Cornelius N. Bliss; secretary, James P. Archibald.

CHARLES A. MOORE
CHAIRMAN

WILLIAM H. FARLEY
1ST VICE-CHAIRMAN

CORNELIUS N. BLISS
TREASURER

JAMES P. ARCHIBALD
SECRETARY

The following constitute the General Board:

On the part of the Public:—

FELIX ADLER (Professor, Columbia University).
CORNELIUS N. BLISS (Ex-Secretary of the Interior).
NICHOLAS MURRAY BUTLER (President Columbia University).
JOHN B. CLARK (Professor, Columbia University).
RALPH M. EASLEY (Chairman Executive Council National Civic Federation).
RT. REV. JOHN M. FARLEY (Archbishop Roman Catholic Church).
R. WATSON GILDER (Editor Century Magazine).
HAMILTON HOLT (Editor Independent).
ALEX. C. HUMPHREYS (President Stevens Institute).
V. EVERIT MACY (Capitalist).
EMERSON McMILLIN (Banker).
WALTER H. PAGE (Editor World's Work).
ROLAND PHILLIPS (Managing Editor Harper's Weekly).
RT. REV. HENRY C. POTTER (Bishop Protestant Episcopal Church).
C. T. ROOT (Editor Dry Goods Economist).
ALBERT SHAW (Editor Review of Reviews).
OSCAR S. STRAUS (Member of the Court of Arbitration at the Hague).
FRANCIS B. SWAYNE (Lawyer).
H. C. WATSON (Editor Dun's Review).
THOS. F. WOODLOCK (Editor Wall Street Journal).

On the part of Employers:—

W. D. BALDWIN (President Otis Elevator Company).
EMIL L. BOAS (General Manager Hamburg-American Line).
JOHN COOPER (The Cooper-Wigand-Cooke Company).
OTTO M. EIDLITZ (Chairman Board Governors Building Trades Employers' Association).
WM. GREEN (Chairman New York Typothetæ).
J. ALEXANDER HAYDEN (Chairman Association Interior Decorators and Cabinetmakers).
HENRY C. HUNTER (Commissioner New York Metal Trades Association).
REGINALD H. JAFFRAY (R. H. Jaffray Company).
EDGAR L. MARSTON (Blair & Co.).
MARCUS M. MARKS (President National Clothiers' Association).
CHARLES A. MOORE (President The Shaw Electric Crane Company).
THOS. M. MULRY (Thomas Mulry & Son).
HOSMER B. PARSONS (Vice-President Wells, Fargo & Co.).
WALTER L. PIERCE (Lidgerwood Manufacturing Company).
CHARLES A. SCHIEREN (Charles A. Schieren & Co.).
LOUIS B. SCHRAM (President Associated Brewers).
C. W. SWEET (Sweet, Orr & Co.).
CHARLES W. TERHUNE (Edwin C. Burt Co.).
BENJAMIN D. TRAITEL (Traitel Bros. & Co.).
CHARLES WILHELMS (President United States Lithographers' Association).

On the part of Wage Earners:—

JAMES P. ARCHIBALD (Brotherhood Painters and Decorators).
A. J. BOULTON (Stereotypers).
JAMES DALY (Dockbuilders).
CHARLES DELANEY (Granite Cutters).
SAMUEL B. DONNELLY (Typographical Union).
WILLIAM H. FARLEY (Mosaic and Encaustic Tile Layers).
J. J. FLYNN (Metal Polishers).
M. J. FORD (Machinists).
EDWARD GOULD (Teamsters).
JAMES P. HOLLAND (Stationary Firemen).
W. LONG (Lithographers).
FRANCIS J. McKAY (Boilermakers and Iron Shipbuilders).
EDWARD A. MOFFETT (Editor Bricklayer and Mason).
ROBERT E. NEIDIG (Housesmiths).
GEORGE E. PEPPER (President Amalgamated Association St. Railway Employees, New York Division).
HERMAN ROBINSON (Retail Clerks).
HENRY WHITE (Garment Workers).

A summary of the advantages derived from membership in a local union is set forth by J. O. Carson, of Indianapolis, in "The Carpenter," in a manner that may appeal also to craftsmen of other trades. He gives importance to the training in parliamentary law and the preparation for taking part in miscellaneous public gatherings. The use of the referendum accustoms members to appreciate their individual responsibility for their votes. These are influences distinctly educational and promotive of good citizenship. The clearance card assures a welcome in other localities. The funeral and disability benefits encourage that feeling of independence and security which follows investment in a safe form of insurance. The minimum wage scale, which prevails in the Carpenters' Union, is adduced as a method by which the least efficient workman is enabled to make a livelihood, while not interfering with the greater rewards that are due to the sober, industrious and reliable. The support of trade journals tends to technical education. An economic proposition is involved in the claim that as unions raise the scale of wages, they increase the purchasing power of the greater part of any population. Such argumentative methods of forwarding the organization of labor are commendable, especially when they are directed to show that unions should strive for the mutual benefit of employer and employed.

THE GREAT LAKES DEADLOCK.

A Report of the Special Committee of the Cleveland Civic Federation Upon a Recent Important Industrial Controversy.

(From the Cleveland Leader, June 9.)

The report of the special committee elected by the Cleveland Civic Federation to investigate the deadlock existing between the Lake Carriers' Association and the American Association of Masters and Pilots has been submitted.

It is an interesting document of some 5,000 words. It reveals some of the inside history of the trouble and closes by saying that the committee is powerless to adjust the difficulties.

The testimony given at the hearings of the committee is not given in full in the report. It is simply outlined, and some deductions are made from the information obtained. The committee is composed of Hon. John C. Hutchins, chairman; James A. Reynolds, secretary; W. H. Hunt, Colonel J. J. Sullivan, Hon. Elroy M. Avery, W. H. Canniff, E. W. Oglebay, Harry D. Thomas and Peter Hasenphflue. It was elected May 26, and the first hearing was held on May 31.

The whole of that day was devoted to receiving written and oral statements from the two associations, both of which willingly responded to the request of the committee for information. Many questions were asked by members of the committee, and the proceedings were taken down by a stenographer. On the next day the lake carriers' representatives were heard separately and later the masters and pilots, and both positions were gone over with the greatest freedom.

Efforts Toward a Settlement.

The report says that the result of these various [illegible] perfectly manifest to the committ[illegible]t could not, probably, be arrived [illegible]n settlement of the difficulties. [illegible]mittee in executive session voted to authorize the chairman to select two special committees of three members each to wait upon the two warring factions separately to determine whether or not the chief points of difference could not be smoothed over in such a way as to make it possible to bring about a settlement.

These committees, the report says, worked earnestly toward this end, but were obliged to report back the failure of their efforts, as both sides claimed that the questions involved contained important principles which neither side could yield with safety.

The report then gives the history of the organization and the personnel of the two opposing associations. It says that the Masters' and Pilots' Association was organized a year or more ago and that, as such association, negotiations and working agreements were had with it in a greater or less degree, by the Lake Carriers' Association during the navigation season of 1903, and that preparatory to the season of 1904, some time this spring the lake carriers began again to renew negotiations with the Masters' and Pilots' Association.

The unexecuted agreement is given containing section 11, "that all members of the lake carriers will pay their masters and pilots the same salaries as were paid during the year 1903." The history of the hitch on this section is given and the different interpretations of the break in the negotiations are stated.

The Lake Carriers' Contention.

The report states that while the evidence shows that the two associations had up to this point endeavored by meetings between representatives to harmonize their differences, at no time since has the Lake Carriers' Association manifested a disposition to deal longer in any way with the Masters' and Pilots' Association. The reasons of the lake carriers are given as follows: (1) that past experience with the Masters' and Pilots' Association has convinced them that they can no longer recognize the association in any way; (2) that the masters occupy a unique position to the government in that there is no principle applicable to any class of skilled or unskilled service which is in any degree applicable to them; (3) that the government has placed certain restriction upon the masters and given them certain privileges; (4) that the relation of a master to his ship is that of general agent with possibly the broadest powers known in the laws of agency. He has the power in case of necessity even to sell the cargo or the ship, for the proper exercise of judgment in this respect the owner is responsible.

On this last ground the carriers maintain that they cannot negotiate with an organization in which the masters are associated with their subordinates in such proposition that the latter can outvote them and are oath-bound to rules beyond and inconsistent with the rules prescribed by the government and the full performance of their duties to the ship, the owner, and the public. The lake carriers say that because of the peculiarly close relationship between the owners and the masters they cannot deal with an association of masters and mates. They insist that such a compound organization is inconsistent and unreasonable, and say they are willing to deal with two organizations composed each of masters and mates, and will aid in the formation of such associations.

Masters' and Pilots' Side.

The masters and pilots deny this stand, the report says. They claim the double organization is not inconsistent because from year to year mates become captains and captains become mates. They claim that the carriers would, in event two organizations were formed, use one to disrupt the other.

On this rock the negotiations were wrecked, the carriers refusing to deal with the masters and mates in joint organization, the latter refusing to change their association. The report says that the committee believes that growing out of the change, which has been going on so rapidly, which has resulted in the passing of the ownership of lake vessels from individual and private hands to corporate and syndicate ownership, various abuses have crept in of which the masters and mates have reasonable ground to complain. But the committee believes that many, if not all of these grievances, would be corrected by the present management of the various lake fleets; that representatives of the Masters' and Pilots' Association also believe this.

"We further report," says the committee, "that while the different associations are divided upon a number of propositions, these differences could be adjusted if the two contending parties could see their way clear toward meeting and negotiating these differences."

In view of the foregoing facts the committee decides that no effort on its part would avail, and asks to be discharged. The report closes with the following words:

"In view of the determined attitude assumed by both associations as indicated above, all the efforts which this committee could, by any possibility, put forth to settle their differences, were from the beginning foredoomed to failure."

AN EVIDENCE OF UNION WISDOM.

(Labor World, Pittsburg.)

The sympathetic strike is no longer a necessary part of trades unionism. This fact was fully demonstrated the other day by President Dolan, of the United Mine Workers. The pilots now on strike on the lakes recently joined the American Federation of Labor. Because of this they became possessed of the notion that other organized bodies identified with the A. F. of L. would, if required, join in the strike. Thus it was that the miners who mine coal for the lake trade were asked to strike against mining any coal for that trade.

President Dolan very pointedly stated that no such strike would be inaugurated by the miners, and he added that he could not see the justice of entering on any such conflict.

This declaration ought to silence Parry and his friends who never tire of asserting that the sympathetic strike is one of the leading features of trade unionism. [illegible] are strongly [illegible] the worke[illegible] difficult on [illegible] who resolved to strike in the Pittsburg district simply because seamen were on a strike hundreds of miles away. The difference between the seamen and their employers has nothing whatever to do with the mine operators of Pennsylvania or Ohio. The relationship between the miners and their employers is of the most harmonious kind, and there is no trouble whatever between them. Hence the unfairness both to the public and to the operators of the miners inaugurating a strike because the pilots are in conflict with their employers.

The refusal to participate in this sympathetic strike is a definite indication of the intelligence and moral advancement of trade unions. Not many years ago the request of the pilots would almost certainly have been granted. This sign of progress prompts all classes to have a greater regard for and a stronger faith in organized labor.

SYMPATHETIC STRIKES.

The Longshoremen's President Dwells Upon the Importance of Holding to Agreements.

President Daniel J. Keefe of the International Longshoremen, Marine and Transport Workers, in his latest report made the following statement on sympathetic strikes and the necessity of strict observance of trade agreements:

"The so-called sympathetic strikes cannot be countenanced by our organization. When deserving we can lend our aid and moral support. Yet we must not forget that our honor and manhood is involved in the obligations of our contracts and agreements. The influence and respect we to-day command as an international union is due to the fidelity and faithful performance of each and every agreement entered into.

"Labor long ago complained, and justly so, of the gross injustice practiced on them in the past. Now when we are dignified with the consideration and public approval of just cause, we can ill afford to be swayed by the inexperienced and unthinking portion of the movement, who have but recently been made aware of the existence of a union.

"It has taken years of patient struggle and sacrifice to build up our organization, and the wisdom of the best minds who have suffered in the past contend that unless the provocation is very great should we order a sympathetic strike. The past policy of this organization has always been to exhaust all means to arrive at a satisfactory settlement and only when every other means failed, to strike, and then do so with a full knowledge and appreciation of what the contest means, and be prepared to endure all the conflict entails.

"But the great secret of the success of our organization has been due to our ability to meet with our employers and have them see where our labor has merited and is entitled to increased wages and better conditions. * * *

"Public sentiment is sure to be with us, if our cause is right, and deserves public support, and our every act should be a studied effort for its approval. Public sentiment to-day exacts that the contracts or agreements of labor be free, as contracts for commodities, under fair and just agreement for services rendered, to the end that the wageworker shall not be obliged to make contracts or terms not acceptable to him. And public sentiment will hold the party who violates an agreement or declines to resort to conciliatory methods of arbitration, morally responsible for all the ill effects growing out of contest or strike."

The label must be respected by union men themselves, and this only will be done as a good mechanic is respected—by making it the emblem of excellence in workmanship.—"Union Label Magazine."

National Civic Federation

MONTHLY REVIEW

VOL. I. No. 6 NEW YORK, AUGUST, 1904 TEN CENTS

A SHORTER WORK-DAY WITH AN UNRESTRICTED OUTPUT.

VIEWS OF MANY EMPLOYERS UPON A PROPOSITION TO OFFSET FEWER HOURS OF LABOR WITH UNRESTRAINED EXERTION BY EMPLOYES.

The discussion of the desirability and practicability of a shorter work-day in the United States has centered about the eight-hour bill in Congress. That measure, now under consideration by the Department of Commerce and Labor, proposes to limit to eight hours a day all labor performed for the government by contractors and sub-contractors, with exceptions provided as to emergencies and as to goods bought in the open market, and carries with it the machinery for its enforcement. But the proponents of the bill, including the American Federation of Labor, candidly avow that its design is to bring about a uniform eight-hour work-day in all industries in all the States, which Congress has not the constitutional power to require.

The discussion, therefore, has gone beyond the proposition embraced in the eight-hour bill for public contracts. It has extended to the social and economic philosophy of the shorter work-day and has elicited a mass of testimony from both employers and representatives of labor as to its practicability. It has included consideration of various statutes in States regulating hours of labor under public contracts and upon material for public use and regulating the employment of women and children. Finally, quite aside from the criticism, favorable and adverse, of the eight-hour bill, it has brought to the public consciousness a realization of the fact that the progress of our national civilization has been accompanied by an actual, though gradual, reduction of the hours of labor in virtually all pursuits, and that the movement for a still further reduction is so general and so powerful that probably it cannot successfully be resisted or long stayed. Back of this movement lies a growing perception that the economic result of the shorter work-day is increased consumption of manufactured products, through the gradual elevation of the masses and the simultaneous multiplication of their wants. But this elevation can be ensured only by proper use of increased leisure. So that, on its social side, the discussion has recognized the importance of providing the workers the opportunity and the guidance to utilize for their mental and physical culture the added time freed from gainful toil, and to prevent Satan from snatching the new leisure for his proverbial activity in finding mischief "for idle hands to do."

The discussion has included consideration of voluntary trade agreements for a shorter work-day, extending throughout an industry, and including the removal of arbitrary restrictions upon output. Cannot the desire of the employer to be rid of such restrictions be matched against the desire of the employed for shorter hours of toil? Cannot one be made the quid pro quo of the other? In fact, that idea was incorporated in the agreement made in 1900 between the National Metal Trades Association and the International Association of Machinists.

This idea of making the length of the work-day uniform throughout an industry is of prime importance, because of competition. A ship-builder is concerned chiefly with the cost of labor to other ship-builders. If hours and wages are uniform in all ship-yards, competition is transferred to skill in buying and assembling the materials produced by many contributory industries, and in construction. So in mining, an operator is interested only in the length of the work-day in mines so far as it affects the cost of coal to himself and his competitors. He is not concerned directly in the hours of work in ship-yards.

The proposition to make reduction of hours gradual is of equal importance, because it relates to the supply and equipment of labor and sometimes to existing contracts. It may involve the training of more apprentices in a given craft. The president of the Wholesale Clothing Manufacturers' Association has furnished a concrete illustration in saying: "Speaking for myself, I would rather see the clothing business of this country upon an eight-hour than a nine-and-a-half hour basis, if it could be brought about gradually and uniformly throughout the trade. But a proposition to go to eight hours in thirty days is revolutionary and could not be considered for a moment. In the first place, it would call for an increased number of cutters, and they could not be obtained, for we barely can get enough for our business now. But, if we had the increased number, we would have no room for them in our factories as

MEMBERS NATIONAL EXECUTIVE COMMITTEE.

GROVER CLEVELAND,
Ex-President of the United States.

HENRY PHIPPS,
Director U. S. Steel Corporation.

SAMUEL GOMPERS,
President American Federation of Labor.

ANDREW CARNEGIE,
Capitalist.

AUGUST BELMONT,
President Interborough Rapid Transit Co.

JOHN MITCHELL,
President United Mine Workers.

now arranged. We also have contracts for future delivery which are based on the nine-and-a-half hour schedule. There must be plenty of time to adjust to the new condition."

The National Civic Federation has made an effort to ascertain the drift of opinion among employers upon that subject, and will follow that effort with another to ascertain the disposition among workmen to grant, in return for a shorter work-day, the removal of arbitrary restrictions upon output. A circular letter addressed to a list of manufacturers, none of less than $500,000 capital, contained the following question:

"Do you regard it a practical proposition to gradually reduce hours by voluntary uniform agreement through a given industry, providing the employes agree to abandon any arbitrary restriction upon the output?"

To this question there were nine hundred and twenty answers, of which six hundred and seven said "yes" to the proposition, coupled with opinions as to its practicability, varying from unqualified assent to extreme doubt. **The Monthly Review** obtained the consent of a large number of the writers of these answers, which in the first instance had been confidential, to their publication. Out of these as many have been selected for presentation as space would permit, and as would afford fair representation of the various opinions expressed.

These opinions readily divide themselves into groups, according to the point of view, the conditions of an industry, commercial and social theories and the attitude of the writers toward organized labor. It will be observed that there is a general prevalence of assent to the desirability of shorter hours as an abstract proposition. Those who object on the ground of increased cost of production and the restriction of business expansion are offset by those who propose a proportionate reduction of wages as a consideration in addition to unrestricted output. The purpose of both these considerations is identical—lower cost of production. One trade condition that opposes itself to shorter hours is when the industry requires continuous work, carried on by shifts, or tours. The two-shift system means a twelve-hours' day. There could be no reduction of hours short of the three-shift system, or an eight-hours' day. This, it is urged, would be too violent a change; although there is one instance cited of its economical operation.

There is a considerable group of replies that express a fear of foreign competition, if the American work-day is shortened. In contrast, another group declares that the demand of the home market, for some products and in active periods, is in excess of the supply, thus creating a need for labor that would only be aggravated by shorter hours. Some manufacturers perceive a tendency toward shorter hours, not by industries, but by localities, beginning in the larger cities and influenced to some extent by time consumed in transit to and from work.

Many employers would welcome removal of arbitrary restrictions from output in return for shorter hours. But some of these regard such restriction as unsound morally and therefore not negotiable. Others raise the questions of both the responsibility and good faith of trades-unions in keeping such an agreement. Still others regard such an agreement as only possible of enforcement when an association of employers is strong. Another group holds that shorter hours can be attained only through the aggressive efforts of unions.

Those who believe that shorter hours would result in better social conditions far outnumber those who fear the abuse of more leisure. There are some who maintain that present hours of labor are not excessive, neither impairing the health nor denying reasonable opportunity for self-improvement.

The answers representative of these opinions follow.

J. P. Brophy, Cleveland Automatic Machine Co., Cleveland.—My idea of changing the hours of labor in this country is that if the labor unions as a whole in any particular industry would ask for say a nine-and-a-half hour day instead of ten hours, and agree to lose the wages while the manufacturer lost the output of his factory for this particular half-hour, and have this take place universally, I have not the slightest doubt that all manufacturers in this country would agree to this proposition because it would look to them as though the working-man was willing to sacrifice something in order to gain this shorter day. I also believe that in a short time his wages would come back to normal, or about as it is to-day. I also believe that after this nine-and-a-half hour day was universal and all the manufacturers on the same footing, then the nine-hour day would come about in the same way and this without any great contention. I believe that if the working-men were educated up to this point by the leaders of unions a great many of the strikes that we now have and bitterness that these strikes cause would be eliminated, and that the employer and employes would get along very smoothly, and would not have any bitterness in connection with this change in the working hours; but as I understand it the working-men in asking for a nine-hour day with ten hours' pay, are demanding something that is very unjust, especially when this demand is not universal. As you well know, to any company that has got to grant this concession, it means about 20% of loss in their business. Bear in mind that this company as tool builders have very sharp competition, and if we should be forced to a nine-hour day with our competitors working ten hours, it would almost be necessary for us to close up our factory. It is well understood that there are very few manufacturers in this country that are making as high as 20%, and for this reason it is very easily understood that if we have got to compete, working a nine-hour day, the loss of output for this hour and the extra wages to our men would bring us to a standstill. We could not possibly advance the price of our machines because this price at the present time, owing to competition, is down to rock bottom, and it is very easily understood that if we had to raise the price of our machines, with our competitors working ten hours, this would drive us out of business. If the nine-hour day was brought about in the manner above described, it would, in my opinion, prevent all this bloodshed and trouble that we now have; and before a great length of time it would be the means of bringing together much closer than they are at the present time employers and employes. There is no necessity, in my opinion, for the great and disastrous labor troubles that we have at present.

—

C. W. Hubbard, Ludlow Manufacturing Associates, Jute and Hemp Goods, Boston.—We would like to see a shorter day in a business which, like ours, employs so many women and children, but at the same time it is a great handicap to economical manufacturing and the success of our business to have a very large and expensive plant operated shorter hours. The writer hopes in future to see some arrangement of double shifts of short hours in place of the present system of one shift of long hours; this would require one shift starting early in the morning, and another ending late in the day, and outside the hours now allowed under Massachusetts laws. Laws which may require the shortening of the hours of labor, and yet prevent double shifts, may work very seriously with concerns competing with other States or countries not so handicapped. We are strongly opposed to any restrictions upon output.

—

N. E. Whitaker, Whitaker Iron Co., Wheeling.—The proposition to reduce hours by voluntary and mutual agreement is thoroughly practical, especially if arbitrary restrictions are removed and abandoned, provided based upon equitable conditions of compensation, but we do not regard the proposition practical, expedient, or equitable, if involving the same compensation for a less number of hours.

—

F. A. C. Perrine, Stanley Electric Manufacturing Co., Pittsfield, Mass.—It is our belief that it is a practical proposition to gradually reduce the hours by voluntary and uniform agreement, throughout any given industry, provided that no restriction be placed upon output and providing, of course, that the reduction of hours be limited to a point where the output from a given shop shall be the greatest. As the number of hours is decreased, the output of men, not largely dependent upon tools, is increased; but the output of all large tools and of all automatic tools is decreased. There is a point where these two curves' will cross and give a maximum total output. Beyond this point, hours cannot be economically reduced, but up to this point it would be a gain both for the men and the manufacturers to reduce them.

—

Nathaniel French, Bettendorf Metal Wheel Co., Davenport, Iowa.—In most branches of work we regard it a practical proposition to gradually reduce the hours of work, being of the opinion that a workman in these branches can expend, without injury to himself, all his daily working force in less than ten hours. In other words, he can do as much work in nine hours as in ten, and possibly in eight hours. An agreement to abandon arbitrary restrictions will be of some value, but it will be broken with great frequency, till the workman learns that he cannot

CORNELIUS N. BLISS,
Ex-Secretary of the Interior.

E. E. CLARK,
Grand Chief, Order of Railway Conductors.

FREDERICK P. FISH,
President American Bell Telephone Co.

receive more than he produces, that limitation of production must also in the long run prove a limitation of wages, and that increase in production makes possible a higher wage rate.

—

Thomas Hoopes, Wheels and Wheel Material, West Chester, Pa.—I think it desirable that the hours of labor be gradually decreased, and believe that with the improvements going on in machinery and methods, it is possible to do this and still produce all the goods that are needed.

—

Thos. H. Williams, A. A. Griffing Iron Co., Steam Warming Apparatus, Jersey City.—This question of hours of labor per day resolves itself in the writer's mind to a question as to whether a shorter day becomes the universal practice or not. As long as all competitors in our line work nine hours a day it makes no difference to any of them, as the relative position of each one to the others remains the same. If, however, the shorter day prevails to such an extent that it is carried to all other lines, then it becomes a matter of national policy, since it would directly affect the ability of this country to compete in the world's markets. In order that the conditions should remain the same as between one country and another, it would be necessary that all countries adopt the same length of working day. What we fear is that this shortening of hours and thus curtailing of product produced would increase the cost to such an extent that it would curtail the demand, and all this is based upon the fundamental principle of supply and demand.

—

R. D. Reed, The H. B. Smith Co., Iron Founders, Westfield, Mass.—I personally believe that the hours of labor will be reduced probably eventually to eight hours in all lines of manufacture, but I have been led to believe that the reduction in the hours of labor will not follow given industries. It has already started in the large cities, and no doubt next year most of the cities of the first class will in all lines of industry be reduced to eight and nine hours; and I feel that it is just that it should start in the larger cities, on account of the length of time it takes the workmen to get to their respective places of work. I feel that a general reduction of the hours of labor throughout the country will not be attained, and it is not best that it should be attained, until times are much different than at present. It seems to me that the labor leaders should consider that at the present time, when nearly every line is pushed to its utmost, that this is not just the time to reduce the hours of labor. No doubt in the future all lines of manufacture will not be so pushed, and I have every reason to believe that a good many of the manufacturers themselves will voluntarily reduce the hours which constitute a day's work. I am satisfied, however, that in the lines of manufacture which I am familiar with, the reducing of the hours of labor will actually reduce the output with present methods, but I do believe it is the duty of each employer to himself to consider this matter seriously, and prepare himself for this reduction in the hours of work of his employes.

—

E. W. Peck, Co-operative Foundry Co., Rochester, N. Y.—The chief restriction is as to the number of apprentices. We deem this feature the most objectionable and tyrannical, and our experience this year has been such as to arouse our strongest antipathy to it; more especially in the unions connected with stove manufacture are young men prevented, through restrictive apprenticeship rules, from learning the trade. We should not look with disfavor upon a uniform and voluntary reduction of hours by the employers, provided the union would agree to some modification of apprentice rules to the end that there might be enough mechanics to fill requirements of the trade, as now there are not, in our particular line, and the situation is growing worse monthly. If, in addition to this, hours of labor were shortened, a very serious condition of affairs would quickly ensue.

—

E. A. Mallory & Sons, Fur Hat Manufacturers, Danbury, Conn.—There are all sorts of restrictions put upon us, as to limit our production, methods of work and use of machinery. Those we consider the most serious. The men are limited as to maximum and minimum wages they can earn. We are handicapped in putting in machinery, and changing methods of work in order to make savings. We are also limited as to the number of apprentices we can teach, to such an extent that we cannot at times fill our shops with necessary workmen for the business we have to do, and the union does not supply this demand. In unskilled jobs we have to pay 30c. per hour, which is entirely too high.

—

C. B. Orcutt, Newport News Shipbuilding and Dry Dock Co., New York.—It may be practicable to gradually reduce the hours of labor, but this can only be done successfully in large plants with a system of supervision so complete that there can be no doubt as to employer getting the full benefit of the hours actually worked; the cost and difficulty of securing proper system of supervision makes one hesitate to state that the proposition is a practical one.

—

Theo. Bollmann, The Hoefinghoff & Laue Foundry Co., Cincinnati.—We are heartily in favor of the reduction in hours provided the employes will agree to abandon the arbitrary restrictions of output and the apprentice question.

—

E. L. Shuey, Lowe Bros. Co., Paint, Dayton, Ohio.—We believe it possible to secure reduced hours with comparatively small reduction in output if employes meet the employers' offer in the right spirit and recognize his desire to be just to all interested.

—

F. E. Wheeler, International Heater Co., Utica, N. Y.—As a general proposition, reducing the hours of labor means increasing the cost of production. Increased costs means higher prices, and a consequent curtailment of trade. But to leave entirely out of the question the policy of a reduction in hours, or to concede for the moment that the hours of labor are to be reduced in any particular trade, then the most practical manner of doing this is by a voluntary, uniform agreement throughout that trade, made through an association of employers which is large and powerful enough to control the situation, and who, when granting the concession will at the same time insist upon the removal of all limitations as to the number of apprentices employed, and all restrictions as to the amount of work done by any employe, in any given time.

—

G. C. Sherman, St. Regis Paper Co., Watertown, N. Y.—In our industry several of the best mills are running 144 hours a week, with three sets of men instead of two, and this with the consent of the union. We think the mills refusing the shorter hours gradually lose their best men to competitors, who grant shorter hours at the same rate of pay. If eighty per cent. of the mills are running uniformly and twenty per cent. the other way, we should feel we were not suffering if we were in with the majority. On the other hand, if the percentage operating at the shorter hours was reversed, of course it would be necessary for us to adopt the short hour system and the lower rate of wages. The men understand, of course, that it is up to them to insist upon the short hour system, as otherwise the union would not be controlling.

—

Salling, Hanson & Co., Lumber, Grayling, Mich.—We believe it practical by national legislation to gradually reduce laboring hours from ten to eight hours a day, but this can only be done by national legislation, for the reason that if laborers are allowed to work ten hours in one locality for a day's work and nine in another and eight in another, the employers working only eight and nine hours could not compete with those working ten hours. We firmly believe that eight hours a day would provide a good living for the people of the United States and put 20% more of our laboring forces to work, and in a measure avoid idleness and over-production. We realize, however, that we have to compete with the rest of the world in our pursuits for a livelihood, and unless we can in some measure fortify ourselves so as not to come in competition with foreign labor, we would be practically a failure.

—

T. I. Hickman, Graniteville Manufacturing Co., Cotton, Augusta, Ga.—Hours of labor, sixty-six per week. We would be perfectly willing to reduce this to sixty hours a week if other cotton manufacturers would conform to the same rule; or we would favor a universal ten-hour law for cotton factories. I think that ten hours per day is enough for any person to work, but of course we cannot work ten hours while our competitors in the same field are working eleven.

—

F. C. Caldwell, H. W. Caldwell & Co., Engineers and Machinists, Chicago.—If an agreement were made which, as you state, would be voluntary and uniform, and would cover an entire industry, such an agreement would certainly be effective. Our idea of the question of shorter hours is that in so far as the reduction of hours is for the purpose of improving the social condition of the employe, the reduction can be brought about; but if the hours are shortened for the ulterior purpose of requiring the employment of a greater number of men, such action would be economically wrong and certainly would fail in the end.

—

Fred F. Smith, Ferracute Machine Co., Bridgeton, N. J.—We have always believed that the world could work with many less hours than now practised, if all would agree to it, and if there was no great amount of waste. At present we do not think it wise to change the number of working hours to less than ten in our line of business. In some kinds of business, where the men are exposed to great hardships or unusual strains, the hours should be less, but owners of factories and each set of employes should decide these matters themselves, as it is impossible for outside "delegates," who are not always men of experience, to decide arbitrarily a number of these details. We certainly do not favor a restriction upon

OSCAR S. STRAUS,
Of The Hague Court of Arbitration.

FRANCIS L. ROBBINS,
President Pittsburgh Coal Co.

JAMES DUNCAN,
Secretary Granite Cutters' National Union.

output, "for the sake of protecting the poor brother." Every one should produce all he can properly, and the world would then be richer.

H. Wittenberg, Pacific Coast Biscuit Co., Portland, Oregon.—The conditions in America are changing each year. Free schools, public libraries, and on all sides higher degrees of civilization are having their effect upon the workmen of our country. They are becoming more intelligent and observant, and have a good understanding of what their rights should be and how they should be treated by their employer. With a better condition and higher education comes a desire for more luxuries and more time for recreation, just the same as the operator, or employer, who, starting early in life, works late and early, practises every possible economy in his effort to accumulate and increase his worldly goods. This he continues until he has reached a certain point in life where he feels that he can take a little more comfort and reduces his hours of labor. Now, if this is the plan of the employer, why should not the employes have the same object in view, and why should it be denied to them? We can see no good reason for a counter argument. The people of this country, both as individuals and tax-payers, furnish the ways and means to improve the condition of the general public, and as they furnish them such means they should expect that the workmen, or general public, in securing such knowledge, should desire to profit and improve their condition, and in doing so, better pay and less hours of labor is required to satisfy their desires and new conditions. The only danger that presents itself in the labor situation in America, in my opinion, is whether labor will use good judgment in adapting itself to its new conditions. Not having the same experience and, if you please, the cool, conservative judgment which the employer in general has learned through years of contact with the business public, the employe is apt to overstep the bounds of prudence and injure himself many times over, before he has learned it is only by slow degrees that he can further improve his condition. Let us hope that the employe will realize that the interests of his employers should be safely guarded by him; that he should feel an interest in his employer's business, for only through the success of such business can he hope to secure further benefits. When such a policy will be adopted by the working men of this country, there is no doubt that the acme of good feeling and pleasant relations will have been reached.

Several establishments, compelled by the nature of their business to run consecutively, point out that they are confronted, not with the proposition of a gradual reduction in hours, but of a sudden reduction from twelve to eight hours:

H. J. Brown, Berlin Mills Co., Lumber and Wood Pulp, Portland, Me.—Most of our works run continuously, the day crew working from 7 to 6, six days in the week, the night crew working from 6 until 7, five nights in the week, each man having an hour's intermission, but his work being kept along by his mates. There can be no modification of this, except the jump to an eight-hour day, the men working through the eight hours without any time for meals, except to eat a lunch alongside their work. We do not see how this change can be brought about gradually. It might, however, be brought about by an agreement to all go on to this system at a fixed day sufficiently far in the future to allow present contracts to run out and new ones to be made on the new basis. The only restrictions in our business are that the men in the paper mill will not work extra for extra pay at seasons of the year when we need to have them. This would be obviated by an eight-hour day, which would keep the mill running the entire week excepting Sunday.

Fox River Paper Co., Appleton, Wis.—It will be necessary for us to substitute three tours of eight hours each for the present two tour system in order to make any reduction of hours to those working, and in this connection it is well to say that we do not believe that our tour workers would favor the three tour system, as they recognize that if put in practice it must be a reduction of diem pay, and also that it would increase the number of skilled hands, which in dull times would make it more difficult for the individual to obtain work.

But another paper company, which made the change, writes:

F. L. Moore, Raymondville Paper Company, Watertown, N. Y.—Part of the mill is working on the three tour system, and part on the two tour system. In changing part of our mill from the two to the three tour system, making a day of eight hours, we found we could cut off a few extra men and that the same work could be accomplished with fewer men, and they would work harder and take more interest in their work than when working twenty-four hours in two shifts. We find in doing this our production is somewhat larger and the men are better satisfied with the hours.

Several replies object to shorter hours on the ground that they would increase cost on the amount produced and would retard business expansion:

Arthur E. Barlow, Newark, N. J., Malleable and Gray Iron Castings.—The foundry business cannot profitably be run on shorter time than nine hours per day. The only productive part, strictly speaking, is the time when they do the molding, and if an eight-hour work-day were enforced it would allow only six or six-and-one-half hours for molding; therefore, nine hours per day is the minimum time for a work-day in a foundry.

B. L. Stowe, Eureka Fire Hose Co., Jersey City, N. J.—We do not find that people will do as much work in fifty-five hours as in fifty-nine, as is sometimes claimed, and actually Saturday forenoon is not as valuable as other forenoons. The shorter week, therefore, places us at some disadvantage in competition with our competitors who work fifty-nine hours, but we have no intention of increasing our time.

The Bain Wagon Co., Kenosha, Wis.—We do not regard it practical to reduce the hours of labor; our goods are sold to the farmer almost exclusively. With nature for his master, the farmer must work such hours as are necessary to meet natural conditions, that is, he must sow his grain in the right season or it will not come to fruition; he must harvest it at the proper time or nature will waste it. Any attempt on our part to add the cost of reduced hours of labor to the product he consumes would be met by the sternest kind of opposition from him, and in our opinion ten hours per day is no more than the laborer's share of time to be expended in the production of our goods, when compared with the hours of labor that the farmer must spend in producing his crops.

Schofield, Mason & Co., Carpets, Philadelphia.—We do not doubt it might be practicable to gradually reduce hours by voluntary, uniform agreement throughout a given industry on the conditions you name, but we should deprecate such action in our business, as our machinery will only produce a certain amount of work, and to reduce the time 10% would be to reduce our output that much, and make our plant 10% less valuable.

Several establishments held that there is not always enough labor supply to warrant reduction in hours. These are frequently in industries having seasonal demand for their products. But the following replies were written before the present period of comparative industrial laxity:

C. H. Smith, Western Wheeled Scraper Co., Aurora, Ill.—When men are scarce I would not regard it as practicable to reduce the working hours to eight, or even nine. Our business has been restricted because we could not get help enough to turn out the work offered.

G. H. Schulte, Milwaukee Harvester Co., Milwaukee, Wis.—We have no objection to shorter hours, if the reduction can be brought on gradually and simultaneously throughout our line of business. We object to restrictions upon output for the reason that there is not enough labor to be hired at times to produce our output even at ten hours a day.

Wm. A. Lynch, The Aultman Co., Oil Engines, Canton, Ohio.—When the production is equal to or exceeds the demand, we would favor a gradual and general reduction of hours of labor, so as to keep all workmen employed a part of the time, but to reduce the hours of labor say from ten to nine hours in a period of great activity would be a loss to the productive capacity of the whole country.

C. G. Hussey & Co., Pittsburgh Copper and Brass Rolling Mills, Pittsburgh.—We doubt if we are competent to make reply, having had practically no experience with union labor, but we think it doubtful if your proposition would work satisfactorily for the reason that the labor employed, say this year, in all probability would not be to the extent of 50% of the same employed two or three years later, when it might be proposed to carry out the scheme and put any restrictions upon the output. The labor employed, say three years later, might object to these conditions, if the labor were non-union.

H. E. Hardin, Acme Harvester Co., Peoria, Ill.—The number of hours which employes are expected to work should be optional with the employer, especially if he shows a disposition to be fair, and should be a matter of mutual agreement before the employe goes to work. Conditions are such, especially in our line of business, that an iron-clad rule limiting the number of hours of labor to eight or nine per day would work as a great hardship

(Continued on Page 12.)

CHARLES W. ELIOT,
President Harvard University.

HENRY G. DAVIS,
Coal Operator.

DANIEL J. KEEFE,
President International Longshoremen.

WHAT IS WELFARE WORK?

ESPECIAL CONSIDERATION FOR PHYSICAL COMFORT, RECREATION AND MENTAL DEVELOPMENT OF EMPLOYES.—CONDITIONS OF SUCCESS AND CAUSES OF FAILURE.

The announcement of the formation of its Welfare Department has brought to the National Civic Federation various inquiries as to the nature of the subject with which that department deals.

Welfare Work.

Welfare work involves special consideration for physical comfort wherever labor is performed; opportunities for recreation; educational advantages; and the providing of suitable sanitary homes; its application to be measured by the exigencies of the case.

Before discussing the several divisions of this definition, a brief statement of the theory underlying welfare work will be advisable.

The first essentials to the welfare of the employe are steady work, an equitable wage, and reasonable hours of labor. It is an economic truth that employment without interruption is of the first importance to the prosperity of the wage earner. The employer, however exacting, whose foresight and good management make steady work possible is a greater benefactor than can be the employer, however benevolent, whose business is of spasmodic activity. Hunger is only a fortnight behind the average worker thrown into idleness.

The payment of the market wage creates in the mind of the worker confidence in the justice and fair dealing of the employer. This confidence is absolutely essential to the prosecution of welfare work, which must fail whenever the workers are led to suspect that its cost is taken from their wages. It is difficult to explain to employes that the total cost of welfare work in any establishment, if distributed among them, would be individually an infinitesimal amount.

The relation of the hours of labor to welfare work lies in their effect upon the physical health of employes and in the opportunity they leave, especially where there is much "overtime," for recreation and education after the close of the day's work. It is recognized that, where competition is keen, a reduction in hours can only be brought about by agreement involving practically all the competitors in a given industry.

Each Industrial Establishment a Separate Problem.

In the application of welfare work, every industrial establishment presents in itself a separate problem, requiring special study. Every beginning is an experiment. Every general rule has its exceptions. Nevertheless, while the welfare work in any single establishment can not as a whole be applied to another, various features can be adapted to the special conditions peculiar to a particular concern. Welfare work has proved of value in small as well as large establishments.

Special Supervision of "Welfare Manager."

A general rule for all welfare work in large concerns is that its successful conduct requires the employment of a welfare manager. This manager should not only possess tact, executive ability, common sense, acquaintance with local jealousies and sometimes with racial prejudices, but a knowledge of industrial subjects. He must recognize and in no way interfere with the authority of the superintendents, who are responsible for the successful operation of their departments, the administration of labor, and the maintaining of discipline. He must gain in advance their full approval of each effort, and use every proper method to enlist their full co-operation. He must have the patience to endure the slow realization of his plans. In time it will become evident that they are for the benefit of all, of the employer and of the executive chiefs as well as for the mass of employes.

Many employers would introduce welfare work into their establishments were it not for the time and trouble needed for its organization. The employment of a welfare manager removes this obstacle. Successful prosecution of welfare work requires concentration of responsibility. All of its branches must be under the supervision of one person, or efforts in different directions may conflict, or special and, perhaps, pressing needs may escape attention. Pressure of daily business routine usually relegates welfare work to the last consideration. This is another reason why in large establishments it should receive the entire time and attention of one person. Welfare work has sometimes been started enthusiastically, but has afterward failed because there was no one person to keep its operation active and apace with daily needs.

Participation of the Employer.

The part of the employer in welfare work invites special comment. His active participation and that of the executive heads of the business in the work is a prime requisite to its success. The employer should not expect demonstrations of appreciation or expressions of gratitude for his fulfilment of a moral obligation. He has within his control influences that affect the physical, moral and mental development of the human beings in his employ. It becomes then clearly his duty to direct these influences for their welfare. Nor should the employer expect welfare work to avert a strike against unjust conditions.

The question is often asked whether the employer should take the initiative in welfare work or await suggestions from employes. In practice it is found that whenever an initial step is taken by the employer to meet an urgent need, abundant suggestions for his consideration of further betterments will follow from employes. It is essential in taking this initial step, however, that confidence in the employer's motive should be unquestioned by the employes.

Confidence in the Employer's Motive.

The employer must show that his interest in the welfare of the employes is genuine. An agreement with executive heads as to plans and purposes will ensure an understanding of his sincerity which will be helpful in reaching the rank and file. In securing confidence of employes at the outset of welfare work, it is necessary in unionized establishments to explain its purposes to the union officers; and in non-union establishments it is important to obtain the co-operation of selected committees of the employes. This may sometimes be promoted by the printing of placards in different languages.

Should Not be Used for Advertisement.

The employer, it has been shown, should not pervert welfare work into an advertisement for his business. This impugns his motive and discredits the plan. When publicity is inevitable, there should be care that the subject is treated in a dignified manner.

Paternalism and the Democratic Plan.

The spirit of welfare work must not be that of condescension, nor have the appearance of thrusting benefits upon subordinates, nor rob the worker of self-respect. But any effort at welfare work may be regarded as more or less paternalistic. A resort to direct paternalism, however, is necessary or desirable only for recent immigrants who in their native lands have been accustomed to the guardianship of superior authority. Going to the other extreme, in the so-called democratic idea, is also to be avoided. When their confidence has been gained, employes will generally prefer to entrust the direction of welfare work to the employer. The need of relaxation and the natural impulse homeward should not be denied or checked during intermissions or at the

JOHN IRELAND,
Archbishop, Roman Catholic Church.

H. H. VREELAND,
President N. Y. City Railway Co.

P. H. MORRISSEY,
Grand Master, Railroad Trainmen.

close of the working day by too much committee work. It must be borne in mind that the chief purpose of committees of employes is advisory and to enlist their interest, rather than to initiate or execute welfare plans. Committee work is also valuable in developing among the employes a spirit of helping one another, while it is, in its very nature, educational.

Some Causes of Failure.

Especial inquiry has been made into cases of failure in welfare work, in order to ascertain its causes. One cause of failure has been found in its too rapid introduction. As a general rule improvements should be adopted gradually, so that the workers may become accustomed to them. For example, if an employer were suddenly to erect a fine club-house at an impressive expense, the workers might conjecture that its cost was to be in some way taken out of their own pockets. If a library is not patronized by employes, its failure may be caused by the absence of interesting catalogues for leisurely inspection in the homes, or by lack of special effort to overcome diffidence in frequenting the library building. Prices charged for luncheons may be too high for wages in a given industry. A lunch room may not be patronized because it is untidy, or unattractive, or too small, or because there is no place for men to smoke. Elaborate toilet facilities with cold water only and no soap may be scorned for the drilling compound which does remove oil from the hands. In brief, failures are usually traceable to insufficient preliminary study of the particular need to be met. This study may often be forwarded by enlisting the co-operation of committees of the employes. There have been some failures of welfare work not justly chargeable to its conduct. These have been brought about by a change of management in the establishments concerned, the new management showing opposition to what had been done before.

Physical Welfare of Primary Importance.

The beginning of all welfare work must be directed toward meeting the pressing necessities for the physical well-being of the employes in their place of work. These most pressing needs are provisions for cleanliness, pure drinking water, adequate toilet rooms, ventilation, light, separate lockers for outdoor clothing and dressing rooms. In some industries, provisions for cleanliness should include especial attention to the relief of men whose toil induces profuse perspiration. There should be free laundries for washing their working clothing. Baths will be of benefit and will be much used. Ventilation in factories should include devices for removing dust. Much suffering in such superheated places of labor as rolling mills, foundries, and forge shops can be relieved at comparatively small expense, while more attention should be paid to damp substructures and unnecessarily cold and and drafty places. Abundant light is important to cheerfulness as well as to health. Besides rest-rooms for women, it is important to have, when the task permits, fixed rest periods, even if brief.

All of the details that have been specified are primary. They are literally the first letters of the alphabet of welfare work. Yet these very things, simple as they seem, are of the utmost practical value to the employer. The one provision for cleanliness alone, for example, improves the spirit of every worker as well as the health, and raises the moral tone of the force, even improving discipline. Taken altogether, all the separate provisions that have been noted have the effect of attracting to any establishment a higher and more constant class of labor. Workers everywhere enjoy and will seek improvements in the surroundings in their hours of toil.

A further step toward physical welfare of employes is the establishment of lunch rooms. The importance of the midday meal to health and vigor is obvious. Also, forenoon luncheons and breakfasts are valuable, especially when the breakfast at home, through lack of appetite or haste in starting for work, has been skimped or skipped entirely, and when there are several shifts. Luncheons in overtime are important. Any establishment should at least provide a place to keep from spoiling or drying the prepared food brought from home. A still further step will be care for the sick and injured. It is but humane to furnish a couch on which a prostrated woman may be restored, instead of permitting her to lie on the floor or on two chairs. Wherever serious accidents in a factory are likely to occur, a doctor should be continually present, and an emergency hospital is necessary. Under this head also would fall the guarding of machinery.

Protection for Women Workers.

In applying these primary beginnings of any system of welfare work, several moral questions are encountered. In factories where both men and women are employed, it is desirable, though unfortunately not always possible, to separate by a period of three or five minutes their times for beginning and quitting work. This simple precaution for the protection of the feminine element among the employes of any large establishment has the effect of preserving respect for womanhood. Experience shows that, where this system prevails, the establishments soon acquire a higher tone. An additional protection is the employment of a matron, who will also be a confidential adviser and render temporary relief in cases of illness. When the general morale of a factory is not in good repute, it is difficult for the employer to induce desirable working-women to accept employment.

Recreation.

After providing for immediate physical needs, the recreation of employes is the next step in welfare work. Here again the peculiarities of individual establishments must be considered. A gymnasium, for example, would be desirable only in establishments where the work is more or less sedentary, so that the employes are in need of exercise, or for the young men and women employed in factories. A gymnasium would be superfluous in a place where the work itself involved severe bodily exertion. Athletics, both indoor and outdoor, are highly desirable. They may involve organizations. In large establishments, the plan of recreation may include a club-house, with rooms for theatricals, dancing, entertaining and for games. The entertainments may include music and, perhaps, lectures, which approach a further development of welfare work—that looking to the education of employes.

The question of vacations is important. Where the industry is located in a large city nearby camps in the country for laborers and their families may be conducted. Information as to the location of summer resorts, rates and transportation, is especially desired by clerical workers.

Educational Efforts.

The possibility of extending welfare work to the education of employes is contingent upon the hours of labor. A scheme of education may begin with technical classes for the younger men, and may include instruction designed to replace the loss of earlier schooling. Women employes may be taught to help themselves in such ways as in millinery, dressmaking, cooking, and all household affairs; and in some pursuits they may also profitably receive technical instruction. In a large settlement a kindergarten may be provided. The instruction of children becomes a direct contribution to better citizenship when the parents employed are largely immigrants. A reading-room or circulating library, or both, will be of great benefit. A company may publish with advantage a periodical in the several tongues used by the workers. Sometimes an establishment may be so large that its plans of education may come into co-operation with the municipality, or may even assume all the functions ordinarily performed through municipal agencies. This has been the case in towns which have been created for the industry, where the company has been obliged to provide public schools as well as churches and social halls.

Homes of Employes.

Welfare work concerns itself also with the housing of employes. The two purposes to be kept in mind in this branch of the work are the health and the self-respect of the employe. The reflex social and moral influence upon the people of a community in encouraging attractive home-making is of far-reaching consequence.

Plans for Saving and Lending Money.

Mutual plans for saving and lending money have proved highly beneficial to employes, through protecting them in times of stress, when desperation forces agreement to any terms, against the extortions of the "money-shark." To avoid encouraging the tendency to borrow, any plan for lending should be conditioned upon a system of saving.

Insurance and Pensions.

Beneficial insurance societies are quite commonly included in welfare work, both compulsory and voluntary plans having been tried with varying degrees of success. Related to these are pension plans, in which there is a growing interest. This entire class of projects requires more original research and experiment than any other phase of welfare work, as their inception and successful operation are complicated by many problems.

GERTRUDE BEEKS,
Secretary Welfare Department.

HENRY C. POTTER,
Bishop, Protestant Episcopal Church.

THEODORE J. SHAFFER,
Prest. Amal. Ass'n I. S. & T. Workers.

SAMUEL MATHER,
Great Lakes Shipper.

THOUSANDS OF WAGE-EARNERS TO SEE THE WORLD'S FAIR.

THE WELFARE BUREAU AFFORDS EMPLOYERS AN OPPORTUNITY TO ENCOURAGE WORKERS TO ENJOY ITS EDUCATIONAL ADVANTAGES WITH COMFORT, ECONOMY AND GUIDANCE.

The Welfare Department of the National Civic Federation has established a bureau at the St. Louis Exposition for the convenience, comfort and guidance of the thousands of wage-earners in the United States, for whose instruction a systematic study of special exhibits and observation of the World's Fair as a whole are highly desirable. Large employers of labor already show appreciation of this opportunity to add to the intelligent productivity of workers. To a number of such employers the following letter, which explains itself, has been addressed by H. H. Vreeland, chairman of the Welfare Department:

"On behalf of the National Civic Federation, I beg to call your attention to the unequaled advantages offered for the mutual benefit of the employer and employe through attendance at the Louisiana Purchase Exposition.

"It is generally conceded that in very many respects this Exposition surpasses anything of the kind in history. The sum of $50,000,000 has been spent in construction, and its exhibits represent over $800,000,000 in value. It is safe to assume that this generation will never have another opportunity of viewing such a stupendous exhibition of the world's latest and best achievements in industry and science.

"The Executive Council of the National Civic Federation recognizes that it would be most unfortunate were not every possible effort exerted to place within the power of each wage-earner, where practicable, the opportunity to visit this Exposition. It is convinced that the superintendents, foremen and other leading workers in every manufacturing plant or commercial institution should enjoy the educational advantages presented at St. Louis. With the object of helping to solve the problem of how to visit the World's Fair to the best possible advantage, the National Civic Federation has, with the hearty approval and support of the Exposition management, authorized its Welfare Department to establish a World's Fair Bureau in the Transportation Building, on the exposition grounds.

"This bureau will be glad to arrange, free of all charge, for economical accommodations through responsible agencies, to prepare and furnish itineraries for the systematic observation and study of objects of special interest in the various departments, and otherwise to do everything possible to contribute to the profitable enjoyment of those who visit the Exposition under its auspices. It will undertake to engage lodgings in hotels, private houses or tented cities, meet parties at trains, and guide them to their stopping places.

"As experience demonstrates that the attendance at all expositions increases in the closing months, it is obvious that more favorable terms can be obtained now than later. We would therefore urge the advisability of making your arrangements at the earliest possible moment. Exclusive of railway fares, the visitor can spend six days in St. Louis and see the Exposition comfortably at a total expense of $15 for lodgings, meals, car fares and admissions

"There is enough instructive entertainment in the main exposition palaces, the United States Government Building, State buildings, and the pavilions of foreign countries, to all of which admission is free, to occupy attention for a much longer period.

"One of our Illinois members is arranging to bring 6,000 of his employes in groups to the Exposition, and an Ohio member will bring 2,500, while others are arranging for from 100 to 500 foremen and superintendents from more distant sections. In some cases employers pay part of the expenses; in others, they help in securing low railroad rates; and in one case, the employer has advanced the money, deducting a stated amount from the weekly wage. One large manufacturer states that he regards it as a good business investment for both employer and employe—and he is defraying one-half the cost.

"If this subject interests you, our World's Fair Bureau will be glad to furnish any further information desired."

CONFERENCE COMMENDED.

President Covell Advises the National Metal Trades Association to Encourage Trade Agreements Consistent with Fundamental Principles.

A liberal attitude of organized employers toward organized labor was the subject of a portion of an address delivered by H. N. Covell, president of the National Metal Trades Association, to the sixth annual convention of that body, in Philadelphia. President Covell said:

It is not my purpose to enter upon a theoretical discussion of the great subject of capital and labor. You will find all the printed matter on every hand that you will be able to read on that subject, written by learned and wise men. It is not theory, but facts, with which we have to deal. This association is created to deal with men who hold no theories save that they are after all they can get. They should obtain all they are entitled to, but no more.

The question of our relations with organized labor is a most important one. I believe that the tendency is growing to a more liberal spirit; that is, that more employers have come to view the situation in a broader and less conservative manner, and have eradicated from their minds, the idea that all is absolutely bad in organized labor and, conversely, wholly good on the employer's end.

More lasting, ultimate good may be accomplished by an endeavor to correct the abuses of organized labor than by crushing it (if such a thing were possible).

I am of the opinion that no harm will be done, but that much good would ensue, by occasional conferences with representatives of organized labor. We cannot ignore the fact that organized labor is prominent in our nation's affairs. Were it not that labor is organized, this association would not be organized; and, therefore, in the mere fact of our own organization, we recognize the organization of labor.

The use of the word "recognize" as applied to labor organization, is, perhaps, not a happy one. To use the word from the labor union standpoint, would mean the adoption of the closed shop, minimum rate, hours work, limitation of apprentices, and, throughout, the whole category of labor union restrictions; which is a condition strictly contrary to our Declaration of Principles, and is in no sense to be considered by this association. But, using the word "recognize" in a broader sense, we cannot deny the fact of their existence. We recognize the fact of their existence, hence recognize them to that extent; and this is something we cannot avoid.

Organized labor has rights and a standing in the community, whether we like it or not. If through conference we can impart some of our ideas, and we certainly can, it will be sowing seed which some day may take root and grow and thrive. If two persons disagreeing upon a matter, should stand upon opposite sides of a street and hurl epithets, stones and sticks at each other, no good will be done to either. Surrounding property and passersby would be liable to receive injury. The more stones thrown the more angry would they become. It would be infinitely more sensible if both sides should conclude to come to the middle of the street and talk it over.

And so it seems to me that the National Metal Trades Association should meet organized labor in conference. I am a firm believer in national agreements. I do not mean any agreement, but agreements which must be based upon our fundamental principles and this without any infringements of our rights as employers, citizens of the United States or members of the association.

It is not logical that we should disparage or disapprove of agreements with organized labor as a body when component parts, as represented by local associations, make local agreements, and are, in numerous instances, successfully operating under them to-day; and, in fact, using as a basis of the agreements a form officially sanctioned by this association.

MONTHLY REVIEW

OF THE

National Civic Federation

Offices: 281 Fourth Avenue, New York City

RALPH M. EASLEY, Editor

The Editor alone is responsible for any unsigned article or unquoted statement published in THE MONTHLY REVIEW.

Ten Cents per Copy; One Dollar per Year.

The National Civic Federation

THE OPEN SHOP AN OPEN QUESTION.

The organs of the "Smash the Unions" employers' associations unite in making much ado about the pronouncement by Judge Adams of Chicago, that a closed shop is illegal and criminal. Those anti-union organs persist in ignoring the fact that Judge Adams' declaration was not a decision but a dictum, and that the consensus of opinion of able members of the bar is that it stands the test neither of law nor of logic. Experience, not dicta, will solve the case of the open vs. the closed shop.

For that case is one of practice, not of principle. But it is a case that must be decided in accordance with principle. That principle is the principle of liberty. In turn, liberty must accord with the interests of society as a whole. The despot and the anarchist each has his definition of liberty. Neither can be right. Liberty does not mean freedom to do as one will with one's own. Liberty imposes duty. That is the duty to direct conduct and to use property for the common weal. The gain of the individual, whether from the use of capital or the increment of earnings, must not mean the loss of society.

It is the interest of society that the relations between employers and employed be such as to encourage the active and profitable use of capital so as to leave a margin for improving processes, and that they be such as to elevate continuously the condition of the great body of workers, so as to increase consumption. Anything that checks this progress opposes civilization and must be removed.

Apply this principle to practice in the case of the open or closed shop. The union is a means for securing the rights and bettering the conditions of labor. It is, therefore, wrong for the employer to discriminate against the union. The employer who aims to make the open shop mean a shop closed against the union, occupies an untenable position. On the other hand, the employer is responsible for the successful conduct of his business. Only such conduct makes possible the employment of labor and the betterment of wages and conditions. It is, therefore, wrong for the union to wrest from the responsible employer the control of his business. The union that dictates to the employer whom he shall vest with executive authority or whom he shall hire or refuse to hire, occupies an untenable position, and the employer is warranted in trying to smash it in self-defense. If all the workers in any establishment belong to the union, that is in effect a closed shop regardless of any specific contract. Should any one or several prefer not to join the union that is their right. But the union has also the right to refuse to work with any outside its membership. Such refusal does not deny the right of the non-unionist to seek employment, or the right of the employer to employ whom he pleases.

Whenever the employer discriminates against union workers because the union is the organized force that he confronts, he compels the union to fight for the closed shop as a necessity of self-preservation. The union then has the right to make that fight, because it is a fight for its life. It is idle for the "Smash the Union" employers' associations to attempt to deceive the unions or to mislead the public upon this issue. Their orators may prate upon the rostrum about the right of labor to organize and may protest that they do not fight the principle of unionism, but its excesses. But their insincerity is betrayed by their boasts in private of how they will break this or that union through the open shop. Such men force upon the union the issue of life or dissolution.

While the union has the undoubted right to strive for a closed shop, the employment of any form of coercion must be unequivocally condemned. If the union can convince the employer that the closed shop means a steady supply of superior labor, it will have won its purpose by demonstrated merit. The closed shop upon any other condition would be intolerable.

CRITICISM AND FACT.

The animus against organized labor of some editorial writers for the daily press leads them occasionally into inconsistencies that are amusing. They are also instructive, as disclosing a disposition upon the part of these writers not to credit trades unions with evidences of growing self-restraint, self-respect and enlightenment, that are to be found in the record of facts published in their own news columns.

A typical newspaper critic of unions recently made these editorial remarks:

> Labor cannot divest itself of responsibility for the excesses, the oppression, the cruelties and the crimes of individuals and organizations until it finds courage to disown the leadership and teachings of demagogues and agitators, and to relegate to obscurity men who, in executive control of trades-unions, have made them dangerous to the public interest. . . . If wage-earners by thousands are willing to march in public procession under the leadership of a convicted bribe-taker and barroom bully during a brief interval from deserved incarceration in State prison, . . . they have only themselves to blame if they are misjudged and saddled with a very large share of responsibility for the misdeeds of individuals and organizations.

This is a misstatement of fact. The same newspaper was more accurate at the time of the occurrence, leaving to others the distortion contained in the above quotation. When the convicted Parks was released from prison through a certificate of reasonable doubt, this same journal said editorially:

> Judge Sewall acted within his rights. . . . Judge Sewall thought him entitled to a new trial, and he will have it. . . He [Parks] is entitled to his rights, but the fewer honors he receives, the better for the interests of labor.

Despite this recognition that the convicted Parks had been restored to civil rights pending a new trial, but quite in accordance with its own advice, the news columns of the same journal during that week afford voluminous evidence that the great body of organized labor turned its back upon Parks and his political patron of that period. Of the 150 different labor crafts in New York City, only thirty involved in the building trades considered the Labor Day parade. Of these thirty, the twenty-three that had signed the arbitration agreement with the employers quickly turned it down. Of the other seven, supposed to be under Parks' influence, five of the largest also revolted, leaving only the two unions to which Parks belonged. As a matter of fact, only a small fraction of those two unions joined in the parade, the rest of his following being Devery heelers. On September 8 this critical journal thus headed its report of the Labor Day parade: "Labor Day Fizzle. Only 8,593 Men in Line, as against 25,000 Last Year." Editorially the same issue observed:

> What promised to be the largest parade organized labor had ever had in New York was spoiled by the fatal mistake of placing Parks at the head of it. . . The most hopeful feature of the whole unhappy and deplorable incident is that so many unions refused to parade under such leadership, and that of those which were not permitted to refuse so many self-respecting men remained at home.

Later, when Parks was apposing bitterly the negotiations that finally resulted in the arbitration agreement between the building trades unions and the employers, President Samuel Gompers and 1st.-Vice-President James Duncan, of the American Federation of Labor, came to New York and investigated the situation. As a result, these two labor leaders issued a letter to the unions advising those who had been locked out or were on strike to sign the plan of arbitration. This was in effect a clear repudiation of Parksism, whose influence was recognized as the one obstacle in the way of restoration of harmony in the building industry. These national labor leaders explicitly recommended the plan of arbitration which Parks was fighting. These facts were published by this same journal on October 14, under the caption, "Arbitration Plan Urged by Gompers." Surely, this was finding "courage to disown the leadership and teachings" of a demagogue and agitator, as it was a step "to relegate to obscurity" one of the "men who, in executive control of trades-unions, have made them dangerous to the public interest." Editorial criticism should be made to accord with news history.

THE "MUGWUMP" AND THE "SCAB."

Adherents of political parties heartily hate the "mugwump." The regular partisan rates the "mugwump" as the personification of dilletante selfishness. He beholds the tomahawk of the "mugwump" brandished against every nomination that does not please his personal taste. With all the hard physical and mental labor of forming national, State, county, city, ward and precinct organizations, of attending caucuses and primaries, of attracting allegiance of voters, of awakening interest in public issues, of educating citizens to their meaning, of all the toil involved in the control of conventions, the making of platforms, the conduct of campaigns,—with all these varied, incessant activities, without which there could be no republican form of government, the "mugwump" will have nothing to do. He holds aristocratically aloof from association with a political organization whose workers devote themselves to its extension in the interest of specified principles. Nevertheless, the partisan beholds the "mugwump," while thus escaping the hardships, the self-denial and the exacting efforts of partisan conflicts, enjoying, in common with other citizens, and accepting with irritating complacency the benefit of whatever progress in good government is the outcome of party competition for public approval.

There is a striking parallel to this partisan view of the "mugwump" in the attitude of the union worker towards the "scab."

Like the political party, the union is formed for the realization of certain ideals. These include higher wages, shorter hours, and generally better conditions of labor. These objects can be attained only through organization, as they could not be brought about by individual workers. To form and maintain 150 national and international craft organizations, 45 State federations, 1,200 city federations, and 25,000 local unions requires infinite effort and incessant self-sacrifice. Their officers must be chosen through all the machinery of caucuses, conventions and elections. Dues must be paid. There must be picnics, excursions, and all kinds of entertainments to awaken interest. There must be meetings, lectures, speeches, debates. Every member must face, with heroic fortitude, the prospect of suffering for the cause. These are some of the unescapable burdens of the loyal unionist. They are not lightly borne.

But in their bearing, according to the unionist, the "scab" takes no share. In securing the results severely attained by organized labor, he takes no part. He pays no dues. He robs his leisure of no hours for the elevation of his industrial group. Like the "mugwump" in politics, the "scab" holds selfishly, scornfully, hypercritically aloof. Nevertheless, while thus escaping hardships and self-denials necessary to win, through organization, by conflict or negotiation, from the employer better conditions for the employed and more rightful relations between them both, the "scab" shares all the benefits won by the systematic struggle of organized labor. Thus it is that the scorn of the regular party adherent for the "mugwump" is equaled by the scorn of the unionist for the "scab." The parallel suggests that an appropriate definition of the "scab" would be the industrial "mugwump."

If organization is essential to good government, it becomes the patriotic duty of every citizen to enter a party organization and seek to make its policy and conduct conform to conscientious conviction. If organization is essential to advance the cause of labor, it becomes the duty of every wage-earner to enter the union of his craft and to eliminate from its conduct everything detrimental to the attainment of its purpose. But neither "mugwump" nor "scab" should be coerced into his organization by ostracism or bludgeon.

THE SHORTER WORK-DAY SYMPOSIUM.

The question of a shorter work day is very much alive. It is an issue of active current discussion and of present importance. The eight-hour bill, long pending before Congress, was referred by that body to the Department of Labor and Commerce, which is preparing a report upon the probable effects of its enactment. The American Federation of Labor has included the support of this measure among the questions that it is asking every candidate for Congress to answer. For these reasons, the opinions of employers upon this subject, presented in this issue of THE MONTHLY REVIEW, are of interest and value.

EXECUTIVE COMMITTEEMEN.

The countenances that look forth from the pages of this issue of THE MONTHLY REVIEW are those of members of the Executive Committee of the National Civic Federation. These are citizens representative of three groups, the general public, employers and employed, united by a common public spirit and devoted to the promotion of rightful relations between labor and capital. To that cause they unselfishly and patriotically give their time, their talents and their zeal.

INDUSTRIAL WAR AND PEACE.

Strikes are industrial war. They wake the echoes with discordant din and arouse public attention as they affect public interest.

Controversies between employer and employed. so long as they are kept within the pacifying scope of conciliation and conference, receive usually the notice only of the parties directly concerned. If a third party, by mutual agreement, is called in to arbitrate the difficulty, little more outside attention is attracted. It is when a controversy has exhausted or rejected these methods of industrial peace and reaches the stage of a strike that general public attention is excited. Idle cotton mills in New England and riots in Chicago stock yards distort the perspective. The great body of undisturbed industry is ignored.

The failures of conference and of arbitration, thus made conspicuous, are really of less importance than their successes, which are too quickly forgotten. The imagination shrinks from the paralysis of industry and the halting of transportation that would have followed the threatened bituminous strike, so happily averted through conciliation; while the pacific outcome of conferences in the tin and sheet iron and the 'longshoremen's industries is of incalculable value, although unnoticed because of its silent calm.

International diplomacy also has its ruptures. The Hague Court of Arbitration had its inception in the advocacy by the present Emperor of Russia of that method of deciding disputes between governments. Yet Russia and Japan to-day, despite the strongest, most earnest and persistent efforts of civilization to avert war, fill the Orient with the clash of arms, while their peoples suffer the expenditure of blood and treasure. But the world waits only the favorable moment when the good offices of some power may be invoked for the restoration of honorable peace. There is no reason to despair of the eventual settlement of industrial conflicts, even when they are most bitter and passionate.

A COLORADO OPINION.

The Man Who Pays the Militia Believes that the National Civic Federation Could Have Averted Trouble.

Sheldrake, N. Y., July 25th, 1904.

To the Editor of the Monthly Review:

Sir.—As a citizen of Colorado, where for more than twenty years I have been a large employer of labor, I have been keenly interested in the work of the National Civic Federation. I have studied its literature about its purpose and scope, which you courteously furnished at my request, and I feel that I must express to you my conviction that the methods advocated by your organization form the one avenue of avoidance, in this country, of violent collision between the forces of capital and labor.

I write during a vacation in the east, which has afforded me opportunity of getting a new perspective upon the spectacle, presented in my own state, of the overthrow of normal civil processes and the substitution of military rule.

I write also as a member of Governor Peabody's administration, having been elected State Treasurer upon the same ticket with him.

Many things have occurred in Colorado, in the enforcement of law, that are to be deplored, and that probably would not be justified under ordinary circumstances, but the general policy of the Governor undoubtedly meets with the approval of most of our law-abiding people.

But that a military alternative should be presented to the executive authority of any state in the Union is itself an evidence that the public services of your voluntary organization, conciliatory and educational, are absolutely needed to insure the pacific fulfillment of the mutual obligations of social order.

The organization of labor is a necessity of self-defense, arising from the selfishness of human nature. In Colorado, this system of self-defense has developed into aggression, which has grown from defense against capital into assault upon capital in its physical property and in its independent employment of labor. This, in turn, has excited reprisal, itself a method of defense against anarchy, which in its turn has become a usurpation, temporarily essential, of the authority exercised under normal conditions by the courts and police. This extreme exercise of executive power is warranted only by necessity. The necessity is that of upholding the social order, recognized and beloved throughout all of the United States.

The intelligent and farsighted citizenship of Colorado has no desire to set up a system of government within its borders different from that of any other state. But to restore a condition harmonious with that of the other Commonwealths of the Union, a reconciliation between the forces of capital and labor must be brought about. The men arrayed on each side must be made to see that the law is supreme, and that it must be obeyed by each alike. The men on each side must also be educated to perceive that harmonious co-operation between capital and labor is essential to profitable industry, because it is essential to both production and consumption. When this economic fact is brought home to opposing minds, they will become reconciled, if only through self-interest.

I believe that if the National Civic Federation had established a branch organization in Colorado two years ago, all of the blood-shed, riot and loss in wages and in the earnings of capital that have marked the dire months of 1904 could have been avoided.

Truly yours,

WHITNEY NEWTON.

The man who has nothing to sell but his services may be taught differently by demagogues and fanatics, but his interest in the maintenance of law is greater than that of most men who have great possessions of money, lands, buildings and securities. The rich man can get away from disorder. The poor man must stay and face it and stand the consequences.—"Chicago Chronicle."

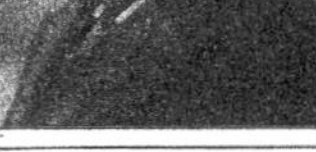

DAVID R. FRANCIS.
President La. Purchase Exposition.

CHARLES A. MOORE.
Manufacturer.

JAMES O'CONNELL.
President International Association Machinists.

THE EMPLOYER AND TRADE UNIONISM.

THEIR RELATIONS, ADJUSTED TO CERTAIN PRINCIPLES, SAYS LOUIS D. BRANDEIS, WOULD BRING ABOUT AN ERA OF PEACE AND PROSPERITY.

"The Employer and Trades-Unions" is the subject of an address delivered recently at the annual banquet of the Boston Typothetæ by Louis D. Brandeis, Esq. This address has taken rank as a brochure remarkable for its high purpose as well as for its keen analysis and lucid statement of the several duties and responsibilities of the employer and of organized labor. Its quality is the reason for reproducing here the general part of the address.

Mr. Brandeis reviewed the history of a rupture early in 1904 between the Boston Typothetæ and the Boston Typographical Union, resulting in a strike, during which the Union induced pressmen and feeders to leave their work, which action was enjoined by the Supreme Court. The strike was finally declared off by the President and members of the Executive Committee of the International Typographical Union. Taking this as an instance of erroneous leadership in a local union and as a lesson of experience, Mr. Brandeis said:

Mr. Brandeis' Address.

So much for the past: what shall the future be? What should you do to make it an era of peace and prosperity? The answer involves a discussion of certain broad principles which, in my opinion, should govern the relations of employer and employe in all branches of industry, though in their application they would, like every rule, be subject to exceptions more or less temporary, dependent upon the peculiar facts of the individual case.

First. Prolonged peace and prosperity can rest only upon the foundation of industrial liberty. The peace which employers should seek is not the peace of fifty years ago, when the employers were absolute masters of the situation. The peace which the employes should seek is not the peace of mediæval guilds, with their numberless restrictions. Industrial liberty must attend political liberty. The lead which America takes in the industrial world is no doubt due to our unbounded resources; but of these resources none are so great as the spirit and the ability incident to a free people. We lead the world industrially, not so much because the resources of nature are unbounded, as because the faculties and aspirations of men are comparatively unfettered. The prosperity of New England—this poor rich country—is ample evidence of this. We must have therefore for the development of our industries, as for the development of our citizens, the highest degree of liberty attainable. Industrial democracy should ultimately attend political democracy. Industrial absolutism is not merely impossible in this country at the present time, but is most undesirable. We must avoid industrial despotism, even though it be benevolent despotism. Our employers can no more afford to be absolute masters of their employes than they can afford to submit to the mastery of their employes, than the individual employes can afford to have their own abilities or aspirations hampered by the limitations of their fellows. Some way must be worked out by which employer and employe, each recognizing the proper sphere of the other, will each be free to work for his own and for the common good, and that the powers of the individual employe may be developed to the utmost. To attain that end, it is essential that neither should feel that he stands in the power—at the mercy—of the other. The sense of unrestricted power is just as demoralizing for the employer as it is for the employe. Neither our intelligence nor our characters can long stand the strain of unrestricted power. Every business requires for its continued health the memento mori of competition from without. It requires likewise a certain competition within, which can exist only where the ownership and management, on one hand, and the employes, on the other, shall each be alert, hopeful, self-respecting, and free to work out for themselves the best conceivable conditions.

Second. The right of labor to organizé is recognized by law, and should be fully recognized by employers. There will be in most trades little probability of attaining the best conceivable conditions unless in some form a union of the employes exists. It is no answer to this proposition to point to instances of trade union excesses and of the disasters which attended them. We believe in democracy despite the excesses of the French Revolution. Nor are claims of the trades-unions disproved by pointing to the instances where the best results have been attained in businesses in which no trace of unionism existed. Wise, far-seeing employers act upon the spirit or the hint of union demands instead of waiting to have them enforced. "A word to the wise is sufficient." The steps in advance have been taken often for the express purpose of preventing trades-unionism from finding a lodgement, often, unconsciously, as a result merely of the enlightenment which comes with the necessary thinking that trades-union agitation compels. Such successful businesses are, indeed, the greatest triumphs of unionism; and their marked success is due in large part to the fact that they have had all the advantage of unionism without having to bear the disadvantages which in their imperfect state attend the unions. We must not forget the merits of unionism in our righteous indignation against certain abuses of particular unionists.

Most people admit the immense service which the labor unions have rendered to the community during the last twenty-five years in raising of wages, shortening of the hours of labor, bettering of conditions under which labor is performed, and protecting women and children from excessive or ill-timed work; but the services which the labor unions can render in the future are even greater than they have been in the past. The employer needs them "to stay him from the fall of vanity"; the employes need them for their own protection; the community needs them to raise the level of the citizen.

Strong, stable trades-unions can best serve these ends. The leaders of strong unions only will adequately feel the terrible responsibility resting upon them. The leaders of stable unions only can get the experience essential to an adequate performance of their duties; and experience almost invariably makes the leaders reasonable and conservative. Only long service as a labor leader can give that knowledge of the employer's side of the controversy which is essential to its just and proper settlement. Peace and prosperity, therefore, are not to be attained by any attempt to weaken trades-unions. Our hope lies rather in their growing strength and stability.

At all events, the employer, whether he wills it or not, has in most trades to reckon with the union. What shall his attitude be?

Third. Employes are entitled to be represented by union officers. A short time ago it was common for an employer not to "recognize the union." That is, although he knew a large number of his employes were members of the union, he refused to negotiate in matters relating to the employe with its officers, on the theory that the employer should deal directly and only with his employe, and may not brook the interference of an outsider. This plausible but unsound theory has yielded generally to facts and to reason. One hears little now of employers arbitrarily refusing to deal with the chosen representatives of union employes. But, of course, recognizing that union officers are the proper representatives of the employes in any matter requiring consideration by the employer does not mean yielding to union demands, any more than recognizing a customer means conceding his demands.

FRANKLIN MACVEAGH,
Franklin Macveagh & Co.

ISAAC N. SELIGMAN,
Banker.

JOHN TOBIN,
President Boot & Shoe Workers.

How, then, shall the employer deal with the union's representative when a demand is made to which he feels he cannot accede, or a controversy has already arisen? Many are ready with the answer: Arbitration; others again say: Conciliation. Arbitration and conciliation are each at times wise, but each involves the intercession of third parties. In arbitration it is the referee; in conciliation, the common friend. Ordinarily, neither is needed.

Fourth. Employers and employes should try to agree. A very able man, who taught the law of partnership at Harvard, once asked the class, "What shall be done if a controversy arises between partners?" The students suggested one legal remedy after another,—a receiver, an injunction, a dissolution. "No," said he, "they should try to agree." In the most important sense, employer and employe are also partners. They, too, should try to agree; and the attempt made in a properly conducted conference will generally be successful.

Nine-tenths of the serious controversies which arise in life result from misunderstanding, result from one man not knowing the facts which to the other man seem important, or otherwise failing to appreciate his point of view. A properly conducted conference involves a frank disclosure of such facts, —patient, careful argument, willingness to listen and to consider.

Bluff and bluster have no place there. The spirit must be, "Come, let us reason together." Such a conference is impossible where the employer clings to the archaic belief commonly expressed in the words, "This is my business, and I will run it as I please." It is impossible where the labor representative, swaggering in his power to inflict injury by strike and boycott, is seeking an unfair advantage of the employers or would seek to maintain even a proper position by improper means. Such conferences will succeed only if employer and employe recognize that, even if there be no so-called system of profit-sharing, they are in a most important sense partners, and that each is entitled to a patient hearing, with a mind as open as the prejudice of self-interest permits.

The potent force of right reasoning in such conferences can hardly be overestimated. If applied with tact and in the aid of right action, it is almost irresistible. But it must be used only in the right spirit and in the aid of right action.

Fifth. It is necessary that the owners or the real managers of the business should themselves participate in the conferences, partly because the labor problem requires the best thought available and the most delicate treatment, and partly because the employes feel better satisfied and are apt to receive better treatment when they are dealing with the ultimate authority and not with an intermediary. Such conferences are necessarily time-consuming, but the time cannot be better spent. They are as instructive to the employer as to the employes. We must remember that there are no short cuts in evolution.

The greatest obstacle to the success of such conferences is the suspicion of the labor representatives,—a suspicion due partly to ignorance of the employer's actual attitude, partly to knowledge of individual acts of unfairness of other employers, and partly also to a belief, which is frequently erroneous, that the employer will get some advantage through his supposed superior skill and ability. Suspicion yields only to experience; and for this reason, among others, the conferences are most successful when participated in by labor leaders of long standing. The more experienced the representative, the better.

But conferences, though wisely conducted and with the best of intentions on either side, do not always result in agreement. Men fail at times to see the right; and, indeed, what is right is often in doubt. For such cases arbitration affords frequently an appropriate remedy. This remedy deserves to take its place among the honorable means of settling those questions to which it properly applies. Questions, however, arise, which may not be arbitrated. Differences are sometimes fundamental. Demands may be made which the employer, after the fullest consideration, believes would, if yielded to, destroy the business. Such differences cannot be submitted to the decision of others. Again, the action of the union may appear to have been lawless or arbitrary, a substitution of force for law or for reason.

What, then, should be the attitude of the employer?

Sixth. Lawless or arbitrary claims of organized labor should be resisted at whatever cost. I have said that it is essential in dealing with these problems that the employer should strive only for the right. It is equally as important that he should suffer no wrong to be done unto him. The history of Anglo-Saxon and of American liberty rests upon that struggle to resist wrong, to resist it at any cost when first offered rather than to pay the penalty of ignominious surrender. It is the old story of the "ship money," of "the writs of assistance," and of "taxation without representation." The struggle for industrial liberty must follow the same lines.

If labor unions are arbitrary or lawless, it is largely because employers have ignominiously submitted to arbitrariness or lawlessness as a temporizing policy or under a mistaken belief as to their own immediate interests. You hear complaint, too, of lawless strikers in the legislature and in the city council; but, if lawlessness and corruption exist there, it is largely because the great corporations and moneyed interests have forgotten the good old maxim, "Not one cent for tribute, but millions for defence."

Who bribed Sam Parks? The rich contractors—pre-eminently the huge corporations on whose boards of directors sat many of the leading financiers of the country. They corrupted Sam Parks or fed his corruption, corrupted him either to get an undue advantage over their employes or over their competitors, or as a seemingly inexpensive way of meeting what they deemed to be unreasonable and extortionate demands. At last employers, employes, and a large part of the community paid the penalty. Fortunately, the world is so ordered that we must pay the penalty for our sins, be they sins of commission or omission, of doing wrong or of suffering wrong to be done unto us.

You may compromise a matter of wages, you may compromise a matter of hours,—if the margin of profit will permit. No man can say with certainty that his opinion is the right one on such a question. But you may not compromise on a question of morals, or where there is lawlessness or even arbitrariness. Industrial liberty, like civil liberty, must rest upon the solid foundation of law. Disregard the law in either, however good your motives, and you have anarchy. The plea of trades-unions for immunity, be it from injunction or from liability for damages, is as fallacious as the plea of the lynchers. If lawless methods are pursued by trades-unions, whether it be by violence, by intimidation, or by the more peaceful infringement of legal rights, that lawlessness must be put down at once and at any cost.

Likewise industrial liberty must rest upon reasonableness. We gain nothing by exchanging the tyranny of capital for the tyranny of labor. Arbitrary demands must be met by determined refusals, also at any cort.

In our international relations we are told that the best assurance of peace lies in preparedness for war. This is equally true in the industrial world. The union has its strike fund. The employer must also pay in some form the premium for insuring an honorable peace. He has adopted long since the guaranty fund for his credits, the depreciation fund for his machinery. He should now adopt another reserve fund to guard him against the losses attendant upon strikes, and, above all, should so organize his business as to be less vulnerable to them. Known weakness invites arbitrary attack, as opportunity makes the thief.

These are the principles by which alone the labor problem can be satisfactorily solved. They are broad, indeed; for they are the eternal principles of

Liberty, Fraternity, Justice, Honor.

JAMES SPEYER,
Banker.

CHARLES H. TAYLOR, JR.,
President Am. Newspaper Pub. Association.

JOSEPH F. VALENTINE,
President Iron Moulders' Union.

A SHORTER WORK DAY.

(Continued from Page 4.)

at certain seasons of the year. An employe, who has the interest of a company at heart, should not, in our opinion, be averse to making an extra effort to help them out at such times as it is really necessary, and should not take advantage of such conditions to force the payment of double his regular wage for all overtime.

A large number of answers emphasize foreign competition as a serious obstacle to shortening hours:

C. O. Bartlett, The C. O. Bartlett & Snow Co., Mill and Labor Saving Machinery, Cleveland.—If the hours of labor are reduced, it will be to the detriment of our business. We have already lost nearly all of our foreign trade, of which we had quite a large one worked up. Germany and England have taken it practically all. This is chiefly on account of paying high prices for castings and other materials going into our machines.

C. W. Post, Postum Cereal Co., Ltd., Battle Creek, Mich.—We would like to see a universal eight-hour day in all countries, but it is very plain that if we reduce the amount of labor two hours per day out of ten, equivalent to 20%, we must either increase the producing capacity or stand a 20% handicap in the markets of the world. Foreign buyers are not going to pay a 20% increase in the cost of our goods in order to supply us with an eight-hour day. I would like to see the hour system take the place of the day, and if some plan could be devised by which a man would be permitted to work ten or even twelve hours if he saw fit, and thereby earn an increased amount of money, it would be more in keeping with the American idea that a man should be allowed to earn all he can. On the other hand, I hope to see the day when under the hour system, or some other practical plan, wage earners will not be compelled to labor over eight hours per day. To restrict a man's energies by force or to compel him to labor beyond a reasonable time seems un-American.

Asher Miner, Colonial Pure Cereal Foods, Wilkes-Barre, Pa.—The hours of labor of the engineers, firemen, millers and oilers is twelve, of laborers, teamsters, etc., ten, and the office force, nine. We do not consider it a practical proposition to gradually reduce the hours, as a considerable portion of the output in flour and corn mills is for export, and the business is done on an exceedingly small margin. If the hours of labor were reduced the cost of milling would be so great as to wipe out all profit.

J. H. Webster, Assignee, The Variety Iron Works Co., Cleveland.—Reduced hours of labor mean large increase of fixed charges in capitalization, salaries, real estate, machinery, etc. An industrious man naturally inclines to labor from sunrise until sunset. It has been so ever since labor began. A uniform agreement throughout a given industry can never be reached until that agreement extends to all civilized nations whose products of labor can come in competition. Making it uniform throughout the United States would not prevent the competition of the Old World except by building the wall of tariff still higher. Are we ready to do it? An agreement of employes to abandon any arbitrary restrictions upon output is as hopeless as it is fantastic.

M. E. Clow, J. B. Clow & Sons, Cast Iron Pipe, etc., Chicago.—We do not believe it practical to reduce the hours of labor unless it is the intention of American manufacturers to follow the example of England. If we are to maintain the position we have taken as the greatest manufacturing nation on earth, we must maintain the same reasonable conditions that exist in other countries, and if men are well treated and properly cared for, there is no reason why they cannot work ten hours.

T. H. Thieme, Wayne Knitting Mills, Fort Wayne, Ind.—Foreign competition must be taken into account, and a ten-hour work-day to my mind is the only safe stand to take. Even if a given industry under present conditions would be safe adopting an eight or nine-hour schedule, conditions through competitive industries or tariff changes may seriously injure such an industry working on a shorter workday. In our industry we are just able to compete with foreign competition, we needing ten-hour schedule, and with possible tariff changes shorter hours would receive no consideration on our part. The question of imposing restrictions upon output by employes or labor was settled in our factory a year ago at the close of a two-months' lock-out, when we put a minimum capacity on every machine with penalty of discharge for non-delivery of required product. This seemed hardship at first, but when our employes got accustomed to their larger pay envelopes, they showed every indication of being satisfied with the change.

F. A. Wilde, Nordberg Manufacturing Co., Engineers and Machinists, Milwaukee.—We regard it as entirely practical to "gradually reduce hours by voluntary, uniform agreement throughout a given industry provided the employes" abandon all restrictions upon the output. Indeed, we sincerely believe the shortening of hours to be most desirable and, therefore, to be earnestly striven for by employers everywhere. But in order to reduce the hours of labor of all, without diminishing the earnings,—the enjoying of the comforts of life—it is absolutely necessary to increase the product of each worker in even a greater ratio than that of the decrease in hours. This increase is to be accomplished by improved machinery, better processes and methods and greater ability on the part of each and every employe.

R. D. Wood & Co., Philadelphia.—My impression is that the hours given to any employment can best be arranged by the character of employment, rather than try to have a uniform rule covering all work. In other words, there are some duties at which people can comfortably work only six hours, and some where twelve hours is not too long. This question of eight hours finally resolves itself into simply whether mankind is going to be satisfied with what they can produce in eight hours instead of what they can produce in ten hours' work, or confining the question to the United States, the question is, will not some other countries work longer hours and take our export trade from us?

J. E. Mooney, American Oak Leather Co., Cincinnati.—Its effects would be to increase cost of production to the extent of reduction of the availability of the plant, plus the proportion of tax, insurance and maintenance, placing home production to a fatal disadvantage for international and domestic trade, as compared with the production of other countries. In other words, arbitrary restrictions on the output of plants or on individual workmen would, we believe, be a fatal economic error.

A few establishments consider that the short hour movement must begin, if at all, in districts and cities, and not be general for a line of business, as:

W. D. Sargent, American Brake Shoe and Foundry Co., New York.—We regard it as a practical proposition to reduce hours where the employer finds he can do so without seriously interfering with his rate of production or his profits; but conditions differ so much over the country that we doubt if a shorter work-day can be brought about uniformly throughout the country, and feel that it must come by districts, and that each district should demand from its employes the abandonment of arbitrary restrictions as suggested in your question, before consenting to the shorter day.

Several establishments regard restriction of output by workmen as not a matter for compromise but as wrong in itself, and not to be taken as a basis for agreement:

Samuel Moyer, The Lunkenheimer Co., Brass and Iron Steam Specialties, etc., Cincinnati.—We believe it practical to gradually reduce the hours of labor by voluntary, uniform agreement throughout a given industry, but we cannot afford to diminish the hours of labor in our shop unless all of our competitors do the same. As regards making an agreement with the employes to abandon any arbitrary restrictions upon output and giving them, in return, reduced hours of labor, would say that, looking at the matter in an abstract way, we cannot consider any such proposition, and any manufacturer who would, had better sell out his business. No manufacturer should recognize the right of any union to place restrictions upon the output, and, if we found that such a case existed in our shop, we would go out of business rather than permit its continuance; hence we do not consider this feature any element in connection with any labor organization, it being non-arbitrable.

G. O. True, Northern Engineering Works, Detroit, Mich.—In reference to an agreement with the employes to abandon restrictions upon output, in exchange for shorter hours, we do not believe the questions are on the same moral plane. We employ our men on a basis of hours and wages mutually agreed upon: under this agreement the workman owes his employer a fair day's work. If he limits his output he cheats his employer. Your proposition implies the gift to the workman of an hour or so a day, in consideration of a promise of the workman to quit stealing his time. We doubt the wisdom or morality of such a bargain.

L. B. Keiffer, Keiffer Bros., Shoes, New Orleans.—We think the only practical manner for the reduction of hours is by voluntary, uniform agreement throughout a given industry. We should not be willing to admit that employes had a right to restrict the output.

CHARLES FRANCIS ADAMS,
Publicist.

DAN R. HANNA,
M. A. Hanna & Co.

JAMES M. LYNCH,
President International Typographical Union.

A large number of those who oppose a reciprocal agreement of this kind give as one of their reasons their belief that unions would not live up to their agreement:

S. W. Watkins, Christensen Engineering Co., Milwaukee.—If this question had been written "Provided employes abandon arbitrary restrictions upon output," our answer would have been, Yes. As written, "Provided the employes agree to abandon restrictions upon output," would answer, No.

—

T. C. Wood, The Ball & Wood Co., Automatic Engines, New York.—We do not regard it as a practical proposition, first, because the conditions surrounding the different shops vary so greatly that it will be impossible to obtain the consent of all the employers in any given industry; and second, because employes could only make such an agreement through their union, and as these are irresponsible, no such agreement can be enforced.

—

H. D. Sharpe, Brown & Sharpe Manufacturing Co., Machinery and Tools, Providence.—It is difficult to say whether such a proposition is practical, but it would in no way depend upon what the employes agree. "Restrictions upon output" is not a matter of agreement but one of disposition on the part of both employer and employe. The solution of the question depends upon the proper working together of both.

—

E. T. Gilbert, Michigan Bolt and Nut Works, Detroit, Mich.—We believe it is practicable to gradually reduce hours by voluntary agreement. Would have no objection to such a movement if it was universal and if we obtained in return a real abandonment of restriction of output.

—

H. F. Wanning, Birmingham Iron Foundry, Derby, Conn.—We do not think it is a practical proposition to gradually reduce the hours. In fact, we started to do this as members of the National Metal Trades Association, but when the arrangement with the International Association of Machinists was repudiated, we went back to ten hours, after winning the strike. It will be necessary, in our opinion, to tie down the membership of unions in some manner to make them live up to their promises in regard to the restrictions of output. If there were really no restrictions whatever, it would be very easy to make up for a nine-hour or even an eight-hour day in contrast with the present ten hours.

—

G. W. Fuller, A. S. Cameron Steam Pump Works, New York.—Our plant is now operated on the nine-hour basis, or fifty-four hours a week, instead of ten hours as formerly, but on the same rate of pay per day as before. In other words, ten hours' pay for nine hours' work. We do not regard any further reduction in hours, voluntarily or otherwise, as a permanently practical proposition, for we do not believe there would be any increased volume in the output that would compensate for the added cost of labor due to the reduction in time, which would include payment at the same rate per day; and we would look upon a removal of "restriction upon output" as a specious offer, and one which past experience has proved the fallacy of.

R. M. Downie, Keystone Driller Co., Beaver Falls, Pa.—We do not believe it is a practical proposition to gradually reduce hours by voluntary, uniform agreement throughout a given industry for the simple reason that labor organizations are not chartered, are not responsible, and it has been our experience that an agreement cannot be made with them which will hold over night if they are disposed to break it. We have tried this and failed. If an agreement is made and a workman finds that he can get more money elsewhere he goes—which, as a matter of fact, is proper and right, but it prevents the possibility of making an agreement in advance which will bind workmen to stay with you any length of time at any given wages. We believe it is wholly useless to try to bind employes to agree to abandon arbitrary restrictions upon output because in so doing the unions would abandon their whole theory of procedure. Their limiting of apprentices is arbitrary, i. e., not founded upon any defensible right or principle of justice. Their limitation of hours is arbitrary and contradicts all personal freedom and even natural law. Their limiting the number of automatic machines a workman may watch is, likewise, arbitrary, and all are urged for one central purpose—the limitation of product. Our large factory to-day lies a heap of scrap iron and ashes because, after all offers to arbitrate had been refused, we presumed to permit apprentices and regulate hours without the consent of the union. We don't see how we could unite comfortably in any agreement whatsoever with that which ignores the common rights of all men.

—

J. H. Day, The J. H. Day Co., Machinery, Cincinnati.—We have no confidence in any agreement made by labor unions, and particularly with regard to restrictions upon the output. There are undoubtedly restrictions upon the output in our shops. We know this and see it almost every day, and the only way that hours of labor could be reduced without restrictions upon the output would be by the "premium" or "piece" work system. Several of our workmen have told us that they could easily do the ten hours' work which they are now doing in eight hours, and we believe it, but we found when we reduced the time from sixty hours per week to fifty-seven hours per week that the output was reduced even in a greater proportion.

—

G. C. Murphy, East Liverpool Potteries Co., East Liverpool, Ohio.—We would deem it a practical proposition to gradually reduce the hours of labor by voluntary, uniform agreement, providing the employes agree to abandon any arbitrary restrictions upon output. But we have very little confidence with any contract with employes, as our experience has taught us they will not live up to any contract, and are never satisfied. Any proposition of this kind we would not consider binding.

—

Some replies maintain that shorter hours can only be attained through the efforts of organized labor:

N. O. Nelson, N. O. Nelson Mfg. Co., Bath Tubs, Brass Goods, etc., St. Louis.—I don't regard it a practical proposition to gradually reduce hours by purely voluntary consent of the employers. Only after long agitation, repeated demands enforced by more or less strikes, can uniform agreements for reduction of hours through any given industry be reached. The employers look at a reduction of hours as an increase in the cost. Even when a demand is made upon all similar employers in the same industry, they do not see that it simply raises the price and does not injure their profit. Commonly, the demand does not come in this shape, but affects one employer or one city or locality by itself. In that event, it is a direct invasion of the employers' profits. The building trades' hours were reduced from ten hours to nine and to eight by local demands and strikes continued throughout many years. The shortening of factory hours from ten to nine is now going on, and is possible only by the more complete national union organizations and the American Federation of Labor. The Civic Federation Industrial Department will also lend itself to the shortening of hours, by bringing employers' associations and National unions together. Restrictions upon output need not be considered an obstacle. It is not a union principle or a union demand except in a local and sporadic sense. It is not countenanced by the general authorities.

—

Everett Morss, Simplex Electrical Co., Boston.—We do not consider it practicable to reduce the hours in our particular industry on the basis mentioned. Our principal business is the manufacture of insulated wire, and with the most of our competitors the business is complicated by being in each case a department only of a much larger industry. We do, however, expect that within a few years the probable working hours in our works will be reduced to fifty-four per week, and that it will be quite general in manufacturing work. We do not believe that eight hours per day will be adopted except in special trades which are in the nature of a labor trust.

—

Some establishments hold that only a national law or uniform State laws can bring about reduction of hours:

Jacob Stephans, W. H. Haskell Mfg. Co., Bolts and Nuts, Pawtucket, R. I.—As to reducing the number of hours, were this to be a national law so that all branches would work a certain number of hours, we certainly should be in favor of it, but we are decidedly against an eight-hour law that is not a National law. A law that is made for government employes, or for any particular branch of trade, is certainly a detriment to business.

—

Thos. F. Parker, Monaghan Mills, Greenville, S. C.—We hardly regard as practicable to greatly reduce hours of labor by voluntary uniform agreement among mill men. While we favor a reduction to what may be reasonable and right hours, we however think that this will have to come through the education of public opinion and legislation.

—

A considerable number of replies indicate that there are social evils which follow on shorter hours:

Kalamazoo Corset Co., Kalamazoo, Mich.—The question of the benefits to be obtained by a reduction of the hours of labor is a very large one. Unless the character of the work is of such a nature as to make large drafts upon the strength of the employe, we think shortness of hours may prove to be a positive damage because of the tendency to bring on habits of idleness with all its attending evils. In other words, we believe it is best for every one to keep busy.

JOHN G. MILBURN,
Lawyer.

WILLIAM D. MAHON,
President Street Railway Employes.

MARCUS M. MARKS,
Prest. Nat. Ass'n Clothing Mnfrs.

H. M. Kinney, Winona Wagon Co., Winona, Mich.—We do not think it wise to have a loafing period morning and night for the men who are inclined that way to drop into saloons on their way to and from work, and we believe they will be happier and more prosperous, and their employers will be better able to give them continuous work, on the ten-hour per day plan.

—

E. D. Johnston, P. H. & F. M. Roots Co., Rotary Blowers, etc., Connersville, Ind.—We do not regard it a practical proposition to gradually reduce hours by voluntary, uniform agreement, because if the employes agree to abandon any arbitrary restrictions upon output, we could not force them in any possible way to turn out as much work in eight hours as in ten. Generally speaking, we believe it is better for a laboring man to be employed ten hours than eight. It might be all right for some of the more intelligent class, but for the average laborer, he is better at work ten hours than eight. We believe if there was a general movement to adopt the eight-hour system, in ten years we would have more crime and drunkenness and, generally speaking, a lower order of intelligence among our laboring classes than if we adhere to the ten-hour rule.

—

F. B. Cole, Cole Manufacturing Co., Saw Mills, Engines, etc., Newman, Ga.—We do not favor reducing the hours of labor. We still believe in the doctrine that an idle mind is the devil's workshop, and in our forty years of manufacturing we have never noticed that any man's health was injured by ten hours' work.

The following reply is typical of a considerable number that maintain that the hours worked in their establishments, which are usually ten, are not excessive:

F. H. Stillman, Watson-Stillman Co., Hydraulic Machinery, New York.—Relative to the reduction of the hours of labor by voluntary agreement, I would say that machine tools as used in the shop do not get tired, nor do I believe that in our line of business the attendants upon them are over-wearied by a sixty (or a sixty-six hour week, when the residence is convenient to the shop), and I believe the fifty-four hour week the shortest that is possible at present rate of wages.

OTHER EMPLOYERS' EVIDENCE.

Opinions Favorable to Universal Shorter Hours Gathered by a Hostile Agency.

In the course of its campaign against the eight-hour bill in Congress, the National Association of Manufacturers addressed to employers a series of questions which included: "What are your general views as to the wisdom or unwisdom of the shorter work-day principle?" The inquiry was successful in developing opposition to the eight-hour bill. Nevertheless, it elicited many responses favorable to a universal shorter workday, irrespective of the specific proposition to limit to eight hours all work on government contracts. A few of these replies are quoted:

Barry Lumber Co., Poley, Ala.—If universal and not permitting two or three shifts, we think it would affect us favorably.

Lathrop Hatten Lumber Co., Riverside, Ala.—We could not compete, unless all are on eight-hour basis.

California Cotton Mills Co., Oakland, Cal.—We would like to see a national enactment, applicable to every State, making a nine-hour day a full day's work.

California Fig Syrup Co., San Francisco.—We favor an eight-hour day, because you can work men for that time at higher speed and accomplish more.

California Barrel Co., San Francisco.—We hope to see the actual number of hours of physical labor shortened gradually. We believe that this is a natural process . . . and that with the gradual introduction of labor-economizing appliances, the actual hours of physical labor will be curtailed. We are rather doubtful that the time has as yet come rendering it possible to limit generally the day's work to one of eight hours.

Pacific Tank Co., Los Angeles, Cal.—A universal eight-hour law would suit us well.

Denver Engineering Works, Denver, Col.—The shorter work-day principle is all right, but we think this is a matter to be settled between the employer and the employe.

The Billings & Spencer Co., Machinists' Tools, Hartford, Conn.—We are willing to concede that the nine-hour work-day is of advantage to the workmen and of no great disadvantage to the employer, provided it is made universal.

The Bullard Machine Tool Co., Bridgeport, Conn.—We believe that a shorter work-day is desirable, but it should not be forced upon the manufacturers by law in such a manner that they cannot regulate their own shops to the best advantage.

E. A. Mallory & Sons, Danbury, Conn.—If it were compulsory on all manufacturers in our line, we would all be in the same boat; hence it wouldn't affect us much.

Lobdell Car Wheel Co., Wilmington, Del.—Excessively long working hours necessarily not only impair a workingman's vitality, but detract from the social engagements to which he and his family are justly entitled. A ten-hour day requires a man's wife or family to be up early and late, and the trite saying that a woman's work is never done is fully exemplified.

Southern Spring Bed Co., Atlanta, Ga.—If universal, it would make no difference except in cutting short one-tenth or one-fifth of our product.

A. Rossi & Co., Lumber, Boise, Ida.—If universal in the United States, it would not affect us.

American Electric Telephone Co., Chicago.—We believe eight hours best if generally adopted; also we believe in a minimum wage and age scale.

Burson Knitting Co., Hosiery, Rockford, Ill.—Shorter hours are bound to come, but should come as the result of economic conditions and not of legislation.

The California Mfg. Co., Doors, Chicago.—It would in our opinion be better for the greatest number in the country to run uniform length of time, and even at eight hours' labor we believe American skill and machinery would fairly compete with outside products.

Rockwell & Rupel Co., Filing Cabinets, Chicago.—From actual experience, the writer, after careful observation, considers that a man working forty eight hours a week can do a great deal more work than the man working sixty hours a week, or even longer, for the reason that he has more time for recreation and is fresher.

Acme Milling Co., Indianapolis.—The writer believes that an eight-hour day would be a good thing providing we could induce our men to be content with the short day.

J. A. Everett, Publisher, Indianapolis.—Let us have a ten-hour day and a five-day week, rather than eight-hour days and six-day weeks.

Haugh Noelke Iron Works, Indianapolis.—We believe that if an eight-hour law for all labor should prevail throughout the United States, that it then would be equitable to both employer and employe.

Topeka Milling Co., Topeka, Kan.—Short-hour days should not be compulsory.

American Steam Gauge and Valve Co., Boston.—Unless the law were universal, we could not compete.

American Optical Co. Southbridge, Mass.—We take the position that if the short day is to be adopted, it should be by national legislation, and to affect the entire country.

Covel Machine Co., Fall River, Mass.—This law has got to be a uniform law throughout the nation to be just.

A Massachusetts Manufacturer of Iron Pipes (name not stated).—We are thorough believers in a short day, but not an eight-hour day. We recognize the economical advantages that have come from shortening the day, but there is a point beyond which these advantages will not be gained.

Hastings Wool Boot Co., Hastings, Mich.—We would not object to it, if it could be applied to all classes of business and in all sections of the country.

The Michigan Stove Co., Detroit.—If eight or nine hours became a universal law, we could stand it.

Michigan Brass and Iron Works, Detroit.—We believe the shorter work-day is coming, but we do not believe it is wisdom for the government to enforce it at this time.

Michigan Bolt and Nut Works, Detroit.—We think shorter hours are likely to come. We think they will come slowly, and that the economic conditions of the country will secure it in good time.

Northern Engineering Works, Detroit.—If eight or nine hours could be universally adopted, both here and abroad, we would favor it, provided the Saturday afternoon holiday could be maintained during the summer.

The Walsh De Roo Milling Co., Holland, Mich.—Shorter days of work would have to be a world-wide practice, or those factories working shorter hours would be at a disadvantage.

The Millers' Exporting Co., Omaha, Neb.—Can see no objection to the eight-hour system, provided that all use it.

J. H. Bawden & Co., Grate and Fender Work, Freehold, N. J.—We are in favor of the eight-hour system, as we are able, under it, to obtain better results from our men than on the ten-hour run; but we cannot compete with other shops that run their men ten hours.

A. F. Griffing Iron Co., Radiators, Jersey City.—We can say that there are only certain industries

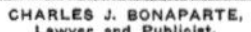

CHARLES J. BONAPARTE,
Lawyer and Publicist.

WILLIAM H. PFAHLER,
Stove Manufacturer.

DENIS A. HAYES,
President Glass Bottle Blowers.

which cannot be successfully conducted upon fixed hours, shorter days and half-holidays.

Newark Rivet Works, Newark, N. J.—If it were universal, it would not affect us more than others, but under present conditions it would be disastrous.

A New Jersey Manufacturer of Woollen and Worsted Goods (name not stated).—We believe a shorter work-day will gradually spread throughout the industrial world, and only because of its world-wide extent can it be successful or desirable.

Geneva Optical Co., Geneva, N. Y.—A general eight-hour law placing all manufacturers on the same basis would not injure us.

Hecla Iron Works, Brooklyn.—We think that any man ought to be able to earn a living by working eight hours a day.

Ithaca Calendar Clock Co., Ithaca, N. Y.—I have been long of the opinion that the eight-hour day is coming, not only in government work, but in all work, and it will be the standard day, the same as ten hours has been.

The Weber Piano Co., New York.—We think well of it, if all in our line would do so.

The Akron Belting Co., Akron, O.—We do not object to a voluntary eight hours a day law.

The F. H. Lawson Co., Household Goods, Cincinnati.—If an eight-hour day law was made in each State, we would not have to pay labor any more than our competitor would; so it would give us better labor, if laborers in general had more time to improve themselves in every way.

The Lunkenheimer Co., Engineering Specialties, Cincinnati.—If every concern in the land would work but eight hours per day, it would be all right; but such a thing is out of the question at the present time.

O. H. L. Wernicke, Furniture, Cincinnati.—I think it is bound to come; therefore, the wise man will be on the outlook for offsets.

The American Pulley Co., Philadelphia.—It is our general impression that when men are working at their very best, on piece-work, fifty-four hours a week is about enough.

H. Belfield & Co., Castings, Philadelphia.—We would not object to a nine-hour day, if universal in every department of trade.

Thomas Devlin Mfg. Co., Castings, Philadelphia.—We favor a universal eight-hour day.

Falkenau Sinclair Machine Co., Philadelphia.—From a broad point of view, we believe that if an eight-hour day were universal, it would be a benefit to mankind.

Merritt & Co., Iron and Wire Ropes, Philadelphia.—I think the eight-hour day will come in time, but should not be forced.

W. T. Smith & Son, Textiles, Philadelphia.—We feel satisfied that in the future there will certainly be a curtailment of the hours of labor.

Chicago Brass Co., Kenosha, Wis.—We believe that the times are tending toward an eight-hour day, and undoubtedly it will come, and we would prefer it to come in a manner which makes it universal rather than haphazard.

Gold Metal Camp Furniture Mfg. Co., Racine Junction, Wis.—The time is coming when the eight-hour system will be generally observed and the writer feels the sooner the better.

Hoffman & Billings Mfg. Co., Brass and Iron Goods, Milwaukee, Wis.—We favor a universal eight-hour day.

Thomas B. Jeffery & Co., Automobiles, Kenosha, Wis.—I think that it will be in a few years the prevailing rule, and think that the arrangement would be a wise one, but do not approve of any law which interferes with free and independent contracting for services.

ANOTHER TEAMSTERS' STRIKE AVERTED.

Representatives of the Teamsters' Brotherhood and of the Contractors' Protective Association Form a Trade Agreement at the Rooms of the New York Civic Federation.

The past month has witnessed another avoidance of strife between teamsters and employers and the formation of a trade agreement, between the International Brotherhood of Teamsters and the Contractors' Protective Association of New York City. This agreement is the second to be made in this city between employers and the organized teamsters, the previous one having been consummated in June with the Truck Owners' Association, through the mediation of the Conciliation Committee of the New York Civic Federation, thereby averting a threatened strike that would have caused incalculable loss and inconvenience.

The members of the Contractors' Protective Association are engaged chiefly in excavating work, including those at work on the subway. In all, they employ about 8,000 men. There had been for some time a spirit of discontent among the organized teamsters with irregular rates of pay. This feeling displayed itself early in July, when the teamsters employed by Clarence Smith refused to work. They would not treat with Mr. Smith directly, but referred him to the officers of their International Brotherhood. A meeting of the Contractors' Protective Association was promptly called. It was considered that the strike at Mr. Smith's stable was probably the beginning of a series of demands for uniform wages, to be made upon one contractor after another. Some members of the Association suggested that this method warranted retaliation by a lock-out. But it was pointed out that such a course might involve many other contractors, particularly those in the building trades, in a conflict with the teamsters in their employ, and that, furthermore, through sympathy, all the wheeled carrying trade of the city might be tied up.

Accordingly, negotiations were opened with the Teamsters' Brotherhood. It was found that the formation of an agreement was not difficult, after the associated contractors had decided to confer with representatives of the union. The teamsters' representatives showed a spirit of fairness in assenting to the requirement that all drivers help load their trucks in cellar work and also whenever teams are crowded at loading points, in order to break the jam. The maximum work-day was fixed at twelve hours, the hours to be adjusted to suit business conditions of the employer, overtime to be paid in proportion to a uniform wage-scale. This scale made a slight average increase of pay. The question of "open shop" was met by the stipulation that "Preference shall be given, in hiring new men, to competent members" of the union. A clause provided for the reference of differences between employer and employe to a board composed of an equal number of teamsters and members of the contractors' association, with power, in case of disagreement, to select an umpire, "whose decision shall be final and binding." Pending that decision, no lock-out or strike shall be ordered, and the union binds itself to order no sympathetic strike. The agreement is in force until June 1, 1905.

The agreement was put into final form and signed by representatives of the two parties at the rooms of the New York Civic Federation on July 7. The agreement is signed on behalf of the Contractors' Protective Association by A. McC. Parker, Patrick Reddy, Edward J. Galway, John L. Keating and Hugh Thomas; and on behalf of the International Brotherhood of Teamsters by Edward Gould, James M. Brady, Michael J. Rogan, George W. Prescott, John Martin and John P. Brannigan.

CO-OPERATION IN MASSACHUSETTS.

The State Arbitration Board Welcomes the Boston Branch of the National Civic Féderation.

In its eighteenth annual report to the Legislature, the Massachusetts Board of Conciliation and Arbitration states:

"The Board at the end of its eighteenth year reports that the confidence of employer and employed, so necessary to a tribunal of voluntary resort, continues to increase. The attention which the public has ever given to the Board's work is manifested by invitations to address clubs, societies, schools and religious organizations, and by the requests of students and teachers, writers and speakers, for information concerning its work. This interest, which is one of the most encouraging signs of the times, was manifest when the transportation strike of 1902 was brought to a speedy close through the timely aid of public-spirited men of this State. In its efforts to secure the speedy termination of the strike and to prevent its recurrence during the month following the settlement, the Board was heartily assisted by the secretary of the National Civic Federation and its members. It is gratifying to note that these men, devoted to the promotion of peace between industrial parties, contemplate a branch of their organization in Massachusetts."

OTTO M. EIDLITZ,
Chairman Building Trades Employers.

RALPH M. EASLEY,
Chairman Executive Council.

HENRY WHITE,
United Garment Workers of America.

HOW LABOR UNIONS HURT THEMSELVES.

When Internal Labor Quarrels Disturb the Public, Trades-Unionism Suffers.

(Editorial, "N. Y. Evening Journal," July 22.)

The threatened strike in New York City's underground railroad illustrates strikingly and unpleasantly one of the greatest difficulties in the progress of union labor.

There are two rival unions of painters, "The Amalgamated Society of Painters and Decorators," and "The Brotherhood of Painters." Both of these associations consist of union men, both seek employment for their members. The agents of each association, of course, do only their duty in protecting the members whom they represent.

But unions quarreling among themselves should find a way to settle their difficulties without exposing the public to great inconvenience, and without attacking the interests of any innocent third party.

If this strike of painters should prevent the opening of the underground railroad, millions of people would be inconvenienced.

There is nothing more damaging to the interests of union men, nothing that so much undermines respect and sympathy for union labor as these quarrels between the men themselves, in which they sacrifice the interests of innocent parties—employers and the general public—to carry on internal rows.

When an individual employer or city is willing to hire union men, willing to pay fair wages, it is preposterous for the unions to say the work cannot go on, that a man's business must be ruined, or the public imposed upon, because the union men are fighting among themselves.

Let them fight among themselves if they want to. Problems of unionism, like other problems, must be worked out through struggles and misunderstandings.

But let rival unions fight each other, and pay the cost of their own fights, instead of making the public or the innocent employer pay the bill.

Perhaps the union men will ask: "Haven't the unions a right to quarrel and fight with each other, the same as the great corporations? Don't the corporations get into rows and fight to the death?"

Yes, the unions have a right to fight as much as they please and imitate, if they choose, the most elaborate cut-throat methods of the trusts and the big corporations. But, in the first place, the fact that a trust or a great corporation does harm certainly does not excuse evil-doing on the part of a labor union.

In the second place, and what is more important, when the trusts and the big corporations go to fighting the public is benefited.

But when unions fight, instead of fighting each other, they fight the public or their employer, threatening ruin to one or inconvenience to the other, and that is foolish childishness.

It is nonsense to say that the questions cannot be arranged without making the public suffer.

Suppose Belmont, the builder, should have a misunderstanding with McDonald, the contractor, and lock out all the men and delay the tunnel indefinitely pending an agreement. Would the public stand that kind of nonsense?

It would not, and there is no reason why it should stand the nonsense that results from a fight between the unions.

Unions are the most important factor in modern life. They alone stand between the working people and the unlimited greed of the corporations.

They alone, by compelling the payment of fair wages, can bring about at least a partial distribution of wealth.

The good that they can do is enormous, and intelligent working men should see that they are not damaged in the public estimation by foolish fights between brothers.

FAULTY SHOP MANAGEMENT.

Mr. Du Brul Iterates and Explains His Statement That a Large Percentage of Strikes are the Fault of the Employer.

The statement made by E. F. Du Brul, commissioner of the National Metal Trades Association, before the National Association of Manufacturers, that "eighty per cent. of the strikes in this country are the fault of the employer" is repeated by him, together with the following explanation, in the "Boston Transcript":

"Strikes and labor troubles are the fault of the employer to a very large extent because the employers, whom one would naturally expect to be more intelligent than their workmen and therefore more familiar with industrial conditions, have not studied questions of labor. They are too busy to read things about labor, and too busy to bother about many things that go on in their own shops. It is the employer's fault if he has a foreman or superintendent who treats the men unfairly, thereby giving an excuse for the agitator to come in and work on the prejudices of the workmen, drawing away their loyalty from the employer to the organization. His fault is probably one of omission rather than of commission.

"Many strikes in their last analysis are demands for better shop management, and it is a fact that shop management is being reduced to a science; the abuses where they have [illegible] in the piece-work system are caused by a [illegible] definite knowledge on the part of both emp[illegible] employes as to how long a job should take, and so, too, with many other things. It is the employer's fault that employers' associations were not formed long ago to control strikes."

PUBLIC SENTIMENT THE ARBITER.

The President of the Employers' Association Points the Way to Peace with Unionism on the Basis of Justice.

In a recent communication to the National Civic Federation, in relation to a contemplated meeting, Mr. Phil. R. Tell, President of the Kansas City Employers' Association, expressed the following sentiments:

"We believe unionism and contra-association of employers are products of necessity; that both per se are right; that the tendency of the employers' association will be to educate unionism, and aggressiveness on the part of the unions will tend to eliminate selfishness and unjustness on the part of the employer; and that the product derived will be happiness, prosperity and peace; that the American people can be depended upon to act as arbiter between the two, and that public sentiment, to which both appeal for a verdict, will decide in favor of justice.

"Unionism was born from necessity, that necessity being the selfishness of humanity in the guise of the employer. Employers' associations were born from a necessity, that necessity being arbitrary restrictions, unjust demands and violations of law on the part of unionism. Employers must recognize the justice and demands of employes, and employes must not make unreasonable nor restrictive demands upon the employer. Both sides must recognize justice and neither must attempt to cast the mote out of the other's eye until they have removed the beam that is within their own.

"On both sides of the question we have too many who will not recognize the justice of the other's position, and until this condition is remedied, we may expect industrial disturbances."

The London Society of Compositors, with 11,2[illegible] members, has a reserve fund of $361,000. Nearly $80,000 was paid to the unemployed last year. The society maintains 330 superannuated members, who received for the year $33,000 from the general treasury. The funeral benefits for the twelve months totaled $11,740.

When violation of contracts through sympathetic strikes is declared by the official representative or agent of labor organization to be harmful, dishonorable, and not to be tolerated, obedience must be rendered by the local unions which compose its membership, or discipline is lost.—Tampa "Union Label."

National Civic Federation

MONTHLY REVIEW

Vol. I. No. 7 | NEW YORK, SEPTEMBER 15, 1904 | Ten Cents

A SIGNAL VICTORY FOR FACE-TO-FACE CONFERENCE.

A STRIKE ON THE GREAT INTERBOROUGH SYSTEM AVERTED THROUGH MEETINGS BETWEEN CORPORATION OFFICERS AND LABOR REPRESENTATIVES.

The partisans of organized capital, the adherents of organized labor and the interested general public may all rejoice in the establishment of peace between a great corporation and its army of employes. The significance and the consequences of the contract just signed between the Interborough Rapid Transit Company and its organized employes cannot be exaggerated. The attainment of that contract meant the avoidance of a strike whose enormous inconvenience to the public was in the mind of every one, while its extension to all the railroads centering in New York, through the action of the railway brotherhoods, was only the beginning of a chain of possibilities that would have agitated the whole country.

But these dangers, now happily banished, were physical. It is the moral effect of the success of the candid conferences between employer and employed that invites emphasis and the earnest attention of all students of the ever-present labor question. The Interborough is the largest public service corporation upon this continent, if not in the world. Its business of urban transportation employs thousands of wage-earners, whose number is to receive a large addition through the operation of the new subway. That corporation found itself confronted by certain demands backed by three national organizations of labor and their local branches—the Amalgamated Association of Street and Electric Railway Employes, and the Brotherhoods of Locomotive Engineers and Firemen.

This largest employer in its line of business in the United States did not reply to these demands with the old-fashioned answers that it would "manage its affairs in its own way"; that it would not brook the "interference of outsiders"; that it would "meet only the men in its employ"; that there was "nothing to confer about"; that there was "nothing to arbitrate." Instead, it accepted, through an enlightened directorate and its president, August Belmont, that method of round-the-table conference whose efficacy in securing industrial peace has been practically demonstrated elsewhere, and whose promotion is the main object of the National Civic Federation.

AUGUST BELMONT,
President Interborough Co.

WILLIAM D. MAHON,
President Amalgamated Association.

WARREN S. STONE,
Grand Chief Brotherhood of Engineers.

CHARLES A. WILSON,
Vice-Grand Chief Brotherhood of Fireman.

The consequences of this agreement, it is hoped, will be far-reaching. Thousands of other employers will be impressed with this object lesson of the effectiveness of the plan of having representatives of two clashing interests meet face to face and through verbal interchange make each thoroughly acquainted with the claims, the beliefs and the desires of the other. By this method a middle ground, perhaps of compromise, perhaps of mutual conviction of what is fair and just to both capital and labor, can be reached. This method receives the force of influential example from the list of directors who stood behind Mr. Belmont in its adoption. Their well-known names are: E. P. Bryan, Andrew Freedman, James Jourdan, Gardiner M. Lane, John B. McDonald, Walter G. Oakman, John Pierce, Morton F. Plant, William A. Read, Alfred Skitt, Cornelius Vanderbilt, George W. Young.

The adjustment of the difficulty between the Interborough and its employes is of great and general importance to both the capital and labor employed in all parts of the country, particularly in and near the centres of population. The change on the Elevated from steam to electric power was a visible forerunner of the predicted similar change on all railways carrying suburban traffic, as well as for local trains along their systems. This meant much to members of the Brotherhoods of Locomotive Engineers and Firemen, whose occupation would become that of motorman, still ranking as skilled labor, but not requiring much of the technical training requisite to run and manage a steam locomotive. In this change labor was naturally anxious to protect itself against a reduction of wages, while capital perceived an opportunity to urge that less expensive service should accept lower wages, and perhaps longer hours.

Without doubt, the use of the method of conference was made easier in the case of the threatened strike on the Elevated by the fact that contractual relations already had been established last year between the company and the men, through conferences brought about by the New York Civic Federation. When the Elevated passed into the control of the Interborough company at that time, a union including practically all of its employes had been formed. This branch of the Amalgamated Association made demands upon the Interborough which were put into the form of an ultimatum. That would have meant a strike, or surrender. But the Conciliation Committee of the Civic Federation persuaded the executive committee of the union to delay, brought the International President of the Amalgamated Association into conference with the new management of the road, and thus effected a settlement without a strike.

The existence of this contract, between the Interborough company and its employes, was a substantial precedent for the negotiations as to the terms and conditions of employment upon the subway. The reader is freshly familiar with the series of conferences between the president and executive officers of the Interborough ,company and the representatives, national and local, of the three labor organizations concerned, at Mr. Belmont's residence, his private office and the office of the company. That series of conferences culminated in the now famous conference between the representatives of the company and of the employes in August Belmont's office at 23 Nassau street on September 6.

Both sides felt that this conference was crucial. While hopeful of its success, each side had made grim preparations for its failure. The labor leaders had arranged for the men to quit work on the entire Elevated system at a moment's notice. The company had fitted its car barns with cots and cooking utensils, and had garrisoned them with a small army of strike breakers. With the diplomats of both sides striving for peace, they were ready for war. The entire police force had been ordered on full time duty, sleeping in the station houses, ready at an instant's warning to preserve public order. The city was pervaded by a feeling of the keenest anxiety. A large portion of its population went to bed on the night of September 6 not knowing the result of the conference. Not until they saw the reassuring headlines in the morning papers of September 7, did thousands know that their daily journey downtown would not be interrupted.

Thus all the circumstances and conditions whetted and concentrated public attention upon the consecutive phases of the prolonged negotiations. The demands of the men, their justice or extravagance, the attitude of the company and every strategical move by either side were all eagerly and critically discussed.

It was not, however, of general public knowledge that, throughout this time of anxiety, the Conciliation Committee of the National Civic Federation was holding innumerable conferences with both sides of the controversy. The fact that the president of the employing corporation and each of the national labor leaders involved are members of the Executive Committee of the Federation, and the fact that it was that organization that had previously been successful in bringing about the existing contract on the Elevated, rendered its good offices peculiarly acceptable to both parties.

At one stage of the negotiations the entire subject of dispute came near to being submitted to arbitration. The plan proposed and favorably received by all concerned was that Mr. Belmont should select from the labor group of the Executive Committee of the National Civic Federation John Mitchell, President of the United Mine Workers of America, and E. E. Clarke, Grand Conductor of the International Brotherhood of Railway Conductors; and that Messrs. Mahon, Stone and Wilson select from the employers' group of the same committee Lucius Tuttle, President of the Boston and Maine Railroad, and Frederick D. Underwood, President of the Erie Railroad. In case these four could not agree, they were to select from the representatives of the general public upon the Executive Committee of the National Civic Federation a fifth arbiter, whose decision should be accepted as final. Had the final conference of September 6, between Mr. Belmont and the labor leaders, not been successful, arbitration would have been the only resort to prevent a strike.

It was on the very day of this final conference that members of the National Civic Federation, realizing its grave importance, made a special effort to smooth the way for a successful outcome. At noon of that day, Charles A. Moore, Chairman of the Conciliation Committee, Oscar S. Straus, Emerson McMillin, Louis B. Schram, Ralph M. Easley and S. B. Donnelly, met the interested parties at luncheon. This social gathering was devoted to a final analytical review of the progress of the negotiations up to that hour and a critical examination of every demand on the part of the men. In fact, there was a general and thorough threshing out, around the luncheon table, of every question involved. The result was that all those directly concerned went to the formal conference of that afternoon in a conciliatory and judicial frame of mind, calculated to go far towards bringing about an agreement which, if not wholly satisfactory to either side, would ensure harmonious relations between the company and the employes.

It is notable that at the time when the question of the "closed shop" was the crux of almost every other labor difficulty, in this case it was never mentioned.

Summarized, the demand of the men was that preference be given to Elevated employes in manning the subway; that the hours and wages in force on the Elevated be extended to the subway; that seniority of service on the Elevated be counted in making promotions in the subway; that the medical examination of applicants for work be not what is known as the "standard railway" test, but one called the "practical" test, which is much less severe. The demand as to wages would have meant \$3.50 and a nine-hours' day for motormen in the subway, the same as is paid under the existing contract on the Elevated. When these demands were first made publicly known, on August 20, President Pepper of the local branch of the Amalgamated Association claimed that the extension of the Elevated contract to the subway and the preference to Elevated men in appointments to subway positions were part of an oral agreement made sixteen months ago between his organization and officers of the Interborough company. The company's officials denied knowledge of such an understanding. But from the outset Mr. Belmont expressed his belief that all the differences between the employes and the company would be satisfactorily adjusted.

In fact, Mr. Belmont made epigrammatic expression of his confidence in the method of conference, when he replied at a critical stage of the negotiations to a query whether he would grant yet another hearing to the representatives of the employes:

"Certainly! I will attend a hundred conferences if necessary, if only they will bring about a peaceful solution."

But this faith in the ultimate peaceful solution of the difficulty did not make the company's officials unmindful of the company's obligation to the public convenience. Their precautions, in the contingency of a strike, against a tie-up of the Elevated system, were both prompt and energetic. Knowledge of these precautions did not lessen the determination of the labor leaders to stick to their demand. At the same time it impressed them with the importance of exhausting every possible means of settlement, before resorting to a strike.

An alliance between the Amalgamated Association and the two railway Brotherhoods brought into the field three national labor leaders,—President W. D. Mahon, of the Amalgamated, and Grand Chief Warren S. Stone of the Engineers' and Vice-Grand Chief Charles A. Wilson of the Firemen's Brotherhoods. Before their arrival there had been conferences between General Manager E. P. Bryan and Superintendent Frank Hedley of the Interborough, and Presidents George Pepper of the local branch of the Amalgamated and William L. Jencks of the local division of the Engineers' Brotherhood. These local leaders, with their executive committees, also participated in the conferences that followed directly with President Belmont, the General Manager and the Superintendent of the Elevated.

The direct conferences with Mr. Belmont began on August 31 and continued until the final meeting of September 6, and the subsequent formulation of details of the agreement on September 7, and its signature on September 9. The conference of August 31 was inconclusive. It looked as though the company and the men were dead-locked on the question of wages and hours. But the arrival at this juncture of President Mahon and of Vice-Grand Chief Wilson opened the way for the conference of September 3.

At that conference a proposition was formulated which was acceptable to the company, as it provided for a wage of \$3 for a ten-hours' day in the subway, while it embodied various concessions to the Elevated employes, including retention of seniority.

But this proposition was rejected by all the local committees of the men. Not only was it rejected, but new demands were made, including that for a modified medical examination, to which reference has been made. Rumors of a strike were rife. President Mahon demonstrated, however, that the local radical spirits in the Amalgamated Association could be held in check by the national organization, and he was able to hold together also, for still further conference, the grand chiefs of the Brotherhoods. It was this spirit on the part of the labor leaders that resulted in the final and successful conference of September 6. In a letter agreeing to this conference, Mr. Belmont had excluded from its discussion the question of wages and hours. But although they knew that this question absolutely could not be excluded if a strike was to be prevented, the labor leaders accepted the terms of Mr. Belmont's letter, having faith that when once more face to face with the officers of the company, the question of wages and hours would naturally come up. As one of them said: "These interchanges of letters may be very well for international diplomats, but I believe in talking face to face." The outcome proved the wisdom of this counsel, since the final conference did adjust hours and wages. The agreement was for \$3.50 for a ten-hour day. Its other conclusions, relating to the modified seniority and minor details, retained the standard railway examination.

After the final conference, Mr. Belmont said: "I am glad that all of our long, hard tedious work has not been in vain. I am more than ever convinced of the soundness of the policy advocated by the National Civic Federation. We ought to be too civilized in this day and age for capital to refuse to meet organized labor in conference. This present experience confirms my belief in meeting the representatives of employes face to face."

In speaking of the adjustment of the difficulty, Mr Mahon said: "This conference, with its successful outcome, reflects vividly the wisdom of the policy of conciliation of the National Civic Federation. It was through the intervention of the Civic Federation more than a year ago, that the national and local representatives of the Amalgamated Association and the officers of the Interborough company were brought together and made acquainted. That was the beginning of a candid interchange of views that has been uninterrupted ever since. There never has arisen an occasion when both President Belmont and General Manager Bryan have not been as willing as ourselves to meet and discuss any subject of controversy.

"The great value of these conferences is that they bring the men of two sides face to face, when they can talk over, informally, all the features of a case in dispute. That is a far better method than the exchange of formal, written communications, or the making of demands and counterdemands through the press. When one side draws up a letter, its effort is to present as strong a case as possible, without any suggestion of compromise. In preparing a reply to any proposition made in that manner, the opposing side will also, naturally, try to frame as strong a document as possible. Each side is afraid to concede anything whatever in writing. So the two parties in negotiation, instead of getting together, may get farther and farther apart.

"But in a personal conference, where men sit together in one room, it is possible to create a mutual belief in a common purpose to arrive at a satisfactory settlement. In spoken conversation, misunderstandings are cleared away and each side begins to see the way open to reach ground on which both can stand. The officers of the Interborough never have raised any question of 'recognizing' the union, and as a result all fear and suspicion in dealing with them have been removed from the minds of the leaders of our labor organization. As to the agreement we have reached, I have only to say that it is satisfactory to us, as was shown by its unanimous ratification by the members of the New York Division of the Amalgamated Association."

Mr. Stone said of the conferences: "This is my first contact with the National Civic Federation, as I have only just become a member of that body. I am certainly pleased with its method of operation. I commend highly the spirit shown by Mr. Belmont and the officers of the Interborough throughout the conferences, and I am highly gratified at their successful conclusion. Without a doubt, there is great advantage to be gained by having representatives of the two sides, in any controversy about labor, meet and talk over every phase of the difficulty. That prevents misunderstandings and brings out the facts. Misunderstandings are the frequent cause of keeping apart interests that should be harmonious. The success of our conferences illustrates these statements."

Mr. Wilson said: "The officers of the three labor organizations involved in the controversy worked hard to hold the men back from striking. A strike would have been a public calamity, but when we arrived here it needed only a match to fire a strike. The officers of the unions are to be congratulated for their conservatism and deportment through many long and trying hours. So are the officers of the company, who met us squarely and courteously on every issue. We all deplore strikes, and believe in exhausting every resource before striking. The present is an impressive example of the value of getting together and talking things over. If we had conducted negotiations at a distance, our differences could not have been adjusted so rapidly, if at all. The agreement is the best that I ever helped to frame. It will form the basis for dealing with all future developments in the subway. It is unprecedented in that it is an agreement for wages, hours and conditions of labor on a railroad not yet in operation."

THE COUNTRY ESCAPES ANOTHER ANTHRACITE STRIKE.

THE MOST NOTABLE SYSTEM OF CONCILIATION AND ARBITRATION SAVED FROM A BREAK-DOWN, THROUGH REFERENCE OF A DISPUTE TO JUDGE GRAY.

"I regard this reference as preventing a repetition of the anthracite strike, with all its resultant disaster to the country."

That was the comment of Carroll D. Wright upon the reference to Judge George Gray, by the Anthracite Conciliation Board, of a deadlock in the Board which, if not relieved, would have set aside an award of the Anthracite Strike Commission, would have smashed the machinery of arbitration which it had created, and would have plunged the country, at the end of summer, into the woes of another strike throughout the anthracite regions of Pennsylvania. It would have been a moral disaster as well, for it would have shattered the confidence of the industrial world in the principle of arbitration of which this Anthracite Board is the most conspicuous example in history.

This is an event the more impressive because of the magnitude of the interests thus retained in harmony, in contrast to a period when labor troubles were unusually frequent. All of these troubles were made conspicuous in the daily press, while comparatively little attention was paid to the prevention of a threatened rupture more serious than all the existing strikes combined. This avoidance of a repetition of the disastrous anthracite strike of 1902 was made possible by the willingness of the miners' representatives in the board to acquiesce in the manner of reference of the question at issue to Judge Gray. The representatives of both interests in the board have expressed their determination in advance to abide by the decision of Judge Gray, so that the prevention of a strike upon this question is not temporary, but probably permanent. The expectation is that this action will result in eliminating entirely from the anthracite industry a knotty problem that has been fraught with danger,—that of the payment of check weighmen and check docking bosses.

The existence of this Board of Conciliation, it will be recalled, grows out of the award of the Anthracite Strike Commission, appointed by the President of the United States, October 16, 1902, at the request of both the operators and the miners. The report of this commission, made March 18, 1903, included the following award:

That any difficulty or disagreement arising under this award, either as to its interpretation or application, or in any way growing out of the relations of the employers and employed, which cannot be settled or adjusted by consultation between the superintendent or manager of the mine or mines, and the miner or miners directly interested, or is of a scope too large to be so settled and adjusted, shall be referred to a permanent joint committee, to be called a Board of Conciliation, to consist of six persons, appointed as hereinafter provided. That is to say, if there shall be a division of a whole region into three districts, in each of which there shall exist an organization representing a majority of the mine workers of such district, one of said Board of Conciliation shall be appointed by each of said organizations, and three other persons shall be appointed by the operators, the operators in each of said districts appointing one person.

The Board of Conciliation thus constituted shall take up and consider any question referred to it as aforesaid, hearing both parties to the controversy, and such evidence as may be laid before it by either party; and any award made by a majority of such Board of Conciliation shall be final and binding on all parties. If, however, the said board is unable to decide any question submitted, or point related thereto, that question or point shall be referred to an umpire, to be appointed at the request of said board, by one of the Circuit Judges of the Third Judicial Circuit of the United States, whose decision shall be final and binding in the premises.

The members of the Board of Conciliation are, on the part of the operators: W. L. Connell, chairman, of Scranton; S. D. Warriner, of Wilkes-Barre; R. C. Luther, of Pottsville. On the part of the miners: T. D. Nichols, secretary, of Scranton; W. H. Dettrey, of Hazleton; and John Fahy, of Pottsville. The accompanying cut is reproduced from a photograph of the board in session at the time of the reference to Judge Gray, Mr. Luther being absent.

W. L. CONNELL, Ch'man, Scranton — W. H. DETTREY, Hazleton — JOHN FAHY, Pottsville — S. D. WARRINER, Wilkes-Barre — T. D. NICHOLS, Sec'y, Scranton

THE ANTHRACITE BOARD OF CONCILIATION

The reference of the particular question in controversy to Judge Gray, who served as chairman of the Strike Commission, it is thus seen, was an act entirely beyond the provisions for arbitration contained in the award. It was a voluntary, mutual act, to whose outcome both sides are pledged to adhere. It was performed after the official umpire, Carroll D. Wright, had rendered a decision adverse to the operators, to the effect that the wages of the check-weigher employed at the request of a majority of the workers in any mine must be deducted from the wages of all the workers in that mine. The representatives of the operators upon the Board of Conciliation declined to accept this decision as official, claiming that it had not been made at the request of the Board, but at the request of one of its members, Mr. Nichols. Thereupon the representatives of the miners offered to refer the entire interpretation of the subject of check-weighers and dock bosses (involved, as will be explained, in the fifth award of the Strike Commission) to Judge Gray. The operators' half of the Board would not agree to this unrestricted reference. Instead, they insisted upon the following form of reference, to which the miners on the Board finally assented:

The question at issue is whether the resolution of the Conciliation Board of July 9, 1903, conflicts with Mr. Wright's findings in the case of grievance No. 106, concerning this question, and if the resolution still remains effective; or whether it was annulled by the declaration of Mr. Wright in the case of grievance No. 106, and in order to settle this question, and to avoid any further delay or friction, the operators' and miners' representatives now propose to refer the question at issue to Judge Gray.

If, after a proper presentation of the facts to him, he will find that the resolution of the Conciliation Board of July 9, 1903, is still effective, then, in order that the whole text of the Anthracite Strike Commission's 5th award relating to check weighmen and check docking bosses shall receive a proper interpretation, the operators and miners agree that the said 5th award shall be submitted to Judge Gray, and if his interpretation shall be at variance with that given by the Board of Conciliation, in its unanimously adopted resolution of July 9, 1903, the operators and miners agree that the said resolution shall be formally withdrawn and that a new resolution of the Board of Conciliation will be adopted in conformity with Judge Gray's finding.

There was an interesting colloquy at the meeting of the Board next following this reference. Col. Wright, the umpire, was present, and at the conclusion of hearing several cases submitted to him for decision, remarked informally: "I am highly gratified by the action of the Board in referring the check-weighing matter to Judge Gray. I do not regard that action as reflecting upon my decision in the premises. I still hold that for me to have decided otherwise would have vacated the award of the Commission, and that I could not bring myself to do. I regard this reference as preventing a repetition of the anthracite strike, with all its resultant disaster to the country."

"Oh, our objection to your decision," exclaimed Mr. Warriner, a representative of the operators on the Board, "was not as to its merits, but as to its application. The operators would not impugn your opinion. We shall abide by the decision of Judge Gray, whatever it may be."

"Yes, we also shall abide by his decision, whatever it may be," responded Mr. Nichols, of the miners; "but I do not hesitate to say in the presence of Mr. Warriner, now that the reference to Judge Gray has been made, what I would not say before, lest it be construed as a threat, and that is that the situation was very serious—far more serious than Mr. Warriner apprehended."

The following is the text of the Commission's fifth award, whose disputed interpretation and application caused the danger of another anthracite strike:

That whenever requested by a majority of the contract miners of any colliery, check weighmen or check docking bosses, or both, shall be employed. The wages of said check weighmen and check docking bosses shall be fixed, collected, and paid by the miners, in such manner as the said miners shall by a majority vote elect; and when requested by a majority of said miners, the operators shall pay the wages fixed for check weighmen and check docking bosses, out of deductions made proportionately from the earnings of the said miners on such basis as the majority of said miners shall determine.

The difficulty arises out of the method of paying the wages of check weighers and check docking bosses. As they are employed in the interests of the miners, it is conceded that the miners should pay their wages. But should the minority of the miners in a colliery, who do not care for this protection, be forced to pay for it? And how shall the money be collected? If all the miners are to pay, can a proportionate assessment be legally withheld from the wages of the minority without their assent? If the minority refuse to make an assignment to the company for this purpose, should they be protected in their refusal by the operators? Or should they be required to make an assignment as a condition of employment? Would such a requirement be legal? If not, could the assent of the miners to the award of the Commission be regarded as waiving their constitutional rights to the extent of its terms?

The operators' side of the case that has been referred to Judge Gray is stated by Mr. Warriner, of the Conciliation Board, and superintendent of the Lehigh Valley Railroad Company, to be based upon two facts, viz.:

First—The Board of Conciliation at one time passed upon the check weighmen question, and its action gave sanction to a plan which was then and is now pleasing to the operators. That plan was to collect the wages for a check weighman from the men employed at a colliery who requested the appointment of said check weighman.

Second—The operators object to the opinion of Umpire Wright, which reverses the above plan and sustains the contention of the United Mine Workers that the wages for the check weighman should be collected proportionately from all the men at any colliery where the majority of the men request it The objection of the operators is that in the first place the check weighman question has been dealt with, decided, and is therefore dismissed by the Board of Conciliation, and secondly, that the opinion furnished Mr. Nichols by Umpire Wright was a personal one at the solicitation of Mr. Nichols, and was not asked for by the Board, and hence is not to be considered binding.

The resolution adopted by the Board of Conciliation on July 9, 1903, to which Mr. Warriner refers, provided that the person elected by the miners as check docking boss should be accepted by the operator, and that his wages "shall be paid by the miners requesting such appointment"; and that for this purpose the employer "will make the deduction from the earnings of such miners as make a legal assignment."

Mr. Nichols, of the miners' representatives in the Board, claims that the position of the operators would in effect vacate the award of the Strike Commission. He submits that the Board is itself in the nature of an umpire; that the Board had not limited its action to a technical detail in another case, that of Coes Bros. & Co., but had passed upon points not submitted to it, so that it was inconsistent for the operators to object to Umpire Wright's decision on the ground that it went beyond the specific point submitted to him. Mr. Nichols argued that the entire interpretation of the fifth award of the Commission should be referred to an umpire, and that it should not be restricted to the technical form presented on behalf of the operators. He held that the question at issue was the observance of that award; that the agreement of the miners to abide by the decision of the Commission would absolve the operators from legal responsibility for making a deduction from the wages of all miners to pay check weighers elected by the miners. In conclusion, Mr. Nichols says: "We believe that we have done all that we can, consistent with the responsibility of taking care of the interests of the miners, to bring harmony out of disagreement."

With these arguments, the case went to Judge Gray.

WILL LABOR MAKE CONCESSIONS FOR A SHORTER WORK-DAY?

ITS LEADERS AND EDITORS DISCUSS GRANTING TEMPORARILY LOWER WAGES OR UNRESTRICTED OUTPUT FOR FEWER HOURS OF TOIL.

The voice of organized labor, in answer to questions relating to the proposed shorter work-day, is heard in a collection of opinions, here presented, of its leaders and of editors of labor periodicals. These opinions are a response by wage-earners to the symposium of employers upon the same subject which appeared in the August number of The Monthly Review. That symposium revealed a prevalence of assent among employers to the desirability of a shorter work-day as an abstract proposition. Most of their qualifications or objections were based upon the assumption that fewer hours of labor would increase the cost of production. Many employers urged that workers, as a consideration for fewer hours, should reduce this assumed increase in cost of production either by accepting temporary lower wages during an adjustment of trade and prices to the new condition, or by removing what the employers claimed to be arbitrary restrictions upon the quantity of production.

Labor's response to the employers was obtained by asking its prominent leaders and guides the following questions:

"Do you believe that organized labor should be willing to make the concession, either of temporarily lower wages or of unrestricted output, in return for a shorter work-day?"

"Do you believe that a shorter work-day lessens production, or increases the labor cost of production?"

The collection of opinions thus gathered is of great value and interest. The symposium reveals a high order of thought and a widely diffused understanding of the philosophy of the shorter work-day in its relation to production, consumption, domestic and foreign markets, wages, prices, legislation, trade agreements and the standard of American citizenship. It is a valuable contribution to the current discussion of the desirability and practicability of the shorter work-day which, at first centering about the eight-hour bill for government contracts, now under consideration by the Department of Commerce and Labor, has extended to the social and economic aspects of fewer hours of daily work and has developed the existence of a demand on the part of employes for fewer hours that cannot be denied recognition.

Out of the replies received, some fifty have been collated, representing many distinct national industries and, of course, a far greater number of crafts and a vast multitude of wage-earners. The editorial expressions range from New England to the Pacific. The representative character of these replies will be perceived by a mere glance at the titles in labor organizations and the callings of the writers. A perusal of the text of the replies will be necessary to appreciate their pertinence and acumen and, with few exceptions, the spirit of amity and the desire to attain the highest good of the community at large that animates them all. They are a notable evidence of the absence of enmity toward capital or of class hatred among the leaders of labor.

An analysis of the replies indicates that approximately 36 per cent. of their writers are willing to make, in return for a shorter work-day, the concession either of temporarily lower wages or of unrestricted output. Only ten replies would refuse any concession whatever. It is to be noted that this result is to some extent affected by a misunderstanding of some of the writers as to the purpose of the suggestion of temporary lower wages. That purpose was intended to be understood as purely tactical, with the idea that the concession, at least in some industries, might increase the willingness of employers to grant the shorter day, and with the further idea that existing wages would be restored as soon as the industry had adjusted itself to the new condition.

To confusion upon this point may be attributed the fact that about half of the replies oppose, and a few of them bitterly, any reduction of wages whatever. For this denial, a variety of reasons is advanced. Several writers assert that the present rate of wages is barely sufficient for existence; that even now many wage-earners are forced to deny themselves a full allowance of the necessities of life; that lower wages would lower the standard of living below the physical welfare and self-respect of the American working-man. Others assert, more moderately, that the present wage for a day of nine or ten hours would be only a fair equivalent for eight hours' work. An allied opinion is that the present margin of profit upon production is so large that the employer should rightly bear the entire additional labor cost, if any. Others argue, from experience in industries where the eight-hour day already prevails, that the shorter day increases production and lessens its cost, so that there would be no reason for lower wages. Another argument offered is that lower wages would lessen consumption, wage-earners constituting 95 per cent. of the consumers; and that this would result in over-production and injury to the employers. Coupled with this is the theory that lower wages, through diminishing the home market, would force manufacturers more than ever to enter into competition in foreign markets.

About a score of writers favor temporary reduction, all insisting that it must be only temporary.

Several would make the concession only where lower wages would not reduce the earnings of the worker below the comfort line. Others regard this as a proposition to be answered according to the conditions in each industry. Several regard the permanent benefit of a shorter day as worth a temporary sacrifice, which would forward the movement. One writer esteems leisure as an asset; and another declares that where eight hours now prevail, the workers would prefer a reduction of wages to a return to the longer day for the same pay.

The other suggested concession, that of removal of arbitrary restrictions of output, evoked at least a dozen denials, several of them very emphatic, that such restrictions exist in the writers' crafts, together with declarations that it is the sincere policy of unionism to place no limit upon the amount to be done by any worker in a given time.

But nearly a score of replies declare that restrictions (thus assuming them to exist) should be removed for economic reasons. They pronounce restriction short-sighted, because increased productivity is essential to higher wages. One writer remarks that only ordinary "gumption" is needed to perceive that union workers should strive "to produce the most in the least time possible." "The only limit should be the normal capacity" of the worker, remarks another. But these advocates of unrestrained energy protest against the "pace-maker" among workers, that is, against pitting workers against those of exceptional skill, strength or swiftness. Others believe that restriction will voluntarily disappear, because of the greater energy and willingness of workers. Only one writer advances the theory that restriction is necessary to prevent throwing large numbers out of work through over-production.

About three-fifths of the replies declare that the shorter work-day will not increase the labor cost of production. In support of this claim, the most important argument is that which cites the proof of experience in industries where the eight-hour day prevails, notably in the building trades. The replies from these trades have been grouped, and the especial consideration which they merit is given them further on.

Other reasons urged why the cost of production would not be increased are because of the greater zest of the short-day worker; because (in some industries) machinery would be run longer hours, by more shifts, thus lessening fixed charges on plant; because the total output would be greater; because the refreshed workers will welcome the sound of the morning whistle; because the manhood of the worker would spur him to do his utmost for the employer who had granted a boon. The writers who urge that the shorter work-day would increase the number employed, thus creating the same output as in the longer day, of course contradict those who assert that the same number of workers will produce in eight hours a result equal to their output in ten.

Only ten replies admit, more or less distinctly, that the shorter day would increase the labor cost of production. One reason adduced is that machinery is already speeded to the limit, and fewer hours would necessarily mean less product per worker. Against this is the claim that the output would be greater but that its cost would at first be higher, pending adjustment of the industry. One writer declares that the higher cost of production would be offset by increased purchasing power of the home market. Another avers that decreased output would remedy present over-production and cause steadier employment.

A few writers volunteer the opinion that a uniform eight-hour day can be accomplished only by legislation. One writer favors legislation because the shorter work-day is of the same public policy as the public schools and the statutory regulation of child labor. Another believes that unions should debate political questions and vote for candidates who favor an eight-hour law. Several advocate national voluntary trade agreements, so that the shorter day would be uniform, and to that end favor more thorough organization of both employers and employed. One writer discusses at length the history of the battle for the prevalent eight-hour day in the building trades and its effect upon wages, output, cost and morale.

With notable enthusiasm, several dwell upon the social and moral effect of fewer hours of toil. They point to better, brighter, more attractive homes, an uplifted citizenship and consequent national prosperity. Several of them take pains to contradict the notion that workers would abuse added leisure, and declare that long hours mean ignorance, poverty, drunkenness and a degraded citizenship.

BEST SERVICE, NO LOWER WAGES.

W. R. Fairley, Member National Executive Board, United Mine workers of America:—I am glad to notice that the prevailing opinion among employers of labor is in favor of a shorter work-day as an abstract proposition. But they claim that it will increase the cost of production and urge that workers as a consideration for fewer hours should reduce this increased cost of production either by accepting lower wages or by removing what the employers claim to be arbitrary restrictions upon the quantity of production.

I believe that organized labor should be willing to remove any arbitrary restrictions on outputs to secure the shorter work-day, that they ought to render the best service of which they are capable, so that outputs would not be decreased and thereby increase the cost of production. I am not in favor of lower wages, even temporarily, to secure a shorter work-day.

After years of close observation and experience, I do not believe that shorter hours lessens production. If it does, it is only temporarily until the system adapts itself to the changed condition created, and therefore does not increase the labor cost of production.

RESTRICTIONS MUTUALLY INJURIOUS.

John D. Pringle, Editor of The Labor World, Pittsburg:—In answer to the first of the two questions you forward me, I beg to state that I certainly deem it right that organized labor should grant unrestricted output in return for a shorter work-day. This concession would apply more to time workers than to piece workers. Under present industrial conditions, restrictions that are put upon production by some of our labor unions are injurious to trade and react disastrously to both employer and employed. Experience has led me to believe that a reduction in wage is not necessarily requisite for a shortening of the work-day.

Your second question is comprehensive, and brief statements must suffice for arguments. I do not think that a shorter work-day "lessens production," and therefore does not increase the cost of production. The natural course of industrial evolution has proven this to be true. Except in rare cases shorter hours of work have actually resulted in increased production, increased profits and wages and cheaper commodities. The history of various trades proves this.

In the mining industry, even before machinery was introduced, the highest per capita output of the English miner was when his work-day was shortest. The same holds good, as a rule, in this country. A shorter work-day without any artificial restrictions on the output tends to supply the workman with a motive to do his best, and particularly when he works "by the piece." It is the motive that maintains the standard and keeps down cost of production.

AN ARGUMENT FROM EXPERIENCE.

William S. Carter, Grand Secretary-Treasurer Brotherhood of Locomotive Firemen:—I believe that with the introduction of improved methods, a shorter work-day does not lessen production or increase the labor cost of production. If a like cause will produce a like effect, we may reasonably expect the reduction from a ten-hour day to an eight-hour day to produce the same result that the reduction from a twelve-hour to a ten-hour day produced. Then, why not simplify an intricate problem by reducing an unknown quantity to a known quantity, and ask: "Do you believe a shorter work-day did lessen production or did increase the labor cost of production?" I believe that with a shorter work-day came increased production and decreased labor cost of production.

You also ask, "Do you believe that organized labor should be willing to make the concession, either of temporarily lower wages or of unrestricted output, in return for a shorter work-day?" I have said that the shorter work-day neither lessened production nor increased the labor cost of production. Then why should have organized labor accepted lower wages? Wages are not lower with the present ten hour day than they were with the former twelve-hour day. Then, why should wages be lower with the coming eight-hour day than with the present ten-hour day?

Now, what is meant by "unrestricted output"? If it is meant that a locomotive engineer should be permitted to operate his engine until, exhausted by continuous labor, he falls asleep and hurls to destruction a train laden with passengers or with fellow-employes, I do not believe that organized labor should make the concession.

If it is meant by "unrestricted output" that a task shall be set by an employer for a hundred employes to perform, which task is fixed by the ability, strength and endurance of the ablest and strongest of that hundred, I do not believe that organized labor should make the concession.

If it is meant by "unrestricted output" that employes should not place a maximum limit to the amount of work performed in a given time, I believe that organized labor should not only make the concession, but prohibit such practice, should it exist, among members of labor unions.

Continuous improvements in "labor-saving" machinery have reduced the labor cost of production until a comparatively small number of shoemakers can produce more shoes than our eighty millions of people can consume. There can be no doubting that modern machines have "saved labor"—but for whom? For the laborer himself only as the work-day has been shortened. For the employer, as he has added to his wealth. For the consumer, as he has obtained the product cheaper.

Since labor-saving machinery has performed its part in the development of this country, the employing class has profited so greatly that the world now stands amazed at the accumulated wealth of the "American Trusts." Since labor-saving machinery has performed its part in the development of this country, the American consumer has learned to class former luxuries as every-day necessities. Since labor-saving machinery has performed its part in the development of this country, the American workingman finds that his labor has been "saved," that his work-day has been shortened only as his trade union has possessed the power to extort from the employing class.

The working-man has now turned to the law-making body of the nation for some of the good things which that body has so lavishly bestowed upon others. They have asked that the United States Government stipulate in all contracts entered into with manufacturers that working-men shall be employed only eight hours per day in prosecuting those contracts. So far, the law-making body of the nation has denied working-men this request.

FAIR EMPLOYERS DESERVE NON-RESTRICTION.

W. C. Platell, National Vice-President Metal Polishers, Buffers, Platers, Brass Molders, Brass and Silver Workers' Union of N. A.:—In reply to Question 1, I will say that this is a very broad question, and a great deal depends upon the fairness which may be displayed by both sides in the controversy. I honestly believe that where the employer shows a disposition to be fair in the matter, organized labor should not restrict the output in any shape. But it has been my sad experience in a number of cases that where the output was restricted it was in cases where the men worked by the piece.

I would therefore frankly say that where any employer is fair enough to establish a shorter work-day, without any reduction in wages, the employes should in turn do all they can in the way of getting out as much work for such an employer without killing themselves, and thus show to him that they are at least willing to play fair.

In reply to Question 2, I will say that I do not believe that the shorter work-day lessens the production, and I do not believe that in the end the cost of labor is increased. Here again it depends upon the fairness and spirit of good will shown on both sides, for it has been my personal experience—and I have enjoyed the shorter work-day for over three years—that where men work short hours, and they are treated fairly and like human beings, that before the end of the first year they will produce as much or nearly as much as they did under the ten-hour system. Men who are only required to work eight or nine hours per day without having their pay reduced will, if they have any manhood in them at all, work for the interests of the employer granting them the shorter work-day, and show to him in many ways that the concessions he has granted his employes are not thrown to the winds. A man working shorter hours feels more like working when the whistle blows in the morning than the ones who do not enjoy the shorter hours, and when the whistle blows at night he is happy in the thought, knowing that he has dealt fairly and honestly by his employer, and he hastens home to spend a couple of hours of daylight at least with his wife, sweetheart or family. As one who enjoys the shorter work-day, I find that instead of production being lessened, in the end it will almost be as much as it was before the hours were reduced, and the cost of labor will be no more considering the amount produced in less hours of labor. Hasten the shorter work-day, give us fair and humane employers, and the organized employes will in more ways than one show their appreciation.

NO RESTRICTION, IF NO PACE-MAKER.

Edgar A. Agard, Member Executive Board, Glass Bottle Blowers' Association of the United States and Canada:—I believe in the highest possible standard of life for the workers. To secure and maintain this standard, a shorter work-day is necessary. If it is impossible to reduce the hours of labor in any given industry and still leave the employer a fair profit, without corresponding reduction in wages, then I believe that labor should concede a lower wage scale in return for a shorter work-day: Provided, however, that the lower wage does not fall below the comfort line. Any enterprise which demands the entire time of those employed therein, at a wage so low as to make it impossible for them to save something for a time of future idleness, without denying themselves present comforts, is a curse to organized society and has no right to live.

I would also favor an unrestricted output, not only as a means toward the securing of a reduction in the hours of labor, but at all other times, if manufacturers will cease their pitting of the man of exceptional strength, skill and swiftness, like a gladiator, against the willing worker who is simply the average man.

Where the hours of labor are destructively long, that is, of such length that human endurance goes to the limit each day, I do not believe that shortening the work-day will decrease production or add to the labor cost thereof. Upon the other hand, if the hours are more humane, I certainly am of the opinion that a shorter work-day means an increased labor cost, because of a decrease in production.

I further believe that ultimately a shorter work-day will be more greatly to the advantage of the employer than to the employe. That it seems to be a vexed question I will admit, but if the parties who are primarily interested will get together for the purpose of agreeing upon some plan to bring about its consummation, and not for the purpose of proving that it cannot be done, or that the other side is illogical and unfair, I am sure that a plan could be agreed upon without any great difficulty, which would be injurious to none, but fair and beneficial to all.

LEISURE AN ASSET.

John A. Dyche, General Secretary-Treasurer International Ladies' Garment Workers' Union:—I believe that organized labor should be willing to accept lower wages in return for a shorter work-day. Leisure, even if it possesses no exchange value and one cannot deposit it with the banker, is yet as useful as any other form of wealth. A demand for a shorter work-day at the same rate of pay means not only a demand for increased pay per hour, but such a demand may also involve a rearrangement in the factory which may cause more inconvenience to the employer than an increase of pay. The resistance on the part of the employer may be such that the game may not be worth the candle. Wherever a shorter work-day will increase the cost of production—and this will probably be the case in a good many instances—the increase will only be temporary.

The restriction on production practised by some unions is to my mind quite unjustifiable. It is the result of a short-sighted policy on the part of the organizations pursuing it. Some of our unions seem to forget that the increase of the productivity of labor is the most important factor in a permanent increase of wages. I believe, however, that the restriction of the hours of labor by legal enactment to be more economically advantageous and socially useful than by voluntary agreement between manufacturers and employers. Voluntary restrictions of the hours of labor will give an opportunity to the sweater and tenement-house employer to compete with the regular manufacturer by working his hands abnormally long hours; while under legal restrictions competition can only be carried on by adopting better methods of production and by introducing new machinery which must lead to the concentration of capital and the elimination of the sweater and tenement-house worker as a factor in production.

INDIVIDUAL CAPACITY GAUGES OUTPUT.

J. E. Mulkey, Editor of The Advance Advocate, Official Organ of the International Brotherhood of Maintenance-of-Way Employes:—Where the wages of labor are sufficient to enable the worker to submit to a temporary reduction of wages without depriving his family of the ordinary comforts of life, if the hours of labor are such that the worker does not have reasonable time for rest and recreation, it would be proper and beneficial for him to submit to a reasonable reduction of wages in return for a proportionate reduction of hours.

In regard to output, that should be limited only to the normal capacity of the worker, and one worker's capacity should never be gauged by that of another.

Where a man is required to work longer hours than his physical nature will stand, a reduction of hours would tend to increase his output per hour until his normal capacity for endurance is reached. To assert in a general way that shortening the working-day would increase the output of labor would be equivalent to saying that the greatest output would result from no labor at all. This applies also to the labor cost of production.

NO LIMIT TO AMBITION.

John F. McNamee, Editor Locomotive Firemen's Magazine:—In reply to your two questions would say: First—It is a question of considerable importance to determine to what extent laboring men could sustain a reduction in their earnings, and yet provide themselves with the necessities of life at the present prices of those articles which they require for their subsistence, and this is a question that should call forth the best thoughts of our political and industrial economists. While it might be politic on the part of organized labor in order to secure the benefits of a shorter work-day to temporarily endure a reduction of earnings and run chances for securing subsequent restorations to the former standard, it is an indisputable fact that such a course would work a decided hardship upon a large majority of wage-earners. In view of the immense fortunes that are being built up all about us as the joint result of the investment of capital and the expenditure of labor, it would seem that the public welfare could best be subserved by the burden of this change being sustained by the employing classes.

As to the subject of unrestricted output, I will state it as my belief that the welfare of organized labor would be best furthered by unrestricted output under any and all conditions. There may be reasons for restricting the capacity of the laborer in certain trades of which I have no knowledge, but it would seem to me to be contrary to the ultimate well-being of any organized craft to place restrictions upon the ambitions, skill and attainments of its individual members.

Second—It is my opinion that a reduction in the number of hours of daily labor would have but a temporary effect upon the volume of production, if it would have any. Perhaps it might partially disorganize some branches of industry until the new conditions could be so systematized as to produce the maximum results with the amount of effort expended. The individual laborer with more time at his disposal occasioned by the shorter work-day would undoubtedly have greater opportunity to give thought and attention to the development of his skill and ability, and as a natural consequence invest greater vigor and productive effort in his work during the shorter day than when the hours are long and wearisome.

PRODUCE MOST, IN LEAST POSSIBLE TIME.

John L. Britton, Member National Board, United Mine Workers of America:—Do you believe that organized labor should be willing to make the concession, either of temporarily lower wages or of unrestricted output, in return for a shorter work-day? Answer: No, to temporarily lowering the wages. The wages are too low already in lots of trades and callings, and to bring them lower temporarily would not help matters or bring the results that organized labor is aiming at, viz., a living wage.

There should be no restrictions on output, because, if intelligence or gumption rules—and it ought to rule,—we as progressive trade-unionists must aim to produce the most in the least time possible.

Do you believe that a shorter work-day lessens production or increases the labor cost of production? Answer: No to first paragraph of this question, because, with the advancement made by machinery, there is specializing in most every branch and up-to-date methods in most every calling or trade. I believe it can be shown that these increase production, and if it can be shown it answers the second paragraph, for if we can produce more in a given time, it must necessarily lower the cost of production.

UNIONS DO NOT RESTRICT OUTPUT.

W. D. Mahon, International President Amalgamated Association of Street and Electric Railway Employes of America:—No, the shorter work-day does not increase the cost of production at all. As to the restriction of output, there is no such a thing practised by the trade-union movement. The trade-union seeks the reduction of the hours of toil, but in no way does that interfere with or restrict the output. We say at the present time, eight hours should be the work-day. This does not in any way interfere with the shop, factory, or any other business, so far as the output is concerned.

We represent street and electrical railway workers. Some years ago we labored fourteen and sixteen hours per day. We have brought the work-day down in many cases to a nine-hour work-day, but the shorter work-day does not interfere or restrict in any way the operation of the roads. When a man has completed his nine-hour work-day, the car goes right on and is operated by another. It is true that during these past years wages have from time to time increased, but that does not affect your question. That has been due to the increased cost of living and other environments and conditions that surrounded us. The charge that the trade-union interferes and restricts the output is a proposition raised by those who are either ignorant of the subject or else by those who are seeking some pretext to destroy the trade-union movement.

THE CHEER OF SHORT HOURS.

S. M. Sexton, Editor Mine Workers' Journal, Indianapolis:—In reply to both questions would answer, No. The questions are so entwined that it is hard to disintegrate them so as to answer clearly. For instance, Question 2 implies a doubt as to the proposition in the latter part of Question 1. I state with all confidence that shorter hours do not lessen production; therefore, to accept lower wages for the same or larger output is giving something for nothing, a proposition not based upon equity.

When the coal miners worked twelve or fifteen hours per day the average tonnage for the days worked was a little over three tons. To-day, in the same mine, same height of coal with the same tools, the same men average over four tons.

Under the long-hour system the miner had to take his small sons to help him. Under the shorter hours he does the work himself and sends his sons to school.

I do not pretend to analyze the mental process which makes a man readier to attack a large and difficult piece of work when he knows that he will not have to toil from sun to sun, and the hesitation and disinclination the same man exhibits when he attacks similar tasks when he knows that he must toil from the "rising of the sun until the going down of the same." But the fact exists, and the cheerful and hearty manner in which the short-hour man sets himself to work and keeps to work more than overbalances the advantages he gains from the same pay.

The short-hour man is rested; his muscles and brain have become refreshed; he is eager to begin his task; gives it better attention and is able, from physiological reasons, to give it better attention. The long-hour man has not recovered from the toils of the previous day. He is stiff and sleepy, unconsciously careless. His body has not fully recuperated from the exhaustion of the previous day's toil; therefore, he is not as fit to render the same services as the short-hour man.

The overwhelming fact in favor of the shorter hour, the one that clears away all doubt as to whether hours lessen production, is the fact that the piece workers, like pick miners, printers, machinists, and bricklayers are the most urgent in the demand for shorter days.

If these men were not fully convinced they could earn more under the short-hour system they would not advocate it. If a printer could set 10,000 ems during a ten-hour day, the natural deduction is that he would set but 9,000 ems during nine hours. But the fact remains that since the nine-hour system has been adopted he sets nearer 11,000 ems.

Again, when the pick miner with the aid of his son could dig and load a little over three tons per day during the twelve hours, it seems a mathematical fact that he would mine and load a little over two tons with the hours reduced to eight. Yet the fact remains, impregnable to successful assault, that a reduction of hours increased his output.

Were a man a machine capable of being geared up to a certain number of revolutions per hour, of course the less number of hours he ran the less revolutions he would perform. But a man is not a machine, but a living, breathing, thinking, sentient being, and improves in health, morals, citizenship, manhood, when he is not used as a dumb, driven brute.

FEWER HOURS FOR EMPLOYER'S BENEFIT.

Thomas Taylor, Secretary Fall River Loom Fixers' Association:—In answer to your first question, I would say that where it was proved to the employe that such change was causing financial loss to his employer, so far as to make his business unprofitable, a mutual arrangement might be made where wages could be adjusted for the time being, until the normal balance of business that might be disturbed by the change could be restored.

If such an arrangement as the above could be carried out with regard to shorter hours, I believe the question of restricted output would settle itself, inasmuch as the working-man would then be an interested party as well as the manufacturer, and would naturally give his best service to secure the higher rate of wages.

With regard to your second question, I would say that I thoroughly believe in the shorter working-day as ultimately being to the advantage of the employer and employed. It would be conducive to the working-man's benefit, morally, socially and physically, and in my opinion the employers would eventually reap the benefit in a larger output and of better quality.

CONCESSION CONSIDERED FAIR.

C. E. Layman, Member Board of Directors, Order of Railroad Telegraphers:—I believe that organized labor should be willing to make the concession, either of temporarily lowering wages or unrestricted output, in return for a shorter work-day.

I do not believe that a shorter work-day lessens production or increases the labor cost of production.

EIGHT HOURS NEAR AT HAND.

J. L. Feeney, Editor "The International Bookbinder," Washington:—I believe that the eight-hour day will be the universal work-day in all branches of skilled labor before many years have passed away. In our branch of trade, bookbinding, our craft has received the eight-hour day in several cities, and it is expected that a general demand will be made for same on or before January 1, 1906.

I do not believe that any local union of our International Brotherhood will be allowed to concede a decrease in wages for the shorter day. It cannot be denied that the eight-hour day will lessen production, but not to the great extent that some manufacturers believe it will. A slight increase in the price of a manufactured article where there is a minimum profit will more than compensate the manufacturer for granting the shorter day to his workers.

There are but very few trade organizations that limit the output of its members, and such trades, we believe, are now enjoying the eight-hour day, but where there is a restriction upon the quantity of production in any branch of trade where the workers are now under the ten or nine-hour schedule, we believe a slight increase in the output should be conceded, but no decrease whatever in wages.

TEMPORARY REDUCTION; NO RESTRICTION.

John B. Lennon, General Secretary Journeymen Tailors' Union of America:—In reply to Question 1, I deny positively and without reservation that the trade-unions restrict output. It may have been true to some extent a number of years ago, and there may even be isolated unions where it is still practised to some extent, but as a rule the trade-union movement does not stand for the restriction of output by its members. I believe that where the hours of labor are reduced that there should be a temporary reduction in the wage until such time as the industry can adjust itself to the new conditions that come with the establishment of an eight-hour work-day.

In reply to Question 2, I believe unquestionably that, as applied to industries in general, the reduction of the hours of labor to eight means less product by the same number of employes as were previously employed ten hours a day. Were this not true, one of the greatest of all the reasons for the demand for the eight-hour work-day would disappear, to wit, an opportunity for the unemployed to secure work.

As to whether the cost of production is increased or not under the eight-hour work-day, I am not prepared to answer specifically. Some employers with whom I have talked, who should be experts on this phase of the matter, have stated that it did not increase the cost; others have held to the contrary. A careful investigation would probably demonstrate the truth as to this phase of the question.

LESS HOURS, GREATER SPEED.

Albert Hibbert, General Secretary United Textile Workers of America:—So far as the textile workers are concerned, the cost of labor would not enter the question so much as in other industries, because of the fact that a very large percentage work by the piece. I believe in a shorter work-day, and am of the opinion that in a day of eight hours, if in universal practice, no industry would suffer.

I do not believe that a shorter work-day, unless carried to extremes, decreases production. In 1892 the hours of labor were reduced in the State of Massachusetts from 60 to 58 per week, and the production is greater to-day than when the operatives worked 60 hours. Of course, the difference is accounted for by the extra speed put on the machine.

PAY WORK FOR ITS QUALITY.

J. E. Schwarz, Vice-President Retail Clerks' International Protective Association:—I do not think it is necessary for labor to reduce wages on the unrestricted output, for I feel that good workmen should be paid according to their work, and if they can produce more than the poor men, they should naturally be paid accordingly. I feel that the manufacturers in co-operation can readily regulate the matter of higher salary being put in the product manufactured even if he has to pay more, and at the same time get more for his goods.

It naturally would appear that a shorter work-day would mean an increased cost of production; but if labor is unrestricted, I think the difference could be made up.

LESS HOURS FOR MEN, MORE FOR MILLS.

James F. Fitzgerald, International Representative, Brotherhood Paper Makers, Pulp, Sulphite and Paper Mill Workers:—I do not believe that organized labor could accept a reduction in wages as a return for the eight-hour day, and I do not see why it should be asked when it has been clearly demonstrated by several manufacturers of paper that the eight-hour work-day ensures better dividends to them. For example, in our line, pulp and paper-making, the working days per week are from Monday, 7 o'clock A. M., till Saturday, 6 o'clock P. M., there being no work done Saturday night, Sunday or Sunday night, and the working hours for the mills giving the eight-hour work-day are from 7 o'clock P. M. Sunday night till 7 o'clock A. M. Sunday. In other words, the manufacturer giving his employes the eight-hour work-day is able to run his mill 24 hours more per week than on the long day, thereby lessening to a great extent the fixed charges on his plant. While I do not believe that the employes could accept a reduction in wages, I am in favor of running the pulp and paper mills more hours per week for the manufacturer giving his employes the eight-hour work-day. I have found that where the employes work the eight-hour day, the manufacturers generally agree that he is able to do enough extra and better work to offset the hours reduced from his day, and I have found the management of mills operated on the eight-hour day so well pleased with the results, both financially and in workmanship, that they could not be induced to return to the long hours per day.

I believe that the eight-hour day increases production, and decreases the cost of production, and I also believe in our line of business that we should increase the working days per week for the eight-hour manufacturers, over the long-hour-day manufacturers, which we are ready and willing to do.

TEMPORARY INCREASE OF COST.

George Preston, General Secretary-Treasurer, International Association of Machinists:—Replying to question No. 1, I beg to reply in the affirmative. Wherever it can be shown that the reduction of hours will increase the cost of the production I believe it would be good policy for the organized employes to accept a corresponding reduction of wages, believing as I do that said reduction of wages would only be temporary and would show a tendency to rise as the market became adjusted to the new conditions. As to the restricted output, this is not a feature in our organization, no man being limited to the amount of work he can perform in any one day.

Question No. 2. Do I believe that a shorter work-day lessens production or increases the labor of production? My answer to the first part of this question is No. In fact, I believe that the shorter work-day will have a tendency to increase production; first, because the workers, having more time for recuperation, will be handled more energetically while employed, and they will be apt to perform more effective labor than under the reduced hours. In reply to the second part of the question I would like to say that I believe reduction of the hours of labor will in a majority of instances increase the labor cost of production. The effect, however, would be only temporary, inasmuch as new methods and improved devices in productive work are more apt to be introduced under the shorter work-day than they are in the longer hour day.

FEWER HOURS, GREATER EFFICIENCY.

Thomas M. Nolan, Editor of The Union Label Magazine, Boston:—While answers to your questions must in some cases be governed by local conditions, I believe an eight-hour day would prove satisfactory to employer and employed.

It has been stated in trade and other papers that in some unions there is a rule for the restriction of output per hour or day. I do not know of such an arrangement in any industry in New England. It does not prevail in the printing or publishing trades.

As to what arrangement or concession might be made by members of different crafts in return for a shorter work-day, it would be based, as suggested, upon peculiar conditions applying to each trade which it would be difficult to cover in general terms. In securing the nine-hour day in the book and job branch of the printing trades there was no general curtailment of wages, in the greater number of cases the same wages being paid for nine and a half and nine hours as formerly prevailed for ten hours, and since the adoption of the shorter work-day (nine hours) there are cases in which wages are paid greater than those prevailing under a ten-hour day. While some employing printers have taken position against further shortening of the work-day, the time is not far distant when they will adopt the eight-hour day.

Another important point is that the general morale of the craft has advanced as the hours have decreased. Temperance, morality and a general uplifting tendency has been observed to a greater extent among the rank and file of the printing crafts This is referred to, because of criticism expressed by certain employers, and their solicitude whether it would be dangerous to reduce the hours, as the men would then be inclined to spend the time in saloons. This has been disproven so many times it seems those using it are at desperate straits for arguments against the shorter work-day.

Where agreements cannot be made between employer and employed upon a national basis—this by far being the better way, as is obvious—it would be well for both parties to arrange conferences providing for a gradual reduction in the hours to eight per day, and if the shorter work-day can be secured in no other way employes might accept a reduction for a certain time to be mutually agreed upon, pending its universal adoption that is, providing wages already were not below a living rate. The shorter work-day is the "ultima thule"—given that, the question of wages will adjust itself.

So far as I have observed in my own and other trades decreasing the hours has not lessened production nor increased the labor cost to the employer.

GREATER ACTIVITY, EQUAL OUTPUT.

B. A. McCormick, Correspondent Div. 332, Amalgamated Association Street and Electric Railway Employes of America:—In my experience, both as an employer and employe, better results can be obtained by the granting of shorter hours than ten per day, and the paying of such wages that will permit men to live comfortably and so conduct themselves as to gain the respect of the community. While often money is the root of evil, it is also the source of much good, and the good wife of a man earning fairly good wages will make his home so attractive that he will shun places to which the poor man frequently resorts for an extremely unhealthy change of scene.

With an eight-hour work-day the employe feels that his efforts in his employer's behalf are appreciated, and this will produce harmony and good-fellowship between what I may call (apologetically) the two classes, and certainly lengthen the life of a piece of machinery which has become a valuable adjunct in the shop or mill.

NO LESS PRODUCTION, NO GREATER COST.

Philip Christ, Member Executive Board, National Brotherhood of Coal Hoisting Engineers:—In reply to your first question, I would like to say, Yes. In our business the employes have worked under the eight-hour system for nearly five years, and I am firmly convinced that should the time come when they should be compelled to choose between longer hours for the present wages or a reduction in wages but the shorter hours, they would certainly accept the reduction in wages.

In reply to the second question, I beg to say that in my personal experience the shorter day did not lessen the production, nor do I think that it has increased the cost of production. We are producing more under this eight-hour system than we did under the ten or twelve-hour system. We who have had a chance to try both systems do not agree that ten hours' work is as good as eight for an employe There is no more drunkenness now than prior to the change; less, I think.

STEADIER EMPLOYMENT, EQUAL OUTPUT.

C. E. James, Member General Executive Board, Boot and Shoe Workers' Union:—I am very much interested in the work of the Civic Federation, and believe that much benefit will result to both employers and employes through its efforts. I read with much interest the views expressed by various large employers of labor in your last issue as to the desirability of a shorter work-day, and am not surprised that most of them are favorable to a shorter work-day as an abstract proposition. This method of ascertaining the views of both employers and employes seem to me to be the very best means of starting a crusade for a shorter work-day.

As to your first question, I have no hesitancy in saying, that I believe that the most practical way of bringing about a shorter work-day (under the existing conditions) would be for organized labor to make the concession of temporarily lower wages, excepting of course, in those industries working under the piece price plan.

If both employers and employes were so well organized that a general eight-hour day could be arranged, so that the same condition would prevail in all industries, and no employer would be placed at a disadvantage because of his competitor being able to work his employes for a longer period, this would not be necessary. But under the prevailing condition I believe there are many employers who would be willing to grant a shorter work-day providing they could do so without their labor cost being greater than their competitors. In those industries where the piece price plan prevails this is not necessary, as whether the work-day is eight hours or twelve, the labor cost is equal.

(Continued on pages 9, 10, 11 and 12.)

MONTHLY REVIEW
OF THE
National Civic Federation

Offices: 281 Fourth Avenue, New York City
RALPH M. EASLEY, Editor

The Editor alone is responsible for any unsigned article or unquoted statement published in THE MONTHLY REVIEW.

Ten Cents per Copy; One Dollar per Year.

THE SHORTER WORK-DAY.

The attitude of organized labor toward the proposition to grant some concession in consideration of a shorter work-day, and the consensus of opinion of organized labor as to the economic and social effect of fewer hours of toil, are disclosed by the symposium presented in this issue. In the August number, the opinions of many large employers upon the same subject were published. It was shown that there is a general disposition among employers to assent to the desirability of the shorter work-day as an abstract proposition. Their objections were in the main based upon their belief that production would be lessened or its cost increased.

The desire of organized labor for the shorter work-day has no exceptions. That universal desire, it is now shown, is accompanied by a considerable willingness to quicken its realization by a temporary reduction of wages, or by the pledge of unrestricted output, when restriction is admitted. The belief is held by the majority of wage-earners that fewer hours of work would neither lessen production nor increase its cost. The experience of the building trades, where the eight-hour day has prevailed almost universally for several years, is cited as proof positive of this assertion.

The history of the eight-hour movement in the building trades shows that its initiation and progress have been the result of strikes. The import of the views of labor leaders and editors now is that the time is at hand when the movement can be extended in other trades through negotiation, without the use of the strike. They find apparent basis for this hope in the general recognition among employers of the economic benefit of the shorter work-day, if only it can be brought about gradually, so as not to disturb violently production and trade; uniformly, so that the innovation shall bear equally upon all; and upon such terms as shall not impair seriously the present margin of profit. The response of labor shows a disposition to meet these demands, where their necessity to business prosperity can be demonstrated.

Economists, leading publicists and journalists will next be invited to elucidate the general principles involved in the movement for fewer hours of toil. The purpose is to gather their well-considered thought upon the philosophy of the shorter work-day and its relation to industry, production, consumption, wages, and the cost and standard of living. Their disinterested judgment, following the expressions of both capital and labor, may be received as representing the attitude of the general public toward this subject.

STATISTICS THAT DO NOT APPLY.

Widespread comment and some criticism have been stirred by the bulletin of the Bureau of Labor at Washington, analyzing data of retail prices of food, wages and hours of labor, from 1890 to 1903. Partisan motives, sharply accentuated by a Presidental campaign, have caused both attack and defense of these data. From their economic consideration, these motives may be wholly excluded. The welfare of the individual wage-earner and its relation to the prosperity of the country at large may be considered quite apart from these arguments for or against the legislative and administrative policies of any political party.

What should interest labor and capital alike upon scientific ground, is the patent fact that this report of the Labor Bureau has no pertinent bearing upon the present capacity of wage earning, or upon the present cost of living; nor does its compiler claim that it has. Its figures, in that view, are properly subject only to such criticism or defense as professional statisticians may make of the method of their collection and classification. They share the fault, perhaps inevitable, of all governmental statistics. They may enlighten retrospect, but as to the immediate present they are out of date. Even more disappointing examples of delay are reports of State Commissioners of Labor. A report upon the "Growth of Industry in New York" has just made its appearance; yet this document is a part of the report of the Commissioner for 1902, and its statistics are no later than the year 1900.

The national labor bureau was confronted, while carrying forward its compilation, by an exceptional and sudden change in commercial and industrial conditions. It was as if the smooth pathway of its calculations had encountered an abrupt downward curve in prices and business activity that left its figures in the air.

The sharp midsummer panic of 1903, known as the "Wall Street panic," or "The millionaires' panic," had the wholesome effect of squeezing the water out of securities. To such dimensions had grown the rush to organize and reorganize industrial enterprises that their capitalization at that time was estimated at $6,000,000,000. The collapse of some, such as the shipbuilding trust, and the disclosure of the limitations of others, such as the steel trust, caused a shrinkage of prices that extended throughout almost the entire list of securities. These financial phenomena were not alone distressing to over-confident investors. They checked the activity of capital in many industries.

Of these, the most familiar is that of transportation. Railroad companies that a year ago regarded large additional facilities as necessary to their traffic suspended new construction, throwing into idleness many thousands of workers. Iron, steel and coal were affected along with transportation. The trade year began with the acceptance by the bituminous miners of a cut in wages of 7½ per cent. Among steel workers there was a cut of from 15 to 30 per cent. in the wage scale, while at the present time there is a strike in this industry against a cut of from 25 to 60 per cent. The 'longshoremen on the Great Lakes accepted a reduction of 10 per cent. in their wages. Almost simultaneously the textile industry encountered speculative values for raw material and a shrinking market for its product. The consequent effort to reduce wages closed New England cotton mills. The metal trade industries, employing molders, machinists, boilermakers, blacksmiths, etc., because of reduced orders began laying off men. Officers of the international unions of these trades became alarmed, and sent circular letters warning against demands for higher wages and expressing the hope that workers would be satisfied if they were able to maintain existing wages.

These are but the more conspicuous events directly affecting wages. But as it is a rule that in hard times lower wages are the economy of last resort, it is not surprising that the official figures for 1903 fail to disclose the lower earnings which did not become prevalent until about January, 1904.

The danger of a misapprehension of statistic· that do not apply to the present lies in its possible encouragement of mistaken tactics on the part of labor. For a series of years previous to 1903 there had been great business activity and large profits. Public opinion had strongly sympathized with the demand of organized labor that it share with capital the prosperity of the boom. Thus the captains of the wage-earners had been able to wrest many concessions from the captains of industry. When the period of shrinkage and depression arrived there was danger that the captains of wage-earners might not appreciate the changed conditions confronting them. The deciding factor in the ceaseless adjustment of the relations between capital and labor, public opinion, now recognized the fairness of a reasonable revision of wage scales. To continue demands for higher wages, which two years ago might have been warranted, was to fly in the face of forbidding circumstance. To strike against moderate reductions, as in the case of the meat strike, was to invite defeat in a contest most inopportune.

Conversely, there was danger that capital, with the opportunity to urge business necessity as a reason for economies, might push its reduction of wage scales to an unreasonable degree.

These are the reasons why both sides have been urged to moderation and to mutual forbearance, which would go far to secure the respect and future good-will of both. The belated official statistics of the labor bureau do not impair this counsel and should not change the policy of caution adopted generally last winter by leaders of labor and considerate employers.

UNIONS AND THE MILITIA.

An incident occurred during the recent convention of the International Typographical Union at St. Louis that has entirely escaped the notice of the daily press. Great prominence has been given to the isolated case at Schenectady, where a worker was expelled from a radical local union, because he was a member of a militia company. A committee reported adversely to the convention a resolution that "no member of the Typographical Union shall enlist in the service of any state in the United States as state guard, militiaman or ranger, under the penalty of expulsion and being barred from reinstatement."

A few advocates of this resolution tried to have the convention reverse the action of the committee and adopt the resolution. The chairman of the committee, Delegate Anderson, of Macon, Ga., defended its report. In the course of his remarks he quoted the lines of Sir Walter Scott. "Breathes there a man with soul so dead, Who never to himself hath said, This is my own, my native land." The quotation threw the convention into a tumult of enthusiasim and the resolution was rejected, amid cheers, by an overwhelming majority.

Surely this is an act by an international body of organized labor that merited as prominent publicity as was accorded to the lamented and local art of stupidity at Schenectady. It is in accordance with the opinion expressed by Samuel Gompers, President of the American Federation of Labor, who made the following reply to an inquiry:

Yes, a member of the State militia can be seated in a trade council. In fact the matter is so obvious that it ought not be open for discussion at all.

A man who is a wage earner and honorably working at his trade or calling to support himself and those dependent upon him has not only the right to become a citizen soldier, but that right must be unquestioned.

The militia, i. e., the citizen soldiery of the several States in our country, supplies what otherwise might take its place—a large standing army.

The difference between the citizen soldiery of the United States and the large standing armies of many European countries is the difference between a republic and a monarchy—it is the difference between the conceptions of liberty and tyranny.

Practically no mention was made in newspapers of the overwhelming rejection by the annual convention of the United Garment Workers of America of an anti-militia resolution. Had these events been more widely published, the prevalent but erroneous impression that unionism is opposed to the militia might, in a measure, be corrected.

INFORMATION FOR EMPLOYERS.

The Welfare Department of the National Civic Federation is prepared to furnish, upon request, a consulting agent to study the especial needs of employes in a given plant, advise the best methods of introducing such features of welfare work as may be deemed most essential, direct their installation, and, when required, recommend a permanent agent or "welfare manager" to administer the work.

A central bureau is maintained at the headquarters of the Welfare Department for the exchange of experiences by employers. Information with reference to the latest efforts by employers to give especial consideration to the physical or mental welfare of their employes may there be obtained. Some of the subjects covered are:

[illegible] Work [illegible];
[illegible];
[illegible];
[illegible];
Recreation;
Educational Efforts;
Housing of Labor;
Pensions;
Insurance Associations.

AGAINST SYMPATHETIC STRIKES.

The International Miners' Congress Side-Tracked a Perilous Proposition.

Suppose that a strike occurred in Austria, Belgium or Wales, what justification would that be for the miners of the United States to break their contracts? It would, as urged, "show that the miners were a world power," and it would also show that reason had been dethroned and folly had usurped its place. It would have been more to the point to have entered upon a scheme to render mutual financial aid. It was due to the eloquence and sound reasons advanced by Messrs. Mitchell and Dodds that the chimera was side-tracked.—"United Mine Workers' Journal."

A DRASTIC LABOR LAW.

An old labor law of England, in force 121 years ago, would satisfy the most radical member of the Manufacturers' Association. It contained the following six clauses:

1. Any tailor who joined a union was to be sent to jail for two months.
2. Tailors must work from 6 in the morning until 8 at night.
3. Wages were not to be higher than 48 cents a day.
4. Each tailor was to be allowed 3 cents for breakfast.
5. Any tailor who refuses to work was to be imprisoned for not more than two months.
6. If any employer paid higher wages he was to be fined $25, and the workmen who took the increase were to be sent to jail for two months.

Intelligent workers the world over favor voluntary arbitration for the settlement of trade difficulties, rather than being forced to submit their grievances to professional arbitrators.—"International Wood-Worker."

CONCESSIONS FOR SHORTER DAY.

(Continued from page 7.)

As to granting concessions as to unrestricted output possibly my experience in the labor movement has not been extended enough to answer that question intelligently. However, I do not know of any organizations who sanction the restriction of the output. Certainly they do not in my organization, and I am sure that as a general proposition organized labor does not attempt to restrict the output.

As to your second question, I do not believe a short work-day would lessen production. Undoubtedly the individual would not be able to turn out as much work as under a longer work-day (although the difference would not be as much less in proportion to the number of hours worked), but there would be less idle people. The opportunity of obtaining employment would be greater, and in most industries there is a long period of idleness, and I believe a shorter work-day would result in more steady employment, and the same amount of output would result.

WAGES SOON RESTORED.

Thomas O'Donnell, Secretary Fall River Cotton Mule Spinners' Association:—My people would be willing to work less hours with a corresponding reduction in wages, as it would only be a short time when the wages would be restored to their former rate.

WORK UP TO THE LIMIT.

J. L. Sullivan, General Secretary Bartenders' International League:—In my opinion, organized labor should, in the first place do all in its power to attain the eight-hour day, and it should be willing to sacrifice the wage to obtain the effect; for in obtaining the eight-hour day, the dawn of a new era will be a fact instead of a fancy, and it will be but a short time when the employers will begin to realize that more can be accomplished by the eight-hour day than could be by the former long day. When the laborer can feel like working right up to the limit, he will be able to accomplish more, and do it better. This will be the result of the new order of things,—eight hours to work, eight hours of rest, and eight hours to play.

As for the other question, No, for I believe that any working-man can do as much work in eight hours as he can in ten.

GREATER VIGOR WILL MEET LABOR COST.

[illegible] Atwood, Editor Union Labor News, Los [illegible]:—Organized labor should not, in [illegible] a concession in wages [illegible] more [illegible] The cost [illegible] ter allowing for [illegible] Not as is now done, [illegible] forcing the cost down so [illegible]

As to the unrestricted output, will say frankly, that I know of no union regulation in any organization that restricts the output.

I am of the belief that a shorter work-day will not materially decrease the amount of production nor will it increase the labor cost after a short period when the workman has begun to get the full benefit of a more vigorous body and mind made possible by longer hours in which to rest and recuperate.

THE MUSICIANS' TENDENCY.

Owen Miller, Secretary American Federation of Musicians:—I am a representative of a business that cannot be classed as productive, but will say that in our business, since we have been organized, the tendency has been to reduce the hours of labor without reducing the price, as for instance: Formerly, we played from eight o'clock until five o'clock in the morning for $5.00. That was reduced to 4 a. m. for the same price. Now, most of the musical unions in the country have adopted a system of charging $4.00 for a ball until 2 a. m. and $1.00 per man per hour for each hour thereafter. This would make a ball until 5 a. m., pay $7, $2 more than formerly for the same time, and until 3 a. m., the price would be $5. Therefore we receive just as much now for seven hours' work, as we formerly did for nine hours' work, but of course we cannot apply the manner in which the musicians do business to any other class of labor.

WORKERS SHOULD AID EMPLOYERS.

Homer D. Call, Secretary-Treasurer Amalgamated Meat Cutters and Butcher Workmen of N. A.:—When an employer is willing to grant the eight-hour day, I believe that organized labor should be willing to assist him in his efforts to adjust his business to those conditions, even if it does in some instances necessitate a slight reduction in wages. We all fully understand that the large industries of the country are operated under certain systems, which are based upon the ten-hour day and that they can not be successfully changed without some injury to the employer in some cases, and where those contingencies arise, I believe that organized labor should use judgment and be willing to meet the employer half way in his efforts to conform to the eight-hour day.

I do not believe that in the long run the shorter work-day would lessen the production or increase the labor cost. It might possibly temporarily, but I feel confident that a body of workmen after having become familiar with the workings of the eight-hour system would make an extra effort and be successful in producing fully as much in eight hours as they do under the present economic system in ten.

—

WAGES AND RESTRICTIONS MAY VARY.

Bert H. Beadle, President Watch Case Engravers' International Association:—I am heartily in favor of the eight-hour day. While of the opinion that this point cannot be gained all at once, I think that it is only a question of time until it will be granted. It is a question that cannot be taken up by one here and there, but one that will require the combined efforts of all manufacturers. Let them all agree to the eight-hour day, and you may be sure that when it comes to the workman he will not be lacking in his efforts to do his part. As to a reduction of the wage, that is a question that would require the consideration of those to whom it would apply directly; that is, to unions as unions, and is therefore a question that would be very hard to answer. It would be the same in regard to the restriction of output.

As to the increasing the cost of production, I do not think it would. The average man of to-day would, I think, if he be given an eight-hour day, more than do his share toward the betterment of himself and his employer, and would in no way throw stumbling blocks in the way of those who through this means had at least tried to aid him in bettering his condition.

—

A UNIVERSAL DATE SUGGESTED.

John F. Ream, Member National Executive Board, United Mine Workers of America:—To your first question, will say that as a matter of justice the wage-earners should be required to make no concessions for the purpose of making their work-day shorter. If, however, the work-day cannot be shortened without some concessions from the laborer, he should not hesitate to accept slight reduction in wages which, as your question implies, would not be permanent, for the purpose of shortening his day's labor. But it appears to me that with its strong combinations capital could easily shorten the [illegible] labor and still maintain the [illegible]. I say this, because the [illegible] would be fixed by the wages paid to work[illegible] increased [illegible] would make the [illegible] prices for their goods. The principal [illegible] about securing the adoption of this great and much-needed reform is that each corporation employing workmen fears that it will be the first one called upon to make the concession, and will thus be placed at a disadvantage with its competitors. What is wanted to bring about the transition from a long work-day to a short one is for every man who works for wages to enroll himself a member of the union of his trade, have all trades affiliated with the American Federation of Labor, and let that organization meet representatives of the employers of labor and fix a date on which eight hours shall, throughout the country, constitute a day's work.

To your second question, will answer that in many, perhaps in most trades the shorter work-day lessens production, nor do I regard the lessening of production per capita for the workman now employed as an evil.

—

NO LOSS UNDER NATIONAL AGREEMENTS.

Charles O. Sherman, General Secretary United Metal Workers' International Union:—I am not unmindful of the fact that the various labor organizations are endeavoring as fast as they believe it is feasible to shorten the hours of labor and I am quite familiar with the arguments made against the policy by the employers. In a sense, both sides are correct. There is no doubt but what the argument holds true that by shortening the hours of labor from nine to eight hours it would make an increase in the expense of production, but past experience has demonstrated that the increase in cost is not as high in percentage as quoted by those who object to shorter hours of labor.

In your second paragraph you ask "do I believe that organized labor should be willing to make concessions?" In reply to the same I will say that I have known of specific cases where labor has made concessions in the way of accepting lower wages, which would practically balance the difference when receiving the shorter work day and feel that it might be necessary for some industries to grant such concessions temporarily.

From my observation of the shorter work-day, I feel that the greatest drawback in securing the same is through the employers who are not willing to have their labor organized. If any industry carried on in the United States is thoroughly organized and in a position to make a national agreement with all of the employers engaged in that industry, I cannot see where any loss could be brought about on any employers, for, if they all employ labor on the same basis of remuneration and the same number of hours work, it leaves them at liberty to go into the competitive market and every individual has an equal opportunity. Where the difficulty comes in and where the good employer is punished or suffers through the shorter work-day, is not through the fault of the union or the members, but it is the fault of the unfair employer who objects to his men being organized and does not permit them to place themselves in a position to move forward with other union men in the same industry.

I am the last one to consent to reduced wages in any trade, as I feel that I am quite well posted on the cost of production of most of our products in the United States and I am quite positive that there is a wide difference between the cost of production and the price placed on the same when put in the market and there are very few goods produced in the United States but what there is not a good, fair and, in some cases, large profit made from them. I am opposed to reduction in wages, as I cannot see what would warrant the same when taking into consideration the cost of everything that is used by the human family.

—

LOWER WAGES IMPOSSIBLE.

John E. Bruner, President International Union of Steam Engineers:—I give you my views from the standpoint of one who has been in close touch with both employer and employe.

To your first question I will say that under no consideration would I approve of a lower wage. The workmen of to-day, comparatively speaking, are receiving a lower wage than ever. Statisticians may collect a vast amount of data on this question, and attempt to prove by their figures that the workmen of to-day are receiving a better wage than ever before recorded, but the wage-earner himself will tell you that under the existing conditions, he and his family must more than ever deny themselves the actual necessities to keep body and soul together.

I am of the opinion that every workman should give value received for his wage, and under that condition there will be no restricted output.

To the second question I will say that this question is broad in its scope. In cases where employers are working their men eighty-four hours per week, there is no doubt but that the cost of production will increase if the hours are reduced to fifty-six. But is it not a fact, that it is inhuman to insist that a man spend over one-half of his existence in the shop or factory, so that the margins of the employer may not be reduced? In the shop or factory where the hours were reduced from ten to nine, there has not been a lessened output. Conditions are changing so rapidly, and improved machinery is increasing the output of man to such an extent that the manufacturers' margin is as great, if not greater than ever.

The building trades are an object lesson to the employer as well as the wage-earner. The reduction of hours in these crafts has not lessened the output of the man. The work is more satisfactory and cost of production has not increased.

—

FOR UNIONS TO WIN.

George H. Taylor, General President International Glove Workers' Union of America:—I do not believe that organized labor should, or would agree to accept a reduction in wages for a shorter work-day. In fact, the very reverse is in the minds of men who toil; the "slogan" of labor for years past, and which is stronger and louder to-day than ever is, "Less hours and more pay."

As regards the apprehension of those employers who pretend to take such an interest in the moral welfare of their employes, as to where they would spend their extra hours of leisure, if such were granted, if they would look around and be willing to be convinced, they would find that long hours means ignorance, poor wages, poverty, drunkenness, and naturally poor citizens.

A shorter work-day would mean, a greater intelligence, a higher standard of manhood, better wages, more time for study and recreation, a chance to enjoy the pure air in the sunshine every day in the week instead of Sunday's only, and an opportunity to become acquainted with one's wife and family.

That the eight-hour day will succeed the ten-hour is certain, but working-men will have to fight and get it for themselves; it is human nature to wish for better conditions, and it's the labor unionist who is fighting for a better future, and a better nation; not only for himself, but also for those unfortunates who seem to have lost faith in mankind, and are willing to drift down with the current of events, a drag on their fellows, yet always willing to share in any benefits that may be secured without any sacrifice to himself.

The supposition that the union restricts the quantity of production of a member's day's work is fallacious, and in my opinion arises from greed and thoughtlessness on the part of the employer. There appears to be a general impression, that a union man conceals a portion of his vitality, and it seems an impossibility to disabuse the minds of certain employers that such is not the case. As to what constitutes a day's work, a wide different opinion exists. The employer claims there is not enough work being done and the employe declares he is doing to much already. So far as my experience goes, it is the employer, and not the union who sets the task which constitutes a day's work, and in general, the task is based upon the quantity of work which the strongest and most speedy man can turn out; and when the average man is compelled to keep the pace thus set for him, anyone can imagine his physical condition at the end of ten hours' labor.

These, and other evils are created through the helplessness of unorganized labor, and later, when the men form a union, and as a body demand a voice in the matter as to what conditions they shall work under and insist upon different treatment, immediately a protest is raised by the employers against what they term the tyrannical and arbitrary conduct of the union.

—

CAPITAL INVESTED AT HIGHER INTEREST.

W. Macarthur, Editor "Coast Seamen's Journal," San Francisco:—I do not think it advisable or necessary that organized labor should accept lower wages in return for a reduction in the daily hours of labor. To do so would be to negative the benefit of the shorter work-day and to impose a positive and permanent loss upon the employers; whereas, under the system of maintaining wages at the old figure the loss to the employer, if any, is only relative and temporary. From the purely economic point of view, the purpose of reducing hours is to increase the consuming power of the worker. A reduction of wages would lessen the consuming power. In other words, to reduce the hours and keep up wages is to invest so much capital at an increased rate of interest; to reduce both hours and wages is to withdraw so much capital from the business and leave it entirely idle.

As to the question of conceding unrestricted output in return for shorter hours, I am unable to speak, for the reason that I know of no instances of restriction in that regard. Probably such instances exist; in which case I am inclined to believe that they are based upon exceptional circumstances, of which only those personally concerned are competent to speak.

Generally speaking, it may be conceded that the reduction of hours lessens production and, where wages are maintained at the rate paid for the longer work-day, increases the cost of production. But that is merely saying that any improvement in industrial methods increases the initial cost. In the end, however, the most efficient labor, like the most efficient machine, is the cheapest—that is to say, it brings in the largest returns. The shorter work-day may cost more in wages, but it also brings back more in the form of an increased demand for the products of labor. If long hours means profitable production, we should find the American worker outstripped by the coolies of Asia and India. If lower wages is a natural or necessary accompaniment of the shorter work-day, we should find that wages generally are high as hours are long. As a matter of fact, we know that the opposite of these conditions is the universal rule.

—

"THE MEN BEHIND THE GUNS."

John Bradley, Chairman Executive Board, Iron Molders' Union of North America:—I do not believe in temporarily lowering the wage scale for the following reasons: The history of the wage-earner proves that when once lowered it is a difficult matter to have the employers agree to a restoration of wages to the former scale. Another objection is the increased cost of the necessaries of life and a lowering of the present wage scale is likely to lead to untold miseries among the working classes, bringing on discord, strikes and lock-outs. These, I believe, we should avoid.

An unrestricted output in return for a shorter work-day would meet with my approval, providing the men in shops, "the men behind the guns," receive the encouragement given to the superintendents and others higher up, who, at the end of a successful year's business, are called before a board of directors and presented with diamond pins and voted handsome increase of salaries. This rarely occurs to the working-men, no matter how large may be the output.

That a shorter work-day lessens production or increases the labor cost of production, I do not believe, as in all instances coming under my observation where the change has been made to a shorter work-day, the output has not been diminished nor has the cost of production been increased.

A CURE FOR OVER-PRODUCTION.

John Roach, General Secretary-Treasurer Amalgamated Leather Workers' Union of America:—There seems to be a great difference of opinion as to the probable effect of the shortening of labor's work-day. Some contend a shorter work-day will lessen cost of production, and as evidence of this assumption compare the greatly cheapened cost of all manufactured commodities to-day, when we work less hours, with what they were two score years ago, when the extremely long work-day was in vogue.

I do not believe the shortening of the work-day will decrease the cost of production. I do not believe the average laborer will expend as much muscle or brain power in eight hours as he did before in ten. I do not believe that he intends doing it, or that intelligent people who have kept apace with improvements in production expect the worker to work as hard to-day as he did in days of comparatively crude methods of production.

I believe the very idea of the shorter work-day is to lessen the laborer's burden by giving idle hands, unemployed hands vainly seeking employment, a part of his work to do. If as much work is performed in eight hours as was formerly done in ten, manifestly none of the unemployed will gain relief through the shorter work-day. I believe in the philosophy of the shorter work-day if it means a rest for the worker, a lessening of the expenditure of energy. The great evil all the civilized nations suffer from to-day is, not that they do not manufacture enough, but rather they make too much, so that a foreign market must be found for the surplus.

—

OUTPUT INCREASED WITHOUT CONCESSIONS.

James Cliffe, Secretary Operative Mule Spinners' Association of Rhode Island:—I believe the hours of labor should be reduced in our cotton mills, and favor a universal nine-hour law for cotton operatives Of course, we could not expect our manufacturers in the North to run their mills nine hours while their competitors in the South are running from ten to twelve.

I do not believe that organized labor should be willing to make concessions of either temporarily lower wages or of unrestricted output. It is an admitted fact that whenever the hours of labor in our mills have been reduced, the output has always increased.

—

PRODUCTION AND COST UNCHANGED.

Thomas McDowell, Member Executive Board, Glass Bottle Blowers' Association of the United States and Canada:—I believe that a shorter work-day would result in better social conditions, but no concessions for lower wages. I don't believe in an unrestricted output.

A shorter work-day will not lessen production in this age of machinery, nor will the labor cost of production increase, for this has already been proven by manufacturers who have adopted this system. The manufacturers of glass bottles in connection with their employes have been working this way for twenty years, and would not make a change.

—

LOWER WAGES WOULD CHECK CONSUMPTION.

John P. Le Point, 3rd Vice-President, International Brotherhood Paper Makers, Pulp, Sulphide and Paper Mill Workers:—I do not believe that organized labor should be willing to grant any concession, temporarily of a lower wage, for in my opinion the laboring class are the greater in number, and therefore said class are the greater consumers, and if deprived of the consuming power by accepting a lower wage would certainly flood the markets and consequently the employers would restrict the output of their manufacture in order to retain their prices. Therefore, the laborer must suffer from both sides and in my opinion it would be disastrous both to employer and employed.

I do not believe that a shorter work-day lessens production, because if a man turns out as much work in eight hours by paying close attention to his work as in ten hours, how can it increase the cost of production? I know of instances in the paper industry of shortening the hours from seventy-seven per week to sixty-five hours, and with one machine less, and less help, and said mills are turning out more production than ever before. Therefore, I believe the shorter work-day would lessen the cost of production by causing less wear and tear on machinery, instead of increasing the cost, and in such cases the employers as well as the employes have been satisfied and work to a much better advantage.

—

HOPE AND VIGOR SAVE MONEY.

Arthur E. Holden, of "Monthly Journal," International Association of Machinists:—I do not like the way this question is put. In the first place, there are two questions, that require a division. In the second place, there is a clumsy invitation to make an admission (concerning restriction of output) which I refuse to acknowledge with the bulk of the trade-unions in the United States. First, I believe that if organized capital is at all sincere and really desires to know how to obtain a shorter work-day without great loss, they should be willing to meet their organized employes and let each figure the question out scientifically and fairly, and let whatever losses might occur (and I believe they are largely in the imagination) be equitably shared by the employer and the employe. They will soon find out with a fair, honest experiment what they are, and remedies will soon be forthcoming, by the ingenuity of men who are conscientiously trying to accomplish an honorable task.

The restricted output talk is mere bosh and bugaboo; it is not general, and never was, only to this extent: when a man has to get up in the morning at 6, rush to work by 7, rush at his mid-day meal like a half-famished wolf, rush for a car at night and hang on by a strap for another hour before he gets a square meal for the day, putting in 13 hours instead of 8, all under a strain and exhausting on nerve,—this makes a natural and unavoidable restriction of output, that all the worrying, and all the driving and nagging of modern industrialism cannot replace. It is positively out of the question; human flesh and blood are not equal to it. It is the most horrible reflection upon the results of several generations of training in the American schools and universities that we have not been able to muster enough intelligence to direct affairs industrially without putting in all the hours of the day, and many that properly belong to the night, in order to be able to make a living for the bone and sinew of the land.

As to your second question, I can draw from an experience which has covered thirty years in some of the largest machine shops in this country and that of England. I have also worked for some of the largest corporations in positions of trust, where mechanical accuracy and production were required of a high grade.

During that time I have found that the shorter work-day lessens production as a total product. The amount that was produced in ten hours is less than what is produced in eight hours. The proportionate amount that is produced in one hour on the ten-hour basis is not as much as that produced in an hour on the eight-hour basis, because of the human fact mentioned in the previous answer, which is this: Men are fresher and brighter; as a consequence they have more vim and vigor, they are better tempered, there is more energy left for work and less required for brooding. This affects the supervising force equally with the underlings. Any business man can therefore see the saving of fixed charges, less coal, less gas, less friction on machinery, less everything which makes the cost of production high.

What is wanted more than anything else at this time is a little more common-sense and less passion. None are exempt; we are practically all alike; but a suggestion to the man with the dollar may not be out of place. Let him exercise a trifle more human thoughtfulness, let him become more confiding and less suspicious, let him put more trust in the honor of the toiler who may be only a drudge. He can save many dollars on what now goes to waste by the extraordinary effort to increase the number of non-producers, like clerks and foremen, who make more trouble than what is avoided, and make the path ready for tedious labor fights that are scarcely ever necessary beyond the fact that these meddlers presume it is necessary for them to earn their pay by making trouble.

Friction, worry, suspicion, envy and jealousy are the poorest kind of investments. They injure the worker, spoil the boss, and deteriorate the product. Substitute hope, sunshine, vigor, fairness and honor. They pay. I have had many chances to put them in practice for men who have made millions, and there are millions left to be made by sensible men who will read these few words from a humble worker and get some stock, which cannot be purchased on any stock exchange, but which can be personally manufactured by all.

—

THE ARGUMENT OF EXPERIENCE.

James P. Archibald, President New York District Council, Brotherhood of Painters, Decorators and Paperhangers:—Temporary lower wages may in some cases be conceded as a method of getting the shorter work-day. Restriction is already rare. No, the shorter work-day will not increase cost of production nor lessen output.

I have prepared some observations upon the history of the achievement of the shorter day in the building trades and its result.

It is an important fact that the eight-hour day now obtains throughout the building trades in the United States. The history of how this condition was brought about is pertinent. The first practical step was taken in 1866, when the first National Trades Congress, held in Baltimore, adopted a resolution favoring the eight-hour day and appealing to the unions in the several States to agitate the cause and to obtain official bureaus of statistics to prove its practicability. In the same year the Journeymen Stone Cutters of North America ordered strikes for the eight-hour day. They were successful, and that is the single trade that has maintained the eight-hour day, without interruption, from that time to this.

The movement progressed in other trades with varying success. The agitation was reflected in the introduction of eight-hour bills in Congress, the first of which was presented by Representative George Julian of Indiana in 1867. In 1871, the local organization of painters in New York City struck for the eight-hour day. This strike soon involved nearly every union in the city, the length of the day then prevailing being from ten to eleven hours. Many mass meetings were held and several bloody riots occurred. Year after year saw May Day demonstrations for the shorter day. These kept the subject before the public in all the large cities.

In 1866, the American Federation of Labor formally declared in convention at Cleveland in favor of the universal eight-hour work-day. There was a rivalry among the affiliated national unions for the distinction of leading in the fight. The Cleveland convention selected the Brotherhood of Carpenters to head the movement. That Brotherhood ordered many local strikes, which were so successful that within a year or two many strikes occurred in other building trades. By 1890 the movement had progressed so far that the eight-hour day had become established throughout many building trades, although in some, where the ten-hour or longer day had been the practice, a compromise on nine hours was effected. From 1890 even these exceptions grew more and more rare, until by 1896 it could be said that eight hours had become practically universal throughout the building trades in the United States. There are, it is asserted, not more than a dozen towns of noteworthy size where the old longer day still holds.

"Inferior habits are as much the cause as they are the result of lower wages," wrote John Stuart Mill. "Reducing the hours of labor acts more directly on the habits of the people than any other measure heretofore proposed." How far is the truth of these propositions proved by the actual experience of the building trades in New York City?

The habits and the standards of life among all the 800,000 workers, of all grades, in the building trades in New York City have been visibly and materially elevated since 1886. This is clearly the result of the shorter work-day, which has enabled the heads of families to devote more time to all phases of their education. The consequent elevation of thought causes a more refined home life, improved dwellings and a higher standard of morality.

I wish to emphasize the fact, also, that higher wages have followed the shorter day throughout the building trades. For example, wages of marble-cutters, electrical workers, carpenters, painters, structural iron-workers, varnishers, have doubled or nearly doubled, while the wages of all other building trades have been largely increased. The statement that less hours of labor means less wages is historically untrue and is based upon a false theory of the law governing wages. If wages were regulated by the number of hours of work, then wherever the day's work is longest wages would be highest, and where the day's work is shortest wages would be lowest. Exactly the reverse is true. Civilization follows the line of the shorter work-day, and means the highest purchasing power of a day's labor.

The assertion is frequently made that restricted output prevails in the building trades. I have ascertained that quite as much and in many cases more work is now accomplished in these trades in eight hours as was formerly done in ten. As to arbitrary restrictions, I have made an investigation which shows that there is but one union among the building trades in New York City that fixes a limit to the amount of work that a man may do in a day. That is in the plasterers' union, which has a trade agreement, satisfactory to the employers, limiting the quantity of a day's work for each man. But in that case, the standard is fixed so high that it not infrequently happens that a journeyman fails to reach it; and it is the custom for his faster fellows then to make up his deficiency.

—

OUTPUT HAS NOT BEEN LESSENED.

J. C. Skemp, General Secretary-Treasurer, Brotherhood of Painters, Decorators and Paperhangers of America:—Organized labor considers the shortening of the hours of labor a matter of the most vital importance, and is prepared to make many sacrifices to secure the shorter work-day. A reduction in wages may appear to be the most practical method of securing the consent of the employers to the desired change, but as the wages paid to 90 per cent. of the wage workers are barely sufficient to enable them to exist, the adjustment of the matter by a reduction of wages is impossible. It would mean the lowering of the standard of life below the point necessary for the maintenance of the physical welfare and self-respect of American working-men. I feel confident that should any employer who advocates this method of adjustment temporarily confine his expenditure to the income of the average wage worker minus 20 per cent., he would agree with me that a reduction in the wages commensurate with the shortening of the hours of labor is out of the question.

I believe in removing arbitrary restrictions upon the quantity of production, which, if they exist at all in the United States, do so to a very limited extent. In the building trades with which I am most familiar, there are no such restrictions. They have been attempted in one or two instances locally, but have never been enforced or advocated by any national organization of the building trades.

In the building industry the adoption of the eight-hour day has not lessened the amount of work accomplished. Keen competition has resulted in every man upon a building being compelled to perform as much labor as he is physically able to do, and in many instances more work is now performed in the eight-hour day than ever was done when the ten-hour day was in vogue. I believe this same condition prevails in every trade where the labor of the worker is not regulated by the machine he operates. Of course, men who operate machines can not perform as much labor in eight hours as they can in ten hours unless the machinery is operated proportionately faster, but in such industries it is unprofitable to run a machine faster than it can be properly attended to by the man in charge of it, and he is compelled to regulate his work and reserve his strength so that he may be able to complete his day's work. If he has to work ten hours, he will expend his energy so much more slowly than he would if he knew his labors only lasted for eight hours.

Consequently it is my belief that the shorter workday would lessen production in but few instances, and would not increase to any considerable extent the labor cost of production.

Personally I believe in the regulation of the hours of labor and the fixing of a minimum wage by law. This has been done successfully in the Australian colonies and New Zealand, and although this is denied by many newspapers opposed to governmental regulation of such matters, the fact remains that the people of Australia would not consider for a moment the repeal of the eight-hour laws which have been in effect for a number of years.

This sentiment is not confined to trades-unionists, but is the sentiment of the entire people, and is the best kind of proof that these laws are effective and beneficial.

If, as a matter of public policy, it is wise to maintain public schools, to support which every citizen is taxed, whether he has children to educate or not,—if for the national welfare we are justified in regulating the age at which children shall be employed and the hours and conditions under which women shall work, is it not equally to the national interest to guard the physical welfare of our wage-working citizens, and to ensure to them sufficient wherewith to feed, clothe and educate themselves and their families in a manner befitting the citizens of an enlightened country?

NO REDUCTION, NO RESTRICTION.

Frank Buchanan, President International Association of Bridge and Structural Iron Workers:—It is generally conceded that the eight-hour day in labor is productive of the best results to the country, in that it gives the laboring man a chance to have a part of his time to the improvement of his own mind, and takes him out of the category of the draft horse.

The objections upon the part of the employer to the eight-hour day are based upon (1) the increase of the cost of production, (2) that it restricts the output.

To the first of these objections, I would say that the work produced by men working eight hours a day would fully equal the work produced by men working ten hours. Because of the added rest and the renewed zest of the employe, a man working steadily and consistently for eight hours will accomplish more than the man who drags through ten hours, just as the fresh draft horse will draw more than the overworked draft horse.

Aside from this, it is well known that there is an over-production in all industries, and the result is frequent shut-downs. By the eight-hour system the work would be more continuous and the result the same. Again, I would say that while the hours are shortened, the wages should not be reduced, because, as I have stated, the amount of work produced by men working eight hours would equal, or nearly equal, the amount produced by men working ten hours; and moreover, it must be remembered that if the eight-hour system is uniformly adopted by all employers, it eliminates this item of the cost of production from competition and affects all alike, so that if it should be added to the cost of production, as is always the case, it would necessarily come out of the general public, of which the working man goes to make up the bulk, and if any one has cause to complain it would certainly not be the employer.

So far as foreign competition is concerned, the tariff has always seemed to be able to take care of that. Moreover, the increased facilities of machinery and modern labor-saving inventions has increased the working capacity of the men a great many times, so that a man working eight hours today can produce a great many times the amount that a man working ten hours could produce a few years ago, and there is still room for improvement.

In regard to the restriction of the output, no fair-minded union man objects to unlimited production. The vital question affecting the output is the amount of consumption, and necessarily always will be.

In this brief synopsis I have eliminated the moral and humanitarian view of the subject, about which I could write a volume.

NO RESTRICTION IN PRACTICE.

James Duncan, National Secretary-Treasurer Granite Cutters' National Union:—It is a healthy sign of the times that many employers not now using the shorter work-day, or what we call the eight-hour system, are looking with more favor upon it than heretoforé, but when they offer new thought on that subject simply as a condition that workers shall consider the removal of restrictions upon the quantity of product, they are dealing with a practical versus a theoretical situation. I have endeavored to set forth in as strong language as I could, that in as far as our trade is concerned and those with which we are closely allied, there is no such thing as a limit to production. It is true that both employers and employes are taking more kindly in recent years to the day work system than to piece-work, but wherever the piece-work system is a practical feature in the output of a manufactured article, employers have the option of hiring either by the day or by the piece, as they see fit. If workers are employed by the day, the trade agreement, which in importance should be considered along the lines of a Magna Charta or our own Declaration of Independence in this country, names a minimum wage rate for the established work-day, and employer and individual workman may agree for as much more than that per day as may be mutually arranged.

If piece-work is followed, the trade agreement is right there with its practical utility. The piece scale suggests the pace, and the workers employed are paid according to the amount they produce. It is not true that at any time the trade-union movement calls upon or requires employers to pay the same price to a slow workman that is paid to a fast workman.

Experience proves beyond question of doubt that the eight-hour work-day is not detrimental to the amount of output, and thereby causing an increase in the cost of production. Practical management and the desire of the workmen to perform a day's work adjusts these matters, so that employers in my own trade, for instance, will promptly aver that granite cutters are doing as much per diem on the eight-hour day as they were previously doing on the nine-hour day. All told, the reduction to eight hours is beneficial both to employer and employe. It gives additional opportunity of social intercourse to both, and the more that is enjoyed, the better both become. I desire, therefore, to be quoted as urging, as far as possible, the fullest introduction of the eight-hour work-day and as giving bona-fide evidence that the shorter work-day does not increase the cost of the finished product.

NO CONCESSIONS AND HIGHER COST.

Alfred See, Vice-President Branch 3, Amalgamated Society of Carpenters and Joiners:—Question 1 implies that there is a reserve of energy not yet put forth by American wage-earners, which certainly does not apply to the building industry, in which eight hours already prevails in the United States. It is equivalent to getting "net" quotations and then expecting discounts. No! I do not believe that organized labor would, or should, be willing to obtain shorter hours by the concession of lower wages or attempting to keep pace with record-breaking specialists, bell-horses, or by whatever term those hacks of the sub-contractor and lumper are known.

Question 2. Messrs. Woods, Jenks & Co., of Cleveland, O., in 1890 conceded the nine-hour work-day, the operatives in planing-mill undertaking to produce the same amount as under the ten-hour day, which condition they were unable to fulfil. The reasons are apparent. Wherever machinery is applied, manual labor is brought into competition with, instead of co-operation with, a social product which should be socially used for the betterment of the largest part of society, not for its demoralization. Therefore, this question, relating as it does to actual practical methods of production, must be answered in the affirmative: Yes! I do believe, and know, that a shorter work-day lessens production in all cases where machinery is running, and time is a more important factor than in the case of mental operations. Will a shorter work-day increase the labor cost? Yes! It would and should, is the opinion of most labor students.

A MATHEMATICAL ILLUSTRATION.

James F. McHugh, General Secretary-Treasurer Journeymen Stone Cutters' Association:—I note that the shorter work-day has many friends among the larger employers. They appear to dread, though, that the eight-hour day will increase cost of production. I do not see how this could enter into the matter as the men are employed by the hour, and are only paid for the number of hours worked. I do not think the unions should lower their wages in order to secure a shorter work-day, and should not ask for nine hours' pay for eight hours' work.

I do not believe that the short-hour-day lessens production, for if an employer has a piece of work to perform within a limited time, he will increase his force, and that is the real reason that the worker strives for the shorter working day. It furnishes employment to a larger number of men, and at no increase of cost, for if an employer had twenty men working ten hours to complete a job in one week at 50 cents per hour it would cost $600. At eight hours a day twenty-five men would be employed whose wages would amount to $600. This same rule would apply whether twenty men were working or 20,000.

PUT HEART INTO WORK.

Lawrence H. Fitzgerald, General President, Journeymen Stone Cutters' Association of North America:—Where the employer has various interests (for instance, the manufacturer who has accepted orders for goods in advance of any knowledge of extra cost of production on the part of the workman), I believe it would be only showing the proper spirit on the part of employes to accept temporary reduction in wages, except in cases where the wage is so small that further reduction would work a hardship on the employe. In such a case I believe it would be not only fair on the part of the employe, and justice to the employer, but that it would redound to the mutual interest of all concerned.

As a general proposition, I have always favored and so advised the organization desiring to secure the eight-hour day to first secure the reduction of the hours of labor, and that in due time the wage question would regulate itself. To illustrate this by a case in point: The stone-cutters of New York City some thirty-five years ago made a demand for an eight-hour day. The employers refused to yield, but made the offer to raise the ten-hour scale from $4 to $5. This offer the stone-cutters refused to accept, but agreed to accept $2.50 as the scale for an eight-hour day. The result was that a year from that date the wage had so regulated itself that the stone-cutters were receiving the ten-hour scale for an eight-hour day.

As to the cost of production: There are certain kinds of labor where the brain and muscle are taxed to produce, where it has been proven that the same amount of work is now produced in eight hours as was produced when the ten-hour day was in vogue. This is a recognized and an acknowledged fact in the building trades.

As a general proposition, better results will accrue to all concerned by recognizing the short-hour workday. The employe now working the ten-hour day very often becomes so fatigued that he loses heart in his work long before the hour for quitting has arrived. Give him the eight-hour day and he will put his heart in his work. Combined with the energy and force that he sometimes grudgingly spent on his ten-hour task will now be focussed on the one point, with the one end in view, to produce in eight hours what he formerly produced in ten.

WITH CONCESSIONS, OUTPUT NOT LESSENED.

T. E. Burns, 1st Vice-President International Shingle Weavers' Union:—I do believe that organized labor should make some concessions for a shorter work-day, both in reduction of wages on men receiving over 20 cents an hour and in unrestricted output.

I believe that an eight-hour day would not lessen production to a great extent, as many factories and mills would run 16 hours where they only run 10 now and 24 hours where they run 20 now. I believe it will increase the labor cost of production very little.

No doubt agreement evasions, and subterfuges, reward, more or less, those indulging in them, with the self-satisfaction that they got the best of the other fellow, but the practice is invidious and is simply carrying on the strife, in another way, that the agreement aims to get rid of. Whether indulged in by workers or employers, agreement evasion and subterfuges are not only wrong but injurious, and often cost more than the gain expected from them.—"Shoe Workers' Journal."

More than 100 labor unions in Cleveland, Oho, will be united into one great organization, to be known as the United Trade and Labor Council. A large building will be erected for the organization, to be used exclusively as a labor temple.

TRADE AGREEMENTS APPLIED TO OPERA AND THE DRAMA.

ORGANIZED THEATRICAL MANAGERS, MUSICIANS AND STAGE EMPLOYES CONVERT "DISCORD" INTO "HARMONY," PREVENTING "DARK" PLAYHOUSES

Lovers of music and those who enjoy theatrical performances will be interested in the introduction into that field of formal trade agreements between organized labor and organized employers. These agreements are between the musicians' union of New York, known as "Local 310," the Theatrical Protective Union, and the Association of Theatre Managers of Greater New York. In addition to their novelty, these agreements are of interest because of the negotiations which led up to their formation, as they illustrate throughout the value of candid conference between the authorized representatives of opposing interests. It is certain that had not the two sides in this controversy been organized and had not these conferences been held, the resulting harmony would not have been attained. Instead, the relations between the orchestras and the managers would have been "jangled and out of tune," millions of habitual theatre-goers would have been deprived of their accustomed entertainment, the business of the managers would have suffered and the employment of thousands of artists, actors, singers, stage hands and others dependent upon the prosperity of public entertainments for their livelihood would have encountered serious and costly interruption, not only in the metropolis, but throughout the United States. For the controversy in its possible developments, had it not been thus converted into an agreement, might have involved every play-house in the country, from the Metropolitan Grand Opera House to the rural "one-night stand."

ROLAND PHILLIPS

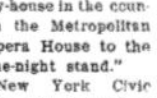

HEINRICH CONRIED

The New York Civic Federation was invited to exercise its good offices in harmonizing the differences between the musicians and the managers as to rates of payment, substitutes, rehearsals and minor details, because of its success in bringing about an agreement between the managers and the Theatrical Protective Union. That union is composed of mechanical and other stage employes. Through the Civic Federation, Mr. Phil Kelly, representing that union, was brought into communication with the managers.

JOSEPH WEBER

A conference was held, on May 12, at which all the managers in the city, with a few exceptions, who were out of town, were present; while the union was represented by Messrs. Kelly, John H. Cunningham and John J. Taylor. The managers presented a series of rates of wages and conditions of employment. To these demands the union representatives demurred, pointing out that there had been no increase in their wages for many years. They presented the reasons for their attitude, which explained away many details which the managers had considered as grievances. This conference was so satisfactory that at its conclusion many of the managers voluntarily expressed themselves as satisfied with a continuance of existing arrangements, and as impressed with the intelligence and diplomacy of the union representatives. Subsequently, in Milwaukee, in July, this arrangement was commended by the national convention of the Theatrical Protective Employes. Certain special arrangements desired by Manager Conried for stage employes in grand opera were left open for adjustment later in the season, with every prospect of amicable arrangement.

In the meantime, Manager Conried had become so interested in trade agreements that he attended the conference upon that subject, held on May 7, at the Fifth Avenue Hotel, under the auspices of the National Civic Federation. He listened attentively to the addresses of Francis P. Robbins, John Mitchell and others. When invited to speak himself, Mr. Conried said emphatically: "I did not come here to make a speech, but to learn how to apply the principle of trade agreements to the production of grand opera, through a rational arrangement with musicians and theatrical employes."

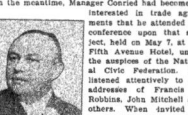

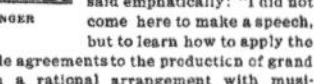

A. L. ERLANGER

The Musical Mutual Protective Union of New York City had been for thirty-five years an independent local body, chartered by the Legislature, without connection with any national organization save for a brief association with the National League of Musicians. It had held aloof from other organizations in the belief that, as artists, its members could command a market of their own and that their service and skill would be sufficient to secure from managers the rates of payment fixed by their local union. But an officer of the union says that experience demonstrated that some managers would pay individual musicians as little as their circumstances might force them to accept. It was found, says this officer, that the union scale of rates for musicians was maintained in only three or four theatres in the city, while in several theatres members of the union were playing for less than the wages of unskilled manual laborers.

MAURICE F. SMITH

This condition convinced the members of the Musical Mutual Protective Union that only through connection with organized labor as a whole could they secure a scale of wages, both living and uniform, and also commensurate with their artistic worth. They therefore sought affiliation with the national body, the American Federation of Musicians, which is itself affiliated with the American Federation of Labor. This was accomplished through amalgamation with "Local 41," the New York branch of the national body. The reorganized union was designated "Local 310" of the American Federation of Musicians; and thus, in July, 1903, the former Musical Mutual Protective Union became a part of national organized labor.

HENRY W. SAVAGE

In August, 1903, "Local 310" appointed a committee to visit the theatrical managers one by one and make with them individual agreements, thus causing the union rates to prevail in every theatre. These negotiations were successful, although prolonged into the autumn. But the individual managers, after making these concessions, determined to combine on their side, and formed "The Association of Theatre Managers of Greater New York."

One incident of the season of 1903-4 that attracted much public attention, while contributing to the antagonism felt by at least some of the managers to the musicians' union, was the enforcement of a rule that its members should not perform with non-members. This was a rule of long standing. But as women artists were not eligible to membership, in the old union, this rule did not apply to them; so that a lady harpist, for example, could be accompanied by union musicians without difficulty. But qualified feminine artistes were eligible to membership in the reorganized union, as a part of the American Federation of Musicians. This brought them under the operation of the old rule, from which they had been exempt. Accordingly, the union, to be consistent, felt itself obliged to insist that a lady harpist, before being accompanied by any of its members, should herself become a member, after passing the regular examination as to her professional capacity.

JAMES BEGGS

Early in April, 1904, the Association of Theatre Managers issued what was regarded as an ultimatum. So far as this related to the Theatrical Protective Association an agreement was reached as previously narrated. A preliminary conference was held on May 13, relating to the terms and conditions of the employment of musicians. It was decided then to postpone the subject until after the national convention of the American Federation of Musicians, which met in New York on May 16. That convention authorized Local 310 to confer, through a committee, with the organized managers. The managers' ultimatum set forth a list of what they held to be grievances. The union welcomed the prospect of a conference, and appointed a committee of five to meet the managers. The committee of the New York Civic Federation, which was invited to join in the negotiations, was composed of Roland Phillips, chairman; R. H. Jaffrey, Samuel B. Donnelly, Henry White, Charles Delaney, V. Everit Macy and James P. Archibald. The committee representing the musicians' union consisted of Frank Evans, Frank J. Hauser, Ernest H. Clarke, Maurice F. Smith and James Beggs. The executive committee of the managers authorized A. L. Erlanger to meet the committee of the musicians together with the committee of the Civic Federation. Previous to this two conferences had been held with Mr. Erlanger which produced no definite result, and the negotiations might have ended there, had not the Conciliation Committee of the Civic Federation persuaded Mr. Erlanger to agree to the appointment of a special committee of as many managers as there were members of the union's committee. Accordingly, the managers sent as their representatives to

OSCAR HAMMERSTEIN

PHIL KELLY

the next conference A. L. Erlanger, Marc Klaw, Oscar Hammerstein, Henry W. Savage and Al. Hayman. These committees took up one by one the list of the concessions demanded from the union by the managers, and the list of prices and conditions demanded of the managers by the union. As these discussions went on, it became evident that progress would be more rapid if the committees were somewhat smaller. Accordingly, the union formed a committee of three—James Beggs, Maurice F. Smith and Edwin Walther. With them acted Joseph Weber President of the American Federation of Musicians. To confer with them the managers deputized Messrs. Erlanger, Savage, Hammerstein and Hayman.

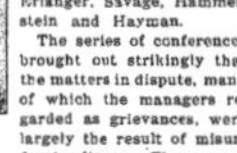

AL. HAYMAN

The series of conferences brought out strikingly that the matters in dispute, many of which the managers regarded as grievances, were largely the result of misunderstandings. There was much complaint on the part of the managers of various acts which they considered as discourtesies and as interfering with the effective and harmonious presentation of public entertainments. It was disconcerting, for example, when an individual player had become familiar with his part to have a green substitute suddenly appear in his place at a rehearsal or a performance. The managers required that no substitutes should come to the theatre without the previous consent of the leader. They were surprised when it was pointed out to them that the union itself made this very requirement, Section 6 of its by-laws reading as follows:

Any member accepting an engagement from another member and disappointing him, shall be fined to the amount of the engagement, and it shall be deemed an offense equal to a disappointment, and fined accordingly, for a member to take an engagement and send a substitute, without the consent of the person that engaged him.

EDWIN WALTHER

Several causes of dispute were also quickly adjusted when mutual explanations were made. In short, the progress of these conferences was a continuous demonstration, to both the committees of the two sides and to the committee of the Civic Federation, of the effectiveness of frank discussion, face to face, between men whose interests had been at variance through many years, and who had now been brought together for the first time.

Upon point after point agreement was reached. At the final conference there remained but one question in dispute,—that of free or paid Sunday rehearsals. Each side made an extreme demand. The union asked payment for all Sunday or evening rehearsals, to be limited to four hours. The managers wished Sunday rehearsals to be free, day or night, but assented to their limitation to four hours. The musicians urged that many of them had opportunities to earn money through private engagements on Sunday evenings. A compromise was reached by which the union granted a free Sunday rehearsal once every six weeks, from 3 to 7 p.m., payment to be at the rate of $1 per hour after 7.

FRANCIS L. ROBBINS

In consideration of the acceptance of the union rates by the managers, the union representatives agreed to a special schedule for the production of grand opera in English. This was because it was shown to them by Manager Savage that the receipts must be less than for grand opera in a foreign language, while the large number of persons employed in a representation of "Parsifal" in English made the concession of special rates of payment essential to the reasonable pecuniary success of the enterprise. It was agreed that higher rates of payment were warranted for the musicians engaged in Manager Heinrich Conried's productions.

A comparison of the two sets of demands, as they stood at the beginning of these conferences, will show how far apart they were then. The differences related to grand opera in English, to dramatic musical comedies, extravaganzas and comic opera; and to vaudeville, burlesque and popular price houses.

JOHN MITCHELL

The managers made the following propositions, applying to all these classes of performances:

All members have the right to engage their musicians and leaders, subject to the rules and discipline of the house in which musicians perform. No substitutes will at any time be permitted, unless agreed to by the managers. No extra pay when required to play behind the scenes. The manager shall have the right to engage extra musicians for appearance before an audience. No extra charge for Sunday rehearsals, day or night. No rehearsal longer than four hours in duration.

The counter proposition of the union for all classes of performances was:

Agent or leader engaging musicians must be member of the organization. Have no objections to rules and discipline of the house in which musicians perform, provided such rules are not at variance with above conditions. The question of substitutes rests between the manager and the leader solely. No extra pay when required to play behind the scenes. (This does not apply to grand opera.) Musicians appearing before an audience, such as stage bands, etc., must be engaged by agent or leader who is a member of the organization. Sunday or evening rehearsals must be paid. No rehearsal over four hours in duration.

Yet these opposing propositions were reconciled, through patient conference, into an agreement which, it is hoped, will result in harmony, without as well as within the play-houses.

RACIAL LABOR STATISTICS.

Professor Walter F. Willcox, of Cornell University, has made an exhaustive study of the census negro statistics, and presents some valuable information bearing upon the industrial situation in the Southern States. One fact relating to the future labor supply in the South is that the negro population is not increasing as fast as the white, in that part of the country. The increase among the negroes in twenty years, from 1880 to 1900, was 33.1 per cent., while for the same period the increase in white population for the same section was 56.5 per cent. Moreover, the rate of increase among the negroes is constantly declining. Of interest to cotton growers is the increasing tendency among the negroes to leave the rural regions for cities, although the great majority of the race still live in the country districts. The percentage of negroes engaged in gainful occupations to the total negro population was in 1900, for the entire country, 45.2, against 41.1 in 1890. For the Southern States the percentage in 1900 was 44.7 against 40.7 in 1890.

No contract should be more sacred than the trade agreement of organized labor. It is a matter of honor between the contracting parties that is neither circumscribed by surety companies' bonds nor by compulsory edicts which enslave the body or dwarf the mind. It is regrettable that in too many instances these principles are violated both by the unscrupulous employer and by ignorant or unadvised workmen; but such mistakes should not be viewed as the failure of the labor movement any more than the collapse of a business venture should be considered a slap to civilization.—James Duncan, Secretary Granite Cutters' Union.

STRUCTURAL BUILDING TRADES ALLIANCE.

A New International Combination of National Unions, Designed to Promote Industrial Peace Through Trade Agreements and Arbitration.

A new international labor organization has been formed, called the Structural Building Trades Alliance of America. It is designed so to regulate the organized building trades as to bring about harmony between employers and employed throughout that industry, to encourage the investment of capital in structural operations, to substitute arbitration for strikes or lock-outs, and to make impossible anywhere such a situation as has existed of late in the building trades in New York City. The General President of this new organization is Frank Buchanan, President of the International Association of Bridge and Structural Iron Workers.

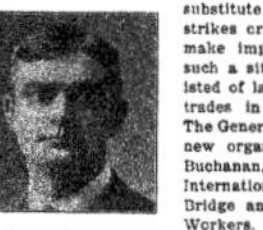

FRANK BUCHANAN

Mr. Buchanan said of this new combination of unions: "We hope for the co-operation of employers in the building trades who are friendly to labor in carrying forward this movement. The Building Trades Alliance will say to such employers, who will organize, we hope, on their side, if they will enter into trade agreements affording fair conditions to the building-trade craftsmen of the country, we will see that your work proceeds regularly, without stoppage. We desire to create a status of stable harmony that will free capital from any hesitation as to investment in structural operations, because of fear of troubles with labor. This is a new step in national labor organization. We wish the step to be at a walking rather than at a running pace. We would make haste slowly. While we are progressing, we would invite suggestions from employers. We wish their comradeship in this advance toward industrial peace and we shall welcome friendly advice."

The recent history of this movement begins with an informal meeting at Indianapolis on August 18, 1903, attended by George Gubbins, then president of the Bricklayers' National Union; Michael Carrick, secretary of the Painters, Decorators and Paperhangers of America; Frank Duffy, secretary of the Carpenters' and Joiners' International Brotherhood; Herman Lillian, president of the Building Laborers' International Union; and Frank Buchanan. These men considered plans to unite the national organizations of the building trades, with fair terms as to membership and allotment of work and with the general idea of formulating methods as to prevent industrial war. Their meeting sent communications to the national organizations of building trades, requesting them to send three delegates each to a convention at Indianapolis on October 8, 1903. That convention was attended by delegates from the national organizations of bricklayers, carpenters, painters, hoisting engineers, plasterers, building laborers, bridge and structural iron workers and electricians. They formed a preamble and constitution, which were referred to the several organizations for approval and which were formally adopted, at the first regular convention of the Alliance, held at Indianapolis on August 8-11, 1904.

The preamble to this constitution declares that its purposes are: The establishment of local and international boards of arbitration to settle disputes without strikes; to give international sympathetic support, when necessary, to all trades affiliated, when local boards fail to adjust difficulties; to safeguard the interests and to protect the autonomy of the trades represented; to keep agreements with employers inviolate; to avoid strikes by substituting arbitration; to annihilate dual and rival bodies and assist only unions affiliated with their respective national and international unions; to maintain fraternal relations with central bodies and to emphasize the necessity of a centralization of organized wage-earners.

A local union is just what the members make it. If it isn't right don't kick, but go to work in an earnest manner to make it right. That's the way to accomplish something.—"Union Label."

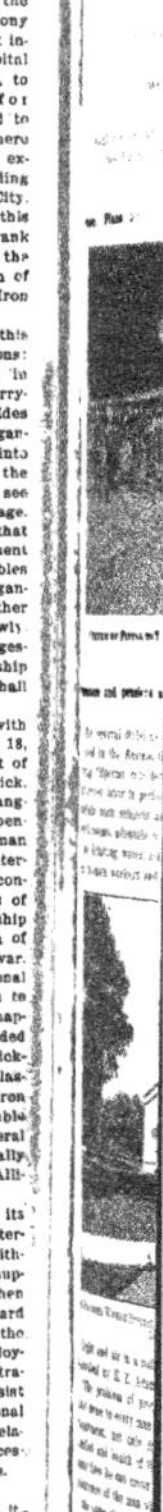

WELFARE WORK INVOLVING PROVISION FOR PHYSICAL COMFORT.

I.—VENTILATION OF THE FORGE SHOP AND ROLLING MILL, AND LIGHT WORK ROOMS FOR FACTORIES, WITH PRACTICAL ILLUSTRATIONS.

In the August issue of The Monthly Review a general discussion of Welfare Work appeared. It was defined briefly as follows:

Welfare Work.

Welfare work involves special consideration for physical comfort wherever labor is performed; opportunities for recreation; educational advantages; and the providing of suitable sanitary homes; its application to be measured by the exigencies of the case. Plans for saving and lending money, insurance and pensions are also included in welfare work.

SYSTEM OF PIPING TO THROW FRESH AIR IN THE FACES OF THE MEN OCCUPIED AT THE ROLLS.

The several divisions of welfare work will be discussed in the Review, the first to receive attention being "Special consideration for physical comfort wherever labor is performed." This discussion will include such subjects as ventilation, light, sanitary work-rooms, adequate toilet facilities, baths, lockers, pure drinking water, rest rooms, lunch rooms, seats for women workers and emergency hospitals.

A FACTORY WHERE SPECIAL ATTENTION HAS BEEN GIVEN TO PROVIDING LIGHT WORK ROOMS.

Light and air in a rolling mill and forge shop are described by E. E. Adams, Superintendent:

"The problem of proper ventilation is one that must come to every man in charge of a large forging department, not only from the standpoint of the comfort and health of the workman, but as to how many fires he can crowd into a given space, and the endurance of the man who is to work in that space. In the same class with proper ventilation, comes the problem of properly lighting the department.

"No one will argue that a satisfied, healthy workman is not the best investment for the employer, and with a man as with a plant, nothing produces health and strength like good air and daylight. They practically mean life to the workman, and he is certainly entitled to them if there is any way of getting them for him.

"In the rolling mill and forge in which the writer is superintendent, we have never ceased experimenting along this line. In the rolling mill, time and time again we have had men give out at the rolls, and at times in very hot weather were obliged to shut down the entire mill, the workmen thereby losing their wages and ourselves the product of their work.

"About three or four years ago we hit upon the plan of putting a large suction fan outside of the mill building, and blowing the air through a large galvanized iron pipe, with which was connected smaller pipes so as to cover the space each workman occupied at the rolls. Since this fan was started we have not lost a single day or an hour on account of the workmen being unable to perform their duties.

"These fans were immediately put into the forge department, but on account of the large number of open fires, the sulphur smoke still bothered the workmen, and this smoke also developed the problem of proper light.

"To give them better light we cut large sky-lights in the roof, but in a few days they were covered with soot and smoke, and our shop was as dark and grimy as ever. This led to a plan that has been the most successful of any that we have tried. We took out the sky-lights, and covered these openings with sliding doors, which can be operated from the inside of the shop. We now have unobstructed daylight, and I might say here that I have never seen our men appreciate anything as they do this, and, in addition to the light, these openings seem to act as flues and draw every bit of the smoke out of the shop, together with the hot air.

"The company feels more than repaid by the satisfactory working of the shop during this hot weather, and I repeat that I have never known anything to be so thoroughly appreciated by the workmen."

With reference to light work rooms in a factory, E. F. Olmsted, the Welfare Manager, says:

"Our building is of steel, with just enough brick to cover the girders, the balance of the wall space being devoted entirely to windows. Each window is double glazed in order to exclude the dust and smoke. The fan system is used for ventilation, the air being changed in the manufacturing section automatically every fifteen minutes, and in the offices every seven and one-half minutes. It is brought in from a tower two hundred feet above the ground and is conveyed to the first floor of the building, where in the winter it is heated and then forced throughout the building. Electric thermostats regulate the temperature."

Ventilation is discussed by W. E. Nazro, Welfare Manager of a large mill:

"We installed a modern system of ventilation, which has given most satisfactory results. The air is taken from out-doors by large fans, and, in winter, is forced over coils of steam piping. When heated, the air is forced through ducts to the floors above. The windows are dropped at the top, and the bad air has a chance to get out, thus making a complete system of ventilation. During the summer months the air is taken from out-doors by the same system, but, of course, it does not pass over steam pipes. The mill thus ventilated in summer is from three to four degrees cooler than in our No. 1 mill, where the system is not installed. In rooms where dust or fumes accrue, they are removed by a system of exhaust fans that helps materially to keep the air clean and pure."

John H. Patterson, president of a company whose plant has light work rooms, says:

"Attention is given to the hygiene of the factory. Large windows admit plenty of light and sunshine. The ventilation and heat are properly looked after. Every fifteen minutes the air in the factory and offices is changed by means of a fan system."

A GRINDING ROOM, SHOWING EXHAUST SYSTEM TO REMOVE DUST FROM THE EMERY WHEELS.

The value of light and well ventilated shops is emphasized by L. A. Osborne, vice-president of a large manufacturing company:

"The floor area of the works used for manufacturing purposes comprises, approximately, one million eight hundred thousand square feet. Natural illumination for this area is obtained by means of skylights and side windows, the total area of the former being 250,000 square feet and the latter 212,000 square feet.

"Artificial illumination in the works is obtained through the use of the Bremer arc, incandescent and Nernst lamps, which are sufficiently numerous and carefully placed to give an even effusion and a minimum of fatigue to the eyes of the operatives. The interior of the buildings is finished in white. The force of painters constantly employed upon this work is sufficient to give the surface two coats of paint each year.

ANOTHER FACTORY WHERE THE CONSTRUCTION INSURES LIGHT WORK ROOMS.

"The buildings are heated by hot air, drawn from apertures in the roof through coils of steam pipe. The heated air circulated throughout the works maintains a temperature of about 70° F. The fans are kept in service during the hot days of summer for air circulation. The general ventilation is further assisted by means of adjustable side and roof windows, controlled from the ground floor."

A TRADE AGREEMENT INTERPRETED.

A Notable Decision by Emerson McMillin as to Arbitration of a Request for Higher Wages, under the Lithographers' Contract.

An interesting feature of the conferences that were held last spring, under the auspices of the Conciliation Committee of the New York Civic Federation, Emerson McMillin of the committee presiding, was a controversy between the representatives of the allied unions of employes and the National Lithographers' Association as to the use of the words "changed" and "reduced." These words occurred in relation to wages in the highly important trade agreement in that industry, which was the successful outcome of many arduous days and nights of earnest conferences. In commenting upon the character of these conferences, Mr. McMillin observed: "One paragraph of the contract drawn on behalf of the employes provided that the rate of wages should not be 'reduced' during its life. The employers' contract in the corresponding clause used the word 'reduced.' Of course, the employes would prefer that word to their own, and vice-versa. Each side wanted the word of the other. The word 'reduced' was finally adopted."

EMERSON McMILLIN,
of the Civic Federation Conciliation Committee.

This incident was the prelude to a recent serious controversy as to the interpretation of this clause of the agreement, which was submitted to Mr. McMillin for decision. Thus unexpectedly he was called upon to decide a serious question, affecting the entire trade, growing out of a phase of the framing of the contract that at the time caused laughter. His decision, rendered on August 16, virtually involves arbitration concerning arbitration. The question was referred to him by W. D. Coakley, General President of the Lithographic Apprentices' and Press Feeders' Association, and Charles Conradis, representing the Lithographers' Association, West. Its reference and decision are an interesting example of the peaceful settlement of a dispute by a rational method, thus preventing the rupture of an agreement and a resort to hostilities.

The question at issue arose out of a request of the Cincinnati Press Feeders for an increase of wages. The trade agreement, framed with so much care, contained a section (2) providing that wages should not be reduced, and a section (4) providing that only such matters as were not specifically covered by the agreement could be arbitrated. It was the contention of the representatives of the employers that this debarred from arbitration the request for an increase of wages, while the representatives of the union hold that the intent of Clause 2 was to provide only against lower wages, and not against an increase.

The essence of Mr. McMillin's decision is in his statement: "A scale of wages to obtain throughout the life of the contract was not specifically provided for in the agreement, and therefore a request for an increase of wages to be paid to any of the employes may under the provisions of Section 4—properly be submitted to a joint commission, and if necessary, to a board of arbitration, for final settlement."

A bald statement of the case would seem to carry its own answer. The agreement had been drawn with painstaking care, every word and sentence being weighed by adepts in the use of the English language. "Nevertheless," says Mr. McMillin in his decision, "one is compelled to concede that there are grounds that warranted the raising of the question at issue."

The employers made the following quotation from a colloquy between Mr. Conradis and Mr. Parker, of the union, as follows:

Mr. Parker: If we are to interpret that the rate of wages should remain the same—that is entirely satisfactory?
Mr. Conradis: Absolutely.
Mr. Parker: And that is not necessary to be arbitrated?
Mr. Conradis: Not at all.

This passage, in connection with other remarks by Mr. Parker, was held by the employers to show that the whole question of wages was settled by the agreement.

The employers also referred to a colloquy about the use as synonymous of the words "changed" and "reduced," as indicating that they were binding themselves not to reduce, while they asserted that it was mutually understood that wages could not be increased, because of the condition of the trade.

The contention of the employes was that the intent of Clause 2 was to protect employes against reduction of wages, but to leave open the question of increase; that the word 'reduced" was adopted after careful consideration in preference to the word "changed," which latter would be required if it were the intention to exclude the wage question in every form from arbitration; that the Cincinnati employes had asked for an increase months before the adoption of the agreement; that it was a representative of the employers who withdrew the word "changed," which he had offered as a substitute for "reduced"; that the employers wanted stability, and to guard against the enforcement of a demand for increase by strikes; that the ratification of the agreement by the local employes' associations was obtained only through representations that it contained nothing to prevent an increase of wages; and that the right to ask for an increase had been conceded, and an increase granted, by the Lithographers' Association of the Pacific.

The decision of Mr. McMillin carefully dissects and reviews these contentions, and arrives at the conclusion quoted, thus opening the way to a judicial determination of the equity of any request for higher wages in the lithographers' industry.

ARBITRATION IN PRACTICE.

President Lynch of the International Typographical Union, in his report to the convention of that body, made the following statement as to the working of the arbitration agreement with the American Newspaper Publishers' Association:

"The arbitration cases have been conducted and completed harmoniously and satisfactorily. Of course, the use of the word 'satisfactorily' does not mean that in the few cases where the verdict has not been favorable to local unions, these unions have been wholly contented. But the agreement has preserved the peace, and whether the verdicts have favored the union or the publishers, work has continued, and strikes, friction and disaster have been averted. The continuance of present relations with the vast majority of the great newspapers of this country is worth something, and when the cases that we have won and the cases that we have lost are taken together and the results averaged up, it will be found that we have made considerable progress."

The practice of union men anywhere to hire professional "wrecking crews" and two-by-four entertaining committees" to "put men to sleep" or "out of commission," as has been and is in some instances still being practised in one or two cities, is a blot and disgrace on the historical pages of trades-unionism that trades-unionists everywhere must expose and cause the punishment the abominable crime merits. —"Labor Compendium."

MEDIATION ENDS A STRIKE.

The Good Offices of Louis B. Schram Mend a Rupture Between Labor and Capital that Threatened Serious Consequences.

A strike of firemen in the Heurich brewery in Washington, D. C., which threatened to involve a large number of other employes, with possible complications in other cities, has been brought to a peaceful end, through the mediation of a representative of the National Civic Federation, Mr. Louis B. Schram. Curiously enough, it was a conflict between rival forces of capital that caused this difficulty with labor. The Heurich Brewery company was engaged in a trade war with four other concerns. The competition became so fierce that the employes feared that one or more of the rival breweries would be driven to the wall, thus throwing many innocent persons out of work.

Accordingly, the firemen in the Heurich brewery struck, to enforce their demand that the rival breweries make peace. Their action brought all mechanical operations in the brewery to a standstill.

Timothy Healy, President of the International Brotherhood of Stationary Firemen, was summoned to take charge of the strike, to which the New York branch of the Brotherhood offered financial support. After looking the situation over, he held a conversation over the long distance telephone with Mr. Schram, who is chairman of the labor committee of the United States Brewers' Association, and an officer of the India Wharf Brewing company of Brooklyn.

LOUIS B. SCHRAM,
of the Civic Federation Conciliation Committee.

As a member of the Civic Federation, Mr. Schram perceived an opportunity to restore peace. He went at once to Washington and quickly convinced both Mr. Healy and the local union that the strike had been precipitate and that its purpose could be attained through pacific and business-like methods, while to persist in the strike would only invite the brewing company to stubbornness in its trade policy. Mr. Schram then held a conference with Mr. Heurich, whom he induced to take a conciliatory attitude. He agreed, if the firemen returned to work, to make no discrimination against the union. At the same time, the trade war between the breweries was put in process of settlement. Both the firemen and Mr. Heurich expressed their satisfaction at the conclusion of the controversy.

Justice and fair dealing must ever be a prominent part of the policy of trade-unionism. Without this none of us need hope for the permanent success of organized labor. Deference to the rights of others must be a guiding light, and if this be so there will not be an over-eagerness at any time to inaugurate "sympathetic strikes."—"Labor World," Pittsburg.

If you make your services indispensable the wage question will not be a hard one to solve.—"Advance Advocate."

National Civic Federation

MONTHLY REVIEW

Vol. I. No. 8 NEW YORK, OCTOBER 15, 1904 Ten Cents

AN INTERNATIONAL CIVIC FEDERATION TO BE FORMED.

AN IMPRESSIVE ASSEMBLY OF REPRESENTATIVES OF EMPLOYERS, OF WAGE-EARNERS AND OF MANY NATIONS DISCUSSES WORLD-WIDE INDUSTRIAL PEACE.

The formation in other countries of bodies similar to the National Civic Federation in the United States, with their affiliation with an International Civic Federation, was the central idea of a luncheon at the Hotel Astor, in New York City, on September 26. At this luncheon, the Executive Committee of the Federation were the hosts, and the guests were delegates to the Interparliamentary Union, selected because of their interest in industrial affairs. These delegates are all members of the parliaments of their respective countries. Other foreign guests were the delegates from French organizations of labor and industrial corporations, sent by the French government to study industrial conditions in the United States.

This was the first international gathering in history in which employers, employed and the general public were all represented.

The purpose of the Interparliamentary Union is the maintenance of international peace through the reference to arbitration of differences between nations that diplomacy fails to adjust. At the time of the luncheon, the Interparliamentary Union had concluded at St. Louis the first session that it had ever held in this country. Both the time, therefore, and the personnel of the company coöperated to bring out in the speeches at the luncheon a parallelism between international peace and industrial peace; between the processes of diplomacy and the methods of conciliation and conference between representa-

THE INTERNATIONAL CONFERENCE ON INDUSTRIAL PEACE.

tives of capital and labor; between the proposed substitution of international arbitration for war and the utility of voluntary arbitration of differences between capital and labor, in preference to the final resort of strikes and lock-outs.

The speeches also brought out the fact that compulsory arbitration is a plan not acceptable to organized labor in this country.

The following is a list of those present at the luncheon:

Members Interparliamentary Union.

America :—Hon. Richard Bartholdt, President Interparliamentary Union; Hon. T. E. Burton, of the Committee of Congress on the Interparliamentary Union; Hon. S. J. Barrows, Secretary of the same Committee; Hon. James Rupert, Member of the Committee.

Austria :—Vladimir Ritter Ladislaus V. Gniewosz, Member of Reichsrath.

Belgium :—X. Houzeau de Lehaie, Senator; Emile Vandervelde, Deputy.

England :—W. Randal-Cremer, M. P.; Thos. Lough, M. P.; Fred. Maddison, ex-M. P.; W. P. Byles, ex-M. P.; Dr. G. B. Clark, ex-M. P.; Corrie Grant, M. P.; Col. Pryce-Jones, M. P.; Dr. E. C. Thompson, M. P.; John Wilson, Secretary Durham Miners; Jeremiah Jordan, M. P.; D. V. Pirie, M. P.; J. Bryn-Roberts, M. P.; William O'Doherty, M. P.

France :—M. Paul Strauss, Senator; M. Dr. Delbet, Deputy; M. Noel, Deputy.

Germany :—Prof. Hoffmann, Member of Reichstag; M. Dr. Hauptmann, Member of Landtag.

Hungary : — Count Albert Apponyi, President Chamber of Deputies; Andre Gyorgy, Deputy.

Italy :—Prof. E. Coccotti, Deputy; M. F. Di Palma, Deputy; M. Edoardo Daneo, Deputy; M. G. Cerruti, Deputy; M. Marquis di San Guellano, Deputy.

Netherlands :—M. Tydeman, Deputy.

Norway :—M. John Lund, Deputy.

Roumania :—Stanislaus Cihcski, Deputy.

Sweden :—John Olsson, Deputy; Ernst Beckman, Deputy.

Switzerland :—Alfred Brustlein, Deputy; Dr. Albert Studer, Deputy; Herman Greulich, Statistician.

Delegation of French Labor Representatives.

M. Albert Metin, Professor of Political Economy in the Colonial and Naval Cadets Schools, and the representative of the French Minister of Commerce; L. Benoist, Technical School of Shoemaking, Nice; H. Buisson, a Director of Le Travail, Co-operative Union of Painters and Glaziers, Paris; H. Dugue, Federal Union of Ironworkers, Havre; A. Fouclause, Director of the Co-operative Union of Musical Instrument Makers, Paris; C. Gignoux, Director of the Co-operative Union of Printers and Typographs, Nimes; E. Hyolet, Hat Makers' Union, Paris; M. Jaquet, National Union of Post and Telegraphers, Paris; J. Le Blanc, National Federation of Engineers, Le Vallois; J. Malbranque, National Union of Railway Workers, Amiens; Charles Rousseau, Director of the Union of Painters, Puteaux; E. Martin, member of the Wool Spinners' Union and a member of the State Superior Council of Labor; Charles Vulete, Director of the Co-operative Union of Industries of Precision, Paris; A. Manoury, of the Central Union of Co-operators of Paris.

Members of the National Civic Federation.

Representing Labor :—Samuel Gompers, President American Federation of Labor; E. E. Clark, Grand Chief Conductor, Order of Railway Conductors; P. H. Morrissey, Grand Master, Brotherhood of Trainmen; John J. Pallas, President New York State Federation of Labor; Edward A. Moffett, Editor "Bricklayer and Mason"; James P. Archibald, Brotherhood of Painters and Decorators; Samuel B. Donnelly, Typographical Union; Edw. Gould, Teamsters; William H. Farley, Mosaic and Encaustic Tile Layers; J. W. Sullivan, Typographical Union; P. F. Quinn, President Central Federated Union; Herman Robinson, Retail Clerks; George E. Pepper, President Amalgamated Association Street Railway Employes, New York Division.

Representing the Public :—Cornelius N. Bliss, Ex-Secretary of the Interior; Oscar S. Straus, Member of the Court of Arbitration at The Hague; John G. Milburn, Lawyer; C. R. Miller, Editor "The Times"; St. Clair McKelway, Editor "Brooklyn Eagle"; Isaac N. Seligman, Banker; Oswald G. Villard, Editor "Evening Post"; Bradford Merrill, Editor "New York World"; James Speyer, Banker; Hamilton Holt, Editor "The Independent"; Charles Stewart Smith, ex-President New York Chamber of Commerce; Roland Phillips, Managing Editor "Harper's Weekly"; H. C. Watson, Editor "Dun's Review"; Warren H. Page, Editor "World's Work"; Lyman Abbott, Editor "Outlook"; John Finley, President College of the City of New York; Ralph M. Easley, Chairman Executive Council.

Representing Employers:—August Belmont, President Interborough Rapid Transit Co.; W. A. Clark, President United Verde Copper Co.; Charles A. Moore, Manning, Maxwell & Moore; Isidor Straus, R. H. Macy & Co.; H. H. Vreeland, President New York City Railroad Co.; John D. Crimmins; Francis L. Robbins, President Pittsburg Coal Co.; B. J. Greenhut, Treasurer Siegel-Cooper Co.; William Green, President New York Typothetæ; Louis B. Schram, President Associated Brewers; John Cooper, President Iron League; John S. Huyler, President Huyler's; J. Alexander Hayden, Chairman Association Interior Decorators and Cabinetmakers; Edward A. Filene, Treasurer William Filene's Sons Co.; Charles W. Terhune, Edwin C. Burt Co.

The speech-making was introduced by Oscar S. Straus, who performed the duties of chairman, proposing "the health of all the sovereigns whose distinguished representatives are in this country in order to promote the good cause of international peace." This toast was followed by another to the health of the President of the United States, proposed by the Hon. Thomas Lough, M. P., of Great Britain. All responded to these toasts standing, amid hearty enthusiasm.

The Chairman, Mr. Straus, then addressed the assembly as follows:

"Gentlemen of the Interparliamentary Union and Distinguished Guests:—It becomes my privilege and pleasure to thank you on behalf of the National Civic Federation for your presence here to-day. We have every reason to congratulate you upon the initial success that has attended your great cause for the good of mankind in the prompt decision on the part of the President of the United States to summon a second International Conference in order to further strengthen and complete the work of the Hague Tribunal and to bring 'the future of humanity under the majesty of the law.' (Cries of "Hear, hear," and great applause.)

"National happiness is the best guaranty for international peace. National good-will—the welfare of the people in the respective countries—is, at the best, an international good-will and an international peace. It is for that reason that we have asked you gentlemen of the Interparliamentary Union to come here and in this informal way discuss with us the best means for promoting the harmonious relations between the great forces of our industrial life.

"When we organized the National Civic Federation we recognized that the relationship between the forces of industry is one that closely touched the whole people. In following that idea we determined that in order to bring the representatives of the whole people together we should divide them into three groups, all of which are equally interested in the country's welfare and in the harmonious relations between the industrial forces. These three groups are the employers on one side, the employes on the other side, and standing between the two, the great public. At the head of the group representing the general public we have placed our most distinguished private citizen, Ex-President Grover Cleveland. (Applause.) At the head of the employers' group we have placed that man whose name and fame is known in every land, and who from his deep interest in the cause of international peace has dedicated to the world a temple where the Court of Peace shall be held. I mean Mr. Andrew Carnegie. (Applause.) At the head of the third group we have placed a man who wields as great power for good as any private citizen in this land. In the council chamber of our National Civic Federation, in which he has always participated, we have seen from day to day surest evidences of his conscientious and deep devotion to the great cause of industrial peace—at the head of that group stands Samuel Gompers, the President of the American Federation of Labor. (Applause.)

"I will not take up time in discussing the triumphs and defeats that the International Civic Federation has met with since its organization three years ago. But I will say that we have succeeded and are succeeding in cementing the relations between the great industrial forces by bringing about a better understanding and by accustoming them to consider the great questions around a council table on an equal plane, with an equal interest in harmonious relations.

"The great problem of industrial peace I know is one that confronts the people under the governments which you represent here. We have inaugurated a plan—the best that we have been able to discover—and that it is not perfect no one is more conscious than we. Expansion of commerce marks the spirit of our day. Commerce means peace. It travels along the highroad of peace. It is based upon mutuality, and brings happiness to both sides. The great labor leaders, recognizing this expansion of commerce, are beginning, and have already begun, to organize their associations internationally. So have many of the large corporations controlling large interests; they have passed beyond national lines and have international interests. I ask you, has not the time arrived when the forces that make for the harmonious relations of the great industrial enterprises should also cross national lines, and that you may carry home with you, and also bring back to us, the idea that is embodied in our National Civic Federation?

"We will heartily join hands with you in cementing a mighty power for securing Industrial Peace; uniting the wage-earners and the wage-payers, the employers, the employes and the general public; confederating the industrial forces of our several countries for their peoples' welfare, happiness and peace, under an International Civic Federation.

"I now call upon the Honorable Richard Bartholdt, a Representative in the Congress of the United States, and President of the Interparliamentary Union." (Applause.)

Mr. Bartholdt said:

"Mr. Chairman and Gentlemen:—Permit me to congratulate the National Civic Federation upon the noble work in which its members are engaged. The endeavor to lay the foundation for industrial peace is worthy of the efforts of the best and noblest of all nations. Centuries have passed with our present industrial system in vogue, and during all this time the so-called social question has been the subject of study and thought of all civilized nations. No remedy has as yet been found for the occasional differences between capital and labor, but at last the light seems to be breaking in,—the light which will illumine the pathway leading to industrial peace and tranquility. We have finally come to the conclusion, and fortunately both sides to the controversy seem to agree upon the proposition,—that an appeal to the spirit of conciliation and mutual concession, and if that fail, an appeal to the principles of arbitration, are the right remedies. (Applause.)

"A bill is pending in the Congress of the United States providing for industrial arbitration, and it has been referred to the Committee on Labor, of which I have the honor to be a humble member. This bill would have been considered even in the last session, had it not been for the fact that the eight-hour bill consumed practically all of the time at the disposal of that committee. For me, I am frank to state here and now, that if the great Civic Federation, in whose judgment I have implicit confidence, and in which both sides are properly represented, will say to me that they are in favor of such legislation, I am ready to support it in the next session of the House of Representatives.

"In view of the gigantic growth of the industrial forces in our country, it has always seemed to me that organizations on the part of labor and also organizations on the part of capital should not only be tolerated but encouraged. A method must then be provided to enable the representatives of both sides and in the several industries to meet and by amicable agreement fix the hours of labor and the amount of wages for a certain period of time. If no agreement upon these conditions is possible, then both sides should invoke the great principle of arbitration, for which a machinery should be provided by law. It must be remembered that in all industrial controversies there are not only two sides but actually three. There are the employed and the employer, but there is also the general public, which in cases of great strikes is even a greater sufferer than either of the contending parties; which I submit is an additional reason, and certainly a very strong one, why in the interest of our common good these conflicts should be averted if possible.

"The Interparliamentary Union, of which I have the honor to be president, is striving not to abolish war 'with one fell swoop,'—because that is impossible,—but to starve to death 'the dogs of war,' by promoting a policy of mutual agreement between the nations entered into in times of peace, and submitting any controversy which may arise to arbitration.

"Every man who favors such a policy in our international relations is bound to favor a policy of arbitration in the industrial arena. Law must be substituted for physical force wherever it can be done. This is the demand of the interests of civilization and humanity, and the condition sine qua non of social peace and general prosperity."

In introducing the Hon. W. Randal-Cremer, M. P., Mr. Straus said:

"Mr. Cremer is par excellence a 'Prince of Peace.' He stands as the pioneer of arbitration, of conciliation and of the harmonious adjustment of the relations of men, both nationally and internationally. To him was awarded the great Nobel prize as the most distinguished promoter of international peace,—a prize of eight thousand pounds,—which was immediately devoted by him to the cause to which his life has been consecrated."

Mr. Cremer said:

"My forte is not speaking, but working. I have done a great deal more working than speaking in my now fairly long life, and I am not going to break my record by attempting to make a long speech this afternoon.

"I can only account for the fact that I have been not merely invited but almost compelled to speak by the mandate of our chairman by the fact that I am, I think, the oldest man in the assembly, and certainly I am the oldest member of any organized body of the industrial classes. I have been for nearly fifty years a trades-unionist, and my life has been spent amongst the people with whom I was born and reared and with whom I have shared their aspirations and their hopes and desires. I have seen, Mr. Chairman, during the fifty years of my connection with trade-unionists of the United Kingdom of Great Britain, and with my co-workers on the continent of Europe, some very remarkable changes.

"I have been engaged in two or three industrial wars; the first, in 1859, perhaps one of the most severe conflicts that ever took place between capital and labor. For nearly five months 100,000 working-men in London were locked out by their employers, and for nearly five months we struggled with our employers to succeed in the objects which we demanded from them. For the time being we failed, but in the end we triumphed. But one of the morals that I learned upon that occasion, and which was subsequently burned into my memory by other struggles in which I have been engaged, was that it was an act of folly, if not of madness, almost, on the part of either employer or employed to engage in conflicts of that kind. (Applause.)

"The amount of suffering on the part of the poor, the loss of capital on the part of the wealthy, each was such as scarcely any of us could calculate. I learned the great lesson many years ago, and I have tried to give effect to it ever since throughout my life by doing my very best to remedy those conflicts by arriving at a peaceful solution of the problem of the difficulties between capital and labor.

"It is because I have found that this great movement of yours, the National Civic Federation, is built up on such peaceful lines that I am glad to have the opportunity of being present to-day, and especially of renewing my acquaintance with my old friend, Mr. Gompers, with whom I was associated—not too well but only slightly, I regret to say—but whom I learned to admire because of his heroic efforts in the United States nearly eighteen years ago.

"Mr. President, we have been trying—and the lesson I learned in the trades-union world and in the industrial world was that we should try—to introduce into industrial life and industrial strife the same principle for which we are contending and which we are trying to introduce into political life amongst the nations of the globe.

"I have said a great deal more than I had intended. I told you my forte is not speaking, but working; and all I can say in closing is that I hope the Civic Federation, under whose auspices we are assembled here to-day, will be as successful in preventing social and industrial wars as the Interparliamentary Union has been in providing for the future discouragement of war between the various nations of the earth." (Applause.)

Mr. Straus then called upon Samuel Gompers, President of the American Federation of Labor, to speak for the National Civic Federation.

Mr. Gompers said:

"Perhaps, gentlemen, I ought to wish that I could have been advised that I was to address this meeting to-day, so that I might have been enabled to give to the subject some little more mature thought. Let me say, in supplement to the most eloquent welcome that has been extended by our honored toast-master, that we also welcome the delegates of the French working-men who come here by the authority of the government of France to investigate conditions of American industry, commerce and civilization.

"I cannot permit the opportunity to pass without saying a word or two in regard to my old friend—my young friend in spirit and heart, though many years have crept upon him, but they have left no indelible impression other than maturer and riper judgment—our friend Cremer. It is now seventeen years ago when he, in company with Sir Lionel Playfair, came to the United States and sought to fulfil the mission which he so eloquently describes. I remember, too, that there were but very few men who met him in a spirit of cordiality. There were very few men in our country who bade him good cheer and Godspeed in his mission, but the gentleman to whom our toastmaster has referred as heading the representatives of the employers in the National Civic Federation—Mr. Andrew Carnegie—gave his unqualified support to the movement at that time. (Applause.) It was very pleasing—aye, more than pleasing; exceedingly gratifying—to find that he has been a consistent friend and advocate of international peace from that day to this; and I think our friend Cremer will agree with me, too, that the organized working-men of America at that time were those who gave the strongest impetus to the movement of any of our fellow citizens in the United States. I am proud to recall the fact that Mr. Cremer and Sir Lionel Playfair came to the American Federation of Labor held at Baltimore, and a resolution was unanimously passed pledging the organized labor movement of America to international peace.

"Assembled here this afternoon are not all the great Englishmen, are not all the great Frenchmen, are not all the great Irishmen, are not all the great Norwegians, nor Scandinavians, nor all the great Americans; but I think it goes without saying that the gentlemen assembled here this afternoon are of the best types of our respective countries. You are constituted of the best men of your countries, because you have done something, and not only done something but done something useful for humanity. The men who work, the men who pave the way of commerce, the men who pave the way for civilization give it its fullest and amplest opportunities for development.

"I am one of those who believe with Mr. Bartholdt, Member of Congress and honored President of the Interparliamentary Union, in favoring the organization of capital and the organization of labor. I don't believe that in our time it is possible for the fullest development of all the abilities of our people, except by the concentration of effort and by the association of men.

"I believe, too, in arbitration of the industrial problems that cannot be solved by these two contending forces of capital and labor. I am free to say, however, without attempting to inject any spirit of controversy into these proceedings, that I must dissent from his expression of opinion when he says that in the last analysis the government should determine the condition of labor, the payment of wages by the employer, or the reception of wages by the employe. I would not mention this except that my silence might be construed to be an assent to that proposition.

"Let me say that the National Civic Federation undertakes to do the thing in industry that ought to be done. It is the voluntary mediator, which undertakes to bring about a better relation between the employer and the employe, and it has done much more than that for which it is already given credit. It has alleviated distress, avoided and averted contests and controversies and conflicts—many more than is known to the world. It has done much to bring men together who formerly looked with disdain upon one another and who could not, by reason of their positions in life, meet each other around the table and discuss their respective interests. It has made possible in our country a condition of affairs by which the largest employers of labor—a number of whom are at this table, and grace it,—can meet with the representatives of organized labor and discuss the relative interests that are involved in a controversy which may be pending, or a controversy which is contemplated, avert them and bring about a feeling between the men of lasting desire at least to do no harm to each other.

"The National Civic Federation represents, as our Chairman, Mr. Straus, has so well said, not only the employers, but its members are the employers themselves; not only the representatives of labor, but the employes themselves; and also the public, by a portion of the public itself; and by meeting and discussing the great problems of the day as well as the problems of the future, tries to find a way out by which no man will lose his interests, by which no man will lose his honor, or have his dignity impaired. But after all we shall have to depend for our success in establishing peace, both industrially and internationally, upon the growing intelligence and humanity of our peoples; for unless it rests upon that growth of intelligence and spirit of humanity it cannot be successful, no matter how it may be writ in law.

"We want to change ourselves, we want to improve ourselves; and in the same degree that we shall improve ourselves we shall by example improve our fellows. We are making for industrial peace, despite the conflicts that arise here and there; and deplorable as is the disturbance of the international peace which we now observe, I think we all agree that we are nearer the time when international peace will be the realization of our dreams and our hopes, our prayers and our work; that is, if all make an effort; and he who does this not only does himself honor, but benefits his fellow-man."

The Hon. Dr. Hauptman, Member of the Prussian Landtag, who was next introduced, spoke in German, which was translated as follows:

"I have never regretted in all my life more than now that I am unable to speak the English language, as I would like to properly express my gratitude for the many evidences of American hospitality I have received since arriving here.

"The European visitors, including myself, have received very many object lessons in our tour through this great country; one of them being the apparent equality of the classes, which proves to me that democracy here is not an empty word, but is a reality. We have all learned something this afternoon about the efforts which are being made in this country by the National Civic Federation to conciliate and bring about a harmonious understanding between capital and labor. I think the proper way to do this has been chosen by you, namely, to bring representatives of both factors together so that they may discuss and understand the principles underlying these controversies, and, better yet, to understand each other, and that their mutual interests lie along the line of mutual concession and harmonious relations. This is not only the best way, but is also the easiest way to settle these differences.

"I thank the Civic Federation for the invitation and the hospitality extended to my colleagues and myself on this occasion, and I wish to express my gratification that our people who come to this country—the German-Americans—have become such loyal American citizens, although they have not forgotten their mother tongue or the great lessons learned from German literature and philosophy." (Applause.)

The Hon. Paul Strauss, of the Senate of France, spoke in his native tongue as follows:

"In the name of the French people I will say that I am particularly pleased to be be able to concur in the sentiments which have been expressed here this afternoon in regard to the promoters of this interesting meeting and the organizers of the Interparliamentary Union. I am also pleased to say that there are here not only the representatives of the universal suffrage of Europe and the United States, but we have the good fortune to have among us those who are representatives of the working-men and of the associations of Frenchmen—representatives of both labor and capital; and if the time had been given us, and if you should have opened your doors, you would have not only representatives of these French associations, but also representatives of all European working-men.

"I want to express the wish that the International Civic Federation shall become a unit of harmony, and that in its meetings there will be not only representatives of organized labor, but also members representing capital, both taking an active part in the deliberations to bring about a harmonious result. The ground was broken and this work was really begun by the Berlin Convention, in which the first bill was passed for the protection of women. I hope that the plan submitted to the International Conference at Basle, in Switzerland, will be followed, and that next year we shall be permitted to see the beginnings of international legislation for working people, which will be welcomed by both the members of parliament and the members of unions representing working-men and capital as well.

"The peace between capital and labor—industrial peace—is the necessary beginning of a general peace of nations." (Applause.)

Prof. E. Coccotti, of the Chamber of Deputies, Italy, spoke as follows:

"I did not expect that I would be invited here to speak, and because I admire your language and your great poets, I would not speak that which would offend your sensibilities. I would speak in my own great Italian, but because I want to be understood—perhaps I would be better understood if I spoke in Italian—I will try to express myself in English.

"Mr. Chairman and Gentlemen, I am a Socialist, but I am, too, a practical man. (Laughter.) I hope to be more and more a practical man. I learned to be a practical man in America. You teach so many things to the world here, that you teach the Socialists, even, and others, to be practical. I agree with you in every wish and hope that we will alleviate these contests. I believe with the great English poet, Charles Algernon Swinburn, that this reality must be brought about by the worker, and that when the contest between employer and employe shall be settled, that may be the moment in which we may expect to see final human justice.' (Applause.)

Charles Stewart Smith, for many years President of the Chamber of Commerce of New York, was next introduced. He said:

"I have no mandate here to speak for the Chamber of Commerce; at least I have not been sent here as a delegate. I am indebted for my presence here to the friendship of Mr. Straus. But I assure you that I am very glad to be here.

"I have been very much gratified by the speeches made here to-day, and I have been also very much instructed. It seems proper that I should speak on this occasion, because I recognize in your first speaker, Mr. Chairman, my old friend Mr. Cremer, a gentleman who came here seventeen years ago, and when I chanced at the time to be President of the Chamber of Commerce and had the honor of inviting him to our annual banquet on that occasion. He made us one of the very best speeches that we had that evening. He was received with glorious applause, and he gave great impetus in that presence to the association of which he was a delegate.

"Now, gentlemen, I think I may say that the Chamber of Commerce is in full sympathy with all the views I have heard expressed here to-day. (Applause.) We have passed resolutions in favor of the utmost reciprocity with the different nations of Europe. We believe that it is perfectly right for both capital and labor to organize in the most efficient way possible. We believe it is their right, and not only their right, but their duty. But if I were permitted to express an opinion in conflict with my old friend Gompers, who is an expert on all questions of labor, I would ask him to consider the proposition whether he was not ready to advise his friends to organize in corporations, so that they would give the laboring class the same power with the capital class, so that they can approach these questions with a larger organization behind them—an organization which would guarantee their contracts, which would give them power distinct from the people; and I should be very glad indeed to see labor organizations take that position.

"Now, I have said that the Chamber of Commerce is in favor of reciprocity. I believe that is one of the most important questions that can affect international peace. Reciprocity involves acquaintance between the great nations of the world. Trade goes always for peace, and if we have mutual reciprocity and mutual relations we cannot fail to have peace. Merchants always oppose war; men of commerce always oppose war, and the labor unions, I think, Mr. Gompers, are equally opposed to it. Consequently, what I want to see is labor unions made strong, and I believe their organization into corporations would give them power which they do not have now. They could speak with authority then; and I am very much in hopes that my friend Mr. Gompers will advocate that system for the people whom he so ably represents.

"Now, Mr. President, only a word more. I believe the question between capital and labor is the greatest question, the most enormous problem, that confronts industrial peace, not only in the United States, but in all industrial nations. It has not been solved yet, and I hope that this National Civic Federation, which is represented here to-day, is on the right track. I believe it is, and that it is on the way to solve that question in accordance with the highest ideals of rectitude and justice. If that can be accomplished, I think that we may look for commercial prosperity such as we have never seen before. Look at the enormous amount of money lost in strikes, both to capital and labor, which may be saved if the principles which you are advocating so bravely and earnestly can be universally adopted and carried out! And I sincerely hope that that may be the end, and that your organization, Mr. Chairman, may have this effect. If it does, you will certainly earn and receive the gratitude of the civilized world." (Great applause and cries of "Hear, hear.")

The Hon. Emile Vandervelde, Deputy from Belgium, said:

"In speaking to you I must say that I am a little embarrassed because I was not prepared, and secondly and mainly because I have not a commission to speak in the name of the whole Belgium delegation, because it is composed of men of different opinions, partly Conservatives and partly Socialist. I myself am a member of the Socialist party, and I am afraid I will be considered by some here a 'black-faced sheep.' But all the Belgium delegates agree to be grateful to the President of the United States for his initiative in a second Hague Conference, which we must recognize is to prevent war, but which we must say is not sufficient, because to have international peace we must have national good-will and peace of labor. Peace to be stable and sincere must be founded on justice, and perhaps here we differ not only in the principle but in the application which we make of this principle.

It must be understood that the question of work must not be resolved by bloody conflict, but by peaceful conciliation. Class struggle is not necessarily class war. I am in favor of arbitration and conciliation, and I am pleased to see how much that view has progressed in the big Democracy of the United States to-day.

"Social peace is only possible with strong and well organized labor unions, and nowhere is capital so well organized as in the United States or working-men so well organized as in the federations of labor in the United States.

"To-day we see the greatest industry in the world in this country, where everything is larger than anywhere else, but the best remembrance of the liberty of this country which I shall keep is that we have seen in the City of New York twenty or thirty thousand organized people; and in a few days, when we will be on the other side of the ocean, we will say to the working-men, 'Be organized as the Americans are organized.' And why is this possible? Because the United States are a republic, because the Statue of Liberty is at the entrance of the harbor of New York, and because that is not a lie but a reality. (Applause.)

"I hope it will be permitted me to again see the United States of America, and not only that but in the near future to see the United States of Europe, and I hope the moment will come when New York and London and Paris and Berlin will be united, and we will be able to toast the United States of the World." (Applause.)

The Hon. Andre Gyorgy, Deputy from Hungary, said:

"It is not many years since in England the name of Mr. Morley was immortalized by these agitations between capital and labor. We are trying all over the world to settle these differences, but just now Mr. Vandervelde told us that there should be and must be conciliation and arbitration between capital and labor, and our efforts must be directed to this. We have in every nation and country of Europe these arbitrations, and I am very sorry to find that you have not in the United States, but you are before the continent of Europe in this—you are doing what we are trying to do.

"We are trying in the Interparliamentary Union to bring about arbitration, and you are trying to do the same thing between capital and labor,—and I was told very successfully.

"You are trying to bring about peace before arbitration, and I think it should be the greatest glory of the National Civic Federation when you shall be in a position not to want any arbitration bill, but shall be able to settle all the disputes between capital and labor in a social way, by way of your Civic Federation—not to have any arbitration bill or any legislative interference between those social divisions." (Applause.)

The Hon. John Olsson, Deputy from Sweden, said:

"I was not notified before that I would have to say some words here, and therefore I am in the same predicament as my friend the Italian professor. I am sorry that I cannot speak much to you in your own language, because I speak the English but very imperfectly. Therefore you will please allow me to be very short and only to make one remark.

"We in our land have also organizations between labor and organizations between employers, and I think this National Civic Federation is just in the right way. This Federation, as I understand, is trying to help, and permanently help, the conciliation of labor with capital. I think that is the way for all countries to go forward, to get arbitration between capital and labor.

"Now, Mr. Chairman, I am not able to speak more because I cannot speak the English language, but you will allow me to express for myself and my Swedish companion our great thanks to this Civic Federation for your kindness in inviting us to this splendid entertainment." (Applause.)

The Hon. Alfred Brustlein, Deputy from Switzerland, addressed the assembly in French. The following is a translation of his remarks:

"I am the only Swiss man here, and that is why I have the right to speak in the name of my country. But in speaking I will remember one thing that I have learned while I was in France, and which exists, perhaps, also in England. It is the brief poem which says you have two eyes and two ears but only one mouth. I have drawn from this verse the lesson that when arriving in a foreign land you must mainly open the eyes and ears and speak the least possible, because the little that you would say might seem stupid, as the sentiments are so different in one country from another.

"In this country, capital and labor are engaged in a real struggle, although not a bloody one. That is because the two classes may meet readily. You have not in America the difference of classes, and that is why, very likely, in America events will take a different turn from that which we have in our own country. You sit at the same table, and you speak the same language all over the United States. It is not the same in our country. The struggle between the classes has deeper roots; and it is in our home, not in America, that the struggle between the classes has been discovered.

"There is a great difference between the relations between nations and the relations between labor and capital. The relations between nations are affected by the difference of language, while the difference between labor and capital lies in the difference between two classes; and consequently they can be reconciled only through a reign of justice which must be open to all.

"Your President, Andrew Carnegie, in his beautiful book on the use of riches, has said that a man who gains riches with only the idea of transmitting them to his heirs will not be worthy of having them. And that is why, feeling this sentiment, I think we should have before us many good years of peace and love; and although we have some differences now, in the final end of things we will be united. And that is why I shall now shake the hand of your president." (Applause.)

The Chairman introduced Professor Albert Metin, as the head of the delegation of French workingmen. Professor Metin spoke in English:

"We members of the delegation of working-men sent by the French government appreciate highly this beautiful reception you have given us, and also the magnificent welcome we have received to this Empire City.

"Allow me to present to you the fourteen members of the working-men's delegation sent here by the French government. These gentlemen have been nominated by the French government from the working-men's associations to which they severally belong. They are partly corporators and partly members of the unions, but it is not necessary to observe very closely to see that the members of the corporations are in favor of the unionists and that the unionists are in favor of the corporation. We have among us some members representing the different corporations. They are secretaries of the corporations for production and consumption—administrators or directors or secretaries of the associations or syndicates; at the same time they are administrators or secretaries of what we call universities or popular institutions of education. We also have among us two members who represent what we call the State Superior Council of Labor. These are composed in part of some functionaries, or officials, nominated by the government and in part of labor members—working-men—returned by the unions for the purpose of looking after social legislation.

"It is needless to say we are great admirers of America. We admire it from two points of view; because here we get lessons of democracy and we also get lessons of industry. We are learning much in New York, and we hope to learn much more in our trip through the United States. We admire your institutions because we find in them many useful lessons, and we also know by experience the magnificent qualities of the people of the United States. We know, too, that the people of the United States are ready to do the same justice to the old nations of Europe. It is a pleasure for me to unite in the same sentence the names of the Presidents of the American and French Federations of Labor.

"I toast to the better organization of our working-men and to the friendship of our nations and people and Democracy all over the world, for social progress and for union and peace." (Applause).

Francis L. Robbins spoke as follows:

"I would invite the attention of our foreign guests to some practical methods of preserving industrial peace now in operation in this country.

"Probably the most conspicuous example of a trade agreement in practical operation is that between the bituminous coal miners and operatives. The method of settlement in that industry is reached through a joint conference held each spring in Indianapolis. We leave nothing to arbitration, believing that we are better able to agree between ourselves as to wages and conditions of labor than anyone could agree for us.

"In the last convention it was unanimously resolved that any agreement made must be kept inviolate and that no sympathetic strike and no other cause whatever could be an adequate reason for breaking the contract. The company of which I have the honor to be the president, employing nearly 75,000 men in mines, on docks, in transportation and in selling agencies, has not to-day a single dispute with an employe. This is due largely to the conservatism of those labor leaders with whom we have relations, notably, John Mitchell, President of the United Mine Workers of America, and Daniel J. Keefe, President of the Longshoremen's International Union.

"The Pittsburg Coal Company, shortly after its organization, inaugurated a method to enable the employes to share in its profits. It formed an employes' association through which the employe can purchase the preferred stock of the company by the payment of $1 per share per month, the company carrying the loan at 5 per cent. interest. This plan has been the means of permitting a great many of the company's employes to make savings that otherwise they would not have made. The plan has interested them also in the success of the company, and its indirect effects are everywhere visible in the spirit of industry prevailing among the workers and in their attitude toward their employer. The company has also inaugurated a death and accident association, with a lodge at each mine, the expense of which is in part borne by the company. We have also established an old-age pension fund, to which the company contributes aid and co-operation.

"We regard our plan of profit-sharing, of accident insurance and of pensions as a practical and satisfactory solution of the problem which arises with the present tendency to concentrate the control of the management of business in large corporations. In this process there is a constant increase in the percentage of those whose only interest in the business is their daily, weekly or monthly wage allowance. This tends to widen the separation of the employer and the employe, without some such reuniting factor as the Employes' Association of the Pittsburg Coal Company. The organization of the lodges sharing in the insurance and pension benefits is voluntary at each mine. No lodge is organized until the majority of the operatives of the mine agree to be governed by the general by-laws adopted at a convention of the employes, at which each of the company's mines was represented by delegates elected by the men. The treasurer of the Coal Company is treasurer of each of the lodges. All disbursements, therefore, are made from the company's general office by the treasurer of the employes' association.

"The dues paid by the men are at the rate of 40c. per month per man. The benefits are graded into seven classes, ranging from $150 for a fatal accident while at work, of which the company directly contributes one-half, down to benefits of $5 per week for minor accidents. The pension fund received at the start a contribution of $10,000 by the company. This fund is invested in the preferred stock of the company, and is to remain intact and grow for a period of ten years. At the end of that time the principal and earnings of the fund in excess of $100,000 may be used in the payment of pensions to operatives who have paid into the fund continuously for a period of ten years and who through old age, accident or sickness are not able to earn their livelihood. All expenses of the employes' association are paid by the company. It is believed that the development of such a movement in such practical lines is a source of strength and progress, and students of social economy have stated that the furtherance of this movement goes a long way towards solving the problem of industrial peace."

In bringing the occasion to a close, Mr. Straus said:

"I have endeavored to call on a representative from each country. I should be glad to have it called to my attention if I have omitted to call upon a gentleman from any country represented here.

"I thank you again on behalf of the Civic Federation for the honor you have done us by your presence. I trust that you will carry with you the mission of peace which we place in your hands, with the hope that the work in which we are all engaged will contribute to elevate the standards of life and bring happiness and contentment to the peoples of our several lands."

THE EDUCATION OF UNIONS.

Sound Advice as to the Social and Intellectual Utilization of the Winter Evenings.

The desire among trades-unions to promote education among their members is strikingly illustrated by the following editorial from the "Machinists' Monthly Journal," the official organ of the International Association of Machinists:

The shortening of the days and the increasing coolness of the nights will remind the local committees who have been appointed to look after the entertainment and educational features of their respective lodges that the time has come when they must show their greatest activity. If these committees have been alert and active and with a due appreciation of their duties and what was expected from them, they will have their work well in hand and everything prepared for the winter's campaign of education. The importance of this work is very great, for the whole success of the local lodge as an educational factor depends upon its thoroughness. Nothing should be omitted from the plan of education, and no subject of an economic nature, however small, should be considered unworthy of consideration. The range is wide and the field is great, and no one will fail to gain additional knowledge—no matter how perfect may be his learning—when a subject is discussed with intelligence and moderation and an honest desire to get at true solutions.

When subjects are under discussion their success, which is really their value, will depend in a great measure upon the tolerance shown for the opinion of others by those who participate. Every one has the right to think, though every one doesn't always think right, and it is only when our mistakes are pointed out and we receive enlightenment which shows us our error, and we acknowledge and see that we have been in error, that our true education begins. It is, therefore, wise for all of us to refrain from considering ourselves above criticism until our thoughts and theories have run the gauntlet of honest discussion. Then, if no great flaws have been discovered in them, and they have been strengthened in their weak places, we may feel assured that not only have we added a little to our own knowledge, but we have contributed to the knowledge of others. Any subject that cannot bear honest investigation and honest discussion is not worth while considering, and can not be of educational value. It will be the educational committees' duty to see that the time placed at their disposal is not wasted in fruitless theorizing or profitless discord. It ought also to be seen to that no member be considered too intellectually insignificant to give expression to an opinion. All have a right to be heard, and the man who says least may think most, so that when he does speak he may solve a difficult problem. Wisdom isn't always the attribute of the man who talks loud and long, neither is it the mark of wisdom to show impatience and intolerance when a quiet man has the temerity to express a difference of opinion. Upon the education committees' work and the intelligence therein displayed will depend the success or failure of the local lodges of the International Association of Machinists to aid in the intellectual development of their members or add to their economic education.

AGAINST SYMPATHETIC STRIKES AND FOR ADHERENCE TO TRADE AGREEMENTS.

SOME PRACTICAL POLITICAL ECONOMY LUCIDLY DISCUSSED BY THE HEAD OF A STRONG INTERNATIONAL UNION.

The annual address of the President of the International Longshoremen, Daniel J. Keefe, discusses several subjects of interest and importance to both capital and labor. He makes an ingenious comparison between war and strikes:

"Universal Reason does not yet understand the Arts of Peace. Divine Providence has seemingly postponed the emancipation of Nations. War and Conquest are still popular. The world still sings the Song of War. But humanity is not without hope, commencing with the abolition of slavery, and advancing over the ruins of aristocracies and thrones, the White Angel of Peace will ere long teach that standing armies are a paralysis of humane activities, and their maintenance the wanton waste of the nations' bone and sinew and the pillage of the sweat and blood of labor.

"Under the head of strikes let us think of war, let us pause and contemplate the terrible object lesson now being presented by the Russian and Japanese War. The frightful loss of life and wealth that must ensue to both the victor and vanquished. This enormous loss to be sustained in greater part by the masses of the people, and represents the patient toil, the misery, and privation of generations, not to speak of the cruel sacrifice of thousands of lives.

"This great waste of millions of the wealth of both nations, if economically applied in the alleviation of the misery of the masses of these countries, would be productive of relieving want and poverty and creating a paradise on earth, by the uplifting of these vast hosts, now chained down by oppression, ignorance, and superstition; and whose abject condition on earth to-day is akin to hell. Yet, these miserable wretches furnish the sinews of war and ''twas ever thus.'

"Strikes are but another species of war, industrial war—so-called. But humanity is being fast converted to the idea of conciliation and arbitration, as a method of settling the disputes and differences between nations and between the forces of capital and labor. Strikes are like war, part and parcel of our civilization, and must be dealt with on broad lines of public policy, through an enlightened public conscience.

"As modern war owing to the invention of modern appliances for the destruction of life and property becomes more terrible, so also does the strike of to-day become more serious, owing to the great strength and intelligence of the forces of labor; and the loss to the victor and vanquished correspondingly heavy.

"Let us try and consider the meaning of a strike in the United States, where the entire force of organized labor was arrayed against capital. The mere contemplation of such a crisis makes my blood run cold. Imagine for a moment what this would mean. It would mean nothing, if not war. But let us hope that such a contingency will never arise. While strikes at times are unavoidable, as, for instance, when the soulless and sordid greed of a coal baron sneers at labor with the hiss 'that he has nothing to arbitrate.' Whose impious utterances cause the human soul to shiver with the cold-blooded blasphemy of the Divine Right' for the exploitation of humanity. Happily, the Baers are but few, and the employers, as a general rule, are ready and willing to meet labor half-way.

"While the strike is labor's only weapon to resist the unjust oppression of greedy capital, it should be employed only when all other means of settlement has been exhausted and failed to avert it. Under these conditions a strike may be justified, yet the so-called sympathetic strike should not be thought of.

"Sympathetic strikes should never be countenanced or sanctioned by this organization. We may give our moral support, or we may lend financial assistance, where the same be merited and the cause found worthy. But our honor and integrity as an organization is bound up in our contracts and agreements, and our very manhood at stake; to violate those contracts by a sympathetic strike would be suicide and dishonor. Public sentiment says that arbitration is the most equitable medium for the solution of differences and disagreements between the industrial forces.

"'With public sentiment,' said Abraham Lincoln, 'nothing can fail; without it, nothing can hope to succeed.'"

Upon the relation between wages and cost of living, Mr. Keefe makes the following remarks:

"The question of wage agreements must be based on the standard of life of the American wage-worker.

"It is the purchasing power of our labor that should be the real basis, that should determine the rate of wage.

DANIEL J. KEEFE,
President International Longshoremen's Ass'n.

"To make this more clear, let me say, that in Alaska gold fields, where labor is paid $10.00 per day, and where the cost of a flannel shirt is $10.00, and everything that goes to sustain life in the same proportion, no rational man will believe that the laborer in the Philippines, whose wage of fifty cents per day, that will provide him with the necessaries of life for three days, is not better off physically, and the purchasing power of his labor greater than the fellow in Alaska with his $10.00 per day. And any reference to the low wages of Europe can have no force or effect in arriving at an equitable and just compensation measured by our standard of living.

"This question of the cost of living in its relation to wages should be studied carefully and its importance duly considered. The wage-worker has only one thing to sell, the skill of his hands and brain, and he never claims a price which will destroy his employment by destroying his employers' profit.

"As a preventive of labor disputes and strikes, and the great and ultimate factor in the solution of the industrial problem, annual trade agreements between employer and employe will, in my judgment, not only accomplish this, but will in the near future establish an economic unity of interests between the two great contending forces, that will eventually become co-operative in its broadest sense, and the final relations will be that of business partnerships.

"My experience is that no bond or surety furnished by the worker will inspire the confidence, or guarantee the satisfaction that trade agreements have produced.

"The acceptance of a moral obligation of the workers by our employers, is certainly a glowing tribute to the fidelity, the honor, and integrity of any labor organization, and our contracts should be revered and held as sacred as our lives.

"He who prevents an epidemic or an illness, is the greater physician; so also are trade agreements the greater moral force in the solution of the question; they eliminate industrial strife, in so much as they prevent or render strikes, lockouts, etc., impossible.

"The cost of labor, or rather the current rate of wages that can permanently exist depends on, or should depend on the cost and necessary expenses of living; and those expenses depend—in turn—on the condition of the worker.

"Hence, other things being equal, the more educated, morally and intellectually elevated, any community of workers become, the higher will be their standard of living, and of necessity, their wages must correspond to the standard. The higher the American standard of life attained by labor, the greater the benefit to the nation.

"Although wages rise and fall with the general rise and fall of the commodities, they do not in equal proportion. For nearly all products there is both an actual and speculative value or present demand; and no one speculates in wages. The price of any commodity or merchandise may rise to a very high point in value, yet no person ever claimed that the wages of labor in those particular lines advanced in proportion. As, for example, when the price of steel went soaring a few years since, no writer on economics has ever contended that wages rose pro rata; the miners of iron ore, the longshoremen, and all engaged in the transportation of the iron ore, never felt their wages swell in proportion to the increase in the price of steel. The same is true of cotton, and those whose labor puts it on the market; in fact, the same is true of all speculative commodities. While it is true that our wages have advanced with the prosperity of the last eight years, yet, the cost of living has advanced and continues to advance in the face of a general decline.

"The wants of the wage-worker have immensely increased and the standard of living will continue to rise, and the workers' necessities to-day may have been luxuries a few years past; and absolutely unknown a generation ago; and it is upon these points that great stress must be laid in making our annual agreements; and it behooves each and every member to study the question thoroughly, so as to be able to meet with intelligence any and all phases of the question relative to wages.

"In the making of contracts, or annual agreements, we must clearly understand our rights, and at the same time recognize the necessity of respecting the rights of those with whom we are dealing. The real point to contend for is simply the adjustment of our relations on a basis of mutual interest and justice, with no desire to kill the goose that lays the golden egg."

Mr. Keefe pronounces organization of labor to be "the greatest moral force of the century" and declares that it has accomplished the following things:

"Organization removed the child of tender years from the mill and mine, and brought sunshine into the lives of the little ones.

"Organization has limited women's toil in the sweat-shop and improved the surroundings and sanitary conditions.

"Organization has promoted economy and encouraged sobriety, taught the worker not to waste his opportunities, has removed ignorance and prejudice.

"Organization has been a positive force in the awakening of a higher duty in the parent in the education of his off spring; that they may be better equipped to fight the battle of life.

"Organization has eliminated many of the burdens and evils that were the inheritance of centuries.

"Organization has made us better men and to-day our actions are controlled by sentiments of justice, equity, and humanity, promoting peace, comfort and happiness."

NEEDS OF THE NEW ENGLAND COTTON INDUSTRY.

AN ADDRESS URGING THE STUDY AND SOLUTION OF THE LABOR PROBLEM, AND THE ADOPTION OF IMPROVED METHODS.

Herbert E. Walmsley of New Bedford, Mass., President of the New England Cotton Manufacturers' Association, in his address to the semi-annual meeting of that body in September, dwelt upon the importance of industrial peace. He also declared it to be an economic principle that no industry that depends for its life upon undue restriction of wages, in order to atone for loss caused by failure to employ the most modern methods, has a right to exist. Mr. Walmesley said:

"First and foremost of all questions for consideration and elucidation is, without doubt, the so-called labor question; the standard of prosperity of the cotton trade in New England, depending so largely upon the presence or absence of a correct and good understanding between employer and employed.

"In the spirit in which the concerns of a great industry ought to be conducted, and on the principle that we are totally and absolutely opposed to strikes and lock-outs, favoring on the other hand an equitable adjustment of differences between employer and employed by conciliation or any amicable method that will preserve the rights of both parties, I do not hesitate, as president of this association, to again submit that the question of industrial peace is a perfectly legitimate topic for investigation and discussion by this association. At the same time, let me say that I am not unmindful of the fact that one must expect to have one's motives scrutinized and one's every word sifted with no ordinary jealousy and with no sparing criticism, when attempting to deal with the subject.

"As you are aware, the cotton trade of this country is one of the very important, if not the most important of our great staple industries, some millions of our population being directly or indirectly dependent upon it. Its dislocation or stoppage brings in its train every kind of disaster without parallel; its prosperity is the guarantee of comfort and well-being to an enormous section of our people, and is to be earnestly labored for.

"Is there any man who does not see the extent of the burdens placed upon the industry and the community through the disastrous and ever-recurring conflicts between employer and employed, with their desolating effect, destroying as such conflicts do, hundreds of thousands of dollars of capital taken from the profits of the mills and the thrift of the workers, benefitting our competitors to the lasting and permanent injury of New England, imperilling the very existence of the trade?

"Is there anyone who does not acknowledge that it is a matter of intense concern to all of us that the smooth working of the great cotton manufacturing industry of New England should, if possible, be insured? Surely not! Let us then endeavor to infuse the genius of common sense into the question.

"Is there anyone among us, any employer of labor, who does not fully realize the absolute necessity of harmonious co-operation and combination between employer and employed? Who does not recognize the fact that the road to trade prosperity lies through the region of mutual understanding?

"There is small need to point out or recount reasons which demonstrate the evils of strikes or lock-outs; at best they are a clumsy, uncivilized and outrageous remedy. The pity is that such occurrences so often become inevitable. We can ill afford these wretched conflicts, entailing such severe loss upon capital and such untold misery and suffering upon labor; these 'fights to a finish,' jeopardizing the very existence of the cotton industry, are to be deprecated and discountenanced, dislocating the trade and driving much of it into the hands of our competitors Recognizing, therefore, to the full, the dangers of future strife, provision should be made for the settlement of disputes, in an amicable and broad-minded manner.

"A trade quarrel is an occasion, not for a mere display of endurance, but for argument, for statistics, for careful investigation of facts and principles. There must be union if the cotton trade is to prosper.

"All must admit the desirability of conciliation in the place of the violent methods of the past; the evolving of some definite method of adjusting disputes which would preclude the possibility of extreme measures and even make disputes a remote possibility. The common sense, no less than the common interest of both parties, should supply any want so apparent. Let both sides do what they can to agree upon the principles upon which they alone are competent to speak.

"With a reasonable security against strikes and lock-outs over long periods, the possibilities of a permanent return upon capital would be more stable than they are at present; panic competition would be checked, and the maintenance of our markets rendered more secure; more capital would thus be

HERBERT E. WALMSLEY,
Prest. New England Cotton Manufacturers' Ass'n.

attracted to the industry with added security for the investment; production would be strengthened with beneficial results all around.

"The matter is one of public concern, and it should therefore be the great effort of all alike to establish a permanent industrial peace, so that, united, we may all the longer withstand the unequal competition of longer hours and lower wages, and preserve for New England the inestimable advantages of the great cotton manufacturing industry that has served New England so long and so well.

"Is there anyone holding any position of authority and responsibility in our great hives of industry who is not prepared to concede and admit that labor, in asking for what is moderate and just—in asking for what is necessary for the protection of its interests, without inflicting unnecessary injury upon capital—is not perfectly within its rights?

"Let us without reservation concede to labor its legitimate and indisputable claim as an important factor in the situation. It is incumbent on each to respect the rights of the other, for both have their respective rights.

"The point desired to be made is, that there must be combination of purpose between employer and employed, that the laborer is worthy his hire, that labor is entitled in all equity and expediency to as fair and full return as circumstances permit of.

"With respect to the hours of labor in the cotton mills of New England and the rate of wages to be paid the operatives. As regards the former, the hours of labor, or the working hours per week. Fully realizing the force of Southern competition and its daily increasing severity, it is perfectly plain that the cotton industry of New England, in view of this rapidly increasing competition, cannot afford to have its power of successful competition further weakened by reducing the hours or having any further burdens whatsoever imposed on it. There can be no two opinions as to this. On the other hand, however, it is equally perfectly plain and certain that the working hours in the New England workshops cannot and will not be increased beyond the present legal and lawful limit. No retrograde movement of any such character is possible in this twentieth century, no matter by whom contemplated or thought of. Any suggestion of this nature may be at once dismissed without further words or consideration.

"As to the rate of wages. Far better look this problem squarely in the face also, and equally, freely and candidly admit that the normal or standard rate of wages in the New England cotton mill never can nor will be brought down to the level of the Southern standard. The difference in the cost of living alone, between these two sections of the country, makes such a thing impossible. I do not hesitate to say, in the most emphatic manner, that in my judgment any such reduction or levelling down is neither desirable nor necessary. Rather should we aim for higher standards in the interest of the well-being, advancement and prosperity of the entire community, regarded from any and every point of view. The real and true self-interest of the employer will not permit of any forced and continued attempt to reduce wages below a normal or legitimate standard.

"Good wages are not incompatible with our position in the world's market. Such, at least, is my deliberate judgment of this delicate and vexed question.

"It is high time to speak plainly and without equivocation. The time for smooth words and evasion has gone by. Where conditions have arrived at such a pass that mills are in such an unfortunate and unenviable position that they cannot any longer be run with any degree of profit, let them close down and go out of business altogether, and the sooner the better. They are nothing less than a demoralizing and disturbing element in what would otherwise be a healthy, vigorous and satisfactory situation. Mills of this undesirable character,—and, unfortunately, it is to be feared there are too many such in New England,—could not compete with the well-equipped Southern mills, even were they to pay the same wages and run the same number of hours, from the fact and for the simple reason that their machinery is antiquated, fit for little else than the scrap-heap. They are in no condition to meet any kind of competition on any class of work, or under any circumstances. In the face of it, on their own admission, they cannot compete with their worn-out, obsolete machinery, barely able to make even the cheap low-grade goods they have so long and so blindly persisted in making and still continue to make, and for which there is not a sufficient demand at anything like remunerative prices. No such short-sighted policy can nowadays succeed in New England, or anywhere else for that matter. If to-day the management of any individual mill or of any particular group of mills in New England will still persist in the production of such yarns and fabrics, in which particular line of product, competition is the keenest, and margins are the narrowest, they inevitably invite defeat and disaster, which they can alone expect and will surely encounter.

"If again the cotton industry of New England or any particular section of the industry has arrived at such a pass, such a stage in its history, that all that can be done in the endeavor to make ends meet is to reduce wages below a legitimate standard, below what is fair, equitable, humane or expedient, by all means, let such portion of the industry leave us, and go elsewhere, we want none of it. Such condition is sufficient to warrant, to demand drastic action. There is no hope for them."

MONTHLY REVIEW
OF THE
National Civic Federation

Offices: 281 Fourth Avenue, New York City
RALPH M. EASLEY, Editor

The Editor alone is responsible for any unsigned article or unquoted statement published in THE MONTHLY REVIEW.

Ten Cents per Copy; One Dollar per Year.

The National Civic Federation

AN INTERNATIONAL CIVIC FEDERATION.

The projected formation of an International Civic Federation was the natural outcome of the luncheon tendered by the National Civic Federation to members of the Interparliamentary Union and to representatives of labor organizations and industrial corporations and societies sent to the United States by the French Government. Civic Federations are now being organized in England and Canada. The nations represented in the Interparliamentary Union are those in which constitutional government is most developed. Its purpose of promoting international peace is in essence dependent upon the good will of peoples, to which national prosperity is essential; and that in turn depends upon industrial peace in each country. The establishment of industrial peace is, therefore, precedent to the discouragement of war. General industrial conditions would also be affected, if treaties of arbitration should cause any large degree of disarmament, through a material increase in the world's productivity. The extension throughout every industrial nation of a systematic betterment of the relations between capital and labor would increase the world's consuming capacity.

An International Civic Federation could perform work that would accord perfectly with the mission of every society that favors the abolition of war, which has been an ideal for centuries; while its deliberations might contribute valuable additions to world economics if not to world politics.

LABOR CANNOT DO IT ALL.

The editorial spirit of the "Wall Street Journal" on labor matters has been notably fair and broad. That paper has not hesitated to criticise employers or capitalists whenever it thought they were unfair, and it has been generous in its treatment of the shortcomings of organized labor. The following paragraph from a recent article, however, contains a proposition that even its editor, we think, will admit is rather untenable:

> If organized labor would drop its programme of monopoly and would strive for the uplifting of the industrial classes by intelligent education, and agitation, by methods of co-operation, by plans for insurance against old age, sickness and accidents, and by the establishment of schemes of fair adjustment of differences with employers, it is safe to say that nearly every wage-earner in the United States, as well as thousands of broad-minded employers, would hasten to join the unions.

The fact is that organized labor is more and more striving to do these very things. It must be granted that for one of them,—"the establishment of schemes of fair adjustment of differences with employers,"—labor is constantly making its share of effort. But how absurd it is to expect organized labor to accomplish this alone. The very statement of that ideal relation implies co-operation by the employers. Yet the head of the Manufacturers' National Association openly declares: "This is not the time to talk conciliation. Neither is it the time to talk arbitration or trade agreements. To arbitrate questions of wages and hours is to introduce artificial methods," etc.

Why should organized labor be enjoined to work out this scheme alone? What would it be worth to Wall Street, to all industry, and to society generally, to establish "schemes of fair adjustment of differences with employers"? And yet, the "Wall Street Journal" asks: Why does not organized labor bring this about by itself? If, as the editor of the "Journal" will doubtless admit, the purpose of organized labor is to secure better conditions for wage-earners, should it not have the hearty support and co-operation of employers, bankers, and in fact of all of the "non-producing classes"?

Indeed, organized labor has had to struggle for the improvement of the mass, not only alone and unaided, but against opposition, even against persecution. It is a far cry from the collared serf of the dark ages to the upright, free workman of to-day. The march upward from the market place at Magdeburg in 1301, where ten handiworkers were burned alive for resisting the oppression of the patriciate, from Cologne where thirty-three weavers were executed in 1371 after losing a strike against the ruling families, through wholesale massacre and exile, through the nights when the tramping journeymen were required to have masters present at their tavern meetings to prevent the crime of making demands for better treatment, through the years when men were thrown into jail for the heinous offense of mere membership in a union, through the slow conversion of public opinion to the acknowledgment of the right to organize, has traversed centuries of time and has endured an infinitude of suffering. The way has continually led over the worse to the better. Brentano well summarizes this halting advance: "The dawn of every new epoch of progress has been accomplished by steps backward."

This march has been made the harder because labor has had to evolve its own leadership. It has made all the mistakes of unskilled generalship and of undisciplined following. It makes them still. Its successes have been won despite the follies of its own ignorance.

But the time has come when employers and public-spirited citizens, who have some understanding of the awkwardness, blunders and misdirections that hamper the advance of labor, and who realize that the betterment of labor is the betterment of the entire social structure, are lending a helping hand; and we are glad to state that the editor of the "Wall Street Journal" is one of them.

WHAT CAUSES RAILWAY ACCIDENTS?

Everybody shares the shock of reading daily agonizing reports of fatal railway accidents. Everybody is interested in any effort to learn and to eliminate, if possible, their cause. The charge has been made that the frequency of preventable accidents is a decadence in the personnel of trainmen, brought about through the destruction of ambition by the rule of seniority. But the agreements between the principal railway companies and the brotherhoods show in their text that seniority is theoretically coupled with ascertained merit in making promotions. This is confirmed by statements from both railway officials and representatives of brotherhoods, presented on page 16. They suggest a comparison with the operation of the rule of seniority in the civil and military services.

OUR ENEMIES.

The National Civic Federation promotes industrial peace through securing rightful relations between employer and employed. Any organized effort to array employer and employed in hostility must oppose its mission. Hence the employers' associations and citizens' alliances, formed to war upon organized labor, and the socialists, organized to war upon capital, join their voices in similar criticism of the Civic Federation. Diametrically opposed in their ultimate purposes, they share a common opposition to the only organization that would bring labor and capital into harmony.

It is an officer of the Citizens' Industrial Association of America who said that employers were to be delivered "from the bondage of organized labor, not by continuing the policy of organized labor's colleague, the National Civic Federation, which is the greatest menace to industrial peace now in existence."

The President of a socialist railway organization in a confidential letter advised his organizer to stimulate public sentiment

> against capitalism and the Gompers faction, which is working in harmony with Marcus A. Hanna and the infamous Civic Federation to keep down the masses.

A report in the Chicago *Tribune* of a meeting to form a federation of employers' associations contained the following:

In the evening a majority of the delegates gathered in an informal meeting and talked over the general situation. It was then that the National Civic Federation was condemned for its policy of "conciliation and arbitration."

"Our association has nothing to do with the Federation," began Secretary Job. "One reason why we are to meet in October is to overcome the influence of that body."

"The Federation is made up of politicians who are looking for their own interests," said J. West Goodwin.

"What do they represent anyway?" asked Secretary Du Brul of the metal trades. "I have found them a lot of meddlers."

"The Federation is a costly plaything," was the comment of Secretary Marshall of Dayton. "Chicago was its birthplace, and the city has been paying the penalty for the last two years."

"The whole question is this," began President Parry. "Has a body a right to institute an arbitration court to take precedence of the courts of the land and tell the people—the workers, the business men—what they should do?"

"Stalking back of it all is the ghost of the Homestead riots," said another, and that ended the first attack the Federation has received from an organized body of employers.

Of the same meeting, the Chicago *Record-Herald's* account said:

President Parry paid his respects to the National Civic Federation, which he styled a "mutual admiration society of 'butters-in' with a $10,000 a year secretary," by saying that it was a question whether the Federation shall decide the laws of the country and tell men what to do, or leave the interpretation of the laws to the courts.

The national leader of the socialist party, Eugene V. Debs, brandishes this red flag at the Civic Federation:

The time is not far when the socialists will be in the majority in the trades-unions, and they will rescue the union movement from the withering hand of the leaders who dominate it, and from the blighting control of the Civic Federation, which has entered into an unholy alliance—the slaughterers of the laborer and those leaders in joint conspiracy against the union man.

The "Call to Arms" of the New York section of the socialist labor party says:

Betrayed by the Civic Federation and the labor fakir, or defeated by the Parrys in every big conflict, finding the pure and simple union a hollow reed to lean upon, the workers are beginning to turn to the socialist labor party.

The *People*, the organ of the socialist labor party, says:

Led by the late Mark Hanna, who saw the necessity of keeping the working class in line while a commercial conquest was made of the world, the ultra-capitalist class formed an alliance with the "labor leaders," the Gomperses, Mitchells, Keefes, et al. The result was the Civic Federation and the various agreements recognizing the Gompers type of unionism. . . . It was no miracle that D. M. Parry first became famous through his attacks on Hanna and the Civic Federation.

The platform of the socialist labor party declares that the Civic Federation and the American Federation of Labor "threaten to throttle the labor movement," and says that they have become "one of the strongest obstacles in this country to socialism."

The *Brauer-Zeitung*, a Cincinnati socialist paper, pays us this compliment:

The National Civic Federation, the most infamous, cancerous ulcer which has been inoculated upon the trades-union movement of this land.

and predicts that the time is coming

when the capitalist influence of the Civil Federation will be condemned and spurned by the workers and eradicated.

These quotations sufficiently show that the Civic Federation receives the vituperation of the socialists simultaneously with the criticism of their foes.

The socialists seek to excite class hatred and to inflame the minds of wage-earners against the Civic Federation. They aim to grasp control of trades-unions and pervert them from a purely economic force into a political army, as is shown by their futile efforts to capture the American Federation of Labor. Mr. Debs says: "I welcome the assaults upon unionism by David M. Parry and his kind, because Mr. Parry is doing as much to array class against class as any other individual, although he aims at the opposite effect."

The bulk of the membership of employers' associations will be surprised to learn that their leaders are regarded as allies by the socialists; but these quotations speak for themselves.

A FALLACIOUS COMPARISON.

It is a frequent but misleading statement that organized labor includes only a small minority of the wage-earners of the country. The purpose of the statement, which is based upon a deceptive comparison, is to give force to the claim that it is monstrous tyranny for the small minority to dictate to the great majority of workers the wages, hours, and conditions of their toil. Figures are cited that, on their face, prove that labor organizations contain only 8 per cent. of all wage-earners. But it is only in trades where the union has included nearly all the workers that it is strong enough to become a potent factor. In such cases, the mass of unorganized labor does not figure. If a union contains 95 per cent. of the skilled workers in its craft and demands better conditions, it is no argument to say that the farm hands or the washerwomen are not organized.

Whatever one's attitude toward labor organization, it is well to have a correct perception of its strength. The comparison most frequently quoted credits organized labor with a membership of about 2,400,000, which is only 8 per cent. of the more than 29,000,000 persons engaged in "gainful occupations" in the United States in 1900. But an analysis of the "gainful occupations" shows the fallacy of the comparison. These 29,000,000 include: In agriculture, 10,000,000: domestic and personal service, 6,000,000; the professions 1,200,000. Practically none of these are organizable, and they should be excluded from the comparison. Trade and transportation engaged 4,700,000 persons. But from these should be deducted bankers, brokers, merchants, officials of banks and corporations, bookkeepers, commercial travelers, agents, accountants, foremen and overseers, hucksters and pedlers, livery stable keepers, undertakers, and miscellaneous workers.

Moreover, in most cases, this considerable minority has the sympathy and following of the unorganized majority. There is a distinct community of purpose between the union and the non-union man. Shorter hours, higher wages, and improved conditions are just as much desired by those without as by those within the unions. Occasional brutal combats do not impugn this broad truth.

When 6,000 union strikers went out of the Fall River cotton mills, they took with them 24,000 non-unionists. The two are standing shoulder to shoulder, the families of the non-union strikers being supported from the treasury of the union, to the best of its ability. The 8,000 anthracite union miners who struck in 1900, were joined by 140,000 non-union miners. When the railway brotherhoods contemplate a strike, they submit the question to a vote of all the employes, non-union as well as union, the vote of every man counting equally. So that, in many occupations, the potential strength of organized labor is far greater than its exact enrollment, while in some crafts it represents 95 per cent. of the workers.

A LESSON FOR NEW ENGLAND.

All who have investments and all wage-earners in textile industries will be directly interested in the address of President Walmsley to the New England Cotton Manufacturers' Association, which we present on another page. The address will be of interest as well to all those whose prosperity is associated with the continuance of an industry that is "the guarantee of comfort and well-being to an enormous section of our people."

The critical stage that cotton manufacturing has reached in New England, in its competition with Southern mills, is frankly recognized in this address, and the establishment of industrial peace and the introduction of the most improved machinery and processes are pointed out as essential to maintain the Northern industry. Conflicts between employer and employed, with the loss they entail to both capital and labor, injure New England and benefit its competitors.

There is a lesson to be learned from the agreement between the operatives and operators in the North of England cotton trade. There committees of both organized employers and employes determine the wage-scale, subject to change at any time by mutual consent. The way is left open, in case of failure to agree, to the lock-out or strike. But the agreement has worked so well that the scale that went into effect in 1892 has undergone but one change, when an advance of 2½ per cent. was made in 1898. Old England thus shows New England a trade agreement, with a provision for joint consideration of a scientifically adjusted scale, that in practice has produced a long period of peace.

It is profoundly true that no industry that depends for success upon taxing wages for the greater cost of defective or antique processes deserves to survive. That is a law of civilization that cotton manufacturers should face with a courage equal to the candor with which it is recognized.

PARALLEL METHODS OF PEACE.

The sessions of the Interparliamentary Union in St. Louis and of the International Peace Conference in Boston developed a remarkable parallelism between international peace and industrial peace. The speeches of their delegates, with little paraphrasing, would apply as well to the solution of the world-wide labor problem as to the establishment of world-wide peace. The terms of the methods of securing each are readily interchangeable. The proposal that an international parliament shall consider periodically questions of international law parallels the proposition to form an International Civic Federation, in which representatives of employers, employed and the several peoples may formulate conclusions of importance to the entire industrial world, regardless of national boundaries.

A PRESCRIPTION FOR LABOR DIFFICULTIES.

By "Dr." Marcus M. Marks, President of the National Association of Clothing Manufacturers.

R:

ice for the excited.

pins for the sluggish.

brains for the stupid.

light for the prejudiced.

Mix thoroughly and administer at least once a day in conciliation conferences until the head and the hand work harmoniously.

P. S.—Perhaps ice should have been written with a capital I, as it is the most important ingredient in the prescription.

If rightly conducted, unionism may be made a force helpful alike to its members and to society in general. Standing on sound principles and wisely led and guided, it will encounter more help than hindrance from employers and from the public. If its course is marked by foolish and unjustifiable strikes, it will encounter only opposition and ultimate defeat. In precisely that danger unionism now stands. An often offended and sometimes outraged public is rapidly forming itself into a national jury, on whose verdict the fate of unionism will depend.

Both parties to industrial conflicts, employers as well as organized employes, are now on trial. A vast problem is in process of solution, and the fate of unionism is in its own hands.—New York "Sun."

The motive of industry is money making. The motive of life is good-will. That which one cannot justly do, another cannot justly require. When the requirements of justice are understood and complied with strikes will cease to be with us.—"Public Policy."

"A LABOR DEPARTMENT."

ITS IMPORTANCE IN EVERY LARGE INDUSTRIAL ESTABLISHMENT.

Its Need Caused by the Loss of "Personal Touch" Between Employer and Employes—Its Personnel and Its Work to Establish Just Relations.

BY CHARLES U. CARPENTER.

CHARLES U. CARPENTER

Every great industrial establishment should maintain a distinct department of labor, with a special head for its administration. The purpose of this department would be the avoidance of friction and the adjustment of the relations between labor and its management. It is a fact that grows more and more surprising with consideration that while every large business has its executive heads of departments, who are selected for their especial fitness, labor alone has rarely received such treatment. Yet the cost of labor is a factor in the cost of production and the price at which the product can be put upon the market. The necessity of meeting competition, therefore, should make obvious the importance of a special department of labor.

The necessity of this department is increased by the loss, in this day of huge corporations, of the former "personal touch," which exists now only in the small shop. There is seldom trouble in the small shop, because difficulties are usually met by the employer himself before they can grow into unwarranted importance. Why not adopt a plan, in the case of the large corporation, which will insure the meeting of difficulties in the same manner?

What work requires more specialized and more continuous and practical attention than does the handling of the labor question? And yet, upon whom does this delicate and difficult problem actually fall? Is it handled by a department composed of men especially fitted for this question by their education and broad study of labor and knowledge of conditions in every country? By men selected for their fair-mindedness and practical experience in handling large bodies of men and of such character as to gain the confidence of the workmen; and by men of experience in making labor contracts, who know where the rights of labor end and the transgressions of the rights of capital begin?

No! this is seldom the case. The active, actual every-day policy of handling labor, the part that is vital to the workingman and the manufacturer, is dictated not by him but by his foremen.

The superintendent is usually so loaded down with duties and responsibilities that it is almost impossible for him to give the subject the close attention it deserves. Again, he is often in the same condition as the higher officials. He is seldom in close touch with the workers. The foremen who are superintending the departments are exercising the direct and consequently the real potential influence over the men for good or bad. No matter what the manufacturer may desire to do for his men, no matter what his actual policy may be, their feeling toward the firm is governed more by their feeling toward the man who has them in daily control than by any other factors. If this man is weak, the workmen will impose upon him and the company. If harsh, unjust, or inclined to "play favorites," they will be discontented. The foreman will either augment or annul the effect of any good action or purpose of the employer.

"The time to stop trouble is before it begins." Some plan of organization must be adopted to make this possible. Some method should exist whereby employer and men could get together and discuss their mutual difficulties before trouble begins. When once trouble does arise and it has become so acute as to require the attention of the employer, the feelings and prejudices of all who have attempted to handle the proposition have, by that time, been aroused to a high pitch.

Workmen may often make a proposal too absurd for the employer's consideration. But, embittered by delay in consideration by foremen, the workmen may at times insist upon its acceptance. Or the employer, who might have granted some fair demand if it had reached him directly, may feel obliged to stand by his subordinates who have refused it. This means trouble that might have been avoided.

These considerations emphasize the necessity for a special labor department. This department should be in control of the labor question, with full authority to settle all questions that the men and foremen cannot settle. There should always exist a right of appeal to this department on the part of either workmen or foremen. It should be its constant aim to settle all questions before they reach an acute stage and assume an unwarranted importance. The questions should be considered directly with the employes affected. The department should also investigate those practices of the workmen which are unjust to the foremen, and endeavor to have them corrected. In actual experience great good has been accomplished by the investigation and taking up with the workmen such matters as restriction of output, opposition to improved machinery, unjust wage demands, unreasonably high wage rates, demands for a shorter work-day, unreasonable opposition to justifiable discharges, etc. The writer's experience has been with several large factories, and especially with one concern employing four thousand men. In that factory there were represented eleven international organizations, twenty-four local unions, and thirty-eight shop committees. These local organizations were new and undisciplined. They restricted output and the employment of men, and caused the greatest difficulties in discharging incompetent men. The success of the policy outlined has been proved by a change in the attitude of the workmen. The men now seem to try to limit their complaints to those which are fair.

A standing advisory committee should be formed, composed of men who are highest in authority in the company, before whom shall be brought all important matters of labor policy and any very serious affairs that cannot be satisfactorily settled. This advisory board should be called together by the labor department on emergencies, and also for monthly reports, which should indicate clearly the nature of the troubles settled and the progress made.

This work should not be undertaken in a spirit of hostility to the workmen. It should be carried out along lines of justice to all concerned, coupled with firmness in demanding and insisting that that which is right should be granted, and that which is wrong should not be tolerated.

The labor department is as valuable in a non-union as in a union factory. It is as important in one as in the other to establish relations of confidence; to give the men opportunity to earn a fair wage and to have their complaints heard, and in no other way can this be satisfactorily accomplished.

Thorough investigation, prompt action, just decisions, and a firm stand for what is right should mark the work of the labor department.

It can do nothing more important than to establish a just and scientific wage system, both to satisfy the workmen and produce work with the greatest economy. The lack of attention to this matter causes much of the trouble between employes and the employer.

This department can, with great advantage, watch for undue shrinkage in output or any tendency toward its limitation.

The important questions of "employment" and "improving the personnel of the factory force" have a most important connection with efficient production. That the efficiency of the factory force can be largely increased by scientific methods is a fact not generally recognized. Systematic steps for the separation of the poor workmen from the efficient for their education and improvement, or, in case they prove totally inefficient, their discharge, are important factors in improving the factory's efficiency. In a properly systematized factory, it is not difficult to obtain accurate information concerning the character, ability and earning capacity of different workmen, even though they number thousands. Such data are also valuable in checking up discharges, as any discharge for an unjust cause can be noted at once.

The labor department should investigate and have installed such improvements in sanitary and working conditions as experience has found to be practical.

An acquaintance with legal decisions bearing upon the rights of capital as well as of labor and with the associations of labor and capital and the conditions of both throughout the world is necessary.

The work of the labor department will be largely ineffective unless it has the support and co-operation of the foremen or men who are in direct charge of departments. These men should be brought into sympathy with its aims and purposes. Generally the responsibility for this labor question is something which they will gladly relinquish, but the seeming interference with their preconceived ideas of the boundaries of their own authority, which this work must involve, will be at first resented. Nothing, however, need or ought to be done to interfere with the necessary authority of a foreman.

These foremen must be instructed in the best methods of handling men; most effective ways of increasing their working efficiency, in a manner not detrimental to their health; of increasing their interest in their work, and, especially in union shops, the most effective methods of securing the best results for the company and the men under union conditions.

In order to gain the desired results, weekly meetings of all the foremen and assistants for the purpose of discussing these problems and difficulties, are of the utmost importance. Their discussions will give

A LABOR DAY CELEBRATION IN AN INDUSTRIAL COMMUNITY.

SOME RESULTS OF WELFARE WORK SHOWN IN A FAIR, WITH EMPLOYES' EXHIBITS, MUSIC AND ATHLETIC SPORTS.

Labor Day is observed in one manufacturing community in New England as nowhere else in the country. The peculiar observance of this national holiday there is an outcome as well as part of organized welfare work. Labor Day has there become an annual holiday of the most wholesome, instructive and inspiring nature.

The central features of its observance are a Fair, containing exhibits of fruit, flowers, vegetables, fancy work, poultry, and various domestic products; work of the kindergarten, manual training and cooking schools; Athletic Sports; a Baseball Game; a plenitude of music by the Employes' Band, and unrestrained social freedom throughout the day.

Hitherto this popular celebration has been entirely under the executive direction of the Welfare Manager. This year various committees of employes were entrusted with the preparations for the exhibits and the arrangements of the sports, in accordance with the general plan outlined by the Manager. This participation in the work of making the celebration a success by the employes was suggested to the Welfare Manager by an address delivered by the Chairman of the Welfare Department of the National Civic Federation at its conference in New York last March.

More than ten thousand employes and their families attended the fair and its adjuncts this year. The exhibits were collected and arranged in a large tent erected at one side of a wide athletic field. The exhibits were remarkable for their own excellence as well as for the taste and ingenuity displayed in their arrangement.

An official of the State, whose duty it is to visit all the county fairs, declared that this Labor Day fair was surpassed by only two other fairs in New England. It is interesting to observe that some of the exhibits shown here, especially of poultry and eggs, have acquired such a reputation as to command particularly high prices, thus adding materially to the prosperity of the employes. There were so many applications from the employes to present exhibitions of highly bred fowls that there was not room to receive them all.

The athletic field stretches before the exhibit tent, a rolling expanse of green, beyond which is a lake surrounded with the lawns and attractive homes of many of the wage-earners. Throughout the morning there were run a wide variety of races, stimulating a wholesome rivalry in athletics, and exciting the keenest interest and applause, for the victors, among the spectators.

While the athletic sports were in progress during the morning, the official judges were inspecting the exhibits in the tent and awarding prizes.

At noon, when the sports were over, the tent was thrown open to the populace. The signal for this was the blowing of a whistle by the Welfare Manager, and an example of the careful organization of the plans for the day was shown by the celerity with which a force of men removed, as in the twinkling of an eye, from the athletic field all the paraphernalia that had been used in the races.

The scenes in the tent during the examination of the exhibits were most animated. It was pleasing to observe that the highest official of the company was as much interested to see whether the vegetables from his garden had taken a prize as was any of the workmen.

The centre of interest in the afternoon was the baseball game. This is a spirited contest every year, the local nine being always matched against a visiting team worthy of its prowess. This year, although the visiting team was defeated, there came back from their town subsequently expressions of the most cordial recognition of their treatment by their manly hosts.

During the sports, both morning and afternoon, the thousands of men, women and children scattered over the grounds all the miscellaneous debris incident to such an occasion. No objection whatever was made to this, but a force of men was kept constantly at work gathering this scattered rubbish into buckets and taking it away. This process afforded an object lesson in cleanliness to all the people.

When the concourse was assembled for the ball game, Gideon F. Holmes, Treasurer of the Company, awarded a cup offered by the Welfare Manager to the member of the nine who had made the highest all-'round average during the season previous to Labor Day. His encouraging remarks concerning the success of the exhibition and the enthusiasm displayed in the field sports were warmly applauded. There was evident appreciation, also, of his outline of the origin and progress of baseball.

The visitors at this fair were especially impressed by the happy faces of the throng, men, women and children all seeming to be filled with the most hearty spirit of enjoyment and interest. The assembly presented a cosmopolitan appearance, because of the different nationalities represented among the employes.

The entire success of the celebration is an evidence of the executive ability of W. E. C. Nazro, the Welfare Manager. His thoughtfulness also had provided every facility for the visitors to observe each phase of the day's amusements, and had made every provision for their material comfort.

---

relief to the views of the most radical and disseminate the ideas of the more conservative. Thus there is developed a tendency toward harmonious action and uniform policy among the foremen. They will learn much that will result in direct economies in their departments. There will also be developed a desirable esprit de corps among the foremen themselves.

Where union conditions exist, workmen should be encouraged to attend their union meetings, and to act as officers and members of union committees. In many cases, foremen are found making it so unpleasant for union shop committeemen that only the worst and most radical men, who are continually stirring up trouble, will serve. The conservative men, bound by their obligations, and by the company's acceptance of unionism, are compelled to follow the lead of these men whenever trouble arises. It should always be kept in mind that these committees are not only representatives of the men before the company, but also practically the representatives of the company before the unions.

More will depend upon the ability, character and experience of the man at the head of the labor department than upon any other factors. He should have had a wide experience in the handling of large bodies of men, both union and non-union. He should have an acquaintance with the heads of existing manufacturers' associations and prominent labor leaders, as well as a thorough knowledge of union methods. He should be thoroughly informed on modern factory systems and methods, especially as applied to wage systems. Mechanical experience is very desirable. Inasmuch as many of the disputes that will arise will concern the question of wages and output, he should be able to devise methods of ascertaining the output that could be fairly expected from any job. He should be capable of introducing methods of increasing the interest of workmen in their tasks. Such work requires a combination of tact, good judgment, experience in handling men, executive ability, and firmness. In short, the man guiding such a department, formed to undertake such work as a safeguard to the company's interests, should possess no small degree of ability.

No work is more worthy of the close attention of those high in authority in the company. It is indissolubly linked with the highest and most important interests of the employer. The commercial success of any business depends not only upon the securing and developing of markets, and the development of the economic possibilities of the factory, but also upon the existence and continuance of satisfactory relations between employer and employe.

A UNIQUE BEQUEST.

A Permanent Fund Created for Employes out of Work.

Herman Stursberg, who died recently, in disposing of his large fortune, placed in the hands of two sons, his executors, $10,000, and expressed a wish that it be used by them in a manner that they might deem best for the benefit of the operatives of the Germania Mills, of Holyoke, Mass., especially at times when the mills might be shut down. He suggested that they invest the principal and use the income from it for this purpose.—"New York Herald." October 5, 1904.

AGRICULTURAL INTEREST IN INDUSTRIAL PEACE.

THE FARMER'S PROSPERITY DIRECTLY RELATED TO HARMONY BETWEEN CAPITAL AND LABOR, WHICH SHOULD "GET TOGETHER AND BE REASONABLE."

By JOHN M. STAHL, Secretary of Farmers' National Congress.

The final verdict in contentions between employer and employed will be written by public opinion. If wise, both employers and employed will be concerned about the rights and the attitude of the public. In labor wars it is frequently the case that the innocent public suffers almost or quite as much as the belligerents. I would speak as special representative of the most important element of the public—the farmer.

Who is this farmer that asks to be considered in your contentions? Not the man depicted by stale newspaper wit and cartoon. The remarkable increase in the use of machinery and of force other than human energy to farming has made it a light employment, and the farmer, of necessity, a student and skilled workman. The farmer to-day takes full advantage of the telephone in his house, of the daily delivery of mail, of up-to-date business methods, and is in close touch with social and economic affairs.

Of our population "at least ten years of age, engaged in gainful occupations," more than one-third are engaged in agriculture. Farmers employ more than twenty billion dollars of capital—and it is actual wealth, not watered stocks—in their business. Our annual corn crop alone is worth on the farm more than three times the value at the mine of all the coal mined in this country per year, and of our exports farm products are much more than twice the value of all others combined. Of the population of this country, we own more homes than all others combined, we own more homes free from debt than all others combined, and we have fewer mortgaged homes and less than one-third as many hired homes as the rest of the population. And consider that the farm home is not merely a house, but a house with other buildings and broad acres.

We have a direct interest in disputes between employers and employed, as when such disputes will not permit the handling or transportation of freight. Then our grapes must rot on the vines and our vegetables become unmarketable, and our other products cannot reach the place of demand. But our concern about the relation of employer and employed comes from a broader view, the conception of a fact that employer and employed too often ignore, that our industrial life has become so complex and our economic interests so interdependent that any violent disturbance in one field of labor ultimately injures those in all others. For example, every strike or lock-out lessens the capacity of laborers to buy farm products from their wages and of employers to buy farm products from their profits. An enforced lower plane of living in the city means lower prices and a duller market for the products of the farm. On the other hand, the farmer profits by the increased purchasing power of urban people resulting from the steady, peaceful employment of capital and labor. The strike or lock-out that reduces the trade of merchants reduces their purchases of the products of manufacturing capital or labor and of agricultural capital or labor. Neither employer nor laborer can hurt the other without in the end hurting himself and others. "No man liveth unto himself."

It may be profitable to consider the opinion of that class that in itself combines the employer and the employed as none other does, and that is farthest removed from the scenes of industrial conflicts and presumably is the freest from prejudice. We farmers would offer a solution of what are termed labor troubles in just five words:

"Get together and be reasonable."

It is unfortunate that the development of the factory system and of the corporation has to such degree differentiated the employer and the employed and has put them so far apart. The first step in securing better relations between employer and employed is to correct this separation by coming together for discussion. Each side will gain respect for the other. This will be all the more certain if back of each is a compact organization—an organization not created to fight, though it will if need be, but to make more effective the results of conference or arbitration.

There is no inherent antagonism between employer and employed. Their interests are antagonistic only as the interests of buyer and seller are antagonistic. There is really no more ground for the buyer and the seller of labor to quarrel than there is for the buyers and the sellers of shoes or lumber or hay to quarrel.

If conference fails, then arbitration. Compulsory arbitration is linking two contradictory words.

JOHN M. STAHL,
Secretary Farmers' National Congress.

Leaving aside any constitutional hindrances, I doubt the advisability or the possibility of enforcing a law that will take from either employer or laborer so much of his liberty as to compel him to go to a third party to settle differences. Certainly, before we attempt to enforce such a law we would better see if we cannot accomplish as much by other means.

Even though the parties to labor controversies were forced to submit their differences to arbitration, it might be found impossible to compel them to abide by the decision. You cannot compel a man to carry on a business against his will, nor can you compel a man, as a general statement, to work for some one he does not wish to serve.

Undoubtedly the laborer in private employment may, as a general proposition, quit work when he pleases and for whatsoever cause he pleases. It is a corollary that trades-unions ignore—something to which the public will not much longer remain indifferent—that the same freedom of action must allow a laborer peaceably and without violence or harm, to work when he pleases and for whomsoever will hire him to his satisfaction.

This much for what is termed private business. The public has the right to demand that such things as the mails, the telegraph service and transportation by railway shall not be stopped to the great public injury by any strike or lock-out. These things enter too closely into our lives, they are too essential to our livelihood and the public welfare, for them to be at the mercy or the whim of a narrow-minded stubborn capitalist or labor leader. Would it not be feasible to have the laborers of all grades in these lines of activity enlist for, say, a year, their desertion from service being a misdemeanor if certain facts are ascertained by the courts, and they being secure from dismissal except for certain causes? As no one would be compelled to enter this service, there would be no dangerous invasion of personal liberty of action.

The certainty of uninterrupted mail, telegraph and transportation service would greatly aid business and increase the general prosperity and welfare. Those enlisted in this public service would constitute a grand army, soldiers of peace, men valiant, not in destruction, but in service. Years of faithful service would be indicated to the public and would secure hearty public approbation. Those who, by unusual ability and fidelity, became captains and generals of this host, would be esteemed even more highly than the captains and generals whose business it is to destroy.

If the union man does not wish to labor with the non-union man, he has a right to labor where only union men are employed. But the American believes in fair play, and the violence and brutality inflicted on non-union workmen have done much to draw public sentiment away from organized labor. It would be strange if, among the hundreds of thousands of organized laborers some were not brutal and lawless; and probably many misdeeds are wrongfully charged to organized labor. But the public, not forgetful of the thousands of law abiding union laborers, cannot fail to note that the brutal beating of non-union workmen has not been denounced by organized labor, and that labor organizations have not made enough effort to have punished those guilty of lawlessness in their name. Undoubtedly when, as in cigar-making or tailoring, the union label is evidence of not only competent workmanship, but that the manufactured goods are not disease-carriers, the union label shall mean union labor; but the public does not believe that a union painter in Chicago should refuse to work on lumber from Arkansas until assured that it was manufactured by only union labor. The public has grown heartily tired of some of the preposterous stands made by union labor in this particular, as it has of the sympathetic strike, sometimes three degrees removed! Furthermore the public believes that the man who takes the risks and pays the bills should have a considerable voice in the management of the business.

A gradually increasing disrespect for law has reached such degree that public sentiment is shaking off its sleep. It is beginning to move. Woe to him, employer or employed, that defies it. In the industrial field it will be true that they that draw the sword shall perish by the sword. The American people are aroused concerning lawlessness. It is not so safe as it was to buy city councils, state legislatures or the officers of the law.

Of all people, we should most respect the law. We are the law-makers. If our laws are not what they should be, we have only our apathy or prejudice to blame. The law is our sleepless servant and our only protector. It is so faithful and unobtrusive that we do not regard it. It fences about our fields and shops and homes with security. It locks our doors against the intruder, it guards the sleeping households in city and country. It pays the laborer his wages, the seller for his goods. It broods over our homes. The law touches with kindness and help our daily, commonplace, homely life at a thousand points. We have no arbitrary power to help or harm us—only the laws we ourselves have made. Let us consider what the law is to us, what it does for us, and we will exclaim, the Law and our Liberties forever!

PACKERS AND BUTCHERS BOTH LEARN LESSONS FROM THEIR CONTEST.

A STRIKE THAT FAILED TEACHES THE WORKERS CONSERVATISM AND THE EMPLOYERS GREATER CONSIDERATION.

Luke Grant

Lessons for both capital and labor, in the underlying causes and inner history of the strike against the meat-packers, are summarized herewith by Luke Grant, Chicago Secretary of the State Board of Arbitration of Illinois, and labor writer for the Chicago "Inter-Ocean."

On the surface the unions lost the strike, and it was probably the best thing that could happen to them that they did lose. They will build up stronger and better organizations for the experience, after they recover from the immediate hardships which must invariably follow great strikes.

Looking at it with a view to the permanency of the butchers' organization and its possibilities to do good to its members, the union has gained, and that fact will be generally recognized within the next twelve months.

The packers will never again return to the old system of dealing with their employes that prevailed before the formation of the union. Of that there is no danger; the experience has been too costly. A more liberal policy will be adopted by the packers in treating with their employes than ever before, and this policy will continue to grow more liberal as time goes on, not for any sentimental reason, but simply as a business proposition. Strikes are expensive, and the packers have learned that fact.

On the other hand many of the petty and annoying exactions that the unions have demanded in the past year or two will be stopped, as they should be. The shop stewards and business agents have been brought to a realization of the fact that their powers are not supreme, as they supposed, and that the packers are to have something to say about the conduct of their own establishments.

But did the packers ever seriously consider the causes of this usurpation of power on the part of the unions which they so much resented? It is fair to assume that they did not. They have been accustomed too long to regard wages as mere "fixed charges" and their employes as part of their machinery. In that respect they were no different from many other large corporations, who, while paying the strictest attention to every detail of their business, fail to notice the social unrest in the world that is constantly throbbing around them on all sides. They have applied scientific methods to every other part of their business and overlooked the most important part of all—their wage workers.

The organization of the men, the attaining of power through that organization, the strike and all its attendant suffering, were simply a reaction from conditions that preceded it.

The packers justly complained of the limitation of output exacted by the unions. In some instances production was curtailed 50 per cent. from what it was before the men were organized. This, taken in connection with the increased wages granted the men, made dividends dwindle. Contrary to the general belief, the profits of the packers have not been enormous in the past few years.

But what caused the unions to restrict the amount of work to be done in a day? Was it not the pace-maker employed in the old days who forced men to work at a nerve-racking speed almost beyond the limit of human endurance? The limitation of output, while wholly indefensible, was simply a reaction from the pace-maker. The excesses of the packers and their foremen paved the way for the future excesses of the unions.

With the attainment of power the unions ran to excess. The limit of production was not placed at a fair day's work for a fair day's pay, but at an amount that could be easily accomplished by the most inefficient. Those conditions are certain to result in an open rupture as soon as an opportunity arises.

The pace-maker is inhuman and in the long run unprofitable; the restriction of output is economically unsound and indefensible from any standpoint, and neither one should be tolerated in an establishment where labor is dealt with on a scientific basis. The late strike has in all probability abolished both, and for that reason alone it will prove a blessing in disguise to both sides. After all the "world does move."

As to the strike itself and the manner in which it was conducted, the public is familiar. The immediate cause is also well known, but it is the underlying causes that are interesting and should be studied if good is to come out of the experience.

Many have condemned Michael Donnelly for calling the strike in the first place in the face of an offer to arbitrate. The excuse was made that arbitration was not offered until the strike order had been issued and it was too late to stop it. That was not the real reason for calling it, however. Donnelly could have stopped the strike had he chosen, but if he had he would, figuratively speaking, have signed his own death warrant at the same time.

Had Donnelly tried to stop the strike on an indefinite offer to arbitrate, even though his own judgment told him he should do so, it would have been taken as conclusive evidence by the radical element that he was a packers' man. It would have caused a revolt and aroused a wave of mistrust that might have been fatal to the organization. Of all the ungrateful human beings in the world the members of labor unions are the worst. They are always ready to mistrust their leaders, and are usually so blind that they cannot see one day ahead.

That was the case with the stock-yards men. They wanted to strike, and would have done so without orders. Secretly Donnelly was not averse to a short strike, as he believed it would prove a revelation to the packers that would be useful in future dealings with them. In that he was not mistaken, for the spontaneity with which the men walked out took the breath of the packers away and made them anxious to settle. The strike was orderly and well conducted during the first week, and everything appeared satisfactory when the first settlement was made. Had it been observed by the men it would have proved a decided victory for them.

But the day following the settlement the same radical element had to be heard. Donnelly was unmercifully scored for making the settlement. His honesty is well known to every one who has ever come in close contact with him, but even that was questioned by some of the radicals who were not sufficiently chastened by the ten days' strike. So they determined to ignore the settlement and provoke another strike if possible.

Donnelly is sensitive to harsh criticism. He knew in his heart that the settlement was a good one, and he did not like to have his motives impugned when he knew there were no grounds for it. So he weakened at the supreme moment, when he should have stood firm, and, listening to the advice of radicals, he ordered the second strike.

It was one of the most gigantic mistakes ever made during a strike, and Donnelly realized it before the message had reached its destination, but he was in an excitable frame of mind and still smarting under the unjust accusations that were made against him by some of his own members.

Had he stood firm it would probably have resulted in a revolt against his authority, but he would have had the consolation of knowing that he was right, even if it meant his resignation. The men, however, had to be well beaten, and they were not beaten at the time the first strike was settled.

The packers knew also that the men had to be thoroughly beaten, and they set about it. The result was never in doubt after the second week of the second strike. Had the packers given in to the radicals they could not have continued in business because of the conditions that would have been imposed on them. That would have meant another fight later, and that is why it is a good thing for the men themselves that they did not win. The men have learned that the packers can operate their plants without the unions, even if it is a costly and unsatisfactory experiment, and it is well that they have learned that lesson.

There are times in the history of every labor organization when success is more to be feared than defeat, and the butcher workmen had reached that stage. Now it is past, although at great cost; but it had to come. Each side has been brought to a realization of the fact that the other side has rights in this great question. Neither side will be so anxious to force another fight and each will have a wholesome respect for the fighting qualities of the other. That may maintain the equilibrium for several years.

When an employer exercises his authority to the point of tyranny there will surely be a revolt, and the same is true of labor unions. A union is sometimes apt to exercise its power to the point of tyranny until it has been chastened by a good beating. Then it goes steadily on making for progress without running to excess.

After the allied trades were drawn into the fight and the management of the affair partially left the hands of Donnelly the conduct of the strike was one series of blunders. There is not enough space here to recount them, and, besides, the subject is too painful, although it is due Donnelly to say that he was opposed to most of the foolish things done. The calling out of the men from the independent plants and the boycotting of meat are but two of the illustrations where "too many cooks spoiled the broth."

The struggle presents so many interesting phases that it is impossible to treat with more than one at this time. From a sentimental point of view the fight the skilled men made to protect the unskilled workers is one of the most remarkable things in labor history. The improved standard of life among the workers since the organization was formed furnishes one of the most striking examples of the benefit of trades-unions that the country has ever seen.

The most advanced students of the question are agreed that the joint trade agreement and arbitration as a last resort when conciliation has failed, is the best method so far found for maintaining friendly relations between employers and employed. That agreements are sometimes violated by both sides, and that strikes sometimes occur in spite of offers to arbitrate, should not be taken as conclusive proof that the joint trade agreement plan is a failure.

The trouble is that neither employer, trade-union, nor the outside public is educated up to the point where the joint trade agreement can be successfully put in operation in every case. But all are slowly becoming better educated on the subject, and every big strike helps along the work, even if such education proves exceedingly costly.

Too much is often expected of the joint trade agreement, and when it fails extreme radicals on both sides are ready to declare the whole scheme a failure. But it is not.

When a trade-union violates an agreement the whole country hears of it in short order. When an employer violates an agreement the country does not hear of it quite so readily, if at all; but employers sometimes do it, nevertheless. And it frequently happens that when an agreement is violated each side accuses the other of being the guilty party, and strange as it may seem, each side may be acting in entire good faith in making the accusation.

THE SHORTER WORK-DAY.

ITS ECONOMIC REQUISITES AND EFFECTS.

Mankind May Take the Benefit of Greater Productivity in Either Larger Income or in More Leisure, but Prosperity is Essential to Either, Says Professor F. W. Taussig of Harvard University.

To most workmen the shorter work-day presents itself simply as a form of higher wages. For less hours of work, they wish as high pay, or higher pay. To most employers it presents itself in the same way. It means to them that for the same wages they get less output.

It is true that in some trades and under some conditions there may be shorter hours and yet the same

F. W. TAUSSIG,
Professor in Harvard University.

output. The pace may become faster. Whether work is done by the piece or by the day, some gain in this direction can probably be achieved in most industries. Where there has been an understanding among workmen, tacit or explicit, for a restriction of the amount to be accomplished by them in a given time, there is now more clearly a possibility of such gain. Whatever is secured in this way brings greater leisure for the workmen, very rarely, if any, excessive intensity of labor, and no less for employer or for the community.

But there is a limit to this possibility, and not a very wide limit. At bottom, and in the long run, the shorter day means higher wages; the same pay, or higher pay, for a less amount of work. The demand for a shorter work-day raises the same questions in the main as are raised by a demand for an increase of wages. This broad fact must be frankly faced in any discussion of the topic.

In any particular trade, better terms for the workmen, whether in the form of less hours or of higher wages, can sometimes be secured at the expense of consumers, sometimes at the expense of employers. The conditions of a trade for the moment may be such that the prices of goods are less than the demand would permit, or that employers are getting less profits, to have their capital and management normally secure.

But a general rise in wages, or a general shortening of hours, depends on other conditions. Such a general increase is what chiefly interests the economic student, and obviously is of most importance to the workmen and to the community. It can take place, to any substantial extent, only in consequence of a general advance in material prosperity. It can come if industry is more productive. Improvements in the arts, inventions, good management, intelligence and willing spirit among laborers, rich natural resources,—all the factors that promote prosperity tend to raise wages. And a considerable, general rise can come in no other way. The actual industrial income of the people must be greater. Trade-unions may enable workmen to secure the benefits of a general advance in industry more quickly, perhaps more fully, than would otherwise be the case, but the basis of the advance must be there, in diffused productiveness of industry.

As the arts progress, and labor becomes more productive, mankind may take the benefit in two ways: in greater income, or in shorter hours and more leisure. Or something may be taken in each of the two directions,—both higher returns for labor and lessened hours of work. The great advance in material prosperity which the enlightened world has made in the last century, and especially in the last half-century, has brought gain in both directions. Similar gain is probably in store for the future. We are likely to see both higher wages and less hours.

Shorter hours of work are a natural and beneficent outcome of the forces of civilization. The great mass of men need not only an increase of income, but an increase of leisure,—leisure for rest, for play, for education, for happier and higher living. No doubt leisure is sometimes abused; but in the main it is a needed means of raising the sum of happiness. Therefore, the short-hour movement should have the sympathy of every friend of humanity. But it must be remembered that it rests on the same forces that underlie all prosperity. It cannot come, as a general change from restriction of output, from redistribution of work among laborers, from mere pressure on employers. It can come only if employers and workmen unite in making industry as efficient as possible.

Like any general change in industrial conditions, this one has not come in the past, and will not continue in the future by a simultaneous movement all along the line. It takes place by a succession of steps, one here, one there, each apparently independent; yet possible as a whole only because industrial conditions are favorable, while the change in each case seems to depend on the conditions of the particular industry for the time being, it depends even for the particular industry on the causes that affect industry at large. It rests on widely different prosperity, it rests also in some degree in the attitude of the persons directly conserved. It comes more easily and quickly if employers are fair-minded and public-spirited, and desirous of doing what is in their power to promote the well-being of their workmen. And it comes more easily and quickly if employes are moderate and considerate, do their best to make industry efficient, and ask no more than in reason can be granted.

Harvard University. F. W. TAUSSIG.

OPEN SHOP DISCRIMINATION.

A Statement that it Injures Union Workers in the Ladies' Garment Industry.

JOHN A. DYCHE

The assertion is frequently made on behalf of employers that the closed shop means such a loss of control of their business as to be ruinous, while the open shop means the fair employment of both union and non-union men. John A. Dyche, General Secretary of the International Ladies' Garment Workers' Union, makes to The Monthly Review a statement showing that in that industry the closed shop is essential to the maintenance of prices and of fair treatment, while the open shop gives opportunity for such discrimination as to make it in practice a shop closed against all union workers. Mr. Dyche says:

"Nine-tenths of the workers in our trade are employed in making ladies' cloaks and skirts. The rest make ladies' wrappers, waists and underwear. The nine-tenths are almost wholly piece work. The bulk of the prices are fixed twice a year, at the beginning of the spring and fall seasons, according to the samples then designed. But in our business, styles are constantly changing. Any shop may be making from fifty to three hundred styles at the same time, and in the course of a season there may be five hundred styles. Thus it is that there is a constant higgling over prices running through the season. Prices for work must be agreed upon for each new style.

"A worker's earning capacity depends not so much upon these prices as upon the kind of work that the foreman gives him to do. Some fabrics are easier to handle and finish than others. Again, if a worker has a single style to make constantly, or goods of one color to make, he can accomplish much more in a given time, than if he is compelled to make frequent changes. Thus it is possible for the foreman, who gives out the work, to cause a favorite to earn as much as $10 or even $15 a day, while he can cause a worker whom he dislikes to earn less than $1.50 a day.

"It is to the interest of a foreman to run a shop as economically as possible, so as to please his employer. In a non-union shop, when the question of price for a new style arises, the worker is afraid to hold out for a figure that will be in proportion to the general scale fixed at the beginning of the season. The foreman may say to him, 'You take a lower price for this garment. It is a style that will run steadily and I will see that you get plenty of it, without changes.' If the worker refuses to accept a reduction, he is known as a 'sticker out' and the foreman can, as we say, 'freeze him out' by 'troubling' him. That is, he can arrange his work so that he can make only starvation wages, while the man next to him, although no better a workman, will be making high pay. This makes the non-union shop a place of scramble for 'cream.' This discrimination is exercised in the open shop against a worker who is known to belong to the union, or who is suspected of membership. Conditions are made so intolerable for him that he must quit that shop or starve.

"The following quotation from a Chicago correspondent shows how the open shop works in our trade there: 'Wherever an abuse was to be remedied, the manufacturer increased the amount of work in the open shop and decreased it in the union shop. In the so-called open union shops, the union had no power and worked for less money, so that the saying was: If you want a good price, go to a union shop with no work. If you want work, go to an open shop at a small price.'

"In the union shop the purpose is to see that the earning capacity of a worker does not depend upon the amount of 'cream' he gets. Any discrimination would at once be called to the employer's attention and justice would be secured. The prices agreed upon at the beginning of the season would be maintained. No worker would be afraid to refuse a reduction at the whim of the foreman. Any change of price would be because the employer and the representative of the union had agreed upon its fairness. The result is harmony, justice and mutual satisfaction. Just as soon as non-union labor is introduced in a union shop in our trade, a stampede begins. The union workers will either leave the shop or leave the union, for the non-union workers will at once begin to get the 'cream.' The union men who work in open shops do so either because their membership is secret or because their skill is such as to make them indispensable to the employer."

The union, like the corporation, is a natural product of civilization. Evolution has brought the time when collective bargaining cannot be avoided. The time came when business on a large scale, like continental railway construction, could not proceed without combination of capital, and the corporation was a necessity. The time is here when business cannot be done without collective bargaining and the union is equally a necessity.—"Labor News," Los Angeles.

It is impossible to revolutionize the customs of years in a day, but the time will come when honest capital and honest labor will meet upon common ground, and reason together, and when that day comes the labor question will have solved itself.—Portland "Labor Press."

In demanding justice from employers, let us be sure that we are just to them ourselves. Let us practice what we preach.—"Labor Compendium."

TRADE UNIONS ARE FOR PEACE.

They Advocate Conference and the Honorable Adherence to Trade Agreements.

BY JAMES DUNCAN, SECRETARY GRANITE CUTTERS' NATIONAL UNION, AND MEMBER CIVIC FEDERATION.

The time is fast approaching when the great majority of corporations, as quite a number have already done, will realize that the proper and businesslike way is to meet the representatives of organized labor to discuss and agree upon properly defined working rules and carefully prepared wage scales. Distrust and misunderstanding are the two greatest disorganizers of modern industry, and as long as the two great factors, capital and labor, stand aloof and fire at long range, that long will indiscriminate and unfriendly acts be perpetrated by each toward the other. Trade-unionism stands for peace and prosperity. In crafts where it is strongest and best administered, conditions for the worker are the most desirable and the greatest amount of industrial tranquility is obtained. Capital is there found to be in its soundest realm. Great financial bonanzas may not be visible, but neither do we find the misery

JAMES DUNCAN.
Secretary Granite Cutters' National Union.

and despair of the poorly organized worker or of the non-unionist.

No contract should be more sacred than the trade agreement of organized labor. It is a matter of honor between the contracting parties, that is circumscribed neither by surety companies bonds nor by compulsory edicts which enslave the body or dwarf the mind. It is regretable that in too many instances these principles are violated both by the unscrupulous employer and by ignorant or unadvised workmen; but such mistakes should not be viewed as failure of the labor movement any more than the collapse of a business venture should be considered a slap to civilization. The bar has members with a peculiar itching in the palm of their hands, which only unearned greenbacks will soothe; the church has within its fold men who fall by the wayside or hear the voice of God calling them to a larger salary, and the labor movement has its bribe takers. The more is the pity that such should exist, but those who expect the trade-union to be perfect, while to that extent complimenting it, are expecting too much for the time in which we live.

Again, asserting that the economic movement is one of honor, words fail to express sufficient contempt for the official who barters the confidence of his fellow workmen, either for lucre or for other personal preference. Such a man may revel in notoriety for a brief time, but honest and practical procedure will assert itself and, distrusted both by bribe-giver and by his old constituents, the dishonored official will be relegated to the rear and will be remembered only as one recalls a disease. So much for the individual. No organization can long maintain the respect necessary to success, a majority of the members of which permit an agreement to be openly violated or even casually disrespected, and in the trade-union movement the young organizations, which have not yet learned to follow the lead of older unions in that particular, cannot do better than pattern after such of them as have by experience proved that a fair and square observance of craft settlements is an essential and fundamental principle of the labor movement.

That such violations sometimes occur is true, but it is also true that in every such instance a great mistake has been made. Sometimes the cause is found in hasty action by the oppressed or over zealous workman, but often employers in a mad desire to outdo some competitor, inflict unbearable conditions on workers which arouse their antagonism and retaliation, and thereby violate the spirit of the agreement as fully as the other case, and both causes are equally reprehensible. This feeling will be in evidence on both sides as long as either retains the idea that the other has no rights to be respected,—but if the up-to-date method fostered by trade-unionism and advocated by the Civic Federation, of each conceding that the other has inherent rights and that both should meet and adjust their differences in conference if possible, and if not by arbitration, is followed, ninety per cent. of the labor disputes causing suspension of production and inconvenience to the public would be prevented. Along this line of thought the moral effect of such a body as the industrial department of the Civic Federation, standing as preceptor for the logical, rational and pacific adjustment of commercial affairs, will go a long way toward bringing otherwise discordant elements in unison. It is not only essential to provide or suggest a way to adjust affairs of this kind after trouble has ensued, but they will be statesmen indeed, of the highest rank, who can formulate and put into use either customs or rules which will bring employers and representatives of labor together to formulate new agreements a month or more before the expiration of the old ones. Men's minds are then cool and calculated to reason well, but when the excitement of a change is at its height, ill digested advantage takes the place of better judgment and less satisfactory settlements are obtained.

In conclusion, a word on limitation of production may not be out of place. Unless in a few instances where physical endurance is at stake, organized workers do not limit production. In their collective bargain they declare for a minimum wage rate and leave the individual to produce what he can. Too often, however, the minimum rate in the bargain is considered a maximum rate by the employer, and the public is thereby led into a misconception of conditions, and trade-unionism is again required to bear a burden which should be on the other fellow's shoulders. If law will continue to tolerate the sweating system, for instance, sapping the vitality of men, women and children in their effort to earn a mere pittance, it becomes a question of practical consideration if trade-unionism should not supply the deficiency, as it does others, by seeing to it that human beings shall not be treated as mere machines, and be ground to death at the behest of a false commercialism.

THE DUTIES OF FOREMEN.

Fairness, Impartiality and Firmness in Discipline Will Beget Loyalty and Harmonious Co-Operation Among the Employes of a Great Corporation.

Edward E. Loomis, vice-President of the Delaware, Lackawanna and Western Railroad Company, delivered an address at a recent dinner of the mining and engineering staff of that company, at Scranton. A portion of his address, as to the delicate and important responsibility of those in immediate command of the body of employes, is here reproduced:

"The duties of a successful foreman are somewhat complex in these days of competition and strife. I first wish to call your attention to the fact that from time almost immemorial, the Delaware, Lackawanna and Western Railroad Company has enjoyed the reputation of dealing justly with its employes. We desire this same course of treatment to be continued. All men, whether their complaint be real or fancied, are entitled and should receive a courteous hearing. Much trouble can be avoided in handling men by the little things receiving their full measure of attention. We are all liable to error, and the employe may not be wrong all the time, and if one of you is placed in a position of doubt, the man should be given the benefit of it.

"You should not, however, construe this as in any way interfering with discipline, which is most necessary for the successful handling of any concern employing a large number of men. You can be fair and impartial, and yet firm. Your position calls for tact and judgment.

"In a majority of cases the foreman is reflected by his employes, and loyalty on the part of the foreman will induce a loyalty on the part of the employe. No one can hope for advancement in any line of business, unless he gives to it his unquestioned loyalty. And it should be the endeavor of each foreman to cultivate the best that is in each employe, and aid them to realize that the company has a personal interest in each of them, and desires to be their friend.

"Hence, I say, in all your dealing be fair, equitable and impartial. Such treatment, you will find, will cause every man to reciprocate that harmonious feeling that should exist between employer and the employe; friction will be avoided, and the results that follow will be the best.

"Again, in selecting your workmen, we desire that you select only such men as will in your estimation merit promotion. Look well into the person's qualifications; for instance, when an ashman is hired, question yourself as to whether or not he will eventually prove to be such a man as you can trust as a fireman, pumpman, or engineer. Merit should always receive recognition and promotion when the opportunity arises, and the man who does not desire promotion, who does not care whether he merits praise or condemnation, is not a good man to have in any position, at any price.

"A man to succeed to-day must excel in the work assigned to him. A man without courage and ambition, or a man satisfied to work as few hours as possible, without the real interests of his employers at heart, need never expect promotion. He is getting all he deserves.

"We trust that no necessity may arise whereby a repetition of 1902 will occur; and that your course will be such that harmony and good feeling will be the rule amongst not only the superintendents and foremen, but that it will reach to and exist between you and all the employes, and you all will extend that hearty co-operation without which we cannot succeed. We also trust that your course will be so wisely planned; your judgment so equitable, that no necessity will be found to call upon the services of any board of mediators to sit in arbitration, but, should any questions arise, we confidently expect that your course will be such as to merit approval and the endorsement of the management of our company."

One of the incidents of the Mining Congress at Paris, to which President Mitchell and Secretary Dodds of District 5 are delegates, was the offering of a resolution that when a strike occurred in Europe among the miners a sympathetic strike should be started in the United States and vice-versa. It is hard to comprehend the state of mind which could evolve such a phantasm. It was the pinnacle of folly. Suppose that a strike occurred in Austria, Belgium or Wales, what justification would that be for the miners of the United States to break their contracts? It would, as urged, "show that the miners were a world power," and it would also show that reason had been dethroned and folly had usurped its place. It would have been more to the point to have entered upon a scheme to render mutual financial aid. It was due to the eloquence and sound reasons advanced by Messrs. Mitchell and Dodds that this chimera was side-tracked. The two have won renown for themselves and shed lustre upon their organization for the sensible, manly and wise course they have pursued upon all questions discussed.—"Miners' Journal."

RAILROAD ACCIDENTS AND SENIORITY.

HAS THE PERSONNEL OF TRAINMEN UNDERGONE DETERIORATION?

A General Denial of that Suggestion by Both Employers and Employes, who Speak from Experience.

Public attention is attracted and public apprehension is excited by the many recent horrible railway accidents. The figures of the Inter-State Commerce Commission show that during 1903 there were 11,006 persons killed on American railways, and 89,872 injured. During the year ending June 30, 1901, there was a record of 8,455 killed and 53,339 injured.

The last quarter of 1903 exceeded all records in its disasters. The number of passengers killed during that period was three times as great as in any previous equal period.

What is the underlying cause of these accidents? A recent article in the New York "Sun" quoted a prominent railroad official as saying:

The fault lies with the employes. In spite of everything discipline is lax. The tone of the men is deteriorating. There was a time twenty or twenty-five years ago when every railroad employe was right up on his toes trying to do the best he could because promotion was on merit. . . . But now promotion is not made on the basis of merit but according to seniority. The labor unions have done this. They have made seniority alone the basis of promotion. There is no chance now,—at least on roads where the men are thoroughly organized,—for a spectacular career. There is no chance to rise through alertness and faithfulness. And so the men have no interest except in getting the biggest day's pay for the smallest day's work.

How far is this assertion true? This inquiry has been put to several railroad officials, as well as to several editors of railway periodicals and officers of the railway brotherhoods, in an endeavor to ascertain the facts.

President L. E. Johnson, of the Norfolk and Western Railway, says:

The rapid and unprecedented increase of traffic throughout this country in the past few years may have temporarily impaired the standard of employes in railroad service, but on the whole I believe the personnel of railway service has improved to a greater extent than that in any other class of business.

President Frank N. Finney, of the Missouri, Kansas and Texas Railway Company, made the following statement:

I believe that the rule of promotion by seniority is one that should be subject to certain modifications. Everything else being equal, I think it should be the rule, but in a great number of cases, perhaps in the majority, mere seniority would not secure the best men for promotion. I think all offices should be filled by the very best men that can be secured, and that ability and fitness for the positions should be the requisites upon which the appointments should be made. There is no question but that the esprit de corps on railroads is not as high as it used to be, and I think that the reason for this is that the employes feel that their chances for promotion are so limited by this rule of seniority that they have no ambition nor incentive to do their best. In my opinion the labor unions should look upon this matter in this light, so that they might work in harmony with the best interests of the companies they serve. Labor unions are all right when led by men of sense and good judgment, and instead of hostility between labor and capital there should be the greatest friendship and good feeling. When this exists the best results will be insured. I have always been and am thoroughly in sympathy with the laborer and desire nothing more strongly than to bring labor and capital into the closest relations that will establish peace and prosperity for both.

President, F. D. Underwood, of the Erie Railroad, said:

I think the causes of the increase in the number of railroad accidents are susceptible of being divided into three grand divisions:

First: Increase in the speed and weight of trains and engines with the attendant increased number of train miles run, resulting in an increase in the percentage of accidents. This must continue to increase with the increase in the number of trains operated.

Second: Inability to apply remedy through lack of knowledge of the causes.

Third: Lack of esprit de corps among employes.

President George W. Stevens, of the Chesapeake and Ohio Railroad Company, said:

While the unions do, to a certain extent, dwarf individual ambition, yet it is within the power of the appointing officer to distinguish between merit and mere seniority; in other words he is only compelled to recognize seniority when other things are equal.

An examination of trade agreements, or of the regulations in force upon the principal railroads of the country shows that almost without exception the rule of seniority is accompanied by some such statement as "other things being equal" or "merit being taken into consideration."

The representatives of the brotherhoods deny entirely the theory that deterioration of service through operation of the rule of seniority is responsible for an increase in railway accidents.

John F. McNamee, Editor of the Locomotive Firemen's Magazine, writes:

Nothing but blinded prejudice could charge railway accidents to the personnel and morale of the men employed in the railway train service. The efficiency of train service men to-day is much advanced over the conditions that prevailed under the old system of promotion by the method of personal favoritism, and the improvement has been brought about largely by the railway labor organizations. The standard examinations through which railroad men are required to pass before being promoted have made it necessary for these men to become thoroughly informed upon all subjects pertaining to their business. Seniority only secures for the men the right to be examined for promotion in their regular turn, and a failure to pass the standard examination adopted by the railway company means no promotion. In the days before the labor organizations brought about the rule of seniority, the travelling public was at the mercy of trainmen, engine men who were promoted without the form of an examination and solely upon the personal choice of some railway official, who had authority to place whomever he might see fit in a position.

H. D. Perham, Chief of the Brotherhood of Telegraphers, said:

I have had exceptional opportunities during thirty years for observing the growth and development of railway employes. There are few, if any, experienced railway men who will disagree with me when I say that the personnel of railway employes, especially those connected with train movements, has improved steadily in that period, and intelligent management and employes' organizations are responsible for it.

Thirty years ago railway employes were notoriously a reckless roving class who cared little about their positions or anything else. The organizations came with their discipline in regard to temperance and their seniority rules, and the result was that the men had to stick to their jobs to work their way up to desirable positions. Those who years ago were living a hand to mouth existence perhaps without family or other responsibilities, have changed places with men who have families to provide for, a stake in the country, and a home of their own. Considering the risks in their calling, they constitute the most careful, conscientious, right-minded, sane and sober set of citizens any country ever produced.

There is no such thing as straight seniority in the railway service. The oldest man in the service does not, by reason of being the oldest man, get promotion. He has to be capable, and his superior officer always reserves the right to be the judge of capability. Even the contracts that the employes have mutually agreed upon with the officials, provide for that supervision.

In my opinion the growth of traffic in the country has outstripped that of the installation of safety devices. The desire for economy in operating railways very often leads to an appalling disaster. In one place we find the track walker's services dispensed with to save $50 per month, and a passenger train crashing through a bridge with its abutments undermined by a torrent. In another place we find a signal report man with too many signals to look after and keep in order, and the train gets into a block where it had no right to be. In many instances we find signal towers and telegraph offices operated by mere children working for half wages. This feature is a most prolific source of danger. There are exceptions to the rule, but it may be stated without fear of successful contradiction that motives of economy are responsible for a large majority of the railway accidents in the United States.

John T. Wilson, President of the International Brotherhood of Maintenance of Way Employes, said:

In 16 years' experience as an officer of a railway brotherhood, I have never seen a single trade agreement between the officials of a railway and their organized employes in which seniority was made the sole basis of promotion. On the contrary the stipulation always runs in words of similar import to the following: "other qualifications being equal the employe longest in the service of the company shall be promoted to fill any vacancy in rank above him." In one agreement I find the following statement which is well understood and accepted by the railway brotherhoods generally as admitting of no contention: "The responsibility in the operation of the road rests on the Management, and they will therefore pass upon the question of the competency of the employe in line of promotion."

Judge Caldwell, of the United States Circuit Court, in a decision rendered April 5, 1904, stated: "Two of the ablest railroad managers ever in the service of Union Pacific System, and probably as able as any this country has ever produced,—Mr. S. H. H. Clark and Mr. Edward Dickinson,—testified that these labor organizations on this system had improved the morals and efficiency of the men and had rendered valuable aid to the company. The managers testified . . . that their efforts have been seconded and materially aided by the labor organizations."

In 1892 one passenger was killed for every 1,491,910 carried in the United States, while in 1902 there was one killed for every1,883,706 passengers carried. This shows an actual decrease in the ratio of fatalities to the number of passengers.

I do not dispute that many serious accidents have occurred, which might have been avoided by the exercise of official prudence in various ways, but I do not know of a single instance where the labor unions have arbitrarily forced an incompetent employe into a position where his subsequent blundering has caused disastrous results.

CONCILIATION AND ARBITRATION.

A Permanent Tribunal to Adjust Labor Differences Established at Hamilton, Ont.

A plan for the adjustment of disputes between employers and wage-earners has been organized in Hamilton, Ont. In its development, the example of the National Civic Federation in promoting better relations between employer and employed in the United States was cited as an edifying and encouraging example. The plan consists of a permanent tribunal of conciliation and arbitration, formed by the joint action of the local Trades and Labor Council and the Hamilton Board of Trade. The tribunal has been organized in accordance with the recommendation of a joint committee of those two bodies, ratified by them:

"That the Board of Trade appoint a permanent committee of seven, to be known as a 'Board of Conciliation and Mediation,' out of which there shall be selected from time to time a committee of three to co-operate with a similar committee to be appointed by the Trade and Labor Council, which shall constitute a board, which, at the initiative and upon the request of any employer of labour or any body of wage-earners, shall offer its services to secure the adjustments of disputes as they may, from time to time, arise."

This is the outcome of an original proposal by the Trades and Labor Council that there should be formed a committee of conciliation, composed of three or five members of the Board of Trade, and the same number from the Trades and Labor Council; this committee to be ready at all times to tender its services whenever a strike or lock-out should be threatened or should have occurred.

This proposal was submitted by the Council merely as a basis for conciliation, with the statement that it would be happy to appoint a committee to confer with a similar committee of the Board of Trade.

The Board of Trade expressed immediate concurrence with this suggestion, and appointed a special committee of three members to confer with the committee of the Council. The scheme of organization now in operation was evolved at a series of conferences between these committees. Their joint report made special reference to the proceedings of the National Conference on Industrial Conciliation, held in New York under the auspices of the National Civic Federation, and observed that the public, the employers and the wage-earners were there represented by many of the most notable public men in the United States. The words of the late Senator Hanna as to the supreme importance of bringing labor and capital into closer relations were quoted, as were several of the recommendations adopted by the conference, including the following:

That all the industries in the United States should establish boards of conciliation within the several and varied interests, to which boards of conciliation all differences and disputes arising between employer and employe, if not readily adjusted between the immediate interests concerned, may be referred for settlement.

"The Labour Gazette," issued by the Dominion Department of Labor, notices prominently the movement in the United States, under the auspices of the National Civic Federation, for industrial peace through conciliation and conference.

National Civic Federation

MONTHLY REVIEW

VOL. I. No. 9 — NEW YORK, NOVEMBER 15, 1904 — TEN CENTS

THE VOICE OF THE CHURCH RINGS OUT FOR LABOR.

THREE WORLD-WIDE ECCLESIASTICAL BODIES DECLARE THEIR SYMPATHETIC, UP-LIFTING ATTITUDE TOWARD WAGE-EARNERS.

The growth of interest in the moral and social aspects of the labor question is indicated by the increasing attention paid to that subject by churches. Both the Protestant Episcopal and the Congregational Churches have made inquiries into the subject through committees and their reports just made public are highly instructive. Pope Pius X, through an official letter, repeats the interest in labor expressed by his predecessor.

"The organization of labor is essential to the well being of the working people," is the conclusion of the Standing Commission on the Relations of Labor and Capital, of the Protestant Episcopal Church, after three years' investigation.

The members of the Commission are: The Bishop of New York, Henry C. Potter; the Bishop of Massachusetts, William Lawrence; the Bishop Coadjutor of Chicago, Charles P. Anderson; the Rev. R. H. McKim, D.D.; the Rev. George Hodges, D.D.; the Rev. C. D. Williams, D.D.; Samuel Mather, Jacob Riis, and George Pinckard.

Concerning the causes of industrial disturbances, the Commission reports:

"We are agreed in the conviction that the causes of the violence of the past three years in Pennsylvania, in Colorado, and in Illinois, are not so much economical as moral.

"The strike commonly begins in distrust. The reason at the heart of it is that the master has as little confidence in the good will of the men as the men have in the good faith of the master. The employer and the employed, separated by our industrial conditions at such a social distance as to make fraternal understanding difficult, make their bargain one with another, under these conditions, not as partners, but as competitors. Where distrust and antagonism are well founded, there is nothing for it, so far as the Church is concerned, except conversion. They who are at fault are to be admonished, on the one side against prejudice and passion, and on the other side against covetousness and the sins which proceed from the inordinate love of riches.

HENRY C. POTTER,
Bishop, Protestant Episcopal Church.

WILLIAM LAWRENCE,
Bishop, Protestant Episcopal Church.

SAMUEL MATHER,
Manufacturer.

JACOB A. RIIS,
Sociologist.

"Where distrust and hostility are unfounded, the Church may afford an opportunity of conference. The capitalist and the laborer are alike sons of the Church. They may not sit in the same seat, or even in the same building; that is largely a matter of locality. But there is as much loyalty to the Church and to the Divine Head of the Church in the one class as in the other. The voice of the Christian religion reaches both capital and labor. The Church helps to remove the moral causes of industrial strife when she brings these different members of her family into better acquaintance.

Concerning the "aim and spirit of labor organization," the report says:

"We perceive among our clergy and laity alike, much ignorance (frankly confessed and deplored) as to the principles which are involved in the conflicts of the industrial world. At the same time, it is plain that an enlightened public opinion is one of the determining factors of the situation. Every industrial dispute involves three parties,—the employer, the employed, and the public; and the public eventually casts the deciding vote. Thus a serious social responsibility rests upon every Christian citizen and, more especially, upon the Christian minister.

"We call attention to the analogy between certain offenses of the union, and like offenses, past or present, of both the capitalist and the churchman. Thus the employer's black-list corresponds to the union's boycott, and both are akin to the major excommunication. The lock-out and the strike are of the same nature, and there is no great difference between such endeavors to employ the argument of famine and an interdict which deprives a people of the blessings of spiritual life. The question of the closed shop is like the question of the closed state. Men whose Puritan ancestors strove to maintain a state whose privileges should belong only to members of the church ought to be able to understand the [illegible]

(Concluded on page 14.)

PRESIDENT ELIOT OF HARVARD ON UNIONS AND EMPLOYERS' ASSOCIATIONS.

THE RIGHT OF WORKERS TO CONFERENCE ASSERTED AND THE UNION PRONOUNCED INDISPENSABLE IN GREAT INDUSTRIES.

President Charles W. Eliot of Harvard University delivered an address before the Economic Club of Boston, on Nov. 16, in which he declared it to be the right of workmen to advise employers about the conduct of business, and pronounced the maintenance of unions to be essential. He would test the worth of employers' associations by their regard for variety of industries, for personal and public liberty and for good will. The following is a verbatim report of Dr. Eliot's address:

Employers Forced to Organize.

Since the first meeting of the Economic club the most striking fact in the development of the industrial combat—for combat it has been—is the organization of the employers. The employers were forced into these compact organizations. They found the force that could be exerted by the organization of labor; they found that these labor organizations could defeat any single employer.

They found that their only safety was to organize firm, trustworthy associations, and these associations have been formed in great number all over our country. They are, of course, various, because the interests and needs of the different trades and industries are various, and we cannot expect that the employers' association has a uniform policy.

The effort after the uniform policy which characterizes the labor-unions is, in my view, a dangerous one, whether for the unions or for the employers' associations. The diversities in the industries and occupations of the country are so great, the different conditions under which different industries are prosecuted are so widely different that I think we may reasonably distrust any efforts at universal policies, universal legislation—policies which cover a great variety of trades, or policies and legislation which are intended to produce the same rates of wages, the same hours of labor, etc., all over wide areas of our country.

I think we may reasonably distrust, I say, legislation or policies which aim at universal application. It is clear that a mode of conducting one industry which is almost indispensable to it may be entirely inapplicable in another industry, and these diversities extend to rates of wages, to the hours in a day's work, to the distribution of the hours of work through the 24 hours of the day. I look, therefore, to see the employers' association generally acting against uniform legislation affecting either wages or hours.

How should the employers' policies be characterized in general? Are there any tests which we may apply to them to distinguish the good and safe policies from the dangerous or evil policies? That is a very interesting inquiry, because the efforts of the employers' associations are becoming very strenuous,—they are becoming keenly directed against the labor unions and their policies, and it is all-important that the employers' policies should as a rule in all their diversity command public confidence and approval.

Monopolies Unwelcome.

I need not say that it is the effort after a monopoly of labor in a given trade which characterizes the fundamental policy of the labor-union. Now, if the employers show that their effort is after all directed to the attainment of a monopoly, they will lose, not command, public confidence in their efforts. Monopolies are no more welcome to the free people of the United States to-day than they were to our English ancestors 400 years ago.

The contest against monopolies granted by the sovereign for the profit of his government was one of the great steps in the development of public liberty; and it is a striking thing that under free institutions there should have arisen in our day such elaborate efforts toward the seizing of monopoly, first on the part of bands of working people, and second on the part of bands of capitalists.

Now, public confidence can be no more commanded by men seeking the first sort of monopoly than by men seeking the second sort of monopoly—the monopoly of labor on the one hand of a given trade or the monopoly of capital on the other hand. Therefore, employers' associations must acquit themselves in the public view of the suspicion that they are searching for monopoly and the means thereof.

But again, is there a test by which a rightful employers' policy may be recognized? I believe there is. And I should state it thus: An employers' association is rightful if it clearly appears that in the prosecution of that policy a single employer or the great association of employers are tending toward the development of private and public liberty.

But if the employers' policy is tending the other way—toward the restriction of either private or public liberty, the chances are that that policy is wrong, not right, dangerous to the public weal, not beneficial.

Employers' Objects Analyzed.

Let me illustrate what I mean by this test. I have here a list of the objects of the Boston employers' association, formed within the last six months. They state their objects in this way:

"First—No closed shop.

"Second—No restriction as to the use of tools, machinery or materials, except such as are unsafe.

"Third—No limitation of output.

"Fourth—No restriction as to the number of apprentices and helpers when of proper age.

"Fifth—No boycott.

"Sixth—No sympathetic strike.

"Seventh—No sacrifice of the independent workman to the labor-union.

"Eighth—No compulsory use of the union label."

Eight objects are thus stated. Do they tend toward liberty or toward the restriction of liberty? "No closed shop." That means contending against the effective weapon of the labor union toward the establishment of a complete monopoly. This, then, is a measure toward freedom.

CHARLES W. ELIOT,
President Harvard University.

"No restriction as to the use of tools, machinery or materials." There again clearly the effort is to prevent bonds being put upon the development of the trade, or the introduction of improvements. It tends toward freedom.

"No limitation of output." That principle not only tends toward freedom, but it tends to the development of independent, different powers in the individual workman, and that is indeed a most important element of individual liberty. It tends, of course, against the most demoralizing doctrine and practice of the labor union.

"No restriction as to the number of apprentices and helpers when of proper age." Is that a policy which tends toward freedom or towards the restriction of freedom? In education we should not for a moment doubt that that policy tended toward freedom. Even Napoleon stated, and stated very briefly, the liberty which this policy tends to promote—"Every career open to talent."

"No boycott." A boycott is an illegal attack on individual traders or workers or producers. It of course is a great attack on liberty, so that this policy also works toward freedom.

"No sympathetic strike." Here again the tendency is to resist the use of a powerful weapon to promote the boycott or to cripple the producing power of a single firm or factory.

"No sacrifice of the independent workman to the labor-union." I need not say that employers have until within times still recent neglected extraordinarily the observation of the principle here stated. Here in Boston, for instance, we have seen strikes in industries the continuity of which was very important to the owners, non-union men called in to occupy the factories in spite of the strike, but in a few weeks the strike was settled, all the non-union men that had been called into the factories were driven out and the entire body of strikers reinstated.

We have seen that right here in our city repeatedly. Now is it not clear that such a policy as that on the part of employers works directly in restraint of liberty?

Is it not clear that it is the duty of every employer suffering from a strike not only to protect every man who comes to his help, but to make sure that that man continues to be employed?

Trivial Strikes Rebuked.

Is it not sure that one of the great causes of the frequency of strikes for trivial reasons—very trivial reasons even,—is the assured belief on the part of the strikers that they are only to be out a week or a few weeks, or at worst a few months, and then that they would all return to their jobs?

That is, I believe, the fundamental reason for the frequency of strikes and for the inconsiderateness with which they occur. If only this principle of this new association of employers can be enforced, "no sacrifice of the independent workmen to the labor-union," we shall see that men will strike only for serious reasons and when they feel that in striking they are endangering their jobs permanently; that they are putting themselves at risk, making themselves liable to a complete change of residence, for example,—making themselves liable to a change of occupation. I know no more valuable principle or method for the promotion of industrial liberty than this principle, "No sacrifice of the individual workman to the labor-union."

Finally, "No compulsory use of the union label." Is that a regulation which tends toward liberty?

Let us observe that the union label is, after the closed shop, the most effective weapon for securing to the labor union in any trade a complete monopoly.

The union label is an effective weapon and it is directly for the promotion of a monopoly, for the securing of monopoly, holding it up, and for enforcing the penalty of disobedience to the union.

Importance of Liberty.

I find every one of these principles to be in defence of private and public liberty. They bear that test, and I conceive that this test is one we should always apply to any proposed employers' policy. It is not in industrial affairs alone that this test may be as I conceive safely and wisely applied. I am sure it should be applied to every educational policy. It is only when the policy of school government, college government, university government tends towards liberty, that is, tends to give play to the free spirit of youth, that the policy will have any hope of living or much hope of conferring practical benefit on the community.

So with our wars and with governmental policies. Are there any wars which other generations remember with gratitude or praise except those out of which came some increase, some development of public liberty? Are there any policies safe, prudent even, except those which do away with restraint of freedom or give freer play to the native human instinct for liberty?

Good-will the Highest Essential.

But there is another test which I conceive should be applied to all employers' associations. Do they tend to promote good-will between employers and employed? After all, the great thing to be done to make the industries of any people productive is to secure the good-will of the men that labor in those industries. What is the reason that slavery is notoriously unproductive and costly? There is no good-will in it. What is the reason that any man working as he feels for himself and for the benefit of his family will work a great deal harder than a man will who has no such belief?

It is all a question of good-will. If the unions of work people in our country to-day all felt that they were working with a will for their own benefit, for their own uplifting, for their own happiness, the productiveness and efficiency of labor in this country would amount to an inconceivable height. The ultimate question, therefore, is the promotion of good-will.

Now, must we not all desire that all the employers' associations and every individual employer should constantly bear in mind this test of his own tendency, of the association's tendency—Does it tend towards good-will between the employer and the employed?

How can these tendencies be secured? Only by thoughtfulness, by considerateness, by sympathy, by constant care for the right relation between the employer and the employed.

How can these feelings be expressed? Not by any form of benevolence or condescension, not by the giving of privileges or favors, but by the giving of rights, by the giving of earned privileges.

(Concluded on page 10.)

A YEAR SAVED ON THE SUBWAY BY A SANE TRADE TREATY.

HONORABLE ADHERENCE MAKES EFFECTIVE A TRADE AGREEMENT BETWEEN ORGANIZED CONTRACTORS AND ORGANIZED CRAFTSMEN.

"We saved a year," said John B. McDonald, the general contractor for building the New York Subway. "If it hadn't been for the labor agreement between the Rapid Transit Contractors' Association and the Central Federated Union, the public wouldn't have ridden in the Subway before October, 1905."

Amid all the oratory and congratulation that celebrated the opening of the New York Subway in October there could be found not a reference to the part that the trade agreement named by Mr. McDonald performed in its construction. Yet the history of its building is a signal illustration of what can be accomplished by amicable conference between capital and labor, and of the influence of a trade agreement in preventing, with one exception, industrial disturbances and in encouraging good relations between employers and employed.

All the skilled labor employed in the actual construction of the Subway was union labor. The terms of its employment were defined by a truly collective contract, since the two parties were each composed of a number of constituents.

The smooth and successful operation of this contract excited amazement among large employers in all parts of the United States. Contractors who were having trouble with labor wondered at the reports that reached them of the steady progress of work, day and night, upon the Subway in New York. Many of them wrote requests for copies of the agreement which produced results so enviable.

This device for industrial peace was born out of discord. After the contract to build the Subway for $35,000,000 had been awarded to John B. McDonald, and he had divided the work among sub-contractors, it became evident that mutual co-operation among them would be needed. This need became more and more apparent every day after the first spadeful of earth had been turned on March 24, 1900. The sub-contractors had acquired widely different methods of dealing with labor, through their experience in various states, with various bodies of workmen, and in various kinds of work. Co-operation was needed also among the various organizations of labor, representing many trades, employed in the tunnel. The machinery for united action among the labor organizations already existed in the Central Federated Union, a body composed of delegates from constituent trades-unions.

The general contractor, John B. McDonald, sought some corresponding method to harmonize the different ideas and methods of the sub-contractors. Work on the tunnel had not progressed far before it became evident that divers systems were developing in the several sections into which the total length of the Subway had been divided. These clashing systems threatened to become fertile sources of discontent and trouble. Labor was quick to compare its treatment on one section with its treatment on another. Complaints and friction multiplied until they culminated in a strike involving several of the unions employed on the line. It was plainly necessary to extend over the entire line of the tunnel a system that should be uniform in every section, and that should protect equally and equitably the rights of all the contractors, while securing fair treatment to all the trades employed.

JOHN B. McDONALD,
Prest. Rapid Transit Contractors' Association.

WILLIAM C. DOUGLAS,
Sec'y Rapid Transit Contractors' Association.

JOHN J. PALLAS,
Prest. New York Federation of Labor.

JAMES P. ARCHIBALD,
Of Painters, Decorators and Paperhangers.

Accordingly, Mr. McDonald called a meeting of all the sub-contractors, and the Rapid Transit Contractors' Association was organized on June 4, 1901. Its officers were John B. McDonald, President; and William C. Douglas, Secretary and Treasurer. Its members were Degnon-McLean Contracting Co.; Holbrook, Cabot & Daly; Ira A. Shaler; Naughton & Co.; William Bradley; Capt. John Shields; Farrell, Hooper & Co.; John C. Rodgers; McCabe Brothers; John B. McDonald; Rufus C. Hunt; Terry & Tench Contracting Co.; E. P. Roberts; Sicilian Asphalt Paving Co., and United Building Material Co.

This Association entered at once into negotiations with the Central Federated Union for the purpose of forming an agreement which should apply to the entire construction of the Subway and include, so far as practicable, all the crafts employed. The drawing of this agreement involved considerable discussion and many conferences between committees representing the two organizations. The agreement was finally perfected and formally signed on June 4, 1901. Thereafter it was the chart by which the relations between the contractors and the unions were guided until the Subway was finished. The violations of this contract were rare, and they served to increase on both sides the appreciation of its practical value in averting trouble and securing justice. The contract provided that no strike was to be declared during the progress of the work, that if at any time there were differences that could not be decided by the Joint Committee of the Contractors' Association and the Central Federated Union, they were to be referred to arbitration. But during the years of its operation there never was a resort to arbitration, the Joint Committee succeeding in settling any disputes referred to it.

This agreement provided for the employment of union skilled labor, with the exception of foremen and master mechanics; for the eight-hour day, in accordance with the New York statute relating to public work, and for the adjustment and arbitration of grievances. The total number of organized skilled wage earners affected by the contract varied from 2,000 to 3,000. The variety of skilled labor involved is indicated by the list attached to the agreement, which includes:

Architectural Iron Workers; Plumbers and Gasfitters; Sheet Metal Workers; Pavers; Rammers; Blue Stone Cutters; Flaggers; Bridge and Curb Setters; Marble Cutters; Polishers and Helpers; Coppersmiths; Electrical Workers; Eccentric and Standard Engineers and Firemen; Safety Engineers; Steam Fitters and Helpers; Granite Cutters; Painters; Tile Layers and Helpers; House Movers and Shorers; Double Drum Hoisters; Machinists; Pipe Caulkers and Tappers; Rock Drillers and Tool Sharpeners; Tar Felt and Waterproof Workers; Forgers and Blacksmiths.

The contract was signed on behalf of the Contractors' Association by George W. McNulty, Frederick Holbrook and E. J. Farrell, and on behalf of the Central Federated Union by William J. O'Brien, Edward Friday and John J. Pallas.

The members of the standing Joint Committee on Grievances for which the contract provided were three on behalf of the contractors—Messrs. McNulty, Holbrook and Farrell. On behalf of the unions there were also three members, who, at various times, were John J. Pallas, William J. O'Brien, James P. Holland, Edward Friday, [illegible], James P. Archibald and John A. [illegible].

(Concluded on page [illegible].)

PRESIDENT GOMPERS' ANNUAL MESSAGE TO ORGANIZED LABOR.

THE HEAD AND THE SECRETARY OF THE AMERICAN FEDERATION ANNOUNCE GREAT GAIN IN MEMBERSHIP DESPITE ADVERSE CONDITIONS.

The address of President Gompers to the annual convention of the American Federation of Labor contained many important statements relative to the strength and the policies of that organization. Of its spirit, Mr. Gompers said:

"The immediate future is pregnant with good or ill for the people of our country. It devolves upon the organized labor movement to determine by its course the form which it shall assume.

"The constant improvement in machinery, the division, subdivision, and specialization of labor, the wonderful development in industry, and the concentration of wealth, give to the wealth possessors such extraordinary power, which, when coupled with the cunning and greed for gain, unless intelligently and comprehensively met by a well organized labor movement, will tend to the deterioration of our race, the destruction of all our achievements, and the dissipation of all our hopes.

SAMUEL GOMPERS,
President American Federation of Labor.

"On the other hand, if we are faithful to the history and traditions of the struggling masses in the past, if we shall prove true to the interests and the welfare of the hosts of labor of our day, the power calculated to injure will be diverted to the common weal, and thus open up vistas of larger opportunities and a broader conception of human rights and ennobling aspirations.

From workshop, factory, mill, and mine comes the appeal to you for comfort, aid, and relief. The yearning cry of the children of labor for emancipation from the drudgery of incessant toil to the freedom of home, the playground, and the sunshine is not heard in vain by you. The sufferings of the past, the struggles of to-day, and the hopes for a brighter and a better day for all are represented by the united and federated labor movement of our time and of our country.

"While the eyes and hearts of our fellow workers are fervently turned toward this convention, hopeful and confident that the broadest and best interests of the working people will be safeguarded and forwarded, the scrutinizing vision of our opponents and antagonists is concentrated upon our gathering and our work, ready to turn to our disadvantage and discomfiture any error of judgment of speech and action. May we not hope so to conform our course as to satisfy and gratify our friends, confound and disarm our would-be despoilers?"

The address thus treated the growth of the movement:

"The law of growth in organized labor is little understood. From the formation of the first bona fide trade-union movement in modern times it has grown with each era of industrial activity and receded to some degree with each industrial depression, but with each recurring revival in industry the degree of growth has been greater, and with each recurring period of depression it has receded to a lesser degree than its immediate predecessors. All students of our movement appreciate these facts and count with them. The antagonists and the ignorant view these natural economic changes with exultation or alarm.

"When it is borne in mind that the trade-union movement of America is, comparatively speaking, still in its infancy; when there is taken into consideration the vast extent of territory as well as the makeup of different nationalities speaking foreign tongues, the great development in industry and the concentration of wealth, using its powers to prevent or crush out organizations; when all these things are given due consideration, that we have brought about any degree of fraternity and homegeneity should be counted to our credit rather than to our detriment.

"It is not necessary here to recount the advantages which have been secured by our movement in the interests of our fellow workers. Not only are our records of achievements available to all, but the better results in the home, the more material improvement, the social and moral advancement, as well as political independence, and the character and manhood of our working people, are the best attestation, demonstration, and proof of the efforts, the work, the aims, methods, and ennobling purposes of our movement.

"Our opponents must lamentably fail to prove to the toilers that their freedom is curtailed or impaired in becoming organized when the workers themselves have the indisputable proof of their enjoyment of larger vision, occasioned by fewer hours of daily, burdensome toil, as our antagonists must also fail to impress upon the wives and the children of workmen that the freedom of action of their husbands and fathers is impaired when they themselves enjoy the fruits of brighter homes, more material improvements, and the opportunities of leisure and education.

"But, despite the destructive purposes of labor's antagonists, I am in a position to report that there has been a sum total of great gain in the membership of the organizations affiliated to the American Federation of Labor."

Mr. Gompers discussed the economic effect of resistance to wage reductions:

"In former periods when an industrial reaction was manifest, employers generally viewed the situation from their own immediate standpoint only, without regard to their own broad interest or the general good. Their first recourse was to that which to them seemed the easiest course to continue the operation of their plants—to find markets. They reduced wages. Reduction of wages followed in quick order; the consuming power of the masses was curtailed and still more limited, entailing wholesale discharges of workmen who were formerly employed in producing the things the masses, the workers, formerly consumed, inducing and giving the further cause to still further entailment of consumption and production and still more discharges of workmen, until millions were unemployed; the wheels of industry and commerce paralyzed; until men were walking the highways and byways of our country in idleness, while poverty, hunger, and misery stalked through our land.

"It is held now that there can be no real natural famine in the world because of the easy facilities with which the remotest corners of the earth can be reached. Surely if this be true, and no informed, sane, reasonable being disputes it, there is an utter absence of excuse for non-employment, hunger, poverty, or misery in our land, a land so richly and bountifully blessed. When idleness and its consequent misery are permitted to come among our people it is due entirely to rapacious, sordid avarice, mismanagement, and incompetency on the one hand, or to ignorant indifference and culpable pliancy on the other. The employers generally typify the one and the workers formerly typified the other.

"If the employers followed their policy of wage reductions in previous years as a supposed way out of industrial stagnation, and thereby simply accentuated the situation and made it worse, is it not a logical inference that the same ruinous policy would be pursued in the present era?

"Are all the dire experiences and sufferings of our people to go for naught? Should we permit ignorant indifference on our part to make us culpable for a repetition of the awful conditions which followed in the wake of the former mischievous and wrongful course of our employers, or shall we continue the course which we last year declared when we had the prescience to foresee the danger with which we were threatened? Organized labor then called a halt and declared the entire policy of wage reductions unwise, wrongful, and dangerous to the well-being of labor and of all our people.

"We were fully aware that it would be impossible to prevent all wage reductions, but we can view the result of our last year's declaration of policy of resistance to wage reductions with satisfaction and pride. We can challenge our critics and opponents to compare the past year, when we were confronted with an industrial reaction, with a year of a similar industrial situation, and it will demonstrate beyond cavil or doubt that

"First. Wage reductions have been checked.

"Second. The industrial situation has not become acute, as was the uniform course formerly.

"Third. Much idleness, poverty, suffering, and misery have been prevented.

"Fourth. The era of industrial stagnation, as compared with former like conditions, has been shortened.

"Fifth. The prospect for a revival in industry and commerce in the future is brighter, as compared with any similar previous period.

"Sixth. There is less acute feeling of unrest among workmen and employers generally, business men and all our people.

"Seventh. There are more workmen and employers in agreement and understanding.

"Eighth. There is a more general effort to bring about more rightful relations between workmen and employers.

"Ninth. There is a better conception of the rights and duties of man to man, a more general satisfaction among our people with the present, and a more gratifying and hopeful outlook for the future.

FRANK MORRISON,
Secretary American Federation of Labor.

"The results of labor's policy are our best justification.

"It is a science becoming more generally understood by labor to know when to strike and when not to strike; to know for what to strike and for what not to strike. It is said that it is not wise to strike on a so-called 'falling market.' It can not, however, successfully be gainsaid that a strike or preparedness to strike in resisting an offer of wage reduction will prevent the market from falling still lower. It may not be, and undoubtedly is not, wise or prudent to strike for wage advancement on a downward industrial trend, yet it is better that even this economic error be committed than a complacent acceptance of wage reductions.

"At the risk of criticism I repeat last year's paraphrase that in the offer of wage reductions it is better to resist and lose than not to resist at all. The resistance will at least demonstrate that labor is an equation and factor which must not be ignored in the material, economic, industrial, commercial, and social affairs and welfare of our people and our country.

Mr. Gompers declared "preparedness to strike" to be "the determining factor to bring about industrial peace on a more equitable basis," and said:

"We would abolish war, industrially as well as internationally; but its abolition must come, and it will come from conscious power, intelligent and broader humanity. May the day never come when peace is proclaimed or maintained because of the inanition of the workers. Peace, to be desirable, to be lasting, advantageous, and humane, must come from a virile and intelligent manhood. We want no peace, and there will never be peace, founded upon the servility and degradation of the workers.

"The vantage position now occupied by labor was not brought to it on a silver platter, but was contended for and won by the unity of the workers, by the burdens which they have borne, and the sacrifices they have made. More thorough organization, a greater

(Concluded on page 16.)

THE THREE CONSPICUOUS FOES OF ORGANIZED LABOR.

THE TASKS OF UNIONISM ARE TO CONVERT "PARRYISM," TO RESIST SOCIALISM AND TO CORRECT ITS OWN INHERENT WEAKNESSES.

(By the Editor.)

Organized labor is triply beset. It is assailed by its two outward foes, "Parryism" and Socialism, and is at the same time endangered by its own inherent weaknesses. It is the purpose of this article to analyze the methods of each of these outward foes and to examine the inward weaknesses of trade unionism which must be corrected if it is to survive assault from without. All society must be interested in these three perils, if in truth the movement represented by organized labor is in the interest of civilization. That is the truth that organized labor must incessantly demonstrate, for therein lies its right to live. Unless it can maintain this warrant for its existence, organized labor must be overthrown by assault or disintegrate from essential errors.

There are organizations of capital that seek and find the establishment of honorable business relations with corresponding organizations of labor. These are composed of employers on the one side who represent the greatest investments of capital in the United States in the basic industries, such as mining, and the manufacture of iron and steel and fabrics, in the metal trades and in transportation by rail and ship; and of unions on the other side, in which the great mass of organized wage-earners is enrolled. While there are sometimes serious conflicts in these industries, the ultimate purpose of their organization is to bring about and encourage peace through negotiation. This characteristic is only emphasized by the fact that some of these organizations were formed originally to fight the unions, but have learned from experience the superiority of trade agreements to trade battles.

THE ASSAULT BY "PARRYISM."

There are other organizations of capital whose present aim is to "smash the unions." Sometimes this policy is boldly avowed, sometimes it is disguised. "Parryism" is a coined word that has grown into current use to describe the uncompromising hostility to organized labor that inspires this class of employers' associations and "citizens' alliances." These have not been formed to negotiate with labor, since they aim to destroy all organization of labor with which negotiation is possible. It is conceivable that these societies may appeal to employers whose experience has been restricted to the arrogance, excesses and brutalities of some particular union or labor leader, and who feel a natural impulse of hatred and revenge against all organized labor in general. But this attitude becomes inexcusable on the part of employers when they have looked beyond these incidental outrages and have learned to comprehend the history and philosophy of unionism. Such employers are able to understand that the organized effort to uplift labor is as distinct from labor's intolerance as is the church from the tortures inflicted in its name by the Inquisition.

"Parryism" discloses its purpose through its literature. It is a peculiar literature. Its characteristics are adroitly disguised misstatements, studied persistence in associating unionism with crime, socialism and anarchy, and, above all, constant pretense of friendship to organized labor, while advocating every conceivable plan for its disruption and disbandment. This literature, while professing friendship, is in reality the propaganda of war. It extends one hand to labor in pretended amity, and with the other would stab it in the back.

The bulk of this literature is addressed to employers, but it is designed also to deceive all of the so-called non-producing classes, and to convey to a miscellaneous audience the impression that organized labor is a foe to republican institutions and that it must be destroyed if constitutional government is to be preserved. This literature is in the form of periodicals, newspaper reports of speeches, reports of employers' associations in pamphlet form, and inflammatory circulars. Even fiction is to be employed as an agent of excitement; for a new periodical has appeared, which announces that it is "conducted under the personal guidance of David M. Parry, President of the Citizens' Industrial Association of America," and "devoted to the interests of free and independent labor; opposed to organized lawlessness, Socialism and Anarchy." A prominent feature is a serial by Mr. Parry, entitled "The Scarlet Empire." This serial essays to treat of the relations between capital and labor "as they might become." Its lurid title suggests a red-handed reign of terror, when the "brutal tyrant," organized labor, shall have overthrown the republic and shall wave its sceptre over a wholesale massacre of capitalists, lighted by a universal conflagration of property.

"Parryism" voices incessantly the cry, "Organize." Its one perception is that of the power of well-disciplined combination. Its aim is to organize the employers of the country as a class. Its entire spirit and purpose are to inflame a class warfare. Since the class spirit is un-American, its literature is un-American.

It is both singular and lamentable that this noxious growth of appeal to selfishness and hatred should spring up at the very time when the trade-unions are growing more and more conservative. The persistent preaching of all those union labor leaders who have appreciable influence is against violence and in favor of obedience to the law. All of them oppose strikes, except as a last resort; all of them discountenance violence whenever a strike does occur; all of them advocate the establishment of industrial peace through conciliation, conference and trade agreements. But those employers' associations whose officers and organs oppose this policy aim to reduce the individual wage-earner to the lowest standard of living that can be forced upon him when he shall be deprived of the benefit of collective bargaining. They would conquer the peace of an industrial Warsaw. Despotic power can not long maintain peace. The enforcement of such a relation between capital and labor could only be followed by an outbreak of abnormal virulence.

The literature of "Parryism" runs the gamut from extravagant, outright denunciation to sly insinuation.

An example of the bold, open style of assault upon organized labor is that employed by John Kirby, Jr., an officer of the Citizens' Industrial Association of America. This is a sample of the Kirby manner:

"No organization of men, not excepting the Ku Klux Klan, the Mafia, or the Black Hand societies, has ever produced such a record of barbarism as has this so-called organized labor society which, through misdirected sympathy, apathy and indifference has been permitted to grow up to cripple our industries, and trample in the dust the natural and constitutional rights of our citizens."

The following is another example of the extravagant language of Mr. Kirby:

"The labor leaders are trying to force upon the American people a universal system of slavery even more degrading and more damnable than that to which the Negro was subjected."

It is to prevent this weird and impossible culmination that this violent pleader would have all employers organize to make war upon what he calls a "Turbulent body of hoboes and aliens, who must not be permitted to turn America into a Bedlam."

President Parry of the same organization is responsible for this statement:

"Carried to its final analysis, the theory of unionism would be that if all capital were destroyed and men dug the soil with their fingers to raise the crops of the world the millennium would be here and wages would be at the top notch."

But usually the form of attack upon organized labor is more insidious. It is cloaked in the garb of solicitude for the welfare of the workingman. A pamphlet of advice as to how to organize associations of employers declares it to be the duty of the employer "to deal honorably, justly, generously with each employe." But this excellent advice is coupled with the admonition "to decline to accede to any and every demand made by officers or committees representing organized labor." Generosity is to be extended only to the individual who is willing to trust all of his interests to the tender care of the philanthropic employer. The employes must not organize. The employers must organize and their organization must, forsooth, be the sole court of appeal for questions of wages, hours and conditions of toil!

A monthly magazine published at St. Louis in the interest of the Citizens' Alliance movement, devotes many pages to a recital of all the outrages committed by or charged against the socialists of Colorado. The apparent purpose is to convey the impression that this is a proper arraignment of organized labor in general. One writer says suavely: "No one denies that labor has rights," and from this seemingly friendly premise leaps to the statement that when union by-laws "conflict with the constituted government of this country, they should be swept aside." That is absolutely true, but the implied assumption that union by-laws do conflict with constituted government is wholly unwarranted. Yet the effect of such writing upon the mind of the careless reader is to create the belief that they do. A similarly insidious method is employed in an editorial which groups in one phrase "unions, socialism, crime"; which attributes to the closed shop contract "intimidation, assault, dynamiting, assassination"; which makes the sly statement: "The union man may be an ex-convict; the independent workman may be a gentleman"; and which wishes that "all Governors would enforce the law as Governor Peabody did," in order to make the open shop universal. That is, this writer advocates militarism in order to prevent the legal exclusive contract! In some comment upon disorder in Chicago, a similar suggestion is made: "If the law officers will not act, remove them and put in officers who will enforce the law. It can be done anywhere. It should be done in Illinois. It has been done in Colorado." Here is an extremist who would imitate "everywhere" the "citizens' alliances" in Colorado that presented to a sheriff his resignation and a noose and bade him take his choice of signing the one or hanging by the other; that deported citizens without trial and that burned co-operative stores.

Another article, addressed to "The Farmer," asks him to study what unionism means, and undertakes to tell him by asking such questions as this: "Suppose your barns and haystacks were burned, or suppose that some neighbor's conflagration lighted up the sky every evening?" To this supposition, the farmer is expected to reply that the only remedy would be a soldier in every barnyard and a vidette in every pasture,—all because of the grotesque spectre of a farmhands' union that would carry the torch through the agricultural counties of the United States!

The National Association of Manufacturers is issuing a series of what may be called "fire-alarm" circulars designed to frighten employers into taking out insurance at $50 a year. One of these quotes the advocacy of certain legislation by the American Federation of Labor and states:

"The labor organizations gained 1,024 new unions last year, embracing a membership of 300,000 individuals. Where is it going to end?"

Another circular calls attention to the use of organizers by the American Federation of Labor, and thus seeks to disturb the dreams of the pacific manufacturers:

"You may be at peace with your workmen now, but the organizer comes like a thief in the night. You go to bed in fancied security; you say boastingly 'I never had any trouble in getting along with my men. Please let me run my own business. I have been doing it for twenty-five years and I guess I am able to continue it.' This kind of talk makes the organizer laugh. You wake up out of your dream and you have a strike on your hands. The organizer has been at work while you were asleep."

If this does not frighten the manufacturer who is on friendly terms with his employes into declaring his factory in a state of war, another circular employs cunning to alarm him. The careless eye, upon glancing at this circular, would convey to the brain the inference that the American Federation of Labor had adopted a rabid socialist resolution, declaring for the "overthrow of the wage system and the establishment of an industrial, co-operative democracy." The words quoted are in big type. Only close scrutiny discovers the statement, in smaller type, that this resolution "came within four hundred votes of being adopted." The fact is omitted that the vote was taken upon an amended resolution, from which the socialist proposition had been stricken out. The rest of the circular proceeds upon the assumption that, unless all employers make war against organized labor, "Chaos and anarchy" will come "from a proposition to seize the private property of individuals,"—a proposition that the American Federation of Labor has repeatedly and overwhelmingly rejected, repeating its rejection in its recent convention.

One of the circulars with which employers are being flooded sets forth the purposes of the Dayton Employers' Association as follows:

"To protect its members in their right to manage their respective businesses in such lawful manner as they may deem proper."

This is a smooth paraphrase of the fallacious proposition that every one may do as he will with his own, without regard to the general welfare. This doctrine is the acme of selfish sordidness, and is repudiated by broad-minded employers.

"The adoption of a uniform legitimate system whereby members may ascertain who is and who is not worthy of their employment."

This is a disguised way of saying: "To form a black-list of all employes who for any reason are disliked by any employer."

"The investigation and adjustment . . . of any question arising between members and the employes."

This means the settlement of questions exclusively

by one of the interested parties, organized into an employers' anti-union union.

"To make it possible for any persons to obtain employment without being obliged to join a labor organization, and to encourage all such persons in their efforts to resist the compulsory methods of organized labor."

This is the equivalent of a declaration of discrimination against members of labor-unions, on the ground of their alleged "compulsory methods."

The circular exultantly states that as a result of the "aggressive and defiant" action of this Citizens' Association, the Labor Day parade dwindled from 9,000 in 1900 to 1,914 in 1903. It advocates a "non-union policy" which will "enforce a reorganization of trades-unionism," whatever that may mean.

But even in this circular of defiance, the pretense of friendship crops out. It declares the belief that "it is the right of labor to organize for the purpose of improving the condition of wage-earners, and that organization for the purpose of promoting the real interest of the workingmen of the country will subserve public welfare." Yet its entire programme is that of actual antagonism to unionism. It professes approval of its theory, but advocates methods whose undoubted effect would be to break up organized labor. It exults in the evidence it adduces of the loss in union membership.

The circular concludes by advocating a National Federation of Employers, which "can meet the American Federation of Labor on its own ground, defeat its unlawful undertakings, counteract its baleful influence and restrain its evil tendencies."

The Rev. William H. Boeteker is described as "a personal representative of D. M. Parry" and the editor of a publication of the Citizens' Industrial Association. A report of a recent address delivered to a "secret" meeting of manufacturers, merchants, contractors, and professional men at Evansville, Indiana, quotes him as declaring himself "the earnest friend of the workingmen, and as saying:

"The Citizens' Alliance consists of both employers and employes. It is secret because in secrecy is its greatest strength. It has signs of recognition, passwords and signs of distress.

"The organization is friendly to workingmen. In nine days I saw in one city 1,200 union men reduced to 62, and join the Citizens' Alliance. We are not opposed to unionism as such. They have a perfect right to organize. The unionist says the world owes every man a living. He never thinks that he owes something to the employer as well. We believe a man ought to get good wages because he earns them, not because he belongs to the union."

It is appropriate that such a hodge-podge of self-contradictory pretense of friendliness to unionism and frank declaration of hostility to its purposes should be addressed to a "secret" meeting. It would have run the risk of correction in an open meeting, which might have been attended by some one more accurately informed as to the philosophy and history of organized labor and its true relation to wages and conditions of work. Pretense accompanied by flagrant misstatements of fact can never withstand the light of day or the illumination of free speech.

Herbert George, President of the Citizens' Alliance of San Francisco, boastfully emphasizes its especial antagonism to the trade agreement:

"Up to date we have not lost a single fight we have gotten into, nor has there been a trade agreement signed up to our knowledge since the first day of May."

Some of the "alliance" literature advocates various plans, characterized by legal ingenuity, to undermine organized labor. The "Bulletin" of the National Metal Trades Association publishes a form of agreement with individual employes which is an adroit anti-union device. It makes the employe agree that "he will not quit such employment during the life of this agreement because of the grievance of any other person or persons, or in the furtherance of any strike or demand of any other person." That is to say, the contracting employe who is a member of a union binds himself not to strike, if his union orders a strike. To secure the keeping of this pledge, the employer credits each contracting worker with five cents for each ten-hour day, and the worker agrees to the deduction of an equal amount from his wages, also to be placed to his credit. The total of this accumulated joint fund is to be paid to the worker at the end of the agreement, provided he has kept all its terms. The effect of this arrangement is that in case a worker should strike, or should vary one jot or tittle from shop rules, he would lose both the accumulated deduction from his wages and the equal sum placed to his credit by the employer. He both loses a premium and incurs a penalty. The two sums in the course of a year would amount to $30. In order to clinch legally the employer's hold upon this fund, the agreement makes the employe responsible for $40 as liquidated damages to the employer from any breach of the contract. These damages are to be paid out of any wages due and from the joint fund previously described. The union man who signs such a contract would thus sign away his right to strike upon any issue whatever; and would sign a lien upon any balance due him in wages to an amount greater by $10 than the possible accumulation of the premium-penalty fund in the course of a year.

Incidentally, the employer would make a substantial gain. If he employed 5,000 men, he would have deducted from their earnings at the end of a year the tidy sum of $75,000. For nine months he would have the use of $18,000; for six months of $37,000; for three months of $56,000—all without interest and with the opportunity of absolute confiscation at his caprice. Such a fund would be a constant temptation to provoke a strike against unendurable conditions.

Advocates of the "smash the unions" policy are encouraging a subtle plan to undermine the influence of organized labor. Taking advantage of a period of industrial depression, which has increased the number of unemployed and lessened the strength of unions in negotiating terms of labor, employers' associations have established employment bureaus in various trades. The management of such a bureau in Chicago asserts that it is not formed to fight the union, and yet admits in the same breath that no man can hold one of its certificates and be loyal to his union. The pretended friendship of such employment bureaus to organized labor can not be taken seriously.

The method of these employment bureaus is to issue certificates to applicants who meet their approval. The bureaus require that those who receive these certificates must have worked at least one year in their present employment, or at least sixty days during a strike. The certificates are to show that the holder has rendered faithful service to members of an employers' association "at certain times"; commend the holder to all employers' associations, and promise "to permanently take care of the men who have worked for members of the association during labor troubles."

The true purpose of such a bureau is disclosed in the latest report of the Commissioner of the National Metal Trades Association, who stated:

"The Association has established a certificate system for tried and true workmen, who have been faithful to us during strikes. While the number of these certificate men is not large, it grows with each strike, and we shall soon have quite a body of these men whom we know can be depended upon in case of trouble."

There is no hypocrisy about that statement. It is the frank announcement of a tactical method in industrial war.

This discrimination is warmly urged upon employers by F. C. Nunemacher, of Louisville, who said in an address to the United Typothetæ of America:

"The open shop means much to the non-union workman, and as he is the only helper that the employer has in preserving his own individual rights in his own plant, there is no question as to the duty of the employer in the premises. He must, as a true man, see that these non-union men who have been his helpers in time of trouble are at all times treated with greatest consideration and given all needed protection."

A conspicuous feature of the new organ of 'Parryism" is an "Independent Labor Bureau." This is announced in this language:

"Independent or free labor is as much entitled to employment as union labor. In fact, if the whole truth be told, it is more entitled to employment than union labor. As union labor takes the position that independent labor shall not be employed, it cannot complain if it finds that it itself is the kind of labor discriminated against instead of independent labor. Simple justice dictates that those who are denied their rights should receive special consideration at the hands of all who have employment to offer."

Are not all these devices and declared purposes direct incitements to organized labor to fight for the closed shop? Are they not direct appeals to employers to discriminate in favor of the non-union worker? If all fear of such discrimination could be dissipated, the question of the closed shop would work its own practical solution in the various crafts. But when the open shop is openly declared to mean special consideration for non-union men, it is equivalent to a declaration of war against the union. It is but natural that the union should fight for its life.

—

THE ASSAULT BY SOCIALISM.

It has been shown that the "smash the union" class of employers' associations and citizens' alliances assail organized labor with every variety of language, from extravagant denunciation to insinuation veneered with pretended friendship.

But organized labor faces another foe. That foe is Socialism.

It is a favorite charge of the agents of the hostile associations of employers that the trades-unions are synonymous with socialism.

There is no doubt a widespread confusion of mind as to the relation between trades-unionism and socialism. They are in fact absolutely antagonistic in both doctrine and method. The socialists and the unionists understand this well. The general public does not, because not one in a thousand clearly knows what socialism means. The average mind confuses socialism with its antithesis, anarchism, or with half a dozen other isms, most commonly perhaps with the public ownership of such utilities as gas and water works and street railways.

If a clear definition of socialism be made, the reason for its enmity to the labor union will be plain.

Socialism, in its own words, (in the platform of the Socialist Labor party) demands "the restoration of the land and all of the means of production, transportation and distribution to the people as a collective body, and the substitution of the co-operative commonwealth for the present state."

Eugene V. Debs, the Socialist candidate for President, went about the country shouting these sentences:

"The tool-less worker is an industrial slave."

"The tool-owning capitalist is an industrial master."

The socialist, through political action, would turn over to the state the factory, the machinery it contains, the land on which it stands.

This is wholly opposed to the programme of the trades-unions, which would negotiate for the employes just terms with the employing owner of the factory.

The socialist would eliminate the employer and confiscate his property. This purpose is stated by the "International Socialist Review," in a manner especially interesting to the anti-union employers' associations: "Socialism will not ask for shorter hours or a few cents more wages, but will ask the whole produce and point the way for the employer to pass down and out of the industrial field. . . . They (the socialists) ask no arbitration. They do not recognize that the employer has any rights to arbitrate."

The Trade-Unionist would treat with the employer for the development of his factory for a fair share in the profit of its productivity.

The programme of trade-unions is strictly economic.

The programme of socialism is economic and political.

The two theories are absolutely opposed. The two methods are absolutely contradictory.

Hence, the socialists logically seek to destroy the trade-unions, either by outward assault or internal perversion, and to gather their distintegrated membership into a political party, to whose programme of confiscation their suffrage is essential.

Socialists regard every benefit to wage-earners, achieved by organized labor, as a palliation of discontent and a postponement of the revolution that they hold to be necessary and inevitable. The socialist is always painting the picture of society in the darkest colors. The trade-unionist assents as to existing evil, but contrasts that with the past and shows that the picture of to-day is brighter than the picture of yesterday. The socialist abhors every present betterment of industrial conditions. The unionist exults in such betterment. The socialist denounces what he calls industrial slavery; the unionist asserts that he represents industrial freedom.

The union leaders recognize this incompatibility. Delegate White said at the Boston Convention of the American Federation of Labor:

"To throw our movement into the political arena would be injecting a firebrand of discord that would soon scatter it to the four winds of heaven. When it is so difficult to get the workingmen to agree upon the simply every-day issues, how can you expect to get them to agree upon the complex propositions that political action involves?"

The socialists have two methods of attacking organized labor. One is to assail it from without, the other is to pervert its membership; to sink its ship by "boring from within."

The method of assault from without is exemplified by the platform adopted by the socialist labor convention, which declares that:

"The bulk of what is called the Trades-Union Movement of America now threatens to throttle the Labor Movement, and as such has become what the capitalist 'Wall Street Journal' triumphantly greeted it with,—'one of the strongest obstacles in this country to socialism.'

"Gompers Unionism befogs the workingman's intellect with capitalist economics and it hounds Socialist or working class economics out of its camp, under the false pretense that such economic teachings are 'politics' and that they 'divide the working class.'

"Gompers Unionism acts as a parachute to the downward course of Labor's condition, rendering the decline insensible and even seeking to conceal it.

"Gompers Unionism is a prop of capitalist society; it is a wheel in the machinery of capitalism; it is essentially the revamped guild of capitalism in the days of capitalist infancy; it is a job-trust, and as such has no part in the Labor Movement."

The same declaration suggests also the organization of straight, out and out socialist unions, to fight the present labor unions:

"We consider it the duty of the militant socialists of the land to join to their political endeavors the economic endeavor of promoting the industrial organization of the working class into unions that shall remain true to the class struggle spirit that gives unionism its birth, instead of degenerating into handmaids of capitalism."

The Socialist party of Texas adopted a plank pronouncing the American Federation of Labor a futile failure and declaring:

"There is one form of trade-unionism, and only one, that can be made to subserve the interests of the working class. This kind of union must be committed to the program of the international movement for the emancipation of the working class, and must be in the nature of a training school for the political expression of that movement. It is already taking form in what is known as the Socialist Trade and Labor Alliance of the Socialist Labor party in the East and in the American Labor Union allied with the Socialist party of America in the West."

This expression was hailed by the "People," the organ of the Socialist Labor party, as heralding the time when, "as the rushing of mighty streams, the socialists of the East and of the West will join indissolubly and, a resistless torrent, crash through all the fakir out-posts of the capitalist class (The labor unions) and sweep capitalism out of existence.".

The Socialist Labor party issued a "call to arms" for the recent campaign that throws some interesting light upon its attitude toward unionism. This "call" declares that the workers are "finding the pure and simple union a hollow reed to lean upon" and announces that now "is the psychological moment of which the Socialist Labor party must avail" itself. A part of its campaign plan is thus stated:

"Wherever dissatisfaction exists amongst members of pure and simple trades-unions in consequence of sell-outs by the fakirs, lost strikes, or other causes, let no stone be unturned to make these men acquainted with the Socialist Labor party position on trades-unions and with the Socialist Trade and Labor Association, by distribution of suitable literature, meetings, personal contact, and in every other way that can be devised.

"The systematic distribution of leaflets at factory gates, morning, noon, and night, and in workingmen's districts on Sunday mornings, is working well in New York State. On with the war against Capitalism."

A recent instance of the quickness with which the socialists seize a lost strike as an opportunity to invade the field of organized labor occurred in the Chicago stock-yards. Promptly after the end of the meat strike, socialists began forming in the stock-yards organizations antagonistic to the Amalgamated Association of Butchers, a branch of the American Federation of Labor. They distributed a circular reading:

"Why have you lost your strike? Your union was affiliated with the American Federation of Labor, which boasts of 2,000,000 members. You have suffered the most crushing defeat in the history of organized labor. Why? You are not properly organized. The whole mass is loosely connected with the American Federation of Labor, which is absolutely powerless to make a united successful fight against anything and whose leaders hobnob with your enemies in Civic Federation."

The "People" gloated over the diminution of the Labor Day parade this year as much as did the unfriendly employers' organs:

"Despite the big expectations of the Central Federated Union fakirs and their cringing Kangaroo trades who have deserted May Day to cater to the pure and simple by taking part in a capitalist Labor Day parade, yesterday's turnout of the 'marching hosts of labor' was not so vast and glittering a cavalcade."

But the most dangerous effort of the socialists against organized labor is that directed to its disintegration from within. It is the votes of the unionists that the socialists are after. Jack London, a socialist writer, has defined, in the "Independent," the partisan aim of socialism, with an open candor whose almost brutal frankness bespeaks the confidence of fatalism:

"This revolt in the form of demands for an increased share of the joint product is being carefully and shrewdly shaped for a political assault upon society. . . . The leaders intend to direct the labor revolt to the capture of the political machinery of society. . . . With the control of the police, the army, the navy, and the courts, they will confiscate, with or without remuneration, all the possessions of the capitalist class which are used in the production and distribution of the luxuries and necessities of life. They mean to apply the law of eminent domain to the land and to extend the law of eminent domain until it embraces the mines, the factories, the railroad and the ocean carriers."

The "insidious," instead of the violent, method of disrupting the unions is described by the same writer:

"The socialists turned their energies upon the trade-union movement. To win the trade-unions was well-nigh to win the victory.

"Instead of antagonizing the unions, the socialists proceeded to conciliate the unions. 'Let every good socialist join the union of his trade! Bore from within and capture the trade-union movement.'

"To-day the great labor-unions are honey-combed with socialists. At work and at play, at business meeting and council, their insidious propaganda goes on. Night and day, tireless and unrelenting as a mortgage, they labor at their self-imposed task of undermining society.

"The battle plan of the socialists is to organize the working class and those in sympathy with it into a political party, with the object of conquering the powers of government and using them for the purpose of transferring the present system of private ownership of the means of production and distribution into collective ownership by the entire people."

This is the "insidious" campaign that the leaders of organized labor are fighting, and successfully. Year after year, the American Federation of Labor, in its convention, rejects socialist resolutions. Its convention last year in Boston defeated a socialist resolution, upon a clear-cut issue, by a majority of 10,000 to 1,000. That the leaders of the American Federation of Labor thoroughly realize the hostile animus of the socialists was shown in the speech delivered by Samuel Gompers in Faneuil Hall, Boston, at its twenty-third annual convention. Mr. Gompers said:

"I shall not refer at this time to their very many detailed acts of treachery to the trade-union movement; but I shall show you that though they may believe themselves to be trade-unionists, they are at heart, and logically, the antagonists of our movement.

"When the socialists formed the American Labor Union in rivalry to the American Federation of Labor, I took occasion to continually say in the "American Federationist" that it was but another attempt to form another Socialist Trade and Labor Alliance, without its practical courage to openly declare its enmity to the American trade-union movement.

"I want to tell you, Socialists, that I have studied your philosophy; read your works upon economics, and not the meanest of them; studied your standard works, both in English and German—have not only read, but studied them. I have heard your orators and watched the work of your movement the world over. I have kept close watch upon your doctrines for thirty years; have been closely associated with many of you, and know how you think and what you propose. I know, too, what you have up your sleeve, and I want to say that I am entirely at variance with your philosophy. I declare it to you, I am not only at variance with your doctrines, but with your philosophy. Economically, you are unsound; socially, you are wrong; industrially, you are an impossibility."

This year's convention of the American Federation of Labor in San Francisco defeated another socialist resolution by a majority so overwhelming that its advocates did not even ask a roll-call. A socialist anti-militia resolution was also overwhelmingly rejected.

But despite these rebuffs, socialism continues to strive for the overthrow of the trade-union movement, both by bitter denunciation and by luring it into a political morass with the ignis fatuus of a "co-operative commonwealth."

As politics is said to make strange bed-fellows, the common antagonism to the unions of the socialists and the radical employers' associations has brought them into apparent alliance. The "People," the daily socialist paper, heartily endorsed the speech of President Parry at New Orleans, quoted in the previous chapter, in this language:

"President Parry is right. An equitable arrangement of wages and hours can not be effected by the 'artificial' method of arbitration or conciliation. An 'equitable arrangement' can only be effected by allowing the class struggle full scope, and as a means to this end nothing is so much to be welcomed as the 'straight-out tactics' of the anti-union employers' associations. Socialism will triumph as a result."

Eugene V. Debs said recently in Faneuil Hall, Boston: "Parry is doing a better work for us than we could do for ourselves. As Mr. Pure-and-Simple Union Man is crushed, his eyes are opened to the fact that he must transfer his efforts to the political field."

That this friendly feeling of the socialists is reciprocated is indicated by the following complimentary statement by President Parry in an interview in the Indianapolis "News" just after the presidential election: "The great personal magnetism of Mr. Debs also counted for much in the large vote polled for him. As a labor leader he has kept himself clean and above suspicion in every way. While I can not approve of the methods used by him in the railroad strike, yet all fair-minded men must admit that he has much ability and force of character. Naturally, such a man is bound to have a large following."

THE INHERENT PERILS OF UNIONISM.

These assaults by "Parryism" and Socialism make it the duty of those who are convinced that the movement of organized labor is in the interest of civilization to aid in perfecting its discipline. If it is to win success it must discover its own weaknesses and remove them. What, then, are the inward weaknesses of organized labor? What measures are its leaders and its councillors taking to correct them, and with what success?

Some of the perils that sharply beset organized labor may be discerned in the attacks of its enemies, who naturally direct their assaults against its weakest points. Its most bitter assailants select for their attack violence during strikes; venality among officers of unions who are authorized to deal with employers; and failure to stand by trade agreements.

Now, every one of these indictments can be supported in individual cases. Every one of them is an admitted wrong, whenever and wherever it occurs. Every one of them is indefensible. It is no defense to say that violence is exceptional and may be provoked; that there is vastly more "graft" in politics and in commerce than in the unions; that vastly more agreements are violated in the world of business than in the field of labor. Neither can arbitrary and unreasonable restrictions be defended on the ground that there are some restrictions that can be justified. Nevertheless, these indefensible evils are not in themselves the greatest weakness of organized labor. Rather are they symptoms of weakness, and they will progressively diminish only as the weakness that causes them is overcome.

The real, underlying weakness of organized labor is the apathy of the mass. In that respect unionism suffers as does every other organized movement. The leaders of political parties have no greater task than to overcome apathy in recurrent campaigns. It is apathy of citizenship that makes possible malfeasance in public office. It is moral apathy that permits the growth of "graft" in business. The church itself incessantly struggles against apathy in recruiting and maintaining its membership. Now and then there is an upheaval of sentiment that substitutes energy for this apathy, as in the culmination of a political campaign, or when political "graft" and business corruption are exposed, or when a religious revival sweeps thousands into the fold of the church, At such times, these organized movements exhibit their greatest strength. They have made real progress only if the pendulum does not swing all the way back to its extreme former position.

Because of the nature of its constituency and because it is nearly a pure democracy, the labor-union is peculiarly susceptible to this weakness. A chilling inertia often characterizes its membership. This is born of the lack of self-assertion, which is the natural characteristic of the average son of toil. By inheritance he is accustomed to his lot. Even in a land of opportunities, it is hard to overcome this temperamental inertia and arouse the worker to the actual practicability of improving his condition through organized effort. The real work of the union, it must be remembered, demands constant effort. But this necessity is often not realized by members. Moreover to maintain that effort is an addition to the necessary burdens of the day that it is a strain to meet. The temptation is constant to shirk the obligations of the union in attendance upon meetings, in activity for mutual improvement, and in payment of dues.

It is this apathetic inertia that every now and then permits the management of a local union to fall into the hands of a ring. The rough, boisterous element may attend its meetings. The better element, including the married men, may stay at home. The result is that the reckless gain control, and an unwarranted strike may follow, under turbulent leadership. Violence will be widely advertised and the blame charged against the whole body of organized labor. Or instead of recklessness, crafty cunning may gain control; and then a Parks or a Weinsheimer is evolved. Or men without moral fibre or education in business honor may break a trade agreement; and then the "faithlessness" and "lack of responsibility" of unionism will be proclaimed.

Another outcome of this apathy is the poor financial condition of many unions. The contrast between British and American unionism in this respect is familiar. The British unions have developed systems of payments of benefits for out-of-work, for traveling to places where work is available for injury or sickness and for death, simultaneously with maintaining a "defense" fund in anticipation of strikes. While similar systems exist together with insurance, in some bodies of labor in this country, as in the railway brotherhoods, the cigar-makers' union and the typographical union, in many crafts they are still to be brought into extensive and efficient operation. The American workman is keenly suspicious about the financial conduct of the union. "What becomes of my dues?" is his jealous query, that can be answered only by the regular publication in the journal of his organization of detailed financial reports. This spirit is wholesome in so far as it compels honestly conducted treasuries; but it adds to the inertia to be overcome. Again, the average worker does not always comprehend the actual pe-

(Concluded on page 16.)

MONTHLY REVIEW
OF THE
National Civic Federation

Offices: 281 Fourth Avenue, New York City
RALPH M. EASLEY, Editor

The Editor alone is responsible for any unsigned article or unquoted statement published in THE MONTHLY REVIEW.

Ten Cents per Copy; One Dollar per Year.

ARBITRATION TREATIES AND LABOR.

The natural sympathy between the movements for international peace and for industrial peace, illustrated by every speaker at the luncheon tendered to members of the Interparliamentary Union of the National Civic Federation, receives further recognition in the preparations for the mass meeting in New York in the interest of arbitration treaties. The executive committee in charge of that meeting, appointed by the chairman of the American Conference on International Arbitration, includes men prominent in the movement for industrial peace. The recent announcement that the terms of an arbitration treaty have been agreed upon by the representatives of the United States and Great Britain is significant of the spirit that views with pitying horror the enormous sacrifices of war and that encourages the adjustment of international disputes by the very methods of conciliation and arbitration that are invoked to settle controversies between capital and labor.

PRESIDENT GOMPERS' ADDRESS.

Conservatism and intelligent enterprise characterized the proceedings of the twenty-fourth convention at San Francisco of the American Federation of Labor. Socialism met its overwhelming annual defeat. Its proposed overthrow of the wage-system and its opposition to membership of wage-earners in the militia except by conscription after the Swiss plan, were rejected overwhelmingly. This action by delegates representing 1,676,200 workers should carry conviction to the public mind that organized labor repudiates industrial revolution and associates patriotism with humanity.

With these victories there deserves to rank an affirmative declaration. That is the exhortation to the rank and file of organized labor to devote a large share of the time spent in local union meetings to studies and lectures upon economic subjects. The adoption of this resolution for education will go far to refute the assertion,—which is now made seriously by but few employers,—that the shorter work-day will mean abuse of added leisure by the mass of wage-earners. The prevailing spirit among the toilers of the land is that of self-helpfulness; there surely will not fail a response of encouraging reciprocity from those who work more with the brains than with the hands to this self-reliant determination to supplement manual skill with mental expansion. Education, as is pointed out elsewhere, is the best correction for that inertia of the mass which is common to all democratic organization.

The address of President Gompers is marked by breadth of view and economic insight. He makes a strong argument in support of the policy, which many question, of resistance to wage-reduction in periods of industrial depression. He exults in the progress of agreement and understanding between employers and workmen and in the extension of effort to bring about more rightful relations between them.

There will be surprise at Secretary Morrison's announcement of an increase in membership cf 210,400, during a year of adverse conditions. Such a growth during such a time indicates sturdy increase in a movement that requires wise leadership and invites thoughtful counsel.

FOR ECONOMIC EDUCATION.

The Department of Industrial Economics of the National Civic Federation has been formed to extend education in the subjects that are vitally associated with the relations between capital and labor. These topics are largely economic, and require the most thorough elucidation. Even conscientious students of the labor question, who approach it from the point of view of either the capitalist or the wage-earner, are liable to deception by plausible fallacies. Editors, scholars and publicists are sometimes puzzled to detect the flaw in an ingenious proposition. Speakers from platform and pulpit and learned college professors have been known to enunciate as *ex cathedra* doctrines which are open to debate. The keen interest in these topics is indicated by the ready acceptance of the invitation to join in their consideration.

This Department promises to be the most comprehensive and far-reaching movement for education upon industrial topics ever inaugurated in this country. It aims at the evolutionary rather than the revolutionary method of dealing with capital and labor. It enlists as co-operative forces the metropolitan press, the labor press, the magazine and book, the bar, the platform, the university and the church.

DR. ELIOT FOR UNIONS AND CONFERENCE.

President Eliot of Harvard University, in his address which we publish upon another page, advances two propositions of the highest importance as bearing upon the relations of employers and employed. This eminent scholar and thinker recognizes that workingmen "have a *right* to confer with" their employer and 'advise him about the rules of the works." This advanced view discards absolutely the old-fogey notion that the employer may do as he will with his own and that he may run his own business in his own way with utter disregard to the feelings and the welfare of the human beings who work with him as well as for him. Dr. Eliot's other notable declaration is: "It is essential that the organizations of the workpeople themselves should be maintained and should be recognized by the employer and the associations of employers." These words are a clear-cut and definite rejection of the design of certain employers' associations to destroy the unions. Dr. Eliot's approval of the avowed objects of one local employers' association arises from his insistence upon the preservation of individual liberty, of which some sacrifice is implied in all organized effort for the up-lifting of a social group. The eight objects which he avers are consistent with the maintenance of individual freedom are in large part debatable questions of detail which, with the two chief policies established, that Dr. Eliot advocates without reserve, would soon work out their solution in practice. They are objects that we will undertake to discuss in detail in the next issue of THE MONTHLY REVIEW. He well estimates as "inconceivable" the effect upon productivity of those two methods of establishing good-will between organized employers and wage-earners.

THE SOCIALIST VOTE.

There is a misapprehension in certain quarters of the significance of the vote cast for Eugene V. Debs, the Socialist candidate for President. Some of the "smash the union" employers' associations would add to this misapprehension by efforts to confuse Socialism with organized labor.

The vote for Debs is not a true measure of the growth of Socialism. Its estimated total of 500,000 in 1904 seems impressive at first glance, when compared with Debs' 97,730 votes in 1900. But it is of general knowledge that a large number of citizens cast their vote for Debs as a negative protest. A large fraction of the Debs vote is not, therefore, indicative of a growth of Socialist sentiment, but is expressive of the discontent of certain radical groups with the principal parties. For instance, in Chicago the Single-taxers, who are Individualists, not Socialists, openly exhorted their followers to vote for Debs.

In Massachusetts, where the election of Douglas was a conspicuous result of scratched ballots, Socialism lost ground, its vote falling from 33,629, in 1902, to 20,000 in 1904. It is especially significant that in a State where Socialism has elected several mayors and members of the legislature, its lack of administrative and legislative ability has been such as to forfeit whatever political positions it had gained. The theory of political Socialism did not stand the test of practice.

In Colorado the "labor vote" was undoubtedly largely cast for Adams, as the direct way of getting at Peabodyism. It was Peabodyism, not Socialism, that was the issue in Colorado. The Socialist leaders themselves recognize that they cannot claim the increase in the vote for Debs as an increase in the vote for Socialism. The Debs organs are exhorting their readers to make special efforts to make real Socialists out of the various groups of the discontented whose votes for the Debs ticket may be lost to that party another year.

A WELFARE DEPARTMENT CONFERENCE.

The conference of members of the Welfare Department, held in New York City on November 15, was characterized by consideration of several specific subjects. The papers and their discussion were of such importance as to warrant their verbatim publication in pamphlet form. Many inquiries addressed to the Welfare Department are evidence of widespread interest in these and kindred subjects. The paper upon "Railway Provident Institutions," of which the first instalment appears in this issue of THE MONTHLY REVIEW, presents the views of one qualified to write as an expert upon that subject. The Assistant Comptroller of the Pennsylvania Railroad Company, Max Riebenack is a member of the Advisory Committee and Chairman of the Supervisory Committee of the Relief Department, and Secretary of the Board of Officers of the Pension Department. He has been largely instrumental in maturing and promoting the provident undertakings of that railway system. He was selected by the Permanent Commission of the International Railway Congress, whose membership is recruited from the highest officials of the leading railways of the world, to report upon "Railway Provident Institutions," for discussion at the seventh session of that Congress, to be held at Washington, D. C., next May. In another paper, E. H. Perley describes interestingly the operation of an employes' bank in a newspaper establishment. Its purpose is to enable faithful employes to escape loan sharks when emergency causes their expenses to exceed current income.

AN INTERESTING DISAVOWAL.

The call for the fourth annual meeting of the National Executive Committee of the Civic Federation pointed out that the organizations of employers having the largest investments of capital in the United States in the basic industries sought and found honorable business relations with organized labor. But the call also stated:

There are other organizations of capital whose present aim is to smash the unions. Sometimes this policy is boldly avowed; sometimes it is disguised. Uncompromising hostility to labor inspires this class of employers' associations and citizens' alliances. These have not been formed to negotiate with labor, since they aim to destroy all organization of labor with which negotiation is possible.

To this statement, exception was taken by David M. Parry, President of the Citizens' Industrial Association of America and of the National Association of Manufacturers, in whose behalf the following reply was published:

We know of no organization of employers whose aim is to smash unions, and if this passage is aimed at us it is altogether wide of the mark. We certainly do not aim to smash the unions, and have no hostility to unions as such. We are opposed, however, to the principle of coercion or force in unions and believe that unions which are conducted properly are not only not a disadvantage, but may be a benefit to the workers. At the same time we have not, like the Civic Federation, a Bishop or a Gompers or a Mitchell in our body, and we do not invite the general public to mix in our affairs.

This announcement that the "smash the union" shoe does not fit Mr. Parry and that the organizations of which he is President have "no hostility to the unions" is news as welcome as it is surprising. It is possible that an erroneous impression of the purposes of his organizations has been caused by the great mass of utterances concerning organized labor that have been attributed to Mr. Parry and his associates. Certainly his announcement is in welcome contrast to statements here quoted selected at random from several hundred. The Rev. William J. H. Boeteker said at Evansville, Ind.:

The Citizens' Alliance consists of both employers and employes. It is secret, because in secrecy is its greatest strength. It has signs of recognition, passwords and signs of distress.

The organization is friendly to workingmen. In nine days I saw in one city 1,200 union men reduced to 62, and join the Citizens' Alliance. We are not opposed to unionism as such. They have a perfect right to organize. The unionist says the world owes every man a living. He never thinks that he owes something to the employer as well. We believe a man ought to get good wages because he earns them, not because he belongs to the union.

The reverend speaker was introduced to the meeting to which he addressed these remarks as "a personal representative of D. M. Parry" and the editor of a publication of his Association. In view of this relation, Mr. Parry's denial that any Bishop belongs to that body appears rather technical. It is true that the Rev. Mr. Boeteker has not yet attained the rank of a Bishop, but his activity indicates that he is not devoid of ambition.

But surprise grows into amazement upon reading the following, ascribed to Mr. Parry himself:

This is not the proper time to talk conciliation. . . . An attitude of conciliation would mean an attitude of compromise with regard to fundamental convictions. . . . Neither is it the time to talk arbitration or trade agreements. To arbitrate questions of wages and hours is to introduce artificial methods. . . . An equitable arrangement as to either cannot be effected artificially. . . . Arbitration is only putting off the day of reckoning.

Amazement becomes astonishment, when the Chairman of the Executive Committee of the Citizens' Industrial Association, John Kirby, Jr., is quoted as saying to his annual meeting:

The only way to settle a controversy with organized labor is to have absolutely no dealings with it.

Astonishment becomes wonder when Mr. Kirby also says:

No organization of men, not excepting the Ku Klux Klan, the Mafia, or the Black Hand Society, has ever produced such a record of barbarism as has this so-called organized labor society which, through misdirected sympathy, apathy and indifference, has been permitted to grow up to cripple our industries, and to trample in the dust the natural and constitutional rights of our citizens.

And still the wonder grows when "American Industries," the official organ of the National Association of Manufacturers, of November 15, quotes Mr. Kirby:

The fact is that the fundamental basis of all such joint agreements is recognition of the union, and there would be no recognition if there were no coercion and no restriction upon the employer's lawful rights. Once you are in the toils of the union you are its victim, to be tossed about at its dictation.

Thus Mr. Parry and his friends abolish conciliation, arbitration, trade agreements, the unions themselves as worse than the Ku Klux, Mafia and Black Hand societies, shut the door in the face of the impertinent general public and reject every method that civilized society has yet devised for treating the problem of capital and labor. Otherwise, the English language has lost its meaning.

UNION PAYMENTS FOR BENEFITS.

The annual report of Secretary Morrison of the American Federation of Labor shows benefit payments of various kinds by sixty-six International Organizations during the past year of $1,739,796 could not include the amounts, in many cases larger, paid in benefits by local unions.

For example, Secretary Morrison's report credits the International Typographical Union with $38,925 for death benefits. But this represents probably less than half the total expenditure for death benefits alone in that Union. The New York local, "No. 6," pays an additional death benefit of $80, making with the $70 paid by the International a total of $150 for each death benefit. The same local union paid $46,000 last year for out-of-work benefits. Its members also maintain voluntary shop sick benefit associations; a bed in every hospital in New York City and are constantly making contributions for charity at every meeting of the union. None of these expenditures appear in the financial statement of the International. The future collection of these local data would go far to prove that the benefit treasury of organized labor is larger by far than its war chest.

FOR INTERNATIONAL ARBITRATION.

A mass meeting will be held in Carnegie Hall, New York City, on the evening of December 16, to give expression to public opinion in favor of the ratification of the arbitration treaties which have been and are now being negotiated between the United States and other Powers. This movement is under the general direction of the Executive Committee of the American Conference on International Arbitration, of which ex-Secretary John W. Foster is chairman. The New York executive committee, which is to conduct the meeting, is composed of the following:

John Crosby Brown, Hon. Oscar S. Straus, Hon. George B. McClellan, Prof. John B. Moore, Dr. Leander T. Chamberlain, Francis Lynde Stetson, Hon. Nicholas Murray Butler, Morris K. Jesup, Hon. Cornelius N. Bliss, Hon. John W. Griggs, Hon. Carl Schurz, Charles A. Moore, Hon. Stewart L. Woodford, Hon. Lyman J. Gage, Hon. Charles S. Fairchild, John A. McCall, James Stillman, Horace White, John E. Parsons, Spencer Trask, John D. Rockefeller, Jr., George Haven Putnam, James Speyer, Andrew Carnegie, Hon. Whitelaw Reid, Hon. Elihu Root, Robert C. Ogden, Samuel Gompers, Jacob H. Schiff, Melville E. Stone, Hon. George L. Rives, Ralph M. Easley, Dr. John H. Finley, Edward M. Shepard, Hon. Charles E. Schieren, Alexander E. Orr, George Foster Peabody, Hon. John E. Bigelow, John J. McCook, Harry Payne Whitney, John Jacob Astor, Cornelius Vanderbilt, Hon. John G. Carlisle, I. N. Seligman, Chandler P. Anderson.

ANNUAL MEETING AND DINNER.

The Executive Committee of the National Civic Federation Will Transact Important Business and Entertain all Its Departments.

The fourth annual meeting of the Executive Committee of the National Civic Federation will be held in New York City on December 15. It is expected that this meeting will be the most important in the history of the organization. The Executive Committee will hold two business sessions in the morning and afternoon, and in the evening will entertain at its annual dinner the members of all the Departments of the organization. Among the speakers at the dinner will be Andrew Carnegie, Archbishop Ireland, Bishop Potter, August Belmont, Cornelius N. Bliss, Oscar S. Straus, John Mitchell, Samuel Gompers and E. E. Clark.

The Department of Industrial Economics will hold its first meeting for organization, prior to the annual dinner.

The business of the Executive Committee will include the election of a president to fill the vacancy caused by the death of Senator Marcus A. Hanna. The selection of his successor was entrusted to a sub-committee of twelve, representing employers, wage-earners and the general public.

Reports will be received by the Executive Committee from the Chairman of the Executive Council, and from the Departments of trade agreements, conciliation and arbitration, welfare work, publication, and organization. An international committee will be named to form an International Civic Federation, the suggestion of which has elicited encouraging responses from England, Canada, France, Belgium and Germany.

The call to the members of the Executive Committee contains the following:

"The country is at the threshold of a new era of industrial activity. It is to be hoped that all producers, including both capital and the wage-earners, as well as all consumers will share in this revival of prosperity. This new era succeeds a period of depression which has had at least two wholesome results. The 'water' has been 'squeezed' out of inflated securities and a sounder measure of values has been reached. Organized labor has gone through an almost parallel succession of inordinate expansion and reformation. During the boom period that preceded the recent depression, labor had its organizers everywhere, and pressed aggressively its demands for a larger share in the increased profits of production. When the industrial reaction came, organized labor found itself extended beyond a sound basis, and unable to avoid its share of the hardship caused by industrial depression.

"But for both capital and labor the outlook is now more hopeful. When the National Civic Federation was organized four years ago, the country was going through the craze of indiscriminate trust capitalization. Direful predictions of resistance, which might go even to the point of revolution, were heard on every side. Within six months of that time the greatest of these trusts, the United States Steel Corporation, encountered its first great struggle with organized labor, and no revolution followed. There have been similar experiences in other encounters between organized capital and organized labor. As in the anthracite strike, they have been guided to a sane and sound conclusion. In all the United States, but one city, Fall River, to-day suffers from an industrial struggle of any moment."

DEPARTMENT OF INDUSTRIAL ECONOMICS OF THE NATIONAL CIVIC FEDERATION.

A MOST COMPREHENSIVE AND FAR-REACHING MOVEMENT FOR POPULAR EDUCATION UPON FACTORS IN THE PROBLEM OF LABOR.

INDUSTRIAL ECONOMICS.

The initial membership of the new Department of Industrial Economics of the National Civic Federation is herewith published. A perusal of the list will show that it is composed of editors of the daily press, and of politico-social magazines, trade papers whose readers include all the great employing interests of the country, and labor journals that reach millions of wage-earners; and of economic and legal authors, lecturers, the heads of the departments of political economy in universities and representatives of the pulpit.

The National Executive Committee of the Civic Federation will tender an informal dinner to this Department, following its annual meeting in New York City on December 15. Prior to this dinner, the members of the Department will be called together to organize and to define its mode of procedure at future meetings.

This Department represents the most comprehensive and far-reaching movement for popular education upon industrial subjects yet inaugurated in this country. Its members are to meet at informal dinners to discuss such practical topics as "Trade Agreements," "Wages and Cost of Living," "The Shorter Work-Day," "The Open and Closed Shop," "The Minimum Wage," "Restriction of Output," "Piece-Work and Day-Work," "Arbitration," "Apprentices," "Introduction of Machinery," etc. That these discussions will have both practical and scientific value is apparent from the character of the participants. All of them are instructors of the public, each in his own field, and all of them are able to teach and to learn from one another. Besides the reports of these gatherings by the Associated Press, a special summary of their proceedings, in the form of a syndicate article, will be furnished to 5,000 newspapers. A verbatim report will be published in THE MONTHLY REVIEW.

The following have accepted membership:

ABBOTT, LAWRENCE F. Editorial Staff Outlook, New York City.

ADAMS, HENRY C. Professor Political Economy, Ann Arbor, Mich.

ADLER, FELIX, Professor Columbia University, New York City.

BAINE, C. L. Editor Shoe Workers' Journal, Boston, Mass.

BOARDMAN, W. H. Editor Railway Gazette, New York City.

BOWKER, R. R. Editor Publishers' Weekly, New York City.

BRAMWOOD, J. M. Editor Typographical Journal, Indianapolis, Ind.

BRANDEIS, LOUIS D. Corporation Lawyer, Boston, Mass.

BRIGHT, F. D. Editor Railway World, Philadelphia, Pa.

BROOKS, JOHN GRAHAM, Lecturer, Cambridge, Mass.

BUTLER, NICHOLAS MURRAY, President Columbia University, New York City.

CALL, E. PAYSON, Publisher New York Commercial, New York City.

CASSIER, LOUIS, Publisher Cassier's Magazine, New York City.

CEASE, D. L. Editor Railroad Trainmen's Journal, Cleveland, O.

CLARK, E. E. Editor Railway Conductor, Cedar Rapids, Ia.

COMMONS, JOHN R. Department of Political Economy, Wisconsin University, Madison, Wis.

CONANT, CHAS. A. Treasurer Morton Trust Company, New York City.

COOK, FREDERICK H. Author and Lawyer, New York City.

DAVIS, BEN. I. Editor Amalgamated Iron Workers' Journal, Pittsburg, Pa.

DONNELLY, SAMUEL B. Typographical Union, New York City.

DOYLE, REV. A. P. Editor Catholic World, New York City.

DUNCAN, JAMES, Editor Granite Cutters' Journal, Quincy, Mass.

ELIOT, CHARLES W. President Harvard University, Cambridge, Mass.

ELY, R. T. Professor Political Economy, University of Wisconsin.

ESTERBROOK, HENRY D. General Counsel Western Union Telegraph Co., New York City.

FAIRCHILD, E. M. Editor Daily Trade Record, New York City.

FARNAM, HENRY W. Professor Political Economy, Yale University, New Haven, Conn.

FISKE, AMOS K. Editorial Staff, New York Journal of Commerce, New York City.

FORD, E. A. Editorial Staff New York Tribune, New York City.

FOSTER, FRANK K. Typographical Union, Boston, Mass.

FREEMAN, REV. JAMES E. President Hollywood Inn, Yonkers, N. Y.

FREUND, JOHN C. Editor Music Trades, New York City.

FREY, JOHN P. Editor Iron Moulders' Journal, Cincinnati, O.

GIDDINGS, FRANKLIN H. Head Sociological Department, Columbia University, New York City.

GILDER, R. WATSON. Editor, Century Magazine, New York City.

GLADDEN, WASHINGTON, Author, Columbus, O.

GLEED, CHARLES S. Attorney-at-law, Topeka, Kan.

GOMPERS, SAMUEL, Editor American Federationist, Washington, D. C.

GREEN, JOHN, Editor Bradstreet's Journal, New York City.

GUNTON, GEORGE, Editor Gunton's Magazine, Washington, D. C.

HARVEY, G. B. M. Editor North American Review, New York City.

HOLT, HAMILTON, Editor New York Independent, New York City.

HOWLAND, EDWARD C. Economic Writer, New York City.

IRELAND, JOHN, Archbishop, St. Paul, Minn.

JENKS, J. W. Professor Political Economy, Cornell University, Ithaca, N. Y.

JUDSON, FREDERICK N. Attorney, St. Louis, Mo.

KEEFE, D. J. International Longshoremen's Association, Detroit, Mich.

KIRCHHOFF, C. W. H. Editor Iron Age, New York City.

LENNON, JOHN B. Editor The Tailor, Bloomington, Ill.

LORIMER, GEORGE C. Editor Saturday Evening Post, Philadelphia, Pa.

MAHON, W. D. Editor Motorman and Conductor, Detroit, Mich.

MARTIN, T. C. Editor Electrical World and Engineer, New York City.

MERRILL, BRADFORD, Editorial Staff New York World, New York City.

McGRAW, JAMES H. President McGraw Publishing Co., New York City.

McKELWAY, ST. CLAIR, Editor Brooklyn Daily Eagle, Brooklyn, N. Y.

McNAMEE, JOHN F. Editor Locomotive Firemen's Magazine, Indianapolis, Ind.

MILLER, C. R. Editor New York Times, New York City.

MILLER, FREDERICK I. Editor American Machinist New York City.

MITCHELL, JOHN, President United Mine Workers of America, Indianapolis, Ind.

MOFFETT, EDWARD A. Editor Bricklayer and Mason, New York City.

MOODY, JOHN, Author of Moody's Manual, New York City.

NEILL, H. H. Editorial Staff New York Mail, New York City.

O'CONNELL, JAMES, Editor Machinists' Journal, Washington, D. C.

PAGE, WALTER H. Editor, World's Work, New York City.

PATTISON, W. J. Publisher Evening Post, New York City.

PECK, GEORGE R. General Counsel, Milwaukee & St. Paul Railroad, Chicago, Ill.

PHILIPS, ROLAND, Managing Editor Harper's Weekly, New York City.

PIERCE, D. T. Editor Public Opinion, New York City.

POTTER, HENRY C. Bishop, New York City.

QUICK, L. W. Editor Railroad Telegrapher, St. Louis, Mo.

RAINSFORD, WILLIAM S. Clergyman, New York City.

RIECK, W. C. Executive Manager New York Herald, New York City.

RIIS, JACOB A. Sociologist, New York City.

ROOT, C. T. Editor Dry Goods Economist, New York City.

SALMONS, C. H. Editor Locomotive Engineers' Journal, Cleveland, O.

SEXTON, S. M. Editor United Mine Workers' Journal, Indianapolis, Ind.

SELIGMAN, EDWIN R. A. Head Department Political Economy, Columbia University, New York City.

SLEICHER, JOHN A. Editor Leslie's Weekly, New York City.

SHAW, ALBERT, Editor Review of Reviews, New York City.

SKEMP, J. C. Editor Painter's Official Journal, Lafayette, Ind.

SINCLAIR, ANGUS, Editor Locomotive Engineering, New York City.

SULLIVAN, J. W. Editor The Unionist, New York City.

TAUSSIG, F. W. Department Political Economy, Harvard University, Cambridge, Mass.

TAYLOR, C. H., JR. President American Newspaper Publishers' Association, Boston, Mass.

TAYLOR, GRAHAM, Editor The Commons, Chicago.

THOMPSON, SLASON, Chief Statistician Railway Managers' Association, Chicago, Ill.

TOBIN, JOHN F. Editor Shoe Workers' Journal, Boston, Mass.

VANDERLIP, FRANK A. Vice-President City National Bank, New York City.

WARDMAN, ERVIN, Editor New York Press, New York City.

WATSON, HENRY C. Editor Dun's Review, New York City.

WHEELER, E. J. Editor Literary Digest, New York City.

WHITE, WILLIAM ALLEN, Author, Emporia, Kan.

WILLIAMS, TALCOTT, Editorial Staff Philadelphia Press, Philadelphia, Pa.

WOODLOCK, THOMAS F. Editor Wall Street Journal, New York City.

WRIGHT, H. J. Editor The Globe, New York City.

PRESIDENT ELIOT'S ADDRESS

(Concluded from page 1.)

Welfare Work and Good-will.

Of course, we all believe that the arrangements called "Welfare" arrangements tend in the direction which I am now speaking of, but the welfare arrangements should never be presented as if they were a benevolence. They are really means of promoting efficiency, means of promoting productiveness,—above all, they are means of promoting the natural good-will, the natural co-operative effort between employer and employed. All health arrangements come under this head. The great incubus that weighs on all our industries is ill-health, sickness, premature death, the failure to take care for the body of the workman.

Then there are various contrivances for making the workman feel as if he had a share in the industry. We need, however, many more inventions in this direction. There is the premium method, the commission on sales method, the sharing of a profit with the employes. All these are experimental; they have their ups and downs, and there is a difficulty with all of them, namely, that method which works well when the establishment is profitable may work very ill when the same establishment is unprofitable. I say, therefore, we need inventions in this direction to promote the sense of common interest between the employer and the employed.

But we must go much farther than this if we are to manage wisely these delicate relations. We must see the employer interesting himself, not only in the efficient productiveness of his workmen, but in their social surroundings and their opportunities for pleasure. There is no separating this general physical and mental well-being from the problem of establishing good-will. I hope you have all seen, as I have, industries where all these conditions have been thoughtfully worked out, where even the state of the town enters into the thoughtful calculation of the employer, where municipal well-being is made a part of the industrial well-being.

The Workers' Right to Confer.

There is another place where the employers' constant attention can be profitably applied. It is in the region of discipline, of works or shops. IT IS A REASONABLE EXPECTATION ON THE PART OF THE WORKINGMEN WHO FEEL THAT THEY ARE IN PARTNERSHIP WITH THE OWNER THAT THEY SHOULD HAVE A RIGHT TO CONFER WITH HIM AND ADVISE HIM ABOUT THE RULES OF THE WORKS. IT IS A REASONABLE EXPECTATION THAT COMPLAINTS SHOULD BE PROMPTLY ATTENDED TO AND HEARD, LISTENED TO BY THE RIGHT PERSON AND NOT BY THE WRONG PERSON. THIS EXPECTATION, I SAY, IS THOROUGHLY REASONABLE. AND, MOREOVER, SINCE THESE THINGS ALL TEND TO THE ESTABLISHMENT OF GOOD-WILL IN THE WORKMEN, THEY WILL BE HIGHLY PROFITABLE IN ANY COMMERCIAL OR INDUSTRIAL ESTABLISHMENT.

I find then, three tests which may be applied to the policies of employers—

Do they take sufficient account of the immense variety of industries, shops, stores, employments, occupations? Uniformity is not to be expected.

Second, Do they promote personal and public liberty?

Third, Do they promote good-will?

The Union Indispensable.

NOW, ONE THING I WANT TO SAY FURTHER, NAMELY, THAT IT IS PERFECTLY CLEAR THAT IF THE BEST RELATIONS ARE TO BE ESTABLISHED BETWEEN EMPLOYER AND EMPLOYED, PARTICULARLY IN THE INDUSTRIES WHICH EMPLOY THOUSANDS OF WORK PEOPLE, MEN AND WOMEN, IT IS ESSENTIAL THAT THE ORGANIZATIONS OF THE WORK PEOPLE THEMSELVES SHOULD BE MAINTAINED AND SHOULD BE RECOGNIZED BY THE EMPLOYER AND THE ASSOCIATIONS OF EMPLOYERS. THE UNION IS INDEED INDISPENSABLE IN THE GREAT INDUSTRIES, AND IT IS A FACILITY FOR THE EMPLOYERS AND FOR ASSOCIATIONS OF EMPLOYERS THAT THEY EXIST, AND EXIST IN A FIRM AND JUDICIOUS FORM. WHAT WE HAVE TO REGRET IS, NOT THE EXISTENCE OF THESE ASSOCIATIONS OF WORK PEOPLE, BUT THAT THEIR POLICIES HAVE IN SEVERAL IMPORTANT RESPECTS BEEN MISDIRECTED. WHAT WE HAVE TO HOPE IS THAT OUT OF THIS CONFLICT BETWEEN THE ASSOCIATIONS OF WORK PEOPLE ON THE ONE HAND, AND OF EMPLOYERS ON THE OTHER THERE WILL ARISE TWO SAFE, PRUDENT, WISE LINES OF POLICY,—ONE IN THE ASSOCIATIONS OF WORK PEOPLE, THE OTHER IN THE ASSOCIATIONS OF EMPLOYERS.

WELFARE DEPARTMENT OF THE

National Civic Federation

OFFICERS.

H. H. VREELAND, Chairman.
CYRUS H. McCORMICK, First Vice-Chairman.
JOHN H. PATTERSON, Second Vice-Chairman.
EDWARD A. FILENE, Third Vice-Chairman.
CORNELIUS N. BLISS, Treasurer.

EXECUTIVE COMMITTEE.

George W. Brown (Treasurer United Shoe Machinery Company), Boston, Mass.
W. A. Clark (President United Verde Copper Company), Butte, Montana.
Ralph M. Easley (Chairman Executive Council, National Civic Federation), New York City.
G. E. Emmons (Manager Schenectady Works General Electric Co.), Schenectady, N. Y.
Edward A. Filene (Treasurer Wm. Filene's Sons Co.), Boston, Mass.
Frederick S. Fish (Chairman Executive Committee, Studebaker Bros. Mfg. Co.), South Bend, Ind.
W. C. Fish (Manager Lynn Works General Electric Co.), West Lynn, Mass.
G. Watson French (President Bettendorf Metal Wheel Co.), Davenport, Iowa.
Orrin S. Goan (Manager National Biscuit Co.), New York City.
Wm. C. Greene (Treasurer Peace Dale Manufacturing Company), Peace Dale, R. I.
B. J. Greenhut (Treasurer Siegel-Cooper Co.), New York City.
F. R. Hazard (President The Solvay Process Co.), Syracuse, New York.
H. J. Heinz (President H. J. Heinz Co.), Pittsburgh, Pa.
Edwin M. Herr (Vice-President Westinghouse Air Brake Co.), Wilmerding, Pa.
Charles W. Hubbard (Treasurer Ludlow Manufacturing Associates), Boston, Mass.
Charles H. Hulburd (President Elgin National Watch Co.), Chicago, Ill.
John S. Huyler (President, Huyler's), New York City.
M. E. Ingalls (President C., C., C., & St. L. Ry. Co.), Cincinnati, Ohio.
John F. P. Lawton (Assistant Treasurer & Secretary Gorham Mfg. Co. of Rhode Island), Providence, R. I.
Arthur T. Lyman (Treasurer The Boston Manufacturing Co.), Boston, Mass.
W. G. Mather (President Cleveland Cliffs Iron Co.), Cleveland, Ohio.
Cyrus H. McCormick (President International Harvester Co.), Chicago, Ill.
L. A. Osborne (Vice-President Westinghouse Electric and Manufacturing Co.), East Pittsburgh, Pa.
John H. Patterson (President National Cash Register Co.), Dayton, Ohio.
A. J. Pitkin (President American Locomotive Co.), New York City.
Thomas G. Plant (President Thomas G. Plant Company), Boston, Mass.
Ellison A. Smyth (President Pelzer Manufacturing Company), Pelzer, S. C.
Nathan Straus (R. H. Macy & Co.), New York City.
H. H. Vreeland (President New York City Railway Co.), New York City.

Miss Gertrude Beeks, Secretary

A WELFARE DEPARTMENT CONFERENCE.

Papers and Discussions Upon "Railway Provident Institutions," "Banks for Employes," "The Labor Department," and "A Factory Lunch Room."

A conference of members of the Welfare Department of the National Civic Federation was held in New York, Tuesday, November 15. The Chairman, H. H. Vreeland, presided. Papers were read by M. Riebenack, Assistant Comptroller of the Pennsylvania Railroad Company, upon "Railway Provident Institutions"; by E. H. Perley, Secretary of the Globe Employes' Bank, Boston, on "Banks for Employes"; by C. U. Carpenter, Vice-President of the Herring-Hall-Marvin Safe Company, on "The Labor Department"; and Edward F. Weston, Secretary of the Weston Electrical Instrument Co., delivered an extemporaneous talk on "A Factory Lunch Room." Those who participated in the discussions were: H. H. Vreeland, President, New York City Railway Co., New York; R. E. Danforth, General Manager, Rochester Railway Co., Rochester, N. Y.; George R. Elder, Manager, The Ingersoll-Sergeant Drill Company, Easton, Pa.; W. C. Fish, Manager, General Electric Company, West Lynn, Mass.; Frederick C. Fletcher, Treasurer, Pocasset Worsted Company, Boston; B. J. Greenhut, Treasurer, Siegel-Cooper Company, New York; George H. Harries, Vice-President Washington Railway and Electric Company, Washington, D. C.; H. Gilbert Hart, President, Hart & Crouse Company, Utica, N. Y.; T. H. McInnerney, Siegel-Cooper Company, New York; Charles T. Page, Treasurer, Page Belting Company, Concord, N. H.; Edward F. Weston, Secretary, Weston Electrical Instrument Company, Newark, N. J.; Arthur A. Fuller, Superintendent, Providence Engineering Works, Providence, R. I.; George W. Brown, Treasurer, United Shoe Machinery Company, Boston; Thomas G. Plant, President, Thomas G. Plant Company, Boston; M. Riebenack, Assistant Comptroller, Pennsylvania Railroad Company, Philadelphia; E. Horace Perley, "The Globe," Boston; C. U. Carpenter, Vice-President, Herring-Hall-Marvin Safe Company, Hamilton, O.; Mr. Anderson, Pennsylvania Railroad Company, Philadelphia; Charles W. Hubbard, Treasurer Ludlow Manufacturing Associates, Boston; Edward A. Filene, Treasurer, William Filene's Sons Co., Boston.

All of the papers and a verbatim report of the discussions will be published in pamphlet form. The paper of Mr. Perley appears upon a subsequent page of THE MONTHLY REVIEW. The paper of Mr. Riebenack will be published in two parts. The first, which treats the subject generally, follows; the second, relating particularly to the Pennsylvania Railroad, will appear in the next issue.

RAILWAY PROVIDENT INSTITUTIONS.

Their Status in the United States Reviewed and their Statistics Analyzed.

By M. Riebenack, Asst. Comptroller, Penna. R.R.

The principal avenues of provident effort in which the railways of the United States are interested on account of their employes may be enumerated as: Insurance and Relief Provision, (embracing (a) regular or commercial insurance, (b) insurance societies and organizations conducted exclusively by railway employes, and (c) the relief departments created and conducted wholly by the railroad companies); Superannuation Funds; Pension Funds; Savings Funds; Hospital Service, (including (a) hospital departments, (b) contractual hospital service, (c) emergency stations, (d) ambulance crews, (e) "first-aid" relief, (f) hospital cars); Libraries and Reading-Rooms; Young Men's Christian Association Railway Branches; Co-operative Stock Sharing Plans; Public and Private (Outside) Provisions; and Miscellaneous Provision.

Eliminating the independent or outside insurance and relief organization with which employes are affiliated, and confining attention to the strictly Railroad Relief Departments, it is found that, unlike the practice commonly obtaining with roads in foreign countries, membership is purely *voluntary*.

Relief Fund Statistics.

Out of upwards of twenty-four roads conducting insurance plans of different kinds in which their employes participate, nine are interested in strictly Railway Relief Associations, the others being concerned, under varying conditions, in (a) regular life and accident insurance, (b) mutual insurance, (c) endowment insurance, and (d) employes' relief associations or societies, and are not under the direct control nor operated as a department of the railroad companies.

The nine purely relief department roads represented an aggregate of 31,000 miles of roadway, or about 15 per centum of the total railway mileage of the country, with employes numbering 318,000, or about 24 per centum of the total number of railway employes in the United States, and an insurance membership of 206,000 employes, or practically 65 per centum of the total number of employes identified with the roads involved, and this membership percentage would be largely increased were the computations based by excluding non-membership employes who are so because of ineligibility for membership, owing to age or physical disqualifications. The average annual disbursements of these departments aggregate $2,230,000, while their combined disbursements since organization reach close on to $37,150,000.

Superannuation provision is confined exclusively to the Pennsylvania System East of Pittsburgh and Erie, Pa.

Railway Pension Funds.

Railway Pension Funds in the United States originated with the pension feature of the Baltimore and Ohio Railroad Company, instituted October 1, 1884, participation in which is based on four years' membership in the Company's Relief Department, of which the pension feature is an auxiliary. The operations of the Baltimore and Ohio Fund were originally on a small scale. The Company's annual appropriation up to July 1, 1900, was $31,000 (consisting of an annual appropriation of $25,000, and use of the $6,000 reserve fund of the Relief Department when the same was not needed by that Department); on the date named, however, the annual appropriation by the Company was increased to $75,000, with reversionary interest in the $6,000 reserve fund of the Relief Department. It will therefore be apparent that the present standard of the Pension Fund operations dates practically from the year 1900, from and after which year all of the funds were established on the prevailing scale of allowances.

The objects of the pension departments are to provide for compulsory or involuntary retirement from service at ages sixty-five or seventy years, with service ranging from ten to thirty years, on a fixed allowance, usually computed at 1 per centum of the average pay for each year of service, and voluntary retirement, growing out of incapacitation, between ages sixty-one and sixty-nine years, with a specified period of service.

Data on pension undertakings furnished by eighteen different roads show sixteen pension funds in operation, and two practically ready for introduction, while, besides, several roads announce plans either under consideration or in course of preparation, the lines of the "Vanderbilt System" being in the latter category.

The roads reporting pension funds embrace upwards of 50,000 miles, or about 24 per centum of the total railway mileage of the country, and close to 500,000 employes, or about 38 per centum of the total number of employes of all roads in the United States.

These funds represent an aggregate annual appropriation not to exceed $1,350,000, when necessary to make payment of pension allowance, while eight of the roads set aside originally, as the basis of pension or working funds, an amount aggregating about $600,000. Twelve of the funds have expended since organization an aggregate of $2,500,000, and the same roads, at the end of the year 1903, were carrying on their pension rolls the names of 3,200 pensioners, while the aggregate mortality among pensioners, since fund organization, had been 1,150.

A prominent characteristic of the railway pension fund is that the undertaking is wholly financed and supported by the railway company concerned, the beneficiaries making no contribution whatever thereto. The financial demands of the fund are sometimes met by setting aside originally a certain amount as an investment, the interest accruing therefrom constituting a pension or working fund, this amount being in some cases supplemented by provision for a maximum appropriation when necessary; in other cases the railway company simply assumes responsibility for a maximum annual disbursement.

Railway Saving Funds.

Saving Funds have not found widespread foothold among the railroads of the country, the three now in operation being identified with the Baltimore and Ohio Railroad Company and the Pennsylvania System of the lines East and West of Pittsburgh and Erie, Pa.

The Baltimore and Ohio Saving Fund differs from the Pennsylvania System Funds, in that it provides that the wife, mother, or child of an employe, or the beneficiary of a deceased member of the Relief Fund, may deposit under the same terms and conditions as employes, and the Fund, which was established in August, 1882, also has an important adjunct known as the "Loan Feature," which enables employes members of the Relief Fund to borrow money at a reasonable rate of interest and on easy terms of repayment for the purpose of acquiring and improving homesteads.

The combined total of depositors for the three roads as of December 31, 1903, was 14,807, and depositaries 1,895, their deposits and withdrawals since organization having aggregated respectively $14,877,724.99 and $10,047,776.47.

Recapitulation of results from investigations made shows that the railroads of the United States are interested in insurance, superannuation and pension undertakings on a very extensive scale, and that these roads represent a mileage aggregating 73,351.76 miles, or 35.8 per centum of the country's total railway mileage, and employes numbering 646,690, or 49.3 per centum of all railway employes, while the combined disbursements, for the features named, run well up into the millions of dollars annually.

Railway Hospital Service.

Hospital service was one of the earliest forms of relief adopted by the railroads on behalf of their employes, the first Hospital Department, as conducted at the present time, having been organized in conjunction with the Southern Pacific Railway, in California, in 1868.

The average monthly contributions by members are 25 and 50 cents, while the railway company usually furnishes the hospital building and other quarters, also free transportation to and from the same, and not infrequently assumes responsibility for financial deficiencies.

Many roads, particularly in densely populated sections, rely upon State, municipal, and private hospital service, and to that end have agreements with such institutions for the treatment of their sick and injured employes on reasonable terms.

There is also in vogue provision for extending first-aid relief to injured persons, consisting of the "First-Aid Packet" and the "Emergency Box"; while the hospital car and the "system of furnishing baggage, wrecking, and maintenance-of-way cars with stretchers" are finding general adoption.

A list compiled from data supplied by **thirty-five**

railroads with distinctive hospital organizations, represents an aggregate of about 70,000 miles of roadway, and employes numbering upwards of 360,000, the number of cases treated annually approximating 275,000.

Libraries and Reading-Rooms.

Upwards of fifty roads, representing over 100,000 miles of roadway and nearly 800,000 employes, were on record on December 31, 1903, as being interested in library and reading rooms for their employes, these features being very largely associated with the railway branches of the Young Men's Christian Association, the number of volumes involved being about 250,000.

Two notable instances of libraries conducted exclusively by railroads, and wholly dissociated from Association railway branches, are the Baltimore and Ohio Railroad Company's Circulating Library, with 15,000 volumes, and the Pennsylvania Railroad Company's Mechanics' Library at Altoona, Pa. (at which point are located the principal car and machine works of the Company), with 35,000 volumes.

Association Work.

The Young Men's Christian Association first found lodgment in America at Montreal, Canada, November 25, 1851, and in the United States at Boston, Mass., December 29, 1851.

The Railroad Department of the Association has its principal and most exclusive standing in the United States, the work having started on the Cleveland, Cincinnati, Columbus and Indianapolis Railroad, at Cleveland, O., in the fall of 1872.

On December 31, 1903, roads representing 79 per centum of the total railroad mileage of the country recognized and supported the Association. Investigations concluded for the same year resulted in forty odd roads advising of direct and active operation and promotion of railway branches, embracing, in round numbers, upwards of 100,000 miles of roadway and 785,000 employes, quite 55,000 of whom were identified with the branches, whose annual operative cost approximated $500,000. The railroads covered by these figures are regular contributors to the movement. There are many others, however, which while not directly identified with the work, are systematic subscribers thereto.

Membership rates are purely nominal, ranging from $3 to $5 a year for the privileges extended. The bulk of expenditure is, however, borne by the railroads concerned.

Educational courses, conducted for the most part throughout the fall and winter months, and which are evidencing pronounced increase in the variety and usefulness of the studies comprehended, are growing in popularity and value. These courses embrace in their curriculum those commercial and railroad branches a knowledge of which is of prime importance to the ambitious and progressive employe, and particularly to those employes who would otherwise be debarred from enjoying that encouragement and opportunity for general intellectual training and improvement which experience has shown to be essential for individual advancement in any chosen vocation.

Tuition rates are nominal, while the classes are in charge of specialists of well known ability and highest endorsement.

It is to be noted that one of the prominent features in the success of the movement rests on the fact that it is free from sectarian complications, the religious work being of such a broad general character that it can be participated in without intrenching upon denominational affiliations—being based upon the simple principles of morality that are accepted and recognized by all Christian people.

Stock-Sharing Plans.

Co-operative Stock-Sharing Plans are in operation with the Illinois Central Railroad and the Great Northern Railway Companies, representing an aggregate of 9,500.10 miles of roadway and 64,010 employes, in 1903.

Illinois Central employes are enabled to purchase the Company's capital stock upon an easy payment basis, receiving a fixed rate of interest during the time payments are being made for the shares. An employe may subscribe for one share at a time, payable by instalments in sums of $5 or any multiple of $5, on the completion of which the Company delivers to him a certificate of the share registered in his name on the Company books; and he can then, if he wishes, begin the purchase of another share on the same plan. The rate of interest allowance is 4 per centum per annum. Any officer or employe making payments under the plan, and for any reason desiring to discontinue them, can have his money returned with accrued interest, by making application to the head of the department in which he is employed.

Under the Great Northern plan provision is made for investments by the employes. A certain number of shares of stock was originally issued by the Company's Board of Directors, to be handled by a specially created Employes' Investment Association. Certificates are issued against these shares, in multiples of $10. The Company guarantees 6 per centum interest on certificates taken out between dividend dates, from the dates of such certificates to the next following dividend date (interest being paid in the form of quarterly dividends); and also guarantees the same rate of interest on certificates redeemed from the last dividend date to the date of such redemption. Between dividend dates the Company guarantees that the holder of a certificate shall receive the same percentage and interest on his certificate as the Company pays in dividends on its stock. At the present time there is outstanding about $710,000 worth of these investment certificates, and the amount is gradually increasing.

SOME PARTICIPANTS IN THE WELFARE CONFERENCE

Outside Provident Endeavor.

Public and Private (Outside) provision represents provident endeavor through the intervention of capital or its equivalent emanating from sources other than those directly identified with active railway interests. In this class may be enumerated "The Andrew Carnegie Relief Fund," effective January 1, 1902, based upon an endowment of $4,000,000, the interest on which is applied in providing relief for employes of The Carnegie Company in all its works, mines, railways, shops, etc., injured in its service, and for those dependent upon such employes as are killed; also to provide small pensions or aids to such employes as, after long and creditable service, through exceptional circumstances, need such help in their old age, and who make good use of it.

Another instance is "The Moses Taylor Hospital" (established March 29, 1882; incorporated July 22, 1884), located at Scranton, Pa., and endowed by Mr. Moses Taylor, Sr., and Mrs. C. A. Taylor, the endowment principal being invested in such manner as to net an income sufficient to take care of all operating expenses. Cost of building and equipment was $355,233.05, and total cost of operation to close of 1903, $450,524.92; while 3,293 surgical and 1,170 medical cases had been cared for up to the end of the same year. This hospital is conducted principally in the interest of the employes of the Delaware, Lackawanna and Western Railroad Company and the Lackawanna Iron and Steel Company. The Iron and Steel Company having removed from Scranton, Pa., to Buffalo, N. Y., another hospital, known as "The Moses Taylor Hospital of Buffalo," was opened in the latter city during the present year.

The late J. Edgar Thomson, a former President of the Pennsylvania Railroad Company, provided in his will that the net income from the estate, after the decease of his wife, was to be used for the education and maintenance of female orphans of railway employes killed while in the discharge of their duties on the Pennsylvania Railroad, as well as on other railroads of the United States, as far as the net income will permit.

In 1882, Mrs. Lavinia F. Thomson, under the will of her husband, started the St. John's Orphanage in Philadelphia, where have been domiciled a number of orphan girls, who have been cared for and given the privilege of a good education. Since her decease in 1903 the Orphanage has been under the supervision of the trustees of the estate.

Efforts of Allied Companies.

In the course of investigation it was deemed advisable to examine into and discuss the methods pursued by Express Companies, Sleeping Car Companies, and the Railway Mail Service, on account of the provident undertakings already mentioned. These interests are closely and inseparably identified with the railways, and are therefore properly subjects for consideration in this relation.

Six Express Companies in the United States,—the Adams Express Company, the American Express Company, the United States Express Company, the Southern Express Company, the Pacific Express Company, and Wells, Fargo & Company,—representing an aggregate mileage operated of 198,503 miles, and 62,574 employes, as of December 31, 1903, are interested in insurance and pension measures, also Young Men's Christian Association Railway Branches and Libraries and Reading-Rooms, on behalf of their employes.

One of the Express Companies,—Wells, Fargo & Company,—has libraries located in five of the principal cities of the United States and in the City of Mexico, carrying a total of 15,523 volumes, and also provides what are known as "Terminal Libraries" at twenty-two points, through the territory traversed by its service.

The Pullman Company, operating over 175,761 miles of roadway, and with 20,398 employes, as of December 31, 1903, encourages its employes to carry good insurance, and has under consideration a pension plan in their behalf. This Company conducts a "merit system" for its transportation men, under the operation of which employes with over five years' service to their credit are rewarded with having placed conspicuously upon their service uniforms "meritorious marks" indicative of their years of service with the Company. This feature is highly appreciated by the traveling public, as the presence of these evidences of special distinction inspires confidence and security, in that they grow out of long and faithful discharge of assigned duties.

BANKS FOR EMPLOYES.

By E. Horace Perley, Secretary of the Boston Globe Employes' Bank, Boston, Mass.

When I became an employe of the Boston *Globe*, nearly twenty-three years ago, one of the first things that impressed me was the very general practice of borrowing money. Some would get their wages advanced from week to week by some fellow-worker, some would borrow a sum that would tie up their wages for weeks at a time, while some made a practice of borrowing to such an extent that they could never draw their own wages.

Looking around, I found that the same state of affairs existed in all the newspaper offices. As time went on, and I asked questions here and there, I found that to be a condition which existed in almost every establishment where there is a large body of employes. There is always a large class willing—yes, anxious—to borrow, and a smaller class willing to lend—for a consideration. The department stores have it. Among the factories, the shoemakers especially, are noted for it. I know quite a number who derive a considerable income from fellow-workmen on the railroad.

But to get back to my own field. I soon found that the borrowing capacity was unlimited, many taking all they could get, on any conditions; in fact, no questions were asked usually as to interest rate. If a loan could be obtained at ordinary rates it was a "cinch" for the borrower, but the lender was considered anything but bright. The usual rate was five per cent. per week—in fact, I knew one man who, at that time, kept out at that rate between $600 and $700 continuously. Ten per cent. per week, however, had no terrors for many, and I think I could have then named persons with quite a number of hundreds of dollars out at that rate.

The newspaper grew rapidly in public favor, and with its growth there was a corresponding increase in the working force, which meant an equal increase in the number of borrowers. When I joined the force there were about a hundred, I think, while now we number nearly an even thousand.

The foregoing will, perhaps, give an idea as to how I have arrived at the conclusion that the workingmen, when they want to borrow, *will borrow*, actually giving no thought to, or seemingly caring nothing about, the cost. Their one aim is to get some money.

About the time I began to form definite ideas on this subject, I took out some shares in a co-operative bank, and, as I grew accustomed to the bank methods and purposes, I advanced quite a stage in my reasoning. I began to ask why it was not possible to get the men to establish a fund and borrow their own money. I argued that they seemed to care nothing about what they paid in the way of interest. Therefore, they would pay a pretty high rate of interest to the fund. That being received, a substantial dividend could be paid from the earnings at stated intervals, and a substantial dividend would be a sufficient incentive to cause the deposit of a dollar or more each week by quite a number of men.

MAX REIBENACK

My argument bore fruit. A dozen or more formed an association, and by the end of the first year we had about sixty members. This was about twelve years ago. Now we have 275 members, and the business has grown until now we loan on the average about $800 each week, and receive as deposits on an average about $900 each week.

I was, at the outset, chosen as working executive; that is, all the detail of the business devolved upon me, and has continued to ever since. With experience, I evolved a system of keeping accounts that seems to fill the bill perfectly and give satisfaction to all.

Our plan of operation is, in some respects, similar to the co-operative bank, except that we do business weekly instead of monthly. They sell the use of money at auction, and we fix an arbitrary scale. Any employe can join or withdraw at pleasure, the only prerequisite being the payment of the first deposit.

When one joins he agrees to deposit a certain sum each pay-day. He must deposit the same sum, no more, no less, each pay-day. Failure means a fine of two cents on each dollar which should have been paid, and a double payment on the next pay-day. The earnings are divided each six months pro rata, according to the number of dollars each member has on deposit when the books are closed.

To accommodate the borrower who wanted money only for a week, a rate of one cent on a dollar was established. At first $100 and over was loaned at 12 per cent. per year, $200 and over at 9 per cent., $300 and over 6 per cent. Now, experience has proven it is better to have an arbitrary graduated scale, not based on a regular percentage. $1 to $25 is 1c. to 25c. per week; $50 is 33c. per week; $100, 38c.; $150, 42c.; $200, 45c.; $250, 48c.; $300, 52c., etc.

The men seem to have no care how much interest they pay, and the only way to attract and keep them is to pay good dividends. These rates have enabled us to pay an average, for eleven and one-half years, of 12 per cent. per annum. Net earnings the last semi-annual term were about $1,200, and total deposits average more than $800 each week.

At present we receive, as a deposit, not less than $1 per week, nor more than $5 per week. A dividend is paid on nothing above $350, and no one is allowed to borrow more than $200 above what he has on deposit, except, as provided by a recent amendment, that he give real estate security. The treasurer is executive in making loans, and the secretary makes all collections and keeps all accounts and records. Deposits are placed in bank so as to require the signatures of both president and treasurer for withdrawal. A depositor wishing to borrow more than $20 above what he has on deposit can do so only with the approval of a majority of the thirteen directors.

Security is largely the character of the borrower; sometimes the treasurer has the right to draw the man's pay, sometimes a legal assignment of the man's wages is made, in some cases life insurance is assigned, and, if the borrower is married, the note must bear the wife's indorsement. This latter practice has a tendency to prevent some classes of needless borrowing—husband and wife having a mutual knowledge of the transaction.

As I have said, the men will borrow. Our aim is to control their borrowing, and let them have back the proceeds. The membership has increased constantly and steadily from the beginning. The president receives $1 per week, the treasurer $3 per week, and the secretary $6 per week, the latter volunteering to give the association half of the time necessary for keeping the accounts.

The bank is governed in every particular by the employe members, though in the outset the employers showed approval by assisting financially, becoming depositors during the first two years.

There is a board of three auditors. At least two of them must thoroughly examine all accounts once a month. Each auditor receives $2 each time he officiates.

The losses have been very few, especially when this method of loaning and the lack of security are considered.

When money comes in faster than it can be loaned, advantage of the dividend period is taken to scale down the capital, returning the surplus cash pro rata to the depositors. Several times the capital has been scaled down a quarter or a third, and once about a half.

When a borrower's deposit, on dividend day, amounts to a sum equal to his loan, the deposit must be withdrawn and the loan paid.

Casually, perhaps, this plan would seem to indicate that the dividends returned did not compensate for the high rate of interest paid. Still this can be logically accounted for. The average amount out at loan is about $20,000, and as it is divided among 250 men, it will be seen there must be many of what we call large loans, and therefore at the lower rates of interest charged. ($250 pays 48 cents per week—10 per cent. per annum.) The "large loans" hardly pay the dividends, therefore, which, as I have said, average 12 per cent. per annum. The small and temporary loans, that is, the $1, $2, $5, $10, and even $20 loans, to be paid usually in a few days, which pay one cent for each dollar borrowed, pay the profits of the business, and really reap very little of the benefits—except in the way of accommodation.

All employes are invited and urged to join the bank, that is, become depositors, and participate in all its privileges. There is no let or hindrance to them. They may join at pleasure and withdraw their funds at will. If a loan of more than $20 is obtained, the borrower must become a depositor. Then if he does not share in the earnings, he alone is to blame. The only rule to be observed is this: "All money that has been on deposit for the three months next preceding the day of the dividend shall receive its pro rata share of all money earned during the six months the dividend day closed." The membership of the bank is coming and going all the time. Some obtain membership that they may borrow for four or five weeks, withdrawing as soon as the loan is wiped out. Many utilize the bank as a place of deposit, because they find themselves unable to withstand temptation to spend when money is in pocket, and then withdraw as soon as they have laid enough away to attain some object.

E. HORACE PERLAY

In fact, withdrawals will average $250 per week. Many times a borrower will say he does not care for the dividend; what he wants is the *money* when he *wants* it. He borrows, pays weekly, and withdraws, repeatedly. Yet I have made it a rule to point out, whenever withdrawal is asked, the loss of dividend by such action, so that all may act with eyes open. These transients will borrow any way and anywhere; if we do not furnish the opportunity, they will go elsewhere and pay five times as much for the privilege. In their coming and going some stick, and the membership grows. We urge the savings idea, and if a borrower, we compel it as long as he borrows. In the several applications, the value becomes gradually apparent, to some sooner, to some later. Of course, there are a few apbank, even some of these change their methods and parently incorrigible. But when they awake to the fact that the transients really pay the running of the join the majority, who benefit.

At the last dividend, no depositor had the limit allowed on deposit. Ten or a dozen had $300 in, and so received $18 dividend, which was more than they had paid as interest during the term. From my working knowledge of the bank, I estimate that these borrowers who made their deposits regularly during the six months and did not withdraw any portion of their deposits, received a dividend that would average equal to from one-half to two-thirds of what they had paid in interest during the term.

The bank has taught many to save who never before saved anything. It has been of great benefit numberless times to men hard pressed who could not possibly get money anywhere else. In a number of cases the savings here have been the nucleus of home-buying. Many save here for the larger expenses that come periodically during the year. The chronic borrowers in very many cases, learn gradually the folly of their extravagance. The bank has many times, in promising cases, where a man was nearly overwhelmed with his many obligations, taken his affairs in hand, paid his debts, and let him work it out from week to week until he was again a free man—and the lesson has generally proved salutary and profitable.

The only objection I ever heard to our methods was our high rate of interest. I believe, as I have already said, that the high rate is a necessity. But, to see if others had a similar opinion, I questioned our officers and many members. They were unanimous in saying that the large dividend is a necessity—it is what draws in the deposits, is to some the sole incentive in beginning to save. Even with the prestige of nearly twelve years of success, with all that that implies, only one or two thought it would be safe to reduce the interest rate on even the small weekly loans—those of from $1 to $25.

The establishment of an association on the lines of ours, I believe, cannot fail to do much good in any large body of employes.

[The discussion of this paper developed the fact that a Bank for Employes backed by the employer could be operated at a nominal cost and that such a plan would permit lower interest charges for short time loans.—The Editor.]

AN INTERESTING QUESTION ANSWERED.

The following request to the Welfare Department was received from a molder who asked that his name be regarded as confidential:

"Can you not agitate through your publication the necessity of providing relief for molders in the foundries? If the union's business agent approaches the employer on this subject, in our district, he thinks the agent is only trying to stir up trouble and will not listen. For instance, we had considerable trouble because one of our business agents asked to have windows replaced to prevent colds.

"The molders should be enabled to change their working clothes. It makes a great difference in the health of all the men. You can especially notice that the young men age very rapidly, as their clothes are constantly wet with perspiration, and they do not have the opportunities or facilities to bathe."

A reply secured from the National Cash Register Company:

"We think the request of this molder is worthy of the careful attention of every company which has such men in its employ. We believe the moral effect of pleasant environment, which we are trying to establish, is a benefit to both employer and employe, and therefore it should be promoted as a good business policy. With this belief we have made a great effort to improve the working condition of our employes, and we feel the results accomplished show that our endeavors have been appreciated. This acts as an incentive for a continuation of our policy.

"Lockers have been provided for all the foundry employes. Shower baths, with plenty of hot and cold water, have been established; also a number of troughs for those who have not the time or inclination to use the showers. Towels are furnished free by the Company. Ten minutes are allowed at noon and fifteen at quitting time for changing clothes. We have separate baths and lockers for the colored employes.

"A large ice-box has been placed at the disposal of the foundrymen, in which they keep their lunches. Before this was put in use, great difficulty was experienced in keeping lunches free from the dust which prevails in all foundries.

"A milkman supplies his product to those who desire it, settlement being made at the end of each week.

"Employes are permitted to lunch at any time provided they do not abuse the privilege.

"The men in the sand room are furnished with respirators which fit closely over the mouth and nose, effectually excluding the small particles of sand which otherwise would be inhaled. We used a great many windows in the construction of our foundry, both on the side of the building and on the roof. These afford plenty of light and make good ventilation possible. A number of fans are used to aid the circulation. Each furnace has ample space,—a provision which has modified somewhat the extreme heat to which all melters are subjected.

"The effects of this Welfare work are distinctly apparent. The men enjoy better health, they are more content, and therefore give the Company much better service. In no department of our factory has Welfare Work brought better results."

The barons Alphonse, Gaston and Edmond de Rothschild, of the Rue Laffitte, Paris, went recently to M. Trouillot, the Minister of Commerce, to inform him that they would devote the sum of 10,000,000f. to the building of workmen's dwellings, healthy and cheap, and that the income from these dwellings would be employed in social improvements.

THE VOICE OF THE CHURCH.

(Concluded from page 1.)

brethren to maintain a shop in which no man shall serve except a member of the union. They may not agree with these brethren, but they ought to appreciate their self-sacrifice. The laborer has learned from the capitalist to despise order and break law. He has learned from the churchman to pursue the dissenter with menace and violence. The recent tragedies in Colorado do not follow at a far distance the massacres which in the sixteenth century ensued upon the withdrawal of Holland from the ecclesiastical union.

"While, then, we condemn the tyranny and turbulence of the labor union, and call upon the law to preserve the liberty of every citizen to employ whom he will and to work for whom he will, we deprecate the hasty temper which, in condemning the errors of the unions, condemns at the same time the whole movement with which they are connected. The offenses of the union are as distinct from the cause for which the organization of labor stands, as the Inquisition is distinct from the Gospel.

"In the face of a prejudice and an hostility for which there are serious reasons, we are convinced that the organization of labor is essential to the well-being of the working people. It is based upon a sense of the inestimable value of the individual man. 'The cause of labor is the effort of men, being men, to live the life of men.' Its purpose is to maintain such a standard of wages, hours, and conditions as shall afford every man an opportunity to grow in mind and in heart. Without organization the standard cannot be maintained in the midst of our present commercial conditions.

"This report is designedly general in its terms, but there is one matter which we are constrained to commend in particular to the consciences of Christian people. We do not undertake to say how much of the blame of child labor belongs to the employer and how much to the parent. But we do say this, that the employment of children in factories and mills depresses wages, destroys homes, and depreciates the human stock. Nothing is so important in any community as a human being. Whatever interferes with the education of a child, contradicts the best interests of the nation. We call, then, on Christian employers as on Christian parents to endeavor after such betterment of the local and general laws as shall make the labor of children impossible in this Christian country.

"In the name of our common Master, we ask the attention and energy of the Church to the removal of this and other crying evils. Thus shall we assist in setting forward the kingdom and obedience of our Lord and Saviour, Jesus Christ."

The Pope and Labor.

The following letter, signed by Mgr. Merry Del Val. Papal Secretary of State, and addressed to the International Society for the Protection of Workmen, indicates the interest taken by Pope Pius X in labor;

"My sublime master, the pontiff, desires me to express to you that, like his predecessor, Pope Leo XIII., he is in hearty accord with all movements intended to benefit workmen.

"The pontiff, in particular, desires it understood that he favors with all his heart any lightening of the burden of the men and women who work with their hands. Work should be so regulated as to conform to the physical ability of the workmen; it should be regulated to fit the sexes; it should be regulated to permit of the stoppage of all work on Sundays.

"The workman should be protected against employment and employers that have no regard for his dignity as a man and a citizen. That endangers his morality and interferes with his family life.

"The holy father trusts that you will devise peaceful means to realize the above ends. If you do, your efforts will be crowned with success, and all good governments will regard them with sympathy. On his own part, the pope will be happy to assist you with advice and prayer."

The National Congregational Council.

The report of the Labor Committee of the National Congregational Council recounts the inquiries into the industrial situation by its members, David N. Beach, Washington Gladden, William J. Tucker and William A. Knight, Secretary. Their investigation has included much correspondence, the study of industrial strife in the field and attendance upon a convention of the American Federation of Labor and a conference of the National Civic Federation. The Committee recommends the appointment of similar committees by each state organization of the church and affiliation with kindred committees of other denominations and with non-ecclesiastical bodies that work for industrial betterment.

Upon the industrial situation, the Committee reports:

"We have a labor problem because we have large freedom, education, democracy, in which aggressive and acquisitive human beings are struggling for personal and social expression and betterment. The deep tendencies and the surface conditions of modern industry result in that consolidation of the forces of the employed, and the forces of the employer, that express themselves in the former instance in unionism, and in the latter in the various types of employers' associations. Apparently unionism is something more than that valuable phase of present-day industry, collective bargaining, for unionism stands for the introduction of democracy into industry, the right of representation in the conduct of business. More fundamental than any other practical question, such as the closed shop or freedom of contract is this underlying demand of representation in the conduct of industrial enterprises. To achieve it is the core of intelligent unionism, which seems fast passing into industrialism, and to resist it is the purpose of much of the counter organization of employers. The result appears on the surface in suspicion, resistance, lawlessness, violence,—the common hard features of much of the present industrial struggle. It is not our part to discuss this phase of the question. We simply state it, as a primary and inevitable element in the present contest.

"We believe that organization of labor and organizations of capital are inevitable, and that these forces are to be dealt with intelligently and humanely, and that any policy that means the utter subversion of one force to that of the other is certain to result immediately in intensifying the already ominous tendency to class division and class warfare. Constructive policies, under the forms of law and tempered by the justly critical force of public opinion, are being framed by conservative leaders on both sides, and for these results we can hopefully wait.

"We urge upon trades-unionists and upon employers in the meantime the right use of power and the cultivation of such a sense of responsibility as will conserve social well-being for the present and for the future. The spirit of the marauder, by whomever shown, should be checked, and industrial organizations both of employes and employers, should become as they may become, strong forces in behalf of law and order."

A YEAR SAVED ON THE SUBWAY.

(Concluded from page 3.)

An example of the good faith with which the agreement was kept, under exceedingly difficult conditions, was its absolute maintenance throughout the six months of general strike in the building trades in New York in 1903. During all that time, when building was at a complete standstill all over the city, owing to labor troubles, the work on the Subway, in which the building trades were largely employed, went steadily and rapidly on.

Again, in May, 1903, there was a strike of all the unskilled laborers, excavators and others, employed in the Subway. These workers, who were not represented in the Central Federated Union and who were not included in the contract, sought the aid, in their strike, of the unions of skilled labor. The Contractors' Association declined to admit the laborers into the agreement, but offered to arbitrate the questions in dispute. The laborers refused to arbitrate. The unions, while presumably sympathising with the demands of the laborers, stood by their agreement, and the strike of the laborers collapsed.

Experience in the practical operation of the agreement showed that most of the grievances that were brought by unions before the Joint Committee originated with acts of the foremen and other subordinate overseers of labor, such as employing non-union men, or refusing to pay union wages. In every case, the Joint Committee through their secretary, Mr. Douglas, ascertained the facts by thorough investigation. Whatever was found to be wrong was set right; and if the grievance had no substantial basis, it was dismissed. If a union showed symptoms of recalcitrance, the labor members of the Joint Committee acted with the contractor members in insisting upon its compliance with the agreement. Comparatively few unwarranted complaints, however, from either contractors as to unfair union exactions, or from the unions as to attempted violations of the agreement or oppression by the foreman, received the support of a majority of either of the two organized parties to the agreement, which was necessary to bring any grievance before the Joint Committee. That committee adjusted many questions of wages. This was because the rate specified in the agreement was subject to modification from time to time, owing to changes in the nature and conditions of the work in a given craft. The settlement of such questions grew more and more easy as the contractors and the unions gained mutual confidence in the sincerity and judical fairness of the Joint Committee. As a result of this feeling not a few of the claims of the unions were waived upon the representation of the Joint Committee that they were unreasonable.

The value of personal conferences received many illustrations. A grievance relating to certain work among the sections caused the Joint Committee much perplexity, until they brought the controversy to the attention of the sub-contractor himself. The sub-contractor went to the heart of the matter at once and corrected the trouble, which had its origin in some arbitrary and unreasonable rule by a foreman. "This is the first I have heard of this matter," said the sub-contractor; "why did you not come to me before?" "Oh, we didn't want to bother you," was the reply of a labor member of the Joint Committee. "But I wish to be bothered about any such trouble. Come to me whenever you think anything is wrong, and if there is a real wrong, I will make it right." announced the "big" boss.

One union largely engaged in the work of the Subway was not a party to the general contract. This was the Housesmiths' Union, which was not represented in the Central Federated Union. Its members drove, with compressed air machines, the millions of rivets that bind together the structural iron work of the tunnel. With this union, the contractors had a separate verbal agreement. Whatever difficulties the contractors had with the Housesmiths, therefore, cannot be charged to any breakdown of the agreement with the Central Federated Union.

The most serious difficulty encountered in the history of this collective contract, and which did not occur until late in the construction, was caused by the interference of a third party. This was the Building Trades Alliance, formed and at that time dominated by Philip Weinseimer, its president. This Alliance admitted to its membership the Amalgamated Painters, a local independent union, not affiliated with the Central Federated Union. To the National Brotherhood of Painters, which was affiliated with the Central Federated Union, the Contractors' Association was compelled to give, under the agreement, the work of painting the Subway or at least the permanent coat. The Building Trades Alliance demanded that the Amalgamated Painters' should have half of the painting, and called a strike to enforce its demand. This call was obeyed in the Subway by about 1,000 carpenters, electrical workers, plumbers, plasterers and tile layers. The failure of the Central Federated Union to discipline these unions for violating the agreement is the only blot on the escutcheon of organized labor during the life of that contract.

The strike called by the Alliance was brought to an end in most of the trades affected through Mr. McDonald's firm attitude. He received a committee of the strikers and told them that he would stand by the Central Federated Union, as that body had stood by its agreement with the Contractors' Association. He maintained that an outside organization, such as the newly-formed Building Trades Alliance, must adjust its grievances through the existing agreement, which had served its purpose admirably and equitably ever since it was signed.

It is calculated that this strike, called by Weinseimer, delayed the opening of the Subway possibly three weeks.

All the members of the Joint Committee, both the representatives of the Contractors' Association and of the Central Federated Union, were throughout the operation of the agreement in thorough accord with the general contractor, John B. McDonald, in the one great purpose of completing the Subway as rapidly as possible. As the chairman of the Labor Committee during more than three years, Mr. John J. Pallas, now President of the Workingmen's Federation of New York State, held frequent conferences with Mr. McDonald.

Mr. Douglas, the Secretary of the Contractors' Association, also served the Joint Committee as its secretary. Many matters were settled by him without the necessity of calling together the Joint Committee, and in those which had to be adjusted by the Joint Committee, his tact and patience usually smoothed the way to an amicable and satisfactory understanding.

Mr. Pallas, the present President of the Park Board, for many years a delegate to the Central Federated Union devoted much of his time to the harmonious working of the agreement.

The constant efforts of the Joint Committee were to forward the progress of the work, so as to remove as rapidly as possible the obstructions to surface traffic along the line of the route. The members always responded promptly and faithfully to the demands upon their time when any question arose that required detailed investigation. Throughout their work they were aided by the support and confidence of their respective organizations. The meetings of the Joint Committee promoted the good fellowship of the representatives of both sides and conduced largely to a unity of purpose to bring this most difficult engineering work to a prompt and successful conclusion. After the opening of the Subway both parties to this agreement pronounced it the most successful collective contract ever made between capital and labor.

A DISSENT FROM SOME SWEEPING ATTACKS UPON UNIONISM.

ITS WHOLESALE CONDEMNATION NOT WARRANTED BY ITS OCCASIONAL ERRORS NOR IN ACCORD WITH ITS BETTER LEADERSHIP.

(By RALPH M. EASLEY, Chairman Executive Council, National Civic Federation.)

A series of articles upon the labor question by Mr. John Keith, recently published in *Harper's Weekly*, has been of special interest because they are typical of a mental attitude toward this subject that has become unfortunately frequent among magazine and newspaper writers. The prevalence of this mental attitude is not hard to explain. Up to the time of the anthracite-coal strike the public had paid little more than passing notice to the labor question. The direful possibilities when zero weather loomed up before the nation with empty coal-bins at that time set everybody thinking, talking, or writing on the great labor problem. About the same time some of the most conspicuously offensive incidents in the labor movement cropped out, such as Sam Parksism in New York; picketing funerals in Chicago; expelling union men for belonging to the State militia in Schenectady, etc., etc. These occurrences naturally gave the new students of unionism a very unfavorable impression, as their trenchant pens have since given innumerable evidences. Mr. Keith, in his very interesting articles, whether one of the old students or of the new, evidently was not searching for trade-union virtues; and if there were any excesses he overlooked I do not now recall them. If the view were restricted to the array of hostile witnesses he summons, the reader would be quite ready to believe his conclusion:

"It may be set down as a general truth that the labor-union acts in no way as a spur, but in a thousand ways as an obstacle to the development of the country along the most scientific lines of economic advancement."

But suppose this method of criticising labor-unions were applied to other social institutions, what would be the conclusion? Only the other day there was a hurry call for the police reserves to a restaurant to prevent students of Columbia University from pounding one another into bloody insensibility during a class fight. The week before the daughter of a president of a college in Illinois was dragged out of bed by a gang of hazing students. Only a short time before that, in another institution of learning, a young man was taken out at night, hammered until several bones were broken, and thrown into a pond. Is it fair to single out such instances and to say that, therefore, higher education "acts as an obstacle to the development of the country"?

Again, many writers lay undue stress upon the fact that in isolated cases labor-unions have broken "solemn" agreements with employers. Every trade agreement has in truth all the solemnity of a contract. It is no defence of the gravity of such a condition to point out that "gentlemen's agreements," which railroad officials openly state are "solemnly" made between themselves, are often broken just as quickly as some of the officials can reach the telephone; or that when goods are sold for future delivery and the price falls a large number of buyers—about seventy-five per cent., as stated recently by a prominent wholesale merchant—break their "solemn" contracts through some pretext or other. The point is that while the breaking of contracts by labor-unions is a most serious matter, its occurrence is much less common than the public is led to believe. Where one labor-union breaks a contract there are five hundred broken contracts with which organized labor has nothing to do.

Much stress is also placed upon the assumption that organized labor is opposed to the militia. This assumption is based upon the expulsion from a local union, controlled by radicals, of a member of the New York militia; a similar isolated act of folly in Michigan; and the unsupported testimony of a local witness in Boston. If true, this would be a serious charge. A special point is made of the New York statute forbidding discrimination against members of the National Guard, causing the inference that it was passed to meet an unpatriotic phase of unionism. The fact is not stated, however, that this law was equally directed at employers who had discharged or docked their employes for joining the militia and absenting themselves from business to atend to their sworn duties to the State.

Further investigation would show that many labor organizations have repudiated all spirit of antagonism to military service. For instance, the International Typographical Union voted down an anti-militia resolution by an overwhelming majority.

The rousing demonstration of patriotic enthusiasm that followed the speech of the chairman of the executive committee, a printer from Georgia, in closing the argument against the resolution, would have excited, I am sure, the approval of the most severe critic of organized labor.

Still higher authority was the reply made by Samuel Gompers, president of the American Federation of Labor, to a member who asked if a union man could be a consistent member of the State militia:

"Yes, a member of the State militia can be seated in a trade council. In fact, the matter is so obvious that it ought not to be open for discussion at all.

"A man who is a wage-earner and honorably working at his trade or calling to support himself and those dependent upon him has not only the right to become a citizen soldier, but that right must be unquestioned.

"The militia—*i. e.*, the citizen soldiery of the several States in our country—supplies what otherwise might take its place—a large standing army.

"The difference between the citizen soldiery of the United States and the large standing armies of many of the European countries is the difference between a republic and a monarchy—it is the difference between the conceptions of liberty and tyranny."

The critics of labor-unions rarely omit the regulation statement that organized labor includes only a small minority of the wage-earners of the country. The estimate generally quoted to give force to the claim that it is "monstrous tyranny for the small minority to dictate to the great majority of workers the wages, hours, and conditions of their toil" is that labor organizations contain only from eight to twelve per cent. of all wage-earners. But if a union containing ninety-five per cent. of the skilled workers in its craft demands better conditions it is no answer to say that the farm-hands or the washerwomen are not organized.

The comparison most frequently made credits organized labor with a membership of about 2,400,000, which is only eight per cent. of the more than 29,000,000 persons engaged in gainful occupations in the United States in 1900. But an analysis of the gainful occupations shows the fallacy of the comparison. These 29,000,000 include: In agriculture, 10,000,000; domestic and personal service, 6,000,000; the professions, 1,200,000. Practically all of these are unorganizable and should be excluded from the comparison. Included also in the 29,000,000 are the 4,700,000 engaged in trade and transportation. But among these are bankers, brokers, merchants, officials of banks and corporations, bookkeepers, commercial travellers, agents, accountants, foremen and overseers, hucksters and pedlers, livery-stable keepers, undertakers, and miscellaneous workers, who are also unorganizable, and should be excluded from the comparison.

It is repeatedly asserted that there is no community of purpose between the union and the non-union man. The fact is that shorter hours, higher wages, and improved conditions are just as much desired by the non-union workers as by the unionists. Occasional brutal combats do not impugn this broad truth.

When the 6,000 union strikers went out at Fall River a few weeks ago they took with them 24,000 non-unionists, and the two are standing shoulder to shoulder, the families of the non-union workers being supported from the treasury of the union to the best of its ability. When John Mitchell called out his 8,000 members at the time of the anthracite-coal strike in 1900, the 140,000 non-union miners went with them. When the railway brotherhoods contemplate a strike they submit the matter to a vote of all the employes, non-union as well as union, the vote of every man counting equally.

Such experiences are common, and yet many writers would have us believe that unionists and non-unionists are natural antagonists.

Organized labor is charged with "defiance of the mandates of the courts," because Samuel Gompers, in connection with an injunction issued by Judge Friedman of New York, "against interference with non-union cigarmakers," was quoted as saying, "I am here especially to violate the injunction."

What is there in this charge? It may be said that Mr. Gompers was misquoted. But waiving that point entirely, Mr. Gompers would have been clearly within his rights if he had uttered the words imputed to him. As a matter of record, the injunction in question was not "against interference with non-union cigarmakers," but forbade locked-out cigarmakers to contribute to their union treasury or to pay money out of their union treasury to assist cigarmakers who were in distress. The injunction was overruled as soon as it was brought before a higher court, thus sustaining Mr. Gompers.

Whether or not the injunction was sound, it is plain that in disputing its soundness, Mr. Gompers was exercising only a right that is brought daily into use in the courts. Was it a "defiance of the law" for President Baer of the Reading Railroad to refuse to obey a judicial order to testify before the Interstate Commerce Commission, until the Supreme Court had decided that he must? Did the promoters of the Northern Securities Company "defy" the law when the government of the United States was obliged to appeal to the Supreme Court to establish the constitutionality and pertinence of the anti-trust law? Unquestionably they, as well as President Baer, were within their legal rights. Any citizen may test the constitutionality of a law, whether in the form of a judicial mandate or of a statute, by appeal even to the highest court in the land. To assume otherwise would be to assume the infallibility of single court or of a legislative body. To assume otherwise would be to blot out in an instant all the appeals for which judicial machinery is devised.

In considering here the familiar charges against the unions of broken contracts, tyranny of a minority, antagonism to the militia, and defiance of courts, it is not intended to minimize by omission the array of crimes growing out of violence during strikes, ranging from petty assault to women-beating and murder, or the cases of corruption that have been exposed. But these deplorable offences are as opposed to the true philosophy of unionism as were the *auto da fe* and the sale of indulgences to the spirit of Christianity.

Granting all the charges brought against labor-unions to be true, and multiplying them a hundred-fold, what is the result? They would prove that some labor-unions and some labor leaders have committed grave offences against society and against themselves. That proposition is admitted.

But it remains none the less true that the trades-unions of this country, no matter what per cent. of all the wage-earners they include, or what incidental crimes they have committed, have a fundamental purpose which all will admit to be for the benefit of society as a whole. They are striving to improve the condition of the working masses. Organized labor has been struggling for this end, not only alone and unaided, but against the general opposition of employers, individual and organized, and against the misrepresentations of prejudiced critics, when, in fact, it deserved the friendly co-operation of them all. Labor has constantly had to evolve its own leadership. It has made all the mistakes of unskilled generalship and undisciplined following. It makes them still. But the time has come when those who have some understanding of the hardships and misdirections that hamper the advance of labor are extending the sympathetic aid of their superior intelligence.

There are associations of employers who would beat down the advance of labor with a bludgeon. There are other associated employers who would come to terms of mutual understanding. This second method, I am glad to say, receives more and more the approval of leaders of public opinion and of humane and intelligent employers. In the multiplication of concrete examples of relations between employer and employed that are harmonious because they are just, can be discerned a brightening outlook in the entire industrial situation. In this view national prosperity will be coincident with the uplifting of organized labor, so that its admitted errors may become fewer and its sincere co-operation with capital in increasing productivity more frequent. Some hopeful phases of the mutual progress of organized capital and labor in this direction I shall illustrate in a subsequent article.

INFORMATION FOR EMPLOYERS.

The Welfare Department of the National Civic Federation is prepared to furnish, upon request, a consulting agent to study the especial needs of employes in a given plant, advise the best methods of introducing such features of welfare work as may be deemed most essential, direct their installation, and, when required, recommend a permanent agent or "welfare manager" to administer the work.

A central bureau is maintained at the headquarters of the Welfare Department for the exchange of experiences by employers. Information with reference to the latest efforts by employers to give especial consideration to the physical or mental welfare of their employes may there be obtained. Some of the subjects covered are:

Sanitary Work Rooms;
Wash Rooms and Baths;
Hospital Service;
The Luncheon Room;
Recreation;
Educational Efforts;
Housing of Labor;
Pensions;
Insurance Associations.

[T]HREE FOES OF ORGANIZED LABOR.

(Concluded from page 7.)

iary gain to himself, in higher wages that may be ured through effective organization. If the Chi-o teamsters could have known in advance that ir union would succeed in raising their wages m $7 to $18 or $20 a week, it might not have been 'cult to induce them to pledge to the union fund much as twenty-five per cent. of the increase. the average contribution to the union in time of peace is only nominal.

Jurisdictional disputes are another source of weakness. These disputes between unions, each claiming exclusive right to do certain branches of work, arise with almost every improvement and invention. They are, however, recognized as a source of weakness. The Executive Council of the American Federation of Labor thus frankly dealt with this weakness two years ago:

"The Executive Council regrets to state that much of its time has been unavoidably taken up with the settlement or attempted settlement of jurisdiction disputes. Despite the fact that your body in convention assembled has repeatedly declared for peace between the unions, and has advocated the submission of all matters in dispute to the arbitrament of third parties, the jurisdiction disputes seem to grow in number and in intensity. We regret to state that while many of the unions so engaged in controversies over jurisdiction are willing to accept any reasonable arrangement arrived at, a number of unions refuse to abide by the decision of an impartial arbitrator and insist narrowly upon their own interpretation of the boundaries of their trade.

"The Executive Council feels called upon to issue to the unions composing this body a solemn note of warning as to the dangers which lie in the continuance of jurisdiction disputes. Many of the unions appear to be more engrossed in the problem of securing new adherents from unions already existing, or to extend the work of their members at the expense of other organizations, than they are in resisting the aggressions of employers, or securing higher wages, shorter hours, and better conditions of work."

Since that time, several important jurisdictional fights have been settled, but there are yet some irritating cases, especially when capital is tied up while two unions, so completely organized as to monopolize the craft, battle as to which shall do the work.

The contest between autonomists and industrialists has been a menace to organized labor. The autonomists would organize each craft in national unions. The industrialists would organize in one body all the craftsmen engaged in a single industry, which method proved a failure in the case of the Knights of Labor. Socialists and socialist writers have thought that they saw in this contest a possible wedge to split in twain the American Federation of Labor, and with that motive have urged industrialism with vehemence. But this controversy is adjusting itself in accordance with special and local conditions.

The boycott, the union shop and the sympathetic strike are targets for the shafts of the enemies of unionism. These are questions that are in the process of solution through the evolution of experience. For instance, the boycott ranges from the "white list" of the Consumers' League, composed in part of wealthy society women, which is a negative blacklist, to such extremes as the organized persecution of a physician who ministers to the needs of a dying non-union man, or of the druggist who sells the doctor medicine, or such as parading with a denunciatory banner before a grocery that offers for sale a brand of soap whose wrapper was printed in a non-union shop. Somewhere between these extremes lies the freedom of action that may be justified by its motive. The courts are progressing toward a determination as to how far it is legal to make effective a force that is recognized wherever men associate together for a common object.

But the most perilous internal weakness of organized labor is the apathy of the mass. That is a peril that must be met and overcome if unionism is to endure the stress of concentrated assault or to resist insidious disintegration. The one obvious process of overcoming that apathy, with its evil results, is education. That is necessarily a slow process, demanding patience and persistence on the part of those who teach and awakened interest and faithful attention on the part of the taught. These are the very qualities essential to the life of any democratic movement; and in its development, unionism is industrial democracy.

Organized labor is doing much on its own account to remove its weakness of apathy. There are indications that the number is increasing of those who work for the cause, not spasmodically, or only in times of excitement, but steadily, faithfully, throughout the year. When a question was submitted to the referendum of the International Typographical Union, four years ago, the returns showed that only one member in four in the New York local voted. But in another referendum this year, over 30,000 votes out of a membership of 42,000 were cast. This showing is the more encouraging, because it is more difficult to poll such a vote in a large city than in a smaller community. The cigar-makers' union shows a similar increase in the active participation of its members in its affairs. This participation is encouraged by the development of benefit funds, which stimulate individual interest. It is also true, as a general proposition, that the greatest advance in overcoming apathy is made in the skilled crafts. The more unskilled the calling, the greater the need of education and the greater the difficulty of stimulating ambition among the workers.

That the vital importance of its own education is realized by unionism is shown by the adoption of the following resolution at the last convention of the American Federation of Labor:

"Whereas, it is evident that this Nation is destined to take the lead in this grand struggle for better conditions and higher culture; therefore, be it

"Resolved, That we hereby recommend to all organizations affiliated with the American Federation of Labor to have their members study the economic conditions; to have lectures upon these subjects in their lodge rooms, homes, and in meetings set apart for this purpose, and to do everything in their power for the enlightenment and intellectual advancement of the proletariat."

There are other evidences that the unions appreciate the necessity and are gaining the advantage of education. The official periodicals of the railway brotherhoods contain technical articles upon the practical work of engineers, firemen and trainmen. The same statement is true of the stationary engineers' publication, and of the journals of the building trades and of other mechanical callings. Many of these articles are illustrated by diagrams and are sufficiently lucid and simple to interest the lay reader. Moreover, the constant discussion of various phases of the labor question in these and other publications can not fail to enlighten the mass of their readers upon social and economic questions.

An example that merits imitation is that of the International Union of Steam Engineers, that conducts a regular winter course of lectures in New York City. The official journal of that union states: "The prime object of these monthly lectures is to educate our men in all the latest electrical and mechanical devices, so as to fit them to perform their duties in the most efficient manner. It is also our desire to teach the employer that a union engineer, while asking for the eight-hour day and the prevailing rate of wages, wants to give in return a class of service of which the non-union engineer is incapable." That is an illustrative method of how to win the "closed shop" through superior union merit; and it is a practical method also of substituting interest for apathy in the membership.

The organized laundry workers of Chicago have arranged a course of lectures this winter, covering a wide range of subjects. Many of these lectures, like those delivered in the evenings in some of the public schools in the larger cities, are illustrated with stereopticon views. The lectures are so arranged as to stimulate systematic reading at home. The legislation authorizing this use of public school buildings received the earnest support of organized labor.

Other efforts at education aim to encourage the reading of papers and the conduct of debates upon the social and industrial topics at the regular meetings of local unions. This is a movement that the labor press generally favors, and it deserves to receive the approval of all friends of organized labor. The more advanced members of a local union have in this method an opportunity for the guidance of the more backward. It is method of self-help that, properly directed, must result in mental development and in improving the capacity of the mass. It is a method that should go far to meet the cynical assumption that the average wage-earner will abuse the additional leisure that a shorter work-day would grant.

Another force at work for moral education among the unions is their machinery for discipline. Almost every offense for which labor organization provides a penalty is an offense against morality. Its prohibitions are directed against disorderly conduct; intemperance; fraud; non-payment of debts; untruthfulness. The trials of such offenses, especially where there is an appeal from the decision of a local union to a higher body, should afford good parliamentary practice.

Thus do we see that, more or less unconsciously, organized labor is striving to overcome its most dangerous weakness through education and through the establishment of systems of benefits. It is the task of education, as endless as the generations, that organized labor should not be left to perform alone. Labor has had to struggle upward, not only alone and unaided, but through centuries of opposition, even of persecution. But, although its progress has been impeded, it has now reached a point where it is receiving the helping hand of those who realize that the betterment of labor is the betterment of the entire social structure.

As Edgar Gardner Murphy has well said: "The problems of labor and capital, like the problems of science and religion, yield to no precise formulæ; they are problems of life, persistent and irreducible. And yet they are subject to approximate adjustments, increasingly righteous, intelligent and effective, and yielding an increasing measure of social peace, of industrial co-operation; of individual freedom and happiness. . . . Toward the establishment of such a working adjustment of any national problem, it is well to labor, in order that the problems of American life may become the occasions of a keener and more widely distributed sense of social obligation, a larger and saner political temper, a purer civic devotion, rather than the occasions of national demoralization."

PRESIDENT GOMPERS' MESSAGE.

(Concluded from page 4.)

willingness to accumulate funds in the unions, the spirit of fraternity and solidarity, will bring their own reward and the recognition not only of employers, but of the world. It may be safely asserted that as a rule, in our time, those who have no power to insist upon and maintain their rights have no rights to maintain."

Of the advantage of trade agreements, Mr. Gompers said:

"The division and subdivision of labor and its specialization, brought about by inventions of machines and new tools of labor, have robbed workmen of their power of individual freedom of contract with their employers. Their only opportunity for anything like fair or advantageous terms under which to sell their labor is in associating themselves with their fellow workmen in making a collective bargain, a working agreement; in other words, a union and a contract by the union with employers for their labor and the conditions under which it shall be sold."

He thus stated the attitude of organized labor toward international peace:

"True to the highest and best conception of human life the trade-union movement, from its first inception, has been opposed to war. It recognizes that though others may fall, the brunt of war is borne by the working people; not only upon the battlefield itself, but the burdens thereafter which war entails. We cannot be indifferent to, restrain our feeling of horror at, nor withhold our sympathies from, the slaughtered thousands of human beings, even in the far east, regardless of the country toward which our predilections lie.

"International wars have become so destructive of human life and property that the world is shocked from centre to circumference at the holocausts now witnessed in battle. While it may not be a practical proposition to ask for immediate disarmament of all countries, the time and the intelligence of our peoples surely demand that the extraordinary increase in the armed naval and military forces be limited and restricted rather than expanded and extended. We welcomed the establishment of the International Court of Arbitration at The Hague. We recognize that in the last analysis, and in order to prevent any reaction that may lead to greater and more repeated wars and bloodshed, the success for international peace by arbitration must come from higher intelligence and a better conception of the sacredness of human life. Out of these well-springs will flow that kindred and humane spirit that will recognize the best maintenance of our own rights by conserving the rights of others. In the broad domain of human activity there is no force so potent and which will be so powerful to establish and maintain international peace and human brotherhood as the fraternization of the workers of the world in the international labor movement."

The report of the Secretary, Frank Morrison, contained a statement of the numerical progress of the organization that was a surprise to those who had assumed that adverse industrial conditions had lessened its membership. The report said:

"The growth of the American Federation of Labor has been phenomenal; particularly so in many localities. Where organizations spring up within a few months, it must be expected that in adjusting the members into unions, the membership must decrease somewhat from the highwater mark which it reached during the time that the organization wave held sway. . . . My report last year showed an average membership of 1,465,800, while the average membership this year is 1,676,200, clear gain of 210,400. A remarkable increase, when you consider the number of strikes that have taken place, and the organized effort of the citizens' alliances to retard organization and disrupt unions now in existence."

The total receipts were $307,009; expenses, $203,991, leaving a balance on hand of $103,018.

The 109 international organizations composing the American Federation of Labor reported 1,806 strikes, involving 245,174, and costing $2,860,620. The report asserts that these strikes benefitted 121,340 persons and failed to benefit 18,829.

Sixty-six of these international organizations reported payments for death benefits, death benefits to members' widows, sick benefits, traveling benefits, tool insurance, and unemployed benefits, amounting to $1,739,796.

National Civic Federation

MONTHLY REVIEW

VOL. I. No. 10 NEW YORK, JANUARY 1, 1905 TEN CENTS

AN HISTORIC GATHERING TO PROMOTE INDUSTRIAL PEACE.

THE THEME OF AN ASSEMBLY REPRESENTATIVE OF CAPITAL, LABOR, LETTERS, SCIENCE, PRESS, BAR, PLATFORM AND CHURCH.

An event of such character and of such promise of benefit to industry and all society as to make it of high historical significance was the annual dinner of the National Civic Federation, in the Park Avenue Hotel, New York City, on the evening of December 15. The striking characteristic of the gathering was its comprehensive democracy. Its vibrant keynote was that of confidence in progress toward industrial peace. Its democracy was illustrated in the composition of the assembly. Both the presiding officer, Samuel Gompers, the head of the largest labor organization in the world, and August Belmont, the capitalist and employer, whose election to succeed the lamented Marcus A. Hanna as President of the Civic Federation was warmly supported by its labor element, pointed out that in no other country in the world could such a gathering be brought together. Only the democracy of American institutions made possible the commingling in unconscious equality and in conscious co-operation for a common purpose representatives of billions of capital, of millions of wage-earners, of scholarship and letters, of the bar, the press, the platform and the church. The list of speakers is a catalogue of active workers for better relations between capital and labor in the United States. The utterances of men eminent in widely different fields of thought and experience concurred in confidence that the era of industrial peace, with all that it implies for national welfare, is not a dream, but can in a measure be realized. The significance of such

ANNUAL DINNER OF THE NATIONAL CIVIC FEDERATION.

a conviction shared by such a constituency is tremendous. Its importance cannot be exaggerated.

It was in itself an impressive spectacle to behold this aggregation of capital and enterprise, labor and thrift, learning and literature, presided over by the President of the American Federation of Labor. Democracy was literally in the chair. It was significant of the prestige which this movement for industrial peace has attained, that the President of the United States should commend in virile terms the work of the organization and express ardent hope for its continued and wider success. Happily appropriate was the President's heartfelt tribute to the patriotism and mentality of the late Senator Hanna, who had made the realization of the purpose of the National Civic Federation the highest aspiration of his life. The modest dignity with which August Belmont, in accepting his unanimous election to its presidency, pledged his "best effort"; and the experience of the other officers who are to uphold his hands, are signally auspicious. Andrew Carnegie, who had shown his interest in the organization by coming from a sick bed to the meeting of the Executive Committee during the day, made a notable contribution. His address was replete with shrewd and philanthropic wisdom garnered in a lifetime of experience as one of the largest employers of labor in the world.

THEODORE ROOSEVELT
PRESIDENT OF THE UNITED STATES.

The record of this historic evening is herewith presented verbatim:

Samuel B. Gompers, 1st Vice-President, in calling the meeting to order at the close of the dinner, said:

"I do not know that I can open any remarks that I may desire to make, or that the duty devolves upon me of making, or that I may take pleasure in making, better than to address you as 'fellow-Americans.' On behalf of the National Civic Federation, permit me to bid you a hearty welcome around this festive board. There are a number of gentlemen with us this evening whom, I am sure, you will be much more interested in hearing than you would be in hearing me discuss anything I could say to you to-night. But I feel confident that you would not permit me, in the capacity of acting Chairman and Toastmaster this evening, to take my seat without a few observations.

"Let me say to you this, then, my friends, that I am deeply impressed, as no doubt you all are, at this splendid gathering here tonight. It is doubtful in my mind whether a gathering of this character, with the types of men that are represented round this festive board to-night, could be brought together in any other country on earth. (Applause.) Men in all the proféssions, men representing the public, men in public office, men high in the churches of our country, great captains of industry and business and of finance, and men of labor,—all are assembled here in social and intellectual communion. Many of you have traveled more than a thousand miles,—busy business men, busy labor men,—to be here and mingle with the men of affairs of America.

"A few months ago a number of foreign gentlemen called upon me at my office at Washington. They were sent here by their respective governments to make inquiries into the industrial conditions of our country; incidentally, also, to make investigations into the National Civic Federation, its work and its methods. They asked me how they could institute organizations of a similar character in their own countries. And inquiries of this character are frequently made. My answer was this: that it is not an easy matter to form an association such as this. It was not brought about in a day; it was a matter of growth and development, not only in industry, but in intelligence; that it was not only these, but it was the outgrowth of the possibilities of the institutions of our country. (Applause.)

"Men of capital, men of large wealth, employers of large numbers of men, recognize in the National Civic Féderation an honest effort to arrive at just results. (Applause.) The representatives of labor recognize in the National Civic Federation an honest effort to attain just results, and to accord fairness and honorable conditions to all. (Applause.) Before a National Civic Federation was possible in our country, it was just as essential that the contests and contention should have occurred in our industries as it seems to be one of the essentials for infantile growth into youth and manhood that the child should fall and stumble; and the growths and the falls and our contentions have resulted in both sides having a higher regard and a more mutual respect for each other.

"In other countries, the employers of labor have become accustomed to look upon the workmen, not only as their financial inferiors, but as their social and political inferiors. (Cries of 'No! No!') My friends, I do not know that I ought to allow that to interrupt my train of thought, but I will, for a minute, to demonstrate the truth of what I say, even in England. England is a country, among other countries, in which the workmen have evolved from slavery to serfdom and wage labor, and the traditions and legends of old are not yet dead, even in free England. The workmen, on the other hand, with the history and the traditions of the past, have not yet been able to free themselves from their mental state of looking up to their employer. In the United States, with our Republic, theoretically, if you please, yet declaring that all men are born free and equal, the workmen have been fed upon that declaration and believe it. (Applause.) In becoming part of, and associated with, this National Civic Federation, no employer, no workman, surrenders his right or his independence. It is, however, an effort on the part of the representatives of employers, meeting with the representatives of labor, and in council with representatives of the public. These come together and, as my friend Marks has so often and appropriately stated, meet around the round table where men do not sit opposite each other. Men do not occupy opposite seats, but they are all round the table, and we discuss and endeavor to find a way out of the difficulties and the problems by which we are confronted, and a solution of this great labor problem,—the problem of the age; aye, the problem of the ages,—with which all former problems in the history of men sink into comparative insignificance. We do not undertake to solve, nor do we imagine that it is possible for us to solve, this labor problem by our National Civic Federation. We realize that, as we meet and endeavor to solve the problems of today, we shall be confronted with new problems to-morrow, and to-morrow, and to-morrow's morrow; but that each problem solved makes us jointly better qualified to meet and to solve the new problems as they daily arise. (Applause.)

"There are a number of men whose hearts yearn for a solution of this great problem, with all the difficulties, and something of the dissensions and disturbances that arise, and that often are incidental thereto; but the men who have laid the foundations of this National Civic Federation, and have been constantly and intimately associated with every effort, know that we do not undertake too much. We realize that any effort to undertake too much, to realize too much, to accomplish too much, will simply lead us into dismal and lamentable failure. We try to be of some assistance to our fellow-men. (Applause.) We know that if an employer of labor, who may have heretofore looked with suspicion upon any organized or associated effort of the working-people, will come to know our men in the labor movement better, he will not have so profound a feeling of hostility and antagonism to them. We feel, and know, that as we have the opportunity of meeting the representatives of the employers, face to face, discussing with them the great questions which interest us and the great public,—we know that the employers are not such modern monsters as they are often painted. (Applause.) We come to look upon each other as human beings, as men with strength of character, with manhood, and integrity, and faith, and an honest purpose to serve our fellows; and when men meet under such circumstances, it cannot but prove to the advantage of all, not only of our day, but of days to come. (Applause.) We are building day by day.

"I welcome,—and when I say 'I,' in this sense, I speak advisedly for the representatives of organized labor,—we welcome the associations of employers. We believe that in modern industries, and under modern industrial conditions, the best results can be and are achieved by associated efforts of employers and organized efforts of the wage-earners. There has been this difference between the associations of employers. Those who, for instance, will brook no interference whatsoever, will regard every overture for consideration, every attempt for advancement, every objection to deterioration, as an effort to be stifled, and who will undertake or attempt to undertake, in our day, to deal with organized workmen or with workmen as if we were living in the medieval ages when a man applied himself to his work with the commonest tools and by hand labor;—on the other hand, the associations of employers who recognize modern industrial conditions and developments as they have come to be in our age, and who recognize that the best interests of all are served by conciliation and agreement.

"The National Civic Federation has done much to cultivate this idea. It has done much to polish down the rough edges of bitterness and antagonism of both sides, and, as I said at the outset, it has made possible this large gathering of representative men in all the walks and professions in our country, around a festive board such as this is to-night.

"I shall not detain you further with any remarks, but I have been asked to read to you to-night the letter of President Roosevelt, which was read to the meeting this morning. (Applause.) And, since the letter is equally addressed to the participants at this dinner as it is to those who participated in the conference to-day, it is wholly applicable."

Mr. Gompers then read the letter of President Roosevelt, as follows:

"White House, Washington, D. C.,
"Dec. 14, 1904.

"Mr. Samuel Gompers, 1st Vice-President National Civic Federation, New York City:

"I greatly regret that my duties here do not admit my attending the annual meeting of the National Civic Federation which will be held in New York City on Thursday the 15th inst. But though I cannot take part in the conference or be present at the dinner in connection therewith, I assure you that I am in hearty accord and sympathy with the purposes of the National Civic Federation in its effort for the establishment of 'more rightful relations between employers and employes.' It is a movement so praiseworthy and so thoroughly American in conception that it should as a matter of course receive the earnest support of all good citizens who are awake to the vital needs of our nation.

"Views upon economic and sociological problems often differ. There can be, however, no division of opinion that the highest aim of all should be toward establishing on an ever closer basis of mutual respect and friendship the relations between employers and workmen.

"The men associated in the National Civic Federation have already done much in the direction of settling labor difficulties on a basis of conciliation and just dealing. Among those most prominent in this work and largely and intimately associated with all your work was the late Marcus A. Hanna, President of the National Civic Federation, a large employer of labor, a man of extraordinary force of character and great mental strength, who devoted much of his time and efforts to the material improvement of the wage-workers, not only without injury to employers, but to their marked benefit, as well as to the benefit of the people generally. When he attended the last meeting of your body his condition was such that a less consideration of the interests of others would have prompted him to stay away in the interests of his own life and health. But when he saw what he deemed a high duty he never paid any heed to his own physical welfare.

"You are about to elect a President to fill the vacancy caused by his death, and I am sure your wise judgment will enable you to choose some man able to carry on in his spirit and with his power the great work of your association.

"Again permit me to assure you of my entire sympathy with your organization, which has done so much, and which if rightly conducted will, I am confident, achieve so much more in the interests of the people of our common country.

(Signed) "THEODORE ROOSEVELT."

At the conclusion of the reading of the letter, three cheers were given for President Roosevelt.

The Chairman:—Gentlemen: This morning, attending our Executive Committee, was Mr. Andrew Carnegie. I am informed he is rather indisposed this evening and is unable to be with us. I am sure that you share the regret we feel at his enforced absence, and trust that his health may be improved and his life spared for many years more of the useful and good work with which his name is associated. Mr. Carnegie was invited to address you this evening. He prepared his address, and I now have the pleasure of presenting to you Mr. Ralph M. Easley, Chairman of the Executive Council, who will read Mr. Carnegie's address." (Applause.)

Mr. Easley read the following address by Mr. Carnegie:

Mr. Carnegie:—"I have been furnished with an admirable text,—'Industrial Peace.' This is the day of Peaceful Arbitration Treaties among Nations to promote 'International Peace,'—a beneficent change, even although these agreements reserve two kinds of disputes for the arbitrament of war in the last resort.

"We should always remember with satisfaction that peace reigns in six-sevenths of the industrial world. There are only seven out of twenty-two millions engaged in gainful pursuits, in mechanical and manufacturing occupations. Now, we hear nothing of war in the agricultural branch, which of itself has more than ten millions of workers. The farmer and his farm-hands co-operate peacefully, and their relations are satisfactory, as we safely infer from the absence of quarrel between them. In domestic service, comprising five and one-half millions, all is peace; perhaps in this department the relations of employer and employed are most satisfactory of all. How very few are the homes with servants in which we do not find several old retainers, old nurses or old butlers, old coachmen, old gardeners, who pass their old age in comfort as part of the household and valued friends.

"These facts lead us to the cause of much of the tension and strife found in the manufacturing and mechanical departments. It rests just here: the former bring in the personal equation, and into the latter nowadays that scarcely enters. It is these personal relations, the knowledge of the virtues of the employer and employed revealed to each other, creating mutual regard, that establish the reign of peace in agricultural and domestic service.

"Small manufacturers and contractors, employing each a few men, rarely have trouble with each other. Each man knows the qualities of the employer and the employer knows his men. Naturally they become interested in each other, and mutual esteem, often ripening to affection, ensures not only peace but good-will. Eliminating the class of small employers, there remain out of the seven millions engaged in manufacturing and mechanical pursuits, probably not more than three million of the seven, from whom the blessings of peace are often swept away by industrial war. That is, out of twenty-two millions of workers, six-sevenths may be assumed to have industrial peace. Only one-seventh employed in huge numbers at the large works or mines are exposed to successive and disastrous outbursts of war, and this chiefly for the reason that employers and employes are strangers to each others' good qualities. It is, therefore, to this class,—employers equally with employes, we of the Civic Federation require to devote most of our thoughts and efforts. I am persuaded that quarrels arise quite as often from the employer's ignorance of the fine qualities of his employes as from ignorance of the workmen of the good qualities of their employers.

"As far as the largest manufactories and mines are concerned, I think the great corporation engaged in a dispute with its men makes a mistake if it adopt the policy, or even consider it, of running the works with new men. First, the best workmen are not idle, and to employ the only class that can be obtained is to lay the foundation of serious future trouble. It does not pay to lose a body of excellent workmen and sober, respectable men, nor to employ the class of workmen whose services can be obtained to fill their places. There is another consideration of much weight. Just in proportion that the workman is earnest and efficient in his pride in his work, he feels that the tools he operates or the furnace he works are in a sense part of himself. He has a personal interest in them and in his job. To compel him to stand by and see an outsider,—almost sure to be his inferior both as workman and as man,—take his place, is to subject him to a trial he should be spared. That the support of his wife and children depends upon his labor, of which he is deprived by another, is the most excruciating thought of all. This is a trial to which no workman should be subjected.

"Even when the employer succeeds in running the work with new men, his victory is really a defeat He will ultimately lose more by the change than he would have lost had he patiently awaited a settlement with his own men. The fact that there are in any works thousands of men who began there in youth and are now middle-aged, all proud of the works and fond of their owners, is the best preservative of peace and successful operation. It is such works that break records.

"If, in case of a strike, the employer promptly informed his men that they need have no apprehension about their jobs, that he would not have any but his own men and knew that he could not get such men as they, and therefore would wait for them until their unfortunate differences were settled, all would soon be well. I think employers should make this an invariable rule,—never to employ new men in case of a strike, but to wait patiently for the old men.

"In special branches this policy is impossible, such as in street and other railways and wherever the daily wants of the public are concerned. No doubt new men in extreme cases must be employed, but it is a sad necessity, to be avoided whenever possible. In these cases, public sentiment plays a potent part and hastens a settlement.

"We have another branch to deal with, much in evidence in New York. I am told that a contractor building a residence here employs men from no less than thirty-eight trade-unions. In recent years one or more of these have been constantly at war. Seldom are the thirty-eight all enjoying industrial peace. Saddest of all sights, it is often against each other,—union against union,—that war is waged. Union fighting union must surely give the great fiend exhilarating rapture.

"I have no personal experience in this matter, but such information as I have been able to acquire from

AUGUST BELMONT,
President National Civic Federation.

CORNELIUS N. BLISS,
Treasurer National Civic Federation.

SAMUEL GOMPERS,
1st Vice-President National Civic Federation.

OSCAR S. STRAUS,
2d Vice-President National Civic Federation.

some fair-minded employers is to the effect that the fair, competent and quiet workmen do not yet give proper attention to the management of their unions, and that, consequently, these have been hitherto left to the extreme men. This is a stage which organized labor always has to meet, but it often passes that stage, and as the necessity for prudent action is realized, the moderate, open-minded and fair men finally obtain control. In organizations like the Locomotive Brotherhood and other unions of railroad men, we have proof that there is evolved a safe, conservative, fair management, which renders strikes a very rare occurrence indeed. It is not the able, educated workman that favors demands or violent action, but the

ANDREW CARNEGIE,
Capitalist.

ignorant, and just as men become intelligent, there will be greater harmony.

"It were idle to expect that differences between buyer and seller of labor will not arise, for these characterize every kind of exchange. It is naught, sayeth the buyer. It is invaluable, says the seller; and in one point of view the workman sells labor and the employer buys. It is wholesome that capital should be made to pay well for labor, and to pay very high for it when profits are high, and it is inevitable that wages will fall when profits fall, so that we must expect, and not be alarmed at, repeated demands and repeated rejections from both employers and employes from time to time. These are healthy signs. What the Civic Federation should aim at is that strikes or lock-outs should be prevented, and for these I can see no cure so effective as a trade agreement providing for arbitration, after every effort has been exhausted to settle the difference by the employer and his men themselves, as friends co-operating in a vast enterprise to whose success both must contribute, and in the prosecution of which capital and labor are not foes but allies.

"I would not call these conferences ended between employers and employes until not one ray of hope existed, for employer and employed agreeing between themselves is the best proof of mutual respect, esteem, yes, and of regard,—surest foundation of all upon which any enterprise can rest. The employer who does not estimate the cordial co-operation of employes, because their hearts are with him, as worth a very considerable advance in wages does not share my opinion.

"Gentlemen, the most cheering feature in the relations of capital and labor is that there seems a law at work which rejects the extreme men of both employers and employes and slowly evolves the reign of the fair-minded element which continually makes for industrial peace. The mission of our Federation is to bring these together in friendly conference and prove to them that there are always two sides to all disputes, and also many kindred virtues and an earnest desire for harmony upon both sides; that there are fair employers as there are fair workmen, and that it is a bad day for both capital and labor when they fail to settle themselves peacefully any dispute that arises between them."

The Chairman read the following telegram from Chauncey H. Castle, President of the Stove Founders' National Defense Association:

"Your association is accomplishing great things by nearly ideal methods. I regret that I cannot attend."

The Chairman read also the following letter from the Rev. Washington Gladden:

"Columbus, Ohio, Dec. 12, 1904.

"Mr. R. M. Easley, Chairman Executive Council, National Civic Federation:

"I am very sorry that it will be impossible for me to attend the reception and dinner of the 15th inst. To meet the distinguished men whom you announce, and to hear what they will have to say, would be a great gratification.

"From the abuse which extremists and destructionists on both sides are heaping upon the Civic Federation, I judge that it must be doing some good work for industrial peace. There are, it must be confessed, a good many people in this country who do not want industrial peace; who will be satisfied with nothing less than the subjugation of those with whom they find themselves at variance. There is an element among the workingmen of whom this is true; and there are, I am sorry to say, quite a number of employers who are so unjust and unfair that they are ready to deny to their employes the liberty they claim for themselves. I trust that against both these contending tyrannies the counsels of the men of good will may ultimately prevail, and I hope that what is done at your supper may have the effect to make the Christmas bells tell a little more clearly of Peace on Earth.

"Very truly yours,
(Signed) "WASHINGTON GLADDEN."

The Chairman:—"To-day I was informed that I made a very eloquent presentation and argument and urgent appeal to our reverend friend, Archbishop Ireland, and found, after I had concluded my address, that he was not present. However, he is here with us to-night in the flesh and in the spirit, and I ask our friend, Archbishop Ireland, to address this gathering now."

Right Reverend Archbishop Ireland:—"I believe I can, in all truth, address you all as fellow-workers and fellow-Americans. Upon those two titles I would willingly build arguments that would lead to a pacific settlement of all the difficulties arising between labor and capital. I have supreme faith in America—(applause),—in her institutions; in the spirit which her institutions create and foster; I have supreme faith that those problems that can be solved by men, will be solved; and if any social question cannot be solved and is not to be solved in America, I despair of its solution anywhere.

"Fellow-workers,—we are all fellow-workers. I have contempt for a man who does not work, who does not believe that his first duty here on earth is to do something for the general good. (Applause.) It matters not what be the precise nature of the work: the important thing is that it be work conducive to the welfare of his fellow-men. It is a maxim of highest philosophy, as well as of highest religion, proclaimed by the great St. Paul, 'If a man does not work, neither shall he eat'; and this formed the truest social philosophy, in theory assuredly, if it were not always carried out into practice, of the old and the mediæval times when it was laid down as a vital principle that a man who owned the property and who lived from his property owned it only in order that he would have greater leisure to serve his fellow-men. We should be all workers. Let it be the work that cleans our streets, let it be the work of him who makes use of his pen for the general information of mankind, let it be the work of him who is seated in the President's chair, or who leads the armies of his country in its de-

FRANCIS L. ROBBINS,
President Pittsburgh Coal Company.

fense. Work because it is work, and because it is serving the general good, is honorable.

"It seems to me that this gathering is an indication, Americans and fellow-workers, that those problems which at times seem to affright people are surely on the road to solution. The two things needed most for the solution of those problems are here made manifest,—intelligence and sympathy for one another. The problems that come before us in the name of capital and labor are the result of a hundred social complications. It is only by serious thought that we can reach the root of the difficulties. It is only by large-mindedness that we can see the trend of difficult problems. Those problems are to be solved mainly through principles, and it takes mind, it takes thought, to study out and investigate those principles.

"To-night we have with us the representatives of thought in America. I salute with very great pleasure the new Department of the National Civic Federation opened to-day: that of Industrial Economics. We have the representatives of the journals and the professors. They are the ones who give thought to all these questions, who study them in all their relations to put them before us in living form.

JOHN MITCHELL,
President United Mine Workers' Union.

I believe supremely in intelligence, and the hope of the day is this: that the humblest laborer to-day is a man of intelligence. We have educated our people; it is largely because they are educated that they see the difficulties under which in the past labor has often suffered. But the same intelligence will lead them on to seek practical remedies for those conditions which they are anxious to remedy. Let us all approach the study of these questions with thought, with calm, dignified thought, and then let us approach them with sympathy for one another. This is the lesson of America: that a man is a man, and manhood in him demands respect. Whoever he is, we should feel a brotherly love for him, and see that all his family is provided for. We should look one another in the face. This is the great result of the National Civic Federation. Were this meeting of to-night multiplied a hundredfold, or a thousandfold, through the country, it would be well for the country. For this is a meeting which brings men of all kinds together, in which the poorest laborer, because he is a man, is received as a brother by the richest employer,—a meeting in which we are all brothers, whatever otherwise be for the moment our social conditions.

"It has been said that this meeting could be with difficulty reproduced in other countries. There is much truth in the statement, and one of the difficulties in other countries is this: that classes are divided one from the other; that in one class men do not know, do not come to another class, do not shake them by the hands, do not look them right into the eyes; and here is where the democracy of America is accomplishing wonders. It has taught us that it is no crime to be poor, and no crime to be rich. It has taught us that property is to be respected, because property is the very life-blood of the individual. It is the output of his own energies, his own talents. The respect for manhood in America has opened the way for us to meet and believe in brotherhood, and in love for one another. When we do come to honor them, and feel that we cannot build up our own interest without building up the interest of the laborers, we are very near victory. We must realize that we live not merely for ourselves, or for our immediate fellows,—we live for our country. We must know that it is our God-given duty to build up the whole social structure, and no country is safe, no country is prosperous, where there is not a livelihood for all. No country is safe where any one class of citizens has a reasonable grievance, a reasonable cause for complaint; so, the more we know one another, the more all those so-called causes of division disappear. Who among the employers, with a heart in him, is not anxious to know that his fellow-American has a comfortable home, and wife and child growing up to the possession of American liberty and American opportunity? (Applause.) And who among the laborers does not understand that his own interest is linked with the talent and the energy of the employer? We all know that society is a complex institution. It is an army:

some must lead, some must follow, and the more intelligence we have, the more we understand this complexity of society. I am very sure that the soldier marches to battle with much more hope and confidence when he knows that he has as a leader an officer who is sympathetic, who is skilled, who watches out for opportunities of victory; and so it is with the representatives of labor. They are not jealous of their employers; they know they must have employers; they know that they must put men in the front to seek out openings for capital; otherwise there would be no industry, no occupation, for the laborer. And when we work together, we all know that there must be safety for our

JOHN IRELAND,
Archbishop, Roman Catholic Church.

earnings, whatever they are. We talk sometimes of capital as belonging to an especial class. Why, I trust there is not a laborer in America who is not a capitalist. I think there are few industrious workingmen who have not an account in the bank. Well, the workman with a bank account is a capitalist, and if he attacks capital in others because, perhaps, he thinks the others have more of it than he has, he attacks by that his own capital. He loses for his own arm, for his own energy, the protection of the law. I mingle much myself with capitalists and the laborers, and sometimes the question is strong, Whither are we drifting in America? Well, from my knowledge of the laborers of America, I have not much fear of the menace of anarchy. (Applause.) I know very well that each laborer wishes protection for his own little cottage, and to feel that his savings belong sacredly to himself and to his family. If there were some danger of this wild socialism, it would come from those who are not industrious, who do not respect themselves; and it is the duty of the employer and the more powerful elements of society to reduce the number of those who own nothing, who have no stake in the country. I know no better solution for all these threats of anarchy or socialism than this: to teach them all to love and revere the Star Spangled Banner. (Applause.) This is a great and blessed country. Those who are employers to-day were themselves employed yesterday. The richest among us, whose name has been applauded,—Andrew Carnegie,—says that the time was when he worked hard for a few dollars. Now, this is the country of opportunity for all. All cannot possibly be in the front, but all may aim at being in the front, and none can say that hard-drawn classifications held them back. We are watched by all the nations of the world; watched with love and watched with fear. We are watched with love by those who cherish the institutions of liberty. There are those who would wish to see America torn to shreds, because America's freedom is a menace to conditions in their countries which they would fain maintain. It is our duty to hold ourselves as exemplars before the whole world. Throughout all nations it is said the one peril of America is the labor question, because there the labor people, having universal suffrage, understanding their power, would be willing to tear down the institutions of America to satisfy their own personal ambitions and greed. We who know the American laborer have no such fear. At the same time capitalist, laborer, writer, minister,—every one,—should feel that one of the great questions of the day is decidedly this of industrial peace, and should bind himself with the best instinct of his soul to its solution.

"Before all else, we are fellow-men, brothers, and fellow-Americans. And with those titles thoroughly understood, and the meaning of them permeating our minds and hearts, we can look up at the flag of our country and rejoice that it is lifted over a great democracy, over a government of the people, by the people, for the people. May that flag ever wave over free men and over happy men and over men whose motto is Peace and Brotherly Love." (Applause.)

The Chairman:—"Gentlemen: The next gentleman who will address us is a man also well known to the people of our country,—aye, to the world,—a great financier, a large employer of labor, one of the employers of labor who, by his assistance and co-operation in agreement with organized labor, made it possible to save a year in the construction of that great engineering work, our Subway of New York. I have the pleasure to present to you the Honorable August Belmont. (Applause.)

Mr. August Belmont:—"Mr. Chairman and Gentlemen: You have called upon me to say something. On the rolls of our Association I am designated an Employer. I take it, therefore, I am expected to speak from that standpoint. Of the thirty years I have been in active business, my association with transportation companies as an executive officer, dated my commission back only fourteen years. I see around me this evening many veterans of great experience, to whose superior wisdom I bow; and recognizing their grasp of affairs and knowledge of conditions, I address you with diffidence from the standpoint of an Employer.

"One idea has impressed me, this evening, more than all others,—the unequalled value of American citizenship. WE must recognize that citizenship is evolution. Its distinctive merit and qualities are the product of social, industrial and political conditions fostered, nurtured and made possible by social, industrial and political institutions which are peculiar and individual to our nation. These find their roots in the principles of democracy; indeed, they are the outward and visible signs of democracy, and, therefore, when revealed in the practical affairs and contacts of life they present in American citizenship a picture *of* life as shown nowhere else in the world. In no other country, I venture to say, would it be possible to bring together in an unrestrained atmosphere of equality, such a company as we find here assembled. Here are the representatives of Scholarship and Science; Capital and Labor; Enterprise and Thrift.

"Our national life, our national character, our national wealth, our national progress, stand as a structure upon what YOU represent. This company typifies the great democratic idea of co-operation between citizens in all walks of life, that in the end the betterment of all society may be attained. In this idea,—the betterment of all society,—is the inspiration of the Civic Federation. It aims to bring together citizens of every vocation,—all who are interested in 'life, liberty, and the pursuit of happiness,' so by a united effort it may be possible to improve the relations between the so-called Employer and Employed. It enlists the support, and I am fully convinced, the enthusiasm of all gathered about these tables to-night, and draws to its banner from distant points, thousands concerned in great and diversified interests.

SAMUEL MATHER,
Great Lakes Shipper.

"It has been well said, 'Blessed is the nation that has no history.' Unfortunately, history is too often the record of war, of turbulence, of disaster. What is most prized in Peace! Statesmen of all nations unceasingly labor to maintain Peace,—Peace with Honor. To that end the Civic Federation labors in the industrial world. It is patent to all, employer and employed that nothing so profits labor and capital as Peace with Honor. 'One of the methods advocated by this organization for the prevention, and when required, the cure, of industrial controversies which threaten a breach of Industrial Peace,—the prolific mother of Misery,—is a Conference having in view *new*, or *revised* trade agreements, and it further stoutly maintains that such trade agreements must be conscientiously lived up to by the signatories. Good faith and honest dealing are the basic principles upon which such trade agreements must rest to be enduring and such contracts must be equally binding upon employer and employed.

"I am glad to testify to the efficacy and efficiency of face to face conferences with honorable employes. I pronounce it a practical method of reaching a common understanding upon points in controversy, from which harmonious agreements are possible; and, if I may refer to my own experience, from such conferences, over controverted points, followed a better understanding and a harmonious

DANIEL J. KEEFE,
President International Longshoremen's Association.

agreement in the conduct of a great public service corporation.

"Brains and Muscle; Money and Material are the essentials of a successful transportation company. There are those who find the ways and means for construction, equipment and operation; those who provide engineering, mechanical and technical skill; and those who furnish labor. Capital, labor and material must lie dormant until utilized by brains and muscle, which, controlled and regulated by executive ability provide the energies essential to the profitable employment of capital and labor.

'In the great business of transportation, human beings can only be conveyed from one place to another by the co-operation of other human beings. Human energy, or labor, therefore, is as essential as steam or electricity. This labor is divided between the executive on one hand, which assumes the responsibility for invested capital, for faithful service, and the regulation of subordinates;—and the great army of employes on the other, who discharge their important duties in their respective functions. These two divisions, representing capital and executive management on one hand, and labor on the other, are bound by a common tie,—the success of the corporation. For success implies the capacity to earn wages and pay for the use of invested capital. From which I mean to say the relations between employer and employe are *reciprocal*.

"Trade agreements, or by whatever name contracts between employer and employed may be designated, should be entered upon in good faith, and maintained by each with scrupulous integrity. The employer, by reason of this contract embarks the capital of the investor, and the employe *his* capital,—namely labor. Each is essential to the other. Neither is independent. From profitable co-operation flow the conditions which convert the desert into a garden, and confer blessings of life, liberty and happiness. Such contracts are binding alike on employers and employed, and they should be so regarded. They may be likened to a promissory note, which involves the credit of the maker and endorser. Employes making contracts for labor should establish their credit by living up to their contracts,—and it goes without saying,—employers must be equally punctilious.

"It is a pleasure to believe that organized labor is learning more and more the lesson that its share of responsibility for a contract is equal to that of capital. The dignity of labor equals the dignity of capital, where labor adheres as strictly as capital must adhere, to the obligations of a trade agreement. I would emphasize to the leaders of organized labor the prime importance, the absolute necessity, of fidelity to contracts. When they have made a collective bargain, it should be impressed upon all workers whom they represent that the individual honor of every man is pledged to abide by the terms and spirit of that contract. When employers feel assured that the making of a contract with organized labor is as reliable as any of the transactions in the business world to which they are accustomed,—as I am glad to learn is becoming more and more the case,—then the trade agreement will carry its own recommendation, as an effective solution of the labor problem.

"Gentlemen,—I thank you for your courtesy and attention." (Applause.)

The Chairman:—"Gentlemen, I desire to divert your attention for a few moments to a formal matter which I think will be agreeable to all here assembled. At our former meeting a committee was appointed, and the number of that committee was augmented by the executive committee meeting today. The committee was entrusted with the important mission of submitting the names of gentlemen for the officers of the National Civic Federation for the coming year. The chairman of that committee is Mr. Franklin MacVeagh of Chicago, and I ask Mr. MacVeagh now, and in the presence of this assemblage, to make a report to this committee." (Applause.)

HENRY PHIPPS,
Director U. S. Steel Corporation.

Mr. Franklin MacVeagh:—"Mr. Chairman: I am directed by your committee on nominations, a committee of twelve, to make their unanimous report, first for the position of President of the National Civic Federation. They have considered this nomination with a complete sense of the very great importance of having just the right man to fill it, and their unanimous nomination for the presidency is Mr. August Belmont." (Applause.)

The Chairman:—"For the moment, we shall enfranchise all those assembled and empower you all to vote."

Mr. McVeagh:—"If you will permit me then, Mr. Chairman, I move the election of Mr. August Belmont."

The motion was seconded by William D. Mahon, President of the Amalgamated Association of Street Railway Employes of America, and by Warren S. Stone, Grand Chief of the International Brotherhood of Locomotive Engineers.

The Chairman:—"It has been moved and seconded that Mr. August Belmont be elected president of the National Civic Federation. I shall ask you gentlemen to vote by rising. All in favor of the nomination will signify by standing."

The motion was unanimously agreed to by a rising vote.

The Chairman:—"I take pleasure in announcing the election of Mr. August Belmont as president of the National Civic Federation for the ensuing year." (Applause.)

President Belmont:—"Gentlemen: This honor has come to me as a great surprise, and the sense of its responsibility I feel very deeply; more so, when I think of my predecessor, the great work which he did, and the position which he occupied with you and throughout the country. I can only say that I will lend to this work my best effort. I do not exaggerate when I say to you that I hardly feel myself capable of filling it in the manner in which I think it should be filled; but it being your desire, I cannot refuse, and I thank you and appreciate the honor gratefully." (Applause.)

Mr. MacVeagh:—"Mr. Chairman, I now report to you the nominations for the remaining positions:

"First Vice-President, Samuel B. Gompers; Second Vice-President, Oscar S. Straus; Chairman Ways and Means Committee, Henry Phipps; Treasurer, Cornelius N. Bliss; Chairman Conciliation Committee, Charles A. Moore; Chairman of Welfare Department, H. H. Vreeland; Chairmen of the Trade Agreement Committee, Francis L. Robbins, John Mitchell; Chairman of the Executive Council, Ralph M. Easley; Secretary, Samuel B. Donnelly.

"Mr. Chairman, I move the election of these gentlemen."

The motion was seconded, and the question being put, the above-named gentlemen were unanimously elected to fill the respective offices.

The Chairman:—"Having disposed of the election, I think I may assume the function for a moment to say to you who are not members of the Executive Committee that you are disenfranchised herewith. (Laughter.)

"We have had gentlemen address us this evening, who have been accustomed to bear great responsibilities and deal in large affairs, men who have shown their capacity, and their faithfulness to duty to their fellow-men. I now have the pleasure of presenting to you one who has had dealings with large affairs, and large interests affecting his fellow-men, one who has proven his worth by his work. I refer to Mr. John Mitchell, President of the United Mine Workers of America." (Applause.)

Mr. John Mitchell:—"Mr. Chairman and Gentlemen: I esteem it a very great privilege to be afforded this opportunity of speaking to you, however briefly, upon the question of the relationship of capitalists and laborers. It has been my fate, or my duty, to take part in many of the disagreements, as well as the agreements, between employers and employes, and because of my experience and because of my observations, in the industrial affairs of our country, I am here.

"I am glad to be a part of this peace movement. (Applause.) I think it must be obvious to every observant person that we have in America a labor question; that in some departments of industry the relationship between these two forces of our society has become strained almost to the breaking point. It must be apparent to every good citizen of our beloved country that there is a duty devolving upon every man who cares for the progress and the perpetuity of this republic that something be done to bring into closer and more harmonious relation these two apparently antagonistic forces.

"I am very glad to be here for another reason. It is just four years ago to-night since the Civic Federation was born. Four years ago to-night a small committee, some six or seven in number, met in the city of Chicago and proposed the formation of a Civic Federation,—proposed a movement that they believed would do something to minimize the labor disturbances, to lessen the number of strikes, and reduce the number of lock-outs. Even the most optimistic among the number who gathered there had no idea that the Civic Federation would grow in influence, that it would prosper as it has done, and that four years later we would meet here with the representative men of every walk of life in America. I say the Civic Federation has done well. Its work, its efforts and its purposes should commend it to every man who cares for industrial peace.

"I sincerely hope that all those who have met with us to-night will do something, however little, to establish peace within the industries of our country. I want to say to you that from my observations and my experience, it requires something more than resolutions; that resolutions, however eloquent, will not settle the labor question. If the labor question is to be settled at all, it must be by men having courage and honest purpose. It must be settled by men who will not stand upon their supposed rights. It will not be settled by men who are unwilling to give credit to the other man for honest purposes and to concede to him what is his just due.

"I am a firm believer in the trade agreement. I have had many years' experience in the coal industry. I want to say to you, gentlemen, that where the representatives of the employer, the coal operator, have met with the representatives of our association, where we have sat down and talked the matter out, where we have reasoned together, we have been able to avert strikes; we have been able to maintain peace, peace not by surrender on the part of capital, not by surrender of the part of labor. There has been no surrender of fundamental rights. We have met and talked it out. We found, gentlemen, it was better to talk for a week than strike for a year. (Applause.)

"I wish to emphasize, if it is necessary, this fact: I do not think that any employer or any workman will accuse me of being afraid to strike or of not striking hard enough when we have to strike; but, gentlemen, there are many methods better than striking. Peace is preferable to strikes, although, as I have stated in these meetings before, I hope the time will never come when the workmen of this country will surrender their right to strike. (Applause.) I hope the time will never come when the employers of labor will surrender their right to close their mines, their mills, or their factories. I believe the best safeguard, the greatest assurance of peace, is our ability to fight. (Applause.) But strikes, lock-outs, black-lists and boycotts should never be resorted to so long as there are other methods of maintaining peace.

"I hope, gentlemen, to live long enough to see the time when we shall understand each other's rights sufficiently well to be willing to concede those rights. I hope to live long enough to see the day when strikes and lock-outs and black-lists and boycotts will be unknown. I believe the Civic Federation, denounced as it is by some, not only capitalists, but laborers, is doing more to establish confidence, to bring into closer and more rightful relations the interests of capital and labor, than any other institution in this country.

"It is growing late, gentlemen; there are a number of other speakers. I thank you for the attention you have given me, and I sincerely hope in closing you will join with the Civic Federation and its Executive Committee in making this the recognized tribunal of peace in the industrial affairs of America." (Applause.)

The Chairman:—"The next gentleman who will address you is one well-known in our own country and the world over, conspicuous in his efforts for international peace and the high science and art of diplomacy, and who is using and has used for a number of years past his high gifts and attainments to contribute much to establish peace in the industrial affairs of America. The gentleman who will address you now is the Honorable Oscar S. Straus." (Applause.)

P. H. MORRISSEY,
Grand Master, Railroad Trainmen.

Hon. Oscar S. Straus:—"Mr. Chairman and Gentlemen: I have only a word to say. We have been engaged in our meetings and in our conferences since half-past ten this morning. I have had occasion to say everything that I ought to say, and I will say very little to-night. The great American who stands very high in my calendar of saints made the wise statement, 'What are all these strifes and struggles about but for larger dishes and bowls of porridge?' He was Roger Williams.

"Our object is to lessen the struggle between man and man and, instead of that struggle, to unite in a struggle against the unrelenting forces of matter. That is the object of our Civic Federation. The object is to teach the man who stands at the head of great employing forces to have a wider conception of the relations of man and man than may be gathered from the size of dividends, and at the same time to teach the labor leader that he has a larger responsibility than may appear to him from the four walls of his workshop,—the responsibility to the community at large. And it is for this reason that we have constituted the Civic Federation, composed of three groups, the one group representing the employers, the other group representing the wage-earners, and the third group representing the general public. And if we can harmonize the interests of these three groups, we have solved the problem of industrial peace.

"We are doing our best in that direction. We have often succeeded in bringing about peace, and there are times when we have lamentably failed. But we ask you to be patient with us. It was only recently that the Civic Federation entertained the members of the Interparliamentary Union, who visited this country for the purpose of international peace, especially those members who were at the same time particularly interested in industrial peace. We conferred together for the purpose of learning from them, and if possible, teaching them, the best methods of preserving industrial peace. I can tell you here that these Parliamentary delegates from the fifteen most enlightened countries in the world, and members of high standing in their Parliaments, were of one accord that they had not discovered a better method to work out this problem than the one that has been evolved by the National Civic Federation. (Applause.) Criticise as you will—and we welcome criticism; find fault as you will,—and we are conscious of committing fault. But when you do criticise, we ask you to give us a better method than this one, which is not entirely satisfactory, the one that we have adopted in the Civic Federation. We are searching for it.

"We have to-day organized a department of scholars, of writers, of the leading contributors to our magazines and newspapers, to help us work out the great problem that we have assumed, and in all modesty we ask them for their co-operation and for their aid, in educating the public,—the laborer and the capitalist, and the general public,—in understanding our work, and in contributing whatever they can in order to throw light upon our path. This is our object and this is our aim, and it is for this that we are groping along. If we could present you to-night the result of a year's work, and you could know the scores of important industrial conflicts that we have peaceably brought to an adjustment, I think

CHARLES W. ELIOT,
President of Harvard University.

you would feel some encouragement with me in the work that we have undertaken. It is only the tragic cases, the cases that resolve themselves into strikes, that make an impression upon the public mind, which does not know the scores of cases that are quietly adjusted by bringing together around our council table leaders of industry and leaders of labor, and looking into each other's eyes and plainly setting forth their grievances and their complaints. It is in this way that we have brought about the preventive methods which in so many cases have avoided serious and important industrial conflicts. This is the part of our work that we cannot make public, because it is very often upon the pledge of silence that we can bring the two sides together; but we have established a platform, a natural platform, that no man who wishes to do justice is afraid to come to. There he will receive equal treatment without conceding anything, or without lessening his position, until he finds he can do so in justice and in agreement and in accord. This is the main work, the work of conciliation, and not, as is generally believed, of arbitration, that the Civic Federation performs.

"Finally I wish to say this. Deeply as I am committed to and, of course, interested in industrial peace, there is no surer guarantee of international peace than contentment among the nations themselves. In other words, industrial peace is one of the greatest guarantees for international peace. (Applause.) In the name of the National Arbitration Conference, that is to assemble to-morrow night at Carnegie Hall for the purpose of making known to our Senators in Congress the deep feeling of the peace-loving people of this great country for international peace, and in order to let the Senators know that the treaties of arbitration that our government has negotiated and is negotiating with the civilized powers of the world, which will soon be laid before them by the President of the United States,—that they will be interpreting the mandate of the peace-loving people of this great country, not only to confirm them, but to confirm them expeditiously. I invite you heartily, most cordially, to be present at that meeting to-morrow night at Carnegie Hall. Mr. Andrew Carnegie is to preside, and our Mayor, Mr. McClellan, is to be the temporary chairman, and distinguished speakers will present the subject to you. I feel entirely justified, Mr. Chairman, in connecting the two subjects together at this great gathering of peace-loving, patriotic citizens, laborers and employers of labor and the representatives of the general public, that with the inspiration of this meeting they will come to the meeting to-morrow night and unite with us in the great work of international peace." (Applause.)

The Chairman:—"The next gentleman who will address us is one who also has been for a number of years entrusted with large affairs connected with an important branch of the railroad industry. Without further ado, I have the pleasure of introducing to you Mr. P. H. Morrissey, the Grand Master of the Brotherhood of Railroad Trainmen." (Applause.)

Mr. P. H. Morrissey:—"Mr. Toastmaster and Gentlemen,—Being notified but a short time prior to the assemblage of this evening that it would devolve upon me to fill a place in the program, I feel somewhat like the colored gentleman who was recently tried in a United States Court. He had been charged with selling liquor without a license. The government had made a pretty strong case against him, and his attorney turned to him and asked him if he cared to go on the witness stand in his own defense. The son of Africa replied: 'Boss, I think I had better remain neutral.' (Laughter.) And so, after the very able addresses to which we have listened, I think I had better remain neutral.

"The organization which I represent is committed to the policies and principles enunciated by the National Civic Federation,—(applause),—viz., conference, conciliation, mediation and arbitration. Mutual conferences between employer and employe, with feelings of confidence that should always be evident, form the very keynote of industrial peace. Organized labor has come to stay. No matter what its errors may have been in the past, no matter whether or not it may have been at times economically and ethically wrong, out of this turbulent past it has evolved into an industrial factor which is recognized by thinkers everywhere, and which fixes its permanency in our industrial life. It must be satisfying to every workman who has identified himself with a labor organization to know that no less a person than the President of all our people so recognized the influential force of association and organization among workingmen, that he saw fit to make it an important part of his last message to Congress and the American people.

"Labor organizations will be approved or disapproved by the press, by the public, by our government, and by the courts, just as they conduct themselves. If they are law-abiding, if they show as respectful a regard for the rights of others as they demand for themselves, they will be recognized; but when they evolve themselves into a force that becomes unlawful, they will be disapproved not only by the law-making bodies of the country and its courts, but by that always present factor known as public sentiment. We of the railroad have in the years of the late past tried the Civic Federation's method of solving these differences, and they have been in the main successful. You have not heard of many strikes on railways in the past ten or twelve years. We had not entirely tried the Mitchell formula of talking the strike idea to death,—(laughter),—but we have met each other face to face, established terms of mutual conference, represented in trade agreements, whether known as contracts, schedules, agreements, memoranda, or in whatever form.

"I am glad, indeed, as a representative of organized labor, to add a hearty endorsement of Mr. Belmont's estimate of the duties of organized labor toward the employers in relation to trade agreements and trade contracts. In years gone by, when organized labor was in a more crude state than it is now, we used to accept all of the advantages that would go with organization in increased wages, shortening of hours, and other helpful conditions, and when a difference arose, it was hard indeed to find the responsible party. When labor was called upon to make good its side of the contract, there was considerable evasion and pleas of expediency. Much sentiment was indulged in, and it got to be a serious question with employers whether or not a labor agreement amounted to anything. But out of that came labor's guarantee that its word was good, that a contract made by it would be kept inviolate, for we realized that any other course meant nothing less than labor's dishonor.

"I do not know of any place where you could find as cosmopolitan a set as is assembled here to-night, unless it might be on an elevated train or on the Pike at St. Louis. The gentlemen who have assembled here this evening, coming from the different walks of life, all have influence in their respective spheres. We sincerely hope and trust that with the guarantees that have been given to you to-night of the purposes and desires of the Civic Federation, it will receive your hearty and unqualified support. We believe that it is one of the forces that make for good in our industrial life. We do not expect that it will prove to be a panacea for all of our industrial ills, but as its principles are extended, and as the things that it stands for become fixed in the public mind, we have no doubt that its influence will spread accordingly. As organized labor forms a section of it, we ask you to treat it for the good it promises. It cannot be questioned but organizations properly conducted are helpful agencies in a country like ours; that any movement that is for the betterment of human kind, that will build men up morally, and teach them the requirements of good citizenship, that will make their labor less oppressive and more remunerative, must surely be for the welfare of the whole people, and as such should receive substantial encouragement." (Applause.)

The Chairman:—"Gentlemen, among those here assembled there is perhaps no one who has been called upon to deal with such large affairs in industry and public life as the gentleman I have in mind. It is true he has not come as a public speaker, but I am sure even a few words from him will be welcomed by you and by us all. I refer to Mr. Henry Phipps, of Pittsburgh—and elsewhere." (Applause.)

Mr. Henry Phipps:—"During the evening I have thought of some of my own experience in business. I remember going out with Mr. Carnegie one afternoon, late in December, to see some of the workmen, and talk over the matter of adjustment of wages for the coming year. One of the men took me aside, and said: 'Now, Mr. Phipps, it seems very hard that in this season of the year, when we ought all to be

WILLIAM D. MAHON,
President Street Railway Employes' Association.

happy, we are most anxious and alarmed. And do you not have the settlements the first of January in order to reduce us in our wages or to keep us from getting better wages?' I told him it was a very fair inquiry, but if he heard the facts of the case, I thought he would not entertain that opinion. I told him the rails were ordered usually in the autumn of the year, and were distributed over some eight months. We bought our ore in the autumn, so they would dig the ore during the winter, and we had to provide money for that. We could not sell our rails unless we knew we had the ore; we could not get the ore unless we had the labor, and we were just as helpless as we could be. He said: 'I never understood it before, Mr. Phipps; I have a better opinion of the employers than I had before.' I only mention this to show how often misapprehension will arise between us when there is really no reason for it. A little explanation will remove it.

"I cannot leave you to-night without expressing the very great gratification I have had in being with you. I cannot help thinking how much nicer it is to be in business to-day than it was when I was a young man. Then it was war. We did not know what was going to happen on a July or January settlement. Now we know there is arbitration, and that there will be peace; that no anger will start up and impulsive action taken. It is real civilization. The other was barbarism. (Applause.) I do not know when my heart has been more touched than at this meeting. I feel that we are really a band of brothers, and I hope we shall each think of the interests of the others as well as ourselves. I thank you very kindly for this opportunity to make these very few remarks, and my heartfelt wishes go out to this gathering." (Applause.)

The Chairman:—"We are all of us more or less eloquent, even those who are supposed to be unable to say anything. We have just had a demonstration of how eloquent one can be. (Applause.) I regret that we cannot sit here in a sort of perpetual session, or take an adjournment and meet some other time. There are a few more gentlemen upon whom I wish to call, and I trust that you will all be enabled to remain with us until the close of the meeting. I take pleasure in presenting to you now a gentleman who is very largely interested in industrial affairs, who has traveled a very great distance to be with us and to spend part of the day and evening with us. I refer to the Hon. James Kilbourne, President of the Kilbourne & Jacobs Manufacturing Company, of Columbus, Ohio." (Applause.)

Mr. James Kilbourne:—"Mr. Toastmaster and Gentlemen,—I am an optimist on the labor question. For more than a third of a century I have been manager of a company between whom and its employes, both union and non-union, there never has existed even the slightest difficulty. When they march together on Labor Day, they carry a banner that has upon it two clasped hands and the words 'Capital

(Continued on page 9.)

MONTHLY REVIEW
OF THE
National Civic Federation
Offices: 281 Fourth Avenue, New York City
RALPH M. EASLEY, Editor

The Editor alone is responsible for any unsigned article or unquoted statement published in THE MONTHLY REVIEW.

Ten Cents per Copy; One Dollar per Year.

The National Civic Federation

OFFICERS.

August Belmont, President.
Samuel Gompers, First Vice-President.
Oscar S. Straus, Second Vice-President.
Henry Phipps, Chairman Ways and Means Committee.
Cornelius N. Bliss, Treasurer.
Charles A. Moore, Chairman Conciliation Committee.
H. H. Vreeland, Chairman Welfare Department.
Francis L. Robbins, } Chairmen Trade Agreement Com-
John Mitchell. } mittee.
Ralph M. Easley, Chairman Executive Council.
Samuel B. Donnelly, Secretary.

EXECUTIVE COMMITTEE.

ON THE PART OF THE PUBLIC.

Grover Cleveland, ex-President of the United States, Princeton, N. J.
Andrew Carnegie, capitalist, New York City.
Cornelius N. Bliss, ex-Secretary of the Interior, New York City.
Oscar S. Straus, member of the Court of Arbitration at The Hague, New York City.
Charles W. Eliot, President Harvard University, Cambridge, Mass.
Archbishop John Ireland, of the Roman Catholic Church, St. Paul, Minn.
Bishop Henry C. Potter, of the Protestant Episcopal Church, New York City.
David R. Francis, President Louisiana Purchase Exposition, St. Louis, Mo.
Isaac N. Seligman, of J. & W. Seligman & Co., New York City.
James Speyer, of Speyer & Co., New York City.
Charles Francis Adams, Publicist, Boston.
John G. Milburn, lawyer, New York City.
V. Everit Macy, capitalist, New York City.
Charles J. Bonaparte, lawyer, Baltimore.
Ralph M. Easley, Chairman Executive Council, New York City.

ON THE PART OF EMPLOYERS.

Henry Phipps, director United States Steel Corporation, New York City.
August Belmont, President Interborough Rapid Transit Company, New York City.
Lucius Tuttle, President Boston & Maine Railroad, Boston.
Frederick P. Fish, President American Bell Telephone Company, Boston.
Francis L. Robbins, President Pittsburgh Coal Company, Pittsburgh.
Henry G. Davis, Coal Operator, Elkins, W. Va.
H. H. Vreeland, President New York City Railway Company, New York City.
Samuel Mather, of Pickands, Mather & Co., Cleveland.
Charles A. Moore, Manning, Maxwell & Moore, New York City.
Franklin MacVeagh, of Franklin MacVeagh & Co., Chicago.
Charles H. Taylor, Jr., President American Newspaper Publishers' Association, Boston.
Dan R. Hanna, of M. A. Hanna & Co., Cleveland.
Marcus M. Marks, President National Association of Clothing Manufacturers, New York City.
Otto M. Eidlitz, Chairman Board of Governors, Building Trades Employers' Association, New York City.
William H. Pfahler, former President National Founders' Association, Philadelphia.

ON THE PART OF WAGE EARNERS.

Samuel Gompers, President American Federation of Labor, Washington.
John Mitchell, President United Mine Workers of America, Indianapolis.
E. E. Clark, Grand Chief Conductor, Order of Railway Conductors, Cedar Rapids, Iowa.
James Duncan, General Secretary Granite Cutters' National Union, Washington.
Daniel J. Keefe, President International Longshoremen, Marine and Transportworkers' Association, Detroit, Mich.
Warren S. Stone, Grand Chief International Brotherhood of Locomotive Engineers.
P. H. Morrissey, Grand Master, Brotherhood Railroad Trainmen, Cleveland.
William D. Mahon, President Amalgamated Association of Street Railway Employes of America, Detroit, Mich.
Theodore J. Shaffer, President Amalgamated Association of Iron, Steel and Tin Workers, Pittsburgh.
J. J. Hannahan, Grand Master Brotherhood Locomotive Firemen, Peoria, Ill.
James O'Connell, President International Association of Machinists, Washington.
John Tobin, General President Boot and Shoe Workers' Union, Boston.
Joseph F. Valentine, President Iron Molders' Union of North America, Cincinnati.
James M. Lynch, President International Typographical Union, Indianapolis.
Dennis A. Hayes, President Glass Bottle Blowers' Association of United States and Canada, Philadelphia.
William Huber, President United Brotherhood of Carpenters and Joiners of America, Indianapolis.

PRESIDENT AUGUST BELMONT.

August Belmont, the new President of the National Civic Federation, has been associated with its work for two years, during which time he has shown his active interest by prompt response, by day and by night, to every request for his aid in putting its principles into practice. He was first attracted to the New York branch through the quiet effectiveness with which it averted a controversy and brought about an agreement with employes at the time the Elevated railroads in New York passed into the ownership of the Interborough Rapid Transit Company. At the semi-annual meeting of the Executive Committee last May, Mr. Belmont accepted the chairmanship of the Ways and Means Committee. Since then, he has had personal experience, during a critical period on the Elevated relating to terms and conditions of employment in the new Subway, of the practical value of conference in adjusting labor difficulties. His attitude throughout that controversy so combined dignified insistence upon the rights of the company with patient discussion of the claims of three national labor organizations, presented by more than a score of representatives, as to command for him the respect and confidence of both capital and wage-earners; while at the same time he showed a keen sense of his official responsibility for the public convenience. It was this happy combination, together with his modest but earnest share in the successful efforts of the National Civic Federation to prevent industrial discord in a number of other highly important cases, that attracted the unanimous support of his name, for President of the organization, of all its three groups. It is significant that his nomination was seconded by two of the national labor leaders with whom, as an employer, he had conferred. Mr. Belmont's speech of acceptance, with its appreciative reference to the high character and standing of his devoted predecessor, is filled with the spirit of quiet and effective executive ability.

FOUR YEARS OF PROGRESS.

A higher and broader conception of its mission was conspicuous throughout the fourth annual meeting of the Executive Committee of the National Civic Federation. All of its proceedings were inspired by this wider view and a determination to put into operation plans to realize larger possibilities. Incidentally, it became evident that there is growing to be a more accurate public understanding of the purposes of this organization. The popular misconception that the sole end of the National Civic Federation was to settle strikes and lock-outs, that it was to be a kind of voluntary tribunal of arbitration, is yielding before the persistent reiteration that arbitration is not one of its functions as a body, although its individual members may upon request act as arbiters; that its ultimate aim is industrial peace; that such an ideal state can only be approached in the great industries through a series of adjustments; that the trade agreement has proved the most practicable method of securing harmonious relations between capital and labor; that, in general terms, the National Civic Federation would examine the underlying causes of industrial conflicts and search for their remedies.

Its definite aim,—the promotion of more rightful relations between employer and employed,—it has become apparent, involves the entire field of industrial economics,—a science so far-reaching as to extend into every department of human life and endeavor, and at the same time so technical as to demand the closest study for the correct ascertainment of facts and the keenest analysis to determine their inter-relations and their interpretation.

The past year has witnessed much work accomplished by the Departments of Trade Agreements and Conciliation and Arbitration in encouraging collective contracts and in avoiding labor troubles. The Department of Welfare Work has been organized, and is in active and practical operation. The reports of these Departments, which appear elsewhere, speak for themselves.

The members of the Executive Committee expressed their confidence that the new Department of Industrial Economics will be a most effective educational agency. Its periodic meetings, which will discuss specific topics, will be reported verbatim in THE MONTHLY REVIEW, and will thus evolve a body of industrial literature of distinctive quality and high value. The participation in the discussion by economists, sociologists, professional writers and speakers and hard-headed men of affairs must bring about a combination of theory and fact that should confirm or modify recognized principles. The membership of this Department is of a character that warrants its high aims.

The proposed Trade Sections, whose task will be to consider the best solution of especial problems relating to the employment of labor in particular industries, will produce definite results through special investigations and conferences. These technical studies may be carried into all of the great industries.

The formation of an International Industrial Committee may have a practical bearing upon the internationalization of great industries and the development of international unions. Oscar S. Straus suggested an association between this movement and the prevalent desire for arbitration treaties when he said: "Industrial peace is one of the greatest guarantees of international peace."

The four years that have passed since the birth of the National Civic Federation have brought to its founders and promoters ample reasons for faith in a future of progressive usefulness. The organization has endured all the strains which both the scoffing and the doubtful predicted. The labor leaders have found that some of their demands have been defeated, and large employers have learned the necessity of concessions, in the various disturbances with which the body has had to deal. Yet each element has adhered to a movement that has survived the period of excessive sentiment as well as of decided reverses, and that is to-day stronger than ever in the confidence and support of the general public.

AN EVENING OF MEMORABLE ADDRESSES.

The speeches delivered at the dinner of the National Civic Federation were worthy of the occasion and of the highly representative gathering to which they were addressed. In their complete form, as presented in this issue of THE MONTHLY REVIEW, they will reach a wider audience. The address of Andrew Carnegie may well rivet the attention of employers everywhere upon his conviction, born of experience, that "the great corporation engaged in dispute with its men makes a mistake if it adopt the policy, or even consider it, of running the works with new men." The reasons he recites for this proposition are at once humane, sympathetic and business-like. In truth there are victories so dearly bought as to be defeats.

The Toastmaster, Samuel Gompers, whose graceful and pertinent introductions served to place the speakers and the hearers upon reciprocally agreeable terms, thus evinced a singular adaptability. He infused the spirit of good cheer, mingled with high philosophy, into a brilliantly democratic social evening with as much tact and readiness as he displays when, as President of the American Federation of Labor, he directs the annual proceedings of the delegated representatives of nearly 2,000,000 organized wage-earners. The retired ironmaster and active philanthropist and the aggressive leader of the largest labor organization of the world, are but two of the striking figures that by turns dominated the profound attention of an unparalleled assembly. An appreciation of that gathering can best be gained by a glance through the list of those who accepted invitations to the dinner. It is an array of names that made inevitable the comment that in no other country in the world would such a gathering be possible. It is remarkable for the variety of successful achievement that it represents.

TWO IMPRESSIVE WITNESSES.

Representing the largest employing corporation of its kind in the world, whose business of mining and transporting fuel extends from the Great Lakes to the Gulf, enlists $135,000,000 of capital and employs 75,000 men, Francis L. Robbins, President of the

Pittsburgh Coal Company, gave the eloquent testimony of facts, at the dinner of the National Civic Federation, in favor of the trade agreement. He cited the agreements of his company with the miners' and the longshoremen's unions as typical contracts between a combination of capital and organized labor, accompanied by a system of profit-sharing, insurance and pensions and productive of peace and prosperity throughout a vast industry and a territory imperial in extent.

Representing the largest labor union in the world, whose membership of half a million delves and toils above and below the surface of nearly every State in the Union, John Mitchell, President of the United Mine Workers of America, matched the testimony of capital with the testimony of labor in favor of the trade agreement. Each of these striking witnesses dwelt upon the necessity of conference as a prelude to agreement, and each recognized good faith and mutual respect as essential to conference. Mr. Mitchell expressed the wish that labor would never surrender its right to strike or employers their right to lock-out; but he put a fundamental trait of human nature into his epigram: "The best safeguard of peace is our ability to fight."

THE CONCILIATION DEPARTMENT.

The report of the Committee on Conciliation, presented by its Chairman, Charles A. Moore, to the Executive Committee of the National Civic Federation, was a striking exhibit of effective prevention of industrial conflicts during the past year. The record is one for congratulation. The work involves such confidences and affects such delicate relations that its publication might impair the future effectiveness of the committee.

AN HISTORIC GATHERING.

(Continued from page 7.)

and Labor.' I believe that fully represents the feeling which has always existed between us, and I know of no reason why, if just consideration is given by one to the other, these relations should not be those of labor and capital everywhere.

"I do not believe at all in this theory of an irrepressible conflict between them. I am happy in the belief, on the contrary, that industrial peace in this country is more nearly at hand than is generally supposed. There will always, doubtless, be differences more or less acute between individual employers and their employes, but such serious and widespread disturbances as have occurred during recent years, threatening the general peace and welfare, will, I believe, in the not distant future, become a thing of the past in this country.

"I also believe that the accomplishment of this result will be largely due to what, in the opinion of many, was the chief cause of the violent disturbances referred to, viz., the organization of labor. Before the time when labor became thoroughly organized, wages and working hours in this country were far from what they should be, and the conditions which then surrounded working men and women would to-day be deemed intolerable. Perfection has not yet been attained,—far from it. Labor will ultimately receive a still larger share of the joint proceeds, and capital will have to content itself with less; but a great advance has been made.

"Organized labor has increased wages to the benefit, not to the injury, of the general public; it has shortened the hours of work, not to the advantage of working men and women alone, but of the community at large; it is fast doing away with child labor, to the ultimate improvement of the race, both physically and morally; it has caused the enactment of laws which make it comparatively safe to work in factory and mine when formerly death was always waiting for its victim; it has, in many of the States, amended the fellow-servant law so that the responsibility for death or injury by accident is placed where it rightly belongs. It has so educated public opinion that it is no longer reputable for one man to buy the labor of another as he would merchandise, at the lowest obtainable price, with no other restriction than the supplying of the means of bare existence; it has, in a hundred ways, improved the conditions of working men and women.

"I say that organized labor has done these things. They would have, perhaps, been done in time without it, but the progress would have been slow and halting, with many a backward step.

"As it is, organized labor, while its work is not completed, and perhaps never will be, has removed or greatly lessened the most serious causes of discontent, and thus made possible an industrial peace which otherwise could not and should not exist. It has also demonstrated to the employer that it is neither wise, profitable, nor safe to defy a public opinion which demands for the workers safe and healthful surroundings and a fair day's wage for a fair day's work.

"In bringing about these results, its methods have not always been commendable; quite the contrary has at times been true. But it is better in the end that disease should be eradicated even by unnecessarily harsh methods. I believe thoroughly that, notwithstanding all the strife and bitterness and injustice that has at times marked the course of organized labor, it has paved the way for an early coming of industrial peace in this country which, but for it would be long delayed.

"That this is so is owing in no small degree to the able, honest, and unselfish leadership of some of its representatives present here to-night. (Applause.) God grant that they may be strong enough and big enough to put aside all personal ambition, all thought of personal aggrandizement, and continue to use the power their position and the devotion of their followers gives them to seek only the right, with charity, and so hasten the end of strife.

"Amongst the obstacles in the way of an early establishment of industrial peace, there are two which seem to me of prime importance, and in speaking of these I may give offense to some of those present. One is the insistence upon the part of some unions for what is commonly known as 'the closed shop.' I know that these unions say that is a misnomer, but it represents the conception by the general public as to what is demanded. It is not my purpose to discuss this matter now, but merely to read the statement of two members of organized labor as reported some time since in the public press, which statements seem to me to breathe the true American spirit and to be unanswerable. One of these is reported to have been made by a member of the Brotherhood of Locomotive Engineers, and the other by Mr. Warren S. Stone, Chief of that Brotherhood, who is present, and can correct the statement if he he is incorrectly reported.

"A representative member of the Brotherhood of Locomotive Engineers is quoted as follows in an interview given to the 'New York Tribune':

> We wish it to be distinctly understood that the Brotherhood of Locomotive Engineers takes the stand that, as our forefathers gave us all equal rights, we have no right to decide that we will not work with non-union men. The Brotherhood of Locomotive Engineers or its members as a body never said that they should work with none but members of the Brotherhood. What we have insisted on, and will always insist on, is that the standard of union wages be observed all along, whether the men be union or non-union men. We hold that a non-union man has as good a right to work as a union man, if he gets the same wages.

"This declaration was supplemented by the following statement by Mr. Warren S. Stone, Grand Chief of the Brotherhood:

> That is true, and it applies not only to the Engineers but also to the four railroad Brotherhoods. In this respect we differ from most of the other trade and labor assemblies. The Constitution of the United States guarantees every man a right to work, and the railroad Brotherhoods have never objected to working with non-union men so long as they were paid union wages and worked under union conditions.

"Now, there is one thing I would like to say right here. In my early manhood I passed a great deal of time in the Hocking Valley, and I saw a great deal of the miners, and was very much interested in their conditions. I made up my mind then, and the conviction has grown with the years, that however it might be elsewhere, so far as the mines were concerned it was better, not only for the miner but for all the operators, that every workman in the mines in this country should be a member of the miners' union.

"The second obstacle in the way of peace to which I referred is the veiled, but in my judgment apparent, purpose of some—not all—of the several employers' associations to disrupt and break up entirely labor organizations. None of them, so far as I know, openly avow such a purpose at this time,—they sometimes, indeed, deny it,—but it is impossible to read their literature and the speeches of those most influential in their organizations without being convinced that such purpose, however concealed for the present, nevertheless exists.

"Any effort in that direction, in my judgment, will be futile, and should be. When united action of the workers is no longer necessary to secure justice, unionism will cease; but that time has not yet arrived. While public opinion is improving and is coming more and more to the laborer's side, while instances multiply of just and kindly relations existing between the employer and the employed, proving by their results the benefits to each of the recognition of the rights of the other, and making in some cases unions unessential; yet in a majority of cases union organization is still necessary in order to secure just wages, and what is of equal, if not greater, importance to American workingmen, the acknowledgment of equal manhood. (Applause.)

'As I said some years ago upon an occasion similar to this, the onward march of labor cannot be permanently prevented. The overwhelming weight of public opinion is on its side, and will be as long as it seeks its rights in lawful ways. Let the laboring man remember that liberty under the form of law is his greatest earthly inheritance; of more importance to him than it is to the rich. Let him be careful, as careful of the rights of others as he is of his own, and in the end he will surely be triumphant, helping the coming of that day, which may God speed, when strikes and lock-outs shall be no more, because all men shall recognize the obligations that pertain to the universal brotherhood of man." (Applause.)

Mr. Chairman:—'I am sure we shall all be interested in hearing a few remarks from a representative of, I think, the largest holding of mining in this or any other country,—a gentleman who believes in trade agreements, and who has done much to help reach the full fruition of the idea for which the National Civic Federation stands. I refer to Mr. Francis L. Robbins, President of the Pittsburgh Coal Company." (Applause.)

Mr. Francis L. Robbins:—"Mr. Chairman and Gentlemen: I am not going to attempt at this late hour to make a speech, and yet if I did not say something it might be misunderstood. Jointly with Mr. Mitchell, as Chairman of the Joint Trade Agreement Committee, of the National Civic Federation, and having represented for a great many years the mining industry on the part of the operators, as he has upon the part of the miners, and therefore speaking not as a mere theorist but from actual practice and actual knowledge, I believe that the interests of capital and labor are reciprocal, and that they are best served by combinations of capital and by organizations of labor. I believe so, because I think it is far more advantageous, far more profitable to deal with the leaders of organized labor than with the rank and file. Leadership tends to conservatism. It makes men think, and because of that, because of the conservatism of the leaders who have preceded Mr. Mitchell,—and none of them was his superior,—the joint trade agreement between operators and miners stands to-day as the most representative trade agreement of this or any other country. I can bear witness to the fairness with which we have met Mr. Mitchell and his colleagues. The interests have been very large. At times there has been a great tension, but at no time was there ever an intimation on the part of either side that the other was not desirous of doing what, in his interest, he felt represented his rights.

"There is another organization which we meet in like manner,—the 'Longshoremen's union, of which Mr. Keefe is the worthy president. In each organization, by unanimous vote, it has been declared that any agreement that was reached should be inviolate, and that under no pretext whatever should any sympathetic strike occur.

"As far as our companies are concerned, the old saying that corporations have no souls is certainly not true, because we have endeavored to and have introduced the profit-sharing system with our employes, which has been most favorably received and has been of great benefit. We have also aided in a death and accident association, in which the company and the men jointly provide for death and accident funds. We are also jointly building up a pension fund, so that to-day in our great army of employes, stretching from Pittsburgh to New Orleans, in every port, and on nearly every craft upon the river, and stretching over all the Great Lakes and in every important port of all the Great Lakes, there is not to-day a single disagreement between the company and its employes. (Applause.) In this way we have endeavored to do our share in wiping out that scathing indictment,—scathing because it is true: 'Man's inhumanity to man makes countless thousands mourn,' and we have supplied the other doctrine in place of it: 'Peace and good-will to our fellow-men.'" (Applause.)

The Chairman:—"Gentlemen, as I stated a few moments ago, we have a number of gentlemen from whom, of course, we should all like to hear, but the hour is growing late. There is one gentleman who has traveled all the way from Detroit to be with us this evening,—a representative of labor,—and I shall call upon him now. He is a gentleman who is dealing with a most important industry, or rather a most important traffic, Mr. William D. Mahon, president of the street railway men's organization of America." (Applause.)

Mr. William D. Mahon:—"I want first to correct the Toastmaster. I did not travel from Detroit. I left New Orleans to attend this meeting, and I put in some forty-eight hours' hard riding to try and be present at this meeting, and arrived here late to-night. With a great deal of anxiety I traveled all this day, and I want to assure the Archbishop that I fasted all day, because we missed our connection and had no diner. (Laughter.) My reasons for wanting to be present were that I have been connected with this organization for some time, and I had an anxiety as to its future. We have lost our distinguished president, Mr. Hanna, since the last meeting that I attended, and I was worrying as to who would lead this organization in the future. It so happened that the late president was a street railroad man, and I worried about the future of the organization for fear they would not select proper officers. But when I arrived here to-night I was highly satisfied. I found they had chosen another railroad man to direct the future of the organization. (Applause.) So my anxiety was all for nothing. But I think it was due to my prayers during the day, while I fasted, that the committee made their wise decision, and selected the gentleman they have to represent us during the coming year.

"I realize that the hour is late; but it is a little later than this that we street car men usually hold our meetings. We usually hold them until four

HENRY C. POTTER,
Bishop, Protestant Episcopal Church.

o'clock in the morning. So I am prepared to hold you here from now until four o'clock. (Laughter.)

"I am pleased to be at this meeting and to have listened to the gentleman who preceded the last speaker, Mr. Kilbourne. I remember, years ago, the first attempt that I made to address a public meeting in defence of trade-unionism. The distinguished gentleman, Mr. Kilbourne, was chairman of that meeting. He expressed the same sentiments then that he has to-night, and it is gratifying to find such men engaged in this work. (Applause.) The world has not gone to pieces yet. There are some men, on both sides of the fence, who are interested in its future welfare, and they are working hard for it.

"I was told, after coming here to-night, that the subject for discussion was the question of industrial peace. I was gratified to know that was the subject up for discussion. I was also gratified to hear the president-elect say, 'peace with honor.' I assure you, upon the part of those I represent and the trades-union men of our nation, we are interested in industrial peace, the industrial peace with honor to all alike, regardless of whether we are captains of industry or the toilers of the land. Archbishop Ireland said that it was no disgrace to be poor, but those of us who happen to be on that side of the line find it, sometimes at least, disagreeable. Yet with all of that, with all our environments, we never forget that we are American citizens, striving, not for wealth, not for riches, but to improve our conditions as American citizens; and I assure you, upon the part of the wage-earners of this country, of whom I know something, and whom, in my lifetime, I have come in contact with, and worked with, that the great army of labor is also interested in industrial peace,—interested in seeing the wheels of progress roll on, and men rise higher and higher to better conditions.

"So my friends, I congratulate this organization to-night upon its good work in the past. The Civic Federation has done a good work, and at this time, when there are rumors of war and of strife between men of capital and the men of labor, this organization stands out as a bright star, pointing the way to true industrial peace. I have not time to relate the good work which I know the Civic Federation has done for the cause of labor and the cause of capital jointly, but it is doing a noble work, and upon the shoulders of the men engaged in this movement rests the future, under the circumstances and conditions that now surround us, of leading both capital and labor to a better understanding, and the establishment of industrial peace in our country.

"I have just come from a long campaign. Seven weeks ago I left my office, and I have been among the workers of this nation from that time until to-night. Once in a while we condescend to associate with you captains of industry, and this is one of the occasions. (Laughter.) There are times when we would hesitate to meet you. I know something of the feelings that exist. A few nights ago, after closing an address at a public mass meeting largely attended, there came to my room in the hotel a committee of earnest men. They came to talk of the industrial conditions, of the threatenings of the Citizens' Alliance. I listened to their story attentively, and when they had got through I said, 'Gentlemen, now be collected; do not have any alarm. First of all, realize this fact: We have got our organizations; we have established them after a long and hard-fought battle. They are here. They are here to stay. We have not only our organizations, but we have our labor press. Every organization controls—or almost every one—a journal. We have got our batteries back of us to defend our position. We have established them in the face of opposition, and they are here to stay. You cannot remove them.' Their proposition was that, on account of the alarming situation, we form secret organizations and do battle against the opposition. I said, 'Gentlemen, no. We want no secret organizations. We are American citizens. Our rights are clearly prescribed by the Constitution of our land. We are interested in its welfare. Every act, and all we do, we have no objection to any man knowing. Our doors are open. We lay everything bare to the world. We need not establish any such organizations, and I will tell you why: Because, gentlemen, the leading men of industry are not engaged in any such a movement. They recognize in this industrial age, in this industrial hour, the necessity of an organization. They form their organizations, and the broad-minded men, the broad-minded representatives of capital, recognize and concede to us the right to organize. That is the organization that will lead and will direct the forces of capital and the forces of labor, and it will go on with its work, its influence and its efforts when the Citizens' Alliance shall sleep in its unknown and forgotten grave.' (Applause.) So I said to them, 'Gentlemen, do nothing of the kind, but stand up for the rights of your organization. Stand up as manfully in the future as you have in the past. Let the leaders of your organization direct its affairs, and you will find them around the consultation boards settling the questions with the leading representatives of organized capital in this nation.'

"So I say to you, my friends, this is my faith in the Civic Federation, and that is the work that is before it to-day. And that is the work it is doing. I doubt if half of you realize the great work that has been done by the few men in this organization,—such men as my friend Kilbourne, such men as MacVeagh and others have done, secretly and unknown. The good work has gone on, and I say to you, if we all determine here to-night to put our shoulders to the wheel, to work as men interested in the welfare of our nation, in the welfare of our homes and our firesides, we will bring industrial peace with honor that will be a credit to this great nation, and the great people that we are so proud of, that we are part and parcel of. There is work, let me say, for all of you, whether you are on the side of labor or of capital. We only want what is fair; we only want what is just.

"I have not time, nor would I take it at this late hour, to attempt to tell you the work of the trade-unions. I know what they have done. I read one article, which I commented on in a speech the other night, which told me volumes as to what the trade-unions are doing, and I thought of it when my friend representing the coal mining industry was speaking a moment ago. The other day it was announced that 2,500 children, under the legal age of 14 years, would be taken from the mines of Illinois and forced to go to schools. (Applause.) I wish that such a law might have been in effect thirty years ago, and then I might have had an education, and I might have been a Belmont, or something like him. (Laughter.) My friends, we have volumes to argue in favor of trades-unions and our organizations and their movement. Do not misunderstand us. We are going to stand by them and, if forced to, we are going to fight for them; but, on the other hand, we stand ready as the representatives of our organizations, as business men and as citizens of this great republic, to meet you around the consultation board, and there to represent our organizations, and,—let me say to Mr. Kilbourne and others,—there to fight out the question of the open or of the closed shop. We do not come to fight it out here. We will discuss that with our employers. We will settle that question with them. The press of this country, the pulpits—no one else can settle that. We will settle that within our own organizations, and with our own employers, around our consultation boards. (Applause.)

"I say to you, friends, again, we are standing for peace, as the chairman of this meeting said, 'honorable peace'—the peace that shall be granted to American citizens, men striving for the rights of their homes and their firesides. That we stand for in our organizations. That we shall insist upon—a fair interpretation of all that peace means. And when that is granted to us you will find us side by side—you, the representatives of capital; we, the representatives of labor. We recognize that the great army of men and women must always be the hewers of wood and the drawers of water, but we insist upon civilized conditions for them, and when that is granted you will find us in harmony with you for peace." (Applause.)

The Chairman:—"As I have already indicated, I shall call upon a gentleman well known to us all, one whose great attainments and whose great work commend themselves to our earnest consideration,—the great president of that great seat of learning, the University of Harvard, President Eliot." (Applause.)

President Eliot:—"Mr. President and Gentlemen: I am very sensible that I have been listening to oratory on this subject for thirteen hours to-day,—(laughter)—and therefore I propose to be extremely

JAMES DUNCAN,
Secretary Granite Cutters' National Union.

brief. I have the honor to represent in the constitution of the National Civic Federation a vague body known as the public. (Laughter.) It is, however, a body very much larger than all the labor-union men and all the employers in the country. (Laughter and applause.) It is a body at the lowest estimate five times as large as all the union men and all the union men's families and all the employers and all their families. (Laughter.) The total number of the employers, the union men, and their families, in the United States does not exceed 20,000,000. The population of this country approaches, if it does not surpass, 80,000,000. I say, therefore, that I have the honor to represent three-quarters of the American people. (Laughter and applause.)

"Now, I have heard all day and many days before about this strife to which one-quarter of the American people seems to be committed, but where did these two combatants get their power to fight? Where did they get it? They got it exclusively from the fact that free institutions have been created in this country. (Applause.) It is only about fifty years since the first corporation was established in England with limited liability in industry,—only about fifty years. The first American corporation with limited liability,—and that is the root of all corporate action, of course,—was created a few years earlier in this country. But it has only been about fifty years since the liberty was given which has created the army of the employed and the opposing army of the employers. This is a very recent phenomenon, indeed, in the history of the world, and this power of association came to us out of the public liberties of England and America.

"Now, I say that we want something more than industrial peace as the result of the conflicts between these two minorities of the American people; and we want something more than peace with honor, the honor of the combatant: we want peace with liberty. (Applause.) Now, the closed shop and the boycott and the union label will never give us peace with liberty. (Applause.) Never! Those are the means of building up the monopolies. The monopoly of a labor-union is perfect when the union has succeeded; the monopoly of a trust is perfect when it has succeeded. And we have conspicuous examples of the perfect success of both these monopolies in this country. I say, therefore, speaking for the American public,—three-quarters of the American people,—that we want to get out of this Civic Federation peace with liberty, as well as peace with honor. Liberty gave you, the combatants, your chance to fight. Let liberty regulate freedom. Let liberty regulate monopoly. There are a great many natural and inevitable monopolies, and there are a number of gentlemen in this room who are creating with all their might artificial monopolies. (Laughter.) Now, let liberty,—which we all, I trust, love,—deal with those monopolies.

"In the little State of Massachusetts we have

learned how to deal with some monopolies,—railroads, for example,—steam railroads, electric rail roads, gas companies, electric light companies. We have learned, I say, how to deal with them. Now, free institutions must learn to deal with all monopolies which are concerned with the necessaries of life. These necessaries are plainly food, fuel, light, transportation,—we have got to learn to deal by the national government with all these monopolies, and because the monopolies themselves are national in scope. And I am very thankful to see that the present government of the United States is beginning to think how it can deal with a monopoly—the monopoly of transportation. There is the way in which progress lies. There is the way where peace lies, and honor, and freedom." (Applause.)

H. H. VREELAND,
President N. Y. City Railway Co.

The Chairman:—"Gentlemen: May I ask your indulgence for a moment? I desire to make just one remark which I believe I ought to make, and that is that the laborer for centuries has been a slave until he has developed into a wage-earner and a free American citizen; that any associated effort that shall give the laborer a shorter work-day,—which means larger leisure, more opportunities for the cultivation of his mind and his body, more opportunity to devote his attention to the well-being of himself and his fellows and his family,—any associated effort that shall tend to the uplifting of the wage-earner must of necessity tend to the improvement of the conditions of all the people; and that this means larger liberty and opportunity; that there is no such thing possible as the improved material conditions of the working people involving slavery or the loss of freedom; that freedom, as Heine has put it, is bread; that bread is freedom, and that without bread there is no such thing as freedom and liberty. I would not feel called upon to say this, were it not that the statement made this evening was a repetition of one made to-day, upon which I felt then called upon to express my dissent. I have at this time nothing further to say, and regret that I even felt the necessity of making the remarks that I have.

"I want to thank you for your attendance here this evening. It is good that even these differences of opinion should come up. An exchange of opinion, even though we differ, brings forth the best that is within us and leads to a better conclusion. I am glad and proud of my citizenship in this republic; proud of President Eliot,—(applause)—proud of his independence and his freedom to express his views as he holds them. I am proud of my right as an American citizen to express my dissent from the views of so profound a scholar and thinker.

"Again I want to thank you all for your attendance this evening. I am sure that this assemblage this evening, and our meeting to-day, will contribute much toward the bringing about of better relations between not only the employer and the worker, but between all our people; and after all, that is the great purpose for which we are associated.

"I thank you all for your attendance, and bid you all good-night." (Applause.)

EXECUTIVE COMMITTEE BUSINESS.

Proceedings at the Fourth Annual Meeting of the Central Body of the National Civic Federation.

The Executive Committee of the National Civic Federation held its fourth annual meeting in the Park Avenue Hotel, Dec. 15, 1904, amid circumstances of unusual interest. The meeting attracted general attention because of the growing appreciation on the part of the public of the scope and work of the organization. There was wide popular interest and some concern as to the selection of a President to succeed the lamented Marcus A. Hanna. The business transacted by the Executive Committee disclosed an extension of the activities of the Civic Federation in many directions, and developed broad plans for the future. Andrew Carnegie received warm greetings upon this, his first attendance at a meeting of the Executive Committee, since his election last Spring.

The Executive Committee received and referred the reports of the Chairman of the Executive Council and of the Chairmen of the several Departments; elected August Belmont as President, to fill the vacancy caused by the death of Marcus A. Hanna, and elected the other general officers; discussed favorably the formation of the new Department of Industrial Economics; amended the by-laws so as to define the Executive Council as consisting of the officers and heads of departments, having the direction of affairs of the National Civic Federation between the meetings of the Executive Committee. The recommendations in the various reports, referred to the Executive Council, included the appointment of a special committee to study the situation presented by the simultaneous expiration in 1906 of the trade agreements in the bituminous and anthracite fields; an inquiry and public report into alleged conspiracies against the public interest in the building trades; the formation of Trade Sections for the special study of labor questions in particular industries; the organization of branches in seven industrial centers, covering the entire country; the employment of conciliation commissioners, an organizer, a business manager for the MONTHLY REVIEW and a Secretary of the Department of Industrial Economics, and the creation of an International Industrial Committee. The financial report was referred to the Ways and Means Committee, and an auditing committee, consisting of V. Everit Macy, Franklin MacVeagh and Daniel J. Keefe, was appointed, at the request of the Chairman of the Executive Council, to examine the accounts of his office.

The following resolution, presented by Marcus M. Marks, was, on motion of Oscar S. Straus, referred to a committee composed of Mr. Marks, Charles W. Eliot, John Mitchell, H. H. Vreeland and Mr. Straus:

"WHEREAS our practical experience has proven that most labor troubles originate from misunderstandings caused in many cases by misconception of the terms in ordinary use in the labor world by either employers or workers, or both; and believing that education is the greatest power in helping to solve the labor problem,

"RESOLVED, That the Executive Committee of the National Civic Federation recommend that the schools throughout the country add to their curriculum, as soon as feasible, a short course of instruction on the labor question, and that free lectures on this subject be generally encouraged."

The Executive Committee transacted its business at morning and afternoon sessions, at which nearly all the members were present. The election of officers was effected during the annual dinner in the evening, the guests participating in the election, which was unanimous. The Committee on Nominations, appointed at the semi-annual meeting of the Executive Committee in May, was composed of the following:

Employers—Franklin MacVeagh, Francis L. Robbins and Charles H. Taylor, Jr.

Labor—John Mitchell, Daniel J. Keefe and P. H. Morrissey.

Public—Right Rev. Henry C. Potter, Isaac N. Seligman and V. Everit Macy.

To these were added, at the morning session of the Executive Committee on December 15: Employer—William H. Pfahler; Labor—Warren S. Stone; Public—Archbishop John Ireland.

The complete list of officers reported by this committee and unanimously elected appears in the report of the dinner.

Among those who addressed the Executive Committee, during its morning and afternoon sessions, were Samuel Gompers, 1st Vice-President, who presided during the business sessions; Samuel Mather, of Cleveland; P. H. Morrissey, Grand Master Brotherhood of Railroad Trainmen, Cleveland; Andrew Carnegie, New York; John P. Freye, Editor of the "Iron Molders' Journal," Cincinnati; Charles A. Moore, New York; William H. Pfahler, former President National Founders' Association, Philadelphia; Oscar S. Straus, 2nd Vice-President, New York; Francis L. Robbins, President of the Pittsburgh Coal Company; James O'Connell, President of the International Association of Machinists, Washington; Warren S. Stone, Grand Chief International Brotherhood of Locomotive Engineers, Cleveland.

By invitation there were present several members of the Executive Committee of the Welfare Department, including John S. Huyler, President of Huyler's, New York; Harold F. McCormick, Vice-President International Harvester Company, Chicago; B. J. Greenhut, Treasurer Siegel-Cooper Company, New York; Edward A. Filene, Treasurer William Filene's Sons Company, Boston; Henry L. Higginson, head of the banking firm of Lee, Higginson & Co., Boston; James Kilbourne, President The Kilbourne & Jacobs Manufacturing Company, Columbus, Ohio.

The several reports received by the Executive Committee of the National Civic Federation appear in this issue of THE MONTHLY REVIEW.

INDUSTRIAL ECONOMICS.

Organization of a New Department of the National Civic Federation for the Study and Elucidation of Industrial Problems.

The formal organization of the Department of Industrial Economics was begun at a meeting of its members, immediately following the afternoon session of the Executive Committee. In adjourning that body, Vice-President Gompers announced the first meeting of the new Department, and at his suggestion Dr. Charles W. Eliot, President of Harvard University, was made the Chairman of the preliminary meeting. Oscar S. Straus explained that the purpose of the meeting was to consider the possibilities of the Department and to take steps toward its practical operation in the elucidation of industrial problems.

WARREN S. STONE,
Grand Chief Locomotive Engineers.

Dr. Eliot said in part:

"This Department, as is obvious from its composition, is intended to give instruction to the public, in the first place, as to the facts of industrial strife. I have always felt that one of the calamities attending this strife was the secrecy of it; the separation of the public from the discussions and debates which take place among the separate contending parties, until the strife actually breaks out in view of the public. Now, this Department of the Civic Federation is going to be the means of giving great publicity to all the elements of industrial strife, and I for one believe that the Civic Federation, in its Executive Committee to a man, believes that publicity will be an enormous gain for the general movement in promoting industrial peace. We see in this Department a strong means for a just and rational publicity. We also see in this new Department the means of educating public opinion in the reasoning of the trade-union on the one hand and of the employers' association on the other. The conditions of the industrial strife are very new since the Civic Federation came into existence. The organization of employers is now attended with the firmness and comprehensiveness which before characterized the organization of labor-unions. Under these new conditions, the public needs to be informed concerning the reasoning and the sentiments of both parties to this strife. Here are a hundred or more men in this Department, who will have the means of putting before the public both reasoning and sentiment, and thereby leading public opinion on this greatest of public questions,—far greater than any political question now before the country, far greater than any probable or discernible question of foreign warfare, because this warfare is at home, and because it touches in the most intimate way the very truest interests of human society."

It was announced that there had been received one hundred acceptances of membership in the Department, but that it had not been practicable to gather all the members at this preliminary meeting. Upon motion, the acting Chairman of the meeting, Dr. Eliot, was authorized to appoint an executive committee to take charge of the work of the Department, and to arrange the time of holding the meetings and the topics to be discussed.

Prof. E. R. A. Seligman, head of the Department of Political Economy in Columbia University, in response to a request for his view of the work of the Department, said:

"It is the fact that the great ideas which guide a

movement are not always realized at the time. Mr. Straus in his remarks spoke of modesty on the part of the Executive Committee and of the Federation in general. So far as I venture to represent the guild of economists, of which there are far more prominent representatives here to-day, I would say that we are much more inclined to be modest, because it is precisely in dealing with these great questions of industrial economics, of the relations between capital and labor, that economists have in the past perhaps made their most significant and signal blunders; and now, perhaps, we have been recalled to a sense of what is a little more near the truth, so that I think it will be found that the economist is willing to learn from men

CHARLES A. MOORE,
Manufacturer of Machinery.

of affairs and practical men on both sides.

"In all great industrial questions there are two points. One is a knowledge of the facts,—something which is absolutely necessary to the solution of any problem, economic or otherwise. The other point is the attitude. What attitude are you to take as to the facts? Now, the great value of economists, as I understand it, and the only excuse for their presence in such a body as this, is that they are not themselves conversant with the facts, but must learn them from the men intimately acquainted with the question,—the employers and the employes. But what the economist and thinker can do is to give you an attitude, a way of looking at things which comes from their habit of regarding every action in industrial and social life from the point of view of what has happened before, namely, the historical point of view.

"If there is anything that is borne in upon the student of the labor problem, it is that all changes come by imperceptible gradations. Those who live in a certain age are almost unable to see the changes that are going on. It is only after the lapse of a decade, or a century, or a period, that we can see that we have really made great progress; and that is the reason the economist is declared to be a conservative, for it is born in the fact that from his study of history he perceives that all changes are the result of small and almost imperceptible steps."

C. T. Root, Editor of the "Dry Goods Economist," and John A. Sleicher, Editor of "Leslie's Weekly," dwelt upon the value of publicity in elucidating industrial questions.

Prof. F. W. Taussig, of Harvard University, expressed his confidence that economists can approach the subject from the point of view of what conduces to the prosperity of the community. He said that economists in dealing with the labor question are hampered by a lack of familiarity with the constantly changing facts and rapid development of the situation; but that they have one advantage, and that is the sincere desire to contribute to the welfare of the whole community. That should be the constant purpose of this Department.

Chairman Eliot, in adjourning the meeting, stated that he would announce the Executive Committee of the new Department after careful consideration.

REPORT OF CHAIRMAN EXECUTIVE COUNCIL.

By Ralph M. Easley.

The past year has been the most successful in the history of the National Civic Federation. It has witnessed marked progress in the growth of the organization and a higher and wider conception of its scope and plan. Moreover, it has been a year of recovery from depression in the industrial world. A revival of production, consumption and exchange now brightens the skies of the future. We meet amid conditions in sharp contrast to those of a year ago. Then the outlook was oppressively gloomy. A large part of our discussion turned upon the prospect of general reductions of wages as well as a threatened increase in the number of the unemployed, during a period of general depression whose effects were already apparent. But that period has passed without serious or general disaster. The tide of industry has turned toward prosperity, and material reasons multiply for making still more numerous contracts of peace such as have successfully withstood the trials of the recent past.

What progress has been made since a year ago in the general cause of industrial peace? I believe that it has been such that it would rejoice the soul of our late President could he be with us to-day.

Never before have there been so many evidences of the growth of a spirit of broad conservatism on the part of large employers and on the part of organized labor. The recent convention of the American Federation of Labor throughout its proceedings presented to the country the spectacle of the chosen representatives of nearly 2,000,000 wage-earners repressing radicals and fanatics and giving to the serious questions involved in the labor problem, not the limited view of partisans, but the broad, careful consideration of economists. This is a high estimate to make of any body chosen from the ranks of a very large and democratic organization, subject to all the prejudices of locality and the inherited resentments of past conflicts and laboring at the same time under the necessity of maintaining a militant attitude. But that the estimate is not exaggerated will be acknowledged by any candid observer of the actions of that convention, as indeed it has been generally conceded by a not always unprejudiced press. The millions of lives dependent upon the vigilant efficiency of more than a million enginemen, trainmen, signalmen and trackmen are made safer by the discipline and conservatism of the great railway brotherhoods.

On the other hand, the employers who have to deal with large masses of workers in the great basic industries and in the largest enterprises exhibit a constantly growing disposition to approach questions of labor in a spirit of justice. Such employers relax not a whit the zealous fidelity with which they administer vast investments. But these great captains of industry appreciate that intelligent and fair adjustment of the relations between capital and labor is not inconsistent with the prosperity of their enterprises, but actually conducive to their success. The report of our Department of Trade Agreements, whose membership represents on one side hundreds of millions of active capital and, on the other side, millions of wage-earners, affords concrete results of this spirit. The report of our Department of Conciliation reveals a most gratifying readiness among large employers to respond to its overtures for face-to-face conference as a method of adjusting or averting controversies with bodies of employes.

The report of our Department of Welfare Work shows a growing appreciation among employers of the importance and the obligation of improving the physical, mental and moral conditions of workers. Many employers have come into touch with the National Civic Federation through this Department, who would not have become affiliated through any other branch of its work. That antipathy to our general policy has been changed into sympathy through this Department will be indicated by the presence of several such employers at our annual dinner to-night.

Our conception of the mission of this organization has widened. We have all learned that the great purpose of the National Civic Federation is not alone to settle strikes and lock-outs, but to reach and disclose the sources of industrial disturbances and to search for their remedies. The settlement of a strike or lock-out may not prevent its recurrence; but the process is educational to all the participants. Fundamental truths should be our further aim. We strive for peace, but we would ascertain and make clear the underlying causes of war. We must study the phenomena of incessant readjustment of wages, profits and prices. Behind these lie economic laws, whose reading varies widely from different points of view. It is our task to examine first the facts and to make deductions afterward. These studies should be for the elucidation of the public at large as well as of those directly concerned.

It is a significant and encouraging sign that from all sides rings a demand for economic education. This cry comes from the extremists as well as from the conservatives. Those associations composed of employers hostile to trade-unions and "citizens' alliances" prone to the vigilante method of settling honest differences of opinion are incessantly proclaiming the importance of education. Simultaneously, the American Federation of Labor has formally adopted the policy of introducing systematic instruction in social, political and industrial economy throughout its 25,000 local unions; while the periodicals of the railway brotherhoods and of the mechanical occupations are filled with valuable technical articles designed to enhance the practical skill and earning capacity of their readers. All of the crusade against child labor, as well as the movement for the shorter work-day, have the importance of education, as well as of sound physique, as their primary justification.

This demand for education must be met. But with what meat shall this hunger for knowledge be fed? Shall it receive the fads, vagaries and utopian theories of sentimental sociologists and unsound economists? Or shall it receive the sound and nutritious pabulum of whatever economic science the experience of all civilization has been able to evolve?

The relations between capital and labor must be studied through their phenomena; but it would be superficial to observe only the concrete fact without discovering its relation to a general and controlling principle. A fact that excites frequent and vehement objection is the placing of artificial restrictions by union labor. Many of these restrictions may appear arbitrary, unfair, and even ridiculous, but there is back of nearly every one of them a reason, whether good or bad, that has its root in some fear that the permanence of and compensation for employment are imperiled. For example, the limitation of apprentices is to prevent the overcrowding of the craft. In other words, the impulse against destructive competition underlies this restriction. But when we thus arrive at competition, we advance from the single fact of restricted apprenticeship into a wide range of phenomena.

JAMES KILBOURNE,
Kilbourne & Jacobs Mfg. Co.

That excessive competition is an evil is recognized by every one when it occurs in his own business. It is recognized by capitalists, by farmers, by the professional classes and by wage-earners. The epithets used to describe it testify to the dislike of it. Excessive competition is "destructive," "unfair," and "cut-throat." The "price-cutter," "underseller," and "rebate giver" are as unprincipled in the eyes of the merchant and railroad manager as the "non-unionist" and "scab" in the eyes of the trade-unionist. When excessive competition occurs in the field of capital, it shows its havoc by depression of trade, long and risky credits, bankruptcy, and "demoralization." When it occurs in the field of labor, its consequences are the sweating system, long hours, low wages, the "exploitation" of labor, unsanitary and dangerous work places, miserable homes and other phases of poverty. And the two series of results are usually found together, for the ruin of the employer's business means the destruction of employment and the exploitation of labor means the survival of the unscrupulous employer.

Volumes might be filled with accounts of the efforts and methods both of capitalists and laborers to do away with destructive competition. And interesting enough is the fact that the methods of the two classes are similar. They all agree not to compete with their fellows beyond a certain point and to deal effectively with those who will not join in the agreement. The capitalists call themselves an "association," an "exchange," a "pool," a "corporation," or a "trust," and the workmen commonly call themselves a "union." The capitalist organizations, of course, differ widely in details, but so do the unions. All originate in what they consider the absolute necessity of preventing ruinous competition, and all are open to the temptation of carrying their methods, which originate in self-protection, over into monopoly and public menace. They have all been legislated against in varying degrees of penalty. They have been haled before the courts, and the courts have handed down hopelessly contradictory decisions. They have been sustained in one State and overthrown in another, and the same courts have reversed themselves, leaving the ultimate policy of the country toward combinations unsettled. Whether they are criminal is not our present concern. We are exercised only with the economic fact that they have sprung into being to meet the real evil of mutual destruction through over-competition.

Thus we have seen that an isolated fact,—the restriction of apprentices,—when its relation to an underlying motive is discovered, leads to the operation, in both capital and labor, of a tremendous and far-reaching principle. If we were to treat of such other isolated facts as the open or closed shop, or the boycott, or the restriction of machinery, or piece-work and day-work, or the shorter work-day, or wages and cost of living, or trade agreements, we would arrive at the more general and immensely more important problem presented by the operation, throughout our industrial and social system, of the same principle.

It may well be asked, in view of these universal efforts to regulate or eliminate competition, What is to be the outcome? and, What should be the policy of the general public toward combinations? We may ask, Shall all combinations be suppressed and all industries be compelled to submit to the unregulated competition of anarchism? or, Shall these combinations continue to grow and competition be entirely eliminated in the state of socialism? If neither of these extremes should be followed, what shall be the middle ground where competition may continue without being destructive and where the public shall not be exploited by monopoly of capital or monopoly of labor?

WILLIAM H. PFAHLER,
Stove Manufacturer.

The eternal presence of these questions, so vital to all society and to the progress of civilization, invites the most searching and devoted study. If they are insoluble and irreducible, there may be found adjustments that would prove effective so far as they accord with principles. It is for the ascertainment of these principles that the new Department of Industrial Economics has been organized. This addition to our educational agencies should prove the most comprehensive and far-reaching movement ever inaugurated for economic education. Its membership comprises the editors of the daily press and of politico-social magazines, trade papers and labor journals, economic and legal authors, the clergy, lecturers, financial and commercial experts, and university professors of political economy. Their interchange of thought will lead them, as they in turn will lead the public, to a better comprehension of the interwoven problems that they will examine.

Trade Sections.

I wish to renew my recommendation of last year for the working out of trade sections. I am more and more convinced, as I examine this subject, that along that line is going to be some of our most valuable constructive work.

In the metal trades, the problems that arise receive a significance of their own from the fact that there is an intimate connection between the methods of production in this country and the limitation to our so-called invasion of Europe, of which we are hearing so much.

In the building trades, or the public service corporations, the question of competition with Germany and England is not important, but in the surplus manufactured products which must win in competition with the rest of the world, there must be care that no handicaps are to be placed on the manufacturer at home.

This does not mean that the American machinist and molder and blacksmith and boilermaker, and other metal trade craftsmen shall be rushed to death by pace-makers, or shall compete in wages with the low-priced labor of Europe.

But it does mean that any arbitrary restriction whose purpose is to increase the number of jobs, should be removed.

There is so much to be said on both sides of the problems arising between employe and employer in the metal trades, that only conferences of men thoroughly familiar with all the technical conditions can make much headway in dealing with the evils, real or fancied.

The labor problems to be met and treated in the manufacture of textiles are totally dissimilar from those in the building trades, or in the metal trades, or in the street railway service, or in mining, or in the reduction of iron and steel. The construction of a building necessitates industrial relations whose adjustment is especially delicate and difficult. There are involved as many as thirty-seven highly organized crafts and an equal number of employers' associations. There must be considered the interdependent relations of the several crafts, including jurisdiction of disputes that arise with almost every improvement and invention and that concern the masters as frequently as the men. The thorough organization of both employers and workers in the building trades in all large cities places their relations in a distinct class. The relations of labor to public service corporations are of peculiar importance. An engineers' strike in a gas or electric plant may plunge a city into darkness. A strike on a street railway may throw into confusion the commercial and social activities of a community. It is expected that the technical studies of these sections will ultimately be extended to all important lines of industry.

Organization.

In regard to local branches, I wish to state that the experience we have had in the past year shows conclusively that it is not a practical proposition to rush out and organize local committees indiscriminately in the large cities.

Eventually I believe that we can have branches all over the country, but it must be worked out slowly and thoroughly. There must be an especially equipped first-class organizer in charge of the work, and this organizer must not only keep closely in touch with every local branch, but keep everlastingly at it.

Instead of attempting to scatter local organizations promiscuously, I would recommend that we establish branch offices at seven large industrial centers, covering as many general divisions of the country. Each center should have a paid secretary, whose whole time should be devoted to the work of organization. As for instance, Boston is naturally the center for New England, and that territory is ripe for organization; preliminary work has already been done. New York is another natural center, including New Jersey and Connecticut. Pittsburgh is the center of the great iron industries. From Chicago as a center, Indianapolis, Detroit, Milwaukee, Kansas City and St. Louis can be dealt with. At Denver we strike the mining world. The growth of transportation in north and south lines parallel to the Mississippi makes New Orleans a center of increasing influence radiating through the South. San Francisco is geographically and commercially a center for the Pacific Coast.

From these centers the question of local committees can be worked out. When once organized, the educational possibilities are great. For instance, the Industrial Economic Department can work out a programme for each center and furnish the ablest speakers in the country, and, if necessary, draw on the Old World. But there is a surprising amount of talent in every locality which could be utilized in such an educational movement. A local organization in a city where they are having practically no strikes, feels that it has nothing to do; but the development of the work of industrial education by these branches will be far more in accordance with the purpose of the National Civic Federation.

International Industrial Committee.

I invite your consideration to the projected formation of an International Industrial Committee. There is progress in the formation of international organizations of labor, and there is also an increasing tendency to the internationalization of production. Some employing members of this organization have plants in a number of countries. The correspondence at our headquarters includes a steadily growing number of inquiries from foreign countries concerning our work and many requests for our publications. The interest thus manifested in our methods found further and sympathetic expression when members of the Interparliamentary Union were your guests in this city on September 26. The nations represented in the Interparliamentary Union are those in which constitutional government is most developed. Its purpose of promoting international peace is in essence dependent upon the good will of peoples; and that in turn depends upon industrial peace in each country. The establishment of industrial peace is therefore precedent to the discouragement of war. The present activity in negotiating arbitration treaties and the organized movement in this country for their ratification, which includes many distinguished citizens who are in accord with the National Civic Federation, have drawn attention to the striking parallelism between prevention of international war through diplomacy and arbitration and the prevention of industrial war through conciliation, conference and arbitration. The [illegible] of trade agreements is consistent with the [illegible] of international treaties. The terms of diplomacy and of industrial conciliation are, with slight modifications of verbiage, etc., interchangeable. Movements for the organization of Civic Federations are making progress in England, France and Germany, and in Canada. Their success might logically lead to the creation of an international body to improve the condition of wage-earners and their relations with employers and to forward economic education throughout the world.

REPORT OF DEPARTMENT OF TRADE AGREEMENTS.

By Francis L. Robbins and John Mitchell, Chairmen.

The Department of Trade Agreements, which was organized at the conference upon that subject held in New York City last May, is able to report a growing appreciation of the trade agreement on the part of both organized employers and wage-earners as a practical method of securing and maintaining industrial peace. There have been several important additions to the more than fifty trade agreements already existing in great national industries, and an extension of their local application. It should be observed that as trade agreements are frequently the outcome of conciliation and conference, the work of the Department upon those subjects is closely associated with the work of this Department.

JOHN F. TOBIN,
President Boot and Shoe Workers' Union.

The experience of this Department has confirmed our conviction that there is nothing so important for the future of this country as the trade agreement as a method of reaching harmonious relations between capital and labor. The trade agreement, in our opinion, offers the most practical way to avert difficulties, dangers and possibly disaster in the industrial world.

Quite as important in some of the great industries as the creation of new collective contracts is their preservation under strong temptations to their dissolution. There was no more important industrial event of the year than the renewal by the organized bituminous mine workers in the four States of Pennsylvania, Ohio, Indiana and Illinois of their agreement with the operators' associations. The acceptance by the miners' organizations of the compromise as to wages, that had been rejected and then submitted to a referendum by the Indianapolis conference, made a red-letter day in the calendar of the current history of the relations between capital and labor in the United States. Not only did the renewal of that agreement prevent a strike that might have literally stopped all the wheels of transportation and production in the country, but it taught the lesson, itself of incalculable moral value, that organized labor has the business sagacity to accept a reduction of wages, forced by lower prices for the product and other adverse conditions of the trade. No longer need silence meet the allegation that the trade agreement, when put to the test, would prove to be an arrangement that would work always in the direction of a share for the employe in larger profits of an industry, but never in the acceptance by the employe of his share of the privation caused by smaller profits. Against that allegation can now always be cited the conspicuous example of the acceptance of a sacrifice by the miners' organizations after they had been convinced of the necessity of the reduced scale.

The conference which resulted in this bituminous agreement was itself an unusual body. Upon the side of the operators were men who, while standing firmly for what they maintained were the rights and necessities of capital, asserted freely their hope that the interstate agreement might not be terminated. Upon the side of the miners were delegates whose appearance and manner bespoke the constant uplift of education, and whose words were sustained arguments, of course in support of their contention, but in large degree animated by a response to the friendly expressions of employers and inspired by an apparent desire for co-operation. In the debates over the terms of the agreement there were moments of dramatic earnestness, when none might tell how a passionate utterance, a misplaced word or a verbal collision might have widened the breach that it was the effort of the conservative leaders on both sides to bridge.

The agreement between the dock managers at Lake Erie ports and the International Longshoremen, Marine and Transport Workers' Association was

FRANKLIN MACVEAGH,
Franklin MacVeagh & Co.

strengthened this year by a resolution adopted at the annual conference between the representatives of those bodies. That resolution thus emphasizes the inviolability of collective contracts:

"That any and all contracts made between the local manager and the men directly involved shall be held inviolate for all work not specifically covered in exhibits attached to and made part of this contract, and that any one trying to break such agreement, or in any way interfering with its performance, shall be barred as a representative, and shall not be permitted to work under this contract, and in all cases work shall not be interrupted on any account."

This agreement covers an immense territory, and embraces thirty-nine divisions of trade. It is not only for the navigation season of 1904, but includes winter work until May 1, 1905, when every influence of this Department will be exerted for its renewal, as this contract has proved conspicuously effective in preventing strikes and lock-outs.

Members of this Department attended many of the protracted and arduous conferences between representatives of the Lithographers' Association and of the employed crafts, which resulted in a national trade agreement that includes practically all of the industry. After the formation of that agreement, a dispute arose at Cincinnati and San Francisco over its construction, which was referred to a member of this Department. Both sides accepted his decision as satisfactory. A second contention arising under the same agreement in St. Louis, Chicago and Cleveland, each side selected a different member of the Civic Federation, and they chose a third member. This arbitration committee rendered a decision mutually satisfactory to the contestants.

A somewhat difficult and highly interesting case to handle was that growing out of the controversy between the Theatrical Managers' Association and the Musical Protective Union. The conference in this matter extended over a period of several months, frequently resulting in no progress, but finally the members of the Conciliation Committee handling the matter succeeded in bringing the two sides to an understanding which resulted in the introduction of the trade agreement into the new field of the production of grand opera, other musical entertainments and the drama. This trade agreement, national in effect, extends to every place of public amusement in the United States. Here the value of frank and free discussion was disclosed by the fact that when the parties came together many of their grievances proved fanciful. For instance, the managers complained that at rehearsals and performances green substitutes frequently appeared in place of players familiar with their part. They were surprised to find that the union itself had provided in its by-laws against this evil. As they had never before conferred with the union leaders, the managers did not even know of the existence of those by-laws, which afforded them an instrument to correct the evil.

A member of this Department is the chairman of the labor committee of the United States Brewers' Association. This committee was formed to deal with all the labor difficulties arising in that industry. It has already formed several trade agreements with unions, and is preparing to sign others. Its chairman has been active in adjusting differences as to agreements in Washington, D. C., and Buffalo, N. Y.

A threatened strike of organized teamsters that would have stopped the wheels of every truck in New York City, and have caused inconceivable inconvenience as well as distress throughout the city during the past summer, was not only prevented but was converted into the first trade agreement ever entered into between the parties concerned. This agreement was signed at the headquarters of the Civic Federation by representatives of the New York Truck Owners' Association and of the Teamsters' Brotherhood and witnessed by a member of the Department.

This Department recognizes that trade agreements are not without defects. One of these is an occasional provision that an employers' association shall employ only members of the union, who in turn shall work only for members of the employers' association. Such exclusive reciprocity can not survive adverse judicial decisions. The agreement between the Journeymen Stone Cutters' Association and the Employing Stone Cutters' Association, recently decided by a magistrate in New York City to be a conspiracy in violation of the penal code of the State, is an example of an effort to restrain trade for the mutual profit of the interested contractors and craftsmen, at the expense of the public. This agreement, according to the admitted facts submitted to the court, actually provided for a "rake-off" of 10 per cent. upon all contracts and the distribution of 10 per cent. of the "rake-off" among the union workers on the day before Christmas. Bids for contracts were compared; and only those above an established average were allowed to be submitted. The Stone Cutters' Union was used under this agreement to force independent contractors to join the association, contribute to its treasury and share in its methods of bidding, under penalty of a strike. The union was also used to force an employer to pay his alleged debt to another.

This Department is ready at all times to promote the formation of legitimate collective contracts and to furnish to that end to any intending negotiators the information which it has collected concerning their terms and their operation in many industries. Applications for such information are constantly received and answered. Recently a large employers' organization sent its secretary to our headquarters to study the various devices for arbitration contained in these agreements.

REPORT OF THE WELFARE DEPARTMENT.

By H. H. Vreeland, Chairman.

It will be remembered that practically the last official act of President Hanna's life was the appointment of a committee to organize the Welfare Department as authorized by this National Executive Committee, in the belief that its efforts to better the relations between employers and employes would be materially aided by the promotion of Welfare Work. In a personal conference, Senator Hanna requested me to act as Chairman for at least the first year. I was led to consent, because I had had to do with work in the ranks and had gained an experience, upon both steam and street railways, which had a certain value with reference to Welfare work.

The first meeting of the committee on organization was attended by representative employers from various sections of the country, and it developed that that was the first time employers giving especial consideration to the welfare of their employes had been brought together. The interest in the exchange of experiences was so great that the entire day was spent in discussion, and it was necessary to await an adjourned meeting a month later to determine upon a plan of work for the Department.

As a result of the first invitation to employers to accept membership in this Department, we have over one hundred and twenty-five members. When I can say to you that we find employers "not only willing but anxious" to become members, you will understand the enthusiasm that is being shown in this work. We have not limited the membership to employers who are promoting Welfare work, as we desire to extend the influence of the meetings to those who have not yet given it consideration.

Under its plan of work the Welfare Department undertakes to educate the public as to the meaning and value of Welfare work, which is understood to involve especial consideration for physical comfort wherever labor is performed; opportunities for recreation; educational opportunities; and the providing of suitable sanitary homes. Plans for saving and lending money, insurance [illegible] pensions are also included in Welfare work.

The Department interest[illegible]ers to give especial attention to the phy[illegible]mental welfare of their employes, through [illegible]es, the publication of reports, and of illustra[illegible]es in THE MONTHLY REVIEW.

Upon request, a consulting agent is furnished to study the peculiar needs of employes in a given plant, to advise the best way of introducing such methods of Welfare work as may be deemed essential and to direct their installation. When desired, a permanent agent or Welfare manager to administer the work is recommended.

A central bureau is maintained to furnish information relative to the success or failure of experiments in Welfare work, the causes of either, and with reference to the latest efforts of employers in this direction. Some of the subjects covered are: Sanitary Workrooms; Washrooms and Baths; Hospital Service; Luncheon Rooms; Recreation; Educational

ISAAC N. SELIGMAN,
Banker.

Devices; Housing of Labor; Pensions and Insurance Associations.

Conferences and Educational Work.

We have held two conferences this year, their great value lying in the fact that those who participated in the discussions were practical workers and employers promoting Welfare work.

The first conference gave a general view of Welfare work, and the report, which contained illustrations of practical efforts, has not only proven a great revelation, but has stimulated many to undertake similar work. An interesting illustration of the value of this report came from one employer who requested eighty copies to distribute among his foremen, who had been inclined to "knock" all his efforts along this line, the employer having found that those who had read his copy had radically changed their views.

Our second conference dealt with specific subjects, such as Insurance Associations, Banks for Employes, and the Labor Department; and this plan will be continued. In addition, plans have been made for holding local conferences in large cities where we have a number of members, this being by special request and to give publicity to such work in those communities.

In response to appeals from members of different trades-unions, we have begun a series of articles in THE MONTHLY REVIEW on the needs of employes in certain industries. The purpose of these articles is also to show employers how Welfare work has been carried forward in such industries, with beneficial results. Marked copies of such issues are sent to employers in these trades.

For instance, one of the business agents of the International Iron Molders' Association appealed to us to emphasize the necessity of providing relief for molders, stating that any effort on the part of the union to secure these physical comforts was regarded by employers as only an effort to stir up trouble in the absence of any other excuse. He pointed out the need of a place for the men to change their clothes, and how they suffer in the winter, when they are obliged to work in places where there is no heat and there are broken windows, because the work necessitates the removal of their outer clothing. He dwelt upon the desirability of providing baths, and of an opportunity to change the clothing, stating that when the men are through casting, no matter what the temperature may be, ordinarily they have to leave the shop wet with perspiration, simply throwing on an overcoat, and that the outer air strikes them with a deadly chill.

The following letter from a business agent of the Bridge and Structural Iron Workers' Association will illustrate this point:

"There has never been any work looking to the interest of the first trades that are employed in the erection of buildings and in such structural iron work as bridges and viaducts, where no other mechanics are employed. The other trades are in a

measure looked after, inasmuch as a building generally has taken some definite shape before they are long at work, and a room can be set aside within the structure for storing their street clothes in the day and their gloves and overalls at night. Wage-earners in the iron industry would be grateful to your worthy organization if you would get some of the largest contractors to supply us with portable rooms in which to store our street hats and coats in the day time and our gloves and overalls at night. This is our first need, as our clothing is constantly stolen. Second, a place to wash up with sanitary toilet accommodations; and third, an emergency hospital room."

JAMES O'CONNELL,
President International Association of Machinists.

A business agent of the International Association of Machinists has gone so far as to prepare a list of questions, which has been sent to unions throughout the country, asking the men what conveniences have been furnished them. He has appealed to us, however, to aid in securing these comforts, which, from the answers to these questions, seem to be pressing needs.

A high officer of the International Association of Pulp and Paper Makers, has represented to this Department that the sanitary conditions of the wage-earners in his industry in many mills in this country are exceedingly bad, and has asked that his statements be confirmed by an investigation. The purpose of the inquiry would be to bring friendly influence to bear upon employers to improve the conditions, if they are found to be such as reported. This investigation will be made.

A very large corporation, whose operations cover a great extent of territory and employ a variety of nationalities, has, during the last year, had on its hands a serious strike. Despite this fact, which might be expected to create animus against the corporation, a prominent labor leader came to the office of this Department and personally urged the publication of a report prepared by an officer of the corporation on its Welfare work. This labor leader was broad enough to urge that the publication of such an article from such a source would exert a far-reaching influence in encouraging the introduction of the work elsewhere, and would be of benefit to unknown numbers of employes. This union speaker was especially appreciative of the educational features of Welfare work, which he desired to be as widely extended as possible by example.

Information Furnished.

Our Secretary, who has had practical experience in Welfare work, has been called for consultation to a number of large plants.

In one plant, with 11,000 employes, the plans for a luncheon-house, capable of accommodating 1,000 persons, were developed in detail.

Two months were spent in an establishment employing 7,000, investigating the needs of the employes and making recommendations.

Detailed help was extended to a manufacturer who has 10,000 employes, in formulating plans for housing hygienically a large proportion of the employes.

In another manufacturing community all the recommendations made by the Secretary of this Department were adopted.

In one large city visits have been made to establishments, each employing several thousands, for the purpose of giving advice as to the application and administration of Welfare work; while in another, advice has been given with reference to initial steps for Welfare work in several factories. In both cities the Secretary has been requested to pursue the work further.

A prominent manufacturer who had heard of this Department only through its bureau at the Louisiana Purchase Exposition, wrote a request for counsel during his erection of an entirely new plant, his purpose being to provide facilities for Welfare work in every department and also to erect sanitary houses for the families of his employes upon satisfactory terms.

We have furnished a large mining company with accurate information as to the introduction and conduct of savings banks by other employers, this company desiring to act upon the lessons taught by their experiences.

The management of a department store requested similar information in regard to the experience of others in the same State in creating insurance funds as well as in establishing savings banks.

In response to a request we have supplied a Welfare Manager, who is a woman, to supervise the Welfare work in a department store having 4,000 employes. It is believed that the success of the Welfare work in this instance will lead to its introduction in many of the 1,400 other department stores in the United States.

In response to a request from the management of a factory where there are 10,000 employes, we have recommended another Welfare Manager, in this case a man.

One manufacturer obtained the first idea of organizing a Men's Welfare League, and thus making the work of his company less paternalistic,, at one of our conferences; and our Secretary was not only able to recommend to three of the men, sent on for consultation, immediate work, but she personally conducted two of them through some plants where these recommendations found support in practice.

In addition to this we have not only supplied various written suggestions where requested, and photographs of luncheon-rooms, workers' houses, bathrooms, club houses, and other features of Welfare work, but innumerable consultations have been held at our headquarters.

It is impossible to enter into a detailed report of the assistance that has been rendered along this line; and that we have gone into even a wider field is illustrated by a request from a large manufacturing town for advice in formulating a plan of work for a committee of citizens who desire especially to promote social welfare work in their community.

World's Fair Bureau.

A unique effort of this Department was the promotion of a World's Fair Bureau. Circulars were sent to employers throughout the country, informing them as to how their employes could visit the World's Fair within their means, and giving a tabulated statement of daily expenses under our plan. In addition to this, agents of the bureau at St. Louis met arriving employes at the trains and conducted them to their lodgings. They were also furnished with a six days' itinerary that their expenses might not be swollen by losing time in trying to learn what to see. In this way large numbers of wage-earners were enabled to receive the educational benefit of the great Louisiana Purchase Exposition.

Future Work.

Aside from continuing the policy of promoting conferences, both national and local, and our educational work through THE MONTHLY REVIEW, we shall respond to requests for illustrated lectures in such cities as Boston, Baltimore, Philadelphia and New York. We shall also continue to build up our Bureau of Information at the Civic Federation Headquarters. Only to-day we have had a letter in which the employer says, "I am desirous of doing the right thing by our people, but do not know just where to begin." It is just such requests as this that are constantly received at our Bureau.

The work of the Welfare Department represents the humane as well as the human side of industrial economics. Nevertheless, its conduct must be intensely practical. It is a realization of the necessity of preserving this practical characteristic that has made of our conferences assemblages of business men, who, while not insensible to sentiment, are thoroughly aware of the practical results of Welfare work in improving the physical, and elevating the mental and moral conditions of the mass of wage-earners. Welfare work is essentially altruistic, but those engaged in it have had repeated to them through experience again and again the lesson that Welfare work is also intensely practical.

LIST OF ACCEPTANCES

For Dinner of National Civic Federation.

EMPLOYERS.

Henry Phipps, United States Steel Corporation, New York.

August Belmont, President Interborough Rapid Transit Company, New York.

H. H. Vreeland, President New York City Railway Company, New York.

Francis L. Robbins, President Pittsburgh Coal Company, Pittsburgh, Pa.

C. A. Coffin, President General Electric Company, New York.

Albert J. Pitkin, President American Locomotive Company, New York.

Adolph S. Ochs, Proprietor New York Times; Philadelphia Ledger; New York.

Frederick P. Fish, President American Bell Telephone Company, Boston.

H. L. Higginson, Lee Higginson & Company, Boston.

Franklin MacVeagh, Franklin MacVeagh & Company, Chicago.

Harold F. McCormick, International Harvester Company, Chicago.

Louis Stern, Stern Brothers, New York.

E. W. Winter, President Brooklyn Rapid Transit Company, Brooklyn, N. Y.

H. T. Ambrose, President American Book Company, New York.

Heinrich Conried, President Metropolitan Opera and Real Estate Company, New York.

Isaac Guggenheim, Treasurer American Smelting and Refining Company, New York.

F. W. TAUSSIG,
Professor in Harvard University.

S. B. Chase, Treasurer, King Philip Mills, Fall River.

Chas. A. Moore, Manning, Maxwell & Moore, New York.

Robert C. Ogden, John Wanamaker's, New York.

P. F. Sullivan, President Boston & Northern Street Railway Company, Boston, Mass.

F. R. Hazard, President Solvay Process Company, Syracuse, N. Y.

William P. Clyde, Clyde Steamship Company, New York.

Anthony N. Brady, Consolidated Gas Company, New York.

J. B. Greenhut, President, Siegel-Cooper Company, New York.

Wm. C. Greene, Treasurer Peace Dale Mfg. Company, Peace Dale, R. I.

William H. Pfahler, Former President National Founders' Association, Philadelphia.

Royal Robbins, Treasurer, American Waltham Watch Company, Boston, Mass.

Frank Tilford, Park & Tilford, New York.

Frederic S. Clark, Talbot Mills, North Billerica, Mass.

George H. Harries, Washington Railway & Electric Company, Washington, D. C.

Thos. F. Parker, President Monaghan Mills, Greenville, S. C.

H. B. Graves, Standard Optical Company, Geneva, N. Y.

Eugene S. Benjamin, Alfred Benjamin & Company, New York.

Wallace Downey, President Townsend-Downey Shipbuilding Company, New York.

C. W. Terhune, Edwin C. Burt Company, New York.

John B. McDonald, Conntractor, New York.

G. E. Emmons, General Electric Company, Schenectady, N. Y.

Benedict J. Greenhut, Siegel-Cooper Company, New York.

J. W. Miller, Fall River Lines, New York.

Festus J. Wade, President Mercantile Trust Company, St. Louis, Mo.

Chas. T. Page, Page Belting Company, Concord, N. H.

James Kilbourne, Kilbourne & Jacobs Mfg. Company, Columbus, Ohio.

Emil L. Boas, Hamburg-American Steamship Line, New York.

Robert M. Donaldson, American Lithographic Company, New York.

Maurice Fels, Fels & Company, Philadelphia.

W. M. Pratt, Goodell-Pratt Company, Greenfield, Mass.

C. W. Sweet, Sweet, Orr & Company, New York.

J. A. Campbell, Trenton Potteries Company, Trenton, N. J.

Luddington Patton, Patton Paint Company, Milwaukee, Wis.

Wm. H. McCord, President Post & McCord, New York.

James Talcott, American Hosiery Company, New York.

Irving T. Bush, Bush Terminal Company, New York.

George Haven Putnam, President G. P. Putnam's Sons, New York.

Charles T. Wills, Builder, New York.

John Atkinson, Builders' Exchange, Philadelphia.

James J. Ryan, Builders' Exchange, Philadelphia.

Thos. F. Armstrong, Builders' Exchange, Philadelphia.

Theodore Starrett, Thompson-Starrett Company, New York.

Otto M. Eidlitz, M. Eidlitz' Sons & Company, New York.

Benjamin D. Traitel, Traitel Bros. & Company, New York.

John Cooper, Cooper, Wigand, Cooke Company, New York.

George R. Elder, Ingersoll-Sergeant Drill Company, Easton, Pa.

C. H. Ludington, Jr., Curtis Publishing Company, Philadelphia.

H. A. Tenney, President Herring-Hall-Marvin Safe Company, New York.

T. F. McCarthy, New York Truck Owners' Association, New York.

J. D. Robinson, Libbey Glass Company, Toledo, Ohio.

Wm. Butterworth, Deere & Company, Moline, Ill.

Harry B. French, Smith, Kline & French Company, Philadelphia.

Irving Smith, The Crescent Watch Case Company, New York.

W. O. Fayerweather, First National Bank, Paterson, N. J.

F. C. Fletcher, Pocasset Worsted Company, Boston, Mass.

Louis B. Schram, India Wharf Brewing Company, Brooklyn, N. Y.

T. H. McInnerny, Siegel-Cooper Company, New York.

John F. McClain, Remington Typewriter Company, New York.

Robert Perkins, President Hartford Carpet Corporation, New York.

Wm. C. LeGendre, Newburgh, Dutchess & Connecticut Railroad Company, New York.

Frank H. Scott, Publisher Century, New York.

J. D. Dort, President Durant-Dort Carriage Company, Flint, Mich.

Samuel Mather, Pickands, Mather & Company, Cleveland, Ohio.

Foster Milliken, Milliken Bros., New York.

Edward A. Filene, Wm. Filene's Sons Company, Boston.

Marcus M. Marks, President National Association Clothing Manufacturers, New York.

Wm. J. Rogers, President Borden, Condensed Milk Company, New York.

Edgar L. Marston, Banker, New York.

John S. Huyler, President Huyler Company, New York.

H. F. J. Porter, Nernst Lamp Company, Pittsburgh, Pa.

E. P. Bryan, Interborough Rapid Transit Company, New York.

J. H. Sternbergh, President American Iron & Steel Mfg. Company, Reading, Pa.

B. F. DeKlyn, Huyler's, New York.

James E. Brown, Geneva Optical Company, Geneva, N. Y.

Chas. Wilhelms, Sackett & Wilhelms Lithographing & Printing Company, New York.

Wm. Miller, Henry Disston & Sons, Philadelphia.

W. H. Pouch, Vice-President Orange County Traction Company, Newburgh, N. Y.

James H. Nutt, Republic Iron & Steel Company, Youngstown, Ohio.

Frank Huyler, Huyler's New York.

N. H. Colwell, President The National Novelty Corporation, New York.

W. L. Clause, President Columbia Chemical Company, Pittsburgh, Pa.

Lee Kohns, L. Straus & Sons, New York.

H. W. Ashley, Assistant to the President Wabash Railway Company, St. Louis, Mo.

David Huyler, Huyler's, New York.

S. W. Bowne, Scott & Bowne, New York.

Arthur A. Fuller, Providence Engineering Works, Providence, R. I.

V. A. Wallin, Wallin Leather Company, Grand Rapids, Mich.

John R. Butler, Simpson-Crawford Company, New York.

Frank C. Spinney, Faunce & Spinney, Lynn, Mass.

A. Houghton, Sr., Glass Manufacturer, Corning, N. Y.

William R. Farrand, Farrand Organ Company, Detroit, Mich.

Oliver Gildersleeve, Brown Wire Gun Company, New York.

Alexander Ferris, Ferris Brothers, Printers, New York.

Berkley R. Merwin, Merchant Tailor, New York.

D. E. Titsworth, Potter Printing Press Company, Plainfield, N. J.

Herman Younker, Younker Brothers, Des Moines, Iowa.

Orrin S. Goan, National Biscuit Company, New York.

William Smith, President The Standard Optical Company, Geneva, N. Y.

J. B. L. Hornberger, Comptroller, Pittsburgh Coal Company, Pittsburgh, Pa.

Leo Arnstein, Nathan Mfg. Company, New York.

James L. Bowlby, President Master Teamsters' Association, Boston, Mass.

Frank H. Clark, Townsend-Downey Shipbuilding Company, New York.

N. A. Dingwall, Townsend-Downey Shipbuilding Company, New York.

H. C. Hunter, Secretary New York Metal Trades Association, New York.

Manfred K. Heynemann, California.

Nathaniel B. Borden, Treasurer Barnard Manufacturing Company, Fall River, Mass.

W. F. Shove, Treasurer Pocasset Manufacturing Company, Fall River, Mass.

Edmund B. Osborne, President American Colortype Company, New York City.

Frank Leake, President Star & Crescent Mills, Philadelphia.

J. Lindsay Little, Master Builders' Exchange, Philadelphia.

H. E. Cary, President Lluvia de Oro Mining Company, New York.

Sol. G. Rosenbaum, National Cloak & Suit Company, New York.

George D. Selby, The Drew-Selby Company, Portsmouth, Ohio.

Edwin H. Wolf, Rogers, Peet & Company, New York.

Samuel H. Wolverton, Gallatin National Bank, New York.

Felix M. Warburg, Kuhn, Loeb & Company, New York.

Julius Liebmann, Brewer, New York.

James T. Sargent, The American Washboard Company, Cleveland, Ohio.

Joseph C. Baldwin, President New York & Boston Dyewood Company, New York.

THE PRESS.

Charles R. Miller, Editor New York Times, New York.

Bradford Merrill, Editor The World, New York.

Albert Shaw, Editor Review of Reviews, New York.

G. B. M. Harvey, Editor North American Review, New York.

R. Watson Gilder, Editor Century Magazine, New York.

Charles W. Knapp, President The Republic, St. Louis, Mo.

Herman Ridder, President Staats-Zeitung, New York.

St. Clair McKelway, Editor Brooklyn Eagle, Brooklyn, N. Y.

Ervin Wardman, Editor The New York Press, New York.

Rev. J. M. Buckley, Editor Methodist, New York.

Henry L. Stoddard, Editor Mail & Express, New York.

John Bancroft Devins, Editor New York Observer, New York.

Charles H. Taylor, Jr., President American Newspaper Publishers' Association, Boston, Mass.

Talcott Williams, The Press, Philadelphia, Pa.

James C. Bayles, New York Times, New York City.

Walter H. Page, Editor World's Work, New York.

Henry Harmon Neill, New York Mail, New York.

S. W. Meek, Business Manager, The Cleveland Leader, Cleveland, Ohio.

H. J. Wright, Editor The Globe, New York.

R. C. E. Brown, New York Tribune, New York.

C. A. Rook, President Dispatch Publishing Company, Pittsburgh, Pa.

F. D. Bright, Publisher Railway World, Philadelphia.

Frederick J. Miller, Editor American Machinist, New York.

John A. Sleicher, Editor Leslie's Weekly, New York.

R. R. Bowker, Editor Publishers' Weekly, New York.

C. Kirchhoff, Editor Iron Age, New York.

Lawrence F. Abbott, The Outlook, New York.

Horace White, New York Evening Post, New York.

H. C. Watson, Editor Dun's Review, New York.

James H. McGraw, President McGraw Publishing Company, New York.

John P. Frey, Editor Iron Molders' Journal, Cincinnati, Ohio.

Hamilton Holt, Editor The Independent, New York.

C. H. Salmons, Editor Brotherhood of Locomotive Engineers' Journal, Cleveland, Ohio.

S. M. Sexton, Editor United Mine Workers' Journal, Indianapolis, Ind.

John C. Freund, Editor Music Trades, New York.

D. L. Cease, Editor Railroad Trainmen's Journal, Cleveland, Ohio.

E. W. Fairchild, Daily Trade Record, New York.

E. R. A. SELIGMAN,
Professor in Columbia University.

Roland Phillips, Editor Harper's Weekly, New York.

Ray Morris, Editor Railroad Gazette, New York.

Thos. F. Woodlock, Editor Wall Street Journal, New York.

Amos K. Fiske, Journal of Commerce, New York.

Edward Payson Call, Commercial, New York.

John Green, Editor Bradstreet's, New York.

Chas. T. Root, The Dry Goods Economist, New York.

Angus Sinclair, President and Editor Railway and Locomotive Engineering, New York.

John F. McNamee, Editor Brotherhood of Locomotive Firemen's Magazine, Indianapolis, Ind.

Albert Halstead, Washington Correspondent, Washington, D. C.

D. T. Pierce, Editor, Public Opinion, New York.

C. L. Baine, Editor Boot and Shoe Makers' Journal, Boston.

W. P. Hamilton, Wall Street Journal, New York.

Kellogg Durand, Boston Transcript, Boston.

REPRESENTING PUBLIC INTERESTS.

Andrew Carnegie, Capitalist, New York.

Cornelius N. Bliss, Ex-Secretary of the Interior, New York.

Oscar S. Straus, Member Court of Arbitration at The Hague, New York.

Chas. W. Eliot, President Harvard University, Cambridge, Mass.

Archbishop John Ireland, of the Roman Catholic Church, St. Paul, Minn.

Bishop Henry C. Potter, of the Protestant Episcopal Church, New York.

Isaac N. Seligman, J. & W. Seligman & Company, New York.

Frank A. Vanderlip, National City Bank, New York.

Chas. A. Conant, Morton Trust Company, New York.

Chas. S. Hamlin, Attorney-at-Law, Boston, Mass.

Leander Chamberlain, Clergyman, New York.

Hon. Stewart L. Woodford, New York.

Hon. Carl Schurz, New York.

V. Everit Macy, Capitalist, New York.

A. B. Hepburn, President Chase National Bank, New York.

F. W. Taussig, Department Political Economy, Harvard University, Cambridge, Mass.

Spencer Trask, Banker, New York.

Henry Seligman, J. & W. Seligman & Company, New York.

Robert F. Herrick, Attorney-at-Law, Boston, Mass.,

Frederick H. Cooke, Lawyer and Author, New York.

J. J. Sullivan, Chamber of Commerce, Cleveland, Ohio.

Edwin R. A. Seligman, Head Department Political Economy Columbia University, New York.

Dunlevy Milbank, Capitalist, Jersey City.

John J. McCook, Lawyer, New York.

Charles Dana Palmer, M[...]usetts State Board of Conciliation and Arbitration, [...] Mass.

[...]nson Weil, Lawyer, New York.

[...]ayes Robbins, Economic Writer, Boston.

[...]H. M. Garlick, President First National Bank, Youngstown, Ohio.

Richard T. Ely, Professor Political Economy, Wisconsin University, Madison, Wis.

Rev. James E. Freeman, Rector, St. Andrews' Memorial Church, Yonkers, N. Y.

Charles S. Gleed, Attorney-at-Law, Topeka, Kansas.

Henry W. Farnam, Professor Political Economy, Yale University, New Haven, Conn.

Chandler P. Anderson, Lawyer, New York.

Wm. C. Douglas, Secretary Rapid Transit Contractors' Association, New York.

Warner Van Norden, Banker, New York.

Edward M. Shepard, Lawyer, New York.

Ralph M. Easley, Chairman Executive Council, New York.

Wm. H. P. Faunce, President Brown University, Providence, R. I.

Rev. W. S. Rainsford, St. George's Protestant Episcopal Church, New York.

Bishop Chas. H. Fowler, Methodist Episcopal Church.

Rev. F. M. North, Methodist Episcopal Church.

John G. Milburn, Lawyer, New York.

Franklin H. Giddings, Head Sociological Department Columbia University, New York.

Hayne Davis, Lawyer, New York.

Slason Thompson, Chief Statistician Railway Managers' Association, Chicago.

George M. Fuller, American Museum, New York.

E. C. Howland, Economic Writer, New York.

John Moody, Author Moody's Manual, New York.

Joseph Silverman, D.D., Rabbi Temple Emanuel, New York.

Dr. William Jarvie, Brooklyn.

William H. Allen, Association for Improving the Condition of the Poor, New York.

Frank L. Hall, Lawyer, New York.

Henry M. Leipziger, Board of Education, New York.

William H. Maxwell, Superintendent of Schools, New York.

Royal L. Melendy, Newark Social Settlement Association, Newark, N. J.

Rev. Howard H. Russell, Mt. Vernon, N. Y.

Wm. Belahay, Secretary Amalgamated Society of Engineers, New York.

L. H. Severance, Vice-Moderator, General Assembly Presbyterian Church, New York City.

Charles Sprague Smith, People's Institute, New York City.

J. W. Jenks, Professor Political Economy and Politics, Cornell University, Ithaca, N. Y.

LABOR MEN.

Samuel Gompers, President American Federation of Labor, Washington, D. C.

John Mitchell, President United Mine Workers of America, Indianapolis, Ind.

James Duncan, General Secretary Granite Cutters' National Union, Quincy, Mass.

D. J. Keefe, President International Longshoremen's Association, Detroit, Mich.

P. H. Morrissey, Grand Master Brotherhood Railroad Trainmen, Cleveland, Ohio.

Warren S. Stone, Grand Chief International Brotherhood Locomotive Engineers, Cleveland, Ohio.

James O'Connell, President International Association Machinists, Washington, D. C.

John Tobin, General President Boot & Shoe Workers' Union, Boston, Mass.

Wm. D. Mahon, President Amalgamated Association Street Railway Employes of America, Detroit, Mich.

Denis A. Hayes, President Glass Bottle Blowers' Association of United States and Canada, Philadelphia.

William Weihe, Former President, Amalgamated Association of Iron, Steel and Tin Workers, New York City.

J. W. Parker, Poster Artists' Association of America, New York.

J. W. Bramwood, International Typographical Union, Indianapolis, Ind.

Geo. E. Pepper, Amalgamated Association Street Railway Employes of America, New York.

Herman Robinson, Organizer American Federation of Labor, New York.

J. P. Archibald, President New York Council International Brotherhood of Painters, New York.

Thos. B. Lavey, Iron Molders' Conference Board of New York and Vicinity, New York.

Wm. H. Farley, Tile Layers' Organization, New York.

Edward Kelly, Electrical Workers, New York.

Samuel B. Donnelly, Typographical Union No. 6, New York.

Edward Gould, International Brotherhood of Teamsters, New York.

James Daly, Dockbuilders' Union, New York.

Lawrence O'Keefe, Vice-President Iron Moulders' Union of North America, Detroit, Mich.

James B. Wilson, International Association of Machinists, New York.

A. B. Madden, Amalgamated Association of Street & Electric Railway Employes of America, New York.

E. A. Pickett, Amalgamated Association of Street & Electric Railway Employes of America, New York.

Thomas Martin, International Brotherhood of Teamsters, New York.

W. H. Ashton, International Brotherhood of Teamsters, New York.

James P. Holland, International Brotherhood of Stationary Firemen, New York.

C. Oberwager, Printers, New York.

J. H. Hatch, United Upholsterers' Union, New York.

C. Schmidt, Upholsterers' Union, New York.

James McCabe, Gold Beaters, New York.

Henry S. Hand, Carriage and Wagon Workers' International Union, New York.

M. McConville, Stationary Engineers, New York.

Alfred J. Boulton, Stereotypers, New York.

Robert C. Neidig, United Housesmiths and Bronze Erectors' Union, New York.

Jess P. Larimer, Bridge & Structural Iron Workers' Association, New York.

John F. Gunshanan, Chairman Workingmen's Free Reading Room Association, Hartford, Conn.

George L. Cain, International Association of Machinists, Lynn, Mass.

Patrick Grimes, Plasterers' Union, New York.

James Nilan, Plasterers' Union, New York.

D. C. Doris, Bricklayers' Benevolent and Protective Union, New York.

Alfred Sager, International Brotherhood of Teamsters, New York.

George Bridge, Plumbers' Union, New York.

James Beggs, Musical Protective Union, New York.

Philip Kelly, Theatrical Protective Union No. 1, New York.

Maurice F. Smith, Musical Mutual Protective Union, New York.

P. J. Mulligon, Bricklayers' Union, New York City.

The National Civic Federation Review

Vol. I. No. 11 NEW YORK, FEBRUARY 1, 1905 Ten Cents

ANOTHER GREAT LABOR CONFLICT AVERTED BY CONCILIATION.

OFFICIALS OF THE GREATEST RAILWAY CORPORATION IN THE WORLD SOLVE DIFFICULT PROBLEMS BY FACE-TO-FACE CONFERENCE WITH ORGANIZED EMPLOYES.

ANOTHER conspicuous example of the value of the method of joint conference, between representatives of employers and wage-earners, in solving a great labor problem, was the success of the recent negotiations that averted a strike on the Pennsylvania Railroad. There are some employers, whose pay rolls include perhaps hundreds of men and whose business demands thousands of capital, who still cling to the obsolete notion that they will have nothing to do with any but their own men about hours or wages or conditions of work. But here we have the spectacle of the executive officers of a corporation whose railway system, with its alliances, represents a capitalization of nearly two billions of dollars, a mileage that would nearly girdle the earth and employs men in army corps numbering hundreds of thousands, holding conferences day after day with the officers of an organization of labor, not confined to their system, but embracing in its membership employes of all the other railroads of the country.

Even after these conferences had been protracted to the point where they seemed to have reached a deadlock, the General Manager of the Pennsylvania Railroad, W. W. Atterbury, welcomed a request for their continuance from P. H. Morrissey, Grand Master of the Brotherhood of Railroad Trainmen. Mr. Atterbury did not say to Mr. Morrissey, "You are not an employe of our company; we will manage our own business in our own way." Instead, the conferences were resumed and repeated until an agreement was reached, satisfactory to both the corporation and the vast number of its employes. The conferences illustrated also the practical value of this method in reaching the truth as to disputed questions of fact. As will be seen, it was widely varying assertions as to the effect of a regulation upon earnings that greatly complicated this difficulty. But when the truth was made plain, the way to agreement was cleared, again illustrating the fact that most labor troubles have their root in needless misunderstandings.

It is needless to say that had not these conferences resulted in agreement, the consequent strike, probably involving all the other employes as well as the trainmen, would have tied up the entire Pennsylvania system, causing enormous loss to both the largest railway corporation in the world and its army of wage earners, as well as incalculable inconvenience to the public and costly interruption to commerce.

This outcome was prevented entirely through the conferences between General Manager W. W. Atterbury, of the Pennsylvania Railroad, and representatives of the Brotherhood of Railroad Trainmen. The main point at issue was the requirement by the company that the forward brakeman on freight trains should go into the engine cab to assist the regular fireman during the pulls up heavy grades. This had long been the custom on the Pennsylvania, which employed one more brakeman per train for that purpose than was the practice on other roads. But with the adoption of air-brakes on 50 per cent. of its freight trains, as required by law, the Pennsylvania had found the employment of the extra brakeman for firing no longer necessary and had issued a regulation that the regular forward brakeman should assist the fireman up grades whenever required by the engineer.

A. J. CASSATT, President Pennsylvania Railroad Company.

P. H. MORRISSEY, Grand Master Brotherhood Railroad Trainmen.

W. W. ATTERBURY, General Manager Pennsylvania Railroad.

W. G. LEE, First Vice-Grand Master Railroad Trainmen.

Members of the Brotherhood of Railroad Trainmen objected to this requirement because they claimed that it exposed the forward brakeman to extremes of heat and cold, and because they regarded the increased pay of the brakeman for firing as inadequate. The company, on its side, claimed that the sanitary objection was more fanciful than real; that the increased pay was fair; and offered to add the time served in firing to the seniority of brakemen when promoted to be firemen.

There were involved other questions relating to the wage scale of trainmen in large yards and near terminal points.

These questions had been a subject of futile discussion for months between minor officials of the company and local representatives of the Brotherhood. A demand was formulated and presented by W. G. Lee, Vice-Grand Master of the Brotherhood of Railroad Trainmen, to Mr. Atterbury. This demand, which related chiefly to extra pay for brakemen when required to assist firemen, was preceded by a referendum vote of the trainmen east of Pittsburg and Erie upon the question of whether or not to strike if the demand were refused. By 8,365 to 611 the trainmen voted in favor of a strike in that contingency.

This vote precipitated a critical situation. Had the vote meant immediate action, 10,000 trainmen would have been affected directly. It was claimed that the first strike order would have paralyzed the freight service. But had a strike been declared by them, it was thought probable that all other employes of the road would be at once called out. It was at this juncture, on January 18, that both sides to the controversy began preparations for the threatened rupture. A corps of electricians equipped the Philadelphia office of General Manager Atterbury with special telegraphic wires, connecting directly with all points on the Pennsylvania system east of Pittsburg and Erie. At the same time, Vice-Grand Master Lee sent to officers of each of the eighty-five locals of the Brotherhood in the territory affected explanations of cipher telegrams directing the action of the men under various anticipated conditions. This action was taken by Mr. Lee in conjunction with the Committee of Adjustment, composed of sixteen members of the Brotherhood from as many divisions of the road. A strike could be ordered only by their vote and the signature of the Grand Master.

But just at this time it became known that the heavy vote of the trainmen in favor of a strike might not have been cast had the exact status of the negotiations been more generally known. This lack of knowledge was not caused by concealment on the part of any of the negotiators, but by the fact that proposals and counter-proposals had been exchanged with such rapidity that their final form had not become fully understood by all the trainmen throughout the system when the vote was taken.

Grand Master P. H. Morrissey, of the Brotherhood of Railroad Trainmen, was notified at his home in Cleveland by long-distance telephone of the crisis. He started at once for Philadelphia, informing Mr. Lee that he had in mind a compromise suggestion. The day before Robert Pitcairn, first assistant to President A. J. Cassatt, was summoned from Pittsburg to Philadelphia for consultation with Mr. Cassatt.

In order that all trainmen might understand the position of the company, Mr. Atterbury had his latest proposition, which he regarded as more liberal than had been understood, printed and posted on the bulletin boards at every terminal and station and distributed to the employes.

Mr. Lee made public a general review of the issue. He pointed out that the brakemen dress to withstand cold weather, and "when compelled to alternately brake and fire, they subject themselves to the risk of contracting pneumonia, or, at least, heavy colds." It was also stated that the increased pay offered by the company would in many instances net the brakeman serving as firemen only $1.50 a month. Subsequent calculations showed that Mr. Atterbury's proposal would cause an average increase in the earnings of such brakemen of $6 a month. The clearing up of this fact doubtless did much to bring the subsequent negotiations to a successful result.

Grand Master Morrissey reached Philadelphia on the night of January 19, and arranged for a renewal of conferences with General Manager Atterbury.

Both Mr. Morrissey and Mr. Atterbury openly expressed their desire to prevent a strike if possible, and their determination to exhaust every means of reaching an agreement. Mr. Morrissey made the reopening of negotiations possible through suggesting that the company place firemen's helpers at points along the road where the services of brakemen as firemen were needed.

The subsequent negotiations consumed many hours on January 20 and 21 and were concluded on Monday, January 23, when Mr. Atterbury and Mr. Morrissey issued the following formal joint statement:

> Mr. Atterbury has accepted Mr. Morrissey's proposition on the Jersey City situation, increasing the wages of the conductors and brakemen in the Jersey City, Harsimus Cove, Greenville, Meadows, Newark and Waverly yards, to the standard rates of New York harbor, together with other working conditions.
>
> Mr. Morrissey has accepted Mr. Atterbury's proposition of January 7, as amplified by the results of the conferences of the last few days, in regard to brakemen assisting the firemen, both to go into effect as of January 1, 1905.
>
> Mr. Atterbury will, in addition, take up and put into effect within a reasonable time such other measures of relief, not only to the brakemen, but also to the firemen, as have been discussed and offered by Mr. Atterbury and suggested by the committee.

Mr. Morrissey said, after peace had thus been declared:

"The concessions are accepted in the generous spirit with which they have been tendered. Mr. Atterbury has given his word that the relief of the firemen from unusual strain will be his first regard.

"The stationing of extra men at ash pits, which, I understand, are about thirty miles apart on the middle division, the putting to work at junction points of men who have been laid off, when need for such extra services shall be demonstrated; these are some of the concessions made by the company.

"It was my first meeting in conference with Mr. Atterbury, and I was much impressed by his kindness and his disposition to hear patiently and judge fairly."

By increasing wages for trainmen within a radius of twelve miles of New York harbor, the Pennsylvania company accepts the higher scale recently adopted by the New York Central, Lackawanna, Staten Island, Long Island, Central Railroad of New Jersey and Lehigh Valley. It is estimated that the total increase amounts to more than $300,000 a year and affects about two thousand men. The negotiations resulting in this increase have been in progress between Messrs. Morrissey and Lee and officials of the several roads since early in December.

ARBITRATION AND CONCILIATION RECOGNIZED IN THE COTTON INDUSTRY.

GOVERNOR DOUGLAS, OF MASSACHUSETTS, MANUFACTURERS AND LABOR REPRESENTATIVES GET TOGETHER IN ENDING FALL RIVER'S ORDERLY, HISTORIC, TEXTILE STRIKE.

"I REGARD the recognition of the principle of arbitration as the most important element in the settlement of the Fall River strike," was the significant statement made by Gov. W. L. Douglas of Massachusetts, when that long struggle between the owners and the operatives in the cotton mills of that city was brought to an end, through his mediation, on January 18. Gov. Douglas expressed the hope that the seed of arbitration, thus planted, would grow in a few years to a strength that would prevent a "recurrence of these demoralizing and pitiful strikes." The agreement for the end of the strike was signed by Gov. Douglas, Nathaniel B. Borden, on behalf of the manufacturers, and James Tansey, President of the Textile Council of Fall River, on behalf of the operatives.

NATHANIEL B. BORDEN,
Cotton Manufacturer.

W. L. DOUGLAS,
Governor of Massachusetts.

JAMES TANSEY,
President Textile Council, Fall River.

The arbitration, whose introduction Gov. Douglas regards as so hopeful, relates to the future adjustment of the wages of the operatives to the margin of profit between the cost of raw cotton and the selling price of manufactured goods. An annual adjustment similar to this has long been made in the cotton manufacturing districts of England by committees representing the manufacturers and the organized employes through conference, although there is a provision for arbitration in case of a failure of the representatives of the two sides to agree. The arbitration exercised by Gov. Douglas relates to an average margin between the cost of raw material and the price of the product, upon which the manufacturers are to pay a dividend of 5 per cent. upon the wages earned between the date of the end of the strike and April 1. If this arbitral decision prove satisfactory to both sides, it may result in the introduction into the textile industry in New England, and ultimately in the United States, of the principle of the sliding scale. That principle has proved successful in this country in the manufacture of iron and steel and in coal mining.

One of the manufacturers was quoted as saying:

> The reduction has been accepted and the strike has been declared off. We have simply done to-day what we have been prepared to do at any time; that is, to treat with the operatives on future wage advances if market conditions warranted it and we could afford to do it. The labor leaders have conceded that we could not pay more wages under conditions prevailing July 25 and that is what we have contended for. In my opinion we will be able to do something about a permanent marginal scale of wages as a result of what has now been accomplished.

The Fall River strike is historic. The latest bulletin of the State Bureau of Statistics of Labor (December, 1904) pronounced it "unparalleled in the history of the textile industry in Massachusetts, which ranks as the first State in the Union in the number of operatives employed in the cotton goods industry, having about three times as many employed as any other State. * * * No single strike in the textile industry in this State has reached such proportions as to duration, number of operatives thrown out of work, financial loss to employes and employers, and such large disbursement of aid from organized labor and from sympathizers all over the country."

The strike began July 25, 1904, the date of the 12½ per cent. reduction in wages. The strike was ordered by a vote of the five textile unions. That vote was 1513 for a strike and 396 against. About 25,000 operatives, of whom less than one-fifth were members of the unions, thus followed the lead of 1513 organized workers.

The State Labor Bulletin said: "The Fall River strike stands by itself in the manner in which it has been conducted. On all sides the labor leaders have been characterized as being intelligent and conservative men. The mill operatives have proved themselves to be law-abiding citizens. There have been no riots, mobs or acts of violence, such as have been attendant upon all strikes of such magnitude throughout the country."

The strike affected 33 corporations, closed 72 mills; tied up $21,665,000 of capital and caused a weekly loss of wages of $150,000 and to the corporations of $23,000.

"THAT VAGUE BODY KNOWN AS THE GENERAL PUBLIC."

ITS MEANING AND ITS RELATIVE IMPORTANCE DEFINED BY REPRESENTATIVES OF VARIOUS WALKS OF LIFE.

MUCH comment was caused among professional scholars and writers, as well as among labor leaders, by the remarks of President Eliot of Harvard University, at the annual dinner of the National Civic Federation, concerning "a vague body known as the public." He estimated this body to be "five times as large as all the union men and all the union men's families and all the employers and all their families." He added: "The total number of employers, union men and their families in the United States does not exceed 20,000,000. The population of this country approaches 80,000,000. I have the honor to represent three-quarters of the American people."

Among those who seemed perplexed by this utterance was a Chicago member of the Carpenters' Brotherhood, who wrote this question: "According to this, I am not a member of the public because I am a union man. But did not the coal strike affect my bin just as it did Dr. Eliot's? When the street car strike was on in Chicago, I had to walk just like Dr. Harper of Chicago University. Just who compose the vague body known as the public?"

This carpenter's inquiry, accompanied by Dr. Eliot's remarks quoted above, was sent to a number of the readers of THE MONTHLY REVIEW, with a request for answers for publication. Some of the most pertinent replies are herewith presented. The varied interests represented by the writers indicate the wide concern felt in a question that some regard as abstract, or even finical, but whose economic importance is generally appreciated. Definitions are of first importance in discussion. Agreement upon terms is essential to profitable debate. This symposium, including the opinions of both theorists and practical men, representative of both parties to the industrial struggle and of its critical observers, therefore deserves the perusal of economic students.

—o—

THE PUBLIC ARE THE OUTSIDERS.

H. C. Watson, Editor Dun's Review, New York:—While the word "public" in itself possesses no ambiguity the peculiar application in connection with industrial or financial problems is calculated to confuse, and it is not surprising that the Chicago carpenter felt neglected. As used in relation to the Civic Federation, the word "public" is intended to apply to the bystanders or non-disputants in the industrial strife; those who get no direct benefit from the higher wages obtained by a protracted strike, but who suffer all the inconveniences during the controversy. The public differs from the bystanders in that it is possible for the spectator to vacate the scene if the bullets fly too thickly in the case of a street fight, but there is no avoiding the suffering that follows suspension of coal mining.

Strictly speaking, I should think that the carpenter was of the public when there was a coal or street-car strike, but not when his particular craft was holding up a job on a building. It is to be hoped that the Chicago carpenter will not get the impression that those who represent the "public" on the various committees of the Civic Federation are not "workers." Probably the third class works harder than the organized laborers; certainly its hours are much longer, but it finds time to help keep the peace and to protest against injustice. The "public" often lacks intimate knowledge of facts in regard to many disputes, which leads it into erroneous judgments, but the growing tendency toward publicity is making the conditions much better in this respect.

—o—

THE UNION MOVEMENT ALL-COMPREHENSIVE.

John B. Lennon, General Secretary Journeymen Tailors' Union of America:—The remark of President Eliot made at a recent dinner in New York that he represented a body known as the public five times as large as all the union men and all the union men's families, and all their employers and all their employers' families, struck me as a strange remark as soon as I read it. I wondered if old Harvard had departed from that sound democracy upon which her foundation was laid, and had taken up in lieu thereof a belief in class distinctions to separate and divide the people into different sections in this the United States of North America as they are divided in some of the other older countries of the world.

There is no such thing as a general public that the trade unionists and the employers of the country are not a part of. President Eliot himself is a part of the trade-union movement, and from it he cannot escape. It is education that has made our modern trade-union movement as effective and successful as it is. Where ignorance reigns supreme there is no labor movement like we have in the United States, and so long as Harvard University and the other colleges and universities of the country, together with the public schools, continue to enlighten not only the children, but all the people of our country, the trade-union movement will continue and will become more and more successful; and whether we will it or not, we are all a part of the great labor movement of the world, for there is no other movement that from the earliest dawn of civilization has worked for progress, for enlightenment and for a higher life. No matter what form it may take, whether it be that of the plebeians in ancient Rome, or of the serfs in the middle ages, or of the trade-unions at the present time as the foremost factor of this labor movement, there is no possibility for any one to escape being a part of it. While our friend President Eliot may think that he repsents some distinct entity from the trade-unionists of the country and from their employers, your humble servant thinks he is mistaken, and that he only repretsens in part the great mass of the people of our common country.

—o—

"THERE IS NO OUTSIDE PUBLIC."

George Gunton, Economic Author:—Much is said about the interests of society being superior to the interests of either labor or capital, but this is more sentiment than fact. Competitive struggle between large and small corporations for survival and supremacy, and the contest between laborers and employers over wages and conditions, is not limited to the particular contestants in a given struggle, but includes the interests of like units and all the active economic elements of the country. Those who speak of society as something superior seem to imagine that there is a great world constituting an overwhelming majority of the nation outside of the economic elements interested in the industrial contest. Such is not the case. The so-called public not interested directly or indirectly in the profits and conduct of business, on the one side, or the income and conditions of labor, on the other, is too small to be considered. Outside of office-holders, teachers and professional persons, no such public exists. Of course, the purchasers of coal are affected by a coal strike, but these are all either laborers or employers, or people depending upon laborers or the income from the profits from industry. This struggle may be to-day in the coal mines, to-morrow in the cotton factories; or it may be to-day with the railroad corporations, to-morrow with the iron or steel or cotton or woolen or other corporations; but every struggle for industrial adjustment is a part of the general struggle of all society, and there is really no such thing as an outside public. Therefore, it is not true to say that the interests of the public are more important than the interests of capitalists and laborers. There is no public that has any such preponderant interest.

—o—

A QUESTION OF INDIVIDUAL AND PUBLIC RIGHTS.

Thomas F. Woodlock, Editor Wall Street Journal, New York:—Every individual is a component part of the public. His social and business life largely consists of an adjustment of conflicting rights, as against other individuals, taken singly or in common. The public has some rights against him as an individual, and he has some rights as against the public. When there is a question as to the public rights against him, he is not one of the public. When there is a question of his rights as against another individual, the public is not concerned. When there is a question of the rights of the public against an individual other than himself, he is then part of the public.

—o—

THE INTERESTS OF ONE THE INTERESTS OF ALL.

R. R. Bowker, Editor and Publisher Publishers' Weekly, etc., New York:—On the inference that out of our 80,000,000 population 20,000,000 are engaged in or dependent upon occupations in which union men constitute the great body of workers, it is of course evident that the whole 80,000,000, as consumers, constitute "the public" in the economic sense, of which three-fourths are affected only as consumers and citizens by the relations of unionism with industrial activity, prices and public order, while the other fourth are concerned both indirectly as consumers and directly as wage earners. So far as unionism tends to increase prices by increasing wages, all consumers are affected alike, and one of the most notable features in strikes has been the willingness of union men in other occupations, as part of the consuming public, to bear, with cheerful self-sacrifice, their part of the deprivation or burdens resulting from the strike of fellow workmen in another industry. It is not to be taken for granted that a rise in wages means an increase in prices, for though this may be the immediate result, the ultimate consequence of raising the standard of living and of productive skill may be, and should be, to decrease cost and prices. The economic mistake of unionism, from which it is probably emerging, has been in restricting the output of the increased productivity of the more skilled or more competent workers, so that the economic good results of labor organizations have been in some part offset by the ill results of restriction. It is evident, here as everywhere, that the interest of one is the interest of all, and that the union man, as a member of the general public, must share whatever benefits or disadvantages come from union policy. When prices, whether of rent, fuel, food or other necessaries of life, rise in disproportion to the increase of wages, as has perhaps been the case in this country in recent "boom" periods, the result is hardest on people of small earnings, and the man who earns $600 a year instead of $500 is no better off if it costs him $600 for what before cost him $500. It is the whole public of 80,000,000 people, including union men, who suffer by any mistakes of the unions; it is the whole public, outside as well as within the unions, who should benefit by wise and uplifting policy on the part of labor organizations.

—o—

EVERY MAN, WOMAN AND CHILD.

C. A. Rook, President The Dispatch Publishing Company, Pittsburg:—Who is the public? Why, the public is the public—every man, woman and child is the public. The union man, the non-union man, the working woman, girl and boy. The boys and girls who have rich fathers and mothers and who can lie in bed until noon and stay up all night and never have to give a thought as to where they will eat and sleep, they are the public. The poor little boys and girls with hearts and ambitions as big and great as other boys and girls, but who know not where they will eat and sleep, if at all, they are the public. The man or woman who is trying to get a fair day's pay for a fair day's labor, whether union or non-union, is the public. In fact, the whole 80,000,000 persons who live and labor in this great and grand country of ours, whether he is employed or unemployed, capitalist or laborer, is the public. If I were an employe instead of an employer I would belong to that great public which is called union. If the employes of this great United States would follow the Golden Rule, there would be but little need for unions. When President Eliot of Harvard, either through error or intention, excluded the union men from among the public, then President Eliot makes one big, grand mistake, for they are and will remain a part of our public.

—o—

THE PUBLIC MEANS ALL CONSUMERS.

Edward J. Wheeler, Editor Literary Digest, New York:—My understanding of Dr. Eliot's words is that he included in "the public" the Chicago carpenter and all the rest of the population; but inasmuch as the employers and employes have *special interests* that may be supposed to transcend in their cases the general interests common to all "the public," he did not assume to represent them, but to represent the rest of "the public" not affected by the special interests. For industrial purposes, "the public" consists ordinarily of the entire body of consumers of industrial products. That means everybody.

—o—

RIGHTS OF THE PUBLIC NOT PARAMOUNT.

D. L. Cease, Editor Railway Trainmen's Journal, Cleveland:—Who compose the "vague body known as the public?" can be answered by saying, the general people. What are the rights of the public? which I think is the question wholly in keeping with the source of the first inquiry, seems to need more of explanation.

It is admitted that one-fourth of the people, or that percentage of the "vague public," is affiliated with the organization of labor, either as master, workman, or dependent upon either. A body so large naturally deserves consideration, regardless of the fact that it is not in the majority.

If we will eliminate from the calculation those engaged in agriculture and domestic service, who have not been reached by organization, we will find that one-fourth of the public, so far as its organized representation is concerned, to be materially increased. If we add to this increased body that other portion of the "vague public" which is receiving higher wages and shorter working hours, secured by labor organization action, we will find that at least one-half of the "vague public" is either thus represented or indirectly affiliated.

If it were made known to the "vague public" that only such employes as were affiliated with the labor organizations would receive the wages and hours that had been granted through labor organization effort, the one-fourth of the "vague public" now allotted to organized labor would visibly swell, and, I believe, would become three-fourths. There are some employments that have not been directly reached by labor organization. Farm and domestic labor has not profited from direct organization of each class, but both classes have benefited from the increased wages of the other occupations, because higher wages must be paid to hold them in their class of service.

I believe that when the entire question is figured out that, aside from the "submerged tenth," the representative portion of the public that stands for itself and apart from the labor organizations will not be three-fourths by any means.

And now as to the rights of the public. This, I take it, means to what extent can the other man make his fellow serve him, and under what conditions can he quit his service without disturbing the rights of the "public."

This question naturally involves service and the leaving of it. A strike naturally inconveniences the public; this includes those on strike just as much as it does those who are not; it disturbs business, embarrasses the employer and perhaps makes the striker suffer from want. But in the question of his responsibilities toward the public, let it be understood that the man who leaves the service does not do so for the purpose of hindering or injuring his employer; he does not aim to inconvenience the rest of the public; he seeks to better his own condition; his relation, or duty, to the public is absorbed in the question of defending that part of the public with which he has been classed from the impositions of another part of the public, or his employer.

If this were a world wherein men sought to assist each other at the expense of themselves, this condition would not maintain; it could not exist; there would be no reason for it. But it is a condition governed altogether by self interest, in which no part of the public rightfully can be expected to sacrifice its well being for any other part. It must be the judge of its duty toward the remainder of the "vague public," and it is asking too much to expect that one part of the general people will sacrifice its welfare for the benefit of the remainder. If this were done, as the question of the duty of labor organizations toward the public is sometimes understood, we would very soon pass from the period of self sacrifice to that of the branding iron, the ball and the chain, in which case the three-fourths of the "vague public" now standing aside would join in the "public" demand for a better condition.

—o—

VAGUE TERMS UNDESIRABLE.

James E. Freeman, Rector St. Andrew's Memorial Church, Yonkers, N. Y.:—There is so much vagueness and ambiguity about many of the trite terms and phrases that we employ in every-day speech that we need to exercise greater caution in our utterances. For instance, we talk about that misty, difficult-to-be-defined corporate body, which we call the "public," as though it were a something that were capable of exact limitations. Again, we speak about "Public Opinion" or "Public Sentiment," as though it were an arbitrary and definite object, susceptible to analysis.

We take it that a reasonably clear and adequate definition of what constitutes the "public" is that *whole* body of people of every sort and kind, without reference to occupation or station, who, in the aggregate, make up the body political and the body social. A "public interest" is one that is coterminous with every near and remote concern of our corporate life. We venture to think that it is a somewhat dangerous thing to segregate our people by undertaking to classify them, thus making it appear that their interests are in any way divorced or inimical.

If I understood Dr. Eliot correctly, he was seeking to emphasize, for the purposes of discussion merely, the several elements involved in a common cause; he was not seeking to emphasize points of difference, but rather points of resemblance. Our whole people, of whatever sort or kind they may be, constitute segments in that corporate wheel we call the "public," and the more this cardinal fact is emphasized and understood, the greater will be the responsibility of each, and the more secure the prosperity and peace of all.

—o—

A QUESTION OF USE OF WORDS.

Amos K. Fiske, Editorial Staff, Journal of Commerce, New York:—It seems to me that the National Civic Federation has by its own organization established a certain distinction between employers, wage-earners and the public, not meaning that employers and wage-earners are not included in the public in a general sense, but meaning by the latter the mass of those not comprised in the two classes named and having a somewhat different interest in the controversies between capital and labor, or between employers and union workmen in particular. In that sense, it seems to me there is a distinction, which is that recognized in the representation of the Civic Federation and that intended by President Eliot, and the question of the Chicago carpenter appears rather carping. Of course, "the vague body known as the public," strictly speaking, includes all producers and consumers alike, just as producers include consumers and consumers include producers, but there may be parts of that body which not only have interests different from those of other parts, but interests different from the mass of those who do not belong to those particular parts. In so far as employers of labor, having control of capital, are able to arrogate to themselves any special advantage or any special or excessive part of the common product of labor and capital in their particular industry, and in so far as wage earners by organization are able to arrogate to themselves any special advantage or any arbitrary portion of that common product, they establish interests apart from those who are not included in their own ranks, and may impair the fair share of the rest who do not control productive capital and who are not organized, and may encroach upon their rights.

—o—

CONTESTANTS ARE OF THE PUBLIC.

Frederick H. Cooke, Lawyer and Author, New York:—I find that in my treatise of "Trade and Labor Combinations," published in 1898, I had substantially anticipated the phrase used by President Eliot, for I there speak (p. 17) of "that vague combination known as the public," adding, "that is to say, the inhabitants of a given town, city, state or country, as the case may be, or even of a region not limited by mere political boundaries." It is said elsewhere that the word public "may refer to the whole body politic, that is to say, to all the inhabitants of the state, or to the inhabitants of a particular place only" (23 American and English Encyclopedia of Law, 2d ed., p. 303).

This being, I take it, the ordinarily accepted meaning, the Chicago member of the Carpenters' Brotherhood, referred to in your letter, is right. The "public" affected by the coal strike constituted, generally speaking, the entire population of the United States; likewise the "public" affected by the Chicago street-car strike, constituted, I take it, the entire population of Chicago. In each case the Chicago union carpenter was one of the "public."

The real question of difficulty I understand to be whether, in case of a contest affecting the public interests of a given community, the parties to the contest are, if themselves inhabitants of such community, to be regarded as a portion of the public affected. This is a question of words rather than substance. I am inclined to think that they are to be so regarded. Ordinarily, however, the interest of such a person as party to the contest is by him, at least, regarded as far more important than his interest as a member of the public.

—o—

DR. ELIOT SUSTAINED.

Henry D. Estabrook, Solicitor The Western Union Telegraph Company, New York:—President Eliot's use of the word "public," to distinguish the people generally from those belonging to unions, was a correct use of the word. Every individual is himself one of the public as a whole, but if he wishes to distinguish himself from the people en masse he would use the words "I and the public." A corporation composed of thousands of stockholders would do the same, and a union composed of millions of adherents would do the same. The purpose is to distinguish a particular or individual interest from a general or universal interest.

—o—

"FOUR-QUARTERS OF THE PEOPLE."

Henry W. Farnam, Professor of Political Economy, Yale University:—The question seems to me simple. The word "public" includes in general four-quarters of the people. If, however, one-quarter consider their special interests to be more important than the general interests of the people as a whole, a man who speaks for these general interests would naturally only claim to *represent* the remaining three-quarters.

—o—

MILITANT UNIONS SEPARATE FROM THE PUBLIC.

Charles T. Root, President Textile Publishing Company, New York:—If the Chicago union carpenter feels afflicted by President Eliot's intimation that the unions and the public are distinguishable bodies, he and his associate unionists have themselves to thank for the impression thus indicated. When the unions set themselves apart not as a merely peaceable, mutually helpful association of individuals, but as a militant, quasi-governmental institution demanding universal obedience, willing or unwilling, to all its edicts, and ever ready to turn the homes of non-combatants into the battlefield upon which they wage their desolating struggle for supremacy, they cannot complain and should not wonder at the growth of the feeling that they are, from the industrial point of view, no more the public than the Russians and Japanese are Manchurians.

Whenever, and in so far as the unions themselves feel themselves to be vitally related parts of the public body and not themselves the "whole show," to whom injuries of the public body are of inconsiderable concern, compared to the enforcement of their own rules and demands, then the state of affairs indicated by President Eliot and recognized by the National Civic Federation in the form of its own organization will give place to actual solidarity in which, in its highest and best sense, the injury of one will be the concern of all.

—o—

LIBERTY AND LAW BEFORE THE UNION.

Slason Thompson, Manager of News Bureau, Railway Exchange, Chicago:—There is nothing to the query of your Chicago member of the Carpenters' Brotherhood. President Eliot said that he represented a vague body known as the public, which he estimated to be five times as large as all the union men, etc. Subsequently he divided the public into 20,000,000 union and 60,000,000 non-union. The union had been represented by the speakers who preceded him to the neglect of the non union portion of the public. He undertook to speak for the three-fourths of the public, which had not been heard from, and also for the whole public, which included union and non-union.

In any republican assembly the man who speaks for three-fourths is entitled to speak for all. In my opinion President Eliot spoke on behalf of liberty for the Chicago member of the Carpenters' Brotherhood as well as for those of the great majority who agree with every word he said.

Yours for liberty, law and union,
But for liberty and law, union or no union.

—o—

ONLY DIVISION ONE OF INTEREST.

J. W. Jenks, Professor of Political Economy and Politics, Cornell University:—Members of trade-unions are, of course, members also of the "vague body known as the public," unless, by their actions, they put themselves in opposition to the interests of the public. In that case, they should for the time being be considered no longer members of that body. It can be readily seen that the interests of the member of a union may for the time being be greater in the acts of his union than in his association with other members of the body politic. The unions should keep continually in mind the fact that they are members of the body politic, and so far as possible should make the acts of the union beneficial to the whole of the body politic as well as to the members of the unions themselves. In my judgment, they very generally do keep this in mind, but sometimes they certainly do not. It was doubtless some instance of the last case that President Eliot had in mind in his address.

—o—

ALL PURCHASERS AND CONSUMERS.

Franklin H. Giddings, Professor of Political Science, Columbia University:—President Eliot's use of the phrase "the public" was, I think, misleading and unfortunate. From the standpoint of any given individual, combination of individuals or corporation, "the public" is simply everybody else, and there are as many "publics," therefore, as there are individuals and combinations thereof. President Eliot set "the public" over against the corporate employers and their wage-earning employes; but from the standpoint of any one of the farmers or shopkeepers making up President Eliot's "public" the corporations and their employes are themselves a part of a "public." Speaking in terms of economics, it would be approximately true to say that "the public" consists of everybody considered as a purchaser and consumer, as distinguished from everybody considered as a producer. It would not do, however, to push such a definition to far, or to construe it too literally.

—o—

AN HISTORIC COMPARISON.

S. M. Sexton, Editor United Mine Workers' Journal:—The only parallel to the statement of Dr. Eliot that he represents three-quarters of the American people can be found in an incident that occurred in London in the latter part of the eighteenth century. The people and politicians were greatly disturbed by a manifesto which demanded certain radical reforms. The manifesto began with: "We, the people of England," and had it the support of a considerable body must have borne serious results. But an investigation revealed that "We, the people of England," consisted of "Three Tailors of Tooley Street," and they were snickered down by the whole city. It is highly probable that President Eliot has magnified matters as hugely as the "Three Tailors of Tooley Street."

—o—

A UNIONIST ACCEPTS DR. ELIOT'S TERM.

Frank K. Foster, Typographical Union, Boston:—While each person making up our 80,000,000 of the population is undoubtedly an integral part of the "public," yet President Eliot is also fully justified in using the word "public" in the sense he did by the Civic Federation itself, a portion of whose executive committee is selected "on the part of the public."

—o—

THE PUBLIC IS EVERYBODY.

Hamilton Holt, Managing Editor The Independent, New York:—I would say that my idea of the "public" is everybody—employers and employed, "scabs" and middlemen, etc; but I suppose in the sense of the National Civic Federaton, the "public" is all that remains after deducting the representatives of organized capital and the representatives of organized labor from the whole population of the United States.

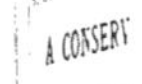

A CONSERVATIVE APPEAL TO THE UNITED MINE WORKERS OF AMERICA.

PRESIDENT MITCHELL, TRIUMPHANTLY RE-ELECTED, REVIEWS THE COAL INDUSTRY AND ADVISES HIS CONSTITUENTS TO STRIVE FOR PEACE IN NEXT YEAR'S CRISIS.

THE re-election of John Mitchell as President of the United Mine Workers of America, announced at its sixteenth annual convention in Indianapolis, proclaims the continued confidence in its chief leader of the largest body of organized labor in the world. It sets the seal of approval by that body upon the policy of President Mitchell last year in advising the bituminous miners to accept the compromise reduction of 5.55 per cent in wages offered by the operators at the Indianapolis conference.

Other general officers elected are:

Vice-President, T. L. Lewis (re-elected); secretary-treasurer, W. L. Wilson (re-elected). Delegates to the American Federation of Labor—John Mitchell, T. L. Lewis, W. L. Wilson, W. D. Evans, Patrick Dolan, John Fahy, John Dempsey. Delegates to International Mining Congress—W. H. Haskins, H. C. Perry.

JOHN MITCHELL,
President United Mine Workers of America.

The importance of this convention is widely recognized, because of the fact that a year from next April the biennial contract with the bituminous operators' association and the award of the anthracite strike commission expire simultaneously. The annual report of President Mitchell thus spoke of this impending situation:

"It may not be amiss at this time to call your attention to the fact that one year from next April our joint agreements expire in practically every coal-producing district—both bituminous and anthracite—in the United States. Reference to the reports of commercial agencies and trade journals seems to indicate an approaching revival of business and a period of industrial activity. If these predictions are realized, we should be able to regain the loss in wages sustained one year ago and to improve conditions of employment in those districts in which no reductions were forced upon us. It is, of course, unnecessary to say that our ability to make further advancement—or even to retain our present standard of living and wages—will depend in no small degree upon the strength and solidarity of our union, and in making preparations for that time we should not only strive with all our energies to perfect our organization numerically, but we should also make provision for the maintenance of our people, should we be so unfortunate as to become involved in a strike.

"I am, of course, hopeful that we shall be able to reach a satisfactory settlement upon the expiration of our present contracts, but, nevertheless, there is always the possibility of disagreement, and as far as I am personally concerned, I have determined that—under normal conditions—the present scale of wages, the present standard of living among the coal miners of this country, shall never be lowered with my consent. There are times when workmen are called upon to and should share in the loss of profits which follows periods of industrial depression, but there is a standard below which men cannot maintain themselves and their families, and below this point the wages of organized workmen cannot be permitted to fall.

"A reference to the financial report of your secretary-treasurer will impress you more forcibly than any words of mine could do, with the necessity of providing funds for the maintenance of strikes. In the words of Washington, 'To be prepared for war is one of the most effectual means of preserving peace.' And you should bear in mind that those organizations which are best prepared for strikes are called upon least frequently to engage in them. Whatever the causes, the strikes that have taken place during the past few years have established a precedent which cannot well be departed from, and when men strike now we are compelled, within certain limitations, to provide them with the necessities of life. The funds for this purpose can come only from one source—unless our membership provide us with the money, we cannot supply it to those who are on strike. And if we are to make adequate preparation for our next interstate convention we must have a large fund at our disposal, so that we may in the interim, resist any attempts to reduce wages in the outlying districts or any efforts to weaken the strength and influence of our union."

Mr. Mitchell declared that the acceptance of the compromise bituminous agreement last year, involving a reduction in wages of 5.55 per cent., was "a monument to the sagacity of the members of our organization and proves that government, whether of unions or of nations, is safe in the hands of the people." He believed that the union is "in a far better condition now than it would be had a strike been inaugurated."

The average membership for 1904 was 251,096. This was an increase of less than 4,000 over 1903, while membership for December, 1904, showed a decrease of 24,900. This decrease is based upon the tax received for the month and is explained by the exemption from dues of about 25,000 miners then on strike.

Mr. Mitchell showed that the operation of the Anthracite Commission's sliding scale had caused an increase of 7 per cent. in the pay of mine workers during the last three months of 1904.

Of the federal injunction, Mr. Mitchell said:

"Every year that passes emphasizes more strongly the iniquity of the federal injunction as applied in labor disputes. During the past year injunctions have been issued in every coal field in which a strike has been inaugurated, and members of our association have been confined in jail because of alleged disregard of these injunctions, notwithstanding the fact that after our people had remained in prison for considerable time, the very judge issuing the injunction has reversed his own action and declared that when the injunction was issued his court was without jurisdiction in the case.

T. L. LEWIS,
Vice-President United Mine Workers of America.

"It is difficult to speak in measured tones or in moderate language upon this subject. It is apparent to every one who is acquainted with the facts that many of these injunction judges—and especially Judge Jackson—are totally unfit to perform the functions of their sacred office. In numerous instances members of our union, when brought before these judges, have been treated with indignity and have had such abuse heaped upon them as should be countenanced by no man of impartial mind or of judicial temperament.

"I wish to emphasize the fact that we ask no special privileges over other citizens or other associations; we seek no immunity from the law, but we do demand and insist upon the exercise of all the rights and all the privileges that are guaranteed us by the constitution and enjoyed by other citizens of our common country. If any member of our union violates the law he deserves to be and should be arrested, tried, and convicted for his offense; but when judges issue orders restraining trade-unionists from doing that which they have a perfect moral and legal right to do, and which would be no offense if done by other citizens, and when these same judges incarcerate our people without trial, without hearing, because they refuse to surrender their constitutional liberties, then, I say, it is time to call a halt.

"For several years past a bill has been pending in the United States Congress defining the word 'conspiracy,' and limiting to its proper and constitutional function the authority of these federal judges. This bill will again be under consideration at the present session of Congress, and it seems to me that no effort should be left untried to secure its passage. To that end, I recommend that your president or your executive board be given authority to employ one or more representatives to go to Washington and lobby in the interest of this bill."

DANIEL J. KEEFE,
President International Longshoremen's Association.

DANIEL J. KEEFE ON ORGANIZATION AND CONTRACTS.

The Leader of the Longshoremen Emphasizes to Employers' Associations the Beneficence of Trade Agreements.

Daniel J. Keefe, president of the International Longshoremen, Marine and Transport Workers' Association, delivered an address to the recent convention of the Licensed Tugmen's Protective Association at Detroit, in which he dwelt upon the importance of developing organizations of both employers and employed. Mr. Keefe said in part:

"There is no war between capital and labor, no real hostility, simply the desire of each to get as good a bargain as possible for his side. When both recognize that each is essential to the other, with a mutual recognition of the rights of both, which must be decided upon a basis of equity, where justice will rule, then will begin the era of the Golden Rule, but the conditions we hope for will not come by our sitting down and idly dreaming. We all must, and are expected, to do our part. Every man has it in him to contribute his share and can aid in spreading the gospel of perfect organization.

"A few years ago, in speaking of the late Senator Hanna, I inadvertently referred to him as a 'professional man.' 'Dan,' said he, 'I am a worker, and a worker for wages and profits, the same as any other man in my employ; and let me tell you,' said he, 'when any man working for our company ceases to regard himself as a wage worker, and fails to realize that he is so regarded by me, his usefulness to this company is at an end.' (So much for professional labor.) I accepted his rebuke and now understand the one great element in his character that went to make Senator Hanna great among the modern captains of industry, and one of the great men of progress of our generation. Let us then strive to so shape the laws of this land, socially and politically, so that we may obtain a reward for our labor equal to its full value."

In an address to the Lake Carriers' Association, also in Detroit, Mr. Keefe congratulated that body upon having been the pioneers in leading the way in observing the moral obligation of organized labor to carry out its contracts.

THE CAUSES AND PREVENTION OF RAILWAY ACCIDENTS.

A BROTHERHOOD CHIEF AND TWO BROTHERHOOD EDITORS DISCUSS THE RESPONSIBILITY O EMPLOYES AND OF DEFECTS IN ADMINISTRATION AND EQUIPMENT.

THE shocking totals of death and injury from railway accidents and their cause and remedy continue subjects of keen public concern. The following articles are from contributors familiar with the employes' views of their cause, and continue the discussion begun in the October issue of THE REVIEW. The editor has arranged for further articles, expressing the opinions of high executive officers of several large railway systems, one of them the president of a trunk line.

AN EXPERIENCED EMPLOYE'S OPINION.

By E. E. CLARK, *Grand Chief Conductor, Order of Railway Conductors.*

Much is now being said in the public press relative to the frequency with which fatal accidents are occuring on the railroads of the United States. That such accidents have occurred with alarming frequency and

E. E. CLARK,
Grand Chief Order Railway Conductors.

appalling results none will doubt or deny. No one will question the importance of discovering the cause or causes which contribute to such disasters and of applying the necessary remedy, however drastic, it may be.

It seems to me unfortunate that those who publicly discuss those questions are so prone to lay all the responsibility at the door of some one condition which they hold an antipathy for, or a condition which they claim would be corrected by the adoption of some idea or device in which they are interested.

On one hand we see a disposition to attribute the whole trouble to penurious management, and strong appeals are made to the already existing prejudice against railway companies.

On another hand, we find an energetic effort to make the people believe that insubordination among the employes, encouraged and supported by the labor organizations to which they belong, is responsible for the accidents of which every person hears and reads with horror.

Again, we find the correspondent who attributes it all to the alleged fact that railway officials habitually require employes to remain on duty excessively long hours and after-exhaustion renders them unfit and unsafe. This is answered by some railway official who claims that if men are on duty long enough to be exhausted it is because of their own desire and demand to be allowed to earn more money.

As a matter of fact most of the casualties can be clearly and directly traced to carelessness, neglect, forgetfulness or exhaustion on part of some employe or employes. In a list of fourteen accidents cited by Mr. Slason Thompson no less than five were caused by improper or negligent flagging and three were the result of conductors and engineers forgetting opposing trains or of failure to properly comply with orders relative to meeting of trains.

The working agreements between the railway companies and their employes in the train and engine departments provide that after continuous service of a certain number of hours the employes may demand rest before again being required to go out. The burden of compliance with this proper provision rests with the employe as he is permitted to be the judge of whether or not he needs rest. Everyone who is at all well informed on the subject knows that there are instances in which employes are required to work against their wishes and in which they are permitted to work in accordance with their wishes when, because of physical exhaustion, they are not in a safe condition.

It is idle to argue that the universal adoption of any particular device would avert the possibility of a recurrence of these sad accidents. Signaling devices depend largely upon human agencies to operate them and even if they did not so depend, the fact would still remain that perfect safety under them would depend upon observance of them by men who are made from the same material as are other men.

Some representatives of the railways assert that the unions have bred and encouraged a spirit of insubordination and that they have enforced a system of promotion by seniority under which ambition is smothered and the worthy and the unworthy, the competent and the incompetent, the bright and the dull, are all placed on a common level.

This, to my mind, is the most unfair and incorrect of all the statements so far made. It is not true that the organizations composed of train and engine employes encourage insubordination in the slightest degree. No instance can be cited in which they have taken the position of arbitrarily upholding their members in violation of the rules of the company by which employed. They teach loyalty, not disloyalty, to their members.

It is true that the practice prevails of generally promoting the older man in the service who is in line of promotion. This is commonly called "seniority," and many would have it appear that the unions are wholly responsible for the practice and that its provisions are inflexible. A reference to a file of working agreements between railway companies and their train or engine men will disclose the fact that the rule for promoting men in accordance with seniority in service is always qualified with the specific provision "all things being equal," or "merit, ability and competency being equal." All men promoted are obliged to pass examination prescribed by the company and at the hands of officials of the company.

The practice of promoting men by seniority is as strongly favored by railway officials as it is by employes, and the managements have contributed as much to its establishment as have the employes.

I offer no excuse for neglect or carelessness or indifference on part of railway employes. They occupy positions of great responsibility and in no other employment can the disastrous results of error or omission be so far-reaching. They have much to account for and, considering the immensity of the industry and the imperative demands of their employ-

D. L. CEASE,
Editor Railroad Trainmen's Journal.

ment, as well as the feverish impatience of our people as a whole and the insistence upon faster and still faster movements, they render a remarkably good account.

The railway employes will be glad to be judged at the bar of public opinion when the public properly understand the true facts.

SOME EXACTIONS OF TRAIN SERVICE.

By D. L. CEASE, *Editor of The Railroad Trainme Journal, Official Organ of the Brotherhood of Ra road Trainmen.*

That employes are responsible for many railw wrecks is true; that much of the system of train ope tion is also responsible is equally true.

There are any number of matters co-incident w the operation of trains that do not appear on the su face, but which are largely responsible for ma collisions.

Regardless of the manner of train that is being ru there is the mandate following it from the time leaves until it reaches its terminus, "make time." make time and escape the ever pending inquiry a reprimand, or something more severe, the tra employes are encouraged to take chances.

This leaves room for very many lapses in perfect tra

JOHN F. M'NAMEE,
Editor Railway Firemen's Journal.

management, and it is not surprising that serious re sults follow. The majority of these wrecks are charge to the men, but really should be charged properly to th lack of intelligent official operation.

I believe that back of this can be found too muc technical method, and too little of practical knowledg of the needs of the service. Trains cannot be run switched and safely controlled by the lead pen only.

The demands made upon the men are conducive t forgetfulness, for there is a limit to human endurance The hours are very often too long; the work at best i nerve exhausting, tiring out the employe mentally an physically. Every railroad has its "drags,"—long freights, that are started out with the certainty tha they are going to work overtime,—how long wil depend upon circumstances. Men can only remai alert for a given time, after that they are worn out Men will drop asleep on the field of battle. Is i strange, then, that men with the wearying stretch o hour after hour on a locomotive or a train will grow dull or sleepy?

The "drags" are generally so long, and the me employed are so few, that intelligent communicatio between the members of the crew is out of the ques tion. The engineer is almost a mile away from th hind end of the train. It takes the fireman and th head brakeman to do the firing; the engineer becaus of the build of the engine is by himself on many of th heavy engines, and is not seen by the other men o the engine unless they climb up where he is; the con ductor, looking after his many clerical duties, is o the hind end, or he ought to be, and the flagman i generally back somewhere riding on the followin train. Rear end wrecks are not so frequent, by an means, as head end ones. The man behind has al of his attention on his work.

Railways lay particular stress upon their safety equipment and bring it to their defense in freight train wrecks. There are any number of railways that still depend upon the hand brake in handling their train

(*Concluded on page 8.*)

EMPLOYERS' POLICIES TOWARD LABOR.

Declaration in Favor of Encouraging Employes to Join Unions.

By EDWARD A. FILENE, *Merchant, Boston.*

(*Extract from an Address before the Economic Club.*)

American employers have won their success largely by their open-mindedness, by their willingness to change the good for the better. It has been well said that a good measure of the superiority of American manufactures is the greater size of their scrap heaps of displaced machinery as compared with the scrap heaps of manufacturers of other countries.

EDWARD A. FILENE.

But ideas of policies grow out of date as well as machinery, and the successful employer must have an intangible scrap heap of ideas and policies larger than the visible one of machinery. The time has now come to add to that heap some of our policies toward our employes, toward trades-unions.

When the unions were young and weak, and their management and policies so uncertain that that stability which is necessary to the maintenance and growth of business enterprises could not be guaranteed by them, then we fought them in defence of our property and rights; but now the evidence that the union has come to stay is so indisputable that all clear-sighted men admit it, and employers must recognize that the question is not, "How can the union be annihilated?" but "What shall our policy be so that the unions can be made to help us in helping themselves? What kind of bargain can we make with our employes, with the union?" remembering that every bargain to be a good one must be mutually advantageous.

The chief difficulty of the past no longer confronts us. That difficulty was that we did not admit at first that the union had come to stay. If I criticise that position, I do it most sympathetically, for I believe, as human nature runs, and recognizing how industrial principles and rights are evolved through contest, that no other position toward the organized form of the new demands of our employes than that of opposition was possible at the beginning.

Be that as it may, the time has now come when clear-sighted men admit that the unions have come to stay, and that only by organization of employers and of employes can best conditions be brought about.

Employers must be better and more strongly organized and unions must be better and more strongly organized in order that the needless part of industrial strife be averted.

If, then, the unions are to stay, how are they to be made more serviceable?

For it is undoubtedly true, and admitted by wise union leaders, that their policies must also be changed, at least in part.

How *are* these policies to be changed?

The answer is forced upon us that the first and most necessary thing to do is to change our own policies—our employers' policies. In the past, harassed by the unions, we have believed that this harassing would be weaker, would be less, if we kept the unions weak. This is the great, the fundamental mistake we have made. To-day we know from bitter experience that it is the weak union that does the most damage to us—the union controlled by radical, short-sighted men, because larger numbers of our more conservative employes are not active members.

This is a truth we have learned very slowly, and at great cost, and as far as our policies bear witness we have not yet wholly learned it. Otherwise it would be our policy distinctly and definitely to encourage our best employes to go into the unions.

At present our policy towards the existence of trades unions is at best not more than neutral. I urge with all my power that the time has come to change this policy to one of definite purpose to make the unions better by encouraging our best and most valuable employes to join them, and to become active workers in them.

What will happen if we do this?

The first and most important result will be that much of the struggle that has hitherto been fought out to our great loss in our plants will be fought out in the union meetings.

For our best and most valuable men are not only good workers, but they are broader minded than the average; see conditions more clearly than the average employe; and therefore know our difficulties better than the weaker employes. And so when the employes' policies are decided in their unions, these broader-minded, clearer-seeing employes, adding their numbers to those that are already in the unions, will have the greatest weight in determining the union policies toward employers and will help to determine them with more consideration for us and our difficulties.

If we adopt this policy, it will eventually follow that many of the questions that are now "debated" (God save the mark), with strikes, boycotts and lockouts in our shops, will be really debated and fought out in the union meetings.

This policy must and will bring about better things for us. It is an open secret that the wisest and most far-seeing union leaders have often failed to carry out their more liberal policies for lack of the support which this new employers' policy would give them.

More than this. Our new policy would send many of the harmful union policies to the scrap heap, in company with some of our own.

What are these?

To be concrete, let us take a pair of the competing forces: The closed shop and the open shop. As long as employers believe their interests are best served or least harmed by a weak union, so long will the union fight as for its very life for the closed shop.

For as long as we hold that belief, so long will the unions believe—and in many cases believe rightly—that we will use the open shop to weaken the union by dropping the union men in preference to non-union men, as the need of men grows less with slackening work.

Personally I believe that if we adopt this new policy, the unions will soon cease to fight for the closed shop, for it will no longer be necessary.

If employers adopt this new policy of favoring strong labor unions, then the unions will change their policy in regard to apprenticeship. For the further reason that there will then be no longer any attempt to weaken unions by substituting an undue number of apprentices in place of skilled union workers as is done by some at present.

In a word, many of the union policies are war measures adopted to meet our war policies. If from our experience we now see our way clearer, and send these war policies to the scrap heap, the unions will do the same with many of theirs, out of self-interest, if from no higher motive.

For this new policy of ours will help to bring about that which is the most valuable to us for business success—the stability of labor conditions.

Is it not true that we can afford to pay any reasonable wages, or cut the hours of work down any reasonable amount, providing these wages and hours are the same for all our competitors; and are so stable that we can count on them with certainty in making our selling prices? Such stable conditions can only be brought about by strong labor unions.

Is it not true that our interests as producers or distributors are best served by having as consumers employes so highly paid as to be able to make a profitable demand for our wares? Is it not true that one man earning $20 a week is more valuable as a profitable consumer than twenty men earning $6 a week?

I am not unmindful that the general public has also its interest and rights in this question of wages and hours, as they affect the cost of production.

But the public can be amply protected, if necessary, through the tariff and other means.

On these final grounds our interests as employers are in accord with the interests of our employes, and the time has come to adjust our policies to these mutual interests.

The virtues of war are the vices of peace. We can change our policies without being ashamed. These policies were called for in the era of individualism that was the chief mark of the century just gone. But the larger men this era has bred have in turn bred larger, better policies, and *noblesse oblige* American employers will adopt them.

But I hear some one say, "If we strengthen the unions, they will run away with us, ruin us!" Of course I do not urge the policy of making stronger, better unions without taking for granted at the same time the necessity of stronger employers' associations. This need is too self-evident to require urging.

I have already pointed out that as a matter of fact, many of the excesses of the unions are due to their weakness, and by putting in our better men, and in other ways helping to strengthen them, we will stop these excesses. But, more than this, the surest way to make a conservative of a radical is to give him power—to make him assume responsibility. The unions are no exception to this truth, which I know to be a truth from many years of practical experience.

A NEW DEBS SCHEME.

Socialists to Organize to Fight the American Federation of Labor and the Railway Brotherhoods.

Chicago News, Jan. 10.

Plans were secretly laid in Chicago last Saturday at a conference of labor leaders from various parts of the country to organize a new great labor body in the United States and overthrow the American Federation of Labor. News of this became public to-day when the promoters of the new organization issued a "manifesto" outlining its purposes and calling for a convention to be held in Chicago June 27. Back of the movement is Eugene V. Debs. Among the labor organizations which are said to support the plan to overthrow the American Federation of Labor and supersede the American Labor Union are international unions affiliated with both of these.

The scheme contemplates the uniting of all wage-earners in the land under one general organization, whose trend shall follow the teachings of Socialism.

After attacking the present system of labor organization and prohibitive initiation fees the declaration is made that "class divisions foster political ignorance among workers, thus dividing them at the ballot box as well as in the shop, mine and factory." Continuing, the manifesto says:

"Craft unions may be and have been used to assist employers in the establishment of monopolies and the raising of prices. One set of workers are thus used to make harder the conditions of life of another body of laborers. Craft divisions hinder growth of class consciousness of the workers, foster the idea of harmony of interests between employing exploiter and employed slave. They permit the association of the misleaders of the workers with the capitalists in the Civic Federation, where plans are made for the perpetuation of capitalism and the permanent enslavement of the workers through the wage system.

"Previous efforts for the betterment of the working class have failed because limited in scope and disconnected in action. Universal economic evils can only be eradicated by a universal working-class movement. Such a movement of the working class is impossible while separate craft and wage agreements are made favoring the employer against other crafts in the same industry, and while energies are wasted in fruitless jurisdiction struggles, which serve only the personal aggrandizement of union officials.

"A movement to meet these conditions must consist of one great industrial union embracing all industries, providing for craft autonomy locally, industrial autonomy internationally and working-class unity generally. It should be founded on the class struggle, and its general administration should be conducted in harmony with the recognition of the irrepressible conflict between the capitalist class and the working class.

"It should be established as the economic organization of the working class, without affiliation with any political party.

"All power should rest in the collective membership.

"Local, national and general administration, including union labels, buttons, badges, transfer cards, initiation fees and per capita tax should be uniform throughout.

"Workingmen bringing union cards from foreign countries should be freely admitted into the organization.

"All members should hold membership in the local, national or international union covering the industry in which they are employed, but transfers of membership between unions, local, national or international, should be universal.

"The general administration should issue a publication representing the entire organization and its principles, which should reach all members in every industry at regular intervals.

"A central defense fund, to which all members contribute equally, should be established and maintained."

The document is signed by the following:

Thomas J. De Young, of the United Brotherhood of Railway Employes, Houston, Texas.
Thomas J. Hagerty, of the American Labor Union, Chicago.
Charles O. Sherman, of the United Metal Workers, Chicago.
Fred D. Henion, of the United Brotherhood of Railway Employes, Minneapolis.
M. E. White, of the American Labor Union, Denver.
Ernest Untermann, Chicago.
W. J. Bradley, Minneapolis.
W. J. Pinkerton, of the Switchmen's Union of North America, Argentine, Kan.
Frank Krafft, International Union of United Brewery Workers, Chicago.
A. G. Swing, of the American Federation of Musicians, Cincinnati.
A. M. Simons, editor, *International Socialist Review,* Chicago.
J. E. Fitzgerald, Fort Worth, Texas.
Wade Shurtleff, of the International Musical Union, Cleveland.
William D. Haywood, of the Western Federation of Miners, Denver.
"Mother" Jones, Chicago.
Frank M. McCabe, Chicago.
John M. O'Neill, editor, *Miners' Magazine,* Denver.
Charles H. Moyer, of the Western Federation of Miners, Denver.
William E. Trautmann, of the International Union of Brewery Workmen, Cincinnati.
W. L. Hall, Chicago.
Joseph Schmitt, of the International Union Bakery and Confectionery Workers, Chicago.
Clarence Smith, Chicago.
John Guild, Chicago.
Daniel McDonald, Chicago.
Frank Bohn, New York City.
George Estes, Chicago.

A permanent executive committee was appointed, with William D. Haywood as president, W. E. Trautmann, secretary, and Clarence Smith, W. L. Hall and A. M. Simons as members. An office will be established in Chicago about February 1.

The Labor World of Pittsburg thus interprets the purpose of this movement:

> Of course the chief aim, in fact, the only aim, of this proposed movement is to destroy or injure the American Federation of Labor and all other movements designed to perpetuate industrial peace. To accomplish this Debs wants the wild theories of a many-sided socialism put before the wage workers in hopes that they may be led from the paths along which they have so safely and materially progressed. In this he will be aided by "Comrades" Parry & Co. The latter will be more than delighted at the move of Debs, in fact likely enough Parry & Co. are aiding Debs in his project, for they are working for the same air, viz., the destruction of trade unionism.

A unique union has been formed by Louisville carpenters. It will be known as Independent Carpenters' Union No. 1. Its objects are the open shop, no walking delegates, and no members except first class mechanics, and to prevent strikes and lockouts. It will be independent of all central organizations, and will not affiliate with the international body, but will accept all recommendations made by the Employers' Association, and work in harmony with that body—*American Industries.*

THE CIVIC FEDERATION OF BOSTON AND VICINITY.

THE NEW ENGLAND CENTER ESTABLISHED WITH GENERAL OFFICERS AND AN EXECUTIVE COMMITTEE REPRESENTING EMPLOYERS, WAGE-EARNERS AND THE PUBLIC.

THE New England Civic Federation was organized at a meeting in Boston on Monday, Jan. 23, attended by representatives of employers, wage earners and the general public. Major Henry L. Higginson, of Lee, Higginson & Co., bankers, presided and E. H. Walcott, Secretary of the Boston Merchants' Association acted as secretary. This organization is to be the center of the work of the National Civic Federation throughout New England. Its formation is in accordance with the plan by which the entire country is to be divided into seven sections for that work, each having a center.

The New England organization was effected by the election of officers and an executive committee. The officers are: President, Lucius Tuttle, President Boston and Maine Railroad; First Vice-President, Frank H. McCarthy, President Boston Central Labor Union; Second Vice-President, Louis D. Brandeis, attorney-at-law; Treasurer, Charles H. Taylor, Jr., Boston *Globe;* Secretary, E. H. Walcott, Secretary Boston Merchants' Association; Recording Secretary, Henry Abrahams, President Cigarmakers' Union.

The following constitute the Executive Committee:

On the part of the Employers: Amory A. Lawrence, President Merchants' Association, 89 Franklin Street; Lucius Tuttle, President Boston and Maine Railroad, North Station; Frederick P. Fish, President American Bell Telephone Company, 125 Milk Street; W. C. Winslow, 30 Congress Street; Arthur T. Lyman, Treasurer Boston Manufacturing Company, 50 State Street; Charles H. Taylor, Jr., Boston Globe.

On the part of the Public: Charles Francis Adams, publicist, 23 Court Street; Rt. Rev. William Lawrence, Protestant Episcopal Bishop of Massachusetts, 1 Joy Street; Major Henry L. Higginson, of Lee, Higginson & Co., 44 State Street; Hon. Charles S. Hamlin, 14 Beacon Street; John Mason Little, 74 Boylston Street; Louis D. Brandeis, attorney-at-law, 161 Devonshire Street.

On the part of Wage Earners: Dennis D. Driscoll, Central Labor Union, 93 E. Newton Street; Henry Abrahams, Cigarmakers' Union, 11 Appleton Street; Frank K. Foster, Typographical Union, 116 Eliot Street; Frank H. McCarthy, President Central Labor Union, 95 Regent Street; James R. Crozier, 25 Blue Hill Avenue, Roxbury; John F. Tobin, General President Boot and Shoe Workers' Union, 434 Albany Building.

Several of those present addressed the meeting. Lucius Tuttle said that he could name no one who knew just how to settle the labor question. But he was sure that nothing had done so much good as a free exchange of views between the employer and employes. Wrong ideas and misunderstandings were not provocative of disputes. It conduced to calmness to turn the hot tea of controversy into the cooling saucer of confidence. Mr. Tuttle said that, as a railway president, he gave the committees of employes, with whom he conferred, type-written figures of the business of the road in the same confidence as he gave them to the directors. The employes had never violated this confidence.

Henry Abrahams, as a representative of labor, greeted President Tuttle as made of the proper metal, for he was an employer willing to meet his employes. Most strikes resulted from the acts of superintendents and foremen, when the employes could not reach the head executive. If the Civic Federation did nothing more than to extend the practice of conference, it would have done a great work.

Charles H. Taylor, Jr., said that the Civic Federation was not intended to settle the whole labor problem, nor did any of its members believe that it could. The idea of the New England organization was to encourage conciliation and conference, and to lessen through fair discussion, the probability of conflict.

LUCIUS TUTTLE,
President New England Civic Federation.

CHARLES H. TAYLOR, JR.,
Treasurer New England Civic Federation.

FRANK H. M'CARTHY,
First Vice-President New England Civic Federation.

HENRY ABRAHAMS,
Corresponding Secretary New England Civic Federation.

CAUSES OF RAILWAY ACCIDENTS.

(*Continued from page 6.*)

down heavy grades; other roads are asking to be relieved from using safety appliances, and to be permitted to use an appliance that is neither fit for service nor emergency use. Train wrecks do occur because of insufficient or defective appliances.

To sum up the situation, I believe that wrecks are the result of carelessness, forgetfulness, long hours, heavy trains, the hurry-up system with discipline when time is not made, too many duties exacted from one employe, lack of a safe system in train running, and the failure to use safety appliances.

BROTHERHOOD HAS IMPROVED SERVICE.

By JOHN F. MCNAMEE, *Editor Locomotive Firemen's Magazine, Official Organ of the Brotherhood of Locomotive Firemen.*

Twenty years ago the majority of railroad men had no incentive to superior effort, and their principal object was to make a stake. They changed employers almost continually and were hired without any preliminary examinations whatever nor much if any regard to their past record. Their employment was insecure and uncertain, promotions were the result of personal favoritism. They had no source of appeal or hope of redress when unjustly treated as the result of personal dislike on the part of petty officials or from other causes. Almost every payday there were discharges at every yard office and roundhouse for drunkenness (something rarely, if ever, heard of nowadays). Men were no better off as far as prospects for promotion were concerned after years of service than they were when newly hired and the term "railroader" was synonymous with that of "floater."

While it is a fact that many thousands of dollars are annually expended in equipping railway rolling stock with safety devices and improvements, these advantages to the men are more than counterbalanced by the greater exactions on the part of railroad companies as to the amount of work to be performed per man in the train service departments; many roads having single track twenty years ago have four tracks now; locomotives now are three times as large as they were then, and have three times the hauling capacity; where twenty cars was an average train then, a drag of seventy-five cars in one train is no unusual thing at the present day; where a freight car of twenty tons capacity was considered large twenty years ago, it pales into insignificance beside the fifty-ton cars that are in use to-day; where a hundred miles or less constituted a division and a day's work back in those good old days, the men are now often required to haul these greatly increased trains over divisions of from 150 to 200 miles in practically the same number of hours; there are certain modern conditions which greatly jeopardize public safety.

Men are not admitted to the Brotherhoods haphazard. A probationary period in railway employment of from nine months to a year is an essential requirement for the determination of their eligibility to the organization representing their occupation. If at the end of this period they are still in the service and the investigating committee finds them morally eligible, they are accepted as members. Under the vigilant eyes of their superiors and their associate employes their possession of any physical or moral defects liable to incapacitate them from the proper performance of their duties will be quickly detected and the delinquents weeded out before becoming eligible for membership in the Brotherhoods. The Brotherhoods have come to stay. They are a fixture and must be reckoned with. They are universally respected, and railway managements, appreciating their usefulness and conservatism, recognize and encourage them. As business institutions they are conducted on a basis that defies adverse criticism.

SOCIALISM VERSUS UNIONISM.

A Disclosure of the Ulterior Purpose of Industrial Revolutionists in Entering Trades-Unions.

The following correspondence concerning the hostility of Socialism to unionism has been exchanged between the editor of *The Worker*, a Socialist weekly, and the editor of THE MONTHLY REVIEW of the National Civic Federation:

THE WORKER, NEW YORK, November 23, 1904.

To the Secretary of the Civic Federation, New York City.

SIR: From the call for the fourth annual meeting of the Executive Committee of the Civic Federation I quote the following:

> Another foe simultaneously assails organized labor. That foe is Socialism. Although Socialism is the avowed foe also of capital, it regards as an aid to its cause the radical type of employers' organizations, because of their common hatred of unionism. Socialism sees in unionism a means of bettering the condition of the masses that must postpone indefinitely the confiscation of all the machinery of production and distribution. Before Socialism can deliver its assault upon all capital it must remove from its way the self-improving organization of the wage-earners.

Your organization, Sir, professes to seek a basis for social and industrial peace. Do you think that this purpose is to be served by the publication of such unqualified falsehoods as that contained in the paragraph I have quoted? Or is it possible that, with the means at your disposal, you have made so superficial a study of the question that you can believe what you say in that paragraph? In either case, you deserve a rebuke proportionate in severity to the eminence of the men composing your Executive Committee and to the professions of devotion to the public welfare which they have made.

I speak, Sir, as an authorized spokesman of the Socialist party that has just cast half a million votes in this country, doubling its record of two years ago. I speak whereof I know when I tell you that the Socialists of this and other lands regard the trade-unions as their allies in the attack on capitalism, the movement for industrial democracy; that we rejoice in the victories of the trade-unions and do all in our power to render those victories more frequent and more complete; that our party, by formal resolutions in its national and international congresses, has repeatedly expressed its sympathy with the unions and advised its adherents to join the unions of their respective crafts; that the majority of our organized party members and the great majority of our candidates and party officers are trade-unionists; and that our party organization and its press has again and again raised funds to assist the trade-unions in their days of need. For proof I refer you to the proceedings of the International Socialist Congresses held at London in 1896, at Paris in 1900, and at Amsterdam in 1904; to the proceedings of the national conventions of the Socialist party held at Rochester in 1900, at Indianapolis in 1900 and 1901, and at Chicago in 1904; to the files of the numerous Socialist papers; and finally to the records of such Socialists and trade-unionists as Eugene V. Debs, Benjamin Hanford, James F. Corey, Frank A. Sieverman, Morris Brown, J. Mahlon Barnes, Max S. Hayes, Robert Bandlow and C. A. Hoehn.

I invite you, Sir, and through you the Civic Federation, to retract the false statement quoted, or to stand convicted of wilful mendacity.

Sincerely yours,
ALGERNON LEE,
Editor of *The Worker*.

OFFICE OF THE MONTHLY REVIEW,
NATIONAL CIVIC FEDERATION,
NEW YORK, December 1, 1904.

Mr. Algernon Lee, Editor The Worker, New York City.

SIR: I have before me your letter of recent date, in which you assert that a statement, given out by me as part of a call for the fourth annual meeting of the National Civic Federation, is an "unqualified falsehood," in so far as it describes as hostile the attitude of Socialism toward unionism; and you express your opinion that I merit a severe rebuke for either mendacity or ignorance.

In thus addressing me you claim to "speak as an authorized spokesman of the Socialist party that has just cast half a million votes in this country." You surely must advance that claim in a Pickwickian sense, since you must know that the Socialist party cannot truly claim as belonging to its ranks the 500,000 votes that were recently cast for Mr. Debs. You are well aware that many Single-Taxers and other radical groups, who have no more liking for Socialism than for smallpox, voted for Mr. Debs as a protest against the platform or candidates of the two great parties, or as a tribute to his personality. You have recognized in your own paper that the vote for Debs was enormously greater than the membership of the Socialist party. You have lamented that the number of your party members is less than 5 per cent. of the number of your voters (or less than 25,000), because your vote has increased in a larger ratio than your party membership. You have exhorted Socialist leaders to devote particular attention to the States where there was the greatest increase of the Debs vote and to do their utmost to get those who had cast their first "Socialist" vote this year really into the party organization.

You cannot, therefore, "speak as an authorized spokesman" for half a million voters. But you can and do speak as the editor of *The Worker*, a leading organ of what may be termed, for popular understanding, the Debsite Socialists.

In my statement I used the words "Socialism" and "unionism" in their broad, general sense. I freely confess, as you intimate, that I am not thoroughly familiar with the refined shades of distinction between the "fifty-seven varieties," or more of Socialism. Perhaps I would have been more technically correct had I stated that all of the DeLeon Socialist party and a large section of the Debs Socialist party are opposed to the American Federation of Labor and the Railway Brotherhoods. Those two varieties of Socialists are not opposed to all unions because, in fact, they have organized unions of their own to fight the American Federation of Labor and the Brotherhoods. Their names are, respectively, the Socialist Trade and Labor Alliance (the DeLeonites in the East), the American Labor Union (the Debsites in the West), and the United Brotherhood of Railway Employes, which is affiliated with the American Labor Union, and therefore a Debsite organization. The current Socialist literature furnishes incontestable evidence in support of these statements.

In denying my proposition that "Socialism" is inimical to "unionism," you adduce in your support statements that the Socialists regard the trade-unions as their allies in the attack on capitalism; that Socialists rejoice in the victories of the trade-unions, and do all they can to make them more frequent and complete; that your party, "by formal resolutions in its national and international congresses, has repeatedly expressed its sympathy with the unions, and advised its adherents to join the unions of their respective crafts"; that most of your party members, officers and candidates are trade-unionists, and that your "party organization and press have raised funds to assist unionists."

All these professions of friendship and support have an alluring sound, but their charm is somewhat shattered by the delightfully frank disclosure of the sinister object of the Socialists in going into the trade-unions. Mr. Jack London, a Socialist writer, in an article published in the New York *Independent*, in October, 1903, declared:

> This revolt in the form of demands for an increased share of the joint product is being carefully and shrewdly shaped for a political assault upon society. . . . The leaders intend to direct the labor revolt to the capture of the political machinery of society. . . . With the control of the police, the army, the navy, and the courts, they will confiscate, with or without remuneration, all the possessions of the capitalist class which are used in the production and distribution of the luxuries and necessities of life. They mean to apply the law of eminent domain to the land and to extend the law of eminent domain until it embraces the mines, the factories, the railroads and the ocean carriers.
>
> The Socialists turned their energies upon the trade-union movement. To win the trade-unions was well nigh to win the victory.
>
> Instead of antagonizing the unions, the Socialists proceeded to conciliate the unions. "Let every good Socialist join the union of his trade! Bore from within and capture the trade-union movement."
>
> To-day the great labor unions are honey-combed with Socialists. At work and at play, at business meeting and council, their INSIDIOUS PROPAGANDA goes on. Night and day, tireless and unrelenting as a mortgage, they labor at their self-imposed task of undermining society.
>
> The battle plan of the Socialists is to organize the working class and those in sympathy with it into a political party, with the object of conquering the powers of government and using them for the purpose of transferring the present system of private ownership of the means of production and distribution into collective ownership by the entire people.

This revelation by Mr. London is supplemented with brutal candor by Mr. Debs, who must be accepted as a really "authorized spokesman" of his party, since he was its nominee for President. In his speech in Faneuil Hall, Boston, just before the November election, Mr. Debs said:

> Parry is doing a better work for us than we could do for ourselves. As Mr. Pure-and-Simple Union Man is crushed his eyes are opened to the fact that he must transfer his efforts to the political field.

Why does Mr. Debs welcome Parryism? He tells his audience the reason. It is because the success of Parryism would mean the crushing of Mr. Pure-and-Simple Union Man. If that is not an expression of hostility to unionism, what is it?

The Indianapolis *News*, published in the home town of Mr. D. M. Parry, president of the National Association of Manufacturers, and of the Citizens' Industrial Association of America, calls attention to a remarkable tribute to Mr. Parry by the *Social Democratic Herald*. That official Journal of the Socialists of Wisconsin published on its front page an interview with Mr. Parry, accompanied with the words, in display type, "COMRADE PARRY!" and "WAS FIGHTING FOR US!" The *United Mine Workers' Journal*, the official organ of a labor organization containing twenty times the membership of the Socialist party, made the following comment on this economic mesalliance:

> The *Social Democratic Herald* is edited by Victor L. Berger who made a scandalous attack upon Messrs. Mitchell and Gompers. What tie binds Berger, Parry, Hayes, et al., in their warfare upon trades-unions? They eulogize Parry, call him "Comrade," and he in turn eulogizes them and calls them true men. It is a strange spectacle to see Parry and Berger link arms and denounce trades-unions, and is a cause for some deep thinking upon the part of trades-unionists. Here Parry denounces trades-unionists as murderers, incendiaries, thugs, grafters and other scandalous epithets, and then Berger, Debs, Hayes, et al., call him "Comrade." Reflect upon this, Mr. Trades-Unionist, and see if there are not ample grounds for a complete divorcement. If "Comrade" Parry, why not "Comrade" Peabody, as the latter only puts into practice what Parry preaches. "Comrade," forsooth!

To return to the attitude of the Socialists toward the American Federation of Labor, there can be no more competent witness than Mr. Samuel Gompers, who has just been re-elected president of that organization. You may read Mr. Gompers' speech in opposition to a Socialist resolution, delivered in Faneuil Hall, Boston, in November, 1903, upon pages 196-197 of the Official Report of the Proceedings of the Twenty-third Annual Convention of the American Federation of Labor. Upon that occasion Mr. Gompers said:

> I shall not refer at this time to their very many detailed acts of treachery to the trade-union movement but I shall show you that though they may believe themselves to be trades-unionists they are at heart, and logically, the antagonists of our movement.
>
> When the Socialists formed the American Labor Union in rivalry to the American Federation of Labor, I took occasion to continually say in *The American Federationist* that it was but another attempt to form another Socialist Trade and Labor Alliance, without its practical courage to openly declare its enmity to the American trade-union movement.
>
> The secretary of the Socialist party has severed his connection with the reformed (?) Socialist party, because of his being opposed to the hostile tactics of that party to the trade-unions; and, being at heart a trade-unionist, he was forced out of his position. Since that time be has given to the world the real reasons why he was forced out,—because he dared to stand up in defense of trades-unions and against the policy of antagonizing the trades-unions and hoisting up the American Labor Union.
>
> I want to tell you, Socialists, that I have studied your philosophy; read your works upon economics, and not the meanest of them; studied your standard works, both in English and German—have not only read but studied them. I have heard your orators and watched the work of your movement the world over. I have kept close watch upon your doctrines for thirty years; have been closely associated with many of you and know how you think and what you propose. I know too what you have up your sleeve and I want to say that I am entirely at variance with your philosophy. I declare it to you, I am not only at variance with your doctrines, but with your philosophy. Economically you are unsound; socially, you are wrong; industrially, you are an impossibility.

I trust, Brother Editor, that I have adduced sufficient evidence to establish the truth of the statement that you have, I fear, too sweepingly denied. If the testimony I offer does not seem to you sufficient, I refer you to an article in the November issue of THE MONTHLY REVIEW of the National Civic Federation, which I herewith take pleasure in sending you, and which sets forth in more detail the hostile purposes of the twin foes which unionism faces—Parryism and Socialism.

Sincerely yours,
R. M. EASLEY,
Editor MONTHLY REVIEW.

LABOR PRAISES OSCAR S. STRAUS.

The Motorman and Conductor.

(Official Journal of the Amalgamated Association of Street and Electric Railway Employes of America.)

We doubt if there is a man among the many friends of the Amalgamated Association that is entitled to more appreciation at the hands of the Amalgamated railway men of American than Oscar S. Straus. Not only has he assisted from time to time the international officers to secure conferences with the various companies and bring about peaceful settlements of disputes that were threatening to lead to serious contentions and strife, but it was he as arbitrator in the San Francisco dispute of 1903 that gave to the street railway men of America the highest general rate of wages ever established for surface railway men.

The situation in San Francisco had become critical. Mr. Calhoun, representing the company, and Mr. Mahon, representing the organization, failed to agree upon the wage question. It was finally agreed that the matter should be submitted to arbitration, and the Hon. Oscar S. Straus was selected as arbitrator. The company spent many thousands of dollars employing the best of lawyers that the country afforded, and in preparing their evidence to, if possible, establish a lower wage rate than the one which at the time prevailed. On the other side, the Association, through the direction of that tireless and fearless advocate and friend of trades-unionism. Hon. Edward J. Livernash, of San Francisco, prepared their evidence at heavy expense and with much labor, and after many weeks of preparation the entire matter was submitted to Mr. Straus, who, after a careful consideration of the facts, established the wage at 26¼ cents per hour for the first two years, and after that time 27½ cents per hour; thus establishing the highest general rate of wage that had ever been established by the street railway workers throughout the country.

We doubt if the importance of this decision has been considered or truly appreciated by the great mass of our people, but here is the position that it places us in: Here is a wage rate established not by strike, or lock-out, or by force of any kind, but by a careful consideration of the entire conditions surrounding the occupation, and then by a man unbiased and in no way in touch with either side; again, by a man who has a world-wide reputation for his fairness as an arbitrator. The result of this decision is bound, in the future, to be referred to, and to have the effect of assisting the men in other cities, where the wages are much lower, in establishing a reasonable and living rate. So, a moment's consideration of the work done by Mr. Straus cannot help but be appreciated by the great army of Amalgamated Railway Workers throughout the entire continent.

THE NATIONAL

Civic Federation Review

Offices: 281 Fourth Avenue, New York City

RALPH M. EASLEY, Editor

The Editor alone is responsible for any unsigned article or unquoted statement published in THE CIVIC FEDERATION REVIEW.

Ten Cents per Copy; One Dollar per Year.

THE BODY KNOWN AS "THE PUBLIC"

"The Public" is a term with which some of those who discuss economic subjects would conjure a vision of some supreme and distinct body, separate and apart from the industrial struggle. That struggle is incessant, but varies in intensity. When it assumes an acute phase, because of precipitated conflict over wages or hours or conditions of work, it is a common experience to hear of the interest, the inconvenience, or the suffering of "The Public."

What is this "Public"? Is it possible to differentiate it sharply from the actual participants in any industrial war? Are the non-combatants separate and distinct from those who fight? Is their interest paramount?

It is evident that there does prevail a conception of such a body. It is often stated, for example, that the success or failure of a strike depends largely, if not mainly, upon public opinion. To that opinion employers and employed continually appeal, whenever they are at strife. Its moral force is tacitly recognized in every utterance, in every strategic move of the combatants. But how shall the body, whose verdict is thus regarded as vital to any cause, be defined?

The collection of opinions published in this issue of THE CIVIC FEDERATION REVIEW is interesting, in that it reflects divers methods of using the term, coupled with ingenious efforts at its definition; and it is of value, in that it goes far to confirm the conclusion reached by one writer, that in the industrial struggle "there is no such thing as an outside public." Practically everybody in the community is interested in the profits of capital and the earnings of labor, for these are factors in all production as they are factors in all consumption. The infifluences and the effects of any industrial struggle are so far-reaching and so interwoven with the structure of all society that they cannot be dissected out of the body politic. A coal strike concerns every fireside; a cotton strike touches every wearer of fabrics; a railway strike affects everything that is carried, and transportation enters into almost every article that human beings use.

But thus "vague" as the general public may be, it undeniably exists. Because it is inseparable, it is none the less real. The important question is whether its interest is paramount. Is not its interest in any industrial strike purely selfish? "The Public" is usually apathetic to the conditions of workers in mines, in factories, upon railways. But when revolt comes, "the Public" is first awakened, through the inconvenience it suffers, to what may be cruel wrongs. The mass of people, preoccupied with a myriad pursuits, practically all workers, whether with hands or with millions, has little time or inclination to disturb itself about the profits of any single business, however great, or about the hardships or income of any class of toilers, however numerous. But let a clash come, let the smooth, everyday relations of supply and demand be interrupted, and the general community is rudely jarred out of indifference into interest whose intensity is likely to be proportionate to the degree of inconvenience caused or the increase in the cost of a product. Then ensues the process of forming public opinion upon a subject probably novel to most of those whose thought is thus aroused. In this way a strike, or a crisis in some industry, may be widely educational. "The Public" learned more in 1902 about the business of mining coal, about hours and wages and transportation and risks and profits, than it ever knew before. In contrast, "the Public" took but a languid, though wide and sympathetic, interest in the strike in the Fall River cotton mills, because the prices of manufactured cotton were not affected. The rise and fall of speculative fortunes in the market of raw cotton was more dramatic; and the recent spectacle of burning cotton in bales in the South has served to make many consider the relations between crops and demand, and to realize the economic crime of attempting to enhance prices by destroying natural wealth.

Thus "the Public" is painfully and expensively instructed. In time the larger lesson may be learned that it is the duty of "the Public," that is, of every one, to take active interest every day in the questions involved in the relations between capital and labor, instead of permitting attention to wait upon disturbance.

THE RIGHTING OF INDUSTRIAL WRONGS.

Recent events in Russia and the strike in the coal mines of Germany illustrate to labor in the United States the vast difference between Socialism abroad and Socialism in this country. They make it manifest that the reason why Socialism makes so little headway here and is a negligible force in both politics and economics is that under republican institutions all of the people already have the civil and political rights which are denied to the mass of the people in many foreign countries. Socialism thrives upon the denial of rights. Socialism is puny in a land of equal justice to all and of mutual regard for the business success of employers and the welfare and fair reward of wage-earners.

In Russia the demands of the strikers, as formulated in the petition which they sought to present to the Czar, were so elementary, so absolutely essential to "life, liberty and the pursuit of happiness," as to seem shocking to the American mind. To the free citizen of this Republic it seems incredible that tens of thousands of workingmen should ask for a wage sufficient to sustain life; should beg for relief from a compulsory day of eleven hours; should humbly ask for laws applying alike to all classes; should seek representative government; should ask for the right to organize and that it be not a crime to choose delegates to present their grievances to employers. When labor has been so oppressed that death is preferable to life, the only alternatives are revolution or extermination. Even in Germany, a land of constitutional government, 270,000 men are described as working naked in water for 96 cents a day, fatally affected by worm disease because their lives are daily in darkness, cursed by the overseers as lazy, required by an antiquated custom of militarism to stand at attention and click their heels together the moment a foreman approaches a subterranean gang, and forced to the gloomy query: "What difference, whether we starve or perish fighting?" To this outcry the only answer of the employers is: 'Return to work, or under the law we will mulct you six days' wages."

It is conditions such as these that make Socialism abroad a political and social force of moment. It is able there to appropriate to itself the advocacy of social and industrial reforms that appeal to the fundamental instincts of self-preservation and self-respect.

But the weakness of Socialism in America is the absence of such monstrous wrongs as still prevail in the lands of class separation. This is not to say that we have attained or even approached social and industrial perfection in the United States. Many wrongs are yet to be righted, many crooked things are still to be made straight. In all movements for industrial betterment, organized labor is performing its share with increasing intelligence and efficiency. Particularly of late is it addressing its efforts toward educational advancement.

It is only in abuses that the root of Socialism can flourish. Frequently it seeks to mingle and confuse its propaganda with the advocacy of reforms noble in themselves. In such efforts, wage-earners and well-meaning reformers should be alert to discriminate between their own cause and Socialism, which often assumes the mask of rectitude to disguise its presence in the midst of the righteous.

SOME SELF-ANSWERED CRITICS.

The Editor has received a letter from an employer who is a member of the Citizens' Industrial Alliance of America, and several clippings from papers owned by branches of that organization, finding fault with an article in the November number of THE REVIEW under the caption of "Three Conspicuous Foes of Organized Labor." The burden of the complaint is that this article was "extremely partisan," "unfair," "unjust," etc. We have gone over the article line by line in search for justification for this criticism and confess that our search has been in vain. On the other hand, we cannot believe from the nature of their comments, that our critics have read the article in its entirety.

The purpose of that article, as its heading indicates, was to show just who the foes of organized labor are; the contention being that, while beset with "Parryism" on one side and Socialism ("Debsism") on the other, the most dangerous foe of Unionism ("Gompersism," as it is termed by Citizens' Alliance folk) is its own inherent weaknesses. No offense was intended in using the word "Parryism" as embracing that class of employers' organizations whose real animus against organized labor is openly avowed. We are informed by friends of Mr.

ry that he is proud of the title, and therefore there be no personal offense to him in the term. The criti- m of the official journals of these employers' associa- s is expected, as it was from these same journals that evidence of the real purpose of the Industrial Alli- e movement was cited. Nor are we surprised that the cialists attacked the article as "unjust" and "unfair." another column will be found the correspondence ween the Editor of the official organ of the "Debsite" cialists and the Editor of the CIVIC FEDERATION RE- w, which speaks for itself. The response of the cialists is much franker, however, than is that of the arryites." The Socialists make denials in detail, but r other critics hide behind glittering generalities and ore entirely the specific allegation that their move- nt is a foe to organized labor.

Here is the point, and the whole point: Did or did t the President of the National Association of Manu- cturers and of the Citizens' Industrial Alliance of nerica, as alleged, formally declare?—

This is not the proper time to talk conciliation. . . . nce the principles and demands of organized labor are solutely untenable to those believing in the individual- ic social order, an attitude of conciliation would mean attitude of compromise with regard to fundamental nvictions. . . . Neither is it the time to talk arbi- ation or joint agreement. To arbitrate questions of ages and hours is to introduce artificial methods of termining what they shall be and an equitable arrange- ent as to either cannot be effected artificially. . . . rbitration is only putting off the day of reckoning.

Did or did not the Chairman of the Executive Com- ittee of the Citizens' Industrial Alliance make, as leged, the following declarations?—

No organization of men, not excepting the Ku Klux lan, the Mafia, or the Black Hand Society, has ever oduced such a record of barbarism as has this so- lled organized labor society which, through mis- rected sympathy, apathy and indifference, has been per- itted to grow up to cripple our industries, and to ample in the dust the natural and constitutional rights f our citizens.

Did or did not the same officer announce this dic- m?—

The only way to settle a controversary with organized bor is to have absolutely no dealings with it.

Did or did not a preacher, described as a "personal epresentative of D. M. Parry" and as the editor of a ublication of the Citizens' Industrial Alliance, state to a ecret meeting of manufacturers, merchants, contractors nd professional men, at Evansville, Indiana?—

The Citizens' Alliance consists of both employers and mployes. It is secret because in secrecy is its greatest trength. It has signs of recognition, pass words, and igns of distress. . . . In nine days I saw in one city ,200 union men reduced to 62 and join the Citizens' lliance.

If these representatives of the "Citizens' Alliance" ovement did not make these statements, or if they have hanged their minds since they did make them, or if the nglish language has to them a meaning different to its omprehension and use by all others, the columns of HE REVIEW are open to their denial, recantation or xplanation.

But, after all, is it worth while to try to discuss seri- usly industrial questions with the members or the fficial organs of a body of men who, in spite of the idely published fact that the American Federation of abor had rejected Socialistic resolutions at its Boston onvention by a majority of 13,000 to 1,000, and again t San Francisco, so overwhelmingly as to make a roll all superfluous, deliberately declared in their call for heir recent annual convention?—

Insidious and socialistic doctrines as preached, pub- ished and practiced by so-called labor leaders have of ate so dominated labor unions as to preclude the exer- ise of free and independent thought on the part of in- elligent members of labor unions, and have become a indrance to business and a menace to society.

Or with men who, in the face of the widely published act that the San Francisco convention, representing ,000,000 wage-earners, had rejected, by an overwhelm- ng majority, a resolution opposing service in the militia, ts President, Samuel Gompers, emphatically declaring it he positive duty of every able-bodied wage-earner to ncourage the citizen militia in convention assembled, eliberately adopted and published this declaration?—

Whereas, Organized labor throughout the country eeks to discourage and practically prohibits membership n the militia.

We hardly think it is.

THE "AGE LIMIT."

Official Testimony Contradicting the Current Assertion That Two Great Corporations Discharge Employes When Thirty-five Years Old.

The *Labor Compendium*, of St. Louis, official organ of the International Building Trades Council, on January 1 contained the following:

"Will the Carnegie Steel Company now rescind the rule which, according to reports, it had adopted against the hiring of men over thirty-five years of age in some departments and over forty years in another? Surely, the address of Andrew Carnegie to the National Civic Federation would indicate a new and more humane policy to be inaugurated in 1905 than has been promulgated in 1904."

It can be stated authoritatively that Mr. Carnegie does not own a single share of stock in the Carnegie Steel Company and that he has no more to do with its management or with its policy as to labor than has the editor of the *Compendium*.

The main point, however, is as to the "age limit." The statement has been going the rounds not only of the labor press, but of the daily press for months, that the Carnegie Steel Company and the Pennsylvania Railroad Company had made it their rule to discharge all employes as soon as they reach the age of thirty-five. These two corporations have been linked in many a paragraph of bitter denunciation.

Last year's files of the NATIONAL CIVIC FEDERATION contain correspondence, which THE REVIEW has permission to publish, that discloses fully and exactly the facts as to the policy of both these companies. They show that the "age limit" relates only to the employment of new men. In response to letters of inquiry from the Secretary of the Welfare Department and from the chairman of the Executive Council, letters were written by W. H. Corbett, Paymaster of the Carnegie Steel Company, and by Max Riebenack, Comptroller of the Pennsylvania Railroad.

The relation between the age limit and the pension fund is more fully discussed in Mr. Riebenack's article upon "Railway Provident Institutions," which appears elsewhere in this issue.

Mr. Corbett's letter states:

"It is not true that our men are discharged when they reach the age of thirty-five years, or any other age for that matter, so long as they can give satisfactory service. To my personal knowledge there are several hundred men over *fifty* years old, some few over *sixty*, and about two years ago one of our stationary engineers died in active service who was *eighty*. Of course the latter is an exceptional case. He had been in continuous service for about twenty-five years, and when the Carnegie Relief Fund was started, arrangements were being made to place him on the pension list.

"From their rules I quote: 'Any employe of a constituent company of the Carnegie Company which has been ten years with the Carnegie interests who shall have reached the age of sixty years, shall have been at least fifteen years continuously in the service of the company and who claims that he is, or should his employing officer consider him, incapacitated for further service, may make application to be retired and the Advisory Board shall decide whether or not he shall be placed upon the pension list.'

"From this you will note that even after they get to be sixty years of age they are cared for if they have seen fifteen years of active service.

"In taking on new men, preference is always given to younger and more able-bodied men for the reason that if we were to take on men well up in years the relief fund would soon be overtaxed on the age limit, and it is of course good policy to arrange for care of those now in the service who, when they arrive at pensionable age, are entitled to the benefits

"Regarding the savings fund, its principal object is to allow employes to save enough for a foundation to obtain their own homes, which many have done, by using this fund to save until they had enough to buy a lot and then the company would, through trustees of a fund for that purpose, lend enough money to build a comfortable house, which could be repaid in monthly instalments, which would amount to perhaps a trifle more than rent.

"In this way many of our best employes gained homes and became permanent residents of the vicinity, and thus established themselves as permanent employes.

"Regarding men who leave service of this company to go to work elsewhere, and for any reason return later and apply for work again, it could not be expected they would get back their former position, as promotions had been made when they left, and upon their return would certainly not be entitled to consideration other than as new men. Such leaving and reinstatement, however, would not debar them from pension allowance provided not more than two years have elapsed, but would be deducted in computing length of service. Leave of absence, suspension, temporary lay-off on account of reduction of force or disability, are not deducted in computing length of service.

"Our older employes, if not eligible to pension fund, are usually given light work, such as cleaning up the yards, drying sand, carrying oil for lubricating machinery, oiling cars, etc.

"Many of our stationary engineers are men of much experience and some of them are over fifty years. In that position much valuable machinery is under their care and requires men of judgment and experience that are not always obtainable in the younger men, and as the position is not hard manual labor, they can perform their duties satisfactorily."

Mr. Riebenack wrote:—"I would advise that copies of the original circular issued by the president of this company in regard to the age limit for employment in the service on and after January 1, 1900, is not available. I give you below, however, a transcript of what was embodied in the circular, and amended as of February 27, 1901, bearing upon this feature. The amendment covers the addition of the fourth clause, in regard to the interchange of service between the lines east and west of Pittsburgh, or from one company to another, associated in the administration of the Pension Department.

"'As amended and approved by the Board of Directors of the Pennsylvania Railroad Company at their meeting held February 27, 1901, and concurred in by the Boards of Directors of the other companies associated in the administration of the Pension Department.

"'No person shall be taken into the service of the company who is over thirty-five years of age, except that, with the approval of the Board of Directors—

"'First—(a)—Former employes may be re-employed within a period of three years from the time of their leaving the service, or former employes of any other company associated in the administration of the Pennsylvania Railroad Pension Department, may be employed within a period of three years from the time of their leaving the service of such company;

"'Second—(b)—Persons may, irrespective of age limit, be employed where the service for which they are needed requires professional or other special qualifications:

"'But:—

"'Third—Persons may be temporarily taken into the service, irrespective of age limit, for a period not exceeding six months, subject to extension, when necessary to complete the work for which engaged, and

"'Fourth—Persons in the active service of any company associated in the administration of either the Pennsylvania Railroad Pension Department or the Pension Department of the Pennsylvania Lines west of Pittsburgh, may, irrespective of age limit, be transferred to and employed in the service of any such company.'

"This age limit has been in force for nearly five years, and we have not experienced any difficulty in carrying out its provisions. The conclusion which led to its adoption was that by restricting the age limit for entrance into service to thirty-five years, all employes upon reaching the pensionable age (sixty-five years) would have been thirty years in the service, which latter is a requirement in order to be pensioned at that age."

A SOCIALIST CRITIC PILLORIED.

The Civic Federation, the organization whose object is to make the slaves satisfied with their lot, has just elected August Belmont, the Rothschild agent, its President! How the Rothschilds do love the working mules! And the mules listen to such men!—*Appeal to Reason*.

Since Mr. Belmont was elected President of the Civic Federation the editor of the *United Mine Workers' Journal* has made diligent inquiry about him among his employes and finds that Mr. Belmont is a fair-minded, liberal employer, who meets committees from labor unions, holds conferences with them, pays union wages and insists upon union conditions. He employs nearly 15,000 men in various occupations and has wage agreements with nearly all of them. He was at the head of the movement which built the great New York Subway, costing $35,000,000, most of which is a tunnel nearly ten miles long. With the single exception of the few blows of a pick struck by ex-Mayor Van Wyck not a stroke of work was done upon that gigantic enterprise by non-union labor, and it is a monument to the skill of union labor. Mr. Belmont insisted upon that point. W. D. Mahon, President of the street car workers' organization, testified that Mr. Belmont is a fair, liberal man to deal with, and has, upon several occasions, settled strikes or prevented them when the matter was brought to his attention, and keeps the agreements both in spirit and letter and pays the highest wages in the country. Others state that if every member of a labor union would patronize the union label as strictly as Mr. Belmont does, sweat shops and unfair manufacturers would soon vanish.

That is one picture. Here is another: The editor of the *Appeal to Reason* is A. J. Wayland. He is the man who calls the men who made the United States great "working mules." Elegant classification. Well, in 1902, Mr. Wayland's employes asked for an advance in wages. Did he grant it? No; he would not receive a committee of its employes, and locked them out and filled their places with scabs. The *Appeal to Reason's* wage scale showed that the girls got $3 per week. Mr. Wayland nearly ruined himelf by his lavish generosity. Now which, August Belmont, receiving his employes, listening to their grievances, adjusting them fairly and honorably, paying the highest wages, or A. J., locking out his $3-a-week girls? Which more truly represents the spirit of American manhood? Which could a bona fide trades unionist respect the most? No wonder, with his aggregation of scabs, that he terms working people "mules." Perhaps his are.—*United Mine Workers' Journal.*

WELFARE DEPARTMENT
OF
The National Civic Federation

THE NEW PROFESSION.

Five Welfare Managers Describe Their Duties and the Growth of Their Departments.

Five directors of welfare work in different industrial establishments contribute to this issue of THE CIVIC FEDERATION REVIEW articles descriptive of their duties, and of the progress they have made in organizing and making effective their departments. In each case the writer is at the head of a distinct Welfare Department. The articles illustrate, therefore, first of all, the prime importance of devoting to the supervision of welfare work in large establishments the entire time and attention of one person. It has been shown by actual experience that even when an employer is willing and anxious to put welfare work into operation, if its direction is entrusted to any official already charged with special duties the pressure of his daily business routine relegates the welfare work to the last consideration. These articles prove that welfare work has been successfully prosecuted when responsibility is concentrated, and all of its branches are placed under the direction of one person. Otherwise, efforts by various heads of departments to be found in any organized business may conflict, or special and, perhaps, pressing needs may escape attention.

The general rule for all welfare work in large concerns, that its successful conduct requires the employment of a welfare manager, has created a distinct profession. Moreover, the profession of welfare manager is new. For example, the writers of these articles are among the first to be placed in charge of Welfare Departments, and yet the oldest of them has been performing his duties less than five years.

It has been shown that the qualifications of a welfare manager, welfare director or welfare superintendent—whichever term may be preferred—while exacting, can be met successfully, This welfare worker should not only possess tact, executive ability, common sense, acquaintance with local jealousies and sometimes with racial prejudices, but a knowledge of industrial subjects involved in the relations between employer and employed. The manager must acquire a comprehensive and definite understanding of the field that welfare work covers.

How can this preliminary but essential knowledge be acquired? After reading all the available literature upon the subject, it will be necessary for the beginner to learn from conferences with welfare workers of experience of their actual successes and failures and their causes. It is highly desirable that one entering this work should have comparatively expert mastery of some one specialty, such as medicine, mill engineering, architecture, domestic science or trained nursing. Equipped with such a specialty the welfare worker will know how to make a definite beginning with confidence. From the point of vantage thus gained, the new manager may take up one by one the most pressing needs and respond to the most obvious opportunities for extending the work. The practical experience gained in meeting these will prove an educational process that will develop the manager's ability to met the various and larger demands upon these qualities of character that alone can make one adapted to the profession.

It is necessary that the welfare manager, at the outset, should become familiar with the business conditions that confront the establishment in which the work is being applied. The welfare worker must be patient to endure the slow realization of plans. Keen competition or the rapid growth of a business may either retard or temporarily prevent the execution of plans whose desirability is recognized.

One of the difficulties that this new profession encounters is the adjustment of its delicate relations to the superintendents. There must be a gradual process of convincing them that the presence in an establishment of a welfare manager will not interfere with their discipline or lessen their responsibility, but will bring about in time a gain in results of intelligent and harmonious co-operation.

GERTRUDE BEEKS.

A VAST FIELD OF ENDEAVOR.

By R. W. CORWIN, M. D.,

Superintendent Welfare Department, The Colorado Fuel and Iron Co., Pueblo, Col.

The welfare work of the Colorado Fuel & Iron Company is organized under the title of Sociological Department. Its field covers forty properties consisting of coal, manganese, and iron mines, coking and steel plants, rolling mills and two railroads. These properties are scattered through portions of four States and give employment, when in full operation, to nearly 17,000 men, who, together with their families, make a total of well nigh 80,000 persons. This population is settled in many small communities and comprises thirty-two nationalities speaking twenty-seven different tongues, not to mention a variety of dialects.

In a field of such magnitude and highly different topographical conditions, concentration of effort is impossible. What might be done with comparatively little effort and expense were these families all concentrated in one city, becomes at once a much more difficult and expensive task with conditions as they actually exist. For the successful prosecution of the work the Welfare Department enlists the services of a superintendent and assistant superintendent, a superintendent of kindergartens and domestic science, thirteen kindergartners, the superintendent and matron of our Normal and Industrial School, managers and presidents of clubs, directors of reading rooms, teachers of night schools, a director of an orchestra and two directors of bands.

The educational work of the department begins with the kindergartens, of which there are thirteen. The work is peculiar in that many of the children enter with no knowledge of English; nevertheless, the little ones learn to speak and sing in our language with astonishing quickness. At Christmas time there are joyous entertainments in each kindergarten when gifts and candy are provided for all the children. In spite of the strike disturbances of last winter, surprisingly little difference was seen in the attendance at the kindergartens. Even when the strikers were compelled to keep off the company grounds, the mothers would bring their children to the picket lines and pass them through to school, thus showing their confidence in the teachers. Now that the strike is over the attendance is larger than at any previous time in the history of the schools. The same is true to a much larger extent of the social and industrial clubs and mothers' meetings.

R. W. CORWIN, M. D.

Wherever there is a kindergarten teacher, groups of the older boys and girls are organized for social and recreative purposes, and other groups for industrial education. The smaller children find interest in games and stories that inculcate patriotism, courage, kindness, and gentleness; the older girls and boys in club swinging, dancing, basket-ball and target shooting. Light refreshments add attraction to the club meetings. One of the clubs edits and publishes a little bi-monthly newspaper, the children having their own printing press.

Instruction in simple cooking is given the children at a number of camps, including the use of ordinary utensils; the proper preparation of vegetables, meats, eggs and fruits; the care of cupboards and housekeeping. Similar classes are also conducted for the women of the camps in which cooking, sewing, basketry, child study and literature are the topics discussed.

Separate houses are provided for the use of the kindergarten teachers. These are simply and inexpensively furnished and serve as standards of taste and economy of expenditure for the housekeepers in each community. At the same time they become centers for social work.

Once a month the kindergarten teachers meet in Trinidad, Colorado, under the direction of their superintendent for conference, instruction, and suggestions. Some special phase of the work is taken up at each conference. Thus, the teachers are helped individually and a healthful *esprit de corps* is established.

The department works in very close co-operation with the public schools in the camps. The local school boards have been assisted in securing good teachers, and architects' plans for proper buildings have been furnished. Where the public school funds have been exhausted teachers are being carried on our pay-roll. The yards of three of the public schools have been equipped with play apparatus for children and two more yards are to be so furnished at once. The play is made free and unrestrained and is encouraged, not checked, by the teachers.

Night schools are conducted at several of the camps and also at our Normal School building in Pueblo. In fact, such schools are organized wherever there is a demand. The school at Rouse was composed almost entirely of Japanese.

The commodious lounging, reading, and lecture rooms in our Normal School building at Pueblo are occupied by a polytechnic association, composed of civil, mechanical, and electrical engineers, superintendents of departments and managers of metal producing plants. Smokers, lectures, and social events diversify the winter.

In Pueblo, where our steel plant is located, giving employment to six or seven thousand men when at full capacity, a company hospital is also located, which Dr. Lorenz, of Vienna, has pronounced to be the finest hospital in America. Here is established likewise, our normal and industrial school, in which an evening course in the elementary branches is conducted during the winter months, and a six weeks' normal course in the summer to instruct and train teachers and workers of the department in their peculiar duties. At the first term of the normal school sixty-seven teachers were in attendance from four States. Besides the regular normal course there were classes in sociology, domestic science and physical culture. This school greatly increased the efficiency of the camp teachers. The building is also used as a dormitory and social center for steel workers and others.

The instruction given the kindergarten teachers in cooking, sewing, and basketry has by them been imparted to the classes in the camps. Especially popular are the classes in sewing. The girls have learned to do fine stitching, hemming and embroidery, and this winter they are being taught to make skirts, shirt waists, and dresses.

The work of the Normal School was supplemented last summer by sending a party of our teachers to the St. Louis Exposition. The expenses of the teachers to St. Louis were paid by the company on condition that the teachers remained there at least two weeks; that they visit the educational exhibit at least three mornings each week, and that they submit to the Sociological Department before September 1st, a thesis upon some phase of the exhibit. Every morning throughout June some twenty teachers were busy in the Educational Building with note books and pencil. Their studies resulted in the production of about twenty essays, each upon a specific subject studied at the Exposition, which have been roughly bound and are now being circulated from camp to camp so that each teacher may have the benefit of the work of all the others.

The local surgeons stationed in each camp give semi-monthly lectures in the school houses for the benefit of pupils, teachers, and parents, and these lectures are often supplemented by the use of the stereopticon. These lectures are followed up by a series of monthly bulletins in the form of a leaflet of four pages devoted to such subjects as "Milk and Its Care," "Consumption," "Foods," "Liquor Problem," etc. Each bulletin contains practical information and useful suggestions upon vital life and health problems. Scientific names and unfamiliar terms are eliminated or avoided as far as expedient. These bulletins are free to all employes and the teachers explain their contents to their pupils and the local physicians do the same for the adults.

Dances and dramatic entertainments by home talent, under the direction of company officers, are popular forms of entertainment in several camps.

A circulating library is kept traveling between stations throughout the territory. This library is increasingly popular. In one camp a long line of children is always waiting when the time for exchanging books arrives. This library is contained in forty-five boxes, of which twenty-nine are devoted to English books for adults, twelve to juvenile works and four to works in Italian. There is also a circulating collection of art. This comprises thirty sets of twelve pictures each. The pictures are accompanied by a typewritten description or interpretation of their meaning, together with a brief survey of the artists, school or type. Several hundred dollars contributed by interested individuals have been expended for casts and framed pictures to adorn the interiors of school buildings.

At several of the larger mining communities we have erected recreation halls and club houses for the men containing card and game rooms, bar and hall for entertainments.

A new club house for men at Segundo contains reading, card and billiard rooms, a barber shop and bath room. No liquors are served. Another men's club contains a lounging room and well stocked bar in addition to the attractions mentioned above. The reading rooms are supplied with popular weekly and monthly magazines and daily papers, the latter in English, Italian and Slavonic. These rooms are easily accessible from the card rooms and furnish an attractive place of rest after enjoying the shower and tub baths in the basement. Once a month this club house is thrown open to the wives and daughters and visiting friends of members.

A "no treating" rule encourages temperance in the use of liquor, and all soft drinks are served at a nominal cost.

The plans for our Industrial Home are yet in their incipiency and the experiments thus far made have not been successful. Mattress making has proven too heavy work and just the right occupations have not been hit upon.

Especial attention is paid to the sanitary laying out of new camps; the construction of model dwellings; the renovation and improvement of old houses and general sanitary improvement, such as cleaning wells and cisterns and providing for the systematic disposal of refuse.

The new dwellings, usually from three to six room cottages, are comfortable and convenient. Many of

them are furnished with water and electric lights. The variety of architecture and color transforms an unattractive coal camp into a most picturesque and attractive village.

A fine new church has been erected at Primero at a cost of $7,000. Its seating capacity is about three hundred, and under its bell tower, a gallery affords ample room for choir and pipe organ. A large chancel contains a robing room and vestry. In the basement is a hall designed for a club room, reading room and lodge room. In its free use the people can enjoy every privilège not inconsistent with the church work and the welfare of the community.

In the other camps the Sociological Halls and school houses are used for Sunday School, Christian Endeavor and church services.

At the Recreation Hall of our hospital at Pueblo, chapel services are held every Sunday morning for convalescents, nurses, doctors and visiting friends. Brief addresses by prominent speakers from various parts of the country and varied walks in life frequently add to the helpfulness of these services. It is planned shortly to add to the attractiveness of the service by the addition of a vested choir.

This winter it is planned to extend the bathing facilities afforded our men by erecting a series of showers, wash basins, and clothes lockers for the miners at Primero similar to the equipment for the coke pullers at Redstone, but on a much larger scale. As rapidly as possible this equipment will be extended to all the camps.

No account of the work of the Sociological Department would be complete without reference to the Company Hospital at Pueblo, but an entire article would be necessary to do it justice, for no completer hospital is to be found in this country. The Medical Department treated last year 63,141 cases at the hospital and camps.

The work of the Sociological Department has received pleasing recognition at the St. Louis Exposition, inasmuch as our Kindergarten work and Industrial class work were each awarded a gold medal and our system of workingmen's dwellings received a silver medal.

WISE EMPLOYMENT OF LEISURE

By Mary E. Hamson,

Welfare Superintendent in a Large Manufacturing Community.

A French writer has said: "Oh, if I could discover how best to employ the leisure of men! Labor in plenty there is sure to be, but where look for recreation? The daily work provides the daily bread, but laughter gives it savor."

Miss Mary E. Hamson.

Only men are employed in our works. The company, after having provided for their welfare and comfort during working hours, decided to extend the welfare work into their leisure time and to include their wives and children, believing that what is done for a man's family is a help to the man.

Much of this outside welfare work centers in a commodious Guild House, to which is attached a Guild Hall, containing modern improvements, including electric lighting, a stage, equipped with all the accessories for amateur theatricals, dressing rooms, a coat room for men and a cloak room for women. The main floor of the assembly room in Guild Hall will seat six hundred, and a gallery at one end will accommodate an additional number of people. This auditorium is available to the employes, for social entertainments, concerts and so forth, at a nominal price.

On the first floor of the Guild House are parlors and sitting rooms used as class rooms; reading rooms; a circulating library; and a thoroughly equipped kitchen.

For the purpose of encouraging out-door sports among its employes and their children, the company enclosed a five-acre plot situated between the office building and the Guild House. This athletic field has tennis courts and a running track. A portion of the space is used for baseball or football, according to the season of the year.

This year, to meet the growth of the work, a thoroughly modern gymnasium has been constructed, a system of baths being included. Besides the salary of the Librarian, the company contributes $25 a month toward the purchase of books. There are contributors from other sources. A separate building is being erected for library purposes, so great has been the appreciation of this side of the work.

The class work begins in October, and extends through May, making a working year of eight months.

On Monday afternoons there is an embroidery class for girls between eight and fourteen years of age. They may either buy their own material or be furnished with work, in which case the worker may buy the finished article at cost. Some one reads aloud while the girls work.

On Tuesday evening there is a class for the mothers and older sisters. The instruction is free, and there is an annual December sale of embroidered articles.

An art class meets on Monday afternoons. This year they are doing water color sketching under a competent instructor. Each member of the class furnishes her own materials, and pays ten cents a lesson for the instruction.

A class in piano instruction has been started. The charge is twenty-five cents for a half hour lesson.

The senior cooking classes are attended by those whose age enables them to make a definite and immediate use of the learning acquired. Each class partakes of the results of its own modest labors, sitting down to a meal attractively served upon a carefully laid table, thus giving an opportunity for table setting and serving. The junior cooks take home part of their results for parental approval. A trained instructor is hired to teach these classes. The cost to each girl is twenty-five cents a month, payable in advance, for one lesson each week.

A class in bead work meets on Saturday afternoons. Each member pays the cost of the beads used.

The basket making clubs on Tuesday afternoons are for girls; Thursday afternoons for boys; and Saturday mornings for advanced workers, both boys and girls. The cost to each is the price of the material used. For home work, two or three cents' worth of material is sold to a child. In June comes a basket exhibit, at which the fathers and mothers are invited guests.

The sewing school, which meets on Friday afternoons, includes fifteen classes of twelve pupils each. These classes are taught by volunteers from among the wives of the officers and head men of the company. A carefully graded course is followed. The stitches learned are applied by each girl in the making of aprons and undergarments for herself. The work for the graduating year is the cutting, fitting and making of dresses. In the dressmaking department each girl furnishes the dress material used. An experienced teacher has charge of this work.

To relieve the tension for the younger girls part of the sewing time is devoted to instruction in housekeeping. The object of this is to teach the girls to work neatly and intelligently at home with the utensils and materials there provided.

On Friday nights there is a class for advanced pupils in dressmaking. Here a charge of twenty-five cents a month is made, payable in advance, one lesson each week.

One of the most popular events of the week is the Wednesday evening dancing class for younger children. Two instructors and a pianist are furnished. The charge is five cents a week, except for hops, when it is ten cents.

On Thursday nights, the older people have a weekly dance. The music is the piano and violin. The admission is ten cents for ladies and fifteen cents for men.

The social clubs on Monday nights and Tuesday afternoons are for girls; on Thursday and Friday nights for boys. Prompt and full attendance attests their enjoyment and appreciation. The members of each club confer weekly with a director who receives suggestions, makes suggestions, and helps them to carry out ideas for mutual enjoyment. At the close of the club year the girls entertain their brothers and cousins. The boys also have a special party once a year.

Each gymnastic class meets once a week. The cost of these classes includes the use of soap and towel for the bath. The yearly charge is $3 for seniors; $2.50 for intermediates, and $2 for juniors. The instructor is on duty each night from five until nine. The girls and women are as enthusiastic and faithful in attendance as the boys and men.

The company is constantly extending its outside welfare work because its beneficial results are increasingly obvious.

GRATIFYING RESULTS ACCOMPLISHED.

By W. E. C. Nazro, B. A. S., S. B.,

Welfare Manager in a Large Manufacturing Community.

Sympathy between the employer and the employe is the keynote to industrial peace. In the early days it was very easy for the employer to keep in touch with his men and to prevent neglect of things necessary to their welfare. But to-day the larger area that our plants cover, together with the vast amount of work, makes it impossible for the heads of the business to keep close inspection over the property, the factory and the people. Such problems have brought about the position of Welfare Manager, a position, however, which can never be made a success unless the heads of the business are in thorough accord with the work, and unless, upon large fete days or other social entertainments, they attend and lend their personal interest to the occasion. It was through this perfect sympathy of the treasurer of a large manufacturing plant that I was engaged to fill the position of Welfare Manager.

My first tour of inspection brought to light many little things that required immediate attention, such as cleaning up rubbish about the mill and houses. The grounds about the houses especially required the use of the hoe and shovel.

Systems of collecting ashes and carrying away garbage were inaugurated, also a system of visiting the houses every few months was carried on until all the little repairs and leaks had been attended to. A remark was made by one of the men a little while after I had taken up the work, "that it was really the first time that the people thought that the company cared how they lived, and that they appreciated the step that the company had taken in providing some one to listen to their wants."

Not only did we try to improve their home life but endeavored to make their daily life about the factory more wholesome, procuring for them the best sanitary appliances, ventilation, drinking water, and many minor betterments.

We then started upon a plan to improve the exterior of our plant. New roads were built, good drainage systems constructed, grass plots laid out and vines planted.

The development of this side of the problem was very interesting to watch, because we had expended this amount of money in the hope of showing our people how grounds should be kept up, or at least to give them an interest to try some of the methods upon their own places. I may say that we felt great gratification to learn that on the first Saturday afternoon after these improvements the employes took home the lesson that we had taught them, and began edging their walks, cutting their grass, etc. Thus it was that our first efforts to show the people how to better their surroundings had been eagerly accepted. It is with this proof in view that I am led to believe that the employes' environment has much to do with developing their character and increasing the happiness of their lives.

So this principle of showing by example has been carried through our different branches of welfare work in our library, dining hall, kindergarten, and other institutions, with the hope of encouraging our employes to strive toward higher ideals.

I was once asked, "Are you not getting your buildings a little too good for your men?" As they were not at all lavish, I did not think so then, and time has proven that I was right. If the buildings are better than they had been accustomed to, the men proved their capacity of self-development by their appreciation.

There are always a few men whose clear perception and other superior qualities have placed them in positions of power and responsibility. These captains of industry should now lend a helping hand to develop the power of perception and appreciation in those who are less fortunate and who are working with them to increase the output and to make the product of each the best of its kind in the market.

W. E. C. Nazro.

How are you to arouse this ambition in the workingman to better his condition? The condition of the laborer at the end of his daily toil, which has taxed both body and brain, often is likely to be that of discontent with himself and his surroundings.

To stimulate the ambition of the laborer, there should be put in his way opportunity for physical recreation and mental rest through social enjoyment. It is for the employer to offer these opportunities, because the average wage earner can not make them unaided. Such opportunities will keep awake the universal instinctive desire to rise above discontent. There is special recreative pleasure for employes in sports that bring them in competition with their fellow men. There is also a stimulus to ambition in the pride of their home life. This pride in making their little homes attractive is most real and is not dissimilar to that of the employer in his own estate.

It has been said to me, "What is the use of providing them with better homes? Workingmen do not appreciate them." My experience disproves this assertion. I have seen many tenants move from old homes to new and better ones built by the company. The test of the reality of their pride came in whether or not they used the opportunity thus offered for improvement. In every case these tenants took better care of their lawns and flowers, and in a dozen details increased the cheerfulness and beauty of their homes. For instance, muslin curtains displaced shawls and ragged hangings in the windows. Why did not this neat and attractive condition exist before? Because the houses were of the old, old type with no lawns or gardens; their environment was not of the character to awaken pride. But with their new environment, where the houses were surrounded by grass plots, with a little garden attached and well made walks, their ambition was immediately aroused.

It has been said to me, "This voluntary improvement might appear in your community, but it would not occur with us." This inborn desire for better conditions is not confined to our community, but its awakening needs the encouragement of example. No employe who has worked all day in or about a factory surrounded with rubbish and tin cans can be expected to decorate his home or keep clean its surroundings. Then again, the employes may have neither the knowledge nor the time to seek out ways and means of improvement. This lack may be supplied by the employer through literature or talks on the subject, and through extending to the employes opportunities for better homes.

My contention is that employes will grasp the opportunity for physical and mental recreation and generally to improve the conditions of their family life, if only the chance is given. They will read, not always the best books, but better ones, because of guidance in their selection. Their children will be better clothed and the workmen will be more orderly and of a higher degree of intelligence than those without such opportunities.

One caution is necessary. These opportunities for the workingmen should be kept free from patronage. The self respect of the workmen must not be offended by causing them to feel under obligation. Employes feel more manly if they can pay a certain share of the cost of welfare work. For some things the employer must pay entirely, such as better ventilation, better sanitary conditions and a plentiful supply of wholesome drinking water. But such forms of welfare work as schools, baths, lunch rooms, reading rooms, gymnasiums, and clubs should be managed on business principles.

The activities under my direction include the construction of mills and houses; landscape gardening, employing draughtsmen; a library, with a librarian and assistant; a dining hall, with a manager and necessary help; a kindergarten, with two teachers; a store, with a manager, four men and three teams; a band; a baseball team; a drawing school, with two teachers; a sloyd school and a school of basketry, each with one teacher; a department of baths with two employes; an athletic club; a hospital, with two trained nurses, and the supervision of an annual fair and celebration on Labor Day.

The results of these efforts have clearly shown that the wage-earner aspires to become something more than a mere machine, that there is readiness to improve when the opportunities are offered. Therefore, is it not the duty of every captain of industry, who controls the lives of men, women and children, to find some method of work and education that can be applied to his community to educate his employes, to make better citizens of them and to inspire them toward higher standards?

The large industrial plants and enterprises throughout the United States, controlling as they do somewhat the lives of the people, contain, if properly fostered, the seed for one of the greatest educational processes the country has ever known. They reach a vast class of people that the public school and college systems never can. They can be made to implant in the younger generations a pure and high perception of American citizenship, American life and American ideals.

GREAT PROGRESS IN ONE YEAR.

By Anna B. Doughten,

Welfare Manager, the Curtis Publishing Company, Philadelphia.

The welfare work of the Curtis Publishing Company has been in charge of a Welfare Manager for little more than a year. Before its supervision was entrusted to me there was a place where women employes could eat the cold lunches that they had brought from home and obtain, without charge, coffee, tea or milk. There were also a room for rest and reading for women, and a Saving Fund Society for both men and women, which now offers its members insurance in the form of an endowment policy at a low rate.

At the outset of my work a new and attractive lunch room for the women employes was opened, where hot lunches are sold at the lowest possible prices. It is expected to be self-supporting in time. I was engaged to manage this lunch room and to extend the welfare work as I should learn the needs of the employes.

As a starting point, the lunch room gave an opportunity of enlisting the interest of the employes without arousing their antagonism. Several months were required to gain the sympathy of the employes and the co-operation of the heads of departments. Until that is gained there can be little tangible work. An advisory committee on the lunch room has been of considerable help.

A Voluntary Mutual Benefit Society has just been formed. Other new efforts are a circulating library and a hospital room in connection with the girls' rest room. A men's lunch room is under consideration and a smoking room is being fitted up. The first steps in the formation of a woman's club have been taken, and we have started a system of suggestion boxes. We are also preparing to make our wash rooms and dressing rooms adequate.

There is ceaseless opportunity for work in gaining the confidence of employes, in helping them in illness and in need, in being ever ready to talk over their affairs and in sustaining constant interest in their welfare, thus making them realize that the firm takes a real interest in them as human beings. So many and varied are these opportunities for usefulness that I feel that the days are not half long enough for what I wish to accomplish. My occupation has been one of continuous and progressive education in the work itself.

EXTENSIVE AND THOROUGH APPLICATION.

By C. T. Fugitt,

Welfare Director, National Cash Register Co., Dayton, Ohio.

The National Cash Register Company made its first move toward betterment of the working conditions of its employes in 1894. Prior to that year the employes of the company were subjected to the usual unpleasant surroundings found at most factories. It was believed, and correctly so, as developments proved, that in the betterment of the conditions surrounding the workers, mutual benefits would result both to the employer and to the employe. As our President, Mr. John H. Patterson, aptly expresses it: "We do welfare work because it is right, and because it pays."

C. T. Fugitt.

From a very modest beginning in 1894, when small gas stoves were provided in the women's departments for heating coffee, welfare work has become an important factor in the company's organization.

A Welfare Department has been created and maintained in the belief that those conditions which affect the working man and working woman in their daily routine should be given first consideration. In carrying out this idea we have devoted considerable time and money to the problems of light, heat and ventilation. We feel that we have solved them in a satisfactory manner. The buildings are well lighted, 140,000 panes of glass having been used in their construction. They are connected by bridges and tunnels. This facilitates trucking and avoids the necessity of employes undergoing a change in temperature in passing from one building to another. Much unpleasantness and some sickness is prevented in this manner. By means of an efficient ventilating system the air in the buildings is changed every fifteen minutes.

The small particles of brass found in most brass polishing rooms form a disagreeable feature which we have practically eliminated. The dust from each buffing wheel is carried away by a pipe to a building on the outside. This is effected by the use of a suction fan arrangement.

The molders have also received attention. Considering the character of their work they should be given much more consideration than is usually accorded them in some factories. The acid fumes, a very unhygienic feature of their work, are carried out by suction fans. The gas room has been provided with all possible safe-guards. The ventilation and light are all that could be expected.

Well equipped bathrooms have been installed in different parts of the factory. The company gives all employes twenty minutes a week in winter and forty minutes in summer for baths, and in addition furnishes soap and towels. This privilege is much appreciated. Many take advantage of it.

Rest rooms in charge of a trained nurse have been provided for the women. These rooms are furnished with easy chairs and couches and with the accessories necessary for giving simple treatments. Girls are permitted to retire to these rooms if indisposed or in case of fatigue. It is gratifying to be able to say that the privilege is rarely, if ever, abused.

Emergency rooms have been arranged for the different men's departments.

In all women's departments high back chairs and foot rests are in use. We find that by the use of these simple comforts the women are capable of much better work.

At 10 A. M., and at 3 P. M., they are given a ten minute recess. Part of this time usually is devoted to physical development exercises. A competent teacher has given them instructions in this work and in the correct manner of standing, sitting and walking. They arrive at the factory one hour after the men and are permitted to leave ten minutes earlier at night. This was done not only to give them shorter hours but to facilitate their transportation to and from the plant.

Aprons and sleeves are furnished to the girls, and white suits to the janitors. The company launders these articles free of charge.

Another important branch of welfare work is our Domestic Economy Department which serves over a thousand warm meals each day. Separate dining rooms have been provided for the women and the office force, while the heads of departments with their assistants and the foremen meet for luncheon at the Officers' Club. These dining rooms afford an opportunity to discuss matters pertaining to the factory and of general interest. They also enable employes to hear addresses made by many of the prominent visitors to the factory. Meals are furnished at cost. When employes are requested to work overtime, lunches are furnished at the expense of the company.

The N. C. R. Library contains volumes on fiction, history, science, mechanics, and many other books of an educational character. These are supplemented by the leading newspapers of the country and most of the magazines. Portable libraries are being used for the conveyance of books to the respective buildings. We found that the men in the making departments would not take the time to go to the library, so books are taken to them. One cent a week is charged for books taken home.

Great interest is centered in our factory classes for employes. This year instruction is being given in English, cooking, dancing, physical development, sewing, first aid, health and Bible study.

Many of our employes go to and from work on bicycles. Sheds have been provided in which their wheels may be kept during the day. Provision is also made for inflating the bicycle tires.

At the N. C. R. factory Saturday is a half holiday the year around. This affords an opportunity for any shopping the employes may wish to do.

Welfare work has had a beneficial effect on those living in the vicinity. This has been evinced by the formation of clubs for betterment work. The results accompanying their efforts toward neighborhood betterment have been most encouraging.

A plat of land is set aside for boys' gardens. All the neighborhood boys are given an opportunity of caring for a small garden. Prizes are given each year for the best garden and for the best products raised. The boys show their appreciation of this opportunity by their faithful work.

Two independent clubs have been formed by the employes — The Men's Welfare Work League and the Women's Century Club. The women's club was organized in 1896 with 205 members. To-day it has an enrollment of 625. This club has been an important factor in promoting the principle of co-operation here. Its object is to aid in the betterment of those conditions which surround most working women.

The men's league is composed exclusively of the men employes of the N. C. R. Company. Although scarcely a year old the results already accomplished would do credit to much older organizations. It has fostered the spirit of welfare and good-fellowship among its members. It is active in the support of all matters educational. By the successful management of picnics and athletic sports and by monthly dues funds are procured for carrying on its work.

SECRETARY OF THE WELFARE DEPARTMENT.

Miss Gertrude Beeks, Secretary of the Welfare Department of the National Civic Federation, has had long preparation for welfare work and wide experience in the new profession. Her previous activity in business, in organizing business luncheon clubs and in the earliest sociological work of the Civic Federation, involving much personal investigation, prepared her for the formation of the Welfare Department of the McCormick Harvesting Machine Company in Chicago, employing 500 women and 6,000 men. She was in charge of this Department during several years. Later, after studying the plant and the needs of its employes, also numbering about seven thousand, she outlined a plan for the welfare work of another division of the International Harvester Company, to cover matters requiring the greatest attention, and which would need time to develop completely. Some of these recommendations have already been put into effect. She has traveled extensively in this country, visiting plants and studying the causes of the notable failures and successes of welfare work. In her capacity as Secretary of the Welfare Department of the National Civic Federation, Miss Beeks is frequently called into consultation by employers as to the application of welfare work, both in large industrial establishments and communities, and in more limited concerns.

Miss Gertrude Beeks.

RAILWAY PROVIDENT INSTITUTIONS.

Their Development and Application Upon the Pennsylvania Railroad System.

By Max Riebenack, *Comptroller of the Pennsylvania Railroad Company.*

[The following is the closing instalment of Mr. Riebenack's paper upon "Railway Provident Institutions," read at a conference of the Welfare Department in New York City in November. The first instalment was published in the November number of The Civic Federation Review. The author of this paper, the Comptroller of the Pennsylvania Railroad Company, is qualified to write as an expert upon this subject. In his official capacities he has been largely instrumental in maturing and promoting the provident undertakings of that railway system. Mr. Riebenack was selected to report upon "Railway Provident Institutions" to the seventh session of the International Railway Congress, composed of the highest officials of the leading railways of the world, to be held in Washington, D. C., next May. —EDITOR'S NOTE.]

I may be pardoned for speaking directly on the efforts made and the plans adopted by the Pennsylvania Railroad Company in its endeavor to further the welfare of its employes, for the reason that I am more familiar with its plans and operations and practical workings, also on the ground that the policy pursued in the conduct of its provident undertakings has been largely followed by other American roads. Its status in this relation may therefore be taken as a fair indication of the drift of sentiment on the part of the railroads of the country toward providing institutions and measures for the benefit of their employes.

For operative and administrative purposes the System is divided into two distinctive organizations, one styled the "Pennsylvania System East of Pittsburgh and Erie," including the lines east of those points, and representing 5,852.44 miles of roadway with 117,928 employes, of which the roads associated in the administration of the Relief and Pension Departments represent an aggregate mileage of 5,209.87 miles of roadway and 110,502 employes, respectively; and the other the "Pennsylvania System West of Pittsburgh and Erie," embracing the lines west of those points, and representing 5,061.45 miles of roadway with 49,202 employes.

The provident institutions and undertakings now conducted comprise well-defined plans, and their relative importance warrants the following grouping:

Relief Fund and Superannuation Feature;
Pension Fund;
Saving Fund;
Hospital Service;
Libraries and Reading Rooms;
Young Men's Christian Association Branches.

Both parts of the System employ very similar methods for the benefit of their employes, but as those operated on the lines east come more directly under my observation, detailed remarks will be confined to that territory.

RELIEF DEPARTMENT.

The subject of providing some manner of aid for employes in case of disablement or death was first brought to the attention of the management of the Pennsylvania Railroad Company in 1874. An exhaustive canvass of the field culminated in the establishment of the present "Pennsylvania Railroad Voluntary Relief Department," in February, 1886. While many of the features of the original Baltimore and Ohio Railroad Relief Association, in operation at that time, were given full consideration and served as guides in preliminary work, the Pennsylvania Railroad Relief Department represents a purely distinctive organization, built up on the basis of the ascertained requirements of the employes.

The affairs of the Department are under the control of an Advisory Committee, consisting of the General Manager of the Railroad Company, as member *ex-officio* and chairman, and fourteen members, seven of whom are elected by the contributing members, the other seven being appointed by the several interested Boards of Directors. Each member serves for a period of three years, the elections and appointments being made triennially, in different years, and in such manner as to provide for there always being on the committee a majority of members who have served thereon for a period of time sufficient to afford them practical familiarity with the workings of the Fund.

Employes not over forty-five years of age may be enrolled upon making proper application and passing a satisfactory physical examination. Membership contributions, payable monthly in advance and collected by deduction from wages on payrolls, are made in accordance with a graduated scale, based on wages earned, and are, respectively, beginning with the first class, 75 cents, $1.50, $2.25, $3.00 and $3.75 per month for the five classes.

The benefits of the first class are: For sickness, after the first three days of disablement, 40 cents per day for a period of 52 weeks, and 20 cents per day thereafter during continuance of sickness; for accident, 50 cents per day for 52 weeks, and 25 cents per day thereafter while disabled. Other class benefits are proportionately higher. The death benefits are, respectively, beginning with the first class, $250, $500, $750, $1,000 and $1,250. Additional death benefits may be secured by payment of fixed monthly rates over and above regular contributions, the limit of such benefits being governed by class membership; the highest amount being for the fifth class, members of which may take five additional death benefits, with $250 as the benefit unit, or a total of death benefits, including that of their class, amounting to $2,500. The monthly rates of contribution are, for each additional death benefit of the first class ($250), when taken at age not over forty-five years, 30 cents, when over age forty-five and not over sixty years, 45 cents, and over sixty years, 60 cents.

The Company gives the Department free use of its offices and other facilities; defrays all expenses of operation and administration, including the salaries of the two officers in charge, the eighty-nine medical examiners, and ninety-six other employes directly identified with the conduct of the Department; agreed at the outset to make good any deficiency that should arise in any period of three years, which assumption of responsibility was subsequently made a part of the Fund regulations; and also arranged that any surplus arising during any triennial period should be set aside as the foundation for a Superannuation and Pension Fund.

A summarization of eighteen years' operation of the Fund, for the period ending December 31, 1903, presents the following results:

RECEIPTS.

Contributed by members	$11,672,717.39
From company	2,544,348.11
From other sources	422,027.04
Total	$14,639,092.54

DISBURSEMENTS.

Superannuation allowances	$148,662.15
Operating expenses	1,815,641.54
For sickness	4,455,618.80
For accident	2,246,454.10
Death from natural causes	3,527,818.27
Death from accident	1,323,616.61
Total	$13,517,811.47

During these eighteen years benefits were paid for 469,000 cases of disablement, for periods ranging from one day to seventeen years, while 8,531 families of deceased members received death benefits varying in amount, from $250 to $2,500, according to class membership. The membership as of December 31, 1886, was 19,952, while at the close of 1903 it numbered 76,507, or about sixty-nine *per centum* of the total number of employes, and included nearly all those who, by reason of age and physical condition, were eligible to membership.

The value of the protection provided by the Fund may be better understood when it is stated, that members may draw for disablement in 52 weeks as much as their contributions would aggregate in about sixteen years, and that the death benefit, which may become payable at any moment, is equal to the contributions of twenty-eight years.

SUPERANNUATION FUND.

The formation of the Superannuation Fund (which became operative January 1, 1900, simultaneously with the inauguration of the Pension Fund) was brought about by the establishment of the pension feature, when it was decided that members of the Relief Fund, upon retirement from active service, should receive monthly a proportion of the surplus on the basis of their relative contributions. This basis is one cent per month per class for each month of membership.

The Company's liberal policy in meeting all expenses growing out of the operations of the Relief Fund, as well as making up deficiencies at the close of any three-year period, made possible the accumulation of a Surplus Fund of $751,256.25.

The original plan of payment of superannuation allowances involved that the interest accrued upon investments should be used for the purpose. After four years' operation under this plan, it was found that the interest returns were inadequate to meet the demand, whereupon the Company, preferably to making a reduction in the basis of payment, caused the Relief Department regulations to be amended, as of January 1, 1904, to provide that, in addition to the interest derived from the investment of the Surplus Fund, at the end of each three-year period the money not required to discharge the liabilities of former periods shall be applied directly to the payment of superannuation allowances instead of being transferred to and becoming a part of the Surplus Fund; if, however, at the end of the next ensuing three-year period there shall be a balance in the Superannuation Fund, it is to be transferred to and become a part of the Surplus Fund. On the other hand, the Company holds itself responsible to pay any deficiencies in superannuation allowances up to January 1, 1907.

Retired employes receiving superannuation are permitted, upon paying the proper rates of contribution, to retain title to death benefits in the Relief Fund.

PENSION FUND.

The pension plan was started January 1, 1900, and, as finally approved by the Company's stockholders, provides that the Company shall contribute all money necessary for the payment of pension allowances, and for the operation of the Department; also that the maximum amount disbursed for pension allowances under existing regulations shall not exceed in any one year the sum of $390,000. Department operations are controlled by a Board of Officers, consisting of the following officers of the Railroad Company—namely, the Vice-Presidents, the General Manager and the Comptroller, vested with full power to make and enforce Department rules and regulations.

All officers and employes upon attaining the age of 70 years are retired and placed upon the pension payroll, while those of ages between 65 and 70 years, after 30 years' service, are retired and pensioned, either at their own request or upon the recommendation of the proper employing officer, if found to be permanently incapacitated by a Board of Company Physicians. Retirement is based on age, and pension allowance on service and pay; that is, for each year of service one *per centum* of the average monthly pay for the ten years immediately preceding retirement.

During four years' operations, ending December 31, 1903, there was paid in pension allowances the sum of $1,224,087.59, the expense of operation for the same period having been $20,134.78.

Up to the end of 1903 there had been retired and granted pension allowances to 2,126 employes, while 527 pensioners had died. Of the total number retired, 456 were between ages 65 and 70, and 348 of these were relieved at their own request with the approval of the proper employing officer, which indicates that the number of requests to be relieved originating with the employes themselves was in the proportion of three to every one emanating from the employing officers.

RELATION OF AGE LIMIT TO PENSION FUND.

Provision is made that persons beyond the age of 35 years will not be admitted into the Company's service (the exceptions being in cases of former employes, whom the Company may desire to re-engage within a period of three years from the time they were last in the service, or of professional men or specialists). Employment in the service is generally understood to be permanent, and the Company, so viewing the matter, made provision accordingly in the organization of the Pension Department, by limiting the age to 35 years.

The motive for establishing this age restriction was to provide a basis of Department operation under which employes in the future, after the starting period, would be retired from the service and carried on the pension roll at age 65, with thirty years' service. In other words, under the present workings of the Fund it will be merely a matter of a few years when the application of this age limitation feature will bring about a condition under which all pension beneficiaries will have been in the Company's service for not less than thirty years previous to their retirement on pension allowances; and will, in consequence, receive not less than thirty *per centum* of their average wages for the ten years next preceding such retirement.

SAVING FUND.

Mature deliberation, growing out of appeals made by employes identified with the service of the various divisions and branches of the Company for saving fund advantages, resulted in the creation of the "Pennsylvania Railroad Employes' Saving Fund," as of January 2, 1888. The Fund is conducted as a separate department, in charge of a Superintendent, under the supervision of a Board of Trustees, three in number, the members of which are directors or officers of the Railroad Company. Custodianship of all moneys and securities of the Fund is vested in the Company, which assumes responsibility for the proper return of all securities in which Fund surplus may be invested, also the return of membership deposits, together with a fixed rate of interest thereon, which at the present time is three and one-half *per centum per annum*. Fund regulations provide that no change shall be made in the rate of interest allowance on deposits without six months' previous notice to depositors, thus insuring against sudden fluctuations in the earning power of savings.

Employes whose regular monthly wage compensation does not exceed $300 may become depositors, upon making due application at any of the depositaries. No employe is, however, permitted to carry a balance in excess of $5,000, nor deposit more than $100 in any one month. Report of Fund operations for the year ending December 31, 1903, shows 9,494 depositors; deposits, $1,260,229.50; withdrawals, $796,204.22; interest allowed depositors at three and one-half *per centum*, $127,587.09, and balance of $4,010,116.88, equivalent to an average *per capita* credit balance of $420. On the date named there were 1,102 depositaries, located at station agencies most accessible to the employes, and of which the general clearing house is the Company's Treasury Department.

Statistics for the period since establishment of the Fund to the end of 1903 furnish the following results:

Deposits	$9,334,945.08
Withdrawals	6,400,892.71
Interest allowed depositors	1,058,676.97
Number of applications for deposit books	20,133

Fully ninety-five *per centum* of the total amount on deposit is invested in first-class securities averaging an annual return of three and one-half *per centum*.

HOSPITAL SERVICE.

The Railroad Company does not conduct a Hospital Department, there being no absolute necessity therefor, owing to the fact that it is conveniently and reasonably enabled to avail itself of the numerous public and private institutions of this character located in the different cities and towns along its lines. There is, however, a well established corps of surgeons, the members of which are assigned to points on the road where they can be reached by quick summons, also the corps of medical examiners allied to the Relief Department, the members of which are assigned to special territorial districts, with offices at vantage points where they are ever ready to give in emergencies needed medical advice or attendance to employes, regardless of Relief Fund membership.

To render prompt assistance to those who may meet with accident or are seized with sudden illness on its lines, the Company has numerous devices, the foremost being the "Hospital Car," which is especially constructed to meet all requirements, and thoroughly equipped with necessary paraphernalia for emergency use.

FIRST AID TO INJURED.

For some years the Company had under consideration the establishment of a system of "First Aid to the Injured," but the actual inauguration of the plan was deferred pending the development of Relief Fund operations to a stage at which adequate equipment and working machinery could be commanded. The plan was launched on October 1, of this year, since which date the medical examiners have been giving lectures to employes selected to perform this work. The arrangement comprises the following features: The "First Aid Packet," containing small packets in a tin box, hermetically sealed, which, in turn, is enclosed in a sealed wooden box, these boxes being placed in every engine and caboose, and at principal stations, and the "First Aid Emergency Box," which is placed at large stations and agencies, with full instructions as to the use of contents, which, in a general way, include medicines, bandages and plasters, and surgical instruments. The Company also has in operation a systematic arrangement for supplying stretchers to all baggage, wrecking and maintenance-of-way cars. General orders have been issued requiring the giving of instructions to all trainmen and others concerned, on extending first aid to the injured.

LIBRARIES AND READING ROOMS.

Germane to the work of the Young Men's Christian Association Railroad Departments, and in many instances going hand in hand with it, is the plan of providing libraries and reading rooms at various points on the lines of road at which trainmen and others are required to collect in the discharge of their duties.

Numerous reading rooms are located on the lines of the Pennsylvania System East of Pittsburgh and Erie, at various division terminals; also at other points, where trainmen begin and end runs. These rooms are currently furnished with daily papers, magazines, periodicals and miscellaneous reading matter, the literature supplied being of such character as to be entertaining and instructive, thus enabling advantageous employment of enforced time off duty. Permanent libraries are scattered throughout the System, with a large *clientele* of employes. The growth of the library system has been steady, and at the end of 1903 it comprised 62,973 volumes.

Y. M. C. A. RAILROAD BRANCHES.

The Pennsylvania Railroad Company was among the first of the large trunk lines to realize the practicability of embracing a plan which would place before its employes of all classes broader and higher educational opportunities and advantages, and at different times during the preliminary consideration of the question endeavored to pave the way for the introduction of a permanent branch of the Association. Efforts in this direction did not meet with what might be termed signal success until the completion of the railroad branch located at West Philadelphia, Pa. This branch was finally organized November 18, 1886, although originally undertaken May 1, 1876; it was fully housed in 1893, when approximately $140,000 had been raised and disbursed through the combined efforts of nearly 6,000 railroad men and their friends, together with the substantial co-operation of the Railroad Company.

The Pennsylvania Railroad Department Young Men's Christian Association of Philadelphia is the largest on the Pennsylvania System of Lines, and also holds the enviable distinction of being the largest railroad branch in the world in point of membership (which on December 31, 1903, numbered about 2,500), equipment, and variety and extent of work.

The demonstrated benefits accruing to employes enjoying membership in these branches have enlisted the enthusiastic and continuous support of the Company and its principal officers.

President A. J. Cassatt made the statement:

> "I am in full sympathy and accord with the work which is being so successfully carried on by the Railroad Department of the Young Men's Christian Association. From observation I am satisfied that excellent results, from the standpoint of the employes as well as of the Company, are being accomplished through this agency."

At the close of 1903 there were thirty-one Association branches, with a total membership of 12,732 on the lines of the Pennsylvania System East and West of Pittsburgh, to which the Railroad Company extended financial upport. Some of these branches own the buildings they occupy, but the larger number are located in buildings belonging to the Company.

SUMMARY OF EXPENDITURE DURING YEAR 1903.

The details of the annual expenditure for the various provident features of the two parts of the System, during the year ending December 31, 1903, show a total of $943,618.23, as follows:

	Lines East.	Lines West.
Relief	$262,777.37	$91,614.09
Pension	363,629.29	130,381.81
Hospital	18,370.00	2,197.50
Saving Fund	8,417.93	4,537.76
Y. M. C. A. and Libraries and Reading Rooms	53,351.36	8,341.12
Total	$706,545.95	$237,072.28

REMARKS ON PROVIDENT FUNDS.

A few remarks may be appropriately made on certain prominent characteristics of railway relief and pension funds as conducted in the United States.

The real consummation that has grown out of efforts made by the Pennsylvania Railroad Company in the provident fields of sickness, accident and pension, may be summed up in the statement, that all employes of the Company are, at the present time, given ample opportunity to provide for themselves in case of sickness or accident, and for designated or proper beneficiaries in the event of death, through the instrumentality of the funds—a co-partnership maintained jointly by the members and the Company, and later, when the prescribed time for retirement from active service is attained, either on the ground of old age or permanent incapacitation, the Company, absolutely from its own revenues and without any contributions or other form of support from the employes, grants to all employes entitled thereto, liberal pension allowances, while these monetary provisions are still further ncreased by a supplmental payment from the Relief Fund, in the form of superannuation allowances, on a fixed basis in proportion to the amount of contributions during Fund membership.

COMPULSORY MEMBERSHIP ILLEGAL.

Relief Funds may be properly styled "mutual benefit associations," as under their operations each member practically contributes for the joint welfare of himself and fellow members, and with company co-operation the duration of mutual assistance is unlimited. Membership is purely voluntary. As a matter of fact "compulsory" membership is prohibited by the United States Arbitration Act of June 1, 1898. It is sometimes held that membership is nominally voluntary but practically compulsory. This view undoubtedly arises from the circumstance that the companies, in accordance with the principle observed by all large business undertakings requiring the constant employment of large numbers of men, exercise the generally conceded right to decide upon the physical fitness and general qualifications of applicants for positions in their service. In carrying out this principle the discriminations made between applicants may appear to the uninformed to indicate a disposition to enforce "compulsory" membership, but this is an entirely erroneous conclusion, as such a course is of paramount importance with railroads for safeguarding the interests of the public as well as their own.

The question of joining the Fund is laid before new employes without the slightest pressure one way or another, and there are no cases on record to my knowledge where an employe has been dismissed from service simply because he refused to become a member of the relief fund, or rejected for employment on account of his declining, if employed, to become a member of the organization. It is entirely optional with the employe after he has become a member of the Relief Fund to resign from it at any time he may see fit, and his status with the company as an employe is not affected by such action on his part.

The stability of relief departments is based altogether on the extent to which the railroad companies assume responsibility for their operations and are willing to guarantee their financial obligations. The members are thus doubly protected, first by their own contributions and next by the promise and ability of the companies to make up any deficiency which may occur. There is, therefore, a direct mutual interest between the members and the companies. There is no encroachment on other plans of relief or insurance which may have enlisted the support of employes.

Contributions are intended primarily for the purpose of assuring sick or disabled members of a designated monthly income at a time when most needed, and in providing this income promptly.

The payment of death benefits is an incidental feature of the plan, whose presence stands for a logical constituent of the chief factors—sickness and accident, from the fact that it insures deceased members respectable burial, and intervenes to prevent the possible immediate impoverishment of their families.

No provision is made for the return to members of the Relief Fund, leaving either the service or the Fund, of any proportion of their contributions, for the reason that during their connection with the Fund they have been protected against sickness and accident at a minimum cost, and to make repayments would necessitate an increase in rates, which would mean an added expense to all the members. It is also a fact that the laws of some States prohibit the continuance of fund death benefits after employes leave the service of the corporation, as being an infringement upon State Insurance statutory enactments.

ADVANTAGES OF RELIEF FUND MEMBERSHIP.

The advantages of membership in the Relief Funds may be thus recited:

(a) Indemnity in case of disablement from accident or sickness, and death from accidental or natural causes, at a minimum cost; the protection extended for death being particularly advantageous to employes occupying hazardous positions, as many of the regular-line insurance companies will not insure them, and those that do demand largely increased premiums over the ordinary risk.

(b) Free surgical attendance in case of disablement from accident while in the performance of duty; also the furnishing of artificial limbs and other appliances.

(c) No payment for membership or medical examiners' fees.

(d) No special dues or taxes, and no extra assessments.

(e) Exemption from contribution during disablement, after that made for the month in which the disablement originates.

(f) Protection against possibility of forfeiting title to benefits for non-payment of dues; the practice of collecting contributions on the pay-rolls obviating this so long as members are on duty.

(g) No assessments for administration, all expenses being defrayed by the associated companies.

(h) Benefits are not susceptible to hypothecation, and death benefits cannot be diverted for any purpose, being confined exclusively to payment to designated beneficiaries, who must be members of the family.

(i) Relief from making contributions to their fellow-employes or their families in destitute circumstances; solicitations in this direction were of common occurrence before the funds were established.

LEGAL RIGHTS OF MEMBERS.

An important point in connection with the operation of relief funds is the question of a member's right to have recourse to action at law against the interested railroad companies in lieu of accepting accident benefits extended by the funds. To understand this point it must be borne in mind, primarily, that the applicant for fund membership enters into an agreement with the fund to accept, in the event of sustaining disablement injury while in the service and in the performance of service duties, the accident benefits specifically prescribed in fund regulations. This is a distinct agreement, with a good and valid consideration, made between proper contracting parties, and, therefore, invested with due legal status. By becoming voluntarily a party to the agreement the applicant should live up to its terms, any overt or serious violation of which should, and does, result in relinquishment by the violating party of the benefits that would otherwise have accrued to him thereunder. The companies by reason of guaranteeing that all obligations of the funds will be met, also paying their deficiencies, and contributing the entire amount necessary in the conduct of their operations, clearly assume responsibilities which warrant them in asking employe applicants to enter into the agreement referred to. By entering into such contract the member is invested with a fixed and certain rate of compensation, while the companies are always in position to determine the extent of their financial obligation, and accord each case prompt and systematic treatment. The object contemplated by the agreement is the safeguarding of both the funds and the associated or interested railroad companies, by the introduction of provisions that are plainly set forth and as well serve equally the best interests of both parties to the contract. This manner of fund agreement does not deprive the member from instituting legal proceedings instead of taking the rate of compensation offered by the fund. It does provide, however, that where the member disregards his plain obligations under its terms, he thereupon forfeits his rights to fund benefits, and the question of company compensation will then depend wholly upon the merits of the case from a purely legal standpoint.

REASONS FOR AGE LIMIT.

The establishment by the railroad companies of an age limit for admission into the service was for the purpose of making it possible, when the retirement age is reached, for employes to receive a return for services rendered an allowance equivalent to a fair proportion of their average pay.

The adoption of this provision does not, however, preclude the re-employment of former employes, who are over the age of 35 years, for the reason that this privilege is accorded to them, provided they have not been out of the service for more than three years and that the companies have positions in which they could be employed. This period is deemed sufficient for employes to decide whether or not they desire re-employment, and at the same time such absence from the service does not destroy the feature of the employes at the retiring age, having been in the service such a number of years as to give them the benefit of a fair pension allowance.

MOTIVES AND RESULTS.

Too much praise cannot be accorded the railway officials of the United States for their broad-minded and liberal treatment of the subject of conferring pension allowances upon employes. In providing for extension

(*Concluded on page 20.*)

THE VOICE OF THE PRESS DECLARES FOR INDUSTRIAL PEACE.

THE AIMS AND METHODS OF THE NATIONAL CIVIC FEDERATION WARMLY APPROVED BY EDITORS THROUGHOUT THE COUNTRY.

THE following four pages are filled with extracts, some of them reproduced photographically, from the publications, daily and periodical, lay, professional, technical, economic and reigious, that have been stirrred to comment upon the proceedings at the fourth annual meeting and dinner of the National Civic Federation. Comparatively few of these comments are reprinted here, but their publication will be continued. They have been selected at random, and without regard to their favorable or qustioning tone. They serve to show that the progress of the Federation is critically scrutinized by millions of observers, and thus wil impress those in sympathy with the promotion of rightful relations between employers and employed with the vast public responsibility that is involved in their joint and individual efforts for industrial peace. They afford convincing evidence that this movement has won that general support throughout the country which warrants its vigorous prosecution and wider expansion:

GOOD ACCOMPLISHED BEYOND EXPECTATION.

Locomotive Engineers' Journal.

The National Civic Federation has expanded equal to the fondest hopes of its principal promoter, the late Senator M. A. Hanna, and the scope of good it has accomplished has exceeded the most sanguine expectations of all interested in it; and now is reaching out by adding a new department of Industrial Economics, composed of prominent educators, heads of departments of political economy in universities, representatives of the pulpit, editors of the daily press, politico-social magazines, trade and technical papers, whose readers include all the great employing interests, among whom are those most antagonistic to organized labor, and more than twenty editors of papers and magazines which are read by millions of wage-earners.

We believe the organization of the new department will be specially beneficial to the latter class, for it gives opportunity to present the attitude of labor organizations, causes that make them necessary and the good they are doing, not only for those who are members, but that the bettered conditions they bring are not only not injurious to the public, as Parry and many others say, but are decidedly beneficial.

About one hundred editors were invited to join, and nearly all accepted and attended a meeting of the National Civic Federation on December 15, and we believe every one felt that in bringing together every class of interest, so they could get better acquainted, enter into the discussions of the various phases of this greatest subject now before the American public, it would be of great benefit to all concerned, correcting many erroneous opinions and modifying extreme views, and we believe these associations, with their attending education influences, will eventually leave very small space in public opinion for such men as Parry and his association, organised for the purpose of destroying organised labor.

The permanent organization of this department will be effected at the next meeting, when the *Journal* will give space to the subjects which come before this body, and a synopsis of the discussion, and point out with such ability as we possess the direction of the influence exercised by it.

HARMONY PREDICTED IN THE PIANO TRADE.

Music Trades.

It will be well if employers of labor, and particularly those who have large manufacturing plants, will take the trouble to read carefully the account in this issue of the *Music Trades* of the convention of the National Civic Federation, which was held in this city on Thursday of last week.

The eminence of those engaged in this work, and the absorbing interest of the speeches made by the heads of great corporations, as well as by the great labor leaders, should be sufficient to warrant a careful perusal of the proceedings; but there is a further and greater reason why the men engaged in these industries should take a deep interest in the work of the Civic Federation. In the event of there being labor troubles in this trade, and especially in the piano industry, the Civic Federation stands prepared to use its best efforts to bring the contending parties together, and as these efforts are put forth by conciliation committees, composed of men of the highest standing in the world of labor, as well as in the world of capital, it can be readily seen that a force will be brought to bear to bring about an adjustment of differences on a reasonable and fair basis that cannot well be resisted.

With the Civic Federation in the field, represented by men to whom industrial peace is a labor of love, who leave their vast interests to serve the public without hope of even that reward which comes from publicity, it is not likely that this trade will ever again be disturbed by labor troubles as it has been in the past.

GREAT STRIDES TOWARD CONCILIATION.

Locomotive Firemen's Magazine.

At the banquet, which was held after the adjournment of the meeting, Mr. Samuel Gompers acted as toastmaster. In his opening remarks he referred to the growth of the Civic Federation and said that as new problems are continually arising, and as the Federation solved them one by one, it puts itself in a position for the more ready and able solution of the next to come. He said that labor had discovered, through the instrumentality of the Federation, that employers are not the "modern monsters" which they were regarded as being in the past, and that he welcomed, advisedly, for labor which he represented, the organizations of employers.

The name of the late Senator Hanna was greeted with cheers when mentioned by the speaker, as was also the name of Mr. Andrew Carnegie, when Mr. Gompers, stating that indisposition kept him from attending, wished for his speedy recovery. Mr. Gompers then introduced Mr. Ralph Easley, Secretary of the Federation, who read Mr. Carnegie's address. Mr. Carnegie, as is well known, is an extensive employer of labor, and speaking as the result of a life's experience in that capacity, he sets forth in his address very clearly the great disadvantages resulting to corporations engaging in disputes with their men which culminate in strikes, and the advisability of their seeking, by every fair and honorable means, to avoid all such contention. Mr. Carnegie's address clearly set forth the provocations and trials experienced by workingmen who, in a just cause, are compelled to stand by and witness low, degraded, unprincipled and incompetent loafers usurp their places—fellows who, under normal conditions, are idle the better part of their time through lack of merit on their own part, and who seek work only when specially lucrative opportunities are offered through open warfare between capital and labor. He showed what a hardship it was for honest, competent wage-earners to see the work in which they had always taken such a pride being botched by such incompetents, and they themselves, deprived of the revenues resulting from its performance, whereby they had been enabled to support those dearer to them than life itself. An acknowledgment of this kind from such a source is a striking indication of the efficacy of the great work of the Civic Federation. The vivid portrayal by Mr. Carnegie of the feelings of the striking wage-earner, and the public expression of his opinion that employers, partly out of consideration for the men who create their wealth, and partly with a view to the protection of their own best interests, ought "never to employ new men in case of any strike, but to wait patiently for the old men," is, in itself, evidence of the great strides that have been made in recent years in the work of conciliating labor and capital through the influence of that vigorous, sane and healthy sentiment being developed through the instrumentality of such agencies as that powerful organization.

BROAD AND ENLIGHTENED VIEWS.

American Machinist, New York.

It has been Mr. Belmont's habit to recognize the rights of the men who work under his administration and the completion of the new subways in New York within the time in which it was accomplished is credited largely to what is described as his broadminded and fair methods of dealing with labor questions. At any rate, few could ask for a more liberal or more enlightened expression of views than he gave in his address, and it is altogether probable that his promise to give the affairs of the Federation his best efforts means very much. And certainly the fact that a man of such large wealth, one who is so busy and possesses such a large measure of administrative ability is willing to devote his time and talents to such work is of itself significant. Another significant point in connection with it is that the many prominent labor leaders who are members of the Federation and who were present at the meeting and banquet very heartily endorsed Mr. Belmont's nomination and election.

Besides the letter from President Roosevelt, expressing the most hearty sympathy with the objects of the Federation, there was an address by Andrew Carnegie, the most notable feature of which was a declaration of his belief that where differences arise between an employer and his employes it ought to be announced by the employer that no effort would be made to get a new body of employes, but that operations would simply await the reasonable settlement of the difficulties.

John Mitchell made a manly and clean-cut address, in which he said.

"I hope the time will never come when men will surrender their right to strike or employers give up their right to close their mines or their mills, and I hope to live long enough to see the day when lock-outs, strikes and boycotts will be unnecessary, and when the American Civic Federation will be the recognized tribunal of peace in the industrial affairs of America."

Mr. Belmont's declaration to the effect that he had found face-to-face conferences the best, and, in fact, a practical and satisfactory means of avoiding or of settling labor difficulties was heartily endorsed by others, notably by Mr. James Kilbourne, of Columbus, Ohio, a manufacturer who seems to have been able to remain upon entirely friendly terms with his employes throughout the troublous recent period and who, in his address, gave the most emphatic testimony as to their faithfulness and fairness when approached in the right spirit, and treated with the consideration to which he claimed American citizens are entitled.

A GATHERING OF "FELLOW-AMERICANS."

The Christian at Work, New York.

That was a notable gathering last week when the Civic Federation met for the first time since the death of its former head, Senator Hanna, and elected Mr. August Belmont president. The Federation, representing men equally prominent in the world of Finance and the world of Labor, is a movement prompted in the interest of both the great parties, to secure, if possible, a common working basis with a view of preventing strikes, and, when they do occur, of reaching a common agreement. So far no iron-clad rules of procedure have been adopted, if indeed, such rules are possible. The effect of the meetings of the Federation so far has been to bring the parties together for conference, with the result that by this means some strikes have been averted and others adjusted. Not only capital and labor, in the generally accepted meaning of the term, were represented among the 300 diners, but art and education, all had standard bearers there. So vast and diverse were the interests which mingled at the tables that Samuel Gompers, the first vice-president of the Federation, who acted as chairman, could think of no more specific term in which to address his audience than "fellow-Americans."

FOR INDUSTRIAL PEACE.

The Dry Goods Economist, New York.

The National Civic Federation, which held its fourth annual meeting Thursday in this city, is probably the most important organization in the world that has for its object the lessening, and ultimately perhaps the extinction, of industrial strife through education and conciliation. The importance of the organization is attested by its steady growth, by the character and caliber of the men who stand foremost in its councils, and by the work already accomplished along the line of its avowed aims.

It is a hardship upon the Federation that the details, and even the outlines, of its most successful achievements cannot be made public for the reason that the parties to impending contests usually stipulate, before meeting under the conciliatory auspices of the Federation, that the facts of such meeting shall remain a secret. Of what the institution has done, however, enough is already known to increase the general respect and confidence it has inspired, and to make it apparent that the National Civic Federation is to be a permanent, or semi-permanent, factor in the great work of bringing peace into the American industrial field.

A novel and significant spectacle was the array of capitalists, employers, labor leaders and representatives of the professions and the great institutions of learning, who sat promiscuously about the tables at the banquet.

When such men as Andrew Carnegie, John Mitchell, Henry Phipps, August Belmont, President Charles W. Eliot, of Harvard University; Oscar S. Straus, Samuel Gompers, Archbishop Ireland, James O'Connell, of the machinists; P. H. Morrissey, of the trainmen; Franklin MacVeagh, St. Clair McKelway, of the Brooklyn *Eagle;* Warren S. Stone, of the Brotherhood of Locomotive Engineers; H. H. Vreeland, president of the Metropolitan Traction Company; Professors Taussig of Harvard, and Seligman, of Columbia, and literally hundreds of others of similar prominence in the mental and physical activities of the country—when such men, we say, come together, not perfunctorily, but with a serious and sympathetic purpose, good results to labor, capital and to the public will surely follow.

In handling the complicated problems, social, financial and industrial, involved in what is called the "labor question," at least two important factors must always co-operate; first, the personal equation—the skill, tact and persuasiveness of the men who draw together and finally conciliate opposing forces—and second, the knowledge of actual facts and principles relative to the subject, which furnishes a basis for conciliation and agreement.

The Federation has already shown in a satisfactory measure its possession of the first of these requisites. It now proposes to provide the second by the formation of a Department of Industrial Economics, the organization of which was completed on Thursday, with President Eliot, of Harvard, at its head. As now equipped, and with August Belmont as successor to the late Senator Hanna in the president's chair, the National Civic Federation enters upon its new year with bright prospects of rendering illustrious service not only to labor and capital, but to the entire community.

A TRIBUTE TO PERSONAL WORTH.

Harper's Weekly, New York.

During the recent political campaign the person most frequently referred to as "a Wall Street man" was August Belmont. The term is usually meant by those who use it to be opprobrious, but we question whether Mr. Belmont himself would so regard it. He really is a Wall Street man in the sense that his office is in that vicinity, as was that of his distinguished father before him. In those days an honorable banker was considered to be as reputable as any other citizen. Times have changed somewhat in this respect, but a pleasing indication that they have not gone wholly awry was afforded last week by the unanimous election of Mr. Belmont to succeed the late Senator Hanna as president of the National Civic Federation. He not only did not seek the position, but was naturally very reluctant to accept it, and would not have done so but for one fact, in which lies the significance of his selection, viz., that the suggestion came from the representatives of labor in the Federation. That it was a meritorious choice is well known to everybody familiar with the admirable manner in which Mr. Belmont has sustained the reputation of an honored name, but that it should have been made by the courageous spokesmen of an element supposed to regard the Wall Street man with horror is clearly indicative of growing breadth and tolerance on the part of both labor and capital. The personal tribute to Mr. Belmont is surpassed only by the credit won for themselves by Mr. Mitchell, Mr. Gompers and their associates.

APPRECIATED BY ORGANIZED LABOR.

The Independent, New York.

Last week Mr. August Belmont was elected to the presidency of the National Civic Federation, to succeed the late Senator Hanna. Mr. Belmont has yet to prove his ability in this position, but his modest speech in accepting the office would seem to show that he realizes the responsibility conferred upon him and the high order of work required. It is no small honor for a great Wall Street financier to have the confidence of the leaders of organized labor, as was evidenced by the unanimous vote cast for Mr. Belmont. Even Mr. Carnegie, who declined the presidency before it was offered to Mr. Belmont, admitted that it was the greatest honor that had ever come to him, especially in view of his supposed connection with the Homestead affair. The National Civic Federation in its four years of existence has amply justified itself. Leaving radical and Utopian solutions of the capital and labor problem to others, it confines itself to the immediate difficulties between employers and employed, and uses its good offices to settle these difficulties in the most practical manner possible. As such it has done more than any other agency to bring about peace in the industrial world. No wonder it is bitterly hated by the uncompromising Socialists on the one hand and by the so-called "Parryites" on the other. At the annual dinner last year one of the representatives of the employes brought down the house by asking what the people whom he represented could expect from an organization harboring two such eminent politicians in its membership as Senator Hanna and Grover Cleveland. The labor element, however, has found that it pays to work and confer with the representatives of the other classes, and we believe that there is not a labor leader of any importance in the country who does not now acknowledge the value to organized labor of the work of the Federation.

A PECULIARLY FIT CHOICE.

Pueblo (Col.) Chieftain.

Universal satisfaction is expressed over the election of Mr. August Belmont to the presidency of the National Civic Federation. Mr. Belmont is peculiarly fitted in many respects for the position, and there is little doubt that there could have been no wiser selection for Mr. Hanna's successor. Mr. Belmont is an authority in the financial and political world and in the management of his vast interests he has had ample opportunity to acquire the knowledge that will prove useful to him in directing the affairs of the Federation. In his relations with his army of employes he has shown himself ready at all times to hear the other side, and by his sense of justice complications have been avoided that might have been most disastrous in their results. He has earned the confidence and respect of the men under him, and in his election the representation of all the elements was united and enthusiastically harmonious.

PRESIDENT BELMONT AND TRADE AGREEMENTS.

Ironton (O.) Register.

It is to be hoped that Mr. Belmont will not only be able to prove himself a good president but that he will be able in some real measure to carry out the large purposes of good and industrial peace which the former president thought so much of.

In his speech of acceptance he spoke of the work of the Federation as being for the good of all society, and that it must accomplish its end by teaching "good faith and honest dealings as the basic principles upon which trade agreements may rest." If agreements once entered into are faithfully carried out there will not be the trouble of making agreements what they should be for each side concerned.

SEES STRIKE REMEDY

CIVIC FEDERATION HAS SYMPATHY OF ROOSEVELT

NATIONS MAY JOIN CIVIC FEDERATION

August Belmont Will Head Civic Federation

AUGUST BELMONT MADE PRESIDENT

CARNEGIE ON PEACE

GOMPERS PRESIDES.

BELMONT IS CHOSEN

HE SUCCEEDS MR. HANNA

PRESIDENT PAYS TRIBUTE TO LATE SENATOR HANNA

BELMONT MADE THE NEW HEAD

SEES MUCH GOOD IN FEDERATION

BELMONT CHOSEN

BELMONT NAMED AS PRESIDENT

THE PRESIDENT LAUDS MARK HANNA

PRAISE FROM THE PRESIDENT.

INTERNATIONAL CIVIC FEDERATION COMING

Prophecy at Annual Meeting of Organization in New York.

GREAT GOOD

Accomplished by the Civic Federation.

LIKE BELMONT AS HANNA'S SUCCESSOR

Majority of Labor Leaders Think He's Right Man for Head of National Civic Federation

IMPORTANT LETTER IS READ

BELMONT AS PRESIDENT

BELMONT HEAD OF CIVIC FEDERATION

SAMUEL GOMPERS

BELMONT HEADS CIVIC FEDERATION

CAPITAL AND LABOR ANNUAL DINNER

PLEADS FOR HIGH WAGES

PEACE AND HONOR

Keynote of Civic Federation Speeches

THE NEW PRESIDENT.

FLOOD MR. BELMONT WITH TELEGRAMS

SAMUEL GOMPERS ADDRESSES NATIONAL CIVIC FEDERATION

CARNEGIE ADVISES EMPLOYER AND MAN

SAYS THEY SHOULD BE BETTER ACQUAINTED

August Belmont Is Elected President of the National Civic Federation—Archbishop Ireland Declares Labor Problems Should Be Settled on the Basis of Intelligence and Mutual Sympathy

BELMONT'S VIEWS ON LABOR MATTERS

BELMONT IN SEN. HANNA'S PLACE

KEEP OLD HANDS SAYS CARNEGIE

HE SUCCEEDS HANNA

WILL LEAD TO A WORLD-WIDE BODY

THE FEDERATION IS IN SESSION

ROOSEVELT PRAISES CIVIC FEDERATION

TRIBUTE TO HANNA FROM ROOSEVELT

PRAISES WORK DONE BY HANNA

DOESN'T PAY

BELMONT CHOSEN HANNA'S SUCCESSOR

CARNEGIE DISCUSSES LABOR

GET CLOSER TOGETHER

DAY OF PEACE IN INDUSTRIAL WORLD NEAR

GREAT CIVIC FEDERATION

CARNEGIE OPPOSED TO STRIKEBREAKER

CARNIEGIE SEES REMEDY FOR STRIKES

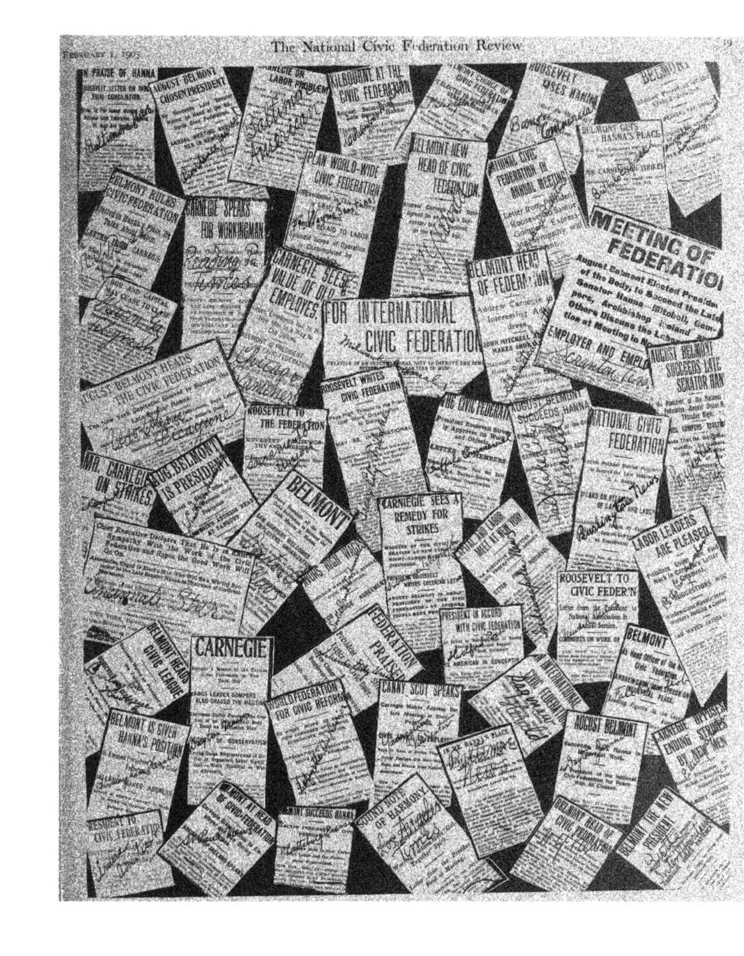
IN PRAISE OF HANNA
AUGUST BELMONT CHOSEN PRESIDENT
CARNEGIE ON LABOR PROBLEM
KILBOURNE AT THE CIVIC FEDERATION
ROOSEVELT USES HANNA
BELMONT GETS HANNA'S PLACE
PLAN WORLD-WIDE CIVIC FEDERATION
BELMONT NEW HEAD OF CIVIC FEDERATION
NATIONAL CIVIC FEDERATION IN ANNUAL MEETING
BELMONT RULES CIVIC FEDERATION
CARNEGIE SPEAKS FOR WORKINGMAN
MEETING OF FEDERATION
CARNEGIE SEES VALUE OF OLD EMPLOYES
BELMONT HEAD OF FEDERATION
FOR INTERNATIONAL CIVIC FEDERATION
AUGUST BELMONT SUCCEEDS LATE SENATOR HANNA
AUGUST BELMONT HEADS THE CIVIC FEDERATION
ROOSEVELT WRITES CIVIC FEDERATION
ROOSEVELT TO THE FEDERATION
THE CIVIC FEDERATION
AUGUST BELMONT SUCCEEDS HANNA
NATIONAL CIVIC FEDERATION
MR. CARNEGIE ON STRIKES
AUG. BELMONT IS PRESIDENT
BELMONT
CARNEGIE SEES A REMEDY FOR STRIKES
LABOR LEADERS ARE PLEASED
ROOSEVELT TO CIVIC FEDER'N
PRESIDENT IN ACCORD WITH CIVIC FEDERATION
FEDERATION PRAISED
CARNEGIE
BELMONT HEADS CIVIC LEAGUE
BELMONT
WORLD FEDERATION FOR CIVIC REFORM
CANNY SCOT SPEAKS
BELMONT IS GIVEN HANNA'S POSITION
AUGUST BELMONT
PRESIDENT TO CIVIC FEDERATION
BELMONT AT HEAD OF CIVIC FEDERATION
BELMONT SUCCEEDS HANNA
SOUND NOTE OF HARMONY
BELMONT HEAD OF CIVIC FEDERATION
BELMONT THE NEW PRESIDENT

PRESIDENT ROOSEVELT'S LETTER TIMELY.

Review of Reviews, New York.

In certain trades there has been a marked disposition on the part of the labor unions to carry their methods to the extreme of tyranny and dictation, while, on the other hand, there has been a disposition on the part of certain capitalists, working through employers' associations, to do everything in their power to crush out labor organizations altogether. As between these opposing tendencies, the wiser and more experienced labor leaders on the one hand and the more thoughtful and public-spirited employers on the other have found themselves during the past year subjected to a sharp cross-fire. It was therefore a particularly timely supplemental utterance of President Roosevelt that appeared in the form of a letter to be read at the annual meeting of the Civic Federation in New York, on the 13th of December. The National Civic Federation is an important body in which labor, capital, and the general public are equally represented. Its great practical mission is to bring men together in close relations and to promote industrial peace by conference, with conciliation and arbitration in the background. There are extreme labor leaders who oppose the Civic Federation in all its views and methods. There are organizations of employers which are even more bitterly opposed to the good work of the Civic Federation, for the Federation gives the fullest credit to the value of labor organization, and believes in a general way, that not only the best interests of the workers themselves, but also those of American citizenship at large, are advanced by a union of men in various callings for the improvement of their conditions.

The form in which the Civic Federation has found that industrial peace can best be conserved in this country is the form known as the "trade agreement," under which employers and employed meet directly through their accredited representatives and make their relative proposals, try to understand one another's point of view, learn to recognize one another's fundamental rights, and then settle by "give and take" those practical questions which are matters of bargaining rather than of conscience or conviction. As Mr. John Mitchell says, it is better for employer and employed to get together and talk a week than for them to fight by means of strike or lockout for a year. This is what the Civic Federation stands for, and it is most cheering to see how heartily the leaders of labor and the representatives of capital, meeting in this public-spirited organization, have come to esteem and respect one another. At the annual dinner of the Federation in New York, where President Roosevelt's wise and sympathetic letter was read, Mr. Samuel Gompers ably presided as the head of the American Federation of Labor, while among the speakers whom Mr. Gompers presented to a great company of representative men were capitalists and employers like Mr. Henry Phipps, Mr. August Belmont, Colonel Kilbourne, of Ohio, and Mr. Robbins, of Pittsburg. Among the scores of talented leaders belonging to the ranks of labor besides Mr. Gompers himself, were such speakers as Mr. John Mitchell, of the United Mine Workers, and Mr. Morrissey, of the Railway Trainmen, and as representing the general public were President Eliot, of Harvard, Archbishop Ireland, and Mr. Oscar S. Straus. Mr. Andrew Carnegie had been with the Federation through the day, and was represented at the banquet by a paper read for him by Mr. Ralph Easley, the organizer and executive officer of the body. The vacancy in the office of the president caused by the death of the late Senator Hanna was filled by the election of Mr. August Belmont, the New York banker and capitalist, who is also at the head of the New York Underground Railway, and in that and other capacities has come into relationship with organized labor. Last fall, questions and disputes of various importance relating to the hours, wages, and other conditions of men employed in the Subway were finally settled by direct conference, in which Mr. Belmont himself took a leading part. His remarks at the Federation dinner were manly and to the point, and he promised in brief language, but with evident sincerity, to use his best efforts for the success of the work of the Civic Federation and for the promotion of these principles for which it stands.

The great doctrine for which Mr. Roosevelt in many an utterance has made a strong plea, and which he set forth again in an address to the members of his own church, Grace Dutch Reformed, of Washington, on December 25, is the doctrine of brotherhood. While it is perfectly true that lofty generalizations alone will not settle the hard workaday problems that men meet in the carrying on of their business affairs—and while it is doubtless true, as John Mitchell holds, that for the present, in matters industrial, the best safeguard for peace may lie in the ability to fight—the man who does not see how valuable it is to establish kindly personal relations, and to cultivate a love for justice and a sense of mutual regard, is a man not only of low conscience, but of narrow and meager mental development. There remain some heads of great corporations and some large employers of labor in this country who regard with distrust, and even with abhorrence, the leaders of organized labor; yet no impartial judge at the Civic Federation dinner would have assigned to the labor leaders any lower rank either in character or capacity than the capitalists and financiers who sat at the same table with them, or the numerous representatives of the press, the church, and the university. Undoubtedly, in directness and in force, the labor leaders were better public speakers than any of the other elements that made up the body.

AN AID TO ORGANIZED LABOR.

United Mine Workers' Journal.

Every man possessed of a lucid mind and whose thoughts are not gangrened with saturnine political bias hails the work of the Civic Federation with emotions of delight, and knows that the cause of organized labor is stronger, far better equipped to present its case favorably to a hostile or indifferent public when backed by such forces as met that night. The Civic Federation will not hesitate in its glorious career simply because Messrs. Hayes, Parry, Berger and Kirby do not approve. The Civic Federation stands for industrial peace. It would disarm hostile forces, it would bring distrusting employe and employer together, and have them get acquainted, free their minds from mutual aversion and upon the grounds of justice arrive at an amicable solution of their contentions. It would substitute arbitration for the strike, conciliation for the lock-out, the hand-clasp for blacklist, friendship for the boycott. In a word, it would remove the causes for the present industrial strife and bitterness and use common sense and equity in their settlement. That would bring industrial peace. But "Comrades" Hayes and Parry do not want peace. "Comrade" Hayes wants strikes, riots, bloodshed; he wants to embitter the hearts and minds of working men against their employers. He preaches Christ and practices satan. "Comrade" Hayes' great desire for industrial turmoil arises from the fact that through some devious mode of reasoning he comes to the conclusion that the bitterness necessarily arising will swell the ranks of his political cult. "Comrade" Parry desires the same thing, but for a different purpose. He would have these belligerent exhibitions so that the armed forces of the State could be summoned to strangle organized labor, and thus crush out the last hope save revolution. It is quite evident that "Comrade" Hayes never was personally concerned in a strike. He evidently knows nothing of its appalling results upon the women and children. It was a noticeable fact that those labor leaders of whom "Comrade" Hayes speaks so slightingly—Mitchell, Mahon, Keefe, Moffitt, Tobin, O'Keefe *et al.*—have led the greatest and fiercest industrial wars of a generation. When these warriors who know what such things mean, have seen them, been in them, led them, gladly welcome a course which will prevent their recurrence, it is not of the slightest import what figurative warriors such as Hayes and Parry think or say about them. Was "Comrade" Hayes ever in a strike? Was he ever blacklisted? Were his thoughts ever haunted by day and his dreams at night of a wife and little brood desolate, perhaps dead? Did he suffer an eviction, face the winter's storms, hungry, ill-clad, a stranger in a strange town? Did he ever face a Pinkerton, a servile sheriff or an angry militiaman? It is prima facie evidence that he never did any or all of those things, else he would not so glibly advocate their continuance.

The Civic Federation, despite the sneers of the Hayes-Parry cults, have prevented more strikes, which would have involved more men than the aggregate of membership in both cults. And it is going to go on in its grand mission, will be successful, will give peace and dignity to employe and employer. The twin-cults will doubtless assail Mr. Belmont, the new President, just as they caricatured, lampooned and villified the first President with equally fruitless results.

A PLATFORM FOR EXCHANGING VIEWS.

The Outlook, New York.

The National Civic Federation held its annual meeting in this city last week. The large and representative attendance of members and guests, the interest displayed in its department conferences and committee meetings, and the significant quality of the speeches at the successful social dinner which closed the three days' gathering, seem to indicate that the Federation is a sound organization and is likely to have a permanent usefulness. It was established about four years ago, for the purpose of dealing in a large and fundamental way with the labor question. Its aim is to bring together in counsel the three parties of every labor conflict—the employer, the employe, and the public. In accomplishing this aim the officers of the Federation have been surprisingly successful, for the list of those actively interested in its conferences and work includes the names of some of the most distinguished capitalists, labor leaders, and public men in the country. The late Senator Hanna was its president from 1902 until his death, and it has seemed to *The Outlook* that perhaps he performed the very best work of his public career in its organization and direction. The Federation has done something more than to collect and publish facts regarding the labor question, or to hold conferences, or to furnish a platform for the expression of opinion; it maintains a Department of Welfare, which concerns itself with the physical and social conditions of working men and women; and through its Department of Conciliation it has been able to settle some labor disputes which have never come to the knowledge of the public, and which, without such a settlement, might have developed into disastrous labor wars. Admirable as this practical work is, *The Outlook* is inclined to think that not the least important function of the Federation is, after all, to provide a platform upon which men with vital interest in the labor problem, but with varying and often radically antagonistic opinions about it, may meet one another and exchange views. The annual dinner was a picturesque illustration of what may be done in this direction. August Belmont a great railroad capitalist and operator, and P. H. Morrissey, a railroad brakeman, now Grand Master of his union; Henry Phipps, a great steel master and employer of an army of steel workers and coal miners, and John Mitchell, a coal miner himself and a master-mind of trades-unionism; President Eliot, of Harvard University, and Samuel Gompers, originally a cigar maker and now a national leader of organized labor—all these sat at the same table, ate together and talked together, without in the slightest degree sacrificing their own independent views, but entirely respecting one another's personality and opinions. As Mr. Mitchell said in his after-dinner speech, "It is better to talk a week than to strike a year." A very large proportion of labor conflicts spring in the first instance from personal misunderstandings and their consequent irritation and friction. When men are willing to try to understand one another, such controversies can very often be adjusted by a little patient discussion.

IN A PEACEFUL WAY.

Staats Zeitung, New York.

An undertaking as represented by the National Civic Federation is, of course, utterly impossible in Germany, where only a few years ago an official representative of a manufacturers' association in the course of a discussion of reform propositions, said that the "captains of industry" would never consent to meet the workmen on an equal basis. . . . It must be acknowledged that the association rests upon the fundamental principle of social equality of employes and employers, and thereby has already removed from its sphere of activity contrasts existing in other places and has made to a great extent compromises superfluous.

The solution in a peaceful way of the existing questions in dispute between the two economic parties is thereby really being put into practice. What has been stated at the banquet, which followed the annual meeting, shows how the association—by means of the aid of that fundamental principle of equality—has been productive of much good in many directions. Having contemplated at the beginning only the paving of the way for a mutual understanding and appreciation, as the principal aim of its activity, the object of the association has been, meanwhile, enlarged. Credit is due for this, partly to the committees, who have made efforts to solve practical questions in practical ways, and to remove dissensions wherever they appear. This activity of mediation is supplemented by an educational one carried on by speeches and writings, and the agitative activity resting on the establishment of sound conditions of agreements between employers' associations and trades-unions, as well as on suitable changes of existing laws, seeks to prevent the breaking out of differences, and especially the disadvantages of economic struggles.

ONLY POSSIBLE IN A DEMOCRACY.

The Western Laborer, Omaha.

We have received the National Civic Federation MONTHLY REVIEW, containing a full report of the meeting, banquet, business transacted and addresses delivered after the dinner in New York. In this age of sharp practices, commercialism and fierce struggles between the contending forces of capital and labor, it is a pleasure and begets hopefulness for industrial peace in the minds of those interested enough to note the progress being made by the National Civic Federation.

The meeting was such an assembly (as was tersely remarked by Samuel Gompers, August Belmont, Archbishop Ireland and others) as could not be gathered together in any other nation or under any other flag in the world. Such a meeting is only possible in a democracy and under such institutions as ours. The members of that gathering were all "men of affairs," embracing in their representative character capital, labor, letters, science, bar, press, platform and church, and through the whole deliberation of the meetings there was an atmosphere of earnestness, honesty of purpose and a sincere desire to arrive at a basis whereby the disturbances which affect our industrial life so disastrously from time to time could be lessened and our social life amended for the benefit of all our people.

President's Roosevelt's duties prevented his being present, but he sent a letter of regret in which he voiced his hearty accord, sympathy and hopes for the practical success and full recognition of the principles for which the federation is earnestly working.

A letter from Andrew Carnegie on the objects, aims and plans of the organization was also read, in which that hard-headed Scotchman gave utterance to more honest truths than have ever been credited to him before; the letter being replete with sound advice acquired by stern and costly experience.

Take the meeting for all in all it was a parliament of the world, as its work will affect the world beyond the seas and become an agent for international peace abroad as well as industrial peace at home.

When this organization was proposed it was pooh-poohed by the great dailies, the subsidized organs of corporate monopolies, but the time is not far distant when it will crystallize more public sentiment in a given direction than all the big newspapers in the United States, bearing full tribute to the genius of the late M. A. Hanna, who conceived and founded it. This is one of the instances where the genius of the dead lives on to work for the living and his country. These meetings were addressed by men of all classes, making no special pleas for their class; they met on a plane of perfect equality, a perfect democracy, where the capitalist, Belmont, listened to the coal miner, Mitchell; where the archbishop, Ireland, and the Protestant bishop, Potter, paid respectful and earnest attention to the arguments of the longshoremen, the street-car men, the printer, bricklayer, etc., and where all these many classes of our industrial life in perfect good faith listened to the views of the builder, the banker, the college professor, the editor, the churchman, and all the other classes in our social life represented there; where no "class consciousness" was to be seen or felt anywhere, and where a common mutual confidence and honesty of purpose pervaded the entire atmosphere.

MR. AUGUST BELMONT IN A NEW ROLE.

New York Times.

The unanimous and even enthusiastic election of Mr. August Belmont to the presidency of the National Civic Federation, an office made vacant by the death of Senator Marcus A. Hanna, is a gratifying indication that the work of that body commends itself to the approval of men of affairs who are much too busy to have leisure for dilettante trifling with economic and social problems. That his nomination was so obviously acceptable to the labor men who took part in the election shows that they are outliving class prejudice, and that the possession and management of great wealth does not disqualify a man for their respect and confidence.

In this instance there is no reason why it should. Mr. Belmont is a workingman of great industry. The wage-earner who had to carry a tithe of the cares and responsibilities of this organizer and manager of great enterprises would feel himself burdened beyond his strength. Mr. Belmont's sympathy with honest toil may be assumed from the fact that he earns his rest, when he has it, by the most systematic devotion to business. As one of the largest employers of labor in New York he has had intimate contact with the problems it constantly offers for wise and intelligent solution. His success in averting troubles threatened from time to time in the operation of the railways for which he is responsible shows that he does not lack patience or discretion. Finally, his willingness to undertake the duties of the presidency of the Civic Federation and to promise their faithful performance shows an unselfish and broadly humanitarian purpose to make his activities and his experience of benefit to others.

We wish him satisfactory success in every effort to promote industrial peace. That he will not be a figurehead, leaving to others the work for which he assumes responsibility, those who know him are assured.

APPROVED BY LABOR AND EMPLOYERS.

Indianapolis Sentinel.

Among the labor organizations of the East, as well as in the councils of the most level-headed and conservative employers of the industrial centers, great satisfaction is expressed over the elevation of August Belmont to the head of the National Civic Federation, the great organization in which employer and employe are so well represented.

The action of the national organization at its annual meeting and banquet at the Park Avenue Hotel, on Thursday evening, is looked upon as the forerunner of a better order of things and a step toward the great work of bringing about more amicable relations between capital and labor. In the presidency of the organization, which was so well filled by the late Senator Marcus A. Hanna, August Belmont, it is believed, will do all in his power to bring both great factions in the industrial life of the nation toward that goal when each will give due recognition to the rights of the other, while carefully safeguarding its own. In no uncertain manner Mr. Belmont has announced his views on the labor problem. He declared plainly in his address to the body that elected him its president, that he is "a believer in organization," and that he sees hope for the settlement of all American labor troubles through the medium of conference between representatives of organized employes and organized employers.

This conviction on the part of a man who is head of one of the greatest financial firms in the world, and who is himself a director in no less than thirty-five great corporations employing thousands of men, is regarded as a rebuke to those extremists among the employers of the country who believe that "organized labor ought to be given no quarter."

MR. CARNEGIE'S TRUTHFUL ANALYSIS.

Boston Herald.

It is an interesting point that Mr. Carnegie makes in his communication to the Civic Federation, calling attention to the fact that while labor disturbances break out at frequent intervals in the manufacturing and mechanical occupations, nothing of the kind ever occurs in agriculture, which employs more than ten millions of workers. Mr. Carnegie accounts for this by saying that the relations of the farmers and the farm hands are always personally pleasant. They become interested in each other, and mutual esteem, often ripening to affection, insures not only peace, but good will. There's lots of truth in this analysis.

RAILWAY PROVIDENT INSTITUTIONS.

(*Concluded from page 16.*)

of the allowances absolutely without cost to the employe and wholly from the revenues of the roads concerned, no distinction has been drawn as to rank or condition of employment. All employes, from the chief executive down to the man holding the humblest position in the service, are, one and all, amenable to the governing provisions. Generally there has been no distinctive classification of employes into "salaried officers" and "wage-earners," as is the practice in other countries, but, instead, all share alike, in accordance with their service status, in the benefits growing out of Fund operation.

These provisions for sick, injured and aged employes, and designated beneficiaries in the event of their death, in conjunction with the various opportunities for mental, physical and spiritual betterment, are actuated by truly humane and benevolent purposes and in their continuous development are bringing about a reciprocal feeling of mutual regard and respect between capital and labor. Conditions are being improved and at the same time energy is being vitalized and ambition stimulated among the rank and file of railway employes.

The National
Civic Federation Review

Vol. I. No. 12 NEW YORK, MARCH, 1905 Ten Cents

LABOR WRESTS VICTORY FROM DEFEAT.

NATIONAL LABOR CHIEFS CHAMPION THE SANCTITY OF CONTRACTS AND INSIST UPON THEIR PRESERVATION BY SUBORDINATE BODIES.

"THERE will be no strike," said Grand Chief Warren S. Stone, of the Brotherhood of Locomotive Engineers, to August Belmont, President of the Interborough Rapid Transit Company, two weeks before the strike. "You need not hesitate to go away on your vacation. If any disagreement arises between the management of the road and our local committee, it will be referred to you and me. If we cannot agree, we will refer the dispute to an arbitration committee of six, each selecting three." To this Mr. Belmont replied: "All right, Mr. Stone, and if we get to that point you can name all six of them."

This colloquy closed an interview between Mr. Belmont, Mr. Stone and a local member of his organization concerning the negotiations then pending between General Manager Hedley of the Interborough and representatives of its employes over a new schedule and other questions. Mr. Belmont had said that he was anxious to make his annual trip South, which he had already delayed two weeks, but that he did not wish to go away if there was to be any trouble between the company and its employes.

That Mr. Belmont had ample cause for asking whether he could go away on his vacation without feeling that there was danger of interruption to the public service of the corporation of which he was the responsible head must have been clear to any observer of incidents prior to that interview. As long ago as January [illegible] there had been loud talk of a strike unless certain concessions were made. A conference was brought about between Vice-President Bryan, General Manager Hedley and the employes' grievance committee. This committee included Messrs. Jencks, Pinney and Pepper, the heads, respectively, of the local branches of the Engineers' and Firemen's Brotherhoods and of the Amalgamated Association of Street and Electric Railway Employes of America. The demands presented were for the re-employment of a subway motorman, who had been dismissed after his train had crashed into another at the Worth Street Station; for the reemployment of three other discharged motormen; for automatic signals on local tracks; for a new schedule, and for various changes in the methods of employing men. This conference adjourned for two days, Mr. Hedley announcing that everything had been discussed amicably, although nothing had yet been settled. When told of this statement, Mr. Jencks said testily to the reporters, "Mr. Hedley gave you a sweet talk, and he may think that everything is all right. But I tell you that things are much more serious than he would have you think, and he will find it out at the conference next Thursday. Our grievances will have to be settled. The unions will stand by several motormen who have been discharged." The conference was resumed on January 26. At its conclusion it was announced that the cases of the discharged motormen had been adjusted satisfactorily, and that a new train schedule was to be made. Messrs. Pepper, Pinney and Jencks all said that they were "satisfied," and naturally were in high glee at what they considered a victory over the management of the road. "All our demands were granted, down to the right of seniority in appointments and the fifteen minutes' rest after every trip," proclaimed Jencks.

Several days of quiet ensued. But suddenly more trouble arose. The new schedule was put into effect, but it did not please the men. Under its contract with the city, the Interborough Company was required to run trains at a speed of thirty miles an hour. This speed could not be attained until its men had learned thoroughly the handling of the trains. It was intended to increase the speed gradually until it should reach the required maximum. As the three years' contract with the motormen named no number of miles to be run within the specified ten hours' workday, General Manager Hedley in his new schedule added one run a day for each train, by increasing the speed. This schedule had been in effect only a few hours, when Mr. Pepper called up Superintendent Merritt on the telephone and in a peremptory manner demanded: "What does this extra trip mean? This is inhuman. It increases our runs to [illegible] miles a day. Unless that schedule is taken down there will be something doing. The men won't stand for it." Mr. Pepper was told that he would have to see General Manager Hedley, as the superintendent has no authority to change schedules.

Accordingly, the next day a committee representing the Interborough employes demanded of General Manager Hedley that the new schedule be taken down, Mr. Jencks declaring publicly, before the conference: "Unless the officials change their schedule to-day, there will be a

(Continued on page 9.)

WARREN S. STONE,
Grand Chief, Brotherhood of Locomotive Engineers.

WILLIAM D. MAHON,
President, Amalgamated Association Street and Electric Railway Employes of America.

SAMUEL GOMPERS,
President, American Federation of Labor.

JOHN MITCHELL,
President, United Mine Workers of America.

AN ECONOMIC EXHORTATION TO ORGANIZED LABOR.

EMPLOYES SHOULD INCREASE EARNINGS BY UNRESTRICTED INDIVIDUAL OUTPUT, SEEKING STEADY WORK AND STUDYING CONDITIONS OF THEIR PARTICULAR INDUSTRY.

An address by LOUIS D. BRANDEIS *to the Boston Central Labor Union.*

TRADE unionism has made great advances within the last three years. The growth in membership has been large, but the change in the attitude toward unions both on the part of the employer and of the community marks even greater progress. To this result the anthracite coal strike, so wisely led by John Mitchell, has largely contributed. That struggle compelled public attention to the trades-union problem in a degree unprecedented in this country.

The arbitrary attitude of the presidents of the coal and railroad companies was an object lesson which made clear to many employers the unreasonableness of the position that an employer "must be free to run his own business in his own way."

From this warning example many employers learned also that one may deal with employes otherwise than directly or individually, and that the representatives of unions may be recognized without impairment of usual business honor. Since then it has become far more common for enlightened employers, whether their shops be union or open, to discuss labor problems with the representatives of the unions as freely as they would discuss other problems with other business connections.

The people at large who had no special interest in contests between employers and employes learned also through the coal strike much about unions. Sympathy was generally with the men as against the coal trust. Even among employers there were many who realized that their interests lay with the workingmen as against the great aggregations of capital.

IN THE MAIN COMMENDABLE.

Sympathetic attention being drawn to the unions, many people realized that the aim of the unions was in the main commendable, even if particular measures of unions or acts of individual unionists deserved condemnation—for who could deny that the work of the unions in seeking to improve the conditions and to shorten the hours of labor, to raise wages—to protect children and women—made for good citizenship and the general welfare of the community? The attitude of the American Federation of Labor in opposing socialism is also gaining for the unions support from the most conservative classes.

A substantial advance has thus been made by the unions in the estimation of working men, of employers and of the public.

The achievements of the unions in improving the lot of the labbrer are not to be measured solely by conditions in the union shop or even in the non-discriminating open shop.

Unions may well point, as their greatest triumphs to certain establishments where no unionist is to be found, but where the conditions of labor are far in advance of the standard ordinarily prevailing. Those are instances where wise, far-seeing employers have acted upon the spirit or hint of union demands.

These steps in advance have been taken often for the purpose of preventing trades unionism from finding a lodgement, often unconsciously as a result merely of the enlightenment that comes with the necessary thinking that trade-union agitation compels.

So the unions have already achieved much, both directly and indirectly, in shortening the hours and in improving the conditions under which labor is performed, and in raising wages.

How far can this increase in wages be carried, and how shall it be accomplished?

LABOR'S RIGHTFUL SHARE.

First—The unions should strive to secure for the workingmen all the earnings of a business except that part which is required to get for it the necessary capital and managing ability.

Into most businesses three elements enter:

1—The capital.

2—The ordinary labor.

3—The special labor, usually called the "management."

The owners of capital are comparatively few in number; the possessors of the special ability to manage business still less in number; men competent to perform the ordinary labor very numerous.

Obviously in our country we should strive to conduct our industries as we do our government; that is, to secure the greatest good for the greatest number. The employes being the greatest number, should get of the fruits of the business as much as possible. This is clear. The question is merely, What are the limits now possible, and how can those limits be extended?

It is absolutely essential upon any scheme of division of the fruits of industry among employer, capitalist and employe that the business should be profitable. By "profitable" I mean not merely that the business shall not be run at a loss, but that the business shall be run under such conditions that the owner of the capital on the one hand is willing to risk his capital in the business, and the possessor of that special ability which is required to organize and conduct a successful business will be led to use his greatest efforts in that direction.

Unless the profits of businesses are such as to tempt capitalists to risk their money, the money will seek, not participation in business, which necessarily involves great risks, but will be put into classes of investment where there is supposed to be no risk whatever.

Unless men of exceptional business ability have the promise or possibility of large rewards they will not be led to develop or use those special talents or capacities which we find in the leaders of great businesses—the men who have made or managed them.

What the exact amount of profit is which is necessary to make men risk their money in business, and how great the rewards must be in order to develop the leaders of industry are, of course, matters which cannot be decided by any general rule.

STRIVE TO INCREASE EARNINGS.

Second—The employes should strive to make the earnings of any business as large as possible.

There can be no greater mistake for the workingman than to restrict the output of the individual.

LOUIS D. BRANDEIS,
Lawyer and Publicist, Boston.

You must make the total earnings of the business in which you are engaged the largest possible. By earnings in this connection I mean the aggregate fund available for paying workingmen, capitalists and managers. Make that aggregate large and there will be plenty for all among whom it is to be divided.

The most potent factor in securing large profits is the avoidance of waste, and the greatest source of waste in the industrial world is unused, undeveloped or misdirected human effort. To the correction of that evil trade unions should direct their attention.

Let every one engaged in the business work with the greatest possible efficiency and diligence consistent with maintaining himself in good condition to work thereafter, and leaving himself the leisure necessary to the performance of his duties to his family, to his state and for his own development and pleasure.

The hours of labor should be reasonably short; but during working hours each individual should work hard and earnestly, and under conditions leading to the greatest possible efficiency.

Any restriction upon the output of the individual reduces the fund of profits available for distribution, besides demoralizing the man who is so restricted.

It follows also that differences in efficiency between different individuals must be recognized and rewarded; and that those who can work faster and better than others must not be retarded by the less efficient. The industrial superiority of America is largely due to the absence of restriction upon individual effort; to the encouragement of the individual by giving him the fruits of his efforts.

Your federation opposes socialism, but to ignore the difference between individuals would lend strength to socialism and communism.

LIMITATION IS WASTE.

A limitation of the production of the individual is pure waste. The business is merely rendered less profitable, and the man whose production is restricted is injured also.

Nor does the restriction of the output of the individual make more work for others. The amount of work to be done is, in a country like ours, in no sense fixed; for the amount of goods or service men buy is not fixed. The amount bought is as a rule limited only by the ability to buy.

If you waste human effort you make the product cost more. If you raise prices without increasing incomes you have simply limited the amount that will be bought. You have not made work for more people. You have merely given people less for their money.

Another great factor of waste in most businesses is the cost of inspectors, foremen and assistant foremen—men whose services are, in large part required only because so many employes work, not as hard or as well as is possible but only hard enough or well enough to pass the inspector or foreman.

Every man should look out for himself, should do the work without inspector or foreman watching him like a policeman. The dishonor and the expense of unnecessary inspectors and foremen should be avoided.

Trade unions have already done much for the manhood of the workingman. They should teach him that it is a disgrace to manhood to require watching.

WORK SHOULD BE STEADY.

Third—The unions should demand for the workingman steady work.

In order that the pay of the individual may be large it is necessary not merely that the business as a whole be profitable, but also that the individual be given full opportunity to work for his share of the profit.

Most controversies between employers and employes have arisen upon claims for what is called higher wages; that is, for a higher rate per day or per piece. But the rate per day or per piece is only one of the factors which go to make up wages.

The important question is not how much a man is paid per day nor how much per piece, but how much can he earn in a year. He may have high wages and an opportunity of working only half the year.

For instance, it appeared in the anthracite coal strike inquiry that the men worked only about 18[illegible] days in the year. Speaking roughly, men should work 300 days in the year.

Lack of earnings is only a small part of the evil which results from irregularity of employment. It is the uncertainty as to a job which produces a large part of the care of a workingman's life, and the days of enforced idleness which lead to most of the bad habits.

Every man should have the opportunity of working every day in the year excepting Sundays and holidays and such time as he properly wishes for a vacation. In some trades this is impossible, but in many trades where the irregularity of work is accepted as a necessity, it would be found that if the effort were duly made the amount of slack time could be greatly reduced.

Where men are engaged in trades which on account of the physical conditions can be followed only during a part of the year, there ought to be found for them work at some other trade for the remainder of the year.

PROVIDE AGAINST IRREGULARITY.

No industrial condition can be satisfactory which does not tend to remove the thing called "day labor," which does not seek to make the work of the workingman as steady as that of the clerk or salesman.

No adequate effort to provide against irregularity of work has been made. If the unions once formulate demands for steady work and co-operate with employers to secure it, an immense improvement on these lines will undoubtedly result.

Steadiness of work is nearly as important to the employer as to the employe. For instance, the great aim of the manufacturer must be to run his factory full all the time. Many factories can earn their profit only if they do. If the factory runs all of the time and the employes work all of the time, it is obvious that the owner can be satisfied with a much smaller rate of profit and the men can be satisfied with a smaller rate per day or per piece than they would

(*Concluded on page* 11.)

GREAT CAPTAINS OF INDUSTRY AND OF LABOR IN JOINT CONFERENCE.

OFFICIALS OF A GREAT RAILWAY CORPORATION CO-OPERATE IN ADJUSTING JURISDICTIONAL CONFLICT BETWEEN TWO POWERFUL LABOR ORGANIZATIONS.

IT IS a pleasure to record another triumph for the method of direct conference between the representatives of a great employing corporation and of its organized employes in preventing industrial strife and public inconvenience. The value of this method found signal illustration in the avoidance of the threatened strike on the New York, New Haven and Hartford Railroad. The danger of this strike arose not from any dispute about hours, wages or conditions of work between the company and the employes. The question at issue was a dispute between two highly organized bodies of employes, each of them entirely friendly toward the company, but contending with each other over their representation before company officials in cases of discipline. The two organizations thus opposing each other were the Brotherhoods of Locomotive Firemen and Locomotive Engineers, and the dispute between them threatened to extend from the New Haven to every other important railway in the country.

The absence of a direct issue between the company and the employes makes all the more striking the patience and care which the company exercised in treating with the firemen and the engineers. It makes peculiarly significant the fact that a man of such large affairs and intense daily occupation in business as J. Pierpont Morgan, together with the other members of a directors' committee, Charles F. Brooker of Ansonia, Professor George J. Brush of Yale, and William Skinner of Holyoke, should willingly upon two different occasions spend several hours in conference with representatives of the firemen. It makes more conspicuous, also, the long period during which the officials of the company exhausted every effort to bring about an adjustment of the dispute between two organizations which officially and theoretically were not recognized by the company.

The trouble arose out of the claim that members of the Brotherhood of Locomotive Firemen who had been promoted to be engineers, but who retained their membership in the firemen's brotherhood, were neglected in cases of appeal by the engineers' adjustment committee. In other words, the firemen claimed that the engineers' adjustment committee was not taking up with the management cases of engineers who desired to appeal unless those engineers were members of the engineers' brotherhood. Therefore, the firemen's committee claimed that it should be permitted to represent before the officers of the road the engineers who were members of the firemen's brotherhood. This complaint was made to the general manager of the company as long ago as June, 1903. The claim being denied by the general manager, the firemen's committee appealed successively to the first vice-president and to President Mellen. Mr. Mellen, after earnest consideration, confirmed the preceding decisions, and pointed out that should the Brotherhood of Locomotive Firemen at any time have in its organization a majority of the engineers employed by the company, the question would undoubtedly settle itself.

Mr. Mellen explained: "The company has no objection to labor organizations, and is absolutely indifferent as to whether an employe belongs to a labor organization or not. The employes of different classes meet the officers of the company for purposes of making agreements, settling disputes, etc., through committees selected by them from among their own number. Thus there exists an engineers' adjustment committee. Naturally, if the members of the Brotherhood of Locomotive Engineers are in the majority among the engineers, the adjustment committee is likely to be composed of brotherhood men. If the non-union engineers (of whom the road employs about 1501) were in the majority, they would presumably control the committee, and if most of the engineers belonged to the firemen's brotherhood it would be probable that the committee would be composed of men of that brotherhood. This, however, is an internal matter, with which the company has nothing to do." After further conference with Grand Master J. J. Hannahan, of the Brotherhood of Locomotive Firemen, and A. P. Kelly, chairman of the firemen's general adjustment committee, President Mellen again reviewed the subject carefully with the general committee of adjustment of the engineers, asking that committee if it could not possibly assent to the demands of the firemen's committee, thus releasing the company from that particular phase of its agreement with the engineers. The engineers' committee could not see its way clear to assenting to this suggestion. The committee of engineers was agreeable to arbitration, but this was declined by the firemen's committee on January 13 and 16 last.

First Vice-Grand Master Timothy Shea, of the firemen's brotherhood, stated: "The firemen are asking for nothing more than their rights. They have in their membership many engine drivers who have retained their allegiance to the firemen's organization after becoming drivers. These men believe they have a just right. We had an agreement with Mr. Hall, formerly president of the company, which lasted one year and three months. Recently the drivers have made an agreement with the company which gives them alone the right to negotiate for the drivers. This leaves those drivers in the Firemen's Brotherhood out in the cold."

In reply to this, President Mellen said: "The first vice-president, on investigation, was not only positively assured by the engineers' general committee in adjustment that it had and would in the future take up before the officers the cases of all engineers, irrespective of their union affiliations, if the cases were proper, but also produced evidence to show that all proper cases had so been taken up. The first vice-president furthermore communicated with former President Hall, who stated that in March, 1903, at the urgent request of the firemen, he had heard their committee in an individual case, that of Engineer Fox, but denied emphatically that he had made any such agreement for the future or in any other case."

J. PIERPONT MORGAN,
Financier.

CHARLES S. MELLEN,
President, N. Y., N. H. & H. R. R.

WARREN S. STONE,
Grand Chief, Brotherhood Locomotive Engineers.

J. J. HANNAHAN,
Grand Master, Brotherhood Locomotive Firemen.

Conference after conference followed, and time after time the same ground was patiently gone over without reaching an agreement. The question of a strike was submitted to a referendum vote of all the firemen, union and non-union, employed on the system, and the resulting vote was strongly in the affirmative. From First Vice-Grand Master Shea, of the firemen's brotherhood, came the suggestion of the appointment of a second adjustment committee of engineers, to be composed of members of the firemen's brotherhood. This plan was declined by the company as impracticable, because it would be in violation of its agreement with all its engineers, and because the plan would require the appointment of a third adjustment committee to represent the non-union engineers, and would compel the road to distinguish between its employes in the same class of work but belonging to different organizations.

The subject was then brought by the firemen's general committee before a directors' committee of five, of which Mr. Morgan was chairman. This action, constituting an appeal from the chief executive of the corporation virtually to the corporate [illegible], was itself a most extraordinary proceeding. The receiving of this appeal and its careful consideration illustrate the willingness of these representatives of large interests to exert every effort to treat labor considerately, the utmost desire to attain fairness, and they are an example, also, of the diligence of directors who really direct.

The conferences of the directors and general committees resulted in sustaining the president's decision. After this decision Grand Master Hannahan and Grand Chief Warren S. Stone of the Brotherhoods of Locomotive Firemen and Engineers reached an agreement which is expected to heal a breach between the two organizations that was widening throughout the country.

COMPREHENSIVE AIMS OF TRADE UNIONISM IN GREAT BRITAIN.

MARKED PROGRESS IN THE COLLECTIVE CONTRACT, CONFERENCE AND CONCILIATION, AND IN ORGANIZING, HOUSING AND EDUCATING UNSKILLED WAGE-EARNERS.

By JAMES WIGNALL, *of Swansea, Wales, General Organizer of Dockers' Union; Fraternal Delegate to the American Federation of Labor.*

THE main difference that I observe between the development of trade unions in our country and the United States is that the movement in England has for its broad aim the accomplishment of all things that are for the benefit of all the people. Thus, while higher wages, shorter hours and better conditions of labor are primary objects, the English trade movement also concerns itself with the social life and with the education of the workers and with everything, in short, that its constituents believe will contribute to the prosperity of the country. The movement endeavors to cultivate among the masses self-respect, and to teach constantly the lesson that any individual good must come from self-exertion.

There has been among British employers much antagonism against trade unions. Some employers have looked upon the movement as an unmitigated evil; some other employers have become reconciled and have thought it something to be conciliated temporarily, that in time would pass away; other employers and, I am glad to say, a large majority of them, have now come to realize the right of labor to the collective bargain, the right of labor to sell its commodity, through combination, at the best price that can be obtained. This change has grown progressively, and chiefly during the last ten years. During that period both sides have learned much. There have in the past been too many strikes and too many lock-outs, because both parties have been anxious for industrial strife rather than industrial peace. But experience has gradually taught that it is far better to resort to conciliation than to the bitter arbitrament of strikes or lock-outs. Thus there has been evolved a large number of courts or boards of arbitration. The result is that now about 70 per cent. of all the disputes between employers and employed in England are thus adjusted without trouble. For example, in the mining industry, there is a Board of Conciliation, composed of an equal number of representatives of the mine workers and of the mine owners. If this Board fails to agree, there is an independent chairman, to whom the case is referred. He hears the arguments on both sides, and his decision is always accepted. This method has averted trouble in the mining industry for several years.

The tin plate industry—once nearly ruined by the American tariff, but now, through the recovery of markets in other parts of the world, in a better condition than ever before—was formerly notorious for its labor troubles. But five years ago a Board of Conciliation was created, composed of representatives of both sides. This Board has made yearly agreements. Its agreements are now in their sixth year and during that time the industry has had only one slight dispute, which was settled by arbitration.

Another example is the agreement in Bristol between the dock-workers and the merchants. Under this agreement, each side deposits £600 with two elected trustees. This deposit is a security that each party shall carry out the agreement. Upon only two occasions has there been any dispute, which, in each case, was decided by an umpire, the decision including the amount of the deposit to be paid as damages. In one of these cases the agreement was violated by the men, and in the other by the employers. There is every probability of an indefinite continuance of peace under this agreement.

The question that I have observed as uppermost here—that of the open shop—has also troubled us during the past ten years, although under a different name. With us the open shop means the "Free Labor Association." Out of the efforts of that organization have grown great suffering, dislocation of trade and loss of money. I have seen its efforts supported at the point of the bayonet, when soldiers and police were protecting non-union men at work. But in every case the struggle, after two or three months, has collapsed and amounted to nothing. The "Free Labor Association" has upon the whole not resulted in a gain for the employers, but rather in a loss. For every shilling in labor cost that they have saved, they have spent a pound in trying to carry out, and without avail, their program.

Our general attitude is this: We recognize that the employers have a right to employ the cheapest labor they can find in the market. We ask the same right, to get the best price that we can exact for our labor. We find it the best plan to bring these two rights into harmony by sitting around a table and winning the battle one way or the other by the force of argument and reason instead of resorting to physical strife.

Previous to the last fifteen years there was practically no organization in England among the unskilled workers, such, for example, as the dock-workers and the general laborers; but after the London dock strike of 1889, a great wave of organization of unskilled labor swept all over England. The success of this movement has been wonderful. In my own town of Swansea, fifteen years ago, the dock laborers were hanging around all hours of the day and night waiting for work. Rarely did they see the merchant with whom this work originated. It was passed down from him through one middleman after another until it reached the dock foreman. This dock foreman invariably kept a saloon. Only the man who would drink at his saloon could get a job. The man who could hold the most, who had the longest string of check marks behind the door, could get the best job. When the man was paid at the end of the week he would be paid in a saloon. One pathetic result of this system was the spectacle on every Saturday night in the market street of Swansea. There you would see scores of women waiting about hour after hour with their baskets. A stranger would ask in wonder what were these shivering, half-clad creatures doing. The explanation was that their husbands were all in the public houses, waiting for their pay. The saloon keeper and foreman would be busy serving his customers and he would delay paying the men as late as possible. He would even keep them waiting until the legal hour of closing. Then many of them were often

JAMES WIGNALL,
General Organizer, British Dockers' Union.

turned out without a cent to give their wives for food, and in debt for the coming week.

When the dock-workers organized it was resolved to bring this system to an end. Before they asked for higher wages, or shorter hours, or better conditions, they first made one demand. This was that the workmen should be employed directly by the principal; that no saloon keeper should be an employer; that no workman should be paid from a saloon, and that no worker should be kept out of his money after Saturday midnight. The result of granting this demand has been that the wages of the dockworkers have increased, on the average, 100 per cent. over fifteen years ago, and at the same time, the cost of labor to the merchant is not a cent more, because of the elimination of the middleman.

The next step of our union was to begin to teach the men, many of whom could not even read or write, in the evening classes. Gradually the workers began to understand that they were real human beings quite like others, and that their children were like the children of others. The result of this discovery was a change in their lives that seems incredible. They had emerged from degradation. In our town alone, the Dockworkers' Union has had one mayor, one alderman, seven members of the City Council, two members of the Harbor Board, fourteen members of Boards of Guardians, and one auditor. These changed conditions in Swansea only illustrate an equal change in many other towns and cities in England.

Meantime our trades unions undertook a war against slumdom in many cities. We argued that if you wish to have good people it is necessary to give them good surroundings. We discovered that the wretched quarters in slumdom were returning enormous profits to the owners. The conditions in the alleys and tenements were such that their inhabitants were practically living in the saloons, which were bright and warm. We held meetings, appointed investigating committees, and secured tabulated statements. In this way we caused existing laws to be enforced. Then we secured the passage of a law authorizing city councils, in cases where the towns owned suburban land, to build houses in the country and to run cars for workingmen for a through fare of one penny between the hours of 5 and [illegible] A. M. and 5 and 8 P. M. Many cities have done this, and now have in the beautiful country workmen's cottages containing six rooms and a bathroom. When it was first proposed to put bathrooms in the workmen's cottages there was a great outcry. "Bathrooms for dockers! How absurd! They won't use them." But we said, "Only try them and see." The result is that now hundreds of families, born and reared in slumdom, own beautiful, bright homes in the country. The infinite good that this has done and is doing to the rising generation is one of the boasts of our trades unions. It is producing a better type of manhood and womanhood, and has infused great communities with a better spirit. All this has been accomplished in the last fifteen years.

The English trades unions have fought everywhere for good schools, furnished with the best teachers and the most beautiful and complete equipment. It frequently happens that the most beautiful school is situated in the poorest district of the city. Our Trades Union Congress is fighting persistently to increase the school age. This we have raised to fourteen years, and hope to increase it in another year to fifteen. Our Trades Union Congress discusses all social economic questions, and promotes such legislation as it believes will be for the benefit of the entire community. Our labor representation committee is an offspring of our Trades Union Congress. It aims to secure labor representation in all municipal boards and in Parliament. Each member of the organizations represented in the Trades Union Congress contributes one shilling per annum toward the expenses of representation in the House of Commons. In that body we now have fourteen members, and we have forty candidates ready to go to the country whenever Parliament is dissolved. In this way we have created a labor party in Parliament distinct from either of the other parties, which is constantly working to secure legislation for the good of the whole country.

As a further step we have brought about the Workmen's Compensation Act. This legislation was necessary because of defects in the former Employers' Liability Act, which caused the non-suiting of ninety-nine out of every one hundred actions, on the ground of "common employment," or of contributory negligence. Under the new law any injured employe may receive during life not over £1 a week, or, in case of death, from £150 to £300 to go to his dependents. This money is welcome enough to those injured, or to the heirs of those killed. But of far more value than the money is the effect of the law in causing the employers to take every precaution against accidents. The act has proved efficient in preventing accidents, and has reduced immensely the number of working people killed or injured in the course of the year.

NEWSPAPERS POINT THE WAY TO PEACE.

(Concluded from page 5.)

then the president of the International Typographical Union guarantees the subscribing publisher against strikes, boycotts, and any concerted interference with the peaceful operation of his office.

"In very many cases this contract has operated to prevent serious labor disturbances, and, conversely, to prevent the granting of unreasonable demands for the increase of wages. Therefore, there is every desire to continue the contract in force at least until its expiration, May 1, 1907.

"A similar agreement with the International Printing Pressmen's and Assistants' Union dates from 1902. We have had no friction in carrying out this agreement. In nearly every case expiring individual contracts have been renewed by conciliation, while in only one case has it been found necessary to resort to arbitration.

"As the printing trades are more thoroughly organized than almost any other in the country, the skilled men in those trades, outside of the union, are to say the least not plentiful. Therefore, as to the question of the open shop, it is a condition and not a theory that confronts us. The scarcity of non-union printers practically compels the publisher to deal with the unions. Before the existence of these contracts the question asked by the unions was 'How much wages can the employer be forced to pay?' The rule of arbitration now decides what it is reasonable to pay in each case under all the circumstances."

GREAT AMERICAN NEWSPAPERS POINT THE WAY TO INDUSTRIAL PEACE.

THE OPERATION OF THE LONG-TERM CONTRACTS BETWEEN THE AMERICAN NEWSPAPER PUBLISHERS' ASSOCIATION AND THE TYPOGRAPHICAL AND PRESSMEN'S UNIONS.

THE nineteenth annual convention of the American Newspaper Publishers' Association, which closed its proceedings in New York City with a dinner on the evening of February 24, was notable for the harmonious celerity with which it dispatched a large volume of business. The following addresses were delivered: "The Newspaper Man," Postmaster William R. Willcox; "The Newspaper," Colonel George Harvey; "The Newspaper in Politics," D. Cady Herrick; "The Man Upstairs," William H. McElroy; "The New Member," Lafayette Young, and "Breaking Into the Business," William McM. Speer.

These officers were elected: President, S. S. Rogers, Chicago *Daily News*; vice-president, W. L. McLean, Philadelphia *Bulletin*; treasurer, E. P. Call, the New York *Commercial*; executive committee, W. P. Weston, Seattle *Post-Intelligencer*; C. H. Taylor, Jr., Boston *Globe*; Colonel Cabiness, Augusta *Chronicle*, and C. H. Herrick, San Francisco.

The harmonious nature of this convention of an employers association was chiefly due to the existence of a trade agreement with two corresponding organizations of employes, the International Typographical Union and the International Pressmen's and Assistants' Union of North America. Before the existence of these contracts a large proportion of the annual meetings of the publishers was devoted to the discussion of labor troubles. But with the smooth operation of the local and national machinery of conciliation, conference and arbitration which these trade agreements provide, the business of publishing the great dailies of the country progresses with regularity as assured as the almost human-like operation of type-setting machines and lightning presses. More than $90,000,000 of capital is represented in this publishers' association, while the membership of the unions with which it deals numbers hundreds of thousands.

These contracts rank among the other most conspicuous and important trade agreements in the United States, such as those between the interstate organizations of bituminous operators and the United Mine Workers of America, between the anthracite operators and miners under the award of the Anthracite Strike Commission; between the Lake Carriers' Association and the International Longshoremen. These are the agreements involving the greatest amount of capital, the largest number of wage earners and that have exhibited the highest degree of success in adjusting differences through conferences, with a resort to arbitration in the background. The agreements between the Newspaper Publishers' Association and the two unions of employes are most elaborate in their provisions for arbitration. The agreement with the International Typographical Union, as does that with the Pressmen's Union, combines three features designed to make secure the result of arbitration. These are a pledge by both parties to accept the decision as final and binding; a pledge that there shall be no strike or lockout pending the decision; and a penalty for refusal to abide by the decision.

These agreements provide for a graded system of appeals from local boards to a national board of arbitration. The typographical national board consists of the President of the International Typographical Union and the Commissioner of the American Newspaper Publishers' Association, or their proxies. In the event of failure to agree, these select a third member in each dispute, who acts as chairman of the board. The finding of the majority is final, and must be accepted as such by both parties to the dispute. When the two original members of the National Board differ as to the interpretation of the trade agreement, the difference is referred to a Joint Conference consisting of the three members of the Executive council of the unions and the three members of the special standing committee of the publishers' association. If these disagree, to quote the code of procedure: "The selection of the seventh member shall be referred to the National Civic Federation. The decision of the arbitrator shall be final and binding upon the Joint Conference and upon the members of the National Board of Arbitration."

Thus there is established a system of appeals up to the highest body of national conferees, with a further provision for the settlement of any dispute, akin in judicial procedure to a pure question of law to be determined only by the Supreme Court, to still another body, with provision for a final arbiter to be selected by an outside disinterested body, itself composed of representatives of employers, of wage earners, and of the general public. In the last resort all the elements of the community, which as a whole is interested in the uninterrupted output of the daily press, exert a combined influence in the decision.

The argument most frequently advanced against the trade agreement as a method of industrial peace is that the trade union cannot be held legally responsible for the fulfillment of its part of a collective contract. But in addition to its pledges against strikes or lockouts, and to accept the result of arbitration as final, the typographical agreement provides that, "in the event of either party to the dispute refusing to accept or comply with the decision of the National Board of Arbitration, all aid and support to the firm or employer or local union refusing acceptance or compliance shall be withdrawn by both parties to this agreement. The acts of such recalcitrant employer or union shall be publicly disavowed, and the aggrieved party to this agreement shall be furnished with an official document to that end." Although the form for local contracts does not contain this provision, it does pledge the International Union to protect the employer in case of violation of the agreement of the local union. This is a strong re-enforcement of the other features to ensure acceptance of the result of arbitration, namely, the mutual pledge in advance to abide by the decision, and the abstinence from rupture during the settlement of a controversy.

One outcome of the typographical contract is that a representative of the International Typographical Union usually attends, by invitation, the annual meeting of the publishers' association, and, conversely, a representative of the publishers is usually present at the annual convention of the union. This interchange of courtesies tends to promote mutual confidence between the two organizations in their respective good will and intention of fair dealing. The task of representing the publishers at the conventions of the union and in all matters relating to questions of labor and the formation and interpretation of local contracts rests with Frederick Driscoll, who has been commissioner of the publishers' association since its formation of the standing committee on labor in 1900.

Commissioner Driscoll says of the history and operation of these contracts:

"The association created at its annual meeting in 1900, after some severe experiences with strikes and labor troubles, a special standing committee to establish a bureau of labor. At that time about 80 per cent. of our publishers had trade relations with local unions. It became evident at once that it was necessary to make our arrangements with the International Union, which alone had power to regulate the locals and keep them in check. Accordingly a plan of arbitration with the International Typographical Union, covering the composite room, stereotype, mailing, and photo-engraving departments, was ratified by the publishers' association and also by the International Typographical Union. After a year's satisfactory experience with this plan, it was mutually agreed that it should be extended for five years from May 1, 1902, and that its scope should be enlarged so as to cover arbitration of wages and hours.

"It is important to observe that the plan of arbitration provides that whenever any one of the publishers agrees by individual contract with the International Typographical Union that he will arbitrate all labor differences

S. S. ROGERS.
President, American Newspaper Publishers' Association.

CHARLES H. TAYLOR, JR.
Ex-President, American Newspaper Publishers' Association.

JAMES M. LYNCH.
President, International Typographical Union.

MARTIN P. HIGGINS.
President, International Pressmen's Union.

(Concluded on page 42)

A NEW ENGLAND CONFERENCE OF EMPLOYERS UPON WELFARE WORK.

ITS VARIOUS PHASES DISCUSSED AND ITS APPLICATION ILLUSTRATED BY PRACTICAL EMPLOYERS AND WELFARE WORKERS.

Boston Herald, Feb. 28.

THE Welfare Department of the National Civic Federation held a notable local conference to discuss welfare work, at Young's Hotel last evening. H. H. Vreeland, President of the New York City Railway Company, and Chairman of the Department, who presided, although he arrived late on account of a railroad accident, spoke on "How to Make Good Foremen—The Labor Department." "Men's Clubs" was considered by Rev. James E. Freeman, Chairman of the Board of Directors, Hollywood Inn Club, Yonkers, N. Y.; "Welfare Work in a Mill Town," by W. E. C. Nazro, Welfare Manager, Plymouth Cordage Company, North Plymouth, Mass.; "Should Manufacturers Attempt Welfare Work for the Benefit of their Employes?" by C. W. Hubbard of

NEW ENGLAND WELFARE CONFERENCE DINNER, YOUNG'S HOTEL, BOSTON.

Boston; and "Loyalty and Fair Dealing," by Frederick P. Fish, of Boston, President of the American Telephone & Telegraph Company.

Miss Gertrude Beeks, the Secretary, gave an interesting talk on the work of the Welfare Department, illustrated by the stereopticon. This department embraces a large number of employers who are voluntarily giving especial consideration to the physical, mental and moral welfare of their employes.

In the course of his remarks Mr. Vreeland declared that one of the most regrettable results of great industrial combinations was the disappearance of sympathetic association between the operatives and administrators of these giant concerns. This altered relationship, considered historically, seemed to be a natural outcome of modern industrialism wherein, with its high organization and specializing tendency, an executive has little opportunity, however humane he may be, to consider his operatives except as a single unit. This necessity of dealing with labor as a unit has developed the importance of the foreman both economically and morally to a point where his task is greater even than that of the chief executive. In his keeping, to a very large degree, is the welfare of those whom he represents before the executive. If he is merely commercial he comes to regard the mass of human beings organized under him as a mere machine out of which he is to express so much finished product for a given stint of wage. If ambition tempt him to ignore moral obligations, trouble is bound to ensue, because there is little toleration among workingmen of a system that tends to merge them into mass for treatment. This resentment to being individually obliterated, Mr. Vreeland said, he knew to be strong among workingmen, despite all the unionizing tendencies of labor.

He emphasized the importance of broadening the view of foremen as the means of communication between the great mass of laborers and executive heads, and he pleaded for greater intimacy and sympathy between foremen and laborers. In this, more than in any other way, could the frequent causes of misunderstanding be diminished. The modern foreman's delicate duty is to truly present the point of view of the operative to the executive, and then, no simple task, he has to explain the point of view of the executive to his men. He stands in a sort of judicial and patrimonial relation between these two. Only moral inspiration will give him the courage and the ingenuity to correct a growing and deplorable tendency in the development of great industrial concerns.

Rev. James E. Freeman, of Yonkers, who had twelve years' experience with Cornelius Vanderbilt, which brought him into close contact with the men along the New York Central Railroad, said in part:

"We need something that at least hints at heaven here and now, and there is no place where this needs to be so largely emphasized as where for six days men and women are toiling for their bread. What is needed to render our operatives immune from that most corrupting curse, the saloon, is a kind of club environment that will give the men a place for necessary and legitimate recreation. The head of a large industry in a Southern State told me that the presentation of such a club scheme to his fellow directors was received by them at the outset as an indication of his own mental derangement. My friend was so determined to make the test that he undertook the enterprise without the full consent of his board. In one year he had fully demonstrated the wisdom and commercial value of his proposition."

W. E. C. Nazro, of the Plymouth Cordage Company, said:

"Health and physical comfort are cardinal considerations for the welfare of the great number of employes in our large factories. Under the division of physical comfort, in our works, we have established modern systems of ventilation, light and heat, sanitary work rooms, wholesome drinking water, wash rooms, fire protection, seats for women, rest rooms, hospital and resident nurses, and lunch rooms. Under the division of recreation, we have established the social hall, athletics of different kinds, field day contests, lectures, private theatricals, and bath department. For education, the first monument was that of the Loring reading room, while there followed classes in cooking, sloyd, basketry and cane-seating, lectures, kindergarten, and a periodical issued by the company. Prizes are awarded for gardens, house surroundings, poultry, and other products, at our Labor Day exhibit. In the division of housing, modern houses have been built, with open and sanitary plumbing, with attractive grounds for the development of lawns, walks, etc. Under a miscellaneous head is improved environment of the mills by the planting of shrubbery and road building."

C. W. Hubbard, Treasurer of the Ludlow Manufacturing Associates, after pointing out that both duty and self-interest demand that large employers of labor do welfare work among their employes, said:

"It seems to me that there is too little thought of the harm of giving too much publicity to welfare work. It is not wise for the beneficiaries of welfare work to find themselves exploited in the public press. It would be well if the public could be interested in the general subject, leaving the details for quiet study by those intending to practice them.

"The need and difficulty of this work are greater in America than in England or in France, where one has to deal with a permanent community of one nation and one language. We ask the public to recognize this need and to demand of our large employers that they also recognize it, and that they use their brains and their money in some organized effort to improve the lives of our laboring population. We also ask the public to remember that we have before us one of the toughest problems of the race—that of forming character. We ask the public to be slow in passing judgment, and to be charitable, if in our efforts we make mistakes."

Frederick P. Fish traced welfare work to the natural spirit of co-operation and of friendship that always exists wherever men are associated together for a common purpose and in a common work, with all the inequalities of position inevitably involved. This spirit, which he said permeated the army, the crews of ships, bands of explorers, the founders of governments, and the industrial associates, was not philanthropic, though containing an element of philanthropy; not charity, but primarily loyalty to the work and to the men associated in the work. "The man above expects and exacts loyalty from those below; the men below expect and exact loyalty from those above. Herein is the root of the movement represented here to-night. The purpose is to find a way, through organization and through method, to disclose to employes this feeling of loyalty on the part of employers." Mr. Fish continued:

"There are many ways in which this can be done. One is by the spirit of fairness, which the chairman has expressed as one of his cardinal principles of doing business. If there is a spirit of fairness at the top, it permeates the whole organization and is known to the man at the bottom, and he appreciates it and instinctively reciprocates it. Another is to make the conditions of the work just as favorable as they can be. Another is to see that the wages are on the right basis. They cannot be excessive, or enterprise would be ruined. But they can be meager and inadequate, and where they are, the employer is absolutely failing in this fundamental duty of loyalty and friendship to the men who work for him.

"Now, we in this welfare work, as I understand it, are endeavoring so to shape our organization, so to regulate our affairs, and so to establish our relations in an enormous aggregation of men, as to permeate the whole system with this spirit of fairness, frankness and co-operation.

"The interesting exhibits of applied welfare work that we have seen on the screen to-night illustrate methods of showing the employed that employers have thought for their comfort and welfare. Furthermore, they tend to create a standard for which the wage-earner should work in other relations and ultimately will bring up the standard of living in the community. For when we consider the cheapness of such sanitary appliances, the day will undoubtedly dawn when every artisan will demand them in his own home because he has them in his factory.

"All movements for social betterment are equally significant. What is the purpose of annual fairs in industrial communities? It is not merely for casual amusement, but to give the working people to understand that employers regard them as attached by the tie of a common enterprise and a common purpose.

"Take the business in which I am engaged. All through this country I have occasion to go into telephone exchanges from Maine to California, and wherever I go it delights my soul to find that the exchange manager shows me with more pride the retiring room for the girl operators, the bath facilities, the racks for their clothes, the hospital beds, the lunch counter, the cooking apparatus, than anything else in his whole establishment; and he feels that pride because he recognizes that therein he is carrying out, not the philanthropy nor the charity, but the spirit of friendship and loyalty which employers and employes naturally feel toward each other, unless their relations become artificial and strained, as is too apt to be the case under modern conditions.

"I personally believe that the importance of this welfare work cannot be exaggerated, because it is almost the only obvious and tangible expression that is open to us under modern conditions of the feeling on the part of employers, which should be and must be cultivated to the greatest possible extent, that they are the friends, the loyal friends, closely interested in the affairs of their employes."

Those present at the dinner were:

H. H. Vreeland, President New York City Railway Co., New York City.
James E. Freeman, President Hollywood Inn Club, Yonkers, N. Y.
Augustus P. Loring, President Plymouth Cordage Co., Boston, Mass.
James Logan, Chairman Executive Committee, United States Envelope Co., Worcester, Mass.
Frederick P. Fish, President American Telephone and Telegraph Co., Boston.
Frederic S. Clark, Treasurer Talbot Mills, North Billerica, Mass.
Charles Dana Palmer, State Board of Conciliation and Arbitration, Boston.
W. E. C. Nazro, Welfare Manager Plymouth Cordage Works, North Plymouth, Mass.
George W. Brown, Treasurer United Shoe Machinery Co., Boston.
G. E. Emmons, Manager Schenectady Works, General Electric Co., Schenectady, N. Y.
Charles S. Dennison, Treasurer Dennison Mfg. Co., Boston.
Thomas G. Plant, President Thomas G. Plant Co., Boston.
J. G. Taylor, President The Taylor-Burt Co., Holyoke, Mass.
Franklin W. Doliber, Mellin's Food Company, Boston.
B. Preston Clark, Boston.
W. C. Fish, Manager Lynn Works, General Electric Co., West Lynn, Mass.
Charles W. Hubbard, Treasurer Ludlow Manufacturing Associates, Boston.
Preston B. Keith, President The Preston B. Keith Shoe Co., Campello, Mass.
Louis Krumbhaar, The Solvay Process Company, Syracuse, N. Y.
Everett Morss, President The Simplex Electrical Co., Boston.
H. H. Wells, New York City.
J. F. P. Lawton, Gorham Manufacturing Co., Providence, R. I.
Charles T. Page, Treasurer Page Belting Company, Concord, N. H.
F. R. Maxwell, Thomas G. Plant Company, Boston.
W. M. Pratt, Treasurer Goodell-Pratt Company, Greenfield, Mass.
P. W. Power, Manager Stanley Electric Manufacturing Co., Pittsfield, Mass.
Frank C. Spinney, Faunce & Spinney, Lynn, Mass.
Winthrop C. Winslow, Manager Metropolitan Coal Co., Boston.
John E. Stevens, Agent Ludlow Manufacturing Associates, Boston.
Frederick C. Fletcher, Treasurer Pocasset Worsted Co., Boston.
E. H. Clement, Boston Transcript, Boston.
Rev. Edward Cummings, Boston.
Wm. C. Greene, Treasurer Peace Dale Mfg. Co., Peace Dale, R. I.
R. A. Robertson, Treasurer Providence Engineering Works, Providence, R. I.
George F. Willett, President George F. Willett & Co., and President United Printing Machinery Co., Boston.
C. J. H. Woodbury, American Telephone and Telegraph Co, Boston.
T. King, President Eureka Silk Manufacturing Co., Boston.
E. J. Bliss, Treasurer The Regal Shoe Company, Boston.
E. P. Brown, United Shoe Machinery Company, Boston.
F. Alexander Chandler, New England Hardware Dealers' Association, Boston.
H. S. Dennison, Dennison Manufacturing Co., Boston.
Franklin W. Hobbs, Treasurer Arlington Mills, Lawrence, Mass.
W. H. Gleason, Revere Rubber Co., Boston.
Elbridge L. Howe, President Howe & Stetson Co., New Haven, Conn.
Louis P. Howe, President S. H. Howe Shoe Co., Marlboro, Mass.
Chas. W. Hughes, President Men's Club, Lorraine Manufacturing Co., Pawtucket, R. I.
M. W. Alexander, General Electric Co., West Lynn, Mass.
John Brooks, Page Belting Co., Concord, N. H.
Charles H. Eastman, General Manager Howe & Stetson Co, New Haven, Conn.
A. Lincoln Filene, Wm. Filene's Sons Co., Boston.
T. B. Fitzpatrick, Brown, Durrell & Co., Boston.
W. S. Forbes, The Forbes Lithograph Mfg. Co., Boston.
William D. Hartshorne, Agent Arlington Mills, Lawrence, Mass.
Wm. W. Blades, Lorraine Manufacturing Co., Pawtucket, R. I.
John P. Jewell, Page Belting Co., Boston.
M. B. Kaven, United Shoe Machinery Co., Beverly, Mass.
D. King, Treasurer Eureka Silk Manufacturing Co., Boston.
W. H. McElwain, W. H. McElwain Company, Boston.
Charles A. Morss, The Simplex Electrical Co., Boston.
Hayes Robbins, General Secretary New England Branch National Civic Federation, Winchester, Mass.
William Brooks, Kidder, Peabody & Co., Boston.
John Daboll, Mellin's Food Company, Boston.
R. C. Southwork, Wm. Filene's Sons Co., Boston.
E. H. Walcott, Merchants' Association, Boston.
Henry Clayton Metcalf, Professor Political Science, Tufts College, Boston.
George R. Nazro, Boston.
Rev. Edward S. Travers, Rector Trinity Church, Boston.
G. M. Thompson, Boston.
Arthur A. Adams, Director, Dennison Mfg. Co., Boston.
Frank G. Allen, Winslow Bros. & Smith Co., Boston.
Philip R. Allen, F. W. Bird & Son, East Walpole, Mass.
Matthew J. Fox, Wm. Filene's Sons Co., Boston.
P. C. Brown, Dennison Manufacturing Co., Boston.
T. O. Peterson, Wm. Filene's Sons Co., Boston.
Preston Pond, Director Dennison Mfg Co., Boston.
Louis Vose, Hollingsworth & Vose, Boston.
Charles E. Hall, Dennison Manufacturing Co., Boston.

WAGES ADJUSTED TO PRICES.

[The following extract from an address by James F. Williams, of Streator, Ill., was published by the *Industrial Independent*, official organ of the Citizens' Industrial Association, with its approval and the advice that we present to our readers Mr. Williams' "sound common sense." We are happy to comply.—Editor's Note.]

Let me say that there are just three ways in which a man may increase his wages, three possible sources out of which an advance may come. I will summarize them briefly:

1. It may come out of the pocket of his employer; that is, wages may be increased at the expense of profits.

2. It may come out of the pocket of the consumer; that is, wages may be increased by raising the price of the product either by artificial combination or otherwise, and charging it up to the buyer.

3. It may not come out of anyone's pocket; in other words, wages may be increased by enhanced skill and efficiency in production, by which the sum total of the goods produced may be increased and thus more wealth created, which can be divided as wages or profits.

Corresponding to these three ways of increasing wages there are three stages of trades-unionism. In the first stage the workman thinks his wages come out of the pocket of the employer and he is all the time fighting to get more. He does not realize that the employer is only a middleman who stands between him and the market, and that even if he could compel him to give up all his margin it would not make him rich. He does not remember that the margin of the employer is made up of small profit on the work of many men; so that if he can make ten cents on the labor of a thousand men it will give him a profit of a hundred dollars a day; and yet so small is the profit on any one man that if the laborer could get all of it, it would not make the difference between comfort and poverty. As long as the laborer is in this stage of unionism he will always be fighting the employer and trying to take his profit away from him; and we shall have local strikes, lock-outs and all manner of industrial strife as the outcome. Mind, I am not saying that the employer may not be claiming an excessive profit, and that he may not be even less enlightened than the men but, be that as it may, there is no hope that this stage of unionism will ever bring permanent peace. It will always be a primitive and barbarous stage in which attack on the one hand and reprisal on the other will be the rule, and the law of the highwayman, "That he may take who has the power, and he may keep who can."

Men pass out of the first stage into the second stage of unionism by enlarging their combination and by changing the point of attack. Instead of attacking the employer, they attack the market—that is to say, the consumer. In this way they make the employer a friend of unionism instead of an enemy, and together they present a united front against the common foe—who is the man who buys the goods. In order to make this co-operation possible, the union must be so extended as to include every competitor in a given industry. It must be made co-extensive with the competitive area; otherwise, it will fail, and the union will return to the first stage, where it fights the employer and not the consumer.

This point is well illustrated by the experience of the miners of Illinois, who, prior to their national organization, were spending their energy fighting their employers and impoverishing both themselves and the community. If the glass blowers, the coal miners, or the clay workers of Streator, were to confine their union to this town alone, the result is so obvious it would be a waste of time to discuss it. They would be at the mercy of a competitive market and would have to accept such wages as the market allowed or go out of business. The same thing is true of any workmen, skilled or unskilled. If they do not organize on a large enough scale to control the market, the competition of non-union producers will soon drive them to the wall. In this connection the situation of unskilled labor, with its unlimited and uncontrolled supply, presents a difficult problem. Speaking quite frankly, it seems to me the most promising plan of organization for common labor is to unite itself with the skilled labor in the same trade, and to be enabled to take part in making a uniform scale that shall be binding on everybody in that industry. So doing, they will get on a common ground with the employer and present a common front to the enemy; who is, in this case, the innocent and often unconscious consumer. They will thus pass from the first to the second stage of unionism, from chronic war to comparative peace. For in the second stage the friction between employer and workman is greatly reduced, joint agreements take the place of strikes—and the millennium is one step nearer.

But we are not yet at the goal of unionism. There is a third stage, which is as far in advance of the second as the second is ahead of the first. It is the stage in which the laborer refuses to use his power to plunder either the employer or the consumer. I was discussing the relation of the union to the consumer with an intelligent Northumberland miner this summer, and he put it with such clearness that I can not do better than reproduce his argument.

"Who is the consumer?" said he; "the consumer is my fellow-workman. If I can force up the price of a ton of coal by combining with my fellow-miners, who pays for it? Why, even the mason, hod-carrier, the factory girl, even the poor widow who is struggling to bring up her fatherless children."

"But," I suggested, "suppose all men and all women in every trade were unionized."

"Then," he replied, "we would all be just where we were before. For suppose there were 25 per cent. added to the wages of every worker in England. What would be the result? Why every one of us would have to buy, and we would be no better off. It's like traveling in a circle; you get no further ahead." * * *

No union that hopes to increase wages by lessening production or by appropriating some other person's earnings can hope to ultimately succeed. You cannot create wealth by refusing to produce it; you cannot increase wages by diminishing the source from which they must be paid. Restriction is folly. Scamp work cheats nobody as much as the laborer. * * * A catchpenny motive is just as sordid in a union as in a capitalist; and a mean, grasping spirit is the more contemptible in so far as the union professes to occupy a higher plane and to appeal to higher motives. You cannot rear a broad structure on a narrow foundation. Nothing less than industrial peace, social solidarity, the subordination of selfish and class interests to the rule of ethical and economical law, can be the ultimate aim of unionism. Only such an aim can arouse or justify social enthusiasm or hope to make a permanent contribution to the solution of the labor question.

The Northumberland Miners organized two bodies with legislative and judicial powers, that might roughly be compared to our upper and lower houses of Congress. They called one the "Board of Conciliation," and the other the "Joint Committee," and they gave them jurisdiction over any dispute that might arise, and invested them with power to enforce any decision they might arrive at.

They agree on a wage basis that should bear a certain relation to the market price of coal, and they made

(*Concluded on page 8.*)

THE NATIONAL

Civic Federation Review

Offices: 281 Fourth Avenue, New York City

RALPH M. EASLEY, Editor

The Editor alone is responsible for any unsigned article or unquoted statement published in THE CIVIC FEDERATION REVIEW.

Ten Cents per Copy; One Dollar per Year.

The National Civic Federation

OFFICERS

AUGUST BELMONT, President.
SAMUEL GOMPERS, First Vice-President.
OSCAR S. STRAUS, Second Vice-President.
HENRY PHIPPS, Chairman Ways and Means Committee.
CORNELIUS N. BLISS, Treasurer.
CHARLES A. MOORE, Chairman Conciliation Committee.
H. H. VREELAND, Chairman Welfare Department.
FRANCIS L. ROBBINS, JOHN MITCHELL, } Chairmen Trade Agreement Committee.
RALPH M. EASLEY, Chairman Executive Council.
SAMUEL B. DONNELLY, Secretary.

EXECUTIVE COMMITTEE

On the Part of the Public.

Grover Cleveland, ex-President of the United States, Princeton, N. J.
Andrew Carnegie, capitalist, New York City.
Cornelius N. Bliss, ex-Secretary of the Interior, New York City.
Oscar S. Straus, member of the Court of Arbitration at The Hague, New York City.
Charles W. Eliot, President Harvard University, Cambridge, Mass.
Archbishop John Ireland, of the Roman Catholic Church, St. Paul, Minn.
Bishop Henry C. Potter, of the Protestant Episcopal Church, New York City.
David R. Francis, President Louisiana Purchase Exposition, St. Louis, Mo.
Isaac N. Seligman, of J. & W. Seligman & Co., New York City.
James Speyer, of Speyer & Co., New York City.
Charles Francis Adams, publicist, Boston.
John G. Milburn, lawyer, New York City.
V. Everit Macy, capitalist, New York City.
Charles J. Bonaparte, lawyer, Baltimore.
Ralph M. Easley, Chairman Executive Council, New York City.

On the Part of Employers.

Henry Phipps, director United States Steel Corporation, New York City.
August Belmont, President Interborough Rapid Transit Company, New York City.
Lucius Tuttle, President Boston & Maine Railroad, Boston.
Frederick P. Fish, President American Bell Telephone Company, Boston.
Francis L. Robbins, President Pittsburgh Coal Company, Pittsburgh.
Henry G. Davis, Coal Operator, Elkins, W. Va.
H. H. Vreeland, President New York City Railway Company, New York City.
Samuel Mather, of Pickands, Mather & Co., Cleveland.
Charles A. Moore, Manning, Maxwell & Moore, New York City.
Franklin MacVeagh, of Franklin MacVeagh & Co., Chicago.
Charles H. Taylor, Jr., ex-President American Newspaper Publishers' Association, Boston.
Dan R. Hanna, of M. A. Hanna & Co., Cleveland.
Marcus M. Marks, President National Association of Clothing Manufacturers, New York City.
Otto M. Eidlitz, Chairman Board of Governors, Building Trades Employers' Association, New York City.
William H. Pfahler, former President National Founders' Association, Philadelphia.

On the Part of Wage Earners.

Samuel Gompers, President American Federation of Labor, Washington.
John Mitchell, President United Mine Workers of America, Indianapolis.
E. E. Clark, Grand Chief Conductor, Order of Railway Conductors, Cedar Rapids, Iowa.
James Duncan, General Secretary Granite Cutters' National Union, Washington.
Daniel J. Keefe, President International Longshoremen, Marine and Transportworkers' Association, Detroit, Mich.
Warren S. Stone, Grand Chief International Brotherhood of Locomotive Engineers.
P. H. Morrissey, Grand Master Brotherhood Railroad Trainmen, Cleveland.
William D. Mahon, President Amalgamated Association of Street Railway Employes of America, Detroit, Mich.
Theodore J. Shaffer, President Amalgamated Association of Iron, Steel and Tin Workers, Pittsburgh.
J. J. Hannahan, Grand Master Brotherhood Locomotive Firemen, Peoria, Ill.
James O'Connell, President International Association of Machinists, Washington.
John Tobin, General President Boot and Shoe Workers' Union, Boston.
Joseph F. Valentine, President Iron Moulders' Union of North America, Cincinnati.
James M. Lynch, President International Typographical Union, Indianapolis.
Denis A. Hayes, President Glass Bottle Blowers' Association of United States and Canada, Philadelphia.
William Huber, President United Brotherhood of Carpenters and Joiners of America, Indianapolis.

LESSONS OF THE INTERBOROUGH STRIKE.

"Labor organizations must keep their part of agreements if they expect success."

"No labor organization can break its contracts or aid others to break theirs and live."

In those two sentences, Warren S. Stone, Grand Chief of the Brotherhood of Locomotive Engineers, and William D. Mahon, President of the Amalgamated Association of Street and Electric Railway Employes of America, summarized the greatest lesson of the needless, unwarranted strike on the lines of the Interborough Rapid Transit Company. All that labor has gained, all that labor expects to gain, in wages, hours and conditions of work, is the result of the organization being stronger than the individual. If, then, the results of this greater strength through organization are to be retained, and if such further gains are to be made as the business conditions of industry may warrant, the collective contract must be held by labor in as high respect as is the contract between individuals. This is the doctrine that the chief leaders of organized labor, as well as its disinterested friends and advisers, have been constantly preaching to the mass. Now this doctrine has been driven home by a concrete object lesson so impressive that it will reach every local union from Maine to California. It should also impress every employer in the country with a new sense of the responsibility and conservatism of the national leaders of organized labor, whom some employers habitually denounce. To take its charter away from a local union for violation of a contract seems a drastic measure; but be it said to the credit of the organization of which Mr. Stone is the head, he would himself have been called to account at its annual convention, and his own head would have fallen had he failed in this instance to enforce its laws. The promotion of trade agreements between employers and wage earners is one of the primary purposes of the National Civic Federation. But work to this end would be futile indeed, had organized labor upheld the precipitate action and unreasonable conduct of the local leaders of the three organizations involved. The heroic action in this case of the national chiefs of organized labor gives renewed hope to all who are interested in promoting industrial peace.

The second great lesson of this conflict is that labor organizations must vest the decision of vital issues in their national officers. This principle has been recognized by many of the unions and is embodied in the constitutions or by-laws of many national labor organizations; but in New York City some local organizations have too long been permitted to treat this principle as a dead letter. In fact, they have frequently and openly defied the national authority on the pretext that metropolitan conditions made them a law unto themselves. Some such action as that of Messrs. Stone and Mahon was necessary to bring these locals to their senses. A great deal of trouble in the building trades has arisen from this disposition on the part of the New York unions to ignore or openly defy the authority of their national bodies.

The enforcement of this national authority in labor organizations is of the utmost importance to employers and to the general public, and should receive their cordial approval. The establishment of such large and responsible authority makes for all the approved methods of attaining industrial peace, including trade agreements and arbitration. Equally important with the establishment of this authority to wage earners everywhere is it to awaken their rank and file to the necessity of electing sane, responsible and honorable men to positions of local leadership.

These lessons were forcibly put by Samuel Gompers, President of the American Federation of Labor, in a speech which he delivered at Baltimore, the day following the end of the Interborough strike, to an audience of labor men, who heartily applauded his remarks:

"The most important object in the labor organizations to-day is the honor of agreement between employe and employer. The strike in New York involved the violation of agreements, and if the leaders of the New York unions had considered the agreements the strike could have been prevented. It was a simple case of the members of the local unions flying off half-cocked and not taking the advice of the men who have made the labor organizations in the United States what they are to-day. I want to impress upon you, fellow unionists, the importance of living up to your agreements and contracts."

William H. Farley, of the Tilelayers, one of the more experienced of the local leaders in the building trade, said:

"The labor men of New York feel that this strike and the stand that the national officers took has done more for the labor movement than anything that has happened within the last ten years. It has proved to large employers that the national leaders intend to hold trade agreements sacred, and local leaders in the future will not be so quick to get into fights of this kind without first consulting their national officers. The possibility of strikes will be reduced to a minimum, and instead of strikes we will have arbitration. The members of organized labor will then lose no time during the arbitration, and employers of labor will be willing to arbitrate as long as they know that the national leaders will be able to hold the local unions in line.

"After one conference during the strike, one of the representatives of the Amalgamated Association, who had been in the labor movement less than two years, said that he learned more of that movement in an hour's talk with Thomas I. Kidd, Vice-President of the American Federation of Labor, and William D. Mahon, President of the Amalgamated Association, and with some of the local leaders, than he ever knew before. This goes to prove the value of education of local unions as a preventive of strikes. The result of this strike is a lesson to union men everywhere, and especially to building trades men who seem to ignore their national officers and have caused many strikes that should never have been ordered."

The conclusion of the Interborough strike thus presents an interesting paradox: While many arguments in favor of the trade agreement by its advocates were nullified in this instance by the headstrong local leaders, the upholding before all the country of the responsibility of labor for its contracts is a lesson so valuable in itself and so beneficial to the cause of industrial peace as to make the outcome of defeat in reality a victory. This lesson is well worth all its cost.

WAGES ADJUSTED TO PRICES.

(*Concluded from page 7.*)

it the business of the Board of Conciliation to adjust the scale every three months. They made it the function of the Joint Committee to sit on all internal questions that might arise in the daily operations of the mines, and settle them forthwith. This body is in almost constant session, and like the Board of Conciliation, is composed of an equal number of miners and owners, and presided over by an outside chairman or umpire. Both associations maintain a staff of salaried officers, who are experts on all matters pertaining to the coal trade. * * *

Wages go up and down with the market; there is no maximum and no minimum. During the great depression the price went so low that the scale was abandoned in some of the poorer mines, and men were allowed to work for whatever the mine would yield; and during a spell of very high prices the miners once volunteered to accept a reduction to check the upward tendency and to save the industry from the effort of a reduction.

LABOR WRESTS VICTORY FROM DEFBAT.

(*Concluded from page 16.*)

not only of my good offices, but also those of President Gompers, of the American Federation of Labor; President Mitchell, of the United Mine Workers of America; Vice-President Kidd, of the American Federation of Labor, and President Healey, of the International Brotherhood of Stationary Firemen, were inconsiderately rejected.

"Nothing now remains for me to do but to declare that the present strike is neither authorized nor approved by the Amalgamated Association of Street and Electric Railway Employes of America, and I therefore advise all our loyal members to report for duty at once. To maintain their organization, which has done so much for the betterment of their material and moral conditions, and by the result of their present experience avoid such errors in the future; in that effort I shall be glad to assist to the fullest."

LABOR WRESTS VICTORY FROM DEFEAT.

(*Continued from page 1.*)

strike, to go into effect Saturday morning at the rush hour. Every train in the Subway will come to a standstill, and there will not be a wheel turning on the Elevated. This order is final."

Mr. Pepper also announced: "Unless Hedley rescinds his schedule I will tie up the whole road."

When Mr. Pepper was asked whether, before striking, it would not be necessary for him to get the consent of President Mahon of his national organization (the Amalgamated Association), he defiantly replied: "We don't need any teaching from Mr. Mahon. We can strike when we like, and when we do, we won't waste any time."

Another member of the employes' committee was quoted as saying, after the conference: "The situation was so tense during the conference that several members of the committee were in favor of granting the Interborough officials just fifteen minutes to grant their demands."

In vain did Mr. Hedley explain to the men that the new schedule had not received a fair trial, because it had been subject to the sudden increase of traffic in the Subway caused by the severest storm in New York in twenty years, which had almost paralyzed travel on the elevated and surface roads. He asked that the schedule be allowed to stand for a week, in order to allow it to be tested under normal conditions. This request the committee peremptorily refused. He asked the men to appoint a sub-committee of three to join with him in making a schedule. But the men would listen to no proposition whatever, and issued an ultimatum that unless the new schedule were taken down by 11 o'clock the next day, they would tie up both the Elevated and Subway. This demand was carried to President Belmont, who ordered the schedule taken down.

Mr. Pepper's exultant remark was: "The men have obtained all they ask. We'll get all the rest we want."

Mr. Jencks declared: "We got everything we went after."

Thus ended the preliminary encounter. The local chiefs had threatened and blustered to their hearts' content. The company's officials, in order to avoid a rupture, had humbly accepted the orders of Messrs. Pepper, Jencks and Pinney, and gone back to the former schedule, with the understanding that a new schedule was to be arranged before March 1. The company thus had every intimation that could be conveyed by abusive language and an intolerable spirit of dictation that the local leaders were plotting trouble. It was evident that if the men continued in this spirit a clash was inevitable, for no quasi public corporation under heavy obligations to furnish safe and rapid transit for the millions of people of a great city could long endure such a situation.

The New York Civic Federation at this juncture appointed a special committee of fifteen to tender its good offices if need for them should develop. This committee was composed of the following:

Representing the Public:—Oscar S. Straus, Rt. Rev. H. C. Potter, Albert Shaw, Roland Phillips, Thomas F. Woodlock.

Representing Employers:—Charles A. Moore, Frederick D. Underwood, Emerson McMillin, Louis B. Schram, Marcus M. Marks.

Representing Wage Earners:—Samuel B. Donnelly, Edward A. Moffett, A. J. Boulton, Herman Robinson, James P. Archibald.

Both the Interborough officials and the employes' committee were apprised of the appointment of this committee and its willingness to aid in every possible way in preventing a fupture. While the ill-natured talk of the local leaders of the three unions involved had given notice to the Interborough officials of what they might expect on the 1st of March, it gave warning also to the national officers of these unions that there was need of a restraining hand to be placed on the local leaders. The national officers took hold at once with such apparent success that Chief Stone felt safe in making the statement to Mr. Belmont appearing at the beginning of this article.

The Civic Federation committee also quietly sounded the situation and was assured by the local leaders that prior to March 1, when the Amalgamated contract on the Elevated road would expire, they would send a committee to the Interborough offices and present a schedule calling for increases in the wages of a number of the trainmen, some of whom were getting as low as $1.40 a day. They said that while there was a handful of radicals who wanted an eight-hour day, the executive committee knew that this was impracticable and would not ask for it. They promised, however, in the event of a disagreement with the local management, to take the matter up with the Civic Federation committee along the lines of conciliation and arbitration.

The Civic Federation committee in the meantime sounded the Interborough Company far enough to feel assured that there would be no hitch over the wage question, as the demands were not regarded as unreasonable. It seems, however, that the operating department of the company, after its experience in the conferences in February, was determined to take no more chances of being held up at the last moment by impossible demands, and took precautionary measures.

As late as February 27, Grand Chiefs Stone and Hannahan, respectively of the engineers and the firemen, being in conference with Civic Federation members on another controversy, gave the information that everything seemed to be going along all right on the Interborough, they having received such information from their local organizations.

Even on Saturday, March 4, both Messrs. Pepper and Jencks announced in the papers that the people of New York need not worry; that there would be no strike, but that if any differences arose they would be dealt with in a businesslike manner; that if they could not come to an agreement with Mr. Hedley, they would go to Mr. Bryan, and if they could not agree with Mr. Bryan they would go to Mr. Belmont.

On Monday, March 6, however, it seemed as if this conciliatory talk had been largely for public consumption. The local leaders had instructed the men to vote on Monday on authorizing the committee to call a strike in case their demands were not granted.

Up to this time the engineers and firemen had publicly kept out of this last controversy, rightfully stating that their organizations had three-year contracts and no grievances that could not be taken care of in a regular manner. But at 3 o'clock that day, when the Amalgamated committee appeared at the Interborough offices for an answer to their demands, the engineers and firemen joined it, and at this time the engineers renewed all the demands they had not secured in their three-years' contract last September, utterly repudiating that document.

Manager Hedley stated that these new demands contained propositions that he had no power to grant, and urged the employes' committee to take their demands above his head to the proper authority—first, Vice-President Bryan, and then, if necessary, President Belmont, who, although in Florida, could be reached on the telephone at any time.

This idea the men refused to consider, saying, in effect: "You are the General Manager and it is your business to have all the power necessary to grant our demands or else get it from somebody who has. We are here to get action, not delay."

Together with their written demands, the men presented another paper containing the name and home address of each member of the committee. "There are our demands, and there are our addresses, where you must send your answer, yes or no, before 11 o'clock to-night," they said as they departed.

The spirit of reckless irresponsibility of the local leaders was glaringly exhibited that afternoon in other ways. "Let us talk to him ten minutes and no longer," said Mr. Jencks to Mr. Pepper, as they approached Mr. Hedley's office. "If they want to throw down the gauntlet, we'll pick it up," Mr. Pepper responded. Again Mr. Pepper was asked whether he could order a strike without the consent of the national officers of his organization, particularly of William D. Mahon, President of the Amalgamated Association.

"That's my business," replied Mr. Pepper, amid the laughter of the local committeemen surrounding him.

After the conference in Mr. Hedley's office, which lasted half an hour Mr. Pepper stated: "We made our demands. They are final. We are to get an answer, yes or no, by 11 o'clock to-night, and then something will happen."

Meantime a sub-committee of the Civic Federation committee, consisting of Messrs. Schram, McMillin, Marks, Moffett and Donnelly, undertook to intercept the employes' committee as they left the Interborough offices at 4 o'clock, but failed to reach them. The members of the employes' committee scattered to their respective headquarters, with the exception of the Amalgamated members, who, with local President Pepper at their head, went to the Clarendon Hotel to have a talk with their National President, W. D. Mahon, who had reached the city during the day. Mr. Mahon pleaded with them to abandon their rash plan, and stated that the national officers were ready to take up any grievances they had and were satisfied that they could secure a fair adjustment. He pointed out to them further that under the by-laws of the national organization they could not have the support of that organization without having first submitted the questions at issue to the national executive committee and obtaining its approval; and that the by-laws of the organization provided that arbitration should be offered by the employes and refused by the company, before a strike should occur. But this all fell upon deaf ears. In so many words they notified their national officers to keep their hands off, and to the statement that arbitration must first be offered, they replied: "We will strike first and arbitrate afterwards."

Messrs. Donnelly and Moffet, as a sub-committee of the Civic Federation committee, visited the headquarters of the Amalgamated local, where the vote was being taken, and tried to prevail upon the local officers either to extend the time twenty-four hours, or to offer, as a last resort, a proposition looking to arbitration. They practically guaranteed that if either were done the Civic Federation committee could bring about an amicable adjustment and save the New York public the great inconvenience that would follow a strike and at the same time protect the contracts between the Interborough and the unions. But the local leaders rejected all peaceful overtures. In the first place, they were absolutely certain that before 11 o'clock that night, "Hedley would be on his knees to them," and that if by any possibility he did not grant all their demands and risked a fight they would "bring him to his knees by noon the next day." They utterly disregarded National President Mahon's official warning that he would not sanction the strike.

In the meantime, Grand Chief Stone, of the engineers, who had been notified of the part his local organization was taking, at once wired Mr. Jencks that if the motormen went out on strike without following the by-laws of the national organization, they would find themselves outside the brotherhood; and as he had an important engagement elsewhere he telegraphed Assistant Chief E. W. Hurley, who was at New Haven, Conn., to take charge of the situation. Mr. Hurley reached New York at 11.30 that night, and at once sent for Mr. Jencks. Mr. Hurley used every argument to have the local leader retrace his steps; he threatened Mr. Jencks with expulsion from the order; pointed out to him the sad facts that many of the men were too old ever to get back on another railroad; that they would lose their insurance and bring disgrace upon their organization. To all of these entreaties Mr. Jencks replied that the men had voted to go out, and that he could not recall them. Assistant Chief Hurley then wanted Jencks to issue an order authorizing him to use Mr. Hurley's name instead of his own, recalling the men, but Mr. Jencks declared that it was too late.

Thus, despite all efforts, the strike was on.

The next duty of the Civic Federation committee, under the by-laws of its organization, was to endeavor to bring about peace between the company and the strikers. The committee was called together, Chairman Straus presiding.

It was clearly perceived that the local unions were in open rebellion against their national officers, and as the local officers were declaring that they would "accept nothing but a complete surrender of the company," which was impossible, the first move decided upon was to bring the local and national leaders into working relations. In this task it was evident that only the labor members of the committee could be of any practical value, and until there was an occasion for opening negotiations with the Interborough Company, the main work of the committee would devolve upon them.

A sub-committee consisting of Edward A. Moffett of the Bricklayers, A. J. Boulton of the Stereotypers, William H. Farley of the Tilelayers, Herman Robinson, General Organizer of the American Federation of Labor, Robert Neidig of the Housesmiths, [illegible] Gould of the Teamsters, Frederick Lemon, [illegible] Elevator Constructors, and James P. Archibald, of the Painters, was appointed to call upon President Mahon of the Amalgamated Association at the Clarendon Hotel, and Vice-Grand Master E. W. Hurley of the Brotherhood of Engineers, at the Grand Union Hotel, and tender their services, which were accepted. A sub-committee consisting of Wm. H. Farley, A. J. Boulton and Frederick Lemon then called on the joint executive committee of the strikers to invite them to a conference with their national officers. This effort was but partly successful, as only the Amalgamated members would accept. President Pepper appointed a committee of three, Messrs Madden, May and McCormick, to attend the conference. In addition to the full local committee named, the conference included President Mahon, Vice-Grand Master Hurley, Thomas I. Kidd, Vice-President of the American Federation of Labor; James Hatch, of the Upholsterers, and President of the Central Federated Union, of New York, and Timothy Healey, National President of the Brotherhood of Stationary Firemen.

This conference lasted four hours. One reason advanced by the strikers' committee for precipitate action was that the Interborough Company had been collecting strike breakers in New York from other cities, and that every hour's delay tended to make a strike ineffective. In reply to this, it was pointed out that it was only a question of two or three days at any time for the company to collect strike breakers; that from that standpoint, it would be good tactics to let the company go on accumulating strike breakers; that so long as the men kept at work, the company was put to the expense of maintaining an army in idleness, and that this very factor would soon become a potential influence with the company for peace. This argument was not one of theory, but was drawn from experience.

This conference broke up at 10 o'clock Wednesday night, the sub-committee appointed by Mr. Pepper being thoroughly convinced that they had made a mistake in calling a strike without the sanction of the national officers. They thought they could convince the whole executive committee of the strikers of their error by 11.30 o'clock and bring about a full conference at midnight. They reported at 12 o'clock, however, that they had not been successful, but thought they would be able to report favorably by 10 o'clock the next morning.

In the meantime the sub-committee of labor members of the Civic Federation had called upon Grand

(*Continued on page 16.*)

VITAL QUESTIONS AT ISSUE BETWEEN EMPLOYERS AND WAGE-EARNERS.

HOPEFUL INDICATIONS THAT THEIR RIGHTFUL RELATIONS CAN BE ATTAINED THROUGH SANE METHODS OF PROVED SUCCESS IN THE GREATEST INDUSTRIES.

By Ralph M. Easley. *Reprinted by permission from The Bankers' Magazine.*

ONE of the subsequent assets, if it may be so expressed, of the great anthracite coal strike has been the general awakening of interest in the industrial question. The "empty coal-bin" carried it home to practically every citizen. Prior to that strike, the view of the labor problem taken by the public was more or less academic and generally colored by local conditions. The rapid development of industry during the past fifty years has so revolutionized methods of production and distribution that innumerable and most intricate problems have arisen which only some such tremendous jolt would bring to public view. The great coal strike turned the inquiring mind of the public toward the questions lying back of industrial disturbances, such as "fair wages," "arbitration," "shorter hours," "the open shop," "boycotts," "black lists," "piecework," "restriction of output," "opposition to machinery," "minimum wage," "apprentices," "sympathetic strikes," "recognition of the union," "trade agreements," "integrity of contracts," "jurisdictional quarrels between unions," etc. These it found to be not only burning practical questions with every employer and employe, but also interesting from a general sociological and scientific point of view.

THE PIECEWORK SYSTEM.

Take the simple question of piecework, which has caused so many strikes, and which is a potential cause of more. The public hardly knew what the question meant. A most scholarly and eminent citizen wrote it "peace-work." But in the manufacturing world they would never think of spelling it that way! The Machinists' and Boiler Workers' Unions oppose piecework, while the Hatters' and Glove Makers' Unions will fight for it. The International Association of Machinists is so pronounced in its hostility to piecework that one of its annual conventions voted to refuse to work by that system after July 1, 1904, although a contest was afterward postponed by a referendum vote. The Industrial Commission gave a list of twenty-eight national labor organizations that prefer piecework and twenty-two that forbid it. In general there have been more strikes to secure piecework than to prevent it. Similar difference of opinion exists among employers, some being willing to order a lockout, if necessary, to force piecework in their establishments, while others insist upon day labor, believing that system to yield a better quality of work. Back of each of these positions there is an apparently good reason. The bitter hostility of some unions to the piecework system springs from the fact that after fixing a scale of prices for work by the piece, employers, when not checked by a union, often arbitrarily reduce the scale of prices for work upon finding that some of the men are making what they consider too high wages. Here the union comes in and says in effect to the swiftest workers, "You must slacken your speed. By employing all your energy you do not help yourself, for you are reduced at once by your employer, while you are forcing those less speedy to a starvation basis or to over-exertion that destroys their health."

This tendency of the employer thus arbitrarily and selfishly to reduce the scale of wages is so pronounced and recognized by employers themselves that a new plan is being introduced by some manufacturers called the "premium system," which undertakes to remove all cause for the fears of the workingman, and at the same time secure to the employer the benefits held out by the piecework system.

THE OPEN SHOP.

The open versus the closed shop is another question that has especially come into prominence the past year; and from the fiery speeches made by the leaders of the opposing sides, one would judge that there is no way out short of the utter annihilation of the unions, if the open shop should prevail, or the extinction of the non-union man, if the closed shop should be adopted. As both Mr. Gompers and Mr. Parry state the matter, there seems to be an "irrepressible conflict;" but, while theoretically the open or closed shop problem seems to be impossible of solution, practically it is being worked out every day. There are closed shops which are working satisfactorily and they are not criminal conspiracies against the public; and there are open shops operating successfully, and the unions accepting such have not gone to pieces, but are stronger to-day than they ever were.

Is there not a great deal of fustian put out on both sides of this question? We are told with ponderous eloquence that it is "unconstitutional," "un-American" and "infamous" for an employer to agree to employ only union men. We are told on the other side that an employer who should discriminate against union men would be violating every principle of justice and equity, and in some States the penal code. Is it not possible that both are overstating the case just a little? For instance, many employers insist on emphasizing vigorously the liberty and rights of the non-union man, and those rights should be fully protected; but are there not also some rights, and some liberty of action, due the employer? For example, if he wanted a hundred men to perform a certain piece of work, and thought he could secure better service by employing only non-union men, or only union men, only Germans, only Irish, only Catholics, or only Methodists, would it not be his right to so discriminate? And would it be anybody's else business? This, of course, does not apply to labor employed by the Government—City, State or National—but to an individual employer.

Is there not a great deal of human nature in this open shop question? When a union leader goes to an employer and says, "If you don't discharge that 'scab' in an hour, we will tie you up," or "If you employ any non-union men, we will call a strike and put you out of business," the old Adam at once arises in Mr. Employer and he frequently responds by kicking Mr. Agent out of the office. But suppose this same agent should go in and say: "Mr. Employer, we want to make a contract with you to do your work. You want your work performed in a good workmanlike manner, under such conditions and at such rates as we may mutually agree upon. Now, we don't object to working with non-union men, but if you will make an exclusive contract with us, it will put us in a position to discipline and control our men so that we can enforce our contracts, and we can guarantee you better and altogether more satisfactory work." In other words, does not that place the proposal on a business basis? What freedom of contract, or what liberty of action, would be violated by such an agreement? What essential difference is there between that proposition and the common everyday agreement made in the mercantile world between manufacturers and dealers wherein the manufacturer says to the dealer, "If you will handle our goods exclusively, we will make you a discount;" or, as testified to by a manufacturer in a case recently, "If you will make the statement every ninety days that you have sold no goods made by our competitors, we will allow you a discount of ten per cent?"

When Smith lets a contract for a house, the contractor, of course, hires all the men. Smith may never see them, nor does he know whether they are all Catholics, Protestants, Germans, Irish, union or non-union men; and in fact he has nothing to do with it, and cares nothing about it. In the case of the Longshoremen and the Great Lake carrying companies, the union contracts with the employer in just about this manner.

A good illustration of the human nature that crops out in this question came under my notice recently when a conciliation committee, which had worked for a week to settle a strike involving several thousand men, finally secured an agreement upon everything except the disposition of five non-union men. They had been taken in during the strike. The employer said that under no circumstances would he discharge those men at the command of the union. The union emphatically said it would not go back to work until the "scabs" were discharged. Consultation developed the fact that these particular five men were incompetent and undesirable in every respect, but the employer stood on the principle involved and justly refused to "throw them down," as he put it. The committee prevailed upon the union to give up its contention and go back to work with these men. When the union finally yielded, the leader called up the manufacturer and said, "Well, we will go back to work to-morrow morning." The answer, delivered in a tone as snarling and bitter as it could be made, was: "Well, you will have to work with those non-union men if you do." "All right," was the leader's reply, in his best "Sunday voice," "there won't be any trouble about that." On reaching the shops the next morning they found that the employer had discharged every non-union man.

When an employer makes a demand for an open shop on the public pretense of securing liberty for the non-union man, but privately announces that with the open shop he will "smash" the union, it can hardly be expected that the union will submit. If, as some employers claim, the open shop means the death of the union, one certainly cannot blame the union for fighting for its life. On the other hand, if a closed shop means the absolute control of all the business of the shop by the union, leaving the employer only to pay the bills Saturday night, then the employer cannot be blamed for wanting to "smash" the union. However, these extreme positions, I believe, are both unnecessary evils, which patience, tact and forbearance will remove in time.

While I believe the employer has the absolute right to make an exclusive contract with the union, I have just as strong a conviction as to the legal rights of the non-union man to determine for himself, without coercion, whether he shall belong to a union, or not, and to work without molestation wherever employed. There is no legal conflict between these two rights.

The bitter feeling toward the non-union man in this country is marveled at by the trades-union leaders of England. In many of their contracts there is a clause stipulating that they work with non-union men; but this state of affairs did not always exist. The English unions passed through the bitter stage several generations ago, and doubtless the broader spirit will eventually control in our unions. It is hard to believe, when one now sees the tolerance and fraternizing of the various religious denominations, that at one time they were burning one another at the stake on account of differing views.

THE RESTRICTION OF OUTPUT.

The question of "restriction of output" is one that has called forth strong denunciations of unions and has been the cause of much friction. Many of the union leaders indignantly deny the charge, but they speak from their own craft experience only. There are unions that deliberately place a limitation on work and do it openly in their by-laws, and, generally speaking, all the union rules and methods, whether governing membership, apprenticeships, working with non-unionists, the minimum wage, piecework, machinery or output, are in some form a restriction upon the employer, and have come into vogue to protect the members at some point where they feel that competition will be destructive. But this natural desire to prevent destructive competition is so universal that it is not fair to stop the inquiry with the labor union. It is common to capitalists, farmers, the professional classes, and merchants as well.

The merchant who cuts prices is just as reprehensible in the eyes of the other merchants as is the non-unionist who cuts wages in the eyes of the unionist. The tactics employed in the mercantile and in the labor worlds to deal with the common enemy, the price or wage cutter, are almost identical. Purchasers of holiday books will doubtless remember finding a printed slip in each one containing the following:

> In accordance with the agreement of the American Publishers' Association, which went into effect May 1, 1901, this book must be sold at retail at the published price without discount.

Now, back of that simple little statement there is a history of a combination between 95 per cent. of the publishers of all kinds of books and magazines in the United States, and about 90 per cent. of the wholesale and retail booksellers. The publishers made an iron-clad agreement among themselves that they would refuse to sell books to any booksellers who cut prices. This combination between the publishers and the booksellers was so advantageous that the sellers helped to compel the independent publishers (the "scabs") to join the publishers' organization. As these organizations have existed only four years and include practically all the old-established publishing houses in the United States, I will quote verbatim from the official circulars produced in court:

> By special agreement entered into with the Organization Committee of the American Publishers' Association, the members of our association are bound not to buy, not to put in stock, nor to offer for sale the books of any publisher who shall finally decline to co-operate with us in the maintenance of the net price system by joining the American Publishers' Association and issuing books under the net price system. Inasmuch as the publishers have carried out their part of the agreement upon which our contract was conditioned, it now becomes necessary for us to preserve our part of the agreement. We had sincerely hoped that you would be pleased to join the American Publishers' Association and co-operate with us through it in the maintenance of the net price system; and if you will take the matter into consideration at the present time, we are confident that you will now join the Publishers' Association and not compel us to take final action in this matter. We inclose a copy of the last issue of the Booksellers' Bulletin. By referring to page 6 of the Bulletin you will see that one publisher has already been cut off by the members of our association. We sincerely hope it will not be necessary to extend the list. Very truly yours,
>
> American Booksellers' Association.

The resolution on which the above notice was based is as follows, adopted by the American Booksellers' Association June 17, 1902:

> Whereas, All publishers of trade books still remaining outside of the Publishers' Association have been repeatedly invited by us to join the organization and through it co-operate with us in the maintenance of the net price system; and,
>
> Whereas, Such publishers of general trade books as still remain outside of the Publishers' Association are continuing to sell their publications to the few persistent price-cutters, and thus encouraging them to continue their opposition to the net price system; therefore,
>
> *Be it Resolved*, That we, the American Booksellers' Association, in convention assembled, do hereby instruct our secretary to give final notice to such publishers that it is our intention to

apply Reform Resolution No. 1 unless they immediately join the American Publishers' Association and co-operate through it with us in the maintenance of the net price system; and therefore,

Be it Resolved, That should any such publisher on receiving such notice decline to co-operate with us by failing to make application to the American Publishers' Association after receiving final notice, the secretary shall promptly issue notice to all members that Reform Resolution No. 1 is thereafter to be applied to such publisher, and all members shall discontinue handling the books of such publishers, as provided by Reform Resolution No. 1, until further notice.

As a further illustration of the methods adopted and the success with which they were carried out, the following extracts are given from a circular letter sent out by one of the publishers:

Several things have already been demonstrated of interest to the entire trade in connection with the "no cut rate" movement.

1. The substantial loyalty to the association of all dealers. In only one case (up to date of this letter) has there been any cutting of price—one large department store in New York City.

2. The vigor and promptness of the association to punish those who violate its regulations. The association immediately took steps to assure itself that the cut in price was deliberate and intentional. The entire wholesale publishing trade was at once notified not to sell a *book of any kind* published by members of the American Publishers' Association to the offending concern. There is every indication that this order will be loyally carried out by all publishers and wholesalers.

The two organizations above referred to claim they took the only course open to prevent the "demoralization of the trade" by department stores, "home library" and "mail order" agencies, but the methods are strikingly similar to those of the labor unions.

Everyone is familiar with the bitter warfare that has gone on for years between the "cut price" drug stores and the wholesale dealers and manufacturers of proprietary remedies. In fact, the whole commercial world is honeycombed with definite organized efforts to prevent what each trade would term destructive competition, and, in conducting the various fights on these propositions, the boycott, spies, and, in some cases, physical attacks, have been employed. Even the recent disgraceful conduct of the livery drivers in Chicago, where burial of the dead was interfered with, finds its parallel but not justification in the conduct of the "coffin combination," which in many cities has carried its fights against the independent coffin companies to the same disgraceful limit. In one Western city, the fight became so bitter that attachments were taken out for the corpses by the rival companies, and, in another, because a man had had an undertaker who handled independent coffins, he could not secure a hearse nor a public conveyance and had to take the body to the cemetery in a grocery wagon.

While the limitations and restrictions by unions have caused wholesale condemnation, little or no attention is paid to the regular meetings of manufacturers and dealers at which they openly discuss and agree upon prices and limitations of output. The New York *Commercial* of January 2, 1904, contained the following statement, which is certainly to the point:

The power of the Steel Corporation has been demonstrated by its ability to maintain high prices for its finished material in the face of a falling off of something like 60 per cent. in the demand for steel, and reductions ranging from 40 to 50 per cent. in the price of pig iron. This has been accomplished through the various pools which have been formed for the purpose of regulating prices and output. Practically all the pools met last December and decided to maintain the 1903 schedule. The iron and steel industry is now controlled by various associations, among them the billet manufacturers, steel rail manufacturers, structural manufacturers, steel plate manufacturers, tin manufacturers, and pig iron manufacturers.

In fact, when one strikes the iron and hardware world, it is difficult to find anything that is not in a pool or combination of some description, where prices are arbitrarily fixed and in some instances output prorated. I do not claim that these pools and combinations are not necessary to maintain stability in the market and, therefore, stability in employment; but I simply desire to call attention to the fact that what is accepted as an every-day matter of necessity on one side ought not to be too harshly condemned on the other. When a union man observes how readily the public acquiesces in the demand of all railroad corporations that their "fixed charges" be provided for beyond any peradventure, he wonders why the union man's "fixed charges," that is, his cost of living, should not be as surely provided for by the employer. Thus the "minimum wage" demand is nothing more or less than what the unionists claim to be their "fixed charges."

Limited space forbids reference, even by name, to the hundreds of combinations one may find upon investigation that restrict prices or limit output. In fact, it can be said that there is scarcely an industry that is entirely free from combinations of capital or combinations of labor in some form. There is an infinite variety in the methods of these different combinations, but there is a general similarity in their efforts to regulate competition and bring pressure to bear on persistent "competitors," "price cutters" and "non-unionists." It may well be asked, in view of the universality of this effort, What is to be the outcome? and, What should be the policy of the general public toward combinations? We may ask, Shall all combinations be suppressed and all industries be compelled to submit to the unregulated competition of individualism? Or, shall these combinations continue to grow and competition be entirely eliminated in the "ideal state" of socialism? If neither of these extremes should be followed, what shall be the middle ground where competition may continue without being destructive and where the public shall not be exploited by monopoly of capital or monopoly of labor? Shall these combinations be left to work out their purposes, or shall the courts and legislatures be called upon to deal with them?

CONFERENCES AND TRADE AGREEMENTS.

Whatever the destructive forces that are finally brought to bear on this phase of the situation, there are some constructive forces whose great potentiality gives us hope that progress is being made, not the least being the trade agreement. While here and there these joint trade agreements between small bodies of employers and employes in a given craft have resulted in conspiracies against the public, now being dealt with by the courts, the great majority of them have proven of immense value in preserving the stability of industry. Such employers' organizations exist in over one hundred different industries, like the Stove Manufacturers' Association, the American Publishers' Association, and the Bituminous Coal Operators' Association, which meet annually in joint conference with the Iron Molders' Union of North America, International Typographical Union, and the United Mine Workers, respectively, and consider in a businesslike way the conditions of the trade, conditions of labor, and all matters pertaining to the special industry as well as the position of the general public.

The elevating effect of the joint trade agreement system upon the intelligence and character of the union leaders is clearly shown in a statement by Mr. Francis L. Robbins, President of the Pittsburg Coal Company, referring to the sixth annual joint convention of the operators and mine workers of the interstate bituminous field, held at Indianapolis, in February, 1903. He says:

Looking back over the recent convention, and comparing it with the conventions held at the inception of the movement, one is struck by the change in the *personnel* of the miners' delegates Instead of seeing flannel shirts, hob-nail shoes, no vests and often no coats, you meet a body of men as well dressed as any body of men gathered from the middle class in any Eastern city. There has been a corresponding change in the intelligence, as shown in the faces of the delegates, and particularly perceptible to those who have argued scale questions before these meetings for the past fifteen years. It is a critical audience of practical workmen, who are quick to detect sophistry or misleading statements.

Mr. Robbins did not so state, but it is equally true that the tone and breadth of view of the operators who met these men correspondingly improved. Page after page of testimony could be recited showing that the educational side of these joint conferences is important. Recently the Amalgamated Association of Iron, Steel and Tin Workers, the organization which deals with all the large iron and steel companies, met in special conference with the employers to consider abandoning certain artificial restrictions which had grown up in the trade and had become "vested rights." After a week's discussion the union leaders recommended that the restrictions be abolished; a referendum vote was taken by the organization, and the recommendation was accepted. At the same time, the organization of its own volition, in consideration of the trade conditions, offered a cut of 10 per cent. in the wages of its men notwithstanding the fact that the organization had a contract which still had months to run.

EMPLOYERS WHO DESIRE TO DESTROY THE UNIONS.

But there is another class of employers, which, under the banner of "law and order," "free labor," "individual liberty," etc., is organized primarily to "smash the unions." These employers refuse to consider the history, purpose and benefits of trades unions and see only the coercive, brutal and lawless methods which have too frequently been indulged in by the newer and cruder unions. Some of these same employers' associations had no sooner become organized than they adopted identical methods of warfare. It is openly boasted by one organization of employers in a city of something over 100,000 inhabitants that they compelled every employer to become a member; and that where they found any employer reluctant, they got the banks to shut off his credit and the wholesale houses to refuse supplies.

The attitude of this extreme class of employers and employers' associations is quite similar to that of the extreme wing of the labor movement—the Socialists. Socialists denounce the unions and the leaders of the unions for entering into agreements with employers, just as extremists among employers denounce all movements looking toward dealing with unions. The Socialists affirm that the class struggle is irrepressible, and that the workingmen must fight their employers to the bitter end and make no compromise. There are also a few labor organizations controlled by the Socialists which take similar ground respecting employers. The community of sentiment between the Socialists and this class of employers' association appeared plainly in an editorial in the Socialists' *Daily People* (New York, April 7, 1903.) commenting upon the annual address of the president of the National Manufacturers' Association. The Socialist editor says that the president is correct in holding that an "equitable arrangement" cannot be effected by the "artificial" method of conciliation or arbitration. An "equitable arrangement," he says, "can only be effected by allowing the class struggle full scope; and as a means to this end nothing is so much to be welcomed as the straight-out tactics" of that association. "Socialism," the editor concludes, "will triumph as a result."

If these two extreme wings of irreconcilables had their way, the outcome would be either arbitrary control by labor or arbitrary control by capital. If all employers stood for intolerance and bigotry, or if all unions stood for tyrannical and unreasonable methods, the end would necessarily be a revolution. But the American people, as a whole, are not willing to enter upon such a permanent warfare of "capital" and "labor." They have enough practical sense to recognize conditions as they exist, and they have the courage and patience to deal with them.

I believe that rightful relations between employers and employes will eventually be worked out in this country, in spite of the Socialists in the wage-earners' camp and the anarchists in the employers' camp.

AN ECONOMIC EXHORTATION TO ORGANIZED LABOR.

(*Concluded from page 2.*)

have to get if the factory and the employes were idle part of the time.

The manufacturer and the men will get less per piece, but more in the aggregate, and if you can keep the price low the demand for the article, whatever it may be, will be increased.

That is, if you can get your goods cheaper and yet have the men who make them earn in the aggregate as much as when the price of the goods was higher, you are increasing the amount of work, not diminishing it. In other words, it is by increasing the output per man, not by restricting it, that you give work to more men.

And therefore every bit of efficiency that you can add to the ability of an individual, and every bit of waste that you can avoid and thus enable the goods to be turned out cheaper, will increase the number of consumers, and increase the number of men employed, and increase your own means of comfort and improvement.

STUDY THE CONDITIONS.

Fourth—The unions should adapt their demands to the conditions of a particular business.

In order to determine how large a part of these earnings of any business you can properly demand, it is essential that your representatives should understand the conditions of the business.

It is not sufficient that you should make a demand and have that demand assented to or refused. Your representatives must be able to understand the needs and the possibilities of the business you are engaged in.

John Mitchell was successful in the anthracite strike because he understood the conditions of the businesses of the employers and they did not understand the workingman's side of the question.

Your representatives must understand not merely the general line of the business, but the possibilities and the necessities of the particular business in which your demands are to be applied. Concerns engaged in the same line of business in one part of the country and in another, or even in the same community, have varying possibilities and necessities, and your demands must be tempered by those possibilities and necessities.

The possibilities of employers' businesses vary like the employes' capacities. If you attempt to apply rigidly a uniform rule to all you may kill the goose that lays the egg; and except in extreme cases the goose must be kept alive whether the egg be golden or not.

Don't assume that the interests of employer and employe are necessarily hostile—that what is good for one is necessarily bad for the other. The opposite is more apt to be the case. While they have different interests, they are likely to prosper or to suffer together. Like in the case of dealer and customer, co-operation and a mutual regard for the other's rights are essential to continued success.

This is the lesson unions should teach.

There is no trade union that has a higher average of intelligence or whose management is marked by a higher degree of business sagacity and forethought than the typographical. It never forgets that prosperity in the printing business can only be assured by conditions that justify good wages. In the matter of contracts, a typographical union keeps faith with the employing party. The rules are carefully drawn to prevent hasty and ill-considered strikes. The Socialistic element is kept in safe subordination.—*Washington Post.*

Armies are necessary evils, but for my part I prefer a procession of trades-unionists to the marching by of armed regiments and the simple and homely garb of a worker to the tawdry trappings of men of war. I respect a man who honorably fulfills his calling as a soldier, but he is no better in my eyes than the man who honestly labors in other and more peaceful vocations.—*London Truth.*

A review of the past twenty years goes to show that the labor problem, like the poor, is always with us. It is a chronic condition. It is the result of the eternal struggle of man to better his condition.—*Wall Street Journal.*

PROFIT-SHARING, INSURANCE, PENSIONS.

The Working of a Successful Plan to Promote Thrift and Relieve Distress Explained for the Information of Employers.

IN the article that follows, Francis L. Robbins, President of the Pittsburg Coal Company, the largest corporation of its kind in the world, describes and explains the plan of profit-sharing, insurance and pensions, as carried out through its Employes' Association. Mr. Robbins presents this plan for the information of other employers, after the experience of more than four years has demonstrated its practical success from the points of view of both the company and the wage-earners. His treatment of the subject reflects the aid that a willing employer may receive from the suggestions of an assistant especially devoted to the development of such a plan.

J. B. L. Hornberger, Comptroller of the company, and president of the Employes' Association, to whom President Robbins gives credit for originating and extending the plan, contributes these interesting observations:

"Our plan had in part its origin in the knowledge that the average wage-earner does not think it worth while to save, because he cannot save much; but we made it as simple and easy as possible for him to save. We organized our work with a view to encouraging even the earners of the lowest wages to save something. The plan operates exactly like a building association, only in our case the investment of the money is altogether in the Pittsburg Coal Company's preferred stock.

"The Employes' Association has a double purpose: To encourage the men to save money, and that might be called the humane side of it; and to get them to become stockholders of the company, and that might be termed the practical side, since when they serve the interests of the company, as stockholders, they serve themselves.

"Many of the wage-earners have taken stock. They are as yet a comparatively small percentage of the whole; but at this time there are nearly 2,000 out of about 50,000 employes who are becoming stockholders. Since September there has been a very marked increase in the purchase of the stock.

"A large percentage of the employes are foreigners, cannot speak English, and are suspicious of the company, and these do not understand our methods and fail to appreciate the spirit of the organization that is intending to help them. They are very prone to give their earnings to some agent of a foreign bank, or to some self-styled banker, such as a grocer, who takes their money and promises them a good rate of interest. In many cases they make good, and in many cases they make away with the deposits. These defaults have made the men suspicious, and have made it more difficult for us to gain their confidence. Some of them carry their money on their persons. I remember one man who took off a belt he had been wearing next his skin, and he had $800. His wages probably averaged $500 or $600 a year.

"We had, also, to encounter the suspicion caused by the business failure in the past of some small employers, causing the loss of savings entrusted to them by wage-earners. But we were aided here by the size and solidity of our corporation."

PLAN FOR SELF-HELP AMONG EMPLOYES.

By Francis L. Robbins,
President of the Pittsburg Coal Company.

The plan of profit-sharing, benefits and pensions that is carried out through the Pittsburg Coal Company Employes' Association is in harmony with a wide recognition of the necessity of adjusting social relations to new conditions created by modern industrial development. This plan represents a broad spirit of comradeship and affects many thousands of employes. It is also noteworthy, because after four years it has long passed beyond the experimental stage, and is a thoroughly demonstrated practical success. This demonstrated success is important to students of industrial providence, since the company is the largest producer of coal in the United States. The employes of all kinds number 50,000, and are to be found from the mouth of the Mississippi to every port on the Great Lakes and in the mines of many intervening States.

FRANCIS L. ROBBINS,
President, Pittsburg Coal Company.

The Pittsburg Coal Company is an example of the present tendency to concentrate business under the control and management of large corporations. Its plan of profit-sharing, employes' accident insurance and benefits, has proved a practical and satisfactory solution of a serious problem that arises out of the tendency to concentration. In the new order of things, the percentage of managers and operatives, whose capital, as well as their brains and hands, is employed in a given business, is largely reduced; and there is a greater increase in the percentage of those whose only interest in the business is the daily, weekly, or monthly wage earnings. The new order, without some such factor as our Employes' Association, means eventually a wider separation between the employer and the employe, and a corresponding indifference on the part of the employe to the interests of the employer, while the latter may lose that paternal interest in the welfare of the wage-earner that existed under the old regime, when individual contact was common. It was with the purpose of preserving this interest and to encourage the employes in habits of sobriety and thrift, as well as of assisting them in emergencies and old age, and of perpetuating under the new order the incalculable benefits of service by loyal and disinterested employes, that the plan here described was put into operation in the latter part of 1900. I have found this plan most available to put into practical operation a broad and generous policy toward the great body of the company's employes. It is my hope to see its beneficial results, if not its exact form of operation, extended to the yet larger number of employers and employed that are represented in the Joint Interstate Convention of miners and operators, which annually works out and agrees upon the wage scale and the conditions under which more than half a million mine workers and others dig and ship the bituminous output of Western Pennsylvania, Ohio, Indiana, and Illinois.

The plan is in accordance with the injunction of the greatest of all leaders of men: "Whatsoever ye would that men should do to you, do ye even so to them."

The operation of the Association proceeds under two heads—first, investment; second, insurance and pensions.

The Pittsburg Coal Company Employes' Association makes contracts with employes to sell them preferred stock of the company at cost, the stock being bought on the open market by the officers at such times as the funds of the Association and the condition of the market may warrant. Employes pay for this stock at the rate of $1.00 per month per share. They have the privilege of withdrawing from their contracts at any time upon thirty days' notice, and when such withdrawals are made employes receive back the full amount of their payments, together with interest at the rate of 5 per cent. per annum. A new series of stock purchase contracts begins at the first of each month.

Since December 1, 1900, therefore, there have been some fifty series of contracts, the first nine of which matured at intervals of one month beginning on May 1, 1904. The dividends paid on stock held by the Association to fill its contracts with employes are divided pro rata among the several series. The net earnings thus accumulated by the Association amounted, up to Jan. 31st, 1905, to $129,240.20; and the portion of these earnings falling to the series which have matured was sufficient to net a return to the employes holding those series, based upon the market value of the preferred stock, of more than 20 per cent. per annum on their monthly payments. The Association has purchased a sufficient quantity of stock at the low prices then prevailing to enable it to close out the next ten or twelve series of contracts on about the same basis as those which have already matured. The first nine series of contracts embrace 2,460 shares, leaving in force 2,280 contracts, covering 17,222 shares.

While it is true that a large percentage of the Association's contracts are with heads of departments, superintendents, clerks and the more intelligent class of employes in the general offices, at the mines and the various docks and selling agencies of the company on the Great Lakes in the West and Northwest, and in the Hocking district of Ohio, yet it is a significant and encouraging fact that the percentage of purchasers among the miners and day laborers at the company's mines and shops is steadily increasing. Not a few of these latter, who never before accumulated any savings, are now taking upon themselves the dignity and bearing of men who have a financial interest in the company's operation; an element of conservatism and fairness, and a disposition to repress radicalism and lawlessness, are becoming more and more manifest among the men.

The great fall in stock values which began last year and affected Pittsburg Coal Company stocks along with others, together with the general business depression of the first months of the year 1904, which resulted in closing down a number of the company's mines and curtailing very materially the company's gross output, checked the growth of the Association. With the great improvement in the company's business, however, incident to the opening of lake navigation and the general resumption of operations at the mines early in June, the number of stock purchase contracts began to increase and is increasing daily. It is confidently expected that the operations of the Employes' Association will eventually place a large portion of the company's preferred stock in the hands of the people who are digging, handling and selling the company's coal, building its tipples, cars and docks, and keeping its accounts.

Up to this time the company's insurance and pension benefits accrue only to workers in its mines. These benefits are conducted through branch lodges of the Employes' Association. These lodges are organized at practically all mines of the main company, and their organization is rapidly extending to mines of the subsidiary companies, such as the Monongahela River Consolidated Coal & Coke Company, the New York and Cleveland Gas Coal Company, Mansfield Coal & Coke Company, and the New Pittsburg Coal Company, operating in the Hocking district of Ohio. The organization of a lodge is voluntary at each mine, but no lodge is organized until the majority of the operatives at the mine agree to be governed by the general by-laws adopted at a convention of the employes, at which each of the company's mines was represented by a delegate selected by the men. One of the features of these by-laws is that every employe at the mine is to be protected by the benefits and pay dues. Each lodge is governed by an executive committee of three, selected by the men, and this committee passes upon all claims for benefits and issues all warrants. The treasurer of the Pittsburg Coal Company Employes' Association, under the by-laws, is elected treasurer of each of the lodges; all disbursements, therefore, are made from the company's general offices by the treasurer of the Employes' Association.

INSURANCE DUES AND BENEFITS.

The dues paid by the men are at the rate of 40 cents per month per man; the benefits are graded into seven classes: First, for a fatal accident while at work, $150, of which the company directly contributes one-half; second, death of an employe through natural causes, $100, paid altogether by the men; third, death of an employe's wife or father or mother, if the employe is the sole support in such cases, funeral fund of $75, paid altogether by the men; fourth, death of an employe's child over two and under twelve years, a funeral fund of $25, paid altogether by the men; fifth, non-fatal accident of a serious nature, benefits $10 per week, one-half paid directly by the company; sixth, non-fatal accident of a less serious nature, benefits $7.50 per week, one-third paid directly by the company; seventh, minor accidents, benefits $5 per week, paid altogether by the men.

The conduct of the relief department employs a manager (J. E. McDonald, secretary and treasurer of the Association), one staff surgeon, one adjuster of claims, three bookkeepers, one stenographer, and clerical service, and includes payment for postage, etc., etc., at all mines, shops and agencies.

It should be specially noted that all expenses of the Employes' Association are paid by the company.

START AND GROWTH OF PENSION FUND.

The pension fund had its start in a contribution of $10,000 by the company. Its growth and maintenance are provided for by monthly portions of 2 cents per man of the 40 cents dues paid by the men, to which is aded 1 cent per month per man paid by the company. This accumulating fund is invested in the preferred stock of the company and under the by-laws is to remain intact and grow for a period of ten years; at the end of that time the principal and earnings of the fund in excess of $100,000 may be used in the payment of pensions to operatives of the company who have paid into the fund continuously for a period of ten years, and who, through old age, accident or sickness, are not able to earn a livelihood.

MANY THOUSANDS PROTECTED AND AIDED.

There are at this time about 20,000 employes paying dues into the various lodges of the Association. A large percentage of these are married men with families. If an average of two is allowed for each man (a wife and one child, a father and mother and sister), it will be seen that 60,000 people in the Pittsburg district are protected and helped in emergencies by the relief department of the Employes' Association. The benefits paid up to and including January 31st, 1905, were $188,891.54, and there had been accumulated in the pension fund on the same date $32,671.87.

APPROVAL SUCCEEDS LOCAL OPPOSITION.

The organization of these lodges met with resistance at first from radical elements in certain communities, but this opposition has all melted away and evidences are not wanting of a growing appreciation of the wise and beneficent measures taken by the company to minister to the welfare of its employes.

The *United Mine Workers' Journal*, the official paper of the largest body of organized labor in the world, after analyzing the last annual report of the Employes' Association, said editorially:

> These figures tell clearer than words what Messrs. Robbins, Hornberger and Jones are doing to relieve the "labor question" of its rancor and turmoil. Read the report, consider the purpose and intent of the Pittsburg Association, and you can clearly see the pitiable meanness, the whole grotesque humbug lurking under the term Parryism. There is a great corporation, the largest of its kind in the world, officered by men who, in the multitude of perplexing duties, have hearts and minds for the men who toil for them. The sordid side of wealth has not appealed to these great business men. The merciless struggle for dividends has not deadened their manhood or their sense of equity and justice. These shares are not froth and bubbles on an ocean of watered stock. Behind them stands $75,000,000 of tangible property, managed by men of brains and integrity, whose fortunes are linked with the miner-shareholder. Then behold the Death and Accident Association, in all of its beneficence, its mercies and goodness. The 19,250 men who contribute to its funds have an anchor against the surges of trouble's seas. Hurt in the mines? You are not left to the mercies of charity. You do not have to grovel and cringe for necessaries or medical attention. Why? Because the Pittsburg Coal Company inaugurated a system backed it with its dollars, officered it with men of commanding ability, and helped you erect a barrier against want and woe in the time of death or disaster. It is such things as these that rob the anarchists and the Parryites of their power to poison the minds of workingmen against their employers and cause them to stand as a bulwark against the assaults of the demagogues.
>
> It also teaches, practically, how by thrift and industry the workingmen themselves may easily work for themselves instead of others rather than by chasing rainbows and chimeras. It is a wholesome object lesson against the ravings and industrial insanities far too prevalent at present.

It is obvious, of course, that the benefits of the company are indirect at the best, but, nevertheless, the management is thoroughly of the opinion that the plan has a definite value for the company, and this is understood clearly by the men.

Patrick Dolan, President, and William Dodds, Secretary and Treasurer of District No. 5, United Mine Workers of America, have both heartily approved the plan from the standpoint of the employes. That they were not particularly favorable to the plan at its inception makes their commendation of especial interest and effectiveness. Secretary Dodds, who was associated with John Mitchell, President of the United Mine Workers of America, in attending several international meetings of labor representatives in Europe last year, authorizes this statement:

> In my opinion the Pittsburg Coal Company, through the opportunity for their employes to become partners in the business and share in the profits, is to be commended to all large corporations in the United States, and there is no doubt in my mind that in the future the employes of this country will better understand the interests that can best be served by the co-operative policy embodied in the profit-sharing through the stock held by the employes.
>
> The fund which the Pittsburg Coal Company has established amongst their employes, to take care of them and their families in case of sickness or accident, is certainly to be commended and encouraged, and employers would do well to put themselves in touch with the Pittsburg Coal Company and secure information through the by-laws and have similar institutions established in their different industries, and I certainly appreciate the efforts of the officers of the company who have been instrumental in giving opportunities and protection to their employes, who are in a large measure unable to take care of themselves in case of accident and death.

It is important to note that, in the face of original opposition by some of the men at the mines to this plan of profit-sharing, benefits and pensions, the management of the company persevered. Other employers who undertake welfare work of this description may also encounter at the beginning suspicion and even aspersion of their motives. I would advise them also to persevere. Any sincere effort for good will bear fruit somewhere, sometime. Sooner or later the persistent showing of humane, sympathetic interest will evoke a response that will promote industrial peace and prove for the mutual advantage of both employers and employes.

WHY EMPLOYES OBJECT TO RAILROAD RELIEF DEPARTMENTS.

By E. E. CLARK.

Grand Chief Conductor, Order of Railway Conductors.

In his paper, "Railway Provident Institutions," which appeared in your issues of November, 1904, and February, 1905, Mr. M. Riebenack presents comprehensively the "provident effort in which the railways of the United States are interested on account of their employes."

All large employers of men have, and should have, an interest in the health, welfare and contentment of their employes. It is not too much to say that the railways are in the front rank of employers in this regard. I am not one of those who are unable to see anything good in what the employer does or wants. Human nature is human nature, however, and whether or not it be the impelling motive there is a strong motive of self interest in or behind every move made by an employing corporation which involves the expenditure of the corporation's funds.

It is unfortunate that improvidence is so general a trait of human nature. Seemingly the average person believes in literally applying the scriptural injunction to give no thought to the morrow. There are altogether too many men who are content, if left to their own inclinations, to continue in most hazardous employment and to grow old knowing, if they ever think of it, that it is merely a question of time when they or their families, or both, will be dependent upon charity. And so, influences and education which encourage and teach reasonable thrift and providence must work good to present and future generations.

Self respecting, steady, reliable and thrifty employes are greatly to be desired by a railway company. The man who spends his hours off duty in procuring full amount of necessary sleep and in reputable amusements and reading is a more reliable and efficient and valuable employe than if his habits were of a more questionable nature. He is less apt to make mistakes; is less likely to antagonize patrons; less apt to be injured himself and he sets a good example for his fellows. It is, therefore, a good investment from a purely business standpoint for the employing company to assist in affording opportunity for employes to so occupy their time by contributing to reading rooms, libraries, etc. The services of an intelligent employe are always of more value and prove most economical in the long run.

The railway employes are quasi public servants. Those employed on trains face dangers more appalling than the average person dreams of. A President of the United States, in recommending to Congress legislation intended to afford them more safety in their employment, called attention to the fact that the men in service on the freight trains of the country were in greater danger of being killed or injured in the discharge of their duties than were the average soldiers in time of war. The latest official records show that in the year ending June 30, 1903, one in every 123 of them was killed and one in every 10 was injured, and this record is not materially different from the average of the ten years preceding it.

I do not wish to belittle or underestimate the spirit which has led some railway companies to provide pensions for employes who have worn themselves out in their service. No occupation is so exacting as railroading. No workmen have such irregular hours and none, with the possible exception of sailors, are obliged to expose themselves to the extremes of weather to the same degree. If a man lives to be sixty-five or seventy years old in such work and has been a faithful employe, as he must have been, he has certainly earned a pension and it should be viewed more in the light of according something which is his due than as granting him some special consideration in the form of a gratuity. And when we consider the public character of the corporation and the growing interest in its affairs by the general government it does not require a very wild stretch of imagination to imagine a time when such care of worn out employes as is given through pension funds will be imposed by legislative requirement.

Any reasonable assistance which the employing company can render or any fair inducement which it may offer in the direction of thrift and saving on part of employes is good work in a good cause.

Hospital departments have been maintained, to the support of which employes have been required to contribute, with benefit to both employes and employing companies. This has been especially true in the less thickly populated regions of the far West. Except in isolated cases where someone charged with management failed to inspire or to hold the confidence of the employes, they have contributed to this department willingly and cheerfully.

Stock-sharing plans have behind them the theory and belief that if an employe owns even a small interest in the property he will be a better and more valuable employe who will take greater interest and care in the discharge of his duties. This is a rational theory and it would be a splendid thing if the employes of every railway owned enough of its stock to insure against having the property managed and operated with an eye principally to the stock market.

Mr. Riebenack says that there are nine "roads" which conduct purely Relief Departments, representing 31,000 miles of railway. I wish he had named the "roads" to which he referred. Systems of railway are made up of several "roads," each having [illegible] porate name, but when we speak of the Penn[illegible] railway the average person understands that w[illegible] of the system. It is well known that the [illegible] vania, the Baltimore and Ohio and the Bur[illegible] systems conduct relief departments. The mileage of the Pennsylvania system, covered by the relief department, as given by Mr. Riebenack, is 10,271 miles. The mileage of the Baltimore and Ohio system, taken from official guide, is 4,410 miles, and that of the Burlington system, taken from the same authority, is 8,442 miles. We, therefore, have 23,123 of the 31,000 miles accounted for in these three systems, and it would hardly be fair in discussing such a subject to bewilder the average reader with distinctions in technical names of roads which for all purposes in which the public are interested lost their identity when they became part of the system.

In a little further analysis of Mr. Riebenack's figures we find that he gives the total number of the employes of the "nine roads" as 318,000, and that 159,704 of them, or just about half, are on the Pennsylvania system.

Information is not at hand as to the date upon which the Baltimore and Ohio relief department was established. It was, however, at a considerably earlier date than that on which the Pennsylvania system instituted its relief department, viz., February, 1886. The Burlington relief department was organized about 1887. It will thus be seen that the establishment of such departments is not appreciably on the increase and that they are not maintained by many railway systems. It is well known that in some instances railway companies have proposed to their employes the institution of such departments and that the employes have promptly and emphatically negatived the proposal. It should be here remarked that in many others of the lines of provident effort referred to by Mr. Riebenack railway companies are receiving cordial support from their employes in their general and increasing interest and efforts in those directions.

OBJECTIONS RAISED BY EMPLOYES.

And now we come to the question of why the employes object to relief departments. There are two principal objections. One is that, despite the fact that the word "voluntary' is included in the official name of the department; despite the fact that it is emphasized and italicised; despite the fact that a United States statute prohibits compulsory membership on part of employes, or discrimination against applicants for employment, because of their unwillingness to join such department, the employes of the companies which conduct such departments in speaking where they are not afraid to speak plainly generally express the conviction that in so far as an employe who is a member of the department is concerned, he feels that if he should withdraw from it he would incur the displeasure of his employers, and that, when the opportunity offered, a fellow employe who retained membership in the department would be given preference over him, and that so far as applicants for employment are concerned, the man who is not ready and willing to join the relief department, is not needed and does not secure employment. In reply to inquiry as to how the practice followed affected applicants for employment, an old and reliable employe of one of these companies recently said: "An applicant for employment is required to fill out an application for employment, which also contains application for membership in the relief department. He then goes to the examining physician, who is also the physician for the relief department, and if he is accepted as an employe he at the same time becomes a member of the relief department." It would be interesting to know how many men who did not become members of the relief department have been given employment within the past five years by the several important systems of road that conduct such departments.

If membership in the relief department carried with it nothing more than the requirement that certain reasonable sums be paid periodically as a condition of being entitled to certain specified sick, disability or death benefits, the objections entertained by the employes would not be so strong or so well founded. If that were all that the department undertook to do the men would feel that in paying their contributions they were providing for their fellows as well as for themselves and were removing the necessity for circulation of subscription papers for the purpose of relieving or burying unfortunate fellow employes.

If the relief department simply undertook to require men, through mutual or co-operative means, to provide some financial assistance for themselves and their families in the hour of sickness or injury or death and did not attach conditions to the acceptance of the benefit, for which the employe has, in fact, paid full or practically full value, which conditions operate wholly in the interests of the employing company and against the injured employe, there would not be such general distrust of, and opposition to, them on part of the employes. Neither would there be such broad and justifiable ground for criticism of the relief departments as now presents itself.

The applicant for membership in a relief department is required to execute a contract that, in the [illegible] of his being injured in the performance of his [illegible] and of his accepting the benefits provided in the department for such cases, he thereby releases the employing corporation from all liability under the statutory or common law. This means that if a member of the department is injured through neglect of the company or of its agents and, believing that no permanent disability is to ensue, he accepts the first month's benefits provided by the relief department and tendered by the company, and, later, finds that he is disabled for life or his death ensues, all efforts to recover damages from the company are frustrated by the company pleading the contract which the employe signed when becoming a member of the relief department.

Instances of this kind have not been rare and a sufficient number of them, accompanied by distressing conditions and surrounded by facts which clearly demonstrated the injustice involved, occurred in the State of Iowa to lead the Legislature to place upon the statute books of that State a law which specifically provides that such contract is and shall be null and void.

The fact that the company insists upon such a contract is sufficient evidence that the relief thus afforded to it from legal liability is one of the strongest reasons for its interest in the relief department. The fact that the department is thus made a shield against liability which would otherwise attach to the company leads one's thoughts away from the idea that the company's interest is purely philanthropic.

Mr. Riebenack furnishes figures which show that in the eighteen years of the existence of the Pennsylvania system's relief department the company has contributed to it the sum of $2,544,348.11, and that the cost of management has been $1,815,641.54. The company has, therefore, contributed $728,706.57 more than the cost of management. And the cost of management is entirely within the control of the company.

But if we dismiss from consideration the cost of management we find that in eighteen years the Pennsylvania system, containing 10,271 miles of railway covered by its relief department, on which are employed 159,704 men, has paid as its contribution to this fund—and this includes the purchase of relief from legal liability as above mentioned—$2,544,348.11, or a fraction over $15.93 for each employe. Considerably less than one dollar per year per employe. I quote figures for the Pennsylvania system because they are the ones at hand, having been furnished by Mr. Riebenack.

Mr. Riebenack argues that the contract under discussion is a legal and voluntary agreement. Its legality is not here questioned. It has been sustained by numerous courts. It was found necessary in Iowa to enact legislation clearly making it illegal. The contract is voluntary in this: That the employe and the seeker for employment sign the agreement believing that if they do not do so they will have to go elsewhere for employment.

All men who work for railways are not fully informed as to their legal rights. Most railway employes find it difficult to lay up much against the rainy day and hence find it almost absolutely necessary to accept the assistance which the relief department provides. The railway employes of the country generally object strongly to relief departments being made agencies through which the corporations evade liabilities which the law places upon them and which they should not be permitted to thus escape.

THE HOMESTEAD STRIKE RECALLED.

Some Inside History Showing Andrew Carnegie's Favorable Attitude Toward Conference.

THE memorable address of Andrew Carnegie at the annual dinner of the National Civic Federation having revived an interest in the Homestead strike, our attention has recently been called to an article written by Edward W. Bemis, at one time Professor of Political Economy in the University of Chicago and now head of the Water Department in Cleveland, in the administration of Mayor Tom Johnson. This article appeared in the *Journal of Political Economy*, published by the University of Chicago, for June, 1894, and dealt with the causes leading up to the Homestead strike, and the history of its conduct and conclusion, based upon a thorough personal investigation by Professor Bemis. The extract from that article which follows recalls a chapter of the strike not generally understood:

Only once in twenty-six years of personal management has Mr. Carnegie, in a single one of his works, had any stoppage from strike or lock-out, but when difficulties were likely to arise, he had shown a disposition to "sit down and wait" till an agreement could be reached rather than to call in new men.[1]

1 Note—In 1886, he wrote in the *Forum*: "I would have the public give due consideration to the terrible temptation to which the workingman on a strike is sometimes subjected. To expect that one dependent on his daily wage for the necessaries of life will stand by peaceably and see a new man employed in his stead, is to expect much. This poor man may have a wife and children dependent upon his labor. Whether medicine for a sick child, or even nourishing food for a delicate wife, is procurable, depends upon his steady employment. In all but a very few departments of labor, it is unnecessary and, I think, improper to subject men to such an ordeal. In the case of railways, and a few other employments, it is, of course, essential for the public wants that no interruption occur, and in such case, substitutes must be employed; but the employer of labor will find it much more to his interest, wherever possible, to allow his works to remain idle, and await the result of a dispute, than to employ the class of men that can be induced to take the place of other men who have stopped work. Neither the best men as men, nor the best men as workers, are thus to be obtained. There is an unwritten law among the best workmen, "Thou shalt not take thy neighbor's job." No wise employer will lightly lose his old employes. Length of service counts for much in many ways. Calling upon strange men should be the last resort.

* * * In this connection there are certain hitherto unpublished facts to be taken into account. On the first Sunday (July 17th) following the arrival of the militia at Homestead, two gentlemen, prominent in labor circles, came to Homestead and urged Mr. O'Donnell, chairman of the Advisory Committee, to go to New York and secure, if possible, the intercession of some prominent man, for the purpose of inducing Mr. Carnegie to order Mr. Frick to re-open conference with the men. On the unanimous vote of the Advisory Committee, Mr. O'Donnell set out. On reaching New York and consulting with a few labor leaders it was decided to approach Mr. Whitelaw Reid, who, as candidate for the vice-presidency on the Republican ticket, was assumed to be interested in maintaining peace in a tariff-aided industry. In the office of one of the editors of the New York *Tribune* the letter given in the note below was dictated by Mr. O'Donnell, but dated from Homestead and dated back a couple of days.[2]

2 Note. Homestead, Penn., July 16, 1892.

Hon. Whitelaw Reid,
New York N. Y.

Dear Sir: I address you in behalf of the 12,000 inhabitants of Homestead, Pennsylvania. In their name I ask that you interest yourself in the unfortunate controversy still pending between them and the Carnegie Steel Company by whom the majority of the adult population of the town is employed.

In presenting this matter to you, I have no desire to dwell upon the merits or demerits of the conflict. I am looking toward the future, not the past. With the past I assume you are fairly well informed; sufficiently well, at all events, to make it unnecessary for me to supplement your knowledge at this time. It would be foreign to my purpose to do so. I simply therefore lay before you the situation as it exists to-day.

A borough, not only one of the most prosperous in Pennsylvania, but in the entire Union, whose population represents to the highest degree the thrift, industry, intelligence and morality—in short, the best tendencies of the American people, is at present practically under martial law. The entire State militia, numbering 8,000 or more, are in control of the place at an expense to the commonwealth of $22,000 a day. The spirit of peace and progress has been supplanted by one of intense bitterness and discontent. It is in the interests of no one that this state of affairs should continue; that it should not, there is but one, and only one, course to pursue. I say only one, and I speak advisedly. That course is an honorable settlement on the lines that I shall presently indicate.

But before submitting my proposition permit me to say a word in reference to the course of procedure which appears to be in the minds of the Carnegie Company. I mean their express determination to put non-union men at work in the places of our people by the aid of the State authorities. I am not going to discuss the question of the right of the company to do so. I simply want to point out the practical effect of that action, which in my judgment may be briefly summed up in the statement that it will precipitate an unending internecine strife at Homestead. It must be borne in mind that a majority of the present employes own their own homes. All their interests center there, and they will never surrender them without the most determined effort, and one that will be made regardless of all that can be said or done to the contrary. In brief, owing to the peculiar conditions of this strike which I have indicated here, the trouble will, in my judgment, only begin in earnest when the mills are set going by the men who will take the places of the old employes.

I am sure that you agree with me in saying that it is not desirable to have this come to pass. It is not desirable that the present situation should continue, nor is it desirable that the men who have by years of patient toil acquired a little homestead should be cut off from their employment if it can be prevented in any honorable way. It can be prevented easily and without the sacrifice of honor or dignity upon either side. How shall it be done? Simply let the Carnegie Company recognize the Amalgamated Association by re-opening the conference doors, and I have no hesitation in saying that when that is done the end of the strife is at hand. I am warranted in saying that there is no disposition on the part of the employes to stand upon a question of scale, or wages, or hours, or anything else. The spirit that dominates them is conciliatory in the extreme, for they deplore the recent sad occurrence as much as any other class of people in the whole country. I assure you that they will do all in their power to bring about a re-establishment of harmonious relations.

I ask you to interest yourself in this matter because I believe you are in a position to render more effective service than, perhaps, any other man in this country. I do not think that it is necessary for me to dwell upon this point, nor state the reasons why this is true. That it is true is sufficiently clear to my mind to cause me to ask you to do what you can in every honorable way to bring about an amicable settlement.

My appeal is not in the name of any political party, nor in the name of organized labor, but for the sake of the men, women and little children that make up our present distressed community.

Sincerely and respectfully yours,
HUGH O'DONNELL.

Mr. O'Donnell states, as did President Weihe, on July 6th, that there was "no disposition on the part of his employes to stand upon a question of scale, or wages, or hours, or anything else." All that was wanted was a "re-opening of the conference doors."[3]

3 Note—The information here given on this point is derived not only from Mr. O'Donnell, but also from very high and absolutely reliable authority, entirely disconnected with the Carnegie Company or with organized labor. Inquiries addressed to the Carnegie Company have brought no reply.

Mr. O'Donnell, having been charged by the Carnegie officials with murder in connection with the events of July 6th, hastened back to Homestead on the promise that Mr. Reid would cable Mr. Carnegie. Mr. O'Donnell surrendered to the authorities and was held in prison five days. Then (July 25th) he was released on $10,000 bail. Meantime Mr. Reid, in response to Mr. O'Donnell's letter cited above, had applied to Mr. Frick for Mr. Carnegie's address in order to telegraph him—Mr. Carnegie being at that time absent in Scotland and his address not being known to any one in this country except his business associates. Mr. Frick refused to give the address; whereupon Mr. Reid obtained it from our Consul General in London, John C. New, and then cabled Mr. Carnegie, urging a speedy and amicable settlement. An answer was received by cable from Mr. Carnegie in which he accepted the terms proposed by Mr. O'Donnell and urged that Mr. Frick be seen immediately with a view to effecting the settlement.[4]

4 Note—Copies of these cablegrams cannot now be obtained.

By this time the New York anarchist, Alexander Berkman, without the knowledge or recognition of the strikers, had made his attempt on Mr. Frick's life (July 23), so that when the gentleman who undertook the mission of reconciliation reached Mr. Frick he found him confined to his bed with the injuries he had sustained. My informant (whose name is withheld) goes on to say: "Mr. Frick was obdurate. He refused to consider the matter at all, denounced the strikers as assassins and declared that if Carnegie came in person, in company with President Harrison and the entire cabinet, he would not settle the strike."[5]

5 Note—My informant adds: "There is a well-defined rumor that since Mr. Carnegie's return he has written Mr. Reid, expressing regret that Mr. Frick did not agree to O'Donnell's proposition as forwarded to Mr. Reid.

Mr. O'Donnell writes: "Thus it would seem that the bullet from Berkman's pistol, failing in its foul intent, went straight through the heart of the Homestead strike."[6] Disclaiming the idea of having intended to make political capital out of the New York trip, he asserts the purity of his motives.[7]

6 Note—Mr. Frick's previous refusal, July 7th, to confer with President Weihe and the strikers, as well as his refusal to give Mr. Carnegie's address to the editors of the New York *Tribune*, throws some doubt on the probability of Mr. Carnegie's order being followed, even if Berkman had not made his attempt.

7 Note—He says, in a letter written in February, 1894: "Believe me, I was actuated with but one desire, and that was the happy termination of our troubles, and to have restored to our own prosperous little borough a peace and repose that had formerly blessed its humble homes. Mine has been the sacrifice. To-day, in reward for my efforts, I am misunderstood and maligned by the unthinking crowd—a modern Ishmael doomed to wander in the desert of ingratitude."

THE VOICE OF THE PRESS DECLARES FOR INDUSTRIAL PEACE.

EDITORIAL APPROVAL OF THE AIMS AND WORK OF THE NATIONAL CIVIC FEDERATION FROM MANY VARIED SOURCES.

A METHODIST EDITOR'S COMMENDATION.

Rev. Dr. James M. Buckley, in the Christian Advocate.

Mr. Gompers presided and made an appropriate speech. He is a very slow speaker, but clear and forcible. Mr. Carnegie was present in the afternoon and was to have been present in the evening, but found himself too weary to attend. But he sent a most pertinent address, in which he stated that industrial peace reigns in six-sevenths of the industrial world. He recommended employers to keep their old men; declared that when the employer succeeds in running the works with new men his victory is really a defeat. He believes employers should make it an invariable rule never to employ new men in case of a strike, but to wait patiently for the old men.

After Mr. Carnegie's address Archbishop Ireland was called upon. We had long desired to have an opportunity of hearing the archbishop, as his reputation for fervid oratory is world-wide. Long ago in France he delivered an address in the French language so interesting as to be rapturously applauded, not alone for what he said, but for the admirable French in which he spoke it. As we sat near him the opportunity was afforded of asking him something of how he acquired his mastery of the French tongue. He responded that he spent eight years of his youthful life in that country. In conversation he is very attractive and animated. His address was a genuine oration of the old type, built upon two pillars—fellow Americans and fellow workers. All the problems could be solved by intelligence and sympathy for one another. One passage was directed against those who endeavor to break down the social structure.

Next came August Belmont, who testified to the efficacy of face-to-face conferences with honorable employes. He affirmed that it is a practical method of reaching a common understanding, and from his own experience testified that conferences over controverted points were followed by a better understanding and an harmonious agreement in the conduct of a great public service corporation. John Mitchell made a pleasing speech, in which he declared that he had not promoted strikes for the sake of strikes, and never would. James Kilbourne, of Ohio, read a very carefully prepared address. Mr. P. H. Morrissey, of the Railroad Trainmen, had only a little previous notice, but he made such a rational, calm, and well expressed speech as to secure universal applause. Mr. Oscar S. Straus gave a full statement of the number of labor disputes which had been settled by the Federation during the past year.

The National Civic Federation seems to us an admirable institution, for it tends to substitute calm discussion for acrimonious controversy. We are also convinced that the only thing in the way of "industrial peace with honor and liberty" is the attempt to prevent non-union men from working, which is equivalent to preventing employers from securing work unless labor unions consent to it. One of the speakers admitted that his union went upon the principle of making no trouble with non-union men who worked for union wages. We had framed a favorable estimate of the motives of those who established the National Civic Federation, and have appreciated everything good that we could trace to it in the struggles of the last few years. Our estimate of it was greatly enhanced by the proceedings at this dinner.

BRIDGING THE CHASM.

Address by John T. Wilson, Grand President International Brotherhood of Maintenance of Way Employes.

A potent factor in the partial elimination of strikes and lockouts during the past few years has been the National Civic Federation, which is endeavoring to substitute conciliation and arbitration in lieu of the wasteful and barbarous strike and lockout so frequently resorted to in the recent past as a result of disputes between employers and employes. The Federation is composed in equal numbers of representatives of employers of labor, representatives of employes and representatives of that large public interest which unjustly bears the brunt of each industrial conflict. Especially worthy of mention in this connection is the efforts made by the Monthly Review of the National Civic Federation to bridge the chasm which divides the classes by giving each interest an impartial hearing through the columns of the Review, thus allowing the public to judge of the reasonableness of each contention from the facts and the arguments submitted, rather than by appealing to class prejudices and arousing class hatreds, and thus widening the gulf between the representatives of capital and the representatives of labor.

AN INDUSTRIOUS EXECUTIVE.

Boston Herald.

Mr. August Belmont is getting some very handsome compliments, apropos of his unanimous and enthusiastic election to the head of the National Civic Federation. The New York Times, for instance, calls him a workingman of great industry, adding that the wage earner who had to carry a tithe of the cares and responsibilities of this organizer and manager of great enterprises would feel himself burdened beyond his strength. Mr. Belmont's sympathy with honest toil may be assumed from the fact that he earns his rest, when he has it, by the most systematic devotion to business. He is now one of the largest employers of labor in New York, and he gets on amicably with all his employes.

GOOD WILL THE WAY TO CONCORD.

Chicago Record-Herald.

Strikes and lockouts are costly, uneconomic, wasteful, and American capital and labor are too sensible and practical to prefer them to the pleasant ways of confidence and peace. Hence, as President Roosevelt said in his letter to Mr. Gompers, "The highest aim of all should be the establishment on an ever closer basis of mutual respect and friendship of the relations between employers and workmen."

Where the proper disposition is wanting, where distrust and suspicion and bitterness prevail, no mere machinery of arbitration will insure industrial tranquility. Where there is what a great philosopher has called the highest product of human development, a good will, no obstacles can long obstruct the way to concord and understanding. The essential condition is that each side should not only place itself on a basis of reason and fairness, but should believe the other side to be equally willing to reach a settement conceived in reason and fairness. The Civic Federation, in reporting encouraging progress in all the departments of its work, demonstrates the efficiency of friendly discussion, conciliation and arbitration as cures for industrial ills.

A HIGH STANDARD OF LEADERSHIP.

Boston Transcript.

The National Civic Federation has come to stay. That at least seems assured by the enthusiasm, increased definiteness of purpose and notably representative character of the fourth annual meeting of this unique institution just held in New York. From the beginning the Federation has been subject to superficial criticism from those who were not, and from an outside standpoint could not be, aware of the solid, practical work that has lain behind the more general aspects in which from time to time it has come into public notice. The annual meeting with the numerous conferences, the sessions of the executive council, and the detailed reports on the various phases of practical work during the past year, conciliation, trade agreements, "welfare institutions," etc., furnish probably the best reply to unfriendly criticism that could be offered. The movement has passed the experimental stage.

The gravity of the issues the Federation is called upon to face demands a high standard of broad-gauged, tolerant, sagacious leadership. That it had in Senator Hanna; and in his associates, whose active co-operation will be given now to Mr. Belmont, the new president. Mr. Belmont's election seems to have been the result, largely, of the somewhat new light in which he came before the public in the important conferences which prevented the threatened strike on New York transportation lines last summer. As the fruit of that experience, he is decidedly persona grata to large labor interests, and presumably will not need any intervention to get a respectful hearing among the captains of industry and finance. It is to be hoped that the experience of the coming year will justify in even increased measure President Roosevelt's estimate of the Federation, in his letter read Thursday night, that it is "a movement so praiseworthy and so thoroughly American in conception that it should as a matter of course receive the earnest support of all good citizens who are awake to the vital needs of our nation."

LIVE AND LET LIVE.

New York Mail.

All that was said at the banquet of the National Civic Federation, and all that was implied by the fellowshipping of employers and employed over the mahogany, was in a sense an amplification of the text given by President Roosevelt in a lay sermon at Washington the same evening: "The one all-important necessity of our social, industrial and political life is the necessity of the realization of what brotherhood means." It means that each man must "recognize in his fellow man his brother whose interest he must have at heart."

Men must live and let live; that is the principle of industrial peace. The extreme men on both sides are being relegated; that is the cheering sign under which both sides move to a better understanding.

GOOD INFLUENCE EXTENDING.

San Francisco Chronicle.

The main source of the influence of the Civic Federation is the great prominence of all prominently concerned with it. They are among our most eminent men. The late Senator Hanna was president, and the vacancy caused by his death has been filled by the election of August Belmont. The first vice president is Samuel Gompers. That the body is of recognized national importance is shown by the fact that the President of the United States deems it proper to address a sympathetic letter to the annual meeting, sent, by the way, through the hands of Vice President Gompers. The influence of the body is great and is extending. Federations on similar lines are forming in other countries. The entire work of the association is to assure industrial peace by promoting industrial friendship. Friends will not fight each other.

CONFIDENCE IN HANNA AND BELMONT.

Buffalo News.

August Belmont's election to the presidency of the National Civic Federation meets with general approval. Mr. Belmont is a man of great ability and ambition and will undoubtedly make a creditable figure in his new role. The office to which Mr. Belmont is chosen is the one left vacant by the death of Senator Hanna. That men of wealth like Hanna and Belmont should have proved acceptable to the labor men of the Civic Federation is in itself a gratifying fact, tending to show that while there may be classes in this country there are no class barriers. Workingmen gave Hanna and Belmont their confidence, and rightly, too, for Hanna knew and Belmont knows industrial conditions and the lot of the toiler.

BELMONT AND GOMPERS.

Los Angeles Express.

"Belmont and Gompers." This is a legend which, without further explanation, might serve as caption for a stirring story of encounter between capital and labor, but in these mild days when amity seems to be a universal watchword it merely conveys the intelligence that the New York banker, sportsman and representative of Rothschild and the leader of America's greatest industrial army are in friendly association as president and vice-president, respectively, of the National Civic Federation. Much good must be predicted from this harnessing of Belmont and Gompers, even if they find occasional difficulty in trotting in unison. Such action tends to lessen apparent extremes, and often it is successful in proving that real differences are non-existent.

MR. CARNEGIE'S SYMPATHETIC STUDY.

Baltimore Herald.

The ablest labor leaders are statesmen, recognizing the force of public opinion and guarding against the handicap of a decision by the Civic Federation against them. The letter addressed by Mr. Carnegie to the meeting can only promote a better feeling all around. It is a plea for a better understanding between the men and the employer, for patience in dealing with the differences between them, for a regard by both sides for each other's good points. His paper discloses the man with vast experience in employing labor who has studied the question with a large sympathy.

WAIT FOR THE OLD EMPLOYES.

Milwaukee Sentinel.

It amounts to commendation of Mr. Carnegie's thoughtful address read at the meeting of the Civic Federation to say that extremists like D. M. Parry, who are at odds with the spirit and methods of the Federation, will find in it little to approve. To illustrate, the great ironmaster made the at first view rather startling assertion that a large corporation makes a mistake when it adopts or even considers the policy of employing new men when its old employes are on strike. Mr. Carnegie qualified his statement by adding that, of course, in special branches, as street and other railways, where unbroken continuance of a public service is imperative, his rule could not apply. But his general principle is that large employers will best serve their own interests by waiting patiently for the old men to return in case of a strike, though the rule must have its exceptions.

It is not difficult to deduce from Mr. Carnegie's view an argument for the organization of labor where employed in large masses. The physical difficulties in the way of direct personal contact between employers and workmen under such conditions are obvious. But indirect contact and thereby a degree of mutual acquaintanceship, so necessary to mutual reasonableness and sympathy, can be obtained by resort to the representative principle. But even such contact is impossible between large employers and a host of unorganized and therefore unrepresented workmen. The only medium of contact possible is the representative body created as a result of labor organization. Unionism should make for industrial peace and equity—if only the men selected to lead and represent are well and wisely chosen and are really and honestly representative of the collective interests they are supposed to stand for.

A WELL DESERVED HONOR.

Buffalo Times.

Hon. August Belmont of New York, has been elected president of the National Civic Federation to succeed the late Senator Mark A. Hanna, and the honor is well deserved. Mr. Belmont employs a large number of men and he has always taken a deep interest in the affairs of the Federation, believing it to be an organization through which great good may be accomplished in the mutual interests of capital and labor. In the construction of the New York subway Mr. Belmont won the friendship of the employes by his eminent fairness and justice in dealing with them. As president of the Federation he will have an opportunity to do much toward solving the problems involving capital and labor, and that he will improve it, all who know him are confident.

INDUSTRIAL WAR USUALLY AVOIDABLE.

Philadelphia Inquirer.

So far Mr. Belmont has never figured in any of the labor troubles of the country, although he is financially interested in many corporations. He is a quiet, unassuming man of much force of character and his selection, while a surprise, may prove to be one of the happiest possible. It is certain that the Federation is constantly achieving much, not only in the settlement of actual disputes, but in preventing strikes and in a larger way educating the people up to the knowledge that such industrial wars are usually disastrous to all concerned, and usually avoidable. The career of the new president will be watched with the greatest interest.

MR. CARNEGIE'S INDUSTRIAL DIPLOMACY.

Detroit Tribune.

A new school of industrial diplomacy is being fostered by Andrew Carnegie, whose address at the dinner of the National Civic Federation in New York was characterized by its good sense. He approaches the problem in much the same manner as he has approached the question of international war, the more portentous threats of which have been time and again averted by the offices of diplomats. "A corporation engaged in a dispute with its men makes a great mistake if it adopts a policy of running its works with [illegible] Carnegie [illegible] here become responsible [illegible] idea is possibly wholly [illegible] and advanced for a motive that [illegible] material gain, nevertheless it is an [illegible] with profit to everyone. In the [illegible] of industrial strikes there are skilled men with whom [illegible] of idle, when [illegible] available, labor cannot compete. Each new man is as much a potential striker as the old. A strike is a difference to which there is a possible agreement, rather than a revengeful warfare.

MR. CARNEGIE AGAINST STRIKE BREAKERS.

Detroit Times.

Andrew Carnegie, in his speech at the National Civic Federation, an organization conspicuously in contrast with the convention of Parryites, which met in New York recently, declared that a victory over labor, won by the employment of new men, is a defeat in reality. He declared the method unjust to the men and their families and disastrous for the employer because of the necessary inferiority of men employed in time of labor trouble to take the place of old employes. Mr. Carnegie did not mention labor unions in his speech, but his words apply so perfectly to those situations where union men are opposed by strike breakers that their meaning loses no force from that fact. As a criticism of employers' associations and a support of the contention of unions that the men opposed to them in the ranks of labor are inferior workmen, no higher testimony could be adduced.

MR. CARNEGIE DEPLORES INTOLERANCE.

Pittsburg Press.

Mr. Carnegie has been until recently one of the largest employers of labor in America. It is, therefore, significant that he believes thoroughly in the mission of industrial reconciliation, rather than in the efficacy of the spirit of violence. This, we take it, Mr. Carnegie deplores, whether it be manifested by lawlessness on the part of strikers or intolerance on the part of employers (such for instance, as the employers' association, represented by D. M. Parry, whose motto appears to be "War to the knife, and the knife to the hilt"). In addition to the Carnegie letter, the Federation listened to a letter from President Roosevelt, who made it plain that industrial conciliators have his entire sympathy. The Federation has already done a great deal to promote industrial peace. Representative American citizens could find no worthier work. August Belmont, who was elected, to succeed the late Senator Hanna as president, has not been known to the country as a special friend of the cause, but he has the ability and the influence to fill the position acceptably.

A GREAT OPPORTUNITY AND RESPONSIBILITY.

Saratoga Springs Saratogian.

August Belmont has taken part in many works of great public moment and in many ways his career has been a good example of what men of brains and wealth may accomplish toward the world's good. But never before has there been shifted to his shoulders a greater opportunity or a larger responsibility than has come with the headship of the Civic Federation bestowed by the ballots of his fellow members. The work of that organization toward a closer fellowship and understanding between capital and labor was one of the great moving forces in Senator Hanna's life. How dearly he cherished the plan and how hopeful he was of the results to follow, only his intimate associates knew. But he left much of his inspiring faith behind and it is to be hoped that Mr. Belmont will feel its influence and will seek to carry forward the same ends with the same high and unselfish purpose that prompted his dead predecessor in the past.

INDUSTRIAL PROBLEMS AS SEEN BY LABOR CARTOONISTS.

Iron Molders' Journal

Clearing the Path

International Hod Carriers' Journal

Journal of the Amalgamated Meat Cutters

INDUSTRIAL PROBLEMS AS SEEN BY ANTI-UNION CARTOONISTS.

"A Square Deal—No More, No Less"

Industrial Independent

YOUTH UNDER THE BAN

UNION LABOR—"THE DOOR IS CLOSED. FOLLOW THE ROAD."

Industrial Independent

The Modern Procrustes

Industrial Independent

LABOR WRESTS VICTORY FROM DEFEAT.

(*Continued from page 9.*)

Chief Stone, of the Engineers; Samuel Gompers, President of the American Federation of Labor; and John Mitchell, President of the United Mine Workers of America, for assistance, and they were on the ground Thursday morning. At 10 o'clock that morning, no answer having been received from the joint executive committee of the strikers, Chiefs Stone and Hurley, of the Engineers; President Mahon, of the Amalgamated; President Samuel Gompers, President John Mitchell, and Herman Robinson, met in conference to decide on the course of action. At 12 o'clock there was still no answer from the strikers' committee and President Mahon telephoned the local Amalgamated officers that unless he had an answer by 2 o'clock in person he would issue a statement repudiating the strike. Chief Stone meantime drafted his statement to the public, but agreed to hold it back out of courtesy to the committees that had been trying to bring about a conference. At 3 o'clock the sub-committee of the Amalgamated Association appeared at the Clarendon Hotel and reported to Mr. Mahon that while the Amalgamated members of the joint executive committee were willing to call in the national officers, the engineers and firemen had outvoted them and therefore none of them could accept.

Chief Stone then read his letter to the committee and it was heartily approved and given out to the public. It is as follows:

"The Brotherhood of Engineers have no differences between their organization and the Interborough Company at the present time that could not have been adjusted at the present time in a proper manner.

"The present strike now going on by men claiming to represent the Brotherhood of Engineers is in direct violation of our orders. It is not recognized, nor will it be supported by our organization. The contract entered into in September, 1904, between the Interborough Company and the Brotherhood of Locomotive Engineers we recognize to be as binding to-day as it was when signed, and loyal members of the Brotherhood of Engineers are instructed to at once report for duty to comply with the requirements of the agreement. Members refusing to do so will be expelled from membership in our organization. It has been reported to me that many of our members have been misled by statements that the grand officers have given consent to this strike. This is not correct. No request was made or granted, nor were the officers of the Brotherhood of Engineers consulted in the present situation. This is the first time in the history of the Brotherhood of Engineers that our members have repudiated their agreement with any railroad. Labor organizations must keep their part of the agreement inviolate if they expect success. Had our laws been complied with conditions as they now appear could not exist on the line of the Interborough Rapid Transit Company."

Mr. Mahon's statement soon followed and was:

"The present strike of Local Division No. 332, of the Amalgamated Association of Street and Electric Railway Employes, was undertaken without consulting the responsible officers of the general organization, without their consent or approval.

"Last Saturday a telegram was received at my Detroit office stating that 'the situation in New York City is critical,' and my presence was essential at once. I reached this city on Monday morning and was astonished to learn that the request for my presence here was made on personal responsibility and not at the instance of the local division.

"A copy of the demands to be presented to the Interborough Railway Company on Monday afternoon was shown me, and I strongly advised against their presentatioin, for, in addition to the demands for better conditions, the document contained the endorsement of the local division of engineers (motormen) which violated the agreement that organization had with the company.

"I had reason to believe there would have been little or no difficulty in obtaining from the company better conditions, but our organization is strongly committed to the maintenance of its own agreements with employers, and was in honor bound not to encourage the violation of an agreement which another organization had with the employer of its members.

"Under our laws our local unions have no right to strike in violation of any agreement they have with the employers, and surely then they can have no right to strike to support another organization to do an act which they themselves have no right to do.

"It seemed to me that without resorting to drastic measures I might yet give whatever assistance my experience and position offered to advise a way out of the difficult and questionable position in which our men and our local division were placed, to try and bring about an honorable adjustment in the establishment of better relations between the men, the organization, and the company; however, the repeated tender

(*Concluded on page 8.*)

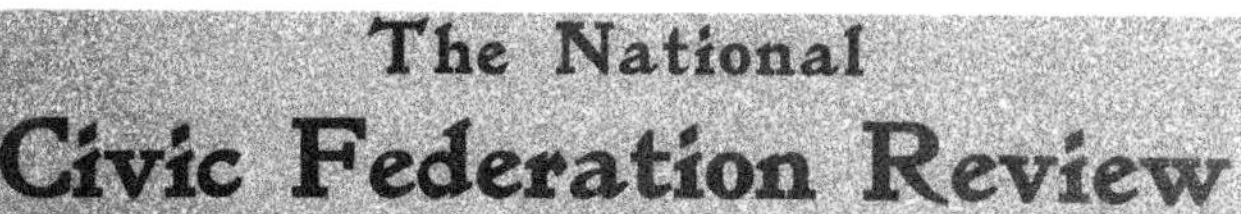

The National
Civic Federation Review

Vol. II. No. 1 NEW YORK, APRIL, 1905 Ten Cents

IS COMPULSORY ARBITRATION PRACTICABLE?

SHOULD CORPORATIONS RENDERING PUBLIC SERVICE BE REQUIRED TO ARBITRATE ALL DIFFERENCES WITH EMPLOYES?

COMPULSORY Arbitration, with special reference to the practicability of its application to quasi public corporations, was the special topic discussed at the second annual meeting of the Civic Federation of New York and Vicinity on April 4. This subject was directly suggested by the recent strike on the lines of the Interborough Rapid Transit Company, which presented a number of problems, both interesting and [illegible] bearing upon the [illegible] between similar [illegible]

[illegible]

individual injured another, it was regarded as an individual affair, and the individual injured was remitted in a very inchoate way to his right for redress. As law developed, a new theory also developed upon [illegible]

takes up the question; and the public prosecutor assumes the power of the state in order to correct the injury that the public has received.

Now, analogously, we may say, that if a difference arises between a public service corporation and its employes, it is no longer a question solely between the public service corporation and the employes, but the larger interests of the general public that are to be passed upon. [illegible]

HON. SETH LOW,
Ex-Mayor of New York City.

HENRY C. POTTER,
Bishop, Protestant Episcopal Church.

EVERETT P. WHEELER,
Lawyer, New York City.

JAMES P. ARCHIBALD,
[illegible] N. Y. Brotherhood Painters and Decorators.

[illegible] subject, but wishes rather to [illegible] to the lines of thought that [illegible] the discussion here to-day. [illegible] development of law if one

which today [illegible] law of [illegible] namely, that if one [illegible] another [illegible] most serious infraction [illegible] results [illegible] disturbing public peace. It is [illegible] theory of law that the public

[illegible] thing could [illegible] No one is able to suggest [illegible] except through arbitration [illegible] arbitration is spoken of [illegible] munity, it is apt to be challenged by both sides. The capitalist says: "Compulsory arbitration is unfair, because labor is not responsible;" and labor says: "Men are not slaves: they cannot be compelled to work against their will."

I venture to submit, however, that at one point capital and labor stand in precisely the same position before the law; and that, at this point, if it is desirable, compulsory arbitration may be insisted upon, and may be made practicable. Without the privileges given by statute, neither capital nor labor, as illustrated in corporations and trade unions, can lawfully combine. In the eye of the common law, such combinations as a corporation and a labor union were both conspiracies. In other words, in order to combine at all, in such forms, both capital and labor have to ask the same privilege at the hands of the State.

The State can certainly say, if it will: "Yes, you may combine, but only upon the condition that all disputes between you shall be arbitrated." And the State can as certainly, secure the acceptance by both parties of the award of an arbitration, by providing that a failure to arbitrate, or to abide by the award of the arbitration, shall work a forfeiture of the privilege of combining. In the case of a corporation, it would, in that event, lose its charter; and in the case of a trade union, which is an association of individuals, each individual would become amenable to the criminal law against conspiracy. Such a provision would probably be equally effective as to both labor and capital; and it would be equally fair to both, because it would apply to both equally for the same cause; that is to say, because of a failure to observe the conditions upon which the statutory privilege of combining had been granted.

Of course, in this paper, I am not attempting to deal with the details of legislation. It would be altogether possible, I believe, instead of depriving a company of its charter, to deprive the responsible officers and directors for a term of months or of years, as the statute might provide, of the privilege of being officers or directors in any corporation within the State; and, similarly, if a trade union were at fault, [illegible] the officers or the men responsible for the fault [illegible] be deprived, as in the other case, for a term of months or of years, as the statutes might provide, of the privilege of belonging to any trade unions within the State. [illegible] not helpless. [illegible] rather is why should it not [illegible] legis[illegible] in the first instance, to public service corporations, where the evils felt by the community are greatest.

It may throw some light upon the problem to try to show the philosophy of the present situation. For many centuries the best men of the race, the world over, have been struggling to secure for the individual man equality before the law and freedom of opportunity. In this country, and at this time, these results have been achieved more generally than ever before. On the other hand, as we observe what is going on about us in the field of industry and commerce, it seems as if the individual capitalist was disappearing in the corporation, and the corporation itself in the trust; while the individual laborer is disappearing in the trade union, and the trade union itself in the brotherhood or federation. What does all this signify? Does it mean that, in this large field of human activity, the loss of individuality is threatened by the force of combination? I think not. It means, on the contrary, as I conceive, that we have reached, in human society, the era of combination simply because we have first succeeded in individualizing each man as to his legal rights and as to his social privileges. In other words, what has happened in society may be illustrated by the art of printing. Until each type had come to represent a single letter only, the era of limitless combinations of types did not appear, and there could be no art of printing. When every type had been individualized, then, and then only, the era of limitless combination was attained and the art of printing was born. This, I think, is what has happened in our day of our times, the inference from it is important. Nobody thinks of antagonizing the force of gravity. Everybody simply takes it for granted, and adjusts his actions to it. Just as soon as, in a free community, the movement towards combination on the part of both labor and capital is recognized as a movement in response to a law as universal as the law of gravity, the bitterness of antagonism between capital and labor will tend to moderate. Each will take for granted the position of the other, and each will strive, as wise men always strive, so to adjust themselves to universal law as to get from it the greatest possible advantage. Then the effort to destroy the trade union, on the one hand, and the trust on the other, will give place to the wiser effort to regulate both so as to do away with the abuses of which each is capable.

This power of combination in industry and business, while of slow growth, in its recent manifestations is almost like the discovery of a new force. It has taken more than a century since the steam engine was invented for men to learn how to make the use of steam as effective and as safe as it is now; and yet, even now, from time to time, boilers explode and loss of life takes place. No one should be surprised, therefore, and no one need lose heart, if progress in learning the limits of safety in the use of the power of combination, on the part of both capital and labor, is slow, and if, in the process of learning, much injury is done. It is only through experimentation that men learn what can be done and what cannot, when they are put into possession of a new power. Especially must this be the case when the same power is put at once into the hands of men who occupy competing relations as to its use. The first impulse of human nature, when given control of a new power, is to use it to its utmost; and it is only as experience shows what are the limitations of its usefulness, that such limitations are accepted. Capital, in combination, has sometimes imagined that it could do anything that it wished. Labor, in combination, has often yielded to the same idea. Both have found, when they have carried their ideas to the extreme, that forces exist in society with which they are obliged to reckon, and which put a limit upon what they are able to do. In the first stages of the struggle growing out of the efforts of both capital and labor, each to secure for itself, by combination, a larger proportion of the joint products of both, resort was almost uniformly had to main strength. The appeal to justice and the appeal to the community's sense of right seemed to be unnecessary when one side or the other apparently had power enough to have its own way, no matter what people thought. I think it may fairly be said, speaking broadly, that this stage of the matter has been passed in the so-called conflict between capital and labor nowadays. At the beginning of every such controversy, both sides now put forth a statement of their positions, in the endeavor to secure the favor and help of public sentiment. This they do because both have discovered that seldom, if ever, can either side win, in such a dispute, unless it has public opinion with it. From this I infer that the time is ripe to urge that no breach of relations between employer and employe should ever be allowed to take place without a resort to arbitration.

When arbitration is urged in any controversy, one side or the other is pretty certain to say, "There is nothing to arbitrate." This phrase always has one of two meanings. First, it often means, on the part of the employer, that he does not admit the right of his employes to any voice in the decision of the points under discussion; or, second, it may mean, either on the part of the employer or on the part of the employe, that he feels himself so strong that he does not want to arbitrate. Men often say, with a great deal of force, that the finding in almost every arbitration is a compromise. The weaker side is always ready to arbitrate, because it feels that, while it may not get everything that it wants, it is pretty sure to get something. The stronger side, for the same reason, is unwilling to arbitrate, because it feels that, while it may not have to give everything that is asked, it will have to grant something, and it does not want to grant

[illegible] poration receives from the State two very vital privi[illegible] leges—first, that of limited liability, and, second, th[illegible] of indefinite life. The State may well demand [illegible] people who receive such privileges at its hand, th[illegible] they also shall conduct their business in ways th[illegible] are consistent with the public interest. Were it wor[illegible] while, it might be shown that the argument in fav[illegible] of arbitration, even as between the business firm, [illegible] individuals and their employes, is only less stron[illegible] but the amount of business likely to lead to labor di[illegible] turbances, carried on under these forms in these day[illegible] is so small as practically to be negligible in this di[illegible] cussion. It may be said, therefore, that it is ver[illegible] seldom indeed, if ever, in our day that the capitali[illegible] is justified in saying that there is nothing to arbitrat[illegible] because he is unwilling to admit that his employ[illegible] are entitled to a voice as to the conditions upon whic[illegible] they will work for him.

Turn now to the second sense in which that phra[illegible] is frequently used, "There is nothing to arbitrate; that arbitration, after all, is merely a form of unwe[illegible] come compromise. Is it certain that this is an arg[illegible] ment against it? I perceive that the round world [illegible] kept in place by an opposition of forces, and it ma[illegible] easily be that the best possible arrangement, as b[illegible] tween employer and employe, is the arrangement, [illegible] they fail to agree, upon which a fair-minded arbitrat[illegible] would decide. That is to say, the equilibrium betwee[illegible] the demands of the opposing forces, so establishe[illegible] may be, upon the whole, the best possible adjustmen[illegible] for the time being. Such a practice would certainl[illegible] tend to adjust the relations between employer an[illegible] employe upon the basis of reason and good will, instea[illegible] of by force and compulsion. Relations established wit[illegible] good will are not only likely to be more permanent, b[illegible] also more mutually advantageous, for my busines[illegible] experience convinces me that no business relation[illegible] are enduring that do not involve advantage to bot[illegible] sides.

There are certain lessons vital to this argument [illegible] be drawn from the recent strike in New York [illegible] upon the Subway and Elevated roads. From [illegible] moment that the breach occurred, and the publi[illegible] read the statement of the two sides on the [illegible] involved, there was never a moment's dou[illegible] public opinion would be against the men, [illegible] public sympathy would go to the railroad. Fo[illegible] two things were evident to the most casual re[illegible] First, that there was no issue at stake that ju[illegible] such immense injury to the public as was done b[illegible] strike; no issue, indeed, that could not have [illegible] easily adjusted by arbitration; and, second, that [illegible] section of the men, at any rate—the motormen—[illegible] gone out in flat violation of their agreement. Eve[illegible] friend of industrial progress through industrial peace when he became aware of the facts of the situation must have felt a sinking of heart, because it is perfectly evident that organized society cannot prospe[illegible] when men will not keep their faith. Most happily the day was saved by the good sense and the courag[illegible] of the national labor officials, by promptly and pub[illegible] licly repudiating the locals who had broken faith. I[illegible] is, therefore, now more clear than ever, that th[illegible] more responsible labor leaders and the more respon[illegible] sible labor unions are to be trusted when they hav[illegible] once given their word. As long ago as when th[illegible] Book of Psalms was written, the writer said that th[illegible] just man was he who kept hi[illegible]th, although he ha[illegible] sworn to his own hurt. It i[illegible]cause the laws o[illegible] nature are uniform that [illegible]e in the worl[illegible] subject to those laws; and [illegible] because the [illegible] mass of men, in their [illegible] faith that [illegible] [illegible] it was disco[illegible] [illegible]y of men as the moto[illegible] [illegible]t strike should absolutel[illegible] [illegible], it was, on the other han[illegible] [illegible] this action should be [illegible] [illegible]ly repudiated by the officials [illegible]

Mr. Wheeler:

Mr. President and Gentlemen: You know there are two sorts of lawyers—one, the lawyers who make a specialty of seeing how not to do it and the other who make a specialty of seeing how things can be done.

I see here a portrait of a man who was one of the ablest of us all, Mr. Simon Sterne, whose specialty was to see how things could be done, and I believe, among all the members of the bar in his time, there was not one who was more successful or more suggestive in that direction. My endeavors have been to follow his example in that line, and I suppose it is for that reason that you, as an old friend, have appreciated that I am honored by being asked to speak.

Now, it does seem to me that compulsory arbitration is entirely practicable and that it might take this form: Let an act be passed by the Legislature making it unlawful for employers to lock out their workmen or for the workmen composing a union to strike until the subjects in difference between them have been previously submitted to the arbitration of a competent and impartial tribunal which would be provided by the law. That is all you need, as it seems to me, to accomplish the result. Practically I would say that such a law should apply, in the first place, to what we sometimes call public utility corporations—to common carriers especially—who perform a public function that in many states is performed by the state itself. In Europe most of the railroads are managed by the respective kingdoms or republics, and managed to the satisfaction of the public as well as to the advantage of the state itself. In this country, on the contrary, with the single temporary exception of the railroad across the Brooklyn Bridge, I am not aware that any city or state has undertaken to manage and direct a railroad. But it certainly is perfectly competent for the states of this Republic, or the cities under the authority of the state, to do it. We have thought it advisable up to this time in general that railroad corporations should be organized under the direction of the state. But certainly they are subject to the control of the state that creates them and vests them with a public franchise and function. There is not, I apprehend, any serious difficulty in compelling performance by a railroad of the award of such a tribunal. That is not seriously contested, and, if i[illegible] experience which again I say Mr. Sterne so often [illegible] procuring the appointment of a receiver of a delinquent railroad corporation, who very often managed the corporation quite as well as the board of directors did, would meet the difficulty and would show that the corporations were certainly amenable to such a tribunal

All we ask is to establish another court. The present courts of justice in effect enforce compulsory arbitration. If my client has a contract, and the other party to it refuses to perform, there are many cases already under which the court will decree specific performance and will enforce it. There have been receivers appointed, not only of railroads but of newspapers, and of many other lines of business, who have carried on the business, whatever it was—and I don't say always carried it on well; sometimes carried it on very badly; but it has been carried on, and in many cases has been well carried on. So I think we may pass from the side of the corporation.

Let us look at the labor side. The objection is made that to compel the performance of an arbitration tribunal would be to create an involuntary condition of servitude. Let us look at that seriously from the practical and not from the theoretical side. Practically, what is it? One thousand men or ten thousand men make an agreement voluntarily. You don't compel them to do it. Nobody compelled the motormen, for example, or the trainmen, or any of them to enter into their agreement with the Interborough Rapid Transit Company. It was perfectly voluntary. There was no compulsory servitude there. Do you mean to tell me that it is compulsory servitude if a court obliges a man to keep his contract? In what book, in what decision of a court, can any authority be found for that proposition? Look it squarely in the face. It is said that it is involuntary servitude to compel a man to keep a contract he has voluntarily made. The objection is absurd.

What, after all, is it that leads the great majority of men to make contracts to do something—to do a piece of work, to manufacture a given article? Why, it is the necessity of life. It is the Lord Almighty that creates that condition of servitude—we must work or starve. There is sometimes accumulated capital; but that is the accumulation of the labor of some one. All capital, after all, when you look at it, is the accumulation of labor in the past and that labor was voluntary labor. And you get it in that concentrated form, as it were. So then we are under that necessity. We want to live. We want to have food and clothing and shelter, and to get that somebody certainly has had to work for it. That is the necessity. That necessity lasts and that necessity compels in itself the performance of the work.

Go a step further. What is it in effect that makes a strike? Why, it is the decision of the leaders. The men who are in the union elect certain leaders. It is those leaders as a rule that decide upon a strike. The men follow them. We all know, and cannot help but admire, the loyalty of the men. The leaders are amenable to the process of the court. If they commit a crime they can be punished for it, and if it is a punishable offence to violate the judgment of an arbitration tribunal, why cannot the law punish the leaders for that offence as it would for other offences? And if they are punished, the strike of necessity goes to pieces. If there had been such a law as that, and the leaders of this late strike had sought to do what they did and had been arrested on the charge of violating the law, the strike would have gone to pieces from the first. It never had any life except from the action of the leaders and the loyalty of the men. If the state should interfere and say, "You must do this; it is as much an offence against the public to initiate such a strike without arbitration as it is to pick a man's pocket," and the state proceeds to punish that offence, that would be the end of the strike. And why should anybody complain that society compels members of it to perform contracts which are made for the public benefit? I confess I have tried very hard, Mr. Chairman and gentlemen, to see the objections to that proposition, and I fail to see them.

I would like to say this one thing in conclusion. We are, after all, a law abiding people. We are too much given to making laws, and many laws are made undoubtedly that are not enforced. I am willing to admit that. But when in your experience has a court, after a fair hearing, decided and rendered a judgment, that the judgment has not been obeyed? You may say you can appeal. Very well, you appeal. But when the final court has rendered its judgment, who can give an instance where that judgment has not been regarded? Take this notable case of the Northern Securities Company. There, the richest, most powerful persons in this country were involved. The interests were mighty. We all remember the struggle and the keen competition that resulted in that famous Northern Securities agreement. Those people have been obliged, by the law of the land, to submit this controversy to the judgment of the court, and the court has annulled their agreement. They had another controversy, as to how the result of all that combination should be divided, and the court has decided that. They are going to obey the decision. Is there anybody, from the greatest to the least, that was connected with that combination who is not going to submit peacefully, without a struggle, to the decision of the court? Will it be necessary to order out the marshal or the United States troops to enforce the decision? Not at all. That is ingrained in the American people. I think I can truthfully say—I am sometimes called an optimist—but I think I can truthfully say that the disposition of our people is to submit to the decision of the court when it has been rendered after a fair and impartial hearing. I don't believe you would need any compulsion. I don't believe, when such a tribunal has rendered its decision, there would be any occasion to put anybody in prison or take any method of enforcing that decision.

May I refer to my own experience in this connection? Every man's experience ought to be worth something to himself, and it is out of the combined experience of many individuals that we ought to learn something, at least, of a useful lesson for the conduct of life. I have been practicing law in this city for forty years. I can only remember three occasions in all the cases I have tried, and I have tried a great many, where it has been necessary to resort to the compulsion of the sheriff or marshal to enforce the orders of the court, and one of those cases was the case of a defaulting trustee. If even out of one thousand cases there were three where you had to call in compulsion, would that be a serious defect? I submit that such a law as I have suggested could be devised which would do justice to all parties, which would provide a fair and impartial court, the decision of which would be respected and would be greatly in the interest of the public, because it would prevent these social wars which we call strikes. (Applause.)

The Chairman: I shall now call upon a gentleman to speak on the other side, a representative labor leader, Mr. James P. Archibald, who I believe has given considerable thought to the other side of this question. (Applause.)

Mr. Archibald:

The general objections to compulsory arbitration, based upon political, social and economic grounds, apply to the specific phase of the question here under consideration, which would limit the application of compulsory arbitration to differences between employes and employing corporations chartered to perform service, essential or important, to the public convenience, comfort and welfare. Despite that limitation, it will be found that nearly all, if not every one, of the broad reasons that can be adduced against legislation to make industrial arbitration compulsory will hold good as against the proposition to employ compulsory arbitration only in differences between employers and employed engaged in quasi-public service. Furthermore, this is true even if we admit at the outset that the corporation engaged, for instance, in transportation, owes to the state a duty, more or less defined and restricted, in requital for its charter, and that the employes of such a corporation are in a sense public servants who, in accepting employment, have incurred on their side the duty of exerting every effort to secure the safe and prompt conveyance of goods and passengers. Even to place thus in a category by themselves such a corporation and such employes, does not exempt them from the operation of universal principles.

The first of these broad objections to compulsory arbitration, to my mind, is that it must tend, in its practical operation, toward control of industry by the state; that is, toward Socialism. The very definition of arbitration, whether compulsory or voluntary, implies a surrender of control of any industry to which it is applied by either of the two parties whose co-operation is essential to its success and to their share in its prosperity. Arbitration is defined by the Industrial Commission as the authorized decision of an issue, as to which both parties concerned have failed to agree, by some person or persons other than those parties. That is, the decision thus reached may be unsatisfactory to either or to both of the parties. If each has agreed in advance to abide by the decision, whatever it may be, that agreement involves only a voluntary and temporary self-sacrifice by one or the other or by both. But if the state is empowered to compel obedience to the award, to which each party is enforced to submit, the outcome would be, in case the parties should refuse either to carry on the business or to work, that the state would assume the conduct of the industry; that is, if its continuance were essential or conducive to the public welfare. It is not necessary here to enter into a discussion of Socialism further than to say that opposition to Socialism thus implies opposition to compulsory arbitration, whose ultimate tendency toward Socialism is clear enough in theory and not to be measured by any experience.

The next broad objection to compulsory arbitration is that it is unnecessary. It is a general principle that legislation should be framed only to meet requirements. Needless laws cumber the statute books and are a burden to society. The maxim that the best government is that which governs least may be carried to an extreme, but it is certainly true that no one would seriously contemplate a large extension of our judicial machinery without a clear demonstration of its necessity. Now, in the regulation of industry there has been no such demonstration of the necessity of the creation of a court of arbitration, to which either party to a dispute could cite the other at will or caprice, and from whose decision, reached without reference to a jury, there could be no appeal. The advocates of compulsory arbitration are keenly aware of this vital objection. They usually preface their argument by statements designed to picture the United States as in an incessant ferment of industrial war, and at least one of them has gone so far as to apply the famous definition of war to the relations of capital and labor as a whole. But a calmer view will show that the normal and usual condition of industry is one of peace, and that war is the exception. So distinguished and experienced an observer as Andrew Carnegie recently remarked that "peace reigns in six-sevenths of the industrial world." Mr. Carnegie reached this conclusion by pointing out that out of 22,000,000 engaged in gainful pursuits only seven millions are in mechanical and manufacturing occupations. Outside of these, in agriculture and domestic service, peace reigns. Out of the seven millions engaged in mechanical and manufacturing pursuits, he estimates that not more than three millions, or those having relations with large employers, are often disturbed by industrial war.

The strikes, then, that do occur, nearly all involve directly less than one-seventh of the total wage earners of the country, and only a fraction of them at one time.

Official figures show that of the 22,783 strikes in the twenty years from 1880 to 1900, the industries most affected, in the order named, were the building trades with 4,440 strikes; the coal and coke industry, with 2,512; the metal and metallic goods industry, with 2,079; the clothing industry, with 1,536; the tobacco industry, with 1,509, and, least of the six, transportation, with 1,262. Of the total 22,783 strikes, 58.09 per cent. were in these six industries. In the number of establishments involved, transportation also takes lowest rank, few more than 5,000 establishments being involved in the twenty years, as against 41,910 in the building trades; 19,695 in the clothing industry and 14,473 in the coal and coke industry.

In this connection, it is to be noted that this lack of necessity for compulsory arbitration is progressively decreasing. The methods of conciliation, conference and voluntary arbitration are largely responsible for this decrease of industrial war. No one can fail to be impressed with the fact, of common knowledge, that there has been no strike of serious consequence upon any of the great railway systems since 1893, or for more than a decade. This, it has been pointed out, is due to the increase of organization among railway employes. Strikes upon such public service systems as gas or water works are so rare that they may be left out of account. There remain, then, only the strikes upon street railways in centers of population to be considered in relation to the necessity for compulsory arbitration, and as to them the necessity is yet to be demonstrated. In their case, it is not the capital or the number of employes involved that becomes important. It is the inconvenience of the public and the dislocation of the business of a community that cause the outcry for a drastic remedy or an effective prevention. The gravity and the reality of these public grievances cannot be minimized or obscured. Yet it is none the less true that their occurrence is local, though intense; their endurance temporary, though acute; their effect limited in time, though accompanied by an appreciable increase in danger of operation. These are not adequate causes for introducing an innovation into our judicial machinery.

The organization of employes, accompanied by the organization of employers, is a constantly increasing cause of industrial peace, and a constantly increasing argument against the necessity of compulsory arbitration. If, then, we accept the organization of labor as socially and economically desirable, as tending to elevate the mass and increase its power of consumption, we must oppose compulsory arbitration as inimical to the development of unionism. A primary object of unionism is the negotiation of trade agreements, otherwise collective bargaining with employers, organized as corporations or associations. Nearly every labor organization in the country is opposed to compulsory arbitration because of the conviction, that is shared by many professional economists, that its adoption must, in the words of Carroll D. Wright, "inevitably result in the destruction of trade unions." A decision in a contest adverse to a union would render that union liable to whatever penalty would be contingent upon disobedience. A violation of the decree of the arbitration court by the union would probably be followed by the imposition of a money fine or the loss of its charter and its dissolution. The only alternative, obedience to the decree, if the decree were against the sense of justice and therefore against the sense of self-respect of the employes, would amount to working for specified wage under compulsion, or, in other words, to involuntary servitude, forbidden by the Thirteenth Amendment to the Constitution of the United States.

The ready answer to this is that the operation of compulsory arbitration in New Zealand has not there destroyed the trade unions, but has strengthened them, just as it has promoted unions of employers. That may be in part because the New Zealand system is accompanied by the preferential employment of union labor under the terms of an award, accompanied by the requirement that the unions admit all competent workers, without ballot and upon the payment of a nominal fee. But, aside from that explanation, which implies a national closed shop in all industries, as well as making dependents of workers incompetent to earn the minimum wage and yet able to earn their living if permitted, the conditions of life and labor in New Zealand are so radically different to those in the United States as to make inapplicable to this country the lessons of the experiment in New Zealand. That experiment, moreover, has not reached conclusive results even in its own territory and under its peculiar conditions. Its strongest adherents have confessed their inability to transfer it to this country. The report of the Anthracite Strike Commission said: "Apart from the apparent lack of constitutional power to enact laws providing for compulsory arbitration, our industries are too vast and too complicated for the practical application of such a system."

It is precisely the belief that the awards, or the bulk of awards, of a court of compulsory arbitration would be adverse to wage earners that impugns in advance the efficiency of this device. It is an essential precedent to voluntary arbitration that each disputant shall feel confident that his interests will receive the same consideration as those of his opponent. Each must have faith that the award will be guided by a spirit of perfect fairness. But when the element of compulsion is introduced, this essential element of confidence disappears. It is impossible, as men are constituted, to guarantee the fairness of a tribunal of arbitration clothed with power to compel the hearing of disputes and to enforce its conclusions. It is a condition that must be taken into account that the belief largely obtains among wage earners that state-created courts or boards are generally, if unconsciously, on the side of capital or invested interests as against the more indefinite influence of labor.

Another general objection to compulsory arbitration is that it involves a surrender of the right to strike and of the corresponding right to lock out. These are weapons that neither self-respecting capital nor self-respecting labor can afford to surrender. The abandonment of the power to fight would make for the peace of subjection, for the craven submission of one side or the other. The possession of the weapons of war makes for peace in industry as surely as it does in international affairs. The arguments for an effective military force as an insurance of national security against foreign offense and of foreign respect for the rights of a nation abroad are quite parallel to the arguments for retaining an inalienable right to refuse to work or to refuse to employ, reinforced by thorough organization. The mutual respect of employer and employed is essential to harmony. The abandonment of liberty to fight for conviction of right would impair and ultimately destroy that mutual respect. It would be a confession of inability to reconcile mutual respect with a manly compact of peace.

I have enumerated all these general objections to compulsory arbitration as applicable to the specific class of public service corporations and their employes. It is for the advocates of compulsory arbitration to prove that they are not so applicable. It is for them to show that the injury to the public convenience and safety or to the conduct of business is so frequent, so serious, so important as to warrant an innovation that is repugnant to republican conceptions of liberty.

But, it is said, it may be possible to create a method of compulsory arbitration that will stop short of compelling either employers to continue a business or employes to continue to work. Let us see how any conceivable plan of non-compelling compulsory arbitration would work in practical application to a system of rapid transit in a great city.

The chief purpose of such a plan would be to prevent, under any and all circumstances, the interruption of service. The first essential, then, would be to forbid by law either strike or lockout on the railroad, pending the submission of a dispute to the court of arbitration. Assume that the corporation on the one side and the employes on the other have been deprived by law of this weapon. The decision of the court follows. It is regarded, we will say, as unjust by the employes, who then enter upon their deferred strike. Pending the decision of the court, would the corporation be in contempt if it gathered an army of strike breakers? The strike breaking remedy is not immediately effective in preventing delay and interruption to traffic, and it involves danger to the traffic. The only alternative would be for the state or municipality to operate the road with police or military. If there were to be no interruption nor danger to traffic, the members of these forces would have to be trained to render instant and efficient service as motormen, trainmen, signal men and in all other capacities necessary to the continuous and safe operation of the road. Is the public prepared to include these accomplishments in the list of requirements for service in the police or army?

It has been suggested also that, as the final court of appeal in all industrial disputes is public opinion, a court might be created with power to compel the production of all testimony, persons and papers, and to render its decision. It is argued that under present conditions public opinion cannot learn the truth in industrial controversies; that it is bombarded with contradictory, ex parte statements and confusing and ill-informed reports in the press, and that the creation of a court empowered to ascertain and publish the truth would make conclusive and morally compulsory, because necessarily right, the verdict of that highest court of arbitration—public opinion. Strictly speaking, this proposition is not compulsory arbitration, but compulsory investigation, with submission of the finding to the verdict of the community.

This proposition is based upon the assumption that public opinion, if correctly informed as to facts, is infallible. But what basis is there for this assumption? As to the ascertainment of facts, the historic conundrum, "What is truth?" is persistently pertinent. Especially does it apply to an industrial inquiry as to which only experts, not laymen, would be qualified to arrive at a just decision, and even experts might disagree. A task difficult for such a select body would assuredly be confusing to the judgment of that vast, indeterminate jury known as the general public. Even in cases of litigation, carried to the highest courts of appeal, in the States and in the Federal Government, judicial decisions now divide the bench and fail to command by far the unanimous approval of public opinion. Yet those decisions are reached in accordance with procedure elaborated through centuries and with principles evolved through the teaching of all history. But judicial inquiry into industrial questions would explore unknown fields, would meet novel questions, involving both expediency and principle, would evolve new principles and in the absence of any body of industrial jurisprudence, would make of such a court in practice a legislative as well as a judicial agency.

Be it noted, the element of compulsion is still present. If there is to be a candid inquiry into the existing facts of an industry, the status quo must be preserved. If the industry be that of transportation, the employes must keep the trains running and the corporation must discharge none of its discontented employes, pending the inquiry. Each antagonist must appear in the judicial arena with hands tied. The contest must be reduced to statement and argument. It must be a battle of witnesses and counsel.

The objection to this procedure is that it is against the normal processes of human progress. The race does not emerge from barbarism by argument, but by deeds. Valor, not eloquence, wins battles. In the long run, right, truth, justice must win, and they must be demonstrated. But they cannot stand unsupported against the ever powerful forces of wrong, untruth, injustice. It is only by fighting, or by the power to fight, that the weal of society is advanced through the adjustment of relations between its component parts. Remove this ability to fight by compelling peace while the issue is submitted to a tribunal, and that tribunal will inevitably and unconsciously be swayed by adherence to the old away from digression into the new. It must ever be kept in mind that the struggle of labor for betterment is not merely a question of here and now. It is eternally a question of the future, and not to be a combatant, at least potentially, would be for labor to turn its face backward.

There is a conspicuous illustration of these facts, which are facts of human nature, in the outcome of the anthracite coal strike. That was a struggle that in time came to affect the public convenience, comfort and health as vitally as could the paralysis of any public service corporation. That struggle was brought to an end through adjudication by a tribunal of inquiry. Very well; but be it observed that the battle preceded the inquiry. Had there been in existence a tribunal empowered to pronounce a verdict upon the issues between the mine workers and the operators, it never would have made an award so favorable to the advance of civilisation among the mass of inhabitants of the anthracite region as was made by the Anthracite Strike Commission, for the reason that there never would have been made the demonstration by the workers that they were so terribly in earnest in their conviction that their demands were just, that they were willing to go hungry and even to see their wives and children suffer, rather than work upon oppressive terms. There has existed for generations in Russia an office-holding class whose function was that of an industrial judiciary. Against industrial adjustment by this bureaucracy, it was a crime for workers to organize for appeal. The result was the evolution of industrial conditions so shocking as to be incredible to occidental minds and to cause a revolt in demand of rights that our civilization has grown to treat as axiomatic and to take for granted. Establish in the midst of our civilization such an industrial tribunal as proposed, and retrogression would ensue, perhaps slowly, but surely, toward the suppression of the toilers whose hands are tied.

The Chairman: Gentlemen, if there are any questions suggested by the discussion that any here wish to ask any of the three speakers, they are in order. Will Bishop Potter say a few words?

Bishop Potter: I would like to ask a question. I would like to ask my friend Dr. Low and my friend Mr. Wheeler how they propose to get this commission of compulsory arbitration appointed. Is it to be selected by the state or is it to be appointed by the two sides?

Mr. Low: I haven't attempted to work out the details of such a scheme, very largely because I don't believe myself entirely competent. The only thing that I presented was the reasonableness of such a method of settling disputes and the practicability of it. The point I endeavored to present for purposes of discussion was the reasonableness of settling disputes of this kind and its practicability if it was found to be desirable to do so. I assumed that if public sentiment desired, a law could be framed which would constitute such a tribunal in either of three ways—by perma[illegible]es, by temporary judges appointed by au[illegible] voluntary arbitrations are carried out, by the choice of an arbitrator throughout the parties concerned.

Bishop Potter: Mr. Easley, how far would a board of arbitration created by the state be able to go?

Mr. Easley: There are boards of arbitration and mediation in several states. They have no power to do more in some states than to compel attendance of witnesses and the production of papers. They then make a report. They have no power to compel compliance with the report.

Bishop Potter: My friend Mr. Archibald's suggestion to you of the value of force and collision in settling industrial disputes emphasizes my difficulty in reconciling the terms "compulsory" and "arbitration," and while I desire to make my acknowledgment publicly of what has been said by Dr. Low and Mr. Wheeler, I am bound to say that they have neither of them made that point clear. The value of arbitration, as I understand it, is the voluntary note in it. The moment it loses that note it loses its value. And while I quite agree with Mr. Wheeler that we are a law abiding people and disposed to acquiesce in judicial decisions, yet what I should like information about would be, How are you going to make, for example, a body of men who are on strike in connection with a railway company, go back and take their places and do their work unless you invoke, as Mr. Archibald very admirably told us, the military element? And then I should like to inquire how you are to avoid the inevitable tendency of such a system of government as it applies to labor and to travel, and to all the labors of life that strikes involve—the tendency of such a system toward what we call militarism and are very properly afraid of?

I don't believe the ordinary misapprehensions that grow up between workingmen and the employers of workingmen are the result of deliberate misleading on the part of labor leaders, though I am bound to say that there is no greater opportunity for enlargement of intelligence and information which underlie the relation of employer and employed than at that particular point.

What I think we want to-day is not so much a law creating a board which shall apply to the labor classes compulsory arbitration, as a commission which shall interpret the terms on which the workingman and the employer of the workingman are related to one another. Dr. Low has stated the substance of the whole question when he has reminded us that it is impossible for such a relation to exist unless it is plainly mutually advantageous. What you want is when the workingman comes into collision with a condition, which is usually what happens to him, some such help as will translate to him the terms on which he works and shall translate to the employer the terms on which he pays, and I believe the solution of our labor difficulties, so far as they exist in America, is exactly that point—to get a commission—

(*Continued on page 13.*)

TRADE AND INDUSTRIAL SCHOOLS IN THE UNITED STATES.

AN EMPLOYER, AN EDUCATOR, AND TWO LABOR LEADERS DISCUSS THEIR NECESSITY AND ECONOMIC EFFECT

THE following group of opinions upon the advisability of encouraging trade schools in the United States, and upon their relation to organized labor, has been collected as a result of the present agitation of the subject in Massachusetts. Governor Douglas, who officially recommended the creation of a State Commission to examine and report upon the subject, presents an argument in their favor. R. Fulton Cutting regards their necessity as following upon the disappearance of the apprentice system and cites the operation of the New York Trade school as an example of their practical usefulness. On behalf of wage-earners, Frank K. Foster, representing the Typographical Union and many other unions in Massachusetts, argues against them, but does not object to an inquiry by a commission on which labor shall be represented. John F. Tobin, President of the Boot & Shoe Makers' Union, favors their introduction in that industry.

TRADE SCHOOLS, COMPETITION, WAGES.

The following is the condensed argument of Governor William L. Douglas, of Massachusetts, advocating the establishment of trade schools.

In my official capacity I have called the attention of the General Court to the necessity of considering the advisability of establishing trade schools. I notice that there is some opposition to the project by the workers, on the ground that it would create a surplus of skilled labor, and that graduates from such schools would go to other parts of the country and lend their talent to the building up of competition. These reasons are not altogether well founded.

The object of the industrial and trade school is, first, to benefit the individual—the person who is compelled to earn his living by the work of his hands. It is intended by the establishment of these schools to teach the person not only how a thing is done, but why it is done, and to broaden his knowledge of the entire industry in which he is engaged so that when he has served a sufficient time he will be capable of purchasing the raw materials, converting them into a finished product and possess some knowledge of marketing them.

The second object of the trade school is to provide a sufficient amount of skilled labor to enable the manufacturing industries of the commonwealth to keep in the lead in its several lines of manufacturing. Thus could Massachusetts capital be employed to advantage in the manufacture of a large part of the goods now imported into this country, which in turn would mean the better employment of our work people and the prosperity of those communities in which the industries were located.

I have every reason to believe that the opposition to the movement will be less when the question is better understood. Our country is far behind other nations in the establishment of industrial and trade schools.

There has been urged upon the legislative committee on education the wisdom of reporting a bill authorizing the appointment of a representative commission to consider the whole matter and report to the General Court its findings and recommendations, together with some practical plan whereby the system of trade schools for all our industries may be established in the commonwealth. Surely there should be no opposition from any source to our endeavor to learn all we can about the subject.

To those who have given the subject but limited study it is apparent that the future of Massachusetts is dependent almost wholly upon the success of her manufacturing industries.

The method of conducting trade schools in Germany and the thoroughness of the education are the best in the world. Germany saw the need of such schools many years ago. Trade schools were organized, graduates sent out and the effect was so marked on the industrial situation that other countries were attracted by the progress made, and finally realized that Germany was distancing them in the excellence of her manufactured goods. Germany with her technical schools and army of educated workers has demonstrated the great economic principle that finer and better goods can be manufactured at a less cost than by uneducated and unskilled labor. Throughout the empire of the Kaiser trade schools are to be found in all the cities, towns and large villages. New factories are springing up everywhere, and Germany is increasing her export trade wonderfully.

I wish also to call your attention to the fact that in Berlin, as well as in most German cities, trade schools for shoemaking, tailors, carpenters, metal workers, masons, etc., are being conducted with friendly relations with the labor unions, and in many cases the boards of inspection have upon them members of the trade unions.

England, too, has schools teaching 60 trades. These schools are in operation and doing good work in all the cities, towns and larger villages. France is making great strides in the trade school movement. Belgium, Italy and Switzerland are also endeavoring to teach their young men to become expert mechanics. In Geneva, where the best watches are made, a young man must serve a five years' apprenticeship in order to get his education. He must make five or six of the best watches, make every part and put the watch together before he can receive a diploma which certifies that he is a practical, skilled workman.

The schools of technology, the textile schools and nautical training school of Massachusetts are doing a great work.

The Boston School of Technology has turned out mining engineers who have revolutionised the business. Twenty-five years ago a mine that would not yield from $20 to $30 worth of gold to a ton of ore could not be worked, because it cost $10 to get the gold out of it. Now, thanks to education, a ton of ore can be worked profitably that does not contain over $2 worth of gold. Under the Elmore process a ton of ore can be worked and 98 per cent. of the gold extracted at a cost of 10 cents a ton. Twenty-five years ago only about 25 per cent. of the gold could be saved. This shows what education can and does accomplish in our own country.

WILLIAM L. DOUGLAS.
Governor of Massachusetts.

The shoe industry is greatly handicapped by a lack of expert workers, especially in the cutting departments. Forty per cent. of our cutters do not perform the amount of work they should, owing to the lack of training to use quick judgment in placing patterns on the leather. In a trade school such as is proposed a competent instructor would teach pupils how to place patterns to the best advantage. By this lack of proper training the manufacturer loses, because the shoes cost more to cut; he loses because the workman is not able to produce as much work as an expert in the same number of hours. He also loses because the unskilled workman does not always put the right piece of leather in its proper place in the shoe.

The shoe manufacturer is also handicapped because the skilled workman is levelled down to the unskilled workman in the quantity of work done. This method of levelling down in the last five years has largely increased to the manufacturer the cost of cutting shoes. The cost in sole leather rooms, owing to unskilled labor, has also been increased by this levelling down process, and these conditions are growing worse every day. If these handicaps are not remedied it practically builds a barrier against the worker, which will prevent him from bettering his condition or in wages. The method in vogue to-day prevents any possibility of a young man's advancement, takes away his ambition, and places him in a position where he can see no hope for the future.

The shoe manufacturer is also handicapped because of the men who run machines, not more than 25 per cent. know how to keep their machines in thorough working order to produce the best results. Men have to be hired to do this work for them. A large corps of sub-foremen have to be employed to see that the work is kept up to a proper standard to meet competition. All this makes it harder and harder every day to meet competition.

With a thorough system of technical education, where a man would serve an apprenticeship and learn all parts of the business, our goods would be produced at a less cost and the workman would receive higher wages. When a young man thoroughly learns a trade and receives a diploma from a trade school, he is sure to get employment.

When our young men are all taught a trade, the problem of the unemployed will be solved. Those who are out of employment to-day are men who have very little knowledge of the work to be performed in any of our industries.

There will also be an opportunity for girls to learn a trade. In the factories owned by my company 500 women are employed. Trade schools would furnish an opportunity for girls after leaving school, between 14 and 17 years of age, to prepare themselves for employment. There has already been established in Boston a school for the education of girls where they are taught dressmaking, millinery and how to operate machines. They secure employment immediately after they receive a diploma from the managers.

The apprenticeship idea cannot meet the requirements of the present factory system. It has been outgrown. We must find a broader, larger way to assist the young man who desires to learn. The school for the many who may learn at once must take the place of the master who formerly personally taught his apprentices.

In the last generation the position of Massachusetts as a manufacturing state has greatly changed. Skill in workmanship will decide the future of Massachusetts, and only by the use of the best skilled labor can we compete with the Germans, English and French.

The skilled labor necessary to Massachusetts industries should be furnished not by skilled labor imported from abroad and other states, but by the young men from 15 to 21 years of age who are to become citizens of this state. We take away their birthright when we refuse them the positions of skilled laborers which we give to others, and equally so when we refuse to assist them in obtaining the knowledge which will enable them to compete with other skilled labor in their own state.

THE NEW YORK TRADE SCHOOL.

By R. FULTON CUTTING, *President of Trustees of the New York Trade School.*

The Trade School is the scientific method of trade education. The old apprentice system, now extinct, while narrow and unfair in some particulars, possessed practical qualities. The contract between master and youth embodied a mutuality of interests that supplied the inducement for the observance of its provisions. The master, taking the apprentice into his home and family, could only compensate himself by making him efficient and of good behavior. The more rapidly he could teach the apprentice his trade, the sooner would he become remunerative; and he looked to the last three years of his seven years of apprenticeship to compensate him for the cost of the young man's board and lodging during the whole term. It was always to the interest of the apprentice to acquire the trade as early as possible, as opportunities of earning a little money for himself were frequently afforded during the last years of his apprenticeship. The principal objection to the system, and that which led to the repeal in 1814 of the Act of Elizabeth, which with few modifications had been the law for four hundred years, was its practical restriction of the number of apprentices. The long term of the indenture and the exclusive methods of master workmen kept down the supply. In the middle ages the collusion between great land owners and the trade guilds was a serious abuse—the former desiring always to maintain a large supply of unskilled labor that they could hire at a low wage during the harvest seasons, and the latter, jealous of the privileges of their organizations, found common interest in shutting the door of opportunity to the unskilled.

Since the disappearance of the true apprentice system, there has been nothing discovered to replace it, in this country at least. The so-called apprentice of to-day learns as he can from the journeyman with whom he happens to work; he is really not taught at all. The journeyman, intent upon his own duties and under no obligation to the apprentice, makes what use he can of the latter, but gives nothing in return. Of course, in not a few individual instances, the kind heartedness of the journeyman induces him to give the apprentice occasional hints and suggestions; but however sympathetic may be his inclination, he has little opportunity to act as a teacher. Moreover he has himself learned his trade in the same "rule of thumb" school. He knows the "how" of his trade, but rarely the "why." Manual dexterity must, of course, be acquired, and the really ambitious student can learn much from books, but [illegible] ordinary measure of ambition that comes from an intelligent apprehension of the scientific basis of trade is lacking.

The New York Trade School, in a course of four months and with sessions of seven or eight hours a day, can actually teach a trade. It is difficult to comprehend how thoroughly trades can be taught in a school until a study is made of the system of instruction which prevails at this institution. In all departments each student is required to follow a prescribed course, starting with the basic principles and advancing, as skill is acquired, until all details from simple to complicated work are mastered. The students are of the proper age to insure excellent results, the general average being between eighteen and twenty. They are sufficiently mature mentally to realize the value of a trade and old enough to determine along just what line their aptitude lies. They are full of zeal and determined to succeed, and it is an inspiring sight to see them at work in the school shops. As serving to illustrate the practical character of the instruction, an outline is here given of the course in house painting:

(1) Name and use of tools, care of brushes, manner of keeping pots clean; (2) Painting new wood, priming, puttying and sandpapering, second and third coats; (3) Burning off paint when advisable; (4) Painting brick work; (5) Treating plastered surfaces in both kalsomining and oil; (6) Mixing paint, materials required; (7) Use of various stainers; (8) Color mixing in oil; (9) Color mixing in kalsomine; (10) Contrast and harmony of colors; (11) Painting doors and sashes; (12) Painting in two and three shades; (13) Flatting and painting with a glass; (14) Stippling; (15) Staining; (16) Varnishing; (17) Treatment of hard wood; (18) Enameling; (19) Gilding; (20) Preparing stencils and cutting same; (21) Laying in panels; (22) Applying ornaments; (23) Bronzing; (24) Graining; (25) Marbling; (26) Paper hanging.

During the progress of the course lectures bearing on the scientific features of the trade are given to the class.

It is true that these young men need from six months' to two years' practice and experience to make them fully equipped journeymen, but when they have had this they possess not merely the manual dexterity, but the scientific knowledge of their calling. They will have passed an examination, in graduating from the Trade School, of a nature that would floor many journeymen of this city who have spent years at the trade. Of course this does not mean that they are already as efficient as such journeymen, but it does mean that they possess possibilities of development and growth such as the ordinary craftsman does not.

The trades unions object to the school. It threatens to increase the number of journeymen too rapidly. The economic loss involved in spending five years in learning a trade that can be acquired in two or three does not appeal to their reason. They have spent five years as apprentices and the coming generation should not expect easier conditions. Of course, limitation of the number engaged in any trade is the fundamental objection of the trades unions to what they regard as an artificial method of increasing the supply, and one must remember that the journeyman who is no longer young does not wish to accelerate a movement that threatens to diminish his prospects of employment. The union fears its scale of wages cannot be kept up with an increased supply of skilled labor. But one factor in this question of supply and demand does not receive adequate attention by the American journeyman. Every spring hundreds of tradesmen flock to this country from various parts of Europe. They are usually very competent workmen—most of them have learned in European trade schools and technical institutions. They belong to the unions—they take advantage promptly of the demand for skilled labor which in good times exists all over the country during the season of pleasant weather. When the autumn arrives they sail back across the ocean, taking with them out of this country the earnings which should have gone to American tradesmen. This has been going on for years—the trade unionists of this country fighting against the education of their own children so that trade employment may be enjoyed by foreign craftsmen.

In the learned professions the tendency has been altogether the other way. It is true the general standard has been raised and it is necessary to acquire more learning to qualify, but the colleges and similar institutions have arranged their systems of study in such a way as to make it possible to acquire professional education under the most favorable conditions. That the professions have not suffered from this policy can readily be demonstrated. As far as efficiency is concerned, our professional men are second to none in the world. This is not the case with trade unionists. While the intelligence and energy of the American enables him to attain an excellence in the crafts that is astonishing when we remember his opportunities, yet in many trades the best men we have are foreign taught. They are the product of trade schools.

There can be no question but that trade schools tend to elevate the handicrafts by bringing into them men who are carefully and thoroughly taught, and who by reason of such training can undertake every branch of their trade. Proficiency and capability should be the passport into the ranks of journeymen and not simply the service of a stipulated term of years. The general run of apprentices under present conditions cannot become first class all round mechanics.

SOME OBJECTIONS OF WAGE-EARNERS.

The following are the views of Frank K. Foster, of the Typographical Union, as expressed to the Education Committee of the Massachusetts Legislature, upon the proposed commission to investigate trade schools:

"We are not lacking in gratitude to our friends, the professional educators, and other disinterested philanthropists, who desire to expedite the manufacture of

FRANK K. FOSTER,
Typographical Union, Boston.

craftsmen by state aid. We cheerfully assume that they have but the single purpose of the future welfare of the state in their propaganda for trade schools. We deem it but just, however, that the public shall be informed as to certain reasons why trades unionists cannot be expected to share this enthusiasm.

"The great economic fact confronting us, from the trade union standpoint, is that there are hundreds of thousands of wage-earners in this state whose life capital is their knowledge of a craft. They have listened very patiently of late to the frequent accusation that Massachusetts workmen possess comparatively little of this knowledge. This may or may not be true—incidentally, we don't believe it is true—but whether it be true or not, it is not germane to the point under consideration.

"But here our friends will doubtless interject the plea of the mobility of labor—that if a man cannot do one thing he can another. Would that this were true in general, as it may be true in especial instances. But every practical craftsman knows that the average man loses 50 per cent. of his earning capacity when divorced from his trade. It takes years of adaptation, of ad-

JOHN F. TOBIN,
General President, Boot and Shoe Workers' Union.

justment of sight and touch, of the acquirement of those deft details which are essential to skilled workmanship, to make the expert mechanic. You may as well say to the manufacturer whom you crowd out of business by flooding the market with the commodities he manufactures: 'You can go into some other field of business. The general welfare demands it.'

"No, gentlemen, you must consider the craft and the craftsmen as a whole, for the craftsman must practically depend upon conditions in the craft in which he has been bred. Here is a vested interest, so to speak, which legislators may not consistently disregard.

"I take it that it will quite generally be granted that the wage rate of Massachusetts mechanics is none too high, bearing in mind that these mechanics are taxed upon almost everything consumed by their families, assumedly for their own protection. What regulates this wage rate? How many times have we been taught and told that it is the law of supply and demand, i. e., that wages will go up when the supply is less than the demand, and down when the demand is less than the supply?

"Now, while the trade unionist would modify this teaching of the economist by the assertion that the causes which make the wage rate are complex, and may be modified by the will power of the labor seller himself, they yet recognize the truth of the general proposition that two employers hunting after one man give an upward tendency to the wage rate, and vice versa.

"If, then, you propose by this commission to recommend that the commonwealth shall increase the quantity of the supply of the commodity of craft skill in any given craft beyond the normal supply drawn in through competitive demand among employers, how can you expect the trade unionists to wax joyful over a course of action which, according to your own economics, will have a tendency to break down the rate of wages?

"May we be pardoned for insisting that public attention shall be called to this possibility, and that, if the associations of labor are to be dragged at the chariot wheels of a so-called educational and philanthropic movement, they shall not be compelled to profess ignorance as to just what kind of a performance they are going through?

"Despite all this, we are not in an attitude of hostility to the appointment of this commission, provided that the industrial class be given its equitable share of representation upon it, and that the conditions of service be such that these representatives can afford to serve upon it. We believe that the present resolve is defective in that it provides for but one representative from the large class most directly concerned, and that it provides for gratuitous service, which would bar out all wage earners from accepting positions on the commission.

"We are not opposed to industrial education, in its broad sense. We are opposed to the proposition of trade schools which would virtually place the state in the position of a recruiting agency for certain manufacturers, which the normal conditions of the labor market force to pay higher wages for skilled help than they desire to pay."

A LABOR LEADER'S APPROVAL.

John F. Tobin, General President of the Boot and Shoe Workers' Union, is a prominent labor leader who has declared unequivocally in favor of trade schools and unlimited apprentices in his industry. The following letter states his position:

Boston, Mass., March 8, 1905.

Editor The Shoe Retailer, Boston, Mass.:

As a result of the recommendation of Governor Douglas in his inaugural address, the subject of trade schools has become a live question in the State of Massachusetts.

I confess that when the subject was first approached I was very much opposed to the proposition, having in mind the barber schools, where they profess to turn out skilled barbers in a very few weeks, and which has resulted in the five cent barber shops, coupled with groans and scars sufficient to make trade schools of that kind decidedly unpopular.

Shoe manufacturers and other advocates of the trade school dwell at length upon the necessity of more skilled workers in the trade, if we are to develop a foreign market and hold it against countries where trade schools flourish.

They also dwell upon the necessity of men learning the various branches of the trade, so that they become not only skilled workmen, but have the necessary qualifications to make foremen and superintendents.

Germany is said to be a dangerous competitor because of the existence of trade schools, and I understand that in that country apprentices at the different trades are obliged to spend a certain portion of their time in attendance at the trade schools, and no person is eligible to attend the trade school unless they are employed at the craft which they seek to learn in the school.

I would, therefore, suggest that trade schools be established and that shoe manufacturers have unlimited scope in the number of apprentices they shall employ, who shall be indentured for a period of not less than three years, and they shall spend at least one-third of their working time in attendance at a trade school and two-thirds in the factory of their employer, thus acquiring a practical and technical knowledge of the craft in all its departments; the trade school to be maintained at the expense of the state, and the employer to be compensated for the time the apprentice spends at the trade school through his superior skill because of the technical training.

Respectfully yours,
JOHN F. TOBIN, General President.

CHURCH FEDERATION AND ITS RELATIONS TO CAPITAL AND LABOR.

A GREAT INTER-CHURCH CONFERENCE WILL EXPRESS ITS INTEREST IN INDUSTRIAL PROBLEMS —MINISTERIAL DELEGATES TO LABOR UNIONS.

By E. B. Sanford, D. D., *General Secretary of the National Federation of Churches and Christian Workers.*

AMONG the great movements of the present time one of the most hopeful and important is the drawing together, in closer fellowship and co-operation, of Christians of every name who hold to Christ as the Head of the Church.

It is significant that the basis upon which they find they can clasp hands and plan together in facing common difficulties and meeting common needs, is that of ministration and service. It is in the recognition of the great truth of the brotherhood of men, a truth that found its highest expression in the life and teachings of Jesus of Nazareth, that the fact is manifested that all Christians are one in Christ. In proportion as this fact is translated into terms of life, the Church is true to its mission and brings men to the recognition of their right relations to one another.

In the autumn of this year, for the first time in the history of the Protestant Churches in the United States, delegates appointed by the highest ecclesiastical assemblies or conferences of bodies, representing denominations whose aggregate membership is over seventeen millions, will meet in New York City for mutual counsel and federated action regarding matters of common interest.

This great Inter-Church Conference will directly and indirectly represent a considerable proportion of the

E. B. SANFORD, D.D.
Gen. Sec. National Federation of Churches.

home and family life of our country and their religious affiliations. If the number of employes and those connected with labor unions, found in the membership of the churches represented in this Conference, could be correctly enumerated, it would be a surprise to many.

Its message touching the relation of capital and labor cannot fail, therefore, to interest the entire community. That it will hold up a high ideal of brotherhood and plead for the spirit of the Christ in solving the difficult questions that grow out of present industrial conditions, we cannot doubt.

These questions, in spite of all representations to the contrary, rest heavily upon the thought and heart of those who have official and ministerial leadership in the churches. This has been shown in the action of great denominational bodies in the past year. We quote first from the message signed by Bishops of the Methodist Episcopal Church, a communion having a membership of over three million.

This message which forms an important part in the record of the General Conference held at Los Angeles, California, in May last, says: "Assuredly one of the burning questions of to-day is the relation of employes and employed. It may smolder here or there for a time, but somewhere it breaks forth in volcanic eruption and now and then it shakes the whole social fabric like an earthquake. The workers with brain and the workers with hands are often in hostile camps between which sharp collisions are alarmingly frequent and disastrous.

"Situations leading to such enormous waste and so fomenting evil passions, cannot fail to command the intense attention of the Church of God, which was founded by Him who died to save all sorts of men from their sins and from such frightful consequences of sin. The Church must come in between these vast contending forces, holding aloft the banner of the cross, to which both must bow, and offering to both the Sermon on the Mount as the charter of the rights and the duties of both. Never, until the Church shall lay the Golden Rule upon the conscience of capitalists and laborers, will the golden millennium of industrial peace be assured us.

"In all this contention it need hardly be said that the sympathy of the Church must to a large extent be with those concerning whom Abraham Lincoln quaintly said, 'The Lord must like the common people, else He would not have made so many of them,' doubtless having in mind the fact that when Jesus was on earth 'the common people heard Him gladly.'

"In spite of all the blunders made by labor leaders, and the indefensible acts of their followers philanthropic men must wish them success in every lawful effort to better their condition and secure their rights. But they must learn from their real friends that every act of violence hurts their cause and that law and order must be maintained at all hazards. We recognize as significant and hopeful the recent movement led by certain capitalists to settle by arbitration all disputes between labor and capital."

At the last session of the General Assembly of the Presbyterian Church held in Buffalo, May, 1904, the report of a committee of which the R. F. Coyle, D.D., of Denver, was chairman, was adopted that closed with these words:

"The Presbyterian Church has always believed and does now and most profoundly believe that the principles of the religion of Jesus Christ are the only basis upon which any true and lasting peace can be established between nations or between men in their industrial and other relations; and so believing the Church offers its earnest prayers and devotes its consecrated energies to the universal establishment of these principles, knowing that when the nations have received and adopted them they will learn war no more, and when men have embraced them they will dwell together as brethren: the employer, remembering that his employes are brethren, will treat them justly and righteously, and employes will remember [illegible] has rights which must be respected; and [illegible] the Church rejoices in the efforts [illegible] apply these principles [illegible]

"Believing that the [illegible] and the Arbitration Council are working along the lines of these principles, and for high and righteous ends, we [illegible] heartily commend their efforts and offer our prayers for their success. Gladly will we hail the day when nations shall settle their differences and men their industrial contentions in the arena of calm, just council and arbitration."

The vigorous and thoughtful reports on capital and labor adopted by the General Convention of the Protestant Episcopal Church, and the National Council of the Congregational Churches have already been published in the pages of this "Review" (Nov., 1904).

In view of these utterances and those we have quoted we have reason to expect that at the Inter-Church Conference to be held this year a message and plea in the interest of brotherhood and industrial peace will be sent forth, the influence of which will be far-reaching and fruitful.

THE PRESBYTERIAN CHURCH AND LABOR.

The Practical Success of a General Movement in that Denomination to Establish Cordial Relations between the Pulpit and Unionism.

The Presbyterian Church has been fostering for more than two years a movement to bring about a more cordial relationship between the church and organized labor. Those especially interested in this effort agree in reporting that the thoughtful labor leaders welcome the movement and urge their followers to co-operate. The result is already evident in the fact that much opposition to the church formerly existing among workingmen has changed into a spirit which makes it possible to carry the idea of co-operation between the church and trade unions, in the movement to better the conditions of wage-earners, farther than would have been at all possible two years ago.

A practical manifestation of this movement, which has received the full sanction of the Presbyterian Church, is the exchange of fraternal delegates between Ministers' Associations and Central Labor Unions. This plan has been carried into operation in about a dozen cities, with such good results that a special effort is now being made to extend it in many more cities. Only last month the Brooklyn Central Labor Union admitted a representative of the Brooklyn Presbytery. As this plan has been devised and carried out by Rev. Charles Stelzle, the special representative of the church in the interest of workingmen, its first step is to secure the interest of the President or the Secretary of a Central Labor Union. It has been found that this is easily accomplished, as soon as it is intimated that the delegate of the Ministers' Association is not bent upon preaching at the members of the Union, but that he wishes to learn, for his own benefit and that of the other ministers, something about what the organized labor movement in that city stands for.

The delegate minister does not ask for any of the privileges of regular members of the Union, but only for the privilege of the floor, when opportunity offers to make practical, helpful suggestions in the spirit of brotherhood.

It is regarded as important that the delegate minister should come to the union meetings unpledged to secrecy, the men trusting in his honor as a Christian gentleman not to disclose matters that, for business reasons, it may be wise not to give to the general public. This understanding relieves the delegate minister of embarrassment, and makes a better impression upon the community. In turn, the delegate sent by the Union to the meetings of the Ministers' Association is also unpledged and trusted with equal confidence.

To employers in the church, the suggestion is made that it is quite as proper for a minister to be associated with an organized movement that embraces great classes

REV. CHARLES STELZLE.
Labor Representative, Presbyterian Church.

of people as it is to be identified with associations or clubs composed almost exclusively of employers. This work is not primarily evangelical, but provision is made for meetings of that nature. Industrial problems are discussed at conferences between ministers and labor leaders. A considerable amount of literature is circulated upon topics connecting the church with labor, some of the suggestive titles being: "Jesus Christ and Rich Men;" "Class Spirit in America;" "Has the Minister a Closed Shop?" "The Relation of the Church to the Labor Movement;" "Labor Leaders in the Church;" "Not Missions but Churches for Workingmen."

This movement is opposed to Socialism, understanding that, while there may be Christian Socialists, Socialism is avowedly materialistic and that its leaders strive to make it a substitute for the church. But it concerns itself with the great host of workingmen who are not Socialists, and recognizes that the wage-earners of this country who are organized practically control the labor situation. The Rev. Mr. Stelzle says:

> With the increasing struggle and influence of [illegible] and the growing organizations of [illegible] interests, America has before it the biggest [illegible] problem she has ever wrestled with. The Church cannot [illegible] to this problem. There is rarely a strike or a lockout [illegible] Church or its ministry are in some way [illegible]. As a church and as ministers we must make our position clear to the men who misunderstand us.

Rev. John Dixon, D. D., who in an official capacity is especially familiar with the prosecution of this work, says:

> I have no doubt that the practical success with which this movement is meeting will have a [illegible] attitude toward the great questions involved in the relations between capital and labor of the representatives of the Presbyterian Church at the great conference of [illegible] Church Federation to be held in New York City next November.

The Rev. Mr. Stelzle is a machinist by trade, having been employed for years in a large manufacturing establishment before entering the ministry, and he still carries his union card.

THE NATIONAL

Civic Federation Review

Offices: 281 Fourth Avenue, New York City

RALPH M. EASLEY, Editor

The Editor alone is responsible for any unsigned article or unquoted statement published in THE CIVIC FEDERATION REVIEW.

Ten Cents per Copy; One Dollar per Year.

The National Civic Federation

OFFICERS

AUGUST BELMONT, President.
SAMUEL GOMPERS, First Vice-President.
OSCAR S. STRAUS, Second Vice-President.
HENRY PHIPPS, Chairman Ways and Means Committee.
CORNELIUS N. BLISS, Treasurer.
CHARLES A. MOORE, Chairman Conciliation Committee.
H. H. VREELAND, Chairman Welfare Department.
FRANCIS L. ROBBINS, } Chairmen Trade Agreement
JOHN MITCHELL, } Committee.
RALPH M. EASLEY, Chairman Executive Council.
SAMUEL B. DONNELLY, Secretary.

EXECUTIVE COMMITTEE.

On the Part of the Public.

Grover Cleveland, ex-President of the United States, Princeton, N. J.

Andrew Carnegie, capitalist, New York City.

Cornelius N. Bliss, ex-Secretary of the Interior, New York City.

Oscar S. Straus, member of the Court of Arbitration at The Hague, New York City.

Charles W. Eliot, President Harvard University, Cambridge, Mass.

Archbishop John Ireland, of the Roman Catholic Church, St. Paul, Minn.

Bishop Henry C. Potter, of the Protestant Episcopal Church, New York City.

David R. Francis, President Louisiana [illegible] sition, St. Louis, Mo.

Isaac N. Seligman, of J. & W. Sel[illegible] York City.

[illegible]

[illegible] the Part of Employers.

Henry Phipps, director United States Steel Corporation, New York City.

August Belmont, President Interborough Rapid Transit Company, New York City.

Lucius Tuttle, President Boston & Maine Railroad, Boston.

Frederick P. Fish, President American Bell Telephone Company, Boston.

Francis L. Robbins, President Pittsburgh Coal Company, Pittsburgh.

Henry G. Davis, Coal Operator, Elkins, W. Va.

H. H. Vreeland, President New York City Railway Company, New York City.

Samuel Mather, of Pickands, Mather & Co., Cleveland.

Charles A. Moore, Manning, Maxwell & Moore, New York City.

Franklin MacVeagh, of Franklin MacVeagh & Co., Chicago.

Charles H. Taylor, Jr., ex-President American Newspaper Publishers' Association, Boston.

Dan R. Hanna, of M. A. Hanna & Co., Cleveland.

Marcus M. Marks, President National Association of Clothing Manufacturers, New York City.

Otto M. Eidlitz, Chairman Board of Governors, Building Trades Employers' Association, New York City.

William H. Pfahler, former President National Founders' Association, Philadelphia.

On the Part of Wage Earners.

Samuel Gompers, President American Federation of Labor, Washington.

John Mitchell, President United Mine Workers of America, Indianapolis.

E. E. Clark, Grand Chief Conductor, Order of Railway Conductors, Cedar Rapids, Iowa.

James Duncan, General Secretary Granite Cutters' National Union, Washington.

Daniel J. Keefe, President International Longshoremen, Marine and Transportworkers' Association, Detroit, Mich.

Warren S. Stone, Grand Chief International Brotherhood of Locomotive Engineers.

P. H. Morrissey, Grand Master Brotherhood Railroad Trainmen, Cleveland.

William D. Mahon, President Amalgamated Association of Street Railway Employes of America, Detroit, Mich.

Theodore J. Shaffer, President Amalgamated Association of Iron, Steel and Tin Workers, Pittsburgh.

J. J. Hannahan, Grand Master Brotherhood Locomotive Firemen, Peoria, Ill.

James O'Connell, President International Association of Machinists, Washington.

John Tobin, General President Boot and Shoe Workers' Union, Boston.

Joseph F. Valentine, President Iron Moulders' Union of North America, Cincinnati.

James M. Lynch, President International Typographical Union, Indianapolis.

Denis A. Hayes, President Glass Bottle Blowers' Association of United States and Canada, Philadelphia.

THE ORGANIZED AND THE UNORGANIZED.

Letters from both employers and wage-earners are frequently received at the headquarters of the National Civic Federation bearing upon its attitude toward organized and unorganized labor. Several employers have asked why the representatives of wage-earners in the organization include only members of labor organizations. Why, they ask, is there no representation of the great mass of non-union wage-earners?

The answer to this query is simple. There really is no way to select a representative of unorganized labor, even if desirable, because that is composed wholly of individuals, each worker representing solely himself in his relations with any employer. To this reply, one employer made the rejoinder that non-union labor should be formed into an organization and representation given it. The fallacy of this suggestion is, however, apparent; for as soon as any number of non-union workers are organized, they cease to be "non-union" men, and their representative would not be a representative of unorganized labor.

A contrasting inquiry frequently made in various forms by members of trade unions may be thus summarized: "Why does the National Civic Federation include in the employers' branch of its membership some who do not employ union men, or who do not recognize union labor? If the Civic Federation believes in the organization of labor, why doesn't it expel all such members?"

This question involves a misconception of the character and scope of the National Civic Federation. Its by-laws define its purpose "to be helpful in establishing rightful relations between employers and workers." That broad statement does not restrict its mission to association of either employers or of workers. Again, its by-laws express the belief "that at all times representatives of employers and workers, organized or unorganized, should confer for the adjustment of differences." This language does not conf[illegible] representatives of [illegible] [illegible] Civic Federa[illegible] at the formation of [illegible] branches. But in every instance the labor members reached the conclusion that it is wise to include such employers in the movement. The reason they gave is that it enlists the interest, good will and intelligence of even the anti-union employer in a cause continually educational to all of its advocates. In one city there was at first objection to an employer as a member of the local branch of the Civic Federation, because he was then actually on a union's "unfair list." But further consideration caused the labor men to say: "Why, this is the very man we want to meet. We do not want to know only our friends; we want to make converts by showing that the leaders of organized labor are not agitators and grafters, but are devoted to the objects of unionism because they believe that their attainment is essential to the welfare of the human race."

There was a spirit akin to this in the response made by one large employer to an invitation to join the Civic Federation: "If to join the Civic Federation," said he, "means that I endorse all the radical acts or theories of organized labor, I will not accept membership; but, if it means that I recognize the labor problem as the greatest of the age, requiring the best that is in us all to work toward its solution through interchange of thought and experience, instead of through fighting, then I will gladly join in the effort."

SOME ANTI-BOYCOTTERS' BOYCOTTS.

The boycott is rated high among the crimes and misdemeanors imputed to organized labor by the anti-union employers' associations. This fact lends peculiar interest to the quotation that follows from an address by the chairman of the executive committee of the Citizens' Industrial Association, and to two remarkable examples of employers' association boycotts against independent employers in San Francisco. The quotation is made more refreshing by its opening exhortation, to those who "bitterly abhor" the "tyranny" of the union labor movement, to be "consistent in all things":

"Be ye consistent in all things," is a charge worthy of the consideration of all men. But let us see how consistent men are in some things relating to the labor-union movement, the tyranny of which they bitterly abhor.

The *American Federationist* is the official organ of the American Federation of Labor. It is edited by Samuel Gompers, the President of that organization. Its issue for July, 1903, contained 125 advertisements; its September, 1903, Labor Day issue, 490; its July, 1904, issue, 102, and its September, 1904, Labor Day issue, 431 advertisements, representing manufacturing and mercantile concerns, transportation companies, etc., and why were they there? Simply for lack of moral courage to say No! or, worse yet, because of a desire, prompted by selfishness, to stand in with the unions.

Have we not had experience sufficient, and is it not time now that men of common sense, men of honor, and men of ordinary patriotism, capable of reading the "handwriting on the wall," quit feeding their money into a cause which contemplates the destruction of an industrial and social system under which we, as a people, have prospered so well? If not, then when shall it be?

The Citizens' Alliance of San Francisco has threatened to boycott employers who do not join fight against the cooks, waiters and allied unions. This group of unions had agreements with the Restaurant Keepers' Association, fixing wages, hours and conditions of work. The Citizens' Alliance formed a new employers' organization, known as the Amalgamated Restaurant and Hotel Keepers' Association. When a committee of the allied unions attempted to renew the yearly agreement it encountered a flat refusal.

In the meantime, the President and Secretary of the Citizens' Alliance sent circulars to restaurant and hotel men urging them to join the new employers' association, which had declared "that no more contracts would be signed between its members and the unions." This was reinforced by the following formidable bit of literature:

OFFICE OF PRESIDENT.

THE CITIZENS' ALLIANCE
OF SAN FRANCISCO.

HERBERT GEORGE, President. 'Phone—Main, 966.

My Dear Sir: Mr. A. W. J. Gibbs, General Manager of the Amalgamated Restaurant and Hotel Keepers' Association, reports to me that you (for some reason best known to yourself) think it best not to identify yourself with the Amalgamation. The Citizens' Alliance is deeply interested in making the movement a unanimous one so far as the hotel and restaurant keepers are concerned, to the end that it may be spared the cost of a long and expensive strike. I believe you are intelligent enough to realize that we live in an age of organization, and the only way for you to protect your business is to forget that there are big and little restaurants and accept the fact that everyone in your line of business has the Cooks' and Waiters' Union to deal with. We trust you will need no further hint than this one to ally yourself with the new Association that Mr. Gibbs represents, because this new Association is simply an auxiliary of the Citizens' Alliance, and the Citizens' Alliance is backing it. I suggested the plan, and I feel sure that every man who belongs to this new Amalgamation of hotel and restaurant keepers will realize before the end of the year that for every dollar he pays into it he will get $10 back. We are not looking for trouble, and the only way to head off trouble is for all of us to get together and work in harmony. Above all things, I aim to avoid using the flour, meat, poultry, oyster and milk interests (which we have organized and now have in working shape) to coerce anybody. We are not in that sort of business and think the boycott is as un-American when practiced by our side as it is when practiced by the other side; but we are interested in the upbuilding of this new association for the protection of hotel and restaurant keepers, and it must succeed. The membership to-day is large and growing rapidly, but we want to make it absolutely complete to the end that its completeness will prevent the unions from breaking through our ranks.

We realize that many are hanging back believing they can get something for nothing by so doing. That is to say, they are perfectly willing that we should fight their battles with the unions while they stay outside and profit by the victory that follows. It is not our intention to let any man enjoy any such privilege. The membership is secret, and everyone must join and do his share. That is what the Citizens' Alliance is for. It is not fighting unions as much as it is fighting that class of people in its own ranks who refuse to do what they know is the right thing to do, believing that by hanging out they can play to both sides and thereby secure a little mean advantage over their neighbor.

"A word to the wise is sufficient!" You would greatly oblige me if you would call upon Mr. Gibbs and identify yourself at once.

Very truly yours,

HERBERT GEORGE, President.

As if this threat were not enough, another circular warned employers who were still reluctant to make war on the cooks and waiters that "We are now busy with the bakers, who are forming a strong organization"—thus adding bread to the other supplies that the association threatened to cut off from any hotel or restaurant persisting in dealing with the unions. This circular added the ominous information: "I have been compelled with the asistance of the Citizens' Alliance to commence suit against three restaurants for signing with the unions." To the threat of the boycott is thus added the vague terrors of the law for daring to make contracts with unions in defiance of the edict of the Citizens' Alliance!

Another employers' association in San Francisco, styled the Butchers' Exchange, places the union button under the ban and decrees the substitution of the "open shop card," enforcing its ukase with threatened penalties in the following circular:

SAN FRANCISCO BUTCHERS' EXCHANGE,
628 MONTGOMERY STREET.

Room 22, 3d Floor. Telephone—Bush, 131.

SAN FRANCISCO, March, 22, 1905.

The attention of the San Francisco Butchers' Exchange has been called to the fact that certain shops are taking advantage of trades union conditions to gain trade by the displaying of signs and the wearing of union buttons by employes; it has been therefore

Resolved, That no shop shall display cards or advertisements having any bearing on the labor question, or allow their employes to display union buttons while on duty, or any other insignia of unionism.

Any infraction of this rule will be punished by suspension, or fine, or by both.

The only sign or placards to be used shall be the regular Open Shop Card, which must be displayed in a prominent position.

L. B. WIELER, Secretary.
By W. A. SAMUEL, Assistant Secretary.

The *Labor Clarion* publishes a fac-simile of an official notice by the Butchers' Exchange that two butchers had been suspended, because they had refused to pay an assessment of the Butchers' Exchange, on the ground that they were not members. One of them tore up the open shop card. As a penalty, the *Clarion* states, these two butchers discovered the next day that they could buy meat from the Butchers' Exchange only by paying several cents a pound more than their competitors.

TWO CONSERVATIVES DISAGREE.

(*From the Iron Age.*)

While the management of the strike on the Interborough system in New York was admirable, one minor mistake was made, which we trust will not be repeated in any part of the country. An offer of employment was made to students at Columbia University, which was accepted, largely as a lark, by quite a number of the boys. Newspaper reports indicate that some of the professors of the university rather encouraged the students to enter employment which could at best be only temporary, since the boys are supposed to be engaged in preparing for a profession—a work which, as it is, suffers from only too many distractions. We do not blame the students when they seize upon an opportunity for excitement and for attracting public notice. But it was a serious mistake on the part of the college authorities to permit the boys to become strike breakers, because it fosters a class feeling, which should be studiously avoided. The pupils of an educational institution must not be placed in the position of participating in an industrial struggle. The day of learning the management of men must come to many of them when they enter upon their life work, but until they have left the university they should not be allowed to intervene as students, whatever they may do as individuals during their vacations. In the eyes of a very large proportion of our citizenship a certain odium attaches to every strike breaker, and our highest institutions of learning should not go out of their way to fasten that odium upon themselves.

We hold the belief, too, that the managers of the Interborough system made a tactical mistake when they invited engineering students to accept such employment, because it was obvious on the face of it that those who responded to the call could do so for only a very brief period. It gave strength to the conviction which the strikers themselves generally hold that strike breakers are employed for only a brief emergency and that few of them settle down as regular employes who permanently occupy at least some of the places of the strikers.

(*From the Wall Street Journal.*)

The organ of the American Federation of Labor comments with severity on the action of a number of Yale students in offering to take the place of strikers in case of a strike on the New Haven road. During the recent subway strike in this city a number of students offered their services as motormen, conductors and ticket sellers. The *American Federationist* does not think that the students are bad, or that they would knowingly injure the cause of organized labor, but says that "they must be misled by such attacks on trades unions as President Eliot, of Harvard, is in the habit of making." The spectacle of students taking the place of strikers is in its opinion "disgusting, shameful and dangerous."

This is laying down a rule that when a body of men give up their jobs in order to force a corporation to pay them higher wages or grant them shorter hours of labor, other men have no right to take their places. In other words, jobs are sacred to members of the American Fed-er[illegible]n of Labor, and nobody else has any right to them. [illegible] is not the American idea. The spirit of this [illegible] is free labor for everybody. Let everybody have [illegible] to work, and if he does not want to work for [illegible]ges which are paid him, he has the liberty to stop [illegible]rking; he has the undoubted right to strike. But there is no moral or legal obligation on the part of other men to prevent them from taking the places of those who choose to strike.

The bulk of the young men who go into our colleges come from families possessed of moderate incomes. To put them through college means a hard financial struggle. It involves sacrifice of many pleasures and rigid self-denial. Many of our young men pay their way through colleges. They are glad, therefore, of the opportunity to find places where they may earn something that will enable them to continue their college course. That they should take the opportunity of a strike to secure remunerative employment, instead of being disgusting and shameful, is in the highest degree creditable to them. It shows that they are willing to work and work hard in order to get ahead in the world.

The American Federation of Labor cannot erect a fence around the jobs in the United States and put up a sign, "No Trespass." There can be no such a thing as monopoly in labor very long in this country, and we believe that the same thing is true of capital.

HON. SETH LOW ARBITRATES THE CLOSED SHOP.

THOROUGH MASTERY OF TECHNICALITIES RESULTS IN AN AWARD WITH WHICH BOTH SIDES EXPRESS SATISFACTION.

ONE objection urged against arbitration generally by employers is the danger of calling in as an umpire some high-minded representative of the public, who, not being able to grasp the technical complications involved in a controversy, may render a decision that will be satisfactory to nobody. Both employers and unions are generally agreed that there are certain questions of principle that are not arbitrable, such as the question of the closed shop. To each of these propositions a conspicuous exception is found in a decision rendered, as an arbitrator, by the Hon. Seth Low. He evinced a remarkable capacity for mastering the most intricate details of the highly skilled printing industry; rendered a decision that proved satisfactory to both parties, while the decision was peculiarly important in that it related to the question, usually excluded from arbitration, of the closed shop.

The fact that this decision was satisfactory led to a subsequent request for Mr. Low's services in another case in the same trade, in which the representatives of the Typothetæ and of the Typographical Union joined in this expression:

"Your decisions in the settlement of the strike at Little's, though applying to only one office, have served as a precedent in every similar case that has arisen, and have been so accepted by both parties to the controversy, which can be said of but few arbitrations of individual cases; so that both committees are naturally very desirous that you should accept. We know that you are a very busy man and that we are crowding in on time already fully occupied, but we hope that you will see your way clear to oblige us."

The strike in the job rooms of J. J. Little & Co., in 1896, ordered by the Typographical Union and supported by the Pressmen's and Electrotypers' unions, threatened to involve the entire printing trade of New York. But the men returned to work under an agreement to refer the eight demands to a joint committee of ten, with Mr. Low as arbitrator. Five of these demands were adjusted by the committee. Of the three submitted to Mr. Low for decision, he found in one case in favor of the union and in the other in favor of the Typothetæ.

The demand for a "closed shop" was in this form: "That book and job rooms shall be recognized as card offices." Mr. Low's decision, delivered at a time when the "closed shop" was not a subject of such acrimonious discussion as now, follows:

This is a question ordinarily decided by power. If the union is strong enough to carry its point, an office is made a card office. If the employer is strong enough to maintain his position, he declines to have his office made a card office. I have shrunk not a little from attempting to pass, as arbitrator, upon a question of this nature; but, upon reflection, I have thought that a fearless discussion of the question by one in a position to look at it with impartiality might prove of sufficient advantage to justify the attempt. In a word, I think the contention of the union has in it an element of right; but in its entirety it involves two points that I am unable to sustain.

As one detail of this question in its application to the office of J. J. Little & Company, it is urged by the union that Mr. Little at one time became a member of Typographical Union No. 6, and in so doing pledged himself to give preference in securing employment to union men. Mr. Little admits that he did join the union thirty years ago; but claims that the incident has no relation to the present question. As it bears upon the matter in arbitration, I am constrained to treat the incident as having no decisive weight.

A card office, in the meaning of the union, is an office in which only union men are employed, and which is organized into a chapel, so-called, presided over by a chairman on behalf of the union. It is clear that such a condition of affairs may exist in an office as matter of fact, without its being recognized as a matter of policy by the employer. The union claims, for example, that in the office of J. J. Little & Company the press department, the electrotypers' department, and the stereotypers' department are all card offices. J. J. Little & Company aver that they have never been recognized by the firm as such. It appears to be the case throughout the trade at large that more than a few offices are considered card offices by the union which are not so considered by the employers.

In support of its demand, the union alleges that it is unwelcome to union men to work in the same office with men who receive the benefit of the union scale and generally profit by the attitude of the union, but who decline to share with the union the burden of securing and maintaining these advantages; and that it is especially unwelcome to union men to work side by side with men who, having been at one time members of the union, have been expelled therefrom for one cause or another. The union deems, therefore, that for this reason, among others, it is justified in asking that Little's book and job rooms should be recognized as card offices, in view of the fact that most, if not all, of the employes of the office in those rooms at the present time are union men. It further urges this conclusion in the interest of the compositors, in order that the compositors may be upon the same basis, as it claims, as the stereotypers, electrotypers, and the pressmen in the same employ. The union urges it also because such a condition, in its judgment, is absolutely necessary to the faithful carrying out of the provisions agreed upon in the present settlement, as well as of those to be determined by this arbitration.

The Typothetæ object to the claim of the union that the book and job rooms of J. J. Little & Company be recognized as card offices, for a number of reasons, the most fundamental of which are:

1. That J. J. Little & Company have successfully withheld this recognition for many years, "particularly in 1887, when not only that office, but nearly every office in the city of New York successfully resisted such a demand, although enforced by strike;" and that, as matter of fact, the demand is to-day as obnoxious as ever to that firm.

2. Because they claim that "in the office of J. J. Little & Company no distinction is made as to union or non-union, Jew or Gentile, American or foreigner, black or white; qualification being the only test."

3. Because of the character of the control claimed by the Union in an office that is admittedly a card office.

It is apparent from this *resume* that the questions at issue in this demand are very fundamental.

So far as the Typothetæ hesitate to recognize the union as the representative of the union men in their employ, I think they are mistaken. I think they are justified, on the other hand, in objecting to certain incidents that would flow from the recognition of the book and job rooms of J. J. Little & Company as card offices. As I view it, an employer is at liberty, if he pleases, to employ none but union labor. He is at liberty, also, if he pleases, to employ only non-union men. There are, in fact, printing houses of both types in the city of New York, although, as I judge, many more of the former than the latter. In the book and job trade, I understand that most of the offices are what are known as "open offices;" that is to say, employment in them is open to union men and to non-union men alike. I understand the office of J. J. Little & Company, as to its book and job rooms, to be such an office at the present time. It does not follow, it seems to me, because an employer employs both union men and non-union men without discrimination, that he is therefore at liberty to disregard the connection of his union men with their union. When a man employs members of a union, knowing them to be union men, or having good reason to suppose that they are union men, he must take them, it seems to me, with all that their unionism implies. In other words, I think that J. J. Little & Company, having book and job offices which are composed largely, if not altogether, of union men, may reasonably be expected to recognize the union in all negotiations upon which it may enter in behalf of the union men in their employ. To this extent I think the union is right in its present demand.

There are two points involved, however, as matters now stand, in the recognition of an office as a card office, which, it seems to me, cannot be sustained by argument, however they may be enforced by power. No one can compel union men, without their own consent, to work with non-union men. But it is a different thing to demand that an employer shall not be free to employ any but union men, and that I understand to be involved in the demand under consideration. It is no more reasonable, I think, for the union to demand that J. J. Little & Company shall not be free to employ non-union men, than it would be for non-union men to demand that the firm should no longer be free to employ union men; or, than it would be for J. J. Little & Company to demand that the union should be deprived of its freedom to take in new members at its own discretion. Employer and union alike ought to be free to determine what is for their own advantage in such matters. No arbitrators, I think, could find that an employer should be constrained, against his will, to shut his office either to union men or to non-union men. The other point at which I stumble in the consideration of this demand is this. In a card office, under the regulations of the union, a dispute between the employer and his employes is determined by the Executive Committee of the union. The representatives of the union have urged with great force that this tribunal in Typographical Union No. 6 has shown itself in many cases to be an impartial tribunal; that it has, as matter of fact, decided in favor of the employer perhaps as often as in favor of the employe. This may be conceded; but it remains a fact, nevertheless, that it is a one-sided tribunal, and because it is a one-sided tribunal it does not afford such a provision for the settlement of disputes between employer and the employe as would

(*Concluded on page 12.*)

HOW THE AMERICAN TELEPHONE AND TELEGRAPH COMPANY PROVIDES FOR THE WELFARE OF ITS EMPLOYES.

(From a Contributor.)

When telephone central stations were first established, the work of attending to the wishes of the subscribers was done exclusively by young men, who stood while at their work, but it soon became evident that the needs of the service could best be fulfilled by women, and their transference to these positions took place rapidly. With these later conditions of help, active measures were initiated for furnishing them with the most beneficial means for their comfort. As it is to-day, so from the very first, every endeavor of the telephone company was concentrated upon methods whose sole purpose was to secure the permanency of the telephone service by housing the central apparatus as far as possible in fireproof buildings, equipped with every desirable safeguard, to make the construction of lines as stable as possible, and also to lay the wires in cities underground. While limiting conditions require varying means for the comfort of the operators, yet every effort has been made from the first to obtain the highest efficiency of the service by the use of the best apparatus at the time being, only to renew it, even if it be in good order, to substitute later improvements, which were rendered necessary by the destructive agency of inventions, and in order to secure the manipulation of this apparatus with the highest degree of efficiency, it was essential that the operators should be selected from intelligent young women, who could be well trained for their duties with environment which would conduce to health and contentment, for it is wholly desirable that good telephone operators should be retained in the service as long as possible, without intermittent breaks in daily attendance.

The care for the welfare of the operators differs in various cities according to the facilities which it is feasible for the company to adopt. These are modified locally

ADJUSTABLE CHAIRS WITH FOOT RESTS, BOSTON.

by the space available for such purposes and by the distances of the operators' homes from the exchange. The amount of travel is minimized by assigning them to central offices as near to their homes as the requirements of the service permit. In snow storms so severe as to stop street car service the company has often provided quarters for the operators for the night at a nearby hotel under the chaperonage of the matron. In other cases the company has sent operators to their railway stations in carriages.

When one visits the telephone offices, which are generally in the top story of fireproof buildings, away from the noise of the city, one is at first struck with the quiet which prevails in the room where a babel might be expected; for an operator need speak but little and that in a low tone of voice in the performance of her duties.

LIGHT.

Such rooms are lighted during the day for the most part by monitor roofs, which divert the glare of the polarized rays which are so trying to the eyesight, and a system of curtains as elaborate as those of a photographer's studio provides for agreeable illumination during the day. At night the face of the switchboard is illumined by incandescent lights, screened from direct vision by reflectors, which cast rays on the face of the board in such directions that the accuracy of the hand is never impaired by shadows.

VENTILATION.

Although there is necessarily a great concentration of occupancy of such rooms, health and comfort are secured by means of forced ventilation, and the temperature is frequently controlled by thermostatic appliances. The continuous use of an operating room requires far more efficient ventilation than does an office or a workshop occupied less than one-third of the twenty-four hours. Therefore great care is used in the ventilation. The air is drawn from a place either at the rear or on the roof of the building, as far as possible from direct contamination of the streets. Nevertheless, this method of forced ventilation would necessarily bring an excessive amount of dust into the room, were not this air filtered through tubular screens of cloth. An analysis of this dust, thus extracted in large quantities from the air, showed it to contain:

Moisture	.20
Magnesia	2.18
Alkalies and other undetermined substances	8.95
Lime	12.82
Alumina	13.70
Silica	22.85
Carbon, organic matter, etc.	39.30
Total	100.00

This material has also been found to contain a large amount of iron, evidently worn by attrition from horseshoes and wagon tires, although the inlet to the air supply was in the center of a large block. Microscopical examinations show that the material is mainly composed of particles of soot, scales of mineral matter, spores of mould, shreds of wool and cotton, and bits of hair. The removal of such foreign and unnutritious material must contribute to the hygienic properties of the air as well as render the building cleaner.

In certain western cities, where the use of bituminous coal is universal, the air is actually scoured by sprays of water, and the excess of moisture is removed by subjecting it to a rapid rotary motion, which throws out the water as a centrifugal extractor separates the milk from cream. In winter, the air is humidified to an extent which renders it soft and equable, and has mitigated the throat difficulties which result from excessively dry air, which prevails under the usual conditions of artificial heating in northern temperatures.

These methods of sanitation were devised for the purpose by persons connected with the company, and the result has been so successful that they have been widely adopted elsewhere and also form the subjects of lectures in several medical schools.

SEATS FOR WOMEN.

The chairs provided for the operators are adjustable, both as to the height and the foot rests. Their shape was selected after careful experiments, in which those who were to occupy the chairs took a prominent part; and, before adoption, this type of chair received the approval of physicians whose services were secured for this purpose.

REST AND READING ROOM.

Connected with each telephone office is a retiring room, in which each operator has a ventilated locker, usually of enamelled iron, for outer garments and other paraphernalia. This room is also furnished with easy chairs, lounges and tables, and provided with books and papers. The care and management of reading matter is under a committee of the operators, and the expense is usually divided between the company and a payment by the operators of about 5 cents a week. In some instances books are cirmulated as in the case of a reading club, the last person receiving the book in alphabetical order of name retaining it as her own. The lounges in this room are of plaited bamboo and of a shape selected by the advice of physicians.

TOILET AND LOCKER ROOMS.

These retiring rooms are under the charge of a matron, who has a few simple remedies for cases of slight indisposition. If illness sufficiently serious occurs an arrangement is made with neighboring physicians to respond to any call for immediate attention.

Connected with the retiring room are toilet and bath rooms, as well as lavatories. There are clothes dryers heated by steam, so that damp garments and umbrellas may be thoroughly dried.

LUNCH ROOMS.

Telephone offices are equipped with lunch rooms, which are provided with steam tables for heating lunches and with refrigerators for cooling them. In many instances the telephone company supplies, without charge, coffee or chocolate to supplement the cold lunches brought by the operators; and in some places, at nominal cost, a light lunch, including soup, one or two cold meats, fruit, bread and butter, and tea, coffee or milk.

PRIZES.

In some cities where there is a large number of switchboards a record is kept in each office of the rate of answering calls, speed of answering, percentage of errors, number of complaints, and regularity of attendance of the operators. The office making the best record for the month receives as a prize a picture or other gift appropriate for the retiring room.

REST AND READING ROOM, NEW YORK.

FIRE PROTECTION.

As in the case of schools or other places, where there is a dense occupancy, the tendency to panics, which otherwise would be inevitable on exposures to fires or smoke from other parts of the building, is reduced by fire drills, which are held at irregular intervals and without warning. There have been numerous instances where an operating room was filled with smoke from fire which threatened no actual physical hazard, yet was naturally alarming; but any destructive results which might have followed a panic among the operators were averted by the discipline of the drill.

CLASSES FOR INSTRUCTION.

The selection of an operator is attended with the utmost care. It involves the usual recommendation as to character, information as to general intelligence, and a medical examination by a woman physician—particularly as to the voice and hearing. Before taking permanent positions at the switchboard, they are under instruction, and also under pay, in a school where the operation of the telephone switchboard is explained and to a great extent its principles illustrated by means of models specially constructed for the purpose. The learners are also given practical experience in the operation of the switchboard.

One company employs a man to give talks to the operators, which are not merely technical, but treat of travel or topics of literary interest. The appreciation of these efforts on the part of telephone companies for the benefit of their operators is indicated by the fact that it is customary for them to come earlier than their duties require or remain later for the sake either of reading in these retiring rooms or attending to sewing or other feminine handiwork.

WORKING CONDITIONS.

Hearing is not impaired by the use of the telephone, but on the contrary, as is the case with musicians—particularly those playing the violin, or other instruments requiring tuning by the performer—the auditory sense is developed to a point of great acuteness. Operators use identical receivers and transmitters, and when one leaves her position at the board, after a period of not over three hours, her instrument is hung upon a numbered hook; a substitute in turn uses instruments which are reserved for her own use.

Women operators are directly under a woman supervisor, although in the large offices the whole operating room is under the supervision of a man. The service at the switchboard is broken up by recesses, and an operator can at any time obtain a temporary substitute by telephoning to the lady supervisor in the room.

In addition to the manipulation of the telephone service at the central station, there are in large business houses private branch exchanges in such numbers that in large cities, such private branch exchange operators exceed the number of central operators. While the conditions surrounding these private branch exchange operators are like those of stenographers or other first-class office help, yet such positions are considered desirable because in most instances the hours are very short and the duties light, although requiring such a high order of experience and intelligence that these operators are usually selected from the most efficient of those in the central telephone offices.

The telephone company exercises especial efforts

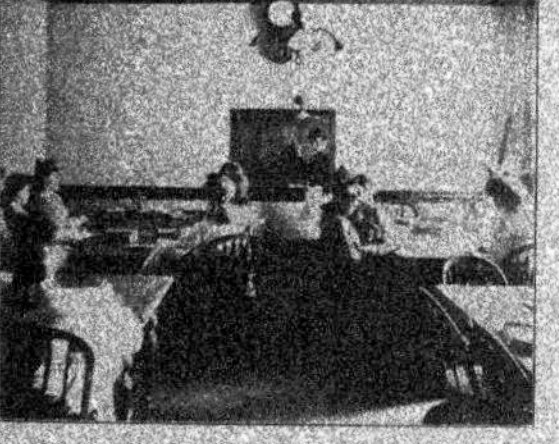

SCHOOL FOR BEGINNERS, NEW YORK.

for the welfare of its men employes, who are obliged to face the exposure of weather and various hazards incident to their work. The duties of many linemen being to a certain extent intermittent, some place or room is always provided for them when not on active outside duty.

There are many methods of insurance, varying in detail. One organization has a fund of $19,000 accumulated from its annual balls; another insurance association has relatively large reserve funds. Generally a person's membership continues for a year after leaving the service of the company, and in some instances membership is retained as long as the annual dues are paid. These associations include benefits which award a larger amount for death by accident than by disease, as well as a larger weekly stipend in case of disability from accident than from illness. In all cases the telephone company adds large contributions to the monthly assessments paid by the men. Various meetings of a social and improving nature are held in connection with these insurance and benefit associations.

CLOTHES DRIERS, HEATED BY STEAM, BOSTON.

(This view shows one drier pulled out for the purpose of hanging the damp clothes therein. Frequently in stormy weather employes are obliged to remain in damp clothes all day where they have been obliged to walk long distances to work. This is a very essential provision for health.)

STATE INSURANCE IN GERMANY.

(Reprinted by permission from *Scribner's Magazine* for April.)

[The following is an extract from the fourth of a series of articles by Frank A. Vanderlip, appearing in *Scribner's Magazine*, under the general caption, "Political Problems of Europe." The subject of the April article in *Scribner's* is "Paternalism and Nationalism," and the extract here reproduced deals especially with State Insurance in Germany. The author's treatment of this subject makes a fitting climax to previous articles that have appeared in THE CIVIC FEDERATION REVIEW upon allied topics, namely: by Max Riebenack, Comptroller of the Pennsylvania Railroad Company, upon "Railway Provident Institutions;" by E. E. Clark, Grand Chief Conductor of the Brotherhood of Railway Conductors, upon "Why Employes Object to Railroad Relief Departments," and by Francis L. Robbins, President of the Pittsburg Coal Company, upon "Profit-sharing, Insurance and Pensions."—EDITOR'S NOTE.]

In any examination of European political and economic institutions, the attention of an American would at once be attracted to the subject of workingmen's insurance. He would find it a subject not only of vast importance in European political and social life, but one presenting to him novel considerations, because the institution is practically without parallel of any sort in this country. Nothing that I have seen in Europe has interested me more than the effect of workingmen's insurance. On the Continent one finds it, measured from any point of view, one of the most important subjects that is presented in the whole array of affairs. As a rule, I think Americans have little conception of the extent to which the system has developed, and of the marked effect which it is producing upon national economy and upon social conditions.

Workingmen's insurance conducted as a government or semi-government institution is confined to the Continent. In Great Britain there is no Government activity in this field, the development there being wholly within the ranks of the friendly societies, or else in the direction of the provisions which are made by the great railway corporations for pensioning in part their superannuated servants. The weight of political sentiment in Great Britain is violently opposed to the adoption by the Government of any position which might lead to national responsibility for workingmen's pensions. On the other hand, in the ranks of the working men, and particularly in organized labor, there is a growing disposition to force the question upon the attention of Parliament.

It is on the Continent that we find the governments intimately related to the subject of workingmen's insurance. There has been an interesting development of semi-public, semi-government insurance institutions in Germany, France, Italy, Austria-Hungary, Belgium, Sweden, and Denmark, and in all of these countries the movement has assumed proportions of political importance, and the workings of the systems have already produced marked sociological effect.

It is in Germany that there is to be found, by all odds, the highest evolution of workingmen's insurance. In that country a social experiment has been conducted on a vast scale, and I think the movement may fairly be said to mark the most interesting recent social legislation that is to be found anywhere in the world.

The significance of the movement in Germany will be better understood when it is noted that 17,000,000 German workmen are contributing to and enjoying the benefits of the pension system. That significance is emphasized when we learn that since the inception of the system, in 1885, the total receipts have reached $1,750,000,000. At the present time the annual receipts are in excess of $130,000,000, an amount sufficient to make us consider with much interest the economic consequences of the plan.

ADMINISTRATION OF INSURANCE FUNDS.

Especially is it noteworthy to find that this vast sum has been administered with absolute integrity. The administration of the insurance funds of Germany offers one of the best indications in the world to-day of the possibility of a successful state control of important institutions, even when enormous sums of money are involved. The demonstration, however, has more than integrity to its credit. The collection and disbursement of these great funds have been carried on with an economy which is admirable. In considering the cost of administration of the German insurance funds it should be remembered that collections are made from 17,000,000 individuals, as well as from the employers of those individuals, and that in making disbursements, particularly of the sick and accident funds, there is a care and intelligent supervision exercised which must make the cost of disbursement quite as great as the cost of collection. There are, therefore, reasons for a much higher ratio of expenses than would be essential in such a system of life insurance as we have in America. But, as a matter of fact, the cost of administration of American insurance funds makes sorry comparison with the expense of administration in Germany. It is a monument to the economy of the German administration to find that less than eight and one-half per cent. of the total income is used up in the cost of administration, and that ninety-one and one-half per cent. is paid out in benefits to the insured. A showing like this, so greatly in favor, apparently, of the economy of government administration, would seem to raise the inquiry as to whether Germany has not found a better plan for the administration of insurance funds than we have evolved in this country.

Nothing like a full consideration of the subject of workingmen's insurance is to be given in the course of a magazine article. I believe it is a subject worthy of the deepest consideration. Certainly it is one that offers many difficulties before a clear conclusion can be reached as to its effect and advisability. There are arguments of great weight on both sides of the subject. I believe, however, that it is a subject which in due time will come before us in America for consideration and action.

Any exposition of even the German system of insurance alone is too complicated to be presented in a brief study of the subject. The system in Germany is an evolution, and in its present form probably none of its friends would suggest that it is an ideal system. Anything like a complete understanding of its provisions is complicated by the fact that there are three distinct forms of insurance—insurance against sickness, against accident, and insurance to provide old-age pensions. An explanation of the system is further complicated by the fact that the administration of these three distinct and separate insurance funds is in many different hands, although all are under the supervision of the general Government. The sick insurance fund is administered by more than 23,000 sick clubs. The accident insurance is administered by nearly five hundred managing boards, which represent various state and municipal communities and various trades and industries. The old-age pension system is in the hands of some thirty-one distinct insurance institutions. An understanding of the details of German insurance administration is, therefore, difficult, but some general considerations of its provisions, and effect are easily possible. All the insurance funds are contributed to in about equal proportion by employers and by the insured, and that total is augmented by a subsidy from the empire. Employers pay in about forty-seven per cent. of the total, the workingmen less than forty-six per cent., while the subsidy from the Government provides between seven per cent. and eight per cent.

EFFECT OF DEEP SOCIOLOGICAL INTEREST.

The effect of the institution, as seen in Germany, is of far wider significance than are merely the admirable efforts in alleviating distress caused by sickness, by accident, or by poverty in old age. The results which have been attained in the accident insurance field, for example, are far broader than the mere indemnification in some measure for the suffering and loss which accidents have entailed, and it is likewise true in the other branches that the provision which has been made for the payment of pensions in lieu of wages lost in case of sickness has been only a part, and one might say almost a minor part, of what has been accomplished in that field.

The results of the German workingmen's insurance embrace considerations of the deepest sociological consequences, on the one hand, and of a most significant effect on the national health and physique, on the other. The Germans have gone at the whole subject with their characteristic thoroughness, and the whole world will in time be forced to give attention to what is being accomplished.

ACCIDENT INSURANCE.

The German system of workingmen's insurance is founded on a very general belief that the change which has been going on in Germany, transforming that country from an agricultural into an industrial state, and the evolution which has been proceeding in industry, resulting in a great specialization of work and the high development of the factory system, have made necessary an enunciation of some new principles in regard to the duty of the community toward the individual, principles which are fundamental in their character. The intricate and complicated modern system of industry has left the industrial population economically dependent, no matter how free it may be politically, the Germans argue, and the development of that system has brought the industrial population into a position where it is difficult for the individual to extricate himself from his misfortunes should he be overtaken by accident, sickness, or old age. In this new industrial order the liability to accident is greatly increased, and new means for meeting the condition which that fact has brought about are demanded.

Various nations have recognized the increased liability to accident which has come with the present-day development of industry, and have taken diverse means to meet the new condition. Germany offers the most notable example of a development of accident insurance. France, on the other hand, has undertaken to meet the demands which industrial workers make for some adequate provision for indemnity by passing most rigid and far-reaching legislation, fixing upon the employer the liability and making provision so that the injured workingman may easily enforce that liability in the courts.

EMPLOYERS' LIABILITY LEGISLATION.

In America there not only has been little legislation passed on this subject, based on broad principles of humanity, such as have actuated the German legislation, but there has been little progress toward more definitely fixing the liability of the employer, and making it easy for the injured person to enforce a claim. Instead of that, there has arisen here a system of so-called employers' liability insurance, which is in effect organizations of strength with which to combat weakness, organizations the object of which is not to indemnify the worker for injuries, but rather to indemnify the employer for the cost of fighting in the courts the claims of the injured persons. The purpose of this system is not to put the insurance company in the position of a fair employer who will make payment of a just indemnity. Its purpose is accomplished rather by fighting each individual case with all the skill which its organization, made up of experienced adjusters and sharp attorneys, enables it to pit against the feeble efforts of an injured workingman who is attempting to enforce even the inadequate legal rights that our legislation has thus far accorded him. If statistics were presented dividing the receipts of these insurance organizations so as to show what amount they expended in actually paying indemnity to injured persons, and what amount they used in fighting claims and paying dividends, the comparison which those figures would make with the humane institution of accident insurance as developed in Germany would be anything but to our credit.

Germany has accomplished most admirable results in the way of providing indemnity to persons injured in industrial occupations. The work accomplished by accident insurance however has been of far wider usefulness. Accident insurance as developed in Germany has really been an insurance against accident, not merely the providing of indemnity. There has been evolved there, as a result of the study which employers and employes who have been managing these insurance funds have given to the subject, a system of laws and of regulations providing for safeguards which have gone far to reduce the number of accidents, and to remove the danger from industrial callings. In the last few years the effect of these safeguards has been to reduce one-half the frequency of accidents. Viewed from an economic standpoint alone the saving which has resulted to the national economy has been a vast sum. In the United States we seem as extravagant of life as of resources. There is no single line in our national statistics that is read in Europe with such startling surprise as the one which shows 60,000 fatalities and injuries on our railroads in a single year. In other industrial fields we are as careless of life. It seems to be regarded as more economical to fight damage suits than to provide safeguards, and dangers that do not interfere with dividends frequently receive little attention.

SAFEGUARDS AGAINST ACCIDENT INTRODUCED.

It is noteworthy that German employers have willingly accepted the burden they are charged with on account of workingmen's insurance. That it is a very considerable burden there is no denying. The Krupp Steel Works alone, for example, contributed more than $2,000,000 for the purposes of workingmen's insurance within the period from 1885 to 1902. The amount which employers are paying, compared with the total wages paid, is showing increases as the operations are extended in the various fields of insurance. The actual contributions to the insurance fund have, too, been only part of the expenses that the administration of the insurance laws has charged the employers with, because they have been forced to spend great sums of money providing safeguards against accident, and putting their works in the best possible hygienic condition. The general disposition among employers, so far as I have ob-

FRANK A. VANDERLIP,
Vice-President, National City Bank.

served, however, is to regard these expenditures as having been made with good value received, because of the increased efficiency and better health of their workmen, and their contentment and fair attitude toward capital.

DISEASE PREVENTED AND STEADY EMPLOYMENT SECURED.

There have been almost as great indirect benefits connected with the administration of the sick insurance fund as has been the case in the field of accident insurance. Remarkable results have been attained in the prevention of the spread and in the cure of contagious diseases. The sick insurance administration has by no means stopped at the point of giving care and financial aid in cases of sickness. More and more its aim has been to seek, with the utmost energy, every means for avoiding the disturbance in the wage-earning capacity of the workingmen which sickness entails. It has sought to ascertain the principal causes of sickness, and to combat with organized and scientific efforts the various enemies of public health. The organs of the workingmen's insurance committees have done a great work in educating the people in hygiene, and particularly in reducing the scourge of pulmonary diseases. This has been done through prompt and effective measures of isolation and treatment, and in directing special attention to the question of the hygiene of workingmen's dwellings. The administration of the sick insurance, instead of being confined to rendering assistance to the sick and the invalid, has sought to cure them, and make them fully capable again of earning their former livelihood. In the development of that work the Germans have characteristically gone to the very foundation of the question, and are doing as important service in effectively preventing sickness as they are in curing it or relieving the distress which follows from it.

The effect upon the general level of the national health has been enormous. In the field of hygiene, as in the field of education, the German Government seeks to make of each individual the most effective economic unit it is possible to develop. In doing that, the aid which has been rendered by the direct and indirect results of workingmen's insurance in improving the physical condition and increasing the power of resistance to diseases, and in promoting the recovery and full return to health of those who are ill, has been beyond all calculation.

HARMONIOUS RELATIONS BETWEEN EMPLOYERS AND EMPLOYES.

There is one phase of the benefits which workingmen's insurance in Germany has conferred that is not to be measured by statistics nor weighed with exactness by definite evidence, but it is, nevertheless, one of the most noteworthy of all the influences that have grown out of this great social experiment. There has been accomplished a service of the very first importance in the direction of bringing about more harmonious relations between employers and employes. There is growing to be a better and better mutual understanding between capital and labor, and the administration of these insurance funds has furnished a common ground upon which the two interests can meet and discuss those questions which affect both. The committees that have the administration of all the details of the collection and expenditure of these great funds are made up in part of employers and in part of workingmen. In serving on these committees, employers are brought to a better understanding of and a closer sympathy with their employes, and workingmen have been given a clearer comprehension of economic possibilities in the field of industry, and have come better to understand their employers' point of view. I do not mean to say that Germany has reached a millennium, and that there is complete harmony and understanding between capital and labor there, but I do feel that the labor situation offers some sharp contrasts to conditions in other countries, and that those contrasts are favorable to Germany. I have frequently spoken of the spirit which pervades so many of the institutions of Germany, the spirit of making each individual member of the commonwealth the most efficient of industrial and economic units.

HON. SETH LOW ARBITRATES.

(*Concluded from page 9.*)

commend it to the approval of disinterested men. A tribunal, to command such approval, ought to be composed of an equal number of representatives of both sides, with provision for arbitration in the event of inability to agree. Section 125 of the General Laws of the International Typographical Union appears to me to recognize this position. This section reads: "When disputes arise between subordinate unions and employers, which cannot be adjusted after conference between the parties at issue, the matter may be settled by arbitration." Indeed, the present proceeding, in my judgment, is a type of what ought to be the uniform method of procedure in cases of dispute between union men and their employers. My observation, founded upon an experience of ten years in business life, leads me to believe that all business arrangements, to be permanent, must involve the element of mutual advantage. A relation that permanently favors one party to a transaction at the expense of the other, is, in the nature of things, short-lived.

Accordingly, if my functions as arbitrator permit me to pass upon this demand only categorically, I am obliged to find that the demand that the book and job rooms of J. J. Little & Company be declared card offices should be denied. If, on the other hand, I am at liberty to say, with hope of its acceptance, what I think is fair in all the circumstances of the case, my finding would be this: That J. J. Little & Company recognize Typographical Union No. 6 as the accredited representative of the union men in their employ in their book and job rooms, and that permanent arrangements be made for the arbitration of all differences between the firm and the union upon the general lines of the present arbitration.

Such an agreement as I have in mind has been recently entered into between the Lithographers' Association of the Metropolitan District and the New York Subordinate Association of the International Lithographers', Artists' and Engravers' Insurance and Protective Association of the United States and Canada. This agreement is spread out at length in the history of the recent lithographers' strike, pages 27-30 inclusive. Another form of permanent arbitration, which has behind it the record of ten years of success, is to be found in the agreement between the Masons and Builders' Association and the Bricklayers' Union of the City of New York. The lithographers' agreement provides for a temporary board of arbitration to dispose of each dispute as it arises. The masons' agreement provides a permanent board of arbitration, and contemplates an agreement to be revised and renewed in all its details each year. It is naturally impossible for me to say which form of agreement is best adapted to the printing trade. In one form or the other, however, I wish to throw whatever authority or influence I have, as the arbitrator in this controversy, in favor of this method of settling all disputes hereafter in the book and job rooms of J. J. Little & Company.

IS COMPULSORY ARBITRATION PRACTICABLE?

(*Continued from page 4.*)

and I believe that commission would be of incomparably greater value if it were a voluntary commission and not a commission elected or appointed by the Legislature, but a commission representing trained minds like that of our friend, Mr. Carroll D. Wright and others, who have made a life long study of this enormous subject. That is the only word that I should like to leave before we adjourn, that while on the whole we have made during the last quarter of a century enormous progress in the betterment of the condition of the workingman and the betterment of the understanding of his relation to labor and capital, there are yet in that direction much land to be passed, many fogs to be cleared away, much illumination to be furnished, and with a commission of interpretation, if to-day we could create that everywhere to construe the contract, the relation, whatever it is, between the workingman and his employer—that would be of supreme value. (Applause.)

On the day following the above discussion, Mr. Wheeler addressed the following letter to Bishop Potter:

New York, April 5, 1905.

My dear Bishop Potter:

May I answer the question that you put to Mayor Low last night?

My proposition would be that the members of such an arbitration tribunal as I propose should be appointed by the President of the United States, and selected from among the judges and ex-judges of the Federal Courts, and that their jurisdiction should extend to all interstate commerce cases. A similar tribunal in this State I would have appointed by the Governor, and selected from the judges and ex-judges of the Supreme Court of the State.

It does seem to me that Mr. Archibald's objections are very like those that used to be taken a hundred years ago or more, to the giving up of duelling. This was a sort of private war, but experience has shown that we can do very well without it, and that questions, even of a very delicate and even sacred character, can be safely adjusted by the courts. I cannot see that the questions that arise between capital and labor are any more sacred or difficult than those which arise between husband and wife; and yet when all efforts at conciliation in the latter instance have failed, it is better to have a judicial tribunal to give some decision than to leave the decision to the contention of the two parties concerned.

At any rate this is the judgment which I have formed as the result of forty years' experience in court.

Yours faithfully,
EVERETT P. WHEELER.

INTERNATIONAL NON-ARBITRABLE QUESTIONS.

The following letter from the Professor of International Law in Columbia University, who is recognized as the highest authority in this country upon that subject, sheds light upon questions excluded from international arbitration:

Editor National Civic Federation Review:

Sir:—I have your letter of the 7th instant, in which you ask, "What questions, if any, arising between nations, are considered by common consent, or in international law, or usage, as essentially non-arbitrable?"

If we consult the history of international arbitrations during the past hundred years, we find that it is impossible definitely to answer this inquiry. By this I do not mean to convey the opinion that the use of force in the conduct of international affairs is likely soon to be abolished; but I do mean to say that phrases such as "national honor" and "national self-defense," which have been employed in describing supposed exceptions to the principle of arbitration, are of little value as indicating what questions may or may not be arbitrated. Questions of honor and of self-defense are, in international as in private relations, matter partly of circumstances and partly of opinion. When the United States, in 1863, first proposed that the differences that had arisen with Great Britain, as to the fitting out of the *Alabama* and other Confederate cruisers, should be submitted to arbitration, Earl Russell rejected the overture on the ground that the questions in controversy involved the honor of her Majesty's Government, of which that government was, he declared, "the sole guardian." Eight years later there was concluded at Washington the treaty under which the differences between the two governments were submitted to the judgment of the tribunal that met at Geneva. This remarkable example serves to show of how little value are mere descriptive phrases, when we are dealing with practical questions.

The extent to which international arbitration can be carried depends chiefly upon the dispositions of the parties to the dispute. A nation could not be expected to submit to arbitration the naked question of its own independence; and yet a dispute which in one form might appear to involve independence, in another form might not appear to do so. In other words, the dispute might, by patient negotiation and mutual concession, springing from a desire to reach an amicable settlement, be reduced to a form in which the issues would be clearly arbitrable. I may observe that the project of an arbitration treaty adopted by the Pan-American Conference in 1890 provided that arbitration should be obligatory in all cases except those which, in the judgment of one of the parties to the controversy, might imperil its independence; and even in these cases it was provided that, while arbitration should for such nation be "optional," it should be "obligatory upon the adversary power." This treaty never became effective. Had it been put into operation it is altogether probable that the clauses which have just been quoted would, when they came to be applied, have given rise in some cases to a wide divergence of views; and this divergence would have furnished a proof of the correctness of the opinion that the limitations of arbitration cannot be precisely fixed by general restrictive phrases. Roughly speaking, it might perhaps be agreed that "vital interests" and "national independence" may properly be excepted from an international agreement of arbitration, where such agreement takes the form of a general and positive obligation. But we should still have to determine in each case whether the particular difference fell within or outside those categories.

Very truly yours,
JOHN BASSETT MOORE.

April 10, 1905.

SOME QUESTIONABLE ASSUMPTIONS.

(*By the Editor.*)

The discussion of compulsory arbitration of industrial disputes, as thus far developed, proceeds largely upon two assumptions: First, that all questions that may arise between employers and wage earners are arbitrable; second, that neither party to an industrial dispute can win without the support of public opinion, and that public opinion is infallible. It may clarify the further consideration of this subject if we examine these two assumptions and ascertain whether they are wholly warranted.

Disputes between nations arise as do disputes between employers and employed. Voluntary international arbitration has been applied successfully to the settlement of some disputes between nations. But the method of international arbitration provided in The Hague Convention, the most advanced product of the efforts of civilization to secure peace, clearly recognizes that there exist questions that no nation would consent to submit to the decision of an arbitral court. The most casual thought will make it apparent that among the disputes between nations that diplomacy may fail to adjust, there are some that, if they are to be settled at all, can be settled only by the stern arbitrament of arms. It is not conceivable that any question involving, or appearing to involve, the existence of a nation or the continuance of its form of government, or its honor, could be submitted to arbitration. The Hague Convention in express terms provides that "powers who accept arbitration will sign a special act, clearly defining the scope of the arbitrators." Not content with this limitation, the United States Government, in becoming a signatory to the treaty, made this declaration: "Nor shall anything contained in said convention be so construed as to require the relinquishment by the United States of America of its traditional attitude toward purely American questions."

Thus we see, in the concrete outcome of the Universal Peace Conference of 1899, the existence of non-arbitrable questions recognized both generally and specifically.

It could not have been possible for the first French Republic to have consented to arbitrate the effort of the Alliance to restore the Bourbon monarchy. Within our own time and in our own country, the impossibility will be recognized at once of arbitrating the issues of the "irrepressible conflict" that were settled by our civil war; or the Cuban question that, despite the most painstaking efforts of diplomacy, made inevitable our war with Spain; or any issue involving the Monroe Doctrine, or the exclusive right of the United States to construct the Panama Canal.

Similarly, in the industrial world there are questions which one side or the other could not consent to submit to arbitration, because they involve principles strikingly parallel to those that debar some issues from international arbitration. The right of a man to belong to a union or the right of an employer to hire a non-union man are questions that neither employe nor employer would consent to arbitrate, because there is involved what each side regards as an intolerable surrender of individual liberty.

When the Chicago Metal Trades Association (employers) proposed to the International Association of Machinists (employes) to arbitrate a dispute involving apprentices and handy-men, the answer was a refusal on the ground that the questions placed in jeopardy the very existence of the union, and a strike ensued.

When a union, through its organized efforts, has secured certain general conditions, such as an eight hour day, it refuses to arbitrate a demand to return to a nine hour day, on the theory that it will not risk losing what it has already established.

The Building Trades Employers' Association of New York City (the largest organized body of building trades employers in the country), recognizing that the union would not arbitrate questions involving working with non-union men, or the lengthening of hours, excluded these two questions from arbitration in their celebrated compact.

John Mitchell has instanced the eight hour day, which has prevailed in the bituminous mining fields for years, as a subject never to be submitted to arbitration.

The International Association of Bridge and Structural Iron Workers, in its contracts with employers, stipulates: "None of the definite agreements of this contract shall be subject to arbitration."

This same idea is put in the most extreme form and made to apply to any use of arbitration in a recent speech by John Kirby, Jr., chairman of the Executive Committee of the Citizens' Industrial Alliance of America:

> Arbitration has proven a failure over and over again. If I am held up for my belongings and I refuse to surrender them, why should I submit the question to arbitration and take my chances on having to surrender half of what I have. Then, on the next hold-up, surrender half of what I have left, and so on until everything I ever had is gone.

In fact, people who have had practical experience in arbitration in the industrial world are constantly running against exceptions until, in some cases, it seems that it is hardly possible to find anything that both sides are willing to arbitrate. For instance, in the controversy between the lithographic employers' association and the five allied national unions, representing 95 per cent. of the capital invested and the labor employed in that industry, the employers demanded a trade agreement that should bind the unions to submit all questions that might arise to arbitration. The unions contended that there were certain questions that they could not, with justice to themselves, so submit. These were the three great issues of wages, hours and the closed shop, which they maintained must be definitely established in any trade agreement, and arbitration employed only for any remaining questions. Conversely, the employers, while demanding wholesale arbitration and an absolute abandonment of strike or lock-out, contended that the ratio of apprentices should be made larger and should not be subject to arbitration.

In the operation of a public service corporation, such as an electric street railway, the corporation regards an entire class of subjects as impossible of arbitration, because they involve the safety of the traveling public. For instance, the motormen of the Interborough objected to a medical examination, claiming that what they called a "practical road test" would be just as effective in ensuring safe service. But it was pointed out that the medical examination was necessary to test the heart action, for its susceptibility to electric shock; the hearing and vision, for quick and accurate understanding of signals; and the respiration, to guard against the chance of unconsciousness while running a train at high speed. Questions of discipline in such a service are also regarded as non-arbitrable, because they also relate to the safety of the public; just as in marine transportation, the absolute authority of executive officers at sea is not to be arbitrated.

Sympathetic strikes present issues that are not arbitrable. The last great railway strike in this country, that of 1873, is an illustration. The original trouble was a strike in the manufacturing shops of Pullman Car Company. An effort was made to tie up every railroad in the country that hauled Pullman cars, out of sympathy. The railway companies were under contract with the Pullman Company to haul its cars. To the suggestion of arbitration, they replied: "We have nothing to arbitrate. We have done nothing to cause you to strike. We would be penalized if we broke our contracts with the Pullman Company. Your affair is with them, not with us."

On the other hand, a labor organization does not regard provisions of its constitution or by-laws as arbitrable. Thus the constitution of the American Federation of Musicians forbids its members to play with non-union musicians, fining them for the first and second offenses and expelling them for the third. Accordingly, last winter, the local union of musicians in New York declined to play with a lady harpist until she joined the union. This was not a question of gallantry, to be arbitrated by a commission expert in artistic etiquette; it was a question of the union's constitutional law, that left no ground for arbitration.

These examples might be multiplied indefinitely. They serve to show that there is a considerable range of questions, varying in different industries, that are regarded by either employers or wage-earners as outside the scope of arbitration.

The second assumption of the advocates of compulsory arbitration, that the verdict of the public is necessarily infallible, is not surprising. That assumption is extremely common and ancient, as is indicated by the saying, "Vox populi, vox dei." No one will deny that in a broad sense this is true, even though it is commonly said that all majorities have at some time been wrong. All progress means emergence from darkness toward light, a growth out of error toward the truth. All progress, in its origin and growth, is a process of conversion of popular belief.

But this long process of historical evolution cannot be applied to the public opinion whose judgment, quickly, almost instantly, formed, may become the basis of action upon present issues.

A little reflection will show that the opinion of the public, even of its most intelligent portion, is subject to the influences of as much bias, prejudice and emotion as is the opinion of the individual, and is as discordant as are the opinions of parties to any dispute. Thus, in the long period of debate, both economic and passionate, that preceded our civil war, the church itself was rent asunder upon the moral aspect of slavery, while the bar was divided upon its legality and the Nation was torn over the constitutional right of secession. The bulk of the most learned opinion in England, after the growth of the factory system, stood aghast at the proposition to restrict the hours of labor, to require sanitary conditions, to regulate the employment of women and children. These, it was asserted, were invasions of individual liberty; while the economists gravely argued that unless the cost of labor were kept to the lowest point consistent with the existence of the laborers, foreign competition would ruin British industry. It required years for the minority demanding these industrial reforms to become the majority.

It is pertinent to recall the state of public opinion during the anthracite strike of 1902. The public was widely divided in opinion as to the right and wrong of the struggle between the mine workers and the operators. Public opinion was unanimous only upon two points: People wanted their coal bins filled, and they protested against the cost. These were points of agreement, because they touched the common need. Had public opinion been of a judicial cast it would have suffered cheerfully the deprivation, discomfort and expense, because these should be endured in the cause of right, either of the strikers or the mine workers.

Political contests afford the most familiar examples of the fallibility, not to say gullibility, of public opinion.

Large results sometimes hinge upon incidents, essentially trivial, but distorted and exaggerated for political effect. The "roorback" is a familiar weapon of the closing days of important campaigns.

The perspective of history illustrates vividly the changing public conception of the characters of men in political life. To-day, the American Nation reveres the name of the Father of His Country. But in his own time, a considerable portion of the citizens of the Thirteen States believed the denunciations of George Washington heaped upon him by his partisan opponents.

Was it not public opinion that forced Galileo to recant, under oath, his discovery that the earth moves around the sun? Andrew D. White answers that question by saying: "The supporters of what was called 'sound learning' declared his discoveries deceptions and his announcements blasphemy." It was a century before modified opinion permitted the removal of his bones from a dishonored grave. Even nearer our own day, the same authority tells us, the great Cotton Mather published a book "thanking God" for the burning of witches at Salem; "and his book received the approbation of the Governor of the Province and the President of Harvard College." Even Christ was crucified in obedience to an outburst of public opinion.

But granting that public opinion is not infallible, the advocates of compulsory arbitration would provide a method for its education, through a commission of "high-minded, disinterested citizens" to investigate and report upon industrial disputes. The assumption here is that a body of such a character can always be trusted to arrive at the truth in any controversy. But do the conclusions already reached by the expert wisdom of the Bench wholly verify this assumption?

Civilization has evolved elaborate codes of law and systems of jurisprudence. Yet the highest court in the land renders decisions upon which the justices are almost evenly divided; the decisions are themselves subjects of popular debate.

The Dred Scott decision settled nothing and plunged the Nation into violent controversy. Nothing could show a more hopeless tangle of judicial intellects than the decision as to the Philippines; scarcely any two of the justices following similar lines of reasoning. Expediency, rather than conviction, favored its general acceptance.

Industrial disputes are essentially questions for prompt decision. But there exist no formulated principles of industrial ethics such as have been established, through centuries of experience, in legal jurisprudence.

Any tribunal would have to summon to its aid expert testimony relating to a tangle of confusing interests and peculiar conditions. The experts would contradict one another, as handwriting and medical experts do now in the courts. Is there any certainty that a conclusive result, carrying in its terms conviction of its justice, would be reached by such a process? And is there any assurance that subsequent public opinion would sustain the decision?

So strong has grown to be the distrust in the assured justice of the decision of a dispute by any outside judgment, whether of an umpire, a court, or ultimately of the general public, that many trade agreements, especially in England, now provide that disputes shall be referred to a joint committee, composed of an equal number of representatives of each side, and prohibit the employment of any umpire, as well as the rendering of any compromise verdict. The bricklayers and other organizations in this country have a similar provision in their by-laws. A provision for conference, instead of arbitration, with equal representation of each side, is an increasingly frequent feature of trade agreements.

There is a striking parallel to this resort to an evenly balanced conference committee in industrial disputes in preference to arbitration in the method by which the controversy over the Alaskan boundary was settled. In that instance, it was the effort of Great Britain to make it appear that the boundary dispute was referred to "arbitration." But in fact, the word "arbitrate" was stricken from the treaty at the request of the United States, whose attitude was that its right to the Alaskan coast strip was too well established for arbitration. The treaty accordingly provided that the six members of the tribunal, three appointed by Canada and three by the United States, were to act as "impartial jurors." John W. Foster, ex-Secretary of State, thus defined the method of settling this international dispute: "The treaty does not entrust any American territory to the adjudication of arbitration, but creates a commission of three American and three British experts to determine where the line should be drawn between Alaska and British Columbia."

It is urged that the state may exact, as a condition of any corporate franchise, that the company bind itself to arbitrate any difference with its employes. One objection that employers instantly suggest is that such a requirement would amount to a standing invitation to the employes to seek or to invent or to exaggerate grievances, and to demand arbitration in the confidence that the award would not injure them, and might better them. The chance that the arbitrator might be an elective office-holder or other politician would tend to increase this temptation. Even more serious, employers claim, is the objection that this plan would be compulsory upon the corporation but not upon the employes. No device has yet been contrived that would enforce compliance with an award by the employes. Neither bonding, nor incorporation of the unions seems practicable. But even if they both were, there exists no means to compel men to work effectively against their will. There was a recent impressive illustration of this fact in Italy, where the Kingdom operates the railways. But a dispatch from Rome describes the employes, during a period preceding a strike, as adopting a novel means of pressing their demands upon the authorities:

They observe the regulations in their minutest details, and lose as much time in the process as possible, with the result that the entire railroad system is disorganized, and the official time table has no relation to the running of trains. The method employed by the "obstructionists," as they are termed, instead of strikers, is as follows: When a passenger arrives in a railway station and asks an employe where the ticket office is, the man is as long as he can possibly be in giving the desired information. Arrived at the ticket office, the employe there scrupulously tests every coin handed him by the passenger before accepting it. The porter who handles the baggage saunters along the platform at a snail's pace, and with exaggerated care arranges the hand luggage in the compartment. The trunks are piled with mathematical exactness on the truck and leisurely conveyed to the baggage car. As the train is about to leave the station it is discovered that the engine is short of coal, or water, or that the wheels of the train have not been tested for hot boxes, and so on, until the passengers are exasperated beyond measure. In the beginning the men had the sympathy of the public, but this they have lost by their erratic proceedings.

At Milan some tourists fell upon the employes and beat them with their canes. The large number of English and American tourists who visit Italy at this season are the main sufferers from the present state of affairs, and many are leaving the country for other lands by the waterways.

Even under a monarchy and under state operation here is illustrated the power of recalcitrant employes to nullify the possible regulations established by an arbitral tribunal.

ANNUAL MEETING OF THE NEW YORK CIVIC FEDERATION.

INDUSTRIAL DIFFERENCES HARMONIZED THROUGH ITS CONCILIATION COMMITTEE—AUGUST BELMONT REAFFIRMS HIS FAITH IN TRADE AGREEMENTS.

THE second annual meeting of the Civic Federation of New York and vicinity made a special feature of its proceedings a discussion of Compulsory Arbitration as a method of preventing industrial disturbances, particularly in its application to public service corporations and their employes. The discussion of this topic, which was suggested by the recent strike on the lines of the Interborough Rapid Transit Company, is published in full upon preceding pages of this issue of THE REVIEW. The other business of the meeting, which was held in the rooms of the Board of Trade and Transportation on April 4, consisted of the receiving of reports and the election of a General Board, which will elect general officers.

In calling the meeting to order, Oscar S. Straus, Second Vice-President of the National Civic Federation, stated that he had been called to take the chair, in the absence of Charles A. Moore, President of the New York Civic Federation. Mr. Straus said:

"A great deal of the work that is done by the Civic Federation is of a confidential nature; often so confidential that even the Secretary's report refrains from touching upon it. However, there is considerable work of which many of you are more or less conversant which will be presented. When the Civic Federation was formed, it was the opinion of a great many that our main work would be arbitration. But it has proved that the Civic Federation, as such, has never arbitrated a single case. There have been here and there members of the Civic Federation who have been called on in their individual capacity as arbitrators; but the Civic Federation, as such, has never acted as an arbitration board. Its function has been confined almost entirely to conciliation and to a method of adjustment that is even subsidiary—to bring together the disputants. We have often found that troubles have arisen between employers and employes which were not due to any fault on the part of either, but rather due to the lack of understanding among the employers. There were certain concessions which the employes demanded which the employers would have been glad to concede, but the employers, being all competitors, one with the other, and not on the most friendly relations, and by reason of severe competition, never came together; and the result was, while some of the employers would have been very glad to grant some concession, they were unable to grant it because their competitors would not grant the same concession. This happened in several important cases. The mere fact of bringing employers of a certain line together has in several instances contributed to an adjustment of serious differences that would have lead to lockouts and to strikes." The Secretary, James P. Archibald, read the report of the Conciliation Committee of the New York Civic Federation for the past year, which was received and placed on file. The report follows:

"Much of the work of the Conciliation Committee of the New York Civic Federation, like that of the similar committee of the National Civic Federation, is of a confidential nature and cannot be disclosed to the public. Not that there is anything in the settlement of these disputes that would not bear the closest scrutiny and the widest publicity, but neither employers nor employes as a rule care to have their disputes or differences between themselves aired in the press. If our conciliation committee should give to the press every case it takes up, both employers and employes would feel that we were simply running a publicity bureau for the purpose of exploiting our own work. One of the great assets of our organization is the confidence both employers and employes repose in our good faith and disinterestedness in tendering our services. There has not been a week in the past year in which the officers of this body have not been asked by either employer or employe to bring them in touch with the other party.

"There are cases, however, where the parties in interest announce the connection of the Civic Federation with their work. It is only such cases that we feel free to refer to as illustrations of the work done by the committee.

"Just a year ago to-day there began a series of conferences brought about through the efforts of this organization between the employing body of lithographers known as the National Lithographers' Association and the five allied organizations representing the different crafts of employes. These conferences were continued for eight consecutive days, beginning at ten o'clock in the morning and lasting from six to ten at night. These conferences resulted in an agreement covering hours and wages for one year. As this contract is about to expire, the organizations are again in conference looking to the making of a contract for the ensuing year. With this present conference the Civic Federation has no connection, its services being entirely unnecessary. This very fact is a gratifying proof of the efficacy of the trade agreement as a basis for establishing negotiable relations between employing and wage earning organizations.

"This situation was attained in the lithographic industry only through the patient application, to a vexed and complicated problem, of methods of conciliation. The negotiations between these two forces covered a period lasting from October, 1903, to the middle of April, 1904. They involved the exercise of the utmost tact and patience; a gradual process of education, each side learning much from the other; a constant avoidance of all appearance of interference from an outside source, coupled with persistent efforts to bring the contending parties face to face, and the necessity of creating mutual confidence in the good faith of both parties. Not only did these negotiations cover a long period; they also enlisted the time and energy of disinterested persons, as well as of the representatives of the employers' association and of the organized unions, to such an extent that several of the conferences were prolonged to the point of mental and physical exhaustion.

"A highly interesting and somewhat difficult case, in which the offices of the Civic Federation were enlisted, was that resulting first in the settlement of differences between the Association of Theatre Managers of Greater New York and the Theatrical Protective Union, composed of mechanical and other stage employes, and afterward in the agreement between the Managers' Association and the musicians' union of New York, known as 'Local 310.' This trade agreement, approved by the American Federation of Musicians, is national in effect, extending to every place of public amusement in the United States. The value of conference was signally illustrated in the highly satisfactory result of the very first meeting between the representatives of the managers and of the stage employes' union. Mutual explanations of grievances and demands resulted in an agreement that was subsequently commended by the national convention in Milwaukee of the Theatrical Protective Employes. This initial success led directly to the opening of negotiations between the Managers' Association and the musicians' union. Conference between the representatives of the managers and of the musicians' union extended over a period of several months, frequently resulting in no progress, but finally the members of the Conciliation Committee succeeded in bringing the two sides to an understanding which resulted in the introduction of the trade agreement into the new field of the production of grand opera, other musical entertainments and the drama. Here the value of frank and free discussion was disclosed by the fact that when the parties came together many of their grievances proved fanciful. For instance, the managers complained that at rehearsals and performances green substitutes frequently appeared in place of players familiar with their part. They were surprised to find that the union itself had provided in its by-laws against this evil. As they had never before conferred with the union leaders, the managers did not even know of the existence of these by-laws, which afforded them an instrument to correct the abuse. The special committee of the Civic Federation, which by invitation took part in these conferences, was composed of Messrs. Roland Phillips, chairman, V. Everit Macy, Samuel B. Donnelly, and James P. Archibald. The controversy between the musical union and the Marine and other governmental bands was brought to the attention of this organization by a threatened strike in Brooklyn. A sub-committee, with Roland Phillips as chairman, was appointed to take up the trouble. While the threatened rupture in Brooklyn did not materialize, the committee began an investigation of the whole subject involved in the controversy, which has been breaking out periodically for many years past. This report is not ready to-day, but will soon be presented. Suffice it to say that the committee did not find the subject such a simple one to deal with as had been anticipated. On the contrary, it involved some very serious problems.

"Mutual conferences, arranged through the efforts of the New York Civic Federation, succeeded last May in averting a strike of organized teamsters, that would have brought to a standstill every truck in New York, causing untold mid-summer inconvenience and distress throughout the city. Furthermore, out of these conferences was evolved a satisfactory trade agreement, the first one ever made between the organized New York truck owners and teamsters. At least one of the issues considered at these conferences was so delicate that only the earnest argument and tactful persuasion of the chairman of our special committee, Marcus M. Marks, reinforced by the efforts of Messrs. Donnelly and Archibald, secured their continuance and successful outcome. The month of July witnessed another avoidance of strife and the formation of a trade agreement, through the mediation of this committee, between the International Brotherhood of Teamsters and the Contractors' Protective Association of New York City.

"Our conciliation committee is frequently called upon in the adjustment of difficulties in towns up the State. It is at present working on a matter which was brought to its attention last December, involving directly not over a thousand men, but indirectly a very much larger number. The controversy had gone to such an extent that a strike vote had been taken and the men had almost unanimously decided to go out unless they could secure a hearing and a modification of certain alleged grievances. On account of the extreme sensitiveness of some of the parties in connection with the matter names cannot be here reported. Suffice it to say that after much effort a conference was finally brought about ten days ago, and two members of this body, one representing the employer and one representing the employe groups, were invited to use their good offices in effecting a settlement. They have spent two days taking the statements of one side of the case and next week will hear the other side. They are quite confident that they will be entirely able to establish satisfactory relations.

"In February a jurisdictional controversy arose between the engineers and firemen on the New York, New Haven and Hartford R. R. While only the employes on that one line of railroad were directly involved, if a strike had occurred it would doubtless have involved other systems, as the dispute was one of long standing. The Civic Federation was asked to exercise its good offices by the officials of the Brotherhood of Firemen, after their committee had exhausted its own resources with the company, appealing first from the superintendent to the president and from the president to the executive board. Our committee held conferences first with the firemen and then with the engineers. Finally they were brought together and reached an agreement.

"The unfortunate strike of the employes of the Interborough Company, on March 7, 1905, in many ways was a severe disappointment to the friends of trade agreements and conciliation. In fact, some of our members felt on the morning of the strike that the general cause of industrial peace had encountered a serious check. Having been instrumental in bringing about the conference in 1902 that resulted in the first agreement ever made on that line between its officials and employes, and having followed that initial success with the pacific settlement of one or two subsequent controversies, our committee had every hope that it would be able to prevent the recent break. As the details of the work done before and during the strike have been published in our MONTHLY REVIEW, we will not take the time of the meeting in recounting them here. Suffice it to say that, despite the earlier apprehension of the committee, the outcome of the strike was in reality a victory for the principle of trade agreements and a demonstration of the respect for their inviolability which animates national organizations of labor. Many problems arose during the progress of this controversy, some of which will be discussed here this afternoon."

At the conclusion of the report, the chairman said:

Gentlemen, we have with us Mr. August Belmont, the President of the National Civic Federation, and perhaps he may have something to say upon the subject of the report, especially the portion of it referring to the recent strike on the Interborough lines and the inviolability of trade agreements:

Mr. Belmont: I feel somewhat embarrassed in being obliged to address you as President of the National organization. It will be impossible for me to speak upon the subject of the strike without alluding to it in a measure from the point of view of the organization which I represent; but I hope and trust that what I do say—and I will not go into much detail about it—will not be construed in any way as a bid for a decision for or against the position which the company assumed. I will simply refer to it as bearing upon my own position with respect to trade agreements as outlined at the time I had the honor of being elected President of the National Civic Federation: and I wish to say that those remarks were prepared before I had any idea of assuming any official position in connection with this organization, and, therefore, they expressed at that time my personal position on that subject; and I have no reason, in the light of what has occurred, to change my views.

I stated then that I believed in the trade agreement but that it should be observed and kept inviolable by both capital and labor, and scrupulously so.

The agreements which were made with the Interborough Company were broken, as is proved by the attitude which the national labor officers assumed with relation to them, and I think it speaks well, as your secretary's report stated, for organized labor, that the position of these national officers was so promptly assumed on the side of what was right. The details of this controversy and the question of hours of labor and wages had no bearing upon the importance of the point at stake, which was the observance of the agreement between the company and its employes.

What has occurred was deplorable. But a public service corporation has no choice about the question of continuing in operation or ceasing in the same way that a manufacturing concern has. It is under contract to give service uninterruptedly. Any manufacturing concern follows its own interests in the matter. So that the Interborough Company was compelled, under its duty to the public, to be prepared for a disagreement, which, unfortunately, it had some reason to foresee, and which it was its duty to provide against. And it could not do it in a manner which would have involved simply a temporary operation of the road. It had to provide for its permanent operation in any case, and, therefore, the company, in turn, entered into an agreement with individual employes, whom it took into its service, that their positions should be secure as long as they should give proper service and satisfaction. So that, when it became possible for the company to take back some of its old employes, it could take only as many as it had vacancies for. It welcomed them. There was no antagonistic attitude on the part of the company toward the freedom of the men to affiliate with trade organizations. There was no question in regard to that. There was no interference with the freedom of labor affiliation. The men who were taken back are employed on the same terms as they were before.

I state that, because there has been some misapprehension on the part of those who choose to interpret the attitude of the Interborough Company as unfriendly to organized labor. If that had been the case, in taking back any of its old employes it would have discriminated against organized labor, which it did not do.

In the course of a conversation with some of the representatives of the Central Federated Union, I find that it is stated that I expressed myself as in favor of compulsory arbitration. That must be qualified. The statement was based simply upon this: That I was asked the question, and I answered that that could not be possible unless both sides to the controversy could be held to the result of the arbitration. That was all I said, or intended to convey.

The following were elected members of the General Board:

ON THE PART OF THE PUBLIC:

Cornelius N. Bliss, Ex-Secretary of the Interior.
Nicholas Murray Butler, President Columbia University.
W. C. Douglas, Attorney at Law.
Ralph M. Easley, Chairman Executive Council, National Civic Federation.
Charles S. Fairchild, Ex-Secretary of the Treasury.
Rt. Rev. John M. Farley, Archbishop Roman Catholic Church.
R. Watson Gilder, Editor *Century Magazine*.
Hamilton Holt, Editor *New York Independent*.
Seth Low, Ex-Mayor of the City of New York.
V. Everit Macy, Capitalist.
Emerson McMillin, Banker.
John A. Sleicher, Editor *Leslie's Weekly*.
Walter H. Page, Editor *World's Work*.
Roland Phillips, Managing Editor *Harper's Weekly*.
Rt. Rev. Henry C. Potter, Bishop Protestant Episcopal Church.
C. T. Root, Editor *Dry Goods Economist*.
Albert Shaw, Editor *Review of Reviews*.
Oscar S. Straus, Member of the Court of Arbitration at The Hague.
H. C. Watson, Editor *Dun's Review*.
Thomas F. Woodlock, Editor *Wall Street Journal*.

ON THE PART OF EMPLOYERS:

Emil L. Boas, General Manager Hamburg-American Line.
John Cooper, The Cooper-Wigand-Cooke Company.
Otto M. Eidlitz, Ex-Chairman Board of Governors, Building Trades Employers' Association.
William Green, Chairman New York Typothetae.
J. Alexander Hayden, Chairman Association Interior Decorators and Cabinetmakers.
Henry C. Hunter, Commissioner New York Metal Trades Association.
Edgar L. Marston, Blair & Co.
Marcus M. Marks, President National Clothiers' Association.
Thomas F. McCarthy, President New York Truck Owners' Association.
Charles A. Moore, President The Shaw Electric Crane Company.
Hosmer B. Parsons, Vice-President Wells, Fargo & Co.
Walter L. Pierce, Lidgerwood Manufacturing Company.
Herman Ridder, Manager *Staats Zeitung*.
Charles A. Schieren, Charles A. Schieren & Co.
Louis B. Schram, Chairman Labor Committee, Associated Brewers.
A. Beverly Smith, U. S. Lithographers' Association.
C. W. Sweet, Sweet, Orr & Co.
Charles W. Terhune, Edwin C. Burt Co.
Benjamin D. Traitel, Traitel Bros. & Co.
Charles Wilhelms, President United States Lithographers' Association.

ON THE PART OF WAGE EARNERS:

James P. Archibald, Brotherhood Painters and Decorators.
A. J. Boulton, Stereotypers.
William O. Coakley, Lithographic Press Feeders.
James Daly, Dockbuilders.
Charles Delaney, Granite Cutters.
Samuel B. Donnelly, Typographical Union.
J. J. Flynn, Metal Polishers.
William Fyfe, Amalgamated Carpenters.
Edward Gould, Teamsters.
Timothy Healy, Eccentric Firemen.
James P. Holland, Stationary Firemen.
Jesse Larimer, Housesmiths.
Philip Kelly, Theatrical Protective Union.
Fred Lemon, Elevator Constructors.
William Long, Lithographers.
Edward A. Moffett, Editor *Bricklayer and Mason*.
Robert E. Niedig, Housesmiths.
John W. Parker, Poster Artists.

A LABOR LECTURE TO LABOR.

Here is what is sometimes found in the labor movement: Selfishness, greed, grafting; jealousy of the leaders, no real co-operation; neglect of the meeting, indifference as to the label, the button and the card, knocking, trivial differences magnified into open quarrels, disputes, cliques, who run the whole thing for personal ends, lack of cohesion, consequent failure of many strikes and generally slow progress toward the ultimate success of the movement. Here is what should prevail: Broad-minded consideration for each other—no selfishness: absolute integrity—no grafting; confidence in well selected leaders—no jealousy; every union to help every other union—no lack of co-operation; large and enthusiastic meetings—no neglect; a vigorous campaign for the label, the button and the card—no indifference; boosting—no knocking; conferences and arbitration—no quarrels; the referendum and action by the whole union—no cliques; concentration of aims and work—no lack of cohesion.—From the *Pattern Makers' Journal*, Official Organ of the Pattern Makers' League of North America.

At best restriction of output by a particular class of workmen is a most selfish principle and therefore cannot truly be a trade union principle. The aim of this restriction is to benefit those who adopt the principle at the expense of their fellow producers in other crafts and callings. So that besides being economically false it is morally bad.—*Labor World*, Pittsburg.

THE NEW ENGLAND CIVIC FEDERATION ESTABLISHES HEADQUARTERS.

ITS RELATION TO THE NATIONAL ORGANIZATION AND ITS SPECIAL FIELD OF ACTIVITY AND USEFULNESS.

(From Bulletin No. 1 of the Civic Federation of New England.)

HEADQUARTERS for the newly-organized Civic Federation of New England have been opened on the tenth floor of the Paddock Building, 101 Tremont street, and with the much deliberated question as to who should be secretary settled by the selection of Hayes Robbins, for several years a writer on economics and labor questions, the Boston branch of the organization is now in a position to fulfill its mission of bringing about a better understanding between the wage earners, the employers and the public. The headquarters are not pretentious; they consist of an office for the secretary large enough for ordinary business conferences if desired, and an outer office for a stenographer. But the secretary's room will soon become a virtual library of labor publications, for Mr. Robbins is gathering the labor reports of all the New England States, and already receives most of the economic and labor periodicals of the country at large.

The New England organization can hardly be called a branch of the national body, after all. It is allied with the national organization in purposes and methods, but is independent in action and influence. It has now practically perfected its organization, its lists of officers are substantially complete, its by-laws are in print, and the secretary will issue a series of bulletins which will state the aims and objects of the organization in detail and serve as a medium of communication between the executive committee and the members or others interested in the Federation's work. This is the first bulletin.

The Federation is a voluntary association composed of three general groups, one representing employers, one representing wage earners, and one representing the general public not directly identified with either of the other bodies. These three groups are also represented equally in the executive committee of thirty, which directs the general policies and work of the organization. The condition of membership is acceptance of the general purposes and methods of the Federation as stated in the by-laws, and expressed willingness to support the work by personal influence and, if possible, active co-operation when necessary. There is no membership fee. The work is maintained entirely by voluntary contributions.

It is desired to remove any possible misunderstanding of the objects and practical work of this organization. It is not an "interference committee." It does not attempt to entangle petty shop disputes, nor, for that matter, to intervene in any industrial difficulty except by request or consent of both parties. It does not pretend to know more about the details of a disagreement or the peculiar problems and special point of view of each side than those engaged in it. Its chief work is not with strikes and lockouts, but with the preventable causes thereof. What the Civic Federation has accomplished for good on that line in the national field is well known, but it does not pretend to have any final and complete "solution of the labor problem." Neither is it organized to promote [illegible] indirectly any eccentric scheme of social [illegible] reorganization. It has no political affil[illegible] interests. It does not concern itself with [illegible] nor in any way antagonize or interfere [illegible] work of state boards of arbitration. Being jointly controlled and directed by representatives of employers, wage earners and the general public, in equal numbers, it is not and cannot be at the service of any special interests to gain advantage over any other interests involved in a controversy.

But the Civic Federation does stand for positive ideas, positive principles, positive work. A movement is sometimes assumed to have no principles unless it is "anti" something, or takes sides on special or local issues. That may be principle, or it may be simply short-range partisanship. The Civic Federation is neither "anti" nor partisan. It stands squarely on the proposition that our present industrial system, based on individual enterprise and free labor, is inherently sound and full of promise, in spite of many defects and abuses; that it is not a failure because of industrial strife; on the contrary, that the discord and hardship are survivals, not new growths, and are diminishing instead of increasing; that they are incidents in the slow and painful upward movement of the race, and not the result of any crafty scheme of labor exploitation, supposed to render the lot of the wage earners hopeless except through social revolution.

The Whole design of the Civic Federation rests on the principle that there is no "inevitable" conflict between the interests of labor and capital. That the two are not engaged in a hopeless struggle to divide a certain fixed product, but in a common effort to make nature yield a constantly increasing return; so that practically the whole issue between capital and labor is one of fair division of a product which, with the progress of invention, skill and intelligence, may become larger for both.

The strife that does occur is not the fault of our industrial system as such; it is due very largely to preventable causes, to misunderstandings, lack of the spirit of fairness, hasty conclusions, poor organization, unwise leadership on one or both sides, lack of self-control in the use of power, arbitrary demands, arbitrary refusals to confer, lack of correct information, failure of one party to appreciate the special problems, view point, difficulties and motives of the other, lack of personal acquaintance and of frank businesslike relations between the representatives of the interests involved on both sides. Realizing these facts, broad-minded and farseeing men directly concerned in the problem from the standpoint of employers and of wage earners, and indirectly from that of the general public, have sought to provide, in the Civic Federation, a common meeting ground where as much as possible of this needless misunderstanding may be cleared up, and the elements of friction and prejudice taken out of the situation.

Men who have occasion to know of the good results of personal acquaintance and a better understanding between employers and employes have often remarked: "If the Civic Federation did nothing more than promote just that, it would be many times worth while."

Various doctrines of social upheaval are represented throughout the country to-day by active organizations, zealously at work encouraging class antagonism, destroying faith in the general scheme of our institutions, and

HAYES ROBBINS,
Secretary New England Civic Federation.

building up sentiment for this or that radical social experiment, guaranteed to bring in the millennium. The insistent propaganda of these movements works its way into a surprisingly large variety of important groups—social, religious, philanthropic, labor, educational, political. Its results are constantly cropping out in quarters least expected, and supplying the advocates of these doctrines with fresh ammunition. Naturally, the most determined efforts are being made among wage earners; it is a little appreciated fact that the trade union movement, on the whole, is to-day bearing the brunt of the attack. Thus far, it has proved one of the strongest bulwarks of our industrial society at what has been generally thought of as its most exposed point.

One of the most telling arguments made use of in this crusade is the fact of industrial strife—the hardship, loss and suffering that go with it. It should not be necessary to argue the question, therefore, whether it is worth while to develop a practical method of lessening the strife, or to maintain an organized means of rallying, at the danger points, the enormous reserve of public sentiment which is all the time in favor—if only passively—of industrial peace under free democratic institutions, and believes in progress through evolution rather than revolution.

The general educational influence of such an institution is probably its most important service,—more important even than the sum total of specific labor troubles it succeeds in averting or settling. In the nature of the case, the value of the work can never be measured by any tabular record of the number of such disputes adjusted; it must be estimated chiefly by the general preventive influence it steadily exerts in the community, against industrial strife on the one hand and revolutionary movements on the other, and by its practical work in building up, little by little, the habit of resorting to peaceful rather than violent methods of settling differences.

The general officers of the Civic Federation of New England are as follows: Lucius Tuttle, president; Frank H. McCarthy, first vice-president; Louis D. Brandeis, second vice-president and chairman conciliation committee; Charles H. Taylor, Jr., treasurer; Henry Abrahams, recording secretary; Warren A. Reed, vice-chairman conciliation committee; Hayes Robbins, secretary.

The following compose the executive committee, which directs the general affairs of the Federation in the New England States:

ON THE PART OF THE PUBLIC:

W. Murray Crane, United States Senator, Dalton, Mass.
Charles Francis Adams, Publicist, Boston.
Henry L. Higginson, of Lee, Higginson & Co., Boston.
Bishop William Lawrence, of the Protestant Episcopal Church, Boston.
Bishop William Stang, of the Roman Catholic Church, Fall River, Mass.
Charles S. Hamlin, Lawyer, Boston.
Louis D. Brandeis, Lawyer, Boston.
John Mason Little, former President Real Estate Exchange and of Associated Board of Trade, Boston.
Horace G. Wadlin, Librarian Public Library, former Chief of Bureau of Statistics of Labor, Boston.
Hayes Robbins, Secretary Civic Federation of New England, Boston.

ON THE PART OF EMPLOYERS:

Lucius Tuttle, President Boston & Maine R. R. Co., Boston.
Frederick P. Fish, President American Telephone and Telegraph Co., Boston.
Amory A. Lawrence, President Merchants' Association, Boston.
Arthur T. Lyman, Treasurer Boston Manufacturing Company, Boston.
Edgar Van Etten, Vice-President [illegible], Boston.
Charles H. Taylor, Jr., of the Bos[illegible]
P. F. Sullivan, President Boston [illegible], Boston.
W. C. Winslow, of the Metropol[illegible]
Wallace L. Pierce, President [illegible], Boston.
James Logan, Chairman Executive Committee, U. S. Envelope Co., Worcester, Mass.

ON THE PART OF WAGE EARNERS:

Frank H. McCarthy, President Boston Central Labor Union, Boston.
Henry Abrahams, International Cigar Makers' Union, Boston.
Frank K. Foster, International Typographical Union, Boston.
Francis J. Clarke, President State Branch American Federation of Labor, Brockton, Mass.
[illegible] D. Driscoll, Secretary-Treasurer [illegible] Federation of Labor, Boston.
Edmund F. Ward, Vice-President Boston Central Labor Union, Boston.
John J. Connolly, State Organizer International Association of Machinists, Boston.
P. F. Sheehan, President Street Railway Employes' Union, Brockton, Mass.
William H. Frazier, Secretary-Treasurer International Seamen's Union, Boston.
Peter W. Collins, International Brotherhood of Electrical Workers, Boston.

The conciliation committee was organized in part on March 13, 1905, with the following membership:

ON THE PART OF EMPLOYERS:

Lucius Tuttle, Boston.
Charles H. Taylor, Jr., Boston.
Simeon B. Chase, Treasurer King Philip Mills, Fall River, Mass.
Herbert T. Drake, Superintendent Douglas Shoe Company, Brockton, Mass.
James L. Bowlby, President Master Teamsters' Association, Boston.
Edward C. Mead, of Mead, Mason & Co., Building Contractors, Boston.

ON THE PART OF THE PUBLIC:

Louis D. Brandeis, Boston.
Hayes Robbins, Boston.
Judge Warren A. Reed, Brockton, Mass.
Rev. Denis T. O'Sullivan, Boston College.
Dr. Carroll D. Wright, President Clark College, Worcester, Mass.
Professor John Marshall Barker, Boston University.
Hon. Charles S. Hamlin, Boston.

ON THE PART OF WAGE EARNERS:

Frank H. McCarthy, President Boston Central Labor Union.
Henry Abrahams, International Cigar Makers' Union, Boston.
John F. Tobin, President Boot and Shoe Workers' Union, Boston.
Peter H. McNealy, President Joint Council Teamsters' Union, Boston.
James Tansey, President Textile Council, Fall River, Mass.
James Duncan, Secretary-Treasurer Granite Cutters' Union, Quincy, Mass.
William Shields, New England Organizer Brotherhood of Carpenters, Jamaica Plains, Mass.

The National Civic Federation carries on its work through six general departments: Trade agreements, conciliation and arbitration, welfare work, industrial economics, trade sections, and organization, and the New England organization will proceed in the same way. Under the head of industrial economics the educational work in this section will be promoted by public meetings, from time to time. The first of these is planned for April 26, when the organization hopes to get together representative men from all over New England. There will be a dinner, and some addresses by prominent Federation leaders.

Governed as we are by public opinion, the utmost care should be taken to preserve the purity of the public mind. Knowledge is power, and truth is knowledge; whoever, therefore, propagates a prejudice, willfully saps the foundation of his country's strength.

The National Civic Federation Review

Vol. II. No. 2 NEW YORK, MAY 15, 1905 Ten Cents

PEACE WITH LIBERTY AND JUSTICE.

EMPLOYERS, WAGE-EARNERS AND PUBLICISTS DISCUSS RESTRAINTS UPON INDIVIDUAL LIBERTY CAUSED BY ASSOCIATIONS OF CAPITAL AND OF LABOR.

EMPLOYERS, wage-earners and scholars were the participants in a discussion that marked the first [illegible] meeting of the Department of Industrial Economics of the National Civic Federation. The meeting was made the occasion of a dinner at the Park Avenue Hotel, New York City, on the evening of April 25. This meeting was the beginning of a series of similar gatherings to be held for the purpose of bringing to bear upon [illegible] issues connected with the relations between capital and labor the experience of men familiar with the interests of employers and of wage-earners and the convictions of ripe scholars in economic science. The design is that these meetings shall cause a clearer understanding by the participants and by the general public of some of the questions that directly concern the industrial world and that are of general importance.

The question discussed at this first meeting was: "How far does associated effort in industry involve the curtailment of individual liberty?" This question was the outgrowth of a spirited exchange between Charles W. Eliot, President of Harvard University, and Samuel Gompers, President of the American Federation of Labor, at the annual meeting of the National Civic Federation last December. Dr. Eliot then declared that what the country needs is "peace with liberty," which he held could not be attained with combinations of either capital or labor that aim at monopoly; while Mr. Gompers asserted that there could be no liberty for the workingman without his material prosperity, to which union is essential.

Those who took part in the discussion were August Belmont, President of the National Civic Federation, who acted as chairman; President Eliot, who opened, and President Gompers, who closed the debate; Edwin R. A. Seligman, *Professor of Political Economy in Columbia University*; Frank K. Foster, representing the Typographical Union and other labor organizations in New England; Louis D. Brandeis, lawyer and economic author, of Boston; Francis L. Robbins, President of the Pittsburg Coal Company. A verbatim report of their addresses follows:

SCOPE OF THE NEW DEPARTMENT.

Chairman Belmont:—

Gentlemen: It is with pleasure I perform this evening an act of official duty, that of presiding at the first regular meeting of the Department of Industrial Economics. It is a new Department of the National Civic Federation—one that is natural and logical.

At the outset the National Civic Federation was met by a very general misapprehension of its mission. I[illegible]

THE FIRST DINNER OF THE DEPARTMENT OF INDUSTRIAL ECONOMICS

was commonly and erroneously believed that it was organized to avert or settle strikes and lockouts. Our position is now better understood. We strive for industrial peace and more rightful relations between employer and wage-earners. In doing this, we look beyond the strained relationships to the causes which induce them. Inquiry, discussion, education are important factors in the settlement of vexatious problems, which are sociological as well as industrial; and this new departure in the work of the organization admits of a broader conception of the possibilities and opportunities afforded by intelligent review, research and agitation. It is not my belief that any one man, at any one time, will be able to solve these vexed and ever changing problems, but it is my belief that a step in the right direction can only be taken after the most free, full and thorough discussion.

We must place ourselves in the attitude of students, of earnest seekers after Truth. We must examine the economic laws and understand their application in special localities. We have before us, from time to time, industrial agitations, and it is our duty to discover what sub-surface conditions produce them. Economic laws govern. It is for us to read them in the relations between employers and employes, in the scale of wages,

CHARLES W. ELIOT,
President Harvard University.

in prices, cost of living, in production and consumption, combinations of capital, limitation of apprentices, restriction of output, open and closed shop, piece work, the shorter work-day, regulation of child and woman labor, the requirement of sanitary conditions of work, the restriction or distribution of immigration.

We hear in all directions a cry for economic education. On the one hand, we cannot read the publications of associations of employers without encountering an incessant emphasis upon the necessity of education. The larger employers, in transportation and in the basic industries, have in some instances advanced beyond the preaching of education, and are making systematic efforts for its actual extension among the workers. On the other hand, organized labor perceives that education is essential to its own maintenance and advancement. The American Federation of Labor has undertaken to introduce regular instruction in social, economic and industrial topics throughout its 25,000 local unions. The trade union publications contain an increasing proportion of reading matter devoted to technical subjects, all designed to increase the efficiency and productive capacity of the individual worker.

The very life of democratic institutions will be profoundly affected by the character of the information that is to be disseminated throughout the mass of the body politic. It becomes, therefore, of immediate importance that economic science be presented with convincing force and attractive clearness. To this end is this new department formed, and I cannot conceive a more useful function or a work more patriotic.

The special subject to be discussed to-night was suggested by the short debate at the last meeting. It is one of vast interest: "How Far Does Associated Effort in Industry Involve the Curtailment of Industrial Liberty?" We will this evening hear the question debated; therefore, I will not detain you by further or extended

Gentlemen, I, being a Harvard man, must be permitted to state that we have here to-night the man who stands at the head of the greatest educational institution in the country, (laughter and applause), and I will introduce, therefore, President Charles W. Eliot, of Harvard College. (Applause.)

INDUSTRIAL PEACE WITH LIBERTY.

President Eliot:

Mr. President and Gentlemen: Before we enter on the discussion of the precise subject which has just been read by your president, it has seemed to me that it would be useful to make a brief statement concerning the fundamental importance in industries, and productive industries, of this principle of individual liberty, the curtailment of which is threatened by industrial combinations, whether of capitalists on the one hand, or of laborers on the other.

For brevity's sake I have written out what I wish to say on that subject. It is, of course, a theoretical presentation, but it might be indefinitely illustrated by practical examples.

The foundation of American prosperity and progress is not cheap land, or fresh mines, or flowing oil wells, or virgin forests. The real foundation is the efficiency of the American at work. By different philosophers this efficiency is attributed to various causes—to strong food, to the stimulating climate, to a native alertness and eager energy, to an intense desire to possess, to a readiness to study and try things new, and doubtless these causes all contribute to American efficiency; but there is another cause, which Americans apparently think about but little, and of late often completely ignore—namely, American freedom for the individual, the freedom which feeds hope and ambition. This freedom is of many kinds—all fruitful.

When the Pilgrims sought at Plymouth freedom to worship God they planted a great tap-root of American efficiency. Religious liberty not only makes accessible to every thoughtful soul its congenial nurture, but also prevents the wastes and destructions of religious strife, evils which history teaches have been both widespread and intense. Europe still wastes a deal of force on religious contentions.

American political liberty is another source of American efficiency; for it is founded on a broad suffrage which enlists the interest and effort of every citizen capable of making a choice between parties or policies, no matter whether the choice be determined by reasoning, or by inherited or acquired sympathies and feelings. It takes the voter out of the narrow round of his personal or family affairs, and makes him think of the larger interests of the commonwealth. In other words, it develops not only the intelligence but also the co-operative spirit of the masses of the people.

Another very precious source of efficiency is the free access for all competent children to a prolonged education. This is a characteristic American opportunity which has much to do with the efficiency of the population. It secures for the many children, born in humble stations, but endowed by nature with exceptional gifts, access to their most appropriate and productive life-work. In this way free education makes an immense contribution to American efficiency.

The setting free of women for a variety of productive employments has greatly increased the collective efficiency of the nation; and we have much yet to expect from this emancipation which has followed from comparatively recent improvements in the education of women.

The perfect liberty to travel or migrate, without government passport, permission, or even inquiry, also promotes collective efficiency; for it permits both capital and labor to go where they can earn most. Indeed, parts of the laboring population are too migratory; for the nomad makes no home.

Again, American social mobility promotes efficiency; since any improving and growing man or woman readily rises from the social level at which he was born to any higher level which his early education, his trained capacities, and his experience make congenial to him. This rise is a stimulating prize for efficiency—all the more effective because his children may share it.

The very evils which accompany the present day doings of unions and trusts are only abuses of precious liberties not yet two generations old—the liberty of association, and the liberty of incorporation with limited liability. To be sure, the potent agencies created through the exercise of these new liberties have practically become, in the keen pursuit of pecuniary and especially of monopolistic advantages, enemies to the liberty of the individual, the combinations by a fatal or inevitable development always trying to absorb or destroy independent outsiders. Nevertheless, it is great liberties given by legislation which are thus temporarily perverted to the restriction of individual liberty. Undisturbed by the adverse phenomena of the moment, let us ourselves see clearly, and declare as persuasively as we can, that the chief source of American efficiency is the personal liberty of the individual workman.

If I needed any confirmation of this doctrine I should find it in the history of American education, where a new liberty for the individual has been the chief source of progress, ever since Thomas Jefferson began to design the University of Virginia.

Now, in the industries of our country this principle of liberty for the individual ought to be the chief promoter of good-will and content in labor and therefore of efficiency. What prevents this natural felicity? The opposing interests of workmen and employers prevent, and the consequent organization of labor on the one hand and of capital on the other for attack and defense. Whenever large bodies of men organize to fight, individual liberty goes to the wall. For effective fighting implicit obedience to leaders, self-sacrifice, and passionate zeal for the common cause are indispensable, and individual interests must be subordinated. Every workman who joins a fighting union, and every capitalist who joins a fighting employers' association makes a sacrifice of personal liberty, and both act thus with the same object in view—namely, to win in a fight. These fighting unions and associations all dislike and try to prevent competition. Unions and associations alike seek to establish and maintain controlling monopolies, and some of them succeed. Thus they strike another blow at industrial liberty by destroying free competition.

The only way to prevent these sacrifices of that individual liberty which is the mainspring of industrial efficiency is to stop the fighting and the monopoly-grabbing. This is not a job likely to be finished to-morrow or next year; but it is just what the National Civic Federation, and particularly this new department of the Federation, is trying to do. What are the recognized preventatives of fighting between nations, classes or individuals? Are they not better mutual acquaintance between opponents, frank discussion of differences, publicity for evils and wrongs on either side, and agreements to abide by the decisions of previously accepted tribunals? In all labor and capital contentions the ultimate tribunal is the public opinion of the great body of consumers. Sooner or later that public opinion will regulate these new monopolistic powers, the sudden rise of which has taken courts, legislatures, and consumers by surprise. But legisla-

SAMUEL GOMPERS,
President American Federation of Labor.

tion follows slowly after public opinion, and judicial interpretation follows legislation. For the enlightening and crystallizing of public opinion concerning the industrial strife which has often seriously embarrassed particular factories or trades and general business, and has even threatened to cut off the supply of absolute necessaries of urban life, what better combination of forces can we imagine than that here assembled? This assemblage represents immense and various forces for promoting the better acquaintance of employers and employed, the discussion of industrial contentions, and the publicity which compels attention to evils before they cause war, and forms a public opinion capable of leading to beneficial legislation. The press as a whole is not likely to lose sight of the fact that the most fundamental and characteristic cause of American efficiency has been and still is American individual liberty. Industrial liberty is not to be lost; it is only impaired temporarily. Trades unions and associations of employers or capitalists are natural and useful products of democratic society, and any nation which harbors one of these forms of industrial combinations must harbor the other also. They will endure; but they will create great disturbances and do much harm until they give over the pursuit of monopoly, recognize that competition is indispensable to industrial and social progress, and see in liberty for the individual the mainspring of efficiency.

Therefore, I say again, as I said at the preliminary meeting of this department of the Civic Federation—what we want is industrial peace with liberty. (Applause.)

—

Chairman Belmont: Gentlemen:—We have with us Prof. E. R. A. Seligman, of Columbia University, who has made a special study of the questions which interest us most and part of which are to be discussed to-night, and it affords me much pleasure to now call on him. (Applause.)

AN ANALYSIS OF ECONOMIC LIBERTY.

Professor Seligman:—

Gentlemen: Individual liberty, as an economic concept, is the result of a slow evolution. The ordinary picture of the freedom of the untutored savage is as fanciful as the rest of the fairy tales of our youth. Primitive man lacked freedom in three ways—he was in abject dread of nature, of his stronger comrades, and of the social group. In his ignorance of natural phenomena he was subject to all kinds of fear and superstition, an easy victim of the sorcerer or medicine man. Living in a state based upon brute strength, he was at the mercy of the more stalwart savage. Dependent upon the group or clan for existence he was hemmed in by social customs that could not be infringed and by group prohibitions which it would be folly to evade. Civilization and not primitive nature is the creator of liberty. Knowledge has emancipated man from superstition. Law and order have protected him from the oppressor. Social progress has evolved in every phase of life a sphere of liberty evermore secure from the encroachments of absolutism. Economic liberty, like political liberty; freedom of thought, like freedom of speech, is the product of a most advanced stage of society.

FREEDOM OF INDIVIDUAL ACTION.

As opposed to the theories of ancient and mediaeval absolutism, with its continual interference in the economic life of the individual, the modern doctrine is that a man can commonly be depended upon for utilizing his opportunities and turning his own energies to the best account; that an adult of sound mind usually knows what is most advantageous for him, and that in making the most effective use of his own abilities, he will ordinarily do the best for the community. It involves the substantial identity of private interest and public welfare, and it is to-day, almost everywhere in the civilized world, either an accomplished fact or a cherished ideal.

FRANCIS L. ROBBINS,
President Pittsburg Coal Company.

If we look more closely, however, we shall find that liberty is more than the mere absence of restraint from interference. In contrast to this mere negative conception of liberty as adopted by the average man, we must put the positive conception as elaborated by recent thinkers. Economic freedom is not an attribute of primitive man, but has been hammered out by centuries of toilsome effort. Individual liberty is the product of social effort. If it is to be a constructive rather than a destructive force; if it is to minister to social progress rather than to social dissolution, it must be accompanied by two other conditions. Of these the first is equality.

ECONOMIC EQUALITY THREEFOLD.

By equality we do not mean absolute equality. A certain degree of inequality inheres in the nature of things. Men are born with an inequality of physical, mental and moral attributes which no amount of care can eradicate. As soon as private property develops, these natural inequalities inevitably produce their results in inequality of possessions. The real equality that is important for economic purposes is threefold:

First—Legal equality, or the certainty that one man is as good as another before the law, and that his economic rights will be protected.

Second—Equality of opportunity in the sense that no man is shut out by legislation or social prejudice from free access to any vocation or employment for which he deems himself fitted.

Third—Such a relative equality, at least in the conditions of bargaining, as not to put one party to the contract at the virtual mercy of the other.

Without such a threefold equality freedom becomes illusory, for liberty based on gross inequality means the liberty of the stronger and more unscrupulous to impose his force on the weak. Liberty without equality is the power of the one and the subjection of the other. The liberty to invest one's capital in slaves was stoutly defended by the ante-bellum Southerner, but his liberty involved others' slavery.

SOCIAL SOLIDARITY.

In addition to equality, the growth of competition and the complexity of modern economic life have brought into prominence the second condition of liberty. The enormous power exerted to-day by accumulations of capital as well as by combinations of labor is in the present stage of human development peculiarly susceptible of abuse. These abuses may be within the margin of the law and yet none the less socially reprehensible. Unless great power is tempered by responsibility it is apt to run wild. We are beginning to speak of the responsibilities of the rich, but the adage "Noblesse oblige" applies to all forms of economic power, whether represented by wealth or not. What is needed, and what is gradually being developed is the sense of social solidarity, the conviction that no one can really disassociate himself from his neighbors' welfare, and that his every action must be judged by its influence on society at large. It was this idea that found vague expression in the "fraternity" of the French Revolution. It is the same idea that is again more forcibly advanced to-day under other names. The application in the economic sphere is no less strong than in the others. Liberty without responsibility is license.

LIBERTY AS A POSITIVE CONCEPT.

Real economic liberty, therefore, is constructive. in that it implies not simply restraint, but such a complex of conditions resting on law and custom as to insure to the greatest possible numbers the opportunity of a full development of their faculties. Liberty when based on equality and responsibility means wealth for the individual and progress for society. Liberty without equality and responsibility may mean advance for the few and retrogression for the many. Liberty as a negative concept is disruptive. Liberty as a positive concept harmonizes society and the individual. The one is a menace, the other an aid to lasting economic progress.

Let us now apply these criteria to the various forms of economic freedom:

First:

FREEDOM OF MOVEMENT.

In the middle ages the right of internal migration was often restricted. Under the settlement laws of England, for instance, it was virtually impossible for a workman to leave his native parish. In modern times, the growth of freedom has brought the right not only of internal but of international migration. Restrictions on emigration still existing in Russia are a relic of mediaevalism. On the other hand, the prohibition of immigration which is sometimes found in modern countries must be judged in the right of liberty as a positive concept. Chinese immigration into the United States, for instance, is forbidden. Cheap Chinese labor would undoubtedly help in developing the resources of the Pacific slope, but the vital objection is the lasting inequality between the Chinese and the American workman. Immigration in general is to be welcomed because even though the standard of life of the immigrant may be lower than that of the native, he or his children will soon reach the American level. The Chinese, however, refuses to assimilate and will not adopt the American methods. He retains and perpetuates his lower standard, and will, if present in sufficient numbers, inevitably drag the American standard down to his own level. Freedom of immigration, which in this case means prosperity for the employer and comparative comfort for the immigrant, implies permanent degeneration for the American workman, that is, ultimate economic decay. It is a specious liberty because based on inequality. When, however, there is any prospect of speedy equality, interference with the freedom of immigration is uneconomic.

Second:

FREEDOM OF OCCUPATION.

The right of choosing one's profession was in former times hedged in by all manner of barriers. At its worst, the system of caste and custom prevented progress because it put men into vocations for which they were not fitted. Freedom of competition insures as far as possible the right man for the right place, and thus leads to enhanced production and better distribution. The only restrictions which modern society permits are the evidence of fitness in those occupations where incompetence would imply irresponsibility and involve injury to others as well as to one's self. The certificates required from doctors, dentists, engineers, plumbers, pilots, and the like, are not a hindrance but an aid to true liberty. The apprenticeship regulations of the trades unions, however, are sometimes good, sometimes bad. Where they are designed to secure good work or even to prevent the degradation of wages and the workers' standard of life through the irruption of large numbers of underpaid apprentices, there is much to be said for the practice. But where the object is simply to keep out competent workmen and erect a monopolistic close corporation, as in the older stages of the mediaeval guilds, the limitation is clearly indefensible.

Third:

THE FREEDOM OF ASSOCIATION.

The chief forms of association, for economic purposes, are combinations of labor and combinations of capital. In classic Rome as in modern Russia, where both political and economic aims were sought, we find a stern repression of labor associations. Even after the right of political and religious association had been secured, however, combinations of labor were prohibited. Under the modern factory system such combinations have assumed the form of trade unions. The legitimacy of trades unions, as such, is now accepted, because it is recognized that they tend to secure real freedom for the laborer. The individual workman in a large factory is at a clear disadvantage in dealing with the employer. The union restores equality by securing the right of collective bargaining.

In the same way, the right of free association by capital in the form of the corporation and other combinations has been acquired only in the past half century. It is only when liberty of association results in restraint of trade or virtual monopoly inimical to the general interests, or when the enterprise is conducted without any sense of social responsibility, that the community is justified in curbing its excesses. The greatest care, however, must be observed in the analysis before the infringement of the right of association can be conceded. To abandon liberty because of mere apprehended, but imaginary, inequality would be to sacrifice both liberty and equality. A clear case must be made out before the law should be invoked against combinations of either labor or capital.

Fourth:

FREEDOM OF PRODUCTION.

This includes freedom of contract and enterprise.

Here again the emphasis has been shifted in modern times. The world has outgrown the time-worn conception of the citizens as the children of an all-wise and benevolent paternal government. It has been realized that governments are not always benevolent, and never all-wise, and that with the growth of capital and competition better results can be secured by the repeal of conflicting and even contradictory provisions, which thwart

FRANK K. FOSTER,
Member of the Typographical Union.

production and check individual initiative. It was this which the French manufacturers meant when they told the Minister, "*Laissez-nous faire*," and this paved the way for a celebrated phrase. There was indeed the necessary destructive process of pulling down the barriers which impeded progress, because they checked equal opportunity. It has been requisite, however, in recent times to modify both the theory and the practice of "Laissez faire" in order to safeguard the interests of the various classes of society. The complex requirements of modern life have necessitated a governmental regulation of many business enterprises in behalf of producers, consumers, investors and the general public. The difference between mediaeval and modern interference is to be found chiefly in the fact that the one sought to prevent competition while the other endeavors to enlarge its domain and to raise its level. Factory laws give the operatives a fair chance, railway regulation attempts to secure equal treatment of shippers, supervision of banks and corporations is intended to enforce financial responsibility. In all these cases, interference is justified only as leading to surer and greater general liberty. We have to deal with the positive, not the negative concept.

Fifth:

FREEDOM OF TRADE.

This is virtually included under the last head, since trade is a species of production; but it forms so important a part of the subject that it is generally treated separately. The modern age has seen the emancipation of internal trade from mediaeval restrictions on the part of governments. The great controversy to-day centers about international trade. Here, again, the general hypothesis must be in favor of freedom. But freedom is not necessarily and always beneficent. When the relative inequality of two countries in the production of a certain commodity is great, free trade may hinder, in the weaker country, the growth of an industry which might become comparatively profitable and even highly necessary. Under such conditions, protection, by building up the industry to the point where there will be a domestic competition, may help in creating that relative equality between the domestic and the foreign producers which will ultimately redound to the interests of the consumer as well. Such a policy is defensible, however, only when protection increases and not diminishes real productive efficiency, and when the undoubted intermediate economic loss does not outweigh the ultimate advantage. Only then is interference with freedom legitimate, because only then is it in the interest of a more real and beneficent ultimate freedom.

We see, then, that modern liberty does not mean absence of restraint. Absence of restraint is license, not liberty. All social progress is a result of a certain repression of liberty of some in the interests of all. These restrictions are imposed by custom, by voluntary association, or by law. Good manners and social usages which prevent men from doing what they like are a mark of civilization. Associations like the church, the club and the business union, lay down rules to which each member must conform. The government enacts many laws the wisdom of which is unquestioned, and obedience to which is compulsory. In every case there is necessarily an infraction of liberty in the crude sense.

Moreover, especially in industrial matters, the cry of individual liberty often becomes a mere shibboleth, invoked by individuals against others instead of themselves. The railway magnate restricts his own liberty by pooling arrangements, but objects to interference by the shipper. The manufacturer demands protection against his foreign competitor, but objects to factory laws. The cotton grower acclaims the rise of prices brought about by manipulation on the exchange, while the spinner decries the liberty of speculation. The employer joins the selling bureau which restricts output

EDWIN R. A. SELIGMAN,
Professor in Columbia University.

or fixes prices, but objects to the "tyranny" of the labor union. The labor union adopts provisions relating to apprenticeship, the open shop, and the boycott, but opposes lockouts and trusts. The lawyer refuses to consort with the "shyster," and the doctor with the "quack," because they wish to maintain the standard of their professions; but they sternly reprobate the effort of the trade unionist to prevent the "scab" from similarly reducing the level of his occupation.

Liberty, then, must be looked at from the social as well as from the individual point of view. The individual has become what he is largely through associated effort. This, however, implies a certain subjection of the individual to the group. The liberty that is compatible with social progress involves the readiness of the individual to work for a common end. If this readiness is not voluntary, it must be developed by persuasion or by force.

THE USE OF ASSOCIATION.

All association involves a certain sacrifice of independent action. The question, therefore, whether the sacrifice of independent action, which is involved in the idea of association, means a curtailment of that liberty which is really advantageous for society, depends on the use that is made of the association. If the association has for its object or incidental result the general welfare, we applaud it; if it has for its object only the advantage of the particular group at the expense of the rest of the community, we decry it. If capital is combined so as to save expenses and reduce costs, and if the advantages incidentally accrue to the community, in the shape of lower prices or better service, we cannot reasonably object to it. If the combination, on the other hand, becomes a monopoly and secures its high profits only through higher prices, we seek to restrict it. If a labor union endeavors to maintain monopoly advantages by shutting out intending members, if it unduly restricts output or unreasonably interferes within the shop, it inevitably increases cost, curtails production and raises prices. But if a labor union uses its power to prevent starvation wages, to raise by reasonable regulation the standard of life and to promote the real efficiency of the workman, the laborer may ultimately become, and has often in the past actually become, so much more efficient a workman that his higher money wages represent a lower real cost and therefore lead to lower prices for the community. In both cases, we have a sacrifice of one kind of independence to secure the economic liberty which rests on the possession of wealth; but in the one case it involves a disadvantage, and in the other case an advantage, to society as a whole. In the one case, the enlarged opportunity of the group is purchased at the cost of the community; in the other, it goes hand in hand with the general interests of the community.

REAL ECONOMIC FREEDOM.

All liberty then is a balancing between the forces of anarchy and tyranny. The individual freedom that is oblivious of the rights of others, or of the best interests of the majority, leads to the destruction of real liberty. Group restriction that is forgetful of the possibilities of the individual leads to a tyranny that is equally destructive of real liberty. But associated action, which in helping the group also subserves the interests of general social progress, is none the less defensible because it implies a certain curtailment of the freedom to do as one likes. In a socially complex society, one must learn to like that which is best for society as a whole. From the economic point of view, only that is real freedom that is calculated to reconcile the greatest possible production in the group with the greatest possible consumption of every individual within or without the group. The liberty of one, therefore, must not endanger the economic progress of the others. Economic liberty implies at least economic opportunity, and economic opportunity depends on a certain degree of equality and responsibility. Economic liberty, in the last analysis, is the result of action, not of inaction. It is a social, not an individual, product.

—

Chairman Belmont: I have the pleasure of introducing as the next speaker the editor and proprietor of one of the leading labor organs and authorities, Mr. Frank K. Foster.

A LABOR VIEW OF LIBERTY.

Mr. Foster:—

Gentlemen: Those of us who speak for the philosophy of the shop are somewhat peculiarly placed in a discussion like this. Our argument springs not from an elastic and tenuous abstraction, but from the concrete fact. The work-a-day world, moved by instinct, guided by experience and driven by necessity, has sought liberty along the lines it has found good. In doing this it has disproven former economic postulates and disarranged old economic philosophies. The why and the wherefore has therefore been subordinated to the imperative Is.

The manual laborer has always possessed liberty to starve. His ambition, expressed through his craft association, is for liberty to live. Without this, nothing.

That the application of the principle of association, even upon voluntary lines, involves the surrender of more or less personal liberty, is conceded by all of those who have contributed to this discussion. But even the opponents of unionism have not the hardihood to assert that the social relationship itself could exist if this principle were eliminated. The real question in the industrial world is to find that happy medium which shall produce a maximum of good with a minimum of ill effects.

RESTRICTION OF COMPETITION.

There is no single, separate fact in the world of industry affecting prices and wages, whether on the side of capital or on the side of labor, that does not imply some degree, and often a large degree, of the surrender of individual liberty. That is the general principle to which the analysis of any such fact must surely lead. Let us take, for example, one such fact in the labor world—the demand for the limitation of apprentices, with which is involved the union objection to the trade school as a substitute for the training through apprenticeship. It will not profit us to observe exclusively this isolated fact. We must discover its cause, its motive. This restriction of apprentices and the associated opposition to trade schools spring from the underlying fear, warranted or not, that a craft may be overcrowded. In other words, these are efforts to prevent destructive competition between its wage earners in a given trade.

Thus we have advanced from the limitation of apprentices to the large question of excessive competition. Any of the other measures taken by organized labor to meet and overcome whatever retards or prevents their aims of higher wages, shorter hours and better conditions of work will be found to involve efforts to restrict competition. Thus the unions procure the aid of legislation to prevent wage reduction by woman or child labor. They seek by organizing the immigrant to prevent his becoming a wage reducer. The fight for the union shop is a fight to erect a barrier against nonunion labor or to force all labor in a given craft to become unionized so as to maintain a wage scale.

All of these efforts to restrict competition are efforts of association, and every one of them implies some sacrifice of individual liberty of action for a common purpose. But in competition, we have reached the cause of a vast range of phenomena, extending throughout the world of industry and manifested by capital as well as by labor.

EVILS OF EXCESSIVE COMPETITION.

Competition, it is said, is the life of trade. Yet every one recognizes, almost instinctively, that excessive competition in his own occupation spells ruin. Capitalists, farmers, professional men, all feel its danger, as well as wage earners. "Destructive," "ruinous," "unfair," "cut-throat" are adjectives applied to excessive competition by all whom it affects. The rebate-giver, the discount shaver, the under-seller, the doctor who accepts fees below a standard, are as offensive in their roles as is the "scab," or the working wage reducer, to the trade union man. Excessive competition in the world of capital works the havoc of reduced dividends, depression of trade, long and risky credits, the vanishing of confidence, business demoralization, bankruptcy and panic. Excessive competition in the field of labor brings the dire evils of the sweat-shop, starvation wages, unsanitary factories, unprotected dangerous machinery, wretched homes, ignorance, poverty, despair and crime. These consequences are reciprocal; for the ruin of the employer means an increase in the unemployed, and the ruthless cutting of earnings following wage rivalry means the driving out of business of all but unscrupulous employers.

PARALLEL RESTRICTIVE DEVICES.

The devices to prevent excessive competition between organized capital and between organized wage earners are almost numberless, and are impressively similar in that they all restrict individual freedom. All of them involve agreement between the members of an organi-

LOUIS D. BRANDEIS,
Lawyer and Publicist, Boston.

zation not to sell transportation or manufactured articles or labor or the use of money, or any other commodity, below a minimum price. The arrangement between capitalists may be called an "association," a "gentlemen's agreement," a "pool," an "exchange," a professional society, a "corporation," or a "trust;" the arrangement between wage earners is known as a "brotherhood," an "amalgamated association," or a "union." Upon both sides these associations of capital and labor vary widely in their methods. But they all have the object of preventing ruinous competition; and they are all subject to the danger of carrying the regulation of competition to the extreme of monopoly, of exploiting the consumer of exacting unreasonable demands from the employer, of conspiracy against the public interest. Many are the attempts to regulate these combinations by legislation. Many and contradictory are the decisions of state and federal courts affecting them. With their moral aspect, this department need not concern itself. Its interest lies in the economic causes of their evolution and in the principles that should guide efforts to restrict competition, based upon the instinct of self-preservation, along lines that shall not run counter to industrial prosperity and the welfare of employers, wage earners and all consumers.

Throughout the commercial and manufacturing world we encounter these combinations, everywhere seeking to regulate prices, from the raw material to the finished product. The most familiar of these, the pool, affords a notable example of the surrender of individual liberty. The pool is an unincorporated association of manufacturers, who agree to maintain a schedule of prices and to limit production for that purpose. Each manufacturer is allowed to produce only a certain percentage of the whole output, proportioned to the capacity of his plant. To prevent violation of the agreement a money deposit is often required from each, forfeitable to the association. If one manufacturer sells more than his allotment, a fine is imposed, while members selling less than their share receive a bonus from the common fund.

EXAMPLES OF COMBINATIONS.

These pooling associations are most familiar in the iron and steel industry. Prices of ores are regulated as soon as they are dug. Price agreements among associated furnace men regulate the price of pig iron, of steel rails, and of all the immense variety of products resulting from successive treatments of the original raw material. As to competition in the larger of these prod-

(Continued on page 15.)

THE TRADE AGREEMENT ENTHUSIASTICALLY ENDORSED.

DISTINGUISHED SPEAKERS ADVOCATE COLLECTIVE CONTRACTS AS A METHOD OF INDUSTRIAL PEACE BEFORE THE NEW ENGLAND CIVIC FEDERATION.

THE first general meeting of the Civic Federation of New England, held at the Quincy House, Boston, on the evening of April 26, was devoted to a discussion of "Trade Agreements." A reception and banquet, attended by about 150 prominent business, professional and labor men and students of political and industrial economy, preceded the discussion. Among the speakers were Lucius Tuttle, President of the Civic Federation of New England, Boston; August Belmont, President of the National Civic Federation, New York; Samuel Gompers, President of the American Federation of Labor, Washington; Wm. H. Pfahler, former President of the National Founders' Association, Philadelphia, and John F. Tobin, General President of the Boot and Shoe Workers' Union, Boston. All of the speakers advocated the trade agreement as a practicable method of advancing toward industrial peace, but emphasized the importance of adherence to collective contracts between employers and employed by both parties.

The Boston *Globe* published the following report:

PRESIDENT TUTTLE'S ADDRESS.

Mr. Tuttle, in opening the discussion, said:

Gentlemen: I think we may all congratulate ourselves and each other and the Secretary of the New England Civic Federation upon the successful gathering of so many people to-night interested in the great subject which the National Civic Federation began to discuss and to educate itself upon some years since, and which the New England branch has recently undertaken to study and to help work out in this section of the country.

We have no panacea for what is called the labor problem, and I doubt very much if there is any labor problem as such. What is known commonly as the labor problem is a great economic question confined more or less to this social problem, which has been working itself out from the earliest dawn of written history down to the present day.

It has had in ancient and in modern times fluctuations upward and downward, and in acute stages there has been great excitement, many difficulties to overcome, and probably many people have looked upon the question as insoluble and as presenting difficulties which were in the end perhaps to lead to a general break-up of society.

There are, it is true, many discouraging and troublesome questions in connection with this matter, as there are in connection with every other great economic problem; but I think those who have given the most thought to the subject have never at any time felt that there were any other dangers in it than those that might be overcome by a careful consideration of the whole problem as one having various conflicting elements in its nature.

BETTER MUTUAL UNDERSTANDING.

The Civic Federation has undertaken mainly, as I understand it, to get those who are called employers and those who are called employed to understand each other better.

I doubt if there has ever been a serious labor problem so called, or a serious outbreak of labor difficulties, unless there was a great lack of intelligence or understanding of the subject matter, either on one side or on both sides; and I think it is the purpose of the Civic Federation and all of its branches to endeavor as rapidly as possible (and with a full understanding that the movement must go slowly) to get each to understand the other side of the problem.

It is just as important from my point of view that the man who is called the employer should reason with the men who are called the employed and give them a complete and thorough knowledge of his side of the case as it is that those who are called the employed should be asked to develop the other side of the case.

I have studied somewhat this subject, and I feel that my knowledge of it is still very limited, and yet I have discovered this—that with practically all classes of the employed, or on the part of all classes of the employed, collectively and individually, there is a desire to be trusted, and I believe that one of the things which the Civic Federation is endeavoring to bring about is a willingness on the part of the employer to trust his employe with the facts of his business and to endeavor to procure a fair and satisfactory division of the results produced by the joint effort of the employer and the employee.

There can be no prosperity in this world anywhere unless there is a fair division of results between all of those who produce the results; and it is my belief that whenever from the efforts of the Civic Federation or in any other way the men who work—and I think we all work—can get together over the problem, reason it all out, show all sides of it, show in the end that the division which the employer is willing to make with the employed is a fair and reasonable division of the results of both, I think you have gone a long way on the road toward the settlement of any difficulty that may arise.

CONFERENCE PRODUCES AGREEMENT.

If, on one hand, the employer says, "that is your part and this is mine, and there is a wall between us, and nothing can be done on either side of that wall except that I will do what I please on my side, and you may do what you please on yours," so long as that plan of dealing with the question lasts so long there will be trouble.

But when it can be understood that there is a common interest taken in every man who works, and that the employer may come up collectively, or through his committee, state his case and have it heard, and the employe can come to his committee and state his case and have it heard, I think you have begun to solve the labor trouble in that particular instance, and there will be little difficulty in reaching ultimately an agreement which will be reasonably satisfactory to both sides. (Applause.)

Now in a word that is the purpose of the Civic Federation everywhere. It does not intend or attempt to lay down for the employer any rules or for the employe any rules, but it undertakes to put in the hands of each the olive branch of peace and to say that peace is more valuable than strife. When that shall have been accomplished, there may not be anything more for the Civic Federation to do, but it can certainly retire with honor then and rest securely upon its laurels. (Applause.)

THE FIRST DINNER OF THE NEW ENGLAND CIVIC FEDERATION.

I now take great pleasure in introducing to you Mr. August Belmont, President of the National Civic Federation, in the first place, and incidentally of the little corporation known in New York as the Interborough Rapid Transit Company. (Applause.)

PRESIDENT BELMONT'S ADDRESS.

Mr. Belmont spoke as follows:

Mr. President and Gentlemen of the Civic Federation of New England: Your topic this evening is "Trade Agreements." I am requested to address you in my capacity as an employer, and that I will cheerfully undertake to do.

At the threshold of our inquiry I desire to impress upon you: First, that corporations face problems in relation to labor peculiar to their own special classification as industries; and, secondly, that public service corporations in their relation to labor widely differ from private corporations engaged in mining and manufacture. A public service corporation deals in a daily necessity. Its activity must be constant. It creates and supplies in the same instant. It has no reserve, no accumulation to draw upon.

In many industries, as mining and manufacture,

AUGUST BELMONT,
President National Civic Federation.

employers may decide to stop or continue as their judgment guides them; but no corporation chartered to render public service has such freedom of choice. The corporation derives its life from the state. Failure to perform its chartered duty or service works its forfeiture.

Referring to the distressing conditions attending the strike on the Interborough Company's lines, I want to say publicly to the honor of the men who went out, that among the twenty odd individuals now under indictment and facing conviction and imprisonment for forcibly interfering with the operation of the elevated and underground roads, not one was a striker; they were all outsiders, either sympathizers or hoodlums.

MR. CARNEGIE'S ADVICE.

Our respected and admired friend, Mr. Andrew Carnegie, to whom, in many things, we are willing to concede much, has recently given some advice, the wisdom of which I am compelled to question.

Mr. Carnegie advises when the employes "go out," to wait patiently for the old men to return to work, and not to fill the places with new men. This course of action may, to a limited extent, go beyond the manufacturing and iron industries, even to the steam railways, as freight trains may be delayed for a reasonable time without serious loss and inconvenience. But in a great city where the demand is for the transportation of human beings, I assert the advice would spell ruin.

The question of the open or closed shop which is involved in some trade agreements does not present itself in the operation of steam railroads. I have not encountered it in the railroad world as an employer. In the steam railroad industry what are virtually trade agreements with the brotherhoods exist. They permit members of the brotherhoods to work with non-union men, provided only all are accorded alike the conditions specified in the agreements with the brotherhoods. This question—that of the open or closed shop—did not enter at all into the former contract between the Interborough Rapid Transit Company and the Amalgamated Association of Electric Railway Employes.

The only difference before and after the strike, so far as the open shop was or is concerned, related to the proportion of union and non-union employes. At no time has the Interborough Company taken an antagonistic attitude toward the freedom of the men to affiliate with labor organizations. This I recently stated at the meeting of the New York Civic Federation. I now desire to say that since the strike the men who have been taken back were re-employed without discrimination as to their membership in labor organizations.

At a time when I had no expectation of being honored as the President of the National Civic Federation I expressed myself, solely as an employer, in favor of trade agreement. I again declare for it. I maintain that trade agreements afford a practical method toward the establishment of industrial peace, whether in transportation, manufacturing, mining or other industries.

TRADE AGREEMENTS SHOULD BE INVIOLABLE.

But such trade agreements must be held inviolable by both contracting parties. They are equally obligatory on the signers, both employer and employe. In all such contracts the officers of the corporation in behalf of an association of employers sign for one side, and the officers of the union in behalf of an association of employes sign for the other side. Such an agreement, cautiously and deliberately entered upon, becomes binding upon the honor of every individual affected, as well as upon each body, whether company or union, as a whole. The national organization, affected by the strike on the Interborough, by its officers gave convincing proof that such is its belief and its practice. Its action must be considered to the credit of organized labor.

We must bear in mind that the union labor movement is an evolution. Progress has been made slowly, but not with the assistance or sympathy of employers. Have we a right to demur because self-government in all of the 150 organized crafts has not become a perfected system? On the contrary, I claim that it is to the credit of organized labor that its faults are not more numerous.

In the matter of trade agreements every contest may develop new problems for our department to consider. For example, the recent deplorable strike on the Interborough lines in New York stimulated general discussion of such topics as compulsory arbitration; the incorporation of unions: the licensing of railway employes and other propositions more or less suggested by experiments in New Zealand and elsewhere, amid conditions vastly different from those in the United States, and which, even there, have yielded no conclusive results.

THE DISCIPLINE OF LABOR.

From the union standpoint there has developed the question involving the power of officers of national organizations to enforce contracts in the face of a rebellious and defiant local organization. What practical means can be devised to enforce the discipline of labor by labor? If the government of Italy cannot force its employes to work upon the railways, we should not expect the national officers of a labor organization to be able to compel several thousands of its local members to work against their will. Possibly the contract between the International Typographical Union and the American Publishers' Association may point the way to answer this question. That contract, I understand, is underwritten by the national officers of both those organizations. If it is violated by a local union, the national union at once fills the places of the strikers with other union men, expelling the offending local. The longshoremen, I understand, have such a proviso in their contract with the Great Lakes shipping interests, and they have exercised this discipline, going as far on one occasion as to fill the strikers' places with non-union men. I am glad to say that not only the national leaders, but the most representative local leaders of organized labor, are in favor of similarly drastic methods of compelling adherence to contracts.

I am not one of those who would cite an occasional broken contract, either by employers or by labor, as an argument against the Trade Agreement. Rather would I point to the encouraging record of honorable observances and successful operations as a vindication of the good faith and common sense of both employers and wage earners.

PRESIDENT GOMPERS' ADDRESS.

President Tuttle then introduced Samuel Gompers, who spoke as follows:

I am very much impressed with not only the work which the National Civic Federation has performed for, after all, the actual achievements are of less consequence than the lessons which it has inculcated upon the minds of all our people.

We may look the whole world over and fail to find anywhere an effort of this character. It is true that in Germany about half a century ago Mr. Schulz-Delitsch undertook to bring about what he declared to be harmony between capitalists and laborers. It was in another way, what we understood to be the Manchester school of concrete or perhaps speculative political economy.

AGREEMENT AND HARMONY.

I do not know that there is any considerable number of men in our country and our time who believe that it is possible in our day or even in the near future to bring about harmony between the employers and the employed. I am not satisfied that such a condition would be either right or even natural.

There has not been entire harmony in this world between the buyers and sellers of a given thing; and after all, in the cold blooded consideration of the relations between the buyer and the seller of labor, it is a business proposition, when stripped, of course, of any element of humane feeling. And there has not always been, there is not now, and I doubt that the future will develop entire harmony between the buyers and the sellers of any particular thing.

There may be mutuality, there may be a common understanding that for the sake of convenience during a specified time there shall be agreement, there shall be understanding, there shall be a common effort to continue industry, transportation, the distribution of wealth, under the term commerce.

With the increased ability to produce the wealth of the world, due to all the pent-up genius of all the ages that have gone before; with the possibilities of the improvements in our day upon the conditions of the past, the world of workers asks this question: Are we to be constantly in the condition of our forefathers or of the present day? Are we not entitled to be sharers in the great industrial advancement and development of our time?

LUCIUS TUTTLE,
President New England Civic Federation.

We ask whether it is fair, whether it is just, whether it is wise that the hours of daily toil which have prevailed in the past shall continue despite the fact that wealth is produced in our day a hundred fold to what it was half a century ago?

We ask that with the great material progress and mental advancement of all others in society, larger opportunities should be opened up to our children that they may be the better prepared to meet the problems and to bear the burden of modern industrial conditions.

THE DEMAND OF LABOR.

Labor makes a demand upon modern society for better conditions. It asks for more leisure, a shorter workday that shall give men leisure to live, leisure to love, leisure to enjoy their freedom, leisure to develop the best that is in them and in their wives and in their children.

Of course those who take a position antagonistic to this demand that labor makes may fancy themselves in a security by that opposition. There have been instances in the history of the world where the possessors of wealth have lulled themselves into a fancied security against such demands, but they have never enjoyed either the safety of the security supposed to come from the effort to maintain that position. For, no matter whether the organizations of labor continue to exist, or whether they by any possible effort could be swept out of existence to-morrow, you could not destroy the yearnings in the human heart, or these aspirations in the human mind.

If the workingmen had continued in slavery as in bygone ages, if they had not been taught the alphabet and the three R's and something beyond them, you employers of labor might have continued to be masters of the situation. But owing to certain conditions that are not necessary to enumerate now, the workingmen have tasted freedom. They have learned the importance of the A, B and C, and the other letters of the alphabet. They have learned to conjure with those letters. They have learned that certain of the letters spell "liberty," and having learned that, it is neither wise, nor sane, nor economic to try to dispel that understanding and conception. (Applause.)

THE INTEREST OF EMPLOYERS.

I have every reason to believe, judging from the history of the people of our country, that there is not any problem which may confront us that we cannot solve. We have our organizations of labor; we have grown immensely in numbers; we have grown even in greater proportion in the feeling of fraternity among those who are organized and even among the unorganized workmen there is the general concession that the hegemony and the progress and the interests of labor are represented by the organization of the labor movement.

Yet this growth that has taken place in numbers, in intelligence and in feeling has not been confined to our own ranks. It has aroused the intelligent consideration of the employers of our country to a very large extent.

And I say to you, gentlemen, that up to this year of grace it has not been possible until now to bring about an association such as exists in our country where the employers of labor can meet with the representatives of organized labor to discuss the relative interests and try to find a way out where the mutual interests of both may best be conserved. (Applause.)

What do we find as the result of the much vaunted individual agreement between individual workman and employers? An agreement entered into between them is reached, where? Usually at the entrance of the factory, the workshop, the store, the mill or the mine or an office established for that purpose by some public service corporation. And what are the consequences? If there are fifty men who may be required, if there be ten men who may be required, what is the basis upon which wages and hours and other

WILLIAM H. PFAHLER,
Former President National Founders' Association.

conditions of labor shall be fixed? The man or the men in the group of applicants for that employment compete with each other for the positions. Those whose poverty is direst, whose needs are most immediate, are those who not only secure the employment, but by reason of their immediate necessities and their impoverished condition, set the wages, hours and other conditions of labor for themselves, and for others not so immediately driven.

The trade agreement transfers the employment and the determination of the conditions of the employment from the mouth of the mine, the door of the factory or shop, to where the conditions are to be determined, not by the direst necessity, but where, after discussion, the average intellect obtains and a committee stand between the employer and the employed to determine what is just and equitable under the conditions.

MR. PFAHLER'S ADDRESS.

William H. Pfahler, of Philadelphia, former President of the National Founders' Association, was introduced as the man who, with the late Mark Hanna, had been largely instrumental in founding the National Civic Federation.

He first commented on the progress which is being made from year to year in the settlement of labor problems, through a better and clearer understanding of their causes, and especially because of the fact that employers and employes were more and more willing to discuss their differences.

He then cited three examples of associations of employers which had been formed, in each of which the trade agreement had been found of distinct advantage for a time at least. One of these associations had each year for thirteen years made agreements with employes which had been respected and which had prevented strikes, while wages had been fixed each year according to the conditions of the trade. These agreements were successful, he thought, because in the case of this particular association the agreements dealt solely with wages.

The other two organizations had not been as successful as this first one, largely because they attempted to deal with too many problems. In the case of the National Founders' Association the question of apprentices had for years been laid one side as a problem upon which agreement could not be had until within a few months when it was deemed expedient to take the matter up and settle it.

Mr. Pfahler felt that this was the spirit in which agreements should be made—go slowly and settle the problems as they arise one at a time. He felt that the National Civic Federation and the subordinate bodies like the Civic Federation of New England, would do a great deal toward furthering the trade agreement idea and toward settling all disputes in a deliberate and at the same time effective manner.

MR. TOBIN'S ADDRESS.

John F. Tobin spoke of the best means of reaching trade agreements and making them effective. He said there was no doubt but there had been many violations of agreements by employers as well as by employes—the wonder, when all things were considered, was that there had not been more of the latter, but he thought the tendency was more and more every day to live up to these agreements.

In his own experience he had seen conferences for agreements broken up on trivial grounds too often, but he was glad to testify there was a growing disposition on both sides to forget bygones and act from the present necessities.

His observation had led him to believe that there was as large a percentage of employers unreasonable in their demands as of workmen or trade unions that were unreasonable. It would be the work of the Civic Federation to aid and further trade agreements and to point out the best ways of making and continuing such agreements.

In his own experience with trade agreements in the shoe trade those had been the means of practically abolishing strikes in an industry in which strikes had been of frequent occurrence.

It was the policy of the Boot and Shoe Workers' Union to impress on the unions the necessity of adhering to agreements and of living up to obligations or suffer the consequences. His organization was pledged to that principle. The result was that peace had been established through trade agreements. And as a necessary consequence this peace meant the union or closed shop which he pointed out was necessary in order to enforce the agreement. If agreements are broken in a shop the union fills the places of strikers regardless of consequences. Mr. Tobin felt that the trades union was necessary for the preservation of liberty.

LIST OF ACCEPTANCES.

Following is the list of those who accepted invitations to the banquet of the Civic Federation of New England:

EMPLOYERS.

Adams, Charles E., President Massachusetts State Board of Trade, Lowell.
Ackerman, J. E., Ackerman & Brummel, Manufacturers of Cut Soles, Boston.
Alexander, M. W., General Electric Company, Lynn.
Aldrich, John G., General Manager New England Butt Company, Providence, R. I.
Belmont, August, President Interborough Rapid Transit Company, and of the National Civic Federation, New York.
Brummel, Max, Ackerman & Brummel, Manufacturers of Cut Soles, Boston.
Bowlby, James L., President Master Teamsters' Association, Boston.
Bowker, William H., President Bowker Fertilizer Company, Boston.
Balls, J. Arthur, Barber Asphalt Paving Company, Boston.
Billings, L. C., James Wilkinson & Co., Electrical Contractors, Boston.
Berry, W. F., Second Vice-President Boston & Maine R. R., Boston.
Burrowes, E. T., Manufacturer of Burrowes' Screens, Portland, Me.
Barnes, Frank L., Barnes Electric Company, Boston.
Chapin, H. D., Traffic Manager N. Y. C. & H. R. R. R. Company, Boston.
Capen, Samuel B., Torrey, Bright & Capen, Merchants, Boston.
Chandler, F. Alexander, Secretary N. E. Hardware Dealers' Association, Boston.
Cordingley, William R., Wilcock & Cordingley, Wool Merchants, Boston.
Covel, A. S., Treasurer Tremont & Suffolk Mills (Cotton), Lowell.
Crapo, Hon. William W., President Wamsutta Mills (Cotton), New Bedford.
Cumnock, A. G., Treasurer Appleton Company (Cotton Mills), Lowell.
Chase, Simeon B., Treasurer King Philip Mills (Cotton), Fall River.
Clemence, M. B., Hyde Manufacturing Company (Shoe Knives, etc.), Southbridge.
Daniels, George F., President New England Shoe and Leather Association, Boston.
Drake, Herbert T., Superintendent Douglas Shoe Company, Brockton.
Ellis, George H., Printer and Publisher, Boston.
Eaton, Charles A., Shoe Manufacturer, Brockton.
Fox, Charles K., Shoe Manufacturer, Haverhill.
Filene, Edward A., William Filene's Sons Company, Merchants, Boston.
Filene, A. Lincoln, William Filene's Sons Company, Merchants, Boston.
Frank, Philip, Boots and Shoes, Boston.
Fosdick, Frederick, President Fitchburg Steam Engine Company, Fitchburg.
Fish, W. C., Manager General Electric Company, Lynn.
Fuller, J. E., George A. Fuller Company, Building Construction, Boston.
Field, J. Howard, Charles A. Eaton Co., Shoe Manufacturers, Brockton.
Gleason, W. H., Secretary Revere Rubber Company, Boston.
Hoyt, George B., President Employers' Association, Boston.
Hutchinson, George, Treasurer Clark-Hutchinson Company, Shoe Manufacturers, Boston.
Houlihan, M. J., Master Builders' Association, Providence, R. I.
Hills, George H., Treasurer Durfee Mills (Cotton), Fall River.
Houghton, George C., Secretary New England Shoe and Leather Association, Boston.
Howe, Louis P., Vice-President E. H. Howe Shoe Company, Marlborough.
Harriman, Henry I., Cotton Machinery Manufacturer, Readville.
Jones, E. C., General Manager Central Vermont Railway, St. Albans, Vt.
Knight, Arthur O., Secretary and Treasurer [illegible] Wire Cloth Company, Worcester.
Kimberly, [illegible], [illegible] Manufacturer, [illegible].
Logan, James, Chairman Executive Committee United States Envelope Company, Worcester.
Lawrence, John S., [illegible] Lawrence & Co., Commission Merchants, Boston.
Logue, Charles, Building Contractor, Boston.
Lee, Charles E., Assistant General Manager Boston & Maine R. R., Boston.
Lyman, Arthur T., Treasurer Lowell Manufacturing Company (Cotton), Boston.
Miller, John L., President Granite Manufacturers' Association, Quincy.
MacColl, J. R., Lorraine Manufacturing Company (Worsteds), Pawtucket, R. I.
Milne, Andrew, Miller & Chalmers, Granite Manufacturers, Boston.
Myers, S. A., Myers & Andrews, Clothing Manufacturers, Boston.
Mead, Edward C., Mead, Mason & Co., Building Contractors, Boston.
Marsh, E. A., American Waltham Watch Company, Waltham.
Procter, Henry H., Procter-Ellison Company, Leather Manufacturers, Boston.
Pillsbury, R. W., W. S. & R. W. Pillsbury, Shoe Manufacturers, West Derry, N. H.
Perry, G. U., Treasurer [illegible] Company [illegible], Boston.
Plunkett, W. C., Manager W. C. Plunkett & Sons (Cotton Manufacturers), Adams.
Plunkett, C. T., Secretary Berkshire Cotton Manufacturing Company, Adams.

JOHN F. TOBIN,
General President Boot and Shoe Workers' Union.

Pierce, Wallace L., President Walworth Manufacturing Company, Boston.
Pfahler, William H., former President National Founders' Association, Philadelphia, Pa.
Penniman, Edwin G., Master Builders' Association, Providence, R. I.
Rust, Nathaniel J., President Boston Storage Warehouse Company, Boston.
Robinson, H. C., Superintendent Southern Division Boston & Maine R. R., Boston.
Richards, James L., Boston Consolidated Gas Company, Boston.
Smith, H. G., Fore River Shipbuilding Company, Quincy.
Stott, Charles A., Belvidere Woolen Manufacturing Company, Lowell.
Shepard, Frank R., Treasurer Employers' Association, Boston.
Shove, W. F., Treasurer Pocasset Manufacturing Company (Cotton), Fall River.
Sumner, Charles P., Agent Cunard Steamship Company, Boston.
Sherwin, Thomas, President New England Telephone and Telegraph Company, Boston.
Taylor, Charles H., Jr., The Boston Globe, Treasurer Civic Federation of New England.
Tapley, Henry F., Amos P. Tapley & Co., Shoe Manufacturers, Boston.
Tuttle, Lucius, President Boston & Maine R. R. Co., and of the Civic Federation of New England, Boston.
Winslow, W. C., Vice-President Metropolitan Coal Company, Boston.
Walcott, S. H., Secretary Boston Merchants' Association, Boston.
Wyman, Charles D., Stone & Webster (Street Railway Interests), Boston.
Washburn, Charles G. (Steel and Iron), Worcester.
Wright, John G., Wool Merchant, Boston.

REPRESENTATIVES OF LABOR.

Abrahams, Henry, International Cigar Makers' Union, Boston.
Agnew, Philip, Hotel and Restaurant Employes' Union, Providence, R. I.
Baine, Charles L., General Secretary-Treasurer Boot and Shoe Workers' Union, Boston.
Bradford, R. H., Brotherhood Electrical Workers, Boston.
Birmingham, M. J., Brotherhood of Electrical Workers, Boston.
Cain, George L., International Association of Machinists, Lynn.
Cameron, Colin W., Agent Carpenters' District Council, Boston.
Coogan, Hugh J., International Cigar Makers' Union, Boston.
Cohen, Edward, Third Vice-President Massachusetts State Branch American Federation of Labor, Lynn.
Crosman, W. J., Typographical Union, Boston.
Cooke, Herbert W., Typographical Union, Boston.
Cunningham, William J., International Association of Tube-workers, Somerville.
Collins, Peter W., President Central Labor Union, Boston.
Connolly, John J., International Association of Machinists, Boston.
Davis, Arthur L., Typographical Union, Boston.
Dyer, W. R., Metal Trades Council, Boston.

(Concluded on page 15.)

THE LAW AND THE CLOSED SHOP CONTRACT.

THE ATTORNEY FOR A CITIZENS' ALLIANCE REVIEWS JUDICIAL DECISIONS AND REACHES A CONCLUSION FAVORABLE TO COLLECTIVE BARGAINING.

[The following are extracts from a pamphlet entitled, "The Law Relating to the Closed Shop Contract," by Walter Drew, of Grand Rapids, Mich. The fact that Mr. Drew is the attorney for the Citizens' Alliance of that city makes his narrative, analysis and conclusion in favor of the legality of the closed shop and of the desirability of complete combination of labor and of collective bargaining especially noteworthy.—Editor's Note.]

A closed shop for the purposes of this article may be defined as a "shop" in which none but members of a certain union or unions can secure employment. "Shop" is a general term for any business requiring the employment of labor. A closed shop in itself is a mere condition, and cannot properly be spoken of as lawful or unlawful. The law, however, will look to the active forces by which the condition known as the closed shop is brought about or maintained and will determine if those forces in their purposes or workings be lawful or unlawful.

A closed shop contract is a contract the immediate purpose of which is to secure or maintain the condition known as a closed shop.

Such contracts are susceptible of division into several classes according to the parties to them.

(1.) Contracts among the several members of a union in which they agree not to work in a shop where non-union men are employed. These contracts are usually in the form of by-laws.

(2.) Contracts between a union and an employer by which none but members of the union are to be employed in the employer's shop.

(3.) Contracts between a proprietor and a contractor by which the contractor is to employ none but union labor upon work to be done for the proprietor.

Such contracts may also be classified as public and private. A public closed shop contract is one which a public corporation, such as a city, county, or Board of Education is a party. A private contract is one all of the parties to which are private persons or corporations.

The courts have unequivocally condemned public closed shop contracts as unlawful and void upon constitutional and other grounds, and with no diversity of opinion.

The legal history of trades unions, their conduct, incidents and agreements, is in large measure a history of the application to labor combinations of the common law of conspiracy. It seems to have been true under early English common law that workingmen had no right to combine for any purpose connected with labor conditions and that their mere combination was a criminal conspiracy. The restrictions upon the right of workingmen to act in combination have been more and more removed, until, at the present time, there is no substantial difference from a legal standpoint between a labor combination and any other combination. The old common law restrictions upon combinations of workmen in general also applied to combinations of masters, the courts viewing with distrust any combined effort to influence or control trade conditions. This removal of restrictions or grant of greater freedom to act in combination may be called the development of the "right to combine."

All the different legal questions connected with trades union activities are directly or indirectly connected with this so-called right to combine. The right to strike is the right of men to combine to quit work in a body. The right to boycott is the right of men to combine to refuse to deal with another. So too the closed shop contract is related to the right to combine, for it is the act of men in combination, and expresses the terms upon which they have combined. The right to make such a contract necessarily presumes the right to combine.

Besides the greater recognition by the courts of the workingmen's rights to act in combination, there are two other doctrines associated with recent judicial views upon labor questions. One is the comparatively recent doctrine that labor is a commodity to be bought and sold in the market in like manner as any other article of trade. The other is the right of individual contract, which, by the development of the view of labor as a commodity, has gained a new meaning or application in labor matters. The workingman like the merchant has something to sell, and has the right of individual contract in regard to the terms of sale. The fact that his commodity is labor, and not goods, has ceased to make any difference in the methods he may use in his bargaining. Undoubtedly these views have influenced the attitude of the courts toward labor combinations and have had much to do with the judicial recognition of the workingmen's right to combine.

The development of the right to combine, or rather, the greater recognition by the courts of the right to combine, from the time when a combination of workmen for any purpose connected with labor matters was held to be a conspiracy, to the present, is summed up and expressed in the modern definition of a conspiracy. A conspiracy at common law has now come to be generally defined as a combination to do an unlawful act, or to do any act by unlawful means. In other words, mere combining is no longer criminal. It must be further shown that the combination has an unlawful purpose in view, or contemplates the employment of unlawful means.

With the former restrictions upon the right of workmen to act in combination in mind it becomes clear that the question of the validity of a closed shop contract must be a comparatively recent one. Under the early doctrines such a contract would have been not only void, but also evidence of a criminal conspiracy. Does the right to act in combination as now recognized justify or legalize the closed shop contract?—is the question to be answered.

In this country the right to combine on the part of workmen has been fully established and recognized by the courts without the coercion of any statute. This right to combine was not recognized by the common law at the time our country was separated from England, and English common law became American common

WALTER DREW,
Attorney Grand Rapids Citizens' Alliance.

law. The action of the American courts, therefore, in recognizing this right on the part of workmen, though not so stated, has been in the nature of a departure from the early English common law and has amounted to a grant or creation of a right not before enjoyed. Of course there are cases to be found where our American courts have followed to a greater or less extent English precedents. These cases, however, have been more and more discredited until it may be considered as firmly established in this country that there are no restrictions whatever upon the laborer's right to combine, other than that the combination shall not be for an unlawful purpose or employ an unlawful means.

We come now to the discussion of the closed shop contract as affected by the recognition by the courts of the right to combine within the limits of the law of conspiracy.

Every contract starts with a presumption of validity. It may be said, therefore, that a closed shop contract is valid unless its purposes be unlawful or it be secured or enforced by unlawful means. But no closed shop contract which has ever come before the courts has stood this test. There is no case at law or in equity holding such a contract valid; there are many and some most recent holding such contracts void.

A closed shop contract, the purpose of which is to establish or foster a monopoly of the labor market, is contrary to public policy and void.

The rule that a contract, the purpose of which is to secure a monopoly, is void, is a familiar one. In its application to closed shop contracts two classes of cases arise: (1) Where the court hold that it is apparent on the face of such a contract that its manifest purpose and inevitable tendency is to establish a monopoly, and, therefore, that such a contract is per se void. (2) Where the courts do not hold such a contract void per se, but inquire whether under the facts of each case the purpose of the particular contract is to secure a monopoly. In the first class of cases no outside or extrinsic evidence is necessary. In the second, outside evidence is considered in order to make clear the purpose of the particular contract in question.

The purpose of compelling non-members to join the union against their will is unlawful. Closed shop contracts having such a purpose, are, therefore, unlawful, and the attempt to enforce such a contract to the injury of persons, not parties to it, is an actionable wrong.

This is practically the same rule as the one preceding, except that it is stated from the standpoint of the non-union man. Evidently the ultimate purpose of compelling non-union men to join the union is to create a monopoly of the labor market. From the standpoint of the public, as we have seen under the previous rule, this purpose is contrary to public policy. From the standpoint of the non-union man sought to be coerced, this purpose is not only unlawful, but if attempted to be carried out to his injury, it gives him a right of action.

The agreements or conduct of combinations must have a legitimate and proper motive. The injury of third persons from mere malice, or without any justification, is an actionable wrong.

Under this head come chiefly cases involving attempts to enforce or perform closed shop contracts and the rights of third parties affected thereby.

Ordinarily, the act of an individual done with malice involves no greater legal liability than one done without malice. So long as the individual stays within his strict legal rights his motive is immaterial. Many judicial utterances may be found to the effect that the same rule applies to combinations, and the question has been much debated. It may be said, however, that the later authorities, and the present weight of authority, is to the effect that malice or other improper oppressive purpose on the part of a combination resulting in injury to a third party, confers a right of action upon the one injured. In other words, malicious conduct on the part of a combination is unlawful when it would not be so on the part of an individual.

A closed shop contract must be the voluntary act of all the parties to it, both in its inception and in its performance.

This is a most important limitation upon closed shop contracts. It means that closed shop by-laws or closed shop agreements with an employer, adopted by a majority vote of the union, do not bind the minority. It means that the vote of a majority ordering a strike or boycott to enforce a closed shop by-law or contract, does not bind the minority. It further means that if the assent or co-operation of the minority is secured by means of any coercive measures such as fines, forfeitures or other penalties, the contract becomes unlawful, and its enforcement to the injury of others becomes an actionable wrong.

If this article shall have made it clear that the closed shop in and of itself is not an unlawful thing, and has further clearly defined the limits set by the courts upon efforts to secure or maintain the closed shop, it has accomplished its purpose. The question of the closed shop contract, and the other labor questions now of such acute interest, are but different phases of an epoch in industrial history through which we are passing. The epoch started with the entry into the labor world of the spirit of combination. The epoch may be called "The Epoch of Incomplete Combination."

The very fact that combination on the part of labor is partial and incomplete, makes inevitable strife and war and legal questions. If there were 1,000 carvers in the United States, all of whom belonged to a union, it could not be said that such a union was trying to gain a monopoly, or to injure non-union men in any agreements it might make. Such a union could carry on its "collective bargaining" with the employer unhampered. It could name any wage or other conditions it saw fit, and the employer would have no option but to accede or go without the services of its members. Unreasonable demands would thwart their own purpose, for the public would arrange to do without services for which a wage not warranted by trade conditions was insisted upon. In other words, complete combination of labor secured and maintained would do away with the present epoch of strife, with its attendant bitterness and legal questions. It would bring an era of "collective bargaining" when the different questions at issue between labor and capital would be settled more than ever before by the laws of trade and not by the laws of the courts.

It is the belief of the writer, and his justification for introducing economic considerations into a legal article, that the courts are more and more recognizing the above fact; that they look upon complete combination of labor as a good and not as an evil; and that within the limitations already set they will put no unnecessary obstacle in the way, but that their attitude toward labor in combination will be broad and liberal.

THE GREAT CONFLICT IN THE BUILDING INDUSTRY ENDED.

EXPERIENCE EVOLVES A NEW ARBITRATION PLAN COMMANDING THE CONFIDENCE OF BOTH EMPLOYERS' ASSOCIATIONS AND UNIONS.

AN event of the highest importance in the building industry was the adoption, on April 22, of a new joint arbitration plan, between the Building Trades Employers' Association and the unions of the Building Trades of New York City. While this plan is local, yet it is of national consequence, since disturbances in the building trades in New York City have affected the execution of contracts from Maine to California. The plan is expected to maintain peace between about 5,000 employers and nearly 100,000 wage-earners, organized in thirty-two trades. The New York plan, moreover, may serve as a guide in bringing about peaceful conditions in the building industry in other large and growing cities.

This plan was brought about through a convention composed of three representatives of each employers' association and of each union which was held in March. At this convention, Otto M. Eidlitz, of the Mason Builders' Association, was Chairman, and James Hatch, of the Upholsterers' Union, was Vice-Chairman. A committee of ten, five representing employers and five representing unions, was appointed to draft the plan. The members of this committee, to whose assiduous work, extending through four weeks, the unanimous adoption of the plan at the second meeting of the convention on April 22 was largely due, were:

Employers—J. R. Strong, Electrical Contractors' Association; Otto M. Eidlitz, Mason Builders' Association; Benjamin D. Traitel, Grate and Mantel Association; Lewis Harding, Master Carpenters' Association; George A. Suter, Master Steam and Hot Water Fitters' Association.

Labor—James H. Hatch, Upholsterers; Daniel J. O'Mahoney, Steam Fitters; Jess P. Larimer, House-smiths; Julius Gerher, Sheet Metal Workers; William Keating, Marble Workers.

DANIEL O'MAHONEY,
Vice-Chairman General Arbitration Board.

This new plan replaces the arbitration plan adopted on July 3, 1903, which had proved in many respects a failure in practical operation, as was shown by the number of strikes and lockouts occurring during 1904. The important changes from the old plan are the result of experience, and for that reason, it is hoped, will prove effective. In the convention that adopted the plan, the representatives of all but four of the thirty-two trades were empowered to act. These four trades were the stonecutters, the cement masons, tile layers and bricklayers. But the representatives of these trades voted as individuals with the others in favor of the new agreement. Their action was afterward ratified by their four local unions.

The prominent features of the new plan will be indicated by an explanation of the important changes from the old. The plan is based upon an unqualified surrender on each side of the right to strike and the right to lock out. That is, it provides for the peace of disarmament, all disputes between employer and wage-earner to be settled through the machinery provided for arbitration. The old plan provides that no unions should strike and that no member of the Employers' Association should lock out "before the matter in dispute has been brought before the General Arbitration Board and settled."

The important section providing for the "closed shop" reads as follows:

> The employers, parties to this arbitration plan, agree to employ members of the trade unions only, directly or indirectly, through subcontractors or otherwise, on the work and within the territory described in Section 1 of this plan.

(Section 1 defines this territory as "all the territory known as Greater New York, unless otherwise specified in trade agreements.")

This is far more definite than the corresponding provision in the old plan, which permitted the employment of non-union men, in case a union "is unable to provide sufficient workmen, who shall become members of the union, if competent." Under the new provision, a non-union workman must join the union of his craft before he can find employment; and the unions, by their own rules, are obliged to admit any competent workman of good character, thus removing an arbitrary restriction that some unions had before imposed.

OTTO M. EIDLITZ,
Chairman General Arbitration Board.

Sections 4 and 5, relating to the General Arbitration Board, are entirely new, and follow:

> There shall be a General Arbitration Board, consisting of two representatives from each employers' association affiliated with the Building Trades Employers' Association and two representatives from each union recognized as a party to this plan.
>
> The General Arbitration Board shall exercise the powers delegated to it by the several provisions of this plan; shall determine the manner of adjustment of any dispute which is not specifically covered by this plan; shall adopt and amend a code of procedure, and shall determine the manner in which and by whom the expenses of special arbitration boards shall be paid.

Under the old plan, the employers' associations and the unions each elected two representatives to the General Arbitration Board, to serve six months; but there was no provision for substitutes in case of absence. The new plan provides for two alternates, and, in case of necessity, the association or the union may appoint a temporary substitute. The old agreement specified that "the arbitrators from the unions shall not be business agents." These words are stricken out of the new plan, but, nevertheless, business agents cannot act as arbitrators, for it is provided that "all representatives of the unions shall be working at their trade."

SAMUEL B. DONNELLY,
Secretary General Arbitration Board.

The officers of the General Arbitration Board are a Chairman and Vice-Chairman, elected by and from its members semi-annually, one to be an employer and the other an employe; and a General Secretary, to be elected by the Board for a term of one year. These officers, who serve until their successors are elected, are: Chairman, Otto M. Eidlitz, employer; Vice-Chairman, Daniel J. Mahoney, employe; Secretary, Samuel B. Donnelly, former President of the International Typographical Union. There are regular monthly meetings of the Board. Special meetings may be called by the Chairman or Executive Committee, and shall be called upon the filing with the Secretary of a written request from five of the organizations represented. A majority vote carries any question in the Board; except a member call for a division, when a majority vote of each side present and voting is required. In case of inability to agree upon a motion, a conference committee shall be appointed, which shall report a motion or motions to the meeting. All these detailed provisions are new and replace what proved to be troublesome indefiniteness in the old plan.

Important new provisions are these:

> The cost of maintaining the headquarters of the General Arbitration Board, including the salaries of the secretary and his assistants, shall be divided equally between the Building Trades Employers' Association and the unions collectively.
>
> The headquarters of the General Arbitration Board shall not be the meeting room nor the club rooms of any association of employers or employes.

Under the old plan all the expenses of the General Board were paid by the associated employers, and its officers were in the Building Trades Employers' Club. This arrangement proved repellant to members of the unions, who felt that the General Board was thus, at least in appearance, unduly subject to the influence of the employers, and who also felt a certain embarrassment and hesitancy in bringing their business affairs to the headquarters of the employers. This difficulty is eliminated by the establishment of the arbitration offices in a neutral place. No difficulty or objection is anticipated on the part of the unions in bearing their half of the necessary expenses.

JAMES H. HATCH,
Vice-Chairman of Convention Upon New Plan.

The old agreement provided simply for an Executive Committee of the General Board, with power to appoint special arbitration boards. But the new plan is specific and elaborate in its provisions regarding the Executive Committee. This is to consist of twelve members, elected equally by the employers' and unions' representatives in the General Board, to serve six months. These are divided at the outset into six classes, serving one, two, three, four, five and six months, respectively, so that hereafter this Executive Committee will be a continuous but gradually changing body. The Committee, which meets once a week or upon call of the Secretary, has control of all receipts and expenditures, acts as a Board of Conciliation and exercises all the powers of the General Board between its meetings, except the power to amend the Code of Procedure and fix the expenses of the Special Boards. All its decisions are to be final and binding, subject to review by the General Board at the written request of an employers' association or a union, endorsed by a majority vote of the representatives of either side present and voting.

(Concluded on page 15.)

THE NATIONAL

Civic Federation Review

Offices: 281 Fourth Avenue, New York City

RALPH M. EASLEY, Editor

The Editor alone is responsible for any unsigned article or unquoted statement published in THE CIVIC FEDERATION REVIEW.

Ten Cents per Copy; One Dollar per Year.

The National Civic Federation

OFFICERS

AUGUST BELMONT, President.
SAMUEL GOMPERS, First Vice-President.
OSCAR S. STRAUS, Second Vice-President.
HENRY PHIPPS, Chairman Ways and Means Committee.
CORNELIUS N. BLISS, Treasurer.
CHARLES A. MOORE, Chairman Conciliation Committee.
H. H. VREELAND, Chairman Welfare Department.
FRANCIS L. ROBBINS, } Chairmen Trade Agreement
JOHN MITCHELL, } Committee.
RALPH M. EASLEY, Chairman Executive Council.
SAMUEL B. DONNELLY, Secretary.

EXECUTIVE COMMITTEE

On the Part of the Public.

Grover Cleveland, ex-President of the United States, Princeton, N. J.
Andrew Carnegie, capitalist, New York City.
Cornelius N. Bliss, ex-Secretary of the Interior, New York City.
Oscar S. Straus, member of the Court of Arbitration at The Hague, New York City.
Charles W. Eliot, President Harvard University, Cambridge, Mass.
Archbishop John Ireland, of the Roman Catholic Church, St. Paul, Minn.
Bishop Henry C. Potter, of the Protestant Episcopal Church, New York City.
David R. Francis, President Louisiana Purchase Exposition, St. Louis, Mo.
Isaac N. Seligman, of J. & W. Seligman & Co., New York City.
James Speyer, of Speyer & Co., New York City.
Charles Francis Adams, publicist, Boston.
V. Everit Macy, capitalist, New York City.
Ralph M. Easley, Chairman Executive Council, New York City.

On the Part of Employers.

Henry Phipps, director United States Steel Corporation, New York City.
August Belmont, President Interborough Rapid Transit Company, New York City.
Lucius Tuttle, President Boston & Maine Railroad, Boston.
Frederick P. Fish, President American Bell Telephone Company, Boston.
Francis L. Robbins, President Pittsburgh Coal Company, Pittsburgh.
Henry G. Davis, Coal Operator, Elkins, W. Va.
H. H. Vreeland, President New York City Railway Company, New York City.
Samuel Mather, of Pickands, Mather & Co., Cleveland.
Charles A. Moore, of Manning, Maxwell & Moore, New York City.
Franklin MacVeagh, of Franklin MacVeagh & Co., Chicago.
Charles H. Taylor, Jr., ex-President American Newspaper Publishers' Association, Boston.
Dan R. Hanna, of M. A. Hanna & Co., Cleveland.
Marcus M. Marks, President National Association of Clothing Manufacturers, New York City.
Otto M. Eidlitz, Chairman Board of Governors, Building Trades Employers' Association, New York City.
William H. Pfahler, former President National Founders' Association, Philadelphia.

On the Part of Wage Earners.

Samuel Gompers, President American Federation of Labor, Washington.
John Mitchell, President United Mine Workers of America, Indianapolis.
E. E. Clark, Grand Chief Conductor, Order of Railway Conductors, Cedar Rapids, Iowa.
James Duncan, General Secretary Granite Cutters' National Union, Washington.
Daniel J. Keefe, President International Longshoremen, Marine and Transportworkers' Association, Detroit, Mich.
Warren S. Stone, Grand Chief International Brotherhood of Locomotive Engineers.
P. H. Morrissey, Grand Master Brotherhood Railroad Trainmen, Cleveland.
William D. Mahon, President Amalgamated Association of Street Railway Employes of America, Detroit, Mich.
Theodore J. Shaffer, President Amalgamated Association of Iron, Steel and Tin Workers, Pittsburgh.
J. J. Hannahan, Grand Master Brotherhood, Locomotive Firemen, Peoria, Ill.
James O'Connell, President International Association of Machinists, Washington.
John Tobin, General President Boot and Shoe Workers' Union, Boston.
Joseph F. Valentine, President Iron Moulders' Union of North America, Cincinnati.
James M. Lynch, President International Typographical Union, Indianapolis.
Denis A. Hayes, President Glass Bottle Blowers' Association of United States and Canada, Philadelphia.

AN UNPRECEDENTED OPPORTUNITY.

The new plan for arbitration between the associated employers and the unions in the building trades in Greater New York commands confidence in its successful operation chiefly because its provisions are the fruit of experience with the former unsatisfactory plan. There is a wider interest, however, in the practical outcome of this elaborate device of arbitration. Under it, the members of some thirty-two unions have obtained three leading demands of organized labor: The eight hour day; the highest average wages paid to craftsmen in the world, and the closed shop.

Here is an unprecedented opportunity for organized labor to exhibit to its critics a broad and high-minded standard of conduct. Having won these substantial gains, it would be the height of folly for the local leaders of these unions to allow trivial or limited subjects of dispute to become sources of rupture. The unions now have equal representation throughout the machinery of arbitration. Their rank and file should be careful to select representatives capable of meeting in a spirit of fairness the representatives of the employers, and of cultivating a mutual desire to maintain peace with justice in the great building industry. Thus will they set an example inspiring to organized labor throughout the country, not alone in the building trades, but in all industries. Moreover, they have now an opportunity to disprove the assertion frequently made by enemies of organized labor, that the granting of any of its demands will only whet its appetite into insatiable greed.

Great credit is given to all those leaders, among both employers and craftsmen, whose joint efforts have culminated in this latest device for industrial peace. Without invidious discrimination, it is but fair to say that no employer in the country has worked more earnestly, patiently and devotedly for the establishment in practice of the principle of trade agreements than has Otto M. Eidlitz, the Chairman of the New General Arbitration Board, and a member of the Executive Committee of the National Civic Federation. The Secretary of this organization, Samuel B. Donnelly, while Secretary of the former Arbitration Board, whose expenses were wholly paid by the associated employers, although a loyal veteran in the trade union movement, was subject during two years to the angry criticism of every union disappointed in obtaining all of its demands. His unanimous re-election as Secretary of the new Board is a merited tribute to clear-headed fairness and indefatigable industry.

RESTRICTED INDIVIDUAL FREEDOM.

The verbatim report of the papers and addresses at the first general meeting of the Department of Industrial Economics, presented in this issue of THE REVIEW, is a body of literature of such interest and value to economic students, that it has been decided to republish the matter, with supplementary comments, in book form. A single meeting of this department will thus result in placing in every economic library in this country and abroad a volume that will go far to dissipate the confusion about "personal liberty" and "constitutional rights" that some opponents of organized labor have injected into the discussion of trade agreements and of the open and closed shop. Convincing evidence is here accumulated that any associated effort in industry must and does involve the curtailment of individual freedom. The welfare of society, as a whole, is pronounced the general measure of the extent to which this surrender of freedom ought to be carried. Further discussion may discover a more specific and immediate test.

THE NEW ENGLAND CIVIC FEDERATION.

Notable for its representative character and for its atmosphere of serious earnestness was the first general meeting of the New England Civic Federation, of which an account appears elsewhere in this issue of THE REVIEW. The gathering will extend a wider understanding of the purposes and methods of the national organization and of the associated local organizations, which will in time be formed in the industrial centers of large divisions of the entire country. The speakers, both employers and wage-earners, were unanimously in favor of the trade agreement as a method of industrial peace, while they did not fail to emphasize the equal responsibility upon both parties, for the inviolability of the collective contract.

AN IMPORTANT DISTINCTION.

It is too bad that the National Civic Federation has degenerated into an apologist for the Standard Oil Company. The high character of the gentlemen connected with that organization has led us to expect that its energies would be directed to better ends.—*Wyoming Sentinel.*

Several Western papers have published similar comments. They evidently confuse the Civic Federation with a new organization, recently launched by Francis B. Thurber, President, styling itself the Civic Association of New York. The National Civic Federation has absolutely no relation to the latter organization.

THE C. F. U. ATTACK.

It has been pointed out in a former issue of THE REVIEW that the work of the National Civic Federation is opposed by two foes, whose enmity is natural and logical. These two foes are the militant socialists and those employers' associations which, under the false cry that the rights of American citizens are in peril, would destroy every union.

The Civic Federation would promote better relations between employers and employed by methods which both its foes oppose, some employers because they wish the peace of subjugation, and the Socialists because they wish revolution. It is especially disconcerting to the Socialist programme of the seizure of all industries by the State to behold employers, labor leaders and publicists coming together around a table in social intercourse and search after Truth, the solvent of the most difficult problems. Such association, some of the Socialist publications protest, counteracts the radicalism of organized labor. They mean that such commingling is fatal to the class hatred which they openly and insidiously ferment; that it makes more and more impossible their "self-imposed task of undermining society."

Outside of their partisan publications, the Socialists can express their hatred of the Civic Federation only by making speeches and offering resolutions in a few unions, or in some central bodies, where the radical element, including both Socialists and anarchists, is in a majority. In only two or three such bodies in the United States is this the situation, but the radicals never miss an opportunity to push forward a resolution condemning the Civic Federation. For example, one local branch of the United Mine Workers of America adopted a resolution demanding that John Mitchell, their President, withdraw from membership in the Civic Federation. When this resolution came before the national convention of the Mine Workers, it was hooted out of hearing. Once the radicals passed a resolution in the national convention of the Iron Moulders' Union, taking advantage of a slim attendance in the closing hours, requiring its President to withdraw from the Executive Committee of the National Civic Federation. The President called for a referendum vote of the union throughout the country, which resulted in the overwhelming repudiation of the resolution.

A more recent attack of this nature was made in the Central Federated Union of New York City. The radicals, although really in a minority in the New York Central Federated Union, sometimes are in temporary control, because of a light attendance of conservative delegates. It was such a meeting that passed a resolution, some weeks ago, calling for the withdrawal of all its members from the New York Civic Federation. Those labor representatives in the New York Civic Federation who belong to unions not affiliated with the Central Federated Union of course paid no attention to this resolution. Members of unions that are affiliated ignored the order to resign and demanded that a committee be appointed to investigate the charges, made when the resolution was adopted, that the labor membership in the Civic Federation was detrimental to the cause of organized labor.

This committee, consisting of Delegates Lorimer, of the Housesmiths' Union; Richter, of the Musical Union; Morton, of the Amalgamated Woodworkers; Green, of the Rock Drillers and Tool Sharpeners' Union, and Hand, of the Eccentric Engineers' Union, none of whom are members of the Civic Federation, spent two weeks in an investigation, which included a visit to the Civic Federation headquarters, where all records were placed at its disposal, and which also included fruitless efforts to extract any testimony whatever from the delegates who had made the charges, or, more properly speaking, the innuendoes. The committee finally reported unanimously that the work of the Civic Federation was altogether beneficial to the movement of organized labor and that not a single delegate who had alleged to the contrary, could be found with the courage to come into the light in support of the assertion. Among the witnesses who did testify were Samuel Gompers, President of the American Federation of Labor; John Mitchell, President of the United Mine Workers of America; William D. Mahon, President of the Amalgamated Association of Street and Electric Railway Employes of America; F. J. McNulty, Grand President Electrical Workers of the United States; Joseph Weber, President of the American Federation of Musicians; Frank Buchanan, President International Association of Bridge and Structural Iron Workers, and others.

Mr. Gompers addressed the following letter to the committee:

New York, April 28, 1905.

To the Committee of the New York Central Federated Union:

Dear Sirs and Brothers—

It is not a question with me to praise either the National Civic Federation or the work it has done or can do: in my judgment as an association it is and can be made an instrument of good. What it has accomplished is history, and regardless of carping criticism or malicious misrepresentation, those organizations of labor which have been brought into contact with its representatives, those who have been benefited by its aid, must of necessity be the best witnesses to the good that it has done.

With other representative trade unionists, I have held, that the National Civic Federation, *without a well-organized, thoroughly alert trade union movement, would be absolutely futile*, and perhaps its very existence unnecessary: but with the growth in our movement, the greater intelligence our membership manifests, the higher and deeper the interests of our fellow-workers in the success of the cause of labor, in that same degree will the National Civic Federation be helpful to us in attaining the purposes for which we are organized, and to attain them with the least possible friction or contest.

After all, what is the National Civic Federation? It is not an arbitration body, it does not foist itself either upon organized labor or upon employers. It undertakes to bring workmen and employers into a full, fair, free and fearless discussion of the views or interests that each represents, and by that brings a more intelligent understanding on both sides of the real industrial situation. It undertakes to bring representatives of organized labor in conference with employers with whom there is a dispute as to wages, hours of labor, or other conditions of employment, and by such conferences to come to an agreement by which a strike or a lockout may be avoided and averted.

When a strike or lockout has occurred, it not only holds itself in readiness, but by reason of the desire to further the interests of both, has brought and does bring the representatives of both sides together in conference, with a view of arriving at an adjustment of a conflict; and since the formation of that organization, in not one instance has any such conference resulted in anything but to the advantage of the labor interests.

Of course, when the Civic Federation undertook to be helpful to maintain industrial peace, or to bring about peace when strife had occurred, some over-zealous friends and more opponents undertook to say that all differences would be settled, that all strikes would be avoided, that organized labor would lose its power and potency to defend and promote the interests of the workers; but this was neither in the minds of those who organized it, nor of those who are still participants therein. Each man strongly and stoutly defends his convictions, the interests of his class, everywhere and under all circumstanes. Disussion in its broadest sense, the bringing of men to argue and defend their convictions and the faith that is in them, must of necessity tend to bring a better and a higher conception of the rights to which labor is entitled. This has been a marked result of the conferences of all sorts which have been thus far held, and has helped to place the demands which organized labor makes upon modern society upon a decidedly higher plane.

It is impossible in the brief time I have to note the individual cases in which the Civic Federation has been of practical advantage to our movement, but it may not be amiss to mention a few cases which are typical of others too numerous to mention now. Conferences were held between the representatives of the United Mine Workers and others of organized labor with the mine operators of the anthracite region, and though the strike occurred, the efforts were continued throughout to bring about an honorable adjustment of that controversy. These efforts, which contributed in the final termination of the strike and the advantages which were secured for the miners, have not been written and cannot yet be written. Ask the representatives of the Housesmiths' Union of New York, the Lithographers' Union, the Textile Workers of Fall River, the Street Railway men of San Francisco, and other centers throughout the country; the building trades of New York, Chicago and elsewhere, the printing trades unions, the Structural Iron Workers, the Paper Makers, and many others, and they will surely and gladly acknowledge the valuable assistance rendered, both in the avoidance of conflicts and others brought to an honorable conclusion, and all of them with advantage to labor.

It is neither my desire nor duty to pronounce an eulogy upon the Civic Federation. It is an association made up of representative men in the ranks of labor, and a great number of large employers of labor, with some representatives of the general public. It discusss economic problems affecting the workers and people, and it aims to be helpful in bringing about more rightful relations between workmen and their employers with the least possible amount of friction, strife and conflict. No decisions are rendered binding any one to surrender his judgment or convictions or independence of his position. It aims to bring representative men in all ranks of life together to be helpful to their fellows. It has made conferences possible when, without it, many of them would have been impossible. It has been helpful in preventing strikes and paving the way for the adjustment of difficulties, and in no instance have either strikes or conflicts been avoided or adjusted when they have been other than helpful to labor.

Without more ado and simply based upon this statement, it must convince the most skeptical that the Civic Federation has not been detrimental, but on the contrary, has been of advantage to labor and the cause of labor, the great cause with which we have the honor to be associated. Fraternally yours,

(Signed) Samuel Gompers,
President, American Federation of Labor.

THE USES OF ADVERSITY.

There have always been much unhappiness and suffering in this world. Every effort to lighten the burdens of the race is humanitarian. But the Socialists, who would aggravate discontent, and their close allies, the sentimental exaggerators, would make it appear that all travail is unalloyed evil and a symptom of progressive social degeneracy. The apostles of despair are incessantly presenting the admitted evils of the tenement sweatshop, the horrors of child labor, the wretchedness of the slums and every kind of distress incident to crowded centers of population, with sensational distortion, as if they were warnings of approaching cataclysm. To those whose minds may thus be turned toward pessimism, we commend a perusal of the following article, by Prof. E. E. Slosson, of the University of Wyoming, published in the *Independent:*

When modern science began to examine critically the ladder by which man has climbed to his present position, it was found that every step was stained with blood; that life was war and suffering the common lot of all; that animals preyed upon plants and man upon animals and bacteria upon man, a cycle of suffering; that every species was an Ishmael; that birds and butterflies were not the careless, joyous things the poet thought them, living only for beauty and pleasure, but were engaged in a terrible struggle for existence; that the song of the birds was a war-cry and the adornment of the butterfly was merely war-paint. It was found that there was an awful waste in nature, waste of time, waste of work, waste of life. Of a million seeds sown by the wind only one lived. A thousand eggs were cast upon the waters to produce one fish. A hundred men labored and sweat that one might rise. It was an awful revelation, that of science fifty years ago. No wonder that it drove men insane; made them pessimists, atheists. If science had stopped here it would have been a gospel of despair.

But it did not stop; another step changed it to a gospel of hope. It was discovered that this suffering, that looked to a casual glance like an impediment to progress, was really its cause; that pain was the mainspring of the universe; that war was the mother of all things, as the Greek had said long ago; that the rod of affliction was the modeling tool by which God created all living things; that there could have been no happiness now if there had been no suffering in the past; that joy is the offspring of sorrow, out of war comes peace, and through death comes life. This changed the whole view. It put optimism in the place of pessimism. Man could see the uses of adversity. There was a time when there was no suffering in the world. But that was when there was no life; when the earth was without form and void and darkness was upon the face of the deep. With life came suffering, and increase with it. Progress may be defined as increase in the capacity for suffering. A stone does not feel pain, probably a plant does. Ancient animals suffered less than their descendants. The gigantic saurians that used to creep across the Rocky Mountain plains were as big as a house, but their brains could have been put into a tea-cup. Not much chance for pain there. And finally man came, a creature built upon a new and improved plan; but his chief endowment was that he was able to suffer more. Several new kinds of suffering were invented expressly for him. He alone of all the animals suffers in anticipation of coming perils, and grieves over the errors of the past. It is the greater capacity for suffering that has made men what they are. These are they who have come up out of great tribulation.

The earliest animals were built to avoid suffering. They were as big as an animal could be, and walk. The sensitive parts were protected, as in our modern iron-clads, by defensive armor as thick as could be carried; hide and scales almost impenetrable. Now these animals are all extinct. They were beaten in the struggle for existence, and by what? *By little animals with the nerves on the outside.* The animals that were easiest hurt conquered those that were most protected. Now our museums are filled with the relics of these obsolete forms, models of inventions that did not work well, and on the walls are hanging the armor of the knights of the Middle Ages, who were beaten by men without armor. The best protected animal now in existence is the clam; the least protected is the man. To try to escape suffering is not a good plan. It has been tried on a large scale, and it does not work.

There was a time when there was no death in the world. This was long after the creation of living beings; if by death we mean a definite and certain period of life. The infusoria, the simplest organisms, are immortal. They do not die a natural death, although they can be killed. These tiny specs of protoplasm grow and divide, but we cannot say that one part is the parent of the other. It is the same individual, only separated into two parts for convenience. It lives and grows as long as the proper conditions prevail; not merely for three score years and ten, but for thousands of years. In fact, the first created speck of protoplasm is living yet, divided into innumerable parts. Later there came beings that died—spontaneously, at the end of a given time. It was apparently a great disadvantage that an animal should die when it had acquired the strength and skill of maturity, and that a new individual should have to pass through the period of helpless infancy. But the animals that died progressed and developed, while those that did not die remained stationary. Death came into the world that we might have a fuller and completer life.

Now we see more clearly what is meant by the many mysterious sayings in the Bible, that benefits arise from afflictions, that good comes out of evil, and life comes from death. People used to believe these statements; yes, they were doubtless true, but in some hazy mystical sense, nobody knew how. Now we know that they are not imaginative, but plain statements of fact; they are not figurative, but literally true.

We now know something of the benefits of suffering in the past, but why do we have to suffer? We hear that the whole creation groaneth and travaileth in pain till now, because it has brought forth US—but why does the labor continue? Here is man; intelligent man, who knows some things and thinks he knows it all; civilized man, except for occasional lapses into barbarism; man who stands erect, except when he crawls into some meanness; man with the moral law written in his heart, which he follows whenever he thinks it is good policy; man who knows God and prays to him whenever he gets into trouble; man, proud man, looks up to his Creator and says, "Here am I, the end and aim of all, Thy creation. I am worth all the pain and suffering that I have cost other beings, but do not carry this any further. Let us have peace."

This is no caricature. You will find substantially this view of the position of man in dozens of theological and scientific works. Of all created beings man is certainly endowed with the greatest capacity for conceit.

PRESIDENT MAHON'S GOOD SHOWING.

The report of 1904 of William D. Mahon, President of the Amalgamated Association of Street and Electric Railway Employes of America, shows that over 10,000 members, in 23 out of 137 divisions, have received increased wages of from one to three cents per hour. Nowhere have wages been reduced. Hours have been shortened in fourteen divisions, and nowhere lengthened. The organization paid a total of $43,297 for sick and death benefits during the year and but $13,130 for strike benefits; while $17,488 were contributed to other unions. Sixty-nine divisions are working under written agreements, an increase of four, and there is a growing disposition among companies in favor of written rather than verbal contracts with the Amalgamated Association.

CHAIRMAN VREELAND TELLS PHILADELPHIA EMPLOYERS ABOUT WELFARE WORK.

He Narrates His Experience and Emphasizes the Importance of Selecting Judicious Foremen.

The Hardware Merchants and Manufacturers' Association of Philadelphia recently evinced its interest in "welfare work" by extending, through its President, Thomas Devlin, an invitation to H. H. Vreeland, Chairman of the Welfare Department of the National Civic Federation, and President of the New York City Railway Company, to address its members upon that subject. Mr. Vreeland's address is here presented, both because of its inherent value and as an example of the widening circles of interest in "welfare work" among employers:

I understand that I am invited to address you in a dual capacity—as Chairman of the Welfare Department of the National Civic Federation, of which the President of your Association, Mr. Thomas Devlin, is a member; and as an employer having experience in the practical operation of "welfare work" among some 15,000 employes. I shall begin, therefore, with a brief statement of the scope and methods of the Welfare Department.

The very first meeting to organize this Department was attended by representative employers from various parts of the country. This was the first time that employers giving especial consideration to the welfare of their employes had been brought together. The extraordinary interest in their exchange of experiences at the outset indicated the educational possibilities of the Welfare Department, which have been more fully demonstrated by the literature resulting from the several conferences between employers, and between welfare managers, that have been held during the past year. There are now over one hundred and fifty members in the Department, and the enthusiasm and membership are growing, while the practical results are multiplying.

The educational work of this Department relates to the meaning and value of "welfare work."

The great value of our conferences lies in the fact that those who participate in the discussions are practical, successful, business men, who frankly state their failures as well as their successes in the work; or the welfare workers, specially employed to supervise welfare work. We maintain a central bureau at the headquarters of the National Civic Federation to furnish information relative to the success or failure of experiments in "welfare work." Upon request, a consulting agent is furnished to study the peculiar needs of employes in a given plant, to advise the best way of introducing such methods of "welfare work" as may be deemed essential. When desired, a permanent agent or welfare manager is recommended.

RESULTS OF PERSONAL EXPERIENCE.

Let me turn now to my own experience, and the way in which I became acquainted with the need of "welfare work," with some of its applications and its results.

At eighteen years of age I went to work in a railroad shop. In the course of time I became foreman, and step by step have filled every grade of position from foreman up to president of a street railway. In those years I did a good deal of thinking about the condition of employes.

Every man who becomes financially successful has an inclination to help his fellow men. As I became successful, I determined that my money and my personal efforts should go to aid the men engaged in the work that had been my profession.

Thousands of young men work in and about railway terminals, many of them having homes in other cities. When I was young I was in that position, and I did not know what to do with my evenings. Many of my fellows spent their leisure time in the saloons, simply because they had no other place to go.

As a result of that early experience, we have in New York a large club room, equipped with billiard tables, gymnasium, library, cigar stand and numerous other facilities; while at the power stations and terminals there are shower baths, toilet rooms and lunch rooms. At our club there are seldom less than five hundred men each night, and at the special monthly meetings, which the officers of the company attend, and at which they freely discuss every topic which may interest the wage earner, between one and two thousand workmen are present.

THE PERSONAL EQUATION.

In nine years I have been absent from only two of these meetings. I believe the attendance of the President and other officials at these meetings to be the keynote of success in this work. I keenly appreciate that it is this personal equation between officials and workmen that influences the latter, and I am careful that nothing shall disturb that friendly feeling.

There cannot be any want or serious trouble among our men or their families without our knowledge. It is the duty of every foreman to report to the head of his division every morning any case of emergency, such as might be caused by a fire, or by sudden illness. Any need for money to buy medicine, or to procure shelter, or for the care of a physician, is thus promptly met. It is especially gratifying to me to be able to state that not a single name among the employes of the company I represent has ever appeared upon the list of beneficiaries of any public charity, while so employed.

THE SELECTION OF FOREMEN.

Half of the labor troubles in all large industrial establishments are caused originally by foremen who do not know how to handle men. There is a vast difference between the small employer of half a century ago and the head of a great industrial enterprise of the present day, with its thousands of employes, where the directing heads may rarely come into personal contact with the men who perform the details of physical labor. In inspiring and creating good will, no single factor is of such consequence as the judicious selection of those who are put over and have immediate direction of the employes.

The selection of properly trained foremen is, then, a most important factor in the conduct of an industry. The old method, which still too often survives, was to select a foreman chiefly or alone because of his ability to get the most work out of the force, and with little or no regard to the question, "What are his qualifications for handling men?"

We test a foreman as to his ability and methods of discipline, but we also carefully investigate his attitude toward the employe. If he is a man calculated to antagonize the labor, we do not want him. Every foreman makes a report to me at the end of the month, telling me how many men he has discharged and his reason for doing so in every case. If foreman A discharges fifty men in a month and foreman B discharges five, we start an investigation in A's department to ascertain the cause of the trouble. If the foreman is at fault, he speedily modifies his conduct, or else we dispense with his services. By means of a table of percentages, the manager can tell at a glance what each foreman is doing in this direction.

The effect of this good treatment of employes is apparent. Several years ago, when I established a rate of pay based upon the length of time men had been in our employ, I found that only five per cent. of them were on the payrolls for five years or more. That was the effect of the old regime. To-day eighty per cent. of our employes have been with us five years or more. Every business man will appreciate the effectiveness of the latter force as compared with the former.

THE WELFARE DEPARTMENT TO WIDEN ITS OPERATIONS.

The Executive Committee Approves the Secretary's Report and Listens to Papers and Addresses Upon Welfare Work by Prominent Employers.

The Executive Committee of the Welfare Department of the National Civic Federation, at a luncheon at the Fifth Avenue Hotel, April 25, Chairman Vreeland presiding, listened to the report of the secretary upon the work of the past year and upon plans for the future. The Committee unanimously approved the report and adopted its recommendations, looking to the enlargement and extension of the operations of the Department. The papers read and addresses delivered at this meeting are published in this issue of The Review.

The report of the secretary included the following summaries:

CONFERENCES HELD.

1. Of Welfare Workers, March, 1904. Provided general view of the Welfare Work of twenty companies in the United States. Report widely distributed.
2. Of Members, November 15, 1904.
   Subjects discussed by experts:
   - Relief Associations.
   - Banks for Employes.
   - Labor Department.
   - Lunch Rooms.
3. First Local Conference, in Boston, February 27, 1905. Attended by seventy-five prominent New England employers.
   Subjects discussed:
   - How to Make Good Foremen—The Labor Department.
   - Men's Clubs.
   - Welfare Work in a Mill Town.
   - The Welfare Work of The American Telephone and Telegraph Company throughout the United States.
   - Stereopticon views of practical features in Welfare Work were shown.

RESULTS OF CONFERENCES.

A gratifying demand for further information including plans for sanitary appliances; photographs and special advice on club houses, employes' homes, etc.

Also the recommending of Welfare Managers upon request, and the provision of special agents to install such features as lunch rooms, smoking rooms and rest rooms.

FUTURE CONFERENCES.

Sectional conferences of employers are being arranged for Cleveland, Pittsburg and Chicago.

An annual conference of Welfare Managers will be held in June, upon request from a number who feel that such exchanges of experiences are invaluable to them.

LECTURES.

By request of Thomas A. Devlin, President of the Hardware Merchants and Manufacturers' Association, Chairman Vreeland spoke on the work of the Welfare Department of the National Civic Federation, at Philadelphia.

T. H. McInnerney, of the Siegel-Cooper Company, described its Welfare Work before the Monday Club of New York. The Secretary of the Welfare Department also gave stereopticon illustrations of Welfare Work in different industries throughout the United States.

Among others, lectures were given before the:
- Baltimore Club of Social Workers.
- School of Philanthropy, two lectures.
- Y. M. C. A.—Business Economy Class.
- And the C. W. Club of New York.

FUTURE LECTURES.

Foundrymen's Association, Philadelphia, June 7—Stereopticon Talk, showing special features for the benefit of molders.

Jewish Chautauqua Society at Atlantic City, N. J.

School of Philanthropy, New York.

Shoe Manufacturers' Association, Lynn, Mass., and others.

EDUCATIONAL WORK.

In addition to the publication of Reports of the Conferences, articles on different phases of Welfare Work have been widely distributed through the National Civic Federation Review each month.

The Department has undertaken to stimulate various State Bureaus of Labor to investigate and report upon Welfare Work, with very gratifying results.

PLANS FOR FUTURE EDUCATIONAL WORK.

Further articles are to be published in the REVIEW, with illustrations, on the following subjects:

Provision for Physical Comfort of Workers.
Recreation.
Education.
Housing.

Picture pamphlets will be published, with short descriptions of views of Welfare appliances in special trades, to show by example what may be done for the employes of railroads and street railways, in the line of terminal facilities, as well as for the employes in:

Paper Mills.
Theatres.
The Rubber Industry.
Foundries; and for
Bridge and Structural Iron Workers.

BUREAU OF EXCHANGE.

Much valuable data have been collected, including literature, architects' plans, photographs and stereopticon slides. The policy of building up this Bureau will be pursued. Many employers, planning to put in certain features of Welfare Work, have obtained the experience of other employers through this Bureau of Exchange.

Among the subjects covered for inquiring employers have been:

Relief Associations and Pensions.
Savings Plans.
Money Lending.
Profit Sharing.
Wash Rooms and Toilet Rooms.
Changing House for Miners.
Rest Rooms.
Lunch Houses and Lunch Rooms.
Laundries.
Fire Protection.
Club Houses and Recreation Halls.
Libraries.
Schools for Employes.
Housing.
Reorganization of Welfare Departments.
The Labor Department.

WELFARE MANAGERS.

The following workers have been placed:

Samuel T. Stewart, General Electric Co., Lynn, Mass.
Mrs. J. J. Spencer, Siegel-Cooper Co., New York.
Miss Anna D. Mitchell, National Cash Register Co., Dayton, O.
Miss Laura Mitchell, National Cash Register Co., Dayton, O.

Several employers have since requested our assistance in securing such workers for their institutions, and recommendations have been made.

GENERAL INFORMATION.

Very much general information has been given, both through personal interviews at headquarters and through correspondence, to employers, prominent foreigners, prospective welfare managers, factory inspectors and others, who are interested in promoting the work.

WELFARE WORK OF THE SIEGEL-COOPER COMPANY.

By B. J. GREENHUT, *Treasurer; read before the Executive Committee.*

Ever since the firm of Siegel-Cooper Company, New York, started, we have made a special feature of doing something for our employes; but it is only within the last few years that the subject has been given especial attention. Ours was the first among the large department stores in this country, we believe, to adopt Welfare Work systematically.

To begin with, we have an Employes' Association, the directors being employes; but naturally, they are among some of our most important men and women, as we impress upon our employes the importance of having their affairs managed by those most capable.

We do not make it compulsory upon employes to join, but I do not recall the case of a single employe not a member; for the association gives such advantages at so small a cost that, as soon as its plan and purpose are explained, no employe hesitates to join. The dues are nominal, ranging from ten to forty cents per month. In addition, the firm gives the association all fines imposed upon employes for whatever cause, and these fines average about [illegible] per month.

The employes derive financial benefits from the association. In case of sickness they receive half pay, and a doctor's services and medicines without charge. The death benefit is $100. Sometimes, in case of a death in the family of an employe, when circumstances warrant, the association sends the employe from $25 to $50. The association makes loans to its members ranging from $25 to $200. A committee investigates each application, both as to the worthiness of the applicant and the object of the loan. No interest is charged and repayment is made in weekly or monthly instalments.

A loan of from $100 to $200 has several times been given to employes whose health required a permanent change of climate, usually because of consumption, to pay for their transportation and care until they could find suitable work in their new homes. When our physician reports that an employe's condition is so depleted as to make a complete rest and change of surroundings necessary, we send the patient to a farm to enjoy out-door life in the country. Only those are sent who do not need medical attendance, but simply to get away from the city; and their expenses are paid for as many weeks as the doctor recommends.

The summer cottage at Long Branch for girls is one of the most attractive and valuable features of our welfare work. About four years ago, the firm bought this cottage, with its surrounding grounds, which it had previously rented each year, and presented it to the Employes' Association, with the statement that the association should conduct the establishment, all expenses being paid by the firm. The instructions were to spare no expense in procuring the best comforts and food, and the committees in charge of the cottage carry out their instructions literally. Not a penny of expense to the girls is involved, from the time they leave the store on Saturday afternoon, until they return the following week. Transportation is provided. Each week's party is personally conducted and is met on arrival by our welfare secretary, who acts as hostess throughout the summer.

The cottage accommodates about 55 girls per week. All the rooms are light and airy, well and neatly furnished, each having a single bed, so that the guests of the association feel independent. A corps of servants leaves nothing for the girls to do but enjoy themselves thoroughly. Something is provided for their amusement and recreation nearly every moment, including sea bathing, trolley rides, coaching and sailing parties, clam bakes, and theatre and lawn parties. The large grounds are well shaded with trees, beneath which are hammocks, swings, croquet grounds, and tennis courts. Thus each girl in our employ has in the summer one week of continual wholesome pleasure. At the outset of this experiment there was some natural hesitancy among the girls in accepting this hospitality, but the initial experience caused every one to express enthusiastic appreciation. We have yet to hear a single complaint from any of these guests.

B. J. GREENHUT,
Treasurer, Siegel-Cooper Company, New York.

I have often found it advisable in reprimanding employes to point out to them the right course to pursue in order to succeed in their work. Invariably this advice was appreciated. But my time was so taken up that I could not devote this attention to our people individually. The necessity therefore impressed itself upon me of having a tactful representative who could gain the confidence of our employes and do for them that which I could not find time to do myself. I think that we have such a person in Mrs. Spencer, our welfare secretary, who does not make the employes feel that she is there to help them, unless they wish her help. Experience has shown that the mere knowledge that there is such a person causes our people to seek her counsel voluntarily. Her effort is to help our employes to help themselves. As our business employs so many people, it has been impossible for our managers and heads of departments to bestow much attention upon the individual person. When the work was not performed satisfactorily, it was the custom simply to dismiss such an employe and engage another. This continual change proved often to our disadvantage, as we found the new person often not as capable as the one discharged. I believe that when work is unsatisfactory, there is some reason for it. It is the function of the welfare secretary to examine carefully into each case, giving the delinquent good advice and encouragement. It is often a lack of encouragement that causes lack of success. In a rapid age and surrounded by others who enjoy luxuries and occupy more enviable stations in life, it is easy for employes to become discouraged when they do not meet with quick success in their work. Yet all mercantile business has repeatedly illustrated the fact that there is always room at the top. With a few exceptions, those occupying the best positions and even members of firms are those who started in the lowest grade, and who exercised energy and perseverance. The possibilities of advancement are as great to-day, if not greater, than ever before. It is impossible for people with energy, ability and a desire to work for the best interests of their employer not to receive recognition sooner or later. But the employe may not receive this recognition as soon as expected. It is possible that discouragement at such a time may cause an employe to give up trying, with the result of utter failure. Our welfare secretary tries to instill in each employe the feeling that all have equal opportunities and that recognition will surely follow individual effort, application, energy and perseverance.

Many of our employes who now occupy positions of high pay and of trust started at the very bottom. This is true of both girls and men. I believe the best people are the cheapest. The firm is willing to pay liberally for value received. Nothing should be done to give the employes the impression that they are dependent upon the firm. Try to make them independent and exercise their own judgment. If this is properly done a large percentage of the employes will work loyally for the best interests of the employer, almost unconsciously.

Sometimes the welfare secretary discovers interesting reasons underlying apparent shortcomings in work. We have found instances where an employe, because of sickness at home and inability to employ proper attendance, was obliged to spend the greater part of the night in housework and in helping the sick. Such a person, because of loss of rest and because of worry, could not put the mind upon the work at the store during the day. This state of mind was aggravated by the fear of losing the position which was sorely needed for the payment of rent and supplies. By relieving such a person from worry, through proper help at home, she is able to apply herself to the work. But this must be done delicately, as often such a person will make any sacrifice rather than accept charity.

Within a few months a branch of the New York Public Library has been established for the convenience of our employes. Their appreciation is shown by its rapid growth.

In one corner of the employes' reading room is a manicure parlor. The woman employed there is paid by the association, in addition to which she receives a small charge of ten or fifteen cents from those availing themselves of her services, thus making them independent in taking advantage of this opportunity for personal neatness.

Recently my attention was called to a school of salesmanship. Investigation showed that this school would materially help those who could take the course; but it appeared that its cost might be beyond the reach of many. The managers of the school, however, were induced to make a special price for a large class of our employes. The firm assumed part of this payment, and thus was able to present to our salespeople the opportunity of taking a course at a cost of $20. The firm advanced to the employes any part of this sum desired, allowing its repayment in weekly instalments, in some cases as low as 25 cents per week. It is yet too early to know the results that will accrue from this experiment, but I feel confident that they will be most beneficial.

More recently our attention was brought, by the Welfare Department of the National Civic Federation, to the excellent work of a lady in giving instructions in physical culture in factories where girls were employed. She showed the girls how they could, during their regular duties, by proper breathing, standing, sitting and walking, exercise the different muscles of the body. This conduces greatly to their good health. We were so favorably impressed with the demonstration given by Mrs. Rouland, that the association has employed her to give our girls the benefit of her instruction. They are enthusiastic over the innovation.

IMPORTANCE OF STEADY EMPLOYMENT.

A Member:—

I am very glad to endorse the sentiments of Mr. Greenhut as to the gradual development of the employe, rather than his discharge for minor offenses. While it is necessary to discharge at times and for serious offenses, I believe that this practice is indulged altogether too commonly. In many instances if the employe is given a little help and encouragement, he will overcome the fault for which otherwise he might be discharged. In this way, two good purposes are accomplished: (1) The employer secures a better employe, and (2) the employe is moved a step further on in his proper development. All inexperienced people have much to learn and are at first of little value to an employer. They will make many mistakes but the better and more intelligent, as a rule, do not make the same mistakes twice. To discharge for a given mistake only means that another inexperienced employe will take the place of the first, and probably make any the same mistakes. Hence, so long as the disposition of the employe is right and his intentions good, it is likely to result much more satisfactorily if the employer will exercise a reasonable amount of patience and either personally or through his assistants endeavor to give such instruction and encouragement as will in time qualify the employe to perform all of his duties satisfactorily. I believe that the authority to discharge should be vested only in heads of departments and other high-class superintendents, who should possess patience and be free from prejudice and the inclination to act upon quick impulse.

It may be well to speak here also of the responsibility which rests upon the employer to make the employment regular and constant. A man who has a regular income, even though it be a small one, say of $10 per week, can adjust his expenditures accordingly. But, if a man is employed at $15 a week, naturally with the expectation of regular employment, he will calculate his living expenses on that basis; and, if he is then put on short time of four or five days a week and his income perhaps reduced to $9 for several weeks instead of $15, he will begin to run behind and his condition will soon be worse than if employed at $9 in the first place. Short time not only disarranges the workman's plans, but I regret to say it may also disarrange his habits. Idleness may beget dissipation. Factories producing perishable goods or seasonable goods are frequently obliged to adjust their output to a varying demand. But, certain industries should have no difficulty whatever in arranging for a continuous output proportionate to the requirements. During the season when sales are light, a reserve supply can be accumulated which can in turn be drawn upon when the demand is larger than the output, and in this way the total annual output can easily be made equivalent to the total demand. It seems to me that there are many employers in such lines of business who, if their attention were called to it, would appreciate the benefits which would accrue to their employes from regular and constant employment and who doubtless could be persuaded to arrange their work accordingly.

Would it not be well for our National Committee to consider this question?

WELFARE WORK IN A COTTON MILL.

Remarks made by G. Gunby Jordan, *President Eagle & Phenix Mills, Columbus, Ga., before the Executive Committee*

At the Eagle & Phenix Mills we manufacture colored cotton and woolen goods. Our employes number about 1,850. That you may correctly understand our location, I will explain, that these mills are in Columbus, Georgia, a city of about 25,000 inhabitants. The Chattahoochee River is the boundary line between Georgia and Alabama at this point. Immediately West of Columbus, and located in Alabama, are two villages, incorporated; one known as Phenix City, the other as Girard.

So far as I am advised, ours is the first cotton mill which undertook to do absolutely free welfare work for its help. Since I became president, we have taken up a few improvements, believing it would result in good for both the millowners and the operatives. Primarily, our intention was solely to help the operatives; and incidentally, if we made better people of them and made them more comfortable, we would indirectly receive some advantage, and certainly the consciousness of a duty well performed.

Beginning with the children of our operatives, we have established free kindergartens.

Columbus has the distinction of being the first city in the South to establish graded public schools. It also was the first, if I remember correctly, to establish a manual training school, and certainly was the first to establish a primary industrial school.

I am one of the trustees of the Public Schools of Columbus. It is the intention of the Board of Education soon to establish a secondary industrial school at this point, which will be largely self-sustaining. Our population being mainly a manufacturing one, this will, with a splendid system of free kindergartens inaugurated and sustained by the free-will offerings of the noble women of Columbus, the Primary Industrial School, Manual Training School, and graded Public Schools, give all the children—both white and black—of that community exceptional privileges to become independent bread-winners.

The Alabama side of the river is not so well situated because the incorporating act of these two villages limits the taxation to one-half of one per cent. As very many of our operatives reside in those villages we have established free kindergartens for our operatives' children. These we have tried to make as good as the best. The buildings are specially constructed and all that could be done in the way of simple ornamentation, perfect heating, good ventilation, large and roomy yards with plenty of flower and vegetable gardens, gymnasiums and mechanical devices for diversion have been supplied. The best teachers that we could procure are surely and certainly directing the minds of these children in the right channel.

It is our intention to follow the plan adopted by the Board of Education in Columbus and establish a Secondary Industrial School, on the Alabama side, where these kindergarten children will receive further training which will thoroughly fit them for their duties in life.

We have found the children educated in these kindergartens and the Primary Industrial School more alert and bright than others; and as they become old enough to begin work in the mills they show an aptitude and a discernment for colors and designs and other things incident to the manufacture of high-grade colored goods, which is valuable to the mills themselves and must be comforting and satisfying to the children.

Our corporation established the first club in the South, and I believe the first in the United States established by any cotton mill, which was exclusively for the use of its work people. It embraced a lyceum, gymnasium, free circulating library, bowling alleys, free baths with an attendant, and all innocent games which this character of people would be liable to desire to amuse themselves with. Certain nights in the week are devoted to dances and receptions of the members' friends. This club is based on the plan of the Hollywood Inn, at Yonkers.

Several of the teachers in Columbus cross the river five or six nights each week to give lessons to women employes in domestic science, basket weaving and other useful household arts. These classes meet in a house recently fitted for the use of the Young Women's Christian Association, with the aid of some of the good ladies interested in that work.

We hope that our success in welfare work may encourage other corporations to improve upon what we have done.

THE NEW DEPARTMENT GREETED.

Labor World, Pittsburg.

That the new industrial department of the Federation can be utilized in accomplishing a grand work no person who has thought the question over will dispute. Of

G. GUNBY JORDAN,
President Eagle & Phoenix Mills, Columbus, Ga.

course it has its opponents and objectors, just as the Civic Federation itself has. Some people contend that a department made up of a membership entertaining the most conflicting opinions regarding the claims of capital and labor cannot be a success, and it will fall of its own weight. We do not think that there is any force in an argument of this kind, indeed, it seems to us a most powerful reason for the existence of such an organization. These opposite and contrary opinions can be put against each other and there will then be a better chance of the false disappearing. One error will rub against another until truth is evolved. As Buckle says, it is not discussion that we should dread; it is that inertia that keeps us going along in the ruts and grooves of our forefathers. If intelligent representatives of capital and labor can be brought together, as members of one organization, to discuss methods of harmony and betterment, depend upon it good is sure to result in some way.

There is a growing desire among employers of labor to assist in putting methods of industrial peace into operation. This means organization both on the part of capital and of labor. This desire is growing despite the statements of men like Parry and the Socialists. It is a most hopeful sign and by all means none should be more anxious to encourage this growth than the wage workers. So that it can be deemed to a great extent a matter of duty for trade unionists to help in the developing of the Industrial Economic Department of the Civic Federation.

There is no reason whatever to doubt the sincerity and honesty of purpose of the leading employers of labor who are actively identified with the Civic Federation. No men can be more in earnest in their work and desire to do good than are such men as Francis L. Robbins, of the Pittsburg Coal Company, Marcus M. Marks and Oscar S. Straus, of New York. Whatever detractors of the Federation may say regarding it, the fact remains that it is a power for good. It has proven itself such, and every additional year of its existence is finding it better qualified to fulfil its mission.

There is nothing dogmatic about the Federation and this is one of its best recommendations. It is educational and is founded on the idea that costly strife between capital and labor is not necessarily inevitable. Education will lead to a broader, a truer and more humane conception of each other's interests. This is the education that the Civic Federation is spreading, and with the aid of friends of industrial progress, hopes to spread more than ever. It aims at friendly methods of adjusting disputes and is always prepared to suggest methods that are fair and practical.

A PLEASED UNIONIST DINER.

Bulletin of the Clothing Trades.

The dinner of the Civic Federation at the Park Avenue Hotel last week was a disappointment. It disappointed those outside chronic critics who, after a previous dinner meeting mistakenly but loudly lamented the non-union things eaten and done on the occasion. It disappointed those timorous caretakers of union sensibilities who expected the lordly capitalists present to manifest their displeasure by listening to expressions of union sentiment with black frowns. It disappointed those bold soldiers of the union ranks who suspiciously expected that the unionist orators would be mealy-mouthed. It disappointed the virtuous absent extremists who foresaw that the labor men present were to be led captive into the capitalist camp. Above all, it disappointed the waiting crowds of various sociological complexions throughout America who anticipated their joy of soul on reading again that President Eliot had roared defiantly, "The scab is a hero and a saint on earth!"

None of these lucky happenings for the get-it-all-quick revolutionists or the to-sheol-with-every-union Parryites came to pass. Cigars, coffee-rolls and waiters were properly decorated with union labels and buttons. Samuel Gompers and Frank K. Foster gallantly sent the union eagle soaring. Professor E. R. L. Seligman, of Columbia University, boosted it yet higher. Louis D. Brandeis, employers' association attorney of Boston, mounted to a lofty height in a grand strain of union praise. Francis L. Robbins, the greatest of coal barons, wrote a letter that would have done credit to a walking delegate bent on leaving his competitors out of sight. President Eliot—well, that most illustrious professor of Harvard, surpassed the others by going clear up into the clouds and staying there.

Before the evening was half over the union crowd present had caught on to the chain of events that was occurring in their favor. The orators who were to have devoted their innings against them were batting the ball high and slow their way, every hit an easy catch. The union auditors felt sure of their own spokesmen who were to follow. The feature of the evening having the greatest significance was the hearty applause given all along the lines of tables for sound union talk, and it grew tumultuous when Frank Foster sat down after a peroration in which he re-established his reputation as a brilliant speaker. The hearty manifestations of approval for much that was said eulogistic of unionism by all the speakers was balm upon all the sore spots in the hearts of the battered business agents present.

At the close of the speaking a dozen well known union representatives talked with President Eliot, and tried to argue him into being entirely good. He didn't come over in all respects to the domains of progressive unionism, but his opening words to the group after he had shaken hands with them went far toward satisfying their appetite for his conversion. He said: "Gentlemen, there has been a misunderstanding as to my attitude. I want you to know at once that I am in favor of trade unions."

There wasn't a labor man present who didn't go home with the feeling that labor had lost nothing that night through the Civic Federation.

UTILITY AND COMMON SENSE.

Dayton (O.) Journal.

The National Civic Federation has issued a tiny compact pamphlet which can be carried in the pocket and yet gives all the necessary details as to the purpose, scope and work of the organization. A study of the fifty or so small pages will convince the most skeptical of the utility and common sense of all the aims of the Federation. It has rarely, if ever, meddled in any labor controversy without quickly bringing peace. The active work of averting or settling strikes and lockouts is conducted by the department of conciliation. This body refuses to act without the consent of both sides to a controversy and its whole business is to bring the two parties together. Sometimes this can be done easily, but often it is the result of endless effort and consultation. But the one hundred and fifty-six cases already handled by the conciliating department prove how much better prevention is than cure. When the strike has not yet been declared, there are many chances for obviating trouble which disappear when the affair has come to an open rupture. A new department of the Federation is that of industrial economics, in which thoughtful men of all professions, especially editors, are associated for the study of industrial topics.

THE TRADE AGREEMENT ENTHUSIASTICALLY ENDORSED.

(*Concluded from page 7.*)

Driscoll, J. F., Bricklayers' Union, Boston.
Driscoll, Dennis D., Secretary-Treasurer State Branch American Federation of Labor, Boston.
Evans, Alfred J., Journeymen Barbers' Union, Providence, R. I.
Foster, Frank K., Typographical Union, Boston.
Frazier, William H., Secretary-Treasurer International Seamen's Union, Boston.
Golden, John, General President United Textile Workers of America, Fall River.
Gompers, Samuel, President American Federation of Labor, Washington, D. C., and First Vice-President National Civic Federation.
Huddell, A. M., Steam Engineers' Union, Boston.
Haverty, M. W., Typographical Union, Boston.
Isaacs, Harry, United Garment Workers' Union, Boston.
Isaacs, Samuel, Cigarmakers' Union, Boston.
Kimball, L. W. E., Brotherhood of Electrical Workers, Boston.
Kneeland, Fred. J., Brotherhood of Painters, Decorators and Paperhangers, Boston.
Lovely, Collis, General Vice-President Boot and Shoe Workers' Union, St. Louis, Mo.
McNulty, F. J., National President Brotherhood of Electrical Workers, Washington, D. C.
McDonough, F. C., Agent Waiters' Union, Boston.
Morris, Charles, Secretary Hatters' Union, Boston.
McLaughlin, John J., Brotherhood Electrical Workers, Boston.
Maloney, Robert S., Central Labor Union, Lawrence.
Myers, S., Cigarmakers' Union, Boston.
McNealy, Peter H., President Teamsters' Joint Council, Boston.
McCarthy, Frank H., Ex-President Central Labor Union, Boston.
Nolan, T. M., Typographical Union, Boston.
Olin, Carl, Brotherhood of Electrical Workers, Charlestown.
Potts, J. E., Brotherhood of Carpenters and Joiners, Boston.
Pratt, Thomas L., Boston.
Reed, Stewart, Field Organizer American Federation of Labor.
Sheehan, P. F., President Street Railway Employes' Union, Brockton.
Shields, William J., New England Organizer Brotherhood of Carpenters, Boston.
Sweet, Philip H., Fourth Vice-President State Branch American Federation of Labor, Boston.
Stirling, Charles R., International Association of Machinists, Boston.
Standcumbe, William, President New England Label Conference (Cigarmakers), Boston.
Skeffington, H. J., Ex-Secretary Boot and Shoe Workers' International Union, Revere.
Tagen, George F., Upholsterers' Union, Boston.
Taylor, Thomas, Secretary Loom-Fixers' Association, Fall River.
Thayer, P. B. S., Typographical Union, Boston.
Thormer, Max B., Atlantic Coast Seamen's Union, Boston.
Tansey, James, President Textile Council, Fall River.
Tobin, John F., General President Boot and Shoe Workers' Union, Boston.
Ward, Edmond F., Secretary United Brewery Workmen, Boston.

REPRESENTING PUBLIC INTERESTS.

Barker, John Marshall, Professor of Sociology, Boston University, Boston.
Bell, A. D. S., Real Estate, Boston.
Brandeis, Louis D., Lawyer, Chairman Conciliation Committee Civic Federation of New England, Boston.
Crocker, Hon. George G., Chairman Boston Transit Commission, Boston.
Commons, John R., Department of Political Economy, University of Wisconsin, Madison, Wis.
Cushman, S. H., City Editor Evening Record, Boston.
Dubuque, Hugo A., Lawyer, Fall River.
Elder, Samuel J., Lawyer, Boston.
Fahey, John H., Editor and Publisher Boston Traveler, Boston.
Farley, William H., Bureau of Industrial Statistics, Providence, R. I.
Goldstein, David, Economic Writer, Boston.
Gardiner, Robert H., Lawyer, Boston.
Hallowell, N. P., President National Bank of Commerce, Boston.
Harrington, John H., Proprietor The Lowell Sun, Lowell.
Hamlin, Hon. Charles S., Lawyer, Boston.
Kimball, Rev. Thatcher R., President Church Association for the Advancement of the Interests of Labor, Boston.
Long, Hon. John D., Ex-Governor of Massachusetts, Hingham.
Lawrence, Rt. Rev. William, Bishop of Massachusetts, Boston.
Metcalf, Henry C., Professor of Economics, Tufts College.
O'Sullivan, Rev. Denis T., S. J., Boston College.
Pritchett, Dr. Henry S., President Massachusetts Institute of Technology, Boston.
Robbins, Hayes, Secretary Civic Federation of New England; Boston.
Rich, Edgar J., Lawyer, Boston.
Reed, Hon. Warren A., Judge Police Court, Brockton, Mass.; Vice-Chairman Conciliation Committee Civic Federation of New England.
Stang, Rt. Rev. William, Bishop Roman Catholic Church, Fall River.
Storrow, James J., Lee, Higginson & Co., Boston.
Taussig, F. W., Department of Economics, Harvard University, Cambridge.
Thomson, Professor Elihu, Swampscott.
Tracy, Frank B., Editorial Department Boston Transcript.
Tafft, H. J., City Editor Boston Journal.
Webb, George H., Commissioner Bureau of Industrial Statistics, Providence, R. I.
Wadlin, Horace G., Librarian Public Library, Boston.
Walker, Hon. Joseph H., Worcester.

THE GREAT CONFLICT IN THE BUILDING INDUSTRY ENDED.

(*Concluded from page 9.*)

If a decision of the Executive Committee be disapproved, the General Board must dispose of the question.

The first members of the Executive Committee are:

For the employers: James R. Strong, electrical contractors; D. W. O'Neill, manufacturing woodworkers; Frederick Usher, mason builders; R. F. Tucker, cement masters; C. G. Norman, metal covered door and window manufacturers, and Charles Kelly, mosaic employers.

For the unions: D. J. O'Mahoney, steamfitters; William Nason, marble cutters; John Issing, modellers; Charles Dinsmore, cement masons; G. H. Reed, metal lathers, and William A. Parsons, journeymen plasterers.

The busy, as well as delicate, nature of the Secretary's office is indicated by the provision that "all complaints shall be addressed to the Secretary, who shall endeavor to adjust them, and report them to the Executive Committee."

When a trade agreement exists in a given trade, all disputes are to be settled by a Trade Board of Arbitration, with an umpire, if necessary. Should there be failure to agree upon an umpire, or should either side fail to abide by the decision of the Trade Board or the umpire, the General Arbitration Board is to act within twenty-four hours. Disputes in trades where there is no trade agreement are referred to the General Board.

The old plan referred all questions as to jurisdiction of trades to the General Board, it being understood that such kinds of work already recognized as in possession of a trade were not subjects of arbitration. The new plan deals far more elaborately with this subject, providing for a conference, called by the General Secretary, between the unions and employers' associations interested, to settle the dispute by conciliation or arbitration.

Refusal or failure to adjust brings the subject before the General Board or Executive Committee, which may refer it to a special board, if conciliation still fails. Work heretofore recognized as in possession of a trade is not arbitrable.

The new plan defines the unskilled trades and provides that any difficulty arising in them shall be adjusted through the mechanics of the trade in which the unskilled are working. If the mechanics of a trade repeatedly refuse to file a complaint, it may be presented upon the written request of five organizations.

The new plan provides for Special Arbitration Boards of not less than four members, selected from members of the General Board, to meet within twenty-four hours, when notified by the General Secretary.

The representatives of any union or employers' association in the General Board may select the members of a special board to act for them, but no general arbitrator can act when the dispute is in the trade which he represents. If there is failure for two weeks to select special arbitrators by any party, the Executive Committee shall select the special arbitrators.

The old provisions as to arbitration papers are made much more detailed. They must be drawn by the General Secretary, specifically state the issue, and provide that all parties agree to abide by the decision of the Special Board or umpire, who must be selected before the case is opened. If any party refuses to sign the papers, the Executive Committee is to determine, from the papers in the case, the specific question to be arbitrated. Hearings are stenographically reported, each party receiving a copy. A majority vote must include at least one representative from each party. A verdict so reached, or by decision of an umpire, shall be final and binding. No decision by the General Board, Executive Committee or a Special Board can be amended by an organization of employers or employes. Members of Special Boards are guaranteed re-employment when their duties as such cease.

The new plan excludes lawyers from all proceedings. The reason for this is that experience with legal counsel in trade arbitrations has not proved satisfactory, it being the duty of counsel to gain every advantage through legal subtleties, while those familiar with the trade itself are more likely to reach a just conclusion through the knowledge gained by experience and the exercise of practical common sense.

A MESSAGE OF PEACE.

Edward J. Wheeler in Homiletic Review.

The best two Christmas messages which the year has brought to the United States, come to us, one by way of the office of the Secretary of State at Washington, the other by way of the National Civic Federation. The former message consists of the successive announcements of the signing of arbitration treaties. The second Christmas message to which we refer is also an announcement of provisions to avert war, but in this case industrial war. If "war is hell," industrial war is at least purgatory. The number of strikes chronicled in the annual report of Samuel Gompers, President of the American Federation of Labor, for the year ending September 30, is 1,806. The direct cost of these strikes to the men in the Union is given as $2,864,642.13. Of these strikes, 1,193 were won by the employes, 194 were lost, 233 compromised, 178 pending. Such statistics tell us something, but they cannot tell us of the suffering, the violence, the passions unchained, the waste of time and destruction of property, the moral deterioration, the privations of women and children—all the deplorable adjuncts that go to make up so many of the strikes. There is not a great labor leader in the country, there has not been one for many years, who does not regard a strike as a deplorable, even if necessary, method of settling labor difficulties. Now comes the National Civic Federation with its Christmas message. In a little pamphlet dated "1905," it tells what the organization has done, is doing, and hopes to do, to secure "Education, Conciliation, Industrial Peace." Last year a conference was held in New York City under the auspices of the Federation, which "elicited an unanimous expression of opinion that trade agreements afford the most practical method yet devised for securing harmonious relations between employers and wage-earners." In consequence of this conference, a Department of Trade Agreements was formed by the Federation, the object of which is not to arbitrate but to avert labor difficulties. . . . According to the pamphlet from which we take the above instances, there are fifty other examples of trade agreements or collective contracts in operation to-day through as many industries, including the highly important agreements between the railway corporations and railway brotherhoods. If there is to be heard anywhere in America any better echo of the angels' song of "peace to men of good will" just at this time, we have missed hearing it.

PEACE WITH LIBERTY AND JUSTICE.

(*Continued from page 4.*)

ucts, the past few months have witnessed the effort to bring together companies classed as outside the pool or as independent, through the so-called Southern Iron Merger.

The hardware trade affords interesting examples of these pools, which are characterized by nearly all the general features that have been enumerated.. Some of the lines of hardware industry, however, are not included in the pools, but in what are called "gentlemen's agreements." These pools and agreements as a rule take in all the manufacturers in a given line. Their whole purpose is to prevent hardware merchants from selling goods to their local customers as they please. So elaborate is the machinery of combination necessary for this end that there now exist eighteen state organizations of retail hardware dealers, extending from Connecticut to Colorado, that fix the price of every article on the shelves.

Ninety per cent. of the drug trade in the United States, from manufacturer to the corner store, is controlled by a combination whose whole object is to restrain the man behind the counter from selling at as low a profit as he pleases. This control of the trade begins with the mammoth Wholesale Druggists' Association and extends to local associations of retailers that reach every town in the country. New York City was the last of the greater centers of population to be brought into this combination, through a mass-meeting that organized practically all the retail druggists in the metropolis. The union between wholesalers and retailers is made more complete by the organized manufacturers who have a system of distributing their products to retailers by direct contract and by serial numbers, so that the most petty transaction can be traced.

The freedom of the press is one of the vaunted accompaniments of constitutional government. But free as may be the thoughts expressed, the price at which they must be read in book form is severely regulated. Probably every buyer of a book has seen within its covers a printed slip bearing the terse statement:

"In accordance with the agreement of the American Publishers' Association * * * this book must be sold at retail at the published price without discount."

That printed slip means that there is a combination between 95 per cent. of the publishers of all kinds of books in the United States and about 90 per cent. of the wholesale and retail booksellers. The publishers made an ironclad agreement to sell no books to booksellers who cut prices. All this was to prevent the freedom to sell literature at less than a fixed price; thus placing an embargo upon thought itself.

How much individual liberty now remains to the railway president? How far is he permitted to run his road to suit himself? In the case of railroads restriction of competition has come to be recognized as so necessary that government regulation is demanded. "No competition," says the Interstate Commerce Commission, "is so destructive as that between railways." Hence that commission has recommended that railway pooling should be legalized. It is a general contention on the part of railway managers, however they may differ as to method, that something must be done to put the railroads on a basis of equality to prevent ruinous rate competition, which, it is claimed, is the root of rebates, drawbacks, underbidding and all the other practices that are not only inimical to corporation earnings, but are detrimental to the interests of unfavored shippers. The development of the "community of interest" idea is an evidence of the gradual working of the natural law of self-preservation, without, thus far, the artificial aid of legislation. Yet whole communities are demanding strict government regulation of railway rates, fearing the effect of free competition (or individual liberty) upon their industries and population.

THE CENTRAL PROBLEM.

Thus we see to what a large problem the tracing to its cause of a single phenomenon in the field of labor leads. Any other such phenomenon as the centralization of banking, the merging of railway systems, the reduction of the acreage or the burning of cotton, the opposition to labor-saving machinery, the closed or open shop, the boycott, piece work and day work, the shorter workday, the regulation of immigration, or child labor—any of these we shall find, when analyzed, to be associated in some way with this instinctive effort to restrict or remove ruinous competition through the voluntary abdication of individual action. How, then, shall that effort be made to yield the largest good, instead of the greatest evil, to all society? Shall the answer be found in forbidding all combinations and in unbridled competition between individuals? Or in abandonment of all individuality through the control of all industry by the State? Or in some ground between these extremes, where there shall be found neither excessive competition, ruinous alike to employer and wage earner, nor monopoly of capital or of labor, grinding the face of the consuming public?

Just one word as to the nature of liberty. The question presents itself to my mind as a question of results. It was not until the associations of labor learned the lesson taught them by the captains of industry and discovered the power of association that this extreme solicitude for the preservation of liberty as an abstraction arose and in such large degree possessed the public mind and the minds of our teachers during the past few years. We take exception to the classification of the associations of labor with the trusts; the motive is not the same. The contention of the seller of labor is for larger liberty and larger life; for a higher standard of living; for a wider education. And we point to the handwriting on the wall. that where the trade union is there comes the broader education, the more comfortable home and the higher standard of living. The man who protects himself through the association of labor does not water his stock; he does not defraud by legalized preferment any portion of the community. Those who are bound down by the iron bands of circumstance in the work-a-day world have been for generations and centuries struggling and struggling and struggling for liberty, and the whole inspiration of the labor movement of the world is for liberty, not as I said at the outset, that abstraction which can be defined and interpreted in various phases, but that real liberty which means better sustenance, more care for those dependent upon the wage earner and those things which make life better worth the living.

The work of our American Federation of Labor, with its vast host of affiliated organizations, speaks for itself. It has taken from the child the liberty to work in the factory and placed it in the school room; it has protected the breaker boy in the mines; it has safeguarded the life and limb of the worker in dangerous occupations; it has raised the school age, even against the protests of our State Board of Education in my own commonwealth; it has in every way given larger opportunity for the seller of labor to develop those faculties which God has given him, by giving him that greater equality which is the equality above all most desired in the association of labor, that equality of opportunity, either in bargaining for the sale of the commodity of labor, or in laying hold of those things in life which make for higher civilization.

—

Chairman Belmont: Gentlemen:—Whatever be our theories, when we put them in practice, if that practice involves something new, ultimately the law will have to pass upon them, and it is therefore fitting that we should hear from the law, and I introduce to you one of the leading members of the Bar, the Hon. Louis D. Brandeis, who will address you.

THE DESIRABLE INDUSTRIAL PEACE.

Mr. Brandeis:—

Gentlemen: We do want industrial "peace with liberty", but in this country, at least, material well-being is an essential condition of liberty. In most trades some form of union of employes is required for the attainment or preservation of this liberty. The single workman, standing alone, is in the power—at the mercy, of his employer. The union, while it works for liberty in curbing the power of the employer, necessarily restricts in some measure the freedom of its members. This is an inevitable incident of organization. To secure the benefits of society, including political and civil liberty, we surrender to society a large part of the rights and privileges man would be free to exercise in a state of nature. The trade union exacts from its members no more.

It is not true that the "success of a labor union" necessarily means a "perfect monopoly". The union, in order to attain or preserve for its members industrial liberty, must be strong and stable. It need not include every member of the trade. Indeed, it is desirable for both the employer and the union that it should not. Absolute power leads to excesses and to weakness: Neither our character nor our intelligence can long bear the strain of unrestricted power. The union attains success when it reaches the ideal condition, and the ideal condition for a union is to be strong and stable, and yet to have in the trade outside its own ranks an appreciable number of men who are non-unionists. In any free community the diversity of character, of beliefs, of taste—indeed mere selfishness—will insure such a supply, if the enjoyment of this privilege of individualism is protected by law. Such a nucleus of unorganized labor will check oppression by the union as the union checks oppression by the employer.

THE UNION SHOP AND LIBERTY.

The cause of industrial liberty will ordinarily be best subserved by an open shop in which a strong union has a predominating influence. But it is not true that the closed shop—that is, the shop open to all willing to become union men, and to such only—will never give us peace with liberty. The union shop is not necessarily prejudicial to industrial liberty; its adoption may, at times, be indispensable to the attainment or preservation of liberty. The conditions in a trade may be such that the union must, temporarily, endeavor to enforce the union shop by every legal means in its power.

Such a condition arises, for instance, where the employer, while pretending to run an open shop, is actually and insidiously discriminating against union men. It may arise even if the employer's attack be an open one. In such cases, adoption of the union shop becomes a proper war measure. It may possibly, even in the absence of direct attack by the employer, be at times an instrument which it is desirable to use temporarily in order to secure for the union the strength necessary to enable it to exert a predominating influence in the trade. The analogy to the tariff protection of infant industries suggests itself.

NON-UNION COMPETITION.

Again, if the conditions of a trade are such that non-union labor can find a fair field for employment, the existence within that trade of shops which are open only to union men may be most conducive to the general welfare. The union then works out its regulations and demands under the spur of the competition of non-union shops. The non-union employer works out his relations to labor under the spur of unionism, the knowledge that only very enlightened self-interest can prevent the union from finding lodgment in his establishment, or the loss of his best employes attracted elsewhere by conditions secured in union shops.

If then, the union shop may be at times an effective measure for securing the existence or the efficiency of the union, which is in itself essential to the industrial liberty of the employes, its introduction should not be condemned absolutely and without qualification, unless it be that the union shop is necessarily illegal as infringing some fundamental inalienable right of the employer or of non-union workmen. There are indeed a few cases in some of our inferior courts which seems to declare that agreements with employers to establish the union shops are illegal as interfering with the employer's "right of contract", as unjustly discriminating in favor of one class, and thereby interfering with the workman's "right to work", and as tending to create a monopoly. None of these positions seem tenable.

THE RIGHT OF CONTRACT.

It does not interfere with the employer's right of contract to induce him to enter into a certain contract. Every contract which any person enters into interferes in some way with his future freedom of contract or other action. That is the very purpose of entering into a contract. The "right of contract" is the right to restrict one's freedom of action. This sacred right of contract is limited only by the requirements of public policy as expressed either in rules of the common law or of statutory prohibition. The privilege for which employers have most strenuously contended in the past is the right to employ, that is to contract with, whom they please—union or non-union men. The employer exercises this privilege when he elects from day to day to employ union men. No sufficient reason suggests itself why he should not be permitted to agree in advance for a limited time, or until further notice, that he will employ only union men.

It is not an unjust discrimination against certain workmen, or an interference with their right to work, for a private employer to employ only persons of a certain class. Nor does an agreement to make his selection on such lines, however capricious or unreasonable, interfere with any one's rights. A discrimination between two classes of workmen cannot be unjust unless there is a right not to be discriminated against, in other words, a right to equality of treatment. So far as relates to private employment, there is no such right. The right to work for a private employer is merely the right to be allowed to work if one can find a willing employer.

An agreement to employ union men only undoubtedly tends in some degree to a monopoly, but the tendency ordinarily would be very slight and remote. It certainly is not the law that every contract which tends however slightly towards the creation of a monopoly is unlawful. If it were, no large manufacturer could contract to increase his plant, for such a course tends inevitably towards securing a larger share of the market, thereby driving out competition and to that extent tending towards a monopoly.

In the case of strikes, employers usually assert with much vehemence that in the absence of intimidation, violence, or coercion, the places left vacant by union strikers could be readily filled by non-union men. It is conceivable that the union control in one or all branches of trade might become so great, or be exercised in such a manner as to present the evils attendant upon monopoly and call for intervention by law. But if that time should come there would be no occasion for agreements to employ exclusively union men.

EXPERIENCE MUST TEACH.

Experience—the natural law in the industrial world—will alone teach us the best course to be pursued, and that course, when laid out, will doubtless follow eventually the lines of liberty:

In the first place, liberty on the part of the employer to agree with the union for a closed shop whenever the inducements offered are sufficient to lead him to voluntarily renounce for a time his absolute freedom to choose such workmen as he pleases. Then, a recognition by the unions that their interests will be best subserved by omitting all attempts to restrict the choice of the employes, and devoting their efforts to increasing the attractions of unionism for the workmen, and to removing the incidents of unionism most objectionable to the employer. The wisest labor leaders have already taken this position, and have among other things declared the policy that the union label must be regarded as a valuable privilege to be acquired through assent to the closed shop, but that where such assent and hence the union label are withheld, the union workman may still work side by side with his non-union brother.

The union label means to-day—goods made in a union shop. It may come to mean goods made under union conditions, whether produced in a closed or an open shop. Whichever its meaning in a given case, the label is the most appropriate means of conveying information to which every citizen in a free conuntry who is interested is entitled. It is an instrument of persuasion, not essentially differing from the manufacturer's trade mark, under which he seeks to induce customers to buy only a certain brand—"None genuine without our label." The Consumers' League adopts the same method of informing the public what articles are made under conditions it regards as fair and wholesome, and urging special favor for such goods by the consumer. To prohibit the use of such means of conveying information would appear to be an appreciable abridgement of the right of free speech. To prohibit American citizens from acting upon such information would be a serious infraction of their liberty.

We want industrial peace with honor—not the honor of the combatant, but that honor which "is the finest sense of justice that the human mind can frame" and which in a democracy must include something of fraternity as well as liberty.

In such a peace—with liberty, justice and fraternity—and hence with honor, the public is profoundly interested; because it involves the whole future, the success or the failure, of democracy. And the public which is so interested is not "three quarters of the American people" but the whole.

—

Chairman Belmont: It will interest us, gentlemen, now, to hear from one to whom the subject is more a question of practice than of theory; a man standing at the head of large industrial interests and who makes it a part of his daily life to adjust in that industry, which is one of great importance, the different questions which divide the laborer and the employer. I call upon Mr. Francis L. Robbins.

I have just been informed that for reasons Mr. Robbins cannot be present, but has sent a paper to be read, and I will ask Mr. Easley to read it to you.

TRADE AGREEMENTS AND INDIVIDUAL LIBERTY.

By Francis L. Robbins, *President Pittsburg Coal Company.*

In considering the query presented to us this evening, "How far does associated effort in industry involve the curtailment of individual liberty?" I have been led to the general reply that no associated effort in any field of human activity is at all possible without the voluntary surrender or modification of some measure of individual freedom of action. This proposition is supported by all human experience in attaining progress in any direction. Whether it be in the formation of governments, from the family to the clan, the tribe, the township, the county, the state; whether it be in the promotion of a religion, through missions, parishes, dioceses, national and international ecclesiastical bodies or federations of denominations; whether it be the sustaining of national autonomy and rights against other powers, through the ramifications of diplomacy or by war, with all its sacrifice, discipline and many branches of organization; whether it be the advancement of morality, the prevention of crime, the reformation of the depraved, the rescue of the oppressed—whatever the effort, from the elimination of the "white plague" to the creation of a new republic, both history and current activities show the instinctive resort of all humanity to the union of many units for a common purpose.

INDUSTRIAL ASSOCIATION REQUIRES SACRIFICE.

Our topic is confined to the restraint upon individual liberty involved in association in industry; and to my mind, observation and experience both show that industrial association involves, for its success, a considerable degree of willing sacrifice of the theoretical right to do as one pleases, so long as one does not infringe upon the rights of others. This is true, whether the association be one of employers or of wage earners; and it becomes conspicuously true in the collective contract between organized employers and organized wage earners in any industry, or group of allied industries, known as the trade agreement. Any such contract involves a series of acceptances of restraint of individual freedom, beginning with the individual employer or the individual shareholder in an employing corporation on the one side, and with the individual wage earner and his local union on the other. This series of successive waiving of individual freedom proceeds in the case of an employing industry, from the formation of a simple partnership to the organization of a corporation and to the merging of several constituent corporations. It proceeds in a parallel way in the case of the employed in an industry, from the acceptance of mutual obligations by individual wage earners in a local union to the combination of such unions in city, state, national and international federations. At every step, on either side, there must be some acceptance of restriction of individual liberty for the sake of concerted action for the common benefit.

TRADE AGREEMENTS DEFENDED.

There undoubtedly exists a good deal of misunderstanding as to this necessity of the curtailment of personal rights through trade agreements. There are some employers who still protest that the signing of a trade agreement regulating hours, wages and conditions of work infringes on his personal right to conduct his business as he sees fit. Such an employer forgets that he is continually making contracts, other than with labor, and entering combinations, that restrain and modify his conduct of business.

An example of this adverse attitude to the trade agreement is found in the following quotation from a recent issue of the *Industrial Independent*, the official organ of the national organization, that practically opposes all dealings with organized labor:

"The trade agreement would form a monopoly of employers, and a monopoly of labor, and induce them to make terms with each other to the advantage of both monopolies. It would deprive the individual of his constitutional right to work for whom and what he pleases, compelling him to surrender his allegiance as a free American citizen before he could work and live. The right to do with one's labor as one pleases is guaranteed by this free government of ours, but under trade agreements this guarantee would not be sufficient. It would have to receive the stamp of organized employers and employes before it would be considered good."

This is an exaggerated and perverted statement. The trade agreement involves no "surrender of allegiance as a free American citizen," and deprives the individual of no constitutional rights. The individual exercises his constitutional right, whether an employer or a wage-earner, when he enters voluntarily into association with others for the attainment of advantages which he could not secure by individual effort. When two such associations deal with each other, it is for the purpose of increasing the efficiency and productivity of an industry, which necessarily implies that their agreement is for the good of all the community.

It is indeed the benefit of society at large that inspires and justifies sacrifice of individual liberty. I regard the trade agreement, involving as it does a voluntary adjustment of personal freedom to the common weal, to be of the highest importance to the future of the country as a method of reaching harmonious relations between capital and labor.

THE BITUMINOUS AGREEMENTS.

In no great field of industrial activity, enlisting billions of capital and employing a vast army of men, is there a more signal example of benefit to the general social welfare than in the operation of the trade agreements between the Bituminous Operators' Associations of Western Pennsylvania, Ohio, Indiana and Illinois and the wage earners organized as the United States Mine Workers of America. These agreements would be impossible did not each of the parties to the contracts recognize that the exercise of individual liberty must be made to accord with the interests of society as a whole.

These agreements are formed biennially at a convention composed of representatives of the operators' associations and of the organized mine workers. The agreements are worked out in detail and by localities. Upon them rests the stability of the production, transportation and marketing of fuel. Only their existence and the fidelity to their obligations of the wage earners themselves prevented the immeasurable disaster of a strike of the bituminous workers in 1902, simultaneously with the anthracite strike. Only the recognition of the mutual advantages of these agreements led the operators to propose a compromise scale at the convention of 1904, and led the miners to accept, by a referendum vote that compromise, although it involved a reduction of wages. The appreciation of the value of these agreements could have no more convincing evidence than their withstanding this dual test—that the associated employers should propose a reduction far less than they believed to be warranted by the conditions of trade then existing, and that the mine workers should accept a share of the burden of decreased profits due to adverse market conditions.

Now, who are the parties to these agreements, whose value I have but cursorily indicated? On the one side, they are the organized operators of four states, on the other, the organized mine workers. But they are individual operators, whether in business as persons, firms or corporations. They cannot form themselves into the four state associations without some sacrifice of their individual liberty to do as they please with their own properties. The owner of one mine, producing coal of a peculiar quality, or enjoying special facilities of transportation, or having measures worked with particular economy of labor, might find temporary advantage in refusing to enter into an association with other operators that would destroy or lessen these fortuitous advantages in competition. But looking beyond his immediate, temporary personal advantage, he surveys the whole range of the industry and extends his prospect over a period of a year or two years. He takes into consideration the superior advantage in the long run of being assured a steady market, of the absorption of a reasonably continuous output, and of the opportunity to enter a joint agreement that will enable him to calculate with some assurance of certainty the great factor of labor cost entering into his production and sales.

In case the operator is a corporation, its officers carry into this joint agreement the waiving also of the individual liberty of its shareholders. This statement applies, indeed, to the business transacted by all corporations. The confusion that would arise, should every individual shareholder demand the exercise of individual liberty of judgment as to every act by and on behalf of a corporation, is indescribable. Indeed, it is plain that in the modern business world no transactions between corporations or between corporations and persons would be possible unless shareholders waived their individual liberties of action and entrusted them in block to directors and executives.

MUTUAL CONCESSIONS AND RISKS.

But to return to the interstate bituminous agreements. The other party to them is the union of mine workers, as represented in the interstate convention. According to the theory of individual liberty, every mine worker in the bituminous field of the four states concerned has the right to sell his labor to the owner of the mine where he works, upon such terms of wages, hours and conditions as he pleases. He surrenders that right when he joins the union, in order that he may share in the advantages of a collective contract, even at the risk that errors may be made in that contract that will work during its term to his disadvantage. The employer makes a similar surrender and takes a corresponding risk. It is conceivable that in some cases local conditions may make the union scale less than the individual mine worker might be able to exact from an individual employer. It is equally conceivable that in some cases other local conditions might make it possible for an individual operator to impose the acceptance of a lower scale than that agreed upon between the association operators and the miners for that district. But both the miner and the operator have learned by experience that there is a larger and a more permanent advantage in the subordination of individual liberty to joint agreement through the chosen representatives of their two organizations.

STABLE TRANSPORTATION ASSURED.

All that I have said applies also to trade agreements between shippers and the wage earners organized under the title of the International Longshoremen, Marine and Transport Workers' Association, with whose representatives we meet yearly and make contracts covering the terms and conditions of hauling and transporting coal from every port in the Great Lakes to the mouth of the Mississippi. These contracts mean the stability and prosperity of transportation, throughout a territory imperial in extent, of fuel, ores, lime, lumber, stone and grain. It is these contracts, taken together, that make the capitalists and the wage earners interested in the production, transportation and marketing of bituminous coal the leaders, during the past seven years, in the actual accomplishment of peace in their own industry throughout an immense area of this country, and affecting favorably in turn all the other industries of transportation by land and water, and of manufacture, that consume fuel. The mine operators realize that this result, with its benefits to invested capital, could not be attained without restraint of their individual freedom of action. The mine workers realize that in their corresponding individual sacrifice labor is concerned all along the line—the labor of the man who delves, the labor of the mine worker above the ground, the labor of those who load and unload vessels and cars, the labor of the vessel crews and trainmen, the labor of the men who deliver the fuel to the consumer.

Thus, with all their faults of detail, trade agreements in principle and in practice are the very embodiment of far-reaching benefits to employers, wage earners and the general public, through the voluntary surrender of individual liberty. (Applause.)

Chairman Belmont: The next speaker, gentlemen, and the last on this subject, needs no introduction to you. He is Vice-President of the National Civic Federation and President of the American Federation of Labor, Mr. Samuel Gompers. (Applause.)

"LIBERTY IS BREAD."

Mr. Gompers:—

Mr. Chairman and Gentlemen: I feel that I have deep cause for regret that I have not had time and opportunity to write down carefully what I would like to say to you to-night. With a large number of others, I am engaged in the fight; and it is not often that one who is fighting has much opportunity to write, without interruption, in calm moments, thoughts that occupy his mind. I had even little opportunity to acknowledge the receipt of the letter from Chairman Easley asking me to speak at this meeting to-night.

The work in which this Civic Federation is engaged is to my mind exceedingly important. It gives the opportunity of bringing together men who differ widely upon important features and facts regarding this great industrial problem. I think we owe a debt to President Eliot for his utterances at the last meeting of the Civic Federation, which led to the response that at the moment I felt impelled to make, because he brought conspicuously to the attention, not only of the members of this Civic Federation, but of the thinking active men in the worlds of labor, business and education, how it is possible for men to draw from a given state of facts diametrically opposite inferences. President Eliot then said, and repeated to-night with emphasis, that what we want is "industrial peace with liberty."

No man having any regard for the welfare of the human family will dispute the proposition that we want peace with honor, peace with justice, peace with liberty. But when there is strife or discord, when conditions are such as to make conflict inevitable, is it not true that we modify our conceptions of honor to the exigencies of the contest, or to the nature of the question at issue? Is it not true that we are constantly changing our concept of justice? Is it not true that there is a modification of what was generally accepted by the term "liberty"?

SOME HARDSHIPS OF LIBERTY.

The conditions of industry as they existed when the workman emerged from the state of feudalism into what was known as the free competitive system of society, and which brought in its wake the introduction of machinery, followed by the discovery of gas, so that the machines could be operated by night as well as by day—the conditions of the working people during those periods cannot be read by investigators, by sympathetic men and women, without touching them to the very core of their being. And yet we had then the highest conception of the liberty of the workingman. The workingman was untrammeled by organization. He did not yield one jot of his liberty to his fellows in a union. He enjoyed liberty to the full. That liberty spelled for the workman long hours of daily toil, scanty wages, a miserable hovel for a home, unsafe and unsanitary workshops, factories, mills, and mines.

During the early period of our present system of industry there went forth from some of the work people of Great Britain, particularly those in the textile industries, a demand upon Parliament for the establishment of a twelve-hour work-day. That demand was resisted as strenuously then as is the demand of organized labor to-day for a nine or an eight-hour work-day, and always, then as now, upon the two-fold ground: (1) that industries could not afford it, and (2) that it invaded the individual liberty of the worker. Despite these objections, despite hostility, despite antagonism, the organizations of labor continued to grow in Great Britain. And they have grown here. They are not, as some people imagine, importations. They are the result of our conditions in the United States. They showed their first living existence in Massachusetts and New York, where workmen went on strike as early as 1806 to enforce their demand for a reduction in the hours of labor. The shipwrights and the tailors struck even at that early day, when they found that there were no other means to secure any consideration of their rights. But the organization of labor could not grow in the United States, so long as this was overwhelmingly an agricultural country. Nor could they grow fully, so long as slavery was one of the institutions of our country. But with the cessation of the Civil War, the great impetus of industry, the factory system, the concentration of production, the invention and introduction of new machines—all these applications of new forces to industry tended to bring about organizations of labor. For the workmen observed that industry was becoming specialized, divided, subdivided, and that they were becoming as a mere atom in the great industrial hives—only one little factor in the great industrial plants.

UNION RESTORES INDIVIDUALITY.

I beg to submit this condition to our friends who oppose the organization of labor, and who assert that in its union men lose their individuality. Counter to that I present this statement: That in modern industry, with its great machines, which have specialized and subdivided labor, the workman is deprived of his individual liberty the moment he enters a modern industrial plant; and that the individuality which the workers have thus lost has been regained in the economic and social importance which they have achieved by association, that is, in their unions. It is true, if we accept liberty to mean some fanciful thing with which to conjure, if we imagine liberty to mean that we may run riot, that we may totally disregard our own interests and that we may make our actions prejudicial to the interests of our fellows—it is true that the workmen lose their individuality and liberty by becoming members of a labor union. We all of us surrender to society certain things that are sometimes called liberty. We surrender them in order that we may be the better safeguarded in the exercise of our natural rights and of our true liberty.

I quoted at the last meeting Heine as saying: "Freedom? Freedom is bread. Bread is freedom." I am in entire accord with Heine. He did not mean simply the piece of bread such as this in my hand, that one may eat, but all that the term implies. Liberty can be neither exercised nor enjoyed by those who are in poverty. Material improvement is essential to the exercise and enjoyment of liberty.

Any one may say that the organizations of labor invade or deny liberty to the workmen. But go to the men who worked in the bituminous coal mines twelve, fourteen, sixteen hours a day, for a dollar or a dollar and twenty-five cents, and who now work eight hours a day and whose wages have increased 70 per cent. in the past seven years—go tell those men that they have lost their liberty, and they will laugh at you. Go to the wives who have received the benefit resulting from this higher wage and the companionship of their husbands; go to their children and compare them with the children who were deprived from going to school and have grown up to become miners and miners' wives, and see the difference in the standard of education and of morals; say to these miners' wives and children to-day that their husbands and fathers have lost their liberty by joining the union! Go to the bricklayers who worked formerly ten hours a day, but who for the past several years have enjoyed the eight-hour work-day with higher wages, with greater comforts, with larger enlightenment and social activity—tell these bricklayers that their liberties have been invaded! Go to the workers in the clothing trades, who worked in the sweatshops, whose very homes, even whose bedrooms were the factories where they toiled, and who organized and fought and won and lost and won and lost again and again, until that healthier public judgment was formed that abolished sweatshops—go to them and tell them that their liberties have been invaded by the unions! And so, through all the gamut of industries that I might enumerate. And then again go to the other industries in which you find little or no organization among the working people, and note there the comparatively long hours, low wages, misery and poverty. If those working people only had the power to speak their minds, if they had only the semblance of an organization that would give them the opportunity to exercise their freedom of speech, they would tell you in such thunderous tones that you would hear the echo and re-echo that their hope of liberty is through unions.

We hear much of the strike due to organization. But, pray, what say you of the strike of the unorganized workmen? Indeed, much of the larger number of strikes occur among the unorganized workmen. The fact is that organization is the workman's protection and secures for him, generally, many of the advantages that he enjoys, without the necessity of striking. But what would you do with the unorganized workmen who strike? Would you outlaw their effort because of lack of development, their failure of preconceived associated effort, the simultaneous movement that impels them, in desperation, to protest against their constantly deteriorating condition?

THE SUPREME COURT AND THE BAKERS.

We are told to make our appeals to the law and there find the means to secure our rights as workmen, or to find relief from onerous conditions. May I call your attention to a recent occurrence? The United States Supreme Court has just declared the ten-hour law for the bakers in the State of New York unconstitutional. It is neither my desire nor my purpose to criticise the highest judicial tribunal of our country, for which I entertain the highest respect; but one cannot always defer even to the judgment of that tribunal, and particularly when we see the court, divided by a vote of five to four, declaring as unconstitutional an act that was the result of decades of discussion and of an aroused public conscience; an act that had been tested and upheld as constitutional through the various courts of New York, and only decided to be void when it was brought before the Supreme Court of the United States.

Without discussing the merits or demerits of that decision, let me call your attention to the fact that the four dissenting judges designate the majority decision of the court as the most far-reaching that has been handed down in over a hundred years. There is now no law upon the statute books of New York limiting the hours of labor of the bakers. Let me call your attention to a few of the conditions that obtained in the bakery trade before the passage of that law. It seems a peculiar incident in human life that bakers were always required to perform their work underground and facing a great furnace, perhaps to remind them of what awaits them hereafter (laughter). It was a rule that bakers were always required to board and lodge with the boss baker. Their trade, therefore, set a premium on single blessedness; it was a practical prohibition against marriage. The bakers worked every day in the week, every week in the year. They would sleep anywhere. Sometimes, as one said facetiously, they would "lie down on the dough and rise with it" (laughter). They suffered more than any other workmen.

BETTERMENT BY EVOLUTION.

Now, the Supreme Court has decided a law to relieve such conditions unconstitutional. Assuredly, the boss bakers had some purpose in mind when they incurred the expense and the trouble of carrying their appeal to the highest judicial tribunal of the land. It is only fair to assume that they want the spoils of their victory. In other words, they will want the bakers to toil more than ten hours a day. I ask our friends who speak so eloquently of the liberty of the workmen, and who advise the workmen never to enter an association because they will surrender their liberty—I ask these gentlemen to answer themselves the question—What are these bakers going to do? Go back to the old conditions? Work eleven, twelve and more hours per day? I don't know what any one else may think, but so far as I am concerned, when that test shall come, and there is no other means to prevent it, I will urge these bakers to strike, and to strike hard, to enforce the ten-hour day for themselves.

No one believes for a moment that conditions to-day are perfect. No one imagines that there shall be no progress, that there shall be no improvement economically, socially and morally. Every one of us has his day dream and believes that in a year, or ten, or fifty, or a hundred, or a thousand, or a million years, a better day is coming. The question with us is whether, in our own time, if we are agreed that there is a better day coming, we shall work toward that day. I do not believe in an ultimate, absolute finality of anything—not even of life. If there is a division of opinion as to how the better day is to be attained, we must, nevertheless, work gradually and naturally and rationally toward its attainment. There are some who would have the better day come within our time, in a decade, immediately, or, perhaps, sooner. (Laughter.) But it behooves us to do our share in our time to help in the evolutionary process that shall go to make up a better life for all our people. The question is with us, not whether an improvement is going to occur or not. It is going to occur. We find that this movement of discontent, with existing conditions, is world-wide. It is a question whether it shall take the form, as in Russia, of bloody revolution, or the plain, modest American evolutionary method of attaining betterment through the trade-union movement.

As for us workmen who have so far developed as to surrender the fantasy of so-called liberty (the sort our opponents have in mind); we believe in the American method of the trade-union movement. You can look the whole country over, look the whole world over, and you will find that wherever there has come the organization of labor, in that same degree has depravity and misery and poverty disappeared.

CIVIC EDUCATION OF UNIONISM.

We speak of our great sovereignty of American citizenship. Yet we know that every right-thinking public man is concerned because there exists even to any extent the pollution of the ballot box through the purchase or influencing of votes. Let me tell you, my friends, that in the industries that were unorganized you could always tell the political opinion of the workmen when you knew the political opinion of the employer. You will find that to be true to-day in our country wherever organization does not exist. But you cannot make voting cattle out of eight-hour workmen. Workmen who toil eight hours a day have time and opportunity to acquaint themselves with the current questions that affect the people of our country. They earn wages at least sufficient to warrant them in expressing contempt for any one who may, for any financial reason, desire to influence their vote. The organizations of labor help not only to raise the economic and material standards of the workmen and of their families, but also their manhood, their character, their independence and their citizenship. When an organization does that, not only for one class of workmen, but for all who participate in the benefits resulting from organization, that is not curtailing liberty, but is giving a new meaning to the word liberty through the enjoyment and the fullest fruition of the benefit which comes from an enlightened mind and a broadened sympathy for all fellow men. (Applause.)

Chairman Belmont: It has been suggested that before this meeting adjourn there may be some gentlemen present who would like to address the meeting, and, with that end in view, any one desiring to do so would be recognized by the Chair—but limited to five minutes in making such address, and a real five minutes, with the request not to exceed it.

I will therefore ask if there is any one present who would like to speak upon the subject which has been before us to-night and which is of interest to us all.

If not, as I see that no one has volunteered, I desire, on the part of all, to thank the speakers who have entertained us this evening, and bid them and all of you good-night. (Applause.)

THE DISCUSSION REVIEWED.

A Critical Observer's Reflections on the Debate Before the Industrial Economic Department.

By J. W. Jenks, *Professor of Political Economy in Cornell University.*

While at the meeting of the Department no resolutions were passed, and while there was no formal agreement upon any of the points under discussion, it seemed, nevertheless, that in the addresses given, certain points were made on which there was unanimous agreement.

I. It was generally conceded that association, both of capital and labor, was necessary and desirable.

II. It seemed likewise to be conceded that this association on both sides did of necessity involve a certain degree of curtailment of individual liberty. The association of capitalists necessarily, and to a certain degree properly, curtailed the individual liberty of action of its members, in order to produce better results for all; and likewise the members of labor unions very properly and wisely gave up some of their individual liberty of action in certain ways in order to secure to better advantage their other individual interests and their liberty of action in other ways.

The question as stated, "*How far* does associated effort in industry involve the curtailment of individual liberty?" was not the main question discussed. But one could gather from incidental expressions of nearly all of the speakers that, as a matter of fact, the associations of capitalists on the one hand and of laborers on the other do often actually curtail individual liberty as much as they think necessary to secure the accomplishment of their ends, provided they have the power. It was intimated by several of the speakers that this curtailment of individual liberty for the purpose of securing these ends was sometimes carried so far on both sides that it was contrary to the general interests of society.

The main question actually discussed may, perhaps, be stated in this way: "How far *ought* associated effort in industry be permitted to curtail individual liberty in carrying out the purposes of the organizations?" An attempt to answer this question regarding the degree of curtailment of individual liberty that ought to be permitted, was made by two of the speakers, while there was an intimation in President Eliot's remarks that such interference ought not to go far, certainly not to the use of the boycott or of monopoly. In Mr. Robbins' paper it was suggested that these associations might properly restrict individual liberty so far as that could be done without infringing upon the *rights* of others; and Professor Seligman, in his address, implied that these associations might properly restrict individual liberty so far as this restriction was consistent with the promotion of the public welfare, but no further.

It will be evident to any one that these tests, while very suggestive, in shaping our ideals, and quite possibly sound, are nevertheless of little practical value in the settlement of any individual dispute. When, for example, an employer attempts to restrict the liberty of action of any of his employes, he invariably says, and generally believes, that he is going no farther than is necessary to secure his own rights, and that he is not infringing any proper rights of the laborer; whereas, the laborer, with equal sincerity, declares that he is asking only his own rights and that the employer's demands are wrong and unjust. If, instead of the word "rights" we use the word "justice" there will be found the same difference of opinion in applying the test.

Or, again, if we adopt Professor Seligman's principle, which is clearly sound, we shall find scarcely less difficulty in its application. At the time of the coal strike, certain sympathizers with the strikers did not hesitate to say that the strike could not be won unless pressure were brought to bear upon the strike breakers, which amounted to threats of physical violence against individuals, and they would not have hesitated to say that it would be in the public interest to employ violence rather than to lose the strike, if violence were necessary as they thought probable. The leaders, so far as I know, discouraged violence. On the other hand, the sympathizers with the nonunion man believed that any such invasion of individual liberty was directly contrary to public interest.

Can there be found, then, any test that is practicable in its application in individual disputes by which one may determine the degree of restriction of individual liberty that ought to be allowed? If any such test can be agreed upon by employers and laborers it will serve a useful purpose as a starting point for further action, even though the test be very imperfect in itself.

In the long run public opinion, it is generally conceded, settles all such questions, and we believe that in the long run it settles them right, although it may temporarily, in answering a specific question, be wrong. Now, is there any way in which public opinion can give an answer which is in any way direct and positive in specific cases? The only way in which public opinion has any official expression is through the acts of government as expressed in law. We may have a hazy belief as to what the public thinks upon any subject from reading the newspapers, from talking with friends and acquaintances, and from judging others by what we ourselves think; but any such judgment is likely to be doubtful, and there certainly can be many differences of opinion regarding it. On the other hand, the government exists to carry out the will of the people, and any act of the government, whether moral or immoral, wise or foolish, is an official expression of the public will. Until that declaration is reversed by other governmental action, either of the Legislature or of the courts, it stands, and must stand, among all civilized peoples, as the expression of the people's will. May we not then find in law—which is the concrete expression of the people's will—a practicable test by which, for the time being, we may agree that the limitations which may be placed upon individual liberty by the action of associations of either capital or labor shall be determined? This agreement will not prevent our working toward other ideals. The principle may perhaps be stated as follows: Associations of capital or of labor are be permitted, in the carrying out of the purposes for which they exist, to curtail the individual liberty of others, whether capitalists or laborers, so long as they act clearly within the law. As soon as they violate the law their acts ought to be universally condemned.

It will be noted that this test does not claim to be as high a test as that of justice or of rights or of public welfare, and these ends should be sought always; but existing law is a practicable test that can be immediately applied to specific cases.

It must be noted again that in suggesting this test it is by no means considered that either associations of capitalists or trade unions must depend upon law to attain their ends. They must in all probability in most cases depend upon their own actions applied directly instead of through the Legislature, but in so acting they must not go beyond their legal privileges.

Mr. Gompers, in his address, called attention to the fact that the Supreme Court of the United States had declared unconstitutional the New York act, limiting the hours of labor of the bakers to ten; and he asserted that he should consider it his duty to urge upon the bakers to strike, should it prove necessary, in order to secure a ten-hour day, and not to wait until an act should be passed which would be declared constitutional. In that assertion, Mr. Gompers was not going beyond the principle laid down, so long as the bakers in their strike should do nothing contrary to law. It was undoubtedly right for them to attempt to secure a ten-hour day, through act of the Legislature, but it would also be entirely practicable under this principle, for them, if possible, to secure the same result through an agreement with their employers, brought about by a strike or the threat of a strike, so long as they did nothing illegal. The observance of law on the part of both employers and laborers in their dealings with one another, and with the public, does not seem to go very far. It ought to be a matter of course, but, in fact, it would be a decided advance over present conditions. Associations of employers and of labor often accuse each other of violations of law, and, sometimes at least, on apparently good grounds.

If, now, this test is to be considered practicable and useful, then, the whole doctrine may, perhaps, be summed up as follows:

1. Associated effort in securing its purposes may from this point of view take any action that is not contrary to law.

2. If the law restricts the action of associations to an extent that they think unwise and unjust, it is proper and best for them to attempt to have the law so amended as to give them greater liberty of action in restricting individual liberty.

3. It is usually, if not invariably, more detrimental to the public welfare to secure even a just end by illegal means than to wait until justice can be secured under the law, either by amendment to the law or by some change in the methods employed which are still legal.

a. Is the above suggested test a practicable one?

b. Is there any other test that is practicable?

c. Will associations of employers and of laborers now abide by such a test?

The observance of law would not hinder work toward an ideal that is beyond existing law.

Comments of an Observer Who Would Eliminate Coercion from the Problem.

By Marcus M. Marks, *President of the National Association of Clothiers.*

The statement of President Eliot draws a sharp distinction between industrial peace with honor and industrial peace with liberty. I fail to see, however, where the line can be drawn between these conditions. To my mind there can be no true industrial peace without honor nor without liberty; other so-called peace is slavery. It is the peace of the brute creation, enslaved to man—not the peace of noble manhood.

We must all agree that in joining a union or an employers' association, individual liberty is to a certain extent surrendered. Workmen and employers have the liberty to surrender their liberty, but should not be *forced* to do so. This, to my mind, is the crucial point. *Coercion* is the destroyer of industrial peace—there is no true peace under its screw. Coercion embitters employer and employe. What causes its use? Lack of patience—brutal pleasure in the triumph of superior force. If labor and capital would work for better conditions along the lines of least resistance, patiently and persistently, they would reach permanent improvement, real industrial peace, with honor and with liberty, much sooner than by force. Furthermore, the results of force are apt to be temporary and followed by reaction.

The great bone of contention just now is the closed shop. Omit coercion and let missionary work on the part of the unions bring about the union shop, where conditions warrant, and the trouble is practically over. The unions should *legitimately* strengthen their own ranks and not force men into the union, nor try to compel the employer to make unwilling converts to their cause. Many employers would cease their opposition to unionism if they did not fear being compelled to say to a workman, "join the union or starve!" I know many employers, and gladly state that I am one of them, who are strongly in favor of workingmen's unions, but who consider it just as vicious for an employer to be compelled to coerce a workman into joining a union as it would be for the union to be compelled to coerce an employer to join the employers' association.

It may seem that this theory, while correct, is difficult to carry out in practice, but I have great faith in leaders in high authority; their very positions are apt to raise them to the level of lofty ideals and give them strength to live up to and carry them into practical effect.

If it be true that evolution, not revolution, voluntary agreement, not coercion, will bring about the healthiest and most permanent conditions of true industrial peace then indeed is the work of the Civic Federation most important, to prevent, or at times end, clashing between labor and capital. How? By substituting patience for temper, persuasion for coercion, conference in place of strike and lockout. May the influence of the Civic Federation in this direction grow and grow.

LIST OF ACCEPTANCES.

The following accepted invitations to the dinner of the Department of Industrial Economics:

Allen, William H., General Agent Association for Improving Condition of the Poor, New York.
Arnold, C. K., Philadelphia.
Archibald, James P., President New York Brotherhood of Painters, Decorators and Paper Hangers, New York.
Belmont, August, President Interborough Rapid Transit Company, New York.
Bright, F. D., President The Railway World, Philadelphia.
Brown, Roscoe C. E., New York State Civil Service Commission, New York.
Buchanan, Frank, President International Association Bridge and Structural Iron Workers, Cleveland, O.
Buchanan, Joseph R., Labor Editor New York American and Journal, New York.
Butler, John R., Simpson Crawford Company, New York.
Beggs, James, American Federation of Musicians, New York.
Brandeis, Louis D., Lawyer, Boston.
Baine, C. L., Editor Shoe Workers' Journal, Boston.
Baldwin, Joseph C., President Boston and New York Dyewood Company, New York.
Cooke, Frederick H., Counselor at Law, New York.
Call, Homer D., Secretary-Treasurer Amalgamated Meat Cutters and Butcher Workmen of North America, Syracuse, N. Y.
Cease, D. L., Editor Railroad Trainmen's Journal, Cleveland, O.
Chamberlain, Leander, Director Federation of Churches and Christian Organizations, New York.
Colwell, N. H., President National Novelty Corporation, New York.
Conant, Charles A., Treasurer Morton Trust Company, New York.
Colton, Olcott B., The Smith Worthington Company, Hartford, Conn.
Coakley, W. O., Lithographic Press Feeders' Association, New York.
Cooper, John, President Iron League, New York.
Corning, Edward, New York.
Cullingworth, George R., New York.
Cunningham C., Brooklyn.
Davis, Hayne, Counselor at Law, New York.
Delaney, Charles, Granite Cutters' National Union, New York.
Devins, John Bancroft, D.D., Editor New York Observer, New York.
Donaldson, Robert M., Treasurer American Lithographic Company, New York.
Donnelly, Samuel B., International Typographical Union, New York.
Doyle, John J., Brooklyn.
Daly, J., Dock Workers' Union, New York.
Eaton, Allen B., New York.
Eidlitz, Otto M., Marc Eidlitz & Son, New York.
Eliot, Charles W., President Harvard University, Cambridge, Mass.
Emmons, G. E., General Electric Company, Schenectady, N. Y.
Estabrook, H. D., General Counsel Western Union Telegraph Company, New York.
Fairchild, E. M., Editor Daily Trade Record, New York.
Farley, William H., Assistant Commissioner Bureau of Industrial Statistics, Providence, R. I.
Filene, A. Lincoln, William Filene's Sons Company, Boston.
Filene, Edward A., Treasurer Wm. Filene Sons Co., Boston.
Finlay, John H., President The College of the City of New York, New York.
Fiske, A. K., New York Journal of Commerce, New York.
Foster, Frank K., Typographical Union, Boston, Mass.
Flynn, John J., Brass Polishers', Platers' and Buffers' Union, New York.
Friedman, Henry, retired, New York.
Fyfe, William, Amalgamated Society of Carpenters and Joiners, New York.
Garrigues, W. A., Levering & Garrigues Company, New York.
Garvin, George K., The Garvin Machine Company, New York.
Gildersleeve, Oliver, S. Gildersleeve & Sons, Gildersleeve, Conn.
Gilder, R. Watson, Editor The Century, New York.
Gean, Orrin S., Manager National Biscuit Company, New York.
Goldman, William, Clothing Manufacturer, New York.
Gompers, Samuel, President American Federation of Labor, Washington, D. C.
Graff, C. L., Secretary Retail Dry Goods Association, New York.
Graves, H. B., Secretary and Treasurer Standard Optical Company, Geneva, N. Y.
Greenbaum, Samuel, Judge, New York City.
Greene, John, Editor Bradstreet's, New York.
Greene, William C., Treasurer Peace Dale Manufacturing Company, Peace Dale, R. I.
Greenhut, B. J., Treasurer Siegel Cooper Company, New York.
Greenhut, J. B., President Siegel Cooper Company, New York.
Grimes, Patrick, Operative Plasterers' Society, New York.
Gunshanan, John F., Chairman Workingmen's Free Reading Room Association, Hartford, Conn.
Goodwin, John A., Secretary and Treasurer Brotherhood of Painters, Decorators and Paper Hangers of America, White Plains, N. Y.
Hamilton, W. P., Wall Street Journal, New York.
Hammill, Joseph P., President Central Federated Union, New York.
Healy, Timothy, Eccentric Association of Firemen, New York.
Heidelberg, Isaac N., Clothing Manufacturer, New York.
Hatch, James H., President Upholsterers' Union, New York.
Havemeyer, J. C., Capitalist, Yonkers.
Herman, Julius, New York.
Hillard, George B., President Paper Box Makers' Union, New York.
Hogan, C. M., Siegel Cooper Company, New York.
Holmes, William J., Assistant Secretary Building Trade Employers' Association, New York.
Holt, Hamilton, Editor The Independent, New York.
Hochschild, Berthold, American Metal Company, New York.
Holzman, Benjamin M., Banker, New York.
Hornberger, J. B. L., Comptroller Pittsburg Coal Company, Pittsburg, Pa.
Hubbard, Charles W., Treasurer Ludlow Manufacturing ciates, Boston, Mass.
Hunter, H. C., Commissioner New York Metal Trades' Association, New York.
Hunter, William, Blacksmith and Engineering Works, Hoboken, N. J.
Huyler, John S., Huyler's, New York.
Jenks, J. W., Professor Political Economy and Politics, Cornell University, Ithaca, N. Y.
Kelly, Philip, Theatrical Protective Union, New York.
King, D., Treasurer Eureka Silk Manufacturing Company, Boston, Mass.
Kohns, Lee, L. Straus & Sons, New York.
Kohn, Emil W., Jeweler, New York.
Kohn, Robert D., Architect, New York.
Kohn, Harry D., Clothing Manufacturer, New York.
Korn, Albert R., S. W. Korn Sons & Co., New York.
Korn, Harold, S. W. Korn Sons & Co., New York.
Kuhn, Ferdinand, Clothing Manufacturer, New York.
Larimer, J. P., Structural Iron Workers' and Bridgemen's Union, New York.
Lauterbach, Edward, Lawyer, New York.
Lavey, Thomas B., Iron Molders Conference Board of New York and Vicinity, New York.
Leake, Frank, Star & Crescent Mills Company, Philadelphia.
Leipziger, Henry M., Supervisor of Lectures, Board of Education, New York.
Lippmann, Leopold, Clothing Manufacturer, New York.
Lively, James M., Federal Bond and Surety Company, New York.
Long, William F., President Subordinate Association No. 1, Lithographers' International Protective and Beneficial Association, New York.
Lord, Hartley L., Chicopee Manufacturing Company, Chicopee Falls, Mass.
Lord, J. C., Editorial Department, Record and Guide, New York.
McAinsh, John, Proprietor Mitchell Company, Engineers and Boiler Makers, New York.
McCarthy, T. F., President New York Truck Owners' Association, New York.
McCormack, P. H., Typographical Union, New York.
McCook, John J., Attorney at Law, New York.
Mackay, Clarence H., President Postal Telegraph Cable Company, New York.
Marks, Marcus M., President National Association of Clothiers, New York.
Marks, Frederick W., Clothing Manufacturer, New York.
Mather, Samuel, Picands, Mather & Co., Cleveland.
Maxwell, William H., City Superintendent of Schools, New York.
Melendy, Royal L., General Secretary Newark Social Settlement Association, Newark, N. J.
Merrill, Bradford, Editorial Staff The World, New York.
Messiter, Richard P., Minot, Hooper & Co., New York.
Miller, W. W., Attorney at Law, New York.
Miller, Frederick J., Editor American Machinist, New York.
Moffet, E. A., Editor Bricklayer and Mason, New York.
Moore, Charles A., Manning, Maxwell & Moore, New York.
Morgenthau, Henry, Capitalist, New York.
Morse, Raymond P., Brooklyn.
Morris, Ray, Managing Editor Railroad Gazette, New York.
Murphy, John P., Boot and Shoe Workers' Union, Boston.
Michener, C. C., Secretary Industrial Department, Young Men's Christian Association, New York.
Nazro, W. E. C., Welfare Manager Plymouth Cordage Company, North Plymouth, Mass.
Neidig, Robert E., Structural Iron Workers' and Bridgemen's Union, New York.
Neill, H. H., Mail & Express, New York.
Nichols, George, New York.
Nichols, John W. T., Minot, Hooper & Co., New York.
Parker, J. W., Poster Artists' Association, New York.
Phillips, Roland, Managing Editor Harper's Weekly, New York.
Phipps, Henry, Director U. S. Steel Corporation, New York.
Pringle, John D., Editor The Labor World, Pittsburg, Pa.
Ridder, Herman, New York Staats-Zeitung, New York.
Root, Charles T., Root Newspaper Association, New York.
Salmons, C. H., Editor Brotherhood of Locomotive Engineers' Journal, Cleveland, O.
Sargent, James T., American Washboard Company, Cleveland.
Schell, Philip L., Dry Goods, New York.
Schmid, August F., Upholsterers' Union, New York.
Seligman, Edwin R. A., Head Department Political Economy, Columbia University, New York.
Seligman, Isaac N., J. & W. Seligman & Co., New York.
Sinclair, Angus, President and Editor Railway and Locomotive Engineering, New York.
Silverman, Dr. Joseph, Rabbi Temple Emanuel, New York.
Sleicher, John A., Editor Leslie's Weekly, New York.
Smith, A. Beverly, Secretary Lithographers' Association (East), New York.
Smith, Harris W., New York.
Speyer, James, Speyer & Co., New York.
Stark, George, Treasurer Harlem River Lumber and Wood Working Company, New York.
Stern, James, Real Estate, New York.
Stoddard, Henry L., Editor Evening Mail, New York.
Stone, Warren S., Grand Chief Brotherhood Locomotive Engineers, Cleveland, O.
Stuart, John C., New York.
Straus, Oscar S., Member of the Court of Arbitration at The Hague, New York.
Sullivan, J. W., Editor Garment Workers' Journal, New York.
Suter, G. A., G. A. Suter & Co., New York.
Sweet, Clinton W., Sweet, Orr & Co., New York.
Traitel, Benj. D., The Traitel Marble Company, Long Island City, N. Y.
Terhune, C. W., Edwin C. Burt Company, Brooklyn.
Thomas, Bond, Tiffany Studios, New York.
Thomson, James, New York.
Thompson, Robert, United Brotherhood of Carpenters and Joiners of America, New York.
Thompson, T. B., Vice-President Eureka Silk Manufacturing Company, Boston.
Tobin, John F., President Boot and Shoe Workers' Union, Boston.
Ullman, Joseph, Lawyer, New York.
Underwood, F. D., President Erie Railroad Company, New York.
Valentine, Joseph F., President Iron Molders' Union of North America, Cincinnati, O.
Vreeland, H. H., President New York City Railway Company, New York.
Watson, H. C., Editor Dun's Review, New York.
Wells, Henry H., Attorney at Law (Barnum and Wells), Brewster, N. Y.
White, Horace, New York Evening Post, New York.
Westergren, M. F., President M. F. Westergren (Incorporated), New York.
Wheeler, Edward J., Editor Literary Digest, New York.
Wilhelms, Carl G., New York.
Wilhelms, Charles, Sackett & Wilhelms Lithographing and Printing Company, Brooklyn.
Williams, J. R., New York.
Wolf, Simson, Attorney at Law (Wolf, Kohn & Ullman), New York.
Wolf, Edwin H., Rogers, Peet & Co., New York.
Wolff, Max, New York.
Wright, H. J., Editor The Globe & Commercial Advertiser, New York.
Younker, Aaron, Dry Goods, New York.
Younker, Herman, Dry Goods, New York.

THE NATIONAL SOCIOLOGICAL ASSOCIATION.

Cincinnati Volksblatt.

It is a somewhat free translation which we use for the name of the association known as the National Civic Federation, and yet we believe it to be the proper one. The term "civic" does not relate only to matters pertaining to civil life; its meaning is broader, embracing every citizen's activities toward society. The study of such matters comes under the heading of sociology.

The organization whose object we are endeavoring to describe etymologically is deserving of a detailed account. If it is at all possible to reach an understanding between capital and labor, it can be expected from this organization, whose members are prominent capitalists, labor men, scientists and philanthropists. Social peace can only be attained through such men. Labor and capital formulate their demands, science determines their justice, and philanthropy endeavors to lessen the rest of the problem that cannot be solved.

The greatness of the powers that co-operate in the Sociological Association constitutes a welcome contrast to the opposing society, the Manufacturers' Association, whose one-sided point of idea has condemned it to fruitlessness, and whose actions are annoying rather than appeasing.

The latter consists not only exclusively of manufacturers, but of those who hold the most extreme ideas, and who are led solely by selfish gain, consequently failing to appreciate advantages which are in their interest. Comparing the speeches and articles of Parry, President of the Manufacturers' Association, with the speeches and articles of the Sociological Association, one notices immediately the distinction between men adhering to a one-sided point of view, and men grasping the problem in all its greatness and seeking to solve it in a calm way. This contrast has acquired a personal phase, adding much to the characterization of the Manufacturers' Association. The latter has termed the Sociological Association a feasting organization, whose sole purpose it is to awaken in the workingmen hopes of things to which they are not entitled. In saying this, the Manufacturers' Association stamps every endeavor to represent the rights of the workers as a hostile action.

The meeting of the Sociological Association which has just come to a close demonstrated that the Federation does not limit its activities to banquets, but is eagerly laboring to establish social peace. As proof of this, we regard the announcement that the Federation has undertaken steps to connect itself with similar organizations in Europe. That is equally as wise a step as it is just, which recognizes a heretofore disregarded fact, that the labor question needs international co-operation in order to settle it successfully. If in one country the average working hours are eleven, and in another nine, if in one country women and children toil unhampered and in another such labor is restricted, the conditions of production are at such variance that progress seems impossible. The conditions of labor must be nearly the same throughout the world, if the position of the working people is to be improved.

A remarkable paper was the one of Mr. Carnegie, who distinguished himself by his intimate knowledge of the subject he treated, and hence it was instructive and elucidative, seemingly making it appear that the Federation will soon reach its aim. In equally an interesting and convincing way Mr. Carnegie explains that the labor problem exists in this country actually only for one-seventh of the entire population of workers. For the 10,000,000 workingmen who pursue an agricultural career, there is no hindrance of the social peace known as strikes; the same applies to the 5,500,000 persons who busy themselves with housework. Small manufacturers have no difficulties with their employes. Deducting the number of smaller establishments, there are left, of the 7,000,000 industrial workingmen, only 3,000,000 who do not enjoy the blessings of continuous peace. This difficult problem is thereby reduced to such an extent that of the 22,000,000 workingmen of this country, only 3,000,000 employed in large industries and in the mines, are to be satisfied in order to establish harmony between capital and labor. Mr. Carnegie explains how this is to be accomplished. As the first condition, he suggests that good wages should be paid whenever business conditions make it possible. This suggests the logical thought that employes cannot demand higher wages than such as are justified by business conditions. Mr. Carnegie notices nothing alarming in the fact that workingmen ask for higher wages and employers refuse to grant them; to him this appears natural, just as though goods were for sale. The buyer makes his offer, and the seller insists on his price. Not being able to agree on the price, there is no reason for animosity. In the relations between capital and labor a different state exists, causing a suspension of production when the two parties cannot reach an agreement. For the purpose of preventing such a state of affairs Mr. Carnegie suggests the introduction of arbitration boards. This suggestion recommends itself because it will cast aside men of extreme ideas on both sides, who are known to be the main causes of strikes. Practice has sufficiently demonstrated that the plan possesses much practical value.

Industrial peace has been by such means practically established in one of the most important industries—in the coal mines. This point of view is strengthened by Mr. Carnegie, by an observation which is remarkable to the highest extent. He tells the manufacturers of the Parry type, whose principle consists in an unconditional surrender of the toilers, that a manufacturer can add no greater injury to his business than to part from his experienced employes, so as to save on wages by employing new men. Whatever he saves on wages on one side, he loses double the amount on the performed labor on the other side. The meaning of this observation, therefore, is that the employer has a greater interest than the employe to prevent strikes. Such a view is held by every sensible manufacturer. Mr. Carnegie furnishes a psychological contribution to the labor question, when he seems to justify acts of force by striking employes, saying that the indignation of the experienced worker can be easily explained, when he is replaced by a less able person and thereby deprived of the means of subsistence both for himself and for his family. A workingman should not be exposed to such torture. In so far as employes are advised to prevent strikes, this view is unquestionable. Of course, the right to commit acts of force cannot be recognized.

The reader will share our view, that Mr. Carnegie's speech does not only bear an element of enlightenment, but also furnishes proof that the establishment of good conditions between capital and labor is not one of the problems that cannot be solved.

SAUCE FOR GOOSE AND GANDER.

Wall Street Journal.

The less interference with economic law, the better. More freedom of trade, less tariff restrictions; more competition, less monopoly; more liberty, less legislation and governmental interference—those are ideals to strive for and work towards. But we are always in danger of going to an extreme in the advocacy of any principle. Freedom is so desirable that we must have it at any cost, but too much freedom means anarchy. Law is essential to public order and justice, but too much law becomes tyranny. The highest human happiness lies somewhere between the two extremes of tyranny and anarchy. Mr. Parry pleads for industrial freedom. To that we say "Amen." But too much industrial freedom would lead to industrial anarchy.

Order and justice must rule in our industrial relations. The danger is that measures taken to secure order and justice may lead to industrial tyranny. Somewhere between monopoly and unrestricted competition, lies the point of highest "economic" efficiency and national prosperity.

But the thing that we would especially call attention to, is that Mr. Parry in his appeal for "industrial freedom," limits that beneficent principle to labor. He wants freedom for labor. But how about freedom for capital? He is much concerned about economic law in its relation to labor, but how about economic law and capital? What is sauce for the goose is sauce for the gander.

One of the mightiest developments now going on in the world of business is concentration of capital. We are told that concentration is a result of natural economic law, and that any interference with it would be followed by the penalties which always visit violation of law. This concentration, however, is working toward the wiping out or reduction of competition which is freedom. It is working for regulation of production, and maintenance of stable rates and prices, and such regulation is interference with the law of supply and demand.

What is trades unionism but another phase of concentration? May not labor copy capital? When we begin to talk about law and freedom, let us be sure that we mean law and freedom for everybody alike, both master and servant, employer and employed, capital and labor.

Incidentally we may remark that Mr. Parry is doing the cause he advocates more harm than good, and the labor unions might help themselves by contributing to Mr. Parry's campaign expenses.

EXTREME MEASURES; EVIL RESULTS.

Staats Zeitung, New York.

The "Citizen's Industrial Association," assembled in convocation in this city, has formulated its demands, which sound well at first reading and appear justifiable at a glance, but which are not entirely sincere. If it is said that the association's sole object consists in creating freedom for labor, and in preventing a wage-worker's idleness because he is not a member of a trades union, then it does not coincide with the utterances of the president of the association and of other speakers who spoke at this and at previously held conventions. It is, furthermore, entirely wrong to condemn as a whole the legal regulation of hours constituting a work-day. The principle maintained by the association, that the freedom of individual agreements should not be curtailed, is out of date.

As a matter of fact, this association does not intend to solve the so-called social question in a peace and sensible way. On the contrary, the associati is organized to combat demands of laborers; garding the form in which they are presented, as w shown by the unmeasured attacks made upon Civic Federation. That has at least a noble ob The "Industrial Association" is controlled by fan of the worst kind, who seek to conceal their motives when they say that they do not desire make any distinction between organized and ganized workers. Its real object is to destroy trades unions, without regard to their constitu form. So often and emphatically has this been stat at its meetings that it can no longer be denied. A yet, this association does not realize that an emplo ers' association cannot claim any more reasons f its existence than an organization of employes.

The last demand of the association consists in short sentence: "The enforcement of laws." W this we coincide fully. Its meaning is, however, mo significant than one thinks. What the associati really demands is not only that the existing la shall be enforced, but that they shall remain u changed. There can be no such thing. Legislati measures that were enacted when factories were pra tically unknown are not sufficient, now that th United States has evolved into an industrial state the highest order. We will have to follow the examp set by all other civilized countries, in that new la will have to be enacted which will meet the chang conditions of the working people. Every observ of conditions knows that the old laws are insufficie they are just as burdensome to the employer as t the employe.

He who obstructs the process of evolution pour oil on flames. He adds nothing to the solution of continuously fiercer growing battle, but embitters He himself becomes an obstacle to progress, a increases the danger of a nearing flood by his attempt to stem it. It is beyond doubt that trades union have committed grave sins. Underlying all of thei movements are their just and reasonable demands fo the enactment of new laws which will meet change conditions. The fanatic who desires to obstruct th attainment of those wishes embitters the case. Mutu recognition and regard are necessary, and this can not be demanded by one party if it refuses to gra them in the same measure to the other party. A solution by force will be the result of strengthenin the extremes and inciting trouble. It is doubtfu whether such a solution, if brought about by the fanaticism displayed by the "Citizen's Industrial Asso ciation" will be of advantage to the manufacturers.

OPENING OF EMPLOYES' CLUB ROOMS.

(From *Store Notes*, official organ of the Howe & Stetson Department Store Employes' Association.)

The new club rooms in the Moses Building, which will be ready for opening shortly, have been planned and arranged for use by our president and general manager, Messrs. Howe and Eastman, and Miss Matae B. Cleveland, who has come to New Haven especially to look after the work of instalment. Miss Cleveland is an expert in this line of work and comes here through the Welfare Department of the National Civic Federation.

So much interest has been manifested in these club rooms, and so much anxiety has been shown for their existence, that the news that they are nearly ready for use will be hailed with delight. The employes will especially welcome the announcement that the serving of lunch in the large dining room, in accordance with the plans, will so soon begin. The dining room will accommodate as many as one hundred at a time. It is intended to divide the working force of the store into four divisions, the first of which will go to the dining room at 11.30 and the last at 1 o'clock. Everything has been planned to permit quick service and it is hoped that the clerks will thus be enabled to take a little stroll, after luncheon, and still get back for their duties within the allotted half hour.

Upon one side of the dining room will be placed the reading and resting room, furnished with library tables, lounges and chairs, and provided with newspapers and other literature. On the other side will be the smoking room, while the kitchen will take up a large space across the rear of the big hall.

Even before completion, the hall and adjoining rooms will be dedicated to future social uses by a dance, under the management of the entertainment committee of the Employes' Association.

The prevention of strikes or lockouts by the National Civic Federation is a new proposition to both employer and employe, yet, in its comparative infancy, it has to its credit a splendid record of prevented breaks between capital and labor. It is to be hoped, and it is expected, that the men who are really interested in the question of industrial peace and who are in touch with the National Civic Federation will do much toward adjusting many controversies that, without their kindly offices, might result in disagreement to the point of separation. —*Labor Clarion*, San Francisco.

194

The National Civic Federation Review

VOL. II. No. 3 NEW YORK, JUNE, 1905 TEN CENTS

IS THERE AN IMMIGRATION PERIL?

THE POPULAR IMPRESSION THAT THE SCUM OF EUROPE INVADES THE UNITED STATES VIGOROUSLY COMBATED BY QUALIFIED EXPERTS.

THE growing volume of immigration and its relation to American industry was the general topic discussed at the quarterly meeting of the Civic Federation of New York and vicinity held on June 19 at the rooms of the Board of Trade and Transportation, 203 Broadway. Special questions considered in relation to the subject were: What is the net annual gain in the population of the United States from this source, and what is its character? Is there any practicable and desirable plan for distributing the immigrants throughout the country? What percentage of the arrivals is undesirable, and what, if anything, can be done to reduce this? What proportion of the 64 per cent that arrive at Ellis Island remains in this city? What industries does this affect, and how?

The participants in the discussion all spoke with the authority of expert knowledge. The information that they presented and the opinions they expressed were such as to correct much popular misapprehension upon this subject; such as, for example, that a great majority of the arrivals are from the jails, asylums and poorhouses of Europe. They were also of such a nature as to emphasize the importance of the topic. For that reason, a resolution was adopted requesting the National Civic Federation to appoint a committee to give especial consideration to the relation of immigration to American industry, including particularly methods of its distribution and existing and proposed legislation; the committee to be composed of men of national reputation and to make a public report as soon as practicable. Among the illustrations accompanying this report are reproductions of photographs of immigrants, selected by the officials at Ellis Island as typical both of those admitted and of those deported. A verbatim report of the proceedings follows:

Charles A. Moore, President of the New York Civic Federation, in calling the meeting to order stated succinctly the scope of the discussion. He introduced as the first speaker Nathan Bijur, President of the State Conference of Charities and Vice-President of the United Hebrew Charities.

Mr. Bijur:—

Mr. Chairman and Gentlemen.—I doubt whether I can say more than a word or two on one or two of the suggestions contained in the invitation, as the subject is so broad as to be impossible of thorough treatment in the short compass of a few informal remarks.

As a lawyer I take the liberty of advising my friends that it is impossible to discuss a problem unless we know what the problem is.

It is a very common thing to hear of the evils of immigration and the misfortune brought upon the United States by the immigrant, and of the hardships and burdens of the immigrant. Personally, I have no knowledge of these burdens; personally, I have not seen the evils as the term is applied particularly to immigrants, and I have searched in vain for a categorical and clear statement of what the trouble may be. I know that we have in the United States, and particularly in New York City, a great many poor people. That is nothing new. It simply carries out the prediction contained in the good old book. I presume we shall have those poor with us for a long time to come. I have no knowledge whether there were poor people when the original Americans monopolized the inhabitancy of this country, that is, the North American

ALIENS WAITING FOR TICKETS AT RAILWAY TICKET OFFICE, ELLIS ISLAND STATION.

Indians, but so far as our civilized history goes, we have had the poor among us ever since the first immigrant landed here, in the person of Columbus.

Now, in regarding the question of the immigrant—not the evils of immigration, but the question of the immigrant—we are frequently furnished with statistics. Let me say a word about statistics. Statistics should never be gathered by an advocate. Statistics should be gathered by a statistician. You know the old joke about three kinds of lies: Lies, and blank lies, and then statistics. That is a very unfair characterization of statistics. Statistics, if gathered by a statistician, do present the pictures of fact. After we have the statistics we may honestly determine whether we are an advocate or an opponent of the particular question which the statistics elucidate. The trouble with very much of the statistics gathered on the subject of immigration is that they have been sought after with a view of proving or disproving some previously conceived theory.

Now, when we look at the question broadly, what have you here about immigrants and immigration? That there is such an enormous number of immigrants coming into the United States at the present time. I have taken the trouble to look up some figures, in fact they have been collated by a number of men interested in the subject, and some of these have been published. A very interesting tale is the one prepared by Mr. R. P. Falkner and published in the *Political Science Quarterly* for March, 1904. Taking the decades from 1821 to 1900, 1821 to 1830, 1831 to 1840, and so on, he shows the relation of the total number of immigrants to one thousand inhabitants of the initial population. That is, the relation of the number of immigrants coming in during each ten years to the number of inhabitants of the United States then present in the United States. Now I will read this relation of the number of new immigrants to the actual population by decades:

1821 to 1830, 15 to the 1,000.
1831 to 1840, 47 to the 1,000.
1841 to 1850, 100 to the 1,000.
1851 to 1860, 110 to the 1,000.

And now in subsequent decades, 73, 73, 104, and in the decade from 1891 to 1900, 59 to the 1,000.

In other words, not only is the ratio of increase by immigration not growing, but it is actually diminishing. That is to say, the number of immigrants who came in between 1891 and 1900 is very much fewer to the general population than the number of immigrants who came in in 1841 to 1850, 1851 to 1860, 1881 to 1890, and the other periods that I have named. So that this tremendous inrush of immigrants is something that is tremendous in its absolute figures but very small in its relative figures to the general population of the United States.

Now, when you remember that the State of Texas, which is larger than Germany, is alone capable of feeding a population and holding a population very much larger than Germany, which is, I think, some fifty-five million, and that the total number of inhabitants of Texas is about three and a half million, you will see that there is room, at least in some parts of the United States, for an increase of population, whether by immigration or otherwise.

But when these figures are presented we hear another objection to immigration, namely, this: It is true we need two hundred million, or we can stand two hundred or three hundred million more population, but we want them in the West and we want them in the South, and they should not come in the great cities; but that is where the immigrant flocks.

Now, it is equall- interesting in that relation to see what the growth of urban population has been in the United States in recent years. From 1891 to 1900 the increase of population in the United States as shown by the last census was 13,000,000. That is, new inhabitants of the United States, whether born here or coming here as immigrants. Now, out of the 13,000,000 the growth of population in the urban communities was 7,600,000; in the semi-urban communities 2,000,000, and in the rural communities, 3,400,000. That is, the urban and semi-urban population grew 9,600,000 while the rural population grew 3,400,000. The total immigration during that period was but 3,600,000. It is perfectly evident, therefore, that the tremendous growth of the urban communities was not due to the immigrant at all, or at least was only due to the immigrant to the same extent that it was due to the native. The people from the country have come to the city, because either they liked it better, or thought there were greater opportunities in the city. If we are going to shut out from our city, because of some rule that we arrogate to ourselves the power to make, the people who now live in the country who prefer to live in the city, we should have to shut out the Vice-President of the National Civic Federation, Mr. Oscar S. Straus, and we should have to keep from our city lines a gentleman who has recently distinguished himself, named Mr. Thomas F. Ryan. There are other men you might think of who have come from rural communities to the cities and have not been a great burden upon the city institutions or upon the charity of the rich.

Now, what other general objection do you hear to the immigrant? You hear this, as I have said: First, there are too many of them. Well, the figures do not seem to show that, proportionately considered. Next, they flock to the cities more than the native does. That does not seem to be borne out by the figures. But, you are told, the immigrant in particular becomes a burden upon the community by occupying the charitable and the penal and the reformatory institutions which the public have established. Then you are told that there are two kinds of immigrants—desirable and undesirable, the desirable being those that are designated as the ones who are kin to us in race or blood or habits, and the undesirable are all the rest.

But an analysis of the figures, which it would be altogether too voluminous a task to undertake here will indicate that while it is true that the alien and the foreign-born furnish a large proportion of the census of our charitable institutions, it is not true that the undesirable, so-called, that is, the south and the eastern European furnishes that larger proportion. On the contrary, an analysis of our criminal and of our charitable statistics will show that the so-called desirable aliens from northern and western Europe, occupy—well, nearly double the amount of room in our charitable and penal institutions that is occupied by the so-called undesirable immigrant from southern and eastern Europe. I want to say a word after all about this occupancy of our charitable institutions. The immigrant comes here and generally for the first ten or twenty years, until the new generation is on its feet, the immigrant is poor; the immigrant takes what we might call the laboring oar in the community. Is it any wonder that he occupies our hospitals and our insane asvlums? Not at all.

You see, statistics must always be regarded from a comparative standpoint. You must differentiate, you must classify.

If you compare the statistics of accidents that happen in the City of New York and pick out, say, the firemen, you will find the proportion of accidents is much larger among firemen than among other people. It is their duty to meet with accidents. And the same might be said of the police. If you pick out the immigrant, who is generally the worker, it is quite natural you will find more immigrants in the hospitals than natives, because

MAIN BUILDING, ELLIS ISLAND.

IMMIGRANT CHILDREN ON ROOF GARDEN, ELLIS ISLAND.

PAUPER ALIENS—DEPORTED.

ROVING SERVIAN GYPSIES—DEPORTED.

TYPICAL SLOVAC WOMAN.

TYPICAL HOLLAND DAMES.

the immigrant is the man who takes up the employment which brings about the accidents; he takes up the employment in which the work is hard and dangerous. It is no wonder that he breaks down, and it is no wonder that he is injured.

On the question of intelligence I have never heard the immigrant criticised. There is a vague notion that the immigrant is illiterate. That is not true. Moreover, whether the original immigrant be illiterate or not, his children are more literate than the children of the native American.

I was very much startled to find a little set of figures that gave these facts: Natives of foreign-born parents who could not speak English in New York State, according to the 1900 census, 2,500; in Wisconsin, 5,000; in Minnesota, 2,740, and in Pennsylvania there were natives born of native parents who, nevertheless, the children, could not speak English to the number of 19,000.

Now, there is nothing significant in this; there is no conclusion to be drawn from this. I cite it merely to dissuade rapid judgment from insufficient figures. I know of no inference that can be drawn from this. But you go about and you know from your own experience that the children of the immigrant are the most ardent citizens and the most ardent students in our schools and colleges.

We have a notion that the immigrant comes here poor and that, therefore, he is a burden on the community.

What would we do without the poor? Somebody has got to do this work. The history of the United States has been that in every irruption of a large number of immigrants the people who have been here before have been, as I think some politician once expressed it, kicked up into a higher place. It has been the history of this country since 1821 that every time a poorer class comes in, it takes the last economic strata of the community and pushes it up a peg. And that is going on to-day exactly as it did in 1830 and in 1840.

If we establish a purely economic or financial basis for immigration I am afraid we would be apt to exclude a great many gentlemen who are to-day quite a factor in the community—we would have excluded them, one of whom I see sitting here now, another of whom has become famous the world over as the greatest ironmaster, and yet when he came here he was quite incapable of getting in by a show of cash in hand.

There is a different question, not the question of anti-immigration, but the question of sifting the immigrant who comes in. When it comes to the question of keeping out the diseased, the actually pauperized, the actually criminal, who, gentlemen, come here, I think, not of

STALWART SPECIMENS FROM ROUMANIA.

their own accord, but because they are sent here—that is a different question. Anything that we can do to protect ourselves against the burdens that probably belong in other communities we should do. Whether we can do that by imposing a money penalty upon the immigrant that comes in I doubt very much. Whether we charge a $2 a head tax or a $25 a head tax, it is my impression it will make no difference. I think the community—I do not mean this as applying to Germany or France—but I think the community in Germany or France or Austria or England, or wherever it is, will pay the $25 to get a pauperized immigrant in here. But the honest immigrant, who deserves to come in and who may have only $10, will be kept out. Financial bases for immigration are very artificial and very dangerous.

I do not know that I can add anything more—excepting to say one word: There is something in this question of immigration altogether outside of figures and dollars and cents. The United States is great, not because of any one class of its population, but just because it represents an amalgamation of various types. There have been brought to us all the forms of activity that have made modern civilization what it is, and the United States has become on that account a microcosm. We have got our love of art from the Italian; we have a lively and active spirit, perhaps from the French and from the Irish; from the German we got our love for music. From all these continental nations we are beginning to learn how to rest. Now, why do we want to keep these elements out? What is the matter with them? From the Russian we are getting an idealism to which we ourselves have been strangers for decades. Do we want to go back to the old humdrum, or do we not want to have all these elements?

And then here is one other consideration. I need not go into the history of the United States to say that if the United States stands for anything, it stands for political and for religious freedom, and I think I voice the sentiments of the American people in its true sense if I say that so long as there exists a man or a group of men in any part of the civilized world who are persecuted or oppressed because of peaceable political or religious beliefs and purposes, so long the doors of the United States will have to remain open. (Applause.)

The Chairman.—The Chair will call on Mr. A. W. Sullivan, editor of the *Weekly Bulletin of the Clothing Trades*.

Mr. Sullivan:—

Mr. Chairman and Gentlemen.—Being asked a few days ago my views on immigration, I replied, "Exclusion." Thereupon I was invited to come here and outline my position.

TYPICAL ROUTHENIAN WOMAN.

FROM ROUMANIA TO MICHIGAN LUMBER CAMPS.

The transatlantic steamship lines, almost exclusively non-American, in the last three years, coming and going, have carried wage workers in migration to the number of more than three millions; any one may compute for himself how nearly the gross earnings of these companies from this traffic have approached one hundred million dollars. If the average of the railroad and steamboat fares spent within this country by these migrants has been ten dollars, the inland American transportation companies have garnered from them about thirty millions dollars. If the manufacturers and mine owners and the employing classes in general have availed themselves of one-tenth of this providential supply of cheap labor, in substituting it for labor previously better paid by 10 per cent., they have saved in the three years in wages a matter of fifty million dollars. Crumbs sufficient to keep them alive falling from this traffic have also been picked up by some thousands of contractors, padroni, employment agents, slum landlords, and dealers in small patches of "our" undeveloped resources. If in America it could occasionally happen that lawmaking should result from pull and steering, the not somnolent interests mentioned might perhaps be tempted to try their turn in asking Congress for something good. Having overstuffed the

CHARLES A. MOORE,
President New York Civic Federation.

cities to a point of acute indigestion, they might come forward and suggest a project for loading up the hinterland.

Among the numerous articles afloat on the ocean of print during the last year or two advocating government aid in distributing the arriving millions, none has suggested a clearly considered, specific, detailed plan. "Kansas announces its need of forty thousand agricultural laborers for the coming harvest;" "the South is always calling for more field workers;" "immigrants have reclaimed many abandoned New England farms;" "healthy new communities can be nurtured from the bosom of Nature itself;" "land is offered everywhere on desirable conditions;" "plenty of room in our West, Northwest, South and Southwest"—these glittering pearls, borrowed from the phraseology of the real estate boomer, have been dangled before us, but out of it all we have been given no definite project.

To what part of this country can the coming poverty-stricken swarms be sent where they will surely benefit themselves and the community?

Shall we recommend the Pacific Coast? For twenty years rural California has been the gleaning ground of thousands of roving, homeless white blanketmen and of great gangs of yellow and brown men, whose movements depend on the successively ripening crops on large plantations in various parts of the State. To-day the entire Pacific Coast is in the throes of an agitation for the exclusion of all Asiatic laborers. The San Francisco *Chronicle* says that there are now in California thirty-five thousand Japanese, and on the whole length of the Coast fully one hundred thousand, the majority having arrived in the last five years, and a former agent of the Industrial Commission reports that "the number of Japanese in California alone is greater than the total number recorded at all ports of the United States in ten years."

Shall we send immigrants to the Northwestern States? The last number to hand of the Butte (Mont.) *Reveille* redescribes the remarkable movement of American citizens to Canada. It says the number going this year will be fifty thousand; Collier's counts on a hegira of one hundred thousand a year. Why don't these people stay and develop the alleged virgin riches of the country they are deserting?

Next, Colorado. Are we to send a hundred thousand more laborers to that noble State. Last year the United Mine Workers spent nearly half a million dollars in the Rocky Mountain region supporting moderate union demands and came to grief. But perhaps there are other vast mining districts only awaiting the "magic hand of labor" for their needed development. There's Illinois, the State of Mr. Joseph Leiter, having, Professor Commons tells us, thirty-seven thousand coal miners, 60 per cent. being foreign born, the majority, arriving since 1894, having taken the places of Americans and Americanized miners from Western Europe. There's West Virginia, the scene of a long series of strikes, still on, many of the non-unionists newly arrived foreigners and the union men being described in the United Mine Workers' *Journal* this month as living under a reign of terror, the victims of lawless opponents. There's the Alabama mine district, where the United Mine Workers have recently had eight thousand men out, but where convicts have long been busily employed. There are the anthracite regions of Pennsylvania, where the Slavs and their descendants number one hundred and ten thousand, if we may believe Dr. Peter Roberts, of Mahanoy City, a systematic observer of the subject.

It is no longer proposed that immigrants adapted to the work be sent to the New England textile mills, which now largely employ not only French Canadians, but Armenians, Greeks and Portuguese, with remnants of the English and Irish who two decades ago pressed in on the American employes. None are to go to the iron and steel mills of Western Pennsylvania, where the callous indifference to their swarming foreign human life has recently moved the Austrian, German and Italian Consuls to seek an investigation. Skilled immigrants are not to be assigned to communities according to their trades—for example, potters to the pottery towns, packed with importations from England; glassworkers to the middle West, over-run with Belgians who came under inducements; quarrymen to Vermont and Massachusetts, where the union organ is printed in four languages. Are our beneficent railroads still clamoring for more foreign construction hands? Or are there really not enough half-employed Italian gang laborers in this country now? The Ninth Special Federal Report (p. 29) put the percentage of the unemployed unskilled Italians in Chicago at 56.97. Dr. Peter Roberts writes that after the great anthracite strike, when the mining industry was rushing, the collieries did not average more than two-thirds time.

What region or occupation in America is not already over-supplied with cheap foreign labor?

Ah, agriculture! Every farmer needs a hired hand! Five million farms; five million hands wanted! Five years more of business for the steamship companies before our vast national stomach shall be crammed to the throat. Unsophisticated persons there are who still echo the marvellous tales told about farm help somewhere growing rich on harvest-hand wages. And what is the big, broad, blanket-like fact that covers the entire proposition? It is this: For fifty years the average yearly earnings of the American farmhand have been the lowest in the entire national wage scale. From 1860 to 1890, except during part of the Civil War, the annual farm wages was variable in but the slightest degree. Aside from the census, the Department of Agriculture has made repeated investigations, one official conducting five of them within twenty-five years, and always finding this same state of facts. The census of 1900 reported a small increase, but the late Dr. Spahr, making special inquiries in '99 as correspondent of the *Outlook*, found that general farm wages in Arkansas, for example, had fallen from $18 a month to $10 within fifteen to twenty years. Those excellent citizens who find mental recreation in belittling the laboring classes sometimes indulge in agreement on a fallacious prejudice according to which the working man shuns the country and loves the city's lights. The fact and principle involved are otherwise. America's labor, following the line of least resistance in striving for the American standard of living, cannot be expected to remain contented at an occupation whose rewards do not include a united family life, a home or wages above that of the day laborer. As to the attractions of the South and Southwest, continually advertised during the last quarter of a century, the foreigner believes them to be counteracted by competition with the negro, who, acclimatized, disciplined to subservience, by nature a season worker, presents to the world an example of the survival of the fittest.

But, "the immigrant is to buy land," "the era of the small farmer is at hand," "suitable acreage can be had on most desirable terms." Reply: The three hundred thousand Southern Italians, Hebrews and Poles arriving last year landed with an average capital of $13 per person. The Industrial Commission in 1900 gave the average for these nationalities for years as respectively $8.84, $8.67 and $9.94. Our immigrants reach here on the brink of want, the general average of their capital in 1904 being $25.70. Nearly all are untaught in American methods of agriculture and of selling produce. The barrier between the $10 foreign capitalist and the independence of an American farmer's life is mountains high—his need of food, clothing and shelter until he can surely produce a paying crop, his need of at least a part of the purchase price of his land, his ignorance of our language and commercial methods.

Where, in the name of horse sense, is there to-day a dearth of common labor in America? In what region will not brawn and backbone, of itself, appear, ready and willing, whenever a living wage is offered? In 1900, the census tells us, the percentage of those engaged in gainful occupations who were unemployed during some portion of the year was for the whole country 22.3; in 1890 it was only 15.1. In agriculture the percentage was 20.7.

[At this point the speaker said that to deliver his entire address would overrun his time; he therefore asked leave to print. Granted.]

One quarter there is to which the non-English speaking creatures with but $10 between themselves and pauperism can count on being rushed posthaste to work. It is where there is a strike or lockout. In one occupation they are given an indulgent trial for the passing hour by solicitous employers. It is as strikebreakers. Unrestricted immigration is unlimited government aid to union wreckers.

The cry now is for "distribution!" The unemployed are already well distributed in every State of the Union. The many great strikes of the miners the last two years should be deeply significant to those who urge sending the laborers out away from the cities. That is where the miners are. The miners are diggers, delvers, laboring men, as closely related to farm workers as any other class. If really any rural part of this country wants labor, underpaid, partly employed mine workers

ROBERT WATCHORN,
Commissioner of Immigration at Port of N. Y.

are so distributed by the thousands that it is strange they do not respond to the demand.

The problem of immigration admits at its present stage of only two modes of interference.

The first mode is further to extend the present policy, which, ostensibly that of assistance to the immigrant, is really a costly and indulgent paternalism toward parasites on the American people. Further steps in its pursuance will provide for more dividends to foreign corporations subsidized by European governments, possessed of ships convertible to war uses, and developed with the intent to drive our American marine from the seas in peace and in war. These further steps will also call for more rackrent for slum landlords, more rakeoffs for contractors, padroni and foreign agents of transportation, more voting cattle for our political stockyards, more blood for real estate sharks more non-unionists for manufacturers' combines, more outlay for every charitable and penal institution in this country, and incalculably more misery for America's wage earners.

Shall I illustrate by facts?

Not alone more riches and power for foreign steamship companies, but help to foreign governments. We read only last week that the Royal Steamship Company of Great Britain, built up by a subsidy of a million dollars a year, is to establish a line between America and the Mediterranean ports. We are informed that the English Government has a sovereign interest in the great new convertible Cunarders. The advertised present activity of the Italian Government in supervising emigration greatly results in keeping in Italy conscripts for the military service. The long continued practice of deporting public dependents has been astutely permitted by foreign governments to be shifted to a new form of insurance company. Professor Edward T. Devine writes that at Bremen and other points of embarkation are agencies with offices in many parts of Central and Southeastern Europe which contract for a price a safe landing in America or a free return to all comers. In this transaction the hand of neither government nor steamship company can be seen. But steamship officials are not always so modest. On January 26, 1897, the restriction bill being up in Congress for a vote, a German steamship official telegraphed to doubtful members threatening them with defeat at the next election if they voted for the act—if we may believe the Restriction League, which prints the telegram,

...ing names, in one of its leaflets. Mr. Lodge declared [i]n the Senate, without contradiction, that another tele[gr]am had been sent at the time to every American [ne]wspaper carrying the company's advertising.

More fees to steamship agents! Stimulating emigra[ti]on to America is in Eastern Europe a recognized pro[fe]ssion. A representative of the United States Treas[ur]y Department investigated the subject in the summer [o]f 1903. He found that in Europe drummers for steer[a]ge passengers to America included school teachers, [n]otaries, postmasters, pedlars, peasants, and even priests. [M]r. Ward assures us that the seven thousand steam[sh]ip agents scattered throughout Italy have succeeded [i]n persuading many thousands to come here who other[wi]se would have remained at home.

More success to Italian padrone and American con[tr]actor. For example, Rome, New York. That city [l]et out to the lowest bidder certain public works. He [s]ent to New York for a gang of two to three hundred [It]alians. They came and did the work at wages rep[re]senting a degenerate level for Americans. They lived [in] shacks, ate animal food, wore foreign clothing, lived [ch]eaper than at home, for economy's sake. They saved [th]eir full share of the $45,000,000 annually sent to Italy [b]y New York's Italian banks. To the town shopkeep[er]s they brought little or nothing; to the State, no taxes; [to] the jail, assault cases; to the public schools, itch and [tr]achoma. The city of Rome, N. Y., had numerous [w]orkingmen who would have been glad of the work. [B]ut, as in ancient times, foreign serfs labored on the [m]unicipal improvements while Rome's proud citizens [sto]od idly by. In this respect the history of Rome has [be]en repeated in a hundred American cities.

NATHAN BIJUR.
President State Conference of Charities.

To the employers' combines that are engaged in the [cr]usade against trade unionism the hordes of fresh im[mi]grants have been an inestimable blessing. These [co]mbines are invariably composed of intense Ameri[c]ans, bound by hooks of steel to every American tradi[ti]on save traditional American wages. They'll drive the American wage workers out of a trade, and when [th]eir foreign non-unionists purge themselves and join [th]e unions, will upbraid them for their un-Americanism.

An example, the clothing trade. The New York [St]ate Department of Labor (p. 43, Report of 1902) has pronounced the sweatshop a result of immigration. Dr. George C. Stiebling, of St. Mark's Place, New York, thus defines sweatshops: Workshops "in which [c]lothing is manufactured and which serve at the same [ti]me as dwelling rooms to the bosses, their families and boarders"—"overcrowded, ill ventilated, over heat[ed], full of dirt, filth, vermin and stench," consequently, "unwholesome, health destroying and disease breeding." Joseph Barondess two weeks ago publicly stated that [ne]ver were sweatshop conditions worse than at present [o]n the East Side. In 1904, the immigration bureau re[po]rts, 23,908 tailors arrived. Besides, a benevolent [so]ciety maintains schools for tailors on the East Side. [La]st summer the wholesale ready-made clothiers' com[bi]ne, with philanthropic intent, established another [sc]hool and union blacklisting employment bureau in [As]tor Place. This combine's organ, the "*Daily Trade Record*" (March 28, 1905), thinks well of the proposed [El]lis Island great exhibition hall. It wants there, as [a] part of it, a big clothing factory, in which arriving [im]migrants could note the class of tailoring work to [wh]ich they are best adapted. "Agents could be stationed [th]ere to direct them to the concerns in different markets [m]ost in need of their service. In this way considerable [la]bor trouble would also possibly be averted." True, [fo]r the Chicago special order tailoring unions charge [th]is combine with boldly violating its trade agreements, [an]d refusing to submit the point to arbitration, because [un]controlled immigration permitted it to lock out its [Sc]andinavians, Germans and naturalized Hebrews hav[in]g $100 apiece, and lock in Bohemians, Poles, Italians and greenhorn Hebrews possessed of $13 apiece, less immigrant fare to Chicago.

Can the Ellis Island officials guarantee that the incoming hosts booked for the suburbs will not stray to the cities? The federal inspectors, obeying the recent reform laws relating to pauper, insane, criminal, diseased and contract labor immigrants, last year deported the largest proportion ever known—and that was less than 1 per cent. The law's guarantee to protect us from these classes is plainly worthless. There's hardly a skilled trade in America, there's no industrial center employing highly specialized labor—from wood working to chemistry, from musician to cloth dyer—that cannot bear overwhelming testimony to violations of the contract labor law. The Federal Census Bureau reports that while the native born inmates of American insane and charitable institutions are 3 to 1,000 inhabitants the aliens number 30 per 1,000. Dr. Shively has estimated that 23,000 tuberculosis immigrants were landed in New York in 1902. The State of New York alone has 6,000 aliens in its public insane asylums. Of the 44,985 aliens in the insane, penal and charitable institutions of the United States, 19,764 are insane. Goodwin Brown, a specialist in lunacy statistics, predicts that in ten years the alien insane will cost the United States $50,000,000 a year. A writer in the Brooklyn *Eagle* has recently estimated that the cost to New York State of its foreign born poor is annually $12,000,000. Of 2,595 cases cared for by the New York Lying-in Society only 315 were patients native born. Multitudinous are the phenomena that government inspectors cannot either see or foresee. And astonishing are the things they are unable to do. The New York State Free Employment Bureau, with a million job seekers to experiment on, found places last year for about 7,000. The State Commissioner of Labor, when his inspectors last January captured in Elizabeth street tenements numerous bundles of men's clothing being finished in unlicensed dwellings contrary to law, refused to make public the names of the manufacturers owning the goods, since the statute gave them that discretion.

Good reasons, and many of them, in all the facts just mentioned for not enlarging the powers of labor bureau officials over Europe's impoverished millions thrown overboard in New York Harbor.

The second mode within sight of dealing with the immigration question is exclusion. As President Roosevelt said in his message, let us welcome the desirable and reject the undesirable. I submit that every immigrant who cannot pass an illiteracy test and prepay an insurance of $50 against becoming a burden to this country, to be used for his deportation if necessary, is undesirable.

I also hold that a period of total suspension may become a necessity. This is conservative as compared with a decision of the United States Supreme Court, rendered in May, 1895. This was: "The power of Congress to exclude aliens altogether from the United States, or to prescribe the terms and conditions upon which they may come to this country, and to have its declared policy in that regard enforced exclusively through executive officers, without judicial intervention, is settled by our previous adjudications."

The illiterate among the immigrants over fourteen years of age, coming from Eastern and Southern Europe, were in 1900, 38.8 per cent.; in 1901, 46; in 1902, 44.3; in 1903, 40; in 1904, 43. The State Department of Labor reports that "the two countries having more than 50 per cent. of illiterates furnish one-fourth of the whole number of New York's aliens."

Reject the illiterates, require the fulfillment of the obvious obligation insisted on in wise New Zealand, that the foreigner shall not become a public burden, and the results will stagger the imagination. The colossal European marine leeches will no longer get drunk on both foreign and domestic blood; the discontented democratic hosts of Europe will be strengthened through the retention of their brothers at home; the working men of America will soon begin to pour out money to our business men, for their advancing wages will at once absorb a fair share of the enormously increasing product of the country. An authority in the New York building trades equal to the best recently told me that with immigration suspended common labor in this city would be $3 a day within one year. The clothing trade unions would quickly proceed to enlist every garment worker, Hebrew or Gentile, in Greater New York, and their label would insure the well attired classes that no consumption sputum infected their coats.

Have no fear that the foreign born wage workers now here will not, after a brief campaign of education, favor exclusion. Why is only one immigrant in eighty a Frenchman, one in forty an Englishman, and one in several hundred a Swiss? It is because the masses of those intelligent nationalities are already educated in the fact that, all things considered, the economic level of the American wage earner is but a bare notch or two above that of their own land. The 10 per cent. of immigrants returning disgusted to Europe teach them that point. The immigrants now in this country can on humanitarian grounds repel the charge of selfishness in voting for exclusion. As one of the speakers said when the United Hebrew Trades voted for suspension of immigration for five years, "We are in a trap here; let our brothers at home keep out of it." When the unions of the State of New York voted, two hundred to two, for suspension, it was avowedly done without prejudice of nationality or race, but purely for economic causes, and in the belief that governments owe it to themselves to work out their special problems of poverty within their own boundaries.

The Chairman.—Gentlemen, this is what the Governor of the State of North Carolina says to you here in a letter:

State of North Carolina,
Executive Department.

Raleigh, June [illegible], 1905.

Charles A. Moore, President New York Civic Federation.

Dear Sir.—It is with deep regret that I have to write you that it is impossible for me to be with you on June [illegible] to attend the immigration meeting. Our State at this time is offering the very highest inducements to [illegible] who will make good laborers, and also to farmers. Our farmers are willing to furnish the land, the stock, the necessary working tools, and give the party furnishing the labor *half of all that is made*. I wish it was so I could be with you and extend an earnest and open-armed invitation to all to come to our State, but am compelled to send my regrets.

Yours very truly,
(Signed) R. B. Glenn,
Governor.

The Chairman.—The next speaker will be Dr. Joseph H. Senner, ex-Commissioner of Immigration:

Dr. Senner:—

Mr. Chairman and Gentlemen: We do not propose here to have a college debate dealing in generalities of all kinds. We propose to fall back on the specific points mentioned in the two circular letters received. The second letter I want to mention first, because it contains the stupendous statement that the great majority of the arrivals, which is more than two-thirds of a million, are from the jails, asylums and poorhouses of Europe. I wish, gentlemen, that statements of this

J. W. SULLIVAN.
Editor Weekly Bulletin of the Clothing Trades.

kind would be entirely dropped from the discussion of the immigration question. There may have been some isolated cases in immigration of persons coming from poorhouses or jails, but I can positively state that no number of such cases has been or is among the arrivals at Ellis Island. And further I can state that if they exist they are not among the steerage passengers, but they are among the first and second cabin passengers. (Applause.)

We have here to consider the question of what is the net annual gain in the population of the United States from immigration, and what is its character?

The net annual gain in figures has been treated of by the first speaker, but the gain in numbers, gentlemen, is very little as compared to the gain in wealth to this country by any immigrant arriving here.

If with me you pride yourselves upon the fact that we have the greatest home market of any empire in the world, you must not forget the fact that it is no doubt due to immigration. It is immigration that has made possible the immense development of our industries.

Having had the opportunity to witness in tens of thousands of cases and with my own eyes to see the immigrant arriving upon this shore, poor, destitute, more than simple in all his make-up, and a year after to have seen the same immigrant, whether a man or a woman, come to Ellis Island again to call for her sweetheart or for her husband or for children or for a friend, the difference, gentlemen, between the parties as they arrived and the parties as they appeared within a few months is simply wonderful. They have entirely changed; all their clothes are American and their new make-up is quite respectable. It is absolutely wonderful to any one who remembers their condition when they arrived. Our great home market, with its feeding of millions and millions of skilled laborers, was only made possible by immigration.

In the same way it was only by immigration that we could build up such a wonderful network of railroads, many of whom had to go into the hands of receivers every time immigration came to a standstill, or because the constructors of such railroads had been rather visionary as to the time which would be necessary to fill up their country.

There is the net gain for our country which has been secured from immigration, not to speak of the fact that without immigration the number of our population would be immeasurably smaller than it is now, because our immigrants do not believe in race suicide.

Is there any practicable and desirable plan for distributing the immigrants throughout the country?

When I was Commissioner of Immigration at this port I conceived first the idea that the problem of immigration will in time be solved only by the proper distribution of immigrants all over the country into those places where they can be of the most good to themselves and to the country they live in. I then suggested in the immigration investigation report of 1895 that a clearing house should be established in Ellis Island for that purpose. I am very glad indeed that the present Commissioner General about two years ago took up the very same idea. I admit it appears rather impracticable for sometime, but only because our laws forbid instructions to immigrants about the benefits and advantages of sections of this country by any kind of advertisements or educational work abroad. This clause of the law would have to fall first. But then, with the previous education of emigrants given to them partly in their own homes before they make up their minds as to where to go,

EMIL L. BOAS,
General Manager Hamburg-American Line.

partly on board of the steamship and finally on Ellis Island itself, such education I believe would be practicable and would finally lead to the point that immigrants could settle in places for their own welfare and for the welfare of the country, instead of being allured as to-day by all kinds of incidents or by the glowing accounts of some interested person.

A great deal is also said about the inducement of emigration by the steamship companies. I have no reason, whatever, as you know—I suppose most of you know—to be in any way interested, directly or indirectly, in or for the steamship companies. But do you believe that the zeal of the steamship companies or of their European agents to induce emigration has been smaller during my term of office, when only 250,000 to 400,000 immigrants used to land annually, than it is now, when 1,000,000 immigrants land? Just the opposite. You may rest assured that at that time when immigration was only 250,000 to 400,000 a year they worked much harder than they do now when immigration, so to speak, falls into their lap. It is the hundred million dollars spent right here in the neighborhood of New York on tunnels, it is the agency of all those people who prosper and write about it to their friends abroad, it is this that creates immigration and not any agency, which would be actually helpless in the case of dull times such as we had in the middle of the nineties.

The first thing we have to do under all circumstances is to exclude all and every undesirable immigrant. But in speaking about a desirable or undesirable immigrant I beg to differ from the first speaker, who classified them according to races or origin. Every immigrant in himself, his individuality, his personality, has to be judged and appraised in order to determine whether he or she is desirable or not. (Applause.)

Every one who, for any reason whatsoever may appear to be undesirable is to be rigidly excluded. And I am glad to state that under the present regime this is absolutely and conscientiously done.

Now this is the first axiom of treating the immigration problem. The second, however, is in my opinion and my conviction: Don't place any unnecessary hardships or obstructions in the way of any desirable immigrant that desires to come to the land of the free. And the third axiom is this: When they are found desirable endeavor to place them by governmental assistance and by the assistance of all private associations and corporations, in such localities, in such environments, where they will find a good future for themselves and where they will benefit the country to which they have come. I thank you for your attention. (Applause.)

The Chairman.—The next gentleman I desire to call upon is Mr. Emil L. Boas, the General Manager of the Hamburg-American Line.

Mr. Boas:—

Mr. Chairman and Gentlemen.—I do not want to make a set speech. I simply want to mention a few figures and correct impressions that have gone abroad for a long time.

It is said, first, that this country annually increases by immigration from 700,000 to 1,000,000. But first of all, sight is lost of the fact of how many leave every year. Now, in this city alone, in the City of New York, we had last year 571,000 arrivals in the steerage, but 323,000 left in the steerage. So there was an actual increase of only 56 per cent. And so it is in the other ports, so that in the four ports of the North Atlantic, Boston, New York, Philadelphia and Baltimore, there were 693,000 arrivals, but 359,000 departed in the steerage. So that there was an actual increase only of one-half of this number. Now, I want you not to forget this whenever the newspapers or any persons speak of the enormous increase. Sight should not be lost of the fact that half of the number go out of the country.

A Voice.—Do they take back any money with them?

Mr. Boas.—I do not know. They do their work during their stay here and have actually earned whatever they take back. (Applause.)

Besides, I wish to call attention to the fact that one of the speakers has said that the poverty stricken hordes of Europe come over here. Now, according to the figures of the Commissioner General of Immigration the immigrants that arrived last year were first of all thriftier than ever before; they showed up no less than twenty millions of dollars in coming over (Applause), and that was four million dollars more than the larger number that arrived the year before. So they are not a poverty stricken horde.

Mr. Sullivan.—The figure was $25.78 per head.

Mr. Boas.—That is only what they are showing up on the request of the Commissioner.

The Commissioner's official report states that the immigrants showed up the amount mentioned, and if this is only $25 per head, and if that were all that they possessed upon arrival, it must not be forgotten that it costs them something to break up their homes, that they have to pay the railroad fare to the port of departure, Hamburg, Bremen, Antwerp, Rotterdam, etc., and the steamship fare from the continental port to the American port which is at present at least $36 per head, so that adding up all the traveling expenses alone, they must have between $60 to $70 for each person, which, with the $25 shown upon arrival, makes $85 to $95 each. A family of six must, therefore, have had before starting over $500! These are average figures. Now, do you call a man in this country who has put away over $500 for a rainy day as belonging to the "scum" and to "poverty stricken hordes?"

The money which these immigrants bring is, however, by no means their whole addition to the wealth of this country, for it has been computed by political economists that the economical value of every able-bodied male immigrant over twenty years of age represents on an average the sum of $1,125 actually added to our working capital; in that way the wealth of this country is annually increased by hundreds of millions of dollars.

I only wish to remark again that the steamship lines are not scouring Europe to bring over immigrants. I want to refer to the very able article written by Mr. Whelpley in the *North American Review* of this month, in which he makes the statement that the laws of European governments are made with the view to retaining the population there. They don't want to lose it. And the steamship lines are not allowed to scour Europe and distribute circulars that point in glowing colors to the advantages of America. All they are allowed to do is to announce their sailings, and if they do anything else they are severely punished. The greatest emigration agent is the United States mail, the letters that are sent from here, the letters sent home from this country, that say what a man makes when he works, that is the immigration agent that brings the people to this country. (Applause.)

These letters bring information upon which implicit reliance is placed, and cause the people in the old home to sever their connection with that which is dear to them and go to the strange country beyond the sea. An emigration agent could talk till doomsday before he would have the same effect. These conditions will never change as long as the advantages are greater in this country than in Europe. There is no better barometer of the business conditions than the number of immigrants that come to this country. If times are good they will come.

Mr. Sullivan.—May I interrupt to ask one question? May I ask you whether it is correct, as Prof. Devine says, that in Bremen and in numerous other quarters about Europe there are insurance companies which will insure the coming emigrant that he will be landed here, and if not landed here that he will be brought back? A gentleman of the Treasury Department says to-day there are 7,000 agents, and that even the priests are among the agents. I very much regret to interrupt you.

Mr. Boas.—I cannot possibly speak for the numbers of people who consider themselves emigration agents in Europe, and those are figures that are assumed. I cannot controvert them. Anybody can make a statement of that sort, that priests are emigration agents or that there are 7,000 agents, or any other number. I speak for the steamship line that has been charged with scouring Europe to bring the poverty stricken hordes over here. That is absolutely untrue. It is not allowed by law, and I wish to say the steamship companies and their agents are lawabiding citizens. We abide by the law here and abroad. Here is the Commissioner of Immigration, he can say what we do to conform to the American law.

One of the speakers referred to $10 immigrants. The steamship lines had a war last year and rates went down to a very low basis, and the newspapers announced that in consequence of these low rates hordes, thousands, hundreds of thousands would come over here. Statistics have shown that last year during the lower rates fewer arrived than the year before, and fewer than this year when the rates are high. That only shows that the passage money has absolutely no influence on immigration at all. (Applause.) There is another point I wish to make: It is again the same old story, if times

JAMES P. ARCHIBALD,
Secretary New York Civic Federation.

are better here the immigrants are bound to come, and who comes? It is the energetic man who has the courage to break away from the ties that bind him, it is the intelligent man who can appreciate that his condition will be better here than on the other side and who can cut loose from his ties and come across to the unknown country, and it is the man with savings who can afford to go—that is the man who comes, and the poor, the ignorant, the scum, the people who are not energetic, they stay behind. They do not come to America. So I wish to contradict again the statement that it is the poor, the uneducated, the criminal horde that come over here. We have laws that restrain the criminal from coming to this country. Here is the Commissioner of Immigration; it is his business to exclude every one that is undesirable. The steamship lines do not bring the undesirable here, and if any should slip in there is the man to keep them out, and he does keep them out, too. He observes the law, and so do we. That is all I wish to say, gentlemen. (Applause.)

The Chairman.—Permit the Chair to suggest this, that any gentleman present who is interested, and I presume every one here present is interested in this great question of immigration—if any one has not visited Ellis Island and observed the immigrants landing, I ask him to take the opportunity of doing it at the first available moment. It will be the greatest education to him as to these "hordes," these "pauperized people." You will see as bright, intelligent figures, capable looking people, as you will find in the same number of their class anywhere in the world. I think this is a subject that should interest every thoughtful American, whether a property owner to a little or a great extent, who employs labor. And if he will go over there and take the courtesy of the Commissioner of Immigration, he will be surprised as to the people who come here as immigrants, and at the manner of handling immigrants.

In the last few days a prominent railroad man told me it would be impossible for the West to have kept its tracks in condition to run over them if it had not been for immigrants, absolutely impossible.

The man who is going to speak next is the man who, in my judgment and from my observation, is the best qualified to tell us the truth as to the character of the immigrants, and to answer any questions about them.

I am going to call on the Hon. Robert Watchorn, Commissioner of Immigration at Ellis Island. (Applause.)

Commissioner Watchorn:—

Mr. Chairman and Gentlemen.—When I assumed charge of Ellis Island I stated to a committee that called on me to participate in some meeting of this or similar character, that I did not believe that a Commissioner of Immigration had any business to participate in the discussion of questions of immigration; that I believed it was his business to enforce the law as it now stands and leave it to the good judgment of the people of this country and Congress to alter the law when it ceased to be satisfactory. I have concluded since I sat here this afternoon that, notwithstanding the very handsome manner in which the invitation to be present here this afternoon was framed and delivered to me, that I made a mistake in departing from that conclusion.

I am quite sure from what I have heard this afternoon that the subject is very thoroughly understood without any information from the Commissioner of Immigration, and I am not quite sure in my own mind that there are not some people who know more about the practical enforcement of the law than I know.

It is not for me this afternoon to say to you whether I believe the law as it stands to-day is satisfactory or not. There is just one thing that prompted me to come here this afternoon more than any other, and that was that I might be able to state to you on my honor that at the present time the law, as it is, is being rigidly and

DR. JOSEPH H. SENNER,
Ex-Commissioner of Immigration.

honestly enforced. I have been told and have seen quoted in the newspapers that there is very great room for improvement, and I have no doubt that some people might improve on conditions at Ellis Island from their own point of view, but I do not believe that a man who stands for a wide open policy, who would let everybody in because his sympathetic feelings get the better of him would be the proper man to enforce the law; nor do I believe that a man who has concluded, for reasons best known to himself, that there are already enough people in this country, and for that reason and that only, no more should come, that he would be a fit and proper person to administer the law.

I do not agree with some of the speakers here this afternoon that the law as it now stands is all that it ought to be. I think there are some people coming into this country to-day who ought not to come in. But I think the law is inadequate to keep them out as it now stands. I do not undertake to say to you how far this tendency to exclude should be extended, but I will give you one or two points for your consideration, and I leave it to you to judge whether what I suggest ought to be given serious consideration.

I have heard a great deal about the term "undesirable." Now, what constitutes an undesirable person? When you begin to discuss that one phase and turn it over in your mind you will follow the process of elimination until you get down to a point where the number will be very small comparatively and somebody will be apt to dispose of the whole question for you by still further reducing it; and if you leave it to all those who are actively interested in this question, there will not be many that will fall under the ban of undesirable. What is needed, in my opinion, is a drastic law which shall state specifically what is desirable and what is not desirable.

Now, let us take a case in point: An immigrant steps off the boat and the doctor takes him in hand, looks him over as to his mental capacity and and as to his prospective physical endurance, what he is likely to stand, at what point of pressure he will break down and become a burden to somebody who will support him, voluntarily or otherwise, and the doctor says he will probably break down very soon, and for that reason he should not be allowed to come in; and the inspectors, acting upon their best judgment under the law, will decide that he should be deported; then there will come forward some of the very best citizens of this land who will undertake to prove to the government that it is utterly impossible for such a person to become a burden on the community, and they will bring such pressure to bear and file such proofs with the authorities at Washington that even such a person will be admitted, no matter what the inspectors may do in the premises. Now, I would like to point out, so far as I am concerned, that when a certain standard of test has been established and it is proven by all the tests that may be applied that that person is liable to break down at a certain point and somebody will have to support him, whether that somebody be public or private, there should be very good reasons assigned why such a person should be admitted, and Congress ought to stipulate that he ought not to come in.

One of the speakers representing the steamship lines said that they were obeying the law. I believe they are, but it is because they are compelled to. (Applause.) If you were to relax the rules and leave it to their good judgment and patriotic sentiment, undesirable immigration would increase in contrastive proportion to said relaxation. The power to exclude and the power to deport is just in proportion to the power to fine or punish for violating the law. Now, I have no fault to find with the steamship companies as such. I think they are endeavoring to obey the law. Not because they have any special scruples about violating it, perhaps, but because they do not like the punishment that is meted out to them for not observing it. This is probably rather a serious stricture to make on some of them, but my good friend, Dr. Senner, who preceded me, knows that since his term as Commissioner the power to punish has been very largely increased, and in proportion to that power to punish, an increased respect for the law has been demonstrated.

Now, gentlemen, I should like to ask you all to come to Ellis Island. What concerns me now most is this: I want you all to know, and I want you all to believe, that just as the law stands and is interpreted by the courts and other competent authorities, it is being rigidly and honestly enforced, and if, after you have discussed this matter to your satisfaction, you believe that the law can be improved, as I believe it ought to be, all you have to do is to make that known to Congress. Get the law amended, and I assure you that the government has ample machinery and satisfactory facilities for enforcing it effectively.

Whether the great number that are coming in are a detriment to this country or a benefit is not for me to say. My chief function at the present time is to see that the quality is just what the department and the courts have decided it should be. As to the quantity, I do not think that you will expect me to deal with that. I do not think it would be proper for me to deal with it. But I do hope that those of you who wish to be more thoroughly informed of the difficulties encountered by the Bureau of Immigration in enforcing the law, would come to Ellis Island and exchange views with those officers with a view to getting the law intelligently amended in order that we may still further eliminate those from the incomers that are likely to be a detriment to this country in part or in whole.

I am quite sure that from the Chairman down, there are those here, as I stated before, who are amply qualified and able to discuss that feature. So far as getting acquainted with the practical end of it is concerned, none of you will need a pass to come to Ellis Island. You will all be welcome, and if you can point out to me where the present system of enforcing the law can be improved I shall most cheerfully welcome your suggestion. (Applause.)

The Chairman.—We have here this afternoon with us Mr. M. V. Richards, Land and Industrial Agent of the Southern Railway Company, who has done a great deal to build up the Industrial South. I was at Washington a short time ago and the president of the road pointed to a map, and speaking of the change that had occurred since he came in charge, showed that on three hundred miles of that system three hundred cotton mills have been erected.

Mr. Richards:—

Mr. Chairman and Gentlemen.—I come to you to-day quite in sympathy with the foreign immigrant; I mean the immigrant who comes to our shores for the purpose of bettering his condition and is willing and competent to avail himself of the great opportunities our country affords those seeking a competency and desiring to conform to the splendid rules and regulations which go to make this the leading nation in the world. I have no sympathy with the immigrant who is not capable of appreciating the privileges extended to the homeseeker. I would uphold a most rigid investigation of immigrants before they are permitted even to purchase tickets to the United States. We can, in my opinion, well afford to strengthen immediately the Department of Commerce and Labor, so that it can organize its forces in Europe sufficiently to carefully investigate immigrants seeking admission into this country. It is our duty as Americans to throw safeguards around our shores, and while we welcome the thrifty progressive and substantial newcomer, we should strongly fortify ourselves against the undesirable class.

The trend of immigration to this country has been to the West through the ports of New York, Boston, Philadelphia and Baltimore. Until within the last few years foreign immigration into the Southern States was limited. The last census shows that the States of Virginia, Kentucky, Tennessee, the Carolinas, Georgia, Florida, Alabama and Mississippi, all of which I have the honor to represent by reason of the railroad I am connected with, having lines running through or to those States, had only 1½ per cent of the total foreign-born population of the United States, or 156,884. These States occupy a very peculiar position in reference to immigration. Since the Civil War the South sent about two and one-half millions of white people into the North and West and received from all sources less than one-half that number of immigrants. One State alone sent out to other sections 415,000 people and received only 190,000, showing a net loss of about 230,000. Massachusetts sent 300,000 people to other States, but received 845,000 from Europe alone.

The reason for this movement from the South to the West and North is well established. It will be interesting to note that no section of the United States has advanced more rapidly during the past ten years in agriculture, manufacturing and commerce than the Southern States. This advancement has been made under many disadvantages. It is well known that not many years ago the South was without money, without credit, and—as has been shown—immigration was pouring out, rather than coming in. The results accom-

M. V. RICHARDS,
Land and Industrial Agent, Southern Railway.

plished by the South under these conditions have at last attracted the attention of the outside world. The South is now recognized as one of the desirable fields for people with limited means and for the employment of capital. A few years ago the railroads, state authorities, manufacturers and farmers in the South found that their country could be best advanced through increased immigration. A systematic campaign has been carried on, and to those who have labored earnestly, seriously and persistently in promulgating information concerning the South, it is very gratifying to observe that the South to-day is in the minds of people throughout the North, Canada, and many parts of Europe, as a field for settlement and investment.

We have established numerous factories throughout the Southern country. You will be interested to know that over 2,300 manufacturing enterprises were located within the last three years upon the line of the Southern Railway. These factories each give employment to anywhere from five people to 2,000 people. A large percentage of the employes in these factories were drawn from the farming sections. The immigration into the South has not been equal to the migration of people from the farms of the South to the factories. While we have progressed remarkably well in our agricultural development, if we could have kept all of our farmers on the farms, induced immigrants to come in, open up and develop more farms and accept employment in our factories, our agricultural development would have been far greater and our factories would be larger to-day than they are.

We have appeals to us from farmers and manufacturers in all parts of the South for laborers. We can accommodate several million people. They can be provided with pleasant homes and profitable employment. The future of the immigrants locating with us, I do not for a moment doubt, will be in line with their desires and necessities.

We have systematically laid the foundation for the introduction of a foreign population by securing Germans, Scandinavians, Italians, French, Bohemians and Polanders from the Northern States. We are now ready to receive the raw immigrant from Europe. We

(Concluded on page 10.)

THE NATIONAL

Civic Federation Review

Offices: 281 Fourth Avenue, New York City
RALPH M. EASLEY, Editor

The Editor alone is responsible for any unsigned article or unquoted statement published in THE CIVIC FEDERATION REVIEW.

Ten Cents per Copy; One Dollar per Year.

THE IMMIGRATION PROBLEM.

It is a noteworthy discussion of a problem of the highest national and economic importance that we present to our readers, in the verbatim report of the consideration of Immigration in Its Relation to American Industry, by the Civic Federation of New York. The opinions of the speakers at that meeting are well worthy the careful perusal of both employers and wage earners, as well as of students of the economic questions involved in the absorption of an influx of aliens into our population and its ultimate effect upon production and consumption.

The most impressive and, probably to many, the most surprising feature of this discussion, is its refutation of the widely prevalent impression that the tide of immigration is choked with the social debris of Europe, contributed from its jails, asylums and poorhouses. The evidence of both statistics and observation adduced at the meeting went to dissipate this alarmist misapprehension. Upon the contrary, it was shown that an accumulation of capital, to an amount that would cause a similar saving by the family of an American workingman to be regarded as a result of unusual thrift, must precede the migration of a European family to the United States. Impressive also were the statements as to the unsatisfied demand for labor in the South and West and the suggestion as to the distribution of the newcomers away from the ports of arrival. Conversely, the plea of those who believe that the interests of American labor demand the restriction or exclusion of immigration was forcibly presented.

The National Civic Federation will comply with the request of the New York branch to appoint a national committee to consider this question and to report its recommendations to a general conference to be held in the fall. The composition of this committee, which will be of a character commensurate to the importance of the subject, will soon be announced. Its investigation and report may be expected to have a direct and practical bearing upon the solution of the problem.

SOCIALISM AND REVOLUTION.

We present upon following pages an exposition of the new campaign of "scientific Socialism," which is cunningly designed to captivate the support of minds more sympathetic than thoroughly trained and more susceptible to emotion than solidly grounded in the fundamental and unshakable principles of political economy. If we have appropriated considerable space to this recently developed strategy of Socialist leaders, it is not because we consider their creed of revolution really dangerous to republican institutions. There is no occasion to view with alarm a movement which openly and flagrantly proclaims its purpose to "undermine society"; for, in this free country, the absence of repression makes of the most violent of its utterings mere vaporings. But it does appear to be well worth while to place clearly before the public, and particularly before those who take special interest in current economic developments, the real ultimate design of these Socialists who pose as would-be benefactors of the working mass, whom they classify as the "proletariat," of whom they are themselves not a part, whose true aspirations and growing capacity of self-elevation they do not comprehend. The real representatives of the working mass have repeatedly rejected and denounced the apostles of social despair and revolution as the most dangerous enemies of those who would maintain the honor and elevate the living conditions of American labor.

There is another reason for this arraignment of those who avow their sympathy with Socialism as a remedy for economic evils and who would instil its deceptive doctrine into the minds of collegiate and graduate students. Just as the popular conception of Socialism is inexact, often confusing it with many causes plainly worthy or entitled to respectful consideration and debate, ranging from the restriction of child and woman labor to governmental ownership of public utilities, so it is possible that some of the personally estimable signers of the call for an "Intercollegiate Socialist School" may not have realized the true purpose of the cult with which they have identified their names. The very processes of unconscious exaggeration of industrial evils, of incessant contemplation of the most lamentable social distress, which they would employ to convey the sympathetic impression that modern civilization is a failure, may have wrought more upon the imagination than the reason of these self-proclaimed Socialists. It is possible that some of them may be amazed at the revelation that what they have regarded as an altruistic and harmlessly esoteric theory exhales, noxiously if innocuously in this land, the spirit of treason. There can be no half-way position for these men. They must array themselves either as patriots or as open enemies of the institutions of the one country that stands pre-eminently in the history of mankind for the development of democracy.

There is a mental temperament predisposed to champion the creed of a minority. Its argument is that every great cause that has ultimately triumphed in history was at its initial stage the cause of a minority, and that, therefore, the minority must always be right. The defective logic is obvious. Nevertheless, there is a fatuous charm to a vanity that would fain believe itself a part of the "saving remnant," ignoring the fact that a "remnant," instead of being "saving," may be the vilest shoddy. The Socialist minority in this Republic is neither admirable nor formidable, but its advocates, whether malignant or self-deceived, should be paraded in their bald attitude of revolutionists.

A QUESTION OF DISCIPLINE.

We have a letter from a Connecticut employer asking us to give a list of men expelled from unions for assaulting non-union men or for participating in mob riots during strikes. Our correspondent admits that labor leaders denounce these offenses in their speeches, but says that he has never heard that a union expelled a member for such lawbreaking.

We can give no list of names, although a union in Chicago did assist last year in the prosecution of one of its members for violence and did expel him upon conviction. There may be other similar instances. We have asked the same question of labor leaders and their answer has been in substance this:

"We cannot expel these men except through regular processes provided by our by-laws and constitution. We must have the evidence to convict."

Any man who commits such an act will deny it, and his particular friends will shield him just as every accused person is shielded in the courts every day. When violence is committed and arrests are made, the organization cannot act until after a conviction, and then it does act. The same obstacles arise when demand is made for the expulsion of members from a church. How many churches to-day are expelling men whose rascality in "high finance" has been exposed during the last two years? Take a list of them and one will be surprised to find how prominent some of them are in ecclesiastical organizations. But, so long as nothing is proved against them in the courts it would be most difficult for a church committee to prove anything which the regularly constituted authorities, with their machinery for convicting of crime, cannot prove. If public prosecutors cannot find evidence, how much less can the trustees of a church or the trustees of a union find the evidence to expel their respective members?

STRIKES AKIN TO WAR.

From the Chicago Tribune.

While so many are working for international peace, it would be well if more were working for industrial peace. A strike may be as great a calamity as a battle, and the public sentiment should be educated to realize that strikes, like wars, should be measures only of the last resort. This does not mean that working people should not try to better their condition. That, of course, will be their ceaseless and proper effort. Nations continually strive to strengthen their international positions. But they no longer resort to war, except for the gravest and most fundamental reasons, and when all hope of settlement through negotiations, arbitration, or compromise has been exhausted. The cost of even victorious war is so great as to destroy by anticipation many of the benefits which it brings. So with the strike. The men who get better wages or better hours through strikes rather than through negotiations, arbitration, or compromise, lose in advance many of the benefits which spring from their improved condition.

On the other hand, employers who refuse to treat reasonably with their men, and so bring about strikes, lose a great deal through even the strikes they win.

SOCIALISTS SEEK TO INFLAME THE MIND OF AMERICAN YOUTH.

A PROPOSAL TO INCITE COLLEGE STUDENTS TO REVOLUTION—ORGANIZED LABOR REPUDIATES THESE FOES OF AMERICAN INSTITUTIONS.

(By the Editor.)

SOCIALISM schemes to plant its germs of discontent, despair and revolution in new fields. Its advocates, having failed to capture the mass of wage earners, have projected a campaign beyond them, planned to pervert the minds of the professional classes and of the younger and more impressionable recipients of higher education. The new venture in behalf of Socialism is in part revealed in the following call, published early this month, and addressed to college men and women, for the formation of an Intercollegiate Socialist Society:

In the opinion of the undersigned the recent remarkable increase in the Socialist vote in America should serve as an indication to the educated men and women in the country that Socialism is a thing concerning which it is no longer wise to be indifferent.

The undersigned, regarding its aims and fundamental principles with sympathy, and believing that in them will ultimately be found the remedy for many far reaching economic evils, propose organizing an association to be known as the Intercollegiate Socialist Society for the purpose of promoting an intelligent interest in Socialism among college men, graduate and undergraduate, through the formation of study clubs in the colleges and universities and the encouraging of all legitimate endeavors to awaken an interest in Socialism among the educated men and women of the country.

The call was signed by J. G. Phelps Stokes, Thomas Wentworth Higginson, Charlotte Perkins Gilman, Oscar Lovell Triggs, Clarence S. Darrow, B. O. Flower, William English Walling, Leonard D. Abbott, Jack London and Upton Sinclair.

THE LATEST DESIGN OF SOCIALISM.

An "Intercollegiate Socialist Society," which would stand committed by its very title to the advocacy rather than to the study of a doctrine, is directly in line with this latest scheme of Socialism to extend its propaganda toward the so-called "upper social classes." Thus "The Collectivist Society" is the title of an organization in New York City, whose object is definitely stated by The Worker, an official organ of the Social Democratic party, to be that "of disseminating Socialist literature among the professional classes, persons not ordinarily reached by the party propaganda, particularly." This organization, according to the same authority, first recruited its membership by appearing in the guise of "a sort of American 'Fabian Society;'" that is to say, a kind of go-slow, conservative-radical body. But it speedily advanced beyond this stage, and, as was announced in connection with its second general dinner, on November 19, 1904, now "frankly accepts the fundamental tenets of scientific Socialism." By "scientific Socialism," it may be explained, the Socialists mean the out-and-out Karl Marx uncompromising school of revolution.

The Publication Committee reported at this same dinner that "ministers, Catholic priests, secretaries of the Y. M. C. A., physicians and instructors and seniors in the various colleges are the groups at which this propaganda has been mainly directed." These Collectivists issue a general invitation to sympathizers "to encourage the Society in its determination to assist in strengthening the Socialist party by making propaganda for Socialism in quarters not ordinarily touched by party agitation."

CHARACTERISTICS OF SOCIALIST AGITATORS.

It is interesting to observe that the promoters of the proposed Intercollegiate Socialist Society and of similar movements, inspired by self-imposed solicitude for the toiling masses, are almost never workingmen, and have nothing in common with the interests of laborers. This statement is true of 90 per cent. of all the Socialist writers, workers and open-air orators. Their roster is largely made up of briefless lawyers, pulpitless clergymen, professional writers, ex-professors whose usefulness in college faculties has ceased to exist, sentimental exaggerators in social settlements, faddists, economic freaks, and here and there some man of wealth, whose capital has come to him through inheritance or marriage and whose vanity is tickled by being called a "millionaire Socialist, devoting his wealth to the uplifting of the downtrodden masses."

This heterogeneous aggregation is earnest, persistent and fanatical. In Russia, such devotees would develop under restraint into terrorists and include bombs in their political arsenal. But in a country of free speech, free press and free ballot, their fulminations usually expend themselves in the heated atmosphere of street corner harangues, or in the academic excitements of social coteries that flutteringly aspire to sensationalism, or in perfervid literature.

The serious pose of these apostles of the impossible has its counterpart in the antics of the quarreling professional agitators, who expend their force in mutual denunciation. One Socialist organ makes these remarks concerning the candidate for Mayor of an opposing Socialist faction in a large city:

Who is this man?

First, he is not a workingman.

He is a smooth, political huckster and grafter of the rankest type, besides leaving behind him, when he left Minneapolis, a record well known to the Republican boodlers in Minnesota, back in the 90s.

I met this man at the last national disgraceful convention at Chicago, where grafters and boodlers flocked in majority numbers. I could not help but regard him as I did, as he strutted about the convention hall dressed in broadcloth and silk stockings, buckled up with a one-eye glass and a gold chain dangling from the glass, tied in the button hole of a ten dollar silk vest, and his ten dollar silk slouch hat.

No workingman delegate of the fifty-two Socialists dared to speak to this gentleman worker of the workers.

Another evidence of the esteem in which these social "purists" hold one another's capacity for hastening the millenium by the revolutionary route is this excerpt:

The Socialists who have been trying to rid the Debs party of its fleas and barnacles are about tired of trying. Organized as it is, with grafters, traitors, and spies, from Maine to California, and from Minnesota to Florida, and with state constitutions and platforms drafted in such a way that a man or woman cannot be a member unless they are grafters and old party politicians.

In fact, a perusal of the organs of the factions of Socialism in this country would show that each Socialist believes every Socialist of another brand to be a liar, fakir, boodler and traitor. They preach "class-consciousness" and exhibit an amusing variegation of self-consciousness. They do not denounce all society and capitalism with more virulence than they denounce one another. They would create a new social order. And yet they display nothing but disorder in their own ranks. Their constant tempest in a teapot is in itself a demonstration of their utter incapacity for public affairs and an indication of the confusion, leading inevitably to anarchy, that would follow the inauguration of their impossible regime.

WHAT IS SOCIALISM?

But just what is this Socialism, with which these highly respectable gentlemen announce their sympathy and which they propose to promote? Let the following utterances, culled from the official organs and recognized spokesmen of Socialism, answer:

Far be it from me to deny that Socialism is a menace. It is its purpose to wipe out, root and branch, all capitalistic institutions of present-day society. It is distinctly revolutionary and in scope and depth is vastly more tremendous than any revolution that has ever occurred in the history of the world.—*Jack London.*

We give the capitalist class due notice of the possibility of volcanic eruption—we mean the real article, not the kind they have in New York. In every upheaval a terrible retribution would be enacted on the capitalist class. The French Revolution and the Paris Commune ought to serve as warning examples. —*Social Democratic Herald.*

The Socialist party is a party of revolution, not of reform. No reform of the present order of society, however radical or sweeping it may be claimed to be, will satisfy its class-conscious supporters.—*Eugene V. Debs.*

Desperation is born in poverty, and hunger will fire the heart and nerve the arm of rebellion.—*Socialist Magazine.*

The war between the capitalist class and the working class is bound to grow in intensity and to continue until one or the other is destroyed.—*The Worker.*

The proletariat will possess itself of the government, apply democracy to industry, abolish wages, which are merely legalized robbery, and run the business of the country in its own interest.—*Jack London.*

To large numbers of people the earth is little better than a dungeon—they are simply serving time on earth at hard labor, in order that an imperious few may lead butterfly lives.—*Social Democratic Herald.*

Such measures of relief as we may be able to force from capitalism are but a preparation of the workers to seize the whole powers of government, in order that they may thereby lay hold of the whole system of industry and thus come into their rightful inheritance.—*Socialist National Platform.*

This revolt in the form of demands for an increased share of the joint product is being carefully and shrewdly shaped for a political assault upon society. * * * The leaders intend to direct the labor revolt to the capture of the political machinery of society. * * * With the control of the police, the army, the navy, and the courts, they will confiscate, with or without remuneration, all the possessions of the capitalist class which are used in the production and distribution of the luxuries and necessities of life. They mean to apply the law of eminent domain to the land and to extend the law of eminent domain until it embraces the mines, the factories, the railroad and the ocean carriers.

The Socialists turned their energies upon the trade union movement. To win the trade unions was well-nigh to win the victory.

Instead of antagonizing the unions, the Socialists proceeded to conciliate the unions. "Let every good Socialist join the union of his trade! Bore from within and capture the trade-union movement."

To-day the great labor unions are honeycombed with Socialists. At work and at play, at business meeting and council, their insidious propaganda goes on. Night and day, tireless and unrelenting as a mortgage, they labor at their self-imposed task of undermining society.—*Jack London.*

The employers' associations that fight the unions will soon recognize that Socialism is a movement that will call a different strike from that of any trade union—that will not ask for shorter hours or a few cents more wages, but will ask the whole product and point the way for the producer to pass down and out of the industrial field. * * * The Socialists ask no arbitration. They do not recognise that the employer has any rights to arbitrate.—*International Socialist Review.*

INNOCUOUS THOUGH INFLAMMATORY RHETORIC.

Let no reader be alarmed at these quotations. The tropical rhetoric of these solicitious guardians of helpless American labor, in their "self-appointed task of undermining society," through debauching the mind of youth, cannot flourish under the temperate atmosphere of democracy. Familiarity with the virulence of Socialism makes it ridiculous. There is no danger in a parade of words whose very violence proclaims their impotence. Yet there is something offensive to patriotism in the spectacle of respectable citizens declaring their "sympathy" with doctrines that strike at the very foundations of the institutions of our country. While the ultimate aims of the Socialists and the Anarchists are antithetical, they follow precisely the same method and use the same material in preparing the minds of their hearers to adopt their theories. Both of them rail violently against existing institutions. Both of them denounce in unmeasured terms the present constitution of society. Both of them dwell upon the most extreme and exaggerated evils. The burden of the street corner speech of a Socialist agitator could not be differentiated with a microscope from that of a foaming Anarchist. The one would excite the passions of a pliant nature to the frenzy of murder as thoroughly as the other. At the time of the assassination of President McKinley, the Socialists were loud in their condemnation of the Anarchist murderer. Yet Socialist oratory alone would have inflamed the hatred of a disordered mind as hotly as did any of the Anarchist literature that Csolgolz read.

Are these seditious teachings of class hatred and social revolution to be made a part of the college curricula? Are the more or less distinguished signers of the call for an "Intercollegiate Socialist Society" really willing to stand before the fathers and mothers of the college youth of the country as the sponsors of such teachings to their children? The authorities of the University of California were incautious enough to permit one of the signers of the call, Jack London, to address a meeting of the student body of which he was at one time a member. This is what he gave them:

"You are drones that cluster around the capitalistic honey-vats. Your fatuous self-sufficiency blinds you to the revolution that is surely, surely coming, and which will as surely wipe you and your silk-lined, puffed-up leisure off the face of the map. You are parasites on the back of labor." One capitalist among London's auditors interrupted. "Do you know what will be the result of your revolution?" he asked. "Anarchy, civil war, death and crime will be the results of the revolution you are prophesying." "I know it," shouted London; "but what are you going to do about it?"

STUDIES OF THE ABNORMAL.

But not all of the verbal batteries employed in the campaign of Socialism are directly vituperative and revolutionary. The projected "Intercollegiate Socialist Society" would hardly fail to include in its course of instruction excursions into another kind of literature that is used as a subtile ally to franker propaganda, through inspiring a mental protest against the present social and industrial system. This literature exists in abundance in two forms. One is the dark and gloomy description of all the nether strata of society; the other consists of sensational and exaggerated statements in newspapers concerning such recognized abuses as work in sweatshops, child labor and unsanitary tenements. The first and more pretentious of these forms is devoted to hideous, horrific pictures, drawn with revolting realism, of all that is pitiful, abnormal, shameful, vicious and criminal in the most degraded slums of the great cities. The effect upon the mind of any reader of this literature, of an average amount of sympathy, is most depressing. Its effect upon a nature supersensitive, either by temperament, by youth, or by temporary adversity is so unwholesome, that within the past month newspapers have reported two suicides, one of a man and one of a young girl, both attributed to the mental despair caused by reading these Socialistic studies of human degradation. Without questioning the scientific value and importance of learning all the ills that afflict the modern social structure in order to seek their remedy, it must be admitted that an exclusive concentration of the attention upon these painful phenomena, especially when they are pictured with sensational rather than philanthropic intent, must destroy correct perspective in the social outlook. If an ornithologist were to confine his studies and lectures to the habits of the buzzard, he would convey to his students the impression that all bird-life was sustained by carrion. The keeper of a prison, whose days and nights are spent among convicted criminals; the superintendent of an asylum in whose ears continually ring the ravings and wailings of the demented; the caretaker of a pest-house, whose eyes are constantly filled with the spectacle of the human body when afflicted with the most loathsome plagues—if these persons, useful and honorable as are their several offices, were continuously and persistently to exploit their painful and shocking experiences before the public as representative of prevalent conditions, they would create a tidal wave of pessimism. Indeed, it is a familiar fact that the reflex action upon those too long and constantly surrounded by such environments not infrequently has dire and even fatal effects upon the strongest minds and most resistant wills, leading to melancholia and suicide. The atmosphere surrounding the social settlements, steeped with appeals to sympathy and pity, has a disheartening effect upon some of the young college dwellers, whose fine enthusiasm has led them into the midst of squalid misery, exciting socialistic impulses. A surgical clinic may be of the highest scientific value when conducted in the amphitheatre of a medical school; but if held upon a street corner it would be degraded into an excitant of morbid fascination.

SOCIOLOGICAL EXAGGERATIONS.

Exaggeration, not always wilful or malicious, but based upon superficial inquiry into conditions wholly novel and necessarily unfamiliar to the observer, is available material for the Socialist orator. Not long ago a conservative newspaper in one of the largest American cities contained a long article, headed in striking type: "Women Inspect Sweatshops. Members of the State Federation Clubs Appalled by Awful Conditions Found Here. Making Men's Pants at 28 Cents a Dozen. Stitch, Stitch, from Dawn to Dark." The article, which is typical of its class, described the visit of a group of fashionable club women, who had become interested in the "study of sociology," to a slum tenement. It told with gloating detail how these social explorers discovered forty families upon two floors, "herded together like cattle. In one foul, rank room, two women, with wan, drawn faces, were sewing on men's trousers. They were mother and daughter. Born almost with a needle in her fingers, neither had ever known what it was to rest." Questioned by one of the compassionate club women it was "learned" that the women were paid 28 cents a dozen for "making" trousers; and that each of them, "by stitching incessantly from dawn to dark," could by the utmost effort "make" two dozen pairs a day. Hence the glaring head-lines.

It happened that this sensational article so stirred the compassion of a certain philanthropist that he employed a trained investigator to make an inquiry. Observe the result: A thorough search at the address given failed to discover any forty families crowded like cattle upon two floors. Instead, the dwellers were housed in fair comfort. The two sewing women were found, cheerful and contented. Instead of "making" trousers, they were finishing trousers upon which all the heavy work had been done by machinery in a factory. It was further learned that the husband had steady work and good wages; that the mother and daughter were sewing merely to earn a little extra money; and that this sewing was quite incidental and did not interfere with their housekeeping and the care of three young children. It is needless to say that the philanthropist did not find occasion for his charity.

All this is not to minimize the deplorable evidence of poverty and distress in city tenements. Nor is it to disparage the efforts of the good men and women who devote time and energy to praiseworthy and often effective social service. Neither is it to obscure the value of legislation and of rigorous public administration in elevating the social, industrial and sanitary conditions in congested centers of population. But it must be admitted that the article quoted, especially as it was published in a conservative journal, would spread broadcast an impression far from the truth and quite available for those who would stimulate discontent.

A conspicuous and recent example of sociological exaggeration is a book entitled "Poverty," by Robert Hunter. Ever since its publication last winter, this book has been advertised by Socialist organs as one of the "great works" of the day. The preachers of despair fairly revel in Mr. Hunter's assertion that there are 10,000,000 people in the United States in the grasp of poverty. Yet this assertion has been discredited by all those whose training, experience and opportunities of observation qualify them to estimate the true value of such figures; and even Mr. Hunter admits that he is "largely guessing."

The Socialists acclaim this book as written by one who has come down from the "upper walks of life" into the slums and made a series of shocking but scientifically accurate discoveries. They never betray their knowledge that this author belongs to their own school, but always convey to the reader the inference that he is an unprejudiced observer. They have even published "A Review by John Spargo," which would lead the reader to assume that the book had won the approval of a severe critic; whereas, the criticism was merely that of one Socialist patting another on the back.

An assertion of this same socialistic sociologist that 70,000 children in New York City went breakfastless every morning to the public schools was advertised all over the country, being exploited by the sensational press in every large city. The Board of Education, after a special investigation, declared Mr. Hunter's statement to be grossly exaggerated and without foundation in fact; while the Health Department could find, out of 275,000 school children examined, only 825 improperly fed.

Further remarkable evidence of his reckless exaggeration is afforded by the experience of the Salvation Army. No one will accuse that organization of any disposition to minimize the existence of distress. The Salvation Army undertook to supply free breakfasts to the "70,000 suffering little ones." In reply to an inquiry as to the result of this charitable enterprise, an agent of the Salvation Army made this report:

> That the conditions as represented by Mr. Hunter were very much exaggerated; that the Army established in all nine or ten stations in different parts of the city; that they never had more than 500 children apply at the total number of stations in one day, and this number only the first two or three days; that the number gradually dwindled down, necessitating the gradual closing of the stations, until they were reduced to one or two, and then no one having applied for a day or two, these last stations were closed; that the Army had soup, cocoa, coffee and rolls for the applying school children, but that the children stated they did not care for the soup or cocoa, and preferred merely the coffee and rolls; that if a child who had coffee and rolls for breakfast was considered breakfastless, then there were many thousands of such in New York City. This would apply equally to thousands of business men and capitalists.

Another choice bit of morbid rhetoric by the same imaginative "sociologist" follows:

> In the Chicago stockyards are 50,000 on the verge of pauperism. They are in practical slavery. I have seen children of ten years of age working all day in great vats of blood. Incurable rheumatism before the age of twenty-five is reached is a common result, and tuberculosis even among the children is extremely prevalent. They have nothing to look forward to but death.

In fact, no such condition as described exists in the Chicago stockyards. The statement quoted was denied as promptly as possible and its absolute falsity was exposed. But no denial is as sensational as an accusation, and it is not to be expected that this denial will ever catch up with the swift circulation of the original children-in-vats-of-blood fiction.

Space permits but one more example of this nature, out of thousands that could be arrayed. A professional woman, having exceptional opportunities for observing the life of workers in the tenements, recently published the following statements:

> Every garment worn by a woman is found being manufactured in tenement rooms. The coarsest house-wrappers to the daintiest lace gowns for a fine evening function are manufactured in these rooms. All adornments of woman's dress, the flowers and feathers for her hats themselves—these I have seen being made in the presence of smallpox, on the lounge with the patient. All clothing worn by infants and young children—dainty little dresses—I have seen on the same bed with children sick of contagious diseases, and, into these little garments is sewed some of the contagion.

Her statement, whose accuracy is not questioned, unintentionally conveys the impression to the average reader that such repulsive and dangerous conditions are prevalent, instead of exceedingly rare and necessarily corrected as soon as detected. Her peculiar use of the words "every garment worn by a woman," and "all clothing worn by infants and young children," leads to an unconscious inference that is startling. The official records of the Board of Health show that during the past two years there have been not more than seven or eight cases of smallpox per year in all Greater New York. In fact, the sanitary authorities consider the disease so rare, in proportion to the population, as to be practically eliminated.

Now, in their "self-imposed task of undermining society," the Socialists eagerly seize this kind of literature and exploit it to the fullest extent. Jack London, in his speech at the University of California, quoted freely from the hysterical assertions of Mr. Hunter about poverty, in order to impress his college hearers with the notion that the world outside groans in a state of universal, abject misery, whose only salvation is "revolution." If the "Intercollegiate Socialist Society" were to succeed in carrying out this part of its programme, mischief might result.

The effect upon the young mind of such distorted pictures, accompanied by an appeal to its generous impulses, can only be conjectured. The student, carefully trained for serious and important work in the world of which he knows so little, might thus be perverted into advocacy of a doctrine, presented to him as a panacea, but whose ultimate significance he is too immature to perceive.

DECEPTIVE TRICKS OF SOCIALISTS.

These promotors of "intelligent interest in Socialism" would doubtless cajole the students in their projected intercollegiate society with tricks similar to those habitually employed by the professional agitators of the cult. For example, the vice-president and actuary of an insurance company recently delivered an address claiming Socialism to be the phenomenon of the 20th century. Thereupon the Socialist organs heralded this address as an acknowledgment from a Wall Street capitalist that Socialism is inevitable, wholly suppressing the fact that this self-same Wall Street capitalist, strange as it may seem, has been a Socialist for twenty years, treating the address as if it were a tribute from an enemy, instead of being the plea of a partisan advocate. They printed it in pamphlet form and published this advertisement:

> That first lot of leaflets giving the remarkable setting forth of the philosophy of Socialism by Vice-President Weeks, of the New York Life Insurance Company, went off like hot cakes. We were whipped out of them almost before we knew it. Order early if you want any of the new lot. Ten copies for a dime, one hundred for 35 cents and a thousand for $2.50.

It is one of the stock tricks of the Socialists to deceive the public as to the strength of their following. Immediately after every election, when official returns of the balloting for the candidates of the various minor parties are not at hand, they announce tremendous gains in their vote. For example, directly after the last Presidential election their party officials gave the statement to the newspapers that the popular vote for Debs had increased to 600,000. This was accepted by the public as a statement of fact. Subsequently official data reduced the Socialist vote to less than 400,000 and it was admitted that the enrolled party membership was less than 25,000. But this revised and corrected statement reached only a few. The original claim of 600,000 Socialist voters in the Nation remained unchallenged and furnished the text for many an excitable editor, who swallowed the Socialist figures at their face value and wrote a post-election article "viewing with alarm" the remarkable "percentage of increase" in the Socialist vote.

LABOR LEADERS DENOUNCE SOCIALISM.

But it may interest some of those who profess such solicitude for the "working class" to learn what the genuine, hard-headed workers themselves think of their revolutionary theories. How do the proposed beneficiaries look upon their doctrinaire would-be benefactors? They may be astonished to learn that there is not to-day a representative officer of any important labor organization in the country who does not, upon every occasion, denounce the Socialist propaganda of these silk-stocking faddists who would propose to force an entrance into the college lecture rooms. The American Federation of Labor, which contains the largest number of organized wage earners in the world, has defeated every effort of the Socialists to commit it to their cause, at its annual conventions for the past four years. So overwhelming, indeed, was the Socialist defeat in its last annual convention, held in San Francisco, that most of the Socialist leaders have openly abandoned this form of attack and declare that they no longer wish to capture the American Federation of Labor.

Instead, they now plan to destroy it. Thus the leaders of organized labor are actuated by two motives in their antagonism to Socialism. They are opposed to its creed, because it is wholly opposed to the spirit and operation of American institutions. They also fight it as the openly recognized enemy of the trade union movement. The call for an industrial convention in Chicago on June 27, to form a new national labor organization, was signed only by leading Socialists. That movement was promptly denounced as "treason" by Samuel Gompers, President of the American Federation of Labor, in the following language:

> 'Tis treason, gentlemen! The defensive actions of the rank and file, as well as advocates and defenders of the trade union movement, do not seem to commend themselves to the callers of the Chicago convention, nor have they commended themselves to the other Socialists, who are either openly aiding or encouraging the effort to destroy the trade union movement, while a number of other Socialists are hoping against hope that the destructive work may be crowned with success.
>
> Do the convention callers or their friends imagine for a moment that the trade unionists will sit idly by and see the great organizations which they have builded to protect and promote the workers' interests, and which are the bulwarks of defense and opportunities for progress and advancement—see these attacked, maligned, and sought to be divided or destroyed without a word of dissent or protest?
>
> The official journals of the Western Federation of Miners, the *American Labor Union*, the *Socialist Review*, and all other Socialist publications, are virulent in their malicious abuse of the active trade unionists, professing friendshp for the American Federation of Labor, and yet proposing to supplant it by the call they have issued.
>
> When any man or set of men mask behind the pretense of friendship for labor, then attempt to undermine or to open fire upon the most successful general organization of labor that the world has yet seen, the American Federation of Labor, we say, "This is treason, gentlemen; it is treason."

President Gompers gave a good example of the straight-from-the-shoulder fight that trade unionism makes upon Socialism, in the following forcible conclusion to a speech against a Socialist resolution, delivered in Faneuil Hall, Boston:

> I want to tell you, Socialists, that I have studied your philosophy; read your works upon economics, and not the meanest of them; studied your standard works, both in English and German—have not only read, but studied them. I have heard your orators and watched the work of your movement the world over. I have kept close watch upon your doctrines for thirty years; have been closely associated with many of you, and know how you think and what you propose. I know, too, what you have up your sleeve, and I want to say that I am entirely at variance with your philosophy. I declare it to you, I am not only at variance with your doctrines, but with your philosophy. Economically, you are unsound; socially, you are wrong; industrially, you are an impossibility.

John Mitchell, President of the United Mine Workers of America, itself the largest single labor union in the world, is equally emphatic in his denunciation of Socialism:

> I advocate not industrial revolution, but industrial progress. The deadening blight of Socialism would wither progress. The virile, active forces of industry, enlisted in the wage system under the form of capital and labor, can be brought to work mightily, through sane and rational agreement, for that progress of industry which means the advancement of civilization and the lightening of the burdens that still oppress humanity. This progress can be stimulated by negotiation and, when necessary, by conflict. The Socialists abhor all such progress and denounce every method that has been discovered, including the trade agreement, for its encouragement. That is why the Socialists seek, either by assault or by "boring from within", to destroy or to disintegrate the trade union movement, because its aim and its effect are the betterment of society as a whole. The instinct of individual self-improvement is the life-blood of labor unionism. The control of all industry by the State, being against that instinct, could result only in either anarchy or despotism.

If any of the dilletante triflers with revolution are still in doubt as to the estimate in which their plan to undermine society is held by labor leaders, let them inquire of such men as the following:

James Duncan, General Secretary Granite Cutters' National Union, Quincy, Mass.

E. E. Clark, Grand Chief Conductor, Order of Railway Conductors, Cedar Rapids, Iowa.

Daniel J. Keefe, President International Longshoremen, Marine and Transport Workers' Association, Detroit, Mich.

Warren S. Stone, Grand Chief International Brotherhood of Locomotive Engineers, Cleveland, Ohio.

P. H. Morrissey, Grand Master Brotherhood of Railroad Trainmen, Cleveland, Ohio.

Theodore J. Shaffer, President Amalgamated Association of Iron, Steel and Tin Workers, Pittsburgh, Pa.

J. J. Hannahan, Grand Master Brotherhood of Locomotive Firemen, Peoria, Ill.

James O'Connell, President International Association of Machinists, Washington, D. C.

Joseph F. Valentine, President Iron Moulders' Union of North America, Cincinnati, Ohio.

James M. Lynch, President International Typographical Union, Indianapolis, Ind.

William D. Mahon, President Amalgamated Association of Street Railway Employes of America, Detroit, Mich.

Denis A. Hayes, President Glass Bottle Blowers' Association of the United States and Canada, Philadelphia, Pa.

George W. Perkins, President Cigarmakers' International Union of America, Chicago, Ill.

Frank Buchanan, President International Association of Bridge and Structural Ironworkers, Cleveland, Ohio.

Max Morris, International Protective Association of Retail Clerks, Denver, Col.

John B. Lennon, General Secretary, Journeymen Tailors' Union of America, Bloomington, Ill.

In short, let these poseurs as friends of labor address the entire roster of the 125 chief officers of the national and international unions. Among them all will not be found more than a half-dozen who will not tell the advocates of Socialism that their programme is foolish and unwelcome and that it would be regarded as dangerous were it not known to be utterly weak, contemptible and incapable of making headway against the common sense and sound economics of the captains of organized labor.

THE SOCIALIST ANTI-UNION PLOT.

These labor leaders are men who cannot be deceived as to the ulterior purposes of the Socialists. They are acquainted with all their treason, strategem and wiles, for they have been fighting the Socialists for years, not only in national and international trade unions, but in state and city federations of labor, as well as in thousands of local unions. In ninety-nine out of a hundred of these contests, the leaders of organized labor have completely routed the Socialists; yet they do not relax their vigilance of Socialist tricks nor lessen the vigor of their denunciations of Socialism itself. Every friend of the recognized methods of attaining industrial peace, such as conference, conciliation and arbitration, and who has had experience in dealing with strikes and lock-outs, has learned how to identify the Socialist. He is generally the loud-mouthed blatant agitator, whose every word is directed against the settlement of any controversy between capital and labor, because he does not wish peace, but revolution. A recent article from the pen of Luke McKenny, of the Wire Lathers' Union, published in a labor magazine, states the situation so truthfully and succinctly that we quote it here:

> Their active workers are led by men who are both vengeful and unscrupulous. Expressing principles that are directly antithetical to trades unionism, and down in their own hearts bitterly opposed to trades unions, they are, nevertheless, found ever at the forefront in labor matters.
>
> Seek for the prime mover in some abortive and disastrous strike—you will find a Socialist.
>
> Look for the sponsors of arbitrary boycotts, defamatory and insulting resolutions denunciatory of employers; in fact, anything that will tend to besmirch the name of labor or involve it in difficulties and you will come upon a Socialist in ninety-nine cases out of a hundred.
>
> It cannot be gainsaid that in the rank and file of the Socialist party there are many conscientious but mistaken union men, and even among the leaders there are a few men of unimpeachable character. But reeking to heaven as a stench in the nostrils of organized labor is the "party" with its vicious and irresponsible—even corrupt—leaders and labor can never assert itself; can never meet nor expect to meet its employers upon fair and equitable terms until it has thrown off this noxious burden for good and all.
>
> Equitable agreements with employers, collectively entered into, and arbitration, that will be entered into in good faith by both sides, as a means of settling differences, is the ideal system, in my opinion, for the future relations of Capital and Labor. But in our own ranks we must inculcate a vital principle: that trade agreements honestly entered into shall be honorably and inviolably kept and respected during their life. But, in order to effectually maintain this principle, the party Socialist, to whom an agreement with Capital is more honored in the breach than in the observance, must be relegated to the rear for good and all.
>
> But now the question presents itself to us: "How can we the soonest rid ourselves of this nuisance?" I would answer: By following in our local and central unions the same methods invariably used by the Socialists themselves. This, in brief, means regular attendance at our meetings and united and aggressive action against this disturbing element at all times. In our local bodies you will seldom find the Socialist absent. He is there to answer the roll call, not, you may be sure, for any particular love he bears for his union, but to be ready to exploit his visions of Utopia; he is there in force on election nights and he lets the conservative element indulge in petty electioneering for practically unimportant positions, while he sees to it that the delegation from the local to the central body is of his own stripe, as a unit, if possible. Once he is in the central body he follows the same plan of campaign. If the central organization publishes an official paper, the "red-buttonite" sees to it that, by manipulation at each election, his party furnishes the staff and controls its policy. And the paper under its "red button" management gives about three-fourths of its editorial space to the advancement of "class conscious propaganda," while the balance is given to comment upon existing labor troubles, usually containing such vicious and unwarranted abuse of employers that troubles which might have been adjusted are prolonged indefinitely, to the great hardship of the workmen involved and to the Satanic delight of the "class conscious" freak who edits the paper, who uses two or three columns of space to point the trouble out as "an object lesson, showing the necessity of voting the Socialist party ticket at the next election."
>
> See to it that no Socialist is sent to a central body or to a convention as a delegate. It may seem arbitrary advice, at first thought, but when we consider the fact that we are endeavoring to combat insidious and unscrupulous foes, whose very existence in our ranks is a constant menace to us, we should stifle all such wandering thoughts, use "the big stick" and use it effectively.

We have endeavored to group some of the salient

(Concluded on page 15.)

THE WANTON, INHUMAN, INDEFENSIBLE CHICAGO STRIKE.

FRANKLIN MACVEAGH LOOKS BEYOND ITS EXCESSES TO THE GREAT UNDERCURRENT OF UNIONISM INDISPENSABLE TO CIVILIZATION.

(Address by Franklin MacVeagh before the Cincinnati Commercial Club.)

MR. CHAIRMAN AND GENTLEMEN:

You may question an appearance of impartiality toward labor unions, by a Chicago man lately escaped from a state of street ruffianism and a general mix up of brickbats, lumps of coal, glass bottles, stones, brass knuckles and the rest of the familiar equipment of disorder and slugging incident to Chicago strikes.

And you may not welcome Chicago suggestions about labor unions; our city being considered a high-roller in labor matters. Chicago's labor ferment, however, it is fair to say, is but part of the wider ferment, because of which many of the problems of our national development are finding their chief forum in Chicago and this Middle West.

Doubtless our teamsters' strike has not heightened Chicago's authority. But you must admit that it is a credit to our originality. For it is unique as a finished example; being an unprecedented combination of every mistake and every abuse which unionism has so far

FRANKLIN MAC VEAGH,
Merchant and Publicist, Chicago.

evolved. One may study in this one strike all the defects, excesses and deplorable features of the labor movement—and with the brilliant effect undimmed by any of its virtues.

It was at first sympathetic, though the teamsters had agreements specially prohibiting sympathetic strikes.

They struck for the garment workers, but only when the latter had long lost their cause. And they did not strike against the employers of the garment workers, but, like lightning from a clear sky, against houses with whom their own relationships, and those of all other unions, were satisfactory and unruffled. They struck only such houses as had never, to their knowledge, seen a garment worker in their lives—with the single exception of one house who had as a side show of their business nineteen tailors, and who didn't care a penny if they did not have one. The houses with whom the garment workers had their strike were not molested. They were exempt. They were prime favorites. The teamsters never turned their eyes their way.

It was not merely a sympathetic strike, and sympathetic by pretense; but it immediately became also a reckless criminal boycott, with automatic alternations of strike and boycott that could not stop short of involving, in the end, every employer in Chicago whose business used a team. And yet, so fatuous and ill-considered were their plans that the strike leaders expected to restrict the strike.

The strike has broken every contract it could lay its hands upon, and as nonchalantly, and almost as frequently, as the leaders take a drink.

It has picketed, not legitimately, or in self-defense, but maliciously and to terrorize.

It has blockaded the streets with union teams, though less than formerly, because comparatively few teamsters sympathize with the strike.

It has slugged at every turn and at every distance.

It has disregarded the courts, both state and federal, and has loudly resented any legal restraints.

By common belief it was not a genuine strike at all, but "conceived in sin and born in iniquity," with sympathy as a pretense, and with revenge and cupidity hopelessly confused in inconceivable motives.

It has broken the peace into little bits, and has resented and resisted protection, even by the police, for the legitimate and necessary business of the employers.

It has terrorized the retail merchants throughout the city.

It has driven the unwilling union men from their jobs, denied non-union men the right to work, and the employers the right even to attempt to do business.

It encouraged hideous strikes of children.

It has done everything it could find to do that would forfeit the good will of the public, and it has raised up against itself a nearly unanimous public opinion from ocean to ocean.

It is a strike and boycott of an oligarchy of unfit leaders, who have sacrificed with impartial indifference the rights of the employers, the citizens, the teamsters and the union cause. It is a strike which the rank and file have had little to say about, which has had no cause to fight for and no reason to fight, which is wanton, wasteful, inhuman, deplorable and unnecessary from any and every point of view. A Philadelphia lawyer could not find a word to say in its defense. It has closed the mouth of apology.

The initial blunder of the oligarchy was taking it for granted that the employers would have no scruples against buying immunity, or would have no principles or self-respect for which they would fight. It is unsafe to count upon the pusillanimity of peaceful American citizens.

Such is the latest dire experience of Chicago. But even this does not shut Chicago's eyes to the underlying just positions of unionism. Because war breaks out between Japan and Russia we do not forget the permanent values of civil government, nor the fruitful progress of the years and areas of peace. All through the injustice of this guerilla warfare, Chicago's employers and press have more than ever pledged themselves to a fair field for unionism. And the present is particularly a juncture for holding on to the just habit of discrimination between fundamental unionism itself and its wretched excesses.

For with all its faults—and its faults are grievous and many—unionism is a great movement. It is far too great; it relates its fortunes far too surely to every section of our national life and society, and it concerns far too vividly the far-reaching issues of present civilization, for us to confine its sphere to its own membership and its own leadership. Evidently its fortunes are bound up with those of the employers. But its relationships extend immensely further, even to the limits of present human society. The union labor movement is no mean part of the whole movement—industrial, social, intellectual and spiritual—that now has the stage of the world. For good or ill it is a significant part of the big life of the time. It is part of that greater human union which is carrying forward, and I believe upward, the general movement of mankind.

Unionism has so much power for good and so many possibilities of evil, that it must not be dealt with by employers as a mere enemy, or with habitual impulses of belligerency, notwithstanding those undeniable occasions when unions must be fought relentlessly to a finish. For the situation is permanent. It is childish to think we can abolish labor unions, for the public opinion of all nations has accepted them as fixtures. We must develop, not abolish them. And the employers, as sure as there is moral responsibility anywhere in the world, must assume a distinct share of the responsibility for the increase of their usefulness and for the correction of their faults. And we come a long way toward progressive unions whenever employers deal with them as friends.

But final friendly acceptance of labor unions, either by employers or the public, will not take place until all of the unions have definitely abandoned two wholly revolting and abominable methods which it is impossible for the American people ever to condone. I mean physical violence and the breaking of contracts. Other methods may be debatable. Even the open shop is not a closed question. But the breaking of contracts and the breaking of heads are not in the nature of subjects for debate.

There is a controlling fact about violence that should be made clear and prominent. I mean the fact that it is never a private offense. It is a public offense, wherever and whenever committed. It is always an act against the government. Crime is crime.

The violence committed by strikers and their sympathizers does not differ from any other crime. It is simply crime. Such violence therefore takes issue not with employers, but with the public authorities, and the issue is taken up by the government necessarily as its own.

The important thing to notice is that this crime is no part of the strike. It is extraneous and incidental, and as external as if committed at another time.

A strike is a test of whether an employer can run a business to his satisfaction without the strikers, or whether the strikers will have to be called back. Everybody agrees as to that. And it must be agreed that this test cannot be made without a fair field, and that there is no suggestion of violence or disorder in the

(Concluded on page 15.)

WELFARE DEPARTMENT
OF
The National Civic Federation

OFFICERS

H. H. VREELAND, Chairman.
CYRUS H. McCORMICK, First Vice-Chairman.
JOHN H. PATTERSON, Second Vice-Chairman.
EDWARD A. FILENE, Third Vice-Chairman.
CORNELIUS N. BLISS, Treasurer.

EXECUTIVE COMMITTEE

George W. Brown, Treasurer United Shoe Machinery Company, Boston, Mass.
W. A. Clark, President United Verde Copper Company, Butte, Mont.
Frederic S. Clark, Treasurer Talbot Mills, North Billerica, Mass.
Ralph M. Easley, Chairman Executive Council, National Civic Federation, New York City.
G. E. Emmons, Manager Schenectady Works General Electric Co., Schenectady, N. Y.
Edward A. Filene, Treasurer Wm. Filene's Sons Co., Boston, Mass.
Frederick P. Fish, President American Telephone and Telegraph Co., Boston, Mass.
Frederick S. Fish, Chairman Executive Committee, Studebaker Bros. Mfg. Co., South Bend, Ind.
W. C. Fish, Manager Lynn Works General Electric Co., West Lynn, Mass.
G. Watson French, President Bettendorf Metal Wheel Co., Davenport, Iowa.
Orrin S. Goan, Manager National Biscuit Co., New York City.
William C. Greene, Treasurer Peace Dale Manufacturing Company, Peace Dale, R. I.
B. J. Greenhut, Treasurer Siegel-Cooper Co., New York City.
F. R. Hazard, President The Solvay Process Co., Syracuse, New York.
H. J. Heinz, President H. J. Heinz Co., Pittsburgh, Pa.
Edwin M. Herr, Vice-President Westinghouse Air Brake Co., Wilmerding, Pa.
Charles W. Hubbard, Treasurer Ludlow Manufacturing Associates, Boston, Mass.
Charles H. Hulburd, President Elgin National Watch Co., Chicago, Ill.
John S. Huyler, President Huyler's, New York City.
M. E. Ingalls, Chairman Executive Board C., C., C. & St. L. Ry. Co., Cincinnati, Ohio.
G. Gunby Jordan, President Eagle and Phenix Mills, Columbus, Ga.
John F. P. Lawton, Assistant Treasurer and Secretary Gorham Mfg. Co. of Rhode Island, Providence, R. I.
Wm. W. Lobdell, President Lobdell Car Wheel Company, Wilmington, Del.
Arthur T. Lyman, Treasurer The Boston Manufacturing Co., Boston, Mass.
W. G. Mather, President Cleveland Cliffs Iron Co., Cleveland, Ohio.
Cyrus H. McCormick, President International Harvester Co., Chicago, Ill.
L. A. Osborne, Vice-President Westinghouse Electric and Manufacturing Co., East Pittsburgh, Pa.
Thomas F. Parker, President Monaghan Mills, Greenville, S. C.
John H. Patterson, President National Cash Register Co., Dayton, Ohio.
A. J. Pitkin, President American Locomotive Co., New York City.
Thomas G. Plant, President Thomas G. Plant Company, Boston, Mass.
Albert L. Pope, Vice-President Pope Manufacturing Company, New York City.
Francis L. Robbins, President Pittsburgh Coal Company, Pittsburgh, Pa.
H. A. Sherwin, President Sherwin-Williams Company, Cleveland, Ohio.
Ellison A. Smyth, President Pelzer Manufacturing Company, Pelzer, S. C.
Nathan Straus, R. H. Macy & Co., New York City.
H. H. Vreeland, President New York City Railway Co., New York City.
J. H. Williams, Vice-President J. H. Williams & Co., Brooklyn, N. Y.

Miss Gertrude Beeks, Secretary.

CONDITIONS UNDER WHICH FOUR THOUSAND EMPLOYES WORK AND LIVE IN BOURNVILLE, ENGLAND.

By Edward S. Thackray.

Bournville is about five miles from Birmingham and lies in one of the beautiful Worcester valleys, through which runs the pretty river Bourn, in a district largely wooded and pastoral. Close by the station the factory of the Cadbury Brothers, Limited, cocoa and chocolate manufacturers, was erected some twenty-six years ago, and was one of the first factories in England to move from the city out into the country, where now about four thousand employes enjoy the beautiful surroundings.

WORKING CONDITIONS OF EMPLOYES.

The entrance by the lodges to the office and factory buildings is through a rock garden, having a pathway arched by bowers covered with flowering creepers. Close to the entrance are the cycle houses, where the employes can leave their machines and have them thoroughly overhauled and ready for use when leaving at mid-day or evening. Between the blocks of buildings the grounds are laid out in gardens, planted, in the winter months, with evergreens, and in the summer, with flowering plants. The walls of the buildings themselves are covered with creepers.

The work hours are based on the eight-hour day. The women usually arrive at 9 and leave from 5 to 5.30, having a break of an hour for luncheon and recreative purposes at 12.30. On Saturdays the factory closes at noon the year round.

The work rooms are so arranged that the temperature is kept even, ventilators being freely used. During the cold months, heat is obtained from the hot steam-pipe system, over which the fresh air from outside is thrown. All the rooms are exceedingly lofty, and the numerous windows and skylights furnish a means of drawing off excessive heat.

ENTRANCE TO THE OFFICE AND FACTORY BUILDINGS.

In the card box department special appliances have been installed for drawing off the fumes which rise from the heating of glue, so that the rooms where this process is going on are absolutely free from any suspicion of odor which would in any way affect the health.

The employes wear white uniforms. The first one is supplied free by the company to each employe. The second is paid for, half by the company and half by the employe; but after that, each employe pays for the uniform, but buys the material through the company at 25 per cent. less than cost.

Every facility is provided for the employes to sit at their work, if they choose. In each room throughout the factory, drinking fountains are installed, also telephones, suggestion boxes and other incidentals to make the work pleasant. Plants are profusely distributed throughout the interior of the works, adding considerably to the home-like aspect of the work rooms.

A complete ambulance system is in vogue. There are in each room ambulance boxes which are in charge of several accredited persons. Three nurses, a doctor, and a dentist, whose services are free to employes, hold office hours daily for those who may be poorly, and they also attend to any individual cases of minor disorder on the premises.

Separate retiring rooms for the men and the women are provided, and these are well equipped with beds, couches and easy chairs.

The dining room for girls, which is distinct from that for men, accommodates some two thousand, food being

A LOFTY WORKROOM.

APPLIANCES FOR DRAWING OFF FUMES.

provided daily, at cost prices. A cup of coffee, tea, cocoa or a glass of milk may be had for a ha'penny; a large basin of soup with bread for a penny; a plate of meat, vegetables and pastry for a four-pence. Fresh fruit is brought in daily from the fruit growing district around the factory, and is often consumed in the dining rooms within two or three hours after it has been gathered. An expert is employed to select only the best and brightest fruit for the dining rooms. In the general laboratory of the establishment all food supplies are subjected to analytical tests for purity. The entire time of some thirty employes is occupied in connection with the kitchen and restaurants.

There is also a large heating chamber provided, into which the employes may put the lunch which they have brought from home. The doors of the chamber are then pulled and within an hour the lunches are hot.

The forewomen have their own separate dining room, fitted up with easy chairs and couches and supplied with all the current magazines and newspapers, so that they may have their rest where they can secure the needful quiet for the better carrying out of their duties.

RECREATION.

All of the employes have a fortnight holiday in the summer, and the management arranges with the railroads to run cheap trains to the seaside places all along the coast. The works are closed for a week at Christmas time and five days at Easter, which is a few days longer than is customarily given in England by other large firms.

The recreation grounds for the employes are very extensive and are divided into distinct sections, one for the women and the other for the men. The grounds for the women are laid out in tennis courts, net ball grounds, croquet grounds, and also large sections for swings and other games. The trees are many and of noble proportions; among them inviting seats have been arranged for those who prefer to take their rest quietly and read or chat together.

Bournville Hall, the old family mansion which belonged to the estate, is utilized as the women's club house, and associated with this club are many societies for the general welfare of the girls.

A girls' bath house is now being completed, containing swimming and other baths for the exclusive use of the female employes. Before the erection and completion of this building, architects were sent to the various countries on the continent to procure the best plans for the efficient installation of these baths. There is a large swimming pool in the center, and in the gallery around are private baths of every description.

A gymnasium is provided for the girls. This affords accommodations for the classes, which all the girls not over sixteen years of age are obliged to attend twice a week, to receive instruction in various exercises for physical development.

On the other side of the lane from the girls' recreation grounds are the recreation grounds for the men. The cricket field is sufficiently large to run four full counter-matches at one time. In connection with this cricket field are open air swimming baths, fishing pools, bowling greens and tennis grounds, so that all tastes are satisfied. A gymnasium pavilion is also provided for the men, which is filled with all the appliances associated with athletics. There are also two large football fields.

Associated with the outdoor sports are walking clubs, whose members take rambling tours, looking up old cathedrals and other buildings of historic interest, and enjoying the beautiful scenery along the road. There are also harriers, or groups of men in light silk suits, who start out and run for some twenty miles over fields, fences, walls and brooks, with no particular goal in view. This is a favorite sport in the winter months.

During the summer months the brass band gives performances in the recreation grounds and in the parks, and in the winter the orchestral and choral societies give various concerts in the large dining hall of the works.

EDUCATIONAL.

The intellectual side is not overlooked. A large library in the room adjoining the girls' dining room is at the disposal of all. Connected with this department are classes in plain sewing, fancy work; also lectures in cooking, ambulance work and other subjects which will be helpful to them in connection with their home life. No fees are charged for these lectures and classes.

There is a large youths' club house, which is used by any of the employed men who are not over nineteen years of age. In connection with this, there are a library and lecture rooms. Bagatelle boards, chess and whist rooms are provided.

Another building is utilized for a club house for the clerks, where there are billiards and other games, with reading rooms and a lending library.

EMPLOYES' HOMES.

Adjoining the works is the beautiful village, which is the result of Mr. George Cadbury's loving and philanthropic heart and head. When a youth, associated with Sunday School work in Birmingham, and especially with neighborhood work, as he visited the poor living in wretched, so-called homes, he made a vow that should wealth ever be vouchsafed to him, he would devote a large portion to improving that state of affairs. This desire has been fulfilled, and Bournville is now an object lesson to the world, showing that beautiful homes can be secured by even a man of low wages at small cost.

Many of the homes built on the estate rent at from four to six shillings per week. These houses contain two or three bed-rooms, sitting room, small kitchen, bath and washing conveniences, and all have a kitchen-garden attached. Some of the larger houses, renting at from seven to eight shillings per week, are most artistically arranged. The effect on the dwellers generally has been to bring about a desire to make their homes beautiful; and thus is spread abroad an influence for keeping the husband, wife and family to their own hearth, rather than, as is the case elsewhere, allowing wretched surroundings to drive them to frequent saloons or other places which tend to blunt all that is highest and best. In many cases, individual persons, after seeing the bright interiors of some of the houses, have not rested until they themselves have arranged their rooms along similar lines; and in this way the general tone of house decoration has been elevated. From this has sprung a desire that their children shall be neatly clothed and they themselves dressed with care and cleanliness.

By the trust deed the garden must be at least three times as large as the area covered by the house, so that enough vegetables may be grown to supply a family of six. At the end of each garden a fruit orchard is planted, containing apple, pear and plum trees, currant bushes and other small fruits.

Playgrounds are provided for the children and the gardener overlooks the children to see that they come to no harm. These grounds are away from the main roads.

The roads of the village are all laid out with the object of taking advantage of triangular and other

GIRLS' BATH HOUSE AND SUN REST HOUSE.
(The latter so arranged that the gardener can revolve it during the day.)

LUNCH ROOM FOR TWO THOUSAND GIRLS.

small sections of land for parks. Along all the roads trees are planted and each road is named for a tree, such as Elm or Sycamore.

VILLAGE SCHOOLS.

There is now building on the estate a system of the most perfectly equipped schools in the country, which is costing Mr. Cadbury over twenty thousand pounds. These will be for the benefit of those living on the estate as well as for others living in the neighborhood.

CARE OF THE SUPERANNUATED.

The late Mr. Richard Cadbury, whose interest in the welfare of the community was great, caused to be erected a number of almshouses, fitted up with every comfort. These almshouses are occupied by those who have been associated with the works, if any such need the help; also by others who may be nominated, and whose character is thoroughly satisfactory. The almshouses surround a quadrangle of beautiful lawns and gardens, so that their environment is wholesome and cheerful. Each house contains a bedroom, sitting room and small kitchen. By the side of each bed is a bell pull communicating with the next house, so that in case of sickness, assistance can be easily called. The furniture is of solid oak, and every thought has been given to make conveniences such that the occupants have every comfort. The almshouses accommodate about one hundred.

MEN'S RECREATION GROUNDS.

STOVE FOUNDERS AND IRON MOLDERS AGREE.

A Year's Demonstration of the Peace Resulting from the Enforcement of Collective Contracts Leads to a New Agreement.

The annual report of Chauncey H. Castle, President of the Stove Founders' National Defense Association, is a notable recognition, from the employers' standpoint, of the practical value of trade agreements, and of the increasing respect for their inviolability among both employers and wage earners. The recent convention of the association ratified the new agreement made by its Conference Committee with the Iron Molders' Union, a prominent feature of which is an increase in the ratio of apprentices. The following are extracts from President Castle's report:

This is the twentieth annual meeting of the Stove Founders' National Defense Association, and while your officers have, during the last year, had a large number of grievances to adjust, none of them were of a very serious nature. This may be accounted for by the fact that the officers of the various organizations with which we have agreements have become more familiar with the objects and intents of the agreements and impressed with their importance and value in the settlement of questions in dispute. I am pleased to be able to say that in all cases the letter and spirit of the agreements have been carried out, so that peace and harmony have prevailed.

The number of cases of general importance that have been adjusted during the last year is 71. Of this number those involving the molders were 36; mounters, 28; polishers, 7. In six instances the molders quit work and were, in accord with the agreements, obliged to return before consideration could be properly given their grievances. In the same number of cases the mounters who had gone out on an independent strike were, under agreements, obliged by their officers to resume their work pending adustment. In one or two cases our members shut out their workmen through error, but on being admonished by us opened the shop to them while the grievances were being taken up and adjusted under the agreements. In all instances the questions were adjusted without difficulty, with little expense and in full accord with the intent and purpose of our agreement.

COLLECTIVE BARGAINING.

Its Successful Growth and Application in the Highly Sub-Divided Shoe Industry.

(*Shoe Workers' Journal.*)

COLLECTIVE bargaining is manifestly the most economic method of disposing of the wage, hour and conditions problems between employer and employes. The development of sub-divisions of labor and specialization in our industries has introduced seventy-five or more divisions and sub-divisions of the work formerly done by one individual.

There are few industries in which this process has been carried on to a greater extent than the shoe manufacturing industry. Formerly the negotiations between the employer and employe were for the price of the shoe made complete, but now there is a separate and distinct bargain for each of the many operations into which the work has been divided and specialized. In the past the shoe manufacturing industry was confined almost entirely to one section of the country, but it has gradually branched out until it is conducted to-day in all sections. The industry, the labor and the product have undergone great changes. From the small shop of the proprietor-worker to the immense factory; from a few hundred factories located mainly in one section to fifteen hundred scattered throughout the country; from practically one system to a thousand; from the individual making the shoe complete to seventy-five individuals performing as many different operations; from the segregated workers to thousands of associated workers under one roof; from hand work to machine work; from a comparatively few styles of shoes to a great variety of styles the shoemaking industry has steadily progressed. The development from the old to the modern method of shoemaking has introduced an immense variety of details in the accounts and managements of the factory and a consequent increase of expenses. These details and the expense thereof are minimized by collective bargaining. The saving does not end there, but extends to every department of the factory. Collective bargaining introduces a closer mutual relationship, a spirit of helpfulness among the workers, which eliminates disharmony and unnecessary interference with each other, points out unnecessary obstacles and wasteful methods and installs the most economic systems of distributing and getting out the work. When there are incentives and inducements to the workers to co-operate to facilitate and promote the work of each other a saving in space, time, labor and money results to the employer. The concentration of capital, labor and management have effected wonderful economics, and the concentration of bargaining (collective bargaining) is their economic corollary. When unions first engaged in collective bargaining they were inexperienced, and at times evinced a disposition to be arbitrary, and did not always employ the best specialist or the best and most business like methods.

Often the tactics of the old form of organization were applied to an entirely new and different form, a business form, of relationship between employer and employes. In fact, methods that would not pass business scrutiny and would be suicidal in other lines of bargaining were indulged in by both employers and unions. The same tolerance, restraint, recognition and courtesy which influenced the relations between buyers, sellers or bargainers in other lines of commodities, business or trade, did not mark the relations between employers and unions in their bargains. This, coupled with the opposition of the employer and the inexperience of the union in conducting the business of collective bargaining, often resulted in waste rather than economy. Unfriendly relations, prejudiced, selfish and unwise opposition and wrong methods of execution did not affect the principle of collective bargaining or disprove its just claim to be the most economic and just arrangement for the adjustment of prices, hours and conditions of labor, although it detracted from its utility and efficiency. With the development of more reasonable relations between employer and unions and the adoption of sound methods, collective bargaining has been perfected along business lines and established its economic value in a variety of directions. It has introduced the union and arbitration agreement which fixes the price, hours and conditions of labor subject to change by mutual consent, thus limiting the bargains and bargainers and adjustment of disputes to the union representative, and the bargaining time to a fixed date. The whole matter is often settled and the question disposed of for the period stated in the agreement in one and usually in a few interviews between employer and representative of the union. It tends to impartial treatment and impartial wage scales as uniform as conditions will permit. It affects the economics before mentioned, accruing from a closer relationship and mutual helpfulness among the workers. It is the economic principle of associated effort, which enables one man to act for many, given a new application. It embodies the economics of simplification, systematization and concentration. It developed the most economic processes of doing the work and is the practical originator of the best factory systems in vogue to-day, systematized by the employer.

THE WANTON, INHUMAN, INDEFENSIBLE CHICAGO STRIKE.

(Concluded from page 11.)

proposition. Indeed, the suggestion of violenee would destroy the proposition. And it would destroy strikes themselves, for it is inconceivable that a strike could be instituted if it proclaimed violence as a part of its proposition. If violence or disorder occurs it is wholly foreign to the test. It is "pure cussedness," and a refusal to fight fair. To consider violence a factor in a strike, and to hold the man struck against responsible for it, would be like putting two wrestlers in a fair ring and then let the friends of one of them break into the ring, slug the other and fix the blame for the slugging on the man slugged.

The intellectual confusion which makes the maintenance of public order a part of a strike issue must be cleared up. Striking is one thing. Breaking laws is another thing. But many people are honestly, and others not so honestly, confused as to this plain distinction, including, especially, in the two classes mayors, aldermen and those well-meaning people whose sympathy for the workingman is never baked quite through.

Such people think that the police are a part of the employers' advantage, instead of what they are—a burdensome imposition upon their business. Certainly a man who is attacked by robbers is not taking an unfair advantage if he allows the police to rescue him. Now, no policeman ever guards a wagon or place of business except to ward off crime. No strike calls the police. Only crime calls them.

As to breaking contracts, labor unions are in no different case from anybody else. There is no moral exemption for any man or body of men that breaks contracts. Nor is there any hope of public or private respect for a contract breaker. A contract breaker is an utter misfit either as a citizen or a business man. There is no help for him except to be born again. And until contracts become sacred with all unions, until the public mind believes union contracts to be as good as gold, unionism will not be finally accepted by either the employers or the people. Happily, however, the strong and honorable men who are rising to the highest positions in the union movement understand as well as we do that it is vital for unions to keep faith.

One of the finest things ever done by a union man was the action of John Mitchell, when he resisted the sympathetic strike of the bituminous coal men while his anthracite strike was on. They could not strike without a violation of contracts, and he not only would not accept help through a breach of faith, but used every influence of his personal authority and that of every friend he could rally about him, to avert what he considered the dishonoring of his people. That example is celebrated, but there are abundant examples less conspicuous, by other tried labor leaders who are helping to make unimpeachable the contracts of the unions.

But much remains to be accomplished. The inviolability of contracts and the stern discountenancing of violence must become universal articles in the very creed of unionism. And these articles must become seasoned and confirmed before the American people will give its full endorsement to a cause and an institution that it is nevertheless anxious to adopt.

What would be the effect upon the fortunes of the labor unions, of the radical elimination of violence and broken contracts from their records? What could result but strength, success and progress?

First, there would be a new good will and co-operation on the part of the employers. Employers and workmen would soon come into cordial relations. That of itself would add immensely to the facilities of the unions.

But a more powerful ally than the good will of the employers is the good will of public opinion. With that as an ally everything is possible. Without it nothing is possible.

Public opinion will work for the working man if it can at the same time be just and moral. It is eager to be upon his side, and can be discouraged only by the conduct of the unions. It backs the honest man; but it will back him all the sooner if he works for wages. Nothing, however, can persuade it from despising and hating a contract breaker or a slugger.

There are various issues between employers and the unions, beside the sacredness of contracts and the maintenance of peace. But they are mostly debatable issues, respecting which final settlement may be a long time deferred but may always be expected. These issues require far more consideration and discussion than they have yet received. Much more experience and much more knowledge is needed for their final solution. But the two indispensable eliminations will make it possible to treat these other issues fairly, and in the end, wisely.

But not only are there issues to be settled. There are reforms to be effected in the labor movement. And all must help.

The unions, in frequent instances, suffer prodigiously from corrupt, incompetent or brutalized leadership, though it should exalt the pride of the American people that in so short a time so many of the highest places in the unions are filled by men who are an honor to the American name.

The unions are suffering too from the insufficiency [illegible] their government. Their government is an attempt at the extreme democratic form of the town meeting, and it frequently produces instead of a democracy a [illegible]rous oligarchy. Some modification of this form [illegible]vernment, or some evolution from it, or some [illegible] safeguards and checks, are necessary to prevent [illegible]nning of many of the unions by their parasites—[illegible]afters, the demagogues and the fools.

[illegible] needed reforms in whatever direction will take time. But what I want to say, with particular em[illegible], is this: that for these reforms the workingmen [illegible]elves can never be wholly responsible. [illegible] employers must accept a share—an important [illegible]—of this great responsibility.

And unionism makes large demands on our intelligence as well. In the first place there is the obligation to train ourselves to discriminate between the permanent values and meanings of unionism and the excesses incident to the first growth of an immense new power. The evolution of wise leadership and conservative membership in a new movement of workingmen must be slow. And it must be made at the cost of strange misconceptions of rights, of wild and illegal notions of self defense, of hostile mistrust of employers, and of deplorable disregard of the sanctities of law and order. Any man who will calmly and competently reflect upon this great matter will see for himself both that these phenomena are inevitable, and that they are entirely apart from the fundamental meanings, intent and values of the labor movement. They produce deplorable, and sometimes horrible facts and conditions; but they are, after all, superficial and might be temporary. It is our duty, substituting reason for feeling, to learn and understand the true significance of these excesses; and while dealing with them as they deserve to be dealt with, to always have a mind that looks beyond them into the depth of the great undercurrent which can, eventually, carry the whole American working world forward to calm prosperity.

We must accept the fact, too, that great changes in the conception of personal and property rights have come or are coming, as part and parcel of the democratic evolution. And among these is the acknowledgment—partly already legal and partly only as yet intellectual—that in employment matters there are two parties instead of one. A man who used to say I will run my business to suit myself, has to modify that exclusiveness. Some of us feel sometimes that we should be outrageously happy if we had even half to say about our business. In some respects a man can, it is true, run his own business—but in other respects public opinion, and not infrequently public law, steps in and limits his exclusive control.

But the chief requirement, after all, is that we shall believe that labor unions are indispensable to the advancement of mankind and to the growth of its civilization, for therein lies their profoundest claim. That is the great reason why we must not be halted by their present excesses, their present injustice, their present brutalities. That is why the movement must be purified, humanized and made wise and progressive. And that is why the labor movement—a large factor in the progress of the nation and the world—does not wholly rest upon the shoulders of the workingmen, but is a responsibility of yours and mine.

It is mere idleness to talk of an advancing civilization which doesn't include the advancing civilization of the workingmen. The development of only you and me, the rising comfort and manners, the rising intelligence and education, the rising character and morality, the rising altruism and ideals, the rising imagination and thought of only you and me and the few, would be a poor fruitage in that great garden of God where mankind has been placed to plant, cultivate and harvest the developments of progress and civilization. To leave out of the count vast sections of the people would be to defeat all the human purposes of Heaven.

And we cannot leave them out of the count. They will not be left out. For, why are the imperishable instincts and impulses of development and progress implanted in the race if they are not to carry forward and upward the whole people and not merely a small fraction of the people? What is there to satisfy, as a finality, the human intelligence, the human imagination, the human spirit, but the progress of the whole people?

But, how in the world, under present industrial and social conditions, can the workingmen of America hold their place, or how can we employers help them to hold their place, in the slowly but surely advancing columns of the army of civilization without the protection—the only protection—of their self organization? It would not be possible. It would not be conceivable. They would fall by the wayside—helpless victims of the vicissitudes of a cruel and inordinate competition. Where else but in this self protection is there even a breakwater, to moderate those high waves of immigration that are forever rolling in upon our working people from remoter and remoter Europe, where wages and the standards of living are miserably lower and lower?

The problems are difficult enough even with labor unions, for the unions are imperfect enough to suit their most fastidious critics. But without the unions the problems would be hopeless.

Therefore, for the larger reason that without the unions there would be the chaos of modern progress and the travesty of modern civilization, and for the immediate reason that the unions need, above all, right direction and development, their claim upon all who care, within the unions and without, for the fate of all orders of men, is a claim with the highest sanctions.

I know how comparatively few there are as yet among union men themselves who relate the union movement to the general interest of society. The motives of union men necessarily are mainly selfish and interested. And the disinterested view appears imaginative to many employers who experience the aggressiveness of the unions. And treating the present problems—some of them very sordid problems—with intellectual sympathy, patience and hopefulness, may well look like optimism. But optimism isn't the blackest crime in the calendar. At least men are sometimes hung for worse crimes than optimism.

And to go, in conclusion, a step further along the path of cheerfulness and hopefulness—availing myself for a moment more of the opportunity of an exceptional audience—I shall let myself believe that this nation, which is the first that has had both the purpose and the free opportunity to accomplish the impartial development of its people as a whole, will not fail in this its distinctive and incomparable mission. Speak of optimism! Speak of idealism! There is no optimism and no idealism, there is no sane dream, that exceeds the accepted and grounded national propositions of the American people. Our foundation creeds revel in magnificent imagination. But not one article of those creeds lies outside the realm of the rational and the practicable.

The persistence of the centuries has broken the bondage of the individual man—and the American nation is the expression of this triumph. But democracy, under whose banner the slow and tenacious progress was made, had one steadfast dream—the development of all the people. It broke the vested privilege of the monarchs and the nobles, that all men together might rise steadily and forever, step by step, with the upgrowths of civilization. And the American nation, which speaks to the world, as no other nation is commissioned to do, in the name and with the voice of democracy, will not let its enfranchised individual carry his liberties so far as to defeat the interests of his fellow men! and will not replace the abolished privilege of the nobles with a new privilege of the rich. Neither will it weakly turn as a refuge from plutocracy to the negations and the paralysis of socialism. But, avoiding both, America will gladden humanity with the spectacle of a whole people advancing in happiness and civilization by an honest enforcement of the policies of "a square deal."

SOCIALISTS SEEK TO INFLAME THE MIND OF AMERICAN YOUTH.

(Concluded from page 11.)

phenomena of the Socialist program which its advocates now seek to inject into the systematic instruction of the higher institutions of learning. It has been pointed out that the varied and eccentric constituents who make up the "57 varieties" of Socialism, together with the revolutionary doctrines themselves that they announce, constitute a menace more ridiculous, in this free land, than grave. But this effort to distort the social vision and inflame the misguided ardor of youth against existing institutions, if it were permitted full and unchecked scope, might have a deleterious effect upon some of those who are in training for the leadership in the thought and action of the future. But it is shown simultaneously that the real toilers of the land, as represented by the leaders of organized labor, reject and repudiate these apostles of gloom and revolution, for whose welfare these "scientific Socialists" display such concern in their fantastic campaign.

These millions of wage earners can rely upon the solid support of the uplifting, progressive and patriotic forces of the Republic—the pulpit, the press, the colleges, the leaders of public thought—in nullifying the doctrines of despair and class hatred, whose advocates openly boast their purpose to undermine society and overthrow the institutions of free, popular government.

There is no more worthy or better publication in circulation to-day than the Monthly Review of the National Civic Federation. The Review takes the position that it is not only wrong but is foolish for employers to undertake the destruction of the trade union movement. It urges upon both employer and employe the necessity of coming together in friendly conference and settling their differences. Where they cannot agree The Review urges the next best thing, which is arbitration.—*Cooper's International Journal.*

The Civic Federation is composed of the representative men in the business world, the labor movement and the philanthropic life of this nation, and much good has been accomplished by the organization in harmonizing the relationship between capital and labor.—Louisville *Journal of Labor.*

IS THERE AN IMMIGRATION PERIL?

(Concluded from page 7.)

can place him in neighborhoods in which are successfully established people of his own nationality. We do not doubt but what we will be successful.

Not many years ago I remember we established the first settlement of Germans in a State on our line. The forerunners of this settlement were brought from the congested sections of your city, New York. They were followed by German-speaking people, friends of friends and acquaintances of acquaintances. There are now several hundred German families in that section and more are wanted, and as they come, properly establishing themselves, they will be successful. In the same section we have colonies of Bohemians, Hungarians and some Scandinavians, all of whom are being joined by friends from the North and Europe. Recently we established a colony of French-Canadians. These people came from Canada to the United States, and after working around the mills in New England for a time found that they would be better satisfied if engaged in agricultural pursuits. They purchased farms in the South, at practically their own terms. They are satisfied and are being joined by other French people. We now have French colonists coming to us from Europe. True, the number is limited, but the foundation for an increased immigration is being laid. We have many Scandinavian farmers and business men located with us, and more are coming annually.

Recently I had the pleasure of making an extended trip through the South with the Italian Ambassador, Baron Mayor des Planches, at which time he studied several of the Italian colonies located on our system. These colonies were found most prosperous and contented. There is abundant room for many thousand Italian families on Southern farms and in Southern mills. We have to-day applications from not only farmers, but manufacturers as well, for Italian laborers. They will be given steady employment, and those desiring to own homes of their own will have no difficulty in being accommodated. We visited one settlement of Italians numbering about 175 families. Each family works from 20 to 30 acres of land for which they pay rental. They are furnished equipment, seed and supplies, as well as houses to live in. The statement of their net earnings shows that no farmer earned less than $350—some of them as much as $1,375. This was accomplished without any capital, and no investment whatever on the part of the Italian family, excepting the labor. I note this to show that the family without capital can succeed in the South.

It would seem appropriate for me to make the following suggestion as an aid to the solution of the problem:

Of the many thousands of immigrants now domiciled in your city, a considerable proportion come from farms in Europe. They come to this country to better their condition, to secure a home in free America. They are without any knowledge of the country beyond your city limits. They are not assimilating with our people, and I question whether they will; at least not as rapidly as they would, if placed in the rural districts. To distribute and establish these people we must have a location and money. With land, some money and people much can be accomplished. We have these three factors:

1. Desirable lands in the South at low prices.
2. Capitalists in the City of New York, in the North, and some in the South.
3. The people in congested districts.

Let us bring these three together.

The Commissioner of Immigration of the United States has, in my opinion, wisely recommended, that he be authorized to permit the various States to establish on Ellis Island, bureaus of information, the purpose being to reach the immigrants before they are permitted to enter the United States, and direct them to suitable homes, sending them direct thereto from Ellis Island. We are anxious to have many of these people in the South, and are ready to consider taking them; we believe we could aid materially in relieving the situation here in New York if we were permitted to go among these immigrants, making our investigation and selection, that is, giving the immigrant reliable information concerning the advantages we offer, the opportunities existing in the South, so that he can intelligently consider the proposition we would make. This done in advance of the immigrant having an opportunity to taste metropolitan life would, we believe, send more people away from the city than are going at this time. I would further suggest that the various organizations in your city interested in the caring for and protection of these immigrants be given sufficient support to properly connect themselves with people throughout the United States, likely to be interested in securing immigrants, thereby enabling these societies to do considerable more good work in directing people to suitable homes.

The Chairman:—Gentlemen, this is a national subject, and time will not permit of much further present discussion to-night. We have some gentlemen from the West here whom I would like to invite to show the immigrants the advantages of the West. Somebody is evidently getting men who want to work, for I can't get farm hands out on my farm twenty-five miles away. There is a scarcity of labor in the country, and I do not know whether they go South or where [illegible] go, but I can't get them.

Mr. James P. Archibald:—

Mr. Chairman and Gentlemen: It was my in[illegible] to read a paper here to-day from the labor sta[illegible] and to endeavor to express the feelings of the [illegible]ing people in regard to the question of immi[illegible]. I feel that it would have settled some of the as[illegible] that have been made here to-day in regard to u[illegible] desirable immigration.

I will detain you but a few moments, Mr. [illegible]man, but I want to get square with you because [illegible] not read my paper, but I will endeavor to [illegible] it printed in the proceedings of this meeting. [illegible] paper that I prepared ten years ago. When I was invited to address this meeting, I read over this old paper and found that it expresses my views now just as if I had written it yesterday.

Way back in 1892 the Central Labor Union of New York interested itself very much in immigration, and I was one of the committee that was then selected to investigate and report to the Central Labor Union. We did so, and our conclusion at that time was that no desirable man should be prevented from landing in this country. That is my opinion. I am amply satisfied that the interests of the labor people will be conserved, at this port at least, because of the fact that the Commissioner at this port to-day is a man in whom all of us who have the pleasure of his acquaintance have unqualified confidence. (Applause.)

As this question is likely to give rise to discussion all over the country, and perhaps compel the attention not only of our State Legislature, but of our National Government, I believe it behooves the Civic Federation to be in a position to put itself on record as to its attitude towards this great question, the principal part of which I believe is the distribution of the immigrants in the country. Mr. Chairman, I move you that the Civic Federation of New York and Vicinity request the National Civic Federation to appoint a committee composed of men of national standing to investigate this question of immigration and report to the National Civic Federation at as early a date as possible.

The resolution offered by Mr. Archibald was adopted unanimously and the Chairman declared the meeting adjourned.

The following is the paper submitted by Mr. Archibald:—

It should be clear, in our opinion, to every thinking man that a course of public policy which would diffuse labor all over the country is the great necessity of our times. Every year, and in their tens of thousands, there come to us men and women whose life experiences have been wholly connected with farming. They come from countries where militarism and landlordism eat the substance of the people, where taxation and rents have reduced them to an almost entirely impoverished condition. Hence, when they reach our ports, they have little or no money; they are ignorant of our resources; they do not know where to go; and if they did they would not have the means to defray the cost of transportation.

The result is that they remain just where they first land. They crowd the districts which are already overcrowded. Want and misery, filth and disease are the inevitable concomitants of such unnatural conditions. Hunger must be at least partly appeased. The "sweater" comes to offer something for its appeasement, or the employer of "scab" labor is at hand to give work for starvation pay, or the employer of union labor is besieged with applicants for work until, even were he a philanthropist, he could not find places for all. The remainder go to the wall. They go down and down. Public and private charity are next taxed to the last degree of endurance. A standing army of paupers is created. Trampdom is filled to repletion. The criminal classes are increased by many, at first, unwilling recruits. Public health is endangered. Public appreciation of man's inherent dignity is lessened. Public morality is assailed in a vital part, while the multiplication of suffering by tens of thousands of able-bodied men and women tends to destroy the finer feelings of humanity and to create a brutal hard-heartedness in the stead of Christian love and fraternal sympathy. Meanwhile the South and West are calling loudly for the very class of labor which most abundantly discharges itself on our shores. But there is no organized means to supply it. The poor immigrant is unable to help himself or place himself within the reach of fair opportunity for work.

Now, why is this not remedied? And is it not apparent as the noonday sun that the means of our remedy are in the hands of our Governments, both national and state?

And is it not equally clear that the whole country would be improved and the condition of workers everywhere be ameliorated if an effective remedy were applied? So far as our State Governments are concerned, it seems to be wholly within their power and entirely within their province to maintain labor commissioners at this port, whose duty it would be to hold constant communication with the national officials of immigration, and take concurrent action with such officials to take charge of the immigrants in directing, divesting and transporting them to a place where labor is required. If credence is to be given, as no doubt it should, to the press of the South, they are more in lack of labor than of capital in those fertile States. The want of farm labor fetters the farmers, who cannot increase the areas of improved and cultivated lands because they cannot find laborers to do the work. Good pay awaits the sober, industrious laborer. Plenty awaits the able-bodied workers if they only get there. But unadvised and unaided, our European immigrants cannot and do not get there. Vast treasures of national wealth remain undeveloped while vast additions to national poverty are made with each new influx of what might be manipulated to public and private good.

Nor is it in farming alone that the South, Southwest and West are calling for more workers. Alabama and Georgia cry out for more mechanical labor every day. Tennessee is rich in mineral wealth, while her soil has but to be scratched for abundant results. Florida calls for fruit growers. Louisiana offers great sugar opportunities. Arizona, the Dakotas, Nebraska, the wonderful State of Washington, Montana, Texas—but why further enumerate?—all these States require the industry (and have ample opportunities for its exercise) of millions yet to come; and it only remains for us to distribute and transport our immigrants where they are most needed. Such action would stop overcrowding. The general good would be promoted, and in the general advantage of the States the whole country would share. The organs of plutocracy may shriek "paternalism" as much as they may when dealing with this feature of the labor problem; they may desire to the top of their bent that there shall be yet more overcrowding in our already congested districts, so that concentration of capital may find a defenseless, impoverished concentration of mere human machinery at hand to be dealt with according to the dictates of soulless greed; but to this great policy of adequate, intelligent and well-directed distribution of labor the country must come.

Nor are we without example and precedent, in a limited degree, in this matter. One of the greatest governors of Massachusetts, the long-headed, far-seeing, wise and patriotic Andrews, once sent one hundred respectable, well-educated daughters of that State to the extreme West. They had been educated to an employment then crowded. There was nothing before them but starvation or the indescribable infamy of the streets. At the expense of Massachusetts they were saved from either of these awful alternatives. Provided with suitable escort, they were removed to a part of the country where their education, labor and thrift were most needed. They were placed where they could be of efficient help to themselves and to those about them. The result proved the wisdom of the great Andrews, and what he caused to be done for those one hundred young women can be done by our National and State Governments if they but rise to the height of the occasion in behalf of our immigrants.

It may and will be objected that the State has no right to interfere with individual liberty, and that such direction and transportation of immigrants would infringe on their individual rights; that they have a right to further congest the labor supply in our large cities if they choose; that they have a right to further overcrowd the already overcrowded tenement house districts if they wish to do so; that they have a right to increase the fierce competition for means of mere existence and further add to the burdens of labor in places where its superabundance is the superinducing cause of cheap wages and consequent hardship to the community. But such objection cannot stand the test of logical examination. It is self-evident that the State has the inherent right to protect itself against pauperism and its consequence, heavy taxation. It is not upon the barons of monopoly the burdens of taxation fall. It is the industrious poor of New York, with outrageously high rents flowing into the pockets of the landlord class, whose evicting propensities out-Herod the Herods of Ireland, who bear the burden of taxation for almshouses, houses of correction, penitentiaries, city hospitals and prisons. When trouble comes in financial circles thousands are thrown out of employment, and when the unemployed are brought to utter destitution the State or the municipality must come to their relief.

The idle and profligate are among us, but what shall be done with those who are only anxious for work, and the morality of whose lives under the most wretched conditions excites the admiration of every Christian or philanthropic observer, be he in religious belief or what he may? If the State has the right to organize for punishment, it must have an equal right to organize for guardianship. To prevent further overcrowding in this and other large cities would seem to be one of the highest forms of guardianship the State can exercise; and we hope that in due season, before the evil becomes unbearable, our statesmen and legislators will cease for a season their selfish scramble for place and power, and give to the question of labor distribution their best thought and action. By so doing they will urge forward the car of American progress, create tens of thousands of American homes, cause civilization to bloom over trackless prairies, build up a citizenship that shall be a tower of strength to the Republic and invoke on our statesmanship the benedictions of Him before whose all-seeing eye the humblest workingman stands the equal of the wealthiest capitalist.

The National
Civic Federation Review

VOL. II. No. 4 NEW YORK, JULY—AUGUST, 1905 TEN CENTS

WELFARE WORK AND THE PANAMA CANAL.

THE COMMISSION SECURES EXPERTS FROM THE WELFARE DEPARTMENT OF THE NATIONAL CIVIC FEDERATION TO REPORT UPON RECREATION.

TWO experts in Welfare Work, furnished by the Welfare Department of the National Civic Federation, sailed for the Isthmus on July 20, in the company of Chairman Shonts of the Isthmian Canal Commission and Chief Engineer Stevens. These men are W. E. C. Nazro, Welfare Manager of the Plymouth Cordage Company, North Plymouth, Mass., and Edward A. Moffett, editor of the *Bricklayer and Mason*, New York.

These experts were engaged by the Canal Commission especially to investigate the needs and opportunities on the Isthmus for the recreation of the workers engaged in canal construction, to put their conclusions in the form of definite recommendations, and to arrange to have carried into effect such plans as are adopted. The whole purpose is to secure the physical and mental welfare of the thousands of employes of the United States Government who, for years to come, will work and live in a climate and amid environments wholly different from their previous surroundings. These employes include heads of departments and chiefs of bureaus, clerks, stenographers, and a large number of engineers and rod-men, many of whom are college graduates, steam dredge men, high-class firemen, machinists; many hundreds of locomotive drivers, yardmen, steam drill operators, carpenters, bricklayers, plumbers, and mechanics.

Before sailing, Chairman Shonts thus explained, on behalf of the commission, the introduction of recreation into the work of canal construction:

"We have appreciated the necessity of doing something in the way of providing recreation for employes on the canal, and we have decided to take steps in

DEPARTURE FOR THE ISTHMUS OF WELFARE EXPERTS ON STEAMSHIP MEXICO.

that direction at once. It is absolutely true that down there our American employes have had no means of amusement. We are going to provide tennis courts, baseball parks, and perhaps fields for such other athletic sports as are suited to the climate. These opportunities for wholesome open air exercise and amusement will be especially valuable and welcome to the clerical force, and others whose work is largely sedentary. We intend, also, to have club houses erected, with every facility for reading and for all kinds of games and indoor amusements. In connection with these clubs and their various rooms, there will be reasonable opportunity for men to spend money in a proper way, who wish to do so. Before undertaking this plan we consulted with officials

W. E. C. NAZRO,
Welfare Manager, Plymouth Cordag[illegible]

of the National Civic Federation. The [illegible] partment of that organization has put [illegible] [illegible] two experts that the Nation[illegible] Federation has furnished to look over the field [illegible] pare definite plans.

"These plans will [illegible] also better houses and quarters for the me[illegible] problem of housing is highly important, an[illegible] rs for immediate consideration.

"We recognize th[illegible] ernment employe down on the Isthmus is e[illegible] a habitation and surroundings in keeping [illegible] American standard of living. These addition[illegible] preliminary plans may impede the actual work on the canal a little, but the delay will not be serious. It is far better to attend to this need in advance, and insure a contented and well housed army of employes, than through neglect to invite discontent and lack of enthusiasm in the work, not to speak of the sanitary question.

"Again, we are going to take steps to improve the food, and see that it is provided at the lowest possible figure. When we have accomplished these things, I believe the storm of complaints about the situation on the Isthmus will have ceased, that everybody will be contented, and that we shall in the end make a great gain, because of these preparations for recreation and wholesome living. With healthy underlying conditions we shall accomplish infinitely more, with less cost and less friction."

The experts furnished by the Welfare Department of the National Civic Federation are well qualified to prepare these desired plans for recreation. Mr. Nazro graduated from Harvard University in 1897, with the degree of B.A.S. upon landscape architecture, the laying out of recreation grounds, etc. In 1898, he received the degree of S.B. in architecture, having made a special study of all recreation buildings, such as club houses, gymnasiums, etc. After leaving college, Mr. Nazro traveled through England, France, and Italy, devoting most of his time to the study of these subjects. After returning from Europe he spent two or three years in practical work along the line of architectural and mill construction, and studying particularly the adaptation of sanitary conditions, light, etc., in the construction of mills, to the needs of employes. He was for a time with a large engineering firm, which made a specialty of mill construction. From there he went to the Plymouth Cordage Company as Welfare Manager, to take up their work of mill architecture, landscape improvements, homes for employes, a library, lunch-house, recreation hall, athletic association, and the development of other Welfare features. Mr. Nazro has carried on this work successfully for four years, and won the gold medal for his specialty at the St. Louis Exposition.

Mr. Moffett, as the editor of the official journal of [illegible] ca, has [illegible] ed with [illegible] ades, of [illegible] on the [illegible] us. In his capacity as a national representative of labor, he will make a thorough study of the pros[illegible]e conditions that will surround the mass of em[illegible] on the canal. He will thus be able to render valuable assistance to Mr. Nazro in preparing a report to the Isthmian Commission which, it is hoped, will clear away a great deal of the popular misapprehension upon that subject.

Upon completing their investigation, Messrs. Nazro and Moffett returned to New York, where, after their arrival on the eve of THE REVIEW's going to press, they made the following preliminary statement:

"Inasmuch as we are to make an official report to the Isthmian Canal Commission upon our investigation into what has been done and may be done to make the Canal Zone more habitable for employes, we obviously could not say anything that might anticipate our findings and recommendations.

"Speaking generally, it is well known that conditions on the Isthmus have been unfavorable for the employment of labor. Yet at the same time, our investigation warrants our saying that they are not as bad as they have been represented. In undertaking this stupendous enterprise, our Government has from the first met with most difficult problems, not the least of which has been the proper housing, etc., of the employes. Still, it must be said that the officials engaged in canal construction are making conscientious efforts to mitigate the hard physical conditions with which the employes have had to contend. It is plainly evident

EDWARD A. MOFFETT,
Editor *Bricklayer and Mason.*

that the Commission is determined to remove the slightest ground for whatever dissatisfaction may have existed. At the same time, we should say that the Isthmus with its tropical climate is no place for a man who expects to find all of the creature comforts to which he is accustomed at home. A man unaccustomed to the rough side of life, or at least unwilling to meet it, has no place on the Isthmus.

"We believe the efforts to better the conditions of employment on the Isthmus are to be continued with more intelligent direction. A day or two before we left, it was announced that Chairman Shonts, of the Commission, and Chief Engineer Stevens had issued a mandatory order to the effect that all work on the Canal should cease forthwith save the work of providing ample accommodation for employes already on the ground and for those yet to come."

NATIONAL IMMIGRATION CONFERENCE.

A Representative Gathering, at Our Largest Port of Entry, to Discuss a Problem of Inter-Continental Importance.

[illegible] Conference upon Immigration will be [illegible] York City, December 6 and 7, under the [illegible] the National Civic Federation. The de[illegible] the investigation of this subject a national [illegible] followed the many and widespread manifestations of interest in the discussion, at the midsummer meeting of the Civic Federation of New York, of the growing volume of immigration and its relation to American industry.

Invitations have been sent to the Governors of all the States to appoint each ten delegates to the National Conference. The responses have been prompt and favorable, and it is already assured that practically every State in the Union will be represented by delegates familiar with the needs and desires of their localities as to influx of population and with its relation to their industries. The following is the formal invitation:

SIR: Your Excellency is invited to appoint ten delegates to represent your State at a National Conference on Immigration, to be held in New York City, December 6 and 7, under the auspices of the National Civic Federation.

Some of the questions to be discussed under the general head are:

What is the character of the net increase in the population of the United States from immigration?

Should existing legislation looking to the elevation of this character through the exclusion of undesirable elements be extended and made more effective?

Should there be any change in the system of inspection, such as having it made at ports of departure, or at the home sources of emigration, or at both?

Are there any external influences tending to stimulate the volume of immigration?

What are the nature, extent, and locality of the demands in the United States for more labor?

What domestic industries and what labor crafts are most affected by the influx of alien labor, and in what ways?

What percentage of European immigration remains in the ports of arrival, such as New York, Boston, Philadelphia, and Baltimore?

What practical method can be devised of distributing immigration, especially for agriculture, to points where it may be needed?

What will be the effect of the distribution of large numbers of immigrants in the South upon the problem of industrial education and social betterment of the negro race?

Should the exclusion of Chinese coolie labor be made more rigid, and should it be extended to Japanese and Corean labor?

How shall the admission of exempted classes of Asiatics, such as scholars, merchants, and tourists, be regulated?

In fact, any topic related to immigration and its effect upon our national life and industries that the Conference wishes to consider may be included in its proceedings.

Yours respectfully,
(Signed)

August Belmont, Samuel Gompers, Oscar S. Straus, Bishop Henry C. Potter, John Mitchell, Archbishop John Ireland, William D. Mahon, Charles A. Moore, Warren S. Stone, Ralph M. Easley, Samuel B. Donnelly, *Committee.*

At the request of the Committee, the following were appointed by the Civic Federation of New York to cooperate in the preliminary arrangements; in the reception and entertainment of delegates, who will come from all parts of the country; and in making every effort conducive to the success and public value of this national gathering:

William H. Allen, General Secretary Association for Improving the Condition of the Poor.
J. Willis Baer, Secretary Board of Presbyterian Home Missions.
Nathan Bijur, President State Conference of Charities.
John N. Bogart, President Trades' Union Social Club.
Michael Brayer, Cloth Finishers' Union.
William O. Conkley, Lithographic Press Feeders.
John Cooper, The Cooper-Wigand-Cooke Company.
James Daly, Dock Builders' Union.
Charles Delaney, Granite Cutters' National Union.
Edward T. Devine, President National Conference of Charities and Correction.
Otto M. Eidlitz, Building Trades Employers' Association.
R. Watson Gilder, Editor *Century Magazine.*
Edward Gould, International Brotherhood of Teamsters.
B. J. Greenhut, Treasurer Siegel-Cooper Company.
C. L. Graff, Secretary Retail Dry Goods Association.
J. H. Hatch, United Upholsterers' Union.
James P. Holland, International Brotherhood of Stationary Firemen.
Daniel F. Jacobs, Cigar Makers' Union.
Arthur P. Kellogg, Assistant Editor *Charities.*
Philip Kelly, Theatrical Protective Union.
B. A. Larger, United Garment Workers.
Thomas B. Lavey, Iron Molders' Conference Board of New York and vicinity.
Edgar L. Marston, Blair & Company.
E. A. Moffett, Editor *Bricklayer and Mason.*
Charles A. Moore, Manning, Maxwell & Moore.
Thomas M. Mulry, Thomas Mulry & Son.
Eliot Norton, President Society for the Protection of Italian Immigrants.
Robert C. Ogden, President Southern Education Board.
Jacob A. Riis, Sociologist.
Charles A. Schieren, Charles A. Schieren & Company.
Louis B. Schram, President Associated Brewers.
Joseph H. Senner, Ex-Commissioner of Immigration.
Thomas R. Slicer, Clergyman.
Andrew J. Smith, Clothing Cutters' Union.
Maurice F. Smith, Musical Mutual Protective Union
Frederick Boyd Stevenson, Sunday Editor Brooklyn *Eagle.*
Dr. George W. Stoner, Medical Officer in charge United States Hospital Service, Ellis Island.
A. Beverly Smith, Sec'y, National Lithographers' Association
J. W. Sullivan, Typographical Union.
William Williams, Ex-Commissioner of Immigration.
C. E. Weisz, Superintendent of Public Charities, New York City.

TRADES UNION SOCIAL CLUB.

A New York Organization, Containing National Labor Leaders, Plans a Dollar Dinner on Labor Day.

The Trades Union Social Club of New York is composed, as its name implies, of officers and representatives of trade unions in that city, and also includes a goodly number of the officers of National and International organizations of labor. It maintains a club

A COMMISSION TO INVESTIGATE PUBLIC OWNERSHIP AND OPERATION.

THE NATIONAL CIVIC FEDERATION INITIATES AN EXHAUSTIVE INQUIRY, AT HOME AND ABROAD, TO LEARN HOW FAR THEY ARE DESIRABLE.

THE Executive Council of the National Civic Federation, upon request of its Departments of Industrial Economics and of Trade Agreements, has decided to appoint a Commission to make a thorough investigation, in this country and Europe, of National and Municipal Ownership and Operation of Public Utilities.

The current discussion and acute agitation of this subject indicate its hold upon the popular mind and the necessity for its analytical and comprehensive examination. Its present debate is often inconclusive, because of contradictory or unsatisfactory statements of fact. It is intended, therefore, that this investigation shall disclose the actual results of public ownership and operation as far as they have been undertaken in the United States, and of their more extensive practise in foreign countries. The ascertainment of these facts will afford a solid basis upon which to found discussion and conclusions for the guidance of future policy.

The scope of this inquiry will cover the relative advantages of Public Ownership and Operation, as compared with Public Ownership and Private Operation and Private Ownership and Operation. Each system will be examined with regard to its effect upon, among other topics:

Wages, hours, and conditions of labor;
Collective bargaining;
Cost and character of service;
Political conditions, civil service, spoils system, and municipal corruption;
Financial results;
Taxation.

The Commission will meet early in the fall to determine upon its program and methods of work. Among those appointed are:

Melville E. Ingalls, Big Four R.R., Cincinnati, Ohio.
Isaac N. Seligman, Treasurer Citizens' Union, New York City.
Oscar S. Straus, Merchant, New York City.
Albert Shaw, *Review of Reviews*, New York City.
Franklin MacVeagh, Merchant, Chicago, Ill.
Alexander H. Revell, President Chicago Civic Federation, Chicago, Ill.
Walter L. Fisher, Secretary Municipal Voters' League, Chicago, Ill.
Robert W. De Forest, Attorney at Law, New York City.
Wm. D. Foulke, Attorney at Law, Richmond, Ind.
Edward Rosewater, Editor *Bee*, Omaha, Neb.
Charles W. Knapp, Editor *The Republic*, St. Louis, Mo.
Frederick N. Judson, Attorney at Law, St. Louis, Mo.
Austen W. Fox, President City Club, New York City.
John G. Agar, President Reform Club, New York City.
Ambrose Swasey, President Cleveland Chamber of Commerce, Cleveland, Ohio.
Alfred F. Potts, President The Commercial Club, Indianapolis, Ind.
H. W. Goode, President General Electric Co., Portland, Ore.
Frank A. Vanderlip, Vice-President National City Bank, New York City.
W. D. Mahon, President Association Street Railway Employes, Detroit, Mich.
John Mitchell, President United Mine Workers of America, Indianapolis, Ind.
Samuel Gompers, President American Federation of Labor, Washington, D. C.
Daniel J. Keefe, President International Longshoremen's Association, Detroit, Mich.
E. E. Clark, Grand Chief, Brotherhood of Railway Conductors, Cedar Rapids, Iowa.
James Duncan, General Secretary Granite Cutters' National Union, Boston, Mass.
John F. Tobin, President Boot and Shoe Workers' Union, Boston, Mass.
Timothy Healy, President International Brotherhood Stationary Firemen, New York City.
F. J. McNulty, President International Brotherhood of Electrical Workers, Washington, D. C.
F. W. Taussig, Harvard University, Cambridge, Mass.
Edwin R. A. Seligman, Columbia University, New York City.
J. W. Jenks, Cornell University, Ithaca, N. Y.
Henry W. Farnam, Yale University, New Haven, Conn.
Frank J. Goodnow, Columbia University, New York City.
Leo S. Rowe, University of Pennsylvania, Philadelphia, Pa.
Carroll D. Wright, Clark College, Worcester, Mass.
John R. Commons, Wisconsin University, Madison, Wis.
Henry C. Adams, University of Michigan, Ann Arbor, Mich.
Hugo Meyer, University of Chicago, Chicago, Ill.
J. H. Hollender, Johns Hopkins University, Baltimore, Md.
John H. Gray, Northwestern University, Evanston, Ill.
Alexander Humphrey, Stevens Institute, Hoboken, N. J.
Edward W. Bemis, Superintendent Water Works, Cleveland, Ohio.
William J. Clark, General Electric Co., New York City.
Walton Clark, Vice-President Traction Co., Philadelphia, Pa.
Samuel Insull, President Edison Company, Chicago, Ill.
P. F. Sullivan, President Boston and Northern Street Railway Company, Boston, Mass.
Charles L. Edgar, President The Edison Electric Company, Boston, Mass.
Thomas Lowry, President Twin City Rapid Transit Company, Minneapolis, Minn.
Horace E. Andrews, President Cleveland Electric Company, Cleveland, Ohio.
J. C. Hutchins, President Detroit United Railway Company, Detroit, Mich.
George F. McCulloch, President Indiana Union Traction Company, Indianapolis, Ind.
Hamilton Holt, Editor *The Independent*, New York City.
Lawrence F. Abbott, Editor *The Outlook*, New York City.
Graham Taylor, Editor *The Commons*, Chicago, Ill.
Talcott Williams, Editor *The Press*, Philadelphia, Pa.
R. R. Bowker, *Publishers' Weekly*, New York City.
Milo R. Maltbie, Franchise Expert and former Editor *Municipal Affairs*, New York City.
T. C. Martin, Editor *Electrical World and Engineer*, New York City.
D. L. Cease, Editor *Railroad Trainmen's Journal*, Cleveland, Ohio.
John P. Frey, Editor *Iron Molders' Journal*, Cincinnati, Ohio.
John F. McNamee, Editor *Locomotive Firemen's Magazine*, Indianapolis, Ind.
Edward A. Moffett, Editor *Bricklayer and Mason*, New York City.
C. H. Salmons, Editor *Locomotive Firemen's Journal*, Cleveland, Ohio.
S. M. Sexton, Editor *United Mine Workers' Journal*, Indianapolis, Ind.
Louis D. Brandeis, Attorney at Law, Boston, Mass.
Edwin Burritt Smith, Attorney at Law, Chicago, Ill.
Edward A. Filene, President City Club, Boston, Mass.
Towner K. Webster, President City Club, Chicago, Ill.
George E. Hooker, Secretary City Club, Chicago, Ill.
Frank Parsons, President National Public Ownership League, Boston, Mass.
W. D. P. Bliss, Sociological Author, New York City.
George C. Sikes, Municipal Voters' League, Chicago, Ill.
Charles A. Conant, Morton Trust Company, New York City.
V. Everit Macy, Capitalist, New York City.
Marcus M. Marks, Manufacturer, New York City.
Slason Thompson, Railway Managers' Association, Chicago, Ill.
James F. Jackson, Chairman Massachusetts Board of Railway Commissioners, Boston, Mass.
F. L. Barker, Chairman Massachusetts Board of Gas Commissioners, Boston, Mass.
H. B. F. Macfarland, President Board of Commissioners District of Columbia, Washington, D. C.
William Wirt Howe, former President American Bar Association, New Orleans, La.
Clark Howell, Editor *Constitution*, Atlanta, Ga.
George H. Harries, Vice-President Washington Railway and Electric Company, Washington, D. C.
J. W. Bramwood, Editor *Typographical Journal*, Indianapolis, Ind.
Homer D. Call, Secretary-Treasurer Amalgamated Butchers' Association, Syracuse, N. Y.
Amos K. Fiske, Editor New York *Journal of Commerce*, New York City.
Charles S. Gleed, Attorney at Law, Topeka, Kan.
John Green, Editor *Bradstreet's Journal*, New York City.
S. W. Meek, the *Cleveland Leader*, Cleveland, Ohio.
Bradford Merrill, Editor New York *World*, New York City.
James H. McGraw, President McGraw Publishing Company, New York City.
James O'Connell, President International Association of Machinists, Washington, D. C.
William F. White, Vice-President North American Company, New York.
J. W. Sullivan, Editor *Clothing Trades' Bulletin*.
William H. Brown, Secretary Civic Federation of Chicago.
Roland Phillips, Editor *Harper's Weekly*, New York City.
C. A. Rook, President Dispatch Publishing Company, Pittsburg, Pa.
Angus Sinclair, Editor *Locomotive Engineering*, New York City.
Clarke B. Firestone, Editorial Staff *Evening Mail*, New York City.
Henry C. Watson, Editor *Dun's Review*, New York City.
James P. Archibald, Brotherhood of Painters and Decorators, New York City.
John A. Sleicher, Editor *Leslie's Weekly*, New York City.
Charles Kirchhoff, Editor the *Iron Age*, New York City.
Edgar H. Van Etten, Vice-President New York Central Railroad Company, Boston, Mass.
Thomas F. Woodlock, Editor *Wall Street Journal*, New York City.
O. R. Young, General Manager *International Steam Engineer*, New York City.

Up to date, acceptances of their appoin[illegible] been received from nearly all of the above [illegible] has been requested to indicate the most [illegible] time for him to attend the first meeting, bet[illegible] tember 15 and October 15.

It is not expected that the entire Commission can devote its time to such an investigation, but it is believed that subcommittees can be appointed which, with experts, will examine the various phases of the general subject and report their findings to the full Commission. It is hoped that such a subcommittee of nine will make a three months' investigation of conditions in European cities.

JOHN N. BOGART.

room as a social center for the local labor leaders and as a rendezvous for visiting representatives of unions, and holds meetings to discuss economic subjects.

An illustration of the activity of this club is found in its recent decision that there should be a revival of interest in Labor Day, which was first made a legal holiday in New York State, and that its observance, in addition to a pleasurable picnic, should include some consideration of the higher purposes of this annual celebration of organized labor. The club voted to have a dinner on the evening of Labor Day, with appropriate addresses. A committee of arrangements was appointed, composed of William F. Long, of the lithographers; Morris Carmody, hatters; Francis J. McKay, boilermakers; Jesse Larimer, housesmiths and bridgebuilders, and Captain William Bruce, of the Sandy Hook pilots. The committee met immediately and determined that it should be a dollar dinner, and that two hundred of the representative New York labor leaders should be brought together around the banquet tables.

Many of the veteran members of the club were delegates to the old Central Labor Union when, twenty-two years ago, the resolution was adopted declaring (three years before there was any law on the subject) that "the first Monday in September of each year shall be designated and recognized by the workingmen of New York City as a holiday, and be called Labor Day."

The club comprises in its membership Samuel Gompers, President, and Thomas I. Kidd, Vice-President of the American Federation of Labor; William D. Mahon, President Amalgamated Association of Street and Electric Railway Employes; George Preston, General Secretary International Association of Machinists; James Wilson, President International Patternmakers' League; John S. Henry, General Secretary International Wood Carvers' Union; William H. Frazier, General Secretary International Seamen's Union; John J. Pallas, President New York State Workingmen's Federation; James P. Archibald, ex-President Central Federated Union; Herman Robinson, Secretary Central Federated Union, and fifty of the leading business agents and other officers of New York unions.

JOHN B. MCNERNEY.

Its officers are: President, John N. Bogart, organizer American Federation of Labor; Vice-President, Edward A. Moffett, editor of the *Bricklayer and Mason*; Recording Secretary, John B. McNerney, International Secretary, Patternmakers' League; Financial Secretary, Frank A. Corbett, business agent Job Press Feeders' Union; Treasurer, Eugene A. Johnson, delegate Musicians' Union, 310.

A SOCIALIST ATTACK CRUSHED.

The Boston Central Labor Union Welcomes the New England Civic Federation, and the Cigar Makers Honor Its Officers.

Organized labor in Boston, through its highest and most authoritative body, the Central Labor Union, has expressed cordial approval of the formation of the Civic Federation of New England, and the earnest sympathy of the trade union movement with its plans for promoting industrial peace. Simultaneously, organized labor has discovered and repudiated a temporary victory of the Socialists in the local branch of the Cigarmakers' Union. It was, in fact, the temporary success of the Socialists in passing resolutions, in a meeting of the cigarmakers' local, when they were momentarily in the majority, that led to the subsequent enthusiastic commendation of the Civic Federation by the Central Labor Union, and virtual repudiation of the resolutions by the cigarmakers themselves.

The first general meeting of the Civic Federation of New England, held in the Quincy House on April 26, was devoted to the advocacy of trade agreements. The trade agreement is a method of attaining pacific progress in industry that is most abhorrent to Socialists. Among those who attended that meeting were Frank H. McCarthy and Henry Abrahams, respectively First Vice-President and Recording Secretary of the New England Civic Federation. Mr. McCarthy was also a former President of the Central Labor Union, of which Mr. Abrahams is Recording Secretary. Both are members of the Cigarmakers' Union, No. 97, of Boston.

At a meeting of that union, on May 10, when there was but a slim attendance, the Socialists carried the following resolutions by a vote of 147 to 105:

Whereas, The daily press of April 27 printed the names of several of our members as being present at a banquet given by the Civic Federation, and

Whereas, The printing of such names as members of the Cigarmakers' Union would lead the public to believe that they were present at that banquet as representatives of Cigarmakers' Union No. 97, and

Whereas, The Civic Federation, an organization founded for the purpose of continuing capitalistic control in the industrial world by keeping the workers unorganized and offering their services during times of strike to bunco them, as, for example, the Boston Teamsters' strike, and

Whereas, The president of the Civic Federation stands for the scab shop as against the union shop, and who, by his actions as president of the Interborough R. R. demonstrates that he bitterly opposes the efforts of the trades union, be it

Resolved, That we, in meeting assembled, do not allow any

(Concluded on page 4.)

Christensen versus People not on this question

CHIEF JUSTICE PARKER ON LEGAL RIGHTS OF UNIONS.

A DECISION BY THE HIGHEST COURT OF NEW YORK THAT OFFSETS A MUCH-QUOTED DECISION IN MASSACHUSETTS.

UNFRIENDLY critics of organized labor, in the daily press and in periodicals, have been making much ado over a recent decision of the Supreme Court of Massachusetts, in the case of *Berry versus Donovan*. This decision was, in brief, to the effect that a labor union commits an illegal act when it causes the discharge of any worker for the reason that he is not a member of the union. The decision even held that such action was not justified by the fact that the employer had previously agreed with the union to employ its members exclusively.

The facts leading up to this decision are that a non-union shoemaker sued an officer of the Boot and Shoe Workers' Union for procuring his discharge from employment. This discharge was enforced under a contract between the union and a firm, the firm voluntarily agreeing to employ only members of the union and not to maintain in its service any non-members. The Supreme Court held that the contract between the union and the firm (whose legality was not before the Court) did not justify the union officer's demand for the plaintiff's discharge, and that the latter was entitled to damages.

This decision is cited extensively in connection with a recent decision by the Supreme Court of Illinois, to the effect that members of a labor union could not legally compel, by threats, a contract for the exclusive employment of fellow-members. This opinion incidentally advanced the dictum that the closed shop contract is "illegal and criminal." That dictum was, however, no part of the decision, as that question was not before the Court.

The effort is made to create an impression in the public mind that these decisions, rendered by the highest Courts in Massachusetts and Illinois, go far to establish first, that a union commits an illegal act in causing the discharge of non-union men by a strike, or by a threat to strike; and second, that the closed shop contract is a violation of law. The fact is ignored that the Massachusetts decision, even though of the highest Court in that State, is directly controverted by the highest Court in New York, the Court of Appeals, in the decision rendered by Chief Justice Alton B. [illegible] the case of the *National Protective Association* [illegible] *Cumming*. The fact is also ignored that the [illegible] Court of Illinois sustains the decision of [illegible] court in the case of *Christensen versus People*, upon grounds wholly aside from the legality of the closed shop contract, which, as stated above, is no way involved in this decision.

It is pertinent, therefore, to recall the decision rendered in 1902 by Chief Justice Parker; for that decision, by the highest Court of New York, should in fairness be held before the public eye as conspicuously as the contradictory decision by a court of only corresponding rank.

Indeed, this New York decision goes even further in upholding the right of a union to demand, and to take measures not in themselves illegal to compel, the exclusive employment of their members than does the Massachusetts decision in denying that right. The official report of Chief Justice Parker's decision (New York, 170) thus summarizes its scope and significance:

> A labor union may refuse to permit its members to work with fellow servants who are members of a rival organization, may notify the employer to that effect and that a strike will be ordered unless such servants are discharged, where its action is based upon a proper motive, such as a purpose to secure only the employment of efficient and approved workmen, or to secure an exclusive preference of employment to its members on their own terms and conditions, provided that no force is employed and no unlawful act is committed. If, under such circumstances, the employes objected to are discharged, neither they nor the organization of which they are members have a right of action against the union or its members.

The history of the case culminating in this decision is brief. Charles McQueed, being refused admission into a union entitled the Enterprise Association of Steam Fitters, organized another union, which was incorporated as the National Protective Association of Steam Fitters and Helpers. Delegates of the older union, among them Cumming, ordered strikes wherever the members of the National Protective Association were employed, resulting in the discharge of the latter. McQueed procured an injunction against the Enterprise Association, which appealed to the Appellate Division of the Supreme Court. The Judges there vacated the injunction. The Protective Association thereupon carried the case to the Court of Appeals, which sustained the Appellate Division.

In giving the opinion of the Court, Chief Justice Parker recognizes "the right of one man to refuse to work for another on any ground that he may regard as sufficient, and the employer has no right to demand a reason for it," and continues:

> But there is, I take it, no legal objection to the employe giving a reason, if he has one, and the fact that the reason given is, that he refused to work with another who is not a member of his organization, whether stated to the employer or not, does not affect his right to stop work, nor does it give a cause of action to the workman to whom he objects because the employer sees fit to discharge the man objected to rather than lose the services of the objector.
>
> The same rule applies to a body of men who, having organized for purposes deemed beneficial to themselves, refuse to work. Their reasons may seem inadequate to others, but if it seems to be in their interest, as members of an organization, to refuse longer to work, it is their legal right to stop. The reason may no more be demanded as a right of the organization than of an individual, but if they elect to state the reason, their right to stop work is not cut off because the reason seems inadequate or selfish to the employer or to organized society. And if the conduct of the members of an organization is legal in itself it does not become illegal because the organization directs one of its members to state the reason for its conduct. . . .
>
> Some things may be treated as the subject of a grievance, namely, the desire to obtain higher wages, shorter hours of labor, or improved relations with their employers, but this enumeration does not, I take it, purport to cover all the grounds which will lawfully justify members of an organization refusing, in a body and by prearrangement, to work. The enumeration is illustrative rather than comprehensive, for the object of such an organization is to benefit all its members and it is their right to strike, if need be, in order to secure any lawful benefit to the several members of the organization, as, for instance, to secure the re-employment of a member they regard as having been improperly discharged, and to secure from an employer of a number of them employment for other members of their organization who may be out of employment, although the effect will be to cause the discharge of other employes who are not members.
>
> And whenever the Court can see that a refusal of members of an organization to work with non-members may be in the interest of the several members, it will not assume, in the absence of a finding to the contrary, that the object of such refusal was solely to gratify malice and to inflict injury upon such non-members.

ALTON B. PARKER,
Former Chief Justice N. Y. Court of Appeals.

Justice Parker made an important point in his decision regarding the influence upon safety of life of a trade union requiring a system of examination and a certificate of qualification for work. He argued "So long as the law compels the employe to bear the burden of the injury" due to the "negligent acts of a reckless coemploye . . . it is clearly within the right of an organization to provide such a method of examination and such tests as will secure a careful and competent membership, and to insist that protection of life and limb requires that they shall not be compelled to work with men whom they have not seen fit to admit into their organization, as happened in the case of the plaintiff." Upon this point Justice Parker further said:

> I know it is said in another opinion in this case that "workmen can not dictate to employers how they shall carry on their business, nor whom they shall or shall not employ," but I dissent absolutely from that proposition, and assert that, so long as workmen must assume all the risk of injury that may come to them through the carelessness of co-employes, they have the moral and legal right to say that they will not work with certain men, and the employer must accept their dictation or go without their services.

Entirely aside from this question of safety of life, the decision entered into the question of motive. Justice Parker said that he does not assent to the following proposition, laid down in the earlier case of *Bowen versus Matheson*:

> If an organization strikes to help its members, the strike is lawful. If its purpose be merely to injure non-members, it is unlawful. If the organization notifies the employer that its members will not work with non-members, and its real object is to benefit the organization and secure employment for its members, it is lawful. If its sole purpose is to prevent non-members working, then it is unlawful.

The following is the most sweeping portion of Justice Parker's decision:

> The defendant associations, as appears from the findings quoted, wanted to put their men in the place of certain men at work who were non-members working for smaller pay, and they set about doing it in a perfectly lawful way. They determined that if it were necessary they would bear the burden and expense of a strike to accomplish the result, and in so determining they were clearly within their rights, as all agree. They could have gone upon a strike without offering any explanation until the contractors should have come in distress to the offices of the associations asking the reason for the strike. Then, after explanations, the non-members would have been discharged and the men of defendant associations sent back to work. Instead of taking that course, they chose to inform the contractors of their determination and the reason for it.
>
> It is the giving of this information, a simple notification of their determination, which it was right and proper and reasonable to give, that has been characterized as "threats" by the Special Term, and which has led to no inconsiderable amount of misunderstanding since. But the sense in which the word was employed by the Court is of no consequence, for the defendant associations had the absolute right to threaten to do that which they had the right to do. Having the right to insist that plaintiff's men be discharged and defendant's men put in their place if the services of the other members of the organization were to be retained, they also had the right to threaten that none of their men would stay unless their members could have all the work there was to do.

A SOCIALIST ATTACK CRUSHED.

(*Concluded from page 3.*)

> of our members to attend as members of Union 97, any meeting that is held under the auspices of the Civic Federation, and be it further
>
> *Resolved*, That we consider the Civic Federation unworthy of our support and to be condemned by Organized Labor.

In adopting this resolution, the Socialists ignored a letter from the Teamsters' Union of Boston, denying that the Civic Federation had "betrayed" them in their strike.

The same local union of cigarmakers held an election of officers on June 13. Mr. Abrahams was a candidate for Recording Secretary and Mr. McCarthy for delegate to the Central Labor Union. Elated by their success in smuggling through the above resolution, the Socialists announced that they would defeat both these men. But the effort failed, both being elected by substantial majorities. The total vote of over 1,600 for officers indicates how slender was the attendance at the meeting which adopted the hostile resolutions, and demonstrates that the Socialists are, in fact, in a minority in the cigarmakers' local. Its action in honoring the two men whom the Socialists opposed, because of their official connection with the Civic Federation was, in effect, a repudiation of the resolutions of May 12.

The Boston Central Labor Union, however, went still further, and on May 21 adopted the following:

> *Resolved*, That the Boston Central Labor Union expresses its approval of the establishment of a branch of the Civic Federation in Boston, believing that the basic principles underlying the conduct of that organization merit the cordial endorsement and hearty cooperation of men and women identified with the American Trade Union movement.
>
> *Resolved*, That we, the delegates to the Boston Central Labor Union, in regular meeting assembled, express on behalf of the organized trade union movement of Greater Boston profound appreciation of a movement based upon a full, free understanding of controversies between employer and employee, whose efforts toward substituting mediation, conciliation, and arbitration for the drastic weapons of strike, lockout, and boycott should receive the fullest commendation of American wage earners.

In commenting upon this action of the Central Labor Union, its President, Peter W. Collins, wrote to Hayes Robbins, the Secretary of the New England Civic Federation: "Only those who were in attendance at our meeting can appreciate the sincerity of the Central Labor Union. The hearty cooperation it intends to accord the Civic Federation was very strongly and unanimously expressed, not only by the resolution of confidence, but by the very hearty approval of the sentiments it contained by the rank and file of labor."

BOTH SIDES WOULD AVERT A GREAT COAL STRIKE.

A COAL DEALERS' PANIC EFFECTUALLY QUELLED BY THE STATEMENTS OF PRESIDENTS DAVID WILLCOX AND JOHN MITCHELL.

THE speaking tour of John Mitchell, President of the United Mine Workers of America, in the anthracite regions of Pennsylvania has been accompanied by a series of sensational rumors and reports that another coal strike, involving both the anthracite and bituminous fields, was imminent. The sources and the terms of those reports were suggestive of a deliberate effort on the part of some large dealers in coal to scare the consuming public into heavy and general buying in anticipation of a famine. These tales dwelt with particular emphasis upon the threatened peril of a great coal strike this fall; whereas it is a well known fact that the miners, both bituminous and anthracite, are working under trade agreements which have withstood every strain, and will not expire until March 31, 1906.

That no such present danger exists, and that there is on both sides an absence of desire for a conflict when the bituminous and anthracite agreements expire simultaneously for the first time in their history, is shown by the utterances both of one of the largest anthracite employers and of Mr. Mitchell, speaking on behalf of his union. The employer is David Willcox,

DAVID WILLCOX.
President Delaware & Hudson R.R.

President of the Delaware and Hudson Railroad Company, who contributes to the August issue of the *North American Review* an article entitled "Present Conditions in the Anthracite Coal Industry."

President Willcox thus summarizes his own article (the emphasized type is our own):

"The existing conditions have, therefore, all been the result of arbitration in which both parties were represented. They have secured to the employes a rate of wages which the Commission held to be proper when the 'prepared' or domestic size of coal sell at $4.50 per ton with an advance as the price increases, and have also provided machinery by which all grievances have been adjusted and which will be equally available for that purpose in the future.

"**The employers have no desire to disturb these results, which have been so painfully and expensively reached by Arbitration, and are perfectly willing to continue the present arrangements indefinitely.** There is no association of the employers generally, such as is attempted in the case of the employes; indeed, either one would probably incur the charge of illegality under the anti-trust acts. The Supreme Court of Massachusetts has just held that an attempt to exclude non-members of a union from employment violates the prohibitions of monopoly, and other courts have made similar rulings. As already pointed out, everything suggested as the subject of a general contract between the employers and employes has been secured by the award. Therefore, no contract with the union is necessary for the protection of the employes; the Commission held that nothing of the sort would be admissible save on conditions which the union has failed to carry out, and any such arrangement would tend to defeat the award of the Commission and the decisions of the courts establishing the principle that employment must be open to all irrespective of membership of trade unions or otherwise.

"It is, indeed, a misnomer to call such arrangements contracts, for, as Mr. Mitchell says in his work on Organized Labor (p. 347), the union no more guarantees that any particular man will work than the employer guarantees that work will be provided for any particular man. Manifestly, there can be no contract where nobody is bound to anything. The illogical and illegal scheme of having all the labor organized in a great industry controlled by one organization and compelling all the employers to enter into contracts with that organization, rather than with their own employes, is rapidly passing away, and agreements of employment are fast reverting to their natural form of arrangements between the parties concerned.

"It may be added that the anthracite coal industry has been under investigation by the Interstate Commerce Commission, unhampered by the rules of evidence (194 U. S., 25) for two years and a half, without result. Although no formal decision has yet been made by the Interstate Commerce Commission, it is not too much to say that the manifold charges which have been made with such resonance and iteration for so many years past against those engaged in the industry have collapsed under investigation.

"The present state of the industry is, therefore, exceptional. All the existing conditions have been settled by arbitration, to which the employes were parties, **and the machinery has been successfully provided through the Conciliation Board for adjusting any future questions.** The methods of transacting business have been fully investigated and have not been found objectionable in any respect. **What possible ground can exist for disturbing this situation and subjecting the country to the hazard of another anthracite strike?"**

President Mitchell, in an interview at Scranton, was thus reported in a dispatch to the New York *Herald* of July 31:

"I believe some apprehension was caused by a report originating in Pittsburg that I had sent T. L. Lewis, Vice-President of the United Mine Workers, to arrange with the officers for a general strike which was supposed to offset a lockout on the part of the anthracite operators. The strike was alleged to involve the bituminous and anthracite miners, and to be effective in a month or two.

"There was no truth whatever in that statement. Mr. Lewis was in Pittsburg on other business. All the bituminous miners in Arkansas, Missouri, Illinois, Indiana, Ohio, Michigan, Western and Central Pennsylvania and some other points have agreements with the operators' association until April 1, when the award of the Anthracite Coal Commission expires. It is only natural that when so many men are released from contract obligations the public would feel some anxiety. And regardless of the fact that both operators and miners may be, and I believe are, desirous of renewing these contracts as they are now, or modifying them as the conditions of the coal trade may warrant, there is, of course, an element of danger that they may not agree. There is the same risk in our affairs that there might be in any other.

"But the attitude of our organization is simply this: We want to be in a position to make a contract that will be as advantageous to our people as possible. Personally I am satisfied that we will be able to negotiate another contract in the bituminous district, which will insure a continuance of the relations now existing between operators and miners in that field, and I am hopeful of like results in the anthracite region. I am sure that whatever differences may exist between the anthracite operators and the mine workers can be readily adjusted if the two interests will make any efforts to come together in a spirit of fairness."

Mr. Mitchell spoke as if he had no doubt whatever of such a result.

"I feel," he continued with deliberation, "that the last strike of 1902 was a lesson not soon to be forgotten by miners or operators. It is, of course, natural that the miners and operators of the anthracite districts should make such preparations as are necessary to *defend* themselves against any emergency that may arise next spring. Both miners and operators are doing this, the former by organizing their men, the latter by stocking coal. But these preparations do not necessarily mean there is any danger of a conflict. They are the precautions of prudent men. In our case the indications are that every miner in the anthracite field will be in the organization by April 1. They are joining now in thousands."

THE ANTHRACITE SITUATION.

(Editorial in *Wall Street Journal*, August 4.)

Referring to the article in the current number of the *North American Review* on the anthracite coal situation, written by Mr. Willcox, President of the Delaware & Hudson Company, the *Sun* points out that Mr. Willcox on behalf of the coal operators considers the present agreement with the miners entirely satisfactory, and is willing to have it continued. Mr. Willcox says:

> "The employers have no desire to disturb these results, which have been so painfully and expensively reached by arbitration, and are perfectly willing to continue the present arrangements indefinitely."

The *Sun* thinks that Mr. Willcox undoubtedly speaks with authority, and that it is impossible to believe that he would speak in this fashion if the operators contemplated any steps in the direction of changing the present position to the disadvantage of the miners. It professes to see, in the steps taken by Mr. Mitchell to strengthen the union, evidence that the miners intend to fight for something better than present conditions. It is unable to account for the activity of the union on the theory of self-defense merely because, as it says, "where no attack is contemplated no defense is necessary."

This strikes us as ridiculous. What would the *Sun*

JOHN MITCHELL.
President United Mine Workers of America.

say if the government of the United States, placing in evidence the declarations periodically made by representatives of foreign countries, that the one thing that foreign countries desired at all times was peace with the United States, were then to announce that as foreign countries contemplated no attack upon the United States, no defensive measures were necessary? We can imagine the screech with which our neighbor would greet a message from the President proposing to abolish the navy and dismantle the coast defenses. Yet it is precisely this that it expects of Mr. Mitchell as the head of the Miners' Union. It proposes that, on Mr. Willcox's statement that the operators are satisfied with present conditions, Mr. Mitchell should at once abandon his efforts to strengthen his union.

If we mistake not our neighbor is a firm believer in the advice to "speak softly, but carry a big stick." Can any one blame Mr. Mitchell for doing the best he knows how to maintain a strong union of mine workers in the anthracite regions? Does any one suppose that present wages and conditions would rule in the anthracite region if there had been no union? If there were no union in the anthracite regions to-day how long would present conditions last? We believe that there can be but one answer to these questions. Admitting that the union has been directly responsible for many infamous outrages, and regretting that unionism in general can not divest itself of direct responsibility and therefore guilt in this respect, we must, nevertheless, take things as we find them. And facts being facts, Mr. Mitchell is perfectly warranted in preparing for war so as to assure peace.

If the operators desire to enlist the public on their side of the case at the start, they can do so by formally and officially notifying everybody that they are willing to extend the present agreement in the regions. The public will then want to know from Mr. Mitchell where he stands, and why he stands there. But meanwhile no fair-minded man can find fault with Mr. Mitchell for looking after the future of his organization.

TRADE AGREEMENTS FORMED IN FOUR GREAT INDUSTRIES.

TYPICAL EXAMPLES OF THE SUCCESS AND INCREASE OF COLLECTIVE CONTRACTS BETWEEN LARGE EMPLOYERS AND LABOR ORGANIZATIONS.

THREE important national trade agreements, tending to secure harmonious relations between labor and capital in the great industries of iron and steel, inland water transportation, and iron molding, have recently been formed. These agreements are of importance even wider than these industries, since they affect favorably, because of their interwoven relations, many other spheres of production, and have a direct tendency to ensure stable conditions in every branch of trade. In addition to these, the Chicago, Burlington & Quincy Railroad, which has refused to recognize organized labor since its bitter and noted strike in 1886, has resumed the policy of conference and collective contracts with its employees.

IRON, STEEL AND TIN.

The assurance of peace in the iron and steel industry during the coming year, accompanied by the abandonment of the restriction of output by the Amalgamated Association of Iron, Steel and Tin Workers, is the highly important result of conferences in June and July between delegates of the organized wage earners

HENRY PHIPPS,
Director U. S. Steel Corporation.

and representatives of two of the largest employing corporations in the country. These are the Republic Iron and Steel Company, with which an agreement was reached at Detroit on June 9, and with the American Sheet and Tin Plate Company, which was signed at Pittsburg on July 3. Among those active in the negotiations on the part of the Amalgamated Association were its President, Theodore J. Shaffer, its President-elect, P. J. McArdle, and its Secretary and Treasurer, John Williams. The Republic Iron and Steel Company presented its terms through its President, Alexis W. Thompson, and its Vice-President, Archibald W. Houston; while on behalf of the American Sheet and Tin Plate Company, the scales were signed by its President, John A. Topping, and its First Vice-President, C. W. Bray. The new scale fixes eight hours as a day's work in finishing mills working three turns, which is to be done wherever practicable; and eight hours are to be a day's work in tin and black plate mills.

The Amalgamated Association also made the important concession that the rebate on tin plate for export, after August 1, 1905, shall be changed, should business conditions demand, from the present rate of 1½ per cent. to 3 per cent.

This is a concession involving such an intimate knowledge of trade conditions that the arrival at an equitable conclusion could result only from their frank and full discussion between representatives of the employing corporation and of the workers. In this case, organized wage-earners have agreed to reduce the labor cost of a product so that it could be sold as cheaply as by a foreign competitor. This product, tin plate, is bought in large quantities by the Standard Oil Company, for making cases in which oil is shipped abroad. Before the rebate in wages was granted, the American company was unable to compete with the tin plate makers of Wales. This concession was made originally only after months of investigation by the Amalgamated Association, which decided that this rebate should come out of the wages, not of the workers in tin sheet mills alone, but should be distributed among all members of the union, and be paid out of its national treasury.

In general terms, the wage scale of 1904-05 were adopted for the coming year in the agreement with the American Sheet and Tin Plate Company. The importance of this agreement is enhanced by the fact that its terms were immediately adopted by practically all of the independent employers.

In the agreement with the Republic Company, the workers secured a restoration for boiling iron of the scale of 1903-4, which the *Amalgamated Journal*, the official organ of the Amalgamated Association, says "is generally regarded as being the best scale that the boilers ever worked under." The muck scale was advanced at the same rate, and there were other minor advances. Of this agreement, the *Amalgamated Journal* says:

> The Republic company and the Amalgamated Association can well afford to give their respective representatives a vote of thanks for bringing to pass such an honorable and amicable settlement. It will undoubtedly result in knitting the company and the Association closer together, making each more willing to make concessions when conditions and circumstances demand.

It will be remembered that a symposium upon the Shorter Work Day, published in THE REVIEW for September, 1904, contained the opinions of a large number of representative wage-earners and editors of labor papers upon the advisability of granting certain concessions in return for fewer hours of work, among them being the removal of restrictions of output. At least a dozen of the writers in that symposium denied that such restrictions existed in their crafts, and declared that it is the sincere policy of unionism to place no limit upon the amount to be produced by any worker in a given time. But nearly a score of writers, admitting that restrictions do exist, declared that they should be removed for economic reasons. They pronounced restriction short-sighted, because increased productivity is essential to higher wages.

Still others, while agreeing with this general economic proposition, defended restriction of output in certain callings, as a protection to labor against excessive strain caused by "pace-makers," or against physical conditions of unusual hardship, or as an insurance of greater safety in construction upon whose soundness or stability human life depends, such as bridges, buildings, and ships.

The Amalgamated Association is a union that has hitherto been one of the conspicuous adherents to the restriction of output, on the ground that the labor in the manufacture of iron and steel is especially severe, and that, unless some limit were agreed upon, physical exhaustion and injury would result. The operation of the new plan in this industry will be observed with interest, both as to its results in the labor cost of production and in the welfare of the workers.

The *Amalgamated Journal* says:

> The new scale was negotiated under the most trying circumstances. The American Sheet and Tin Plate Company had determined upon certain departures from past conditions. The conferees representing the Association put up a strong fight against the Company's proposition, and it is safe to say that if arguments could have won the convention scale, it would have been accepted by the officials of the company. The conference committee deserves only praise from the rank and file for the strenuous fight they put up for the convention scale, and it was only when it became apparent that the officials of the American Sheet and Tin Plate Company were set in their purpose of acquiring the changes set forth in their proposition, and had been fortifying their position to press their claims to the point of operating their plants non-union, did the Association's conferees yield in as graceful a manner as possible. Circumstances were against declaring a strike at this time to sustain the convention's demand.

The *Labor World* of Pittsburg says of the agreement:

> The very fact that a union agreement has been made is a matter of great public moment and is of the utmost importance to trade unionists all over the country. It will tend more than anything else to aid in the re-strengthening of the A. A., and this is something that is of infinite worth to the Amalgamated Association and to all organized labor.
>
> Probably the most important feature of the new agreement between the A. A. and the American Company is the abolition of the limitation of the output rule. This is not only a step in the right direction, but goes toward removing one of the most damaging objections to so-called trade union policy. This limitation of output rule has for years been a blemish on the economic wisdom of the association. It has afforded argument, and powerful argument, to the bitterest foes of trade unionism. It has always, in view of the fact of a limitation of hours of work, been utterly devoid of the support of logic and argument. It has caused immeasurable trouble, and has, in fact, almost brought the association itself to complete destruction. It will require years for the A. A. to redeem the injury that the folly of this rule has imposed upon it.
>
> Now that this limitation of output rule has been obliterated, do not let us overlook the fact that it is due to President Shaffer more than to anyone else that the absurd condition has been discarded. He has valiantly and ably opposed the rule within the ranks of the association. While he could have made his advocacy more public, and thus more forcible, he has yet preached an unpopular proposition with vigor among his fellows. For years it has been a decidedly unpopular work among the rank and file of the organization to oppose this limitation of output rule. At the recent annual convention of the A. A. the continuance of the rule was upheld by a large majority, and even in face of the opposition to it of President Shaffer. So that let the retiring president have all of the credit due him for the disappearance of an exceedingly mischievous and highly unsound rule.

The *National Labor Tribune*, also of Pittsburg, another labor journal, takes a somewhat different view of the industrial result of the removal of restriction:

> The agreement reached between the A. A. conference committee and the representatives of the American Sheet and Tin Plate Company in this city on Monday, is one of the most momentous in the history of the Amalgamated Association. This is not only because it averts a strike, but because of the terms of the agreement itself, which provides for the abolition of the limit on output. There has been no article in the constitution of the Amalgamated Association that has been more stubbornly adhered to than this one. The refusal to remove the limitation has resulted in numerous lockouts of late years. It has probably lost the association a number of the mills controlled by the combine, and it looked very much as if a continued adherence to the limitation would provoke an early fight with some of the largest independent manufacturers, who claimed that they could no longer afford to stick to the association scale on this account. There has undoubtedly been a powerful combination of circumstances pressing the association to recede from its former position.

THEODORE J. SHAFFER,
President Amal. Asso. Steel & Tin Workers.

> While for some time foreshadowed, therefore, the removal of the limitation is still somewhat of a surprise. Its ultimate consequences are hard to foresee. It is, of course, a material advantage to the manufacturer. It means that the men in the mills will be subjected to a greater strain than ever, and the man who cannot do a yeoman's work will not long survive the increased severity of the struggle. There will probably be a very considerable increase of production at once, and we think it reasonable to suppose that in the end the workers will be doing a great deal more for a good deal less pay. Naturally, too, the increased average output per man will decrease proportionately the number of men for whom there is employment.
>
> It is the old story of machinery replacing labor over again, and it is not necessary to follow the matter further here. We are told that the machinery which displaces labor always requires more labor than it displaces. This seems paradoxical, but let us hope it will prove true in the present case.

GREAT LAKES SHIPPING INDUSTRIES.

This year has witnessed a renewal of the annual agreement between the International Longshoremen, Marine and Transport Workers' Association and the Dock Managers at Lake Erie ports. This has proved one of the most successful of trade agreements in the United States, in preventing strikes and lockouts, while it is one of the most far-reaching in its pacific effects. The Longshoremen's Association, of which Daniel J. Keefe is President, covers more territory than any other labor organization in the world, extending throughout the inland commerce of Canada and the United States and into the ports of two oceans, the Gulf of Mexico and Central America; while it maintains fraternal relations with corresponding organizations in Great Britain and Europe. It was organized by Mr. Keefe in 1882, and its wage-scales have been advanced an average of 60 per cent. since 1895. Its agreement with the Lake Erie dock managers covers thirty-nine divisions of trade, but its essential provisions are uniform.

This agreement is reached at an annual conference between representatives of the union and of the organized employers. The delegates from both sides to this conference are vested with full power, so that no confirmation of their conclusions is required. A marked characteristic of this conference is that the various subjects to be included in the agreement are previously referred to committees of the union. Before these committees, union men present the employers' side of the case. By this method, the union conferees, when they meet the representatives of the employers, are prepared to discuss every article of the proposed contract, both from their own and the employers' point of view. This preliminary process conduces greatly to the dignity and harmony of the annual conference. Every demand advanced by either side has been thoroughly discussed in advance, and the labor delegates are not likely to present demands to the employers whose justice they have not been able to prove before a committee of their fellow-craftsmen. In the conference, each article of the contract is first adopted by a majority vote and then confirmed by a unanimous vote. In this way the will of the majority is made binding upon all. Any subject not covered by the agreement, and any dispute as to its interpretation is subject to arbitration, and work must continue pending the decision, which both sides are pledged to accept. The principal contract and the local contracts formed in accordance with its provisions are neatly printed in compact form, and every worker is furnished with a copy, so that he may refer at any moment to its exact language.

This conference is also noteworthy for its yearly emphasis of the inviolability of the contract. The Longshoremen's Association is often cited by employers as one of the best examples of the responsibility of unions for keeping contracts. Any local union violating its contract is subject to expulsion. Not only has

H. COULBY,
Chairman Lake Carriers' Association.

this penalty been rigidly enforced, but in the case of one recalcitrant union, the Longshoremen's Association, being unable to furnish all the union labor required, sent non-union men to fill the places of the men who had been expelled for striking in violation of the agreement.

One article provides for cases of unusual work in these words:

> It is understood that occasionally when any unusual work arises in isolated cases not covered by this agreement, the men, when called upon, shall perform such labor, and the compensation therefor shall be determined and adjusted between the representatives of the local organizations and the dock managers or owners, and in event of any disagreement shall be arbitrated.

The joint conference this year adopted a resolution declaring that the principle covered in this article is:

> That any and all contracts made between the local manager and the men directly involved shall be held inviolate for all work not specifically covered in exhibits attached to and made part of this contract, and
>
> That any one trying to break such agreement or in any way interfering with its performance, shall be barred as a non-conformist, and shall not be permitted to work under this contract, and in all cases work shall not be interrupted on any account.

Resolutions were also adopted requiring all grievances or suggested changes in the contract to be submitted to the chairman of the dock managers and the president of the union prior to the next conference; and that any future addition to the contract must receive the two-thirds vote of the delegates of the conference.

The agreement is for the navigation season of 1905, and also covers winter work from December 1, 1905, until May 1, 1906. Wage schedules are attached as part of the contract. All employes are to be members of the local organization whenever such men can be had who can perform the work. When such men can not be had, the dock managers have the right to secure any other men who can perform the work satisfactorily, until members of the union can be secured. No man shall be discharged without just cause, and any man discharged shall be notified of the cause.

If any controversies or grievances can not be settled by the local representatives of the union and employers, they shall be arbitrated by choosing a third disinterested man, the decision of any two to be final. "If the representative of the local organization and the representative of the dock managers or owners can not agree upon a third man, then each side shall choose a disinterested man—the two disinterested men thus chosen to choose a third disinterested man, and said three men shall constitute a board of arbitration, and the decision of a majority of said three shall be final, and all parties shall abide thereby." This board must meet within ten days after the difference arises.

No beer or intoxicating liquor shall be brought upon the property of the dock managers. No man under the influence of liquor shall be permitted upon their premises. No employe shall leave the dock during working hours without permission. Pure and fresh drinking water with oatmeal and ice shall be provided on the dock.

STOVE-MANUFACTURING INDUSTRY.

One of the most important of the national trade agreements, which has been ratified with one important modification for the coming year, is that between the Stove Founders' National Defense Association and the Iron Molders' Union of North America. The modification relates to the ratio of apprentices, which has long been a subject of debate between the organized employers and the union. This year, the representatives of the Molders' Union, in conference with a committee of the Founders' Association, agreed to a considerable increase in the ratio.

As its name indicates, the National Defense Association was formed to fight. That was twenty years ago. Since then, while still militant for the rights of its members, the association has demonstrated that the trade agreement, with its provisions for arbitration, is efficient in preventing strikes and lockouts, or in affording a method for adjusting troubles when they do occur.

In this industry, the organizations of both employers and wage-earners have shown a progressive appreciation of the inviolability of contracts. During the last year, for example, seventy-one disputes were adjusted through the method provided by the national agreement. In twelve of these cases, the molders and the mounters had struck, but in accordance with the terms of their agreements were obliged by their national officers to resume work before their grievances could be adjusted. In two cases, employers suspended operations, and they, also, were compelled by the officers of the National Defense Association to cease their lockouts while their complaints against their men were being adjusted under the terms of their agreements. All of the other cases were settled without even temporary resort to either strike or lockout. In the words of Chauncey H. Castle, President of the Founders' Association: "In all cases, the letter and spirit of the agreements have been carried out, so that peace and harmony have prevailed. This is because the local as well as the national officers of the unions have become more and more familiar with the objects of the agreements, and more and more impressed with the prime importance of their strict observance; while upon our side, we have admonished our members against resorting to the lockout in violation of the trade agreement."

Joseph F. Valentine, President of the Iron Molders' Union of North America, declares: "Our trade agreement proves every year a practicable and efficient method of promoting peace in our industry, through the adjustment of grievances, by conference between representatives of the organized employers and workers, and, when necessary, by arbitration."

To these two Presidents are first referred for settlement disputes as to subjects not covered in local agreements, when a majority of the molders in the foundry concerned are union men. In case the two Presidents can not agree, the dispute is referred to a permanent conference committee of six, composed of three members of each side, the decision of a majority to be binding.

A NEW RAILWAY AGREEMENT.

The Chicago, Burlington & Quincy Railroad Company is a recent example of the conviction on the part of a large employing corporation that it is a sane and wise policy to enter into contractual relations with organized labor. Ever since the great strike on its system in 1888, this company had ignored the national brotherhood organizations of railway employes. But during six weeks, from the middle of June until the end of July, a board composed of representatives of the Brotherhood of Locomotive Firemen formulated their propositions and held a series of conferences in Chicago with officials of the Burlington corporation, which resulted in the signing of a schedule, covering wages and conditions of work for the ensuing year, satisfactory both to the corporation and the employes.

The Chicago *Chronicle*, a journal severely and usually adversely critical of organized labor, said in its report of the successful conclusion of these conferences:

"So quietly did this organization of locomotive firemen attend to their business during this meeting that few guests of the hotel were aware of its presence. The members were in the halls, in the restaurants, and everywhere in the hotel, but neither by word nor act did they disclose their identity or the object of their mission.

"The impression this board made on those familiar with its work was that if labor unions and officials of corporations met in the same friendly spirit that actuated this body and the representatives of the company that the millennium in the labor world would be at hand, and that strikes and their attendant riots would be at an end.

"The board, after completing its schedule, met in conference for several days with the officials of the Burlington. The schedule was thoroughly discussed and the arguments were sometimes exciting, as might have been expected. However, it was clear sailing from the start when Mr. Daniel Willard, Second Vice-President of the Burlington system, said:

"'I am not opposed to labor unions, and I was a member of one myself. I was a member of the Brotherhood of Locomotive Engineers before any of you men were here. I am familiar with most of the questions that bring you here.'

"This remark was followed, in an equally generous spirit, by N. C. Allen, chairman of the board, who said:

"'We have been fair both to ourselves and to the company, and followed the policy of our organization along the line of conservatism. We think that, after due

DANIEL J. KEEFE,
President Longshoremen's Association.

deliberation, we have decided on rules that will be a benefit to the men and also to the company. It is the policy of our organization if we find men that will not look out for the interest of the company the same as if it were their own organization, we will not stand for them.'"

The Burlington at the various conferences was represented by Mr. Willard, Mr. Holdridge, Mr. Gruber, Mr. Clark, Mr. Torrey, Mr. Smith, Mr. Judson, Mr. Byron, Mr. Ross, and Mr. Nutt.

The protective board represented the 1,700 firemen who are employed on 9,000 miles of railroad, and whose compensation monthly runs from $80 to $140 each. The members of this board were:

> N. C. Allen, Chairman; Norman Allen, J. Hannahan, Grand Master of the Brotherhood of Locomotive Firemen; Willie Hannahan Finley, J. S. Ford, secretary; Otto Schultz, vice-chairman; Maurice Larson, alternate, secretary and treasurer; W. K. Hess, F. O. Paulus, M. J. Houlihan, William McCormack, O. A. Brouse, W. S. Bixler, J. M. Barber, A. M. Deen, J. E. Cambronn, Howard Timmel, Frank Armstrong, C. W. Tillen, A. O. Cockingham, F. L. Bradley, Thomas J. O'Neill, R. V. Brook, Thomas Flock, R. E. Tucker, C. W. Reisinge.

The conferences ended with a display of good feeling between the officials of the Burlington company and the representatives of the Firemen's Brotherhood. The protective board adopted resolutions expressing its appreciation of "the invaluable services rendered by our worthy Grand Master, John J. Hannahan, in obtaining the best pay schedule west of Chicago." Mr. Hannahan is a member of the Executive Committee of the National Civic Federation.

There can be no hope for winning untimely and irrational strikes. A just cause always meets a responsive public sentiment, without which no strike can be won, and for which an irrational strike can not appeal, and it is necessarily lost. Such was the Interborough strike. It was apparently an unnecessary and untimely strike, and did not appeal to the public. It was lost.—*Motorman and Conductor.*

ORGANIZED LABOR AND THE ISTHMIAN CANAL.

PRESIDENT GOMPERS, OF THE AMERICAN FEDERATION OF LABOR, INSISTS UPON HUMANE CONDITIONS AND PROTESTS AGAINST EMPLOYING COOLIE LABOR.

THE President of the American Federation of Labor, Samuel Gompers, delivered an address recently before the Trades Union Social Club of New York, upon the relation of organized labor in the United States to the construction of the Isthimian Canal. This address was delivered upon the evening of the day of the sailing for the Isthmus of the two Welfare experts. This official adoption of Welfare Work by the United States Government received the hearty approval of the President of the American Federation of Labor.

Mr. Gompers spoke as follows:

Mr. Chairman, and Members of the Trades Union Social Club:

You will understand the pleasure it is for me to be here and address you, especially on a subject of such importance as the one to consider which this meeting is held. It is not necessary to criticize the formal selection of the Panama route for the construction of the canal. I don't know that we would change the route even if we desired. I don't know that it is desirable, or, even if desirable, whether we can with advantage even discuss it. I think it is agreed, however, that the greatest difficulties in the construction of the canal will be met upon the Isthmus of Panama. Its climatic conditions, its geographical situation, the well-known diseases, the ills and the ailments, to which the men who go there are subject, are known to every one.

It is claimed that there is no obstacle so great that the American people can not cope with and eventually overcome it. And, in truth, there is a long line of achievements to the credit of our people. We might look to many of the tropical countries, some of which have come under the jurisdiction of our government, in which in former years and under the old régime diseases of this same character marked their victims by the thousands; and as soon as we have entered those regions, we have, if not entirely eliminated the germs of these great awful climatic diseases, reduced them almost to a minimum, and the possibilities for their future elimination seem promising, so that they may be as free from them or very nearly so as we are free from them in the main land of the United States.

The construction of the canal, all men are agreed, [illegible] world's great progress. That it [illegible] to industry and commerce, bring [illegible] who are now remote from each [illegible]ser proximity, by reason of being able to reach each other more readily; that it will be beneficial to the country's great commerce—to the carrying of the great commerce of the world more readily—is easily understood and accepted by all; that it will make for better opportunities and conditions and tend to the uplifting of the world, I think is also agreed. But in the building of the canal, great as its opportunities will be when completed, largely contributing toward the world's progress as it will, wonderful with its potentialities as it will be, there is one thing that must not be lost sight of. The coral reefs are very wonderful; but the millions and millions and millions of insect lives that have perished in making those reefs must not be repeated or duplicated in the loss; in the sacrifice of human lives in the building even of the interoceanic canal. There are some achievements that are too costly in human life even to be ventured.

The organized expression of the American people, our Federal Government, has undertaken this task. I am always glad of things that may be helpful. I believe to-day that in the great undertaking we must be careful in our adverse criticism, lest we overstep that which is fair, which may result in harm to our own integral life, and lay us open to the criticism of the peoples of other countries.

I think we are all agreed that in the industries of our time there are too many lives lost and too many limbs hazarded, and the health of too many of our people placed in jeopardy; and I think we also believe and hope and are confident that, as the workingmen of our country and our time shall organize, and as we shall impress upon the minds of our fellow-citizens the necessity for more humane conditions under which labor shall be performed, there shall be greater precautions for the health and life and limbs of our fellow-workmen. We shall make greater progress upon these lines. That we have accomplished much, all of those who have studied, as well as those who have lived during the industrial progress and development of the organization of labor, will agree. But yet, one can almost count with a degree of accuracy the number of men who lose their limbs, whose health is undermined and even destroyed, who even lose their lives, by reason of our modern methods of industrial and commercial life. And we aim to improve the conditions of labor so that it shall not be so hazardous to either our lives or limbs or health.

We don't undertake to say that we shall stop industry because it involves the loss of life or of limb or of health even to as large a degree as it does now. We insist that there shall be better protection against machinery; that there shall be better sanitation; that there shall be better hygienic conditions; and shorter hours of labor, giving us liberty and more leisure and time for the recuperation of our health and of our strength; and that we shall have higher wages with which we may buy the things that contribute to our health and our strength, physical, mental, and moral.

I want to approach the subject of the Panama Canal and in its construction in the light of that thought that I have tried to express. We want the canal; we are agreed upon that. At this time, there is no choice as to the route. The Panama route has been chosen. We are committed to that. And as long as there is, I suppose, a fair chance for the prosecution of the work, though under adverse influences, there will be no change in the route. In Panama, and throughout that great miasmatic country through which this canal has to be dug, life is not congenial. The conditions

SAMUEL GOMPERS.
President American Federation of Labor.

are not such as contribute to health and comfort; are not such, I imagine, as would allow one to regard it as a health resort. In the Convention of the American Federation of Labor two years ago, a resolution was passed, and I think unanimously, declaring that the construction of the canal is a great world's benefit; and then it was declared that the preference should be given to the laborers of America. Now, if we want the work, I take it that we shall be compelled to submit to some of the privations, some of the difficulties, and that we shall also enjoy some of the advantages and pleasures that come from organized society and civilized labor. No man has the right to assume to take employment on the Panama Canal and expect that every Sunday he can visit Coney Island. It won't do for our men who may take this work to expect to go to a roof garden in the evenings. The man who undertakes work of that sort must realize that for the work in which he is engaged he will have to make some sacrifices of what we in our civilized lives expect to enjoy as a recreation after our day's work is done. I don't want any one to imagine that I harbor in my mind the idea that the condition of the American workman is such that he enjoys invariably Coney Island and roof gardens and all that sort of thing; but I have tried to put it rather extravagantly, so as to emphasize my thought.

I want to repeat that the lives of our American workmen are too valuable to be sacrificed upon the scheme of building the canal, and, further, that the conditions of labor in and around the canal for the workmen must be such as to make life and the conditions of life at least tolerable, and that no man shall feel that he in his zeal for the world and for our civilization has made his life a burden and not worth living.

I have been in correspondence with a number of people employed near and on the canal. I want to be entirely frank with you and say that the date of the last letter which I received is more than two months ago, and of whatever change in conditions may have occurred between then and now, I can not speak. I can only speak of the conditions up to date of the letter which I last received. I want to read that letter to you:

> I read a florid interview with one of your labor union friends in which he told me of the arrival of the two Bates brothers in Chicago and of their coming to Panama. I believe that at the time he said that he would overrun the Isthmus with union men at salaries of $190 and $165 per month, with bonuses of $1 per cubic yard for every yard over 125,000 per month which their shovels excavated.
>
> If you want to have some facts in regard to the situation here, listen to the following: The union should not rush men down here with the idea that they are going to get high wages and an easy snap. Every man should have his contract hard and fast before he comes here.
>
> In regard to the Bates brothers. The steam shovel engineer received $190 and the crane man $165 per month. There are only two other engineers and two other crane men receiving such salaries in the whole Isthmus. The six men are, outside the heads of departments, the highest salaried men in the employ of the Commission. In the Rocky Mountains, where they operate their shovels, they will be very lucky if they get out even 20,000 cubic yards per month.
>
> The steam drill men who work with the shovels receive $50 per month. The pit men receive $75. A foreman of drillers receives $75. A fireman on the steam shovel receives $75. These salaries do not compare very favorably with the ones in the States.
>
> There are other disadvantages. Board at Culebra, the station where the excavating is being done, is $21 per month. Quarters are provided by the Commission in all except a few cases.
>
> All except the professional men and officers work ten hours per day. Ten hours here means starting at 6 o'clock in the morning and keeping at it in the hot sun until 11.30. The afternoon hours are from 1 to 5.30. Salaries are but little better in the States, and the hours are hardly what can be called a union scale. In Panama and Colon the rates of board are even higher. The men are not provided with quarters, but are given an allowance of 8 per cent. of their salaries for that purpose, which is in all cases inadequate. Rents are increasing weekly.
>
> An experienced machinist, blacksmith, boiler-maker, plumber, carpenter, mason or such, receives 45 cents per hour and works under the same conditions. He will not be given transportation to or from the States, and will be paid only for the time he works.
>
> A general foreman, and there are not a half dozen on the Isthmus in these trades, gets $150 per month. An ordinary foreman gets from $83.33 to $125, and an assistant foreman gets from $50 to $75 per month.
>
> The above wages are paid in gold, and only to Americans. Subordinate employes are paid in silver, which is $2.16 silver for $1 in gold. Not a few Americans are on the silver pay roll.
>
> In the mechanical and building trades the foremen get 60 cents per hour in silver. An assistant foreman gets 50 cents, an artisan gets 25 to 40 cents. Ordinary laborers get either 15 or 17½ cents silver per hour.
>
> No union man should come down here with the hilarious idea that he is going to get high wages and an easy time. If he has a contract he may be all right. Most of them, even with contracts, are dissatisfied and anxious to get back.
>
> I have not mentioned the malaria, which every one gets, the yellow fever, which comes to more than a few, the scorpions and the tarantulas, and many other things which give local color to the country.

I can not understand why there should have been any question raised as to whether the eight-hour law of the United States should apply to the work in the digging of the canal. Is it not agreed, at least among a large portion of our fellow-citizens, that the eight-hour day for Government work is long enough? Not even the worst antagonist of organized labor has made any attempt to change the law and practise of the eight-hour workday in the Government employes. If eight hours' work a day is sufficient in the United States, with its comparatively advantageous climate, how much more essential is it that no longer than eight hours should constitute a day's work on the Isthmus of Panama?

Organized labor has given me an opportunity of visiting several parts of this world, and among them Cuba and Porto Rico. They are considered as a part of the tropics, and yet any one who knows, who has been there, in either of those islands, knows that one of the great causes of the enfeebled condition of the workingmen, heretofore of Cuba and still of Porto Rico, is due to the fact that they work abnormally long hours. And a climatic comparison between Cuba and Porto Rico on the one hand, and the Isthmus of Panama on the other, is as like our seashore and the climate of the netherlands. While men work and live, and till the ground from which come lethal fumes, surely eight hours ought to be enough to constitute a day's work.

And now, I want to speak in regard to the employment of Japanese and Chinese on the canal. I have no antipathy to the Chinaman. In fact, so far as he is a man, I have no antipathy to him at all. The objection that I, in common with all members of organized labor, in common with every thinking citizen of our country, entertain to the Chinaman is this—that he is a cheap man, and that he and his fellows are entirely incompatible with the civilization of the people of our country.

I don't want now to discuss this Chinese problem. It is too big to discuss in a few minutes. But I want to say a word or two regarding the so-called Chinese boycotts of American made goods. A few months ago a committee of American merchants called upon the

(Concluded on page 20.)

THE IMMIGRATION PROBLEM.

A SYMPOSIUM TREATING OF SOME OF IT'S IMPORTANT PHASES BY WRITERS OF WIDELY VARIANT VIEWS AND DIVERSE CONCLUSIONS.

WE present upon the following pages a collection of articles bearing upon The Problem of Immigration. Each of the writers has approached that subject from his individual point of view, and it is inevitable that each should arrive at his own conclusions. When grouped together in this way, the articles afford an interesting opportunity for the economic student to compare opposing premises, different methods of reasoning, and several plans of treatment proposed. It is to be observed that the writers are all agreed in their recognition of the importance of their problem and in their patriotic desire to find a sound solution.

BISHOP POTTER ON IMMIGRATION.

He Regards Equity and Freedom from Racial Prejudice Essential Elements in its Restriction.

BISHOP HENRY C. POTTER, of New York, in an interview on August 6, declared that the question of immigration ranks as one of four great civic problems uppermost just now in the minds of thinking citizens, the three others being municipal ownership, the relation of labor and capital and the negro question. The Bishop, who is a member of the "general public" section of the Executive Committee of the National Civic Federation, thought that the restriction of immigration is a subject to be "sifted mentally apart from bias and partisan conviction" at the National Conference in December, called by that organization. The Bishop further said:

"The question of the restriction of immigration is one which, so far as the constituent principles of our American republic are concerned, touches the foundations. Originally the republic was declared to be a refuge for the downtrodden and oppressed of every nation, race, and creed. Of late years in the interests of particular classes of labor we have enacted certain restrictive laws which have had in them conspicuous elements of injustice, and which are now, in the boycott of American products, which is almost universal in China, producing their appropriate results.

"There has not been in the history of American politics a more dramatic illustration of the punishment of a political party or parties for special legislation than this. A much larger interest, and one which at the same time is inexplicably allied to the labor interest, is to be punished for the folly of a special legislation which aimed to protect a particular class.

"The questions which now confront the American people are twofold: Whether (a) there should be any restriction to immigration, and (b) if so, upon what that restriction shall be based. It is not only perfectly competent, but perfectly equitable for a nation to restrict its immigration in its own interests. Self-preservation, we are wont to say, is the first law of nature. The American Republic exists for the illustration and propagation and the maintenance of certain ideals of civic government and of personal freedom. The invasion of a race which would destroy these would be a sufficient ground for resisting such invasion and excluding the invader, and no less would this be true of moral standards. The basis of high political ideals is a moral basis. The nation rests upon the cornerstone of the eternal righteousness, and a race which by its moral or religious standards would assault these would strike at the foundations of the Republic. Therefore, some restriction of immigration has in it the essential quality of equity.

"But, the moment this has been said, it should be remembered that this restriction can only be equitable when it is impartial. Its basis should be certain requirements which demand equally of all and every race certain qualifications for American citizenship. I believe that a common law which bore equally upon all those various races and peoples that are knocking at our doors would command the sympathy of the Republic and the votes of the upright men; but any proposed legislation must have in it the essential notes of equity and absolute freedom from racial prejudice."

HOW SHALL WE SELECT OUR IMMIGRANTS?

An Argument in Support of Proposed Additions to the Classes now Excluded.

(By Robert De C. Ward, of Cambridge, Mass.; Republished by permission of *Charities*.)

WE are now witnessing an annual immigration of about a million people, taken largely, as formerly was not the case, from countries that are strangers to the institutions and traditions on which our republic was founded. When present methods of transportation are further developed, we may see the annual arrival of two or three times that number, largely derived from countries still more remote and alien to our methods of government. In the face of such facts it is only those who seem to the writer to be optimistic beyond the bounds of reason, or the hopelessly incautious, or those selfishly interested, who do not say to themselves that the stream must be further checked and regulated.

We can not justly charge with prejudice against the alien those who wish a more careful selection of the fathers and mothers of future American children. We can not count as un-American those who, with the late Gen. Francis A. Walker, believe that this stream of "pipe line immigration" will, if left to itself, flow on "as long as any difference of economic level exists between our own population and that of the most degraded communities abroad." We can not justly call those narrow or inhuman who see the danger of having our future standard of citizenship, and the future physical condition of our people, determined by the greed of a few transportation companies.

HENRY C. POTTER
Bishop, Protestant Episcopal Church.

We still welcome, as we have always welcomed, those immigrants who, however humble, add to the health and to the sum of good citizenship of our country, but we have the undoubted right to restrict, regulate, or prohibit any alien immigration that proves a menace to the standard of living of our wage-earners or a danger to our democratic form of government, an influence tending to pull down rather than build up our national health and physique.

In trying to effect a solution of this problem, it is obvious that we must bring about united action, on the part of those who believe that the time has come for something to be done. As a step in this direction the writer has given below a brief explanation of a number of measures that have most strongly recommended themselves to those who have within the last few years given study and labor to the subject of practical legislative remedies and to their application.

Means should be taken to assist in the more complete enforcement of our present laws. Most of these laws are excellent so far as they go, and so far as they can be enforced by officials, hitherto largely unsupported by the public in the face of interested and often unscrupulous opposition. * * * Our only safeguard against endless fraud, dishonesty, deceit, and political pull is popular support of those who are trying to administer the laws. No body of Federal officials deserves as hearty support as do the men of the United States Immigration Service. Nor is there any body whose work should be watched with more jealous care.

Our immigration laws should be amended, and there should be further additions to the excluded classes. Many suggestions have been made concerning further restriction. Some, such as consular inspection abroad, or the admission of aliens on a five-year probationary period, would be clumsy, expensive, and largely ineffective. Other measures, such as a large head-tax of $50 or $100, are open to criticism as carrying exclusion too far. Others, such as a wholesale distribution of aliens over our country districts, are palliatives rather than cures, and can not of themselves solve the immigration problem. No one can doubt that a well-directed and intelligent distribution of aliens of strong physique over farming districts where they will find work which they are fitted to perform, and where they are wanted, should be encouraged. But it must be remembered that the immigration which we most need to check is made up of people who are not fitted for an agricultural life; that our agricultural communities do not desire a wholesale and indiscriminate invasion of Slav, Latin, Hebrew, and Asiatic immigrants, but want something else; that the effect upon the sections in which the distribution takes place is not always for the best, and that the immigration which we are now getting is crowding out the class of immigrants who used to be in the majority, and who went readily into the country. In the corn belt of the West, as has recently been shown, the newer immigrants, because of their lower standards of living, have an advantage over the native-born farmers. Again, the immigration of Italians and other alien laborers into the South will doubtless cause a migration of the negroes to the cities—a result which those familiar with the conditions of negroes now congested in cities can not fail to view with apprehension. Further, to attempt to relieve our slums by dispersing their inhabitants, without at the same time further restricting the numbers of newer aliens who will pour in, is like trying to keep a boat bailed out without stopping the leak.

No distribution of immigrants should be thought of if the States to which they are to be sent do not welcome them. A canvass of the different States, made within six months, brought forth from the officials to whom the inquiries were sent a vigorous protest against the shipment of southern and eastern Europeans from the city slums into their States. In the South to-day there is need of pickers in the cotton fields in some sections, of skilled workmen in factories in others, and of mine laborers in others. The demand for "cheap" labor without regard to the effects which the wholesale importation of "cheap" laborers will have upon the community comes from a comparatively limited number of capitalists, and from certain Southern railroads. The majority of the thinking people of the South, who know something about the evils which have come in the train of the newer alien immigration in the [illegible] look with favor upon the wholesale [illegible] cheap and ignorant alien labor. [illegible] might, it is true, give a temporary relief [illegible] bring in its wake, in the future, [illegible] complex problems which the South has not yet had to face. * * *

1. *The head-tax should be raised.* The act of March 3, 1903, increased this tax to two dollars. This money is paid by the steamship companies, and is simply added to the price of the passage ticket. The immigrant himself knows nothing of the payment. The head-tax is paid into the United States treasury, forming what is known as the "immigrant fund," and is spent in maintaining the immigration service. This head-tax should be increased to twenty-five dollars. The chief reason for advocating such an increase is that we have no other means of keeping the steerage passage rate to the United States at a figure which brings it somewhere near the rate to South America and other countries to which immigrants are likely to go. When a steamship war is on, the steerage rates may drop to ten dollars, or even less, as they did in the summer of 1904, and as they seem likely to do again. Such a reduction immediately brings a large influx of desperately poor and generally undesirable aliens, as was the case last year. An increased head-tax means a larger "immigrant fund," and that means more effective administration of existing laws and better care of the immigrants. It is objected to an increased head-tax that the honesty and character of an immigrant do not depend upon his ability to pay a certain sum of money, and that undesirable persons, criminals for example, might easily pay the tax. In answer to this objection it need only be pointed out that the higher head-tax is not to be substituted for the other restrictive clauses of existing law; it is to be added to them. Criminals are already excluded by law. They would be excluded—if detected—even if they could pay the extra passage money necessitated by a larger head-tax. An increased head-tax is intended as a means—the only means within our reach—of keeping the steerage passage above the level of pauper rates, and is one of the few practicable methods of reducing the flow of undesirable immigration to a point where it can be properly assimilated. The United States should not be chosen by an immigrant, as it now often is, because it is the cheapest country to go to. It should be se-

(Continued on page 15.)

this investigation are outlined in the announcement made in the newspaper press and published upon another page of THE REVIEW, while the personnel of the Commission is an assurance that the inquiry will be conducted in the interest of no one school, party or faction, but will be directed to placing argument upon a solid basis of fact.

The general subject readily divides itself into various systems, under each of which an accurate comparison is practicable of various economic, industrial and civic results. The question is so large that the examination of its several phases will doubtless be assigned by the Commission to subcommissions, carefully chosen with a view to educing "the truth, the whole truth, and nothing but the truth." It is expected that one subcommission, composed of about nine members, will spend at least three months in Europe, upon a thorough study of the results of Public Ownership and Operation. The collection and publication of these reports will be a substantial aid to the crystallization of sound opinion upon one of the greatest questions affecting the industrial, financial, and moral welfare of communities and nations.

THE IMMIGRATION CONFERENCE.

For the first time since the earliest colonists set foot upon the land destined to become the United States of America, a National Conference, composed of officially designated representatives of these States, is to consider the problem of immigration in its relation to our industrial and social prosperity. The response to the call for the Conference from students of this problem reveals an expert appreciation of its growing importance and a confident expectation that the gathering that will convene at our largest port of entry on December 6 and 7 will make intelligent progress toward its solution. In its promotion of this Conference, the National Civic Federation, as an organization, has committed itself to no attitude of approval or opposition as to any of the propositions concerning the regulation, restriction, suspension, exclusion, or encouragement of immigration that have been advocated. The Conference will be an open forum for debate by the best thought of the country in the hope that an earnest thrashing out of every phase of the subject may result in definite recommendations of far-reaching consequence and value to our present and future national welfare.

The Governors are accepting the invitation to appoint delegates to the National Immigration Conference in such number as to make it certain that practically every State in the Union will be ably represented. Their letters indicate the intention of many Governors to attend in person with their delegations.

We present in this issue a symposium of informatory articles upon the immigration problem by writers whose studies of several of its phases have led them to widely different conclusions.

WELFARE WORK ON THE ISTHMUS.

The Isthmian Canal Commission has received general and merited commendation for its decision to introduce Welfare Work into the stupendous enterprise which the Government of the United States has undertaken. In fact, under the general title of Welfare Work may be grouped practically all of the preliminary preparations, in the way of sanitation, housing and commissariat, for which operations in the actual construction of the Canal have been temporarily halted. It is conceded that the delay incident to these end the Commission engaged two experts, furnished by the Welfare Department of the National Civic Federation, to investigate the needs and opportunities in the Canal Zone for the recreation of the workers, and to embody their recommendations in a report. The Welfare experts selected, W. E. C. Nazro and Edward A. Moffett, were peculiarly fitted to render the Government this valuable service.

The importance of the realization of this purpose upon the Isthmus was forcibly presented to an audience of representatives of organized labor in a recent address by Samuel Gompers, which we publish in this issue. The President of the American Federation of Labor utters a broad and high recognition of the importance of the canal to the commerce of the world; but he would have a due regard for the wholesome living of the workers and for the protection of occidental civilization accompany the bisecting of the Americas.

ANTHRACITE AND OTHER AGREEMENTS.

That the present conditions in the anthracite industry are pacific, and that sincere efforts will be made, on the part of both operators and workers to maintain peace when both the anthracite and bituminous agreements expire simultaneously, is indicated clearly by the statements of David Willcox, President of the Delaware & Hudson Railroad Company, and of John Mitchell, President of the United Mine Workers of America. The significance of President Willcox's statement, that the anthracite employers "are perfectly willing to continue the present arrangements indefinitely," is equaled by that of President Mitchell that a great strike would be "criminal," "without first exhausting every conceivable effort for a peaceful adjustment."

In connection with the process of conference and conciliation between operators and miners that is here suggested, we invite the attention of President Willcox, as well as of other large employers, to the accounts, in this issue of THE REVIEW, of typical trade agreements that have been formed this year in four great industries. These agreements are cited as representative of the growth of collective contracts. They are convincing witnesses to the success and the increase of that method of industrial peace. Such facts are not in harmony with President Willcox's view that "agreements of employment are fast reverting to their natural form of arrangements between the parties concerned." Every year sees more employers who prefer to enter into contracts with organizations rather than with individual employes. We doubt that President Willcox really meant all that his language implies. He, of course, well knows that every large railroad in the country makes agreements with the railway Brotherhoods instead of with individuals, his own road being no exception.

A highly successful conference of Welfare Managers and Special Welfare Workers—those who have charge of any particular phase of Welfare Work, such as men's clubs, technical schools, lunch houses or relief departments—was held in Atlantic City, on July 25. An account of the proceedings will be published in the next issue of THE REVIEW.

The June number of THE REVIEW quoted an extract from an article by Luke McKenny, of the Wire Lathers' Union, setting forth the opposition of organized labor to Socialism. That article was originally printed in *The Mechanic*, New York, to which esteemed labor periodical we omitted, through an oversight, to give due credit.

THE ORIGIN OF "THE INTERCOLLEGIATE SOCIALIST SOCIETY" DISCLOSED.

ITS DEFENSE BY THOMAS WENTWORTH HIGGINSON, IN "HARPER'S WEEKLY," ANALYZED AND REFUTED.

(BY THE EDITOR.)

THE "Intercollegiate Socialist Society" will not capture American universities for revolution and anarchy. Its scheme would have been impossible in any event, and it did not threaten any real danger to our social and political structure.

But that men whose names are generally accepted as standing for culture and good citizenship should be permitted deliberately to announce such a project without rebuke would have been to ignore their public challenge to patriotism. It was necessary to consider that there are people in this country who esteem at least some of the signers of the call for the formation of a society to teach Socialism as serious, disinterested, high-minded philanthropists. It may be conceded that the signers are endowed with a large share of these qualities, but with them is now revealed the added fact that in so far as they are Socialists they are opposed to the institutions of this Republic.

A multitude of letters, received from university and college presidents and professors, from ministers of the gospel and from representative men in the professions, have thanked THE REVIEW not so much for its disclosure of the real aim of the projected society, which is generally ridiculed, but for its information as to the vigorous and successful opposition of organized labor to Socialism.

That exposure has called forth another kind of response—a response of mingled consternation, evasion, and abuse. The revelation in cold type of the unequivocal and undeniable purposes of Socialism has caused a fluttering among the flock of dilettante sympathizers with the effort to "undermine all society"; to "enact a terrible retribution upon the capitalist class, comparable to the French Revolution and the Paris Commune"; to "fire the heart and nerve the arm of rebellion"; to "confiscate all the possessions of the capitalist class"; etc., etc.

It was to be expected that the signers fully committed to the creed of Socialism would respond with vicious attacks upon the article. It was a plain, straightforward exposition of the doctrines which such a society would undertake to instill into the receptive minds of American youth, in the course of training for positions of leadership in the rising generation. It placed the signers of the call in the position of subscribing to those doctrines, since its language explicitly stated that the "undersigned" regarded the "aims and fundamental principles" of Socialism "with sympathy" and believed that "in them will ultimately be found the remedy for many far reaching economic evils."

But it is not what most of the signers may say that concerns the general public. The one man in the list whose signature was a surprise to those familiar with his standing in the literary and ethical circles of New England was Thomas Wentworth Higginson.

It is alone with his reply to a criticism in *Harper's Weekly* that we shall deal in this article. We reprint in full his response:

DUBLIN, N. H., *July* 14, 1905.

To the Editor of Harper's Weekly:

SIR,—I observe in a recent number of your valuable journal an expression of surprise that my name should be united with others in the formation of an "Intercollegiate Socialist School" which "aims to imbue the minds of the rising generation with Socialistic doctrines." This last phrase is your own, for I at least am connected with no organization for the purpose you here state. As to the names with which mine is united I am not concerned; as Theodore Parker used to say, "I am not particular with whom I unite in a good action." As to the object in view it is clearly enough stated in the call itself; the movement does not aim to produce Socialists, but to create students of Socialism.

It is based on the obvious fact that we are more and more surrounded by institutions, such as free schools, free text-books, free libraries, free bridges, free water-supplies, free lecture courses, even free universities, which were all called Socialistic when first proposed, and which so able a man as Herbert Spencer denounced as Socialism to his dying day. Every day makes it more important that this tendency should be studied seriously and thoughtfully, not left to demagogues alone. For this purpose our foremost universities should take the matter up scientifically, as has been done for several years at Harvard University, where there is a full course on "Methods of Social Reform—Socialism, Communism, the Single Tax," etc., given by Professor T. N. Carver. This is precisely what the "Intercollegiate Socialist School" aims at; and those who seriously criticize this object must be classed, I fear, with those medieval grammarians who wrote of an adversary "May God confound thee for thy theory of irregular verbs!"

I am, sir,

THOMAS WENTWORTH HIGGINSON.

We regret, Mr. Higginson, to be compelled to prove that most of the statements in your letter are wholly incorrect. We shall give you credit for not knowing the facts when you wrote it. The whole scheme of the Intercollegiate Socialist School—as you should have known before you signed that call—is promoted in this country by the Collectivist Society, whose purpose is not the scientific study of Socialism, but "the spread of its propaganda among the professional classes." The scheme has its root among Socialist groups that day and night are plotting revolution in European cities, as we shall proceed to show you.

First, as to the origin and purpose in this country of the Intercollegiate Socialist Society:

Upton Sinclair, a Socialist writer, whose name appeared with that of Mr. Higginson as one of the signers of the call, recently wrote a letter to the editor of the New York *Worker*, an official organ of the Socialist party, with the request that it be reprinted promptly by "the rest of the party press." His letter strips all disguise from the purpose of the proposed Society:

To the Editor of The Worker:

I beg to say a few words to the comrades concerning the Intercollegiate Socialist Society, a call to which was sent out recently. The work of this Society will be the **organizing of those college men and women who believe in Socialism,** to aid in **propaganda clubs at our colleges**, to select and distribute literature, to furnish speakers, and to aid in every way the work of inducing college students to take an interest in Socialism. That this is a most important movement, capable of wide growth and usefulness, **all comrades** must admit.

In commenting upon this letter, the *Worker* remarked:

While the majority of the students in the colleges and universities are probably children of capitalists, large and small, and while the majority of the children of capitalists are either fanatical believers in the Gospel of Getting-on or else hopeless devotees of the Senior Prom. and the Sophomore Cotillion, yet there remains a number of real men and women—young and full of energy and capable of great things—who **belong of right to the Socialist movement.**

Again the *Worker* published on August 5 a call "addressed to all those interested in the formation of an Intercollegiate Socialist Society"—addressed, therefore, to Mr. Higginson. This highly interesting document reveals that it is intended to send the original call for the formation of the Society to "the secretary of every institution of learning, with request to put on bulletin." The announcement continues:

Here is submitted an outline of the ideas of those who have been instrumental in sending out the call:

"The Society should be open to all who are or ever have been students in any American college or are engaged in educational work.

"Its purpose should be the interesting of college students and teachers in the subject of modern Socialism.

"Its methods should be the bringing together in one body of all persons interested in this work, the discussion of plans, the establishing of an agency for their prosecution.

"**The forming of clubs for propaganda work in all college and high schools.**

"The selection and distribution of **literature suitable for college men.**"

In reply to this communication kindly state name and address, college and high school and year; Socialist organization of which you may be a member, dues you would feel able to pay, any work at which you could help; speaking, organization, correspondence; a list of all persons who would be interested in this plan."

(Signed) M. R. HOLBROOK, Secretary,
P. O. Box 1663, New York.

An application was addressed to the Secretary for information and literature. Promptly in response came several Socialist pamphlets, all issued by the Collectivist Society, and revealing that its Secretary and headquarters are the same "M. R. Holbrook, P. O. Box 1663, New York." Among the enclosures was a printed request for a contribution, with this added assurance of a secrecy quite appropriate to a conspiracy to "undermine society": "No mention, except by permission, will be made of the name of any one who writes to us." This was signed, as above stated, "The Collectivist Society," with the same address as was affixed to the "Intercollegiate" call. The identity of interests and purposes of the two organizations is thus clearly established.

As to the Socialism of the Collectivist Society, let us again quote the *Worker*. The recognized mouthpiece of the Debs Socialists stated the purpose of the Collectivist Society to be that of "disseminating Socialist literature among the professional classes, persons not ordinarily reached by the party propaganda, particularly. Originally a kind of Fabian society, this organization **has since proclaimed itself as frankly accepting the fundamental tenets of scientific Socialism**"—a term of the cult which signifies outright revolution.

So much for the relation between the Collectivist Society and the Intercollegiate Socialist Society; so much, also, for Mr. Higginson's denial that he is connected with an organization that "aims to imbue the minds of the rising generation with Socialistic doctrines." His denial is thus brought face to face with the official announcement of the purpose of this Society: "The forming of clubs for **propaganda work in all colleges and high schools;" "the organizing of those college men and women who believe in Socialism, to aid in forming propaganda clubs at our colleges."**

But this proposition to hold what Mr. Higginson would have considered as a harmless academic discussion, in peaceful college class-rooms, of Free Bridges, Free Water, Single Tax, and Irregular Verbs assumes another aspect when its real origin is disclosed. This scheme was not conceived amid the tranquil shades of Cambridge nor yet at a tea-party of the Collectivist Society. It is in reality a cis-Atlantic outcropping of an ambitious international enterprise, whose purpose is to sow the seeds of Socialism in all the universities, colleges, normal schools and lecture-rooms of the world. This movement has manifested itself in the form of three international Congresses of "Socialist Students and Graduates" at Brussels, Genoa, and Paris. At the last Congress, students were present from universities in Russia, Poland, Bulgaria, Armenia, the West Indies, Belgium, Holland, Italy, Denmark, Hungary, Germany, Austria, and France. A report of this Congress in the *International Socialist Review* says:

"The Socialist students of the great American universities, Harvard, Columbia, Brown, and Chicago, had joined the Congress. These comrades showed great activity during several months, and even established an intercollegiate Socialist bureau. For reasons unknown to us, they could not, as expected, be directly represented."

Prof. Enrico Ferri, now of the University of Palermo, Italy, addressed the Congress upon the question of "how to bring into Socialism the greatest number of students." A recent Socialist publication describes this professor as "undoubtedly the greatest living figure in the Socialist movement," and adds the uncomfortable statement that he received, not long ago, "a sentence to sixteen months' imprisonment for a political offense, in the name of the King of Italy." His advice to the Congress may, therefore, be accepted as that of an expert in teaching Socialism both in the lecture-room and the cell. Prof. Ferri said:

"We should introduce Socialism into the students' minds as a part of science, as the logical and necessary culmination of the biological and sociological sciences. **No need of making a direct propaganda which would frighten many of the listeners. Without pronouncing the word Socialism once a year I make two thirds of our students conscious Socialists. Among workingmen it is necessary to add the Socialist conclusions to the scientific premises, because the workingman's psychology permits it, and indeed requires it; before an audience of bourgeois intellectuals, it is necessary to give the scientific premises alone, and let each mind draw its own conclusions.**"

This Congress made a formal call, says the *International Socialist Review*, "on the groups of Socialist students **to make an active propaganda among normal school professors, who will, in turn, transmit their Socialist convictions to the teachers they will have to train, and who thereby may do a work of capital importance throughout the country.**"

A further evidence of wily strategy appears in the following resolution adopted by the Congress:

"**That the best means of propagating Socialism in the universities is to organize, along with clearly Socialist circles where they are possible, neutral circles for the study of social sciences.**"

M. Boucher, in a report presented to the Congress in the name of the Group of Collectivist Students in Paris, invited:

"**The Socialist students to enter the People's Universities, either as professors or as voluntary critics; there is, apparently, the real battle-field for the Socialist students, there is the role which is most suitable to them in the whole range of the movement; that which will excite the least antagonism, and where they will be the most useful.**"

The announcement was made at this Congress of the forthcoming of the *Socialist Student*, edited "by our Brussels comrades," and "designed as the international organ of Socialist students." Doubtless this valuable periodical would be included in the "literature" which Mr. Higginson's proposed Society would consider "suitable for college men."

Here we have, stated in detail, the program of the international organization of "Socialist Students and Graduates." This program includes precisely the insidious device of forming "neutral groups" for the study of social sciences, which Mr. Higginson would

(*Concluded on page 20.*)

WELFARE DEPARTMENT OF The National Civic Federation

OFFICERS

H. H. VREELAND, Chairman.
CYRUS H. McCORMICK, First Vice-Chairman.
JOHN H. PATTERSON, Second Vice-Chairman.
EDWARD A. FILENE, Third Vice-Chairman.
CORNELIUS N. BLISS, Treasurer.

WELFARE WORK IN MERCANTILE HOUSES.

Previous articles in this Department have shown what can be done for the welfare of employes in large factories. It is now proposed to show by typical examples how Welfare Work has been introduced in both large and small mercantile houses. This statement must be more or less general in its scope, but detailed information in reference to the work described may be had upon application to the Welfare Department of the National Civic Federation. The articles that follow are supplied by officials of the several establishments

A CHICAGO EXAMPLE OF WELFARE WORK.

The distinctive characteristic of the Welfare Work of Marshall Field & Co., Chicago, is to be found in the pervading spirit of the place. To have the several thousand employes "intelligent, loyal, happy, and progressive" has been the company's primary aim. Just dealing with the employes has established relations of genuine friendliness.

This design is well and concisely expressed in the following rule:

[illegible] with and purpose of [illegible] love, no [illegible] the position [illegible] gotten or [illegible] instead every [illegible] is on the pay roll shall be recognized as a part of this great force, and that individual effort shall be carefully and frequently considered by the one above in authority.

Several methods are actively used to appeal to the intelligence and enlist the interest of all the employes without regard to their length of service. Little leaflets are freely distributed containing useful information, attractively presented, for their direction and encouragement. One of them, for example, contains terse precepts gathered from memoranda of meetings between the manager and the heads of departments and their assistants. Another is the letter written by Marshall Field to a prominent clergyman upon "The Virtues that make for Commercial Success." The idea is that the readers may find something peculiarly pertinent to themselves or to their work.

The pay envelopes which employes receive each week are variously imprinted with suggestive quotations bearing upon some of the most familiar and essential practical rules of conduct in daily life. One enumerates more than twenty reasons "Why He Was Not Promoted," some of the statements being:

He watched the clock.
He was willing, but unfitted.
He didn't believe in himself.
His stock excuse was, "I forgot."
He learned nothing from his blunders.
He chose his friends among his inferiors.
He never dared to act on his own judgment.
He did not think it worth while to learn how.
He did not learn that the best part of his salary was not in his pay envelope.

Another explains the "Value of a Mistake," while a third gives a table showing the way savings and interest accumulate when systematic deposits are made. Here and there in the rooms devoted to the employes are posted attractive placards setting forth injunctions helpful to those struggling for self-improvement, and homely but pertinent proverbs. One containing the caption "DEVELOPMENT" reads: "Push steadfastly against the boundary lines of to-day's limitations and your scope will be wider to-morrow"; and another headed "SALESMANSHIP" states: "The essentials are: integrity, courtesy, tact, knowledge of merchandise, judgment, accuracy, energy, personal appearance, and dignity."

In order to develop initiative and bring about improvement in details, the firm invites criticisms from all employes upon any point in system and method, in either their own sections or elsewhere which, in their judgment, can be bettered. Whenever such suggestion is regarded as practicable by the manager and is adopted, a reward of one dollar is paid. This system, besides bringing to the firm the improvements caused by accepted suggestions, causes the employes to be watchful, studious, and interested in the general improvement of the store. Section managers or assistant managers are not rewarded for suggestions for improvements regarding their own sections, as such suggestions are regarded as included in the duties of their positions. The firm pays a reward of one dollar for all corrections of errors (other than typographical) in its advertisements. It is considered an error in the advertisement when there is any exaggeration; when the price is wrong; when a word is misspelled; when the language is grammatically incorrect; or when a false statement occurs. The effect of this is to increase the interest of employes in the advertisements, and to cause them to be able to answer intelligently questions asked by customers, whether the goods inquired about are in the employe's section or not.

YOUTHS' GYMNASIUM. GIRLS' GYMNASIUM.
EMPLOYES' WRITING AND READING ROOM. GIRLS' MUSIC AND RECREATION ROOM.
EMPLOYES' LUNCH ROOM.

The educational work includes, during the busy months, beginners' meetings to which all, employed mornings, are sent at four o'clock each afternoon. A little talk is delivered relative to the business methods of the house and its policy and wishes concerning the employes. These talks are illustrated with charts.

It is endeavored to throw about the girls employed in the establishment an atmosphere of protection. To that end the young men begin work at 8 a. m. and the girls at 8.30, while the girls leave at 5 p. m. and the young men at 5.30.

An abundant supply of drinking water that has been twice filtered conduces to the health of the employes.

The toilet room facilities are exceptionally good.

One entire floor, the ninth, is devoted to the interests of employes.

There is a large lunch room where they may eat their luncheons brought from home, or may be served at the lowest possible cost.

An adjoining room is fitted with individual wire lockers.

A hospital, also on this floor, affords speedy relief for any one who has met with an accident or who has been taken ill suddenly.

There is a boys' gymnasium with shower baths, and also a gymnasium for the girls. This serves as a playroom for the young girls, who thus do not disturb the more mature, when occupying the resting and music room adjoining the gymnasium.

There is a library and reading room, with writing desks, for the use of all employes. All the daily papers are on file, as well as magazines selected because of their probable interest to the readers, and there are two cases filled with books. The firm signs slips which entitle the employes to the use of all books which they desire to draw from the Chicago Public Library. A subscription bureau enables the employes to enjoy the benefit of special prices for periodical literature which the firm is able to obtain.

Employes may purchase goods for their own use at special prices, the discount ranging from six to twenty per cent.

Employes detained at home because of illness receive half pay.

A vacation of two weeks is allowed, each summer, to those employes who have been with the firm twelve consecutive months, beginning before September 1, and one week is allowed those who have been employed six consecutive months, beginning before March 1.

When men employes are called upon for jury service, as they frequently are, the firm protects them against financial loss. They are expected to spend all spare time, during business hours, at the store, as jury duty rarely requires the entire day. All jury vouchers are turned over to the paymaster. The pay for jury service is $2 a day. Those whose wages are less than this sum receive the full amount of jury money. Those whose pay exceeds jury wages are paid the difference by the house. The time given to the business by employes during their term of jury service is also recognized by the manager.

The firm encourages enlistment in the militia, and allows, to the young men who join, the extra week necessary each summer for the annual encampment, at half pay.

New features of Welfare Work are added from time to time, the company aiming to do all in its power for the general good.

SCOPE OF THE WORK IN A NEW YORK DEPARTMENT STORE

About three thousand five hundred of the five thousand employes of R. H. Macy & Co., New York City, patronize its lunch room daily. The employes' lunch room occupies a large space, of which one portion is partitioned off for the men. It is possible to buy all that appetite demands for eight cents. A sample menu contains:

Tomato Soup	3c.
Beans and Pork ...	3c.
Potato Salad	3c.
Sandwich	4c.
Quarter of a Pie ...	4c.
Ice Cream	3c.
Tea, Coffee or Milk	1c.
Oranges .....2c. or	3c.
Different kinds of Cakes 1c., 2c. or	3c.

In the winter roast beef and other hot dishes are served. Fruit may be purchased at cost.

Tea, coffee, or milk is given free to all minors, such as cash girls, bundlers, and stock girls. All are expected to buy tickets for other articles on the menu desired, unless they are without money. Then upon application the minors receive free tickets for lunches. Whatever is left in the lunch room at the close of the day is supplied free to the night porters.

Employes are allowed to eat in the lunch room their lunches brought from home, and to supplement them with anything for sale. Very few, however, do this, as they can get lunch so cheaply that they prefer to buy it. The allowance of time for luncheon is three-quarters of an hour. The employes go to luncheon in shifts which begin at 11 a. m. and extend to 2.30 or 3 p. m. The first shift numbers usually about seven hundred, and is the most popular because many employes are hungry as early as eleven o'clock, and some of them think they will be better served then than later; this, however, is an erroneous impression, as the same quality of food is served to the last as to the first shift.

Large locker rooms are provided containing wire lockers. Two employes share a locker, and each pays twenty-five cents for a key upon taking employment with the company. When the employe leaves the service, the money is refunded upon the return of the key.

There are separate toilet rooms on evry floor for the men and women. Each contains wash bowls, closets, and shower baths which may be used at any hour by obtaining permission. The baths are more in demand in summer than in winter. Facing the shower baths are curtained, individual dressing-rooms.

The company supplies soap and towels, and there are two fine large mirrors in each toilet room. The individual wash bowls are provided with special cans made to granulate the soap.

There are drinking fountains throughout the store, the water being filtered and cool.

Special elevators are provided for the use of the employes.

Fire apparatus is placed throughout the building. Drills are held upon short notice to ensure their efficiency in the event of an actual emergency.

Three rooms are set apart as hospitals on different floors in the store. In attendance are two doctors, one of them a woman, and there is a trained nurse to assist. One of the hospital rooms is adjacent to the recreation room, where the Secretary of the Relief Association is in constant attendance. She refers all cases requiring treatment to the physicians. The man doctor visits the homes of all who are ill, and is required to make a formal report upon every case. From five to seven thousand cases a year are treated. Sometimes the physicians will have from fifty to one hundred cases a day, perhaps for a week, and then there will be fewer for a period.

Improvident employes were generally the ones who failed to join the relief association when membership was voluntary, and it has recently been made compulsory. When urged, the employes were glad to join, because they have known so many who have been helped through the association. The dues are nominal.

The mechanism of the association is such that no employe can be ill without the fact becoming known and immediate relief being extended. Every employe has a postal card, addressed to the company, which must be mailed as soon as illness occurs. If an employe is absent for a single day, the company sends a representative to see the absentee.

Under the former system a case occurred where an employe was very ill and unattended in a lodging house for three days. She did not belong to the relief association, but the company sent to inquire the reason for her absence, and learned that she had been entirely alone and that, consequently, nothing had been done to provide relief or food.

A recreation room accommodating three hundred at one time is set apart. The [illegible] tables in the room are well filled with reading matter. The floor is covered with large rugs, and there are comfortable chairs.

Upon the top floor there is a beautiful exhibit hall where the company contemplates giving employes dances.

WASH ROOM.

LOCKER ROOM.

EMPLOYES' LUNCH ROOM.

RECREATION ROOM, WITH HOSPITAL ADJACENT.

In the summer the company entertains all of the junior help—the cash girls, stock girls, bundlers, and packers—in the country. It makes arrangements with churches of the various denominations represented by the affiliations of the employes, maintaining summer recreation homes, such as Sea Cliff, and others on the Hudson. The company pays the board of each for one week. It also bears the cost of transportation and cares for their baggage from the time of departure from home until their return. When these parties start on their vacations, a luncheon, an orange, and a box of candy are provided for each traveler.

From three to four hundred go each year in parties of from twenty to fifty between July 1 and September 1.

Every employe who has been with the firm for a year is entitled to a vacation of one week with pay.

The company presents to every married employe a Thanksgiving turkey weighing from twelve to fifteen pounds.

Each of the junior help receives a Christmas remembrance of one dollar and a box of candy.

Every three and every six months premiums are paid, in addition to the regular salaries, upon all sales exceeding the amounts of sales by the individuals concerned in the previous year. This distribution of time brings one of these premium payments at the Christmas season and one at vacation time. An interesting illustration of its operation shows one sales girl who was quite overwhelmed with joy at Christmas when she found $55 in her envelope, and another starting on her vacation with $116.

Twice each week at 9.30 a. m. one of the superintendents gives a talk of twenty minutes to employes from the various departments. Sometimes as many as three hundred are in attendance. A notice is sent to each head of a department requesting that as many of the employes as can be spared shall be present on a certain morning. In the course of a few weeks every employe in the store will have had the benefit of one of the talks. The superintendent, who delivers them, discusses all complaints that have been received from customers, and makes special reference to such topics as the appearance of the employes, tardiness in arrival, courtesy to customers, how to keep stock in good condition, and the requirements for successful salesmanship.

Other talks are given frequently to the floor walkers and the heads of departments. They are delivered in the recreation room at 6.30 p. m., lasting ten minutes. Included are such topics as attention to customers, discipline, personal appearance, leaving counters or floors without permission, and other defects in service and their remedies.

The hours of work are from 8 a. m. to 6 p. m. Upon a stormy morning the company does not insist that every employe must arrive exactly at 8 o'clock. Any one in the store may have permission to go home at four o'clock, upon application, for any reasonable cause, without loss of wages.

The company believes that good discipline can be maintained without fines. The only fine inflicted is for lost checks, if occurring twice. For losing checks a third time the penalty is dismissal. The money collected from these fines goes into a fund for the bundlers, used to make up losses. While such losses are charged against the employes for the moral effect, they are never obliged to pay.

A PHILADELPHIA EXPERIENCE.

In the Philadelphia establishment of John Wanamaker, emphasis is placed on commercial education.

The young people in the store are organized into three classes which, united, are known as the John Wanamaker Commercial Institute. These classes typify a systematic effort to meet responsibility for the future of the junior employes.

What is styled "The Cadet Corps" includes girls up to about seventeen years of age, and boys, other than cash boys, from sixteen to eighteen. Into this corps cash boys go by promotion. With the exception of the Christmas season, the cash boys average two hundred in number and the cadets four hundred, of whom about one hundred are girls.

Besides excellence in school work, cultivation of good manners, neatness, elevated personal habits, and efficiency in store service are elements considered in promotion, and are emphasized by a system of monthly averages. To illustrate: Each of the cash boys has his record card which he must carry for a month and keep in a state of cleanliness. A sign of progress is an increased average whiteness. The boy reverences and guards this card. On one side are rules to be committed to memory. On the other is an array of spaces to be filled with weekly ratings by his department manager for neatness, promptness, truthfulness, etc.; a weekly rating at morning "inspection" by his general chief; daily strokes of the pencil for misconduct or neglected duty, called by the boys, without levity or disrespect, "blues"; and the monthly figures for school work. Protest against an undeserved "blue" is accorded a patient hearing. The average of all ratings is the "store average," and misconduct marks reckon so much off. Upon the store average depends promotion and increase of salary. If the first upward step is not taken within two months, the conclusion is reached that the boy is unfitted for the business and dropped from the ranks.

These record cards secure discipline without the harsh word and impulsive discharge. They are carried home for inspection and signature by parents and guardians.

The six hundred young people which include the cash boys and cadet corps are assigned to duty in the various divisions of the business according to their natural aptitude and fitness, and are under the direction of their respective department heads; but always, also, and until graduation from the cadet corps, they are under the care and discipline of the chief of the corps and a woman assistant. The young people are not lost sight of individually, but are known and studied by the managers with view to advancement.

They are placed as early as possible where some distinct branch of the business or class of merchandise will be learned thoroughly. Stock boy, salesman, stock-head, buyer's assistant, is the usual line of advancement. Development in clerical lines makes the bookkeeper, the auditor, the office assistant, the stenographer. In trades lines grow up, for example, the milliner, the dressmaker, the paper shade and flower worker, the plate engraver and printer, the designer, show-card painter, draftsman, decorator, and the mechanic to repair bicycles. Exceedingly numerous and varied are the paths open, and, in so far as possible, an early and definite selection and patient, reasonable progress along some one of them is insisted upon. Their natural abilities, however, are not found sufficient to bring about normal development, unless trained and added to by knowledge in the common branches of education. It has been found practicable, therefore, to bring into the business lives of the young people most of the activities usual in the schools.

The smaller boys are organized into school and military companies. Each company assembles in the school room on the fifth of the store building two mornings in the week where regular instruction is given in arithmetic, grammar, spelling, writing, composition, and singing. On two other mornings they have setting-up exercises and military drill, with some other features of physical culture. The boys elect their own military officers, except their chief, and these officers become successful diciplinarians. A fife, bugle and drum corps of these boys has been pronounced the best junior organization of the kind in the city.

The girls also have a school organization, each division being taught two mornings in the week. In addition to the branches taught to the boys, the girls are instructed in business correspondence, stenography and typewriting and bookkeeping. Attention is given to singing and physical culture. An elocution class and a mandolin club are successful outgrowths of this branch of the store school.

The older boys, numbering about three hundred, have supper in the store, and remain for their school two evenings in each week. The branches taught are arithmetic, spelling, writing, commercial correspondence, English, stenography, bookkeeping, the metric system, mechanical and free hand drawing, and rapid calculation. Military and gymnastic training is given. Among these boys are a club for debate and literary exercises, an orchestra, a field music band, a mandolin club, a glee club, an elocution and dramatic class and a minstrel troupe.

A monthly report of the standing and progress of each pupil is made to the parents.

Each of the three branches of the school has its separate annual commencement. The graduates receive certificates which have a double significance. They testify to the attainment of a certain standard in the school work proper, and also to the actual number of years of satisfactory service in the business with promotion from the cadet corps to positions in the regular ranks of the store's departments.

Thus there has grown up in practice a system of civil service promotion. The higher positions are being filled continually with those who have grown up in the business from childhood. It sometimes happens

EDUCATIONAL CLUB, CHRISTMAS.

VACATION COTTAGE.

that a young man fits himself for a high position before there is an opening here, and assumes one elsewhere, with the approval of the firm; but a faithful worker need not look outside for a business future.

The graduates of the school have organized alumnae and alumni associations which maintain, in addition to their social features, a debating and literary club, a dramatic club, and a mandolin class.

Other features in the Welfare Work are separate lunch rooms and resting rooms for women and men.

In the lunch rooms, besides service a la carte at low rates, a special luncheon is served each day for ten cents, consisting of meat, one vegetable, bread and butter, coffee, tea or milk, and dessert.

A porch connecting with each of the lunch rooms gives opportunity for rest in the open air, where the men may smoke.

The resting room for women is fitted with numerous couches, easy chairs, and a piano.

There is a private room for the sick in charge of a matron, with a trained nurse, who can be called if required.

A beneficial association provides for the care of those who are ill, and it includes death benefits.

Two savings funds are conducted, one for men and women, and the other for boys and girls of the establishment.

The library for the employes, in charge of a librarian, contains about five thousand volumes.

A "Women's League," composed of a large number of the women employes, was organized for social and educational purposes. It carries on classes for chorus singing, physical culture, dancing, sewing, and instruction in English, German, French, and the mandolin.

There is a baseball club consisting of young men.

The firm maintains at Island Heights, N. J., camping grounds and a headquarters house. The boys enjoy an annual encampment at this place, and the house is used by such of the women employes as care to arrange club outings there during their vacation.

All employes receive two weeks' vacation with pay.

WHAT HAS BEEN DONE AT KANSAS CITY, MO.

The George B. Peck Dry Goods Company, at Kansas City, Mo., maintains a lunch room for employes, in charge of a competent man and woman, with a force of assistants. An abundance of wholesome food is served at the lowest possible cost.

The store is equipped with an ample number of wash rooms. There are provided also lockers for the employes' wraps.

A physician is regularly employed at a fixed salary to attend any employes when ill, either at the store, at their homes, or at his office. The firm furnishes the greater part of the medicines used.

A rest room and a library adjoin the lunch room. Books are taken from the library without fee on a ticket and retained for two weeks, or renewed, as desired. This library contains all the standard works of fiction, and is supplied from day to day with current publications as they are received.

The cash boys and girls are organized in an "Educational Club." Its members attend a school each morning, where they are instructed in the regular elementary branches by a competent teacher. All books and supplies are furnished free.

Every summer the cash girls and boys and all the younger help are sent for a vacation, with pay, to a camp in one of the large suburban parks. The camp contains a cottage, in charge of a competent matron, which is equipped with conveniences for comfortable and happy summer life. This camp is highly appreciated by the employes, and has proved of great benefit to them.

The sales people and other employes, who are not sent to this camp, are allowed vacations with pay, according to the number of years they have been in the company's service.

There are also various summer excursions.

WOMEN'S RESTING ROOM AND LIBRARY.

Every Christmas there is a Christmas tree for the cash girls and boys' educational club.

SACRAMENTO AND SAN FRANCISCO.

In the stores of Weinstock, Lubin & Company, at Sacramento and San Francisco, there are good lunch rooms and rest rooms, the latter being provided with magazines, newspapers, and small libraries.

There are modern wash and toilet rooms.

EMPLOYES' RESTING ROOM.

All work rooms are well lighted, have plenty of window space, are well ventilated, and are thoroughly sanitary.

Above the San Francisco store there is a roof garden.

All employes between fourteen and eighteen years of age are organized into classes for systematic instruction in the usual common school branches.

There is a savings plan for employes. The firm allows interest at four per cent. on ordinary deposits, which the depositor may withdraw at any time. Upon term deposits, requiring a notice of six months before they can be withdrawn, six per cent. is allowed. There is a profit-sharing plan which applies to all heads of departments.

THIRTY YEARS OF WELFARE WORK.

In the establishment of Bloomingdale Brothers, New York, Welfare Work has been developing continually since the formation of the firm thirty years ago. Its distinctive feature is the education of the employes with a view to their promotion in accordance with demonstrated merit. This difficult task is met by constant instruction in their respective duties. Upon a large blackboard are written, daily, instructions, rules and regulations, alternately addressed to sales clerks, floor walkers and others. There is ample proof that these notices are productive of good results. They are the subject of conversation each day among the employes, who often make suggestions of new topics to be placed upon the blackboard.

Prominently placed and accessible to all employes is a box wherein they may drop suggestions. It is labeled "Suggestion Box to Encourage Suggestions from Employes." It is a medium through which injustice may be righted, while those who are thoughtful and ingenious enough to make useful suggestions may thereby receive their first and immediate introduction to the firm and secure early recognition.

An employes' merchandise department enables them to purchase goods and pay for them in weekly instalments. The weekly payments required are determined by the amount of the purchase and the salary received. This has proved a blessing to hundreds who have been in the employ of the firm a reasonable time, and were thus entitled to make necessary purchases, upon easy payments, avoiding instalment houses which extend credit, but charge exorbitantly. This convenient method also saves the time necessary to make trips, in the limited leisure of employes, to the instalment houses.

The firm encourages employes to save, beginning with pennies. There is in the store a branch of the "Penny Provident Fund." The clerk required by this branch and the necessary space is furnished the Provident Association without charge by the firm. Any employe who has saved one hundred pennies may begin making deposits with the banking department, receiving 4 per cent. interest. Occasionally texts are written upon the blackboard to encourage saving for "rainy days."

The "Bloomingdale Brothers Employes' Mutual Aid Society" was instituted in 1881 and incorporated in 1888. Its officers are the heads of various departments throughout the store. Before the formation of this Society, it was necessary to bring all cases of sickness and distress to a member of the firm for financial aid, always generously extended, but now these cases are cared for through the machinery of the Society.

All employes are members. There are three grades of membership: Employes in the first grade pay monthly dues of ten cents, entitling them to $2.50 per week sick benefit, and $30.00 death benefit.

In the second grade dues of thirty cents entitle them to $4.00 a week sick benefit and $40.00 death benefit.

(*Concluded on page 20.*)

THE IMMIGRATION PROBLEM.

(*Continued from page 9.*)

lected because it is the best, and by those who want the best. A head-tax of twenty-five dollars was not desirable years ago. It becomes more and more necessary as the increasing facilities of land and water transportation make it easier and cheaper to come here. The tax would not act as a permanent and insuperable barrier to desirable aliens, for a hard-working and ambitious man or woman who wanted to come here could earn the extra money. It would doubtless deter many of the shiftless and incompetent, and it would prevent such shipments of paupers and criminals as are now known to have been made with the connivance, if not at the expense, of the authorities abroad.

2. *"Assisted" immigration should be further restricted.* * * * Congress some years ago very properly recognized the danger in "assisted" immigration when it debarred from landing "any person whose ticket or passage is paid for with the money of another, or who is assisted by others to come." But in order to make it possible for the members of a family to send for one another, the following words were added: "But this section shall not be held to prevent persons living in the United States from sending for a relative or friend, who is not of the * * * excluded classes." The motive of Congress was excellent, but the phrasing of the law is too loose to meet present conditions. At present about fifty per cent. of our total immigration is "assisted," and, for an "assisted" immigrant, any one is a "friend," and any one up to a fifth or sixth cousin several times removed is a "relative." The time has come, with our present enormous immigration, to restrict to the immediate family the privilege of "assisting" other aliens. As a rule, it is safe to say that the less desirable immigrants are those who can not pay their own passage. We should certainly allow fathers and mothers, and brothers and sisters, and husbands and wives and children to prepay each other's passage. Beyond that, "assisted" immigration should be stopped. Therefore, the clause concerning "assisted" immigration should be followed by some such words as these: "But this section shall not be held to prevent *citizens* of the United States from sending for their fathers or mothers, wives, sisters or brothers, or minor children who are not of the excluded classes." A bill introduced by Senator Lodge into the Fifty-eighth Congress (S. 1376) embodied an amendment along these same lines. In his last annual report as Commissioner of Immigration at the port of New York, Hon. William Williams said on this matter: "I believe that assisted immigration should be prohibited, subject to reasonable exceptions in cases of very close and otherwise eligible relatives, such as fathers, mothers, children, brothers and sisters of responsible aliens who have already resided here a sufficient length of time." There would be no permanent hardship in such a provision, because any alien, otherwise admissible, could come as soon as he had been able to pay his own passage money.

3. *We should debar immigrants of poor physique.* The immigration question is racial, rather than economic. One of the most potent factors in decreasing the American birth-rate has been the immigration of aliens of lower standards of living. American fathers and mothers, as the late Gen. Francis A. Walker pointed out, and as leading authorities have since reiterated, naturally shrink from exposing their sons and daughters to competition with those who are contented with lower wages and lower standards of living, and therefore these sons and daughters are never born. The stronger the competition, the greater the effort to maintain and raise the standard of living and the social position, and the greater the effort, the greater is the voluntary check on population. * * * It is of the utmost importance that we should keep the new blood pure, and that we should keep up the American race standard.

One of the essential points in regard to our recent immigration is that much of it is not voluntary in the true meaning of that word. It is an artificial selection by the steamship companies of many of the worst elements of European and Asiatic populations. Steamship managers and agents deny this most emphatically, but those who have had to do with immigration matters have learned to be very cautious about accepting any evidence which is given by steamship people, railroad officials, and other "interested" persons. In such matters the statements of our own Government officers are the sole evidence which is trustworthy. The social responsibility which rests upon this country in this matter is overwhelming. We may decide upon what merits, physical, intellectual, or moral, the fathers and mothers of American children shall be selected. But we have left the choice almost altogether to the selfish interests which do not care whether we want the immigrants they bring, or whether the immigrants will be the better for coming. Steamship agents and brokers all over Europe and eastern Asia are to-day deciding for us the character of the American race of the future. * * *

4. *The Illiteracy Test.* No plan for further selecting immigration has had more general support than the illiteracy test. This requires that adult immigrants, with exceptions in favor of wives, minor children and parents, shall be able to read a few lines in their own language. * * *

There is no danger that the exclusion of illiterates would cause a scarcity of labor in this country. If there is a demand for laborers, the supply will be forthcoming from Europe. If the steamship companies can not bring illiterates, they will fill their steerage with aliens who can read. And with the stimulus thus put upon education, the illiteracy in many of the countries of Europe would soon show a notable decline. There is plenty of labor now in our cities which would be better off in the country, where there is great need of farm "help." But the cities attract, and the farmer waits for his help. So it would be under the illiteracy test.

It is urged that our native population, as well as the better class of immigrants, will not do the hard work needed to build our railroads and develop our mines, and hence we must continually import lower grades of aliens to do this work. The usual course of reasoning in this matter is fallacious. Americans abandoned the harder kinds of manual labor, not because they despised these occupations, but because they found that these occupations brought them into competition with aliens whose standards of living were much lower than their own. The same is now true of the Irish, who have largely been replaced by the Italians, and will later be true of the Italians, when other newer immigrants come in whose standards of living are so low that the Italians will not wish to associate with them. But meanwhile, if we continue to admit lower and lower grades of immigrants in this fashion, the general standards of living of the whole community must inevitably also be lowered. It is often said that the crowding out of native Americans and of the older nationalities of immigrants is all for the best; that they all go up into higher occupations. This is not so. While some doubtless do rise in the social scale as the result of being displaced, some are crowded out and move elsewhere, and many are crowded down, becoming paupers and swelling the army of American tramps. * * *

To sum up: We need intelligent distribution from our congested districts of physically fit aliens over the country districts, where these aliens are wanted, and where they will be given work which they are physically and mentally qualified to perform. We need a public backing for our immigration officials in enforcing the laws we now have. We need new legislation to sift the immigrants whom we receive. We need a higher head-tax: a restriction of the privilege of "assisting" immigrants to come here; a physical test. And we need that limit to the present unwieldy numbers of immigrants which would be best furnished by an illiteracy test.

G. GUNBY JORDAN,
Cotton Manufacturer.

THE SOUTHERN NEED OF LABOR.

Several Governors Propose Concerted Action to Divert the Tide of Immigration.

(From an Address by G. Gunby Jordan, before the Georgia Industrial Association.)

I AM aware of the fact that very many of the older mills are making large and important improvements in their properties, adding more, and substituting new for old machinery. But in thoroughly new textile enterprises, the South seems to be now at a standstill.

The main cause of all this is that we have exhausted the available labor of the South which is capacitated by birth and adaptation for textile work. Hence there is in several of the Southern States much idle machinery. A telegram from New Bedford, Mass., in the last few days conveys the intelligence that the Mississippi Mills, at Wesson, Miss., has just made a contract with one hundred or more weavers at New Bedford, and is moving them to Wesson because weavers could not be found in Mississippi.

This telegram further vouchsafes the information that these weavers are under a contract for a year at $2 each for each working day.

Speaking solely for our corporation, as a matter of certainty I can truthfully say that there are now, and have been for some months, a good many openings unfilled for competent mill help. Information which I believe to be reliable convinces me that practically all other mills South are in like condition. We, therefore, are to-day discussing a condition, not a theory.

No investment in manufacturing can ever prove attractive so long as there is any large portion of the machinery idle. It is a fact beyond controversy that idle machinery in the South at the present time is caused solely by the lack of competent labor.

I have just read in a New York newspaper under a headline which says: "Louisiana calls for 100,000 men," a communication saying that there is an absolute labor famine in Louisiana, and that there is employment enough waiting now for 100,000 men who are able and willing to work.

Clerks, bookkeepers, and people seeking for soft jobs, wholly within the shade, are not needed there, as probably they are not needed at any place, because there always seems to be a large surplus of people willing to work at such vocations in the South and North, the East and the West. But people who are willing to go into the fields, the factories and the mines to do manual labor, are needed in Louisiana and in Georgia as well.

South Carolina, recognizing this condition of affairs, has established a Bureau of Immigration, and has an actual office in New York looking toward the movement of immigrants to that State.

A cablegram from London, April 30, says that Donald Rose, General European Representative of the Illinois Central Railroad, has just returned from a trip to Austria and Italy, where he met the governmental authorities, with whom he discussed the possible diversion of Italian and Austrian settlers in the United States from the Eastern to the Southern States.

Mr. Rose states that he does not represent his railroad in this matter, but the governors of the States of Louisiana and Alabama.

The Italian government has thought sufficiently of this matter to have her Ambassador make a personal visit of investigation into the Southern States for the purpose of reporting upon the welfare of forty settlements of Italians already in the South, and asking for his recommendation as to the further movement of Italians to that section.

His report has been quite favorable, and with very few exceptions, advises that Italians do better by going on lands in the South than in Eastern States as miners and as laborers. This is upon the theory largely that in the South the Italian becomes a permanent land owner where land is cheap.

It is understood from high authority that the governors of several of the Southern States propose to carry on a propaganda of education respecting their several States, with a view to inviting European immigrants to them.

We learn that the manufacturers of South Carolina have met together and resolved for their own protection, and for the purpose of starting up idle machinery, that they will furnish representatives of their own to try to divert some of the immense hordes of immigrants now landing in this country to their own State.

Recently in interviews with the representatives of the Southern railway lines, Commissioner Sargent expressed himself as anxious to distribute the immense throngs of immigrants which are reaching our shores in a scientific and sensible manner, and that he believed, with the representatives of the Southern roads, that very many of these immigrants, so badly needed by it, could be diverted to the South.

Among his recommendations, which he will urge before Congress, is an appropriation sufficient to have attractive buildings on Ellis Island arranged so that each State in the Union can have a display of the products of the soil, of the manufactories and the mines, and, if desired, a capable representative to explain these and the other attractions of the respective States to immigrants, so that they can intelligently make up their minds as to the point that they may eventually choose as a permanent home.

As it is now, the ports of Alaska receive scores more of people than do all the important ports in the State of Georgia, and we certainly have two very important ports in this State—one of them sufficiently so to receive this year about 1,750,000 bales of cotton.

In the five years since the last Federal census was taken there has been an increase of the population of this country, as shown by the monthly estimates of the Treasury Department, of 6,613,000 people, for on May 1, 1905, the estimated population of this country was 83,026,000.

Of this increase during the past five years over one-half, say 3,255,000, came from Europe.

By 1910 it is easy to see that this country will have 90,000,000 of population.

We need not anticipate; but taking what has already occurred during the past five years, we see that the gain is 8.7 per cent.

Even as discerning and conservative men as manufacturers generally are do not take sufficient account of the increased population when estimates are made of the business outlook, for every addition to our population adds just so much to the consumptive demand upon every productive industry.

It is a fair estimate to presume that the average amount needed by every person to maintain life in this country is about $200 a year. Then, the actual increase in the United States, as based upon the last five years, means an annual increase of the consumptive demand of $264,000,000.

This fact alone sufficiently explains the enormous vitality displayed by this country, its immense power of recuperation and the constantly growing and intense pressure upon its producing energy.

It may interest you to know that either Michigan or Minnesota, in this good year of 1905, has more foreign born population than fourteen Southern States combined: that either Pennsylvania or Illinois has twice as many as these fourteen States, and that New York alone has four times as many as the whole of the fourteen States named. That in the State of Massachusetts there are forty-five cities of 10,000 inhabitants or more, and that the entire Southern States have only thirty-eight: that it would take several Southern States in population to equal that of New York City or Chicago alone.

There were 23,000,000 immigrants in round figures received in this country up to the year 1905, and these all, or nearly all, went to the Northern, Eastern, and Western States. This has been one of the great underlying causes of the failure of the South to develop in an adequate way.

For comparison let us take for a moment our own State of Georgia and that of Iowa. In selecting Iowa for an object lesson, it is done mainly because the area is almost identical with that of Georgia, Georgia being larger, however.

First, Georgia was one of the original colonies, and hence one of the original thirteen States.

Iowa was not admitted to the Union until 1846. In the census just prior she had 43,112 people within her borders. Georgia at that time had 691,000 people, of which 407,695 were white. To-day Iowa has outstripped Georgia in population, and hence in all other commercial and financial advantages.

To emphasize this fact, let us compare Georgia with Illinois:

	Georgia.	Illinois.
Square miles	58,980	56,000
Population	2,216,331	4,821,550
Density	37.6	86.1
Agricultural products, value	$104,304,476	$345,649,611
Agriculture, per capita, value	$47	$72
Manufactured products, value	$106,654,527	$259,730,168
Manufacturers, per capita value	$48	$261
Engaged in agriculture	522,848	462,781
Engaged in manufacturing	85,385	481,550

In other words, if Georgia had as many persons to the square mile as Illinois, its population would be now 5,080,000, or about twice the present population.

But this comparison is valuable in that it shows how rapidly this large population in Illinois has increased the agricultural products instead of decreasing their values, as some of our misguided friends fear. In other words: In Georgia we receive $47 per capita and Illinois $72 per capita for the value of agricultural products.

The contrast in manufacturing products is still more intense, being $48 in Georgia and $261 in Illinois.

There are, with all this immigration into Illinois, 60,000 more people engaged in agriculture in Georgia than there are in the State of Illinois, and on the other hand nearly 400,000 more engaged in manufacturing in Illinois than in Georgia.

There can be no race question in any country where the intelligent race is largely in numerical excess. If no other incentive existed than this, every white man in Georgia should be desirous of bringing into his State good, sound, white immigrants from any section and from any country.

Let us then take up the two decades beginning in 1880 and ending in 1900. In that time in agriculture, the balance of this country increased 65 per cent., the South 72 per cent.; in manufactories the balance of the country 242 per cent., the South 348 per cent.; in the value of manufactured products the balance of the country 135 per cent., the South 219 per cent.

In mining, lumbering, railroad building, and general industries the South stood much higher than did the balance of the country. And to-day West Virginia mines more coal than does Belgium, nearly as much as France, and these two European countries have the reputation of being great mining countries.

To-day Alabama is showing a vitality and growth in the production of iron, steel, and coal which prophesies that in the next twenty-five years she will exceed the Pittsburg district in this regard.

In 1880 the South consumed one-seventh only of the cotton spun in this country. In 1900 and since she has consumed 50 per cent. of it. All of this in the face of the fact that the Southern States were increasing in population, and hence in human energy, only through the natural birth rate.

Let us take our own State for example. Where 46.7 percentage of the population is negro or of negro origin, it is a lamentable fact that the last census shows that during the preceding ten years the population of Georgia increased at a less rate than the birth rate in the State. Out of the American born population of 2,203,928, only 193,520 were natives of other parts of the country, while at the same time 412,453 natives of Georgia were living in other States, 78,000 Georgians being in Texas alone.

Thus there was a balance in the exchange of 218,933 against Georgia, which was diminished but very slightly by the incoming of only 12,403 persons born in foreign countries.

So that it is true that we are not holding our own, even from the increase that nature gives us.

Adam Smith says there are only two factors known to produce wealth—land and labor. Within our State there are millions of unused acres of land. What we need is the labor to till them.

The South has grown rich from enormous crops, so that the prodigality of nature has left much for

JOHN WILLIS BAER,
Secretary Presbyterian Board of Missions.

investment in banks, in manufactories, in opening mines and developing the wonderful natural resources in the Southern States.

Now we have reached the apex of that development, unless we bring in people sufficient to continue the work. Machinery can not operate itself. Mines are not automatic in their development. People are needed, and from some source and from somewhere they must come.

If we continue to progress, these people must be brought within our borders. Cotton consumption has doubled in the world in the past fifteen years. By 1920, if things remain in a normal condition and the peace of the world is assured, the annual consumption of cotton should be equal to twenty-five millions of bales.

The thinking men of the South have long ago concluded that it was suicidal for the bulk of this crop to leave our shores in its crude condition. The markets of the world are open to us, and manufactures should increase in the South more rapidly than in any other section of the world.

OUR GREAT ALIEN INVASION.

Its Regulation, Distribution and Evangelization Measures of High Interest and Duty.

(By John Willis Baer, Assistant Secretary Presbyterian Board of Home Missions, in the *Christian Herald*.)

"Breathes there a man with soul so dead,
Who never to himself hath said:
This is my own, my native land?"

THERE may have been a time when men who could not give a hearty "Amen" to that sentiment were called men "without a country." If ever true in its full meaning, and I doubt it, it is not true to-day. Let me remind you that there are loyal and royal citizens of the United States who gladly give full allegiance to the Stars and Stripes, who are not "to the banner born." America is not their native land; it is the land of their adoption.

Let us together look into this subject of Emigration and Immigration. It is now an international problem. That man who views the situation from an exclusively national aspect needs to broaden his horizon. Don't you remember the old truth familiar to our boyhood days—"What goes up must come down, upon the head or the ground"? By the same natural law the tide of migration must find its level. The tide goes up in one place, it goes down in another. I believe that nationally we are too selfishly concerned about what comes upon our head and upon our ground. We give too little constructive thought to the other fellow's head, and the other fellow's ground.

Let me at the beginning declare my position on Immigration from our own national standpoint. I am with President Roosevelt, who said in one of his messages to Congress: "We can not have too much immigration of the right kind, and we want none of the wrong kind." I had occasion to write that sentence in a letter recently to Mr. Jacob A. Riis, and in reply by letter, among other things, he said:

> I agree with you thoroughly, and further, the "wrong kind" of immigration is in my mind easily identified with the kind that wants to do wrong, not with any class or race. I know no better material for the true American than the one who came from abroad, but with appreciation of what freedom may be made to mean for the race.

Jacob A. Riis is such a one, and Jacob A. Riis is right. Now go back in our thoughts to this great restless force moving upon the map of the world. Let us consider some facts, some figures, some fears.

Whelpley, in his new book just from the press, *The Problem of Immigration*, says:

> Like a mighty stream it finds its source in a hundred rivulets largely in Northern, Southern, and Eastern Europe. It's an army moving at the rate of nearly two millions each year, and is invading the civilized world. Its tongue is polyglot; in dress all climes, from pole to equator, are indicated; all religions and beliefs enlist. There is no age limit; young and old alike travel side by side. There is no sex limitation, for the women are as keen, if not more so than the men. The army carries its equipment on its back. Throughout Europe the word America is synonymous in all classes with freedom, prosperity, and happiness. The desire to reach America is the first sign of awakened ambition; the first signal of revolt against harsh environment; the dream of age and youth alike.
>
> Gaining in volume and momentum each year, without apparent regard for the law of supply and demand, the pressure of this army has already made itself felt upon communities in which it finds its destination. The cry of protest has gone up from those who find themselves crowded from their occupations and their homes by the new arrivals, and the peoples are asking also: What steps are to be taken to check this alien invasion?

Personally, I should be glad to see this whole question taken up seriously and constructively by the governments of the world. Would that President Roosevelt, the great international policeman and peace-compelling executive, might take the initiative in calling together such an international conference.

A writer in the *Fortnightly Review* has suggested some such programme as this for such a conference. Give it careful thought:

> First, To encourage a high moral, physical, political, and educational standard of admission into any country.
>
> Second, To guard against the spread of disease from one country to another.
>
> Third, To check undue activity on the part of transportation agents.
>
> Fourth, To maintain a world-wide system of police identification and restraint of criminals.
>
> Fifth, To persuade each nation to live up to its full responsibilities in the care of its deficients.
>
> Sixth, To induce the amelioration of political or economic wrongs in given areas. Such influences are driving people from one country to another to the discomfort of the latter.

By all means let us have such a conference. This great question of migration is viewed by some with too much alarm, when they consider it purely from a selfish and national standpoint. It demands "team work" by the nations of the world. The people of the United States gladly welcome the choice of Europe; Europe desires to retain its worthy sons. Europe, however, is willing to miss from among its numbers its undesirable citizens. The United States very properly objects to receiving them, and vice versa. At present it is a great game of chance—a game of give and take. Many of the world's governments are aroused—some are passing laws restricting immigration, others making laws restraining emigration.

Now for some figures. This ever restless moving from one land to another; this apparent all too easy snapping of national ties—let us view it from our own shores. The United States received during the fiscal year ending June, 1904, a total of 812,870 aliens, 30,000 of these came to us through Canadian ports—a decrease of 80,600 over 1903, which was the year registering the largest number of immigrants ever received into our country. You ask very naturally, "From whence did these aliens come?" Let me quote from the government's official report as follows:

> A striking and significant feature of these figures is that the chief diminution in immigration for the year was shown in the arrivals from Austria-Hungary amounting to 28,855, and from Italy to 37,326. These two countries aggregating 66,181, or twenty odd thousand more than the total net decrease of the fiscal year 1904. The countries of Northern and Western Europe, with one notable exception, show increases, Great Britain's increase being 18,643. The one exception to the foregoing statement is shown by the decrease of 18,265 in the arrivals from Sweden.
>
> It appears that during the year there arrived 549,100 males and 263,770 females, an increase in the females as compared with last year of 19,870, and a decrease in the males of 64,046. As respects age, 109,150 were under 14 years; 657,155 were between 14 and 45, and 46,565 were 45 or over. 3,053 could read but not write; 168,903 could neither read nor write. In

presumed the remainder, 640,014, could both read and write. It also appears that 103,750 of these aliens had already been to this country. That 95,375 brought with them fifty dollars or more each, while 501,530 brought each less than fifty dollars. The total amount of money shown to officers by these 812,000 aliens was $20,894,383, or $4,776,870 more than was brought by the 857,000 of the year before. This fact, taken in connection with the circumstance already referred to as to countries from which the increase of the year under consideration came, furnishes assurance of a marked improvement in the character and thrift of the more recent immigration. The 28,451 English immigrants brought with them, in 1903, $1,405,000. This year the 41,479 of the same race brought $2,736,000. The 35,366 Irish had $796,000, while the 37,000 Irish this year showed [illegible],000,000. 71,700 German immigrants last year had $2,480,000, this year, 74,790 possessed in hand $3,622,000.

It is further shown that there were excluded at the seaports of the United States during the year a total of 7,994, indicated as follows:

Idiots	16	Women for immoral purposes	9
Insane	33	Assisted aliens	38
Paupers	4,798	Contract laborers	1,501
Diseased persons	1,560	Anarchists	1
Convicts	35	Procurers	3

While considering our own national immigration statistics, let us have in mind the movement to and from Canada. Keep in mind, too, that Canada has more land than the United States, though we still have millions of acres to be occupied by the immigrant after irrigation has done its ecessary work of transforming the desert into a garden. Canada now has a population of about six millions, and more than three millions and a half square miles of area. Canada has more area than the United States, but we have a population of more than eighty millions. I am informed from good authority that the emigration from Canada during the last one hundred years or less has been one million. Her immigration last year was 100,000, fully half of it going across the imaginary line from the United States. Seventy-five per cent. of her total immigration is from the agricultural classes of foreign countries.

Now, what are the real reasons for this great movement of peoples from our shores to North America? The reasons are very well stated by Whelpley, to whom I have already referred.

Leaving out of consideration the movement of all undesirable people, such as criminals and paupers, Whelpley refers to four distinct causes of migration.

First, the *natural* cause which arises from the restlessness and ambition of youth and middle age, apparent in all peoples. As a rule, these people make acceptable citizens.

Second, the *economic* wrongs that are causing the exodus from Italy, and in a less degree from Austria-Hungary. Sicily is practically depopulated. From some of the Italian villages over eighty per cent. of the people have come to the United States, to escape what really amounts to slavery and mental and bodily starvation.

Third, the *political* cause is best illustrated in the case of the Hebrews of Russia (permit me to say, however, that we can afford to drop the curtain over Russia at this time. It's as bad to hit a nation as it is to hit a man, when that nation is down.)

Fourth, the *artificial* cause is the abnormal activity of Transportation Companies to secure business.

Now, for some fears viewed also from our own national standpoint. I prefer to state them in the language of Commissioner Sargent. He says:

It is impossible for any but the most recklessly and foolishly optimistic to view the situation without realizing very seriously its bearing upon our well being. It is not alone that virtually nearly a million aliens have been added to our population within the short space of one year. I think that fact is one of large dimensions. All the constituent elements of this great army of invasion are to be considered—their individuality, character, and capacity for useful work, their respect for law and order and their ability to stand the strain, moral, physical, and mental, of the life of their new surroundings. In other words, the power to assimilate with people of this country, and thus become a source of strength for the support of American institutions and civilization, instead of a danger in periods of strain and trial. To doubt that they possess such ability is to discredit unvarying human experiences. The problem presented, therefore, to enlighten intelligence for solution is, how may the possibility—nay, probability—of danger from an enormous and miscellaneous influx of aliens be converted by a wise prevision and provision into a power of stability and security?

Now for some remedies, to be summed up in two good words, distribution and evangelization.

First.—As to the practical question of distribution, take in the words of an expert. "These congested alien centers within our cities and States become a menace to physical, social, moral, and political security." As Commissioner Sargent has said, "These colonies become hotbeds for the propagation and growth of those false ideas of political and personal freedom whose germs have been vitalized by ages of oppression under unequal and partial laws, which find their first concrete expression in resistance to constituted authority, even the occasional assassination of lawful agents of that authority. Above all, they are congested places in the industrial body which check the free circulation of labor to those parts where it is most needed, and where it can be most benefited. Do away with them, and the greatest peril of immigration will be removed."

The problem of the distribution of immigration must be carefully thought out. Commissioner Sargent suggests that the government establish a Bureau of Information. A splendid suggestion, when we take into consideration that thirty-two per cent. of the immigrants remain in New York. This problem of distribution is not, however, to be easily settled at the seaport where the immigrant lands. It must be handled at the point of his debarkation. Thus, again, I believe I am proving that the whole general question is one of international importance, and demands most careful consideration by accredited representatives from various governments.

The question of evangelization, thank God, is now being taken up by many of the evangelical denominations and societies having headquarters in our own land. We must keep in mind, however, the fact that a very large proportion of this alien population, whatever their life may have been politically or socially, as compared with our own, is composed of loyal adherents of Christianity as expressed in various forms. The steerage of many a ship contains devout Christian men and women, loyal to the work of God, whose motive power is swayed by the deep fundamental truths of Christianity. My heart often burns with indignation when many a speaker unconsciously, in his appeal, which often seems self-righteous eloquence, urges that the Gospel of Christ be carried to these immigrants as they come to us, assuming that they are pagan, and that Christianity is unknown to them. We must give the Gospel to those who do not have it, and we must surround with proper influences those who have already espoused it in their home lands, and thus strengthen and deepen their faith.

Unless the question is thoughtfully considered and the problem solved, the alien invasion into this country of ours "may be the rift within the lute which, slowly widening, will make the American music mute." Instead, however, of placing undue emphasis on the menace of this invasion, I consider it a mission, not only for the loyal disciple of Christianity,

WILLIAM S. WAUDBY,
Special Agent U. S. Bureau of Labor.

but a mission for every loyal American. We must Americanize the immigrant, or he may Europeanize us. We must lift him up, or he may pull us down.

SHALL THE UNITED STATES SUSPEND IMMIGRATION?

(By William S. Waudby, Special Agent U. S. Bureau of Labor.)

Nearly two-thirds of the entire immigration of the world is directed to the United States!

The invasion and successful capture of the United States has been accomplished. None of the horrors of war were visible, and we provided the means of transporting the millions of invaders to our hospitable shores during the past decades. These invaders are very skilfully disguised under the form of "immigrants," and the railroad and steamship companies make a profit of $50,000,000 per annum in landing them.

Financial and industrial depressions in Europe, and prosperity in the United States, increases year by year the number of these invaders.

"Restriction" has been tried for twenty years, and still the immigration increases year by year, until it has arrived at that period in the country's history when it becomes not a question of "restriction" that confronts this nation, but the question of exclusion (for a term of years at least) of these immigrants. It is now the question of self-preservation.

The influence of immigration upon wages is large and complex, and there is no doubt at all that wages have fallen since the great tide of immigration set in; the only thing that has acted as a counterbalance being the solidarity of the labor organizations in resisting wholesale reductions in wage rates. Immigrants do make, and have made, first-class trades unionists, but in too many instances these migratory personages have been brought into the country for the purpose of taking the places of native labor, and are without trades union affiliations.

The first immigration law was passed by Congress in 1864, and was for the purpose of encouraging immigration—being entitled "An Act to Encourage Immigration." This act was repealed in 1868. From that time until 1882 (August 3) there was no statute bearing upon immigration.

After much discussion and agitation upon the part of the labor organizations then in existence, the local Federation of Labor of the District of Columbia (Washington City) succeeded in having a bill passed by Congress, which took effect February 26, 1885, and was the first step taken for protection against the "pauper labor" of Europe, and was known generally as the law "to prevent the importation of foreign labor under contract to perform labor or service of any kind in the United States."

Under this law it has been almost impossible to apprehend contract laborers in the casual examination to which they are subjected at the various ports of entry—and they are only arrested after they are actually engaged in the labor for which they have contracted to perform. The law has never been sufficient to accomplish the object of its enactment.

The United States has full power to exclude aliens altogether, as the Supreme Court has decided that question beyond all controversy. In May, 1895, Justice Harlan delivered this opinion of the Court: "The power of Congress to exclude aliens altogether from the United States, or to prescribe the terms and conditions upon which they may come to this country, and to have its declared policy in that regard enforced exclusively through executive officers, without judicial intervention, is settled by our previous adjudications."

Each of the leading steamship lines has several thousand agents engaged in working up immigration traffic.

In one of the Senate committee investigations it was shown that the Italian bankers of New York City send to Italy in an average year from $25,000,000 to $30,000,000. This is a permanent injury to the labor and capital of the United States surely.

The Italians were the first to be exploited by the "padrone system"—now all nationalities are fair spoils; employment agencies (?) now take the place of the padrone in the large cities. It is possible for a contractor to secure any number of Italians or other laborers, at short notice, at about one-half the wages of the American standard, for sewer, railroad, mining, clothing trades, etc. Thus native labor suffers many hardships by this displacement. This system exists among the Poles, Hungarians, Greeks, Armenians, Russian Jews, and others. Many Armenians and Greeks are employed in the cotton mills of New England, especially in Massachusetts, having been brought in to break strikes and to reduce wages.

The immigration question is a national one.

"Immigration" is an economic as well as a political question.

In one day in May (the 8th) ten steamship companies landed 12,039 immigrants at Ellis Island. Never before have so many steerage passengers come into this port. During the month of March, 1904, the [illegible] ber of immigrants was 78,225—or an avera[illegible] of 2,523. For the month of March, 1905, [illegible] was increased to 126,932—or an average da[illegible] of 4,094.

Where do they all find work? The labor market can not expand rapidly enough to provide for all of these new arrivals, so that the labor already here must either be displaced or compete with this daily influx and at pauper labor rates.

The monthly statements issued by the Bureau of Immigration are well worth the careful study of every class of our citizen voters, and especially that of every workingman. The statistics therein are clearly set forth as to the nationalities represented, and it is readily observable how few are the English-speaking arrivals. These reports also indicate the occupations and probable destination of the immigrants, and give a mass of information that is of great value to the student, as well as to the investigator after knowledge.

In the March (1905) report of this bureau, out of 126,932 arrivals for the month, there were 97,786 from Austria-Hungary, Italy, and the Russian Empire alone. Norway, Sweden, and Denmark threw in 7,334, with 1,433 from Finland as good measure. Greece contributed 349, and Bulgaria, Servia, and Montenegro's quota was 295. Should the March average hold out we will have a record for 1905 of a million and one-half immigrants, or double that of the highest period (1903), with its score of 857,046 arrivals.

By decades the problem stands as follows:

1820-1830	128,392
1830-1840	539,391
1840-1850	1,423,337
1850-1860	2,799,423
1860-1870	1,964,061
1870-1880	2,834,040
1880-1890	5,246,613
1890-1900	3,694,298
1900-1904	3,255,149

It will be noticed that in the first half of the last decade the immigration nearly approaches that of the entire 1890-1900 decade.

At a recent meeting of the patrons and members of the Home for Aged and Infirm Hebrews, New York City, Edward Lauterbach made the statement that 90,000 Russian Jews were preparing to emigrate to the United States, "turning their backs on tyranny and persecution, and coming to the land of freedom and liberty. The time is coming, and you engaged in charity work necessarily must face it, when the care of thousands of your Russian brethren will be in your keeping."

Is it not time for the nation to take serious thought over this vital matter? Why waste so much time over trifles like "tainted money" or "frenzied finance," when questions like this immigration problem confront us?

AN INTERNATIONAL CONFERENCE.

Departures and Arrivals Should be Regulated by Countries of Origin and Destination.

(By Gino C. Speranza, Lecturer on Italian Immigration.)

IT has been justly said that the United States immigration law is "the most far-reaching measure of its kind in force in any country," and a most competent foreign observer has recently declared that "it is thoroughly and intelligently enforced."

Why then, despite such severe statutory provisions and their strict enforcement, do our immigration laws fall short of their purpose and leave much to be desired? The answer seems simple enough, yet it appears to have escaped many of our sociologists and legislators. *Our immigration laws fall short of their purpose because they seek to control by national means such a movement of population as can be disciplined only by international action.*

It has been generally recognized that the *source of supply* is the strategic point for the control of immigration; yet we have centered our efforts in pushing back the migratory tide *after* it reaches our shores; in other words, after it has reached this point where it is hardest to check it, and where, at times, we must resort to methods savoring of cruelty in order to enforce the letter of the law.

But it will be argued that our laws can have no extraterritorial application; that we can not legislate for people not subjects of our government and outside of our jurisdiction. This is true, as far as it goes. But to-day the old international demarcations are becoming obliterated. Commercial interests and improved methods of transportation and communication are not only drawing countries into a closer community of interests, but increasing the causes and occasions for international action. Shipping has been, from ancient times, regulated by international agreement. The apprehension of fugitives from justice has necessarily been the subject for international conventions or treaties. To-day international cooperation is resorted to not only where commercial interests are involved, such as posts, telegraphs and patents, but in the interest of health, such as quarantine regulations and the enforcement of laws [illegible] adulteration of certain food stuffs.

[illegible], recognizing that the problem of the immi[illegible] international one, and having many striking [illegible] for joint action among different countries, have we made little, if any, attempt to reach some international agreement?

I say it with the utmost respect, but with no less serious conviction, that it is because we have allowed certain preconceived notions and prejudices to blind our judgment and our powers of observation. We have allowed the notion to gain currency that foreign governments were using our land as a dumping ground for the worst elements of their population, and that they were, directly or indirectly, encouraging such noisome exodus for their benefit and to our detriment. With such notion firmly established in the popular mind, we approached the problem of the immigrant in a spirit, if not of prejudice, certainly of narrowness. Our legislators sought legislative measures which savored more of *defense* against an invading horde than of adjustment of what is, in its essentials, a natural phenomenon; so, likewise, our officials enforced those provisions more in a spirit of suspicion against probable evaders of our statutes than as impartial magistrates.

This is not said in a spirit of criticism. It is set forth rather as showing one of the causes that have prevented international action. For, obviously, if we think, for instance, that Austro-Hungary or Italy is dumping her refuse here, how can we even propose that those countries agree to certain regulations to be mutually enforced? So we send Secret Service men to spy on officials of friendly Powers to get at their "plots" for exporting their *Mafiosi* and their incapables, instead of sending or inviting delegates in an open, frank, businesslike manner *as we should do if we wished to arrange about our postal rates, or the protection of our trade marks.*

I plead in all earnestness for a juster attitude, and one more in harmony with the facts, toward the problem of the immigrant, as only thus can we pave the way for that international action which alone can be effective in the solution of such a problem. More in harmony with the facts I say, for we must free ourselves of the idea that the problem of the immigrant is a problem only for us, and not for the country of the immigrant's origin. We must recognize the fact that any large movement of population, such as that represented by the annual flow of aliens to our shores, is not, and can not be, looked upon with pleasure, still less encouraged by the countries of origin. Italy, for instance, can not well afford, in the long run, to loose thousands of her able-bodied sons every year. Sicilian wheat fields are becoming pasture land from lack of hands to till them; the old men left at home can not take care of the farms. Italy needs strong men in her factories, in her fields, and for her army.

Looking upon the problem in this light, What are the chances for international action?

I can only speak as regards Italy, and yet the example of Italy may be most instructive. Even to-day the Italian government allows American medical examiners at Italian ports of departure. This of itself is some evidence against the popular belief that that country seeks to evade our laws on immigration. Her Emigration Department, about which so little is known here, exercises a positive check rather then an encouragement to emigration. The Italian emigration law has been called the finest example of modern social legislation, and if it were better known here many popular ideas regarding governmental encouragement to emigration would be quickly disposed of. Official documents are on record showing a serious desire on the part of the Italian government to have our immigration laws respected. The annual reports of its emigration department, and its official instructions to the mayors of Italian cities, might be cited. A circular of the Minister of Foreign Affairs, issued last April at Rome, reaffirms an earlier provision that no passport be issued to an intending emigrant who would be excluded by the laws of the country to which he intends going. "It is in the public interest," reads the circular, "that a

GINO C. SPERANZA,
Lectures on Italian Immigration.

migratory current should not be tainted by elements considered undesirable by the country of destination." The last annual report of the Italian Emigration Department makes a strong appeal to Italian emigrants against crowding in American cities, and urges their settling in agricultural States. Recently, while in Italy, I had many interviews with political men and leaders of thought, such as journalists, writers, professors, and magistrates. Their opinion was practically unanimous that Italy would consent to cooperate with us in the regulation of her emigration, provided the subject were approached in the proper way.

In that last statement lies, in my opinion, the secret of successful international action. If we approach a foreign government in a spirit of suspicion, treating it as an inferior who is trying to evade our laws or as a poor cousin who wants to burden us with its numerous and incapable children, our endeavors are foredoomed to failure.

But let us call an international conference as between political equals, inviting delegates and asking for suggestions and frank discussion; let us bring together men really cognizant with existing conditions and laws, instead of relying on peripatetic observers who give us picturesque but superficial observations, and we can be tolerably sure of achieving some substantial results regarding the regulation of immigration.

In conclusion I would suggest:

First—That foreign legislation regarding emigration, and its enforcement, be more carefully studied with a view to reaching a juster idea of the attitude of foreign countries toward emigration, its regulation, and control.

Second—That an international conference on immigration be called by our government, to which delegates from every European country be invited to discuss international regulations of the movement of population between different countries.

Third—That, in the meanwhile, as regards Italy, closer direct relations be established between our immigration department and the Italian emigration department, looking especially to the possibility of a rational distribution of Italian immigration.

As regards this last suggestion, the Italian government is officially on record as desirous of cooperating with Commissioner General Frank S. Sargent in his plans to induce Italians to settle in our Southern States, where there is a great demand for farm hands. This would be an excellent beginning in that cooperation which would result in benefit both to ourselves and to the strangers within our gates.

CHINESE BOYCOTTS AND EXCLUSION.

An Historical Review of our Legislation against Asiatic Immigration.

(By Earle Ashley Walcott, in *Collier's Weekly*.)

ON both sides of the Pacific there appears to have arisen an organized attempt to break down the exclusion policy that shuts out the Chinese from free admission to the United States.

"Boycott American goods," or the Chinese equivalent, has been raised as the war-cry of China's commercial leaders, if we may believe the despatches from China, and under official encouragement has united the dealers and consumers in a non-importation league for the punishment of America. Even the Chinese Chamber of Commerce of Manila passed the boycott resolution, but on second thoughts rescinded it The reason for this attempt to cut off America's growing trade in the Orient is said to be the indignation roused by the American policy of excluding certain classes of Chinese.

Simultaneously with the boycott agitation in China, a chorus of complaints has been raised in the American press against the harshness with which the exclusion laws are administered. The examination of merchants, students, and travelers of Chinese birth has been criticised as on a level with the examination of a suspected criminal seeking to enter the country. The case of a Chinese, claiming to have been born in this country, denied admission by the immigration bureau, and refused relief by the Supreme Court of the United States as a matter outside its jurisdiction, has also been used to excite sympathy for the excluded Chinese and to cast discredit upon the exclusion policy.

The demand for the exclusion of the Chinese took its rise in the hard times that followed the panic of 1873. There had been sporadic agitations before, but they had no force. With the hard times, employment became scarce and business suffered. The pinch came, as usual, hardest on the laboring man. He looked about him for a cause of his troubles, and saw the Chinese, employed, prosperous, growing in numbers. Every steamer from the Orient brought a thousand or more immigrants from China. In 1872, 10,642 came; in 1873, 18,154; in 1874, 16,651; in 1875, 19,033; in 1876, 16,879. These added to a city whose population was less than 200,000, and to a State whose population was less than 800,000, produced industrial disturbance. Chinatown grew and prospered while the white men were in distress, because the Chinaman could live and thrive on wages that would not support a white man.

The workmen of California, having decided upon the cause of their woes, promptly organized to demand the exclusion of their competitors. They made such a noise about it that Congress sent out investigating committees, who took much testimony that is buried in the cellars of the Capitol. The committees found that the Chinese roused hostility by both their virtues and their vices—the virtues being a little ahead in the competition.

The testimony of both friends and foes of the Chinese justified the following conclusions: The Chinaman is of extraordinary industry, docile, faithful to a bargain, not addicted to intoxicating liquors. He worked for low wages, lived in quarters that a white man could not occupy, was content with a little boiled rice and a cup of tea when he could get nothing better, and was able to master any industry known to the white man. Hence the Chinaman was employed while the white man was left idle.

Possibly the difficulties of the white laboring man under Chinese competition would have excited but indifferent sympathy had it not developed that the competition of the Chinese against the American employer was quite as keen and successful as that against the American workman. The American shoe manufacturer, for instance, who filled his factory with Chinese workmen to cut down the wage bill, presently found that a Chinese manufacturer had learned the business from him and was running a plant on a closer margin than he himself could afford. Having taught the business to the Chinese, a Chinese capitalist, with Chinese foremen, Chinese laborers, and a Chinese office force, was underselling him in his own market. The same was found to be the case in a number of other lines—notably ready-made clothing and cigar making, which were largely controlled by Chinese. It was evident that under the operation of the natural laws of trade a large part of the manufacturing and commercial business of the city would eventually pass to the yellow man as the one best fitted to survive in the struggle for existence. There-e employers as well as employed became vigorous ponents of Chinese immigration.

Besides economic objections there were others. The ge Chinese population of the Pacific Slope was med almost exclusively of young men; and these n, removed from the influence of home ties and ditional public sentiment, developed a combination Oriental and Western vices demoralizing to the mmunities about them. The importation of women immoral purposes early became a recognized traffic at forty years of vigorous effort on the part of the icers of the law has scarce sufficed to stamp out. mbling and opium-smoking are ineradicable vices the race, and they have introduced the opium habit iong the white people with lamentable results. ackmail and murder are a recognized business in inatown. Large organizations live by collecting oney from merchants, gambling houses, and haunts vice. They enforce their contributions by the knife, e hatchet, and the revolver. Private disputes are so settled by murder, the Highbinders, so-called, atnding to the business for a cash payment. The price r killing a man runs from $50 to $2,500, according his social or business position. These crimes have e saving grace that they are committed by Chinese on Chinese for Chinese. It is rare for them to atck a white person. But within their own quarters ey have a large number of bold and desperate crimils, requiring an extraordinary police service to aintain order.

Thus, from all causes, the friends of the open door licy in California were reduced in numbers to those spired by the duty of saving the Chinaman's soul, d the large landholders who found Chinese labor, hich could be hired in gangs for a few months in the ar and turned off to shift for itself for the rest of e time, the only labor that could make the great nches profitable. So when it was put to a vote in alifornia, in 1879, only 883 voted for Chinese immiration, while 154,638 voted against it.

All these matters were laid before Congress, and ongress sympathized. Impressed by the deadly earestness of the Pacific Slope, the legislative body beame dimly conscious that there was a real danger to hite supremacy in the outposts of our own land. So 1878 both Houses passed the Fifteen Passenger bill, miting the number of Chinese that could be brought y any one vessel to fifteen. President Hayes vetoed , and advised a treaty with China as the first step in estricting immigration.

In 1880, James B. Angell, John F. Swift, and William H. Trescott were sent to China and negotiated treaty agreeing that the United States might limit r suspend the coming of Chinese, but might not proibit it.

Then in 1882 Congress passed a bill suspending the oming of the Chinese for twenty years. President Arthur vetoed it on the ground that the twenty-year imit was prohibition, not suspension. Congress cut lown the limit to ten years, and Arthur signed the ill. The act forbade Chinese to enter after ninety lays from the passage of the act, but permitted the Chinese in America to re-enter the country after reurning to China. They were required merely to take ut return certificates on leaving the United States, and present them on re-entering.

The act came up against a hostile court and was unched as full of holes as a sieve. It was held that he act applied to those who left the country between he adoption of the treaty of 1880 and the ninety days fter the passage of the act, when it went into effect; and as it was impossible for these to have obtained eturn certificates, they should be permitted to enter upon parol evidence of prior residence. Court proedure became wonderfully simplified. Chinese seekng to enter the country without certificates were lenied landing by the customs officers. A writ of abeas corpus was thereupon issued by the Federal Court, returnable before a court commissioner. The Chinese were thereupon landed, taken before the comnissioner in express wagons without guard. A few questions were asked as to the geography of San Francisco and the time they had lived here. The oaching was not very good, and the answers were often ridiculous, but the commissioner usually reported to the court that they were prior residents. The District-Attorney would protest, and the court would sign an order turning them loose. Under this procedure 8,031 were admitted in 1883. It was a ource of bubbling indignation to San Francisco. The press roared. The United States District-Attorney said to me one day with tears of anger in his eyes: "Every day I go to the limits of contempt of court, but nothing I can say will move those men to enforce the law." The three judges were kept busy ordering discharges under habeas corpus writs.

The protest reached Congress, and in 1884 the law was amended to make the return certificate "the sole evidence" on which a Chinese laborer could establish his right to land. The Federal Courts paid no attention to this enactment. The act by its terms admitted the right of all who had left after the ratification of the treaty of 1880 to return, and the judges held that the provision that the certificate should be the only evidence to entitle laborers to land did not apply to those who left before certificates were issued. Therefore they continued to hear parol evidence, and to land Chinese on testimony that was for the most part flat perjury.

But the perjury of the bogus "prior resident" was not the only ground of complaint. It soon became evident that the certificate business itself was being overdone. Investigation showed that certificates were articles of merchandise. Every Chinese who left America took out an authorization to return, and promptly sold it to some one who wanted to cross the water to make his fortune. Brokers bought up certificates, schools were maintained in Hong Kong and even on shipboard to teach the Chinese immigrant to answer the few questions that were asked by the customs officers. Then a "ring" was uncovered in the custom house itself that had been issuing forged certificates by the thousand, and selling them to the Chinese brokers. Some of the gang were sent to prison. The others fled. With "prior residents," forged certificates, and other devices for evading the law, coolie immigration grew rapidly—7,704 in 1885-86, 11,162 in 1886-87, 12,816 in 1887-88.

The indignation roused by these exposures brought the passage of the Scott act of 1888. The circumstances were these: In March, 1888, the Senate requested the President to negotiate a treaty with China, providing that no Chinese laborer should thereafter enter the United States. The treaty was negotiated through the Chinese Minister and sent to the Senate on the 17th of March. The Senate added a provision that Chinese laborers who had left this country and had not then returned should not be permitted to return, even though they held return certificates. The treaty was sent to China for ratification, and on the report that it had been rejected by China a bill carrying out substantially the same provisions was brought into the House on September 3, passed at once without division, and sent to the Senate, passed by that body on September 7, and was signed by the President when official confirmation of the rejection of the treaty was received.

This measure cut off all the frauds of the "prior resident" testimony, the sale of certificates, and the forgery of certificates. The pleas under which a laborer could make his way into the country by sufficient perjury were reduced to two—the first being to swear that he was a "native born," who, under the court rulings, could establish his birth in San Francisco by parol evidence and enter as an American citizen, and the second was to play successfully the part of a merchant. Some hundreds dribbled in by these chinks in the exclusion wall.

Then in 1892 the whole subject was opened afresh. The Restriction Act of 1882, on which all subsequent legislation hung, expired by limitation in May of that year, and fresh legislation was sought. The famous Geary Act was framed by a Congressman from California, and in modified form was accepted by the Senate. It continued all former legislation for another period of ten years, made illegal entry into the United States a crime punishable by imprisonment and deportation, ordered all Chinese lawfully within the United States to take out certificates of identification, and made failure to produce such certificate a cause for deportation. The intent of these severe provisions was to make it easy to identify the smuggled Chinese who were drifting across the northern and southern borders in large numbers, lack of a certificate being presumptive evidence of unlawful entry into the country. Bail was by this act forbidden in habeas corpus cases. Congress modified the act in 1893 to permit the Chinese to comply more readily with the provisions for registration, and to strengthen the administrative features of the act.

This legislation ended most of the abuses against which the upholders of the exclusion law had contended. By the successive acts the handling of the Chinese seeking admission had become committed almost exclusively to administrative officers. The grounds on which a landing could be sought by the habeas corpus route had been so cut away by the successive enactments that the courts found little opportunity to interfere.

China, however, was not satisfied with this final legislation, and in 1894 sought a modification of the restrictions that had been thrown about the movements of her subjects. A treaty was framed permitting a Chinese having wife, child, or parent in the United States, or owning property to the amount of $1,000, or having solvent credits to the same amount, to take out a certificate, giving him the privilege of return within one year after leaving the United States. This treaty was made for the period of ten years, and at the end of that time China signified her wish to abrogate it.

In 1902 the Geary Act expired by limitation, and was re-enacted with a few additional provisions to strengthen its administrative features. It extended the restrictions of the law to the island possessions of the United States, required the Chinese in the Philippines to register, and provided that the island Chinese should not be permitted to come to the mainland. Then, in 1904, when China denounced the treaty, it became necessary to re-enact all prior legislation, and this was done without change. Here the legislative history ends, with China seeking a new treaty that shall reopen the doors to her people.

If the Chinese stand firm in their reported resolve to forego the advantage of buying the goods they want in the cheapest market, and shall decline to sell their products to Americans, no part of the United States will regret their policy more than the Pacific Slope. We are counting on the development of Oriental commerce as one of the chief elements in the future growth of our cities and the establishment of our manufactures. But if we must choose between the loss of this valuable trade and the surrender of white to yellow civilization in the Western seaboard States, we will relinquish the trade rather than sacrifice the ultimate interests of our land and our race.

THE IMMIGRATION PROBLEM IS SERIOUS.

But Serious for the Foreign Countries, Not for Us.

(Editorial in New York *Evening Journal*, June 8.)

Small-sized Americans, so much excited about the arrival of immigrants in this country, would be enlightened if they knew the attitude of the foreign countries toward emigration to America.

Every one of the foreign countries is doing its best to PREVENT such emigration.

Years ago, in South Germany, the newspapers printed dark and gloomy warnings, inspired by the government and intended to frighten the peasants.

These warnings told how emigrants to America were lured into barber shops here and had their throats cut—the chair and the murdered one subsequently sinking through the floor. Much ingenuity was used to convince the would-be emigrant that a trip to America was suicide.

In Spain, whence emigration has increased very rapidly, the newspapers and the government are much disturbed and are making every effort to keep the population from moving to America.

A similar crusade is made in Hungary, in Austria—in fact, everywhere throughout Europe.

The European nations, who lose the citizens that come here, are well aware that EMIGRANTS TO AMERICA ARE AMONG THE BEST CITIZENS OF THE VARIOUS COUNTRIES.

The emigrant has imagination, enterprise, and will power—otherwise he could not make up his mind to tear up his home, however humble, and move to an unknown country.

It is the character of the immigrants who reach this shore that has made the character of the American people.

If we are a nation of inventors, a nation of nervous activity, working on new lines—IT IS BECAUSE THE OLD COUNTRIES HAVE SENT THOSE QUALITIES TO US, giving us the best of their citizenship.

The Americans that oppose immigration are narrow-minded and ill-informed. It is proper to keep out professional criminals, diseased classes and idiots, since selfishness is the first law of "civilization."

But practically the entire body of immigrants add to the wealth of the country, the wealth of everybody in it.

We have untold millions of acres of land uncultivated. We need people to cultivate them.

All the people of the United States could live in comfort in the single State of Texas—and there would be room and food there for eighty millions more, even under our inferior processes of agriculture.

The United States needs a thousand millions of inhabitants. It needs more HUMAN BEINGS, as a great farm of the West needs horses and agricultural implements.

The country is lucky in having the enterprise, courage and manhood of the Old World to draw upon.

Remember that we get from Europe not only some of our best workers, some of our men of strongest ideas and personality, but also men BEST FITTED TO LIVE IN A REPUBLIC AND MAINTAIN A REPUBLIC.

Europe sends millions of men who know by experience what it is to live in a land where men are not free. These immigrants know by experience what the ballot means and what it should be worth.

Their influence is needed in a country where already republicanism is becoming a matter of course and the ballot more or less of a joke, a mere question of partisanship or financial advantage.

The European countries know that every immigrant arriving here is a loss to them and a gain for us. And we should be intelligent enough to realize that also.

But leaving out all question of gain, what right has the United States to act like a great international dog in the manger and presume to reserve this great section of the earth's surface for a small population, less than one-tenth of the number it can comfortably support?

LABOR AND THE ISTHMIAN CANAL.

(*Concluded from page 8.*)

President to discuss with him the possibility of Chinese reprisals or of possible Chinese animosity toward us, the danger to American manufactures and American commerce if this policy of ours of excluding Chinese labor is not changed in some way or other. I don't believe they mentioned the possibility of the repeal of the exclusion law, but it was openly hinted at in the newspaper interviews immediately following, and was so known to every observer.

We all know our very genial Ambassador from China to the United States, who returned to that country about a year ago, Mr. Wu Ting Fang. He was said to be very "charming" in his way in cajoling Americans, in telling them funny stories, and in trying to impress on the people of the United States that all the Chinese were of the mental caliber of the Ambassador. That Mr. Wu was a clever man, all the Americans who talked with him say. He judged the temper of some of our American methods at the first glance. And there is not a particle of doubt in my mind that this bright heathen Chinee, when he went back to China, carefully planned this scheme of a pretense to boycott American goods with the end to secure first, action such as is indicated by the issuance of the President's recent order, and second, to stimulate an agitation with the view of the repeal of the Chinese exclusion law.

In an address delivered recently by the Secretary of Commerce and Labor, he referred to an increase in the exportation of American manufactures and mechanical and agricultural implements to China of nine millions of dollars in the last year. I ask any candid man, with this fact in view, whether there is good ground, even taking the dollar as the only consideration, to change the policy of our country in regard to Chinese immigration and exclusion? There is not even that semblance of an excuse. I deny that this is sufficient ground, even if China should cut off every dollar of Chinese business. American manhood and American civilization are too dear to us, too sacred to us, even to take a chance at what Mongolian immigration into our country would mean.

You and I in New York can not tell what Chinese immigration is, in spite of the fact of Pell Street and that little district there. They say that comparisons are odious under any circumstances. It is impossible to make a comparison between Chinatown in New York and Chinatown in San Francisco. The Chinatown of New York and the Chinatown on the Pacific Coast stand in direct opposition to each other. Can you imagine for a whole mile around in the heart of the city, three stories underground, people living, living there the whole day and night, the whole night long, some of them never coming up to the surface at all? The entire place is unlike what we have here. Thousands are living there—not living, but ex-[illegible] But even that could be endured if there [illegible] possibility of their ever becoming American-[illegible] to understand Chinese life and Chinese im-[illegible], you have to understand this fact, that the [illegible] regards himself as possessing an entirely higher civilization than ours; that what we have is what they call barbarism, and our commercialism is entirely at variance with their considerations of human life. I shall not undertake to discuss whether ours is ideal or perfect. Every man agrees that it is not; but they think that their civilization is far above and beyond ours. I take it we don't want to become Chinaized, no matter how much more they may believe in their civilization than in ours.

The settled policy of the American people is that Chinese laborers, whether skilled or unskilled, must not come to the United States. Inasmuch as the Federal Government has by solemn treaty declared that the canal strip in the Isthmus of Panama belongs to the United States, the Chinaman must not come to Panama to build the canal. The danger of their coming by millions to the United States and undermining or overwhelming our civilization, not in my time—well, think what it means for others outside of you and me. We love our children; we love our country; we hope to perpetuate and improve this civilization which our forefathers have developed, and which we have brought to its present stage, and hope to make the conditions such that our children and our children's children shall make of this fair land of ours a haven for life and liberty and right and justice and humanity, which shall be manifest to every people everywhere.

The Executive Council of the American Federation of Labor has discussed this very question, and we have had several interviews with the Panama Canal and other Federal authorities. I want to say that you, of course, know—at any rate some of our enemies make it quite conspicuous—that I am a member of the Civic Federation. It is my pleasure to help in the suggestion of things that may be useful to the interests of labor. Those representing other interests have able men enough to look after their own interests. Whenever there is anything that can be said, or done, or suggested, in the interests of labor, that is my chance; and I have never permitted it to pass without taking advantage of it and turning it to the account of labor.

We all know that Brother Moffett is a splendid fellow. We are all proud of his friendship, his sterling qualities, and character; and we all have the feeling that his appointment to visit the Canal district and make an investigation and suggest improvements will be productive of great good; will convey useful knowledge to laborers all over the United States, as well as to the workmen who shall go to Panama. We shall learn the truth from him. He will be helpful to us and to the Commission. He is going to tell them what he believes to be true, and he will have wonderful opportunities of observation. He goes with the good will of organized labor everywhere.

I may say that the appointment of Mr. Moffett and the appointment of Mr. Nazro is the result of an idea of the welfare of labor in industrial plants wherein we have been helped whenever that idea came to the front.

We want the Canal built and built well, under American conceptions of right, justice, and humanity. So that when completed without tears or wails it may stand as another perpetual monument to the skill, the genius of American science, American labor, American manhood and grit.

STATE MEDIATOR R. W. HAWTHORNE.

Robert W. Hawthorne, recently appointed the New York State Mediator of Industrial Disputes by Commissioner of Labor P. Tecumseh Sherman, is a native of New York City, where he has been actively employed

ROBERT W. HAWTHORNE.
N. Y. State Mediator of Industrial Disputes.

since leaving school. After valuable experience as Executive Secretary to Judge Greenbaum, he was for several years engaged in reporting important cases in the courts. Three years ago he became Assistant Secretary of the National Civic Federation and Secretary of the Conciliation Committee of the Civic Federation of New York. In those capacities he developed unusual tact and readiness in averting and settling disputes between labor and capital, participating in several important negotiations. Commissioner Sherman selected him for his present public position entirely because of these qualifications.

WELFARE WORK.

(*Concluded from page 14.*)

In the third grade dues of fifty cents entitle them to $6.00 a week sick benefit and $50.00 death benefit.

All fines, the total never amounting to more than $200 a year, are turned over to the Society.

The regular sick benefits are paid upon receipt of the attending doctor's certificate.

To all members living in Manhattan the services of a physician are free.

The physician employed by the Society devotes two hours daily to medical attendance of the employes in the store. He is provided with a well equipped office for immediate dispensary work. This is proving of great benefit. Prompt attention to illness in its first stage often prevents its serious development.

To any member in urgent need the president of the Society may give outright a sum not exceeding $25.00. Thus everyone throughout the establishment knows that any honest case of genuine want can be immediately relieved without red tape or delay.

The Society loans to a member when pecuniarily embarrassed, temporarily, an amount not exceeding $50.00. This loan, without interest, must be paid back in weekly instalments.

The benefits of the Mutual Aid Society extend, under its by-laws, only to members in good standing, but the Society administers the "Fannie Myers Fund," which is devoted to the assistance of the families [illegible] employes who are not members, and, therefore, [illegible] not entitled to aid from the Society. Its beneficiaries include ex-employes and members of the Society, wh[illegible] have received all the benefits to which the [illegible] entitle them.

Thanksgiving Eve, every employe who desires [illegible] presented by the Society with a fine turkey.

The restaurant for employes has ample space, [illegible] and light. Moderate prices are charged to enable the lowest as well as the highest paid employes to [illegible] luncheon, and the restaurant is used each year by [illegible] increasing number. It is conducted at a loss to the firm.

An annual ball, with a special entertainment, is [illegible] by the Mutual Aid Society. This ball is one of the prominent features of the winter season, and is highly popular.

The junior help is not permitted to attend the an-nual ball. For the entertainment of the juniors and of their friends, the firm gives a May Party on Deco-ration Day. This party is in charge of about one hundred chaperons, women and men employes, selected because of their fitness. The young people who at-tended the last May Party consumed one thousand quarts of milk, five thousand sandwiches, four barrels of sweet crackers, and three hundred and fifty quarts of ice cream. To add to their enjoyment, there were distributed five hundred bean bags, two gross of rubber balls and two gross jumping ropes.

Women employes who have been with the firm for one year or longer are sent every summer for a week's vacation to a hotel at Far Rockaway, L. I. Sometimes in the case of girls of more delicate physique this vacation is extended to two weeks. They are paid their full salary; receive their transportation to and from Far Rockaway, and their board is paid, while many amusements are provided free of expense. Among these is a weekly Tally-Ho ride through the beautiful surrounding country. The increasing popularity of these free vacations is shown by the fact that three hundred and fifty are listed for this year, while two hundred and fifty enjoyed the trip to the country last year.

The chaperons who gave up a day of rest and pleasure to attend and entertain the junior employes at the May Party on Decoration Day are remembered with a special outing on Labor Day. They are then the guests of the firm at Far Rockaway, where they are entertained at breakfast, dinner and luncheon and enjoy a ride in the Tally-Ho.

The term "Welfare Work," in the view of the firm, has proved most happy, in that it conveys no suggestion of charity. Many employes avail themselves of advantages offered who would never accept them in the form of personal charity, which was the only method of rendering benefit before the present system was organized.

"INTERCOLLEGIATE SOCIALIST SOCIETY."

(*Concluded from page 11.*)

persuade himself and his perturbed friends is a wholly innocuous form of mental culture. In its systematic treachery, the plan is in thorough accordance with the Socialist plot to scuttle the ship of organized labor by "boring from within." Socialist students are to be stimulated to "enter the people's universities" [illegible] spreading their propaganda in dark and devious ways that will "excite the least antagonism," just as Socialist workingmen are urged to join the unions of their crafts, there to promote, in the phrase of one of Mr. Higginson's fellow-signers, their "insidious propaganda." Teachers are to imitate the example of Prof. Ferri, who does not "frighten" his listeners with frank, plain language; who does not whisper before timid youth the startling word "Socialism," but [illegible] instills into their ears all the poison of its creed of revolution.

We think that Mr. Higginson can no longer complain that the editor of *Harper's Weekly* overstated the case in saying that the Intercollegiate Socialist Society "aims to imbue the minds of the rising generation with Socialist doctrines."

Assuredly, Mr. Higginson can no longer plead ignorance of the facts as an excuse for his surprising association with an organization whose purposes and whose origin are utterly at variance with his distinguished record as an American soldier and patriot.

The Civic Federation of New England has issued a bulletin setting forth its scope and purposes. This association, although an independent body, is patterned after the National Civic Federation, and hopes to be of assistance in settling industrial disputes in its particular locality. Frank K. Foster, of Boston, one of the International Typographical Union delegates to the American Federation of Labor, is a member of the executive committee of the federation.—*Typographical Journal.*

Under the agreement system the best judgment on each side will control the situation; under the rough-and-tumble system the most pugnacious element will control.—*Coast Seamen's Journal.*

The National Civic Federation Review

Vol. II. No. 5 NEW YORK, SEPTEMBER—OCTOBER, 1905 Ten Cents

CONCILIATION'S GREATEST VICTORY.

ITS SUCCESS IN PRODUCING THE PEACE OF PORTSMOUTH STRENGTHENS ITS POTENCY IN THE ADJUSTMENT OF GREAT INDUSTRIAL DISPUTES.

THE principle of conciliation and conference has received the most profoundly impressive exercise that the world has ever seen in the signing of the treaty of peace by the plenipotentiaries of Russia and Japan.

The historic event at Portsmouth, N. H., on September was the successful culmination of an effort, pronounced without precedent, to end war and restore peace through their employment. This effort was made in the name of civilization and humanity. The race has been incalculably benefited, and its moral and material progress has been immensely forwarded by the cessation of the terrible and disastrous conflict between Russia and Japan, brought about through the initiative and dignified endeavor of the President of the United States.

The results to humanity and civilization are not only of immediate but of cumulative benefit. Not only are the waste of blood and treasure and the interruption to economic production brought to an end, but it has been demonstrated to every government on this planet that it is practicable to adjust international disputes amicably, through frank discussion between their authorized representatives around the conference table, instead of upon the battlefield. The demonstration has all the lasting force and weight, not only of the theories of students of international relations, but of practical execution. This concrete result appeals to the imagination of the world and impresses itself as a fact accomplished that must influence all the future evolution of human history.

The lesson goes even further. If war, with all its grim enginery in full activity, with all its passions fiercely inflamed, with all its energies at their most intense strain, can thus be ended, if armies can be halted in the very midst of murderous combat, if their guns can be silenced and their charges checked with hand upon lanyard and with sabers in air, if the bristling area of carnage can be converted into a smiling region of peace, all through a verbal process between plenipotentiaries, then surely the peoples of the world, upon whose productive capacity the burdens of all wars fall, should be increasingly open to the conviction that it is possible to settle industrial wars through similar processes of negotiation.

THEODORE ROOSEVELT
THE GREAT CONCILIATOR.

International diplomacy thus points the way that industrial diplomacy should tread. As humanity has paid in the blood and tears of centuries the frightful cost of the "last argument of kings," so have "countless thousands" mourned because of the inhuman elements enlisted upon either side in the perennial dispute between capital and labor over their just shares in the product of their united efforts. If national conciliation and conference can lessen the red stain of battles upon the pages of history, it is an irresistible inference that the application of the same methods [illegible] in increasing ratio [illegible] attending the necessary adjustments between employer and employed, and that the progress of civilization, which must include simultaneously greater economy of production and a higher standard of living, can be carried forward with fewer of those industrial battles known as the lockout and the strike.

In the world of industry, when capital and labor are at war, it has been demonstrated repeatedly that personal, face-to-face conference between their representatives, when duly authorized and clothed with power to treat, has no equal for establishing mutual respect and confidence and bringing about a settlement which, without such a conference, would have seemed impossible. The terms of such a settlement are often formulated in a trade agreement, which thus may be entitled an industrial treaty, which representatives of both capital and labor declare should be held sacredly inviolate.

In the world of international politics, diplomacy has for centuries striven to prevent or to provoke wars, as the policy of sovereigns might dictate; but diplomacy has been always the channel through which war was prevented or peace restored. The foundation of diplomacy is communication or conference between the direct representatives of sovereign powers; and its most pacific results are embodied in treaties, which are the highest law [illegible] the participating countries.

When conflict actually exists between capital and labor in an industry there is as much opportunity for the exercise of methods of conference as there is in war between nations. The opportunity in each case is strikingly similar. Who is to act as conciliator? Who is to persuade the belligerents, whether national or industrial, to consent to a conference, with a view to the cessation of hostilities and the restoration of peace? Obviously, if neither party to the war is crushed, it must be some outsider; and that outsider must be possessed of certain qualities. The outsider, if his attempted mediation is not to be rejected peremptorily and resentfully by one or the other or by both the combatants, must first of all be disinterested. His motive must be above suspicion. He must also possess a dignity and prestige that entitle him to the most distinguished consideration of each side. He must command respect as well as confidence.

These were precisely and essentially the conditions that surrounded the action of the President of the United States which resulted in the cessation of the war between Russia and Japan. He impersonated a government of strict neutrality. It could not be suspected of self-interest. There was historic warrant for confidence in the disinterested and sincere friendship of that government for each of the warring powers. Simultaneously, the Government of the United States commanded the respect of each. Its intervention was in behalf of the largest "general public," that is, of humanity and civilization. All this was represented in the identical note of the President to Russia and Japan:

"The President feels that the time has come when in the interest of all mankind he must endeavor to see if it is not possible to bring to an end the terrible and lamentable conflict now being waged. With both Russia [illegible] the United States [illegible]ed ties of friend[illegible]oodwill. It hopes [illegible]rosperity and wel[illegible]ch, and it feels that the progress of the world is set back by the war between these two great nations.

"The President accordingly urges the Russian and Japanese Governments, not only for their own sake, but in the interest of the whole civilized world, to open direct negotiations for peace with one another.

"The President suggests that these peace negotiations be conducted directly and exclusively between the belligerents; in other words, that there be a meeting of Russian and Japanese plenipotentiaries or delegates without any intermediary, in order to see if it is not possible for these representatives of the two powers to agree to terms of peace. The President earnestly asks [the two governments] to agree to such meeting. While the President does not feel that any intermediary should be called in in respect to peace negotiations themselves, he is willing to do what he properly can if the two powers concerned feel that his services will be of aid in arranging the preliminaries to the time and place of meeting.

"But even if these preliminaries can be arranged directly between the two powers, or in any other way, the President will be glad, as his whole purpose is to bring about a meeting which the whole civilized world will pray may result in peace."

The student of industrial economics and the student of international relations may read this letter with the same eyes and may read it above, below and between its lines with the same conclusion. That conclusion is that there has been applied, with a success without precedent, but with a success that establishes a precedent, the identical methods of conciliation and conference between warring states that have been proved to be most efficient when invoked to end conflicts between capital and labor. These mighty forces within the boundaries of any country should find in the President's illustrious achievement the inspiration to infuse renewed energy into efforts for just reconciliation of industrial differences through mediation.

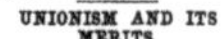
M. Witte. Baron Rosen. The President. Baron Komura. Minister Takahira.
FIRST MEETING OF THE PEACE NEGOTIATORS ON BOARD THE MAYFLOWER.

ADVANTAGEOUS TO LABOR OFFICIALS.

Their Participation in Civic Federation Gathering Conduces to the Interests of Unionism.

(*The Shoe Workers' Journal.*)

There isn't a class of men in the country to-day whose duties bring them into public prominence whose actions are more closely scrutinized than so called labor officials. This is especially true of those officers of labor organizations whose unswerving fidelity to the workingman's cause for years has given them national prominence. They have been pilloried by the opponents of trades unionism and emissaries and hirelings, but by none more severely than the unreasoning and unreasonable element within the ranks of unionism. The objects of the labor movement are the same, but changed conditions and changed sentiment change its direction.

The change in sentiment is most notably illustrated in the formation of such an organization as the National Civic Federation. These changes, so closely related to the labor movement, naturally introduce changes in the work and duties of or adds new work and duties to prominent labor men. In the opinion of the writer a most profitable work in the interests of the trades union movement is the thorough education of the public to its real work and objects. The National Civic Federation is promoting this work, and an organization of this nature demands the membership and presence of labor's ablest advocates. It is to the interests of the workers that their friends and advocates be heard at the meetings of this organization, and it is in the interests of the workers that they are there.

Where the cause of labor is given every opportunity to be heard it never suffers, and it has been ably defended and advanced by its representatives in the National Civic Federation and at its meetings. However, the unreasonable element within trades unions takes occasion after each one of these meetings to raise the utterly nonsensical cry that labor officials attended a non-union meeting. Labor officials attend non-union churches, walk on non-union streets, and drink non-union water, and breathe non-union air. Non-union conditions demand the presence of labor's advocates; it is there that their greatest and best work is done. It is from the non-union places, the non-union condition[illegible] situations and the non-[illegible] workers that the ran[illegible] unionism are recruited. [illegible] duties of labor officials [illegible] them into non-union factories and work places fully as much as into union shops. They can not preach or teach the doctrines of trades unionism from afar, but must carry it to the non-union places. If it could be shown that their presence in those places was opposed to or not in the interests of unionism, there would be some sense in criticizing their union principles. At a recent dinner of the National Civic Federation the question, practically, of the relations of organizations of labor or capital to individual liberty was discussed. Employers, unionists, lawyers, educators, and publicists took part in the discussion. It would be to the advantage of the unreasonables to devote considerable time to reading and pondering over the addresses delivered on the above question.

The labor officials who attended that dinner accomplished then and there more in the interests of unionism and the workers than the unreasonable element of objectors.

UNIONISM AND ITS MERITS.

(*Chicago Chronicle.*)

Without abating in the slightest degree the opposition which is due to lawlessness under the cloak of trades unionism it is fair and proper to concede the advantages of unionism without lawlessness.

The business houses which are taking back their old teamsters are doing so because the old men are more efficient than the temporary substitutes who were hired during the strike. There can be no doubt of that.

Membership in a union involves a certain sense of responsibility, and while this responsibility has been disregarded by a proportion of unionists it is recognized by a larger proportion of them.

Union men are, as a general thing, actual citizens and permanent residents of the places where they are employed. Non-union men are more likely to be unsettled in their habitation and consequently less to be relied upon in the long run.

This is a free country, and every man is entitled to earn his living whether he is a union man or a non-union man. There is no reason why the open shop principle should not be accepted by unionists because, other things being equal, the unionist will always enjoy an advantage over the non-unionist in securing and retaining work.

This is one of the benefits of organization. The average employer will prefer union labor because, if the union be wisely and honestly conducted, he has to deal with a centralized, responsible authority instead of with individual workmen who are responsible to no one save themselves.

THE DIGNITY OF LABOR ESSENTIAL TO NATIONAL MORALITY.

ITS ORGANIZATION NEEDED TO SECURE REASONABLE HOURS, JUST WAGES AND ADJUSTMENT OF RELATIONS WITH CAPITAL.

(ADDRESS BY WILLIAM J. BRYAN, AT OMAHA, ON LABOR DAY.)

INSTEAD of delivering a set speech, I desire to submit a few suggestions which seem to me appropriate to the day. In the first place, I am glad to participate in a labor day celebration because I believe it to be the duty of all of us to emphasize in every possible way the dignity of labor. No sentiment is more dangerous to the nation or more destructive to the morals of the people generally than the belief that labor is a dishonorable thing from which men should seek to divorce themselves and their families. We should lose no opportunity to propagate the idea that labor is respectable, and that idleness ought to be despised. The young man who, with brain and muscle, adds something to the wealth of the country and contributes to the welfare of his fellows is engaged in a worthier work than the young man whose only ambition is to spend the money that some one else has left him. Our schools have sometimes lent themselves to the theory that education ought to lead one away from manual labor. The result has been that many have gone out from school ashamed to come into contact with dirt and dust, and have sought only that kind of work which enables them to wear good clothes all the time. A contempt for manual labor is naturally followed by indifference toward those who engage in manual labor. The establishment of classes in society is largely due to this antipathy toward labor. Carl Hilty, an eminent Swiss statesman, in a book recently published, presents the theory that labor is necessary to health, and Tolstoy is a champion of the doctrine that bread labor—actual contact with the soil—is necessary to restore sympathy between man and man. The first suggestion, therefore, that I desire to leave with you is that the doing of something useful ought to be the ambition of every life and that the idler should be shunned rather than envied.

I am also glad to take part in your exercises to-day because I believe in organized labor. I do not mean to say that organized labor will always abstain from mistakes or will always be wise in its decisions. To expect that would be to expect perfection, and perfection is not within the reach of any of us. But I believe that organization is not only necessary for the protection of labor's rights, but useful for the advancement of the interests of those who toil. While it may be the primary object of members of labor organizations to secure benefits for themselves, it is impossible for them to confine the benefits of their organization to themselves. Those outside of the labor organization, even those laboring men who most bitterly oppose the labor organization, profit by the organization. When organized laboring men secure better wages, shorter hours or improved conditions for themselves, they secure them, as a rule, for those engaged in the same work outside of the organization. This point was brought out in the Chicago street car strike. The union men insisted that only union men should be employed and the employers insisted that they ought to be allowed to employ non-union men. The union men replied that they would consent to the employment of non-union men provided the non-union men were employed at the former rate of wages, while the union men received the advanced rate which the strike had secured. The employers said that that was impossible, because they could not get non-union men to work at a less rate than that received by the union workers.

There are certain things which the laboring man has a right to ask of society. Let me enumerate a few of these. First, he has the right to ask for reasonable hours, and I believe that the eight-hour day is a reasonable requirement. When we remember that eight hours are required for sleep and something like an hour and a half for eating, and a considerable time for going to and from labor and removing from the person the stains of labor, it will be seen that an eight-hour day does not, after all, give a man an unreasonable amount of time with his family. The wage-earner is not a beast of burden; he is a human being. He has his family, and time must be given for association with his family. Besides, he is an intelligent being, and time must be allowed for mental recreation. He is a political factor also, and time must be allowed him for preparation for the proper discharge of his political duties. He is also a moral being and a member of society, and he has the right to claim a sufficient time for the discharge of his obligations to his fellow men and to his Creator. We can not expect the laboring man to be what he ought to be physically, mentally, morally, socially, and politically if he is driven from his couch to the shop and from the shop back to his couch. While this question primarily affects the laboring man, it in a broader sense affects us all, for we are so knit together that we can not separate ourselves from each other, or without danger to ourselves, neglect any portion of the community to its injury.

The laboring man has the right to ask for arbitration of differences between labor and capital. This phase of the labor question is not fully appreciated on the farms and in the smaller towns, for the reason that there is a sympathy between employer and employe which regulates the conduct of both, where the number of employed is so small that there can be personal acquaintance. But where one man employs a thousand, or ten thousand, personal acquaintance is impossible, and the sympathy that rests upon acquaintance is likely to be absent. There must be some way of establishing justice between employer and employe, and arbitration is the only method that has been proposed. The employer who arbitrarily insists that he has the right to run his own business without consulting his employes does not state all of the case. So long as in running his business he does not attempt to regulate the lives and the conditions that shall surround his employes, nobody will question his right, but when he includes in the

WILLIAM J. BRYAN.
Editor of The Commoner.

running of his business the right to determine the material, the social, the intellectual, and the political standing of his employes, he is claiming that which he can not defend. There ought to be in every city, in every State and in the nation a permanent arbitration board with power to investigate and report upon any labor trouble at the request of either party or upon its own initiative. The compulsory investigation of a labor trouble must be distinguished from the compulsory enforcement of the finding of the board. It is far more important that the investigation shall be compulsory when either party desires it than that the finding shall be binding, because public opinion will surely enforce a fair and impartial finding.

I believe that this plan can be applied to differences between nations. We are all rejoicing that our nation has, through the efforts of the President, been instrumental in bringing peace between Russia and Japan. We have won more moral prestige by playing the rôle of peacemaker than we could have won in a generation by wars of conquest. If we had an international board of arbitration, with an agreement that all the leading countries would submit their differences to the board for an impartial investigation before entering upon war, nearly if not all wars would be avoided.

The laboring man also has a right to ask for reasonable compensation, and the reasonableness of compensation must depend upon the conditions which surround him. When the cost of living increases he has a right to expect increased wages; if his business requires a high order of skill he has the right to expect a larger pay than when engaged in work that requires less skill. The longer the preparation for work, the higher the compensation as a rule. Then, too, a business in which one can engage but a portion of the time must furnish a larger per diem than a business in which the work is constant. These are only a few of the conditions that enter into the determination of wages.

Having mentioned some of the things which the laboring man has a right to demand, let me add that society also makes demands upon the laborer. Our obligations in this life are mutual ones. None of us stand in a position where we can demand without making return. The laboring man owes faithful service to his employer, and the labor organization will commend itself to the employers in proportion as its influence upon the members tends to increase their efficiency.

As public opinion is the all-controlling force in this country and the powerful factor in any country, the members of any labor organization will find the public inclined toward them in proportion as the organization proves its claim to the public confidence and respect. While a man's right to a reasonable wage and to reasonable hours is a legal one that ought to be recognized no matter what use a man makes of his money or of his time, still the laboring men will find that their claims will be reinforced in proportion as they demonstrate the usefulness of the organization in promoting virtue and character among its members. A few members who make a bad use of surplus money or surplus time throw discredit upon the order, and such waste of time and money will be used to answer the demand for increase of wages or more leisure.

The members of the labor organizations also owe to society a respect for law. No one can afford to be lawless, and no one can long expect public sympathy who attempts to substitute force and violence for reason and persuasion in any controversy. The labor organization ought to be swift to punish violations of the law among its members, for such violations, when unpunished, bring odium upon the entire body. The laboring men might point to some distinguished instances of lawlessness on the part of men who are quick to find fault with labor organizations. For instance, the Chicago Board of Trade recently repealed a rule which provided for the expulsion of a member who violated the law against grain gambling. If a labor organization were to announce, as the Chicago Board of Trade virtually did, that it would not require the expulsion of a member for the violation of the criminal law, there would be a loud outcry against the lawlessness of the labor organization, and there will be an outcry against the lawlessness of the Chicago Board of Trade. A bad example like that is better rebuked than followed.

It is natural that the members of a labor union who tax themselves and contribute from their earnings to improve the conditions of labor, should complain if the very ones who profit by their action act as strike-breakers and attempt to defeat the plans and purposes of organized labor. And yet, irritating as this is, the laboring man must remember that he is not the only one who is sometimes thwarted by the persons whom they try to benefit. That is the common lot of those who try to improve the world, and the laboring man must content himself with making such progress as he can by the use of moral suasion. Force may seem attractive to one who is angry, but the peaceful methods of example and argument commend themselves to those who will consult their better natures and take time for reflection. Progress is often slow. Those who are most eager to do good are apt to be most impatient. Satisfied of the righteousness of their own efforts, it is hard to understand how others can be indifferent or even antagonistic. But patience and persistent effort accomplish much. The labor organization has contributed mightily to the welfare of the wage earner. It has won him the confidence of the public generally, and in its coming contests it can count upon increasing support as it proves itself a worthy champion of worthy men and women.

LABOR DAY DISTINCTIVE

(American Federationist.)

The trade union movement may well look to it that the first Monday in September is maintained with its distinctive characteristics of demonstration and power, protesting against wrong, and agitation in the demand for right. Otherwise it, like many other holidays, will lose its distinctive characteristic and simply become a holiday for jollification without other purpose or design.

The newspapers of the country for several days in advance of Labor Day, Labor Day itself, and particularly the day following, devoted pages concerning local and general demonstrations and observances of Labor Day, and, incidentally, discussions of the aims and purposes of organized labor. If Labor Day was observed simply by holding meetings at which addresses were made, does any one imagine that so much space and attention would be given it?

The Sabbath preceding Labor Day is becoming more and more devoted by ministers of the different denominations to preaching sermons upon the significance of Labor Day, the rights and wrongs of labor, and the purposes of the labor movement.

WHAT JOHN MITCHELL REALLY SAID TO ANTHRACITE MINERS.

AN ACCURATE REPORT OF A TYPICAL ADDRESS WHICH HAS RECEIVED MISINTERPRETATION AND CAUSED UNWARRANTED APPREHENSION.

Many of the reports published in the daily press of the speeches delivered by John Mitchell, President of the United Mine Workers of America, during his tour of the anthracite fields, have represented him as either predicting or urging a strike, and as appealing to the mine workers to present to the operators an "ultimatum." In order that our readers may know exactly what Mr. Mitchell is saying to the miners, THE REVIEW presents the following verbatim report of an address which he made to a mass meeting of miners at Shamokin, Pa., September 16:

You are, of course, aware that I have been in the anthracite region for the past three months, assisting your district officers and our international representatives in the work of perfecting the union and making preparation for any contingency that may arise upon the expiration of the award of the Anthracite Coal Strike Commission. During these months I have addressed fifty-three meetings in various parts of the anthracite field, at which I have spoken to approximately 190,000 people. It is a pleasure to report that, largely as a result of these meetings, the organization has increased in numbers, and that the prospects are that before the close of the year our membership will be greater than at any previous time in the history of coal mining in the anthracite regions.

It is, of course, a source of keen regret to me, as I know it is to every loyal and constant member of the union, that so many of our fellow-workers who sacrificed and suffered uncomplainingly during the long, weary strike of 1902, should at its termination, when victory had been achieved, disconnect themselves from their organization, and abandon the movement which had done so much to raise to a decent standard of life the multitudes of people dependent upon the coal industry.

I have sought in every manner possible to ascertain the cause which prompted the wholesale desertions that followed the strike and continued up to the middle of this year, but, so far, I have been utterly unable to find a man who could give good reason for his action, and, indeed, very few offered any defense at all.

I have tried constantly to inculcate the world-widely accepted principle enunciated by the immortal Washington, that "To be prepared for war is the most effectual means of preserving peace:" and in the elucidation of this idea I have consistently announced my earnest desire to see such a relationship established between the workmen and their employers as would insure peace and tranquillity in these anthracite fields. But I have discovered that owing to misconstruction of the arguments I have presented, the press of the country has interpreted my language to mean that an ultimatum was delivered, and that we would refuse to maintain peace except upon terms dictated by ourselves.

I have no hesitancy in saying that those who are familiar with my views, or those who know the policies I advocate, have given little credence to the erroneous reports sent broadcast through the country by the public press. I am now—as I always have been—unalterably opposed to the issuance of an ultimatum until every reasonable effort has been made to reach an agreement and to adjust relations by conference, conciliation, or other honorable and peaceful means.

It is true that I have presented the conditions upon which I believe a permanent peace to be possible. I have said that, in my judgment, permanent industrial tranquillity could not be maintained until the union is recognized as a contracting party with the employers and until an eight-hour workday is established in these fields. I repeat and reiterate these views now, but by no fair construction of language can these views and expressions be interpreted to mean that an ultimatum as to our position has been delivered. Both of these principles are fundamental to trade unionism; they are not exclusively the desires of the men in the mines; they are the demands of the workers of the entire civilized world. And so far as I am concerned, I shall continue to advocate their adoption so long as I am connected with the United Mine Workers of America.

I, of course, recognize the fact that we can not hope in a few short years to remove all the wrongs and correct all the abuses which have accumulated during the past half century; but I hope that we shall be able to present such arguments to our employers, when we meet them again, as will convince them of the justice and equity of our position.

In some of my addresses I have called attention to the fact that labor is practically the only commodity on the market upon which the purchaser names the price. In drawing the analogy between labor and other commodities, I have used this illustration: If a man went to Mr. Baer and said to him, "Mr. Baer, I desire to purchase a hundred (or a thousand or a million) tons of coal," Mr. Baer would very courteously say, "All right. The price is $4.50 a ton on the first day of April; $4.60 a ton on the first day of May. It will increase ten cents per ton per month until it reaches $5, where it will remain stationary for six months. How many tons shall I send you?" If the purchaser were disinclined to pay the price named by Mr. Baer, he would be told that coal was for sale only at a fixed figure; he could take it or leave it. In my arguments to the miners, I have said that if labor were as well organized as capital it could, with equal consistency, say to the employers, "Here's our labor, it's worth so much. We've fixed a price upon it just as you fix a price upon coal. If you want it at our price it will be sold to you, if not, we shall keep it until you need it badly enough to pay our price for it."

In using this illustration of the difference between labor and other commodities, I have simply sought to demonstrate the idea that human labor is entitled to at least as much consideration as coal or other inanimate products. But either through misunderstanding or design, the impression has been conveyed to the public that we were going to New York next spring, and walk up to Mr. Baer and his colleagues and defiantly assert: "Here, Mr. Baer, we have the labor of 150,000 men to sell: we want so much wages for it; you can take it at our price or leave it alone; we'll keep it until you need it badly enough to pay our price for it;" while, as a matter of fact, our whole ambition is to be able—when we do meet the anthracite operators for the purpose of negotiating a new agreement—to say, "We are here as the spokesmen and representatives of all the men and boys employed in the anthracite mines; we wish to confer with you upon the question of our joint relations. We are desirous of entering into an agreement fixing wages, hours of labor, and other conditions of employment. We have certain claims which we desire to present, among them the recognition of our union as a contracting party and the establishment of a maximum eight-hour workday." If we are in a position to speak for all the employes of the various coal companies, I am quite sure we shall be able to negotiate a better agreement than if we represent only a portion of the men.

JOHN MITCHELL,
President United Mine Workers of America.

Now, ladies and gentlemen, I have gone into this matter in detail, not because I care particularly for the criticisms of myself, but because I am desirous that the cause of organized labor shall not suffer through misunderstanding or through misrepresentation.

At no time in my life have I felt so keenly the gravity of the labor situation in the anthracite fields. While it is true that I hope for an adjustment of our relations with the anthracite operators upon a basis that will be satisfactory to us and at the same time fair to them, there are, nevertheless, many evidences that the employers are preparing either for an aggressive movement against us or to resist any reasonable demands we may make upon them. Our organization in these fields is honeycombed with spies employed by the Thiel Detective Agency. In the early part of last month fifty of these emissaries were shipped from Chicago and have been distributed among the local unions of the entire region. These men were supplied with transfer cards fraudulently obtained from our locals in various States in the Central West. We know where they are located and we know the work they are doing.

The operators have also attempted to nullify the mine certificate law. This law was enacted by the legislature some years ago, and was intended to protect the life and limb of the man in the mines. It is indicative of their lack of regard for the welfare of their employes when the operators seek by subterfuge to remove this safeguard, which affords us some small protection against the hazard of our employment. It may be important at this time to say that there is no employment in America more dangerous than that of mining coal. And if the operators are permitted to employ the careless and incompetent to fill the responsible positions now held by those who have demonstrated their ability by passing a rigid examination, it will result in a further increase in the number of men who shall be killed and maimed in the anthracite mines.

It is my earnest hope that the coal mine workers of America will unite in one solid phalanx, being prepared to defend what they have gained, and, when opportunity presents itself, constantly to ask for more.

To those unfamiliar with the conditions of our life and labor, it may appear that we are unecessarily or unreasonably extravagant in the demands we make, but, my follow workmen, we should not cease our efforts until the coal mine workers of our country are in such a position that their earnings shall be sufficient to enable them, by the exercise of reasonable frugality, to supply themselves and their families with all the necessities of life, to live in comfortable homes, properly to educate their children, and to make provision for their own declining years. There is nothing that I can imagine so sad as to see an old man, after a whole life of industry, and when he is no longer able to work, cast adrift to become an inmate of the almshouse or a burden upon his friends.

The task we have before us may seem stupendous, but if each man will do his part I have no fear as to the final result. It is, of course, unreasonable to suppose that at times we shall not meet with repulses; there have been and there will ever be victories and defeats, recessions and progressions; but we must see to it that every forward movement carries us further on than the preceding or the succeeding step may carry us back. We should ever keep in mind those two well-known Americanisms, "Eternal vigilance is the price of liberty," and "An injury to one is the concern of all."

The trade union movement has proved itself to be the greatest institution ever founded among men. It has raised wages, reduced hours of labor, taken the child from the mill and the factory and sent it to school. It has elevated the manhood and the womanhood of the working people of the world: it has raised the standard of citizenship, sobriety and integrity of the workingmen of our own country.

(*Concluded from page 16.*)

population of either. Yet Wisconsin and Minnesota have been largely settled by what are known as the "desirable" Germans and Swedes. New York is preeminent for the large number of "undesirable" Italians and Russians; but the "undesirables" seem to be more fond of and better able to grasp the English language.

Now, the final generalization is an appeal to racial pride. The Germans and the Irish who came over in the '40s and '50s were of "our" Anglo-Saxon stock, or kin to it. But the Italian and Slav are entirely foreign elements. Moreover, they come from conditions at home which are so miserable that they are unfit for our social and industrial life! But, alas for the argument, the conditions from which the Irish came in the days of their great immigration were infinitely worse than those of the Slav and Italian of to-day. Descriptions of Ireland during the days of the famine show that the people were living at the very lowest possible level of existence. And still more striking is the fact that the Know Nothings of the '40s and '50s made the same arguments against the Germans and Irish that are now being made against the Slav and the Italian: yet to-day the German and the Irish are "desirable" and the Slav and Italian are said to be "undesirable."

The truth is that modern ethnologists do not recognize the racial differences made by the opponents of immigration, and in fact they say that these so-called races have been so blended in Europe that the racial influence is very difficult of discovery or determination. But, above all, as was so tersely said by M. Taine, the three great influences in history have been environment, epoch, and race. Whatever racial traits are brought to us are so strongly molded and modified by our environment and the spirit of our times, by the influence of our political institutions, by the effect of individual manhood and self-reliance which these institutions have created, that year by year the immigrant is swallowed up in the body politic. After a while he becomes an American, that American who has been made up out of the blend of all Europeans, and who will continue to grow greater and greater as the new blood constantly filters through his veins.

"MUTUAL GOVERNMENT" OF INDUSTRY BY ORGANIZED EMPLOYERS AND EMPLOYED.

EQUAL POWER IN CONFERENCE ENABLES CAPITAL AND LABOR TO ADJUST DIFFERENCES WITH RARE RESORT TO ARBITRATION.

(BY A. BEVERLY SMITH, SECRETARY LITHOGRAPHERS EMPLOYERS' ASSOCIATION.)

THE history of industrial conflicts shows that there are three methods by which the contending parties reach a conclusion. These are (1) abject surrender by one side or the other, without an open rupture; (2) opposition leading to open conflict, which continues until one side is exhausted; (3) preventive measures, which derive their effectiveness from equality and fairness.

The first of these methods usually and logically leads to the second, which has resulted in the many upheavals in business and checks to general prosperity which have occurred in the past. The conclusion reached by either the first or the second method is never permanent, but is always upset by a recurrence of hostilities as soon as the losses of conflict have been recouped. This statement applies equally to the forces of capital and labor.

Efforts to regulate the relations between capital and labor have lacked a practical plan of execution. These efforts, when exerted on the part of individual employers and individual unions, have, indeed, wrought betterment, but not as generally as could be wished. Arbitration has appealed for approval as a universal method of settling industrial disputes. But trials of arbitration have found it wanting, because arbitration as heretofore practiced almost always results in compromise; and no one respects compromise, especially of questions of right and wrong. Arbitration is a last resort, and it should be preceded by the exercise of mutual and equal power by capital and labor in an organized process of adjusting industrial conditions. It is this process that is termed Mutual Government.

Mutual Government involves: *first,* joint action between capital and labor upon any disputed question, in which each has equal representation, influence, and power; this joint action being broader in scope, as will appear, than a trade agreement; *second,* arbitration, to be employed only when joint action has failed to solve the difficulty. Both of these actions are to be employed **before any difference between capital and labor has developed into strained relations**; it being trite, but none the less true, that prevention is better than cure.

In the practical application of this theory in any industry, both capital and labor reach a preliminary agreement that during a certain period the conditions of the trade shall be determined equally by both parties. For this purpose, business offices are established on the part of the employers, who must have an organization with power to enforce its policies and decisions upon members; and on the part of unions organized with corresponding power. To these offices are committed the enforcement and administration of all agreements, so as to prevent any difference from growing into open war, or even disturbing friendly relations; it being kept in mind, above all, that in the adjustment of every question capital and labor are accorded equal weight and power.

Under this system an individual or local question is taken up at once by the business representatives with equal representation from those concerned. If the effort to adjust the difficulty is successful, the subject is considered by the organizations of both capital and labor to be finally settled.

Should a question arise between the two organizations, or of paramount interest to the industry at large, even though of individual or local origin, a joint commission is formed, consisting of an equal delegation from the organizations of employers and of workmen. No one is eligible for membership in this commission who is personally or directly interested in its decision, other than in its general relations to capital and labor. The business agents of the two organizations, as attorneys, present their sides of the case, with evidence and arguments. The commission decides the issue by vote. Usually this vote is unanimous, although provision may be made that a majority vote shall be decisive. In the practice of Mutual Government in the lithographic industry, into which it has been progressively introduced during more than three years, there have been less than six cases which were not decided by a unanimous vote of the joint commission.

Should the joint commission fail to reach a decision, the case is referred to a board of arbitration, consisting of three arbitrators, one selected by each organization, and these two selecting the third. The arbitrators selected by the organizations of employers and of workmen are not connected with the industry, although they may be employers or workers in another industry. Either side may refuse to accept an arbitrator selected by the other, if there has been any attempt to make such arbitrator a partisan. The decisions of a board of arbitration thus constituted are not compromises. It decides the question upon the arguments and evidence presented upon a purely business basis, all sentiment being excluded upon the principle that the object sought is the conservation of an industry which affords the means of livelihood to both employers and employed.

In 1902, the employing lithographers of the East and of the Pacific coast, representing about 75 per cent. of the entire industry, formed an organization to carry into effect this plan of Mutual Government. The seven unions then in the trade had for ten years dominated the industry, having met with only sporadic or individual opposition. The employing lithographers began a campaign of education, which resulted in the establishment of Mutual Government early in 1904.

As showing the conservative power and force of Mutual Government in the handling of delicate or important questions the experience of the trade in meeting the question of the shorter work week is valuable. In the lithographic trade the organizations of employers and of unions have agreed that this is a question to be presented to a national joint commission, its decision is to be final and binding on both parties. Thus this question, which has disturbed other trades, is well in hand in the lithographic industry. While decided opinions upon the advisability and practicability of the shorter work week are held by each side, the question is not to be allowed to interfere with the livelihood of all concerned. It is probable that a national joint commission will decide this question this year or early in 1906. Meanwhile, the lithographic industry, under Mutual Government, is undisturbed by the turmoil surrounding it. Thus in San Francisco, during a typographers' strike, in July, 1903, for a shorter work week, the lithographic departments of the printing establishments were entirely unaffected. This was in accordance with the unanimous decision of a joint commission for the lithographic trade, sitting for San Francisco, that this question was national, not local, and should not be taken up at that time. This experience was repeated in a strike of the typographical unions in San Francisco in July, 1905.

A. BEVERLY SMITH,
Secretary Lithographers Employers' Association.

Hundreds of cases in the lithographic industry are decided every year. Nearly all individual grievances are readily adjusted by face to face conferences between those immediately concerned, aided by the business representatives of the two organizations. Of the questions that have been brought before joint commissions since May 1, 1904, only one failed of settlement there and went to arbitration. The decision in that case was against the employers, who put the decision into effect immediately upon its verbal announcement, without waiting for its receipt in written, official form.

Convincing evidence of the success of Mutual Government is found in the fact that no question decided under its methods of procedure has ever again become a source of contention. Moreover, all parties concerned have not only abided by every decision, but have uniformly expressed satisfaction with its results.

The millennium has not arrived, but common sense is always with us. The unanimous judgment of a body, equally representative of both sides, on any question must be closer to the truest interest of all concerned than can be the opinion of any individual or group arrayed on one side alone. The way to see both sides of the shield is to reach a point of view whence both sides are visible.

Such are the general results of Mutual Government in the lithographic industry. One of its applications, not originally contemplated, is to the education of apprentices, a question that lies at the root of any trade.

The apprentice left entirely to the control of the employer is too often a subject of exploitation for profit. Although all employers are deeply concerned in the evolution of workingmen of good ability, but few interest themselves in this aspect of apprenticeship, and workmen's organizations have not attempted to interfere. Thus, in every line of trade, skilled craftsmen are scarce, the great bulk of apprentices becoming most commonplace artisans.

The apprentice left to the control of workingmen, whether individual or organized, is too often treated as an interloper, and his development hindered under the mistaken idea that he will rob the workingman of his livelihood. This has a deleterious effect upon the ability of the apprentice when he becomes a workingman.

These two adverse influences have hindered the progress and increase of many industries.

In lithography, Mutual Government has established a joint apprentice system. A joint apprentice board, with subordinate local boards, controls the apprentice during his entire term. It is the prerogative of the employer to nominate the apprentice. After his nomination, the apprentice belongs to the entire trade that must support him and in turn derive from him its continuance.

The nominated apprentice must present to the joint board a physician's certificate as to general health and an oculist's certificate as to eyesight, with particular reference to the branch of the industry he elects to pursue. This being satisfactory, he is admitted to a probationary period, at the end of which he is again examined as to progress. If that comes up to the standard, he is indentured, with the proviso that the joint board may cancel the indenture at any time. During his entire term, the relations between apprentice, employer and workmen are under the control of the joint board, whose object is to secure for him full instruction and protection, and for the employer willing service and due diligence. Under this system, future lithographic workers will be both skilled artisans and good citizens; for lukewarmness, laziness, and bad personal habits in the apprentice are not tolerated by the joint board. This one result alone more than repays to the trade all the expense and trouble of Mutual Government.

PRESBYTERIAN INTEREST IN ORGANIZED LABOR.

The new Department of Church and Labor, of the Presbyterian Church, of whose formation and purposes. *The Review* has published an account, now represents over seven thousand ministers and over one million members. There was manifested special interest in the work of this new department during the recent General Assembly of the Presbyterian Church in the United States, at Winona Lake, Ind., which adopted unanimously the following resolution:

"Appreciating the increasing importance of the industrial problem, and realizing that the labor question is fundamentally a moral and a religious question, and that it will never be settled upon any other basis, we recommend that the Presbyterian Home Mission Committees appoint subcommittees for the purpose of making a systematic study of the entire problem in their respective localities.

"These committees shall cooperate with the newly-organized 'Workingmen's Department' of the Board of Home Missions, thus establishing, in connection with the organized Presbyterianism of every city in America, a Board of Experts, who may be able to inform the churches with respect to the aims of organized labor, and to inform the workingmen concerning the mission of the Church.

"These committees shall also assist in the already successfully inaugurated plan of securing for the churches fraternal relationships with workingmen in their organizatons; become responsible for the distribution of the literature issued by the board for the membership of the Church and for the great mass of workingmen outside of the Church, and to push aggressively whatever methods may bring about a more cordial relationship between the Church and labor."

SOME CURIOSITIES OF THE SOCIALIST PROPAGANDA.

EXCERPTS FROM ITS LITERATURE, WHICH "THE INTERCOLLEGIATE SOCIALIST SOCIETY" WOULD DISTRIBUTE, RANGE FROM REVOLUTION TO INANITY.

(BY THE EDITOR.)

Thomas Wentworth Higginson, whose name among the signers to the call to form an Intercollegiate Socialist Society excited surprise among the admirers of his distinguished and patriotic career, was conspicuously absent from a recent meeting at which some of his fellow signers and a group of sympathizers with that call, representing even more than "fifty-seven varieties" of socialism, formed an organization. It is reasonable to attribute to his absence a certain significance. He may be representative of others who have innocently lent the weight of their names to a movement of whose sinister origin and unpatriotic purpose they had been ignorant.

It was quite fitting that this aggregation of "impossibilists," "revolutionists" and all-round economic freaks should elect "eat-'em-alive" Jack London as their president. He is the "barker" who invites the crowd to walk inside and feast upon garish cataclysms eclipsing "The Fall of Babylon" or "The Destruction of Pompeii." Hear him at the gate:

> Socialism is distinctly revolutionary and in scope and depth is vastly more tremendous than any revolution that has ever occurred in the history of the world.
>
> I know that anarchy, civil war, death and crime will be the results of the revolution I prophesy; but what are you going to do about it?

The rest of the official staff of this organization are: First vice-president, Upton Sinclair, newspaper writer; second vice-president, J. G. Phelps Stokes, settlement worker; secretary, M. R. Holbrook, secretary of the Collectivist Society; treasurer, Owen R. Lovejoy, secretary of the National Child Labor Committee.

It has been shown in a previous article that the origin of this dilettante cult of revolution is foreign. Its sinister source lies among those who plot in European cities to overthrow governments. The chief activity of this imported school finds vent in printed matter. This constitutes the "literature suitable for college men," which it is the purpose of the new society to distribute. It will be interesting to look at a few samples of this literature, of which these disciples aspire to become collegiate apostles. It ranges from violence to inanity, and of its making there seems no end.

Few persons outside the circles of avowed socialism are aware of the zeal and ingenuity exerted to multiply the productions of its pens and presses. The *International Socialist Review*, the most pretentious periodical of the movement in this country, is published monthly by a cooperative house. The same house publishes much other Socialist literature, including a series of more than forty booklets. The house is in debt, and each issue of its *International Review* contains an appeal for stock subscriptions, together with an acknowledgment of subscriptions received. Some of the names in the list are of well-known persons, who, as have been the friends of Mr. Higginson, may be surprised to learn to what end their subscriptions are devoted. One of the recent appeals reads:

> America is ripe for Socialism. Whether genuine international Socialism is to come at once to the front, or whether we are to have a long and painful siege of opportunism, depends largely on the amount and the kind of Socialist literature circulated in the near future, and this again depends to a very considerable extent on the financial position of this publishing house. Comrade, it rests with you to say whether the growth of our work shall be rapid or slow.

A few extracts from the literature provided by this cooperative house will suffice to indicate its character, which the Intercollegiate Socialist Society would consider "suitable for college men." The editor of the *International Review*, in the course of an address to the Socialist convention held in Chicago last June, to form an organization to fight the American Federation of Labor, said:

> The proletariat of America stands ready to grasp any weapon, **the ballot, the strike, the boycott and the bullet, if necessary.**

The cheers that greeted this outburst encouraged him to add:

> **This is the beginning of the greatest battle in history.**

The following are some excerpts from issues of the *International Review*:

> The Socialist movement differs from Trades Unionism in this, that per se it has nothing whatever to do with anything short of the Revolutionary solution of the labor or industrial problem.
>
> The only hope of an adequate representation of the Socialist movement in the field of journalism is the establishment of a Socialist press, frankly revolutionary.
>
> While Tolstoi would have peace even at the price of liberty, Socialists prefer war for freedom to the peace of slavery.
>
> The Social tinder now on hand needs only some violent clash of classes to strike the spark to ignite it, and with the ruling classes ready to fan the flame, we have all the elements essential to a Social conflagration.
>
> The coming revolution will be much less of a sudden uprising against the authorities than a long drawn out civil war.
>
> All indications point to the probability that American Socialism will be the champion who will batter down the walls of capitalism.
>
> The Socialist party of America stands in the most intelligently revolutionary and uncompromising position of any Socialist party in the world.
>
> Three interesting epochs in the story of the world are the English revolution of the 17th century, the French revolution of the 18th century, and the approaching World Revolution of the 20th century. The third will see the final overthrow of the autocratic, aristocratic and plutocratic forces of government.
>
> There is no Socialism that is not Revolutionary Socialism. This is a Revolutionary Ideal to be attained by a Revolutionary Class, preaching a Revolutionary Propaganda, through the agency of a Revolutionary Party, and by which the workers are to secure the general ownership of the means of production and distribution for all the people.

Interspersed through some of the other literature distributed by publishers of the *International Review* are such gems as the following:

> From Ferdinand Lasalle: The revolutionary method, terrible as are the drawbacks with which it is accompanied, has in spite of them the one advantage of attaining speedily and energetically a practical result.
>
> The Rev. T. McGrady, of Kentucky: The assassin of Humbert is an angel of innocence compared with those who elect Bryan or McKinley.
>
> From Eugene V. Debs: The day of crisis is drawing near and Socialists are doing all in their power to prepare the people for it.
>
> From the *Communist Manifesto*: The Communists everywhere support every revolutionary movement against the existing social and political order.
>
> The Communists openly declare that their ends can be attained only by the aforesaid overthrow of existing social conditions. Let the ruling classes tremble at the Communistic revolution.

When the reader has ceased trembling at these fulminations, it will be a diversion to turn to the other extreme of grand and lofty tumbling. The most freakish of Socialistic publications, which would possibly add to the gaiety of the moments of relaxation in Socialist classrooms, is *Wilshire's Magazine*. This periodical attempts to increase its circulation through making its subscription price ten cents a year, twenty-five cents for three years. This low price, its editor frankly explains, is only possible through receipts from advertisers, and its advertisements are, of course, solicited from the abhorred capitalists. In a recent issue, the editor publishes a page advertisement of his own headed: "Have you Money to Invest? 17 per cent. and Socialism." He announces that the advertising receipts will be such as to promise this highly capitalistic return to all who will buy stock, and makes this delicious argument:

> What better can a Socialist do than to invest his money in a Socialist magazine that is paying a profit? Every dollar invested in a capital concern helps perpetuate capitalism. **Every dollar invested in *Wilshire's Magazine* helps to kill capitalism.**

The editor makes, of course, the quantity of his circulation the basis of the advertising rates, which are to furnish the sinews of war against capitalism. As a highly finished "nerve proposition," this may be said to merit a medal. "Kindly give me your gun and I will use it to blow off your head" would be a parallel proposition.

This extraordinary phase of a Socialist business policy leads to some amusing and embarrassing complications. One of the advertising supporters of this organ of Socialism is the president of the Citizens' Industrial Association of America, an organization formed to destroy trade unionism. As Socialism also plans to destroy the movement of organized labor, there is a natural alliance between the two in their common hatred of a force of industrial conservatism and progress. Just how the president of the Citizens' Industrial Association squares his avowed detestation of Socialism with his financial support of a Socialist publication is not clear, unless it be the result of their common enmity to organized labor. But this alliance places the editor of *Wilshire's* in a ludicrous position, whence his efforts to extricate himself form one of the most amusing exhibits in the Socialist performance.

In order to sow the seeds of Socialism among the unions, this editor seeks subscribers among their members. Some of these subscribers complained at his publication of the advertisements of a foe to labor unions. The editor thus explains:

> I replied to the complaints that it must be taken for granted that all our advertisers are advertising with us to make money out of our subscribers, and not to subsidize *Wilshire's* in order to advance Socialism. If I should attempt to look into the politics of our advertisers and only insert their advertisements upon the result of such investigations, I would probably find that every one was dead against Socialism, and, therefore, would be compelled to either stop the publication of *Wilshire's* altogether or run it at a very heavy loss, for it can only be published at the present price by running the advertisements of capitalists, who are logically naturally averse to Socialism.
>
> Everybody should know that Mr. Post is the most violent opponent of trade unionism in the United States, so there is no danger of any one buying his goods under any misapprehension of his politics. Therefore, when we run his advertisement in this journal, no one can make a mistake in the matter. However, as before stated, we must have the money of capitalist advertisers in order to run this journal at the present price of 10c. per year. The question to decide is whether it is better to advertise capitalist goods and propagate Socialism or refrain from such advertising and give little or no propaganda, remembering always that the people of the United States are mostly bound to buy goods made by capitalists because nobody else can make them. We ourselves think it would be foolish to stop the publication of this journal for any such silly sentimentality.

Another Socialist writer whose essays its advocates would spread before college students is Clarence S. Darrow, himself one of the signers of the call for the Intercollegiate Socialist Society. He teaches:

> To violate law is often the highest, most sacred duty, that can devolve upon the citizen.
>
> Some of you people are perhaps plying the profession which is called burglary. . . . It always requires experience and education for this profession, and people who fit themselves for it are no more to blame than I am for being a lawyer.
>
> All prosecutions are malicious, and all judgments are meted out in anger and hatred. Our own judges are constantly showing this.

Such statements as these are in accordance with the broad assertion by George Bernard Shaw, a Socialist author whose works the new society would present to collegiate students, in one of his plays that the convicted criminal, when listening in court to his sentence, may regard the judge as guilty as himself. The same play, Mr. Shaw himself defiantly states, "contains an explicit attack on marriage as the most licentious of human institutions."

The ingenuous mind of youth might leap to the conclusion that it is the mission of juvenile chivalry to save society from the slavery of wrongful statutes by constituting itself a generic John Brown. Similarly, the clever flippancy of a Shaw might pervert a callow mind into indiscriminate disrespect for the entire judicial system; or his wanton attack upon the domestic unit of civilized society, revolting though it be, might shake the faith of youth in the sanctity of the home and impugn the divine command to "honor thy father and thy mother."

The keynote of most Socialist literature is that of despair. It leaps from individual cases of social wrong to general denunciation of the entire social system, and advances revolution as the only remedy. The evil and impractical theories favored by the Intercollegiate Socialist Society may appropriately be relegated to the shelves sought only by explorers into the esoteric curiosities of literature or the imaginative ingenuities of the fourth dimension.

EXPERT ECONOMISTS APPRECIATED.

Rochester, N. Y., Times.

The trend toward municipal ownership is interestingly evinced in the determination of the executive council of the National Civic Federation to investigate the movement. If the declared purpose of the Federation in examining the subject is fulfilled to the letter, a valuable contribution to economic progress will have been made.

It is encouraging to find in the list of members of the commission appointed to investigate the subject such able, sincere, and thorough political economists as Professor Frank Parsons, of Boston; Professor Edward W. Bemis, of Cleveland; Professor John R. Commons, of the University of Wisconsin, who occupies the only trades unionism pedagogical chair in the United States, and Albert Shaw, editor of the *Arena*. They have a valuable especial knowledge on the subject which ought to make a strong impression upon the prominent corporation lawyers, business men, and conspicuous captains of industry on the commission, naturally against limiting private enterprise, if the latter sincerely seek for light and are capable of a broad conception of public interest.

EVERY INTEREST REPRESENTED.

Scranton, Pa., Scrantonian.

The Civic Federation, recognizing the widespread interest now manifested in the problem of municipal ownership, has decided to investigate the whole subject, and with that end in view has appointed a large, representative commission, which will begin work early in the fall. The commission consists of capitalists, manufacturers, labor leaders, lawyers, educationalists, engineers, etc., and that the subject will be probed to the bottom and thoroughly discussed from every point of view, may be taken for granted, as every conceivable interest is represented on the committee by men who are both able and willing to express opinions.

Municipal ownership is an easy and pleasant thing to talk about, but in the United States its adoption involves so many other considerations that it is well to look before we leap.

Samuel Gompers, John Mitchell and other noted labor leaders have been appointed on the commission to look after the industrial interests, and nothing that is worth while considering is likely to escape their notice.

A man is morally bound to waste no time and to do his work right whether the boss is looking or not. To shirk or to do work wrong is stealing, though the wrong be undiscovered.—*The Carpenter.*

Trade unionism nowadays can take no harm in the broadest of economic discussions. The full and free presentation of the truth is what the best friends of trade unions desire most.—*Labor World*, Pittsburg.

THE SMASH-THE-UNION MOVEMENT OFFERS TO SAVE THE NATION.

IT ASSUMES MONOPOLY OF PATRIOTISM, LIBERTY, ET CETERA, AND MAGNANIMOUSLY VOLUNTEERS TO RUN THE GOVERNMENT.

(BY THE EDITOR.)

What is generally termed the smash-the-union element in the employing world has been indulging of late in a series of manifestoes designed to prejudice public opinion through misinformation. No economic doctrine can flourish, however persistently advocated and however strong its financial backing, which is based upon misstatements of fact, and whose purpose is not for the greatest good of the greatest number. The group of writers who assail the movement of organized labor tacitly recognizes this truism in its attempts to make it appear that the admitted misdeeds of members of labor unions are universal instead of exceptional; that all labor leaders are radical advocates of violence; and, above all, that the trade agreement, the most practical device that modern industrialism has evolved for peaceful relations between capital and labor, is destructive of the constitutional rights of the individual citizen. While asserting that they favor organizations of wage-earners that are "properly conducted," these writers betray the fact that their idea of "proper conduct" is absolute surrender to the will of the employer, and that they would deprive the labor union of all power to elevate the condition of its members by dealing with employes only as individuals, and never in a body. They oppose violently the closed shop, but they reveal that their conception of the open shop is a place where no union men can work and live.

This anti-union school of writers puts forth its literature in its own periodicals and in the form of addresses and advertisements in the daily press.

A characteristic of this type of literature is its brazenly complacent appropriation of all the virtues of patriotism and all the glories of American history.

To the great number of economists, divines, publicists and editors who encourage and seek to guide the self-helpful efforts of wage-earners to elevate themselves through organization; to the largest employers in the United States, who make collective contracts with organized employes—to all these, this literature would deny any of those virtues and glories, while it accuses organized labor itself, not merely of a lack of patriotism, but of downright treason.

The typical writer of this literature wraps himself in the American flag, asserts exclusive possession of the Constitution, if not of the Decalogue, and claims to have a monopoly of that spirit of liberty which maintained with arms the Declaration of Independence, freed the slaves while saving the Union and expelled Spanish oppression from Cuba. He would pose as a Washington, a Lincoln and a McKinley all concentrated in a living model of perfect Americanism. By contrast, he would have the reader infer that the 2,500,000 citizens who are enrolled in the American Federation of Labor and the great railway Brotherhoods are composed of Arnolds, Booths and Weylers; that they are enemies of their country and foes of civilization. He would deny to them all patriotism, all love, not only of country, but of humanity; all allegiance to the Flag and all respect for the organic law framed by the fathers of the Republic.

This extravagance should defeat its own purpose. If there were a scintilla of truth in these charges or insinuations, the entire movement of organized labor would have been withered in its infancy by the burning blast of public condemnation. It could have no more chance of survival and growth in a land of self-government than has anarchy or polygamy. The very progress of organized labor in both strength of numbers and intelligence of policy, the very respect which it has won from the largest and best-informed employers, the very consideration it receives from economic scholars and writers form a body of convincing evidence that the movement is recognized as an important social force, meriting critical study, to be credited with having accomplished much in uplifting the mass of wage-earners and capable of increasing both the producing and consuming capacity of the nation. It is because the malicious and indiscriminate verbal assaults upon this movement could not find entrance into the news or editorial columns of reputable journals that they are frequently forced into the advertising columns, when they are paid for at so much a line.

These smash-the-union writers attempt to class the labor organizations with the most unpopular trusts, and accuse them with being conspiracies to increase the cost of living. They collate with an industry worthy of a better cause the most remote, abnormal and exceptional misdeeds of individual members of labor unions. They claim that the purpose of "citizens' alliances" is to create "a national power for general peace." But they would establish the peace of extermination. The Socialists say, "We have nothing to arbitrate with the employer; we would abolish the employer." So these writers say in effect: "We would not negotiate or arbitrate with the unions, but destroy them." And this program they seek to justify by such exaggerated statements as these:

> Tens of thousands of American citizens have been assaulted and hundreds have been murdered by these labor trusts in their bloodthirsty efforts to force all the rest of humanity to implicitly obey their orders.
>
> What about the thousands of decent white men and women, tied hand and foot, unable to work, move or act, except by contribution to and with consent of the trust? Human liberty and constitutional rights of an American citizen are denied them.
>
> Men who have regard for the sacred mantle of liberty fought for, won and handed down to us, are patriots enough to stand together and save this fair America from chaos.
>
> This is not the proper time to talk conciliation. Neither is it the time to talk arbitration or joint agreement. To arbitrate questions of wages and hours is to introduce artificial methods of determining what they shall be. Arbitration is only putting off the day of reckoning.
>
> No organization of men, not excepting the Ku Klux Klan, the Mafia, or the Black Hand societies, has ever produced such a record of barbarism as has this so-called labor society.
>
> The labor leaders are trying to force upon the American people a universal system of slavery even more degrading and more damnable than that to which the negro was subjected.

An official journal of one of the organizations that would thus promote peace by invective and misrepresentation is not content with arrogating to itself all the patriotism and achievements of American history. It assumes that the functions of the American Government have now been paralyzed by the labor unions, and it magnanimously proposes that this anti-union organization shall take to itself all executive, legislative and judicial functions. It calmly announces:

> This association is composed of citizens of the United States, organized for mutual protection of person and property.
>
> It is based upon the same fundamentals [as the United States Government] and seeks to insure the personal liberty of the individual guaranteed by the Constitution.
>
> This subsidiary organization of the people has been made necessary by the impotence of many local municipalities to furnish adequate protection and make good the constitutional guarantee.

This publication, after incidentally charging the "labor trust" with "setting up much actual slavery and robbing vast numbers of people of their liberties," naively remarks:

> The judicial mind will inquire why the people are not now thus protected by the Government set up and maintained for their protection.
>
> Theoretically they should be, but bitter experience proves that they are not, for the machinery of the Government is slow, inert and clumsy and its movements interfered with by the manipulations of the [labor] trusts until we see great damage done before its machinery gets into operation.

"All of the 780 citizens out of every 800 who are not members of any trust" are invited by this custodian of our liberties to join his would-be substitute for the political machinery that has been running since George Washington took his first inaugural oath. It must be news to 779 out of these 780 citizens that the Government at Washington does not still live, or that the State, municipal and township systems have broken down. Is it then possible that the nation has been plunged into anarchy by the labor unions and is all unconscious of its state of woe? Is the United States a lawless mining camp, in need of this proposed national vigilance committee to save its women and children from butchery and its property from destruction?

The attempt thus to inflame class hatred reaches the height of absurdity, when it does not sound the depths of misrepresentation and malice.

For instance, one of the stock charges of these assailants of organized labor is that the labor leaders and the labor press continually incite the unions to acts of violence. This is a libel, pure and simple. There is not a labor leader of any standing in this country, nor is there a labor journal, outside of the Socialist organs that are apparently acting in alliance with the anti-union agitators, that does not persistently exhort union wage-earners against the employment of force in strikes and advance earnest arguments to prove the folly of that criminal policy.

As an illustration of a labor lecture to labor, the *Typographical Journal*, the official paper of the International Typographical Union of North America, published a long article upon the lessons of the teamsters' strike in Chicago, of which it said the principal one is:

> It is unwise, inadvisable and dangerous to pin faith in the outcome of a strike by relying on force and outlawry. . . . The attempt to win a strike by the pugnacious arguments of educational committees who rely on brick throwing and pop-bottle suasion as a method of demonstrating that the striker is right and the employer wrong, will sooner or later come to grief. . . . When a union declares no other man can work under penalty of death, it assumes a position that sooner or later will become its undoing. . . . Life, liberty and the pursuit of happiness can be as well applied in union constitutions as in the Declaration of Independence. This is good unionism enough for a true American citizen by birth or adoption. . . . Unions that devote their energies to making union men instead of killing off the non-union ones are the organizations that are doing business with greater results and less trouble.

Another way in which organized labor has formally and collectively arrayed itself in the ranks of law and order is through its action as to membership in the militia. Great publicity has been given to a few isolated cases where local and ignorant unions have forbidden members to belong to military organizations. A convention of one of the anti-union societies even went so far as to adopt and publish this declaration:

> *Whereas*, Organized labor throughout the country seeks to discourage and practically prohibits membership in the militia.

This was in face of the fact that the convention of the American Federation of Labor at San Francisco, only two weeks before the anti-union convention rejected by an overwhelming majority a resolution opposing membership in the militia; and in face of the further fact that President Gompers of that Federation, which exults in its title "American," has emphatically declared it to be the duty of every able-bodied wage-earner to encourage the citizen militia. Both this action and this utterance were published broadcast. The resolution of the anti-union convention, therefore, could not have originated in ignorance but must have been founded in malice.

Another example of the wise counsel against all forms of coercion that organized labor is receiving from its own ranks is the contribution by Frank K. Foster, of the Typographical Union, to a symposium upon Labor Day, which we reproduce upon another page from the *American Federationist*, the official magazine of the American Federation of Labor, whose President, Samuel Gompers, is its editor.

The object of these vigilantes is the dissolution of organized labor and the reduction of wages to the lowest point consistent with the continuance of the race. Poverty, discontent, ignorance and crime would be the inevitable fruit of their propaganda, which is therefore unpatriotic as well as unphilanthropic.

The inspiration of the movement of organized labor is the elevation of the physical, mental and moral condition of the great mass of wage-earners. The movement has progressed from the medieval days and nights when workingmen were forced to meet in secret, subject to penalties for "conspiracy," up to the present time, when labor's right to organize for its betterment has undisputed legal status and when the unions make technical and general education, not violence and law-breaking, a part of their regular usages. This great advance has been long and tedious. Those who have done the marching have had to discover their leaders among themselves. Their progress has hitherto been made in the face of discouragement, derision, denunciation and even persecution. Until within a few years they have encountered the solid opposition of employers. If their aim be recognized as one for the benefit of all society, surely it behooves every element of society to stretch out a guiding and a helping hand to those who halt and stumble in their struggle upward. This is a duty that impresses itself with growing force upon educated employers, whose larger opportunities imply greater responsibilities toward the welfare of the mass. Labor should not be left to uplift itself alone and unaided. Yet more should it not be subjected to the rebuffs of would-be oppressors.

Organized labor is here and there guilty of law-breaking. Yet in every case its sins of violence react upon its own head. The lessons taught by its most advanced leaders are thus reenforced by bitter experience. There can be no doubt that labor is learning respect for the law. No one need doubt that it will use with growing wisdom the larger liberty, including just wages and proper leisure, for which its organization strives.

Assuredly, it is more in accordance with the spirit and the principles of American institutions to encourage than to repress an organized movement whose growth depends upon the development of individual character, including the qualities of self-control, self-improvement, fraternal aid and the care and elevation of the home. If organized labor makes for all these desirable ends, it is a factor for good citizenship. For wholesale denunciation of the movement because of errors incident to its progress, it would be more patriotic to substitute efforts looking to the correction of those errors, leading to a lessening of their repetition, and to guidance in the direction of those just and enlightened relations between capital and labor which experience has proved to be of most benefit to both and to the community at large.

A HEAD TAX DESIRED.

Poughkeepsie, N. Y., Eagle.

As we read the report of the debates upon immigration, initiated by the Civic Federation, we are more and more impressed with the value and importance of our own pet suggestion, namely, the imposition of a head tax upon the immigrants. It seems to us that that will furnish restriction of the undesirable. It will furnish a fund to be expended in the care of the dependent, in the distribution of useful information, and in the general supervision of the work.

TRADE ASSOCIATIONS AND THEIR REGULATION OF PRICES.

HOW EFFORTS TO PREVENT DESTRUCTIVE COMPETITION LEAD TO PARALLEL METHODS IN LABOR UNIONS AND MERCANTILE COMBINATIONS.

Much is said nowadays about the monopolistic tendencies of labor unions. Their critics charge that they are arbitrary and even tyrannical in their enforcement of such methods as placing restriction upon output; limiting the number of apprentices in a given craft; demanding the minimum wage; opposing the introduction of labor-saving machinery; boycotting employers who resist their demands; refusing to work or to have any relations with brother workmen who do not subscribe to their doctrines and conform to their practises.

It is not our purpose here to deny the truth of any of these general allegations, or to discuss the measure in which they may be defended or should be condemned. Accepting them, for the sake of argument, as facts, we would point out that each of them is the symptom of an underlying fear—the fear that excessive competition may impair for all or destroy for some the living wages or the steadiness of employment. The root of this fear of destructive competition lies as deep as the instinct of self-preservation. The limitation of apprentices arises from the fear that a craft may become overcrowded, inciting mutually destructive underbidding of wages to obtain work. The underlying motive becomes equally obvious upon scrutiny of each of the union practises of which complaint is made.

There is much less current comment upon the manifestations by capital of this same underlying motive—the fear of destructive competition. Nevertheless, precisely the same principle reveals itself in the proceedings of capitalists, large and small, who seek to regulate the market, both as to supply and price, in practically every branch of industry and trade in the United States. These methods vary widely in their details and their operation in practise, which are modified to meet the requirements and conditions peculiar to various markets and products. But they are all alike in their common object—the prevention of destructive competition. Their avowed purpose is to insure living profits (the union's "living wage") to manufacturer, wholesaler and retailer. Their evolution involves the formation of pools, "gentlemen's agreements," trade associations and other combinations. Here and there is involved resistance, through artificial devices, to the simplification of the machinery of trade on the ground that it would decrease or destroy the business of middlemen, such as jobbers. This corresponds to union opposition to the introduction of labor-saving machinery. Combinations to maintain prices through agreement between manufacturer and wholesaler to furnish goods only to retailers who belong to the organization, correspond in many respects to the union demand for the closed shop. The boycott to punish those who do not subscribe to such agreements is employed freely and openly by mercantile associations. There is little or no concealment of these operations, and their wisdom or legality need not concern us here. They are facts of economic importance, analagous to the corresponding set of facts manifested by some organizations of labor.

Examples of these systematic efforts to prevent destructive competition in business can be found in the press almost daily, and to describe them in detail would require more than a complete issue of this REVIEW. But there are here grouped, as illustrative of the general principle, brief accounts of the methods of regulating prices in use in the drug, the hardware, the dry goods and the grocery trades:

PROPRIETARY DRUGS.

The most persistent efforts are made and the most elaborate machinery is devised to maintain the prices of proprietary drugs, or so-called "patent medicines." The total sales of these goods in the United States in one year amount to between $80,000,000 and $100,000,000. They constitute from 60 to 65 per cent. of the drug trade. Three organizations undertake to regulate prices. These are the National Wholesale Druggists' Association, organized in 1882, representing 90 per cent. of the wholesale jobbing trade; the Proprietary Association of America, composed of the manufacturers; and the National Association of Retail Druggists, composed of delegates from affiliated State associations and local branches. The retailers' organization has been greatly extended, the most recent local branch formed being that in New York City. It now embraces 516 associations, comprising 39,915 druggists.

The three organizations named cooperate in their efforts to prevent price cutting through agreement to cut off supplies of goods from any cut-rate house.

A recent example of the rigor with which cutting of prices is disciplined is the case of McKesson & Robbins, a wholesale drug firm of New York. The case illustrates both the working of the plan and its frank and open recognition. The National Association of Retail Druggists placed the firm upon its "cut-off list," in other words, boycotted the firm. This was openly announced in the newspapers of May 26, and was admitted by the firm. This process resulted in a complete and costly surrender by the firm, which was announced in the New York *Commerical* on August 14 under the headlines: "Big Drug Firm Makes Amends—McKesson & Robbins Pay for Error. Result of Bad Sale. On the Black List for a Time, but is Again in Good Standing—Explains to Trade. Carload of Patent Medicine Shipped to One House but Destined for Another Known as a Cut-Rate Concern—Goods Recovered After a Hot Fight and Expensive Litigation. Retailers with the Manufacturers of the Medicine Win a Notable Victory. Cordial Business Relations Resumed Between the Innocent Parties."

All this is stated in the most matter-of-fact way, implying the tacit recognition that the boycott is an every-day weapon in the mercantile world to compel adherence to prices, just as unions strike against or boycott employers who cut wages. The article goes on to explain that a contract existed in this case between the manufacturers, the wholesale firm, and a retail firm, C. H. Loveland & Co., of Binghamton, N. Y., which bound the parties to sell no goods to any druggist who cuts prices.

It appears that McKesson & Robbins shipped a car load of medicine to Loveland & Co. The size of the shipment aroused the suspicion of the manufacturer. Investigation revealed that the medicine was really intended for another and a cut-rate firm. The boycott and surrender followed. The terms of settlement showed the completeness of the surrender. They included the return of the goods, the repayment of cost of shipment, the payment of costs of litigation and expenses of storage, the payment of a fine to the Retail Druggists' Association, and the publication of a most contrite apology by the boycotted firm.

The most ingenious device in the drug trade for maintaining prices is called the Serial Contract or Serial Numbering plan. This plan involves an exclusive system of distribution. Only authorized wholesale houses handle the goods, and they are under contract to sell only to the retail agents of the company. Every retail dealer, before he can purchase the goods, must sign a contract by which he becomes an agent of the manufacturer, and agrees not to sell the medicines to any other dealer who is not an agent at any price whatever, and to sell to others only at the authorized retail price. Each dozen of bottles sent by the manufacturer to the wholesaler is numbered, and is accompanied by a postal card bearing the same number. When the wholesaler sells that dozen bottles, he mails the card to the manufacturer, with the name and address of the retailer to whom sold. The retailer must not dispose of a bottle until his firm name has been written or printed upon each wrapper. Thus the sale of a bottle anywhere at less than regular prices can be traced, and the cutter, by the terms of the contract, makes himself liable to the manufacturer for specified liquidated damages.

The *Pharmaceutical Era* of May 11, 1905, declared:

> The plan has shown its ability to accomplish the purpose for which it was designed, i. e., the prevention of price demoralization. The more of these proprietary goods that are placed upon the market with the restrictions embodied in the plan, the better it will be for the retailers, for they are thereby assured of a profit on their sales, and consequently all branches of the trade are benefited.

No more effective plan has been devised for the enforcement of the minimum wage.

A pending suit has been brought by A. G. Loder, a retail druggist in Philadelphia, for $100,000 damages against the National Association of Retail Druggists. The complainant avers that he has been blacklisted by the association for cutting prices, and that his business has been damaged by the boycott. He states that he is not even able to keep books, lest the association learn the names of those who sell him drugs, and boycott them also. This allegation could hardly be exceeded by any union boycott against an "unfair" employer, nor could any union carry further a system of espionage.

THE HARDWARE TRADE.

Especial efforts are made to control the price of products in the hardware industry by means of pools or "gentlemen's agreements." Estimates of the amount of the output of the entire industry, whose prices are thus controlled, vary from 60 to 95 per cent. This is remarkable, when it is considered that there are at least 500 different lines of goods in this trade.

"Price Restriction" was the subject of keenest interest at the joint meeting, early in June, at Hot Springs, Va., of the Southern Hardware Jobbers' Association and the American Hardware Manufacturers' Association. Coupled with this topic was the effect upon prices of manufacturers' selling goods directly to retailers, instead of through jobbers. The report of the proceedings of these two bodies, published in the *Iron Age* of June 15, shows that not only persuasion, but the more drastic method of the boycott is to be employed to prevent cutting prices in the hardware trade.

As to direct selling from manufacturers to retailers, the Southern Association took the position, conveying the threat of a boycott, that:

> *If* the manufacturer thus ignores the legitimate channel of distribution through the jobber to the retailer and the consumer, the jobbers should hesitate about distributing the products of such manufacturer, even though he be not a distributing factor in their immediate locality. It was pointed out that when unoccupied territory has thus been taken possession of and the manufacturer becomes well established as his own distributor, it will be more difficult to correct the disturbance than if action were taken in time. The spirit of the suggestion was that if the manufacturers ignore the jobbers, they could hardly expect the active support of the jobbing trade.

The same report said:

> A strong sentiment apparently pervaded the meetings of the Southern jobbers in favor of manufacturers extending the system of restricted prices with a view to not only permitting, but it might almost be said, **constraining the jobbers to market goods at a profit.**

A joint meeting of the two associations was addressed by W. W. Webber, on behalf of the jobbers, who said:

> All of you are advised that we want you, where it is at all feasible, to arrange your methods of handling your product to the end that the jobber will be compelled to make a reasonable margin when he makes a sale. . . . Those of us who have no desire to make money should be compelled to cease our bushwhacking tactics to the end that those who do want to succeed may do so with some degree of comfort and pleasure and to an extent commensurate with the energy and annoyance required. Some of us have no more conception of commercial ethics or of the correct principles of money-making than has a hog of a holiday or a Senegambian of "Paradise Lost," and **these are the fellows for you to handle. You will not be able to do so by any milk and water policy, but must make up your minds that nothing short of a lignum vitae club, loaded to scatter, will suffice in some cases.** . . . To embark on the restricted system you must give all concerned to understand that there are to be no subterfuges, that you intend to be alert and firm in policing your plan, and that we all look alike to you; that you will not play any favorites, nor condone offenses, but that he who strays from the straight and narrow path in this particular will wander into the bogs and brier patches of your displeasure **to the tune of the exact amount of rebate due him, plus a good, stiff fine. The fine might consist of a stated amount of "Uncle Sam's Illuminated Anguish Plaster" or, better still, drop the offender from your list.**

The report of the executive committee of the Southern Jobbers' Association, as summarized by the *Iron Age*, said that:

> One of the most important subjects was a satisfactory arrangement between the manufacturer and the jobber for the **enforced maintenance of stipulated prices upon a profitable basis.**

A joint convention of these two associations was held last year at Atlantic City, when an article upon the subject of "Price Maintenance" was read by T. W. Williams, Vice-President of the Bissell Carpet Sweeper Company. He defined "Price Maintenance" as meaning:

> An honest, equitable system of uniform prices, that is based upon the sound principle that the manufacturer, the jobber, the retailer, are justly entitled to a fair margin of profit on the sale of any article and that the quality of an article can only be maintained so long as all parties concerned in its sale cooperate and rigidly maintain uniform prices.
>
> The system of price maintenance carried out in this particular line depends for its legality upon the right of a manufacturer of a patented article to fix the retail price on his product. This right has been sustained by judicial decisions in both the United States and England.

Mr. Williams further said:

> I want to point out a significant virtue of an honest system of Price Maintenance, namely: that while protecting and conserving the best interests of the manufacturer, the jobber, and retailer, it reaches out and fully protects the consumer by insuring to the purchaser a high standard of quality in the article, and a reasonable price. On the contrary, price cutting is a species of commercial debauchery that rests upon the relentless doctrine of the survival of the fittest; upon the narrow, cold-blooded principle that merchandising is a sort of commercial warfare; that "all's fair in war" and "the devil take the hindermost." Price cutting lowers the commercial standing of the manufacturer, jobber, or retailer who practises it, destroys profits, breeds distrust, fosters prevarication, and finally robs the consumer by debasing the quality of the commodities, upon which prices are cut, if not actually driving many of them from the market.

Could any union leader make a stronger argument in favor of the closed shop?

DRY GOODS JOBBING TRADE.

The National Dry Goods Association is also fighting to preserve the business of the jobbers from extinction through direct sales from manufacturers and commission houses to retailers. Its executive committee has declared that if these direct dealings are permitted, the business of the jobber "will not be worth continuing."

The semi-annual meeting of this association was held in New York City on June 8, behind closed doors. No manufacturers nor commission merchants were present. After the adjournment, the official announce-

(*Concluded on page 11.*)

LABOR LEADERS DISCUSS THE SIGNIFICANCE OF LABOR DAY.

THEY CONTRIBUTE A SYMPOSIUM TO THE "AMERICAN FEDERATIONIST," PRAISING WAGE-EARNERS' ACHIEVEMENTS AND URGING CONSERVATISM.

The official magazine of the American Federation of Labor, the *American Federationist*, published in its September number a symposium of articles upon the significance of Labor Day, which has now been made a legal holiday in practically every State in the Union, and which is recognized by the National Government in its dealings with wage-earners. Extracts from this symposium are here republished, as examples of the kind of literature that the thoughtful, conservative leaders of labor are producing for the guidance of their readers:

WORLD-WIDE TRADE AGREEMENTS.

(By James Duncan, First Vice-President American Federation of Labor.)

LABOR DAY is an American product; yea, it is of trade union origin, and therefore abiding and utilitarian.

There is a semblance of a May day demonstration in a portion of continental Europe, but it too often takes the form of discussing political vagaries some of them similar to the expressions heard on Sunday afternoons on Boston Common, week nights on "Growlers' Corner," Washington, and almost perpetually in "Bug House Row," San Francisco. Invariably the European celebrations take place at night or on the nearest Sunday to May 1, and have not the importance or prestige of our Labor Day. Our date is logical. May 1 is associated with heated discussions incidental to introduction to new trade agreements, which suggest partisan or technical debate. The first Monday in September calls for mature, cool-headed reasoning in which the speakers are untrammeled from ordinary shop talk, and by inspiration rise to the sublime in setting forth the philosophy of the economic evolution we are well into and in suggesting practical methods to be used for the betterment of mankind.

If this point is clear the suggestion follows—as night follows day—that at the coming convention of the American Federation of Labor next November in Pittsburg, action should be taken to send a message to organized labor of the world to adopt the first Monday in September as Labor Day, the same to be a holiday set apart for the dissemination of economic instruction, to the end that a correct entering wedge can be instituted to hasten and direct the way to the brotherhood of man.

To associate a universal holiday with one of the tenets of trade unionism would forever keep the purpose in healthy thought channels. The sequence, therefore, suggests "*the trade agreement*," and particularly that part of it which, when entered into provides the way for pacific adjustment by conference or arbitration of disputed points as a modus operandi for the ultimate reduction of strikes to a minimum. This subject would serve two purposes: First, suggesting constructive procedure, and second, disabusing the international mind of a bugaboo that unions are formed to cause strikes. Here, then, we have concrete material with which to greet labor everywhere, and the coming convention can do no better thing than to vitalize this spark and set in motion the universal labor movement, through and because of which the organized workers can become acquainted and the unorganized may be shown a development of their true interests, from which they could not long remain aloof.

When history is written our "trade agreement" idea will be given place in importance alongside of the Magna Charta and the Declaration of Independence. It partakes of the best in both without the shortcomings of either. It aims at getting the best possible conditions [illegible] possible injury to either employer [illegible]ently elastic to move with the [illegible] obsolete or hamper progres[illegible]n." It does not eliminate strik[illegible] be a species of slavery, but it comes near do[illegible] in that by voluntary action disputes can be [illegible] by conciliation and arbitration which would [illegible]ise require force, ending in favor of those best [illegible]sist, whether or not they were in the right.

In this di[illegible] American Federation of Labor—that is, tr[illegible]nism—leads the world. The Hague notion of [illegible]nternational ruptures is copied from the adjus[illegible]use of our trade agreements, only that we [illegible]ick minus red tape, while The Hague machine [illegible] red tape, plus what they copied from our trad[illegible]ents. We agree to give disputes arising under a trade contract to five or seven practical men, with assurance we will abide the result, and we place in the paragraph a proviso that pending adjustment there shall neither be a lockout, strike, or suspension of work. Practice crowds the fact upon us that settlement of disputes can sooner be reached, and with better results, if all hands are working than during a suspension.

If these suggestions mature, our next international circular should be top-heavy with universal eight-hour workday propaganda. Watch for action along those lines by the Pittsburg convention.

COERCION CONDEMNED.

(By Frank K. Foster, of the International Typographical Union, Boston.)

THE recent decision of the Supreme Court of Massachusetts in the case of Berry vs. Donovan, which decrees that the agent of a trade union is personally liable in a suit for damages for his action in securing the discharge of a non-unionist working under contract, brings up the question as to whether the permanence of unionism is necessarily dependent upon what may be called a physically coercive policy against non-unionists.

Personally, I do not believe that such is the case, and my opinion is not based upon consideration of any theoretical injustice which may be done the industrial non-conformist, whose moral obligation, we all concede, is to join with his fellow craftsmen in their endeavors for craft betterment, but solely upon the question of the best general policy for the unions themselves.

If we are to maintain our own legal "right to work how, when, and where we please," and voluntarily choose to submit to the dicta of collective bargaining for the determination of this how, when, and where, does not the inevitable logic of our position appear to be that we should concede the non-unionist an equal *legal* right to do the same thing? If, as in the case above cited, the particular non-union man is working under contract, and does not choose to be a party to the collective bargain for labor, how, without inconsistency, can we demand that he be forcibly deprived of that right which we insist upon for our own members?

It is a truism that a man convinced against his will is of the same opinion still, and the trade union movement has had ample opportunity of observing that the mere possession of a union card by no means makes its holder a genuine unionist. It is also true that in war times forced drafts are sometimes necessary, and the forced recruit is all too numerous in the union ranks, where he is apt to mutiny on the firing line, as did the unhappy conscripts of the Russian Czar during the battle of the Japan Sea.

There has been of late an unfortunate increase of the custom of compelling employers to act as union organizers, using them as agents for driving men into unions, a custom as reprehensible in principle as that practiced by other employers who instruct their foremen to disorganize unions by discharging union men. The unions have asked, and in many States have obtained, legislation for preventing discrimination of this latter kind. If we really believe in equality before the law, how are we to consistently object if the courts decree that what is sauce for the goose is sauce for the gander?

So much for the purely legal aspect of the question. As an economic policy the coercive method has injured unionism in two ways: It has been the prolific source of the sympathetic strike on the part of the workmen, and the cause of much of the outcry raised against the union shop, or the so-called closed shop, on the part of the employers.

Whatever sentimental virtue the advocates of the sympathetic strike may claim for it, as a practical instrument of economic warfare it has proven itself wofully deficient as a means for achieving practical results. It would, perhaps, be an extreme statement to say that the sympathetic strike is never justified, but most impartial unionists must confess that the history of the sympathetic strikes which have taken place in this country is not such as to warrant the expectation that this method can be safely relied upon as an efficient way by which to accomplish the purposes of trades unionism. The recoil of this industrial blunderbuss has commonly kicked over the man behind the gun, while the humming-bird aimed at has gotten away unscathed.

The label shop or union shop is one of the proper and rightful objective points of trade union endeavor. Its stable establishment must rest upon its business feasibility. The argument for the union shop, however, can be made sufficiently strong without compelling the employer to violate contracts with his employes. The trade agreement follows naturally in the wake of efficient organization of the sellers of labor commodity, and it is up to the wage earner himself to bring about this organization.

There may be those among us who hold that the attitude of the public toward trade unionism is a matter of slight moment and not worth bothering about. This opinion may be correct as applied to some specific instance in trade union activity, but is not true as a general proposition. The organization of labor has won a wide public recognition for its useful industrial and social service, and won it, moreover, in the face of an early prejudice against it. It is idle to say that either individuals or associations can afford to disregard the way in which they are looked upon by the great mass of the people. The union has a character to maintain as well as the individual, and there is always weight to be attached to the criticism of unbiased observers.

But the main point after all is as to whether the dependence of trade unionists upon coercive methods of propaganda does not weaken the moral fibre of the movement. Our liberalized age has repudiated the coercive policy in theology and politics. We no longer approve of the practice of burning people at the stake for non-conformity in religious belief. We protest vigorously against employers of labor who attempt to coerce their employes into voting for a certain party. Why not carry this same principle of freedom into our own movement, and rely upon moral suasion rather than upon the big stick for our converts? It may be possible that a slight numerical loss would result from the adoption of this plan, but numbers are not everything, in unionism as elsewhere. The ideal trade unionism, therefore, appears to me to be a purely voluntary association composed of members who are unionists because they believe in unionism, and who have been enrolled by appeal to their judgment and their enlightened self-interest, rather than by pressure upon their selfish fears.

SOME UNION ACHIEVEMENTS.

(By George W. Perkins, President Cigarmakers' International Union.)

IN contemplating the progress of labor in the past twenty-five years, we find wonderful improvement, which, under the circumstances with which we have had to contend, makes its splendid achievements the most remarkable accomplishments in the annals of human effort in this or any other country. Go to Ellis Island, N. Y., or any other large port of entry, and watch the never-ending inrushing flow of immigrants which sweep the country like an avalanche, and deny this statement if you can; consider the habits and customs of people coming from all quarters of the globe, some with a low and inferior standard of life; some with ideas entirely at variance with the trade union movement of our country; some with anarchistic ideas, others with socialistic leanings, and others with ideas peculiar to all points of the globe, and all at variance with ours, with no knowledge of the hopes, ambition, and aspirations of our trade union movement of this country, knowing little and caring less for our institutions and standard of life, and you have some idea of the heroic effort of the past and the stupendous task that lies before us and the effort made and to be made to organize the workers.

The task of organizing the raw recruits of the world into trade unions has been and is a stupendous one, and deserves the highest commendation of all lovers of freedom, and a better and higher social and economic state.

The obstacles, the obstructions, failures, and disappointments have been many and trying, but, despite them all, the movement under the leadership and guidance of the American Federation of Labor has grown in the time mentioned from 13 small national and international unions to its present magnificent proportions of 117 national and international unions.

This wonderful growth has no parallel in the history of the civilized world in this line or any other human endeavor, and should challenge the admiration of all students of economic endeavor.

Wages have been increased and hours reduced, the truck system and shop tyranny abolished, better sanitary conditions and more independence of the workers achieved in keeping with the onward march of our movement; in short, the whole world and the workers have been made better by the success of the trade union movement.

The splendid results and success of the American Federation of Labor and the trade unions affiliated therewith is not due to mere chance, but rather to the indomitable will and pluck of those who first had faith in the trade union movement, and, secondly, the courage of their convictions.

It is indeed fortunate for the workers and the future of our movement that those intrusted with its destinies and guidance have resolutely stood by the good old ship of trade unionism, and always kept its course in the channel of pure trade unionism and free from the rock of partisan politics and other isms upon which so many movements have been dashed to destruction.

THE NATIONAL
Civic Federation Review

Offices: 281 Fourth Avenue, New York City

RALPH M. EASLEY, Editor

The Editor alone is responsible for any unsigned article or unquoted statement published in THE NATIONAL CIVIC FEDERATION REVIEW.

Ten Cents per Copy One Dollar per Year

METHODS OF INTERNATIONAL AND INDUSTRIAL PEACE.

The rulers and peoples of the world have paid adequate tribute to the broad statesmanship exercised by the President of the United States, with the beneficent result of ending, through conference, a most destructive war. They have all recognized both the present and the future importance to peace in international relations of this brilliantly successful employment of mediation. To the realm of industry, this great event conveys a lesson as important as that which it introduces into world politics. The potency of face-to-face conference in adjusting the relations between capital and labor could receive no more emphatic illustration than in the same principle put into practice in the negotiations culminating in the treaty signed at Portsmouth.

It is not to sound a note of discord in the joyous acclaim that greets this achievement, to point out that the probability of future international wars is not entirely ended, even though it be greatly diminished; and, correspondingly, that the more frequent employment of conciliation between representatives of employers and employed cannot wholly eliminate conflicts from the world of industry.

It is natural that enthusiasts who cherish visions of permanent, world-girdling peace should hail the successful issue of the Portsmouth conference as a substantial basis for the realization of their beatific aspiration. But it should not be forgotten that this world is stern and practical. It is no discouragement to the increasing employment of conciliation and arbitration, to direct attention to the fact that their compulsory establishment, in either international or industrial relations, is but a dream. There are questions that cannot be arbitrated. So high an authority as John Bassett Moore, Professor of International Law in Columbia University, has written in this REVIEW that "'vital interests' and 'national independence' may properly be excepted from an international agreement of arbitration." The latest example of agreement through conference, which averted the threatened war between Norway and Sweden, explicitly excepts from arbitration matters of dispute which affect the independence, integrity or vital interests of either. Similarly, there are in the industrial world subjects which neither capital nor labor could submit to arbitration without incurring the surrender of matters of principle that are involved in the successful conduct of business or in the elevation of the standard of living.

It would not tend to strengthen the human race, either physically or morally, if all possibility of conflict between nations, or between capital and labor, were removed. All progress involves struggle. The ability to struggle is commensurate with the ability to fight. To relieve humanity from the stern necessity of eternal vigilance would be to cast away the price of liberty. The discipline of resistance to aggression is essential to advancement. The blood of martyrs is the seed of every righteous cause.

The capacity to fight, even when latent, is an essential element to national progress, just as it is to the advancement toward the adjustment of the relations of capital and labor which shall be most advantageous to civilization. The very statesman who receives the plaudits of the world for restoring peace between Russia and Japan is a most persistent advocate of a powerful navy and army, trained to meet the emergency of any moment. There is in this no inconsistency, since the known effectiveness of armies and navies is the surest guarantee of peace and the strongest moral support of diplomacy. In a similar way, those who are most prominent in advocating industrial peace are the most ardent in encouraging the organization of both capital and labor, so that negotiations between them may have the greater prospect of success through mutual respect. Upon that basis, the incessant readjustment of their shares in production can proceed with the best assurance of that equity without which there can be no peace. The demonstration of approximate equality of power upon each side, coupled with confidence in mutual good faith, will forward the settlement of any issue. Despite the hard logic of the fact that all life involves contest, such an achievement as that of Portsmouth tends to lessen the asperities of conflict and to convey far-reaching moral encouragement to common-sense methods of conciliation.

REGULATION OF OUTPUT AND OF PRICES.

"Regulation and Restriction of Output" is the subject of a special report of the Commissioner of Labor, just published and prepared during the incumbency of Carroll D. Wright. This report is of great importance and value to students of industrial phenomena, and is unique in that no other official inquiry into its subject has been made, either in this or in other countries. The materials for the report as to the United States were in the main collected and prepared by Professor John R. Commons, now of the University of Wisconsin; while the portion relating to Great Britain was prepared by John H. Gray, Ph.D.

Now that this exposition of restrictions imposed by labor has been made, it would be appropriate for the Department of Commerce and Labor to make an investigation of the restrictive methods in use by combinations of capital and of employers. Like the restriction of output, the regulation of price has its origin in the desire to prevent destructive competition. There is a wide field for such an inquiry, for the practise exists, in one form or another, and is accepted as an every-day familiar fact, in practically every branch of trade and transportation. In an article upon another page, we have collated some illustrative examples of this practise. These might be multiplied indefinitely. The examples we cite in the drug, the hardware, the dry goods and the grocery trades could be amplified, for instance, by the traffic agreements between railroads; the anthracite railway pool; the iron and steel pools; the restriction of acreage in cotton-growing and the effort to maintain a maximum price for that material; the attempt by associated publishers to prevent the sale of books at cut prices; the farmers' organizations formed to force upward prices of the great staples; and all the list of conspicuous trusts. An investigation of these phenomena, widely variant in their manifestations but all alike in their purpose, would throw light upon the interesting question, How far is it economically wise to employ artificial methods to regulate competition in trade, as well as in production?

THE COAL SITUATION.

A portion of the newspaper press is sounding a note of alarm as to the probability of a great coal strike next spring, for which we find no warrant in present conditions. It is represented that John Mitchell, President of the United Mine Workers of America, has been making a series of fire-brand speeches throughout the anthracite fields, and that the mine operators, on the other side, are collecting vast stores of fuel so as to be prepared for a suspension of production. These are cited as omens of war. Rather are they to be interpreted as preparations essential to negotiations for peace. This is not a prediction but an interpretation of the present.

A perusal of the correct report of the address delivered by Mr. Mitchell at Shamokin, which we publish upon another page and which is in effect a summary of the motives and the utterances of his tour, will show that its tone, if firm, is most temperate. He advances a straightforward business proposition, for which his effort is to gain the practically unanimous support, in their own interest, of the anthr[illegible]. That support can be given only t[illegible] President Mitchell should be [illegible] leader, and if the union should [illegible] tenth of the mine workers, he wo[illegible] in no position to appear as their representative [illegible] the operators. But if he represents nine-tenths of the workers, the operators could not refuse to consider his presentation of their demands. His recruiting [illegible] union membership, from the miners' standpo[illegible] necessary preliminary to negotiation.

Conversely, the operators would be [illegible] with equal wisdom if they were accumulating stor[illegible]. They, too, must be in a position to present with firmness whatever agreements they may have as to the relation between the union demands and the prosperity of the industry of producing, transporting and marketing fuel. Equality of position is a condition precedent to any fair bargain; and in no industry has the principle of collective bargaining been carried into effect with more far-reaching benefit and with more signal examples of good faith maintained under strong temptation to violate agreements than in that of mining coal.

PUBLIC OWNERSHIP INVESTIGATION

The announcement that a Commission upon Public Ownership and Operation, under the auspices of the National Civic Federation and composed of experts and representatives of all interests, would make a thorough investigation of that subject, both at home and abroad, has been received with many public expressions of approval. This approval, moreover, is accompanied with evidences of confidence that the findings of the Commission will clear up many disputed questions of fact that now confuse the current debate upon this many-sided and far-reaching question of public policy. The organization of this Commission and the allotment of its work are assurances that the inquiry will be pursued with system and vigor, and that it will be animated by an impartial determination to ascertain the whole truth.

The first meeting of the Commission will be held Thursday, October 5, at 10:30 a. m., in Earl Hall, Columbia University. An informal preliminary meeting at the headquarters of the National Civic Federation, on September 18, to discuss tentatively the scope of inquiry and the method of procedure, was attended by seventeen members. The fact that practically every shade of thought in the general Commission was represented at this meeting, gave it peculiar interest. This preliminary discussion brought out such questions as: Shall the foreign inquiry confine itself to such public utilities as gas, water, electric power and lighting and street railways? Shall it include Government ownership of railroads, telegraph, telephone, parcel post, postal savings banks, etc.? Shall it further include what comes under the general head of "municipal trading," such as municipal markets, abattoirs, bakeries, laundries, playhouses and tenements?

A unanimous sentiment was reached that it would be unwise to undertake to cover so many topics with one sub-Commission; that those subjects, however, should all be taken up eventually, but by different sub-Commissions; and that the first sub-Commission should confine itself mainly to municipal ownership and operation of gas, water, electric power and lighting and street railways. A report of this informal non-committal discussion was sent to the entire Commission.

NATIONAL IMMIGRATION CONFERENCE

The representative character of the Conference upon Immigration, to be held in New York City on December 6 and 7, under the auspices of the National Civic Federation, is indicated in advance by the number and the nature of the responses to the invitations. The Governors of all the States are appointing delegates, with a view both to their acquaintance with the general subject and to their particular knowledge of the needs and the desires of their own localities and industries in connection with the problems growing out of the admission of alien labor. The replies have disclosed an interest as wide and as diversified as the continent, and the personnel of the delegations is such as to ensure illuminating discussions and conclusions of value to the entire [illegible] of national consequence. One phase [illegible] problem, the agitation for and [illegible] Asiatic labor, is of such growing [illegible] Committee on Arrangements proposes to assign [illegible] consideration one entire day, which may have the [illegible] of continuing the conference upon December 8.

The copies [illegible], Vol. I, of The National Civic Federation [illegible] are desired at this office. Twenty-five cents per [illegible] will be paid.

The unions [illegible] have a decent regard for the rights and [illegible] of employers and the general public are the ones which make the greatest and most permanent headway.—*Cigar Makers' Official Journal.*

There is no difference between the man who "kills time" the moment his employer's back is turned and the man who steals a dollar from the cash drawer.—*Clothing Trades Bulletin.*

ADVICE TO MACHINISTS

Their President Upholds Agreements, Deprecates Strikes and Tells How to secure the Union Shop

(From the Biennial Report of James O'Connell, President International Association of Machinists.)

We should see to it that our organization is not made the tail to anybody's kite, political or otherwise, neither should it be allowed to be used as the stepping stone for impracticable ideas, wild theories, or unsound, unbusinesslike methods. The trade union principles as promulgated by our association should be first and foremost in all things, and the deliberations of those assembled at our conventions should be practical, not theoretical, real, not phantom.

The success of our organization up to date can be largely accredited to the splendid discipline throughout our ranks, but there is still improvement to be made in this direction.

First of all our members must be taught to respect to the full letter every agreement made by our organization. We must be in a position at all times to prove that violations of agreements are not made by our members. Where charges of violations have been made heretofore, we have been able to prove that they were the result of a misconstruction placed upon the agreement, and upon closer investigation it has been proven to my satisfaction that the employers are more liable to take advantage of a technicality, and thus create dissension, resulting in the best interests of both parties being lost sight of.

JAMES O'CONNELL,
President International Association of Machinists.

Our local lodges must see to it that our members obey the constitution in every particular, and those who wilfully or maliciously violate the principles for which our association stands should be summarily dealt with.

The willingness with which our members enter into strikes is a question of more than passing importance to this convention. It is, therefore, necessary, in order to secure the highest type of discipline among our members, that the laws governing strikes, etc., etc., must be more fully observed by our membership at large, and it is even the duty of the delegates to this convention to strengthen the position of the Grand Lodge by amending our laws so that trivial and unnecessary strikes will be avoided.

The employers' associations are leaving no stone unturned to misrepresent the position of the trade unions relative to what is commonly known as the union shop. They insist upon reserving the right to be the judges of all applications for employment, but refuse a similar right to the wage workers to say whom they shall work with. The open shop is purely a bugaboo. There is nothing to it but the imaginary restrictions thrown around the so-called union shop by the trade unions.

We do not interfere with the right of any individual mechanic to seek employment where he will, but we do reserve the right to say with whom we shall work. If we secure, through our efforts, better conditions of employment, we have a right to say that mechanics enjoying the results of our labors should contribute to the success of our organization in maintaining the improved conditions secured by us.

If the machinists throughout our jurisdiction would organize as they should, the open shop proposition would rapidly disappear, because the employer would quickly realize that the best mechanics, the most intelligent workmen, and the most industrious citizens could only be secured through the union. Thus we would protect our rights as union men, strengthen our position as an organization, and prove to those who have given little thought to the question, that the trade union stands for the best interests of the wage workers of our country.

There is absolutely no fear from the so-called open shop. It is only the unfair employer who is advocating the open shop and the abolition of the union, because the open shop, as the employer understands it, means that the union must go out of existence. I am pleased to report that, notwithstanding the persistent effort on the part of the employers' associations to enforce the so-called open shop, the trade union movement is growing more powerful and influential day by day.

(Concluded from page 8.)

ment was made that there had been a discussion of the evils of direct selling. The ominous statement was added:

Everything possible will be done to arrange matters amicably, and not until conciliatory methods have been exhausted will aggressive action be taken. The Association puts its purchasing power at $400,000,000, and this lever may ultimately have to be used in self-protection, although it is hoped that any action of this kind will not be necessary.

In other words, a boycott is threatened by this "purchasing power."

GROCERY JOBBING TRADE

A special effort has been made this year to prevent price-cutting in groceries to save the business of jobbers, by discouraging direct sales from manufacturers to retailers. "To condemn the practice of some manufacturers going directly to the retailer with a portion of their business" was the expressed purpose of the first National Convention of Wholesale Grocers held in Milwaukee, June 29 and 30. This convention appointed an executive committee, which was instructed to use "all legal means to induce the manufacturers of food products to refrain from selling the retail trade except through jobbers." Upon occasion, this committee is to call in additional members and resolve itself into "a Special Action Committee for any particular service in this line."

This convention, it was estimated, represented an annual business in the United States of $1,000,000,000. It applauded, however, as if it were a labor convention listening to a union leader, such remarks as the following by its chairman, William Jordan, of Grand Rapids:

Merchants and retailers will respect a rational unionism among merchants for purposes of mutual improvement. We must not indulge in excuses, but we must firmly hold on to the just habit of insisting upon maintaining our rights as legitimate distributors.

It should be the wish of every wholesale grocer to strongly condemn the practise of some manufacturers going directly to the retailers with a portion of their business.

Rational unionism is no mean part of the whole human movement, industrial, social and intellectual, and I believe it will surely carry us forward and upward.

In the course of an address to this convention, J. A. Van Hoose, President of the Southern Wholesale Grocers' Association, related amid applause the following narrative of the penalty of the black list inflicted upon a salesman who had dared to cut a price:

There was a complaint made to me that a man had cut the price on cottolene. The investigation developed that that salesman sent in a sworn affidavit to the effect that he had not. He lied to his house, lied to his God, lied to his conscience. When it was proven that he had, under the czar, dictatorial power given me, I decided that only one of two things was permissible—dismissal without recommendation or that he should pay $50 out of his own pocket. The house replied that they would take the first and not the second; that no man should take a grip out of that establishment for them who thought no more of the honor of that house than to trample it into the mire of the State of Arkansas.

That man to-day is a wanderer on the face of this earth, without a job, because he has no recommendation; and the pathos is that he lost the home which he had paid for. It had to be done. There were 5,000 other salesmen in that territory who were trying to make their living like men and gentlemen, and for their honor and protection, and the safety of their own integrity in business, it had to be done.

Compare the plight of this salesman with the grievance of the non-union man who is discharged at the demand of a union having a contract for the exclusive employment of its members.

TEAMSTERS' BENEFIT ASSOCIATION

The "Liberty Dawn Association" is the title of the beneficial feature of the New York [illegible] of the International Brotherhood of Teamsters. It is the motto of the parent body, "United to Protect, not Combined to Injure." Its benefit feature provides through moderate dues for the free services of a physician and for sick benefits, for benefit to dependents in case of death of a member and for benefit to a member in case of the death of a wife. The report of President James Kenney and of Secretary-Treasurer Edward Gould shows the financial condition of this Association to be prosperous. Its official leaflet contains some worthy exhortations to the members, such as:

Be faithful to your employers; Be courteous to their customers; Be kind to their horses; Be kind one to another; Don't report late in the morning; Don't patronize saloons.

WELFARE DEPARTMENT
OF
The National Civic Federation

OFFICERS

H. H. VREELAND, Chairman.
CYRUS H. McCORMICK, First Vice-Chairman.
JOHN H. PATTERSON, Second Vice-Chairman.
EDWARD A. FILENE, Third Vice-Chairman.
CORNELIUS N. BLISS, Treasurer.

EXECUTIVE COMMITTEE

George W. Brown, Treasurer United Shoe Machinery Company, Boston, Mass.
W. A. Clark, President United Verde Copper Company, Butte, Montana.
Frederic S. Clark, Treasurer Talbot Mills, North Billerica, Mass.
Ralph M. Easley, Chairman Executive Council National Civic Federation, New York City.
Charles L. Edgar, President The Edison Electric Illuminating Co., Boston, Mass.
G. E. Emmons, Manager Schenectady Works General Electric Co., Schenectady, N. Y.
Edward A. Filene, Treasurer Wm. Filene's Sons Co., Boston, Mass.
Frederick P. Fish, President American Telephone and Telegraph Co., Boston, Mass.
Frederick S. Fish, Chairman Executive Committee, Studebaker Bros. Mfg. Co., South Bend, Ind.
W. C. Fish, Manager Lynn Works General Electric Co., West Lynn, Mass.
G. Watson French, President Bettendorf Metal Wheel Co., Davenport, Iowa.
Orrin S. Goan, Manager National Biscuit Co., New York City.
William C. Greene, Treasurer Peace Dale Manufacturing Company, Peace Dale, R. I.
B. J. Greenhut, Treasurer Siegel-Cooper Co., New York City.
F. R. Hazard, President The Solvay Process Co., Syracuse, New York.
H. J. Heinz, President H. J. Heinz Co., Pittsburgh, Pa.
Edwin M. Herr, Vice-President Westinghouse Air Brake Co., Wilmerding, Pa.
Charles W. Hubbard, Treasurer Ludlow Manufacturing Associates, Boston, Mass.
Charles H. Hulburd, President Elgin National Watch Co., Chicago, Ill.
John S. Huyler, President Huyler's, New York City.
M. E. Ingalls, Chairman Executive Board C., C., C. & St. L. Ry. Co., Cincinnati, Ohio.
G. Gunby Jordan, President Eagle and Phenix Mills, Columbus, Ga.
John F. P. Lawton, Assistant Treasurer and Secretary Gorham Mfg. Co., of Rhode Island, Providence, R. I.
William W. Lobdell, President Lobdell Car Wheel Company, Wilmington, Del.
Arthur T. Lyman, Treasurer The Boston Manufacturing Co., Boston, Mass.
W. G. Mather, President Cleveland Cliffs Iron Co., Cleveland, Ohio.
Cyrus H. McCormick, President International Harvester Co., Chicago, Ill.
L. A. Osborne, Vice-President Westinghouse Electric and Manufacturing Co., East Pittsburgh, Pa.
Thomas F. Parker, President Monaghan Mills, Greenville, S. C.
John H. Patterson, President National Cash Register Co., Dayton, Ohio.
A. J. Pitkin, President American Locomotive Co., New York City.
Thomas G. Plant, President Thomas G. Plant Company, Boston, Mass.
Albert L. Pope, Vice-President Pope Manufacturing Company, Hartford, Conn.
Francis L. Robbins, President Pittsburgh Coal Company, Pittsburgh, Pa.
H. A. Sherwin, President Sherwin-Williams Company, Cleveland, Ohio.
Ellison A. Smyth, President Pelzer Manufacturing Company, Pelzer, S. C.
Nathan Straus, R. H. Macy & Co., New York City.
H. H. Vreeland, President New York City Railway Co., New York City.
J. H. Williams, Vice-President J. H. Williams & Co., Brooklyn, N. Y.
Rufus K. Wood, Maryland Steel Co., Sparrows Point, Md.

Miss Gertrude Beeks, Secretary.

WELFARE WORK.

A Comprehensive, Compact and Philosophic Review of Its Growth and Practice.

(By H. H. Vreeland.)

H. H. Vreeland, Chairman of the Welfare Department of the National Civic Federation and President of the New York City Railway Company, delivered an address upon Welfare Work before the New England Cotton Manufacturers' Association, at Atlantic City, September 20.

Mr. Vreeland opened his address with the statement that there had been no time for fifteen years when there were less than 15,000 men on his pay-roll directly, and indirectly 15,000 more, and that, therefore, he had nothing theoretical to present, but appeared as a practical man with a message to practical men.

He spoke of the necessity of carrying on Welfare Work in a coöperative way with the employes, making them a part of it, and said that the mistake which had been made in the past was the placing of Welfare Work on a charity basis, when it would never succeed.

Mr. Vreeland continued:

It is encouraging to those who are giving their thought and time to the promotion of Welfare Work to have that cause recognized by an invitation to present an argument in its favor before so influential a body as the New England Cotton Manufacturers' Association. A membership which is not only national but international presents a channel through which it may be possible to attract the attention of employers to the value of Welfare Work to a degree that may be of incalculable benefit. It is with a full realization of the opportunity presented to the Welfare Department of the National Civic Federation that I shall attempt to enlist your deep interest in the work which we are promoting.

The Welfare Department is a branch of the National Civic Federation, devoted entirely to efforts to interest employers in giving especial consideration to

HERBERT H. VREELAND.

the physical, mental, and moral welfare of employes in all industries. Membership in the Welfare Department is confined to employers.

In extending the practice of Welfare Work, the department has found of especial value conferences of employers, held under its auspices in different sections of the country, for the interchange of experiences. Successful Welfare Work, when pictured by practical business men in connection with their own industries, exerts an influence toward gaining the application of similar ideas by other employers. Thus you will see that through our organization, Welfare Work is not advocated by theorists.

Care for the welfare of employes is by no means novel, although its exercise is becoming more and more scientifically understood and extensively practiced. One of the earliest problems in the development of factory life was that of the housing and of the social environment of the inhabitants of mill towns. Such towns were, at the outset, of artificial creation. Their location was determined by that of the new factory, which was, in turn, dependent upon circumstances of power and transportation. Nearly a century ago, therefore, the management of such a mill was confronted with the question of how to build houses for the workers at a cost which would afford a return for the investment while keeping the rent within its proportion of the cost of living of the wage earners. This question of housing was accompanied by the correlative necessity of providing for these communities schools for the children, and churches, which should in some measure be the social centers of the towns, in addition to their moral influence and training.

Indeed, some of the first efforts in the United States to introduce Welfare Work were begun by manufacturers of cotton goods. One "corporation boarding house," as it was called, at Lowell, Mass., afforded evidence, not only of the employers' interest in regulating the price of board, but of the necessity of housing in order to secure the necessary operatives.

The growth of the municipality and the introduction of electric rapid transit, making possible homes in the country, have now rendered unnecessary some of these corporation boarding houses. The five corporations that manufacture cotton goods in Lowell still contribute toward the maintenance of a hospital and a technical school.

One of the members of our Welfare Department and one who must be closely associated with you, Mr. Arthur T. Lyman, of Boston, should be listed among the pioneer Welfare Workers in this country, not only in caring for the needs of employes at Lowell but also at Waltham. The Welfare Work at Waltham has been persistently maintained and developed. Aside from the well-lighted, well-ventilated watch factory, with good cloak rooms and an emergency room for those who may be ill or exhausted, and seats for women workers who were previously supposed to hold "walking jobs," the company still maintains an interest in the social life of the employes, even though the town has grown into a municipality. The company joins the community in maintaining the band, which is now a private enterprise. The company still supervises the women's boarding house, although that for the men has been sold. There is a benefit association, and the company lends money to employes in times of stress to prevent the "money shark" evil. These do not exhaust the list of Welfare activities.

As the manufacture of cotton goods has extended to the South, mill villages in several notable instances have there been developed along broader lines than in the cotton mill towns of New England. The surroundings of the mills and the houses are beautified, flower seeds are distributed annually, and prizes are awarded for the most attractive and best kept gardens. There are kindergartens and classes in domestic science to teach the proper preparation and serving of food, how to buy groceries, the desirability of cleanliness in the home, and how to make comfortable and economical clothing. It goes without saying that a good, wholesome meal will make a more contented and efficient worker, and that the disappearance of slovenliness from the household will make the fireside an attractive and winning competitor to the saloon when the day's work is over.

The question of recreation also receives consideration, and opportunities for enjoyment, through athletic sports, indoor games, stereopticon lectures, and other methods, are opened to the operatives.

Before leaving the subject of the mill village, I would invite your attention to one of the finest examples in the United States of Welfare Work in an isolated community. This is to be found at Vandergrift, Pa., a town wholly sustained by the steel industry. Here the drainage system, piping for gas, paving, curbing, and pure water supply, were installed before the great shop was completed. A system for saving and lending money was promoted by the employer, to enable the men to own their homes. The several religious beliefs were recognized by the erection of eight churches—each with its pipe organ—and there were built school houses, an inn and a social hall. An athletic field was also supplied. In the works, there was installed the most complete emergency hospital to be found in any shop in this country; whil[illegible] satisfy the material needs [illegible] of local trade.

A more recent [illegible] Work is its applica[illegible] ploying both large [illegible] numbers, [illegible] cities. Here the co[illegible] are reversed. The factory, instead [illegible] the creator of the city, is one [illegible] adjuncts and constituents. [illegible] problem in its beginning relates [illegible]ectly to the factory itself, and to [illegible]mediate surroundings of the d[illegible]. Physical welfare, in the stress [illegible] strain of city life and in the toil [illegible]ctory itself, becomes of initial im[illegible]. The providing of facilities fo[illegible], the furnishing of toilet rooms, the supplying of pure drinking water, are all elementary steps toward the health and comfort, as well as the efficiency of the workers. Many details, such as seeing that these facilities are easily available, and that they are not abused by the careless or indifferent, are involved in even these primary applications of Welfare Work.

STATIONARY FIREMEN'S SHOWER BATHS, WASH AND LOCKER ROOM, BOSTON.

THE OLD WAY OF HEATING COFFEE, DAYTON.

In the work rooms themselves, ventilation and light are of first importance. These, of course, can best be secured when a new plant is built.

Another forward step in the city factory would be the furnishing of a place for the midday meal. This may be merely a room where the employes may eat in the midst of comfort and cleanliness the luncheons they have brought from their homes, or it may be a lunch room where the midday meal is prepared and served.

Some other considerations will be seats for women, [illegible] service for women, rest rooms or emergency hospitals, fire protection, transportation facilities, relief associations, pensions, and employes' banks for savings and loans.

Welfare Work in large cities may be extended also to careful, sympathetic and unobtrusive efforts to brighten the homes of the workers. It has been said that it is impossible to extend the influence of Welfare Work into the homes of employes in cities. My own experience refutes that assertion. When I installed a library in the club rooms of our Employes' Association, it was my purpose to reach the families. I stated at a meeting where there were 6,000 of our employes with their families that it was the desire of the management that the catalogues of the library should go into the home of every married employe. I made it clear that we wanted the wives and sons and daughters of the employes to read the books. I also announced that if there were a man who had a son or a daughter working for an education—technical education, perhaps—and special text books or books of reference were needed, the books would be bought and put in the library upon application. The library is, so to speak, a family concern, and it was turned over at [illegible] three the best [illegible] we had. It was [illegible] to see the high grade of literature that was taken out.

One Relief Association provides for a man in case of illness or accident, a pension in old age and at the time of death a fund for burial. I have found that the wife of the average laboring man will always land on her feet, if she is tided over for a few weeks, when the husband dies suddenly. All these benefits lead us into the home life again.

My own experience as a wage earner having taught me that the unmarried man has no place to go evenings, except a hall bedroom cold in winter, led me to establish club rooms for the men employed on the street railways in New York City. A large percentage of the ten thousand men employed by our company lives in boarding houses. Many are from the country. Thirty years ago, as a brakeman on a steam railway, I was in the same position, away from home and forced to live in a boarding house, such as the railroad terminals and my wages could afford. There was absolutely no place for me in the evenings, where it was warm, except the saloon and the pool room. I said to myself, "Here my own experience shows me something our men need." The club rooms we established include an auditorium, where monthly entertainments are given, a library, a pool room, and a physician's office. They were used immediately and extensively, and a chance visitor will find the rooms filled every night in the week.

GIRLS' LUNCH ROOM, DAYTON.

In another city and in another industry, in Chicago and in a factory where there are seven thousand employes, entrance into the home life of the employes has been successfully accomplished by having a trained nurse visit the workers when injured or ill. The superintendent of a large rolling mill in Cleveland is chairman of the visiting committee of the Relief Association, and, by visiting the homes every Sunday morning with the other members of the committee, it has been possible to vastly improve the sanitary conditions. The superintendent has gained much information through these visits which has been beneficial to the business as well.

OLD AND NEW WAY OF EATING LUNCH AT A CHICAGO FACTORY.

It is, of course, impossible, in a large city where the employes live in widely distributed districts, to promote frequent evening entertainments, but the plan of taking a large hall, which is pursued by many large employers in New York and other cities, for an annual entertainment or ball, has become quite customary. These entertainments are much enjoyed by the employes, their sweethearts, and families. In my own experience I have never been able to secure a hall large enough to accommodate all who desire to attend. Several companies in large cities maintain club rooms which are not only patronized nightly by employes who desire to use the game rooms or library, but the auditoriums are used frequently for dancing parties by the different sets or cliques. It goes without saying that this is a decided improvement upon the saloon dance hall.

A notable instance in Pittsburg shows an auditorium in the center of the factory where the employes are taken once a week at the noon time, which is extended for the purpose, to enjoy a vaudeville performance, which is often supplemented by an educational courses of instruction relating to the work to be performances by employes in the evenings, for Christmas entertainments for them and their families, and for other methods of enjoyment.

With the exception of the establishment of primary schools, which will be unnecessary in a city, the employer may advantageously initiate for new employes courses of instruction relating to the work to be performed, a portion of each day being devoted to this purpose. If the hours are not so long as to weary the worker to a degree which will render it impossible for study after the day's toil, evening classes may be conducted for older employes.

With philanthropists making donations, and voluntary organizations giving consideration to the solution of the tenement house problem, the city employer has not found it necessary to house those who work for him. This is a question, however, which should be given more consideration by employers in cities. In Philadelphia and New York, at least, there is need for the establishment of good boarding houses, particularly for women workers, where both sleeping rooms and good food should be furnished at reasonable rates. The custom obtaining in the women's boarding house at Waltham which permits the use of the several sitting-rooms without compromise, by the young women to entertain privately their men friends should be adopted.

While it is not necessary in a city for an employer to initiate each individual effort to meet the social needs of employes, he may contribute to their satisfaction by aiding in the promotion of such movements as social centers in connection with public schools.

Indeed, the Welfare Manager in a large Chicago establishment has found one of her chief duties to be the creation of a bureau through which employes could be informed of the existence of gymnasiums in connection with public schools, domestic science classes, night schools, and art museums. The employes not only did not know of the possibility of using these opportunities, but did not feel free to do so without some form of invitation which would make them feel

STREET RAILWAY EMPLOYES' LIBRARY, NEW YORK CITY.

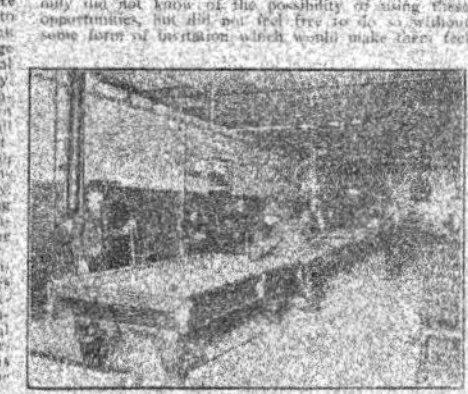

STREET RAILWAY EMPLOYES' POOL ROOM, NEW YORK CITY.

WOMEN'S REST ROOM, BOSTON.

welcome. City employers will find it especially advisable to provide for summer outings, and many already maintain vacation homes for that purpose. One city factory has adopted the unique plan of giving the employes two weeks' vacation with pay.

All the Welfare activities enumerated for the city factory are applicable to the mill village. It is also possible to secure helpful suggestions through Welfare Work for railroad men. They are the largest single class of workingmen, and it is not too much to say that some of the railway corporations are in the front rank of employers who are giving consideration to the welfare of their employes. Here you will find rest rooms for trainmen, containing clean beds for use during the hours of uncertainty at the end of their runs while they are waiting for the return of their trains; baths, game rooms, libraries, etc., and in the engine cabs cans for drinking water. The Relief Department of railroad companies has been imitated by some manufacturing concerns.

But the needs of the employes of a railroad, a department store, or a mining camp may not entirely coincide with those of manufacturing plants, and the needs of the latter may vary greatly.

There will have to be considered the nationality of the employes, whether they are skilled or unskilled workers, as well as many other contingencies.

One may take two manufacturing establishments in the same line of work in a city but located in different districts, and find a luncheon room, for instance, required in one but not in the other. The reason is that, with an hour for luncheon in one instance the employes may go to their nearby homes and become much rested by their outing, while in the other district, the employes' homes are so remote that a luncheon room is an absolute necessity.

This brings me to a point which I desire to emphasize. This is a day of specialization. To meet this problem of what shall be done for the welfare of employes under different conditions, our Welfare Department has established a bureau which has enabled us to supply experts, who may study such conditions and recommend efforts for the benefit of the employes. A notable example of the recognition of the need of such specialized effort has been the call upon us by the Isthmian Canal Commission for two men to investigate the needs and opportunities for recreation of the employes of the Government engaged in the construction of the Panama Canal, and to make definite recommendations. The Government found it essential to provide recreation for the men in addition to sanitary measures. It was discovered that, with nothing of interest to occupy their leisure time, the men become lonely and depressed, and subject to the diseases of the tropical climate. To secure a happy, contented, permanent set of men, the Government sought the advice of experts upon plans for recreation. Our force gives constant thought to this subject of Welfare Work in different industries, and, by concentrating the attention upon this one great subject and constantly studying the experiences of employes in different industries, employers may initiate Welfare Work with our assistance with less likelihood of making mistakes than has been possible in the past.

It is not possible in a talk of this nature to enter into a discussion of methods. A special essay would be required for any one of the subdivisions of Welfare Work.

It may be stated generally that employes will welcome all efforts properly introduced to provide for their physical, mental, and moral welfare. An employer who is noted among his employes for fair dealing need have no fear in introducing Welfare Work after a careful study of conditions has been made. That is to say, after recognizing the first needs of employes to be steady work, an equitable wage, and hours as short as competitive conditions will permit, the employer may successfully install Welfare Work, if proper attention is given to its introduction. A clean, attractive lunch room with wholesome food at prices within the reach of the employes, will succeed; its opposite will not. Shower baths for molders in a basement room where the temperature is lower than

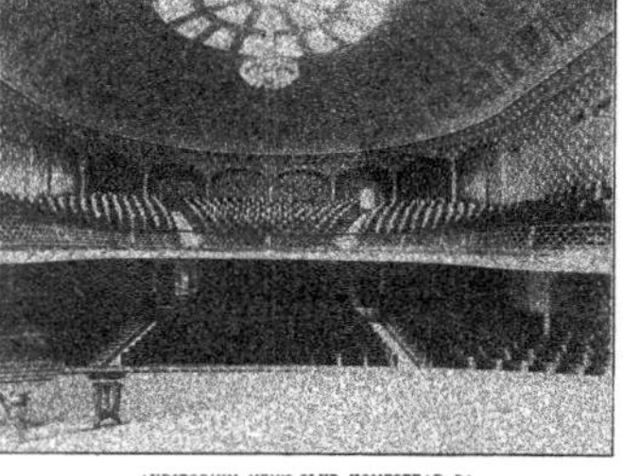

AUDITORIUM, MEN'S CLUB, HOMESTEAD, PA.

in the foundry will not be utilized. On the other hand, shower baths easily accessible to the molding room with a temperature which will not be a shock to the system, kept in cleanly condition, and supplied with towels and soap and an attendant, will be not only a great comfort to the men, but an advantage to the employer, as the health of the men will thus be promoted and skilled workmen will seek employment where such comforts are provided.

An employer who gives no attention to the elimination of inequality in wages, but constantly cuts piece prices, without studying their fair adjustment, will find the employes unwilling to patronize a club house, which should afford much enjoyment, because of their suspicion that its cost has been taken from their wages.

This was well illustrated when, by the merest chance, the president of an overall manufacturing concern in Iowa found it necessary to cut the wages the very day of the opening of a lunch room which he had equipped. It is scarcely necessary to say that the employes would not go near it.

The successful prosecution of Welfare Work once installed depends upon its constant supervision. The employer and his executive force in the average concern is too much engaged with the routine business to study the needs of the employes or to oversee the conduct of the work which must receive constant attention to ensure interest in its continuance. And so, there has appeared what is called in different institutions the "Welfare Manager," "Welfare Superintendent," and "Welfare Secretary," who serves as an intermediary and helps to secure the personal touch which otherwise would be lost in our large business organizations of the present day.

One of the obstacles to the successful prosecution

HOMES RENTED TO EMPLOYES IN LUDLOW, MASS.

PHYSICAL CULTURE ON ROOF DEPARTMENT STORE NEW YORK CITY.

of Welfare Work is the tendency of the average foreman to "knock" all such efforts. Naturally, the foreman, whose especial business is to turn out manufactured material at the lowest possible cost, is not impressed with the value of what may have appeared to be sentimental propositions. Recently the president of a company with 25,000 employes asked us to supply a stereopticon exhibit of efforts of other employers to secure the cooperation of his foremen. He invited them to a dinner at one of the principal hotels, after which this subject was presented, when their minds were free from business cares. The evening was opened by the employer, who expressed his interest in the general subject of Welfare Work—and let me say that the active participation of the employer is essential to its success. It was astonishing to note the surprise and interest of these men when they observed views of efforts promoted by many employers throughout the country, and found that Welfare Work is not a fad, but that it includes practical features, with good sanitary conditions as the first object. Naturally, foremen can not be expected to give a great deal of their time to Welfare Work, but they can, if not in sympathy, prevent its forwarding.

Foremen's meetings held periodically constitute one of the most valuable features of Welfare Work. The education of the foreman is essential to peace in the industrial establishment. There is nothing which causes so much disturbance as the narrow, overbearing, martinet foreman. Justice and fair dealing must be the basis of all Welfare Work.

The motive of the employer is one which comes before us constantly. While the economic value of Welfare Work must be admitted, it is pleasant to find that the average employer promotes Welfare Work from the humanitarian standpoint. It is not difficult to prove that it is desirable from a mercenary point of view. One may enumerate such advantages as the attracting of skilled employes who will seek work where the conditions are best; good discipline and self-respect, which may be secured through opportunities for cleanliness; a permanent set of employes as against a constantly changing force which requires effort to train, and necessitates the loss of much material wasted; and a happy, contented class of workers.

May I close by quoting Dr. Eliot, who has stated: "Happiness is a state of mind much more than a state of body, provided that the elementary necessaries for the well-being of the body are at hand."

PROPERTY OUTSIDE COMPANY'S CONTROL, LUDLOW, MASS.

THE CIVIC FEDERATION OF NEW ENGLAND.

MANY REPRESENTATIVES OF ITS THREE ELEMENTS EXPRESS THEIR REASONS FOR SUPPORTING ITS METHODS OF PROMOTING INDUSTRIAL PEACE.

(FROM THE BULLETIN OF THE CIVIC FEDERATION OF NEW ENGLAND.)

THE membership roll of the Civic Federation of New England, including officers and members of general committees, now numbers within a few [illegible] of three hundred. New members are being steadily added, but it has seemed desirable to publish the acceptances received thus far, together with as [illegible] as possible of the voluntary expressions accompanying such acceptances, both as evidence that the Civic Federation is not a secret organization, whose members are taking a position they do not dare avow, and for the further reason that a list representing, as this does, a large portion of the strongest and most influential employers and labor interests of New England can not fail to give genuine encouragement to all friends of sane and just methods of industrial peace.

This membership plan is one of the most important factors in the educational work the Federation is carrying on. It brings a definite body of representative men to the support of the ideas and methods for which the movement stands, and every addition to the list strengthens the influences that are going out through the industrial community in behalf of fair-minded and reasonable methods of dealing between employers and employes. The object in view is to build up a "prevailing sentiment" of this kind, to the point where the instinctive first step in case of a threatened dispute will be to seek a peaceable adjustment of the trouble through whatever particular methods the special conditions may suggest, rather than to rush into hostilities at once, as has so often been the custom.

By this it is not implied that a member is committed to some fixed, specific position in this or that dispute or delicate complication that may arise, but simply that he stands, so far as may be practicable, for the just and rational methods of conference and direct agreement in industrial dealing. New members, brought into closer touch through the conferences, reviews, and bulletins of the work, with others of similar views successfully applied, find that whatever is being done is on the lines of common-sense, practical experience, and as far as possible from any visionary or theoretical "panacea" plan of social or industrial upheaval.

Much of this influence is necessarily indirect and impossible to trace or make exact record of, but the [illegible] of efforts on these lines, from whatever sources, is to be seen in the increasing tendency to adjust labor difficulties by the conference and agreement method, without special intervention or suggestion from mediating agencies of any kind. It is to promote just this habit or practice, in advance, rather than to interfere in local disputes that have passed into the stage of open conflict, that the Civic Federation devotes its principal efforts in the field of relations between employers and employes.

Typical paragraphs from letters of acceptance follow:

I beg to assure you that as far as time will permit I shall [illegible] to carry out the noble objects and purposes of the Federation.—[illegible] Stang, Bishop of Fall River.

It will give me great pleasure to join the Civic Federation of New England, and to have you use my name in support of the principles and practical aims for which the movement stands.—[illegible] A. Pope, Pres't Pope Manf'g Co., Boston.

I am willing to do anything that will tend to push forward the work of the Civic Federation, and the principles to which it is committed.—John Golden, Gen'l Pres. United Textile Workers of America, Fall River.

I believe any movement which will bring labor and capital to understand intelligently the position which one must assume to the other is a movement which will be conducive to good in the future.—Frederick C. [illegible], Treas'r [illegible] Worsted Company, Boston.

I shall be very glad to be counted one of your members.—Curtis Guild, Jr., Lieut.-Governor of Massachusetts.

I feel assured that there is no more potent force in the community of greater value than the Civic Federation, and the work it will be possible to accomplish, under its wise and careful supervision, will be inestimable.—Frank W. Collins, Pres't Central Labor Union and Agent Bro. of Electrical Workers, Boston.

It is certain that the true relations between the employer and the employed must be those of mutual respect, mutual confidence, consideration, and good will. I am heartily in accord with the principles for which the Federation stands, that the industrial system based on individual enterprise and free labor is inherently sound, and that differences between employers and employes should, and in most cases can, be settled directly between the parties themselves.—Thomas Sherwin, Pres't N. E. Tel. & Tel. Co., Boston.

Anything that I can do to bring the relations between the employer and the employe closer together I shall be more than glad to do.—[illegible] H. [illegible], Sec'y-Treas'r International [illegible] Union of America, Boston.

I believe both employees and employers will benefit by such a [illegible] of education as you propose.—[illegible] H. Carroll, Commissioner of Labor, Concord, N. H.

[illegible]

[illegible] a strike, when at the beginning they were opposed to a strike—had actually been chosen by the union to represent it because they were known to be reasonable, conservative men.—Arthur [illegible] Davis, Typographical Union, Boston.

My experience has been very limited, and I have had an opportunity of testing my theories, which accord with yours, but once, on which occasion they seemed to work very satisfactorily, and I feel sure you will, in your larger field, find the same principles hold good.—S. Parker Bremer, Treas'r Monadnock Mills, Boston.

It is perhaps too much to expect that strikes, lockouts, and other kindred evils will be eliminated altogether, but that there is room for improvement in the relations of employer and employe at the present day is a matter of common knowledge. Both have problems to face, and should be equally tolerant of each other; ready to give and take, and to respect mutual trade agreements above all things. In accepting your offer of membership, I may add that any service I can render to help the good work along, no matter how slight, will be cheerfully given.—Thomas Taylor, Sec'y Loom Fixers' Ass'n, Fall River.

I shall be glad to assist in the work of the Federation, so far as I am able to.—Samuel Bowles, Editor Springfield *Republican*.

I should be glad to be of assistance where possible in the matter of forwarding the work of the Federation.—Charles H. Wilson (Woolen Manufacturer), Pittsfield.

In time I look to see great results come from your body, provided you can keep men with brains and hearts at the head of the organization, and I guess you have got about the right people at present. Of course some of us "agitators" hear about all the good, bad, and indifferent qualifications of an employer, but up to date I have heard of nothing but good words for President Tuttle, and I know hundreds of men who quietly look to him, feeling they will get justice if they have any reasonable grievance.

Everywhere I have been so far I have explained the aims and objects of the Civic Federation, and you can read the expression of approval in about 99 per cent. of all the countenances. It is really the mediator between capital and labor.—Park Mitchell, Pres't New Hampshire State Federation of Labor.

I am in hearty sympathy with your aims and tendencies.—Edward Moll, Managing Director American Oak Leather Company, Boston.

The purpose of the Federation meets with my hearty approval, as I believe it should and will with the people at large. I believe it will tend to the better understanding between the public and the buyers and sellers of labor.—Lloyd J. Smith, Sec'y Bro. of Carpenters, Brookline.

Of course I shall be glad to be numbered among the friends of your great movement in any way you consider helpful to the cause.—E. H. Clement, Editor Boston *Transcript*.

The *Traveler* will be pleased to do what it can at all times to forward this good work.—John H. Fahey, Editor Boston *Traveler*.

I feel sure that such an organization as the Civic Federation can do the greatest amount of good, and if its object is attained will leave its mark in the history of the world. I am anxious to see the unsettled condition of the industrial system change so there may be a reign of peace and safety in its stead. The movement will have the support of the Maine State Federation and its affiliated bodies.—Eugene Brawn, Pres't Maine State Federation of Labor, Ellsworth, Me.

I am in sympathy with the purpose which the Federation represents, namely, to prevent, so far as possible, strife between labor and capital.—Samuel B. Capen, Torrey, Bright & Capen Co., Boston.

It seems to me that the Civic Federation is something to which every man of sense ought to lend his favorable influence. If you see anything that I can do to advance the interests of the association, please let me know what it is and I will cooperate.—Gordon Woodbury, Editor the *Union*, Manchester, N. H.

I am most heartily in accord with the purposes and the methods of the Federation.—Henry Hopkins, Pres't Williams College.

It would be impossible for a man situated as I am, brought in contact with the engineer, the contractor, and the laborer, not to be interested in the solution of the industrial problems which confront us. I can ill spare the time for a new organization, but I feel that I cannot well stay out of this one.—Henry S. Pritchett, Pres't Mass. Institute of Technology.

I am and have been heartily in accord with its object.—J. F. Frawnino, Pres't The S. M. Howes Company, Boston.

I freely admit that too much of an arbitrary spirit is shown by both sides at times, simply because in the narrow minds of some, labor and capital should be opposed to each other in all things. This idea is wrong and should not be tolerated, and I believe, through the good offices of the Federation, a great deal of this feeling can be removed, and both sides brought into the path that will lead to industrial peace.—Thomas O'Donnell, Sec'y Cotton Mule Spinners' Ass'n, Fall River.

I believe in its principles, and what little I can do to aid the cause I shall be glad to do.—Louis P. Howe, Vice-Pres't The S. H. Howe Shoe Company, Marlboro.

Its principles and aims indicate that it will accomplish much.—Charles K. Fox (Shoe Manufacturer), Haverhill.

I believe in an organization such as you represent, where employer and employe can meet. Many times, if both parties could meet, trouble would be avoided.—A. M. Haddell, Steam Engineers' Union, Boston.

The purposes of the Federation which, I know, are intended to bring about better relations between capital and labor and to improve industrial conditions, appeal to me very strongly, and I am most happy to become a member.—Henry Cabot Lodge, United States Senator.

If I had no other motive, I should wish to be identified with your work in order to show the workingmen that the church is not only not indifferent to their interests, but intensely eager to serve them in all peace-making, uplifting ways. Equally does the Christian Church desire justice for employers.—Daniel A. Goodsell, Resident Bishop, Methodist Episcopal Church, Brookline.

I am in hearty sympathy with the aim of the Federation.—Edward A. Taft, Pres't New York and Boston Despatch Express Company.

You are creating the public sentiment which will one day hold capitalists accountable to their duties to the state. On the other hand, the working class must be brought to an intelligent understanding of the immorality of intensifying class antagonisms, [illegible]

[illegible]

I can not express my views better than to quote your [illegible].—Edward P. Mason, Pres't Mason & Hamlin Company, Cambridge.

I deem it a great privilege to become [illegible] with a movement which I believe marks a distinct epoch in this [illegible] century, and which can not but redound to the [illegible] advantage and greater happiness and prosperity of all the people of our great country.—Thomas M. [illegible], Typographical Union, Boston.

It is a noble work, and it will be a gratification to have even an humble part in it.—A. E. Winship, Editor *Journal of Education*, Boston.

Having read the aims and objects of the Federation, and knowing something of its work, I would [illegible] as a trades unionist and workingman if I did not endorse them.

I believe in conciliation rather than in arbitration as a means of settling disputes. I believe that most [illegible] can be accomplished by conference between employers and employes, provided both meet in an open, straightforward spirit, with the aim to settle disputes and avoid an outbreak of trouble. But I believe that arbitration is vastly preferable to strikes and lockouts. In its proper place, as a court of last resort, it has much to commend it.—Herbert W. Cobb, Typographical Union, Boston.

I believe in the sort of work which is being attempted, from my experience both as a wage earner and employer, for if wisely done it must result in the common good, which we are all after.—B. Preston Clark (Trustee), Boston.

I am convinced that the association is approaching great questions at issue between capital and labor in a reasonable and practical manner, and that through the means [illegible] by it, these questions will gradually form less of a barrier to the continuous prosperity of this country. I take pleasure in pledging to the association my earnest endeavors to contribute in every possible manner toward the measure which we so much desire.—Robert B. Treat, President, Manufacturers' Fuel Company of Rhode Island, Providence, R. I.

A grand feature you have, that all fair-minded men will accept, is the conciliation part. This is a vital point to organized labor, as it has a tendency to avert strikes and lockouts, and does away with a good deal of the radical ideas that do and will exist in all bodies of men, whether employers or employes.—J. E. Potts, Agent United Brotherhood of Carpenters and Joiners, Boston.

If I can be of any service in the general good proposed by your organization, I am glad to have my name proposed for membership.—Samuel N. Brown, Pres't Fairbanks Co., Boston.

It is a privilege to be identified with those who are broad enough to have devoted themselves to the development of the idea for which the Civic Federation stands.—[illegible], Dennison Manufacturing Company, Boston.

Were the workers, through their representatives, allowed to approach their employers with the thought that their requests would be listened to without jeopardizing their livelihood, better results would be attained, and less friction would occur.

In referring to your honorable body's existence, I believe that it is a step in the right direction in bringing about such conditions, and a possibility of showing to all parties concerned a probability of bringing about the desired ultimatum.—Edward Cohen, 3d Vice Pres't Mass. State Branch, American Federation of Labor, Lynn.

We are heartily in sympathy with any movement which will bring capital and labor in closer touch and promote general harmony and welfare.—W. S. Forbes, Forbes Lithograph Manufacturing Co., Forbes.

The lines of work which you have laid down ought to be productive of a better feeling than has been the case up to this time.—F. B. Towne, National Blank Book Co., Holyoke.

It is a well known fact that if the employers and employes could be brought closer together it would do away with a good many strikes and lockouts, and it would do away with the annoyance to the public in general, who are, as a general rule, the greatest sufferers when war is raging between employer and employe.—Max B. Thrower, Delegate Atlantic Coast Seamen's Union, Boston.

That something must be done to better the relations of employer and employe is admitted by all who give the subject any thought, and I am surely in sympathy with any rational movement with that object in view.—T. M. Perry, Pres't Massachusetts Pink Granite Co., Milford.

I have always believed it to be an organization that was very necessary to help in bringing about industrial peace. I can not do better than endorse its purposes.—William [illegible], Cigarmakers' Union, Boston.

We think the object of your Federation a worthy one, and we hereby apply for membership in the Civic Federation of New England.—J. F. Fuller, Manager George A. Fuller Company, Boston.

I am in hearty sympathy with your work.—J. P. MacColl, Lorraine Manufacturing Co., Pawtucket, R. I.

I fully agree with the plan as I understand it, and regard the idea as wise and worthy of support.—Charles E. Rickard, Treas'r Cranston Worsted Mills, Bristol, R. I.

It seems to me easily one of the most important influences now acting to lessen the friction in industry.—John Graham Brooks, Pres't American Social Science Association, Cambridge.

In my experience in labor organizations I believe many times troubles could have been avoided if we could only have got in touch with the people who really employ us, and laid before them our grievances, and talked the matter over with them in a businesslike manner. Therefore, I am willing to lend a hand to bring about an amicable settlement of [illegible] questions.—Philip H. Sweet, 4th Vice-Pres't Mass. State Branch, A. F. of L., Boston.

I should be very glad indeed to become a member of the New England Civic Federation, and to support its good work to the best of my ability.—Henry L. [illegible], Readville.

I am now and have been a firm believer in the method laid down by the Civic Federation, in establishing an organization made up of representatives of all the elements who may be affected by any industrial upheaval, by creating a common meeting ground, where employer and employe may [illegible] thus giving all a clearer understanding of this great question of labor, the result of which must naturally greatly diminish the probability of industrial strife.—Charles R. [illegible], International Ass'n of Machinists, Boston.

[illegible]

ARGUMENTS FOR AND AGAINST THE RESTRICTION OF IMMIGRATION.

TWO OPPOSING VIEWS FORCIBLY PRESENTED BEFORE THE NATIONAL CONGRESS OF FARMERS—THE RELATION BETWEEN ALIEN LABOR AND AGRICULTURE.

The following addresses before the Farmers' National Congress, at Richmond, were delivered on September 14 by two recognized experts upon the question of Immigration. They are cogent summaries of phases of the current discussion of the topic to be considered more exhaustively at the National Immigration Conference, to be held in New York on December 6 and 7, under the auspices of the National Civic Federation:

IMMIGRATION AND FARM LABOR.

(Address by Robert De C. Ward, of Cambridge, Mass.)

The large cities of the North and East find themselves greatly overburdened with the many problems which have grown out of the enormous and very indiscriminate alien immigration of recent years. It has become perfectly clear that the only remedies for existing conditions are, first, a considerable restriction of immigration, so that only the more desirable aliens shall be admitted; and, second, the distribution of the present congested slum populations throughout the less thickly settled parts of the country, in the West and South. While the philanthropic people of these great cities are thus preparing to unload some of their alien burdens upon the farming districts, and in this effort are naturally receiving every possible assistance from the railroads, which see in this scheme of distribution a large source of revenue to themselves, the farmers in some parts of our country are in need of farm help, and are asking that some of this great tide of inflowing aliens be turned away from the cities and out over the fields and farms.

The American farmers at present hold the key to the immigration problem. If they say: "We want anybody we can get to work for us; if we can not have an honest, strong, intelligent, skilled laborer, we will take one of low vitality, poor physique, mentally deficient, unused to outdoor work, dishonest," then the charity workers in our cities and our railroad companies will send all sorts of aliens who are generally regarded as "undesirable" into the farming districts.

If, on the other hand, American farmers clearly recognize the fact that our present immigration laws make it possible for thousands of aliens to land here every year who are not likely to be a benefit, but an injury; who are weak and sickly; who have come because they were inveigled into buying a passage ticket by a steamship agent, or were given the ticket by a charitable society, in order that they might become a charge upon the United States rather than upon the home country. If American farmers regard the welfare of their own country instead of considering only their own financial gain, then they will insist on having none but honest, industrious, healthy, and fit immigrants. Such aliens there are in abundance in the large cities, who would be far better off in the country. These are the ones whom the farmer wants. Dishonest, shiftless, sickly, and unfit immigrants there are also in abundance in our large Northern cities. These the farmer does not want. Neither do the Northern cities want them. Yet they continue to pour in on us because Congress has not yet properly dammed the flood. To send out from the large cities of the North thousands of aliens who are not desired in the country districts, simply because charitable agencies think they can thus relieve themselves of an unpleasant burden, is much like throwing one's weeds over one's neighbor's fence into his garden.

Such a wholesale distribution of aliens who are not desired on the farm would prove a burden to the country districts, and would not relieve the pressure in the cities. "To relieve the pressure in the cities without restricting the number admitted only opens the way for a still larger immigration." Europe has ten persons ready to fill each place thus vacated in our city slums. . . .

It is evident that much of our present immigration is as unfit on the farm as in the city; that it is of low vitality, poor physique, very ignorant, often diseased, mentally deficient and of criminal tendencies, by reason of its much lower standard of living entering into unhealthy competition with American labor. The immigration which we most need to check is made up of people who are not fitted for an agricultural life. Long generations in the ghettos of Europe have unfitted the Jews for farming, and they are singularly unsuccessful at it. Armenians take naturally to certain kinds of indoor labor; Greeks become peddlers of fruit or work in factories; Syrians are oftenest peddlers. And so it is with many other races who now make up a large part of our immigration. Further, our farming interests, whenever they have been asked their opinion, have not desired a wholesale and indiscriminate invasion of Slav, Latin, Hebrew, and Asiatic immigrants, but have expressed very distinct preferences for people from northern and western Europe. And, finally, it is clear that the immigrants whom we are now getting in such large numbers from the cities of Russia, and from other countries of eastern and southern Europe, are crowding out the better classes of immigrants who used to be in the majority, and who went readily of their own choice into the farming districts. The United States Industrial Commission, only three or four years ago, made a careful study of the need of farm labor in all sections of the United States, sending out many letters of inquiry to representative farmers, and found that the most successful immigrants were those who are skilled in intensive farming. The nationalities noted as the best along these lines were the Scandinavians and Germans; also the Dutch and Bohemians. Of the races from southern and eastern Europe, the Italians alone were mentioned in this list of the more successful. Considerable numbers of Italians have proved satisfactory as laborers on the large sugar and cotton plantations of Louisiana, Mississippi, Texas and other Southern States, and also in truck farming, but there are many Southern planters who are not satisfied with Italians, and it is reported that large numbers of these farm laborers are already flocking to the Southern cities. A recent canvas of many representative State officials of the South showed a decided preference for farmers and farm laborers of Scandinavian, German, and British origin. These are the people who have the energy, skill, intelligence, and industry needed on an American farm to-day. Immigrants from southern and eastern Europe and from Asia, as a rule, crowd into the large cities, and huddle together in the tenement districts. They do not go out on to the farms, and I believe they are not wanted there, certainly not in large numbers, because of their low standards of living and of their foreign habits and tendencies, which do not improve the tone of a healthy, educated, and self-respecting American rural community. I have recently had the pleasure of reading an admirable letter from a gentleman who is an honored member and an officer of this organization. In this letter the case is put so clearly that I can not do better than quote, as follows:

"Farming, especially in the upper Mississippi valley and beyond, has been revolutionized during the past fifteen years. The successful farmer must now be a man of unusual intelligence, one able to grasp the meaning of such terms as bacteriology of the soil, feeding coefficients, protein compounds, etc., and it is safe to say that a very small percentage of the immigrants from southern Europe are capable of this. Their immediate descendants will be little more capable."

The American farmer is now in a position to exercise a determining influence upon the character of the future American race. The railroads are ready to distribute over our agricultural districts many unhealthy, shiftless and unfit aliens from our Northern city slums, and are planning to carry on this distribution on a vastly larger scale, by taking the newly arrived immigrants directly from the steamships. If such a wholesale and indiscriminate distribution is allowed to go on without a protest on the part of the farming communities, our railroads and trans-Atlantic steamship lines and European governments will have good reason to congratulate themselves. But you must realize that such a distribution of undesirable aliens will not give you the labor you need; will injure the quality of the American race of the future; will spread more widely the evils which result from exposing our own people to competition with the lower classes of aliens. Hence this congress should become a strong supporter of any reasonable measure of further selection of immigration, for it can not fail to see that the continued influx of hundreds of thousands of unhealthy, shiftless, and unfit immigrants is a burden upon, and a detriment to, the whole country. We need and want none but honest, industrious, intelligent, healthy, and fit immigrants. Any reasonable legislation which shall improve the quality, physical as well as mental, of our immigration, and reduce the quantity to the point of proper assimilation, should be supported. I believe that American farmers have everything to gain and practically nothing to lose by advocating a higher head-tax, the exclusion of aliens of poor physique, and an illiteracy test.

ARGUMENT AGAINST RESTRICTION.

(Substance of address by Nathan Bijur, of New York.)

The opponents of immigration have for a number of years relied on statistics, but unfortunately for them these statistics do not seem to have stood careful analysis. A set of figures prepared in Massachusetts indicated a high rate of criminality among the Italians and Russians and a low rate among the Irish and English. This was cited to show that the Irish and English were desirable immigrants and the Russians and Italians undesirable, but when it was pointed out that in these statistics all crimes arising from intoxication had been omitted, and that the inclusion of these crimes reversed the order, the argument turned in favor of the present immigrant. This is but an example.

Then when accurate statistics seemed to fail, resort was had to the citation of large figures. The public was to be startled by learning that the number of immigrants had grown from, say 200,000 in the '50s and 400,000 in the '70s to 800,000 in recent years, and the cry was "How shall we absorb these strangers?" But again the analyst came forward and showed that in proportion to the total population of the United States at the various periods named, the immigration had actually fallen off, and that while the ratio of immigration to the thousand of initial population between 1840 and 1860 was from 100 to 110 per thousand, in 1891-1900 it has been but 59.

This, however, is not all. The opponents of immigration have talked only of the number who came. They have never told of the numbers who return every year. While something like 800,000 immigrants came to this country in 1904, some 325,000 steerage passengers left our ports, so that the net immigration is not a very startling figure.

Then we were told that statistics gathered by the Bureau of Immigration had shown that there were 45,000 aliens in the penal, reformatory and charitable institutions of the United States, and that their care was a great burden. Further examination, however, developed the fact that only 21 per cent. of these 45,000 had been in this country less than five years, 50 per cent. had been here from five to thirty years, and 22 per cent. over thirty years. The recent and "undesirable" arrivals, therefore, could not be responsible for this "burden on the community."

Moreover, finally, people began to ask what was meant by the term "alien" in these statistics, and as yet that question is unanswered. Is it an alien as opposed to a naturalized citizen, and if so does the taking out of naturalization papers render a man less likely to disease or accident or insanity? And how about women and children? When are they aliens and when do they cease to be such? Thus, again, the talking in big figures came to nothing.

When it is remembered that the "alien" must necessarily be a foreigner, and the foreigner, therefore, a comparatively recent immigrant, and that the immigrant is the man who takes the hard and laboring oar in the production of wealth in the community, and engages in the arduous and dangerous occupations, it is no wonder that there should be a greater proportion of sickness and incapacity in that class of the community than in any other, but that has nothing to do with the problem of immigration. It is the result of poverty, and so long as we have poor people we shall find a greater proportion of incapacitated individuals among them.

The latest phase of opposition is appeal to generalization. Gen. Francis A. Walker is cited as having said that the arrival of so many immigrants willing to work at comparatively low wages has rendered native parents unwilling to have children to compete at these wages, and that therefore the immigration is responsible for the decrease in the birth-rate. A reference to Gen. Walker's own articles shows that he admitted that the reverse might be true, namely, that the decrease in the birth-rate had made a place for immigrants, only he said *that he thought it more reasonable and likely* that the immigration had been the cause of the decrease in the birth-rate, rather than the result.

Of course, any one is entitled to the opposite view. In trying to reach a conclusion I am led strongly to believe that Gen. Walker's opinion is unwarranted, when I recall the notoriously low and declining birth-rate in France, which certainly can not have been brought about by immigration, since there is none there.

Then we are told that an illiteracy test should be applied. That this would exclude "undesirable" people. But since the immigrant comes here to labor, the exact connection between valuable manual work and literacy does not appear. In fact, even the advocates of this test admit that a man may be a most excellent laborer and still may be illiterate. On the other hand he may be a consummate scoundrel and be able to read and write many languages.

Moreover, illiteracy is not confined to the immigrant. Any citizen who refers to the census of 1900 will be astounded at the number of illiterates among native Americans. When it comes to the children, they are the ones that interest us. The census shows us that the children of native born parents are illiterate to the extent of 5.7 per cent., while the children of foreign born parents are illiterate only to the extent of 1.6 per cent. It is evident that the illiterate foreign parent learns quickly the advantage of education, and sees to it that his children enjoy it.

There are twice as many native born children of foreign parents in each of the States of Wisconsin and Minnesota who can not speak English as there are in the State of New York, which has nearly four times the

(Concluded on page 4.)

NEWSPAPER COMMENTS UPON THE NATIONAL IMMIGRATION CONFERENCE.

THE PRESS UNANIMOUSLY COMMENDS THE ACTION OF THE CIVIC FEDERATION AND ANTICIPATES CONCLUSIONS BENEFICIAL TO SOUND PUBLIC POLICY.

IMMIGRATION CLIPPINGS.

A GUIDE TO CONGRESS.

Chicago Chronicle.

THE BEST BLOOD WANTED.

Boston Transcript.

MEN AND MERCHANDISE.

WOULD EXCLUDE ILLITERACY.

NEW JERSEY WELCOMES NEW COMERS.

Trenton, N. J., True American.

A VITAL AND PREGNANT TOPIC.

Brooklyn Daily Eagle.

A TOPIC FOR CAPITAL AND LABOR.

DISTRIBUTION RATHER THAN RESTRICTION.

Wall Street Journal.

THE PRESIDENT INTERESTED.

Pittsburg Press.

A PUBLIC SPIRITED EFFORT.

SEEK ROOM AND OPPORTUNITY.

AN ILLUMINATING CONVENTION.

EUROPEAN ECONOMISTS INTERESTED.

DISTRIBUTION THE PRACTICAL PROBLEM.

(Concluded on page 20.)

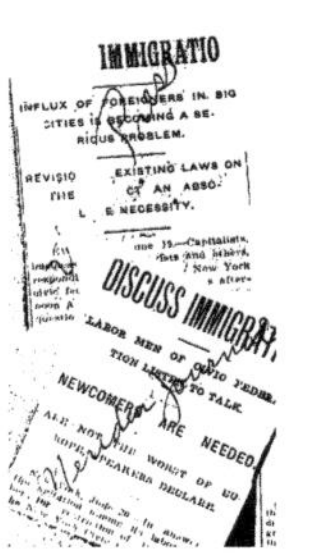

IMMIGRATIO
INFLUX OF FOREIGNERS IN BIG
CITIES IS BECOMING A SE-
RIOUS PROBLEM.
EXISTING LAWS ON
AN ABSO-
NECESSITY.
DISCUSS IMMIGRA
LABOR MEN OF CIVIC FEDER-
TION LISTEN TO TALK.
NEWCOMERS ARE NEEDED.
SPEAKERS DECLARE.

PUBLIC OWNERSHIP A QUESTION OF EAGER CURRENT DISCUSSION.

NEWSPAPERS WELCOME THE INVESTIGATION, AT HOME AND ABROAD, OF A SUBJECT NOW ACUTE IN MANY MUNICIPALITIES.

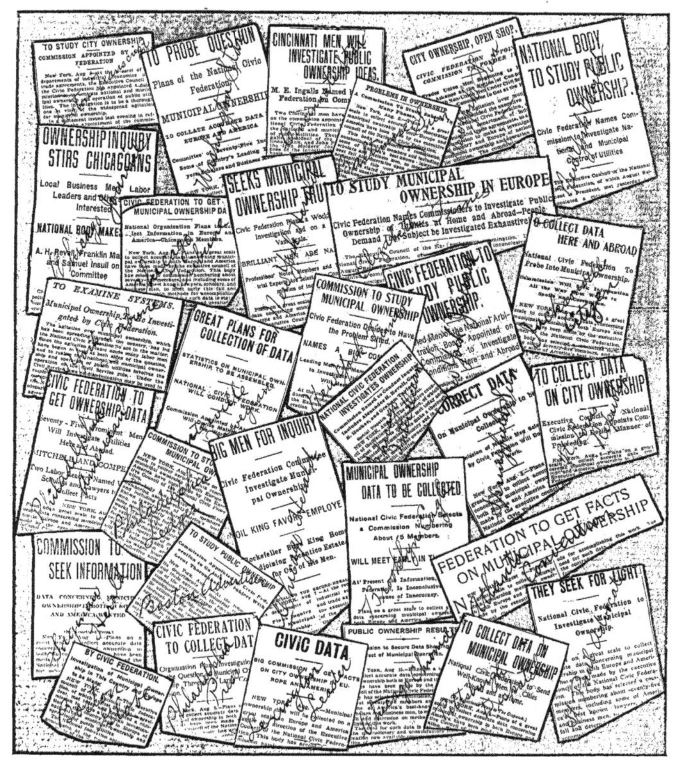

TO STUDY CITY OWNERSHIP

TO PROBE QUESTION

Plans of the National Civic Federation.

CINCINNATI MEN WILL INVESTIGATE PUBLIC OWNERSHIP IDEAS.

CITY OWNERSHIP, OPEN SHOP.

NATIONAL BODY TO STUDY PUBLIC OWNERSHIP.

Civic Federation Names Commission to Investigate National and Municipal Control of Utilities

OWNERSHIP INQUIRY STIRS CHICAGOANS

SEEKS MUNICIPAL OWNERSHIP TRUTH

TO STUDY MUNICIPAL OWNERSHIP IN EUROPE

CIVIC FEDERATION TO GET MUNICIPAL OWNERSHIP DATA

TO COLLECT DATA HERE AND ABROAD

TO EXAMINE SYSTEMS.

COMMISSION TO STUDY MUNICIPAL OWNERSHIP

CIVIC FEDERATION TO STUDY PUBLIC OWNERSHIP.

GREAT PLANS FOR COLLECTION OF DATA

CIVIC FEDERATION TO GET OWNERSHIP DATA

CORRECT DATA

TO COLLECT DATA ON CITY OWNERSHIP

BIG MEN FOR INQUIRY

MUNICIPAL OWNERSHIP DATA TO BE COLLECTED

COMMISSION TO SEEK INFORMATION

FEDERATION TO GET FACTS ON MUNICIPAL OWNERSHIP

THEY SEEK FOR LIGHT

CIVIC FEDERATION TO COLLECT DATA

CIVIC DATA.

PUBLIC OWNERSHIP RESULTS

TO COLLECT DATA ON MUNICIPAL OWNERSHIP

BY CIVIC FEDERATION.

(*Concluded from page 17.*)

admitted. The present rate of immigration is generally regarded as unprecedented, and in an absolute sense it is; but these speakers dwelt on the fact "in proportion to the population immigration has been decreasing." The vast majority of the new comers, it was argued, were in every way desirable people, and there is no foundation for the statements so often made regarding the "emptying of old-world poorhouses and jails" to dump the inmates on American soil.

The convention to be called will, therefore, direct its attention chiefly to the practical question of the distribution of our immigration, while giving an opportunity to those who believe that restriction is quite as essential as proper provision for the meeting of supply and demand of alien labor.

A BUREAU OF INFORMATION.

Omaha Bee.

The National Civic Federation has brought out the statement, preliminary to its coming conference on immigration, that there is a serious scarcity of labor in some industrial centers. Is it practicable to effect such a distribution of immigrants as is manifestly desirable? The Commissioner of Immigration has suggested a plan which very many believe would have good results and it ought to receive the careful consideration of Congress. It is simply to provide for giving trustworthy information to immigrants as to where there is a demand for labor and where the most favorable opportunities for settlement are to be found. Such information could be supplied by the government without very much expense, as the States would undoubtedly supply a great deal of it. That it would prove of very great value is not to be doubted. Having such information, thousands who now congregate in the large cities would go into the country places, to the material benefit of the latter.

Additional restrictions upon immigration are not needed. The existing regulations are ample if properly enforced. The real question is to effect a distribution of the immigrants where labor is in demand and they can be most useful.

SEND ARRIVALS WHERE NEEDED.

Pittsburg Gazette.

The National Civic Federation will discuss from various points of view the question of the distribution of immigrants. Commissioner Watchorn earnestly declares that the law is being rigidly enforced, but the law is not stringent enough to keep out many who are undesirable to any part of the country. However, the question to be discussed by the Federation is distribution, not restriction, as it is felt that under present conditions the only thing to be done is to guide the tide of immigration so that those unsettled portions of the country will get what benefit there is to come from an added population. It is hardly necessary to say that no hard and fast rule has been discovered that will coax the new comers into those sections of the country where they are needed. That may come later, however, when the government decides to take it up.

A FRIEND OF RESTRICTION.

Rochester, N. Y., Chronicle.

The Civic Federation's conference on immigration, no doubt, will throw a flood of light upon this question. The reports of consular officers, of State and municipal institutions—penal and charitable, of steamship companies and of the Immigration Bureau of the government, will be focused on that gathering and discussed intelligently and systematically. The results can not fail of affording great assistance to Congress in formulating a plan for the better regulation and control of immigration.

This country would not suffer in its material development—on the contrary, it would be benefited—if the great bulk of immigration now pouring in on it like a mighty tide of turbid and polluted water should be restrained and turned back for years, if not permanently. The population we now have is fully equal to the further material development of the continent, and what it would lose in quantity by restricting immigration would be more than counterbalanced by the quality of our people after a few years of normal growth under American influences.

PROBATION BEFORE NATURALIZATION.

Brooklyn Standard Union.

The discussion upon immigration, under the auspices of the National Civic Federation, is proving both educational and valuable. One point brought out is that a large percentage of immigrants, amounting to something like 40 or 45 per cent., return to their native lands after remaining here for a while, so that the apparent increase, based solely on the figures of arrivals at our various ports, is far from being a permanent one. But there is plenty of room here for the healthy, virile, industrious immigrant, whose intent is to be self-supporting, law-abiding, and finally to become a loyal American citizen. Only he must not remain in the already overcrowded cities. The farms, the wheat fields, and the mining camps will welcome his presence, and a thousand other occupations invite his activities. Distribution of immigrants, however, is a prime essential, while concentration is a menace. There must be manifest sympathy with American civilization and ideals before the alien can be safely admitted to citizenship. It is the potentiality of a foreign education and environment that constitutes the real peril in permitting millions of men to vote on questions which it is impossible they can properly understand. The present law should be promptly and radically amended. While permitting all immigrants now here to be admitted to citizenship as soon as they shall have complied with existing regulations, a time ought to be fixed after which no alien should be allowed to take out final papers unless he shall have resided here for at least ten years—fifteen years would be better. Also, after a certain prescribed period, no foreigner should be admitted to citizenship unless he can read and write the English language. With these safeguards, the danger involved in large annual additions to our population from foreign lands would be reduced to a minimum. The public schools and an American environment would do the rest.

SOME MISAPPREHENSIONS CORRECTED.

Pittsburg Post.

The information sought by the Civic Federation is most desirable and enters largely into the repeated discussion of the immigration subject by citizens generally, and serves to correct much popular misapprehension, that a majority of the arrivals are from jails, asylums, and poorhouses. This is far from being the case, and the information will be received with satisfaction and contentment.

There are many poor people in the United States and in New York City, but this does not imply, by any means, that a majority of the immigrants are outcasts and unfortunates. There were always poor people in the country. We have had poor among us since the first immigrant landed here in the person of Columbus, or with the Pilgrim fathers, or the Cavaliers at Jamestown. There has been a tremendous rush of immigrants at different periods in our history, but it is very small in its relative figures to the general population of the United States. The State of Texas is larger than Germany, and is capable alone of feeding a population very much larger than that of Germany, which is some fifty-five millions.

It is fallacious to attribute the great increase of the population of cities and towns in the United States to immigration. Statistics show that the great increase of the urban population in this country is due to the fact that the people have come from the country to the cities because they like the life and opportunities of the city best. We arrogate very much when we attempt to shut them out from the cities, and besides that it is impracticable and un-American.

The immigrants for the first ten or twenty years, until the new generation is on its feet, take what may be called the laboring oar of the population. They are poor and industrious. If more immigrants are found in hospitals than natives, it is because they are more pressed into hazardous occupations.

Allegheny County maintains well on to a hundred thousand immigrants, and they are certainly the most industrial and frugal of the population. Compare them with the negroes! What would our mills and furnaces and mines do if deprived of their willing hands and great labor capacity? The United States is great and this industrial hive is great not because of any one class of population, but because it represents an amalgamation of various types. In the form of immigration there has come to us all the forms of activity that have made modern civilization. Immigration of the past hundred years has been the basis and source of our prosperity and advancement in science, industry, and invention. No sensible or observing man or woman can vote or declare immigration a peril. The wars of the Republic have declared it otherwise, and the progress of the country proves it the reverse day by day.

GOOD RESULTS ANTICIPATED.

Los Angeles, Cal., Herald.

That there is a decided trend of sentiment in favor of a general overhauling of the immigration laws is shown clearly in the call which has been issued by President August Belmont, of the National Civic Federation, for a general and quasi-official conference on the subject, to be held December 6 and 7 in this city.

The conference will be under the auspices of the Civic Federation, and the Governor of each State in the Union has been requested to name ten delegates to represent his State at the meeting. In addition to this, the call for the meeting includes a set of questions which the various delegates are expected to answer for their respective States.

With an organization such as the National Civic Federation taking hold of this great problem, and at a time when the sessions of Congress are about to be resumed, it is believed much general good can be accomplished.

INVESTIGATION OF PUBLIC OWNERSHIP AND OPERATION APPROVED.

EDITORIAL OPINIONS INDICATE WIDE INTEREST IN THE SUBJECT AND UNANIMOUS CONFIDENCE IN THE WORK OF THE COMMISSION.

A NON-PARTISIAN INQUIRY.

Washington Post.

The announcement that the National Civic Federation proposed to collect accurate data concerning municipal ownership in Europe and the United States will be accepted as indicating an honest and non-partisan effort to obtain facts upon an important subject. The question of the wisdom and practical advantage of municipal ownership is one that is just now thoroughly engaging public attention. It is true that the skyrocket which ascended when Judge Dunne was elected mayor of Chicago has come down as a stick, but the advocates of the alleged reform do not seem to be discouraged. On the contrary, they assert that the failure of their ideas to materialize in Chicago is merely a temporary and not a permanent backset to their cause.

The names of the distinguished gentlemen who are to represent the National Civic Federation in its inquiries are a sufficient guarantee that practical results will be obtained. It is worth while, however, to note that during the past three or four years there have been no more active propagandists of the municipal ownership idea than a coterie of United States consuls in England and Germany. If the suggestion did not seem absurd, it could easily be intimated that these officials were acting under instructions. They have written industriously and enthusiastically upon the subject, and their reports have been given wide circulation through government agencies. Within the past few weeks the Bureau of Statistics has issued another volume of consular reports, devoted entirely to details of experiments in municipal ownership in Austria, France, Germany, England, and Canada, and the consuls, in nearly every case, take occasion to express their hearty approval of what has been accomplished. It is, at least, a curious coincidence to find these consuls sounding the praises of the new system.

What is the meaning of this sudden and universal chorus of acclaim regarding municipal ownership Why are these consuls, in every part of the world, viewing the new system through rose-colored spectacles? We are loth to believe that society is being revolutionized, despite the mass of evidence officially promulgated, and for this reason we are glad to see the inquiry undertaken by the National Civic Federation. If it shall be found that the United States consuls are reporting facts and that a long step toward governmental millennium has been taken, a great work will have been accomplished. Up to the present time, however, we must be content to express our surprise that our consuls, for some reasons or other, have failed to discover a single fly in the ointment of municipal ownership.

MAKE THE INQUIRY THOROUGH.

Chicago Tribune.

The agitation in behalf of municipal ownership has attracted the attention of the National Civic Federation. It has decided to appoint a committee to investigate thoroughly the national and municipal ownership and operation of public utilities. This is no summer vacation job. If the committee be thorough and go over the entire ground in Europe and America, it will have to put in many months of hard work.

If the committee of the Civic Federation will investigate all the elements of the question and present in bold relief the essential differences between municipal government at home and abroad it may do some good. The incorrigible municipal ownerites will not be convinced. They will say that the report is the work of a "capitalistic organization." Mr. August Belmont, who is at the head of the federation, is identified with corporations controlling some of the public utilities the municipal ownerites would like to lay hands on. They will fall back on their solitary argument, that an American city can do anything a European city does.

There are many men who have not waded deeply into the swamps of municipal ownership and operation and whose brains are still above water. A searching, complete inquiry into the boasted virtues of municipal ownership would do them good. It would show them why there are some things which European cities can do and American cities can not. It might lead them to the conclusion that the greatest need of American communities is the divorcement of politics from local administration. If English cities can do that and thrive because of it, why can not American cities?

A STUDY OF MUNICIPAL PROBLEMS.

Boston Transcript.

Whether inspired with that evangel of municipal ownership, Mayor Dunne, or whether acting on its own unprompted initiative, we know not, but the National Civic Federation has been making elaborate plans to collect accurate data bearing on that problem, both in Europe and America. To this end it has selected a commission of about seventy-five members, including some of the best known lawyers, scholars, and business men in the country, to meet early the coming fall and outline methods for pursuing the work. It is intended, according to the purpose stated in its circular, that this investigation shall disclose actual results of public ownership and operation, so far as they have been determined not only in this country, but in all countries.

UTILITIES AND TAXATION.

Cincinnati Enquirer.

The National Civic Federation has appointed a commission of seventy-five members to collect data on municipal ownership in this country and in Europe. This is a subject on which there is now a great need of reliable and well digested information. Those who have gone mad in the United States on the subject of municipal ownership have relied on a few European examples which have been apparently successful, but have failed entirely to consider the differences in form of government. Because street cars are run by the municipalities in Europe the conclusion is quietly drawn that all municipalities in the United States can do the same thing—that all they have to do is to do it on the same general plan that Horace Greeley proposed for resumption of specie payments. The information should be thoroughly digested, and especial trouble should be taken to learn how the public is to acquire the utilities without overwhelming the people with taxation.

A WELCOME MOVEMENT.

Boston Globe.

There are so many contradictory and unsatisfactory statements concerning municipal ownership of public utilities it is gratifying to learn that the executive council of the National Civic Federation is formulating plans to collate accurate data on this subject here and abroad. This plan of the federation will give great satisfaction to the officials of municipalities, as well as to all citizens. All people desire their local government conducted in the most economical manner, but they are bewildered by all the current arguments for and against municipal ownership. Nor is it strange they are puzzled because most speakers say more about the theory of municipal ownership than they do relative to its practical workings abroad.

Municipal ownership works well in some foreign communities, chiefly because the conditions there are favorable. In many parts of Europe where this system is established it is satisfactory and successful because the national or imperial government is behind it, having more to say about the management of cities than do the state governments of the United States.

In some foreign cities most of the local officials, from the mayor down, are unpaid, and the national government has so much power over the finances of the communities that local difficulties are reduced. Hence it is easy to utilise the cheapest methods of conducting the affairs of a municipality.

Most of the public utilities can be and are managed by those foreign cities because there are no outside corporations interested in them. The general government, and not corporations, deals directly with the cities.

Glowing accounts reach America of the success of municipal ownership abroad, but this commission of the Civic Federation can ascertain the actual facts in each case.

It can investigate and inform us concerning wages, hours, and conditions of labor, collective bargaining, the cost and character of services, political conditions, civic service, the spoils system and municipal corruption, and, most important of all, the financial results and taxation. This data will be of vast importance and settle all doubts as to the actual financial value of municipal ownership methods.

SEEKING LIGHT SENSIBLY.

Pittsburg Dispatch.

It will prove gratifying to those who have for years felt that municipal ownership of public utilities would solve city franchise problems to learn that an exhaustive investigation of the subject, both in this country and abroad, is being undertaken by the executive council of the National Civic Federation at the instigation of its departments of Industrial Economics and Trade Agreements.

There are few in this country who have given the subject any study who are convinced that municipal ownership will not result in an expansion of present evils rather than a solution of them. Political conditions are so different in the United States compared with European municipalities that even those who have placed in successful operation abroad public utilities under municipal, and even government guidance, have been forced to admit after an American investigation that political machines and the opportunity for graft would be strengthened by the addition of municipal corporations with their heavy revenues and their armies of employes who would add to the campaigning strength of the rings and bosses.

The National Civic Federation, however, is seeking light in the most sensible way. It has selected a committee whose report will be above reproach and whose conclusions can be regarded in no other light than that of wise conservatism. Nothing of tangible and practical worth to the various municipalities may result from the investigation, but the careful study of the great and growing question by men of such ability and standing as those selected can not but result in a wider knowledge of the subject and of undoubted good. It is certainly a step forward in reaching a practical understanding of a problem which has threatened for some time to become a national issue.

The National
Civic Federation Review

Vol. II. No. 7 | NEW YORK, DECEMBER 1, 1905 | Ten Cents

THE GREAT PROBLEM OF IMMIGRATION.

OFFICIAL DELEGATES FROM EVERY STATE IN THE UNION WILL HOLD THE FIRST NATIONAL CONFERENCE UPON THIS SUBJECT.

THE first National Conference ever held in the United States upon the subject of Immigration will convene in Madison Square Garden Concert Hall at 10:30 o'clock, Wednesday morning, December 6, under the auspices of the National Civic Federation. The sessions will continue during December 7 and 8. One feature of the Conference will be a visit to Ellis Island, where the delegates will be entertained at luncheon, the food and its preparation being identical with that provided the alien arrivals after leaving the steamships and while awaiting inspection. Steamships due to reach this port at that time should afford the delegates an opportunity to witness the arrival, inspection and disposition of approximately five thousand immigrants.

Those composing the Conference on Immigration will be delegates appointed by the Governors of States and Territories, and representatives of commercial, economic, ecclesiastical, labor and agricultural organizations. The participants have been selected because of their interest in the general subject and their expert knowledge of some of its social, economic, moral and industrial phases as manifested in their own localities. Because of this composition of the Conference, the Committee of Arrangements has not presumed to prepare a complete program. Through correspondence with delegates the Committee will be able, however, to facilitate the discussion by outlining the several topics and in some cases by suggesting an opening speaker for a subject.

The Conference will consider the problem of immigration in its relation to our industrial and social prosperity. The discussion will include the effectiveness of the administration of existing legislation and propo-

ELLIS ISLAND, THE PRINCIPAL GATEWAY FOR INCOMING ALIENS.

(Concluded from page 17.)

admitted. The present rate of immigration is generally regarded as unprecedented, and in an absolute sense it is; but these speakers dwelt on the fact "in proportion to the population immigration has been decreasing." The vast majority of the new comers, it was argued, were in every way desirable people, and there is no foundation for the statements so often made regarding the "emptying of old-world poorhouses and jails" to dump the inmates on American soil.

The convention to be called will, therefore, direct its attention chiefly to the practical question of the distribution of our immigration, while giving an opportunity to those who believe that restriction is quite as essential as proper provision for the meeting of supply and demand of alien labor.

A BUREAU OF INFORMATION.

Omaha Bee.

The National Civic Federation has brought out the statement, preliminary to its coming conference on immigration, that there is a serious scarcity of labor in some industrial centers. Is it practicable to effect such a distribution of immigrants as is manifestly desirable? The Commissioner of Immigration has suggested a plan which very many believe would have good results and it ought to receive the careful consideration of Congress. It is simply to provide for giving trustworthy information to immigrants as to where there is a demand for labor and where the most favorable opportunities for settlement are to be found. Such information could be supplied by the government without very much expense, as the States would undoubtedly supply a great deal of it. That it would prove of very great value is not to be doubted. Having such information, thousands who now congregate in the large cities would go into the country places, to the material benefit of the latter.

Additional restrictions upon immigration are not needed. The existing regulations are ample if properly enforced. The real question is to effect a distribution of the immigrants where labor is in demand and they can be most useful.

SEND ARRIVALS WHERE NEEDED.

Pittsburg Gazette.

The National Civic Federation will discuss from various points of view the question of the distribution of immigrants. Commissioner Watchorn earnestly declares that the law is being rigidly enforced, but the law is not stringent enough to keep out many who are undesirable to any part of the country. However, the question to be discussed by the Federation is distribution, not restriction, as it is felt that under present conditions the only thing to be done is to guide the tide of immigration so that those unsettled portions of the country will get what benefit there is to come from an added population. It is hardly necessary to say that no hard and fast rule has been discovered that will coax the new comers into those sections of the country where they are needed. That may come later, however, when the government decides to take it up.

A FRIEND OF RESTRICTION.

Rochester, N. Y., Chronicle.

The Civic Federation's conference on immigration, no doubt, will throw a flood of light upon this question. The reports of consular officers, of State and municipal institutions—penal and charitable, of steamship companies and of the Immigration Bureau of the government, will be focused on that gathering and discussed intelligently and systematically. The results can not fail of affording great assistance to Congress in formulating a plan for the better regulation and control of immigration.

This country would not suffer in its material development—on the contrary, it would be benefited—if the great bulk of immigration now pouring in on it like a mighty tide of turbid and polluted water should be restrained and turned back for years, if not permanently. The population we now have is fully equal to the further material development of the continent, and what it would lose in quantity by restricting immigration would be more than counterbalanced by the quality of our people after a few years of normal growth under American influences.

PROBATION BEFORE NATURALIZATION.

Brooklyn Standard Union.

The discussion upon immigration, under the auspices of the National Civic Federation, is proving both educational and valuable. One point brought out is that a large percentage of immigrants, amounting to something like 40 or 45 per cent., return to their native lands after remaining here for a while, so that the apparent increase, based solely on the figures of arrivals at our various ports, is far from being a permanent one. But there is plenty of room here for the healthy, virile, industrious immigrant, whose intent is to be self-supporting, law-abiding, and finally to become a loyal American citizen. Only he must not remain in the already overcrowded cities. The farms, the wheat fields, and the mining camps will welcome his presence, and a thousand other occupations invite his activities. Distribution of immigrants, however, is a prime essential, while concentration is a menace. There must be manifest sympathy with American civilization and ideals before the alien can be safely admitted to citizenship. It is the potentiality of a foreign education and environment that constitutes the real peril in permitting millions of men to vote on questions which it is impossible they can properly understand. The present law should be promptly and radically amended. While permitting all immigrants now here to be admitted to citizenship as soon as they shall have complied with existing regulations, a time ought to be fixed after which no alien should be allowed to take out final papers unless he shall have resided here for at least ten years—fifteen years would be better. Also, after a certain prescribed period, no foreigner should be admitted to citizenship unless he can read and write the English language. With these safeguards, the danger involved in large annual additions to our population from foreign lands would be reduced to a minimum. The public schools and an American environment would do the rest.

SOME MISAPPREHENSIONS CORRECTED.

Pittsburg Post.

The information sought by the Civic Federation is most desirable and enters largely into the repeated discussion of the immigration subject by citizens generally, and serves to correct much popular misapprehension, that a majority of the arrivals are from jails, asylums, and poorhouses. This is far from being the case, and the information will be received with satis and contentment.

There are many poor people in the United States and i York City, but this does not imply, by any means, that jority of the immigrants are outcasts and unfortunates. were always poor people in the country. We have ha among us since the first immigrant landed here in the pe Columbus, or with the Pilgrim fathers, or the Cavaliers at town. There has been a tremendous rush of immigra different periods in our history, but it is very small in its figures to the general population of the United States. State of Texas is larger than Germany, and is capable al feeding a population very much larger than that of Ge which is some fifty-five millions.

It is fallacious to attribute the great increase of the pop of cities and towns in the United States to immigration. tics show that the great increase of the urban population country is due to the fact that the people have come fr country to the cities because they like the life and opport of the city best. We arrogate very much when we atte shut them out from the cities, and besides that it is imprac and un-American.

The immigrants for the first ten or twenty years, un new generation is on its feet, take what may be calle laboring oar of the population. They are poor and indus If more immigrants are found in hospitals than natives, because they are more pressed into hazardous occupations

Allegheny County maintains well on to a hundred thousa migrants, and they are certainly the most industrial and of the population. Compare them with the negroes! What our mills and furnaces and mines do if deprived of their hands and great labor capacity? The United States is and this industrial hive is great not because of any one of population, but because it represents an amalgamati various types. In the form of immigration there has co us all the forms of activity that have made modern civili Immigration of the past hundred years has been the bas source of our prosperity and advancement in science, inc and invention. No sensible or observing man or woma vote or declare immigration a peril. The wars of the Re have declared it otherwise, and the progress of the co proves it the reverse day by day.

GOOD RESULTS ANTICIPATED.

Los Angeles, Cal., Herald.

That there is a decided trend of sentiment in favor general overhauling of the immigration laws is shown clea the call which has been issued by President August Belmo the National Civic Federation, for a general and quasi- conference on the subject, to be held December 6 and 7 i city.

The conference will be under the auspices of the Civic eration, and the Governor of each State in the Union has requested to name ten delegates to represent his State meeting. In addition to this, the call for the meeting inclu set of questions which the various delegates are expect answer for their respective States.

With an organization such as the National Civic Fede taking hold of this great problem, and at a time when th sions of Congress are about to be resumed, it is believed general good can be accomplished.

INVESTIGATION OF PUBLIC OWNERSHIP AND OPERATION APPROVED.

EDITORIAL OPINIONS INDICATE WIDE INTEREST IN THE SUBJECT AND UNANIMOUS CONFIDENCE IN THE WORK OF THE COMMISSION.

A NON-PARTISIAN INQUIRY.

Washington Post.

The announcement that the National Civic Federation proposed to collect accurate data concerning municipal ownership in Europe and the United States will be accepted as indicating an honest and non-partisan effort to obtain facts upon an important subject. The question of the wisdom and practical advantage of municipal ownership is one that is just now thoroughly engaging public attention. It is true that the skyrocket which ascended when Judge Dunne was elected mayor of Chicago has come down as a stick, but the advocates of the alleged reform do not seem to be discouraged. On the contrary, they assert that the failure of their ideas to materialize in Chicago is merely a temporary and not a permanent backset to their cause.

The names of the distinguished gentlemen who are to represent the National Civic Federation in its inquiries are a sufficient guarantee that practical results will be obtained. It is worth while, however, to note that during the past three or four years there have been no more active propagandists of the municipal ownership idea than a coterie of United States consuls in England and Germany. If the suggestion did not seem absurd, it could easily be intimated that these officials were acting under instructions. They have written industriously and enthusiastically upon the subject, and their reports have been given wide circulation through government agencies. Within the past few weeks the Bureau of Statistics has issued another volume of consular reports, devoted entirely to details of experiments in municipal ownership in Austria, France, Germany, England, and Canada, and the consuls, in nearly every case, take occasion to express their hearty approval of what has been accomplished. It is, at least, a curious coincidence to find these consuls sounding the praises of the new system.

What is the meaning of this sudden and universal chorus of acclaim regarding municipal ownership? Why are these consuls, in every part of the world, viewing the new system through rose-colored spectacles? We are loth to believe that society is being revolutionized, despite the mass of evidence officially promulgated, and for this reason we are glad to see the inquiry undertaken by the National Civic Federation. If it shall be found that the United States consuls are reporting facts and that a long step toward governmental millennium has been taken, a great work will have been accomplished. Up to the present time, however, we must be content to express our surprise that our consuls, for some reasons or other, have failed to discover a single fly in the ointment of municipal ownership.

MAKE THE INQUIRY THOROUGH.

Chicago Tribune.

The agitation in behalf of municipal ownership has attracted the attention of the National Civic Federation. It has decided to appoint a committee to investigate thoroughly the national and municipal ownership and operation of public utilities. This is no summer vacation job. If the committee be thorough and go over the entire ground in Europe and America, it will have to put in many months of hard work.

If the committee of the Civic Federation will investigate all the elements of the question and present in bold relief the essential differences between municipal government at home and abroad it may do some good. The incorrigible municipal owner-ites will not be convinced. They will say that the report is the work of a "capitalistic organization." Mr. August Belmont, who is at the head of the federation, is identified with corporations controlling some of the public utilities the municipal owner-ites would like to lay hands on. They will fall back on their solitary argument, that an American city can do anything a European city does.

There are many men who have not waded deeply into the swamps of municipal ownership and operation and whose brains are still above water. A searching, complete inquiry into the boasted virtues of municipal ownership would do them good. It would show them why there are some things which European cities can do and American cities can not. It might lead them to the conclusion that the greatest need of American communities is the divorcement of politics from local administration. If English cities can do that and thrive because of it, why can not American cities?

A STUDY OF MUNICIPAL PROBLEMS.

Boston Transcript.

Whether inspired with that evangel of municipal ownership, Mayor Dunne, or whether acting on its own unprompted initiative, we know not, but the National Civic Federation has been making elaborate plans to collect accurate data bearing on that problem, both in Europe and America. To this end it has selected a commission of about seventy-five members, including some of the best known lawyers, scholars, and business men in the country, to meet early the coming fall and outline methods for pursuing the work. It is intended, according to the purpose stated in its circular, that this investigation shall disclose actual results of public ownership and operation, so far as they have been determined not only in this country, but in all countries.

UTILITIES AND TAXATION.

Cincinnati Enquirer.

The National Civic Federation has appointed a commission of seventy-five members to collect data on municipal ownership in this country and in Europe. This is a subject on which there is now a great need of reliable and well digested information. Those who have gone mad in the United States on the subject of municipal ownership have relied on a few European examples which have been apparently successful, but have failed entirely to consider the differences in form of government. Because street cars are run by the municipalities in Europe the conclusion is quietly drawn that all municipalities in the United States can do the same thing—that all they have to do is to do it on the same general plan that Horace Greeley proposed for resumption of specie payments. The information should be thoroughly digested, and especial trouble should be taken to learn how the public is to acquire the utilities without overwhelming the people with taxation.

A WELCOME MOVEMENT.

Boston Globe.

There are so many contradictory and unsatisfactory statements concerning municipal ownership of public utilities it is gratifying to learn that the executive council of the National Civic Federation is formulating plans to collate accurate data on this subject here and abroad. This plan of the federation will give great satisfaction to the officials of municipalities, as well as to all citizens. All people desire their local government conducted in the most economical manner, but they are bewildered by all the current arguments for and against municipal ownership. Nor is it strange they are puzzled because most speaker more about the theory of municipal ownership than the relative to its practical workings abroad.

Municipal ownership works well in some foreign com ties, chiefly because the conditions there are favorable. many parts of Europe where this system is established satisfactory and successful because the national or im government is behind it, having more to say about the ma ment of cities than do the state governments of the U States.

In some foreign cities most of the local officials, from mayor down, are unpaid, and the national government h much power over the finances of the communities that difficulties are reduced. Hence it is easy to utilize the che methods of conducting the affairs of a municipality.

Most of the public utilities can be and are managed by foreign cities because there are no outside corporations inte in them. The general government, and not corporations, directly with the cities.

Glowing accounts reach America of the success of mun ownership abroad, but this commission of the Civic Feder can ascertain the actual facts in each case.

It can investigate and inform us concerning wages, h and conditions of labor, collective bargaining, the cost and acter of services, political conditions, civic service, the system and municipal corruption, and, most important o the financial results and taxation. This data will be of importance and settle all doubts as to the actual financial of municipal ownership methods.

SEEKING LIGHT SENSIBLY.

Pittsburg Dispatch.

It will prove gratifying to those who have for years felt municipal ownership of public utilities would solve city fran problems to learn that an exhaustive investigation of the su both in this country and abroad, is being undertaken by executive council of the National Civic Federation at the gestion of its departments of Industrial Economics and T Agreements.

There are few in this country who have given the subject study who are convinced that municipal ownership will not in an expansion of present evils rather than a solutio them. Political conditions are so different in the United S compared with European municipalities that even those have placed in successful operation abroad public utilities municipal, and even government guidance, have been forc admit after an American investigation that political machine the opportunity for graft would be strengthened by the add of municipal corporations with their heavy revenues and armies of employes who would add to the campaigning stre of the rings and bosses.

The National Civic Federation, however, is seeking ligh the most sensible way. It has selected a committee whose p will be above reproach and whose conclusions can be regard no other light than that of wise conservatism. Nothin tangible and practical worth to the various municipalities result from the investigation, but the careful study of the and growing question by men of such ability and standin those selected can not but result in a wider knowledge of subject and of undoubted good. It is certainly a step for in reaching a practical understanding of a problem which threatened for some time to become a national issue.

The National
Civic Federation Review

Vol. II. No. 7 NEW YORK, DECEMBER 1, 1905 Ten Cents

THE GREAT PROBLEM OF IMMIGRATION.

OFFICIAL DELEGATES FROM EVERY STATE IN THE UNION WILL HOLD THE FIRST NATIONAL CONFERENCE UPON THIS SUBJECT.

THE first National Conference ever held in the United States upon the subject of Immigration will convene in Madison Square Garden Concert Hall at 10:30 o'clock, Wednesday morning, December 6, under the auspices of the National Civic Federation. The sessions will continue during December 7 and 8. One feature of the Conference will be a visit to Ellis Island, where the delegates will be entertained at luncheon, the food and its preparation being identical with that provided the alien arrivals after leaving the steamships and while awaiting inspection. Steamships due to reach this port at that time should afford the delegates an opportunity to witness the arrival, inspection and disposition of approximately five thousand immigrants.

Those composing the Conference on Immigration will be delegates appointed by the Governors of States and Territories, and representatives of commercial, economic, ecclesiastical, labor and agricultural organizations. The participants have been selected because of their interest in the general subject and their expert knowledge of some of its social, economic, moral and industrial phases as manifested in their own localities. Because of this composition of the Conference, the Committee of Arrangements has not presumed to prepare a complete program. Through correspondence with delegates the Committee will be able, however, to facilitate the discussion by outlining the several topics and in some cases by suggesting an opening speaker for a subject.

The Conference will consider the problem of immigration in its relation to our industrial and social prosperity. The discussion will include the effectiveness of the administration of existing legislation and propo-

ELLIS ISLAND, THE PRINCIPAL GATEWAY FOR INCOMING ALIENS.

sitions for new legislation. Especial consideration will be given to the relation of alien labor to domestic crafts, the industrial progress of the negro and other questions growing out of the distribution of incoming aliens. One day will be accorded for a particular discussion of the Asiatic phase of the problem.

The Conference will be called to order by August Belmont, President of the National Civic Federation. Addresses of welcome will be delivered by Governor Frank W. Higgins, of New York State, and Mayor George B. McClellan, of New York City. The national Government will be officially represented by Frank P. Sargent, United States Commissioner of Immigration.

The importance of this Conference and its potential influence upon public policy toward a problem of far-reaching importance to the racial composition, the present and future industries and the political and social institutions of the nation have been widely and significantly recognized. The call for the Conference, issued by the National Civic Federation, has been followed by a continual debate upon various phases of the question that has served to clear the way, to some extent, for the proceedings of the Conference itself. Valuable papers upon the theme have been published in many periodicals, including THE NATIONAL CIVIC FEDERATION REVIEW.

In this preliminary debate, the newspaper press has taken a lively part. The comment has concerned itself with the comparative quality of various elements in the incoming stream of aliens and with methods proposed for its modification. The discussion has brought out plans for more thorough inspection, at ports of arrival and of embarkation, and at original sources; for a higher head-tax; for more rigid educational requirements, and even for suspension or absolute exclusion. There has been much examination into the correct significance of statistics.

The National Civic Federation, as an organization, has taken no attitude for or against any of the propositions that have been advanced for the regulation, restriction, encouragement or exclusion of immigration. The Conference will be an open forum for debate by the best thought of the country, in the hope that its conclusions may be an efficient aid in forming a sound and consistent policy that will safeguard the social and industrial welfare of the United States, while conducing to the fullest development of its prosperity and the furtherance of its destiny as a member of the great family of nations.

At the date when this issue of THE REVIEW went to press, nearly all the Governors had appointed delegates to represent their States, and of these several have signified their intention to be present with their delegations. Some of the names of these delegations were not received in time for insertion in this issue of THE REVIEW. Here follows a list of the delegates appointed by the Executives of States and Territories:

ALABAMA.

Appointed by Governor William D. Jelks.

Hon, Robert R. Poole .... Montgomery.
Hon. W. H. Seymour .... Montgomery.
Hon. W. W. Screws .... Montgomery.
Hon. Erwin C. Craighead .... Mobile.
Col. Frank Y. Anderson .... Birmingham.
Hon. Wilson Brown .... Birmingham.
Hon. R. A. Mitchell .... Alabama City.
Hon. Eli S. Shorter .... Eufaula.
Hon. Ross C. Smith .... Birmingham.
Dr. Louis Edleman .... Huntsville.

ARKANSAS.

Appointed by Governor Jeff Davis.

Capt. E. A. Darr .... Atkins.
R. J. Wilson .... Russellville.
Dr. Love .... Dardanelle.
Ad. Bertig .... Paragould.
Dr. Wallace Carter .... Ozark.
B. A. Hardy .... Monticello.
J. H. Pryor .... Hamburg.
Hon. Jake Shaul .... Marianna.
Hon. W. H. Harvey .... Ponte Ne.

COLORADO.

Appointed by Governor Jesse F. McDonald.

Hon. Wilbur F. Cannon .... Denver.
Judge Frank T. Johnson .... Denver.
D. C. Packard .... Denver.
Dr. F. K. Dabney .... Denver.
C. E. Wantland .... Denver.
Joseph G. Brown .... Denver.
John T. Burns .... Denver.
J. L. Donahue .... Denver.
R. A. Morrison .... Denver.

CONNECTICUT.

Appointed by Governor Henry Roberts.

Rev. Joel Ives .... Hartford.
Hon. Wm. D. Parker .... Meriden.
Hon. F. Clarence Bissell .... Willimantic.
Hon. Robert A. Griffing .... Hartford.
Hon. John H. Perry .... Southport.
Hon. Henry H. Bridgman .... Norfolk.
Hon. Waterman R. Burnham .... Norwich.
Rev. Watson L. Phillips .... New Haven
Rev. Clarence F. Bacon .... Middletown.
Rev. Olcott B. Colton .... Hartford.
Hon. Lynde Harrison .... New Haven.

DELAWARE.

Appointed by Governor Preston Lea.

Hon. John Hunn .... Wyoming.
Hon. Ebe W. Tunnell .... Lewes.
Hon. George Gray .... Wilmington.
Hon. Anthony Higgins .... Wilmington.
Henry B. Thompson .... Wilmington.
Thomas H. Savery .... Wilmington.
George A. Harter .... Newark.
Willard S. Meredith .... Wilmington.
Harry A. Richardson .... Dover.
Samuel H. Messick .... Bridgeville.

DISTRICT OF COLUMBIA.

Simon Wolf .... Washington.
W. V. Cox .... Washington.
James F. Oyster .... Washington.
William F. Downey .... Washington.
George Truesdell .... Washington.
Ellis Spear .... Washington.
L. G. Hine .... Washington.
M. I. Weller .... Washington.
W. F. Gude .... Washington.
F. S. Hight .... Washington.

FLORIDA.

Appointed by Governor N. B. Broward.

Irving H. Welch .... Jacksonville.
H. S. Gateskill .... McIntosh.
W. R. Fuller, President Tampa Board of Trade, Tampa.
R. S. Hall .... Tampa.
Z. C. Chambliss .... Ocala.
J. R. Saunders .... Pensacola.
George F. Miles .... St. Augustine.
William M. Brown, President Miami Board of Trade, Miami.
Capt. C. E. Garner, President Jacksonville Board of Trade .... Jacksonville.

GEORGIA.

Appointed by Governor J. M. Terrell.

Hon. G. Gunby Jordan .... Columbus.
Hon. J. E. Page .... Wrightsville.
Hon. Crawford Wheatley .... Americus.
Hon. S. F. Parrott .... Macon.
Hon. I. C. Wade .... Cornelia.
Hon. T. M. Cheatham .... Broxton.
Hon. J. P. Billups .... Atlanta.
Hon. W. G. Cooper .... Atlanta.
David Robinson .... Atlanta.
Dr. B. Wildaur .... Atlanta.
Hon. Pleasant A. Stovall .... Savannah.
Hon. Thomas G. Hudson, Com. of Agriculture, Atlanta.
Hon. William S. West .... Valdosta.

IDAHO.

Appointed by Governor Frank R. Gooding.

Hon. R. M. McCracken .... Blackfoot.
Hon. Avery C. Moore .... Weiser.
(The names of the additional delegates will be announced later.)

ILLINOIS.

Appointed by Governor C. S. Deneen.

A. H. Revell .... Chicago.
F. W. Mathieson .... La Salle.
Charles H. Williamson .... Quincy.
Charles Ridgely .... Springfield.
Charles E. Kiler .... Champaign.
John M. Stahl .... Chicago.
E. A. Bancroft .... Chicago.
W. G. Edens .... Chicago.
Charles H. Wacker .... Chicago.
George Parsons .... Cairo.

INDIANA.

Appointed by Governor Frank Hanley.

John Halliday .... Indianapolis.
(The names of the additional delegates will be announced later.)

IOWA.

Appointed by Governor Albert B. Cummins.

B. Annundsen .... Decorah.
Edward A. Steiner .... Grinnell.
V. Lyngby .... Cedar Falls.
W. R. Patterson .... Iowa City.
Rev. J. F. Nugent .... Des Moines.
O. H. Cessna .... Ames.
C. F. Wennerstrum .... Des Moines.
Charles Grilk .... Davenport.
A. L. Urick .... Des Moines.
E. E. Clark .... Cedar Rapids.

KANSAS.

Appointed by Governor Edward W. Hoch.

Hon. F. D. Coburn .... Topeka.
Hon. C. C. Carver .... Pratt.
Hon. A. E. Case .... Marion.
Hon. John E. Frost .... Topeka.
Hon. J. H. Stewart .... Wichita.
Hon. H. J. Smith .... Ottawa.
Hon. W. L. A. Johnson .... Topeka.
Hon. James A. Orr .... Weir City.
Hon. Archie Fulton .... Lansing.
Hon. D. J. Hanna .... Hill City.

KENTUCKY.

Appointed by Governor J. C. W. Beckham.

Geo. L. Sehon, Pres. Children's Home Soc., Louisville
F. A. Burgess .... Louisville.
Dr. B. F. Laird .... Covington.
Col. John R. Allen .... Lexington.

LOUISIANA.

Appointed by Governor Newton C. Blanchard.

Senator S. D. McEnery .... New Orleans.
Senator Murphy J. Foster .... New Orleans.
Congressman Adolph Meyer .... New Orleans.
Congressman Robt. F. Broussard .... New Iberia.
Congressman J. T. Watkins .... Minden.
Congressman J. E. Ransdell .... Lake Providence.
Congressman Samuel M. Robertson .... Baton Rouge.
Congressman A. P. Pujo .... Lake Charles.
Hon. E. F. Kohnke, Pres. Board of Trade, New Orleans
Hon. M. J. Sanders, Pres. Progressive Union, New Orleans.
Hon. W. E. Glassel, Pres. Board of Trade..Shreveport.
Dr. John P. Scott, Pres. Progressive League, Shreveport.
F. L. Maxwell .... Mound.
Hon. Thomas C. Barrett .... Shreveport.
Mayor A. A. Forsythe .... Monroe.
Hon. J. B. Lee .... Mansfield.
Judge R. R. Reid .... Amite City.
Hon. R. H. Snyder .... St. Joseph.
Hon. Paul Capdevielle .... Baton Rouge.
Hon. W. W. Duson .... Crowley.
Hon. John Marks .... Napoleonville.

MAINE.

Appointed by Governor William T. Cobb.

Edwin Riley .... Livermore Falls.
Robert McArthur .... Biddeford.
Hayward Peirce .... Frankfort.
Jasper Wyman .... Milbridge.
F. E. Wheet .... Rumford Falls.
H. E. Dunnack .... Augusta.
E. S. Clark .... Bar Harbor.
Charles L. Fox .... Portland.
D. N. Beach .... Bangor.
George K. Walker .... Millinocket.

MARYLAND.

Appointed by Governor Edwin Warfield.

Fabian Franklin .... Baltimore.
Norval E. Foard .... Baltimore.
Theodore Marburg .... Baltimore.
George E. Barnett .... Baltimore.
Richard M. Venable .... Baltimore.
Frank K. Carey .... Baltimore.
John M. Glenn .... Baltimore.
Charles J. Fox .... Baltimore.
Rev. C. E. Redecker .... Odenton.
Dr. D. F. Penington .... Baltimore.

MASSACHUSETTS.

Appointed by Governor William L. Douglas.

Charles F. Pidgin .... Boston.
Joseph Lee .... Boston.
John Graham Brooks .... Cambridge.
Frank K. Foster .... Boston.
Henry Abrahams .... Boston.
Max Mitchell .... Boston.
Prescott F. Hall .... Boston.
Frank B. Hall .... Worcester.
Frank W. Merrick .... Boston.
Augustus P. Gardner .... Hamilton.

MICHIGAN.

Appointed by Governor Fred M. Warner.

William F. Bird .... Ann Arbor.
S. T. Fairbanks .... Saline.
Allen B. Morse .... Ionia.
Hamilton Carhartt .... Detroit.
Edward C. Hinman .... Battle Creek.
Frederick B. Smith .... Detroit.
F. A. Peavey .... Port Huron.
Gilbert W. Dickson .... Detroit.
Stephen Corvin .... Bay City.
Paul Merin .... Grand Rapids.
Mathew H. Walters .... Wegaunee, Mich.
William H. Longley .... Kalamazoo.

MINNESOTA.

Appointed by Governor John A. Johnson.

Hon. Adolph Bydal .... Crookston.
Hon. Alex. C. Johnson .... Minneapolis.
Hon. R. E. Burbridge .... Minneapolis.
Hon. R. S. Odell .... Marshall.
Hon. John E. Burchard .... St. Paul.
Hon. B. F. Beardsly .... St. Paul.
Hon. John M. Dahlby .... Moorhead.
Hon. W. D. Washburn, Jr. .... Minneapolis.
Hon. Wiley Tindolph .... Thief River Falls.
John H. Hoeschen .... Melrose.

MISSOURI.

Appointed by Governor Joseph W. Folk.

S. A. Huges .... St. Louis.
Frederick N. Judson .... St. Louis.
Charles L. Meriweather .... Louisiana.
A. B. Newland .... Holden.
H. H. Weaver .... Rush Tower.
Guy Murray .... Richmond.
Alexander New .... Kansas City.

(Continued on page 4.)

15

TYPICAL EXAMPLES of
ADMITTED ALIENS
COSSACKS For COW-BOY PLAINS
NO RACE SUICIDE HERE
ROUMANIAN SHEPHERDS Bound For THE NORTHWEST
TYPICAL EXAMPLES of
EXCLUDED ALIENS
A BAND of ROVING GYPSIES
A PAUPER FAMILY
LACKED REQUIRED FUNDS

(Continued from page 2.)

O. L. Munger .... Greenville.
W. S. Anthony .... Farmington.
G. D. Harris .... New London.
W. B. McRoberts .... Monticello.

MONTANA.
Appointed by Governor Joseph K. Toole.

L. P. Benedict .... Helena.
Martin Maginnis .... Helena.
T. H. Carter .... Helena.
J. H. Calderhead .... Helena.
John MacGinniss .... Butte.
J. D. Ryan .... Butte.
W. A. Clark .... Butte.
William Walsh .... Butte.
S. T. Hauser .... Helena.
Edwin Norris .... Dillon.

NEBRASKA.
Appointed by Governor J. H. Mickey.

Sophus Neble .... Omaha.
Peter Jansen .... Jansen.
Hon. F. E. Anderson, Editor *Posten* .... Omaha.
B. V. Kohout .... Wilber.
S. F. Nichols .... Beatrice.
John Rozicky .... Omaha.
J. F. Hanson .... Fremont.
Rev. J. E. Nordling .... Swedehome.
Paul Getzschmann .... Omaha.
Henry Wehn, Editor *Freie Presse* .... Lincoln.
T. R. Evans .... Norden.
V. Michaelson .... Omaha.

NEW HAMPSHIRE.
Appointed by Governor John McLane.

Hon. Jacob H. Gallinger, U. S. Senate, Washington, D. C.
Hon. Henry E. Burnham, U. S. Senate, Washington, D. C.
Hon. Cyrus A. Sulloway, House of Representatives, Washington, D. C.
Hon. Frank D. Currier, House of Representatives, Washington, D. C.
President William J. Tucker, Dartmouth College, Hanover.
Hon. Henry B. Quinby .... Lakeport.
Col. William Marcotte .... Manchester.
Hon. John M. Mitchell .... Concord.
Hon. Seth M. Richards .... Newport.
John W. Kelly, Esq. .... Portsmouth.

NEW JERSEY.
Appointed by Governor Edward C. Stokes.

Ruford Franklin .... Summit.
Grinnell Willis .... Morristown.
Hon. Wood McKee .... Paterson.
Rev. Adolph Roeder .... Orange.
Dr. Bleecker Van Wagenen .... South Orange.
Mrs. Caroline B. Alexander .... Hoboken.
Mrs. Emily Williamson .... Elizabeth.
E. J. Ellis .... Plainfield.
Hugh Fox .... Plainfield.
Rev. James A. Reynolds .... Red Bank.
Mrs. H. E. Mott .... Elizabeth.
William Perry .... Newark.
Clinton Mackenzie .... Elizabeth.

NEW MEXICO.
Appointed by Governor Miguel A. Otero.

W. B. Bunker .... Las Vegas.
Alfred Grunsfeld .... Albuquerque.
J. W. Bible .... Hanover.
Granville Pendleton .... Aztec.
S. B. Grimshaw .... Santa Fe
John W. Poe .... Roswell
James G. McNary .... Las Vegas.
Charles Springer .... Springer.
Martin Lohman .... Las Cruces.
L. O. Fullen .... Carlsbad.

NEW YORK.
Appointed by Governor Frank W. Higgins.

Hon. Charles A. Schieren, ex-Mayor of Brooklyn, New York City.
Adolph Strasser .... Buffalo.
Adna F. Weber, Chief Statistician, State Department of Labor .... Albany.
P. H. McCormick, Pres. Typographical Union No. 6, New York City.
James H. Hamilton .... New York City.
A. J. Boulton, Register of Kings County... Brooklyn.
Jacob A. Riis .... Richmond Hill.
Albert T. Fish .... Buffalo.
Charles Sprague Smith, Director People's Institute, New York City.
John Kirkpatrick, Pres. State Association of Superintendents of Poor .... Patchogue.

NORTH CAROLINA.
Appointed by Governor Robert B. Glenn.

W. E. Faison .... Raleigh.
Z. P. Smith .... Raleigh.
F. W. Hossfield .... Morganton.
W. C. Ervin .... Morganton.

NORTH DAKOTA.
Appointed by Governor E. Y. Sarles.

F. B. Chapman .... Buford.
J. A. Johnson .... Fargo.
J. D. Bacon .... Grand Forks.
B. Prom .... Milton.
J. L. Cashel .... Grafton.
H. S. Oliver .... Lisbon.
L. A. Simpson .... Dickinson.
J. B. Sharpe .... Kulm.
Ole Serumgard .... Devil's Lake.
J. F. Selby .... Hillsboro.

OHIO.
Appointed by Governor Myron T. Herrick.

Hon. D. P. Rowland .... Cincinnati.
Dr. Thomas C. Minor .... Cincinnati.
E. E. Wright, the *Youngstown Telegram*.. Youngstown.
James R. Hopley, the *Evening Telegram* .... Bucyrus.
E. P. Hawley, Pres. Trades Labor Assembly, Columbus.
W. D. Brickell .... Columbus.
Col. J. J. Sullivan, Chamber of Commerce .. Cleveland.
Warren S. Stone, Grand Chief Brotherhood Locomotive Engineers .... Cleveland.
A. D. Alderman, the *Register* .... Marietta.
Jesse Taylor .... Jamestown.

OREGON.
Appointed by Governor George E. Chamberlain.

James Hutchinson .... Union.
James Ingland .... Union.
C. T. Blumenrother .... Bandon.
W. E. Grace .... Baker City.
Paul Wessinger .... Portland.
N. H. Bird .... Portland.
C. H. Gram .... Portland.
Grant McDonald .... Portland.
H. G. Kundret .... Portland.
H. B. Nicholas .... Portland.
Newton McCoy .... Portland.
Samuel Kafka .... Portland.
Harry Gurr .... Portland.
H. G. Thomas .... Portland.
James Foley .... Portland.
Thomas Whalen .... Portland.
H. Wolf .... Portland.
M. Ostrow .... Portland.
L. Greenburg .... Portland.
K. Bromberg .... Portland.
H. Abraham .... Portland.
M. Gale .... Portland.
M. Rybke .... Portland.
Jos. Sheminski .... Portland.
M. Blatt .... Portland.
M. Davidson .... Portland.
N. Horn .... Portland.
A. Gale .... Portland.
M. Sugarman .... Portland.
I. Weinstein .... Portland.
M. Wolf .... Portland.
A. Miller .... Portland.
S. Hochfield .... Portland.
D. Nemerosky .... Portland.
M. Rein .... Portland.
J. Rosencrantz .... Portland.
M. Wax .... Portland.
L. Robinson .... Portland.
H. Gerson .... Portland.
J. Lesser .... Portland.
L. Friedman .... Portland.
I. Gevurtz .... Portland.
Philip Gevurtz .... Portland.
W. Fest .... Portland.
A. Flechman .... Portland.
I. Friedman .... Portland.
S. Julius Mayer .... Portland.
J. Nuddelman .... Portland.
M. Simon .... Portland.
I. Morris .... Portland.
Jos. S. Whiteside .... Portland.

PENNSYLVANIA.
Appointed by Governor Samuel W. Pennypacker.

Hon. Wm. M. Kennedy .... Pittsburg.
C. B. Price .... Pittsburg.
Prof. L. S. Rowe .... Philadelphia.
Hon. Robert Adams .... Philadelphia.
Dr. Carl Kelsey .... Philadelphia.
J. F. Warne .... Philadelphia.
Edward Tingle .... Philadelphia.
Hon. Vance C. McCormick .... Harrisburg.
James M. Lamberton .... Harrisburg.
Stephen Collins .... Pittsburg.
C. C. Latus .... Pittsburg.

RHODE ISLAND.
Appointed by Governor George H. Utter.

John F. P. Lawton, Gorham Mfg. Co. ..... Providence
Joseph E. Fletcher, Mapleville Worsted Co., Providence.
Webster Knight, B. B. & R. Knight Co..... Providence.
Thomas F. Kearney, President Rhode Island Building Trades' Council .... Providence.
George B. Sullivan, Pawtucket Typographical Union, Pawtucket.
Prof. James Quayle Dealey, Brown University, Providence.
Prof. Henry B. Gardner, Brown University.. Providence.
David S. Barry, Editor *Providence Journal*.. Providence.
Arthur W. Barrus .... Providence.
John W. Saunders, M.D. .... Shannock.
George H. Webb, Commissioner of Industrial Statistics .... Providence.
George Lewis Smith, Chairman of the Board of State Charities and Corrections, Providence .... Nayatt.
Walter R. Wightman, Agent of State Charities and Corrections .... Providence.

SOUTH CAROLINA.
Appointed by Governor D. C. Hayward.

E. J. Watson .... Columbia.
A. G. Furman .... Greenville.
A. J. Matheson .... Bennettsville.
W. E. Lucas .... Laurens.
A. G. White .... Spartanburg.
Geo. Bell Timmerman .... Lexington.
James A. Hoyt, Jr. .... Columbia.
John S. Wilson .... Lancaster.
Col. Henry Schachte .... Charleston.

SOUTH DAKOTA.
Appointed by Governor Samuel H. Elrod.

Sen. R. J. Gamble .... Yankton.
E. W. Martin .... Deadwood.
John Gray .... Terraville
T. J. Grier .... Lead.
O. H. McCarty .... Huron.
W. A. Beach .... Sioux Falls.
M. F. Greeley .... Gary.
W. H. H. Beadle .... Madison.
Hon. August Frieberg .... Beresford.
Hon. J. J. McLaury .... Milltown.

TEXAS.
Appointed by Governor S. W. T. Lanham.

James F. Grimes .... Houston.
(The names of the additional delegates will be announced later.)

UTAH.
Appointed by Governor John C. Cutler.

Simon Bamberger .... Salt Lake City.
Abel John Evans .... Lehi.
W. C. Spence .... Salt Lake City.
J. Reuben Clark .... Salt Lake City.
Fred J. Pack .... Salt Lake City.
Will Ward .... Salt Lake City.
John Sears .... Salt Lake City.

VERMONT.
Appointed by Governor Charles J. Bell.

Cassius Peck .... Burlington.
James K. Curtis .... Georgia.
George H. Terrill .... Morrisville.
H. M. Farnham .... East Montpelier.
C. A. Bump .... Salisbury.
E. W. Johnson .... Ludlow.
G. W. Young .... St. Johnsbury.
L. M. Craigin .... Springfield.
C. W. Cram .... Williamstown.
W. R. Bell .... Lunenburgh.

VIRGINIA.
Appointed by Governor A. J. Montague.

Joseph Bryan .... Richmond.
James M. Quicke, Jr. .... Petersburg.
R. H. Beazley .... South Boston.
W. H. Bond .... Wise.
John M. Chalkley .... Big Stone Gap.
A. Moore, Jr. .... Berryville.
R. C. Blackford .... Lynchburg.
G. W. Koiner .... Richmond.
W. H. Aston .... Meadow View.
R. L. Dibrell .... Danville.
Archer Anderson .... Richmond.
Lucien H. Cocke .... Roanoke.
Theo. S. Garnett .... Norfolk.
G. M. Serpell .... Norfolk.
A. A. Phleger .... Christiansburg.
James L. Tredway .... Chatham.

WASHINGTON.
Appointed by Governor Albert E. Mead.

A. J. Ferrandini .... Bellingham.
Col. T. M. Fisher .... Walla Walla.
W. B. Estell .... Seattle.

WEST VIRGINIA.
Appointed by Governor William M. O. Dawson.

William S. Foose .... Wheeling.
Frank C. Cox .... Wheeling.
Hon. B. F. Meighen .... Moundsville.
A. H. Winchester .... Buckhannon.
John Nugent .... Charleston.
J. A. Springer .... Flemington.
Hon. George C. Sturgiss .... Morgantown.
Hon. George A. Laughlin .... Wheeling.
Hon. John T. McGraw .... Grafton.
John R. Foster .... Charleston.
Hon. I. V. Barton .... Wheeling.
T. J. Edwards .... Montgomery.

(Concluded on page 12.)

AN INTERNATIONAL INVESTIGATION OF PUBLIC OWNERSHIP.

EVERY SHADE OF OPINION AND ALL INTERESTS CONCERNED ARE REPRESENTED IN THE COMMISSION APPOINTED BY THE NATIONAL CIVIC FEDERATION.

THE Commission appointed by the National Civic Federation to investigate the ownership and operation of public utilities is now organized and prepared to prosecute its inquiry into selected divisions of that subject. The general Commission on Public Ownership, as it is called for sake of brevity, held its first meeting in Earl Hall, Columbia University, New York City, October 5. The Commission spent the entire day in a discussion of the scope and method of its work. A verbatim report of this meeting was published in a special number of The National Civic Federation Review.

The impartial attitude of the National Civic Federation, in providing that the investigation should be a purely scientific inquiry, was made clear in a letter written by President August Belmont, who was unable to be present because of serious illness. In his absence, Samuel Gompers, First Vice-President of the National Civic Federation and President of the American Federation of Labor, presided at the first session of the Conference. The letter of Mr. Belmont, addressed to Mr. Gompers on the day before the meeting, follows:

"There is no function which it has ever been my privilege to exercise, and no duty I ever more desired to perform, than that of presiding at the first meeting of the Public Ownership Commission, which is entrusted by the National Civic Federation with the duty of selecting committees to seek abroad and at home information on the subject of municipal ownership and operation of public utilities.

"My physicians have forbidden me to postpone an operation which they have prescribed for me, and I will be compelled to subject myself to their treatment. Therefore it is a matter of personal satisfaction to me that you are here in New York to take my place.

"The subject of municipal ownership and operation of public utilities is forcing itself upon the attention of all thoughtful persons. Unfortunately, the very lack of comprehensive and authoritative data and information leaves the discussion to theorists on both sides who often advance arguments which can neither be accepted nor rejected, for the very reason that no authoritative data exist. The National Civic Federation, through this Commission, will now try to obtain true and reliable facts to guide the student and legislator in seeking the best means to establish peace and maintain cooperation between capital and labor. To the accomplishment of this purpose, I have encouraged this movement and advocated the missions of the subcommittees.

"The relations of capital and labor are vital to the prosperity of the individual and to the State. It is proper, therefore, that arguments should be based on correct facts and known conditions. The Civic Federation has no greater work among its varied duties than to secure these data. The committee, which this Commission proposes to send abroad, will represent every shade of thought and opinion on the subject. This committee, when it returns, will report to a larger commission of men at home, likewise drawn from every part of the country and representing every phase of life. The Civic Federation has no interests to serve and no arguments to make on the subject, but to present the facts and conditions as they may exist abroad and at home, for the use and benefit of the entire country, without respect to party and without respect to special interests.

"Believe me, had I been able to attend the meeting, I would certainly have been present, and I trust that I may regain my health and strength at an early date, in order that I may cooperate in every way in the furtherance of the great object of the gathering over which you are to preside to-morrow."

At the conclusion of the reading of Mr. Belmont's letter, John Mitchell, President of the United Mine Workers of America, moved that a letter of acknowledgment be sent to President Belmont, of the National Civic Federation, expressing regret for his illness and earnest wishes for his speedy recovery.

MELVILLE E. INGALLS,
Chairman Commission on Public Ownership and Operation.

JOHN MITCHELL,
1st Vice-Chairman Commission on Public Ownership and Operation.

JOHN G. AGAR,
2d Vice-Chairman Commission on Public Ownership and Operation.

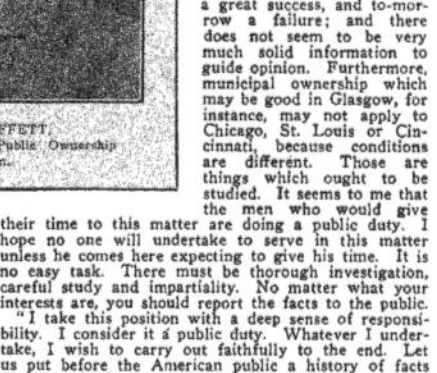

EDWARD A. MOFFETT,
Secretary Commission on Public Ownership and Operation.

Prof. Frank Parsons, President of the National Public Ownership League, Boston, moved that the letter also state the Commission's appreciation of the impartial spirit, breadth of view and desire to bring out the facts manifested by President Belmont and the National Civic Federation throughout the organization of the Commission.

Mr. Mitchell accepted the amendment and the motion was unanimously adopted.

In his opening remarks, Chairman Gompers thus emphasized the impartial character of the investigation:

"The municipal ownership of our street railroads and other public utilities is a great impending question occupying the attention of the people of the cities of our country; and it is well that it does. I am sure the advocates of municipal ownership will have no cause of complaint if a rigid, full, and analytical investigation is undertaken, so that the real facts may be ascertained and clearly, impartially, and without bias presented to the people of our country in such form that they may understand that the truth is before them, unvarnished and untarnished by individual predilections. I am sure that those who may be opposed to municipal ownership should have their minds in such a receptive condition, that when the presentation of facts is made, these facts will find a ready lodgment."

As a result of the day's discussion, the Commission decided to restrict the initial investigation to the comparative results, in America and abroad, of public and private ownership and operation of gas, water, electric power and lighting, and street railways—those utilities being at the present time most prominent in the public mind. The general Commission elected the following officers:

Chairman, Melville E. Ingalls, Chairman Board of Directors, Big Four Railroad, Cincinnati;

First Vice-Chairman, John Mitchell, President United Mine Workers of America, Indianapolis;

Second Vice-Chairman, John G. Agar, President Reform Club, New York City;

Secretary, Edward A. Moffett, Editor *Bricklayer and Mason*, Indianapolis.

In accepting the chairmanship of the Commission, Mr. Ingalls said in part:

"This is a time when it is especially important that every man ought to do what he can to try to solve questions of importance to the common weal. There is a tremendous pressure all over the country on the question of municipal ownership; one side wants one thing, and another the opposite. You will find people who say that public ownership is the beginning of socialism, and that it will be the ruin of the country. You will read to-day in the newspapers that municipal ownership is a great success, and to-morrow a failure; and there does not seem to be very much solid information to guide opinion. Furthermore, municipal ownership which may be good in Glasgow, for instance, may not apply to Chicago, St. Louis or Cincinnati, because conditions are different. Those are things which ought to be studied. It seems to me that the men who would give their time to this matter are doing a public duty. I hope no one will undertake to serve in this matter unless he comes here expecting to give his time. It is no easy task. There must be thorough investigation, careful study and impartiality. No matter what your interests are, you should report the facts to the public.

"I take this position with a deep sense of responsibility. I consider it a public duty. Whatever I undertake, I wish to carry out faithfully to the end. Let us put before the American public a history of facts as they exist in this country and abroad."

The general Commission elected an Executive Committee and a Committee of Twenty-one on Investigation. The latter was authorized to investigate the phases of the subject which have been specified, to

(*Concluded on page 9.*)

(*Continued from page 2.*)

). L. Munger ... Greenville.
V. S. Anthony ... Farmington.
. D. Harris ... New London.
V. B. McRoberts ... Monticello.

MONTANA.
Appointed by Governor Joseph K. Toole.

. P. Benedict ... Helena.
fartin Maginnis ... Helena.
. H. Carter ... Helena.
. H. Calderhead ... Helena.
ohn MacGinniss ... Butte.
. D. Ryan ... Butte.
V. A. Clark ... Butte.
Villiam Walsh ... Butte.
. T. Hauser ... Helena.
dwin Norris ... Dillon.

NEBRASKA.
Appointed by Governor J. H. Mickey.

ophus Neble ... Omaha.
'eter Jansen ... Jansen.
Ion. F. E. Anderson, Editor *Posten* ... Omaha.
. V. Kohout ... Wilber.
. F. Nichols ... Beatrice.
ohn Rozicky ... Omaha.
. F. Hanson ... Fremont.
lev. J. E. Nordling ... Swedehome.
'aul Getzschmann ... Omaha.
Ienry Wehn, Editor *Freie Presse* ... Lincoln.
. R. Evans ... Norden.
. Michaelson ... Omaha.

NEW HAMPSHIRE.
Appointed by Governor John McLane.

Ion. Jacob H. Gallinger, U. S. Senate, Washington, D. C.
Ion. Henry E. Burnham, U. S. Senate, Washington, D. C.
Ion. Cyrus A. Sulloway, House of Representatives, Washington, D. C.
Ion. Frank D. Currier, House of Representatives, Washington, D. C.
'resident William J. Tucker, Dartmouth College, Hanover.
Ion. Henry B. Quinby ... Lakeport.
ol. William Marcotte ... Manchester.
Ion. John M. Mitchell ... Concord.
Ion. Seth M. Richards ... Newport.
ohn W. Kelly, Esq. ... Portsmouth.

NEW JERSEY.
Appointed by Governor Edward C. Stokes.

uford Franklin ... Summit.
rinnell Willis ... Morristown.
Ion. Wood McKee ... Paterson.
lev. Adolph Roeder ... Orange.
)r. Bleecker Van Wagenen ... South Orange.
Irs. Caroline B. Alexander ... Hoboken.
Irs. Emily Williamson ... Elizabeth.
. J. Ellis ... Plainfield.
Iugh Fox ... Plainfield.
lev. James A. Reynolds ... Red Bank.
Irs. H. E. Mott ... Elizabeth.
Villiam Perry ... Newark.
linton Mackenzie ... Elizabeth.

NEW MEXICO.
Appointed by Governor Miguel A. Otero.

V. B. Bunker ... Las Vegas.
lfred Grunsfeld ... Albuquerque.
. W. Bible ... Hanover.
ranville Pendleton ... Aztec.
. B. Grimshaw ... Santa Fe
ohn W. Poe ... Roswell
ames G. McNary ... Las Vegas.
harles Springer ... Springer.
Iartin Lohman ... Las Cruces.
. O. Fullen ... Carlsbad.

NEW YORK.
Appointed by Governor Frank W. Higgins.

Ion. Charles A. Schieren, ex-Mayor of Brooklyn, New York City.
dolph Strasser ... Buffalo.
dna F. Weber, Chief Statistician, State Department of Labor ... Albany.
. H. McCormick, Pres. Typographical Union No. 6, New York City.
ames H. Hamilton ... New York City.
. J. Boulton, Register of Kings County ... Brooklyn.
acob A. Riis ... Richmond Hill.
lbert T. Fish ... Buffalo.
harles Sprague Smith, Director People's Institute, New York City.
ohn Kirkpatrick, Pres. State Association of Superintendents of Poor ... Patchogue.

NORTH CAROLINA.
Appointed by Governor Robert B. Glenn.

V. E. Faison ... Raleigh.
. P. Smith ... Raleigh.
. W. Hossfield ... Morganton.
V. C. Ervin ... Morganton.

NORTH DAKOTA.
Appointed by Governor E. Y. Sarles.

F. B. Chapman ... Buford.
J. A. Johnson ... Fargo.
J. D. Bacon ... Grand Forks.
B. Prom ... Milton.
J. L. Cashel ... Grafton.
H. S. Oliver ... Lisbon.
L. A. Simpson ... Dickinson.
J. B. Sharpe ... Kulm.
Ole Serumgard ... Devil's Lake.
J. F. Selby ... Hillsboro.

OHIO.
Appointed by Governor Myron T. Herrick.

Hon. D. P. Rowland ... Cincinnati.
Dr. Thomas C. Minor ... Cincinnati.
E. E. Wright, the *Youngstown Telegram* ... Youngstown.
James R. Hopley, the *Evening Telegram* ... Bucyrus.
E. P. Hawley, Pres. Trades Labor Assembly, Columbus.
W. D. Brickell ... Columbus.
Col. J. J. Sullivan, Chamber of Commerce ... Cleveland.
Warren S. Stone, Grand Chief Brotherhood Locomotive Engineers ... Cleveland.
A. D. Alderman, the *Register* ... Marietta.
Jesse Taylor ... Jamestown.

OREGON.
Appointed by Governor George E. Chamberlain.

James Hutchinson ... Union.
James Ingland ... Union.
C. T. Blumenrother ... Bandon.
W. E. Grace ... Baker City.
Paul Wessinger ... Portland.
N. H. Bird ... Portland.
C. H. Gram ... Portland.
Grant McDonald ... Portland.
H. G. Kundret ... Portland.
H. B. Nicholas ... Portland.
Newton McCoy ... Portland.
Samuel Kafka ... Portland.
Harry Gurr ... Portland.
H. G. Thomas ... Portland.
James Foley ... Portland.
Thomas Whalen ... Portland.
H. Wolf ... Portland.
M. Ostrow ... Portland.
L. Greenburg ... Portland.
K. Bromberg ... Portland.
H. Abraham ... Portland.
M. Gale ... Portland.
M. Rybke ... Portland.
Jos. Sheminski ... Portland.
M. Blatt ... Portland.
M. Davidson ... Portland.
N. Horn ... Portland.
A. Gale ... Portland.
M. Sugarman ... Portland.
I. Weinstein ... Portland.
M. Wolf ... Portland.
A. Miller ... Portland.
S. Hochfield ... Portland.
D. Nemerosky ... Portland.
M. Rein ... Portland.
J. Rosencrantz ... Portland.
M. Wax ... Portland.
L. Robinson ... Portland.
H. Gerson ... Portland.
J. Lesser ... Portland.
L. Friedman ... Portland.
I. Gevurtz ... Portland.
Philip Gevurtz ... Portland.
W. Fest ... Portland.
A. Flechman ... Portland.
I. Friedman ... Portland.
S. Julius Mayer ... Portland.
J. Nuddelman ... Portland.
M. Simon ... Portland.
I. Morris ... Portland.
Jos. S. Whiteside ... Portland.

PENNSYLVANIA.
Appointed by Governor Samuel W. Pennypacker.

Hon. Wm. M. Kennedy ... Pittsburg.
C. B. Price ... Pittsburg.
Prof. L. S. Rowe ... Philadelphia.
Hon. Robert Adams ... Philadelphia.
Dr. Carl Kelsey ... Philadelphia.
J. F. Warne ... Philadelphia.
Edward Tingle ... Philadelphia.
Hon. Vance C. McCormick ... Harrisburg.
James M. Lamberton ... Harrisburg.
Stephen Collins ... Pittsburg.
C. C. Latus ... Pittsburg.

RHODE ISLAND.
Appointed by Governor George H. Utter.

John F. P. Lawton, Gorham Mfg. Co. ... Providence
Joseph E. Fletcher, Mapleville Worsted Co., Providence.
Webster Knight, B. B. & R. Knight Co. ... Providence.
Thomas F. Kearney, President Rhode Island Building Trades' Council ... Providence.
George B. Sullivan, Pawtucket Typographical Union, Pawtucket.
Prof. James Quayle Dealey, Brown University, Providence.
Prof. Henry B. Gardner, Brown University ... Providence.
David S. Barry, Editor *Providence Journal* ... Providence.
Arthur W. Barrus ... Providence.
John W. Saunders, M.D. ... Shannock.
George H. Webb, Commissioner of Industrial Statistics ... Providence.
George Lewis Smith, Chairman of the Board of State Charities and Corrections, Providence ... Nayatt.
Walter R. Wightman, Agent of State Charities and Corrections ... Providence.

SOUTH CAROLINA.
Appointed by Governor D. C. Hayward.

E. J. Watson ... Columbia.
A. G. Furman ... Greenville.
A. J. Matheson ... Bennettsville.
W. E. Lucas ... Laurens.
A. G. White ... Spartanburg.
Geo. Bell Timmerman ... Lexington.
James A. Hoyt, Jr. ... Columbia.
John S. Wilson ... Lancaster.
Col. Henry Schachte ... Charleston.

SOUTH DAKOTA.
Appointed by Governor Samuel H. Elrod.

Sen. R. J. Gamble ... Yankton.
E. W. Martin ... Deadwood.
John Gray ... Terraville
T. J. Grier ... Lead.
O. H. McCarty ... Huron.
W. A. Beach ... Sioux Falls.
M. F. Greeley ... Gary.
W. H. H. Beadle ... Madison.
Hon. August Frieberg ... Beresford.
Hon. J. J. McLaury ... Milltown.

TEXAS.
Appointed by Governor S. W. T. Lanham.

James F. Grimes ... Houston.
(The names of the additional delegates will be announced later.)

UTAH.
Appointed by Governor John C. Cutler.

Simon Bamberger ... Salt Lake City.
Abel John Evans ... Lehi.
W. C. Spence ... Salt Lake City.
J. Reuben Clark ... Salt Lake City.
Fred J. Pack ... Salt Lake City.
Will Ward ... Salt Lake City.
John Sears ... Salt Lake City.

VERMONT.
Appointed by Governor Charles J. Bell.

Cassius Peck ... Burlington.
James K. Curtis ... Georgia.
George H. Terrill ... Morrisville.
H. M. Farnham ... East Montpelier.
C. A. Bump ... Salisbury.
E. W. Johnson ... Ludlow.
G. W. Young ... St. Johnsbury.
L. M. Craigin ... Springfield.
C. W. Cram ... Williamstown.
W. R. Bell ... Lunenburgh.

VIRGINIA.
Appointed by Governor A. J. Montague.

Joseph Bryan ... Richmond.
James M. Quicke, Jr. ... Petersburg.
R. H. Beazley ... South Boston.
W. H. Bond ... Wise.
John M. Chalkley ... Big Stone Gap.
A. Moore, Jr. ... Berryville.
R. C. Blackford ... Lynchburg.
G. W. Koiner ... Richmond.
W. H. Aston ... Meadow View.
R. L. Dibrell ... Danville.
Archer Anderson ... Richmond.
Lucien H. Cocke ... Roanoke.
Theo. S. Garnett ... Norfolk.
G. M. Serpell ... Norfolk.
A. A. Phleger ... Christiansburg.
James L. Tredway ... Chatham.

WASHINGTON.
Appointed by Governor Albert E. Mead.

A. J. Ferrandini ... Bellingham.
Col. T. M. Fisher ... Walla Walla.
W. B. Estell ... Seattle.

WEST VIRGINIA.
Appointed by Governor William M. O. Dawson.

William S. Foose ... Wheeling.
Frank C. Cox ... Wheeling.
Hon. B. F. Meighen ... Moundsville.
A. H. Winchester ... Buckhannon.
John Nugent ... Charleston.
J. A. Springer ... Flemington.
Hon. George C. Sturgiss ... Morgantown.
Hon. George A. Laughlin ... Wheeling.
Hon. John T. McGraw ... Grafton.
John R. Foster ... Charleston.
Hon. I. V. Barton ... Wheeling.
T. J. Edwards ... Montgomery.

(*Concluded on page 12.*)

AN INTERNATIONAL INVESTIGATION OF PUBLIC OWNERSHIP.

EVERY SHADE OF OPINION AND ALL INTERESTS CONCERNED ARE REPRESENTED IN THE COMMISSION APPOINTED BY THE NATIONAL CIVIC FEDERATION.

THE Commission appointed by the National Civic Federation to investigate the ownership and operation of public utilities is now organized and prepared to prosecute its inquiry into selected divisions of that subject. The general Commission on Public Ownership, as it is called for sake of brevity, held its first meeting in Earl Hall, Columbia University, New York City, October 5. The Commission spent the entire day in a discussion of the scope and method of its work. A verbatim report of this meeting was published in a special number of The National Civic Federation Review.

The impartial attitude of the National Civic Federation, in providing that the investigation should be a purely scientific inquiry, was made clear in a letter written by President August Belmont, who was unable to be present because of serious illness. In his absence, Samuel Gompers, First Vice-President of the National Civic Federation and President of the American Federation of Labor, presided at the first session of the Conference. The letter of Mr. Belmont, addressed to Mr. Gompers on the day before the meeting, follows:

"There is no function which it has ever been my privilege to exercise, and no duty I ever more desired to perform, than that of presiding at the first meeting of the Public Ownership Commission, which is entrusted by the National Civic Federation with the duty of selecting committees to seek abroad and at home information on the subject of municipal ownership and operation of public utilities.

"My physicians have forbidden me to postpone an operation which they have prescribed for me, and I will be compelled to subject myself to their treatment. Therefore it is a matter of personal satisfaction to me that you are here in New York to take my place.

"The subject of municipal ownership and operation of public utilities is forcing itself upon the attention of all thoughtful persons. Unfortunately, the very lack of comprehensive and authoritative data and information leaves the discussion to theorists on both sides who often advance arguments which can neither be accepted nor rejected, for the very reason that no authoritative data exist. The National Civic Federation, through this Commission, will now try to obtain true and reliable facts to guide the student and legislator in seeking the best means to establish peace and maintain cooperation between capital and labor. To the accomplishment of this purpose, I have encouraged this movement and advocated the missions of the subcommittees.

"The relations of capital and labor are vital to the prosperity of the individual and to the State. It is proper, therefore, that arguments should be based on correct facts and known conditions. The Civic Federation has no greater work among its varied duties than to secure these data. The committee, which this Commission proposes to send abroad, will represent every shade of thought and opinion on the subject. This committee, when it returns, will report to a larger commission of men at home, likewise drawn from every part of the country and representing every phase of life. The Civic Federation has no interests to serve and no arguments to make on the subject, but to present the facts and conditions as they may exist abroad and at home, for the use and benefit of the entire country, without respect to party and without respect to special interests.

"Believe me, had I been able to attend the meeting, I would certainly have been present, and I trust that I may regain my health and strength at an early date, in order that I may cooperate in every way in the furtherance of the great object of the gathering over which you are to preside to-morrow."

At the conclusion of the reading of Mr. Belmont's letter, John Mitchell, President of the United Mine Workers of America, moved that a letter of acknowledgment be sent to President Belmont, of the National Civic Federation, expressing regret for his illness and earnest wishes for his speedy recovery.

Prof. Frank Parsons, President of the National Public Ownership League, Boston, moved that the letter also state the Commission's appreciation of the impartial spirit, breadth of view and desire to bring out the facts manifested by President Belmont and the National Civic Federation throughout the organization of the Commission.

Mr. Mitchell accepted the amendment and the motion was unanimously adopted.

In his opening remarks, Chairman Gompers thus emphasized the impartial character of the investigation:

"The municipal ownership of our street railroads and other public utilities is a great impending question occupying the attention of the people of the cities of our country; and it is well that it does. I am sure the advocates of municipal ownership will have no cause of complaint if a rigid, full, and analytical investigation is undertaken, so that the real facts may be ascertained and clearly, impartially, and without bias presented to the people of our country in such form that they may understand that the truth is before them, unvarnished and untarnished by individual predilections. I am sure that those who may be opposed to municipal ownership should have their minds in such a receptive condition, that when the presentation of facts is made, these facts will find a ready lodgment."

MELVILLE E. INGALLS,
Chairman Commission on Public Ownership and Operation.

JOHN MITCHELL,
1st Vice-Chairman Commission on Public Ownership and Operation.

JOHN G. AGAR,
2d Vice-Chairman Commission on Public Ownership and Operation.

EDWARD A. MOFFETT,
Secretary Commission on Public Ownership and Operation.

As a result of the day's discussion, the Commission decided to restrict the initial investigation to the comparative results, in America and abroad, of public and private ownership and operation of gas, water, electric power and lighting, and street railways—those utilities being at the present time most prominent in the public mind. The general Commission elected the following officers:

Chairman, Melville E. Ingalls, Chairman Board of Directors, Big Four Railroad, Cincinnati;

First Vice-Chairman, John Mitchell, President United Mine Workers of America, Indianapolis;

Second Vice-Chairman, John G. Agar, President Reform Club, New York City;

Secretary, Edward A. Moffett, Editor *Bricklayer and Mason*, Indianapolis.

In accepting the chairmanship of the Commission, Mr. Ingalls said in part:

"This is a time when it is especially important that every man ought to do what he can to try to solve questions of importance to the common weal. There is a tremendous pressure all over the country on the question of municipal ownership; one side wants one thing, and another the opposite. You will find people who say that public ownership is the beginning of socialism, and that it will be the ruin of the country. You will read to-day in the newspapers that municipal ownership is a great success, and to-morrow a failure; and there does not seem to be very much solid information to guide opinion. Furthermore, municipal ownership which may be good in Glasgow, for instance, may not apply to Chicago, St. Louis or Cincinnati, because conditions are different. Those are things which ought to be studied. It seems to me that the men who would give their time to this matter are doing a public duty. I hope no one will undertake to serve in this matter unless he comes here expecting to give his time. It is no easy task. There must be thorough investigation, careful study and impartiality. No matter what your interests are, you should report the facts to the public.

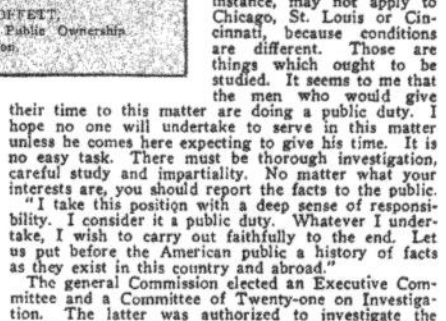

"I take this position with a deep sense of responsibility. I consider it a public duty. Whatever I undertake, I wish to carry out faithfully to the end. Let us put before the American public a history of facts as they exist in this country and abroad."

The general Commission elected an Executive Committee and a Committee of Twenty-one on Investigation. The latter was authorized to investigate the phases of the subject which have been specified, to

(*Concluded on page 9.*)

STREET RAILWAY EMPLOYES VINDICATE PRESIDENT MAHON.

THEIR NATIONAL ORGANIZATION UNANIMOUSLY APPROVES HIS REPUDIATION OF THE INTERBOROUGH STRIKE.

THE true attitude of national organized labor toward the strike on the New York Subway last March is clearly and forcibly expressed in the report which William D. Mahon, President of the Amalgamated Association of Street and Electric Railway Employes of America, made to the national convention of that organization at Chicago, October 2. The keynote of that report is the inviolability of contracts. It is of great significance that the malcontents with the action of President Mahon in repudiating the strike on the Interborough signally failed in a movement for his defeat in the convention. That movement dwindled into insignificance, the result being the enthusiastic and unanimous adoption of his report, while only sixteen votes were cast against his reelection. The other officers of the Association, also reelected, are: First Vice-President, A. W. Morrison; Second Vice-President, Benjamin Commons; Third Vice-President, J. C. Colgan; Fourth Vice-President, J. J. Thorpe; Treasurer, Rezin Orr; Chairman Executive Board, D. L. Dilworth.

Besides treating of the Interborough strike, President Mahon's report dwelt upon the tendency among the organized street railway employes to increase sick and death benefits; the satisfactory settlement of a number of disputes by arbitration, without inconvenience to the public; and the increasing number of trade agreements.

President Mahon's report upon the Interborough strike follows:

"I desire to submit to you a full history of the New York Subway strike, which took place on March 7, 1905, that you may understand my attitude in connection with the same. A great deal of criticism has been heaped upon your officers and the officers of the American Federation of Labor because of our attitude in connection with this strike by persons who had no true information as to the facts or who never sought to obtain the true situation, but have misrepresented and lied about the facts in order to belittle the trade union movement and magnify and exploit their own particularisms.

"In order to give you thorough information concerning the Elevated and Subway organization, it will be necessary to refer back into the early history of this organization.

"In November, of 1902, Mr. Herman Robinson, the Organizer of the American Federation of Labor of New York City, decided to organize the Elevated railway men. An attempt showed Mr. Robinson that he could not approach an individual man, because they were all afraid to discuss with him the question of organization. So after a consultation between Mr. Robinson and myself it was decided that a letter should be drafted and published, and this letter be forwarded to each and every employe whose name Mr. Robinson could secure, and invite them to send him their applications by mail, pledging them that the names would be kept an absolute secret until enough could be gathered together to form an organization. This policy was adopted. After four months of hard work on the part of Mr. Robinson a sufficient number of names were secured to establish the organization, and on March 4, 1903, Mr. Robinson and myself called the men together and organized Division 332. The organization being once established, the men upon the service very rapidly enrolled themselves as members, and in the early spring of 1903 they made requests upon the Company for improved conditions of labor and an increase of pay. Results of their conference with the Company were unsatisfactory, and when I arrived in New York I found them on the verge of a strike. Through the assistance of the Civic Federation I was able to secure a conference for myself and the committee with the officials of the Company, and after several conferences we succeeded in securing a very satisfactory settlement; so satisfactory that it was accepted by almost the unanimous vote of the membership.

"Matters then moved along until the Subway trouble in September, 1904. Prior to this trouble, however, I had received a communication from the organization saying that they had secured a satisfactory understanding concerning the operation of the Subway when it would be opened for travel. However, on or about the first of September I received a telegram urging me to hasten to New York because of threatened trouble. I arrived in that city to find that the Brotherhood of Locomotive Engineers had made demands on the Company concerning the conditions of labor when the Subway would be open for travel. The Company had refused their demands, and they had sought the assistance of the Locomotive Firemen and Division 332 of our Association. I found that a written agreement had been entered into between Grand Master Stone of the Brotherhood of Locomotive Engineers and Division 332, in which our Division had pledged itself to strike upon the Elevated if the Engineers did not secure a satisfactory adjustment of the Subway trouble. I again took up this matter with the Company and after several conferences we succeeded in reaching a settlement satisfactory to the Engineers and Firemen. This agreement was for three years, and covered the conditions of the motormen in the Subway, who were members of our Association.

"I speak of these matters, so that you may understand that we had always been able to secure a satisfactory adjustment with the Company of any dispute when approached in accordance with our laws and rules.

"As to the late trouble, the first knowledge I had that the situation was serious was on Saturday, March 4, when I received a telegram from Secretary Madden, requesting me to come on to New York at once. I was at that time in Columbus, Ohio. I returned to the General Office immediately, and left Sunday afternoon, arriving in New York City at about noon Monday. Shortly after my arrival I was met at the Clarendon Hotel by Secretary Madden and Vice-President May, of Division 332. They informed me that they were on their way then to the Company's office to attend a joint committee meeting. This committee was composed of members of Division 332, of the Locomotive Engineers and Locomotive Firemen. In our discussion of the situation they showed me a copy of an ultimatum that it was the intention of the joint committee to present to the Company. I asked them if they had not already presented copies of an agreement embodying the conditions which they desired for the next year. They stated they had, but, at a later conference between the organizations, they had agreed upon this ultimatum.

W. D. MAHON,
President Amalgamated Association Street Railway Employes.

"Now, the ultimatum set aside all existing agreements that had been made by all three of the organizations and made entirely new demands. In this ultimatum they gave the Company until eleven o'clock that Monday night to concede to their demands. If not, they informed me they had decided to strike.

"I argued with these two representatives strongly against any such policy, and tried to persuade them not to present the ultimatum to the Company. They both seemed to agree with my position and promised to discuss the matter with the committee when they met. Secretary Madden then told me that no one knew that I was in the city; that I had not been officially called; that it was not the intention of the other officers to notify any of the International representatives as to what was taking place, and he asked me to keep my presence a secret and not to inform any one. He advised me, however, to wait at the hotel until the committee would adjourn at the Company's office, and then they would let me know what the results of the conference had been. I waited until about five o'clock in the evening, when Vice-President May accompanied by President Pepper of Division 332 returned to my room. They informed me that the ultimatum had been presented to the Company.

"I argued with them against any such a course, and pointed out to President Pepper that it was contrary to our laws and rules and that the International Organization would have to repudiate any such action. Mr. Pepper stated that he knew it was contrary to our laws, and that he expected we would repudiate, but he stated that before we could repudiate the strike, it would be won, and they didn't care what we did. An investigation of the situation showed that the joint committees had prearranged everything, and that no meetings were to be held upon this evening. The men were then voting upon the proposition of a strike, and they were coming individually to the headquarters for that purpose. After a long discussion with Mr. Pepper, I was unable to change his views at all. So I gave up any hopes in that direction, and set to work to see if it was possible to get in touch with the organization. I then called up Mr. Edward Moffett, Editor of the *Bricklayer and Mason*, and met with him and several other representatives of organized labor of New York, and had them assist me in trying to locate the committee of the Division, with the hope of changing their views. We were unable, however, to find any meeting. However, Mr. Moffett met President Pepper, but could do nothing in influencing him against the policy that he was then prepared to carry out. So after working until one o'clock that night, we gave up any hopes of heading off this rash and unconstitutional strike.

"The Company refused their ultimatum, and at five o'clock on Tuesday morning the strike took place. I remained in New York during Tuesday, but I was unable to do anything. On Wednesday I got in communication with the representatives of Division 332, and on Wednesday night met with their committee jointly with a number of representatives of the different trade unions of New York City. We argued with them against the position they had taken, and advised them to call in their International Officers, and seek to get a settlement of the matter. The committee agreed with our position and returned to their headquarters with the hopes of having the joint committee agree with the same, but in this they were unsuccessful, and so notified me later in the night, but asked that I wait until Thursday morning to see what could be done.

"In the meantime, President Gompers, Vice-President Mitchell and Vice-President Kidd of the American Federation of Labor arrived in the city and extended to me an offer of their assistance to bring about an adjustment of the trouble. When I again met the representatives of the committee, I communicated this fact to them, and told them to lay that proposition also before their joint committee. These representatives of the committee went back and forth before the joint committee, and consultations took place until six o'clock in the evening, when they informed me that the joint committee had decided that they would not accept the assistance of any of the International Officers or the Officers of the American Federation of Labor. They stated that if any overtures for a settlement came from the Company, they must be made directly to them, the joint committee; that they would not seek any settlement. After this statement as to their position, I prepared and submitted to the press the following statement of our position, which I now submit to you just as it was published at that time.

"'The present strike of Local Division 332 of the Amalgamated Association of Street & Electric Railway Employes was undertaken without consulting the responsible officers of the General Organization, without their consent or approval.

"'Last Saturday a telegram was received at my Detroit office stating that "the situation in New York City is critical," and my presence was essential at once. I reached this city on Monday morning, and was astonished to learn that the request for my presence here was made upon personal responsibility and not at the instance of the Local Division.

"'A copy of the demands to be presented to the Interborough Company on Monday afternoon was shown me, and I strongly advised against their presentation, for in addition to the demands for better conditions the document contained the indorsement of the Local Division of Engineers (Motormen), which violated the agreement that organization had with the Company.

"'I had reason to believe there would have been little or no difficulty in obtaining from the Company better conditions, but our organization is strongly committed to the maintenance of its own agreements with employers, and was in honor bound not to encourage the violation of an agreement which another organization had with the employers of its members. Under our laws our Local Unions have no right to strike in violation of any agreement they have with employers, and surely they then can have no right to strike to support another organization to do an act they themselves have no right to do.

"'It seemed to me that without resorting to drastic measures I might yet give whatever assistance my

(*Concluded on page 7.*)

A PROGRESSIVE TRADE UNION'S EDUCATIONAL ENTERPRISE.

NEW YORK STATIONARY FIREMEN FORM CLASSES TO INSTRUCT FELLOW CRAFTSMEN, BOTH WITHIN AND WITHOUT THE ORGANIZATION.

FREQUENTLY nowadays trade unions find useful functions beyond the mere struggle to secure or maintain standards of living wages and hours. These unions, having safeguarded with strong, protective organization the material interests of their members, set about to supply other needs—educational and benevolent.

The educational branch of this policy received the emphatic approval of the convention last year of the American Federation of Labor, which adopted a resolution recommending study and lectures upon appropriate subjects in lodge-rooms and in the homes of members.

A commendable example of putting this policy into practise is afforded by New York Local No. 56 of the International Brotherhood of Stationary Firemen. This Local has started a School of Instruction which will accommodate as many of its 4,000 members as care to embrace this opportunity to improve their knowledge of the technical equipment with which they have to deal while at their work. Both day and evening classes will be formed, so that the fireman who works either during the day or through the night may enjoy the advantages of this progressive plan. The number of classes and instructors is to be increased as the demand requires. This school is conducted in the large room in old Military Hall, on the Bowery (at No. 193), where as long ago as 1868 general conventions of labor and reform representatives were held. Susan B. Anthony tells of being at a convention in Military Hall in that year whose object was to organize the sewing women of New York and improve their condition.

STATIONARY FIREMEN'S SCHOOL OF INSTRUCTION.

The Firemen's School of Instruction will be supplied with charts and blackboards for illustrations and drawings to augment the lectures. The scheme of instruction includes engineering, and will not only teach the fireman all about handling boilers and fuel for either steam or electrical energy, but will prepare him incidentally for the promotion in the engine room that all good firemen aim to attain. Non-union firemen are also welcome to attend these lectures.

This technical education supplements the regular efforts of the union to make its members temperate and thoroughly reliable for loyal service wherever they are sent by the organization, which, moreover, holds each of its members to a strict accountability as to the performance of his duties. The employer is thus aided by union discipline to be assured of responsible service.

Stationary Firemen's Local 56 is nineteen years old. During the past ten years it has had no strike nor lockout to interrupt its steady and prosperous growth. Every threatened trouble has been averted by conference and conciliation, or settled by arbitration. No. 56 has benevolent features which are met by the small dues of 50 cents per member a month, showing careful and economical management of the funds. On the death of a member in good standing $100 is paid to the dependents, and on the death of a member's wife the organization contributes $50 toward the funeral expenses.

The union maintains a business office, and a waiting and reading room for the unemployed at No. 193 Bowery. The reading tables are supplied with newspapers and periodicals and also magazines containing useful information concerning the engineering craft.

Local 56 is one of the 215 unions in the International Brotherhood of Stationary Firemen, whose jurisdiction over the United States and Canada is under the direction of President Timothy Healy, of New York, the man to whom credit is generally awarded for building up the local union which is the subject of this sketch. Mr. Healy has been twice elected by the International Brotherhood without opposition as its general president. The President of Local 56 is James Carroll and its Business Agent is James P. Holland.

The International Brotherhood maintains a headquarters and a suite of offices for its general secretary at Omaha, where also a monthly magazine is published as the official organ of the brotherhood, and is sent to every member's home.

The 50,000 members of this Brotherhood, in the United States, Canada and British Columbia, are employed under trade agreements which include provision for arbitration in the electric lighting plants, street railway power houses, paper mills, large office buildings, breweries, packing houses, ice-making plants, the great manufactories, hotels and theaters.

(*Concluded from page 6.*)

experience and position afforded to advise a way out of the difficult and questionable position in which our men and our Local Division were placed, to try and bring about an honorable adjustment and the establishment of better relations between the men, the organization and the Company. However, the repeated tender not only of my good offices, but also those of President Gompers of the American Federation of Labor, President Mitchell of the United Mine Workers of America, Vice-President Kidd of the American Federation of Labor, and President Healy of the International Brotherhood of Stationary Firemen, they inconsiderately rejected.

"'Nothing now remains for me to do but to declare that the present strike is neither authorized nor approved by the Amalgamated Association of Street & Electric Railway Employes of America, and I therefore advise all our loyal members to report for duty at once, to maintain their organization which has done so much for the betterment of their material and moral conditions, and by the result of their present experience avoid such errors in the future. In that effort I shall be glad to assist to the fullest.

"'(Signed) W. D. MAHON,
Street & Electric Railway Employes of America.

"'New York, March 9, 1905.'

"I now submit the report of this case for your consideration and approval or disapproval, as you may decide, but in connection with the same I desire that my position shall be clearly understood by this Convention, for if this organization is to be a success its laws, rules and agreements must be strictly adhered to and carried out by its membership, and so long as I am an officer I shall adhere to that policy; and were the same conditions confronting me to-day I would act exactly as I have acted in this case."

The unions that live up to their agreements, written or verbal, are the ones that enjoy the respect and confidence of the general public and accomplish the greatest good for the greatest number all the time.—*Label Bulletin.*

TIMOTHY HEALY,
International President Stationary Firemen.

JAMES CARROLL,
President Stationary Engineers' New York Union.

JAMES P. HOLLAND,
Business Agent Stationary Engineers' New York Union.

THE NATIONAL

Civic Federation Review

Offices: 281 Fourth Avenue, New York City

RALPH M. EASLEY, Editor

The Editor alone is responsible for any unsigned article or unquoted statement published in THE NATIONAL CIVIC FEDERATION REVIEW.

Ten Cents per Copy One Dollar per Year

PUBLISHED MONTHLY BY

The National Civic Federation

NATIONAL CONFERENCE ON IMMIGRATION.

The first National Conference upon Immigration ever held in this country, when it convenes in New York City on December 6, under the auspices of the National Civic Federation, will find itself a body representative of practically every State in the Union and of every interest, ethical, civic and industrial, concerned in a problem of many phases and of the highest importance. The program, so far as it could be prepared in advance for a body that is sure to be inspired by its own initiative, is attractive and instructive. The visit of the Conference in a body to Ellis Island will enable many of the delegates to witness for the first time the actual arrival, inspection and disposition of some 5,000 aliens; to partake of the same food served to them, and to comprehend accurately how the most important gate to the Republic and its citizenship is kept. The discussions of the Conference will not be confined to a rigid syllabus, but will be elastic in their range, in the hope that the utmost freedom of expression may result in conclusions of benefit to the national welfare.

THE FACTS OF PUBLIC OWNERSHIP.

There is solid ground for confidence that the people of this country, who are showing keen and wide-spread interest in the ownership and operation of public utilities, will within a reasonable time be placed in possession of the entire facts as to that question, so far as they can be discovered from experience in the United States and other countries. The Committee of Twenty-one appointed by the National Civic Federation to investigate this subject passed upon a plan for its inquiry on November 27. This plan was elaborated by a subcommittee, whose composition indicates the thoroughly representative character of the larger body. Its members are: Professor Frank J. Goodnow, of Columbia University; Walter Clark, of the United Gas Improvement Company, Philadelphia; Edward W. Bemis, Superintendent of the Cleveland Water Works; J. W. Sullivan, Editor of the *Garment Workers' Journal;* and Milo R. Maltbie, franchise expert. Here are represented the most diverse interests and the most divergent opinions. But this subcommittee has worked harmoniously in planning a comprehensive and searching investigation because of its unanimous agreement upon the desirability of ascertaining the entire truth about public and private ownership and operation; thus furnishing a basis for debate between the advocates of conflicting theories, out of which a satisfactory public policy may be evolved. Such harmony of purpose warrants expectation of agreement upon facts, regardless of differences as to their general interpretation or local applicability.

ANOTHER BLOW TO SOCIALISM.

In simultaneously adopting resolutions condemning Socialism and commending the methods for industrial peace advocated by the Civic Federation of New England, the State Federation of Labor of Massachusetts has made an exemplary demonstration of the progressive wisdom that is growing to rule the councils of organized wage-earners. It is noteworthy that the author of the anti-Socialist resolutions was David Goldstein, who was once himself a leading advocate of Socialism, but who was impelled by years of conscientious study to reject its theories as unsound. The workingmen of Massachusetts, once a hotbed of Socialism, are arrayed upon the side of rational and equitable relations between the productive forces of industry.

RECREATION ON THE ISTHMUS.

The official report to the United States Isthmian Canal Commission upon the needs and opportunities for recreation of Government employes engaged in canal construction, published in this issue of THE REVIEW, presents the carefully considered conclusions of two Welfare experts, recommended for that purpose, at the request of the Commission, by the Welfare Department of the National Civic Federation. This report outlines plans designed to secure the content, and consequent health and efficiency, of many thousands of men engaged in the prosecution of the greatest engineering work in the world's history, amid tropical conditions and far from their usual surroundings. Already some of these plans have been put into effect by the Commission and others have been approved.

The recommendation in the report that the sale of beer and light wines be permitted in employes' club houses raises a question of growing importance in all large industrial establishments. Does it conduce to the welfare of employes to allow the use of beer and light wines of assured purity at cost prices in the lunch rooms or club-rooms of such establishments? Or should employes who desire such beverages be left to buy them in nearby saloons? These queries open a broad social and moral proposition, which has strong advocates and opponents. They will form one of the main topics of discussion at the annual meeting of the Welfare Department, to be held in New York City in January.

Another noteworthy recommendation of the experts is the establishment of the Saturday half-holiday, in order that the workers on the Isthmus may have opportunity to enjoy the recreative features that are designed.

WHO PAYS THE LABOR BILL?

Directly contradictory statements have recently been made, concerning the question of wages and of who ultimately pays the labor cost of production, by the President of the American Federation of Labor and by the President of the Citizens' Industrial Association of America. The first declares that high wages are both a cause of general prosperity and a preventive of industrial and commercial depression, because they increase the purchasing power of the mass, making consumption so great as to maintain production at its highest point. The other claims that the cost of higher wages must be paid ultimately by the consumer, so that the worker really gains nothing by an advance of wages, since he has to pay a higher price for every article he buys.

The wage-earners being the mass of consumers, this is a question of vital interest to them. It involves directly the relation between wages and the cost of living. Is the one to determine the other? There was a concrete presentation of this question the other day between a Chicago employer and the Wagon Drivers' Union. These teamsters asked an advance of their wages above $2 a day on the ground that they could not live on that sum. They presented this interesting schedule of the daily expenses of an average city worker's family:

Rent	$0.50
Food	.75
Fuel	.30
Light	.07
Carfare	.10
Extra meal	.25
Total	$1.97

If correct, the figures of this schedule leave three cents a day for clothing, medicine, and minor household needs. The reply of the employer to this representation was also interesting: "No, I could not live on $2 a day, and I don't believe that you can. But I can get plenty of teamsters who are willing to work for that price. That is really what governs wages more than the cost of living."

This incident suggests the further queries: Why can these other teamsters live on less than $2 a day? What do they do without, that the teamsters who find $2 a day too scant count as necessary to healthful living? If the rate of wages were thus to be determined by competition alone would the result to society at large be desirable? Or would the tendency be to degrade the American workingman to the condition of the coolie laborer?

The Industrial Economic Department of the National Civic Federation will devote a meeting to the consideration of the questions involved in this problem.

The merging of *Charities* and *The Commons,* now in charge of the newly formed Charities Publication Committee, is the concentration of policies common to each, and will give to the cause they represent a national periodical with greatly increased resources. The union brings into effective cooperation the two editors, Edward T. Devine and Graham Taylor, both recognized authorities in their special fields, the one being the head of the Department of Sociology in Columbia University and the other conducting the Institute of Social Science and Arts of the University of Chicago.

MASSACHUSETTS WAGE-EARNERS DENOUNCE SOCIALISM.

THE STATE FEDERATION OF LABOR REPUDIATES ITS PROPAGANDA AND STRONGLY APPROVES THE CIVIC FEDERATION OF NEW ENGLAND.

THE Massachusetts State Federation of Labor, at its annual convention held in Pittsfield in October, adopted resolutions denouncing Socialism as antagonistic to the trades union movement, and pledging its cooperation in the work of the Civic Federation of New England.

This is the first aggressive declaration against Socialism that this State organization has made in the twenty-five years of its history, its conventions hitherto having been content with a successful defensive attitude against the recurrent attempts to cause the adoption of Socialist resolutions. Consistent with this action was the simultaneous approval of the New England Civic Federation by the State Federation of Labor.

The *Boston Transcript* published the following editorial under the title "Organized Labor against Socialism":

"If the Socialist contingent carries out its threat of withdrawing from the State Federation of Labor because of the resolutions adopted at Pittsfield this week, it will certainly appear to the outside public as a most fortunate thing for legitimate unionism. It will relieve the trade union movement proper, in this State, of a cantankerous, disrupting element which has been making the lives of conservative labor leaders miserable for many years, frequently nullifying their efforts to hold union policies and methods within the limits of sound judgment and fair-minded moderation. The Socialist propagandists have no love for unionism as such; their connection with it is for the sole purpose, often frankly avowed, of capturing the labor movement by 'boring from within,' and converting it into a revolutionary crusade against the existing social and industrial order, which is held, regardless of the facts of steady improvement, to be destined only for abolition, root and branch.

"In denouncing this propaganda as 'intellectually unsound, impractical from an economic standpoint, and demoralizing to the general wellbeing of society,' the State Federation renders a public service which should be frankly acknowledged even by those who see little to admire in either the principles or policies of unionism. It is a service that has been rendered on many previous occasions, and cannot therefore be described as a new departure, but it becomes increasingly important as the Socialist agitation spreads. The growing disposition of organized labor bodies to ally themselves with the broader, constructive interests of the whole community, seeking progress along the lines of evolution rather than revolution, was further indicated in the resolutions strongly indorsing the Civic Federation of New England, in which respect the convention followed the action of the Boston Central Labor Union last May. It is one of the most significant signs of the times that trade unionism, whatever its shortcomings in leadership here and there, or mistakes of policy in special cases, is to-day one of the main bulwarks against the inroads of socialistic radicalism in the very quarter where those inroads would otherwise prove most effective—that is, among the wage workers of the country."

The anti-Socialist resolutions, presented by David Goldstein of Waltham and adopted by the convention, follow:

Whereas, the American Federation of Labor, now entering upon its twenty-fifth year of work, has, by its principles and policy, gained for itself a place of usefulness and of honor within the body politic.

Whereas, trade union principles are those universally recognized as the basis of economic and civil society, namely, the right of private property in capital, the right of buying and selling potential labor, the right of free association, the right of personal protection under the law.

Whereas, the primary object of the trade union is to maintain and to advance the standards of American living, to maintain and to advance the wage earner's position relative to the economic and political progress of our nation.

Whereas, our experience—as an organization founded upon the general lines of trade autonomy—has demonstrated our tactics, high dues, collective bargaining, trade labels, trade agreements, adjustment of trade differences by conciliation and arbitration, and as a last resort the boycott and strike, to be effective in the progressive attainment of the end we have in view; and also to be sound by having won for unionism a place of well deserved importance in American institutions.

Whereas, the American Federation of Labor has for many years been harassed and is now under the assault of men holding to opposite principles, and employing contrary tactics, whose aim it is to convert unionists to socialism, that the economic power of our organization and the political power of our members may form an adjunct to social propaganda, and an accession to socialist party strength.

Whereas, the principles of socialism are intellectually unsound, impracticable from an economic standpoint and demoralizing to the general well being of society.

Therefore be it resolved, That we, the Massachusetts branch of the American Federation of Labor, in convention assembled at Pittsfield, October 9, 1905, do hereby denounce as detrimental to our progress, as destructive to our good fame, as disruptive of those personal and civic virtues, which it is our duty to cultivate, any attitude of sympathy toward socialist propaganda within our ranks.

Be it further resolved, That we recognize as the most despicable attack yet made upon the life of our national body, that organization launched in Chicago, July, 1905, known as the industrial workers of the world; headed by men of international reputation, namely, Eugene V. Debs, late presidential candidate of the socialist party; Daniel De Leon, editor of the *People*, official organ of the social labor party; A. M. Simons, editor of the *International Socialist Review;* ex-priest Thomas J. Haggerty, Messrs. Haywood and Moyer, president and secretary, respectively, of the Western Federation of Miners, and many other socialists of national reputation.

Be it finally resolved, That we condemn, *in toto*, this organization, and that we resist by all lawful means its encroachment upon our rightful territory, the labor world of the United States.

The debate over these resolutions consumed several hours. Among those who opposed Mr. Goldstein were James Kelly and James McCabe, Socialist delegates from Brockton, and Patrick F. Mahoney, Socialist candidate for lieutenant-governor. After the resolution had been adopted by a vote of 71 yeas to 28 nays, Mr. McCabe called upon all Socialists to leave the hall. None followed him, and he later resumed his seat.

The resolutions approving the New England Civic Federation, offered by Thomas M. Nolan, were as follows:

Resolved, That the Massachusetts State Branch, American Federation of Labor, conveys to the New England Civic Federation earnest approval of the efforts made and in contemplation by that organization, in bringing about a condition in which both employer and employed will more fully recognize the rights of the other, and whose work of educating the public upon the value of mediation and conciliation as preferable to strikes, lockouts, boycotts and other similar methods, deserves the loyal and hearty support of the American trade union movement.

Resolved, That the secretary be and is hereby instructed to convey to the New England Civic Federation, the purpose of the Massachusetts State Branch to cooperate with it in every way that will make for the happiness and advancement of the wage-earners of America.

The report of the Pittsfield *Journal* says:

Patrick Mahoney, of Boston, took the floor at the completion of its reading by Chairman Frank Foster, at once wildly gesticulating. Recognized by the chair, he read first a magazine article of the most disparaging sort upon the late Mark Hanna, and touching also August Belmont. He then characterized the Federation as of no account. He reflected upon the integrity and honesty of the union labor men connected with it, and characterized the work of the Federation as of no account and the reading and adoption of such a resolution foolish and uncommon and stated that he would oppose it to the end. Frank Foster, in the most brilliant speech yet heard in the convention, replied to Mr. Mohoney. With no attempt at eulogy, he showed what Mr. Hanna had done. He characterized the efforts of Mr. Mahoney as detrimental to trade unionism, and pointed out to the convention by many examples the great good accomplished for trade unionism in New England through the assistance of the Civic Federation in Massachusetts, and closed with the assertion that the Civic Federation was brought about through the efforts of Samuel Gompers and other noted labor union men, and not through capitalists, and that it was doing good work, and what was good for him should be good for any union man.

Peter Collins, of the Electrical Workers' Union of Boston, followed Mr. Foster. He showed by actual cases what the Civic Federation had done—how it had opened doors to trade union organizations which previously were closed to them because of the influence of its members securing hearings for unionists on matters of importance to them. He cited the case in particular of the American Bell Telephone Company, where advantageous five-year agreements with the electrical union had been entered into by this company, where a lockout seemed certain, owing to the kindly administration of the Civic Federation.

The debate was resumed on the following day. The Springfield *Republican's* report says:

Peter Collins told of meeting the officials of the American Telephone and Telegraph Company through the Civic Federation and of the results attained. He said that the successful outcome of a difference between the electrical workers and the American Telephone and Telegraph Company could never have been reached had it not been for the Civic Federation. He desired to refute the allegations made against the Federation by Patrick Mahoney, of Boston, Tuesday, and wished to be recorded as standing first, last and always in accord with the Civic Federation. He believed those principles will cement the labor movement in this country and provide a common ground on which capital and labor can meet in conjunction with representatives of the public and arrive at a lasting peace with just and honorable conditions for both parties concerned.

Mr. Mahoney again attacked the Civic Federation, which he said would strip organized labor of its strength. If the workingmen were organized as they should be they could enforce their demands themselves without the necessity of calling in the assistance of the Civic Federation, which would in itself be an acknowledgment of weakness.

Frank McCarthy, of Boston, spoke warmly in favor of the Federation. He said that it was formed solely to assist in arriving at some understanding between employer and employe without the necessity of resorting to strikes or lockouts. It was not organized to settle strikes and has no authority to do so; its services can only be exerted upon request of the parties involved. Its avowed object is to bring together parties who could not be brought together for a conference through any other means, and it has accomplished this object on numerous occasions. The principles of Civic Federation are in line with those of every bona fide labor organization in the country. If federation was not indorsed, laboring men will be accused by the people of the country of being afraid to stand up and openly avow these principles.

The resolution was adopted by an overwhelming majority, its opponents not asking for a roll-call.

(*Concluded from page 5.*)

add to its members and to subdivide itself, employ experts when in its judgment necessary, and to allot its work as it sees fit. This Committee of Investigation is to report its final conclusions to the general Commission.

Since the appointment of the Committee of Investigation, a special subcommittee, appointed immediately after the adjournment of the general Commission on October 5, has been occupied in preparing a series of questions, calculated to facilitate, for purposes of precise comparison, the simultaneous ascertainment of facts in this country and in others. Its members are Prof. Frank J. Goodnow, Walter Clark, Edward W. Bemis, J. W. Sullivan and Milo R. Maltbie. This special subcommittee has held at this writing four meetings, each consuming an entire day, while its members have devoted much time to individual consideration of the questions. Its report was submitted to a meeting of the Committee on Investigation on November 27, when plans for prosecuting the inquiry, comprehensively and analytically, were elaborated. The conclusions of this meeting and subsequent steps will be presented in future numbers of THE REVIEW.

The following are the members of the Executive Committee:

The officers of the General Commission, *ex-officio*, and
Alexander H. Revell, Merchant, Chicago, Ill.
E. E. Clark, Grand Chief Brotherhood of Railway Conductors, Cedar Rapids, Iowa.
Isaac N. Seligman, Banker, New York City.
E. Rosewater, Editor the *Bee*, Omaha, Neb.
William Wirt Howe, Lawyer, New Orleans, La.
Samuel Insull, President Chicago Edison Co., Chicago, Ill.
V. Everit Macy, Capitalist, New York City.
John Bancroft Devins, Editor New York *Observer*, New York City.
Frederick N. Judson, Attorney, St. Louis, Mo.
George Harvey, Editor *North American Review*, New York City.
Carroll D. Wright, President Clark College, Worcester, Mass.
Hamilton Holt, Editor the *Independent*, New York City.
Walter Macarthur, Editor, *Coast Seamen's Journal*, San Francisco, Cal.
D. L. Cease, Editor *Railroad Trainmen's Journal*, Cleveland, O.
Franklin MacVeagh, Merchant, Chicago, Ill.
Henry M. Farnam, Yale University, New Haven, Conn.
George H. Harries, Washington Railway and Electric Company, Washington, D. C.
Louis D. Brandeis, Lawyer, Boston, Mass.
Marcus M. Marks, Manufacturer, New York City.
James O'Connell, President International Association Machinists, Washington, D. C.
Lawrence F. Abbott, Editor the *Outlook*, New York City.
Alexander C. Humphrey, President Stevens Institute, Hoboken, N. J.
J. W. Jenks, Cornell University, Ithaca, N. Y.
John F. Tobin, President Boot and Shoe Workers' Union, Boston, Mass.
Frank A. Vanderlip, Vice-President National City Bank, New York City.

The following are the members of the Committee on Investigation:

M. E. Ingalls, Chairman Directors Big Four Railroad, Cincinnati, O.
Dr. Albert Shaw, Editor *Review of Reviews*, New York City.
Talcott Williams, Editorial Writer the *Press*, Philadelphia, Pa.
W. D. Mahon, President Amalgamated Association Street Railway Employes, Detroit, Mich.
Frank J. Goodnow, Columbia University, New York City.
Walton Clark, United Gas Improvement Co., Philadelphia, Pa.
Edward W. Bemis, Superintendent Water Works, Cleveland, O.
John H. Gray, Northwestern University, Chicago, Ill.
Walter L. Fisher, Municipal Voters' League, Chicago, Ill.
Timothy Healy, International President Stationary Firemen, New York City.
William J. Clark, General Electric Co., New York City.
H. B. F. MacFarland, President Board of Commissioners, District of Columbia, Washington, D. C.
Daniel J. Keefe, President International Longshoremen's Association, Detroit, Mich.
Frank Parsons, President National Public Ownership League, Boston, Mass.
John R. Commons, University of Wisconsin, Madison, Wis.
J. W. Sullivan, Editor *Garment Workers' Bulletin*, New York City.
Leo S. Rowe, University of Pennsylvania, Philadelphia, Pa.
F. J. McNulty, President International Brotherhood Electrical Workers, Washington, D. C.
Albert F. Winchester, General Superintendent City of South Norwalk Electric Works, South Norwalk, Conn.
Charles L. Edgar, President Edison Electric and Illuminating Company, Boston, Mass.
Milo R. Maltbie, Franchise Expert and Former Editor *Municipal Affairs*, New York City.

WELFARE DEPARTMENT
OF
The National Civic Federation

RECREATION FOR GOVERNMENT EMPLOYES ON THE ISTHMIAN CANAL.

Club Houses; Athletic Fields; Sunday Excursions; Sea Bathing; Saturday Half Holiday; Fourth of July Celebration; Schedule of Activities.

THE following is the report to the United States Isthmian Canal Commission of two experts in Welfare Work, upon the needs and opportunities for the recreation of the workers occupied in canal construction. The experts, W. E. C. Nazro and Edward Moffett, were engaged by the Commission, upon the recommendation of the Welfare Department of the National Civic Federation. This report embraces their conclusions, after a thorough study of the conditions between and including Colon and Panama. They are designed to promote the contentment and happiness, conducive to the health and effectiveness, of thousands of Government employes in a trying climate and amid novel environments. The publication of this report in THE NATIONAL CIVIC FEDERATION REVIEW has been authorized by the Isthmian Canal Commission.—EDITORIAL NOTE.]

NEW YORK CITY, August 28, 1905.

To the HONORABLE THEODORE P. SHONTS,
Chairman of the Isthmian Canal Commission,
Washington, D. C.

SIR:

We have the honor to submit the following report as to the necessity and opportunity for wholesome recreation for employes of the United States Government in the Canal Zone upon the Isthmus of Panama. It is proper to state that our inquiries into this subject have been thoroughly facilitated by yourself and your executive officers as well as by the civil and military officials within the region upon the Isthmus controlled by the United States. We enjoyed the advantage, also, of making our investigation at a time when the great body of employes was welcoming with enthusiasm what was understood to be a new régime.

Club Houses.

After a thorough inspection of the Canal Zone, we reached the conclusion that the first and most obvious method of providing for recreation is to build club houses at suitable points along the entire route. We believe that these club houses will prove both useful and popular.

We found some plans for the club houses already drafted which, with additions and modifications, appear well calculated for their purpose.

We would recommend that there be three classes of club houses, which for convenience we may designate A, B and C. These several types are recommended to bring about the greatest adaptability of the club houses for the enjoyment of those who will naturally use them.

Class A club houses would be designed for the recreation of army officers, engineers, architects and employes who are graduates of colleges or technical schools, or who have received such a measure of higher or professional education as would cause them to be of common tastes and sympathies.

Class B club houses would be designed for skilled workmen.

"A" AND "B" CLUB HOUSES AND EQUIPMENT.

A single type of club house, as suggested in the plan marked Exhibit A-B, may be used for both classes A and B. This type of house would include in its features the following:

Swimming pool and shower baths;
Reading and writing room;
Bowling alleys;
Billiard and pool room;
Buffet;
Card room (cards, checkers, chess, dominoes, shuffleboard, etc.);
Social hall.

In the equipment of the building, all the verandas should be covered with mosquito netting and provided with rattan chairs, couch chairs, hammocks and small smoking tables.

In the billiard room there should be stands for serving cool drinks and seats for the players and the spectators, in addition to the requisite paraphernalia.

The social hall should contain a piano with a self-playing attachment, as well as chairs and tables.

The refectory should be fitted for the service of sandwiches and other light refreshments, including beer and light wines, but not spirits.

The room for shower baths, toilet arrangements and lockers should be equipped in accordance with the plan and supplied plentifully with soap and towels.

The bowling alley should be equipped with seats for the players and the onlookers.

In the reading and writing room there should be desks with an abundant supply of stationery, tables, chairs, lounges and also well-kept files of periodicals and newspapers from the States.

Chairs, tables and the usual appurtenances should be provided in the card room.

In the grounds of the club house provision might be made for tennis courts, golf-croquet, rifle ranges, archery and handball.

"C" CLUB HOUSES AND EQUIPMENT.

Class C club houses would be intended for the use of the unskilled laborers. These houses should be commodious, and simple in construction. The principal feature should be a large hall, called a recreation and smoking room, with an overlooking office. In the recreation room there should be billiard, pool and card tables, equipments for other harmless and simple games, and an abundance of plain wooden chairs.

On the verandas, covered with mosquito netting, should be plenty of smoking tables and plain wooden chairs.

The demand for reading matter in these club houses would not be as great as in the others and would be partly supplied from their surplus material. It would also be advisable to furnish popular periodicals in foreign languages.

Each Class C club house should also include a swimming pool with locker and toilet rooms, as suggested by the plan, marked Exhibit C, on which possible shower baths are also indicated.

—SECOND FLOOR PLAN—

SWIMMING POOLS.

The recommendation that club houses of each class should be provided with a swimming pool is made subject to approval by the Sanitary Department of plans for their construction, water supply and drainage. It is necessary, if these swimming pools are to be installed, that arrangements should be made to keep the water constantly in motion in order to prevent the breeding of mosquitoes. If such an arrangement is not possible, we would advise, on account of the sanitary conditions, the elimination of swimming pools. If it is decided that there can be no swimming pools, it would be wise to install shower baths in Class C as well as the other club houses.

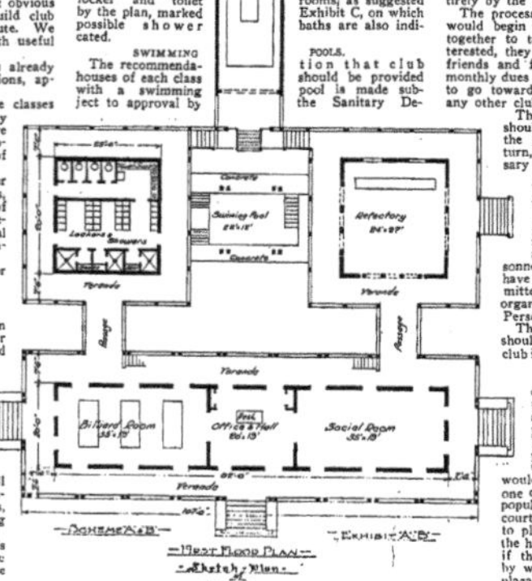

—First Floor Plan—
—Sketch Plan of Club House—

READING MATTER.

We recommend that an effort be made to obtain contributions of newspapers, periodicals and books from the people of the United States for the use of these Isthmian club houses. Such contributions could be sent to the Commission in New York City, whence they could be readily shipped to the Isthmus. The effect of the giving and receiving of this reading matter would be most beneficial in making it evident to the employes, far removed from the United States, that their labor and hardship are the objects of friendly and encouraging popular appreciation at home.

LOCATION OF CLUBS.

We recommend the erection, at the earliest possible moment, of club houses for either Class A or Class B, or both, at points upon the route where there already is, or apparently there is likely to be, a considerable concentration of those classes of employes: for example, at Corozal, Empire, Culebra, Gorgona, Cristobal and Colon.

Understanding that it is the general policy not to encourage the concentration of employes in the city of Panama, we do not recommend the erection of a club house within its limits. If, however, there is need for a club house in that city, the dwelling now used by officers of the Commission, if available, might be put to that use.

Class C club houses should be erected wherever the work of construction is most active. If the places of greatest employment of unskilled labor are to be shifted from time to time during the progress of construction, it would be practicable so to construct Class C club houses that they could be taken apart and moved from place to place with trivial expense.

MAINTENANCE AND ORGANIZATION.

All club houses should be built and equipped entirely at the expense of the Government.

The maintenance of club houses in Classes A and B should be provided only in part by the Government, the balance of the cost of running them to be borne by voluntary organizations. It may be possible to make Classes A and B self-sustaining.

The maintenance of Class C should be borne entirely by the Government.

The process of forming clubs for Classes A and B would begin with calling two or three of the men together to talk over the matter. On becoming interested, they could bring together a number of their friends and form an organization. There should be monthly dues in clubs for Classes A and B, the receipts to go toward defraying the running expenses, as in any other club.

The members in clubs of Classes A and B should be consulted as to the appointment of the paid supervisor for each club, who, in turn, would be expected to employ the necessary service.

The club supervisor in Class A should be appointed by a committee *elected* by the members.

In clubs of Class B, the supervisor should be appointed by a committee of members *selected* by the proper representative of the Bureau of Quarters and Personnel in the locality. It will be advisable to have the Government represented on this committee by one or more persons from the organization of the Bureau of Quarters and Personnel.

The Bureau of Quarters and Personnel should appoint the necessary supervisor for each club in Class C.

Athletic Fields.

We recommend that the project to lay out an athletic field at Corozal be pushed through. In every way this location seems to be more adapted to such a purpose than any other along the route. Upon one side of the railroad at this point there is a large hotel to which the Government is making additions. We would suggest that a band stand be added to one of the wings of the hotel, to be used for popular concerts. Instead of the lawn tennis court now planned, which it is contemplated to place on the grounds directly in front of the hotel, we recommend the making of lawns; if that be impracticable, some other means by which this place can be kept as an open plaza for the people to walk about and enjoy the concerts should be provided.

—EXHIBIT "C"—
—FLOOR PLAN—

SKETCH PLAN OF CLUB HOUSE.

On the opposite side of the railroad is an open, level ield, spacious enough to accommodate all open air thletic features. In this field should be constructed racing track for ponies. Beside the track for onies, there should be constructed a cinder path, for hose who like running sports, equipped with running nd jumping bars, etc. Within this track tennis courts nd a band stand may be located. Other spaces in he field may be set apart for a rifle range, a place or the practise of archery, grounds for golf-croquet, tc. Thus would be afforded a suitable opportunity or outdoor exercises for women, as well as men.

At one side of the track should be built a club house, he type marked Exhibit A-B, of extra large size, to e used by both Class A and Class B employes Saturday afternoons. In this connection we suggest the uture development of Corozal as a principal athletic enter, the result of the Saturday Half Holiday whose stablishment we recommend at another place in this eport. This club house should include a commodious afe which could be conducted by the caterer in the otel. It might be possible to have this club house or the regular daily use of the members of the Class B local club, if that type is needed at Corozal. If the ituation should be such that Class A employes should se it as their regular club house during the week, t would be necessary to have some rooms reserved for heir special use on Saturdays. In other words, an ffort should be made to avoid the necessity of aving this club house in addition to a club house A nd a club house B at Corozal.

At Corozal, we recommend that regular evening oncerts be given at the hotel and that the employes ow invited to go in to Panama to hear the band lay on Sunday evenings be invited instead to these oncerts at Corozal. There appear, to our judgment, everal reasons why this commendable diversion hould be offered to the employes at Corozal rather han at Panama. Among these reasons may be specied two:

(1) The inviting of a large number of employes o the capital, whatever the occasion, is not consistent vith the evident policy to keep as many of the emloyes as possible away from the city and its centers f fever contagion.

(2) Along the route from the railroad station at Panama to the plaza where the band now plays, visors are exposed to many temptations; while at Corozal, after the concert it would be but a step to he train, and the surroundings would afford no inucement to detain any employe from returning home romptly. This plan would in no way interfere with he present popular Sunday evening concerts furished in the capital for its people by the band of he Panama Government.

BAND OF THE EMPLOYES.

We believe that the Bureau of Quarters and Personnel could organize a band of the emnloyes. If this can not be done, a band should be provided by the Government.

FREE TRANSPORTATION.

The employes at every point along the canal route should be provided with free transportation to and from the Sunday evening concerts and the weekly athletic meetings.

ATHLETIC FIELD AT CRISTOBAL.

It may be feasible and advisable in the future to duplicate this athletic field, including all its features, at Cristobal, when the number of employes warrants. In this way there would be two centers for general recreation, one near Panama and one near Colon, available respectively for each half of the route.

A suggested lay-out for this field is presented in the plan, marked Exhibit D.

Sunday Excursions.

We recommend that the excursions that have been run from Panama to Toboga at irregular intervals be hereafter continued regularly, if possible, on each Sunday. At present there is much complaint because of the irregularity of these excursions, which are highly popular, and because of the inconvenience of carrying food for the day, most of the excursionists being able and willing to buy luncheons at a reasonable price. We, therefore, recommend that some arrangement be made by which a steamer can be chartered regularly for each Sunday so that the uncertainty of these excursions will cease; and that a caterer be permitted to sell light luncheons and soft drinks on board, under the supervision of the Bureau of Quarters and Personnel. The steamer should be used on alternate Sundays for employes paid in gold and for employes paid in silver. The present plan of issuing free tickets to employes for these excursions, until the capacity of the boat is reached, should be continued.

Sea Bathing.

We believe that facilities for sea bathing at Colon should be provided for employes who make occasional excursions to that place. At present the fear of sharks deters employes from entering the sea. The beach at Colon is well adapted for surf bathing. There should be constructed small and inexpensive bath houses as an experiment, with a view to their enlargement should they prove popular. Separate bath houses for those employes who are paid in gold and those who are paid in silver should be erected.

It would be necessary to protect those portions of the beach assigned to bathing from sharks by means of closely driven piles connected with coarse wire netting or some similar device.

Bathing suits should be provided at a nominal rental.

A paid supervisor, employed by the Bureau of Quarters and Personnel, should look after the maintenance of the bath houses, the cleanliness of the beach, the care of bathing suits and towels. Under his authority there should be an attendant qualified to teach the bathers to swim, the entire system of instruction and the insurance of safety being similar to that now employed in the municipal baths at American seaports.

Saturday Half Holiday.

If the methods of recreation we have the honor to recommend are to be provided, either in whole or in part, sufficient time should be allowed employes to make them available. Sunday alone, in our judgment, does not afford sufficient leisure for adequate recreation. Even though there were no other uses to which employes might desire to put their weekly day of rest, it would not be well, in our opinion, to crowd into that day all the opportunities for recreation which we have recommended. If employes were to devote their Sundays almost wholly to the proposed athletic field, or fields, or to the amusements in the club houses and grounds, there would be no intervening time for rest and recuperation for the week's work which begins on Monday morning.

Moreover, many of the employes desire to devote a part of their Sundays to purposes other than either rest or amusement, including religious services, writing letters home and mending clothes.

In talking with many employes of all classes upon various subjects connected with recreation, there was brought to our attention a prevalent and spontaneous desire for the Saturday Half Holiday.

The consideration of the Saturday Half Holiday involves, we are aware, some rearrangement of the present weekly schedule. In order to secure the Saturday Half Holiday, it would not be feasible to add to the hours of work for five days in the week, inasmuch as the climatic conditions are such that the men should not work more than eight hours in any one day. This would necessitate a reduction of the weekly working hours which we believe to be warranted by the conditions.

Considering the amount of physical energy burned up in the work, we believe that the Government would be the actual gainer by the Saturday Half Holiday. The Government would apparently lose weekly the three (or four) hours' time of the salaried employes, plus the three (or four) hours' output of the larger body of employes paid by the hour. This loss of the Government would be offset by the fact that there would be introduced into the working force the element of stability, thus reducing to a minimum the continuous loss consequent upon the hiring and training of new workmen. On the other hand, the employes paid by the hour would lose weekly three (or four) hours' pay which, we believe, they would be willing to sacrifice.

We know of no other one proposition, outside of those considerations relating to shelter and food, so well calculated to make the mass of workers on the Isthmus contented and happy as the Saturday Half Holiday. The climate of the Isthmus is such as to make this weekly half holiday important, not only for recreation but, what is more important still, for health. The Saturday Half Holiday will, moreover, afford a distinct opportunity to bring together for outdoor sports and other recreation employes from places scattered along the route, thus encouraging a feeling of communal interest throughout the zone in the social life of all its communities and in the prosecution of the enterprise that binds them all together in a common purpose.

We regard this recommendation of the Saturday Half Holiday throughout the Canal Zone as of great importance. We most respectfully bespeak for it your earnest and full consideration as a measure that would conduce to the comfort, the health and the efficiency of the working population of the Isthmus.

Fourth of July Celebration.

We found abundant and enthusiastic evidence among the employes that the celebration of the Fourth of July this year was highly appreciated, and we recommend its continuance.

W. E. C. NAZRO,
E. A. MOFFETT.

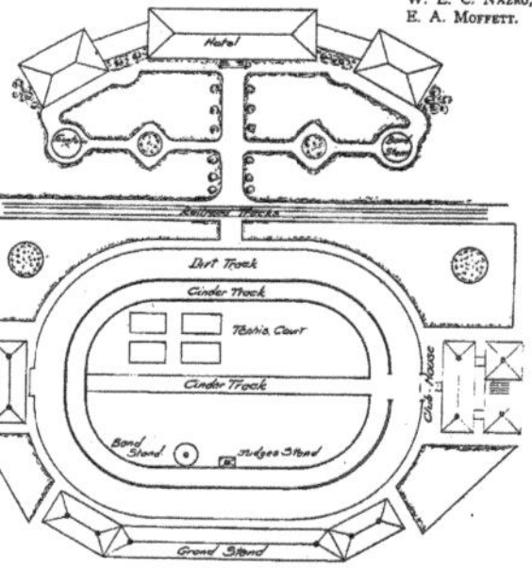

—EXHIBIT "D"—

SKETCH OF LAYOUT OF ATHLETIC FIELD AT COROZAL.

(Concluded from page 4.)

O. C. Edwards .... Montgomery.
George H. Child .... Harper's Ferry
J. R. Thomas .... Charleston.
I. Schwabe .... Charleston.
B. H. Blagg .... Point Pleasant.
James A. Oldfield .... St. Mary's.
R. Ad. Hall .... Weston.
Hon. John H. Holt .... Huntington.
Howard Sutherland .... Elkins.
Hon. P. W. Morris .... Parkersburg.
Hon. S. F. Reed .... Clarksburg.
Dr. M. S. Holt .... Weston.
Thomas A. Dennis .... Lewisburg.
D. G. Lilly .... Bluefield.
Rev. J. W. Telford .... Lewisburg.
Prest. D. B. Purinton .... Morgantown.
Hon. William G. Worley .... Kingwood.
Capt. J. K. Thompson .... Raymond City.
U. B. Buskirk .... Logan.
Hon. F. H. Evans .... Williamson.
Hon. George C. Baker .... Morgantown.
A. L. Craig .... Richwood.
Hon. Henry G. Davis .... Elkins.
Hon. S. B. Elkins .... Elkins.
Hon. James S. Lakin .... Terra Alta.
Phil. C. Adams .... Spencer.
Dr. J. D. Schmeid .... New Martinsville.
E. C. Gerwig .... Parkersburg.
M. P. Shawkey .... Charleston.
F. C. Bishop .... Morgantown.
William H. Prichard .... Wheeling.
Perry D. Burton .... Fairmont.
Hon. F. M. Gallagher .... Hinton.
Robert H. Williamson .... Huntington.
J. D. Prim .... Clarksburg.
T. M. Spaulding .... Raymond City.

WISCONSIN.

Appointed by Governor Robert M. La Follette.

Prof. John R. Commons .... Madison.
Rev. Frederick Edwards .... Milwaukee.
Rev. H. H. Jacobs .... Milwaukee.
Edward W. Frost .... Milwaukee.
Hon. P. B. Nelson .... Racine.
Hon. Burt Williams .... Ashland.
John Humphrey .... Milwaukee.
Hugh Carney .... Milwaukee.
Mark E. Bruce .... Stevens Point.
Ivar Kirkegaard .... Racine.

HAWAII.

Appointed by Governor G. R. Carter.

A. L. C. Atkinson, Secretary of Hawaii, and President Territorial Board of Immigration...... Honolulu.
(The names of the additional delegates will be announced later.)

The following have been appointed to represent the organizations preceding their names:

American Academy of Political and Social Science, Philadelphia.

Dr. Karl Kelsey, Assistant Professor of Sociology, University of Pennsylvania .... Philadelphia.
Dr. F. J. Warne, Editor of the *Railway World*, Philadelphia.
Dr. George Mangold, University of Pennsylvania, Philadelphia.
Dr. Walter E. Weyl, University Settlement. New York City.
Dr. William H. Allen, New York Association for Improving the Condition of the Poor..New York City.

Farmers' National Congress, Chicago.

Hon. E. W. Wickey .... Ocean Springs, Miss.
W. L. Ames .... Oregon, Wis.
Hon. Levi Morrison .... Greenville, Pa.
George M. Whitaker .... Boston, Mass.
John M. Stahl .... Chicago.

Trans-Mississippi Congress.

Theo. B. Wilcox .... Portland.
Herbert Strain .... Great Falls.
John W. Noble .... St. Louis.
Ed. F. Harris .... Galveston.
A. E. Carlton .... Cripple Creek.

Atlanta Chamber of Commerce.

S. D. Jones, President Atlanta Chamber of Commerce, Atlanta.
Marion M. Jackson, Lawyer .... Atlanta.
Col. B. F. Abbott, Lawyer .... Atlanta.
Forrest Adair .... Atlanta.

Detroit Board of Commerce.

M. J. Murphy .... Detroit.
George H. Barbour .... Detroit.
F. B. Smith .... Detroit.
W. P. Harris .... Detroit.

Japanese and Korean Exclusion League, San Francisco.

Walter Macarthur .... *Coast Seamen's Journal.*

New York Board of Trade and Transportation.

Albert Plant .... Manhattan.
John M. Peters .... Manhattan.
Ludwig Nissen .... Manhattan.
Charles E. Hanseit .... Manhattan.
Nils Poulson .... Brooklyn.

Chamber of Commerce of the State of New York, New York City.

A. Foster Higgins .... New York.
William Coverly .... New York.
James A. Wright .... New York.
John B. McDonald .... New York.
Marcus M. Marks .... New York.

American Economic Association, Cambridge, Mass.

Horace White, First Vice-President Economic Association .... New York City.
Professor H. W. Farnam, Yale University, New Haven, Conn.
Professor H. A. Garfield, Princeton University, Princeton, N. J.
Professor Willard Fisher, Wesleyan University, Middletown, Conn.
Professor G. A. Kleene, Trinity College, Hartford, Conn.

The Philadelphia Museums, Philadelphia.

William S. Harvey .... Philadelphia.
Daniel Baugh .... Philadelphia.
Henry R. Edmunds .... Philadelphia.
William W. Supplee .... Philadelphia.
Dr. W. P. Wilson .... Philadelphia.

St. Paul Board of Trade, St. Paul, Minn.

R. A. Durkee, President Board of Trade, St. Paul, Minn.

The American Bankers' Association, New York.

W. L. Moyer, President of the National Shoe and Leather Bank, Chairman .... New York City.
G. S. Whitson, Vice-President of the National City Bank and Vice-President of the American Bankers' Association .... New York City.
Homer W. McCoy, of MacDonald, McCoy & Company, Chicago, Illinois.
John L. Hamilton, Vice-President Hamilton & Cunningham and President of the American Bankers' Association .... Hoopestown, Illinois.
W. P. G. Harding, First National Bank, Birmingham, Ala.
Col. F. H. Fries, Wachovia Loan & Trust Company, Winston-Salem, North Carolina.

The Taxpayers' Association of Paterson, New Jersey.

W. O. Fayerweather, President .... Paterson.
Hon. Francis Scott, Judge Circuit Court.... Paterson.
Thomas P. Graham, Lawyer .... Paterson.
Joseph W. Congdon, President Phœnix Silk Manufacturing Company .... Paterson.
Isaac A. Hall, Manufacturer .... Paterson.

The Trades' League of Philadelphia.

Mahlon N. Kline .... Philadelphia.
Coleman Sellers, Jr. .... Philadelphia.
William McAleer .... Philadelphia.
Charles J. Cohen .... Philadelphia.
N. B. Kelly .... Philadelphia.

Baltimore Board of Trade.

Henry G. Hilken .... Baltimore.

The Commercial Club of Indianapolis.

Hon. John W. Kern .... Indianapolis, Ind.
(The names of the additional delegates will be announced later.)

The Merchants' Association of New York.

Henry A. Caesar .... New York City.
William F. King .... New York City.
George Frederick Vietor, Chairman, of Vietor & Achelis, New York City.
George C. Boldt, the Waldorf-Astoria, New York City.
Henry Sidenberg .... New York City.

Board of Trade of Jacksonville, Fla.

A. J. Mitchell .... Jacksonville.
Dexter Hunter .... Jacksonville.
D. C. Ambler .... Jacksonville.
Theo. G. Eger .... Jacksonville.
Geo. W. Haines .... Jacksonville.

The Portland Chamber of Commerce.

Dr. Stephen S. Wise .... Portland.
A. L. Mills .... Portland.

Board of Trade of Elizabeth, N. J.

James C. Connolly .... Elizabeth.
Lovell H. Carr .... Elizabeth.
Jos. McManus .... Elizabeth.
Elias D. Smith .... Elizabeth.
William F. Groves .... Elizabeth.

RHODE ISLAND WELCOMES THE CIVIC FEDERATION.

AN ENTHUSIASTIC MEETING AT THE PROVIDENCE BOARD OF TRADE ROOMS APPROVES ITS PURPOSE AND ITS METHODS.

(From the Providence *Journal*, October 28.)

The work of the National Civic Federation, especially in the "welfare department," was ably expounded and illustrated to the edification and interest of a good-sized gathering at the Providence Board of Trade last evening, the meeting being preliminary to the organization of a local branch in this State. Gov. Utter made a brief introductory address and Lieut. Gov. Jackson, as President of the Board of Trade, presided. The purpose and progress of the Federation were explained by Ralph M. Easley, Chairman of the executive committee of the organization, and Miss Gertrude Beeks, Secretary of the welfare department, the meeting being devoted principally to this feature of the work.

The fact impressed by the speakers, that the work of the Federation was designed to bring about harmony between capital and labor, among its other purposes, was well illustrated in the attendance at last evening's meeting. The gathering included representative business men, manufacturers and representatives of labor, among those present being Joseph Fletcher, Charles Sisson, of the Hope Webbing Company; J. F. P. Lawton, of the Gorham Manufacturing Company; John W. Danielson, of the Wauregan Mills; Hon. Augustus O. Bourne, of the Bourne Rubber Company; Charles Rockwell, of the Cranston Print Works; Jesse Metcalf, of the Wanskuck Mills; Henry C. Dexter, of Green and Daniels; Stephen A. Jenks, of the United States Cotton Company and the Fales & Jenks Machine Company; Arthur W. Dennis, of the Elmwood Mills; Jere Campbell, of the Eastern Coal Company; George E. Brady, International President of the Jewelry Workers; R. A. Ripley, Secretary of the Electrical Workers; Union; James Coleman, business agent of the Plumbers' Union, and Thomas F. Kearney, President of the Rhode Island Building Trades Council.

Lieut. Gov. Jackson called the meeting to order, and with a few introductory remarks presented Gov. Utter, who likewise spoke briefly, as he had another engagement and was obliged to leave early. In part he said:

"I feel that I can scarcely do more than act as curtain raiser for the principal speakers of this evening, but I want to express my admiration for the movement of which you are to hear a description. When I was a young man there used to be in Westerly a lawyer, of whom, when he died, the Providence *Journal* said: 'Nathan F. Dixon may have done very little toward making legislation, but he did a great deal to prevent bad legislation. He was a good lawyer and he always did what he could to keep his clients from getting into court, to avert needless litigation.' In other words, his effort was ever to maintain harmony, a purpose that actuates this Civic Federation.

"It is natural for a man to look first to the welfare of his own family, but men should teach their children that not only does their responsibility lie toward the family but to the people at large. Selfishness is absolutely essential to the welfare of the world, but the selfishness that looks only to self is a detriment. Any organization that can enable men to see things with a common eye, without conflict, can accomplish great good for a community. It seems to me that this is the work being done by the Civic Federation. It is regrettable that we have not had a definite form of this line of work in this State, and I sincerely hope that this meeting tonight may result in the organization of a local branch of the National Federation."

The Governor was greeted with hearty applause as he rose to speak, and again as he concluded his remarks. The Lieutenant Governor then introduced Mr. Easley, who explained the purposes of the organization he represents as follows:

What is the purpose of the National Civic Federation? What terms accurately define its mission, its scope and its methods? These questions are pertinent, for the reason that the prominence accorded to a single branch of its work has so attracted attention as to convey to the public mind an erroneous impression of the real scope of the organization. The organization has been especially active during the past three years in advocating rightful relations between capital and labor, as a means of promoting industrial peace. Hence has arisen, quite naturally, a prevalent conception of the National Civic Federation as a body dealing exclusively with strikes and lock-outs and with the questions underlying these industrial disturbances; whereas this work is confined to certain of its Departments. A part has thus come to appear greater than the whole. Again, it is not infrequently described as a Board of Arbitration, which is as far from the fact as possible.

The broad and original purpose and scope of the organization are thus set forth in its by-laws, as adopted in 1901:

"The purpose of the National Civic Federation is to organize the best brains of the nation in an educational movement toward the solution of some of the great problems related to social and industrial progress;

"To provide for study and discussion of questions of national import;

"To aid thus in the crystallization of the most enlightened public opinion; and, when desirable,

"To promote legislation in accordance therewith."

The present activities of the Civic Federation, of which the above definition permits further extension, are exercised through the following agencies:

Public Ownership Commission.
Immigration Department.
Conciliation Department.
Industrial Economic Department.
Welfare Department.
Taxation Department.

There exist, with results of acknowledged benefit and usefulness, organizations of farmers, mine operators, manufacturers, wage-earners, financiers, merchants, lawyers, scientists and other distinct but interacting elements of society. All these hold meetings for discussion of affairs peculiar to their own pursuits and callings. The National Civic Federation, in addition to its Departments for the elucidation of specified subjects, provides a forum where representatives of all these industrial, professional, commercial, scientific and other societies may meet to discuss national problems in which they have a common ethical, social or economic interest.

The membership of the National Civic Federation renders its auspices especially appropriate to such a forum. It is drawn from practical men of affairs whose acknowledged leadership in thought and action makes them typical representatives of the various elements that voluntarily work together for the general good. Its national executive committee is constituted of three factors: the general public, represented by the church, the bar, the press, statesmanship and finance; employers, represented by the heads of great corporations, large manufacturers and chiefs of employers' organizations; and labor, represented by the principal officials of national and international organizations of wage-earners in every great industry.

The actual benefit to the entire community of public discussions initiated and conducted by the Federation has been thoroughly established by the practical results of five national Conferences which have already been held under its auspices.

The first of these, the Conference on Primary Election Reform, was held in New York City in January, 1898. This was the first National Conference ever held on this subject. Its discussions brought out in vivid relief both existing evils and their appropriate remedies. Direct results were the improved primary election laws of New York and Illinois and the formation of a national organization to promote this specific reform in other States. Another Conference upon this subject has been called to meet in New York, January 15 and 16, 1906. Its discussions will embrace such topics as ballot reform, primary election reform, corrupt practises acts and naturalization.

The second, known as the "Saratoga Conference on Foreign Policy," was held at Saratoga Springs, N. Y., in August, 1898. Its date was most felicitous, being almost coincident with the advance of the United States Government to the rank of a great world-power, and with the advent of its extra-continental expansion. Public men of widely divergent views participated in its debates during two days, when they were able to agree upon a memorial. Its presentation to President McKinley elicited the following response:

"I heartily congratulate the Civic Federation upon the success of its conference. It came at a time when its able discussions and conservative resolutions did much to point the way for the nation."

This memorial asked the President to instruct the representatives of the United States at the first Hague Conference, called by the Czar, to urge the establishment of a court of international arbitration and to obtain a declaration in favor of the protection of private property at sea in time of war. It is now an historical fact that the proceedings of the first conference at The Hague were along these lines.

The third Civic Federation Conference, known as the "Chicago Conference on Trusts," was held in September, 1899. Its sessions, covering four days, were attended by more than five hundred delegates, appointed by Governors of States and by organizations representing commerce, labor, agriculture, finance, economics and the professions. Its discussions, published in book form, have furnished the basis for much of the subsequent literature upon the subject.

The fourth Conference, on "Conciliation and Arbitration," was held in Chicago in December, 1900. Its participants included official representatives of all the organizations of employers in the United States, and of practically all the national labor unions. After two days' discussion of the relations between employers and wage-earners, which brought out clearly the principle of conference and conciliation, with the trade agreement as their object, this Conference took action which resulted in the organization of an Industrial Department of the National Civic Federation. It was the first annual meeting of this Department, in New York City, in 1901, that attracted the attention of the public to this one phase of the work of the Federation—the promotion of industrial peace.

The fifth national Conference, that upon "Taxation," was held in Buffalo, N. Y., in May, 1901. More than three hundred delegates, appointed by thirty-one Governors, attended. The call for this Conference, issued by the National Civic Federation and signed by many men prominent in legislation, economics, finance and commerce, set forth the necessity for considering the problem of taxation as no longer local, but as involving the mutual relations of localities and communities as well as the complications of interstate taxation. The two days' discussion dealt with such subjects as the interstate taxation of public service corporations; the taxation of personal property; the taxation of mortgages; the separation of State and local revenues; the taxation of the farmer; the equitable assessment of real property; the inheritance tax; the taxation of corporations; the franchise tax; the income tax. The published proceedings of this Conference have afforded valuable guidance for legislation affecting sources of public revenue. A Department on Taxation, organized at this Conference, has issued several educational bulletins looking to uniformity of legislation.

At the present time the National Civic Federation is engaged, in addition to its continual departmental work, upon the subjects of Public Ownership and Operation, and of Immigration.

It has formed a National Commission to make a thorough investigation in this country and abroad of the ownership of public utilities. This Commission held its first meeting in Earl Hall, Columbia University, New York City, on October 5, 1905. The Commission elected also an Executive Committee and a Committee of Twenty-one on Investigation.

The current discussion and acute agitation of this subject indicate its hold upon the popular mind, and the necessity for its analytical and comprehensive examination. Its present debate is often inconclusive, because of contradictory or unsatisfactory statements of fact. It is intended, therefore, that this investigation shall disclose the actual results of public ownership and operation, as far as they have been undertaken in the United States, and of their more extensive practise in foreign countries. The ascertainment of these facts will afford a solid basis upon which to found discussion and conclusions for the guidance of future policy.

The scope of this inquiry will cover the relative advantages of Public Ownership and Operation, as compared with Public Ownership and Private Operation, and Private Ownership and Operation. Each system will be examined with regard to its effect upon, among other topics:

Wages, hours and conditions of labor;
Collective bargaining;
Cost and character of service;
Political conditions, civil service, spoils system, and municipal operation;
Financial results;
Taxation.

The Committee of Twenty-one which will report to the general Commission has divided itself into two Subcommittees, which will carry on simultaneously the domestic and foreign investigations. The initial inquiry will be restricted to the comparative results of private and public ownership and operation of gas, water, electric power and light and street railways.

A National Conference upon Immigration will be held in New York December 6, 7, and 8, to which the Governors of the various States and national, commercial, economic and ecclesiastical organizations will send delegates.

The problem of immigration in its relation to our industrial and social prosperity will be considered. In its promotion of this conference, the National Civic Federation has committed itself to no attitude of approval or opposition as to any of the propositions concerning the regulation, restriction, suspension, exclusion, or encouragement of immigration that have been advocated. The Conference will be an open forum for debate by the best thought of the country in the hope that an earnest thrashing out of every phase of the subject may result in definite recommendations of far-reaching consequence and value to our national welfare. The discussion will include the effectiveness of the administration of existing legislation and propositions for new legislation. Especial consideration will be given to the relation of alien labor to domestic crafts, the industrial progress of the negro and other questions growing out of the distribution of incoming aliens. One entire day will be devoted to the consideration of the Asiatic phase of the problem.

Three departments of the National Civic Federation are devoted entirely to the so-called labor problem. These are the Conciliation Department, the Industrial Economic Department and the Welfare Department.

The Conciliation Department deals entirely with strikes, lock-outs and trade agreements. In averting or settling strikes or lock-outs, the services of this Department, during the last four years, have been enlisted in about 500 cases, involving practically every conceivable problem or phase of a problem interwoven with or underlying an industrial controversy. Out of this experience, the lesson has been well learned that in the great majority of cases thus treated publicity is not desirable. This is usually true both during and after the negotiations in relation to any labor trouble. The work of the Department is often of so delicate a nature that publicity during its progress would defeat its very purpose; and even after its successful conclusion it has been found that both employers and employed are often averse to having the private adjustment of their relations paraded before the public. A report of the work of this Department could be made very impressive if it were to enumerate names and dates; but in most cases the statement would be displeasing to both parties concerned. Out of the 500 cases treated, probably 100 have been made public by one or the other or both of the parties; but only when publicity originates with one of them does information reach the press. Thus the public, which always receives an abundance of information, more or less accurate, about a strike, may hear nothing at all about the inner negotiations resulting in its settlement; or the public may be wholly uninformed about the quiet but effective measures taken to prevent a strike which, had it occurred, would have filled columns of the newspapers, while causing enormous inconvenience and incalculable loss.

The usual method of procedure by this Department is greatly facilitated by the character of its membership, which extends to every industrial center, and includes representatives of both practically all the organizations of employers and the organizations of wage-earners in the country. Through this membership information of any threatened trouble between capital and labor usually reaches the headquarters, from one side or the other, in advance of any public rupture. The headquarters thus serves as a clearing house where industrial news is focalized. This early intelligence is of the utmost value, since the best time to adjust a dispute is before a rupture occurs. In accordance with this information, usually two members of the Conciliation Department, who are likely to be personae gratae to either or both the employer and the employes, are assigned to the case—an employer to the employer's side and a labor representative to the employes' side. These two members, exercising special precaution against any suspicion of meddlesome interference, unobtrusively get into touch with the situation, personally and unofficially. The two investigators then consult, usually with a view to bring about a conference between representatives of the two sides. When it can be ascertained that a conference will be granted by either side, the other side is usually willing to make the request. Sometimes at such a conference the committee of our Department is present, and sometimes not. That depends entirely upon circumstances and the temper of the opponents. In many cases, the parties in interest could not entertain the idea of inviting any outside person to be present. They avail themselves of the services of the committee up to the very point of a conference; but when that has been arranged, the two sides feel competent to discuss their affairs without further aid, and the members of the committee are only too glad not to be needed. In some other cases, their presence at the conference is desired, and is found useful in allaying temper, soothing the pride of obstinacy or pointing the way to compromise without impairing self-respect or wounding dignity. In one controversy a year ago, between two organizations representing respectively 95 per cent. of the capital invested and 95 per cent. of the labor employed in an entire industry, the Chairman and Secretary of the Conciliation Committee acted in these capacities at a conference running through eight consecutive days, and lasting frequently from 10 o'clock in the morning until from 10 to 12 o'clock at night. This conference resulted in an annual national trade agreement, which was renewed last spring. Other conferences have resulted in trade agreements for a year which, upon expiration, have to be worked out afresh.

A concrete example of this method occurred only last week. The members of one of the great railway brotherhoods employed upon a street railway system in one of the largest cities in the United States, believing that they were suffering serious grievances, were on the very verge of a strike that would have tied up immense traffic and caused great inconvenience to many thousands of passengers. The national chief of the brotherhood involved, being a member of the Civic Federation, brought the threatened trouble to the attention of the Conciliation Department. One of its members promptly arranged a face-to-face conference between the chief of the brotherhood and the president of the corporation, and the difficulty was quickly adjusted. Not one of the daily passengers upon that road ever heard of the impending strike, although it was averted by a margin of only a few hours.

At all times the Conciliation Department advocates the making of trade agreements, having a special committee for their study and encouragement. Their advocacy is warranted by experience in their operation in both the United States and England during more than fifty years, which has proved them the best practical method where organization exists, of reducing industrial disturbances to a minimum. Trade agreements now obtain in practically all the great basic industries, such as coal, iron, lumber and transportation, between employers and national organizations of labor. Each party to these agreements has at various times undergone successfully the strain of granting higher wages on the one side and of accepting lower wages on the other. The honorable maintenance of these agreements in the great industries is an object lesson that is aiding much in the education of other employers and labor organizations into a realization of the inviolability of the collective contract. The use of trade agreements is extending among the building trades, the great daily newspapers and manufacture in many industries.

In averting or settling controversies upon the great railway systems with the brotherhoods of engineers, firemen and trainmen, thus affecting the industries dependent upon transportation in practically every State of the Union; in promoting agreements between the longshoremen and vessel-owners, vitally related to all the industries in shipping, such as coal, iron, steel, lumber and the elevator interests; in adjusting street railway troubles in San Francisco, New Orleans, Chicago, Pittsburg, New York, Newark and other cities; in averting troubles in the teaming industry in several large cities; in improving relations and averting strikes in many branches of manufacture, such as textiles, garment-making, boots and shoes, the metal trades, including machinists, molders, steel and iron workers, structural steel and bridge workers, blacksmiths, etc.; in promoting agreements between coal operators and miners; in bringing about contractual relations between the thirty-four crafts grouped as the building trades and the corresponding associations of employers; in establishing agreement between theatrical managers and musicians and actors throughout the country; in securing more than two hundred conferences, at the request of one side or the other, thus checking as many controversies at their incipient stage—in these and in many other directions the Conciliation Department has exerted an influence repeatedly effective for peace in industries widely diversified and of national magnitude. There have arisen cases where the spirit of antagonism on both sides has been so aroused, and where the issues presented were so utterly irreconcilable, that there seemed no recourse but to fight it out.

The Department of Industrial Economics was formed to meet the plain necessity for more light upon the principles underlying the ever recurring problems that are encountered in the work of the Conciliation Department. When once representatives of employers and employed are brought into conference for the purpose of making a trade agreement, these problems invariably arise in multifarious forms. They demand knowledge among the negotiators of such industrial subjects as "Wages and Cost of Living," "The Shorter Work-Day," "The Open and Closed Shop," "The Minimum Wage," "Restriction of Output," "The Ratio of Apprentices," "The Introduction of Machinery," "Piece-Work and Day Work," "Arbitration," etc. The drawing of any collective contract implies contact with any one of these or many other questions. For example, in the joint convention of 1904 between the organized bituminous operators of Illinois, Indiana, Ohio and Pennsylvania, and the United Mine Workers of America, the whole controversy revolved around the question of wages. The operators advanced the industrial depression then existing as making necessary a reduction of wages of 10 per cent. John Mitchell, speaking for the Union, said: "If you reduce the wages of our 500,000 members, you will reduce correspondingly their consuming power, thus making the business situation worse, instead of better." Francis L. Robbins, speaking for the employing operators, replied that if that were sound philosophy, the thing to do when panic threatened was to double the wages of workingmen. Many other instances might be cited where able disputants have differed about fundamental principles. In most cases, out of their debates light has been evolved.

To further earnest, intellectual discussion of practical economic problems, the Department of Industrial Economics was formed in 1905. Its membership is composed of leading economists, including the heads of the departments of political economy in universities, lecturers and economic and legal authors; editors of the daily press, of politico-social magazines, of trade papers and of labor journals; representatives of the pulpit; large employers and representatives of labor. This Department will soon announce a program for the discussion, by the ablest experts to be procured, of each of the vital and frequently irritating questions that arise in the Conciliation Department.

The Welfare Department is devoted entirely to efforts to interest employers in giving especial consideration to the physical, mental and moral welfare of employes in all industries. Membership in the Welfare Department is confined to employers. While the work in the other Departments deals with controversies and may be itself controversial, as in the Industrial Economic Department, the dominant note in the Welfare Department is that of the highest altruism; yet is its work intensely practical. In extending the practise of Welfare Work, the Department has found of especial value conferences of employers, held under its auspices in different parts of the country, for the interchange of experiences. Conferences for a similar purpose are also held between Welfare Managers. Successful Welfare Work, when pictured by practical business men in connection with their own industries, exerts an influence toward gaining the application of similar ideas by other employers. Thus Welfare Work is not advocated alone by theorists and philanthropists. The Welfare Department maintains a bureau at the National Civic Federation headquarters, where information about the work is furnished and exchanged. The Department also undertakes to supply, upon request, experts qualified to examine industrial establishments, make suitable recommendations for the introduction of Welfare Work and, if required, superintend its installation. Recently, for example, the Department, at the request of the Isthmian Canal Commission, furnished two Welfare experts to investigate the needs and opportunities for the recreation of the workers engaged in canal construction. Their report, which has been made to the Commission, is designed to promote the contentment and happiness, conducive to effectiveness, of thousands of Government employes in a trying climate and amid novel environments.

The Welfare Department gives special consideration to the following topics:

Light and Ventilation;
Drinking Water;
Locker and Wash Rooms;
Seats;
Laundry;
Lunch Rooms;
Rest Rooms;
Fire Protection;
Elevators;
Street Cars;
Suggestions;
Recreation;
Educational;
Boarding Houses;
Housing;
Pensions and Relief Associations;
Banks.

The chief mission of the National Civic Federation being educational, it presents accounts of much of its work in a monthly periodical, entitled The National Civic Federation Review. This publication is now recognized as a valuable contribution to the economic literature of the world. It is sent to the principal libraries and educational institutions of every country; to the executive and departmental officials of every nation; to the headquarters of all professional, literary and scientific societies; to organizations, both national and local, of employers and of employes; and to thousands of editors, clergymen, educators and other leaders of thought in the professions, commerce, finance and industry. The Review has become a far-reaching educational force in the elucidation of all great public questions.

It is hoped that this statement will make clear the broadly educational purposes of the National Civic Federation and that it will enlist the earnest cooperation of those who are interested in elucidating vital social and industrial problems whose thorough comprehension is essential to national progress.

Miss Beeks was then introduced and was greeted with applause. Her talk was entirely of the work of the welfare department, and was accompanied by more than 100 fine stereopticon views showing actual conditions in scores of factories and industrial concerns of various kinds. The wonderful improvement made in provision for the comfort, health and pleasure of employes in many places was admirably illustrated, and among the model places shown were views of what has been done in this line by several local concerns, notably the Gorham Manufacturing Company and the Brown & Sharpe Manufacturing Company.

The views as illuminated by the speaker's explanations proved highly instructive, and the remark of Mr. Jackson at the close to the effect that "the world, as well as the sun, do move," was undoubtedly echoed by all present. The Lieutenant Governor said that he wished that Infantry Hall might have been filled with all classes of men and women to see the work that has been accomplished. Miss Beeks was given a rising vote of thanks at the conclusion of her talk.

Last evening's meeting was held largely through the efforts of Col. George H. Webb, Commissioner of Industrial Statistics, who in his forthcoming annual report will have a chapter devoted to what has been accomplished in this State along the line of work followed by the welfare department of the Federation. It is probable that within a week or two a local branch of the National Civic Federation will be formed in this State. Messrs. Joseph Fletcher, Rowland G. Hazard and J. F. P. Lawton are already members of the organization.

A GRAPHIC TALE OF FUTILE EFFORTS AGAINST RUINOUS COMPETITION.

CAPITAL, LABOR AND MERCHANTS SUFFER COMMON INJURY THROUGH THEIR UNIQUE ATTEMPT AT ARTIFICIAL REGULATION OF AN INDUSTRY.

The eleventh special Report of the United States Commissioner of Labor, upon "Regulation and Restriction of Output," is a volume of nearly one thousand pages. Yet its bulk is not sufficient to permit of a really exhaustive treatment of a subject whose ramifications are exceedingly numerous and complex. But so far as it goes, this Report is of great interest and value to the student of both industrial and commercial conditions. It is a work of experts. It was prepared, when Carroll D. Wright was Commissioner of Labor, in the main by Prof. John R. Commons, now of the University of Wisconsin, assisted by John H. Gray, Ph. D., who collected the data for England; Walter E. Weyl, Ph.D., who dealt especially wth the anthracite industry; and several special agents, including Ethelbert Stewart, Walter B. Palmer and Henry T. Buffington. The introduction to the report frankly states that it is impossible to present a complete summary of the evidence, "for the conditions are so widely different in various industries and in different localities in the same industry that a summary would be misleading." It has been thought best, therefore, for the purpose of conveying to the readers of THE REVIEW a conception of the method and results of the investigation into this subject, to republish the entire chapter upon the Window Glass Industry, which stands by itself as an absorbing narrative of attempted combination between manufacturers, jobbers and wage-earners, with its effects upon all three interests.

THE WINDOW GLASS INDUSTRY.

THE conditions in the manufacture of window glass have peculiar features not found in any other industry investigated for this report. It is the only industry where the workmen, through their organization, have attempted to join with the employers to regulate the total output of the industry according to the varying states of the market. By reason of thus entering the province of the manufacturer the history of the restrictions on output in this industry is a history of the alliances of various associations of employers with associations of workmen. More than this, the associated jobbers and wholesale dealers have become parties to the agreements, and the regulation of output has been temporarily determined by the joint action of skilled workmen, manufacturers and jobbers. The varied interests, internal dissensions, and changing market conditions have caused kaleidoscopic changes in these arrangements, and at the present time (March, 1904) alliances are broken and the output is unregulated as far as joint action of the three interests is concerned. But for more than twenty years some form of regulation, alternating with unrestricted competition, has been going on.

It is firmly believed by all parties in the trade that the peculiar nature and situation of the industry made regulation and restriction of output necessary. They point out in the first place, that the market for window glass is wholly inexpansive or inelastic. That is, consumers can not be induced, even by the most extreme concessions in prices, to take a larger stock than they will take when prices are held up. This is because the market is almost wholly that furnished by the building trades, and the amount of window glass that will be purchased depends on the amount of building construction that is going on. The cost of the window glass for a building can scarcely exceed 1 per cent., or 2 per cent., of the total cost of the building, and an extreme change in the price of so small an item has no appreciable effect on the amount of construction. A concession of 50 per cent. in the price of window glass will not stimulate owners to construct more buildings, neither will a doubling of the price restrain them. Retail dealers and local builders can not be tempted to lay in a stock at low prices in anticipation of a rise, because they do not know how much or what sizes they will want. The building industry is itself largely speculative, and therefore subject to extreme fluctuations. The annual demand for window glass in recent years has fluctuated from 4,000,000 to 6,000,000 boxes, irrespective of prices, so the jobbers and manufacturers say. Now, the manufacturing capacity of the country, amounting to 4,000 pots, is enough to supply this demand in three or four months. Owing to the restriction on membership and apprenticeship imposed by the organizations, there are only about 2,500 window glass blowers in the country, so that 1,500 pots are idle on that account. Yet this number of blowers is enough to supply the country's demand in four to six months, their output being about 1,000,000 boxes a month when they are all at work. Altogether the consequence is that while the factories are working, the output is beyond the current demand for building, and the stock is piling up in the hands of the manufacturers, unless they can get the jobbers to help them carry it. In either case the carrying charges are heavy, and the weaker manufacturers, if they are compelled to sell, must do so at a destructive sacrifice, the jobbers not being willing to take their product when the consumers are not ready to buy. Price cutting at such times becomes utterly reckless, and, frequently, the weaker producers go to the wall. Frequent repetition of these experiences has firmly convinced the trade, all the way from workman to jobber, that restriction, or what they call regulation, of output is necessary for the protection of all. In general this regulation has been brought about in three ways, namely, by limiting the maximum output per week of each blower, by limiting the number of blowers, so that there are not enough to operate all of the pots and pot capacity, and by alliances of the unions with leading manufacturers to force a shut down of the independent manufacturers when stocks accumulate.

The window glass workers' organization began its restrictive policies in 1879, instituting the July and August shut downs. In the spring of 1879 the union passed the law restricting the output of workmen while at work, this restriction to take effect September 1, 1879. Curiously enough, this was the first year of wage agreements with the employers; and it is stated that the restrictions grew out of the demoralized conditions of trade. The manufacturers had failed to prevent destructive competition, and as a solution of troubles occurring in 1877, the union undertook to unify conditions to the extent at least of fixing the running time of all plants alike, settling an equal

JOHN R. COMMONS,
Professor Political Economy, University of Wisconsin.

amount of output per blower, and hence per pot capacity, for each; and in addition to this it gave a differential to the localities where coal was most expensive, so as to even up conditions as much as possible. Prior to 1879 the length of fire had been a go-as-you-please, and so had the output of the workmen. There was a summer vacation tradition in the industry, and few houses attempted to run without a stop. These stops varied in length and occurred sometimes in winter, when the men could work best, and then the plant would run during the summer, when the work was hardest on the blowers. The union set the limit at ten months of work, and required all plants to close from June 30 to September 1. A few of the larger plants objected to this, but it was accepted without strike. This was changed later to read: "From June 15 to September 15;" and in recent years the length of fire is fixed annually and made part of the wage-scale agreement.

At the outset of restriction (1879) the summer shut down was made a constitutional provision by the union and was intended to make a uniform working period for the men and factories, and incidentally to limit production. In practise it is found necessary to close down each year for needed repairs and changes. Especially is this true in pot furnaces, and all were pot furnaces in those days. July and August are especially disagreeable months for the working glass blower, and since shut downs were necessary it was decided that they must occur and all repairs be made during these months. With the increase in productive capacity in the United States the shut down became more and more a means to reduce the general output. The fire of 1885 was the last ten months' fire in the industry as a whole. The constitutional provision was changed to read: "Blowers or gatherers shall not work from June 15 to September 15," thus shortening the fire to nine months. With the opening of the gas fields and the increase in furnaces, and especially with the organization of manufacturers into associations, came the further shortening of the fire.

There are four trades in the window glass workers' organization which, prior to 1880, were organized in separate trade unions with unrelated sections known as east and west. In 1880 these unions were consolidated in one organization, Local Assembly 300, Knights of Labor, and this organization remains to the present time as the only strong union among glass workers that has retained its allegiance to the Knights and has refused to go over to the American Federation of Labor. The four trades referred to are the blowers, gatherers, flatteners, and cutters. The gatherer takes the molten glass from the pot or tank; the blower shapes it in long "rollers"; the flattener smooths out the sheet in a hot oven after the snapper has cut off the ends to form a cylinder and has slit it down the side, and the cutter cuts it into commercial sizes.

On the side of the manufacturers the leading combinations in recent years have been the American Glass Company, organized in 1895 and reorganized as the American Window Glass Company in 1899. This corporation was a consolidation of the more prominent survivors of the preceding period of price war. As a result of the shortage of men the company entered into a contract with Local Assembly 300 by which a block of stock, whose par value was $500,000, was placed in trust for the union, to be paid for out of accruing dividends, and the union was to have representation upon the board of directors of the corporation. The whole transaction was conditioned upon Local Assembly 300 furnishing this corporation an adequate number of skilled men to run its plants to their full capacity during the "length of fire" agreed upon each year. The Assembly accepted the stock and elected its president, Mr. Simon Burns, as its representative on the board of directors. The attempt to carry out this arrangement disrupted the union and caused the formation of another organization, which at first contested for the right to the title Local Assembly 300, Knights of Labor, but, being defeated in this contention, took the name of "Window Glass Workers' Association of America." This organization immediately advocated longer fires and a fair show for the independent manufacturers. Had it not been for this split in Local Assembly 300 the independents would have been deprived of a large proportion of their workmen. As it was, their plants were manned by the new organization, and at a later date Local Assembly 300, being unable to fulfil its part of the contract, forfeited its block of stock and its representation on the board of directors.

The independents being able to continue in business, a bitter war of price cutting was kept up. Jobbers took more glass than consumers could handle, and their business also suffered heavy losses. The jobbers were organized in an association which was closely affiliated with the American Company, and, indeed, was created on the suggestion of that corporation. The independents, thus threatened with a loss of their workmen on the one hand and a loss of their markets on the other, and fighting between themselves, were forced to unite in a pool to protect themselves. This they did in December, 1900, and then the American Company, "realizing the folly of senseless competition, joined with them in a share-and-share-alike agreement."

The Independent Glass Company was not a manufacturing corporation, but a selling agency, designed to regulate the output of its members. Each firm subscribed for as many shares of $300 each as its pot capacity, which thereupon became a pledge or forfeit, binding the firm to obey the orders of the board of directors. The entire product of each firm was turned over to the company and paid for at a rate agreed upon. It then became the property of the company, to be sold, marketed, and handled with the product of the other firms. Each firm retained the management of its plant as before, except that the board of directors of the parent company had authority to designate, by a majority vote, the time for starting in the fall and shutting down in the summer, thus regulating the output for all. The board of directors was composed of one representative from each firm. This form of organization to control output was similar to that of the American Glass Company, which had preceded the American Window Glass Company. It was to expire by limitation in January, 1903.

These two combinations of manufacturers controlled about 90 per cent. of the window glass capacity of the country.

The workmen were also divided into camps, like the manufacturers — operating, respectively, the plants of each combine. Local Assembly 300, Knights of

Labor (hereafter called the old organization), manned the plants of the American Company, with a contract to furnish an adequate supply of competent workmen, while the Window Glass Workers' Association (hereafter called the new organization) manned all but three of the plants of the Independent Company. The American Company had an agreement with the old organization for a seven months' fire ending April 15, 1901.

The jobbers were organized as the National Wholesale Glass Jobbers' Association, with a New Jersey charter, the organization including every important jobber in the country. Each jobber took stock in the association to the amount of $1,500, and the board of directors had authority, in case a jobber violated the rules regarding prices, to call for his stock, refund his money, and thus drop him from the organization. The association employed a president, on a salary, to attend to the purchase and apportionment of glass. There were two committees, a Western and an Eastern, dealing with the president. The object of the jobbers' association was to make their purchases in a lump from the manufacturers and then apportion the boxes among themselves. The first purchase was 750,000 boxes, in January, 1901, at a price 30 per cent. in advance of the preceding unregulated scales, and this was furnished by the two companies of manufacturers in a proportion agreed upon between themselves. The second purchase was made in March, when 1,000,000 boxes were taken at a further advance of 25 per cent. The jobbers' association became practically the sole selling and distributing agent of the two combines. A jobber not a member of the association, or expelled from it, could nominally purchase glass from the combines, but he would be in the position of a small purchaser at higher prices, which practically shut him out of business. Such jobbers could look only to the small number of manufacturers outside the combines, and these were not then in a position to deliver a large amount of glass.

But new conditions rapidly developed. The increase in prices was a strong motive to outsiders to build new factories, and the shortening of the fire alarmed many of the ablest and most responsible workmen. The latter went in considerable numbers into a new movement which had heretofore been experimented upon in a few cases successfully, namely, the building of cooperative factories. The workmen put in a certain amount of capital, secured a loan of the balance and elected one of their number manager. As the cost of a twelve-pot furnace—the usual size—is but a moderate figure, this form of independent action extended, until at the present time (1904) there are forty-three cooperative factories in different parts of the Middle West. Other outsiders started up, and in January, 1902, the American and Independent Companies were operating but 60 per cent. of the total number of pots in actual operation.

The cooperatives were opposed to an early stop, but an arrangement was made in 1901 by which practically all of the factories were shut down in May. It was found that both the jobbers and the manufacturers could not dispose of their stocks, and an agreement was made with the unions to advance wages 10 per cent., if they would close three-fourths of the outsiders in May. The cooperatives were placated by a contract to purchase their product for the next year, and were paid $250 per pot as a bonus in lieu of the profits they expected to make by running to the end of June. This agreement was carried out, and by the first of June, a month earlier than the regular close, not only had the combines shut down, but the unions had withdrawn their men from practically all of the outside factories, notwithstanding in the wage scale they had agreed to work until the end of June.

The wage scales agreed upon at this time for the fire of 1901-02, besides the 10 per cent. advance, provided for an eight months' fire, beginning September 15 and running to May 15. Before the date for starting, it became evident that consumers were not buying sufficient glass to warrant a start on the date arranged, and the two combines decided to postpone it to November 1. The American paid its men one-half "market money" to hold them till that time, and the cooperatives were persuaded to postpone starting till October 15. A small number of factories and workmen could not be restrained from starting the last week in September.

During the course of this season's fire the Independent Company, which was manned by the new organization whose men had declared for longer fires, announced its withdrawal from the restrictive agreement. There followed one of the most remarkable of industrial battles. The American Company joined forces with the cooperative factories, which had now in their turn organized a selling agency called the Federation Window Glass Company, which was designed to regulate output in a manner similar to that followed by the Independent Company. These cooperative factories were manned by members of the old organization (L. A. 300). This year it was agreed to shut down the factories manned by the old organization on May 24, the consideration being another increase of 10 per cent. in the wage scale for the year 1902-03. The old organization fulfilled its part and shut down the majority of the outsiders as well as three factories belonging to the Independent Company. The new organization of workmen had made an agreement with the Independent Company to work full nine months, but did not, however, secure the 10 per cent. advance granted by the American and the Federation Companies.

In the season of 1902-03 a still greater surplus stock of glass accumulated in the hands of the companies and jobbers. An early closing seemed necessary and, while the agreement of Local Assembly 300 provided that the blast should terminate May 27, 1903, the three combines shut down on or before April 18, and the old organization adopted a resolution inviting or ordering others to do the same.

The general business conditions became serious during the year 1903 and the conflict between the two labor organizations, after a temporary truce, broke out afresh. The contention turned solely on the question whether the unions should assist the manufacturers in restricting output, the old organization favoring such a policy and the new one opposing it. Wage scales were made and the members violated them by private agreements. The scales were then cancelled and lower ones accepted, and the old union made an agreement to go 5 per cent. below the wage scale of the new organization "no matter how low they go, said reductions to take effect on same day and date as their reduction." The manufacturers no longer maintain their agreements and are selling directly to jobbers as best they can, and the jobbers' association has suspended activity and stopped expenses.

This much of the recent history of the window glass industry has seemed to be in place in order to show definitely the peculiar policy of the union for the time being in going beyond the ordinary forms of restriction on output and joining with the manufacturers in attempting to control the commercial side of the business. As already stated, such a policy has not been found in any other industry. In this case it disrupted the union, caused many of its best members to venture their savings in cooperative experiments, produced an oversupply of factories, many of them projected for speculative purposes, and finally ended in reductions of wages and a suicidal wage-cutting war, exactly similar to the price-cutting war of the manufacturers.

SECRETARY OF THE EXECUTIVE COMMITTEE.

Theodore Hardee, who has been elected Secretary of the Executive Committee of the National Civic Federation, comes to that position from Portland, Oregon. There he was assistant to the President of the Lewis and Clarke Centennial Exposition, his duties including the care and entertainment of distinguished guests, and the arrangement of social functions of an official character. Mr. Hardee's previous experience has developed his qualities of tact and executive ability. After a tour of South America, he read law in California, and in 1900 became an official in the Post Office Department. He accompanied President McKinley during his visit to the Pacific coast. Afterward he was detailed as assistant secretary of the United States delegation to the Pan-American Congress in Mexico, where he was also special correspondent of the New Orleans *Times-Democrat.*

THEODORE HARDEE.
Secretary of Executive Committee.

In 1902, Mr. Hardee was assigned to accompany John Barrett, Commissioner-General of the Louisiana Purchase Exposition, on a tour of the world to confirm to foreign rulers, in person, the invitation of the President of the United States for their countries to participate in the World's Fair at St. Louis. He was made the Special Commissioner to Oriental countries, and in recognition of his labors in China, the Emperor conferred upon him the Order of the Golden Dragon.

Upon his return, Mr. Hardee was appointed assistant to the General Secretary and Director of Exploitation of the Exposition, Walter B. Stevens. In this capacity his activity was devoted principally to securing attention to foreign Commissioners in fulfilment of the promises of the management. At the conclusion of the St. Louis Fair, the management conferred upon him a commemorative diploma and medal, in special recognition of his "active interest and efficient cooperation in the Universal Exposition of 1904."

Mr. Hardee is a grand-nephew of General William Joseph Hardee, of Georgia, author of "Hardee's Tactics," and Commandant of West Point prior to the Civil War. He is a graduate of St. Stanislaus College.

CONSULTING EXPERT OF THE WELFARE DEPARTMENT.

The Welfare Department of the National Civic Federation has engaged as its Consulting Expert W. E. C. Nazro. At the time of his acceptance of this appointment Mr. Nazro was Welfare Manager of the Plymouth Cordage Company, North Plymouth, Mass. He is one of the two Welfare experts whose report to the Isthmian Canal Commission upon the needs and opportunities of recreation for Government employes in the canal zone is published in this issue of The Review. Mr. Nazro graduated from Harvard University in 1897, with the degree of B. A. S. upon landscape architecture, the laying out of recreation grounds, etc. In 1898 he received the degree of S. B. in architecture, having made a special study of all recreation buildings, such as club houses, gymnasiums, etc. After leaving college, Mr. Nazro traveled through England, France and Italy, devoting most of his time to the study of these subjects. After returning from Europe he spent two or three years in practical work along the line of architectural and mill construction, and studying particularly the adaptation of sanitary conditions, light, etc., in the construction of mills, to the needs of employes. He was for a time with a large engineering firm, which made a specialty of mill construction. From there he went to the Plymouth Cordage Company as Welfare Manager, to take up its work of mill architecture, landscape improvements, homes for employes, a library, lunch-house, recreation hall, athletic association, and the development of other Welfare features. Mr. Nazro carried on this work successfully for four years, and won the gold medal for his specialty at the St. Louis Exposition, and honorable mention and a gold medal at the Lewis and Clark Exposition for exhibits of Welfare Work.

W. E. C. NAZRO.

When request is made to the Department by an employer, Mr. Nazro will study the especial needs and opportunities for Welfare Work in an industrial plant, advise the best methods of introducing such features as may be deemed most essential, and direct their installation. For example, Mr. Nazro is at present developing a new mill town at Welland, Canada. His services will be furnished to employers free, the only cost to them being his traveling expenses.

Fair dealing and honorable treatment are the best business policy to pursue, and in this respect the advantages as well as the obligations of fair dealing should be reciprocal. It is not alone the duty of the corporation to be fair to its employes, but in reciprocal measure it is the duty of the employe to be loyal to his employer. —*Electrical Worker.*

The National Civic Federation Review

TEN CENTS

THE NATIONAL CONFERENCE ON IMMIGRATION.*

LARGE AND REPRESENTATIVE GATHERING ENGAGES IN FREE DISCUSSION OF THE VARIOUS PHASES OF THE SUBJECT.

ORE than five hundred delegates, representing commercial, economic, ecclesiastical, labor and agricultural organizations throughout the United tes, gathered in Madison Square Garden Concert l on the morning of December 6. They met in re-nse to the call issued by the National Civic Federa- for a National Conference on Immigration, the : ever held in this country.

President Belmont's Address.

he Conference was called to order by August Bel-nt, President of the National Civic Federation. In lcoming the delegates and outlining the course of ir deliberations Mr. Belmont said:

'As President of the National Civic Federation it be-ies my pleasant duty to call this meeting to order and to welcome you to this Conference, held under its auspices—I repeat and emphasize, under its auspices only. The Civic Federation has no opinions and no policy to advance on the subject you are to consider, but will afford you, under its protection and through its efforts, free, uninfluenced and untrammeled debate.

"It is claimed that a change is taking place in what I may call, in a general way, the complexion or character of the immigration, which causes a very substantial portion of our most intelligent citizens to advance arguments for restrictions. They deny that this country is an asylum for the oppressed and unhappy of other nations. Indeed, they say that if this were the case, changed conditions and our growth compel us to deny what we formerly admitted. Is this really sound? You are to deliver the verdict.

"For years Europe gladly dumped her human refuse in our lap, and we housed, fed and clothed it. Of late, however, a spirit of what we owe to ourselves has come over us. Our Federal Government has become discriminating, if not restrictive, in those matters, and it is asked by some, Do our restrictions go far enough? This is for you to answer.

"Proceeding on the theory that our national character was formed and that we had room enough for all comers, we were taught to believe that by the power of assimilation we would gain—not lose—by this constant and growing alien influx. Has the character of the flood changed, and how? If so, it is right to inquire whether from the standpoint of correct economics and sane care for our national health and mental soundness, it is for good or evil.

"Customs foreign to us and calculated to sap our national vigor are brought to our shores, and if maintained by the people to whom they have become a part of their existence, they destroy the theory of assimila-

* full stenographic report of the proceedings of the Conference will [illegible] by The National Civic Federation.

OPENING SESSION OF THE NATIONAL CONFERENCE ON IMMIGRATION

tion. If it were true—and unfortunately it is not true—that our people only absorbed what was good and rejected what was bad, we would have no cause to fear that menace. If, however, the enhancement of the value of material wealth is the main argument for receiving into our national existence all comers, if this is the paramount consideration, then I say you should discuss this question for the benefit of the country at large and point out a sane and beneficial course to pursue.

"That this fair land of ours, however, is not to be made a receptacle of the human refuse of nations is evidenced by the trend of Federal laws; and that the

HON. ANTHONY HIGGINS.
Vice-Chairman of the National Conference on Immigration; former U. S. Senator for Delaware.

mission of our institutions is not to afford asylum to the intemperate, the habitual beggar and pauper, the insane and the criminal of foreign nations, is well established in our minds. Other phases of this question command your time and your best thoughts. You are to consider legislation as it bears upon immigration, and to inquire whether existing laws are sufficiently comprehensive to exclude all undesirable elements; whether the volume is stimulated by extraordinary influences and whether the system of inspection as now operated is properly conducted.

"Another phase of discussion and inquiry which will be presented at this session is of momentous interest. I refer to the distribution of immigrants from ports of entry to the agricultural districts, and more particu-

JOHN A. HOLLIDAY.
Vice-Chairman of the National Conference on Immigration; President of the Union Trust Company, Indianapolis.

larly to its effect in the South, where the industrial education and social betterment of the negro race are still unsolved problems."

Samuel Gompers.

Samuel Gompers, First Vice-President of the Civic Federation and President of the American Federation of Labor, followed Mr. Belmont. In the course of his remarks he stated the position of organized labor with regard to immigration in these words:

"Speaking primarily for those with whom I have the honor to associate most intimately, those who are usually termed the wage-earners, I know with a peculiar emphasis the conditions from which they suffer by reason of unrestricted and unregulated immigration. Apart from the ordinary immigration, the general tide that may flow toward our shores by reason of some improved economic material condition, we find this artificially stimulated immigration from several sources, one of them those who are interested in the carrying of immigrants; secondly, the employer of labor, who is continually desirous of maintaining an army of unemployed workmen who shall be in continuous competition with those who are employed; and thirdly, those people whom some tyrant monarch seeks to drive out of his country as the safety valve for the maintenance of his monarchical machine. Those causes, and many others which do not now occur to me, contribute to make the condition of the American working man an exceedingly precarious one. Taking this fact, together with the industrial conditions as they obtain in our country, the highest developed machinery, the most wonderfully propelled force and power in driving the wheels with greater velocity than the wheels of any industrial machine the world over; taking again the millions of colored men, who, up to this time, have manifested but very little evidence of a desire to exert themselves to their own material improvement—all these things, my friends, make it essential that the working people of our country first exert themselves, and that you should co-operate with them and they co-operate with you, in order that the economic and material and social problems confronting them in our time may be solved in our own country without our being compelled to bear the additional disadvantage of this overwhelming number of immigrants coming from all shores and from all climes.

"I do not think that we desire to restrict immigration because we fail to appreciate the true meaning of the brotherhood of man. I do not believe that we can

SETH LOW
Chairman of the National Conference on Immigration.

be justly accused, because we desire restriction of immigration, of a failure to recognize the obligation of the fraternity of man. But the principle applies to international contests, to international questions, the same as it applies to the nation, to the family, to the individual, that self-protection is the first law of nature; and let me add this, too, that if the American people shall attempt some practical measure that shall stop to a considerable degree this wholesale immigration of people from several of the monarchical countries where tyranny is the handmaid of poverty and misery, and these people shall be compelled to remain in their own country, it will also compel them to find the remedy for their economic and social ills in their own country, and compel reform and improvement."

Oscar S. Straus.

Oscar S. Straus, Second Vice-President of the National Civic Federation, was then introduced and spoke in part as follows:

"Is it not rather remarkable that of the three gentlemen, including my humble self, who have addressed you, respectively the President, the First Vice-President and myself, two were themselves immigrants and the third is the son of an immigrant father? (Applause.) It has been said truthfully that in this country we are all immigrants; that there is simply a question of a few years between us. And therefore we, best of all, are able to study and to consider this important question and weigh in the balance the human rights, on the great platform of humanity itself. The United States is the greatest immigrant country that has ever been known to the history of the world, and I think I can say without boasting that this is, at the same time, the most prosperous, the most flourishing and the greatest country that the world has ever known.

"I think there is no difference between us upon the question that this country is not to be used as the prison house of the nations of the world. I think that we all agree that there should be some restrictions u[…] the natural immigration. If I have one passion […] love that is stronger than another, it is for the pe[…] who are so ably and so well represented by my predec[…]sor, President Gompers, and for that reason, for […] reason that for so many centuries the laboring […] has been tied to the soil and treated as a chattel belo[…]ing to the soil, that he could not leave without […] permission of his seigneur—it is for that reason tha[…] maintain that, with some limitation, the right of […] human being to move from one part of the earth […] another is a fundamental element of personal libe[…]

"You have heard, so far as the Civic Federatio[…]

HON. W. S. WEST.
Vice-Chairman of the National Conference on Immigration; President of Georgia State Senate.

concerned, from the side of capital and also from th[e] side of labor, and the little I have said is from th[e] side that is neither represented as capital or as labor, bu[t] from the side of the general public; or, if I may pu[t] it in another way, you have heard from the right hand of industry and from the left hand of industry, and I am supposed to represent the heart that unites the two."

Commissioner Frank P. Sargent.

Letters expressing sympathy with the movement in favor of judicious restriction of immigration were read from Cardinal Gibbons and John H. Vincent, Chancellor of Chautauqua, after which the Chairman introduced the Commissioner of Immigration, Frank P. Sargent, who said in part:

WARREN S. STONE.
Vice-Chairman of the National Conference on Immigration; Chief of the Brotherhood of Locomotive Engineers.

"We have just passed the banner year in the history of immigration, with a record of 1,026,499 arrivals. These represented the actual accredited immigration, for which the head tax was payable to the Government, and did not include the large number coming from Canada or from Mexico, citizens of those two countries. The admission of one million people in one year from foreign countries is a large addition to our community. It makes quite a large city of itself. It is important to discover where the greater proportion of them go. You will be interested in knowing something about whence this immigration comes, what it is, where is goes, and what it is worth.

NATIONAL IMMIGRATION CONFERENCE DELEGATES AT ELLIS ISLAND.

"New York, out of this figure 1,026,499, received 315,-511; Pennsylvania, 210,708; Massachusetts, 72,152; Illinois, 72,770; New Jersey, 57,358; Ohio, 49,351. Six States of this Union received 777,748, or 76 per cent of the whole. The West received 43,571. The beautiful and prosperous South, just entering upon a season of great activity, commercial and otherwise, received 46,343, divided as follows: Maryland, West Virginia and Florida, 9,000; Louisiana, 5,000; Texas, 4,000; Kentucky—a glorious State for immigration, offering splendid inducements to good, hardy agriculturists, got 618. (Laughter.) Tennessee, wide-awake and prosperous, opening up some of the grandest iron industries of the South, received 782. North Carolina, a glorious State, blossoming out splendidly, got 183. South Carolina, a good second, got just 328; Georgia, 518; Arkansas, 432; Indian Territory, 438; Oklahoma, 260.

"In the great open country where immigration is required, where the best possible opportunities are offered to the peasantry of Europe to settle and grow into independence, the proportion is hardly noticeable in this great aggregation of immigration.

"Where do they come from? Austria-Hungary led the world in immigration to the United States last year with 275,693; Italy sent 221,479; Russia, 184 897; Germany, 40,574; Norway, Sweden and Denmark, 60,625; England, 64 709; Ireland, 52,945.

THE QUESTION OF DISTRIBUTION.

"Three years ago I made a recommendation, which was probably considered as rather an unusual proposition. I said: 'Let the Government go a little further than it goes to-day, merely deciding the right of the immigrants to enter on Ellis Island, and let it decide where they shall go.' In a little while you will have an opportunity to see the method of the admission of aliens to America. There is determined what? Whether or not the alien shall come; that is all. Nothing is said as to where he shall go, but whenever he has passed the line he has the right to go wherever he pleases. I believe that in addition to telling him he can enter, we could offer, under the auspices of this Government, some information as to where it would be to his advantage to go, that we might be helpful in sending to those localities where immigration is desired a large number of those people who are to-day coming to our shores destined to the very places that are already overcrowded and where there are no opportunities for them.

"If there is any subject to-day that ought to appeal to the humanitarian in this country, it is that of the bringing of these men, women and children, some of whom you will see to-day, who have been denied admission into this country, and who have to be taken back. Why were they brought? Nine out of ten of them have been brought by the solicitation of some agent who wanted to get the percentage from the sale of tickets. In my annual report this year I urge that this subject of such vital interest be made an international one, and that a convention of the several countries be called for the purpose of discussing this subject in the interest of humanity; because if there is any person, I do not care whether he lives under a despot or under a republican form of government, who has not got sympathy for men and women and children under those conditions, I am sorry the Almighty God ever made him. (Applause.) Think that over from a humanitarian point and see if such regulations cannot be made as will provide for such inspection in Europe as will guarantee, barring an outbreak of contagion, the landing of every alien when he comes to the shores of America. (Applause.)

"Put your medical officers at the port of embarkation (applause), and let them determine there whether or not a person is afflicted with a disease that is denied admission into the United States. It is of far greater importance to us to stop the disease at the port of embarkation than to have the paltry sum of $100 turned over to the Government by the steamship company that brings the person and takes him back.

OCCUPATIONS AND WEALTH OF IMMIGRANTS.

"Now, it may be of some interest to you to know the occupations of those who came last year. We had 162,134 agriculturists and farm laborers; you gentlemen from the agricultural districts, who are having such trouble in getting farm laborers, can realize that there was not such a very large number of farm laborers among the million who came. Common laborers, those that work at anything they can get, and get all they can for it, were 287,450. Skilled in the various trades—not all trade unionists, I am sorry to say, but many of them will be—were 180,812. Servants numbered 125,472. And yet any lady will tell you it is almost impossible to get a servant. Men, women and children without occupation were 232,018. Under the age of fourteen years were 114,668; fourteen to forty-five years of age, 850,419; forty-five years and over, 56,412.

"How much money—that is what will interest my financial friends who are present—how much money did these people bring? They brought $25,159,012, an average of $25 per capita. Now, would you like to know how this proportion of money is distributed? The Croatian and Slavonian races, $15 per capita; the English, $57; the German, $44; the Hebrew, $14; the Irish, $26; North Italian, $29; South Italian, $17; Magyar, $15; Polish, $13; Scandinavians, Norwegians and Swedes, $26; the Slavic races, $16.

tion. If it were true—and unfortunately it is not true—that our people only absorbed what was good and rejected what was bad, we would have no cause to fear that menace. If, however, the enhancement of the value of material wealth is the main argument for receiving into our national existence all comers, if this is the paramount consideration, then I say you should discuss this question for the benefit of the country at large and point out a sane and beneficial course to pursue.

"That this fair land of ours, however, is not to be made a receptacle of the human refuse of nations is evidenced by the trend of Federal laws; and that the

HON. ANTHONY HIGGINS.
Vice-Chairman of the National Conference on Immigration; former U. S. Senator for Delaware.

mission of our institutions is not to afford asylum to the intemperate, the habitual beggar and pauper, the insane and the criminal of foreign nations, is well established in our minds. Other phases of this question command your time and your best thoughts. You are to consider legislation as it bears upon immigration, and to inquire whether existing laws are sufficiently comprehensive to exclude all undesirable elements; whether the volume is stimulated by extraordinary influences and whether the system of inspection as now operated is properly conducted.

"Another phase of discussion and inquiry which will be presented at this session is of momentous interest. I refer to the distribution of immigrants from ports of entry to the agricultural districts, and more particu-

JOHN A. HOLLIDAY.
Vice-Chairman of the National Conference on Immigration; President of the Union Trust Company, Indianapolis.

larly to its effect in the South, where the industrial education and social betterment of the negro race are still unsolved problems."

Samuel Gompers.

Samuel Gompers, First Vice-President of the Civic Federation and President of the American Federation of Labor, followed Mr. Belmont. In the course of his remarks he stated the position of organized labor with regard to immigration in these words:

"Speaking primarily for those with whom I have the honor to associate most intimately, those who are usually termed the wage-earners, I know with a peculiar emphasis the conditions from which they suffer by reason of unrestricted and unregulated immigration. Apart from the ordinary immigration, the general tide that may flow toward our shores by reason of some improved economic material condition, we find this artificially stimulated immigration from several sources, one of them those who are interested in the carrying of immigrants; secondly, the employer of labor, who is continually desirous of maintaining an army of unemployed workmen who shall be in continuous competition with those who are employed; and thirdly, those people whom some tyrant monarch seeks to drive out of his country as the safety valve for the maintenance of his monarchical machine. Those causes, and many others which do not now occur to me, contribute to make the condition of the American working man an exceedingly precarious one. Taking this fact, together with the industrial conditions as they obtain in our country, the highest developed machinery, the most wonderfully propelled force and power in driving the wheels with greater velocity than the wheels of any industrial machine the world over; taking again the millions of colored men, who, up to this time, have manifested but very little evidence of a desire to exert themselves to their own material improvement—all these things, my friends, make it essential that the working people of our country first exert themselves, and that you should co-operate with them and they co-operate with you, in order that the economic and material and social problems confronting them in our time may be solved in our own country without our being compelled to bear the additional disadvantage of this overwhelming number of immigrants coming from all shores and from all climes.

"I do not think that we desire to restrict immigration because we fail to appreciate the true meaning of the brotherhood of man. I do not believe that we can

SETH LOW
Chairman of the National Conference on Immigration.

be justly accused, because we desire restriction of immigration, of a failure to recognize the obligation of the fraternity of man. But the principle applies to international contests, to international questions, the same as it applies to the nation, to the family, to the individual, that self-protection is the first law of nature; and let me add this, too, that if the American people shall attempt some practical measure that shall stop to a considerable degree this wholesale immigration of people from several of the monarchical countries where tyranny is the handmaid of poverty and misery, and these people shall be compelled to remain in their own country, it will also compel them to find the remedy for their economic and social ills in their own country, and compel reform and improvement."

Oscar S. Straus.

Oscar S. Straus, Second Vice-President of the National Civic Federation, was then introduced and spoke in part as follows:

"Is it not rather remarkable that of the three gentlemen, including my humble self, who have addressed you, respectively the President, the First Vice-President and myself, two were themselves immigrants and the third is the son of an immigrant father? (Applause.) It has been said truthfully that in this country we are all immigrants; that there is simply a question of a few years between us. And therefore we, best of all, are able to study and to consider this important question and weigh in the balance the human rights, on the great platform of humanity itself. The United States is the greatest immigrant country that has ever been known to the history of the world, and I think I can say without boasting that this is, at the same time, the most prosperous, the most flourishing and the greatest country that the world has ever known.

"I think there is no difference between us upon the question that this country is not to be used as the prison house of the nations of the world. I think that we all agree that there should be some restrictions upon the natural immigration. If I have one passion and love that is stronger than another, it is for the people who are so ably and so well represented by my predecessor, President Gompers, and for that reason, for the reason that for so many centuries the laboring man has been tied to the soil and treated as a chattel belonging to the soil, that he could not leave without the permission of his seigneur—it is for that reason that I maintain that, with some limitation, the right of the human being to move from one part of the earth to another is a fundamental element of personal liberty.

"You have heard, so far as the Civic Federation is

HON. W. S. WEST.
Vice-Chairman of the National Conference on Immigration; President of Georgia State Senate.

concerned, from the side of capital and also from the side of labor, and the little I have said is from the side that is neither represented as capital or as labor, but from the side of the general public; or, if I may put it in another way, you have heard from the right hand of industry and from the left hand of industry, and I am supposed to represent the heart that unites the two."

Commissioner Frank P. Sargent.

Letters expressing sympathy with the movement in favor of judicious restriction of immigration were read from Cardinal Gibbons and John H. Vincent, Chancellor of Chautauqua, after which the Chairman introduced the Commissioner of Immigration, Frank P. Sargent, who said in part:

WARREN S. STONE.
Vice-Chairman of the National Conference on Immigration; Chief of the Brotherhood of Locomotive Engineers.

"We have just passed the banner year in the history of immigration, with a record of 1,026,499 arrivals. These represented the actual accredited immigration, for which the head tax was payable to the Government, and did not include the large number coming from Canada or from Mexico, citizens of those two countries. The admission of one million people in one year from foreign countries is a large addition to our community. It makes quite a large city of itself. It is important to discover where the greater proportion of them go. You will be interested in knowing something about whence this immigration comes, what it is, where is goes, and what it is worth.

NATIONAL IMMIGRATION CONFERENCE DELEGATES AT ELLIS ISLAND.

"New York, out of this figure 1,026,499, received 315,-511; Pennsylvania, 210,708; Massachusetts, 72,152; Illinois, 72,770; New Jersey, 57,358; Ohio, 49,351. Six States of this Union received 777,748, or 76 per cent of the whole. The West received 43,571. The beautiful and prosperous South, just entering upon a season of great activity, commercial and otherwise, received 46,343, divided as follows: Maryland, West Virginia and Florida, 9,000; Louisiana, 5,000; Texas, 4,000; Kentucky—a glorious State for immigration, offering splendid inducements to good, hardy agriculturists, got 618. (Laughter.) Tennessee, wide-awake and prosperous, opening up some of the grandest iron industries of the South, received 782. North Carolina, a glorious State, blossoming out splendidly, got 183. South Carolina, a good second, got just 328; Georgia, 518; Arkansas, 432; Indian Territory, 438; Oklahoma, 260.

"In the great open country where immigration is required, where the best possible opportunities are offered to the peasantry of Europe to settle and grow into independence, the proportion is hardly noticeable in this great aggregation of immigration.

"Where do they come from? Austria-Hungary led the world in immigration to the United States last year with 275,693; Italy sent 221,479; Russia, 184 897; Germany, 40,574; Norway, Sweden and Denmark, 60,625; England, 64 709; Ireland, 52,945.

THE QUESTION OF DISTRIBUTION.

"Three years ago I made a recommendation, which was probably considered as rather an unusual proposition. I said: 'Let the Government go a little further than it goes to-day, merely deciding the right of the immigrants to enter on Ellis Island, and let it decide where they shall go.' In a little while you will have an opportunity to see the method of the admission of aliens to America. There is determined what? Whether or not the alien shall come; that is all. Nothing is said as to where he shall go, but whenever he has passed the line he has the right to go wherever he pleases. I believe that in addition to telling him he can enter, we could offer, under the auspices of this Government, some information as to where it would be to his advantage to go, that we might be helpful in sending to those localities where immigration is desired a large number of those people who are to-day coming to our shores destined to the very places that are already overcrowded and where there are no opportunities for them.

"If there is any subject to-day that ought to appeal to the humanitarian in this country, it is that of the bringing of these men, women and children, some of whom you will see to-day, who have been denied admission into this country, and who have to be taken back. Why were they brought? Nine out of ten of them have been brought by the solicitation of some agent who wanted to get the percentage from the sale of tickets. In my annual report this year I urge that this subject of such vital interest be made an international one, and that a convention of the several countries be called for the purpose of discussing this subject in the interest of humanity; because if there is any person, I do not care whether he lives under a despot or under a republican form of government, who has not got sympathy for men and women and children under those conditions, I am sorry the Almighty God ever made him. (Applause.) Think that over from a humanitarian point and see if such regulations cannot be made as will provide for such inspection in Europe as will guarantee, barring an outbreak of contagion, the landing of every alien when he comes to the shores of America. (Applause.)

"Put your medical officers at the port of embarkation (applause), and let them determine there whether or not a person is afflicted with a disease that is denied admission into the United States. It is of far greater importance to us to stop the disease at the port of embarkation than to have the paltry sum of $100 turned over to the Government bv the steamship company that brings the person and takes him back.

OCCUPATIONS AND WEALTH OF IMMIGRANTS.

"Now, it may be of some interest to you to know the occupations of those who came last year. We had 162,134 agriculturists and farm laborers; you gentlemen from the agricultural districts, who are having such trouble in getting farm laborers, can realize that there was not such a very large number of farm laborers among the million who came. Common laborers, those that work at anything they can get, and get all they can for it, were 287,450. Skilled in the various trades—not all trade unionists, I am sorry to say, but many of them will be—were 180,812. Servants numbered 125,472. And yet any lady will tell you it is almost impossible to get a servant. Men, women and children without occupation were 232,018. Under the age of fourteen years were 114,668; fourteen to forty-five years of age, 850,419; forty-five years and over, 56,412.

"How much money—that is what will interest my financial friends who are present—how much money did these people bring? They brought $25,159,012, an average of $25 per capita. Now, would you like to know how this proportion of money is distributed? The Croatian and Slavonian races, $15 per capita; the English, $57; the German, $44; the Hebrew, $14; the Irish, $26; North Italian, $29; South Italian, $17; Magyar, $15; Polish, $13; Scandinavians, Norwegians and Swedes, $26; the Slavic races, $16.

"I think that the time has come when this Government should positively assert that no convict, no man of immoral character, no man who is escaping from punishment that he rightfully deserves, no pauper, no person afflicted with contagious disease, should be permitted to obtain transportation to America on any line which has the right to enter an American seaport. (Applause.) Make every man who comes to America with his wife and children present some good evidence of his good character and his good citizenship at home. That can be obtained, if it is exacted. Bring about an influence that will prevent this promiscuous advertising and encouraging of immigration in Europe by all the interests which are involved in the carrying trade.

"Exact the most stringent enforcement of regulations for the health and comfort of those who travel by sea, especially in the steerage. Give a little more attention to the steerage and less attention to the first cabin.

"Then find some means to make known to the intelligent immigrant that it is to his advantage to keep away from New York. (Applause.) You, gentlemen, use your influence to open up some of your Southern seaports, and then immigrants can go direct to your own harbors and be landed at the gateway, where you want immigration of the right kind, and where there is plenty of opportunity for them."

Commissioner Robert Watchorn.

The first address of the second day's session was that of Robert Watchorn, Commissioner of Immigration at the Port of New York. Dealing with the subject of the exclusion of the unfit, he urged that the present law be

FRANK P. SARGENT.
U. S. Commissioner-General of Immigration.

amended so as to exclude the feeble-minded as well as idiots and the insane. He also suggested the advisability of legislation which should prevent the recurrence of such painful incidents as the deportation or detention of alien children whose mother, by virtue of marriage with an alien since naturalized, is admitted as an American citizen. His address follows in part:

"The law provides that an idiot shall not enter the United States, and I presume that if ever there was any sound legislation, that may be considered sound. I do not believe that any idiot should be permitted to land on these shores. But the law does not say one word about those who are feeble-minded, or imbecile, and if any one here who is familiar with that subject can point out to me where idiocy leaves off and imbecility begins, I shall be indebted to him for the information, for I have not yet received it. You cannot know the number of people who are recorded by the physicians as being feeble-minded, and yet the social and political pressure that they can bring to bear upon the governing machinery ofttimes effects the landing of such persons. My contention is that persons certified by the medical examiners as afflicted with feeble-mindedness or imbecility should be classed with those certified as idiots. No amount of pressure can effect the landing of an idiot, and you should classify the weak-minded, the imbeciles, in such way as to prevent pressure effecting their landing.

"The only way you can weed out that which is, by common consent, undesirable, is by Act of Congress, for there the opinions of the country are crystallized. The way to weed it out successfully is to do what we have done in Section 9 of the present Act, the Act of March 3, 1903; and that is, summed up in a word, to make it more unprofitable to bring them than it is to leave them. In 1903 for the first time the Government could assess a fine on any steamship company or any carrying company for bringing into the United States a diseased person. Since that time, those who are afflicted with disease have fallen to such an insignificant number that they are scarcely worth mentioning. If this kind of legislation applied to loathsome diseases can so successfully weed them out and keep them on the other side and save them the burden of a journey across the sea, surely we can extend that principle so as to include those who are also considered unworthy and those who would be a detriment to this country."

Prescott F. Hall.

Among the speakers on the topic, "What Shall be the Limitation of Immigration?" was Prescott F. Hall, of the Immigration Restriction League of the

DR. ALBERT SHAW.
Chairman, Conference Committee on Resolutions.

United States, who enlarged upon the dangers of immigration artificially stimulated by foreign steamship companies, and quoted statistics to show that the foreign-born population furnished a much higher percentage of criminals than the native-born. In the course of his remarks Mr. Hall said:

"Fifty, or even thirty years ago the expense of coming here, the hardships of the voyage, acted as a sieve to screen out the undesirable. By undesirable immigrants I mean those ignorant of a trade, lacking in resources, of criminal tendencies, averse to country life and tending to congregate in the slums of the large cities; with a low standard of living and lacking ambition to seek a better; failing to assimilate within a reasonable time and having no permanent interest in this country.

"It is significant that in general immigration legislation was found unnecessary until some years after the present flow of relatively undesirable aliens had begun. The result of this influx is shown in the large number of persons who are diseased, insane and criminal at the time of landing, or become so shortly afterward. Commissioner Watchorn asserts that the general physique

CHARLES RIDGELY.
Vice-President of Ridgely National Bank, Springfield, Ill.

of the immigrant has very much deteriorated in the last thirty years. Among recent immigrants, one Hebrew in forty-two was certified as having serious physical defects, and one Syrian in twenty-nine. Of those certified for minor defects having some bearing upon the ability of the immigrant to earn a livelihood, there was one Italian in twenty-six, one Syrian in twenty-four, one Hebrew in sixteen. The proportion of immigrants sent to the hospital in proportion to the landed, was for Hebrews, one in ninety, for Italians, one in one hundred and seventy-seven. Comparing male prisoners with males of voting age, those of foreign birth and parentage contributed three times as many prisoners as those of native parentage, while the foreign-born contributed more than twice as many prisoners as the native white of native birth and parentage.

"It is often said that, however it may be with the original immigrants, their children become good citizens. That this is a fallacy is shown by the fact that of juvenile prisoners in the North Atlantic division, those of native birth and parentage furnish 855 per million, the native children of foreign parentage 2,7[illegible] per million, and the foreign born 2,252 per million. In certain special regions like the mining regions of Pennsylvania and our large cities, the figures as to criminality are more striking. In the anthracite regions from 1880 to 1890 the convictions increased nearly 10 per cent more than the population, and the proportion of Slav criminals increased nearly 25 per cent more than the Slav population. In Massachusetts the foreign-born population furnishes three times as many prisoners as those of native birth and parentage, and those of foreign birth and parentage furnish ten times as many prisoners as the natives. As regards insanity, the foreign-born furnishes 2 1-3 times the normal proportion of insane. The proportion of paupers who are foreign-born is increasing. As compared with the male population of voting age, the foreign whites furnish 4,6[illegible] paupers as compared with 2,096 of those of native birth and parentage.

JOHN W. KERN.
Representing the Commercial Club of Indianapolis.

"The last danger of the present immigration which I would mention, and perhaps the most important, is its effect, not on those whom it introduces into the country, but on those whom it excludes. It is well known that when immigration becomes of a certain low quality it tends to prevent immigrants of a better quality in foreign lands coming here. Those immigrants are diverted to other places where they will not be brought into competition with the lower grade of immigration. If we wish to have selected immigrants, it does not follow that the first effect of the selection would not be to increase the immigration of the most desirable people. But more important than that is the effect which undesirable immigration has in excluding a certain large class of persons who are never born. It is well known that the native birth-rate and even the birth-rate of more recently arrived immigrants is beginning to fall. It is falling very fast. In Massachusetts the birth-rate of the native part of the population is lower even than in France. And why? Undoubtedly this is due to several causes, but the chief cause is the desire for concentration of advantages, and one of the principal reasons for the desire of concentration of advantages is the desire for people not to have their children obliged to take up a trade and a calling in which they will be brought in close competition with a low grade of foreign labor.

"I believe we should increase the head-tax from $2 to $10 or $15, so as to equalize the cost of coming to the United States with the cost of going to South Africa, Australia and South America. Let us put the United States on a level with these other countries, so that this country will not be the cheapest place to come to, the place that the poorest and least thrifty class shall seek.

"Second, let us absolutely exclude persons of poor physique, that is to say, those mentally and physically weak, defective or degenerates, so that their ability to earn a living in their particular occupation is interfered with.

"Third, I think also we should exclude the illiterates, that is, those who cannot read in their own language."

Professor Morris Loeb.

Professor Morris Loeb, of New York University, said that the spirit which actuated the last speaker was "that which whipped the Quakers out of New England towns, which drove Roger Williams and Ann Hutchinson into the wilderness. It is the spirit of the grandfathers of the present generation, the Know-nothings who attempted to keep out of this country in the 50's those people who saved for the North the State of Missouri. According to the rules which the

HON. W. A. CLARK.
U. S. Senator for Montana.

Know-nothings of that period tried to bring forward, General Siegel, General Schurz, the Germans who fought for the Union in the North, as well as the Irish and the Germans who fought for the Southern States, would have been excluded. (Applause.)

RESTRICTIONIST STATISTICS ATTACKED.

"I object to the introduction of pseudo-science of every kind, and the worst pseudo-science is false statistics, and as a college professor I protest against the misuse of statistics. As an American citizen I protest against the misuse of the United States Government records for the propagation of false statistics. I hold in my hand one of the letters of the Immigration Restriction League in which they objected to the publication by this Civic Federation of certain material which had been read in an open meeting, saying it was a one-sided representation of the facts, and that no one-

HON. ROBERT ADAMS.
Ranking Member of the House Committee on Immigration.

sided representation should go forth before an honest and fair exchange of opinion had taken place. Upward of fifty leaflets have been distributed by the League without the chance of answer. Some of them have not yet come to my hands, but some have, and I would like to show you what are the statistics upon which Mr. Hall and his friends base their aspersions upon the character of the foreign-born. He has read himself statistics about criminality upon the basis of 1,000 people of various births resident in Massachusetts. He states that there are 3.60 per thousand of Germans who have been committed in one year for crime; 5 per thousand of Scandinavians, 5.8 of Scotch, 6 of French, and so on in descending scale, 7 in the thousand for Russians, 10 for Austrians, 16 from Poland, 15 from Hungary and 18 from Italy. Now, gentlemen, that is a serious accusation—eighteen per thousand arrested against a very small proportion, only 3 per cent. of Germans, 5 per cent. of Scotch, etc. I don't like that kind of argument. At the present time, 22.7 per thousand of the members of the United States Senate have been convicted of felony. (Laughter.) Quite a number of other gentlemen are under indictment or at least under suspicion of the commission of felony.

"He suggested that the figures that I have given you here are false, because in giving a list of arrests, for the reason that some of you will understand, arrests for drunkenness have been excluded. The Italians, the Russians and the Poles are not addicted to drunkenness, and if drunkenness had been included in the arrests, the Massachusetts figures would have had quite a different significance. (Applause.)

"We have heard about the number of dependents. Leaflet No. 42 of the Immigration Restriction League gives us the figures for dependents, which have been taken from the Immigration Commissioner's report of 1904. I quote from that leaflet verbatim:

"'Considering only the insane and charitable institutions, it appears that an alien population which is only 1.3 per cent. of the total population furnishes 12 per cent. of the inmates of the institution.' Twelve per cent. of alien inmates! Gentlemen, we have 80,000,000 citizens; 1.3 per cent. of 80,000,000 is about 1,000,000. One million aliens arrive every year. Five times 1,000,000 cannot have been naturalized, therefore, and instead of having 1,000,000, that is 1.3 per cent., he should have stated five times that, about 6.3 per cent. aliens resident in the United States, if we only take into account immigrant statistics themselves. Only a born idiot or a person who is completely blinded by prejudice would have put forth figures like that without looking into it. I give the members of the Immigration Restriction League the choice of the horns of the dilemma."

Z. P. Smith.

Z. P. Smith, of North Carolina, favored an educational qualification for immigrants and thought any man an undesirable immigrant who did not purpose becoming an American citizen. Speaking of his visit to the Immigrant Station he said: "There was one thing that impressed me very forcibly: that Ellis Island ought to be on the other side. (Applause.) I was struck with the injustice that this country is perpetrating upon some helpless and defenceless people, aided and abetted by their mother country. We bring a woman here with a lot of children, and you saw them and I saw them, and we don't know whether they will be deported or not. I have no doubt that the medical examiners perform their duties faithfully and well—there is no question in my mind about that—but the examination given the immigrants is very superficial. The place to examine the immigrants is before they are allowed to get on the plank of the steamship. If you will do that, if this Civic Federation will pass a resolution saying that we demand a rigid, not a superficial medical examination and a physical examination of the man, the woman and the child, I tell you you are going to reduce this immigration a very great deal."

Mr. Carnegie for the Open Door

Andrew Carnegie was introduced as "probably the most distinguished immigrant that ever came to these shores." After remarking that immigration was not among the serious problems of the country, Mr. Carnegie said:

"We have solved the question in the present by the somewhat too drastic law that we have enacted. You heard Mr. Watchorn, and you know that the right man is in the right place. (Applause.) Now, what would this country have been without immigration, and who is there here who is not either an immigrant himself or has not immigrant blood in his veins? (Applause.) It is not a problem for us; it is the problem of the poor, unfortunate countries from which we are draining the best blood. (Applause.) Prince Bismarck declared that the United States was draining the most valuable blood of Germany, and he would pass laws preventing the Germans from leaving their country to swell the growth and the prosperity and happiness of the American people (applause), and he was a wise man.

"Now, I hold the prime test and the only test we should exact is this: Has a man ambition to enjoy the rights of an American citizen? Has he the habits of sobriety and frugality to save the sum necessary for him to reach that port? And is he skillful enough to earn that surplus? I want no better proof or testimony than that. If I owned America, and was running it as a business operation, I would not only look for that man, but I would give every man of that kind a premium to come here (applause), and consider it the best bargain that I had ever made in my life.

"Gentlemen, taking the cost, the value of a man, a woman or a child in this Republic as low as you put the slave, and that was an average of about $1,000, you are getting 400,000 a year, and that means $400,000,000 cash value. And every man who comes here is a consumer, and 90 per cent. of all his earnings—even the most saving of them don't save more than 10 per cent.—every dollar of that goes to employ other labor of some kind. The grossest mistake that labor ever makes—if it ever makes a mistake at all (laughter)—is this, that a man coming in here to work injures others, and that they are all in compartments di-

W. D. JELKS.
Governor of Alabama.

vided from each other. Gentlemen, labor is one undivided whole, as society is one undivided whole, and the prosperity of one branch of labor entails the prosperity of other branches. Every laborer is a consumer, and he employs the labor of others. We are interdependent, and the laboring classes of this country have not only nothing to fear from immigration, but as the country becomes wealthy and grows in population, it will be all the more important that we should have the right kind of immigration. Now, this country is the most prosperous in the world. You will all agree with that. It is also the country that receives the great stream of foreigners. A speaker said something about the purity of blood. It is not purity of blood you want; it is a mingling of different bloods that makes the American. (Applause.)

"This question of immigration is settling itself. The net foreign immigration is about 400,000 a year. Your

HON. AUGUSTUS P. GARDNER.
Representative in Congress for the Sixth Massachusetts District.

native births are 1,500,000 a year. There is no danger of foreign immigrants ever affecting the dominancy of the characteristics of the American people. A gentleman has said here that immigration is to increase rapidly. Never was there a greater mistake. Immigration is at its height now, and it is to fall and fall. Don't trouble yourself about imaginary dangers, and don't lie awake at night over the danger to the American nation from immigration. Consider something real. You have got them here, and let Mr. Watchorn go along with his arrangements and little adjustments that he has talked to us about, and go to bed and sleep. The American Republic does not need you to lie awake on the subject of immigration." (Applause.)

Archbishop Ireland Welcomes Aliens.

Archbishop Ireland's address was an eloquent plea for a liberal immigration policy. In the course of it he said:

"It is now proposed by some to limit immigration. Of course we should limit it to exclude the criminals, to exclude the idiots, to exclude those afflicted with con-

CHARLES W. ELIOT.
President of Harvard University.

tagious disease; but to limit it so as to exclude a man coming attracted by the freedom of America, ready to put his hand to the tiller, or to the plough, ready to be an American, would be to turn back upon all the traditions of the past—would be a mistake. (Applause.) What may be done two or three hundred years hence is another question; but to-day America has not at all the population it should have to develop its resources. It has not at all the population which it should have to be great. We need immigrants. We need them in almost every State in the country; in new States to develop our unbroken lands; in other States to give great impetus to our industries.

"It has been asked, 'But shall they vote?' That is another question. Let us dissociate absolutely the question of voting from that of immigration. When they are here it is time enough for us to say: 'Well, if will

WALTER MACARTHUR.
Representing the Japanese and Corean Exclusion League.

take so many years more or less to entitle them to the franchise.' What we are talking of now is bringing immigrants here to develop the country, and we need them, and we need not fear them. We need all the different elements to build up one great American nation. We need the plodding men of the North, and we need the poetic men of the South. What is making to-day the greatness and grandeur of the British Empire is the fact that the Anglo-Saxon, the Scotch, the Irish, each one with his own element of mind and heart is building up that great empire. This is an age of new things, new nations. We are building up here the greatest and best of nations, a nation that will excel in history, a nation that will excel in art, a nation that will have high ideals as well as practical judgment. And for that we need these different races, each one bringing the best, and out of all a great world uprising that will stand unparalleled in history.

"Gentlemen, be not afraid of immigration. Be assured that the more, as the President says, of the right kind we can have, the better. And if you go selecting here and there, you will drive out the very best. Increase the per capita tax? Why, some of the sturdiest and best are those who have worked hard for years to earn in other countries $30 or $40 to buy tickets, and must we put on $30 or $40 more? We must remember that it is a dangerous thing to pick out the weeds here and there in such a manner as to pick out the good seed as well as the weed."

Congressman Adams on Discrimination.

The Hon. Robert Adams, of the House Committee on Immigration, speaking of his efforts to frame legislation which should discriminate between desirable and undesirable classes and nationalities, said:

"In a conversation with my colleague, Mr. Gardner, of Massachusetts, he made the suggestion, why not limit the number from any given country, and that ought to give the solution? That put into practical form the idea that I had in my mind, and I drafted a short bill, which simply stated that no more (and the number is empiric) than 80,000 immigrants from any one country should enter the United States in any fiscal year. That is all. Now, what is the practical result? Italy sent 232,000 men in 1903. Russia sent 106,000, and Austro-Hungary 202,000. No other nation on the entire continent of Europe sent more than 40,000 immigrants in any one year. So you see

ANDREW CARNEGIE.
Publicist and Philanthropist.

the practical working of this simple bill is that Northern Europe is left to develop from 40,000 up to 80,000; Southern Europe is reduced to 80,000.

"The immigrants that come from Southern Europe do not go out upon the land and fertilize our country; they herd here in cities. I am sorry I haven't the time to give you the facts, which I am sure would have very great weight with you, but I can only say that the Hebrew Charities Association of New York shows that there are 20,000 Hebrews dependent upon charity right here in this City of New York."

Hon. Augustus P. Gardner.

In opening the discussion of "The Method by which Immigrants may be Selected," Congressman Augustus P. Gardner, of Massachusetts, said in part:

"If every law that I have heard suggested for the selection of immigration had been in operation last year, though I cannot prove it, I venture to say that nevertheless last year would have been just the same the banner year of immigration into this country. Even your educational test would not, in my opinion, have substantially reduced the number. The figures are not available, or I have not been able to get them for this year, but taking the last previous year, out of 800,000, 200,000 could not read. There were, however, over 100,000 under the age of fourteen. Therefore it is presumable that a large part of the 200,000 illiterates were minors. But let us assume that 125,000 would have been excluded; that is not such a very big proportion. Is it not true that it would simply have resulted that the padrone or the steamship company, or the agents of the corporation would have been obliged to take Jones and Smith for his passage to America instead of Brown and Green? They would have no difficulty in selecting material to draw from, surrounding the Mediterranean, that can read and write. And I don't believe that that law would substantially restrict our immigration. I don't believe that the steamship companies would seriously object to any of these restriction laws. At heart I doubt if they seriously would object to an educational test, though they will fight it on the principle of keeping us as long at the soup as possible in order to avoid our getting at the meat. Now, if it is selection or distribution that you want, we will do our best, if that is what the people want. I do not underrate distribution and selection, but I want restriction, and if the people want that they have got a fight on their hands, and it is none too soon to begin. You cannot get restriction that really restricts without such a fight.

RT. REV. JOHN IRELAND.
Roman Catholic Archbishop of St. Paul

"Now, if we honestly want restriction—and I confess that I have no idea whether the people of the United States want it or not—if we really and honestly want it, let us go for it, and not waste our energies in long battles over minor issues. Really and seriously, to cut down immigration we need a law drastic in its nature, easy to enforce, independent of human frailty, of the judgment of our officials, and automatic in excluding valueless citizens. And such a measure I believe can be found in a $40 head-tax to be imposed on males alone coming from all countries with the present excepted countries, Canada, Mexico, Newfoundland and Cuba, with, of course, such exceptions as are necessary of a humanitarian kind.

"Now, under a head-tax of $40 it would pay no foreign nation to dump their paupers upon us. It would not be worth while for any contractor to keep a weak

PRESCOTT F. HALL.
Secretary of the Immigration Restriction League.

alien until he paid back that extra $40, and I believe that the padrone would very surely find that the duty on the assisted immigrant was prohibitive."

Dr. Frankel Defends Jewish Immigrants.

Dr. Lee R. Frankel, Superintendent of the United Hebrew Charities of New York, was one of several forceful and eloquent speakers who championed the cause of the immigrant, particularly of the Jewish immigrant. "How," he asked, "are we going to select our coming immigrants in the light of those who have come

(Continued on page 14)

THE HOURS OF LABOR.

EMPLOYERS AND WORKINGMEN DISCUSS THE QUESTION AT THE ANNUAL MEETING OF THE NEW ENGLAND CIVIC FEDERATION.

THE first annual meeting of the New England Civic Federation was held at the Revere House, Boston, on the evening of January 11. The number in attendance exceeded two hundred and included 86 employers, 86 representatives of labor organizations and 41 others, largely representative of the various professions. The subject for discussion was "Hours of Labor." A reception preceded the speaking, and Governor Guild and ex-Governor Douglas cordially greeted the members of the Federation and their guests.

Welcomed by Governor Guild.

Governor Guild was obliged to leave before the formal meeting opened, and, standing in the center of the group of those assembled, he said that he was glad to share with his friend, Governor Douglas, the opportunity to congratulate the Federation on its first year of success.

"We have The Hague Conference to adjust difficulties between nations," he said, "and we now have a no less important organization like this in our midst to adjust and bring peace, law and order in the civil as well as military life of the nation.

CURTIS GUILD, Jr.
Governor of Massachusetts.

"I congratulate you on your work and bring to you the greetings of the Commonwealth of Massachusetts, which has always tried to be somewhere near the front, no matter what party was in control, in matters of justice and equal rights for all men, which should be not merely the Massachusetts, but the American motto."

Secretary Robbins opened the meeting and read a letter from President Lucius Tuttle, who was delayed. First Vice-President Frank H. McCarthy presided.

Ex-Governor Douglas.

Ex-Gov. William L. Douglas was then introduced as the first speaker of the evening, and said:

"Mr. Chairman, I find myself heartily in accord with the purposes of your organization. For some years the community has felt the importance of finding a common ground in industrial matters on which the public, the employer and the employe could stand. It seems to me that you have found it. The fact that so many are here to-night proves that the mutual desire to be helpful in establishing right relations between employer and employe is entertained by a considerable portion of the community, and your success in organizing them into a power for good is apparent. Such an organization as yours would hardly be possible in any other country; it is essentially American; equality and free speech are its basis, and I am sure that as time goes on it will take an important part in establishing the relations of employer and employe.

FORMER OPPOSITION TO CONCILIATION.

"I am not a stranger to the proposition which you represent. Twenty years ago, when the idea of conciliation and arbitration had not been accepted by the public, and at a time when such a flourishing organization as yours would have had no support in the minds of the people, it became my duty on the floor of the Senate to labor for the enactment of a law which should define the policy of this State in labor difficulties.

"The arguments of those who opposed the position which the State then took seem strange to-day. It was claimed that the community had no interest in matters pertaining solely to employers and employes; that it was beneath the dignity of the public to enter into the private affairs of the buyers and sellers of labor, who must be left to fight out their differences alone. The State, it was claimed, had no right to assert itself in any manner, even though its prosperity were at stake. It was only by overcoming a strong opposition of this sort that we are enabled to enter upon a policy which is substantially like the idea which you represent.

"The difficulty of the present industrial situation and the means of handling it are best understood by a study of the evolution of modern forms of industry. Men of my age have lived in all the stages of the development of the industrial system from the time when the employer worked side by side with his journeyman, up to the modern factory with its thousands of employes, whose very names it is impossible for the employer to know. The remedy is simply to replace what has been lost by the change. There was no need for the employer and the employe to 'get together' a generation ago, because they were together all the time.

"The personal relationship, made impossible by the factory system, we endeavor to replace by instituting boards of conciliation in each department of the business, composed of workmen who represent the interests of the individuals and bring to the employer their questions, which we feel bound to consider in the spirit of helpfulness, fairness and justice. In this way the confidence of both parties is strengthened; and by a reasonably conciliatory attitude on the part of both we succeed in many instances in speedily adjusting the matters of difference caused by the ever-changing methods and system of production, which too frequently, by lack of confidence, become the cause of chronic grievances. By means of these boards of conciliation in the different departments we are enabled to reduce the number of causes to be left to arbitration.

"I have endeavored to extend this plan of conciliation so as to embrace groups of local factories in the same industry; and while it is not always successful on that line, still I am sure you will agree with me that this plan, having been adopted at Fall River for the settlement of the six months' strike there, resulted in the establishment, for the first time in that city, of a working basis for the settlement of wage disputes, and the lasting benefits accruing to those concerned are apparent to all.

JAMES DUNCAN.
General Secretary, Granite Cutters' International Association of America.

"Such a plan, of course, requires organization of the workman. No man needs to fear organization of his employes if he sincerely approaches in this way the questions that arise between them. As a workman at the bench, I was a member of all the organizations of my craft and since becoming an employer have always felt that my employes had the same right to belong to labor organizations that I had myself.

"It seems to me that the employes think too much of arbitration and the employer too little of conciliation in industrial matters to-day.

"I notice in the statement of purposes which you have put forward in your by-laws, Mr. Chairman, that you propose to encourage mutual agreements between employers and employes as to conditions under which labor shall be performed, and the faithful adherence of both parties in letter and spirit to agreements so made. I understand that you refer to collective agreements.

WORKINGMEN MUST KEEP AGREEMENTS.

"I believe that this matter of faithful adherence to agreements is the most important phase of the industrial problem now before the public. I wish I could impress upon workmen the importance of unwavering support of contracts which they make. I believe that in the past laboring people have lost more by a failure to keep agreements than by almost any other cause. They have not understood that the employer must know that their agreements can be relied on in order that he may go into the market and make contracts of which he can give them the benefit. Business honor is no more the foundation of mercantile success than industrial honor is the foundation of industrial success. I hope that your Federation will require uncompromising adherence to this provision of your constitution and continually exert an active influence to assist in upbuilding that

WILLIAM L. DOUGLAS.
Former Governor of Massachusetts.

faithful adherence to contracts which you name as one of your purposes. A high standard of honor in such matters, Mr. Chairman, comes by gradual growth. Not at first, but after slow and sometimes difficult progress, do we arrive at a high standard.

"I can see progress in the last ten years. Now, we must not expect to arrive at a high standard in one bound, but rather, while we continually insist with firmness on the necessity of the fulfilment of agreements, we should at the same time be mindful of the importance of the spirit of helpfulness toward those who have not been accustomed to the importance of integrity in agreements. I believe that, in the long run, we shall do more good in this way than by wholesale condemnation of every failure. When an employe is wrong he should be told so; but then, there is such a difference in the spirit in which you tell him. We shall arrive at a full appreciation of the importance of industrial honor more quickly by the helpfulness of which you speak in your by-laws than by denouncing and speaking evil. It is the policy of some to denounce the laboring people for certain shortcomings, which they undoubtedly have, and to minimize the value of the progress already made.

"I have no desire to allow either party to compromise the right and admit that we all have much to learn in industrial relationship; still I believe that the spirit with which we approach new and knotty questions is more important than what we do. An employer who is honest with himself and his employes is not likely to go far wrong if he is determined to meet the questions which arise in a fair spirit; while he who approaches his difficulties with the opposite spirit is not likely often to be right."

A British View—Mr. Mosely's.

Alfred Mosely said in part:

"Eight hours' work, eight hours' play, eight hours' sleep and eight dollars a day. (Laughter.) That is the ideal which I often hear expressed by work people. There are some who would probably place eight pints of beer instead of the eight hours' sleep (laughter), but I venture to think in this country that number is happily small. There are others again who doubt the possibility of this ideal of eight hours all round, including eight dollars a day, and are inclined to view the situation from an economic standpoint.

"There are some trades in which I quite agree that eight hours are more than ample, such as mining, and there are many industries where competition does not enter into the field, where you have safeguarded your

LUCIUS TUTTLE.
President of the New England Civic Federation.

markets against the intrusion of foreign products, and where you are safe from outside competition, such as in the printing trade, say of newspapers. I do not see why, with no fear of competition, providing that the work is sufficiently arduous, eight hours should not be ample in such trades, and there are others that may be enumerated. But as a whole the question arises as to whether eight hours can be made universal for all trades for all countries under all conditions.

"Personally I am one of those who think not. Before you can get such an ideal as that, it is necessary to bring, in my opinion, the labor world under one head. Organized labor must not look alone to this country, but to other parts of the world in order to bring it thoroughly into harmony before you can decide upon a universal standard of hours.

"One great question that you have to answer is—and this is a very important question, gentlemen—does the United States intend to manufacture only for itself, or are you going to try to compete in the neutral markets of the world? How can you hope to compete with eight hours' work if Germany and other countries are going to work nine and ten hours and pay their people infinitely lower wages than you are accustomed to receive in this country? Now, gentlemen, you who are representing the labor organizations, I put it to you as a serious question: Is such a thing possible as eight hours?

"The Civic Federation is an organization with which I am in hearty sympathy. I have seen much of its workings. If you will remember, some years ago I was here with an industrial commission of some twenty-two or twenty-three trade union leaders from Great Britain. The Civic Federation, to whose members I appealed for help, readily came forward and piloted the whole of my commission through the States. Mr. Marcus Marks, who is with us here to-night, kindly came forward and said: 'If I can be of any assistance, I will travel round the country with you.' Mr. Easley appointed Mr. Marks, Mr. Donnelly and one or two others to guide us, and their efforts were devoted to making our trip instructive and easy, and I have to thank the employers of this country for having so liberally opened their doors to our people. It was a great opportunity. It was a great education for our commission, and I feel that I am deeply indebted to the Civic Federation for the courtesy which they showed to my people and to myself on that occasion.

"The Civic Federation, as I understand it, lays itself out for the settlement of labor disputes. It does not wait until a strike has taken place and both sides have taken up a position from which they cannot climb down with dignity, but the Federation steps in before any breach has occurred and gets the employer and employe at a round table conference. Now, gentlemen, we all know if before any bitterness has entered into a struggle; if before any act has occurred from which neither side can recede, if you can only get them at the round table to talk out their difficulties, that as a rule half the trouble is over, and ten to one that they will succeed in finding a way out of the various difficulties presented; and I believe it is often found when they come together that they are really talking about that which each side does not understand. In other words, there is no real difference of opinion; it is only imaginary. The Civic Federation has undertaken this work and has carried it to a triumphant issue. A thousand and one disputes that you hear nothing at all about have been, I believe, settled. It is only here and there, when the Federation unfortunately failed to bring about settlements, that it is bruited about in the papers that there is another strike, or that the Civic Federation has attempted to do something and failed. You hear of their failures very largely, but there are scores of successes they are modestly inclined to say nothing about; and I venture to think that both capital and labor are under a deep debt of gratitude to the Civic Federation, which makes for peace, prosperity and contentment, and I have no hesitation in congratulating you gentlemen upon the splendid work that has been accomplished in the past, a work which is only at its inception; and if you people will try to pull together in the future as in the past, there is no limit to the work that the Civic Federation may accomplish for the good of all concerned and especially for the good of the United States." (Applause.)

Eight Hours Enough—James P. Archibald.

James P. Archibald, District Organizer of the Brotherhood of Painters, New York City, said:

"I do not quite agree with Mr. Mosely when he is perhaps pessimistic as to the outcome of our efforts for the eight-hour day. I have been convinced for a

JOHN MASON LITTLE.
Treasurer of the New England Civic Federation.

great many years that eight hours is at least long enough for any man to labor, and I hope and trust that the American trades union movement will never for a single instant do anything that will impede the progress of that advance and its ultimate consummation in this country.

"The movement has given an incentive to the trades unionism of the country, not alone this country but of

FRANK H. McCARTHY.
First Vice-President, New England Civic Federation.

the entire world. And I do believe that if that were eliminated from our movement to-day it would be hard to keep together that compact and solid mass of men that are coming from all trades to stand together for the purpose of achieving a distinct record in that particular line."

Mr. Archibald said that shorter hours would bring greater opportunities for education and the development of home life, and thus make for contentment and peace between employer and employe.

Marcus M. Marks.

Marcus M. Marks, of New York, spoke as follows:

"That there has been a strong tendency—in fact, a well-defined movement—toward the shorter workday during the past few years will hardly be denied. The

ALFRED MOSELY.
Former Chairman of the Mosely Industrial Commission.

question is, has this movement a logical basis? Is it for the best interests of employer and employe? How can it be regulated so as not to affect industry unfavorably?

"The cry for shorter hours comes invariably from the side of labor. Legislation looking to the shortening of the work day has received its inspiration almost entirely from the same source. Rarely, if ever, have employers inaugurated movements in this direction. In fact, capital as a class has resisted and opposed such efforts.

"Let us see what causes these forces of capital and labor to range themselves in opposing columns in this discussion.

MACHINERY AND SPECIALIZATION.

'Labor asks for shorter hours not on account of a mere whim, nor because the call makes a popular slogan, but because the conditions of employment have been changed so much in recent years that workers feel justly entitled to a shortening of the day. They contend that the introduction of machinery has in a large degree replaced the exercise of the muscles, by the use of the eye and the mind. This causes more strain on the system. They contend further that specialization of labor has taken away the restful variety and change of occupation which formerly diversified the day's employment, and has substituted a regular monotony of daily labor which is much more tiring. For, whilst a workman might contribute his maximum efficiency in working ten to twelve hours per day when strictly physical and variegated effort was required, the greater strain of the present so-called 'improved' condition of labor may now bring about the necessity for a reduction of hours in order to preserve the same degree of efficiency. Of course, different trades and occupations vary considerably in the degree of wear and tear on the workman; some classes of work are comparatively easy and simple, while others are more complex and difficult; so that while an eight-hour day may be proper and economically successful in some, a nine or ten-hour day would be just as natural and not unreasonable in others.

"There is another consideration with prompts the demand on the part of labor for a shorter workday: it is the greater desire for self-improvement. This has been encouraged by the advance in the public school system which affects our younger workmen in particular; also by the multiplication of popular free lectures, public libraries, cheap books and newspapers, etc., that have awakened in the workmen's minds the ambition to lead a better life, possible only in the enjoyment of a reasonable amount of leisure.

"It has frequently been charged by employers that a reduction in hours of labor would mean a corresponding increase in saloon patronage. Is this so? Is it a reason, or an excuse for keeping up the grind? Human nature is very much the same whether a man is clothed in Kentucky jeans or in fine linen. When do you, Mr. Employer, feel the need of a stimulant? When you are fresh and rested, or when you are tired and exhausted? Why should you, then, conclude that your workman is differently constituted? Try him—give him shorter hours if you possibly can, a Saturday, half-holiday if trade conditions permit, and you will find that in most cases he will join his wife and chil-

dren in reasonable healthful recreations. He will take advantage of one of Nature's greatest blessings, the bright warm sunshine, and will from time to time enjoy benefits that will tend to make him a better man, a more useful citizen and a more intelligent worker.

RESTRICTION OF OUTPUT.

"If workmen expect employers to be influenced by the arguments already set forth in favor of a shorter work day, they in turn must give earnest assurance that existing restrictions of output will be withdrawn, with due regard, of course, to the protection of health and maintenance of the quality of labor; that they will do their very best work during the desired shorter hours of employment. I have heard that there are three sorts of day's work. One is a day's work, another, a good day's work, and a third, the best one can do in a day. It is the last that should be forthcoming, and then it may be found that, while the worker has gained, the employer has not lost. For it stands to reason that the quality of the stroke will be better, more energetic and forceful, when the pull is a shorter one. Also, the spirit put into the task when the worker feels that he is being liberally treated and not being made a slave of, should count favorably in the net result of his effort. When machinery is used it will be found that when the man who attends to it has shorter hours there will be fewer repairs required, fewer stoppages, fewer accidents and in other ways many economic advantages.

"When we discuss the question of restriction of output by union regulation, we touch a rather tender spot. The existence of schedules defining and limiting the amount of work a man may do in a day is usually denied by the unions; and it is a fact that such restrictions have latterly not been countenanced by na-

MARCUS M. MARKS.
President of the National Association of Clothing Manufacturers.

tional labor leaders. But the stubborn fact remains that shop regulations frequently do establish them with or without national authorization, and the result is very bad indeed. Many workmen still feel that by 'going slow' the job will last longer and give steadier employment. They forget that they are thus handicapping the employer, and that soon, if they continue the evil practice, he will be unable to give them a job at all, for the competition of other manufacturers, whose men are turning out a full day's product, will slowly but surely drive him out of business. Whatever injures employers soon comes to injure employes as well. Unrestricted production, inventive genius and executive talent have brought Americans to the front rank in the world's industries. If the English 'ca' canny' policy creeps in, there will be danger of our dropping out of our proud place of leadership. In the last message of President Roosevelt, under the heading of 'Labor,' we find the sentiment: 'Unless we continue to keep a quick and lively sense of the great fundamental truth that our concern is with the individual worth of the individual man, this Government cannot permanently hold the place which it has achieved among the nations.'

"Arbitrary restriction of output injures not only the employer, not only the commerce of the country, but, worst of all, it degrades the workman. When a wage-earner does not deliver a full day's work for a full day's pay, he is dishonest to himself as well as to his employer; he loses his self-respect, the safeguard of his manhood. He further fails to develop the best that is in him; his latent energies are not encouraged and die out; and he becomes in time a weary, hopeless plodder.

"There are many considerations in the employer's mind in dealing with the shorter hour question. First and foremost, on account of keen competition, he can not ignore the effect of the possible increase in cost of manufacture. Then the effect of a reduction in output, necessitating the employment of more men to do the same amount of work, frightens the manufacturer. He fears that he will have to build a larger factory to accommodate more help in order to turn out the same product. This would mean more rent, more machinery, more supervision, more wear and tear, more expense generally. These objections may be overcome, if all manufacturers in a trade agree on a basis of hours that will be uniform and therefore work injury

LOUIS D. BRANDEIS.
Chairman of the Conciliation Committee, New England Civic Federation.

to none. It is, however, quite true that in many lines of manufacture, foreign competition must also be carefully taken into account.'

James Duncan.

James Duncan, of Quincy, General Secretary of the Granite Cutters' International Union, said:

"You may take any locality in this or any other country where the hours of labor have changed from ten to nine or nine to eight, and I say that temperance has increased in accordance with that reduction. I had the honor to speak in a meeting in Georgia a short time ago, where the mayor of the town was the presiding officer, and he told me when he first became a municipal officer a great part of the revenue of the town came from fines for drunkenness and disorderly conduct of the working people of the vicinity. The granite industry, with which I am proud to be connected, became busy in that locality, and we began the agitation for the shorter work day. The mayor told me that after we had introduced the eight-hour day—and we

HENRY ABRAHAMS.
Recording Secretary, New England Civic Federation.

were successful, and other trades working nine hours were afterwards reduced to eight—disorderly conduct and intemperance became so little known in the community that the town had to look for taxation in other directions than the saloons in order to meet its necessary expenses.

"The labor movement has proved its position by experience. Take, for instance, the competition that is going on in the building of the two great warships now under construction, one being built by contract under a long-hour work day, and the other being built by Government contract under an eight-hour work day. We are waiting for the results, and we organized workmen have no fear of these results. The figures up to the present time show that the men with the shorter day and higher pay are producing a cheaper job for the Government than the Government is getting by contract under a low wage system. The actual figures for that work can be had through the Department of Labor at Washington, to prove what I say."

Louis D. Brandeis on the Need of Leisure.

In the course of his remarks on the subject, Louis D. Brandeis said:

"Whether in a particular business at a particular time the hours of labor should be materially shortened presents usually a grave question. Such a change, owing to competition direct or indirect, may seriously threaten the prosperity or even the life of the business; or the demand for the reduction of hours may be coupled with other terms or conditions clearly inadmissible. In such cases strenuous resistance becomes the duty of the employer. But however commendable the resistance of the employer to a reduction of hours may be in a particular case, we should all recognize that a short working day is in general essential to the attainment of American economic, social and political ideals, and our efforts should be directed to that end.

"Mr. Gompers quoted some time ago the saying of Heine that 'bread is freedom.' The ancient Greeks, recognizing that 'man cannot live by bread alone,' declared that 'leisure is freedom.' Undoubtedly 'a full dinner pail' is a great achievement as compared with an empty one, but no people ever did or ever can attain a worthy civilization by the satisfaction merely of material needs, however high those needs are raised. The American standard of living demands not only a high

HAYES ROBBINS.
Secretary of the New England Civic Federation.

minimum wage, but a high minimum of leisure, because we must meet also needs other than material ones.

"The welfare of our country demands that leisure be provided for. This is not a plea for indolence. Leisure does not imply idleness. The provision for leisure does not contemplate working less hard. It means ability to work not less, but more; ability to work at something besides bread-winning; ability to work harder while working at bread-winning; and ability to work more years at bread-winning. We need leisure, among other reasons, because with us every man is of the ruling class. Our education and condition of life must be such as become a ruler. Our great beneficent experiment in democracy must fail unless the people, our rulers, are developed in character and intelligence.

"Now consider what, particularly in our large cities, the chance for such development is for men and women who are required regularly to work ten or even nine hours a day. Even a nine-hour work day means, including the noon hour, ten hours at the factory or work shop. That means in Boston for most of those who live in the suburbs eleven or twelve hours devoted to the work shop and getting to and from it. When you add the time necessarily spent at breakfast and supper, dressing and undressing, housework, shopping and sleep, you find that at least twenty-one of the twenty-four hours are devoted to subsistence, and a small fraction of the day is left for living, even if after the long day one is in a condition mentally and physically really to live.

"To attain proper development of character, mind and body a short working day is essential; and the eight-hour day is in most occupations and for most people not too short. For the exceptional occupation and for the exceptional man in any occupation, no general rule is required, and right thinking on this subject cannot

(Continued on page 20.)

THE NATIONAL
Civic Federation Review

Office: 281 Fourth Avenue, New York City

RALPH M. EASLEY, Editor

The Editor alone is responsible for any unsigned article or unquoted statement published in THE NATIONAL CIVIC FEDERATION REVIEW.

Ten Cents per Copy One Dollar per Year

PUBLISHED MONTHLY BY

The National Civic Federation

THE NATIONAL IMMIGRATION CONFERENCE.

The National Conference on Immigration, which assembled in New York on December 6—a synopsis of whose proceedings appears elsewhere in this issue—was a remarkable gathering from several points of view. It was the first of its kind ever called in this country; and that the importance and magnitude of the problem to be discussed by its members was fully appreciated is shown by the fact that more than five hundred delegates attended the opening session. These included representatives of every considerable section of the United States proper, and, in one case, of this country's insular possessions. That so many bankers, merchants, professional men, labor leaders and legislators should leave their callings to take part in this conference argued an intensity of interest which insured a discussion worth listening to. All shades of opinion were represented, from that of the capitalist who desired cheap foreign labor to that of the trade unionist who feared alien competition in wages; from that of the humanitarian who would welcome every strong and willing worker, however poor, to that of the reformer who would raise a higher barrier against the penniless alien. All these and many other views were presented with great fullness and frankness from the floor and platform, the widest opportunity for argument being afforded; so that the resolutions voicing the sentiments of the Conference were finally adopted with practical unanimity.

Apart from the formal results obtained in the framing of these recommendations to Congress, the educational effect of the Conference cannot fail to be of permanent value. The delegates who returned to their homes with a wider outlook upon the subject of immigration will influence their communities in the sane discussion of it; and the Department of Immigration of The National Civic Federation, one of the consequences—and not the least important—of the Conference, will, by its systematic investigation of the questions raised there, furnish a basis for intelligent and practical action upon some of the most perplexing phases of the immigration problem.

GOOD WORDS FOR UNIONS FROM THE "SUN."

Two bits of recent strike history are significant of a growing spirit of fair play in industrial differences. Under the caption of "A Model Strike" the New York *Sun* of January 13, commenting upon the action of the union printers in their contest with the Typothetæ, said:

> So far in its history the strike of union printers against the book and job offices in New York City has differed in one important particular from many previous contests of a similar nature, in that it has been free from violence and outrage. The union men, exercising their undoubted right to quit work, walked out of their employers' shops over a week ago. Since then the employers have borne public testimony to the good order observed by their former workmen and the absence from their campaign of violations of the law.
>
> Too often a strike means bludgeonings, sandbaggings, attempts at arson, the distribution of explosives and similar terrifying tactics. The printers' struggle of 1906 sees the adoption of no such measures, in its early stages at least, and witnesses the use of proper arguments, offers of better treatment and the like, to induce support and win recruits. This policy indicates an understanding among the strike leaders of the public opinion that demands from all, employer and employe alike, strict observance of legal methods in the adjustment of their disputes.
>
> Perhaps it may mean the beginning of a period in which the sober, honest, law-abiding men among the unionists of all trades are to have their way, and the passing of that class of violent agitators who regarded themselves as licensed dictators, the defiance of whose commands justified retaliation by fire and sword.

From the Middle West comes the report of a decision as to the responsibility of a labor union as an organization for the unlawful acts of a minority of its members. The Supreme Court of the State of Indiana has denied an injunction applied for by the Karges Furniture Company, to restrain the Amalgamated Woodworkers' Local Union No. 131 from "picketing, intimidating and otherwise interfering with the plaintiffs' employes." It appears that the Woodworkers' Union of Evansville, numbering about six hundred members, declared a strike for higher wages and shorter hours, and voted to establish an orderly system of picketing the furniture factories, according to a definitely formulated policy.

It was shown by the testimony that fourteen members of the union, despite instructions to the contrary, assaulted the non-union workers and by threats and violence succeeded in closing the plaintiff's factory.

In passing upon the application for an injunction, the Indiana courts, from the lowest to the highest, held that such a prohibition would lie against the actual aggressors only, and not against the union, which had officially discountenanced coercion. Judge Hadley's opinion contains the following passages of practical comment:

> The strike being properly conceived and conducted by the great majority of members, its purposes will not be defeated by the unlawful conduct of a few rowdies and lawbreakers that may be found among them. "Where a combination or association is innocent in its inception," says a recent author, "but is afterward perverted to unlawful ends, only those participating in the conversion are held to be conspirators. . . . Under no circumstances have pickets the right to employ force, menaces of intimidation of any kind in their efforts to induce non-striking workmen to quit, or to induce those about to take the strikers' places to refrain from doing so; neither have they the right as pickets or otherwise to assemble about the working place in such numbers or in such manner as to impress workmen employed, or contemplating employment, with fear and intimidation." . . .
>
> It is, however, generally conceded in this country and in England that workmen when free from contract obligations may not only themselves, singly and in combination, cease to work for any employer, but may also, as a means of accomplishing a legitimate purpose, use all lawful and peaceful means to induce others to quit or refuse employment. . . .
>
> This embraces the right to support their contest by argument, persuasion, and such favors and accommodations as they have within their control. . . . So, in a contest between capital and labor, on the one hand, to secure higher wages, and on the other to resist it, argument and persuasion to win support and co-operation from others are proper to either side, provided they are of a character to leave the persons solicited feeling at liberty to comply or not, as they please.

"Surely," says the *Sun*, from whose editorial columns we quote the foregoing, "no partisan of either side, no matter how violent, can fail to see the fairness of these statements of the court or can find fault with the justice of the decision." And such decisions, in conjunction with the repudiation by the unions of all tactics smacking of violence—and their summary punishment of offenders against a declared policy of fairness—will go far toward the removal of prejudice against unionism on the part of employers as well as the general public.

THE CHURCH AND ORGANIZED LABOR.

In admitting the Rev. Dr. John B. Devins and the Rev. Milton Smith Littlefield as "fraternal delegates" to its meetings, the New York Central Federated Union has taken a step in the direction of a better understanding between the church and organized labor. "Fraternal delegates" have no vote, but are accorded the privileges of the floor when they desire to offer suggestions in the debates of the active members of the organization. In return for the courtesies extended to its ministers in this and other cities, the Presbyterian Church invites labor representatives to the Ministers' Association and presbytery meetings. A week before the admission of these two Presbyterian clergymen to the New York Central Federated Union, the Rev. Dr. J. Howard Melish, rector of Holy Trinity Protestant Episcopal Church, and the Rev. Warren H. Wilson, pastor of the Arlington Avenue Presbyterian Church, were present as fraternal delegates at the meeting of the Brooklyn Central Labor Union.

Three of the great religious denominations are active in endeavors to promote closer relations between the church and organized labor. The general movement of which the appointment of fraternal delegates is the latest manifestation is carried on by the Department of Church and Labor of the Presbyterian Church, whose plans for the study of the labor problem have the official endorsement of the American Federation of Labor. These plans were devised, and for the last three years have been successfully executed in a number of cities by the Rev. Charles Stelzle, the special representative of the church in the interest of workingmen. The

THE PUBLIC OWNERSHIP COMMISSION.

IT ENTERS UPON ITS INVESTIGATION OF THE RELATIVE MERITS OF MUNICIPAL AND PRIVATE OPERATION OF PUBLIC UTILITIES.

THE Public Ownership Commission of the National Civic Federation is steadily proceeding in the work of investigating the relative merits of municipal and private operation of public utilities. Unusual interest has been manifested in the work of this Commission, and it is surprising to see with what willingness persons occupying important positions have given of their time and labor without compensation.

The sub-committee in charge of the investigation has laid out a broad and thorough plan involving the investigation of a considerable number of public and private water, gas, electric lighting and street railway plants in various parts of the United States. Expert accountants are to be employed to investigate the financial records of these systems; well-known engineers of recognized standing will handle the engineering aspects of the investigation; and trained investigators will report upon the history of the plant, the franchises granted, the methods of public regulation and supervision and the political and sociological results of each system of operation. When these reports have been completed to the satisfaction of the committee, they will be collated and analyzed for the preparation of the final report. Indeed, it is planned not to omit a single subject of importance in this investigation, and both municipalities and private corporations have expressed a willingness to aid the investigation in every possible way.

The plan adopted in the United States will be applied to Europe, certain of the expert investigators being taken from the United States because of their familiarity with conditions here and other investigators from Europe because of their better acquaintance with the local conditions to be studied there. The reports made to the various Government departments will be thoroughly examined and tested. If found to be accurate for the purposes of the investigation, they will be utilized; if inaccurate or incomplete, they will be omitted and their inaccuracies pointed out. In this way the ground will be thoroughly covered and a more complete, exhaustive and valuable report prepared than has ever been attempted.

The work in the United States has already been begun, and by the middle of February accountants, engineers and statisticians will probably be put to work upon a number of plans. It is hoped that the work in Europe will be also under way by that time, so that all reports may be presented simultaneously. No date has yet been fixed at which the final report will be published, the unanimous opinion being that the work should be thoroughly done as soon as possible, but that thoroughness should not be sacrificed to haste.

At a meeting held in this city January 10 the report of the sub-committee in charge of the investigation was presented and fully discussed. The meeting was attended by members of the Commission from Boston, Chicago, Cincinnati, Philadelphia, Cleveland, Detroit and several other places who came to New York especially for this purpose. This fact alone shows how widespread is the interest not only in the general question of municipal ownership, but also in the investigation which The National Civic Federation is conducting.

For the purpose of obtaining all the essential facts, three sets of elaborate schedules for each industry have been prepared. One set, relating to the financial aspects of the industries, is to be placed in the hands of accountants. A second set, relating to the engineering questions which are factors in the investigation, will be placed in the hands of engineers. A third set, dealing with the development of the industries, franchise conditions, methods of management, political relations and labor conditions, will be entrusted to statisticians of recognized ability. The persons in whose hands these schedules are placed will be expected to fill them out for each plant investigated.

The schedules for each industry are most complete, and they embody every possible bit of information of use to the Commission. It is impossible to reproduce them here, because of their great length, but a résumé will suffice to show their scope and character. The most important points covered are the following:

History of the plant with special reference to any changes from private to municipal ownership, or *vice versa*.

Local opinion and attitude toward management.

Duration, extent and results of competition.

Public supervision of municipalities.

Methods of taxation.

Systems of granting franchises to private companies.

Franchise restrictions.

Methods and extent of compensation for franchise grants.

Means of enforcing provisions; their success or failure.

Organization of department or company.

Character of officers and employes.

Methods of selecting and discharging employes.

Effect of political considerations.

Efficiency of workmen.

Wages and salaries paid.

Political influence of employes.

Political corruption.

Extent and conditions of free services.

Hours and conditions of labor.

Rules regarding sick leave.

Pensions and profit sharing.

Character of service rendered.

Price of service to private consumer and the city.

Efficiency of the plant and its present value.

Extent of use of service.

Economy of management.

Progressiveness of the industry.

Rapidity with which new inventions are adopted.

Powers of the city relative to acquisition, construction and operation of plant.

Provisions limiting city's power relative to the operation and management of the plant.

Supervision of private corporations.

Methods of incorporating companies and limitations imposed in original charters.

Statutory provisions regarding financial matters, equipment of plant, price and character of service.

Public inspection.

Cost of service.

Treatment of depreciation.

Disposal of profits or payment of deficits.

After these schedules have been filled out and returned to the committee, the results will be tabulated and analyzed. The public records will be examined and all available data used for the preparation of the final report, which will contain all of the special reports prepared under the direction of the Commission, a readable summary of these reports and the conclusions of the Commission. The report in its entirety will be of great value to students of the subject; for no such thorough and comprehensive investigation has ever been undertaken by any Government or organization, either in the United States or abroad.

Protestant Episcopal Church has for four years maintained a standing commission on the Relations of Labor and Capital, one of whose purposes is mediation between workmen and employers; or, to quote the words of the commission, in one of its reports: "The church helps to remove the moral causes of industrial strife when she brings these different members of her family into better acquaintance." The Church Association for the Advancement of the Interests of Labor, which is recognized by the Protestant Episcopal Triennial Convention, has a long history of helpful effort in promoting conciliation movements, the recognition of organized labor and general industrial betterment. Miss Harriette Keyser, its secretary, has been cordially received at meetings of labor organizations, though the society does not seek regular representation at such gatherings. The Industrial Committee of the National Council of Congregational Churches, of which Dr. Frank W. Merrick is chairman, makes inquiries into the industrial situation through its own members, besides urging upon the State organizations of the church the appointment of similar committees and their affiliation with kindred agencies in other denominations and with non-ecclesiastical bodies that work for industrial betterment.

Great mutual benefit should be derived from this freeer interchange of opinions between the church and organized labor. Many ministers of the Gospel know far too little of the point of view of the workingmen among their parishioners, and it cannot be denied that among certain classes of laboring men the influence of the church is *nil*, even if actual enmity to religious teachings does not exist. When the clergy understand the facts in the relations between employers and workingmen, and workingmen see their clerical friends standing beside them in loyal co-operation for the betterment of social conditions, many problems which now vex society, while they may not disappear, will be found easier of solution.

THE DEPARTMENT OF CONCILIATION AND ARBITRATION.

The Executive Council of The National Civic Federation, at its December meeting, elected the Hon. Seth Low as chairman of the Department of Conciliation and Arbitration. Mr. Low's name is almost synonymous with the words "conciliation and arbitration." He was a delegate to the Peace Conference at The Hague, and in addition to having been an arbitrator in a great many cases of industrial disputes, has been connected with all the important movements relating to such work. The full committee is as follows:

Seth Low, Chairman.

Representing the public:

Andrew Carnegie, capitalist, New York City;
Cornelius N. Bliss, ex-Secretary of the Interior, New York City;
Isaac N. Seligman, J. & W. Seligman & Co., New York City;
Louis D. Brandeis, attorney-at-law, Boston, Mass.;
Frederick N. Judson, attorney-at-law, St. Louis, Mo.;
Benjamin Ide Wheeler, President, University of California, Berkeley, California;
V. Everit Macy, capitalist, New York City;
Dr. Albert Shaw, editor, "The Review of Reviews," New York City.

Employers:

Lucius Tuttle, President, Boston & Maine Railroad Company, Boston;
Frederick D. Underwood, President, Erie Railroad Company, New York City;
Clarence H. Mackay, President, Postal Telegraph and Cable Company, New York City;
Frederick P. Fish, President, American Telegraph and Telephone Company, Boston.
Samuel Mather, of Pickands, Mather & Co., Cleveland, Ohio;
Franklin MacVeagh, of Franklin MacVeagh & Co., Chicago;
Charles A. Moore, of Manning, Maxwell & Moore, New York City;
Francis L. Robbins, President, Pittsburgh Coal Company, Pittsburgh, Pa.;
Otto M. Eidlitz, Chairman, Board of Governors, Building Trades Employers' Association, New York City.
Marcus M. Marks, President, National Association of Clothing Manufacturers, New York City.

Representing the wage-earners:

Samuel Gompers, President, American Federation of Labor, Washington, D. C.;
John Mitchell, President, United Mine Workers of America, Indianapolis, Ind.;
James Duncan, General Secretary, Granite Cutters' International Association of America, Quincy, Mass.
Daniel J. Keefe, President, International Longshoremen, Marine and Transport Workers' Association, Detroit, Mich.;
William D. Mahon, President, Amalgamated Association of Street Railway Employes of America, Detroit, Mich.;
Warren S. Stone, Grand Chief, International Brotherhood of Locomotive Engineers, Cleveland, Ohio;
E. E. Clark, Grand Chief, Order of Railway Conductors, Cedar Rapids, Iowa;
J. J. Hannahan, Grand Master, Brotherhood of Locomotive Firemen, Peoria, Ill.;
P. H. Morrissey, Grand Master, Brotherhood of Railway Trainmen, Cleveland, Ohio;
John F. Tobin, General President, Boot and Shoe Workers' Union, Boston, Mass.

This committee will have to do with industrial disturbances exclusively. It will meet in March for the purpose of outlining a plan of procedure. At that meeting it will consider the advisability of adopting the methods of the British Board of Trade in organizing local commissions in all important industrial centers, and will also consider how best to co-operate with the various State boards of arbitration.

NEW YORK CIVIC FEDERATION MEETING.

The annual meeting of the Civic Federation of New York will be held Wednesday evening, February 14, 1906, at the Park Avenue Hotel. The subject for discussion will be "Welfare Work."

Leading New York employers will describe what has been done to better the conditions of employes in several important industries.

The necessity of making such provision for the physical comfort of employes as ventilation for stationary firemen and metal polishers, baths for moulders, sanitary dressing rooms for theatrical employes, the factory lunch room, and emergency hospitals for structural iron workers, as well as the requirements of employes in bakeries, the clothing and other trades, will be presented by leaders of employes' organizations.

"How New York City Cares for its Institutional Employes" and "The Need of Better Accommodations in the Station Houses for Policemen" will be presented by former city officials.

Stereopticon views, illustrating what has been done throughout the country by practical, successful business men in providing for the comfort of employes in the work rooms, for recreation, for educational opportunities, and in the housing of labor, will be shown.

WELFARE DEPARTMENT
OF
The National Civic Federation

A SUCCESSFUL APPRENTICE SCHOOL.

The Theoretical and Practical Training of Boys in the West Lynn General Electric Shops.

The following address by M. W. Alexander, engineer of the General Electric Company of West Lynn, Mass., was delivered before a conference of welfare managers and special welfare workers held at Atlantic City under the auspices of the Welfare Department of The National Civic Federation:

"The Thomson-Houston Electric Company at West Lynn, Mass.—a part of the General Electric Company—organized in February, 1902, an apprenticeship system, under which boys of at least sixteen years of age who have had a grammar school education and are desirous of learning a trade, are indentured as apprentices. The period of apprenticeship lasts four years, during which time the boys are taught the mysteries and arts of the different trades which are practiced at our factory.

"Our aim is not only to make of these boys efficient machinists and tool-makers, pattern-makers and carpenters, iron, steel and brass moulders, instrument makers and electrical workers, but to develop a class of artisans from whom we can choose men for our leading positions in the factory, for assistant foremen, foremen and master mechanics. To hold such positions requires not only a knowledge of all the operations that have to be performed by hand or machine, but also a knowledge of the scientific principles that underlie the work, and of the ways and means of conducting the work in a businesslike manner.

"With this aim in view, we recognized the necessity of educational development of the boys and incorporated right from the beginning in our apprenticeship system a school especially fitted for the needs of our apprentices. The lack of proper educational opportunities in the evening in the city of Lynn, such as, for instance, the city of Philadelphia offers in the Spring Garden Institute, was one reason which prompted our company to start its own school. The other reason was the desire to give to the boys eminently practical knowledge of the very kind which they will need later on as journeymen and foremen. We therefore selected our own engineers, draughtsmen and shop foremen as teachers. These men know the needs of our factory and can impart to the boys the specific knowledge which they require in our own factory and, in a general way, in any manufacturing establishment of a similar character.

M. W. ALEXANDER.
Engineer of the General Electric Company of West Lynn, Mass.

The contact during school hours with the same men who direct them during working hours in the factory has a tendency to maintain better discipline among the apprentices, because school does not then appear to them as a separate institution, but as only one part of our apprentice work.

"The school first met in the evening, when the factory closed; the boys assembled in the school rooms, partook of a light lunch furnished free of charge by the company and received instruction for about two hours. It soon became apparent that after a day's work the boys were too tired to reap the full benefit of the school instruction, and the evening school was therefore changed to a morning school. The blowing of the factory whistle in the morning is now the signal for the commencement of the school. The boys come to the school room physically and mentally rested. Formerly we had difficulty in keeping the apprentices in the school; now we rather experience difficulty in getting them out of the school room into the shop. The improvement in the results has been marked.

"Each boy receives three years of instruction. He enters school after he has been an apprentice for about six months and he graduates from the school several months before he graduates from his apprenticeship. Each school year consists of forty weeks with two sessions of two and one-half hours each per week. The comparatively small amount of time devoted to instruction does not permit us to go very deeply into the various subjects which we teach. In fact, a large part of the teaching is merely a review of some of the grammar school work, but applied to practical factory conditions. Experience has prompted us to devote a good share of the time to this review and to carry it back to the elementary stage of the subjects which we desire to review. The rest of the time at our disposal is devoted to subjects which either have not been taught in the grammar school at all or have been touched upon only in a general way.

"The question will arise: Why should we, who have had no pedagogical training, attempt to review what has already been taught in the public schools by pedagogically trained teachers? With all due respect to our public schools, excellent as they are in the main—and nobody has a higher regard than I for a teacher and his efforts—I find from my years of experience that the public schools fail to teach the boy to think for himself and to think clearly and logically. The school has taught the boy a great amount of knowledge and has committed to his memory many formulas, but when it comes to the application of this knowledge and of these formulas to practical uses, many a boy finds himself blocked, because he has not acquired the faculty of independent thinking. Our review, then, aims to instil in the boy the habit of independent thinking.

"Those of you who are closely connected with the management of an establishment will have experienced the difficulty of finding men who can occupy positions of responsibility as foremen. The head as well as the hand must constitute the foreman's equipment. Our industries require of the men who want to rise above the rank and file this very faculty of clear and logical thinking which we find so often lacking in otherwise excellent artisans. I venture to make this criticism of the public schools, because in it I only give you the benefit of my experience. It does not apply to the schools of any particular locality. Our boys come from all parts of the State of Massachusetts and neighboring States, and we have one or more representatives from almost every State in the Union; my previous activity in the Middle West has shown me that about the same conditions exist there.

THEORETICAL INSTRUCTION.

"There is, however, another aim in our review of grammar school subjects, namely, to give the boy additional knowledge by giving him an insight into technology. To make my point clearer I shall take the liberty to outline briefly the course of study.

"During the first year we teach English and mathematics, devoting one-third of the time to the former and two-thirds to the latter. In English, the spelling of technical terms is first taken up and then followed by short dictations explaining technical processes, describing materials and their properties and various kinds of apparatus. The boy, therefore, becomes acquainted in a general way with all our practical work.

"Mathematics is the second subject which we review during the first year. We start with simple processes of addition, subtraction, multiplication and division, first of whole numbers and then of decimal and common fractions, finishing the year with proportion and percentage calculations. Alternating with arithmetic, we review mensuration.

"Only concrete examples are given by the teachers, who as stated before, must aim to lead the boy on to independent thinking and to make him acquainted with the very technical arithmetic which he may have to use as a shop foreman. It is only a test of the boy's memory if you ask him to solve '3 x 420 x 12,' but it is an entirely different test if you put the same problem in the following manner: 'A factory consists of three rooms; each room is lighted with twelve arc lamps, each of which requires 420 watts of energy. How much horsepower of energy will have to be provided for the lighting of the whole factory if 746 watts equal one horsepower?' In stating such a problem, we explain in the very briefest manner the meaning of 'watt' as a unit of measurement of energy, and we also explain briefly the nature of an arc lamp, showing the outside appearance of the same and the inside mechanism. In fact, whenever a teacher speaks of a piece of apparatus or a part thereof, I insist upon having such apparatus or part shown to the boys, if this is at all possible. The boys will associate the picture with the name of the apparatus and will therefore retain the name better in their memory. I do not expect that the boy will learn fully the meaning of a watt of energy, or a volt of pressure, or an ampere of current, or for that matter, the operation of an arc lamp, the characteristics of an incandescent lamp, or the principles that govern the running of a motor. The terms 'watt,' 'volt' and 'ampere,' 'arc lamp,' 'incandescent lamp' and 'motor' will become, however, familiar to him by frequent usage, and when, later on in the teaching of physics and magnetism and electricity, these same terms are brought before him again, they will appear to him as old acquaintances and will therefore make their study so much easier to him.

"I desire to give one more illustration, taking this time mensuration as my subject. A problem may be commonly stated as follows: What is the weight of a steel rod one-half inch in diameter and fifty inches long? We state the problem in a different manner: 'The machine shop is ordered to produce seventy-five steel pins, each to be one-half inch in diameter and three-quarters of an inch long. These pins are to be cut from a long steel rod and the tool for cutting off the pins will waste one-sixteenth of an inch of material between each two pins. How long a steel rod will be required, and what will be the weight of the same?' This is a problem which we meet in everyday factory life and which involves nothing else than plain multiplication and addition. It is simply a question of multiplying 75, the number of pins, by ¾ inch, the length of each pin, and adding to it 74 x 1-16 inch, which we have wasted by the cutting-off tool. The whole will give the length of steel rod required. Now this length is multiplied by the area of a half-inch circle to obtain the cubical contents, which, when multiplied by the specific gravity of steel (a figure which we give to the boy) will give the total weight.

"During the first part of the second year, two-thirds of the time is devoted to square and cube roots applied to practical problems and to calculations of weights of different materials and machines. The remaining one-third is devoted to English.

"We teach the boy to write 'shop notes,' by which

I mean that we teach him to express himself in a very brief and clear manner and without flourish and frills. To illustrate: if a boy should be unable to finish a piece of work because his machine is worn out and, therefore, cannot be run at the proper speed, I expect him to notify the superintendent of this fact immediately—nothing else than what we would expect of any proper shop foreman. His note should, perhaps, be as follows:

I. F. Baker, Supt.:

I shall be unable to finish the 20 motor shafts by next Friday as promised, because my lathe is in very poor condition and cannot, therefore, be run at the proper speed. I expect to finish the shafts by Monday of next week.

(Signed) N. M. SMITH.

"It is not necessary for the boy to start the letter with 'Dear Sir.' The superintendent knows how 'dear' he is to the right boy without being reminded of it. It is a waste of time for the boy to write and for the superintendent to read a letter like the following:

I. F. Baker, Supt.:

I am extremely sorry to report that I shall not be able to fulfil the promise which I made you a few days ago in regard to the twenty motor shafts which I expected to finish by Friday of this week. The lathe on which I am turning these shafts is in very poor condition. I cannot, under the circumstances, turn out as fast work as I could if my machine could be run at a higher speed. I shall endeavor to finish these shafts by Monday of next week and hope that this delay will not cause you any inconvenience.

I remain, yours very truly,
(Signed) N. M. SMITH.

"Many a good shop foreman impairs his usefulness in a position of responsibility because he cannot write a correct and concise letter.

"During the second part of the second year, English has been dropped entirely, and mathematics is only pursued on alternate mornings; the other mornings are taken up with physics with particular reference to mechanics.

"During the third year, one morning per week is devoted to mechanical draughting, the other mornings to mechanics and mechanism, magnetism and electricity. Again we pursue the policy of speaking in concrete terms and illustrating these terms by the objects of which we speak. Our whole factory is utilized as a laboratory which not only aids in the proper understanding of the subject matter, but also arouses and keeps awake the interest of the boys. Mechanical drawing does not aim at the designing of machinery, but rather at the designing of the tools which journeymen need in the process of manufacturing machinery. We give, for instance, to the apprentice the cover of an arc lamp which has nine holes of different sizes and ask him to sketch a jig or holder by means of which these different holes can be drilled by a machine accurately and quickly without the necessity of laying out each hole separately.

"The last few weeks of the third year are devoted to lectures on factory organization and factory systems. A boy too often acquires the idea, which sticks to him even after he has become a journeyman, that a foreman is after all nothing but a slave driver, whose chief duty is to obtain from the man the last ounce of work. We endeavor to show to the boy that the foreman is only one link, though an important one, in the big chain, which cannot operate if even the smallest link gives out. As soon as the boy begins to realize this, he begins to understand that even his own little efforts have their importance and are needed in the carrying on of the whole work; he will become a supporter rather than an antagonist of the foreman.

"I attach quite an importance to these few lectures and to the effect they should have upon the future working men. An ambitious working man may inquire the reason for doing a certain thing in a certain way. What is the usual answer that most foremen will give him? They will tell him in a more or less polite way that it is none of his business; that he should bother about his own work and not waste time by asking such questions. I believe most decidedly that it is an ambitious man's business to understand, in a general way, the conditions that surround him and the reasons for carrying on work in the way in which he is directed to perform it. A question asked in the right spirit deserves some answer in the same spirit. The man will be benefited by it and the company will be better off for that.

"I think it of sufficient interest to state here a psychological element in our school work. If we ask a boy to figure out the weight of a piece of brass three inches long by one inch in diameter and tell him that he is wrong if his calculation does not give the proper figure, he may assume an attitude of antagonism to the teacher. We give to the boy a piece of brass, let him measure the same and sketch it on a piece of paper and calculate the weight. We then hand to the boy a pair of scales to check his own results. If now the scales tell him that he is wrong, he will feel rather ashamed of himself and re-calculate the problem with the earnest desire of arriving at the proper figure. The boy has, so to speak, a greater confidence in the veracity of the scales than in the veracity of the teacher.

"An examination is held at the end of each term, and only those apprentices who obtain a percentage of 60 or more are allowed to advance to the next school term. Some have been left behind. The knowledge of their failure, however, became quickly known among their shop-mates and had a most stimulating effect on the mental machinery of these boys. The final examination after three years of schooling is a competitive one, wherein everyone who obtains a percentage of 95 or more is presented by the company with a technical book or a useful working tool. The standing obtained in the school is also stated in the 'certificate of apprenticeship,' which is given to the boy at the successful termination of his apprenticeship, together with a cash bonus of $100.

PRACTICAL TRAINING.

"At the same time with the theoretical instruction in the school, practical instruction in the handling of tools was carried on in the shop. We soon recognized, however, that there must be a very close connection between the theoretical and the practical instruction, so that a boy may be stimulated to apply every day to the work-shop what the school has taught him. The difficulty can easily be understood of giving systematic practical instruction in the factory with an equal chance of giving the same training to all boys and yet of taking into account the individuality of every apprentice—the quickness of his mental grasp, the dexterity of his hand.

"The work which apprentices perform in the different shop departments must of necessity be governed to a large extent by production requirements. One department may be very busy to-day and may offer splendid opportunities for the boys, while to-morrow, it may have to work up only a small amount of production of a character, perhaps, which does not give the apprentices a really good chance. Then, again, the practical instruction in the shop is influenced materially by the individuality of the workmen, assistant foremen and foremen, all of whom act as instructors to the boys.

"In order to equalize and improve the conditions it was decided a year and a half ago to concentrate the first practical instruction in a separate department, the apprentice training room, and to make the factory a post-graduate course, for the purpose of acquiring increased speed and accuracy on a greater variety of work. The factory would then not only apply the finishing touches to the boy's practical education, but would bring him face to face with real factory conditions and the emergencies that arise. The apprentice training room is, therefore, a second part of the apprentice school and may justly be called a trade school in contradistinction to the theoretical school which we have just described. The training room is in charge of a man who is not only an expert mechanician with inventive ability, but one who takes an interest in boys and understands how to handle them. This man, therefore, has the responsibility of not only initiating the boys into the trade in such a manner as to lay a solid foundation for their future work, but also of arousing in them the proper interest in and respect for manual labor. He furthermore has the opportunity of studying closely the boy's make-up, so that he may drop from the apprentice course those who do not display the qualities which are essential for a successful career, and he has a chance to develop an inventive capacity in those who by nature are endowed with inventive minds.

"Every apprentice has first to enter the training room, where he will be kept from nine to twelve months, according to his ability. Bench-work during the first month is followed by work on simple machines, such as drill presses, from which the boy advances to work of a more difficult character on different lathes, on planers and shapers, on boring mills and milling machines. Some old machines have been rescued from the scrap heap and placed in the Trade School, in order to afford the boys a chance to make repairs—an excellent training for a machinist and an opportunity to develop the ability to meet emergencies. They are also taught to take care, for a short time, of the stock room, which is a part of the training room, and to perform such clerical work as making out time-cards and order blanks, which is required of every assistant foreman and foreman. During the last few months of their stay in the trade school, the best boys act as assistants to the man in charge, looking after some of the new apprentices.

"The present equipment of our training room is limited, due to lack of sufficient room, so that we can take care in it of only about forty apprentices at a time, while about 150 apprentices are distributed through the shop. As those at the top are graduated into the factory post-graduate course, new freshmen, or, rather, fresh young men are taken in. We expect to move into a large, well-equipped building next spring, when we shall be able to accommodate a larger number of apprentices.

"It is a most gratifying pleasure to me to find this trade school and our whole apprenticeship system so universally endorsed by the large body of our working men, whose sons and relatives are always given preference in the selection of apprentices. The trade school movement is a movement of the present time, which is especially alive in our State of Massachusetts. We have therefore only undertaken what in due time and on a better foundation the State or municipality will undertake, and when the State has established trade schools of the proper character, I think there will be no further reason for a private corporation like our company to maintain its own trade school.

"The object of our whole apprenticeship system, as I have already pointed out, is to develop a very high class of employes. Their technical education should therefore be of as broad a character as possible, because with this better education goes a greater sense of responsibility, a firmer grasp of the work, a better understanding of the business methods. This aim cannot fully be accomplished within the compass of our theoretical school. I have therefore supplemented this school by an apprentice club, where the apprentices may congregate in their leisure hours for social as well as educational enjoyment. Expert engineers lecture to the boys once a week on various subjects which are allied to their business and stand ready to enlighten the boys further by answering any questions which may be asked during discussion. The club has been handsomely furnished by the company, but is conducted by the boys themselves, with a representative of the company on the board of directors. It is very interesting to observe how well the boys conduct the business of their club, which develops in them a business instinct and self-reliance.

"These three institutions, therefore, namely, the theoretical school, the trade school, and the apprentice club, constitute the apprentice school of the Thomson-Houston (General Electric) Company at West Lynn, of which you did me the honor to invite me to speak to you to-night."

THE COST OF THE EXPERIMENT.

At the close of his address Mr. Alexander gave additional information about the school, in response to a number of questions put to him by the delegates. He said that at the present time 148 apprentices had signed the apprentice agreement and that 21 were serving on trial. If these latter prove satisfactory they will be allowed to sign the agreement, otherwise they will be asked to leave the company.

A high standard has been set by the General Electric Company, and only boys who give fair promise of becoming first-class men are wanted in the apprenticeship course. Some time in May of each year a letter is sent to the superintendents of schools through the State of Massachusetts, wherein the opportunities offered to boys at the General Electric Works are set forth, with a request that the superintendents recommend good boys who want to learn a trade. Most of the boys are grammar school graduates, although lately a number have applied who have had either a partial or complete high school training.

Apprentices are paid from the hour when they enter the service of the General Electric Company, even during the trial month, and their wages are advanced at stated periods. Grammar school graduates receive six cents an hour for the first six months; high school graduates receive eight cents an hour for the same period; thereafter all apprentices are advanced two cents per hour after six months and again after six months, and so forth as stated in the agreement. Regular wages are even paid for the hours spent in the school rooms. This means considerable expense to the company, but it is believed that it is fully offset by the appreciation of the boys manifested in the zeal to learn in the school and to apply the knowledge thus gained to the work in the factory.

It has been found more convenient to start the day with school work than to take the boys out of the shop and into the school room during the day. "It is no hardship to the foremen," said Mr. Alexander, "to start certain machines at 9 o'clock in the morning instead of at 7 o'clock. It would be a hardship on the foremen to stop such machines in the middle of the afternoon and start them again at say 4 or 5 o'clock."

The form of agreement under which apprentices are engaged is signed by the apprentice and his father or guardian and binds him to perform satisfactory service for a certain compensation. Mr. Alexander values the contract, not so much from the legal standpoint, as for the moral effect which it carries. He illustrated this point by giving the following example: "Some boy who has been with us for perhaps six months or so thinks that in a pop-corn store at the corner he can make a dollar a week more, and he is therefore very much tempted to make that extra dollar. The agreement holds this boy down until he comes back to his senses and prevents him from taking a rash step and thereby, perhaps, spoiling his future. If a boy, however, shows a disposition to break the agreement, that is taken as sufficient indication of his unfitness for the company's purpose."

In response to a question in reference to the limitation of the number of apprentices, Mr. Alexander said: "There certainly will be a limit to the number of apprentices which can be employed by the company. We have, at the present time, about 7,500 employes, and the works are constantly growing. We consider that we should have 250 to 300 apprentices and figure that, if 25 per cent. of all the apprentices who graduate stay with us, we shall have a sufficient number of trained employes from whom to choose our leaders in the shop. The other graduated apprentices will go to other establishments, which we hope will be benefited by them, and by and by, other establishments will turn out good apprentices who will come to us; so we shall gain about as much as we lose. As stated before, we encourage graduated apprentices to remain with us. At the present time we have graduated eight apprentices, six of whom have remained with us, while two have gone into small machine shops where well-trained men are in demand. I feel sure, however, that these boys will come back to us after a while."

Referring again to the use of old machines in the training room, Mr. Alexander said: "We have placed in our training room a number of old machines which nobody could use, because they were on the point of breaking down. We know that something will happen to the machines as soon as they are started, but we do not tell the boys about it. We have a boy start the machine and run it until something happens. We then instruct the boy how to repair the machine, which sometimes may require a new bearing, or a new spindle, and sometimes the inserting of a new tooth in a gear. When the repairs have been finished and the machine is able to perform work again, it is noticeable that the boy takes a greater pride in his machine and pushes his work along with increased pleasure. In this manner we have not only made some first-class tools out of almost useless machines, at a reasonable expense, but have at the same time taught the boys one of the most valuable things—to meet emergencies as they arise and to overcome the difficulties themselves."

The cost of equipment in the training room has been about five thousand dollars, and an additional three thousand dollars will be spent within the next half year for the purchase of new machines. These machines are a good investment and can be used anywhere in the factory. "The General Electric Company," Mr. Alexander said, "does not believe in letting anything go to waste. No money is spent in a purely sentimental way; there is always a straight business proposition at the bottom of things. If that were not the case I would not care to help in the work."

MILL CONDITIONS AND TUBERCULOSIS.

At the Boston Tuberculosis Exhibition, December 29, the reduction of the death rate from tuberculosis, as the result of modern conditions in the factory and home, was given consideration. Among the papers read was one on "Sanitation in the Textile Industries" by C. J. H. Woodbury, Secretary of the New England Cotton Manufacturers' Association. In the course of his address Mr. Woodbury said:

"Every humane and every commercial motive impels those in charge of others to desire that the people in their service should be in the best of physical health. The sound body is more directly essential for those who labor with their hands than for those whose occupations are mental.

"Changes in mill construction and equipment, I believe, have fulfilled their purpose of contributing to the health and comfort of those employed in the mills. The early mills were low-studded, and, after the days of the stoves, heated by cast-iron pipes, about six inches in diameter, hung from the timbers above, to the discomfort of those employed beneath them, owing to the severe exposure to heat radiating upon the head; the walls were of uniform thickness at each story, and questions of strength limited the size of the windows.

"Sanitary and washing accommodations were such as the ignorance of the time afforded.

"Lighting by kerosene or by gas vitiated the air far more, I believe, than the respiration of the help, and the same was true of whale or lard oils earlier in use.

"In contrast with these conditions, by the inorganic evolution of commercial advancement, the modern mill has displaced the old plant by improvements in which the building and equipment has shared with the machinery in receiving the benefit of engineering skill and invention.

"The more economic distribution of masonry in buttressed wall construction establishes greater rigidity of the structure and also permits larger windows with increased introduction of sunlight, and I believe that a layman is warranted in expressing the opinion that this change furnishes more healthful conditions. A practical measure of the increased sunlight through the large windows of the modern mill is shown by the fact that under the same conditions of hours of labor and class of goods, a new mill requires 300 hours of artificial light a year, and an old mill 450 hours. This also means that the purifying effect of the sunlight is more efficiently applied throughout the day in the new mill, as well as extended 150 hours a year.

"The upper portion of the modern mill window is generally swung on a transom, so that incoming air strikes the ceiling and is diffused throughout the room without being concentrated into rapid currents, producing draughts. The rooms are higher and, if heated by a number of elevated wrought-iron pipes, of small diameter, the heat is diffused without discomfort to those employed beneath them. Many mills are heated by a method which also furnishes ventilation, by blowing warmed air throughout the building, and in later instances, a combination of the two methods produces efficient results with greater economy. The humidity artificially produced in mills, primarily for the removal of the disadvantages of unduly dry air in the textile processes, also furnishes more agreeable and, I believe, more healthful conditions.

"The sanitary and washing accommodations have water-proof floors and are equipped with modern appliances such as were unknown a few years ago.

"The appliances for the removal of dust from the air are of two types. In napping and card rooms it is done, when necessary, by centrifugal extractors which whirl the fine fibres from the air and send it back into the room cleaned. In polishing and grinding rooms the metallic dust flies into hoods from which it is drawn by exhaust blowers to the open air. In both cases, it is evident that the removal of dust from the air conduces to conditions which apply more directly to the purpose of this meeting than the other improvements which merely establish more favorable hygienic conditions."

NATIONAL CONFERENCE ON IMMIGRATION.

(*Continued from page* 6)

here in the past? Shall we establish, as has been suggested, an educational test? Has it any merit? Has it any demerit? Congressman Gardner has stated that of those immigrants who came here in one year 200,000

SIMON WOLF.
President of the Order of B'nai B'rith.

could neither read nor write. But there is a brighter side to this picture. Out of the census reports of 1900 we find that out of the children in the public schools, or rather the children of native parents, 5.70 per cent. were illiterate, whereas of the children of foreign-born parents, 2 per cent. were illiterate. If that demonstrates anything, ladies and gentlemen, it demonstrates that the test of our immigration is not the immigrant. The test of immigration is the American generation. (Applause.)

"Congressman Adams said that there were 20,000 Jews in the City of New York who are at present dependent. They are, to a greater or less extent, because they are driven here from countries where they have been so persecuted that when they arrive here they are, to all intents and purposes, poverty-stricken. But out of those who needed assistance ten years ago, less than 2 per cent. are in need at the present moment. Of the immigration that has come here in the last twenty-five years, less than 2 per cent. of Jews in the city of New York or the United States that require help is native born or the children of the first generation. This is true of Italians and every other immigrant. Given an opportunity, these people no longer remain dependent upon either public or private support.

"Shall we select our immigrants along the lines of race? I think we need not go over this subject again. I think we have been convinced by what has been said to us to-day in particular that we can draw neither racial nor religious lines, and that if anything the citizen of the future, the American of the future, is going to be a composite of the various races that have come into these United States, whether he belongs to the Anglo-Saxon or to the South or East European races.

"Shall we select on volume? The statement has been made here to-day that we should limit it to 80,000 from any particular country, and I am going to ask Congressman Gardner how is he going to know that the first 80,000 are the desirable ones?

"Or shall we adopt the extreme of a head-tax of $40 on males? This means that you are going to debar whom? The wage-earner; and you are going to allow the women and children and those who may become dependents more readily to enter this country in any number they may deem fit or wise." (Applause.)

Broughton Brandenburg.

Discussing the possibility of keeping undesirable aliens from starting on their journey to this country, Broughton Brandenburg said:

"The European districts from which immigration is profuse and dangerous occupy a limited area no larger than the State of New York. Lay these spots off into districts and appoint through civil service a small board for each, with one medical member, all speaking the language, to visit each community once a month, say, and issue certificates to intending immigrants. Secure these from forgery and transfer by photography, or other means. Then, when the immigrant has sold his few belongings and made ready in the time limit of thirty days, let him join a group that shall travel in charge of a courier direct to the nearest large port where they shall be delivered directly on board. On every steamer put an officer and enforce all the present laws for decent treatment, hygiene and cleanliness. I estimate $12 as the average amount grafted off each immigrant before he reaches Ellis Island. Make him pay the heavy cost of his examination with a fee of $5, and, having been safeguarded by the direct delivery and supervision, he will be saved the other seven."

President Eliot Condemns Exclusion.

The address of President Eliot, of Harvard, was as strong in its advocacy of a policy of free and unrestricted entry for sound labor as was that of Mr. Carnegie. He began by saying, in reference to a remark previously made by Mr. Gompers:

"I want to express a doubt that the doctrine of self-protection is one which is going to be useful in the settlement of this question. The word protection has been very much overworked in this country. (Applause.) Self-protection is a natural idea if we are thinking of protection from the elements, from the forces of nature, but the moment we begin to think that self-protection is a sound motive for dealing with men, we are getting on dangerous ground. (Applause.) That is not the nobler thought. That is not the generous thought. And in my opinion it is not a thought that will ever commend itself to the American people in regard to immigration. (Applause).

"I suppose it is wholly useless to talk about the desirability of excluding pauper criminals and imbeciles. There is no difference of opinion about that. There may be better devices than we now have for that purpose, but the present arrangements are very tolerably satisfactory in that respect. When it comes to excluding labor, sound labor, on the ground that it has been induced to come here, we enter upon an altogether different discussion. I have no belief whatever in endeavoring to prevent sound, healthy, moral laborers from coming hither (applause), no matter whether they are induced or not induced. (Applause.) They are welcome, and I think we may all be sure that the American people mean to welcome them, although coming in masses from time to time they may somewhat depress the average rate of wages.

"Moreover, there is another thing going on in this world that needs to be taken into consideration in dealing with this problem; namely, the mobility of capital is becoming greater and greater. It is more mobile than population, than working people—much more mobile. We have seen it moved about in a wonderful way already in our own country, and now we are seeing it move out of our country into other countries where there are laborers and a market. This is a process that is going on more and more and must be taken into account. Do we, on the whole, prefer to have the laborers come here and build up our country, or to have our capital go elsewhere and build up other nations? Trade, commerce, manufacturing are becoming international, in spite of tariffs. Now, we see that even in the names of trade unions. How often we read now of the international union of such and such a trade! Why? Because labor organizations themselves perceive that the industrial problems are transcending national bounds. Let us remember this when we are asking Congress or any other authority to deal with this problem of immigration. Let us remember that capital can take care of itself. It will take care of itself. It is taking care of itself. Just remember, too, that national greatness, after all, depends on the soundness of the brain and the brawn of the people." (Applause.)

Jesse Taylor.

The Conference then passed to a general discussion by delegates (under a five-minute restriction) of the subject,—a discussion which reached its climax in the impassioned declaration of Jesse Taylor, a delegate from Ohio, that if influential Protectionists did not soon advocate some way of protecting the American laboring man against the "riffraff of Southern Europe," there were many people that belonged to the old full dinner-pail Republican party who would "flop over, body, bag and breeches, to the other side." He continued:

"In fairness to the farmers and the laboring people

of this country, if you multimillionaires and owners of factories, with all due respect to you (I am not jealous of you because you have got money and because you wear diamonds by the quart), if you have the right to go into the markets of the world for your labor and bring it into competition with American labor, the riff-raff of Southern Europe that can live on two beers and

AUGUST BELMONT.
President of The National Civic Federation.

a hard biscuit a day, then I say to you the time is coming when the laboring people of this country will assert their right and say to you: 'Down with the high tariff; we will go some place else to buy our goods.'" (Applause.)

Rev. Joel Ives.

The Rev. Joel Ives, of Connecticut, laid special stress upon the undue proportion of immigration received by the New England States. "The early immigration," he said, "moved Westward and merged itself into our life and civilization, and the last census names Dakota as the most foreign State in the Union. But statisticians tell us to-day that Massachusetts is the most foreign State in the Union. The census gives us four cities in Massachusetts and one city in Rhode Island with a larger percentage of foreign parentage than New York City, Chicago or San Francisco. If we are to maintain the New England ideals we have a large proposition on our hands when Southern New England is already 65 per cent. of foreign parentage, and when our towns, our farming communities are so largely depleted of that New England stock. Our common schools must be maintained, and a righteous and honorable press must be maintained, and all the influences both of the press and the school and the church must be of a kind to maintain that New England life which

HON. OSCAR STRAUS.
Publicist.

has sent out its people and its influences from the Atlantic to the Pacific; for it is said to-day that there can be found communities on the Pacific Coast that are more purely New England than can be found upon the Atlantic Coast.

"I am proud of the growing generation of the immigrant. One of our people went into one of the schools in Hartford in a section of the city where very few of the native stock are to be found, and looking into the faces of the school children, the question was asked: 'How many of the school are Americans? Please raise your hands.' Every blessed little hand in the school went up. They were all Americans. They all loved the flag; they all are seeking after the knowledge of the English. I am told that there are not as many newspapers printed in a foreign tongue in New England to-day as there were ten years ago, in spite of the enormous increase of the people of foreign tongue within our borders. And therefore there is every reason for an optimistic view in regard to this large immigration if we can properly distribute it."

Dr. Edward A. Steiner.

Speaking on "Distribution of Immigration," Dr. E. A. Steiner, of Grinnell, Iowa, held that the question of distribution was the question of wages. "If South Carolina," he said, "would offer, instead of the $2 which a man earns here, $2.25 or $2.50, she could have all the immigrants that she could take care of. They will go first of all into the industrial centers because work is ready for them. They will stay largely in the city of New York, not because New York is attractive to them, not because they are used to skyscrapers and electric cars, but because New York pays the highest kind of a wage.

"Has this congested immigrant proved a political menace? It has been said that there are 30 000 illegal citizenship papers in the possession of foreigners in the city of New York. That may be a fact. I have been offered citizenship papers for $10, but by an American. (Applause.) I have seen Polish peasants herded and made drunk and pulled to the polls. They sold their votes cheap for a drink of whiskey, the man behind them swearing that they had been long enough in this country. And it was done not by aliens, but it was done by Americans—in this case by members of the Republican party. (Applause.) If you wish to go with me, I will take you among them here in this city, and you will find that it is that East Side that elected Jerome. It is that East Side which put Low up and Tammany down. It is not the fashionable West Side, but the unfashionable, dirty, congested East Side which has over and over again saved the city of New York. And they are ready to do it everywhere. wherever you find them. Politically, wherever you get them they will rise at least as high as you are.

"Now, gentlemen, I believe in scattering the immigrant as quickly as possible for his own sake and for our sakes. But it cannot be done by resolutions. The fact is that the immigrant who comes here has not much more than his muscle, his strong heart and bellows for lungs. The West calls these men. It wants them to buy land, and they have not the money to buy land with. I could send you 20,000 agriculturists if you gave them five acres of ground to call their own, and they would make the wilderness to blossom as the rose, where some Yankee farmer has been starving on fifty or seventy-five acres. (Applause.)

"I am strongly in favor of a measure which may never be passed, that every alien, who, after three years, becomes a public charge, who is convicted of crime and serves his time in the penitentiary, should be sent back. But let me say that the figures about crime lie; that the men who figured did not lie, or intentionally so. It has been my privilege to walk from penitentiary to penitentiary in all our Eastern and Central Western States. I have conversed with the prisoners and with the wardens. These men who are convicted and imprisoned—a very large number of them —are there for some petty crime. They could not defend themselves, they had no money to hire able lawyers, and, more than anything else, they had no political power, and so they were pushed in, and they stay there."

Hon. R. A. Mitchell.

Speaking for Alabama, the Hon. R. A. Mitchell said: "We live at perfect peace with the negro as a citizen and are trying in every way to elevate him and to make him occupy that condition which his intelligence and standing would justify. But the greater the demand made on the negro for work just to that extent do his efforts relax, until to-day he is not as efficient as he was years ago, and in fact has steadily declined for the past two decades.

"While Alabama is not a large State, her population being approximately 2,000,000, I believe that 75,000 people could find profitable employment there to-day. The farmer, the manufacturer, the railroad, in fact every industry, is languishing for lack of labor.

"We think that the distribution of the immigrant North and South can be furthered by getting Congress to pass laws allowing the different States to appoint their agents to go to Ellis Island and present the advantages of their respective communities. As an Alabamian, as a manufacturer and a native citizen, I wish to say that we do not lay much stress upon the money that an immigrant shall bring. All that we demand is that he be of good character, that he be not a criminal convicted of some crime involving moral turpitude. What we want is a good, healthy, strong man, and it doesn't matter whether he has a dollar or not. He is rich in his brain and his muscle, and there is a place in our section for profitable employment for him. We want all we can get. And we are not particular about nationality. I want to say for one I don't believe all the good things reside in any one nationality. They all have good qualities, and we should be very glad to have you aid us by sending them down to us, where land and living are cheap, and they can get plenty of work." (Applause.)

SAMUEL GOMPERS.
President of the American Federation of Labor.

Ex-Senator Higgins on Asiatic Immigration.

Ex-Senator Anthony Higgins, of Delaware, took part in the discussion of the subject of "Asiatic Immigration," speaking in part as follows:

"The reason that has controlled my judgment in favor of the rigid exclusion of an Asiatic population on this continent is one of a character that if well founded makes, as it seems to me, discussion on any other branch of the subject almost unnecessary; and in what I am going to say I would not for an instant be considered as desiring to exclude those classes whose exclusion seems to have given such umbrage, and just umbrage, to the people of China. I mean their scholars, merchants, travelers, their men of science and all men who do not come here as laborers. But with our nation having the great Pacific shore, to be filled with a great American population, we confront a problem of the utmost importance when they are faced by four hundred millions of Chinese upon the other side of that ocean.

"We have a race question already, and with our experience with that race problem, how should it be possible that any plain American would either welcome or be willing to permit that this country should be vexed and troubled with another? (Applause.) I can say this because the active and militant part of my life has

REV. THOMAS R. SLICER.
Chairman, Conference Committee on Rules.

been much absorbed in making as good a fight as I could for the equality of rights to be given the negro. I therefore feel that I can speak as I shall speak without any reproach from any member of that race. But, saying that, I ask first, What would any sensible, sane American give if no negro, slave or other, had ever landed on our shores? (Applause.) We should have had no negro problem, no North, no South, no slavery, no secession, no rebellion, no war, no destruction of life, no public debt, no pension list, no problem of reconstruction. Should we be willing to invoke another race rebellion? The negro can probably never rise to more than his already demonstrated capacities, but the silent; patient, enduring Chinaman brings into your body other elements that make him absolutely impossible of assimilation. The great problem of America has been assimilation. We have assimilated the Spaniard of Louisiana, we have assimilated the Frenchman of Detroit and St. Louis and all that Western country. It has not been done in a century. But assimilate the negro, except to a certain extent, you cannot. And so you have here this practical problem. It seems to me that it is a great, substantial, abiding reason why there should be the most rigid exclusion of the laboring element of China."

Ng Poon Chew Speaks for China.

Much interest was aroused by the speech, delivered in fluent and forcible English, of Ng Poon Chew, of San Francisco, editor of the only Chinese daily newspaper in the United States. He minimized the danger to American labor and American institutions to be apprehended from Chinese immigration, saying:

"An often cited objection to the Chinese is that we do not assimilate. Assimilating humbug! You don't give us a chance. You throw all the obstacles you can in our way. You pass laws against us becoming citizens of the United States. You have passed laws on the Pacific Coast forbidding us to intermarry with other nationalities. You have passed laws forbidding us to bring our women over, and at the same time you damn us for not helping you to solve the race suicide question. (Laughter.) You say we take money away from the country. Gentlemen, we have taken hundreds of dollars from the country. At the same time we have

ROBERT WATCHORN.
Commissioner of Immigration for the Port of New York.

never taken the money; we never send money out of the country in the form of coin. We do not use gold in China, and we do not use your American dollar. Every dollar here amounts to 100 cents, but if your money goes to China it amounts to 47 cents; therefore we leave every American dollar, whether it is tainted or not, in the country (laughter), and we only send the value of money in the form of goods; and if we do send the value of money in the form of goods it helps this country.

"From 1848 to 1882, a space of thirty-four years of free Chinese immigration, when every grade of labor was open to them, the largest number of Chinese who came in was 106,000. Those 106,000 would not be a great menace to the country. During the same period you got from Europe several million people. I am demanding, not the repeal of the Exclusion Law, but the modification of the Exclusion Law. (Applause.) I demand that you should modify the Exclusion Law so as to admit those who do not in any way interfere with the laboring class of the American people. (Applause.) I am here, gentlemen, twenty-five years; I obtained my education in this country; I own property and I pay taxes, and I have raised a family of five children, and yet I am excluded. I am not deported because I am so insignificant that the Chinese inspector could not find me with a great magnifying telescope, and because I came here before the year 1882. Therefore, as long as I stay in this country I am permitted to stay here, but if I should leave the country I should never be able to return to this land of liberty and human progress.

"The Act excludes everybody except five classes—officials, merchants, travelers, students and teachers. The official is one who holds a commission from the Chinese Government to come here in an official capacity. Therefore, if the Emperor of China or the Empress Dowager ever had the audacity to try to reach this country they would be deported. A teacher is one who teaches the higher branches of learning in a recognized institution of education. A student is one who pursues the higher branches of learning in a recognized institution of learning. A merchant is one who has a fixed place of business in his own name. If he does a million dollars' worth of business a year, and if at the same time he is interested in a hotel like the

CHARLES A. MOORE.
President of the New York Civic Federation.

Waldorf-Astoria, the very fact of his having one dollar's interest in such a hotel would invalidate him as a merchant, and he can be deported. A traveler is one who has all his pockets full of money to support him through his trip, and when he gets through he has to get out of the country immediately. But it is much easier for a rich, fat American millionaire, with all his tainted dollars on his back, to climb to heaven through the fire escape than for a Chinese to come through the ports of the United States. (Laughter.) Therefore, outside of those five classes—an actor, we cannot get an actor over here to amuse us in our leisure hours; we cannot get a minister of the Gospel over here to come and minister to our spiritual welfare, to tell us which way to go to heaven and which way to the hot place; we cannot get a doctor over here to heal us, or to kill us, either way. Here we are; we are supposed to come in, but all those are not.

"Now, I have a letter in my pocket written by a friend of mine of the class of '99 of Yale College, and he went back to teach English in our college in Singa-

AVERY C. MOORE.
Editor of the Weiser (Idaho) *World*.

pore. He taught three years there, and then he taught in other colleges in China, and eight months ago he came over here and tried to take the post-graduate course in philosophy in Columbia University. Eight months ago he arrived in San Francisco; after a month in the detention shed he was deported. I have got a letter in my pocket, and I defy any Chinese immigration official to write a letter in such beautiful English, in such well-chosen diction and in such elegant style as that letter was written by a Chinaman they deported.

"When we wake up from our slumber we will never submit to discrimination. And fifteen years from now, if you want to restrict our labor, that restriction law ought to be universal. Restrict all the unworthy people from all the nations. The Chinese Exclusion Law should be modified, because it is opposed to the American sense of justice. It is opposed to this twentieth century civilization, because in all civilized countries every man is looked upon as innocent of crime until he is proved guilty. But under this Chinese Exclusion Act every Chinaman in the country is looked upon as guilty until he can prove himself, by the aid of at least two creditable white men, to be innocent of smuggling into the country."

Senator W. A. Clark.

Senator W. A. Clark, of Montana, who followed Mr. Chew, spoke in part as follows:

"We have in China alone four hundred millions of people. In India, if India is to be considered, and in Japan, the Philippines and other Pacific islands there are several hundred millions more. If we are to throw down the barriers and allow these people to come to our shores unrestricted, we are in danger of an invasion of those hordes that will practically exterminate and destroy American labor.

"In my opinion, in any exclusion act that may be passed by Congress there should be such provision as will enable us to treat the officials of our neighbors in the East or in the West with some consideration. Under the present law, men high in authority in China and other countries have been treated with the greatest indignity. We are laboring to establish and keep the open door in China, and we will succeed. But while working for this plan, let us not lose sight of the fact that we should establish friendly commercial relations with these people, and I believe that we should in

JESSE TAYLOR.
Representing Junior Order United American Mechanics.

this Exclusion Act, when it shall be passed by Congress, provide that all of the officials who enter this country from any other countries, all persons who are seeking to come here to obtain knowledge from us, all students, all professors who are making a tour of observation and students who come to study our customs and to take places in our schools and institutions, all travelers and all persons of respectability who are not coming here to come in competition with the American laborer should be treated as the subjects of the most favored nation. (Applause.)

"Now we come to the question, Shall the bars be thrown down, and with the restrictions that apply to the reception of immigrants from European countries shall we allow an indiscriminate entrance upon our shores to people from Asiatic countries? I believe that I voice the almost unanimous sentiment of the people of the State which I have the honor here to represent, both employers and employes, that we should not allow what we call the coolie labor to come into this country unrestricted. I think it would be an act of inhumanity to the people who are struggling in this country to secure employment and a maintenance for their families and to build up homes in our midst to allow the immigration of hordes of people who, as the distinguished gentlemen who preceded me recently stated, had no idea of making homes amongst us, who had no idea of assimilating themselves with our institutions."

Walter Macarthur Opposes Japanese Immigration.

The views of organized labor on the Pacific Coast were presented by Walter Macarthur, of California, editor of *The Coast Seamen's Journal*, and representative of the Japanese, Chinese and Corean Exclusion League, who asserted that, so far as Asiatic immigration was concerned, there were no labor men and no capital men in California; all were exclusionists, without exception. Continuing, he said:

"The discussion of the question up to this time has been confined to the Chinese phase. There is another phase which is equally, and in fact more important than the Chinese, and that is the Japanese and Corean phase. The people of the West stand not only for the literal, strict maintenance of the Chinese Exclusion Act, but for the extension of the provisions of that Act so as to exclude Japanese and Corean labor. We take that position because all the objections that may be raised to

PROF. J. W. JENKS.
Professor of Political Economy, Cornell University.

Chinese labor apply with equal and with added force to the case of the Japanese and the Coreans. We object to these classes of labor upon three general grounds; the racial ground, the economic ground and the political ground.

"We object to the Asiatic laborer, whether Chinese or Japanese, because he comes from a different and an unassimilable race; because he comes from the Mongolian as opposed to the Caucasian race. And we regard this problem as a problem of race preservation. We object to these classes of labor upon the economic ground because they tend to undermine, and do, as a matter of fact, undermine the standard of living to which the American laborer is accustomed, and which he desires to maintain.

"We object to them upon the political ground, upon the main ground that, being incapable of becoming citizens of the United States, they are a standing menace to the perpetuity of our political institutions. We cannot afford to have in the United States a class of labor permanently proscribed, permanently denied political rights, because, after all, it is upon the laborer and upon the exercise by the laborer of political freedom that the whole superstructure of our Government rests, and to the extent that the laborer is denied the right to participate in the political affairs of the nation you endanger and undermine the political institutions of the nation. (Applause.)

PROF. H. A. GARFIELD.
Professor of Politics, Princeton University.

"In the State of California and other States of the Union on the Pacific Coast the Chinese and the Japanese have driven the white man off the soil. They have driven the white man out of certain industries, not only the laboring man, but the business man. In some sections of California they are establishing banks and driving the bankers out of business. It is not simply a question of protecting labor; it is a question of protecting all classes of men. Just as sure as these Japanese are permitted to come in here without let or hindrance, they will drive us all across the Rocky Mountains.

DR. EDWARD A. STEINER.
Professor of Applied Christianity, Iowa College.

"It has been assumed in certain quarters that we are enforcing the Chinese Exclusion Act because China was not able to protect herself, because China was not able to insist upon a recognition of her equality with the other nations. And it is now hinted that that time and that conditions are passing, and that the day is near when China will be able to protect herself, will be able to compel the United States to throw down the bars and let in the Chinaman upon the basis of equality with other nations. Now, you can clearly see the suggestion. I am a man of peace, and the men of the West are men of peace, and we are pursuing a peaceful policy. We are pursuing a policy in demanding the enforcement and maintenance of the Chinese Exclusion Act and the extension of that act to the Chinese and Japs; we are pursuing in that respect a policy designed to preserve the peace between ourselves and other nations, and unless that policy is adopted the peace will be broken. The time will come, unless some restrictions are placed in the way, when the people of the West will be forced to take a stand in the defence of their birthright, regardless of the consequences to themselves or others."

PROF. H. W. FARNAM.
Professor of Political Economy, Yale University.

No Modification, Says Avery C. Moore.

Referring to the remarks of Mr. Chew, the next speaker, Avery C. Moore, editor of the Weisor (Idaho) *World*, said that Chinese trade and Chinese exclusion were not kindred subjects; the West was willing to abide by the results of [illegible] to Asiatics. He also said:

"It is the testimony of history that cheap labor promotes social degeneracy and national degradation, and yet it was not a great while ago that a well-known master of transportation stated that what this country needed was cheap labor. But I make bold to say that the problem is not how to secure laborers in foreign lands who will work for less than the prevailing wages, but how to secure better wages for the laborers who are already here. (Applause.) The West does not claim

PROF. JOHN R. COMMONS.
Department of Political Economy, University of Wisconsin.

to have a solution for this problem, but it has reason to know that the free admission of Chinese labor would postpone its solution indefinitely.

"We are opposed to any modification of existing laws on this subject, and 'modification' constitutes the whole program of China. Chinese diplomacy is a subtle science that hides infinite menace in simple words. A few days ago the Chinese Minister to Washington appealed to the Government for a more liberal interpretation of the exclusion laws. He asked that the bars be let down to the professions, as they are now down for students and travelers. But we of the West know the Chinese character—as nearly as it is possible to know the inscrutable and the contradictory—and we see the hidden danger in the word 'professions.' We have learned that the destination of the Chinese 'traveler' is nearly always a cheap labor market, and that the brain

PROF. MORRIS LOEB.
Sociologist and Lecturer on Immigration.

of the Chinese 'student' is too often located in his hands. This, therefore, is our will: Close such loopholes as now exist—and create no new ones."

Hon. A. L. C. Atkinson.

Hon. A. L. C. Atkinson, Secretary of the Territorial Government of Hawaii, spoke of his territory as "facing the full power of the Orient." More than 60 per cent of the population, he said, was Asiatic. "Shall we," he asked, "advance along traditional American lines, as our President says? I am willing to admit that the introduction of say twenty-five or fifty thousand Chinese will mean 25 or 50 per cent more dividends. But shall civilization hold its own, or shall we be driven back and the decay of America commence?

"How we intend to meet this problem, and what the present administration in Hawaii is doing is this: it is our definite policy to Americanize these islands and to prevent them from being Japanized. We have done more than that; we are opening our islands; we are making it easy for the homesteaders to obtain land. Our plantations, or some of them, are giving land to every man who will work a certain length of time.

GEORGE PARSONS.
Secretary of the Conference; Mayor of Cairo, Ill.

They will build the buildings, they will give medical attendance, water and firewood. Our whole idea is that we will domicile our labor. We are opening the Government land and fixing the roads so that while the tropical crop is growing men can obtain employment and thereby support themselves. My present mission to this country is to obtain laborers for that purpose. We want to make and build up an American community out there."

Warren S. Stone.

Speaking on the same subject, Warren S. Stone, Grand Chief of the Brotherhood of Locomotive Engineers, remarked:

"The great question which seems to stand in the background to-day is the boycott, which is only sleeping, they say. The question for you to solve is whether, for the benefit of having American manufactures go into China, you can afford to pay the price by letting down the bars and letting the yellow flood pour in. Do you want Chinese immigration at that price? I think not."

In the course of a paper dealing with the question of employing Asiatic labor in the tropical dependencies of the United States, D. G. Ambler, of Florida, advocated the importation of Chinese coolies for the digging of the Panama Canal, but the proposition excited no further discussion.

The Rev. Dr. Arthur J. Brown, Secretary of the Presbyterian Board of Foreign Missions, premising that he was not arguing for unrestricted Chinese immigration, defended the average Chinaman, testifying to his honesty, industry, frugality and peaceful disposition. The real question at issue, however, was whether Chinese who came to this country, not as uneducated laborers, should be treated with common decency.

President Penrose Defends the Chinese.

President S. B. L. Penrose, of Whitman College, State of Washington, declared himself frankly in favor of the admission of Chinese laborers. He spoke in part as follows:

"The exclusion of the Chinaman costs something to the United States. It costs in undeveloped territory; it costs in the neglect of orchards; it costs in the retardation of our Pacific civilization, because we have not at the present time such a labor supply as to meet the demands of the present occasion. I believe that the total exclusion of Chinese of the labor class from the United States is unwise, because the psychological differences of the Chinaman and the American are not so fundamental as to place him beyond the pale of civilization and the consideration of a decent regard.

"It seems to me there are certain definite things which we should accept with reference to the peoples of Asia. In the first place, we ought to have a fair and honest and impartial examination of all kinds for admission to the United States upon the far side of the Pacific—an honest examination. I have it on very good authority, that of an intelligent, well-informed Chinaman who told me quietly, not thinking that I would ever make use of it in any way, that the fixed price that a Chinaman had to pay in order to get into the United States over on the far side was $60. It seems to me that the United States must have an enforcement of honest laws rigidly and impartially administered. I believe also that we ought to make a distinction between our insular possessions and the land of the United States proper. To insist that the same restrictions upon foreigners, upon labor, shall hold in the Philippine Islands, for example, as in the United States seems to me to be confounding the question by failing to recognize the difference economically between those insular possessions and our own country."

The Committee on Resolutions then submitted a report on Asiatic immigration consisting of four resolutions. The first three were adopted without opposition and were as follows:

"Resolved, That we heartily endorse the position taken by the President that the Chinese exclusion laws forbidding the admission of laborers ought to be maintained and rigidly and honestly enforced.

"Resolved, That a rigid examination of all incoming passengers from the Orient be made at the port of departure, as recommended for incomers at the Atlantic ports, so as to eliminate entirely, if possible, the hardship of detention and deportation.

"Resolved, That we request Congress to provide better facilities for inspection and examinations at the Pacific Coast ports, similar to those provided at Atlantic ports."

The fourth resolution read as follows:

"Resolved, That, in the words of the President's recent message, our laws and treaties should be framed not so as to put Chinese students, business and professional men of all kinds, not only merchants, but bankers, doctors, manufacturers, professors, teachers and the like, in the excepted class, but to state that we will admit all Chinese except Chinese of the coolie class, Chinese skilled or unskilled laborers."

Samuel Gompers.

A *viva voce* vote was taken on this resolution, and the Chairman declared it carried. In view of the fact, however, that Mr. Gompers, as a member of the Committee on Resolutions, had opposed the wording of the resolution, and in view of the desire of many delegates that he should state his objections to the Conference as a whole, the vote was reconsidered, and Mr. Gompers addressed the assemblage. He expressed his reluctance to oppose a resolution containing so large a quotation from the message of President Roosevelt; but, he added:

JAMES P. ARCHIBALD.
Secretary of the New York Civic Federation.

"There is given no opportunity to the President of the United States to understand the underlying causes and motives that lead the American workman and so large a portion of the American people to insist upon Chinese exclusion. The American workmen do not want to keep the Chinese student, or the Chinese traveler, or the Chinese merchant from coming into the United States; but experience has demonstrated beyond question that the deception practised upon our Government in the effort to evade the exclusion law is so great that as a matter of truth the larger portion of those who have been excluded are those who came here under the pretence of being merchants and students.

"It is all very well for our reverend and professional friends to stand up on this platform and tell you that you ought to throw your gates wide open. Some of them have been more cautious than to say that. Some of them have said that we do not want the laborer to come in here; but others have said: 'We want the Chinese laborer to come in here'; less cautious, less adroit. But underneath it all the motive is to let down the bars of exclusion to Chinese labor. You may come to us in honeyed words. We possess neither the polish nor the urbanity that you professional and reverend gentlemen possess, but into our hard heads have been pummelled by experience the devices that are resorted to to trick the workingman into consenting to conditions. (Applause.) The sugar planter of Hawaii, the adventurer in the Philippines, are all of the one stripe in trying to deceive the working American people into the belief that there is a dearth of workmen, and that the only recourse is to the Chinaman. (Applause.)

"To speak of Chinese immigration, to speak of Chinese laborers and to refer to the 72,000 Chinese who are here now is begging the question. It is an insult to our intelligence to refer to the 72,000 Chinese who are now here in the United States and ask us to judge from them, as much as it will be an insult to our intelligence to imagine for a moment that the intelligent Chinese gentleman who occupied this platform can be counted as a criterion for his fellow countrymen who have come here in such large numbers, when there was no law upon the subject."

SAMUEL B. DONNELLY.
Secretary of The National Civic Federation.

A motion made by Professor Commons that the resolution be referred to the Executive Committee of the National Civic Federation was lost. Mr. Corcoran, of Minnesota, then offered as a substitute for the fourth resolution the following, which was adopted:

"Resolved, That our laws and treaties should be so framed and administered as carefully to except Chinese students, business and professional men of all kinds, not only merchants, but bankers, doctors, manufacturers, professors and travelers, from the action or enforcement of the exclusion law."

This closed the warmest debate of the Conference, and in a manner which was apparently satisfactory to all interests.

Dr. Shaw then offered the following resolution, which was unanimously adopted:

"Resolved, That The National Civic Federation is entitled to the commendation of this Conference and the public for the interest manifested in the subject of immigration, and that the thanks of the Conference are extended to The Civic Federation for its painstaking and complete arrangements of this meeting, and the many courtesies extended to the delegates."

RESOLUTIONS ON WHITE IMMIGRATION.

The resolutions on white immigration, which were unanimously adopted, practically without debate, were as follows:

"Resolved, That the members of the National Conference on Immigration heartily endorse the wise suggestions of the President of the United States in his annual message to the Congress, regarding the enforcement and amendment of the laws concerning immigration, and regarding an international conference to deal with the question. They urge upon the Congress the speedy passage of the laws required to put such recommendations into effect.

"Resolved, That the immigration laws should be amended in the following particulars:

"(*a*) By placing in the excluded classes 'feeble-minded persons'; 'imbeciles';

"(*b*) By carefully defining the term 'persons likely to become public charges,' so as to permit the exclusion of those persons of permanently enfeebled vitality, whether this condition is due to accident, inheritance, disease, advanced age or other defect;

"(*c*) By making provision so that the air-space allotted to each person in ships carrying immigrants be not less than two hundred cubic feet, instead of one hundred and ten cubic feet for the main deck, as now provided, and that the space be proportionately increased for the other decks;

"(*d*) By making such provisions as shall compel the service of food at tables with seats, in compartments not used for sleeping.

"Resolved, That the penalty of $100 now imposed on the steamship companies for bringing diseased persons to the United States be also imposed for bringing in any person excluded by law.

"Resolved, That the Government of the United States provide some methods of investigation, examination and certification of foreign immigrants in their home countries, or at the port of departure, so as more certainly to avoid the hardship of deportation by preventing the embarkation of persons excluded by law from admission into the United States.

"Resolved, That in order to prevent the undue concentration of immigrants in some parts of our country, and to encourage their better distribution in sections where conditions may be more favorable, the United States Government afford to the separate States and Territories opportunities to furnish to incoming immigrants at the ports of entry, and also so far as it may be found practicable, before their arrival in this country, trustworthy information regarding the material resources and the conditions of life and labor which confront the followers of different occupations in the various States and Territories.

"Resolved, That we recommend to the Congress that it furnish sufficient means to the Commissioner-General of Immigration to improve the facilities for handling immigration at the South Atlantic and Gulf ports, in order thereby to promote the better distribution of immigration over the undeveloped lands of the South and Southwest.

"Resolved, That on account of the large number of alien immigrants who are admitted contrary to law because of the possession of naturalization papers fraudulently obtained, this Conference recommends that all naturalization certificates should contain a description of the applicants similar to that provided in the case of passports issued by the Department of State.

"Resolved, That we recommend to the Congress the establishment of a Commission with competent authority, to be appointed by the President, to investigate the subject of immigration in all its relations, including the violations and evasions of the present law; and to report to the President the results of its investigations with recommendations.

"Resolved, That we heartily commend The National Civic Federation upon its initiative in calling together this First National Conference on the important subject of immigration; and in order that this work may be advantageously continued, we request the Civic Federation to appoint a standing committee on that subject."

The officers of the Conference were:

Chairman, Hon. Seth Low; vice-chairmen, John H. Holliday, Indiana; Gov. W. D. Jelks, Alabama; Hon. W. S. West, Georgia; ex-Senator Anthony Higgins, Delaware; Warren S. Stone, Ohio; Hon. Frederick N. Judson, Missouri; secretaries, Professor H. A. Garfield, New Jersey; Professor H. W. Farnam, Connecticut; Hon. George Parsons, Illinois.

The committees were constituted as follows:

Rules—Rev. Thomas R. Slicer, New York, chairman; Hon. A. L. C. Atkinson, Secretary of Hawaii; Dr. A. Tilzer, Portland, Oregon; David Robinson, Georgia; D. G. Ambler, Florida; D. J. Keefe, Michigan; Wiley Tindolph, Minnesota; Charles Ridgely, Illinois; Warren S. Stone, Ohio; Prescott F. Hall, Massachusetts; Hon. Adolph Meyer, Louisiana; Thomas Parker, South Carolina.

Resolutions: Members-at-large—J. W. Jenks, New York; John M. Stahl, Illinois; Samuel Gompers, District of Columbia; John F. Smulski, Illinois; John R. Commons, Wisconsin; D. J. Keefe, Michigan; J. J. Sullivan, Ohio; Charles P. Neill, Washington; John Willis Baer, New York; Stephen Collins, Pennsylvania.

State members—Dr. Albert Shaw, Chairman, New York; Ross C. Smith, Alabama; David S. Snedden, California; Frank T. Johnson, Colorado; Rev. Joel S. Ives, Connecticut; Hon. Anthony Higgins, Delaware; M. J. Weller, District of Columbia; D. G. Ambler, Florida; Dr. B. Wildauer, Georgia; A. L. C. Atkinson, Hawaii; Avery C. Moore, Idaho; W. G. Edens, Illinois; John W. Kern, Indiana; Edward A. Steiner, Iowa; John E. Frost, Kansas; George L. Sehon, Kentucky; Geo. H. Smith, Louisiana; Dr. F. E. Wheet, Maine; Dr. Fabian Franklin, Maryland; Frank B. Hall, Massachusetts; Edwin F. Sweet, Michigan; W. D. Washburn, Jr., Minnesota; Samuel A. Hughes, Missouri; Hon. W. A. Clark, Montana; B. V. Kohout, Nebraska; Hon. H. B. Quinby, New Hampshire; Hugh F. Fox, New Jersey; L. Bradford Prince, New Mexico; Z. P. Smith, North Carolina; Hon. E. J. Watson, South Carolina; C. H. Salmons, Ohio; Dr. A. Tilzer, Oregon; James W. Kinnear, Pennsylvania; George H. Webb, Rhode Island; N. F. Thompson, Tennessee; H. W. Fairbanks, Texas; Simon Bamberger, Utah; Geo. H. Terrill, Vermont; Theodore S. Garnett, Virginia; S. B. L. Penrose, Washington; Geo. C. Baker, West Virginia; Mark E. Bruce, Wisconsin.

These vice-chairmen occupied the chair at different sessions of the Conference: Hon. John H. Holliday, Governor W. D. Jelks, Hon. W. S. West, ex-Senator Anthony Higgins and Warren S. Stone.

On the afternoon of the first day the delegates were the guests of Commissioner Watchorn at Ellis Island, where they observed the details of the inspection and disposition of immigrants.

"SMASHING THE UNION" IN AUSTRALIA.

THE CRUSHING OUT OF LABOR ORGANIZATIONS HAS RESULTED IN THE DEVELOPMENT OF A POWERFUL SOCIALIST PARTY.

Hugh O'Neill, in Kansas City Independent.

It was Malcolm Donald McEacharn, ship owner and capitalist, who delivered the Commonwealth of Australia to the Socialists. He is the one Conservative on the continent that the Socialists fight without malice. They are under a debt of gratitude to the shipping millionaire, and the bitterest offence he suffers is the occasional reminder of that fact.

Of course McEacharn didn't want Socialism. He only wanted to break the power of the trades unions. He thought that their exaction had become intolerable, and there was some justification for that view. Strikes were common, and frequently the cause of quarrel was trivial. But the strikers were always successful because the country was being flooded with British money, and the voice of the boomster was abroad in the land. The union leaders were ignorant of all economic laws, and they mistook the existing condition for one of natural prosperity. (That's where they made their mistake.)

McEacharn knew better than that. He knew that the burst would come sooner or later, and he prepared to attack labor on a falling market. He figured to smash the unions and remove the heel of aggressive democracy from the throat of capital. A partial victory was not what he wanted. He was after the whole hog. He got it. (That's where he made his mistake.)

The unionists were lions led by asses. McEacharn knew that. Time after time the shipping union made demands upon his company; time after time he granted these demands with smiling readiness. But day after day he went on building together the units of a force to fight trades unionism that was destined to sweep organized labor out of existence. The plan was colossal, but the solid patience with which in the meantime he bore the galling exactions of the trades was quite as great.

And then one day he loosed his thunders and struck hard and straight and true. He chose the time of battle, the cause of battle, and the place of battle. The unions chose nothing. They were arrogant with riches.

The cause of quarrel was childish, as McEacharn meant it should be. A difference arose between the quartermaster and the steward of one of his coasting steamers over the charms of a stewardess. The captain, to settle the difficulty—as he thought, poor man—discharged the sailor. The union demanded his reinstatement. McEacharn, knowing what the reply would be, offered to put him on another ship. The union demanded reinstatement on the same ship. McEacharn in very courteous terms pointed out that that was impossible. Then the asses who led the lions told him that unless the reinstatement was effected within twenty-four hours they would call the crews off all his ships and order a general strike.

Then, like a flash, McEacharn unmasked his guns. Back went the reply that the unions might strike and be damned.

The strike was ordered. And then there followed a battle grim and great. Union after union was called out, ship after ship was laid up, State after State was involved in the quarrel, until the whole continent stood under arms. In less than four weeks the fires of nearly every coasting steamer were drawn. The trade of Australia was paralyzed. Four hundred thousand unionists were idle, and every man of them was drawing half pay. Also every unemployed man who looked like becoming a free laborer was paid a weekly allowance from the general fund to prevent remanning the ships.

But the Shipowners' Union that McEacharn had organized didn't even try to reman the ships. The land boom had reached its limit, trade was declining, very large coal reserves had been laid up, the funds and membership of the unions were known to a dollar and a man. The shipowners simply sat down on their hunkers and waited.

The trades leaders organized pickets, but there was nothing for them to do. The problem was a new one. They couldn't solve it. The owners were apparently not trying to run their ships at all. Patterson, who owned one fleet, wrote to the strike committee, and in a vein of pawky Scotch humor offered to sell them his ships.

Then it dawned upon the union that the strike had become a lockout. The besiegers were besieged. The weapon of capital was not free labor, but starvation.

Starvation won easily. Ten weeks after the first shot the unions capitulated to the grim foe hunger that before then had bowed the neck of many a proud city. McEacharn had meant to break the unions. And they were broken all right.

Funds gone, membership decimated, courage wilted, the once great trades unions of Australia were counted out.

The capitulation was announced in the biggest public hall the labor leaders could get. John Hancock, big bodied and big hearted—the finest platform man in Australia—rose in that hall of silent hundreds to tell the men that they must return to work on the best terms they could get. It was the shortest and most pregnant speech he ever made in his life. "Friends," he said, "men of Australia, we have not been beaten, we have been starved into submission. Unionism is dead, but anything can happen in a democracy, and from the ashes of the funeral pyre that the shipowners have lighted will rise the phœnix of our liberties."

Nobody knew what he meant. It is doubtful whether he knew himself. But it sounded large and fine, and something with that sort of sound was just what those depressed people wanted that night.

But one year later big John Hancock took his seat in Parliament—the first labor member sent in by the first political labor party in Australia.

Vanquished in the industrial war, the members of the battered trades unions had reorganized their forces on a political basis and sought to win by the ballot the privileges capital had denied them. Someone discovered that where all men have votes and the bulk of men are wage-earners they only have to decide among themselves what they want from the State to get it.

That was only ten years ago. And now they have gotten nearly all they wanted. Think of it. Eleven years ago the unions were battered, dead, done for. To-day their direct lineal successor owns the whole blessed commonwealth of Australia.

They attacked municipal councils first, and enforced the minimum wage and eight-hour days on all of them. They attacked the State Parliaments next and gained factory legislation and old age pensions and compulsory arbitration. No factory in the country can now employ child labor, or work its people more than eight hours per day, or pay less than the minimum wage fixed by the wages board. In two of the six States the Labor party are the Government in office, in two others they hold the balance of power, and in two others they are the direct Opposition.

But it is their success in the Commonwealth Parliament—the national assembly—that marks out Australia as a Socialistic nation.

In the Senate half the members are pledged Socialists—definite servants of the labor party. In the Representatives the direct Opposition are pledged Socialists also—members of the same party. Compulsory arbitration in labor disputes is the law actually operating in two of the States, and the national legislature has passed a law enforcing compulsory arbitration in any labor dispute that extends from one State to another.

McEacharn, the Lord Mayor of Melbourne, the man who smashed unionism, was defeated last year by a labor candidate in the contest for election of a member of the House of Representatives.

Twelve years ago in Australia there were two parties, the Freetraders and the Protectionists. To-day there is one party—the Labor party—and the draggled remnant of another that occasionally totters helplessly before a tired public and tries to get itself taken seriously as the Anti-Socialist party. But it has no power, it never had a policy, and its friends are ashamed to recognize it in the daylight. Some day a man may arise in Australia who will evolve a policy big enough to cover the anti-labor party and those others who at present remain outside, but so far as the writer knows he hasn't sent word of his coming. And the gentleman who precipitated all this on the country has sought his country seat and the tiresome seclusion of a friendless man.

The writer points no moral. But he has heard the suggestion that Socialism was a coming force in American politics treated with derision, and he thinks that perhaps this story may be worth thinking over, because manhood suffrage prevails in America, and the great, big bulk of Americans are wage-earners, too.

THE HOURS OF LABOR.

(*Continued from page 9*)

be aided by reference to such exceptional instances. Most professions, many positions in business and some in trades fall within the class of excepted occupations. Good work in such occupations almost necessarily brings with it joy, because it implies development of faculties and, ordinarily, pecuniary advancement. In every occupation there are such possibilities for the exceptional man. But in most industrial occupations—in the unskilled trades and in many so-called skilled trades—the limit of development and of financial success for any individual is soon reached, and consequently there is little joy in such work except as compared with the hours of idleness, or such satisfaction as comes to the needy in securing the means of subsistence.

"LIVING" AND "SUBSISTING."

"And what is necessary to living as distinguished from subsisting?

"In the first place, bodily health is necessary; that is, not merely freedom from illness, but continued physical ability to work hard. For those engaged in the more favored occupations, like the professions and the higher positions in business and some trades, such health, including the postponement of old age, has been measurably attained by better conditions of living, and notably by outdoor recreation. What has been found necessary for continued health and working capacity for those engaged in these favored occupations we should seek to make attainable for all our citizens. The burden and waste to the community and to the individual, and the suffering attendant upon sickness and premature superannuation, may be and should be lessened by a shortening of hours of labor which will permit of proper outdoor recreation.

"In the second place, mental development is necessary. Massachusetts, recognizing the education of her citizens to be an essential condition of a free and prosperous people, has made compulsory the schooling of her children to the age of fourteen, has prohibited their working in manufacturing or mercantile establishments under the age of fourteen and has withheld the right to vote from illiterate adults as inexorably as from idiots. But the intellectual development of citizens may not be allowed to end at fourteen. With most people whose minds have really developed, the age of fourteen is rather the beginning than the end of the educational period. The educational standard required of a [illegible] is obviously high. The citizen should [illegible]rehend among other things the many [illegible] problems of industry, commerce and [illegible] with us necessarily become political [illegible]. He must learn about men as well as things. [illegible] way only can the Commonwealth be saved from the pitfalls of financial schemers on the one hand or of ambitious demagogues on the other.

"But for the attainment of such an education, such mental development, it is essential that the education shall be continuous throughout life, and an essential condition of such continuous education is free time, that is leisure; and leisure does not merely imply a time for rest, but free time, when body and mind are sufficiently fresh to permit of mental effort. There is full justification for the common practice in trades of charging at the rate of 50 per cent additional for work in excess of the regular hours. Indeed, I doubt whether that rate of pay is not often grossly inadequate to compensate for what it takes out of the employe. An extra hour of labor may render useless those other hours which might have been devoted to development, or the performance of other duties, or to pleasure. The excess load is wasteful with men as well as with horses or vehicles or machinery. Whether the needed education of the citizens is to be given in classes or from the political platform, in the discussion of the lodges, or in the trade unions, or is to be gained from the reading of papers, periodicals, or books, freshness of mind is imperative, and to the preservation of freshness of mind, a short work day for most people is essential.

"Bodily and mental health and development will furthermore tend to promote innocent, rational pleasures and in general better habits of living. Such conditions will tend to lessen the great curse of drink and with it some of the greatest burdens of the individual and of society.

"It is of course no answer to the plea for a shorter work day to say that the leisure resulting from shorter hours may not be profitably employed. The art of using leisure time, like any other, must be learned, but it is certain that the proper use of leisure, as of liberty, can never be attained except by those who have the opportunity of leisure or of liberty. Nor is it an answer to the plea for a shorter work day, to say most working men secure a certain amount of free time through the irregularity of their work. Such free time is literally lost. Such irregular excessive free time presents an even greater evil than that of excessive work.

"Although the reduction of the hours of labor is clearly desirable, it may, as already stated, be impossible on account of competition or other cause to grant the reduction at a particular time in a particular business. But in my opinion employers are apt to exaggerate the resulting loss of earnings, at least in the long run. Greater freshness, better health and mental development that go with shorter hours may be relied upon within reasonable limits to make up in many businesses, at least in part, for a shortening of working time, where the employer receives as he should the co-operation of the employes to secure the largest possible production. Obviously no limitation should be imposed upon the output of the individual, nor any rule be insisted upon by the employes which would hamper the most efficient use of machinery. Such arbitrary restrictions are wasteful and uneconomic at all times, and necessarily act as a brake on the movement toward shorter hours. The natural gain in vigor and working efficiency on the part of the employe should be allowed to show itself in the shop results. If this gain in potential efficiency is nullified by artificial limitations on what and how much a man shall do with the facilities placed at his disposal, the decrease in working time must inevitably mean increased cost, without either economic or moral justification, and under such circumstances the employer has no other course open to him than that of resistance to any attempt to reduce the working time.

"If in any case we should find that despite the fullest co-operation of the employes, the reduced working time results in immediate economic loss, the welfare of our democratic community compels us to work, nevertheless, for a reasonably short work day as a condition essential to the making of good citizens."

President Lucius Tuttle.

Lucius Tuttle, President of the New England Civic Federation, in closing the meeting said:

"As you all know, the Federation does not undertake to command any man or any interest. It does not undertake to arbitrate anybody's difficulties. It simply stands ready to hold out the olive branch of peace whenever strife is in prospect, and in the work it has accomplished during the last year it has more and more proved its efficiency and its value in this whole community.

"The principle of this association is the one that I have been working with for more than twelve years, and successfully, I believe. In the companies which I have the honor to represent there are employed about twenty-five thousand men—a good sized army—and we find many differences to work out and many difficulties to solve; and we have had many weeks, many months, of patient negotiation and discussion, and I take it as one of the proudest things I can say that up to the present moment there never has occurred a difference that has not been honorably and amicably settled to the satisfaction of every interest involved. (Applause.)

"It is that kind of thing which the Civic Federation of New England is trying to work out, and I take to this association the credit of much of the industrial peace that exists throughout New England to-day. There never has been a time within my knowledge when there was so little of strife and so little of threat of strife in the borders of New England as at the present moment (applause), and I believe that to no one instrumentality is more of that condition due than to the work which has been accomplished and the influences exerted by the members of your executive and conciliation and other committees.

"I want to add one word more. No organization is ever a success without having in it one man who is the pivot upon which that success turns, and I wish to say, not because he wants or expects me to say it, that this association has that one man in its secretary. (Applause.) Your secretary has conducted, has originated and has helped on negotiations which have resulted in practical good to thousands of people, but he does it in that quiet, unobtrusive way which almost amounts to self-effacement; yet the work has been accomplished. I know of these things, and some of the other members of the committee know of them, but the generality of the Civic Federation cannot, and I think it ought to reach you who may not know, even though our secretary in his modesty would not like to have me speak of the subject.

"Just this much in closing: Every man who works—and we all work—ought to have and must have an interest in every other man, and particularly in every man who works under his direction. There are, of course, well-meaning people who believe that the work of an association like this is unnecessary, but that is usually due to the fact that they have in their own way in the control of the men who work under their direction carried out the same idea. They have met with no troubles, and therefore they do not see why the Civic Federation is necessary. There are others who in a somewhat slurring way criticize the work of the association, who hint that it is giving the workingmen too much control of the business of the employer. The man who says that as a rule is a man who never had twelve men employed under his direction in his whole life (Applause); and the man who says the way to deal with these things is to 'fight it out' is the man that, if he did have the responsibility of a larger number of men, would crawl under the table the moment the fight began." (Laughter.)

OFFICERS FOR THE ENSUING YEAR.

The following officers were elected for the ensuing year: Lucius Tuttle, president; Frank H. McCarthy, first vice-president; Louis D. Brandeis, second vice-president and chairman of the conciliation committee; John Mason Little, treasurer; Henry Abrahams, recording secretary; Warren A. Reed, vice-chairman of the concilation committee, and Hayes Robbins, secretary.

Twelve new members were added to the executive committee as follows: On the part of the public, President W. J. Tucker, of Dartmouth College; President W. H. P. Faunce, of Brown University; Hon. John D. Long and Alvin W. Sulloway, of New Hampshire; on the part of employers, Hon. W. L. Douglas, C. L. Edgar, President of the Edison Electric Company; T. E. Byrnes and J. L. Richards; on the part of wage-earners, John Golden, President of the United Textile Workers of America; Samuel Ross, Secretary of the National Spinners' Association; P. F. McCarthy, President of the Vermont State Branch of the Federation of Labor, and Thomas F. Kearney, Secretary of the Building Trades Council, Providence, R. I.

A vote of thanks was tendered Charles H. Taylor, Jr., for his services in the office of treasurer for the past year.

Just before adjournment, upon motion of T. M. Nolan, of the Typographical Union, a rising vote of thanks was extended to the officers and committees of the Federation for their efforts in behalf of mediation and conciliation during the past year.

AS AN AUSTRALIAN SEES US.

Octavius C. Beale, of Sydney, New South Wales, was an honorary delegate and an interested listener at the National Conference on Immigration. His visit to the United States was largely due to his desire to investigate the extent of harmful adulteration of foods and drugs and the means adapted by Government and other agencies for its suppression. He is now in Europe on a similar mission. Mr. Beale, who is the head of Beale & Co., Limited, of Sydney, manufacturers of pianos, is not only a large employer of labor, but is President of the Federal Council of Chambers of Manufactures of Australia. This organization may be described as analogous to the National Association of Manufacturers of the United States, so that Mr. Beale speaks as an Australian with the same authority with which Mr. D. M. Parry might discuss the business and trade conditions of this country. There is this marked difference between the two presidents, however: that Mr. Beale carries among his letters of introduction strong credentials from the labor leaders of his own commonwealth.

OCTAVIUS C. BEALE.
President, Federal Council of Chambers of Manufactures of Australia.

(By courtesy of the Music Trades.)

In a conversation with a representative of the REVIEW, the Australian manufacturer spoke with much emphasis of his surprise at the attitude of many American employers toward the question of shorter hours for their workmen. It was almost beyond his comprehension, he said, that in this age and country he should have found so large a number of industrial plants where the day and night shift system of eleven and thirteen hours was in operation, not to mention many cases of a less aggravated nature. He thought it a most serious mistake for any employer to show as little concern as he had seen some men exhibit for the length of the working day; and he was again most emphatic in his prediction that, unless employers in the United States themselves inaugurated reforms in the hours of labor, it was only a question of time when the workingmen of the country would unite and force them to grant an amelioration of present conditions.

Mr. Beale had several interviews with President Roosevelt during his stay in the United States. In one of them the President charged him to advise his Government to encourage immigration, especially from Southern Europe, into the northern part of the island commonwealth.

The National Civic Federation Review

Vol. II., No. 3 — NEW YORK, MARCH—APRIL, 1906 — Ten Cents

REFORM OF PRIMARY AND ELECTION LAWS.

RESULTS OF THE SECOND NATIONAL CONFERENCE HELD UNDER THE AUSPICES OF THE NATIONAL CIVIC FEDERATION.

ONE of the most interesting and important conferences which has yet been held in the interest of Election Reform and of clean government took place in New York City on March sixth and seventh under the auspices of The National Civic Federation. More than one hundred delegates were present, representing nearly all sections of the country from Massachusetts to Georgia and Texas.

The following were among the delegates present:

Joseph T. Alling, Rochester, N. Y.; Dr. Clarence A. Barbour, Rochester, N. Y.; Albert S. Bard, Citizens' Union, New York; Hon. William S. Bennet, M. C., New York; Robert S. Binkerd, Secretary Municipal League, Buffalo, N. Y.; Henry T. Blake, New Haven, Conn.; R. L. Borden, Leader Conservative Party, House of Commons, Ottawa, Canada; Ernest [illegible], Delegate Mayor [illegible], Indianapolis, Ind.; Frank T. Brown, Norwich, Conn.; L. Burton Case, West Side Republican Club, New York; Charles Hopkins Clark, Hartford, Conn.; [illegible] Clark, Jr., Delegate Joseph Howell, M. C., [illegible], New York; Alexander [illegible], President Yale Law School Political Club, Yale U., New Haven, Conn.; Horace E. Deming, Delegate City Club of New York and National Municipal League, New York; Richard H. Dana, Boston, Mass.; [illegible], Secretary National Republican [illegible], New York; Henry M. Doremus, Mayor of Newark, Newark, N. J.; John A. Dutton, Republican Club, New York; Ralph M. Easley, The National Civic Federation, New York; Mark K. Edgar, Director Department of Public Safety, Delegate Mayor Connell, Scranton, Pa.; A. Frank Ferris, Good Citizens Federation, Grand Rapids, Mich.; Walter L. Fisher, President Municipal Voters League, Chicago, Ill.; George L. Fox, New Haven, Conn.; Julius J. Frank, Reform Club, New York; George H. [illegible], Delegate Mayor Timanus, Baltimore, Md.; Richard L. Gay, Secretary Election Laws League of Massachusetts, Boston, Mass.; Prof. H. A. Garfield, Princeton University, Princeton, N. J.; Henry M. Goldfogle, Member of Congress, New York; Henry Juhns Gibbons, Philadelphia, Pa.; Abraham S. Gilbert, 38 Park Row, New York; James W. Hawes, Delegate Republican Club, New York City, New York; Learned Hand, Delegate Citizens' Union, New York City, New York; Hon. Lynde Harrison, New Haven, Conn.; William B. Howland, The Outlook, New York; Richard W. Jennings, State Returning Board, R. I., Providence, R. I.; Edward S. Kaufman, Reform Club, New York; Robert N. Kenyon, Alternate Delegate Republican Club, New York, New York; Irvine L. Lenroot, Speaker of Assembly, Wis.; Hon. Seth Low, New York; Robert Luce, Boston, Mass.; Col. Theo. H. MacDonald, Connecticut Commission on Primary Reform, etc., New Haven, Conn.; Frederick F. Meyer, Jr., Newark, N. J.; James G. Monahan, Madison, Wis.; Hon. Rowell H. Moss, Delegate J. Sloat Fassett, M. C., Elmira, N. Y.; Hon. Franklin Murphy, ex-Governor of New Jersey, Newark, N. J.; William Church Osborn, New York; N. G. Osborne, New Haven, Conn.; John E. Owens, Delegate Mayor Dunne, Chicago, Chicago, Ill.; John H. Perry, Southport, Conn.; Roland Phillips, National Civic Federation; Josiah S. Pumpelly, New York; Josiah Quincy, Boston, Mass.; George L. Record, Jersey City, N. J.; Howard D. Ross, Delegate Mayor Wilson, Wilmington, Wilmington, Del.; George Frederick Rush, Chicago, Ill.; Charles R. Russell, Chairman Committee on Elections, General Assembly, Ga., Columbus, Ga.; Joseph E. Ransdell, Member of Congress, Louisiana; Ralph Curtis Ringwalt, New York; Hon. John O. Sheatz, House of Representatives, Pa., Philadelphia, Pa.; Thomas K. Skinker, Delegate Mayor Wells, St. Louis, St. Louis, Mo.; David S. Snedden, Professor Stanford University, Delegate Commonwealth Club of San Francisco, California; Edward B. Sturges, Scranton, Pa.; Mark F. Sullivan, 215 West 23d Street, New York; Hon. A. W. Terrell, Austin, Tex.; Charles Arthur Tribbie, Elizabeth, N. J.; Col. Isaac N. Ullman, Delegate Mayor Studley, New Haven, Conn.; C. V. C. Van Deusen, New York; William D. Washburn, Jr., Minneapolis, Minn.; William R. Wheeler, San Francisco; Fred H. Whitin, Delegate West Side Republican Club, New York, New York; Oliver Whitson, Delegate Hon. William W. Cocks, M. C., New York; Leighton Williams, New York; Rev. Alfred Wishart, Trenton, N. J.; Clinton Rogers Woodruff, Philadelphia, Pa.

The discussions were listened to with great interest, the speakers being for the most part men who have taken leading parts in the practical solution of the questions under consideration. At the close of the conference, which took up in order the three general subjects of (1) primary laws, (2) ballot reform, and (3) corrupt practices, the following resolutions were unanimously adopted, the purposes being, first, to make provision for the permanent organization of the conference under the direction of The National Civic Federation and, second, to put on record the consensus of opinion of the delegates on the subjects of the purchase of votes and of corrupt practices legislation.

These resolutions were adopted:

First, "*Resolved*, that The National Civic Federation be requested to establish a permanent department or branch of its organization to take jurisdiction of the subjects which the conference was called to consider, all of the members of this conference to become members of such department, and that the Civic Federation be requested to call another meeting of this conference at such future time as may be deemed expedient;" and second, "*Resolved*, that experience shows that existing provisions of criminal law against the purchase of votes are inadequate; that proper corrupt practices legislation should include (1) the publication of all contributions and expenditures; (2) the prohibition of political contributions by corporations; (3) the definition and limitation of permissible political expenditures; (4) provisions for judicial inquiry into election expenditures and existence of corrupt practices, in which proceeding any citizen may participate; (5) the punishment of corrupt practices by further penalties such as disenfranchisement or disqualification for office, in addition to fine or imprisonment."

HON. OSCAR STRAUS.

HON. R. L. BORDEN.

HON. SETH LOW.

The committee appointed to prepare these resolutions as announced by Oscar S. Straus, temporary chairman of the conference, consisted of:

Josiah Quincy, Chairman, Boston, Mass.; Walter L. Fisher, Vice-Chairman, Chicago, Ill.; A. W. Terrell, Austin, Texas; Richard Henry Dana, Boston, Mass.; Richard W. Jennings, Providence, R. I.; John H. Perry, South Port, Conn.; Lynde Harrison, New Haven, Conn.; Wm. Church Osborn, New York; James W. Hawes, New York; Harry A. Garfield, Princeton, N. J.; Henry M. Doremus, Newark, N. J.; Thomas Raeburn White, Philadelphia, Pa. (Henry John Gibbons, proxy); John D. Sheatz, Philadelphia, Pa.; Howard D. Ross, Wilmington, Del.; Geo. R. Gaither, Baltimore, Md.; Percy C. Jones, Toledo, Ohio; Ernest Bross, Indianapolis, Ind.; John E. Owens, Chicago, Ill.; Irvine L. Lenroot, Superior, Wis.; T. K. Skinker, St. Louis, Mo.; D. S. Snedden, San Francisco, Cal.; Charles R. Russell, Columbus, Ga.; Joseph E. Ransdell, M. C., La.; Leo E. Bennett, Indian Territory; A. Frank Ferris, Grand Rapids, Mich.; W. D. Washburn, Jr., Minneapolis, Minn.

The Session on Primary Reform.

In opening the conference, Oscar S. Straus read a paper vigorously denouncing the pernicious system of "boss" rule in our political life. He sounded the keynote of the conference in asserting that a free and full discussion of Primary Laws, Ballot Reform and Corrupt Practices would be a decided step in our progress toward clean government. Mr. Straus said in part:

"Eight years ago in these rooms, on January 20th and 21st, 1898, under the auspices of the Civic Federation, since enlarged to The National Civic Federation, was held the first National Conference for the Reform of Primary Elections.

"The subject was debated for two days, and a committee on permanent organization was elected, and as the chairman of that committee I have the honor to welcome you to this second National Conference, likewise called under the auspices of The National Civic Federation.

"There is no subject to-day of more vital concern to the people of this great democratic Republic, irrespective of party affiliations, than that the principles of popular government which the fathers of our Republic wrested from the grasp of monarchial usurpation shall be handed down from generation to generation pure and undefiled.

"The brave and fearless conflict between honest and dishonest politics has seldom if ever won so signal and precious victories for the moral law as were achieved by Governor Folk of Missouri, by Mayor Weaver in Philadelphia, by Senator Colby in New Jersey, by Jerome in New York, and by the Prosecuting Attorney in Boston, and by similar victories against long entrenched bossism under the stimulating helpfulness and uncompromising attitude of Secretary Bonaparte in Maryland, and Secretary Taft in Ohio.

"The encouragement following these victories has spread far beyond the States and cities in which they were won, so that throughout the length and breadth of our land the "plain people" who love their parties and their country, who by degrees have been literally disfranchised by the bosses, have been aroused to an appreciation of their rights and to a sense of their power; and from this awakening has resulted a renewed effort to break the chains of boss rule and to reclaim their rights as members of their party and as free and independent American citizens. Let us not forget in the discussion of the topics of reform that will come before us, important and necessary as they are, that all these are but means to the end, and that no political contrivance, however minute and drastic, can serve as a substitute for the indifference of the general body of electors, or for the lack of the ever-watchful spirit of unselfish patriotism."

Following the address by Mr. Straus, the Honorable Josiah Quincy, ex-Mayor of Boston, took the chair as chairman of the first session of the conference and introduced Horace E. Deming, delegate of the City Club of New York and of the National Municipal League. Mr. Deming contended for more appointive and fewer elective offices and pointed out what in his opinion are some of the proper conditions and safeguards of candidacy for such offices as are elective.

As it is the intention to have the speeches made at the conference reprinted *verbatim* in pamphlet form, only the briefest résumé of the proceedings can be given in this issue of the Review. Mr. Deming said in part:

"Under the present system, each citizen, in order to influence nominations, must ally himself with a recognized political party organization, and in casting his nominating vote must choose his candidates for national, for State, and for municipal offices all from a list of men bearing the badge of that organization. The individual citizen may appreciate the incongruity of this, but he has no choice in the matter. The nominating election should be a *public* election to determine as to each elective public officer who, as a candidate for that office, shall have the right as the sole representative of a given set of political principles properly applicable to its conduct to have his name

HON. A. W. TERRELL.

appear upon the official ballot used at the general election. Prior to registration day, let every candidate for nomination be announced as such candidate, together with a statement of the platform of political principles upon which he stands, each distinct set of principles being denoted by a short title or phrase; let the names of all candidates for the nomination be printed by the State upon an official nominating ballot delivered to the voter upon a registration day and immediately after registering, and let the voter mark secretly upon it his preference among all the candidates for nomination to each office; let the ballot then be deposited in the ballot-box under exactly the same circumstances as at the general election, and at the close of the polls let the votes be canvassed and the result be announced, as at the general election; upon the official ballot used at the ensuing general election, let only such policies and candidates appear as have successfully passed the two tests set forth above. In this way the local interests of the city could be freed from confusion with national politics; and municipal elections could be fought out by local parties, which would appear and disappear according as local issues did or did not warrant their existence.

"The incongruity and absurdity of having so many elective offices would be brought out clearly, and the day would be hastened when the nine out of ten offices now elective which should be appointive would be taken out of politics."

THE NEW JERSEY PRIMARY LAW.

The chairman then introduced the Honorable George L. Record, Corporation Counsel of Jersey City, who spoke on the New Jersey Primary law. 'The New Jersey law," said Mr. Record, "is a combination of the direct vote and the delegate vote. This law was passed under the Governorship of Governor Murphy, to whom the credit in my judgment almost entirely belongs for placing it upon the statute book. Now, a contest was had in Essex County, New Jersey, in which Everett Colby fought a machine successfully. I will tell you exactly the steps that he took to do it, and in that way you will see the New Jersey law. In each ward of each city and in each township of that county ten Republican voters signed a petition to the local city or municipal clerks something in this fashion: 'To the County Clerk of ——— Township: We, the undersigned ten voters of the Republican party residing in this Ward or Township, petition you, the Town Clerk, to print upon a Republican primary ballot the names of the following men as candidates or delegates to the County Convention of the Republican Party.' Then followed the names of the number of delegates which the law provides shall go to each township or ward. Thus far, you have simply the delegate system. We provided that the delegates next nominated might, if they chose, add a petition, in which they could say, 'We petition the City Clerk when making up the official ballot to group our names together, to put a bracket opposite, and opposite that bracket to put the name of Everett Colby under the words, 'Choice for State Senator.' Then those petitions went to the Town Clerk. Meanwhile, what we will call the Machine put in its petitions too, in which it nominated in each ward its delegates, and these delegates had their names printed upon the official ballot. Now, the Town Clerk or the City Clerk made up the official ballot for the Republican party, and this appeared: 'Official primary ballot for the Republican party. Candidates for the delegates to the County Convention. Vote for six (or whatever number there may be in each ward) by erasing all the names except the six, for whom you wish to vote.' Of course all the other conventions are represented, but I am taking one as a sample. The City Clerk made up the ticket in that way, and he grouped the delegates pledged to Colby in the manner in which I have indicated, and then at the bottom, or ahead of them he put the delegates named by the Machine or by any other group in the party that chose to contest, and there was the ticket. You could buy that ticket under the New Jersey law by depositing money with the City Clerk and distribute it in advance of the election.

"Now, the voter on primary day, which is the first registration day, goes to the polls and there registers and asks for a Republican ticket, gets it, puts it in his pocket, goes into the booth, draws a line through every name except those bracketed opposite the name of Colby, if that is his preference, comes out and unless challenged votes that ticket in the Republican box, there being a ballot box for the Republicans and another for the Democrats. If challenged, he makes oath as to his membership in the party, and if he makes that oath his vote must be received. There is no discretion in the Election Board, but he can be punished for a false oath. At night those ballots are counted; they are certified by certificates to the Town Clerk; the Town Clerk adds them all up and the delegates in the party receiving the highest number to the extent of six, we will say, in each Ward, or whatever the number may be, receive from him certificates that they are elected, and these certificates are their credentials in the ensuing election. If there is any attempt to evade that, we have provisions for appealing to the courts."

One of the points brought out by Mr. Record in explaining the operation of this law was that under the system it required a strong man to defeat such a candidate as Colby; and as the "boss" could not put up a strong man and still retain his supremacy his defeat from the start was pretty certain. He added, however, that in his judgment no such system would be successful if the "blank checks" of corporations as in the Colby campaign were available for the "machine" candidate.

THE MINNESOTA PRIMARY LAW.

William D. Washburn, Jr., delegate from Minnesota, outlined some of the provisions of the Minnesota law as follows:

"The Minnesota Primary Law involves the return to the first principles of Democratic Government.

"Its object is to permit the free citizen to vote for whom he pleases without restraint. The existing law includes the following features:

"It applies to all candidates for all elective, district, county and city officers, and elective members of school board, park boards and library, in all cities having over one hundred thousand inhabitants.

"The Primary Election is held seven weeks before the regular election, and includes the safeguard of the Australian Ballot System under the General Law.

"Political parties must have had at least ten per cent. of the vote cast in the preceding election or such party may appear on the ballot by filing a petition with ten per cent. of the actual vote. New parties may also go upon the ballot by a petition provided under the General Election Law.

"All candidates must file their intention to run with the County Auditor at least twenty days before the election. The fee for filing is ten dollars in one county and twenty dollars for an office covering two counties.

"Two weeks before election the County Auditor must prepare a separate ballot for each party for public inspection. Such tickets must be twice printed in full in a legal paper of the county. Rotation in place upon the ballot is also provided, so that each candidate appears first upon the ticket an equal number of times.

"The City Clerk must also give public notice of the time and place of election, and must post the names of all candidates at each precinct voting place.

"Judges and Clerks are appointed under the General Election Law and each Judge appoints two clerks. Ballot boxes are provided for each party, and one box for such women as wish to vote for the school board. No voter may receive a ballot until he has registered and he is required to cast a ballot of his own party, which must be the party for which he voted at the last election.

"This machinery thus provides that the voter be permitted to cast his vote without any restraint, and while it may possess certain defects, these are inherent in the character of the voter, and not in the system which is provided for the free registration of his vote."

THE NEW YORK PRIMARY LAW.

Hon. Abraham S. Gilbert, of New York, spoke of some of the features and of some of the objections to the New York Primary Law as it now stands. Mr. Gilbert said:

"In our Republican County Committee in the City of New York, the leaders of which were in favor of direct nomination, what happens when a broad and important question is presented? A committee is selected to investigate and report. Why? Because the subject cannot be properly handled by seven hundred and eight men in one room; because a committee of seven intelligent, earnest men can hear the arguments pro and con and get down to the meat of the question, say what, summing it all up, they believe, and then present their conclusions to the seven hundred and eight men for discussion. Now, under the law of New York this is generally the plan, and I will try to point out my objections to our law. Under the present law a man may enroll himself as a member of either one of the dominant political parties, take part in the official primary of the party in which he is enrolled as a member, be elected a delegate to a nominating convention and even take part in the nominating convention, and yet, after the nomination of the party has been made, join in an independent nomination in opposition to the party nominee. I say that this is wrong. I say that when I join a political organization I agree to be bound by the majority decision. Now, here is the trouble. The organization presents the ticket on which we first find in every election district the names of all the delegates to the County Committee, and they run as high as sixty or seventy in an Assembly District, sometimes—the members of the District Committee. You then find a dozen delegates to an aldermanic nominating convention, and so on, and you don't know the men on the ticket. Now, you have absolutely free say. You can vote that ticket or mark another one, but there is your trouble; you have to vote a complete ticket of delegates selected by the leaders. The leader has the selection of all these delegates and he chooses or selects all he knows. That is my objection to the law as it now stands. The delegates are then elected to the convention. I am not at all talking in favor of conventions as they are now conducted, but of conventions properly conducted. These conventions nominate the party candidate. Now, the independent people of New York have the simplest kind of a law, providing that one hundred men in a whole assembly district can sign a petition and nominate any independent man they please for assembly; five hundred for other offices, a thousand for still others. Their names go upon the official ballot. Now, in this city we appreciate that in one block or in half a block there are anywhere from five to six hundred voters. That means a good many thousand people; five or six hundred voters in a block. My contention is and has been for some time that those five or six hundred men ought to have a direct voice in the selection of candidates. My plan is, to have an assembly district cut into small districts; have the enrolled members of the party in an election district select a representative to a district committee, which shall be a powerful organization, and a representative one, one close to the people—as close as you can get it—and let those men, according to the population of the party vote, one or two in an election district, select the candidate for assembly, select the candidate for alderman, and be the delegates to every other convention in the City of New York."

Mr. Gilbert's speech closed the first session of the conference. At the afternoon session of March sixth the Honorable Franklin Murphy, ex-Governor of New Jersey, was introduced by Mr. Reynolds, Chairman of the Committee on Arrangements, and was selected as Chairman of the second session of the conference. Ex-Governor Murphy spoke of the value of the information given by the various speakers and suggested that the Committee on Arrangements adopt the necessary plans to put this information to practical use. The Hon. George Fred Rush, of Chicago, was then introduced and spoke on the Illinois Primary Law.

THE ILLINOIS PRIMARY LAW.

"Many writers," said Mr. Rush, "have stated that most of the evils attending primary elections would vanish if party nominations as such were abolished and placed on the same footing as nominations by individuals, as in England. But this simple method of nomination in the United States cannot, in my opinion, be put into effect here, because the party prizes of government and of office holding are greater here than there. In the experience of Illinois two systems have been tried:

"(1) The indirect or convention system, wherein the law gives to the parties a method which simply ensured that the delegates to the nominating convention were honestly elected and seated.

"(2) The direct system, wherein the law furnished parties a method whereby the members of a party should vote directly on various names to determine the nominee of the party.

"Illinois has progressed beyond the first method and is making fair attempts at the second method. A sound, acceptable, simple and complete direct primary law has not yet been placed upon any statute book, and the Illinois law has its defects.

"Governor Deneen and Mr. Roy O. West deserve great credit for their labors to make good the Republican State platform demand for a compulsory primary law for the whole State. The Governor and his co-workers exceeded their party promises and caused the enactment of not merely a compulsory primary law, but one containing so many features of a direct primary system as to entitle it to the name of a 'direct primary.' Its chief defects of substance are that nominations depend upon a majority vote instead of a plurality vote, and that too many offices are exempted from the operation of the law."

Mr. Rush then noted the main features of a direct primary law drawn by himself for the City Club of Chicago and closed his remarks with a discussion of the rights—or in his opinion the *lack* of rights—of citizens to vote at a party primary.

The Honorable Irvine L. Lenroot, Speaker of the Assembly at Madison, Wis., who followed, spoke on the Primary Law in Wisconsin:

WISCONSIN'S PRIMARY LAW.

"It would be interesting," said Mr. Lenroot, "to detail the history of the contest, waged for eight years, which finally resulted in the adoption of our law, a contest which has no parallel in the political history of this nation. Upon this issue Senator LaFollette was elected governor for three successive terms. Arrayed against him, and the measures he advocated, were every railroad and other public service corporation, every politician without visible means of support, and every interest seeking or enjoying special legislation for private purposes.

"The machine fought every inch of the ground. Nominations by direct vote were promised in three successive platforms of the Republican party, and in one of the Democratic party. But we learned that under the delegate and convention system the power of the machine was greater than the binding force of a party pledge; that with a majority of the members of our State Senate, when they were compelled to make choice of masters, the people or the machine, the machine was chosen, and the honor of the member, the will of the people, counted for nothing. To bring this about every resource of the professional lobbyist, of the corrupter of good government, was employed. Many members served the machine through gratitude for past and present favors, and the promise of others to come. Others served it through fear of railroad discrimination in their business, and financial ruin to themselves if they refused to do its bidding. But to the honor of theypeople of Wisconsin be it said, that few of the men who betrayed their constituents in that great contest are in public life to-day.

"The contest was finally won, and won, it is true, under the caucus and convention system, but it was only through the greatest popular uprising which the State had ever known. It was won in spite of the caucus and convention system, not because of it.

"In 1903 our Primary Law was passed and signed, but attached to it was a referendum, providing for its submission to, and adoption by, the voters at the general election of 1904, before becoming operative. It was adopted by a majority of over 50,000.

"In 1901, seeing that the Primary Bill was beaten in the Senate, its friends proposed a referendum. It was refused and was the subject of savage attack by the machine as being socialistic and revolutionary. In 1903 the machine proposed the referendum, not in good faith, but to postpone the operation of the Primary Law until after the campaign of 1904, and in this it was successful.

"Our law provides that all candidates for elective offices (town, village and judicial officers excepted) shall be nominated at a primary held under the provisions of the act, or by individual nomination papers. One primary for all parties, conducted by the general election officers, at public expense, and so far as possible in accordance with the general election laws, is provided. For general elections the primary is held upon the first Tuesday in September preceding, at the regular polling places in each precinct of the State. Other primaries are held two weeks before the election for which the primary is called. Ample provision is made for public notice of the primary.

"The name of no candidate can be printed upon the official primary ballot, unless at least thirty days prior to the primary, a nomination paper, signed by a certain number of electors, shall have been filed in his behalf. A minimum number of signatures to such nomination paper is prescribed for each office, the smallest being one per cent. of the voters of the party of the candidate, in the case of State officers, based upon the vote at the last preceding Presidential election.

"The names of all candidates appearing upon the ballot are published for three consecutive weeks in at least two, and not more than four newspapers of general circulation in each county.

"Separate tickets are provided for each party, the names of all candidates being placed thereon alphabetically, under the appropriate title of each office. In addition a non-partisan ticket is provided for, and non-partisan nominations may be made in the same way as party nominations.

"The open primary is adopted. The official ballot is made up of the several party tickets, securely fastened together at the top. No person not registered can vote, where registration is required at general elections, but primary day is also a registration day, and the voter may register at that time.

"The voter receives the ballot from the clerks, and retires to the booth. There he selects his party ticket from the ballot, and prepares it in the same way as a ballot is prepared at a general election, making a cross opposite the name of each candidate for whom he desires to vote. After the ticket is prepared he detaches it from the remaining tickets, and folds it. The others, attached together and unmarked, are also folded, and the elector votes the marked ballot, and deposits the remaining tickets in a separate box, designated as the blank ballot box.

GEORGE L. RECORD.

I. L. LENROOT.

ROBERT LUCE.

"The votes are canvassed in the same manner, and by the same officers as at a general election. The person receiving the greatest number of votes is nominated as the party candidate for the designated office, and his name is placed upon the official election ballot. But one ticket can be marked. In other words, the voter must select his party in the booth, and confine his votes to the candidates of that party.

"In each precinct a committee of three is elected at the primary. The person receiving the largest number of votes is made chairman. The precinct committees of each ward or town elect from their number a ward or town chairman, who must be a chairman of a precinct committee; they also elect a member of the county committee. The Assembly District Committee is composed of the chairman of the precinct committees in the district. The State senatorial committees are composed of the chairman of the Assembly District committees in each senatorial district; the congressional committees, of the chairmen of the senatorial district committees.

"Candidates for the United States Senate are nominated at the primary in the same manner as State officers.

"The candidates for the various State offices, and for senate and assembly, nominated by each party at the primary, and the holdover State Senators of such party are required to meet at the State Capital on the fourth Tuesday of September, succeeding the primary, and formulate the State platform of the party. They shall also select a State central committee of at least two members from each congressional district, and a chairman of such committee.

"Penalties are prescribed for bribery and violations of the law.

"This is a general outline of our law. As you have observed, it provides for nominations by a plurality vote. At the next session of our legislature we shall endeavor to secure the adoption, in its general features, of the plan of Mr. Remsen, of this city, providing for the elector expressing his first and second choice for the candidates for the different offices.

"As you have noticed from this outline, the prominent features of our law are:

"1. Nominations by direct vote.

"2. A compulsory primary for all parties, held on the same day, conducted by public officials, at public expense.

"3. The open primary and method of voting.

"4. The selection of party committees and the adoption of party platforms.

"The first and second are the really important features. The others are matters of detail."

DEFECTS IN THE WISCONSIN LAW.

Mr. James G. Monahan, of Madison, Wis., Collector of Internal Revenue for the Western District of Wisconsin, followed Mr. Lenroot and said that, in his opinion, far from being a good thing for the State, the primary election law of Wisconsin contained many features which were both burdensome and bungling. Mr. Monahan said: 'The primary election law of Wisconsin, instead of curtailing the power of the boss, increases it; instead of destroying machines, fosters them; instead of protecting the rights of the people, in many instances takes away those rights; instead of relieving them from taxation, adds to their burdens; instead of bringing the people nearer to the source of power, removes them farther away. To make the objections to the law clearly understood, I will briefly specify some of them. First, it compels the candidate to make two campaigns to secure an office and forces him to waste time unnecessarily and spend more money than he can afford, and, before he can even become a candidate and have his name printed on the primary ballot, he must secure from 1 to 4 per cent. of the voters of his party to sign the petition asking him to become such candidate. This alone will defeat many modest men with but little money from becoming candidates; second, it will practically deprive the farmer vote from a voice in either county or State affairs; third, unnecessary taxation is unjust taxation, and the Wisconsin law will impose a tax approximating $150,000 upon the people every time it is put into operation; fourth, under the provisions of the Wisconsin primary, we have abandoned the system that majorities may rule for one that minorities may govern—a plurality vote nominates; fifth, the Wisconsin primary law takes away from the people absolutely the right to make the platform, and gives the power to the candidates for the various State and legislative offices nominated by each political party at such primary. Sixth, the law makes it impossible to consider location or nationality in the nomination of tickets; seventh, the law in principle is a long step toward the abandonment of representative government bequeathed us by the founders of this Republic; eighth, by indirection, it virtually takes away from the people the constitutional right 'Peaceably to assemble to consult for the common good.' It does not forbid such assembling, but takes away both the incentive and the opportunity."

THE PRIMARY ELECTION IN GEORGIA.

After outlining some of the provisions of the Political Code referring to elections, the Hon. Charles E. Russell, Chairman of the Committee on Privileges and Elections of the Legislature of Georgia, spoke on the Primary Election Law in Georgia. Mr. Russell said in part:

"In a Democratic primary election held in my home county, Georgia, in which I had the honor of being elected to the House of Representatives, the Executive Committee, pursuant to a resolution unanimously adopted at a mass meeting held in Muscogee County, formulated rules and regulations calling for a primary election, very closely resembling the Australian ballot system and deviating therefrom only in the following points:

"The ballot obtained by the voter entering the booth or enclosure must contain the facsimile signature of the Chairman and Secretary of the Committee and, also, have printed thereon the number of votes cast in that booth. This is entered on the polling list by the clerk, so that no fraudulent or corrupt practice can be used to trick the ballot. The rules require that the ticket when folded by the voter shall show plainly the number of the ticket.

"Another rule provided for certain impersonal signs, emblems or characters, to be placed on the left of the name of each candidate, which would easily designate to the illiterate voter the person for whom he desired to vote, a true copy of said ballot being published in all the daily papers prior to the date of the primary. The rules further required that the voter should have one minute after entering booth to prepare the ballot, and no one should be allowed to assist in marking his ballot in any manner whatever.

"There was an ample number of booths and voting places to provide for the registered voters, and this system worked most excellently and satisfactorily to the entire community.

PROF. H. A. GARFIELD.

"Our statutes also make it a misdemeanor for any person to sell or furnish intoxicating liquors within two miles of an election precinct, and the only persons not permitted to vote at a regular election are those convicted of treason against the State, embezzelment of public funds or malfeasance in office, bribery, larceny or any crime involving moral turpitude, unless such persons shall have been pardoned. No voter shall be subject to arrest by a civil officer or shall be served with any writ or civil protest while going to, or returning from, or during his stay at, the voting precinct under a penalty of $500.

"As our party nominations are equivalent to elections, it is the consensus of opinion in Georgia that the will of the voters should be freely and truthfully expressed and accordingly declared."

Following the paper by Mr. Russell, five-minute speeches were made by Messrs. Humphrey, Wadhams, Hendrick, Morse and Allee, the general tone of the addresses being favorable to the enactment of any primary laws which shall have the ultimate effect of making the will of the public the dominating force in our municipal, State and national elections.

The Session on Ballot Reform.

Under the chairmanship of Clinton Rogers Woodruff, of the Ballot Reform section, the first paper on the subject was presented by Albert S. Bard, New York City.

Mr. Bard outlined briefly some historical points referring to the use of the ballot in elections and pointed out that in his opinion the ideal ballot should have seven chief qualifications:

1. Secrecy.
2. Honesty.
3. Simplicity.
4. Fairness to both candidate and voter.
5. Fairness as between different classes of society.
6. Opportunity to vote quickly, and
7. It must be easy to canvass and count.

In describing the three existing methods of using the secret ballot to-day the speaker divided these types into the separate party ballot, the office group blanket ballot and the party column blanket ballot. He laid stress on the differences in the reform of the ballots of the different States and showed, on account of the great variety of conditions under which elections are held in the United States, what a difficult problem has to be faced by those who undertake to study the question of ballot reform.

THE CONNECTICUT BALLOT LAW.

Mr. Henry T. Blake, of New Haven, in outlining some of the provisions of the ballot law in Connecticut, said that in that State a ballot contains only a single ticket, and the State supplies blanks for the ballots at cost to any one who applies, and on these ballots each party or political organization prints its own ticket. Mr. Blake pointed out that, as the State neither prints nor distributes the party ballots, there is no limitation of time within which nominations must be made and the ballots printed. Any organization and any individual may make up such a ballot as he pleases up to the time of closing the polls, and may put it in the field and get as many supporters as he can. This gives free scope for independent tickets if the regular party nominations are not satisfactory and, moreover, the dominating influence of primaries over the election is curbed and the success of the tickets depends largely on the character of the candidates. The speaker pointed out that some of the reasons in favor of the Connecticut form of ballot are that it is simple and convenient; that it secures facility and secrecy in the act of voting; that it is favorable to independent voting; that it is adaptable to changing conditions, and is economical. Mr. Blake admitted that bribery is possible with the envelope system of voting, but contended that it is rare because of the risk involved by all parties concerned.

In presenting Prof. Harry A. Garfield, of Princeton, the Chairman, Mr. Woodruff, stated that, in his opinion, one reason why we have so much straight party voting in this country is the multiplicity of public offices. Referring to the ballot reform law granted by the Pennsylvania Legislature in 1903, he remarked that it is well to scrutinize closely all laws which pretend to reform the ballot, for in Pennsylvania it was his opinion that every "last condition is worse than the first." Prof. Garfield took the ground that what we need is to elect men to public office who do not necessarily represent one idea or one faction, but who are fully equipped to carry out the duties of office. He argued from that the necessity of having a ballot which should enable every voter to express an opinion as between various men on the ticket with the utmost freedom. Referring to the Connecticut ballot, Prof. Garfield said that his objections could be reduced to a single point, viz., that the fundamental principle was in his judgment, wrong, for it really amounted to nothing more than the old "vest pocket" ballot. He contended that such a ballot made bribery a comparatively easy matter and that, in his judgment, the question of economy in printing really did not count. The Connecticut ballot puts a premium upon party voting and does not procure for the individual voter enough freedom of choice.

The next speaker, Mr. C. V. C. Van Deusen, formerly Assistant Secretary of Elections in the City of New York, defended the New York ballot law and the party column ballot as opposed to the Connecticut and Massachusetts type of ballot. The speaker laid down as a premise that the freedom of ballot or the system of voting bears little, if any, relation to or effect upon corrupt practices at elections except that, under certain systems, such practices are more difficult of detection and punishment. In his judgment, the establishment of a course of instruction in all the grades of our public schools would do more in twenty years to purify politics than twenty centuries of legislation has done. "The Connecticut form of ballot," said Mr. Van Deusen, "is practically the same as that in use in New York from 1890 to 1896 without the official envelope. The latter feature does not compensate for the objections raised to the separate party and independent tickets, and certainly the Connecticut and New Jersey systems, which are almost identical, leave the door wide open to the briber." While contending that in States like Massachusetts which have adopted the office group ballot, all candidates except those at the head of the ticket, are slighted, the speaker admitted that certain objections are raised against the form of ballot in New York; first, that it is too complicated in regard to the markings permitted the voters; that it does not lend itself to independent voting for candidates of various parties and independent bodies; and that it is difficult to canvass, thus permitting a loss of a great percentage of the votes cast. Under the New York system, while many votes are returned as blank, such votes are "infinitely less under our form of voting than under the office group system. I contend that with the adoption of a few amendments to our present law, which will simplify the tally sheet and modify the technical bookkeeping now entailed in making out the returns, we will have an almost ideal law."

THE BALLOT LAW OF TEXAS.

Hon. A. W. Terrell, of Texas, former United States Minister to Turkey, and author of the Election Law of Texas, known as "The Terrell Election Law," referred in his paper which followed, on the ballot laws of Texas, to the widely different conditions to be met in solving the problem by States of the North and South. "What the country now needs," said Judge Terrell, "both North and South, is a system of election laws which will tend to diminish the depraved, the purchasable and the reckless class of voters. Any system based on the desire to have what is called 'A full vote' must end in failure. What the country needs is a voluntary and honest vote, and not a vote that is controlled at the polls by the ward heeler, the campaign boss or the machine demagogue."

"What we in Texas require is, first, to make the citizen perform some act for the public benefit each year to evince his desire for good government and to perform that act voluntarily before a political campaign begins and make his right to vote depend upon its performance; second, to protect the citizen against machine politics, convention dictation and corrupt methods at the polls." With regard to the kind of ballot used in Texas, Judge Terrell said: "A uniform official blanket ballot is furnished each voter by the presiding judge on which every party ticket and an independent ticket, if there be one, is printed, and the voter is not permitted to have in his possession when he enters the booth any other ticket or paper to guide him in casting his vote. These and other precautions have caused the work of advancing poll tax money, or otherwise buying a vote, to almost cease, for the purchaser of a vote is careful in advancing money when he has no means of controlling the vote. A direct primary election is required of all organized political parties that cast 100,000 votes at the last preceding general election."

Hon William S. Bennet, of the 17th District of New York City, spoke upon the general subject of direct nominations with especial reference to New York. He said: "Up to a certain point the law in the State of New York in relation to the nomination of party candidates is one of the best in the country. The primaries are held under the direction of State officers on a day fixed by law, are participated in by all parties of any size and the polls remain open for a definite, fixed and extended period. Experience has demonstrated that all these matters are essential to the existence of any proper system of primary nominations." The speaker's objection to the system was that the individual voter, Republican or Democrat, had, as a matter of fact, no voice in nominations, nor the right to have his say in relation to the nomination of any particular candidate without at the same time overthrowing the entire organization of his party in the district in which the candidate is to be nominated. "As I said, the nomination law at present is admirable so far as it goes. It may be readily adapted to direct nominations. The change required would be slight. The simple elimination of the convention and the substitution therefor of the names of nominees on the primary ballots instead of the names of delegates to the convention, would effectuate the change. Should it be desired to extend the system to State officers, the provisions of the Wisconsin statute in relation to the preparation of a party platform by the nominees of the party might be added."

THE BALLOT SYSTEM IN MASSACHUSETTS.

Hon. Josiah Quincy, ex-Mayor of Boston, was introduced by the Chairman, and spoke informally about the merits of the Massachusetts ballot system. The Massachusetts law rests upon the theory that an election is not a choice between parties, but a choice between candidates—between men who are candidates for particular offices. Mr. Quincy said that after an experience of eighteen years in Massachusetts with the Massachusetts ballot law, he was convinced that both in theory and in practice the Massachusetts form of ballot has proved effective as opposed to the party column form of ballot. Under the Massachusetts law the voter is obliged to make a selection between the candidates for each particular office. One objection to the Massachusetts form of ballot is that it constitutes in itself a substantial educational qualification and, therefore, is out of place in States which have not an educational qualification. Mr. Quincy pointed out in answer to this that, in the first place, the educational qualification of Massachusetts is a very limited one, and, second, that any Australian ballot system has in a measure necessarily an educational qualification. Another objection to the system is that it results in the great falling off of the vote. The speaker admitted that this was true. He replied to the objection by calling attention to the fact that under the best conditions only a percentage of the voters exercised the privilege of franchise, and he raised the question whether it is not "exactly as legitimate that the voter who goes to the polls should refrain from exercising his total franchise as it is that a certain proportion of the voters should choose to stay away from the polls altogether."

Following Mr. Quincy, Mr. Richard W. Jennings, Secretary of the State Returning Board of Rhode Island, said that he did not propose to criticise the Massachusetts ballot, but that this system would not be the best for Rhode Island. In Rhode Island the situation on election day is complicated on account, some years, of choosing at one time Presidential electors, congressmen, State officers, members of the legislature, city officials, members of the city council and of the school committee. Further complications arise from the different methods of electing members of the legislature and general assembly. According to Mr. Jennings, the alphabetically arranged ballot, with the names of candidates grouped under each office, produced for a number of years a startling number of blank and defective votes, and, therefore, a large percentage of the voters was disfranchised. The party column ballot is now in use in Rhode Island and, while it has been tested by only one election, the results seem to be satisfactory. The blank and defective ballots have been signally reduced.

The Session on Corrupt Practices.

The fourth session of the conference was called to order by Mr. Reynolds, who introduced, as Chairman of the afternoon, ex-Mayor Low. Mr. Low said: "The subject of corrupt practices at elections has been one that has attracted growing attention in all parts of the country. There has come to be a pretty keen realization of the fact that vast sums are spent (often unnecessarily, often improperly) and people realize with increasing unquietness that the result of an election here and the result of an election there has been determined by the use of money. Further than that, there is a growing conviction that the electorate itself is being progressively debauched, for on every hand those who look into the subject are compelled to realize that constantly growing numbers of men will only vote for their own party when they are paid for it. They may not vote—perhaps could not be persuaded to vote against the side that they want to support by any money [illegible]; as they have come to look upon payment [illegible], as it is euphoniously called, as one of the privileges accruing to citizenship.

"There is a most hopeful movement in progress, as many of you know, to secure publicity [illegible] requirement of publicity as to election receipts and expenditures through the action of Congress, and the same movement is taking place in many of the States. In some States it has already gone so far as to place laws upon the statute books. That is the case in the State of New York, and this year there is a determined effort being made to improve those laws. I think I may fairly say that in the judgment of that association there are at least four points that must in some way be covered.

"The first is this question of publicity, as to which there is very little difference of opinion.

"The second is the prohibition of campaign contributions by corporations. And as to that again there is very little difference of opinion.

"The third is to pass an act that in some form or another shall make it possible to establish by judicial inquiry the fact of bribery, if there has been such in any election district, with a penalty [illegible] of losing the benefit of the votes obtained in that electoral district.

"In other words, we feel that a remedy or *the* remedy for the evil is not to be found in criminal statutes and in fines, but it must be sought along the line of making it unprofitable to the candidate on whose behalf bribery is used, if bribery is to be stopped.

"And in the fourth place, our association at any rate feels that either through the activity of some public officer who is independent of both parties and who will therefore enforce the law against both or through an association which will do for these laws when passed what the Civil Service Reform Association has done for the laws upon that subject—in one form or another these laws must be made effective through such an agency. In other words, no matter how good your law upon the subject is, it won't enforce itself, and there must be behind it a free and well organized and active public opinion expressing itself either through a public official or through an organization established for the purpose to see to it that the laws upon the statute book are enforced fearlessly through the courts."

CORRUPT PRACTICES IN NEW YORK.

Following the address of Mr. Low, Mr. William Church Osborn, Secretary of the Association to Prevent Corrupt Practices at Elections in New York City, outlined briefly the work and plan of the Association to Prevent Corrupt Practices. "At the present time," said Mr. Osborn, "there are three movements in this State for a corrupt practices act, the movement of the Independent League, the so-called Belmont Publicity Bill and the Association to Prevent Corrupt Practices at Elections, of which Mr. Low is Chairman, and of which I have the honor to be Secretary.

"The Independents' bill and the Belmont bill are both publicity bills and are both largely modeled on the accepted form, which provides for the payment of all contributions for election purposes to a definite person, such as the Chairman and Secretary of a county committee, etc.; for the accounting by those committees and officers; and in some cases for a system of procedure to determine whether those accounts so stated are complete and truthful, and whether such expenses are required.

"The Association has also put in a publicity bill which has been developed in accordance with the traditions of

JAMES B. REYNOLDS

CLINTON ROGERS WOODRUFF

ISAAC S. WHEATON

this State as a part of our Penal Code and is similar to our present provisions requiring candidates to file statements.

After outlining these general provisions, Mr. Osborn spoke of the advanced position taken by his Association in the matter of corrupt practices. He stated that in nearly every instance in which the different States have approached the subject they have taken as their method of procedure attacks against individual candidates for corruption of which they may be guilty personally or through agents. The penalty in nearly all corrupt practices legislation is forfeiture of office. Mr. Osborn stated that his Association wished to go one step farther and to hold not an individual but the party responsible for corruption.

CORRUPT PRACTICES IN MASSACHUSETTS.

Hon. Robert Luce, of Boston, contrasted the situation in his State with that of New York, calling attention first to the fact that Massachusetts is a State where the individual is emphasized and where party development does not present one-tenth of the danger evident in New York. Mr. Luce recalled that the essential parts of the Massachusetts Corrupt Practices Act became law in 1892, and so have been tried for fourteen years. The law was inspired by the English act of 1883 which worked a revolution in English politics. The English act sought four things, first, publicity as to contributions and expenditures; second, a definite maximum limit on expenditures; third, prohibition of certain classified classes of expenditure; fourth, forfeiture of office as a penalty. Now, in Massachusetts only one of these things—publicity—was sought. Mr. Luce said that unless a publicity law is so thorough and drastic that it cannot be safely evaded it will accomplish nothing whatever in disclosing what the statutes have declared to be a crime. This has actually been the result in Massachusetts, for not a prosecution has been made under the provisions of the law during the fourteen years of its existence. Is, then, the publicity secured worth while? Mr. Luce answers this query by asserting that "it has not been worth while if its chief or sole purpose has been an immediate and positive check on the use of money in elections. There is no proof whatever that, so far, the Massachusetts law has had such an effect. On the contrary, the use of money in politics was never so great as it has been in the last two years. Yet clear as it is that expenditure has grown alarmingly, apparently in spite of the law, it is equally clear that the publicity secured by the law has been a powerful factor in bringing public opinion to what is now a universal demand that the evil shall be crushed. The effect of publicity then has been that it has secured public knowledge and understanding of the evil and its danger. Perversion of the suffrage can no more be prevented or even checked by public opinion alone than can perversion of commerce or industry or the social relations." Mr. Luce stated, however, that, in his judgment, better practical results will come from a law which does not insist too much upon the detailed statement of small expenditures, such, for example, as personal expenditures of candidates not to exceed $40 or $50.

CORRUPTION IN PENNSYLVANIA.

Following Mr. Luce, Mr. Mark F. Sullivan, of New York City, recounted some of his personal experiences in Greene County, Pa., on the subject of corrupt practices. He stated that in that county it was the usual thing to pay for votes, that by long practice the voters have become accustomed to getting money for their votes and that they count on it as a part of their annual revenue. The evidence against the men who used the money for bribery is practically clear, but they cannot be convicted because of the collusion of the court and the make-up of the grand jury. Mr. Sullivan suggested two remedies, first, to watch the grand jury and its foreman and to get jury laws which provide for a select list of the community so that the mere actual permeation of the machine's influence will not so corrupt the community that a representative grand jury will not indict. Second, to arouse a healthy public sentiment, and, in the case of certain large cities like Louisville, to which the speaker referred in passing, to provide that all the crime of one city will not come before one judge.

CONNECTICUT CORRUPT PRACTICES LAWS.

Mr. George L. Fox, Principal of the University School, New Haven, next spoke of the corrupt practices situation in the State of Connecticut. Mr. Fox said: "If corruption at elections is to be lessened in the United States, the federal congress and the States must enact and enforce laws after the model of the English and Canadian laws which for twenty-five years have been most effective. It is difficult to adapt this law to our conditions because of the very complex character of State and federal government, because of constitutional limitations as to the body who have the final scrutiny of the election and because of the large size of many electoral areas in this country. And yet we should aim to come as near to the English standard as possible by rigorously enforcing without fear or favor existing laws and by strengthening them in every way." Mr. Fox advocated establishing the election court with fearless and rigorous judges; punishing failure to file sworn statements of expenditure by arrest and fine; limiting or abolishing paid conveyance and strictly limiting the number of paid workers; forbidding contributions by corporations and the granting of passes of all sorts to any public officials by any public service corporation, especially in the case of judges; strictly limiting the amount of expenses to a reasonable amount by law determined by the number of electors in an electoral area.

W. D. WASHBURN, Jr.

On the same subject of the Connecticut corrupt practices law the Hon. Lynde Harrison, of New Haven, gave an interesting personal sketch of his part in the framing of the present law and in an informal discussion, in which a number of delegates took part, he outlined the main provisions of the law and stated that, in his opinion, the corrupt practices law, based on the present law in England, would do away with corrupt practices in this country as it has there.

A LETTER FROM HON. PERRY BELMONT.

It was expected that the Hon. Perry Belmont would address the conference on the subject of his corrupt practices bill which he is earnestly advocating at this session of Congress in Washington. Mr. Belmont was unable to be present, however, and sent the following letter:

"I regret extremely that I am unable to attend the Election Law Conference of the Civic Federation, as I find it necessary to remain in Washington to continue the effort to obtain a hearing from the House committee which has the publicity bill in charge. It has been my intention to comply with your invitation to inform you of the progress of the bill.

"The movement had its origin in the last Presidential campaign. The demand upon Mr. Cortelyou and Mr. Taggart for information upon the subject of contributions to the national committees was very insistent towards its close. That demand has been re-echoed throughout the country until it has become evident that before another Presidential campaign, a law will have been enacted, requiring publication of such contributions and expenditures.

"The Armstrong investigation itself has been but one of the important incidents of this agitation. Revelations in regard to insurance companies and their contributions to political campaigns, disclosures before congressional committees of reprehensible pecuniary transactions in regard to the Panama Canal, knowledge of similar sinister influences and considerations in connection with concessions in the Philippines and Santo Domingo have impressed upon the American people the conviction that what may be termed investments in campaign funds for future benefits are constantly growing larger and more threatening to the honest administration of our domestic and foreign policy.

"Last September during the insurance investigation, when Mr. Taggart had made the announcement that 'Neither the Democratic National Committee nor any authorized representative ever asked or received from Mr. McCall, the New York Life, or any other insurance company a single dollar's contribution to the campaign fund.' Mr. McCall himself declared in a public interview that he was in favor of a law prohibiting corporations from contributing and compelling publicity of contributions. He had previously said to me, 'Mr. Belmont, if you knew what I was obliged to do, you would feel sorry for me.' I have often thought of those words since, and the circumstances of his death invite general attention to the evils of the system of which he is regarded as a victim. Those, however, who are mainly responsible and the beneficiaries of that system, should not escape their responsibility.

"The movement for state and national remedial legislation requiring publication of what are now secret political contributions and expenditures has been rapidly increasing in strength and scope. National and state organizations have been formed. Organised labor, by resolutions and petition, is actively and effectively co-operating. Bills have been introduced in Congress and members of the Senate and House of Representatives of both parties are earnestly in favor of a national publicity bill.

"This movement is non-partisan, and the friends of this measure believe that it will continue non-partisan. The controlling elements of the House of Representatives are all-powerful in deciding, under the rules, what bills shall be advanced or retarded. So far, there has been no disposition to delay this measure, and it is to be hoped that there will be none. It cannot be supposed, however, that those who have adopted what is known as the 'stand-pat' policy would care to assist a movement which would bring about radical changes in the manner of collecting and spending campaign moneys.

"If the publicity bill should meet with obstructions, its friends are now so numerous and the question is so important to the people of this country, that a loud protest would be heard against any indirect methods to bring about its defeat."

As a number of speakers at the conference referred to the corrupt practices acts of England and Canada, the address by the Hon. R. L. Borden, leader of the conservative party in the House of Commons, Ottawa, Canada, was listened to with particular interest. Mr. Borden said:

"We have in Canada, as you have in the United States, government by party. Now, there seem to me to be three absolute essentials of Democracy, and particularly of the party system as associated with democracy. One is the honest appropriation and expenditure of money. The next is the appointment of public officials from the standpoint of efficiency and personal character, and not from the mere standpoint of partisan service. And the third is the cleansing of our elections from those corrupting influences which have made themselves manifest, I believe, in all countries which have adopted representative systems.

"As far as our party system in Canada is concerned, it is very much simpler than yours in the United States. The law does not regard parties so far as nomination is concerned. I will speak of the federal system only, which is typical of all systems in Canada, both provincial and municipal. The federal system in Canada permits any twenty-five electors to nominate a candidate for the House of Commons. We do not elect as many of our public officers as you do in the United States. I am not for the moment concerned with the question as to whether our course or your course is the wiser. I am simply telling you what our system is. For example, in the House of Commons the electoral unit is about twenty-five thousand. Twenty-five men nominate the candidate; a ballot is prepared; usually only two candidates are nominated. Behind all this, behind the formal nominations by twenty-five electors, there is the party organization, of course; that party organization is very often pretty thorough, but the people are absolutely at liberty to nominate as many candidates as they like, whether for the Dominion Parliament, the Provincial Legislature, or at a municipal election. You might think that would result in a multiplicity of candidates. That has not been our experience. It is very rare indeed that we have more than one candidate for either of the two political parties nominated either for the House of Commons, for the Provincial Legislature or in municipal politics. We have very elaborate laws against bribery, laws very much the same as I observe you have in the various States. We have laws against the use of money, laws against the provision of refreshments; we have laws closing our hotel bars and saloons upon polling days; we have laws against intimidation; we have laws providing that any person employed by a candidate for money during the course of an election is thereby disfranchised. In respect of all these matters I think we follow pretty much the law which has been followed in the United States.

"Now, about thirty years ago our Parliament gave up the jurisdiction which it had long exercised of dealing with controverted elections to its own body. With us—and I suppose with you—the Legislature was the judge originally of whether or not a candidate had been elected by corrupt practices or had been fairly elected.

"In 1874 or 1875 the Federal Parliament handed that jurisdiction over to the judges of our superior court. We have found the transfer of this jurisdiction from Parliament and from the Legislature to the courts to be eminently satisfactory. But I should like to say what I think we should have in Canada, and to point out to you what I think might be the advantage. In Great Britain they have an officer called the Public Prosecutor, who is charged in that country with the direction of all important public prosecutions. By the English Act of 1883 that officer has imposed upon him very important duties with regard to election petitions. He is bound to attend the trial of every petition. He is bound to attend every application to withdraw petitions, and if evidences of corrupt practices come to him from any division in which no petition has been filed, it is the duty of the public prosecutor to intervene and to make such investigation and to take such steps as may seem to him to be desirable. In Great Britain also the candidate is limited as to his expenditure for purposes which are declared legitimate by statute. We have not that in Canada. I hope that we shall have it, but I hope especially that we shall have very soon the appointment of some officer, some independent public officer having a status which places him beyond the reach of either one political party or the other, upon whom shall be imposed the duty of investigating every election in respect of which a petition has been filed, as well as of investigating every election where he has reason to believe that corrupt practices have been carried on upon any extensive scale. If we had that in Canada, so that we should not have the scandal (because it is a scandal there) of the withdrawal of election petitions by agreement between the two political parties, we would have accomplished a very great result."

"WELFARE WORK" DISCUSSED BY EMPLOYERS AND EMPLOYES.

IMPROVEMENT IN WORKING CONDITIONS THE TOPIC AT THE ANNUAL MEETING OF THE NEW YORK CIVIC FEDERATION.

AT the annual meeting of the Civic Federation of New York, held at the Park Avenue Hotel on February 14, the general subject of discussion was "Welfare Work." In connection with the statements made by leading New York employers concerning what has been done to better the conditions of employes in several important industries, interesting papers were read by former city officials showing how New York City cares for its institutional employes and referring in detail to the need of better conditions in the station houses for policemen. One of the most interesting features of the meeting was the presentation, during the dinner which followed the informal reception, of stereopticon views illustrating what has been done by practical, successful business men in providing for the comfort of employes in the work rooms, for recreation, educational opportunities and in the housing of labor. Special importance is attached to the fact that at this meeting leading representatives of labor were for the first time requested to present the needs of workingmen in their respective industries.

Among the subjects presented by leaders of employes' organizations were papers showing the needs of stationary firemen and hotel employes, a discussion of what may be done for the men in the building industry, as well as for the moulders, metal polishers, theatrical employes and teamsters. It is well to state that, while only a brief report of the many interesting points covered by the various speakers of the evening can be given here, it is intended a little later to have a complete verbatim report published of all the proceedings.

In addressing the meeting as Chairman, Mr. Charles A. Moore, after describing briefly the work and methods of the Civic Federation, spoke of what, in his opinion, was of first importance to the continued pre-eminence and well-being of both employers and employes in America, that is, economy in industrial methods.

Mr. Moore said in part:

"I had on my desk the other day a pamphlet which contained the address of Mr. Stuyvesant Fish, the President of the Illinois Central Railroad—a very thoughtful and good man—and he says, as to the household question, that the people of America are spendthrifts, earning money freely and wasting it to such an extent as to make it proverbial. He says that the sum wasted is enormous. With a population of eighty-five millions, who either save or waste, it is hardly to be believed that any one will either save or waste less than five cents per capita per day. That is a very small sum, from the American point of view, but it would amount to more than $4,250,000 or $1,551,250,000 annually; and yet we think we are just about as smart a lot of people as are produced on the earth. We think we are second to none, and we are not, in general; but some people are so busy getting smart that they omit some of the things that will keep them so. Unless we study economy, unless we utilize these God-given opportunities in a sensible way, the people at whom we are sneering will be taking care of us some time in the future—we may have to suffer the humiliation of falling back on them.

"The other day I had a practical illustration of Welfare Work. A young man had been with me ten or twelve years and had demonstrated pretty well that he had good business ideas. I was thinking about some one whom I could send to Japan to cover that field, and said, here is my man. He was about to be married, and as soon as the ceremony had taken place he came and said he was ready to start. I happened to think a few days before he started: Well, here is a fellow going away off to Japan to look after my interests. Out of the hundred and eighty-five of his associates in the office he might not be able to see more than fifty or sixty to bid them good-bye; so I said to my secretary, go right uptown and see what you can do about arranging a dinner; I want to give this fellow a good dinner as a send-off. It was arranged at the Hotel Astor, and later they called me on the telephone and said, 'How about this dinner?' I said, 'just as good a dinner as the Astor can give.' They said, 'How about wines?' I said, I want to have everything that goes with a good dinner, the best of cigars and everything else. I was asked whom I was going to invite. I said, everyone, the messenger boy who came in last week—the teamsters, packers, shippers, stenographers, bookkeepers and clerks. So I sent formal invitations, and arranged to have the room decorated in Japanese style. I was curious to see whether men who had been with me as long as they had would abuse the privilege; and I want to say to you gentlemen that out of one hundred and eighty-one men there was not a man or a boy that took one drop of wine more than he should have, or who took a cigar and put it in his pocket. I never enjoyed a dinner more in my life, nor felt that I had been with a better average lot of men, nor where there was more enthusiasm

CHARLES A. MOORE.

and interest. One of the best toasts of the night was from the head of the teamsters, who said, 'Here's to Mr. Richards. You go to Japan and get the business, and we will haul the goods for you in prompt time and be back of you solid for the three years you are there.' (Applause.) Now, that spirit seemed to be present everywhere. Richards goes to Japan, not as an individual representative of a concern, but he goes there with the knowledge that all the men he knew in that organization are 'solid,'—just as a man will go to war and know that everyone at home is ready to back him up.

"That is what will result from Welfare Work, and you will all feel that this work is the best investment that one can make."

Mr. Moore said that, in all of his experience as a manufacturer, he had always instructed his superintendents to hand in their resignations the minute they refused to hear a complaint, always going on the theory that about 75 per cent. of the fault was the employer's and 25 the employe's. "But," added Mr. Moore, "they always had to work lively to get rid of their 25 per cent. before I could get rid of my 75.

"I believe that men should meet and understand each other and that is one of the purposes for which The National Civic Federation was founded. It not only helps to prevent controversies but is influential in improving the working conditions through such discussions as we are to have this evening."

Following his address the Chairman introduced Mr. H. H. Vreeland, Chairman of the Welfare Department of The National Civic Federation, who explained the methods of the Department which prepared the program for the meeting, and who then gave an interesting account of the Welfare Work which he inaugurated for the employes of the New York City Railway Company.

John S. Huyler, President of Huyler's, and a member of the Executive Committee of the Welfare Department of The National Civic Federation, endorsed Welfare Work, and stated that in his factory there are 600 employes, about two-thirds of whom are women, and whose regular hours of work do not exceed fifty-four. These are some of the welfare provisions instituted by Mr. Huyler:

The young women wear caps and aprons.

Fire protection has been given consideration, the new building being especially well constructed, and there are many fireproof exits. The floors are tiled. Fire drills are being introduced.

All the employes have seats with foot rests.

There are separate dressing rooms, in which the employes hang their clothes, adjacent to the different departments.

There are individual wash basins and soap and towels are provided by the company.

In the largest dressing room there is a matron who cares for the young women needing her advice or assistance, and who also makes the caps and aprons.

Pure drinking water, which is cooled by having the pipes coiled about the ice, is provided.

There is an emergency hospital with the necessary equipment. There is not much illness, but when employes are indisposed they are paid in full upon the doctor's authorization.

The company recently purchased a brown stone house next to the factory on Irving Place and equipped each floor with dining-room furniture.

At Christmas time the employes who have been with the company over six months get a week's wages. For some time the company gave one week's vacation to the factory employes who had been in its employ for one year with pay. Lately it has increased the vacation to two weeks with pay, Mr. Huyler stating that it was a hardship for them to be without their pay during the vacation period and that the company should be willing, as its profits increased, to share them with the employes.

There is an annual outing, which is usually an ocean excursion. When the employes and their families and sweethearts reach the boat, each person is handed a basket of lunch, every young woman being presented with a box of chocolates in addition. There is a counter for free soft drinks on the boat, and there is a band to furnish music for dancing. Each child is given a toy, and every effort is made to ensure the enjoyment of the two thousand participants.

In introducing Mr. Timothy Healy, President of the International Brotherhood of Stationary Firemen, the Chairman said:

"Now, we are going to hear from a class of men in which I am greatly interested. When you walk around the streets of New York and see that the sidewalk is clear you don't know that you are walking over a powder magazine. Few people realize how much brains and intelligence and loyalty and faithfulness exist among the men who fire boilers and take care of them. Now, I want to tell you the man who does not speak, who does not say anything, is down there under the building firing that boiler, and we would like to hear something about him. I take pleasure in introducing to you Mr. Timothy Healy.

MR. HEALY: Our chairman has just turned my attention to powder magazines. They certainly are powder magazines—very dangerous—and they take men of brains and men who keep their heads clear to operate them. But I regret that the large employers of labor in this city do not encourage these hard worked men. About six years ago there was a law enacted in this State licensing stationary firemen in the city of New York. That law is not enforced. The large employers of firemen, particularly those employing large numbers of them, don't want that law. I don't know what their object is. We do know that when the men ask their superintendents or chief engineers for the letter, which the law requires, to present to the Board of Examiners, they are frequently told that a license is not necessary for firemen, and, in many instances, they have been discharged for daring to ask for that letter. I wish we could bring it home to the large corporations of Greater New York who have ignored this law and try to get them to recognize it. It would result in improving the efficiency of their men. A good fireman is a good man for an employer; he sticks faithfully and takes care of his plant, and he is a safe man to have around it. And if there are any large employers here to-night whose firemen are not licensed, I hope they will take the matter up in the near future. (Applause.)

The firemen of this city have always been neglected. They are a class of men that never had an opportunity of going to the office, or going directly to their employers. When, by chance, a man has gone over the head of a superintendent or engineer to make complaint, he has "had to walk" very soon. His job was ended under that man. The firemen never get any show to make conditions known to the employers. Those men have been for years and years, up to a few years ago, working twelve hours a day for three hundred and sixty-five days a year, with never a Sunday or a holiday or any other time to themselves. If they should take a day off to attend the funeral of some relative, or on account of sickness in their families, when they would report for work they would be told that their places had been filled. This was not the exception. It was the rule, and it is to-day in many places. Now, the conditions under which those men work, no one knows except the man who has done the work and who is doing it to-day. Take, for instance, one of the big sky-scrapers downtown. A man way down two stories under the ground on a hot summer's day has to put in twelve hours there in the awful heat, anywhere from 110 or 115 to as high as 160 degrees—generally 130 or 140—with no system for ventilation. Some of these places are wet and damp under his feet

(*Continued on page 8*)

THE NATIONAL
Civic Federation Review

Office: 281 Fourth Avenue, New York City

RALPH M. EASLEY, Editor

The Editor alone is responsible for any unsigned article or unquoted statement published in THE NATIONAL CIVIC FEDERATION REVIEW.

Ten Cents per Copy One Dollar per Year

PUBLISHED MONTHLY BY

The National Civic Federation

PROGRESS OF WELFARE WORK.

At the annual meeting of the New York Civic Federation on February 14, the proceedings of which are given elsewhere in this issue, Welfare Work was the general topic of discussion. An important feature of the meeting was the opportunity given to labor men to express their views. One of the speakers, representing the teamsters, remarked that he was at first inclined to wonder whether a mistake had not been made, since formerly his organization was not considered worth recognizing. An employer remarked, after hearing the address by the representative of the stationary firemen, that he had no idea the conditions described could prevail, and that, in the hotel of which he is proprietor, he would at once make a thorough personal investigation of working conditions.

This first recognition by The Welfare Department of the right and of the necessity of men who do the work to be heard on the sanitary requirements in their various trades is, of course, only an extension of the idea of personal conference which is a cardinal principle in the work of the Federation. But it marks an era in Welfare Work in opening the way to the dissemination of accurate, first-hand information on working conditions which will be welcomed by a vast number of our most progressive employers.

To carry cut this idea the New York Civic Federation has appointed a committee of sixty which, divided into twenty sub-committees, will report upon the sanitary and general working conditions in as many industries. The reports will include the results of investigations into the Welfare provisions made by the city for policemen, firemen, and letter carriers, and by private employers in such crafts as the bakers, metal polishers, teamsters, and moulders.

ELECTION REFORM.

The Second National Conference on Primary Laws, Ballot Reform and Corrupt Practices was held in New York City March 6 and 7 under the auspices of The National Civic Federation. Delegates representing all sections of the country from Massachusetts to Texas were present, and had the only result of the conference been to bring together such a representative gathering of experts for the purpose of free discussion of what is possible and desirable in election reform, the object of the conference would have been abundantly fulfilled.

But more than this was accomplished. Perhaps the most important result, apart from the information as to the efforts of each State to procure adequate legislation looking toward election reform, was the resolution requesting The National Civic Federation to form a permanent department for a thorough investigation of the topics considered by the conference. The need of such a department is evident. No careful observer will question the growing feeling throughout the length and breadth of the country that our election machinery is too largely controlled by "bosses" and "machine politicians" acting under the direction of great corporations and moneyed interests. To change these conditions, public offices must, *in fact*, be controlled by the people. Now the mere enactment of laws will not bring this result. It is not enough to go to the polls on election day; it is not even enough to go to the primaries. If any considerable change is to be made in the present control of our political machinery the voters must begin further back than the primaries. They must have a voice in the preliminary caucuses; they must join their local party organizations and take an active part in the selection of the ward captains and district leaders. They must take part in the work of these organizations and not make their one political act of the year consist in casting a vote—possibly for a "machine-made" candidate—on election day. This work must be done by the individual voter. It cannot be left to others, and it cannot be shirked. Writing essays or making academic speeches, without work, will not change the name of one delegate to a single convention. On the other hand, good, hard "hustling" and active interest, beginning in the ward and district organizations, will abolish the "money" or other undesirable control of our whole political machinery, and it is the only thing that will.

These ideas were clearly brought out by various speakers at the conference. In organizing the permanent department on Election Reform men will be chosen whose wide experience in practical politics will qualify them to bring these questions home most effectively.

A BROAD-MINDED UNION.

The organization of Eccentric Firemen, which is Local No. 56 of the International Brotherhood of Stationary Firemen, gave its third entertainment and reception of the year on Saturday, April 7, at the Grand Central Palace, New York. It is the admirable purpose of this organization to have every year at least four large social gatherings, including a picnic and outing during the summer, which are attended not only by the members but by their wives and families. These entertainments take the place to a large extent of the theatre or other forms of amusement which many of the members of the union cannot afford.

The meeting on April 7 marked the twentieth anniversary of the founding of the union, and it was made the occasion for a most fitting tribute from the members to their International President, Mr. Timothy Healy. Mr. Healy was recently elected a member of the Public Ownership Committee of Twenty-one, appointed by The National Civic Federation to investigate the operation of public utilities here and abroad. The members of this committee sail for London on May 22. As a practical form of congratulation upon his appointment and appreciation of his wise guidance and long-continued service on behalf of the union, the members presented Mr. Healy with a purse of $1,000 for his personal use while abroad. The address of presentation was made by Mr. John N. Parsons, ex-President of the National Association of Letter Carriers.

Replying to Mr. Parsons's address Mr. Healy said: "It is not the first time that you have shown your appreciation of the little that I have done in the interests of all of you and of our organization. I want to say that I fully appreciate your good will more than I can tell you—far more than the money. I shall continue to do the best that I can, not only for the Eccentric Firemen's Association of New York but for the firemen in Canada and in British Columbia who have honored me by electing me without opposition as their International President. There are some people in this city and in this country who will tell you that a labor organization is a dangerous institution. We can refute that statement by our appearance here to-night. I want to say that a labor organization that is governed by the desire to better the condition of its members and is trying to make the wives and children of the members better is not a dangerous organization. Such an organization as ours is one that will build up citizenship for the protection of our American institutions and make future generations better than they are to-day.

"I should like to say a word about that great organization, the National Civic Federation, which has honored me and the Eccentric Firemen's Association by selecting me as one of the commission to inquire into industrial conditions. That great organization is a friend of the oppressed and downtrodden, no matter what it may be called by people who do not believe in it. It is an organization for the purpose of bringing together people in different walks of life, and there is no better proof of what I say than the fact that Mr. August Belmont is in one of the boxes here to-night. If Mr. Belmont and the other gentlemen of the Civic Federation who are with him did not have the interests of your organization and the interests of labor at heart I do not think that they would have come here. If Mr. Belmont had wanted to see an entertainment he would have gone to his box at the Metropolitan Opera House or to one of the Broadway theaters.

"The National Civic Federation has a great mission to accomplish. If I did not believe that honestly I would not be a member of it. If it were not that I had to be at this entertainment to-night I should be out in Chicago taking part in the investigation by its Commission on Public Ownership, and I would have the same voice in the workings of that commission that anybody else would have. The commission is made up of men in various callings and walks of life who will study the conditions of labor and of public utilities."

"WELFARE WORK" DISCUSSED BY EMPLOYERS AND EMPLOYES.

(*Continued from page 7*)

and filthy all around—just a little hole under the ground. On account of the work that these men have to do, handling coal, perspiring as they do, they have to make a complete change of their clothing when they are going to work and when they are getting off. But usually no place is provided outside of the boiler room where the clothes may be changed or the street clothes kept in cleanliness during working hours. If a man has any distance to go it will take him an hour to get to his place of work, change his clothes and get ready to jump in to relieve his partner. When he is relieved, after working twelve hours, it takes another hour for him to get home. Sometimes the other fellow does not get in to relieve him when his twelve hours are up and he has to stay and work twenty-four hours. We have hundreds of poor, unfortunate men in this city working those long hours for $1.50 a day. Large corporations and the big hotels in this city have not raised the wages of their stationary firemen, except in a few instances, since the plants were built—twelve, fifteen or eighteen years ago. I am sure you will bear with me in the statement that the men who could get along on $2.25 or $2.50 a day eighteen years ago would find it hard to do so to-day, because the living expenses have gone up thirty-five to forty per cent. Very often the salary they are getting is not sufficient to keep nothing on their families. We do not make unreasonable demands, but are trying to establish the three-dollar scale. We hear a great deal about the advantages of a young man. I want to tell you gentlemen if you start to give the young American citizen an advantage you have got to give his father sufficient wages to clothe him and feed him and send him to school and give him a common school education."

The Chairman: The man who thinks that a fireman is not an artist, if he is a good fireman, makes a big mistake—as big a mistake as if he should say that the man who puts shades and lights on a picture is not an artist. The manner of a man's firing—whether he fires with the desire to get the best results out of a pound of coal, or whether he does it in a desultory way—makes a difference, a very considerable saving. But I want to say right here that The Civic Federation is just the place to come and present these cases. (Applause.) It is a fact that there is a great deal of injustice going on, and whether we can regulate it or not is a question of how much zeal we have in our work. We have with us to-night Mr. Thomas B. Lavey, of the Iron Molders' Conference Board, who will treat the subject of "Consideration for the Physical Comfort of Molders."

Mr. Lavey said in part:

"The main complaint of the molders has been and is to-day against the conditions under which they work. Owing to the peculiarities of the trade of molding, due to the excessive hard work in constructing the mold, which first necessitates ramming it into shape and then changing to the finishing with the most delicate tool, the molder goes from the one extreme of perspiring freely, in the first operation of active exercise, to shivering with cold during the finishing of the job. This is due to the conditions of many of the foundries where in the winter the doors are kept open from five to ten and often as long as fifteen minutes while refuse is being carted away, sand is being brought in and flasks removed. The open doors permit the cold drafts to penetrate every part of the shop. The molder who is compelled to work with as little clothing on as possible suffers from these drafts, which often result in colds and serious illness. We have demonstrated the serious effects of this, not only by our actual experience, but by the fact that our organization, which is the Iron Molders' Union, has paid out in the last ten years $1,777,000 to members who are on the sick list, and two-thirds of this is put out between the months of December and the last of March—an awful statement to make. Many of the shops are without glass in the windows and their owners seem to be satisfied to have boards placed in these openings which only partly prevent the drafts. A further objection to the boards is the obstruction of the light which the workmen should have for the proper performance of their tasks. A good deal of this I do not attribute entirely to the owner or the manufacturer. I blame it sometimes on the foremen, who neglect to notify the proper official and have repairs made.

"In one shop there is plenty of light and good ventilation. There are air pipes for the purpose of throwing hot air in the winter and for throwing cool air in the summer through the foundry. These pipes are so arranged that the air is distributed in a way to prevent drafts. The cool air coming in contact with the damp ground makes it the most comfortable foundry in New York in the summer. There are only a few foundries in this vicinity where there are steam pipes. There should be steam heat in the winter, because the men have to work with just as little clothing on as possible. Even where there are fires during the week, they are usually allowed to go out over Sunday,

TIMOTHY HEALY.

JOHN S. HUYLER.

and on Monday it is just as cold in the shop as it is out of doors. I know of one shop in Brooklyn which used to be an old barn, but which has recently been fixed up by putting in windows and closing the doors and having the place heated, so that now it is one of the nicest shops in that vicinity. So it is evident that these old places can be made comfortable. The reason I speak of this is because of the feeling that the men have after such improvements are installed. It doesn't make any difference how men feel otherwise, but when there is an attempt made to bring out a condition in the foundry which is going to benefit and make the men more comfortable, there is a feeling of gratitude in the heart of every man who works in that foundry. (Applause.)

"Now I have in mind one of the finest shops, where the windows are all in good condition, and there is heat in the foundry, but it might surprise you to learn that 110 men are employed and that there is no place for them to hang their clothes.

"Very few shops in this district have lockers—I mean within a radius of thirty-five or fifty miles of the city hall. In some cases an ordinary soap box is used for that purpose. On my way home from work I have frequently known a stir to be created among the passengers on the cars who thought someone was on fire, so thoroughly had the core smoke penetrated the clothes I wore.

"Every one who knows anything about foundries realizes that during the cast, when the melted metal is distributed, there is plenty of heat. The heat is so great that every particle of the men's clothing becomes moistened and often wet with perspiration. In that condition the men often leave the shop for home, after putting on their overcoats which have hung on the damp wall all day.

"They should have places in which to bathe and put on dry clothing. Those who are charged with the responsibility of the care of men, must make their condition such that the robust man to whom we point with pride as the ideal mechanic, the protector of our institutions at all times, must not be superseded by a generation whose standard will be largely traceable to our lack of interest in their welfare."

The Chairman: Now we will have a few words from Mr. Orrin S. Goan, of the National Biscuit Company on "How We Found Space for Welfare Work."

Mr. Goan: We began what we might call our welfare work by thoroughly renovating and rearranging all the dressing rooms. We tore out old lockers, put in shelves for hats, hooks for clothing, and benches with shelves under them for shoes. Then we painted everything thoroughly even to the walls; and, we have continued to paint them every year since, both for the appearance of cheerfulness as well as for cleanliness.

"We also made a plan by which any of our girls could take baths during work hours by arranging with the forewomen in charge of their departments. To show how well these bath-rooms have been appreciated, I may state that out of about eight hundred girls employed in the factory, there have frequently been over fifty baths taken in a day during the hot weather. We naturally followed this up by putting in shower baths for our men. These were placed in the dressing rooms so that a man upon leaving his work could strip off, take a bath and immediately get into his regular clothing. Let me emphasize the importance of having all these things convenient for the help. They should not be required to wash in one place and dress in another. Facilities which are not conveniently arranged may as well not be provided at all.

"About this time we decided to have a restaurant in order to supply our people with good food at low prices. We took some space from another department, put in a small gas stove, a steam soup kettle, urns for coffee and tea, hired a cook and made a start. Our people took kindly to the plan and in a very short time we were obliged to increase our facilities. Our prices we have endeavored to keep on a cost basis. In fact, they have been a little below cost as the restaurant loses a little—but not enough to be a serious consideration.

"These things we consider of prime importance to the health of our people; and, it is a matter of fact that while many of our people work in places where it is very warm in the summer, we have had very few heat prostrations for several seasons past, whereas previously there were sometimes as many as eight or ten in a single day. We attribute this improvement in the general condition of our help to their ability to get proper food at our restaurant and to improved ventilation.

"In due course we decided to make our dining room somewhat more attractive and table linen was introduced, also better dishes. With the table linen came the necessity for a laundry which was soon established. We then took up the question of supplying our men and women with working uniforms. In consideration of their supplying themselves with these uniforms we do all the repairing as well as the laundry work.

"We now come to our roof pavilions and club room. After eating, some men like to smoke, so it naturally followed after the establishment of our restaurant that we should provide a smoking pavilion on the roof. This pavilion, which is about thirty feet square, is provided with seats and covered with a canvas awning. It overlooks the river and is a most delightful place for a rest after the noon-day lunch. After having the benefit of the roof pavilion one summer the advent of cold weather created a demand for some place to smoke inside the building. The demand was met by the establishment of a club room for our men and boys. As we wanted to do as much for the girls as for the men, we provided for them a little roof garden also, near the tower which contains the sewing room. Of course, neither of these pavilions will accommodate anything like our full force, but we find that some employes will go one day and others another so that there is usually room for as many as may wish to go. Of the things which have contributed most to the comfort of our employes, next to the restaurant and laundry, I should place our emergency room. In this room we attend to our sick and injured. It is now in charge of a trained nurse, and we have also a capable man who is very useful in cases of serious accident. By an arrangement with the New York Hospital, any injured employes whom we may send there receive immediate attention. In such cases the expense is borne by the company. Adjoining our emergency room we have a reading room which also serves as a rest room for the women. Among other things it contains a circulating library, which is a branch of the New York City Public Library, arrangements for the same having been made through the kindly assistance of the Welfare Department.

"In addition to the list thus far enumerated, we have recently put into operation a systematic fire drill, which we feel certain will prevent any panic in case we should be so unfortunate as to have a fire. We have also arranged for the women employed on the upper floors of the building to have elevator service. We have, moreover, made a great effort to keep the entire place clean and pleasant by painting and whitewashing the walls and woodwork, hanging pictures and putting window boxes and hanging baskets of plants in the hallways.

"Now a word about the expense. Omitting the restaurant and laundry equipment, as those are 'going' departments, I should estimate that a thousand dollars would cover all that has been invested. This amount represents

THOMAS B. LAVEY.

about one cent a week for each employe for one year and leaves no room, therefore, in our case for the thought that welfare work is done in lieu of wages. This is a very important point and it is also a reason why this work should be done in a modest and unpretentious way. Intelligent employes are likely to assume that if a firm can afford to spend money lavishly in this way, it can afford to pay more wages—and naturally, what working people want above all other things is good wages and more wages. But, granted the wages are just and the hours reasonable, a firm may well expend a few extra dollars and a little time and thought on the comfort and happiness of its employes. Let there be no mercenary motive. Virtue and kindness are their own reward. A good name is always valuable in business as in private life and a reputation for good treatment of working people still tend to attract a desirable class of help."

After the address of Mr. Goan, the following letter was read from the Hon. William McAdoo, who was expected to speak, but was detained at home on account of illness:

"The station houses and the prisons connected therewith in a large number of the precincts of Greater New York are a positive disgrace to the city. Many of the buildings used as station houses and prisons are very old and have been allowed to run down and are in a very bad condition. As a rule the prisons are unsanitary, poorly ventilated, and without modern improvements. In some instances they are heated by stoves in the winter which give out a poisonous coal gas. They are at all seasons of the year damp, gloomy, forbidding, and incapable of being kept thoroughly clean. In winter when the windows are closed and the heat turned on, and the prison filled, some of the prisoners being drunk and incapable of taking care of themselves, the air is poisonous. Many of them are so situated that in summer it is impossible to get fresh air in any quantity into them. The cells in the present Police Headquarters have officially been adjudicated as the worst in the city. It is shocking to reflect that a great city like this has allowed such a place to exist so long. In the administration of justice innocent persons are often arrested, and in more than one instance citizens otherwise decent and reputable have been incarcerated for trivial offences which at the best will result in but a small fine. In the meantime they have suffered the fearful degradation of being locked up in one of these black and filthy holes.

The prisons to be erected should be well ventilated, have modern plumbing facilities, and, above all, should be so constructed as to be capable of being thoroughly washed and hosed and lighted with electricity. In many of the station houses the men sleep in over-crowded quarters, the beds being so close that in some instances they have to crawl over each other to reach them. In some of these buildings the dormitories are old and the walls have sunken, so that the windows are never thoroughly closed. They are freezingly cold in winter, and being unprotected from the sun during the day, are heated like ovens in the summer. In the older station houses there is no proper provision made for heating and ventilating them. The waiting rooms, in which the men spend many hours while on reserve, are as a general rule, dingy, dirty, uncomfortable, noisy, and in every way unattractive. In nearly all of the station houses will be found an insufficient number of chairs for the men to sit on. The common sight is an old rickety table and a few old worn-out chairs, dirty and soiled walls, blackened ceilings and a rough board floor, saturated and stained with years of use. The doormen, as a general rule, do their very best with these houses, but they do not have sufficient assistance, and even if there were a large number of cleaners it would not materially affect the general bad conditions. There are no proper bathing facilities for the men. In the Army and Navy the shower bath is universally used; tubs are dangerous and out of date. Well tiled bath rooms which would admit half a dozen or a dozen men at a time ought to be provided with hot and cold showers. The bedsteads are some of them fifty years old, and are very uncomfortable and of a primitive type. Except that they are higher up, the dormitories are sometimes not much better than the prisons.

The Police Surgeons as a body have condemned a great many of these houses in an elaborate report giving the details in full; the Health authorities have inveighed against them; the Fire Department has protested against the danger to life; humanitarians, philanthropists, State investigators, and leading newspapers have implored the city to do something. My experience with the city authorities in this respect is not encouraging. Last year they cut down the appropriation for keeping these wretched and tumble-down barracks in somewhat decent order. Many of them need painting and cleaning; some of them have panes out of the windows and it is difficult to get the money to replace them. In some cases the city has really no station house at all for the men, but houses them in stables as in the case of the Sheepfold in Central Park. The best part of that building is given to the horses, and the part where the horses could not be put with safety to their health is turned over to the men. A great sewer opening is within three feet of where the men have to eat their meals. Thas the police in New York look so healthy, and are in the main a well-conditioned body of men, is owing to the fact that they spend so much of their time in the open air and are compelled to take exercise. The mounted men, for instance, in Central Park, would probably all have been dead long ago from the sewer gas which pours into the horse barn where they have to spend their time when not in the saddle but for the fact that they get so much fresh air and healthy exercise when on active duty. They thrive just as sailors do at sea who stand the horrors of the fo'castle because they have to spend most of their lives on the deck where the air is the best. Were it not for this the sick list of the police would be appalling. The city authorities have either got to face the question squarely or let the whole thing get worse and worse. You can get votes by building a schoolhouse—a very proper thing to do—but there doesn't seem to be many votes in building a station house; hence some of these people seem to be entirely indifferent. I have appealed in writing and in person constantly since I went to the Police Department, but I never found any response.

It will probably cost two or three million dollars to tear down and reconstruct a number of the station houses and renovate and in some instances radically change the character of the others. A smaller sum would make a beginning. The expenditure of this money could go on, however, over a period of years, but the plan ought to be a systematic one. All of the station houses should be constructed on the same general plan. It is a criminal waste of the city's money to have a lot of architects drawing different sets of plans, some of them perfectly grotesque and foolish. The station house should have a distinctive, individual character so that you would know at once what it was intended for. This is the practice of governments in Europe with regard to public buildings of this kind. The station house should be as distinctive as the green lamp in front of it.

The Mayor should appoint a commission at once of which of course the Police Commissioner should be one, to consider this very important subject. A sanitary engineer, a police officer, a doctor, an architect of the highest character and professional standing, and a practical builder should also be on the commission.

I am very much pleased that the Civic Federation has taken this matter up. It is entirely in line with your work. The city is the employer and it should treat the employe decently, certainly in a half-civilized way at least. If the Federation will investigate this subject they will find that I have not only not exaggerated the conditions, but that I have rather understated them. If I had had the opportunity I would have been glad to have presented to your body fuller details from the official findings with reference to these filthy and broken-down places. Believe me,

Very sincerely yours,
WILLIAM McADOO.

THE CHAIRMAN: We have with us to-night a gentleman who will now tell you something about "How New York Cares for its Institutional Employes"—Mr. Homer Folks, President of the New York City Visiting Committee of the State Charities Aid Association.

MR. FOLKS: I am especially pleased that the Civic Federation has taken up for consideration the condition of the employes of the city. When we have thought and spoken of Welfare Work hitherto we have almost always had in mind the employes of factories and workshops carried on as private business affairs; but there are two very important reasons why we should primarily consider the employes of the city in our talk about Welfare Work. The first is that the city is by far the largest employer of labor in the city of New York. The employes of the city of New York already number, in round numbers, fifty thousand. No single employer in the city of New York employs any such number of people. Probably the largest group of employers—those operating the traction companies—employ perhaps some twenty-two thousand people. And the second reason why we, as citizens and as a Civic Federation, should interest ourselves in the city employes, is the fact that in so doing we are looking after our own business, for when the city employs, we employ. Each one of us is a constituent part of this city, a voting and contributing member of this corporation, and if the city does badly and fails in its duty by its employes, you and I, each one of us, must share in that responsibility.

(While delivering the rest of his address, Mr. Folks exhibited a number of stereopticon views.)

As an employer the City of New York, through its Department of Public Charities, ranges from fair to indescribably bad. Probably in no other branch or department of the city government are such wretchedly inadequate salaries paid as in the city's hospitals and other institutions. It is not so many years ago that prisoners were employed in large numbers in these institutions, and the Department is still in the transitional stage from prison labor to adequately remunerated labor.

In most of these institutions the city provides board and lodgings for its employes, and pays them very low salaries. The munificent salaries of $12, $15, and $18 a month are not at all uncommon. It is true that some of the employes receiving these salaries are ex-prisoners, and that a much larger number are ex-patients, and some are both ex-patients and ex-prisoners,

HON. WILLIAM McADOO

ORRIN S. GOAN

HOMER FOLKS

ANDREW HELLTHALER.

CHARLES P. NEILL.

EDWARD GOULD.

...n the city is not starting them on the road to independence by employing them at salaries which would hardly provide decent clothing.

The city provides board and lodgings such as they ... A few years ago the lodgings were, almost without exception, just about as bad as they could possibly ... Herded together in unventilated, dilapidated, unsanitary, cheerless buildings, with practically none of the creature comforts of life, it was little wonder that these employes soon entered once more the ranks of their prisoners or patients. Progress has been made in some directions. During the administration of Mayor Low a very comfortable dormitory was erected for the male employes of the City Hospital, in place of a wooden rookery which had formerly housed them. This dormitory provides a well-lighted and comfortable living room, a good-sized room for reading, smoking, games, etc., a considerable number of individual rooms, and two well lighted, well equipped dormitories. At the Kings County Hospital a large kitchen and dining room building was erected, providing well lighted, well equipped dining rooms for the various grades of employes, so situated that food can be served quickly, ...ly, and reasonably attractive.

There has been little progress, however, during the last two years beyond the consideration of plans. At the Metropolitan Hospital on Blackwell's Island the quarters for employes are so bad that I can hardly describe them before this audience. Imagine a large ... low ceilinged dormitory, immediately under the roof of a four-story hospital building, with ceilings so ... that there are no windows at the sides, the only light coming in through skylights; accessible by only one small winding stairway (the building non-fireproof); without a closet or other toilet arrangement of any sort; unbearably hot in summer, always dark and dismal—a fire trap—such is the dormitory for female employes at the Metropolitan Hospital on Blackwell's Island. There is a similar dormitory for men. In addition, a large number of the men sleep in a one-story wooden shed, condemned more than a decade ago as unfit for occupancy, in which the plumbing is archaic, the sanitary conditions hopelessly bad, and the sleeping rooms overcrowded. On Randall's Island you will find a large number of male employes sleeping in a prison building, occupying cells constructed years ago for prisoners, but used for the past decade as sleeping quarters for some of the employes of this great city.

I am glad to say that the present Commissioner of Charities is fully alive to the needs of the Department, and that there is every reason to believe that effective measures will be taken for the remedy of these conditions in the very near future.

The Chairman: We will now hear from Mr. Edward Gould, President of the Teamsters' Joint Council, New York City, who will say "A Word for the Teamster."

Mr. Gould: It has occurred to me that there must have been a mistake in getting the word "teamster" connected with some other craft or industry at this meeting, because I had always been under the impression that a teamster amounted to nothing—I was told so often. There is one hardship in particular that teamsters are subject to, and that hardship is insufficient time to get acquainted with their own families. They work such long hours not infrequently that they ... meet themselves going to work in the morning when they are coming home at night. (Laughter.)

In speaking to several of our more liberal employers that have large teaming interests, they have not infrequently told us or told our representatives that it is a modern impossibility to give better conditions to the teamsters; that the competition is so keen and the other fellow works them under such conditions, that no matter how well he might feel inclined, the business would not warrant it. Quite a number of you gentlemen will remember seeing policemen on our mail wagons some short time ago, and possibly the teamster might be harshly criticised that he should put the business people to the inconvenience of not receiving their mail as promptly as they did at other times; and I would like to place the teamster right, as this is the first time in the City of New York when any cognizance has been given to the teamster.

We made several visits to the representatives of the company that moves the mail in the City of New York and asked them for a conference, to see if we could not bring about some slightly better conditions for the teamsters, who were then working fourteen hours a day, some of them for the paltry sum of $1.25 remuneration for fourteen hours work a day and seven days in the week. The manager of the company was from Missouri (Laughter)—he had to be shown. We evoked the sympathy of the Civic Federation. Some of the officers brought about a conference, and I want to say that the teamster was willing to concede many things in the shape of minimizing some of the demands regarding increase in wages.

There are several large trucking interests in the City of New York where a teamster reports for work at five o'clock in the morning, and gets through in the evening at seven or half-past seven o'clock. When he leaves the home in the morning, his children are asleep in bed, and when he goes home at night his children are asleep. Is it any wonder that they refer to their father as "that man who hangs around the house here occasionally?"

We want to bring about a condition where employers can improve the conditions of the teamster, without putting themselves out of business or without bringing a hardship upon them, and I contend that can be brought about, if the employers want to do it.

We have a second reform that is very much needed in the City of New York. A remark made by our Chairman reminds me of it—consideration. The teamster doesn't make long speeches—he is abrupt, very abrupt sometimes, and he is not very complimentary in his language; and if I should forget myself at this time, I hope you will pardon me, because I am not long off the team. (Applause.)

And as you are well aware, we have truckmen in the City of New York that have found out from bitter experience that it takes an artisan to drive a truck and it takes a teamster to load and unload a truck, and why don't they get more consideration in our community? You are dependent upon the teamster to take the earth out of the cellar where your home is built. You are dependent on the teamster to move the stone and material to build your home, and when you have it built, you are dependent on the teamster to carry the necessaries of life and the comforts of life as well; because the private coachman is a teamster, and he brings a great deal of comfort to the homes of some of our more fortunate friends along Fifth avenue. If to-morrow morning the coal teamsters of the City of New York were to go on strike, and the produce teamsters were to go on a strike—those are only two small spokes that make up the wheel of the teamsters in this city—you cannot imagine what a serious inconvenience it would be. Many of our large office buildings cannot carry a forty-eight hour supply of coal; many of our large hotels cannot carry a forty-eight hour supply of coal, and none of our homes have more than twelve hours' provisions. Before you could get 5,000 men into the City of New York to man those trucks, under the most favorable circumstances, we have no conception of the hardship that a teamsters' strike would entail. Our newspapers speak from time to time of a general teamsters' strike the same as if it were going to a football game or going to a race-track. I hope we will never see the day in the City of New York when we will have a general teamsters' strike. (Applause.)

I believe that a great good could be accomplished, if there was some literature printed and distributed among our various teamsters' organizations. It could teach them to be courteous to each other; it could teach them that the fellow with the light load should give the right of way to the fellow with the heavy load. (Applause.) And I want to say that we have need for that consideration as much on Fifth avenue, where we have horses that only do two or three hours' work a day, as we have on West street, where horses work ten or fifteen hours a day and drag four or five or six tons of merchandise for the same length of time.

Third, and not least, we need better sanitary conditions in the City of New York for our teamsters. We want to abate the evil of the necessity of frequenting saloons from time to time (Applause), during our working hours. I feel that the teamster plays just as prominent a part in our city as any other workman does, and I believe that if he does he is deserving of the same consideration (Applause). It would not cost very much money to have some accommodations placed in various parts of the city in a sanitary way that would not compel our men to frequent saloons. (Applause.) I believe, as I heard a clergyman once say, that going to church is a habit. I think it is a good one. And we should get the teamster to cultivate the habit of staying out of the saloon—and I pride myself with the feeling that he doesn't frequent it any more than any other man. But if we do not get encouragement from the men that feel they are so much in the teamster, what can you expect of them?

In conclusion, I heard mention made of libraries. I would like to know what opportunity a teamster has who works thirteen and fourteen hours a day to go to a library.

We have formed a beneficial feature in most of our local unions in this City of New York, and I want to say that our dues compare favorably with any other fraternal organization. In the last two years our organization has paid out over $[illegible] in sick and death benefits (Applause), notwithstanding the fact that it has only been in operation two years, one of the local unions alone having paid out over $15,000; and I want to say, in conclusion, that no teamster, a member of our organization, has ever entered the Potter's Field. (Applause.)

The Chairman: I am greatly interested in the teamsters as I have a great deal to do with them. I have teamsters that have been with me twenty years, and I wouldn't part with them for any men that I ever saw. They are good teamsters and they take a pride in their work. It is just as honorable to be a good teamster as it is to be a good banker or a good merchant. A man should be good at his calling, whatever that calling may be.

We have with us this evening, Hon. Charles P. Neill, United States Commissioner of Labor, who will tell you "Why the Public is Interested in Sanitary Workrooms."

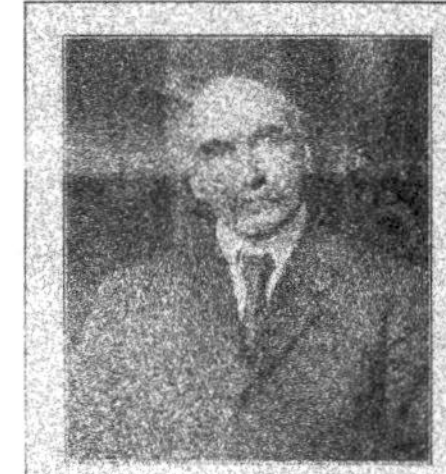

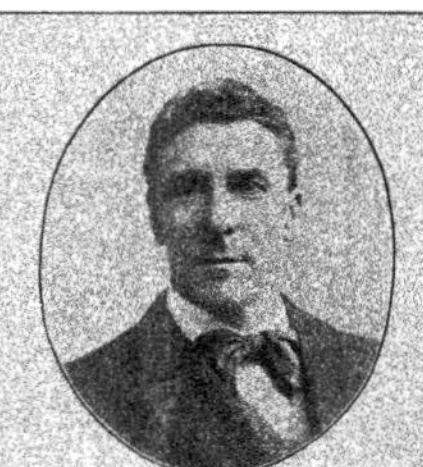

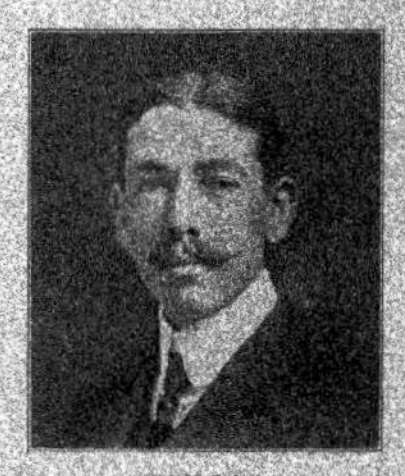

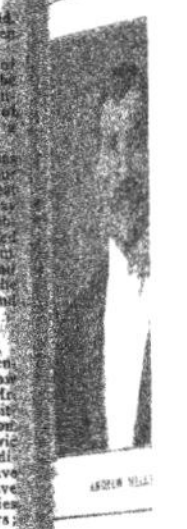

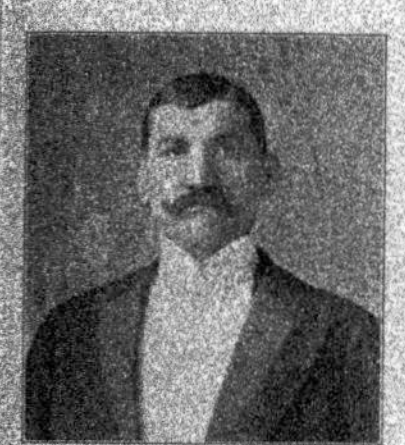

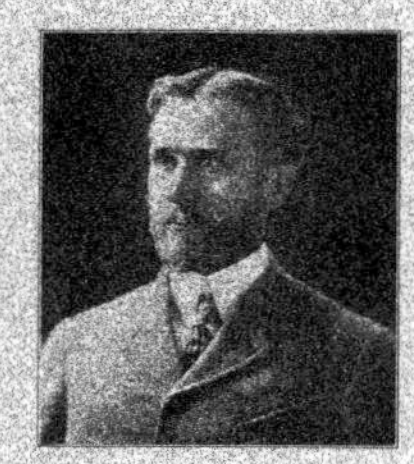

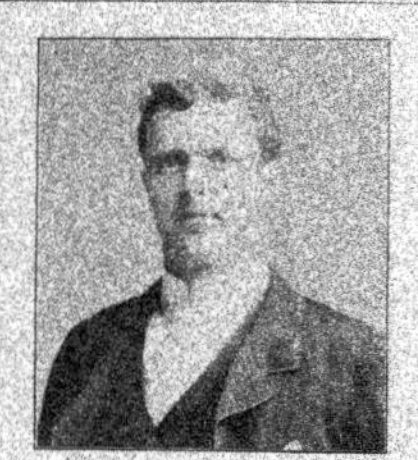

MR. NEILL: To sum up in a very few words the reason why the public is interested in sanitary workrooms, and in every other form of welfare work that makes for the health and comfort of the workers, I might say that it is because the public has a very vital interest in the question of the cost of production. We are all familiar, very familiar, with this term. The employer and the manufacturer know what it means, and they naturally and properly keep a close watch on it—for on this depends much of the success of their enterprises. But this aspect of cost is measured in dollars, and it does not represent by any means the entire cost of production. There is a further element in this cost, and that is the social cost, or in other words, what the production of any given thing represents to society. This social cost, gentlemen, cannot be expressed in terms of dollars; it is expressed in terms of sweat, it is expressed in terms of fatigue, it is expressed in terms of pain, and lastly, as we have heard to-night, in too many cases it is expressed in terms of ruined health and even in loss of human life.

I recall now a single industry, which I need not name, in which the death rate alone—leaving out even accidents that maim or disable workers permanently—is so high that taking thirty years as the term of the working life in that industry, a man has less than one chance in six of escaping a violent death.

This represents one aspect of the social cost of production. In the same way, accident, disease, the dwarfed bodies or the stunted minds of overworked children, and all the evils and misery summed up in the term "sweatshop"—these represent other aspects of the social cost of production. These represent the cost that society pays for the product it consumes.

Now it seems to me that society ought to be as careful and as anxious to reduce its cost of production, this human cost of production, as the manufacturer is to reduce his cost; and it is not difficult to determine what in the long run will be the attitude of any body of workers toward a society which remains indifferent and apathetic while this health cost and life cost run up to exorbitant limits.

We have heard it stated here to-night that there are men working twelve hours and sometimes even fourteen hours a day down under the sidewalks of this city in a temperature of 120 or 140 degrees, for $1.25 or $1.50 a day. If you let them feel that their health and their strength, their opportunity for enjoyment and for home life are a matter of no concern to society at large, can you blame them if they feel no sense of loyalty to a society which permits such things, and in their resentment against it ally themselves at last with radical movements which look to a social overturning?

It seems to me then that society should be very much interested in how the employer takes care of his workers, and in seeing that no class of workers shall be allowed to feel that the people for whom they toil are indifferent to the conditions under which they do their work. (Applause.)

In the last analysis, the public is the real employer. The men who are hired by the person or firm whom we ordinarily denominate the employer, are after all working for that public which consumes their product or enjoys the result of their services. They are the ones for whom the worker is really working, and in this sense they may be said to be the employers.

As I heard that statement about the conditions of work of the firemen in some of the hotels of this city, I must confess I felt personally uncomfortable, and I said to myself that I trust that this room which has been so pleasant and comfortable for all of us to-night is not being kept warm by a man who is putting in his fourteenth hour of work and earning perhaps only $1.25. For after all, that man down in the boiler room is working for you and for me, and we should be interested in the conditions under which he does his work. He himself, may think he is working for this hotel, but at bottom he is not—he is working for us; for this evening, at least, we are as a matter of fact his employers. We, at least in part, are paying his wages just as we are paying the wages for this evening's work of the cook who prepared this excellent dinner and of the men who have served it so well at the table. Of course the hotel proprietor will actually hand the money over to these various workers—but after all isn't he really in the position of the man who collects their wage from us and pays it over to them—perhaps, he doesn't pay them all he collects. (Laughter and Applause.) The public, therefore, has a very direct interest in every form of welfare and betterment work. And I might suggest in conclusion that those of us who believe in the existing social order and wish to maintain it, should realize that by remaining indifferent to the human element in the cost of production, by ignoring this question of the social cost of the things we use and enjoy, we are simply furnishing object lessons and arguments ready to hand for every apostle of Socialism or any other *ism* that aims to supplant the present social order.

THE CHAIRMAN: The Civic Federation, I think, with great forethought and consideration brought into the organization the "public" that it might participate in regulating in a measure the very conditions that are brought to your attention. There are the employer and the employe and there is the public that pays the bill, and it is certainly the great interested party, and I feel that we are wisely organized—more wisely, perhaps, than we thought when we first came together as a body of men. Now, we have with us a gentleman who will respond to another toast, "What Should Be Done to Provide Ventilation," Mr. Andrew Hellthaler, of the Metal Polishers and Architectural Bronze Workers.

MR. HELLTHALER: I speak for an industry in which the death rate—the enormous death rate directly due to consumption and lung trouble is 98 per cent., 80 per cent. of which occurs before the men reach the age of 40 years. That is the condition of the metal polishers to-day. While it is not generally so considered, these facts are ready for proof at any time a committee will visit our international headquarters and see the death claims as they have been paid in years past. My only idea in this matter is that the average manufacturer, considering that the work is so dirty—and I am frank to admit, being a polisher myself, that I believe it is one of the filthiest occupations a man can work at—the manufacturer seeing the men in that filthy condition, naturally picks out the filthiest corner in the factory and throws the polisher in there and keeps him there. I speak from experience which dates directly to the first of this year, and I myself say that I was employed in a factory where there were 65 men

DR. THOMAS DARLINGTON.

on one floor with only six windows for ventilation. Remember, gentlemen, that these six windows for ventilation are not the same as six windows would be here, where there is no dust-producing machinery, where there are no acid fumes floating through the air. These six windows would probably be all right, were there no fumes or dust, but in a polishing room it is one incessant stream of dust from 7.30 to 5 o'clock at night. There are laws on our statute books which provide for exhaust fans to take away the dust from all polishing lathes. In a great many cases these fans are kept in operation, but in a great many others they are not. In many cases they are there so that when the factory inspector comes around the manufacturer can show him that he is complying with the law. The manufacturers' reason why these machines are not running is that they are very fast speeding machines; but everyone who knows anything concerning machinery knows that high speed machinery takes considerable power, so that in order to lessen the expense, the exhaust fans are shut down. If they are not shut down, they are allowed to get in such a dilapidated state that they are not of any use to the men working there. In most factories where metal polishing is done, acids form a principal part of the work. The polisher polishes the plain part, and the part that is chased is dipped in acid to clean it. The fumes of the acid circulate through the factory, and sometimes they are stifling. Now, we want to get as much natural ventilation as we possibly can in all the factories, but we want still more than the natural ventilation. Improved machinery makes it possible to draw all the obnoxious fumes out of the factory. We should have exhaust fans taking the fumes out of the top of the windows and allowing the natural air to come in. I have seen in the factory that I have just left, which was as large as this room, the fumes of the acid and dust so thick that I could not distinguish the people at the further end. When you see the handsome toilet sets and tea sets in the shop windows, you little realize the number of lives that the production of these things has cost; yet the conditions to-day, so far as ventilation and the obnoxious fumes of acid are concerned, are worse in the silver factory than in the cheap brass factory, although the conditions in the latter are miserable. I am deeply interested in the question of tuberculosis, and I only hope that the Welfare committee will take the matter up. I am at their disposal to give them any information they may want and I will go so far as to take them into any factory to verify my statements.

In conclusion, I wish to say that consumption is so prevalent in our industry that the Brooklyn Central Labor Union has bought a plot of ground at Patchogue, Long Island, for which it has paid $1,600, and which is to be devoted to nothing but the curing of the disease. This amount was donated by workingmen and the ministers of Brooklyn have guaranteed to put upon this plot of ground a building to cost $50,000. Some of the ministers have suggested that if the industry really costs such an enormous price of human life, it should be cut out altogether. Of course, we do not take that view. What I wish to suggest is this: if the ministers and the workingmen are interested in this matter I see no reason why the Welfare committee of the Civic Federation should not be likewise. I thank you. (Applause.)

Following the address by Mr. Hellthaler, the Chairman introduced Mr. August Belmont, President of The National Civic Federation.

Mr. Belmont said in part:

"My interest in the subject which you have before you to-night is such as to cause me to disregard my doctor's injunction not to come out. Before leaving, I want to say to you that this subject has occupied the minds of the management of the Interborough Company for some time. It is fair to say that, as an operating corporation, the Interborough will be but two years old next April, having begun the operation of the elevated roads on the 1st of April a year ago, and opened the Subway for operation on the 27th of October the past year—a year ago last October.

"A complete method of insurance was worked out on lines similar to those mentioned by Mr. Vreeland in connection with the Pennsylvania Railroad. The plan was submitted to our men; but for reasons of their own, it was rejected. Taking that as a basis, and attracted by the success of Mr. Vreeland's management of the welfare department of his corporation, our officers have given that subject a great deal of attention, and have conferred—and did confer before there was any idea of our interests becoming identical—with a view to establishing much the same system and improving it by co-operation. We are only waiting for the return of our vice-president, Mr. Bryan, who was obliged to absent himself for a month on account of his health, and then we purpose to put into operation as soon as possible our own Welfare Department.

"In addition to this, it may have escaped your attention that the new corporation proposes to interest itself to a very large extent, and with the subscription of a substantial sum, in a suburban homes movement, the idea being that it may promote, through that agency, the comfortable housing of such of its men as may wish to avail themselves of it. That is in line also with our ideas of Welfare work.

"Thanking you very much for your attention, gentlemen, I bid you good-night." (Applause.)

Following Mr. Belmont's speech, a number of stereopticon views were shown illustrating the needs and accomplishments of Welfare work. As amplifying a point touched upon by one of the speakers the following statement by Mr. Jess P. Larimer of the Bridge and Structural Iron Workers' Association will prove of interest:

"There has never been any effort looking to the interest of the first trades that are employed in the erection of buildings and in such structural iron work as bridges and viaducts, where no other mechanics are employed. The other trades are in a measure looked after, inasmuch as a building generally has taken some definite shape before they are long at work, and a room can be set aside within the structure for storing their street clothes in the day and their gloves and overalls at night. Wage-earners in the iron industry would be grateful to your worthy organization if you would get some of the largest contractors to supply us with portable rooms in which to store our street hats and coats in the day time and our gloves and overalls at night. This is our first need, as our clothing is constantly stolen. Second, a wash room with sanitary toilet accommodations; and third, an emergency hospital room."

Referring to the working conditions of the city's employes an important offer was made by Dr. Thomas Darlington of the Health Department. He expressed his willingness and desire to co-operate in every way with committees of the Federation in providing better working conditions for the employes of the city. He urged continued agitation of this great work and said that his department would be only too glad to be informed of unsatisfactory conditions anywhere in the city; that, if such information were given, he would use, as head of the department, every effort to improve the working conditions of the city's employes.

As a result of the discussion of the evening the following resolution was adopted:

Resolved, That the Civic Federation of New York appoint a committee on Welfare Work, to be composed of employers, labor representatives, and representatives of the general public, to co-operate with the Welfare Department of The National Civic Federation, and that this committee on Welfare Work be requested to appoint sub-committees to give consideration to improving conditions of employes of the city and in the different trades in this vicinity.

THE PROGRESS OF WELFARE WORK.

EMPLOYERS' INTEREST IN IMPROVING WORKING CONDITIONS THROUGHOUT THE COUNTRY

IT is most gratifying to note the constantly increasing personal interest of large employers throughout the country in making practical improvements in the conditions under which their employes work. As an evidence of the widespread interest in this work, and particularly in the progress which is being made by the Welfare Department of The National Civic Federation, it may be noted that within the past few weeks four important meetings have been held, one at Boston, one at Lynn, Mass., and two at Washington, D. C., at which addresses were made referring particularly to the results accomplished and to the methods of the Welfare Department.

At the meeting in Boston, which occurred on February 7, the work of the department was explained to the members of the National Association of Wool Manufacturers at their annual banquet at the Hotel Somerset. More than 200 members listened with much interest to an illustrated lecture by Miss Gertrude Beeks, the Secretary of the department, and at Lynn, Mass., on February 9, the subject was presented at the Oxford Club, the audience including well-known business men and manufacturers.

In Washington two meetings were held at the invitation of Representative and Mrs. Joseph Weeks Babcock, of Wisconsin. Representative Babcock presided at both meetings; and during the two evenings interesting addresses were made by Senator W. A. Clark, of Montana, a member of the Executive Committee of the Welfare Department, on the general work of The National Civic Federation as an introduction to the particular subject of Welfare Work; by Gen. George H. Harries, of the Washington Railway and Electric Company, a member of the Welfare Department, on what his company is doing for the benefit of its employes; by H. H. Vreeland, Chairman of the Welfare Department, on his own experience in Welfare Work, particularly in connection with the New York City Railway Company, and by Miss Gertrude Beeks, who illustrated her paper with a most interesting collection of stereopticon views.

Mr. Vreeland said in part:

"As Chairman of the Welfare Department of The National Civic Federation, I desire to express by appreciation of the opportunity of presenting its work to such a representative gathering.

"First, permit me to give you a brief historical review of the formation of the department. Its organization was authorized for the reason that it was believed that the efforts of The National Civic Federation to better the relations between employers and employes would be materially aided by the promotion of what is called Welfare Work.

"Our first step was to call a meeting at the Hotel Waldorf in New York of representative employers of labor in the eastern and middle sections of the United

MRS. JOSEPH WEEKS BABCOCK.

States. To our great surprise there was an immediate response from many large employers. It developed that it was the first time that employers who were giving especial consideration to the welfare of their employes had been brought together. Each one had an idea that his Welfare Work was an individual effort in his particular locality, and was surprised to find that a great deal of this work was being done throughout the United States."

Mr. Vreeland went on to say that it had been found of special value to employers to bring about conferences for the interchange of experiences; to discuss the question at public meetings; to arrange conferences of the Welfare Workers themselves, and to have assistance given when asked by employers. While it may seem odd that the men successful in business should require assistance in introducing Welfare Work, it should be recalled that this is a day of specialization, and that those who have had practical experience in installing Welfare Work are best qualified to give advice. Further-

H. H. VREELAND.

more, many employers would introduce Welfare Work into their establishments were it not for the time and trouble needed for its organization.

"An employer who is noted among his employes for fair dealing," continued Mr. Vreeland, "need have no fear of introducing Welfare Work after a careful study of conditions has been made. That is, after recognizing that the first needs of employes are steady work, an equitable wage, and hours as short as competitive conditions will permit, the employer may successfully install Welfare Work if proper attention is given to its introduction. All our investigations of failures in this line have shown us conclusively that a just and fair policy of dealing with labor must be the foundation for all Welfare Work. With that foundation, it may be emphatically stated that employes will welcome all such efforts to provide for their welfare."

"Thirty years ago, as a brakeman on a steam railway, I was away from home, forced to live in such boarding houses as the railroad terminals and my wages would afford. There was absolutely no place for me in the evenings where it was warm except the saloon and the pool room. My knowledge of the homelessness of the average railroad employe led me to the establishment of club rooms for the men employed on the street railways in New York City. A large percentage of the 15,000 men employed by the company of which I am President live in boarding houses; many are from the country. The club rooms I established include an auditorium where monthly entertainments are given, a library, a pool room and a physician's office. They were used immediately and extensively, and a chance visitor will find the rooms filled every night in the week. Keeping in mind my own early struggles to gain information and to get the requisite books to read, I determined that, if fortune favored me and I attained a position where I had sufficient control of money and the friendship of those who were interested in the property, I would provide facilities of the character of which I felt the need. The books in the library were not only widely read by the men, but, in many instances, were taken home to be read in the men's families. Another feature of the work is the relief association which provides assistance for the men in case of illness or accident, a pension in old age, and, at the time of death, a fund for burial.

"The success of our work is due to the fact that nothing but illness has ever kept me from the platform of that organization on Saturday night monthly nine months in the year since the society was organized with thirty men in 1893. While a paid Welfare Secretary is necessary to supervise the activities, the participation of the employer is essential to success."

In presenting the general situation in Welfare Work Miss Beeks exhibited views showing what many employers have done in providing for the physical comfort of workers, for recreation, in supplying educational opportunities and in the housing of labor.

"Where ventilation has been given especial consideration, the air is changed completely in the work rooms every fifteen minutes. In the foundry, where the pipes which are used in the winter for heating serve to bring in the cool air in the summer, great comfort is afforded the molders.

"In a rolling mill, galvanized iron pipes carry the fresh air to the faces of the men occupied at the rolls. Previously, in very hot weather, the men were frequently overcome, and sometimes it was necessary to shut down the entire mill, the workmen thereby losing their wages and the company the product of their work. Since the installation of the ventilation system not a single hour's time has been lost because of excessive heat."

"The value of the emergency hospital has been evidenced by the testimony of an employer, who said, 'Our hospital has been a preventive instead of an emergency room as we had anticipated. Instead of patronizing it now and then, the men use it continually. Previously when a man injured his hand he was satisfied to put a piece of waste on it. Blood poisoning followed and he would be laid up for a few days. Now every injury receives immediate attention, and the men are not obliged to lay off for slight accidents.

"Women who have been overcome are frequently able to return to work after resting for an hour or receiving treatment in the emergency hospital."

Reference was made to the effort of an employer to raise the moral tone of a town by providing a social hall. The company furnished pool rooms and bowling alleys in such an attractive manner, and conducted them on such a high plane, that private enterprises in the town were obliged to follow their standard.

Speaking of the homes rented and sold to employes and of the willingness to take advantage of the opportunities offered for better living conditions, the speaker said: "Rents for unskilled laborers in several mill towns, from $7.50 to $10 a month, including bath and furnace, are within the reach of wages of the tenants, and yet give a return upon the investment. Very fine tenements have been provided for skilled laborers at from $16 to $22.

"Cash prizes are offered for the best kept premises and for the best gardens. This has had a salutary effect upon the tenants. When one man received recognition in the form of a prize, his neighbor, who had not previously thought of improving his place, was stimulated to do so, not only because of the desire for a prize, but because he took pride in having his premises look as well as the neighbors'.

Miss Beeks did not confine herself to the workingman's conditions while he is in his prime of useful-

HON. JOSEPH WEEKS BABCOCK.

ness. She exhibited the portrait of a man eighty years of age at work in a shop, and asked the question: "Is it better to pension or give him light work?"

"Many employers have inaugurated systems for supplying funds for employes in illness and old age. The advantage of relief systems for employes was stated to be the assurance of prompt relief in case of illness or accident. The old plan of 'passing around the hat' was apt to work hardship on the employes contributing and did not always reach those in distress.

(Continued on page 16)

THE FACTS OF PUBLIC OWNERSHIP.

ANALYSIS OF THE PLAN AND SCOPE OF THE WORK UNDERTAKEN BY THE COMMISSION ON INVESTIGATION.

BY EDWARD A. MOFFETT, SECRETARY PUBLIC OWNERSHIP COMMISSION.

AS has been pointed out in previous issues of the REVIEW the great work to be accomplished by the Commission on Public Ownership and Operation which was called together under the auspices of The National Civic Federation, is to undertake a thorough and absolutely impartial investigation of all the facts connected with these important questions here and abroad and to present the facts to the public as a practical and efficient aid to the solution of the perplexing problem of public ownership.

Schedules relating to the four subjects to be investigated—Gas, Water, Electric Lighting and Power, and Street Railways—have already been formulated by a sub-committee consisting of:

Frank J. Goodnow (chairman), Columbia University;

Walton Clark, third vice-president United Gas Improvement Company, Philadelphia;

Edward W. Bemis, superintendent water-works, Cleveland;

J. W. Sullivan, editor official journal United Garment Workers, New York;

Milo R. Maltbie, former editor *Municipal Affairs*, New York.

Of this committee two were considered to be in favor of public ownership, two opposed and one neutral. As the duties of this sub-committee involved not only the preparation of the all-important schedules upon which the investigation is to be based, but also the general plan of procedure, the advisability of such representation is apparent.

The best possible idea of the scope, impartiality and thoroughness of the investigation would be given by the presentation in full of all the schedules made up by the committee.

To reproduce in full, however, even one schedule dealing with but one of the four subjects would require more than a single issue of the REVIEW. As the general divisions are the same in each schedule an analysis of the schedule relating to Street Railways will indicate the broad scientific lines upon which the investigation is to be conducted. Such an analysis shows that the investigation of each subject—Gas, Electric Lighting and Power, Water and Street Railways—falls under several general heads, as follows:

(*a*) Historical and General;
(*b*) Supervision of Municipalities;
(*c*) Public Supervision of Private Companies;
(*d*) Franchises of Private Companies;
(*e*) Organization;
(*f*) Political Conditions;
(*g*) Labor;
(*h*) Character of Service and Plant;
(*i*) Financial Matters;
(*j*) Capital Stock and Bonds;
(*k*) Assets;
(*l*) Liabilities;
(*m*) Receipts;
(*n*) Expenses;
(*o*) Profit and Loss.

HISTORICAL AND GENERAL.

Under this head questions are asked intended to trace the history of the particular plant, the dates of adopting special features, and other matters that may assist in reviewing its development. The general sentiment in relation to the present system of ownership and operation, and the attitude of the press, are inquired into. The current objections, if any, to the present system; the degree of interest taken by the citizens in the management; whether or not there have ever been competing companies, and whether there is competition now—all these questions are made subjects of inquiry.

Whether or not private companies have consolidated, with dates and methods required, is a phase that is taken care of by a considerable group of questions.

SUPERVISION OF MUNICIPALITIES.

This separation of the subject deals with the power of municipalities to construct their own street railways without purchasing existing private systems; also whether or not they may condemn private systems under the right of eminent domain. An entire group of questions is devoted to this aspect. The power of the particular city in the matter of raising funds for any such undertaking is then inquired into. In this connection are asked the following questions:

What is the limitation upon the city's taxing power for municipal street railways?

What is the limitation upon the general taxing power of the city?

What is the limitation upon the city's power to incur debt for municipal street railways?

What is the limitation upon the general power of the city to incur debt?

State fully step by step the procedure which MUST be followed and the requirements which MUST be met before the city may construct or acquire a plant; also source of each provision, whether State constitution, statute or ordinance. Note particularly requirements as to initiation of proposal, special action by city authorities before its adoption, mayoralty veto, referendum, publicity, making of appropriations, bond issues, and approval of scheme by courts or State authorities.

Then follow questions on statutory provisions relating to fares and transfers, character and quality of service (method of traction, type of cars, speed, headway, etc.), extensions and general improvements, performance of public work by contract or otherwise, salaries and wages, hours of labor, pensions to employees, strikes and citizenship of employees.

PUBLIC SUPERVISION OF PRIVATE COMPANIES.

This line of the inquiry opens with questions designed to bring out the features of the incorporation of the particular company, with special reference to powers and limitations. As in the case of municipal systems, statutory provisions are examined in detail. A description of defects in remedies and penalties in this relation is also required.

The next questions concretely show the searching nature of the investigation in a most important phase:

What powers of supervision over the construction and operation of the plants of private companies does the city possess?

What provision has the city made for the exercise of its powers of supervision?

How frequently and with what efficiency does the city exercise its powers of supervision?

What provisions have been found impossible of enforcement, and why?

Information concerning taxes paid to State and to local authorities is the object of a considerable number of questions; these conclude with:

Is the company subject to assessment for local improvements?

Are such assessments actually levied?

FRANCHISES OF PRIVATE COMPANIES.

The power of the municipality to grant franchises is here inquired into in detail. Then follow questions to define the legal provisions delimiting the powers of the city as to the insertion of clauses in franchise (a) regarding streets company may utilize; (b) nature of plant and equipment; (c) construction of extensions; (d) adoption of improvements and new processes; (e) duration of grants; (f) forfeiture of franchises; (g) time, method and acquisition of system by city; (h) disposition of plant thus acquired; (i) fares to be charged and transfers to be given; (j) character and quality of service; (k) right of city to regulate operation; (l) taxation; (m) compensation for franchises; (n) paving of streets, etc.; (o) issuance of stocks and bonds; (p) returns to public authorities; (q) transfer of franchise to third parties; (r) labor clauses, and regarding minor features.

Information is then sought to show what penalties and means of enforcing such provisions have been provided, and whether or not they are effective.

The date of issue of each existing franchise, by what authority granted, whether exclusive or competitive, the period for which it has been granted, and approximate mileage of streets conceded—this information is likewise required. Each franchise is further examined in detail, and a full and clear statement of conditions upon which forfeiture may be declared and its possible acquisition by the city, is particularly required. Has the municipality experienced difficulty in forcing companies to live up to the terms of their franchise? is the next inquiry; and this embraces inquiries into the reasons for the difficulty, in case it exists.

The questions that follow trace existing private companies to their very inception, and relate to a most important phase of the investigation. They are:

How much deliberation has usually been given in the granting or renewal of franchises?

Has the exercise of the franchise granting power been attended with public scandal, and if so, in what respects?

How much publicity has usually accompanied the granting or renewal of franchises?

By whom are franchise grants usually drafted?

ORGANIZATION.

The principal questions under this division are intended to bring out how and upon whom the responsibility is placed for the proper maintenance of particular municipal systems; whether or not the authority is divided; how the persons in positions of control are selected and to what extent, if any, political considerations enter into their appointment, and whether or not members of the governing body have technical knowledge. These questions are also designed to determine whether the head of the engineering service is an engineer by profession, and if so, what scope he is allowed in the exercise of his duties, to what extent these duties are executive; and whether or not political considerations affect his appointment or his tenure of office.

It is particularly asked whether or not the office he fills changes with each change in the city administration.

The remaining questions under this head are framed to ascertain to what extent politics may affect the number of employes at any given period; the average length of service; the system of promotion, and whether politics influence the selection or dismissal of wage-earners.

POLITICAL CONDITIONS.

In the questions set down under this head the main object is to ascertain in what measure employes have sought to organize, openly or secretly, their political strength for the purpose of influencing the conditions of their employment, or of exercising similar influence upon city elections; also whether candidates for office have made promises of better wages, etc.

To what extent employes are active in party work is also inquired into; and whether or not they are expected or required to pay political assessments. The question is also asked as to what evidence there is "of the influence of private companies upon the nomination and election of members of the franchise-granting and franchise-controlling authorities."

This division concludes with a series of inquiries designed to show to what extent, in the case of municipally owned systems, free transportation is given, under what regulations, and the possible abuses of this privilege.

LABOR.

Under this important head the opening inquiries seek to ascertain what, if any, significant relations exist between increases of the working force and elections; the wages, maximum and minimum, paid each class of labor; the legal and actual number of hours per diem; pay for overtime, and provisions for sick leave and vacations and holidays with pay. Then follow inquiries in relation to prizes offered for faithful service, profit sharing, and to a possible system of pensions for aged or infirm employes. It is also asked whether or not the employes have local benefit associations and if the funds of these are contributed to by the municipality or company. The question of who makes the payment for badges and uniforms, is inquired into; also the matter of surety bonds and premiums on same; likewise what efforts have been made to provide clubhouses, libraries, toilet facilities, etc.; the frequency and regularity of pay days, the place and manner of payment, and by whom and how wages are fixed.

The succeeding questions relate to the contentedness of the employes, and the answers are to indicate in what manner and to what extent the employes have a part in determining the conditions of employment. These questions are:

Were union rates observed?

If there were trade agreements, state them.

Was there any form of collective bargaining?

Has there ever been any concerted action among employes to have wages raised or hours shortened? Describe.

Were the employes organized in unions?

Was the "closed shop" or "open shop" policy in force?

Was the municipality or company opposed to organized labor?

Has there ever been a strike on the system? If so, describe fully.

How were labor disputes settled?

Were the laws relating to health, employer's liability, and contract labor observed?

Were there any printed or written instructions to employes? If so, enclose copies.

The concluding questions of this division of the subject require a statement of the number of persons, employes and others, killed during the past year; also the statistics with regard to persons injured, and the record of law suits on this account.

CHARACTER OF SERVICE AND PLANT.

The questions that comprise this part of the schedule refer first to those parts of the particular system, municipal or private, that generate and transmit power. The initial inquiries are necessarily of a most technical nature. They seek to determine the general capacity and comparative economy of what is called the power plant.

Then follow questions designed to ascertain the number of lines of the different companies, under and above ground, their types, special features and dates of installation; the number of cars in active service and their character, whether open or vestibuled; the types of fenders and motors; their lighting and heating. Information as to mileage and track data generally is sought, as also information in relation to paving obligations.

Then follow questions intended to obtain a fair appraisal of the particular plant.

Under the sub-division "Traffic," which is the next phase considered, are taken up questions relating to the total number of fare and transfer passengers; the hours at which cars carrying passengers, etc., are run.

Next come inquiries showing the comparison, if there be such, between the legal maximum speed and the actual; headway schedules; the number of transfer points; and whether waiting rooms are provided at such places.

Then follow:

Were passengers kept waiting at points of stopping because cars were run too infrequently?

Were passengers often obliged to stand in cars?

Were the cars crowded?

Were extra cars run during rush hours?

Were the facilities ample to meet the demands of the public at all times?

What types of cars were used?

Were the cars kept clean and well painted?

Were the cars well lighted and ventilated?

Were the cars well heated in cold weather?

Were the guide boards on the cars easily read and plain?

If advertising space was let, state to what extent both inside and outside of cars.

Was service supplied twenty-four hours in the day?

If for part only, how many hours each day?

Are there any engineering tests or experiments being carried on?

Were there frequent complaints about interruption of service?

Has the street railway service ever been completely or partially cut off? Describe instances.

In addition to seeking information as to extension of lines, how extensions are brought about, and particularly the policy of the company (or municipality) in this regard, the questions following go into the matter of street work. On this subject some of the questions asked are:

Were open trenches and obstructions properly guarded?

Is there an up-to-date map showing the location and nature of all street mains and fixtures?

The purchase of supplies by municipally owned lines is next inquired into. The opening questions here relate to the responsibility for the placing of orders, and for the checking of materials purchased. Among the principal questions are the following:

Were contracts advertised?

How did prices compare with those paid by private companies?

Were the dealers supplying materials connected with the city, county or State government?

In practice, did the manager get the types and makes of things he asked for, or was he forced to take something else?

As a general summing up of the questions thus far propounded there appears under the sub-head, "General Matters," a number of inquiries of such manifest importance that they are given without change of any kind. They are:

Is the system adequately equipped to handle the business?

Is the equipment of modern and efficient type?

Is it in good condition?

Will it be necessary to make extensive repairs or alterations in the near future?

Is the plant kept in clean and neat condition?

Are the works adequately ventilated?

Are the pits, shafts and machinery properly guarded?

Are the offices for payments, complaints and other business conveniently located?

Were passengers' complaints promptly and efficiently attended to?

If any parks or other places of amusement are owned or operated by the company, state what and give size, cost and number of visitors annually.

Is there a system of badging or uniforming the employes so that they may be known to the public?

Is the general morale and discipline of the employes good, bad or indifferent?

Are the employes who meet the public polite and attentive?

Are they neatly dressed?

Do the various departments work in harmony? Is there friction or jealousy, and does one department shirk work, leaving it to be done by another?

Is there an adequate system of telephones?

Are the works and offices properly watched at night?

Is there any system of inspection to prevent workmen of other companies or city departments from injuring the underground structures?

Was there a drafting room maintained?

What system was in vogue to take care of the tools distributed to employes?

Were the different classes of workmen equipped with proper tools? Were the tools kept in order?

FINANCIAL MATTERS.

The inquiry into all of the four subjects under investigation ends with a critical examination of matters falling under this head. The professional accountants engaged in this department of the work are under strict orders to exercise the fullest care and are given special instructions as to the scope and bearings of the principal questions.

Capital stock and bonds, assets, liabilities, receipts, expenses, and profit and loss—each of these elements is made the subject of exhaustive inquiry.

Among the detailed questions in this category are those relating to the reduction or increase of fares, to what manner and to what extent the employes have a the proper charging, in the case of municipally owned systems, of each item of expense to the proper account, with particular regard to services rendered by officers of the city government; the keeping of the accounts of the particular plant independent from all others and from the general accounts of the city; the rate of interest paid by the city as compared with the rate paid by private public service companies; the canceling of liabilities, and payment of interest on bonds.

It is also asked whether or not the plant was run at a loss; and if so, how the deficit was met. The manner of auditing is likewise a subject of inquiry, and also a minute examination is to be made of how each issue of stock was disposed of. The schedules end with a résumé intended to show the balance to profit and loss.

As stated above, the schedule of the investigation of Street Railways is typical of the schedules arranged for the investigation of the three other subjects under consideration—Gas, Electric Lighting and Power, and Water; so that even in the brief résumé here given the reader may get a clear idea of the thoroughness with which the work is being carried on. While it is important that thoroughness of the technical side of the investigation should be shown, it is of no less importance that the experts chosen to conduct that side should be named and the manner of their selection indicated.

These authorities were engaged by the sub-committee previously spoken of, and in each instance the choice was unanimous. They are:

GAS—Alfred E. Forstall, New York; J. R. Klump, Germantown, Pa.; Fred C. Burnett, Toronto, Canada.

ELECTRIC—C. E. Phelps, Jr., Baltimore Md.; Theo. Stebbins, Columbus, Ohio; Alton D. Adams, Worcester, Mass.

STREET RAILWAYS—Norman McD. Crawford, Hartford, Conn.*

WATER—Dabney E. Maury, Peoria, Ill.

ACCOUNTANTS—Marwick, Mitchell & Co., New York; Robt. C. James, Wallingford, Pa.

With regard to the actual work already done, a number of American cities have been visited and considerable data has been collected. The work in this country will continue until May 22, when fifteen members of the Commission will sail for London. By that time it is expected that a large part of the technical work in Great Britain and Ireland will have been accomplished. For more than a month past preliminary work has been in progress, under the supervision of Messrs. M. E. Ingalls, Milo R. Maltbie, J. W. Sullivan, and Albert E. Winchester, members of the Commission.

After spending six or eight weeks reviewing the work of the experts, the members of the Commission abroad will return and complete its examination of American plants and finally make its report to the whole Commission.

* Other experts in this line are now being engaged in England.

THE INVESTIGATING COMMISSION IN ENGLAND.

The following cablegram to the "New York Tribune," refers to the work of the Public Ownership Commission of The National Civic Federation, which is now extending its investigation to England:

LONDON, March 10, 1906.

The National Civic Federation of the United States has sent a body of engineers and accountants across the Atlantic to make an exhaustive study of the practical operations of municipal ownership. The commission, headed by Mr. W. J. Clark, Mr. Milo R. Maltbie, Mr. J. W. Sullivan and Messrs. Klump and James has already broken ground in London for systematic work, and within a fortnight will be making a survey of municipal socialism in Glasgow, London, Manchester, Birmingham, Leeds, Liverpool, Sheffield and other large centers of population. As Mr. Maltbie explains the matter, the investigation has been undertaken as a combination movement by interests opposed to municipal ownership and by converts to the progressive policies. Capitalists alarmed by the results of recent local elections in America and politicians and reformers attracted by the scope and spirit of the new municipal activities in England have agreed to unite in an effort to obtain precise information respecting the financial and mechanical achievements of British municipalities as good government clubs. So the commission of engineers and accountants has been empowered to ascertain the facts in an impartial spirit and to report upon them to the National Civic Federation. The commission will be strengthened by new members, and, as its expenses are met by liberal contributions, it will employ additional experts and will be occupied for several months in a thorough examination of the conditions of local government in the most enterprising British towns. The final report can hardly fail to be of exceptional value. Dr. Albert Shaw was the first American writer to direct attention to the trend of collectivism in British towns; but his book was written a decade ago, and there has been subsequently an enormous enlargement of municipal operations. The American Consul at Hull, Mr. Walter C. Hamm, and other members of the consular service have written excellent reports on these municipal activities; and many journalists and magazine writers have contributed freely to the literature of the subject. An investigation by experts uninfluenced by previous bias or prejudice will be of great utility in informing and enlightening American opinion on a matter of supreme importance.

Mr. Maltbie and his associates will not lack prompters, if they are anxious to have cues behind the scenes. There is a powerful association of English capitalists, economists and taxpayers, which has been conducting a vigorous campaign against municipal socialism and has received the support of "The Times." There is also an organized body of representative municipal councillors, which holds an annual congress and brings the town corporations into working relations for mutual benefit. There is "The Municipal Journal," whose former conductor, Mr. Robert Donald, is now the editor of "The Daily Chronicle," and the municipal reformers have in it a most intelligent advocate and capable organ. The Progressive members of the London County Council are municipal socialists; and Mr. John Burns, president of the Local Government Board, has been one of the ablest champions of the new principles of collective responsibilities and investments for the common good. The commission can hear in London all that can be said in favor of the new policies and against them; but if I have correctly understood Mr. Maltbie's explanations it will not be influenced by these special pleadings, but will visit the provincial cities and with the assistance of its own experts ascertain how municipal trading in its various forms is operating, how much it costs in local taxation and what profit, if any, there is from it for the reduction of rates. This method of procedure is one which will be heartily commended by all fair-minded investigators.

NEW OFFICERS OF THE NATIONAL CIVIC FEDERATION.

At the annual meeting of the Executive Committee of The National Civic Federation held at the Park Avenue Hotel on March 26, the following officers were elected for the ensuing year:

AUGUST BELMONT, *President.*
SAMUEL GOMPERS, *First Vice-President.*
OSCAR S. STRAUS, *Second Vice-President.*
ISAAC N. SELIGMAN, *Treasurer.*
HON. SETH LOW, *Chairman Conciliation Committee.*
FRANCIS L. ROBBINS and JOHN MITCHELL, *Chairmen Trade Agreement Committee.*
CHARLES A. MOORE, *Chairman Welfare Department.*
RALPH M. EASLEY, *Chairman Executive Council.*
SAMUEL B. DONNELLY, *Secretary.*

In the election of officers only two changes were made from last year. Isaac N. Seligman and Charles A. Moore were newly elected respectively as Treasurer and as Chairman of the Welfare Department.

In resigning as Chairman of this Department, Mr. Vreeland sent the following letter. Mr. Vreeland's resignation was accepted and a vote of thanks was tendered him for his faithful services as Chairman of the Department.

NEW YORK, March 23, 1906.

AUGUST BELMONT, ESQ.,
President National Civic Federation.

MY DEAR SIR:—Commencing with the organization of the Welfare Department of The National Civic Federation, I have been its Chairman. At the time I was requested to accept the Chairmanship, I advised the Committee that my duties and responsibilities were such that I could not with justice to my business and personal interests accept any additional responsibilities, but in the interest of organization of this Department on lines with which I was more familiar than others, I agreed to accept such responsibilities, and have continued to do so up to the present time to the best of my ability.

The recent developments in connection with the business interests which I represent have increased my duties and responsibilities, and I therefore must request the Executive Officers of The National Civic Federation to relieve me of the duties devolving upon the Chairman of the Welfare Department, and ask that my resignation be accepted, to take effect upon the election of my successor at the annual meeting to be held in New York City on March 28th, 1906.

I shall always be very glad to give to the Department the benefit of my counsel and advice.

With assurances of my support and loyalty to yourself and those associated with you in this important work, I remain, Very truly yours,

(Signed) H. H. VREELAND.

Apart from the election of officers the most important business transacted at the meeting was the appointment of a Committee of Five on by-laws and constitution. This committee was appointed as a result of the suggestion contained in the annual report of the Chairman of the Executive Council to the effect that a consideration of this subject is necessary in order to meet the change in conditions since the adoption of the constitution and by-laws now in force and to keep pace with the enlarged scope of the Federation. This committee, as appointed by President Belmont, consists of Hon. Franklin MacVeagh, Samuel Gompers, Hon. Oscar S. Straus, Rev. Dr. Thomas R. Slicer and Ralph M. Easley, Chairman of the Executive Council. Mr. Easley's report, offering the suggestion which resulted in the formation of this committee and outlining some of the work of The National Civic Federation during the year, follows:

During the past year, The National Civic Federation, in addition to its industrial work, has taken up three new subjects, namely: Public Ownership, Immigration, and Primary Election and Ballot Reform. As the subject of Public Ownership is taken up elsewhere in this issue of the REVIEW the reference to it in this report is here omitted.

DEPARTMENT OF IMMIGRATION.

A Department on Immigration was organized at the request of the National Conference on Immigration held in New York City under the auspices of the Federation, December 6-8, 1905. That Conference was attended by six hundred delegates appointed by the governors of forty States, mayors of large cities, and leading commercial, agricultural, labor, manufacturers, economic, ecclesiastical and educational organizations.

The membership of the new Department is made up of representatives of all those organizations, making a total of one hundred and fifty. A meeting will soon be held for the purpose of organizing and outlining the scope of the Department. The importance of this subject cannot be overestimated. It is claimed that a million immigrants came to this country last year; and the proper distribution and the making of American citizens out of this alien influx is a problem calling for the best efforts of our public-spirited citizens. If the South and West need these immigrants, which are over-crowding the cities, one of the practical problems before the new Department will be their proper distribution. Other important subjects for investigation will be Selection and Restriction of white immigrants and the Enforcement of the Chinese Exclusion Acts.

DEPARTMENT OF PRIMARY ELECTIONS AND BALLOT REFORM.

At the National Conference on Primary Elections and Ballot Reform, held under the auspices of the Federation in New York, March 6 and 7, a resolution was unanimously passed, requesting this body to organize a Department to give consideration to that subject. The Conference was very representative. It was attended by delegates from all parts of the country, appointed by Congressmen, Mayors, and municipal and political reform bodies, representing various shades of political opinion. No more important work could be undertaken by our organization than to help secure clean government, whether national, State or municipal.

CONCILIATION DEPARTMENT.

The work of the Conciliation Department the past year has been confined almost entirely to bringing about conferences, at the request of one side or the other, where there were threatened industrial disturbances. The requests have come from twenty-two States and cover almost every branch of industry. About three-fourths of the Conferences have resulted successfully. In some cases they have been secured without much difficulty, simply by getting the right persons to work toward that end. But, in many other cases, a great deal of patience and tact was required by members of the Department. One advantage resulting from the enlargement of the scope of the Federation has been that members of other Departments were available in different cities to help when necessary.

Within the last month, seven very interesting cases have come to the Department. One was a threatened tie-up on a large elevated railway in a near-by city. The representative of the employes called at headquarters and stated that unless he could secure a conference within twenty-four hours, his men would strike. It was necessary to reach both the chairman of the executive board and the president of the railway, through members of our organization. When the matter was laid before them, they expressed surprise that the trouble had progressed so far without their knowledge. They granted the conference, and the difficulty was amicably adjusted. Both sides wrote to the Department, expressing their thanks for its efforts, but marked their letters confidential.

It is thus kind of quiet, delicate work that has proved most effective. Were these cases to be made public, such action would be resented by the parties interested.

WELFARE DEPARTMENT.

The Welfare Department has made great progress the past year. Its membership now numbers over two hundred employers, each one being committed to the policy of bettering the conditions under which his employes work or live. The progress of the work of the Welfare Department is treated at length elsewhere in this issue.

In pursuing this phase of our work the great problem of child labor and of bettering the conditions under which women work, presents itself to the Welfare Department. It is proposed that the Department shall take up those two subjects, and make investigations, either in co-operation with existing organizations, or independently, as may be deemed wise.

INDUSTRIAL ECONOMICS DEPARTMENT.

The Industrial Economics Department, organized a year ago, held one general meeting at which was discussed the question of Individual Liberty. The Department has mapped out a promising programme for the ensuing year.

The non-union versus the union or, what is commonly called the "open and closed shop controversy"; the injunction; the boycott; and the hours of labor are among the subjects that will be studied.

Some new problems confront us in the open and closed shop controversy, which has become acute in nearly every industry where the employes are organized. It was rare for a union to strike two years ago to secure what it termed the "union shop." To-day the demand for the union shop is the cause of numerous strikes. It is claimed that the reason for this change in policy is that, while, several years ago, the open shop meant a non-discriminating one—that is to say, one in which the union and non-union men were given identical treatment—now the open shop practically means a non-union shop. The unions present much testimony to show that there are numerous employers' organizations whose members, while publicly declaring that they will treat union and non-union men alike, are practically forcing every union man out of their employ. If this be true, then, in fighting for what it calls the union-shop, the union is only endeavoring to preserve its existence.

It will be the duty of the Industrial Economics Department to investigate this subject and present all the facts to the public.

On the question of the injunction, organized labor claims that the courts are lending themselves to the employers by issuing temporary injunctions at crucial moments during strikes, and that although upon a later hearing the injunctions are dismissed they have, in the meantime, served the purpose of the employers to break the strikes. If labor has the right to strike, and no one will deny that proposition, and if the courts are thus made allies of the cause of the employers, it is certainly a serious matter. If it be found true that the injunction is thus abused, the committee investigating this subject will be expected to recommend how the abuse may be corrected without destroying the general principle of the injunction.

Other questions that will naturally come before this Department are: "The Union Label," "Restriction of Output," "The Limitation of Apprentices," "The Minimum Wage," "Piece Work," "Trade Agreements," and "Compulsory Arbitration."

THE CIVIC FEDERATION OF BOSTON.

Following this report Mr. Hayes Robbins, of the Civic Federation of Boston, outlined some of the results of the work of the organization during the year in New England. Mr. Robbins said in part:

The New England Federation organized for business one year ago, with an Executive Committee of 21. This was later increased to 30, and in January last to 42. It was my feeling from the start that we ought to have a definite body of members at large, who should be entitled to attend and vote at our meetings, and feel that they were not merely invited guests, but were officially a part of the work, having some personal concern in its progress and success, and expressly committed to its principles. This last provision was made our basis of membership. We have no financial test; any dues large enough to maintain the work would exclude a large number of our members whose affiliation and influence we desire for other than financial reasons.

It was not an easy matter to pick out the people we wanted as members in the three groups composing the Federation. After a year's campaign, however, we have to-day 547 members, scattered all over the New England States; 239 being employers, 183 representatives of the public, and 125 representatives of labor. Our files of acceptances give us a fairly good index of the strength of sentiment among the broadly representative men of the section, favorable to reasonable methods of industrial dealing.

The fact that our labor membership is smaller than that of the employers is due to the greater difficulty of learning who the influential men are in the large territory covered, but the labor list is steadily growing. The prevailing labor sentiment toward the movement was registered in the emphatic resolutions of endorsement passed unanimously by the Boston Central Labor Union last May, and by the Massachusetts State Branch of the American Federation of Labor last October.

We have also a Conciliation Committee of 15, headed by two of the most capable men in New England for this kind of work—Mr. Louis D. Brandeis and Judge Warren A. Reed, who was formerly Chairman of the State Board of Arbitration, which is perhaps the most effective board in the country, and which was never more so than under his administration.

We are also building up a department of Organization and Education, numbering thus far 41 members, in 32 cities and towns. These members furnish our special points of contact with local situations, and in joining this committee they agreed to give us local information when necessary, and names of people who ought to be interested in the movement.

In the past fourteen months we have had to deal with 24 cases of industrial disagreement, and have taken part in negotiations to prevent trouble where it seemed likely to follow the failure to adjust differences. Details of these cases are on file, but we do not make them public. The difficulty has not been solved in every case by any means, but it may be said of practically all of them that either the trouble has been adjusted or the issue dropped; or, progress has been made toward a possible adjustment after further developments; or, an unforeseen indirect benefit in some co-related matter has grown out of the negotiations; or, the parties have been brought into relations under which the probability of similar friction in the future is materially lessened. President Tuttle testified at our last annual meeting that there never had been a time within his knowledge when there was so little strife or threat of strife within the borders of New England as at present, and expressed the belief that to no one thing was more of that condition due than to the influence this movement has been exerting.

We have held two public meetings, one in April, 1905, and the other in January last. At the latter, our first vice-president, Frank H. McCarthy, of the Cigar Makers' Union, presided, although Mr. Tuttle arrived in time to pronounce the benediction. Governor Guild and his immediate predecessor, ex-Governor Douglas, were both present and spoke; the question of Hours of Labor was discussed by Alfred Mosely, Marcus M. Marks, James Duncan, James P. Archibald, and Louis D. Brandeis. At our meeting of last April we discussed Trade Agreements, Mr. Tuttle presiding, the speakers being Mr. Belmont, Mr. Gompers, William H. Pfahler and John F. Tobin.

We are now forming a new Committee on Workshop Improvement, to rouse interest in that portion of Welfare Work which deals with conditions affecting the health and comfort of employes within the factory or store. Our chairman for that work is Frederick P. Fish, president of the American Telephone and Telegraph Company, and while the members of the Committee proper will be employers, we are forming an advisory board composed of a few selected employers, labor representatives and technical experts, whose advice and help we think will be valuable. The first two lines of work we expect to take up are, enlisting the co-operation of both employers and employes in applying to workshop conditions certain very sane, practical measures that are being successfully promoted by the Society for the Relief and Control of Tuberculosis; and, in another direction, endeavoring to secure better enforcement of the present sanitary regulations of workshops, helping to promote a wider knowledge of what these regulations are, and if possible, getting increased facilities and help for the State police, who are charged with this work.

We have a small office for headquarters, and a considerable amount of current literature and reports on file, bearing on all phases of the industrial situation; this material is pretty fully covered in an Information Index which is consulted more or less by students and others making special study of these subjects.

We have no regular publication, but have issued four special bulletins dealing with various features of our work. Through the courtesy of The National Civic Federation, all of our members receive the CIVIC FEDERATION REVIEW. In some cases we have supplied speakers for outside meetings, and we are especially fortunate in having within reach for such purposes a number of good, practical, fair-minded men who understand the subject and know how to discuss it. We expect to send a fraternal delegate, by invitation, to the State Convention of the Maine Federation of Labor next June.

Among the men who have been most useful to the work are, first of all, our President, Mr. Lucius Tuttle, President of the Boston & Maine Railroad, than whom no man in New England holds a higher place in public confidence and esteem. His status with working men is fairly reflected, without exaggeration, in the statement which is typical, by one of the conductors on that railroad who wrote us that he was proud to belong to anything presided over by a man who is loved by 25,000 whose labor he directs. Mr. Tuttle's influence and cordial personal co-operation from the beginning have been a tower of strength to us. Then we have Mr. Brandeis and Judge Reed, already referred to; Charles H. Taylor, Jr., of the *Globe*, one of the first organizers of the work there, its first Secretary, and Treasurer for a year; John Mason Little, our present Treasurer; Frederick P. Fish, Major Henry L. Higginson, Senator Crane, Bishop Lawrence and a loyal group of exceptionally able labor representatives, including Frank H. McCarthy and Henry Abrahams, of the Cigar Makers; Frank K. Foster and Park Mitchell, of the Typographical Union; John Golden, of the United Textile Workers; John F. Tobin, of the Boot and Shoe Workers; James Duncan, First Vice-President of the American Federation of Labor; D. D. Driscoll, of the Horse Shoers, and Colin Cameron, of the Carpenters.

THE PROGRESS OF WELFARE WORK.

(Continued from page 13)

"Some of the objections of laboring men to insurance plans have been met by progressive employers, who have arranged to return at least a portion of the dues contributed by employes when they leave the service of the company. When a man has been employed from fifteen to twenty years by one company, and has contributed during that period to the relief fund, he may have placed therein all his savings which he can ill afford to lose when his years of usefulness are near an end. A number of employers have abandoned the obnoxious clause which binds the laborer who belongs to the relief society to release the company from legal liability in case of a serious accident.

"There is a growing tendency among employers to encourage thrift by establishing savings funds. It is difficult for employes to patronize the public savings banks, which are open only during working hours, and, furthermore, it does not appeal to a man to spend 10 cents car fare for the sake of reaching a bank where he may deposit 10 cents.

"Employers who have inaugurated a system of lending money to employes in times of stress have discovered a means of eliminating the 'money shark' from their institutions."

On the general topic of the widely growing interest in Welfare Work attention should be called to the action just taken by The Civic Federation of New England in appointing a sub-committee on workshop improvement comprising five officers and an advisory board of thirty-five. Frederick P. Fish, of the American Telephone and Telegraph Company, is the Chairman of the committee and its object is to promote practical interest in the improvement of such working conditions as affect the health, comfort and convenience of employes in factories, stores and other places where labor is performed.

12

The National Civic Federation Review

Vol. II. No. 10 NEW YORK, JULY—AUGUST, 1906 Ten Cents

PUBLIC OWNERSHIP COMMISSION IN EUROPE.

VALUE OF THE INVESTIGATING COMMITTEE'S WORK EMPHASIZED AT THE DINNER OF THE NEW YORK CIVIC FEDERATION.

HAVING practically completed, for the greater part, their study of conditions in the more important American cities as affecting the ownership of such public utilities as gas, water, electric lighting and power, and street railways, members of the Investigating Committee of The Commission on Public Ownership and Operation sailed from New York May 22 on the "Caronia" and are now in Great Britain in the midst of a thorough examination of the facts to be found there bearing upon the various phases of their subject.

The Committee's itinerary during the month of June included Dublin, where the street railway system was investigated; Glasgow, where tramway, electric lighting and gas undertakings were examined; Newcastle, where gas and two electric plants were selected for study; Sheffield, Leicester and Birmingham, where examinations of gas works were made; Liverpool's tramway and electric light undertakings; Manchester's tramway, gas and electric light establishments, and London, where the Committee is now studying tramway, gas, and electric light undertakings, including a trip to examine Bristol tramways, if convenient. The Committee reached London on June 22, where it is to remain until the adjournment of its sessions in England. Headquarters have been established at 9 Arundel Street, Strand, London, in charge of Messrs. Mahbie and Sullivan.

Cable dispatches from Great Britain reporting the progress of the Committee's investigation state that in Glasgow both the "municipality" and the "anti-municipality" in the committee are generally impressed with the compactness and perfection of the Glasgow street railway system. At the banquet to the Committee given by the Glasgow Corporation on June 2, Baillie Alexander, in proposing a toast to The National Civic Federation, asked that the statement that the Glasgow people did not have to pay taxes be contradicted. They paid taxes, he said, but these were more than compensated for by the cheapness of the various public services. Mr. Moffet of Indiana replied that he hoped America would be able to produce such disinterested city councillors as Glasgow had. They had in The Civic Federation a nucleus of this high type. Mr. Parsons of Boston, in proposing a toast to the Corporation of Glasgow, said it was largely a question of civilization. Boston had tried municipal printing and the experiment was not a great success.

Following the Committee's examination of the Glasgow gas enterprises, Chairman Ingalls was quoted in a cable dispatch as saying that he had been much impressed with the success of municipal ownership in Glasgow and thought the same results could be achieved in America if the right kind of citizens would enter public life. He said: "We have the right kind of citizens, but they all seem to be too busy to take part in the affairs of city government." Of the undertakings he had seen in Glasgow he put the tramways easily first, then the gas supply and, last, the electrical supply system. Mr. Parsons said that the facts that had been ascertained in Glasgow would help them greatly to arrive at a decision whether America had the proper conditions for successful municipalization.

At a banquet given by the Glasgow Corporation on June 4, the members of the Committee expressed themselves as delighted by the cordiality of their reception. Prof. Goodnow said that whether or not the members of the Committee were advocates or opponents of municipal ownership or merely perchers on the fence it was a great pleasure to see what Glasgow had done. The advocates of municipal ownership had come to strengthen their arguments, their opponents had come in a vain endeavor to find weakness and those perched on the fence had come merely to ascertain the truth. The Americans, he added, were credited with suffering with swelled head. For himself, since coming to Glasgow, his head had become considerably smaller.

What has impressed all the members of the

Upper Row (from left to right)—John R. Commons, F. J. McNulty, W. J. Clark, Ralph M. Easley, Talcott Williams. Lower Row (from left to right)—John H. Gray, Walton Clark, Frank J. Goodnow, Frank Parsons, Edward A. Moffett.

MEMBERS OF THE INVESTIGATING COMMITTEE OF THE PUBLIC OWNERSHIP COMMISSION

Committee is the remarkably high character of the men constituting municipal governments in Great Britain, who devote as much attention to municipal affairs as men in the United States devote to their private business. At a luncheon tendered to the members of the Committee on June 11 by the city government of Manchester was a councillor who has been a member of the government for twenty-nine years and who retired from business in order to devote all his time and energies to the affairs of the city. The members of the Investigating Committee express appreciation of the kindness and courtesy displayed by everybody with whom they are brought in contact. All the municipal officers and the owners of private concerns show readiness to give them all the facts and figures they desire.

In addition to the Committee's investigation of European cities, an extended examination of municipal conditions has been in progress for some months in the cities of this country, including Chicago, Philadelphia, Pittsburg, Indianapolis, Fort Wayne, Wheeling, Richmond, Allegheny City, South Norwalk, Atlanta, and Norfolk. These investigations of the different cities in Europe and America are being conducted with the sole purpose of collecting the facts—facts that are basal and comparable—as to the ownership of public utilities, and not for the purpose of formulating an opinion as to the wisdom or unwisdom of the action of the various municipalities in adoping the plan of ownership to which each at present adheres.

Various phases of the value and significance of this work of the Commission were emphasized at the New York Civic Federation's dinner to the Commission's Committee on Investigation held at the Park Avenue Hotel on May 21. Hon. Oscar S. Straus presided. Speeches were made by Mr. Straus, Professor Frank J. Goodnow of Columbia University; Dr. Albert Shaw, editor of the *Review of Reviews;* Hon. W. J. Gaynor, of the Supreme Court of New York; Mr. August Belmont, President of the National Civic Federation; Mr. Philip Kelly, of the Theatrical Protective Union; Dr. Talcott Williams, of the Philadelphia *Press;* Mr. Walton Clark, Third Vice-President of the United Gas Improvement Company, Philadelphia; Professor Frank Parsons, President of the National Public Ownership League, Boston; and Mr. Horace E. Deming, Chairman of the Executive Committee of the National Municipal League, New York.

PRIVATE INITIATIVE ON PUBLIC QUESTIONS.

Banquet Address of Hon. Oscar S. Straus, Vice-President National Civic Federation.

THERE is no surer index of a nation's decay than when a people become indifferent to their own welfare, and shift individual responsibility to governmental control. Just as there is a limit to the sphere of individual action in a body politic, so there is a limit to governmental duties.

The very fact that in this country so much work of a public nature is done by private initiative, by private individuals, and by so-called semi-public bodies, is the best evidence that our body politic is sound and healthy. I do not mean to intimate that in this country we are free from the corrupting influences of selfish greed; on the contrary, the crop is plentiful, but so is the vigilance of the upright citizens who are continually on the alert, and wield the scythe with stalwart arms, and fearlessly lop off the deleterious weeds which spring up in the night and grow afield.

In no country in the world has so much been left to private initiative, not only industrially, but even to a greater extent in the benevolent and philanthropic fields. The very fact that in this country the people from the earliest times have been accustomed not to rely upon the State for the support of their religious establishments, has had a large influence in broadening the scope of individual activities and responsibilities. Much work that in the old world was left to government, national and municipal, has, in this country, been initiated, fostered and supported by private individuals. This has developed its good as well as its detrimental sides. Many of our public works in city, state and nation have been undertaken by individuals, often in advance of the need of a people. Often this has proved speculative and hazardous, and often the results have proved marvelously remunerative. This extraordinary enterprise has paved the way to our rapid commercial development, and expedited the movement of our population from the Atlantic to the Pacific, and from Maine to Mexico.

The so-called "unearned increment," if I may borrow a phrase, has grown more and more valuable with the growth of the population of our cities, and it is becoming more and more a serious question to what extent that "unearned increment" should be, and can safely be utilized so as to profit the municipality or State which has a right to hold these valuable franchises in trust for all the people. The question arises, can these franchises be made to return greater advantages to the people if held, developed, and operated in common, or, if held in common and developed and operated by private individuals, or non-governmental bodies.

Many experiments along these lines have been made, some in this country, but more in the greater European cities. The National Civic Federation has taken up the consideration of this subject so far as it applies to public ownership and operation of public utilities in municipalities, confining its investigations specifically to passenger transportation, whether by elevated, surface, or underground systems; to the supply of water, gas, and electricity. For this purpose it has invited men competent, as scientific experts of practical experience, and accountants, to study the subject in all its phases both here and abroad. These men are highly qualified by capacity and experience to make the investigation. Some of these men have large interests in, and represent private ownership, and some of them are pronounced advocates of public ownership and public operation. All sides of this question are fairly represented, so that the investigations will be from all sides, and in no case one-sided. The men who have undertaken this subject deserve to be commended for their public spirit, and we are assembled on the eve of their departure for Europe to extend to them our unstinted appreciation for their commendable public spirit in undertaking this important investigation.

The Committee, consisting of twenty-one members, have already made some investigations in this country, and on their return those investigations will be continued, and a full report covering the entire subject will be laid before the public, with such recommendations as they may be able to agree upon—in any event, the facts as they find them will be presented in detail.

In addition to the economic aspect of the question, there is even a more important side, the comparative effect that public ownership and public operation, as contrasted with private ownership and private operation, has upon our body politic.

We are not blind to the fact that the government of our municipalities is often inefficient and corrupt. Some of them have been a disgrace to our free institutions, and evidence is not lacking that a large share of responsibility for these unfortunate conditions is due to the corrupt influences of private ownership in the securing and in the controlling of public utilities. On the other hand, it is claimed by some of our leading writers both here and abroad, that in a democracy few things are more to be feared than a great increase in the number of those who are in the direct employ of the State or the municipality. Lecky says: "The temptation of the representatives to use public money and public works as a means of electioneering, and the temptation of the electors to use their political power as a means of obtaining trade advantages for themselves, will soon become irresistible, and the floodgates of corruption will be open. . . . Public works are in this respect far more dangerous under a democratic government than under a despotism."

On the other hand, it is claimed by other writers of equally high standing that public ownership and operation carries home to every one the importance of good government, and arrays on its side the strong classes in a community which otherwise would be indifferent, and that municipal government improves as its duties are enlarged.

With these general and preliminary observations, I will call upon the gentlemen who represent the several sides of this question, to address you. These addresses will be entirely informal but, therefore, none the less acceptable.

METHODS OF THE OWNERSHIP COMMISSION.

Professor Goodnow, of Columbia University, Describes the Methods of the Investigating Committee.

SOME time ago I received by the same mail two books on municipal ownership in Great Britain. If one read one of them he could hardly fail to reach the conclusion that the assumption by the British authorities as to the ownership and operation of municipal public utilities was a great success. If upon the other hand, he, by chance, took up the other book, he did not have to go further than a perusal of its table of contents to see that municipal activity along these lines was, in the eyes of the author, a conspicuous failure. In some respects it is true; the conclusions reached by these writers were due to the fact that where disadvantages had to be balanced against advantages, one gave a greater weight to an acknowledged advantage or disadvantage than the other. To that extent the different results reached were due to an honest and perfectly natural difference of opinion. But still, making due allowance for these reasons, for the difference in the final result reached, one could not put these books down without feeling strongly that "some one had blundered." One almost had a suspicion that some one had committed a more heinous offense than a blunder.

Now, this blundering, or worse than blundering, has been, I think, characteristic of most of the literature on the subject of municipal ownership which has as yet appeared. At any rate, this characteristic of the existing literature has been the one which has been most markedly apparent to him who, not blinded by prejudice nor disqualified by interest, has honestly and earnestly attempted to get at the truth. And it was, as I understand it, the purpose of The National Civic Federation in its establishment of the Commission which has entrusted to us the investigation of this most important subject to do what it could to make future blunders less easy and future misrepresentations, if I may so call it, more easy of detection.

The question naturally presents itself, What are the methods which have been adopted to attain the desired end? In answer to this question, I may say, those responsible for the management of The National Civic Federation laid down one fundamental rule which those of us who have been most active in the work of investigation have had continually before us. That rule was that we were to ascertain facts. The adoption of this rule prevented, in the first place, this Commission from meeting and after argument and discussion coming to a determination that, in its opinion, municipal ownership and operation of any specific public utility under the conditions existing in the average American city was better or worse than private management. For the opinions of this Commission, however valuable they may be, are not facts.

We are confined to facts. Now, what are facts? What are the facts of municipal ownership? Not knowing much about the facts of municipal ownership except that, like other facts, they were, presumably, stubborn things, the first thing which we did in order to do the work committed to us was to devise methods by which these facts might be ascertained. We determined that they could be ascertained only through the examination of specific plants and, inasmuch as the means at our disposal were limited, by the examination of selected plants. Now, some municipal and some private plants had a general reputation of being successful. Some, on the other hand, were reputed to be unsuccessful. If we should choose all the alleged successful municipal plants and should set them off against the alleged unsuccessful private plants, or *vice versa*, we should certainly obtain a conclusion of facts—choice facts, they might be called.

But such a method of ascertaining facts we had certainly to avoid. I should not have said we had to avoid this. All necessity for avoiding it was removed by the wise action of The National Civic Federation, which so constituted the Commission that almost every shade of opinion and almost every interest or prejudice was represented on it as well as on the smaller committees which have had the burden of superintending the work of investigation. The result was that when it came to choosing the particular plants to be examined, opportunity was open for making any objection which could be made to a selection, because of the fact that it was unrepresentative or incomparable with other selections. Indeed, the places selected have been selected as the result of unanimous action on the part of the committees in charge of the work. It was in this way, then, that the attempt has been made to secure a fair selection of the places from which our facts were to be ascertained.

After the places to be examined had been selected, the question presented itself as to what things we should look for in these places. We soon found that these things might be grouped under one of four heads: (1) Character of service; (2) Financial results; (3) Political conditions; (4) Social conditions, particularly labor conditions.

Having determined that what we wished was to be found under one of these heads, we had to decide how we would actually get at the facts. We very soon determined that we must have for this purpose men who by education were qualified to do the work, and we therefore selected four classes of experts, viz.: engineers, accountants, those acquainted with labor conditions and those who by training and experience were able most easily to get information with regard to other social and political conditions. In the choice of these gentlemen we have been most fortunate. We did not select any one who was not accepted without objection by every member of our sub-committee. We endeavored, furthermore, to get absolutely the best men available, and we found in these gentlemen a willingness, when they learned of the paucity of our resources, to forego a part of the charges which they usually made for work of this sort. The experts whom we have selected have been engaged, some in England and some in this country, in acquiring the information desired, which will be submitted to the members of the committee before they are called upon to state their conclusions.

This is about all I can say upon our work. I would that I could say more, but the conditions which we have been called upon to examine have been so complex, the records, particularly of the municipalities which have been examined, have been kept in such shape, that it has been exceedingly difficult for us to get the information that we have desired. The result has been that it has been impossible to finish the work in this country as soon as was expected. It will have to be taken up again on our return from Great Britain. The work on the other side, as I understand, has made much more satisfactory progress. This has been due partly to the fact that the information desired has been more easily obtainable on account of the longer experience which municipalities have had in the management of public utilities, partly to the greater detail in which the records of their work, in accordance with the provisions of law, have been kept, and partly to the fact that the investigation has been supervised by two of our number who have been able to give their entire time to the work. Thanks to the indefatigable exertions of Messrs. Maltbie and Sullivan and the gentlemen who have assisted them, so much has been done that we hope the committee will be able to reach conclusions as to the relative advantages of municipal and private ownership in Great Britain after having gone over the field in the time which has by our plans been allotted for this purpose.

OWNERSHIP OF PUBLIC SERVICE CORPORATIONS.

Judge Gaynor, of the New York Supreme Court, Discusses Modern Tendencies.

I HARDLY know what may be appropriate for me to say on an occasion like this; in fact, I feel that bringing any ideas here at all where ideas are the stock in trade, where everybody has ideas, is like bringing coals to Newcastle, where they have more coals than they know what to do with. I feel that I am speaking to philosophers, to men who are considering public subjects seriously, to men who thus far have been of great value to the community.

I think that I may say of this Federation that it has done much in being able to bring together such men as Mr. Belmont on the one side, representing what he represents, and Mr. Gompers on the other, representing what he represents, and that, if The Civic Federation has not made them hail-fellows-well-met, it has disposed them to sit down and discuss soberly important matters between them, and it has thereby accomplished a very great deal for the community. If it had done nothing else it would have done a great deal. Most of the friction in the community on topics which this Federation discusses from time to time on political, industrial and economic subjects, on the topics involving labor and capital and the antagonism between them, arises out of misunderstandings on one side or the other. and from the fact that those representing each side of the subject in this country up to a very recent time have not met together for a discussion with each other; and they could not come to an understanding with each other in any other manner. I say this illustrates the value of The Civic Federation's usefulness to the community in thus being able to bring together these diverse elements.

This Federation is accomplishing a very great deal, and I deem it fortunate that it has now taken up the great subject of public utilities, as to whether or not they shall be owned by the community or by individuals. I deem it fortunate that you have appointed a committee to consider this subject, for the understanding which this committee arrives at will in time be the understanding of this Federation, and that means that it will ultimately become the understanding of the entire community. If this committee can bring in a statement of the facts—not of words, not of rhetoric, but of facts such as we are all so much indebted to Mr. Shaw for in the past—and these facts are presented here and understood by this body, I have no doubt that your final understanding of the matter will "slop over" and become the understanding of the whole community. All great movements spread in that way. If a great masterpiece is produced by an artist some one comes in and sees the work and he perceives that it is a masterpiece, and there is only one person in the world who perceives it. Then he brings in another and he sees it, and so on until at last perhaps twelve persons have seen it and understood it, and their understanding finally prevails and in time becomes the judgment and understanding of all mankind. Now, as to the matter we have in hand, it will be the same way with this committee, so that what they finally ascertain will become the view of the entire country.

The agitation in this country for municipal ownership, and to some extent for municipal management as well, of public service corporations has arisen, in my judgment, out of no hostility toward private management or private capital. We owe much to private management, and it is still a question whether the best service may not be obtained from private enterprise. Private management may in some respects be able to teach us many lessons. But the agitation for municipal ownership has arisen, on the contrary, wholly from the franchises of these public service corporations being overcapitalized or watered, as Mr. Straus has expressed it in his opening address. The community cannot look on this without first a feeling of uneasiness, and then of hostility, and then of open resentment and finally of action against the doubling and trebling over and over of the capital put into these corporations, all of which represents nothing except a perpetual tax by the corporations on the community. We have just seen the corporations in this city bind themselves together in a hard and fast agreement for 999 years on a basis of grossly excessive capitalization, representing the repeated overcapitalization of the constituent companies. Dear me, think of our standing that thing for 999 years! Nine years is more like it. These great gifts, these franchises that are nothing but licenses from the people, are made a drain on the community, by having bonds and stocks issued on them and doubled up, year after year, in all our cities and on our steam railroads as well, until the sum has become colossal enough—I will even say it even in this presence—dishonest enough to shock the moral sense of the people of this country. There is the seed of this hostility, this feeling toward these corporations.

We have just had a great debate in Washington concerning our national railways. There is no resentment in Washington against capital, but there is hostility to the franchises for these public utilities being made a perpetual tax on the people, as though the recipients had the right to do as they pleased with them. What are the railroads but our public highways! They are as much our public highways as the dirt roads which run alongside of them. The public mind has now come to the understanding of this, and you can't rid the public mind of it. The building of these roads was turned over to private individuals, and the trouble is, not that we have any hostility to capital, but that those who have these gifts have come somehow to understand that they own them for their own profit first and for the public second.

It is a horrible crime for the public highways to carry the freight of one man or group of men at half or any lesser rate than that charged to others, to the aggrandizement of one man or set of men and the destruction of another. Go back to the days of toll gates. What do you think would happen if one man were allowed to drive his cattle on the hoof or his teams through for one-half what another man paid? They would tear down the toll gate; and that is what will happen ultimately to these railroad abuses; the people will tear them down. They will do this peacefully if they can, forcibly if they must. There is nothing more certain than that the people have come to the conclusion that this thing will no longer be tolerated either on the highways of the nation or the highways of the city. They demand that the roads shall be managed for the aggrandizement of no individuals, but for the welfare of all. Highways from the twilight of history have always been built and managed by Government. But from 1840 to 1850 when the iron roads came in some governments for some reasons turned the building and operation of them over to individuals. This was the first time in history that public highways were turned over to the management of private individuals, barring the few toll roads that existed. But nevertheless they were made public highways by government; they were licensed as such, to remain as such. What we call a franchise, for the sake of a better word, was given to the corporations to build and manage them as public highways. I need not say to you that government can take private property only for governmental purposes. This great governmental power of taking private property for public use was given and could be given to these corporations only on the theory that they were engaged in a governmental service or function in carrying passengers or freight which, so long as we know history, was a matter regulated or controlled by government.

And I want to invoke a blessing on the man who, as President of the United States, has seen this great question as you would see it through that pane of glass; who has held it up for the country when no political parties dared to make it an issue; who has forced it before Congress and fought for a final issue in spite of all the abuse and recriminations that have been heaped upon him. Not that I think this law will cure all the ills, but the moral feeling of the people is expressed in it.

When this committee comes back from Europe with the cold facts of the experience of Europe—which is a long experience and where municipal ownership and operation is no new thing, and where it has been solved already—I say, when they get back with their report luminous with facts, and you and I are made familiar with their findings, then your opinion will speedily become the opinion of this whole country. In that way they will accomplish a great good, and I am glad to be here to-night to wish them godspeed.

A LABOR VIEW OF THE COMMISSION.

Philip Kelly, of the Theatrical Protective Union, Views the Commission from the Standpoint of Organized Labor.

AS an after-dinner speaker I am a complete failure, which you will discover before I have finished. I hope, however, that when this Committee returns that I will be one of those who will meet them and extend to them a welcoming hand. If their report is entirely satisfactory it will make a very important chapter in the history of this country. If their report is satisfactory to the people, well and good, but if not, they can rest assured that they will be placed on the gridiron and toasted and roasted to perfection.

Gentlemen, the question of municipal ownership is up. There is no use in denying it. It is discussed in the "L" cars, in the subway and on the surface lines. People discuss it going to church and coming home from church. There are thousands of people in this city and in this country who have not yet made up their minds as to whether it would be a benefit to the people or not to have municipal ownership and operation. Now, as far as the idea has any bearing on the workingman is concerned, I do not think they need have any fear. Even municipal ownership would not be a complete cure for all the ills that the workingman suffers from at this time. The employes of the Government are not better paid than those of private concerns. The letter carrier in this city works fourteen hours a day, although the law says that ten hours shall constitute a day's work. But they shift them around and the result is they work fourteen hours. I do not know but what I would prefer to work for a private individual or firm rather than for the United States Government under present conditions. I do not think that municipal ownership could affect the labor organizations one way or the other. They are well able to take care of themselves. If they should decide in favor of municipal ownership I believe it would be accomplished in a very short time. But up to the present time, however, no great labor organization has expressed itself positively. It is true that individuals connected with the organizations have expressed themselves for and against the proposition. A lot will, of course, depend upon the report of this committee when it returns from England and Ireland.

Some people say that it would be a dangerous thing if the Government were to have a large number of employes. Is that a fact? I presume that statement is intended to mean that if the Government employs thousands of people in the Civil Service it would become so strong that it could not be turned out of office. Now, England has more employes than any other country in the world, and yet in no other country in the world are some of the governments so short-lived. The Conservative party has been kicked out of power in a relatively short time and the Unionist party lasted only one month. The idea of municipal ownership has some brilliant advocates.

I believe that the only great bodies in this country that have not taken a stand on this question are the labor organizations. But the question is up. The Commission, when it brings back its report, will find that such report will be discussed in the labor organizations throughout the country, and a great deal will depend upon the kind of a report they bring back. I have the utmost confidence in the men who have been appointed on this Commission; they are capable, brilliant, fearless and honest. I know the labor men on the Commission. They are good, straightforward men. The labor men will know that the report our brothers on the Commission bring back will be worth our study and confidence.

THE REMARKS OF PRESIDENT BELMONT.

Head of The National Civic Federation Officially Explains the Commission.

GENTLEMEN, it was my intention, and it was in fact my duty, to be away from New York at this time, but I set everything aside in order to be with you to-night to have an opportunity of saying a few words with regard to this Commission. The gentlemen who have already spoken to you have confirmed what I intended to say, which was that The Civic Federation's purpose was not to obtain an opinion on the question of municipal ownership, but realizing that the subject was before the people, that it was one that was beginning to be discussed, that ultimately it would be the subject of discussion on the stump during our political campaign, and that it vitally concerned the two elements this Federation has striven to bring together, it desired, if possible, to obtain for the public a text-book on the question. I knew all this would probably be said to you, but from the fact that I am the representative of one of the largest traction systems in the country, if not the largest, I thought that I would like to tell you that myself, because it had nothing whatever to do with my personal interest. At a meeting of the Committee I stated that if the results of this investigation furnished an argument for the acquisition by the municipality of the properties which I have been elected to manage, that that would not deter me. On the contrary, as a citizen I welcome a correct interpretation of this subject. As President of the Federation, it was my duty to try to bring about a proper interpretation of the subject.

I did not expect when I came here this evening that any argument would be advanced on that subject. I do not think that it would be delicate on my part to answer those arguments that have been advanced. I could and I should very much like to do so. I would like very much to have these gentlemen who have preceded me this evening and who have based their arguments on certain alleged facts, to seek those facts as zealously as will this Commission. But I want to repudiate in the most unqualified language the insinuation that I manage or that my associates manage these corporations in any other spirit than that of honesty or of correct purpose, and with any other view than that of complying with every letter of the law. But I do think that every corporation and that every corporate manager is entitled to be heard in court first, and that his action should be tested after the verdict of the court and not before. You know to what I refer and therefore it will not be necessary for me to repeat it, and I am sorry that I have to make this statement.

So anxious was this organization that the report should be absolutely impartial that it took every step to free the Commission from any possible relationship to the Federation other than that it should lean upon the Federation for its expenses. The Federation has directed it in no sense excepting to ask that it ascertain facts on the lines laid down by the Federation. That is all they have asked. They have chosen their own Committee and whatever the result of their work it will bear no hall mark of any special interest and least of all has there been any effort to create an argument against municipal ownership of public utilities, and more particularly of transportation. It would have been more than indelicate for me to have promoted any such movement if its object was other than that which Professor Goodnow has stated to you. That is why I wanted to be here to-night, because it has been insinuated by those who desire to discredit this Committee that there was a purpose to dictate to it. I thank you.

SELECTION OF THE COMMISSION APPROVED.

Dr. Talcott Williams, of the Philadelphia "Press," Commends the Manner of Appointment.

I HAVE been in doubt since I received the notice of my appointment. I do not belong to the college professor class. I am not a capitalist; but I am a Philadelphian. Perhaps this accounts for the reason of my selection as a speaker to-night. In our city we had a government which left nothing to be desired in the way of fraud. We found out that at our elections there were 70,000 fraudulent votes cast; we knew that it was impossible to stop the white slave traffic; we saw our franchises being sold right and left; we stood all that. But there came a May morning about a year ago when it was announced that our gas bills were to be increased, and we arose as one man and demanded reform. The returns of the election showed on that occasion that there were 110,000 voters who were eager for reform. The reform ticket was elected, and we at last began to conduct our own government. At last, it may be said, that we have a reform movement in Philadelphia. Previously we had tried everything. We owned our own gas works and we liked the proposition so little that we gave them up. Then the company we gave them to we liked so little that we decided to take them back.

Gentlemen, I understand that the purpose for which we are gathered here this evening is to wish this Commission godspeed on the eve of its sailing, and to express the hope that it will bring back with it the facts. As has been said by the speakers who have preceded me, it is not a question of private ownership; it is not a question of whether this method or that method is slightly more economical in the governing of a city—it is at bottom a question as to whether at any particular period of our history we would not be happier and healthier by a full consideration of the problems affecting the operation of our public utilities, and a determination to solve those problems in the best light obtainable.

I think this Committee has been selected with admirable judgment. In France a committee selected for such an investigation would necessarily have been drawn from the personnel of the existing party in power. A report from such a commission would, in all probability, have been biased and colored to suit the wishes of the party in power. In Germany a royal commission would have made a report that would have been pleasing to the head of the nation. I submit that this Commission in its method of appointment and investigation has been better constituted than it would have been possible to constitute a similar committee in any other country.

We know that in the preparation of this report and that in its submission to the public it is not so much a question of whether taxes should be raised or lowered, but it is more a question as to what is the best solution for giving the people in our great cities an increase in the number of rooms in which the average family is compelled to live; what will give the greatest amount of pure water in the cities, the most efficient form of lighting, and the best kind of transportation facilities. Some compromise, some middle course, may be necessary, but that, I submit, is the main consideration to be sought.

VIEWS OF JOHN DeWITT WARNER.

Among the letters of regret received from invited guests who were unable to attend the banquet was the following:

New York, May 16, 1906.

Mr. James P. Archibald, Secretary, Committee on Arrangements, 281 Fourth Avenue, New York.

Dear Mr. Archibald: Acknowledging your note with invitation to dinner to be given to the Public Ownership Commission on the 21st instant on the eve of its sailing, I regret that a prior engagement must make me very late, and more probably deprive me entirely of the pleasure of being with you.

I believe The Civic Federation has taken no other step so important as that in which this Commission has been appointed; that it can do no greater service than fully to inform our people of the experience of others in this matter; and that the success with which it does this, and the acceptance by our people of its report as a clear and impartial view is likely long to be its best hold on public confidence.

Sincerely,

(Signed) John DeWitt Warner.

PERSONNEL OF THE COMMITTEE.

The Fifteen Members of the Committee on Investigation Now in Europe Studying Conditions There.

MELVILLE EZRA INGALLS is chairman of the Cleveland, Cincinnati, Chicago and St. Louis Railroad Company, popularly known as the Big Four. He was educated at Bridgeton Academy and Bowdoin College, and was graduated from the Harvard Law School in 1863. He practiced law first at Gray, Me., but soon removed to Boston. A member of the Massachusetts Senate in 1867. First as president (1870) and a year later as receiver of the Indianapolis, Cincinnati and Lafayette Railroad, Mr. Ingalls conducted this company from a bankrupt condition, with aid of reorganization in 1873 and 1880, and put its successor, the Cincinnati, Indianapolis, St. Louis and Chicago, upon a sound footing, consolidating it with other roads into the Cleveland, Cincinnati, Chicago and St. Louis Railroad. From October 1, 1888, until February, 1900, Mr. Ingalls served as president of the Chesapeake and Ohio Railroad. In the Presidential campaign of 1900 he was one of the leaders of the sound money division of the Democratic party. He is president of the Merchants' National Bank of Cincinnati. In 1903 Mr. Ingalls was Democratic candidate for mayor of Cincinnati. In 1905 he served as chairman of the investigating committee of the Equitable Life Assurance Society.

JOHN ROGERS COMMONS is professor of political economy in the University of Wisconsin. He graduated at Oberlin College in 1888, studied at Johns Hopkins University, 1888-90, became professor of sociology in Oberlin College in 1892, Indiana University in 1893 and in 1895 in Syracuse University, resigning in 1899 to become director of the Bureau of Economic Research. He has served as an expert agent for the United States Industrial Commission and as assistant secretary of The National Civic Federation. Professor Commons is the author of "The Distribution of Wealth," "Social Reform and the Church," "Proportional Representation," "Regulation and Restriction of Output by Employers and Unions," "Trade Unions and Labor Problems," etc.

CHARLES L. EDGAR is president of the Edison Electric and Illuminating Company, Boston, Mass. He graduated from Rutgers College with the degree of bachelor of arts in 1882 and later pursued a post-graduate course in electricity at the same college, receiving the degree of master of arts in 1885 and that of electrical engineer in 1887. Soon after leaving college he became associated with the parent Edison company—the Edison Electric Light Company of New York—and remained with this company until 1887, when he went to Boston. He was chief engineer of the New York Edison Company, resigning to become general superintendent of the Boston Edison Company, which was organized in 1886. Mr. Edgar became in turn, general manager, vice-president and president, which latter office he has held for the last five years. Besides being president of the Edison Electric Illuminating Company, Mr. Edgar is president of the Boston Electric Company, the Somerville Electric Light Company, the Woburn Light, Heat and Power Company, the Newton and Watertown Gas Light Company and other central station companies. These companies are closely associated, and supply gas and electricity to Boston and adjacent towns. For three terms Mr. Edgar was president of the Association of Edison Illuminating Companies. He is president of the Massachusetts Electric Lighting Association, chairman of the Boston branch of the American Institute of Electrical Engineers, and was vice-president of the National Electric Light Association in 1890. At the time of his election to the presidency of the National Electric Light Association in May, 1903, he was first vice-president of that organization.

TIMOTHY HEALY has been active in the labor movement for the past twenty years. Was Master Workman of Local Assembly, 6780 Knights of Labor (Eccentric Association of Firemen, New York City) for several years. Represented the stationary firemen of that city in District Assembly 49 K. of L. and the Central Federated Union. Represented the Knights of Labor of New York City in several conventions of the general assembly of the Knights of Labor, and was president of the Knights of Labor of New York State for two years. For the past ten years Mr. Healy represented the stationary firemen of New York City in the conventions of the State Workingmen's Federation, and was elected and served as a member of the Legislative Committee of the Federation. He was elected president of the International Brotherhood of Stationary Firemen in 1903, re-elected in 1904 for a term of two years, and represented the organization in several conventions of the American Federation of Labor. Mr. Healy was largely instrumental in having placed on the statute books of New York a law compelling the licensing of stationary firemen in the City of New York, and is also credited with getting an eight-hour work-day and better conditions generally for a greater portion of the stationary firemen of New York City.

FRANK JOHNSON GOODNOW, professor of administrative law and municipal science in Columbia University since 1883, was graduated from Amherst College in 1879, from the Columbia Law School in 1882, and studied also at the Paris Ecole Libre des Sciences Politiques, at Berlin University. He is a recognized authority on municipal, administrative and constitutional law. Among his published works are: "Municipal Home Rule," "Comparative Administrative Law," "Municipal Problems," "Politics and Administration," "City Government in the United States," etc.

WALTON CLARK is Third Vice-President of the United Gas Improvement Company, Philadelphia. At the age of seventeen years he entered the employ of the New Orleans Gas Light Company, where he continued in various capacities connected with the manufacturing and distributing work until the fall of 1883, when, for a few months, he was connected with the United Gas Improvement Company, working for it in the erection of the gas plant at Pensacola, Florida. He returned to the New Orleans company in the spring of 1884, continuing with them until the fall of 1885, when he entered the service of the Jefferson City (Louisiana) Gas Company, performing the duties of superintendent of that company for about a year. Mr. Clark then removed to Chicago, and was connected for a short time with the United Coal and Oil Gas Company, of New York, the owners of the Hanlon-Leadly patents. In the fall of 1887 he entered the employ of the Kansas City Gas Light and Coke Company, and about eight months later accepted the position of assistant general superintendent of the United Gas Improvement Company, becoming general superintendent, and in 1904 being elected third vice-president. He is also president of the Equitable Illuminating Gas Light Company of Philadelphia, vice-president of the Rhode Island Company, and is officially connected with a number of large gas, electric and street railroad properties. He is a past president of the American Gas Light Association, a director of the Western Gas Association, and director of Franklin Institute of Philadelphia; member of New England Association of Gas Engineers, Pacific Coast Gas Association, the American Society of Mechanical Engineers, the Engineering Club of Philadelphia, member of the Board of Trustees of the Pennsylvania Military Academy and the Chestnut Hill Academy.

J. W. SULLIVAN, until recently Editor of *The Weekly Bulletin of the Clothing Trades*, has been prominently identified with the labor movement in this country during the past twenty years, most of the time serving in different capacities on the editorial staff of labor papers. He is a member of the Typographical Union. From 1892-95 Mr. Sullivan was general lecturer for the American Federation of Labor on the Initiative and Referendum; has served as a delegate to State and national conventions of the American Federation of Labor, and in 1896 was fraternal delegate of the Federation to the British Trades Union Congress at Edinburgh, and affiliated delegate to the International Co-operative Congress at Paris. He was prominent in the United Labor Party campaigns of 1886-7. Mr. Sullivan is the author of "Working People's Rights," "Direct Legislation," "The Trades Union Movement in America," etc.

MILO ROY MALTBIE is assistant secretary of the Art Commission of the City of New York, and a franchise expert. He was educated in the public schools, Upper Iowa University, Northwestern University and Columbia University, in which latter he received the degree of Ph.D. in 1897. He was University Fellow in Administrative Law at Columbia University, 1895-7, professor of mathematics and economics in Mount Morris College, Illinois, 1893-5; secretary of the Reform Club Committee on City Affairs, 1897-1902; editor of *Municipal Affairs*, 1897-1903, and lecturer in various institutions. He spent the summer of 1899 investigating municipal conditions in Europe for the Reform Club, and in 1903 traveled extensively over northwestern Europe for the Art Commission. Among the many committees of which he is a member the principal ones are the Merchants' Association Committee upon Water Supply, National Municipal League Committee upon Uniform Municipal Statistics, Municipal Art Society Committee upon Street Fixtures, Constitutional Home Rule Committee (secretary), etc. Dr. Maltbie has written frequently upon municipal and economic topics, and is now editing a series of books upon municipal problems for the Macmillan Company.

WILLIAM J. CLARK is foreign manager of the General Electric Company, New York City. He served from 1879 to 1887 as postmaster at Birmingham, Conn., during which time he was frequently called upon by the Post Office Department to act as Post Office inspector. In this capacity he made many important investigations, among them the Star Route frauds, frauds in the Brooklyn Post Office, the famous mail robbery of the Chicago and St. Louis Post Office route in 1886,

THE INVESTIGATING COMMITTEE OF THE COMMISSION ON PUBLIC OWNERSHIP AND OPERATION.

1. W. D. Mahon
2. Prof. John R. Commons
3. J. W. Sullivan
4. Walton Clark
5. Daniel J. Keefe
6. Walter L. Fisher
7. Melville E. Ingalls (Chairman)
8. Prof. Frank J. Goodnow
9. Edward A. Moffett (Secretary)
10. Dr. Albert Shaw (Vice-Chairman)
11. Edward W. Bemis
12. Milo R. Maltbie
13. Charles L. Edgar
14. H. B. F. Macfarland
15. W. J. Clark
16. Timothy Healy
17. Dr. Talcott Williams
18. F. J. McNulty
19. Prof. John H. Gray
20. Prof. Frank Parsons
21. Albert E. Winchester

the Jersey City Post Office burglary, and a number of other cases of a similar character. In 1886 Mr. Clark began his street railway career by securing a charter to build a street railway connecting Ansonia, Derby and Birmingham, Conn. The following year he contracted with the Vandepoel Electric Company for the equipment of this line, the first of its kind in New England. This enterprise suggested the reorganization of the Vandepoel Company, and negotiations were conducted, culminating in the sale of the Vandepoel patents to the Thomson-Houston Company. Mr. Clark became connected with this concern in 1888 as general agent of the railway department. He remained in this position until the General Electric Company was formed by the consolidation of the Thomson-Houston and Edison General Electric Companies in 1892, subsequently becoming general manager of the railway department. Later he became general manager of the foreign department, which position he now holds. In the early nineties he effected a reorganization of the British Thomson-Houston Company. He held the title of managing director of this company until the completion of his work, when he returned to the United States. During the present year he has been appointed manager of the General Electric Company's traction department, the recent organization of which has been under his supervision. Mr. Clark was appointed United States Government delegate to the International Railway Congress held at Washington in May, 1905. He is president of the Perforated Music Roll Company of New York and a director in several important concerns. Mr. Clark is also the author of several books, including "Commercial Cuba," published in 1898.

F. J. McNULTY is president of the International Brotherhood of Electrical Workers, with headquarters at Washington, D. C.

FRANK PARSONS is president of the National Public Ownership League, Boston, Mass. He was graduated from Cornell University in 1873; later studied law and was admitted to the bar in Boston. In 1892 he was appointed lecturer on law at Boston University. From 1897 to 1900 he was professor of history and political science at the Kansas Agricultural College, and in 1900 became professor of political science at Ruskin College, Trenton, Mo. He has also been dean of the university extension department there, and has lectured for the University Extension Association of Chicago. In 1901-2 Professor Parsons was an expert witness before the United States Industrial Commission on the public ownership of railroads, telephones and telegraph. Professor Parsons has made a special study of railway systems and co-operative institutions throughout Europe and America. His publications include: "The World's Best Books," "Our Country's Need," "The Drift of Our Time," "Rational Money," "The New Political Economy," "The Power of the Ideal," "The City for the People," "Direct Legislation," "The Bondage of Cities," "The Story of New Zealand," etc. He is an earnest advocate of the public ownership of monopolies.

ALBERT E. WINCHESTER is general superintendent of the electric works of the city of South Norwalk, Conn.

EDWARD WEBSTER BEMIS, superintendent of the Cleveland, O., waterworks, graduated from Amherst College in 1880; was a pioneer lecturer in the University Extension System, 1887-8; professor of economics and history, Vanderbilt University, 1889-92; associate professor of economics, University of Chicago, 1892-5, and statistician of the Illinois Bureau of Labor Statistics. In 1897 he became professor of economic science in the Kansas State Agricultural College and later director of the department of municipal monopolies of the Bureau of Economic Research, New York. His published works comprise: "History of Co-operation in the United States," "Municipal Ownership of Gas Works in the United States," "Municipal Monopolies," "Local Government for the South and Southwest," and numerous papers and articles on municipal government, monopolies, etc.

JOHN HENRY GRAY has been professor of political and social science in Northwestern University since 1892. He was educated in the public schools at the Illinois State Normal University, was graduated from Harvard University in 1887 and in 1892 received the degree of Ph.D. from Halle University, Germany. Studied also at Paris, Vienna and Berlin. Professor Gray was instructor in political economy at Harvard in 1887-9; chairman of the World Congress Auxiliary on political science in connection with the Columbian Exposition, Chicago, 1893; chairman of the Municipal Commission of the Civic Federation of Chicago, 1894-6; vice-president of the American Economic Association; expert agent of the United States Department of Labor, 1902-3, to investigate restrictions of output in Great Britain; in 1902 represented United States Commissioner of Labor at International Co-operative Congress, Manchester, England, the United States at International Congress on insurance of laboring men, Vusseldorf, Germany, and at International Congress of Commerce and Industry, Ostend, Belgium. Professor Gray is the author of many papers in economic publications, especially in reference to gas supplies.

EDWARD A. MOFFETT, secretary to the Commission on Public Ownership and Operation, has been identified with the labor movement in the United States through membership in the Bricklayers' and Masons' Union of America, and for a number of years has been editor of the union's official journal, the *Bricklayer and Mason*. He was one of the two experts in welfare work furnished to the Isthmian Canal Commission by the Welfare Department of The National Civic Federation to investigate the needs and opportunities on the Isthmus of Panama, and to make recommendations for the recreation of the workers engaged in canal construction, as well as to arrange to have carried into effect the plans adopted.

THE GENERAL FEDERATION OF WOMEN'S CLUBS.

SIGNIFICANCE OF ITS RECENT CONVENTION AND IMPORTANCE OF THE PROBLEMS UPON WHICH ACTION WAS TAKEN.

By Helen Varick Boswell.

THE General Federation of Women's Clubs recently in convention at St. Paul is a strong organization. It holds in its membership women belonging to every profession and calling; it represents the brains and the hearts of America's womanhood. The Secretary of the Federation in her report very pertinently asked: "Is there anything in reason that 800,000 earnest and persistent women could not accomplish in the United States, if they set about it with determination?"

It is precisely because they are beginning to unify and use concerted action upon certain measures that the public is taking notice of so mighty a force, that public men have to reckon with it, and that legislators are waking up to the fact that they want this power with them and not against them. It is very obvious that many Senators and Congressmen are keeping tab on what the Federation women are doing. The President of the United States sent the Convention a telegram relative to one of its pet measures—the preservation of Niagara Falls—in which he says: "I cordially agree with your hope for the immediate passage of the bill, and trust that the clubs will do all in their power to secure favorable action thereon by Congress."

The Convention took action, vigorous and immediate action, on the Pure Food Bill, telegraphing many Senators and Congressmen, of whom the members were constituents, that the Convention desired the votes of their representatives in favor of the bill. Many telegrams in reply were received, pledging the votes of those same representatives. It is doubtless a matter of much gratification to the women that several of the measures so strenuously advocated by them have become law. Other measures, which hold over until next session because of stress of business in the closing hours of Congress, will be pushed vigorously by the clubs belonging to the General Federation, which proposes to neither slumber nor sleep until every effort has been made to accomplish what it has pledged itself to do.

In addition to the stand on legislative matters already mentioned, the Convention put itself on record as favoring the eight-hour day for women workers, and pledged its efforts to obtain State laws to that end, as well as to work for Civil Service Reform.

The General Federation stands for much that is good. It is naturally a force in moulding public opinion, and has strong influence in crystallizing that public opinion into legislative action. There are times when perhaps, in the language of the politician, it may be "viewed with alarm" as well as "pointed at with pride" because now and then the conservative element does not bestir itself enough and the very radical element, always ready to be incendiary when occasion offers, gets too strong a hold.

The recent Convention, however, showed that the conservatives are really the large majority, for some rather lurid utterances made by certain members during

SARAH S. PLATT DECKER,
President of The Federation of Women's Clubs.

the conferences on industrial questions were not received with favor, but frowned upon, and the women wanted facts, not imaginative instances.

The Convention compared favorably with any great convention of political parties, and about as much politics is played—in a feminine way of course, and perhaps depending as much on plain common sense and feminine intuition as on parliamentary law, though many of the officers and members are well known parliamentarians—but as one little woman said, "parliamentary law is only the application of the excellent common sense of certain men—let women apply theirs in their own convention."

There can be no gathering of such a large number of delegates without some differences of views on certain questions. Such differences arose, but were so well handled as scarcely to cause a ripple in the Convention proper. The fine work was all done outside.

The thing that stirred the delegates above all else was the question of woman suffrage—should or should it not be allowed to come before the Convention? Several weeks prior to the meeting the industrial advisory committee had sent out to the various clubs a copy of resolutions the adoption of which would practically commit the General Federation to the cause of women's suffrage, a question which the president, Mrs. Decker, has personally pledged herself not to allow presented to the Convention.

Although Colorado (Mrs. Decker's State) is a suffrage State and her State constituency is altogether in favor of woman suffrage, it is a tribute of loyalty to Mrs. Decker and to the Federation that the Colorado women stood just as firm for the prevention of a suffrage discussion upon the floor as did the women of New York and other Eastern and Southern States. All felt that it would hurt Mrs. Decker and might disrupt the harmony of the Federation, and in spite of some misguided efforts on the part of too zealous suffragists, the matter was so well handled that it never had a chance on the Convention floor. Mrs. Decker was unanimously renominated and re-elected, and no woman ever continued in office who held more completely the organization in her hand. Two years of her rule had but whetted the appetite of her great constituency for more.

No woman could hail from Colorado and not have the political instinct, and Mrs. Decker is a true daughter of her State. Her political insight is keen and discriminating. She knows public questions; she knows the relation which her organization can and should sustain to those questions, and is watchful lest it should take an untenable position, led on perhaps by an excess of zeal for the public good which sometimes destroys more than it creates. It is Mrs. Decker's desire that unity and harmony shall prevail in the General Federation of Women's Clubs—the greatest organization of women's interests in the world.

THE IMMIGRATION DEPARTMENT ORGANIZED FOR WORK.

PROMINENT REPRESENTATIVES FROM ALL CLASSES AND SECTIONS ACCEPT MEMBERSHIP ON ITS COMMITTEES.

WHEN the National Conference on Immigration called by The National Civic Federation met in New York City last December, it was the first time in the history of the country that general attention was concentrated upon the problem of immigration. Since then the subject has been brought nearer to the people in innumerable discussions on lecture platforms, in the press and before Congress, so that to-day its growing importance to the welfare of the nation is being pressed home to the citizen. For in this development of various phases of the subject the nation is beginning to realize the meaning and true significance of the immigration problem.

Some idea as to the magnitude of this problem was presented at the National Conference on Immigration by the various speakers. It is reflected in the scope and extent of the subjects there discussed. So numerous were these subjects that it is possible here to indicate only a few of them. They include the character of immigration, assimilation of the immigrant into American national life, the necessity for further restriction, the administration of immigration laws, the distribution of aliens, the demand for immigrants, the effect of immigration upon our industrial, political and broad social life; the part played by the steamship companies, the causes of European immigration, European inspection and examination, proportion of immigrants which become criminal, insane and charitable dependents; effects of immigration upon the native birth-rate, naturalization, the selection of immigrants, Asiatic immigration, etc., etc. This enumeration but faintly indicates the far-reaching ramifications of the innumerable phases of the immigration problem, but at the same time it helps to emphasize the reasons which induced the five hundred delegates in attendance upon the National Conference on Immigration to recommend to The National Civic Federation the formation of a Department of Immigration.

It is in carrying out the formally expressed request of the National Conference, which represented all the States and numerous diversified organizations, that the Federation has established such a department. Its purpose is to undertake a thorough and painstaking investigation of the facts in regard to immigration to the United States. Those who have identified themselves with this very important work as members of the department comprise men prominent in the various walks of life in all States and sections of the country.

The meeting for the organization of the Department was held at the Park Avenue Hotel, New York City, on Friday morning, June 29, and was attended by some fifty members from all parts of the country. Mr. Ralph M. Easley, Chairman of the Executive Council of The National Civic Federation, called the meeting to order and expressed its objects, which were to pass upon the report of the Sub-Committee on Plan and Scope, and to select the officers and committees. Ex-Congressman John DeWitt Warner, of New York, presided and Rev. Dr. Joel S. Ives, of Hartford, Conn., acted as Secretary.

Dr. Leander T. Chamberlain, of New York, as Chairman of the Sub-Committee on Plan and Scope, presented the report of that body. A preliminary report had previously been communicated by mail to all the members of the Department, and some of the suggestions which had come from them were embodied in the Committee's report at the meeting. In presenting the report of this Committee, Dr. Chamberlain reviewed briefly the order of events preceding the meeting of June 29, stating that the Chairman of the Executive Council of The National Civic Federation, acting under instructions of the Federation, had called an informal meeting of the members of the Immigration Department living in the vicinity of New York City for May 4 at the Park Avenue Hotel. Thirty-two members were present, and a sub-committee was appointed to put into proper form certain suggestions concerning the different subjects to be considered by the Department. On May 24 the results of the Committee's work were communicated to all the members of the Department. It was also recommended that the Department meet in New York on some date between June 15 and July 1, and all members were requested to express their views with regard to the recommendations of the Committee. Not far from seventy letters were received in reply. The subjects for the various committees recommended by the sub-committee were cordially approved in these letters, and the date most favored for the general meeting of the department was found to be June 29. Accordingly on June 14 the Chairman of the Executive Council called a meeting for June 29 at 10:30 a. m., at the Park Avenue Hotel. On June 20 the sub-committee sent out its second circular letter reminding all members of the importance of the action to be taken at the meeting of June 29, and soliciting suggestions from those unable to attend, especially suggestions as to the committee on which any

FRANKLIN MacVEAGH, Chairman

member would prefer to serve. To this letter not far from fifty replies were received and the suggestions therein were carefully noted and tabulated.

Dr. Chamberlain next read the concrete results of the sub-committee's labors. The committees provided for in the report are as follows:

Committee on Basal Statistics of Immigration.—While no hard and fast limits can be prescribed for the province of this Committee, it is desired that its verified and rightly tabulated statements shall certainly include those statistical facts which are most important in themselves and most significant as basis of inference. If this Committee succeeds in doing its main work promptly, it may be able to supply to other Committees such information as will greatly aid them.

Committee on the Facts of Supply and Demand.—It is suggested that this Committee set itself primarily to showing the actual relation of immigration to the country's needs, not only as to quantity and quality of supply, but also as to localities to be supplied. Its province will include the facts concerning the sources of immigration, and the distribution of the immigrants. The investigation may well embrace both the past and the present.

Committee on Legislation and Its Enforcement.—As in the case of the Committee on immigration statistics, and on supply and demand, the Committee on Legislation and Its Enforcement will aim to ascertain and present indisputable facts. While expressions of opinion in the form of conclusions are not debarred, the great desideratum is verified, comparable facts. What further is needed in the way of legislation and administrative methods can best be inferred from such premises.

Committee on Naturalization.—The province of this committee includes the history of naturalization in the United States, the legislation which has been passed by the Congress and by the several States and the actual results which have ensued, together with an investigation of the evasions and abuses which have prevented results far more favorable.

Committee on Agencies for Advancing the Welfare of Immigrants.—The primary aim of this Committee also will be statistical—the enumeration and description of all such ameliorating agencies, with the outline of what they have accomplished, are now accomplishing, or are failing to accomplish. Here, too, the exact facts will furnish the best basis for an understanding of what remains to be done. It will be competent for the Committee to investigate agencies which profess to be for the welfare of immigrants, but in reality are shameful frauds.

The International Relations of Immigration.—This Committee will consider whatever action has been taken by other countries with reference to the emigration of their people, and will also consider whether there may not be such international agreements between this and other countries as shall promote the best interests of both the nations affected.

Committee on Oriental Immigration.—On no subject is there more need of verified statistics and authentic facts. This Committee will naturally have to deal with the history of Oriental immigration leading up to the Chinese Exclusion Act, and the effects of the same.

Committee on Finance.—Although the labor of the various Committees is gratuitous, there will still be considerable expense connected with the gathering and publication of the desired information. An adequate fund should be provided.

The officers elected by the Department are as follows:

Chairman, FRANKLIN MacVEAGH of Chicago.

Vice-Chairmen, Dr. LEANDER T. CHAMBERLAIN of New York, President of the Evangelical Alliance of the United States.

N. J. BACHELDER of Concord, N. H., Master of the National Grange.

DANIEL J. KEEFE of Detroit, President of the Longshoremen, Marine and Transportworkers' Association.

THOMAS F. PARKER of Greenville, S. C., President of the Southern Immigration Society.

THEODORE B. WILCOX of Portland, Oregon, former President of the Trans-Mississippi Congress.

L. BRADFORD PRINCE, of Santa Fe, N. M., President of the Historical Society of New Mexico.

Secretary, Dr. FRANK JULIAN WARNE of Philadelphia.

Treasurer, ISAAC N. SELIGMAN of New York.

It was also provided that there should be a State Vice-Chairman from every State, Territory, and the District of Columbia, to be selected by the Executive Committee. This Executive Committee consists of the following members:

Executive Committee.

JOHN H. HOLLIDAY, President Union Trust Company, Indianapolis.

JAMES B. ANGELL, LL.D., President University of Michigan, Ann Arbor.

CHARLES RIDGELY, Vice-President Ridgely National Bank, Springfield, Ill.

Dr. ALBERT SHAW, Editor *Review of Reviews*, New York.

SAMUEL GOMPERS, President American Federation of Labor, Washington, D. C.

JOHN M. STAHL, President Farmers' National Congress, Chicago.

SAMUEL MATHER, of Pickands, Mather and Company, Cleveland.

R. A. MITCHELL, Agent of the Dwight Manufacturing Company, Alabama City, Ala.

G. GUNBY JORDAN, President Eagle and Phenix Mills, Columbus, Ga.

Prof. HENRY C. ADAMS, University of Michigan, Ann Arbor, Mich.

JAMES R. MacCOLL, Lorraine Manufacturing Company of Pawtucket, R. I.

Rev. JOEL S. IVES, Secretary Missionary Society of Connecticut, Hartford.

JOHN DeWITT WARNER, Attorney, New York City.

TERRENCE V. POWDERLY, ex-Commissioner of Immigration, Washington, D. C.

HON. JESSE TAYLOR, Jr., Member National Council of the Junior Order United American Mechanics, Jamestown, O.

C. T. PLUNKETT, Secretary Berkshire Cotton Manufacturing Company, Adams, Mass.

Hon. JOHN W. NOBLE, ex-Secretary of the Interior, St. Louis.

Hon. CHARLES A. SCHIEREN, ex-Mayor of Brooklyn.

WARREN S. STONE, Grand Chief Brotherhood of Locomotive Engineers, Cleveland.

THEODORE MARBURG, Baltimore.

JAMES BRONSON REYNOLDS, Washington.

P. H. MORRISSEY, Grand Master Brotherhood Railroad Trainmen, Cleveland.

Prof. J. W. JENKS, Department of Political Economy Cornell University, Ithaca, N. Y.

F. D. COBURN, Secretary of Agriculture, Topeka, Kansas.

NATHAN BIJUR, Attorney, New York City.

JAMES O'CONNELL, President International Association of Machinists, Washington, D. C.

PRESCOTT F. HALL, Attorney, Boston.

JOHN HENRY SMITH, Utah.

SAMUEL SPENCER, President Southern Railway Company, New York.

Rev. THOMAS R. SLICER, Pastor All Souls' Church, New York City.

J. G. SCHONFARBER, Assistant Maryland Bureau of Statistics, Baltimore.

Rev. ADOLPH ROEDER, Orange, N. J.

S. A. HUGHES, General Immigration Agent St. Louis and San Francisco Railroad, St. Louis.

Z. P. SMITH, Editor *The American*, Raleigh, N. C.

JOHN WILLIS BAER, President Occidental College, Los Angeles, Cal.

Dr. A. J. BROWN, Secretary Presbyterian Board Foreign Missions, New York.

JOHN F. TOBIN, General President Boot and Shoe Workers' Union, Boston, Mass.

JOSEPH E. FLETCHER, President and General Manager Coronet Worsted Company, Mapleville, R. I.

H. W. FAIRBANKS, Secretary and Treasurer Sherman Cotton Mills, Dallas, Texas.

HUGH F. FOX, *New Jersey Review of Charities and Corrections*, Plainfield, N. J.

D. G. AMBLER, Jacksonville, Fla.

JAMES W. KINNEAR, Attorney, Pittsburg, Pa.

GEORGE L. SEHON, Superintendent Kentucky State Children's Home, Louisville, Ky.

J. W. SULLIVAN, Editor *Clothing Trades' Bulletin*, New York City.

L. BRADFORD PRINCE, ex-Governor of New Mexico, Santa Fé, N. M.

JOHN MITCHELL, President United Mine Workers of America, Indianapolis.

THEODORE B. WILCOX, President Portland Flouring Mills, Portland, Oregon.

JOSHUA STRANGE, President State Farmers' Congress of Indiana, Marion, Ind.

THEODORS AHRENS, Capitalist, Louisville, Ky.

Judge NORMAN J. KITRELL, Houston, Texas.

The membership of the various committees, as reported by the Committee on Nominations and accepted by the meeting, follows:

Committee on Basal Statistics.

Dr. WALTER F. WILLCOX, Department of Political Economy and Statistics, Cornell University, Ithaca, N. Y.
Hon. ROBERT WATCHORN, Commissioner of Immigration, Ellis Island, N. Y.
NATHAN BIJUR, Attorney, New York.
Dr. LEANDER T. CHAMBERLAIN, President of the Evangelical Alliance of the United States, New York.
FRED W. ATKINSON, Ph.D., President Polytechnic Institute, Brooklyn.
Dr. EDWARD DWIGHT EATON, ex-President Beloit College, St. Johnsbury, Vt.
Prof. HENRY W. FARNAM, Yale University, New Haven, Conn.
JAMES J. STORROW, Boston.
Prof. GEORGE GRAFTON WILSON, Brown University, Providence, R. I.
Dr. J. H. HOLLANDER, Department Political Economy, Johns Hopkins University, Baltimore.
ANTHONY HIGGINS, Attorney, Wilmington, Del.
Rev. JOEL S. IVES, Secretary Missionary Society of Connecticut, Hartford, Conn.
J. W. SULLIVAN, Editor *Clothing Trades' Bulletin*, New York City.
Hon. CHARLES A. SCHIEREN, New York.
Dr. ALBERT SHAW, Editor *Review of Reviews*, New York.
JAMES SPEYER, Banker, New York.
P. H. MORRISSEY, Grand Master Brotherhood Railroad Trainmen, Cleveland, Ohio.
Prof. EDWARD A. STEINER, Iowa College, Grinnell, Iowa.
HORACE WHITE, First Vice-President American Economic Association, New York.
CHARLES F. PIDGIN, Chief Bureau of Statistics of Labor, Boston.
CYRUS L. SULZBERGER, New York.
KENYON L. BUTTERFIELD, President Rhode Island College of Agriculture and Mechanic Arts, Kingston, R. I.
F. L. MAXWELL, Mound, La.
Dr. WATSON L. PHILLIPS, Clergyman, New Haven, Conn.

Committee on Supply and Demand.

Hon. CHARLES S. HAMLIN, Attorney, Boston.
Hon. EDWIN R. GERBER, Mayor, Reading, Pa.
ELIOT NORTON, Attorney, New York.
W. F. MASSEY, Editor *The Practical Farmer*, Philadelphia.
MAX MITCHELL, Superintendent Federation of Jewish Charities, Boston.

Dr. LEANDER T. CHAMBERLAIN, First Vice-Chairman

ALEXANDER E. CASE, Attorney, Marion, Kansas.
T. K. BRUNER, Secretary North Carolina Department of Agriculture, Raleigh, N. C.
THOMAS F. PARKER, President Southern Immigration Society, Greenville, S. C.
WILLIAM D. MAHON, President Amalgamated Association of Street Railway Employes of America, Detroit, Mich.
FERDINAND STRAUSS, President Leopold Morse Company, Boston.
THOMAS W. SLOCUM, New York.
S. A. HUGHES, General Immigration Agent of the St. Louis and San Francisco Railroad Company, St. Louis.
B. A. LARGER, General Secretary United Garment Workers of America, New York City.
SAMUEL SPENCER, President Southern Railway, New York.
J. G. SCHONFARBER, Bureau of Statistics and Information, Baltimore.
WARREN S. STONE, Grand Chief Brotherhood of Locomotive Engineers, Cleveland.
JOHN M. STAHL, President Farmers' National Congress, Chicago.
JOSHUA STRANGE, President State Farmers' Congress of Indiana, Marion, Ind.
N. J. BACHELDER, Master of the National Grange, Concord, N. H.
J. W. SULLIVAN, Editor *Clothing Trades' Bulletin*, New York City.
F. D. COBURN, Topeka, Kansas.
WILL B. POWELL, Shadeland, Pa.
Hon. WILEY TINDOLPH, Minneapolis.
JAMES J. HILL, President Great Northern Railway, St. Paul, Minn.
JOHN MITCHELL, President United Mine Workers of America, Indianapolis.
Hon. E. J. WATSON, Commissioner Department of Agriculture and Immigration of South Carolina, New York.
T. V. POWDERLY, Washington.

Legislation and Its Enforcement.

Prof. J. W. JENKS, Department of Political Economy, Cornell University, Ithaca, N. Y.
Prof. H. A. GARFIELD, Princeton University, Princeton, N. J.
PRESCOTT F. HALL, Attorney, Boston.
Hon. JESSE TAYLOR, National Council Junior Order United American Mechanics, Washington.
Rev. ADOLPH ROEDER, New Jersey State Civic Federation, Orange, N. J.

DANIEL J. KEEFE, Third Vice-Chairman

THEODORE MARBURG, Baltimore.
Hon. JOHN DEWITT WARNER, Attorney, New York.
SAMUEL GOMPERS, President American Federation of Labor, Washington.
Prof. HENRY C. EMERY, Department of Political Economy, Yale University, New Haven, Conn.
H. W. FAIRBANKS, Secretary and Treasurer Sherman Cotton Mills, Dallas, Texas.
JOSEPH LEE, Boston.
SAMUEL D. JONES, President Chamber of Commerce, Atlanta, Ga.
WILLIAM HUBER, President United Brotherhood of Carpenters and Joiners of America, Indianapolis, Ind.
G. GUNBY JORDAN, President Eagle and Phenix Mills, Columbus, Ga.
MAHLON N. KLINE, President Trades League of Philadelphia.
PARK MITCHELL, State Federation of Labor, Manchester, N. H.
MARCUS M. MARKS, New York.
Dr. ALBERT SHAW, Editor *Review of Reviews*, New York.
HENRY WALLACE, Editor *Wallace's Farmer*, Des Moines, Iowa.
WILLIAM B. WEEDEN, Providence, R. I.
S. W. MEEK, The *Times-Dispatch*, Richmond, Va.
JOSEPH F. VALENTINE, President Iron Molders' Union of North America, Cincinnati.
Prof. JOHN H. MACCRACKEN, New York University, New York.

Committee on Naturalization.

JOHN H. HOLLIDAY, President Union Trust Company, Indianapolis.
Hon. JOHN FITZGERALD, Mayor, Boston.
Rev. ADOLPH ROEDER, New Jersey State Civic Federation, Orange, N. J.
JEFFREY R. BRACKETT, Director School for Social Workers, Boston.
JAMES W. KINNEAR, Attorney, Pittsburg.
Hon. ALEXANDER T. CONNELL, Mayor, Scranton, Pa.
Hon. JOHN E. FROST, Topeka, Kansas.
J. J. HANNAHAN, Grand Master Brotherhood of Locomotive Firemen, Peoria, Ill.
Hon. EDWIN R. GERBER, Mayor, Reading, Pa.
ANTHONY HIGGINS, Attorney, Wilmington, Del.
JAMES P. HOLLAND, Secretary Stationary Firemen, New York.
Z. P. SMITH, Editor *The American*, Raleigh, N. C.
HAMILTON HOLT, Editor *The Independent*, New York.
JAMES O'CONNELL, President International Association of Machinists, Washington.
Hon. L. BRADFORD PRINCE, President The Historical Society of New Mexico, Santa Fé, N. M.
FREDERICK B. SMITH, President Wolverine Manufacturing Company, Detroit.
JOHN F. SMULSKI, City Attorney, Chicago.
Hon. W. D. WASHBURN, Jr., Minneapolis, Minn.
W. L. MOYER, President Mechanics' and Traders' Bank.
W. O. FAYERWEATHER, Paterson, N. J.
L. LAMBERSON, President The Pioneer Loan and Land Company, Warren, Minn.
ADOLPH LANKERING, Hoboken, N. J.

Agencies for Advancing the Welfare of Immigrants.

ELIOT NORTON, Attorney, New York.
JAMES P. ARCHIBALD, New York.
HUGH F. FOX, Member Executive Committee *New Jersey Review of Charities and Corrections*, Plainfield, N. J.
JAMES H. HAMILTON, University Settlement, New York.
RICHARD WATSON GILDER, Editor *Century Magazine*, New York.
Rev. A. P. DOYLE, Boston.
MAX MITCHELL, Superintendent Federation of Jewish Charities, Boston.
GIUSEPPE A. RANDEGGER, New York.
GEORGE L. SEHON, State Superintendent Kentucky Children's Home Society, Louisville, Ky.
Dr. THOMAS R. SLICER, New York.
TIMOTHY HEALY, President International Brotherhood of Stationary Firemen, New York.
DAVID ROBINSON, Editor and Publisher *Southern Investor*, New York.
ROBERT C. OGDEN, New York.
THOMAS W. SLOCUM, New York.
Dr. L. K. FRANKEL, Secretary United Hebrew Charities, New York.
Prof. GEORGE GRAFTON WILSON, Brown University, Providence, R. I.
ANTONI SCHREIBER, Censor of the Polish National Alliance of the United States of North America, Buffalo.
WILLIAM J. BOWEN, President Bricklayers' and Masons' International Union, Indianapolis.
THOMAS M. MULRY, New York.
Prof. T. W. WILLIAMS, Department of History Yale University, New Haven, Conn.
J. W. SULLIVAN, Editor *Weekly Bulletin of the Clothing Trades*, New York.

Committee on International Relations.

Dr. HENRY LEFAVOUR, President Simons College, Boston.
EDGAR A. BANCROFT, Attorney, Chicago.
AUSTEN G. FOX, New York.
E. E. CLARK, Grand Chief Conductor Order of Railway Conductors, Cedar Rapids, Iowa.
OLCOTT B. COLTON, Treasurer The Smith-Worthington Company, Hartford, Conn.
N. B. KELLY, Secretary Trades League, Philadelphia.
DENIS A. HAYES, President Glass Bottle Blowers' Association of the United States and Canada, Philadelphia.
Hon. JOHN M. MITCHELL, Attorney, Concord, N. H.
P. H. MORRISSEY, Grand Master Brotherhood Railroad Trainmen, Cleveland.
Dr. JOSEPH H. SENNER, President The Food Trade Publishing Company, New York.
J. J. SULLIVAN, President Central National Bank, Chamber of Commerce, Cleveland.
ROSS C. SMITH, Commissioner Immigration and Industrial Association of Alabama, Birmingham, Ala.
Dr. WALTER F. WILLCOX, Department of Political Economy and Statistics, Cornell University, Ithaca, N. Y.
Dr. WILLIAM J. TUCKER, President Dartmouth College, Hanover, N. H.
Hon. SIMON WOLF, Washington.

Committee on Oriental Immigration.

JAMES BRONSON REYNOLDS, Washington.
JOHN BANCROFT DEVINS, Editor *New York Observer*.

Dr. FRANK JULIAN WARNE, Secretary

Hon. WILLIAM A. CLARK, United States Senate, Washington.
Prof. J. W. JENKS, Department of Political Economy of Cornell University, Ithaca, N. Y.
JOHN B. LENNON, President Journeymen Tailors' Union of America, Bloomington, Ill.
Dr. A. J. BROWN, Secretary Presbyterian Board Foreign Missions, New York.
HARVIE JORDAN, President Southern Cotton Association, Atlanta.
DENIS A. HAYES, President Glass Bottle Blowers' Association of United States and Canada, Philadelphia.
JAMES R. MACCOLL, Lorraine Manufacturing Company, Pawtucket, R. I.
THEODORE B. WILCOX, The Portland Flouring Mills Company, Portland, Oregon.
R. A. MITCHELL, Dwight Manufacturing Company, Alabama City, Ala.
AVERY C. MOORE, Editor *Weiser World*, Weiser, Idaho.
JAMES B. ANGELL, LL.D., President University of Michigan, Ann Arbor, Mich.
JOHN WILLIS BAER, President Occidental College, Los Angeles, Cal.
Hon. CHARLES DENBY, Chief Clerk Department of State, Washington.
Dr. W. P. WILSON, Director The Philadelphia Museums.
D. G. AMBLER, Jacksonville Board of Trade, Jacksonville.
Hon. CHARLES S. HAMLIN, Attorney, Boston.
DAVID STARR JORDAN, President Leland Stanford Junior University, Stanford University, California.
JOHN W. T. NICHOLS, Minot, Hooper and Company, New York.
O. R. YOUNG, Editor *International Steam Engineer*, New York.

OFFICERS CHOSEN FOR THE INDUSTRIAL ECONOMICS' DEPARTMENT.

NICHOLAS MURRAY BUTLER AT ITS HEAD—LEADERS OF THOUGHT AND ACTION ARE MEMBERS OF THE EXECUTIVE COMMITTEE.

PRESIDENT BUTLER of Columbia University has been chosen by the Executive Council of The National Civic Federation to head the Department of Industrial Economics. Mr. D. L. Cease, Editor of the *Railroad Trainmen's Journal*, is its Secretary. In addition to these officers there is a general executive committee consisting of leading representatives of the large universities, of the bar, the church, capital, labor, the general public and well-known editors of the daily press and of the principal monthly periodicals and reviews. This executive committee consists of the following:

LAWRENCE F. ABBOTT, *The Outlook*, New York City.
C. L. BAINE, Editor *Shoe Workers' Journal*, Boston.
SAMUEL BOWLES, Springfield *Republican*, Springfield, Mass.
LOUIS D. BRANDEIS, Boston.
Rev. J. M. BUCKLEY, Editor *The Christian Advocate*, New York City.
J. A. CABLE, Editor Coopers' *International Journal*, Kansas City, Kans.
HOMAR D. CALL, Secretary and Treasurer Amalgamated Meat Cutters, Syracuse, N. Y.
E. E. CLARK, Editor *Railroad Conductor*, Cedar Rapids, Iowa.
Prof. JOHN R. COMMONS, Department of Political Economy, Wisconsin University, Madison, Wis.
CHARLES A. CONANT, Treasurer Morton Trust Co., New York City.
JOHN BANCROFT DEVINS, Editor New York *Observer*, New York City.
OTTO M. EIDLITZ, Chairman Board of Governors Building Trades Employers' Association, New York City.
Dr. CHARLES W. ELIOT, President Harvard University, Cambridge, Mass.
AMOS K. FISKE, *New York Journal of Commerce*, New York City.
JOHN C. FREUND, Editor *The Music Trades*, New York City.
JOHN P. FREY, Editor *Iron Molders' Journal*, Cincinnati.
RICHARD WATSON GILDER, Editor *The Century*, New York City.
CHARLES S. GLEED, Attorney, Topeka, Kans.
SAMUEL GOMPERS, American *Federationist*, Washington, D. C.
JOHN E. GREEN, Editor *Bradstreet's Journal*, New York City.
GEORGE HARVEY, Editor *North American Review*, New York City.
CLARK HOWELL, Editor Atlanta *Constitution*, Atlanta, Ga.
Most Rev. JOHN IRELAND, St. Paul, Minn.
Prof. J. W. JENKS, Professor Political Economy, Cornell University, Ithaca, N. Y.
FREDERICK N. JUDSON, St. Louis.
D. J. KEEFE, President International Longshoremen's Association, Detroit.
CHARLES W. KNAPP, St. Louis *Republic*, St. Louis.
JOHN B. LENNON, Editor *The Tailor*, Bloomington, Ill.
GEORGE C. LORIMER, Editor *Saturday Evening Post*, Philadelphia.
ST. CLAIR McKELWAY, Editor *Brooklyn Daily Eagle*.
V. EVERIT MACY, Capitalist, New York City.
WILLIAM D. MAHON, President Amalgamated Association of Street Railway Employes of America, Detroit, Mich.
BRADFORD MERRILL, Editorial Staff New York *World*.
JOHN MITCHELL, President United Mine Workers of America, Indianapolis.
C. R. MILLER, Editor New York *Times*.
EUGENE A. PHILBIN, Attorney, New York City.
ROLAND PHILLIPS, New York City.
Rt. Rev. HENRY C. POTTER, New York City.
SERENO S. PRATT, Editor *Wall Street Journal*, New York City.
EDWARD ROSEWATER, Editor *The Bee*, Omaha, Neb.
S. M. SEXTON, Editor *United Mine Workers' Journal*, Indianapolis.
Dr. ALBERT SHAW, Editor *Review of Reviews*, New York City.
JAMES SPEYER, New York City.
Prof. F. W. TAUSSIG, Department Political Economy, Harvard University, Cambridge, Mass.
BENJAMIN IDE WHEELER, President University of California.
TALCOTT WILLIAMS, Philadelphia *Press*.
CARROLL D. WRIGHT, President Clark College, Worcester, Mass.
O. R. YOUNG, Editor *International Steam Engineer*, New York City.

The program and scope of the work for the Department is to be outlined by a sub-committee consisting of Nicholas Murray Butler as Chairman; D. L. Cease as Secretary; Dr. Albert Shaw, James Speyer, Eugene A. Philbin, Dr. J. M. Buckley, Talcott Williams, Prof. Henry W. Farnam, S. M. Sexton, S. S. Pratt, V. Everit Macy, John Greene, and J. W. Sullivan.

The breadth of view and impartiality with which the Department is to approach its investigation of the broad field before it is reflected in the notable address delivered by President Butler, the head of the new Department, at the recent commencement exercises of Columbia University. President Butler said:

"A spirit of unrest is abroad, not only in our own land, but in other lands as well. So far as this unrest has an intellectual foundation, it appears to be the conviction that the eighteenth century formulas and axioms upon which our social and political fabric is so largely built do not work as they were expected to work. So far as this unrest has an economic foundation, it appears to be dissatisfaction with actual and possible rewards for industry. So far as it has a political foundation, it appears to be a perception of easily demonstrated inequalities of power and influence and of an equally easily demonstrated inequality of benefits from Governmental policies.

NICHOLAS MURRAY BUTLER, Chairman

"That this unrest has been and is being used by ambitious men for their own selfish ends and for gain by journalistic builders of emotional-bonfires is certainly true; but it will not do to dismiss this spirit of unrest with a sneer on that account.

"It has passed far beyond the bounds of the dreamers and visionaries, the violent-minded and the naturally destructive. Men accustomed to honest reflections and themselves possessed of property, always the sheet anchor of conservatism, have come under its influence. Policies that not long ago were dismissed as too extreme for serious discussion are now soberly examined with reference to their immediate practicability. What has brought about this change?

D. L. CEASE, Secretary

"An answer is not far to seek. An increasing number of men have come to distrust the capacity of society as now organized to protect itself against the freebooters who exist in it. An increasing number of men believe and assert that law and justice are powerless before greed and cunning, and they are the more ready to listen to advocacy of any measure or policy, however novel or revolutionary, that promises relief. Their imaginations, too, cannot help being affected by the appalling sight, so often called to our attention of late, of that moral morgue wherein are exposed the shriveled souls and ruined reputations of those who have lost in the never-ending struggle between selfishness and service that goes on in the human breast.

"The first duty of the trained and educated mind when it faces conditions such as these and must take a definite and responsible attitude toward them, is not to lose its balance, its poise, its self-control. It is worth while to look back at the majestic figure of Lincoln, crowned now with immortality's laurel, tranquil amid far angrier seas than ours.

"Not much is to be gained by passionate denunciation of principles and men, if there is no clear perception of where the difficulty lies and of what it is that is to be remedied. A first step, then, is an analysis of the conditions complained of and their genesis. I lay particular emphasis upon their genesis, for most rebuilders of society are singularly neglectful of history. Their lip service of evolution does not often carry them to the point of considering our present institutions—social, economic, political—as evolved, and, therefore, as having the weight of years of human experience behind them.

"Looking back over a thousand years or more, it is plain that civilized man has traveled far. An examination of his progress will show, I think, that it rests mainly upon three principles, gradually evolved and erected into institutions: Civil and industrial liberty, private property, and the inviolability of contract. Upon these as a cornerstone rests what we know to-day as civilized human society. That our society has its evils, terrible and dangerous, cannot be denied. That greed for gain holds an appalling number of men in its grasp and that the moral tone of large business undertakings is painfully low are only too evident. But it is quite too rash a conclusion to infer that society must be destroyed and its cornerstone displaced before those evils can be remedied. It may be true—and I think it is—that the difficulty is not so much with the tried and tested principles upon which society rests as with the honesty and intelligence with which those principles are worked. The abounding prosperity of our country with its untold opportunities for material success, the loosening of the hold of some of the old religious and ethical sanctions of conduct, and the weakening of parental control and discipline, have united to place upon American character a burden which in too many instances it has not been able to bear."

The same general topic was touched upon in the address delivered by President Butler to the students of Columbia University at the opening of the last college year. He said:

"Just now the American people are receiving some painful lessons in practical ethics. They are having brought home to them with severe emphasis the distinction between character and reputation. A man's true character, it abundantly appears, may be quite in conflict with his reputation, which is the public estimate of him. Of late we have been watching reputations melt away like snow before the sun; and the sun in this case is mere publicity. Men who for years have been trusted implicitly by their fellows and so placed in positions of honor and grave responsibility are seen to be mere reckless speculators with the money of others and petty pilferers of the savings of the poor and needy. With all this shameful story spread before us, it takes some courage to follow Emerson's advice not to bark against the bad, but rather to chant the beauty of the good.

"Put bluntly, the situation which confronts Americans to-day is due to lack of moral principle. New statutes may be needed, but statutes will not put moral principle where it does not exist. The greed for gain and the greed for power have blinded men to the time-old distinction between right and wrong. Both among business men and at the bar are to be found advisors, counted shrewd and successful, who have substituted the penal code for the moral law as the standard of conduct. Right and wrong have given way to the subtler distinction between legal, not-illegal and illegal; or better, perhaps, between honest, law-honest and dishonest. This new triumph of mind over morals is bad enough in itself; but when in addition its exponents secure material gain and professional prosperity, it becomes a menace to our integrity as a people."

It will be the effort of the Department by means of national conferences and through careful and impartial investigations to throw light on some of the important present-day problems—social, political, and industrial—by giving to the public a sane and unbiased statement of actual conditions. It is believed that such a plan, by presenting the opinions and experiences of authorities and experts on all sides of the problems to be considered, will go far to enlighten public opinion and to assist in arriving at a decision based upon the merits of each case rather than upon *ex parte* argument or presentation. A definite program on plan and scope will be announced later.

THE TRADE AGREEMENT IN FIVE GREAT INDUSTRIES.

ITS PRESENT STATUS IN THE COAL FIELDS, ON THE GREAT LAKES, IN THE IRON AND STEEL INDUSTRY, ON STREET RAILWAYS, AND IN THE FALL RIVER COTTON MILLS.

SOME indication of the value of the trade agreement is shown by recent developments in five important industries of the country—in the coal fields, in the iron and steel industry, on street railways, in the various occupations along the Great Lakes, and among employers and employes of the Fall River cotton mills. These recent events would seem to strengthen the belief of students of industrial conditions that the trade agreement is the only practical present-day method for averting industrial wars. It is true, of course, that the trade agreement machinery is by no means perfect, but it is the only rational method which human ingenuity has devised for regulating the relations between employers and employes. While the progress of events may at some future day bring forth something better, the present hope of the nation for working out some kind of harmonious relations between labor and capital must depend upon this trade agreement machinery.

One of the most important events of recent years tending to emphasize the great value of this conference method of settling differences between capital and labor is the outcome of the negotiations between the anthracite mine workers and the hard coal operators following the termination of the award of the Anthracite Coal Strike Commission. This award was made in 1903 after a five months' investigation of the general labor conditions in the three fields and following the memorable strike of 1902. It was to continue for a period of three years and this expired on March 31 last. Several months previous to its expiration the mine workers and operators held several conferences with the object of arranging some mutually satisfactory basis for a continuance of their working relations. No agreement was reached, however, before the expiration of the Commission's award, and, in consequence, the officials of the United Mine Workers of America ordered a temporary suspension of work in the hard coal fields.. This suspension was brought to a close by an agreement entered into in New York City on May 6 between the representatives of employers and employes in the hard coal industry.

JOHN MITCHELL — W. D. MAHON — P. J. McARDLE — JAMES TANSEY

This agreement provides for a continuance until March 31, 1909, of the award of the Anthracite Coal Strike Commission of 1902 and of any action which has since been taken pursuant thereto either by the Board of Conciliation, which the award created, or otherwise. The Board of Conciliation is continued with three operators and three mine workers as members, and with provision for an umpire in case of a disagreement among the members. Work was resumed in the three hard coal fields on Thursday, May 10, after a suspension continuing through forty days.

As to the trade agreement in the soft coal fields, it will be recalled that for several months preceding March 31 two meetings were held of the Interstate Joint Conference of the central competitive territory, including western Pennsylvania, Ohio, Indiana, and Illinois, and that they finally adjourned the latter part of March without employers and employes in this industry being able to enter into a working agreement for the scale year following April 1. Prior to the adjournment of the last session of the convention leading operators of the western Pennsylvania district consented to grant the compromise wage increase demand of the union officials and, in consequence, for the first time since 1898, a separate agreement without the sanction of the Interstate Joint Conference was entered into in that district. Since then officials of the United Mine Workers of America and representatives of the various operators' associations in Ohio, Indiana, and Illinois have been carrying on numerous conferences in each State for the purpose of renewing the district agreement. In all of these States the mine workers have made concessions as to the conditions of employment, and the operators have restored the wage scale of 1903, which latter carries with it an increase of about five and one-half per cent in wages over those paid the past two years. This, in general, is the agreement signed by western Pennsylvania operators, and such provisions have now been adopted in the agreements signed in the other coal producing States excepting parts of Ohio and the central Pennsylvania district, where the suspension at this writing continues. Thus the officials of the United Mine Workers of America have practically brought to a termination the suspension of coal mining inaugurated in twelve of the coal producing States of the country on April 1, including the four States of the central competitive soft coal fields (western Pennsylvania, Ohio, Indiana, and Illinois), and the States in the Southwest territory, which latter comprise Missouri, Kansas, Arkansas, Indian Territory, and Texas. In all the States approximately 200,000 mine workers have been idle the greater part of the time since April 1.

Advocates of the trade agreement method of agreeing upon wages and conditions of employment were very much discouraged when it was finally announced last March that the Interstate Joint Conference of the middle western coal States had failed in its operation for the first time within the past eight years. So determined was the opposition of some of the operators to a renewal of an agreement which carried with it a wage increase that it all along appeared extremely doubtful if a satisfactory restoration of the principle could be effected. Throughout all the subsequent negotiations and uncertainty, however, the diplomacy of President Mitchell of the United Mine Workers has been a potent factor in keeping intact at least the district agreement. Not only has he been confronted with the determined opposition of certain groups of the employing class, but he has had to face internal dissension within his own ranks. That he has succeeded in carrying his organization through what undoubtedly has been a most critical period in its existence, the trade agreement principle, without losing irretrievably is another tribute to his proved able leadership.

This successful outcome of negotiations between the officials of the miners' union and the operators of the different coal producing States in renewing the district agreement may be regarded as a forecast of an early restoration of the Interstate Joint Conference in both the central competitive and the Southwest territory. So valuable has been this joint conference machinery to the uninterrupted prosperity of the coal interests of the country for the past eight years that it is to be hoped it will again become a potent factor in the future relations between employers and employes in this great industry.

President W. D. Mahon, of the Amalgamated Association of Street and Electric Railways of America, is another labor leader who has recently demonstrated the efficiency of the trade agreement in settling issues between employers and employes. During the past several months he has signed for his organization articles of agreement with the Old Colony Street Railway Company, the Boston and Northern Street Railway Company, and the Scranton Railway Company. Each of these agreements provides in substance that the employing company, through its proper officers, shall treat, when occasion therefor may arise, with those of their employes in their collective capacity who may for the time being be members of said association through the properly accredited officers and the committees of said several divisions, and the officers of the Amalgamated Association. The contracts also cover such questions as wages, hours of employment, suspensions, discharges, extra pay for overtime, free transportation for employes, arbitration of differences between officers of the company and its employes, and like general conditions of employment. An interesting clause in the contract of the Old Colony Street Railway Company provides as follows:

> That the company will do nothing to prevent or discharge any employe from becoming or continuing to be a member of said association, and shall in no way discriminate against a member thereof because of such membership; and that said association shall not discriminate against any person in the employ of said company because of his refusal to join said association or to continue a member thereof; but if any member of said association is expelled or suspended from his membership for a violation of any of the provisions of this agreement, the company, being satisfied that said expulsion or suspension was for such reason and was justifiable, shall dismiss said employe from its service.

The agreement with the Old Colony Railway Company is for a period of four years from and after the first day of October, 1906, with provision as to a consideration and revision of the wage schedule at stated intervals. The agreement with the Boston and Northern Street Railway, which began on June 1, 1906, is also for a period of four years.

A significant feature of the agreement between the Amalgamated Association and the Scranton Railway Company is that it has been made to cover a period of ten years, its date of expiration being April, 1916, and "during that time there shall be no strike or lock-out, provided, however, that on the first day of April, 1909, and on the first day of April, 1912, the question of wages and any other grievances which may be in contention shall be taken up for adjustment." The Amalgamated Association has also recently signed agreements with street railway corporations in East St. Louis, Detroit, Oakland (California), and on both elevated and surface lines of Chicago.

Following a settlement of the strike inaugurated on the Great Lakes May 1 by the International Longshoremen, Marine and Transportworkers' Association for the purpose of securing recognition for the Mates' Union, President Daniel J. Keefe of the Longshoremen's organization has succeeded in entering into agreements with the Dock Managers' Association covering wages and conditions of employment for the ensuing year. The agreement is practically a renewal of last year's wages and conditions. A significant feature of the Longshoremen's agreement with their employers is that it is not subject to ratification by a referendum of its members, it being entered into by representatives of the union who possess full power without restriction. Usually the subjects of the agreement are referred to committees of the union, representatives of the latter themselves presenting to these committees the employers' side of the case. The acceptance of the agreement is by unanimous vote based upon the previous ascertained will of a majority, the rule of the majority thus being made binding upon all members of the Association. Any matter not covered by the agreement as well as disputes as to the construction of the contract are subject to arbitration.

It is, perhaps, true to say that the Longshoremen's Association covers more territory and as many, if not more, different occupations than any other labor organization in the world. While its agreement with employers is uniform, it comprises not less than thirty-nine divisions of trade. This association was organized in 1882, and since 1895, according to its officials, the wage scale of its members has been advanced an average of sixty per cent. The organization includes tugboat captains, engineers, firemen, marine firemen, oilers, water tenders, divers, longshoremen, lumber inspectors, elevator employes, tally men, grain inspectors and others, the wages of individuals of these different classes ranging from about $2 to as high as $15 a day. This is one of the labor organizations whose trade agreement machinery has worked successfully through a period of wage reduction, the decrease having been accepted in the 1903 joint conference.

One of the many interesting phases of the operation of the trade agreement within this organization is that every member of the union is furnished with and carries in his pocket a copy of the contract entered into by his representatives.

A renewal of the agreement between the Amalgamated Association of Iron, Steel and Tin Plate Workers and the Western Bar Iron Association has been effected by President P. J. McArdle and representatives of the employers in a wage conference held at Detroit in June. The scale for the past year was practically renewed, there being but few slight changes, the employers refusing the twenty-five cent increase in wages to puddlers which was voted by the Cincinnati convention of the Amalgamated Association. The slight changes made were in regard to working conditions and customs rather than changes in the wages. The new scale became effective July 1, and attached to it is the continuous working clause. The firms composing the Western Bar Iron Association include such companies as the Shenango Iron and Steel Company, Union Rolling Mill Company, Empire Rolling Mill Company, American Car and Foundry Company, Lake Erie Iron Company, Helmbader Forge and Rolling Mill Companies, Ohio Falls Iron Company, American Rolling Mill Corporation, Vincennes Iron and Steel Company, Highland Iron and Steel Company, Fort Wayne Iron and Steel Company, Youngstown Sheet and Tube Company, and the Interstate Iron and Steel Company.

The Republic Iron and Steel Company, all of whose mills are union plants, was not represented at the Detroit conference and accordingly is not a party to the agreement entered into there, but at a conference with the officials of this company held at Pittsburg later by national representatives of the Amalgamated Association the provisions agreed to were practically those of the Detroit agreement.

President McArdle has also been successful in entering into an agreement for another year with the American Sheet and Tin Plate Company, one of the subsidiary companies of the United States Steel Corporation, covering wages and conditions of employment for sheet and tin plate mills. The wages the past year are continued. At this writing conferences are being carried on between officials of the Amalgamated Association and representatives of the independent sheet and tin plate mills.

Another great industry of the country which illustrates the operation of the trade agreement principle is that of cotton manufacturing in New England. Through negotiations between representatives of the Fall River Manufacturers' Association and President Tansey and other officials of the Textile Council, the latter representing the employes, there has been a restoration of the 1904 wage scale. It will be recalled that in July of that year a reduction in wages of twelve and one-half per cent was made, which was followed by a disastrous six months' strike. Before restoring this wage reduction last month to become effective on July 2, the Manufacturers' Association offered to guarantee to the employes a weekly dividend of five per cent, but this proposition was rejected by the five unions. It provided that until more suitable conditions exist by the cutting of the new crop of cotton, the Manufacturers' Association, beginning June 18 and continuing until October 1, 1906, would guarantee a weekly dividend of not less than five per cent on the present wage, with a further guarantee that if the margin in any one week exceeded this five per cent increase, they would pay an additional dividend upon the same terms as in the agreement of October 30, 1905.

An interesting phase of the Fall River situation is that the sliding scale scheme for wage increases has been abolished, temporarily at least. This was introduced in this industry in October, 1905, with the design of preventing a strike, which it was successful in doing, and it was hoped at the time that the principle would work there as successfully as it has operated in the anthracite industry following the establishment of the sliding scale scheme by the Anthracite Coal Strike Commission in 1903. Whether the sliding scale has been abolished for all time in the textile industry, or merely suspended, will depend on future developments.

SOCIALISM IN AMERICA—WHAT IT MEANS.

AMONG the contributions to the *New York World's* symposium on "Socialism in America—What it Means," published in the issue of that newspaper of May 8, is the following by the Editor of *The Review*, which contains a correction of the widely circulated statements attributed to the late Senator Hanna as to the dangers of Socialism:

To the Editor of *The World*:

I have received your circular letter asking for my opinion as to the meaning of Socialism in America and its relation to American institutions. I observe that it begins with the statement that six years ago Senator Hanna, then Chairman of the Republican National Committee, expressed the conviction that Socialism would be the chief political issue of 1912.

I am aware that this statement of Senator Hanna's, originally published in the Socialist papers, has been going the rounds of the press for a considerable time, notwithstanding the fact that it was often emphatically contradicted by him, and in spite of the fact that his opinion was exactly the reverse. In an interview in the Chicago *Times-Herald*, Dec. 2, 1900, Mr. Hanna, in reply to a question from a man in New York regarding the dangers of Socialism, answered:

> I am not a bit afraid of Socialism, and will tell you why. There are two things that will prevent it. One is the American school system; the other is the Roman Catholic Church. That great Church is just as much against Socialism as the Protestant churches, as I happen to know, and in the last campaign appeals to class hatred were frowned upon by the highest dignitaries and most influential men of the Catholic organization. As long as this restraining force continues to operate you need have no fear of Socialism dominating America.

In addition to the anti-Socialist forces of the Church and the schools Senator Hanna also recognized the transcendent importance of the opposition of organized labor. The Socialists themselves recognize this and are exerting every effort to "capture" the trade unions or to "smash" them.

Mr. Jack London, President of the league organized for the purpose of teaching Socialism to the young men in the colleges, forcibly states this policy when he says:

> The Socialists turn their energies on the trade-union movement. To win the trade unions is well-nigh to win the victory. Instead of antagonizing the unions, the Socialists proceed to conciliate the unions. "Let every good Socialist join the union of his trade! Bore from within and capture the trade-union movement." To-day the great labor unions are honeycombed with Socialists. At work and at play, at business meeting and at council, their insidious propaganda goes on. Night and day, tireless and unrelenting as a mortgage, they labor at their self-imposed task of undermining society.

This "boring-from-within" policy has been adopted by the Debs Socialists. The other branch of Socialists, known as the De Leonites, boldly undertake to "smash the unions" from without by open attacks, in which effort, strangely enough, they are warmly seconded by certain employers' organizations.

But what is more important than the purpose of the Socialists toward the unions is the attitude of the unions toward the Socialists. Out of 125 national organizations affiliated with the American Federation of Labor, representing 2,000,000 wage-earners, it is safe to say that not over five are controlled by Socialists, and these are crafts of comparatively small membership. The great railway brotherhoods of engineers, firemen, trainmen, conductors, etc., are every one strongly anti-Socialist.

The "boring-from-within" faction made its biggest fight to capture the American Federation of Labor in Boston in 1903. On this occasion, at the close of a masterful speech, Samuel Gompers, President of the Federation, dealt Socialism this stinging blow:

> I want to tell you Socialists that I have studied your philosophy; read your works upon economics, and not the meanest of them; studied your standard works, both in English and German—have not only read, but studied them. I have heard your orators and watched the work of your movement the world over. I have kept close watch upon your doctrines for thirty years; have been closely associated with many of you, and know how you think and what you propose. I know too what you have up your sleeve, and I want to say that I am entirely at variance with your philosophy. I declare to you I am not only at variance with your doctrines, but with your philosophy. Economically you are unsound; socially you are wrong; industrially you are an impossibility.

A vote was then taken, resulting in 2,147 for Socialism and 11,282 against. In 1904, at the annual meeting in San Francisco, the Socialists' resolution was so overwhelmingly voted down that a poll was not demanded. In 1905, at Pittsburg, the "borers-from-within" did not even propose a vote.

The De Leonite Socialists have tried all kinds of plans to "smash-the-union" from without, the latest one being to organize an independent labor body to oppose the American Federation of Labor. Neither the De Leonite policy of "smashing-from-without" nor the Debsite policy of "boring-from-within" has had any appreciable influence on the American Federation of Labor.

It is easy to take election returns and make great claims of Socialistic strength. The Socialists well understand that Mr. Debs's vote of 400,000 was a personal, not a Socialist victory. For example, the single-taxers throughout the country, who have no more use for Socialism than they have for smallpox, voted for him. That this is well recognized by Socialists any reader of their papers can readily discover. They lament that the members of their party are less than 5 per cent of the voters, or less than 250,000. One paper has been calling the attention of the party to "the States where there was the greatest increase of the Debs vote," and urging the Socialists to do their utmost "to capture those who were just voting their first vote, in order to get them really into the party."

But what is more significant than Debs's 400,000 votes as bearing on the growth of Socialism is the result of the elections last fall and this spring. In six States which elected one or more State officers last fall the vote fell far below Debs's vote in 1904. Nebraska fell from 7,412 to 3,421; Ohio from 36,260 to 17,795; Pennsylvania from 21,863 to 10,390, etc.; while in Massachusetts, where two or three years ago there were a number of Socialist mayors, to-day there are none, and the Socialist vote is speedily growing less.

The cry of Socialism is "to help the workingman." From a poll made recently by one of the leading labor journals of the men who are doing the talking and writing for Socialism it was found that nine-tenths of them were newspaper writers and men in the professions. The great mass of workingmen themselves recognize that under the regime of Socialism their "last state would be far worse than their first."

R. M. Easley.

New York, May 5.

THE NATIONAL
Civic Federation Review

Office: 281 Fourth Avenue, New York City

RALPH M. EASLEY, Editor

The Editor alone is responsible for any unsigned article or unquoted statement published in THE NATIONAL CIVIC FEDERATION REVIEW.

Ten Cents per Copy   One Dollar per Year

PUBLISHED BY

The National Civic Federation

The Public Ownership Commission. The spirit in which the investigation by the Commission on Public Ownership and Operation has been conceived and brought into existence by The National Civic Federation; the personnel of the Commission; the method of its selection; and the value to the public of the work the Commission has undertaken, were emphasized in the addresses at the banquet to the Commission's Committee on Investigation given by the New York City Federation on May 21. The Commission, as is well known, has taken up the consideration of public ownership and operation of public utilities in municipalities so far as it applies specifically to passenger transportation (whether by elevated, surface, or underground systems), and to the supply of water, gas and electricity. For this purpose it has invited men, competent as scientific experts of practical experience, and accountants to study the subject in all its phases, both in this country and in Europe.

"These men," said Hon. Oscar S. Straus at the dinner to the Investigating Committee, "are highly qualified by capacity and experience to make the investigation. Some of these men have large interests in and represent private ownership, and some of them are pronounced advocates of public ownership and public operation. All views of this question are fairly represented, so that the investigation will be from all sides, and in no case one-sided." As expressing the views of organized labor, Mr. Philip Kelly, of the Theatrical Protective Union, in his address, said: "I have the utmost confidence in the men who have been appointed on this Commission; they are capable, brilliant, fearless, and honest. I know the labor men on the Commission; they are good, straightforward men. The labor men of the country will know that the report our brothers on the Commission bring back will be worth our study and confidence. I believe that the attitude of organized labor toward municipal ownership will largely be determined by the report of the Investigating Committee."

The method of selecting the Commission was endorsed by many of the speakers, this thought being expressed as follows by Dr. Talcott Williams, of the Philadelphia *Press*: "I think this Committee has been selected with admirable judgment. In France a committee selected for such an investigation would necessarily have been drawn from the personnel of the existing party in power. A report from such a Commission would, in all probability, have been biased and colored to suit the wishes of the party in power. In Germany a royal commission would have made a report that would have been pleasing to the head of the nation. I submit that this Commission, in its method of appointment and investigation, has been better constituted than it would have been possible to constitute a similar committee in any other country."

As to the value of the investigation undertaken by the Commission, all the speakers at the banquet referred at greater or less length. Hon. W. J. Gaynor, of the New York Supreme Court, said: "This Federation is accomplishing a very great deal, and I deem it fortunate that it has now taken up the great subject of public service corporations, as to whether or not they shall be operated publicly or privately. I deem it fortunate, and nothing is more certain, than that the understanding which this Committee arrives at and that which will in time be the understanding of this Federation will ultimately become the understanding of the entire country." On the same point Dr. Albert Shaw, Editor of the *Review of Reviews*, said: "This Committee can bring back information that will be very useful. It will bring back information that will inspire a zeal for changing our conditions where changes are demanded, and for further study. * * * The men of this Commission are men of very high authority. The work they will do will be of great value to the country. The Civic Federation is to be highly congratulated on having secured their services. They are as competent a body of men as could be got together anywhere in this country. * * * There are a great many ways, direct and indirect, in which the work of this Committee is bound to be of great value, and I am sure its deliberation will result in untold good to our country."

The value of the work undertaken by the Commission was also emphasized by Hon. John De Witt Warner in his letter to Secretary Archibald replying to the invitation to attend the dinner. Mr. Warner said: "I believe the Federation has taken no other step so important as that in which this Commission has been appointed; that it can do no greater service than fully to inform our people of the experience of others in this matter; and that the success with which it does this, and the acceptance by our people of its report as a clear and impartial view, is likely long to be its best hold on public confidence."

Whatever are to be the definite results of the labors of the Commission, *The Review* believes that the report which is to be made will take a place in the front rank among the powerful forces at work to determine ultimately the issue of this great national question.

Labor in Southern Cotton Mills. Presented elsewhere in this issue is the report of the recent investigation made by Miss Gertrude Beeks, Secretary of the Welfare Department of The National Civic Federation, into the social and industrial conditions of employes of Southern cotton mills. The subjects covered are the conditions under which the operatives work, homes of employes, education of children, recreation, hours of work, and child labor.

The questions involved in the problem of child labor are presented in a most illuminating manner, the investigation revealing important phases of the subject not generally recognized. It shows that children are numerous in one of the three departments of the mills—the spinning room—but the testimony is refuted which pictures the majority of the employes as being emaciated children of five and six years. Elements contributing to child labor, as shown by Miss Beeks, are the desire of the parents, who previously employed their children upon the farms, to have them work in the mills; the extreme scarcity of labor; the difficulty of securing immigrants for the South, and the fact that in the cotton industry the individual wage is too low for the father to support the family by his labor alone. Conspicuous also among these elements must be included the absence of proper State methods of caring for orphans and paupers, and the lack of laws on compulsory education, birth registration, marriage license, and factory inspection, as well as the low age limit of the child labor laws of South Carolina and Alabama.

From the standpoint of Welfare Work, the well-lighted and well-ventilated mills afford comfortable work-places for the employes; and the employers also provide good homes at nominal rentals, recreation in a variety of forms, kindergartens and schools. In fact, their efforts to ameliorate the conditions of the employes demonstrate a realization of the moral obligation felt by the manufacturers, and credit should be accorded them not only for giving food and shelter and an industrial training to the illiterate whites of the South, but also for steadily raising, through their welfare work, the standard of citizenship.

Labors' Political Policy. In a recent issue of the *Railway World* the statement is made, under the caption "Labor Leaders Differ About Politics," that President Gompers, of the American Federation of Labor, appeals to union men to take an active part in politics, while President Mitchell, of the United Mine Workers of America, says that to carry politics into the crafts would be to create discord and endanger the organization. The above is one illustration of the general misinterpretation which has been given to the political program of the American Federation of Labor as being the preliminary step to the launching of a national labor party. It is true the leaders of the American Federation of Labor are appealing to their followers to take an active part in politics, but not as members of a distinct and separate party. As we understand President Gompers's announcement at this stage of the movement, they intend first "to help their friends and punish their enemies" in every case where this is practicable. But in cases where they have only "a choice between enemies," if it is found expedient they will nominate men of their own principles on independent, labor or some other ticket which will lend itself to their interests.

The political policy of the labor leaders is very similar to that of the Municipal Voters' League of Chicago, which has resulted in changing a notoriously bad city council to a fairly representative and decent body. The League only found it necessary to secure the nomination of independent candidates in a very few instances. The idea is a practicable one. It is as legitimate for organized labor to look after its interests as it is for organized employers or any other group interest to work for their own advantage. The National Manufacturers' Association, if one may judge from the literature with which its energetic secretary is bombarding the manufacturers of the country, is carrying on a political campaign along somewhat the same lines.

The Wage-cost of Miners' Suspension.

There are two general statements relative to the recent controversy in the bituminous and anthracite coal fields made by newspapers unfriendly to organized labor which are so palpably absurd that it hardly seems worth while to answer them. One is that the anthracite miners lost $12,000,000 in wages by their recent forty days' suspension. This is not true, because it is well known that in anticipation of a strike so much coal had been mined (for which extra employment the mine workers were paid) that even if there had been no suspension there would have been a lack of employment throughout the summer months totalling at least the number of days covered by the shut-down.

The other point is that the suspension in the bituminous coal fields resulted in no benefit to the unions *"because they only got a restoration of the 1903 scale."* This statement is true but the implication is false. The wage increase was a gain and a very real gain. It meant so much in dollars and cents that the operators were willing to risk a fight rather than grant it. To say that an increase in wages averaging more than five cents per ton and amounting to millions of dollars in the aggregate is not a real gain is ridiculous. A comparison of the money cost to the mine worker of the actual time lost by the suspension with the 5.8 per cent wage increase for two years makes the former amount rather insignificant. What is even more to the point, the mine workers stand to hold the restored rate indefinitely, which at once adds to the importance of the gain.

The Federation's Immigration Department.

Among the dominant forces which have been at work in the upbuilding of the American Republic none stand forth to the present generation in a brighter halo than the resultant operation on these shores of European immigration. We believe this much is conceded by all thoughtful observers of American history. But in the rapid transformations which come about in the development of a nation it is also true that those forces which at one time worked to the nation's upbuilding may operate to the destruction of some of its most prized institutions. This apprehension is held by some as to the present-day effects of alien immigration to the United States and it is finding expression in various channels, conspicuously in newspapers, magazines, and books, and in the formation of organizations having for their expressed objects the further restriction of immigration. Three of these organizations—the Immigration Restriction League, the Japanese and Korean Exclusion League, and the Junior Order United American Mechanics—are explained elsewhere in this issue. Naturally the basis of their operation is their respective interpretation of the effects of immigration.

The real effects of immigration on our industrial, political and broad social life are not easily to be ascertained. In no realm of human knowledge are the facts more elusive. But these facts are just what are absolutely necessary before there can be a correct understanding as to the right solution of such a grave problem. As long as there are disputes as to what are the facts as to immigration we cannot hope for the proper direction on this subject of the energy and ability of those public spirited citizens who strive to find the right way to the advancement of the general welfare. A striking illustration of the widely varying interpretation of the facts relating to immigration to the United States, and that, too, on a point which, it would seem, should be beyond dispute, is at hand. It relates to the character of immigration. In a circular recently issued to members of the Junior Order United American Mechanics by the Dayton Council of that organization is contained the following:

> Will we American citizens allow the Dago, the other riffraff of Southern Europe and the "Coolie" laborers who will work for a matter of nothing and live on the refuse of the cess-pool and the garbage-dump to replace American labor and take our earnings back to foreign lands, or assist more filth and vice to land on our shores? A large per cent. of immigration is made up of outcasts, criminals, anarchists, thieves and off-scourings of the earth, who are forced to leave their own land, and still are allowed to land upon American soil. Isn't it time that we begin to take measures to stop this inflow of foreign scum? Every true American, naturalized or native-born, regardless of nationality, partisan or sectarian affiliation, will answer, Yes!

In direct contrast with the above we have the following word picture from Immigration Commissioner Watchorn, of the Ellis Island immigration station at New York, which we reproduce from an interview in a recent issue of the New York *Times*:

> We cannot have too much of the right kind of immigration; we cannot have too little of the wrong kind. We are seeing to it that we get the right kind—of that I am certain. Consequently I believe that increased immigration of the kind we are admitting to our shores makes for the National weal.
>
> The prime cause of immigration is the letters foreigners in this country write to relatives and friends and to foreign newspapers. These letter writers have thrived, and they spread the news of their success abroad. The result is an influx of bright, ambitious men and women, the brawn and backbone of any country.
>
> Aliens arriving through Ellis Island last year brought with them money aggregating $938,660. Shake more than 800,000 Americans together and send them abroad, and I doubt if they would make as good, certainly no better, showing.
>
> Of the 41,412 immigrants arriving here last January, 34,363 were between the ages of fourteen and forty-four years—formative years of youth and manhood; splendid years. Of the January total 5,272 were under fourteen years of age, and only 1,837 were over forty-four years of age. So what did we get, therefore? Was it not the youth and strength and vigor and ambition of foreign lands?
>
> So far as the steamship companies are concerned I may say that they are very loath to inaugurate innovations, but sooner or later, for one reason or another, they come to our way of thinking. One very important fact that they have lately digested is that it does not pay for them to ship any old sort of an immigrant to this country. The reason why they have come to know this is that we catch the undesirable aliens at this island and make the company take them back at its own expense, plus also the cost of maintaining them while they are in this port. We sent back so many persons in this way that the steamship companies finally issued letters to their agents all over the world saying that it was absolutely useless for them to send on would-be Americans who were ailing in body or mind, or who were otherwise ineligible to land under the immigration laws of the United States. The refusal of steamship companies to carry undesirable immigrants is one of the greatest checks upon pernicious immigration that I know of. Last year, for instance, the various steamship companies refused to bring 20,000 aliens to this country, not through any deep regard for our laws, of course, but simply for their own interests, knowing that we would have sent them back even if they had brought them here.

Not only is the character of our present immigration in dispute, but also innumerable other factors which go to make up the immigration problem. There are controversies, for illustration, as to the exact percentage of immigrants which remains in New York; as to the proportion of aliens in our penal and reformatory institutions, in our almshouses, and in other ways dependent upon public and private relief; as to the ultimate effect of immigration on wages and general labor conditions; and as to the effects of immigration upon the political and broad social life of our cities, States, and even the nation itself. These and other factors of equal importance to the solution of the immigration problem must be known beyond question if we are to control and direct the immigration stream to the advancement of the general welfare. And the one essential to their correct understanding is an organization which seeks these facts, without personal interests of any kind to serve, without preconceived opinions to support, and with the sole purpose of ascertaining those facts which alone are basal and comparable.

It is in this spirit that the Immigration Department of the National Civic Federation, an account of which is presented on another page of this issue, has been organized. The work of the Department will at first be directed along the line of securing basal facts, and to this end seven distinct committees have been created to deal with statistics, supply and demand, legislation and its enforcement, naturalization, agencies for advancing the welfare of immigrants, international relations, and Oriental immigration. The work of these committees will undoubtedly be of great value to a correct understanding of the immigration problem. Possession of the facts which go to make up the immigration issue will present to the nation a starting point for working out by legislation a more satisfactory line of action than is possible at the present time.

Reformers and "Reformers."

Mrs. Martha Moore Avery, in the announcement elsewhere in this issue of the Industrial Bureau which she and Mr. David Goldstein are launching, does well to call attention to the fundamental differences between reformers who want to reform and "reformers" who want to destroy. While we may not agree with all the methods employed by some of the noted journalistic reformers of the day, we can give them credit for honest intentions to really make conditions better. But when we find that a reformer is a pronounced Karl Marx socialist, it is well to scrutinize his statements and methods, because that philosophy teaches that conditions must become worse before they can be made better. It follows, therefore, that his purpose is to make the situation "worse" as fast as possible. One noted socialist "reformer," a member of a number of organizations for ameliorating social conditions, was recently decrying charity organizations when some one said: "Suppose they are not perfect; they are the best we have. Were it not for them a great many working people would starve." Her reply was: "Let them starve. The quicker they starve the sooner will society become aroused at the intolerable conditions and hasten the revolution which will usher in the Socialist State."

Three subjects that furnish a great deal of material for socialist propagandists are tenement houses, sweatshops and child labor. In the last decade great progress has been made in all three fields, but the socialists continue to picture the conditions which existed ten and twenty years ago. It is their fixed policy never to concede progress along any line of activity. With them an isolated case is always typical. However much we may disagree with their philosophy, we must admire their energy and persistence. They manage to become identified with every organization where there is any chance of exploiting their doctrines. Frequently an organization will be found to be shaped and controlled by a group of socialists, although that group may be a very small part of the organization. The public-spirited citizens who compose the larger part of the organization and who furnish all the funds for its work, have no idea that they are being used by socialists, and that they are "rubbing elbows" with people who not only do not believe in the institutions of our country but also are working to destroy them. If the new Industrial Bureau will point out to the country just who these people are it will perform an important public service.

WELFARE WORK AND CHILD LABOR IN SOUTHERN COTTON MILLS.

COMPULSORY EDUCATION AND AUTOMATIC SPINNING MACHINERY WILL AID IN SOLVING THE PROBLEM OF CHILD LABOR.

[For the purpose of learning what manufacturers of cotton goods in the South have done to ameliorate the conditions under which their employés work and live, Miss Gertrude Beeks, Secretary of the Welfare Department of the National Civic Federation, recently visited fourteen cotton mill towns in South Carolina, Alabama and Georgia. This included an inspection of the mills as well as an investigation of the social conditions. The cotton industry having been developed to the greatest extent in South Carolina, the largest number of mills was visited in that State. Children being employed, the question of child labor was naturally involved in the inquiry. While her report shows that there are isolated cases of very young children at work, as well as too many under twelve years, the legal age in South Carolina and Alabama, credit has been given the employers for their efforts to educate the children and to secure proper legislation which would aid in abolishing the evil of child labor. The question has been handled as a broad, economic problem—clearly recognizing the industrial evolution of the South since the destitution left by the Civil War.

This is the first opportunity afforded the general reader to learn from a disinterested, practical investigator, the truth about conditions in the Southern cotton mills. Much literature has been published on this subject, frequently emanating from a source interested in creating socialistic propaganda rather than depicting facts. Miss Beeks not only frankly criticises where the employers are at fault, but also tells of their remarkable, beneficent efforts. The qualifications of Miss Beeks for undertaking such an investigation are unquestioned. Probably no other woman in this country has had as wide, practical experience in dealing with all phases of the problems connected with the employment of labor, and provision for its well-being in stores, mills, factories, mines, on railroads—and in fact wherever labor is employed.—Editor's Note.]

By Miss Gertrude Beeks.

IN reporting upon this investigation the following subjects are covered: Condition under which the operatives work; homes of operatives; education of children; recreation; hours of work; and child labor.

Half a dozen cotton mill villages may be located in one town. Each mill has its group of operatives' homes or village within close proximity. The term "operatives" means employes in cotton mills. While other mill settlements were inspected, trips through the *interiors* of mills were confined to the following eighteen:

Monaghan Mills, Greenville, S. C.
Victor Mills, Greers, S. C.
Pelzer Mills, Pelzer, S. C.
Belton Mills, Belton, S. C.
Cox Manufacturing Co., Anderson, S. C.
Brogon Mills, Anderson, S. C.
Greenwood Mills, Greenwood, S. C.
Grendel Mills, Greenwood, S. C.
Saxon Mills, Spartanburg, S. C.
Olympia Mills, Columbia, S. C.
Saxon Mills, Spartanburg, S. C.
Olympia Mills, Columbia, S. C.
Victoria Mills, Rock Hill, S. C.
Arcade Mills, Rock Hill, S. C.
Manchester Cotton Mills, Rock Hill, S. C.
Graniteville Mfg. Co., Graniteville, S. C.; near Augusta, Ga.
Dwight Mills, Alabama City, Ala.
Massachusetts Mills of Georgia, Lindale, Ga.
Exposition Mills, Atlanta, Ga.
Eagle & Phenix Mills, Columbus, Ga.

A Mill Back Yard

Observations of the general living conditions were made at the villages of the following mills:

Spartan Mills, Spartanburg, S. C.
Drayton Mills, Spartanburg, S. C.
F. W. Poe Mfg. Co., Greenville, S. C.
Granby Mills, Columbia, S. C.
American Spinning Company, Greenville, S. C.
Bath Mills, in South Carolina, near Augusta, Ga.

Front Yard Old Mill Erected in 1845

Langley Mfg. Co., in South Carolina, near Augusta, Ga.
Warren Mfg. Co., in South Carolina, near Augusta, Ga.
Piedmont Mills, Piedmont, S. C.
Lorraine Mills, Gastonia, N. C.
Griffin Mills, Griffin, Ga.

In addition to those mentioned, officials of the following mills were interviewed:

Carolina Mills, Greenville, S. C.
Brandon Mills, Greenville, S. C.
Batesville Mills, Greenville, S. C.
Reedy River Mill, Greenville, S. C.
Capital City Mill, Columbia, S. C.
Richland Mills, Columbia, S. C.
Apalachia Mills, Apalachia, S. C.
Ninety-six Mills, Ninety-six, S. C.
Gluck Mills, Anderson, S. C.
Union Mills, Union, S. C.
Woodruff Mills, Spartanburg, S. C.
Fairfield Cotton Mills, Winnsboro, S. C.
Wylie Mills, Chester, S. C.

Testimony showing the same general conditions at the Avondale and Pell City in Alabama; and the La-

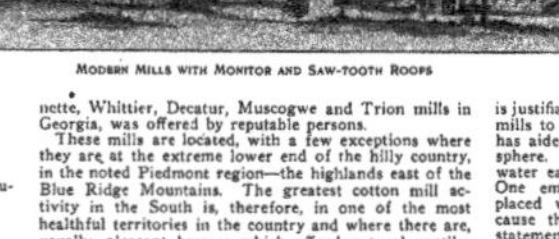

Modern Mills with Monitor and Saw-tooth Roofs

nette, Whittier, Decatur, Muscogwe and Trion mills in Georgia, was offered by reputable persons.

These mills are located, with a few exceptions where they are at the extreme lower end of the hilly country, in the noted Piedmont region—the highlands east of the Blue Ridge Mountains. The greatest cotton mill activity in the South is, therefore, in one of the most healthful territories in the country and where there are, usually, pleasant breezes which afford natural ventilation for mills upon the elevations. South Carolina has the greatest number of spindles. The statistics for 1904 show the leading States to be:

South Carolina......	2,928,000	spindles
North Carolina......	2,192,000	"
Georgia	1,475,000	"
Alabama	820,000	"

In Virginia, Tennessee, Mississippi, Maryland, Louisiana, Texas, Arkansas and Missouri there is some cotton manufacturing but comparatively little, the number of spindles in each State running from 300,000 down to 16,000.

For this investigation mills were selected not only with reference to their relative importance, but a special effort was made to inspect those toward which public attention has been particularly directed in the criticisms of sensational writers.

Spray for Cooling Mill

CONDITIONS UNDER WHICH THE OPERATIVES WORK.

In general it may be said that the mills are unusually well lighted and ventilated, heated in winter and cooled in summer. The saw-tooth roof is used to give a perfectly lighted, modern weave room, and the monitor roof, which insures better ventilation than the flat roof, is found quite often. The employers have been quick to utilize modern devices, such as the exhaust system for the removal of the lint; the cold-water spray instead of the hot-water spray in summer, to humidify the atmosphere for manufacturing purposes; and the blower system for heating in winter and cooling the air in summer. Some, who heat with hot air, use the cold-water spray both winter and summer and have proved by its use that heat is not essential to the successful manufacture of cotton goods. The aim is to keep the temperature at 70 to 75 degrees. That is probably feasible, excepting in a few old mills in the lowlands. But there and in the uplands, in exceedingly warm weather, some progressive employers have cold water sprayed on the roofs or sides of the mills exposed to the sun. The custom at one place visited is to put ice in the chamber through which the fresh air is drawn into the mill, while in another the air is passed through cool water. The claim that the operatives are more comfortable in the mills during the summer than they were when engaged in the hot sun on the farms is justifiable. The introduction of electric motors in many mills to take the place of overhead shafting and belting has aided in reducing the amount of dust in the atmosphere. The custom of having pure, cool drinking water easily accessible in the work rooms, is general. One employer was having the ribbed windows replaced with clear glass, "to please the employes because they like to look out." He supplemented the statement with "I would, too." In two mills there are splendid emergency hospital rooms, with operating tables, and even stretchers. Another mill man goes so far as to provide the trained nurse to visit all families where there is illness in the village, which materially aids in preventing the spread of contagious diseases; and one has an isolation hospital for use during epidemics. Medical attendance, at a nominal fee, is pro-

Something New in a President's Office

From Stereograph. Copyright 1906 by Underwood & Underwood, New York

Carding Department Requiring Men

[furnish]ed quite generally through special arrangements with physicians.

The only points of criticism relative to negligence in providing for the comfort of the employes in the mills are bad ventilation and poor janitor service in connection with the toilet arrangements, and lack of elevator service.

Some of the toilet rooms are in the ends of the mills and are well ventilated by windows and the exhaust system, but others are in the centers of the mills with no provision for ventilation. To explain their unclean condition, it was claimed that the operatives, being migratory and moving constantly from one village to another, only remain in one mill long enough to learn the first lesson in cleanliness. The feeling of discouragement relative to the difficulty of educating what the mill men term that "rough class of people" to the proper use of such conveniences would be amusing to the employer who has had to solve the problem with immigrant labor. It should be comparatively easy to educate the native English-speaking operatives in the southern cotton mills. But the question of janitor service is left to superintendents and foremen. Elsewhere it has been proven that when the expense of janitor service is charged to the various departments, the foremen who are required to keep down the cost of manufacturing neglect their "housekeeping" duties; and that employes will not make proper use of unclean, unsanitary arrangements. When the unclean condition of the toilet rooms, which with one exception was inexcusably bad, was called to their attention, several of the mill presidents immediately undertook to improve the method of caring for them. The system in force in the exceptional mill at Lindale is thorough. Janitors clean the arrangements twice a day, using an antiseptic and a liberal supply of hot soap suds. All the mills have wash sinks which the employes are supposed to use for their ablutions. Until recently such sinks were regarded everywhere as modern conveniences. It was interesting to observe that the employes

[illegible]

want something better. In one mill the operatives have supplied their own individual wash basins which are in rows on the window sills in the work rooms. In another, although the employer has been thoughtful in supplying soap, as usual towels are not furnished and the operatives were observed using the manufactured product in lieu of them.

While the use of elevators to conserve the energy of employes has not become general in this country its need is greater in the cotton mills than elsewhere. The reason is that the spinning rooms, where child labor is found in the main, are usually on the top floors—frequently on the fifth. The employers claim that they have more accidents in connection with the elevators than from the operation of the machinery, but the freight elevators could be guarded so that the employes might be transported safely to the spinning rooms when going to work in the morning and at noontime. The use of the elevator should be given to all employes on the upper floors because the age limit does not exceed twelve years and no young girl between twelve and sixteen years should be obliged to climb several flights of stairs.

Superintendent Who Began Work at Eight Years

At the entrance of a mill located in a large town the immense crowd of "dinner toters," who carry lunch to the members of the family employed there, indicates the need of a lunch room. In a smaller way that need was also evidenced at a mill in a large city where some of the weavers were observed eating their luncheons which were placed on the looms; and one boy was sitting in the wash sink next to the window eating his midday meal and reading a newspaper. The desirability of introducing rest rooms in the mills was made plain

A Group From the Spinning Room

when girls were found sitting upon the landings of the staircases waiting for work. But it may be generally stated that the mills visited are unusually sanitary, comfortable work places.

HOMES OF THE OPERATIVES.

In making this investigation, the criticisms of sensational writers were constantly kept in mind. One of these criticisms relates to the unsanitary homes of the operatives. The writer states:

> Each house was encircled by a wooden veranda, and the order of housekeeping described itself before the eyes, as a whisk of the broom which carried all dirt from the kitchen to the porch, and another whisk which landed it on the ground, bedecked, in consequence, with old tin cans, decaying vegetables, pieces of dirty paper, rags and chicken feathers. The outer room was a kitchen, though it might, except for the stove, have been mistaken for a hen-coop. The chickens pecked their way about the dirty floor, venturing as far even as the table upon which

Spinning Room Where Children Work

From Stereograph. Copyright 1906 by Underwood & Underwood, New York

Weaving Room

> stood the meager remains of the noonday meal. The second and the inner room had each a bed—an unmade bed I was going to say, but, how, indeed, could a bed be made without either sheets or pillows? Two grimy counterpanes were flung in disorder across the mattresses.

To learn the facts relative to such statements, an incessant effort was made to see the worst as well as the best conditions. The village, universally regarded as the worst, was carefully inspected, and it cannot honestly be claimed that the homes of the operatives living there are as unhealthful as those of the inmates of the tenements in our great cities. This village, it is true, was a sad contrast to those of progressive employers who are gradually forcing the others to come up to their standard. The houses are merely clapboarded. The interiors are usually sufficiently spacious. Although the lots are not as large as elsewhere because the mill is in a good-sized town, there is ample space for ventilation. A most serious criticism is the fact that the employer in this village has not provided a general cow shed or pasture, the employes being permitted to keep the cows in their yards—and they insist upon keeping cows, also occasionally, pigs. Sometimes the live stock is directly under the bedroom window. Of course, this is unhealthful and aids in contaminating the well-water. The general aspect of the village is unsightly. The absence of paint, trees, gardens, and other elevating influences makes this village comparatively undesirable. But, while all are not model settlements, the conditions pictured in the paragraph above quoted do not exist in this or any of the other villages visited. It may be stated that generally the premises are extremely neat in the cotton mill villages, and that only in the homes of new arrivals from the primitive districts are the interiors of the cottages unclean. Many a housewife could take lessons in cleanliness from the home of the average

Operatives Going Home to Lunch

Primitive Mountain Home

After Going to the Mill

mill operative. Where they still exist, the old clapboarded houses are being remodeled with weather boarding, or torn down and replaced; some of the new homes are being finished with walls of wood fibre; and where not included in the original plans, porches with railings are now being added, the employers considering that such improvements give greater comfort to their tenants.

The impossibility of gaining a correct impression of conditions by cursory observations was clearly evidenced by the following experience:

The first view of the cotton mill settlements was gained between Gastonia and Greenville, along the Southern Railway, where the homes showed the lack of paint. One of the questions asked the first mill man interviewed was why they had not learned the value of utilizing paint. He replied: "It is the custom to decorate every three years and this is the year for painting." This was shown to be the fact as the investigation was pursued for many of the homes just had been or were being painted.

The moral tone of many of the villages has been greatly improved by lighting the streets with electricity. In some instances the interiors of employes' homes are thus illuminated. Simple bath rooms with zinc tubs have been introduced in some of the houses. Some employers have gone so far as to make ice and deliver it to the homes at low prices.

Unsanitary surface wells, which have been the cause of illness in the past, have been and are being replaced by water systems, and the employers are preparing to make another important improvement, that of the sewer system, although in many villages there are excellent plans for removing the refuse weekly—for example, the pan system of Manchester. One president is expending a considerable sum upon oil each year for the marshy tracts which are gradually being drained and put under cultivation in order to make the village, unwisely located by his predecessor, more healthful.

Some of the villages are exceedingly beautiful, both as to the artistic appearance of the buildings and the landscape effects. In some cases, while the homes of the operatives are comfortable and sanitary, they are built from a stereotyped plan. One president said: "It is much easier to give a contract for the building of homes of one kind, especially when there is great haste to get the mill into operation. It is hard to give time to think of houses when one has to purchase machinery and equip the mill. Besides, it is cheaper, because a builder will take a contract for less than would be possible if he were to attempt to construct different types of houses." But in a number of villages the architecture is widely diversified and individuality is encouraged, notably at Alabama City. Ordinarily the lots are seventy-five by one hundred seventy-five feet. There are garden plots with prizes for vegetables and flowers, and one mill man is planning to erect greenhouses that the employes may keep their flowers in winter. Several of the mill villages are located in beautiful forests, and at other places employers are planting trees annually with a view of securing ample shade within a few years. In one the mud, so disagreeable in that section during the rainy season, has been obviated by the use of chert. The water immediately runs off the walks and roads thus macadamized. Still another public duty has been relegated to the employers, for the last resting place as well as the temporal home is provided by them, and in some of the villages the cemeteries add to their beauty. In one village where the mills have been in operation for twenty-four years, even former employes are permitted to bury their dead in the private cemetery.

The homes are rented by the employers to the employes at two to five dollars a month for houses of four to eight rooms. The rentals meet the cost of repairs, improvements and taxes. One man stated: "We charge rental for the homes because we think the employes respect themselves more." The rents include not only water, vegetable and flower gardens, but in some cases electric light, free cow pastures, cow sheds and pig pens. The people are very timid and will not live in the towns where the mills are located, nor will they attend the general churches. This makes it necessary for the employers to build villages surrounding the mills. Several mill presidents have equipped model tenements for the residences of the Welfare Workers which serve as examples to the operatives. Hotels or "inns," where the price of board is nominal, have been provided for the clerical forces, and, in a few cases, for unmarried operatives. In one village of 1,800 residents, 800 being operatives, the company expended $125,000 upon homes and $20,000 upon social buildings for their benefit. Here, in addition to the $2,000 which the company is taxed for educational purposes, it expends $2,000 annually.

A Mill Village

Operative's Home, Parsonage and Church

EDUCATION OF CHILDREN.

Before going into the cotton mill communities, the operatives could not be reached by civilizing influences. Through the Welfare Work of the cotton manufacturers, the children of Americans of Revolutionary ancestry, largely Tories, have been given the benefits which make for the best citizenship. Through the humane instincts of the mill owners, educational opportunities have been secured to them. These men have either assumed the function of the State by providing educational facilities or have been instrumental in securing legislation for school purposes whereby they are the largest taxpayers. Kindergartens and schools are supported in whole or in part by *all*. The public school system in the South is still in an imperfect condition, and, furthermore, State appropriations are insufficient to maintain the schools longer than four months in each year. In one village where the population is 5,000, 2,200 being operatives, 750 children are being educated at the present time by the mill owner. The salaries paid annually to the twelve instructors, including the Welfare Worker and domestic science teacher who assists her, amount to $7,000. In some other villages the mill owners pay the greatest amount of taxes to support the schools for the regular term of four months, and then, in addition, maintain them entirely at their own expense for an additional four months. In South Carolina one-half of the three-mill tax for education is applied toward schools for negroes, although they do not pay one-half of the taxes. The colored parents send their children to school more generally than the white people, partly because they are more ambitious for them and partly

The Last Mill Tenement

Houses Which Replaced Old Tenements

because there is small opportunity of securing work for colored children.

The employers erect the school buildings in the majority of the villages, as well as the homes for the teachers. The elevating influence of a new kindergarten was illustrated by the good care given the modern conveniences installed in it. This was in pleasing contrast to the conduct of the pupils in the ordinary tenement used for the initial experiment. One president said: "When our kindergartner began the work, the children would throw stones at persons going about the village; now they take off their hats." Frequently, half of the children will go to school for a period, and then alternate with the other half later by working in the mills. The children who attend the entire school period frequently go into the mills during the summer months to permit the other children of the family who are operatives to rest from work. For the children who work in the mills regularly there are night classes in arithmetic, reading and writing. Night classes for feminine employes afford instruction in cooking and sewing.

The overseers, who usually come up from the ranks, as a rule are not sufficiently intelligent to utilize all of the modern appliances. Industrial training on a large scale will be possible within a few months at Columbus, Georgia, where the leading mill president gave a tract of land and a large sum of money to secure, as a part of the public school system, such technical training.

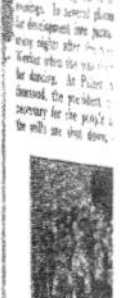

Paint and Trees Absent Contrasting Village

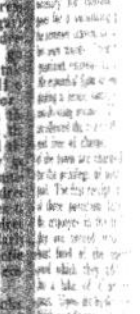

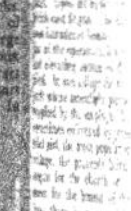

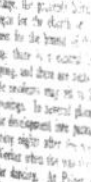

[illegible]artanburg, S. C., there is a Science Hall which was [illegible]owed by one of the pioneer mill men now deceased. [illegible] leading mill president in South Carolina secured a [illegible] of educational stereopticon lectures furnished by [illegible] State of New York, which is loaned to the other [illegible] in that district. These lectures are free and [illegible] attended. All of these movements show the [illegible] efforts made by the mill men to elevate the [illegible]ratives.

There are libraries supplied by the employers and [illegible] for the support of which they contribute en[illegible] or in part, and there are well-patronized savings [illegible]. There are other provident funds, the one most [illegible] being the "Burial Union." The operatives pay [illegible] cents a month and in case of death the family re[illegible] fifty dollars. This also entitles the beneficiary to [illegible] as follows: At the death of a parent over sixty, [illegible] and a child under eight, $10. In one instance the $20 [illegible] paid from the fund in a Georgia mill was for the [illegible] of a mother-in-law in Texas. The death benefit [illegible] the children, does not, as elsewhere, increase child [illegible]. The future value of the child as a wage earner [illegible] of greater importance to the parent than the amount [illegible] the death benefit.

RECREATION.

Included in the general effort to provide recreation [illegible] the employes there are separate social halls or audi[illegible] on the top floors of the school houses, thea[illegible], roller skating rinks, gymnasiums, bowling alleys, [illegible] for the military companies of the operatives, [illegible] rooms for the various lodges and employes' [illegible], halls for Sunday sacred concerts, athletic fields, children's playgrounds with gymnasium outfits, tennis courts, picnic grounds, outdoor dance pavilions and swimming pools. Of course all of the recreative activi[illegible] listed are not in one village, al[illegible] a majority will be found in each. One village was visited on the Saturday which opened the ath[illegible] season. The initial ball game was played by the Monaghan and the Victor teams, and the mill presi[illegible] were as much interested in the outcome as were the operatives. In one town where the employer [illegible] the [illegible] of water necessary for manufacturing pur[illegible] for a swimming pool during the summer season, he was, to quote his own words, "regarded by the prominent citizens as being crazy." He expended $[illegible] in equipment, in[illegible] a fence, seats, spring board and dressing rooms. The operatives are allowed the use of the swimming pool free of charge. The citizens of the town are charged ten cents for the privilege of patronizing the pool. The first receipts met the cost of three porcelain bath tubs for the employes in the mill and now they are [illegible] with an amuse[illegible] fund of the operatives, to[illegible] which they add a [illegible] [illegible]. Another [illegible] a lake of [illegible] mountain water covering six acres. Upon its banks is a natatorium for the employes [illegible]. The dance pavilion has not generally been introduced because of the extreme religious tenden[illegible] of the operatives, but it has proved a very successful and [illegible] source of diversion wherever it has been tried. In one village the pavilion is located in a beautiful park where moonlight picnics are frequent. The music is supplied by the employes' band. Moonlight festivals are sometimes enlivened by prize contests for the most beau[illegible] girl, the most popular man, or the fattest baby in the village, the proceeds being used for a new carpet or organ for the church or toward some other improve[illegible] for the benefit of the employes. In another vil[illegible] there is a central band stand near a bubbling spring, and there are seats under the great trees where the residents may sit to listen to the music Saturday evenings. In several places tracts have been set apart for development into parks. "We limber them up Sat[illegible] nights after the week's work," said a Welfare Worker when she was showing the recreation hall used for dancing. At [illegible], where the population is five thousand, the president [illegible]: "Amusements are as necessary for the people as food." In certain villages the mills are shut down one day of the year for an annual picnic, and although holidays are not as numer[illegible] in this section as elsewhere, it is customary to have a Fourth of July celebration and Christmas entertain[illegible] at which the operatives and members of their families receive gifts.

HOURS OF WORK.

All the employers who were interviewed clearly demonstrated the realization of their moral obligation toward the operatives in their employ. This was fur[illegible] evidenced by their voluntary action in reducing the hours in South Carolina.

At present* the operatives work sixty-six hours a week. At their own request, the work is divided so that they have a twelve-hour day for five days in order to secure the Saturday half-holiday. The village rising bell is rung sometimes as early as 4 a. m. and fre[illegible]quently at 4:30 a. m. for the purpose of awakening the housewives to prepare breakfast for the operatives who are expected to be in the mill by six o'clock. Owing to the long hours, the operatives are too greatly fatigued evenings to avail themselves, to any extent, of the educational classes or the opportunities for recre[illegible]ation. This is thoroughly realized by the mill owners, and it is now proposed in the State of South Carolina to reduce the hours voluntarily. Seventy-three mill presidents determined, at a meeting in Greenville, S. C., June 5, upon a gradual reduction from sixty-six hours a week to sixty, the change to begin July 1, 1906.

CHILD LABOR.

Far too many children were found employed in the mills, but it is necessary to examine the cause before offering criticism. Until industry was organized, child labor was prevalent upon the farms. Labor for the cotton mills was re[illegible]cruited from the farming districts, principally the isolated regions in the mountains. It was only natural, therefore, that the parents should send their children into the mills. In the economic development of the South, remedial legislation has not kept pace with the industrial progress. Nor has public sentiment educated the parents (who have lacked opportunities for education themselves and, therefore, believe that it is unnecessary for their offspring) to the point of sending the children to school instead of the mills.

General Cow Shed Provided by Employer

Live Stock Under Bedroom Window

On observing the general prosperity which has been wrought through the cotton industry the question arose as to *whether it would have been better to have left the people in pauperism and illiteracy* than to have taken them into the manufacturing districts where they could secure an industrial training *with pay* which would insure a livelihood, be uplifted by the elevating influences and secure an education for the majority of their children.

In South Carolina and Alabama child labor laws have recently been secured which provide that no children under sixteen can work in the mills at night, and none under twelve in the day time, with the exception of the child of a widow who furnishes an affidavit to the effect that the support of the child is needed. In that event a child as young as ten may work. In Georgia there is a gentleman's agreement among the mill men which contains the same provisions.

The child labor law in South Carolina has been in existence three years. It increased the age limit gradually. During the first year under the law children were allowed to work at ten; the second year at eleven, and the third year at twelve. The twelve-year limit has been in operation only one year. To make the child labor laws precede compulsory education was to place the cart before the horse. Unfortunately, the child labor laws do not provide for factory inspec[illegible]tors, compulsory education or truant officers. Therefore, they are practically inoperative, largely because of the extreme scarcity of labor and the competition among the mills for families. The unit of labor is the family and not the individual, and in view of the fact that there is no birth registration law, when the parents make affidavit that their children have reached the age of twelve, there is no inclination on the part of the superintendents and foremen—who are responsible for keeping the mills in operation to their fullest capacity—to doubt the truth of such statements. Even where children under twelve are allowed to work there are many idle machines, due to the scarcity of labor.

In reference to this, one superintendent in Georgia stated: "When competitors are working to get help from one mill to another, it is pretty hard to say to a man: 'You shall not work your children.' The only way to handle this question is through compulsory education which will place all the mill men upon the same basis."

Operatives' Wash Basins

At that mill it has been the custom for years to require parents to sign the following certificate when seeking employment for their children:

I hereby certify that my child, ... was .... years old on the .... day of ...., and that I am (or am not) dependent on his (or her) labor for a living. .... attended school for ...... months during the year preceding the date of this certificate, and can read and write.

He said: "While we did not in the past employ children shown by these certificates to be under twelve, or who appeared to us to be under twelve, I shall frankly state that we have not observed that rule since labor became so scarce."

A president in South Carolina gave the following testimony: "Six hundred and fifty children are in our schools at the present time, whereas there should be one thousand, and I want some way of having the parents keep their agreements, made with us when they take employment, to send to school all children between the ages of five and twelve. This plan has been in operation for fourteen years. But it is now impossible to force the parents to keep their agreements, for they can go elsewhere and get work so readily." An inspection of the agreements showed a large proportion signed with the parents' mark. This gave evidence of the probability that such uneducated parents would not realize the value of education for their children.

There was ample testimony to show that, before the scarcity of labor became so extreme, mill men sent families away from their villages when parents refused to send their children to school.

This South Carolina man also said: "More attention should be given to providing adequate primary schools, and funds now diverted to 'colleges,' the equivalent of the ordinary high school, could be more usefully employed for a time, and we should have compulsory education."

In another South Carolina town the most progressive mill man has for some time, in lieu of State statistics, had a census taken twice a year for the purpose of listing births and securing the ages of the children. The object is to keep at the mills the records of all the families, so that children under age may be prevented from obtaining employment.

The situation is further complicated in South Carolina by the lack of a marriage license law. Two young people who enter lightly into the marriage state may separate after the birth of several children. The husband will drift to another mill village and marry again. There is nothing left for the children of the first marriage to do but go into the mills, or the intolerable almshouses. The bigamy, due to the absence of divorce law, brings with it an attendant lessened family responsibility.

That an earnest effort is being made by the mill presidents to improve these conditions is indicated by the passage of the following resolutions, in addition to the one relative to the reduction of hours, at the important meeting previously mentioned:

> That this Conference urge upon all the cotton manufacturers of South Carolina to carefully and faithfully observe the age [illegible] limiting the employment of children to those twelve years of age and older, and forbidding the employment, except under lawful conditions, of children under twelve years of age.

School Children [illegible]

* April, 1906.

A Mill President and Kindergarten Pupils

That this Conference of Cotton Manufacturers earnestly approve the passage of a compulsory school law in South Carolina to apply to all children under twelve years of age, and also recommend the enactment of a law requiring the registration of all births, and also a law requiring marriage certificate before any marriage ceremony can be performed in South Carolina.

That the Chairman of this Conference appoint a committee of seven, who shall prepare a circular letter to be printed and placed on the desk of each member of the Senate and House of Representatives of the South Carolina Legislature, urging upon them the enactment of these three laws.

In Alabama, although there are laws requiring the marriage license and birth registration, as well as the child labor law, there is no factory inspection nor compulsory education and the situation is identical with that in South Carolina. The leading mill man in the State claimed that he has a notary public in each department of the mill who requires the parents to swear to the ages of the children when they go into the mills, and he said: "If we had factory inspection, the parents could be prosecuted for perjury and locked up when they swear falsely."

In South Carolina one informant stated: "Our child labor law has given us a class of children loafing that we do not know what to do with! We sent affidavits from magistrates relative to convictions of youthful criminals who got into mischief when loafing, which enabled us to have the law passed authorizing the establishment of a State Reformatory for boys."

CONDITIONS NOT AS BAD AS DEPICTED.

When inspecting the mills, extreme surprise was occasioned by the invariable statement of the mill men upon entering the spinning room: "Now, *this* is where the *children* are!" This frankness was entirely unexpected, as was the opportunity of free access to every department of the mills. It must be remembered that the mills visited included the ones most severely and frequently attacked.

In making observations the following criticisms of the sensational writers on the subject of child labor were constantly borne in mind:

1. Night work. The "necessity of throwing cold water in the faces of the children to keep them awake." The "wearing of underwear woven in Southern mills where tiny children are allowed to work all night long."

2. "Extreme emaciation of the children. Half starved and deformed."

3. "No child who has worked in the mill can ever learn to read and write."

4. "A child in the mill never talks to anyone."

5. "Children half naked."

6. Discipline. "Children kicked by overseers."

7. Accidents, with the claim of the "loss of fingers by hundreds of children."

8. "Children working through the noon hour."

9. Consumption. "When an autopsy is performed the lungs are found to be filled with lint."

10. "A child walks seventeen miles a day doffing."

11. "Diminutive or adjustable machinery."

These points are discussed below in the order in which they are listed.

(1.) A persistent effort was made, but without success, to find a mill running a night shift. A member of the Child Labor Committee in Georgia *"had been told by a friend who had heard from another leading woman in the State"* that water was thrown in the faces of the children during certain hours of the night at the Trion Mills. As it was not possible to go back to the Trion Mills, a letter was written to the "leading woman" requesting information on the subject, although when investigating in the vicinity of those mills it was learned that there had been no night work in that district for ten years. Her reply follows:

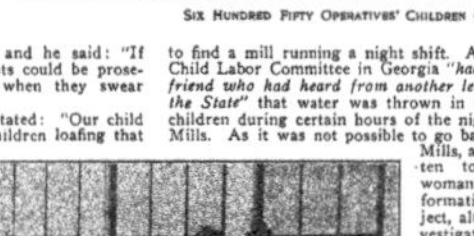

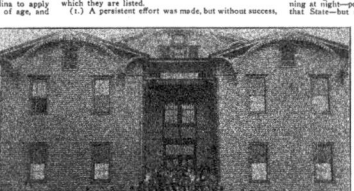

Six Hundred Fifty Operatives' Children in Mill School

A Primary Class

> I am very glad you wrote before quoting me, as your informant was mistaken. I never said anything about throwing cold water in the faces of the children at any mill, much less at the Trion Mill, one of the best regulated in the country. The information got mixed in this way. There was at one time a mill in Rome where I said I had seen a child thrown upon her bed at 10 a. m. in an exhausted sleep because of night work. That mill failed and I think the new management has better regulations.

School Recess

The writer who spoke of "underwear woven by tiny children at night" showed complete ignorance of the product of the Southern mills, which is largely confined to coarse sheetings and drills for Oriental countries, print cloths, fancy white goods for shirt waists, ginghams and outing flannels. There are no fine muslins, lawns or cambrics—the materials used for underwear—manufactured in that section of the country.

In South Carolina leading mill presidents stated that there *might be* some small yarn or knitting mills running at night—possibly half a dozen of the 200 mills in that State—but not a single mill man regarded night work as feasible or profitable, nor was there one operating a night shift. The picture so commonly drawn by sensationalists showing the necessity of dashing cold water in the faces of the children, indicating that to be the general condition, is absolutely false. The general testimony is to the effect that night work is not profitable because it produces too many "seconds," i. e., second-grade quality of goods, and the proportion of output is less because of the drowsiness of the help. In one town the destruction of a mill by fire threw a great many operatives into idleness. The president of another mill adopted night work for the purpose of giving those people employment, but he did not make a cent of profit.

Some of the points raised by mill men against night work were: The machinery gets tired—the particles crystallize and the belting breaks; night work is non-productive because there is so much bad work which cannot be traced to the employes at fault; the night shift leaves the machines in bad condition for the day shift and *vice versa*, because the operatives take no interest in their machines when jointly used, and all of this creates friction among the employes. When a day shift only is run, each operative is responsible for the condition of his machine. A further objection made by an employer was: "Night work is awful from the moral standpoint."

While night work may have prevailed ten years ago—and it must be remembered that the industry has been developed largely within the past ten years—as the size of the mills has been increased night work has been dropped. The leading cotton manufacturer of Alabama,

After School Recess

stated that the reason some mills had it was because a man starting a new mill in a small way with only a hundred thousand dollars in the plant found it difficult to make profits and thought he would realize more out of the investment by running two shifts. The quest for mills running at night was continued up to the end of the investigation without success. It was always a question of hearsay. The scarcity of labor would render the securing of shifts for night work impossible, even if it were desired.

(2.) With reference to the claim that the children are "half-starved, deformed and extremely emaciated," that "their appealing eyes gaze at you from out their pale, bloated brows," that "the memory of faces such as theirs cling in the mind with lingering tenacity; faded masks of withered flesh," and that one "presented the appearance not of a child, but of a gaunt man shrunk to diminutive size," issue must be taken. It is true that children with rosy cheeks are not to be found in the mills, and that they are more or less pale, but there were only two children in the eighteen mills visited who could have been called thin, not in the faces, but their arms were very slight.

The pale complexion, which all mill operatives have, cannot be attributed entirely to work in the mills, but is due largely to the lack of nourishing food. Before leaving the farms, "side meat" and corn bread—a mere mixture of corn meal and water baked—and, as a luxury now and then, molasses, constituted the chief articles of food. As farmers they did well if they had twenty dollars in cash during the year for expenditures. Although their incomes increased, to them fabulously, upon going into the mills, the mother, as well as the other members of the family who could work, was so engaged. With no one to care for the home the family subsisted mostly upon cold canned foods. Domestic science teachers are employed by many of the mill men now to instruct the people how to prepare

A KINDERGARTEN CAKE WALK

properly the food. One employer said: "Our people need more than anything else some system for teaching them how to live."

One of the mill presidents in making an effort to convince a radical that the people are better off in the mill towns than they were in the isolated rural districts, took her for a trip into the mountains. His account illustrates well the conditions under which the primitive mountaineers live:

> I showed her a typical mountain family in which there were eight children. The man had a cabin of one room with no stove, four miles from school and three miles from church. The oldest child was fourteen, had been to school once, and said he knew his letters. The man had three acres and did a little farming, and sometimes hauled timber at fifty cents a day. I asked her what that family would do if the man should die. (I think you must remember that the primary thing in existence is meat and bread). She stated that the people were better off here in the good mountain air than in the mills, and I told her I thought *air was pretty thin diet*.

SHOOTING THE CHUTES AT THE MILL KINDERGARTEN

(3.) That "no child who has worked in a cotton mill can ever learn to read and write" was refuted by families of children where half attend school while the other half work in the mill. This testimony was procured from the children in their homes, in the schools and in the mills. Girls of eighteen to twenty-one who had worked in the mills during childhood were going to the company's night school and learning to read and write. One boy of seventeen was observed in a day school in the primary class making satisfactory progress.

(4.) That "a child in the mill never talks to any one" was shown to be highly absurd not only by the willingness of the children but by their ability to answer all the questions put to them.

(5.) "Children half naked!" That depends on what the term means, but in any event such a radical statement does not describe properly the condition in which the children are found. The majority of the children are stockingless and shoeless when at the mills, but are otherwise very properly clad. The children in the schools are so well dressed as to cause surprise, and when seen on the streets Sundays and holidays all the children are well attired.

(6.) That the children are "kicked and shaken by the overseers" and otherwise severely disciplined cannot be applicable to the general situation. It is always possible that there may be a brute among foremen, but the children in all the mills were exceedingly playful, undisciplined and even destructive. In several spinning rooms they were playing tag around the spinning frames, showing a lack of discipline that would not be tolerated in other districts.

(7.) The picture of the "child of eight which has just had the two larger fingers of the right hand torn from their sockets at the greater knuckles," and the statement that the accident was "but one of hundreds," led to an investigation of the accident records which showed that in one mill where there are 1,400 employes there had been but one accident in four months—a child of eleven lost the first joint of the second finger in picking waste from the gears, which a fellow worker had uncovered, in violation of the strict rules which provide that the operatives shall not clean their machines when in motion. This was pitiful, indeed, but the records showed comparatively few accidents. There is no danger of accident whatever from the part of the machinery upon which the employes are engaged in spinning. In some of the mills the gears have been covered both top and bottom so that it is absolutely impossible for the children to get their fingers caught. This should be done in all the mills, whether there are children employed or not. But it is not fair to say that there are hundreds of cases of children of eight years of age losing their fingers.

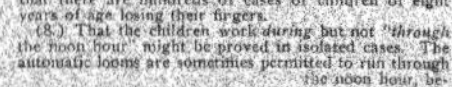

(8.) That the children work *during* but not "*through* the noon hour" might be proved in isolated cases. The automatic looms are sometimes permitted to run through the noon hour, because when the thread breaks the loom will stop and no harm can be done to the product. This, it was admitted, may tempt some of the *weavers*, generally adults, to go back into the mills after taking twenty minutes for lunch because it is piece work, although it was not observed in any mill, and several were visited at that *time* of day. In any event, this could not apply to the children as they work in the *spinning* room and it would not be possible to keep that machinery in operation without a full complement of operatives. There, too, the largest proportion of children are not even *spinners*, but their assistants, *i.e.*, *doffers* who NEVER *work through an entire hour*. The children were found playing about the spinning room at the noontime, at twenty minutes past twelve, and when asked why they did not go home to lunch each replied: "I done been." The shade of the spinning room seemed to be preferable to the noonday sun. The machinery, however, was not in operation.

IN THE KINDERGARTEN VEGETABLE GARDENS

(9.) That consumption has made great inroads upon the health of the children because of the lint in the mills could not be substantiated. In one mill where there are a thousand operatives, reputable persons said that there had been one case of consumption in that village during the last year and the only other case was

KINDERGARTEN MAY POLE

five years ago. In another smaller village there was found one case of tuberculosis, that of a young girl about sixteen. Inquiries were made throughout the trip, but these were the only cases observed; and, in view of the devices for ventilating the mills, it does not seem possible that the lungs can be "imbedded in lint."

(10.) A careful calculation as to the distance which a doffer boy would be required to walk in the performance of his duties during one day, made at one of the largest mills, shows the average to be four miles, and the longest distance he could possibly travel (and he would be going out of his way to do that) to be four and one-half miles instead of the seventeen claimed by the "sensational writer." At a smaller mill the distance does not exceed six thousand sixty feet.

(11.) It has been claimed that diminutive or adjustable machinery has been manufactured expressly for the use of children in the mills. This is an absurd statement made by so-called sociological experts. The machinery in all cotton mills is the size regularly built for adults, and it is impossible that the product could be manufactured otherwise. Quite as preposterous is the statement that the "children are hidden at work in secret places." In the first place, children *were at work in plain sight* in all the mills, and in the second place the different processes of manufacture are so systematised that it would be impracticable to divide any department in order to secrete youthful operatives.

INSTANCES OF CHILD LABOR.

The main processes of manufacture in the cotton mill are carding, spinning and weaving. For the products usually manufactured in the South, the carding and other incidental operations require about one-seventh of the total number of employes, the spinning three-sevenths and the weaving three-sevenths in mills where the automatic looms are used. But there are exceptions to the rule (and so many complex conditions) that a definite statement cannot be made with reference to the proportion of operatives in a single department. In some mills there may be one-third of the operatives in each division. The junior operatives of a mill will be found in the spinning room where they are engaged in spinning, doffing and sweeping, principally the last two operations. When the bobbins upon the spinning frame become filled with the yarn, it is the duty of the doffers to replace them with empty bobbins. Usually this is light work, but in one mill children from ten to twelve doff in the roving room where the bobbins are very heavy. There are youthful sweepers also in the weave room. In one mill they are required to drag the bags of waste a long distance for final disposition. Many of the spinners are over twelve, but children between the ages of ten and twelve are numerous in the mills. In four of the *eighteen* mills inspected, representing a total number of fifteen thousand employes, there were observed seven cases of children undoubtedly under the age of seven years spinning, cleaning bobbins, or putting ends in the balls of yarn. Three of the cases were in one mill which is a financial failure, partly because of the old machinery; and it may be said that two, which were in another, were the only cases of very young children in that mill. The remaining two extreme cases were found in the other two mills—one in each.

The president also made the tour of the first one inspected of these two mills. He said: "Let us go to the spinning room first," and the freight elevator was used for our transportation to the top floor. When it stopped at the entrance to the spinning room, he ejaculated in a surprised tone: "Well!" Right in front of the elevator a little child, who was spinning, was climbing upon the frame to reach the broken threads for the purpose of tying them. When asked the probable age of the child, he said: "Six years." He immediately thereafter inquired of the child its age. The reply came, "Eight." Later, he took the superintendent to task for permitting the child to work. In four additional mills there were some very young children spinning,—one in one mill and a few in each of the others. It would have been impossible to secure the number of children between ten and twelve years in the mills, as it is so difficult to learn the correct ages. The effort was to get a general observation of the situation, and particularly to learn whether or not there was a tendency on the part of the mill men to employ large numbers of children as young as five, six or seven. Clearly this was found not to be the case. It was claimed that very young children are permitted to be in the mills only when the magistrate certifies that "they must work or they would starve,' and that they were either orphans or children of widows. It was also generally claimed that, with the exception of orphans who absolutely required the work in order to secure a living, the young children observed in the mills "were not on the pay-roll, but had gone in to help their mothers, who were widows, or were employed after three o'clock, at the close of school, to help their sisters and brothers." Of course, this adds to the pay envelope of the mother, sister or brother helped, and thus indirectly they were on the pay-roll. The regular operatives were given when thus aided, for instance, eight sides of the machinery to operate instead of six. There are also instances where the children are required by the mothers who are operatives to be in the mill after school that they may thus care for them instead of having them in danger alone at home or on the streets.

When the State has provided no proper way to care for the poverty-stricken, it is a debatable question how far criticism should be offered for their presence in the mills. The following instances were cited by reliable persons, some of whom were and some were not identified with mill interests:

"One child of a widow who was unable to work, seven years of age, paid by a mill man to sweep, although inefficient."

"One little girl in the mill with her grandmother, otherwise she would have to go to the poorhouse, which would be unfortunate, as the almshouses here are exceedingly disagreeable."

Another instance of how the mill men help to take care of the poor, although not a case of a child under age, was given as follows: "There are an old Confederate soldier and his daughter in this village. We let them have one of our homes free and allow the daughter to go to the mill to work intermittently—she cannot leave the old man every day—to enable her to make enough to support them."

Another said: "I have a woman in the No. 1 card room who was left a widow. Her husband died of consumption. She asked to be permitted to have her child

Operatives Bowling

in the mill with her. It was either a question of running her out or allowing her to do this. The woman makes a good living."

Several mill men stated that there would always be some child labor, for "We will always *have to provide work for the poor*"; and that "if we did not let the children work it would be utterly impossible for some men to care for their very large families."

Operatives' Club House

Attacks should not be leveled at the cotton mills alone. Child labor on the farms, in the homes and in the mills always existed, and the condition is the same, generally speaking, to-day, although it should not be.

While there is an obligation on the part of society to render impossible the employment of children of tender age, and the age limit in the South should be higher,—certainly fourteen years—it must be remembered that the majority of the children in the mills are above the age usually pictured by writers upon the subject of child labor. Furthermore, while the spinners must work continuously during the day, the doffers work only twenty minutes out of thirty-five. Non-continuous work must be a point considered when estimating the injury of employment to the child. Very frequently the fifteen minutes usual between doffings in the coarse goods mills are devoted to base ball outside of the mill, the floor superintendent going to the window and whistling for the doffers when needed. Where finer yarns are spun, because it takes longer to empty the bobbins, the rest periods are longer. Outside of one mill the president has a gymnasium bar for the use of the sweeper boys who are not continuously employed.

In the weave room the work is of such a nature that only adults can properly perform it. But among the fifteen thousand employes there were observed weaving in one mill two children who were probably under the age of twelve, and in another two of probably twelve years. The other main operations, in the card and picker rooms, require men.

The superintendent of one of the mills,—a fine specimen of manhood now forty years of age was once a child laborer. He began work in a cotton mill at eight, was a spinner at fourteen, and had charge of the spinning room at sixteen. As other even more successful men in the South to-day, such as merchants, doctors and bank presidents, worked in the mills when young and secured their early education in the schools supported by the mill owners, it would be just as fair to point to this superintendent who began work at eight as typical of the conditions in the cotton mills as it is to take one or half a dozen extreme instances of child labor and make them picture the general conditions. Neither would be true. That the young workers, however, do grow into responsible positions was evidenced by another superintendent who said: "We have a number of fellows who were doffers and have been promoted to high positions. Almost all of our loom fixers were weavers. Many of our boys have gone elsewhere as overseers." In this mill there were three spinners,—girls over fourteen, who had gone into the mill as young children and were the picture of health.

A child of twelve in the spinning room can earn more than its father in the picker room, but the wages of a single member are insufficient to support a family, which is always of good size. In one mill village an interesting family of five was visited. The oldest child was going to school and the next in age was working in the mill, but expressed a preference for school. The two alternate going to school and working. The other children are too young to work. The father is employed in the cloth room of the mill and the mother cares for the home. In another mill there was a splendid boy of fifteen years, who with his mother, another son of nine and an infant had gone to the village two years before. The boy, then thirteen, was put to work in the mill; the family got in debt $75; the nine-year-old boy would go to the agent of the mill and say: "We've nothin' t'eat." The agent took care of them and they gradually paid their debts. The boy-head of the family is pointed to with pride by the agent of the mill, who claims that he will make a head man of him.

SOME OF THE PROBLEMS INVOLVED IN CHILD LABOR.

The farming element, which constitutes the dominating influence in the legislatures, does not yet realize the necessity of providing ample taxation for schools. The resources of the several States visited would permit greater appropriations for the public welfare. Child labor legislation without compulsory education laws has proven inoperative. This is due to the unwillingness of the parents to send their children to the schools in preference to the mills. With inadequate school facilities where the child labor law has been observed, the children become demoralized in running the streets. When convicted of crime they are chained to hardened criminals, and their downward course is assured. Through the influence of club women a reformatory has recently been secured in Georgia and one is authorized in South Carolina, which will prevent the mingling of juvenile offenders and adult criminals in those two states. But until compulsory education, for which *the mill owners* have been agitating more than five years, is secured, with adequate school facilities, the argument that the children are better off in the mills where they gain self-reliance and an industrial training cannot be refuted.

While the vagrancy laws, which the mill men would be glad to see strengthened with "spikes," are practi-

Fourth of July Celebration

[illegible] enforced, the tendency of fathers to live on the earnings of the children has greatly decreased, due largely to the creation of public sentiment against it. Where there are idle fathers, they are chiefly invalids or drunkards.

Child labor has been accentuated by the scarcity of labor due partly to the high price of cotton, which has sent many of the families back to the farms where they rent a few acres for a season; or one crop of cotton, which is mortgaged in advance. They are called "croppers," because as farmers they move annually, and the roving characteristic is so marked that after becoming operatives they move frequently from one mill village to another. Sometimes the employer will be enabled to hold a family by permitting it to move from house to house,—even across the street. This story was told by a jester: "The people change their abiding place so often that when a wagon stops at his door, the man with half a dozen chickens will find them already on their backs with their feet crossed to be tied."

The work people are so independent and quick to move to a mill where their young children will be employed with the other members of the family, that the temptation of the superintendent with idle machines is very great. Undoubtedly the shortage of labor inclines the superintendents to employ more children than they would otherwise. It also causes them, as one put it, to "become rascals by stealing labor from one another." The employers are trying to reach the people to become homemakers by having their living conditions as attractive as possible. One of the three presidents active in bringing about the movement for shorter hours stated: "The need for recreation is very great. At the end of the year after the people have come to the mill, they only know about twenty others in the village. By arranging time and opportunity for recreation so that they will become acquainted, we hope to secure an attachment for the village to decrease the migratory tendency."

When some of the manufacturers were asked why they did not discontinue the building of more mills than could be "manned," the reply came that they make "fill orders" and would take their chances on being able to get enough help by drawing from other mills.

The scarcity of labor is not only caused by the increase in the number of mills, but by the hesitation on the part of immigrants to enter the South. This is due partly to the sensational literature which has painted such dark and unforbidding pictures.* This literature which has been published supposedly in the interest of the children, has operated against them and actually accentuated child labor. The immigrants are further deterred by rumors relative to numerous murders and few convictions. Commissioner Watchorn states this general inclination well when he says: "Immigrants seek places of which they have heard the most favorable all-around reports." Another element contributing toward the lack of a sufficient number of operatives is the rise in wages which has enabled the women to leave the mills and become home-makers. Furthermore, it is claimed that wages have advanced thirty to fifty per cent in five years, more rapidly than have increased the needs of the people. Their needs must be increased to equal the rise in wages to get them to work steadily. Even where the premium plan of adding to the wages for regular attendance has been tried in the spinning room, it has been found ineffective. Of the total number of operatives upon the pay-roll there are always from fifteen to twenty per cent "loafing," as the people can make enough in four days to live six. One president stated that "the people are not sufficiently ambitious to care to work all the time, but as we are throwing about them elevating influences their needs are growing greater and the next generation will be all right." Naturally, the increasing of the needs of the people to the consuming power of their wages would be a slow solution of this problem, even though "the next generation" may be "all right" in some of the long-established villages such as the one mentioned.

* One such effort received the "blue ribbon," in Belgium, as the best Sensational production, and was used by certain interests abroad to discourage immigration to the South.

Swimming Pool

Operatives' Band

Several mill owners estimated that if all the operatives listed upon their pay-rolls would work day in and day out, there would be an adequate supply of labor. When asked why they did not reduce the wages to meet this "scarcity due to higher wages" and thus force the operatives to work full time, it was stated that competition among the mills for labor would not permit.

It must be remembered that wages for *individuals* in the cotton industry are low as compared with other skilled trades, both in New England and the South, and a statement with reference to the present high wages can be only relative. When the mountain people first went into the mills, although the wages were much lower than now, the total amount earned by a *family* so far exceeded its earnings upon the farm that it meant almost fabulous riches. The solution of the child labor problem through a further increase in wages would be a slow process, for the wages of the adults would have to be sufficiently high to permit them to support their families; and taking into consideration cheaper living, the wages are now apparently as high as in New England in the same line of manufacture, but there while the families work in the mills there are greater opportunities for the fathers in skilled trades outside. The Southern manufacturers also claim that they must compete in the world market—with the wages much lower in Italy, France, Germany and England, while in India they are but a small fraction of what is paid elsewhere.

Match Game between Mill Teams

If one of the solutions is immigrant labor, it will have to be *family* labor, owing to the nature of the work. The work in the spinning room, at present so largely performed by children, should be taken up by young women over fourteen; the other adult members of the family being employed in other trades outside or in different capacities in the mills, a living wage would be secured. The *individual* immigrant would not be attracted by the wages which can be paid in the South when he can go to the Northwest and secure a higher rate. Nor does he take into consideration final results due to cheaper living, but he sees the amount of wages paid by the day. Immigrants of few nationalities would mix with the native whites, and it therefore seems that they must go principally to the new mills or to the city mills, thus driving the natives into the country districts.

It was interesting to learn that the greatest scarcity of labor occurs in the spinning room where the children work. For business reasons purely, if for no others, the employers do not desire child labor because the spinning machine is the most delicate and expensive in the mill, and the higher the grade of intelligence to manipulate that machine, they claim the better will be the product and the greater the amount of output. Furthermore, the children are very destructive,—broken bobbins frequently were observed scattered upon the mill floors by the doffers. Again, the loss through wasted material caused by unskilled labor is greater in the spinning room than in the preceding processes because it is so near the finished product. To prove the economic value of older operatives, one employer, who manufactures colored goods, said: "We want children over fourteen because the younger ones cannot tell the difference between the shades." Even the sweeper boys are inefficient because of their youthfulness, and one mill president has introduced negro adults to sweep the floors, while another has substituted superannuated white men. Another said: "It is to our interest to keep the children out of the mills, for otherwise they will not grow up to be strong men." The leading mill men go so far as to say that *they do not believe children should work under the age of sixteen*, that that would be the ideal condition which they would welcome.

The scarcity of labor in the cotton mills cannot be reduced by the use of negro labor. While reliable information shows that negroes are used in the tobacco factories, where they simply have to strip the tobacco leaves, and have made good locomotive firemen and yard switchmen upon the railroads, it has been proved thoroughly that they cannot be used successfully in the cotton mills. While there is no reason why negroes could not be trained to be good operatives, it has been shown that in the cotton mills they could make enough in two days to meet their needs and that they would not work the balance of the week. Furthermore, it is the characteristic of the negro to roam at night. Being drowsy, therefore, during the day, the rythm of the machinery puts him to sleep.

The child labor problem may be met partly by the invention of machinery to displace the children. A letter from the president of the Saxon mills in South Carolina, calling upon The National Civic Federation to aid in this matter is quoted here.

> If your organization can influence the Draper Company or other leaders in inventions to perfect machines to doff the spinning frames and to catch up and insert between the rolls the broken sliver, you will in my judgment be aiming straighter at the mark of the final solution of the child labor problem than any one who has yet interested themselves in it. I wish sincerely that you could put the whole influence of your organization upon an agitation of the need of automatic machinery in the spinning room where the problem is, in the judgment of many, no more difficult than has been solved in both the weaving and drawing-in rooms, and the need is far greater.

He suggested prize competitions to bring the question to the attention of inventors generally. The automatic looms and drawing-in frames are so marvelous as to be uncanny, and surely it is possible to provide for doffing by machinery, which would reduce the number of operatives required for that work. The drawing-in frame takes the place of seventeen girls, and will perform in eight minutes work that used to require about four hours.

The automatic loom, which has lessened the number of operatives required for weaving has an adjustment for supplying mechanically fresh bobbins filled with yarn when those in use have become empty. This operation is not dissimilar to the process of doffing.

One of the greatest needs is the creation of public sentiment in favor of the *modern* legislation required, which at the present time is advocated and understood principally by the employers. Generally speaking, the agitation has been promoted by well-meaning but misguided theorists who have not acquainted themselves with the conditions under which the people work or the business management and financial problems of the mills. The legislation needed in South Carolina is:

Compulsory education with provision for truant officers;

Factory inspection to strengthen the child labor law;

Amendment of the child labor law to increase the age limit from twelve to fourteen years;

Birth registration; and marriage license law.

With the exception of the last two subjects listed, the requirements are the same in Alabama, and in Georgia even the child labor law is yet to be secured.

For the present, the cotton mills are industrial training schools as well as refuges for the unfortunates. Too much praise cannot be given to the mill owners who, in spite of the unfair criticism which has been made, are not only giving food and shelter and an industrial training to the illiterate descendants of the first inhabitants of the colonies, but, through their Welfare Work, are a great civilizing influence and are steadily raising the standard of citizenship.

Dance Pavilion

TO SUPPORT TRADE UNIONISM AND OPPOSE SOCIALISM.

AN INTERVIEW WITH THE FOUNDER OF THE NEW NATIONAL BUREAU AS TO ITS ORGANIZATION AND SCOPE.

FROM recent announcements in the daily press comes the information that a new industrial bureau to uphold trade unionism and oppose Socialism has just been organized in Boston by the well-known writers and lecturers on socialism, Martha Moore Avery and David Goldstein. Mrs. Avery was formerly a socialist and one of the most ardent supporters of the doctrines of the party. For several years, beginning some fifteen years ago, she took an active part, through her writings and from the platform, in advancing socialistic propaganda. Later, convinced of the complete fallacy of socialist principles, she became an out-and-out opponent of all their doctrines. In organizing the Boston School of Political Economy, of which for some time past she has been the head and director, Mrs. Avery inaugurated the movement she had in view of opposing socialism by a broad plan of education.

Mr. Goldstein who, for a number of years, has been associated with Mrs. Avery in her educational work, also began as an ardent supporter of socialism, only later to become one of its most bitter opponents. The reasons for this change in attitude Mr. Goldstein gives as follows in the Preface to his recent book "Socialism: The Nation of Fatherless Children":

> The casual reader would, no doubt, reading in the public press the notice of my withdrawal from the Socialist party, conclude that that action was prompted by the thought of a day. Such, however, is far from the facts in the case. Having for years been interested in the study of economic principles, rather than in the acquaintance of socialist data, I naturally gave my attention, outside of propaganda proper, to acquiring a knowledge of the economic principles which socialism is alleged to rest upon. I came long ago to a realization that the mouthing of the name of Karl Marx was no guarantee of economic knowledge. Seven years ago, together with a few of the then comrades, we organized the Karl Marx class, for the study of his (Marx) work "Capital." Three years ago, having outgrown the work of the socialist master, we changed the name of the class to the Boston School of Political Economy, and took up the study of the original work of the Director, Martha Moore Avery. I know, now, that this was the point at which I began intellectually to move away from the socialist propaganda.
>
> The parting of the ways, from moral standing ground, was more abrupt. The Herron episode furnished the occasion—I resented the attitude taken by the socialist press in regard to George D. Herron's divorce and his "socialist marriage," which had disgusted me—especially for the reason that it could not be denied that he, Mr. Herron, was a socialist leader who was fast mounting to the very top of the ladder in socialist favor. It was at a public meeting held in Boston at which the then editor of the Haverhill *Social Democrat* was the speaker. After he had finished his address in praise of George D. Herron, whom he had lauded as being in power and virtue second only to Jesus Christ, in the discussion which followed, together with Martha Moore Avery and one or two others, the author gave voice to strong condemnation of the lecturer's opinions and to the general tone of the socialist movement throughout the country. It was being sharply forced upon me that that which I had so long fondly believed to be socialism was not socialism at all. It was a severe blow to me—I was cut from my moorings—I could not tell for some months to come whether it was but a personal episode or whether I must in fact regard it is the deliberate position taken in strict accord with socialist philosophy—I had thought my lifework would be given to the cause of socialism, consequently the conflict in my mind and heart was great.

Mr. Goldstein's long experience in the ranks of organized labor qualifies him to speak of socialism in its relation to the great movement of trade unionism. Through close association with socialist leaders on the platform and in "hand to hand fights upon the floor of trades unions," he became thoroughly familiar with the tactics employed by socialists in their persistent efforts to gain control of the trade union movement. He believes emphatically that there is marked evidence to show that upon economic ground the battle to sustain industrial progress will come to an issue between the American Federation of Labor and the railway brotherhoods on the one side, and the socialists' organizations on the other.

It is fortunate that two persons so well equipped as Mr. Goldstein and Mrs. Avery, are to be associated in the work of the new national Bureau to combat the dangerous and disruptive influence of socialism. When asked concerning the organization and scope of the Bureau, Mrs. Avery stated them to be as follows:

> The object of the National Bureau is the creation, collection and analysis of literature which has for its purpose the defense of national principles vs. those of socialism. The promotion and endorsement of reforms, social, commercial, financial and industrial, with the condemnation of the opposing program of revolutionists whether conducted by socialists or anarchists.
>
> Our propaganda has thus a positive and a negative aspect. The defence of the family as against the encroachments of divorce and free love, which issue, ever before us, has been recently emphasized by the Gorky incident.
>
> To defend the principle of individual responsibility, which alone safeguards the integrity of citizenship; as against the denial of free will which lies as a basic doctrine of socialism.
>
> To defend the rights of private property in capital as against the socialist demand that all industrial, commercial and financial capital shall be owned and operated by all the people collectively.
>
> To advance the interests of those trade unions who work upon the principle that the interest of capital and labor may best be promoted by trade agreements, as against the socialist demand for the abolition of the "wages-system."
>
> To inculcate those heroic virtues which come as the fruit of religion, as against the socialist-atheist psychology which is captivating the lesser man under the prospect of material ease.

Foreseeing the necessity of this undertaking the book on socialism above referred to has been published by Mrs. Avery and Mr. Goldstein. It contains quotations from more than one hundred socialists of international standing, these quotations being taken from socialist books, magazines, documents and papers "which are openly hostile to American institutions and which persistently assail those principles which lie as the foundation stones of Christian civilization." This book is receiving the endorsement of men of all classes of society. Mr. Samuel Gompers, President of the American Federation of Labor, wrote to the author as follows: "I beg to say that I have read with keenest interest your book on 'Socialism, the Nation of Fatherless Children,' and have no hesitancy in saying that the book is not only timely, but an excellent contribution to the literature on the labor question and the labor movement. It tears the mask of hypocrisy from

MARTHA MOORE AVERY

the face of those who have long pretended to be friends of the trade union movement, and yet seek its destruction or diversion to an improper purpose. I have found your book a ready reference to the many hostile utterances and action of pretended friends."

"With the Upton Sinclair frenzy at white heat," said Mrs. Avery, "and the Gorky incident not yet faded from the limelight, the time is ripe for the classification of what may be called the 'muckrakers' and for a work which should be undertaken to point out that reformers, however sensational their methods and however interested their personal motives, do not attack the foundations of Christian civilization. Within this limit, because their intention is safe, even illy advised propaganda must be ranked with the sound and sober efforts to perfect our National Institutions, which being grounded upon First Principles are acceptable to all ages.

"On the other hand, this work must show that however seriously some socialists may take themselves or their alleged science, because it is their deliberate intention to destroy what they are pleased to call the 'present system,' namely, private property, the family, the State and religion, they are thus necessarily classed with others of lurid tongue and with bomb throwers. The means employed are indeed different, but Revolution is the object which they all desire.

"No right-minded man can deny the popular cry for Reform,—for something and for many things that shall improve and perfect American institutions, but the principles upon which they are grounded are sound, for God, not men, created them. But it is these principles which it is the express mission of socialism to overthrow. By its very inner constitution the Revolution must first of all strew the human path with the wreckage of faith. Faith in the morality of the individual man; faith in the sanctity of the home; faith in the honor of our native land; faith in the goodness and justice of God must give place to the 'socialist mind' to materialism, to animalism, sugar-coated with idealism. This is the debris of which socialist barricades are building. This was the socialist law, laid down in '48 when Karl Marx with the key of 'Surplus Value,' which unlocks all time and all things, explained the means to the socialist goal. I quote from Karl Marx in 'Secret Societies of Switzerland.' 'We content ourselves at present with laying the foundations of revolutions and shall have deserved well when we shall have excited the hatred and contempt for all existing institutions. We wage war against all prevailing ideas about religion, country, State and patriotism.'

"Reform or Revolution shall be the test, for a reformer though never so extravagant in his speech, does not counsel the overthrow of the existing order. The Revolutionist does.

"The Revolutionist stands against those principles which the greatest minds of all ages have held. Consequently if one would know what a socialist means he must hold the mirror up to that degenerate nature from which free-will and individual responsibility have been taken. For this cult declares that it is environment which creates morals as well as manners; that man is a *non*-moral being. So any vile means to their end may be used. August Bebel, than whom no living man is higher authority in the world-wide socialist movement, defends this policy in these words: 'We want the wounds of the body social kept in a festering condition in order to allow the class distinctions to become as acute as possible.'

"This advice is carried out! Eugene V. Debs while rolling over and over eloquent phrases calls upon American workmen to arm in defense of the working class against capitalism. Our neighbor, Canada, recently barred from her mails the socialist paper containing this effusion, but we allow the Revolution breeder to do its deadly work with a circulation of 300,000. Oppression of the weak exists and it must be righted, but is this the means and is Revolution the end?

"Evidently Mr. Upton Sinclair, the latest socialist star, is of that opinion. He tells with shocking frankness the whole story of how to win the Revolution in his book, *The Jungle,* and how it was written. Its purpose was to 'blow the top off the industrial tea-kettle.' We have his word for it. So long ago as 1903 in the month of May, through the columns of the *Independent*, Mr. Sinclair took the general public into his confidence as though it were his Father Confessor, with this difference, that he was not penitent. By his article entitled 'My Cause' he laid bare his inner motives. They have a first and a second term. First, to sell his intellectual wares, and second, to advance socialist propaganda, the news sensation resting on duplicity.

"Mr. Sinclair has indeed, by his trick, 'got even,' as he said he would, with the literary world; he has choked it with his own stuff for a time. He wanted $1,000 to live on while he wrote his now much talked of *Jungle*. So he created one *Arthur Stirling*, a young poet, who could not find a publisher for his masterpiece. So quite consistent with socialist philosophy he took his life in his hand and went to—hades. Our author perpetuated the scheme of the poet's existence

[...] of his demise upon the general public through the [Ne]w York newspapers. They were betrayed into the [...] by the aid of Mr. Sinclair's friends (socialists [of] course), who reported the imaginary death by the [...] drowning of the imaginary poet. The first [...] had been gained. *Arthur Stirling* had by death [...] a hearing for Mr. Sinclair, who, a few months

DAVID GOLDSTEIN

[lat]er, offered for sale the imaginary *Journal of Arthur Stirling*. Thus Mr. Sinclair found a market for his [...] and a thousand dollars for his pocket.

"But this was not the end! Mr. Sinclair, who had [s]acrificed his honor—that is, a man who does not [h]old the socialist philosophy would have done so—and [th]en he stepped forward to sacrifice his reputation. [W]hen 'My Cause' was published, socialists thought it [g]reat fun and good *means* in reaching the revolution.

"'I knew,' said the author of *The Jungle*, 'that the [h]oax would cost me my reputation and the respect of [a]ll decent people, but that did not matter, for I have [n]ot been favored with the acquaintance of many de[c]ent people, and am not obliged to hear what the [w]orld thinks of me. Besides, I would cheerfully have [r]obbed a house or sandbagged a millionaire had my [t]ask been possible in no other way. My one desire [w]as to raise a sensation, first to sell the book, of [c]ourse, and, second, to give me a standing ground [f]rom which to begin the agitation of my cause.'

"The integrity of his evidence regarding the story [o]f *The Jungle* is as good and no better than the [a]uthorship of *Arthur Stirling*, his life, poetry, death [a]nd *Journal*. For upon the word of Mr. Reynolds not [o]ne of Mr. Sinclair's charges, which were placed be[f]ore the commission to investigate the packing houses, [w]as substantiated. 'Evidence' all coming from socialist [s]ources vanished into thin air when proofs were [w]anted by the Beef Trust Commissioners, Messrs. [N]eill and Reynolds. Disgusting and filthy as the con[di]tions were found to be, and loudly calling for no [l]esser remedy than the recommendation of the Presi[d]ent—for 'inspection from hoof to can'—for the pure [f]ood bill—nothing was found equal to the packing of [d]ead or diseased flesh of cattle, nor comparable to the [h]orror of rendering human bodies into food products.

"But then the motive of the President is Reform, [w]hile that of *The Jungle* and its socialist sources is [R]evolution—there is a difference as wide as heaven [f]rom hell.

"Mrs. Ella Reeve-Cohen-Bloor, a most radical ad[v]ocate of socialism for many years, whose testimony [i]n support of Mr. Sinclair's charges backed out step [by] step as it was pressed for proof after proof, plainly [s]tates her purpose in 'muck-raking' in the concluding [w]ords of her 'Evidence' in the *New York World* of [J]une 3. She says: 'The real remedy will be the [p]ublic ownership of all these great food industries.' [I]n other words, the confiscation of industrial capital; [th]e means, scandal; the end, revolution! Socialists [a]ccept no moral responsibility for breaking down the [b]arriers of truth; anything is all right that will hasten [th]e 'Cause.'

"It is the same with the moral and social relations," [s]ays Mrs. Avery. "Socialism defends a code that is [n]either religious nor rational. As a case in point one [m]ay note the address before Congregational ministers [i]n which Mrs. J. Phelps Stokes advocated socialist [p]rinciples without reserve. For under her treatment [r]eligion utterly lost its identity. She exclaims with [s]omething of dramatic force: 'By what right, whether [d]ivine or human, am I and my sisters compelled to [...] body and soul that other human beings may [be] idle, wealthy and even destroy their own souls in [illegible] 'So right indeed!' But [illegible] is lacking to logic. [illegible] should be the motive [f]or one's work, that other human beings may be idle,

etc., one would thus be a sinner and in grievous need of conviction of repentance and of mending one's ways. This elevated boot is kicking at the wrong fact. It misconceives the character of religion by applying the standard of worldly success to the measurement of Christian grace, since when did religion say that it was a mark of spiritual life to take 'uppermost seats'? For that good men ride in automobiles and that bad men go afoot. As a matter of fact the religion of Jesus Christ is as hard for the rich to practice as for the poor, although for opposite reasons. Now if Mrs. Stokes were as careful of environing 'my sisters' with a moral psychology, as she seems anxious for their material welfare, her defence of the Gorky 'marriage' would not have seen the light of day. But this was a perfectly correct defence of socialist philosophy, and it is by the key notes, or the theme rather, of one's utterance that must give out the understanding as to whether one is for or against national institutions. For quite contrary to socialist theory vanity and lust, not poverty, is the cause of divorce and free love, or if you please the basis of 'socialist marriage.' So not only is the misconduct of some church goers a scandal to the faith in Almighty God, but vastly more so is international socialism which enters the political arena as a means of thrusting out religion and ushering in atheism—or chaos rather. But God is not mocked.

"Our choice is our own, but for those who believe in their home and their country it is worse than folly to support that movement which has for its object the destruction of the family, and the nation. To this end we are pledged, to the analysis of reforms and the revolution."

SOCIALISM ON NEW YORK'S EAST SIDE

From the Jewish Gazette.

HERE is an interesting news-dispatch which appeared on Tuesday morning in several hundred newspapers throughout the United States:

> St. Paul, June 6.—Mrs. Rheta C. Dorr, Chairman of the Industrial Committee of the National Women's Federation, has caused a sensation here by her declaration that in her part of New York, the lower East Side, she did not think she knew "a man or a thinking woman who is not an avowed Socialist or Anarchist."

In one of the several papers in which we saw this item it appeared under the headline:

"ALL EAST SIDERS
ANARCHISTS AND SOCIALISTS."

The statement was made at the convention of the National Federation of Women's Clubs.

Mrs. Dorr, who speaks of "her" East Side, is one of the many "friends" who during the past decade have been intruding into its privacy, destroying its home-ties, causing radical and irreconcilable differences of opinion to arise between parents and children, nullifying the influence of Judaism as a code and guide of life upon the younger generation of Jews, training and developing a breed of "higher dependents," prigs and cads, humiliating the self-respect of the East Side Jew, and grinding our her experiences, experiment, researches and discoveries into highly remunerative "copy" for newspaper and magazine articles and books, in company (or is it in competition?) with Robert Hunter, J. English Walling, Ernest Poole, John Martin, Hutchins Hapgood, John Spargo and others too numerous to mention. In other words, she is one of the self-appointed "uplifters" of the East Side who have degraded its good name.

Mrs. Dorr is a well-meaning woman, no doubt. Her intentions are good, we are sure, but the road to the habitat of Satan is paved with good intentions. The road to new Sheol that is being prepared for the refugee from persecution and massacre—the gate of exclusion—has, undoubtedly, been paved for a goodly distance by just such books as those written by the Hunters and Spargoes and by such statements as that made by Mrs. Dorr.

Needless to say, the statement is absurd on its face. Not only is it absolutely false that all East Siders are Anarchists *and* Socialists, but it is equally absolutely false that any very considerable number are enemies of society or desirous of overthrowing the Constitution of the United States. The facts are quite the reverse; most East Siders are neither Socialists nor Anarchists. Of the latter category there are so few that the proportion could be expressed only in decimal number of the fifth or sixth remove; of the former, the number is variable, according to the improvement of the financial condition of the East Side. As a fact, Socialism is fast losing strength on the East Side.

Of course the lady did not say that all East Siders are Anarchists or Socialists. The unscrupulous telegraph editors and headline writers make that implication. What she said was that she did not think she knew "a man or a thinking woman on the lower East Side who is not an avowed Socialist or Anarchist." We believe her; she met none but these, for the reason that being what she is, an intruder and meddler, she would not meet the thinking Jews and Jewesses of the East Side. She met only the "conscious" and "convinced" of the settlements, and her East Side horizon is bounded by the University Settlement, the College Settlement, the People's Institute and the Corning Clark House. The few Jews and Jewesses whom she may have met are that breed who look up to the "uplifters," and being, in one way or another, dependent upon them, imitate them apishly, and repeat their patter, parrotlike. She did not, could not have met East Siders who represent the heart and spirit of the East Side.

THE WESTERN FEDERATION OF MINERS.

The Socialistic Labor Organization of the West Opposes Trade Union Principles.

AN account of the Western Federation of Miners is presented in *The Outlook* of May 19 by Mr. William Hard, who endeavors to interpret the principles of that organization as expressed through its various channels of operation. The differences between the principles of the Federation and those of most other labor organizations, and in particular of the trade unions, are strikingly presented in a comparison of the Federation, which is composed largely of metalliferous miners in the States west of the Mississippi River, with the United Mine Workers of America, whose membership is confined to coal mine workers. After characterizing the latter as "a business enterprise" and the former as "incidentally a business enterprise but fundamentally a philosophical agitation," Mr. Hard says:

> The United Mine Workers accepts the present industrial system and regards the employer as its partner. The Western Federation of Miners denounces the present industrial system and regards the very existence of the employer as an evil. The United Mine Workers is interested mainly in the division of the proceeds of the present industrial system between itself and its partner, the employer. It wants to increase its own share of the proceeds, and it wants to reduce its partner's share. The Western Federation of Miners, on the other hand, is interested mainly in the elimination of the employer. It wants more wages, of course, but if it should succeed in establishing a scale of even a hundred dollars a day it would still be bound by its principles to spurn the relaxing comforts of prosperity and to nerve itself to a continuation of the struggle.

Referring to the internal policy of the Western Federation and to its attitude toward the trade agreement principle of settling and preventing differences between labor and capital, Mr. Hard says:

> The internal policy of the Western Federation of Miners is consistent with its published principles. The most important part of this policy is an aversion to the signing of contracts with employers. A contract is regarded as a manacle. It binds one union when another union might need its help. Presumably if a contract could be signed by the whole working class of the United States with the whole employing class for the term of a year at a fixed scale of wages, the Western Federation of Miners would not seriously object. But in the absence of such a possibility it seems to the Federation that contracts interfere with the mobility and flexibility of the working class.

In brief, the Western Federation opposes the evolutionary process in the construction of the industrial state and would substitute revolutionary methods for its destruction. It would wipe out in its entirety and by revolution the present industrial state along with all the good it has brought to present-day society, instead of retaining this good through eradicating industrial evils, which can best be done by evolutionary processes. Such socialistic principles (the Federation has openly avowed political action through the Socialist party as the industrial cure-for-all) are fundamentally opposed to all the teachings of history as to the process through which social institutions are best formed. And in consequence they are antagonistic to the orderly and natural development of the broad American social state.

In explanation of the radicalism which prevents the Western Federation of Miners from joining the American Federation of Labor, the central national labor organization with which most American trade unions are identified, Mr. Hard says in part:

> The American Federation of Labor tolerates "craft autonomy." That is, when there are several crafts in the same industry, the American Federation of Labor usually allows the members of each craft to maintain their own union, if they so desire. The teamsters, for instance, in the packing industry have a union of their own; and so have the firemen; and so have the carpenters. These men want separate unions, and the American Federation of Labor consents. The leaders of the Western Federation of Miners believe that such a division into crafts is fatal. They demand that labor be organized, not according to crafts but according to industries.

Since the publication of Mr. Hard's article in *The Outlook* the Western Federation of Miners has held its thirteenth annual convention at Denver, beginning May 28. In their accounts of the convention the Denver newspapers report that 175 delegates were in attendance compared with 300 and 400 delegates in former years. The Denver *Republican* states that "as the roll call of unions progressed it was announced many times that there was no representation." Official reports to the convention, however, stated that a considerable number of unions had joined the Federation since the incarceration of three of its officials in the county jail at Boise, Idaho, for alleged complicity in the assassination of former Governor Steunenberg of Idaho. Among these officials are the President of the Federation, Mr. Charles H. Moyer, and the Secretary, Mr. W. A. Haywood.

This Denver meeting has resulted in a serious split in the Federation over Socialism. It came about through a dispute as to the seating of delegates of the Butte union, the latter being the founder of the Federation as well as its strongest union. The convention seated two members from the Butte union whom the latter had repudiated as delegates because of their Socialistic belief, the Butte union having strongly opposed Socialism. Seven of the thirteen delegates from the Butte union immediately "bolted" the convention and refused to take part in its proceedings.

IMMIGRATION RESTRICTION ORGANIZATIONS.

Objects of the Junior Order United American Mechanics, the Immigration Restriction League, and the Japanese and Korean Exclusion League.

THE recent remarkable growth in the number of immigrants annually coming to the United States has seemingly given an impetus to the activity of those organizations in this country which have to do with the restriction of alien immigration to our shores. These organizations have of late directed much of their influence toward the halls of Congress with the view of securing additional restriction legislation, and are also renewing their efforts along the lines of educating the public to their view of the situation. For the purpose of indicating the objects and principles of these organizations information is presented in this article as to the Junior Order United American Mechanics, the Immigration Restriction League, and the Japanese and Korean Exclusion League. These are not the only organizations that favor additional immigration restriction, as such a policy is endorsed by labor organizations and others, but to our knowledge they are the only ones organized for this definite and distinct purpose.

The constitution of the Immigration Restriction League states the objects of that organization to be as follows:

> The objects of this League shall be to advocate and work for the further judicious restriction or stricter regulation of immigration, to issue documents and circulars, solicit facts and information on that subject, hold public meetings, and to arouse public opinion to the necessity of a further exclusion of elements undesirable for citizenship or injurious to our national character. It is not an object of this League to advocate the exclusion of laborers or other immigrants of such character and standards as fit them to become citizens.

Since the organization of the League in 1894, among its most important activities have been those directed toward embodying in legislation what is known as the educational test. In 1895 it prepared what later became known in Congress as the "Lodge bill," which provided, among other things, for an addition to the excluded classes of "all persons between fourteen and sixty years of age who cannot both read and write the English language or some other language." This bill passed both Houses of Congress, but was vetoed by President Cleveland on March 2, 1897. The League's bill was reintroduced in the Fifty-fifth and Fifty-seventh sessions of Congress, the language of the excluding clause being changed to read as follows: "All persons over fifteen years of age and physically capable of reading who cannot read the English language or some other language; but an admissible immigrant or a person now in or hereafter admitted to this country may bring in or send for his wife, his children under eighteen years of age, and his parents or grandparents over fifty years of age, if they are otherwise admissible, whether they are so able to read and write or not." So far the League's educational test has not been embodied in legislation. The League's other activities include tests made in New York City as to the illiteracy of Hebrew immigrants and the recent conduct of an inquiry as to the need in the South of immigrant labor. Its headquarters are in Boston, and its Secretary and Treasurer is Mr. Prescott F. Hall.

Another out-and-out immigration restriction organization which, however, confines its activities to the problem as presented by Oriental countries, is the Japanese and Korean Exclusion League, with headquarters at San Francisco. This organization has been in existence a little over one year, but it was only on May 6, last, that its principles were formally enunciated in the preamble to a constit[illegible] This preamble sets forth the principles of the League as follows:

> Two unassimilable races can not exist perpetually in the same territory. Contact between such races results in the extermination of that one which, by reason of its characteristics, physical or mental, is least adapted to the conditions of life prevailing in the given territory.
>
> The conditions of life are, in the last analysis, determined by the conditions of labor. Consequently, the question of adaptability, as between two unassimilable races, must be resolved in favor of that race the characteristics of which most nearly conform to the conditions of labor.
>
> The labor of to-day in the United States is a machine, as distinguished from a manual, process. That race, therefore, which by its nature is best suited to complement the machine, as the essential factor of production, is in that respect the superior race, and therefore best adapted to the conditions of American industrial life.
>
> The Caucasian and Mongolian races are unassimilable. Contact between these races must result, under the conditions of industrial life obtaining in the United States, in injury to the former, proportioned to the extent to which such contact prevails. The preservation of the Caucasian race upon American soil, and particularly upon the Western shore thereof, necessitates the adoption of all possible measures to prevent or minimize the immigration of Mongolians to the United States.
>
> With these principles and purposes in view, we have formed the Japanese and Korean Exclusion League, and we urgently invite the active co-operation of all American citizens, to the end that the soil of the United States may be preserved to the American people of the present and all future generations, that they may attain the highest possible moral and material standards, and that they may maintain a society in keeping with the highest ideals of freedom and self-government.

Mr. Walter Macarthur was the representative of the Japanese and Korean Exclusion League, as well as of the State of California, at the immigration conference of The National Civic Federation held in New York City last December.

The Junior Order United American Mechanics, "a loyal, patriotic organization, fraternal and beneficial, strictly non-partisan and non-sectarian," claiming to have 1,600 subordinate councils and over 200,000 members in forty-one States, presents the following in its declaration of principles regarding immigration:

> We recognize the landing upon our shores of the ignorant, the vicious and the lawless of the old world as a constant menace to our institutions, and believe that it should be viewed with alarm by the loyal and patriotic citizens of the entire country.
>
> We announce an honest welcome to all immigrants who come hither seeking to better their condition and intending to become earnest and law-abiding citizens of our country. But we maintain that there is no room in this land for the anarchist, the nihilist or the escaped criminal; or for any one who is not willing to pledge allegiance to our flag and nationality, and to place the allegiance due it above that conceded to any other power, civil or religious. We know our flag to be powerful enough to shield and protect them as well as us in the exercise of both civil and religious liberty.

First place among the four objects of the Order is given to the following: "To maintain and promote the interests of Americans, and shield them from the depressing effects of unrestricted immigration; to assist them in obtaining employment, and to encourage them in business." No applicant shall be eligible to membership in the Order except he be "A white male citizen of the United States of America, born within its then territory or domain, or under the protection of its flag."

For the conduct of a campaign, principally along educational lines, designed to bring about remedial legislation relative to naturalization and a further restriction of immigration, the Order the past year placed in the hands of its National Legislative Committee the sum of $50,000 and appointed a special committee, with headquarters in Washington, to carry on this work in charge of Mr. Jesse Taylor, of Jamestown, O., as its secretary. This committee aims to secure the co-operation of all fraternities, societies and organizations interested in the work. Through this committee the Order prepared a bill (known as House bill No. 17491) which has been reported to the House from the Committee on Immigration and Naturalization. Its general purpose is the restriction of immigration, and it embodies an increase of the head tax, an educational test, heavier fines on steamship companies for violations, more rigid inspection of immigrants, etc. Within the Order there has recently been organized a permanent immigration restriction league.

"TAKE YOUR CHOICE."

From the American Federationist.

NO DOUBT some of our readers have heard thoughtless assertion that certain labor m in the Civic Federation truckle to the e ployers and other men of means, who also are me bers, and these labor men have for that reason be urged to quit that association. Of course, those w know could not very well take issue on the question a do not now. But because that side has been frequen urged and coming upon another view which has be recently published, it is believed that it also will pro "mighty interestin' readin'." The great love (?) wh the Post-Parry Citizens' Alliance has for trade unio and trade unionists is well known. That conglomer tion, impregnated with the virus of trade unio phobia, publish a weekly sheet which they misname t *Square Deal.* In that publication they print an editor which we republish for the benefit of all whom it m concern. It is as follows:

"We quote from a press report of the last nation convention of the United Mine Workers, held in I dianapolis, the following beautiful tribute to the Civ Federation, from the lips of John Mitchell:

> Referring to The National Civic Federatio of which he is a member, President Mitche declared that his association with the gentle men composing that organization had alway been turned to the advantage of the Unite Mine Workers. The Civic Federation, he said was composed of twelve honorable gentlemen who were themselves employers of labor. Th cardinal principles of the Civic Federation wer to maintain friendly relations with organize labor. This organization favored the trad agreement, and in recognizing the trade agree ment had recognized organized labor. "True," he said, "it has men like Eliot, but if we al thought alike there would be no organized labor and no mine workers' organization. There would be no necessity for them." Presiden Mitchell was warmly applauded when he concluded.

While we and other observers must agree with Mr. Mitchell that the Civic Federation is the most useful ally the closed-shop unionists have, we are rather inclined to think that he was "feeling his oats" overmuch when he boastfully proclaimed the fact. Doubtless the most politic Samuel Gompers was filled with chagrined apprehension when he read this ingenious utterance, and realized that it was a most indiscreet exposure, menacing the continued existence of the tinhorn trust of which he and Mitchell are the chief engineers. For Mr. Gompers knows, as Mr. Mitchell ought to, that the Civic Federation can be useful to the labor grafters' guild only in so far as it can make the public believe that it is intended to secure square and fair dealing between the unions and the rest of the world, that it will lose all influence just as soon as the public finds that it is merely the facile instrument in the hands of the closed-shop combine.

That it is that facile instrument in the conspiracy against the free workingmen of America has long been apparent to those who have studied its methods or thoughtfully read its magazine, or who know that in its action the wishes of Gompers and Mitchell are always first consulted and made the governing rule by its executive manager.

There are many good men and true on the various boards and committees of the Civic Federation who owe it to themselves to see that the absolute domination of the labor trust leaders, which makes that organization their creature, is done away with, so that the other side shall at least have a hearing. If they can not accomplish this they should resign. The Federation is doing business under false pretenses. The cunning of Gompers and Mitchell have brought this about. It registers their will and gives the weight of its influence only as they demand. Can any member of the Federation point to a single instance where its action in connection with labor questions had not been dictated by Gompers and Mitchell?

Do not the good men and true—honorable, broad-minded Christian gentlemen, like Dr. Eliot, John H. Patterson, and others, who are advertised as among its official membership, and whose names give it weight; do not these gentlemen know that when a labor question or proposition concerning the relations between employers and workingmen is presented to the executive manager of the Civic Federation his first question is whether it has been put before Gompers and Mitchell, and as to what they think of it, with, when necessary, the positive declaration that nothing will be done by the Federation without the approval of these two men? If these good men and true do not know this, it is time they learned it, for it is a fact well known to others.

The names of the many eminent and patriotic Americans on the official list alone give the Civic Federation weight and influence. That weight and influence is used to promote the conspiracy against the free workingmen of America, at the head of which conspiracy are Gompers and Mitchell.

Would it not be well for these well-meaning persons who have been used by Gompers and Mitchell as stalking-horses to look into things a little?"

The National Civic Federation Review

VOL. II. No. 11 NEW YORK, NOVEMBER—DECEMBER, 1906 TEN CENTS

1. Mr. Thomas W. Waddon (Secretary and General Manager of the Newcastle and Gateshead Gas Company)
2. Mr. A. E. Winchester (General Superintendent City of South Norwalk Electric Works)
3. Mr. M. E. Ingalls (Chairman, Big Four Railroad)
4. Sir W. H. Stephenson (Chairman of the Tyne Improvement Co.)
5. Mr. Timothy Healy (President International Brotherhood Stationary Firemen)
6. Mr. J. W. Sullivan (Editor Clothing Trades Bulletin)
7. Prof. Frank J. Goodnow (Columbia University)
8. Prof. J. H. Gray (Northwestern University)
9. Dr. Milo R. Maltbie (Former Editor "Municipal Affairs")
10. Prof. E. W. Bemis (Superintendent Cleveland City Water Works)
11. Mr. C. L. Edgar (President Edison Electric and Illuminating Company)
12. Mr. Edward A. Moffett (Editor "Bricklayer and Mason")
13. Walton Clark (Third Vice-President United Gas Improvement Company)

PUBLIC OWNERSHIP COMMISSION AT NEWCASTLE-ON-THE-TYNE

THE PUBLIC OWNERSHIP COMMISSION IN GREAT BRITAIN.

IMPORTANT CITIES VISITED, PLANTS INVESTIGATED, OFFICIALS AND EXPERTS INTERVIEWED, AND AN OUTLINE OF THE INVESTIGATING COMMITTEE'S FUTURE WORK.

FIFTEEN members of the Committee on Investigation of the Commission on Public Ownership and Operation of The National Civic Federation, who sailed for Europe on May 22, having completed their work abroad, returned to the United States in August. Their investigation in European cities was facilitated by the itinerary having previously been arranged by Messrs. Maltbie and Sullivan, two members of the Commission, who, with eight experts, had preceded the Investigating Committee three months. The members of the Committee began their work at Dublin and concluded their labors at London.

In all their examinations the Committee consulted with the engineers and accountants. Not only did these technists accompany the Committee upon its visits to the many plants inspected, but they were also engaged—in pairs, the one the nominee of the "pro," the other of the "anti" members—in completing the critical examination of the plants coming under their respective jurisdictions. These experts were: Street Railways—Norman McD. Crawford, of Hartford, Conn.; Gas—J. H. Woodward, of London, J. B. Klumpp, of Germantown, Pa., and Wm. Newbigging, of Manchester; Electric Lighting and Power—A. E. Winchester, of South Norwalk, Conn., and J. B. Klumpp. Messrs. E. H. Turner, of Manchester, and Robert C. James, of Wallingford, Pa., were the accountants.

Labor conditions in the plants chosen for investigation were studied by Prof. John R. Commons, of Wisconsin University, and J. W. Sullivan, Editor of the Clothing Trades Bulletin of New York. Legislation and franchises were studied by Milo R. Maltbie, of New York.

The data these experts were required to obtain had been indicated beforehand in very comprehensive schedules, described in the April number of THE NATIONAL CIVIC FEDERATION REVIEW. The committee will be largely guided by these and the American schedules in framing its final report.

The cities visited and the class of plants examined by the Committee were as follows:

Dublin — Street railways, private.

Glasgow—Street railways, public; electric, public; gas, public.

Newcastle-on-Tyne—Electric, private (two companies); gas, private

Manchester — Electric, public; street railways, public; gas.

Leicester—Gas, public.

Sheffield—gas, private.

Birmingham—Gas, public.

London—Electric, public and private (five plants); street railways, private (two plants); gas, private.

Liverpool—Electric, public; street railways, public.

Norwich—Street railways, private.

At Glasgow the Committee's work was especially promoted by the fact of its having the very friendly cooperation of so noted an exponent of municipal ownership as Manager Dalrymple of the City's Tramways. At London similar assistance was rendered by Sir Clifton Robinson, whose interests in private companies is not exceeded by those of any other man in Great Britain.

Hearings were held at London, at which leading exponents of company management were heard. Among those who attended these hearings were Lord Avebury, Mr. Sydney Morse, President of the Chamber of Commerce; Mr. Emil Garcke, of the Industrial Freedom League; Mr. Dixon H. Davies, Solicitor to the Great Central Railway; Mr. Wm. L. Madgen, and Mr. Robert P. Porter, of the *London Times*. The principal exponents of municipal ownership were also heard. Among the latter were Mr. T. McKinnon Wood, leader of the Progressive party of the London County Council; Mr. J. Allen Baker, Chairman of the London Municipal Tramways; Mr. Robert Donald, Editor of the *Municipal Journal* and Managing Editor of the *London Daily Chronicle;* G. W. Spencer Hawes, Member of the Institute of Electrical Engineers.

From the very beginning great interest was manifested in the work of the Commission. Boards of trade, private companies, city governments, labor leaders, members of Parliament, officials of the Imperial Government, representatives of ratepayers' associations—all seemed interested, and every facility was placed at the command of the Committee.

The general sentiment was that the report of the Commission should be of no less value to the people of Great Britain and Ireland than to the people of America. The fact that so many men drawn from different walks of life, and of such diversity of opinion, could be gotten together and dispatched upon so important a mission, was much commented upon, as was the further fact, that they had set out to determine the actual conditions in each case, by employing a corps of engineers and accountants. In short, the Commission and its sponsor, the National Civic Federation, were warmly commended for having undertaken a work of such manifest importance to cities.

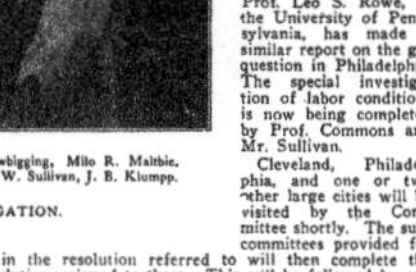

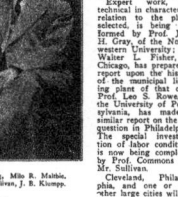

Upper Row (from left to right)—John R. Commons, J. H. Woodward, R. C. James, Wm. Newbigging, Milo R. Maltbie.
Lower Row (from left to right—E. H. Turner, Albert E. Winchester, Norman McD. Crawford, J. W. Sullivan, J. B. Klumpp.

BRITISH AND AMERICAN EXPERTS ENGAGED IN THE INVESTIGATION.

The Committee was entertained by the Lord Mayor and other officials of London, the Lord Provost and heads of departments of the Glasgow city government, and by the several other cities visited. A dinner was also given by the Association of Tramways Managers of Great Britain and Ireland, and a luncheon by Mr. Alfred Mosely. The Hon Whitelaw Reid, Ambassador to the Court of St. James, also entertained the Committee at luncheon. Not only were these affairs highly enjoyable from the social standpoint, but, through the speeches and conversations, they also proved to be the source of much valuable information.

The Future Work of the Committee.

The last meeting held in London adopted a resolution outlining a plan for the accomplishment of the remaining work of the Committee. This resolution provides:

That as schedules are completed copies of same to be promptly furnished members of the Committee; that Dr. Maltbie prepare a history of parliamentary action in relation to the municipal utilities under investigation; Prof. Goodnow, a report on political conditions in the municipalities of the United Kingdom as compared with such conditions in the United States, same to include a discussion of the relation of said political conditions to public and private operation of the particular municipal utilities; Profs. Bemis and Parsons, and Messrs. Walton Clark and Edgar, either jointly or individually, such statements for the plants investigated here and abroad; that the schedules for each plant be collated in a clear, concise statement for the use of the Committee in drafting its report; that the officers of the Committee prepare a general statement of conclusions and recommendations that may be used as a basis of discussion and adoption with such emendation as the Committee may order, etc., etc.

In this country the work of investigation is almost completed. The cities that have been visited are: Wheeling, Allegheny, Indianapolis, Chicago and South Norwalk; a number of other cities have been examined by the experts and by members of the Committee whose work has been specialized. The experts employed in the American investigation are: Gas—Fred C. Burnett, of Toronto, and A. E. Forstall, of New York; Electric Lighting and Power — C. E. Phelps, Jr., of Baltimore, and Theo. Stebbins, of Columbus, Ohio; Water — Dabney A. Maury, of Peoria, Ill.; Accountants— Marwick, Mitchell & Co.

A report upon the Massachusetts method of regulating the electric lighting industry is being prepared by Alton D. Adams, of Worcester, and C. I. R. Humphreys, of Humphreys & Glasgow, New York.

Expert work, not technical in character, in relation to the plants selected, is being performed by Prof. John H. Gray, of the Northwestern University; and Walter L. Fisher, of Chicago, has prepared a report upon the history of the municipal lighting plant of that city; Prof. Leo S. Rowe, of the University of Pennsylvania, has made a similar report on the gas question in Philadelphia. The special investigation of labor conditions is now being completed by Prof. Commons and Mr. Sullivan.

Cleveland, Philadelphia, and one or two other large cities will be visited by the Committee shortly. The subcommittees provided for in the resolution referred to will then complete the duties assigned to them. This will be followed by one or more meetings of the Committee, at which its report will be drafted.

At the present time the work of collating the matter contained in the completed schedules—the data gathered by the experts—in such a way as to make its assimilation more easy, is now being proceeded with.

It is expected that the Committee will be ready to report to the entire Commission about the first of the year.

As the trade agreement has been found to be one of the most important factors in maintaining industrial peace and stability, and in giving the unions a standing which enables them to take part in determining wage rates and shop conditions without continual recourse to strikes and the expenditure of large sums for carrying on an industrial warfare, it is most essential that they should indicate a determination to at all times comply with the terms of their contracts.—*Iron Moulders' Journal.*

PROBLEMS PRESENTED BY INCOMING ALIENS.

STATISTICAL INFORMATION IS CALLED IN QUESTION BY WELL-KNOWN EXPERTS AT THE FEDERATIONS' CONFERENCE ON IMMIGRATION.

STATISTICS generally accepted as representing the facts as to many phases of the immigration problem came in for a vigorous and searching analysis by experts in this branch of knowledge at the annual meeting of the Department of Immigration of The National Civic Federation held at the Park Avenue Hotel in New York City on September 24. All "sides" of the immigration issue, including the two most radical views, were represented, and as a result of the analysis of statistical tables there was a general feeling among those attending the conference, many of them from widely separated sections of the country, that the first and most important work to be undertaken by the Federation's new Department was the correction of much of this alleged statistical information. Franklin MacVeagh, of Chicago, Chairman of the Immigration Department, presided at the meeting. Following the general session there were separate meetings of the seven committees of investigation which are charged with the direction of research work.

Mr. Prescott F. Hall, Secretary of the Immigration Restriction League, in an extended discussion at the general session of the immigration bills now before Congress, alluded as follows to the lack of information: "I think all who have studied this subject for any length of time feel very much the scarcity of accurate statistics on the immigration question. I certainly do. And it is one of the very encouraging things about the formation of this Department that we can hope after a time to get more accurate and reliable statistics. Until that time we have, of course, to take such as we have for what they are worth."

MR. PRESCOTT F. HALL
Secretary of the Immigration Restriction League.

After emphasizing the need and pressing demand for legislation that would further restrict immigration, Mr. Hall analyzed in detail the various sections of measures now pending before Congress. He justified an increase in the head tax, proposed by the Senate bill, from $2 to $5, on the ground that there was need for more money to carry out efficiently the work of the Immigration Bureau. Among improvements in the service needing more money, he referred to better facilities for inspection, additional expenses for the distribution facilities proposed, the cost for medical inspection abroad, better paid and more inspectors, the district-attorneys' offices in enforcing present immigrastations at Southern ports, additional appropriations for district-attorneys' offices in enforcing present immigration laws, the expense of further and more complete statistical investigation and reports, and the need of more money to meet the cost of deportation. In addition to these proposed expenditures justifying an increase in the head tax, Mr. Hall stated that there is the practical argument that if we are interested at all in the reduction of the amount of immigration, an increase in the head tax will have an effect in that direction.

The clauses referring to the excluded classes were discussed and endorsed by the speaker, and the stimulation of immigration was denounced. In this latter connection Mr. Hall said: "The flow of immigration is not entirely normal and is not the natural seeking of our shores by the immigrant, but to a certain extent, and to a large extent, I believe it is artificially stimulated. If that is so, there is more reason why we should on this side take steps to stiffen our existing laws, because the steamship companies will take any person whom they can possibly get through. If we stiffen up our laws they will be driven to seek a better class of immigrants and, therefore, the theory of the present laws, i.e., that the steamship companies practically enforce them, will be carried out more in the way in which it was originally intended to be carried out." The additions to the excluded class provided by the Senate bill include those suffering from tuberculosis, feeble-minded persons, persons of poor physique, children under seventeen years of age unaccompanied by parents, and "any person whose ticket or passage is paid for with the money of another person, or who is assisted by others to come." Of this last provision Mr. Hall said: "Under the present law any friend or relative may send for an immigrant. The object of this clause is to limit the privilege of sending to such persons as are under some legal or moral obligation to support such immigrants after they arrive. It is estimated that upward of fifty per cent of the present immigration is assisted. The effect of this is that a lot of persons come who probably would not come except for that assistance, that is to say, in many cases the more energetic and serviceable members of a family come over, and after getting a footing here, they send for their friends and relatives who probably would not be able to come alone. It goes without saying that a class which is obliged to be assisted to come cannot be the equal of a class which would come of its own accord, and the class of assisted individuals includes a great many persons who sooner or later come upon the public for support in various ways."

Referring to the section relating to the subject of fines upon steamship companies, Mr. Hall said: "Under existing laws a penalty of $100 is imposed upon the steamship lines which bring over immigrants suffering with a loathsome or dangerous disease, if it could have been ascertained at the port of departure that they had that disease. The proposed laws impose fines upon steamship companies in certain additional cases, namely, if they bring idiots, imbeciles, feeble-minded and insane persons, or epileptics. The theory, as I said, of the present law is that the rejection of aliens at the ports on this side will not of itself be a sufficient inducement to the steamship companies to examine immigrants carefully at the port of embarkation or at the time they purchase the tickets. Experience, however, shows that the steamship companies will take everybody that can possibly pass muster, and that in fact they bring numerous diseased persons. This fine was put into the act of March 3, 1903, with the object of stopping that practice as to diseased persons. But in 1904 $31,000 in fines were collected from the steamship companies under this section, and in 1905, after a year's experience, $27,300 in fines were collected, and the Commissioner-General's report for 1905 of the number of diseased persons brought in by the steamship companies shows that this provision, as it stands in the law of March 3, 1903, is not adequate to accomplish the purpose for which it was intended, as there was an increase of forty-one per cent in the diseased persons brought over the previous year. The object of the section in the proposed measure is to extend the classes which the steamship companies should be obliged to weed out."

As to the demand for labor throughout the country, Mr. Hall stated that, while it is true we need more farm laborers in various sections of the country, the same is true with farm labor in England. "It is not purely an American matter," he said, "for in some parts of Europe it is the same. It arises in the United States from the seasonal character of the work. Immigrants are desired a few weeks of the year to harvest the crops, and the rest of the year there is nothing to do, so that the total rate of wages during the year for agricultural work is less than for contract work in the large cities. As long as that is the case it will be impossible to get immigrants to remain permanently in the farming regions. The kind of immigrant who will go to those regions and take his family there and settle there, and who has some means, and who will permanently take up land there, is the kind desired in the various States. That is not the kind we are now receiving to any extent.

"My friend, Prof. Willcox, has recently published an article in which he attacks the proposition that there is a tendency of recent immigrants to congregate in the city slums. I do not consider myself competent to discuss that question without a great deal of study, but I would like to point out that for present purposes of restriction it makes very little difference whether the tendency to settle in the slums is a tendency of persons who come here to remain, or whether it is a tendency to be found there. If you have a large stream of immigrants passing through your large cities there will be an excess of certain kinds in the city all the time. For the purpose of relieving that condition and of considering the question of purely exclusion and restriction, it makes, to my mind, very little difference whether there is in fact this special tendency to stick to cities. The eastern seaport cities will in such a case be overcrowded by a certain class of immigrants in any event."

While approving of medical inspection abroad and the employment of secret service agents, Mr. Hall stated objections to Consular inspection of immigrants. He approved heartily of the proposed educational test in the measure now before Congress. He said that the purpose of this illiteracy test is not at all based upon the view that a man is necessarily a better immigrant because he can read and write, but that, as a matter of fact, statistics show that the class that can read and write is on the whole a better class than that which cannot. He stated that the illiteracy test would not necessarily cut down the volume of immigrants, but that it might do so; it would, however, tend very much to raise the quality; and "if one million

MR. NATHAN BIJUR
Vice-President of the United Hebrew Charities.

immigrants a year are sufficient for us, why not get one million of the best instead of one million less good It is not merely a question of suffrage, although that enters into it, but it is a question of assimilation, as an immigrant who can read has many channels of assimilation open to him which a man who cannot read doesn't have."

Besides the Senate bill there is also before Congress what is known as the Gardner bill. The two are somewhat similar, although the House bill contains one or two provisions not in the Senate bill. One of these defines still further a class of immigrants designated as those "liable to become a public charge," and provides for a money test. This was approved by Mr. Hall.

In calling attention to a number of diagrams reflecting statistical information as to the effect of past immigration, Mr. Hall referred to illiteracy, stating that in 1905 the native white population had an illiteracy of 4.6 per cent; foreign whites of 12.9 per cent. "In other words," he said, "immigration to a certain extent tends to keep people illiterate in this country. Illiteracy has been going down, but it has not been going down as fast as it would if we had had an illiteracy test for immigrants in the last fifty years. One-fifth of those in the country at the present time cannot speak English."

Mr. Hall showed diagrams which aimed to present facts as regards crime among native whites of native parentage, foreign whites, and native whites of foreign parentage. One diagram referred to juvenile prisoners compared with the population of school age, and another showed the male prisoners per million of voting age in 1890. In commenting upon these diagrams Mr. Hall said: "You observe that to a certain extent the children of foreign-born parents are more criminal than immigrants themselves. That means, for a generation or two at any rate, not only is there a great burden upon our penal institutions, but it takes a little while for these unfortunate tendencies to be eliminated. It may be by the fifth or sixth generation this phenomenon will disappear, but for the time being it is in full force, and as immigration is keeping up and increasing, we have that problem constantly before us. That the children of immigrants are more than twice as criminal as the immigrants themselves is due in part to the fact that the immigrants coming into a new country have very often got into hard circumstances and are very largely less favorably situated than the native element. But at the same time, no matter what the cause, the facts remain that they are here and that they constitute that burden.

"In regard to the insane a census bulletin recently issued shows that the foreign-born furnish one and three-quarter times their normal proportion of insane. And another census bulletin shows they furnish three times their proportion of paupers. The fact that the immigrant is a large and increasing burden upon our institutions is evidenced by the testimony of those who come in practical contact with them, namely, the charity organizations. I have recently been in correspondence with the Boards of Associated Charities throughout the country, and I have here a list of endorsements of this Senate bill from widely scattered communities. California, the South, the middle States, and the East alike favor this measure.

"There is one thing upon which my opponents and I can agree, and that is, that we want to get down to definite facts and not rely upon arguments and generalizations. We do not want to argue that, because railroad dividends are high, there is no use in excluding laboring people. We have so far got a certain body of statistics together, such as they are. If they are not correct, we want to improve upon them.

"A great deal has been said about the traditional policy of this country, and just to remove a possible misunderstanding about that I would like to revert to the fact that at the very beginning of this country the people who founded it—Washington, Jefferson and Madison—were all strong restrictionists. As far back as 1826 the State of New York passed a law restricting immigration. Several other States passed laws restricting immigration about the same time. In 1882 the Federal Government took up the subject and since that year has been continuously strengthening the immigration laws. Now, if by a traditional policy is meant the policy of doing nothing, I maintain that that is not the true fact. Our traditional policy has been that of wise and conservative action in regard to such elements as we allow to come in and that is the present status of things to-day. We now exclude sixteen classes of people, and the present Senate bill is not something new of itself, although some of its provisions are new, but is an act calculated to carry out just what the original immigration act of 1882 was passed to accomplish. The present law does not accomplish it. There have been loop-holes. The act of 1891 stopped some. The act of 1893 stopped others. The act of 1903 was still better, but if the Senate bill now pending were to be passed, it would do nothing more than what was originally proposed in the act of 1882, as shown by the debates in Congress. We already have had one elaborate investigation into this subject—that of the United States Industrial Commission—who through its experts have made careful investigations up to the time of publication of their report. We need further data, but to my mind there is no reason for delay in passing what has been characterized as the very mild and moderate measure of these bills. We can at least do that. Then we can study further and see whether anything more is desirable."

THE NEED OF FACTS AS REGARDS IMMIGRATION.

Representative of the United Hebrew Charities Points Out Reasons for Questioning Our Present Immigration Statistics.

NATHAN BIJUR, Esq., Vice-President of the United Hebrew Charities, said that in his study of the question of immigration the first thing that confronted him was the absence of accurate and complete statistics. He said he could not understand how men could draw conclusions and be willing to advocate legislation based upon such conclusions, when at the same time they admit that they have not the facts adequate to the forming of conclusions.

"The question of immigration," he said, "if it be analyzed, I suppose in the last stage comes down to this: Are we getting any benefit, or are we getting any harm from immigration? Not do 16,000 diseased people come to our shores in thirty-six years, because, of course, if you have immigration, you will have diseased immigrants. The specious claim that fifty per cent of the immigrants that come in here are 'assisted' does not impress me a bit; because four-fifths of the whole population is assisted since we have about one male wage-earner to every family of five. There is nothing startling about any statement of that sort when you come to analyze it. If this statement is intended to convey the impression that fifty per cent of the present immigrants are paupers and are 'assisted' to come over by other persons than their relatives,—it is a base calumny. The question is, What has anybody now to present in the way of facts bearing on the benefit or the disadvantage to the country of immigration and of to-day's immigration in particular?" Mr. Bijur said that the only arguments that survived even superficial scrutiny were generalizations like the reference to the competition of the immigrant with the American workingman, and the fear that something might happen some day if the present immigration continues. He referred as follows to some of the more current statements against immigration: "First, we are told that the immigrant is dependent upon public support in greater ratio than any other part of the population. Now, it would not be surprising if he were, because the immigrant is a poor man. He comes here from other countries to improve his condition. He, of course, occupies the lowest financial stratum of the social structure. That is, he is doing the hard work. Of course, you expect to find among the poorest people the greatest amount of dependence. That is nothing wonderful. I know, everybody knows, that the poor are more dependent than the rich. If you want to abolish poverty, take that up, but do not mix up social problems and say they have something to do with immigration unless you think that by keeping out all immigration you won't have any more poverty. I do not think that the experience of any country has brought out facts that would justify any such inference. If you find that the immigrant is more dependent than the rest of the population I should say that would be a very natural thing. But do you find him so dependent that it is really something startling? Do you find him so dependent that you think he is unduly dependent and that you are getting what is known as a pauper class?"

OFFICERS OF THE IMMIGRATION DEPARTMENT OF THE NATIONAL CIVIC FEDERATION.

Mr. Bijur referred to the report of the Bureau of Immigration for 1904 purporting to show the relative proportion of foreign-born and natives in the charitable institutions of the United States, the proportion being 30 "alien" dependents out of each 1,000 alien population compared to 5 out of 1,000 of the naturalized and 2½ out of 1,000 of the native. In commenting upon this, Mr. Bijur says: "That statement has gone through the entire literature of immigration statistics, and it is absolutely a baseless statement. It has not the ghost of a foundation and never had. The first crucial trouble is that it does not define aliens. It is generally understood as referring to people who have been here only five years. It does not say how these statistics were taken which gave the figures 30,000 alien dependents, but I made investigation of both those figures. Now, remember, this is the very basis on which it has been charged repeatedly that the present immigrant is distinguished from the immigrant who came here and was so desirable in the thirties, forties and fifties—and that the present immigrant is so undesirable. Let us see. The census of 1900 shows that there were but 1,000,000 males foreign-born of voting age in the United States unnaturalized, and that is the same number as the 1,000,000 aliens with which the Bureau's report compares the 30,000 alien dependents. In other words, the report referred to has only as many aliens with which to compare the body of dependent aliens with as there are males of voting age, foreign-born, not naturalized, or what we might call political aliens. On the other hand, this 30,000 of alien dependents is made up of men, women and children, and is made up of men, women and children who have been in this country all the way from five to seventy years, as the report of the New York State Board of Charities for 1905 plainly pointed out. They took nine hundred and thirty-nine cases of inmates in the almshouses which were tabulated by the Commissioner-General of Immigration and they found that five hundred and forty-four of these were women and that more than seventy-five per cent of all the cases in the almshouses tabulated in the government report had been in the country five years, and some forty, fifty and sixty years.

"But suppose the figures were correct: suppose someone had been able to get statistics about the whole body of persons in this country less than five years and had found that the people who had been in this country less than five years were more dependent than all the rest of the people. That is of no practical importance at all. The question is, Are the people who have come into this country during the last five years more dependent than the people who came into this country at some other period were during their first five years. It is not pertinent to compare the present condition of people who came here during the last five years with that of people who came here thirty years ago, and who, I hope, now are millionaires. The fact is that the people who came in during the last five years have not had their chance yet. Give them a show. In other words, that whole statement which through repetition has spread broadcast throughout the country the impression that the present immigrant is more dependent than the immigrant who came in the past, is just nothing."

In commenting upon statistics of crime, and in particular as to male prisoners per 1,000,000 of voting population in 1890, Mr. Bijur said: "Now, remember, to begin with, the immigrant is generally over fourteen years of age. The large proportion of immigrants is grown-up. The proportion of children among the immigrants is very much smaller than among the general population. And remember also that the proportion of crime is very much larger among grown-up people than it is among children. Now then, when you find that there is a greater criminality among the immigrants than there is among the rest of the people, that must be so; it follows, as the night the day, that criminality among immigrants must be in higher proportion than with the rest of the population—just assuming the immigrant is like we are.

"Again, what are the crimes included in your statistics? Have you, as was done with some Massachusetts data, excluded crimes arising from drunkenness, so that the immigrant of 1860 should seem to be more law-abiding than the present incomer? What are the 'crimes' for which juvenile prisoners were convicted? Were they the kind of 'crime' for which the children of the poor are always convicted—the petty offenses of throwing banana skins on the street, and of breaking windows in play—all such offenses that go with a poor population. Yes, we know it is that. Moreover, you would expect to find a greater ratio of crime among the poor than among the rich. You are not discovering anything when you discover those things. You are not getting one whit further than the old story that the immigrant is poor,—in fact, he would probably not come here if he were not poor.

"Now, the other side of the picture—the value of the immigrants to the country. To bring up 1,000,000 people to the age of the immigrants coming to us each year would admittedly cost over five hundred million dollars. We are getting five hundred million dollars annually brought to the country through immigration. Does any one pretend that the criminal and dependents among the immigrants cost us five hundred million dollars annually? If we are going to work with statistics, if you think this question can be solved with statistics, then let us have them all. Let us have both sides of the picture. Then, how about the consumption? There are 1,000,000 immigrants and they are consumers; they are not all dependents; they are not all in the almshouses and the prisons. And as consumers they are adding more to the prosperity of the country. Has anybody figured on that? No. No one bothers about that. Here is a daily growing home market which puts into the shade all our eagerly-sought and dearly-bought foreign markets.

"Now, what I hope will be done by this Department of the Federation is that it will gather together all the facts, such as they are, the best statistics available from everywhere and put them down and say: 'Well, so far as we have been able to gather anything, this is what we know,' and then let us sift them and see how reliable they are. When we find a government report which does not mean anything, say so, and say why. When we find statistics of crime which have left out certain classes of criminals, let us say so. Show what the difference would be if they were put in, and go on through and collect all these things and put to the credit of the immigrant all the facts that are to be put to his credit, as well as charge him with all the things that ought to be so charged. Now, that has not been done by anybody. Everyone who has discussed this subject has discussed it from the point of view of the advocate. Let us formulate great general facts. We can formulate a general line of facts based upon fair statistics. Although, of course, we can probably never have statistics isolated and correct in this topic like the ascertained facts in physiology, in chemistry, in geology and in other more or less exact sciences and subjects. I have not had my statement challenged yet, that up to date there have been no arguments to present against our present immigration based upon reliable data."

ASSIMILATION AND IMMIGRATION.

Professor Willcox Calls Attention to Important Phases of Statistics of Crime.

PROF. WALTER F. WILLCOX, of Cornell University, whose analysis and explanation of census statistics has made him one of the leading statistical authorities in the United States, said he felt disposed to accept the principle that the presumption on this question of immigration is in favor of the traditional policy of the country. "The burden of proof," he contended, "must be held to rest with the other side. I believe this for the reason that our policy has worked so well in the past, both for this country and other countries. If we go back, say two or three hundred years, the right to change one's place of residence according to one's judgment of the advantages or disadvantages was not a recognized liberty of the individual. That liberty has gradually established itself in the countries of Europe and in the United States. I take it that no country has done more to establish that liberty than has the United States.

"Now, what about the results of that policy? It seems to me one may say, very briefly, that about one hundred and fifty years ago the population of Europe, according to our best knowledge, was about 130,000,000. It is now 400,000,000. At that time there were practically no people of European stock living outside of Europe. At the present time there are 100,000,000 of European stock living outside of Europe. In other words, the population of the world of European stock has increased 270,000,000 in the last one hundred and fifty years, and a very large part of that increase must be held to be due to the fact that Europeans during that time were allowed to follow the line of least resistance, or to seek their own advantage, even though it called upon them to leave their home or place of residence. We are wont to forget that this is not purely an American question; it is also a European question.

"We are wont to forget that although millions of people are coming to us from Europe, yet the population of Europe at the present time is growing faster than it ever grew before in history. And it is growing faster because of the reaction of these other countries, not merely of the United States but of South America and Australia, which are sending their benefits back to Europe. Practically, this increase of Europe is the whole increase of the population of the world, so far as we can tell, an increase of the people whom, on the whole, we are wont to regard as the leaders of progress.

"It seems to me that these facts establish a strong presumption in favor of the traditional policy of the United States. On the other hand, I think all persons must admit that there might be an excessive immigration into the United States; in fact, it might become so great as to become detrimental to the welfare of this country. Where we would draw the line we cannot say, but if the influx of immigration became, instead of 1,000,000 or so a year, 5,000,000 or 10,000,000 a year, I think most of us, perhaps all of us, would admit that it was too great."

Prof. Willcox stated that what appeared to him to be the central problem was whether or not immigration to our shores is too great. He was inclined to put the question of immigration as being: Is the process of assimilation keeping pace with the process of immigration? In attempting to answer this question, he stated that the first thing to know is how large is our present influx of population, that is, how large is our present current of immigration. This point Dr. Willcox discussed more fully in his paper before the Committee on Basal Statistics, which is presented on another page of this issue.

In referring to statistics which purport to show that the tendency to commit crime on the part of foreign-born people is decidedly greater than on the part of the native population, and that this tendency also manifested itself among the children of the foreign born, Prof. Willcox said: "It should be noted that crime, or rather imprisonment for crime, is much more a city phenomenon than a country phenomenon. I do not mean to say that the city population is more criminal, but that arrest and imprisonment for offenses are more common in the city than in the country. It will, therefore, be expected that those parts of the population living largely in cities would show, in the total population of the United States, a larger proportion of prisoners than those living in the country. Furthermore, the tendency to commit crime is largely a question of age. The criminal age is from fifteen to thirty years: consequently we should expect to find, as we do find, that those elements of the population which, like the children of our immigrants are very largely of criminal age, would have a high criminal tendency. Hence it is not at all surprising to see on the face of the figures that the children of immigrants show a much higher criminal tendency. But I should doubt whether, if you could make your comparison age for age, you would find anything like that difference. The apparent inference then is, first, that the immigrants and the children of immigrants are very largely in cities and the native population largely in country districts; and, secondly, that the children of immigrants are especially of the age when crime is most likely to occur.

CHAIRMEN OF THE COMMITTEES OF THE IMMIGRATION DEPARTMENT.

Mr. Norton is Chairman of the Committee on Agencies for Advancing the Welfare of Immigrants; Prof. Willcox that of Basal Statistics; Mr. Hamlin of the Committee on Supply and Demand; Mr. Holliday on Naturalization; Prof. Jenks on Legislation and Its Enforcement; Dr. Lefavour on International Relations, and Mr. Reynolds on Oriental Immigration.

"You notice that the persons indicated by the diagram are not criminals. We are constantly confusing prisoners with criminals. Suppose a person in New York is arrested for intoxication in the streets. The question whether he goes to prison depends chiefly on whether he has $10 in his pocket to pay the fine. It is very largely true that the statistics of prisoners are the function of the economic standing of the people concerned. If we had the figures, not of all persons arrested for crime, but simply of all who are tried for crime, they would show a difference. I confess I have been unable to find in the figures properly qualified the evidence that there is any considerably greater tendency on the part of immigrants themselves to commit crime than there is on the part of the native population. I think there is a greater tendency on the part of the children of the immigrant as compared with the children of the native."

IMMIGRATION AND HOMICIDE.

Professor Loeb also Points Out Important Statistical Errors as Regards Crime Among Immigrants.

ANOTHER criticism of current statistical information was that of Prof. Morris Loeb, who referred to recent tabulations showing the tremendous effect of Russian, Italian and Slavic immigration upon homicide. "The statistics are really very startling," he said, "so startling that there was evidently something wrong. The presumption was that homicide was taken to stand for criminal tendency, while, as we all know, in New York City for instance, a man who allows a brick to drop from a roof which hits somebody accidentally, that man is arrested for homicide. Homicide was taken synonymously with murder, and I find that homicidal statistics were taken to stand for murder statistics. The conclusions drawn of homicide, when you are unable to differentiate in various parts of the country between accidental killing and murder, are wrong. I do not suppose the foreman of a mine in Arizona can be arrested for homicide if it happens that half a dozen 'Dagoes' or 'Greasers,' as they call them, were blown up by an accidental discharge of dynamite in the bottom of a mine, whereas a foreman in New York would be arrested for any fatal building accident. The question was also entirely eliminated, whether, as in the South, a man would be arrested for homicide if he took part in a lynching bee. And there were no attempts made to discriminate between homicide and murder proper. Nevertheless, within six months those statistics are going to be quoted in favor of restriction.

"But there is another side to it that strikes me very forcibly, and that is this: According to the statistics, which are absolutely erroneous as far as showing actual criminal tendency, the worst offenders were three classes—Italians, Mexicans and Chinese—who stood highest in the proportion per one hundred thousand. It struck me at once that the Chinaman was pretty inoffensive, and the proof came in immediately. Ninety-six per cent of all the Chinamen in the United States are males between twenty and sixty years of age; whereas only twenty-four per cent of the inhabitants of the United States at large are of that age, which has just been shown by Prof. Willcox is the age of crime. Of course, if ninety-six per cent of the Chinamen happened to be of an age when the criminal tendency is strongest, whereas only twenty-four per cent of the entire population of the United States are of that age, you would expect the Chinaman to suffer by a comparison based on these statistics. The same thing is true as regards the Italians and the Mexicans. I was struck by something else, and that was this: In Arizona and New Mexico and the entire territory which was taken from Mexico during our war of 1849, all people are called Mexicans if they speak Spanish, whether they are Mexicans or whether they have been in the United States for two or three generations. Now, all these persons are imprisoned in Arizona and New Mexico and southern California as Mexicans. Nevertheless, there is no way in the United States census to find out how many real Mexicans are in the country, because the United States census disregards the immigration from Mexico as a part of the immigration into the country. Furthermore, among the nationalities which are called very bad on account of this homicidal tendency, I find there are many seamen, and that the man who is arrested on the border, or arrested in a seaport for a crime committed on board ship, or in some low drinking dive on the seashore, will be accredited to that nationality as a criminal, whereas he was never entered as an immigrant. Those figures alone produce such an effect that I cannot see how anybody with a conscience can go ahead and accuse these poor lambs of dirtying the water for the wolf who is drinking upstream."

A LABOR VIEW OF IMMIGRATION.

John Mitchell, the Mine Workers' President, Tells of its Effects in the Coal Industry.

AMONG others who discussed different phases of the problem was Mr. John Mitchell, President of the United Mine Workers of America. Mr. Mitchell stated that he approached the problem not as a student or an expert, but as a practical workingman who has from daily experience observed the effect of practically unregulated immigration. "In this period of unprecedented industrial prosperity," he said, "the people of my trade are given the opportunity to work about 200 days per year. There is certainly something the matter when a man who offers to work 300 days a year is permitted to work only 200 days, and if during this time of great industrial activity, a trade or an industry is only permitted to work 200 days per year, what will they be permitted to work in times of either financial or industrial depression?

"It is a matter of grave concern to the 600,000 men who mine coal in the United States whether or not there is to be some reasonable restriction made upon the admission of aliens into this country. I think that the restriction ought to be upon the broadest possible lines. I think that we should have due regard for those who are less fortunate than ourselves who live in other countries. I think that we should be careful not to permit ourselves to be under even the suspicion of seeking to keep immigrants from landing here because of national or religious prejudices, but I do believe that there ought to be some qualifications, that there ought to be some educational qualifications; that it should be required by our government that those arriving upon our shores should have sufficient money to enable them to select their employment. It is certainly not fair nor just to the American workingman, or to those who have come here some years ago, that a newly arrived immigrant should be forced, by his own necessities, to take the first job offered to him. If this is to be, it means that he takes the job of someone who preceded him here, or who was born in this country. I think it is not unreasonable, with the large population we have and with our own citizens irregularly employed, for us to afford to them who are here the first and best consideration.

"I believe that by fixing a high standard—a reasonably high standard—as a condition of admission to this country, we are not only protecting our higher standards of life and labor here, but we are fixing a higher standard for those who are abroad. If men must have a reasonable education, if they must have a reasonable amount of money in order to be admitted to our country, the chances are that the countries of the Old World will raise their standard to meet our requirements, and in that way we are not only conferring upon our own people that protection to which they, as citizens of this country, are entitled, but we are fixing a higher standard for those who live in the countries of the Old World."

IMMIGRATION AND THE MACHINISTS.

President O'Connell Says the Immigrant Competes for the Place of the American Workingman.

MR. JAMES O'CONNELL, President of the International Association of Machinists, stated that when men are competing for a living for themselves and their offspring, "then we feel it, then we know something about immigration. It is not academic or statistical with us then. I have the honor of representing an organization of 100,000 skilled mechanics, and we feel the immigrant proposition every day. We meet it every day in our own way. We meet the man who comes in every day and stands at the shop door. We have to compete with him. He is not competing with us, we are competing with him, and if we are successful, all right. If we succeed in assimilating that gentleman to our way of thinking, well and good. But if we don't? The question of assimilating the immigrant is one of years and years.

"We are very materially affected by immigration. Our wages, the condition of our families, the way our families are cared for and fed is gauged by immigration; the schooling of our children is dictated by immigration. It is gauged by the fellow who is competing with us and that fellow comes largely, of course, from among the immigrants. We have our own citizens and our own people who are in competition in a way, but it is the man who has come here and is met at the shore by the fellow who is bidding for him—practically by the owner of these men, as is now being done on the greatest public work a government is undertaking—offering so much and so much, selling Chinamen by auction at nine cents an hour. I say, we are the ones who suffer from immigration—our people, our wives, our children; our standard of living is based, is pitted against immigration. We meet immigration here and there and everywhere. In the mining district, in the mechanical trades, in the clothing industry, the allied industries, and in all the industries in which the human being is engaged in our country to-day, we meet with immigration. We feel that our standard of living is kept down. We feel the need of better protection against immigration (not that we have any desire to keep out the desirable immigrant, and I cannot say to you what is desirable immigration to your satisfaction, although I think I know what I mean by that). We want fair opportunities here and we do not want an unfair competition. In other words, we do not want a tariff upon the product and no tariff upon competition with our labor. We want protection from all sides, and I do not say this in a political sense."

THE DEMAND FOR LABOR.

A View of the Situation as Presented by Conditions on the Pacific Coast.

IN discussing the statistics concerning juvenile delinquents, Mr. Hugh F. Fox of New Jersey, stated that as they were sixteen years old he did not think anyone who had studied the question would be willing to base any conclusions upon them. "Sixteen years ago," he said, "juveniles were arrested for all sorts of things that are not considered crimes to-day and they were dealt with in an entirely different fashion; in fact, the whole attitude of the police and the judiciary in regard to the so-called juvenile incorrigible and delinquent of sixteen years ago would to-day be considered semi-barbarous. The whole progress in this question during the last ten years makes the data of sixteen years ago practically the data of the dark ages. I do not think we can base any conclusion that is of value in relation to the immigration problem on such data as was obtained in 1890 on that question."

Mr. Fox referred at some length to conditions in New Jersey with regard to the dependent and delinquent classes and of the agricultural conditions with reference to labor and immigration in New Jersey and along the Pacific Coast. Referring to the hop business in Oregon, Washington and California, Mr. Fox said: "We are now almost at the end of harvesting. Telegrams have been coming to us frantically from all our agents and buyers and brewers interested with us in the ranches, telling us that they have not enough pickers to harvest the crops. This condition has been getting worse each year, partly because the Chinamen who came in before the Exclusion Act have been prosperous, and the Chinaman to-day is successfully competing with the American, the Englishman and the Scotchman as a hop-grower in the Pacific Coast States. He is running large ranches and is himself in many cases employing white labor. Now, I know it is said that that is casual and occasional and seasonal labor. That is true to a certain extent. There is enough of it in harvesting fruit and in the hop and similar industries to keep men employed three or four months. There is ample opportunity to-day for the man who goes there as a seasonal laborer to get small pieces of land, and by farming not only to earn his living during the other nine months but to become in a few years very prosperous. The fact is you cannot separate the immigration problem from the land problem in that part of the country, and I presume elsewhere. Until the last few years that country contained a large number of men who were land poor, because of the policy of the government in giving away quarter sections of extremely rich and valuable land that was very carelessly farmed. I do not attempt to state what bearing this has upon the immigration problem further than this, that it is perfectly clear there are large sections of the country to-day calling for labor and having no prejudice against its nationality, and that it will be a very long time before the country will be so filled up that the demand for such labor will be at all diminished."

IMMIGRATION AN INTERNATIONAL QUESTION.

DR. CHARLES FLEISCHER, of Cambridge, stated that it seemed to him feasible for the Department to start a project for getting the different nations of Europe interested with us in this immigration problem, and thus lifting it to the plane of an international question. "It is not simply the going and coming of many of these immigrants but the fact of the conditions stimulating immigration to America that raises the question to the plane of internationalism. Knowing America as I know her, through history and through personal acquaintance, I see America as a nation somewhat different from other nations in that we are avowedly humanitarian. Therefore, in justice to our national characteristics as well as to our history, it seems to me that we cannot develop an attitude of hostility toward immigration here and at the same time be indifferent to the causes abroad which stimulate this migration. For instance, we cannot say that we have no right to interfere in the internal conditions of Russia and at the same time try to keep out the Russians who are moved to migrate to America by those very internal conditions that obtain in Russia. Such an attitude of indifference to the causes that stimulate migration is false to our history."

A SOUTHERN VIEW OF IMMIGRATION.

MR. THEODORE AHRENS, of Kentucky, presented to the Department a Southern view of immigration. He said in part: "I do not think that this country has reached the point where it does not require further immigration. Speaking for my section of the country, that is, the South, I am sure we do need more immigration. As a manufacturer, I feel to-day the necessity of the absolute want for labor. This condition exists not only in Kentucky, but in Alabama and other Southern States. We could use a million more immigrants a year, but we want them to be of the best kind. I believe we can get one million immigrants a year of the desirable class. I think we ought to throw around our immigration laws such restrictions as the bill before Congress proposes, at least the most of them. I believe that every healthy man, woman or child who comes to the United States, whether they have $25 or not, should be admitted, because this country was built up by just such people. The great majority, such as the Irish and Germans and all other people who came here twenty-five or fifty years ago, never had $25 or $50 that one clause of the proposed legislation provides for. I am in favor of keeping out the criminal classes, consumptives, epileptics and people who are not fit to take care of themselves."

PROPOSED IMMIGRATION LEGISLATION.

REV. ADOLPH ROEDER, of New Jersey, in referring briefly to the point raised as to the effect of immigration upon the number of days employed by the coal miners of the country, stated that it might be possible for this condition to be due rather to the control of coal production and transportation by the railroads. In speaking of the additional restrictions to immigration imposed by the bills now before Congress, he stated that he doubted very much whether the head tax, or the linguistic provision, or other sections of the bill, will seriously interfere with the number of immigrants to the United States. He said: "I think there will be almost as many. I hope there will be. And I think they will be of a better class, which would be good for their own sake, because it puts a lot of people at a disadvantage when they are thrown into a country where they cannot distinguish between liberty and license. In the removal of unintelligent men from the sway of a monarchy where they are well controlled and held well in hand, there is always danger of that removal resulting in the feeling of license and in the increase of the sense of personal liberty which does not exist. Personally, I favor these rather slight restrictions proposed in the bills now before Congress."

Among the other speakers at the conference were Mr. Franklin MacVeagh of Chicago, Prof. J. W. Jenks of Cornell, James W. Kinnear of Pittsburg, Mrs. Florence Kelley of New York, and Mr. D. G. Ambler of the Jacksonville (Florida) Board of Trade.

WELFARE WORK IN POWER STATIONS.

From the Paper Trade Journal, New York.

One of the most interesting phases of modern industrialism is the increasing attention paid by large establishments to so-called welfare work, for the betterment of the conditions under which the employes labor. Activities of this kind are in no sense confined to the rank and file of the employes, but are in many instances broadly beneficial to even department heads. In electric railway circles a great deal has been done along this line to improve the living conditions of employes directly occupied in the handling of cars; companies have fostered esprit du corps and strengthened many a motorman and conductor's position in life by liberal contributions to benefit associations, by supplying various necessities at less than cost, etc. Sometimes the power plant has been overlooked in these commendable activities, and it is the purpose of these comments to point out several ways in which welfare work can be extended to this part of the system.

In far too many plants the chief engineers are unprovided with any sort of office facilities worthy of the name. Of course, a power house is no place for mahogany desks, Turkish rugs and Louis Quinze chairs, but where a man is obliged to prepare careful and regular records of the power cost in detail, something in advance of a nail keg or an oil barrel is sure to be appreciated in lieu of a handsome desk. Again, power houses are sometimes lacking in anything but the most elementary sixteenth century sanitary facilities; lockers are conspicuous by their absence; or there is no place where an engineer or fireman can wash himself and then enjoy a meal which has to be taken when on duty. The provision of hot water for this purpose, a mirror and a few brushes are certainly appreciated by deserving men, and cost little from the company's standpoint. Power plant attendants are not averse to good personal appearance on the way home from work, any more than are the draftsmen in the main office. Another point is worth securing: the provision of enough men so that each power-house attendant can take a day off once in seven or eight days, instead of being hemmed in to continuous service all the year round. Bonuses for reduced cost of power generation are helpful in some plants, and promotions from within when capable men for advancement can be secured from the company's own force are usually much appreciated by employes of the right sort. One or two technical journals supplied by the company ought to be available at the power house for all employes, and all reasonable encouragement should be given to power-house men engaged in night duty or outside efforts of any kind to become more efficient workers. It is in no carping spirit that we mention these points, but in many plants the working conditions may be improved by very simple and inexpensive methods.

OUR GAIN IN POPULATION THROUGH IMMIGRATION.

STATISTICS AFFECTED BY CHANGES IN DEFINITION—ATTENTION DIRECTED TO HUNDREDS OF THOUSANDS RETURNING EACH YEAR TO EUROPE.

By Walter F. Willcox

THE meaning of any statistics depends largely upon the meaning of the unit in which the statistics are expressed. It is a common but fallacious assumption that a word used as the name of a statistical unit has precisely the same meaning that it has when used in popular speech. In the present case the word "immigrant" has had and to some degree still has different meanings, which may be called respectively the popular or theoretical meaning and the administrative or statistical meaning, and these two should be carefully distinguished.

In the popular or theoretical sense an immigrant is a person of foreign birth who is crossing the country's boundary and entering the United States with intent to remain and become an addition to the population of the country. In this sense of the word an alien arrival is an immigrant whether he comes by water or by land, in the steerage or in the cabin, from contiguous or non-contiguous territory, and whether he pays or does not pay the head tax. The essential element is an addition to the population of the country as a result of travel and the word thus covers all additions to the population otherwise than by birth. A person cannot be an immigrant to the United States more than once any more than a person can be born more than once. It is a characteristic of this meaning that it does not alter.

The word immigrant in its administrative or statistical sense is not defined on the reports of the Commissioner-General of Immigration, but from that source and from the instructions and other circulars issued by the Bureau the following statements regarding its meaning have been drawn:

1. The administrative or statistical meaning of immigrant is not fixed by statute law but is determined by the definitions or explanations of the Bureau of Immigration and those are dependent upon and vary with the law and administrative decisions.

2. In the latest circular of the Bureau immigrants are defined as "arriving aliens whose last permanent residence was in a country other than the United States who intend to reside in the United States." This definition seems to agree closely with the popular or theoretical one.

3. But the foregoing definition is modified by a subsequent paragraph of the same circular which excludes from the immigrant class "citizens of British North America and Mexico coming direct therefrom by sea or rail." So the official definition is substantially this: An alien neither a resident of the United States nor a citizen of British North America, Cuba or Mexico, who arrives in the United States intending to reside there.

4. The only important difference between these two definitions is that the statistical definition excludes, as the popular definition does not, citizens of British North America, Cuba and Mexico. As the natives of Canada and Mexico living in the United States in 1900 were 14.2 per cent of the natives of all other foreign countries, it seems likely that the figures of immigration for the year 1905-06 should be increased about 14.2 per cent in order to get an approximate estimate of the total immigration into the country during the year just ended.

5. Perhaps the most important difference between the popular or theoretical and the statistical definition of immigrant is that the former is unchanging and the latter has been modified several times by changes of law or by modifications of administrative interpretation.

6. Until January 1, 1906, an alien arrival was counted as an immigrant each time he entered the country, but since that date an alien who has acquired a residence in the United States and is returning from a visit abroad is not classed as an immigrant. This administrative change has brought the statistical and the popular meanings of immigrant into closer agreement, but in so doing has reduced the apparent number of immigrants more than ten per cent and has made it difficult to compare the earlier and the later statistics.

7. Until January 1, 1903, an alien arriving in the first or second cabin was not classed as an immigrant, but rather under the head of other alien passengers. This change likewise brought the two meanings of immigrant into closer agreement, but also made it difficult to compare the figures before and after that date. By a mere change of administrative definition the reported number of immigrants was increased nearly twelve per cent.

8. Until the same date an alien arrival in transit to some other country was deemed an immigrant, but since that date such persons have been classed as non-immigrant aliens. This change also makes the figures before 1903 not strictly comparable with later ones. About three per cent of those who were formerly classed as aliens have been excluded since 1903. The alteration has brought the two definitions closer together, but in so doing has entailed administrative difficulties which lead the Bureau to favor a return to the former system or at least to favor collecting the head tax from such aliens in transit.

9. An immigrant in the statistical sense is a person liable for and paying the head tax. But to this there are two slight exceptions. Deserting alien seamen not apprehended are liable for the head tax which is paid by the company from which they desert, but such cases are not included in the statistics. Citizens of British North America, Cuba and Mexico coming from other ports than those of their own country are reported as immigrants, but do not pay the head tax. Obviously both are minor exceptions hardly affecting the rule. In the popular or theoretical meaning of immigrant this head tax is not an element.

10. Probably other changes of definition have occurred of recent years. No attempt has been made to exhaust the list. The general tendency of the changes has clearly been toward a closer agreement of the popular and the statistical meanings. But they have probably tended to make the increase of immigration indicated by the figures greater than the actual increase, and to that degree to make the figures misleading. If the Government Bureau of Immigration and Naturalization could make a carefully studied estimate of the extent to which such changes in the official reports really modify the apparent meaning of the published figures, it would render a valuable service.

11. A committee like the present can hardly make such an estimate or go further than to point out that for the reasons indicated the official statistics of immigration are likely to be seriously misinterpreted and are constantly misinterpreted by the public.

The official statistics of immigration being subject to all the qualifications indicated and reflecting so imperfectly the amount of immigration as ordinarily or popularly conceived, the question at once arises, Can any substitute or any alternative be proposed? What the public is mainly interested in, I think, and what it commonly but erroneously believes is indicated by the official figures of immigration, is the net addition to the population year by year as a result of the currents of travel between the United States and other countries.

Alternative figures for the last eight years, a period which closely coincides with the last great wave of immigration now at or near its crest, may be had by comparing the total arrivals and departures in the effort to get the net gain. The results appear in the following table:

Fiscal Year	Total Passengers Arrived	Total Passengers Departed	Total Immigration	Arrivals Minus Departures	Per Cent That Net Increase Makes of Immigration
1898..	343,963	225,411	229,299	118,552	51.8
1899..	429,796	256,008	311,715	173,788	55.8
1900..	594,478	293,404	448,572	301,074	67.0
1901..	675,025	306,724	487,918	368,304	75.5
1902..	820,893	326,760	648,743	494,133	76.3
1903..	1,025,834	375,261	857,046	650,573	75.9
1904..	988,688	508,204	812,870	480,484	59.3
1905..	1,234,615	536,151	1,026,499	698,464	68.1
1898-1905			4,822,662	3,285,372	68.1

The figures indicate that the net increase of population by immigration during the last eight years has been slightly more than two-thirds of the reported immigration. But these figures of net increase should be increased by an estimate of the arrivals by land from Canada and Mexico. As the Canadians and Mexicans by birth residing in the United States in 1900 were 14.2 per cent of all residents born in other foreign countries, this would indicate an influx of 466,000 Canadians and Mexicans, a figure probably in excess of the truth, since the currents have probably been setting Canadaward of recent years. I estimate, therefore, that the net increase from immigration 1898-1905 has been about 3,750,000 instead of 4,820,000, as might be inferred from the Reports of the Bureau of Immigration. The actual increase would then be about 78 per cent of the apparent increase.

[The above article was presented as a paper by Professor Willcox before the Committee on Basal Statistics of the Federation's Immigration Department. It should be regarded as provisional, and is published not alone for its value and interest but also with the hope of eliciting criticisms or corrections.—The Editor.]

WHY THE AMERICAN FEDERATION OF LABOR WENT INTO POLITICS.

THE VIGOROUS CAMPAIGN OF THE NATIONAL MANUFACTURERS' ASSOCIATION AND OTHER EMPLOYERS' ORGANIZATIONS PRACTICALLY FORCED IT.

THE entrance of organized labor into active participation in national politics, the wisdom of which has been seriously questioned by many friends of the labor movement, is the direct outgrowth of the contest which has been waging the past several years between the trade unions, as represented in the American Federation of Labor, on the one side, and manufacturers, as organized in the National Association of Manufacturers and in the Citizens' Industrial Alliance, on the other. The public, while noting here and there in the press indications of this activity of the National Manufacturers' Association and the vehement half-page advertisements of the Industrial Alliance in which organized labor is attacked, nevertheless the public generally realizes but faintly, if at all, what the real extent of this opposition to the labor movement has meant. Organized labor itself, of course, understands it thoroughly and fully measures the strength of this opposition. Its leaders at every turn in Congress meet the officials and attorneys of these hostile organizations, and spend weeks in open combat with them before the committees. The columns of the manufacturers' journals are filled with denunciations of organized labor, its leaders and all its policies.

One feature of the campaign as carried on by the officials of the National Manufacturers' Association has been the sending of letters to their members which, although marked "confidential," do not fail to reach the labor journals, whose editors publish them to show the tactics of their opponents. To show the nature of this kind of opposition, we present some of these letters:

THE NATIONAL ASSOCIATION OF MANUFACTURERS OF THE UNITED STATES OF AMERICA.

General Offices: 170 Broadway (Maiden Lane and Cortlandt Street.)

NEW YORK, Feb. 20, 1904.

Confidential.

DEAR SIR: Our fight against a favorable report of the Eight-Hour bill by the House Labor Committee in Washington is getting warm, and we ask you, as a manufacturer and employer with a vital personal interest as well as a patriotic interest in beating this arbitrary and dangerous socialistic proposition, to help us. Hon ——— — ——— of your State is, as you know, a member of this House Labor Committee. While we understand that he is a brave and patriotic man, who will not be afraid to do what is right in this behalf when it comes to a vote in the committee, we naturally wish to have him supplied with as many *facts, reasons and arguments* against the bill as possible *from home* in order that any such thing as a weakening on his part might be absolutely prevented; for it is not only certain that every vote in the committee will count, but it is of course of the utmost importance that our friends in the committee should realize that they are right, from the beginning of the fight to the end of it, and that they can well afford to stand by the substantial people of their State in helping the fight to be made, in their own time and in their own way of course; for we certainly want to be friendly enough to our own friends not to ask them to expose themselves unnecessarily.

Therefore, if you should write such a letter—the Congressman's address is House of Representatives, Washington, D. C.—and will make it strong and will not hesitate to make it long and full of reasons, and put some of the feeling into it which we believe all manufacturers and employers entertain at the present time in reference to this coercive labor proposition, a most valuable and perhaps a most essential service will have been done. We should all of us very naturally feel chagrined if the member of the committee from your State should fail, on account of a lack of interest from home, to do his part. Kindly do us the honor and the service to write us what you have done in order that we may have as much information as possible and thus may co-operate with you as effectively as possible. Yours most respectfully,

MARSHALL CUSHING,
Secretary.

THE NATIONAL ASSOCIATION OF MANUFACTURERS OF THE UNITED STATES OF AMERICA.

General Offices: 170 Broadway (Maiden Lane and Cortlandt Street.)

NEW YORK, June 15, 1904.

Confidential.

DEAR SIR: We should like first to recall your generous and essential service of last winter; for I assure you positively that our fight for free industrial conditions before the various committees of Congress could not have been successful without the assistance of all our friends everywhere.

There is now a service of vital consequence that you can do for the cause. As you know, the Democratic national convention meets in St. Louis on July 6. It is evident that devotees of Bryan anti-injunctionism and of Hearst eight-hourism—to coin the words—will seek to cause the reaffirmation of the anti-injunction plank of the last two platforms, and, possibly, additional labor planks—for eight hours and almost any kind of socialistic legislation may be endorsed. In fact, it is not safe to assume that these propositions will be kept out of the platform, except by the most diplomatic and resourceful and persistent efforts which you or your association, as an association and as individuals, in common with all of our friends everywhere can make. You have the right to make these efforts; and we ask you, a little more earnestly than we have ever asked anything of you before, to make them.

This labor question is industrial, not political. In your opinion, as well as ours, of course, no party has any business, whether from the standpoint of patriotism or of mere politics to seek to make any such demagogic appeals. I ask you to believe that the whole country feels so nearly as we do on the question, and that public men of both parties are given to feel so nearly as we do on the question, that you are safe in assuming that your efforts, collectively and individually, addressed to any or all of the delegates to St. Louis with whom you are acquainted, or can get in touch, whether on the resolutions committee or not, whether from your State or not, whether known to be friendly to our cause or not, would have the right effect.

These planks will not be left out unless we make the effort. Please do everything on earth that you can, perfectly secretly, without any publicity of any kind, simply scoring with each and every influential person whom you can think of having anything to say about the matter. And please advise me what you have done and are doing, in order that I may co-operate with you as effectively as possible.

Yours most truly,
MARSHALL CUSHING,
Secretary.

THE NATIONAL ASSOCIATION OF MANUFACTURERS OF THE UNITED STATES OF AMERICA.

General Offices: 170 Broadway (Maiden Lane and Cortlandt Street.)

NEW YORK, December 8, 1904.

Strictly confidential.

DEAR SIR: You have not replied to our recent letter. It is our fault; we didn't write you strongly enough.

The simple question is whether your own valued company will not join the other manufacturers of the country in providing *an absolute insurance against destructive and even revolutionary labor legislation at Washington* and at the different State capitals. We believe that you will.

Nobody has ever questioned that it was the National Association of Manufacturers that beat the Eight-Hour and Anti-Injunction bills in Washington last winter. We have got to beat them again this winter, for Mr. Gompers insists that both bills shall be pressed and Senator McComas, of Maryland, agrees.

Not only is the National Association your only guarantee against the enactment of such revolutionary schemes, subversive of the very principles of our government, but the whole tendency towards collectivist and paternal legislation needs to be stopped, and it is this immense and successful movement of manufacturers which alone, apparently, can do it.

I want again to ask you to join us. If we double our strength, we treble or quadruple our power; but we have to be right, and *you can help us to keep right*. We have many friends in your industry. Will you not join them, and us, in the good cause? You will get your money back, anyway, in business advantages.

Please let me hear from you. I won't permit you to be disappointed. Yours most cordially,

(Signed) MARSHALL CUSHING,
Secretary.

THE NATIONAL ASSOCIATION OF MANUFACTURERS OF THE UNITED STATES OF AMERICA.

General Offices: 170 Broadway (Maiden Lane and Cortlandt Street.)

NEW YORK, February 27, 1905.

Confidential.

DEAR SIRS: We take the greatest pleasure in causing to be mailed to you (from this office under Congressional frank) a copy of the Eight-Hour report, so-called, just submitted by Secretary Metcalf to the Labor Committee of the House. As you will doubtless recall, it was managed last spring—at the close of the most remarkable manufacturers' campaign ever seen in Washington—that this whole question should be referred to the Department of Commerce. The Labor Bureau, under the direct supervision of Colonel Wright, has now completed this inquiry. Not only does the report sustain our contention at every point (that the compulsory eight-hour day by act of Congress would be uneconomic and even destructive to the industries of the country and a radical or even revolutionary recognition of a wrong principle of government interference at the behest of "labor"), but the reference of the question itself establishes a precedent which possibly is just as valuable; namely, the possibility of referring such questions for investigation by the proper department itself hereafter, a thing which has never even been attempted until our Association took it up. This matter has already been referred to on the first two pages of our American Industries of February 15, as well as in the editorial columns, to which we respectfully refer you; but we ask you to read and preserve the report itself as one of the most significant industrial documents thus far issued.

The House Labor Committee in executive session Thursday laid this report on the table. Its only friend who was present—Congressman Caldwell, of Illinois, (beaten for re-election)—moved to report the bill favorably, but by the watchfulness of our friends it was laid on the table, and thus the notorious Gompers Eight-Hour bill dies with this Congress. In this, however, as in the Anti-Injunction campaign, the labor lobby may be expected to be just as active as ever in the next Congress. But the Association will also be just as active.

We do not believe there is any calculating in money the value of this work which the Association is doing, which, of course, would be impossible if our individual members everywhere did not follow the work closely and back it up promptly and generously whenever we ask them to do so. In fact, it is always their support without which success could not be attained.

Yours most cordially,
(Signed) MARSHALL CUSHING,
Secretary.

LABOR'S BILL OF GRIEVANCES.

This active campaigning on the part of organizations representing employers and manufacturers became so strong in Congress that in March, 1906, what has come to be known as "Labor's Bill of Grievances" was presented to President Roosevelt, and to the Speaker of the House of Representatives and the Chairman *pro-tem.* of the Senate by prominent labor officials represented in the American Federation of Labor. These grievances grew out of the refusal of Congress to enact into legislation certain demands of organized labor, including the enactment of the Eight-Hour law; legislation to safeguard the American workingman from the competition of convict labor; relief from induced and undesirable immigration; protection of seamen from involuntary servitude; redress from repeated violations of anti-trust and interstate commerce laws; protection from the questionable use of the injunction, and insistence of the right to petition on the part of government employes. In closing their Bill of Grievances the representatives of organized labor said: "Labor now appeals to you, and we trust that it may not be in vain; but if, perchance, you may not heed us, we shall appeal to the conscience and the support of our fellow citizens."

Following this appeal, and soon after the close of the last Congress, the Executive Council of the American Federation of Labor issued an address "to all organized labor and friends in the United States" in which was set forth the political program of organized labor. Following a general analysis of present-day industrial and political conditions, the address quotes a resolution adopted by the National Convention of the Federation as long ago as 1897, as representing the attitude of the organization towards politics. This resolution stated that "the American Federation of Labor most firmly and unequivocally favors the independent use of the ballot by the trade unionists and workmen, united regardless of party, that we may elect men from our own ranks to make new laws and administer them along the lines laid down in the legislative demands of the American Federation of Labor, and at the same time secure an impartial judiciary that will not govern us by arbitrary injunctions of the court, nor act as the pliant tools of corporate wealth." The program stated that "within the past few years claims and promises made in platforms or on the hustings by political parties and politicians, and especially by the present dominant party, have been neither justified nor performed. Little attention has been paid to the enactment of laws prepared by us and presented to Congress for the relief of those wrongs and the attainment of those rights to which labor and the common people are justly entitled and which are essentially necessary for their welfare. Several Presidents of the United States have, in their messages to Congress, urged the passage of equitable legislation in behalf of the working people, but Congress has been entirely preoccupied looking after the interests of vast corporations and predatory wealth.

Congressmen and Senators in their frenzied rush after the almighty dollar have been indifferent or hostile to the rights of man. They have had no time, and as little inclination, to support the reasonable labor measures, the enactment of which we have urged, and which contain beneficent features for all our people without an obnoxious provision to anyone." The relief asked for not having been granted, the program goes on to state that the American Federation of Labor determined upon taking the issue into active politics.

Perhaps the one question above all others that has engaged most strenuously the fighting strength of what may be termed the hostile camps of capital and labor is commonly known as "Government by Injunction." The public generally has little conception of the significance of this issue, being unconscious of the fact that it involves fundamental principles as to the rights of man and the rights of private property. How important these issues are to the future welfare of the nation can best be indicated by presenting a summary of the testimony before the House Judiciary Committee last spring on the anti-injunction issue. Some eight bills treating of this subject were before the Committee. The hearings, however, centered around the bills which aim to limit or define the power of Federal courts in issuing injunctions in labor disputes.

In general, the proposed legislation emphasizes four remedies for the injunction issue. One is the division of contempt of court into two classes—direct and indirect—the latter including an injunction or order of the court, and permitting those accused of contempt who come in this class to have a trial by jury. Another proposed measure makes certain acts innocent; takes certain acts which are lawful for one to do out of conspiracies when done by more than one; that is, it makes legal those acts which are legal for one to do if done by several in a trade dispute. Acts declared to be innocent are not to be restrained or enjoined. One of the proposed measures declares the right to do business to be not a property right.

Another form of proposed legislation provides that the adverse party shall have an opportunity to be heard before an order is granted. This provides that in cases involving or growing out of labor disputes neither an injunction nor a temporary restraining order shall be granted except upon due notice to the opposite party, after hearing, which may be *ex parte* if the adverse party does not appear at the time and place ordered. In support of this bill the railroad brotherhoods have committed themselves, the Brotherhood of Locomotive Engineers, the Brotherhood of Locomotive Firemen, the Order of Railway Conductors, and the Brotherhood of Railroad Trainmen being represented in its behalf at the hearings before the House Committee. Its principal point is that it does not seek in any manner to diminish the power of the court as to the injunction—that is, as to the character of the injunction or as to its power for punishment of violation. It simply goes to the question of the notice before any writ shall be issued. Representatives of the brotherhoods state that they did not regard the Gilbert Bill as a complete remedy for the abuse of the injunctive power by some judges, but they believe it to be a step in the right direction.

The position of organized labor, as represented in the American Federation of Labor, is presented in the testimony of Mr. Samuel Gompers, its president. He contends that there is not now upon the statute books one line that by its fair interpretation is a warrant for the issuance of injunctions in labor disputes. He claims that under the operation of the issuance of the injunctions, the very things they might do as men and as citizens, they are denied the right to do as workingmen. "The injunctions treat us as a class; the injunctions apply to us as workingmen, and apply to no other members of the common country," he says. The enjoining of men from committing any criminal act, Mr. Gompers contends, is an improper exercise of the power of the equity court; "yet some of our opponents," he says, "would have it appear that we favor criminal acts, or that we favor their commission. But we contend that the writ of injunction was never intended to be issued to enjoin men from committing any unlawful or criminal act; that both our country and our States provide for the apprehension and the trial by a jury of persons who commit such acts to ascertain whether such person has been guilty of a criminal act and to punish him if he is found guilty, and that organized civil society has constituted a police force, large or small as the circumstances may warrant, for the apprehension and prevention of any criminal act.

MR. JAMES W. VAN CLEAVE,
President of the National Association of Manufacturers.

MR. SAMUEL GOMPERS,
President of the American Federation of Labor.

MR. MARSHALL CUSHING,
Secretary of the National Association of Manufacturers.

MR. FRANK MORRISON,
Secretary of the American Federation of Labor.

"The representatives of labor appearing for and advocating the enactment of an anti-injunction bill, and an effective one—I want it to be clearly understood—neither directly nor indirectly nor remotely aim to attack the writ of injunction as a writ. We recognize its importance and its value and efficiency and appropriateness and effectiveness within the limits of its original purpose, and that is to protect property rights when there is no other remedy at law."

President Gompers states that what the American workingmen want is an effective bill that shall remove the condition that has selected them as workmen specially to have injunctions issued enjoining them from doing things that apply to no other man, woman, or child. Referring to trespass, unlawful acts, and criminal acts, Mr. Gompers states that no one can defend them and claim honest citizenship in our country. "But the doing, as I say, of the most ordinary things that men do in their every-day lives are more and more coming to be touched upon by injunctions. One injunction was issued—or, rather, many injunctions were issued—prohibiting persuasion, and not even designating what kind of persuasion. We can understand that there is such a thing as persuasion glibly used by the tongue and a club held in the hand; and no one can at all justify such persuasion as that. But even so, in such a case the injunction should not lie, because such an attempt is a threatened assault upon the person, for which there is a law to prevent, to apprehend, to try, and to convict and to punish. But there is a persuasion—that persuasion which is commonly understood in our language—which no man can deny the right to exercise by another. . . . I hold that the workmen have the right to go to any workman employed by anybody, whether in a strike-bound establishment or otherwise, and if such a workman has no legal contract with his employer, and it would not violate the terms of a contract, the associated workmen have the legal right to offer this man inducements to quit his employment and go to work with them in some other establishment, or not to work at all, for the time being. They have the right to 'lure away' and 'wean away' from an employer a workman, and to offer him money inducements, so that he may quit that employment and work for another, or to go idle for a period, in order that a certain lawful, honorable purpose may be achieved. And yet the injunction is issued against workmen for doing that very thing; and for doing it after the injunction has been issued they have been sent to jail."

President Gompers states that organized labor objects to the fact that the courts have read into the law new features. "We are suffering," he states, "from court-made law rather than statute law," and he indicates that the purpose they have in view in offering their bill "is that the law and its purpose shall be as it existed prior to the existence of these modern injunctions in trade disputes arising between employers and employed." He states that his contention is that there has not been one injunction issued that is not in contravention of fundamental rights. He states that he holds that the things which are enjoined and which are in themselves unlawful the courts should not issue injunctions against, because there is already a remedy for them at law. He says further: "We hold that the issuance of an injunction is an extraordinary remedy which is to be resorted to only when the end to be reached can be obtained by no other legal process. That there is a legal remedy for the things which an injunction can enjoin goes without saying, but it is the purpose of the opponents of our legislation on this subject to get rid of the trial by jury in the regular process of the law. Their purpose is to make the judge who issues the injunction both the judge, the jury, and the executioner, and, indeed, to take away from the workman enjoined the constitutional right of being tried before a jury of his peers for any crime or unlawful offence with which he may be charged.

So long as it involves personal liberty Mr. Gompers states that he goes so far as to contend that the courts have not any fundamental power or rightful power to issue an injunction to restrain an unlawful act distinguished from a criminal act. Where it is affecting property Mr. Gompers states that he is in entire accord with the best conception of the writ of injunction; but when it involves personal liberty, the freedom and the exercise of lawful rights guaranteed to the citizen, then he holds that under no circumstances should the writ of injunction apply; and, further, he says it does not apply except to workmen when engaged in a dispute with employers.

"Writs of injunction," he says, "in so far as they enjoin acts forbidden by law, are superfluous, erro-

(*Continued on page 16*)

THE NATIONAL
Civic Federation Review

Office: 281 Fourth Avenue, New York City
RALPH M. EASLEY, Editor

The Editor alone is responsible for any unsigned article or unquoted statement published in THE NATIONAL CIVIC FEDERATION REVIEW.

Ten Cents per Copy One Dollar per Year

PUBLISHED BY
The National Civic Federation

The Federation's Annual Meeting. The annual meeting of The National Civic Federation will be held in the Assembly Rooms of the Park Avenue Hotel, New York City, Wednesday and Thursday, December 12 and 13. The subjects for discussion will be "The Income Tax and the Inheritance Tax," "Government by Injunction," and "Child Labor."

Among the speakers on the first-mentioned subject will be Andrew Carnegie, August Belmont, William D. Guthrie, Charles W. Eliot, President of Harvard University, Archbishop John Ireland, Oscar S. Straus, Samuel Gompers, President of the American Federation of Labor, N. J. Bachelder, Master of the National Grange, Franklin MacVeagh, Melville E. Ingalls, and Nicholas Murray Butler. Other speakers will be Alfred Mosely, who is to present the English tax system, Professor Hermann Schumacker, of the University of Berlin, who is to talk on the German system, and George Foster, ex-Minister of Finance of Canada, who will present the facts as regards the Canadian Income and Inheritance Tax.

"Government by Injunction" will be discussed by John Mitchell, of the American Federation of Labor; H. R. Fuller, representing the Railway Brotherhoods; George R. Peck, ex-President of the American Bar Association, and General Counsel of the Chicago, Milwaukee and St. Paul Railway; Walter Drew, Commissioner of the National Iron Erector's Association; Louis D. Brandeis, Esq., Frederick N. Judson, Esq., and Seth Low.

In the discussion of 'Child Labor" there will be represented the officers of The National Child Labor Committee, representatives of the trade unions from among those occupations in which child labor is most prevalent, representatives of employers' and manufacturers' organizations, labor commissioners, factory inspectors, and representatives of women's organizations.

That these are three vital questions at this time will not be denied. The general demand, finding expression in so many circles, that there should be some curb placed on huge aggregations of wealth, certainly calls for thoughtful consideration by those who believe in the perpetuity of our democratic institutions. Shall we have a graduated Income Tax, and a graduated Inheritance Tax? If so, should there be exemptions, or should every income be taxed alike? Will an Income Tax produce "a nation of liars"? What has been the experience in Europe?

The importance of the problem "Government by Injunction" lies in the fact that organized labor believes that the courts are being used by employers in a partisan way to prevent or break strikes. The employers, while admitting that there may be abuses of the character complained of, claim that the remedy is not along the lines sought by the unions. The merits of the question are fairly well outlined in an article appearing elsewhere in this issue. The question is "Can the abuses complained of, by organized labor be remedied without destroying the beneficial principle underlying the injunction?"

The question on Child Labor to come before the meeting is largely this: What is the real extent of the evil, and is everything being done that is possible to do to meet it? As to the character of the evil there is practically no divergence of opinion; as to its extent there is a wide difference of opinion. Many speakers and writers on the subject declare that there are two million children working in the factories, mines, mills and in mercantile and street trades, etc., under fourteen years of age, and that child labor is on the increase. Others claim that these figures are gross exaggerations, and point to the 1900 census which shows in round numbers 1,750,000 children "under 16 years" of age engaged in gainful occupations. But of this total number the same census shows, it is claimed, that there are 1,065,000 engaged in agriculture, and 500,000 in round numbers who are over fourteen years of age, which reduces the total number which it is sought to protect by legislation, to less than 200,000. It is claimed on the one side that there are twelve thousand boys under fourteen years of age in the anthracite coal breakers, whereas officials of the state of Pennsylvania, after investigating the matter, claim that there are not over 8,100 all told under sixteen, and that with only 760 of them is there any doubt about their being over fourteen,—the age beyond which no attempt is made to prevent employment.

Whether there is a disagreement on the number or not, there will doubtless be an agreement among the speakers at the coming meeting that whatever the number of children of tender years engaged in gainful occupations, they should not be permitted to work if they are under fourteen years of age.

The executive committees of the various departments will meet on the evening of the 12th, and in addition to discussing important questions relating to their respective fields of endeavor, will plan their work for the coming year.

The Conciliation Department will organize its work in a way that will enable it to be in touch with every industrial center and to carry on during the coming year a great deal of educational work along the line of Conciliation, Arbitration and Trade Agreements.

The Executive Committee of the Immigration Department will consider the various projects which have been advanced for the distribution of immigrants and which have in view relieving the congestion of aliens at particular points and at the same time meeting the demands of those sections of the country where immigration is so much desired.

The Welfare Department, in addition to considering the Employers' Liability Act, the question of Safeguarding the Lives of Employes, and Industrial Insurance, will plan its campaign for bettering the conditions of employes in the public service, national, state and local. A special committee the past year has been investigating the conditions under which our public employes work, and will recommend that as active efforts be put forth in their behalf as the Department has hitherto taken in the interests of employes of private establishments.

The Immigration Problem. It was pointed out in the preceding issue of THE REVIEW that widely varying and antagonistic views are being entertained on the immigration question because of the absence of *the* facts. In that issue we quoted opponents of immigration as claiming that a large per cent of immigration is made up of "outcasts, criminals, anarchists, thieves and off-scourings of the earth," and in contrast with this we presented another view by a high authority who claimed our immigrants to be "bright, ambitious men and women, the brawn and backbone of any country." Through immigration, Commissioner Watchorn also said, the United States is receiving "the youth and strength and ambition and vigor of foreign lands."

Another and a much more comprehensive view as to controverted facts on the immigration question was presented by well-known experts in this line of knowledge at the conference of the Immigration Department of The National Civic Federation held in New York City on September 24. Many of the statistics generally accepted as accurate were shown not to represent correctly the actual situation. Some of these statistics—even government statistics which usually go unquestioned—were so vigorously combated that many at the Conference expressed their surprise that thinking people should have gone so long without taking some steps to remedy the conditions. So important was this feature among other objects of the Conference that a number of speakers made reference to it in their addresses. Mr. Prescott F. Hall, secretary of the Immigration Restriction League, expressed his views on this point as follows: "I think all who have studied this subject for any length of time feel very much the scarcity of accurate statistics on the immigration question. I certainly do. And it is one of the very encouraging things about the formation of this department that we can hope after a time to get more accurate and reliable statistics."

Another of the speakers, Nathan Bijur, Esq., Vice-President of the United Hebrew Charities, stated that in his study of the question of immigration, the first thing that confronted him was the absence of accurate and complete statistics. He said: "What I hope will be done by this department of the Federation is that it will gather together all the facts, such as they are, the best statistics available from everywhere, and put them down and say: 'Well, so far as we have been able to gather anything, this is what we know,' and then let us sift them and see how reliable they are. When we find a government report which does not mean anything, say so and say why. When we find statistics of crime which have left out certain classes of criminals, let us say so. Show what the difference would be if they were put in, and go on through and collect all these things and put to the credit of the immigrant all the facts that are to be put to his credit, as well as charge him with all the things that ought to be so charged. Now, that has not been done by anybody. Everyone who has discussed this subject has discussed it from the point of view of the advocate. Let this department formulate great general facts."

The Committee on Basal Statistics of the Immigration Department has undertaken to perform this important service. Prof. Walter F. Willcox, of Cornell University, one of the leading statisticians of the United States, is Chairman of this Committee, and its personnel is made up of other leading statisticians and prominent students of immigration questions. A conception of the character of the work this Committee has undertaken and the scientific spirit with which its members are imbued is indicated in the paper by Prof. Willcox, which is presented elsewhere in this issue. We commend this paper to the thoughtful attention of our readers.

Welfare Work Among Railway Men. Improvements in safety appliances, the increase in block signals, the construction of double tracks, the progress in locomotive and car construction, and the adoption of new devices have all tended the past twenty years or more to minimize the dangers of railway travel. All these mark a phenomenal advance in the direction of safeguarding the traveling public from accidents. At the same time there are not wanting indications which point to the necessity of greater emphasis being placed on the "human" element, especially as regards the men in charge of the trains. Only in very recent years has the attention the subject demands been given to caring for the physical qualifications of engineers, firemen, and trainmen.

In the recent reports of the Interstate Commerce Commission dealing with the causes of railway accidents, the "human" element occupies a prominent place. It is plain that the physical qualities of the men in charge of trains must be in as perfect condition as possible, if accidents are to be prevented. It is upon this principle that many railway companies are now working. They are requiring their men to abstain from alcoholic beverages, from tobacco and the like which scientifically are known to affect the sight, the nerves, and in general the self-possession of the men. Many railroads are also requiring their trainmen to undergo rigid physical examinations. For preserving in their best working order these physical qualities, railway managements are providing rest and recreation houses for the trainmen at various important points along their lines.

In no other occupation is modern welfare work for employes more necessary than among railroad men in charge of trains. Almost any single accident of any importance results in a money outlay on the part of the railway company more than sufficient to provide efficiently for the care of their trainmen, and we believe that if this one fact could be impressed upon the attention of railway officials it would be a sufficient argument to induce them to undertake welfare work to an even greater extent than is now being done.

But it is not the money cost to railroad companies, in the destruction and damage of property and in the expense of lawsuits growing out of railway accidents and wrecks, that is the element of prime consideration when such a vital subject as welfare work among railway employes is up for discussion. Of far more importance is the assurance to the traveling public that by such consideration of the physical welfare of employes, traveling on American railroads, as far as the human element is a factor, is made safer. Such a result is doubly assured by well-organized and well-conducted welfare work among railway employes. An idea of what is being accomplished in this direction by one railroad can be gained from Dr. Latta's article on "Rest Houses for Railroad Men," which appears elsewhere in this issue. It emphasizes two essential factors in successful welfare work—responsible organization and competent management. Similar work among other railroads will be described in succeeding issues of THE REVIEW.

The Ownership Commission Abroad. The announcement in detail on another page of this issue of the investigations of the Commission on Public Ownership and Operation indicates that this very important undertaking is approaching its termination. The article presents an account of the work performed in the important cities of Great Britain, and refers to the social aspect of the Commission's visit, which should be regarded as an important side of the Committee's studies, inasmuch as the social events enabled them to become better acquainted with those experts and officials in Great Britain who are recognized as among the ablest men in the different lines of work coming within the province of the Commission. It is of interest in connection with the Commission's visit abroad to read of the general expressions of approval of the task undertaken by this body, much of the success of the work of the Committee being due to the courtesies extended to the members. For the efforts of the distinguished foreigners who placed every facility at the disposal of the Committee, the thanks of the members are due.

The coming month of December will probably see the completion of all the special investigations of the different cities as outlined by the Commission, with the probability that by the first of the year the Committee of Investigation will be in a position to present its completed report to the entire Commission. As soon as the Commission has passed on the report finally, it will then be made public. We believe it will have considerable effect upon future discussions of the Public Ownership problem, and that it will be a work of reference for many years to come to those concerned in the various questions involved.

Socialism and Trade Unionism. The attention of our readers is directed to the synopsis on another page of this issue of the very able articles against socialism written by Mr. James A. Cable, editor of the *Coopers' International Journal*, and published in recent issues of that paper. It will not only surprise, but we believe it will interest our readers to see how clearly and forcibly a workingman disposes of socialistic doctrines, which presumably are being put forth for his benefit. Mr. Cable sees through the confusion between trade unionism and socialism which has grown up in the minds of many, and is able to distinguish between the two. In fact, Mr. Cable, instead of conceding the two as being identical, clearly shows that there is nothing in harmony between the two, despite the fact that some trade unionists profess socialism. The keynote of the whole discussion may be summarized briefly in the author's statement as follows:

"One of our correspondents challenges us to show reason why the trade-union and the socialist movements cannot be harmonized. The reasons are clear. The two movements are seeking opposite ends.

"By reason of its defects the socialists seek to overthrow the present order.

"By correcting its defects, the trade unions seek to make the present order endurable.

"Now, if the trade unions succeed in making the present order endurable, the aim of socialism is thereby defeated; whereas, if the socialists succeed in overthrowing the present order, the aim of the trade unions is defeated. As the success of the one means the failure of the other, the two are diametrically opposed to each other."

This clearly-stated distinction between trade unionism and socialism is commended to the thoughtful attention of our readers, and in particular do we recommend its study to those who have been in the habit of confusing the two and of regarding them as only different names for the same things.

MRS. J. ELLEN FOSTER, by direction of President Roosevelt, has been detailed from the Department of Justice to investigate the conditions under which women and children work throughout the United States. Mrs. Foster has had years of experience in philanthropic work that peculiarly fit her for this position. She was among the first women of the country to practice law, and most of her clients were moneyless and defenceless women and children. She has been prominent in reform movements and usually has had charge of crystallizing sentiment into practical results.

In 1900 Mrs. Foster was appointed by the late Secretary Hay as a representative of the United States to the

International Red Cross Conference at St. Petersburg. Last year she accompanied the Taft party to the Philippines and made a special report to President Roosevelt on the condition of women and children there. She has but recently returned from a trip around the world, in the course of which she studied the condition of women and children in India and China.

The selection of Mrs. Foster for such work commends itself to the general public, for while full of generous sentiment, she is a student of economics and has the logical mind that looks at all conditions in the light of reason.

MISS HELEN VARICK BOSWELL, well known to club women of the country as a forceful public speaker, has recently been appointed Chairman of the Industrial and Child Labor Committee of the New York State Federation of Women's Clubs. Miss Boswell had charge of the session of this important committee during the convention held at Saratoga the early part of this month, and she was highly complimented for the excellence of her program, and for the fairness with

which it represented the different phases of the industrial question.

Miss Boswell has had some years of experience in public work, having organized numerous clubs, and is always fortunate in holding the confidence of the many club women who are her associates. She completed her law course at the Washington College of Law of the District of Columbia, and has found her legal knowledge of great assistance in her public work.

Miss Boswell is connected with the National Civic Federation and during the winter will give a number of lectures before the women's clubs of the country for the Welfare Department of the Federation.

REST HOUSES FOR RAILROAD MEN.

PENNSYLVANIA'S PROVISION FOR THE WELFARE OF ITS CONDUCTORS, ENGINEERS, FIREMEN AND TRAINMEN.

By Samuel W. Latta, Chief Medical Examiner.

VERY few persons, outside of the railroad people, have any idea what a rest house is or its purpose. I shall explain its origin and the benefits that are derived from it.

In its early days the Pennsylvania Railroad, like all pioneers, experienced great difficulty in not having its train crews where they could be reached readily when needed. This was particularly the case where the men were at the end of the runs and away from their homes. The idea was conceived, therefore, of having rest houses or bunk houses, and they constituted the forerunner of all the welfare work initiated by the company.

The first rest house, as far as I can learn, was established prior to 1875. There was an old hotel building in Philadelphia which our company bought, renovated and fitted up as a rest house for its freight men, that being then a terminus of the freight runs.

Special trains and extra sections of regular trains require special crews. There is no knowing when they will be needed. Emergencies arise, particularly in the night, and it is necessary to be able to locate the men quickly. Freight yards and termini are frequently located at isolated places distant from residential centers and difficult of access to boarding houses. Adequate accommodations are necessary for the crews, arriving and departing at all hours of the day and night, at prices within their reach. In instances, as in Philadelphia, as much as thirty thousand dollars was expended on such a house to allow the men all the comfort and health that is necessary for them to do their work properly.

In many cases the company has rented a room or rooms in private houses, and in some instances an entire house to ensure the comfort and welfare of its employes. In the large yards, situated distant from proper

Library in Philadelphia Rest House. (Pennsylvania R. R.)

accommodations, rooms are furnished with chairs and lounges for the use of the yard men. In large freight and transfer stations rooms in which to wash, and to keep and change their clothes, and places for them to eat their lunch are furnished. Some have reading rooms supplied with newspapers and periodicals.

At many isolated places where only one, or at best a few crews have a lay over, cabin cars are used for the freight crews. These are fitted with six bunks, a stove and utensils for cooking, and answer well as substitutes for rest houses. Every freight train has its cabin, and, whenever necessary, the crews can sleep in the cabin, provided with all necessary means of comfort.

Game Room (Pennsylvania R. R.)

A description of one of the rest houses may give a fair idea of them all. The house in Philadelphia, at 1605 and 1607 Filbert Street, is under the care of a competent number of necessary helpers to make the beds and keep the place plentifully supplied with bed linen, soap and towels, while a librarian looks after the library and game room. Over $30,000 were expended on the site and furnishing of this house; it costs $400 to $500 per month for service, all paid by the company. Everything in this building is absolutely free to the men. The house contains reading, game and diversion rooms, a day bunk room, a room for day lounging, bedrooms, locker rooms, and so forth. There are seventy-two beds for night use; sixteen couches for day use; nine hundred eighty-three individual lockers, wherein the men hang their clothes; fifteen stationary washstands; and eight lavatories on different floors; the library contains 1,286 books circulating among the fam-

Reading Room (Pennsylvania R. R.)

ilies of the men at the rate of three hundred a month; the games furnished are dominoes, checkers and chessmen; the reading room is supplied with Philadelphia and New York newspapers, and various weekly and monthly periodicals. One thousand men avail themselves daily of the privileges of this room; some of them on local runs visit it several times a day. It furnishes a delightful place for rest and recreation while waiting for duty calls. Any one can occupy a couch during the day. Any one desiring a bed for the night must register. He goes to the attendant in charge and states that he is going on duty on a certain train. His name is registered opposite the bed in which he is going to sleep, as well as the time and number of the train for which he is to be called. He is given a check for the bed, and when he goes to the room the colored man in charge allows him to occupy that bed. At the proper time in the morning or during the night he is called for his train. This

Day Bunk Room (Pennsylvania R. R.)

building is sanitarily as near perfect as it can be made. The plumbing is first class; the ventilation is as near perfect as it can be with due regard to dangers of drafts. The beds are taken apart and bedding and rooms are thoroughly aired every day. Every effort is made to render these bedrooms absolutely clean, healthy and safe.

The Pennsylvania Railroad has a rule that everything provided on the road must be of a certain stan-

LOCKERROOM AND NIGHT DORMITORY (Pennsylvania R. R.)

dard; there are a standard track and standard trucks, and so in the rest houses there are standard beds. Each bed is a good iron cot with woven springs; and the mattresses are of excellent quality. The company pays special attention to the cleanliness and sanitary conditions of the rooms. The men take pride in going to them, and they show visitors around and comment upon what is done for their health and comfort.

In some places the rest houses are connected with the despatcher's office by means of electric wires. Those for the wreck-trainmen are all connected in that way. The wreck-train houses are all the property of the company. The operator touches a button which rings a gong in each man's bedroom and in five minutes the train is on the way. (When at their homes the men are reached by callers, their residences being carefully kept in the trainmaster's office and every change promptly noted. When a train is to be made up, the caller is given the names and residences of the men and he calls them for that particular train).

LUNCHROOMS (Pennsylvania R. R.)

At many places the rooms are only used for resting between hours of labor. Then they are equipped with chairs and tables, to make them convenient places for the men to eat luncheons brought from their homes. In some a cook stove makes possible hot coffee. In many small yards, such as are between here and Philadelphia—at Newfield Junction for instance—shanties are provided in which the men keep their clothes and lunch baskets. Each has a key to the building, which is kept locked.

At the large yards we have the big rest houses. Recently there were established very large classification yards at a point called East Altoona, where it was necessary to erect two rest houses. One contains a hundred fourteen bunks for the use of the engineers and firemen, and the other seventy-four beds for the trainmen. I will read you a quotation from a letter that I had from the superintendent of that division: "At East Altoona there are nine rooms fitted up for sleeping rooms. Each of eight of these rooms has eight beds, the ninth room, being somewhat larger, contains ten beds. The beds are made of iron and are single; they are all furnished with Ostermoor mattresses and springs; each bed has two sheets, pillow with pillow case, and blanket; there are a spittoon and chair furnished each bed and at the head there are three hooks in the wall on which to hang the clothes. There is matting through the center of each room and between each bed."

DRINKING WATER CAN IN ENGINE (Pennsylvania R. R.)

This cooler is made of $.80$ inch tank steel; the inside covering is made o .022 inch galvanized iron and there is a space of $1\frac{1}{2}$ inches between the outside and inside cases filled with granulated cork. The bucket fitting inside is made of .022 inch galvanized iron and has a capacity $3\frac{1}{2}$ gallons.

It will be seen from this that on completion of this yard the necessary provisions were made for the comfort of the men.

The needs of the men are closely looked after, and the same consideration for the care and comfort of the men is shown, whether it involves but one crew or more. On the lines east of Pittsburg and Erie there are fifty such places where two thousand men are given free beds every night. It is difficult to give the number of resting or loafing places furnished. Some seventy-five thousand dollars have been expended on furniture and over thirty thousand dollars are spent annually for maintenance. Now, the lines west of Pittsburg are gradually introducing the necessary bunk and rest houses at all points where they may be required.

The men must have means of diversion. Saloons coming into existence to supply it, gave rise to conditions from which serious results often followed and called for means to overcome them. Indeed the moral welfare of the employes, particularly the passenger and freight men, was a matter of great seriousness to the officials of the Pennsylvania Railroad from its very earliest days. The company has on its payrolls about two hundred ten thousand men, counting the lines east and west of Pittsburg, and its operated and controlled lines. To successfully conduct the business the morale of this great army of workmen must be at least above normal.

A clear brain is needed to safely operate trains freighted with precious lives and priceless commodities. In the furnishing of the rest houses, not only did the company supply the essentials, such as the beds, closets for clothes, lavatories and restaurants, but it also furnished means for amusement, such as newspapers, periodicals, libraries, and games. Some of the houses have rooms fitted with mechanical appliances for instruction in airbrakes, and injectors, and instructors are provided to teach the men. This instruction is very useful, for they have to apply that knowledge in their work, and every man who uses them has to undergo examination in the use of airbrakes.

WASHROOM AND Y. M. C. A. REST HOUSE (Pennsylvania R. R.)

From a small beginning the rest houses have grown to what they are at present. Some of them are managed entirely by the company, others by the men themselves, and some are under the care of the Railroad Y. M. C. A. Some of them furnish beds free; others charge a nominal sum, like ten cents a night for the bed, and food is furnished in the restaurants at cost.

Arrangements are made at some places with private parties to furnish meals at small cost within the means of the men. Where that is not possible the cabin car,

Y. M. C. A. REST HOUSE AND HOSPITAL ON ONE OF THE GOULD LINE

equipped with cook stove, utensils and means to prepare food and hot coffee, is provided. At points, such as on the Philadelphia, Baltimore and Washington division, in addition to the bunk rooms we furnish a cook house. This is not unusual where the terminus is at a distance from places where board can be obtained.

In Broad Street Station, Philadelphia, there is a railroad men's dining room, at which a first-class meal is served for fifteen cents. Any employe in uniform can go there and get his dinner. He gets roast beef and two vegetables, bread and butter, dessert and coffee for fifteen cents. So along the road, scattered all over, wherever there are restaurants under the control of the company, special rates are made for trainmen. On a dining car the conductor and crew can get a dinner for twenty-five cents, such as you will receive at a dollar.

The company realizes that anything which provides for the physical and mental welfare of the men, rendering them more content, not only benefits the men, but also the company, in that it receives from the employes better and more loyal service. Where men have left the employ of the Pennsylvania Railroad, engaging with some other company under different conditions, they have returned to our company. An experience of more than twenty years with the railroad has convinced me that the company receives large returns on its investment by the excellent service received from its men and the loyal support that the employes delight in giving.

Interrogations and answers follow:

Q. Is there any compulsory element? Are the men compelled in any way to use the restaurants and rest places?

DR. LATTA: They are obliged to be where the company can put its hands on them. We never had any one raise objection to occupying these rooms, especially when they are free; but I do not think they would regard it as compulsory, except in so far as we want to have the men where we can put our hands on them. If they choose to take board at outside places we do not object. We simply provide these places and, if they choose, they occupy them.

Q. Why do you charge for lodging in some places and not others?

DR. LATTA: I don't believe I can answer that question; I don't know why it is done. I know it is a fact. In some places the houses are managed by the men and are located at the request of the men. It may be that the house is not absolutely necessary there, but is put up for the accommodation of the men, at their request, and they manage it. We provide the heat and light in all cases. I would like to say in this connection that I do not think our men approve of houses not under the control of the company, if it can be helped. I know they would rather that the company or they should manage them than the Y. M. C. A. One of the reasons is that the men they send there to handle them are not experienced; they are not familiar with railroad men. You have to learn to know railroad men—they are not like other people in a great many respects; you have to learn their peculiarities and know how to meet them. A branch Y. M. C. A. is established at some point and given charge of a rest house, and they send some young fellow out there as secretary who doesn't know anything about railroad men; he doesn't know railroad men and he has to learn, and the men don't like that. I suppose one reason is that the company does it for nothing; the company does a great deal for nothing. But no scheme for the benefit of the masses will succeed without responsible organization and competent management. Such essential features have marked the successful progress of the institutions of the Pennsylvania Railroad.

HOW THE RAILROAD MEN REGARD SUCH CONVENIENCES.

Not long ago a locomotive fireman, while in New York City, expressed great enthusiasm for the work of the Welfare Department of The National Civic Federation, but he feared that the railroad workers of the country would perhaps be overlooked by the department, and he had many convincing things to tell as to why special interest should be taken in the work of railroad employes. He said:

"In this railroad world of ours there are a great many men working and working hard for a living, and particularly with engines. As the conditions are which confront the men continuously in this great service, there is one crying need, and that is rest rooms, places where the men can go while waiting for the return of their engines to their initial starting point, that they may have rest sufficient to give them the life that is necessary for them to carry on their work. The rest room should be a place sufficiently warm and equipped with the necessary arrangements to bring comfort to the men, in the way of bathrooms, shower baths, and also individual washbowls.

"When I speak of rest rooms, I mean rooms where bunks could be furnished for the men who have from two to five hours of uncertainty when they are waiting to return with their trains. They should be near the terminals so that the men could be spoken to at any time that it might be necessary in the way of calling them to their work. Some roads have such houses. The Central Railroad of New Jersey has several bunk houses. They have nice, clean cots, and all the facilities in the world for the men to lay over from 12 to 24 hours. They have nice stoves and there is an opportunity for the men to do their own cooking. This is one of the roads which has provided in this way for the comfort of their men.

"The Pennsylvania Railroad does so well by its employes that they are always contented, for they get everything they need. It used to make other men feel bad to think that the Pennsylvania men got everything and we on the other roads got nothing, but other roads do something now. The C. B. & Q., the C. & N. W., Grand Trunk, Union Pacific, Southern Pacific System, Santa Fe System, Central Railroad of Georgia, and the St. Louis & Southwestern Railroad have some rest houses.

"The need for these rest houses is continually felt. I had a remarkable experience last December at one station which is a new freight terminal. Of the six houses at that place, I found four were saloons and two were large boarding houses. All the employes—five divisions—put up in these houses—sixty crews. I never saw such a drunken lot of men in my life. They threw their money away in these saloons, because there was no other place for them to go to eat or sit down. In another town I think it is not too much for me to say that every dollar that the men earn goes to the saloons, because the only places where they can get lodgings are the saloons. As only railroad men go into this particular town, it is very evident that the saloons get their patronage only.

"There are roads in this country where the men start out and do not get back home for a month.

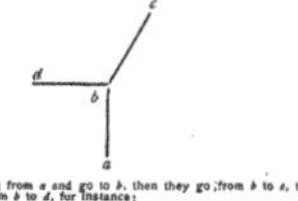

"The men start from *a* and go to *b*, then they go from *b* to *c*, then back to *b*, and from *b* to *d*, for instance:

"There is no use in this sort of thing. The company could manage so that the men would not be away from home so long. It is a matter of arrangement. The Pennsylvania Railroad has a very different method, and it is just as easy to arrange the runs as they have arranged them. The men are often kept out longer than they should be because the motive power has run down and the railroad companies have not kept it up properly. One reason why the work consumes so many hours is because the engines are so large and the fuel is of poor quality, being mixed with snow and dirt often in bad weather."

That the life of the fireman is a hard one and that he needs all that can be done for him in the way of welfare work is graphically shown by another fireman:

"Where the men work fourteen hours a day they have the best jobs. My run is 165 miles every day six days in the week. It is one of the *good* jobs. Only 17 per cent of the men can 'hit the ball,' that is, stand up and do their work. It is only recently that the work has been so hard—all in the past six years. In many of the large engines in the West the fire is so hot and the space so narrow that many of the men require leather blankets from the waist to the knees to protect them—to keep their clothing from burning. The men are subjected to extreme heat and extreme cold. It is said that only one man in six who enters the position of fireman ever becomes an engineer; five fall by the wayside because health fails, or the eyesight is affected from the intense heat and looking into the bright light.

"Railroading has been revolutionized in the last six years and all the work lightened except that of the fireman. That has become almost unbearable.

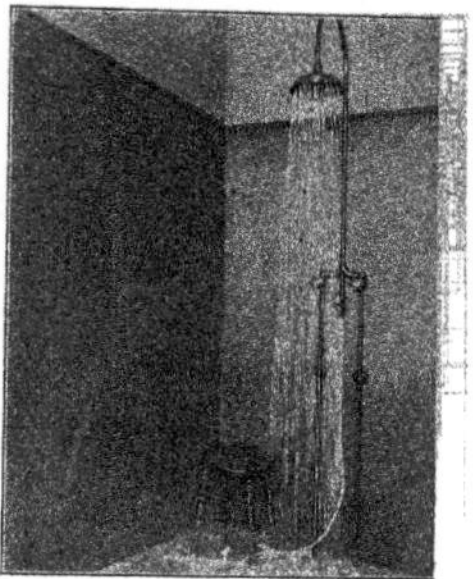

"THE FIRST THING A MAN WANTS AFTER LEAVING HIS ENGINE IS A BATH AND A GOOD SQUARE MEAL"

"Seventy per cent of the men are in the freight service, where the runs are long and uncertain. It is not unusual for them to be out fifty hours, and in extreme cases they have been on duty as many as seventy hours, so you see their comfort especially requires consideration. One of our worst accidents occurred where the engineer on a freight train, who had been on duty thirty-two hours without rest, went to sleep while waiting on a siding for a passenger train to pass. His crew left the train and it slipped down on the main track and was struck by the passenger train."

One of the 'crack'" engineers of the country, who ran a fast train for twenty years, tells that many of the men lie down in their engines to sleep

"Many a time I have slept alongside of mine on the ground. Often the men lie on the hot sand at the roundhouse or in the sandhouse or a handy box car in warm weather will offer the best accommodations.

"One very great need has been a place not only where the men could rest, but where they could clean up and were welcome. Most of our men come in from 8 to 12 P. M. and there is no place to go except the saloons. They are always welcome there.

"In a certain town in Indiana of 900 inhabitants there are thirteen saloons in full blast. In an Illinois town of 3,000 population there are twenty-two saloons. Both are railway terminals. There is not even a place for a man to wash his dirty face and hands when he comes in tired.

"On many roads as soon as the men ask for any conveniences for their comfort the reply comes: 'We pay so much for so much work.' We try to make an employer see it is the best investment which he can make because, if a man coming in from a good hard trip can get a bath, he is refreshed, but if he does not get a chance to change his clothes, a chance to bathe, and a chance to sleep, he starts out again tired. The first thing a man wants after leaving his engine is a bath and a good square meal.

"At many terminals, if the men come in after midnight there is no place to go except the saloons to get a bite to eat. There is a piano going in each saloon

"THE WAY SOME MEN WASH IN ALL KINDS OF WEATHER"

A MODEL WASHROOM WITH VENTILATED LOCKERS

NEW MEXICO REST HOUSE NAMED BY THE MEN, "ROSE COTTAGE"

and it is very attractive to the men. After thirty or forty hours on the road a man has a bad taste in his mouth. Nothing looks well to him. The world is all wrong. Then, if he can get something dainty and well cooked to eat he feels quite different.

"The men worked three years to get a building on a certain road on the promise that one would be put at every terminal if this one should succeed. The company put $12,000 in that building alone. The environment was beautiful and it was a nice building, but it was wretchedly managed. For instance, there was a running brook, and it would have been easy enough to have thrown the refuse into it, but it was simply pitched into the yard, emitting an unhealthful and disagreeable odor.

"Then a man would get dirty coffee which had boiled all day, tough steak and some potatoes that had been cooked in cottolene. He knew exactly what he would get three times a day if he went there. Every Sunday we had chicken for dinner. A man would bet $10 that he would get a wing. I don't know how many wings the chickens had, but I never got anything but a wing!

"In that building they put in nice shower baths, six tubs, a reading room, library, gymnasium, game room, restaurant and beds at ten cents, but they put a young fellow in charge who was entirely unfitted for the position. At first 165 men went there to rest and refresh themselves, but this man did not keep the place clean. The food was not cooked well and the men were made to feel that they were in the road all the time. That grinds in on the soul of a workingman more than anything else.

"It grew worse and worse, and finally the beds were not even made. We got into beds that were not changed sometimes for a week. After a few rounds like that the men said, 'If we have to live in dirt, we might as well go back to the saloons.' Inside of a year that building, which we had tried so hard to get and which had so much that could have been made of benefit to the men, was wrecked purely through mismanagement by the man put in charge."

Another fireman makes a special plea for drinking water. He says: "The men should have cans on their engines for drinking water. They have them on the New York Central. I asked for water cans, and the superintendent said, 'What is it that you firemen don't want?' On another road the company was asked to provide water cans for all engines and to furnish ice

"DUGOUTS." THE WAY SOME RAILWAY MEN SLEEP IN NEW MEXICO

ASLEEP IN HIS ENGINE

"A CAGE IN THE BUNK-HOUSE YARDS OF THE SOUTHERN PACIFIC RAILWAY at an Arizona terminal. Well adapted to the warm climate. Legs of cage in cans filled with water to prevent entrance of bugs. The cages are made of screen on account of mosquitoes and because it is much cooler for the boys to sleep out of doors down on the desert. The men have washstands and bathtubs."

between the months of April and November. The general manager read that paragraph in the proposed contract and said, 'Furnish water and ice coolers! Why not ice cream through the months of July and August?' I told him that would be satisfactory. I got the coolers but not the ice. If the men do not have water they go and fill up on beer at the end of the runs just to quench their thirst."

In regard to rest houses, the fireman says:

"A bad feature about these places generally is that there is no attendant. Wash rooms and lodging rooms are not kept as clean as they should be. I went into one boarding house where a man had died and the room was given to another man without even changing the bed. There should always be an attendant to see to it that the bedclothes are changed. Consumption largely comes from the fact that it is contracted from the bedclothes. In the last four years our death and disability rate has shown a great increase of consumption.

"On our road, with the exception of a bunk room, in one city, which is not near the terminal, the men have no place to sleep except in stock or waste rooms, which are damp and cold. The men simply lie on the floor, with not even a cushion for their heads.

"The men should also have a place to keep their clothes and the rest house should be near enough so they can get to the trains easily. They cannot carry clothes in the engine, especially if the engine cabs leak.

"The work of the firemen is very dirty and frequently they have no place to wash up. They usually have to eat in all their dirt. In one of our roundhouses the men have a small trough with cold water, right out in the roundhouse, but they cannot use this because it is so exposed. They would be obliged to remove some of their clothing in order to wash themselves satisfactorily. Being overheated, they cannot do so except in warm weather, because the roundhouses are cold, and the men would be compelled to disrobe almost in the open air. Besides, the wipers use the wash place in the round house and the water is never drawn—no pretension being made to keep the trough clean.

"Up to two years ago they used to give two pounds of waste a day to clean our *hands* and now we only have a quarter of a pound a day with which to clean the engine *and* our hands and faces. It won't do for the fireman to give his engineer any,—he can't spare it! You are supposed to clean your engine. You have to do *that!* As for wiping your face with it, it is out of the question!

"Another great reform in this work would be if all railroad companies would institute lunchrooms or eating places along the lines where it would do away with the necessity of men carrying food that they are compelled to retain in air-tight pails from ten to fifty hours. Surely after fifty hours this food is unfit to eat."

Another engineer says:

"All engineers and firemen know that the great needs for the betterment of their labor conditions are decent places to sleep, wash, eat and have some simple recreation as an offset to the enticements of the saloon. The continued change of officers on railroads in the last six years has had a tendency to prevent greater improvement in conditions. Every man in the operating department does everything possible to curtail expenses, but even where they are desirous of introducing these beneficial features for the men they have no time to consider them."

A MODEL HOSPITAL CAR.

The hospital car of the Erie Railroad is provided for use when, in case of an accident, passengers or *employes* are injured and the nearest hospital is so far away that operations on the spot become necessary to save life or relieve suffering. It has been pronounced by surgeons to be the most complete and perfect hospital equipment possible in a car.

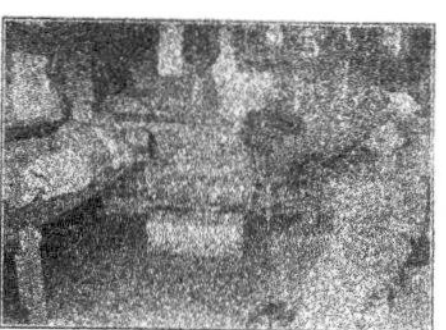

THE ONLY PLACE OF SHELTER FOR THE MEN UPON WHOSE ALERTNESS PUBLIC SAFETY SO LARGELY DEPENDS

The car, which is 60 feet long, is divided into two compartments. It has an operating room 15 feet 10 inches in length equipped with an operating table having a movable head and foot extension in the center, an instrument sterilizer on the right and a surgeon's basin on the left. The car also has two lockers fully equipped with surgical instruments and stocked with bandages, plasters, sponges and all anæsthetics, antiseptics, astringents and other medical and surgical necessities. Sliding doors four feet wide on either side with portable steps permit an easy entrance with a stretcher to the operating room, which has six windows, two windows in each door and a large window in the roof over the operating table. All are of ground glass and provided with white rubber roller curtains. Two 4-flame acetylene gas lights, a single flame over the wash basin and a portable lamp furnish light in the operating room at night. A gravity water system to furnish both hot and cold water from tanks just under the roof of the car is provided. The flow of water can be regulated by a surgeon with a valve operated by the foot, thereby avoiding the necessity of handling any of the equipment. Head lining and inside finish are of a composite board entirely without beading, molding or carving which might serve as places for the collection of infectious matter. White enamel paint is used as a finish and the floor is covered with white rubber tiling.

Two sliding doors with ground glass windows lea to the ward-room. It is 43 feet 4 inches in length, and equipped with 11 brass bedsteads, a lavatory and saloon. It has white rubber tiling on the floor, compoboard sides, painted in white enamel, and white rubber curtains between the beds, which are provided with spring and hair mattresses, rubber sheets, and bed clothing. Equipment boxes underneath the car are provided with crutches, splints, army stretchers, surgical implements, wrecking tools, and other accessories.

There are six-wheel trucks, insuring the utmost freedom from vibration, on which rests the steel underframe. Steel platforms at either end of the car, with gates which can be closed against the curious, are provided. Three-stem couplers and draft gear ease the movement of the car.—*Erie R. R. Employes' Magazine.*

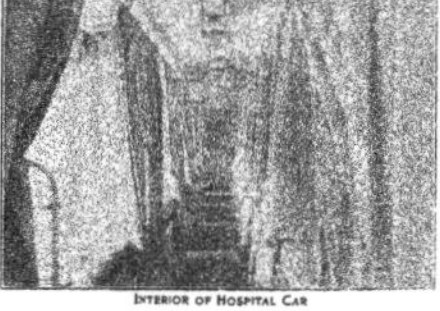

INTERIOR OF HOSPITAL CAR

THE FEDERATION OF LABOR IN POLITICS.

(*Continued from page 9*)

neous, and unnecessary, and they have no function to perform. In so far as writs forbid acts which the law does not forbid they are erroneous and their future issuance should be prohibited." In demanding anti-injunction legislation, Mr. Gompers states that organized labor asks for nothing extraneous, nothing that is unjust or improper. He says: "We want no immunity from the law for any crimes or unlawful conduct of which any man in the labor movement may be guilty. I grant you that here and there some man may be gathered into the fold of a union of labor who, either from a perverted mind or from wrongs which he has suffered elsewhere or here, may do a thing which no man can defend and which no union man will defend. But you must bear in mind that the organized workingmen of America have not always the choice of material."

VIEWS OF EMPLOYERS' REPRESENTATIVES

In addition to the position advocated by representatives of the railway brotherhoods and that taken by the American Federation of Labor, and opposed to these two, is "the other side." This latter is that held generally by employers, and it is in favor of the *status quo*. In advocating this policy before the House Committee, Mr. James A. Emery, representing the Industrial Citizens' Association of America, and other employers' organizations, expressed his belief that "in its actual effect upon the protection of property and personal rights, which we believe an equity court contemplates, the ultimate effect of such legislation, with the moral weight which it would have upon the legislatures of the States, considered merely as a matter of expediency, would be a course of very serious danger by the withdrawal of effectual remedies, adequate protection, which these courts have given during all the time that Federal courts in the operation of Congressional legislation have had jurisdiction of these matters, and would also operate to affect the action of States dangerously."

Because the power of injunction has been abused by the courts is no argument, he claims, for taking away that power, and he states that it is an exceedingly dangerous position to make the chief argument directed in favor of the proposed legislation the abuse of discretion upon the part of Federal judges. He says: "The powers of the court in existence at the present time have been very frequently used because there has been very frequent occasion for their use. There has been an occasion to protect property by virtue of the right of injunction, and of personal rights involved because of the fact that a continuous attack has been made upon those personal rights; and this is not merely the view of the persons who, by virtue of their interests in the offered legislation, might be assumed to be prejudiced, but it is the view of members of the judiciary, of public men who have had occasion to make themselves familiar with the facts, and of tribunals of a moral character, which from time to time have had an opportunity to present their views upon the question.

"In a labor dispute it is continually laid down as though that were a dispute by itself or was to be governed by different rules in morals and in law; that a man has a right to go to another who disagrees with him as to the advisability, the expediency, or the justice of the strike, and on the streets, in the cars, wherever he finds opportunity to approach him, to keep insisting upon his view and compelling the other to accept it. Gentlemen, if we did not have any other jurisdiction of the equity courts except to restrain a nuisance it would at least seem under that that not only was it necessary that such a power should be exercised to restrain it, but it would be exceedingly unwise to adopt legislation that would seem to prevent the issuance of an injunction to prevent the annoyance of another.

"Legislation that would have as its purpose the deprivation of Federal courts of that power which they possess to-day to fit the remedy to the wrong would be a long step in the direction of taking from the courts and throwing into the field of politics, if you please, the essential principles upon which the Republic itself is founded, and those essential principles, the protection and vindication of which are not merely necessary for the protection of this Government, but of all government and all civilized society—the right of a man to work, the right of a man to sell his labor, the right of a man to enter into a labor market and any labor offered freely and willingly to him, the right of a man to live his life free from annoyance, the persecution, the intimidation, the coercion, and even the undesirable persuasion of others—is a right that partakes of the very essentials embraced in our Declaration of Independence—the right of life, liberty, and the pursuit of happiness—which principles were laid down by the fathers of our country as the essential things upon which the Republic rests."

Another bill which representatives of the American Federation of Labor supported before the House Committee is entitled "A bill to regulate the issuance of restraining orders and injunctions and procedures thereto, and to limit the meaning of 'conspiracy' in certain cases." According to the provisions of this bill no restraining order or injunction is to be granted in labor controversies unless necessary to prevent irreparable injury to property or to a property right for which there is no adequate remedy at law. It is further provided that "for the purposes of this act no right to continue the relation of employer and employe, or to assume or create such relation with any particular person or persons, or at all, or to carry on business of any particular kind, or at any particular place, or at all, shall be construed, held, considered or treated as property, or as constituting a property right." In Section 2 of this act it is provided that no "agreement between two or more persons concerning the terms or conditions of employment of labor, or assumption, or creation, or the termination of any relation between employer and employe, or concerning any act or thing to be done, or not to be done, with reference to, or involving or growing out of a labor dispute, shall constitute a conspiracy or other criminal offense, or be punished or prosecuted as such, nor shall the carrying out of any such agreement be restrained or enjoined, unless the act or thing agreed to be done, or not to be done, would be unlawful, if done by a single individual; nor shall the entering into or carrying out of any such agreement be restrained or enjoined, unless such act or thing would, if done or not done, be of the character described in the first section of this act."

ARGUMENTS FOR AND AGAINST THE FEDERATION'S BILL.

Mr. T. C. Spelling, who appeared before the committee as the representative of the American Federation of Labor, stated that this bill was submitted as a substitute for the other bills which the representatives of the Federation had been supporting. The presentation of testimony and the discussions following the submission of this bill centered largely around two points. One was whether the right to do business was a property right, and the other related to the constitutionality of the measure.

On the first-mentioned point, Mr. Spelling argued that no man has anything resembling a property right to carry on business of any kind, or to any extent, anywhere in the world. He claims that a property right is nothing distinct from property. The great dividing line, he says, is between personal and property rights. The right to carry on business is not, in his opinion, a property right when it is divorced from the question of good-will in a particular business. He claims that it is not a fair assumption that any State has decided that the right to do business is property. It is not a final settlement of the matter even if one State or more than one State has done it. He believes that Congress has power to say that the right to do business shall not be considered or treated as property for the purpose of this act. He says: "This being an act to regulate, or limit, the use of Federal process, the questions of the property right under State laws and views of State courts have no relevancy. Congress either has this power or it has not. If it has the power, this enactment is a supreme law of the land There is no question whatever of a taking of property without due process of law. To say that 'for this purpose' certain things shall not be 'considered, held or treated,' as property, is merely to set a definite limit to the power to issue certain extraordinary court process. It is no infringement upon any property right nor the impairment of any State law, nor the invasion of State jurisdiction. Any State courts which hold the right to do business to be property may adhere to that view and enforce it, because we cannot by this or any act control the jurisdiction of functions of State courts." He claims that what is sought under this bill is the lopping off of unwarranted judicial extension of the words "property," or "property right," and "conspiracy." He denies the claim of opponents of the measure that the right to labor is property as much as he denies their claim that the right to do business is property.

Opponents of the measure, most of them representing associations of employers, contended before the Committee that the right to do business is a property right, and it was claimed that the enforcement of such a measure would be in effect to deprive a person of property without due process of law.

Walter Drew, Esq., representing a number of Citizens' Alliances, says the first thing the bill would take away, if it became a law, would be the good-will of the business, "a species of property which in this country is sacred, inviolate, and is protected by our courts." He states that every court, State and Federal, announced the doctrine that good-will is property, subject to contract, to be bought and sold and dealt with as any other species of property. He claims that the right to assume or create the relation of employer or employe has become an established doctrine of our courts, mainly at the instance and behest of laboring men themselves that labor is a commodity to be bought or sold in the open market like any other commodity, and that the right to buy and sell it is a property right, like any other property right, to be protected by our courts. He claims that the bill not only confiscates property, but confiscates the highest kind of property. "As well attack our system of credit," he says, "as to attack the good-will of our business institutions."

Mr. Daniel Davenport states that the measure "assumes by act of Congress to declare that to be not property which by the laws of every State in the Union—I state it without qualification—is property within the meaning, or, as the term is used, in legal and equitable proceedings, and under the recognized system of jurisprudence in force in this country." He claims that any attempt on the part of Congress to declare that which by the laws of the several States is property, shall not be property, when it comes to the question of whether it should be protected by the courts, would be an unconstitutional exercise of authority by Congress.

LYMAN ABBOTT ON SOCIALISM.

DR. LYMAN ABBOTT, editor of *The Outlook*, in an editorial on Socialism, explains what he considers to be its spirit, doctrine and method. After stating that *The Outlook* is in hearty sympathy with the spirit and largely in sympathy with the doctrine of Socialism, Dr. Abbott dissents from its method. On this point he says:

"We dissent from the method and to some extent from the doctrine of State Socialism—that is, of that form of Socialism which would make the State the chief if not the sole employer of industry—for two reasons:

"State Socialism assumes that the evils of society are primarily in the organization of society; so that if the organization were changed, the evils would disappear. In fact, society never will be better than the individuals who compose it. A sound ship can never be made of rotten timber. Individual reformation and social reconstruction must go on together.

"State Socialism assumes that all functions of society should be carried on by one organization, name-

DR. LYMAN ABBOTT,
Editor of "The Outlook."

ly, the State. In fact, society can better perform its various functions by separate organizations. Putting the Church under State control did not make a free Church. It is more free since it has been taken out from State control. Putting industries under State control would not make the industries free. The industries of the free State of Congo are under State control, and industrial despotism is nowhere in the world so bad as it is in the free State of Congo. The Socialist replies that Socialism assumes a democratic State to organize and carry on democratic industries. But in assuming that the State will be democratic when the strong men of the State are incited by covetousness as well as by ambition to control the State, they assume as true what history proves to be false. To take industry out of the hands of a Carnegie and put it into the hands of a Croker would not make industry free, although Croker were kept in power by popular suffrage and Carnegie were not.

"In estimating the value of Socialism the student should keep clearly in mind this distinction between its spirit, its doctrine, and its programme. He should not be ready to accept its programme merely because he believes its doctrine and admires and shares in its spirit."

THE LITTLE MOTHERS' AID ASSOCIATION.

A MOST PRACTICAL AND SUCCESSFUL EFFORT TO LIGHTEN THE BURDENS OF WOMEN AND CHILDREN IN TENEMENT HOUSES.

BY HELEN VARICK BOSWELL.

DICKENS put a great deal of wisdom into the mouth of his quaint character of Chops the Dwarf, and Mr. Chops remarked on one occasion anent Society: "It isn't so much that a person goes into Society, as that Society goes into a person." That is about the way it is with Philanthropy and Mrs. Clarence Burns. She didn't deliberately go into philanthropy, but it went into her so deeply as to take root and blossom forth in the most beautiful welfare work that has ever come to cheer the hearts and better the condition of little daughters of the wage-earning women of the tenements, who have thrust upon them by sad necessity the cares and responsibilities of the mother, when she leaves them to look after the smaller children while she is earning the wherewithal to feed and clothe them.

The Association, of which Mrs. Burns is president, has named this child "The Little Mother." You may see her in the streets, alleys, backyards, and on doorsteps, caring for the baby, amusing her toyless flock as best she can, and you pass her in the street as, with basket or bucket on her arm, she carries food, fuel or beer to her family. Her tiny hands do the cooking, scrubbing, washing, mending; her little feet run the errands and after the toddling babies all the long, weary day.

These children are robbed of childhood's natural heritage of joy—they are unpaid laborers, about whose hardships no sensational writers are filling pages in the magazines, though they are often dwarfed and deformed by burdens too great for their years—but burdens which are cheerfully borne. The other day I noticed one of the little mothers trying to join a group of children who were following a piano organ. The other little girls were dancing and running, and doing all the things she wanted to do, but there around her neck were the arms of that Moloch of a baby—a regular Old Man of the Sea. If she could just follow along and hear a little of the music was all she hoped for, for you can't dance or run carrying a baby, and such a thing as deserting it never entered her loyal little heart. Her faithfulness is often pitifully demonstrated when she is relieved of the burden for a little while and taken out to Holiday House at Pelham Park for a week's rest. Recently a little deformed girl there was asked why she wakened so early in the morning, and why she did not seem to be enjoying herself more, and she timidly said that at six o'clock she always commenced to worry some, thinking of her mother who started out then to scrub offices, and wondering how the other children were getting along without her. She herself had reached the advanced age of nine years.

Another little girl of twelve, also very wakeful in the early morning, told the attendant she was used to waking early, because in hot weather she always got up at four o'clock and took the baby out and wheeled it about from four to six, so it could get some cool air—at six she came in to get breakfast for the others. Oh, those "others," who are always on the faithful Little Mother hearts. Many of these little girls never get any rest until illness actually overtakes them, and they are sent to the hospital. One of these recently told Mrs. Burns, who was visiting her, that it was the "first rest I've ever had"; and like Little Dorrit's poor Maggie she thought an "orspital was a 'eavinly place!"

Now what are some of the practical features of the work which Mrs. Burns and her associates are doing to lighten the load of the Little Mothers and to fit them to do more easily the things they have to do, and later to become useful members of the community?

In the first place the Little Mothers' Aid Association ranks among the five biggest charities of New York City, and while called a charity, and though much money is given to carry on its uplifting work, yet there is no question of pauperizing in the bounty bestowed by it. No child is made conspicuous by her needs, and self-respect and ambition are stimulated. By promptitude, diligence, kindliness, every Little Mother can earn a certain number of good marks at each lesson which she attends at the several houses conducted by the Association, and as these accumulate she is enabled to purchase from the clothing department articles sufficient to supply her wardrobe—she is a purchaser and not a pauper. Fifteen good marks can be exchanged for a pair of stockings, twenty-five for underclothes, sixty for a dress, eighty for shoes. For these marks she gets a certificate, which she uses to make her purchases, and while it might not be exchangeable for silver and bank notes at the United States Treasury, it is a standard medium of exchange at the Little Mothers' Aid Association. Instead of personal things, the marks will buy cooking utensils, and soap and other things for laundry work—and the unselfish "little women" spend many marks in articles of this kind.

MRS. CLARENCE BURNS,
President of the Little Mothers' Aid Association.

The establishments at which the work is carried on are "Happy Day House," 236 Second Avenue, Manhattan; "Pleasant Place," 16 Greenwich Street, Manhattan; "Up-town Branch," 108 Lawrence Street, near 128th Street, Manhattan; "Sunny Side," 84 Pacific Street, Brooklyn.

At each of these houses "Homemaking Circles" are maintained where the Little Mothers of the neighborhood are taught to make and mend their clothes, to purchase, prepare and serve food in an economical, wholesome and appetizing manner—to fix up something really good for "Papa's dinner pail" that doesn't cost any more than the things he used to buy; to care for their health and that of the household. Singing, calisthenics and recitations are also taught. The marked improvement in the morals and manners of the children in these localities has proven the value of the individual training received. Many instances are on record where through the influence of the Little Mother who is getting the benefit of such training, temperance, thrift and integrity have been permanently established in homes, and bad habits overcome with good.

"LITTLE MOTHERS."

The sewing and laundry classes are always well attended and the cooking classes, needless to say, are always full, for the children "eat up" all the plain but good things which they are taught to cook and no feast of Lucullus was ever half so well enjoyed. The teaching of these industries is adapted to the needs and limitations of the humblest homes. Inexpensive decorations for the family table are suggested that beauty as well as thrift may be fostered in the home. Take the record of one year for instance: From October to June 1,568 meals have been served by the cooking classes; in the sewing classes 10,482 lessons were given to the eager little maidens.

At the several houses, the small brothers and sisters are gathered daily in the day nursery while their Little Mothers are learning to be more useful to them. These little ones are clothed and fed and bathed, and kindergarten games are played, and they are a happy lot.

The bright rooms of these houses, where the children, often for the first time in their lives, experience the gracious influences of home and instruction, are a happy refuge from the storms of winter and from the stifling heat during the summer months.

It takes much time, thought, and executive ability to keep such a work going and to aim always to enlarge its beneficence. There are no salaried officers. The only ones paid are the servants, the superintendents and the cooking teachers. A woman physician volunteers her services and goes at certain hours to the houses where the girls can consult her, and often visits them and their families in their tenement homes.

This Association was organized years ago by Mrs. J. H. Johnston, who is its honorary president. Mrs. Burns is the active and untiring and energizing force of the work at present, and her associates marvel always at the amount she accomplishes. No woman in all New York City better knows the needs of the poor, no woman is more thoroughly en rapport with the lives of the tenement dwellers, but years of such work have only sweetened Mrs. Burns' faith in humanity, and belief in the institutions of America. She knows the uplift movement of the times, for she helps to make it, and in herself and as exemplified in the Little Mothers' Aid Association, brings a living refutation to the wails of the Socialist that "whatever is, is wrong."

There is need for a great fund to carry on this work, and every year a bazar is given at the Waldorf-Astoria for which hundreds of interested women work unceasingly, and which nets thousands of dollars. Individuals often do much to give joy to the Little Mothers. Mr. Frank Tilford celebrates his own birthday by giving an excursion to Coney Island each year to seven hundred of them. He gives Christmas festivals to hundreds, and Easter and other holiday festivals are held. At Easter each child is also given a potted plant, which is a source of much interest to the household.

During the past summer 6,335 children were taken on outings. Many ailing and crippled children are kept for weeks at the summer home, Holiday House, Pelham Park, where good food, sunshine, air and proper exercise have done much toward restoring health. Often women of wealth invite to their country places twenty or thirty of these Little Mothers for a visit, and the various Guilds and Fresh Air Funds also help the work.

And the efforts of this Association are not confined solely to the Little Mothers—there are also two clubs designed for the recreation and culture of the parents of the Little Mothers. The afternoon and evening meetings of these clubs are well attended; socially and intellectually they are more than successful, and many are the kindly little deeds done by the parents to show their appreciation of what the Association is doing. So from aged grandparents, of whom quite a number come under the influence of the work, to the infants of the Ex-Little Mothers, of whom many are included, the Aid is a daily blessing and lives up to the motto it teaches the children:

"To do all the good I can,
To all the people I can,
In every way I can."

[The Little Mothers' Association, whose work is described in this article, is fortunate in having as its president one who has led in many other successful endeavors—Mrs. Clarence Burns. Mrs. Burns has been active, among other things, in the women's clubs, in urging the establishment of industrial schools, and is at present organizing a movement to establish a hotel in New York for working girls. As the recently-elected chairman of the Industrial Committee of the General Federation of Women's Clubs, Mrs. Burns represents the combined efforts of eight hundred thousand women to better the conditions for women and children.—The Editor.]

A TRADE UNIONIST'S OBJECTIONS TO SOCIALISM.

REASONS FOR ORGANIZED LABOR'S HOSTILITY TO "AN UNTRIED, IRRATIONAL, UNDESIRABL IMPOSSIBLE, NON-UNDERSTANDABLE THEORY."

IN the five recent issues of the *Coopers' International Journal*, the official organ of the Coopers' International Union of North America, an interesting discussion has been carried on by the editor and certain members of the union on the subject of socialism. It appears that in this union there are a number of socialists who, following out the policy of "capturing the trade-union movement by boring from within, attempted to use the *Coopers' Journal* for free printing and distribution of socialist propaganda. They proposed an amendment to the constitution of the union "to open the *Journal* to a discussion of socialism, giving its advocates equal space with its opponents," which proposition, by the way, has been overwhelmingly defeated. Pending the final vote on the question by the union, the editor voiced the sentiments of the conservative members in a series of articles from which we quote the following extracts. After the preliminary statement that the editor was, for a brief time, a member and secretary of a socialistic section and that "it is due to an impartial study of the subject that he is not now in the socialist ranks, the editor of the *Journal* says:

"No two understand socialism alike. It is not a science, it is an untried, irrational, undesirable, impossible, non-understandable theory which never has been a reality and never will be. As a political threat it may at some time have an effect for good in broadening and liberalizing the policies of dominant political parties, but as to its hopes of overthrowing the present form of government and substituting itself as a government, that will simply never happen, and the man who bases his hopes on such an absurdity is to be pitied for wasting his life's energy in a cause that is hopelessly lost from the very beginning. The American people want a system which offers reward for and opens opportunity to energy, thrift and talent. Whatever claim may be made by the socialists, their theory when analyzed offers nothing of the kind. It is calculated to discourage the possessors of these sterling qualities.

"If the time, money and energy spent in advocacy of this will-o'-the-wisp was devoted to the cause of trade unionism, which is striving every day of the year for actual reforms and improvements in our day and generation, the defects in government could be overcome, and there would be less oppression and more comforts for those who earn their bread in the sweat of their brows here and now. If a socialistic government were instituted to-morrow, we could not get rid of selfish men. We could not hang the selfish for there would not be rope enough. Since we could not get rid of them under a socialist government, it is safe to conclude that as the greedy and the selfish prey upon the less intellectual now, so would they do under socialism. 'If man's inequality is wrong,' says the New York *Mechanic*, 'then find fault with man's Creator.' Socialism cannot cure imperfections created in God's wisdom, and, moreover, men are being born and will continue to be born into the world with these imperfections every day. There being nothing in socialistic theorizing, therefore, which promises to cure man of inequalities and imperfections to which he is heir by nature, it fails, because it approaches no nearer to the seat of man's imperfections than does our present or any other form of government.

"There never was a time in any country when all the people could unite in one political or religious faith. The working people of America, however, regardless of political or religious leaning, can be united in the belief that the hours of labor are too long and the remuneration too small. It is possible for all of them, or at least a great portion of them, to be united on this issue regardless of political or religious differences.

"If the socialists are granted the right to inject their politics into the union, the Republicans and Democrats must have the right to inject theirs. If politics may be injected, so may religion, and if an effort is to be made to inject all these creeds and theories into the trade-union movement, the end of the labor movement is not far off. Instead of being a nation of united working men and women, this would be a nation of political and religious factions, each seeking to undo what the other is striving to do and neither of them accomplishing any good. The man who would steer labor's ship upon the rock of political and religious disaster is not a safe pilot and those who hope for smooth sailing in the labor movement had better beware of such piloting.

"Socialism analyzed means, if it means anything, governmental control of everything, which carries with it abolition of the individual initiative and individual liberty. The history of all countries and all governments, including our own, demonstrates beyond successful contradiction that governmental power is oppression. We in this country, as well as those in other countries, are suffering now from too much governmental power. What we want, then, is not increased governmental power, but less of it, so that we may exercise and enjoy more liberty and freedom.

"Prior to last year's convention it was the custom with the American Federation of Labor to give the socialists all the time and opportunity needed to expound their doctrine and present their theory. So patient was the Boston convention of that body in 1903, that fourteen hours were spent in debating the question of socialism, about ten of which were taken up by the socialists themselves, and after all this talk their resolutions failed of passage by a large majority. Since that

MR. JAMES A. CABLE.
Editor Coopers' International Journal.

time they have been losing strength every year in the A. F. of L. Their oratorical effort, and defeat, at the San Francisco convention in 1904 is accurately described by Luke Kennedy in the following letter to the New York *Mechanic*: 'They put forward their most masterful and brilliant orators, used obstructive and filibustering tactics, in fact resorted to every trick and scheme to accomplish what they had been looking forward to for years—the endorsement of their party by the A. F. of L.—and they were buried beneath an avalanche of "pure and simple votes."'

"As to how strong the socialists were at the recent convention of the A. F. of L. held in Pittsburg, Pa., we will take the word of socialists who were there. The *Cap Makers' Journal* (strictly socialistic) describes the action of said convention on a socialist resolution as follows: 'Suffice it to say here that the last American Federation of Labor convention was a very "harmonious" affair—in fact, so "harmonious" that when President Gompers ruled our resolution out of order on the absurd ground that it dealt with "party politics," there was hardly a delegate to contradict him. All other important resolutions, introduced by delegates Berger, Lavin and others (socialists), were snowed under in about the same fashion, without much ado.'

"The relative positions of the trade-union and socialist movements are very correctly summed up by *Progressist*, of Ticonderoga, N. Y., in the following editorial: 'Organized labor is stronger in America than ever before. The cry for the open shop, and the heated denunciations of the "Parryites" of the boycott, the closed shop and the sympathetic strike is met on every hand by examples of the wisdom of collective bargaining on the part of workingmen when dealing with their employers and the continuance of union shops by cooler-headed employers. Unionists are also coming to understand more fully every day how impracticable are the dreams of the socialist leaders and how fallacious are their arguments.'"

In proof of the statement of the hostility of organized labor to the demands of socialism, the editor of the *Journal* cites the resolutions adopted by the last convention of the Massachusetts State Convention of Labor to the effect that "we recognize as the most despicable attack yet made upon the life of our national body, that organization launched in Chicago, June, 1905, known as the Industrial Workers of the World, headed by socialists of international reputation."

We regret that lack of space prevents quoting in full the opinions of the editor of the *Coopers' Journal* as expressed in this series of articles. On three or four of his telling points, however, we summarize as follows his statements:

"Socialism proposes to solve the problem of wealth and poverty by abolishing wealth and reducing the entire race to a condition of poverty. It proposes to sol the question of righteous living by abolishing Chr tianity and reducing the race to a state of unrighteo ness. It proposes to solve the problems of civilizati by reducing the race to an uncivilized state. In oth words, they hold that since the very inception of h manity, the race has been moving forward on wro lines, and that every step so far taken must be retrac so that under the guidance of socialist minds, whi cannot err, civilization may again come forward right lines and make no mistakes.

"Socialists repudiate municipal ownership just as th do every other reform, because it is 'palliative' a serves to reconcile the people to the present order things, thereby prolonging the coming of the revoluti which they hope for and dream about, which they cla will give to the people complete socialism. Munici ownership is by no means a part of the socialist pl form. Prospective socialists are frequently led to b lieve that it is, but when safely landed in the social bailiwick they are carefully taught that municipal own ship is only a palliative which retards instead of a vances the progress of socialism.

"There can be no fusion between voters who wa reforms in government and socialists who demand t overthrow of the republic, because they are seeking o posite ends. Moreover, the socialist party stands fund mentally pledged against fusion or compromise of a kind. The socialist position is clearly stated by *T. Appeal to Reason* of April 28, 1906, when it say 'There is no such thing as reform. Elimination is t only remedy.'

"The socialists claim that the Church of God havi evolved from capitalistic environment, is a capitalis institution, which with all other institutions of to-d must finally fall when the much-heralded revolution inaugurated. They contend that the Christian religi is an invention of the masters for the purpose of di tracting the minds of the workers from their true co ditions so that they will not rebel against the capitalist system."

The editor of the *Coopers' Journal* points out clear and truthfully the absolute incompatibility of socialis and religion, by quoting as follows from the writin of recognized authorities on socialism:

"Dr. Averling, a socialist of high rank (who was th 'free love' husband of Karl Marx's daughter) accept the world over as an authority on socialism, say 'Whether anything or nothing is done, little that is lasting value can be done until men and women fair face the fact that the terrible condition of our poor due, as are so many other ills, to the two curses our country and time—Capitalism and Christianity. Christianity we see not only a supporter of the great of social evils, but a system that by its fundament principles vitiates human thoughts and distracts the a tention of mankind from the natural and actual.'

"Bax, who is probably recognized as the highest a thority on socialism, in his 'Ethics of Socialism' say 'According to Christianity and the ethics of religion, introspection generally, regeneration must come fro within, must begin in the heart and mind of the ind vidual. The ethic and religion of modern socialism the contrary, looks for regeneration from witho From material conditions and a higher social life.'

"*Avanta*, the organ of the Italian socialists, refers Christianity as the 'dirt heap of modern thought,' a says, 'the civilization of social democracy will never b foul itself with Christianity.'

"*The Comrade*, edited by John Spargo, a sociali periodical published in New York, in its issue of Ma 1903, says: 'Christianity is not big enough, not pu enough, nor noble enough to measure our great worl faith. Socialism-Christianity would be socialism d stroyed.'"

We do not hesitate to say that if these articles we read by every student of the question, there would be much clearer perception of the distinction between trad union principles, which uphold American institutio and the doctrines of socialism, which aim to undermi and destroy them. On this point the editor of t *Coopers' Journal* says:

"One of our correspondents challenges us to sho reasons why the trade-union and the socialist mov ments cannot be harmonized. The reasons are cle The two movements are seeking opposite ends.

"By reason of its defects, the socialists seek to ove throw the present order.

"By correcting its defects, the trade unions seek make the present order endurable.

"Now if the trade unions succeed in making the pre ent order endurable, the aim of socialism is there defeated: whereas, if the socialists succeed in ove throwing the present order, the aim of the trade unio is defeated. As the success of the one means the fa ure of the other, the two are diametrically opposed each other."

ONE OF NEW YORK'S GREAT UPLIFTING AGENCIES.

WHAT THE CHARITY ORGANIZATION SOCIETY HAS ACCOMPLISHED IN RECENT YEARS AS TOLD BY ITS GENERAL SECRETARY.

By Edward T. Devine, General Secretary, New York Charity Organization Society.

DR. EDWARD T. DEVINE.

THE society has obtained from charitable agencies and from private individuals the exact kind and amount of relief which was required for from three to ten thousand families each year since it was founded a quarter of a century ago. It has transformed a fair proportion of those who were, or who might otherwise have become, chronic paupers into independent self-respecting citizens. It has provided for the support of widowed, disabled, infirm, and aged persons, and enabled friends and relatives to do their share toward such support in co-operation with strangers when the latter was necessary.

The evidence of this primary claim, made on behalf of the Society, that it has successfully taken care of the families who applied for assistance or whose needs were made known by third parties can be found, of course, for the most part only in its family records. One who has worked year after year on one of the district committees or as a friendly visitor knows that these things have been accomplished: that the sick have been furnished with medical attention, nursing, medicines, special diet and, when necessary, with protracted convalescent care; that pensions have been raised for widows with dependent children and continued until the children were old enough to work; that absconding male heads of families have been brought back to the discharge of their natural responsibilities; that employment has been procured; friendly encouragement and oversight freely given, not for a day but for months or years; that children and mothers have been sent to the country and to the seashore, and that scores of other similar services have been rendered, some of which require substantial financial outlay while others have demanded that personal attention which in busy New York it is far more difficult to secure.

Ten years ago an experienced charitable worker said to one who was just turning into this field, "Study your case-work. Fix your attention on the individual family." That was excellent advice and any charitable society may rightly be judged only by its success with the individual families who come under its care. What the society has accomplished then, first of all, is to give intelligent, sympathetic, and efficient care to the very large number of individuals and families whose needs are brought to its attention.

In the next place it has cleared the streets of New York of professional beggars. Due credit is to be given to the legislature for its strict laws, to the police department, to the city magistrates for convictions and sentences, to the Workhouse for holding its prisoners, and attempting to give them suitable employment, and to citizens generally for individual co-operation. The Charity Organization Society, however, directed the educational campaign against mendicancy and imposture, made the complaints effective, supplied the information necessary to conviction, and prevented premature discharge for a consideration. It has given a helping hand to mendicants desirous of giving up the shameful life of a parasite and entering on that of self-support and self-respect, and finally, while convincing the whole fraternity of yeggman-panhandlers and ordinary mendicants throughout the country that New York is unsafe territory in which to operate, has yet through its publications and correspondence helped to make other communities less "safe" and has therefore not lessened local burdens at their expense. It has done more for these mendicants individually than has ever before been done for any similar class here or abroad. As the foundation of its work for them and for the city, the Society has insisted that there must be such persistent and intelligent police work that it shall be impossible to live by begging whether from passers-by, at the basement door or by ingenious letters of introduction.

Just now there is a relaxation in the police co-operation owing to the abolition of the Mendicancy Detail—as a part of a general policy of doing away with special details, and there is a corresponding increase in the amount of begging. This reaction will, however, surely be promptly met either by the restoration of this particular detail, which unlike some of the others was engaged in distinctly police work, or by some other plan which the Police Commissioner may devise to take its place.

Verging on and often actually constituting imposture and fraud are the activities of many groups organized in the name of charity. The service which the Society rendered for several years in keeping its members informed as to the standing and management of charitable institutions, and the legitimacy of appeals for support especially from new enterprises, led to the recent establishment of the Bureau of Advice and Information. On request advice will be given to prospective donors concerning plans for founding new institutions; to managers of charitable enterprises regarding needed reforms, new buildings, changes of location and other matters of like character. The Burke Foundation, various hospitals and sanatoria for consumptives, the removal of children's institutions to the country, the organization of charity in Havana, and the relief work in San Francisco may be mentioned as illustrations of the wide range of undertakings upon which such advice and assistance has recently been requested.

The most important achievement of the Society in recent years was the inauguration and carrying through to complete success of the movement for a new tenement-house law and for the creation of a distinct municipal department to enforce its provisions. When the need for advanced legislation was unsuccessfully urged upon the local municipal assembly in the summer of 1899 there was little or no popular interest in the subject, and no outer evidences whatever that the time was ripe for the beginning of an agitation which, within two years, would place upon the statute books a radical and sweeping law by the side of which the Society's original suggestions appear insignificant indeed. The credit for this reform belongs very largely to two individuals: Robert W. de Forest, President of the Charity Organization Society, and Lawrence Veiller, who in 1899 was Secretary of the Society's Tenement House Committee. The Society made an energetic campaign through the public press, before the local and state legislatures, in and through trade unions, settlements, churches, and all kinds of philanthropic agencies, and finally, by means of the tenement house exhibition of February, 1900. As a direct result of these efforts a state commission was authorized by the legislature and appointed by Governor Roosevelt. Of this commission Mr. de Forest and Mr. Veiller were respectively chairman and secretary, and its labors were brought to a triumphant conclusion by the enactment of the laws which they recommended. No changes have since been made except at the request or by the consent of the friends of the law, whose views have been presented when occasion required by the Tenement House Committee, which the Society has kept in existence as a means of co-operating with the municipal department, and, whenever necessary, enlightening the public in regard to proposed beneficent or vicious legislation.

The Committee on the Prevention of Tuberculosis has waged unrelenting war on this preventable disease during four years. Notable as is its publication of the "Handbook on the Prevention of Tuberculosis" and an illustrated "Directory of Institutions" dealing with tuberculosis, the public instruction through the issue of hundreds of thousands of cards printed in several languages with simple directions as to how to protect one's self and others against this disease, has been an even greater service. How to care for the sick and to guard those who surround the patient, and the simple and effective modes of home treatment have been contrasted with the cruel waste and certain detriment from the use of whiskey and other stimulants and of patent medicines. No other class in the community has been more quick to appreciate the import of this work or more prompt and effective in their assistance than the trade unions.

Self help and thrift have been encouraged by the Society through the organization of the Provident Loan Society in 1893, and the Penny Provident Fund in 1889. The former is an independent stock company formed to enforce fair conditions in the business of pawning personal property. Those under the necessity of temporarily raising funds upon such collateral are given a private and respectable opportunity to obtain loans at reasonable rates. It now transacts a business of seven million dollars a year. The Penny Provident Fund has over three hundred branch offices, largely conducted by volunteers and sanctioned by school authorities, through which savings of from one cent upward are received and credited by means of stamps pasted in card-books furnished free and redeemable at regular hours at face value. Last year 90,746 people saved $106,100 in this way. Incidentally, many stores and banks have been influenced to extend commercial facilities at a much lower amount than had formerly been thought practicable and an impetus has been given the project for a post-office bank.

Fresh air work has won recognition and approval throughout the country. One of its earliest successful divisions was the Creche started by this Society in the shadow of the Statue of Liberty for the benefit of mothers with babies whom they could not leave or send away and who could not afford to stop work to accept a longer trip than one day. The Edgewater Creche, a separate organization, has succeeded this work, and now conducts it in conjunction with the Society.

The Charities Directory, a fully-indexed, classified and descriptive guide to the philanthropic, religious, and educational resources of the city, has passed through sixteen annual editions and comes to be more and more used and relied upon. While the mention of a particular institution in the book does not imply endorsement of its purposes, management or methods, still care is exercised to exclude all those about which the Society feels it necessary to warn its members.

The most important of the Society's publications is "Charities and The Commons," the weekly journal and magazine of philanthropy and social advance. The outgrowth of the Society's bulletin of information to members, it now combines six independent efforts at public enlightenment and interest in social righteousness. When at this stage of the twentieth century lunatics are chained to logs in one section of our country, caged naked in sheds in another, and beaten for their imbecility in a third; when an entire large city is scourged with fever bred by neglect; when a great state votes down protection of its future citizenry against lucrative exploitation, there is need of spokesmen and of an organ for them that will stand out sturdily as "Charities and The Commons" has done for new opportunities, new plans, and new hopes for those who are drawn down by their unfavorable environment or heredity.

In order to raise both the standard of efficiency and the standard of remuneration in social work the Society in 1899 started the Summer School of Philanthropy mainly for experienced workers who wished to obtain fresh and broader views of their sphere. It was successful from the first. Three years ago an afternoon course was established to be carried on all winter for the benefit of those at the time actually engaged in work in New York and with especial regard for New York conditions. One hundred and fifty-six employees of the local charities, public departments, settlements, and churches were enrolled. But the plan was found to be insufficient and the endowment of the School by Mr. John S. Kennedy in the following year made possible the adoption of the present plan by which the course has been placed on a professional school basis and the entire time and attention of the students for one year is required for successful prosecution of the course. Fifty-eight students were registered for the last academic year.

A feeling of bewilderment is the first thing that comes to the consciousness of the average good citizen on being approached for alms. What is he to do? Kindly but firmly direct the applicant to the Joint Application Bureau maintained jointly with the Association for Improving the Condition of the Poor. It is open from 9 a. m. to midnight every day of the year for the reception of applicants for aid and the care of the homeless. All homeless people referred to either society are assisted sympathetically and constructively through this bureau. Persons applying for aid may be referred here by anyone, whether a member of the Society or not, and an applicant who calls without reference will be equally well received.

The woodyard and laundry maintained by the Society are nearly self-supporting by their revenues. Both are of great importance to the work as furnishing sufficient and satisfactory tests of the sincerity of earnestness of applicants and temporary occupation while employment is being sought. The salutary effect of remuneration for services is in marked contrast with the giving and acceptance of gratuity even under the best circumstances. The laundry also trains unskilled hands

A TRADE UNIONIST'S OBJECTIONS TO SOCIALISM.

REASONS FOR ORGANIZED LABOR'S HOSTILITY TO "AN UNTRIED, IRRATIONAL, UNDESIRABL. IMPOSSIBLE, NON-UNDERSTANDABLE THEORY."

IN the five recent issues of the *Coopers' International Journal*, the official organ of the Coopers' International Union of North America, an interesting discussion has been carried on by the editor and certain members of the union on the subject of socialism. It appears that in this union there are a number of socialists who, following out the policy of "capturing the trade-union movement by boring from within, attempted to use the *Coopers' Journal* for free printing and distribution of socialist propaganda. They proposed an amendment to the constitution of the union "to open the *Journal* to a discussion of socialism, giving its advocates equal space with its opponents," which proposition, by the way, has been overwhelmingly defeated. Pending the final vote on the question by the union, the editor voiced the sentiments of the conservative members in a series of articles from which we quote the following extracts. After the preliminary statement that the editor was, for a brief time, a member and secretary of a socialistic section and that "it is due to an impartial study of the subject that he is not now in the socialist ranks, the editor of the *Journal* says:

"No two understand socialism alike. It is not a science, it is an untried, irrational, undesirable, impossible, non-understandable theory which never has been a reality and never will be. As a political threat it may at some time have an effect for good in broadening and liberalizing the policies of dominant political parties, but as to its hopes of overthrowing the present form of government and substituting itself as a government, that will simply never happen, and the man who bases his hopes on such an absurdity is to be pitied for wasting his life's energy in a cause that is hopelessly lost from the very beginning. The American people want a system which offers reward for and opens opportunity to energy, thrift and talent. Whatever claim may be made by the socialists, their theory when analyzed offers nothing of the kind. It is calculated to discourage the possessors of these sterling qualities.

"If the time, money and energy spent in advocacy of this will-o'-the-wisp was devoted to the cause of trade unionism, which is striving every day of the year for actual reforms and improvements in our day and generation, the defects in government could be overcome, and there would be less oppression and more comforts for those who earn their bread in the sweat of their brows here and now. If a socialistic government were instituted to-morrow, we could not get rid of selfish men. We could not hang the selfish for there would not be rope enough. Since we could not get rid of them under a socialist government, it is safe to conclude that as the greedy and the selfish prey upon the less intellectual now, so would they do under socialism. 'If man's inequality is wrong,' says the New York *Mechanic*, 'then find fault with man's Creator.' Socialism cannot cure imperfections created in God's wisdom, and, moreover, men are being born and will continue to be born into the world with these imperfections every day. There being nothing in socialistic theorizing, therefore, which promises to cure man of inequalities and imperfections to which he is heir by nature, it fails, because it approaches no nearer to the seat of man's imperfections than does our present or any other form of government.

"There never was a time in any country when all the people could unite in one political or religious faith. The working people of America, however, regardless of political or religious leaning, can be united in the belief that the hours of labor are too long and the remuneration too small. It is possible for all of them, or at least a great portion of them, to be united on this issue regardless of political or religious differences.

"If the socialists are granted the right to inject their politics into the union, the Republicans and Democrats must have the right to inject theirs. If politics may be injected, so may religion, and if an effort is to be made to inject all these creeds and theories into the trade-union movement, the end of the labor movement is not far off. Instead of being a nation of united working men and women, this would be a nation of political and religious factions, each seeking to undo what the other is striving to do and neither of them accomplishing any good. The man who would steer labor's ship upon the rock of political and religious disaster is not a safe pilot and those who hope for smooth sailing in the labor movement had better beware of such piloting.

"Socialism analyzed means, if it means anything, governmental control of everything, which carries with it abolition of the individual initiative and individual liberty. The history of all countries and all governments, including our own, demonstrates beyond successful contradiction that governmental power is oppression. We in this country, as well as those in other countries, are suffering now from too much governmental power. What we want, then, is not increased governmental power, but less of it, so that we may exercise and enjoy more liberty and freedom.

"Prior to last year's convention it was the custom with the American Federation of Labor to give the socialists all the time and opportunity needed to expound their doctrine and present their theory. So patient was the Boston convention of that body in 1903, that fourteen hours were spent in debating the question of socialism, about ten of which were taken up by the socialists themselves, and after all this talk their resolutions failed of passage by a large majority. Since that

MR. JAMES A. CABLE.
Editor Coopers' International Journal.

time they have been losing strength every year in the A. F. of L. Their oratorical effort, and defeat, at the San Francisco convention in 1904 is accurately described by Luke Kennedy in the following letter to the New York *Mechanic*: 'They put forward their most masterful and brilliant orators, used obstructive and filibustering tactics, in fact resorted to every trick and scheme to accomplish what they had been looking forward to for years—the endorsement of their party by the A. F. of L.—and they were buried beneath an avalanche of "pure and simple votes."'

"As to how strong the socialists were at the recent convention of the A. F. of L. held in Pittsburg, Pa., we will take the word of socialists who were there. The *Cap Makers' Journal* (strictly socialistic) describes the action of said convention on a socialist resolution as follows: 'Suffice it to say here that the last American Federation of Labor convention was a very "harmonious" affair—in fact, so "harmonious" that when President Gompers ruled our resolution out of order on the absurd ground that it dealt with "party politics," there was hardly a delegate to contradict him. All other important resolutions, introduced by delegates Berger, Lavin and others (socialists), were snowed under in about the same fashion, without much ado.'

"The relative positions of the trade-union and socialist movements are very correctly summed up by *Progressist*, of Ticonderoga, N. Y., in the following editorial: 'Organized labor is stronger in America than ever before. The cry for the open shop, and the heated denunciations of the "Parryites" of the boycott, the closed shop and the sympathetic strike is met on every hand by examples of the wisdom of collective bargaining on the part of workingmen when dealing with their employers and the continuance of union shops by cooler-headed employers. Unionists are also coming to understand more fully every day how impracticable are the dreams of the socialist leaders and how fallacious are their arguments.'"

In proof of the statement of the hostility of organized labor to the demands of socialism, the editor of the *Journal* cites the resolutions adopted by the last convention of the Massachusetts State Convention of Labor to the effect that "we recognize as the most despicable attack yet made upon the life of our national body, that organization launched in Chicago, June, 1905, known as the Industrial Workers of the World, headed by socialists of international reputation."

We regret that lack of space prevents quoting in full the opinions of the editor of the *Coopers' Journal* as expressed in this series of articles. On three or four of his telling points, however, we summarize as follows his statements:

"Socialism proposes to solve the problem of wealth and poverty by abolishing wealth and reducing the entire race to a condition of poverty. It proposes to sol' the question of righteous living by abolishing Chri. tianity and reducing the race to a state of unrighteou: ness. It proposes to solve the problems of civilizatio by reducing the race to an uncivilized state. In othe words, they hold that since the very inception of hu manity, the race has been moving forward on wrong lines, and that every step so far taken must be retraced, so that under the guidance of socialist minds, which cannot err, civilization may again come forward on right lines and make no mistakes.

"Socialists repudiate municipal ownership just as they do every other reform, because it is 'palliative' and serves to reconcile the people to the present order of things, thereby prolonging the coming of the revolution which they hope for and dream about, which they claim will give to the people complete socialism. Municipal ownership is by no means a part of the socialist platform. Prospective socialists are frequently led to b. lieve that it is, but when safely landed in the social' bailiwick they are carefully taught that municipal owne ship is only a palliative which retards instead of a vances the progress of socialism.

"There can be no fusion between voters who wa reforms in government and socialists who demand t overthrow of the republic, because they are seeking o posite ends. Moreover, the socialist party stands fund mentally pledged against fusion or compromise of a kind. The socialist position is clearly stated by *T. Appeal to Reason* of April 28, 1906, when it say 'There is no such thing as reform. Elimination is t only remedy.'

"The socialists claim that the Church of God havi evolved from capitalistic environment, is a capitalis institution, which with all other institutions of to-d must finally fall when the much-heralded revolution inaugurated. They contend that the Christian religi is an invention of the masters for the purpose of di tracting the minds of the workers from their true co ditions so that they will not rebel against the capitalist system."

The editor of the *Coopers' Journal* points out clear and truthfully the absolute incompatibility of socialis, and religion, by quoting as follows from the writing of recognized authorities on socialism:

"Dr. Averling, a socialist of high rank (who was the 'free love' husband of Karl Marx's daughter) accepted the world over as an authority on socialism, says: 'Whether anything or nothing is done, little that is of lasting value can be done until men and women fairly face the fact that the terrible condition of our poor is due, as are so many other ills, to the two curses of our country and time—Capitalism and Christianity. In Christianity we see not only a supporter of the greatest of social evils, but a system that by its fundament' principles vitiates human thoughts and distracts the a tention of mankind from the natural and actual.'

"Bax, who is probably recognized as the highest a thority on socialism, in his 'Ethics of Socialism' say 'According to Christianity and the ethics of religion, introspection generally, regeneration must come fro within, must begin in the heart and mind of the in vidual. The ethic and religion of modern socialism the contrary, looks for regeneration from withou From material conditions and a higher social life.'

"*Avanta*, the organ of the Italian socialists, refers Christianity as the 'dirt heap of modern thought,' a says, 'the civilization of social democracy will never b foul itself with Christianity.'

"*The Comrade*, edited by John Spargo, a sociali periodical published in New York, in its issue of Ma 1903, says: 'Christianity is not big enough, not pu enough, nor noble enough to measure our great worl faith. Socialism-Christianity would be socialism d stroyed.'"

We do not hesitate to say that if these articles we read by every student of the question, there would be much clearer perception of the distinction between trad union principles, which uphold American institutio and the doctrines of socialism, which aim to undermi and destroy them. On this point the editor of t *Coopers' Journal* says:

"One of our correspondents challenges us to sho reasons why the trade-union and the socialist mov ments cannot be harmonized. The reasons are cle The two movements are seeking opposite ends.

"By reason of its defects, the socialists seek to ove throw the present order.

"By correcting its defects, the trade unions seek make the present order endurable.

"Now if the trade unions succeed in making the pre ent order endurable, the aim of socialism is there defeated; whereas, if the socialists succeed in ove throwing the present order, the aim of the trade unio is defeated. As the success of the one means the fa ure of the other, the two are diametrically opposed each other."

ONE OF NEW YORK'S GREAT UPLIFTING AGENCIES.

WHAT THE CHARITY ORGANIZATION SOCIETY HAS ACCOMPLISHED IN RECENT YEARS AS TOLD BY ITS GENERAL SECRETARY.

By Edward T. Devine, General Secretary, New York Charity Organization Society.

THE society has obtained from charitable agencies and from private individuals the exact kind and amount of relief which was required for from three to ten thousand families each year since it was founded a quarter of a century ago. It has transformed a fair proportion of those who were, or who might otherwise have become, chronic paupers into independent self-respecting citizens. It has provided for the support of widowed, disabled, infirm, and aged persons, and enabled friends and relatives to do their share toward such support in co-operation with strangers when the latter was necessary.

The evidence of this primary claim, made on behalf of the Society, that it has successfully taken care of the families who applied for assistance or whose needs were made known by third parties can be found, of course, for the most part only in its family records. One who has worked year after year on one of the district committees or as a friendly visitor knows that these things have been accomplished: that the sick have been furnished with medical attention, nursing, medicines, special diet and, when necessary, with protracted convalescent care; that pensions have been raised for widows with dependent children and continued until the children were old enough to work; that absconding male heads of families have been brought back to the discharge of their natural responsibilities; that employment has been procured; friendly encouragement and oversight freely given, not for a day but for months or years; that children and mothers have been sent to the country and to the seashore, and that scores of other similar services have been rendered, some of which require substantial financial outlay while others have demanded that personal attention which in busy New York it is far more difficult to secure.

Ten years ago an experienced charitable worker said to one who was just turning into this field, "Study your case-work. Fix your attention on the individual family." That was excellent advice and any charitable society may rightly be judged only by its success with the individual families who come under its care. What the society has accomplished then, first of all, is to give intelligent, sympathetic, and efficient care to the very large number of individuals and families whose needs are brought to its attention.

In the next place it has cleared the streets of New York of professional beggars. Due credit is to be given to the legislature for its strict laws, to the police department, to the city magistrates for convictions and sentences, to the Workhouse for holding its prisoners, and attempting to give them suitable employment, and to citizens generally for individual co-operation. The Charity Organization Society, however, directed the educational campaign against mendicancy and imposture, made the complaints effective, supplied the information necessary to conviction, and prevented premature discharge for a consideration. It has given a helping hand to mendicants desirous of giving up the shameful life of a parasite and entering on that of self-support and self-respect, and finally, while convincing the whole fraternity of yeggman-panhandlers and ordinary mendicants throughout the country that New York is unsafe territory in which to operate, has yet through its publications and correspondence helped to make other communities less "safe" and has therefore not lessened local burdens at their expense. It has done more for these mendicants individually than has ever before been done for any similar class here or abroad. As the foundation of its work for them and for the city, the Society has insisted that there must be such persistent and intelligent police work that it shall be impossible to live by begging whether from passers-by, at the basement door or by ingenious letters of introduction.

Just now there is a relaxation in the police co-operation owing to the abolition of the Mendicancy Detail—as a part of a general policy of doing away with special details, and there is a corresponding increase in the amount of begging. This reaction will, however, surely be promptly met either by the restoration of this particular detail, which unlike some of the others was engaged in distinctly police work, or by some other plan which the Police Commissioner may devise to take its place.

Verging on and often actually constituting imposture and fraud are the activities of many groups organized in the name of charity. The service which the Society rendered for several years in keeping its members informed as to the standing and management of charitable institutions, and the legitimacy of appeals for support especially from new enterprises, led to the recent establishment of the Bureau of Advice and Information. On request advice will be given to prospective donors concerning plans for founding new institutions; to managers of charitable enterprises regarding needed reforms, new buildings, changes of location and other

DR. EDWARD T. DEVINE.

matters of like character. The Burke Foundation, various hospitals and sanatoria for consumptives, the removal of children's institutions to the country, the organization of charity in Havana, and the relief work in San Francisco may be mentioned as illustrations of the wide range of undertakings upon which such advice and assistance has recently been requested.

The most important achievement of the Society in recent years was the inauguration and carrying through to complete success of the movement for a new tenement-house law and for the creation of a distinct municipal department to enforce its provisions. When the need for advanced legislation was unsuccessfully urged upon the local municipal assembly in the summer of 1899 there was little or no popular interest in the subject, and no outer evidences whatever that the time was ripe for the beginning of an agitation which, within two years, would place upon the statute books a radical and sweeping law by the side of which the Society's original suggestions appear insignificant indeed. The credit for this reform belongs very largely to two individuals: Robert W. de Forest, President of the Charity Organization Society, and Lawrence Veiller, who in 1899 was Secretary of the Society's Tenement House Committee. The Society made an energetic campaign through the public press, before the local and state legislatures, in and through trade unions, settlements, churches, and all kinds of philanthropic agencies, and finally, by means of the tenement house exhibition of February, 1900. As a direct result of these efforts a state commission was authorized by the legislature and appointed by Governor Roosevelt. Of this commission Mr. de Forest and Mr. Veiller were respectively chairman and secretary, and its labors were brought to a triumphant conclusion by the enactment of the laws which they recommended. No changes have since been made except at the request or by the consent of the friends of the law, whose views have been presented when occasion required by the Tenement House Committee, which the Society has kept in existence as a means of co-operating with the municipal department, and, whenever necessary, enlightening the public in regard to proposed beneficent or vicious legislation.

The Committee on the Prevention of Tuberculosis has waged unrelenting war on this preventable disease during four years. Notable as is its publication of the "Handbook on the Prevention of Tuberculosis" and an illustrated "Directory of Institutions" dealing with tuberculosis, the public instruction through the issue of hundreds of thousands of cards printed in several languages with simple directions as to how to protect one's self and others against this disease, has been an even greater service. How to care for the sick and to guard those who surround the patient, and the simple and effective modes of home treatment have been contrasted with the cruel waste and certain detriment from the use of whiskey and other stimulants and of patent medicines. No other class in the community has been more quick to appreciate the import of this work or more prompt and effective in their assistance than the trade unions.

Self help and thrift have been encouraged by the Society through the organization of the Provident Loan Society in 1893, and the Penny Provident Fund in 1889. The former is an independent stock company formed to enforce fair conditions in the business of pawning personal property. Those under the necessity of temporarily raising funds upon such collateral are given a private and respectable opportunity to obtain loans at reasonable rates. It now transacts a business of seven million dollars a year. The Penny Provident Fund has over three hundred branch offices, largely conducted by volunteers and sanctioned by school authorities, through which savings of from one cent upward are received and credited by means of stamps pasted in card-books furnished free and redeemable at regular hours at face value. Last year 90,746 people saved $106,100 in this way. Incidentally, many stores and banks have been influenced to extend commercial facilities at a much lower amount than had formerly been thought practicable and an impetus has been given the project for a post-office bank.

Fresh air work has won recognition and approval throughout the country. One of its earliest successful divisions was the Creche started by this Society in the shadow of the Statue of Liberty for the benefit of mothers with babies whom they could not leave or send away and who could not afford to stop work to accept a longer trip than one day. The Edgewater Creche, a separate organization, has succeeded this work, and now conducts it in conjunction with the Society.

The Charities Directory, a fully-indexed, classified and descriptive guide to the philanthropic, religious, and educational resources of the city, has passed through sixteen annual editions and comes to be more and more used and relied upon. While the mention of a particular institution in the book does not imply endorsement of its purposes, management or methods, still care is exercised to exclude all those about which the Society feels it necessary to warn its members.

The most important of the Society's publications is "Charities and The Commons," the weekly journal and magazine of philanthropy and social advance. The outgrowth of the Society's bulletin of information to members, it now combines six independent efforts at public enlightenment and interest in social righteousness. When at this stage of the twentieth century lunatics are chained to logs in one section of our country, caged naked in sheds in another, and beaten for their imbecility in a third; when an entire large city is scourged with fever bred by neglect; when a great state votes down protection of its future citizenry against lucrative exploitation, there is need of spokesmen and of an organ for them that will stand out sturdily as "Charities and The Commons" has done for new opportunities, new plans, and new hopes for those who are drawn down by their unfavorable environment or heredity.

In order to raise both the standard of efficiency and the standard of remuneration in social work the Society in 1899 started the Summer School of Philanthropy mainly for experienced workers who wished to obtain fresh and broader views of their sphere. It was successful from the first. Three years ago an afternoon course was established to be carried on all winter for the benefit of those at the time actually engaged in work in New York and with especial regard for New York conditions. One hundred and fifty-six employees of the local charities, public departments, settlements, and churches were enrolled. But the plan was found to be insufficient and the endowment of the School by Mr. John S. Kennedy in the following year made possible the adoption of the present plan by which the course has been placed on a professional school basis and the entire time and attention of the students for one year is required for successful prosecution of the course. Fifty-eight students were registered for the last academic year.

A feeling of bewilderment is the first thing that comes to the consciousness of the average good citizen on being approached for alms. What is he to do? Kindly but firmly direct the applicant to the Joint Application Bureau maintained jointly with the Association for Improving the Condition of the Poor. It is open from 9 a. m. to midnight every day of the year for the reception of applicants for aid and the care of the homeless. All homeless people referred to either society are assisted sympathetically and constructively through this bureau. Persons applying for aid may be referred here by anyone, whether a member of the Society or not, and an applicant who calls without reference will be equally well received.

The woodyard and laundry maintained by the Society are nearly self-supporting by their revenues. Both are of great importance to the work as furnishing sufficient and satisfactory tests of the sincerity of earnestness of applicants and temporary occupation while employment is being sought. The salutary effect of remuneration for services is in marked contrast with the giving and acceptance of gratuity even under the best circumstances. The laundry also trains unskilled hands ch are capable of earning only one dollar a day at gh cleaning into skilled laundresses for whom there n unlimited demand at from $1.50 to $2.50 a day.

'rom these tests the fit pass on to work which they assisted to obtain. And the unfit? Until recently were borne with more or less grace as a necessary den on either the public treasury or the more special aid of private societies. The Special Employment 'eau of the Charity Organization Society is adjust- the remaining abilities of men who are handi- ped either by a physical or social affliction to cer- kinds of adapted employment. Whatever the m of affliction, such persons find it almost impos- e to secure respectable remunerative occupation themselves. The commercial employment agen- find it too expensive to make sincere efforts in their alf. After five months' trial it may be said that bureau is successful and its continuance will be ranted if friends of the idea will meet the neces- y expense.

Aatrons in the precinct police stations, female fac- y inspectors for industries employing women and ldren, a Municipal Lodging House for wayfarers, ex- sion of legal aid to the poor, the Council of Fresh Charities, inception of the National Child Labor nmittee, and the National Association for the Study l Prevention of Tuberculosis are examples of results omplished by this Society, or in co-operation with ers, which space does not permit me to enlarge upon. The result of the movement inaugurated by this iety and carried to completion by the gift of an indi- ual citizen for a Charities Building to house all the charitable organizations of the city and thus to ure closer co-operation and better understanding sts in handsome and tangible form. Such societies this building was designed to accommodate are espe- lly encouraged to take space in it rather than in a eign environment by reduction of 20 per cent on nmercial rentals.

Although the Society has sought to subordinate its ief rather than to advertise it, the total amount which expends as intermediary has constantly increased. e part which it plays in the support of the depen- it is indicated by the fact that "for the relief of lows and small children" it now annually expends out twice as much as the Society which bears that me and which for more than a century has devoted entire energy and resources exclusively to that thy object. The Provident Relief Fund which was rted by friends of this Society to supply relief to nilies for whom there is no existing special agency s recently become one of its regular departments. e disbursements for relief are at present from three five thousand dollars a month.

It must not be overlooked, however, that these sums present but a small part of the total obtained from urches, national societies, and other co-operators for families under its care.

To summarize the Society's past service and present sition in the community it may be said that it has ught to take an appropriate part in every movement the genuine welfare of the poor of New York City, enever there was any reason to believe that such par- ipation would be of service. It has endorsed and pported state and national measures for social ad- nce, while standing consistently for the maintenance that which has already been secured by individual tiative and normal growth.

THE IDLE RICH YOUNG MAN AND "PARLOR SOCIALISM."

tracts from an Address by Sherburn M. Becker Mayor of Milwaukee.

FEEL like warning young men, whether rich or poor, against the dangers of the fantastic and the treme tenets of Socialism. We have a government at was founded upon good principles largely by young en, and while it has often been threatened with de- uction, it has weathered the storms of over a cen- ry.

I am not in sympathy with what the press has been ased to call "Parlor Socialism," nor any other kind Socialism which contemplates the utter overthrow of r present form of government.

There is great room for reform and we are growing tter every day. Let us not be led astray by the more less attractive pleadings and arguments of theorists ho talk of revolutions. These things come to us incipally through the agency of men who have made failure of life in some country other than our own, d who would be dissatisfied, I believe, no matter at the conditions might be.

The idle rich young man, with proper training, has eat opportunities in all the honorable professions— e church, medicine, the law, the newspaper office, erature, art. If he will identify himself with any e of these he will be producing something and will a working man in every sense that the word implies. e man who shovels in the street is not the only pro- icer and he is not the only man who toils. I could tell u, were I not too modest, of at least one mayor who orks hard and who is known to have labored far into e night for days and weeks that he might fit himself r the laborious duties of his office.

HON. SHERBURN M. BECKER,
Mayor of Milwaukee.

A few weeks ago there came to Milwaukee a young "Parlor Socialist" who informed his hearers in a public address that he had been idle for years; that he produced nothing, and that he had no object in life except to spend the money earned by labor and which did not rightfully belong to him. When I read his address in a paper I felt like saying to him, "Go to work—you have the ability and you are needed—stop talking and do something. Get out of the parlors of the rich if you think you belong somewhere else." And it struck me that a desk in a bank or a newspaper office would be a good place for him. Now I am informed that he is to take a course in agriculture and raise cabbages and turnips, perhaps.

I believe that this young man, Joseph Medill Patterson, means well—that he is honest and sincere, but that he is not the kind of man who makes a success of farming. He has, I understand, the advantages of a college education and the good breeding that goes with it. He was trained in the school of journalism and is an able correspondent and reporter.

Then why should he go to the farm to milk cows or sow grain?

Why cannot he do good in the world with his pen? He can produce something with that as well as others can produce something with the plow or the corn planter. But he probably imagines that he must do manual labor, and toil with calloused hands. He is mistaken. We need intelligent young men in intellectual pursuits to help guide us in the right direction. We need brains as well as muscle, and we must have them. It is within the power of the rich young man to do his country great service. He is not handicapped with poverty and therefore is not tempted to be a grafter while in office. His ambition is not to make money, but to make a name for himself. There might be exceptions to this, but not many.

I do not mean to say that the rich young man is always honest or pure minded or that the poor young man is usually dishonest. What I am trying to do is to demonstrate that there is a place for the idle rich and educated young man, and to show you the things that recommend him. As a matter of fact more poor young men go to the front, I believe, in public affairs, than any other, because the former is forced to do something and in casting about for a calling he seeks public favor at the polls.

LABOR IN BRITISH POLITICS.

American Delegate to British Trades Congress Discusses Labor's Political Future in England.

THE fraternal delegates sent this year by the American Federation of Labor to the British Trades Congress were Mr. Frank K. Foster, of Boston, and Mr. James Wilson, of New York. During his absence Mr. Foster wrote a series of letters, giving his observations on labor matters in Great Britain. One of the most interesting of these, which appeared in the *Boston Globe* of September 27, relates to the much-discussed status of trade unions in politics in the United Kingdom, and includes also an analysis of the real nature of socialist sentiment among British workingmen. In the course of his letter Mr. Foster says:

"Is the British political labor movement liable to continue in its present form? This question I have asked Englishmen of many classes, trade unionists, shopkeepers, lawyers, and at least one cabinet minister. The journalists are discussing it from all standpoints. The politicians are seeking to find its answer. British conservatism is puzzling over it and society as a whole is in a state of mind.

"It all depends. It appears more than likely that while the main policy of seeking labor representation will be followed, there will be a readjustment of the machinery so far used. The general consensus of opinion seems to be that many of the present labor members were elected by the revolt against the Chamberlain protective policy or by Liberal votes as well as by labor votes, and that the concessions which the present government is undoubtedly prepared to grant will greatly weaken the strength of the independent movement should another general election take place. It is nevertheless conceded that even should a satisfactory trades dispute bill be passed, the independent movement would still continue to possess a good deal of vitality.

"There is every indication that Keir Hardie will be supplanted from the recognized leadership of the labor group of M.P.'s when parliament reassembles, and that the extremist policy which he stands for will be likewise dropped. The place will be filled by D. J. Shackelton, M.P., a man of quite a different type—sane, solid, judicial—whose quality of mind and leadership is far more in accord with the British temperament than those of the fanatical and irreconcilable, though more brilliant, Hardie.

"Shackelton, by the way, is one of the fraternal delegates to the American Federation of Labor which meets in Minneapolis in November. He is a socialist, but of the genial and untheoretical type, inspired by temperamental altruism rather than by a vindictive and systematically-stimulated class hatred. This distinction, indeed, may be held to apply to by far the larger portion of the so-called socialists of England. A most eminent authority informed me that not five per cent. of those who called themselves socialists either knew or cared anything about the doctrine of 'the collective ownership of the tools and instruments of production and distribution.' Their creed is a purely opportunist one, demanding practicable reforms.

"Now this kind of socialism finds no great difficulty in fusing and obtaining recognition of all sorts from the old-line trade unionists who make up the rank and file of the British movement. But even here there is on all sides to be observed a suspicion that the trade-union funds are being used to carry on socialistic propaganda under the stimulus of the crisis which came in the last general election. It was felt that unity must be had at all cost, and so trade-union funds are now being paid in to support candidates submitted by the independent labor party elected mainly by trade-union votes, some of whom are not even members of organized labor or wage earners. The trade-union leaders recognize this incongruous state of affairs and meditate a change.

"Another force which the labor political movement will have to contend with is the middle class defense association, which is now rapidly organizing all over London and the provinces. The middle class is the great rate-paying class and is undoubtedly alarmed at the progress of municipalization and unionism.

"The ostensible object of the new movement is the protection of the ratepayer against schemes to raise taxation, and it may easily become directly hostile to the political labor movement. Measuring the various forces in opposition, then, I should be inclined to predict that labor representation in its present form has reached its zenith for some time to come.

"It will readjust itself and continue to be a force of profit, of stimulus, to the political parties. The chances are that the pressing legislative demands of organized labor, the rational demands, will be accorded recognition. If not, then more labor members will be sent to parliament."

Mr. Foster's impressions are confirmed, in part at least, by the following press dispatch, dated London, October 3:

"The labor movement in Great Britain is at present passing through an interesting phase, which is tending to decide the future dominance of one of the two sections of the Labor party in the House of Commons, the Liberal section, led by John Burns, and the Socialist section, led by James Keir Hardie. The Federation of Miners, at a meeting held this week at Swansea, took a ballot which, although official figures are not yet available, is understood to have decided against joining the Hardie section. On the other hand, a conference of the Amalgamated Society of Railway Servants, sitting simultaneously at Cardiff, passed a resolution, after a long and bitter debate, in favor of adhesion to the Hardie section in spite of the fact that their leader, Richard Bell, M. P., was strongly opposed to the railway men submitting themselves to Socialist dictation."

The most successful trade unions to-day are those who believe in trade agreements, and who furthermore believe in maintaining a discipline so effective that no member, or group of members, can violate them with impunity.—*Iron Moulders' Journal.*

When a union is conducted on conservative lines it always has the respect and good wishes of the public, but let the men who act too hastily obtain control and their administration will meet the disapproval of the real union men and bring condemnation upon the entire labor movement.—*Journal of Labor.*

The National Civic Federation Review

Vol. II No. 12 NEW YORK, MARCH—APRIL, 1907 Ten Cents

THE CHILD LABOR SESSION OF THE FEDERATION'S ANNUAL MEETING

The Sixth Annual Meeting of The National Civic Federation was held at the Park Avenue Hotel, New York City, the Five Sessions Being Devoted to Discussions of Government by Injunction, Child Labor, Distribution of Immigrants, the Income and Inheritance Taxes, and to a Review at the Annual Dinner of the Work of the Different Departments of The Federation.

THE CIVIC FEDERATION'S SIXTH ANNUAL MEETING.

TRIBUTES TO ITS SERVICE TO SOCIETY—ELECTION OF OFFICERS—IMPORTANT PROBLEMS DISCUSSED—INVESTIGATING COMMISSIONS CREATED.

EVERY great public gathering for the purpose of discussing pressing questions of the time almost unconsciously develops a thought or idea around which all the proceedings of the meeting are centered. Sometimes this central idea lacks definite expression, but in the case of the remarkable annual meeting of The National Civic Federation held in New York City on December 12 and 13, it was emphasized more than once by different speakers. This central thought, around which all the discussions may be said to have centered and to which was attributed the unbounded enthusiasm which prevailed, was American Democracy. Reference was made to it at the various sessions during the discussion of such widely varying subjects as "Government by Injunction," "Child Labor," and the "Income and Inheritance Tax," as well as by the speakers at the annual dinner held on the evening of December 12.

If the animated discussions of these important subjects left any fear in the minds of the hearers as to the progress of the American Republic amid the whirlpool of dangers which seemed to engulf it on all sides, it is not mere literary effort to say that these fears were set at rest by the speakers at the annual dinner. Conspicuous among these was Archbishop Ireland, who stated that nowhere else in the world was such an organization as The National Civic Federation possible, and claimed that it was one of the powerful institutions at work to conserve and preserve democratic institutions. Referring particularly to the conflict between capital and labor, ex-Mayor Seth Low stated that "the great forces by which we are to settle all these industrial questions is the invisible force of public opinion, which this Federation and other agencies are generating, most fortunately, in all parts of this country." President Samuel Gompers, of the American Federation of Labor, stated his belief that "The National Civic Federation is a common ground upon which we may all meet to discuss the various differences upon which we are divided, and to try to find a middle ground so that the common good of all may be subserved. I believe that this Civic Federation, in its endeavor to work out our common policy and common polity, is the effort to make the principles of the Declaration of Independence the very living factors of our every-day lives. The Civic Federation presents itself as the conservator of peace and progress and of the wealth and belief of our common country." Rabbi Stephen S. Wise stated that he rejoiced in the work of The National Civic Federation, "because the aims of this body imply your faith in the American Democracy, not as an act, not as a process, not as an achievement or consummation, but as a development, as an evolving through education." Other speakers referred in a similar strain to the services which The National Civic Federation was performing in strengthening American institutions in conformity with the progress of American Democracy.

At the annual meeting the following officers were elected:

President—August Belmont, President of the Interborough Rapid Transit Company, New York.

Vice-Presidents—Samuel Gompers, President of the American Federation of Labor, Washington, D. C.; N. J. Bachelder, President of the National Grange, Concord, N. H.; Ellison A. Smyth, President of the South Carolina Cotton Manufacturers' Association, Greenville, S. C.; Benjamin Ide Wheeler, President of the University of California.

Treasurer—Isaac N. Seligman, of J. and W. Seligman & Company, New York.

Chairmen of Trade Agreement Department—John Mitchell, President of the United Mine Workers of America, and Francis L. Robbins, President of the Monongahela River Consolidated Coal and Coke Company, Pittsburgh.

Chairman of Public Ownership Department—Melville E. Ingalls, of the Cleveland, Cincinnati, Chicago and St. Louis Railroad Company.

Chairman of the Conciliation Department—Seth Low, ex-Mayor of New York.

Chairman of the Industrial Economics Department—Nicholas Murray Butler, President of Columbia University.

Chairman of the Immigration Department—Franklin MacVeagh, of Franklin MacVeagh & Company, Chicago, Ill.

Chairman of the Welfare Department—Charles A. Moore, of Manning, Maxwell & Moore, New York.

Chairman of the Taxation Department—E. R. A. Seligman, Professor of Political Economy in Columbia University.

Chairman of the Executive Council—Ralph M. Easley, of New York.

Secretary—Samuel B. Donnelly, 281 Fourth Avenue, New York.

The Committee on Nominations, of which Marcus M. Marks of New York was Chairman, in submitting its report, stated that Oscar S. Straus had felt it necessary to decline re-election as Vice-President on account of his appointment by President Roosevelt as Secretary of the Department of Commerce and Labor. In presenting its nomination for a successor to Mr. Straus, the committee offered the following resolution, which was unanimously adopted: "That in the retirement of Mr. Straus we desire to express our appreciation and thanks for his very valuable services during the past five years of the Civic Federation." President Belmont stated that Mr. Straus's retirement simply meant that he was practically taking a vacation as "he promises to come back to us as soon as the duties which he is now about to fulfill shall have come to an end."

At the close of the discussion on child labor, a resolution was adopted providing for the appointment of a commission to make a thorough investigation of the whole subject of child labor in the United States, the commission to be composed of representatives of various organizations. Provision was also made for the appointment of a commission to investigate the situation resulting from the operation of the Sherman anti-trust law, one on Government by Injunction, and one on the Income and Inheritance Tax.

GOVERNMENT BY INJUNCTION IN ITS VARIOUS ASPECTS.

REPRESENTATIVES OF LABOR AND OF CAPITAL DISCUSS THE CONFLICTING ISSUES OF THE DAY.

AUGUST BELMONT, President of The National Civic Federation, called the annual meeting to order on Wednesday morning, December 12, and extended a welcome to those present. "At this momentous period of our great country's history," he said, "when so many important and perplexing social and industrial problems are pressing for a solution, I regard it as fortunate that there exists such an organization as The National Civic Federation to take a vigorous hand in helping that solution.

"It is timely again to remind you of the purposes of the Federation as stated in its by-laws; they are, to organize the best brains of the nation in an educational movement toward the solution of some of the great problems relating to social and industrial progress, to provide for study and discussion of questions of national import, to aid thus in the crystallization of the most enlightened public opinion and, when desirable, to promote legislation in accordance therewith. The Federation's membership is drawn from practical men of affairs, whose acknowledged leadership in thought and action makes them typical representatives of the various elements that voluntarily work together for the general good.

"Farmers, wage-earners, manufacturers, bankers, merchants, ministers, laymen, economists, and other distinct but interacting elements of society have formed themselves into many useful organizations for the discussion of affairs peculiar to their pursuits and callings, but the Civic Federation, in addition to its departments for the accomplishment of specific purposes, provides a forum where representatives of all these elements meet to discuss important problems in which they have a common interest. Six national conferences have thus far been held, one upon Primary Election and Ballot Reform, on Foreign Policy, on Trusts and Combinations, Conciliation and Arbitration, Taxation, Immigration, and one on Public Ownership. These conferences have, in most instances, been attended by delegates officially appointed by Governors of States, Mayors of cities, and by representatives selected by various commercial, industrial, educational, and religious bodies. The present activities of the Federation are being exercised through six active agencies: The Public Ownership Commission, the Immigration Department, the Conciliation Department, the Welfare Department, the Industrial Economics Department, and the Political Reform Department."

In speaking of the subjects for discussion at the annual meeting, President Belmont stated that the problems growing out of the accumulation of great fortunes were to be considered under the title of the Income and Inheritance Tax, and suggested the hope that the discussion was to result in the appointment of a committee to investigate thoroughly the whole subject and, possibly, to propose legislation, if it is found desirable. "No subject," he said, "can bring greater good to this country, if correctly solved, and greater harm, if, for wise and just taxation, punitive spoliation and the destruction of our boundless spirit of enterprise be substituted through hampering regulations. In contemplating the future of the great and ever-growing needs of our institutions of learning and instruction, our charitable and religious establishments, into whose life and growth have flown a seemingly endless and increasing stream of bequests and donations from great estates and fortunes, such as no other country can boast of, one must pause at the thought of drying up those springs of life. I ask, would popular subscriptions take their place, or, failing that, must a paternal government, to provide them, be the alternative? That is one of the phases of the problem that cannot escape contemplation."

Taking up another subject selected for discussion at the annual meeting—Government by Injunction—President Belmont said: "Seemingly, organized labor and organized employers have come to a deadlock on this question. If I correctly understand it, organized labor does not, as is currently thought, oppose the injunction principle, but it is opposed to what it claims are certain abuses. Organized employers, while largely admitting these abuses, deny that the remedy lies in the direction pointed out by organized labor. When our workmen, however, become imbued with the idea that our courts are used by employers for partisan purposes, so to speak, it is a matter of great moment and worthy of the consideration of this body, and I hope some steps may be taken through the instrumentality of this organization to help solve this apparently insolvable problem.

"Another subject touching our national life, perhaps more closely than any other, because of the sentimental reasons attached to it, in addition to its vast importance as bearing upon our moral and physical development, will be discussed by you at these sessions. I refer to the child-labor problem, up to this time regulated only by the States, but now crystallizing into proposed national legislation. Bills have already been introduced into the United States Senate for its regulation.

"President Roosevelt in his recent message to Congress urges strongly the compulsory investigation of industrial disturbances. I am not sure that such a proposition is advisable in any general sense. In fact, I doubt the wisdom of attempting legislation which will provide governmental interference with every threatened industrial disturbance. If such a policy were to be adopted there would certainly be more justification for its use in the case of quasi public institutions. The public is not vitally affected nor inconvenienced by a strike in a shoe factory or a cotton factory, because there are so many other factories in the same industries that there is no scarcity created by such a strike. In the case of steam railroads, street railroads, electric light and gas plants, the conditions are wholly different. The public, as a whole, is at once inconvenienced and has a direct interest in the controversy."

President Belmont also referred to that part of President Roosevelt's message having to do with amending the Sherman anti-trust and the Interstate Commerce acts in order to meet a certain fundamental conflict between those two laws at the present time. President Belmont said that the attempt to prevent or destroy all combinations, whether good or bad, is unsound in economics and disastrous in the domain of trade. He quoted with approval President Roosevelt's views on this point. President Belmont then introduced ex-Mayor Seth Low as the chairman of the morning session.

IN assuming the chairmanship of the meeting ex-Mayor Low said that it seemed to him to be one of the bright things in our American life that any question, no matter how strongly people feel about it, can be openly and frankly discussed. Continuing he said:

"It certainly is one of the best phases of The National Civic Federation that it offers a platform upon which men of such diverse points of view can meet to discuss every question of interest in the industrial world. I suppose there are very few, if any, questions upon which opinion is more sharply divided at the present moment in the United States than on this question of 'Government by Injunction' so-called. Very likely the feeling is strong, and the difference of opinion is especially marked because the question is not accurately defined, or at least is defined by some men in one way and by other men in another way. It is very much to be hoped that the result of the discussions here to-day will be to enlighten us all, so that we may determine accurately to what extent differences of opinion are based upon differences of definition, differences of interpretation of fact, and to what extent they really represent a diverse judgment upon the same state of facts and the same conditions."

T. CARL SPELLING, general attorney for the American Federation of Labor, was the first speaker on the question of "Government by Injunction." He represented that organization in the discussion before the committee of Congress. Mr. Spelling stated that what is meant by "Government by Injunction" is "that power which has been superadded by the courts of the country to their constitutional power, by which they rule, or are said to rule, despotically upon certain occasions in the matters brought before them in litigation; that is, they rule in excess of their jurisdiction.

"If there be such a thing in this country", he said, "as 'Government by Injunction,' as we believe there is, then it is a most despotic government; that is, it is a government without limitation, without check or restraint, and government exercised by one man without responsibility or liability to account to any other men or to any other power on earth. In our form of government there is no way to reach a judge for his misdeeds except by impeachment, and that has long ago been demonstrated to be a worthless remedy against judicial usurpation."

Mr. Spelling reviewed briefly the judicial history of the country as affecting the subject under discussion, claiming in substance that the effect of "Government by Injunction" was special legislation by an authority other than the properly constituted law-making body. He claimed that the fundamental limitation imposed by the long course of judicial history and procedure was that an injunction shall never be granted except to protect property or property rights. He believed this to be the keynote of the whole issue under discussion. He said that authorities do not distinguish between property, that is, visible and tangible property, and property rights, as regards its bearing on this question. He claimed that the representatives of labor have never insisted that in the case of a trade dispute, if men should undertake to inflict any injury to any property or property rights, for instance, such as trespassing on land, attempting to set fire to buildings or wrecking machinery, anything to which any kind of violence could be offered,—he claimed that they never have insisted that in any such case a writ of injunction to prevent it would not be available. Labor unions, he said, were not trying to abolish the remedy by injunction. "It is not correct to say that never can an injunction issue against strikers or against the working man or in a conflict between capital and labor, because an injunction is always available, and always ought to be used, when anybody, whether workingmen or unionists, or men who do not belong to that class, attempt to inflict any kind of irreparable injury upon property or property rights. We are absolutely safe in assuming and adhering to that position."

Referring to an injunction in trade disputes, Mr. Spelling said: "No court in Christendom has any jurisdiction to restrain me or anybody else from advising any man not to work, not to keep a contract, not to obey the law; you cannot enjoin me in any court for going out and advising men to commit even arson, or murder, or anything else. Now, that sounds harsh, and that is where a great deal of our difficulty has arisen. When anybody proposes to check the usurpation and abuse and excesses of the courts, they say: 'You are advocating violence; you are in favor of disorder.' Now, I admit that it is deplorable that men can be advised to commit crime, to injure people, and to stir up trouble, and put the public to a great amount of inconvenience; but, I tell you, it is more deplorable, it is a thing that will lead to the most disastrous results, if irresponsible men on the bench for life are to be allowed to use their authority above the law and above all the departments of government, to become unrestrained despots, take one side in every trade dispute, become guardians of peace and order and morality in the community, decide ex-parte upon a one-sided showing, that hundreds and thousands of men are about to violate the law, and send forth these special decrees, these enactments of special legislation—for that is what they are—to paralyze and destroy the rights of all these men; I say that is the most dangerous tendency in our government. I do not except the tendency toward monopolization and combination, the suppression of trade; I think that can be remedied. I think that will work itself out. But, I tell you, if these vicious and far-reaching precedents are to be recognized as the law of the land, and the judges are to be encouraged or permitted to go on building more on top of these, that they will soon constitute and erect outside the regular organizations and branches of government a power as despotic as that which destroyed Rome, as that which was exercised in the days of Caligula, as that which was exercised by the notorious and infamous Star Chamber. The liberties of the people of this country are more endangered by that tendency and by that practice than by any other."

Referring to some of the injunctions issued by the courts, Mr. Spelling stated that "they have enjoined men from preventing, by persuasion, or by any means whatever, men from entering the employ of the complainant, that is, the party who went by his attorney before the judge and got out the writ of injunction. They have enjoined men from marching on the public highway; they have enjoined them from meeting in places far from the premises of the employer against whom they struck and from having music and making speeches and presenting their cause to the public. They have done what I call most unwarranted and outrageous things. These things have been done by the courts, exercising all the powers and functions of government on one side in a trade dispute. And you don't hear of any strikers ever going to a court to get an injunction, it is always the other side. Now, the court in such a case palpably and flagrantly takes the side of one party in a litigation, and the stronger party at that, despite the greater numbers of the other side. So long as this power is recognized as belonging to those judges, they will, on a pretense, on a claim and allegation that men are about to resort to violence, prevent them from doing innocent and legal things, and taking the proper steps for the preservation of their constitutional rights. We simply want these usurpations lopped off. If we had the law as it stood before these usurpations began—before a system of precedents was built up in contravention of the ancient and just rule on this subject—we would not demand any legislation. It is not to change the law; all we want is the recognition of our rights as they stood before these usurpations."

WALTER DREW, Commissioner of the National Iron Erectors' Association, stated as his belief that of all the questions involved under the phrase "Government by Injunction" and growing out of the different legislation proposed in Congress, he considered the most vital and the most important to be the restoration of confidence on the part of the rank-and-file of organized labor in our laws and in our courts. After a brief consideration of the theory in practice connected with the use of the writ of injunction, both temporary and permanent, he claimed that, separate from any question of defect in the law or in its administration, the demand that temporary injunctions should not issue in labor controversies becomes a demand that the practice of our courts shall be changed to grant special immunities and privileges to one particular class only and vitally engaged in warfare with another class. "No reason other than this," he said, "exists for discontinuing the temporary injunction in labor cases which does not exist in any other case that might arise. Without its use in such cases, as in other cases, the relation of the parties may be placed in a condition where justice could never be done between them. The very subject matter of the controversy might be dissipated or injured beyond remedy. Organized labor may be aggressive and meet with our approval. It may fight its war with capital if it will, but in that fight it not only must ask but give fair play and a square deal."

Mr. Drew next took up the Pearre bill, of which he said that either it seeks to do away with great and serious evils that exist in our law and its application to labor combinations, or it seeks special dispensations and privileges for labor combinations as a class for the conduct of their so-called war against capital. In this connection he next took up a discussion of conspiracy

Benjamin Ide Wheeler, Vice President
Ellison A. Smyth, Vice President
Samuel Gompers, Vice President
August Belmont, President
N. J. Bachelder, Vice President
Ralph M. Easley, Chairman Executive Council
Isaac N. Seligman, Treasurer
Samuel B. Donnelly, Secretary

OFFICERS OF THE NATIONAL CIVIC FEDERATION.

under the common law and quoted a number of cases as to the rights of labor in combination. He said: "What would be an unlawful purpose on the part of an individual would likewise be an unlawful purpose on the part of a combination. The converse of this statement, however, is not true and what would be an unlawful purpose on the part of a combination might be entirely lawful for an individual, and it is with this fact that the chief fault is found by those who are proposing to change the law. This difference in the law concerning the purposes of an individual and those of a combination is explained by one word—malice. Ordinarily it is of no moment in the eyes of the law whether an individual acts from motives of malice or not, as long as his conduct is confined within the limits of the law. In other words, a malicious motive on his part would not make unlawful that which would otherwise be lawful. A different rule, however, applies to combinations, and a combination, whether of working men or of any other class of citizens, that inflicts intentional injury upon others from malicious motives, while it may not be liable criminally, still it becomes liable civilly and its action is held to amount to a legal wrong. A combination may not wilfully inflict injury upon third persons without lawful justification or excuse, and if such justification or excuse be lacking, its conduct in the eye of the law is deemed malicious and unlawful." Mr. Drew claimed that every principle in the law of conspiracy is applied equally and impartially to all combinations and that in no particular is there any rule or principle enforced by our courts against combinations of labor which is not equally applied to and enforced against other combinations.

Referring to the Pearre bill, Mr. Drew said: "The effect of this measure would be to make lawful and substantiate every method now employed by organized labor except the commission of actual crime. Not only would combinations for the purpose of establishing monopolies, for the purpose of inflicting malicious injury and for other purposes now declared unlawful be legalized, but a systematic use of coercion and intimidation, which have their only strength and danger when used by many against the one, would be beyond the reach of the law. In providing that such combinations should not constitute a conspiracy, not only are they placed beyond the reach of courts of equity, but civil and criminal remedies also are taken away.

"The mere fact that injunctions have been used to a greater extent in recent years than formerly is no proof whatever, without further showing, that they have been misused, but is simply proof that there has been greater occasion for them. Neither is it to be supposed that courts of equity or of law could be infallible in one class of cases more than in others. Courts make mistakes like the rest of us, for the matters upon which they are called to decide must be determined in the light of the judgment, the knowledge and the limitations of the human mind, and it is human to err. But if the mistakes be honest, and if there be no greater number of them in any one class of cases than in any other; the fact that isolated cases might be presented in which the writ of injunction has been improvidently employed, would furnish no more reason for doing away with it altogether in labor cases than in doing away with the whole body of the law and the jurisdiction of all courts.

"With no case made out of discrimination or inequality, either in the law or its administration as to labor combinations, one conclusion only will remain, and that is that organized labor in proposing this legislation seeks special immunities and privileges before the law not enjoyed by other combinations or other classes of the people.

"I shall not enter into an extensive discussion as to the dangers of class legislation. It is not necessary. Not only the history of nations but the fundamental spirit of our institutions alike condemn it, and any class that persists in demanding it will find the face of the great American public solidly set against its efforts. In this case it would be more than class legislation in its results. It would lead to a state of anarchy in labor controversies, for the employing class, finding no protection in the law in their individual fights against combinations using legalized methods of coercion and intimidation against them, would, from the very instinct of self-preservation, seek their protection outside the law and we would have this whole great contest, this war, as it has been termed, between capital and labor, taken out of the pale of civilized methods and of civilized courts."

JOHN MITCHELL, President of the United Mine Workers of America, was the closing speaker on the subject of "Government by Injunction." Among other things he said:

"Do you know that in labor disputes, when the proposition to arbitrate is made, very often—indeed almost generally—the workingmen will make the reservation that the question to be arbitrated shall not be submitted to a Federal judge? I do not share fully in these apprehensions, but the very fact that workingmen do express a fear of the impartiality of the Federal Judiciary is in itself a matter of grave concern, not alone to those who have suffered from the injunction but to the entire people of this country. Men do not lose confidence without cause or at least without the belief that they have cause. So many injunctions have been issued, so many laboring men have been incarcerated because of the violation or alleged violation of these injunctions—not because of the commission of crime, not because they have violated any law of the land, but because they have insisted upon doing those things which they have a legal and a constitutional right to do.

"I wish to say for myself—and I yield to no man living in loyalty to this country—that if a judge were to enjoin me from doing something that I had a legal, a constitutional, and a moral right to do, I should violate the injunction. I shall, as one American, preserve my liberty and the liberties of the people even against the usurpation of the Federal Judiciary, and in doing this I shall feel that I am best serving the interests of my country.

"It is indeed unfortunate that within recent years the courts have gone so far in the exercise of their equity power. It is presumed that injunctions shall be issued only in cases where there is no adequate remedy at law. It is presumed that they are issued in cases where there is danger of the infliction of irreparable injury. In a coal strike in West Virginia, for instance, an injunction is issued; this injunction restrains the men from the commission of crimes and also from the performance of acts which are entirely legal within themselves. The men proceed under direction of their attorneys to do only those things that they have a legal right to do; and they are called into court—they are charged with no crime, they are simply asked, have they violated that injunction? They are permitted to make no defense. They, as truthful men, must plead that they have violated the injunction, that they have walked upon the highway, that they have spoken to the men who wanted to work; the consequence is that they are sentenced to prison, not for violating the law, not for the commission of any illegal act, but because they have done those things which they had a legal right to do; and they are sent to prison without a trial by a jury of their peers. It is to this phase of the injunction that we take exception."

THE EXTENT AND MENACE OF CHILD LABOR.

EMPLOYERS, EMPLOYES AND STUDENTS OF INDUSTRIAL CONDITIONS SHARPLY DISAGREE AS TO THE FACTS AND FIGURES INVOLVED IN THIS PROBLEM.

AT the afternoon session of the first day's meeting the subject, "The Extent and Menace of Child Labor: Is Everything Possible Being Done to Eliminate It?" was discussed. Daniel J. Keefe, President of the International Longshoremen, Marine and Transport Workers' Association presided. He stated that as his organization in no way comes into competition with child labor, he had no desire to discuss the subject, but expressed the opinion that many of the public statements with reference to child labor are very much exaggerated.

SAMUEL McCUNE LINDSAY, Secretary of the National Child Labor Committee, in referring to the claim that gross exaggeration with respect to the statistical enumeration of child labor in this country had been made, said that he didn't think "there is any one who will deny the fact that there have been exaggerations and erroneous statements about child labor. I have seen all sorts of estimates in the papers and magazines, some of them specifying particularly the number of children in particular occupations, and others making mere guesses as to the total number of children employed. I think most persons who read these newspaper statements and have any knowledge of statistics at all, treat them with the indifference that they deserve. I want to say with respect to the measurement of the extent of child labor that I believe it is impossible to measure child labor statistically with any accuracy or with satisfactory results."

After referring to the United States Census as the official source of information, Dr. Lindsay analyzed its methods of securing the data and then referred to the charge of gross exaggeration which had been brought against those who claimed that "two million children are working in the factories, mines, mills, mercantile establishments, etc., under fourteen years of age." Continuing on this point he said: "I presume that such a claim has been made; I would not like to deny it although I don't know anyone who has made it and I don't recall at the present time having seen exactly that claim made anywhere. The National Child Labor Committee has never made such a statement. In a report made a little over a year ago, we said that a conservative estimate for 1905 showed that there were two million children under sixteen years of age engaged in gainful occupations in the United States. This estimate took account of the probable increase since 1900 and always referred to children ten to fifteen years of age on the same basis of calculation as the census itself. That statement was made upon the authority of the National Child Labor Committee. We have had no occasion, by reason of any argument that has been made on the employers' side anywhere since then, to question the accuracy of the statement. I believe it is as true to-day as it was in 1905. The general policy of the Committee has always been to state its case conservatively, to under-estimate rather than to over-state the facts brought out in its work. In other words, we have secured data from private reports, by investigations of our own field agents, from reports of State officials, factory inspectors, school officials, State committees and educational authorities in several of our States, and applying the usual statistical methods of estimating, based upon a proportion, we have come to the conclusion that that estimate of two million children ten to sixteen years of age, in all occupations in the year 1905, is an under-estimate rather than an over-estimate. We could very well make it a little stronger without any danger of going beyond the records that we have at hand.

"Then as to the kind of child labor that represents. No one, so far as I know, has undertaken to say that all those children are the victims of abuse; not at all. No one has undertaken to say that all the kinds of labor represented in the employment of those two million children are necessarily harmful. We do say, that as a general principle, any child under sixteen years of age who is required to work for its living, required to contribute materially to the support of itself or its family, is in a perilous and hazardous condition; that such burdens in childhood are contrary to the spirit of our institutions. It is depriving children of opportunities and bringing about class distinctions that we should seek in this country to avoid. We will say that some forms of child labor represented by these two million children are extremely harmful for children under sixteen years of age and that the labor of many of these children under sixteen years of age should be absolutely prohibited, namely, the labor of all children under fourteen years of age—which represents some 180,000 of these in occupations other than agriculture; that the labor of all the others should be protected, restricted by legal enactment, so that at least all children under sixteen years of age would be prohibited from working in physically and morally dangerous occupations, especially in mines, underground and also at night work, which we believe to be particularly hazardous.

"Now, beyond these statements, and I have tried to make them as definite and as clear as possible, there is nothing in the reports of our National Child Labor Committee that will warrant any further assertions; as to the accuracy of those statements we are prepared to defend them, and to show that they are under-statements rather than over-statements.

"As to the question of the further classification of these two million children according to occupations, first of all we find that most of them are in agricultural pursuits. Understand, I am now taking the Census figures and correcting them as of the date 1905, which means, adding a quarter of a million to the 1,750,000, which gives us 2,000,000. Of this two million a large proportion are in agricultural pursuits. Of the 1,750,000 in the year 1900, 790,623 were under fourteen years of age, and of that number 604,265 were engaged in agricultural pursuits, leaving 186,000 under fourteen years of age engaged in the manufacturing and mechanical pursuits, trade, transportation, domestic and personal services and professional service.

"The point we have made in the use of these statistics has been chiefly this, that 1900 as compared with 1880 showed an increase in the volume of child labor. The Census itself shows, from these figures, that the proportion of working children of either sex engaged in agricultural pursuits and in domestic and professional services was smaller in 1900 than in 1880, while the proportion in trade, transportation and in manufacturing and mechanical pursuits was larger, the movement being rather more marked for female than for male children. That is the essential fact that has been brought out by the Census figures, examined for whatever they are worth. This fact has attracted our particular attention and merited our notice in the work that we are trying to do for the welfare of the children—that in those trades, in those lines of activity where the danger is greatest, the danger to the health, physical development, moral development and education, the increase has been greatest. The figures show some alarming changes in the increase between 1880 and 1900 in these particular trades and industries where the work of children is hazardous. In the next place, we believe that the increase since 1900 has been steady."

Referring to the remedy that is being applied to cure

the child labor evil, Dr. Lindsay detailed the efforts of the National Child Labor Committee in securing prohibitive legislation, both State and National, and endorsed the Beveridge-Parsons bill in Congress. He expressed the belief that in preventing child labor, "we shall remove a very large cause of all our social discontent and many of the causes of the political disturbance of our present day."

OWEN R. LOVEJOY, Assistant Secretary of the National Child Labor Committee, spoke on "The Extent of Child Labor in the Anthracite Coal Industry." He quoted from the 1905 report of Chief Roderick of the Pennsylvania Department of Mines in part as follows: "During the latter part of 1905 a man by the name of Lovejoy made a tour of the anthracite counties inquiring into the ages of boys employed at the mines. In blazing headlines the daily papers published, on Mr. Lovejoy's authority, the statement that ten thousand boys were found at work in and about the breakers who were under the legal employment age of fourteen years." To this Mr. Lovejoy replied in part as follows: "It should first be observed that the statement 'in blazing headlines' was never made by my authority, or the authority of the National Child Labor Committee, that 'ten thousand boys were found at work in and about the breakers who were under the legal employment age of fourteen years.' It was said, discussing the estimate made by Dr. Peter Roberts, 'if the borough we are now studying were taken as a basis for such a generalization, the number of boys under fourteen years of age working in the anthracite coal industry would be 12,800.'"

Mr. Lovejoy referred to other statements as to the number of boys under age employed in the anthracite coal industry, and explained the method of computation by which the representatives of the National Child Labor Committee arrived at their conclusions. The source of much of this information was pointed out as being the public school superintendents. On this point Mr. Lovejoy said: "If the same proportion of child labor prevailed in the entire region which is estimated here by these school superintendents the total number would be six times 2,460, or 14,760 boys working under age, with falsified certificates in the mines and breakers of the region. It is not claimed and has never been claimed by this Committee that the number of boys under age in the breakers is six times the 2,460 estimated by the school superintendents of these seven boroughs. The nearest approach to such a claim has been that if the same percentage prevailed throughout the region as found in these boroughs for which estimates were given by the school superintendents, the number in the *mines and breakers* would be not less than ten or twelve thousand, but estimates of the number have been accompanied always by the contention that 'until some accurate method to determine the age of children has been applied, the exact number will never be known.' The school superintendents, the class of public officials most familiar with the children, complain of the difficulty in determining the age of the children in default of accurate vital statistics."

Mr. Lovejoy argued for the enactment of a law in Pennsylvania which would make sixteen years the minimum age limit for employment in or about any mine, on the ground that coal mining is an occupation dangerous to the life and limb of those employed therein. "If it were true," he said, "that 'if a uniform law, with fourteen years as the minimum, were passed, Pennsylvania would lead all other States and countries in practical and sensible protective legislation on this important question,' then we would be constrained to say that other States and countries where coal mines are operated would be sadly in need of reform. Fortunately, the assertion is erroneous; for Illinois, Montana and Missouri forbid the employment of children under sixteen in mines, while Arizona, Colorado, Montana, Missouri and Utah limit the employment of children in mines to eight hours in the twenty-four. Austria forbids the employment in mines under fifteen years, while both France and Germany, although not having a higher age limit for employment, require that all chilren employed shall have completed the common school course of education."

W. J. RICHARDS, Second Vice-President and General Manager of the Philadelphia and Reading Coal and Iron Company, in his opening remarks stated that, "the cause of my appearance here to-day may be found in the unwarranted statements that have been appearing in the public press for the past six months regarding the employment of child labor in the anthracite fields of Pennsylvania."

"There is in Pennsylvania," he said, "covering the portion of the anthracite fields, a mine law, and in addition special laws have been enacted from time to time limiting the age at which boys can be employed in the breakers and the mines. In the agitation for these laws, the operators have always favored and advocated the highest age suggested. The law now standing on the statute books of Pennsylvania and the age limit fixed thereby was enacted by the Legislature in 1903. That law fixes the age for the employment of boys in the breakers at fourteen years and the age for employment of boys in the mines at sixteen years. These ages have the full approval of all the operators and mining companies in the anthracite regions. The effort of the companies has always been to rigidly adhere to that law. The instructions to all the superintendents and foremen of collieries have been to give close attention to every boy coming to or at work to learn whether he is of the age he is represented to be in the certificate furnished by his parents or guardians.

"To further protect the child and to prevent the employment of any under the legal age the State of Pennsylvania has a compulsory education law requiring the attendance at school of all children under fourteen years of age. To fully enforce its provisions a truant officer is appointed in each school district, whose duty it is to compel the attendance at school of every child under fourteen years of age. This truant officer is a resident of the school district, a man who knows the people and children of his locality. Before the beginning of each school year, he or the district assessor visits from house to house making a complete census of all the children of school age, noting where they are attending school. If any child under the school age has gone to work at any breaker or factory, the truant officer compels the discharge of the child and requires that he be sent to school. Another check is thus provided to prevent the conditions represented by the recent articles of which we have complained.

"Anthracite mining is a large and important industry. We are in every way endeavoring to live up to the laws. We have always led in any effort to improve the advantages and educational opportunities of the boys of the region. There has been no attempt at evasion on the part of the operators. When one of these laws was declared unconstitutional, the operators still continued to enforce the age limit of the law."

Mr. Richards then presented in detail the report of the Pennsylvania Department of Mines, giving the result of a special investigation made by its inspectors in 1905 as to the extent of child labor in the anthracite mines in reply to Mr. Lovejoy's assertion that "the boys working in the hard coal breakers of that State under fourteen years of age number not less than 12,000." Chief Roderick's letter of instruction to the inspectors requested them to "make a strict inquiry as to the ages of boys working in and about the breakers. See whether Section 1 of the Act of May 2, 1905, has been complied with. Insist upon all boys, wherever found, furnishing proper proof of age according to law. You are authorized to enter legal proceedings against all violators of this law, whether employer or employee. Make a report to this department of the total number of boys over fifteen and under sixteen years of age employed in and about each breaker; also give the names of boys of doubtful age, with the address of their parents or guardians." As a result of this investigation, Mr. Roderick stated that "the total number of boys ranging from fourteen to sixteen years of age, employed in and about the breakers, is 8,124. Of this number the inspectors had some doubt as to 760 of the boys having reached the legal employment age, although each of them had presented the certificate required by law, which was on file, showing that he was over fourteen years of age. The boys of doubtful age number a little over nine per cent of the total number employed. It is very probable, however, that many of the 760 classed as doubtful by the inspectors are over fourteen. The difficult thing is to get at the correct age of these 760 boys, as at least seventy-five per cent of them were born in foreign countries."

Mr. Richards stated in conclusion that the company with whose operations he is connected has had a careful examination and investigation made covering its employes between the ages of fourteen and sixteen, and the finding corresponds very closely to that of the State of Pennsylvania. "I am perfectly convinced," he said, "that cases where boys are working under age are very limited."

CHAIRMEN OF THE FEDERATION'S SEVEN DEPARTMENTS.

DR. ROLAND P. FALKNER, a well-known statistician, without attempting to minimize the necessity for eradicating the evil of child labor, at the same time claimed that "the menace to society does not exist unless such child workers are an appreciable factor in the life of the community or of the nation. Society counts with large aggregates; it deals with great masses. To it the question of the extent of the evil is of the utmost importance. It would know whether it has to deal with a sporadic, comparatively infrequent phenomenon, or whether the evil is widespread." He then proceeded to analyze the census results of 1900 in regard to child labor. He said: "They show that between the ages of ten and fifteen years inclusive there were 1,750,178 persons employed in gainful occupations; that they formed 18.2 per cent of the population between the ages of ten and fifteen inclusive, and that they were divided among the groups of occupations recognized by the census as follows: Agriculture, 1,061,971; professional service, 2,945; domestic and personal service, 279,031; trade and transportation, 122,362; manufacturing and mechanical, 283,869.

"Whatever may be our view of child labor, it is clear that not all of this labor would fall equally under condemnation. The labor upon the farm, where the child works generally in assisting the parent or guardian, certainly falls in a different catagory from that in factory, mine, or sweatshop. So little does public opinion condemn such labor that none of the laws designed to throw a protection around the child include it within their sphere. Some of it may be objectionable, but the great bulk of it is so little objectionable that we can throw it out of the reckoning. We have left, then, 688,207 workers in fields other than agriculture."

Dr. Falkner then presented statistics showing the sub-division in age groups, and of a total of 688,207, 310,825 were fifteen years of age and 191,023, fourteen years of age. As to children of these ages Dr. Falkner said that, "it may be in some cases a hardship for a boy or a girl of fourteen and fifteen years of age to earn his or her living, but it is nothing abnormal or unusual. Nor does legislation seek to restrict such labor except in particularly hazardous industries. At this age legal restriction of child labor is the exception rather than the rule. Eliminate the children of fourteen and fifteen years of age and we have 186,259 children at work in 1900 under the age of fourteen who are the proper objects of restrictive legislation. That the number of child workers is so much less than currently reported should not lessen our sympathy with these unfortunates or diminish our efforts to alleviate their condition.

"In face of the evidence presented, how can it be claimed that child labor is a menace to our civilization, a menace growing more threatening as time advances? We may recognize the evil, whether it exists in particular localities or in particular industries. We may and should put forth every effort to diminish it. We should save as many children as we can from the harm which may arise from their employment at an early age, but Why should we malign our democracy with exaggerated pictures of the evil? Why should we condemn our modern industrial system as a whole for an evil which is by no means general? Why should we grow pessimistic over our whole industrial outlook, and looking it in the face see beams in its eyes where there is only a tiny mote?"

CHARLES P. NEILL, United States Commissioner of Labor, stated that there was one very important point that seems to have been entirely overlooked by Dr. Falkner. "If there are 200,000 children this year," he said, "they do not stay fourteen years of age for a lifetime. One-half of these, who are, say, 12½ this year, will be thirteen years old next year. Every year 100,000 go out of the twelve-year-old grade, and another 100,000 children come in; so that, as a matter of fact, it is only a few years before you have got a million citizens who are turned into the body politic with the unfit surroundings of their child labor. I want to submit that the question is not how many are at work this year, but how many children in a reasonable time, within a period of five or ten years, will be at work at the age of twelve or thirteen years. While on the subject, I would like to suggest one further question, that those 200,000 be given two years more of schooling and two years more of childhood, so that if the number is so small in any single year, it will not affect industry to any appreciable extent, but in a given period of ten years it will affect the citizenship of this country to a most material extent."

W. A. MAY, General Manager of the Pennsylvania Coal Company, premised his remarks with the statement that "in order that there may not be a misunderstanding on the part of the public or false conclusions drawn from the magazine articles and newspaper accounts of the conditions existing in the anthracite regions as they relate to the employment of boys in and about the mines," he thought it appropriate "to give facts, figures and arguments which will materially lighten the dark and somber pictures they have drawn. These articles and accounts dwell mainly on single and isolated cases, making them typical when in fact they are not so." Mr. May then told of the efforts made by the employers to get at the ages of the boys seeking employment, so as to comply with the child labor act, referred to the constantly lessening number employed; mentioned instances of money expended for their comfort when employed; discussed the doubtful wisdom of abolishing the boy; and presented several notable examples of what slate pickers, driver boys and car runners have become in after life. "Boys under fourteen," he said, "the age limit fixed [illegible]ch they may be employed at the collieries, are never employed if we know it. We ask for and obtain a certificate, sworn to by their parents or guardian. This was the practice with our companies before the present law, which has for one of its conditions the provision that boys of doubtful age must file a certificate with the employer if given work. What more than this can you ask of us? The boy may be under age, but having taken every precaution, we cannot be held responsible."

Following a presentation of statistics showing the lessening number of boys employed as slate pickers in the breakers of the Lackawanna and Wyoming valleys, where the larger portion of anthracite coal is produced, Mr. May referred to the improvement in slate picking machinery, which eliminated the boy, and stated that "if we could use machinery and clean the coal as the public demands that it must be cleaned we would do so; we would not use boys." He stated that the change as to the employment of boys as slate pickers was great and added "if the use of boys for this work is an evil, it is not a growing one." He referred to the expenditures of the companies in heating the breakers and removing the dust therefrom. He stated that men could not be employed to pick slate because of the lack of supply and because of the character of the work which permitted boys to do it much better than men.

"Is it wise to entirely abolish the boy from our work?" he continued. "One of the speakers referred to the fatalities in our mines. That is true; we have many of them and we shall have them so long as mining is carried on; but will they not be increased by banishing the boy? To avoid accident you must have experience. We need that which comes from training of the hands, the limbs, the eye and the ear. There is no way to get it but by actual work, and how can you get it more quickly, to the greater advantage of the boy when he becomes a man and to his fellow workers, than by putting him at work? I mean a boy fourteen years old and over, because we do not believe it best to employ boys under that age any more than you do. To set the boy at work is the only way, and if you would go into the mines with me, you would quickly see how a boy will get that agility, that alertness, that brightness, which prevent accident. True, boys are killed; and men also are slain; but many more would be sacrificed on the altar of trade and for the sake of public comforts and welfare if they went into the mines without the knowledge gained by actual practice. In other words, we must have apprentices and they must begin young. This is not a false position and it will appeal to any one of you having had experience in practical affairs and in the handling of labor."

JOHN MITCHELL, President of the United Mine Workers of America, said that he was surprised at the statement that men could not be secured to pick slate, because the companies were unable to secure a sufficient number of men to work in the mines. "I dare say," he said, "that with the close of this month and the close of this year the breakers and collieries in the anthracite region will not have operated two hundred days in the year 1906. There are not more than two years in the past twenty when the anthracite miners have been given opportunity of working more than two hundred days in any one year, and if they are permitted to work only two-thirds of the working days in the year, it isn't likely that men are not employed in the breakers because of the inability of the companies to secure men to work in the mines. I quite agree—and I want to be fair about this matter—that men are not as suitable, they are not as well equipped to pick slate as boys. Boys are employed because they are nimble; a man would not work in a breaker; it is work entirely unsuited to him; a boy will work there; and a very large number of the accidents are due to the fact that the boys do run about, that they won't sit constantly at their employment, that at every opportunity that offers itself they want to play, and why wouldn't they? That is why we want this age limit raised, so that the boys may play before they go to the breaker.

"There has been a decided improvement in the conditions of child labor in the anthracite coal fields. Whether that improvement has come about because of the high motives or humane promptings of the coal companies or not, I am not going to say, but I will make this statement: That prior to the advent of the miners' union, there was no effort made to regulate the employment of children; prior to the year 1900, when the coal miners in the anthracite fields first engaged in a strike, there were no adequate laws regulating the employment of these boys, and the men are legion in Pennsylvania who started to work in the breakers when they were eight years of age. There are hundreds of boys of eighteen and twenty years of age there now, who started to work at ten and twelve. The age limit has gradually been raised; it has raised because of increasing intelligence, because of the Americanization of these non-English speaking people, because of the promptings of humanity, but particularly because of the education and influence of the miners' union.

"In justice to the anthracite coal companies I want to say, and I do it gladly, that when the law enacted in 1903, I believe that was the year, which fixed the age limit at which boys might be employed at fourteen and sixteen, was declared to be unconstitutional, the coal companies through their presidents issued orders that the provisions of the law should be continued in force anyway, and they were in most instances continued in force until a new law was enacted. The new law provided that the boys might not be employed in the breakers at less than fourteen years of age, or down in the mines at less than sixteen years of age, but also provided that they must have a certificate from the schools showing they had received a certain amount of education. The coal companies contested that feature of the law, however, and the section fixing an educational qualification was declared to be unconstitutional, so that, notwithstanding the high age limit, it seems to me that they might have left uncontested the law which provided for the educational qualification, because after all it is just as necessary to the future of our American citizenship that men shall be strong mentally as well as physically—that they shall have a reasonable education as well as a strong and robust physique.

"The men employed in the anthracite coal mines constitute only one-half of the miners in Pennsylvania. There are about 150,000 bituminous coal miners in that State, and I presume the children of the bituminous coal miners are about as numerous as are the children of the anthracite miners. The boys may enter the bituminous mines when they are twelve years of age. There is no law that prohibits the employment in the bituminous mine of children above the age of twelve. The only requirement, however, is that the boy of twelve must work with his parents or with a guardian, and inasmuch as there is no employment in the bituminous mines for a boy outside, as there is in the anthracite field, it means that all the boys in the bituminous districts must go down in the ground; they must spend their lives in the earth, not on it; and it seems to me that some law should be enacted for the protection of the sons of the bituminous miner."

ELLISON A. SMYTH, President of the South Carolina Cotton Manufacturers' Association, who has been engaged in the cotton mill industry in that State for the past twenty-five years, stated that "it has been a matter of surprise to those of us in South Carolina who have been trying for twenty years to better the conditions of the working people there, to be antagonized as we have been by the Child Labor Committee." He said that "the statements that they have made and published are so glaringly incorrect that they have excited ridicule and a feeling of antagonism that otherwise would not have existed." Referring to some of these statements Captain Smyth said:

"For instance, there is a statement published by the Child Labor Committee—a general advertisement—in *The Outlook* of November 17, 1906, which says: 'Sixty thousand little children toil in Southern cotton mills; little girls eight years old work through a twelve-hour night.' Now, there are nine million spindles in all the Southern States. The children work in the spinning room. The spinners are paid so much for each number of sides of a spinning frame they run, and every spinning frame has two sides, and a fair average would be one hundred spindles to the side. If you take these figures you will find that not over 15,000 people could be employed in the spinning rooms as spinners, as a spinner will attend anywhere from six to ten sides, and some as much as twelve sides. What I mean by the 'side' of the spinning frame is attending to the spindles arranged along one side of the spinning frame.

"In the census figures of 1905 the statement is given by the officials that in South Carolina there are employed under sixteen years of age—the advertisement referred to says fourteen years—there were employed 9,769 children in all gainful occupations, including those on farms. We have in South Carolina 3,500,000 spindles, over one-third of what are in the Southern States. If you multiply the 9,700, taking that as a figure, and granting that they are all in Southern cotton mills (whereas these figures include children in all gainful occupations, agricultural and otherwise), but assuming that they are all in the cotton mills, you cannot muster over 30,000 in all the Southern States, and yet here is an advertisement which goes out stating that there are 60,000 children working twelve hours a night.

"Now, I happen to be President of the Association of South Carolina Cotton Manufacturers, and we have 110 mills in that Association, representing 3,250,000 spindles, nearly the whole number of spindles in the State. There are only three mills of that 110 that work at night or have worked at night for years. The weaving mills do not work at night. There are only eight spinning mills in South Carolina, and three of them work at night; but the only rooms that they run are the twisting rooms where adult labor is employed and not children. They only work nine hours at night and receive pay for a full day's work.

"Now, Mr. Lovejoy says, in a statement here that was published in *The Independent*—"Child Labor and Family Disintegration"—he says there are Southern cotton mills in which parents sign contracts to send all their children to work upon reaching a certain age. Now, that happens to apply to me individually. Why wasn't he fair enough to make a further statement and give all the facts? What is the contract? 'I (the parent) agree that all children, members of my family between the ages five and twelve years shall enter the school maintained by the Pelzer Company and shall attend every school day during the school session unless prevented by sickness or other unavoidable causes, but all children, members of my family above twelve years of age shall work in the mill and shall not be excused from service therein without the consent of the superintendent for good cause." Now, what are the conditions? That contract dates from 1892. South Carolina to-day has no compulsory school law. South Carolina had no child labor law until 1902. The most of our help that have come into the Southern cotton mills have come from the North Carolina mountains, and the backwoods where they had no school facilities at all. The effect of that contract was to force a compulsory school education upon the children of our mill operatives and to limit the age at which they went to work at twelve years. That was done in 1892, and to-day there is no law in South Carolina affecting compulsory education, and there has been no child labor law until 1902 and which now applies to twelve years of age.

"A committee of South Carolina manufacturers took part in and prepared the labor law that is now in existence in South Carolina and was passed in 1892, and a similar committee of South Carolina manufacturers in 1902 prepared a child labor law that is now in existence in South Carolina and was passed by their advocacy. Now, the National Child Labor Committee took no notice of all those facts, and John Spargo tells us in his book, on the authority of Dr. McKelway, Assistant Secretary of the Child Labor Committee in the South, that Southern mills have adjustable legs or supports to the spinning frames, so that they can be lowered nearer the ground for little children. A more ridiculous and silly mis-statement was never thought of or suggested. The whole cotton mill machinery has to be as rigid as possible. Our floors are four inches thick, with a ceiling of seven-eighths of an inch below and upper floors an inch-and-a-quarter above, the idea being to make as stiff a floor as possible, so that those spinning frames that are running eight to ten thousand revolutions a minute should have a firm foundation and not affect the steadiness of the machinery. It would be absolutely impossible to have an adjustable spinning frame so that legs could be moved up and down; such a thing has never been done, never been seen, never been attempted, and yet that statement was made on the authority of a man who was in the South and is supposed to know and ought to know.

"There has been a great talk and cry about the number of children employed in Southern cotton mills, and when that law went into effect in 1902 in all the cotton mills in South Carolina there were only 53 children that were debarred from working on account of their age. In 1902 our committee of cotton mill manufacturers prepared a very careful statement of statistics as to the schools maintained by the cotton mill corporations. In South Carolina our public school system does not permit—the money raised does not permit—of schools being maintained more than four months in the year. The reason of that is that the white man there has the black man to carry. There are more colored people in South Carolina than there are white. The taxes are paid by the white people and the school fund is divided equally and fairly in proportion to their attendance on the schools. The white man is educating the negro children and he is paying for it and as a result he is unable to give to his own children the full length of time that he would do if his money all went to educate the white children. Now, the cotton mills have their own schools. Those statistics were gathered in 65 corporations in South Carolina. They show that $175,000 have been spent by those mills in school buildings and equipments and that there were 7,433 children in attendance on those mill schools. In some villages children are paid money to attend these schools, they get regular pay envelopes just as if they were working in the cotton mills every month if they do not miss a day at school. Those schools run from eight to nine months in the year and the cost of maintaining those schools amounts to between $25,000 and $30,000 a year, all paid by the cotton mill corporations in addition to special school tax of over $40,000.

"We don't want the children in the mills; it is not economical labor; it is not desirable from any standpoint, apart from any humanitarian feeling on the subject, it does not pay. But our conditions down there are peculiar. We work entirely according to what is called the family system, family help. It is not like in New England where the individual is employed, but a man will agree to hire himself and his family, and if you are not willing to employ his family or give them employment, he will go where he can get it; and for the last three or four years labor has been so scarce, the development of the cotton mill industry has been so rapid, that labor has been very scarce, and no one knows that better than the cotton mill operative and that he can go where he can get employment. That very often forces you to employ a child that is twelve years of age, whom otherwise you would not want, because if you do not take the family they will go to another village where they can be employed.

"Now, our association—that is, the South Carolina Cotton Mill Manufacturers' Association—while in our State we had a law of sixty-six hours a week, we voluntarily reduced in the mills of that association—110 mills—last July the hours of labor to sixty-four and fixed the period when they are going to reduce it to sixty-two and then to sixty. We are doing that in the absence of any demand or request of our employes and in response to no supplication or application or notice from labor organizations, because in the cotton mills of South Carolina there are no labor organizations. This movement is being carried on entirely by the mill managers, because they believe that they will get better results and that it will be better for their people, better for the employes, better for all concerned. It will not come at once, but it was thought it would be better and fairer for both sides that the movement should be gradual and a few months apart instead of being rapidly taken all at once."

J. G. SCHONFARBER, of the Maryland Bureau of Statistics and Information, stated that most of the capital invested in the South in the cotton industry is from the North. "You will remember," he said, "that the Eastern capitalists laid the foundation of great fortunes in the slave trade many years ago, and afterward became Abolitionists. You will also remember that the immense cotton industries of the New England States have been fostered very largely by the employment of cheap child labor. The quickening of the public conscience in the East has abolished the employment of children under fourteen years, and for this and various other reasons the same capitalists have now gone South to exploit that section and avail themselves of the profits to be derived from the employment of children where no laws as strict as those of the East are in existence. We should also remember, in discussing and legislating on this subject, that the South is just now awakening from its industrial inactivity, and that restrictive laws as drastic as those in the Eastern States will retard her progress."

ANNA B. BROWN, Vice-Chairman of the Child Labor Committee of the Tennessee Federation of Women's Clubs, told of her experiences in visiting a number of the cotton mills in the Southern States. From her observation she concluded that: "Unless the States I visited and their churches do more than they have done and are doing for the people in their borders, the educational, industrial and moral redemption of the 'poor whites' and the classes from which mill operatives are drawn will depend for the next twenty-five years, as it depends now, on the Southern cotton mills. Long before we club women, and unions, and labor leagues, and philanthropists plunged into the child labor question, the mill men were already settling it. They are emancipating the children, they are doing it slowly, but they are doing it surely."

D. A. TOMPKINS, formerly a member of the United States Industrial Commission and at present a prominent cotton mill owner, as well as manufacturer of cotton mill machinery, of North Carolina, spoke with special reference to that phase of the child labor subject which relates to the cotton mills of the South. He said in part:

"It is important that some of the antecedent conditions in the South should be understood in order that we may appreciate those in existence to-day. You all know that the end of the Civil War was a calamity for the South, although the most thoughtful Southern people do not believe that the calamity was unalloyed for it ended the institution of slavery, and if the poverty that came were a calamity, the abolition of slavery was in turn a sufficient benefit to balance it; but few realize that the subsequent period of so-called 'reconstruction' was a calamity such as never before was borne by a Christian people. During the twenty years succeeding the war, while the white people sacrificed all else in the fight for Christian civilization, there was absolute poverty for everybody. Every man, woman and child in the South was a veteran of the war.

"The beginning of the cotton mill construction was the end of that desperate poverty, and that beneficent work affected not only the owner, but the operative and the farmer. The cotton mills increased the price of cotton for the farmer and removed the competition of the 'croppers,' who are now operatives in the mills. Through the establishment of this industry came the amelioration of the conditions of all the people of the South. It was not a question of who shall work, but how 'hog and hominy' or 'bacon and greens' might be secured for all to live upon. The effort to help the operatives began at a time when everybody in the South was absolutely on the same level of poverty.

"Immediately after the reconstruction anarchy was ended, and the man on horseback who led, or the one who undertook to build the cotton factory, was simply put forward because he was the right man for the place, and frequently without his consent, to help do the most promising thing for the benefit of the people and the country. The warm ties of friendship generated during the period of reconstruction made every man desirous of doing as much for his operatives as for himself.

"In this work of real reconstruction there came help from unexpected sources. It is to the eternal credit of the New England machinery builders that they gave liberal and long credit to the South which enabled us to make a beginning which has resulted in an industrial development to be brought to a still larger growth for the infinite benefit of the humanity of the South and the Nation. The interest in each other's welfare which was generated during the period of dire distress led the new mill owners among their first undertakings to provide for the education of the operatives by the erection of schools in conjunction with the homes in the mill communities.

"Having established or extended schools, having worked year after year for a compulsory education law, having increased wages fifty to seventy-five per cent, and having brought what to us in the South is great prosperity out of conditions of deepest poverty, through methods which have secured the black man an equal opportunity, we believe that every Southern cotton mill man is doing his utmost to bring about that condition which will enable the limitation of work for profit only for children to fifteen years of age at least. It is not believed that we should undertake to do it arbitrarily, but by continually building up the educational, social and financial forces.

"As long as there are greedy men we must protect children from overwork, but light work in my opinion is not bad for children. In Germany they take a child of ten years and determine its education with reference to the industrial pursuits to be followed; not at twelve, fourteen, or fifteen, but at ten years, and I believe the Germans are correct in their ideas about the proper way to educate children.

"I am engaged in cotton manufacture and machine business. In the latter I have adopted a system of apprenticeship where we particularly desire to have the boy begin at twelve years, for the purpose of education, not for profitable employment. Our apprenticeship contract requires that the boy shall go to school six months in the year, work in the machine shop four months, and we are considering placing in the contract the requirement that he must spend one month of the year in the country, the expense for his board to be borne by our company where the parents are unable to afford it.

"Whatever we do in the way of legislation against child labor for profit, let us not forget that we have a large duty to see that the child when legislated out of the mill shall not be left wholly idle and untrained, but be mindful to provide enough work in school and in some apprenticeship condition to develop a decently trained and educated man or woman. With these conditions I favor raising the age limit of labor for profit to fifteen or sixteen years, but work in the capacity of apprentice for industrial training should begin earlier. I have thought of a graded schedule of apprenticeship work and school attendance, which might well be authorized and controlled by law, for boys and girls in textile pursuits: From 11 to 12 years, three months work in a textile factory may be allowed, but only after an attendance at school of six months; from 12 to 13 years, four months work in a textile factory may be allowed, but only after an attendance at school of four months; from 13 to 14 years, five months work in a textile factory may be allowed, but only after an attendance at school of four months; from 14 to 15 years, seven months work in a textile factory may be allowed, but only after attendance at school three months; from 15 to 16 years, ten months work in a textile factory, but only after attendance at school for two months. This would include official inspection provided by law.

"Instead of enacting laws which totally expel children from that training so essential to their better development as men and women, let us leave the way open for both teaching and training. It is in the period of childhood, I think, that the faculty of mental and physical development may be made most fruitful of permanent results. Very frequently mothers appeal to me to take their boys into our shop when they are too old to make them of any value to us. It is the contact with the actual working conditions,—daily elbow-touch with working humanity, in their early years which is of value in their training. The young apprentice's work in our shop consists in waiting upon the machinists—he gets waste for them, and takes their tools to the blacksmith shop for repair, and does other light work, which secures for him an education through practical contact such as could not otherwise be obtained.

"Weaving is an art and can be carried as high as any of the arts, and it is familiarity with the process of manufacture from very early years which makes the skilled artisan. Why, then, should we legislate in a way which is likely to become too sumptuary and interfere with the higher development of the art? It matters not that a picture has been published recently of a loom showing a bedraggled child operating it, when no child ever did work at a loom, either in this or any other country or period. From time immemorial it has been the custom in the family for the young unmarried women to spin, and the elders to weave—that is where some of you ladies got your name of 'spinster.' To-day, as of yore, the young people do the spinning, and the elders the weaving. The children cannot weave and, therefore, the picture is totally misleading.

"But the Southern cotton mill men want you to realize that we believe that we are doing right and our utmost to raise a totally poverty-stricken country to one of prosperity for all, through constructive efforts, and that we shall continue to work for the greater improvement of conditions in the South."

JOHN GOLDEN, President of the Textile Workers of Fall River, related some of his experiences on a visit to the Southern cotton mills some four years ago, commissioned by his organization and the American Federation of Labor to study conditions there. Speaking of certain portions of the South he said: "I went into the homes of the working people; I lived with them; I went through the mills; I saw their earnings, and when any man tells me that the earnings of the Southern cotton operative are equal to the earnings in

SOME OF THE SPEAKERS AT THE FEDERATION'S SIXTH ANNUAL MEETING.

the North, I am not going to believe it, because I know they are not. And the conditions are not equal; if they were, we would have more people going there during depressions; during some of our big stoppages in the East we would have more people going down South to work; we have had a few, but the only ones that stay are those that either cannot get away or are fortunate enough to become officials.

"I want to tell you in regard to this question of child labor, that I am frank enough to admit it isn't confined to the South alone. There is a lot of it down there. I think the question of whether it does exist has gone beyond the debating stage. We have some of it in the North and East. In spite of many of our humane and progressive labor laws, we have it in Massachusetts, my home State, because I have seen it there. That is mostly on account of the lack of efficient factory inspectorship, the appointing of men as factory inspectors who know nothing about mill conditions, and who are very often appointed to pay off some political debt. It is no use whatever in passing any kind of factory laws, no matter of what humane character they may be, if you do not put in men to enforce them after they are passed. Such is not the case, I regret to say, at the present time in many of our States."

SAMUEL GOMPERS, President of the American Federation of Labor, spoke briefly on child labor conditions with special reference to the South. He related instances concerning investigations of conditions in that section, stating that one of labor's representatives, who went into one of the towns of Mississippi to investigate conditions of the cotton mill operatives, was informed that unless he left the State summarily he would be escorted out by the police, and in fact, he was accompanied on his way beyond the borders of the State by a representative of the city government.

"I know, too," said Mr. Gompers, "that there was pending in the South Carolina Legislature a bill to limit the hours of labor and also to restrict the age of children in the cotton mills of that State, and I have been informed that the resolution of the Cotton Manufacturers' Association of South Carolina to 'voluntarily' limit the hours of labor of children to sixty-six per week was done as an offset to prevent the enactment by the Legislature of that State of a sixty-hour law. The people of Alabama secured the enactment of a law limiting the labor of children to sixty hours per week. In 1895, during a visit to the State, I learned that the Legislature just a day before I arrived in Alabama, repealed the law, and it was plainly stated that it was done for the purpose of inviting the capital of the North, of Massachusetts, to come into Alabama. It seems to me that the very reason given is a condemnation of that repeal. The idea that the State of Alabama, at the instance of its cotton manufacturers, should give them or the Northern capitalists, free play in the labor of the children of Alabama!

"This discussion will do good, and that is after all what we are trying to do. If progress is being made, and I think it is, let us accelerate it and save the children—even save a child—from exploitation and give it the opportunity of going to school and the playground and of becoming a worker, a man or a woman."

DR. J. M. WAINWRIGHT, of the Moses Taylor Hospital at Scranton, Pa., discussed "The Relation of Child Labor to Health," based upon professional experience of six years in the anthracite coal region. He expressed the belief that "our coal fields are just as healthy and happy a community as is any other industrial region in this country, and we very much resent the statement that we are behind any industrial people in the United States in anything that makes for good."

He said: "We have heard a great deal about the boys going into the mines and in a few years developing tuberculosis, dying from the Great White Plague. Now, the facts about that are well stated by Miss Lillian Brandt of the Tuberculosis Society here; she has gotten a table from the last United States Census and classifies fifty-three different occupations, and of these fifty-three, miners and quarrymen were classed together as third from the best in point of mortality from tuberculosis. The only people who have less tuberculosis among them are farmers, planters, and farm laborers, as one class; and bankers, brokers, and officials of companies in the other. There are a lot of such figures available; for instance, in the registration area of the United States, consumption causes 10.6 per cent of all deaths among miners and 16.2 per cent of all deaths among all the occupied males, so that miners are nearly one-third less than all the occupied males in point of view of mortality from consumption. In Scranton for the last ten years consumption caused only 3.37 per cent of all deaths among miners, while among all the occupied males in Scranton it has caused 9.99 per cent, or three times as much.

"Another statement that has been made is that the death rate among the children in the anthracite region is worse than it is in the slums of the cities. Now, I would have felt perfectly free to contradict that statement entirely from my own superficial observation, but the facts in the case as obtained from the United States Census, comparing infant mortality in Scranton with that in other large cities, show deaths in early infancy for 100,000 to be 78.1 in New York, 94.5 in Boston, 78.94 in Philadelphia and only 56 for Scranton. Take children's diseases, measles, scarlet fever, whooping cough, diphtheria, etc.—in New York the average mortality for these diseases is 37, in Scranton 27. So that, coming down to facts, our anthracite center is not only not worse than the slums of New York, but it is much better than the slums, with Fifth Avenue, the bucolic regions of the Bronx and breezy Staten Island thrown in."

EDWIN MARKHAM, author of "The Man with the Hoe," and who has written many magazine articles of late on the subject of child labor, read extracts from a number of letters which he had received commenting upon his articles. Some of these letters, he said, are from persons who are not always heard from, that is, from the workers themselves. "I have also received a number of letters from manufacturers, from those who are employing children, and I am forced to say that the arguments which I have read in those letters are somewhat similar to the arguments that can be found in the books of record about 1820, and so on, when the great problem of child labor was a vivid fact in England. The arguments are about the same. I am told that children enjoy this work, in fact, one writer tells me that after working hours the children sometimes play leap-frog. One gentleman in Illinois has invited me to come out there and see the boys play leap-frog. Well, I am glad of that, because the boys ought to play leap-frog. That is one of their rights.

"Another point is that hardship is necessary for these boys to develop them; it brings out their best qualities. Well, there is some truth in that, and I have been pointed to the illustrious Lincoln as a type of a man who developed himself through hardship. Well, there is a great deal of truth in this hardship argument, but there is not all truth in it by any means. We need a small quantity of hardship, all of us, although we are all flying from it whenever it happens to confront us in the road. Now, we are not all Lincolns. Lincoln had that hardihood and strength of character that forced him through obstacles, but the ordinary child is not equipped with that fortitude that makes its way through obstacles. What the child needs is a proper equalization between work, play and school. No child should be idle. I have been asked whether I thought a child should be coddled and deprived of work. I think a small quantity of work for a small quantity of humanity is very good.

"I am also told that the use of child labor is necessary on account of the necessity, the hard necessity, of trade; that the competitive struggle demands the child, for without him many important industries would languish and possibly go to pieces. This certainly is a serious problem, and for that reason it seems necessary that there should be a national law established in order not to hinder and hamper our national progress.

"The children are the seed corn of the nation, and it was Jefferson Davis himself who announced to his compeers 'we must not grind the seed corn.' The State has a right in this matter because the interests of the State are concerned. Of course, you know that amongst the Greeks the idea of the State took the very first importance, in fact, among the Spartans that position, that the interests of the State were absolutely supreme, took such a definite and sovereign position that they assumed the right even to destroy defective children. In our democracy we do not take so radical a view, but still the same principle holds. It is the opinion of the best thinkers since the beginning of Government that the State has a right to perpetuate its own life, and in saving the children from undue work—work coming upon them at a time when they are simply developing to become citizens—the State is only taking that right which has been accorded to her by the best thinkers of the race."

JAMES H. TORREY, one of the representatives of the anthracite operators before the Coal Strike Commission of 1902, referred to "some statements with reference to child labor in the anthracite region just made by Mr. Mitchell" as being likely "to convey an erroneous impression." He stated that "Mr. Mitchell's claim that prior to the advent of the miners' union and the strike of 1900 there was no effort to regulate the employment of children, is very wide of the mark." Mr. Torrey then reviewed in some detail the various enactments by the Assembly of Pennsylvania since 1891 regarding the employment of children in the anthracite industry previous to the entrance into the region of the United Mine Workers of America. The act of 1891, known as the Mine Ventilation Act, forbade "the employment of any boy under fourteen years or any woman or girl of any age inside the mines, or of any boy under the age of twelve years, or any woman or girl in or about the outside structures or workings of the colliery."

Mr. Torrey referred to the testimony regarding child labor presented before the Anthracite Coal Strike Commission, stating that the gist of the testimony "was to the effect that there was no effort upon the part of the operators to evade the law and that so far as it was not properly enforced and respected it was mainly due to the fact that parents themselves gave false certificates as to the ages of their children for the purpose of securing the benefit of their wages. The cases of the employment of children in the anthracite region which presented the greatest hardship and appealed most strongly to the commission were those where they were employed in silk mills, knitting mills, and other industries which have located in great numbers in the anthracite region for the purpose of securing the benefit of the abundant and cheap labor there to be found." As showing the attitude of the anthracite operators with reference to this matter Mr. Torrey made the following statement by their authority during the sitting of the commission in Philadelphia in January, 1903: "There has been some agitation of this child labor question. It has been up a good many times. There has been some consultation among the attorneys for the operators, and I am authorized to state for all the operators, so far as they could be consulted, and I think it includes them all, that we will heartily recommend and co-operate in any effort to have a law passed forbidding the employment of any children under sixteen years in the bituminous or anthracite coal regions of Pennsylvania." He stated further that through the efforts of the operators there was introduced in the legislature of 1903 a measure which carried out the spirit of this proposition.

"This act," he said, "was attacked in the bituminous regions, and was held to be unconstitutional because two acts of Assembly were amended by one enactment. Nevertheless, the anthracite operators continued, so far as was in their power, to enforce the act according to its letter and spirit."

The act of 1905 relating to child labor, which applied solely to the anthracite region, increased the age at which boys might be employed in the anthracite mines to sixteen years for those inside and fourteen for those outside. "Probably by an inadvertence," said Mr. Torrey, "this act required that every minor employed in or about the mines should be required to furnish an employment certificate and in order to secure an employment certificate certain educational qualifications were required. The effect of this provision, if it had been enforced, would have been to require the operators, under severe penalties, to turn out of their employ all boys between the ages of sixteen and twenty-one who had no education, and thereafter refuse to employ any such. The constitutionality of the act was successfully attacked in the anthracite regions because it required different degrees of educational qualifications for different classes of miners who were practically in the same position."

Replying to Mr. Mitchell's denial of the scarcity of labor in the anthracite region, and his allegation that the record of 1906 will show not more than two hundred days' work, Mr. Torrey stated it to be of such common knowledge and universal complaint, that it is practically impossible to secure men enough to fully operate the mines, that it would appear very strange to any one familiar with the situation that it should be seriously questioned. "There was a six weeks' suspension," he said, "decreed by the union in the spring, covering the period required for it to consent to a continuance of the conditions imposed by the strike commission's award, and the usual number of holidays have been observed by them; otherwise, work has been as continuous and uninterrupted as the conditions and transportation facilities would permit."

EDGAR T. DAVIES, Chief of the Illinois Department of Factory Inspectors, in a letter, stated that 'there is very little child labor in the industrial field in Illinois at the present time; there was considerable under the old child labor law. We have in Illinois what is considered an excellent law. It is quite different from the laws of other States, and applies not only to manufacturing institutions but also to stores, offices, laundries, mercantile establishments, coal mines, concert halls, bowling alleys, theaters and places of amusement. The policy of prosecuting defendants under the law, which has succeeded one of moral suasion, has resulted in a wonderfully increased school attendance and has reduced child labor eighty per cent in three years."

J. C. DELANEY, Chief of the Pennsylvania Department of Factory Inspection, in a letter, stated that "so far as Pennsylvania is concerned, the evils of child labor are not now and I doubt if they ever were so bad as they have been painted." He presented statistics for Philadelphia and Berks counties, comparing 1906 with 1905 as regards minor employes under sixteen years of age, Philadelphia showing a decrease of 6,394, or 34 per cent, and Berks county a decrease of 906, or 30 per cent. "This decrease," he said, "is not to be charged against or credited to industrial decline, for such has not been the fact. It is a direct result of several things working together to the same good end. They are the raising of the minimum age from thirteen to fourteen years by the Legislature of 1905; the vigorous enforcement of the law by the Department of Factory Inspection, and the passing out of the class of 'under sixteen' to 'over sixteen' of a large percentage of minor employes."

VIEWS OF EXPERTS ON DISTRIBUTION OF IMMIGRANTS.

SOME CLAIM THE PROBLEM IS BEING SOLVED THROUGH ECONOMIC LAWS, WHILE OTHERS SUGGEST REMEDIES FOR THE IMPROVEMENT OF CONDITIONS.

FOLLOWING the afternoon session and preceding the dinner on December 12 a special meeting of the Executive Committee of the Immigration Department was held at the Park Avenue Hotel. The special topic for discussion was "Distribution of Immigrants," which many students, lecturers, writers, and practical men of affairs have been emphasizing the past several years as being the crucial question in a proper solution of the immigration problem. Dr. Leander T. Chamberlain, First Vice-President of the Department, presided.

THOMAS W. SLOCUM, Chairman of the Department's Committee on Supply and Demand, was the first speaker. Among other things, he stated that if by any possible way we can direct our immigrants into those sections of the country where they are most needed and away from the congested centers, it would be a step in the right direction. Continuing, he said:

"Within the last year 1,025,000 immigrants came to this country. Of that number, I think 788,000, or practically eight-tenths, came into the port of New York. The best way to settle the matter of having so many immigrants in New York is to do it in the Irish way; the best way to get immigrants out of New York City is not to bring them in; but how are you going to attract immigrants to some other port when eight-tenths of the immigrants last year came into this port because it was to their advantage to come here? The steamship lines made opportunities for them that no other port provided. So long as the immigrants can come here cheaper than they can go anywhere else, they are going to come here, and we have got the problem of distributing them down through the South and out through the West. When it comes to the Italian, who comes in here and can get $2 or $2.50 a day working in New York, there is not very much to tempt him to go down South or out West for less money, although the purchasing value of that money may be greater there than it is here.

"It has seemed to me that we might perhaps make some practical headway if we, representing the Civic Federation, or the Immigration branch of it, could have communication with the steamship lines with the idea of opening up ports through the South, perhaps New Orleans, Charleston, or Savannah, where we could get the immigrants into agricultural pursuits and in manufacturing towns throughout the South."

COMMISSIONER WATCHORN referred to the distribution of immigrants as being like Banquo's ghost, in that it would not down, and said that those who have discussed it in his hearing or whose writings he had read, have invariably taken the view that by delivering immigrants at a certain place and leaving them there, they have solved this problem. He did not agree with such a view. Continuing, he said:

"The thing that will distribute the immigrants on a sound and healthy basis is to establish sound and healthy industrial conditions over very much more widely extended areas. There is no use telling a man who can get $2.50 a day in a crowded city that it would be very much better for him—and perhaps insure his peace of mind, health of body and enrichment of pocket, and all that sort of thing—if he would only go West or go down South where he would get perhaps only $1.15 a day and live under his own vine and fig tree. The thing to do in the distant States in order to attract immigrants, is to offer them as good wages as they can get in New York and until that is done immigrants will continue to avoid such sections of our country. The evils must be corrected where they exist, and then the stream will naturally flow where it belongs. It is useless trying to correct an evil by indirect treatment. The evil of congestion is due to the fact that the immigrants settle where they are best off, as they think, and you will have to show them where they will be actually better off by distributing themselves, before you can induce them to seek pastures new.

"A delegation came from the South to Ellis Island a short time ago, and they told me that they wanted at least 50,000 men and women to go there; that all the industries were languishing for want of help. I said: 'Very well, there are 700 or 1,000 immigrants here now; turn yourselves loose among them and take as many as you can divert from their chosen destinations.' They spent the afternoon trying to coax them to go there, and they could not get one. Why? Because these men knew well enough from the letters they had received from their friends and relatives what they could expect to get when they arrived there. If the report can be truthfully made and duly circulated that conditions in North Carolina are as favorable as they are in Massachusetts, you will have no difficulty in getting immigrants to go to North Carolina; and until conditions are as satisfactory it is no use asking them to go there, and the suggestion that by sending them to any specially selected port as a means of distributing them I think is purely artificial."

PROF. WALTER F. WILLCOX, of Cornell University, said that during the last fifteen years statements have been made frequently and with increasing emphasis that the immigrants are not properly distributed over the country. "My conclusion," he said, "is that the distribution of immigrants is not a serious problem calling for federal intervention and aid. On the contrary, the immigrants, according to the best statistical evidence, are distributing themselves adequately and satisfactorily. They are following the allurements of economic advantage presented to them and going where those advantages are greatest. If this distribution is to be changed, I agree thoroughly with Commissioner Watchorn that it should be changed by changing the conditions, and that there is no evidence that the immigrants are in serious need of additional information regarding the conditions which now exist.

"To these arguments, when presented at a recent meeting of this Department, the answer was made that there was little difference between a tendency to stagnate in cities and a tendency to be found there. To my thinking the difference is radical. If our tenement house quarters of New York and other cities are crowded with foreign born, who linger there indefinitely in a state of hopeless contentment with conditions as they are, the problem might well be deemed a serious one, but if it be true, as I contend, that the population of these sections is in a state of rapid change, the older arrivals passing on to something different, and in the majority of cases, we believe, to something better, almost or quite as fast as new arrivals crowd in, then the whole mental attitude and temper of the population is one of hope, of confidence, of courage. The difference between a stagnant slime-covered pool, the picture usually raised in one's mind by the word 'slum,' is totally unlike the picture of a lake fed at one end by a great stream but kept at the same level and sweet and fresh by the outflow of countless streams of various sizes and in various directions all around its borders. The latter, rather than the former, I believe, is the true picture of our tenement house sections."

S. A. HUGHES, of the St. Louis and San Francisco Railroad Company, speaking for his section of the country and for a solution of the distribution problem, said that in his opinion the agricultural districts offer the solution. He suggested that land propositions be placed before the immigrants before they embark, so that they may be distributed properly on the land to their best advantage and to the best interest of the community. He said further:

"I believe that the immigrants who are coming to this country, allowing you a fair quota for labor in the cities and in the industrial sections, should be attracted to the farm upon this side, and for that reason I had the pleasure of introducing last December in this convention a resolution providing that the Immigration Commissioners' hands should be so strengthened that they would increase the facilities at the South Atlantic and Gulf ports for diverting the business from Ellis Island to the unoccupied and undeveloped lands of the South and the Southwest. But this cannot be done until you have placed your representatives in foreign countries with suitable land propositions, and the question then will arise, Are we not stimulating immigration to this country? I believe that the doors of our country should be thrown open to any able-bodied man, no matter from whence he comes, so long as he is willing to live under our flag and under our constitution. Although he may be illiterate, we will educate him, barring of course Chinese coolie labor as against our American labor."

CHARLES P. NEILL, United States Commissioner of Labor, agreed with the views expressed by Commissioner Watchorn and Professor Willcox. He stated that he had recently been looking into the matter of the distribution of immigrants and that the results of his investigation thus far appeared to confirm Prof. Willcox's statements. Continuing Commissioner Neill said:

"Some good can undoubtedly be accomplished by bringing the resources and advantages of different sections of the country more directly to the attention of our immigrants who have settled on the Eastern seaboard, but we must not lose sight of the fact that the only law that can in any way influence the distribution of immigrants throughout the various parts of the United States is a fundamental economic law and not a legislative enactment. The immigrants who have come to the United States have torn themselves away from their home surroundings and life-long associations, and many of them have crossed the whole continent of Europe in addition to the Atlantic Ocean. Their purpose is largely to better their economic condition, and they are going to settle on the Eastern seaboard or in the South or the West, according as these respective sections offer them the greatest economic advantage. On the whole, they are going where they earn the largest wages. There is, of course, a certain friction that retards their perfectly free movement, but, generally speaking, any considerable difference in wages will bring immigrants from the East to the South and the West. I think what is most needed is to prevent such a large percentage of the immigrants going into the industrial pursuits instead of going on the land and developing our agricultural possibilities. What prevents this, it seems to me, is that such a large percentage of our present immigrants is without the means necessary to take up land. They cannot maintain themselves until their farms are able to support them.

"In a word, I would like to suggest that it is useless to talk about any plan to distribute immigrants, other than the single plan of offering higher wages in the places that want them than they are getting in the places that they are now, or in offering them opportunities to take up land that make the opportunities actual and really within their reach."

REFERENCE was made by Thomas F. Parker, of the South Carolina Cotton Manufacturers' Association, to the practical solution recently attempted in the State of South Carolina with regard to the distribution of immigrants by the establishment of a new line of immigrant steamers to Charleston. Mr. Parker spoke in part as follows:

"In South Carolina our wage scale is just reaching a point where we can commence to bid successfully in the world's labor market. In the last five years the wages in our State, including our mills, have advanced fully 50 per cent. The immigrants to our State for cotton mills in the past have mostly come from the native population of neighboring States. The question of immigration from abroad is very new to us.

"South Carolina is one of the first Southern States to have a Commissioner of Agriculture, Commerce and Immigration, with an appropriation from the Legislature, and his visit abroad and his return on board of the first immigration steamer, the Wittekind, to Charleston, S. C., with 475 immigrants, carefully selected abroad, has attracted considerable attention in the South. We are informed that the results so far have been thoroughly satisfactory to the North German Lloyd Line, and that the indications are that it will permanently establish a line of steamers between Hamburg and Charleston, which would be an important step, as we see it, towards the proper distribution of immigrants.

"We realize that immigrants after arriving in America will eventually drift to where wages and conditions of living are most inviting, but our State prefers selecting the immigrants abroad, and first showing them what inducements the State of South Carolina has to offer, before others talk to them, and we want to save the per capita expense of transportation charges from New York to South Carolina of from $15 to $20. Our idea is that South Carolina has a better chance of keeping permanently people landed in Charleston, than if they were landed in New York or other ports.

"There is no question in my mind that the future development of the South is dependent on immigration from abroad, and that it is time we learn how best to handle this question. Perhaps one of the principal inducements which we can offer is cheap and desirable land. Each family of foreigners that we settle and satisfy is a nucleus around which other foreigners will collect."

JAMES BRONSON REYNOLDS, as Chairman of the Department's Committee on Oriental Immigration, brought before the conference a resolution passed by his Committee authorizing an investigation regarding the economic, social and political conditions of the Chinese, Japanese and Koreans in this country. He said: "We desire to inquire what occupations the Chinese, Japanese and Koreans in this country are engaged in, what compensation they receive and what their hours of labor are. We desire in the second place to investigate their social and political relations where they are found, as is the rule, in communities by themselves. As we are probably all aware, comparatively few of them speak our language fluently, so that the laborers and trades-people of these races are limited to association with their own people. We desire to inquire into their condition under these circumstances and determine what are their actual relations to our own people. We have already inquired regarding the information now possessed on the subject, and find that little exact information is possessed by any one."

JAMES P. ARCHIBALD, Assistant Commissioner of Licenses of New York City, said that to his mind the question of distribution was the most complex phase of the entire immigration problem, and stated his belief that until some elucidation is afforded by hose most interested—the farmer, the manufacturer and the contractor—chaos will still prevail and but unsatisfactory results remain. He gave a number of cases of enforced labor in certain sections of the South, and called for measures to prevent a continuance of such conditions. Continuing he said in part:

"The cases I have here cited are absolutely true and are a fair sample of the treatment which not only illiterates receive in certain parts of the South, but men of more than ordinary intelligence are inveigled into taking these chances, and to them the suffering must be keen indeed. This state of affairs does not apply, as a rule if at all, to agricultural laborers, but does in all its baseness, brutality and deceit, to contractors in particular, to quite a number of unscrupulous manufacturers, who think that this kind of treatment is never heard of outside of the one State where it happens, and presuming upon this, in which they are grievously mistaken, they keep up those vicious practices until it not only gets into the local courts but to the Federal courts. Even President Roosevelt himself has taken notice and has appointed special commissions to stop this practice of peonage in the very localities referred to, many convictions for which have been recently obtained and salutary punishment of both imprisonment and fines has been justly inflicted.

"Thus it is necessary, if those who love the South would develop its great resources, to be satisfied for the time being with less profit on their commercial enterprises, and devise ways and means of bringing the alien closer to the land—the land at present out of use—to give the immigrants a reasonable chance to establish homes and enable them to look into the future and see something in it for them and their offspring. No man will pay from $8.00 to $15.00 for transportation to the sunny South, undergo estrangement from family and friends and be subjected to almost inhuman treatment for $1.25 per diem while there are $2.00 per day and over right here in New York City, where at present there is being spent over four hundred millions of dollars in enterprises of public and private utilities, and where a greater demand for unskilled labor than can be supplied has existed for the past two years."

A REVIEW OF THE CIVIC FEDERATION'S ACTIVITIES.

THE WORK OF THE DIFFERENT DEPARTMENTS SUMMARIZED AND ITS SERVICES COMMENDED BY DISTINGUISHED MEN AT THE ANNUAL DINNER.

VICE-PRESIDENT OSCAR STRAUS presided at the dinner held at the Park Avenue Hotel on the evening of December 12. He referred to the efforts preceding the organization of the Federation in New York City in November, 1901, explaining that the lines of work were undefined and the whole plan tentative when those invited met in the rooms of the Board of Trade, so much so that it was problematical whether there would be a meeting over which to preside. The event brought forth, however, the largest representation of important labor leaders and of capital that had ever assembled in the city. Continuing Mr. Straus said:

"I think that I am not claiming too much for this organization when I say that, since the beginning of its work, a better relationship from that existing hitherto has developed between the labor leaders and the important employers of labor throughout the country. I personally feel a great indebtedness to the Federation. It has been an education to me, and whatever qualifications I may possess for the position to which I have been summoned, I owe (so far as that branch of the department's work relating to labor is concerned) to having come in closer contact with the great leaders of the industrial forces of this country.

"This evening I had one of the most prominent labor leaders of this country say to me—and I repeat his remarks in order to give you an idea of what results the work of the Federation is producing—'When you occupy your position, we feel we can come before you because we have met often before, and that you understand us and that we understand you.' This is no compliment to me; it is a compliment and it is a tribute to the work of this organization.

"Nine-tenths of the troubles between capital and labor result from misunderstanding. I heard a gentleman say this evening: 'It is unfortunate that The National Civic Federation has not been able to prevent two or three of the important strikes that have taken place during the five years of its existence.' Yes, it is unfortunate, but it has been a most fortunate thing, by reason of the existence of this Civic Federation, that many misunderstandings and strikes have been prevented of which there is no public record, but of which the Conciliation Department of the Civic Federation has knowledge and information that would surprise and gratify the community. We have learned how to assemble about the council table and to thrash out differences, and to prepare the common ground to which each side can repair for the purpose of doing everything in its power to avoid a disagreement or a rupture.

"I was told the other day: 'Why, you never can satisfy labor; if you give them eight hours to-day, next year they will want seven; if you give them five dollars a day wages this year, pretty soon they will want seven dollars.' I said: Perfectly true, for, after all, a healthy dissatisfaction, as distinguished from envious discontent, is a stimulus to our civilization. Whenever the desire for improvement is dead, our civilization is dead. For five years I lived in a country where medieval conditions prevailed and there the people were satisfied; there was a stupor of satisfaction, and there was a paralysis of energy. The government had directed to itself every power and every influence, it controlled every business, it controlled every enterprise, and instead of individual energy accomplishing anything, it was through favoritism and fawning that rights were obtained. Yes, healthy dissatisfaction, as distinguished from covetousness, is the very basis of our progress.

"How important is the promotion of industrial peace has only yesterday been illustrated. The great dynamite inventor, Nobel, who died a few years ago and who appreciated peace as perhaps no other man could, for he knew what the destruction of war meant, left an annual prize of $40,000, among a series of prizes, to be distributed to the foremost promoter of international peace; and recently that prize has been given, to the honor and credit of this country, to its chief magistrate, Theodore Roosevelt. The surest foundation for international peace is internal industrial peace, and I am sure that the example he has set in this respect, such as the examples he has set in the 'world's peace,' will have its influence in every civilized country, because in every civilized country they have the same question at issue, namely, the promotion of the good relations between the great industrial forces. And in this connection I can imagine no more important work in which any man could be engaged than the work that is embraced in the scope of The National Civic Federation."

CHARLES A. MOORE, Chairman of the Welfare Department, presented a report of the work done the past year. The Department is now composed of over two hundred and fifty employers in different industries throughout the United States. He explained that opportunities for presenting the subject of welfare work to employers and the public generally through different types of meetings have been taken advantage of the past year. One result of the plan for holding conferences of employers in the different sections of the country for the interchange of experiences to stimulate interest has been the formation in New York and Boston of local committees to promote the work in these places. The Workshop Improvement Committee of the New England Civic Federation has for its object the promotion of practical interest in the improvement of such working conditions as affect the health, comfort and convenience of employes in factories, stores and other places where labor is performed.

He said: "No coercive work will be undertaken by these local committees. The same methods as those adopted by the national Welfare Department are used. When the average employer learns of the improvements which are pertinent to his industry, he is ready to adopt such measures as will afford health and comfort to his employes. This is accomplished again through conferences and literature. Such local work will be promoted in Philadelphia, Cleveland, Pittsburg and Chicago as early as feasible."

Referring to the numerous conferences held the past year Mr. Moore said: "It is interesting to note the effect of the conferences upon our own members. I, for one, after a meeting in New York last February immediately installed proper ventilating devices for metal polishers, and I would defy anyone to-day to claim that our metal polishers are not protected from the dust attendant upon the trade. Mr. Underwood, after the conference with the Chinese Commissioners, at which conveniences for railroad men were displayed by use of the stereopticon, immediately consulted with our Department in reference to rest houses for the trainmen on his road, and he is erecting rest houses which will be far superior to any which have yet been constructed. And, again, Mr. Belmont and Mr. Vreeland, through association with us in the work, have just announced their intention of vestibuling the street-cars of New York City."

Mr. Moore referred to the special investigations carried on the past year by representatives of the Welfare Department, including the charity institutions of New York City, the conditions in Panama, cotton mill operatives in the South, the tunnel workers in New York City, etc. He stated that at the request of labor leaders and others the Department was soon to take up investigations of the tobacco, glass, and paper industries. The methods of the Department in distributing literature, plans, photographs, and architectural designs concerning welfare work were described.

In concluding his report Chairman Moore said: "Questions of such great importance, affecting wage-earners and their families, are before the country to-day that I feel the necessity of recommending the appointment of special committees to investigate and recommend what should be done to meet the needs of workers along the following specific lines: Industrial training; industrial insurance, which includes savings banks, life and accident insurance, building and loan associations, and old-age pensions; public service employes; employers' liability; deleterious trades; eating and ventilation; architecture, and sanitation of work places.

DR. LEANDER T. CHAMBERLAIN, First Vice-Chairman of the Immigration Department, presented a report of its activities the past year. As this department was organized as recently as June 29, 1906, much of the report dealt with the events leading up to its organization, an announcement of its officers, and an analysis of the purposes of its seven investigating committees. Continuing, Dr. Chamberlain said: "One important feature of the work of the Immigration Department to which attention is called was the conference held on September 24. The discussion was participated in by prominent experts whose views and presentation of facts served, partly through the wide publicity given by the press, as an educational force of importance.

"Through the efforts of the Committee on Agencies for Advancing the Welfare of Immigrants, action has been taken resulting in greater protection being thrown around the newly landed immigrant at New York City. It is believed that an effective check has been put upon the increasing number of cases where immigrants have been defrauded. We also have to report that this committee has in preparation a hand-book for immigrants, and that it has also planned to secure from the New York legislature a bill authorizing the licensing of ticket sellers and bankers who have to do with steamship transportation and in the forwarding of immigrants' money.

"The Committee on Basal Statistics has in view the drawing up of a general scheme of statistical investigation.

"The Committee on Legislation and Its Enforcement has in prospect the preparation of a digest of existing laws, departmental regulations, court decisions and department rulings concerning immigration in the United States and foreign countries.

"The Committee on Oriental Immigration has received the sanction of the Department to undertake an investigation of the economic and politico-social conditions surrounding the Chinese, Japanese, and Koreans in this country, including their actual employments, wages received, hours of labor, and their industrial and social condition generally. It is also desired to ascertain their communal relations to people of their own race, or our race, and to public officials in this country. Inquiries also are to be made regarding the effect of civic disfranchisement and ignorance of our language, customs, and laws on their social and moral condition."

ARCHBISHOP IRELAND, in his opening remarks, referred to the pleasure it had given him to be identified with the work of the Civic Federation from its earliest days, and stated that each time he assisted at one of its annual meetings he had found occasion to rejoice at its growth and at its constantly increasing influence and usefulness.

"But never before as this evening," he said, "have I realized what a great institution it is. It is really a wonderful institution. As to the great and good work of the Federation, the reports of the chairmen of committees which you have just heard have given ample evidence. Think of it! Think of how much has been done by the Welfare Department, and think not only of the physical good but of the moral good done thereby. And again our work in the Immigration Department has gone all over the world. A few months ago I was in Europe, and throughout several countries I was asked: 'Tell us something of that great immigration meeting that you had in New York; do you know anything about it?' Well, I was quite proud to be able to say I knew a great deal about it, for I was one of those who took part in that great meeting.

"I believe it is only in America such an institution is possible. And because of the fact of the Civic Federation, I am proud of my country. This fact was told to me in England and France—it is all due to our American democracy, that you can find men of every social position, employers and employes, the rich and the comparatively poor, sitting together around the same table and feeling that we are all equal before the Almighty, all children of the same God, all brothers together.

"Another reason why the Civic Federation is truly an American institution is the fact that we are ac-

Continued on page 13

THE NATIONAL
Civic Federation Review
Office: 281 Fourth Avenue, New York City
RALPH M. EASLEY, Editor

The Editor alone is responsible for any unsigned article or unquoted statement published in THE NATIONAL CIVIC FEDERATION REVIEW.

Ten Cents per Copy One Dollar per Year

PUBLISHED BY
The National Civic Federation

Activities of the National Civic Federation. This issue is appropriately given up to a bird's-eye view of the manifold activities of The National Civic Federation. In it is presented a detailed account of the sixth annual meeting of the organization; a brief report of the second annual gathering of the New England Civic Federation; an account of the Federation's remarkable conference between representatives of capital and labor and the general public held in Chicago at the residence of Mrs. Potter Palmer; and reports of addresses and lectures by officials of the different departments of the Federation before a large number of organizations in various sections of the country.

The sixth annual meeting of the Federation, held in New York City December 12 and 13, was a most remarkable and stimulating gathering. All five of the sessions, as well as the dinner held on the evening of December 12, were largely attended by representative men and women, and marked interest was manifested in the subjects discussed by well-known speakers. These subjects comprised Government by Injunction, Child Labor, Distribution of Immigrants, The Work of The National Civic Federation, and The Income and Inheritance Taxes. In addition to the educational value of these discussions, one of the most conspicuous results was the provision for the appointment of four investigating commissions—one on Child Labor, one on Government by Injunction, one on Income and Inheritance Taxes, and one on the Anti-Trust Laws. The details as to the personnel of these commissions and the plans for their investigations are now being worked out.

The importance of a Commission to inquire into the operations of the Anti-Trust laws is indicated in the fact that those engaged in various governmental relations in enforcing the statutes against combinations in restraint of trade have repeatedly emphasized the need of certain changes of law and policy. The prosecutions and verdicts and judicial decisions of the past ten years, both State and Federal, have completely established the supremacy of law over such combinations and yet, notwithstanding, there is at present a very unsatisfactory situation resulting from a strict enforcement of these laws. This condition is stated by President Roosevelt in his last message to Congress, as follows: "The actual working of our laws has shown that the effort to prohibit all combinations, good or bad, is noxious where it is not effective. * * * It is unfortunate that our present laws should forbid all combinations, instead of sharply discriminating between those combinations which do good and those combinations which do evil. * * * It is a public evil to have on the statute books a law incapable of full enforcement because judges and juries realize that its full enforcement would destroy the business of the country."

No one who reads the conflicting statements and different interpretations of conditions as regards the extent and menace of child labor in the United States, presented in this issue of THE REVIEW, will question for a moment the necessity of an impartial and thorough investigation of the actual situation. This is what the Commission on Child Labor has for its object.

Statements as to the advisability of adopting the Income and Inheritance Taxes differ almost as widely as do those regarding the status of child labor. The speakers at the Federation's annual meeting who discussed this subject, and who have justified the public attaching importance to their statements, disagreed so radically as to the desirability of enacting such laws that an impartial study of conditions by experts specially chosen for that purpose because of their qualifications was provided for.

Another pressing problem of the present day upon which there are widely-varying views is that of Government by Injunction, and the necessity for discovering the exact situation in this connection is as important as in that of the other questions referred to. The close relation of this issue to the conflict between capital and labor makes its study of particular importance.

A comprehensive view of the work of The National Civic Federation the past year was secured for the first time by members and invited guests at the annual dinner in New York City on the evening of December 12. This was presented through brief reports by officials of the different departments, showing what had been accomplished and indicating some of the plans for the coming year. The work of the Conciliation Department, as reported by Ex-Mayor Seth Low, Chairman of that Department, was particularly surprising if not startling in the impression it left on the hearers as to the great value and importance of the efforts of the Federation in preventing what promised at their beginning to be widespread strikes and industrial disturbances. Mr. Low described some of the methods of the Conciliation Department and called attention to a few of the more important cases which had been settled. As the operation of this Department precludes any public announcement of the cases brought to its attention, the greater part of its work is unknown to the public. Attention was called to the other activities of the Federation, through the reports of its Commission on Public Ownership by Chairman Ingalls; of the Department of Immigration by Vice-Chairman Chamberlain, and of the Welfare Department by Chairman Moore. The broader aspects of the Federation's work in the direction of strengthening and preserving American institutions, and in its relation to the progress of American Democracy, were touched upon by many of the speakers, including Oscar S. Straus, now Secretary of the Department of Commerce and Labor; Samuel Gompers, President of the American Federation of Labor; Archbishop Ireland of St. Paul; and Rabbi Stephen S. Wise of New York City.

Two recent events may be referred to here as emphasizing the broader aspects of the Federation's service. One is the increasing success of the Civic Federation of New England, an account of whose annual meeting is presented elsewhere in this issue. The second event is the remarkable "capital and labor" meeting at the home of Mrs. Potter Palmer in Chicago under the auspices of the Federation. In view of the fact that Chicago has been the center of long-waged industrial conflicts between capital and labor the past decade and more, this gathering of representatives of both organized employers and organized employes in that section promises well for the future.

Another view of the Federation's activities, to which attention is called in this issue, comprises lectures and addresses given in various parts of the country by officials of the organization. These lectures have proven beyond question to be a strong educational force—they supplement much of the other work of the organization and are successful in spreading its principles throughout the country.

It is not without its appropriateness at this time and in this place to call attention to the publicity feature of the Federation's activities as represented in THE REVIEW itself. Through its columns great public questions are elucidated by recognized leaders of thought and action and by the publication of reports of special investigations carried on by experts through its various departments. In these and other ways the Federation has made for itself in American national life a place of power and influence.

A new feature of these activities is emphasized in the recent organization of the Public Lecture Bureau of The National Civic Federation. Its purpose is to present to the public different views on important national questions by the best writers and speakers available, including prominent employers, financiers, University presidents, publicists, economists, representatives of the church, bar, labor organizations, etc. Addresses on a number of social and industrial topics have already been given under the auspices of this Bureau in a number of the large cities, including, among others, New York, Boston, Chicago, Philadelphia, Providence, Cleveland, and leading cities of the South; and at the present time arrangements are being made to increase the scope of the work by having prominent speakers deliver addresses on live questions in practically every large city. With the co-operation of the press of the country, which has given considerable space to the lectures delivered so far, a most important educational work is being accomplished. Among the prominent speakers so far engaged by the Bureau is Mr. W. H. Mallock of England, who recently delivered a series of lectures at the leading universities of the country on "Socialism." The speakers who are to follow Mr. Mallock will appear before commercial, religious, labor and educational organizations and institutions.

CIVIC FEDERATION'S ACTIVITIES.

Continued from page 11

customed to listen to one another and to hear men come and state different opinions. Why, if this meeting that we have witnessed to-day had taken place in any country of Europe, there would have been riot before the meeting closed. And when one man would stand up and contradict another, the other would have at once challenged him to a duel. This comes from the fact that in America we are thrown together and that we recognize the manhood of one another. Is it not worthy of America and worthy of religion to hear us all to-day asking, 'What good can we do to the little boy that is away down in some mine of Pennsylvania?' and to hear fellow laborers of that little boy and employers of that little boy say, 'We shall do the best we can for him, for we recognize in him a little brother, a future citizen of this great country.' Is it not beautiful to hear that so wide and grand are the opportunities offered to us all that one who did work as a little boy in those mines died a millionaire?

"Let us not complain that some among us become rich and millionaires. Let us not complain that there are great fortunes. Why, it is all due to America. It is America that has given such opportunities, and if some among us have minds more far-seeing and wills better controlled and more steady to grasp that opportunity, it is to his credit, as it is to the credit of the country that afforded him that opportunity. I always feel proud when I hear that in America there are great fortunes, because the men who have these great fortunes were at one time poor as the poorest among us, and it is because they live in such a great country, the country of opportunity as no other country is, that they have been able to grasp the things that make up these great fortunes. Not that I would have fortunes exercise their power to despoil others of opportunity; not that I would have them absorb the life and liberty of the nation so as to be able to play unjustly with the things in their hands; no, fair play for ever, justice always. But then, if from time to time, out of the shrubs and trees of the forest some do lift themselves higher up in the skies, let us rejoice in the fertility of the soil that gave them the sap that produced these high branches and that rich foliage and let us all see what we may do for our own good; let us not have among us a spirit of jealousy; let us all feel that we are citizens of the same nation; let the rich remember that whatever has come from the opportunities of the country and their own energy, that they are trustees before heaven for what has been placed in their hands to make the best use of it. And let those who have less remember that in a country where all would be comparatively poor, no one could ever hope to lift himself above the small position into which he was born.

"Our workmen are ambitious, hopeful of better things, and consequently are somewhat dissatisfied. It's all the result of America. In other countries they say nothing about the weary, dreary work of every day, and they are satisfied; but every American, poor and hard working as he is, to-day looks up and sees the sun shining for him as for others. He sees, in the flag held ever before him, an invitation to come forward and claim the best. It is only in America that we see workingmen proud of their dignity. But what is best of all, as some become employers and richer than others, they still remember, when they sit side by side with the employes, that they are sitting with fellow citizens and with brothers.

SETH LOW, Chairman of the Conciliation Department, stated that the Civic Federation assumed that the employers of labor and the employes both wish to do what is honorable, and that each asks for himself only what he thinks is right. "Having that belief," he said, "we believe that we can secure conciliation almost always if we can only get the parties to the dispute together in time. That is really the simple method of the Conciliation Department.

"Scarcely a month ago we were fortunate enough to be the means of bringing together two parties to a dispute which affected the welfare of an entire section of this country. It was after the strike had actually taken place, and it is a matter for congratulation on the part of the Federation that its agency was availed of to bring together both sides, neither of whom quite knew how to get together or to make the first advance. When that had been done, the dispute was settled by the parties in interest. I was told, during my recent visit to the South, that the settlement of that dispute was of literally inestimable value to that whole section of the country.

"The Conciliation Department does not do its work through the newspapers. It settles a great many strikes that are never heard of. It prevents more strikes from taking place than it settles, and altogether it is constantly working to bring about a better state of feeling in industrial circles.

"Perhaps the settlement of one strike that was prevented last spring, the manner of it and the method of it, would interest you and will illustrate, as perfectly as possible, the character of the times in which we live, and the character of the country of which we are proud to be citizens. I was at my farm forty miles north of New York, in Westchester county, when the telephone bell rang. I found myself talking to a banker in Philadelphia, who said that his firm were the representatives of a street railroad system, I think in Illinois, close to the Mississippi River; that a strike was threatened; that they were afraid the men would go out before any opportunity could be had to bring about an agreement. Could I, as chairman of the Civic Federation's Conciliation Committee, prevent that disaster? They wanted me to telegraph to the national president, who happened to live in Detroit. I said: 'What can I say? Can I say that you are ready to arbitrate?' 'Well,' he said, 'I don't know that I am quite prepared to say as much as that.' 'Well,' I said, 'may I say that I think I can bring about arbitration?' 'Yes,' he said, 'you may say that.' I called up immediately the office of the Civic Federation in New York City, and in fifteen minutes a telegram was on its way to Detroit to this national officer representing the street railway employes, somewhat to this effect: 'I learn that a strike is probable in such and such a place; I hope that it will not take place until the Civic Federation has had the chance to see whether it cannot bring about a settlement; I think arbitration will be accepted.' Instantly a dispatch in reply came back: 'You may be sure that no strike will take place until the Civic Federation has had a chance to see what it can do. If arbitration is offered on fair terms, it will be accepted.' I ask you to notice how frank, how straightforward, and how explicit, that reply was. Next morning I got my Philadelphia friend in New York City by telephone and told him of this dispatch, and I said: 'What shall I say now?'. After a little discussion it was agreed that I should telegraph, as I did, that the parties in interest here would telegraph to their local representatives to meet the men and settle if possible; that, failing a settlement, they would accept arbitration; and I asked the international officer, in case of need, to communicate with me again. In three or four days the matter was settled by mutual agreement, without any reference to the Civic Federation. I never heard of it again until Mr. Easley received a letter from both sides expressing their gratitude to the Civic Federation for its good offices.

"I never saw a man in connection with the whole business. I talked to a hole in the wall in Bedford, N. Y. The electric current carried the message to Detroit, to the place where the strike was threatened, and the whole thing was actually settled by that method, simply because The National Civic Federation existed, and uses, as the previous speakers have said, such means of getting together both employers and employes. I think that was a splendid illustration of the sort of service this institution is doing all the time; also, as I said, of the character of the times in which we live."

MELVILLE E. INGALLS, Chairman of The Federation's Public Ownership Commission, reported on the work of that body. He said in part: "As chairman of the Municipal Ownership Commission I have been spending three or four months on its work, and the remarkable thing about it is that I got interested in the work. On the committee are twenty other people, the most delightful people, busy men, men of ability, who knew what they were about. They would not postpone the results that they found on a subject, but they would settle it all up before they went to bed, and start next day on something else.

"We have examined the cities in England; we have examined gas plants, street car systems, and electric plants. We have looked into the plants in this country in the same way; and I have to say to you that those twenty gentlemen on that committee have worked harder than you could get them to work for any salary. The only trouble I have had with them was that they worked so hard and they have gone into so many details, that God alone knows when they will be ready to report. But when they do, you will get the whole history of municipal ownership in the kingdom of Great Britain and in this country and will get some facts that will be invaluable, because they have employed experts on both sides; they have had the people in favor of municipal ownership pick their experts and the people against it have selected theirs, and we have prepared questions and tried the case with those experts. We have got the true situation, I think, of the different plants throughout the country, and then we are going to boil that down into the different reports.

"We have divided off the various subjects, so that each member of the committee can do his work, and when they get through, I promise you that they will have a report that will give you valuable information, that will repay the Civic Federation for the large sum of money that they raised for the expenses of this work, for it has been very expensive. We have had to employ the highest talent in the land and it has taken a great deal of money, but the money was put up by friends, as it would not be raised in any other way, a combination of capital which has furnished the money for us, and these gentlemen on this committee have furnished the brains and done the work. All I did was to keep them good-natured and see that they did not quarrel with each other in their anxiety to get ahead, because we have had people in favor of municipal ownership and people against it. It has been a bitter fight after facts, and I believe in the end when we get through, we are going to give you practically a unanimous report upon the general principles of municipal ownership, and when we do, I believe and I hope that it will be a standard for the guidance of the municipalities of this country."

SAMUEL GOMPERS, President of the American Federation of Labor, referring to his membership in The National Civic Federation, claimed to be one of its earliest members, long before it was known as The National Civic Federation. He said:

"I had faith in the idea; I believed it was capable of accomplishing a great deal of good. It seemed to me that the Civic Federation, endeavoring to bring together men of divergent interests, could discuss the questions affecting them and the questions affecting those they represented. I would not take one laurel wreath, one bloom, one leaf from all the grandeur of the results of our united effort, but I would not have one believe that we can solve all problems of our economic life by our Civic Federation. I think that no man surrenders one jot of his opinions or of his rights in becoming attached to the Civic Federation that he holds without membership. I know of a large number of contests contemplated that the Civic Federation has avoided. I believe, though, that the greatest strength of our concerted movement lies in the fact that we strongly hold to the principles and convictions that we held before we became associated with the Civic Federation, and that our best and common interests are conserved by meeting in our Conciliation Department and by our endeavors to bring about a common understanding upon contested points.

"In my endeavor to understand the conditions of labor in the past as well as of to-day, I have come to this conclusion, that the best interests of the working people of America are subserved by their organization, and that through it they are best prepared to defend, protect, and promote the interests of the working people, recognizing at the same time the modern development of organizations of employers in their particular interests as well as in their general class interests. And further, that an organization such as this Civic Federation, composed of the militant representatives of those classes, as well as the representatives of those who are considered in that larger citizen class—those who are not interested in either the one or the other—in bringing them together has demonstrated, as the history of the Civic Federation has proven beyond cavil, that when we have met to discuss the very essence of the interests and the vital points at issue, we have usually been capable of arriving at a common ground.

"These efforts have redounded to the common welfare of all the men and women and children of labor. The industrial workers of our country make constantly increasing demands upon modern society for improved conditions, and these must be considered in the development of our economic and social life. The working people—the wage-earners of our country—are your fellow citizens and mine. They bear the responsibility of sovereignty with you and me. Upon us, as a whole, depends the future of the whole Republic. It is because of this, not only because of our desire to help the children of labor, to protect and promote the interests of the women who toil and of the men who labor, but also because of the common polity upon which the future of our Republic depends, that the organized labor movement of America bases its proposition to benefit all.

"I have an abiding faith in the people of our country and in the institutions of the United States. The Declaration of Independence and all its glowing words are not to me glittering generalities. They imbue me with all the hope I have for the future of my fellow men. They give me an impetus to all that I do and try to do. I believe that this Civic Federation, representing the great captains of industry and of commerce and of learning and of labor—and I do not mention labor last because of its least significance, but because it is the culmination of all—in its endeavor to work out our common policy and common polity is the effort to make the principles of the Declaration of Independence the very living factors of our everyday lives. And it is that hope, it is that desire founded upon experience, that has encouraged the men and women who have toiled long and hard in this work.

"I believe that as there are in the institutions of our country the great powers of energy and of initiative to conserve the common good, so the Civic Federation presents itself as the conservator of peace and progress and of the wealth and belief of our common country."

RABBI STEPHEN S. WISE expressed the hope that The National Civic Federation may become more truly national in its scope and outreaching from year to year. He argued for a standardization throughout the United States of such laws as make for the amelioration of the lot of the worker. Continuing, he said: "I rejoice in the work of The National Civic Federation because the aims of this body imply your faith in the American democracy, not as an act, not as a process, not as an achievement or consummation, but as a development, as an evolving through education.

"You, gentlemen of The National Civic Federation, are doing a great work insofar as you proclaim anew through the gospel of the Federation the message of an American prophet: 'Thy money perish, if it brutalize thy soul.' Alas! it is not the money of the land that will perish if the soul of America be brutalized; it is America itself that will perish. That money may perish, that prosperity and material greatness may disappear were not the worst of events, but greatly to be feared is the passing of the spirit of Americanism. You, gentlemen of The National Civic Federation, appear to understand, and you are seeking to bring to the American people, the essential truth that bigness is not greatness, that 'size is not grandeur, that territory does not make a nation.' Judea was only a little land, not bigger than the Hudson or Connecticut Valley. Greece was a little land, not very much bigger than are some counties in Montana or Texas. But Judea gave us Moses, and Isaiah, and Jesus, and Hillel, and Amos, and Nathan, and Elijah. And Greece gave us Homer, and Socrates, and Sophocles, and Plato, and a mighty multitude of such heroes of the spirit.

"May it be given to you further to develop and to confirm the teaching that the greatest thing in America is not its wealth, not its power, but the American spirit, the spirit of democracy, the spirit of brotherhood—that spirit of democracy which Henry Demarest Lloyd has pithily summed up in the saying: 'The development of all the resources of the land by all the faculties of man for the use of all the people.' May The National Civic Federation ever be privileged to carry this high message to every part of our land. This is a high hope, a noble mission, a great opportunity. May you be equal to it."

INCOME AND INHERITANCE TAXES DISCUSSED.

DISTINGUISHED SPEAKERS ADVOCATE AND OPPOSE THESE METHODS FOR THE DISTRIBUTION OF WEALTH.

IN opening the second day's session of the annual meeting for the discussion of the "Income and Inheritance Tax," President Belmont stated that these forms of taxation have been frequently alluded to as calculated to cure some of our existing and growing evils. "That we should have evils occurring with our national growth is natural," he said, "but it is highly important that we should not attempt to cure them with an improperly considered or wrong remedy. It must also be remembered that our people have been accustomed to and have grown up under a totally different form of taxation. The income tax and inheritance tax are both direct taxes. We are all of us accustomed to pay an unconscious tribute through the form of indirect taxation—our tariff. It is not a question as to whether the tariff is for revenue or for protection. The question is: What is our habit of thought on the subject? For that reason the sentiment with regard to direct taxation is governed frequently by a man's own feelings and habits, and not from the point of view of an economic question.

"As the short remarks I made on the subject seemed this morning in the newspaper to be more or less misinterpreted, I am saying this to you now in partial explanation of what I there intended to convey.

"No one likes the direct tax in this country, and, therefore, in speaking of it, one always refers to it as a form of taxation that for one reason or another is obnoxious. No one likes to have his private affairs made the subject of publication or discussion or inspection. The income tax naturally involves that, and must necessarily involve it, provided there is any difference of opinion as to whether the return is proper or not. We have experienced it. We had the income tax just after the war. We had an income tax within a few years and though that one was declared unconstitutional, many returns were made prior to that, and I personally did make my return at the time, and felt it to be a wise and perfectly proper method of taxation and one which I would be only too glad to advocate and submit to. But since that the other form, which is also in existence in various States—the inheritance tax—has been discussed by many as a method of checking the growth of large fortunes, which threaten, in the minds of some, our institutions and our general economic condition. And when I said that a wise and just method of taxation, and the solution of that in a proper manner, would be of great good to this country, I meant that punitive spoliation must not be resorted to. In other words, that those who accumulate large fortunes cannot do it dishonestly and improperly; it cannot be done; a man will finally meet his fall if such be his method; there may be isolated cases, but that is not the way the accumulation of fortunes in this great country comes about. The existing laws are complete and searching enough; the methods of reaching wrong-doers are sufficient. But that these fortunes, which it is alleged are accumulated in an improper manner all over this country, must be reduced in a punitive spirit, was what I meant should not be done. I did not mean that a tax on inheritance should not be passed, but that it should be done from the point of view of just and wise taxation and on sound economic grounds. That was all I meant to convey."

MELVILLE E. INGALLS, Chairman of the Cleveland, Cincinnati, Chicago and St. Louis Railway Company, referred to three prolific sources of multi-millionaires which are open to criticism. These, he said, were (1) the tariff, (2) illegal favors and contracts given to shippers by the railways, and (3) the production and the securing by questionable means of contracts at nominal prices for the use of the streets of various cities for the purpose of transportation and lighting, and Mr. Ingalls discussed briefly each of these sources.

Mr. Ingalls expressed his belief that the income tax "is the best and fairest tax that can be levied—a tax not for the purpose of destroying property—that would be socialistic—but for the purpose of making property pay its fair share of the burdens of the people. They will tell you that it is a tax difficult to collect, but no more than taxes on hidden or unseen property. I don't believe in a graduated income tax, for I think that would be putting a tax on thrift and energy, but each man should pay upon his income the same proportion—pay it as a tax for the protection of his property. I would tax all incomes of one thousand dollars or over and have a fixed percentage. Under a thousand dollars the income from the tax would not be enough to pay for the cost of collection.

"The inheritance tax has already been taken up by the different States, some of them with a graded tax and others with a straight tax. I am not in favor of a graded inheritance tax any more than I am of the graded income tax, but I am in favor of the inheritance tax as a tax for paying the expenses of the State like other taxes. The question is whether this is not more of a matter for each State to take up by itself and go on as they are now starting. If it cannot be managed in that way, then the national Government should take it up, and the money that is obtained from these sources will enable it to reduce the burden of taxation in places where it is advisable to do so, and will produce income which may be lost from the modification of the tariff.

"I would also enact legislation—or, if it cannot be done under the present constitution, I would get an amendment—that no man should have the right to dispose of his property by will, and that when he dies it shall be divided equally among heirs. I would take away from any citizen the right to tie up any property in trust for one life or two or more. It is simply a continuance of the old law of entail under another form and holds these immense fortunes together, when, if they were divided equally among the heirs, they would soon scatter and be harmless.

"I know that this will be criticised and people will say that if a man has children and some are weak and incompetent to handle the fortune coming to him or her, that the parents should have the right to put them in trust, but that is the very thing that perpetuates some of these large fortunes. Let them be distributed. If some of the heirs waste their inheritance, the public will gain. The property is not lost by distribution, and nothing, in my judgment, will so protect our future against large accumulations of wealth as this. It seems to be a craze with some men to perpetuate after their death the immense fortunes that they have built up, but it is not a thing that the State ought to allow.

"There is danger in the present condition of public opinion that we will drift into a hysteria that will enact legislation that will seriously hurt our business and produce disaster. Especially is this true in reference to the railways, and you must keep in mind that the railways constitute the largest business force in the country. One-fifth of all the population depends upon them for their existence, either as employes or in the business of manufacturing, or supplies, etc. And while we set our face like a stone wall against any of the illegal conditions of the past being continued, we should give them a fair chance to carry on their business in the future and thus prevent disaster to the community.

"The real menace to my mind is the Sherman anti-trust law, so-called. I happen to know that the distinguished author of this law, when it was passed, did not think it applied to the railways in their conduct of their business. In 1895 the joint traffic agreement among the trunk lines was made. I had the honor to prepare that, and it never occurred to me that there was any danger of violating the Sherman anti-trust law, and we drew the agreement so it would aid and maintain the interstate commerce law. But the Supreme Court thought otherwise, and when in 1897 they made their decision that that agreement was a conspiracy and violated the Sherman law, there was then left no power or right among the railways to contract among themselves—to agree upon rates—to sue and be sued. In other words, that decision had the effect of turning them into a sort of Pariah, with every man's hand against them, and no right to conduct their business legitimately among themselves. To-day it is necessary that there should be stable and fixed rates between points—say, between New York and Chicago—and it is necessary that they should be able to enforce those rates among themselves, and they should be allowed to meet and agree what those rates shall be, and which under the present law should be published and maintained. And yet under the construction of the courts if they should so meet and agree, it would be a conspiracy in restraint of trade and subject to fine and imprisonment under the Sherman law.

"I don't believe it is the intention of the people that this situation should exist; I don't believe it is their idea that the greatest industry in the country, employing more than a million of men, could be conducted without regard to law or in defiance of it. There should be co-operation and agreement allowed, but no unfair competition, nor any conspiracy.

"The same reasoning in many cases applies to other classes of business. Almost everything now is construed to be a trust. A trust is nothing but a combination of people for doing business more cheaply and largely. It is the evolution of the corporation; just as the corporation was the evolution of the partnership; and partnership was the evolution of the days of the shepherd when each man tended his own flock. The trust properly conducted is not the enemy of the people, and in the fanaticism of the hour it should not be condemned if properly managed. The law should be taken up and amended to suit business conditions of the twentieth century."

W. D. GUTHRIE, for whom is claimed the credit of defeating the last income tax proposition before the United States Supreme Court, referred to the recent activities for securing graduated or progressive taxation of income and inheritance successions to the property of decedents. He said: "In discussing these principal measures, it should be appreciated that if they become laws, the result, by reason of existing conditions and the general distribution of property throughout the country, will be to exempt the majority of owners of property and the great bulk of property from this form of taxation and to cast the burden upon those who constitute a very small minority of the population. It should likewise be realized that this proposed legislation, particularly as to inheritance, is conceded only a first step, and that increase in the scale is intended and is certain to follow. Indeed the President declares that 'at first a permanent national inheritance tax need not approximate, either in amount or in the extent of the increase by graduation, to what such a taxation should ultimately be.' As the States also have full power to levy similar taxes on inheritances and incomes, it must be manifest that if the scale of graduation adopted by Congress be high, the resources of the States will be correspondingly curtailed and crippled, that they may be embarrassed in securing the necessary revenue for maintaining their governments and performing their functions, and that within a very short time the national Government could appropriate a great part of the property now owned by the residents of the several States.

"The practical questions which are before us as a nation, then, are the following: Is it wise or prudent in a Republic based on universal suffrage to introduce progressive or graduated taxes as a permanent basis for taxation by Congress? Is it a legitimate function of the national Government, or within the scope of any power delegated to Congress, to regulate inheritances or fortunes or to endeavor to force a redistribution of wealth, as a means of solving social problems or lessening supposed moral evils? Ought unapportioned income taxes be levied by Congress in view of the decision of the United States Supreme Court in the income tax cases without first obtaining an amendment to the constitution authorizing such a tax?

"A graduated or progressive tax is necessarily arbitrary, for there is no definite rule or principle to apply. The rate may be reasonable at first, but will ultimately become little short of confiscation. The appetite will grow. One act of spoliation will lead to another. If twenty-five per cent of large fortunes is but a beginning, where will it stop, and who is to determine what is or is not reasonable and the limit beyond which a temporary majority shall not go? There is no limit, no power to check abuses, and we are at the mercy of the irresponsible majority if we once depart from the only safe and consistent rule, that of approximate equality."

Mr. Guthrie held as fundamentally wrong and misleading the claim that the power of our legislatures over inheritances or successions is unlimited; that the right to inherit or to dispose of property on death is not a property right, and that our lawmakers may grant or withhold the privilege at their will and discretion—the grounds upon which progressive and unequal taxation on inheritance are sometimes sought to be upheld. He claimed that the regulation of a succession to the property of decedents, and of the amount of property which any one individual or partnership or corporation may hold, are matters solely within the jurisdiction of the State and not to be interfered with or encroached upon by Congress. He did not believe that the people will ever conscientiously approve and sanction a policy which might deprive the

States of their present source of revenue and the control of the property belonging to their own residents.

As to an income tax, Mr. Guthrie said there was no doubt that any State may levy an income tax. Nor is there any doubt that Congress may levy an income tax provided it be apportioned to population.

Mr. Guthrie did not believe that the cure for existing evils was to be found in any scheme of compulsory redistribution, but rather in the effective and impartial enforcement of the penal laws, in making it dangerous to be dishonest, in severely punishing corporate and individual breach of trust and unlawful discrimination in enacting new laws whenever necessary, in amending the constitution so as to increase the powers of the national Government, but not in assault upon accumulated property or in fomenting hatred, envy and distrust of the rich. In conclusion he said:

"Our malady is not wealth but morals, want of business honesty, brutality in the fierce strife of competition, breach of trust, proneness to corruption, non-enforcement of laws, abuse of office, lack of the sense of civic duty. The breaking up of fortunes will be no cure for these evils. What we want is a re-awakening of the moral sense and a steadfast and consistent determination to enforce the laws and root out dishonesty and criminality. We need incorruptible legislators and public officials. With wealth and honest public opinion permeating the whole fabric of our civilization and demanding constant and vigorous enforcement of laws against individual and corporate dishonesty, all our schemes of legislation will be futile. We cannot make men honest by statute. In the phrase of the Roman, What are laws without morals: *quid leges sine moribus?*"

ANDREW CARNEGIE began his remarks on "The Income and Inheritance Tax" with stating his belief in the saying of Mr. Gladstone that the income tax "made a nation of liars." "There is no tax so pernicious," he said, "not only from an economic but from a moral point of view, as a tax that requires the struggling young business man, doubtful whether the bank directors will pass his note for a thousand dollars to-morrow, to explain his private affairs to some man in the community who may himself be a bank director or who is or may soon be connected with banks. It penetrates business to the core. The nation will never regret anything so much as attempting to collect a tax upon men engaged in business—bees making money for the national hive—and trying to penetrate into all the minutia of their affairs, rendering them liable to have competitors and bank directors and all other classes made cognizant of their position.

"I have always opposed the income tax. I differ with the President strongly upon that, but I am in a very different position in regard to the inheritance tax and to graduated taxation." Mr. Carnegie referred to his position on these questions as stated in his "Gospel of Wealth," written seventeen years ago, in which he advocates graduated taxation and inheritance tax as the best means of getting a better redistribution of wealth than we can by any other means.

"The term 'equality' which my friend Mr. Guthrie uses—he wants equality in everything—is not equality. If a man, a struggling workingman, struggling along at a thousand or two thousand dollars a year, and another man has one hundred thousand dollars a year, and another one million, it is a wrong use of the word 'equality' to say that they should be taxed the same. Adam Smith, an authority which I commend to you, gives us the right solution: 'It should be the object of law makers to derive from every citizen taxation for the support of government in proportion to his ability to pay.' That is the true equality."

After stating that the subject of wealth distribution will not down, and that it is obviously unequal, strangely so, Mr. Carnegie gave some detailed illustrations as to how wealth arises. In one of these wealth came to the possessor of land near New York City through the increase of population, not through ability, foresight, industry, labor. Said Mr. Carnegie: "It grew while the man slept, and probably the best thing in the world that the man could have done about it was to forget he had it; it would have grown just the same, but he might have sold it too soon if he had been thinking of it." Mr. Carnegie answered his own question, Who made that wealth? as follows: "The community, the population, the people. Then you tell me that wealth is sacred. I say that the community was the leading partner who made that wealth. It was hundreds of people, thousands of people settling around there, and we see millions who have toiled not, neither have they spun, spring forth without effort, live idle lives, and die. I am not in favor of touching the bee when he is making honey. Let the bee work, but when he passes away, then I say the silent partner, the community that made the wealth, should receive its dividend—a large proportion."

Mr. Carnegie's comment upon another illustration was to the effect that society makes a huge mistake if it ever interferes with an organizing man in his lifetime. "Such men," he said, "get very little. As a rule, a millionaire is not extravagant. A man who has made money can usually be trusted to keep it. It is more difficult to keep sometimes than to acquire, but his children are not so constituted. They have never known what it was to figure means to ends, to lead frugal lives, or to do any useful work. They are spenders, not producers of wealth."

Referring to the increase in wealth by means of the steel industry, Mr. Carnegie, mentioning one of his former partners, Mr. John Walker, who was in the audience, said: "Now, it was as plain as A, B, C that Pittsburg was the place where a ton of steel could be made cheaper than anywhere else in the world, and that young man and other young fellows—bright, intelligent fellows—took trips to Europe and saw what Britain was doing. Britain was always ahead, you know, in steel manufacture. And they copied her. They found a supply of raw materials essential. They bought up ore mines on Lake Superior. They bought up coke till they could not rest, all around them, forty thousand acres or more; gas territory by the thousand acres; everything conducive to the making of steel. This country's demands for steel increased. Well, now, who made that wealth? The growth of the American people; that's where that wealth came from, and the people are the partners in every enterprise where money is made honorably.

"And I say when these millionaires, as the time comes, lie down with their fathers, the community fails in its duty and our legislators fail in their duty if they do not exact a tremendous share, a progressive share—if he leaves little, little taken. There is no idea of ever making his children poor, nor interfering with an ordinary testamentary apportionment of his property, but these enormous sums of millions and hundreds of millions really should have a different name from what we used to call 'property.' When a man was a 'man of property,' it meant he had enough for himself and his family to live respectably upon, but now we are under changed conditions, and changed conditions require not radically different laws, but that we proceed to change our present laws to these conditions.

"It isn't the millionaire alone who creates wealth. A man who had mines in Montana and made an enormous fortune did not make the ore from which his fortune came. Who made it valuable? The community wished to use that ore, then it became worth while to take it out of the ground and he made a profit. Gentlemen, wealth is based upon the community. Where a nation does not increase in population and is not prosperous, where wealth does not accumulate you will find no millionaires, but where a nation is prosperous, as we are—a new nation, beyond precedent prosperous—there the millionaire and there only they develop."

After explaining the difference in conditions in the United States and England as to enforcing the income tax system, Mr. Carnegie concluded that in this country an income tax is impracticable and would be intensely unpopular.

"I am with the President," he continued, "in regard to a graduated tax, and a heavy graduated inheritance tax, for many reasons. One is that it belongs to the community that made most of the money, and it should come in and get its dues. The second is that excessive wealth left to children is, as a rule, injurious to the child. We don't want to grow up in this community a class whose members are not compelled to render some service to the community to justify that community in giving them all their privileges and their pleasures. There are exceptions every now and then, and here let me say that the millionaire's son who does spurn the coarse pleasures that we see so many of them indulge in and devote himself to the service of the community in any form is entitled to double honor. But we must legislate not for the exceptions, but for the general."

In concluding his remarks Mr. Carnegie said: 'I stand opposed to an income tax as the most pernicious tax that a nation could enact, but I do stand, on the other hand, believing this, that the problem of wealth will never down. The people are becoming intelligent. They see what I tell you is true, that the community makes most of the wealth, and I hope they will persist and tax heavily, by graduated taxation, every man who dies leaving behind him his millions which it was his duty to administer for the public good in his lifetime, and that they will cease to honor any man who does not regard his surplus wealth only as a sacred trust to be administered for the good of the community from which it has arisen."

E. B. WHITNEY, who represented the United States Government before the Supreme Court when the last income tax law was in litigation, followed Mr. Carnegie. He reviewed the attempts by the Federal Government to levy an income tax, and summarized the decisions of the Supreme Court in two cases. Referring to the principle of the graduated tax at the time of our Civil War, Mr. Whitney said that they did not graduate it because they wanted to cut down the large incomes, but because they thought that that made the tax more equal and more uniform. In other words, instead of levying the tax on an absolute rule of so much percentage all the way up from the bottom to the top, they tried to levy it so that the burden as actually felt by the taxpayers should be the same in either case, and that they thought it required to be graduated. When the question of its constitutionality came before the United States Supreme Court, being argued in as many as five different cases, it was decided unanimously that an income tax was constitutional, and that it should be laid on the principle of uniformity over the whole United States. But in 1894 a law, drawn exactly like that of the Civil War period, came before the Supreme Court, which held, by a majority of one, that the law that had been laid down in the first decision was bad constitutional law and that the tax was unconstitutional.

In view of the circumstances surrounding the earlier decisions of the Supreme Court on the income tax, Mr. Whitney stated that the decision in 1894 came as a surprise to the Government. He said: "Now the question is, what is the law? What will the law be if Congress shall pass an income tax statute in the future? That, of course, is going to be a very difficult question, one of the most difficult questions which the Supreme Court ever had to decide. Here are precedents in point, that were unanimous decisions of the Supreme Court, unanimous decisions under the income tax at the time of our Civil War. On the other hand there is a decision which, while not unanimous—a decision on a vote of five to four—is a more recent one. And there are circumstances connected with each that will require special consideration. There was undoubtedly an abler array of counsel in the more recent case. On the other hand, the more recent case was argued with the least opportunity for preparation, and under conditions that were the least conducive to getting the best law, and the best results. It is immensely important that the Supreme Court of the United States should not change its position on questions of constitutional law, because if it changes its position from time to time, then it is the Supreme Court that legislates and not Congress, and we no longer have the distinction between the legislative and the judicial branches of the Government."

In referring to the constitutional amendment as a remedy, Mr. Whitney said: "Do not pass a constitutional amendment like the one that has been proposed, just saying that the income tax shall be levied on the rule of uniformity or anything of that sort. The whole beauty and advantage of the United States constitution is that it deals with great principles and generalizations, and does not go into specific cases." He suggested the right way to amend the constitution is to provide that all taxes shall be uniform throughout the United States; that the present provision should be repealed, and that if there are any taxes to be levied by the States alone, and which the United States Government is not to compete in levying, those taxes should be specified.

PROFESSOR E. R. A. SELIGMAN, of Columbia University, spoke of the general position of income and inheritance taxes in a system of modern finance, and referred more particularly to some of the problems with which any creators of such a system must inevitably deal. Following the statement that "we notice everywhere in modern times, and more especially in democratic countries, an unmistakable tendency toward the adoption or further elaboration of both income and inheritance taxes," Professor Seligman referred to the experience of this and foreign countries in this direction. He believed the question with us is one of special moment because of the universal breakdown of our system of personal property tax.

He said it would be a serious mistake, in considering any question of either income or inheritance taxes, to base the argument on the proposition solely and simply that large fortunes are a menace to society. He conceived this great movement as being an attempt rather to make large wealth pay its equal share of taxation and to reach the fortunes which now virtually escape all taxation. "The only legitimate argument," he said, "on which you can base either income or inheritance taxation is that you are thereby pressing into the service of the treasury aggregations of capital which would otherwise entirely escape. From this point of view, some of the interesting questions which we must all face are these: First, ought an income or an inheritance tax be a federal tax, or should it be reserved to the States? And secondly, what are the particular dangers to be avoided in administration of each system?"

As to the income tax, Professor Seligman did not think it should be a local tax, like our general property tax, and that as far as possible it should apply to the whole country and thus render impossible much of the evasion which takes place under our local tax systems. The income tax might at least be a State tax, and preferably a national tax.

Claiming that the inheritance tax is not needed for national purposes, while in the case of the States it is needed, and needed very badly, he thought the retention by the State governments of the inheritance tax is a matter of very vital importance, and ought to be discussed in detail by any commission that might be appointed.

In referring briefly to some of the problems to be considered in connection with the income and the inheritance tax, Professor Seligman stated that if we ever have an income tax, we ought to frame it in the light of the income tax legislation in other Anglo-Saxon countries. If we are to have inheritance taxes, he said, one of the important problems that confronts the legislature is as to whether the tax ought to be assessed upon the inheritance as a whole, upon the property as such, or whether it ought to be levied upon the recipient of the particular share. Another point, he said, in which the inheritance tax does not stand alone, is the general question of graduation or progression. He said: "The problem here is, does a progressive or graduated rate in the inheritance tax imply a derogation from equality, or is it really the very sum and substance of equal taxation? It will be found, I think, that when we come down into the details of this proposition, there are very interesting arguments and much interesting experience in all countries of the world, which will tend to throw a light upon this proposition and which will lead us sooner or later to the conclusion that graduation, if carefully devised and carefully limited, is not in opposition to the principle of equality, but is rather an embodiment of that principle." These are only a few, he said, of the multiplicity of subtle points of the large number of different problems, on each one of which there is an abundant literature and a manifold experience.

THE system and methods by which the revenues are raised in the Dominion of Canada with reference to the federal power and to the provincial powers, and the place occupied in them by the income and inheritance tax, were described by Hon. George E. Foster, Ex-Minister of Finance of Canada. He explained that the income tax has been tried by only two of the provinces, and these the smaller ones, and that the amount of money received through it is very small compared with the total revenues raised. "With reference, however, to the inheritance and succession taxes," he said, "that has been adopted gradually by all the provinces, so that each province now has a succession or inheritance tax, graded and graduated in a more or less scientific or common-sense way, the exemptions varying from three thousand to ten or twenty-five thousand dollars, and the rate of tax running from one and one-fourth per cent up to ten per cent. Out of these inheritance taxes a very considerable and constantly increasing part of the revenues of the different provinces has been derived. For instance, the Province of Ontario, the premier province in the Dominion of Canada, this year will get $1,000,000 and a little more from this inheritance tax, which is a little more than one-fifth of all the revenues raised by that province outside of the Dominion's contribution."

Mr. Foster indicated the future probable course of development in Canada as regards securing revenue for the State. On this point he said in part: "There is in Canada to-day a live and growing interest in the matter of ownership, control and distribution of what we call public franchises. This has taken a more or less practical shape for the purpose of securing revenue in most of the provinces, and of late in a somewhat striking way. In Nova Scotia, for instance, with its large collieries, every ton of coal that comes to the surface pays a royalty into the provincial treasury. In British Columbia, where there are large mining areas of gold, silver, lead and copper, on the gross output of every mine there is a royalty or a tax which goes to the provincial legislature. In the Yukon district, a royalty is charged upon the output and goes to enrich the federal treasury. In the Cobalt district, the present Government of Ontario has reversed the policy of the preceding Government, which opened the whole district to the prospector and gave the claim to the individual or corporation who staked it, taxing him or it merely a nominal sum for the license and confirmation of title, and then let the possessor have all that he could make from it. The present Government has adopted the principle of reserving certain areas for competition, so that the man who wants to get it has to say to the Government in his offer what he will pay outright for the area or how much bonus he will give for it, and what royalty he will pay besides upon all that is taken out of the mine. Now, that is a radical change in policy, but a change generally approved, and it remains to be seen how it will work out. And then also, they have gone farther, and withdrawn from prospecting a certain amount of territory in which they will grant no individual license, which they are prospecting and propose to work for the benefit of the provincial treasury, either by the Government or under the control of the Government, the profits of which go to the Government.

"Now these are developments along the line of the distribution of franchises and taxation of franchises which set people thinking upon methods and possibilities still open to the State."

THE work of the State Tax Commission of Wisconsin was described by Nils P. Haugen, one of the members of that body. Among other things he said: "As a result of the recommendations of the Tax Commission, we have an inheritance tax law in Wisconsin, and we derive from it considerable revenue. It is not of very long standing, and it is impossible to say as yet what that revenue will average in the long run. We have been successful in securing for the State revenue enough to support the State government entirely independent of local taxation, which is something that has been recommended by economists as generally desirable. The revenues of the State are derived from railroad taxes, which we collect, insurance company taxes, and taxes of other public service corporations of a general character and from the present inheritance tax. I believe that there will be opposition in the States—I am pretty sure there would be in Wisconsin—to the abolition of the inheritance tax for State purposes if the imposition of a federal inheritance tax means that the States will have to abandon it. I say that because I notice the speakers on the question of an inheritance tax have confined themselves largely to a federal inheritance tax.

"Now this inheritance tax question in Wisconsin has been before our Supreme Court. A law was enacted in 1899 which imposed a tax on the inheritance as a whole. Our constitution provides that the rate of taxation shall be uniform, and that taxes shall be levied upon State property as the legislature shall prescribe. The Supreme Court held that first act unconstitutional. It levied the tax upon the inheritance as an entirety. The court said that it was a discrimination between different recipients, although they might be in the same class. It was not uniform within the class. Later, another bill was introduced which is now upon the statute books, which imposed the tax, not upon the inheritance as a whole but upon the share of each recipient. That law has been before the Supreme Court and has been sustained, although it is a graduated tax. Long before this legislation was enacted, our Supreme Court had been somewhat liberal in construing this requirement that the rate of taxation shall be uniform. It had said that it was not necessary that all property in the State should be on a uniform basis, but that all property within a certain class must be taxed on a uniform basis, and it held in the later case of the inheritance tax law that the classification, although it was a graduated tax, was reasonable. The question before the court was whether the classification was reasonable, and the courts sustained the law. So that we now have permanently on our statute books this inheritance tax law."

In speaking briefly of the income tax, Mr. Haugen said he did not know that the income tax would be any more inquisitorial if it is to be enforced than is the personal property tax. "Of course if you shut your eyes to it and do not seek to enforce it, then any system is as bad as any other, but if you try to enforce it you have to be inquisitorial even as to the personal property tax. We have before the legislature this winter, on its second passage, a constitutional amendment authorizing the enactment of a graduated income tax; that is, an income tax law is authorized and the amendment says that it may be graduated. There was some question under our constitution whether such a law would stand the test of constitutionality without some direct provision authorizing it."

A PAPER on the English income tax and its operations prepared by Alfred Mosely was read by Guy Edward Snider of the College of the City of New York. He said in part: "It is intended to tax income derived from every source in the United Kingdom as well as income from abroad received by persons residing in the United Kingdom. It can be said to be, not a single tax but a system of taxes composed of two elements, (1) a tax on income from property, and (2) a tax on income from personal service. The principal strength of the system from a fiscal point of view is found in the stoppage of the revenue at its source, and in the elasticity of the amount of revenue through adjustment of the rate. The tax forms one of the most important sources of revenue for the United Kingdom. In 1903 its total yield was thirty-eight million pounds, or twenty-nine per cent of the total revenue from taxation."

After describing its administrative machinery, the process of assessment, and the operation of the law, Mr. Snider said that the statement that the English tax is not a graduated law, that a man pays on his income from each source, aud that consequently his total income is unknown, needs modification on account of the exemptions and abatements. The tax is graduated but to the point where the abatement ceases, and when a man claims exemption or abatement, he must declare a total of his income from all sources. The paper concluded as follows: "The tax on the income of the individual as distinguished from the tax based on an income producing property forms a minor part in the so-called income tax in England. Even in the case of a tax on salaries and profits the tax is aimed at a source of income rather than at the ability of the individual. Only in the case of exemptions and abatements is there an attempt to regulate the contribution of the individual tax payer with reference to his ability to pay as indicated by the size of his income. The English income tax is based upon the sources of income; it levies on the results of industry at the source. The tax may or may not, according to the circumstances of the case, rest on the individual taxpayer. In effect it is not a tax on the income of the individual, as such; it does not select the individual as a source of revenue, measuring his burden by his ability."

M. W. MEAGHER expressed the belief that a system of graduated income and legacy tax should be adopted primarily for the purpose of preventing a few men from controlling all the wealth of the United States, and not so much for the purpose of deriving revenue. He said that the graduated income tax has been opposed by the preceding speakers on two grounds: That it would induce to lie in order to escape it, and that it would be inquisitorial. "As to the first objection," he said, "it should be borne in mind that lying under oath—which it would be in making false returns on one's income—is perjury; and that as a result of such perjury, the whole community would be defrauded by the perjured. Imprisonment and confiscation of the perjurer's property on which he made no return, or to the extent of concealment thereof by him, would effectually restrain his lying propensity." As to the second objection, that is, that the graduated income tax would be inquisitorial, Mr. Meagher said that is true of every system of taxation except the poll tax. As to the objection that the graduated income tax would remove the incentive to accumulate, Mr. Meagher said that not only should the incentive to such accumulation as is dangerous to our institutions be destroyed, but the power to do so as well. He proposed as a remedy for present conditions a maximum or limitation of wealth, fixed, established and enforced by law, coupled with a graduated income and legacy tax.

EX-GOVERNOR E. BRADFORD PRINCE of New Mexico referred briefly to the claim that the inquisitorial feature of an income tax was an almost insuperable objection. He said that the ability to aid in supporting the Government was the proper criterion for the amount of taxation and that this ability is better shown by the income which a man is receiving than in any other way. "He may have enormous quantities of property," he said, "which produce nothing and which give no present ability. It is the income which gives that immediate financial ability. And yet, while laying that down as a principle, Mr. Carnegie went on to denounce an income tax in general, on account of what he called the inquisitorial character of the information that had to be obtained in order to make an income tax effective." He said that at the present time the listing system for taxation, whereby every man has to produce a perfect list of all his personal property exists in at least thirty-five States, and that in some of the States a list of the man's real estate as well is required as a basis of his taxation.

The claim that it exposes a man's business to the risk of the community and thereby does him a sort of irreparable injury is one, Mr. Prince thought, the contemplation of which in the greater part of the United States, where they have a list system, would be found to be absolutely ridiculous and preposterous. He did not believe there was anything in the objection. He said that the inquisitorial feature was not found to be an insuperable object at the time of the old income tax in the days of the War of the Rebellion, and that no one ever heard of there being any difficulty with regard to a man's having his private matters betrayed to the general public when we really did have an income tax. He characterized this inquisitorial objection as not a practical matter, as entirely theoretical and chimerical; that it is simply a bugaboo, gives no rise to any such objection in the greater part of our country where more than half of the population lives and in seven-eighths of the area where we find that development under existing laws.

FACTS ON IMMIGRATION.

INTERESTING and valuable material on both "sides" of the much discussed question of immigration is contained in "Facts on Immigration," being a report of the proceedings of two conferences on various phases of the problem held in New York City under the auspices of The National Civic Federation.

The introduction is by Frank Julian Warne, who writes of the need for impartially investigated facts, and explains the objects and purposes of the Immigration Department of the Federation. Prescott F. Hall, Secretary of the Immigration Restriction League, discusses various phases of the legislation now pending in Congress. Nathan Bijur criticises many statistics usually accepted as representing the facts as regards immigration. Professor Walter F. Willcox, of Cornell University, analyses immigration statistics and states conclusions as regards our net gain in population through immigration which are strikingly different from those commonly accepted. John Mitchell, President of the United Mine Workers of America, presents a startling view as to the effects of immigration upon coal mine workers, and President O'Connell, of the International Association of Machinists, as vigorously outlines some of the effects among mechanics. Thomas F. Parker, President of the Monaghan Cotton Mills in South Carolina, gives a brief account of the recent experiment in that State in bringing immigrants direct to Charleston from Europe. Charles P. Neill, United States Commissioner of Labor, summarizes briefly some of the results of a recent Government investigation, and Robert Watchorn, Commissioner of Immigration at Ellis Island, gives a clear explanation of what he believes to be the best means for distributing immigrants. There are also other prominent contributors who speak authoritatively on the particular issues they discuss.

NEW ENGLAND CIVIC FEDERATION'S ANNUAL DINNER.

WORKINGMEN'S INSURANCE THE TOPIC DISCUSSED—REPORTS OF OFFICERS REVIEWING THE ACTIVITIES OF THE PAST YEAR.

OF the three general meetings held by the New England Civic Federation since its organization two years ago, that of January 10, marking its second anniversary, held at the Ford Building in Boston, was much the largest and in several respects the most significant. The spirit manifested throughout the proceedings, in which men representing all the different elements included in the Federation took an active part, led one of the guests to remark that if enthusiasm and good feeling mean more after two years of experience with a novel and peculiarly difficult experiment than at the beginning, as we all believe it does, then it is demonstrated that this movement has become a recognized and necessary factor in the industrial welfare of this section.

About three hundred members and guests were in attendance as compared with one hundred and seventy one year ago, and about one hundred and thirty-five at the opening meeting in April, 1905. Opportunity was afforded during the reception hour of meeting President Tuttle and the other officers and speakers of the evening, as well as Governor Curtis Guild, Jr., and Mayor Fitzgerald, who were the guests of honor.

PRESIDENT LUCIUS TUTTLE, in opening the regular program at eight o'clock in Ford Hall, said:

"The Civic Federation of New England appropriately marks by this large assemblage its second anniversary. Of its six hundred members, nearly two-thirds reside elsewhere than in Boston, and while the core of the movement and its main work are in Boston, this widely distributed membership gives satisfactory evidence that it has already become distinctly a New England organization with a constantly widening sphere of influence in that larger field.

"In passing, it may be of interest to note that next Saturday evening a Chicago Branch of the Civic Federation is to be organized under most favorable auspices to carry on in that city and section a work similar in character to that which you are carrying on here.

"In its every act your association has closely adhered to the principles upon which it was founded, by keeping aloof from everything in the nature of partisanship and by never attempting to interfere with the conduct of the business of any interest, whether individual or corporate, and, above all things, it has consistently and persistently refrained from attempting the arbitration of anybody's differences or contentions.

"Its work, which is always quiet and unostentatiously performed, most largely consists in bringing together the representatives of those who labor with their brains and of those who add to the work of their brains that of their hands, and thereby substituting for those wasteful and barbarous methods that are always incidents of the lockout and the strike, the more economical and humane practices of temperate discussion and peaceful negotiation.

"It proceeds upon the assumption that there is no such thing anywhere as an 'irrepressible conflict' between capital and labor, but that the differences and discords that sometimes arise between these two necessary adjuncts of the world's business and progress are nothing more or less than the upspringing of that desire, implanted from the earliest dawn of civilization in every human breast, for a betterment of his or her social and physical condition and environment; and that without this constant and unremitting struggle for individual improvement, which pervades every class of humanity, human progress would cease and civilization lose its virility and become stagnant and senile.

"It does not, however, indulge in any Utopian dreams or theories upon this phase of the world's many-sided social and humanistic problems but, on the contrary, attempts to apply to its solution only the plainest and most common-sense idea that in every disagreement arising between two parties to a common interest, neither may be wholly right or wholly wrong, and that, if the opposing interests may somehow be induced to come together for dispassionate discussion of all the questions at issue between them, each will most likely be brought to a better understanding of the whole subject, and an adjustment become possible that shall make for harmonious action and mutual fruitfulness instead of discord and friction, with the well-known troubles that always follow in their train.

"With these guiding theories, the Civic Federation began and has continued its work, and if its custom permitted, our painstaking and able secretary could give us a long list of many important instances in which his intervention for the Federation, at the crucial moment, has been potential in maintaining industrial peace, and has prevented the outbreak of contentions that would have disturbed, for periods of incalculable length, not only the dominant business of great industrial communities, but would have disastrously interfered with the personal comfort of that great host of outsiders who, under such conditions, are powerless to aid in the adjustment either of the troubles or their causes, and whose only lot seems to be that of irreparable suffering.

"With what has been done in this way during the year I have had but little personal connection, but I know of the many splendid results accomplished by our secretary, and by the members of our committees, particularly those from the side of labor. And I want to impress upon you the work done by the labor men. They have had the laboring oar, and the efforts in behalf of industrial peace have proved many times more effective than could possibly have been the case without their assistance. I know of these things, and out of the fullness of that knowledge I offer you one and all most hearty and sincere congratulations upon the rounding out of the second year of the Federation's useful existence."

LUCIUS TUTTLE,
President New England Civic Federation

JOHN MASON LITTLE, Treasurer of the Civic Federation of New England, followed President Tuttle. Mr. Little said:

"I suppose the reason that President Tuttle introduces me as the only officer to speak is that he wants you all to know me. I will tell you why I think so a little later on.

"With regard to our finances, the fiscal year ends in February, therefore all our funds are not in, possibly, but it is a great pleasure for me to say that our bills are paid to date and there is sufficient money in sight to run the association until the end of the year. The treasurer of an organization like this has to be a gentle beggar, and while I have gone about hat in hand, I have not been unmindful of certain features connected with the work. While the work has been going steadily on, and increasing, the nature of it is so quiet and unobtrusive in many respects, there is not at present an entire understanding in the community, except among you gentlemen, members of the association, and a few others, as to what it is that is accomplished. But it is an interesting feature to call attention to, that while a year ago the former treasurer collected all the money that was collected from thirty-eight individuals, your present treasurer has collected this year's funds, no larger in total amount, from more than one hundred individuals, which is a very important showing because it indicates that our money is coming in smaller quantities from a larger number, and that proves, I apprehend, that we are beginning to be better known.

"Now, gentlemen, we want all the money we can get within reason, because, while it is necessary to meet the expenses of this association, still the work can be very much enlarged if there is more money in the treasury, enough so that we shall feel perfectly comfortable. I have felt perfectly comfortable in one sense because I believed we should raise enough money, but we shall need more money and I think it will come in increasing quantities from more and more individuals as time goes on. That is the reason, perhaps, why the President introduced me, so that you will know me, and when you meet me in the street you will hand me a dollar, or five dollars, as the spirit moves. Because, as you remember, Dr. Holmes said: 'I only want a little more than I can spend.'

"I cannot sit down without saying that although the President declares this is a thankless job I do not so regard it. I consider it a great honor and privilege to do my share toward what I look upon as one of the great works of the beginning of the century."

LOUIS D. BRANDEIS spoke on "Wage-Earners' Savings, Life Insurance and Old Age Annuities," a subject of growing importance among trade unions. Mr. Brandeis said:

"The cost of living, properly considered, involves not merely the expense of supplying adequate food, shelter, clothing, education and recreation, but also such pro rata daily contribution as may be essential to provide against the contingency in the future of diminished earnings or unavoidably increased expenses. The contingency that the future may bring in the wage-earner's family extraordinary expenses or to himself non-employment, sickness or accident, premature death or ultimate superannuation, are ever present facts which must be considered, if the amount of wages to be paid and the disposition of them shall be properly determined. The expense of making such a provision should be recognized by the employer, the employes, and the public, as a fixed charge in reckoning the workingman's cost of living, just as repair and depreciation accounts of machinery are now recognized as fixed charges in the cost of manufacturing.

"In Germany, where this principle is accepted, the workingmen's future is largely provided for through paternal and socialistic measures for compulsory insurance. Compulsory thrift is not in harmony with the American ideas of individual liberty. The American spirit demands that such a provision for the future of the workingman and his family be made voluntarily and be made primarily through his own efforts. Those efforts must be directed, first, to securing wages sufficiently high to leave applicable to such purpose a surplus over the day's obvious needs, and, second, to developing the intelligent self-denial which shall induce the workingmen so to apply that surplus.

"Temporary needs in case of sickness and accident of the wage-earner are now supplied to a considerable extent through the trade unions and other voluntary associations of employes; and in such efforts individual employers have shown a readiness to aid. But adequate provision for the future demands in addition: First, the setting apart of funds which shall be immediately available to meet the proverbial 'rainy day' as in the case of non-employment or extraordinary family expense; second, insurance on the life of the wage-earner to protect the family in case of his premature death; third, an old age annuity or like provision against superannuation.

"Trade unions and other voluntary associations, whether managed wholly by employes or jointly by employers and employes, are admirably adapted for supplying temporary relief in case of sickness or accident, but they cannot be safely used as institutions for savings or to provide life insurance or old age annuities. Their management and membership is necessarily shifting; their officers are generally without the business experience requisite for the safe investment of large amounts; and they are properly without governmental supervision. Institutions which shall receive and invest workingmen's savings and provide life insurance and old age annuities demand necessarily stability of organization, continuity in management, business experience on the part of the managers, publicity of accounts, and governmental supervision.

"The need of proper institutions for workingmen's savings is now adequately supplied in New England, in New York, and in some other States by their system of incorporated savings banks, in which there are no stockholders, and which are managed wholly for the benefit of the depositors by trustees who serve without pay. The record of these savings banks, which are benevolent, quasi-public corporations, has been almost uniformly high. Huge aggregates of the small savings of millions are managed at an extraordinarily small cost. In Massachusetts, the [illegible] of assets of 180 savings banks are managed at a yearly cost of 23/100 of one per cent. In New York, [illegible] of assets are managed at a yearly cost of 28/100 of one per cent. The rate of interest earned on their investments has been such as to enable these banks to pay to depositors dividends of about 4 per cent per annum.

"The second need, proper institutions for providing workingmen with life insurance, does not exist. Pru-

HENRY ABRAHAMS, Vice-President

HAYES ROBBINS, Secretary

JOHN MASON LITTLE, Treasurer

tically the only means of obtaining life insurance open to workingmen are the industrial insurance companies, notably the Metropolitan, the Prudential, and the John Hancock companies, which issue policies in small amounts on which the premiums are collected weekly at the homes of the insured. A vast amount of such insurance has been placed. There were outstanding on January 1, 1906, 16,872,583 such policies, constituting nearly three-fourths of the level premium life insurance policies then outstanding in the United States.

"The result of this industrial insurance has been disastrous to the wage-earner. He is obliged to pay for his insurance at a rate at least double that charged to the holders of ordinary life insurance. For the early periods of the industrial policy, the rate rises to eight times that paid by the insured on ordinary life policies; since in most industrial policies, a provision is inserted that if death occurs within the first six months only one-fourth of the face of the policy will be paid, and if within the second six months after the date of the policy, only one-half of its face.

"The result to the policyholder of this system of life insurance may be illustrated from the following data, based upon the Massachusetts official reports:

"In the fifteen years ending December 31, 1905, the workingmen of Massachusetts paid to the so-called industrial life insurance companies an aggregate of $61,294,887 in premiums, and received back an aggregate of only $21,819,606. The insurance reserve arising from these premiums still held by the insurance companies does not exceed $9,838,000. It thus appears that, in addition to all the interest on invested funds, about one-half of the principal paid by the workingmen in premiums has been absorbed in the expense of conducting the business, and in dividends to the insurance companies' stockholders.

"If this $61,294,887, instead of being paid to the insurance companies, had been paid in to Massachusetts savings banks, and these depositors had withdrawn from the banks the $21,819,606 which they received from the insurance companies during the fifteen years, the balance remaining in the savings banks December 31, 1905, with the accumulated interest, would have amounted to $49,931,548.35; and this, although the savings banks would have been obliged to pay upon these increased deposits in taxes to the Commonwealth more than four times the amount which was actually paid by the insurance companies on account of this insurance.

"Perhaps the appalling sacrifice of workingmen's savings through this system of insurance can be made more clear by the following illustration:

"The average expectancy of life in the United States of a man 21 years old is, according to Meech's table of mortality, 40.25 years. In other words, take any large number of men who are 21 years old, and the average age which they will reach is 61¼ years.

"If a man, beginning with his twenty-first birthday, pays throughout life fifty cents a week into Massachusetts savings banks, and allows these deposits to accumulate for his family, the survivors will, in case of his death at this average age of 61¼ years, inherit $2,265.90, if an interest rate of 3½ per cent a year is maintained.

"If this same man should, beginning at age 21, pay throughout his life the fifty cents a week to the Prudential Insurance Company as premiums on a so-called 'industrial' life policy for the benefit of his family, the survivors will be legally entitled to receive, upon his death at the age of 61¼ years, only $820.

"If this same man, having made his weekly deposits in a savings bank for twenty years, should then conclude to discontinue his weekly payments and withdraw the money for his own benefit, he would receive $746.20. If, on the other hand, having made for twenty years such weekly payments to the Prudential Insurance Company, he should then conclude to discontinue payments and surrender his policy, he would then be legally entitled to receive only $165.

"So widely different is the probable result to the workingman if he selects the one or the other of the two classes of savings investment which are open to him.

"Obviously the present industrial insurance companies are not a proper medium through which the workingmen's need of life insurance can be provided.

"No institution whatsoever exists at present which undertakes to supply the third need of the wage-earners, to wit:—old age annuities, and yet a proper superannuation fund is being recognized as one of the greatest of his needs.

"Life insurance is but a form of saving, and life annuities but a form of insurance. The savings banks manage the aggregate funds made up of many small deposits, until such time as they shall be demanded by the depositor—the insurance company, ordinarily, until the depositor's death. The savings bank pays back to the depositor his deposit with interest, less the necessary expense of management. The insurance company in theory does the same, the difference being merely that the savings bank undertakes to repay to each individual depositor the whole of his deposit with interest; while the insurance company undertakes to pay to each member of a class the average amount (regarding the chances of life and death), so that those who do not reach the average age get more than they have deposited (including interest), and those who exceed the average age less than they have deposited (including interest).

"Savings banks, under the system prevailing in New England and New York, New Jersey and Pennsylvania, are admirably adapted for taking care, not only of savings subject to withdrawal, but for providing life insurance and old age annuities. By extending the functions of the savings banks to these new spheres of usefulness, a remedy will be supplied for the greatest of life insurance wrongs—the present system of industrial life insurance—and a solution will be found for the greatest of workingmen's problems, to wit:—the provision for old age.

"With most wage-earners, the need of life insurance ends at the time that the need for an annuity begins; workingmen require life insurance mainly when their children are young. When the children have become self-supporting, the need of life insurance ceases; and, soon after, the need of superannuation funds frequently arises.

"The savings banks have a goodwill which, if only the opportunity were afforded, would without the intervention of expensive and self-seeking solicitors quickly lead millions of their depositors to become policyholders and prospective annuitants. On the other hand, many of those seeking only insurance or annuities would be led on in the road of thrift, and open savings accounts also.

"If life insurance and old age annuities are furnished under the favorable conditions of low expense rate under which these savings banks operate, small regular payments commenced early and persisted in would suffice to provide the workingman with life insurance during middle age and a reasonable annuity when old age overtakes him. For instance, payments of a little more than $1 a month commenced at the age of eighteen, would be sufficient to provide life insurance to the amount of $500 up to the age of sixty and an annuity of $100 a year after the age of sixty is reached.

"Through no other means can life insurance and old age annuities be so advantageously supplied to the workingman as through savings banks. Neither any other corporations now existing or newly organized, nor the State could supply them advantageously.

"Any other corporation would lack the extensive goodwill which in the savings banks has been developed by nearly a century of noble service; would lack the established traditions of economy which pervade their organizations; and would necessarily be subject to the heavy expense entailed in organizing and establishing a new and independent business. A generation, at least, of efficient service would be required before any new Life Insurance and Annuity Corporation could develop the goodwill which is essential to securing the patronage of the working people and which the savings banks now possess and can utilize without expense.

"Nor could the functions of providing life insurance and annuities be advantageously committed to the Federal Government, the State, or to Municipalities, among many other reasons, because the insurance and annuities reserve could not be invested by any government on a basis higher than the interest it pays on its loans—perhaps 2 or 3 per cent; while the savings banks earn over 4 per cent on their investments.

"The demand for a better system of poviding workingmen's life insurance and the demand for a proper system of old age annuities are imperative. These demands will be met by extending the functions of the savings banks to these new spheres of usefulness."

IN commenting upon Mr. Brandeis's address, Henry Abrahams told of the work which the Cigar Makers' Union had carried on in the way of industrial insurance, strike and sick benefits. To this he attributes largely the success of the Union, and endorsed Mr. Brandeis's plan as an extension of this work. Mr. Abrahams told of the rise and growth of the International Cigar Makers' Union, which was organized after the Civil war and which was regarded as the finest trades union in the United States. It was in 1877 that the union began to develop strength, when the various benefit funds were first instituted that have later made the union a tower of strength. In case of sickness the members of the union got $5 a week; in case of death a sum varying from $50 to $500; when out of work $3 a week; when on strike $5 a week; when serving on committees $5 a week; in case of the death of wife $40; and the death of a widowed mother $40. A man out of work and wishing to go to another city got his railroad fare and fifty cents. In twenty-six years and two months there had been paid out under this last head, $991,777; for strike benefits, $1,092,104; for sick benefits, $2,201,266.43; for death benefits, $1,514,525.99, and for out of work benefits, $1,045,866.11, a total of $6,845,540.66. In 1880 at the Chicago convention the questions of coolie labor, prison labor and tenement house work came up for consideration and were solved by the adoption of a union label, the first union label ever adopted by a trade union body. Since then the eight-hour day had been established and a Saturday half-holiday, and the cigar makers were better paid and happier and there was less intoxication than when they worked twelve and fourteen hours a day under the old system. All the reforms in the trade, he said, had been brought about by the trade union movement.

PROFESSOR F. W. TAUSSIG of Harvard University qualified what had been said of the remarkable system of protection for the wage-earner in Germany. "It is true," he said, "that a lower rate of wages has made it necessary, but it is also true that it has accomplished wonders. It provides for the possibilities of injury, sickness and death, and if there were no other way of doing that except by the suggestion of compulsion which it carries, I should not shrink from something like a German system.

"It is also true that in this matter we must admit we Americans are singularly backward. We are a reckless race; we are a heedless race. Perhaps it goes with the optimism of the industrial strides of the country. The carelessness, both of employers and employes, is a disgrace. Furthermore, the position of ours which places the responsibility on the individual and not on the trade in general is, I think, unsound. We have done an immense amount of insurance in the classes of the well-to-do. We have done singularly little for the workingman, who must bear some fault himself in this matter. We may hope to reach a better solution than that which is given by compulsion in the older countries. Large companies should continue to increase their efforts to provide against old age and injury. The same thing is true of labor unions."

AN interesting contribution to the subject was contained in a letter from Stephen H. Rhodes, President of the John Hancock Mutual Life Insurance Company. He said: "The subject suggested as the topic of the evening is not one for controversy, since any practical movement for the protection and benefit of the wage-earner would meet with earnest sympathy from me and my associates. Any system understandingly inaugurated which would supplement my work of the last twenty-five years, which, with devotion to the interests of a purely mutual insurance company and with a previous intimate knowledge of the underlying principles of insurance, have been spent in the practical service of the wage-earner, would strongly appeal to me."

EDWARD A. MOFFETT, Secretary of the Public Ownership Commission of The National Civic Federation, stated that to his mind the subject under discussion, with the possible exception of the matter of wages and hours, was the most closely related to the welfare of the workingman. "How good, how useful it is to provide insurance upon a universal scale, as Mr. Brandeis's plan necessarily proposes, is indicated," he said, "by the great success which has attended the adoption of such ideas upon the other side of the Atlantic.

"But, as Mr. Brandeis has shown you, the plan of industrial insurance which obtains in this country today has invented itself, has proved itself unsatisfactory and unworthy; for insurance, after all, is nothing less than a social necessity. We must not only provide the means whereby we shall live, but by the same token and with the added scriptural injunction, we should always have in mind, we are also under obligation one to the other to bury our dead. In fact, I feel it would not be too much to say that in a civilized community there should be no poorhouse and no potter's field. But the plan of industrial insurance that prevails now is very much like the Indian's gun, it costs more than it comes to. Until the late insurance developments in New York, the wage-earners were very glad to have the insurance agent come to the door. Now they regard him, although he personally may be an honest fellow, with something of suspicion and distrust.

"I have been asked to state what is the sentiment—the probable sentiment—of workingmen towards this idea of life insurance by the savings banks or through them. For that part of the working class which is unorganized, certainly it would be pretty hard to speak. They hold no conventions, and mouthpiece they have not; but so far as it is my privilege to speak for organized labor, I need say no more than this: That at the Pittsburg convention of the American Federation of Labor a year ago a resolution was adopted to the effect that the United States government should provide insurance—some plan should be adopted whereby insurance should be furnished by the government and no longer by the private companies. This resolution bore no special significance, because at the time of its adoption the people of the country were at a white heat of indignation. Now, whether or not the organized workingmen of the country would prefer to drop that idea and take hold of the one so lucidly and engagingly proposed to us here to-night, would depend, in my judgment, upon what merit Mr. Brandeis's plan would show upon further development.

"Another word in conclusion. I ought to say something about the old age pensions or annuity idea. In no country is there such crying need of relief of that particular kind. In other words, in no other country does a man so quickly reach the limit of the period of his usefulness. This fact is due to several causes, chief among which is, in this country, the fact that machinery has more than in any other way displaced the delicateness and finesse of hand labor. The great demand is rather for agility and youth than for mature age and its correlative skill. People will say: 'Oh, such things have the effect of placing a discouragement on thrift. It teaches men to lean too much on that for the support which in their heyday they should lay up for themselves.'

"I will answer that in a very few words by saying to you that under our present system, in the absence of anything like an old age pension or old age annuity, workingmen fear to grow old. Stating it as mildly as I can, the average workingman who does not lose sight of his social duty, who raises a family, is not in a position to lay up for what has been poetically called 'the winter of life.' I can only hope, as I draw to a close, that the very interesting exposition which you have listened to to-night from Mr. Brandeis, and the added words of the succeeding speakers, will result in giving to the masses of this country a form of insurance—let it include an old age pension if that is possible; I should rather insist on it—whereby the accumulated premiums and usufruct of the same on the part of the working class will find a more economical and beneficial repository than these funds have heretofore found."

HAYES ROBBINS, Secretary of the Civic Federation of New England, in his report of the work accomplished the past year, said:

"It is unnecessary to repeat the detailed statement, offered in last year's report, of the objects, methods and scope of the work; all of which may be summarized to-day as accurately as when the movement was started two years ago, under the head of 'promoting better relations between employers and employes.'

"We have steadily endeavored to keep to that object, without intruding on the field of other worthy organizations or scattering our efforts and resources. We have continued in the belief that any association which begins to fulfil its possibilities of useful service in this particular field can have no lack of work to do, or occasion to make many excursions outside.

"This is not to imply that the movement is a narrow one; to treat it as such would be to defeat its very purposes. On the contrary, one of the most important factors in bringing about this better relation between employers and employes is the promoting throughout the community of a broader understanding of the many-sided industrial problem, with special reference to labor conditions; anything but a narrow task. To this end we bring into one common association men of many diverse interests and view-points—employer, labor, professional, educational, religious, civic, governmental. The object in view is definite and specific, but the methods employed must be broad and co-operative.

"This unique idea of a widely-inclusive membership rests upon an express recognition of the personal equation, as a factor of tremendous importance, far too little appreciated. Personal acquaintance among men representing so many diverse elements in the community means freer interchange of ideas and experiences, larger respect for the 'other man's' position, and a readier disposition to act from motives of reason and fairness than of narrow exclusiveness or mistaken estimates of self-interest.

"During the year we have rendered service, in one way or another, in connection with about thirty trade disputes, many of them of considerable importance. The two most significant were the teamsters' controversy in March, and the longshoremen's in September, both of which involved unusually difficult and complicated negotiations, but thanks to the co-operation of several members of the Federation resulted in satisfactory settlements. Only those closely connected with these matters realized how near this city was, in both cases, to an experience like that of four years ago; and judging from that experience it is safe to say that these two settlements alone represented a very great saving to the commercial and to the labor interests of Boston.

"The other cases with which we had something to do were in connection with street railway service, textile manufacture, electrical work, carpenters, stationary engineers, newspaper mailing, bleachery and dye works, telephone men, carpet weaving, lathing, woodworking, lithographing, paper and pulp making, hat manufacture and metal workers. In the case of longshoremen, and certain other trades named, matters arose in which we were consulted or called upon several times.

"Our second general meeting (first annual) was held January 11, 1906, at the Revere House, taking the form of a reception and smoker, with discussion on the hours of labor. It was attended by about 170 members and guests, and was apparently regarded by those present as entirely successful. In the absence of President Tuttle, the First Vice-President, Frank H. McCarthy, former President of the Boston Central Labor Union, presided; Mr. Tuttle arriving late in the evening in time to make a few closing remarks. Governor Curtis Guild, Jr., extended the greetings of the Commonwealth, and ex-Governor William L. Douglas delivered an address on Fidelity to Agreements. The question of Hours of Labor was discussed by Mr. Alfred Mosely, of London, England; Mr. James P. Archibald, of the Brotherhood of Painters and Decorators, New York; Mr. Marcus M. Marks, President National Association of Clothing Manufacturers, New York; Mr. James Duncan, First Vice-President American Federation of Labor, Quincy, Mass., and Mr. Louis D. Brandeis, of Boston.

"There have been a number of evidences since that this gathering had a good effect, not only in the educational value of the discussion, but in promoting more general personal acquaintance among men from widely

PROF. F. W. TAUSSIG

LOUIS D. BRANDEIS

EDWARD A. MOFFETT

different walks of life, who, without such acquaintance, often misjudge and misinterpret each other's objects, motives and methods. The indirect influence of these meetings is probably greater from the fact that they are not held often enough to become tiresome.

"The attitude of the Boston press has been cordially friendly to the movement throughout the past two years, and it need hardly be said that this is an important factor in helping the industrial results we have in view.

"The new members enrolled during the year, including those connected with the Workshop Improvement Committee only, number 210; the total now being a little under 600. Names of the new members, up to October 1, appear in Bulletin No. 6. About 225 of our members are in Boston, approximately the same number in Massachusetts outside of Boston, and the remaining 150 are divided among Rhode Island, New Hampshire, Connecticut, Maine and Vermont, in the order named.

"The Committee on Workshop Improvement, which was just being organized a year ago, has now fifty-one members. The chairman is Mr. Frederick P. Fish, president of the American Telephone and Telegraph Company; first vice-chairman, Mr. George W. Brown, treasurer United Shoe Machinery Company, Boston; second vice-chairman, Hon. Charles G. Washburn, Slater Mills, Worcester. Bulletin No. 6 contains the names of the other members, except two, who have been added since October—Mr. Horace S. Sears, of Wellington, Sears & Co., Boston, and Mr. Harry W. Smith, president Wachusett Mills, Worcester.

"Bulletin No. 5 (May), on Better Workshops, was devoted expressly to the work of this Committee, and is known to have exerted a considerable influence, direct and indirect, towards the introduction of improvements in sanitary and other working conditions such as affect the health, comfort, and convenience of employes.

"More specifically the services of the committee have been given, sometimes directly and sometimes in co-operation with the Welfare Department of The National Civic Federation, in a number of cases where employers have desired consultation as to the workings and practical value of various improvements of this character, needed or desirable in their own plants.

"Several of these instances are mentioned in Bulletin No. 6 (October), which also contains an account of the work under way for prevention of tuberculosis in workshops. An illustrated pamphlet has been prepared under the auspices of the committee, and approved by five medical experts, on Sanitary Cuspidors for Factory Use, giving descriptions of types approved, care and cleaning, first cost and expense of maintenance, etc. This has been published, for general distribution, by the Welfare Department of The National Civic Federation. The card notices, described in the pamphlet, warning against the practice of spitting on the floor, and calling attention to the fact that cuspidors are provided, is being called for by manufacturers to an increasing extent. The Workshop Improvement Committee supplies these cards, for posting in workrooms, free of charge in limited quantities and at cost of printing in large quantities. Thus far about 1,500 of the cards have been furnished to forty-five employing establishments in New England, the number required ranging from 2 to 100, in one case 500. The list includes manufactories of shoes, cotton cloth, machinery, electrical apparatus, blank books, rubber hose, furnaces, silverware, thread, clothing, paper, chairs, and even ships; showing the wide range of industries in which this important sanitary feature is found necessary. Bearing upon the practical importance of this effort, it is significant that one of the largest shoe manufacturers in Massachusetts has learned, from a recent investigation, that one-third of all the deaths among employes in his factories during the last few years were due to tuberculosis. One large establishment, near Boston, has just arranged for the supplying of destructible paper cuspidors on a scale which will probably call for the use of more than 60,000 a year.

"We have a good Committee on Organization and Education, its forty-eight members being scattered all over New England. It would be well if the Secretary could visit some or all of the members of this committee and personally consult with them on ways and means of extending our ideas and methods in the various sections represented, but it has proved very difficult to get away from the immediate local demands except at considerable intervals. However, new names for membership are secured through this committee from time to time, and occasional information on local conditions, by correspondence.

"Three Bulletins have been issued this season: No. 4, reporting the annual meeting of last January; No. 5, already referred to, outlining details of the Workshop Improvement program; and No. 6, containing more or less detail information about several features of the work, including a history of the longshoremen's strike and settlement, in September; list of new members, etc.

"The State and national bureau reports, and current periodicals of twenty-five or thirty industrial crafts and commercial bodies, kept on file and indexed for quick reference, have been consulted more freely this year than last by people in search of special information. On six occasions speakers for meetings of other organizations have been suggested or arranged for.

"Mr. Frank K. Foster attended the State convention of the Maine Federation of Labor, in June, on our behalf, and addressed the delegates on the aims and work of the Civic Federation. The convention passed resolutions of endorsement, similar to those adopted in 1905 by the Boston Central Labor Union, and the State convention of the Massachusetts Branch, American Federation of Labor. On the other hand, a similar attitude on the part of leading commercial bodies is indicated by the fact that our membership includes the president and secretaries of the Boston Chamber of Commerce, Boston Merchants' Association, National Cotton Manufacturers, and one or more officers of several other trade associations, wool manufacturers clothiers, hardware, etc.

"Recognition should here be given to a fact upon which a very large part of the success of this improvement rests, namely; that many who cannot give money to its support do give time, thought and personal attention. The relatively small amount required to run the machinery of the Federation gives no proper idea of the scope of its efforts or influence, much being done voluntarily by men of prominence and large responsibilities, in all three of the groups represented in the Federation. An active, efficient organization is necessary, both to propagate our distinctive ideas and to furnish a definite means whereby this co-operation and voluntary service of practical men of affairs can be enlisted and made available promptly at the times needed. But it is a significant and optimistic fact that the personal services so rendered multiply by many times the effectiveness of the funds expended for running expenses and general educational propaganda."

CAPITAL AND LABOR MEET IN CONFERENCE IN CHICAGO.

UNDER THE AUSPICES OF THE NATIONAL CIVIC FEDERATION A REMARKABLY SUCCESSFUL MEETING IS HELD AT THE RESIDENCE OF MRS. POTTER PALMER.

THE National Civic Federation held a meeting in Chicago January 12, at the residence of Mrs. Potter Palmer, for the purpose of presenting its work to employers, employes and publicists. It was distinctly an educational meeting, with the view of forming later a branch of the Federation in the central States, having headquarters at Chicago.

The National Civic Federation, which was organized by Ralph M. Easley, Chairman of the Executive Council, was an outgrowth of the Civic Federation of Chicago, of which he was the first Secretary. The Honorable Lyman J. Gage was the first President of the Civic Federation of Chicago, whose object was the promotion of municipal reform, and Mrs. Potter Palmer was the first Vice-President. She was interested in the organization of the National Civic Federation, and it was but natural that she should encourage the establishment of a branch of the organization by holding the initial meeting at her home.

Mrs. Palmer has been long identified with the interests of labor. She was chairman of the Board of Women Managers of the Chicago World's Fair, and through that position secured diplomas for the wage earners contributing toward the manufacture of products whose excellence was recognized by awarding medals to the manufacturers.

There were present over seven hundred prominent citizens, including members of great industrial establishments, financiers, professional men, labor leaders and representatives of philanthropic agencies.

FRANKLIN MACVEAGH, of Chicago, presided, and in his opening address referred to the fact that this meeting of The National Civic Federation was held under most charming surroundings in the most beautiful environments and under most delightful auspices. "That is due," he said, "to the interest which Mrs. Palmer has ever felt in the purposes and objects of the Federation, and to her well known broad and gracious public spirit.

"The object of this meeting is to explain to the people of Chicago the work and spirit of The National Civic Federation. It is necessary for me to say just a word in description of that organization. It is a central body with its offices in New York. It originated in Chicago, but like most things upon which New York prides itself it originated here as a matter of course. But it went to New York when it grew suddenly prosperous; and while you can keep here our people who grow gradually rich, those who grow suddenly rich all go down to New York. In addition to being a general organization, The National Civic Federation is an organization with departments. It has also branches —one in Boston for New England, and it has in New York a local branch dealing with the local situation.

"You may understand it to be an organization dealing purely with labor questions, but that is only one branch of its work. It has an Industrial Department, and that is perhaps its most important single department. It has a Conciliation Department presided over by Mr. Seth Low, who is happily here this evening. The Welfare Department has as its western head our admirable citizen, Cyrus H. McCormick. It is impossible to give you a detailed impression of The National Civic Federation, therefore it was necessary to select some department which would be fairly well represented and they have chosen the Welfare Department, because it is well developed, and of great and general interest. Also because Miss Gertrude Beeks is here, and she has learned, as the executive chief of that department, exactly how to present it to you so that you may understand it."

EX-MAYOR SETH LOW, of New York, Chairman of the Conciliation Department of the Federation, in referring to its work said:

"The Conciliation Department of The National Civic Federation, of which I am chairman, is composed in about equal number of large employers of labor, representative leaders of labor unions, and of citizens who, like myself, are neither one nor the other. So that in all the problems that it has to consider it gets the point of view of the employer, and of the workingman, and of the general public. The object of the Conciliation Department is to bring employers and employes together in such a state of friendship and mutual understanding as to make labor troubles and strikes infrequent; and, wherever possible, to avoid them. You will observe that it is not called the 'arbitration department.' That is not its object. Its object is to conciliate, to bring about good feeling, and to obviate both strikes and the necessity for arbitration.

"The Federation does all of its work in the profound belief that the American men, whether employer or workingman, want to do the fair thing. We know that each one emphasizes his point of view. That is natural. But, after all, we believe that if we can get fair-minded men together and discuss a definite question of disagreement, in ninety-nine cases out of one hundred both sides, with the light that the other can throw upon it, will find the middle path between the two extremes, which all will consider fair. If you really want conciliation it is wonderful to see how often it can be brought about, even when conditions seem to be pretty hopeless.

"Let me give you an illustration of this. Last spring I was called up by telephone at my farm in Westchester County, about forty miles from New York, by a banker in Philadelphia, who told me that he represented a street railway system in one of the southern towns which was threatened with a strike and asked me if I could not communicate with Mr. Mahon, in Detroit, the representative of the street railway employes, and see if, as the head of the Conciliation Department, I could not have this strike put off.

"He said, in answer to my question as to whether I might say that he was willing to arbitrate, that he did not wish to commit himself to that, but that I might say I thought I could bring about conciliation. I called up the office of the Civic Federation in New York by telephone, and in fifteen minutes a dispatch was on its way to Detroit, reading: 'Sorry to learn there is a strike threatened in such a city. I hope it won't be permitted to occur until the Civic Federation has an opportunity to see what it can do. I think we can bring about arbitration.' The reply we received was a model. It said: 'You may be sure no strike will take place until the Civic Federation has had a chance to show what it can do. If arbitration is offered on fair terms it will be accepted.' The result of that was that the trouble was settled without a strike, and both sides wrote to the Civic Federation thanking it for its action. I think that is particularly interesting from the fact that I never saw anybody.

"It is the policy of the Conciliation Department to do its work privately. People often never know the Federation has had a hand in settling disputes that are settled. In the case I am about to tell you of, however, the parties interested gave it to the papers. A strike was in progress on the Southern Railway. Neither side wanted to make the first approach to settlement, because that would have been a sign of weakness. When the situation was brought to my attention I asked for a conference, which was granted. In the course of a conference lasting two days the question was settled honorably, and, I think, satisfactorily to both sides.

"Not so long before that the Department had been called upon by a large paper manufacturer to settle a jurisdictional dispute between two unions, which between them did all the work in his factory. It threatened to hang up the entire business. Through the agency of the Conciliation Department the two unions were brought together. They talked the thing over in good humor and the thing was settled and all trouble averted.

"In another instance a jurisdictional dispute affecting a railway not far from New York was involved. The two unions concerned were invited by the Federation to come to New York. They came to New York, to different hotels, and that was as close as we could get them together. They went home, and after a little while we got them to come back again, this time to the same hotel, and that was the end. When they met they settled the dispute.

"Now, these are illustrations of the sort of things the Conciliation Department is doing all the time. I hope you feel as we do, that it is the kind of work well worth doing. We think that the more widely it is known that there is such an agency, the more industrial disputes can be settled. And if, after hearing of it to-night, you will be led to avail yourselves of this agency, or of the local one here, which will do the same thing, I am sure you will have no cause to regret it.

"It gives me great pleasure to have had the opportunity to tell you this simple story, and to thank your hostess on behalf of the Conciliation Department for giving me this opportunity."

MISS GERTRUDE BEEKS, Secretary of the Welfare Department of The National Civic Federation, illustrated an address on the subject of its work with stereopticon views. She spoke of the scope of The National Civic Federation and referred briefly to the work of its various departments. Portraits of members of the Executive Committee were thrown upon the screen, among whom were August Belmont of New York, Henry Phipps of the United States Steel corporation, Samuel Gompers, John Mitchell, Andrew Carnegie, and former Secretary of the Interior Cornelius N. Bliss.

She stated that the Welfare Department is devoted to interesting employers in improving the conditions under which employes in all industries work and live, and that its activities cover the questions of sanitary work places, recreation, educational opportunities, homes, and provident funds.

After giving consideration to the first essentials to the welfare of the employes—steady work, an equitable wage, and reasonable hours, the employer's attention should be directed toward meeting the pressing necessities for their physical well-being in the work places.

In taking up the question of ventilation, she spoke especially of the conditions under which the stationary firemen work, and said: "Do we realize that these men, especially in our great buildings in the large cities, sometimes, and I am sorry to say, often work without any ventilation? These men," referring to a picture, "are in the second sub-basement in a large building in New York City, where there is no outlet whatever for the foul air except the door which leads into the next sub-basement, where the condition is exactly the same. The temperature reaches as high as 110 degrees in the summer, and it is almost—I might say it is quite—criminal. It is a simple matter, indeed, to provide ventilation for these firemen. Mr. Belmont heard Mr. Timothy Healy, of the International Stationary Firemen's Union, explain at one of our meetings these conditions. He had just finished a large building in New York City, and asked Mr. Healy to meet him the next day to determine whether or not the arrangements were satisfactory for the stationary firemen. Mr. Healy was amazed to find the system of ventilation so perfect in that great building and how well the stationary firemen were provided for by this busy man, who has something else to think about besides the individual employes. When a man who is so busy can do this there is no excuse for any other man forgetting his employes.

"The glass factories also have, many of them, good arrangements for bringing cool air into the faces of the blowers. The metal polishers are also in many instances protected against accident from the breaking of the emery wheel, as well as from the injurious effects of the dust. But the death-rate from tuberculosis among metal polishers, where there is no contrivance for exhausting the dust, is tremendous, and greater attention should be given to the protection of those workers. Fans sometimes are provided for driving out the fumes of the acid used by the dippers in the silver trade and the brass trade, which otherwise would permeate the entire plant and cause a great percentage of illness.

"I have recently been through many of the mines in the anthracite coal fields, and visited the most remote recesses of some in order to find whether the miners get air where they are working, and in a remote corner of this particular mine shown in the picture I found the air better, I am thankful to say, than in many factories of the United States."

Examples of improvements which have been introduced by employers along different lines were contrasted with bad conditions. The many modern conveniences which have been supplied for the benefit of employes were a surprise to all, and as one labor man put it, "Any employer who saw the splendid arrangements which have been introduced by other practical employers would thus be induced to install such improvements, for he would be ashamed not to do so."

(Reproduced by courtesy of the "Chicago Examiner.")

RESIDENCE OF MRS. POTTER PALMER IN WHICH THE CHICAGO MEETING WAS HELD.

PRESIDENT AUGUST BELMONT, of The National Civic Federation, followed Miss Beeks' address. He said in part:

"In 1900, when the Civic Federation was definitely founded, it embraced in the scope of its work a number of subjects of national interest, but the Industrial Department became practically the conspicuous one, because at that time the industrial situation had become so acute that its work in conciliation gave the impression that that was its only office.

"Its object, expressed in general terms, is to promote industrial peace, and there is not one of its departments, as you have been told, but assists in that work. The Conciliation Department finds its work where difficulty in securing an agreement exists. The other departments tend to educate both employer and employe that they may avoid differences.

"A year ago the Municipal Ownership League of New York polled a vote so large that it was apparent that the subject must be studied. The Civic Federation called together about 150 men, representing dissimilar opinions on municipal ownership—those who advocated it and those who opposed; those who had been writing upon the subject and also those interested in transportation and conversant with the operation of public utilities. Their deliberations resulted in the appointment of a committee of twenty-one, charged with the purpose of studying the operations of public utilities both in this country and in Great Britain. They conferred upon a committee of five the preparation of a report on their findings. The Civic Federation did nothing but use its best effort to supply the means to carry out what this committee undertook. It exercised no influence as to the selection, and on that committee were some of the most ardent advocates of municipal ownership of public utilities that we have in this country. They have visited England and have studied the subject in this country. They engaged their own engineers, their own experts, and did their work just as they chose and in whatever manner they thought best, and I am given to understand that within a short time their report will be ready. I understand that it will cover something like 11,000 pages, so you will perceive that a pretty thorough piece of work has been done, and that the Civic Federation folks will furnish teachers and those who are to discuss this subject a proper and thoroughly non-partisan and unbiased text-book. That is only illustrative of how the Civic Federation works.

"I have seen it suggested that a branch of the Civic Federation was to be established here. Of course that must come entirely in a spontaneous manner from you here in Chicago, if you deem such a step wise. In Massachusetts a Civic Federation of New England was organized some two years ago and now is an active and successful organization. They do their work independently of us, but in harmony with us. They have a conference on Thursday to consider this welfare work which has been put before you and the question of old age pensions and insurance of wage-earners. We have taken up that subject in New York.

"I only hope that the suggestion that an active co-operation be started here in Chicago will take form and I am sure with the enormous interests you would have to care for in the Middle West you would soon gain an importance which you can hardly realize and which would tend greatly to solve this subject, so important to our peace and welfare."

WARREN S. STONE, Chief of the Brotherhood of Locomotive Engineers, stated that it was his belief that the question of wages and the labor conditions of our country are the prominent questions of the day. Continuing, he said in part:

"The Civic Federation has enabled capital and labor to sit down and discuss in a friendly way their differences. I am a firm believer in the face to face conference.

"Leaving all question of sentiment out of it, boiling it all down to the basis of dollars and cents—and that is the basis we figure on to-day largely—the Civic Federation has enabled the Board of Locomotive Engineers to make two or three of the best settlements it ever made, and in doing so it has been the means of making settlements that perhaps have brought to our individual members over $300,000. The Civic Federation has done that for us, and I cannot speak in terms too high for the good work that it is doing. It is an educational work all the way through, and when you bring the laboring men together you find that all labor leaders are not demagogues, and that all capitalists are not what they are represented by some.

"I do not believe the time is ever coming when there will be no differences to settle between those who have labor to sell and those who have to buy labor, but I do believe this movement of the Civic Federation will bring us closer together and will enable us to do away with that last resort of the labor organization, the strike. It is a pleasure to me to stand before you to-night and testify to the work the Civic Federation has done."

WILLIAM MAHON, International President of the Amalgamated Street Railway Employes of America, referred to the opposition of certain Chicago labor unions to meeting representatives of capital at Mrs. Palmer's as corresponding to the radicals of the Harriman type in the capitalist class who refuse to go half-way or meet with their opponents. Referring to the trade union movement, Mr. Mahon said that it was here to stay. He said:

"There never has been such opposition against any institution or against any movement, yet the trade union, in spite of all this opposition, has lived. You could not crush it. The whole forces of capital turned against it could not crush it. It is a movement that will not be crushed. You might as well make up your mind to the fact that the trade union is going to live on and on. And to the capitalist and to the man upon the other side I say, you might as well make up your minds sooner or later, as did that distinguished man under whose roof we meet to-night, Potter Palmer, when he told of his struggles against the trade unions by concluding, 'I have changed my mind.' And he came to recognize and deal with the unions, and he found benefit in doing so, and he fearlessly told it to the world in the declarations he made before he died.

"The American workman, schooled in the free schools and taught the rights of American citizenship, realizes that some of the titles to your wealth are as spurious, if you please, as the titles of kings and lords. We recognize that we have the same right to the same conditions, and that as men we are going to have them. We all aspire to have homes like this one if we can.

"The unions have made their mistakes, yes, lots of them, just as you capitalists have made yours, lots of them, but we are going on. We might as well make up our minds to come together to deal with one another and work in harmony and to meet the conditions that are before us. For what is it? The battle of life, after all. What have we gained when we get through by the policy of hoarding and grasping all the wealth there may be? Let us be men, let us realize the battle of life, let us recognize the conditions. You will find the men representing trade unions ready to meet you around the conference board and to take a fair position with you, and they will go more than half-way every time to adjust and settle these disputes upon a broad and fair basis. Meet with them, and by the recognition of them meet the battle of life as it confronts us. Let us deal with it. Let us form our civic federations and our organizations of all kinds that will bring men together.

"When I see the good that the Civic Federation has done, the strikes that it has prevented, the men that it has brought together, and brought peace, I must give it credit for what it has done to assist us in a number of great questions. We have settled a number of strikes that would have been great strikes, that would have involved great cities, and those things no one knew anything about because through the different officers of the Civic Federation those matters have been brought about and settled unknown to the public. And so, when we look at the good it has done, my friends, we are proud of the record it has made along that line.

"Some people say the labor unions want to wipe out the wealth of the world. We want to do nothing of the kind. We want to dynamite the hovels out of existence, if you please. We have no desire to rob you of your wealth. Give us the opportunity with our labor and we will duplicate all the wealth of the world in the next twenty years with our own efforts. I would sooner go down to my grave as poor old Bill Mahon without one dollar to leave my children, and leave a legacy behind of the improved conditions of the street railway men of the country, than to have all the wealth of the Rockefellers, all the wealth of the Morgans, all the wealth of my friend Belmont, rolled up in one pile and doubled ten thousand times."

AN interesting event of the meeting was the action of George A. Schilling, a member of the Coopers' International Union, in calling attention to the remarkable address delivered by Mrs. Potter Palmer at the Columbian Exposition at Chicago. Mr. Schilling stated that the late Governor Altgeld had found the address of so much interest to him that he had re-read it three times. So much of this address was applicable to present day conditions that Mr. Schilling said he was justified in making liberal extracts from it. Some of the quotations were as follows:

"Experience has brought many surprises, not the least of which is an impressive realization of the unity of human interests, notwithstanding differences of race, government, language, temperaments, and external conditions. The people of all civilized lands are studying the same problems. Each success and each failure in testing and developing new theories is valuable to the whole world. Social and industrial questions are paramount, and are receiving the thoughtful consideration of statesmen, students, political economists, humanitarians, employers and employed.

"The few forward steps which have been taken during our boasted nineteenth century—the so-called age of invention—have promoted the general use of machinery and economic motive powers with the result of cheapening manufactured articles, but have not afforded the relief to the masses which was expected. The struggle for bread is as fierce as of old. We find everywhere the same picture presented—overcrowded industrial centers, factories surrounded by dense populations of operatives, keen competition, many individuals forced to use such strenuous effort that vitality is drained in the struggle to maintain life under conditions so uninviting and discouraging that it scarcely seems worth living. It is a grave reproach to modern enlightenment that we seem no nearer the solution of many of these problems than during feudal days.

"It is not our province, however, to discuss these weighty questions, except insofar as they affect the compensation paid to wage-earners, and more especially that paid to women and children. Of all existing forms of injustice, there is none so cruel and inconsistent as is the position in which women are placed with regard to self-maintenance—the calm ignoring of their rights and responsibilities, which has gone on for centuries. If the economic conditions are hard for men to meet, subjected as they are to the constant weeding out of the less expert and steady hands, it is evident that women, thrown upon their own resources, have a frightful struggle to endure, especially as they have always to contend against a public sentiment which discountenances their seeking industrial employment as a means of livelihood. The theory which exists among the conservative people, that the sphere of woman is her home—that it is unfeminine, even monstrous, for her to wish to take a place beside or to compete with men in the various lucrative industries—tells heavily against her, for manufacturers and producers take advantage of it to disparage her work and obtain her services for a nominal price, thus profiting largely by the necessities and helplessness of their victims. That so many should cling to respectable occupations while starving in following them, and should refuse to yield to discouragement and despair, shows a high quality of steadfastness and principle.

"If we now look at the question from the economic standpoint and decide for good and logical reasons that women should be kept out of industrial fields in order that they may leave the harvest for men, whose duty it is to maintain women and children, then, by all the laws of justice and equity, these latter should be provided for by their natural protectors, and, if deprived of them, should become wards of the State, and be maintained in honor and comfort. The acceptance of even this doctrine of tardy justice would not, however, I feel sure, be welcomed by the woman of to-day who, having had a taste of independence, will never willingly relinquish it. They have no desire to be helpless and dependent. Having the full use of their faculties, they rejoice in exercising them. This is entirely in conformity with the trend of modern thought, which is in the direction of establishing proper respect for human individuality and the right of self-development.

"Our highest aim now is to train each individual to find happiness in the full and healthy exercise of the gifts bestowed by generous nature. Ignorance is too expensive and wasteful to be tolerated. We cannot afford to lose the reserve power of any individual. We advocate, therefore, the thorough education and training of women to fit her to meet whatever fate life may bring; not only to prepare her for the factory and workshop, for the professions and arts, but, more important than all else, to prepare her for presiding over the home. It is for this, the highest field of woman's effort, that the broadest training and greatest preparation are required."

MANY letters were received from those who were unable to attend the meeting, some of which are abstracted as follows:

James Duncan, International Secretary-Treasurer of the Granite Cutters' International Association of America—"It is a happy sign of the times that such meetings are being held in our great industrial centers, and the people from the different walks and positions of life and business are meeting on a common level to discuss subjects which make for national business and progress."

Mrs. J. Ellen Foster, special representative of the United States Department of Justice—"I regard The National Civic Federation as a noble exponent of the best thoughts of modern industrialism. I congratulate the representatives of the Federation in the West that so royal a woman as Mrs. Potter Palmer will be its hostess at the beginning of this year."

Homer D. Call, Secretary-Treasurer of the Amalgamated Meat Cutters and Butcher Workmen of North America—"I assure you that my hearty sympathy is with you in the movement, as I firmly believe that The National Civic Federation is accomplishing a great work in harmonizing labor and capital and the uplifting of humanity."

T. J. Dolan, General Secretary-Treasurer of the International Brotherhood of Steam Shovel and Dredge Men—"The organization which your committee represents is a great institution and has done great work in bringing employers and employes into closer relations. In behalf of our organization, I desire to extend the

WILLIAM D. MAHON

MISS GERTRUDE BEEKS

WARREN S. STONE

est wishes and entire support of our brotherhood hroughout the country in its great work."

Michael Colbert, General Organizer of the Internaional Typographical Union—"The question of good anitary conditions is a very important one from an conomic standpoint as well as from the point of view f the health and comfort of the workers. Good light, ood ventilation and good toilet facilities mean that e health and comfort of workers are conserved and ereby greater efficiency in workmanship is secured. ess time is lost through sickness and more work is one. The printing offices to-day, from the sanitary oint of view, are far superior to those twenty years go, and I have noticed in offices where attention is aid to light, ventilation, etc., the printer of to-day is uperior physically to the printer of other days. He is lso more sober and works steadier. The shortening of working hours has had something to do with this, of course, especially in morning paper offices, but improved sanitary conditions account for part of the improvement."

John Mitchell, President of the United Mine Workers of America—"I am so thoroughly acquainted with the splendid efforts that have been made by The National Civic Federation to bring into closer and better relationship the interests of workmen and employers, and indeed the workmen and employers themselves, that I dislike to absent myself from any conference that is held under the auspices of that organization.

"It seems to me that if the best judgment of the capitalists and laboring men would assert itself, assisted by the sympathetic sentiment of public-spirited citizens, much could be done to establish a relationship between these great forces of modern society, which would at least reduce to the minimum the number and severity of industrial disturbances. I believe that this desirable end would be more speedily attained, if there were a fuller recognition by each of the other's rights and responsibilities.

"The time has long passed when either side in the industrial field can say with impunity, 'this is *my* business.' The times has certainly arrived when industries should be regarded as our business. In other words, there must be co-operation and mutual helpfulness in the conduct of business and industry if we hope to have a satisfactory and honorable peace."

The Rt. Rev. Henry C. Potter, Episcopal Bishop of New York—"The Civic Federation began in a high purpose; and has gone forward, as I rejoice to believe, along lines of the utmost value and importance. It has certainly not always (there are some who believe) seen our great social and industrial problems with an infallible eye—but then, you and I don't know any human power that can do that. What it has done, however, has been to help men and women, divided by fragmentary and most imperfect views of their several interests, to see them in a larger light, and with fuller discernment."

RECENT ACTIVITIES OF CIVIC FEDERATION REPRESENTATIVES.

SOME OF THE ADDRESSES DELIVERED BY OFFICERS OF THE WELFARE, INDUSTRIAL ECONOMICS AND IMMIGRATION DEPARTMENTS.

MISS HELEN VARICK BOSWELL has delivered numerous lectures before women's clubs for the Federation's Welfare Department upon the subject of "Welfare Work." Illustrated lectures have been presented to:

A convention of twenty-five women's clubs of Troy, N. Y.

The Woman's Educational and Industrial League of Boston, an organization of large membership, in whose work the leading women of Boston participate.

Civitas Club of Newburgh, N. Y., with an audience of four hundred and fifty men and women; although it is a woman's club, there were present many manufacturers.

The College of Agriculture, Cornell University, Ithaca, N. Y.

The Pine Hills Fortnightly Club of Albany, N. Y., the leading organization of women. The meeting was held at the Urania Club House, the principal men's club, and was attended largely by both men and women interested in public affairs.

During January three lectures were given by Miss Boswell in Washington, D. C., attended by many prominent officials, government employes, and influential residents of that city. The improvements shown as adopted in many of the leading establishments of the country stimulated an interest in such facilities for Government employes as well as those of private enterprises.

The Industrial Session of the State Federation of Women's Clubs of the State of New York, held at Saratoga, was conducted by Miss Boswell. There were other speakers along the same line secured by her.

Lectures were also presented before the Woman's Legislative League, the Woman's West End Republican Association, National Society Daughters of Ohio, and Sorosis, in New York City; the Woman's Republican League of Brooklyn; and the Unity Club at Washington, D. C.

In speaking before the Pine Hills Fortnightly Club of Albany, N. Y., upon "Industrial Conditions of Women Wage-earners," Miss Boswell said in part:

"Every woman in this country is a part of the industrial life of the country, if not through her own efforts, then through those of the men in her family. She should acquaint herself with its conditions, and the fundamentals upon which industrial life is built. We are striving for a higher standard of living. How shall we start to build up that if not by improving the condition of the people who help to create the products of the world? The Welfare Department covers such subjects as apply to the health, the recreation, education, and housing of employes. Under its organization of co-operation employers get together to compare notes, and to plan such improved features as may be worked out. Progressive business men realize the economic strength of their position when they put time, thought and money into the highest development of the conditions surrounding their work-people. Many business men do this without other than their own prompting, but we all know that public sentiment is a great factor in bringing about any needed reform, and it is well that there should be brought before men and women the old and new methods under which work is done, so that we may see improvements, see bad conditions, and judge where judicious suggestions may be made for improvement. Just here is where the clubwomen of this State can, and often do, exert a powerful influence for good by personally looking after the degree of enforcement of laws and endeavor for improving factory and shop conditions. There will be found no greater antidote to the dangerous encroachments of socialism than such welfare work. The cry of the socialist is always that nothing has been done, nothing is being done, and nothing will be done for the amelioration of the working man and woman. To show that much is constantly in progress to improve conditions is the best answer to the socialistic cry, and the way to prevent the making of socialists is to surround workers with such conditions as will make them comfortable in their work, happy in their homes, and appreciative of the form of government under which they live. The real laborers of the country have no socialistic trend. One of the best known leaders, Samuel Gompers, has said: 'I have kept close watch upon your socialistic doctrines and the work of your movement for thirty years, and I am entirely at variance with your philosophy. I am not only at variance with your doctrines, but believe economically you are unsound, socially you are wrong, industrially you are an impossibility.'

"The pessimists of the country have had so much to say of the horrors of our industrial life that I am glad to show some of its brighter sides and to bring before you by means of stereopticon pictures the many advances and improvements that are daily being made for the comfort and health of women workers especially."

MISS GERTRUDE BEEKS, Secretary of the Federation's Welfare Department, has given illustrated lectures on "What Employers in Different Industries are doing to Ameliorate the Conditions of their Employes" before the:

Turn-Verein Von Brooklyn, E. D., at Brooklyn, N. Y.

Institute of the Eighth District of the Pennsylvania Young Men's Christian Association in Philadelphia.

Georgia State Federation of Women's Clubs at Macon.

A meeting of the employers and employes in Chicago, held at the residence of Mrs. Potter Palmer.

The employers of Muncie, Indiana, and their wives, at the home of Mr. F. C. Ball, a prominent glass manufacturer of that city; and before the

City Secretaries of the Young Men's Christian Association at Brooklyn.

Other addresses were before the Massachusetts State Conference of Charities, at Worcester, Mass., on "Welfare Work, a Safeguard to Public Health," and a joint meeting of Women's Clubs under the auspices of the Alta Lita Club of East St. Louis, upon the subject "What Women's Clubs May Do to Prevent Child Labor."

E. STAGG WHITIN, Secretary of the New York Welfare Committee of the Federation, lectured on the topic "Movements for Social Service," before the Woman's Club of Whitinsville, Mass. Mr. Whitin said in part: "The primary institutions, such as the family, the church, the vocation and State, are ever being strengthened and vitalized by many lesser institutions. The industrial revolution brought about changes in these institutions, and created in America many of the more vital problems of our social life today. To their solution, religious agencies, such as missions and other organizations for the 'salvation of souls,' were the first to appear. Gradually, great relief societies have been organized, and the church itself has become socialized. The establishment of the church house and settlement has come as a development out of the earlier forms, and is tending to guide the movement from the religious or salvational to the broader social or educational; thus the extension of public school and other educational agencies to take up the work of social prophylaxis.

"The vocational side, despite its great needs, has been almost untouched by these more social movements. Today, renewed interest in the introduction of welfare work into factories and in industrial education has tended to add a new breadth to the movement, and to point out additional possibilities of advance."

The speaker then showed the recent developments that have been made in this latter type of work; the part the Welfare Department of The National Civic Federation had played in it; how necessary was the work of improving the conditions existing in many factories, and the necessary industrial preparation of those who are to take up factory work now that the increased educational advantages in the schools are tending to bring about a better standard of living.

At the request of the chairman, the speaker answered many questions pertaining to the congested districts in New York City. He showed how exaggerated was the general thought in regard to the conditions existing on the East Side, on account of the many misleading articles which have been written in regard to it. He pointed out that the distribution of the Russian immigrants to other parts of the United States, and the extension of popular education, would very soon relieve the congestion, which is the result of the gathering together of a distinctly foreign population under the influence of Old World customs.

The club honored the speaker with a full attendance for the first time in its history.

J. W. SULLIVAN, of the Typographical Union and a member of the Federation's Public Ownership Commission, in addressing the Home Economics Club, Teachers' College, Columbia University, upon the trade union's attitude toward welfare work, said:

"The trades unionists are observing sympathetically The National Civic Federation's Welfare Department, and its work is upheld by those who understand it. They see that it is discriminatingly promoting certain specific betterments for the working classes, thereby supplementing trade union endeavors and carrying out the good intentions of the enlightened and fair-minded employers who are engaged in the work. It recognizes that the trade unions are chiefly engaged with waves and hours, and the labor laws, and the union regulations associated with wage scales or those laws; that they are busy pushing organization or that they hesitate to bring up with employers new points that may cause friction. Hence they welcome the pacific intervention of a third party. There is a set of betterments for labor in which the employer, seeking to do his full duty by his employes, may engage his energies. I have traveled much over the world in the interests of labor, having been sent out by trades unionists or others, and I am impressed with the general need of well considered forms of welfare work. These betterments, for one thing, result in doing away with shop nuisances, and those inconveniences and burdens of life which factory hands cannot very well take hold of themselves, but through attention to which the employer may make his employe comparatively happy. Working people, laboring separately, may not experience shop nuisances very much, but when brought together by tens and twenties and hundreds and even thousands they find that, in the case of perhaps only one nuisance there may be a menace even to life itself. For instance, drafts of cold air are frequently a source of serious discomfort. The question of whether the window shall be open or closed becomes a vital question in a factory, and factions 'for' and 'against' arise; those far from a window want it open; those near it want it closed. Welfare work suggests a different solution. It brings into play the knowledge of other forms of ventilation.

"Trade unions took part in the establishment of the bureaus of labor. The National Bureau of Labor was not established until the American Federation of Labor again and again passed resolutions in its favor. The State bureaus also came through the unions largely. These bureaus cover the question of factory inspection.

They are also charged to enforce laws as to fire escapes, protection from dangerous machinery, seats for women, weekly payment of wages, abolition of truck stores, the guaranteeing of wages by lien laws, and others. Trade unionists have also proceeded to get the Saturday half holiday, Labor Day, and other holidays. We hold that such reforms were in the main the results of union effort; in any State where the unions are not strong, you do not have them.

"But even after the rules of the unions and the labor laws of the State are in force, something else is needed to improve the conditions of employes.

"The National Civic Federation has gone to the trouble of sending agents about the country, to ascertain what is being done for the betterment of the every-day conditions of the workers without ulterior motive, and one little thing added to another brings up the sum of the betterments in evidence until we have a principle involved that can be recommended highly by union men, a principle that when observed serves to bring about a better spirit and a better relationship between employer and employe.

"Some employers are sincere. Some are self-denying. The most violent radical will concede that much. Employers do not always follow to the bitter end the law of competition. They will stand in the way of it on occasions. They do not even in the majority of cases quote to labor men, 'We can get men just as good as you are at a somewhat lower rate, and men that will never growl.' And on the other hand, union men give full recognition to the good work of considerate and honest-minded employers, and encourage an increase in their number. These two classes of men with hearts, whose pocketbooks destiny has unbalanced, seem to be getting together in the Civic Federation.

"The well-intentioned employer often has to be educated.

"A good man in Chicago said to me not long ago: 'My six hundred garment workers ought to have plenty of ventilation. The air was foul the other day, and I went in and threw up the windows. The next day there were twenty not at work, reporting they had cold.' This was an enlightened man in many ways, but he knew nothing about ventilation.

"Imagine working in a factory where you have not a clean towel except one you may bring yourself, and you have to hide that because some one else may steal it, no soap, no water running regularly, no toilet room, a factory in which you have bad light, poor heat, questionable drinking water, where you must eat your luncheon at your cluttered bench, and where the floors show lack of cuspidors, and the walls covered with clothes for the lack of lockers. It is there that the Welfare Department may aid by representing to the employer what has been done by other employers.

"Certain occupations are open to special forms of welfare work. In the building trades here in New York we have many thousands of men working a bad day like this in the open, with usually no place for storage of their street clothes, and none of the conveniences you would expect in a building. These trades ought to have portable houses for such purposes. Many of the workers are intelligent men, well educated; and there they are working under conditions that take from them their self-respect.

"Trainmen need bunk houses. Formerly, at the ends of railroad divisions, the men had usually no place to go for rest and food but to a cheap hotel. Now bunk houses and railroad club houses are becoming more and more common.

"For molders, gas workers and blacksmiths a necessity is a place for dry clothing.

"In the metal trades, we find this bad example: Sixty-five men in a room with only six windows; the whole force working in acids and amid great machines blowing off an immense quantity of dust. The first question here is not high wages, nor short hours; it is welfare sufficient to make life tolerable.

"My own trade of printing is unhealthful from several causes, yet printing office conditions, in general, continue bad. In a certain office, for example, a linotype machine was in a draft. The man operating the machine contracted a bad cold which ran into consumption. He left the employ of the company. The story was repeated with a second man and a third man. The matter was brought to the attention of the officials and the ventilation of the office improved. If that can happen among printers, what must be the situation as to sanitary conditions among the newly-arrived Russian Jewish garment workers, so much poorer and more helpless? As a fact, it is usually bad in the extreme.

"There is little care taken of teamsters. Many of them in bad weather go into a saloon and get a drink two or three times a day, which is not wise welfare work for themselves. There was once a place in Hudson Street where teamsters could get a cup of coffee for a cent or two while waiting to deliver goods at a near-by freight station—a good plan, which ought to be imitated.

"These examples indicate the room there is for reminders to employers of certain neglected duties in our developing civilization.

"We find as we look into welfare work that with relation to it there are classifications of industrial workers. In this country we have American white working people, the negroes, who are removed from the whites by a gulf, and the immigrants, who are in some cases almost as far from the American whites as the negroes. Three different fields for welfare work.

"I would not say one word for welfare work if I thought the outcome would be to develop in the wage worker a feeling of helpless dependency, or to advertise employing class-charlatans, or to modify one worker's demands through the trade unions.

"Employes can occasionally do an acceptable piece of welfare work for the employer. They can make sure that their representatives tell him the truth when conditions are good, and do not ask impossibilities when they are bad. They can show appreciation when the employer really does well by them. They can mitigate in various ways the unpleasantness of the higgling in the labor market. They can put the employer in a frame of mind in which he will say, 'Well, if I have performed welfare work for you I acknowledge in turn that you are contributing to my happiness, too.'

"Welfare work for boys includes the establishing of athletic fields, bowling alleys, gymnasiums and technical and other schools; and for girls, recreation grounds, light athletics, dressmaking, millinery, and above all, cooking.

"If there is one supreme crying need throughout the world it is for better cooking, how to make food palatable and how to be sure of its wholesomeness. If you are studying all that, young ladies, you are on the way to saintship. You are helping in a radical way to make people better. The roots of your labors run down to the stomach, the boiler of human machinery, and up to man's moral nature, the foundation of Society. If you can help the poorer girls of the hard-working classes to study personal health, household economy and be good housewives, you are engaged in a noble work."

FRANK JULIAN WARNE, Secretary of the Federation's Immigration Department, in addressing the South Carolina Cotton Manufacturers' Association at its recent annual meeting at Spartanburg, S. C., said in part:

"Among the impressions I take away after a most instructive two weeks' trip in various sections of your Southland, is that of the remarkable, almost wonderful industrial development or revolution through which you are passing.

"The unprecedented and rapid growth of your industries has already brought to you many vexatious problems new to this section. The building of your cotton mills, for illustration, has brought about within a period of ten or fifteen years a widespread movement of population from your rural districts to the villages and cities. This movement has been so rapid as to impose upon you with startling suddenness pressing issues of a most intricate nature. While it is true that such problems have already been developed through various stages in other sections of the country, yet it does not follow that the same outcome can be prophesied of your section. These problems, while of the same general character, differ radically because of the varying elements that go to make them up, and it is of these differences and the part they play that public opinion should be correctly informed.

"You have your views, and no doubt your own conception as to how these problems should be solved. But at the same time it is highly important that the public should know your views, and I am convinced that The National Civic Federation can be of incalculable service to you as manufacturers and to your section in the upbuilding of your industrial state, for I take it that in your progress public opinion, not only of the South but of the nation at large, is to be a determining factor. And as captains of industry who have fought to your present position over obstacles which to many seemed almost insurmountable, I am sure you recognize the value of a correctly informed public opinion. 'It is in this connection that The National Civic Federation has its greatest usefulness to you. This organization has 'a decent respect for the opinions of mankind,' be these opinions those of the industrial leaders of the South, or the North, or West. It is a forum where representatives of all interests and all sections can meet and present their views through their leaders. The means which the Federation uses for accomplishing this purpose are conferences for the discussion of questions of public moment. At these conferences all 'sides' are represented and each is given equal opportunity to present its aspect of the issue. As an illustration of this feature of the Federation's work, I call your attention to the recent conference in New York City in December at which the child labor problem, in which you are particularly interested, was one of the questions discussed. You sent able men there to present your views and opinions. I believe that what your representatives said came as a surprise to many who heretofore have not had the opportunity of considering all the phases of this problem.

"In order to give you a general idea of the Federation's work, I might say that the organization is composed of three elements; of employers, representing the larger and more important industries of the country; of employes, representing the great labor organizations, some of them international in their scope; and of representatives of the public, the latter including professional men and public-spirited men from all sections of the country.

"The efficiency and standing of the Federation can probably best be indicated by mentioning the names of some of those who are actively identified in its work. The president of the organization is Mr. August Belmont; one of the vice-presidents is Mr. Samuel Gompers, President of the American Federation of Labor. Up to the time of his appointment by President Roosevelt as Secretary of the Department of Commerce and Labor, Mr. Oscar S. Straus was also a vice-president. Another vice-president is your own fellow-member, Captain Ellison A. Smyth, and another one of your members, Mr. Thomas F. Parker, is Vice-Chairman of the Immigration Department. The officials of the organization also include such public-spirited men as ex-President Grover Cleveland, Mr. Andrew Carnegie, Archbishop Ireland, Mr. John Mitchell, President Eliot of Harvard University, Hon. Seth Low, Mr. Henry Phipps of the United States Steel Corporation.

"In addition to the conference feature referred to, the Federation's work is also carried on through departments organized for the purpose of making special investigations along particular lines. These departments include Immigration, Welfare, Conciliation and Arbitration, Trade Agreements, Industrial Economics, Political Reform, and Public Ownership. The methods under which these departments carry on their work can best be illustrated perhaps by that of the Public Ownership Commission. This body of one hundred men representing public-spirited citizens in various walks of life in different sections of the country was organized more than a year ago to carry on a thorough investigation as to public ownership of such public utilities as water, gas, electric power and light, and street railways. This commission, composed of those who oppose as well as those who favor public ownership, selected a committee of twenty-one to make an impartial investigation and to examine into the conditions and results in this country and abroad of public ownership and operation, public ownership and private operation, and private ownership and operation. Each 'side' selected its own paid experts, and these and the committee of investigation have spent many months in the principal cities of the United States and Great Britain. Such was the attention given to the selection of this important body—every shade of opinion being represented—as to assure an impartial and fair investigation and report, and I believe that when it finally presents its report, it will have a widespread influence in directing public opinion on this pressing issue.

"The other departments of the Federation are selected with the same care and with the sole idea of securing facts that are basal and fundamental. The Immigration Department in which you leaders of the South are greatly interested at the present time is also composed of different elements."

A MOST SENSIBLE VIEW.

WE doubt the efficiency of pity to solve the problem of child labor. A certain value is derived from pictures of the bent shoulders, the contracted lungs, the tired limbs, the sallow faces, the vacant eyes and the dwarfed intellects of those we are banishing from home, playground and schoolroom to the weary tread of our sweatshops, factories and mines. But not all child laborers are "slaves." Those who denounce the evils of child labor in such generalizations as that "two million little, wan and dwarfed child toilers march in the wage-slave ranks of America's industrial army" are a menace to this reform. Intelligent people, seeing many of these two million children who are not "wan or "dwarfed," and who bear no other visible marks of slavery, discount the whole cry against child labor as sentiment. Many of the two million working children in America are between fifteen and sixteen years of age and are in occupations and laboring under conditions not injurious to themselves or to society. Not all glass houses employ little boys at night. Not all coal breakers are dense with clouds of dry dust. Not all telegraph offices employ little children to carry messages at midnight to houses of vice. Not all children in Southern cotton mills work through a twelve-hour night. Some one tells of seeing a little girl in a Southern cotton mill rudely awakened at night by a dash of cold water in her face. Homilies on child labor followed this incident, abounding in graphic descriptions of numberless little girls cruelly awakened night after night by splashes of cold water.

Nothing is gained by exaggeration; much is lost. It is enough that some of the two million are toiling all night in glass houses; that some coal breakers compel little boys of ten years to work in clouds of dust so dense as to completely hide the light and fill the lungs; that some little girls of eight years toil through a twelve-hour night in Southern cotton mills; that some of the little children of New York are crushed in body and soul in the slavery of sweatshop labor. The truth is bad enough. Let the picture be drawn with simple accuracy, and we may hope to arouse, instead of sentiments of pity, the sense of social justice; an appreciation of the relation of this system to our social institutions. A demonstration of the loss to society, the injustice to the laborer, and the dwarfing of the progenitors of our coming generations, will be more effective than specific pictures of little children who suffer from the wrong.—*Owen R. Lovejoy, Assistant Secretary of the National Child Labor Committee, in the New York Independent.*

The National
Civic Federation Review

Vol. III NEW YORK, SEPTEMBER, 1907 1

FOR INDUSTRIAL WORLD PEACE.

SPEAKERS AT MR. CARNEGIE'S HOME DECLARE THIS THE REAL BASIS OF INTERNATIONAL PEACE—A WORLD CONFERENCE PROPOSED.

"HAS not the time come for another international conference, to be held at the instance of the United States, to bring about improvements of conditions surrounding labor and promote industrial peace? I think it has."

In this declaration President Nicholas Murray Butler, of Columbia University, sounded the keynote of the "Industrial Peace Evening" at the home of Mr. Andrew Carnegie, New York City. Of the many conferences that have been held under the auspices of the National Civic Federation to consider the improvement of relations between employers and employes and lessening of industrial strife, this was one of the largest, and in certain respects most significant. The gathering of nearly four hundred representative employers, labor leaders, professional men, educators and publicists under Mr. Carnegie's hospitable roof was in itself a striking illustration of the progress that has been made in recent years toward conditions in the industrial world which now make such a proposal as that of President Butler timely and feasible, as the logical "next step."

Throughout the discussion the analogies of national warfare and industrial disputes were strikingly displayed. Understandings between employers and organized labor are based upon agreements which are in the nature of treaties between the contracting parties. By these quasi-treaties not only are disputes and difficulties terminated but they are also avoided. They are agents of peace not only in fixing the mutual conditions of employment, but in providing a mechanism whereby differences of opinion respecting the contract shall be interpreted.

Equally evident was it that just as good will and kindly intention must necessarily supplement the agreements among nations, so must they animate employer and employed in their mutual relations. It was pointed out that the letter of the contract without its true spirit—a genuine desire to understand and deal fairly with one another—must be ineffective to accomplish good results.

CONFERENCE ON INDUSTRIAL PEACE

THE PROBLEM STATED.

Mr. Carnegie, as host, extended a hearty welcome, in behalf of himself and Mrs. Carnegie, to the guests assembled, and in referring to the coming Peace Congress remarked that peace, like charity, should begin at home.

"Before we begin next week," he continued, "in a greater assembly of a great many people from different parts of the world, striking forth for the world's peace, it is most fitting that we should do something on the home scale for ourselves and neighbors. Making peace at home is the surest way of spreading it abroad. The great object we have in view is arbitration, and arbitration is a principle that works both abroad and at home.

"It is a fundamental point in law that no man shall sit as judge in his own cause. So it should be with trades unions and employers. Neither the men nor the employers should assume to sit in judgment on their own case, because neither sees both sides of the question. (Applause.) It is very rarely, indeed, in my experience, that one party is entirely right and the other party wholly wrong. You must get a disinterested party to judge between them, and all will be well.

"That same principle applies to nations. Nations should no longer be allowed to disturb the general peace of the world, because all nations are now interdependent and much concerned, materially as well as morally, in the preservation of peace.

"So it is in the industrial system. No branch of employers should be allowed to sit in judgment upon their own case and disturb the operations of the community in which all are interested. And the man or the nation that refuses to submit his judgment to disinterested parties is prima facie in the wrong. The man says: 'What, my honor! Shall I allow a man to insult me and not strike back?' No man ever insulted, dishonored, another in the world. No nation can dishonor another. All dishonors from which we suffer are self-inflicted. The principle of arbitration is what laborers should stand for; is what employers should stand for.

"It gives me a special pleasure to meet the representatives of labor. When I look back I think how much pleasure I have experienced with my interviews with workingmen. I could tell you many stories about strikes, and I wish to say this word: It is not wages, as a rule, that cause strikes—no, it is the lack of recognition on the part of the employer [illegible] (Applause.) I remember a serious [illegible] burg. Billy Edwards rose [illegible] upon the whole we don't object to; that is a fair scale, but what we object to is that it is not rightly divided. Now, Mr. Carnegie, you take my job.' I said, 'No, Mr. Edwards, Mr. Carnegie takes no man's job.' They began to laugh, and I laughed, and Billy said, sitting down: 'We won't have any trouble settling this.' And we did not. (Applause.) It is astonishing what a joke will do to settle difficulties that we meet with in life.

"I want to express the genuine, heartfelt happiness of Mrs. Carnegie and myself for this opportunity of meeting the two branches, equal in every respect, who bargain with each other—the one for labor, the other for satisfactory wages; one just as welcome as the other, and both doubly welcome. It is something we will remember with great happiness all our lives, and it is another instance that I will look back to in after years, when I become an old man (laughter and applause), and I will be telling some other audiences what a glorious time I had with the delegates of the Civic Federation Peace Evening. I thank you, one and all, for giving us the pleasure of meeting you here this evening."

THE ISSUE OF THE HOUR.

Mr. August Belmont, President of the National Civic Federation, followed Mr. Carnegie:

"There is no time more important than this for a gathering of this nature. It is very easy to remain at peace during prosperous times, but sometimes times change, and I feel greatly impressed that the unparalleled development of our country and its prosperity have been so extraordinary that it is undoubtedly time to strike a halt, and not wholly undesirable.

"I do not desire to be either a prophet or an alarmist, nor will I discuss the causes which appear to lead to the beginning of it; but it is unquestioned that we should prepare ourselves through just such gatherings as this to understand and solve the problems with which we are at any time likely to be confronted.

"The trade agreement, in my opinion, is one of the most potent factors toward the solution of industrial peace. Only recently, among others, the typographical unions throughout the United States have signed a trade agreement with the newspapers, carrying them through the next five years, and in so doing they have undoubtedly provided themselves in the immediate future with industrial peace. Only yesterday one of the most stupendous movements among our railroad men in the West was brought to a happy issue through the medium of the trade agreement. Our host, as we all know, is greatly interested in the promotion of international peace. There is no more potent ally than industrial peace in the promoting of that movement, and on that subject I shall have the pleasure later of asking President Nicholas Murray Butler, of Columbia University, to say a few words."

THE TRADE AGREEMENT.

Mr. William F. Coakley, general president of the International Protective Association of Lithographic Apprentices and Press Feeders of the United States and Canada, spoke as follows:

"Industrial peace in anything like an absolute sense, needless to say, would be an utopian dream. I take it that we are here this evening not to discuss an idea at once impracticable and illogical. The industrial peace we have in mind does not mean the substitution of ox-like dumb submission to conditions that call for betterment, but rather does it mean a consideration of methods whereby those differences that must inevitably arise in the relation of employer and employe may be equitably and peacefully adjusted. Trade unionists, no less tnan employers, have come to realize that the cost of strikes and lockouts, not only to the parties immediately involved, but also to the unprotected public, means a waste of the nation's wealth; also that such unreason and strife afford welcome opportunity to those doctrinaires who from press and platform preach labor and capital are and must be enemies.

"In this enlightened age, war between labor and capital is no less unholy than war between nations. That this truth is forcing recognition I shall in the few moments at my disposal point out to you several unmistakable signs. Here and there strikes and lockouts do occur, and are made much of by the newspapers; but it is no less true that there is at work a powerful influence for a more rational and more equitable method of adjusting the disputes from which these industrial phenomena arise. The strike and the lockout are being discarded for the trade agreement, that most modern of methods for determining the conditions upon which labor may be bought and sold. Not including the agreement entered into in January at Chicago between the locomotive engineers and the principal railroads of the West, and that equally important agreement effected in Chicago yesterday between the companies and [illegible] train-service employes, during the past six mo[illegible] trade agreements, covering periods varying [illegible]ne to three years, have been drawn up between [illegible] railroad systems and the machinists, molders, [illegible] makers, blacksmiths, pattern makers and other divisions of their employes. And but a few months ago the New York, New Haven & Hartford Railroad signed an agreement with its conductors, trainmen and yardmen; that great organization of workmen, the longshoremen, has made an agreement with the employers; and in most cities throughout the country the street railway employes have entered into similar contracts with the companies that employ them. That large concern, the International Paper Company, and the International Brotherhood of Pulp, Sulphite and Paper Mill Workers have signed an agreement covering all its mills.

"This is but a small fraction of a number of such agreements that have been signed during this period of time. In the great building industry of New York City trade agreements are general; indeed, there are but two or three trades without them. Not only are the many branches of this important local industry governed by trade agreements, but those several agreements are made conformably to a general agreement, one covering the industry as a whole. This general agreement, called the Plan of General Arbitration, through the court of arbitration it has established, has put practically a stop to the strikes and lockouts in the local building industry, which for years has been its chief drawback.

"To say that trade agreements are sometimes broken is to offer no argument against the principle of these contracts. Where is that divinely guarded contract that has not been broken? Men in whatever their relations are limited by their very nature. I am not here to charge that employers break contracts, but I will say that where a violation of contract upon the part of a trade union is pointed out it can be shown that trade unions have been faithful to agreements made with employers even when this honorable course has mightily conflicted with their material interests. Recall the great anthracite strike of four years ago. When the prospect seemed blackest for John Mitchell's men, and when it was apparent that they could win only by calling out the bituminous miners, what did they do? Although engaged in a life and death struggle, reduced to the necessity of depending upon the pennies of their brother trade unionists wherewith to buy bread for their women and children, they said: 'No! Our brothers in the bituminous fields have agreements with the employers. We shall not ask them to join us. Rather than win with dishonor we will fall like honorable men.'

"Labor and capital are interdependent. They are but two different forms of the same thing, the concrete result of human effort directed by an intelligence that is only less than divine. Having the one source they have the one destiny. They must move forward together. Those of us who through choice or circumstances have to do with the relation of the two should strive, as is being done here this evening, to have each understand the other better."

POWER OF PERSONAL SYMPATHY.

Archbishop Farley said:

"I am delighted to see the trend that labor and capital are taking, as evidenced in the union here, under the roof of one of our most hospitable and leading capitalists of the United States. It augurs well. Mr. Carnegie said a few moments ago, in speaking of labor and capital, that much of the trouble comes from lack of recognition on the part of the capitalist. Bearing on that, let me take a tale for my text which will perhaps convey to you what Mr. Carnegie and myself have in our minds as the best solution of these vexed relations between labor and capital. When I was a young man in college a companion of mine told me this story: His father was the employer of some 500 or 1,000 men. Dull times came on, the market was stagnant, material was being turned out by this large body of men and no sales were made. Month after month passed and the conditions promised no improvement. One day the employer was waited on by a delegation of the workers, who stated that they were not contented.

"'What's wrong? Am I not paying you to-day and ever since the dull times just what I paid you before, and you see nothing is coming in?'

"'We know it, but we are not contented, and are sent here to represent the men to make a demand on you in the matter of wages.'

'He said: 'I cannot do anything more for you; I am giving you all I can; I might say I am taking the bread out of my own and my children's mouths.'

"'We know that, and we want you to reduce our wages 20 per cent.'

"Well, this gentleman was completely taken aback, and said: 'I will not do it; you have your families and yourselves to support just as well in dull as in good times.'

"'Very well, then; we will strike.'

"That has stuck in my mind since I was a boy, and it seems to me to contain the solution of a great many difficulties. That man understood his men; he was thoroughly in sympathy with them, and I hold that the source of most of the difficulties between capital and labor, between workmen and employer, is the lack of sympathy. They stand facing one another like two grand armies in battle array, ready to rush at one another; or if it be not that, they stand like two rows of statues in the museum up here, having no sympathy one with the other; whereas there should be a warm current of good, kindly feeling between master and man, since each depends on the other. The capitalist depends as much on the laborer as the laborer on the capitalist. He should, therefore, have a paternal interest in all his employes, in sickness, in health, in death and in life. He should be his men's friend. That was the case in the instance I cited a moment ago. That gentleman was a father to all his workmen, and hence he had their confidence, love and affection. He was willing to make any sacrifice, and they were willing to make one which he would not accept from them.

"Now, I have thought over this problem from time to time, and it occurs to me that the great drawback of the system of corporations (and I recognize the necessity of corporations) is this—that those employed by them never can get at the employer. A corporation has no soul—so it is said, at least—and when a man, or a body of men, have a grievance, they cannot get at the owner, whom they think should feel for them and meet with them. He will always say: 'I cannot do anything in the matter unless it is laid before the board.'

"Now, I hold that if some person in power were given authority, some man with a big heart and a sympathetic nature, to deal with the men as that gentleman I spoke of in the beginning dealt with his men, showing them that he was flesh of their flesh and bone of their bone, that he recognized in them and in their souls the image of God, the same as was stamped upon his own soul, you would hear less of discontent and less of the problems that are vexing the nations to-day between capital and labor. (Applause.)

"I feel that I have a right to speak on this question, and am very happy to have this opportunity of doing so, inasmuch as I am a Bishop of a Church whose supreme head, the Sovereign Pontiff lately deceased, Leo XIII., has put forth the ablest, the clearest and the most solving instruction that perhaps ever has been written on the subject of labor and capital. Doubtless most of you have heard of it. Many of you have read it. There he divides all mankind into two bodies, very properly, workers and employers, and he takes them to task and asks, why should they stand face to face like two armies, ready to fly at one another? He tells the workmen, do not listen to demagogues who promise impossible things which they never can perform. Do no violence to your employer or to your employer's property. Do your work honestly and uprightly. Then he turns to the employer and says: Do not regard your workmen as slaves; do not make capital out of their needs; do not regard their bone and muscle as so much wood and steel to be turned into money. No; and then he touches, as no man I ever heard on the question has touched it, the solution of the wage problem. He says every man is free to make a contract with another; but there is a law of nature more imperious and ancient than any contract between man and man, and any contract that denies a laborer a reasonable and frugal maintenance is an unjust one."

AGREEMENTS IN PUBLISHING BUSINESS.

Mr. Herbert Ridder then read the following letter from Herman Ridder, president of the Newspaper Publishers' Association:

"Arbitration has secured industrial peace for 200 members of the American Newspaper Publishers' Association, employing four-fifths of all newspaper labor. In six years there has not been a strike or cessation of work in any of the union composing rooms of our association. There has not been a single disagreement which has not been amicably adjusted. We are glad to report that agreements just signed provide for a continuance of that happy condition for an additional period of five years. Neither employer nor employe has been subjected to the wasting effects of warfare, both sides have been gainers. The publishers are paying higher wages. The unions are treating the publishers with greater respect, greater caution, greater justice. Both sides are pleased. Our principal gain is not in the troubles we have settled, but in those we have prevented. Our labor commissioner reported that the past year has been the most quiet of our history. There had been steady improvement of labor conditions and an increase of peaceful methods. We know of no other combination of employers which has succeeded in perfecting a great pact with the labor unions, and in maintaining entirely satisfactory relations. The probable explanation of this outcome and our good fortune in the matter lies in the fact that our employes are more intelligent than any other grade of labor, and are more appreciative of what is right. These unions take pride not in the number of strikes they have ordered in newspaper offices, but in the number of days' work they have provided for their members, and in the fact that they have in their ranks many skilled men to whom employers pay more than the scale to retain their services. These unions pride themselves that their word is their bond, and that their treasuries and authority are behind their agreements.

"The American Newspaper Publishers' Association is a voluntary organization of 270 newspapers, covering every considerable city of the Union. It has no power to compel any member to act outside of his own volition. We employ compositors, stereotypers and mailers who work under our International Typographical Union agreement. We employ pressmen who work under our agreement with the International Printing Pressmen and Assistants' Union. We employ photo-engravers who work under an agreement with the International Photo-Engravers' Union. These national agreements with labor organizations are not labor contracts. They simply provide a way by which each individual publisher may secure arbitration without interruption of his business, the national labor organization with which the contract is made by each publisher guaranteeing the performance of all its contracts by unions under its jurisdiction; in other words, it underwrites local arrangements. Those agreements have stood the practical test of time and of wide application under an extreme range of conditions. They are workable.

"At the outset, we recognized labor unions. We dealt with labor representatives. We realized that when we did so, we ceased to recognize the individual, but in doing so we increased the responsibility of the union and the union admitted its obligation. We accepted the closed shop. We substantially accepted the eight-hour day. We assumed that arbitration is possible only when the parties in dispute approach the question in a fair and conciliatory way. We had interests in common and we dealt on the basis that we were not members of hostile classes. We have not wrangled over trifles. We have explained our relative positions and have avoided many difficulties which arise from haughtiness. We have studied patience. We knew that the labor question was full of complications, and that the leaders of the union men must exercise great patience and tact in controlling the men who elect them to office.

"We started out to promote a better understanding between the association and our employes. We established a labor bureau and elected a commissioner with manifold duties. He assisted in settling labor disputes. He worked to secure the appointment of joint national arbitration committees for the adjustment of labor troubles that could not otherwise be settled. He obtained data upon all subjects pertaining to the mechanical work of newspapers. Publishers were thereby equipped to deal intelligently with the unions. We cultivated friendly relations with the organized wage earners. Our commissioner attended their conventions and addressed them every year. Their presidents came to our conventions annually and talked to us. They send to our commissioner regularly the proceedings of their conventions, the copies of their official organ and their reports. Our dealings have been marked with courtesy, promptness and fairness. Disagreements have occurred and diametrically opposite views have been held, but we have always managed to arrive at some sort of understanding which, while not altogether satisfactory, has prevented friction and trouble.

"The first contract became effective May 1, 1901. It was a tentative agreement with the International Typographical Union for one year to settle differences arising from existing contracts. At the end of that period we entered into a second agreement for a term of five years, adding an important provision for the arbitration of wages and hours. In the settlement of each dispute, we arranged to try first conciliation, then local arbitration, and, finally, national arbitration. It is gratifying to report that more than half of the new scales were settled by conciliation.

"Our third agreement, which begins May 1, 1907, and continues for five years, covers wages, hours and working conditions. In it we have attempted a radical departure, new at least on this side of the ocean, though we understand it has been tried successfully in England. We are doing away with the third man in arbitration. We think it is an advance step. Usually the third man has been unfamiliar with the publishing business. His decision has been more or less of a compromise and it has been described as a 'hit and miss' affair. We have now sought to establish perfect equality of both sides in the settlement of any controversy that might arise, the final judgment to be rendered by three representatives of each national body. If this new arrangement meets our requirements, then we will have brought the settlement of industrial disputes to an ideal plane.

"In working out the amicable adjustment of our differences, we encountered in 1903 a difficulty because we did not have a code of procedure which would guide and govern arbitrators in passing upon questions. Ultimately, a draft was formulated and adopted which facilitated work and minimized the occasion for disputes. Later on, we were confronted by the advocates of the sympathetic strikes. It was contended that our contract could not prevail if a newspaper had a dispute with a union [illegible] was affiliated with those under agreement. [illegible] position was taken by the unions, we [illegible] to make any agreement to do other than pay the scale, and because of our firmness in that respect the sympathetic strike idea was abandoned.

"It is true that under arbitration neither side has obtained what it thought it was entitled to receive, but we have maintained friendly relations at all times. We have produced our newspapers without interruption, and our employes have had the opportunity of work uninterrupted by strike or lockout. The recognition of the principle of arbitration has tended to increase the stability of investment in newspaper property. Its chief value has been the means it afforded us for the settlement of minor contentions which formerly caused infinite trouble, often leading to destruction of property, enormous losses of wages and the engendering of passion. Our payments for the maintenance of our special standing committee have been payments for industrial insurance, just as we pay for fire and accident insurance.

"We look forward to the day when the unions will realize that all union men should be proficient in their work and of good moral character in order that publishers may not want other than union men."

INTERNATIONAL ACTION NEEDED.

President Butler, of Columbia University, addressed the Conference as follows:

"Two of mankind's most important interests and activities are government and the production of wealth. The problems of government are primarily political; the problems of the production of wealth are primarily economic. Both, however, rest upon a common ethical foundation.

"The leaders of thought in all civilized countries are now urging upon their governments that concerted efforts be made to reduce the burdens of the world's armaments, to promote peace between nations, and to advance the cause of the settlement of international differences and disputes by the rational and intelligent method of judicial examination and arbitration as a substitute for the rule of force and the exploitation of men's angry passions in war. To this end one great and highly successful international conference has already been held at The Hague, and the governments of the world are now naming their delegates to a second, and, as many of us believe, a more important conference.

"Why should we not seek to promote the cause of industrial peace by methods similar to those which are now making headway in the interest of political or govermental peace? To interrupt the production of wealth by industrial wars is to spread sorrow, suffering and loss over large numbers of the population, those not immediately concerned in the struggle being affected as well as those directly interested. Industrial wars arise from two distinct causes,—first, from struggles between labor and capital, the two necessary and co-operating factors in wealth-production; and, second, from struggles on the part of labor to free itself from limitations and conditions not primarily imposed by capital, but due to outgrown and outworn methods of work and to the traditions of a time which paid little attention to the moral and educational uplifting of those who work with their hands.

"It is often urged that however strong may be the impulse which leads us to favor the removal of these obstacles and restrictions to a better condition for labor, yet not much can be done by one State or one nation alone, because of the fact that the demands of international trade and of competition prevent reforms being instituted in one nation unless others concur and acquiesce.

"If this objection is sound, and indeed whether it be sound or not, if it is seriously urged, why should not the nations of the earth undertake to forward the cause of international peace by formal international conference devoted to that end, at which the nations shall be severally represented by men as able, as thoroughly familiar with the problems and as representative of all parts of the population as are those who are to assemble at The Hague to discuss the problems of political peace? The National Civic Federation could, in my judgment, do no greater service to mankind at this moment than to urge upon the Government of the United States the making of a formal proposal to other nations of the world to assemble at no distant date in international conference on industrial conditions and industrial peace. The same united force which has made such rapid progress in advancing the world's education and the world's science would then be brought into play to advance the world's industrial peace and to improve, not little by little, but more speedily and in large and generous fashion, the conditions which surround labor in its activity in the production of wealth.

"This proposal would not be entirely novel, for at least one such conference has already been held. In the early part of his reign, the enlightened and progressive statesman who is now the German Emperor, turned his thoughts in this direction. Even against the advice of his ministers or in the face of their indifference, Emperor William II called an international conference [illegible] to [illegible] memorandum [illegible] this subject [illegible] workers of the different countries have already established international relations aiming at the improvement of their condition, but that efforts to this end could not meet with complete success until the governments concerned should attempt to come to some agreement on the more important questions relating to the welfare of the working classes. The specific points mentioned in the memorandum upon which international discussion was sought were those relating to Sunday rest, to the restriction of female and child labor, and to the limitation of the length of the working day. When the conference assembled in March, 1890, it met in the Palace of the Chancellor and was as dignified and worthy an assemblage as one composed of trained diplomats or statesmen. The Prussian Minister of Commerce opened the meeting with an important address in which he took high ground as to the necessity of seeking a solution of the human problems presented by industrial competition. Journals of all shades of political opinion supported eagerly the plan for the conference and commented generously and appreciatively upon its discussion. Austria, Belgium, Denmark, France, England, Italy, The Netherlands, Portugal, Sweden and Switzerland were represented, in addition to Germany. Nine years before this Berlin Conference was held Switzerland had made a somewhat similar proposal to the nations of Europe. The conference agreed upon very important recommendations as to work in mines, as to Sunday labor, and as to the work of children and women. It cannot be doubted that these recommendations have had no inconsiderable weight in affecting public opinion and the formal legislation of the nations concerned. Nearly twenty years have passed since the Berlin Labor Conference was held. Long steps forward have been taken in the meanwhile to better the conditions attaching to manual labor. New problems have meanwhile arisen and old problems have taken on new form. Why should we not, then, seek the discussion, and perhaps even the solution of some of these problems through the medium of an international conference on labor and industrial peace?

"If it should be given to our generation to see the public opinion of the world turning from war to peace in the settlement of international disputes and to see it turning from carelessness to solicitous concern in regard to industrial peace and the condition of labor, then indeed would we be able to lay claim to having lived in one of the world's most enlightened eras.

(Continued on page 20.)

PRIVATE VERSUS PUBLIC OPERATION

COMMITTEE ON INVESTIGATION PRESENTS ITS REPORT TO PUBLIC OWNERSHIP COMMISSION—CONCLUSIONS OF COMMITTEE—SCOPE OF THE REPORT

THE full report of the Public Ownership Commission's Committee of Investigation, with all its appendices, is in the hand of the printer, and some of the general results of the inquiry have already been given to the press. The general conclusions of the committee, reprinted here, have attracted the widespread attention which their importance deserves.

Quite as striking as the results obtained were the methods employed to secure them. The care, the patience and thoroughness of the methods of investigation invest the report with a peculiar significance. The committee entrusted with the investigation was thoroughly representative. It was composed of Melville E. Ingalls, chairman (Big Four Railroad), Cincinnati, Ohio; Dr. Albert Shaw, vice-chairman (Editor Review of Reviews), New York City; Edward A. Moffett, Secretary (Editor Bricklayer and Mason), Indianapolis, Ind.; Talcott Williams (Editorial Writer, the Press), Philadelphia, Pa.; Prof. Frank J. Goodnow (Columbia University), New York City; Walton Clark (Vice-President United Gas Improvement Co.), Philadelphia; Edward W. Bemis (Superintendent Water Works), Cleveland, O.; William J. Clark, (General Electric Company), New York City; Walter L. Fisher, (President Municipal Voters' League), Chicago, Ill.; Prof. John H. Gray (Northwestern University), Evanston, Ill.; W. D. Mahon (President Association Street Railway Employes), Detroit, Mich.; Prof. Frank Parsons (President National Public Ownership League), Boston, Mass.; Timothy Healy (President International Brotherhood Stationary Firemen), New York City; Prof. John R. Commons (Wisconsin University), Madison, Wis.; Daniel J. Keefe (President International Longshoremen's Association) Detroit, Mich.; Charles L. Edgar (President The Edison Electric and Illuminating Company), Boston; J. W. Sullivan (Editor Clothing Trades' Bulletin), New York City; Albert E. Winchester (Superintendent South Norwalk, Conn. Electric Works); F. J. McNulty (President International Brotherhood of Electrical Workers), Springfield, Ill.; H. B. F. MacFarland (President Board of Commissioners District of Columbia); Milo R. Maltbie (Member of the Public Utilities Commission), New York City.

All shades of thought were represented in the constitution of the committee, in order that the investigation of facts might be complete in every particular. For it was designed that the investigation be one of facts and not of theories. As a preliminary, schedules of questions appropriate to each class of enterprise to be examined were prepared by a committee, in which divergent opinions were carefully balanced.

From the outset it was recognized that there were two extreme views on the general question, and the policy was adopted of having these views equally represented in all steps of the investigation. Besides the experts who formed part of the committee, it secured the co-operation of technical experts and accountants. In the choice of these experts again "both sides" were represented.

Having laid out its plan and secured its technical aid, the commission proceeded to a personal and searching inspection of plants, both municipal and private. In America 29 plants were visited, and in Great Britain 24. The results of these inspections were placed upon record and form Part II. of the published report. For the guidance of the commission these special reports were made the object of critical reviews by sub-committees. Upon the basis of these reviews, as well as upon the results of the inspection, other members of the committee made special reports on general aspects involved in the question.

In these preliminary reports both sides are vigorously represented; none the less there was found to be much common ground, and this is presented in the general conclusions of the committee. One member only, Mr. Walton Clark, dissents from its conclusions. Two members, Mr. Charles L. Edgar and Mr. William J. Clark, take exception to the form of certain statements, but are in substantial agreement with the body of the report.

The text of these general conclusions is as follows:

REPORT TO THE NATIONAL CIVIC FEDERATION COMMISSION ON PUBLIC OWNERSHIP AND OPERATION.

Your Committee on Investigation beg to report as follows:

After our appointment on October 5, 1905, we met and appointed a sub-committee to prepare a plan of procedure and investigation. It was decided that the Committee should visit a number of undertakings in certain American cities, and then should go abroad and make a similar investigation in certain cities in Great Britain, comparing the methods and results of municipal and private ownership. Much attention was given to the investigation in Great Britain, because it was felt that the American public was not so familiar with conditions abroad as at home, and because in the contests that have been waged for public ownership, allusion has always been made and prominence given to conditions in British cities.

You Committee decided to employ both company and municipal men as experts, so that when investigating a gas plant, for example, there should be ordinarily one expert who had been employed by a private gas company and another to act with him who had been employed by a municipality. A long series of questions was prepared and various special

MEMBERS OF COMMITTEE ON INVESTIGATION IN SESSION AT DETROIT.

reports were called for, some from the members of the Committee who were detailed for this purpose and some from outside experts employed to investigate specific matters. All of these reports and schedules have been carefully prepared and are published herewith.* While it may appear upon a superficial glance that there is too much of this work, we trust it will be appreciated by the student and by those particularly interested, and that these statistics and report will do great good in the future as works of reference upon this important subject.

We wish here, at the beginning of our report, to tender our sincere thanks to the gentlemen in charge of the public utilities in the cities we visited in the United States and Great Britain for their polite attention and thoughtful consideration. Nothing could have been fairer or kinder than the treatment that they gave us. We examined their plants; we asked for detailed reports upon a long list of matters, which were cheerfully given. Whatever may be our opinion of the merits of municipal or private ownership, we are unanimous that no more courteous treatment could have been accorded any one.

It is difficult to give positive answers of universal application to the questions arising as to the success or failure of municipal ownership as compared with private ownership. The local conditions affecting particular plants are, in many cases, so peculiar as to make a satisfactory comparison impossible, and it is very difficult to estimate the allowance that should be made for these local conditions. For instance, in making deductions from the financial conditions of Wheeling, as affected by its gas plant, as compared with those of Atlanta and Norfolk with their private plants, allowance must be made for the presence of natural gas in Wheeling. Again, in comparing the public water works of Syracuse with the private water works of Indianapolis from the point of view of the success or failure of municipal operation, geographical conditions must be taken into consideration. The situation at Syracuse is extremely favorable to the establishment of an efficient plant with comparatively little effort on the part of its management. At Indianapolis the conditions are unfavorable. In Syracuse the water flows to the city by gravity; in Indianapolis it must be pumped. So we might go through the various cities here and abroad that have been visited and show that the results were affected favorably or unfavorably by special conditions applicable to each city.

Further, the difficulty of reaching satisfactory results by the comparative method is not confined to special or local conditions. It is true, as well, of much broader questions. Thus any attempt to compare municipal with private electric light plants in the United States would be fruitless if allowance were not made for the fact that in most cases such municipal plants are confined to street lighting and may not do commercial business. Allowance must be made also for the fact that many municipal plants have had a struggle to exist in the face of unsympathetic public opinion. Again, in England consideration must be given to the fact that the municipal electric light and street railway plants have permanent rights, while the rights of the private companies operating these particular utilities are limited as to the length of their existence, many street railway franchises expiring twenty-one years after they were granted.

Finally, not only must it be borne in mind that the social and political conditions which characterize the two countries find expression in their private and public systems, but we must consider the difference in the nature of the two peoples which causes them to adopt different ideas and views to the expediency of certain things. In other words, a measure of success in the municipal management of public utilities in England should not be regarded as necessarily indicating that the municipal management of the same utilities in this country would be followed by a like measure of success. Conditions are quite different in the two countries, as will be seen from an examination of the various reports that follow.*

There are some general principles which we wish to present as practically the unanimous sentiment of our Committee.

First, we wish to emphasize the fact that the public utilities studied are so constituted that it is impossible for them to be regulated by competition. Therefore, they must be controlled and regulated by the government; or they must be left to do as they please; or they must be operated by the public. There is no other course. None of us is in favor of leaving them to their own will, and the question is whether it is better to regulate than to operate.

There are no particular reasons why the financial results from private or public operation should be different if the conditions are the same. In each case it is a question of the proper man in charge of the business and of local conditions.

We are of the opinion that a public utility which concerns the health of the citizens should not be left to individuals, where the temptation of profit might produce disastrous results, and therefore it is our judgment that undertakings in which the sanitary motive largely enters should be operated by the public.

We have come to the conclusion that municipal ownership of public utilities should not be extended to revenue-producing industries which do not involve the public health, the public safety, public transportation, or the permanent occupation of public streets or grounds, and that municipal operation should not be undertaken solely for profit.

We are also of the opinion that all future grants to private companies for the construction and operation of public utilities should be terminable after a certain fixed period, and that meanwhile cities should have the right to purchase the property for operation, lease or sale, paying its fair value.

To carry out these recommendations effectively and to protect the rights of the people, we recommend that the various States should give to their municipalities the authority, upon popular vote under reasonable regulations, to build and operate public utilities, or to build and lease the same, or to take over works already constructed. In no other way can the people be put upon a fair trading basis and obtain from the individual companies such rights as they ought to have. We believe that this provision will tend to make it to the enlightened self-interest of the public utility companies to furnish adequate service upon fair terms, and to this extent will tend to render it unnecessary for the public to take over the existing utilities or to acquire new ones.

Furthermore, we recommend that provision be made for a competent public authority, with power to require for all public utilities a uniform system of records and accounts, giving all financial data and all information concerning the quality of service and the cost thereof, which data shall be published and distributed to the public like other official reports; and also that no stock or bonds for public utilities shall be issued without the approval of some competent public authority.

We also recommend the consideration of "the sliding scale," which has proved successful in some cases in England with reference to gas and has been adopted in Boston. By this plan the authorized capitalization is settled by official investigation, and a standard rate of dividend is fixed, which may be increased only when the price of gas has been reduced. The subway contracts and their operation in Boston and New York are also entitled to full consideration.

In case the management of public utilities is left with private companies, the public should retain, in all cases an interest in the growth and profits of the future, either by a share of the profits or a reduction of the charges, the latter being preferable, as it inures to the benefit of those who use the utilities, while a share of the profits benefits the taxpayers.

Our investigations teach us that no municipal operation is likely to be highly succesful that does not provide for:

First—An executive manager with full responsibility, holding his position during good behavior.

Second—Exclusion of political influence and personal favoritism from the management of the undertaking.

Third—Separation of the finances of the undertaking from those of the rest of the city.

Fourth—Exemption from the debt limit of the necessary bond issues for revenue-producing utilities, which shall be a first charge upon the property and revenues of such undertaking.

We wish to bring to your consideration the danger here in the United States of turning over these public utilities to the present government of some of our cities. Some, we know, are well governed and the situation on the whole seems to be improving, but they are not up to the government of British cities. We found in England and Scotland a high type of municipal government, which is the result of many years of struggle and improvement. Business men seem to take a pride in serving as city councillors or aldermen, and the government of such cities as Glasgow, Manchester, Birmingham and others includes many of the best citizens of the city. These conditions are distinctly favorable to municipal operation.

In the United States, as is well known, there are many cities not in such a favorable condition. It is charged that the political activity of public service corporations has in many instances been responsible for the unwillingness or inability of American cities to secure a higher type of public service. This charge we believe to be true. However, there seems to be an idea with many people that the mere taking by the city of all its public utilities for municipal operation will at once result in ideal municipal government through the very necessity of putting honest and competent citizens in charge. While an increase in the number and importance of municipal functions may have a tendency to induce men of a higher type to become public officials, we do not believe that this of itself will accomplish municipal reform. We are unable to recommend municipal ownership as a political panacea.

In many cases in the United States the people have heedlessly given away their rights and reserved no sufficient power of control or regulation, and we believe that corruption of public servants has sprung, in large measure, from this condition of things. With the regulations that we have advised, with the publication of accounts and records and systematic control, the danger of the corruption of public officials is very much reduced.

To sum up, certain of the more important of our conclusions are:

Public utilities, whether in public or in private hands are best conducted under a system of legalized and regulated monopoly.

Public utilities in which the sanitary motive largely enters should be operated by the public.

The success of municipal operation of public utilities depends upon the existence in the city of a high capacity for municipal government.

Franchise grants to private corporations should be terminable after a fixed period and meanwhile subject to purchase at a fair value.

Municipalities should have power to enter the field of municipal ownership upon popular vote under reasonable regulation.

Private companies operating public utilities should be subject to public regulation and examination under a system of uniform records and accounts and of full publicity.

The general expediency of either private or public ownership is a question that must be determined by each municipality in the light of local conditions. What may be possible in one locality may not be in another. In some cities the companies may so serve the public as to create no dissatisfaction and nothing might be gained by experimenting with municipal ownership. Again, the government of one city may be good and capable of taking charge of these public utilities, while in another it may be the reverse. In either case the people must remember that it requires a large class of able men as city officials to look after these matters. They must also remember that municipal ownership will create a large class of employes who may have more or less political influence.

EXCEPTIONS.

Messrs. Charles [illegible] and Will[illegible] sent the following exceptions to [illegible] report.

"We the undersigned dissent from [illegible] the Investigating Committee as follows:

"First—The report says:

"'We are of the opinion that a public utility which concerns the health of the citizens should not be left to individuals, where the temptation of profit might produce disastrous results, and therefore it is our judgment that undertakings in which the sanitary motive largely enters should be operated by the public.'

"We dissent from this conclusion as having been proved by our investigations. In our opinion, privately operated water systems were, especially as regards their consideration for the public health, as properly and successfully managed as the public operated water systems.

"Second—The report says:

"'We have come to the conclusions that municipal ownership of public utilities should not be extended to revenue-producing industries which do not involve the public health, the public safety, public transportation, or the permanent occupation of public streets or grounds, and that municipal operation should not be solely for profit.'

"This sentence is so drawn that to a casual reader it implies that the opposite is advisable. From this we strongly dissent.

"Third—The report says:

"'To carry out these recommendations effectively and to protect the rights of the people, we recommend that the various States should give to their municipalities the authority, upon popular vote under reasonable regulations,' etc.

"The words 'under reasonable regulations' were put into the report at the suggestion of Charles L. Edgar, and were intended by him to mean such regulations as would compel deliberate consideration not only by the people, but by their representatives, and would consequently prevent the superficial attractiveness of the scheme from overriding the 'sober second thought' of the people. We strongly dissent from any definition of 'regulations' which does not cover these points.

"Fourth—The second and fifth conclusions in the latter part of the report, being merely repetitions of previous statements, are of course subject to the same dissents."

(Continued on page 19.)

*See "The Facts of Municipal Ownership," Part II. *In Press.*

AN INQUIRY INTO CHILD LABOR:

NATIONAL CHILD LABOR COMMISSION MEETS AND ORGANIZES AT WASHINGTON, D.C. COMMITTEES APPOINTED.

A DEFINITE organization was effected in Washington May 25 of the commission to investigate the extent and menace of child labor in this country.

It will be remembered that the question of child labor was discussed at length at the meeting of the National Civic Federation, last December, by representatives of the cotton manufacturers, coal operators, the National Child Labor Committee, factory inspectors, trade union leaders and others. This discussion developed a very wide difference of opinion on many points; among others, the actual extent of child labor; how many of the supposed two million are under fourteen years of age; what proportion are working in factories and mines, and what proportion on farms; whether there has been a great increase in child labor since 1900, when the census was taken; what the physical effects of mill labor are upon the children; what shall be done with children if taken out of the mills; whether the schooling opportunities are sufficient; what kind of education should be provided for those who expect to enter the mills as soon as the law permits; what measures are feasible to keep them in school until they reach the age limit for employment and so on.

The many differences brought out, both on questions of fact and on the merits of the problems presented, suggested the desirability of a national commission to undertake a comprehensive and unbiassed inquiry into the whole subject. In furtherance of that plan delegates have since been appointed from the National Association of Manufacturers, the American Federation of Labor, the General Federation of Women's Clubs and the National Civic Federation. The members representing each of these bodies are as follows:

For the National Association of Manufacturers: F. C. Nunemacher, president Nunemacher Press, Louisville, Ky. (chairman); C. W. Post, president Postum Cereal Company, Battle Creek, Michigan; D. C. Ripley, president United States Glass Company, Pittsburg, Pa.; D. A. Tompkins, president D. A. Tompkins Company, Charlotte, N. C.; Ellison A. Smyth, president Pelzer Manufacturing Company, Pelzer, S. C.; James R. MacColl, treasurer Lorraine Manufacturing Company, Pawtucket, R. I., and C. H. Pond, president Scranton Forging Company, Scranton, Pa.

For the American Federation of Labor: Samuel Gompers, president American Federation of Labor, Washington; James Duncan, Granite Cutters' International Association, Quincy, Mass.; John Mitchell, president United Mine Workers of America, Indianapolis, Ind.; D. A. Hayes, president Glass Bottle Blowers' Association, Philadelphia; John Golden, president United Textile Workers of America, Fall River, Mass.; B. A. Larger, general secretary Garment Workers' Union, New York City; William B. Wilson, secretary of the United Mine Workers of America; Daniel Harris, Cigarmakers' Union, Brooklyn, N. Y., and Herman Robinson, Retail Clerks' Association, New York City.

For the General Federation of Women's Clubs: Mrs. Sarah S. Platt Decker, Denver, Col.; Mrs. Mary Morton Kehew, Boston, Mass.; Mrs. Phillip N. Moore, St. Louis, Mo.; Mrs. Clarence Burns, New York City; Mrs. Charles A. Dibble, St. Paul, Minn.; Mrs. Josiah E. Cowles, Los Angeles, Cal., and Mrs. A. F. McKissick, Greenwood, S. C.

For the National Civic Federation: V. Everett Macy, treasurer National Child Labor Committee, New York City; Prof. J. W. Jenks, president American Economic Association, Cornell University, New York; Talcott Williams, National Child Labor Committee, Philadelphia, Pa.; Rev. Dr. Thomas R. Slicer, pastor of All Souls' Church, New York City; W. H. Taylor, anthracite coal operator, Scranton, Pa.; Samuel B. Donnelly, member Board of Education, New York City; E. B. Butler, president Illinois Manual Training School, Chicago, Ill.

The following officers were chosen at the meeting of May 25:

Chairman, Ellison A. Smith, of Pelzer, S. C., president of the Southern Cotton Manufacturers' Association; vice-chairman, Mrs. Sarah Platt Decker, of Denver, Col., president of the General Federation of Women's Clubs; secretary, Representative William B. Wilson of Pennsylvania, secretary of the United Mine Workers of America.

The members of the commission visited the White House, after the adjournment of the morning session, and were received by President Roosevelt, who commended the plans of the commission.

A point that occupied much of the attention of the delegates was the relation that should exist between the inquiry it is to undertake and the Government investigation of child labor conditions, authorized last winter, to be carried on by the United States Bureau of Labor. Professor Jenks, in opening the meeting, expressed his belief that the work of each inquiry could be made much more effective through co-operation. He offered the following suggestions:

"It would seem to me that in all probability our most useful work would be in making suggestions to Commissioner Neill as to what we thought might wisely be done in connection with the coming Government investigation of this subject. I suppose he will have machinery to undertake that investigation, and I have no doubt it is the purpose of the Secretary of Commerce and Labor to make the investigation as fair, as broad and as impartial as it can be. I have understood that the chief purpose of this Commission is to secure just that end. We all know there are very great differences of opinion, and the essential thing is that whatever is done by the Government in the way of making that investigation shall be fair, impartial and thorough. It seems to me that all who have experience in the various lines of industry are the ones that can give him suggestions that will help with the investigation.

"It may be, also, that when we have heard from him we shall find that the scope of the investigation at the time being must be limited on account of the funds at his disposal, and it may be possible that along certain lines we can take up work with him. In the nature of the case, I should think co-operation with the Government investigation is something that is extremely desirable."

Mr. Gompers:

"I believe with Prof. Jenks that we should co-operate with the Government in its investigation as authorized by a recent act of Congress, but as the scope of the two investigations are different I am of the opinion that it might not at all be amiss if an independent investigation were made. More than likely some exaggerations have been indulged in with regard to this evil, but I take it that the most acute conditions have been presented, not with any purpose of injury, but for the purpose of rousing the conscience of the people against the continuance of that condition of affairs, even if it is confined to a small number.

"I feel very keenly upon the subject of child labor, and I believe there are few who want such labor simply for the sake of having children in the factories. We are all pretty nearly agreed that it is desirable that children should have the opportunity of growth, development, education and play. There is little room, I think, for division of opinion as to the age limit at which children are allowed to enter upon industrial or commercial pursuits, but none the less that is one of the subjects to which attention should be given."

Mr. Nunemacher:

"I am satisfied that our section of the Committee is in full sympathy with any sane regulation that might be brought about on this question of child labor. I think as a general proposition that the manufacturer from his own standpoint would not employ children under a proper age. I am satisfied that when the matter is fully considered the manufacturer is willing to go as far as anybody in any worthy thing. I had the pleasure of a conversation the other day with Dr. Neill and believe that we will get from him any assistance the government has power to give."

Mr. Tompkins:

"One of the most important things in connection with improving anything is to find its existing status and to begin the improvement from the existing condition. The conditions so vary in different States that I think it very important that the examination which is going to be made by the Government, and which may be made also by this Commission, should indicate how the different conditions may be treated in different sections.

"Take the conditions of living in Philadelphia, where working people nearly all own their homes; again, in the cotton mill villages and in the coal mining districts, where they don't own their homes. In order to bring out the conditions you have to take each one and start from where they are. We all know Mr. Pullman's experience in undertaking to make a model city, the difficulties he met with pointing out just how the balconies for flowers should be arranged and so on. He put in a model sewerage system, model flower yards, model streets, etc. You can regulate people too much.

"None of us wants child labor. Personally I strongly oppose children under 16 years old working in the mills. I think they should be kept in the schools. This subject of child labor is going to involve the subject of education, and I believe there is not a person in this body who would not vote for compulsory education. On the other hand, we must not have legislation that wholly takes from parents the responsibility of their children."

Mr. Ripley:

"There is an important matter to be considered in this investigation, and that is the financial condition of the parents of the children. There are great many families who are not able to send their children to school after they are 14 years old, and a boy that will not obtain a certain amount of knowledge, enough to help him along in his work, by the time he reaches that age never will. From 14 to 16 the way he uses his opportunity will either make a man of him or a loafer.

"To begin with, I am opposed to any children working in a factory under 14 years old; I think they should not become wage earners until their physical condition will justify it. However, there are many boys of 12 years that are better developed than boys at 16 years.

"There has been a great deal said about the wicked glass manufacturers. I forget the name of the man who wrote the magazine article, but he said that the boys were inhaling dust from the glass—you might as well say that you would inhale dust from dough. I don't think that a boy in a glass house is abused at all. Several times I have gone out into the different factories and looked them over, from a little different standpoint than heretofore, and I have not seen boys that have been abused.

"There was a statement made some time ago by a Pittsburg party, who said that he went into a South Side factory and found boys there with their eyes out. Immediately, when I read this, I telephoned the different factories and in an hour's time I got the report that they did not know of any and couldn't find any. Why a statement of that kind should be made I cannot understand. It is not fair, and has the tendency of prejudicing the minds of people against others who are trying to do a fair business. I think that this is a subject to which we all should give a great deal of study."

Hon. Charles P. Neill, United States Commissioner of Labor, addressed the afternoon session as follows:

"I wish that I were able to outline for the committee in a definite way the work which we expect to do in our investigation of child labor. We realize that we have a very hard problem—one of extreme difficulty.

"We have an appropriation of $150,000 to be divided between working women and children. Take $50,000 of that to make an investigation—that would probably allow 25 or 30 investigators—just ask yourselves what kind of a dent that would make in a problem of this kind.

"We are particularly anxious that as far as it goes the investigation be thorough. I feel that if our investigation simply adds fuel to the fire, we would better leave it where it is now. I want to report here and every place I have the opportunity that our object is to get the facts and all the facts, and we are going to show these, no matter what the showing may be.

"I know that an investigation of a subject like this will not escape criticism, but we are absolutely indifferent as to the criticism made, as we propose to go out and get such facts as exist. Now I think that this committee will approve just that kind of a report. It does seem to me that a commission of this kind, representing the biggest organizations, ought to be able to work out the child labor problem. I believe that all of you want the actual facts concerning child labor, and if we can get those in such a way that there is no dispute there will then be no difference of opinion as to what ought to be done. I believe that as the result of the investigation and the result of this committee's work, we shall all join hands on the right kind of policy to correct these evils.

"Child labor is a subject upon which, a year from now, I could probably talk much more intelligently than now. I hope we shall have the co-operation of this committee, and if we have any data or anything that will be of use to this committee to further its investigations we shall be only too glad to give any help or aid we can."

Mrs. Decker:

"In the organization that I represent, the General Federation of Women's Clubs of the United States, we have forty-three State Federations and a vast number of clubs—800 to 1,000—and we have in every state a Child Labor Committee. We are not biassed—we do not wish to discover that there are children working under age—we want to know the truth. Almost every day I get clippings, speeches, etc., setting forth the two sides; we hear first one side and then the other, and we know nothing at all as to the true state of affairs.

"It is not simply statistics that we want. We need a complete investigation of the children working in the mills from the sociological, industrial and educational standpoint. We want to know if working in the mills better their condition; if so, we think that it is better to keep on. Just simply to be told how many children work will not satisfy us—we have been told that. We want to know whether they are better off than they were five years ago, and whether they will be better off five years hence. Now will some one tell how we can also get the real merits of the matter? We are not smart—are not considered so, but we are industrious and are willing to help."

Mr. Neill:

"I fully agree with Mrs. Decker—it is not merely statistics that we want, but to find out if they are better off than they were, and to learn if they are as well off now as they ought to be. I must say that it is perfectly impossible to try to find out the number of children that are working; there may be children working under age, but how can we find that out? Of course, you can get statistics which you may claim are correct; then some one else will take the statistics and claim they are all wrong. As far as we are concerned, there will be very little money and time wasted merely to find out how many children are working.

"I should be very glad to be able to outline a plan whereby we could work together, but it is too early to do so. We want the co-operation of your committee, and we want it understood that everything we are doing is perfectly open. We will be glad to have you come in, singly or collectively, and make any suggestions that you have to offer."

Mr. John Golden:

"I believe that we should work hand in hand with Dr. Neill, but at the same time I don't think we ought to sit still and just act by making suggestions. To put it plainly, I think we are big enough to do something to satisfy ourselves in this inquiry. I believe that this will be a most valuable investigation. We all know that statistics in regard to women and children vary greatly. You can go into the mills in one section of the South and find all good results, and then go farther and find the conditions very much worse. What we want to do is to lay bare these facts ourselves.

"On the question of education the chairman of the Cotton Manufacturers' Association made the reliable statement that in the state of Rhode Island sixty per cent. of the wage workers were in the textile industry, and yet they had not an institution outside of the School of Design, which taught anything about technical matters. All of us would like to see the day when we could keep our boys and girls out of the mills until they are 16 years of age. They would then be more valuable to themselves, and, I think, would be more valuable to the State and to the community.

"In regard to the curriculum of the public schools; would it not be better to teach these boys and girls something that will fit them for their life's work than to fill their little heads full of Latin and Greek? When they are thus cramming their heads they are beginning to wonder how soon it will be before they are 14 years old, so that they can get out. I think that one of the most important phases of this investigation is the subject of education.

"We have here represented several large organizations and we are capable of doing a great amount of good; we all work along our different lines, but I think that when we, as one body, can sit down at one table and plan out a joint line of work we can do some of the greatest work on the subject of child labor in America."

It was suggested that the work of the Commission might well be carried on under different heads, in charge of sub-committees, for example:

Committee on Investigation,
Committee on Legislation,
Committee on Compulsory Education,
Committee on Industrial Training.

An Executive Committee was elected and instructed to prepare a plan of work and submit it to the Commission in writing at a later date. D. A. Tompkins was chosen chairman of this Committee, the other members being Samuel Gompers, Mrs. Sarah Platt Decker, Ellison A. Smyth, William B. Wilson, Prof. J. W. Jenks and Ralph M. Easley.

THE SANCTITY OF AGREEMENTS.

"If there is one thing above all others that should be held sacred by organized labor, it is the strict adherence to all agreements entered into between our International Alliance or our local unions and their employers. No matter if errors have been committed, mistakes made in framing such agreements, they should be held inviolate during the period they were designed to cover. Any breaking of faith on our part only tends to weaken our influence and to strengthen the position of those opposed to us. The best asset of any organization is the honor and integrity with which it observes its obligations, the good faith with which it keeps its pledges."—M. O'Sullivan, general president Amalgamated Sheet Metal Workers' International Alliance.

THE NATIONAL
Civic Federation Review

Office: 281 Fourth Avenue, New York City
RALPH M. EASLEY, Editor

The Editor alone is Responsible for any unsigned article or unquoted statement published in THE NATIONAL CIVIC FEDERATION REVIEW.

PUBLISHED BY
The National Civic Federation

Conference on Trusts and Combinations. In view of the tremendous interest, financial, industrial and political, which now centers in what is termed the "trust problem," the conference on combinations and trusts to be held under the auspices of the National Civic Federation in Chicago, October 22-25, will be one of the most important gatherings of the year. Coming at a time when the whole country is aroused over the many questions involved in the enforcement of the Sherman anti-trust law and the amended Interstate Commerce act, this conference, it is to be hoped, will serve to give direction to public opinion in reaching a final judgment.

Delegates have been named by Governors of forty-one States and Territories and by national labor, agricultural, manufacturing, financial, economic and trade organizations, by chambers of commerce, boards of trade, bar associations and shippers' organizations. Governors, Attorneys-General, members of the Interstate Commerce Commission, members of Senate and House Committees on Interstate Commerce, the Commissioner of Corporations and two members at least of the Cabinet will participate. The delegates appointed by the Governors represent the best interests of their respective States, and include United States Senators, Congressmen, former governors, manufacturers, labor leaders, farmers, merchants, lawyers, clergymen, bankers, etc.

The first day will be devoted to the problems involved in the controversies between State and Federal Government, respecting jurisdiction over interstate commerce, now pending in Minnesota, Missouri, North Carolina, Alabama and Arkansas.

The second day will be devoted to a consideration of the corporation. How should it be constructed? Should there be national corporations as well as State? What should be the basis of capitalization of corporations? their internal control? the provisions looking to the protection of investors and stockholders, as well as fair dealing with the public? Should there be a distinction between public service and other corporations? Should quasi-public utilities, like gas, electric lighting and street railways, be considered natural monopolies to be regulated by the municipality?

The third and fourth days will be devoted to a discussion of the just and practicable limit of restriction and regulation, Federal and State, of combinations in transportation, production, distribution and labor. Shall the Sherman anti-trust act be amended? If so, how?

Hundreds of letters from all classes of people have been received expressing gratification on the calling of this conference, from some of which the following are extracts:

LYMAN ABBOTT, *Editor of "The Outlook"*:

"I am very glad that the National Civic Federation is calling such a conference. It seems to me fundamentally true that the interests of the railroads, the shippers and the general public are essentially one, and that it is of the utmost importance that men representing all three classes should get together, compare views and endeavor to come to some agreement as to the general principles by which those common interests can be best served. I think what we most need on the subject is just what the call indicates this meeting will endeavor to secure—light, not heat. What we need to understand, and what only experience can teach us, is the relation between competition and combination—the one the centrifugal, the other the centripetal force of society. He who believes only in combination will logically be led to socialism; he who believes only in competition will logically be led to nihilism. Neither of these results can possibly furnish the solution of the problems which now confront us. We must learn how to secure the advantages of combination without destroying the individual; to maintain brotherhood in practical forms without sinking, obscuring or belittling personality."

RICHARD WATSON GILDER, *Editor of "The Century"*:

"There is a sign over a shoemaker's shop in the village where I go in Summer which has this inscription above it in large letters: 'CALL IN AND TALK IT OVER.' I am glad the Civic Federation has put that sign up over its shop precisely at this time, and that the subject of talk is to be the burning question of the day—the question of the Trust. So many of the Federation's talks have proved no less useful than timely that I am sure this new talk will help to bring calmness and coolness to the public mind, and Heaven knows it needs them!"

PETER G. GROSSCUP, *Judge U. S. Circuit Court, Chicago*:

"The corporations of this country have grown up as developments of our business life, without much reference to their relations to the people as institutions of, and for, the people. It is time that they be looked into as institutions of, and for, the people. The Sherman act was passed before the regulation of interstate carriers was seriously attempted or foreseen. Now that 'regulation' has come it is time to inquire how far the old 'prohibitions' should remain. The whole matter—corporate reconstruction, and a restudy of the anti-trust act—should be gone over carefully with a view to bringing some kind of order out of the disorder that now prevails!"

N. J. BACHELDER, *Grand Master of the National Grange*:

"I do not know of any meeting more opportune or more needed at this time than the one called by the National Civic Federation at Chicago, October 22-25, to discuss combinations and trusts. The confusion in the public mind to-day is very great on many of the phases of the problem. It certainly is time for serious people to discuss the subject when President Roosevelt and the law officers of the Government, whose duty it is to enforce the Sherman anti-trust act, openly state that the business of the country to-day cannot be done without violating the law."

RT. REV. HENRY C. POTTER:

"I am profoundly thankful to hear of the proposed conference for the purpose of considering the relations of trusts to the public welfare and interest. There is no subject concerning which a wider ignorance, or more curious misapprehension, exists in the public mind, and it is greatly to be desired that, in bringing the whole subject of the administration of corporations into the light, we may be assisted by the best intelligence of the land."

JOHN S. MILLER, *Peck, Miller & Starr, Attorneys, Chicago*:

"If the Sherman act is to remain upon the statute books, it should be amended, if it is to be a beneficent act, and not one hostile and injurious to the industries and prosperity of the country. It should be made specific and definite, so that the men who are conducting the commerce of the country may know from the act itself, or at least have some means of learning with certainty, what acts or conduct is forbidden by the law and made criminal, and what is not. The present law lacks this definiteness. It does not discriminate, in its terms, between that which is good and that which is evil. It furnishes no rule for the guidance of merchants in the conduct of their business. I think the idea of holding a National Conference to discuss this subject and to try and come to an agreement on some general principles will be very valuable."

HAMILTON HOLT, *Editor of "The Independent"*:

"There is no more pressing problem before the business people than what to do with the trusts. If recent developments demonstrate anything, they demonstrate that under modern methods of production and distribution the *laissez faire* policy carried out to its logical conclusion means economic monopoly, business corruption, swollen fortunes and social discontent. The trust question, therefore, at the present moment is a question of how far the American people are prepared to go in the way of regulation, for surely, if regulation fails, the alternative is Government ownership. In my opinion our chief trouble arises from the fact that we have not developed our trust ethics as fast as our trust economics. If the forthcoming Trust Conference of the National Civic Federation can shed any light on the ethical aspect of the trust movement, it will have rendered a lasting service to the country."

JOHN MITCHELL, *United Mine Workers of America*:

"My judgment is that this conference will prove of the greatest interest and will be productive of good results, as it will give opportunity for full and free discussion upon a subject that concerns the well-being of all our people."

CHARLES G. DAWES, *President Central Trust Company of Illinois*:

"I regard the calling of this conference by the National Civic Federation at this time as a highly useful piece of work. It is always wise to say, "Come, let us reason together.' The industrial problems confronting us to-day in this country demand consideration by the best brains of the nation. The commercial, manufacturing, labor, agricultural and financial interests demand a solution of the great trust and combination problem that will protect all the people. Personally, I believe that combinations are absolutely necessary in conducting the business of the country; but they should be restricted and the rights of the people safeguarded by strict supervision and regulation by the Government—State and Federal."

JOHN M. STAHL, *President Farmers' National Congress*:

"The questions to be discussed at the National Conference on Trusts and Combinations are certainly the most important pressing for solution before our people to-day.

1. What is the division of powers under the Constitution between the nation and the State?

2. How should the corporation be constructed and supervised to protect investments of capital on the one hand, and the consumers on the other?

3. What are combinations in restraint of trade? Are labor organizations that seek to fix the price at which they will sell their labor; employers' organizations that seek to fix the price they will pay for labor; farmers' organizations that seek to fix the price at which they will sell their wheat, their tobacco, and their cotton; organizations of buyers that seek to fix the price they will pay for such products; are the innumerable wholesale and retail organizations dealing in all kinds of merchandise that seek to secure what they allege to be fair profits—are all of these organizations, or a part of them only, prohibited by the Sherman anti-trust act? In considering the trust question, we should look at it, not from our own particular interest, but from the standpoint of society as a whole."

SAMUEL GOMPERS, *President American Federation of Labor*:

"I participated in the Civic Federation conference in 1899, and am sure that its educational value was great. The forthcoming conference, I feel sure, will also be productive of much good to the nation, in that it will allow all sides to meet and freely express their opinion on one of the greatest subjects this country has to deal with to-day."

Public Ownership. The publication of the report of the Committee on Investigation to the Public Ownership Commission marks an important step in the discussion of public utilities. The high character and representative composition of the committee give to its conclusions a significance which does not attach to those of an individual investigator. Nor could the latter enjoy the same opportunities for forming a judgment as were possible for the committee. The investigation was extraordinarily extensive, painstaking and impartial. These volumes record the results of personal inspection by a highly qualified body of examiners. The careful study of the plants visited, both by the committee itself and by its technical and accounting experts, gives a high and enduring value to the record and to the conclusions.

The conclusions of the committee are set forth so succinctly at the close of the report that to recapitulate them here would be a needless repetition. No one who reads the report with care can fail to be impressed by the judicial tone, by the careful weighing of evidence, and by the luminous insight into the varying issues of the problem which it reveals. Its measured words are the fruit, not of excessive caution, but of fulness of information. Each of its postulates is capable of an almost indefinite elaboration, and the very compactness of the statements themselves forbids further condensation.

The reception given to the report by the press has been a full recognition of the importance and seriousness of the inquiry. The *Philadelphia North American* designates it as "the most carefully considered and exhaustive report on the subject of municipal ownership ever presented to the American people." The *New York Times* speaks of the report as "a happy surprise and an authoritative contribution to a subject so disputatious that it has seemed really impossible to point to any expression of opinion which should be of determining weight with those unable to make up their minds." The *New York Globe* finds the most remarkable thing in the report is the fact that nineteen out of twenty members of the committee signed, and says: "To have a body of experts practically unanimous is most amazing." The *New York Evening Post* sees in the caution of the committee a proof of "the serious and painstaking nature of their inquiry." Commenting upon what it terms the "real significance" of the report, the *Springfield Union* says: "The report may be accepted as an expression of advanced public sentiment in the matter, a sentiment which is cautious while alive to the progressive tendencies of the times." The *Providence Tribune* expresses the hope "that with this strong and comprehensive report on the subject of municipal ownership by a commission of unquestioned ability that has given a great deal of time and thought to it, there might be an end to most of the loose talk thereupon which has served only to create unintelligent discontent."

The *Saturday Evening Post* believes that "the conclusions about coincide with the sober judgment of the country." *Collier's Weekly* says: "When twenty members of the Civic Federation, including representatives of public service corporations, labor union men, editors and sociologists, went to Europe to study the practical workings of municipal ownership, it seemed impossible that they could reach any sort of agreement. It appears, however, that they have not only accumulated a body of facts accepted by all, but that they have been able to agree with almost perfect unanimity upon certain important conclusions." *Charities* finds that "with its varied membership the committee has offered an interesting example of what might be called investigational psychology. Members of the committee represented oftentimes diametrically opposed points of view with respect to certain phases of public service operation, but when it came to a practical programme of recommendations, the members got together again, and the amount of agreement, considering the make-up of the committee, is marked."

The conclusions of the committee will be placed before the Public Ownership Commission and will no doubt be subject to a searching analysis by the larger body. In the meantime the members of the National Civic Federation may be justly proud of the important public service which has been rendered in the publication of this comprehensive and valuable report.

Conditions in the Canal Zone. An investigation of labor conditions of the employes of the United States Government on the Isthmus of Panama has recently been made by Miss Gertrude Beeks, Secretary of the Welfare Department. It was appropriate that this should be the first undertaking of the new Committee on Welfare Work for Government Employes, whose organization and purposes are fully set forth elsewhere in this issue. Nowhere does the Federal Government employ so large a number of persons under circumstances which impose upon it so great a responsibility for providing proper conditions of life as in the Canal Zone.

It is a large body of workers, some 40,000 strong, which has been gathered there. It includes all grades of skill and experience. It is drawn from all quarters of the globe and includes not only Americans, but Europeans, notably Spaniards, Greeks, Italians, and also West Indian negroes.

The investigation covered a period of five weeks from June 7 to July 12, twenty-three days being spent upon the isthmus. Armed with letters from the Secretary of War to Colonel Goethals, Chairman of the Isthmian Canal Commission, and to the Chief Engineer, Miss Beeks was shown every courtesy by the officials in charge, who afforded her every opportunity to secure the information desired. By means of letters from prominent citizens, including leaders of labor organizations whose crafts are represented on the isthmus, and the Secretary of the Industrial Committee of the Young Men's Christian Association, Miss Beeks was placed in direct communication with engineers, foremen, mechanics, clerks, physicians, nurses and others who represented the viewpoint of the actual workers. The inquiry covered a wide range, including questions of labor, wages, hours, holidays, the houses provided for the employes and laborers, their sanitary arrangements and furniture, the water supply, the food furnished in the eating houses, and that for sale in the commissary department; the general stores, the hospitals, the opportunities for rest and recreation—in short, all the conditions of existence. An account of the results of the investigation will be published in the next issue of *The Review*.

Opposing Forces in the Industrial World The spectacle of reactionaries and radicals alike struggling against the forces of progress is not a new one. Nor is it so incongruous as it seems. The one would fain restore the old order of things and fortify what he deems his prerogatives. The other thrives on discontent and has no patience with solutions which disregard his own special and copyrighted panacea. But the reactionary and the radical are engaged in a futile struggle. They are not the men who make history. It is as fruitless to seek to impede the course of orderly evolution as it is to claim a far-reaching insight into the future and seek to twist the progress of the world to a visionary ideal.

The industrial world just now offers a case in point. On the one hand we find a certain group of manufacturing interests which has banded together for a fight to the finish with trade unions. It would smash them despite the fact that it loudly proclaims its friendship for the "good union." It says, "We believe labor has a right to organize; we believe that through organization labor has accomplished great good for itself, and, therefore, for the people, but"—then comes a string of "ifs" and "buts" that would eliminate every organization from consideration, except those which are dead.

A recent attempt to form a "great federation of national employers' organizations" to bring about "industrial peace" was attended only by organizations which will have nothing to do with unions; in fact, several of them boast that they do not employ union men, when they know it, while one of them insists that every man before going to work for any member of that particular association of employers shall sign a paper resigning "without reservation" from his union, the resignation to take effect immediately, and in the circular letters sent out to the members of that Employers' Organization it boasts of the number of resignations it has thus compelled. This proposed Federation of Employers will not countenance in any way the making of trade agreements with organized labor. It would restore the old-time status of the individual labor contract, which was a one-sided affair dominated entirely by the employer.

On the other hand, we find an element among the laboring men of the country which, though organized in unions, is bitterly opposed to dealing in any manner with employers. We refer to those groups which have been poisoned by the virus of socialism. They denounce trade agreements as "chains forged to fetter the workingman." The Industrial Workers of the World antagonize the American Federation of Labor and the railway brotherhoods on such issues. The Western Federation of Miners, allied with the Industrial Workers, in their recent convention, amended their constitution to prohibit the making of any further contracts with employers. In a speech in Chicago their prophet and martyr, Haywood, told his hearers: "If any of you have an agreement with any employer that compels you to work while the other fellows are out of work, break it. There never was an agreement that was so sacred as to compel one workingman to scab on another, and after you have broken that agreement, let me urge you men not to enter into another one."

We thus have a group of employers and a group of workers who unwittingly in one case and wittingly in the other are struggling to foment discontent. But these two forces, while radical and rabid in their respective attitudes, fortunately do not represent the great body of employers, on the one side, or the masses of workers, on the other. The American Federation of Labor and the great railway brotherhoods represent 95 per cent. of organized labor, and their attitude is voiced by Mr. John Mitchell in the following statement:

"I advocate not industrial revolution, but industrial progress. The deadening blight of socialism would wither progress. The virile, active forces of industry enlisted in the wage system under the form of capital and labor can be brought to work mightily, through sane and radical agreement, for that means the advancement of civilization and the lightening of the burdens that still oppress humanity. The socialists abhor all such progress and denounce every method that has been discovered, including the trade agreement, for its encouragement. That is why the socialists seek, either by assault or by 'boring from within,' to destroy or disintegrate our trade union movement, because its aim and effect are the betterment of society as a whole. The instinct of individual self-improvement is the life blood of labor unionism. The control of all industry by the State, being against that instinct, could result only in either anarchy or despotism."

On the other hand, all the great railway systems, the coal operators, the large building contractors, the great shipping interests that handle the iron, coal, grain, and lumber of the country, 95 per cent. of the daily newspapers of the country, the manufacturers of printing paper, stove manufacturers, the large breweries, and many other employing interests meet with the respective crafts represented in the labor organizations above referred to and form what are known as trade agreements, providing for the hours of work, prices and general conditions of labor, with provisions for arbitration in case of disagreement.

The socialist unions and "smash-the union" employers' organizations heartily agree on three propositions; first, they would like to prevent employers and employees entering into contractual relations; second, they would smash the American Federation of Labor and the railway brotherhoods; third, if they should succeed in the first two efforts, they would like to smash each other.

WELFARE WORK FOR GOVERNMENT EMPLOYES.

CIVIC FEDERATION ORGANIZES COMMITTEE WITH SECRETARY TAFT FOR ITS CHAIRMAN.

THE Welfare Department of the National Civic Federation announces the organization of a national committee on "Welfare Work for Government Employes." The object of this committee will be to create an interest in improving the working conditions of Federal, State and municipal employes.

The officers of the committee are:

Chairman, William H. Taft, Secretary of War.
First Vice-Chairman, John C. W. Beckham, Governor of Kentucky.
Second Vice-Chairman, George W. Guthrie, Mayor of Pittsburg.
Third Vice-Chairman, William R. Willcox, Chairman of the Public Utilities Commission of New York City.
Secretary, Miss Gertrude Beeks.

The committee is composed of State and municipal officials, who have to do with the working conditions of public employes, chairmen of boards of health, heads of departments of public safety, leading physicians connected with public hospitals, heads of charity boards and others.

Some improvements needed are indicated by complaints of public employes and department heads with reference to crowded workrooms, bad light and ventilation, lack of emergency hospitals, of lunch rooms and of proper washrooms. Recreation for employes who not only work but live in State and city institutions, should be provided more generally.

The business of the Government has practically doubled in certain departments within the past five years, which has resulted in unfavorable working conditions. Employes in the Patent Office, for instance, claim that it is not pleasant to be obliged to read of improvements in ventilation devices and other conveniences for which patents are asked, when they are forced to work in close, dusty basement rooms previously used only for the filing of records. In the Winder Building the accumulation of dust since the time of Lincoln, it is claimed, has caused serious irritation of eyes and pulmonary affections of employes required to work constantly among the records. Former Secretary Shaw spoke of the Bureau of Printing and Engraving as "a first-class sweatshop,' the machinery being crowded compactly into the workrooms and the ventilation bad.

New buildings erected by the Government, such as the Library of Congress and the one for public printing, contain modern washrooms and spacious, properly lighted and ventilated workrooms.

Congressman Bennet, who learned at a meeting of the Welfare Department of the National Civic Federation of the emergency hospitals installed in many factories, introduced a resolution of inquiry in the House of Representatives with reference to facilities in Government buildings in the city of Washington for administering first aid to employes. President Roosevelt immediately asked for reports from the various departments, and it was found that such provision was made in only one. An employe of the Government, a compositor in the Department of Public Printing, whose sympathy was stirred by the sight of employes lying on the floor awaiting the arrival of an ambulance for the purpose of carrying them to a hospital had fitted up a small room in which to care for such employes. As there was no

HON. WILLIAM H. TAFT.

appropriation for supplies, he personally paid for drugs, surgical dressings, bandages and other necessities. The Public Printer reported to President Roosevelt that the arrangement had been very beneficial to the employes, as some of the cases were very urgent and need immediate attention; that one thousand two hundred and fifty cases have been treated since this emergency room has been installed; and that previously it was necessary to send out for a physician, and if he were not at home the employe was left lying on the floor of the workroom, or toilet room, suffering until one could be located.

In some of the public buildings there are very good lunch rooms, while in others the employes will be found sitting upon their machines, at their desks or standing outside of the building, eating cold lunches brought from home.

Treasurer Treat doec not hesitate to denounce the conditions in his own department, where scores of women are working in dark, unhealthful basement rooms. The dust and germs where the old money is counted are a constant menace to health.

Many improvements are being made at military posts in providing sanitary arrangements, for gymnasiums and amusement rooms.

In New York, within the past year, through the efforts of Postmaster Willcox, several new postal stations were provided, displacing ill-ventilated, unsanitary workrooms, and in these new structures there are comfortable rest rooms in which the postmen may spend their idle hours reading, smoking or playing games between "swings." Some stations are crowded, unclean and unsanitary and contain swing rooms unfit for occupancy, the corner saloons proving more attractive.

The care of the sick and insane in State and city institutions, with its constant association with suffering and emaciation, is exceedingly depressing to all classes of attendants in such institutions. To maintain health among the men and women helpers periods of rest and recreation are as essential as proper food and sanitary dormitories. Where such provisions for employes are not provided there is a decided disadvantage to the State or municipality in administering the institutions, for only the lowest type of help can be secured.

While connected with some State hospitals there are model dormitories for the employes, and there are club houses, providing wholesome amusement, in many institutions the conditions of the employes not only are deplorable, but a disgrace to communities which should be model employers.

No private employer would be allowed to subject his employes to the unhealthful conditions which have been endured by policemen, notably in the stations in New York City, where they have been crowded into small, unsanitary sleeping apartments. Through the efforts of the Welfare Department of the Civic Federation, the Commissioner of the Police Department recently modified the platoon system, in order to obviate the inhumanly long working hours of the policemen.

There are many type of employes to be benefited by the efforts of the new committee on Welfare Work for Government Employes. Among those employed in the different departments, the navy yards, arsenals, State and city institutions to be affected are: clerks, sailors, soldiers, printers, machinists, carpenters, postmen, firemen, policemen, bricklayers, iron workers, moulders, painters, plumbers, pattern makers, engineers, chemists, blacksmiths, boiler makers, crane men, hospital orderlies and trained nurses.

The subject of pensions, in which all Government employes are keenly interested, will be given consideration. In every department this is a live issue, and there are organizations of Government employes which were formed for the purpose of securing Congressional action.

Mr. Willcox, during his incumbency as Postmaster of New York City, said regarding the question of pensioning postmen after a service of twenty-five years, that sooner or later the Government will have to recognize the fact that, having, under the Civil Service regulations, created a permanent Civil Service force, it will be as necessary to pension such employes as the men who serve in the army. In the matter of pensions, letter carriers should not be segregated from other Government employes, for any man who gives loyal service for twenty-five or thirty years, the best part of his life, and usually for very small compensation, should be given a moderate pension.

A national conference, at which will be discussed the subjects above mentioned, will be held under the auspices of this committee in the Fall.

The Welfare Department of the National Civic Federation is composed of employers in different industries throughout the United States. Its object is to interest employers in improving the working and living conditions of their employes. The topics covered, representing the voluntary efforts of employers

HON. WILLIAM R. WILLCOX.

HON. JOHN. C. W. BECKHAM.

HON. GEORGE W. GUTHRIE.

HON. WILLIAM S. BENNET.

for the benefit of their employes, are sanitary work places, recreation, educational opportunities, housing and provident funds.

The Committee on Welfare Work for Government Employes is the logical result of work already promoted by the Welfare Department for public employes in connection with charity hospitals, for policemen and postal employes. Its importance was also emphasized by the investigation and report of the Welfare Department, two years ago, upon the conditions of the employes of the Government engaged in the construction of the Panama Canal, many of the recommendations being put into effect.

EMERGENCY HOSPITAL, GOVERNMENT PRINTING OFFICE, WASHINGTON, D. C.

IS THE CITY OF NEW YORK A MODEL EMPLOYER?

THAT a great and progressive community like the City of New York should be a model employer will be accepted without argument, but what are the facts? How does it treat the fifty thousand or more human beings which compose its business organization?

HOW DO THE POLICEMEN FARE?

After making a study of platoon systems in other cities in this country and abroad, the New York Committee on Welfare Work of the National Civic Federation felt warranted in asking that the hours of policemen be reduced, and the Sub-Committee on Welfare Work for City Employes addressed the following letter to Commissioner Theodore A. Bingham in October:

"Sir—As it is our desire to see all our municipal employes well cared for, both for their own sakes and for the honor of our city, we have organized a committee of citizens to stimulate improvement in the conditions surrounding our policemen, firemen, letter carriers and institutional employes.

"In your department we find that the hours of service are abnormally long. We learn that in their regular routine men are permitted to go to their homes only for twelve hours every other day, and to be in service for as much as eighteen hours at a stretch—from 6 a. m. to midnight.

"This is in direct antagonism to the spirit of the age, which is favorable to a reduction of the hours of labor that will permit all men to have a fair opportunity for social, intellectual and physical culture; time to be with wife and children, time for religious observance, time for reading, time for exercise and fresh air. Such opportunities make better men, more intelligent in the discharge of their duty, and better citizens. And who should give an impetus to movements in the direction of better citizenship if not the city itself? The city should be the ideal employer; the city should set the example to employers among the people, who, though hampered by the restrictions of competition, will, in a measure, be influenced by this practical example. The city should adopt short hours for its employes and surround them with ideal conditions, both physically and morally. But how New York does fall short of this!

"The present hours we consider criminal from an ethical standpoint, tending, as they do, to degrade the men; and, further, they are not in the line of good policy, for the citizens look to the police for the protection of life and property; they expect good service; and what man can do good service who works such excessive hours? You are undoubtedly restricted by financial considerations in handling the question of hours. Shorter hours mean more men, and your appropriation does not reach.

"The alternative is larger appropriation. The citizens will not object to the extra tax which this will entail. Any man who does is extremely short-sighted and will be overruled by the fair and humane citizens, who are in the majority. Full protection is certainly required. More men working shorter hours will do better service, and only so can safety be insured.

"We have encouraging statistics from the police departments of many other cities, both in the United States and abroad, which show good results from a shorter workday, and we assure you that you will have a strong backing if you endeavor to secure an appropriation which will enable you to bring about a radical change in the hours of service and improvement in other conditions in your department.

Respectfully yours,

Marcus M. Marks, Chairman.

V. Everit Macy, August Belmont, Jr.,
John DeWitt Warner, Isaac Guggenheim,
Samuel B. Donnelly, Charles A. Moore,
E. A. Moffett, Thomas R. Slicer,
Timothy Healy.

The Commissioner gave the matter immediate consideration, and now the policemen work only six hours on tour, giving them twelve hours a day off duty, and every five days they are permitted twenty-four hours off on a stretch.

The Civic Federation undertook to direct public attention to the disgraceful condition of the police stations when former Commissioner William McAdoo was asked to speak at a recent meeting of the organization. Among other things he said:

"In many of the station houses the men sleep in overcrowded quarters, the beds being so close that in some instances they have to crawl over each other to reach them. In some of these buildings the dormitories are old and the walls have sunken, so that the windows are never thoroughly closed. They are freezingly cold in Winter, and, being unprotected from the sun during the day, are heated like ovens in the Summer. In the older station houses there is no proper provision made for heating and ventilating them. The waiting rooms, in which the men spend many hours while on reserve, are, as a general rule, dingy, dirty, uncomfortable, noisy and in every way unattractive. In nearly all of the station houses will be found an insufficient number of chairs for the men to sit on. The common sight is an old rickety table and a few old worn-out chairs, dirty and soiled walls, blackened ceilings, and a rough board floor, saturated and stained with years of use.

"They even cut down the appropriation for keeping these wretched and tumble-down barracks in somewhat decent order. Many of them need painting and cleaning; some of them have panes out of the windows, and it is difficult to get the money to replace them. In some cases the city has really no station house at all for the men, but houses them in stables, as in the case of the sheepfold in Central Park. The best part of that building is given to the horses, and the part where the horses could not be put with safety to their health is turned over to the men. A great sewer opening is within three feet of where the men have to eat their meals. That the police in New York look so healthy, and are in the main a well-conditioned body of men, is owing to the fact that they spend so much of their time in the open air and are compelled to take exercise. The mounted men, for instance, in Central Park, would probably all have been dead long ago from the sewer gas which pours into the horse barn where they have to spend their time when not in the saddle but for the fact that they get so much fresh air and healthy exercise when on active duty. They thrive just as sailors do at sea, who stand the horrors of the fo'castle because they have to spend most of their lives on the deck, where the air is the best. Were it not for this the sick list of the police would be appalling.

"There are no proper bathing facilities for the men. In the army and navy the shower bath is universally used. Tubs are dangerous and out of date. Well tiled bathrooms which would admit half a dozen or a dozen men at a time ought to be provided with hot and cold showers. The bedsteads are some of them fifty years old, and are very uncomfortable and of a primitive type. Except that they are higher up, the dormitories are sometimes not much better than the prisons.

"Dormitories to be erected should be well ventilated, have modern plumbing facilities, and, above all, should be so constructed as to be capable of being thoroughly washed and hosed and lighted with electricity.

"It will probably cost two or three million dollars to tear down and reconstruct a number of the station houses and renovate and in some instances radically change the character of the others. A smaller sum would make a beginning. The expenditure of this money could go on, however, over a period of years, but the plan ought to be a systematic one. All of the station houses should be constructed on the same general plan. It is a criminal waste of the city's money to have a lot of architects drawing different sets of plans, some of them perfectly grotesque and foolish. The station house should have a distinctive, individual character, so that you would know at once what it was intended for. This is the practice of governments in Europe with regard to public buildings of this kind. The station house should be as distinctive as the green lamp in front of it."

Comptroller Metz aptly remarked recently that the shocking conditions of the police stations permitted, for instance, twenty-four men to sleep in a room no larger than his office, and that such treatment of employes by a private employer would place him in jail!

But relief seems at hand, for the Commissioner has taken hold of the problem energetically. An appropriation of two million dollars for the repair of old and erection of new station houses has been made. One is already in process of construction, and plans for two others have been drawn and approved.

EMPLOYES IN THE HOSPITALS.

AN inspection of the condition of the [illegible] one of the hospitals under the De[illegible] Public Charities, made by represe[illegible] of the New York City Visiting Committee of the State Charities Aid Association and of the New York Welfare Committee of the National Civic Federation, two years ago, brought to light ill-ventilated, badly-lighted fire traps used as dormitories for helpers connected with the Metropolitan Hospital on Blackwell's Island. It also revealed poor kitchen and dining-room service, inadequate, unsanitary toilet facilities and an utter lack of recreation.

This led to thorough investigation of all city hospitals, recently, which resulted in a commendatory letter to Commissioner Hebberd, of the Department of Public Charities, upon improvements which have been made since January 1, 1906, with comments on general conditions and suggestions for further developments, in reference to dormitories, dining rooms, work places and recreation. In replying, the Commissioner said: "I am in full sympathy with the suggestions, and shall be glad to do anything that I can toward carrying them out."

COMMISSIONER ROBERT W. HEBBERD.

OLD WOODEN PAVILION, JUST DEMOLISHED.

It is not too much to say that the present needs should have been met ten years ago. Until a few weeks ago, at the Children's Hospital, Randall's Island, for instance, an old shed on the dock was used as a dormitory for forty men. The only washing facilities consisted of a trough at the end, accommodating but two men at a time. Ventilation could be secured only by causing the occupants to suffer from draughts through the windows near the cots. The light being inadequate, reading was impossible, and the men's recreation was merely to gather about the stove and smoke. Through the efforts of Commissioner Hebberd this dormitory has just been displaced by reconstructing an old prison building with cells in which one hundred paid men helpers had been obliged to sleep. The remodelled building contains six light and airy dormitories, making provision for one hundred fifty employes under sanitary conditions.

A new dormitory for men helpers at the Metropolitan Hospital, Blackwell's Island, permits the destruction of some of the unsanitary old wooden pavilions, but this modern structure should be duplicated immediately, for it is a disgrace to the city that human beings should be herded together in

NEW MEN'S DORMITORY, REPLACING WOODEN PAVILION.

cheerless frame shacks, erected at the time of the civil war as temporary shanties. Even more deplorable is the continued use of the skylight attic dormitories, without any windows, in the main hospital building. During the past few months it is true that the number of men and women helpers thus exposed to fire risk has been diminished, but provision elsewhere should be made at an early time.

The single, dark, steep and winding wooden stair leading to each attic would be speedily cut off by fire from below. Slight ladders, some of wood, loosely placed under the small skylights, afford the only other means of escape—to the roof. Smoke would quickly fill these rooms, the ceilings of which range from four to about seven feet in height, and the smoke and flames would soon seek and obscure or render impassable the skylights. The occupants would have the very slightest chance of escape from death by flame or smoke.

Within the past eighteen months the fiscal authorities have made reasonably liberal appropriations in proportion to what has been devoted to benefits for employes in the past.

The first moneys for such modern improvements were awarded during the administration of Mayor Low. Former Commissioner of Charities Homer

INTERIOR WOMEN'S OLD WOODEN PAVILION.

Folks, at that time, undertook to correct the worst abuses. With reference to conditions as he found them, and efforts at reform, he stated at a meeting of the National Civic Federation recently:

"The city provides for the employes' board and lodgings, such as they are. A few years ago the lodgings were, almost without exception, just about as bad as they could possibly be. Herded together in unventilated, dilapidated, unsanitary, cheerless buildings, with practically none of the creature comforts of life, it was little wonder that these employes soon entered once more the ranks of either prisoners or patients. Progress has been made in some directions.

"During the administration of Mayor Low a very comfortable dormitory was erected for the male employes of the City Hospital in place of a wooden rookery which had formerly housed them. This dormitory provides a well-lighted and comfortable dining room, a good sized room for reading, smoking, games, etc., a considerable number of individual rooms and two well lighted, well equipped dormitories.

MEN'S DORMITORY, ERECTED AT TIME OF CIVIL WAR.

NEW MEN'S DORMITORY.

A DISGRACE TO THE CITY OF NEW YORK: ATTIC DORMITORY.

"At the Kings County Hospital a large kitchen and dining-room building was erected, providing well lighted, well equipped dining rooms for the various grades of employes, so situated that food can be served quickly, easily and reasonably attractive."

During the present administration a dormitory for women helpers has been added to the accomplishments at the City Hospital, and contracts have been let for a nurses' home and training school and for additional facilities for women helpers at the Metropolitan Hospital, as well as a staff house for internes and a large and well-equipped dining, kitchen and service building at the City Hospital. Other dormitories, nurses' houses and staff houses are needed at the Children's Hospital, Metropolitan Hospital, City Hospital, Cumberland Street Hospital, Kings County Hospital and Coney Island Hospital.

A modern structure to contain every facility requisite for the proper handling and serving of foods should replace the old kitchen building, and also the dining rooms for the helpers at the Metropolitan Hospital.

The great need of additional accommodations for patients at the several institutions requires large appropriations, but essentials for the humane treatment

ATTIC DORMITORY.

of the employes are just as imperative. This is necessary to aid in securing a permanent class of helpers. At present some of the forces must be practically reorganized each month, the helpers remaining frequently but long enough to draw one month's pay and depart for a drunken spree. No private enterprise could be operated successfully with such a changing force, and it is impossible to give the city's poor and sick proper or economic care under such conditions. Compensation for helpers in the Department of Charities being ridiculously low, contributes largely toward the difficulty in attracting competent, permanent workers. It is worthy of note that the splendid arrangements which have been provided for the convenience of the employes in some city institutions, such as Gouverneur Hospital, are offered in addition to an adequate wage just as they are by employers in many commercial enterprises, and, fair wages and good working conditions combined secure more competent helpers. The economic principle "create a proper environment, and you make for good discipline" also has been thoroughly proved.

INTERIOR OLD WOODEN SHACK, JUST ABANDONED.

Some of the comments and suggestions made to the Department of Charities by the Joint Committee on Welfare Work for Employes of New York City Charitable Institutions follow:

Physical Conditions.

Toilet Arrangements: In the construction of all new dormitories we approve heartily of locating the toilet arrangements, including baths, in separate rooms. Hot water and towels should be provided in addition to soap.

Furnishings: An effort toward having the dormitories homelike and more attractive would be desirable. We believe that there should be some form of decoration, simple but artistic, and it would be very appropriate to call upon private citizens for contributions of pictures for the walls.

Individual Sleeping Rooms: It is desirable where possible to have individual rooms and equipment. While the present low grade of employes may make open dormitories more desirable for supervision, we submit that until individual rooms are provided it

ILL-VENTILATED, BADLY-LIGHTED KITCHEN, METROPOLITAN HOSPITAL.

MODEL KITCHEN, KINGS COUNTY HOSPITAL.

will be exceedingly difficult to secure a higher type of helpers, which in the interest of the patients and of economy is most desirable. Where several occupy one room there is great discomfort; for instance, one will desire to read in the evening, one will wish to sew, and another, especially if not feeling well, will want to sleep, which is impossible with the light burning and the noise from conversation. Such interruption of needed rest naturally causes irritation and ill health, which must prevent the rendering of good service. Another point to consider is that those sleeping near the windows complain of the draft, while those remote will suffer from poor ventilation. Such dormitories afford a miserable existence, not attractive to self-respecting workers, who frequently ask for single rooms.

The use of the present sanitary iron beds should be continued, and we believe that where there are open dormitories there should be not less than one bureau and one wash bowl for two persons, a chair for each and separate lockers for the clothes.

WRETCHED DINING ROOM, METROPOLITAN HOSPITAL.

Janitor Service: In order to maintain throughout the institution the excellent standard of cleanliness obtaining in some, there should be regular janitor service instead of expecting the employes to care for their dormitories and other facilities.

A Comprehensive Plan: We understand that a survey of Blackwell's Island is being made, showing present permanent buildings and contemplated improvements. We commend the idea of having a definite plan for improvements, not only to meet the present needs, but those which must come with the growth of the city, and decidedly do we consider that the sporadic meeting of temporary needs is very uneconomical.

Recreation and Social Conditions.

A systematic study of forms of recreation which would be applicable to the different local conditions should be made.

To aid in securing permanence of employment, the following recommendations are made:

MODEL DINING ROOM FOR HELPERS, KINGS COUNTY HOSPITAL.

Social Halls: There should be special recreation rooms in the dormitories where feasible. If not, special buildings should be erected for that purpose in connection with each of the hospitals.

Writing, Reading, Smoking and Sewing Rooms: In the men's and women's dormitories there should be reading and writing rooms equipped with neat desks, tables and chairs. (At Gouverneur Hospital the end of each corridor, well lighted, with five or six windows, is utilized for that purpose. The writing and rest rooms are especially appreciated by the help during the evenings.)

In the women's dormitories there should be sewing machines and classes for the purpose of instructing the women in dressmaking. In the men's dormitories the reading rooms could be used also for smoking.

Libraries: Arrangements might be made with the New York Public Library for branch libraries in connection with the different hospitals, from which books would be furnished to the nurses and help, working in non-contagious hospitals.

MEN'S READING ROOM, CITY HOSPITAL.

Illustrated Lectures: Illustrated lectures could be provided for the benefit of all employes. The Board of Education might be prevailed upon to supply lecturers and lectures. Some plan of co-operating with the Public Education Department of the State of New York would be worthy of consideration. It has to lend at least eighty lectures, including such subjects as travel, art, science, history and literature. Especially would stereopticon lectures on travel appeal to all classes of employes.

Dancing: In the men's dormitory of the City Hospital we find that the employes now have dancing. If social rooms are provided at all the institutions series of dances can be given.

Physical Culture and Basket Ball: Classes in physical culture could be gradually organized as a further utilization of the space provided for dancing, and there could be basket ball.

Billiards and Bowling: There should be billiard rooms in the men's dormitories and bowling in the general recreation buildings.

NURSES' RECREATION ROOM, CITY HOSPITAL.

Game Rooms: In the women's dormitories there should be game rooms, containing, for instance, checkers, equipment for ping pong or indoor tennis.

Theatricals: The general recreation rooms should be so equipped as to provide for amateur theatricals, as well as the lectures above mentioned. Roller skating also would be enjoyed.

Music: Among the provisions might be included the phonograph and arrangements made for circulating the discs among the different institutions in order that the employes might not tire of the tunes.

Outdoor Games: There should be developed gradually and in so far as feasible, outdoor games such as baseball, quoits and tennis.

Summer Outings: It is hoped that the plan of Summer boating excursions and other outings already inaugurated will be extended.

Verandas: Verandas for lounging should be included in plans for new dormitories, similar to those at the City and Metropolitan hospitals.

Decorations: Citizens might be appealed to for contributions of pictures for the walls of the social rooms, which should be made as attractive as possible without being elaborate. A good utilization of paint, such as dull red walls and Pompeiian green woodwork, beautify with proper simplicity. The buff walls of the recreation room at the City Hospital are very attractive and well hung with pictures.

Clubs: Clubs of employes may be formed and contribute toward the support of recreative places, as has been done in some State institutions. We note with pleasure that the club at the City Hospital of its own initiative purchased a piano, the funds therefor being contributed entirely by club members.

Premiums Upon Length of Service: Series of games such as baseball and handball for the men and other games for the women could be arranged between different dormitories to create a spirit of rivalry. A rule might be made that only employes who have been with the institution for at least six months could compete in the games. This would be one means of encouraging permanence of employment.

A further effort toward securing a more permanent force of employes would be prizes at the end of each year for those who have been the longest upon the payrolls.

Provident Funds: Branches of the Penny Provident Savings Society we believe should be stationed at all the hospitals in places daily visited by the employes, and especially should those branches be easily available to the employes upon pay day.

Arrangements should be made to enable employes to make deposits in savings banks with ease. At the time pay is distributed a properly authorized person might accept deposits.

Welfare Manager: To ensure the successful and continuous operation of the plans proposed under the head of recreation and provident funds, it is essential that there should be one person in the Department of Charities held responsible for the conduct of this phase of its work. His duties would be to plan systematically all such activities for the benefit of the employes, and, when approved, to put them into operation in co-operation with the superintendents of the hospitals. All activities for the benefit of the employes naturally would be included in the scope of the work of the Welfare manager, such as systematic investigations of the dormitories and dining rooms. The operation of the dormitories and dining rooms would be left under the general management of the hospitals, but the Welfare manager could offer recommendations for improvements without in any way entering into conflict with the superintendent's duties.

He could also aid in securing pure drinking water, easily accessible to all employes, the cooling of superheated places, such as the laundries and quarters of the stationary firemen, and the provision of shower baths for stationary firemen, and such other workers as would require them.

It would be very proper for the Welfare manager to organize a more thorough system of securing new employes.

NEW YORK CITY'S POSTAL EMPLOYES.

A STUDY of the postal stations in New York City before the recent resignation of Postmaster Willcox revealed conditions so sharply contrasting as to make it difficult to believe that a single employer—the United States Government—could be responsible for such varying types of work places. Some of the carrier stations are models of perfection, which should serve as a standard to be generally copied. The conditions at others, however, are intolerable, a reflection upon the Govern-

A DAMP, UNVENTILATED BASEMENT LIVING ROOM.

ment and a menace to the physical well-being of its employes. Credit is due to former Postmaster Willcox for an energetic campaign which he waged against the stations in the latter classes. During his administration he succeeded in obtaining new quarters for six of these stations, besides improving the conditions at others. He also gave close attention to the sanitary conditions in the main post office, where improvements have been made which are vital to the health of the workers. The ventilation has been radically improved through the introduction of numerous electric fans, blowers, and fresh air shafts, by which the atmosphere is cooled in Summer and warmed in Winter. In addition to this, large steam radiators have been installed, which greatly add to the comfort of the employes. Systematic watchfulness maintained over workrooms, clothes closets, and in fact, over all parts of the main office, has done much to secure good sanitary conditions at that point. Congestion certainly exists, but this is due to inadequate space, which will, however, be remedied by the completion of the fine new branch post office at the Grand Central Station until the new general post office is erected.

A NEW SWING ROOM

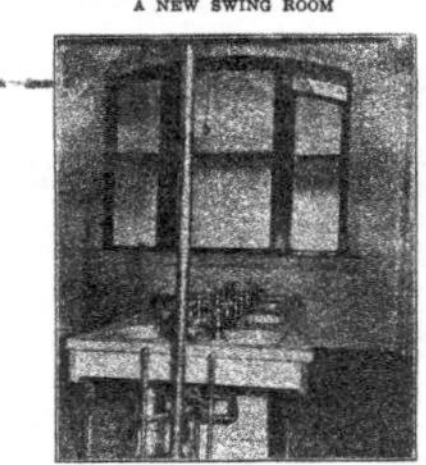

A MODEL WASH ROOM FOR POSTAL EMPLOYES.

What are the especial needs of postal employes? Obviously for the clerks who sort the mail, light and ventilation are of primary importance.

In the performance of this work the men labor with great rapidity and under high tension, and to read the addresses good light is a necessity. Under the present conditions, however, artificial light is necessary in many of the workrooms. Usually it is supplied by having gas jets placed in rows at the tops of the sorting cases, a little above the heads of the men. The gas not only increases the temperature in Summer, as it must be burned the greater part of each day, but its consumption of oxygen serves to vitiate the air to a startling degree. The buildings recently leased or especially erected for use as postal stations are well lighted.

Excellent ventilation is possible in some of the stations which are well equipped with windows and transoms, but in others, especially in basements, radical changes are demanded for the preservation of the health of employes. Perhaps the worst instance is a basement with no inlet for fresh air except the staircase to the floor above. In another case, it is a narrow shaft running to the fourteenth story. Hot water pipes along the ceiling cause such intense heat

WHERE A LUNCH ROOM IS NEEDED; EATING LUNCH ON MAIL SACKS.

in Summer as to add greatly to the discomfort of the men. The purchase of electric fans by the employes in one room illustrates a need of devices to purify the air.

Conspicuous for its wholesome, sanitary condition is a new station equipped with the pneumatic sweeping system. The condition of basement rooms demands greater attention. Dirt collects in them more readily than in upper stories, and only the most scrupulous cleanliness can make such quarters passably habitable. In fact, the extreme cleanliness of some places, and the apparently neglected condition of others, evidence the need of a sanitary corps to maintain a single standard of healthful conditions.

The dirty and dusty condition of mail sacks is applicable to all stations, but this is due to the uses to which such sacks are put in the transporting of mails in cars, wagons, trucks, etc. Except in the case of foreign bags coming from regions infected with cholera or other contagion, there is no provision for the fugimation of mail bags. Employes of the Department know of no provision for ever cleaning the bags, and it is only as they wear out that new, and, for the time being, clean bags are substituted.

GOOD LIGHT AND VENTILATION FOR POSTAL CLERKS.

These old pouches and sacks naturally emit odors far from agreeable, which suggest the existence of dangerous germs. However, the small absenteeism on account of ill health would not appear to confirm this view, and the department is constantly at work replacing old equipment with new.

Drinking water, rendered pure by distillation, will be found in one model station, whereas the lack of such attention to health is shown in an old one where the water is piped from a storage tank at the top of the building with no system of filtration.

For the carriers who are frequently subjected to inclement weather other conditions arise. For instance, no provision is made for the drying of wet garments. It is against the rules for postmen to

POSTMEN PROVIDED WITH OUTSIDE RESTING BENCH IN SUMMER.

linger in the workrooms between tours of duty. During the incumbency of Postmaster Willcox, however, pleasant swing rooms, with tables and chairs, were arranged in some of the stations, in which the postmen may spend their idle moments, although there is no evidence of opportunities for wholesome recreation, or adequate luncheon facilities in any. The most attractive swing room has a high ceiling, is perfectly lighted with four large, outside windows during the day, and groups of electric lights in the evening. It is so partitioned that the men are enabled to read or rest with perfect comfort; this room is finished in oak and tiling. Cleanliness and order prevail. In the rear are ventilated metal lockers. A decided contrast to this is presented in a basement swing room, which receives its only daylight through the grating in the sidewalk. The window underneath was, at the time of the investigation, so unclean as to exclude even such light as might come from that source, and the accumulation of filth in the space outside the window created an environment which would not appear to cause the men to voluntarily seek it. However, this was very materially improved under the direction of Mr. Willcox. The superintendents, who are not allowed to permit the postmen to loiter in the workrooms, find it difficult to force them into the gloomy, damp, basement rest (swing) rooms, where the dilapidated furniture does not invite comfort. That there is a need of combination rest, game and smoking rooms above the basement floor is fully recognized.

In neighborhoods where there are no good restaurants with moderate prices, simple lunch facilities, including cafeteria lunch counters and coffee urns, are needed.

Modern lavatory and toilet facilities, have been introduced in new stations and, with the exception of two of the old ones, health regulations are observed with all devices, although ventilation is inadequate in the majority.

It is the custom for the post office employes to pay for soap, towels, toilet paper and shoe blacking, each man contributing ten cents a month toward this fund. When progressive employers in private enterprises supply free to employes the first three essentials named the question arises why the Government should be behind the foremost in furnishing the "common decencies."

In many cases, locker and dressing rooms are placed in the swing rooms, which makes it impossible to have privacy when changing clothes. Dressing rooms should be entirely distinct from swing rooms as in one of the newer offices.

There is complaint against the rule which requires that the men shall be docked when absent and not be paid for overtime. Consolation may be had in the knowledge that through the persistent efforts of Mr. Willcox salaries, commencing on July 1, were raised. For seventeen years, the law has required new postmen to start at $600, and that the maximum salary should be $1,000. The new schedule makes the minimum $800, which sum he considers to be as little as a man can live upon to-day, and the maximum salary is raised to $1,100. Proportionate increases have been made in the salaries of the clerical force which it is believed will tend to increase the efficiency and satisfaction thereof.

BENEFITS FOR ATTENDANTS IN SOME NEW YORK STATE HOSPITALS.

THE watchword of the Welfare Department of the National Civic Federation, with reference to the desirability of introducing efforts for the benefit of employes is, "Prove by Example!" Somewhat discouraging was the first reply to letters of inquiry lately sent to superintendents of New York State hospitals seeking data relative to dormitories, dining halls and recreation: "The employes of this hospital receive medical and surgical treatment free when required. The facilities of the institution for treating medical and surgical cases are similar to those in the average general hospital."

That such limited consideration is given to all employes of State institutions is disproven by other evidence secured. The excellent arrangements portrayed below, while not introduced generally, pertain to a sufficiently large number of cases to prove their efficiency:

ROCHESTER STATE HOSPITAL.

DORMITORIES.

The Nurses' Home of the Rochester State Hospital is, a new building of three stories, occupying a pleasant portion of the hospital grounds. The building consists of a central portion and an east and west wing.

In the center are rooms for all of the married employes, and five very pleasantly located sitting rooms, used for the benefit and social purposes of all hospital employes.

THE AMUSEMENT HALL, HUDSON RIVER STATE HOSPITAL.

Picture taken at the time of Christmas festivities. Hall used for dances, theatricals and concerts.

Of the two wings, one is used for the unmarried women employes and the other for the unmarried men employes. The wing for the women employes has a girls' writing and sitting room and a large veranda. The centre has four verandas and the men's wing two large verandas.

Married couples are all provided for so that husband and wife room together. Besides these there are some employes who room together, mostly through their own preference. These rooms are all fully equipped for two persons, with two each of beds, dressers, wardrobes, etc.

All the other employes, which constitute about 75 per cent. of the total number, have single rooms, well furnished and pleasant, with lavatories, wash and bath rooms conveniently located.

LARGE BILLIARD, POOL AND SMOKING ROOM, HUDSON RIVER STATE HOSPITAL.

In this room are card tables, checker and chess boards. It is open to employes at all times.

RECREATION.

In the basement underneath the men's wing are located two large and two medium-sized rooms and a hall, which are used for employes' club rooms. One large room is used by the employes for meetings and a card room, the other for a billiard room. Of the

BOWLING ALLEY, HUDSON RIVER STATE HOSPITAL.

In which have been developed teams able to contest with some of the best bowlers in the Hudson River Valley. This is open to the use of employes every evening.

GRAND STAND, HUDSON HIVER STATE HOSPITAL.

On one side of the athletic field. The picture shows a portion of the one-quarter mile track, and a portion of the baseball diamond. On th's field there are ball games, races and contests of all kinds.

PAVILION IN THE GROVE, HUDSON RIVER STATE HOSPITAL.

Where there are held dances, picnics, clambakes and receptions.

smaller rooms one is a cozy room, with a large fireplace in one corner; the other small room is used as a writing and reading room. These rooms have an east and south exposure and are very pleasantly located.

BINGHAMTON STATE HOSPITAL.

DORMITORIES.

The employes have single or double rooms, so that dormitories in the ordinary sense of the word are not in use.

RECREATION.

The men employes have very fine club rooms, consisting of three large connecting rooms, with billiard and pool tables; also tables for cards and other games.

The women have also a club and excellent club rooms, although less extensive than those of the men. Plans have been made, however, for new accommodations for the women, which will be satisfactory in every respect.

INTERIOR AMUSEMENT HALL—GYMNASIUM—TWO ATTENDANTS, MEMBERS BASEBALL TEAM, GOWANDA STATE HOMEOPATHIC HOSPITAL.

CENTRAL ISLIP STATE HOSPITAL.

Thus far the superintendent has not been able to secure a sufficiently large appropriation to carry out all his aims in this direction. He claims no particularly striking features at the institution that pertain to employes' welfare, but makes an effort to furnish what is possible for their entertainment and diversion while off duty.

ATTENDANTS' BAND, GOWANDA STATE HOMEOPATHIC HOSPITAL.

DORMITORIES.

There are two large attendants' homes which house a majority of the employes comfortably.

DANCING AND SKATING.

About two years ago there was completed a large amusement hall, 70x140 feet, in which there are dances several times a week, and on two nights a week it is used as a skating rink. This latter feature has proven a very popular one, and it has been found that, while previously a large number of men and women left the grounds in the evening after duty, they now attend the skating rink.

BILLIARDS.

In one of the attendants' homes and in two of the dormitories there are pool and billiard tables for the amusement of the men employes.

BASEBALL.

For several years there has been one of the best amateur baseball teams in the State, with at least one game of ball each week during the season, attended by the major portion of the employes.

GOWANDA STATE HOMEOPATHIC HOSPITAL.

DORMITORIES.

The hospital employes live in a Nurses' Home somewhat apart from the institution, arranged in the form of a letter "T."

The right and left wings are for single men and single women respectively.

The rear portion of the building is arranged for the married employes.

DINING ROOMS.

The dining room for employes is distinct from the patients' dining room, and is divided into a department for nurses and attendants and another for mechanics and outside employes.

RECREATION.

A room in the basement of the Nurses' Home is used as a club room and smoking room. There is a piano in one of the reception rooms, and it is hoped to supply pool and billiard tables later.

The Amusement Hall, a short distance from the Nurses' Home, is used for entertainments for both patients and employes.

Aside from their dances, the employes have one or two amateur plays during the Winter, while in the Summer monthe they have, as a rule, a baseball team, and in the Fall a football team.

BUFFALO STATE HOSPITAL.

DORMITORIES.

The nurses ,attendants and employes are cared for, with the exceution of a very few who must from the nature of their work be in the main building, in two large homes.

The women's home accommodates about seventy-five persons; the rooms are comparatively large, and two nurses occupy each room.

The men's home contains one hundred rooms; these are single, viz., one for each person.

DINING ROOMS.

The dining rooms for each are located in the main building.

BILLIARD AND READING ROOM AT MEN'S HOME, BUFFALO STATE HOSPITAL.

RECREATION.

The employes have music and reception rooms and the use of the library. They also have a reading room, and in connection with it a billiard room.

ST. LAWRENCE STATE HOSPITAL, OGDENSBURG.

DORMITORIES.

In this institution the employes room apart from the patients, either in buildings wholly detached or in wings separated from the wards. The older employes and those occupying superior positions have rooms alone, others room two together, and in some instances dormitories are provided, accommodating from three to eight or ten.

EMPLOYES' BUILDING.

RECREATION.

In each employes' building there is a sitting room where attendants may spend the evening together.

In addition there is a club maintained by employes, consisting of two large rooms, one a reading room and the other a billiard room. There are provided a number of illustrated magazines and news papers, and the expenses are met by a monthly assessment of twenty-five cents on each employe. The club is self-governing and has a surplus in the treasury. The hospital furnishes light, heat and repairs. The cost of furnishings, rugs and current running expenses are met by the club's treasury.

There is a bowling alley, maintained by the hospital, and dances are given in the Recreation Hall during the Winter. The employes have also the use

WHERE EMPLOYES' DANCES ARE HELD, ST. LAWRENCE STATE HOSPITAL.

of the hall for basketball, there being several organized clubs. No restriction is placed upon the mingling of the sexes when off duty, except very obviously necessary ones.

KINGS PARK STATE HOSPITAL, LONG ISLAND, N. Y.

DORMITORIES.

The Employes' Home is occupied by as many of the employes of the hospital as can be accommodated and spared from the wards, and except those provided with accommodations elsewhere, such as those in clerical positions.

BARBER SHOP, KINGS PARK STATE HOSPITAL.

It accommodates three hundred employes. There are rooms in each wing for single men and women, while the larger rooms in the centre are for married couples.

The third floor of each wing is occupied by night employes, and they are thus removed as far as possible from the noise and other distracting surroundings, the first and second floors being assigned to day employes. There are baths at the end of each wing.

On each floor there is a reception room, with two additional entrance halls furnished as parlors, all being open during the day and until ten o'clock at night for the use of the employes when off duty.

In the basement of the Home is the lecture and recitation room of the Training School for Nurses.

BOWLING ALLEY AND CARD ROOM, WOMEN NURSES' HOME, MANHATTAN STATE HOSPITAL.

RECREATION.

Membership in the organization known as the "Employes' Club," is open to all employes of the hospital on payment of a small initiation fee together with small monthly dues. This entitles them to the use of the club house at all times when they are off duty, and certain additional privileges, such as a late pass Saturday night, a reduction in barber's fees and admission to dances given under the auspices of the club from time to time. They elect their own officers and select their own employes, with the approval of the superintendent.

The building and original furnishings were provided by the hospital. Renewals and additional furnishings are purchased by the Employes Club, which

Continued on Page 17.

TRADE DISPUTES.

THREE METHODS OF SETTLEMENT ILLUSTRATED BY EXAMPLES IN UNITED STATES AND CANADA.

WITHIN the last few months practical illustration has been given, on a large scale, of three distinct methods of dealing with serious differences between employers and employes—direct negotiation, meditation, and official investigation with certain compulsory features. The first method brought about a settlement of demands by the locomotive engineers employed on about forty Western railroads; the second achieved the same result in the case of the conductors and trainmen on the same roads, and has been called into use in the telegraphers' strike; the third was employed with respect to strikes in the Canadian coal mines.

HON. MARTIN A. KNAPP.

The Locomotive Engineers' Settlement.

Of the three, the case of the locomotive engineers attracted the least public attention, perhaps because the methods were the simplest and most direct—nothing more, in fact than ordinary business conferences between the parties immediately concerned. The joint session of the engineers' representatives and railroad managers' committee lasted about two weeks, and a settlement was reached in January which granted certain wage increases to the men and adjusted minor differences to the reasonable satisfaction of both parties. The issues were not easy of solution and the sessions were for the most part day and night affairs, but it was found possible to reach a conclusion without resorting to the mediation of any third party or arranging for arbitration. This is the ideal method of settling industrial disputes.

The Train Employes' Settlement.

The conductors and trainmen employed on these same forty railroads submitted demands for increased wages and shorter hours, and committees representing both sides met in joint conference for many weeks, without making practically any headway toward a settlement. Late in March the railroad companies resorted to the Erdmann Conciliation and Arbitration Act, which empowers the Chairman of the Interstate Commerce Commission and the United States Commissioner of Labor to act in a mediatory capacity when requested, for the settlement of disputes between railroad companies and their employes. Chairman Martin A. Knapp and Commissioner Charles P. Neill went to Chicago and held several sessions with representatives of both parties, finally submitting a proposition which was accepted and signed on April 5 by the committee representing the companies and by Grand Chief Garretson of the Order of Railroad Conductors and P. H. Morrissey of the Brotherhood of Railroad Trainmen.

The settlement includes a guarantee on roads not having mileage limitations in their agreements for passenger men that the mileage will not be increased for the purpose of offsetting the increase in wages, as was done on several lines following the 1903 settlements; and provisions that overtime be allowed for passenger service and that 100 miles or less, ten hours or less, shall constitute a day in

HON. CHARLES P. NEILL.

through or regular freight service. Local freight working time has been reduced to ten hours, or less, on all roads that worked more than ten hours. The day for work trains and helpers will be ten hours or less. On eighty per cent. of the roads it was twelve hours. Many roads had the one-half day minimum in work train service. The principle of pro rata overtime in through, regular, local and work train service was established. The increase in wages will average ten per cent for the entire territory and in certain instances will reach fifteen per cent.

The demand for a shorter working day on all of the lines was dropped, but this feature was also omitted from the settlement made with the yardmen last November and the engineers in January.

At the time of the mediation by Messrs. Knapp and Neill the prospect of making a settlement seemed remote, except perhaps to those whose faith in the admirable methods that have long prevailed in the adjustment of differences in the railroad world was too strong to be shaken by even the discouragements of this prolonged negotiation. It is significant that this settlement, through conciliation, was reached after arbitration offered by the railroad managers had been declined by the trainmen, a circumstance which prompts the Railroad Trainmen's Journal to say that: "It was the sensible thing for the committees to do as they did. . . . . At best the outcome (of a strike) would have left the organizations responsible for whatever would have resulted to business progress. As it is, a substantial increase was secured and many questions brought closer to standard."

The Railway Conductor remarks that: "The method followed in this case is an innovation in the history of railway labor dealing. There were no precedents established by which we could be governed. The very magnitude of the movement itself created conditions with which we had never been confronted and attracted to it public notice and attention that were before unheard of and would have created conditions, had it become necessary to call our membership in that territory out on strike, that would never have had a parallel in the history of the labor movement. The men on the committee took these facts into full consideration, recognizing the interests of the public in the question, and, by their judgment in accepting a settlement below that to which, they believed, they were honestly entitled, fully demonstrated the fact that even when admittedly possessing the power to absolutely enforce their demands they were governed by a spirit of moderation and not by that spirit of tyranny which had usually been ascribed to organized labor when placed under the conditions here outlined."

RAILWAY CONFERENCE.

This photograph, taken especially for the Review, shows the Chairmen of forty-seven Committees of Engineers and the managers of forty-seven railroads just after they had signed their agreement.

Telegraphers' Strike.

Dr. Neill was called in to the telegraphers' strike through a petition having been sent to the President from several commercial organizations. He brought about a settlement which was regarded as fair by the Executive Board of the Telegraphers' Union and accepted by them, but the President of the organization, who was in San Francisco, was not satisfied with the matter and called a strike on the Pacific Coast. Dr. Neill immediately took up the matter again and finally went with the Executive Board to San Francisco and brought about a second settlement of the controversy, which was satisfactory to all parties. Ten days later a strike occurred at Los Angeles, California, which was unauthorized by any officials of the organization. That strike at once spread until the union was involved all over the United States and all the men were finally called out. Dr. Neill at once took hold of the matter, but at this writing it seems as though it will have to be fought to a finish.

The Canadian Coal Mine Strike.

The recent troubles in the mining districts of Canada have attracted widespread attention because of their relation to the "Industrial Disputes Investigation Act," which became a law in March last. This measure provides that "Employers and employes shall give at least thirty days' notice of an intended change affecting conditions of employment with respect to hours and wages," and requires that in the event of any dispute in any industry known as a public industry it shall be illegal to resort to a strike or lockout until the dispute in question has been made the subject of an investigation before a board of Conciliation and Investigation, to be appointed by the Minister of Labor.

During April, before the provisions of the act had become clearly understood throughout the Dominion, strikes occurred in the coal mines of Nova Scotia and in Alberta and in Eastern British Columbia. In the Nova Scotia case, the issue was a demand for the closed shop; in the other, it was on the renewal of a working agreement which had expired in March. In both cases application was made to the Minister of Labor for a board of conciliation and investigation, under the provisions of the new law. In the Nova Scotia case, as the strikers had returned to work before definite steps had been taken under the law to bring about a settlement, no real test of its efficiency was afforded.

In the Western case again, though there was a violation of the law, and an effort on the part of the Government to secure compliance with it, through persuasion, there does not appear to have been any attempt to enforce its provisions. The conference between operators and men during the month of March having failed to come to an understanding, the month of April opened in an unsettled state. Application for a board of conciliation and investigation was made by each of the parties, but technical objections interposed only added to the unrest. Notice of an intended reduction of wages had been posted by some of the companies. Thereupon some of the miners ceased work and by the 21st of April work at all the mines had terminated.

A board of conciliation and investigation was appointed, but in the meantime the Deputy Minister of Labor was sent to the scene. He exerted his utmost endeavors to secure a return to work. He believed that the cessation of work had been due to a misunderstanding of the purposes of the act and so convinced the local leaders, who agreed to put the question of a return to work to a vote of the men. The men, by a vote April 27th, rejected the proposition, but it is pointed out that the negative vote came from places away from the center of the disturbance which had not had the benefit of any of the discussions. The Deputy Minister did not consider the vote in any sense a symptom of open rebellion against the provisions of the act.

Pending the constitution of the official board, the Deputy Minister took the matters of dispute in hand, and by a series of conferences with both parties secured finally an agreement which, after ratification by referendum, went into effect May 5th, 1907. The board adjourned without having organized.

It is to be noted that the negotiations for a settlement were carried on as if the provisions of the law were being regularly complied with in all respects, whereas it had failed in what was supposed to be its vital feature, namely, the requirement that no strike or lockout should occur until the dispute had been finally dealt with by the board. The law expressly provides that:

"In every case where a dispute has been referred to the board until the dispute has been finally dealt with by the board neither of the parties nor the employes affected shall alter the condition of employment with respect to wages or hours, or on account of the dispute do, or be concerned in doing, directly or indirectly, anything in the nature of a lockout or strike, or a suspension or discontinuance of employment or work, but the relationship of employer and employe shall continue uninterrupted by the dispute or anything arising out of the dispute."

Apparently the government was not prepared to test the question of fine or imprisonment to compel the strikers to remain at work, but preferred to ignore the point and work for a settlement as best it might. In fact, this aspect of the law has not been definitely tested. Proceedings were indeed undertaken against certain miners at Texada, B. C., for causing a strike which was initiated March 25, 1907. In the course of the trial it appeared and was brought out that the act was approved March 22, and that the miners at the time of causing the strike had no knowledge of its provisions. Discussions before the Court led to an adjustment of difficulties between the men and their employers and the prosecutions were dropped.

Just what the effect of an enforcement of the law would be it is difficult to foresee. As President John Mitchell, of the United Mine Workers, commenting upon this case in an interview at St. Louis June 7, says: "The question that immediately arises is that of involuntary servitude. If the miner wanted to quit work surely he would be permitted to do so without being fined by the government because he didn't want to work. When a man works at mining who doesn't want to and is forced to do so by the government we would call it involuntary servitude in the United States."

While the Canadian law does not establish compulsory arbitration, in that it does not prohibit a strike or lockout after the report of the conciliation board has been made, but attempts only to compel unbroken relations during the negotiations, nevertheless analysis shows the extreme difficulty of making the compulsory feature workable in any form. Desirable as the object of the law may be on its abstract merits, it is quite possible that an attempt to fine or imprison a large number of workingmen for refusal to remain at work would create a new problem of such magnitude and bitterness and possible social consequences that, by comparison, a strike over the original dispute would drop into significance.

WELFARE WORK FOR GOVERNMENT EMPLOYES.

(Continued from page 16.)

also meets the payment of salaries of the club employes, three in number, man janitor, woman janitor and man barber. The building is in charge of a man and woman, who are selected by the employes with the approval of the superintendent of the hospital. They have general charge of the building, and are responsible for conduct and order. It is open to all until 10 p. m.; Saturdays, 11 p. m.

A small store is conducted at which candy and tobacco are sold. The profits go to the club.

There is a beautiful reception room and a splendid billiard and a pool room. There are reading and music rooms beautifully furnished. The reading room is supplied with daily papers and magazines. Adjoining this room is the hospital library, comprising several hundred volumes, open to both employes and patients.

The Employes' Club House contains a well-equipped barber shop.

THE COUNCIL OF THE GENERAL FEDERATION OF WOMEN'S CLUBS, NORFOLK, VIRGINIA, JUNE, 1907.

1. MRS. SARAH PLATT DECKER, *Colorado.*
2. MRS. PHILIP N. MOORE, *Missouri.*
3. MRS. CHARLES A. PERKINS, *Tennessee.*
4. MRS. PERCY V. PENNYBACKER, *Texas.*
5. MRS. GEORGE WATKINS, *Illinois.*
6. MRS. CLARENCE BURNS, *New York.*
7. MRS. SARAH D. EVANS, *Oregon.*
8. MRS. JOHN DICKINSON SHERMAN, *Illinois.*
9. MRS. GRAINGER, *Georgia.*
10. MRS. W. M. MILLER, *Missouri.*
11. MRS. ELLEN S. CROMWELL, *District of Columbia.*
12. MRS. MAY ALDEN WARD, *Massachusetts.*
13. MRS. GRANVILLE GODDING, *Massachusetts.*
14. MISS VIRGINIA GATEWOOD, *Virginia.*
15. MRS. J. D. WHITTEMORE, *Colorado.*
16. MISS POPPENHEIM, *South Carolina.*
17. MRS. MARY A. LOCKWOOD, *District of Columbia.*
18. MRS. JOSIAH E. COWLES, *California.*
19. MRS. J. H. DIBRELL, *Texas.*
20. MRS. MARY I. WOOD, *New Hampshire.*
21. MRS. EMMA L. FOX, *Missouri.*
22. MRS. J. WASHBURN, *Minnesota.*
23. DR. PORTMAN, *District of Columbia.*
24. MRS. BLAIR, *New York.*
25. MISS KELSO, *New York.*

A meeting of the Council of the General Federation of Women's Clubs was held in June, 1907, at the Jamestown Exposition, Norfolk, Va. Thirty-eight States were represented among the 165 women present, who are prominently identified with the club movements of the country.

While the General Federation of Women's Clubs meets every two years, sessions of the Council are held in alternate years to receive reports from chairmen of standing committees and the committee charged with preparations for the next meeting of the Federation.

Important reports presented to the Norfolk meeting were those of Mrs. J. H. Dibrell, on "Civics;" Miss Anna Lewis Clark, on "Civil Service," and Mrs. Clarence Burns, on "Child Labor." Especial interest was awakened by the report on the co-operation of the Federation with the National Civic Federation and other bodies on the proposed investigation into the problems of child labor.

THE PACIFIC COAST IN LINE

INDUSTRIAL PEACE CONFERENCE AT SAN FRANCISCO PROPOSES TO ESTABLISH BRANCH OF THE NATIONAL CIVIC FEDERATION

EMPLOYERS, labor leaders and citizens one thousand strong by newspaper report, met together in San Francisco on July 24 in an important conference in behalf of Industrial Peace. Professor Adolph C. Miller, of the University of California, was chosen president, and W. J. French, president of the Allied Printing Trades, secretary of the meeting. During the three days of the session there was much forceful discussion of the issues at stake. The representatives of all phases of thought united in expressing the belief that every effort should be bent toward maintaining peace with honor.

The conference was addressed by the Hon. Oscar Straus, Secretary of Commerce and Labor, who urged the formation of a permanent organization in behalf of conciliation. Mr. Straus said in part:

"I had hoped that in this part of the country, where wages are high, where industries are profitable, I would find both labor and capital living in happiness under their own vines and fig trees. I understand they do live under their own vines and fig trees, but, unfortunately, they throw brickbats from the vines and fig trees on the one side to the vines and fig trees on the other side. (Laughter and applause.) I am going to address myself now to the brickbats. I have found among the labor leaders as enlightened and patriotic men as exist among any class of our people. (Applause.) I have found as much ignorance and as much arbitrariness arrayed

HON. OSCAR S. STRAUS.

on the side of capital as I have on the side of labor. (Applause.) We must be willing to make mutual concessions for the sake of right and justice. To demand a higher wage than the industry can afford to pay is to clog the wheels of that industry. In saying that when labor 'makes an uneconomic demand,' those demands deserve to be denied, I am quoting the language of the president of the American Federation of Labor, Samuel Gompers.

"I am told that one division of your labor bodies in this city is not represented here. I am sure that this section of labor, when they find out with what spirit of fairness and what spirit of justice you are endeavoring to find the middle way for the purpose of adjusting these difficulties, will come and join you.

"If it were possible for me to remain here longer I would address myself to that body, and I have never addressed myself to labor without finding a reasonable response to reasonable demands. (Applause.) I hope that the permanent committee that you will name, the organized body that will grow out of these meetings, will confer with all the sections of labor, and I know that they will succeed, even against the advice of some leaders, if such leaders they have, who are misleading them, and that the rank and file will join you in building up an organization and a body that will deal fairly and justly with all classes of labor and all classes of capital regardless of every consideration but of fairness and justice.

"This industrial question must be absolutely divorced from all political considerations (applause). Politics has pitfalls and evils enough without mixing them up with the economic relations between capital and labor. (Applause.) This is in no sense a political question and must not be made the tail of any political fight. This is a humanitarian and an economic question pure and simple. The benefits that result from it are even greater to labor than they are to capital, because they are more in need of industrial peace than the paying class is in need of it."

The constitution of a Conciliation Committee met with favor, and at the conclusion of the conference the Committee on Resolutions, of which Mr. Harris Weinstock was the chairman, submitted a report recommending it. The report was unanimously approved and is as follows:

Whereas, One of the great problems of the hour is how best to maintain industrial peace with justice to employer and employed; and

Whereas, Disputes between labor and capital are serious hindrances to the peace and prosperity of our city and our commonwealth; and

Whereas, It is the consensus of opinion of thoughtful men that the best method for the prevention of such disputes is a better understanding between the industrial forces; and

Whereas, It is imperative that immediate efforts be made to remove friction and to bring into harmonious accord the employer and the employed; and

Whereas, The National Civic Federation, by its disinterested and conciliatory methods, has been eminently successful in averting and adjusting great numbers of strikes and lockouts; be it therefore

Resolved, That we, the representatives of various walks of life, assembled in conference in the city of San Francisco, after the fullest interchange of viewpoints and opinions, firmly believe that great good can be made to follow the bringing into life in our midst of a branch of the National Civic Federation, which shall have for its purposes:

(a) The adjustment and prevention by conciliation and arbitration of industrial disputes which may hereafter arise within our commonwealth.

(b) The furthering of any movement which shall have for its purpose the bringing into closer touch and greater harmony the wage earner and employer.

(c) The investigation of and action in such other matters as may from time to time affect the welfare and the relations between employer and employed; and be it therefore further

Resolved, That the chairman of the conference, with the approval of the executive committee of the Civic League, shall appoint a committee of forty-five members, not necessarily delegates to this conference, fifteen representing labor, fifteen representing employers and fifteen representing the general public, who shall elect a chairman, vice-chairman, secretary, treasurer and such other officers as may be required, and shall draft rules and regulations, and in whom shall be vested full discretionary power in the government of the federation and as to the time when the foregoing purposes shall be carried into effect; and be it therefore further

Resolved, That this conference recognizes that in the organization of labor and capital lies the most effective means of securing and maintaining the objects herein set forth; and be it therefore further

Resolved, That we, the delegates to this industrial peace conference pledge ourselves to give such branch of the National Civic Federation our hearty support.

HARRIS WEINSTOCK, Chairman.
DR. FRANK GALE,
JAMES G. MAGUIRE,
THOMAS MAGEE,
DR. GEORGE EVANS.

The committee, whose appointment was approved, has not yet been announced. Professor Adolph C. Miller, president of the conference, is in consultation with the Civic League in regard to the matter. On behalf of the National Civic Federation Dr. Benjamin Ide Wheeler, president of the University of California, Vice-President of the National Civic Federation, is representing the national organization in its relations to the proposed branch.

PRIVATE VERSUS PUBLIC OPERATION.

Continued from Page 5.

MINORITY REPORT OF MR. WALTON CLARK.

I agree with my associates on the importance of directing attention to the dangers and difficulties attending municipal ownership. I do not dissent from their conclusion that companies entrusted with franchises and charters for the operation of so-called public service industries should be subject to regulation. I write a minority report because, if I correctly understand your instructions to your investigating Committee, the majority report does not, in its form and scope, answer your reasonable expectation, and because I am not able to agree with what I understand to be the meaning of some few of the statements made therein.

Recognizing the almost supreme importance of an adequate and cheap supply of pure water, I dissent from one of the recommendations of my associates, in effect that water works should be operated by public bodies. I dissent for the reason that my study of the report of the water works expert employed by your committee, and my personal investigations, lead me to the conclusion that the water companies have made the more intelligent efforts toward adequacy and purity of supply, and that, all conditions considered, the result of their efforts has been and is a better and cheaper water supply and service than that maintained by the municipal water works departments.

I agree with the majority that such governmental conditions as exist in Glasgow, Manchester and Birmingham are "distinctly favorable" to municipal ownership, as they must be to every urban activity, public or private. The fact that the results of the investigations we have made in these well-governed cities have not led my associates to commend municipal ownership as we have there observed it, or to recommend that our American cities adopt municipal ownership, is pregnant with meaning, and indicates another point upon which we are in accord.

My knowledge of the question, had from personal investigation, and from a study of the reports of the experts employed by the Commission, and of the writings of its members leads me to the conclusion that the city and citizens of Glasgow, Manchester and Birmingham, as well as of the other municipalities investigated, are not so well served by their public service trading departments as the cities and citizens of London, Newcastle, Sheffield, Dublin and Norwich are by companies operating similar trading industries, and that there is no element of blessing in the municipalization of the former cities to compensate for the indifferent character of the service rendered.

I dissent from the statement of my associates that "we take no position on the question of general expediency of either public or private ownership." I come from the study of this question, and from the investigations in which I have had a share, including that of the municipal plants selected as being the most successful in Great Britain and in this country, ready, and with confidence, to take a position on the question of general expediency.

Because the investigation, in which, through your favor, I have had the honor to have a part, has convinced me that municipal ownership has not proven equal to private ownership in benefits to the consumer, citizen or city, I am not able to agree with the majority of the Committee that the way should be left open for any municipality to undertake any trading operation, without special authorization by the Legislature of the State wherein it is located. I cannot believe that the prescribed remedy for any ill should be a worse ill, and I cannot recommend that a municipality suffering, or believing that it suffers, under company administration of a public utility, should be given the right to engage in the operation of such utility for itself, without such a course of procedure as will make sure that the sober second thought of the people shall have ample opportunity for development and expression, before the community is committed to municipal ownership, with the accompanying dangers and difficulties, of which you are warned in the majority report.

Because I believe that the general credit of municipalities should be conserved for the benefit of public and necessary improvements, from which, in the nature of things, private enterprise is excluded; and because I believe that a municipality should not be permitted in any event to engage in any trading enterprise that will not pay its own way, and have the confidence of the citizens as financially sound, I recommend that municipalities be prohibited, by statute, from making investments in trading operations, except with money borrowed on mortgage, or otherwise, the loan being secured by a lien on the plant in which it is invested, and on the right to operate the same, and on these only.

Because I believe that it is practically impossible to secure private funds for investment in an enterprise subject to purchase by a municipality, at a date to be selected by the municipality; and because I believe that the impossibility of so securing private investment may, and often will, work a social harm to a community, I dissent from the opinion of the majority that a city should have the right to purchase, at its option, the property of public service corporations for operation, lease or sale.

I believe in State regulation and protection of public service companies. I do not understand that your Committee was charged with the duty of recommending to you a form of regulation. I know that your Committee made no special study of this subject. Therefore I am not prepared to propose any detailed plan of regulation.

Finally, regretting to be in any degree in conflict of opinion with my associates, I may still satisfy my sense of duty to my fellow-citizens and my sense of obligation to you for the honor of a share in this important work, by recording the conviction I am under at the close of this investigation.

I am convinced that the condition of the British people, individually or collectively, has not been improved by the municipalization of the industries we have investigated.

I believe that political and social condition in the United States are less favorable to the success of municipal ownership than are the same conditions in Great Britain.

I find this conclusion strengthened by our investigation into municipalized industries in the United States.

I am convinced that, under American conditions, the system of private ownership of public utilities is best for the citizens and consumers.

I recommend State regulation and protection of public service companies, provided by statute, and as far as possible automatic in its application and operation.

I realize that in the main the majority and the minority of your Committee are in accord. Wherein we differ, the minority appeals with confidence to a careful reading of the records of your Committee for judgment as to the reasonableness of its conclusions and recommendations.

SCOPE OF COMPLETE REPORT.

The full report of the Commission will appear in two parts, one containing conclusions of the Commission and of individual members, and the other containing the expert reports on plants visited. While the first part will contain more of interest to the general reader, the second will be of especial interest to accountants, engineers, managers of public utility corporations, city officials and members of legislative committees. It will be of special value to those seeking a comparison between American and British conditions.

The contents of each division of the work will be substantially as follows:

Part 1, Volume 1.

General Conclusions of Commission;

British Municipalities, By Frank J. Goodnow, author of "Municipal Home Rule," "City Government in the United States," etc.

American Municipalities, by Walter L. Fisher, Traction Counsel to ex-Mayor Dunne and to Mayor Busse, of Chicago, and author of the franchise plan adopted by the voters of that city.

A Critical Review of the Experts' Reports, in two sections, by Edward W. Bemis and Milo R. Maltbie, and Walton Clark and Charles L. Edgar.

Certain Phases of the Labor Investigation, by John R. Commons and J. W. Sullivan.

Verbatim Reports of Conferences upon Municipal Trading Held at London with Rt. Hon. Lord Avebury (Sir John Lubbock), Mr. Sydney Morse, President of London Chamber of Commerce; Hon. Robert P. Porter, author of "Dangers of Municipal Ownership"; Hon. T. McKinnon Wood, Progressive Leader, London County Council; Hon. J. Allen Baker, Chairman London Municipal Tramways, and Mr. Robert Donald, Editor of the London Daily Chronicle.

Part 2, Volumes I. and II.:

Volume I., the United States:

Reports of Experts on Gas Lighting:
Alf. E. Forstall, Fred Burnett, John H. Gray, John R. Commons, J. W. Sullivan, Marwick, Mitchell & Co.

Special Report on Philadelphia Gas Works, by Leo S. Rowe.

Reports of Experts on Electric Lighting and Power:
Theo Stebbins, Chas. E. Phelps, Jr., John H. Gray, John R. Commons, J. W. Sullivan, Marwick, Mitchell & Co.

Report on the History of Chicago Municipal Electric Lighting, by Marwick, Mitchell & Co.

Report on Water Works Systems, by Dabney H. Maury, John H. Gray, John R. Commons, J. W. Sullivan, and Marwick, Mitchell & Co.

Volume II., Great Britain and Ireland:

Reports of Experts on Gas Lighting:
Milo R. Maltbie, J. B. Klumpp, Wm. Newbigging, Robert C. James, E. H. Turner, John R. Commons, and J. W. Sullivan.

Reports of Experts on Electric Lighting and Power:
J. B. Klumpp, A. E. Winchester, Milo R. Maltbie, Robert C. James, E. H. Turner, J. W. Sullivan, and John R. Commons.

Reports of Experts on Tramways:
Norman McD. Crawford, Milo R. Maltbie, J. H. Woodward, E. H. Turner, Robert C. James, John R. Commons, and J. W. Sullivan.
Report on Taxation of Public Utilities, by Milo R. Maltbie.

A limited edition only will be published. Send advance orders to Isaac N. Seligman, treasurer, 281 Fourth avenue, New York.

The price is:

Part 1, Volume I. (about 500 pages), paper, $1.00; cloth	$2.00
Part 2, Volumes I. and II. (about 1,000 pp. each)	8.00
Complete, cloth	$10.00

Postage prepaid.

FOR INDUSTRIAL WORLD PEACE

(Continued from page 8.)

A PLEA FOR FORBEARANCE.

Mr. T. V. Powderly said:

"I am one of those who have had some experience in the labor world, and the experience gained during that fifteen years of leadership causes me to say that if men on both sides of the industrial question would keep one thing in mind, while we would still have disputes, their settlement would be easy, and when settled hard feelings should not exist; and that is for each man, if he owes a dollar, to pay it, and if he owes a grudge, to forget it.

"During that period I never ordered one strike, although I was engaged in four or five large ones that others ordered; but on going over my books three years ago I found the record of eleven hundred cases settled, each one of which might have been a strike had not common sense—which, by the way, is the most uncommon kind of sense—been called into play before the chip had reached the shoulder. You have read of the four cases that I didn't have anything to do with, but the other eleven hundred cases never broke into print. And if among the things we can do here to-night is to cause the newspapers to give the exact truth (Laughter)—— Wait a moment, this is no laughing matter. I have seen homes made desolate by an ill-considered report in the papers; I have seen men of capital ruined because of matters contained in the papers; and if only the men who write the daily history could be brought to write it truthfully and not exaggerate—there is always enough of the truth to tell—the troubles between capital and labor would be far fewer than they are.

"I feel it to be the duty of every man who has held a position in a labor organization to be ready to respond to the call. Nothing will give me more pleasure than to lend my weight, no matter how little it may be, to the furtherance of industrial peace. One day I met a man with whom we had a controversy, and he said to me: 'Powderly, I don't want to see you at all; get out.' I said, 'You will like me better if you see more of me.' He said, 'I don't want to see you,' and I replied, 'Well, you may think it over. I am stopping at such and such a hotel.' Then he shoved me out of the door, and said things not written down in the Holy Book, and I went away to the hotel. Two hours afterward I got a note and went back; the whole thing was settled in twenty minutes. And here is a caution to some of our labor men and to those on the other side as well: In the struggle you are engaged in, it is not personal. You may think you are working for yourself on the side of capital, but you are not; and you who represent labor are not working for yourselves. No insult, no indignity, and no contumely should find a resting place on you. Wipe them all aside, and keep in view the interests of the great body of people that look to you. And if you remember that, you will always meet the fellow on the other side in the right spirit and in the spirit of rightness." (Applause.)

PEACE AND JUSTICE SYNONYMOUS.

Dr. Lyman Abbott, editor of the Outlook, said:

"What is the proper relationship between the tool owner and the tool worker? What should be the participation of each in the control and in the profits of the common industry? Every demand for a recognition of the union is, at the bottom, a demand to have something to say respecting the control of the industry; every demand for shorter hours or larger wages is, at the bottom, a demand for a share in the profits.

"There are some extreme socialists who hold that the tool owners have no rights, that rent and interest are robbery; and there have been some political teachers on the other side who have claimed that the whole duty of the capitalist was performed when he paid the tool worker a living wage. But I think that both of those classes may be regarded as out of the question here to-night, and the real question before us is: How shall the question of participation in control and in profits be decided? In the past it has been decided by war; not so much a matter of guns and pistols on the one side and dynamite and stones on the other, but it has been war. But, ladies and gentlemen, the lockout and the strike never determine what is right. (Applause.) They only determine who has the greatest endurance.

"War between nations never yet in the history of the world decided which was right; it only settled who was the strongest. The Hague Tribunal means this: We may not in the future appeal to force, but we mean to appeal to the conscience and reason, not to determine which nation is the most powerful, but to determine which nation is right. What we want to do here to-night is to set in motion in matters industrial the appeal to reason and conscience, the appeal which shall determine what is right, and not merely who is powerful.

"If this be done, it should be done by an international gathering, for two reasons: In the first place this is a very complicated, difficult problem, and we need to bring to bear upon it the greatest minds and best thought of the world. Now, Europe needs, I think, the energy, enterprise, initiative and audacity of us Americans; but we must acknowledge that we audacious and enterprising Americans need also the experience of the Old World. We can learn something from Germany, France, Italy and England, and they can learn something from us.

"We are working in this twentieth century not merely toward peace in place of war, but toward the reorganization of a hitherto disorganized world. To bring that about the organization must be not merely political; it must also be industrial, because if we organize politically for peace, and organize industrially for war, we shall have war in spite of all the politicians may do for peace.

"So, gentlemen, I am very glad of the honor of seconding this suggestion which has been made, that the Civic Federation invite a conference that shall stand in the history of the world, in respect to industry, where The Hague conference has stood in respect to international relations. We are fortunate to-night in meeting under the roof of a gentleman whose name, happily, is identified with the cause of international peace—a gentleman whose name I hope may be identified also with the cause of industrial peace throughout all the future, because under his roof and at this meeting there was born that movement which shall secure good will and peace between labor and capitalists. (Applause.)

PREVENTION OF STRIKES.

Hon. Seth Low said:

"I have said to myself always in approaching these industrial questions: If each side will only put itself in the place of the other man and look at it from his side, there would not be half these troubles. I have always felt that if I were a workingman, earning my living by my hands, I would certainly join a union, and therefore I never could understand why the employer was so unwilling to recognize the union. If the employer were to work in the shop I think he would feel that it was a part of what was due to him as a man to have something to say as to the conditions under which he was called upon to work. Children go where they are sent because they are children, but when a man becomes a man he wants to have something to say about the conditions that affect his life, and I have always felt that if the employers would only think of it from that point of view instead of so exclusively from the point of view of the rights of property they would have avoided a great many of the difficulties into which they have fallen. The moment they admit that they are willing to treat with them, and the moment they begin to treat with them, they find out, as my experience goes, that they are a very much more reasonable set of people than they thought when they had never seen them.

"The first time I ever came in touch with a labor dispute was when I was arbitrator between the Typothetae and Big Six back in this city about ten years ago. I remember perfectly well the immense interest I felt in seeing how each side conducted itself, and in what a courteous and reasonable manner, and how cheerfully they both accepted the decision. And from that day to this I have used my influence whenever I had the opportunity to promote arbitration, because it seemed to me an educational process as well as a means of settling most of the disputes much more reasonably than otherwise would be possible.

"The function of the Civic Federation, in this department, is not so much to settle strikes as to prevent them, and it would amaze every one here to know in how many instances serious labor troubles have been averted by bringing together those who have never met before. That, I think, is the best way and the wisest way by which industrial peace is to be advanced, to bring together the disputants and let them talk it out." (Applause.)

The following telegram was read:

"'Kindly express to conference my regret at my inability to attend. I trust that discussion may lead to further progress in establishing industrial peace on lines being followed by National Civic Federation. The trade agreement recognizing capital and labor's rights and obligations assures guarantee of industrial tranquillity. John Mitchell.'" (Applause.)

Before adjournment the entire company arose and sang "America" and "Auld Lang Syne."

INDUSTRIAL ECONOMICS DEPARTMENT.

Appointment of Secretary.

DR. ROLAND P. FALKNER, who for the past three years has been Commissioner of Education of Porto Rico, has been appointed secretary of the Industrial Economics Department, and entered upon his duties August 1.

DR. ROLAND P. FALKNER.

After graduating from the University of Pennsylvania in 1885, with the degree of Ph. B. in the newly organized course in Finance and Economy, he immediately went to Germany, where he studied Political Economy and Philosophy, at the Universities of Berlin and Halle, taking the degree of Doctor of Philosophy at the latter institution, near the end of the year 1887. He thereupon went to Paris, where he spent three months in studying Political Economy at the College de France. While studying abroad he was appointed instructor in accounting and statistics at the University of Pennsylvania, upon announcement of which he returned to Germany and spent the Summer semester of 1888 at the University of Leipzig, engaged in the study of German Commercial Law. His work as instructor at the University of Pennsylvania began in September, 1888. He was made associate professor of statistics in the University of Pennsylvania, in the Spring of 1891, at which time he declined a call to the professorship of political economy at the Northwestern University, Evanston, Illinois. In 1900 he was appointed to a staff position in the Library of Congress. In 1904 President Roosevelt appointed him Commissioner of Education of Porto Rico.

During this period of academic work, in addition to teaching, Dr. Falkner made frequent contributions to the scientific literature in his chosen subject, and was conspicuously identified with two important pieces of public service:

First, as statistician to the sub-committee to the Committee of Finance of the United States Senate, which was charged with the investigation of prices and wages in the United States. The materials for this work were gathered largely through the agency of the United States Department of Labor, but the analysis of the figures was confided wholly to Dr. Falkner, who began the work in the Fall of 1891. The results were the well-known Aldrich Reports, devoted respectively to "Retail Prices and Wages," (three volumes) and "Wholesale Prices, Wages and Transportation," (four volumes). The report is, perhaps, the most important contribution of its kind to the history of prices and wages in the United States, which has been made by our Government.

Second, in the Fall of 1892, Dr. Falkner was appointed secretary of the American delegation to the International Monetary Conference, at Brussels, where he also acted as one of the secretaries of the conference. The translation of the official French text of the proceedings, published as a part of the American report, was prepared by Dr. Falkner and Mr. Smith, the English secretary.

Dr. Falkner has been prominently identified with the American Academy of Political and Social Science, the American Economic Association and other scientific societies. Perhaps the most significant of all was the honor conferred upon him in 1894, when he was elected a member of the International Statistical Institute, whose membership is limited to two hundred, drawn from all parts of the world.

PANAMA EDITION

The National Civic Federation Review

Vol. III. NEW YORK, OCTOBER, 1907 No. 2.

EMPLOYES' WELFARE ON CANAL ZONE.

LABOR CONDITIONS, HOUSING, FEEDING AND SOCIAL LIFE AT PANAMA.

An investigation of the conditions surrounding the employes of the United States Government on the Isthmus of Panama, including arrangements for housing, feeding, amusement, social life and regulations affecting employment, has been made by Miss Gertrude Beeks, secretary of the Welfare Department of the National Civic Federation, and the report has been submitted to Secretary Taft. This effort to aid in improving the condition of the men engaged in our great national enterprise was naturally the first undertaking under the auspices of the Federation's new Committee on Welfare Work for Government Employes. The officers of the committee devoted to bettering conditions of Federal, State and Municipal employes, are:

Chairman, William H. Taft, Secretary of War.
First Vice-Chairman, John C. W. Beckham, Governor of Kentucky.
Second Vice-Chairman, George W. Guthrie, Mayor of Pittsburg.
Third-Vice Chairman, William R. Willcox, Chairman Public Utilities Commission of New York City.

Nearly every feature of life on the Isthmus is touched upon in the report. Many things are highly commended, others are condemned and recommendations are made for the betterment of conditions. The principal topics covered are the climate, housing, drying rooms, walks and roads, street paving, sewerage and water systems, electric light, food, farming, commissaries, laundries, ice plant, bakery, hospitals, rain sheds, recreations, schools, churches, regulation of liquor traffic, jails, passes on the Panama Railroad, transportation service, some of the labor conditions, the "Canal Zone News," a suggestion system and boat service. The investigation covered a period of five weeks from the time of leaving New York, June 7, until the return, July 12, twenty-three days having been spent on the Isthmus.

Lieutenant-Colonel George W. Goethals
(Chairman.)

The opportunity of securing accurate official information was made possible by Secretary Taft. His letter of introduction and recommendation to the Chairman of the Commission assured the investigator the most complete access to facts and documents. The members of the Isthmian Canal Commission, whose cordial co-operation was extended, are: Lieutenant-Colonel George W. Goethals, chairman, Chief Engineer and President of the Panama Railroad Company, and the following, who are heads of the departments enumerated: Major William L. Sibert (Lock and Dam Construction), Major D. D. Gaillard (Excavation and Dredging), H. H. Rousseau, U. S. N. (Municipal Engineering, Motive Power and Machinery, and Building Construction), Hon. J. C. S. Blackburn (Civil Administration), Colonel W. C. Gorgas (Sanitation) and Jackson Smith (Labor, Quarters and Subsistence). Letters were supplied by prominent citizens to friends on the Isthmus and by national labor leaders to members of their respective organizations, those furnishing such credentials being Samuel Gompers, President the American Federation of Labor; James O'Connell, President the International Association of Machinists; Warren S. Stone, Grand Chief, International Brotherhood of Locomotive Engineers; Daniel J. Keefe, President, International Longshoremen, Marine and Transportworkers' Association; John Mitchell, President the United Mine Workers of America and Joseph F. Valentine, President, Iron Moulders' Union of North America. Personal inspection of the many points and features mentioned in the report was supplemented by individual testimony. Information was gathered from officials, superintendents, foremen, mechanics, clerks, nurses, doctors, secretaries of the Young Men's Christian Association, railroad engineers and conductors, their wives and children and in fact every type of resident on the Isthmus, the negroes included. But in no case was testimony sought or received from discharged employes.

It is clearly recognized that never before have there been as good conditions in American construction work, but in view of the climatic conditions, length of time to be consumed in the building of the Canal and the fact that the Government should be a model employer, it is urged that the surroundings of the employes should be made as comfortable as possible. While to a casual reader many of the criticisms and suggestions might seem trivial, Miss Beeks's experience in dealing with employes of many of the largest concerns in the country has taught that it is the accumulation of petty things which causes discontent. The report brings out the fact that it is not alone technical engineering problems—for of course these are not touched upon in it—which confront the United States on the Isthmus. Without a contented force of employes progress in the construction of the Canal must be dilatory and results unsatisfactory. Perfection is not expected, but all the recommendations are for improvements essential to health and good cheer, important factors in promoting efficiency and stability in the working force. In providing for the welfare of its employes, naturally, more can be expected from the Government than from a private employer with limited capital and restricted by competitive conditions.

Marines Preparing for Wall Scaling Contest, Fourth of July Celebration, at Baseball Park, Back of Hotel Tivoli, Ancon.

Some of the recommendations have already been adopted. Secretary Taft immediately requested the Agricultural Department to start a Government farm and made arrangements with Secretary Wilson to have all food stuffs inspected before shipment from the United States; he also authorized the purchase of blankets for the negroes and refrigeration plants for mess halls. A tentative draft of the report was presented to Lieutenant-Colonel Goethals before Miss Beeks left the Isthmus. He at once had plans drawn for drying rooms, and ordered that

THE NATIONAL
Civic Federation Review

Office: 281 Fourth Avenue, New York City
RALPH M. EASLEY, Editor

The Editor alone is Responsible for any unsigned article or unquoted statement published in THE NATIONAL CIVIC FEDERATION REVIEW.

PUBLISHED BY

The National Civic Federation

metal cots be covered with canvas. He has indicated his intention of putting into effect such suggestions as available funds will permit and of calling the more important recommendations to the attention of the Congressional Committee on Appropriations, which will visit the Isthmus in October, with the view of securing funds for their adoption. The Commission also has started the publication of the Canal Zone newspaper and has accepted the services of a representative of the Welfare Department of the National Civic Federation—Miss Helen Varick Boswell—to organize women's clubs and she is now on the Isthmus. The report has been sent officially to the Isthmian Canal Commission for comments, which will be published later. President Roosevelt has requested Miss Beeks to return to Panama within eight months and report upon progress made.

The equipment of Miss Beeks for making such an investigation has been acquired by a wide and practical experience in dealing with all phases of the problems connected with the employment of labor. For the past six years her entire time has been devoted to investigating industrial conditions throughout the United States, and making and carrying out plans for the well-being of men and women in stores, mills, factories, mines and on railroads.—The Editor.

CULEBRA, SHOWING ADMINISTRATION BUILDING, QUARTERS, CLUB HOUSE AND MESS HALL.

CONDITIONS OF EMPLOYMENT AT PANAMA.

By GERTRUDE BEEKS

CLIMATE.

The rainy season extends over eight months, ending about the first of January, the following four being the dry season and said to be most delightful. While there is a short period when, for days at a time, it rains constantly, that is not true during the entire wet season. It rains less at Ancon, on the Pacific Coast, than along the Isthmus, and at some places it is usually clear mornings, but showers are to be expected afternoons. When it does not rain during this season there is, much of the time, a cloudiness which makes out-of-door work quite endurable. Generally there is a good breeze, and nights, mornings and evenings are cool. At noon it is quite warm. Although there is continual moisture, the atmosphere is not oppressive and the climate is much more pleasant than in many parts of the United States in summer. Some also prefer it to snow and ice in winter.

There is something about the light which begets nervousness and the climatic conditions generally cause energy to be sapped, which makes it imperative that there should be vacation periods. With the observance of certain health precautions this is in some ways a more agreeable place to live than certain sections of the United States, but it is felt by some that health would be undermined after an extended residence.

Many who go there expecting to find only marshes have been agreeably surprised. The scenery is beautiful. Colon, on the Atlantic Coast, is quite low, but along the Isthmus there are hills, and they attain quite a height at Ancon, near the City of Panama. The palms are disappointing, but the hills, with their verdure, and, on the coast, the combination of hills and water, and wonderful cloud effects, afford beautiful pictures.

IMPROVEMENTS ADMITTED—MANY COMPLAINTS WARRANTED.

"Things are improving right along!" This sentence was heard constantly, as well as, "There will be no kick coming as long as it can be seen that needed changes are being made." It is recognized that "everything cannot be accomplished in a minute."

Many of the complaints with reference to housing, food and conditions of employment, in addition to those about bad boat service, have undoubtedly been warranted; but it is most gratifying to learn that Colonel Goethals has been energetic in informing himself of the details in connection therewith, since his appointment as Chairman of the Isthmian Canal Commission and Chief Engineer. His policy of making personal investigations of messes and of listening to all complaints of injustice relative to wages, dismissals and other matters, has inspired confidence. There is a general feeling that he intends to do "the square thing," due to the fact that now the men can get a hearing and to the prompt action taken when fully convinced that some wrong condition has obtained.

In view of the changes transpiring at the present time it seems unfair to offer criticisms, but an effort will be made to present conditions as they are today, giving credit for contemplated changes and offering some suggestions for further improvements.

HOUSING.

The camps in the Canal Zone are located along the railroad between the Panamanian cities of Colon and Panama wherever construction work demands a large number of employes. There are seventeen main camps at which the American whites reside and there are forty-six contiguous settlements in which are the barracks of the European and West Indian laborers.

In the settlements there are postal stations, fire departments, telephone service, band stands in front of the hotels and news stands at the railway stations. At several of the large camps Government 'buses meet the trains, while at the stations of Colon and Panama many vehicles will be found for rental by Panamanians and other enterprising individuals.

QUARTERS OF CLERKS, MECHANICS, FOREMEN AND OTHER WHITE EMPLOYES.

The quarters of the employes are of several types. There are houses for married employes, American whites, Europeans and West Indian negroes; barracks (for bachelors who are clerks or American mechanics) which contain several rooms.

each holding from two to four men; dormitory barracks for Europeans, in which there are cot bunks—sixty, seventy-two or eighty-four in each house—and similar separate dormitory barracks for West Indians. Adjacent to the mess halls or "hotels," as

Major D. D. Gaillard.
(Harris & Ewing.)

they are called, there are separate barracks in each camp for the hotel help. At the hospitals, located at Ancon and Colon, there are separate dormitories for bachelors—doctors and clerks—for women nurses, for men attendants, orderlies, maids and other employes.

The newly constructed buildings are exceedingly attractive. There are not many manufacturing villages presenting an appearance so beautiful, and it is certainly an innovation in construction work. Many of the old French houses have been remodeled and painted the standard color used on the Zone—gray with white trimmings, and red roofs. The houses are built on posts. The Government supplies garbage cans, not only for its employes at all the camps, but also throughout the cities of Panama and Colon. Streets and grounds, even under quarters, are kept perfectly free from rubbish of any description. Would that our streets and back yards in the United States were as clean! The settlements are so attractive that one making a short stay upon the Zone, and thus getting a superficial view, would most likely exclaim: "These men are getting all that there is coming to them," which expression was made recently by such a casual observer.

All quarters, both "married" and bachelor, for Americans, have wide verandas. One type of married quarters contains two rooms across the front—one a living room and the other a sleeping room. In the left-hand corner of the rear there is a bath;

Hon. J. C. S. Blackburn.
(Harris & Ewing.)

in the right-hand corner a small kitchen, and between them there is a large open dining room, the end often affording a beautiful view, and being covered with wire screen. The windows and verandas are screened.

The bachelors' quarters, as well as the "married" quarters for Americans, contain shower baths, although with cold water only, and toilet arrangements with modern plumbing. Cold shower baths are not advisable for family use. Tub baths should be installed in all married quarters constructed in future, and it would be well to have for sale at the commissaries movable bath tubs for those who already have shower baths installed. Families may have water heated on their cook stoves. All men cannot use a cold shower bath, for it chills them, especially if overheated at the close of the day's work, and that is the time when the bath is most needed, because shop men, engineers and others find it difficult to remove grease with cold water, and bachelors have no way of obtaining it hot. Even in the morning many men cannot endure the cold water showers. One said: "I wake the boys every morning, 'hollering.' If I couldn't 'holler' I wouldn't be able to get a bath." It would be too much to expect that hot water should now be conveyed to all quarters, but there should be some special bath houses, conveniently located, equipped with hot water for American bachelors.

H. H. Rousseau, U. S. N.
(Clinedinst.)

Colonel W. C. Gorgas.
(Clinedinst.)

All partitions are of wood and the present rule is to stain interior walls a moss green and paint doors and framework white. This is very attractive, pleasant and restful to the eyes in the tropical light. In repainting, it would be well to make it the general plan, if possible.

The Government furnishes quarters, furniture and light free to all. The married employes also receive free fuel, and distilled drinking water is delivered to their homes in some of the camps. It should be provided in all. Ice is carried to each camp from the Colon commissary every morning. It is sold to the employes. There is a great deal of complaint about short weight.

The allotment of furniture for homes and bachelors' quarters is:

Family Quarters.

1 Range.
1 Refrigerator.
1 Double bed.
2 Pillows.
1 Dresser.
1 Bedroom table.
1 Towel rack.
1 Bedroom mat.

Major William L. Sibert.
(Harris & Ewing.)

1 Kitchen table.
2 Kitchen chairs.
1 Dining table.
1 Sideboard.
1 Chiffonier.
1 Bedroom mirror.
1 Mosquito bar.
3 Parlor wicker rockers.
1 Parlor centre table.
2 Porch chairs.

Bachelor Quarters.

1 Single bed.
1 Dresser.
1 Chiffonier (for room two bachelors).
1 20 x 30 table.
1 Rocker (for room two bachelors).
1 Towel rack.
1 Mosquito bar.
1 Student lamp (if no electric light).
1 Mattress.
3 Chairs.

Mission and wicker furniture are used to a great extent in both married and bachelor quarters for Americans. It is agreeably surprising to find the artistic and beautiful thus given consideration. All are required to buy blankets, sheets and pillow cases and pay cost of laundering them. Married employes furnish their own kitchen utensils and china.

The appreciation of the recently arrived housewife upon finding pleasing quarters may be illustrated by the experience of a bride of two months, the wife of a locomotive engineer. This sweet, cultivated woman, previously a school teacher in the State of Ohio, arrived upon the Isthmus the thirteenth of

Jackson Smith.
(Harris & Ewing.)

June, expecting to endure rough camp life. When she entered her pretty cottage, she simply sat and looked at it, "because it was so beautiful"; and yet it was not as attractive as some, for she had golden oak instead of mission furniture.

A Two-Family Flat Building.

To give the impression that all are so agreeably surprised would be incorrect. For instance, a steam shovel man, after the endurance of early hardships and two years of service, took down his family in June. They transported many of their household effects from the States, looking forward to a long residence on the Isthmus, so well satisfied was this man. The wife—a gentle, refined woman—met cruel disappointment, for, in this case, the assignment of married quarters was a box car!

Still, phenomenal changes, during the past two years, have been made, and it is granted by all that even during the last six months there has been great improvement in conditions.

SOME EXPERIENCES OF PIONEERS.

The experience of some of the "pioneers," those who have been there two years, may afford an idea of the transformation which has taken place in that period. To be assigned an old French house, without mosquito netting, without plumbing and with an attic containing bats and rats and all sorts of objectionable creatures which "had a merry-go-round every night," was common, and it was necessary to walk through the jungle, coming in contact with its dangerous fungi and bugs, to reach the house.

The sixth American woman to take her residence upon the Zone stated with reference to conditions two years ago: "In going from Colon to Culebra the train brushed the jungle and the odor from the rank vegetation was sickening. I was away for a time and when I came back and saw the new houses, the sanitary arrangements, the double railroad track, and the jungle cleared away, it seemed miraculous. When I was here the first time I could not even buy such a thing as a wash tub, and one of the carpenters took a crude oil barrel, cut it in two and burned it out for my use. I had the first cook stove, but when it was set up I could not get a stove pipe and so the men made one of solid copper from portions of machinery which had been left by the French. I was fortunate enough to bring with me a meat chopper and it went around the entire Isthmus as a loan. When I went away I sold my effects and everyone was so anxious to get the meat chopper that it was run up to five dollars before I knew what was happening, although I had only paid eighty-nine cents for it, and the rest of the women were all so angry at each other and the lucky purchaser that they would not speak!"

One woman took down a mirror and found that her neighbor, who borrowed it, had not seen her likeness during her residence of three months! Such incidents, both serious and amusing, are related of early conditions. Ice was unheard of, and yet we took down one hundred sets of wire snow brushes for use on the railroad, but, unlike the French, who, it was authoritatively stated, provided snow plows, we were able to put the erroneously ordered utensils to good use in the foundries.

Bachelors, three, and even two years ago, were glad to get quarters at very high prices in the City of Panama or Colon, which would seem to the average individual to be quite uninhabitable. One said: "When I came here, two years ago, I slept on the floor for three nights. Sometimes the men would have to wait fifteen days for mosquito netting. There have been vast improvements." Water was so scarce that it was necessary to pay from forty to sixty cents a can, even for bathing purposes, and to arrange the night before for the morning's bath. The price of board was excessive, and yet one nearly starved. Employes stated that food contained maggots, and eggs had to be fried or scrambled because it was not "safe to boil them." As one superintendent said, "A man was lucky to have a tent in which to sleep. A common remark was, 'We'll never have any homes!' It is a different world now. The only music we heard was, 'Lead, Kindly Light.' I took care of a man three days without knowing that he had yellow fever, and was pallbearer six times in three weeks." As another put it: "To ask for a man and learn he had died from yellow fever the day before was a constantly unnerving experience. The depressing effect of frequent funeral processions caused one to stand on the wharf and think, 'Shall I go or shall I stay?'"

Conditions are, indeed, miraculously changed, but there are improvements yet to be made for health and comfort.

QUARTERS INADEQUATE.

Although the quarters are inadequate, and will be, it is estimated, for a year to come, it is now possible to shelter all Isthmian Canal employes without the use of tents, except in a few instances, and especially when opening up a new piece of work. But it is unfortunate that one thousand men in the construction gangs of the railroad are quartered in box cars, sixteen being the number allotted to each, although it is admitted that more sometimes "crowd in them." It would be expected that small numbers required in maintenance-of-way crews could be quartered in no other way. A few men live in house boats on the old French canal, where there is dredging to be done.

There is great need for additional family houses. Married men are not contented to remain upon the Zone, as a rule, without their families, and through inability to get married quarters there have been lost many competent men. Applications for married quarters still unfilled have been on file for more than a year. Attention was directed by competent investigators to the special need of married quarters two years ago and they should have been constructed in larger numbers more rapidly. It has been proven that the Isthmus is not altogether an undesirable place to live, and many men are anxious to take down their families. There was a rule requiring each

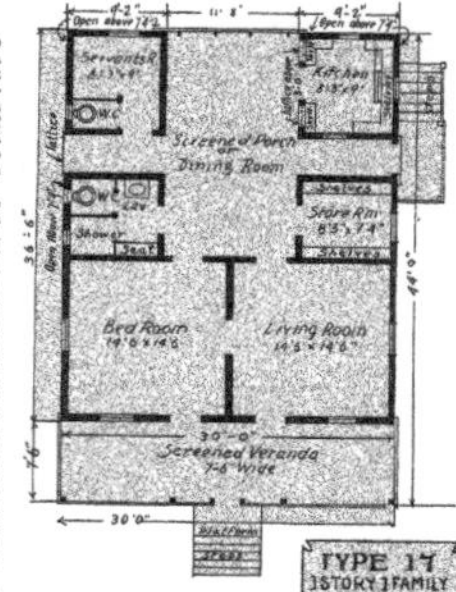

A One-Story Family House.

employe to have an application on file for six months before being awarded married quarters, assignments to be made in chronological order as filed. A new rule has just been adopted permitting the men to make application for married quarters upon taking employment, but its effect cannot be felt for some time unless a supreme effort is made to provide additional quarters, and the notice just posted is not cheering, for it states: "Experience shows that about ten months elapse between applications for and assignment of married quarters."

The outlook is very discouraging owing to the shortage of lumber. One boatload of 1,300,000 feet has just been lost en route from New York. It is estimated that it will take six months to duplicate that shipload, because lumber is in such great demand in the States. The law requires the advertising of proposed purchases and securing of bids. It is necessary to plan six months ahead on materials, for so far it has taken that long to complete transactions and secure delivery. Shortage of materials seems to be due partly to slow methods of purchasing and lack of foresight in ordering; and according to sentiment at Panama the Purchasing Department in Washington too remote to be able to judge of Isthmian needs, has interfered by cutting requisitions. Until we can catch up a little, it would be well if a way could be found to pay the premium which will secure early delivery. As it is, the purchaser in the States gets the preference in deliveries because he is "on the spot," and the seller finds it less disagreeable to be upbraided for failure to deliver on contract time by the Canal authorities two thousand miles away! It is very difficult for the onlooker to have patience with the long delays which are being endured in this and other connections, and how much worse is it for those who are participating in the discomforts attendant!

Dining Room in Family House.

In view of the fact that it must be admitted that the Canal Zone has become a community and no longer simply affords construction camp life, it is urgent to provide adequate quarters for American families and bachelors at the earliest possible moment. It seems as though some extreme measures should be taken to meet this need and that the United States should not be obliged to wait a year to provide living accommodations. It costs the Government large sums to take new men constantly to the Isthmus, transportation fare and wages from time of embarkation being met by it.

To save expense, the present plan in constructing family quarters is to place four flats in a building. It is quite an item of saving, but anything which promotes content is the greatest item of economy, and there is no doubt that all greatly prefer single houses. It is claimed that a building for four families can be constructed for $4,000.00, while a single house will cost $2,000.00. One hesitates to urge the erection of single family houses in the face of that, and yet inferior single houses will be taken in preference to flats, so great is the desire to be alone; and it is not to be wondered at, for there are so many different types and nationalities concerned. It is difficult to find four congenial families in that heterogeneous population. The four-family houses now being constructed contain two flats upon the first and two upon the second floor; and double floors, with felt between, are being laid, thus providing against some of the causes of discomfort to be met in older buildings. In the joint family houses previously built, and necessarily still in use, with no method of deadening noise, several children overhead make life miserable for those underneath. The shrinking of the single floors in the dry season, causing cracks between the boards, makes it impossible to scrub without having water drip into the apartment below.

The need of married quarters is evidenced, not only by the number of married men who desire to take down their families and the number constantly leaving the Isthmus because unable to secure family houses, but by the growing number of bridegrooms and would-be bridegrooms. If the men stay for a few months, they grow enthusiastic about living upon the Isthmus, but they become disheartened and ill when unable to get houses in order to have their families with them. Families happily located encourage their relatives to go down and this helps to secure competent workmen. Many of the families are living better that they ever did in the States and it is a good place for young people to begin housekeeping, not only because of the attractive quarters, but because so much is furnished free that there is opportunity of saving and thus getting a good start in life. But homesick married men and young fellows with sweethearts in the States will not remain indefinitely unless able to establish homes. A man is much more contented in his own home not only because of the sentiment attached to it, but because there is someone to look after his personal needs, to provide wholesome food suited to his taste, and the wife's companionship prevents him from growing discouraged or taking impulsive action when things all seem to go wrong. There is no doubt but that the further development of home life will aid in securing a more permanent force of workers. Men with families there say they "would not stay ten minutes without them!" A man off for his vacation exclaimed: "I have had my application for quarters in since January 7. I'll probably take my family back and rent because I can't stand it sleeping four in a room and no place to keep my clothes free from mold." But the rules will not permit him to obtain the Government rate upon the steamship line until he has secured quarters! An engineer asked, "Do

American Bachelors' Quarters.

ou like it here?" replied, "Yes, I'll stay if I can get y wife down." "How long have you had your ap- lication in?" "Five months." Both had been there x months before applying for married quarters. any such instances could be cited.

MORE BACHELOR QUARTERS REQUIRED.

The first bachelors' quarters to be constructed ave permitted four beds in a room of good size. he recently adopted standard type allows but two a room, which is a great improvement, each build- g containing twenty-four rooms and accommodat- g altogether forty-eight men. But many are sleep- g four in a room. While it must be expected that ome hardships are to be endured in connection with uch an undertaking, at the earliest possible mo- ent it should be arranged that nor more than two en shall occupy a room in any building. It is diffi- ult to place congenial ones together, and "congen- al" there means more than elsewhere, for there are any types of men. One becomes nervous in that limate, and men coming in late at night disturb the leeper. Then again, if one be studious it is trying o be interrupted by companions. It is not agree- ble for one who does not rink to be placed with hose who have more iberal views upon that ubject. If a man be ill in he night he will disturb he others. All this reacts pon the work, for the en cannot be in a cheer- ul frame of mind or in he best condition to labor when so irritated and suf- ering from lack of sleep, ut it seems to be more ecessary to have plenty f sleep in that climate han elsewhere. It helps o prevent nervousness nd ill temper. A few have o objection to sleeping our in a room, but, for he most part, it is obnox- ous. Occasionally a man ill have a room alone, ut very few are so fa- ored. The inclination to e alone is well illustrated y the case of one man leeping in a room containing fleas and bedbugs. Of- ered quarters with four in a room elsewhere, he chose etween the two evils to room with the vermin. achelors who work nights and sleep during the day hould be given quarters remote from the railroad, otably at Paraiso, where they are now very near he tracks and disturbed by the incessantly passing rains. Conductors and engineers in the passenger ervice of the Panama Railroad Company have rooms bove the station at Panama for rest between runs nd an old house a few blocks away serves for the ermanent quarters of some. It is very difficult for he men to secure rest in the rooms above the station wing to the incessant noise, and the permanent uarters referred to are not up to the standard of hose supplied to the majority of the employes. Im- rovement in this connection is desirable. The rail- oad employes, working on passenger, freight and ther trains, live for the most part in the standard ype of quarters.

The hotel helpers—negroes above the type of com- on laborer—sleep three in a room in special dor- itories adjacent to the hotel. The rooms are too mall for three and there is some expressed dissatis- action. Ventilation is not adequate.

QUARTERS FOR HOSPITAL EMPLOYES.

The doctors at the main hospitals have excellent omes and bachelor quarters. One waiting for a ome is the Chief Sanitary Officer, Dr. Gorgas.

The nurses are quartered very pleasantly and com- ortably at the Ancon Hospital; their reception room eing pretty and homelike in appearance. It is un- fortunate that at the Ancon Hospital the women nurses' quarters are across from the fire depart- ment, which prevents them from having the privacy which they should enjoy, for the firemen naturally sit around most of the time outside of their building.

At the Colon Hospital the sleeping rooms are small and the reception room is very unattractive and bare in appearance. The nurses' dormitory at the Colon Hospital should be better protected from rain. During severe storms the apartments on the first floor on the ocean side are pretty well drenched, and on the top floor it was authoritatively stated that nurses have been known to sleep with umbrellas over them because the rain beats in through ventilators.

Better arrangements should be made for nurses on night duty, it being the custom, except in the case of favored individuals, for each to have one month's night duty every four or five months. Since night duty lasts for one month, night nurses could easily move to separate quarters. As it is, they cannot sleep well in day time because of noise. It was claimed at one of the hospitals that two rooms are reserved to which nurses may go if they so desire, but it is certain that the nurses do not so understand it, and, besides, no one would care to go to a room remote from personal effects to sleep. Furthermore, two rooms would not accommodate the number on night duty.

The quarters for orderlies, attendants and maids, which are separate places, are above reproach. The end of each contains a partitioned room, with shower baths and wash bowls, and there is an attendant constantly present to maintain order.

TYPE 18 REVISED 2 STORY BACHELORS QUARTERS

FIRST FLOOR PLAN
SECOND FLOOR SIMILAR

Floor Plan, Bachelor's Quarters.

DRYING ROOMS NEEDED.

The housewife finds her greatest difficulty in combating dampness. The airing of garments and bed-clothing, which soon become moldy and musty, is constantly necessary in the wet season. It is exceedingly disagreeable, if not unhealthful, to lie upon a musty pillow, for instance, and it requires perpetual effort to care for woolen clothing, shoes and other apparel.

It is even a greater hardship for the bachelor, who has no way of drying his wet garments after being at work in the rain daily eight months in the year. The housewife may dry the garments of the husband at the kitchen stove, but the bachelor has no way of caring for his. At the homes of the officials there are drying rooms over kitchens, receiving the heat therefrom. It is vital to health that there should be arranged some system for drying bachelors' clothes. For the American bachelors there might be a shanty constructed, centrally located, and heated periodically for this purpose. It would be better to have in each building where American bachelors reside a room set aside for that purpose. A good arrangement would be ventilated metal lockers with heating apparatus underneath. In this way the garments could be kept locked in individual compartments to

A Bachelor's Sleeping Room.

prevent stealing. The quarters would take a better appearance than now, for, as it is, the clothes are to be kept, if hung at all, on the walls in the sleeping rooms or on lines above the beds. Otherwise they are in trunks. A rule provides that there shall be no clothes' lines on the verandas. A man cannot hang his clothes out of doors and leave them there while at work because rain is almost sure to fall during the day. If left in the quarters damp they soon accumulate mold. The lockers would have to be of material so treated as to endure moisture in the atmosphere. The recommendation relative to drying rooms was presented, with others, to Colonel Goethals and is receiving consideration.

Bedding of bachelors—pillows, mattresses and blankets—should be aired periodically. It grows very offensive from musty odors. Some resort to the sprinkling of perfume upon their pillows at night.

VERMIN.

Another serious difficulty is the existence of bed bugs to such a degree as to cause serious discomfort. A man cannot endure such discomfort at night and be in a contented frame of mind during the day while at work. Cockroaches and fleas are also very numerous in the quarters, and flies are exceedingly troublesome in the mess halls. One wonders if the subject of eradicating vermin in the tropics might not receive such scientific consideration as has been directed to pests which have annoyed farmers. The ordinary methods of fumigation are pursued. The men claim that much of the trouble is due to poor janitor service; that if individuals clean their own rooms bugs go from other quarters in the same building, and that it is only by paying the janitors extra that they secure good service. An illustration given was this: "All the janitors do is to sweep the dirt under the beds and straighten the bed covers. The other fellows have bed bugs and fleas. In our buildings we got rid of them by having our own janitor. He cleans up after the other man gets through each day." Bed bugs are troublesome on the boats also. The presence of scorpions and lizards in the quarters, according to some accounts, is erroneous. They are found sometimes where jungle is not cleared away, but where there is no vegetation they are not frequently seen.

THE SERVANT QUESTION.

During the rainy season mud is accumulated upon the boots to such a great extent as to make housekeeping exceedingly difficult. This necessitates much scrubbing. The difficulty of securing servants among Jamaicans willing to undertake general housework necessitates very hard work on the part of the housewife. If one will wash she will not iron. One who will iron will not cook, etc. By keeping two servants the housework will be lightened, but, as almost all have gone there to save money, or, as they put it, "to make their stake" and be able to take it a little easier when they return to the States, few care to meet the expense of two servants.

It is complained that janitor service is far from satisfactory in the bachelors' quarters. In addition to illustrations given perfectly reputable men [illegible] that a mop had never been used in their rooms. It was stated that there never had been so much cleaning done as during this investigation, and that everybody had been kept "hustling." Such activity was probably due to the introduction of a more rigid system of inspection of camps, i. e., the military system. Owing to the difficulty of securing efficient help, as servants and janitors, through the services of West Indian negroes and of getting good cooks for the mess houses, it would seem desirable to effect some understanding with the Government of Panama, which is always ready to accede to reasonable demands, whereby Chinese laborers might be secured for such work. Then, a corps of janitors might also scrub periodically the married quarters, a charge for such service being made. Wages of Chinese servants might be higher than those of the negroes, but, especially in the matter of janitors and cooks, an extra expenditure would be warranted if necessary. The wives of the high officials, as well as mechanics, are experiencing a distressing time over the difficulty and sometimes inability to secure domestic service of any description.

SHORTAGE OF FURNITURE.

There was much dissatisfaction among American bachelors who were sleeping upon cots. All were promised beds, but many had not yet received them. In some instances when beds have been vacated by men leaving the service those with cots have simply taken such beds, and this custom of "robbing vacated quarters" has also obtained among the married residents. This should not be necessary, with proper supervision of quarters. Promises are made which are as quickly forgotten, it is claimed. Some who have been there for a year have not their full quota of furniture yet. Families have been given houses containing a portion of the furniture required with the assurance that they would get the balance at once, and it is claimed immediately afterward part of what they had would be removed. While it is generally conceded that there always will be grumblers, no matter how great is the attempt to be fair in assigning quarters, many of the conditions existing to-day are certainly unnecessary. Some American bachelors said: "The worst thing is having to sleep on cots;" that "after a hard day's work a man needs a mattress, and after six months' waiting a fellow gets tired of it and leaves."

The hotel helpers have cots. They should have mattresses. It would be very desirable to substitute double deck iron beds for such cots. These helpers rank above common laborers, although negroes, and are entitled to as much consideration as orderlies and attendants in the hospitals who are so well housed.

There is dissatisfaction among Americans because of the inability to get furniture, and it does seem as though when bids are courted bidders should be requested to state whether or not they have stock on hand, to prevent the necessity of waiting until furniture can be manufactured. There were beds, chiffoniers and other articles upon which the contract time for delivery had expired six weeks and two months previous to this investigation, not received. It is to be hoped that the army method of purchasing now being adopted, with the larger corps of inspectors appointed to follow up orders and urge deliveries, may aid in relieving the situation. Again, the idea of paying premiums, as private purchasers do, to insure early delivery, presents itself. Our prosperity has made it difficult to secure the filling of orders made by citizens in the United States, which emphasizes the necessity of special effort on the part of the Government in connection with its purchases for the Isthmus.

An estimate of the amount of furniture which will be required to care for the greatest number of employes, which is now about determined as a permanent force, should be made and furniture for that number secured. In making this estimate additional married quarters to a liberal extent and more bachelors' quarters to obviate having more than two in a room should be taken into consideration.

There must be a poor system of inspection of materials, for types ordered are not received. For instance, copper screen is required in that climate, where everything rusts, and yet iron screen has been received largely. It was observed on new quarters and hospitals to have split in a few weeks. It has been accepted in a spirit of desperation as better than nothing.

Glued furniture cannot be used there because of the moisture, and yet it has been substituted by the best firms for the "knock-down" type ordered, which can be pegged. Even a great drug company has sent adulterated medicines for our sick.

Now, bad screen and furniture are put into temporary use, but contractors are being informed that such goods must be replaced at their expense, with the hope that they will be taught an effective lesson.

COMMON LABORERS' QUARTERS.

European laborers are segregated, and so are the West Indians. The quarters are identical in construction, each house being one large room, containing from sixty to seventy-two and eighty-four cots. According to modern tenement house laws the air space should be not less than four hundred cubic feet for each adult. In only one type of houses has that number been allowed, according to the following estimate:

"At Cristobal, 84 bunks per house, allowing 353 cubic feet per man; at Tabernilla, 72 bunks per house, allowing 412 cubic feet per man; the French Barracks at Rio Grande contain 60 bunks per house, allowing 330 cubic feet per man. It is claimed, and perhaps properly, that it is unfair to make a comparison between city tenements and these buildings having wide openings at roofs, which are supported by posts, leaving a space between the walls and roofs, but this is submitted as worthy of expert advice, especially as those laborers fall such a ready prey to the pulmonary malady of pneumonia.

The bunks or cots are arranged one over the other in tiers of three. The majority of the cots are canvas, but many are made of metal lattice work, the ends of the flat pieces of metal being joined to side rods and front and head rods with springs. The men lie on this metal lattice work with nothing underneath them, and it is about as cruel a system as could be devised. It was officially stated that one thousand metal cots were secured as an experiment, that they have now been adopted as the standard type, and that more metal cots had been ordered. They should be abolished. All the cots are too narrow, and when new ones are purchased they should be wider.

For the purpose of cleanliness the common laborers are obliged to keep their clothes on a wide shelf around the top of the rooms. Sometimes they have them in bags on their cots. It is very desirable that the floors should be kept free to be scrubbed, and they were quite clean invariably, but the clothing should be more accessible. The shelves above are supposed to be reached by ladders, which do not always exist. One of the supervisors, when asked how the men were expected to get their clothes, stated: "Well, that is up to them. They climb over the bunks."

It would be very desirable to have ventilated metal lockers surrounding these dormitories, in which the men might keep their clothes, or to have additions built to the dormitories for that purpose. One of the greatest causes of illness is the wearing of wet garments. The Sanitary Department is urging the men to wear dry clothes. How it can be accomplished under the present conditions it is difficult to understand. By providing a system of lockers, as suggested, steam pipes could be put underneath for drying the clothes frequently, or this could be done in the rooms added for the keeping of the garments. Men who are out in the rainy season and get wet daily, as they do eight months in the year, should be provided with drying rooms for the clothes. The placing of damp clothes in the morning upon the warm body chills it and causes illness. When it was asked if steam could be provided for such drying rooms it was said that it would be impossible. Colonel Goethals, however, took up the matter and found that it would be feasible and had a plan drawn, adding a splendid feature of his own conception for the common laborers. It is to place laundry tubs in one end, where they may wash their clothes. Now they may be observed washing outside their quarters. He agreed that the drying rooms should be supplied. It is to be hoped that there may not be experienced, either due to scarcity of materials or shortage of labor in the building department, the delays of the past, for this is of urgent importance.

There is no furniture whatever, not even benches, on which to sit in the common laborers' dormitories when changing clothes, or when it rains daytimes. It would be well to have wooden benches. Evenings the Europeans are allowed to sit in the mess halls, where they are provided with paper, pen and ink for letter writing, but the negroes have no place to sit.

The common laborers are required to buy blankets, and, consequently, comparatively few have them. In the interest of maintaining health for all the Government should supply such blankets—at least for this class, which must be taught how to live. They should be provided with two blankets—one for underneath the body, which now has no protection from cold, and one for a covering. This is a matter of the utmost urgency. It is hard to understand why a matter of such importance should not have received earlier attention. Aside from its consideration from a humanitarian standpoint, it will be economy in the end. It will save in hospital expenses and in the cost of securing fresh supplies of labor. It is possible that the common laborers are better off than they were in their own countries, but that does not excuse us for neglecting to provide essentials for health.

It is the intention to send the married Spaniards out into the country and give them materials to put up their own quarters. This is an unfortunate move, due, it is said, to an inadequate building force. It is very important that quarters should be constructed by the Government for all, and especially for the ignorant.

A Typical Camp for Laborers.

is not done generally. There is discontent among high officials and other employes because they are obliged to pay so much for quarters in that hotel for the reason that other accommodations cannot be provided. Commutation, amounting to about eight per cent of the salary, was at one time allowed under such conditions, but that was discontinued because, it was announced, there were adequate quarters, which did not prove to be the case.

Employes going to the hotel for separate meals may secure them on the following basis: Breakfast fifty cents, lunch fifty cents, dinner seventy-five cents. For rooms without baths transient rates for employes are from \$1.50 to \$2.50 a day. With baths they are from \$2.50 to \$3.50 a day. In addition meals are two dollars and twenty-five cents a day. This seems absurd in view of the fact that by paying for single meals, as above stated, they would amount to one dollar and seventy-five cents a day. Rooms at the lowest rates are not often available. One official stated that he never goes to the Tivoli with his wife but that it costs him fifteen dollars for the night. The officers of the Marines from Camp Eliot cannot secure rates at the Tivoli unless they own coupon books, which are of no use to them at any other time, and yet, the expense of stopping for a day for such an officer and his wife has never been less than fourteen dollars.

If one were obtaining value received the rates for non-employes would not seem so excessive, but the food was absolutely abominable. For breakfast sometimes there were delicious pineapples to relieve the monotony of cereals miserably prepared, musty eggs and poor quality of breakfast bacon, served day after day. It is not too extreme to say that breakfast coffee was vile. Luncheons and dinners were table d'hote meals with indifferent soups, flat meats, unseasoned canned vegetables and uneatable desserts. After a few days of such meals the mere sight of the food was repulsive and one would involuntarily screw up the face in disgust. It then became a matter of making selections in an effort to get some article which could be consumed. After dinner coffee was good, which demonstrated that there was no excuse for the kind served at breakfast. The drinking water is secured from the steam coming from the water used in cooking utensils. It should, therefore, be pure, but its care must be improper, for it was so unpalatable as to be undrinkable.

The hours of the telephone operator are long. There should be relief for her. The hours of the waiters are from 5:30 a. m. to 9:00 p. m., with an interval of rest in the afternoon. The waiters complain of their quarters, which are the same as at the other hotels, separate dormitories with three crowded in each room.

It is intended that the Hotel Tivoli should be made a congregating place for employes, but it is of small benefit to them in fact. Such a congregating place is greatly needed at that point, especially Sundays and holidays, when employes from down the line visit Panama. If it were made more attractive they would spend less time in the evil resorts of that city.

There is a large hall used Saturday evenings by different social clubs, composed of employes, for dancing, and this is its most beneficial feature. Unfortunately employes of the hotel are not permitted to attend such dances, and, therefore, they have not the opportunity of going to parties because they can never get off duty long enough to go down the line for that purpose. There is a fine billiard room, but there, again, employes receive small benefit as the charge is forty cents an hour for games.

A first-class hotel man should be placed in charge of the Tivoli under such a contract as would ensure certain privileges for the employes.

WALKS AND ROADS.

In the rainy season the mud is not only deep, but exceedingly slippery, and pedestrians fall in going up or down hill where walks have not yet been laid. In speaking of conditions, eleven months ago when he first went to the Isthmus, one man said: "It used to take a tight rope walker to get up to the quarters." Since that time board walks have been widely constructed, some cinder paths have been made and crushed stone has been used for thoroughfares through the camps. The crushed stone is large and uncomfortable to walk upon. Owing to the scarcity of lumber, so much needed for quarters, the question arises as to whether it could be crushed finer and used more largely for new walks, at least until sufficient supply of cinders is assured. The objection to be raised is the expense to the Canal Commission of freight for carrying the stone over the Panama Railway, but it does not seem as though this should be a deterrent. At present cinders are being saved for paths, as it is claimed that board walks rot. It is also said that cinder paths are readily washed away. Therefore it would seem that persistent effort will be required to maintain walks.

Requests were made for a walk in Gorgona from the camp to the shop. It is claimed that there is great danger at noontime in walking railway tracks for trains are traveling both ways at that period.

STREET PAVING, SEWERAGE AND WATER SYSTEMS.

The streets of the City of Panama, not in the Canal Zone, have been paved with brick and a five mile drive has been macadamized from Panama to the summer homes of the first Panamanian families. In Colon, where the city is built in a swamp, houses have been raised for the Panamanians, and many streets paved. The work is progressing in side streets. It is a gigantic undertaking as there must be about two feet of filling. Curbing, filling and paving are being carried on in all the streets. One side of a street will be paved for use of vehicles, a railroad run down the center to carry dirt, and the other side left free to receive the dirt to be used as filling.

There are drainage canals and channels leading to them. No criticism can be justly offered as to an unhealthful condition. Even in the drainage channels water was not stagnant. It was authoritatively stated that this is due to the fact that evaporation takes place night and day, and there are constant fresh rain falls. It may have been a mistake to use

Water Carriers.
(Photographed by Daly.)

macadam, through which it is claimed the moisture seeps, in Colon, but it is claimed that brick can be laid over it. It is but natural that some errors should be made in the various departments where much is experimental in a new country, but there is nothing critical in the situation at Colon, although it is quite likely that the work might have been more expeditiously prosecuted. Paving is one of the contributions to the Panamanian Government for the privilege of constructing the Canal.

A sewerage system has been installed from one end of the Isthmus to the other, all the main work being completed. It will take a year, according to estimates, both in the water and sewerage systems to finish making all connections and the extending of pipes to new camps, but there will be no serious inconvenience on that account.

Water, for all purposes, bathing and drinking, for the majority of the camps, is furnished by four reservoirs, the last one just being completed. At one it is believed that the supply, directly received from the river, will be ample. There are parts of camps where there is no water because of delay in receiving pipe. While it is true that purchasers even in the United States have found it difficult to secure materials, delays seem more vexatious on the Isthmus where nothing can be bought for temporary expedients. As one official said, "It does not matter whether you have \$100 or \$1,000, you simply can't get articles needed."

Although not germane to this subject the following incident affords an interesting illustration of that fact: At Gatun, one of the largest camps, the main cooking for the local hospital was done in receptacles set upon two steel railroad rails, with the fire between them. The loss of the stove ordered for that hospital in a bad fire at the main storehouse was the first chapter in this story. The one ordered by cable to replace it was lost a few weeks ago when the entire cargo of a stranded ship was swept away. To meet the emergency, the City of Panama was scoured, but only two small stoves could be found, which were added to the ingenious device described.

The water supply grew very scarce toward the end of the dry season, but the increase in the capacity of the reservoirs will, it is expected, obviate that inconvenience next year. At the present time there is an adequate supply, although at the new reservoir at Gorgona, the water has been very offensive, due to rank vegetation.

It is not pleasant to drink the water without boiling or distillation any place. In fact, it is quite offensive. It is claimed, however, by the Sanitary Department that it is not unhealthful, and that there is less disease from impure water there than in the States. Typhoid fever at present is confined to the district between the camps of Empire and Gorgona, attributed to negroes drinking from streams into which sewage flows, instead of securing water from the hydrants.

Distillation and sterilizing plants have been placed in some camps to supply pure and palatable drinking water. At the time of this investigation it was the intention to install one system or the other at all camps except where removed from danger of contamination from sewage. Distillation should be adopted in preference to sterilization, and the work of installing distillation plants should be pushed.

In the camps where there are plants for distillation of drinking water it is carried to the married quarters in jugs, each house being supplied by a man carrying a single jug at a time. This seems to be an absurd system, as he is required to walk a considerable distance. It would be well to have carts for this purpose.

Distilled water is supplied in but few instances to bachelors' quarters during the day for their use at night. Employes cannot get drinking water after the evening meals at the hotels, but it would be of little advantage if they could, as the hotels are too remote from the majority of the quarters. Undoubtedly, palatable drinking water at bachelors' quarters would reduce the number of convenient liquor bottles said to be carried to them. It is not difficult to understand the statement that: "If a man can't get water, all he can do is to go and buy a bottle of beer and carry it to his quarters." The Chairman of the Commission stated that a water cooler would be placed upon each floor of the bachelors' quarters and supplied with drinking water, the men to furnish the ice. It is to be hoped that there will be no unnecessary delay in meeting this need.

Drinking water, pleasant to taste, would reduce tea drinking at meals. In a climate where nervousness is so general it is not well for such quantities of tea to be used. It is now placed on the tables in water bottles. In that connection it would be well more largely to use Ceylon tea, which is decidedly better for nerves than other kinds.

Especially should there be drinking water cans on all engines for the engineers and firemen. This is entirely feasible with the use of a little ingenuity. Some have jugs upon the passenger trains, but drinking water is a crying need generally. The Sanitary Department has urged that instead of water upon the engines air-tight barrels be placed a mile apart along the railroad, the ice to come in direct contact with the water. This is not a good plan, as there is danger of contamination in handling the ice, but more particularly because no matter how thirsty a man may be it is not usually possible to stop his train to obtain a drink. The engineers are under orders "to move." Dirt trains must be kept constantly traveling, that steam shovels may be continually in operation. There might be used a bottle now on the market, guaranteed to keep water cold seventy-two hours. It is made of two glass bottles, one within the other, and sealed at the neck leaving a vacuum, which is a non-conductor of heat or cold. It is expensive, but probably would cost no more in the end than other devices which would require cost of labor for handling ice. Tank steel cans, with inside cases of galvanized iron and an interlining of cork, can be used.

There are excellent kegs with faucets for drinking water in the shops, but an effort to secure distilled drinking water at the Gorgona shops has not met with success. It would be well to have a good system of distillation installed in all shops. The Gorgona plan of having the water circulate in pipes around the ice, preventing its direct contact with the water, would be most desirable, for it removes dan-

Family Quarters for Laborers, Near Empire; Having One Room.

Mess Hall for Americans.

ger of cooling water to an unhealthful temperature for men overheated, and of impurities being conveyed. This method is successful in factories in the States, and the failure at Gorgona should not discourage a further effort in that direction.

ELECTRIC LIGHT.

An electric light system was completed two months ago. Some of the camps have all of the houses wired and there are arc lights in some streets. It is intended to develop the electric light plant further, as it is necessary to reduce danger of fire from lamps. It is important that streets in all villages, no matter how remote, should be so lighted in the interest of morality. There is no twilight. When there is no moon the darkness is so dense that it is exceedingly difficult to go about. There is much to be done in connection with artificial lighting and the work should be rapidly pushed. It does not seem as though it should have taken two years to reach the present stage of development, due, it is claimed, to inability to secure delivery of requisite machinery.

FOOD.

The meals which were eaten during this investigation at the various mess houses were good. It was voluntarily stated by many American employes who are eating at the mess houses that the food has greatly improved within the last two months at most of the camps, although not at all. There is reason to believe that the meals were better at some of the places when visits of inspection were made than they are day after day, but it was gratifying to find that the food could be so well prepared. This indicates that there is small excuse for badly prepared meals at those places when plenty of good materials are furnished.

The testimony was ample to prove that before Colonel Goethals began his trips of investigation the meals were exceedingly bad, except at one camp, which is generally conceded to have a first-class mess. Many employes left the Government hotels (mess houses) and now patronize private messes. Their testimony indicates that they were obliged to take such action in order to maintain health. Statements with reference to conditions but two months ago were "rotten meat," food not well prepared, swimming in grease, insufficient served, no variety (steak often tainted, potatoes and red beans daily), no relishes, flies in soup, dishes and table linen unclean, service bad, negroes wiping their faces with dish towels and then using them on dishes, absurdity of paying the Government thirty cents for a poor meal when a good one could be secured at a private mess for twenty-five cents, et cetera.

The Colonel has insisted that there shall not be a "ten-cent meal" sold for thirty cents, and that while an effort will be made to have hotels self-supporting, losses will be cheerfully borne if necessary to provide wholesome food.

The general impression that profits were made at the mess houses is correct. There is no advantage to the Commission in having profits, for such funds cannot be applied toward construction work, but for January, February and March they were considerable.

The profits, beginning with January, for messes and kitchens were:

January	$4,008.04
February	3,118.88
March	10,624.69

The present Commission took charge March 10.

On the first of April orders were given that the mess houses and kitchens would be run on a self-supporting basis.

In April the profits were reduced to $1,193.15.

During May the profits were but $261.09.

There was great dissatisfaction because the sum of $37,000.00 was cleared on food last year, and good food was not supplied.

The mess houses for Americans are attractive and well arranged. Frequently there are separate rooms with table linen for those who eat with coats on, and sometimes the broad, screened verandas are so equipped. In adjacent rooms, men coming directly from shops and other work places may eat in shirt sleeves. There tables are covered with white oilcloth, so that shop grease may readily be washed from it. Kitchens are equiped with modern appliances and large ice chests are provided. Kitchen ranges are usually in dark, unventilated corners.

Dishes are good—even pretty. Silver is of a very cheap grade, is practically unfit for use and possibly a menace to health. There is no economy in buying such cheap ware. Experience in lunch rooms of manufacturing establishments has shown that stocks of high-grade silver seldom need replenishing. A much better grade should be purchased in future.

District physicians are now required to inspect food and kitchens at least three times a week, and this has brought improvement in food and greater cleanliness. There is a certain smokiness in the kitchens, however, which indicates that utensils are not cared for properly. To provide good food there is nothing more necessary than careful attention to kitchen ware. The water in the dish-washing machines at some places was found to be clean and it was very unclean at others. Conditions vary according to the efficiency of the hotel stewards. Linen and dishes are not universally clean and improvement should be made.

Monotonous, cold breakfasts and inability to be served form the burden of a complaint which is general: "Daily egg breakfasts, eggs—eggs—eggs every morning!"

Breakfasts are composed always of a cereal, eggs, bacon, coffee and cakes. There is no reason why they should not be varied. Plenty of foods appropriate for breakfast could be procured.

Those who tip waiters get quick service, and many who have tried to get along without tipping have found that they could scarcely get breakfast. Although there is a rule against tipping, and waiters have been discharged for accepting fees, it is not likely that that system can be changed upon the Isthmus since it has been impossible to enforce such regulations elsewhere. But it should be possible to require the managers of the mess halls to give personal supervision at breakfast time. It is especially complained that they do not appear and that the negro waiters do not care whether they render service or not. The fact is that they could not be expected to do so without guidance.

The following are some of the expressions with reference to breakfasts:

"I do not eat any breakfast at all simply because I can't. The pancakes are so tough I cannot eat them and the coffee is not fit to drink."

"Eggs are cold, the cakes would make good sole leather and the coffee is awful."

"A man will not pay thirty cents for nothing to eat."

"I pay the waiter a dollar a week—God knows I had to get something to eat. The pancakes are hard."

"It is not one time in ten a man can get anything in time to go to work."

It is against the rule for bachelors to prepare breakfast in their quarters, but some do, and claim they are much better off than when obliged to eat the notorious egg breakfast at the mess houses. While there is danger of fire if bachelors have oil stoves and of refuse accumulating as a menace to health, it is too much to expect the observance of this rule unless breakfasts are made less monotonous and service more prompt. It would also be desirable to institute what are called "club breakfasts," as some care for small and others large morning meals. Those who care for little should not be required to pay thirty cents for breakfast.

At the majority of the camps, with the exception of the general complaint about breakfast, such expressions as the following were heard: "The food has been improving for the past two months. Before the new administration took hold it was something fierce."

There is no doubt but that great improvement has taken place. It is equally true that there is still room for betterment.

At one of the camps, where it is claimed that no improvement has taken place in the food, it was said: "You can wait for some improvements, but you can't wait for food. We are getting the same things over and over again. Meat has some kind of sauce, it seems Spanish, over it. Turkey tastes flat and has a queer dressing over it."

At another camp, where it was complained that conditions have not changed, the following statements were made:

"They do not even have ice on the table. You go all the forenoon without water, and then you come in at noon and can't get it cold." "It is a wonder to me that the men keep their health with the food they are getting." That can well be believed in view of the number of complaints offered by perfectly reputable employes, for much of the testimony indicated conditions similar to those experienced at the Tivoli Hotel, which has been under the same management as the mess houses. The lack of nutritious food undoubtedly has been the cause of dysentery and other ailments. Plenty of wholesome food is more essential in the tropics than elsewhere. The body perspires so freely that a generous supply of good fuel is required to replenish waste material. Strength very soon wanes if meals are unsatisfactory. Unpalatable food seems more repulsive there and one soon finds it almost impossible to eat. It is hard to be cheerful under such conditions. The whole world seems wrong and one becomes resentful.

There is one mess, in the opinion of the men, beyond criticism. Engineers will run their engines down to that camp for meals instead of eating where they live. Such expressions as the following were heard: "Why is it they can feed like that at one place and at ours it is impossible to get anything fit to eat?" "That place has been fine for four months, and if every other were as good there would be no kick."

It was learned that at that place the manager was cutting the rations of the negroes short in order to provide such good meals for the Americans. (The supplies for the negro kitchen at that place are sent from the mess hall for whites).

At the Ancon Hospital there is undoubtedly justified complaint with reference to food for employes of the hospital and patients. It is claimed that it is "cold every day in the year." It is cooked in a central kitchen and distributed throughout the grounds to the wards, mess halls and nurses' quarters, patients and employes eating the same food. The vehicles for conveying the food could be improved, and there should be steam tables to warm it at the wards. There is no complaint about food at the Colon Hospital, partly because it is on the Atlantic Coast and secures food fresher, immediately after the arrival of steamships. At Ancon, on the Pacific Coast, cold storage orders must be depended upon entirely, and the trouble is also, as at the mess halls, bad preparation of foods. One of the nurses said: "Tell the President I not only want a 'square deal,' but very particularly a 'square meal.'" At Ancon Hospital it is complained that night nurses have very poor and monotonous midnight lunches, and that in order to get along they must purchase additional supplies and, prepare them.

At present the marines are stationed at Camp Eliot. One of the absurdities is that, owing to the fact that the law requires all purchases for the marines to be made by contract, they cannot be benefited by our commissaries, provided for other Isthmian Canal employes. The marines must eat native beef, even though it costs more than cold storage beef at the commissaries, and purchase bread baked by Panamanians, paying six cents a loaf, whereas, it may be had at our own commissaries for four cents. Potatoes, onions, canned goods and other provisions, are contracted for in the United States and sent down.

EFFICIENT COOKS NEEDED.

Where there is such a variety of tastes it is difficult to please and there will always be some complaints about food, as there is everywhere. But if the food were as well prepared and as neatly served at all messes as at a few popular ones, certainly there would be less grumbling. At such messes there will be found preserves, catsup and pickles constantly on the tables. One steward said that he "could not afford to pursue that plan, as a man would empty a jar of preserves at a meal." That is not the experience of others, and such relishes are greatly appreciated.

Kitchen help at present is principally Jamaican and very unsatisfactory. Chinese are noted for being

Room in Mess Hall Where Americans May Eat Without Coats.

good cooks. They might be secured for such service, and use of the other type entirely discontinued. That health and content cannot be insured without wholesome living arrangements was demonstrated by one foreman, who said: "I have to kinda humor the boys when they don't get good food or comfortable quarters, for they get irritable and fault-finding in the shop." Cooks are paid from seventy-five to one hundred and twenty-five dollars a month. They have quarters free in addition. Six were cabled for in the States at the maximum salary, so thoroughly is the need for good cooks realized. Is it not possible that some of the trained cooks from the army or navy could be detailed to the Isthmus? There should be one chief cook, competent to command a much higher salary than now paid, who would devote his time to supervising and training the cooks, with a view to placing all mess halls on an equally good basis.

MESSES FOR COMMON LABORERS.

The European laborers are fed in separate mess halls, which are splendidly arranged, the dining-rooms containing uncovered tables and benches for seats. They are carefully cleaned daily. Enamelled ware of the appearance of granite makes an excellent type of dishes. Italians, Greeks and Spaniards have their tastes consulted and their favorite foods are furnished. At every plate half a loaf of bread is placed, and each is liberally supplied with a meat stew, macaroni or other vegetables, fruit or other dessert and coffee or tea. Meals are furnished at forty cents a day gold, but Europeans may eat elsewhere if they so desire. They are allowed to take their little bottles of light wine, which they are accustomed to have with meals, to the mess halls.

KITCHENS OF NEGRO LABORERS.

The West Indians, until the first of February, cooked their own food in any sort of fashion, in utensils on the ground, at their barracks. Owing to malnutrition it was decided to erect cook houses and prepare their food, which is now made a part of their wages. Employes file in front of a counter,

EUROPEANS IN FRONT OF MESS HALL.

their rations of meat, vegetables—yams, sweet potatoes or rice—and sometimes fruit are handed to them from the kitchen behind.

This system was recommended by the Sanitary Department a year and a half ago. The delay in establishing it seems as unnecessarily great as do delays in other matters.

Under the old haphazard plan negroes would secure food from the commissaries at noon, usually canned. By the time individual purchases were made, fires built and food prepared the time allowed for lunch and siesta would be consumed. Therefore they were insufficiently nourished, and it was found that when ill in the hospital, after fever had disappeared, they would eat as ravenously as starved creatures.

The new scheme is a great step in advance, but there is still room for improvement. There is no place for them to sit when eating except under their barracks, like animals, or upon the floors in them. Shelters, no matter how simple, should be built and provided with benches and tables.

There is no way to insure cleanliness of dishes, as they are allowed to wash their own crude utensils and leave them at any convenient place. Granite dishes should be supplied. It would facilitate service to have such dishes in the kitchens, some filled and others handy to fill quickly at meal time. They could be carried to the eating shelters recommended, left to be collected after meals by kitchen help and washed.

FOOD SUPPLIES.

There should be a more rigid examination of food supplies before being shipped from the United States. It is inconceivable that any one should be asked to drink coffee which is now sometimes supplied on the Isthmus. Probably it is not coffee at all, and quite possibly not even chicory.

Eggs cannot always be of the best cold-storage type and certainly sometimes there is something radically wrong with cold-storage chickens. Housewives who had delicious chickens, at meals personally enjoyed during the investigation, purchased them from native markets.

During one week of the visit there was no cold-storage meat upon the Isthmus. It was known by the Commission that such would be the case, and it made arrangements, to avoid a repetition of the hardship, with a commercial line of steamers for the transportation of additional lots. Native beef is more expensive than cold-storage beef from the States, and is tough. At a Government West Indian mess it was found to be sickening, but at a private mess of some engineers it was not found to be repulsive.

FARMING SHOULD BE PROMOTED ON THE ISTHMUS.

In addition to needed improvement in transportation facilities between New York and Colon to assure an adequate supply of meats and other eatables, it is recommended that the Agricultural Department should be called upon at an early time to promote farming upon the Isthmus in order to meet the urgent need for fresh vegetables, milk, chickens, fresh eggs and fruit. There is no reason why this cannot be done. Almost anything can be grown upon the Isthmus. The soil is not very good, but it can be fertilized. Some individuals (Americans) at the present time have corn, tomatoes, egg plant and chickens. During the dry season there can be irrigation. This is a matter of such vital importance in maintaining health and content that it should have immediate consideration. The natives do not exert themselves to any extent in farming. There is one mechanic, employed upon the Isthmus, who had experience in profitable farming in the South when with the army, and there are others who are doing a little farming at this time. It would doubtless be possible to enlist the interest of such employes, already familiar with conditions, in farming.

The only dairy is that in connection with Ancon Hospital, it having a few cows to provide milk for patients. The cows of natives are so poorly pastured that they give little milk. Our employes have principally evaporated cream and condensed milk.

No one can know what it means to be deprived of fresh vegetables until obliged to subsist on canned foods altogether. Then an onion, a cucumber or a radish is indeed a luxury. A recent effort to meet this need has been to make arrangements for taking fresh vegetables from Jamaica and New Orleans, but this is not an assured success. There is some likelihood of conveying mosquitoes and germs endangering health from Jamaica. There are no cold-storage facilities on the steamships. It is believed, however, that fresh vegetables may be taken from New Orleans as deck freight, if not too ripe when purchased. The first consignment in June was a loss on that account, and, therefore, an experienced buyer is to be stationed at New Orleans. But there must always be uncertainty if shipments are to be depended upon for the sole supply.

CONSTANTLY CHANGING FORCE OF EMPLOYES.

Successful construction work upon the Isthmus is hampered by the constantly changing force of employes, and there is no doubt but that this is largely due to discontent, resulting from unsatisfactory housing and feeding. Improvements needed will require time for accomplishment. Tactful, considerate attention on the part of the representatives of the Department of Labor, Quarters and Subsistence would do much toward maintaining content under adverse circumstances. If effort were made to explain that everything possible is being done, with the base of supplies two thousand miles away, it is more than likely that the majority would be reasonable and patient. There is no department against which complaint so likely would be aimed as this one, for it has to do with creature comforts. While there is reason to believe that its representatives are interested in the welfare of the employes, and in many respects have striven hard to serve them, it is apparent that obnoxious and arbitrary methods too frequently have been pursued. This is public sentiment on the Canal Zone: "It has not been the rule to explain inability to improve conditions as rapidly as desirable, but to refuse the hearing of complaints and to suggest that the next boat be taken to the States if not satisfied."

Some complaints are favoritism in assigning married quarters, the convenient forgetting of promises to supply full quota of furniture, no memorandum kept of requests made, confiscation of property when on leave, keeping of men on cots for six months or more, refusal to permit private messes or individuals to eat at homes of friends, bad food at hotels, and the upholding of discourteous and unaccommodating managers of mess halls.

The new rule of the commission, in force July 1, enables a man to apply for married quarters when taking employment (assignments to be made in chronological order, as previously), and provides that lists of applicants are to be posted for general inspection. This should prevent suspicion that favoritism is shown if it is made known generally.

The old rule required a man to wait six months after taking employment before making such application. It was made because it was deemed unwise to have men take their families to the Zone until they were reasonably sure of remaining, and to give time to construct quarters. The rule, it is claimed, would have been regarded as reasonable if it had been justly applied. Instead, it is generally believed that recent applicants have been given married quarters in preference to those who have been long upon the list. This has been claimed not only by mechanics, but clerks and men holding high positions.

If specific cases of complaint are taken to higher authorities, it is found that all the papers in such cases have been "lost."

No obligation is felt to care for furniture of married employes on leave, nor have they been notified that their quarters would be given to others. The rule just adopted will help to correct that condition. It provides that such quarters will be held six weeks and notice is given that they may be temporarily assigned. There should be storage facilities for belongings of families and bachelors on vacations.

Property of negroes has been confiscated, but the department recently was required to recompense them for their losses.

A sign posted in quarters of American bachelors requires all to purchase sheets and pillow cases for their beds or they will be removed and "cots supplied instead." That is treating an American of responsible age as though he were a child. Some prefer to sleep next to blankets because of the dampness. It may be essential to require sheets for sanitary reasons, but the request could be more courteously worded.

There has been an obnoxious rule against the securing of table board at private homes by bachelors. One reason that the rule was established was the fear that larger quarters and bigger stoves would be asked for by families having boarders; another was that neighbors would be disturbed. The complaint that a man is now prevented from eating with a family of friends where he would get food more to his taste than he could possibly under the best

INTERIOR EUROPEANS' MESS HALL.

conditions at a public mess, was general, and was regarded as interference with personal liberty. When the statement was made that that rule has been changed expressions of unbelief appeared upon the countenances of the men. This again proves the necessity of having some medium for informing employes of their privileges.

Doubtless many complaints against the Department have been unfair. For instance, where men were found sleeping on cots at one place, beds were stored in the same building awaiting delayed mattresses from the States. Monotonous food may be attributed partly to failure in arrival of supplies, and houses can't be assigned if they are not in existence. The Department has labored under serious difficulties, but its policy of dealing with the human family has been erroneous and is the cause of general dissatisfaction.

COMMISSARIES.

Dry Goods Department.

The main commissary is located at Colon and there are local branches at the largest camps along the line of the Canal Zone. An inspection of the goods at the main commissary revealed a lack of such shoes, overalls, and other goods as would be desired by American workmen. At one of the local commissaries, a cheap and badly made shirt and two pairs of equally poor overalls were purchased. The materials are very coarse and they could not be more wretchedly manufactured. Many of the articles of wearing apparel are purchased in England and do not come up to the standard of the best garments manufactured in the United States. The men claim that the shirts have small sleeves, which readily split, are tight across the shoulders and the collar bands are marked with the wrong sizes. It is especially inconvenient for bachelors to have clothes which tear so easily, as they have no way of mending them. Somehow the Chairman and a few other officials were able to purchase satisfactory shirts at the main commissary, but there were no such garments found at the local commissaries along the line. The general testimony was: "I can get noth-

HOW THE WEST INDIANS COOKED FOR THEMSELVES UNTIL FEBRUARY 1.

ing in the line of shirts which will come anywhere near fitting me," or "I would prefer to pay more and get a good quality of shirts." The stock is not kept up. For instance, white duck suits were found all to be size No. 42, required by few.

A dress suit case was presented to the Secretary by a man just leaving for his vacation. He purchased it at the commissary for five dollars and twenty cents, and when he undertook to buckle the strap it tore out, showing that the case was made of pasteboard, covered with a thin skin.

It is impossible for the Americans to get satisfactory shoes at the commissaries, and they are obliged either to patronize the Chinese merchants along the Zone or go to the expense, as well as loss of time necessary for a trip to the City of Panama, where prices are somewhat higher than in the United States.

When taking vacations, employes make large purchases for themselves and friends for the coming year. One said, on the boat coming up: "I am going to take down eight pairs of high boots. They have some at the local commissary, but they won't stand water because so thin. Why do they sell only ——'s shoes? They do not wear any time." Another stated: "I shall, as usual, take back eighteen shirts, six suits of underwear and three pairs of shoes." The destruction and loss of clothes in the laundering necessitate large supplies of shirts. Heavy rains and inability to dry shoes make several pairs necessary. And this is true of other garments.

Ample stocks of standard makes should be kept at the commissaries. It would seem as though there might be introduced advantageously brilliantine, alpaca or other coats of light materials. It seemed odd to find serge suits worn quite generally.

Good toilet articles are sold at the commissaries, but with that exception, it is very seldom that anything which is wanted by the men can be found.

Furthermore, there are no goods or garments, whatever, for women and children.

TAILORING SHOULD BE UNDERTAKEN.

Linens and woolen goods to be made up there are purchased in better quality and at lower prices from England than the States, and this would be a benefit to the employes if there were tailoring establishments in connection with the commissaries at the large camps. There should be one, not only for the men, but also for the women, where ordinary dressmaking could be carried on. There is no way of having garments made except by natives. It is quite doubtful as to whether the negro tailors with their small shops along the line and in Panama should be patronized by Americans as a matter of danger to health, even if they could render satisfactory service, which is not the case. There are at least twelve hundred American women and children on the Isthmus, and it is decidedly a hardship to be unable to purchase or have garments made. While the need of tailor shops has not received consideration it is recognized by the Chairman of the Commission.

Shoemakers should be encouraged to open shops for repairing, perhaps by giving space at the commissaries.

THE GROCERY DEPARTMENT.

The local commissaries are not always as clean as they should be. The platform at the main commissary, where the cars are unloaded, was exceedingly dirty, smelling from an imbedded accumulation. Meats are delivered along the line daily. For families they are placed in packages which are delivered to the homes by the local commissary wagons.

There is complaint that meats are not always received in good condition, and that they will be left in the sun after being taken from the refrigerator car. It is quite possible that families have been sold bad meat, as the testimony was offered by thoroughly reliable and worthy citizens, and, furthermore, the secretary herself was frequently served with it at the Tivoli, and once at a mess. Some offer no complaint about the meat now, while others say they have received it in such bad condition as to be obliged to bury it. Meats are not properly cut.

It has been suggested that there should be cold storage plants at the large camps and meats for both families and mess halls distributed as from butcher shops. Local commissaries are not equipped with refrigerators for keeping butter and eggs, and purchasers at present must include such articles in cold storage meat orders from the main commissary.

The Panamanians double the charges at their markets when Americans make purchases. Therefore, some housewives send negro servants to their markets, where better chickens may be had than can be secured from the commissary.

PROFITS.

In April the profits of the Commissary Department, including ice plant, bakery and laundry, were $52,000.00. As there is no desire to make anything more than a return on the investment of $300,000.00 in order to reimburse the Government at the end of fifteen years, the prices have just been lowered. There is now no complaint among employes with reference to charges for groceries and meat. It was common to hear: "Since these army officers have taken hold we are getting a square deal."

CHANGES MADE OR CONTEMPLATED.

The management of the commissary has been placed recently under the Panama Railroad Company, and a new man has been put in charge. Attention now is being directed toward improvement in foods, and it was stated: "We shall take up the question of shoes and shirts later."

The objection to black managers of commissaries has been recognized, and whites are being placed in those positions. It is claimed that the wives of American workmen frequently were rudely treated by such colored managers.

The retail portion of the main commissary at Colon, used for both colored and white employes, is very small and at the close of the work day is completely packed. This is to be enlarged and there should be separate counters for negroes and whites. The retail grocery division, although much larger, is inadequate. Blacks and whites should not be required to mix in making purchases at any of the branch commissaries. But they are receiving a thorough overhauling and this change may be under consideration.

In view of the good plumbing in all concentrated camps, it scarcely seems worthy of comment to mention the abominable toilet arrangements at the main commissary, both for women and for men.

NO CASH PURCHASES.

There is no money allowed to be taken for purchases at the commissaries. Employes may buy commissary books, similar to the meal books used at the mess halls, from timekeepers and make their payments at commissaries by tearing off coupons in different denominations.

LAUNDRIES.

There are two laundries. The one at Colon is equipped with electrical appliances, even the irons being heated by electricity. At Ancon the laundry is also a very comfortable work place and the irons are heated by gasoline carried in pipes from one iron to another. The laundries are open at the sides, making the ventilation good, and in every way excellent work places.

They are wretchedly managed. Clothes are constantly lost, torn and frequently returned so yellow as to be unfit for wear. It is undoubtedly difficult to manage and train the negro help, but if satisfactory service cannot thus be rendered Chinese should be taken into this work. Certainly improvement should be made.

The laundries have but lately been established. They are very necessary, owing to the fact that previously along the line clothes were laundered entirely by native women, who wash in the rivers. They beat the clothes upon rocks, causing them to be torn and buttons to be lost. The most unfortunate result of that method is the spreading of garments upon the vegetation to be dried, frequently causing dobbie

THE GOVERNMENT'S BAKERY AT CRISTOBAL. CAPACITY 40,000 LOAVES A DAY.

WEST INDIANS CARRYING FOOD FROM TYPICAL KITCHEN WHERE IT IS NOW PREPARED FOR THEM.

itch. Only those who live near Panama may have their laundry work performed by Chinamen, who give better service, but charge accordingly. The list prices at the Government laundries, if adhered to, would be very fair indeed.

The delay in securing the return of the garments seems to indicate need of increased facilities. Bad work may be due likewise to inadequate plants. Consideration should be given to the establishment of another laundry at an inland point, such as Empire or Culebra.

ICE PLANT.

At Colon there is just being completed a fine refrigeration plant for the manufacture of ice.

BAKERY.

There is a bakery with modern machinery. While the bread is spoken of as being "good," it has not the excellent flavor of the bread baked on the boats. It certainly could be much improved.

HOSPITALS.

The main hospitals are located at each end of the line, Colon and Ancon, the latter being near Panama. They are splendidly equipped. All the men speak enthusiastically of their treatment in the hospitals. The wards are immaculate. The operating rooms are fine. The only complaints which have been made are with reference to the treatment of obstetrical cases, the food and the use of hypodermic needles of extraordinary sizes.

At the various camps there are dispensaries where employes are given medicines if but slightly ill, and there are beds for such patients as must be cared for until they can be taken to the main hospitals. There are also rest camps for common laborers who are not very ill, but who would be more comfortable in beds, with mattresses and bed clothes, than in their barracks on cots without covering.

The hospital at Colon has the advantage of being near the sea, but the environment is not pleasant. The hospital at Ancon is most beautifully located upon high hills, and floral gardening has been introduced, making the premises exceedingly attractive.

The capacity at the Colon Hospital is five hundred and fifty, and it can, in a pinch, be used for six hundred, while that of the Ancon Hospital is six hundred, and it can be made to care for seven hundred and fifty.

Each ward, so designated, means a separate building, containing several dormitories. There are separate wards for Americans, for Europeans, for West Indians and for women, in which also there are both private and dormitory arrangements, and wards for the insane.

There are wire cages in which suspect cases are placed until it can be learned whether or not the disease is yellow fever. The object is to prevent the carrying of contagion, by mosquitoes, from such patients to others. There had not been a case of yellow fever for a year and a half until the first of July, when one was landed at the City of Panama from a boat which had made a stop at a port in the Pacific Ocean, where the disease existed.

In all the wards there are sanitary shower baths, wash bowls and closets.

There are separate mess rooms for nurses, for the different types of patients and for orderlies and attendants. Americans have table linen, while Europeans and Jamaicans have white oil cloth upon the tables. All are neat and well arranged.

At Taboga, an island twelve miles from Panama, where there is no malaria, there is a convalescents' sanitarium.

There is also a colony of lepers in a remote location.

Employes are treated at the hospitals free. If they prefer to remain at home no charge is made for medical visits. It is not understood that married men may remain at home when ill, and complaint was heard on that account. This is another new rule to be explained through the bulletin hereinafter recommended. The remark frequently heard was: "Married men can't stay at home if sick, but are forced to go to the hospital!" The members of the families of the employes making more than fifty dollars a month are treated at the hospitals for one dollar a day in wards, and one dollar and a half a day in private rooms. The members of families making less than fifty dollars a month are treated for thirty cents a day at the hospitals.

In each camp there are emergency physicians, expected to call at the homes in cases of sudden illness, when a charge of one dollar is made.

Quinine is offered free to all at the different messes daily.

The principal ailments are malaria, pneumonia and typhoid fever.

The Sanitary Department is working to prevent the breeding of malaria mosquitoes, which carry the disease from one afflicted person to another. Pneumonia is caused largely by the wearing of damp clothes, which chill the body, and by the lack of proper bedding among the common laborers. Typhoid fever is due to drinking impure water. There are other minor maladies and all kinds of cases of operations.

The highest mortality is among the negroes. During the month of April the total number of black employes of the Canal Commission and Panama Railway was 27,295. There were 114 deaths for that month. The total number of white employes was 10,170, and there were nine deaths. During the month the total number constantly sick in hospitals and sick camps was 822. Quite a number of white employes of long residence who never have been ill there were met.

Just before arriving at Colon the physician on the boat vaccinates all new employes. This is compulsory. It is objectionable to many, and therefore new employes should be informed before leaving New York of this rule, if its practice is continued, for some would not go to the Isthmus under that requirement.

Many suffer extremely and are in no condition to take up new work in a climate where, if one is going to be ill, it is usually within the first three months. Vaccination aggravates, causes nervousness and reduces ability to resist tropical diseases. Very serious cases of bad arms and sides were known to be endured by Americans.

New employes are handed, upon leaving the boat, circulars with reference to the cause of malaria and how to obviate it.

A Ward at Ancon Hospital.

CIRCULAR HANDED NEW EMPLOYES.

WAR DEPARTMENT

ISTHMIAN CANAL COMMISSION,
OFFICE OF THE CHIEF SANITARY OFFICER.

Circular No. 13.

This circular is handed to each new arrival upon the Isthmus for the purpose of instruction as to how to avoid the disease most prevalent in Panama and the Canal Zone—MALARIA. Its cause is now well known and each one, with a little care, can do a great deal toward keeping free from this disease.

It has been proven that malaria is only given to man by the bite of a female mosquito of a certain species (ANOPHELES). This female mosquito must always bite some human being suffering from malaria before she can become infected. In biting she draws blood from the person suffering from malaria, and in the blood thus drawn, she takes in the malarial parasite. Within a few days this parasite infects the mosquito herself, and when she next bites a well person she injects her spittle into the bitten place. In this spittle the malarial parasite is injected, and thus the healthy person contracts the disease.

Now, if every one would use a mosquito bar, so arranged that no mosquitoes could get into the bar at night, much protection would be secured from this disease; for, while it may be contracted during the day time, it is not so likely to be. Probably nine-tenths of the malarial cases contract the disease during sleep, because the malarial mosquito is a night biter and the person is quiet at this time.

Absolute protection from mosquito bites is impossible, but it is known that quinine is a deadly poison to the malarial parasite after it gets into the blood of a human being. If, therefore, every one would take three grains of quinine once a day any malarial parasite that has been introduced during the day would almost certainly be killed. The best time probably to take quinine is before going to bed at night.

W. C. GORGAS,
Colonel Medical Corps, U. S. A.,
Chief Sanitary Officer.

Circulars are issued from time to time in different languages, a sample of the type for negro laborers is quoted below:

Ancon, C. Z., August 2, 1906.

"Our negro laborers are suffering from a very severe form of pneumonia. Pneumonia, like consumption of the lungs, is a disease caused by a very small plant, which takes root and grows in the lung. I speak of it as plant because it has the characteristics of plant life rather than of animal life. It is exceedingly small, very much smaller than the point of a needle, and very much too small to be seen by the naked eye. This plant, as I have just said, takes root in the lung, and the juice which it makes poisons the patient and causes the disease in the lung.

"This plant is very common in the spittle of those who do not have pneumonia; on an average about one-fifth of the people who are not sick carry this plant around in their spittle. Now, if a man having this plant in his spittle becomes much depressed from any cause, such as a bad cold, or attack of malaria, or any other severe exposure, the plant is enabled to take root and multiply very rapidly. When he is strong and in good health the plant when it gets into the lung is destroyed and eaten up by the lung cells themselves, but to do this the lung cells must be in good condition, and to have lung cells in good condition a man must be strong and vigorous."

"One of the most common causes of depression among our laborers is catching cold. He works all day, gets his clothing thoroughly wet with sweat or from the rain, goes to his quarters, sleeps in the same clothing, and as the night grows cool and chilly he becomes chilled and wakes up next morning with a cold. His vital forces become depressed, and the pneumonia plant that is already in his spittle takes root, grows, produces its poisonous juices and gives the man pneumonia.

"To avoid this every laborer when he goes to bed should have a dry suit of underclothing to put on. If he can afford only two suits he had much better keep one dry to be worn at night, and wear his wet one during the day. He is working and exercising during the day and is not near so likely to take cold.

"He should also avoid sleeping in drafts during the midday hour of rest, though he is not so likely to take cold at this time of day.

"Malarial fever is the next most common cause for pneumonia, and is also dangerous in itself. It kills every month a certain number of our employes, both black and white, but is far more fatal to the blacks than to the whites. This disease is not like pneumonia and lung consumption, caused by a plant, but is caused by a very small animal. This animal lives in the blood of a sick man, eats up his blood, and at the same time urinates and defecates into the blood, causing the man to be poisoned. This condition we call malarial fever. This little animal is placed in the veins of a man by a certain species of mosquito. The mosquito puts her bill into a man's vein and injects her spittle just as does the rattlesnake when he bites. Now if this little animal swallows the least particle of quinine it is killed, but quinine does not hurt a man at all. Therefore, if a man will take a little quinine every day—three grains—there will be some in his blood all the time, and when the little malaria animal gets in, it is at once killed.

"These are not theories, but well known facts. A doctor with a microscope can see in the blood of a man sick with malarial fever the malaria animal eating up the blood of the sick man; and so in the spittle of the man sick with pneumonia, he can, with his microscope, see the little plant growing.

"I feel pretty sure that a man who sleeps in dry clothing and takes three grains of quinine every day will not have pneumonia.

W. C. GORGAS,
"Chief Sanitary Officer."

Although malarial fever is "far more fatal to blacks than to whites," mosquito netting is not furnished the former while it is given free to the latter. Other openings are screened, but the doors of the barracks of negroes are not and, as it is not possible to keep the doors closed constantly, they are not protected from mosquitoes.

In one circular issued three grains of quinine daily are recommended to maintain health, while in another not quoted herein it was perplexing to find a daily dose of six grains urged.

CLEARING AWAY JUNGLE.

Vast tracts of jungle have been cleared, principally with the slow and tedious use of the machete and sometimes the ax. The rapid growth of new vegetation is cut with the machete and shears. Only one mowing machine was observed. No scythes are used because the native laborers prefer machetes.

Vegetation preserves moisture and thus creates breeding places for mosquitoes, endangering health. The Sanitary Department has charge of the drainage of damp places, and where that is not feasible oil is poured upon the water. There is constant effort on the part of that department to keep vegetation near quarters reduced. It may be impossible to use mowing machines in marshes, but it would seem that they could be used on many tracts and hills, as they are by farmers in mountainous regions. Surely scythes could be introduced if a serious effort were made to train the natives in their use. The present method is not only slow but requires the uncomfortable posture of constant stooping. The cleaning of streets and removal of garbage are performed splendidly under the Sanitary Department.

Entrance to Ancon Hospital.

STRETCHERS AND EMERGENCY BOXES.

The desirability of having stretchers in the engines of steam shovels and first aid to the injured boxes in convenient places where excavating is going on, as well as in the shops, is worthy of investigation and consideration. Sometimes men have to be carried up hills with great difficulty because stretchers are not near at hand. This is not as serious as it would be if there were not dispensaries at all the camps, but there is no reason why there should ever be any unnecessary loss of blood when emergency boxes are so easily equipped.

RAIN SHEDS NEEDED.

Along the Canal where excavating work is being carried on there should be constructed rain sheds, in which employes could keep coats, and to which they could retire during heavy showers. There are some small sheds on one division, although not enough. Where the main work is being done there are no sheds. One superintendent has been trying for two months to get permission to use old material, where buildings are being torn down, which would be perfectly satisfactory for the construction of such rain sheds, but he has been unable to get any reply with reference thereto. The men become soaked during the storms. This not only threatens health, but, if it occurs mornings, the men go to their quarters and do not return afternoons, which causes delay in the work. This need, with others, was taken up with Colonel Goethals.

RECREATION.

Club Houses.

In some of the camps there are small club rooms above the mess houses, containing billiard and pool tables and dance halls. These are used by voluntary associations which have been formed by the employes and are supported by them. At each of these places there is need of an additional room for library use and of reading matter. There should be appointed a general man to co-operate with the presidents of all the clubs to keep various activities operative and initiate attractive features of entertainment.

There have been four handsome club buildings constructed at as many of the large camps, and they have been placed under the management of the Young Men's Christian Association. These buildings are surrounded by wide verandas, which are screened; the first floor of each contains in one wing a billiard and pool room and in the other a game, smoking and lounging room, while in the rear there is a bowling alley and small gymnasium. In the second story there is a hall, used for dancing and other entertainments, and a library. The use of the social hall is given free to organizations of employes, who arrange their own dancing parties. The Canal Commission has authorized the expenditure of five hundred dollars for books greatly needed for each club house.

These clubs have just been opened and they are much appreciated. Five excellent young men, on duty Sundays and holidays, as well as week days and evenings, are devoting their time in a most enthusiastic and self-sacrificing spirit to this work.

The bowling alleys, which are very popular, are inadequate. Bowling tournaments are held. The gymnasiums are not large enough. The men seem to enjoy boxing, fencing and wrestling, even though they work hard. Up to the present time the greatest effort has been devoted toward organizing chess, checkers, glee and Sunday afternoon "hiking" clubs, as well as camera and dramatic clubs. One minstrel show has been given, with an attendance of two hundred and fifty. Sunday afternoon meetings of a semi-religious character have been held with music and speakers on general topics. Checkers, chess, cribbage and cards are allowed Sundays, but bowling and pool have been prohibited because of the noise.

The present plan is to charge fifteen cents an hour for billiards, two and a half cents a cue for pool and five cents a game for bowling. This is regarded as unfair by some of the men, who claim that otherwise the twelve dollars in dues entitle them only to read and play games, which they can do in their own rooms. It may prove advisable to reduce dues, but the charges for games are reasonable and wise for various reasons.

At present there are about one thousand members in the four associations. Among those who have enjoyed the privileges of the Young Men's Christian Association Clubs the consensus of opinion is that they do not know how they stood it so long without them. Previously there was nothing to do but read, write and play cards in the quarters evenings.

Attractive programmes for a series of entertainments have been arranged, and artists, such as magicians and monologists, are being taken from the United States. Soda fountains are being installed and barber shops and hot baths are contemplated. Sea bathing is under consideration in connection with the club at Cristobal.

There is a good deal of discussion among women who desire to be allowed the privileges of the clubs oftener than the two afternoons a week set aside; especially do they desire opportunities for bowling and to be permitted to attend, in addition to public entertainments, some evenings with their husbands, as well as Sundays. They should be made family clubs as much as possible. Frequently husbands do not care to leave their wives at home alone. Women might be given additional privileges, although debarred from some of the rooms evenings. Wives should be allowed all privileges weekdays when the men are at work. Exception should be made during the two hours' siesta, when the men may enjoy the rooms.

DANCING.

There are plenty of opportunities for dancing Saturday evenings. There are social clubs, such as the Kangaroos, the Red Men, the Texas and the Tivoli Clubs, which hold dances at the Young Men's Christian Association and other club rooms, at the Tivoli Hotel or at the hospitals. There is a scarcity of unmarried women, but the married women enjoy dancing, for they say they "are driven to it, as there is nothing else to do."

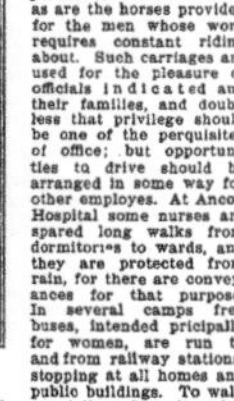

Club for Americans Managed by the Young Men's Christian Association.

BASEBALL.

Several baseball parks have been equipped by voluntary organizations of employes, stock having been sold to create the necessary funds, the Government merely draining the land. Baseball teams have been organized and they compete Sundays and holidays at the parks at Empire and Ancon. There should be practice places at other camps and a park equipped for games at Gorgona.

TENNIS.

There are only three tennis courts—one at Ancon Hospital, one at the Colon Hospital, and one at Empire, where there is also a croquet ground open free to families of employes. Tennis courts should be provided at all of the camps, and it would be quite desirable to light them with electricity. The athletic fields could also be so lighted for practice work.

BOATING.

At Panama there are occasional launch parties for doctors, nurses and clerks. There should be Sunday boat excursions. Different sets of employes could be taken from time to time, thus giving those who enjoy such trips an occasional sea outing. It would not be essential that the boat should land at any place. Such a sea excursion should be arranged for every Sunday and tickets issued to the capacity of the boat. At Panama there is at least one boat which can be so used. A charge to cover expenses of coal and service could be made. All enjoy the opportunity of a trip to the Island of Taboga in the Pacific Ocean. On the Atlantic Coast there are beautiful water trips from Colon. There should be at least one excursion boat there. One small group of employes is arranging to purchase in the United States a sail boat. Some individual might be encouraged to provide boats and opportunities for sailing as a private enterprise at Colon. It may not be impossible for the Navy to furnish one or more boats for the use of the marines at Panama, which could also be placed at the disposal of other employes occasionally. Practice on shipboard would pleasantly interrupt monotony for the marines.

HORSEBACK RIDING AND DRIVING

At Ancon Hospital five nurses own horses and are allowed to keep them at the Government corral at the cost of maintenance—about thirteen dollars a month. Steam shovelmen and other employes have horses and the privilege of boarding them at the corrals is accorded whenever their capacity will permit. But thirteen dollars form a large proportion of the month's salary, of a nurse for instance, to be expended in order to enjoy an occasional horseback ride.

At Panama, where the Government has constructed a five-mile road, affording a beautiful driveway, it should back or in some way encourage an enterprise for renting good riding horses at lower rates than they can now be secured, and thus set the standard of prices within the means of the employes. The establishment of such a livery should include in its plan carriages for rental. The ramshackle vehicles to be rented from Panamanians are unclean and simply better than nothing. The Government very properly places at the disposal of some chief officials at Ancon and Cristobal splendid vehicles left by the French. It is essential that they should be enabled to get about without loss of time, and those vehicles are as necessary to the performance of their duties as are the horses provided for the men whose work requires constant riding about. Such carriages are used for the pleasure of officials indicated and their families, and doubtless that privilege should be one of the perquisites of office; but opportunities to drive should be arranged in some way for other employes. At Ancon Hospital some nurses are spared long walks from dormitories to wards, and they are protected from rain, for there are conveyances for that purpose. In several camps free buses, intended pricipally for women, are run to and from railway stations, stopping at all homes and public buildings. To walk from stations up hill, especially when it rains and there are packages to carry, is very arduous. The bus system is excellent, but it has not been perfected because there are not enough carryalls. Two were ordered more than five months ago but have not been received. Considering the high railroad rates (five cents a mile), an adequately free bus service for all trains would not be undesirable. If rates for employes and families are changed upon the Panama Railway, a general bus service at five cents a ride would be very advisable. It is neither wise nor necessary to give too much.

SEA BATHING.

It has been suggested that sea bathing should be made possible at Colon by the driving of piles and construction of bath houses, and at Panama, toward the savannas, by blasting, thus providing tanks which would be filled with water at low tide. It should be given consideration.

HUNTING.

Some employes enjoy hunting deer and wildcats in the jungle. Hunting parties might be organized.

MUSIC.

There is an Isthmian Canal band, composed of Canal employes, and a marine band at Camp Eliot. They do not supply the need of good music. Probably nothing would be appreciated more than concerts with good artists. This longing is evidenced partly by the private phonographs to be heard along the line evenings. (Phonographs do not last long in that moist atmosphere.)

LABOR DAY CELEBRATION.

It would be desirable to get Damrosch there for an al fresco entertainment Labor Day, or for some future holiday. He goes to Southern States and doubtless could be secured on the Zone. At such an occasion an address by some national leader of the labor movement would be greatly enjoyed. It would be especially appropriate for Labor Day.

FOURTH OF JULY.

The celebration this year was held at Ancon, with the Tivoli Hotel as headquarters. It was gorgeously decorated in the three colors, inside and out. The driveway leading to the hotel was lined on each side with palm leaves upon a framework, there being arches here and there covered with bunting and containing electric lights underneath in red, white and blue.

In the ball park, back of the hotel, there was an address in the morning and there were athletic contests and a ball game in the afternoon. There was contributed by the employes the sum of three thousand dollars for expenses, one thousand dollars being for cash prizes presented to winners of such contests as races of various kinds, tug-of-war, pole vaulting, bucking horse and wall scaling.

The entertainment in the park was free to all. There was an exhibition of the fire department in front of the hotel and at night fireworks were displayed before the conclusion of the celebration with a dancing party at the Tivoli. Music was furnished by the several bands. Special trains were run from all the camps, transportation being free. The day was pleasantly spent and there was no disorder of any description.

RECREATION NEEDED SUNDAYS.

There are baseball games Sundays and the four Y. M. C. A. club rooms are open for reading, chess, checkers, cards and afternoon talks. But comparatively few are provided with recreation upon the one day free for such enjoyment. There should be started a large amusement park, a Coney Island scheme. There could be a hall for dancing, racing track for ponies, with archery and golf croquet inside, a circus ring, bowling alleys, shooting galleries, a small theatre, side shows and possibly a lake for boating. There should be shelters for resting and for light lunches.

Such a scheme undoubtedly can be made a private enterprise, but the initiative must be taken by the Government and some inducement offered, such as land rental free or other concessions to be proposed. There are open spaces such as the Savannas at Panama, La Boca, Empire and Colon which could be utilized.

The Savannas would seem to be the best location because it rains less there; and if the marines are moved to that district, as contemplated, there would be an additional reason for building a street railway line in that section. Doubtless some financier would be willing to make an amusement park a part of a tramway enterprise. Again, boats used by the marines would be convenient for Sunday use of all, if permissible.

La Boca has the advantage of being near the Tivoli Hotel, which could be made a resting place, and that village also is visited with less rain than Empire and Colon.

Empire can be recommended as the centre of population.

At Colon there is so much rain that to locate the entire park there would be unwise, but the ground available might be utilized for some entertainment features, at least during the dry season, one side to be filled in with dirt removed from the other for the formation of a lake with the approval of the Sanitary Department.

It would be necessary to develop transportation facilities from the railroad to either of the tracts available for such an amusement park, and that does not appear at all impossible. It is feasible to run plenty of passenger trains Sundays up and down the Isthmus. In arranging for Sunday entertainments the railroad fare should be reduced greatly, but not until ample recreation opportunities are offered. The present excessive fare to Panama undoubtedly deters many from going Sundays, which is desirable until there are attractions other than the present resorts.

SUNDAY BOWLING AT THE CAMPS.

There should be erected simple structures for bowling and card playing Sundays. At the large camps there should be several alleys and at the small villages at least one. The desire for bowling is so great that such places could be made self-supporting and to pay for themselves in time.

The Young Men's Christian Association has already adapted itself, as far as could be expected, to the peculiar needs of the men at the four clubs under its management. It would not seem fair to ask further infringement upon its rules, but Sunday is the time when the men need recreation and there would be less drinking in Panama and Colon on that day if there were other ways of spending the idle hours, which are very irksome and cause the men to grow restless.

There never was a place in the world where recreation was needed more than on the Isthmus. It is almost impossible to convey an idea of the dreadful monotony of existence. It was interesting to learn that one trades union, now very active in craft matters, was brought into existence for social pleasure primarily.

THEATRICALS.

A stock company with good talent should be induced to spend a season upon the Isthmus, expenses being guaranteed, to go from camp to camp giving dramatic performances. They would be self-sustaining if properly started. At each camp there might be evenings for whites and evenings for West Indians. The halls in the different types of clubs and the lodge rooms could be used, although the scenery would have to be very simple. If additional halls of the kinds mentioned are built, stages should be constructed in them.

A Sunday Ball Game at Empire.

WOMEN'S CLUBS.

One great need is the organization of women's clubs at each camp with definite objects. These clubs could be organized into a Canal Zone Federation of Women's Clubs, to be allied with the General Federation of Women's Clubs in the United States. In the camps where there are Young Men's Christian Association clubs they could co-operate with that organization and hold their meetings in its buildings and in other camps at the general club or lodge rooms. These clubs could organize into "Ladies' Aid Societies" to take an interest in public schools, in the entertainment of patients at the hospitals, in organizing bureaus for meuding bachelors' garments, children's playgrounds and centres for securing servants. There could be study clubs, musicals, card parties, bowling contests, afternoon teas and small groups to entertain bachelors at dinner occasionally and thus give them a little taste of home life. It will be necessary to have a woman give her entire time toward organizing and directing these clubs. If clubs were organized the women would become acquainted and less self-centred, for there would be something interesting to talk about; and they would be a wide influence for content.

RECREATION FOR NEGROES AND EUROPEANS.

In the matter of recreation the negro has been overlooked almost entirely. At Culebra, one of the large camps, they have a dance hall, which is greatly enjoyed, but it is merely a room without decoration and no assistance whatever is given them. There are at least twenty-five thousand negroes. They are very desolate. There is no reason why they should not have simple club houses with dance halls. Work ceases when it rains and such congregating rooms could be used then as well as evenings and Sundays. They would enjoy pool, baseball and cricket and a system of recreation should be evolved for them.

At Gatun, for instance, there are seven hundred Greeks. Forms of amusement suited to them and the other Europeans at the various camps should be introduced. Nothing whatever is done for their entertainment, although they are led to believe, before leaving their countries, that there are plenty of opportunities for recreation. The Southern Europeans, in their native places, largely patronize halls containing tables, at which they sit in small groups to play checkers, listen to music and very moderately drink their light wines.

The marines should be provided with a clubhouse, for which, it is understood, tentative plans have been drawn.

Free libraries containing late books should be placed at the disposal of nurses and hospital employes generally.

SATURDAY HALF HOLIDAY.

The Saturday half holiday cannot be recommended at this time, owing to the lack of adequate recreation. It would be a detriment rather than a benefit, for the time would hang heavily upon the hands of the employes, or they would find a ready excuse to seek the saloon. However, work in that climate, after some length of residence, is bound to sap energy and cause excessive nervousness, and it is important that the Saturday half holiday should be instituted just as soon as recreation can be provided.

A RECREATION DIRECTOR REQUISITE.

It may seem that a very pretentious outline for recreation has been sketched. There is a variety of activities presented for a population of many nationalities, creeds and different tastes. There can be no more cosmopolitan aggregation of people than is now upon the Isthmus.

A permanent force of workers depends largely upon content, and recreation will materially aid in securing it. When asked, "What do you for recreation?" the average man replies, "That's the worst of it; there's nothing to do."

The Young Men's Christian Association is a Godsend to many, and it should be encouraged in every possible way. There are such clubs in but four of the seventeen camps. If that organization is able to hold the interest of the men after the novelty wears off, its field of endeavor should be extended to other camps. Even so, a single club would not accommodate all in any camp, even if that form of recreation were to appeal to every one, and if each were willing to join that organization.

But how can additional activities be secured? Only by organizing a Recreation Department with a thoroughly competent man at the head. He, in turn, might have an assistant especially devoting his energy toward the supervision of athletic sports for which position a man with West Point training would be desirable. There would gradually appear need of other assistants.

A high class recreation director, giving his whole attention to that work, would estimate costs and put into operation gradually a systematic scheme. Only by such special supervision of present and future activities, can they be kept operative.

Every precaution to make life upon the Isthmus as attractive as possible is essential not only to hold those who would return to their homes, where forms of amusement to which they are accustomed may be enjoyed, but to aid in preventing loss in the force through depredations of other nations in that vicinity.

SCHOOLS.

Schools have been established for whites at but five of the camps and for blacks at most of them. Teachers have been brought from the States and wives and daughters of employes have been placed in such positions. At the inception of this work it was very fortunate to be able to secure such assistants. For the colored children the instruction seems to be adequate; for the whites the course is not meeting present needs. Children of all sizes and ages will be in one class under a single teacher, the older children especially not receiving proper instruction.

Inability to educate their children has caused competent men to return to the States, deterred others from taking employment on the Isthmus, and there are those who have had to separate their families, leaving the older children at home in private schools or with grandparents and other relatives. Illustrative of the situation is the large camp of Empire, where there are more than fifty white children and no school has yet been opened for them. One has just been constructed. At some camps the white children have been obliged to receive instruction jointly with the blacks because the location of schools for whites necessitated the crossing of the railroad tracks, which danger could not for a moment be entertained by the parents. Where there are no schools for whites, children could only receive education by going to those for blacks or to other camps, requiring travel by rail with trains so infrequent as to make that course undesirable, were there no element of danger from accident or falling into evil company. Some have placed their children at boarding school in the City of Panama, but progress has been so unsatisfactory that parents are taking or sending the children back to the States. Others have "put up with bachelor quarters and left their families in the States rather than deprive the children of educational opportunities." One touching case on the boat returning was a man who said: "I would rather let the children stay up there and go to school. I ain't seen my family for eleven months and this boat can't go fast enough for me!" Case after case of a similar nature was observed.

The first course of study adopted for the blacks, which includes spelling, language, numbers, physiology and hygiene, meets the requirement. The Superintendent of Education stated that from the beginning there have been added to that elementary course advanced arithmetic, geography, United States history, penmanship and drawing. He also stated that it is contemplated next year to include mechanical drawing, elements of agriculture for boys and needlework for girls, and that the course will be added to by including the more advanced subjects of algebra, elementary geography, physical geography, bookkeeping and Spanish. Unless measures are taken to secure an adequate force of competent teachers and to systematize and grade the work, it is impossible to see how those subjects can be properly taught. Think of one American teacher undertaking to instruct eighty unruly negroes who have no idea of order or discipline!

It has been decided by the Commission to improve the school system by securing teachers entirely through civil service appointments, and a census is now being taken to determine how many white children must be provided with educational opportunities. The Superintendent frankly admits that with the whites no effort for advancement has been made, the object of instruction having been merely to keep the children "from falling behind grades in which they were when they left the States!" The new commissioners recognize that the school question must be thoroughly thrashed out and educational facilities provided for children of American citizens. There is no reason why we should attempt to do more for the Jamaicans than has been offered so well by the British Government in the West Indies, especially when our own are neglected for their benefit. Adult Jamaicans can read and write, frequently, perfect English. It is related that one left the employ of a previous official because he could not "stand his English!" If we provide reading, writing, arithmetic, and hygiene for the colored children our obligation will be fully met, and, apparently, there is no reason why teachers of their own nationality cannot be furnished.

In the program for improvement in the schools there arises the problem of providing proper quarters for teachers. Unless they can reside with private families, in the camps where the schools are located, young women justly cannot be invited to undertake this work. Unless so protected, in that territory, a woman immediately is subject to criticism. School teachers, who live with their parents in certain camps and go elsewhere to instruct are suffering from long hours, for one must take the early morning train, shortly after six o'clock, and return by the late evening train, sometimes reaching home as late as seven-thirty. Passenger trains cannot run frequently without interfering with canal construction work and everything must naturally be subordinated to it. Therefore, it would be impossible to arrange for a special teachers' dormitory and mess at any central point. But this knotty question will be solved as are all others in that "place of emergencies," for the emergency habit is apparent everywhere.

In the school buildings it is complained there are no conveniences for teachers who must spend the entire day therein because of poor train service. The children drink hydrant water and have range closets. The plan for furnishing distilled drinking water should be extended to the schools and toilet arrangements for teachers furnished.

It is imperative that the schools should be improved to attract and keep competent men with families. Family life has become a fixed thing upon the Isthmus. Even though it may be but for a matter of ten years, the Department of Education should be scientifically organized; but it is likely that there will be a permanent result, for a citizenship must be built, perchance with some European race as a basis, for the protection of the Canal when completed.

CHURCHES.

In each large camp the Government has constructed a very attractive building for church services and lodge meetings. The first floor is a chapel and even contains facilities for the use of such denominations as baptize by immersion. The lodge hall above is given free to the Knights of Pythias and other orders, as well as the trades unions.

The Isthmian Canal Commission has upon its payroll ten ministers of different denominations, who give their services at the hospitals in clerical capacities and in the writing of letters.

Hotel Tivoli, Decorated for Fourth of July Celebration.

The duties of a resident hospital chaplain are as follows:

"To hold religious services every Sunday at the hospital to which he is assigned;

To visit all the wards of the hospital at least once a day, giving any patient, who wishes to talk with him, an opportunity of so doing;

To write letters for patients when opportunity is presented therefor;

To hold services, upon the request of the Superintendent of the hospital, over the bodies of all patients dying in the hospitals."

There is one Evangelist who preaches in the different camps periodically; at the Ancon Hospital there is a Catholic Chapel, in which beautiful services are held, and there is an Episcopal Chapel. There is a clergyman sent by the English Government who works among the negroes. There have been church services of some description on the Zone for more than two years. It seems odd to some that various denominations have not directed special effort to that section.

THE REGULATION OF THE LIQUOR TRAFFIC.

On the Canal Zone the Government has gradually reduced the number of licenses from over two hundred to thirty-four. In some of the small camps there are no saloons. The annual license is twelve hundred dollars gold. The requirements are, among other provisions, that there shall be no seats except for the saloon help behind the counter, that the doors shall be left wide open and that there shall be no interior rooms used for drinking. Billiards and bowling alleys must be in separate front rooms also exposed to complete observation. The breaking of such rules is cause for cancelling a license.

In the City of Panama the United States Government has no control of the liquor question. In the City of Colon the Panama Railroad Company owns all but about one hundred lots and, as fast as leases expire, which had been made before the American occupation, new ones require that no liquor shall be sold and no disorderly house shall be allowed.

The testimony from laborers, officials and wives of employes, as well as physicians and the secretaries of the Young Men's Christian Association, prove conclusively that vice and intoxication are no more extensive in this than in any other territory. There is drinking, and undoubtedly, it is a curse, just as it is everywhere, and especially after pay-day, but there is no more orderly a community in the world than that and it is to be regretted that the residents of the Zone as a whole should be misrepresented. There are all types and kinds of men from every section of the world, but those who have been on construction work in other places where there was a certain amount of riff-raff claim there is none there. It is perfectly evident that it would be hard to get together a finer lot of men. An unfortunate result of such misrepresentation is that young fellows are deterred from going to the Zone where they might get a splendid start in life, for salaries in general are good, quarters are free and there is opportunity to save. Some weak young fellows may fall into the habit of drinking on the Isthmus, when temptation would be resisted at home where there are more opportunities to spend idle hours pleasantly; but there are no gambling dens nor resorts of vice upon the Zone, the United States territory where the majority of the employes are located, and it is only possible to go Sundays to the cities of Colon and Panama, which are governed by Panamanian laws. Therefore, anxious mothers with well trained sons need not influence their boys to refuse employment on the Canal Zone, for they will be quite as safe as in any other district away from home influence.

The writer could not better express her feelings on this matter than by saying that she would not hesitate, in so far as this question is concerned, to recommend, in choosing between New York and any other large city and the Canal Zone, that her two brothers should select the last named place.

A splendid fellow who came up on the same boat, after an absence of six years, has since stated: "There is more vice in one block in New York than on the whole Isthmus. If a man had no one in the city for whose respect he cared, he would soon become demoralized."

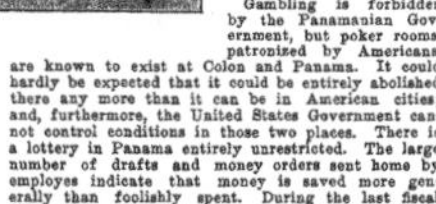

Gambling is forbidden by the Panamanian Government, but poker rooms, patronized by Americans, are known to exist at Colon and Panama. It could hardly be expected that it could be entirely abolished there any more than it can be in American cities; and, furthermore, the United States Government cannot control conditions in those two places. There is a lottery in Panama entirely unrestricted. The large number of drafts and money orders sent home by employes indicate that money is saved more generally than foolishly spent. During the last fiscal year two million dollars were forwarded in money orders alone, according to the figures of the Post Office Department.

Although restrictions for saloon keepers in the Canal Zone are severe, it is difficult to ensure the selling of liquors of good quality. Especially are the Chinese proprietors of rum shops expert in adulterating. Cases of drinking to excess are largely due to the fact that bottles purchased at negro or Chinese rum shops, are carried to lodgings. It was said: "When a man gets started on a bottle he is pretty apt to finish it." While it would be desirable to have prohibition, that is impossible, for there are those who will have liquor and it could be had in Panamanian territory and carried to the Zone were there none to be had in that district. There is no doubt but that as a temperance measure, it would be better to provide good beer and wines at proper rates, under supervision, in the men's clubs. There they would drink a social glass or so and generally stop at that as they do in employes' clubs in certain western mining camps where there is a "no treating" rule and it is required that liquor may not be sold to one in danger of over-drinking. Those clubs have operated to offset the evil influence of the saloon. Gambling is not allowed in such employes' clubs, but billiards, pool, and poker at small stakes—penny ante and ten or twenty-five cent limit—are permitted. The men on the Zone now play poker in their rooms, simply

One of the Stations Built by the Government Along the Line of the Panama Railroad Company.

to pass the time, unrestricted. There would be less danger of unfortunate losses if allowed to play in their own clubs, for while they have been known to play only for meal tickets, or twenty-five cents, others it is said: "Play the sky limit."

A university club which has been organized in the City of Panama and is modestly housed, has among its privileges a bar and billiard room.

Liquors are sold on the boats to and from Colon, but in six days each way not a case of intoxication was observed nor was there an ungentlemanly act on board.

JAILS.

The jails at the camps are of the regular type of Canal construction and sanitary, but the prisoners are required to sleep on wooden beds without mattresses or coverlets. This is unnecessarily cruel. Beds should be provided.

The crimes for which prisoners have been arrested are of the same variety as would be found in any community, the principal ones being violation of sanitary regulations, disorderly conduct, intoxication, petit larceny, forgery, and burglary.

Many arrests are deemed necessary as a form of educating the ignorant foreigners, but they are for very trivial offenses. In May there were five hundred thirty-five, twenty-two being Americans and the balance represented by thirty-eight nationalities. It is believed that order could be as well maintained by making fewer arrests.

There are Supreme and Circuit Courts covering three districts. There is a penitentiary. The number of prisoners in March was seventy-one. The judges do not find enough criminal cases to keep them occupied.

SAVINGS.

The employes are able to and do save large sums. Inasmuch as they pay no rent and have free fuel and light, the cost of living is reduced to the hire of servants and scrub women, the expense of ice and food. Many buy money orders to send home, especially married men who have to support their families in the States, as well as meet their own expenses there. Bachelors, fearing to leave money in their quarters, buy money orders, which are at the rate of thirty cents for one hundred dollars. There should be some system of savings started, enabling the employes to deposit and receive interest at the rate of three per cent., instead of having to pay the Government, their employer, to take care of their savings. It is not likely that employes would have faith in a savings bank plan unless conducted by an American. The International Banking Company, which has an office at Panama, and claims to have but four hundred depositors among Canal employes, is not sufficiently accessible and does not send agents along the line. Many buy drafts from that Company, but there is not a general feeling of confidence in it as a depository for savings.

PASSES ON THE PANAMA RAILROAD.

There has been great dissatisfaction caused by the issuing of passes indiscriminately. It has been particularly aggravating for the mechanic and his wife, without free transportation, to sit next to a clerk and his wife, who have passes upon the railroad. In the clerical department the pass book is handed around every Saturday night and passes indiscriminately issued; whereas, in the track, excavating, transportation and mechanical departments generally, favoritism is shown.

There have been instances where engineers have left their trains at certain stations and had to pay their fares back to the camps where they resided. Until quite recently, conductors, engineers, yard men, and trainmasters had to pay half rate if they wanted to go any place. There is intense feeling against the courtesy shown clerks in preference to mechanics and this unfair provision should be corrected. Passes should be given to all or to none and that fact is recognized by the Chairman of the Commission. It would be very advisable to limit passes to two a month and let all have them. In this way there would be no imposition upon the Government, as has been the case where it was claimed that the wives of the employes have pretty well spent their time riding up and down the road. The plan, above outlined, together with half rates for families of employes, is under consideration.

TRANSPORTATION SERVICE.

There are few passenger trains each way, crossing the Isthmus daily, as they would interfere with the dirt trains and excavation work. Now that there are so many married women upon the Zone it would be very desirable to limit smoking to one car, or at least rear seats, and require that there shall be no spitting upon the floors. Attractive stations have been built at the camps, but at Panama the terminal facilities are so inadequate as to be dangerous. The platform, upon which passengers alight, is altogether too short. It is exceedingly bad to get off in the ditch beyond the platform at seven o'clock in the evening when it is so dark that it is impossible to see. There should be electric lights at that place pending the improvement of the station. One portion of the platform is so high above the car steps and far away that it is very difficult to reach it. It is remarkable that there are not serious accidents. There should be benches under the awnings at all stations, as there is now no place to sit while awaiting trains.

Consideration should be given to the advisability and practicability of inviting capital to build a street car line from Colon to the city of Panama—out to the Savannas for excursions and up Ancon Hill, and to construct the proposed amusement park in connection therewith. Such a traction line would connect homes—enable women to visit—and aid in recreative efforts. As all types ride on the Zone, such a line would apparently be assured patronage. While an electric street car line across the Isthmus might be found impractical by men experienced in such matters, to the lay person it appears to be a proposition no more unreasonable than the erection and operation of the tramways in the Berkshire Hills.

An "automobile" road—for horseback riding and driving across the Isthmus might be too great an undertaking, but it has been suggested for consideration.

SOME OF THE LABOR CONDITIONS.

There are two sets of employes, those of the Isthmian Canal Commission and those of the Panama Railroad Company. The term "laborer" on the Isthmus indicates the type of employe performing the work of a "common laborer." It is not applied to the American mechanic or any other kind of employe. The number of employes is given in the following tabulation:

Isthmian Canal Commission	American clerks, foremen, employes in Sanitary Department and all others not mechanics,	1,000	
	American Mechanics,	4,000	
	West Indian Negroes (Laborers),	25,000	
	Europeans, including Spaniards, Italians and Greeks,	4,500	34,500
Panama Railway	Clerks (Black and white),	1,244	
	Laborers (Black and white),	4,384	5,628
	Total,		40,128

WORKING HOURS AND INEQUALITIES IN VACATION AND SICK LEAVE PRIVILEGES.

A long work day is undesirable in that climate since greater fatigue is felt at the termination of a given number of hours there than in the United States, and yet the majority of the employes work more than eight hours and do not come under the operation of the eight-hour law. It applies to mechanics, and there is comparatively little overtime now for such employes as molders and machinists, except as the shortage of equipment necessitates the repair, after working hours, of steam shovels and locomotives used in excavating. Common laborers are now, according to official statement on the Isthmus, engaged for a nine-hour day but frequently work ten, twelve and fourteen hours. This is a hardship on foremen who must work as long. Construction locomotive engineers work nine and one-half hours at least, with certain compensations, in order to keep steam shovels going eight hours. Judicial decisions have excluded from the operation of the eight-hour law all employes paid by the month. Many monthly employes have a long work day—telegraph operators on the railroad always work twelve hours, track men and yard masters, foremen, clerks in the disbursing and time keeping offices, and others often work ten, twelve and longer hours. Mechanics in the shops of the Isthmian Canal Commission were working on an eight-hour basis, whereas men in the same crafts in the shops of the Panama Railroad Company were working on a ten-hour basis. Both are under one master mechanic and concerned in the construction of the Canal. The President has issued an order requiring the work day in those shops to be made identical and it should be put into effect at an early time, for this inequality has long contributed toward discontent. There are other strange inequalities. For instance, men paid by the hour in the shops of the Panama Railroad Company have vacation with pay and unlimited sick leave. The same type of men among the Isthmian Canal Commission's employes have vacation without pay and sick leave for a definite period, which, however, has but recently been granted after persistent petitioning upon the part of such employes. American employes paid by the month are granted vacation with pay. Monthly men, who are not Americans, feel that it is unfair that they should not be given vacations with pay. They come under the local government of the Canal Zone just as do the natives of Porto Rico employed by that Insular Government who receive a vacation of thirty working days in addition to time for travel between that country and the United States, the same as American employes there. Another inconsistency is the fact that vacation with pay is granted employes of the Panama Railroad Company on the Isthmus and yet captains of the steamships owned by it are not allowed vacation with or without pay although they are on the monthly pay-roll. Since hourly men are paid when required to work overtime and the monthly men are not, it is considered by the Commission as a fair arrangement to grant the latter vacation with pay while denying it to the former. However, as monthly employes are allowed six weeks' vacation* with pay *because the physicians consider an annual change of climate essential for the average man not accustomed to work in a tropical climate*, the hourly men consider that if vacations are necessary for the health of monthly men, they are likewise for them. Americans do not want to work overtime for that is regarded as "blood money." Furthermore, since it is expected that overtime will be limited to emergencies and reduced to a minimum there is of course no guarantee that the income so earned would be a fair substitute for vacation. While monthly men work longer hours, frequently, than mechanics and, sometimes, endure greater hardships, working out of doors, than men protected from sun and storm in the shops and, therefore, may be entitled to special consideration, the reason given for granting vacations to one and not to the other type of employes is certainly open to criticism. Another argument is that all such employes of Navy Yards and Arsenals in the United States, where climate is not a consideration, receive fifteen working days' leave with pay. An additional claim made by the hourly men is that one would be more likely to return from a leave if there were a vacation with pay to look forward to and that it would be economy to offer this inducement to employes to return rather than to be obliged to train "green" men in their places.

Men who live in the western part of the United States object to the change in rules which makes it impossible for vacations to be cumulative for two years except when an employe is prevented by the Government from taking such leave when due. The reasons given are the heavy expenses in taking such a long journey from the Isthmus and the short time to be enjoyed at home when vacation must be taken annually and completed within six weeks. It is the intention of the Chairman to take up such cases individually, but that is not known. Others complain because this change takes away a privilege which was a part of the terms of employment.

There were regulations entitling certain employes to

* This leave of six weeks is considered as an allowance of 12 days for travel to and from the United States and as 30 days' vacation. It may be noted that the usual leave allowance in the United States is 30 *working days* exclusive of Sundays and holidays. The Porto Rican Insular Government allows all employes 30 working days' leave as in the States, and allows 12 days for travel when they visit the States. It would seem well to bring the Canal regulations into better harmony with the rules of the United States by adopting the Porto Rican method.

The Result of a Hard Rain.

thirty days' sick leave, with pay, for each year's service. There was imposition upon the Government by some who were known to take sick leave when not ill. It was stated by employes that after very short service some had indulged in this abuse. To correct this evil a drastic ruling was made in February allowing but fifteen days' sick leave for each six month's service and providing that it should only be granted when the employe had worked ninety-six per cent. of the legal working days or hours. It also provided that no man should be paid for sick leave until after six months' service. This was regarded as a hardship because they claim it is not usual that recovery may be had from an attack of malaria within fifteen days and one may be ill only once during the year. Furthermore, if one were going to be ill, it would most likely occur within the first three months of service and it would be a hardship to wait six months for sick leave pay under such circumstances.

NEW RULES.

A new ruling effective July 1 provides for the payment of sick leave compensation the first pay period after the employe returns to duty, which is an acceptable correction. The following is the present rule:

''To assist the Government in maintaining a skilled force on the Isthmus, all regular employes above the grade of laborer, unaccustomed to a tropical climate, may be granted fifteen days' sick leave with pay for each six months' service, on the certificate of an authorized physician in the service of the Department of Health of the Isthmian Canal Commission that the employe has been unable to work on account of illness contracted through no fault of his own, or because of injury.

This leave may be cumulative to an amount not exceeding thirty days, and payment for same shall be made the first pay period after the employe returns to duty; but no payment shall be made for time lost in excess of the sick leave due at the time of such illness or injury.''

If the intent is to restore the privilege of sick leave for thirty consecutive days at any time during the

A Native Village.

year, the reference to fifteen days for each six months seems unnecessary. Rules often are not clearly stated.

The new rules effective July 1 contain some other changes which will cure certain grievances and others which have generated new ones.

Some of the improvements are:

''A former employe from the United States, who served less than one year, re-engaged for duty on the Isthmus, will receive pay only from the date of his re-entry into service on the Isthmus, and he will be charged the Government rate on the steamers of the Panama Railroad and Steamship Company operating between the United States and Cristobal.''

This is taken to indicate that former employes having served one year will receive pay from the time of embarkation from New York when re-engaged and also free transportation. Employes consider that this should be the case inasmuch as former employes are undoubtedly more useful than new ones who must be trained.

The following is intended to indicate that new employes no longer have to wait six months before putting in application for ''married quarters'' and when this is made plain, it will be appreciated:

''Where practicable and in the best interests of the service, an employe will be provided with such quarters on the Isthmus as may be available from time to time. Family quarters will be assigned when available, assignments to be made in accordance with the date of application. Experience shows that about ten months elapse between application and assignment.''

There is objection to the second sentence in the following because it is felt that it places whites and negroes on the same basis:

''The Commission reserves the right to pay in any money, the value or parity of which is guaranteed by the United States. Being on the gold roll will not in future confer any special privileges.''

It has been the custom to grant a twenty dollar rate on the steamers of the Panama Railroad Company to employes taking vacations. The new ruling simply states that the Government rate shall be granted. Employes object to the uncertainty of expression, believing that the rate may be changed any time.

Employes above the grade of the common laborer, entitled to sick leave, may be granted additional leave on account of injury not exceeding thirty days in any year. Common laborers are granted leave on account of injury and both receive free medical care and attendance at the hospitals.

It has not been the custom to pay mechanics and other hourly employes on the Isthmus for holidays although that is the custom in the United States at arsenals and navy yards. The following, one of the new rules, and an exceedingly liberal proposition, caused satisfaction:

''All employes whose compensation is nxed on an hourly basis and who work on the days prior and subsequent thereto, will be allowed pay for the following holidays:

January 1,
February 22,
May 30,
July 4,
Labor Day,
Thanksgiving Day, and
December 25.

''All hourly employes above the grade of laborer, who render actual service on these holidays will be allowed time and one-half in addition to pay for such holidays.''

It was found that common laborers from other countries did not care for our holidays and were dissatisfied at the attendant lost of pay, therefore, the following is a part of the new regulations making for content:

"If actual service is rendered on the days prior and subsequent thereto, pay will be allowed for the following holidays: January 1, February 22, May 30, July 4, Labor Day, Thanksgiving Day and December 25. If actual service is rendered on these dates double pay will be allowed."

THE WHOLESALE DISMISSAL OF EMPLOYES.

There are also improvements in regulations relative to the assignment of "married quarters" specifically stated but the "straw which has broken the camel's back" in the new regulations effective July 1 is the provision for the wholesale discharge of employes at the end of their next leave period in order to bring all under the same rules and regulations. This is regarded as a breaking of contracts by the Government. The provision reads as follows:

"All provisional appointments will, at the end of each leave period, be so modified as to make such appointments correspond to the then existing rules and regulations of the Commission.

"All appointments made prior to this resolution are hereby terminated, to take effect at the end of the next leave period accruing under such appointment. Conditions of service thereafter will be in accord with the rules and regulations of the Commission.'

It is true that the Commission was entirely within its legal right in making this ruling insofar as employes who have had increases are concerned, because under a decision of the Comptroller, made many months ago, all original contracts are rendered null and void by the acceptance of promotions. It does not seem fair to the men that, because they are raised in pay and accept such increase, all privileges conferred by their first contracts should be lost. All appointments are made "provisionally." If that means that a man is appointed to serve provided he gives satisfaction, it should be so stated but if it means that the appointment is made provisionally in order that the Government may make changes at any time it deems fit, employes feel that it is unjust. Nothing tends to create discontent as much as uncertainty about conditions of employment.

The labor problem is serious with such a changing policy as has been pursued. The men feel that there is no stability and that "they never know when an order is going to be issued with some new provisions affecting their employment." Furthermore, there are those who threaten to take up such conditions with their congressmen and this will still further complicate matters by bringing into general discussion grievances which could be readily adjusted.

There is intense feeling among certain hourly men that they have greater skill than some classes which have recently been awarded an increase in wages. This will doubtless be eliminated by the introduction of a system, now under consideration, by the Chairman of the Commission, under which a certain percentage will be added to the price paid for different types of labor in the United States to make up for discomforts suffered through employment on the Zone.

There has been adopted recently a "longevity plan" providing certain percentages of increase in pay each year for twenty-four types of employes. There is a feeling that it should have been made to apply to others such as time-keepers, and rock drillers, powder men and quarry men, who, although in the most hazardous work, have been overlooked. It is claimed that they work now nine hours for eight hours' pay, compensation being by the month. Others having had verbal promises in the States of rapid promotion, complain because salaries have not been increased, although they have been employed more than a year. There is dissatisfaction because engineers and conductors working for the Commission do not receive overtime pay whereas engineers and conductors working for the Panama Railroad Company do receive overtime. The engineers recognize that certain concessions have been made in lieu thereof but if they have to work overtime, which is not desired, they prefer pay for it.

The marines complain that others in the military service get fifty per cent. increase for colonial service whereas they on the Isthmus get only ten per cent.

Even the captains of the boats, responsible for the lives of so many, receive less than engineers and steam shovel men on the Isthmus and the stewardess receives the pitifully low stipend of twenty dollars a month in service where there is small opportunity for fees.

It is felt that one of the most unfortunate conditions is due to the fact that men are not selected by the employment department in the United States with reference to the positions which they are expected to fill and consequently great injustice has been done both the work and the men employed. For instance, if a man, who is a skilled machinist on civil engineers' gauges is sent down and placed on the repairing of locomotives, he is very likely to be dismissed for incompetency. Men in different lines undoubtedly have been sent away under a cloud when perfectly competent to fill positions for which they applied. Others have, in a few cases, been transferred to positions which they have filled satisfactorily. Many have returned from the States under assumed names or resorted to that means of securing employment at other points on the Zone.

Another cause of discontent is the fact that in the stress of getting men of different types to go to the Isthmus promises have been made prospective employes, which could not be kept. For instance, one might be promised that he would be able to get married quarters in sixty days. Upon complaining that the promise was not kept, it would not appease a man to call his attention to the written contract that such quarters would be given "when available." As one said, "It takes the heart out of a man to be told in the States that he can get married quarters and then he gets here and finds he must have his application in many months before they are assigned."

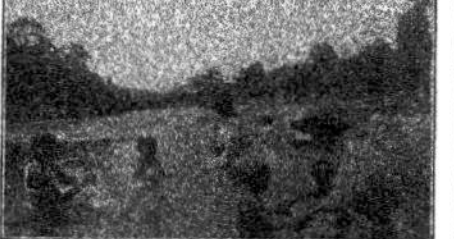

Natives Bathing in the Usual Way.

In the printed matter distributed among Europeans there are misrepresentations; there is a picture of a hotel for American whites which would lead common laborers to infer that they would eat in such buildings; there are mentioned in a misleading way pretty and hygienic houses for workers and the opportunity of taking families and of purchasing clothes at the commissary made in the best factories of the United States as well as alluring statements with reference to recreation and other matters.

Misrepresentations to prospective employes only react against the Government.

There have been complaints at one point that members of the union were discriminated against and this has caused a great deal of dissatisfaction. There seems to be no doubt but that some good men have been dismissed who were members of the union but it is claimed by the master mechanic that non-union men have also been discharged. In other trades in the same shops the men are entirely organized and there is of course no question of discriminating against unionists. Certain it is that the official complained against has tried honestly to live up to his convictions that there should be no recognition of unions on a Government job. While he may have been vexed by leaders who have taken the Government's time in trying to secure members for their unions, it seems to be begging the question of recognition when a committee of boilermakers will be listened to, although not as representatives of the union, as all of the boilermakers belong to the union, and especially when Secretary Taft meets the national officials of these same organizations and confers with them relative to matters concerning their men upon the Isthmus.

There is no general discrimination against unionists on the Isthmus but there is a strong anti-union sentiment among officials and an unwillingness to deal with union committees. There is need of a clear and well defined policy in reference to dealing with committees or representatives of unions.

OPPORTUNITY NOW FOR GRIEVANCES TO BE HEARD.

Great credit is undoubtedly due to the preceding administration for organization work but there was a policy of refusing to hear complaints of any kind which has brought to this administration an accumulation of grievances and serious problems with which to deal.

The Chairman of the present Commission has spent Sundays and the major portion of week days listening to complaints and making personal investigations. Confidence has thus been inspired and there was a general feeling of hopefulness.

A CONCILIATION BOARD AND LABOR COMMISSIONER NEEDED.

Discontent due to bad food, favoritism in awarding "married quarters," uncomfortable bachelor quarters, and such matters as dismissals, inequalities in wages, hours, or vacations, and relative to sick leave provisions, will be reduced greatly without doubt by the forming of a board to consider all labor grievances. Such a board is now contemplated by the Chairman whose intention it is to have upon it a representative of the Commission, a representative of the trade involved, and a representative of the foreman under whom the complainant works.

However, the situation is so complicated that it would be impossible to equalize conditions unless a careful study were made by an expert labor commissioner whose sole duty would be the consideration of labor matters.

In the operation of the Conciliation Board to be established, the principle should be adopted that where a majority of the men belong to a union, that organization shall have the right to be heard by its committee. That principle was established by the Anthracite Coal Commission appointed by President Roosevelt and the same rule has been adopted by many employers' organizations making contracts with unions. Nearly every railroad in the United States has a contract with its engineers, firemen, trainmen, conductors, machinists, molders, blacksmiths, et cetra, notwithstanding the fact that there are non-unionists in every class.

If, in establishing the policy of having grievances heard by a conciliation board an experienced labor commissioner should be employed, many grievances would be adjusted by him in the same manner as they are in the bituminous coal fields, in the building trades in New York, the Newspaper Publishers' Association, and many other organizations. If unable to personally adjust grievances, final appeal could be made to a joint board. The policy and practical operation of such a board could be determined readily by an experienced labor commissioner, after looking over the field. The board contemplated by the Chairman of the Commission could well be made such a body for the final disposition of matters which could not be settled by the labor commissioner.

That the plan of having a permanent conciliation board to which grievances may be taken will allay discontent and resentfulness has already been proved by the result of hearings granted personally by the Chairman of the Commission. This board also would enable him to give more time to construction problems.

Such a conciliation board would prevent interruption of work if it is thoroughly understood that grievances should be presented before and not after "striking" for nine times out of ten they would be adjusted.

Appeal to such a board of conciliation should be final and remove the necessity of distressing the President and the Secretary of War with such details. Furthermore, it is impossible, owing to the length of time which it takes to send communications from the Isthmus and secure replies, to satisfactorily adjust grievances if decisions must be so awaited.

The establishment of a conciliation board with the resultant assurance that justice may be had would serve to attract a good class of laborers, for friends bring friends from the States if conditions are such that they write favorably of them.

SHOP WASH ROOMS.

It was a pleasant surprise to find excellent wash rooms, with individual enamelled iron wash bowls most neatly arranged and hot water wisely provided in the shops; but the wash rooms are located so inconveniently as to make them useless. The men would appreciate the opportunity to wash before going to the noon meal, but, being hungry, due to light breakfasts, they will not climb through inconvenient and obstructed places to do so. These wash rooms should be placed at the exits of the shops, or near the mess halls and roller towels, soap and hot water should be provided.

GROUP OF EMPLOYES AND WIVES.

PROTECTION OF SAWS.

Circular saws should be guarded. There is no more dangerous tool used by workmen, and yet in the carpenter shop visited the saw was unprotected.

EMPLOYERS' LIABILITY.

There were nine men blown to pieces during the investigation. They were employed in blasting where there is excavating. While in this particular case, the best powder foreman was in charge (and was killed), there is feeling that in general such foremen are not proficient. In any event, it brought to mind the query as to whether the Government should provide for dependent families of the injured and killed. Now collections are made among the employes for such funds. Damages are not recoverable from the Government in such cases as they are from private contractors in the United States. As recently as April, one suffering from pulmonary tuberculosis *contracted* in the *service* was denied the amount of compensation for leave *of* absence, when obliged to depart from the Isthmus permanently.

THE "CANAL ZONE NEWS."

There should be published weekly a bulletin, which might be called the "Canal Zone News," in at least English, Spanish, Italian and Greek, in parallel columns. This has been undertaken by private employers advantageously. Through such a channel employes could be informed, for instance, of the loss of a ship containing vegetables, which has just occurred, or the sinking of a ship load of lumber, which likewise has just happened, and of rulings or changes which have been made with reference to mess houses or the assignment of quarters, commissaries or the employment of labor, including vacations, sick leave and other matters affecting the employes. It would be well, through such a paper, to explain exactly the conditions in a trade such as that of the engineers, which called for the raising of wages, and caused feeling that others were not given proper consideration. Those explanations would appeal to the average man. All conversed with were found to be reasonable and if various matters were understood there would be fewer grievances and less complaining. Health suggestions could be made. Care of range closets, explaining to foreigners the result of throwing old trousers, shoes, etc., in them, could be recommended. Danger of drinking water from streams receiving sewage could be explained. Such health suggestions from time to time. would be much more effective than the circulars now issued and placarded in the Post Offices, which cannot be generally read. An illustration of ignorance relative to new regulations superseding objectionable rules was the remark of a high class man who voiced the sentiment expressed by others. It was: "A married man can't stay at home if sick but is compelled to go to the hospital." It is not known that that is not required.

This paper could be supplied with Associated Press dispatches, affording the employes, eager for news from home, something more to relieve the dreadful monotony of that life.

The "Canal Zone News" should be distributed free of charge because it is important to have it read by all.

SUGGESTION SYSTEM.

There should be inaugurated a system of courting complaints and suggestions. "Suggestion boxes" could be placed at railway stations, in the post offices, shops, mess houses and clubs. The fear of the loss of position if complaints or suggestions are offered seems to be justified by past experiences and is so *great* that all asked in giving information that their names should be suppressed. This applies to doctors, nurses and men in *official positions*, as well as mechanics. Through the "Canal Zone News," if established, or some other printed circular, the suggestion system should be outlined explaining just what is requested. In addition to complaints of all kinds, suggestions for improvement in mess houses, quarters, commissaries and in construction work should be asked. Cash prizes might be awarded for suggestions which could be utilized. Valuable points could be culled from many suggestions which doubtless would be useless.

For instance, in one department six-inch boards were greatly needed, but the supply was exhausted; the need could have been met by the loan of such six-inch boards, of which another department had an over supply. The department in distress had plenty of two-inch boards and, failing to secure the loan desired, had to spike them together and the head of the department did not feel very agreeable when later he learned that the ungracious department had had to have all of its six-inch boards run through a planing mill and cut into two-inch boards for which he would have been happy to exchange his two-inch boards.

Another illustration, given by a steam shovelman, is: In the excavating work an empty train, unused because the steam shovel has broken down, could be sent along to another place where it could be used. (Quite recent improvements in the excavation work will prevent such delays in future, it is officially stated.)

The following suggestion, which was made during this investigation and seems worthy of consideration, is offered as an example of what might be received: "Some men lay off a day now and then to rest up and get paid for sick leave. A premium should be put on honesty. For instance, if a man is only away five days ill, he should be awarded as an addition to his vacation a percentage of the balance of the thirty days' sick leave."

BOAT SERVICE BETWEEN NEW YORK AND COLON, PANAMA

The Panama Railroad Company, owned by the Government, operates a line of steamships between New York and Colon, there being five vessels. The conditions under which employes are transported to and from the Isthmus are simply intolerable. The boats are overcrowded, some staterooms poorly ventilated and badly located, the food is awful and some of the ships, undoubtedly, are not safe.

The voyage was made on the "Panama" going, and on the "Colon" returning. They are considered the best boats. The journey from the Isthmus would have been taken upon the "Finance," but it was regarded unsafe. When the question was asked: "How can you afford to take the risk of sending employes to the States on it?" the reply was, "We would not if this were the hurricane season, but it will most probably reach New York safely under the present weather conditions." It is now undergoing repairs and will be put in service again early in August. The sailing time between New York and Colon is advertised to be five and one-half to seven days. The "Finance" takes ten to eleven days and employes so unfortunate as to strike it going upon and returning from vacations have spent twenty-two of their forty-two days upon it. If they live in the Central or Western States, it will be seen that but a short period may be spent at home. It is very doubtful whether this boat should be put into commission again. Its temporary relinquishment cuts down the service to four boats at the vacation season when there were, already, inadequate accommodations. The "Allianca," another doubtful ship, is in dock for repairs and to be somewhat enlarged. The "Brunswick" has been chartered for use until it is released. The "Advance" is the third boat regarded as unsafe.

If objection were raised to the purchase of good English ships when the "Panama" and "Colon" were secured instead from the Ward Line, as is understood, certainly the American people will withdraw such an objection when it is known how the employes suffer; and that the boats are overcrowded and so unfit for service as to be a disgrace to the Nation.

There is constant travel between New York and the Isthmus, due, not only to the securing of new employes, but to vacation trips. It is of tremendous importance that the Government should secure at the earliest possible moment some new boats, improve some now being used and abandon others. Preferable to purchasing boats would be to have some especially constructed for this service were the present needs less pressing. This may be advisable in making plans to meet all future requirements.

Description must be limited to personal experience upon the "Panama" and "Colon," each having cost the Government $650,000.00.

STATEROOMS.

There are staterooms, good in appearance on the steamship "Panama," containing a stationary bowl, two bunks and a couch used as a berth frequently. Each stateroom would be comfortable for two persons if the upper berths were wider and if there were adopted some other means of softening them than the present type of mattress. The lower berths have springs and are comparatively comfortable but better springs should be placed therein. The upper berths are narrow, wooden bunks. One, therefore, not only suffers from a hard bed, but the constant fear of falling out. Were the upper berths so hung as to have the outer edge slightly higher than the inner, instead of being inclined downward, and covered with woven wire springs they could be made usable. They could not be closed, probably, but that would be an advantage really as when put up like a Pullman berth, they cover the ventilating perforations. These berths could easily be made as comfortable as those in the boats plying between New York and Providence or Fall River. The couches, with the exception that there is not the fear of falling from a great height, are just as objectionable, hard and narrow. Even to add the mattress from the upper berth to the one belonging to a couch, as was done by a few so fortunate as to have but two in a room, did not prevent the sleeper from arising with backache and a general feeling of fatigue which at the end of the trip was excessive. Each stateroom should be used for two only, but three are crowded in, causing great discomfort.

However, that is not the worst phase of the sleeping arrangements. On the same deck, which is the upper one, in the stern there are staterooms, each containing six narrow bunks, crowded into the smallest possible space; and there is still a more abominable arrangement, for, on the deck below there are rooms called intermediates, in front of the steerage, there being barrels of potatoes and other unsightly freight between those quarters. Here there are staterooms containing as many bunks as possible, some having no ventilation, some very close to the boilers, which uncomfortably heat them, and others being ventilated by somewhat remote port-holes or an air shaft which carries in cinders. In the last two types of staterooms there is no place to hang clothing.

On the "Colon" the majority of the staterooms are identical. An annex contains a few new ones with comfortable stationary upper berths having woven wire springs. The conditions upon the deck below, however, are even worse than on the "Panama." The bunks in the stern have comfortable springs but the ventilation is poor. These are second cabin rooms, adjacent to the second cabin dining-room. Next are the standee steerage cots upon the open deck. Ahead are the intermediates, partly used by steerage passengers on this trip and quite as bad as the same quarters on the "Panama," with adjacent side rooms containing bunks very narrow and simply made of canvas loosely hung on two iron rods. Six were assigned to one such room containing four bunks. The ventilation was very bad and across there was such an *inside* room with two negroes placed with white men.

Employes on the "Panama" and "Colon" unable to sleep in quarters assigned them, spent the nights lying on deck, in chairs on deck, in the smoking-room and in the social hall upon the seat surrounding it.

There were one hundred and eighty passengers on the "Colon" and it was claimed by one of the chief officials that it was built for eighty. In the Proceedings of the Isthmian Canal Commission, both these boats are claimed to accommodate one hundred first-class and fifty second-class passengers. With forty-two first-class staterooms on the "Colon," accommodating comfortably but two each, it is difficult to reconcile that statement with the conditions.

It has been proven that complaints of employes, who claimed that they had been given steerage quarters, are warranted.

Until the service is improved "first-class" tickets should not be issued to employes who cannot occupy the best type of staterooms. At present such staterooms are assigned until exhausted and then other quarters are given later applicants. All holding tickets *marked for first-class passage* feel that injustice has been practised and that they are entitled to accommodations as good as those secured by others paying the same.

Worthy of attention is the complaint that owing to inadequate service, employes, who have been granted vacation, are unable to secure, immediately, accommodations in returning to the United States. There should be a system of notifying employes, granted leave of absence, that definite reservations have been made. There is a rule requiring applications to be put in ten days in advance of the sailing of the boat selected for the trip. It is officially claimed that, if reservations cannot be made because of previous applications, employes are assigned accommodations on the next boat and that it is a part of the regulations that they shall be so notified, *but that is not done*. This is especially important in the interest of fairness for the Government requires that vacations shall be taken in a country affording necessary change of climate which means the United States and travel upon Government boats unless willing to pay rates on commercial lines. Some lately have paid the fare of $70.00 on a private line rather than endure the hardships attendant upon a voyage on Government boats. Employes granted leave of absence for a particular period are given by the local official of the Department of Labor, Quarters and Subsistence orders for transportation. Many go to Colon the night before the sailing of the boat to be on hand early the next morning in order to secure staterooms. The morning of the sailing of the "Colon," July 6, many who were at the head of the line at nine o'clock were told to return at one and accommodations would be arranged if possible. Such employes saw tickets sold to others in the original line. Some secured good staterooms; others did not know what they had until the boat had sailed and they found themselves in the abominable quarters above described, and some, who had previously been on the boat, accepted bad accommodations with the full knowledge of what they were receiving rather than to postpone going. For instance, a ticket marked room "M" would mean nothing to a man who had never been on the boat, whereas a previous traveller upon it would thus know where he was placed. Some would not have gone had they known that they did not have one of the best staterooms. Several had had applications for vacations on file from six weeks to two months and they had never heard whether they could be accommodated on that boat or not. Such treatment does not make a man feel very agreeable, especially if he has given faithful service for two years and "never been sick a day, nor away except on vacation."

Cases were cited of employes with families, who, after closing their homes and taking their luggage to Colon, were obliged to board at that place or go back to camp and stay with friends until the sailing of the next boat. All who failed to secure accommodations at the first attempt lost at least that day's time. It is claimed by officials that when employes are obliged to wait over for another boat that they are allowed to go back to work, but this is not understood. Some are known to have lost the first five days of their vacation when they would have preferred to be at work and have that time applied upon the period spent in the United States.

Complaint is made that the employe's craft is marked on the back of each steamship ticket, and, when application is made for accommodations the agent immediately looks at that inscription and the clerk is given the preference over the mechanic in assigning staterooms. This is a very general criticism.

The baggage of employes must be checked from the camps to Colon and then re-checked to New York, which causes great confusion at the wharf. If the assignment of accommodations were made before employes leave the camps baggage could be checked through to New York. As it is now, vacations are granted and employes are left to get off as best they can.

It is claimed that it cannot be known until the last moment what may be the ability to accommodate employes as reservations are held for possible South American travellers, but surely it is possible to approximately determine the capacity of the boats in so far as it pertains to employes and to notify them of reservations in advance.

Employes leaving for vacations are given letters to the Isthmian Canal Commission at Washington where they must be sent by employes and orders are forwarded to them wherever they may be visiting. These orders must be presented to the Panama Railway Company in New York. It would seem to facilitate matters if direct orders on the Panama Railway Company were made. As it is, employes frequently must take their chances on reaching New York, of securing return accommodations. Then they will accept anything to get back within the prescribed time, else the vacation pay is lost.

QUARTERS FOR ATTENDANTS.

The sleeping quarters on the boats for the attendants are very bad. The bunks for the waiters are crowded together on the lower decks, inside where it is impossible to get good air. The firemen's quarters are worse, indeed awful, as they are simply packed in the space provided for standee cots in tiers. The sailors have the best ventilated quarters, in the bow of the boats, there being portholes next to their wooden bunks, which have no springs. They are not enclosed; the bunks simply line the bow. The quartermasters have nearby rooms similarly ventilated. They have the luxury of enameled iron wash bowls in sanitary frame stands. The chief cook on the "Colon" has an inside room across from bins of potatoes and cabbages with a port-hole above through which the breezes blow and waft the odors of those vegetables into his sleeping place. He is obliged to take his mattress aft. Many employes of the boat, there being one hundred three on the "Panama" and one hundred seven on the "Colon," carried their blankets to the portion of the lower deck which had wide openings opposite each other, sleeping upon boards, for the purpose of getting air.

There is an inside room containing four narrow bunks for as many cooks and there are but six bunks for seven kitchen employes on the "Colon."

The waiters and cooks, so wretchedly quartered, suffer most during the five days spent between each trip in the dock at Colon where there is little air stirring and they grow ill.

The stewardess has a small inside room upon the upper deck, there being no means of ventilation on the "Colon" except the perforations at the top. On that boat the steward of the second cabin had to sleep on a pile of mattresses on the dining salon floor because he was required to give up his quarters to passengers.

These boats have no bath or toilet accommodations for their captains whose cabins naturally are in the bow on the top deck and they must go to the rear of the deck below no matter how necessary it is for them to be near the post of duty constantly. There is only one bath for women and one for men passengers on each boat. There are shower baths for firemen. It was pleasant to find such consideration no matter how crude the arrangements, but more adequate baths with warm water, soap and towels should be supplied.

It has been suggested that a naval constructor should be assigned to thoroughly overhaul these boats. Long has it been pointed out how staterooms for the top decks could be built and placed in position during a regular layover in the port of New York without encroaching upon a sailing period, it is authoritatively claimed. This would add some comfortable quarters for Isthmian Canal employes, at least, and enable re-arrangements on the lower deck by releasing quarters used for them to be properly prepared for boat attendants and thus to alleviate conditions somewhat until the whole service can be improved.

FOOD ON BOATS.

Complaints with reference to food on all the boats must be justified, for it was exceedingly bad on the "Panama," which is the most popular boat. When in commercial service it was officially stated that the "Panama" accommodated but fifty passengers; and that it is now licensed to carry two hundred. There were one hundred fifty-five passengers on the boat leaving New York June 7. This necessitated three sittings in the dining salon. Those at the third sitting had to take what was left and some never saw a napkin during the entire trip. The table linen at times was so unclean as to be repulsive, at the first table.

Even one so favored as to be placed at the right hand of the Captain and given the best of everything, found it almost impossible to eat. The meats were simply awful, eggs musty, vegetables entirely unseasoned, and the desserts wretchedly prepared. Nuts were stale and oranges were bad. Bread and butter were good and occasionally an article of food was well prepared, but on the whole it was dreadful.

While one might expect to find poor food upon the Isthmus, it seemed utterly inexcusable that a boat just sailing from the port of New York should not supply first-class food in every particular. The table service was bad, the food unsightly and unpalatable; and the employes complained of discourteous waiters. (It is believed that wages are not high enough to attract efficient men in view of the fact that many of the travelers are not in a position to fee liberally.) The dumping of unclean silver into a large pan in the hallway, between the dining salon and serving room, presented a sickening sight.

The drinking water, carried in a tank in the hold, is New York Croton water, unfit to drink without being boiled or distilled and it is not so treated.

Employes who were forced to eat food, either spoiled or not properly prepared, do not reach the Isthmus in the best condition to endure its climatic change.

While many really suffer from the lack of nutritious food, one extreme case is that of a nurse, going to the Isthmus for the first time on the "Colon," who, finding herself unable to eat in the salon, asked to have her food served upon the deck, but was refused that privilege for it is against the rules of that boat, because it is believed that the force of employes is not adequate for that purpose. After attempting to eat unpalatable food for a few days, it is a fact that "one becomes prejudiced against it" the moment the dining salon is entered. (On the "Panama" the stewardess is allowed to serve on deck to those unable to go to the salon.) After four days of struggle, on the part of the aforesaid nurse, a fainting spell convinced the steward of the necessity of yielding to her request and she was served on deck raw eggs, all she could take by that time. Not having good food, on which to build up, after reaching the Ancon Hospital, where she was assigned, she fell a ready prey to malaria and was suffering from that fever during the last week of this investigation.

Returning from the Isthmus some articles of food on the "Colon" were prepared better, but on the whole conditions were the same as experienced going down, except that table linen was cleaner. To many of the employes the food on this boat "seemed good in contrast to that on the Isthmus." Soups and fish were fair. Meats unpalatable, vegetables unseasoned. Bread was good and delicious preserves were served occasionally which, like olives on the "Panama," "helped to cover a multitude of sins." There were also on that boat stale, moldy nuts. Why nuts should be served out of season, it is difficult to understand. It was learned that one purchasing agent furnishes supplies to all the boats so they must fare alike.

In the hallway between the dining salon and serving room on the "Colon," large tin receptacles upon the floor receive unclean dishes and present an offensive scene.

The serving rooms are inadequate and inconveniently placed. The kitchens, below with dumb waiter service, are not supplied with soup or vegetable boilers or (on the Colon) proper bake ovens. The butcher shop on the "Colon," off the kitchen, is entirely unventilated.

RAIL GUARDS, STEAMER CHAIRS, RATES AND DELAYS IN TRANSPORTING PROVISIONS.

Undoubtedly the officials of the boats make all as comfortable as possible with the facilities available.

Not only are doctors, nurses, clerks, and mechanics subjected to bad transportation service, but also wives and children of employes now going to the Isthmus to live, or taking vacations.

At the ends of the lifeboats on the "Colon," the railings leave spaces through which a little child playing on deck could be swept into the sea instantly. Guards should be placed there and other boats inspected with the same end in view. Wire screen, covering the upper deck rails would also be available for the same reason. With the sudden lurch of a vessel a child could easily slip between.

The use of old, rickety steamer chairs should be discontinued and plenty of good ones furnished at a reasonable rate. One of the two chairs required for the trip down had no foot rest and the seat had been repaired by nailing a rough board, a quarter of an inch in thickness, across, making it impossible to sit thereon. That experience led to a written request for two good chairs ten days in advance of embarking upon the return trip. The result was: one cane chair with no foot rest and one framework with separate pieces of canvas on back and seat. The frame seat was so uncomfortable as to make it impossible to use the chair, and yet a bill for $2.00 was presented, but payment was refused. There were some very good chairs but the supply was inadequate.

The Government grants a rate of twenty dollars on its lines to employes on vacations and to adult members of their families, the full fare being ninety dollars. The Government steamship line is a common carrier and required to transport freight and passengers, other than employes, under its charter. It is difficult to explain why it should charge more for bad service than is asked for good service on another line ($70.00) even though its price may be raised to discourage tourists from seeking its service in order to place the majority of the accommodations at the disposal of the employes.

A further point for consideration is the fact that provisions for the Isthmus are carried by these boats and their delivery is delayed frequently because the boats do not reach there on schedule time, due largely to their bad condition.

MEALS OF ATTENDANTS.

In the serving of food the employes of the steamship line are treated much worse than the other employes of the Government, travelling as passengers. One class has a very unattractive, warm, inside dining-room on the lower deck of the "Panama" and "Colon," but sailors and firemen have no place to eat and must simply stand on deck in a most savage and uncivilized fashion, getting their food as best they can from two or three large receptacles.

An employe on the "Panama," who had good credentials, and who had been in the service of the Government for many years, gave a picture of the conditions on the Transports Sherman, Logan, Sheridan and Thomas with reference to care of boat attendants, which affords a severe contrast. He stated that the sleeping quarters are excellent and the mess rooms for the sailors and firemen perfectly white, clean and attractive. If this be a true picture, that standard should be generally applied.

In any event the accommodations on the line operating between the United States and the Isthmus of Panama, are inexcusably bad, both for passengers and boat attendants. It may be asked why they have gone so long unnoticed by officials? The President went to the Isthmus on a special boat and so did the Secretary of War. Special quarters were arranged for commissioners who never took the trouble to investigate those of other employes. The present chairman happened to go down with a Congressional party when, doubtless, special effort was made to have table service good and the question of crowded accommodations for employes would not likely arise under such circumstances. Complaints have been made by employes to superintendents but, if they have been carried to higher authorities, apparently no impression as to their import has been made.

WELFARE DEPARTMENT THE NATIONAL CIVIC FEDERATION

The Welfare Department is devoted entirely to interesting employers in giving especial consideration to improving the conditions under which employes in all industries work and live. In extending the practice of Welfare Work, the Department has found of especial value conferences of employers, held under its auspices in different parts of the country, for the interchange of experiences. Illustrated literature is widely distributed and stereopticon lectures are given. A bureau of exchange is maintained at headquarters, where descriptive matter, plans and photographs relating to betterments in different industries may be obtained by employers.

Some of the subjects involved are:

SANITARY WORK PLACES: Systems for providing pure drinking water; for ventilation, including the cooling of super-heated places, and devices for exhausting dust and removing gases; for lighting work places; and for guarding machinery; wash rooms with hot and cold water, towels and soap; shower baths for moulders and stationary firemen; emergency hospitals; locker rooms; seats for women; laundries for men's overalls or women's uniforms; the use of elevators for women, and luncheon rooms.

RECREATION: The social hall for dancing parties, concerts, theatricals, billiards, pool or bowling; the gymnasium, athletic field, roof garden, vacations and summer excursions for employes, and rest rooms or trainmen's rest houses.

EDUCATIONAL: Classes for apprentices; in cooking, dressmaking, millinery; first aid to the injured; night classes for technical training; kindergartens and libraries.

HOUSING: Homes rented or sold to employes, and boarding houses.

PROVIDENT FUNDS: For insurance, pensions, savings or lending money in times of stress.

In promoting the work of this department it is recognized that the first essentials to the welfare of employes are, steady work, an equitable wage and reasonable hours of labor; but that the employer has a further obligation.

OFFICERS

CHARLES A. MOORE, Chairman.
CYRUS H. McCORMICK, First Vice-Chairman.
NATHAN STRAUS, Second Vice-Chairman.
ELLISON A. SMYTH, Third Vice-Chairman.
ISAAC N. SELIGMAN, Treasurer.
WM. H. TAFT, Chairman Committee on Welfare Work for Government Employes.
S. J. GREENHUT, Chairman Ways and Means Committee.
MISS GERTRUDE BEEKS, Secretary.
DR. THOMAS R. SLICER, Chairman N. Y. Welfare Committee.
ALEXANDER LAMBERT, Physician.
HAYES ROBBINS, Secretary New England Workshop Improvement Committee.

EXECUTIVE COMMITTEE

F. C. BALL, President Ball Bros. Glass Mfg. Co., Muncie, Ind.
JOHN BANCROFT, Joseph Bancroft & Sons Co., Wilmington, Del.
SAM'L J. BLOOMINGDALE, President Bloomingdale Bros., New York City.
CHARLES F. BROOKER, President The Coe Brass Manufacturing Co., Ansonia, Conn.
GEORGE W. BROWN, Treasurer United Shoe Machinery Co., Boston, Mass.
H. M. BYLLESBY, H. M. Byllesby & Co., Chicago.
W. A. CLARK, President United Verde Copper Co., Butte, Mont.
FREDERIC S. CLARK, Treasurer Talbot Mills, North Billerica, Mass.
W. L. CLAUSE, President Columbia Chemical Co., Pittsburg, Pa.
GEORGE OTIS DRAPER, Secretary Draper Co., Hopedale, Mass.
PIERRE S. DU PONT, Treasurer E. I. Du Pont De Nemours Powder Co., Wilmington, Del.

CHARLES A. MOORE, CHAIRMAN THE WELFARE DEPARTMENT.

CHARLES L. EDGAR, President The Edison Electric Illuminating Co., Boston, Mass.
G. E. EMMONS, Manager Schenectady Works General Electric Co., Schenectady, N. Y.
EDWARD A. FILENE, Treasurer Wm. Filene's Sons Co., Boston, Mass.
FREDERICK S. FISH, Chairman Executive Committee, Studebaker Bros. Mfg. Co., South Bend, Ind.
W. C. FISH, Manager Lynn Works General Electric Co., West Lynn, Mass.
HARRY B. FRENCH, Vice-President Smith, Kline & French Co., Philadelphia, Pa.
ORRIN R. GOAN, Manager National Biscuit Co., New York City.
WM. C. GREENE, Treasurer Peace Dale Mfg. Co., Peace Dale, R. I.
S. J. GREENHUT, Treasurer Siegel-Cooper Co., New York City.
F. R. HAZARD, President The Solvay Process Co., Syracuse, N. Y.
H. J. HEINZ, President H. J. Heinz Co., Pittsburg, Pa.
EDWIN M. HERR, Vice-President Westinghouse Electric and Air Brake Companies, Pittsburg, Pa.
CHARLES W. HUBBARD, Treasurer Ludlow Mfg. Associates, Boston, Mass.
CHARLES H. HULBURD, President Elgin National Watch Co., Chicago, Ill.
JOHN S. HUYLER, President [illegible], New York City.
W. B. JANSEN, Vice-President Atchison, Topeka & Santa Fe Railway System, Chicago.
G. GUNBY JORDAN, President Eagle and Phenix Mills, Columbus, Ga.
J. KRUTTSCHNITT, Union Pacific System, San Francisco, Cal.
JOHN F. P. LAWTON, Gorham Mfg. Co., Providence, R. I.
WM. W. LOBDELL, President Lobdell Car Wheel Co., Wilmington, Del.
ARTHUR T. LYMAN, Treasurer The Boston Mfg. Co., Boston, Mass.
MARCUS M. MARKS, President National Association Clothing Manufacturers, New York City.
W. H. MARSHALL, President American Locomotive Co., New York City.
W. G. MATHER, President Cleveland-Cliffs Iron Co., Cleveland, O.
J. R. MacCOLL, President Lorraine Mfg. Co., Pawtucket, R. I.
CYRUS H. McCORMICK, President International Harvester Co., Chicago, Ill.
EMERSON McMILLIN, President American Light and Traction Co., New York City.
CHARLES A. MOORE, Manning, Maxwell & Moore, New York City.
JOHN OMWAKE, President United States Playing Card Co., Cincinnati, O.
L. A. OSBORNE, Vice-President Westinghouse Electric and Mfg. Co., East Pittsburg.
LEWIS W. PARKER, President Victor Mfg. Co., Greers, S. C.
THOMAS F. PARKER, President Monaghan Mills, Greenville, S. C.
C. STUART PATTERSON, President The Western Saving Fund Society of Philadelphia, Philadelphia, Pa.
THOMAS G. PLANT, President Thomas G. Plant Co., Boston, Mass.
ALBERT L. POPE, Pope Manufacturing Co., Hartford, Conn.
H. K. PORTER, President H. K. Porter Co., Pittsburg, Pa.
F. F. PRENTISS, President Cleveland Twist Drill Co., Cleveland, O.
F. W. ROEBLING, JR., John A. Roebling's Sons' Co., Trenton, N. J.
W. L. SAUNDERS, President Ingersoll-Rand Co., New York City.
THOMAS H. SAVERY, President [illegible] & [illegible] Co., Wilmington, Del.
H. A. SHERWIN, President Sherwin-Williams Co., Cleveland, O.
WILLIAM ELIOT SMITH, President Illinois Glass Co., Alton, Ill.
ELLISON A. SMYTH, President Pelzer Mfg. Co., Pelzer, S. C.
THEODORE P. SHONTS, President Interborough Rapid Transit Co., New York City.
NATHAN STRAUS, R. H. Macy & Co., New York City.
WILLIAM H. TAYLOR, President The St. Clair Coal Co., Scranton, Pa.
D. A. TOMPKINS, President The D. A. Tompkins Co., Charlotte, N. C.
H. B. WALKER, President Old Dominion Steamship Co., New York.
GEORGE F. WILLETT, President Geo. F. Willett Co., Boston, Mass.
J. R. WILLIAMS, Vice-President J. R. Williams & Co., Brooklyn, N. Y.
RUFUS K. WOOD, Maryland Steel Co., Sparrows Point, Md.
EDWARD WORCESTER, Vice-President National Tube Co., Pittsburg, Pa.

GENERAL MEMBERSHIP.

ADAMS, EDGAR E., The Cleveland Hardware Co., Cleveland, O.
ALLEN, W. C., The Yale & Towne Mfg. Co., Stamford, Conn.
AMORY, JOHN J., President Gas Engine & Power Co. and Charles L. Seabury Co., Morris Heights, New York City.
ANDERSON, H. M., St. Regis Paper Co., Watertown, N. Y.
APPERSON, R. D., President Lynchburg Traction & Light Co., Lynchburg, Va.
ARNOLD, NEWTON D., Treasurer Rumford Chemical Works, Providence, R. I.
BAKER, A. S., President Baker Mfg. Co., Evansville, Wis.
BAKER, L. K., Treasurer S. S. Stearns Lumber Co., Odanah, Wis.
BALLARD, S. THRUSTON, Vice-President Ballard & Ballard Co., Louisville, Ky.
BANCROFT, WILLIAM P., Wilmington, Del.
BARBOUR, GEORGE H., Vice-President The Michigan Stove Co., Detroit, Mich.
BACHEYTE, WILLIAM, Vice-President Los Angeles Gas & Electric Co., Los Angeles, Cal.

BECKHAM, HON. JOHN C. W., Governor of Kentucky, Frankfort, Ky.
BISSELL, FREDERICK, President The F. Bissell Co., Toledo, O.
BLISS, E. J., Treasurer Regal Shoe Co., Inc., Boston, Mass.
BRADFORD, A. N., Cobb & Drew, Rock Falls, Ill.
BROWN, JAMES E., Geneva Optical Co., Geneva, N. Y.
BUTTERWORTH, WILLIAM, Treasurer Deere & Co., Moline, Ill.
CALDERWOOD, J. F., Vice-President Brooklyn Rapid Transit Co., Brooklyn, N. Y.
CAMPBELL, JERE, President Eastern Coal Co., Providence, R. I.
CAMPBELL, J. A., President The Youngstown Sheet & Tube Co., Youngstown, O.
CAMPBELL, JOHN A., General Manager The Trenton Potteries Co., Trenton, N. J.

Restaurant Seating 900 Employes at One Time, General Electric Company, Schenectady, N. Y.

CARPENTER, C. U., President Herring-Hall-Marvin Safe Co., New York City.
CHASE, C. A., President Syracuse Chilled Plow Co., Syracuse, N. Y.
CHICK, FRANK S., Vice-President John H. Pray & Sons Co., Boston, Mass.
CLARK, CLARENCE M., President East St. Louis & Suburban Railway Co., Philadelphia.
CLARK, WILL L., United Verde Copper Co., Jerome, Ariz.
CORNING, EDWARD, President Edward Corning Co., New York City.
CRADDOCK, JOHN W., President Craddock-Terry Co., Lynchburg, Va.
CROSBY, O. H., Vice-President United States Express Co., New York.
CROSSETT, EDWARD S., Manufacturer of Yellow Pine Lumber, Davenport, Ia.
CROWLEY, L., Superintendent Detroit Stove Works, Detroit, Mich.
CUMMINGS, J. H., Vice-President John B. Stetson Co., Philadelphia.
CURWEN, SAMUEL M., General Manager J. G. Brill Co., Philadelphia, Pa.
DANFORTH, R. E., General Manager Rochester Railway Co., Rochester, N. Y.
DAVIES, H. J., Secretary The Cleveland Electric Railway Co., Cleveland, O.
DEEMS, J. F., General Supt. Motive Power Dept., New York Central Lines, New York City.
DEVLIN, THOMAS, President Thomas Devlin Mfg. Co., Philadelphia.
DORT, J. H., President Durant-Dort Carriage Co., Flint, Mich.
DYER, W. A., Treasurer The Smith-Premier Typewriter Co., Syracuse, N. Y.
EASTMAN, F. E., Eastman Brothers & Bancroft, Portland, Me.
EASLEY, RALPH M., Chairman Executive Council, The National Civic Federation, New York City.
EDWARDS, O. M., The O. M. Edwards Co., Syracuse, N. Y.
ELDER, GEORGE R., Vice-President The Ingersoll-Sergeant Drill Co., Easton, Pa.
ELDRIDGE, CHAUNCEY, Tucker, Anthony & Co., Boston, Mass.
ELLIS CHARLES, President Mutual Fertilizer Co., Savannah, Ga.
FAIRBANKS, H. W., President Sherman Mfg. Co., Sherman, Tex.
FARNSWORTH, JOHN P., Treasurer Providence Dyeing, Bleaching & Calendering Co., Providence, R. I.
FERRAND, WILLIAM R., General Manager The Ferrand Co., Detroit, Mich.
FAY, C. N., President Fay-Sholes Co., Chicago, Ill.
FELS, MAURICE, Fels & Co., Philadelphia.
FIELD, W. B., The L. H. Field Co., Jackson, Mich.

Room for Women Workers, Lunch House, General Electric Company, Schenectady, N. Y.

FISH, FREDERICK P., American Telephone & Telegraph Co., Boston, Mass.
FLETCHER, FREDERICK C., Treasurer Pocasset Worsted Co., Boston, Mass.
FLATHER, FREDERICK A., Treasurer Boott Mills, Boston, Mass.
FORBES, W. S., The Forbes Lithograph Mfg. Co., Boston, Mass.
FORD, J. H., Secretary The Alaska Refrigerator Co., Muskegon, Mich.
FULLER, ARTHUR A., Providence Engineering Works, Providence, R. I.
GEROW, JAMES W., Chairman The United Cigarette Machine Co., Ltd., Lynchburg, Va.
GILBERT, ARTHUR E., General Manager Red Cliff Lumber Co., Superior, Wis.

GRAVES, H. B., H. B. Graves' Home-Furnishing House, Rochester, N. Y.
GRAVES, H. B., Treasurer The Standard Optical Co., Geneva, N. Y.
GREENHUT, J. B., President Siegel-Cooper Co., New York City.
GREEN, R. O., Secretary Green-Wheeler Shoe Co., Fort Dodge, Ia.
GUTHRIE, HON. GEO. W., The Mayor, Pittsburg, Pa.
HANCHETT, BENJAMIN S., Treasurer Grand Rapids Railway Co., Grand Rapids, Mich.
HALL, LUCIEN B., Boston, Hall & Co., Cleveland, O.
HARRIES, GENERAL GEO. H., Vice-President Washington Railway & Electric Co., Washington, D. C.
HART, H. GILBERT, President Hart & Crouse Co., Utica, N. Y.
HAYES, HON. EVERIS A., Proprietor "San Jose Daily Morning Mercury," San Jose, Cal.
HEYBURN, HON. WELDON B., Wallace, Idaho.
HIBBARD, A. S., General Manager Chicago Telephone Co., Chicago, Ill.
HILKER, W. F., Vice-President The Hilker-Wiechers Mfg. Co., Racine, Wis.
HILL, HON. EBENEZER J., U. S. Representative, Vice-President Norwalk Mills Co., Norwalk, Conn.
HOCHSCHILD, M., President Hochschild, Kohn & Co., Baltimore, Md.
HOLMES, G. F., Treasurer Plymouth Cordage Co., North Plymouth, Mass.
HORNBERGER, JOHN B. L., Comptroller, Pittsburg Coal Co., Pittsburg, Pa.
HUTCHINS, J. C., President Detroit United Railway, Detroit, Mich.
INGALLS, HON. MELVILLE E., Chairman Executive Board, C., C., C. & St. L. Railway Co., Cincinnati, O.
JAMES, DR. D. N., Vice-President La Mont Chemical Co., Kane, Pa.
JONES, L. M., President Jones Dry Goods Co., Kansas City, Mo.
KELLER, E. E., Vice-President The Westinghouse Machine Co., East Pittsburg, Pa.
KILBOURNE, JAMES, President Kilbourne & Jacobs Mfg. Co., Columbus, O.
KING, D., Treasurer Eureka Silk Mfg. Co., Boston, Mass.
LAYCOCK, THOMAS B., Treasurer The T. B. Laycock Mfg. Co., Indianapolis, Ind.
LEONARD, CHARLES H., President Grand Rapids Refrigerator Co., Grand Rapids, Mich.
LITTLE, ALEXANDER E., A. E. Little & Co., Lynn, Mass.
LIVERIGHT, ARTHUR K., Liveright Bros., Philadelphia, Pa.
LOCKWOOD, W. N., Treasurer Davidson Rubber Co., Boston, Mass.
LOGAN, JAMES, Chairman Executive Committee, U. S. Envelope Co., Worcester, Mass.
LUDINGTON, JR., C. H., Treasurer The Curtis Publishing Co., Philadelphia, Pa.
LYALL, WILLIAM L., Treasurer Brighton Mills, Passaic, N. J.
McINNERNEY, T. H., Duffy-McInnerney Co., Rochester, N. Y.
MACY, V. EVERIT, Capitalist, New York City.
MATHER, SAMUEL, Pickands, Mather Co., Cleveland, O.
MILES, H. E., President Racine Satley Co., Racine, Wis.
MILLER, IRA M., Treasurer The Aultman & Miller Buckeye Co., Akron, O.

Lunch Room, Wood Mill, American Woolen Company, Lawrence, Mass., Recently Planned by Miss Mary Thaon, Agent of the Welfare Department of the National Civic Federation.

MILLER, WILLIAM, Henry Disston & Sons, Philadelphia, Pa.
MOORE, A. L., Moline Wagon Co., Moline, Ill.
MORRIS, MOSES, Morris & Co., Baltimore, Md.
MORRIS, STEPHEN, Secretary Merritt & Co., Philadelphia, Pa.
MORRISON, V. E., President The Morrison Mfg. Co., Fort Madison, Ia.
MORSE, EVERETT, President The Simplex Electrical Co., Boston, Mass.
MOULTON, W. H., Cleveland-Cliffs Iron Co., Ishpeming, Mich.
NASH, L. R., Stone & Webster, Boston, Mass.
NICHOLS, JOHN W. T., Minot, Hooper & Co., New York City.
OSBORNE, EDMUND B., President American Colortype Co., New York City.
PAGE, CHARLES T., Page Belting Co., Concord, N. H.
PARKER, F. E., Treasurer Mershon, Schuette, Parker & Co., Saginaw, Mich.
PARSONS, H. B., Vice-President Wells, Fargo & Co., New York City.
PASS, JAMES, General Manager Onondaga Pottery Co., Syracuse, N. Y.
PATTON, LUDINGTON, Treasurer Patton Paint Co., Milwaukee, Wis.
PERKINS, JAMES T., Pillsbury-Washburn Flour Mills Co., Ltd., Minneapolis, Minn.
POTTER, M. A., Treasurer E. C. Atkins & Co., Indianapolis, Ind.
POUCH, W. H., Vice-President Orange County Traction Co., Newburg, N. Y.
POWER, P. W., Manager Stanley Electric Mfg. Co., Pittsfield, Mass.
PRATT, EDWARD G., General Manager Milwaukee Gas Light Co., Milwaukee, Wis.
PRATT, W. M., Treasurer Goodell-Pratt Co., Greenfield, Mass.
PROUT, H. G., Vice-President The Union Switch & Signal Co., Swissvale, Pa.
REIDHEAD, F. E., Manager Columbus Railroad Co., Columbus, Ga.
RICHARDS, J. L., President Boston Consolidated Gas Co., Boston, Mass.
RICHARDSON, W. H., Riegel Sack Co., Jersey City, N. J.
RICKER, B. J., Morrison, McIntosh & Co., Grinnell, Ia.
ROBBINS, FRANCIS L., President Monongahela River Consolidated Coal & Coke Co., Pittsburg, Pa.
ROBINSON, J. D., Treasurer The Libbey Glass Co., Toledo, O.
ROCKWELL, CHAS. B., Treasurer Cranston Worsted Mills, Bristol, R. I.
ROOD, CHARLES D., President Hamilton Watch Co., Lancaster, Pa.
SARGENT, JAMES T., General Manager The American Washboard Co., Cleveland, O.
SCALES, JR., W. W., Secretary John M. Stone Cotton Mills, Starkville, Miss.

SCOTT, E. L., Sears, Roebuck & Co., Dallas, Tex.
SEIBERLING, F. A., General Manager The Goodyear Tire & Rubber Co., Akron, O.
SELBY, GEORGE D., President The Drew-Selby Co., Portsmouth, O.
SELIG, A. L., General Manager The Edison Electric Co., Los Angeles, Cal.
SHANTZ, M. B., Button Manufacturer, Rochester, N. Y.
SHORROCK, E., President Northwest Trust & Safe Deposit Co., Seattle, Wash.
SLINGERLAND, G. W., General Superintendent American Express Co., New York City.
SMITH, FREDERICK B., President Wolverine Mfg. Co., President Cadillac Cabinet Co., Detroit, Mich.
SMITH, H. G., Fore River Ship-Building Co., Quincy, Mass.

Emergency Hospital Recently Installed at General Electric Works, Schenectady, N. Y., by G. E. Emmons, Manager, who is a Member of the Welfare Department.

SMITH, IRVING, President The Crescent Watch Case Co., New York City.
SNOW, FRANKLIN E., Treasurer Wells Bros. Co., Greenfield, Mass.
SNOW, W. B., B. F. Sturtevant Co., Hyde Park, Mass.
SPINNEY, FRANK C., Faunce & Spinney, Lynn, Mass.
STARK, O. L. M., Secretary North American Watch Co., Mansfield, O.
STEARNS, E. C., President E. C. Stearns & Co., Syracuse, N. Y.
STEARNS, WAYLAND D., Frederick Stearns & Co., Detroit, Mich.
STOLLWERCK, A. N., Stollwerck Bros., New York City.
STUART, J. C., General Manager Erie Railroad Co., New York City.
STUDLEY, R. L., Goodhue, Studley & Emery, Boston, Mass.
TAYLOR, G. E., President Taylor Bros. Co., Rochester, N. Y.
TAYLOR, J. G., President The Taylor-Burt Co., Holyoke, Mass.
TENNEY, A. B., General Manager Malden & Melrose Gas Light Co., Malden, Mass.
TITSWORTH, D. E., Secretary Potter Printing Press Co., Plainfield, N. J.
TOWNE, F. B., Treasurer National Blank Book Co., Holyoke, Mass.
TREANOR, P. C. J., Woodward & Lothrop, Washington, D. C.
TUFTS, LEONARD, American Soda Fountain Co., Boston, Mass.
VOPICKA, CHARLES J., Atlas Brewing Co., Chicago, Ill.
VREELAND, HON. EDWARD B., U. S. Representative, Vice-President Salamanca Trust Co., Salamanca, N. Y.
WALKER, A. W., President Walker & Pratt Mfg. Co., Boston, Mass.
WALLACE, F. A., President R. Wallace & Sons Mfg. Co., Wallingford, Conn.
WALLIN, V. A., Treasurer Wallin Leather Co., Grand Rapids, Mich.
WARREN, WM. C., S. L. Allen & Co., Philadelphia, Pa.
WELLS, F. O., President Wells Bros. Co., Greenfield, Mass.
WESTERVELT, J. I., President Brandon Mills, Greenville, S. C.
WESTON, EDWARD F., Secretary Weston Electrical Instrument Co., Waverley Park, Newark, N. J.
WHITING, J. H., President Whiting Foundry Equipment Co., Harvey, Ill.
WHITTAKER, BENJAMIN, Treasurer J. H. Williams & Co., Brooklyn, N. Y.
WILKINSON, MELVILLE L., President The William Hengerer Co., Buffalo, N. Y.
WILLCOX, HON. WM. R., Chairman Public Service Commission, New York City.
WILLIAMS, ROGER H., Treasurer The Eaton, Cole & Burnham Co., New York City.

Interior View Lunch House, General Electric Company, Schenectady, N. Y. (The Welfare Department Was Called Into Consultation in Planning These Arrangements.

WILLIAMSON, WILLIAM H., James N. & W. H. Williamson, Raleigh, N. C.
WITHINGTON, P. H., President Withington & Cooley Mfg. Co., Jackson, Mich.
WOOD, E. N., The Denver Dry Goods Co., Denver, Col.
WOODBURY, C. J. H., American Telephone & Telegraph Co., Boston, Mass.
WOODS, FRANK F., Treasurer S. A. Woods Machine Co., Boston, Mass.
YOUNG, WILBER H., President Austin Electric Railway Co., Austin, Tex.

The National
Civic Federation Review

Vol. III. NEW YORK, FEBRUARY, 1908. No. 3

A RECORD OF LARGE UNDERTAKINGS

THE EIGHTH ANNUAL MEETING OF THE NATIONAL CIVIC FEDERATION TERMINATES A YEAR OF ACTIVE EFFORT—A SUMMARY OF ACHIEVEMENT.

PROBLEMS of vital interest to the public welfare, the savings of the people and the prevention of strikes and lockouts, authoritatively discussed by the highest authorities in this country, and a brilliant banquet of nearly eight hundred guests, enlivened by speakers of national reputation, combined to render the eighth annual meeting of the National Civic Federation, held December 16-17, 1907, even more successful than its predecessors. The characteristic note of the activities of the National Civic Federation, the furtherance of mutual interests of capital and labor, revealed itself in all the meetings. As in previous gatherings, a successful effort was made through a careful choice of topics to maintain an open and free discussion from a broad and catholic standpoint, giving equal opportunities for the presentation of the views of all sides.

The discussions which followed the presentation of formal subjects were extremely animated and pointed, betokening a lively interest in the matters before the meeting. Other incidents of general interest were the passage of a resolution on the subject of elastic currency and the election of the Hon. Seth Low as president of the National Civic Federation, in succession to Mr. August Belmont.

"The Protection of the People's Savings," the topic for the first day's discussion, presented two highly important aspects of the banking problem. The morning session was devoted to an argument in favor of such reform of our currency system as should insure the safety of deposits by preventing abnormal and unusual demands upon banks in times of emergency and stress. Among the speakers who

CURRENCY SESSION OF THE FEDERATION'S ANNUAL MEETING.

1. ANDREW CARNEGIE. 2. GRANGE SARD. 3. L. E. HOLDEN. 4. HORACE WHITE. 5. VICTOR MORAWETZ. 6. JOHN MITCHELL. 7. THEODORE MARBURG. 8. ISAAC N. SELIGMAN. 9. JAMES SPEYER.

contributed to the discussion of this subject were: Messrs. James Speyer, Andrew Carnegie, Victor Morawetz, Theodore Marburg, David G. Evans, Horace White and Alfred O. Crozier. The afternoon session was devoted to a presentation of the safeguards which are, or may be, thrown about savings deposits with the view to encouraging thrift and preventing the hoarding of the money of the nation. This involved a discussion of Postal Savings Banks, Mutual Savings Banks and Building and Loan Associations and other agencies designed to gather into a commercial force the small savings of the many and make them available in industry and in commerce. Postmaster General Meyer, Mr. Andrew Mills, Mr. Myron T. Herrick, Mr. James H. Hamilton and Mr. Edwin F. Howell addressed the meeting on several phases of this question.

The second day's sessions were devoted to the subject of "Compulsory Arbitration." The Canadian Industrial Disputes Investigation Act was presented by Mr. S. L. Landers and Mr. G. M. Murray, while the experiences of New Zealand were portrayed by Mr. Hugh H. Lusk. The compulsory features of both laws were sharply criticised by Mr. Samuel Gompers. Mr. Otto M. Eidlitz, Mr. Daniel Keefe, Mr. John Lundrigan, Mr. Rezin Orr and Mr. August Belmont discussed various aspects of voluntary as opposed to compulsory arbitration.

The crowning glory of the meeting was the banquet at the Hotel Astor, attended by nearly eight hundred guests, who enjoyed the presentation of a number of topics of present day social and economic interest in the words of forceful and competent authorities. Gen. F. D. Grant spoke on the "Army Canteen," Mr. John Mitchell on the "Mutual Relations of Capital and Labor," Mr. George W. Perkins on the "Profit Sharing Plan of the United States Steel Corporation," and President Charles W. Eliot upon the "Canadian Labor Legislation, and the Need of Additional Power in the National Government to Cope with Modern Problems." Mr. Samuel Gompers closed the evening's discussion with a forceful statement of the position of labor in the present industrial situation and the purposes, aspirations and achievements of the labor unions.

Too much credit cannot be given to the Committee on Arrangements for the success of the banquet. The committee was as follows:

Marcus M. Marks, Chairman, President National [illegible]ion of Clothiers.
[illegible]verit Macy, Treasurer, Capitalist.
[illegible] Root, Jr., Attorney-at-Law.
[illegible]les F. Delaney, Granite Cutters' Union.
[illegible] John Bancroft Devins, Editor "The New York Observer."
Timothy Healy, President International Brotherhood of Stationery Firemen.
Marcellus H. Dodge, Treasurer M. H. Dodge & Co.
Melville E. Ingalls, Jr., Attorney-at-Law.
Edward Gould, President Teamsters' Joint Council.
Charles A. Moore, Jr., Manning, Maxwell & Moore.
Lawrence F. Abbott, President The Outlook Company.
William H. Taylor, President the St. Clair Coal Company.
Louis P. Schram, United Association of Brewers.
C. U. Carpenter, President Herring-Hall-Marvin Safe Company.
Henry C. Hunter, Secretary Metal Trades Association.
William Fyfe, Amalgamated Carpenters' Union.
Hamilton Holt, Editor of the "Independent."
August Belmont, Jr., August Belmont & Co.
Samuel B. Donnelly, Secretary Building Trades Employers' Association.
Robert E. Simon, Henry Morgenthau & Company.
Edward A. Moffett, Bricklayers and Masons' Union.
T. C. Martin, Editor "Electrical World and Engineer."
Henry C. Watson, Editor Dun's "Review."

The unanimity of opinion which was expressed with regard to the need for an elastic currency led Mr. Isaac N. Seligman to introduce a resolution presenting, in general terms, the approval of the National Civic Federation for the plan of an elastic currency and urging that Congress take some action in the matter. The resolution was referred to a sub-committee consisting of Messrs. Horace White, chairman; N. J. Bachelder, Samuel Gompers, Isaac N. Seligman and Franklin MacVeagh. The introduction of the resolution led to a vigorous protest, lest the Federation by such resolution should commit itself to the scheme of elastic currency issued by the banks. The belief was expressed that the issue of money was strictly a function of government and should not be delegated to banking corporations. When, therefore, the Committee on Currency, through its chairman, Mr. Horace White, presented a memorial and resolution favoring in express words the establishment of an elastic currency through bank issues, based upon assets, the report was not received with unanimous approval. At a later stage of the conference, the report was withdrawn and the original resolution introduced by Mr. Seligman placed before the conference for action. An effort to secure the addition of a proviso to the effect "that the power to expand and contract the volume of currency should be exclusively exercised by the Federal Government and not by banks, clearing houses or private parties," was unsuccessful after it had been pointed out that the purpose of the resolution was simply to endorse the principle of elasticity, but neither to approve nor disapprove of any specific plan to attain that result. The conference thereupon adopted the following resolution:

"WHEREAS, the present financial crisis and the consequent distress has emphatically demonstrated the necessity of some remedial action by Congress as to our currency system;

BE IT RESOLVED, That the National Civic Federation without committing itself specifically to any of the many plans of currency reform, content itself with the declaration that Congress should, after careful consideration, pass as speedily as possible, consistent with security and safety, some measure which will impart to our currency system greater elasticity, so urgently demanded throughout the country."

At an early hour of the session the announcement was made of the appointment of a Nominating Committee, consisting of the following members:

For the Public—V. Everit Macy, New York; Dr. Albert Shaw, New York; Archbishop John Ireland, Minnesota; John M. Stahl, Illinois.

For Employers—Henry Phipps, New York; Franklin MacVeagh, Illinois; Samuel Mather, Ohio; Marcus M. Marks, New York.

For Wage Earners—John Mitchell, Indiana; Daniel J. Keefe, Michigan; James O'Connell, District of Columbia; P. H. Morrissey, Ohio.

The chairman of the committee, before presenting the report, read a letter addressed to Mr. Easley by Mr. August Belmont, expressing his wish to retire from the presidency of the Federation. The letter is as follows:

44 East 34th Street, New York.
December 16, 1907.

R. M. EASLEY, ESQ., Chairman Executive Council,
National Civic Federation.

My Dear Sir:—I am asking with this letter that you request the Committee on Nominations that my name be not considered for the office of president of the Federation, because it will be impossible for me to serve another term.

No work that I have ever been associated with has been nearer to my heart and ideals, but the executive duties of my business compel me to ask relief from an office I prized above all others, but which I cannot fill to do justice to its important requirements.

In retiring, I wish to thank my associates for their loyal support and the unbroken friendly relations that have existed between us during my four years of service. And, as to you, Mr. Easley, I owe a special debt of gratitude for your unremitting labor in promoting the interests of our organization.

I will be none the less interested in the work serving in the ranks, and pledge my loyalty to its future. I remain, yours very truly,

(Signed) AUGUST BELMONT.

The committee then presented as its report the names of the following gentlemen as the officers of the Federation for the ensuing year:

Seth Low, President.
Samuel Gompers, Vice-president.
Nahum J. Bachelder, Vice-president.
Ellison A. Smyth, Vice-president.
Benjamin I. Wheeler, Vice-president.
Isaac N. Seligman, Treasurer.
Victor Morawetz, Chairman finance committee.
John Mitchell, Chairman trade agreement committee.
Charles A. Moore, Chairman welfare department.
Seth Low, ex-officio Chairman conciliation committee.
Franklin MacVeagh, Chairman immigration department.
Ralph M. Easley, Chairman executive council.
William H. Taft, Chairman public employees welfare committee.
Nicholas Murray Butler, Chairman industrial economics department.
Melville E. Ingalls, Chairman public ownership commission.
D. L. Cease, Secretary.

They were unanimously elected.

Mr. Seth Low, on taking the chair, said that he appreciated very highly the honor conferred upon him, that the election carried with it a very unique compliment as a mark of confidence of the several elements represented in the Federation. He said: "I think we must all approach this labor question, as it is called, the question of adjusting the diverse interests involved in it, with some modesty. I used to say at Columbia to the professors, that when they ceased to learn they should certainly cease to teach. It is equally true that all of us who have to deal with this question realize, the more we know, how little we know, and that we must be willing to learn. That is the spirit with which I shall take up the work that you have asked me to assume. Progress has been made in the solution of the problems which have arisen. We have reason to felicitate ourselves as we reflect upon how much progress has been made. The number of employers to-day who are willing to consider jointly with their men and with the organizations that represent their men, the terms upon which the details of their business are to be conducted so far as they influence the employment of wage earners, is very much greater than it used to be, and the number, I think, it greater every year. It is the business of this organization to do all that it can to stimulate that movement.

"We believe in the trade agreement; we believe in arbitration; we believe that there may be a time when a strike is justified; we believe that there may be a time when a lockout is justified; we believe in approaching every definite problem with the best wisdom that we have, and we believe in the wisdom, above all others, in trying to bring together in mutual consideration the diverse interests that have to be harmonized. It is a very great pleasure to me in accepting this nomination to express my high appreciation of the work that has been done by my two predecessors in this office, the late Senator Hanna and Mr. Belmont. I appreciate that each in his own way has set a standard that it will be very hard to live up to. I can only assure Mr. Belmont, in taking the chair which he has resigned, that I shall do the very best I can, and would like to ask for myself a full measure of that co-operation which we have all tried to extend to him."

The motion was then made and carried that the chair appoint a committee of three to draft a suitable set of resolutions to be presented to the retiring president, Mr. August Belmont. Mr. D. L. Cease, the newly elected secretary of the Federation, returned his thanks and spoke briefly of the service which had been rendered to the Brotherhood of Railway Trainmen through the Civic Federation. The chair announced the appointment of Messrs. Keefe, Crozier and Seligman, as the committee to draft and present the resolutions to Mr. Belmont. Call was then made for Mr. Gompers, who made a characteristic speech, and paid a high tribute to the energy and activity of Mr. Easley. He said:

I do not believe that ever was there a gathering brought about such as was assembled last evening, so many people representing so many diverse interests and walks in life, listening to the discussion of great problems. It bodes good for us. I believe in the good, red blood of manhood, that, as we progress, we see more clearly not only our rights, but our corresponding duties. Every time that the people understand better the rights to which they are entitled and have the manhood to stand for them—we may get a little bruised, but there comes from it a better and more enlightened manhood—a better citizenship.

AN ELASTIC CURRENCY

LESSONS OF THE RECENT PANIC—FLEXIBILITY IN CURRENCY WILL MITIGATE FINANCIAL DISTURBANCE—HOW IT CAN BE OBTAINED.

THE general topic for consideration in the opening session was that of Currency Reform. In the absence of President Belmont, First Vice-President Samuel Gompers called the meeting to order. He read a communication from Mr. Belmont and introduced Mr. James Speyer as the chairman for the day.

AUGUST BELMONT regretted that out of town engagements prevented his attending the morning session, and wrote that in a general way he endorsed the recommendations made by Mr. Hepburn last year for a flexible currency. "But," he continues, "whatever method may be adopted to supply the elastic element in our currency system, there

EXECUTIVE COUNCIL OF THE NATIONAL CIVIC FEDERATION.

will remain, if not corrected, a disturbing element to the stability of the money market by reason of the present legal restrictions and limitations placed upon the authority vested in the United States Treasury for placing this money on deposit in the banks. Why should not the Government deposit all its funds not absolutely needed in its Treasury without collateral and protected by the same security that surrounds the ordinary depositor in the national bank?

"Were the Treasury empowered to deposit all its funds in the national banks in its discretion, but regulated by way of precautionary restrictions, according to the capital and surplus of the institutions selected, and at a rate of interest to be prescribed by law, of, say, 2 per cent., such accumulated interest to be set aside in a permanent fund to cover any possible losses as might occur through insolvent depositories, the possible losses would be protected more than twenty-four times over. The losses to depositors in the national bank have not been more than one-twelfth of 1 per cent. annually.

"The Government has an added security as a depositor, by reason of the fact that through its properly constituted officers it has absolute supervision over any of the banks that it chooses to select as depositories. How inconsistent, therefore, is the recent appeal of our Chief Executive, of our public men and bodies in general, that the people should have confidence in the banks and leave their money in their custody, while at that very moment the Government was exacting for its deposits the very cream of the securities our national banks were able to produce as collateral.

JAMES SPEYER on taking the chair at the morning session called attention to the widespread interest in the questions of banking and currency, which had been awakened by the recent financial panic. Continuing, he said:

"An old friend of this Federation said to me the other day, 'No two panics are alike!' This is certainly true, but traced to its ultimate cause this panic, like any other panic, is due to disturbed confidence. To maintain the normal credit necessary for all business and industrial prosperity confidence must not be disturbed by too much governmental activity or interference. The people must have confidence in those at the head of large corporations occupying responsible positions of trust. They must not be disturbed by legislative or other attacks on corporations in whose securities they have invested their savings.

"People must have confidence in each other, and, what is more important, they must have confidence in themselves and their own judgment. When confidence is impaired every one makes an effort to strengthen reserves and resources, to put his money where he thinks it would not depreciate, and where he can put his hand on it. At such a time, when confidence is disturbed, a good and elastic currency will minimize the danger and restore things quickly to a normal basis, while an insufficient and unelastic currency system aggravates the shock. It is then that a great majority of people suddenly awaken to the realization of what they have been told by experts over and over again, that compared with other nations they are laboring under very great disadvantage, that our currency system is not what it should be. Public opinion is now generally aroused and should insist upon Congressional action. The right kind of circulating medium is just as important to the farmer and the workman as it is to the mine owner, the merchant and the banker. The wishes and needs of all classes must be fully considered to arrive at a correct solution.

"It is only a few years ago that the American people settled definitely the most important question in connection with the currency, namely—that the standard of value should be gold, and, personally, I have no doubt, with common sense and with a spirit of fairness and with a desire to subordinate personal preference and prejudice to the common good, we will ere long resolve this question of a proper and elastic circulating medium based on the gold standard; but time is money, and the longer we wait the more it is going to cost all of us. In competing in the markets of the world not only must every producer have the best implements and the best tools, but commerce itself needs the best tools, that is to say, the best form of currency adapted to our needs. Not until we get such a system will the people of the United States take the place amongst the nations of the world to which the wealth of the country, their energy and industry justly entitle them.

ANDREW CARNEGIE stated that our currency system having had a great shock innumerable doctors and quacks were rushing to its relief, some of them with remedies that reminded him of the quack who sold pills warranted to cure earthquakes.

"Let us dismiss from our minds," he said, "the idea that there is any cure possible for financial troubles and panics. They have their root in human nature and are as certain as the tides or the storms or the change from Summer to Winter. They are just as essential for the regulation, clearance and purification of business as are climatic changes for the general health of human life. Prosperity is bound to stretch the lines beyond the breaking point, and dull times are needed to restore them. Let us, therefore, dismiss all panaceas for panics such as we have just experienced, and which was due several years ago, though delayed by an unequaled succession of good crops and strong demands for our products abroad.

"The point that demands attention is that our banking system is unlike that of other countries. Japan tried it, but had the good sense to abandon it, as we shall do some day. The complete change we need is the substitution of gold for our reserves, and currency based upon assets, instead of upon government debt, the false foundation upon which we have built.

'The currency question will never down until it is founded upon correct principles. If there be anything established it is that it should be based upon the assets, viz, trade bills which expand and contract as business does, the reserves being in gold. But this does not seem to be the proper time to urge so great a change as this implies. Congress is in a mood to listen to those who understand banking and currency and to legislate somewhat in accordance with their views. Our first effort should be to get legislation turned from the wrong to the right path by introducing to some extent asset currency. As the people see the advantages of this system we may hope to enlarge its use and gradually to abandon bond security.

"By that means we can substitute gold in our reserves for government evidences of debt and obtain the most profitable form of banking, as proven by the experience of other countries, especially of Scotland. That little country had 1,065 banks in 1902, bringing banking facilities to every village in the land and extending to its small customers these facilities on as favorable terms as to the millionaire in the metropolis. If our farmers and small traders generally knew how much they would be benefited by the Scotch system, we should encounter little delay in Washington.

"Other countries have elasticity of issue of bank notes. We have none. Our system is rigid. This may be illustrated by one elevator which has only the hard rock floor below it, which in its fall is smashed and the passengers injured or killed, and another which, striking a safety air cushion, allows the weight to drop slowly down and avoid serious consequences.

"If our banks had an expanding and a contracting elastic cushion below them, such as banks in any other lands, they would avoid the violent and disastrous shock to which they are now suddenly subjected in the periods of financial distress. In other words, our banks would have it in their power to issue a certain percentage of emergency currency—the soft, pliable cushion, which would break the blow and, as a rule, prevent the loss of confidence that precipitates panic.

"Please note that after the cushion has once served its purpose and been crushed, it must again be filled and put in place exactly as before, prepared to receive and soften the next pressure that falls upon it. So with emergency bank notes. Take one illustration: Every time the crops have to be moved between two and three millions of additional currency are required for this special purpose. Our banks have no power of expansion, and yet, here at hand is an automatic device which would adjust itself without the slightest strain to the task. More than this, our neighbor Canada has proportionately the same demand and is using this device successfully, while our go-ahead country lags behind. European nations all have it.

"Mr. Fowler has shown that our present discreditable banking system involves a loss of at least one hundred and fifty millions of dollars per year from the unusual requirement that currency be secured by Government 2 per cent. bonds costing par. The purchase of these bonds withdraws money from actual banking facilities. Other nations secure their note issues without lessening the banks' power to meet business demands. They make currency notes the first lien upon all other assets, and as banks cannot issue such notes to an amount exceeding their capital, loss by note holders is unknown. Our Government could exact a fund from banks ample to secure the currency, as the two bills now before the country suggest, upon emergency notes. It is estimated that less than one-half of 1 per cent. would be ample, so small is the risk. Our backwardness in this department may be due to prevailing prejudices inherited from the past. They should be overcome. The Civic Federation, representing as it does both labor and capital, is especially fitted to perform a great service here. It is not creditable to our country, foremost in many departments of human activity as it is, that such an old-fashioned, rickety piece of antiquated machinery as our present currency system should be exhibited to the world.

VICTOR MORAWETZ, Chairman Executive Board of the Atchison, Topeka & Santa Fe Railway Company, spoke of the need in a progressive country like ours for a very considerable expansion of bank credits to meet the requirements of business and enterprise.

Recent experience has shown that while the minimum reserves required under the National Banking Act are sufficient in ordinary times they are not sufficient at all times. Bank credits can be kept within the limit of safety and be adjusted to meet the necessities of exceptional conditions only by vesting in some competent authority charged with the supervision of the entire credit situation a power to force a contraction of credit or to allow an expansion when necessary. In England this control is exercised by the Bank of England, by increasing or lowering the rate of interest which it charges on loans and discounts, thereby increasing or reducing the reserves of the bank against its deposit liabilities. In France and Germany the control of the credit situation is exercised by large central banks, through the issue of bank notes, which, however, maintain very large reserves, the Bank of France sometimes keeping a reserve of 75 per cent. and the Imperial Bank of Germany a reserve of 50 per cent.

There is probably no country in the world where the volume of currency in circulation and the demand for bank loans and credits fluctuates more widely than in the United States. The great expanse of country, the annual requirements of the harvest season, the prevailing business activity and enterprise, the rapid and unequal increase of population and business in different sections contribute to this result. There is no country in the world where intelligent control over bank credits and bank reserves is more needed than in the United States, and there is none where it is more conspicuously absent. Each of our six thousand national banks, besides State banks and trust companies, acts in its individual interests independently of the others, with a tendency to expand credits at all times to the limit permitted by law. The establishment of a large central bank, clothed with the necessary duties and powers to supervise and control the credit situation, would not be practical or desirable in the United States.

The beneficial results of a large central bank would be obtained by an association of the national banks in the nature of a large clearing house association, for the purpose of enabling each member of the association to issue notes for the joint credit of the associated banks, depositing a proper cash reserve for the redemption of the notes and securities for the difference between the amount of the issue and the reserve deposited. The minimum reserve should be kept at at least 25 per cent. of the notes, but the managing board should have power from time to time to increase this percentage. The Government should have control over the notes issued by authorizing the Secretary of the Treasury to increase the percentage of the reserves to be kept by the banks. The Government, through the Secretary of the Treasury or the managing board of the joint issue department, representing the judgment of the bankers throughout the country, could at any time force the contraction of outstanding notes and of bank credits generally by requiring an increase of the note redemption fund. To regulate from time to time the percentage of reserve would be the great function of the board of managers. By so doing the board could, to some extent, regulate and equalize the prevailing rate of interest and hinder the export of gold when this is threatened by temporary redundancy of bank reserves.

The plan provides intelligent control over the credit situation through a board of leading bankers under Government supervision and control. It provides a really elastic system of notes with proper reserves. It would avoid the political danger inherent in any plan under which the Government is to lend its credit to the bank. Having regard to the uncertainty of politics and the financial heresies which have prevailed and still prevail in various sections of the country, any expansion of the present system of issuing bond notes upon the credit of the Government would set a very dangerous precedent and probably result in many future schemes for the inflation of the currency.

THEODORE MARBURG, of Baltimore, dealt with the question, "Do we want an asset currency?" The present crisis is largely a question of credit. Industry on its present scale cannot proceed without the aid of credit: Men would want bread while waiting for the products of their labor to be finished and exchanged. However intangible, credit is based upon two very substantial things, capital and money. It is capital that is loaned, but the bank is the agent and money is the language, and to a great extent the the instrument of the loan. The element of flexibility in our currency would have modified undoubtedly the autumn crisis each year, but there is no assurance that even such a salutary expedient would have entirely prevented the crisis. Any device which would have provided a large permanent increase in the currency, other than that based on the money metal, would probably have launched us in the midst of the wildest speculation.

In the consideration of the currency question we must protect the money basis. Gold is at present the money stuff of practically the civilized world and no prominent commercial country can afford to adopt any other than gold as its money basis. Our national bank note, based upon government bonds, is credit currency, and so long as the national bank currency is not too large a proportion of our whole circulation we run no serious risk in continuing the system. United States notes, likewise credit currency, are more dangerous because they offer a temptation to the national legislature to provide funds in an emergency by inflation pure and simple.

A rich country can have its share of gold, and will have just as much gold as its system calls for and no more. The bank note currency passes as money, takes the place of money, and releases so much gold from service. Unless it be taxed to a point where it is unprofitable to keep it in circulation, in ordinary times asset currency is among the devices which must be characterized as dangerous.

Is the experience of other countries conclusive? Canada is cited as an instance, but apart from the fact that the amount of Canadian money as compared with ours is so insignificant, and its trade so small that its experience would be of little value, it may be noted that the supply of gold and silver in the United States was three and three-quarter times as great as the uncovered paper, while in Canada it was less than the paper. If we consult European experience we find the stock of gold and silver in Germany four and three-quarters times as great as the uncovered paper, and in France and the United Kingdom each five times as great as the uncovered paper. To all of this the advocates of an asset curreney in the United States may reply, "What do we want with so much gold anyway; asset currency is cheaper?" Our answer must be that in a country with such a spirit of enterprise, not to say tendency of speculation, as the United States none but the best money is good enough. An abundant supply of gold is in itself an element of national strength. We want safety and uniformity, not only in ordinary times but in extraordinary times, in times of stress and trial. Asset currency would undoubtedly introduce a much needed element of elasticity into our system, but is it the only way or the best way to attain this object? Most of the plans before the country fail to tax the proposed issues heavily enough to cause them to be withdrawn in ordinary times. Making no adequate provision for contraction, they threaten a permanent addition to the currency and a loss in our gold holdings.

DAVID G. EVANS, of New York, presented briefly the plan of securing the deposits in national banks by having the Government act as a trustee of fund formed by the national banks to guarantee such deposits. He proposed that the national banks be taxed about one-twentieth of 1 per cent. of the average deposits to form a fund to be placed in the hands of the United States Treasury Department, under the supervision of the Comptroller of the Currency, which fund should be used to reimburse the national bank depositors in case of the failure of a national bank.

Its underlying idea is that most of the people in the country believe that at present the Government is behind the national banks. When they fail, and the people find that the Government is not behind them, there is disappointment and distrust of the entire system. People familiar with human nature know that when a dark cloud begins to hover over our financial system the people will seek to take their money out of the bank, but if they know that the Government is really behind the banks—our great national Government, with absolutely no politics in this matter—they would not want their money This is human nature. You tell a man he can have it and he doesn't want it.

HORACE WHITE, replying to the arguments of Mr. Evans, stated that, apart from the large deposits in State banks, trust companies, savings banks and in private banks, there were recently in the national banks deposits to the amount of $4,200,000,000. Therefore, the proposition amounts to this, that the United States Government shall assume a demand liability of $4,200,000,000. All the banks in the world could not meet such a demand. It is said that if the Government was behind the banks the people wauld not want their money. Now, in 1893, that is just exactly what they did. Beginning in August, 1893, they continued it for nearly four years. Just as fast as the Government could negotiate a loan they would take their money away, and they continued the run until the Government had paid out $183,000,000 of gold over the counter.

Moreover, such a guarantee on deposits would be a premium on recklessness in banking, for it would relieve depositors from the need of discrimination in the choice of banks in which to make their deposits. The banker could take more risks if his depositors were protected. The morale of banking would be lowered and bad banking methods introduced into our system.

ALFRED O. CROZIER, of Wilmington, Del., stated that the discussion appeared to him rather one-sided. "I consider," he said, "the scheme for an elastic currency a plausible delusion. The plan seemed to overlook the Constitution of the United States, which vests in Congress, the responsible government for the people, the right to provide money for the people. All who have spoken to-day believe that this power should be conferred upon the associated banking interests of the United States. Now, if we farm out the responsibility for our money to a syndicate of bankers and let them handle it, is not it possible that they may use it for the purpose of moving the prices of registered securities up and down like a pump handle? A leading officer in a Wall Street trust company told me the other day that we needed elasticity of our money when the crops had to be moved. My reply was, 'Then provide enough money for the people's maximum requirements.' That is the duty of the Government under the Constitution, but it is not the duty of the Government under the Constitution to provide that as soon as that demand for the maximum amount of money is over there shall exist some power to contract the supply of money solely for the purpose of keeping competition out that would lower the interest rate. The scheme of elasticity is nothing more or less than a scheme to keep up interest rates against the producers of this country."

SARAH S. PLATT DECKER gave a spirited defense of the action of the women of the country during the late financial crisis. During the trouble serious criticism was passed upon the action of women depositors.

The property held by women at present is far beyond any former holdings, and their obligations are the same as men. But the attitude of business men toward the former is wholly different. "If a woman owes her grocer a hundred dollars, even though she may have paid every bill promptly for ten years, he will begin proceedings to collect if there is any financial trouble; while her brother will be allowed to continue in indebtedness for an indefinite period. No care or thought is taken by business men to uphold the women's credit.

"With all this distrust of women in business, it is the rarest instance that a woman or a woman's organization fails or defaults. Thousands and thousands of dollars pass daily through the hands of treasurers of women's organizations with absolute safety and accuracy. All over the land are found women's clubs, solvent, prosperous, managed upon the most conscientious business principles.

"Unfortunately, the lack in the present system of any protection against speculation and improper loaning of banks and trust company funds, and the lamentable fact that old-fashioned moral fiber and business honesty are either in hiding or have disappeared, have combined to render the women of the country suspicious and distrustful."

PROTECTION FOR THE PEOPLE'S SAVINGS

POSTAL SAVINGS BANKS, SAVINGS INSTITUTIONS, BUILDING LOAN ASSOCIATIONS—A RECORD AND A PROMISE.

THE second session of the meeting on the afternoon of December 16, Mr. James Speyer, chairman, was devoted to the subject of "Savings Deposits." Besides the formal addresses reproduced here in abstract, the meeting was characterized by a lively interchange of questions and answers.

POSTMASTER-GENERAL MEYER, in speaking of his plans for the extension of the postal service, called attention to the fact that the postal deficit was steadily decreasing. From being 43 per cent. of the expenditures fifty years ago, it had dropped to 6 per cent. a year ago, and in the last fiscal year, ended June 30, 1907, to 3½ per cent.

The recommendation of the postal savings bank is to encourage economy and thrift among our people and to afford a place of deposit free from any possibility of doubt or suspicion, for vast sums of money which might otherwise be hoarded, but are kept out of circulation through ignorance or lack of confidence. We are annually sending out of the country vast sums of money, which last year amounted to $72,000,000 to European countries alone. Foreigners came over here with preconceived and prejudiced ideas against our institutions. They have confidence only in the Government. They use the Government for their shipments of money abroad because we have a fixed rate of exchange, but what they send abroad represents only a part of their savings, for some of it is retained here. Throughout the recent disturbance people have been coming to the post office and asking the postmaster to take care of their money. When this was refused they have in many cases bought money orders payable to themselves, good for a year. In two States I find the amount of expired money orders over a hundred thousand dollars in each case. This money will not be lost, but it will cause the individual considerable trouble to get it back. The banks of the country are not paying sufficient attention to the encouragement of savings. Ten or eleven States contain 92 per cent. of all savings bank deposits. Furthermore, hundreds of thousands of people live where they have no access to banking institutions of any kind, while the postoffice is at their door.

I have suggested to the Congress that the rate of interest that we pay to depositors be about 2 per cent., and that the limit that any individual or association could deposit shall be $500. The system proposed is a very simple one. The rate of interest is low, that there may be no competition with banking institutions. It will withdraw no money from savings banks or trust companies. The money will come from other sources. The Postoffice Department will seek to get it back instantly into the channels of trade by depositing it in the national banks in the locality of the postal savings bank where the money has been deposited.

You will readily see that we cannot deposit it in any other institution but the national bank, for it is important that the depository should be under the jurisdiction of the Government. We have safeguards through the examinations of the Comptroller of the Currency, and by reason of that fact the Government is a preferred creditor.

If the postal savings bank had existed in the late financial flurry, when small depositors grew frightened and drew their money from the banks and were looking for a safe place to put it, they would have deposited this money in the postal savings banks. Being then instantly deposited in a strong national bank you can see at once that the currency stringency would not have occurred to the same extent that it has occurred.

At the conclusion of Mr. Meyer's address a running fire of questions was kept up which elicited important information in regard to the details of the proposed system. The Postmaster General, in reply to a question, stated that he did not believe the money deposited should be secured by bonds. If the banks were asked to provide collateral security they would be less willing to pay interest upon these deposits.

Mr. Carnegie stated that the postal banks of Great Britain allowed an interest of 2½ per cent., and he would be sorry to see less offered by this country. Mr. Meyer's reply was that the Government to-day borrows money at 2 per cent., and he did not see why the Government should agree to pay more than it could borrow at; that the primary object of the institution was to encourage economy and thrift and not to see how much money could be given in return for deposits. What is wanted is absolute security. If a transaction can be rounded up by which the money boards itself, the Government is put to no expense. The money returns to the channels of trade in such a way that it is not taxed upon the rest of the people. The point is that we should not tax one class to give to another.

The practice of other governments of investing these deposits in government bonds being urged, Mr. Meyer again stated that as the Government bonds, under the present law, were the basis of currency to do anything which might be difficult for the banks to get the Government bonds would result in curreney restriction. One reason, he explained, for drawing the bill in so simple a form was to avoid the question of investment. Previous plans have provided that the money remain in the Treasury, but such an addition to Treasury holdings would be a temptation to reckless legislation. One of the many

PARTICIPANTS IN THE EIGHTH ANNUAL MEETING.

troubles to-day is that too much money is locked up in our Treasury.

A member stated that in New Zealand money could be deposited in one postoffice and withdrawn in another, and asked whether the same provision was contemplated in the United States. The answer was that for the present this was not anticipated, since it would too greatly complicate the system, but the same result can be obtained by withdrawing the money and taking a money order on another point.

The advantage of the system lies in the universality of the postoffice, and it would be comparatively simple to make adjustments which would permit deposits to be made also through the rural free delivery agents.

ANDREW MILLS, president of the Dry Dock Savings Institution, and a member of the committee appointed by the Governor to recommend improvements in the banking laws, gave an interesting account of the operations of savings banks under the laws of the State of New York.

The first institution in this State was established in the year 1819, under the name of the Bank for Savings of the City of New York. Its first prospectus said it was intended to furnish a secure place of deposit for savings of mechanics, manufacturers, mantua makers, cartmen, seamen and laborers; in short, for all who wished to lay up a fund for savings for the benefit of the family or for old age. The institution started nearly a century ago, and is in existence to-day, one of the largest and strongest of them all. Its success encouraged others to follow and to-day we have one hundred and thirty-five in active operation in the State. Prior to 1875 special charters were issued, but in that year a savings bank law was passed which made all charters conform to one standard and brought about new improvements. A savings bank under this law is a philanthropic corporation without capital stock, which pays no dividends except to its depositors, under the management of a board of not less than thirteen trustees, who can have no financial interest in the institution under their charge. The trustee is prohibited from either directly or indirectly borrowing the funds of the institution, or from receiving any fee for his services as trustee. Salaries are paid only to the necessary officers, who devote their entire time to the affairs of the institution.

The maximum amount allowed any depositor is $3,000, exclusive of interest, and if by accumulation his account exceeds $3,000, there can be no interest paid on the excess. The institutions are intended for small depositors only, and this rule discourages those who seek to use them as investments. There is an erroneous impression that the savings banks are used by the rich. The Dry Dock Savings Institutien has 70,000 depositors, with an aggregate deposit of about $34,000,000, or an average of about $468 to the account. A recent examination showed that out of the 70,000 accounts, over 824 had reached the maximum of $3,000, and most of them by a gradual accumulation of what is legitimate savings bank business.

To safeguard investments the trustees are allowed to set apart a small portion of the income each year to form a guarantee fund to provide for any possible loss through deterioration in value of the securities, or otherwise. The fund is limited by law to 15 per cent. of the deposits.

On January 1, 1907, the savings banks of New York showed deposits of $1,362,000,000. Thus the savings bank depositors of the State of New York have enough money in their savings banks to pay the entire debt of the nation and have $84,000,000 left. Of this sum $688,000,000 are invested in first mortgages on real estate. The reserves of the bank were first used to aid depositors to become householders, but many of the mortgages are made to business men supplying the means to erect storehouses, office buildings, apartment houses and tenements, and some loans, and more than would be thought have been made in some of the exclusive residential districts of the city. It sounds strange to say that the tenement house dwellers on the East Side have loaned the millionaire money and taken the house as security, but such is the actual fact.

A large part of the resources—over forty millions—are invested in the bonds of States, cities, counties, villages and school districts. Not long ago statistics were gathered which showed that outside of what is now the Borough of Manhattan, 80 per cent. of the municipal debt of the State of New York was owned by savings banks. Another portion of the resources are invested in the underlying mortgage bonds of a limited number of railroads, an investment which is carefully safeguarded by law. The total cost of administering the care and investment of this vast accumulation in the year 1906 was $4,600,000, or 3-10 of 1 per cent. The savings bank is of the greatest importance to the State, every savings bank book is a policy of insurance against anarchy and social disorder. It is of importance to the individual, it promotes thrift, industry and economy, and helps to make him what every citizen of our Republic should be, an independent man. In these days when everything corporate is the target of indiscriminate criticism and when every officer of a corporaton is, in the minds of many, an object for suspicion, I would have it remembered that there are to-day thousands of men good and honest, conservative men who are giving their time and strength to the care of the interests of the savings banks depositors and that their only possible reward is the consciousness that they are doing something to help their fellow men.

MYRON T. HERRICK, of the Cleveland Society for Savings, said: The Postmaster-General desires to establish postal savings banks to encourage habits of economy and thrift and to afford a safe place for deposit of sums of money which might otherwise be hoarded and kept out of circulation through ignorance or lack of confidence. But are the people suspicious of banks as now constituted, and are they without confidence in the integrity of those who control the banking power of this country? Its banking power is estimated at $16,000,000,000, that of the rest of the world $20,000,000,000. This banking power is made up of the capital, surplus, undivided profits, deposits and circulation of national and State banks of every character. The predominating item in the list is deposits. Is it possible to infer from such a showing that there exists a serious lack of faith in existing financial institutions? Conclusions drawn from savings bank deposits alone are equally impressive. Such deposits in the United States are reported in 1906 as $3,480,000,000, and those of the rest of the world $8,245,000,000. In other words, with a population of about one-twentieth of the world, our savings banks hold considerably more than one-third of all the world's savings, belonging to the thrifty and economical. Does this indicate a lack of confidence? The average savings deposit in this country is $433, more than one-half larger than any other country. Savings deposits per capita in the United States are $41, and are exceeded by those of six nations only. Canada and Great Britain, whose postal savings banks are frequently cited to show the advantages of such institutions, have per capita savings deposits of but $11 and $23 respectively. It is true that a large proportion of the savings deposits of this country is held by the banks of the older and more densely populated Eastern States. This is but a natural condition since the people of the West have use for their funds in the purchase of farms, improvements of all sorts, and in the building of homes. When the time comes that they also have surplus wealth, savings institutions will be established to care for it and the money will continue in its natural channels.

Is there anything in the recent history of banking in this country to warrant the assumption that the existing institutions are not the proper depositories of the people's savings?

The record of mutual savings banks in this country—probably the ideal form of savings banks—for stability and for unselfish devotion to the interests of the depositor, is probably unparalleled in any country of the world. The record of the other class of financial institutions that receive savings deposits, the trust company, while not quite so plain, is still admirable. It is a comparatively new type which has not yet quite found its proper sphere, but serves a real need. It is only a question of a short time before it will rank equally with the older types of financial institutions in conservatism and stability.

It is now proper that we make a hasty survey of the Government's experience in banking. The part which it took in the management of the two United States banks was not altogether to its credit, and yet these two banks were infinitely superior to the Sub-Treasury system that followed, which has ever been a drag to the industrial and financial progress of the country. The Government's management of the currency, properly a banking function, has been equally to its discredit. The issue of greenbacks, the coinage of silver under the Bland law, and the issue of Treasury notes authorized by the Sherman act, are but a few of the unfortunate measures that none but a country of marvelous resources could have withstood. For the people have now finally awakened to the fact that they have borne the burden of the banking operations of the Government, and that their welfare would have been much better served had the Government kept out of the banking business. Are we not, therefore, under the circumstances, justified in concluding that the interest of the nation will be better subserved by leaving the savings of the people where they are?

The Postmaster-General refers to the immigrants who, he says, distrust the integrity of our banks. The class of foreigners who become panic-stricken at the slightest provocation do not possess implicit faith in the beneficent designs of our Government as to either their persons or possessions. About the time they have learned to put their faith in our Government they will also have become convinced that our savings banks are, after all, to be trusted.

Postal savings banks have not been an unqualified success in other countries. A recent issue of the London "Statist" severely criticises Government savings banks, intimating, among other things, that the deposits have not been so invested as to give the depositors a decent return for their self-denial and thrift. Where postal savings have been used to bolster up the credit of the State, the gain of the State has proven the loss of the depositors, and has caused a continuous rise in Government stocks and a corresponding decrease in interest. With all these facts before us, the enormous aggregate of savings in this country, the adequacy and conservatism of savings banks as now organized, the uncertain success of the Government whenever it has undertaken banking functions, to my mind but one conclusion can be reached, that absolutely no need exists for postal savings banks here and that the system would be productive of much more harm than good. Let us settle the currency question first.

One of the basic principles of our form of government is that it shall touch the citizen at as few points as possible, consistent with the preservation of order and individual rights. In recent years there has been a noticeable movement in the other direction, but it cannot be too strongly emphasized that any addition to the power of the Government to interfere with the daily life of its citizens violates our traditions and contracts the field open to individual initiative. Do not let us forget that it was the people who made this government, and not the government the people. Democracy is faith in man, and in man's wisdom and ability to work out his own destiny, and that faith must be preserved, if this country is not to repeat the history of the republics of antiquity, and perish from the face of the earth.

JAMES H. HAMILTON, of the Social Settlement, spoke of the Post Office Savings Bank as an educational institution. He believed that if the Government were to establish such a system that it should be with full recognition of its educational purpose, and not as a commercial undertaking. We recognize the necessity for universal common school education, the great desirability of free public libraries, but the need for appropriate culture on the economic side has not been fully recognized. It is the province of the savings bank, whatever its form, to inculcate and encourage self-denial. If united to industry and ordinary intelligence, it will lead to proprietorship. It teaches the lessons to those who most need them; its students are its depositors, its graduates those whose savings have found investment in stock, public or private, or in real estate securities, or in the ownership of land. Like any other school, it should seek to graduate as many of its pupils as possible, and this should determine its policy. Having in mind the development of a strong economic type in all sections of the country, the post office system has evident advantages over all other plans. The trustee system in America works superbly in spots, but great sections of our country are unfamiliar with the institution. Taking our country as a whole, we may be about as far advanced in savings bank culture as Russia in her common school facilities.

EDWIN F. HOWELL, former president of the New York State League of Building and Loan Associations, presented for the consideration of the meeting a digest of the business of the Building Loan Associations.

There are upwards of 5,500 of these companies in the United States, with a total membership of 1,800,000 persons, and total assets of $700,000. The States of New Jersey, Pennsylvania, Ohio, Illinois, Massachusetts, Indiana, California, Missouri and New York lead in the number of these institutions. They are mutual banks whose funds are invested in one line of securities; namely, mortgages taken upon the property of their own home-seeking members. They have their own place to fill and do not conflict with other financial institutions. Their membership is drawn from the great middle class, and embraces the weekly or monthly wage earner and mechanics, tradesmen and clerks. There is no limit to the size of an association. Its depositors are its members and elect annually their officers and directors. Like other financial institutions, the clientele is divided into a depositor or creditor class, and a borrower or debtor class. Every borrower, however, must also be a depositor and member of the company.

Every home-seeking member who borrows, gives his bond, secured by a first mortgage upon the home he has built or purchased. These loans are repaid in instalments of both interest and principal, such instalments being generally so adjusted that the cost does not exceed the rental value of the mortgaged property. Payments are made weekly or monthly, so that the burden will fall upon the member in the same manner as the rent of a similar building would. To secure the necessary funds to supply demands there must be depositors who are not home owners, and, as the average loan is from $1,500 in the country, to $4,000 in the larger cities, and as the average deposit is about $400, an association is composed of from four to ten depositors to every borrower. The rate of interest on mortgages prevailing in the Eastern States is from 5 to 7 per cent. per annum, and the rate of dividends or earnings to the investing depositor from 4½ to 6 per cent. The principal features, therefore, of a Building Loan Association are the encouragement of home building, the providing of a safe, equitable and certain method of acquiring homes, the payment of indebtedness thereon by weekly or monthly instalments, which take the place of rent, a voice for all in the management of the company, almost absolute safety in the investment of the funds of depositors, and the encouragement of thrift on their part by the regular saving of small stipulated sums. In the savings bank, loans are incidental to its chief idea of hoarding, while in our institutions, the central idea is the creation of homes for our membership and our saving department is incidental thereto. Its funds are as well safeguarded in a properly conducted Building Loan Association as they are in any other financial institution of the country. Its object is commendable and its theory is sound. While the love of home owning exists in the human breast the sphere of its labors and influence will never grow less.

IS COMPULSORY ARBITRATION PRACTICABLE?

WORKINGS OF THE NEW ZEALAND LAW—THE CANADIAN INDUSTRIAL DISPUTES INVESTIGATION ACT—DEFECTS OF COMPULSORY SYSTEMS

THE sessions of Tuesday, December 17, were devoted to the question of compulsory arbitration of industrial difficulties. The morning session was presided over by Mr. Isaac N. Seligman; the afternoon session by Rev. Thomas R. Slicer, who later ceded the chair to President August Belmont. The second session being a continuation of the debates of the morning, the abstract of proceedings is here presented as a whole.

HUGH H. LUSK, of New Zealand, spoke of the compulsory arbitration law of that country. In form the law is not compulsory upon all men, but only upon those who become amenable to it by registering their associations under the law. Since associations, both of workers and of employers, are generally registered, it is and has been for twelve years now past absolutely compulsory arbitration. About six years ago the law was extended to the Commonwealth of Australia, where it is now in force. In New Zealand compulsory arbitration has hitherto been a great success. It has had the effect of preventing all strikes and all lockouts for twelve years in that country until the other day. The history of its extension to Australia has been the greatest tribute that could be made to its success in New Zealand. It has not been in all respects as great a success in Australia as in New Zealand. New Zealand has a million white inhabitants, Australia nearly five million; therefore, by the extension of the law from New Zealand to Australia you have got, as it were, a stepping stone from which you can easily see how far it would be likely to be a success in a country as much greater and as much more pepulous than Australia as is this country.

The law of New Zealand, and now of Australia, compels all associated workers who are registered under the act to submit to the law if they have causes of difference with their employers.

In the first place, they have to go to a member of the Board of Conciliation, one of which exists in any considerable district, and the Conciliation Board failing in its object they can remove the cause into the Court of Arbitration, which passes final judgment.

For twelve years the law operated without serious breakdown in New Zealand. It has been carried on for five years without a serious breakdown in Australia. Now, what is wrong with the Act and its operations? At first the workers were perfectly satisfied with the court because, as a general rule, it was with them. Later on, the court as a rule has been against them. They have been inclined to the belief that the constitution of the court is unfavorable, the court being constituted of two representatives of labor and two representatives of capital, together with one Judge of the Supreme Court, sitting as president or chairman. They have come to the conclusion that it is the fifth man who really gives the decision. The difficulty in such a case as this is that if the representative man who gives his decision has not the confidence of both parties the court fails in its object. It is believed that the decisions are, in general, those of a man belonging to the capitalist class—since laborers do not often find their way to the Supreme Court bench in any country. This seems to be the bottom of the difficulty both in New Zealand and in Australia.

I do not think you could enact a law either as a Federal law or as a State law, to-day, such as the law in New Zealand and enforce it. The people are not ready for it.

The Canadian plan seems to me to be a step, although perhaps rather a timid step in the right direction. The idea there was that they should bring about such a revelation of the facts in each case as would enable the public to understand them and the public to pronounce upon them. The weakness of the act is this, that the public never gets to the length of understanding them until the evil has happened.

In New Zealand the idea was there should be no strike, there should be no lockouts, there should be no interruption of business, there should be no dislocation of society, there should be no suffering of the workers, there should be no loss to the employers until every step has been taken and everything has been done to make known to the public what is really the right in the cause and compel the people to comply with what is just and right according to the findings of unprejudiced persons. The difficulty is to find persons so free from prejudice that their decision meets universal approval. We need a standard of righteousness which not only the court but every one can understand. This can only be achieved when employers understand that the worker is a partner of theirs; that every worker brings his capital when he brings his skill, and that his capital is entitled to recognition in the profits of the business. If you will lay down in your law that the first charge in every business shall be the necessary wages that would be sufficient to keep people in decency, and, on the other hand, the lowest scale of interest which money commands in the country for the capitalists' share, all other profits could be divided on a scale set forth in the law between employers and employes. There would be something upon which a court could act, which would not be a matter of opinion, and after the first returns had been divided, as provided by law, what you have got to do is to say, "How are the profits to go?" They are not all to go into the pocket of the employer, but to be divided fairly between the man who has the capital and the man who has the skill and the labor. I think it can be done. It has been done on a small scale in many individual cases. What you want to do now, so far as I can see, is to advance step by step.

In answer to the question in regard to the recent slaughtermen's strike in Australia, Mr. Lusk said that the strike of the slaughtermen had taken place in New Zealand about a year ago. The Court of Arbitration had decided that the wages should be so much per 100 for killing sheep and lambs, exported in such large quantities from New Zealand. Among the slaughtermen were a number who had come over from Australia, who are supposed to have been responsible for much of the dissatisfaction with the decision of the court. They claimed the court was prejudiced, that the court had not given them as much as it should have done. At one place about one hundred men went on a strike; the employers applied to the Court of Arbitration, which summoned the men to appear before it. The court fined each man $25 for disobedience to the order of the court, and told them that they could not work in their trade in that district, except on the terms set down by the court. As the men had no funds with which to pay the fines, the court was at a standstill. The matter was transferred to the Supreme Court and the men were told that they could go to jail for three months or pay the fine imposed. It ended by the unions paying the fine.

Mr. Gompers asked whether it were not true that on the reference of a matter between the boot and shoe manufacturers and their workers to the court the manufacturers were dissatisfied with the result of the award and went out of business. Such, indeed, was the case.

SAMUEL GOMPERS stated that Mr. Lusk did not appear to be quite so sure of the success and triumph of that magnificent proposition of compulsory arbitration as he was nine years ago. During the last nine years I have tried to keep posted as to what was going on in Australia in the matter of arbitration. There can be no doubt of the magnificent industrial development of these countries, but may we not take a retrospective view of the past twelve years' development of our history. Perhaps it is necessary to do so, since so many would have us believe that the great development that has come in New Zealand and in Australia is due to the great tranquility which has obtained in industry.

What is the object of our activities? No one who has gone through strikes can have anything but a wholesome desire to avoid them. But strikes accomplish oftentimes what could not be otherwise attained. Talk about the Court of Arbitration bringing about a change in the condition of mine workers as was accomplished by their strike; you could not do it in half a century! I would not have employers do as they please; I would not want workmen to do as they please; but I believe that by the organization of industry and by the organization of labor we are gathering forces conscious of their power, which intelligently and wisely wielded, bring forth a spirit of conciliation that no court of arbitration ever yet was able to impose. There is in the United States more genuine conciliation between organized employers and organized workmen than exists in any other part of the world. Now, in reference to our Civic Federation, its unwritten history is its most important work. It has helped to bring men together. The anthracite coal strike is an illustration. Its adjustment was brought about not by law but by the strength of the miners' organization aided by the Civic Federation.

No matter what may be done in another country, whether it be in New Zealand or in other parts of the Australian federation, in the United States we will protect ourselves against any such law that will either practically or actually confiscate property, and, on the other hand, impose slavery on persons as a penalty for refusing to work, or for asserting that the conditions of employment are onerous and unfair. The workers of this country are not only workers, they are citizens. They believe that among their rights is the right to dispose of one's own body; that there is no ownership in man except by himself; that he has the right of free locomotion to go where he pleases, to work or not to work, to sell his labor or not to sell his labor, and you cannot differentiate a man from his labor.

The organized workmen of the United States want to be helpful in creating a higher degree of intelligence among those who are their fellows. We have our public schools for the children, but what institution is educating the emigrants that come here to the number now of a million and a quarter a year, who but the labor organizations of the United States? We are doing a service to this country of which there has been little or no conception. We are going to do our work. Our men want fair treatment, they want a living wage, and if I know anything about the signs of the times, they are going to get it. They are going to insist upon the exercise of their rights to own themselves as men and as workmen, and as citizens they are going to be helpful to their fellow citizens in the country and in the social uplift.

OTTO M. EIDLITZ, president of the New York Building Trades Employers' Association, said compulsory arbitration for the settlement of labor disputes has, up to date, received no very enthusiastic support from any one prominent in the ranks of the employers or the employed. It signalizes the intrusion of the outsider in family affairs, with a possibility of non-consent by those vitally interested in the question at issue. It is a debatable question whether any compulsory method of settlement inaugurated by those outside of an industry could secure the much-desired end of industrial peace with honor.

Perhaps the nearest approach to compulsory arbitration in this country is the present arbitration agreement between the Building Trades Employers' Association of the City of New York and the unions of the Building Trades. It has been characterized as compulsory, for the reason that the Employers' Association compelled the acceptance of the arbitration agreement by a number of unions through the medium of a lockout. Since two years later a convention was held modifying the agreement, the plan may now be properly called voluntary and mutual. During the year ending November 30, 1906, 433 complaints were filed with the secretary of the general arbitration board. Many were adjusted by the secretary, but as many as 247 cases came before the executive committee, and in four cases special arbitration boards were necessary.

Now, the building industry is only one of the many extensive industries in the city, and though perhaps the most complicated in its divisions and sub-divisions, employing the greatest variety of mechanics, all other industries are proportionately complicated. I believe that the capital invested in our New York building industry, the volume of business transacted ploye it does not promote good feeling. With the highest respect for the Canadian judiciary and for the high prelates of the Church, it may be remarked that the most signal failures of the act have been where such personages presided over the board of investigation.

Quite a different procedure was adopted by Prof. Shortt, of Queens University, Kingston, who has presided over no less than four investigations with remarkable success. Proceedings have been had in an ordinary business office, the parties seated around a long table; there has been no suggestion of a court. The board seats itself at one end, with the men appointed to represent the workmen on one side and the representatives of employers on the other side of the table. The proceedings are most informal and lawyers are debarred from them. The side which has called for the investigation is called upon first to state its case, which is answered by the other side, and then the whole matter is treated in a conversational discussion. There are no reporters present. All information given to the press is given by the president of the board. In this way irrelevant matter is excluded, angry retorts and indiscreet remarks do not find their way to the public.

The act has its weaknesses. While its penalties are enforceable against employers it is practically impossible to enforce the act against employes. The employer who declares a lockout may be promptly arrested and fined, but if his workingmen, to a number of a thousand, go out on strike in violation of the act, it is absurd to suppose that they could all be arrested and brought before a magistrate. Moreover, it would be the veriest folly for an employer who is anxious to get his men back to work to have them arrested. The Department of Labor has attempted to smooth this difficulty over by saying that the men did not understand the act. This excuse carried little weight with those who have an intelligent acquaintance with the circumstances. In every case in which the act has been violated the Government has condoned the offence by saying that the men did not understand the terms of the act. But in the only case where an employer has been guilty under the act, that of Mr. Hill, of the Hill Crest Mining Company of Alberta, he was promptly haled before the magistrate and fined $100 a day during the duration of the lockout. Notwithstanding the weaknesses to which I refer, I think the employers, even those who have seen their men violate the act, would be sorry to have it repealed. While the penalties may never be imposed they stand as a wholesome preventive against rash conduct, and so long as it exercises this deterrent effect the employer will regard the measure with favor.

JOHN LUNDRIGAN, of the New York State Board of Mediation and Arbitration, spoke of the necessity of co-operation among such public agencies as State boards or bureaus established for the prevention or settlement of industrial disputes. To this end he believed it advisable that a national or international association be formed of the State officials and others interested in the subject, which might present and discuss ideas, and the information developed and encountered by practical experience, eventually leading up to uniformity in State legislation, making the same more effective and avoiding clashes of jurisdiction.

The great majority of our citizens who occupy the relation of employer and employe are either not informed on this subject, or, what is infinitely worse, are misinformed. I firmly believe that if we can demonstrate it to be the mission and policy of public agencies not to interfere in matters which are the subjects of amicable discussion or negotiation between employer and employe until plainly demonstrated that there will be an interruption of the industry, and that if such interruption does occur, especially in the case of any public service or public utility, there will be a full and complete investigation which will define responsibility and recommend a solution, public opinion will do the rest.

In my opinion most State departments dealing with this subject are limited far short of their possibilities, in other words, not sufficiently equipped in either help or resources to carry out the principle of public investigation, which, if it is to be effective, should not be spasmodic. I believe, however, that public opinion is crystallizing on this subject to such an extent that legislative bodies will treat such departments with more liberality in the future.

At the same time I am of the opinion that, owing to the immense volume of public utilities and public service industries which are positively interstate in character, the Federal Government should continue to exercise the statutory powers or authority now vested in the chairman of the Interstate Commerce Commission and the Commissioner of Labor, which might well be enlarged to the extent of permitting or requiring the Federal authorities to take the initiative, and, if necessary, providing a separate department or bureau charged with its execution, but limiting its powers absolutely to investigation and recommendation.

REZIN ORR, treasurer of the Amalgamated Association of Street Railway Employes, stated that there was probably no industry in the country which, in the event of controversy between the employer and employe, concerned so much the general public as the street railway industry. Those who advocate compulsory arbitration could refer to no other industry in stronger terms than to this, but I do not believe in compulsory arbitration. I do not believe in forcing individuals to do things. I feel the best results can be obtained, not only in the street railway controversies that arise, but in all others, through the instrumentality of this body that is in session here this afternoon. If we establish a system of compulsory arbitration we would be stepping in and interfering with the duties of this body. Much has already been done by it, and should it to-day go on record as being in favor of compulsory arbitration it would be shirking a duty devolving upon it.

We should settle our own controversies. The two parties directly interested—the people who own the property and the men who operate the cars—should sit down together and talk the matters over to arrive at an understanding. If you take the question out of our hands and place it in the hands of others they are likely to forget some of the most vital and important parts to both parties concerned. Finally, a decision is rendered by such a board of arbitration with results that one or the other of the two parties, and possibly both, will not be satisfied with the decision. So my advice on the street railway industry especially is that the Civic Federation should reach out much further than it has already done. There are a large number of employers who are not yet affiliated with the Civic Federation, who do not understand its mission. Instead of going to the legislature and asking for laws to be enacted, let us get right down and do the work ourselves that it has already been demonstrated can be done by this body.

AUGUST BELMONT: It is needless for me to recall the fact that I publicly expressed myself as favoring a trade agreement, and so I do in principle, and in practice, in connection with trade in general, but I have come to the conclusion that it is not the only and safe remedy for difficulties that arise in connection with public utilities.

In this city the elevated railway and the subway were being managed under the operation of trade agreements with employes. There were two unions, and a disagreement between them precipitated a conflict with the management.

The result was the breaking up of the union, and when I was asked some time afterward by one of its heads whether I was definitely opposed to the employment of the union men on the road I said that it was impossible for a utilities corporation to run the risk of a trade agreement, inasmuch as the law could not enforce one. Further, the number of men employed in a great city like this outnumbers so much their associates in other parts of the country that the national organization cannot control them. Now, I have thought if a law could be so drawn, in conformity with the regulations of the national organization, giving a certain amount of time, that there would be an opportunity for conciliation and precipitate action would be avoided. I believe that the law should treat every man entering the service of a transportation line as having, by that fact, entered into a contract to serve the community, and that he must, as an individual, give a reasonable notice of his intentions to leave the service. Of course, you cannot compel a man to remain in the service of a corporation, but the law can say that when you enter the service of a corporation by so doing you make a contract with the community, and must serve them at least a reasonable time before you stop, and you must give them reasonable notice of your intention, let us say, two weeks. But at the present time any man can put down his vehicle, either trolley car or train, before it has reached its destination—he can leave—and that is the end of his obligation. The community, therefore, runs the risk of a breach of a trade agreement without any remedy at all for its protection. The safeguards suggested would be valuable to the national organizations, and I cannot see for myself why they should not be very glad to promote and bring about a regulation of that kind. It would help them enforce their authority, for at the present time they have no remedy except the expulsion of the local unions. That, as you recall, was done, but the result was no better than if it had not been done. The moral effect, of course, was to satisfy the community that the local organizations here had not lived up to their agreements, but the people ran just as much risk of having their transportation lines stop and traffic suspended.

MR. CROZIER: Mr. Bélmont, can I ask you one question.

MR. BELMONT: Yes.

MR. CROZIER: If a company employee enters the employment of a public service corporation at a modest wage and thereby incurs an obligation as a servant of the public should not the corporation which receives the franchise from the public free to use the public streets, free, a franchise which is not property but a mere license, should not they also have an obligation to the public and be prevented from capitalizing that franchise for $100,000,000, and then charging the public higher rates to earn dividends on that capitalization?

MR. BELMONT: Well, that is rather an awkward question—I suppose I must answer that? But then you have stated your question a little incorrectly, I am afraid, and I might, therefore, say it is not, for that reason, answerable, but I will try and answer you. In the first place, you said that these franchises were granted to operate public service in the streets "free." That is not the fact. You will find that the taxation, if you will look into the matter, is very onerous. The franchise tax itself is very heavy, and the real estate and property belonging to these corporations are taxed also.

In the case of the subway, where a contract was made with the city to operate its own property, the city exacted different terms altogether in lieu of taxation, but in the case of the surface lines and the elevated railway the taxation is heavy, and they are not operating free, as you stated, by any means. Now on general principles, it is important for a corporation to have the means required for its development, and those means can only be obtained from investors, and the corporations are obliged—notwithstanding the regulations that are now being exercised over capitalization—they are and will be obliged to seek the investor with the kind of security that he is willing to take; and in most of these large amalgamations that have been effected between stockholders it has been necessary in the past to offer them, in order to induce them to come together, something in the way of future opportunity to earn on their newly created investment. If the investment turns our unprofitably, of course, it may tend to some criticism if you choose to pass on this; but if they do not lose, and frequently they do not, the amalgamation will result in an ability of the corporation to largely increase its usefulness. In the present instance, the great difficulty with the transportation in New York is going to be that the money cannot be obtained to keep it up to its requirements; that the very hostility which is being shown to-day, while this may be justified, nevertheless is so crippling that when the corporations are asked to give additional facilities it may—I won't say it will—but it may be impossible. And I wish to say in this connection that the alternative suggested is that the city take up the question of ownership and operation. In fact, I judge a great deal of this hostility has been based on the assumption that the alternative would be that the city would undertake what the corporation either would not, or could not do. Unfortunately, the city is going to be unable for a long time to do anything of the kind, because the very threat on the part of a certain portion of the press and community that the city should undertake local transportation and should acquire the means for it has had the effect of frightening the investors in the city's own securities. So that neither one nor the other is in a position to do anything.

The plan is based on the fallacious idea that there is such a thing as public money outside of that which is raised by taxation. Money raised through taxation and rentals is the only real public money that is in the treasury, but the moment you go outside of that remember that both the municipality and the Government itself, either State or National or otherwise, have got to go to exactly the same source for their money, which is then only borrowed money—the investor; and there is no such thing as a standing supply of Government funds. It is a fallacy which here locally we ought very soon to explode that there is such a thing as public money other than that which is derived from taxation. Every dollar of any other funds comes from the investor. The proceeds of every Government bond, every municipal bond, come from exactly the same source that the proceeds of your railroad bond comes from, exactly, excepting that the terms offered by the Government may be more attractive and the chances of getting the money may be better; but if the day comes, like to-day, that the investor cannot do anything, then not even the municipality or Government can get what they need. As a result of attacks upon corporations the investor has been guarding himself and keeping his purse strings tight for the past three years, so that the corporations have been obliged because they could not reach the investor, to, in a great many cases, make what are called short time notes. Those were temporary provisions waiting for this investor that I am speaking about to ultimately take their securities off the hands of the corporations. Now, that is the condition of to-day.

I do not mean to say that that is the sole condition operating unfavorably to-day; it is apart from the currency disturbances, but aggravates them. That is one of the features, and after the currency difficulty has passed you still will have that lack of confidence which does not come from mismanagement of corporations, but from an unreasoning hostility to them, and from a fallacy as to what Government can do in case private corporations are either unwilling or unable to do, and you will find that if the investor, as a result of the general attitude of the public and the Government toward his investment remains frightened—if such attacks keep him in his present state—neither the one nor the other will be able to contribute to the improvement that we all need both in our general railroad transportation and in our municipal transportation.

I did not intend to say so much.

THE EIGHTH ANNUAL DINNER OF THE NATIONAL CIVIC FEDERATION

DISTINGUISHED SPEAKERS DISCUSS PERTINENT SUBJECTS OF PRESENT DAY INTEREST

THE eighth annual dinner of The National Civic Federation, held in the Hotel Astor, December 16, 1907, was a notable and remarkable gathering. Nearly eight hundred guests assembled in the banqueting hall of the Hotel. When the cigars were lighted Mr. August Belmont briefly presented as the toastmaster Mr. Melville E. Ingalls.

Mr. Ingalls said that while it was not his purpose to make a speech, but rather to see that others did so, he was proud of the gathering. "Our officials should feel proud that so many men and women from the busy walks of life have come here to-night to consider what can be done and to talk over the various matters that may be presented. The question is, what can be done to better the relations of capital and labor to each other and to the world? The duty of the Civic Federation is not to decide things, but to attempt to get the facts and lay them before the public that the public may decide as it pleases."

GENERAL FREDERICK D. GRANT, commanding the Department of the East, devoted his remarks to the question of the canteen in military posts. Alluding to the fact that he was himself a total abstainer, he had, after noting the effects resulting from the withdrawal of the canteen from military reservations, come to the conclusion that the sale of liquor under restrictions and complete control is a lesser evil than its sale in the low saloons and vile dens of vice which have surrounded army posts since the canteen was abolished. The canteen in the army was the soldiers' club, their resort for social intercourse and innocent amusements. Beer was sold under rigid restrictions. All profits made by sales in the canteen were returned to the soldiers in the form of additions to their rations, to the supply of their reading and writing materials, and secured them a fund from which to draw their amusements and entertainments in general. They were managed by company officers and were conducted in the interests of the soldiers. On the abolition of the canteen soldiers sought their social amusements and diversions in the vile dens and groggeries outside of military reservations.

"When asked to speak here to-night, I happened to have before me for review, proceedings of fourteen court martial cases and noted of these fourteen cases, involving a total of twelve years' imprisonment, three were trials under charges of drunkenness on guard, and nine upon close analysis proved to be cases of offence committed because of drunkenness that would probably not have occurred except for the existence of the anti-canteen law.

"Referring to the annual reports of the Judge Advocate General of the United States Army for the years 1896 and 1907, two years in which the conditions of the service were quite similar, we find that trials for general court martial had increased from 62.6 per thousand men in 1896, to 65.4 per thousand men in 1907. Trials by inferior courts increased from 571 per thousand men in 1896 to 768 per thousand men in 1907. Like results appear in the Department of the East.

"Because of these verified facts I am convinced that the abolition by law of the canteen in the army is a serious disadvantage to the soldiers, and notwithstanding my own inherent disapproval of the sale of any alcoholic drinks in army posts, I believe it is far better to choose the lesser of two evils and grant to the soldiers the freedom of having their clubs, with the privilege of enjoying moderately light drinks under the strict control of those interested in their welfare, rather than have them constantly subjected to the temptations now alluring them in the vile dens and saloons which have clustered as near as possible to the soldiers' barracks. Although a total abstainer, I am an advocate of the canteen in the army until the time comes when the civil authorities abolish those dens near military reservations kept by vicious persons who now tempt the soldiers of our army to their destruction."

JOHN MITCHELL: I conceive it to be the highest obligation and duty upon every man and woman who has at heart the welfare of our country and the welfare of our people to do what they can to preserve among all classes of people a degree of peace and plenty that will make for the good of all. So far as I have been able to control the affairs of my organization, it has been in the direction of peace—of peace with honor. I should be most happy indeed if the time were here when strikes and lockouts and boycotts and blacklists, with their attendant evils and hardships, would be no more. I am not so sure that that time will come within our lives, but is it not better that we reason together and try and see if reason cannot take the place of force? I don't know whether the people of New York, or the people of our country, know how near they came two years ago to becoming involved in greater hardships than they endured in the great anthracite coal strike, but let me say to you now, that had not ten men met together in this city and talked to each other as reasonable men should talk, the great coal strike which occasioned you so much suffering in 1892 would have been repeated. I am proud to say that I found the anthracite coal operators much different when I got to know them than I did when they were talking to me through the newspapers, and I believe that they have a different opinion of those I represent and of myself than they had five or six years ago.

Out of these meetings much good may come. It is especially important now, when our country seems to be entering upon depression and disturbance in our industries, that we try to avoid the experience we had in 1893, and in all periods of depression which preceded it. We who represent labor—and we who represent capital—have it in our power to do more than the men in Congress to return our country to that prosperity it enjoyed for so many years. Financial, and especially industrial, panics cannot be cured by legislation. They cannot be cured at all, but their evils may be materially minimized and their duration lessened if the men who work and the men who employ will do what is right by each other. Experience in the past has not demonstrated that the way to cure an industrial evil is to reduce wages. At a meeting of the Civic Federation four or five years ago, when there was some depression in industry, Senator Hanna, then president of the Civic Federation, suggested to the men of labor who were there that probably the time had come when it would be necessary for the men to give up some of the increased wages which they had secured during the several years before. I suggested that I thought the thing to do was to stand "pat," but the Senator advised that that was not the way to do. It eventually became necessary for the coal miners of America to give up 6 per cent. of their wages. The result was that we demoralized the entire coal industry, and not only made our miners suffer, but destroyed a lot of coal operators. The people who bought from them did not fail to remind them that they had reduced wages, nor did they fail to take from the operators more than the latter had taken from the miners.

I am not so sure that I shall be as active in the labor movement in the future as I have been in the past, but I hope that I shall be permitted to participate in this Civic Federation movement which has done so much to bring influential men and women together. I trust that each person shall feel that upon him rests a share of the responsibility. Let each of us do our part and see if we cannot extricate the country from our present predicament.

GEORGE W. PERKINS, speaking of the profit-sharing plan of the United States Steel Corporation, said the problem that faced the new corporation was this: Would men on salaries and wages carry on this vast organization directed only by other men on salaries, with no proprietorship above them save the vast and scattered body of security holders. The thousands of men employed by the corporation are divided into two classes, those who work with their brains and those who work with their brains and their hands. While the responsibility of the first class of men is, of course, very great, the opportunity of the second class may be of almost equal importance because in the practical everyday working of the thousands of little and big machines and the general handling of material the man who is actually doing the work can, with surprising frequency, suggest this fact or the other improvement which reduces cost, improves quality and increases output. The difficult problem was how to arrive at some method of compensating the officers of the subsidiary companies for the successful management and at the same time compensate the actual workers in the plant.

After much discussion and the examination of many profit-sharing plants, the board of directors, in December, 1902, authorized the announcement of the plan which has come to be known as "The Steel Corporations Profit-Sharing Plan." It is composed of two parts, one of which affects the managers, superintendents and others in positions of responsibility and control. After the company has earned its fixed charges, a dividend in a sum sufficient for maintenance and repairs, a certain sum varying from 1 to 2½ per cent., according to the profits, is set aside. Half of it goes to the participants in cash, the other half in stock, though a part of the latter is not delivered until after five years of continuous service.

The other part of the plan permits the acquisition of stock in the company by all of its employes. The amount which can be purchased may not exceed a fixed per cent. of the salary paid. Stock was allotted at little less than market price and arrangements made for the gradual payment of the stock by deductions from salaries. A reduction from the payments to be made was allowed in the shape of Five Dollars per share for each year in the service of the company up to a period of five years. Title to the stock subscribed for vested in the employe, who thereby gained the difference between the 5 per cent. interest charged him on his deferred payments and the 7 per cent. dividend paid him on the par of the stock.

In January, 1903, when the plan was first announced, 27,000 employes subscribed for 49,000 shares of stock. Almost immediately depression of business came upon us and something over 12,000 subscriptions dropped out during the year, nevertheless. 10,000 of the original subscribers have remained. When the five year period expires next month, they will find that through the difference of interest and dividends with Five Dollars per share credited to their account and sums credited from those who have dropped out, their stock has cost them almost nothing, and is to-day selling for $86.25 per share and paying regular dividends on par of 7 per cent. per annum.

The offer made in 1903 has been repeated in January of each succeeding year with considerable participation on the part of the men.

By the close of this year, when the entire plan will have been in force five years, over $10,000,000 will have been actually distributed through the organization under the various provisions of the plan. It has gone to a very large number of men and has been one of the factors which has helped to form an organization which for loyalty and efficiency is perhaps unequaled in the industrial world to-day.

In these results is there not a form of co-operation of the highest, best and most ideal sort—that makes real partners of employer and employe and yet preserves the right of private preperty—retaining the capitalist's incentive to enterprise while giving the worker a new inspiration for effort—humanizing a vast organization—promoting good will and industrial peace?

DR. ELIOT, president of Harvard University, said that in the National Civic Federation he represented neither capital nor labor, but that great public which invariably pays all the cost of industrial warfare, whether it breaks out openly or is privately compromised; that he had, therefore, the strongest interest in contributing, if possible, to industrial peace. The best legislation that has ever been adopted to promote industrial peace is the Canadian Act of March 22, 1907, called the "Industrial Disputes Investigation Act." Under it no strike is lawful and no lockout is lawful until there has been a public investigation of the causes of the strike and of the lockout. There is no arbitration in it, only investigation, conciliation and publicity, but the primary merit is this, that no strike is legal and no lockout is legal until the public investigation has been held by an impartial authority.

In Canada specified powers belong to the provinces, all others belong to the National Government. It is absolutely the reverse with us, but it is an immense object lesson for the community that these two free countries continue to experiment independently on the conduct of free institutions. But Canada has an enormous advantage. Nearly all of the questions which are now important for the prosperity of our country are new. Not one of them arose at all until more than fifty years after the adoption of the Constitution. How is it possible that that instrument, so wise, so wonderful in its day, should provide the means of dealing with questions never imagined for a moment when the Constitution was made. The Federal Government of our country greatly needs new powers. It is trying to get them by a stretching process and some experiments in this direction have turned out pertty well considering the extremely limited nature of the powers which can be twisted out of the Constitution in this manner. When a corporation has power to carry on business over the whole of these United States—to live and work in many States—can State authorities control it?

The real definition of a good labor union is that it is a commercial association. Now, these commercial associations work over the whole country. Is it to be expected that any power but that of the central Government can control a commercial association of that sort? All the great commercial associations, whatever you call them—trusts, companies or labor unions—are really in search of the same thing, a monopoly. They very seldom get a complete monopoly, but they often approach it. Now, if there is anything in this country that free men in all countries have abhorred and resisted, it is monopoly; and it does not make much difference what sort of a monopoly it is. Now, these great monopolies, broad as the continent, cannot be controlled by any but a central government, and, therefore, I say that Canada has already won a great advantage over the United States, because all these new questions go to their central government.

It is not alone in industrial disputes that we discover the same difficulty. How can the great evil of divorce be dealt with in our land except by the force of the National Government? How can the great evil of child labor be dealt with in this land through the efforts of the State? Take the great source of many of our social and industrial evils, the misuse of corporation and association powers; how can they be dealt with except by the force of the central government? I say, therefore, that we should look forward to an increase of national power in all of these directions. The suggestion goes against our cherished fetish of local government, local interest or local representation. We desperately need, ladies and gentlemen, a revision of our conception of local interest. The interests called local have entirely changed their nature and scope within the last fifty years, and so, I say, we need to revise our idea of local government, and above all, we need to give up our fear of the extension of national power.

The National Government rules to-day a territory really much smaller than New England was sixty years ago. Not only is the territory smaller for administrative purposes, but we can talk all over it on the instant; we can bring news from every part of it on the instant and we can ride across it in five days, whereas, it used to take three weeks for a student to arrive at Harvard College from central New York; as I have heard a student of that day tell, he made the journey in the year 1826, it took him three weeks, and he rode all the way, with all his goods in two saddle bags. So, I say, the National Government rules to-day a much more manageable area than sixty years ago, with infinitely better means of communication. Why, after all from the point of view of a National Government, this continent has become a very manageable place and local interests, what are they? They are continental interests.

In introducing the last speaker of the evening, Mr. Samuel Gompers, Mr. Ingalls called attention to his unique record, in that he had for twenty-six years been elected the chief of his organization and the last time without any opposition.

Continued on page 14.

AS OTHERS SEE US

COMMENT ON ANNUAL DINNER AND WORK OF THE FEDERATION

M. ALEXANDRE ULAR.

ALEXANDRE ULAR, foreign editor of "Le Petit Journal," of Paris, and correspondent of other important journals of the Continent, was a guest of the National Civic Federation at its annual banquet.

"To see capital and labor at a great banquet peacefully discussing social questions was most amazing to me," said M. Ular, "because of my knowledge that discussions in France between the two classes are always unfriendly.

"Above all, I was amazed to see well-known labor leaders on good terms with great capitalists. I could hardly credit the spectacle of John Mitchell, who is considered by his French friends just as revolutionary as our labor leaders, sitting between Mr. Charles A. Moore, a manufacturer, and Mr. Percy A. Rockefeller, the capitalist, and later between Miss Morgan and Mrs. Harriman.

"If a French labor leader were to do this French workingmen would at once believe that he was playing them false, and he would lose influence with them. Here, on the contrary, it seems that laborers want their leaders to maintain friendly relations with capital. It astonishes me to see that the labor men considered their interests identical with those of capital. A toast like the one to which John Mitchell responded would be impossible in France, or at least its sentiments would be regarded as an indication that the speaker was playing into the hands of the capitalists. Mr. Mitchell said that he had always worked for peace between capital and labor, that he was proud of it, and that the prosperity of the working classes was intimately connected with the maintenance of peace between the two classes. Now, the French labor men don't want peace, but strife. They will accept peace only when capital is utterly subdued.

"To a French observer it was indeed a remarkable thing to see Samuel Gompers sitting beside Andrew Carnegie and James Speyer, two of your best know capitalists. You would never be able to bring French labor and capital together for a discussion of labor problems."

Speaking with a representative of the Civic Federation, M. Ular said that what impressed him most was the apparent difference in the mental attitude of the labor leaders of the United States and the workingmen of France. Here, he said, they are practical men, seeking, first and foremost, the improvement of their own economic condition, whereas, in France they are idealists, with the aspiration to reform society, not so much for their own immediate benefit as for the sake of the principles which they believe to be involved. It is needless to say that the principles are those of Socialism. The whole labor movement is permeated with them. For this reason a friendly gathering of employers and workingmen would be impossible in France or in Continental Europe generally.

"LE FIGARO," OF PARIS, December 29, 1907.

PHILIPPE MILLET, of the University of Paris, who is visiting the United States for an extended study of the subject of trade agreements between employers and labor unions, was an interested participant in the annual banquet. His impressions were recorded in a letter to the Figaro, from which the following is taken:—

The eighth floor of the Hotel Astor presented the other night a very animated aspect. The extraordinary thing, even for New York, was the combination of this assembly. Close to men in evening dress and white ties and society ladies in decollete as for the opera, there were many workingmen in their ordinary business suits. At the same tables, elbow to elbow, were Andrew Carnegie, John D. Rockefeller, Jr., Wall street bankers like Isaac N. Seligman, George W. Perkins, August Belmont, together with presidents of miners', railway employes' and building trades unions. I sat myself between the president of Harvard University, Dr. Eliot, and General Grant, who is the son of the celebrated general. At a little distance from my place I saw, comfortably seated between two bankers, Samuel Gompers, the president of the American Federation of Labor, which is—I scarcely dare write it; you won't believe me—the great labor organization of America.

To understand this astonishing combination and the peculiar interest which it offered this evening it is necessary to know the National Civic Federation, of which this was the annual dinner.

It is a private association founded about nine years ago to study problems of national interest and mainly to strengthen social peace by bringing together the employers and the employes. Such initiative is frequent in America. Instead of permitting the State to care for the general happiness, private citizens prefer to take this care into their own hands. It happens very often that they found societies in order to supervise the public powers and prevent the latter from undertaking to promote the general happiness. The National Civic Federation is an association of this kind, one of the largest and most powerful, as it seems, at the present time. The Federation sends to Congress respectfully formulated resolutions, which are very much like those of our General Council, but one feels that the Federation does not expect its salvation from a good legislator and does not believe that the social contest, with its strikes and lockouts, will magically end on the day when an honest Representative will have presented in Congress an excellent law of compulsory arbitration.

Continued on page 17.

34. James Talcott.
35. Joseph R. Buchanan.
36. Horace E. Deming.
37. Robert Mather.
38. Emil L. Boas.
39. Hamilton Holt.
40. C. U. Carpenter.
41. Charles R. Miller.
42. Nathan Bijur.
43. Robert Watchorn.
44. John H. Finley.
45. Lee Kohns.
46. John S. Huyler.
47. Otto M. Eidlitz.
48. Samuel B. Donnelly.
49. John N. Bogart.
50. E. R. Perkins.
51. D. P. Kingsley.
52. Albert McClave.
53. R. H. Swartwout.
54. A. W. Burnett.
55. John C. McCall.
56. Dr. Oscar H. Rogers.
57. Thomas A. Buckner.
58. V. Everit Macy.
59. Marcus M. Marks.
60. Walter H. Page.
61. Arthur Young.
62. W. C. Beers.
63. E. A. Filene.
64. Ernest Graham.
65. T. C. Martin.
66. Grange Sard.
67. Colgate Hoyt.
68. Philippe Millet.

THE NATIONAL
Civic Federation Review

Office: 281 Fourth Avenue, New York City
RALPH M. EASLEY, Editor

The Editor alone is Responsible for any unsigned article or unquoted statement published in THE NATIONAL CIVIC FEDERATION REVIEW.

PUBLISHED BY

The National Civic Federation

The Year's Work. During the past year the work of the National Civic Federation has been more extensive, and has appealed to even broader interests than ever before. It culminated fittingly in the annual dinner at the Hotel Astor, one of the most notable social gatherings of the year. Members and officers of the organization may well be content with so emphatic an expression of the public approval. Everywhere were heard words of commendation for the spirit which marked the occasion. The unique character of the gathering, where so many interests met upon common ground, is reflected in the friendly comment of two visiting French economists and others, which is reproduced elsewhere in this issue of the *Review*.

The consciousness that the National Civic Federation was a living agency for the common weal found further expression in the discussion at the annual meeting of the protection of the people's savings, in its varied aspects of currency reform and the protection of deposits. What in ordinary times is considered a somewhat dry and technical subject became magnetic with life and interest, and the meeting passed a resolution urging upon Congress to provide an elastic currency system. In the discussion of compulsory arbitration the exposition of Australian legislation and of the recent Canadian Industrial Disputes Investigation Act was attentively followed, but the principles of the former awakened no favorable criticism, and there was some disposition to question the compulsory features of the latter.

The report of the Chairman of the Executive Council tells of varied and important activities.

The Conciliation Department has secured many conferences which have averted threatened local disturbances. Proposals are being considered which will strengthen this work through local representatives in every important city of the United States.

Interest in welfare work has been greatly stimulated by numerous addresses of members of the Welfare Department. It has been called upon to aid by furnishing plans for or experts to install conveniences for the health and comfort of employes in large manufacturing establishments.

A specially noteworthy feature was the formation of a Public Employes' Welfare Committee, with the underlying idea that the government—whether Federal, State or municipal—should be a model employer. Important local reforms have already been accomplished. Its principal undertaking was an exhaustive investigation of all the conditions surounding employment on the Canal Zone, which showed much to be applauded, and likewise the need of improvements for creature comforts, in the regulations applying to labor conditions and opportunities for recreation and for the education of the children of the employes.

The report of the Public Ownership Commission has attracted wide attention, and its conclusions are regarded as an authoritative statement of the considerations for and against the municipal operation of public utilities, and its copious and scientific publication will have a permanent place in the literature of this subject.

The National Conference on Trusts and Combinations, which gathered in October in Chicago at the call of the National Civic Federation, was a highly representative body well adapted to reflect the well-considered, sober-minded opinion of the people, and thus to be a sure guide to our legislative bodies. The resolutions of the conference, shortly to be submitted to Congress, point out the way to secure a practical and judicious basis for future legislative enactments.

In the early part of the year Mr. W. H. Mallock, the noted English individualist, visited the United States on the invitation of the Federation, and lectured upon Socialism at some of the leading universities. These lectures, since published in book form, contain a thorough exposition of the Socialist faith and a skilful answer to its claims.

An important educational feature of the work of the Civic Federation is found in its meetings, which bring all classes together for the discussion of the common welfare. Meetings held in New York at the residence of Mr. Andrew Carnegie to discuss industrial peace and one in Chicago at the residence of Mrs. Potter Palmer for a general presentation of the work of the Federation were especially notable.

Every year sees our work broaden. While new activities are being constantly undertaken, they are marked by the same spirit—to promote as far as in us lies the common welfare. Continued public support and interest encourages us to believe that there are still larger opportunities for usefulness in store for the Federation in the future.

EIGHTH ANNUAL DINNER.

Continued from page 11.

SAMUEL GOMPERS: It falls to my lot frequently and yet it is always an unpleasant duty, if perchance I must, to sound a discordant note. I should like at some time to inquire a little further into the profit-sharing proposition. I should like to inquire, had I the time, what are the relative wages of the men employed in the iron and steel industry ten years and more ago, before the profit-sharing system was put into vogue, and what are the wages to-day.

It suggests a little less comfort, but it appears to me a very pertinent question. I doubt that any one listens with deeper interest and concern, but whether it be here at your banquet board or in the hall of discussion, while I am contributing as best I can to the great uplifting of all my fellow men and women, my chiefest concern is for the men and women who labor, and I trust that I may never fail to say a word particularly for them. Gentlemen have come to me and whispered in private conversation, in gentle hints and in knowing innuendoes that after all the workingman of the country must come down in his wages. But let me say the soil of our country is not less valuable than it was yesterday, men's minds have not become dull, men are not less industrious, men are no less willing to work than yesterday, and wherefore is the natural necessity of attacking the wages, the American standard of life, of the working people of our country? You cannot reduce wages without reducing the consuming power of the people, and every time you reduce their consuming power you make your situation worse. Whoever is to blame for the present financial system, the fault is not that of the working people of our country. They have made up their minds that they are not going to be the chief sufferers by reason of an artificially made panic or by the blunders of those who have the affairs of finance and industry under their direction.

If there is one thing upon which I have some pride, not vanity, it is that I think I know something about the labor question and something about the labor movement and something about the history of organization among working people, the history of their struggles through the ages, the history of modern industry, the history of workers in the past century, the history of workers within the past third of a century, with which I have been closely associated; but it has been left for this evening for me to learn that a union of labor is a commercial organization. A trust is a combination of men or persons to control the product of labor; how can there be a trust in a thing that is not produced and will not be produced until it is given to the world? In the very nature of things the organizations of labor cannot be, and are not, trusts and cannot be measured by the same standards.

Nor am I one that have lent my voice to the denunciation or attacks upon the combinations of industry and trust. To me, as a workman, or as a union man, a trust is an employer of labor, and it is either good or bad or indifferent as it accords a fair and square deal to the working people.

With my fellows, I have believed, and still believe, that the organizations of industry in the case of corporations and trusts are in the very nature and order of industrial development. And now a word as to the people. I ask you, my friends, to consider for a moment who are the people. Nothing mythical, I suppose. They are human beings—men, women and children. They are all employers or employed. There is no onerous condition which can be imposed on the working people of any one trade or calling but what it will have its baneful effect upon all who are employed. You cannot improve the condition of any trade or calling, or of the working people of any trade or calling without giving an impetus or tendency to the outward life of all the working people. The strike of the coal miners did more not only to uplift the miners and their families, but it did more than all else could accomplish in half a century of preachments without the strike. Do not for a moment imagine that I am an advocate of strikes. I regard them as a necessary evil, and I do not believe that necessary evils are blessings.

Respecting child labor, I agree that insufficient progress has been made in that line of work, but I think that it is not amiss to suggest the fact that it was the commercial organizations of labor that started and carried on the work to secure even what we now have upon the statute books of our several States that have taken the children out of the factories and workshops and given them the opportunity to be in the schools and kindergartens.

The report of the Chairman of the Executive Council follows:

NATIONAL CIVIC FEDERATION IN 1907

EXTRACTS FROM THE REPORT OF THE CHAIRMAN OF THE EXECUTIVE COUNCIL

THE questions, "Where did the Civic Federation start?" "What was it for?" and "Has it not deviated far from its original purpose?" arise) frequently that a brief account of its origin may ot be inappropriate in this report.

The Federation was organized in 1900, in Chicago, fter a succession of national conferences had been eld upon such subjects as Primary Election Reform, oreign Policy and Trusts and Combinations. It con-isted of an advisory council of five hundred members nd an Executive Committee. On the Executive Com-iittee were several of the members of the present ational Executive Committee, including Franklin lacVeagh, Archbishop Ireland, Samuel Gompers, ohn Mitchell, D. J. Keefe, John W. Stahl and Benja-iin Ide Wheeler. The prospectus, published at the me, stated the purpose of the organization to be as ollows:

" * * * To organize the best brains of the na-on in an educational movement toward the solution f some of the great problems related to social and in-ustrial progress; to provide for study and discussion f questions of national import; to aid thus in the rystallization of the most enlightened public opinion; nd, when desirable, to promote legislation in accord-nce therewith."

Fifteen national subjects were named, and it was xpected that from time to time the formation of ommittees would result having as their special prov-ice the consideration of the subjects suggested.

By vote, it was decided to take up for discussion, hrough national conferences, the three subjects of in-ustrial arbitration, taxation and municipal owner-hip. The first conference, that on industrial arbitra-ion, was held at Chicago, in December, 1900, and re-ulted in the organization of the Industrial Depart-ient, with A. C. Bartlett, of Chicago, chairman. In he following June a national conference on taxation as held in Buffalo, resulting in the formation of the epartment on Taxation, with Edwin R. A. Seligman s chairman. It was the intention to hold the confer-nce on Municipal Ownership in New York the fol-owing December, but in the meantime a number of arge strikes, especially the Steel Strike, the National lachinists' strike and a threatened Anthracite Coal trike absorbed so much of the energy and attention f the active members of the Federation at that time hat the Public Ownership Conference was postponed or the time being.

Through the work done by the committee in con-ection with the coal and steel strikes, Senator Hanna ecame interested in the organization, and in Decem-er of that year was made President of the organ-zation. His selection for that office, together with he appointment of other men of national reputa-ion on the committee, attracted the attention of the ountry to the organization. For two years following hat department was the only one prominent before he public, and its work in the prevention of strikes nd lockouts was naturally regarded as the only pur-ose of the organization. The conferences held dur-ng this period were naturally confined to the subject f conciliation and collateral phases of the work. As ational labor disturbances then became less frequent fter two years of this special work the organization as able to resume its original programme, holding tself, however, in readiness to concentrate its ener-ies on the industrial work at any time the need night arise.

It was at this time that the national conference on mmigration was called, and the Department of Immi-ration organized. After that a national commission n Municipal Ownership was formed, and by that ime the public began to take interest in the broader spects of the organization. Later came the estab-ishment of the Industrial Economies Department, hich has taken up some of the most important prob-ems of the day, including Socialism and Trusts and ombinations. The holding of a national conference n Political Reform resulted in the organization of a epartment especially devoted to these subjects.

While the subjects to be taken up by the organiza-ion are determined by the Executive Committee, he fact is here emphasized that in devoting itself to ther matters than questions relating to strikes and ckouts, the organization has not deviated from, but as returned to, its original lines.

Referring to the activities of the past year, the hairman speaks of the educational value of the eetings held under the auspices of the Federation. he several departments have held important meet-ngs, which are duly noted later. The gathering in lew York at the residence of Mr. Andrew Carnegie, hen 500 persons listened to a discussion of indus-rial arbitration, and one in Chicago at the residence f Mrs. Potter Palmer, attended by 700 persons, when a general presentation of the work of the National Civic Federation was made, deserve especial mention. In all these reunions, leaders of the world of capital and the world of labor have met on friendly terms for the discussion of their mutual interests.

IMMIGRATION DEPARTMENT.

Largely through the work of the Immigration Department, Congress was induced to appoint a Commission on Immigration, which commission has, with unlimited funds at its disposal, undertaken a large part of the work that had been planned by the Federation department. In fact, two members of our department are on the commission and have utilized all the material gathered by the Federation's experts, relating to both white and Oriental immigration. As some of the important evils, however, in the immigration problem are connected with the Port of New York, a committee, with Mr. Marcus M. Marks as chairman, secured valuable legislation at Albany last Winter to protect immigrants from frauds imposed upon them by bankers and ticket sellers. The department, representing all public interests affected by the immigration question, holds itself in readiness to take up any special problems which may remain after the national commission shall have completed its labors.

CONCILIATION DEPARTMENT.

The work of the Conciliation Department during the past year consisted largely of securing conferences at the request of one side or the other in threatened local disturbances. The only national strike of the year was that of the telegraphers, and in that every conceivable organization and influence was brought to bear, and all completely failed to effect any settlement. The same thing was true in the case of the local strike of the longshoremen in this city. It is an organization not affiliated with any other labor organization, and its leaders refused to discuss the matter with any outsiders. In some twenty-six instances conferences were secured by members of the Conciliation Committee that resulted in settlements, the last one being settled on the last day of the annual meeting at the Park Avenue Hotel while the meeting was in progress. This was the case of the New York cab drivers and the team owners' association. In this case the chairman of the New York Conciliation Committee induced seven men from each side of the controversy to meet him at the Park Avenue Hotel, and effected a settlement. In the case of the threatened street railway strike in Philadelphia President Low at the New York end, and Vice-President Gompers at the Washington end set machinery at work in Philadelphia that resulted in a settlement. This case, as well as many of the other cases for the year, brought out very conspicuously the fact that in most cases effective work can only be done through members of our organization who reside in the city where the trouble occurs. It was made perfectly clear in Philadelphia that outside intervention would not be accepted.

If the Committee on Organization, which will be recommended later, is appointed, it should secure membership for the Civic Federation in every important city in the United States. The lack of such members is one of our weak points now, as many of these local troubles arise where we have no one to call upon.

Every member of the Civic Federation, in whatever department, is always glad to respond to any request from the Conciliation Committee.

The importance of studying the questions that produce industrial disturbances was impressed upon the committee in several of the cases, especially the one in the case of the Erie Railroad machinists' strike. It is a straight-out fight on the question of piece-work. The management insists on piece-work and the machinists insist on day work. A committee of business men from points along the line of the Erie Railroad appealed to the Civic Federation to bring about a conference, and one was secured with President Underwood, but the men who have been suffering for several months for lack of work feel that the principle at stake is so great that they cannot afford, under any circumstances, to accept any proposition that even faces in the direction of that method of work. The apprentice question, restriction of output, shorter work-day, union or non-union shop and numerous other questions that underlie the majority of strikes should be taken up by the Conciliation or some other department and earnestly discussed.

The New England Civic Federation has during the past year rendered service in connection with threatened or actual trade disputes in the following industries and crafts: Shoe manufacture, electrical contracting, street railway service, boiler making, paper and pulp manufacture, truck teamsters, excavating, cotton manufacture, machinists, hotel porters, musicians, freight handlers, bookbinders, apparel workers, comb and novelty workers.

The threatened troubles between the big railway systems centering in Chicago and the engineers, firemen and conductors led to the discovery that the Erdman act, which has been on the statutes for some years, could render great service. The engineers settled their troubles with the railway managers without any outside help, but in the case of the firemen and conductors no settlement could be reached, so the railways appealed, under the Erdman act, to the chairman of the Interstate Commerce Commission and the Commissioner of Labor to act as conciliators. They were entirely successful, and prevented what threatened to be the greatest strike in years. The fact that the Interstate Commerce Commission decides, practically, what the railroads may charge for service makes it a logical thing that that commission should pass on the question of wages.

At our annual meeting the head of the New York State Bureau of Arbitration suggested that the Conciliation Committee of the National Civic Federation invite a conference of the various State boards on arbitration, bringing them into relation with its work. Eight or ten States have very good boards, and they have power to compel the attendance of witnesses and production books, etc., which, of course, our committee has not. I think, during the coming year, we ought to adopt the suggestion made.

WELFARE DEPARTMENT.

Among the efforts of the Welfare Department has been the formation of a committee to promote welfare work for Federal, State and municipal employes, with one hundred members throughout the United States, from the Atlantic to the Pacific Coast. Investigations of conditions surrounding Federal employes in the navy yard and in factory and office buildings in Washington, D. C., the post offices in New York and Chicago, the Brooklyn Navy Yard and of the employes on the Isthmus of Panama have been conducted and reported upon with convincing illustrations.

The importance of the work of that committee is shown by the fact that the conditions that were found surrounding the employes in the hospitals in New York City were such as would not be tolerated by a private employer. Commissioner Hebberd, who welcomed suggestions, has already made important improvements, and promises additional reforms as rapidly as funds can be secured by appropriation.

Mr. Marcus M. Marks, chairman of the Committee on Welfare Work for New York City's Employes, took up with Commissioner Bingham the conditions of the policemen with reference especially, to the inhuman working hours and the sanitary arrangements and dormitories in the station houses. Prompt action was taken in the matter of reducing the hours of work and some new station houses are being constructed; but the conditions are very bad, some places being unfit to be used for the stabling of horses, and yet our policemen are allowed to sleep in them.

The result of the investigation at Panama has been to secure many improvements for the benefit of the employes, as is evidenced by letters from and the personal testimony of employes and other visitors from Panama to the headquarters of the Federation, although some of the improvements which are most urgently needed, such as wholesome food, rational recreation, boat service and equitable labor regulations, have not yet received adequate attention.

Assistance Rendered Employes in Private Enterprises.—The department has been called upon to send literature and plans showing what other employers have provided in the way of pension funds, insurance covering accident, death or sick benefits; upon the entire scope of welfare work and specifically with reference to sanitary arrangements, seats for women, drinking water, rest rooms, ventilation, wash rooms, lighting systems, lunch rooms, safeguards for machinery, hospitals, recreation, housing, vestibules for street cars and industrial training.

The following companies have received such aid, either by correspondence or through personal service:

American Woolen Company, Lawrence, Mass.
United Shoe Machinery Company, Boston, Mass.
Colorado Fuel & Iron Company, Colorado.
B. F. Sturtevant Company, Boston, Mass.
United States Playing Card Company, Cincinnati, Ohio.
International Harvester Company, Chicago, Ill.
General Electric Company, Schenectady, N. Y.

Studebaker Brothers, South Bend, Ind.
Westinghouse Machine Company, East Pittsburg, Pa
Butler Brothers, St. Louis, Mo., and Chicago, Ill.
New York City Railway Company, New York.
Champlain Silk Mills, Whitehall, N. Y.
Reliance Automobile Company, Providence, R. I.
O. M. Edwards Company, Syracuse, N. Y.
Herrlinger Cordage & Paper Company, Cincinnati.
Philadelphia Watch Case Co., Riverside, N. J.
Meriden Britannica Company, Meriden, Conn.
Weston Electrical Instrument Co., Newark, N. J.
James Doren's Sons.
Curtis Publishing Company, Philadelphia, Pa.
Paiste & Company, Philadelphia, Pa.
National Railroad Company of Mexico, City of Mexico, Mexico.
Providence Engineering Company, Providence, R. I.
Talbot Mills, North Billerica, Mass.
Ballard & Ballard, Louisville, Ky.
Young Men's Christian Association; various places.
Oneida Community, Oneida, N. Y.
Ludlow Manufacturing Associates, Ludlow, Mass.
Cleveland Hardware Company, Cleveland, Ohio.
Solvay Process Company, Syracuse, N. Y.
The seventeen manufacturers in Greenfield, Mass.
Hood Rubber Company, New York.
Sherwin Williams Company, Cleveland, Ohio.
Deere & Company, Moline, Ill.
Malden Electric Company, Boston, Mass.
Regal Shoe Company, Boston, Mass.
S. D. Warren & Company, Cumberland Mills, Me.
Smith Premier Typewriter Company, Syracuse, N. Y.
Benton, Hall & Company, Cleveland, Ohio.
Commonwealth Steel Company, St. Louis, Mo.
Armour & Company, Chicago, Ill.
F. W. Bird & Son, East Walpole, Mass.
C. M. Clark, president East St. Louis & Suburban Railway Company, Philadelphia, Pa.
J. B. & J. M. Cornell, New York.
William Hengerer Company, Buffalo, N. Y.
Morrison, Mackintosh & Company, Grinnell, Ia.
Pepperell Manufacturing Company Biddeford, Me.
The Western Saving Fund Society, Philadelphia, Pa.
F. C. Huyck & Sons, Albany, N. Y.
L. Abt & Sons, Chicago.
Dexter Yarn Company, Pawtucket, R. I.
Western Corporation.
Stanley G. Flagg & Company, Philadelphia, Pa.
Crews, Beggs & Company, Pueblo, Col.
Farley, Harvey & Company, Boston, Mass.
A glass company in a Central State. (Name withheld because work not completed.)

A few illustrations will serve to show how this work is performed:

American Woolen Company, Lawrence, Mass. The services performed for this company present an interesting illustration of accomplishment through expert advice. Mr. W. M. Wood, the president, having attended a meeting of the woolen manufacturers, at which our stereopticon slides were shown, sent that company's welfare worker to New York to place himself entirely in the hands of the Welfare Department for the purpose of having certain improvements made. An expert was sent, who planned a lunch room for the women and men, trained the manager, selected the equipment, purchased same, and took up other details, which have resulted so successfully that the following letter was received recently from Mr. William E. Hall, treasurer of the Shaw Stocking Company:

"The writer called at your office some months ago and made some inquiry of you relative to welfare work being done by some large manufacturing concerns of the country. I now beg to advise that we are constructing a large building in connection with our factory for the purpose of furnishing meals to our operatives, who are largely girls, and also rooms for those who desire to make their home in the building. Realizing that we are rapidly approaching a point where we desire expert suggestions for laying out our kitchen, dining room, etc., I would be interested in receiving from you, at your earliest convenience information showing what the cost would be to us were we to enter into arrangements with you to have a representative of experience come here, at an early date, and gives us the necessary instruction. The main feature at the present time is the methods of furnishing dinners to about 300 persons during the noon hour from 12 to 1 o'clock.

"The writer understands that one of your lady representatives was given carte blanche at the Wood Worsted Mills, at Lawrence, Mass., in arranging their dining rooms.

"Assuring you that we shall be much interested in hearing from you relative to this important matter, we are."

An expert was sent at once, who has developed the plans, the following letter having been received since:

"I am in receipt of your favor of the 28th inst., with bill enclosed, covering expenses and services of Mrs. Thaon. I assure you that we are more than pleased to enclose herewith our check covering this bill, and beg to advise that we are much pleased with the services rendered by Mrs. Thaon."

A Glass Company in a Central State. At the request of the daughters of the president of that company, the secretary visited the factory, making an inspection and recommendations for improvements. An expert was furnished, who spent three months installing conveniences for the women employes, and plans are under consideration for other beneficial arrangements.

This is an interesting example of the result of the policy of the Welfare Department, which is to do no coercive work. It so happens that the president of the company, who has since become a member of the Executive Committee of the Welfare Department, met the secretary at the time of her visit with the statement that "he had no use for women reformers and would not allow her to enter his factory if it were not for (pointing to his daughter) that girl!" His antagonism is the result of a report made by a Socialist, who included the sentence that at this particular plant "little boys were found carrying red-hot bottles in their naked hands," together with other like occurrences. He attended our meeting at the residence of Mrs. Potter Palmer, in Chicago, and saw upon the screen not only views of ventilating devices such as he had thoughtfully installed for workers in superheated places, but also views of conveniences which have been introduced in various trades, and thus learned that similar facilities for the comfort of the workers might be introduced into the glass industry, since practical employers elsewhere had proven their usefulness. This should have a far-reaching effect, because other employers in that trade are likely to follow his example.

United Shoe Machinery Company, Boston. Mr. George W. Brown, one of our members, secured an expert from us, who completely reorganized the old lunch room and aided in planning a new one for eight hundred employes. It is now in operation. It will be described, with illustrations, in another issue of the *Review*.

Colorado Fuel & Iron Company, Colorado. Thinking that the unusually efficient head of the Sociological Department of that company might be interested, the secretary sent to him the plan of the changing house for miners, which was successfully installed by one of our members, Mr. W. G. Mather, of the Cleveland Cliffs Iron Company, for the purpose of enabling the men to bathe and put on dry, clean garments at the close of the day's work. The result was that during the year the Colorado Fuel & Iron Company constructed such excellent washhouses for its miners and they have been pictured in its annual report.

The B. F. Sturtevant Company, Boston. The publication by this company of plans for the construction of a new mill afforded an opportunity to offer suggestions for modern sanitary arrangements, with the result that the president of the company wrote thanking us for the illustrated pamphlets and stating, "I assure you it will be my purpose to bear the suggestions of your department in mind in the construction of the mill."

One successful piece of work was culminated in March, through the efforts of the Rev. Dr. Thomas R. Slicer, chairman of our New York Welfare Committee, who induced the Interborough Rapid Transit Company to put vestibules on the surface cars in New York.

Lectures have been delivered by members of the Welfare Department at the following places:
Albany, N. Y.—Municipal Men's Club.
Boston, Mass.—Women's Educational and Industrial League.
Newburg, N. Y.—Civitas Club.
Ithaca, N. Y.—College of Agriculture, Cornell University.
Washington, D. C.—Before members of Congress.
Minneapolis, Minn.—National Conference of Charities and Correction.
Grinnell, Ia.—Iowa Manufacturers' Association.
Chicago, Ill.—At residence of Mrs. Potter Palmer.
Brooklyn, N. Y.—The Turn Verein.
Philadelphia, Pa.—Pennsylvania Institute of the Young Men's Christian Association.
Muncie, Ind.—At residence of Mrs. F. C. Ball.
St. Louis, Mo.—Women's Clubs.
Passaic, N. J.—Women's Clubs.
Long Island City, N. Y.—Women's Clubs.
New York City—The Colony Club.
New York City—The Stationary Firemen's Union.
New York City—Speyer School.
New York City—Teachers' College.
New York City—Unitarian Club.
Cambridge, Mass.—School of Inspection at Harvard Medical School.

INDUSTRIAL ECONOMICS DEPARTMENT.

Under the auspices of the Industrial Economics Department Mr. W. H. Mallock, the noted English individualist, visited the United States and delivered a series of lectures on Socialism. The lectures were given at several universities—Columbia, Harvard, Johns Hopkins, Pennsylvania and Chicago. Their keen analysis of the socialistic faith and refutation of its pretensions attracted much attention and the lectures were reproduced extensively in the general newspaper press and in the labor papers. They were published in pamphlet form by the National Civic Federation and have received considerable circulation.

The main achievement of the Industrial Economics Department was the organization of the National Conference on Trusts and Combinations, held in Chicago October 22-25, 1907. It was one of the most successful efforts of the Federation. A large and thoroughly representative assembly, composed of delegates appointed by the Governors of States and a large number of organizations, to the number of nearly 500 persons gathered for the discussion of this most important problem. Without a dissenting voice, the conference passed a series of resolutions calling for an official investigation of the whole subject of trusts by a non-partisan national commission, and indicating some of the lines which such investigation might properly cover. Arrangements have been made for the presentation of these resolutions on March 7, 1908, to the President and to the two Houses of Congress by a large and representative committee.

PUBLIC OWNERSHIP COMMISSION.

During the Summer the Public Ownership Commission made a highly valuable report upon the operation of public utilities by municipal governments and private corporations. The high standing of its members, the representation among them of various shades of opinion, the ample technical and other expert assistance at the disposition of the committee and the personal inspection by its members of many public utility plants had led to the hope that its labors would bear fruit in important and authoritative conclusions. Nor was this hope disappointed. The general conclusions of the committee appended to the report have been most favorably received by the press and by students of this problem as the findings upon the evidence of a highly intelligent jury. These findings gain additional force from the remarkable unanimity with which they are approved by the committee. Out of twenty-one members of the committee only one withheld his consent to the report.

The printed report contains the general conclusions of the committee reports on special topics made by various sub-committees and a detailed account of the various plants visited in the United States and Great Britain. It is published in three large volumes of upward of 2,500 pages.

The conclusions follow:

It is difficult to give positive answers of universal application to the questions arising as to the success or failure of municipal ownership as compared with private ownership. The local conditions affecting particular plants are, in many cases, so peculiar as to make a satisfactory comparison impossible, and it is very difficult to estimate the allowance that should be made for these local conditions. For instance, in making deductions from the financial conditions of Wheeling, as affected by its gas plant, as compared with those of Atlanta and Norfolk with their private plants, allowance must be made for the presence of natural gas in Wheeling. Again, in comparing the public water works of Syracuse with the private water works of Indianapolis from the point of view of the success or failure of municipal operation, geographical conditions must be taken into consideration. The situation at Syracuse is extremely favorable to the establishment of an efficient plant with comparatively little effort on the part of its management. At Indianapolis the conditions are unfavorable. In Syracuse the water flows to the city by gravity; in Indianapolis it must be pumped. So we might go through the various cities here and abroad that have been visited and show that the results were affected favorably or unfavorably by special conditions applicable to each city.

Further, the difficulty of reaching satisfactory results by the comparative method is not confined to special or local conditions. It is true, as well, of much broader questions. Thus any attempt to compare municipal with private electric light plants in the United States would be fruitless if allowance were not made, for the fact that in most cases such municipal plants are confined to street lighting and may not do commercial business. Allowance must be made also for the fact that many municipal plants have had a struggle to exist in the face of unsympathetic public opinion. Again, in England consideration must be given to the fact that the municipal electric light and street railway plants have permanent rights, while the rights of the private companies operating these particular utilities are limited as to the length of their existence, many street railway franchises expiring twenty-one years after they were granted.

Finally, not only must it be borne in mind that the social and political conditions which characterize the

We wish to bring to your consideration the danger here in the United States of turning over these public utilities to the present government of some of our cities. Some, we know, are well governed and the situation on the whole seems to be improving, but they are not up to the government of British cities. We found in England and Scotland a high type of municipal government, which is the result of many years of struggle and improvement. Business men seem to take a pride in serving as city councillors or aldermen, and the government of such cities as Glasgow, Manchester, Birmingham and others includes many of the best citizens of the city. These conditions are distinctly favorable to municipal operation.

In the United States, as is well known, there are many cities not in such a favorable condition. It is charged that the political activity of public service corporations has in many instances been responsible for the unwillingness or inability of American cities to secure a higher type of public service. This charge we believe to be true. However, there seems to be an idea with many people that the mere taking by the city of all its public utilities for municipal operation will at once result in ideal municipal government through the very necessity of putting honest and competent citizens in charge. While an increase in the number and importance of municipal functions may have a tendency to induce men of a higher type to become public officials, we do not believe that this of itself will accomplish municipal reform. We are unable to recommend municipal ownership as a political panacea.

In many cases in the United States the people have heedlessly given away their rights and reserved no sufficient power of control or regulation, and we believe that corruption of public servants has sprung, in large measure, from this condition of things. With the regulations that we have advised, with the publication of accounts and records and systematic control, the danger of the corruption of public officials is very much reduced.

To sum up, certain of the more important of our conclusions are:

Public utilities, whether in public or in private hands, are best conducted under a system of legalized and regulated monopoly.

Public utilities in which the sanitary motive largely enters should be operated by the public.

The success of municipal operation of public utilities depends upon the existence in the city of a high capacity for municipal government.

Franchise grants to private corporations should be terminable after a fixed period, and meanwhile subject to purchaes at a fair value.

Municipalities should have power to enter the field of municipal ownership upon popular vote under reasonable regulation.

Private companies operating public utilities should be subject to public regulation and examination under a system of uniform records and accounts and of full publicity.

The general expediency of either private or public ownership is a question that must be determined by each municipality in the light of local conditions. What may be possible in one locality may not be in another. In some cities the companies may so serve the public as to create no dissatisfaction and nothing might be gained by experimenting with municipal ownership. Again, the government of one city may be good and capable of taking charge of these public utilities, while in another it may be the reverse. In either case the people, must remember that it requires a large class of able men as city officials to look after these matters. They must also remember that municipal ownership will create a large class of employes who may have more or less political influence.

AS OTHERS SEE US.

Continued from page 11.

At the moment a dangerous subject was in the air—the financial crisis. One could not avoid speaking of it, still the most opposed interests were represented in this assembly. There were rich people, who could be considered as having caused the panic, and poor people who suffered by it. How was it possible that the short coat and the evening dress wouldn't quarrel that night? Of course, some very pointed remarks were made. On the side of the evening dress, President Eliot, in spite of his age, showed the greatest audacity. With very quiet disdain of popularity, he maintained that the labor unions, as well as the trades, should be subjected to the control of the Federal Government. A very bold opinion, but the reply of Mr. Gompers was still keener. The external appearance of this famous leader is surely a very pacific one. He always wears a cap, which is very much the same as that of an usher of the College de France; his gray hair is always sweeping the collar of his coat, his nose is armed with golden spectacles, and he looks when on the platform like a good-natured scholar who is going to make a report to the Academy. You wouldn't think at that moment he was the powerful leader of one and a half millions of workingmen, something like the Roosevelt of the American unions. As soon as he speaks, however, he is not the same man. A kind of continual anger seems to possess him, every one of his gestures is a menace, and all his words have a kind of tragical effect. His speech was in an aggressive tone. One felt that behind this little man the working masses were standing, the masses which have not yet expressed their opinion in the general disturbance, but which are going to speak.

MR. TIMOTHY HEALY.

ADDRESSING Local Union No. 56, International Brotherhood of Stationary Firemen, New York, December 21, 1907, Mr. Healy said:

Last Monday night one of the most remarkable gatherings was held in this city. I refer to the dinner of the National Civic Federation, held at the Hotel Astor. It was the largest gathering that the Civic Federation ever had, nearly 800 people being present. There were at the dinner, among others, Miss Morgan, Mrs. Harriman, Mr. Andrew Carnegie, Mr. John D. Rockefeller, Jr., President Eliot, Mr. Samuel Gompers and Mr. John Mitchell. A meeting of labor and capital! Representatives of all walks of life, some of our biggest millionaires and captains of industry, as well as leaders of labor and men representing the "general public," were there gathered together. I want to tell you, my friends, that in no other country could there be such a gathering. It is a great country where capital and labor can sit down and discuss their grievances; and the National Civic Federation is the organization that makes such a thing possible. This organization is only in its infancy. I predict that in ten years from now every one, even the most radical, will be interested in its work.

I want to say that our grievances and the great majority of our strikes and lockouts have occurred because the employer and the employe were too far apart, and if they can be brought nearer together we shall not have the great labor wars that we have had in the past, and both capital and labor will be a great deal better off.

There is a gentleman in England, a great philanthropist, named Mosely.

Mr. Mosely tried to start a branch of the National Civic Federation in England, but it was a failure.

It would not go there. The upper classes in England would not come down to mingle with the representatives of labor. I will just read you an interview with a French editor in last Tuesday's "American," which was published in nearly all the daily papers, who said among other things: "It was indeed a remarkable thing, to my mind, that Samuel Gompers should sit beside Andrew Carnegie and James Speyer, two of your best-known capitalists."

Now, that is the difference between England and America. We are ahead of them in that, and I think that we are the winners. We all know that this is a great country. Boys, let us try to make it greater! We can do it by having more confidence in ourselves and more confidence in those who are higher up.

It will never do to fight all the time, so let us have peace for the great good and the great results that will be obtained in this Republic for our children and our children's children who will come after us.

LESLIE'S WEEKLY.

IN its issue of January 3, 1908, Leslie's Weekly describes the dinner of the National Civic Federation as "one of the most remarkable public dinners of 1907," and, commenting on the Civic Federation, says:—

"The election of Seth Low to the presidency of the National Civic Federation augurs well for the continued usefulness of that organization, which has already done so much to bring the representatives of capital, labor and the general public to a better understanding. Mr. Low is a fine type of the business man, who divests himself of the cares of commerce to give his services unreservedly to the public, as Mr. Low has done in educational affairs, in politics, and is now doing in the cause of industrial peace—thereby performing a service second in importance to none that he has rendered in the past. At the annual dinner of the Federation, given in New York recently, the principles of the organization were illustrated and emphasized by the presence at the same board of such men as President Eliot, of Harvard, and John Mitchell, Samuel Gompers and August Belmont, while members of the Morgan, Harriman and Rockefeller families were elbow to elbow with the wives and daughters of wage-earners. Such social meetings have been made fairly familiar to the American public through the established usage of the Federation, but they seem nothing less than epoch-making to foreign observers, of whom several were present at the dinner in question, and so they are. Well-deserved compliments upon the success of this year's meeting were tendered by the Federation to Ralph M. Easley, the Chairman of the Executive Council, who has for years directed the activities of the organization with consummate tact and efficiency."

TRUSTS AND COMBINATIONS

PROCEEDINGS OF THE NATIONAL CONFERENCE

RESOLUTIONS ADOPTED—DELEGATES APPOINTED

THE National Conference on Trusts and Combinations, held at Chicago October 22-25, 1907, brought together a large and representative body of men for the discussion of one of the most important questions before the American people at the present time. By resolution of the conference, the National Civic Federation was charged with the duty of preparing the proceedings for publication, and a volume of nearly five hundred pages, giving a verbatim report of the entire proceedings, is just off the press. The profound interest aroused by the announcement that the conference would take place is well demonstrated by the large number of delegates appointed by the Governors of the States and by the presidents of commercial, financial, economic, agricultural and labor organizations and other bodies concerned with our national welfare.

The conference was called to order by Dr. Nicholas Murray Butler, chairman of the Industrial Economics Department of the National Civic Federation, who, in his opening address, stated in general terms the problems which were before the conference for discussion. The conference elected the following officers:

Chairman,

NICHOLAS MURRAY BUTLER.........New York

Vice-Chairmen,

SAMUEL GOMPERS....................New York
NAHUM J. BACHELDER..........New Hampshire
DAVID R. FORGAN..........................Illinois
C. P. WALBRIDGE.........................Missouri
D. A. TOMPKINS...................North Carolina
GEORGE LANGFORD.......................Oregon
BROOKS ADAMS...................Massachusetts

Permanent Secretary,

JAMES B. REYNOLDS.................New York

Assistant Secretaries,

HENRY WALLACE..............Des Moines, Iowa
DELL KEIZER....................Topeka, Kansas
HAL H. SMITH...................Detroit, Michigan

The proceedings of the conference were in a high degree interesting and varied. Addresses or papers were presented as follows:

"Present Principles Enunciated by the New Organization of Attorneys-General," Wade H. Ellis, Attorney-General of Ohio.

"State and Federal Jurisdiction Over Interstate Commerce," William P. Borland, Attorney-at-Law, Kansas City, Mo.

"Does the Power to Regulate Rates in Transportation of Commerce Rest with Congress or the States?" A. T. Ankeny, Attorney-at-Law, Minneapolis, Minn.

"Conflict Between Federal and State Courts," David P. Marum, Attorney-at-Law, Woodward, Oklahoma.

"Shall Federal Jurisdiction Be Extended in the Solution of the Trust Problem?" John W. Tomlinson, Attorney-at-Law, Birmingham, Ala.

"Remedies for Monopolies and Their Results," William Dudley Foulke, Attorney-at-Law, Richmond, Ind.

"Governmental Regulation," Theodore Marburg, Baltimore, Md.

"Uniform Federal and State Control Over Interstate Matters," Charles F. Ziebold, President West End Business Men's Association, St. Louis, Mo.

"National Control of Railways," Seth Low, Publicist, New York.

"Powers of the State and Nation Over Corporations and Trusts," Bartlett Tripp, Attorney-at-Law, ex-Minister to Austria, Yankton, S. D.

"The Farmers' Interest in Trust Regulation," Nahum J. Bachelder, Master of the National Grange, Concord, N. H.

"The Trust Situation," Jeremiah W. Jenks, Professor in Cornell University, Ithaca, N. Y.

"The Trust Problem," Isaac N. Seligman, Banker, New York.

"Destruction or Regulation," Edgar A. Bancroft, Attorney-at-Law, Chicago, Ill.

"Overcapitalization," Irving Fisher, Professor in Yale University, New Haven, Conn.

"Trust Philosophy Boiled Down," Frank Parsons, Professor in Boston University, Boston, Mass.

"Corporations as Such," John S. Crosby, Attorney-at-Law, New York.

"The Enforcement of the Sherman Anti-Trust Law," Frank B. Kellogg, Special United States Assistant Attorney-General, St. Paul, Minn.

"Anti-Trust Laws," Peter S. Grosscup, Judge United States Circuit Court, Chicago, Ill.

"Corporate Reforms," Eugene E. Prussing, Attorney-at-Law, Chicago, Ill.

"Labor Unions and Trusts," Samuel Gompers, President American Federation of Labor, Washington, D. C.

"The Sherman Anti-Trust Law," Charles G. Dawes, President Central Trust Company, Chicago, Ill.

"The Evils of Competition," Grange Sard, Manufacturer, Albany, N. Y.

"Regulation of Transportation Rates," Robert Mather, Vice-President Chicago, Rock Island and Pacific Railroad, New York.

"Governmental Regulation of Competitive and Monopolistic Corporations," Allen Ripley Foote, Columbus, Ohio.

"Administrative Regulation of Corporations," Herbert Knox Smith, Commissioner of Corporations, Washington, D. C.

"The Railways and the People," D. A. Tompkins, Manufacturer, Charlotte, N. C.

"Reasonable Agreements Beneficial to Commerce," William Jay Schieffelin, Merchant, New York.

"Newspapers, Their Relation to the Paper Trust and to the Labor Trust," Herman Ridder, Proprietor of the New Yorker Staats-Zeitung, New York.

"Federal Incorporation," Henry W. Palmer, Member of Congress, Wilkes-Barre, Pa.

"The American Society of Equity and Its Need in Our Country," J. A. Everitt, President American Society of Equity.

"What Next," F. W. Taussig, Professor in Harvard University, Cambridge, Mass.

"The Trust Question from Labor's Standpoint," Thomas Carl Spelling, Attorney-at-Law, New York.

"The English Incorporation Act," Hennen Jennings, Washington, D. C.

"The Relation of Industrial Combinations to Export Trade," James H. Gore, Professor in the George Washington University, Washington, D. C.

"The Adjustment of Labor Problems and the Policy of Incorporating Unions," D. C. Seitz, New York.

"Is the Tariff the Mother of the Trusts?" Byron W. Holt, American Free Trade League, New York.

Other participants in the trust discussion who spoke more briefly were: George H. Barbour, Michigan; Warren S. Stone, Ohio; Avery C. Moore, Idaho; Wilbur F. Wakeman and Franklin Pierce, of New York; Charles J. Traxler, Karl Mathie and A. T. Stebbins, of Minnesota; James Bingham and Robert Taylor, of Indiana; J. W. Kinnear and Mahlon N. Kline, of Pennsylvania; Charles W. Needham, District of Columbia; Albert Hibbert, Massachusetts; Thomas V. Wooten, J. Newton Ninde, Henry Othmer, J. E. Defebaugh and S. Westerfield, of Illinois.

As a conference upon the same subject was held in the year 1899 in the same city, under the auspices of the Civic Federation of Chicago, a comparison of the two gatherings is natural. Two marked points of distinction can be observed. First, the larger scope; and, second, the greater unanimity of the latter conference, as compared with the earlier one. It may perhaps be due in part to the growth of the Civic Federation from a local to a national organization that the conference of 1907, called under the auspices of the national body, was so much larger and more representative than that of 1899, and it may be due in part to the growth of public opinion and the spread of information upon the various aspects of the trust question.

Whatever the cause, the results were highly gratifying. A significant evidence of this greater interest is found in the larger number of delegations appointed in 1907 than in 1899. The records show the following:

Delegations.	1899	1907
Appointed by Governors............	33	42
Appointed by national and State organizations......	22	33
Appointed by labor organizations...	7	14
Appointed by local commercial bodies......	33	58
Totals.................	95	147

Furthermore, the attendance of 492 delegates in 1907 might be contrasted with that of 238 delegates at the earlier conference.

To name individually the States whose Governors appointed delegates to this convention would partake of a lesson in geography. Suffice it to say, that official representatives were present from all sections of the country, from Massachusetts to Colorado, and from Washington to Florida. Equally noteworthy was the large representation of organizations which represented interests affected to a greater or less extent by the trust question in its various aspects. The list printed herewith reveals the presence of organizations devoted to the furtherance of such interests as those of jurisprudence, agriculture, banking, manufacturing, labor, commerce in general and wholesale and retail trade.

The conference of 1907 differed further from the earlier body in the adoption of definite and important resolutions. Those who examine the proceedings of the earlier gathering cannot but be struck by the fact that the keynote of its proceedings is the wide diversity of opinion in regard to the economic attributes of trusts and combinations, as well as the legislative measures which should be adopted to cope with them. The Committee on Resolutions of that conference made a prolonged and earnest effort to agree upon definite recommendations, but failed utterly to do so. It may be that at that time the subject of trusts was too new and too vaguely understood for men to be of one mind regarding it.

The situation which confronted the recent conference was materially different. Public education on the subject of trusts has been proceeding at a very rapid rate of late years. Through the investigations of the Industrial Commission, the reports of the Bureau of Corporations of the new Department of Commerce and Labor and the records of several important judicial inquiries, the public now has access to accurate information concerning some of the more important trusts and combinations, where formerly it was obliged to form its opinion upon the unsubstantiated and partial evidence set forth by the critics, and occasionally the defenders, of those organizations. There can be no doubt that public opinion on the subject is beginning to crystallize.

The important service rendered by the trust conference, which was recently held in Chicago was to offer an opportunity for the various interests to give expression to the views which have been slowly maturing in the course of the last few years, and to seek a common ground, if one could be found, on which all these interests might unite. That among so many speakers widely divergent views should be expressed is not to be wondered at. Yet one feature, so characteristic of recent discussions of this matter, namely, the wholesale denunciation of trusts, was conspicuously absent. The recognition of the services to our industrial development rendered by various forms of combinations was general. It varied widely according to the personality of the speaker, between a hearty commendation and a somewhat grudging admission. This attitude, however, willingly or unwillingly expressed, eliminated from the proceedings of the conference the battle which has heretofore been waged between those who would destroy the trusts, root and branch, and those who believe that regulation is not only practicable, but a sound public policy.

So far, though, as it may be possible to gauge the consensus of opinion of such a body, it may be said that the conference was distinctly in favor of the regulation of trusts and combinations, though the details of such regulation presented in the minds of the several speakers a wide variety of form. This difference of opinion as to the proper remedies is, in a measure, reflected in the resolutions adopted by the conference.

The forthcoming volume of the proceedings will be not only a contribution to economic literature, but also to the literature of politics in the larger sense of dealing with some of the fundamental concepts of our national life and government. Were the remarks of the several speakers welded into one, they would appear as a plea for a larger intervention of the national government in the business and commercial life of our people. Not that the strictly business and commercial interests are desirous of government interference, but recognizing under existing conditions the inevitability of government intervention, the desire that such intervention should proceed from the nation rather than the State, was very marked. An increase of the activities of the Federal Government in dealing with questions of industrial life was accepted practically as a matter of course by a large majority of the speakers. Among the legal members of the conference, who gave ut-

OFFICERS AND SPEAKERS, NATIONAL CONFERENCE ON TRUSTS AND COMBINATIONS.

terance to some very acute analysis of the Federal Constitution, there was some diversity of opinion as to whether the increased power needed by the nation to meet the national questions now arising could be obtained by a reasonable interpretation of the clauses of the Constitution, or whether the more cumbersome form of constitutional amendment must be adopted. Here, again, it may perhaps be estimated that the weight of opinion was with those who believed that the nation already has in the Constitution adequate power to meet the situations so far as they can now be foreseen, arising from the prodigious development of trusts and combinations of all kinds in our country.

The general attitude of the conference being thus understood, the resolutions adopted by it assume a great significance. Considering the care devoted to their preparation and the unanimity with which they were adopted, there can be no doubt that they fairly represent the general trend of opinion.

One of the first acts of the conference was to provide for the appointment of a Committee on Resolutions to consist of fifteen members at large appointed by the chair and representatives of each State chosen by the respective State delegations. All persons attending the conference, by whomsoever appointed, were considered part of the State delegation for the purpose of making these selections. The committee thus constituted was thoroughly representative. Dr. Albert Shaw was chosen chairman of the committee and Prof. John H. Gray, of the University of Minnesota, acted as secretary. The members of the committee were:

MEMBERS AT LARGE.

SETH LOW, Publicist....................New York
SAMUEL GOMPERS, President American Federation of Labor....................Washington, D. C.
C. H. SMITH, President Illinois Manufacturers' Association....................Chicago, Ill.
JAMES M. LYNCH, President International Typographical Union....................Indianapolis, Ind.
AARON JONES, National Grange...South Bend, Ind.
GEORGE W. PERKINS, President International Cigar Makers' Union....................Chicago, Ill.
FRANKLIN MacVEAGH, Wholesale Grocer, Chicago, Ill.
A. T. ANKENY, Attorney-at-Law..Minneapolis, Minn.
JAMES O'CONNELL, President International Association of Machinists....................Washington, D. C.
JOHN F. CROCKER, President Chamber of Commerce....................Boston, Mass.
FRANK DUFFY, General Secretary United Brotherhood of Carpenters and Joiners of America, Indianapolis, Ind.
WILLIAM JAY SCHIEFFELIN, National Association of Wholesale Druggists....................New York
DANIEL J. KEEFE, President International Longshoremen, Marine and Transporters' Association. Detroit, Mich.
PROF. J. LAURENCE LAUGHLIN, University of Chicago....................Chicago, Ill.
A. T. STEBBINS, National Retail Hardware Association....................Rochester, Minn.

MEMBERS SELECTED BY STATE DELEGATIONS.

JOHN W. TOMLINSON....................Alabama
G. W. HULL....................Arizona
CHARLES S. THOMAS....................Colorado
IRVING FISHER....................Connecticut
J. HOWARD GORE..........District of Columbia
J. W. ARCHIBALD....................Florida
AVERY C. MOORE....................Idaho
JOHN V. FARWELL, JR....................Illinois
JOHN H. HOLLIDAY....................Indiana
F. L. MAYTAG....................Iowa
JAMES W. ORR....................Kansas
GEORGE L. SEHON....................Kentucky
THEODORE MARBURG....................Maryland
DR. FRED WILLIAM HAMILTON....Massachusetts
GEORGE H. BARBOUR....................Michigan
JOHN W. WILLIS....................Minnesota
ROBERT H. WHITELAW....................Missouri
WALTER L. LOCKE....................Nebraska
NAHUM J. BACHELDER..........New Hampshire
HOWARD H. WOOD....................New Jersey
J. H. BEARRUP....................New Mexico
DR. ALBERT SHAW....................New York
D. A. TOMPKINS....................North Carolina
ALLEN R. FOOTE....................Ohio
DAVID P. MARUM....................Oklahoma
GEORGE LANGFORD....................Oregon
TALCOTT WILLIAMS....................Pennsylvania
J. A. PICKLER....................South Dakota
JAMES S. MEAD....................Tennessee
F. G. HOWLAND....................Vermont
WYNDHAM R. MEREDITH....................Virginia
JAMES C. LAWRENCE....................Washington
JAMES M. PAYNE....................West Virginia
WILLIAM GEORGE BRUCE....................Wisconsin
NELLIS CORTHELL....................Wyoming

The resolutions presented on the floor of the convention, as well as those handed to the secretary, were referred by the committee above named to a smaller committee of nine persons. After a prolonged discussion the sub-committee, upon the basis of the several resolutions before it, drafted a proposition which was submitted to the whole committee, and after considerable discussion and amendment in detail, was adopted by that committee. Upon presentation of its report to the conference at its concluding session there was considerable debate, less in the nature of criticism than for the purpose of bringing out the exact purport of the resolutions. The difficulties suggested being satisfactorily explained, the conference, without a dissenting voice, adopted the following resolutions:

After twenty years of federal legislation as interpreted by the courts, directed against the evils of trusts and combinations, and against railroad rebates, beginning with the interstate commerce act of 1887 and the anti-trust act of 1890, a general and just conviction exists that the experience gained in enforcing these federal acts and others succeeding them demonstrates the necessity of legislation which shall render more secure the benefits already gained and better meet the changed conditions which have arisen during a long period of active progress, both in the enforcement of statute law and in the removal of grave abuses in the management of railroads and corporations. These changes now demanded are:

First—Immediate legislation is required, following the recommendation of President Roosevelt and the Interstate Commerce Commission, permitting agreements between railroad corporations on reasonable freight and passenger rates, subject in all respects to the approval, supervision, and action of the Interstate Commerce Commission.

Second—The enforcement of the Sherman act and the proceedings under it during the administrations of Presidents Harrison, Cleveland, McKinley and Roosevelt have accomplished great national results in awakening the moral sense of the American people and in asserting the supremacy and majesty of the law, thus effectually refuting the impression that great wealth and large corporations were too powerful for the impartial execution of law. This great advance has rendered more secure all property rights, resting, as they must, under a popular government, on universal respect for and obedience to law. But now that this work is accomplished, it has revealed the necessity for legislation which shall maintain all that the Sherman act was intended to secure and safeguard interests it was never expected to affect.

As the next step in executing the determination of the American people to secure in all industrial and commercial relations justice and equality of opportunity for all, with full sympathy and loyal support for every effort to enforce the laws in the past, we urge upon Congress without delay to pass legislation providing for a non-partisan commission, in which the interests of capital, of labor and of the general public shall be represented. This commission, like a similar commission, which proved most successful in Germany in 1870, shall consider the entire subject of business and industrial combinations and report such proposals as to the formation, capitalization, management, and regulation of corporations (so far as the same may be subject to federal jurisdiction) as shall preserve individual initiative, competition, and the free exercise of a free contract in all business and industrial relations. Any proposed legislation should also include modification of the prohibition now existing upon combinations on the following subjects:

1. National and local organizations of labor and their trade agreements with employers relating to wages, hours of labor, and conditions of employment.

2. Associations made up of farmers, intended to secure a stable and equitable market for the products of the soil, free from fluctuations due to speculation.

3. Business and industrial agreements or combinations whose objects are in the public interest as distinguished from objects determined to be contrary to the public interest.

4. Such commission should make a thorough inquiry into the advisability of inaugurating a system of federal license or incorporation as a condition for the entrance of certain classes of corporations upon interstate commerce and also into the relation to the public interest of the purchase by one corporation of the franchises or corporate stock of another.

On no one of these subjects must what has been gained be sacrified until something better appears for enactment. On each, this conference recognizes differences between good men. On all, it asks a national non-partisan commission to be appointed next Winter to consider the question and report at the second session of the approaching Congress for such action as the national legislature, in the light of this full investigation, may enact.

Third—The examination, inspection and supervision of great producing and manufacturing corporations, already begun by the Department of Commerce and Labor and accepted by these corporations, should be enlarged by legislation requiring, through the appropriate bureaus of the Department of Commerce and Labor, complete publicity in the capitalization, accounts, operations, transportation charges paid, and selling prices of all such producing and manufacturing corporations whose operations are large enough to have a monopolistic influence. This should be determined and decided by some rule and classification to be devised by the commission already proposed.

Fourth—The conflicts between State and Federal authority raised in many States over railroad rates being now under adjudication and under way to a final and ultimate decision by the Federal Supreme Court, this conference deems the expression of an opinion on these issues unfitting, and confidently leaves this great issue to a tribunal which for 118 years has successfully preserved the balance between an indissoluble union and indestructible States, defining the supreme and national powers of the one and protecting the sovereign and individual powers of the other.

ORGANIZATIONS WHICH APPOINTED DELEGATES TO THE NATIONAL CONFERENCE ON TRUSTS AND COMBINATIONS

Affiliated presidents and secretaries of commercial and trade organizations.
American Bankers' Association.
American Bar Association.
National Business League of America.
National Association of Clothiers.
National Wholesale Druggist Association.
National Retail Druggist Association.
American Society of Equity.
American Free Trade League.
National Grange Patrons of Husbandry.
National Wholesale Grocers' Association.
National Retail Grocers' Association.
National Retail Hardware Association.
National Association of Agricultural Implement and Vehicle Manufacturers.
Southern Lumbermen's Association.
Yellow Pine Manufacturers' Association.
The Proprietary Association.
National Association of Piano Dealers.
American Protective Tariff League.
National Association of State Railway Commissioners.
National Saddlery Manufacturers' Association.
Western Association of Shoe Wholesalers.
National Association of Stove Manufacturers.
Independent Tobacco Manufacturers' Association of the United States.
National Wagon Manufacturers' Association.
Illinois Lumber Dealers' Association.
Illinois Manufacturers' Association.
Illinois Retail Merchants' Association.
Indiana State Bar Association.
Michigan Manufacturers' Association.
Missouri State Bar Association.
Virginia State Bar Association.
West Virginia Bar Association.
Bricklayers' and Masons' International Union.
Structural Building Trades Alliance of America.
United Brotherhood of Carpenters and Joiners of America.
International Brotherhood of Electrical Workers.
International Union of Steam Engineers.
Glass Bottle Blowers' Association of the United States and Canada.
International Association of Machinists.
International Longshoremen, Marine and Transport Workers' Association.
Brotherhood of Railroad Trainmen.
Order of Railway Conductors of America.
International Brotherhood of Stationary Firemen.
International Typographical Union.
Central Labor Union, District of Columbia.
Syracuse Trades and Labor Assembly.
Chamber of Commerce of Albany, N. Y.
Merchants Association of Boston, Mass.
Board of Trade of Birmingham, Ala.
Commercial Club of Brockton, Mass.
Commercial Club of Cedar Rapids, Ia.
Association of Commerce of Chicago, Ill.
Citizens' Association of Chicago, Ill.
City Club of Chicago, Ill.
Civic Federation of Chicago, Ill.
Commercial Club of Chicago, Ill.
Hamilton Club of Chicago, Ill.
Iroquois Club of Chicago, Ill.
Legislative Voters' League of Chicago, Ill.
Marquette Club of Chicago, Ill.
Business Men's League of Cincinnati, O.
Chamber of Commerce of Cincinnati, O.
Manufacturers' Club of Cincinnati, O.
Chamber of Commerce of Cleveland, O.
Board of Trade of Columbus, O.
Commercial Club of Council Bluffs, Ia.
Chamber of Commerce of Decatur, Ill.
Commercial Club of Des Moines, Ia.
Single Tax Corporation of Fairhope, Ala.
Commercial Club of Fort Madison, Ia.
Commercial Club of Fort Wayne, Ind.
Board of Trade of Grand Rapids, Mich.
Board of Trade of Hartford, Conn.

Board of Trade of Indianapolis, Ind.
Board of Trade of Jacksonville, Fla.
Commercial Club of Kansas City, Mo.
Board of Trade of Lawrence, Mass.
Board of Trade of Louisville, Ky.
Commercial Club of Louisville, Ky.
Board of Trade of Lynn, Mass.
Forty Thousand Club of Madison, Wis.
Merchants' and Manufacturers' Association of Milwaukee, Wis.
Commercial Club of Muncie, Ind.
Commercial Club of New Albany, Ind.
Board of Trade of Newark, N. J.
Chamber of Commerce of New Haven, Conn.
Chamber of Commerce of New York.
Merchants' Association of New York.
Commercial Club of Omaha, Neb.
Chamber of Commerce of Oshkosh, Wis.
Trades League of Philadelphia, Pa.
Chamber of Commerce of Pittsburg, Pa.
Chamber of Commerce of Richmond, Va.
Chamber of Commerce of Rochester, N. Y.
Business Men's Club of San Antonio, Tex.
Commercial Club of St. Louis, Mo.
Manufacturers' Association of St. Louis, Mo.
Merchants' Exchange of St. Louis, Mo.
West End Business Men's Association of St. Louis, Missouri.
Chamber of Commerce of Toledo, O.
Commercial Club of Topeka, Kan.
Board of Trade of Wilkesbarre, Pa.
Board of Trade of Wilmington, Del.
Board of Trade of Worcester, Mass.

PRESS COMMENT ON THE TRUST CONFERENCE

THE PRESS THROUGHOUT THE COUNTRY UNITES IN APPROVAL OF THE PURPOSE AND THE RESULTS OF THE CONFERENCE

FEW of the undertakings of the Federation have attracted so much attention as the National Conference on Trusts and Combinations. The newspaper press throughout the country gave its proceedings wide publicity in their news columns and much sympathetic and approving comment in their editorial columns. From the hundreds of editorials dealing with the matter, a few are here selected as illustrations of the discriminating approval generally expressed:

COMMON SENSE AS TO TRUSTS.

New York Times.

It is fairly to be assumed that the President, before preparing his next message to Congress, will give careful consideration to the recommendations of the Civic Federation at the close of the important conference held last week in Chicago. In that meeting were represented a larger number of interests and classes, we believe, than have ever been brought together for like purposes. The discussion was informing. Many of the addresses were exceedingly able and nearly all of them were in excellent spirit, and this is true especially of some men who have hitherto been prone to excess in denunciation of the trusts. This spirit of moderation and of practical searching for common ground on which to proceed is reflected in the resolutions. These not only call for a commission, but outline the work it would be expected to do, and the general methods by which it should be done.

If the President should come to the same ground, and if he is prepared to submit the whole matter to a fair, nonpartisan, competent commission for study, it would be a good thing, on which the country might be congratulated.

REPEAL THE SHERMAN LAW.

New York Globe.

That progress is being made toward educating the public into a true perception of the true character of the Sherman anti-trust law was shown yesterday at the convention of the National Civic Federation at Chicago. The delegates, many of them economists of national repute, were practically unanimous that the anti-trust law should be repealed—that it is based on a wholly false principle and that attempts to enforce it are necessarily productive of profound business disturbance.

The year 1890 seems destined to be remembered as the birth year of two Diabolic Twins—the Sherman silver purchase law and the Sherman anti-trust law, each a panic breeder. We throttled one of them in 1894, but not soon enough to prevent doubt concerning the integrity of the money base, bringing on a depression. The other is still on the statute books, and for fifteen years practically escaped perception of its true character because unenforced. But its inherent viciousness is now pretty well displayed. As combination is an economic necessity—as our prosperity is dependent on combination—the sound opinion of the country should demand of the approaching Congress the repeal of the Sherman anti-trust law as it did the repeal of the Sherman silver law in 1894.

COMMENDABLE CONCLUSIONS.

Chicago Tribune.

The resolutions adopted by the conference will commend themselves to thinking men. A competent commission should be created by Congress for the consideration of all the great problems which have resulted from the enormous industrial development of the country and from the merger of great railroad and other corporate interests. And it is equally important that there should be legislation along the lines recommended by the President, permitting reasonable agreements between railroads subject to the approval of the government.

TRUST BUSTING HOPELESS.

Buffalo Commercial.

The late meeting of the National Civic Federation in Chicago was made highly significant by the frank opinion expressed by some of the ablest men present that prohibiting, penalizing, dissolution and "trust busting" are hopeless as a means of dealing with the trust problem. This view was advanced by F. W. Taussig, Professor of Economics in Harvard University, an authority of high repute, and was substantially reiterated by others, including Herbert Knox Smith, head of the Bureau of Corporations. What is more, it was formally approved by the conference, which recommended that Congress "without delay" pass legislation providing for a non-partisan commission—such as was organized in Germany in 1880—to consider the entire subject of a general law that will preserve the individual initiative, competition and the free contracts of all industrial relations.

Professor Taussig declares that it is senseless to resist an irresistible economic tendency like that in modern times toward combinations and trusts. Facts must be faced. The proofs of the case are indicated by the railroad situation. In one essential respect our policy toward the railways for the last twenty years has been wrong, he asserts. We have simply caused combination to take new forms, to conceal itself and to become more difficult of supervision. We have not prevented it; we have simply driven it into hiding. We should let railroads combine and co-operate, but they should be made to do it in the open. The principles which are applicable to railway combinations are applicable to the trusts also. The mere act of combination should not be subject to legal penalty. Secret combination should be hounded down.

TO INVESTIGATE TRUSTS.

Chicago Evening Post.

The resolutions which brought the trust conference of the National Civic Federation to a close yesterday admirably express what now may be called the conservative opinion of progressive public men. They do not recommend or, on the other hand, attack the more radical remedies advanced, and in this avoidance provide what may very well be a safe ground of compromise.

The recommendations are of a necessity somewhat indefinite, but not more so than may be welcomed at this time, since there is obvious need of a broad and thorough study of the results of recent legislation in regulation of industrial and commercial activity. The suggestion of a government commission of inquiry was inevitable, and is unobjectionable and even highly desirable if properly constituted and conducted. In this respect, however, the greatest care is necessary. The history of our tariff commissions has not been happy. Partisanship and selfish interest have run riot in them or over them. The just and reasonable conclusions of the best of them have been pointedly ignored by legislators lacking either in public spirit or courage.

FEDERAL CONTROL OF TRUSTS.

Boston Advertiser.

At the conference of the National Civic Federation representatives in Chicago, it is noteworthy that about all the speakers, although discussing the trust question from different points of view, reach practically the same conclusion, which is exactly that at which President Roosevelt arrived in his Provincetown speech—that instead of the Sherman anti-trust law, the country needs more modern legislation, which, while allowing trusts to exist, shall bring them under the supervision of the Federal law. Experience has shown that the tendency of business organizations to-day is to reach closer relations with one another. The law may forbid this, but the same thing is accomplished under cover of law in some roundabout fashion. The President came to the conclusion, therefore, that it was better to recognize the tendencies of the times in a straightforward way, making sure that the public interest should be thoroughly protected.

USEFUL DISCUSSION.

San Francisco Record.

Probably the most notable discussion of recent years in its bearing upon American business and industrial conditions was inaugurated at Chicago yesterday under the auspices of the National Civic Federation.

Discussion of national problems—and this one is most pleasing—has been productive of much good in the past, and there is little doubt that a solution of this one will be found. It is a good sign that the men most interested in the problems that are confronting this nation to-day meet and discuss those problems with a view to finding a remedy that will do equity as between the people and capital. No thinking man can maintain that the present system of trusts and combinations is detrimental to the people at large, by reason of the concentration in the hands of a few of many of the necessaries of life. Nor can any one reasonably maintain that such combinations should not be regulated. Just how that regulation should be done is a matter of wide divergence of opinion that this conference is expected to—and probably will—reconcile.

THE TRUSTS HARD HIT.

Omaha News.

The National Civic Federation's conference on the trusts is over. There were more than 400 delegates present from forty-three states and territories.

Well, what did they DO, these 400 talkers about the trusts?

They asked for NATIONAL LEGISLATION and they asked LOUDLY!

So they asked Congress for a NATIONAL NON-PARTISAN COMMISSION, to represent equally the interest of CAPITAL, LABOR and the general PUBLIC.

They suggested legislation which would interfere LESS with combinations like those among local and national labor organizations and their agreements with their employers as to hours and conditions, associations of farmers designed to secure staple and equitable markets, and business associations or combinations whose object would further the public interest.

They suggested that the work of examining, inspecting and supervising the great producing and manufacturing corporations, already begun by the Department of Commerce and Labor, be ENLARGED so as to give complete PUBLICITY as to CAPITALIZATION, ACCOUNTS, OPERATIONS, TRANSPORTATION CHARGES and SELLING PRICES, and they recommend that conflicts between state and federal authority as to railroad control be turned over to the Federal Supreme Court for adjudication.

Now we shall see how much attention Congress pays to these recommendations.

But don't you think this is a PRETTY SENSIBLE PROGRAM?

BETTER LIGHT ON THE TRUST PROBLEM.

St. Paul Pioneer Press.

The general trend of the proceedings of the recent conference on trusts of the National Civic Federation was toward a broader development of federal regulation. On the one hand, the general opinion leaned toward the extension of governmental control over commerce and on the other hand toward a modification of the requirements of the Sherman anti-trust and the provisions of the interstate commerce laws in respect to pooling. The discussion was significant, in that it was participated in by many of the closest students of the general trust and railroad problem, men who are not influenced by personal or class interests, but who weigh with care and with impartiality both the evil and the good of trusts and combinations and of the laws that regulate them. The desire was not to make the laws more lenient, but to make them more effective by bringing them into harmony with economic forces and with equity. In short, the expressions at the conference reflected very accurately the best thought of the country, which is bound sooner or later to be embodied in national legislation.

TO FORBID OR REGULATE.

Indianapolis News.

The real issue before the country in relation to trusts, as it is presented by the utterances of the speakers at yesterday's session of the National Civic Federation is to forbid or to regulate. Mr. Herbert Knox Smith, Commissioner of Corporations, argued that it was most inconsistent to regulate or to propose to regulate something which you had forbidden. Of course, he is right. If we are going to regulate trusts and supervise their operation it is manifestly absurd to keep in force a law which makes trusts illegal and those connected with them criminals. Governments do not undertake to regulate crime—they simply forbid and punish it.

CONTROL OF CORPORATIONS.

San Antonio (Tex.) Express.

Reviewing the proceedings of the National Civic Federation in Chicago, the Indianapolis News concludes that the old and fierce opposition to trusts, because they are trusts, is swiftly disappearing and that even the bitterest enemies of monopoly are beginning to differentiate between good and bad trusts.

All the speakers at the conference opposed annihilation or destruction in lieu of regulation, and none more strongly than Mr. Gompers of the American Federation of Labor, and the general idea seemed to be that regulation should be by the national government rather than by the state governments.

So it is found that there is a friendlier sentiment being manifested toward great corporations that serve a useful purpose, and at the same time a growing desire on the part of these corporations for federal instead of state regulation, because it would be easier to conform to the mandates of a central commission than to satisfy a number of state commissions that are at variance of views with each other.

LABOR AND THE TRUSTS.

Spokane (Wash.) Spokesman-Review.

If Samuel Gompers, president of the American Federation of Labor, correctly represents the views of organized labor in his public utterances, William Jennings Bryan can hope for little support from that source in his advocacy of the annihilation of all the trusts. At the recent convention of the National Civic Federation no man spoke more strongly in deprecation of any destructive war on trusts than Mr. Gompers, who held that violent denunciation is more harmful than helpful.

Constructive and associated effort, Mr. Gompers declared, must check and correct the abuses which have grown so rapidly in this era of concentrated methods of production and distribution. "We can not, if we would," he said, "turn back to the primitive conditions of industry which marked the early part of the last century. It is idle chatter to talk of annihilating trusts. The trust is, economically speaking, the logical and inevitable accompaniment and development of our modern commercial and industrial system."

A FRUITFUL CONFERENCE.

Muncie (Ind.) Star.

It is generally admitted that the first American trust conference, which met in 1899, rendered the country a great service in emphasizing the duty and need of publicity as regards all affairs of public utility companies and great corporations. The second trust conference, which has just finished its labors in Chicago, has taken several steps forward, profiting by the abundant experience of the last several years and reflecting the decided progress of opinion on the great subject.

A REASONABLE DEMAND.

Grand Rapids (Mich.) Herald.

The demand made at the Chicago Trust Conference, so called, by representatives of numerous nation-wide associations of industries for such amendments to the Sherman law as shall legalize the formation of "legitimate combinations for defense and not offense," thus protecting such associations from harassment, is not unreasonable and should, and probably will, receive attention from Congress in the near future.

NEW ENGLAND CIVIC FEDERATION

THIRD ANNUAL MEETING—EDUCATORS, EMPLOYERS AND LABOR LEADERS DISCUSS THE PROBLEMS OF INDUSTRIAL EDUCATION

THE third annual meeting of the Civic Federation of New England, held January 9, 1908, was devoted to the subject of industrial education. The deep interest felt in this subject is testified to by the large attendance, representing all classes and varied interests.

About three hundred and fifty members and guests accepted the invitation to be present, and, including those in the balconies coming in response to the general public invitation, there were fully five hundred persons present. The meeting began with an informal reception. The Hon. Curtis Guild, Governor of Massachusetts; Hon. George A. Hibbard, Mayor of Boston; the members of the Massachusetts Commission on Industrial Education, and other representatives of the State and local government were in attendance.

In calling the meeting to order Mr. Lucius Tuttle, President of the Civic Federation of New England, congratulated the organization upon its gain in membership, representing an increase of more than 25 per cent., since the last annual gathering, and gave a brief account of the aims and purposes of the organization, in which he said:

"The Civic Federation is a round table at which there is neither head nor foot, and at which all who take part in its deliberations do so upon the plane of absolute equality. It pursues no plans that have in them anything in the nature of demand, dictation, or even arbitration. Its work is wholly educational and conciliatory.

"As is well known, this work of the Federation is unobtrusively, but none the less effectively, carried on; and while it is no part of its policy to publish the details of the different cases in which its assistance is solicited, nor to boast of its successes, enough may be gleaned to give full and satisfactory assurance that results have already been accomplished in the preservation of industrial harmony and peace of paramount social and commercial value.

"One breach of the laws of industrial peace, with its attendant lockout or strike, attracts the attention of whole communities, while hundreds of cases in which prospective and even imminent danger of industrial rupture is adjusted and removed, through the quiet and unassuming efforts of this and kindred organizations in the country, seldom or never become matters of public knowledge.

"I am sure, beyond any question of doubt, that the results of the past three years' efforts of the Civic Federation of New England have been in the highest degree worth while; and that we are justified in entering upon another year of its work with renewed courage and a stanch faith in the efficacy of the methods."

After reading letters from members and guests who were unable to attend the meeting the report of the Nominating Committee was received.

The general officers were unanimously re-elected as follows:

Lucius Tuttle, president; Frank H. McCarthy and Louis D. Brandeis, vice presidents; John Mason Little, treasurer; Henry Abrahams, recording secretary, and Hayes Robbins, secretary.

The following were chosen to constitute the executive committee on the part of the public: W. Murray Crane, Henry L. Higginson, Bishop William Lawrence, Dr. William J. Tucker, president of Dartmouth College; Louis D. Brandeis, John Mason Little, William A. Gaston, William F. Henney, Hartford; Rev. Thomas I. Gasson, S. J.; Frederick P. Fish, W. H. P. Faunce, Charles S. Hamlin, Alvah W. Sulloway, Hayes Robbins. On the part of employers: Lucius Tuttle, W. L. Douglas, Amory A. Lawrence, Charles H. Taylor, Jr., Wallace L. Pierce, J. L. Richards, T. E. Byrnes, C. L. Edgar, J. H. Hustis, P. F. Sullivan, Garret Schenck, Arthur T. Lyman, W. C. Winslow and James Logan. On the part of wage-earners: Frank H. McCarthy, John Golden, Henry Abrahams, Frank K. Foster, P. F. McCarthy, Dennis D. Driscoll, Samuel Ross, Francis J. Clarke, Thomas F. Kearney, Edmond F. Ward, John J. Connolly, P. F. Sheehan, Norman E. McPhail and William H. Frazier.

The chairman announced the subject of "Industrial Education" as the topic for the evening's discussion, and as the speakers, Prof. Paul Hanus, Mr. J. F. Deems, Mr. James O'Connell and Rev. Thomas I. Gasson.

PROF. PAUL HANUS, of Harvard University, chairman of the Massachusetts Commission on Industrial Education, outlined the history of the commission and its work, and said:

LUCIUS TUTTLE.

"One of the most important principles on which our Democratic institutions are based is, briefly stated, equal opportunities for all through education and equal rights before the law.

"We insist that in this country every youth shall have an opportunity to make the most of himself and lift himself to any social level to which he may aspire, and to which his character, capacity and industry may enable him to attain. Yet the school system which has been devised to guarantee this right now fails to reach the great majority of our population.

"Our present provision for public education is inadequate. Its dominant aim is general culture, but it makes no provision for training in some specific usefulness, in some skilled vocation for those who must leave school at the age of 14 or 15, and, therefore, they must face at an early age the momentous question as to what they should do to insure early self-support and progressive well-being as they grow older.

"The majority of pupils leave school at the age of 14. They naturally take advantage of the first opportunity to work for wages that presents itself, and that opportunity usually leaves them stranded at the age of 18 or 19 among the hosts of the unskilled.

"A generation or more ago it was possible for a youth who was obliged to leave school at 14 or 15 to enter one of the skilled vocations as an apprentice and to learn the whole of a trade in the course of a few years. This is no longer possible. The specialised condition of modern industry makes it impossible for the youth to learn the whole of any trade, even when the inclination exists to teach him a trade.

"The progressive development of all high-grade industries requires skilled workmen possessing industrial intelligence and a comprehensive insight and intelligent interest in their several trades as well as their skill, though the present conditions of production are unfavorable to the training of such workmen in the shop or factory, and sometimes render such training impossible.

"Such men, whether workers, foremen or superintendents, are now developed in this country, in general, by chance—and they are then self-made men, possessing the merits, but also the conspicuous shortcomings of their training.

"Meanwhile, boys and girls, young men and young women, are not only not directed toward the trades in our existing schools, but are often actually directed away from them by the bookish education of these schools and their purely academic traditions. Manual training is not industrial training, and should not be confused with it. It may make a pupil generally 'handy,' and hence may serve as preparation for industrial training, but it goes no farther. Industrial training, on the other hand, means vocational training in trades and agriculture. It aims to develop industrial intelligence and skill in particular vocations and does not properly begin until the pupil is at least 14 years old. It does not make a journeyman, but gives each worker at a skilled vocation a training that entitles him to earn a living wage at 18 or 19, and a promise of increasing efficiency as time goes on.

"Boys are not wanted in the industries until they are 16 years of age. The result is, an army of young men from 14 to 16, most of whom are either at work in various kinds of juvenile occupations, in which they learn no trade and are subject to little, if any, beneficial general education. The majority of these children would be in school if that school promised preparation for some life pursuit.

"These years in the life of the child are, however, invaluable for industrial education, but there has been no agency whereby such education is provided, except to a limited extent by philanthropic organizations and correspondence schools. Hence the need of industrial schools to meet this new educational need. Such schools should receive pupils of 14 or 15 years of age desiring to learn a trade. They would, therefore, be parallel to the existing public schools, but must be entirely independent of them. There must be independent schools because their leading motive is vocational training and not general culture. Such schools should offer a course of study covering four years—the first two devoted to general shop instruction, with related drawing, mechanics, natural sciences, the history of industry and commerce, shop and business English, while the last two years should be shop instruction for particular trades and for each trade such drawing, mechanics and other sciences as may be appropriate. It is not likely that such schools can achieve marked success at once, or that they can be founded or carried on without some mistakes. An encouraging beginning has been made. All progress involves some risks. The Commission on Industrial Education desires to make no mistakes, but it also intends to make progress, and to that end it invites the co-operation of all who have the welfare of the wage-earner, the employer, the agriculturist and of the entire commonwealth at heart."

J. F. DEEMS, general superintendent of motive power of the New York Central lines, said: "The only way to get industrial education is by doing the thing itself. The schools cannot replace the constant association of employer and employed. The old system of apprenticeship turned out good workmen thirty-five years ago. The dawn of the present industrial era brought about entirely new conditions. The increased business activity has proved an education in itself. Educators have learned that industrial or commercial training may be as effective as a classical course in turning out broadgauged men. Thus far college course and shop training have only partly adapted themselves to our new conditions.

"It is doubtless true that there are some trades in which the manual training may be largely had in schools. The atmosphere of the trades school, at its best, is not that of the actual shop. There are many trades, however, that, from their very nature, must be learned in a regular shop, and for these trades we must look to apprenticeship, perhaps not the old-fashioned kind, but one suited to our present needs and conditions.

"The problem of securing skilled workmen in machine shops has received much attention from the railroads of the country, and out of this discussion has grown the system of apprenticeship and training which I have been permitted to introduce in the New York Central shops. It went into effect March 1, 1906, its object being to provide a recruiting system which will eventually produce from the ranks a large number of skilled workmen, a number of foremen, as well as draughtsmen, master mechanics and superintendents of motive power. The plan is a purely business proposition. The course of training has been outlined with the intent to educate the boy *in* the trade, and not *out* of it. The general plan is to provide for shop instruction of the apprentice in the trade and for his instruction in a technical way in subjects allied to his trade, during working hours and while receiving pay. The shop instructor teaches the trade in a regular shop and on regular work.

"All of the shop work done by the apprentice is part of the regular shop output. The shop instructor is present to see that each machine is run at its best efficiency, even when handled by a green apprentice. The apprentices are still responsible to the foreman as formerly, and he alone is responsible for shop discipline, but has been relieved from the necessity of instructing the apprentices. Boys are taken on for a probationary period of six months, at the end of which time, if it is discovered that they are not suited to the business, they are discharged.

"The plan is now in operation at the ten larger shops of the system, and already includes over five hundred apprentices. A uniform set of regulations has already been adopted, showing the division or class of work in the shop and the time allotted to each class. These regulations have been made sufficiently flexible to suit various conditions in the different shops, and to insure proper progress of the apprentices. Uniform certificates or diplomas are issued at the completion of the course. Such a system as is here described has its own educational needs, which must be worked out from practical experience, because your work must be brought into living relation with the shop work. The ingenuity of the instructor is taxed to present subjects in an attractive way, so that their vital connection with the whole work may be thoroughly understood. Practical and not theoretical instruction is an essential. The immediate and direct results of the apprentice system have been an increased output (notwithstanding the four hours per week spent in class rooms), less spoiled work, better ability to read drawings and make sketches, better grade of apprentices, and increased interest in work. Local officials have everywhere noted the benefits of apprentice training and are uniformly enthusiastic and interested. One of the immediate results of the opening of the apprentice schools was the request from the foremen and mechanics for educational classes of a similar nature, which resulted in the organization of self-supporting evening classes in several of the shops.

"What can the public school do for the mechanical trades? This is a very large question. It can never teach trades. It can, however, possibly lay a better foundation than at present by simplifying courses, by work in applied arithmetic and mechanical drawing, some presentation of the laws of mechanics. A curriculum might be arranged which would tend to hold in school a boy with a mechanical turn of mind. This, however, is only in the way of preparation. After all has been said, there still remains the fact that the United States must look mainly to apprenticeship for its industrial salvation."

JAMES O'CONNELL, president of the International Association of Machinists, said:

"After the schools have done all that is possible in the preliminary way for the boy the real work begins to properly qualify and equip the coming citizen with all that is necessary to enable him to earn a living and shoulder the social responsibilities that come with mature manhood.

"Books can only help him in part; thoroughness and skill can only be gained by practice. Industrial schools and kindred establishments making claims of ability to instruct the rising generation in all the details necessary to equip fully a practical machinist so that he can hold his own and command the average pay of a journeyman in less time and with less practice than it is done in the machine shop are claiming more than can be accomplished.

"Because of this lack of thoroughness and the attempt to teach by rote, so to speak, the industrial school cannot perform what it promises, and the more the matter is investigated the more conclusive will be the evidence to confirm this view.

"On one occasion I witnessed this remarkable spectacle: About twenty-five young men were being marched from a school to a factory where men had been on strike for several weeks. The young men were headed by a detachment of the State militia, and in the rear of the parade was a squad of city policemen. These young men were marched from the school to the shop in the morning, and from the shop to the school in the evening. The strike was finally adjusted and the boys then remained at their school.

"The industrial school in these cases worked a great injury upon the men on strike, though not nearly as bad as the injury it did to the lads induced to take the strikers' place. To them the injury is well-nigh irreparable. It leaves a stain on their characters that years cannot efface, a stain that will cling to them as long as they attempt to earn a living in the vocation they have chosen, and upon which, in the estimation of their shopmates, they have brought disgrace. No one outside the ranks of labor can appreciate or understand the bitterness of feeling that has been generated among workingmen through the shortsighted selfishness which has taken advantage of boyish enthusiasm and used it to strike-breaking ends. The industrial schools in these cases were used for the vilest purposes, and there can be no excuse or extenuation for those who are responsible or at whose instance it was permitted.

"The workshop is the only place where an education can be gained that is practical and thorough, calculated to fill all the requirements that go to make up a full fledged mechanic. The industrial school merely supplies a veneer of education, which can never compete with the solid practicability of the education acquired in the factory. Its well-rounded thoroughness comes from observation, from intuition, from absorption and all-around hard work that comes with every day application. It can never be acquired elsewhere, or gained in any other way than in the hard school of factory experience. The factory workshop can be depended upon for practical results in the matter of supplying fully equipped mechanics, which can never be expected from the industrial school as long as it is dependent upon itself alone.

"Summing up the whole question of industrial education as it is supposed to apply to the young men, I am firmly convinced that unless every precaution is taken concerning such schools to the end that young men will not be induced or led to believe that after serving a few months, or a year, if you will, in an industrial or trades school, by securing certificates, they are permitted, or even warranted, in going into the industrial field seeking employment as mechanics against the best interests of those who have served a reasonable or legal apprenticeship. To avoid this danger and with views of securing the highest skill, and to perpetuate the supremacy of the American mechanic, I believe that the proper and best methods to be adopted are for employers to establish schools in connection with their factories and workshops for the purpose of giving young men employed by them an opportunity for a few hours' schooling each day, in addition to the practical experience they are securing while serving their time as apprentices. To my mind this idea is best being carried out by the New York Central Lines, as represented by Mr. Deems.

REV. THOMAS I. GASSON, S. J., president of Boston College, said:

"I cannot and never will admit that there is too much education, but will say that there can be misdirected education. There are lines upon which there should be more education, as is shown by the statements of speakers here to-night, who say that when an important position is vacant there is no one to fill it, and when there is an unimportant one, there are battalions to fill it. Take the boy after he has graduated from the grammar school. He will say that he wants to get clean work. He means by that that he doesn't want manual labor. The average boy has the wrong idea. He has a debased idea. Manual work, as we call it, constitutes the backbone of American citizenship.

"When the average boy says he doesn't want to wear overalls and soil his hands with oil he means that he is afraid that he will not be thought a gentleman. He should remember that all labor is clean, and no matter if he has the whitest hands and the finest broadcloth, if there is grime in his heart and his conscience is soiled, then his work is not clean. I believe there is nothing more ennobling than the labor in which the hands are soiled. There is no crown so white as that worn by the laborer.

"Education should bring out what is in the lad, and make the possibility an actuality. Education depends upon circumstances. There may be abuses in the industrial or trade schools, but does that prove that they are entirely wrong? What we should do is to root out these abuses and combine our efforts in lifting up the country to purity of ideals in industrial progress and the promotion of industrial civilization."

PRESIDENT TUTTLE said in closing the meeting:

"I am going to take the liberty of saying one thing from my own knowledge in connection with the industrial school problem as it is being worked out in this commonwealth. There is no attempt on the part of those who have the matter in charge to provide any short-cut to a mechanical education. It is the clear and well understood purpose that there must be thoroughness in the education in so far as they are able to give it in the school, and there is intended to be a survival of the fittest in the course of that education. There is nothing different in this from what we have practised for years in our technical schools. To-day the great technical schools are turning out men who are not absolutely finished engineers or specialists, but who, in their three or four years in that technical school have absorbed the fundamentals of the knowledge so that they begin to be wage-earners from the beginning, and they have learned in those schools what they would otherwise have to learn in three or four years' practice in the field.

"In our commercial schools, in our industrial schools and manual training schools, the chief purpose in mind is to save the boy's time, and time is everything. This is a country of producers, and the producer makes the bone and muscle of the country, and if we can do anything within reason to see that the boy who is coming to be the producer while he is getting general education is taught some of the industrial and mechanical fundamentals, so that he can apply them when he goes to work, we have saved the boy's time and we have done God's service."

EVILS OF HOLDING CORPORATIONS.

Chicago News.

In the opening of the National Civic Federation conference on trusts and combinations, President Nicholas Murray Butler of Columbia University called attention to the fact that the danger in corporations is not due to the large size to which some of them attain. The small corporation, he pointed out, might have such relations to the government as would make it a greater menace than a concern representing larger capital.

President Butler's words on this subject served well to prepare the way for the address which followed. It was by Wade Ellis, Attorney-General of Ohio, and it dealt with the subject of holding corporations. Under the common law, Mr. Ellis pointed out, one corporation has no right to hold the stock of another. This right exists, if at all, by express statutory authority. Some of the states have conferred this authority on corporations; others have not. But the stocks of corporaions in states that have not conferred this authority, nevertheless are purchased and held by corporations organized in states like New Jersey which authorize the purchase by one corporation of the stock of another. In this way, the Standard Oil Company of New Jersey, as a holding company, has obtained control of a multitude of corporations in other states.

JOHN MASON LITTLE.

HENRY ABRAHAMS.

HAYES ROBBINS.

WOMEN'S CLUBS IN PANAMA

CLUBS ORGANIZED THROUGHOUT THE ISTHMUS—THE CANAL ZONE FEDERATION FOUNDED

ONE of the practical results of the work of the Public Employees' Welfare Committee of the National Civic Federation, in investigating conditions in Panama, has been the establishment of a flourishing chain of women's clubs, and their union into a Canal Zone Federation under the presidency of Mrs. George W. Goethals. In her report upon conditions in Panama, Miss Gertrude Beeks called attention to the monotony of life and the isolation of the people in social interests which has been so characteristic of the more or less improvised communities which have sprung up along the line of the canal. Among them there was the lack of common interests such as we always find in older communities, and Miss Beeks pointed out how this might be promoted by establishing women's clubs as central points in which common interest might be focussed.

The suggestion met with the hearty approval of Secretary Taft, and at his request Miss Helen Varick Boswell, of the Welfare Department of the National Civic Federation, visited the Isthmus to organize such clubs. Miss Boswell spent part of the month of October in Panama, and her suggestion met with so appreciative a response that in all of the large centres clubs were established. The Canal Record, which is published weekly under the authority and supervision of the Isthmian Canal Commission, gives in its various issues an interesting account of the inception and progress of this movement. Its underlying purpose is well expressed in a description of a preliminary meeting of the women at Culebra, as follows:

"At the meeting Miss Boswell gave an informal talk, in which she stated clearly her reason for coming down. It was her wish to meet the American women on the Zone and to confer with them, to learn their wishes regarding the organization of clubs. It seemed to her that clubs could be formed in the larger centres, Ancon, Culebra, Gorgona, Empire and Colon, with branches, or separate organizations in the neighboring settlements, each club to be under its own title, all to be affiliated under the title of the Canal Zone Women's League, or other suitable appellation. The club should be for social and educational purposes, to promote social feeling among the women, to enable them, as an organization, to take a part in municipal matters, governing the schools, and matters where a woman's wisdom may be considered to go far, and for the purpose of study, Spanish classes could be formed, a good teacher engaged, and members admitted to the class at club rates. She spoke of the real good that women are doing here, of the influence of the sight of domestic life and happy homes on the young men. While the life of every woman here is a busy one, there is time to be kind. We hear a lot about the 'fatherhood of God,' the 'brotherhood of man.' Let us prove that there is a 'sisterhood of women,' said Miss Boswell. The influence of their development of the social spirit is scarcely to be overestimated. All the women present signified their intention of joining a women's club should one be organized."

The interest which is reflected in this paragraph was shown at the several points along the line where the movement was inaugurated. So successful were the efforts of those interested in the project that by October 12 eight clubs had been organized, seven of which were represented in a meeting held at Ancon for the purpose of establishing a federation. At a subsequent date another club was organized, making in all nine clubs in active operation on the Isthmus.

At the meeting above referred to the Canal Zone Federation of Women's Clubs was formally organized. Mrs. George W. Goethals was elected president, other officers were chosen and a constitution adopted. One feature of the constitution which will undoubtedly prove of interest is the provision for quarterly meetings of the executive officers to be held at different points within the Canal Zone, thus bringing the several clubs into closer relations with each other. Since Miss Boswell's visit the clubs have become important centres of social life and activity in the Isthmus. Every issue of the Canal Record brings an account of their doings. A summary statement from the Canal Record of November 13 indicates the general activities to which the clubs are devoted.

"Each week brings fresh interests in the Women's Clubs in the Zone. New names are constantly being presented, and the scope of work enlarged, suggestions being eagerly seized and acted upon in accordance with the special needs of each individual organization.

"During the past week a number of talks have been given in several clubs on the work of other organizations in the chain, and it was observed that each club took up the points especially adapted to its own community and several new measures of usefulness were adopted.

"The interest displayed in the study of Spanish was universal, and in several of the organizations this promises to be the most useful and prominent feature of club life. In all the communities the club influence is making itself felt in social life, in the increased spirit of contentment and broadening of the lives of the women. In this respect the efforts and work necessarily expended for maintaining the organization are well repaid. One of the most gratifying features of the movement is the interest that the men are taking in it. Not only the unmarried men who greatly appreciate the increased opportunities for social intercourse, but the married men as well, give every encouragement to their wives to take an active part in the work.

"There is a general feeling of satisfaction in the action taken by the Cristobal Woman's Club in the recent resolution quoted in last week's issue of the Canal Record, that the women should unite in fostering favorable instead of adverse criticism of conditions in the Zone and on the Isthmus of Panama. Several of the clubs have already taken action on this and expressed their intention to support the Cristobal Club in this movement.

"A great need is felt for intercourse among clubs which could be brought about in the way of invitations extended from one organization to another for social occasions. This would accomplish, not only the object for which the clubs were organized, i. e., to unite the women in social and educational influence, philanthropic work and musical and literary study, but would afford opportunity for the exchange of ideas, and the study of the methods and work of the other organizations. The general meeting of the Zone Federation of Women's Clubs, which takes place quarterly, different towns being appointed for each meeting, will be beneficial in this respect, but it is greatly desired that the exchange of courtesies among the organizations will be arranged as frequently as is convenient with club work. It is generally understood that business shall be transacted in closed meetings, and that invitations shall be extended for social occasions."

As the foregoing selection indicates, these various activities promise a bright future for these organizations and an important place in the community life. Such activities are as diverse as the varied interests of those who make up the clubs.

In some localities particular attention has already been given to questions affecting the schools. The civil administration is in hearty accord with the interest of the women in promoting the efficiency of the school work.

Where hospitals are located the care of the sick has been a matter of interest to the club members. Nurses from the hospitals have presented papers before the clubs on nursing in the homes and kindred topics, and the clubs themselves have organized committees for the purpose of visiting hospitals and doing what they can to cheer the sick and alleviate their suffering.

Literary entertainments and talks on various maters of general and current interest are also reported.

At other points the "Home Department" of the clubs has developed considerable activity and much attention has been given to the subject of horticulture. Efforts to improve the surroundings of the homes by gardens and experiments with flowers and shrubs which may be suited to the soil are being made.

That the clubs have found so much to do is in itself evidence of their need, and at the same time a guarantee of their usefulness in promoting the interests and welfare of those resident upon the Isthmus.

CANAL ZONE FEDERATION'S FIRST MEETING.

1. Mrs. Lorin C. Collins, First Vice-President and Acting President of the Canal Zone Federation, President Cristobal Club. 2. Mrs. W. C. Gorgas, President Ancon Women's Club. 3. Mrs. F. R. Roberts, President Pedro Miguel Women's Club. 4. Mrs. N. F. Morrison, President Gorgona Women's Club. 5. Mrs. J. C. Barnett, President Paraiso Women's Club. 6. Mrs. F. M. Miracle, President Empire Women's Club. 7. Mrs. J. L. Elliott, Vice-President Gatun Women's Club. 8. Mrs. Charles J. Jewett, Ancon. 9. Miss J. M. Beattie, Corozal. 10. Mrs. J. F. McTyre, Empire. 11. Mrs. F. H. Powell, Cristobal. 12. Mrs. E. S. Waid, Paraiso. 13. Mrs. John Burke, Cristobal. 14. Mrs. M. C. Reddell, Cristobal. 15. Mrs. Ralph R. Wolf, Gorgona. 16. Miss Eunice Browning, Empire. 17. Mrs. Edna Franks, Pedro Miguel. 18. Mrs. S. R. Calvit, Gorgona. 19. Miss Helen V. Boswell.

The National Civic Federation Review

Vol. III. NEW YORK, MAY, 1908 No. [illegible]

SHALL THE ANTI-TRUST ACT BE AMENDED?

EFFORT TO AMEND THE SHERMAN ACT—HEARINGS BEFORE THE HOUSE COMMITTEE ON THE JUDICIARY ON THE CIVIC FEDERATION'S BILL—THE MEASURE EXPLAINED AND DEFENDED.

THE bill prepared under the auspices of the National Civic Federation to amend the Sherman Anti-Trust Act has been considered at length by the House and Senate Committees on the Judiciary. It has been the subject of an exhaustive examination by those bodies. A condensed statement of the hearings before the House Committee on April 4th and April 6th is here given.*

April 4th, Morning Session.

The sub-committee, consisting of Representatives Littlefield, Chairman, Malby and Henry, met on Saturday, April 4, 1908, for the purpose of according a hearing on the bill to amend the Sherman Anti-Trust law. Various members of the Committee on the Judiciary who were not members of the sub-committee were present during the hearing, and some of them took an active part in the proceedings.

On behalf of the bill Mr. Seth Low led the delegation from the National Civic Federation, which included Mr. Samuel Gompers, Mr. W. J. Schieffelin, E. H. Gary, Albert Shaw, Isaac N. Seligman, Charles A. Moore, John S. Huyler, V. E. Macey, William G. Breed, of New York; John Mitchell, Indianapolis; D. J. Keefe, Detroit; Samuel Mather, Cleveland; Henry L. Higginson, Boston; Franklin MacVeagh, Chicago; Frank A. Faxon, Kansas City; Mahlon N. Kline, Philadelphia; A. B. Garretson, Grand Rapids; Theodore Marburg, Baltimore; Prof. J. W. Jenks, Ithaca, and J. W. Kinnear, Pittsburg.

The opposition to the bill was represented by Mr. Daniel Davenport, in behalf of the American Anti-Boycott Association; Mr. Monahan, representing the National Founders' Association; Mr. Henry R. Towne and Mr. Nathan Bijur, of the Merchants' Association of New York, and Mr. Emery, who stated that he appeared in behalf of some 135 associations in opposition to the bill.

Before entering upon the hearings, the Chairman read telegrams opposing the measure.

MR. SETH LOW stated that the Trust Conference in Chicago had adopted resolutions and had authorized a sub-committee to present the same to Congress. In making arrangement for the presentation of the resolutions, the committee met Mr. Jenkins, Chairman of the Judiciary Committee, and Mr. Hepburn, Chairman of the Interstate Commerce Committee. At this conference the suggestion was made that a bill or bills be prepared. The bill now proposed grew out of that suggestion. It is not presented on behalf of the Trust Conference, but on behalf of the National Civic Federation, which called the conference. A careful study was given to the subject and consultations were held with the different interests so far as it was practicable to secure them within the time available for the preparation of the measure.

Mr. Low then read the following statement:

MR. CHAIRMAN and Gentlemen of the Committee:

The problem with which the bill introduced by Colonel Hepburn, and prepared under the auspices of the National Civic Federation, seeks to deal, is not an easy one, but it may be stated very plainly. As a result of a long series of decisions by the Supreme Court of the United States it is at last made clear to everybody doing interstate commerce by the methods of combination which are characteristic of these times that much of such business is done contrary to law. Common carriers, business corporations and business men, labor organizations and labor men have all had it brought home to them, one after another, that under the terms of the Sherman Anti-Trust law a large part of the business done in the United States at the present time is being done contrary to law. Co-operative associa-

*Subsequent hearings, when the opponents of the bill testified, will be reported in the next issue of the Review.

Copyright, 1908, Harris-Ewing, Washington, D. C.
HON. JOSEPH G. CANNON.

HON. WILLIAM P. HEPBURN.

Copyright, 1908, [illegible] Buck, Washington, D. C.
HON. CHARLES E. LITTLEFIELD.

Copyright, 1908, [illegible] Buck, Washington, D. C.
HON. ROBERT L. HENRY.

tions and other associations of farmers are subject to the same statute.

Common carriers should be permitted to combine and to make traffic agreements in proper cases and under suitable governmental supervision; for combination and traffic agreements often mean more effective service to the public. What is wanted is effective public supervision and not an absolute prohibition of the very thing that may secure the best public service. It is singular that a people who have constituted the greatest republic in history by the combination of many States should, even for a moment, deny to its own commercial agencies the opportunity of giving better service by proceeding along the same lines. Regulation, not prohibition, should be our watchword in all such matters. There is scarcely a line of commercial business, if there be even one, in which combinations in restraint of trade are not sometimes desirable in these days in the public interest, no less than in the interest of trade; for modern business is very complex, and its problems are often trade problems, as distinguished from individual problems. Organized labor is built up upon the recognized right to combine, to strike, and to make trade agreements. A law that raises doubt as to these rights for which labor has successfully contended in other countries, when it was a hanging offense to do so, strikes a blow not only at organized labor, but at the whole structure of modern democratic society. The trade agreement, which determines for a fixed period by mutual agreement of employer and of employee the rate of wages to be paid and the conditions of employment, offers the most hopeful metnod which has yet been discovered to promote and to make permanent industrial peace under modern industrial conditions, and to classify such agreements as though they were contracts in restraint of trade would be a public calamity. The attempt of cotton growers, wheat growers, and other producers of farm products, to protect themselves by combination against the combinations that deal in their products is just as certainly unlawful under the Sherman act as the business combinations of which they complain; but even a law of the United States, powerful as this country is, cannot set aside the universal law that leads men in these days to combine, and which leads men to do so precisely in proportion as they are intelligent and free.

As a further aggravation of the situation, the anti-trust law is a penal one. Yet no one is able to be sure as to certain agreements whether they are unlawful or not. Any one making an agreement of such a sort affecting interstate commerce and who does business under it does it at his own risk; and long after the agreement has been made he may find out that he has rendered himself liable to imprisonment as well as to a heavy fine. I respectfully submit that this is a situation which is literally intolerable. It inevitably leads to a wide disregard of the statute upon the theory that "necessity knows no law"; because business to be done at the present time must be done by modern methods and these often involve some restraint of trade. The preservation of our forests, for example, by agreement between the owners as to the amount of timber to be cut year by year is probably impossible under such a law, because such an agreement involves a restraint in trade. Beyond this the statute itself constantly acts in restraint of trade, for the reason that only what is necessary is likely to be undertaken in the face of the penalties which the statute provides. A better method for sapping enterprise could scarcely be devised.

How does it happen that a country like ours, renowned the world over for its freedom of initiative, finds itself in such a condition? If one goes far enough back in history one reaches a time when even so simple a form of combination as a partnership was held to be illegal under the common law. In the interval, especially in this country, we have broken away so far from the original restraints of the common law concerning combinations as to encounter a new set of evils, chargeable, as many think, to the too great absence of restraint. Combinations in this country have been formed upon so vast a scale, and have so efficiently dominated one line of business after another, as to awaken a genuine fear in the minds of multitudes that the end of individual opportunity is in sight. Acting under such an impulse of apprehension, the Sherman Anti-Trust law was passed in 1890. There is little evidence that the popular fear which placed this law upon the statute books has disappeared. The Sherman Anti-Trust law, as interpreted by the Supreme Court, reimposed, as it were, all the ancient restraints of the common law concerning combinations, and as to agreements in restraint of trade imposed even greater restraints, for the common law permitted such agreements as were reasonable, and this law has thus placed us, in fact, in the intolerable position already described. If, then, we cannot endure the ancient restraints of the common law as to combinations nor the large freedom from restraint as to agreements in restraint of trade, which

SETH LOW.

gave rise to the new evils that proved so alarming to the people, what shall we do?

There are evidently several possible courses. (1.) The Sherman Anti-Trust act might be repealed. Every man must judge for himself whether this is possible. To us of the National Civic Federation it seems at the present time out of the question. Popular opinion would not tolerate it. (2.) The Sherman Anti-Trust act might be amended, so that only contracts in unreasonable restraint of trade would be forbidden. This undoubtedly would remove the restraints complained of; but what does it offer to quiet the fears which placed the Sherman Anti-Trust act upon the statute book and which keep it there? By many, such an amendment would be considered the equivalent of the repeal of the Sherman Anti-Trust law. It must be admitted, if such an amendment were made, that it would be difficult to frame a law that would even bring about reasonable publicity. Such an amendment is evidently not in line with the President's recent recommendation. For all of these reasons such an amendment does not seem to us to offer the promise of immediate relief. (3.) It is possible to propose the national incorporation of all organizations doing interstate business. Whether that plan may be adopted or not, in the future, no one can say. It will not be disputed that, to-day, to use one of Gladstone's phrases, "It is hardly above the horizon." (4.) The suggestion that every one doing interstate business should be obliged to take out a national license is another way that has been suggested of dealing with the problem. The National Civic Federation believes that this method, also, is one as to which public opinion is not yet clear. A bill framed upon such lines would doubtless lead to an interesting constitutional discussion as to the precise limits of State and Federal control of commerce, and that would postpone the very relief that is so imperatively needed without delay. It has been said of the bill under discussion that it is in effect a license bill; but the very essence of the license system is that no one can do business who does not take out a license. This bill, on the contrary, is optional, and affects only those who voluntarily place themselves under it. I submit that this is a conservative method of testing how a bill upon new lines is likely to work. If it becomes a law, it is almost certain to lead to a large measure of publicity; and that, in the opinion of many, is likely to be the cure for most of the evils that have brought about too great legal restraint. If so, it will surely lead in the end to greater freedom from such restraint. The advantages of publicity are two-sided. Men whose corporate activities, within proper limits, are to be made matter of public record, are likely to be careful not to do anything that they are not willing that the public should know. On the other hand, much of the criticism of corporations on the part of the people at large is due to the fact that they do not understand corporate methods or corporate procedure. There is much reason to believe that publicity will make the criticism of corporate undertakings more intelligent, and therefore, in the main, more friendly. Rightly or wrongly, people believe that publicity means fair dealing with the public; and they are equally ready to believe, whether justly or unjustly, that secrecy means unfair dealing with the public.

The National Civic Federation fully understands that there may be honest difference of opinion as to the general scheme of the bill under discussion; but while the bill may not escape criticism, we believe it capable of vindication. The reasons why other alternative methods of escape from our present intolerable situation are not available, either now or in the near future, have already been pointed out. Let me now try to make clear the salient features of the Hepburn bill, which is offered as a practicable method of dealing with a situation which is confessedly exceedingly difficult.

(1.) The benefits and immunities offered by the bill are conditioned upon registration; for common carriers, with the Interstate Commerce Commission; for all others, with the Bureau of Corporations; and registration is optional. Therefore the bill affects only those who choose to register.

(2.) Registration can be denied to no one who gives the information called for by the bill; and no one can be deprived of registry arbitrarily; nor for cause without appeal to the courts.

(3.) All corporations and associations affected by the bill are divided into two classes; (a) those for profit and having capital stock; and (b) those not for profit and not having capital stock. The first class must give such information as may be called for by general regulations, to be prepared by the President, as to their organization, their finances, their contracts, and their corporate proceedings. The second class must file their constitutions and by-laws, the address of their head office, and the names and addresses of their officers and standing committees; but this distinction is not arbitrary. Corporations for profit appeal to investors for their money. Corporations not for profit do not. At no other point in the bill is any distinction made between the two classes of corporations or associations. The clause relating to strikes and trade agreements is not an exception to this statement. That clause simply makes clear that certain correlative rights of employes and of employers are not affected by the Sherman Anti-Trust law. The necessity for such a clause I shall speak of later.

What, then, are the benefits to be derived from registration under this bill?

(1.) For the public, reasonable publicity, such as some corporations already give voluntarily.

(2.) For existing combinations and contracts in restraint of trade, the assurance that they will not be attacked by the government, except upon the ground that they are in unreasonable restraint of trade; and as to everything done prior to the passage of the act a statute of limitations of one year is fixed. I ask you to notice, therefore, that this bill does establish the rule of reasonableness as to restraint in trade, so far as the past is concerned. This is fair because many such agreements were made before the Supreme Court had given its wide and sweeping interpretation to the Anti-Trust act; and it is wise, because it will lift a great load of anxiety off men of all sorts who would not willingly do anything contrary to the laws of the country. I doubt if there be any one thing that will do so much to revive business courage and enterprise at a time when both are so much needed.

(3.) For combinations to be formed hereafter, the bill provides that if not disapproved within thirty days (the President in his message suggests sixty days—the precise period is not important) these combinations cannot thereafter be attacked except on the ground of unreasonableness.

(4.) Contracts or agreements in restraint of trade to be made hereafter need not be filed any more than they are now; but if they are filed, the same rule applies; that is to say, if not disapproved within a limited period they can only be attacked on the ground that they are in unreasonable restraint of trade.

I apprehend that this proposed grant to an administrative board or department of the power to disapprove combinations or contracts hereafter to be made is the critical feature of this bill. The first question that will be asked is: Why not adopt the same policy toward future combinations and contracts as toward existing ones, and provide that none shall be attacked except for being in unreasonable restraint of trade? The answer is that such a provision would compel us to go into the future with no other protection than the protection which has proved insufficient, in the past, to avert the very evils which have aroused the strong popular feeling that has placed the Sherman Anti-Trust law upon the statute books and which keeps it there. With such a provision as to future contracts, it is doubtful whether this bill would even bring about publicity; and even if it were to do so, until it is proven by experience that publicity alone is a sufficient protection, it cannot certainly be said that no other safeguard is desirable.

The next question that will be asked is, why should not the government's failure to disapprove be final? The answer is that what is reasonable to-day may become, by the changes that time brings, unreasonable, say five or ten years from to-day. The government should not be prevented from questioning anything that is in unreasonable restraint of trade; but it may properly be compelled, as it is compelled under this bill, to assume the burden of proving the unreasonableness of which it complains.

The third question that may be asked is, what redress have those whose combinations or agreements be disapproved by these administrative officials? It must be frankly said, none. I know of no way to secure a review in the courts of an administrative decision of this character. On the other hand, it must be pointed out that disapproval has no other effect than to leave such combinations and contracts under the Sherman Anti-Trust law as it now stands; that is to say, in the position in which all combinations and contracts in restraint of trade now are. Is it worth while to keep all the business activities in the United States under the harrow because a few combinations or contracts may still be left there, with the possibility at least that they ought to be left there? I think our bill as submitted should be amended at this point, so as to call for a written statement of reasons in every case of disapproval. This would tend to prevent arbitrary action, and it would often enable persons aggrieved by disapproval to modify their agreements so as to secure the withdrawal of the disapproval. Again, it seems worth while to run this risk of executive disapproval for the sake of the gains that accrue if it is escaped. Those wishing to make combinations and contracts in restraint of interstate trade, will learn in this way much more quickly than they can through the courts whether it is safe to make them; and combinations and contracts that successfully run this gauntlet will command a quality of public confidence, including the confidence of investors, not to be had so easily in any other manner. Like all other administrative power, the power to disapprove is capable of being abused, but I ask you to notice the actual safeguards against abuse. First, the administrative officers cannot interfere by inaction. The government must take the responsibility of positively disapproving, and if it is also obliged to give reasons, those reasons will be passed upon in judgment by the whole country. Second, the Interstate Commerce Commission is a body of seven men, trained in exercising such functions. The action of the Commissioner of Corporations must be approved by the Secretary of Commerce and Labor. The Secretary is a member of the President's Cabinet. It is not too much to say, therefore, that the positive, aggressive disapproval of a proposed combination or contract in restraint of trade would form a part of the public policy of the administration, for which it would be held responsible by the country. Inaction can be maintained without sufficient knowledge on which to base criticism; but positive action by a Cabinet officer must be in the open, and must be capable of vindication.

The clause relating to certain phases of trade disputes has been inserted in the bill with the purpose of quieting the fears of organized labor, lest even strikes and labor unions and trade agreements may be declared illegal under the Sherman Anti-Trust act, as in restraint of trade. This fear is not wholly imaginary. Lawyers say, I know, that the Supreme Court in its recent decision has only condemned the boycott; and that, therefore, no such clause as this is necessary; but the members of trade unions scattered all over the country are not lawyers, neither have they lawyers at their elbows, and they are, in great numbers, subject to this fear. Neither are lawyers always right in such opinions; for I remember that many lawyers were confident that the Sherman Anti-Trust act did not apply either to common carriers or to labor unions. But the Supreme Court has ruled that the law applies to both. This clause, therefore, is not only just, but it is in the highest degree important, in order to set at rest the minds of literally hundreds of thousands of men, that their recognized right to strike, to combine, and to make trade agreements with their employers is not open to question. The correlative right of employers to discharge, to combine, and to make trade agreements with their employes must evidently be equally conserved. The precise clause is as follows: "Nothing in said act approved July 2, 1890, or in this act is intended, nor shall any provision thereof hereafter be enforced so as to interfere with or to restrict any right of employes to strike for any cause, or to combine, or to contract with each other or with employers for the purpose of peaceably obtaining from employers satisfactory terms for their labor, or satisfactory conditions of employment, or so as to interfere with or to restrict any right of employers for any cause to discharge all or any of their employes, or to combine, or to contract with each other or with employes for the purpose of peaceably obtaining labor on satisfactory terms." This clause, you will perceive, merely limits the purpose and effect of the Anti-Trust law, and does not assume to render lawful any action that prior to the passage of the Anti-Trust act would have been unlawful. Laborers had no right prior to the passage of the Anti-Trust act to combine or to contract for the purpose of effecting a boycott or of injuring others, and the proposed amendment confers no such right. The only effect of the amendment is to provide that the Anti-Trust act shall not have the effect of preventing employes from exercising their right to strike, that is to say, refusing to work, for any cause; or the right to combine or to contract with each other and with employers for the purpose of peaceably obtaining from employers satisfactory terms, etc. The correlative rights of employers to discharge their employes, and to combine and to contract with each other and with their employes are equally recognized. A boycott or a blacklist or a combination or contract for the purpose of injuring others would continue to be as unlawful as at common law, and would continue to be in violation of the Anti-Trust act if in restraint of interstate commerce.

Supplemental statement of Seth Low, president of The National Civic Federation, made before the Judiciary Committee of the House of Representatives, April 6, 1908:

In reflecting upon the criticisms made upon this bill it seems to me that the scheme of the bill has not been perfectly apprehended. At the present time it is an executive duty, exercised by the Attorney-General, to determine whom to attack under the Sherman law. No one can find out whom the prosecuting department may choose to attack, nor when. Our bill does not change the legal status, under the Sherman law, of any combination or contract in restraint of trade, but it does provide a method by which business men can quickly find out, if they want to, from another executive department, that of Commerce and Labor, whether the Executive is going to attack or not, and while the Executive may change its mind, if time should show that a mistake had been made it can then attack only by accepting the burden of proving that the thing complained of is in unreasonable restraint of trade. Evidently this is not an extension of executive power, but a limitation upon it; and it involves no hardship upon any one, for every one is left free to determine whether or not to apply for such a ruling. It is practically an offer made in return for publicity to define at once the attitude of the prosecuting department toward a particular combination or contract in restraint of trade. This is in the interest of uniformity in the policy of the Government under the Sherman law and is distinctly unfriendly to a policy of selection and persecution which is always possible under the law as it stands.

At the conclusion of the reading Mr. Low was questioned as to the attitude of the bill with reference to boycotts. He replied that it was not the intention of the bill to favor or authorize an interstate boycott or blacklist.

The Supreme Court in the Loewe case condemned the boycott, but it founded its condemnation on three elements: On a strike at the factory; on trade agreements by which seventy out of eighty-two hat factories had been coerced, and then on the boycott of the merchandise all over the United States. The line that we draw in the Civic Federation, so far as I am able to speak for it, is exactly this: We think the Sherman Anti-Trust law should be maintained with reference to boycotts and also with reference to blacklists; but we also believe that it is wise and necessary to make it perfectly clear that the Sherman Anti-Trust law in the future is not to have any bearing on the fact of combinations into unions, nor on the fact of striking, nor on the fact of trade agreements.

The Chairman asked whether he desired to authorize a strike for an unlawful cause, to which Mr. Low replied that it is not the purpose of the measure to define the rights which are now enjoyed. It simply states that nothing in the Sherman Anti-Trust act shall interfere with rights which may now exist.

The Chairman asked whether if, as stated, a large part of the business now being done in this country is being done contrary to law and if anybody has been embarrassed by that condition?

Mr. Low: The Department of Justice has certainly prosecuted some people, but I believe that if the Attorney-General were to attempt to prosecute all who are doing business in restraint of trade it would be like what Burke said was impossible—to indict a whole nation.

We have a law that forbids everything in restraint of trade, reasonable or unreasonable, and it is my opinion, and I think that of a great many, that that is doing injury to the country as long as it remains unmodified. On the other hand, the fear that put that statute on the books still exists, and the question is whether any way out can be found unless it provides some sort of an agency to protect society from the evil results of future combinations and future contracts in restraint of trade, such as have aroused the fear that put that statute on the books. We perfectly well understand that the suggestion that an administrative department should have anything to say about such things is a novel one; but, as regards general business, we have come very closely up to the same point we had reached when the Interstate Commerce Commission was established. I do not myself consider it important whether the decision is given by the Commissioner of Corporations or whether there is a commission created, or whether the whole thing is turned over to the Interstate Commerce Commission. My point is that I do not see any path of progress except along a line that puts up some sort of machinery that can protect the people in advance, instead of trying to right wrongs after they are committed. Whether this is the best plan or not, we have not so much assurance as to assert.

The vital feature of the bill is the question of being upon the registry. Those who are on the registry get the benefits and immunities of the bill. Nobody can be denied registry, and therefore nobody can be denied the benefits and immunities of the bill. If the proposition is made to remove any one from the registry, and the person feels aggrieved, he can only be removed for the causes stated in the bill itself; but if the person feels aggrieved by that proposition, he has an appeal to the Supreme Court of the District of Columbia.

As a result of a somewhat long colloquy between Mr. Davenport and Mr. Low, it appeared that the status of the individual as respects the right to claim damages was not in any way altered by the bill, even though the Government may not prosecute in case the conditions set forth in the bill were complied with.

MR. WILLIAM J. SCHIEFFELIN made a statement in regard to conditions in the drug trade, especially with relation to proprietary goods, or patent medicines. He showed that agreements as to prices had always been prevalent in the drug trade and that this was particularly true in regard to patent medicines, which constitute a large portion of the drug business. These proprietary articles, put up in uniform packages, are sold widely throughout the country. Price cutting among the wholesalers led to agreements with the manufacturers to make fixed

WILLIAM JAY SCHIEFFELIN.

prices. Later, the retailers found that they were subject to the competition of the great department stores, which oftentimes sold these articles at prices less than cost in order to attract the public to the stores and sell them other goods at a profit. The retail druggists formed a national association, with a membership of over 20,000 persons. Probably one-half of the druggists in the United States are members of the association. The retailers made arrangements with the wholesalers by which goods should be sold only to those dealers who charged the regular rates. The effect of this arrangement was to steady prices but not to enhance them.

In certain places the retailers endeavored to draw the line more sharply and to prevent the wholesalers from selling, not only proprietary articles, but sponges, drugs, chemicals and everything to those who cut prices. This was not accomplished in New York, but was in Philadelphia. The Sherman Act was appealed to and out of that unfortunate concession in Philadelphia the whole drug trade has been enjoined from making any three-party agreement—any agreement, that is, between the manufacturer on the one hand, the distributor (the jobber) in the middle, and the retailer on the other hand.

In answer to a question, Mr. Schieffelin stated that in his judgment the Philadelphia scheme was absolutely improper. The complaint of the drug trade is that the terms of the injunction are so sweeping. We would have been perfectly satisfied if any sort of an agreement involving a boycott, involving a blacklist and refusing anything, was enjoined, but the United States Court has enjoined us from making any kind of an agreement and from using any kind of persuasion.

The Chairman of the committee asked a variety of questions from the standpoint of the department stores, leading up to whether legislation was wanted to prevent the department stores from selling to its customers and consumers at prices less than retailers sell for.

This Mr. Schieffelin admitted was the purpose. He believed that the majority should have the right to compel business to be done in the way in which they wanted it done.

It has been said that you cannot indict a whole nation, but here the United States Court has enjoined an entire trade, five or six hundred wholesalers and forty-two hundred retailers. By the terms of the injunction it did not cover members of the association only. It applied to any one who signed these three-party contracts and thus includes practically all the retailers throughout the country.

Mr. Schieffelin: In view of the fact set forth, we desire to propose an amendment. Page 9 of the bill reads in part as follows:

"Anything herein contained to the contrary notwithstanding, all actions and proceedings now or heretofore pending under or by virtue of any provision of the said act, approved July 2, 1890, may be prosecuted and may be defended to final effect; and all judgments and decrees heretofore or hereafter made in such actions or proceedings may be enforced in the same manner as though this act had not been passed."

We ask that there be added to the bill the following: "But no such judgment or decree shall be held to prevent any person whatsoever from taking advantage of the benefits and immunities of this act in reference to any contracts or combinations hereafter made."

After some further questions, which brought out that Mr. Schieffelin, speaking individually, was in favor of the bill as a whole and which repeated further details in regard to the injunction suit already referred to, the committee took a recess.

April 4th, Afternoon Session.

On assembling in the afternoon, after preliminary discussion as to the time for continuing the hearing, the committee heard first MR. SAMUEL GOMPERS, who spoke as follows:

MR. CHAIRMAN and Gentlemen of the Committee: You of course understand that in whatever representative capacity I appear before you it is that as representing the workmen who are organized and who undertake the effort to advance as well as protect the interests of all workmen. I say this now because, before entering into the presentation of the thoughts that I have upon the subject under consideration, I want just to make this remark in passing, and that is that, in so far as the bill presented is concerned, I have had little or nothing to do in the preparation of these features dealing with corporations and associations conducted for profit and owning stock, and also with the common-carrier clauses. Nor am I willing to say that in so far as the construction of the bill is concerned I know enough of it to give the bill per se whatever endorsement that I can——

The Chairman: That is, its legal construction?

Mr. Gompers: Its legal construction; yes, sir. The purposes of the bill in so far as they deal with the associations and organizations and corporations and common carriers have my endorsement, and the fullest possible endorsement that I can give. Such purposes as, for instance, that business men may have full and free opportunity for the growth and the development of their business, and that they may conduct their business upon the assumption that it is fair and reasonable until it is proven and demonstrated that it is otherwise.

Modern business cannot be conducted upon the old notions. Development in industry does not admit of it. Development in transportation does not admit of it. The development and transmission of information does not admit of it. And therefore what may seem to some an anomaly that representatives of large corporations and business interests are here, accompanied by the representatives of workmen, advocating a line of policy to be shaped into law, yet the fact is that labor, or organized labor if you please, has realized for a long time, and realizes now—perhaps clearer now than ever before—the necessity for the fullest and the freest hand in the operation of business and industry and the performance of labor, and that in so far as interference by the Government is concerned, it should be of the least possible character.

Addressing myself particularly to the interests that I in part represent, I may say that, despite the assurances of a number of men, both Senators and members of the House of Representatives, when this Sherman Anti-Trust law was in its tentative and formative state, I still apprehended that lurking within those bills was the feature that covered the organizations of labor, and it was under that apprehension that, with others, I urged upon Congress the adoption of amendments to the then bill in order that it might be specifically stated in the bill that

SAMUEL GOMPERS.

the organizations or associations of labor, instituted to regulate wages, hours of labor and conditions of employment, and with the organizations of farmers and horticulturists, dealing in their own products, shall be excluded from the operation of the law. This is not the language of the amendments which we suggested at the time, but they are substantially the provisions.

Mr. Alexander: Have you got that language with you?

Mr. Gompers: Yes, sir.

Mr. Alexander: Will you put it into the record?

Mr. Gompers: I can read it if you care to have it now.

Mr. Alexander: Yes; read it, and it will go into the record.

The Chairman: You will find it in Mr. Hughes's speech the other day if you do not happen to have it there handy.

Mr. Gompers: I have it in my editorial in the American Federationist. This is the amendment which Senator Sherman made as a proviso to the bill in the Senate, while in the Committee of the Whole, it being an amendment that was drafted and fathered by Senator George, of Mississippi:

AMENDMENT.

"Provided, That this Act shall not be construed to apply to any arrangements, agreements or combinations between laborers made with a view of lessening the number of hours of labor or the increasing of their wages, nor to any arrangements, agreements or combinations among persons engaged in horticulture or agriculture made with a view of enhancing the price of agricultural or horticultural products."

The Senate, in Committee of the Whole, amended it by inserting the words "their own," so that, in so far as it applied to agriculturists' and horticulturists' organizations, that the arrangements, agreements, and so forth, that were made "with a view of enhancing the prices of their own agricultural or horticultural products." In that shape it passed the Senate. Then the entire bill was re-referred to the Judiciary Committee of the Senate, and the committee brought in a reconstructed bill, in which this provision was omitted.

I say again that the assurances were given that in the form that the bill was brought before the Senate by the Judiciary Committee, and as it passed that body, that it was not applicable to the organizations of labor nor the agricultural nor horticultural organizations.

Substantially as it passed the Senate the bill became a law. I want to just repeat the statement that, notwithstanding the assurances that others and myself received, and contending along that line, yet I always was apprehensive that at some time the courts might so decide, that the organizations of labor and of the farmers do come under the anti-trust law. I think Mr. Littlefield will remember that in 1901, I believe, when the Judiciary Committee of the House had an amendment to the Sherman anti-trust law under consideration, the representatives of labor urged the adoption of an amendment which directly and affirmatively excluded the labor organizations from the operations of the then pending bill and of the existing law.

The Sherman anti-trust law either in fact or, as now construed by the Supreme Court in its decision in the case commonly known as the hatters' case, makes it perfectly clear that under the construction the labor organizations come under its provisions.

The Chairman: I have a copy of the opinion here if you would like the opinion itself.

Mr. Gompers: I have it. I am aware that the members of the Judiciary Committee are fully cognizant of the decision of the Court, and I do not want unnecessarily to take time to read the law; but the decision of the Court brings conspicuously to notice Sections one, two and seven of the Sherman anti-trust law; and for a clear presentation—or the best presentation which I can make—I find it necessary to read the three sections of the law which the Court quotes in its opinion:

"Section 1. Every contract, combination in the form of trust or otherwise, or conspiracy, in restraint of trade or commerce among the several States, or with foreign nations, is hereby declared to be illegal. Every person who shall make any such contract or engage in any such combination or conspiracy shall be deemed guilty of a misdemeanor and, on conviction thereof, shall be punished by fine not exceeding five thousand dollars, or by imprisonment not exceeding one year, or by both said punishments, in the discretion of the Court.

"Sec. 2. Every person who shall monopolize, or attempt to monopolize, or combine or conspire with any other person or persons to monopolize any part of trade or commerce among the several States, or with foreign nations, shall be deemed guilty of a misdemeanor and, on conviction thereof, shall be punished by fine not exceeding five thousand dollars, or by imprisonment not exceeding one year, or by both said punishments in the discretion of the Court.

"Sec. 7. Any person who shall be injured in his business or property by any other person or corporation by reason of anything forbidden or declared to be unlawful by this act may sue therefor in any Circuit Court of the United States in the district in which the defendant resides or is found, without respect to the amount in controversy, and shall recover threefold the damages by him sustained and the costs of suit, including a reasonable attorney's fee."

Let me revert back for a moment to Section 1, and call attention to the fact that the law as construed by the Court, and as constructed, makes this fact clear: 'Every contract, combination in the form of trust or otherwise'—and I want to emphasize that word "otherwise," that it need not be a trust, it need not be injurious; but the mere fact that a contract has been made in the form of a combination or in the form of a trust or otherwise. In other words, it makes no difference whatever what the combination may do, whatever contract they may enter into, that shall in any way restrain trade, even though it be to the advantage not only of those who participate in the contract, but be a public benefit, it is still under the law, as construed by the Court, an illegal combination and punishable by the various methods named in the law.

Let me read Section 2, omitting some words, so as to bring out the thought I have, and that I desire to present to the committee:

"Every person who shall monopolize, or attempt to monopolize * * * any part of trade or commerce among the several States, or with foreign nations, shall be deemed guilty of a misdemeanor and, on conviction," punished as already stated.

In other words, an individual who undertakes to enlarge his business comes under the operation of this law. It is a curb upon individual initiative and development. The Court in its decision takes the very evidence of the successful co-operation of employers with employes to maintain industrial peace as the evidence that these combinations or agreements are in restraint of trade. Indeed, Mr. Low this morning, in his address to the committee, called attention to the fact that the Court quoted approvingly that, out of eighty-two manufacturers of hats in the United States, seventy were in agreement with the Union of Hatmakers, as the evidence of the success of the conspiracy between employers and these organizations, the conspiracy of the men in the organizations, the men of labor in their organizations.

May I say here in passing that I am not endeavoring, nor is it my purpose to indulge in such criticism of the Supreme Court or its decision that would directly or indirectly cast any reflection upon either the Justices of the Court individually or collectively. That is not my purpose, nor is it in my mind.

The Chairman: As I understand it, you complain of the statutes and not of the decision?

Mr. Gompers: I complain of the statutes.

The Chairman: You do not criticize the Court; your criticisms are directed to legislation?

Mr. Gompers: To existing law as interpreted by the Court, for until that decision it was an open or debatable question as to whether the labor organizations did come under the operations of the law.

Now, Mr. Chairman, let me say, in a word, that this so-called Sherman anti-trust law is not an anti-trust law, as its very title assumes it to be. It is an anti-combination law. It is a law against associated effort; it is a law something like the law which obtained about 2,000 years ago in Rome that made every form of association or organization which was not approved by the Emperor unlawful and punɔable with all sorts of penalties. Under it I might, ithout expressing my own opinion, for a moment .opt as my own a statement made by an organiza- ɔn of labor having this self-same subject under nsideration:

"Against the dangerous powers of the nobles, wise en of Europe, during the middle ages, nursed the ɔe cities and the guilds. Against the free cities, own too powerful, they raised the power of the ɔole people.

"It would seem reasonable that against the power massed capital such power as may be found in or- .nization of men, as men, might well be used to vantage. With the land monopolized and the in- :uments of production and transportation grown so pensive that they can be owned and controlled ly by the very rich as individuals or by combina- ɔns of capitalists, the owners of such instruments ill be masters, not only industrially but politically— ıy, over life and death—unless the individual free- ɔm of man, as man, is so protected that he may ɔmbine with others in his own interest and for the 'otection of individual liberty and of democratic stitutions.

"As conditions now stand, the worker is without ols and, usually, without land. His inherent neces- ities compel him to seek employment in order that e may live. Capitalists in possession of the land nd the tools of production need the workers to make he former profitable. Surely, the inherent necessity f the worker may be trusted to induce him to labor n conditions that will enable him to live and repro- uce his species. There is no need, and no wisdom, ı converting the law into a lasso with which the ,orker may be caught, led to the employer and ɔade to labor against his will.

"Judge Caldwell, in his dissenting opinion in the xley Stove Co. vs. Coopers' Union, truly says"——

The Chairman: Have you the number of the report f that case, so that we can make the reference?

Mr. Gompers: I have not.

The Chairman: It was in the Federal Reporter, I uppose?

Mr. Gompers (reading): "The only weapon of defense the laborers can appeal to is the strike or the boycott, or both. * * * If these weapons are withheld from them, then, indeed, are they left naked to their enemies. One class of men cannot rely for protection and the maintenance of their rights upon the justice and benevolence of another class who would reap profit from their oppression. They must be in a position to compel respect, and make it to be the interest of their adversary to grant their reasonable and just demands. Laborers can only do this by making common cause—by organization and collective action."

It is not necessary to put in the whole paper. What I just read was from a report made by a committee of the San Francisco Labor Council to that body, and, after a discussion of two evenings, it was adopted unanimously.

Under the law as it now stands construed by the Court, it is apprehended there is nothing which a labor organization can do in furtherance of the interests of labor, nothing which it can do in protection of the rights or interests of its numbers, but what is either enjoinable or punishable both by fine and imprisonment. We contend that equity, power and jurisdiction, discretionary government by the judiciary for well defined purposes and within specific limitations, granted to the courts by the Constitution, has been so extended that it is invading the field of government by law and endangering individual liberty. As government by equity, personal government, advances, republican government, government by law recedes.

I need not say at this late stage of appearing before committees, both this honorable committee and others of Congress, that we favor the enactment of laws which shall restrict the jurisdiction of courts of equity to property and property rights, and shall so define property and property rights that neither directly nor indirectly shall there be held to be any property or property rights in labor, or the labor power of any person or persons.

Mr. Chairman, we have fallen, all of us have fallen, into the misuse of a word in our language that has led to untold confusion. We speak of the working man or the working woman not in those terms, but as labor, labor. And under the confusion into which we have been led by reason of the use of that term—labor as applied to man and woman—comes much of the difficulties with which we have to contend. We all have seen in the press of the past week or two editorials in which the burden finds its expression that there must be equality of treatment of labor and capital. No less than a distinguished member of the present Congress introduced a bill in which there is no provision mentioned in so far as concerns the workman or the workwoman or the organizations of either—neither mentioned nor referred to; and he, too, with his great intellect, and I believe not unkind feeling, says that such a bill would be equal in its provisions to capital as well as to labor.

Now, what is capital? I shall not attempt to give a scientific definition of the term, but simply that which we all understand. It will be good enough for all the purposes of my statement. Capital is the product of human effort, used for the purpose of producing more wealth. It may be inanimate things, and is largely so.

What is labor? Is it an inanimate thing? Taking it in its accepted sense, is labor an inanimate thing? Labor is the effort of the human breathing man and woman. You can take capital and transport it to the other end of the world. You cannot do that with labor. You cannot differentiate the labor of the man or the woman from their breathing, respiring body and heart and brain. It is an abuse of the use of ordinary terms in our language. It is an abuse of the very essence of essential principles to place in the same category capital and labor, labor and capital.

You can make regulations for capital, and the owner of the capital may leave. You may not deprive him of even his own personal liberty, though you make all the regulations you may so far as concerns capital, but you cannot make one regulation in so far as labor is concerned, in the ordinary acceptance of that term, without it affecting the laborer—his heart, his body, his brain and his future.

It is because of this misconception that is so prevalent that we find learned screeds in editorial columns and speeches upon the floor of Congress, and elsewhere, dealing with the subject, with the terminology of which they are entirely deficient. It is because of this that we find editorials headed, 'Labor and Privilege," because we want to have the human rights accorded to us, and to which we are entitled, rights which the workman had before the State—the ownership of himself. With the abolition of human slavery in the dim, distant past, man became owner of himself, and with the ownership of himself and in himself he possessed the inherent ownership of his labor power, and to do with that just as he pleased—to sell it or to withhold it, as best served his purpose and his interests. There may be combinations in the profit of labor, and these may be properly dealt with by the State in order that the rights of the people may be protected and their interests furthered.

I want to say here again that I believe it is the part of unwisdom to attempt to unwarrantably interfere by law in the conduct of business in the interest and for the people of our country and of our time. But there must be a different concept of these two factors in human society—the one not capital, but the owner of capital, and dealing by law with capital, the product of labor; and the other dealing with the human, the man who labors.

I see that there are manifestations of opposition to the passage of this legislation. May I say, Mr. Chairman, that I received a copy of a circular in which this bill or this legislation is denounced as the most dangerous and diabolically ingenious measure yet proposed to Congress?

Mr. Alexander: Who says that, Mr. Gompers?

Mr. Gompers: Mr. James A. Emory, counsel for the National Council for Industrial Defense.

Mr. Emory: Guilty, if your honor please.

The Chairman: He is here.

Mr. Gompers: That is not the only thing, either. This was placed in my hands—I cannot remember how I got it; I know I did not take it. There is only one other species of circulars that are sent through—I do not know whether it is this National Council for Industrial Defense, because this is a new title, or a new organization; I do not know which—but sent out by the same gentlemen, Mr. Emory and his colleague, Mr. Davenport, and some other gentlemen whom it is not necessary to advertise. This circular from which I quoted denounces this bill and this species of legislation. One would imagine that if these gentlemen represented employers of labor who have an intelligent conception of modern industrial conditions and modern commercial conditions, that they would gladly co-operate with the best spirits in all walks of life to try to obtain relief from an intolerable condition. But no. There are some men like that sort of piscatorial creature who swings around in the water and besmirches the entire pool. There is nothing that the labor organizations can aid in securing in the form of remedial legislation to remedy any existing evil but what will meet with the undying antagonism of these gentlemen of the legal profession whose names I have mentioned, and perhaps those whom they represent.

Mr. Emory: Amen.

Mr. Gompers: I want to advertise Mr. Emory just once more by mentioning his name. He has the facility or the adaptability of always butting in when I am talking. I do not know for what purpose; but it is a good confession to make and to have on the record. I want to repeat, that there is not any legislation which the organizations of workmen can advocate to remedy an evil which is not met with their undying opposition, and to that he says "Amen."

Mr. Emory: Pardon me——

Mr. Gompers: Pardon, not now. You may need it worse some time. I cannot give it to you now.

There are some who entertain the hope that the organizations of labor will become disbanded, that their funds will be confiscated or mulcted in damages; that the earnings, the savings of some of the men, little as they may be, will be taken by decrees of the courts, and that the organizations of labor will be swept off from the face of the earth. I do not know what hopes some men entertain in that regard, but I say this, not only advisedly but from a careful study of the past history of the development of the working people of the world and their various forms of organization, and the battles that they have had to make, the obstacles which they have had to overcome—that they were outlawed, that they were criminal, that the men were punished not only by imprisonment, not only by being branded with red hot irons and stamped forever in servitude, but hanged to the gibbet, because they were banded together for the purpose of protecting themselves against the avarice and the tyranny of their employers.

Despite all the laws that outlawed them, despite all the decrees that condemned them, despite all the sentences that sent them to the jail and the branding iron and to the gallows, the organizations of labor still lived, and they will live, they will live. They have done so much to advance the interests of the working men and women and the children of the workers, they have brought so much sunshine into the homes where gloom before prevailed, that you could not drive the spirit and the feeling and the knowledge for and of labor organizations out of the hearts and minds of the working people.

Suppose it were possible that you could drive out of our lives the organizations that have protected us, our wives and our little ones, and done so much for us; suppose you would succeed by an injunction from Judge Gould in prohibiting us from declaring that the Bucks Stove and Range Company products are unfair, supposing you succeed in enjoining us and make that injunction permanent. Supposing you take our funds away by damage suits; supposing you do send us to prison because we believe that we have a right to protect that which we own, namely our power to labor; supposing you do all these things—what then? You may drive us into secret organizations, perhaps not us, but those who will follow. You may drive the men and women of labor into organizations oath-bound and secret; you may drive them into the dark.

There are two things that the American workmen have learned. One of them is some of the declarations of independence. They have been fed upon that. They are not yet satiated with it. They are more in love with it than I think most people are. The next is their organizations of labor. They love our country. They revere our institutions upon which our Republic is founded, and they know that within that Republic are their organizations of labor, their voluntary associations with their fellows that have done so much, and they are going to organize and remain organized—if not in the way that you permit it by law, they will still organize and remain organized, and neither ukase nor injunctions are going to drive the organizations of labor out of this country.

But supposing you force them to do in secret the perfectly legitimate human activities that they have always performed in the open. I need not say to you gentlemen, learned as you are, that men in the open, where they can express their views thoroughly, where they can promulgate to the world their thoughts, their hopes, are always more careful, intelligent and circumspect than they are or would be in considering the same questions in secret, oath-bound; and where they are simply free from the criticism of the general public.

Now, what? Industry has developed, is developing still further and will still continue to further develop. In so far as modern industry is concerned it is largely impersonal. It is a matter of profit, it is a matter of dividends. The human interest in industry, so far as the relations between employer and employes are concerned, is almost absent. Such human interest as the effort which gentlemen of the character and type of Mr. Low, and others, who are trying—and we are helping in our way—to bring about a better recognition of the interdependence of man upon man, whether he be employer or employe—to bring about better relations between them. But in the impersonal character of industry to-day what hope has the workingman to protect his rights and his interests, his wages, to obtain reasonable hours of labor if he, in modern industry, must act as an individual?

I am afraid to give my mind the range of the possibilities of such a condition of affairs—the industries of the country developing and concentrating and the associations of labor gone, and each man acting as an individual and trying to work out his own means of protecting his rights or his interests, without the ability to effectively protect and promote

(Continued on page 19.)

AMERICAN TEACHERS TO VISIT EUROPE

NATIONAL CIVIC FEDERATION PLANS FOR STUDY OF SCHOOL SYSTEMS—A CORDIAL WELCOME PREPARED IN ENGLAND—IMPORTANT COMMITTEES NAMED.

THE National Civic Federation has perfected its plans and made its announcements for a trip to Europe in the fall and winter of 1908-09 for the inspection of schools and teaching which is offered to 500 teachers in the public schools of the United States.

This undertaking, which has been received with great interest by the educators of the country, is a sequel to the visit of 500 English teachers to the United States in 1905-06. Mr. Alfred Mosely, of London, who has done so much to promote a better understanding and a friendly feeling between the two countries by the organization of the Mosely Industrial and Educational Commissions, was the soul of that enterprise. He arranged for the selection and transportation of the teachers, and, aided by committees on this side of the water, provided for the access of the teachers to the schools which they desired to visit, and for their entertainment in the homes of the American teachers, at a very modest cost to those who took part in the visit.

Mr. Mosely is associated with the National Civic Federation in the present enterprise. He has generously undertaken to make all the arrangements for the reception and comfort of our teachers when they reach England next winter, and will secure the co-operation of the various schools which are to be visited. His large influence and his experience in enterprises of this nature insures the successful issue of tne undertaking.

On the part of the National Civic Federation the initiative has been taken by Dr. Nicholas Murray Butler, chairman of the Industrial Economics Department. Through his efforts important concessions in the matter of ocean transportation have been made by the International Mercantile Marine Company. Mr. J. Bruce Ismay, president of the company, is deeply interested in the project. He appreciated the great advantages which accrued to the English teachers from their visit to this country, and, desiring to promote relations which would knit closer the bonds of sympathy and friendship between the two countries, has generously accorded to our teachers the same privileges as were granted three years ago to those of England.

In carrying out the work of planning and arranging for this visit, the National Civic Federation enjoys the co-operation of the leading educators in the United States. The advisory committee, which has been constituted, is thoroughly representative of the varied educational interests participating in the enterprise. Under the chairmanship of Dr. Butler the committee consists of the following:

Elmer Ellsworth Brown, Commissioner of Education, Washington, D. C.

Edwin G. Cooley, President National Education Association, Chicago, Ill.

Frank B. Cooper, President Department of Superintendence, National Education Association, Seattle, Wash.

Edwin B. Craighead, President Tulane University, New Orleans, La.

James M. Greenwood, Superintendent of Schools, Kansas City, Mo.

John R. Kirk, President State Normal School, Kirksville, Mo.

John W. Olsen, Superintendent of Public Instruction, St. Paul, Minn.

Henry S. Pritchett, President Carnegie Foundation, New York City.

Homer H. Seerley, President State Normal School, Cedar Falls, Iowa.

W. H. Smiley, Principal Denver High School, Denver, Colo.

Joseph Swain, President National Council of Education, Swarthmore, Pa.

Henry Clay White, President Georgia State College of Agriculture and the Mechanic Arts, Athens, Ga.

Carroll D. Wright, President Association for Promoting Industrial Education, Worcester, Mass.

The executive secretary is Roland P. Falkner, 281 Fourth avenue.

The conditions of the visit are such as to secure for all who take part in it an ample opportunity to see the work of the schools abroad. They will go on the lines of the International Mercantile Marine Company, leaving the ports of New York, Philadelphia, Boston and Portland during the months of September to December, 1908, in small groups not exceeding ten on any one vessel. The visit will, it is contemplated, last from four to six weeks on the other side. A limited number with a speaking knowledge of the French or German language may visit the continent, landing at Antwerp.

These opportunities are offered to the teachers in the public elementary and secondary schools of the United States. Such varied interests as elementary instruction in all its branches, with special work in music, drawing, manual training and domestic science, as well as work of secondary grade, such as general high school studies, manual training, commercial studies, industrial and trade education, and the training of teachers for elementary and secondary schools will be represented in the visit. Plans will be made to meet the needs of these, and perhaps other interests which may be represented. The places and schools to be visited will be carefully selected to meet the special needs of the visitors.

The project of the visit of the American teachers to Great Britain has awakened a widespread interest and support throughout the country. Mr. Mosely has associated with himself as a general reception committee a large number of influential persons throughout the United Kingdom, representing the various organizations and institutions and social groups which are associated there with the cause of education, and, indeed, with all the forces of social welfare. The co-operation of the leading men of England, as represented by this committee, insures that the visiting teachers will receive a cordial welcome wherever they go, and that whatever can be done for their comfort and for the success of the enterprise will be done. The general committee consists of the following:

The Lord Archbishop of Canterbury.
The Lord Mayor of London.
Rt. Hon. Joseph Chamberlain.
Rt. Hon. R. McKenna, President of the Board of Education in the British Cabinet.
Rt. Hon. A. J. Balfour, late Prime Minister.
Lord Reay, late President of the Board of Education.
Professor T. H. Warren, Vice-Chancellor of Oxford.
The Duke of Sutherland, K. G.
Professor M. E. Sadler, late of the Board of Education.
Sir H. Mortimer Durand.
Professor Osler, of Oxford.
Hon. Whitelaw Reid, the American Ambassador.
The Rt. Hon. Lord Desborough.
The Lord Bishop of Ripon.
Sir Thomas Barclay, LL. B.
Sir Alfred Bateman, K. C. M. G.
Sir John Cockburn, K. C. M. G.
Sir Charles Follett, C. B., etc.
Sir Norman Lockyer, K. C. B., etc.
Sir William White, K. C. B., etc.
The Rev. H. B. Gray.
Professor E. B. Poulton, Oxford.
Principal E. H. Griffiths, of Cardiff University.
Principal H. R. Reichel, of Bangor University.
Lord Ridley, D. L.
Sir Vincent Gaillard, D. L.
Sir Henry Roscoe, D. C. L.
Sir Cecil Clementi Smith, G. C. M. G.
Canon Lyttleton of Eton.
Principal Sir J. Rhys, of Jesus College, Oxford.
Sir Thomas Vezey Strong.
Sir S. B. Boulton, A. Inst. C. E., F. R. G. S.
Sir Edwin A. Cornwall.
Sir William Mather, M. Inst. C. E.
Sir W. J. Collins, M. P.
H. Llewellyn Smith, Esq., C. B.
The Rt. Hon. Charles Booth, P. C., etc.
Sir Alfred L. Jones, K. C. M. G.
Canon H. Scott Holland, M. A.
Dr. W. H. Gaskell, of Cambridge.
The Rt. Hon. J. Austin Chamberlain, P. C., M. P.
The Lord Bishop of Manchester.
The Rt. Hon. Lord Strathcona and Mount Royal, G. C. M. G., etc.
The Rt. Hon. Lord Willoughby de Eresby, M. P.
The Rt. Hon. Sir Herbert E. Maxwell, Bart, P. C., F. R. S., etc.
The Rt. Hon. Lord Viscount Duncannon.
Evelyn Cecil, Esq., M. P.
A. Bonar Law, Esq., M. P.
Col. Sir C. M. Royds, C. B.
The Rt. Hon. The Earl of Malmesbury.
Sir R. L. Morant, C. B., Permanent Under Secretary Board of Education.
Sir Frederick D. Dixon-Hartland, Bart, F. S. A., F. R. G. S., M. P.
Sir Thomas Wrightson, Bart.
The Rt. Hon. Gerald Wm. Balfour, P. C.
The Rt. Hon. H. O. Arnold-Forster, P. C., etc., M. P.
Sir M. Mitchell-Thomson, Bart.
The Hon. Robert P. Porter.
The Hon. T. A. Brassey, M. A., F. R. G. S.
Sir Wm. Reynell Anson, Bart, D. CL., etc., M. P.
George R. Parkin, Esq., C. M. G., LL. D.
The Lord Mayors of : Bradford, Birmingham, Cardiff, Liverpool, Leeds, Manchester, Newcastle-on-Tyne, Sheffield. The Mayors of: Bootle, Brighton, Bolton, Bath, Bangor, Cambridge, Dover, Exeter, Halifax, Leicester, Norwich, Nottingham, Plymouth, Rochdale, Scarborough, Swindon.
Dr. Sir James Crichton-Browne, LL. D., F. R. S.
Professor H. E. Armstrong.
Professor W. E. Ayrton.
A. W. Black, Esq., M. P.
Sir J. W. Benn, M. P.
Dr. J. Rose Bradford.
R. Blair, Esq.
H. Coward, Esq.
G. M. Chamberlin, Esq.
Walter Emden, Esq.
The Rev. Professor T. A. Finlay.
W. C. Fletcher, Esq., M. A.
Dr. T. Gregory Foster.
R. S. Fraser, Esq.
Dr. William Garnett.
H. T. Gerrans, Esq.
Sir W. J. Goulding, Bart.
Edward A. Goulding, Esq., M. P.
J. R. Heape, Esq., J. P.
Professor P. J. Hartog.
Rev. Canon A. W. Jephson, M. A.
Rev. Frank Johnson.
Arthur G. Lupton, Esq.
Professor R. Meldola.
Sir Philip Magnus.
Professor Magnus Maclean.
Dr. T. J. Macnamara, M. P.
T. H. Openshaw, Esq., C. M. G.
The Rev. T. L. Papillon, M. A.
H. R. Rathbone, Esq.
Professor W. Ripper, M. I. C. E.
Charles Rowley, Esq., M. A.
E. A. Ridsdale, Esq., M. P.
A. Rendall, Esq., M. P.
A. E. Spender, Esq.
A. J. Shepheard, Esq.
Mrs. Sadler.
John Whitburn, Esq.

In caring for the comfort of the teachers, Mr. Mosely will be assisted by a special committee headed by Mr. R. Blair, of the London County Council, composed of members of the Mosely Educational Commission of 1903. There has also been formed in each city or town to be visited by the teachers a local committee, generally under the chairmanship of a prominent member of the Board of Education. These local committees have been formed in large part with the assistance of the English teachers who visited the United States some years ago, and will be animated by the desire to reciprocate, as far as possible, the courtesies shown to the English teachers when they visited the United States. These committees have agreed to act as adviser to the American teachers, to introduce them in the schools to be visited, to procure in advance accommodations in boarding houses or hotels, as they may request, to meet the teachers (if desired) on arrival, and to minister to their comfort in every way.

At each of the ports of arrival (Plymouth, Southampton, Liverpool and Dover) the teachers will be met by a member of the reception committee, with whom they can arrange immediately for their accommodations at that port. With these committees they can consult in regard to the schools to be visited and plan out a definite schedule for the trip. The committees will have available specimen routes of travel to meet the needs of the different classes of teachers who may participate in the visit. When the schedule has been determined upon, teachers should then communicate with the chairman of the local committee at the several points to be visited, in order that these committees can arrange in advance such accommodations in boarding houses or hotels, as may be desired. While awaiting information from the committees in the several points to be visited, the schools at the port of arrival can be visited as well as schools in adjoining towns, which are easily accessible. Those persons arriving at Liverpool might very well make that city their headquarters for a week or more, in the meantime visiting schools in Manchester and other nearby cities.

Arrangements have already been made by Mr. Mosely for visiting a large number of schools. The authorities at these schools will throw open their

(Concluded on page 18.)

COMMITTEE ON THE TEACHERS' VISIT TO EUROPE.

FOR SHOP AND FARM

SHALL OUR PUBLIC SCHOOLS TRAIN WORKMEN AND FARMERS?

VOCATIONAL TRAINING ADVOCATED BY HIGH AUTHORITIES IN STATE AND NATION.

THE strenuous demand of the present day for industrial training is being voiced in many quarters. The educational press is full of it. It is attracting the attention of prominent educators. It filled a large place in the programme of the recent meeting at Washington in February of the Department of Superintendence of the National Education Association. The Assistant Secretary of Agriculture, the Hon. Willet M. Hays, made a stirring address upon the subject at one of the large evening meetings of the association. An afternoon session was devoted to the same subject. At another evening session Dr. Andrew S. Draper, Commissioner of Education of the State of New York, touched upon the question in his address on "Desirable Variety and Uniformity in Education." The report of Dr. Draper for 1907 is devoted mainly to this subject. This report and the address of Mr. Hays constitute two of the most important recent declarations in regard to the training of our people for work which have been made, and they are here summarized for the readers of the "Review."

INDUSTRIAL EDUCATION.

HON. ANDREW S. DRAPER.

IN his annual report for 1907, Dr. Andrew S. Draper, Commissioner of Education of the State of New York, in a chapter entitled "Our Children, Our Schools and Our Industries," makes an earnest plea for industrial education. He believes that the schools should hold all of the pupils until they have received a training fitting them for some definite employment. This need is more and more recognized among us from an increased knowledge of what other peoples, harder pressed and more painstaking than we, have done to meet modern conditions. Justice, as well as the progress and strength of the nation, make it necessary to give to the wage earner himself, and to the common industries, such equivalent as we can for what the present schools are doing for the wealthier classes and for the professional and managing vocations. In the early days of our country a knowledge of the "three Rs" was ample for most people. There was one main occupation, that of farming, and the children learned it from their parents. In towns an apprentice system provided for the instruction of the future workmen. Schools went no further than the elementary schools. High schools are a later growth. Universities, supported by public money, are of still more recent origin. The tendency in American education is to lean toward the professional occupations.

Nothing in the common schools leads to a trade. The manual training high schools are too elaborate, too expensive, and lead to nothing other than one of the industrial professions; often they do not even prepare for training any one of these. They are more like schools than shops, whereas they should be more like shops than schools. They are managed by men who are more teachers than workmen, when they should be in the hands of those who are at least as much workmen as teachers. Our system of schools does not train workmen. The unskilled labor in American cities is trained very little in the American schools. American children are taught that they must hold themselves above unskilled labor. The fact that our unskilled labor does not come out of our own schools, joined by the fact that the skilled labor which we have is so largely trained, not only in the schools, but in a very haphazard way in the shop, is disturbing the equilibrium of our factories, impeding our industrial productivity and raising much criticism of the unbalanced curriculum of the schools. The lines in all the schools above the elementary schools are set hard and fast for professional employments and for managing positions in industrial employments. In the high schools, the colleges, professional schools that are independent, as well as those related to the universities; in business and commercial schools, or independent schools of every kind in universities, and even in technical schools of every grade, the whole scheme is to turn out professional men and managers and captains of something or other rather than skilled workmen. From the top to the bottom of the school system the eye is on the school above, and the school above leads to a professional or a managing employment rather than a trade vocation.

Not much beyond the natural growth of existing institutions seems now to be necessary to the professional life of the country. This cannot be said as to the factors which contribute to the industrial life of the nation. In the interest of the common people and of the country the kinds of schools must

HON. ANDREW S. DRAPER.

be multiplied, the educational schemes be broadened, attendance upon schools must be longer and more universal, and the work of the lower schools must have much more bearing upon the labor of the masses. It is commonly assumed that practically all the children who generally go to the high schools finish the elementary schools. But this is not the fact. It is startling to find that certainly not more than two-fifths and probably not more than one-third of the children who enter our elementary schools have finished them, and that not one-half of them get beyond the fifth or sixth grade.

With the development of schools on the literary, scientific and professional sides the indenturing system has practically disappeared. Few boys are now apprenticed to a trade. The increase of machinery has led the older workmen who work with their hands to resist the training of boys for that work in order to avoid more competition. It is even true that there are many less apprentices in the trades than the rules of the labor organizations approve. This leads to a shortage of skilled workmen, and to the complaint of manufacturers that they cannot get competent workmen, and of others that the schools do not fit children for any ordinary duties in stores and offices. The reason why so many leave the elementary schools before finishing the course is not so much because parents need their labor, or because the law says that they may, as because there is too much wandering around in tall grass, too much time wasted in merely incidental matters. It is because the work of the schools is behind the ages of the children. It is because the work which we set to be done by the woman teacher in the fifth grade, and the way we expect her to do it, can no longer be tolerated by a boy passing into his fifteenth year. The hard fact is that we ought to get children well started earlier, and push them along more rapidly than we do, and there is no doubt that we ought to do the work of the elementary grades in at least one year less than we take for it. In any event, we should make it a point of getting children to the end of the elementary schools by the time they finish their fourteenth year. It is monstrous that two-thirds of the children of the State do not go through the elementary. Good citizenship and thrift and morals of the country are dependent upon the mass being trained to skilled work. The successful workman is a happier man and a more reliable citizen, a much larger factor in giving strength and balance to his country, than the unsuccessful or only half successful professional man.

There is nothing which now appeals to the popular fancy in America so much as "industrial training." The newspapers are full of it. Every public audience responds to it quickly. The authorities of charitable and penal institutions are trying to install it. The school boards are all in favor of it, but hardly know how to accomplish it. They do something about it because they dare not do nothing. They do not do much because the pedagogical mind is not very clear about policies and plans, because the professional and capitalistic classes are too often uninformed, uninterested or selfish about it, and because the labor organizations are skeptical about its ultimate effect upon the scale of wages. The confusion and uncertainty are widespread.

We have gone wrong in starting our movements in industrial training at the top rather than the bottom. Other nations have intrenched it at the bottom of their educational system and let the top meet its own needs. The top is more able than the bottom to get what it needs. Whatever the motive or the logic, Germany is educationally more democratic than the United States.

In recent years some special vocations, like stenography and typewriting, and other things relating to office work, have found their way into the public secondary schools. Three or four public vocational schools, of secondary grade, supported by a municipality, or partly by the municipality and partly by the State, like the Washington Irving High School of New York City, the Textile School of Lowell, Mass., and the Central High School of Commerce of Philadelphia, and some of the evening high school of Buffalo and New York City have been established. But their very names prove how far they are from the training of the masses in workmanship.

Private business schools have been more profitable and successful. Some of the great manufacturing or construction companies, like the Westinghouse Electric Company and the Baldwin Locomotive Works, have set up schools of their own, but the enumeration of these agencies shows the general lack of preparation for vocational employments in the United States, and the disconnected, very often unsubstantial, and ordinarily self-interested and sporadic movements to overcome the difficulty, rather than any general plan for meeting a very wide and very imperative demand.

The American public has really done nothing about training the children of the wage earners in industrial vocations. We permitted the very name "industrial school" to become used almost exclusively by institutions of a penal or disciplinary character. The manual training schools are not vocational schools. A number of very excellent trade schools established by benevolent citizens have awakened little enthusiasm, since Americans do not take keenly to institutions which in whole or in part rest upon charity. The American schools which come as near as any to the trade schools of Europe are those which have been established by a few of the great manufacturing works to train workmen for their shops. This movement under private corporations exemplifies the dearth of industrial training in the country. They are unacceptable to labor organizations because the latter think that such schools are created and operated in the particular interest of the employer, and not in the general interest of the employe; and more particularly because such schools provide ways for defeating the aims and methods of organized labor. From the viewpoint of general educational policy, the labor organizations have the better of the contention. We must find a scheme which will involve public proprietorship and be managed in the interest of all the people, or, at least, all with common interests in any trade, before it would be an effective American institution.

The American Federation of Labor, at the recent meeting in November, refused to commit itself to an attitude of antagonism to technical and trade schools, and directed its executive council to examine "established and proposed industrial school systems so that it may be in a position to inform the American Federation of Labor what, in the council's opinion, would be the wisest course for organized labor to pursue in connection therewith."

There can in the end be but one outcome, and I have entire confidence that the wisdom of the labor organizations will lead them to an attitude which is at once sane, patriotic, and promotive of the best good to the children of the masses.

The foregoing consideration which have been very briefly stated from Dr. Draper's able argument, lead him to suggest and recommend a definite programme, which is as follows:

1. Insist upon more complete and always up-to-date vital statistics. Know of the existence of every child, and when he is of school age have him accounted for.

2. Require attendance at seven years of age, instead of eight, and let it continue, in elementary school or trade schools, to seventeen, but excuse from attendance before eight, at the parents' request, on the ground of immaturity, and also excuse from attendance whenever the work in the elementary school and trades school is completed, or after fifteen if the child is regularly at work.

3. Establish schools for teaching trade vocations, the work to begin at the end of the elementary school course, and continue for three years.

4. Let the trades schools be open both in the day time and evening.

5. Establish continuation schools, to be open mainly in the evenings, where the work shall be of a general character, suited to the needs of youth who are employed through the day and are not doing the work in the trades schools. In other words, make our evening schools more general and better. Let the work in the continuation schools go perhaps half way or more through the high school course but with less formalism about it.

6. Shorten the time in the elementary schools to seven years. Take out what it is not vital for a child to know in order to learn or to do other things for himself. Assume that he will learn and do things on his own account if he has the power. Strive to give him power, and expect that through it he will get knowledge. Stop reasoning that mere information will give him power. Stop the dress parade and pretense about teaching, which consume time unnecessarily. Push the child along and aim to have him finish the elementary school in his fourteenth year. When he is fifteen send him to the trades school whether he has finished the elementary school or not.

7. Assume that if the child does not go to the high school, his school work may end with his seventeenth, and not in his fourteenth year.

8. Put into the elementary schools, from the very beginning, some phase of industrial work. Up to the last year or two let it be work that can be done in the schoolroom, at the desks, under the ordinary teachers, and will occupy two or three hours a week.

9. As the child comes to the end of the elementary schools, expect him to elect whether he will go to the high school, to a trades school, or to work.

10. Wherever he goes, expect that the schools will keep track of him until he is at least seventeen. If he goes to the trades school, expect him to get into the possession of the fundamental knowledge and something of the skill of a trade by his seventeenth or eighteenth year. If he goes to work in a store or factory, expect him to come to the continuation school till his seventeenth year is completed. Have him and his parents understand that he is responsible to the schools until he is perhaps eighteen years old.

11. Set up trades schools in spacious, but not necessarily ornate, buildings. Start the particular kind of trades schools that the business of the town and the interests of the trades call for. Let it be understood that wherever there are a sufficient number of children to learn a particular trade there will be a school to teach it to them. Let the trades school partake more of the character of the shop than of the school. Hold to books, somewhat, particularly books which the pupils will be glad to read by themselves, carry mathematics a little farther, lay emphasis upon work with a pencil; let the main part of the work be with the hands; and let the atmosphere of the place be free and comfortable, so that young people will like it. Let the teaching be done by real artisans, who are intellectually balanced and can teach, rather than by teachers who can use tools only indifferently. Above all, have teachers who are not afraid of youth, and so are not under the necessity of brow-beating and badgering them a great deal, but rather who command respect because of what they are, and can lead the way to the pleasure of really doing things.

12. Keep the trades schools open afternoons and evenings. Have their pupils attend from four or five hours to as many hours a week as the pupil can give. Let the training be individual and let the progress of the pupil depend upon himself and upon the time he can give; but allow him to engage in other work for pay if he must.

13. Modify the child labor laws so they will articulate with the plan, and enforce them. Require employers to regulate their affairs so that employes may attend continuation schools or a trades school at least four or five hours per week.

14. Let the trades schools be supported by the town, but give them sufficient State aid to encourage their organization and dispose them to conform to the needs of the situation.

15. Meet any demand on behalf of girls as well as on behalf of boys.

16. Make it quite possible for one in a trades school to go to a manual training high school, and vice versa, but be careful to avoid the inference that one is to prepare for another. Let it be understood that each stands upon its own footing and leads to very different ends.

AGRICULTURAL INDUSTRIES AND HOME ECONOMICS IN OUR PUBLIC SCHOOLS.

HON. WILLET M. HAYS.

OUR country has come to recognize that changed economic conditions, an increase in technical knowledge, and newly devised forms of school work have made it necessary and practicable to broaden our educational machinery so as to give a large place to the industrial vocations. Existing schools must enrich their courses of study along these new lines, so vitally connected with the thought and work of the people, and the newer types of schools especially fitted to the industrial life of the people must be developed so as to meet the new conditions in the largest and best way.

Generally speaking, one-third of our men folks are in agriculture, and one-third in the non-agricultural productive industries; while two-thirds of our women are in the vocation of home-making. Two-thirds of all our people enter these several vocations and nearly all receive their only schooling in our public schools. All will agree that our schools should be fitted in some measure to prepare them for it.

For those who cannot secure in their home schools vocational training along the lines they especially desire, special vocational schools are necessary. For the non-agricultural industries these may best be in the large centres of population, often in the

HON. WILLET M. HAYS.

atmosphere of the vocation for which preparation is sought. Here resident pupils can attend, each choosing that school which best meets his needs. For the agricultural industries these vocational schools should be on the land, preferably near a town or city. Those experienced in agricultural secondary schools designed mainly for young men and young women who are to remain on the farm, or are to change from city to country life, are unanimous in the belief, so far as I know, that these schools will not succeed so well as annexes to city schools as when separate and on large farms. As the school of art, theology, literature or science needs an environment, an atmosphere of its own, made possible by a strong special group of teachers and students in a large institution, or in a separate institution, so the school of an industry needs to be distinctive as a separate school or as a strong unit in a large school. Weak industrial departments in schools mainly devoted to non-industrial subjects have not generally succeeded. No doubt as the industrial subjects are better developed pedagogically, and as the industries are better organized as to the amount and regularity of employment the industrial subjects will oftener succeed, whatever the school environment. But it will always be true that the schools highly developed for special work in agriculture, in the mechanic industries, arts and trades, and in home economics, will establish the highest standards in education in these respective lines. The trend seems strongly to the development of large secondary mechanic arts schools and large secondary agricultural schools as parts of our public school system, and to include home economics in both. There are none, however, so narrow as to limit instruction in these lines to these large special schools. The industrial studies are finding more and more room in the academic city public secondary schools; and especially in the secondary schools of villages, towns and cities not large enough to support separate technical schools. Even short trades courses are finding favor in the public schools of some smaller towns where there is need for expert tradesmen in specific industries. And even the primary schools of our centres of population are giving more and more attention to mechanical and home-making vocational work.

The Davis bill now before Congress (H. R. 534) proposes to give national aid to vocational training It equitably distributes money raised by general taxation and gives its share to every district in the land.

Briefly stated, the terms of the Davis bill provide that Congress shall appropriate annually to each State ten cents per capita for industrial education. Of this sum each city with more than 2,000 inhabitants shall receive its per capita share, the only limitation being that this money shall be used for studies in mechanic arts and home economics in schools of secondary grade. To the population outside of cities the ten cents per capita shall be used for studies in agriculture and home economics in secondary agricultural schools. Both in the city secondary industrial schools and in the agricultural high schools thus established the State or locality must provide the lands, buildings, and also current funds to provide all the necessary general studies to round out strong courses of study.

The bill further provides that Congress shall appropriate one-fourth the sum received by each agricultural high school for a branch agricultural experiment station and requires the State to appropriate an equal sum. This branch station fund will aid the practical teachers to fully understand the soils, crops, live stock, and the plan of farm management suited to the respective districts. It will provide means with which to co-operate both with the State experiment station and with the United States Department of Agriculture in such work as breeding, testing and distributing new varieties of field, orchard and garden crops; in the improvement of the breeds of animals; and in working out systems of farm organization, field management, soil fertilization and crop production.

Following such noteworthy examples as the Minnesota, Wisconsin and Nebraska agricultural high schools and branch experiment station organizations, 300 of these institutions would accommodate 100,000 farm boys and girls, many of whom are not seeking an avenue off the farm. Probably 20,000 would graduate annually, the majority returning to take leading places in their farm communities, a large proportion entering upon teaching as in the consolidated farm schools, in town schools, in normal schools, and in the district rural school, and probably ten per cent. going to the agricultural college.

Following such splendid examples as the St. Louis, St. Paul, and Washington mechanic arts secondary schools, hundreds of these institutions will accommodate hundreds of thousands of city youth who wish to pursue courses in mechanic arts, industries and trades, and girls who wish to have technical training along home making lines. Tens of thousands will annually graduate ready to rapidly gain high efficiency in the expert trades or in the keeping of homes. Not a few will proceed to the engineering or other technical college and the graduates of these schools will eventually grow into the leadership of many of our manufacturing and transportation industries. But the great majority will take the well paid places requiring masterful artisans, places not too often taken from American youth by highly skilled foreigners. These schools, instead of being places to turn out cheap tradesmen, will supply men who, having joined scientific information, school shop experience and actual service in their chosen trades, will set new standards for our expert trades. They will tend to increase wages in these lines, and they will increase the output from labor. Under public management they will treat fairly both the man who has labor to sell and the man who is seeking to employ labor. Many of the women graduates will splendidly build up the home economics instruction in all schools where girls attend, from primary to collegiate, insuring that the housewives and mothers of our land be expert in their work. The improvements which will come through instruction in home economics in the agricultural high schools and in the mechanics arts high schools and by graduates of these institutions carried into all primary schools will pay all the cost to the Federal, State, and local governments as required under the provisions of this bill.

The Davis bill is open to defeat or to improvement and passage. Broadly speaking, it proposed to change our expenditure from, say, $4.00 per capita to $4.10 per capita; and to provide that this added 2½ per cent. of our school expenditure shall be placed under a plan where it can be used only for training in agriculture, in mechanical industries and in home making. We all know that this is the side of our educational machinery which has not kept pace with our needs. The main proposition should be handicapped by amendments.

This enlarged expenditure for teaching the children of our native and recently arrived Americans how to make better homes and to increase their production of commodities has the broadest possible national significance. We are in world competition with nations able and willing to make commodities at lower units of labor charge than we. We must either increase the efficiency of our labor units or be willing to sell them at lower wages. America has charge of the world's highest standards of wage and of living. Industrial education has a place beside a reasonable tariff in keeping America's dinner pail full.

KEEPING THE TRACK IN ORDER

ARDUOUS DUTIES OF MAINTENANCE OF WAY EMPLOYEES ON RAILROADS—SEVERE LABOR AND SCANTY REMUNERATION.

IN a recent investigation of labor conditions on the Southern Railway, undertaken by the Chairman of the Interstate Commerce Commission and the Commissioner of Labor, under the Erdman Act, Mr. A. B. Lowe, President of the International Brotherhood of Maintenance of Way Employes, presented a forcible brief on behalf of the men of his organization. The following extracts give a vivid account of the work of these men and the conditions under which they labor:

To begin with, then, I speak for the men whose duty it is to make possible the rapid transit of trains, passenger and freight, by close inspection of the tracks and bridges, seeing that everything is in good order and making daily repairs which fast and heavy traffic make constantly necessary.

To do this work most economically and efficiently a railway system divides its road into divisions, having its tracks under the supervision of an official usually termed a roadmaster, who probably has charge of 150 miles. The bridges in this or, perhaps a longer division, are under the care of an official called a supervisor, who has charge of the bridges and buildings. The name of the official in charge of either track or bridges and buildings may vary, but this is about the average system, the whole is usually under the charge of a civil engineer, called the engineer of maintenance of way.

The duty of keeping bridges, culverts and other passages in safe condition is entrusted to foremen and gangs of men living in cars and moving as the requirements of the work demand. Their importance in the railway service can be seen by just imagining for one moment any neglect in keeping either the foundations or upper structure of a bridge in safe condition, and the destruction of life and property which such neglect might cause. In addition to the arduous nature of their service and its responsibility it is to be remembered that many of their tools have to be supplied by the employes at their own cost.

A roadmaster's district is divided into sections of varying length, usually not less than six miles, each section being in charge of an employe called a section foreman and from one to six men. Their duty is to inspect daily or as much oftener as may be necessary their entire section, putting in ties, keeping the rails spiked to proper gauge to make the passage of trains safe, keeping the track in good alignment to make easy riding, keeping the surface of the rails level to prevent breaking of the rails by the pounding of the wheels caused by low joints, finding broken rails and renewing the same or worn out rails, keeping the curves properly elevated to prevent derailment of trains by spreading of track, tightening of bolts, keeping the right of way clear of weeds and rubbish, maintaining fences, gates and road crossings; in brief, doing the thousand and one things necessary to make rapid transit safely possible. Often the force to do this is not adequate for the purpose. In prosperous times the men cannot be obtained in many places who will work for the low wages the company offers, and in dull times, when men could be got, the necessity for a small pay roll seems to supersede all other considerations. All the work mentioned is of a laborious character, most of it is done in a stooping position and requires considerable muscular force, and the work has to be done regardless of the weather, and thus we are subject to all the vicissitudes of the intense heat of a Summer's sun reflected from the rails and ballast, and in Winter to all the rigors of Winter's stormiest days of snow and sleet and coldest, deepest frost.

Another point which deserves more than a passing notice is that the worse the weather, the more drenching the rain, the more necessary is it that we should turn out, often in the middle of the night, to make all speed with lanterns and torpedoes to some weak spot in an embankment, or a bridge force must turn out in just such weather to guard some pier that they fear may be undermined and leave a chasm into which a train might leap. To the credit of our craft it is seldom such a thing happens, but the occasions on which the red lanterns and the torpedoes have brought a train safely to a halt before the chasm where a bridge had gone down, an embankment been washed away, or a snow or mud slide had blocked the roadway are of frequent occurrence. As it is all in the line of our duty, not much is said of these things usually, but they are well worthy of a place in the facts connected with this investigation. And as all the risks to trains mentioned are things of daily possibility, I need not say a proper regard for human life requires a class of men in the maintenance of way service of a character that will insure a faithful performance of the means of guarding against such accidents, and the employment of men whose fidelity to duty as well as their skill in its performance can be depended upon. For it must be remembered there is no taskmaster on hand to order these men out when the storms are worst. A roadmaster cannot be everywhere on a division 150 miles long, so it is left to each track or bridge man's sense of honor and his regard for the lives entrusted to his care to send him from the comforts of home out in the dark night's storm.

I need hardly remind you, gentlemen, that every life in the train, from the engineer in the cab to the porter in the rear Pullman, is in the hands of the employes of the M. of W. department. The most experienced engineer may be at the throttle, the most careful conductor in charge of the train, the most skillful despatcher send a correct train order to the most faithful of operators, but all the care and skill of all combined will not save a train from destruction if inefficient or unfaithful men have charge of the tracks and bridges. A careless inspection of the track that fails to detect the scarcely perceptible break in a rail, a little left to chance in the repairs to a bridge, or a lack of watchfulness of a current wearing away the foundations of a pier,

A. B. LOWE.

and, in spite of the utmost care of the most experienced engine and train men, disaster will surely follow.

These facts tell forcibly of the arduous character of the work, the danger to health connected with its performance, the great responsibility resting upon each employe, and the consequences which would assuredly follow even apparently slight neglect of any of our many duties. Believing that I have stated the case fairly, I think I am entitled to claim that men on whom such great responsibility rests should neither be selected from the lowest grade of society nor be the poorest paid employes in the railway service. Each year as heavier locomotives and cars are being introduced into the service, as each new schedule asks for a still faster train service than the last, the responsibility and hardship of the service increases, and as the responsibility and hardship increases certainly the pay should increase proportionately. And if a reduction of expenses ever makes a reduction in pay an actual necessity then the officials at the top, with salaries able to stand a cut, should be the ones selected for the knife, not men whose pay is barely above the point which supports existence. I have said nothing of the increase in pay which should keep pace with the increase in the cost of the necessaries of life, but you gentlemen know that when the cost of living increases if the rate of pay does not correspondingly increase then the wage is cut in the same proportion that the cost of living has increased. On the Southern Railway, although there has been no decrease in the cost of living, the laborers in the track department have had their wages cut ten cents per day, and some are working to-day for the same rate as was paid fifteen years ago. I commend this reduction of ten cents per day of those track laborers to your careful consideration and ask that the pay be restored to at least what it was before the cut was made.

Since March 1, 1907, and as the committee understood to continue for one year, the minimum for section foremen was forty-five dollars and fifty cents ($45.50) per month, the maximum fifty dollars, a few yard foremen getting from fifty-five to sixty dollars per month. Men in the bridge and building department to receive an increase of ten per cent. The minimum of laborers in the track department was ninety cents, the maximum $1.15 per day.

The committee contend this cut was in violation of the agreement between the management and the committee, effective March 1, 1907, while the management claim the laborers were not included in the schedule. There is certainly a misunderstanding between the parties, but I will only refer to it, as I understand the whole matter in controversy between the management and the committee representing the Maintenance of Way employes has been referred to you gentlemen, and I presume you will give a decision on our right to represent the laborers who wish to be represented by us as well as on the question of rates. I would be loath to say the management deliberately broke a contract, as our experience has been that railway managers carry out generously both the letter and spirit of our agreements, and I trust the Southern will be no exception.

This reduction of 10 cents a day brings the minimum down to 80 cents and the maximum to $1.05 per day. I wish I could invent some other word than maximum; it seems such a large word for such an insignificant wage.

We have been hearing a good deal lately about "Frenzied Financiers." Let me call your attention to a class of whom the world has not heard much, but to whom the term may surely well apply. It is the wives of these men who at eighty cents per day of ten hours, having worked twenty-six days in the month, go home to the wife and hand her the envelope with their pay and tell her to provide shelter, food and clothing for the family out of a monthly wage of twenty dollars and eighty cents. If that does not produce "Frenzied Financiers" I can't imagine what would. And yet that is what the Southern management think is sufficient to supply a family with the needed home comforts and pay a man to sacrifice health or life itself if the exigencies of the service call for it, to protect the valuable property and the priceless lives committed to the care of the men in the track and bridge and building departments.

I presume, gentlemen, you understand that the foremen who take charge of sections are brought from laborers trained in the service. There is no other college to turn out graduates capable of performing the duties of a foreman except the hard school of the gauge and spike maul, the pick, shovel and tamping bar. With every passing year heavier, faster train service is demanding a better class of section foremen. Is there any real gain to a railway company in taking the heart out of their employes by paying wages which keeps them dissatisfied and discontented, and only retains them in the service until the first chance of leaving it offers? And as each road must provide its own foreman, what will the character of the future foreman be on the road where they have to be promoted from the men who would remain at track work at either 80 cents or $1.05 per day? In view of the disastrous killing and wounding of passengers and train employes shown by the accident bulletins sent out by the Interstate Commerce Commission, is it permissible, or even, from the viewpoint of dividends, economical, to procure the labor for the Maintenance of Way Department from the flotsam and jetsam, the culls and cast-offs, of the labor market? What else could you get for that price?

I have the utmost confidence, gentlemen, that you will recommend a wage rate for the foremen and men in the Maintenance of Way Department which will be based on our value to the company, the arduous nature of our work, its great responsibility in view of the value of human lives and limbs, and the immense value of the property entrusted to us. I am sure that in estimating a fair living rate for all the employes in the Maintenance of Way service whom I represent the cost of the necessaries of life will come into the calculation and the importance of the rate being such as will bring to the service married men, who will be permanent employes, and a rate sufficient to provide for the comfortable housing, clothing, feeding and educating of our wives and children in a style becoming American citizenship.

SOCIALIST SUNDAY SCHOOLS

THEIR EXTENT AND OBJECTS—MATERIALISM EXPOUNDED TO CHILDREN—SOME APT PUPILS.

THOSE Socialist Sunday schools teaching from the "red catechism" have been refused the further use of the public school rooms in London. But elsewhere throughout the world there seems to have been neither civil nor other effort made to check the education of children in "scientific materialism." In good British fashion the evicted Socialists are resisting the action of the London County Council. Upon civil grounds they stand by their "equal right" to the use of the school rooms with those other Sunday schools whose catechisms are founded upon the Bible. Pedagogically their rights are defended upon the alleged findings of science. They argue if there be such a thing as the soul in the religious sense, it is necessarily the result of a fortuitous concourse of events, in a word, blind force. Consequently the highest possible obligation from man is to man—there is nothing above humanism. As God is the product of imagination, brought into existence to sustain the reign of private property, it is silly to fear Him and idle to love Him. All the heaven worth striving for is made up of little work, more play and much wealth. This triple ascension may be gained by the collective ownership and operation of confiscated capital.

Great demonstrations in the parks of London are being held to compel the authorities to restore the Socialist Sunday schools the use of their erstwhile quarters.

In the United States these schools are not occupying public buildings free of rent, but they are well established and flourishing in all of our large cities.

Decidedly, the American children are shown to be the most apt. From exhibits in "The Worker" (July 20, 1907, the leading Socialist weekly in this country), the doctrine is clearly put forth in six "essays," which were written by the child members "without prompting." They are simplicity itself as to the origin, purpose and end of life.

The pen having already abolished the moral order, there can be no sins to deal with; and as the cause of crime—of killing and stealing—is merely lack of wealth, heaven shall come on earth "when Socialism comes; there will be plenty of food for all, and people will not have to run after food or kill or rob some other man in order to get it,' writes one of these six essayists, Abraham Edelsack.

The dogma of the "social organism" is treated by little Lena Rosenheck, age thirteen. She has been taught that the "science of Socialism" proves that the individual is not yet a responsible being. First, because he is practically non-conscious of the universal ego, and, second, even upon becoming "class conscious," he is powerless to act freely, being the slave of "capitalism." This, of course, applies with equal force to capitalist master and wage slave. When the working class shall have conquered the capitalist class—thus leaving but one class—then a moral code, a moral economy may be resolved in order—not before. So, also, then for the first time in the history of man will there be such a thing as free will.

"A society of men (writes little Lena), like the human body, is made up of different parts. Each part must do its work. A good example we have in the street cleaners of New York. Last week the street cleaners, instead of taking away the garbage every day, went on strike, and the garbage was piled on the streets for five or six days. It smelled very bad. It is believed that many children were taken sick from the terrible smell. The strikers did not win, but it is said they will get what they want." "Science" thus engages to make it plain that no man can do right, or be moral, until all are made to take their places in the "social industries." Domestic economy will die out, for the work of the home will be socialized, and "baby farming" must supplant the mother's care of her children.

The doctrine taught at the "red Sunday schools" is an extension from the premise that "religion is a fantastic degradation of human nature" (Marx). "Socialism must conquer the stupidity of the masses in so far as this stupidity reveals itself in religious observances (Liebknecht). That "we wish * * * in religion, atheism" (Bebel). Modern science having proved that "there is nothing left for Deity to do," clearly there is no reason left to fear God, to love God, or to worship God—"God is a myth."

Another little fellow, Abraham Jacobson, age eleven, deals with the weighty problem of the moral order, or, rather, with a fatalism which has formed civilization in place of the old superstition that there is an universal moral economy to which the individual may conform, or may refuse to conform. "It cannot be different," because "people cannot be kind, true or honest" so long as they work for wages. It is the "capitalist system" which causes capitalists to rob workmen, even if some employers don't want to. Whether we like it or not, the "present order" leads to the revolution, which will cause the workmen to rob their robbers of all the means of production, distribution, and exchange. This robbing will put forever an end to robbery. Because Socialism will be here, and everybody will own everything. And there will be nothing that nobody doesn't own.

These pupils are taught not only "why people are as they are" morally, but how the human body happened to be formed as it is. It was our habits while we were still only animals that made us over into men. Perhaps we shall be obliged to form some other habits that will make us into something other than men. But as yet Socialists are not sufficiently "race conscious" to pretend to give "cook shop receipts" for the conduct of the industries under their own regime, or to aid us in making ourselves over into what we shall be hereafter.

Like the rabbit and the wolf, every structure is made by habits forced upon it. "The rabbit has long ears and his eyes are at the side of his head, because the rabbit has to see what is going on around him."

"The wolf is fierce and his eyes are in front of his head, because he is always chasing the rabbit and trying to get him for food. It is the same way with the people—they are always running after food. * * * If they don't get it they are compelled to rob or kill some one to get food for their wives and children."

These Sunday school pupils have the Socialist dialectic set before them dogmatically. First, physical necessity shaped our necks—not so long as the giraffe's, nor as short as that of the hedgehog—by our prehistoric manner of getting our food supply. That material necessity alone is the master builder of our fate. We are neither good because we will to be and strive to be, nor are we bad because we yield to temptation and dwell in sin. But we are simply thus and so because our environment has made us to be thus and so.

Henry Feigenbaum, age thirteen, has a clear grasp on the doctrine of "class struggle," and also its mission and destiny. The "game of life" has been to "hold as their own social use property" and to keep the "stakes of the game through politics." When Socialists come into power they will "make rules for their own benefit. The working class being in the great majority, the rules they would make would really be for the benefit of all."

The last two of these "essays" tell "What Socialists Want." Jacob Schward is the author of one, and Stella Gillis, twelve years of age, the other. Americanism is ruled out of court, for "Socialists claim that a system like this has no right to exist. It must be changed to a new system of society, where people will not be divided with different interests, but it will be one class with one interest, and this interest will be the good and welfare of society." The revolution having arrived, "class consciousness shall have evolved into "race consciousness"—into the conscious experience of the 'social organism," above which there is nothing.

Bible teaching and Christian standards are not alone out of date, but the "red" catechisms have left behind the principles of logic. The law of contrast—that process by which the identity of each person or thing has hitherto been known because of its difference to all persons or things—is, by their system of thought, not necessary. Of course, their proposed co-operative commonwealth will prove by experience whether it were easier to outgrow the moral code or the law of identity. Though the Ten Commandments have been already curtailed. For some of the "comrades" have, on Boston Common, "Resolved" that henceforth when a man is hungry it is moral to steal.

There is no monopoly in New York of Socialist Sunday school achievement. Chicago is also teaching the "science of Socialism" to its children. The philosophy that "things develop themselves according to some eternal idea" it will not tolerate. Just as from reaching far down into clover blossoms has developed the slightly longer proboscis of certain bees, thus allowing them to survive, "likewise society, as a large organism, has been formed entirely by the economic conditions in which men found themselves. Domestic life, government, literature, architecture and codes of ethics are all outgrowths of social surroundings."

So, also, in Boston the chief aim of the Socialist Sunday school "will be to bring up our children in the ethics of Socialist principles." Boston children are most fortunate, as among the instructors are "some of the heroic ministers who have been promoted from the pulpit to the broader and more strenuous field of international Socialism."

Although admiration for the literary achievement of the New York children spread from ocean to ocean, the Socialist press was keyed up a pitch or more higher in reporting the practical demonstration of those of Omaha. Patriotism was flung in the gutter to make room for the red flag of the world. The heroic act was led on by a "little girl of ten," and a "national reputation" has been made by these children, who tore down President Roosevelt's picture from the walls and hung in its place one of "Mother" Jones. Great exploit this! This incident, says the "Social-Democratic Herald,' of Milwaukee, "speaks volumes for the manner in which these children have been taught the truths of Socialism."

In this free country the spirit of Socialism, even among the children, is intellectual and practical—"truly scientific." While in Melbourne it is somewhat sentimental, devotional. There, too, the doctrine is taught the little ones, but "an earlier step has been taken by the dedication of infants to the cause." Like as of old, Hannibal was sworn upon the altar of Baal always to be the enemy of Roam, so is a "Socialist baptism" given as a dedication to the cause, made a pledge of hatred to all that stands opposed to the oncoming revolution.

Throughout the world the children's literature is fast multiplying. Beginning with "The Young Socialist" there is now added "The Child's Socialist Reader," illustrated by no less an artist than Walter Crane. Tales, poems, pictures and song books are plentiful in supply. All the Socialist papers pay some attention to this branch, while "The Woman Socialist" especially furthers its interests.

Dozens of new schools have been founded during the past year, and while there are no statistics available for our own country, the Sunday school children of the "red internationals" abroad has reached the total of 59,225.

MARTHA MOORE AVERY.

EN ROUTE FOR PANAMA.
(MR. CHILDS ON THE LEFT, MR. BALFE THIRD FROM LEFT.)

MESSRS. WILLIAM CHILDS, JR., and Harry Balfe, members of the Welfare Department of the National Civic Federation, sailed on the S.S. Allianca of the Panama Railroad Company, Tuesday, March 3, at noon, for the Canal Zone to make an investigation for the Government, as experts, on the food served to the men employed in constructing the Canal. This investigation is made under the executive order of President Roosevelt and Secretary Taft. Messrs. Balfe and Childs have been authorized to look thoroughly into the question of improving the food conditions, the inquiry extending into the methods of purchasing, the quality of the food materials, the management of the mess-halls, and the deterioration of supplies in transporting them from the United States to Panama and from the Port of Colon across the Isthmus to the various camps.

The equipment of these gentlemen is evidenced by the fact that they are respectively the President and Manager of the Childs chain of restaurants in New York and Philadelphia, patronized by one hundred thousand persons daily. Mr. Balfe also has charge of feeding the immigrants at Ellis Island.

THE NATIONAL
Civic Federation Review

Office: 281 Fourth Avenue, New York City
RALPH M. EASLEY, Editor

The Editor alone is Responsible for any unsigned article or unquoted statement published in THE NATIONAL CIVIC FEDERATION REVIEW.

PUBLISHED BY

The National Civic Federation

The Washington Meeting. A conference of representative women has been called to meet in Washington, May 11 and 12, to organize the Woman's Department of the National Civic Federation. At the same time there will be a joint meeting of the Industrial Welfare Department and the Public Employes' Welfare Department. President Roosevelt has invited those attending these sessions to meet him in the East Room of the White House, and has consented to address them.

A reception has been arranged at the New Willard Hotel for the evening of the 11th, at which addresses will be made by Seth Low, Samuel Gompers, Nahum J. Bachelder, Sarah S. Platt Decker, Andrew Carnegie and John Mitchell. The next number of the *Review* will contain a full report of the proceedings of these meetings.

Amendment of the Anti-Trust Act. Out of the Conference on Trusts and Combinations held last October in Chicago has grown one of the most important activities in which The National Civic Federation has been engaged—namely, the effort to formulate such an amendment to the Sherman anti-trust law as would permit combinations in business not contrary to the public interest and which shall, at the same time, allay the fears arising from uncertainty as to the scope and application of the present law. It will be remembered that the Chicago conference adopted a series of resolutions declaratory of the existing unrest and of the need for a revision of the Sherman anti-trust act. It provided, moreover, that these resolutions should be presented to Congress and should be urged upon that body by a special committee.

On the presentation of these resolutions to Congress it was pointed out that the resolutions, however important, were not in a form which admitted of legislative discussion, and the suggestion was made by the chairmen of the Interstate Commerce Committees in both the Senate and the House of Representatives that it would be well to suggest definite legislation as a basis for discussion. Inasmuch as the conference at Chicago had not vested in its committee authority to do more than present the resolutions adopted by the conference, it was necessary if any further action were to be taken that it should be done in the name of and by authority of the National Civic Federation itself. Acting upon the suggestion made in Washington, representatives of the varied interests concerned, so far as they could be reached and time permitted, were invited to confer with officials of the National Civic Federation and take part in the drafting of a measure which would meet as nearly as possible the recognized need in legislation. Many conferences were held and the matter discussed at great length from all points of view. In these conferences a measure was finally drafted, in consultation with the Commissioner of Corporations, Mr. Herbert Knox Smith, which was introduced in the House of Representatives by the Hon. William P. Hepburn, chairman of the House Committee on Interstate Commerce. The same bill, slightly amended, was introduced in the Senate by Senator Warner. In both the Senate and the House the bill was referred to the Committee on the Judiciary.

Hearings have been held before both committees. An account is given in this issue of the Review of the first two days' hearing before the House Committee. This record brings into clear relief the constitutional and legal difficulties which are involved in any attempt by Congress to legislate upon the subject of interstate commerce. It shows that tho powers of Congress in the regulation of interstate commerce have not yet had in all respects clear and unmistakable definition by judicial authorities. It would appear that whatever power Congress may have over interstate commerce is in large measure counterbalanced by the fact that the agencies of such commerce are not created by Congress but by the several States. The power of the State over the agency which it creates cannot be questioned. But we have the anomalous situation that the acts of these agents, in so far as they affect interstate commerce, are withdrawn by the Consitution from the jurisdiction of the State. It is equally clear that the acts of these agents affecting interstate commerce are subject to the regulation of Congress. But the authority of Congress to regulate the agencies that do interstate commerce appears to be denied by the Courts.

Probably nowhere else, as in the record of these hearings, can be found in so compact and definite a form a statement of these difficulties. To those who have considered the matter only in an abstract sense, the question here raised as to the power of Congress to secure from corporations information in regard to capital stock and other matters must be highly illuminating. The complex character of our dual control of commerce appears in strong relief. It is evident that remedial measures adequate to relieve the present situation will be hard to find.

This, however, we believe to be merely the superficial view of the case. Constructive legislation is proverbially difficult. It must be borne in mind that the measure under consideration represents the first real effort of a constructive character which has been made, since the passage of the Sherman Anti-Trust law, to deal more wisely with the trust problem. It will not be forgotten that the law itself was the culmination of several years of effort to secure legislation. It should not, therefore, be discouraging if this first effort made by the Civic Federation to amend the law should not be successful. Whatever may be the ultimate fate of this measure, it will have served a highly useful purpose in bringing out this discussion and in placing clearly before the people of the United States the conditions with which legislative measures upon these important topics have to reckon. Time is necessary for the perfecting of such legislation; but we are not among those who believe that the Government of the United States is helpless in the premises, perplexing as the question certainly is. Where the need exists—and the universal testimony is that it does exist—a way will be found.

The Woman's Committee. By the organization of the Woman's Committee the National Civic Federation has taken an important step in rounding out its organization. It is the expressed object of the Federation to organize into effective working groups the varied interests which are concerned in social welfare. It has had from the start the co-operation of prominent men and women in all walks of life. It has lent its aid to various movements in which women have been prominently identified, but has not heretofore made any especial appeal to the women of the country by providing an organization through which they could work in harmony with the general ideals of the Federation.

The need and the opportunity were most happily expressed by Mrs. J. Borden Harriman, president of the Colony Club, at the meeting for the organization of the committee, when she said:

"A decent, wholesome environment for the worker has come, in this progressive age, to be a part of the social and civic obligation of the modern employer.

"The frank recognition of this obligation on the part of employers generally, whether manager, directors or stockholders, not only restores a large measure of the old personal contact which was the best feature of the earlier industrial systems—unfortunately lost sight of too often in the tremendous growth of commercial enterprises—but it also goes far to remove the estrangement and want of sympathy out of which so much social prejudice, distrust and class feeling have grown. There is, perhaps, no better antidote for radical attacks upon present institutions than intelligent, genuine and wisely directed welfare work.

"This proposed Woman's Committee, therefore, furnishes to the women whose co-operation is invited an inspiring opportunity for practical humanitarian effort and, at the same time, for patriotic public service along the lines most needed under present day industrial conditions.

"There is a word for every age, and certainly the word for to-day is Brotherhood; and how better can we live up to the obligation and what this word implies than by trying through this committee to ameliorate the lot of those less fortunate than ourselves?"

The present Woman's Committee has been formed in recognition of the powerful influence which women are in a position to exert. It is, perhaps, true that many of the undesirable conditions of employment which prevail in modern industry are due to the fact that in large measure we are too busy to take note of them. The personal relations which once existed between the employer and his men have largely disappeared in the modern organization of industry. The experience of the Civic Federation has shown, in many instances, that it was only necessary to make employers cognizant of undesirable conditions to interest them in removing them. It seems peculiarly fitting, therefore, that the women of means and position with their greater leisure should be the medium of spreading a knowledge of such conditions. They have given many evidences of administrative and business ability. They are not lacking in sympathy, and thus bring to the study of actual conditions a most helpful and practical equipment. Their aims are thoroughly practical. They are eager to do what can be done for the improvement of social conditions and are not led away by sentimentalism.

There can be little doubt that the organization of this committee will be immensely helpful in promoting that practical understanding of industrial conditions from which the National Civic Federation seeks to evolve the spirit of self-respecting mutual helpfulness.

Teachers' Visit to Europe. The National Civic Federation has undertaken a work of large significance for the cause of education in this country in its plan to send 500 teachers abroad next Winter to visit the schools of England and of the Continent. One of the best means of improving our own work is to observe whether our neighbors are doing theirs differently or more efficiently.

The admirable opportunities which will be offered to these teachers to inspect foreign schools, to observe foreign methods, to become familiar with their forms of school organization, should make an essential contribution to the study of home problems.

The organization of this visit is parallel to that adopted by Mr. Alfred Mosely when the English teachers visited the United States in 1905-6. The selection of the teachers who make this visit will be made by the boards of education and other school authorities. In large part the school authorities will provide that the teachers participating in the visit shall have leave of absence from their home duties without loss of salary. The plan has been received with enthusiasm in the school world. The Department of Superintendence of The National Education Association at its meeting in Washington in February passed resolutions congratulating The National Civic Federation upon the plans made and declared: "The Department believes the cause of education will be helped and advanced by the comparative study of the school systems of foreign countries by competent observers." Many of the larger cities have already provided for sending teachers on this visit, and applications are being received by scores from all parts of the country from teachers engaged in every branch of school work. A considerable proportion of the applications are from principals and others engaged in directive and supervisory work who will be able to put into active practice the suggestions which they may receive from their visit.

The very complete arrangements which have been made for the reception of the teachers in England by Mr. Mosely are set forth in this issue of the *Review*. His consummate skill in the work of organization is the best guarantee that could be made for the success of the enterprise. In addition to the 500 teachers who will go from the United States under the auspices of the Civic Federation, Mr. Mosely expects to have an equal number from the Dominion of Canada.

It is no slight matter to arrange for the selection and comfort of so large a group of individuals, and the educational press has fully recognized the magnitude of the work undertaken by The National Civic Federation and Mr. Mosely and is duly appreciative of the advantages which it offers to the teachers of the United States.

Probably no more opportune time could be chosen for such a visit. Not in years has there been so general an interest in the school world in fundamental problems of methods and organization.

The growing demand in the general public for new forms of education, particularly on industrial lines, has profoundly stirred the educational world. It has led both the advocates of change and the upholders of the old order to a study and restatement of some of the fundamental principles of school organization and school methods. There has been a persistent appeal for a modification of the standard courses of study in order to make room for some form of industrial training. It has been pointed out that our schools were not reaching all of the children for whom they are designed. The illuminating discussion of vocational training by the Commissioner of Education of New York State and by the Assistant Secretary of Agriculture, which is given in the pages of this *Review*, shows how the new educational program may profoundly modify existing schools.

To these demands of the innovator the conservative replies that our elementary schools can not be abbreviated or modified without impairing their efficiency. But the movement has become so strong that the conservative is being placed upon the defensive. He is obliged to demonstrate that the schools are, in fact, efficient and is required to show that the studies pursued in them are essential and that the time allotted to them is indispensable.

The radicals are, therefore, studying school methods with a view to changing them; conservatives with a view to maintaining them. There is abroad, therefore, among the teaching profession a profound interest in methods of study and in methods of school organization. It is universally recognized that in such study comparative methods have the highest value. We may reasonably hope that the experience gained in visiting the schools of sister nations will prove of the utmost value in stimulating in this country educational discussion and school progress.

Justice to Union Labor. A man who feels keenly, thinks deeply and expresses himself vigorously awakens enthusiasm and arouses opposition. Such a man is Samuel Gompers. As representative of the forces of organized labor in this country his voice is heard in no uncertain tones. Beloved by his followers, to whom his sturdy advocacy of their cause endears him, he counts his adversaries by the scores and thousands. Because he feels keenly and is vigorous in expression he is always a radical to many; becaue he thinks deeply he does not satisfy the extreme or socialist element among the workers. He is either radical or conservative, according to the viewpoint of his critics, and his conservatism has been as roundly berated as his radicalism has been abused.

It is strange indeed that there is so little appreciation of the peculiar position of trades unionism in this country. Strange that, in face of the growth of socialistic opinions which are daily forcing themselves upon the public notice, trades unions should still stand in the public eye as the embodiment of radicalism. Strange that every utterance of its leaders should be given at once the most unfavorable construction.

If in seeking their own welfare trades unions appear to be selfish that should not be a reproach. It is not so long ago that an enlightened self-interest was held up as the cardinal motive of all economic activity, and if in these later days we have avoided seemingly harsh terms we surely have not changed the nature of the forces at work around us. The motive power of our industrial organization has not changed. It is behind all the forces that go to make up our complex society. We do not make it a reproach that banks and corporations and trusts and railways seek to influence legislation, to mould public opinion or to favor one political party or the other in the pursuit of their own ends. We expect it and accept it as a fact.

There is, however, a difference, not to be disregarded, between the selfishness of a corporation and that of a trade union, between the selfishness of capital and that of labor. As Mr. Gompers himself says: "We speak of the working man or the working woman not in those terms, but as labor. You cannot differentiate the labor of the man or the woman from their breathing, respiring body and heart and brain. It is an abuse of the very essence of essential principles to place in the same category capital and labor."

Capital is an abstraction, labor a living fact. The welfare of the great masses of humanity lies behind the latter term. And we cannot help but feel that such selfishness as may be exhibited in the effort to ameliorate the lot of the average man should not be judged by the same standard as that which impels the action of the employer.

It cannot, therefore, commend itself to our sense of justice that the daily press should pass over without comment or with sympathetic encouragement the protests of capital against existing conditions and should have nothing but sneers for the voice of labor when it is uplifted in its own behalf.

The attitude of the Federation of Labor toward the courts of the country has been roundly condemned; and yet their attitude is not different from that of any other litigant. The man who goes to law and loses his case abides by the decision of the court, but is not satisfied with it. If the lower court decides against him he is not expected to change his attitude or to abandon his contention until the matter reaches final adjudication. If the court of final resort decides against him he does not cease to be a good citizen if he indulges the hope that at some future time the court may change its decision, or if he seeks to obtain such a change in statute law as will favor his original contention.

When the American Federation of Labor protested against the injunction granted by the courts of the District of Columbia forbidding the further prosecution of the so-called boycott against the Buck's Stove and Range Company they were declared to be in mutiny against the established order of government. This in spite of the fact that the decision was by no means a final one.

The attitude of the press in the recent conflicts between the State and Federal courts over railway rate regulation has been in striking contrast. When the Federal Circuit Court of Minnesota enjoined the Attorney-General of the State and all county attorneys from any attempt to enforce the commodity rates established by Minnesota law pending the decision as to the validity of that law the Attorney-General boldly defied the injunction. He went before a State court and obtained a contrary order. He was haled before the United States Court, judged in contempt, and this action was finally upheld by the Supreme Court of the United States. Yet throughout this contest the Attorney-General was not accused of lawlessness, but his course was in the main commended as an effort to uphold what he believed to be the rights and prerogatives of the State. Can it be that the political rights and privileges which he was seeking to maintain were more sacred than the personal rights and liberties which labor believes to be involved in the boycott case?

Organized labor has been hard pressed by recent decisions of the Supreme Court of the United States. It is fearful lest the inhibitions placed upon its activities be still further extended. Under such circumstances resentment is not unnatural and criticism is human. The protest which has arisen because the American Federation of Labor quite naturally disagrees with the judgment of the court reads as if criticism of our supreme judicial body had never been heard before and as if the protest of labor had been couched in most unbecoming terms.

Before the Judiciary Committee of the House of Representatives Mr. Gompers said:

"I am not endeavoring, nor is it my purpose, to indulge in such criticism of the Supreme Court or its decisions that would directly or indirectly cast any reflection upon either the justices of the court individually or collectively." He stated further that his criticism was directed solely "to existing law as interpreted by the court."

Under these circumstances the American Federation of Labor is directing all its energies to securing such legislation as will relieve the labor unions from the restrictions placed upon them by existing law. In so doing it is following a course of conduct open to every American citizen. Other organized bodies follow a like practice without drawing upon themselves the condemnation of the press.

The newspaper publishers of the country are at the present time engaged in a contest with the paper manufacturers and are seeking a revision of the tariff which they believe will relieve them from the exactions of the Paper Trust. The bankers of the country have been loud in their protest against the currency bills before Congress. The president of the American Bankers' Association stated that the whole force of that organization would be arrayed against the Aldrich financial bill and would use its efforts to punish politically the party which should enact such legislation. Why is it that the efforts of such organizations cause no wave of excitement in the newspaper press? But when Mr. Gompers declares that if the measures urged by labor do not become laws at this session those responsible will have to answer in the Fall election these declarations are designated as threats and menaces. Are not the labor interests of the country equally entitled with other interests to take advantage of public discussion of legislative action and of political contention to obtain their ends?

Another illustration of misrepresentation which is characteristic is to be found in the oft-repeated declarations that Mr. Gompers in the hearing at Washington had threatened that if the demands of labor were not met he would organize a secret organization. Such a statement is cruelly unjust. What he said, as shown by the record, was:

"Supposing you take our funds away by damage suits; supposing you do send us to prison because we believe that we have a right to protect that which we own—namely, our power to labor; supposing you do these things—what then? You may drive us into secret organizations, perhaps not us, but those who will follow. You may drive the men and women of labor into organizations both bound and secret."

Even the casual reader of these lines will observe that it is a very different thing to say that an undesirable organization may arise than to threaten to form one.

Whatever be our personal inclinations in these matters, let us have a fair field and no favor. The struggle between the economic forces, always present, may shift its scene to the courts and to the halls of legislatures, but it is always carried on before the forum of public opinion. In that forum forms and proceedings may lack the ceremonial and dignity of the courts of law, but let us seek to infuse into that discussion as much as we can of the spirit of impartiality which should preside over judicial procedure.

WOMAN'S COMMITTEE OF THE NATIONAL CIVIC FEDERATION

ORGANIZATION OF AN IMPORTANT ADJUNCT—COMMITTEES APPOINTED —THE WORK IN PROGRESS.

The initial step toward enlisting the co-operation of women in the work of the Federation was taken when the following resolution was adopted at a meeting in New York at the residence of Miss Morgan, Friday, March 6, 1908, at 12 o'clock.

Resolved, That the Executive Council of the National Civil Federation be asked to appoint a committee to organize a Woman's Committee of the National Civic Federation.

Mrs. J. Borden Harriman, of New York, presided, and Mrs. Eva McDonald Valesh, of the American Federation of Labor, with headquarters at Washington, D. C., acted as secretary.

There were present:
Mrs. Samuel Mather, Cleveland, O.
Mrs. Joseph Medill McCormick, Chicago, Ill.
Mrs. Cornelius Stevenson, Philadelphia, Pa.
Mrs. Talcott Williams, Philadelphia, Pa.
Mrs. William H. Crocker, San Francisco, Cal.
Mrs. C. P. Orr, Birmingham, Ala.
Mrs. Thomas Sherwin, Boston, Mass.
Mrs. Eva McDonald Valesh, of the American Federation of Labor, Washington, D. C.
Mrs. Archibald Alexander, Hoboken, N. J.
Mrs. Julia K. West, New York.
Mrs. J. Borden Harriman, New York.
Miss Anne Morgan, New York.
Miss Gertrude Beeks, Secretary Welfare Department, and
Mr. Ralph M. Easley, Chairman Executive Council, the National Civic Federation.

Telegrams and letters expressing interest in the movement and willingness to become affiliated with it were received from:
Mrs. Cyrus H. McCormick, Chicago, Ill.
Mrs. J. K. Ottley, Atlanta, Ga.
Mrs. Sarah S. Platt Decker, Denver, Col.
Mrs. Charles Denison, Denver, Col.
Mrs. G. E. Emmons, Schenectady, N. Y.
Mrs. Frederick R. Hazard, Syracuse, N. Y.
Mrs. S. Thruston Ballard, Louisville, Ky.
Mrs. George C. Avery, Louisville, Ky.
Mrs. Marcus A. Hanna, Cleveland, O.
Mrs. A. F. McKissick, Greenwood, S. C.
Mrs. B. Frank Mebane, Spray, N. C.
Mrs. W. T. Harris, Danville, Va.
Miss Ellen D. Smith, St. Louis, Mo.
Miss Eunice Smith, St. Louis, Mo.
Mrs. Richard Wainwright, Washington, D. C.
Mrs. William Corcoran Eustis, Washington, D. C.
Miss Caro T. Field, Boston.
Miss Anna D. Slocum, Boston.

It was particularly gratifying to have for this movement the cordial support of Mrs. Marcus A. Hanna and her daughter, Mrs. Ruth Hanna McCormick, since it will be remembered that the first President of the National Civic Federation was the late Senator Hanna. In promising the heartiest co-operation Mrs. Hanna said she felt a very deep interest in every phase of the work of the Federation because of her husband's devotion to the cause. She stated: "When, in the last general conversation which the Senator had with our son in my presence, the desire of his friends to have him nominated for the Presidency of the United States was discussed, he made the following statement:

"'I would not accept the Presidency if it were offered to me on a silver plate. If I can only be permitted to have ten years more to live, I shall devote that time entirely to carrying out my plans for the National Civic Federation.'" Mrs. Hanna continued: "Its work was the nearest thing to his heart."

Mrs. McCormick said:

"To be able to do anything for my father's work is to me supreme. I call the National Civic Federation his work simply because he meant to give up the remainder of his life to it.

"I am grateful for this chance of fulfilling my highest ideals."

NEW YORK BRANCH FORMED.

On the same day, at 3 o'clock, the New York Woman's Committee was organized at the Colony Club. Mrs. J. Borden Harriman opened the meeting with the following address:

"We are here to-day to organize a Woman's Committee to co-operate with the Welfare Department of the National Civic Federation, because we feel that this organization comes nearer to our ideal than any other operating along these lines. The National Civic Federation, as you know, is an organization composed of prominent employers, labor leaders and representatives of agricultural, financial, economic, bankers', legal and farmers' organizations. The activities of the Federation are exercised through the Conciliation, Immigration, Political Reform, Economic and Welfare Departments.

All of us have an influence and some of us are the wives or sisters of employers of large numbers of factory operatives, or perhaps ourselves are owners and stockholders in companies. Should not the woman who spends the money which the employes help to provide take a special interest in their welfare, especially in that of the women wage earners?

Should we not frankly recognize our own ignorance of the conditions under which they live and work, and seek from those whose knowledge can be relied upon to guide us intelligently to a better understanding of the existing conditions and difficulties?

Neither emotional philanthropy nor ignorant indifference must influence us.

This we can do by taking the trouble to acquaint ourselves with things as they really are, by coming into contact with those whose weakness is a call upon our strength. We will learn to know from actual practical experience what should be done for the betterment of conditions among wage earners, and then we will not use coercive methods undertaking to secure improvements, but will try to find opportunities to offer friendly suggestions to those in power.

Of course, we can only do this by going slowly and after educating ourselves, and one way of doing the latter is to hear from leaders in their specific trades. Some of them will speak to us to-day, and I understand will be willing to tell us of the surroundings and conditions of the workers whom they represent.

This welfare work is not in fact simply a matter of charity. A decent, wholesome environment for the worker has come, in this progressive age, to be a part of the social and civic obligation of the modern employer.

The frank recognition of this obligation on the part of employers generally, whether manager, directors or stockholders, not only restores a large measure of the old personal contact which was the best feature of the earlier industrial systems—unfortunately lost sight of too often in the tremendous growth of commercial enterprises—but it also goes far to remove the estrangement and want of sympathy out of which so much social prejudice, distrust and class feeling have grown. There is perhaps no better antidote for radical attacks upon present institutions than intelligent, genuine and wisely directed welfare work.

This proposed Woman's Committee, therefore, furnishes to the women whose co-operation is invited an inspiring opportunity for practical humanitarian effort and, at the same time, for patriotic public service along the lines most needed under present day industrial conditions.

There is a word for every age, and certainly the word for to-day is Brotherhood; and how better can we live up to the obligation and what this word implies than by trying through this committee to ameliorate the lot of those less fortunate than ourselves?"

Mrs. Harriman presented by-laws for the action of the meeting. It was decided that:

"The object of this committee shall be to use its influence in securing needed improvements in the working and living conditions of women and men wage earners in the various industries and governmental institutions, and to co-operate, when practicable, in the general work of the Federation."

The following officers and chairmen of committees were elected:

Chairman, Mrs. Archibald Alexander.*
Vice-Chairman, Miss Anne Morgan.
Secretary, Miss C. V. R. Delafield.
Treasurer, Mrs. V. Everit Macy.
Chairman of the Committee on the Needs of Workers in Specific Industries, Mrs. J. Borden Harriman.
Chairman of Committee on Welfare Work for Government Employes, Mrs. Julia K. West.
Chairman of Membership Committee, Mrs. F. H. Cabot.
Chairman Press and Literature Committee, Miss Elisabeth Marbury.

On taking the chair Mrs. Alexander introduced as the first speaker of the afternoon Mrs. Eva McDonald Valesh, associate editor of "The Federationist," the official organ of the American Federation of Labor, whose address follows:

MRS. VALESH: Ladies and gentlemen: It gives me a great deal of pleasure to be present at a meeting which promises so much in the way of practical good as this movement that you have inaugurated to-day. I feel perhaps a little embarrassed, having to break the ice on the part of the wage workers, but I have for many years been studying, with somewhat selfish attention, perhaps, the various movements on the part of men and women more fortnnately situated than the wage workers.

I know that the wealthy women of this country have generous and kindly hearts and brilliant intellects, and I know that for years they have wanted to do something for those who were less fortunate. But it required sometimes an experiment to find out what was the practical method of getting at it. It seems to me that in this movement you have inaugurated to-day you have got down to a practical method. If the wife of an employer or a woman who owns stock in factories takes interest enough to find out what are the conditions under which the men and women in that employment work, it then becomes a matter of almost personal pride with her, that if the conditions are not what they should be they shall be improved. And in many cases they are not what they should be—not altogether because the employers are too selfish or too mercenary to do what is right. We have to remember that there has been such a remarkable revolution in industry in the last half century that it is very difficult to keep up with all its effects, and balance it on all hands.

We have advanced from the handworking shop and handworker to the immense factories and establishments, where the worker is not long in personal touch with his employer. The employer, unless he is very much impressed with his responsibility, is apt to hold only an impersonal interest towards his employe. Then, in the new system of industry which has come up, in the rush of accumulating vast fortunes and vast profits, it was very easy to overlook the wage worker, and to forget that he who was contributing so much perhaps was not getting the share that he should. Now the wage workers have done what they can. In fact, it has been incumbent upon them to get what improvements they could by organization; by protests of various sorts. But as a wage worker, I can tell you that one of the most discouraging things about that sort of thing is, that neither the employers nor general public are willing to believe that what we say is true about the conditions of employment. They think we exaggerate it, because we feel ourselves to be a somewhat injured party.

Now that won't be true if the women whose husbands and fathers are interested in business come into this work. The women will go and see for them-

---

*That a wise choice was made in selecting Mrs. Archibald Alexander as chairman of the New York Woman's Committee of the National Civic Federation is demonstrated by the following:

Her father's family was among the first in this country to become identified with the industrial problems, as they then existed. Her grandfather, John Stevens, was the inventor of the first propeller steamboat and designed the first steamboat to go to sea, the voyage being from Hoboken and Philadelphia.

The ferry between Hoboken and New York belonged to the Stevens family for nearly one hundred years, and during that time there never was even a suspicion of a strike.

About 1850 Mrs. Alexander's father built houses for the men in his employ which were far ahead of the times, and her mother built, over twenty-five years ago, one of the first model tenement houses in this country.

At the time Mrs. Alexander and her brother sold the Hoboken Ferry a pension fund for the old employes was the first use made of the proceeds, many of them having worked for their family from thirty to sixty years. They have had for some time in their offices a complete system of profit sharing.

The Stevens family has given to Hoboken three parks, Stevens Institute of Technology, with its endowment; the recreation pier and the land on which now stands the Free Public Library and Manual Training School.

Mrs. Alexander has been for twenty-five years president of a working girls' club, and for many years appointed by the successive Governors of New Jersey as Trustee for Manual Education in Hoboken public schools. For four years she has been appointed by the County Judge Assistant Probation Officer, under her brother, Mr. Richard Stevens, and also is a member of the Executive Committee of the League for Women Workers. Mrs. Alexander has been appointed by several Governors of New Jersey manager of State Institutions. She was recently a representative of the Governor of New Jersey at the International Congress of Mothers held at Washington.

selves exactly what conditions are, and if they make up their minds that there needs to be some improvement, I think that the American women will have their usual success in persuading the American men to do what they want.

Now, I want to call your attention to the fact that welfare work is a good business proposition. Every worker is entitled to perform his or her work in a properly constructed, well ventilated and hygienic factory. The speed of production is such now that an average of eight hours is enough to ask people to work. Those hours are reasonable. Any employer who fails to house his employes properly, who rushes them too greatly, who is not careful, not conscientions about the conditions which surround them, is not getting the work from those people which he should. He is not getting the results. There was at one time somewhat of a feeling in this country that while we had so many wageworkers it didn't matter very much if you did work them out and throw them aside. I don't think that feeling obtains so generally now. I think that there is a very strong public opinion in favor of the more humane and kindly side of things, and in this movement started to-day, I see the strongest illustration of that feeling.

I know from some of the things that I have heard your members say that they propose to study actual economic conditions. Of course, it would not be of much use for you to go around and visit the various industries if you had not some means of finding out whether the conditions you saw were good or not. I believe that economics is a study which will appeal to you, and I think you will find it most interesting and fascinating.

I want to speak a word for the women workers, particularly. I am a bit of a conservative myself. I have been a wage worker from an early age, and at one time was very strongly in favor of many more radical movements among women, but I swung back to the conservative side of things. I think that a woman's place is in the home. A woman ought not to want any better place than that. This sending of girls and women into factories is really rather an abnormal phase of our civilization. But even though that is true, it is a phase that is here to stay for a long time. There is not any doubt that three-fourths of the girls in ordinary poor families—we will say mechanic's families and laborers' families, find it necessary to go out and work in order to earn their own clothing, and to help to support their families. I think that these girls would be appreciative of a kindly interest from those who are more fortunately situated.

Some have said to me that they thought perhaps the working girls would not be appreciative of what is known as welfare work. Personally, I am in favor of accepting the best conditions of work that an employer is willing to offer me. He cannot make my wages too high or surroundings too pleasant to suit me. The better he makes them, the better work I will do for him. I think that is the position of those who look at welfare work reasonably. But I do admit this, there are a great many wage workers who feel, perhaps, a certain sense of pride and independence; they don't wish to be patronized. Welfare work should not be patronage. As I said, it is a good business proposition for the employer. If a man gives employes a well-lighted, clean factory, serves a hot lunch at a reasonable price, and pays good wages, I think that is good for them and will bring him good returns.

If the wives, the daughters, the sisters of large employers would exercise the same tact and courtesy toward the wage workers that they do among ordinary social acquaintances, I think they will find a very kindly and appreciative response. I know that some of you are new in this work, but are very earnest and enthusiastic, and I ask you to keep your eyes open for the occasional talented girl among the workers. There is the occasional girl who has talent, perhaps genius, who has a really artistic soul. You know it is likely to be crushed out of her in the factory or shop. You can do much for the one who is worthy of something far better than a factory or shop. To put even one soul on the road of finding what life really should mean. What greater good could you do? Then, too, there are so many average bright girls, who, if treated in a friendly and frank sort of way, will respond, and go about among their fellow workers and help you to institute welfare work in the way in which it will be most effective.

To have the wife of an employer—I put it in that way as typical of your movement—the wife, sister or daughter of the employer going into her relative's factory or shop and seeing for herself what the conditions are, and if they are not just what they should be, persuading the head of the firm to see that proper reforms are instituted, and taking a really kindly family interest in the workers, is one of the dreams I long have cherished. I hope now to see it fulfilled.

We are a little too hard and commercial in all our manifestations of modern industry. Surely it is about time that the softer and more humane side of life should be touched upon. Then, too, there is this phase of it, the working girls of to-day will be the mothers of the coming generations. We are looking to their children to uphold our institutions in the spirit in which they were founded, and in the spirit in which we hope to see them carried on. If there is some criticism to-day that the tendency is in the wrong direction, the responsibility really rests with those who have the leisure, the intelligence and the ability to set things right. Of course, your welfare work is not identical with my own work as a trade unionist, but to me it seems that there could be nothing finer for the woman who has the leisure, the means and the opportunity, than to get outside of herself; to interest herself in other women less fortunately situated than herself.

I don't know that I could, and, indeed, I have not the time to indicate to you all the various phases which your welfare work may take on. I am sure that you will find out those for yourselves. You will find in this work more and more attractive features than you had ever expected. I don't know that I need to caution you on this point, because I think women sensible enough to take up this line of work are not given to too much emotionalism. But I have sometimes felt in reference to various reform movements, so-called, that I really would like to caution some of the women concerned against that emotionalism which degenerates into a fad or mere sentimentalism. But I don't think that caution is necessary to women who are level-headed enough to see that the work of self-help begins right at home, right at your own door-step, in the factory or the business in which you or your men folks are interested.

I don't think welfare work can go too far. I don't think it can do too much good or is likely to do too much. I will say this one thing on the part of the workers, that welfare work, no matter how generous and kindly in intention, should never deprive the workers of a certain independence which belongs to them. A clean, beautiful, well ventilated factory, with modern improvements, should not be made to take the place of good wages and reasonable hours. Wages should not be charged to the welfare account, so to speak. That has been done occasionally by those who were not wise in their method of going about it. In your study of economics, which I am certain you will soon undertake if you have not already done so, you will find yourselves agreeing with me, that the "prevailing rate" of wages is none too great for any worker, whatever his skill or trade, because the workers are entitled to have sufficient earnings to expend in a fair way of living—they wish to build themselves comfortable homes. They wish to educate their children. Finally, I should say, that welfare work should not be a bar to the trade organization of the workers. It should encourage and supplement the work of organization.

You will find when you come to investigate that there is not as much organization among working women as there should be. One reason for that is that girls who work do not expect to stay long in factory or shop. They expect to be married soon, and have homes of their own. They don't take the interest in organization that men do, who expect to stay in an industry during their whole life. I am sure, as your work progresses you will find the unions among the workers one of the most helpful elements. You will find organized workers the most appreciative, and the most ready to help in carrying out your good work.

I wish to personally assure you of my interest in the work you are so earnestly undertaking and I hope it will be quite as successful as you expect and that its influence for good will be felt in every industry in the country.

The next speaker introduced was Mr. Edward Gould, President of the Teamster's Union.

MR. GOULD: Madam Chairman and Ladies. I appreciate the liberty of coming and bringing to your attention the needs of the many teamsters that are so unfortunate as to follow that occupation in the city of Greater New York.

I believe with the previous speaker that the majority of rich ladies are kind-hearted. I want to say that I have no dislike to wealthy people—absolutely none. I am not an anarchist. I don't know whether I am even a socialist. I believe possibly I might be a Democrat, in the same sense in which George Washington meant it.

I have found in going through the city from time to time, in overhearing conversations, that rich people are possibly a little too prone to unjustly criticize the actions of some of our workmen. I believe that our one great need is consideration. If they would only stop to think and make an investigation as to whether there was not something that caused something that took place! I believe, before we should denounce the actions of any person or any body of people that we should find out whether there was oppression which would warrant rebellion. We have in the Greater New York something like 75,000 teamsters. We have over 30,000 organized. I don't have to come and tell you ladies when you can see the cab driver, but I don't know when you won't see him. You will see him all the time, no matter when you are out. You will meet the baker at 2 o'clock in the morning. I just saw one of their wagons on Fourth avenue. I don't know when they do sleep. But if you were around the extreme East or West Side where those stables are kept, you would find the men are obliged to report as early as five o'clock. I don't know that there are many stables that they don't have to report at before 6 in the morning, and they seldom ever get away before 7 or 8 o'clock at night.

Now, we have library buildings, and we all appreciate them. Let us work to the end that the poor man, who is not able to have the books in his home, will have sufficient time to make a call at the library and get a book, and to take advantage of those great institutions that are built up for our people.

I don't know, if we stop to think, how much we are dependent upon the teamsters. You notice them drawing the earth out of the cellars where our homes are built. They draw the brick and the stone to build those homes. They bring us our meat. They carry our clothes in large boxes down through the city along West street. You ladies who are accustomed to foreign travel have noticed on top of wagons those large boxes going along West street. They administer to your comfort. Think of the poor mail wagon driver who carries the pleasant letters—love letters and sometimes sad news—we had a strike of those poor fellows a few days ago. Well, I believe it was a couple of years ago. It seems such a short time when we look back. There was quite a howl because people were so inconvenienced in not getting their mail at the proper time. When I tell you that those men worked as long as fifteen or sixteen hours every day, including Sunday, I hope that that is a sufficient apology for the little inconvenience that you suffered during that time. The agreement that we reached with the employers at that time was to pay $2.25 for twelve hours' work with a two-horse team, and $1.65—the munificent sum of $1.65—for the privilege of working twelve hours a day for seven days with a one-horse team. Now, what kind of a home can a poor little family have where the income is only $1.65 a day for twelve hours' work? I don't believe that there is a lady sitting in this audience at the present time who would want a man to limit his home to eight or nine dollars a week and bring up two or three little children. For, how much can we expect of them? And the country is dependent upon the poor man's child as well as it is upon the rich.

We have formed the cab drivers' union, which affects the rich—I believe it is a luxury. It is one of the first things, one of the first crafts to suffer in bad times. I am sorry to say that we have four hundred or five hundred men idle at this time owing to the depression in trade. I heard a great many hard things said because those men had to strike five years ago. When we had our first strike, all we looked for was nine hours off—nine hours from the time we left the stable until we would report back again, making it absolutely fifteen hours' work a day. And all we looked for in compensation was $2 per day. We do appreciate the generosity of our patrons in that particular craft, but if it were not for their generosity I believe we would be working shorter hours and possibly getting a greater compensation. But I merely brought that to the attention of you ladies, that particular portion of our teamsters' craft, because that matter is now under arbitration (the final settlement of the recent strike having been referred to an arbitration committee, and that committee has not made its award yet), and all we looked for was twelve hours off and $2.50 per day. I believe there could have been a compromise on the wages, provided that we got the hours.

Now, when New York City has become so very crowded, we are forced to the suburbs. I believe that it is a good thing—that our wives and children ought to have been forced to the suburbs, but it takes an hour to get to our homes. A large percentage of our people work until after 12 or 1 o'clock at night, after the theatre and opera are out, to take the people home comfortably. The transportation is not as regular then as it is in the early hours of the evening, and it takes them generally an hour to get home at night, and an hour to get to work in the morning. With many I don't know how the children know their fathers at all. They are in bed when they leave the house in the morning, and they are in bed when they go home at night. How do they recognize their fathers?

Now, none of you ladies wants that condition to prevail. I believe the object is to try to improve it, and you can do a great deal in that respect. It's all right for a sympathetic lady to find fault with the poor driver trying to hurry his horses along the street, providing she is not waiting for meat for the dinner. That makes all the difference in the world. We find a heavily laden truck this kind of weather, for instance, drawing, possibly, coal, and the team of horses struggling to get along, and the poor driver struggling, and sometimes he uses the whip more frequently than he should. That is because he doesn't know any better. I want to say that the majority of our people are fond of horses. They follow horses because they are fond of horses; it is not because they cannot lay brick or hew stone as well as a mechanic could—it is because they like horses. You can, from your own observation, see that the horse is insufficiently shod. That is not the fault of the driver. If you ask your employer to shoe his horses better, why, he would say, I would do nothing else than pay out my income for shoeing horses. Absolutely none of us wants to see a team of horses struggling with a heavy load.

Some of the officials connected with the New York Humane Society wrote me a communication saying they wanted to have a talk with me on a bill they had pending before the Legislature, and I met some of them and we had quite a talk. They said there was a bill pending before the Legislature at Albany seeking to make the employer responsible when horses are sent out in an unfit condition to work. I don't know how many of you ladies are subscribers to the American Society for the Prevention of Cruelty to Animals, or the New York Humane Society, but it seems pretty hard that we should have to seek redress through legislative measures to place the responsibility where it belongs. A driver is sent out with a horse having a sore back or a sore foot or a sore leg, and the driver is arrested and the driver is punished. It is only two weeks ago that a representative of our mail wagon drivers came to my home around 9 o'clock at night and told me that a man was arrested because the horse was working with a sore back. And I said, "Doesn't the employer take care of them?" And he said, "No." I went to the police station and bailed the man out. He had a wife and four children living out on Long Island, and you can imagine the wife's feelings, and the poor little children's feelings, with their father not coming home at night. They had been accustomed to see him come home every night, because, even though the home may be humble, no matter how humble it may be, there is love in the poorest of our homes equally as well as there is in the wealthiest ones. The following morning I went up to the court, and even then the poor driver did not have the sympathy of his employer. It became necessary to renew his bond to appear in Special Sessions. Now, I claim that the employer is the man who should be punished—not allowed to ask a driver to use a horse in an unfit condition. And I said so to those ladies when I was speaking to them. I said there is a limit of endurance to everybody's patience, and that possibly one day the limit would be reached that way.

Last Summer one of our men had to serve thirty days on the Island, because he was found driving a horse in an unfit condition. I took particular pains myself to make a personal investigation of the matter. I found that the horse had suffered from sores for some time; that it had been drawn to the attention of the employer, and that the driver was told that if he did not want to drive, some other person would. The Society for the Prevention of Cruelty to Animals carries on the prosecution of such cases, placing a penalty upon the poor, unfortunate driver. The result was that we went down to our organization and called a special meeting, and we had a resolution drafted that where a driver is arrested for other than cruel treatment, in the shape of flogging or abusing horses, the employer would be responsible, and that no member of our organization would work for him if he asked any driver to work a horse that was in an unfit condition.

We accomplished more with that particular employer than the Society for the Prevention of Cruelty to Animals had accomplished for the last fifteen or twenty years. That may be saying a good deal, ladies. I said to those people that perhaps some day we would call a mass meeting, or appoint a large committee and wait upon the Mayor, and object to being penalized where we were not responsible. I said, if the teamsters were to cease working as a body in the City of New York, under such circumstances, for forty-eight hours, it would awaken the public to a realization of the wrongs that were heaped upon them. And they said, "Mr. Gould, you would not do anything like that?" Well, now, if I should get three months on the Island for something that my employer is responsible for I don't know what I might do. I don't want to injure an employer, but it is necessary to bring our wrongs to the notice of the public, because that is the bad feature of the American people, they are disinterested until the matter touches themselves—sometimes until the shoe starts to pinch the other foot.

Now, you ladies can do a great deal. All we ask of you is not to censure us until you are thoroughly conversant with the conditions which bring about a state of affairs, whatever it may be. I don't favor strikes myself. I like to avoid strikes as much as we can. But if necessary to protect our own people, even if they are poor, I favor a strike.

Our organization came into existence some four or five years ago. We have benevolent features. Recently I went over our books for the last four years, since the twelfth of July, 1903, and I find that we have paid out in sickness and in death benefits alone over $38,000. Even though the amounts were small, they assisted our families to a great extent.

It was only a few days ago that the papers told of a coal teamster with a heavy laden truck with three horses—presumably about ten tons of coal on the wagon—who was arrested on Fifth avenue and Thirty-fourth street or Thirty-third street, because he could not stop the team the minute the officer put out a finger. I want to say that I am law abiding. Most of our men are. We take pride in it. Some disinterested citizens who were in carriages on Fifth avenue—I presume they must have been responsible—rebelled against the treatment that was accorded that driver, and, notwithstanding their sympathy toward the driver, some of our higher police officials thought they were justified in approving the acts of the officer who arrested him and hurt him. He was hurt. He lay in bed two or three weeks after as the result of the treatment. I merely say that it is utterly impossible for a coal teamster to stop the horses with ten tons of coal suddenly. For one of your private coachmen to stop a spanking team, it only takes a second. That is what we want—consideration. I believe that the traffic rules have done a great deal for our teamsters, and I take pride in saying that organization among our men has accomplished quite a good deal also.

I hope to be accorded the privilege at some future time, after you have continued your work and have become interested in it, to be able to tell you a little more about some of our other teamsters.

When I was a good deal younger I used to go to Sunday School and I read quite some of that big book. It softens my labor quite a good deal when I think of it—that our Saviour was a carpenter, David was a shepherd. I could enumerate quite a number of famous people who were not rich in material goods. See how they are written up. See how they are read by everybody. So I am not dissatisfied that I am poor. I am not ashamed of the fact that I am a poor man, because I can refer to so many poor people who did such great things.

In this work, I want to call your attention to the command that our Saviour gave his Apostles when he told them to go into the byway, to go into the highway and preach the word of God. To help the poor people, and I claim that every man or woman, no matter how wealthy he may be, should feel a pride in doing something for the unfortunate, because we can read "Inasmuch as ye did it unto the least of these, ye did it unto me."

I thank you for your kind attention.

THE CHAIRMAN stated: We do not want to let Mr. Gould leave this platform until those present have had the opportunity to ask questions which may be suggested by what he said:

A MEMBER said: I would like to ask a question. What influence do you exert as an organization to prevent some of your members, chiefly cab drivers, from overcharging by taking advantage, perhaps, of the ignorance of what the municipal tariff is, and endeavoring to get an extra fare, I mean above the legitimate fare? What is the attitude of the organization toward curbing that tendency on the part of some of your cab drivers?

MR. GOULD replied: Madam Chairman, I would state that we don't encourage it by any means, and quite a number of the riding public don't understand it. You can take a cab at the Pennsylvania Railroad from the Pennsylvania Railroad Cab Company and ride to the Waldorf-Astoria for fifty cents. If you get into a Waldorf-Astoria cab the driver is obliged to turn in one dollar, whether you give it to him or not at the Twenty-third street ferry. Now, there is double the charge. The courts have decided thus far—and I don't know to what higher court it has gone—that the livery stables can charge what they like; that it is only the man on the street who is subject to the city rates, and that easily could be remedied if the riding public would acquaint themselves with the city rates, which always are and must be displayed inside of the cab.

We have various charges from various clubs. We find members of the Union Club or members of the Union League Club or members of the University Club can do their riding for fifty cents on the dollar. If I want to get a cab from the same stable, I am charged a good deal more. Yet the organization of cab drivers has absolutely no control over the matter. We have to bring back the price demanded by the employers, and every driver should either exhibit the rate card on being asked, or the riding public should telephone to the stable and get the rates for themselves. We are always willing to give the rates. The unfortunate condition is that disease of getting rich quick, from which none of us is immune. We don't encourage it, I assure you.

The closing address was made by Mr. Timothy Healy, President of the International Stationary Firemens' Union.

MR. HEALY: Lady Chairman and Ladies: It is indeed a pleasure to me to have the opportunity of appearing before you this afternoon and saying a few words relating to my trade, and to working men in general.

I want to say that it is a cause of gratification to me that you ladies are taking an interest in the work of the National Civic Federation. The working men and working women of the City of New York need the assistance of such people as yourselves. It is in your power to do a great deal of good. The National Civic Federation is doing great good all the time, and the working men of this country are beginning to appreciate its good work. I am glad that you are about to be a part and parcel of that great organization.

It takes time to bring working men to realize that an organization such as the National Civic Federation is for their good. When large employers and men in the different walks of life, especially in the upper walks of life, take hold of an institution like that, the working men are naturally suspicious, and they wonder why they are doing it. Is it a pull to control the working men for their own interests? That is what labor men thought at first, when the National Civic Federation was organized, and I might say that I felt a good deal that way myself until I got to know some of the men who were active in it. When I became acquainted with Mr. Easley and others and learned what they were doing to prevent labor disputes, I began to realize that there was something to it, and the more I got in touch with them the more I learned of the benefits resulting from the Federation's work.

It has been said, and truly that the unwritten history of the National Civic Federation is the most important. Now, I intend to lay before you a few things that need the attention of the employers and of the wealthy people of this city, if they intend to do anything in the interest of the working class. There is a great deal to be done, and it is a noble work that you are embarked in, and I hope you will be successful.

The stationary firemen, which craft I represent, are among the hardest working men there are in the City of New York, and in fact the condition is practically the same throughout the country. They are a class of men that we cannot get along without very well, though generally people hear very little of them.

The stationary firemen are employed down in the cellars and sub-cellars all over the City of New York, in apartment houses and great hotels, in office buildings, in factories and power plants and buildings of all kinds. These men have to work for 365 days in the year, never getting a day to themselves, and until quite recently all had to work twelve hours a day and twelve hours a night, week about. Many are still doing so, although the union has secured three eight-hour shifts in the majority of the plants. Now when a man has to work twelve hours a day, or twelve hours a night, whichever it may be, every day in the year and never knows what a Sunday or a holiday is, it is pretty hard. It takes a man nearly an hour to get to his place of business and get ready for his work, as he has to make a complete change of his clothing before relieving his man. At night it will take almost another hour to get home, making practically a fourteen-hour day, and that leaves him very little time for his family. In the places where these men are employed very often there are unhealthy and filthy conditions, bad sanitary arrangements. I have been down in buildings in New York and other cities, where the men have had to work for twelve hours in the Summer time with the temperature as high as 150 degrees. I took Miss Beeks down town a year ago last Summer. I wanted to show her one of the bad places, and we went into a corner where men had to get in and out to work, and the thermometer registered 173 degrees. Now, that is something awful. And those are conditions that in many instances can be changed very readily. Better ventilation is needed. In the new buildings going up we are endeavoring to have more room and to get more ventilation—have more doors and windows, and such like. But in many of the old buildings a change could be made at a comparatively small expense. Just a motor and a few fans would make a big improvement. I am very sorry to say that some of the largest estates in the City of New York have the worst conditions. Some of the large hotels have awful conditions for their men, and there is nobody to say a word for them except our organization, and it cannot reach all places. Where we have reached the employers we have induced them to make necessary changes, to improve the surroundings of the men and make them a little bit comfortable, at least.

There are a hundred and one other things done in a great hotel, for instance, laundry work, the men and women peel potatoes, clean silver, and such like.

in addition to the work of our craft. In some places there are good conditions and in some bad.

Take, for instance, the Hotel Belmont, where Mr. Belmont gave personal attention when the building was going up, and said he wanted the engine room and boiler room, where his men worked so hard, to be as well ventilated as possible. And really, it is a pleasure for a man to work in that plant, though it is sixty feet under ground. And instead of working twelve hours, as in many places, in the Belmont Hotel the stationary firemen have an eight-hour workday, thanks to Mr. Belmont. And I wish we had more Belmonts to take an interest in these particular things. There is a great difference in the working conditions in the large hotels in the city. In one owned by a large estate the men work twelve hours a day in a miserable hole and get 25 per cent less wages. They get $45 a month for this work, whereas in the Belmont Hotel the wages are $60 a month, that amount being really less than a man needs to support a family in New York. However, they have competent men at the Belmont, but at the other place they go to Castle Garden and get immigrants because they get them cheap, although the law requires that men who do this class of work shall be citizens and hold a license from the Police Department. That is the difference between a plant that is taken care of by the employer and one where there is nobody to bother about it.

We had the Legislature pass the law providing that every man who fires a boiler must stand an examination as to his qualifications, and that all men applying for such license shall be American citizens. We thought that under such a requirement the employers would get a better class of men, who would pay more attention to their work and would run the plants more safely than others without any restriction. What do we find? We find the big corporations, the big power and public plants ignoring this law. They ignore it to their shame. They do not want to employ American citizens. No, they would sooner go down to the Spanish and Italian steamboats and pay runners to bring immigrants to be placed in their plants. Thus they violate not only the State law in relation to the licenses, but also the immigration laws of the United States. They are willing to run the risk of the destruction of their property and of the lives of the men who work for them. The danger in having incompetent men is that either too much or too little water will be in the boilers. If the water gets too high, it goes over into the engine and is liable to blow out the cylinder head. If the water gets too low, it is liable to blow up the boilers, destroying property and killing everybody around; but many employers hire cheap men to work around the boilers who do not understand English and therefore cannot interpret the orders given to them by the engineers or others in charge. We have known instances where Italians and others did not know how to start or handle pumps used to feed the boilers. If anything happened to the pumps or the boilers the men generally lost thir heads, and the first thing they thought of was to get to a place of safety themselves. And you ladies, by talking to your husbands or brothers or fathers, as many of you no doubt have, connected with those corporations, may help to stop this abuse, because the heads of the corporations are not always informed of their own working conditions. They do not know the game. It is the people under them, those directly in charge, who are to blame.

I will just give you one of the reasons why they bring these people in. About three weeks ago a number of Italians waited on me and told me that in a certain railroad plant in the city they were abused. Those Italians had taken the places of American citizens who were discharged. The Italians were hired—not because they were any better men, but because they were cheaper. Here are depositions made by some Italians. One ——— makes the following statement: Says he resides at 633 Union street, Brooklyn. He worked for ——— (I am not going to read the name of the company) for three and one-half months since October 4, 1907. He paid the foreman $7—and named him—to get him employment at the power house, and after paying the money he was employed until Christmas, when the foreman asked him to contribute to a fund for the purpose of making the Chief Engineer a present, and told him that if he did not chip in he would be bounced. He did not chip in and he was bounced.

These unfortunate men, who cannot speak the English language, are hired in preference to American citizens because the foreman and superintendent cannot hold the latter up for five or ten dollars whenever they like. That is something that should be looked into.

Now, if those men join a labor union, where they get some protection, they are bounced. I have in my desk downtown thirty-seven affidavits from thirty-seven men, who were recently discharged in one plant in Philadelphia for becoming members of the union. The foreman went up to them and told them that they were members of the union. He found this out through their spy system. They spy on many of our unions. The corporations and the large employers of labor, or the people who are directly under them, hire spies to become members of the union and when they learn that an employe joins the union he is discharged at once. Now, it comes to a pretty state of affairs when men who have been giving faithful service—as these men had—are thus discharged. They had worked from three to twenty-two years for that company, some of them starting in as young men and working until they were bent and old, and they were getting the same wages when dismissed that they had been receiving for twenty years from that corporation, and were working twelve hours a day. The worst of it is, that when these particular men are at work before their roaring furnaces, they have not a shelter of any kind, and have no place to hang their clothes when they come in, and if their clothes get burned, as they often do, through sparks, they get no compensation for that. Now these are things that should be looked into, and they are conditions that make men very discontented. Such things drive men to Socialism. The trades union movement is opposed to Socialism. When we come before you ladies we talk more radically than we do to the members of our own unions. The good trades unionist is always conservative with his own people.

There are other conditions to be criticised. We have our city, state and national governments, which sometimes have worse conditions than the poorest private employer.

I made up my mind this afternoon that I would recite some of those things to you, because, as I have said before, I know that you ladies, many of you, are in a position if you take up this work, to do something. Take, for instance, in the city of New York in the hospitals. The poor girls go into those hospitals as nurses, and they have to work there twelve hours a day and twelve hours a night and relieve each other in shifts. Take a girl in a sick ward at night—she has a whole ward of children down with diphtheria, for instance, to look after. She has to be on her feet all night long. If she sits down to take a little nap or doze off to sleep one of these children is liable to cough up a tube and choke to death. This is the most trying kind of work, and many of the nurses go into consumption from it. There should be at least three shifts there—that is, eight hours on and sixteen hours off duty.

While talking of those institutions, I might say that in Bellevue Hospital, where the poor of our city, when they are sick, are taken, the abuses are such that something should be done. I have been looking it up in the last few days because I wanted to bring this matter to the attention of some of the authorities, though it is outside of my line of business. We find several hundred hospital helpers there working for $10 a month—$120 a year, with board and lodging. They must be able bodied men. Their work is to handle the sick, and to move from ward to ward; to take them off the ambulances as they come in, to help them out and help them around, and remove the dead when they die to the morgue, or wherever they may be sent. In looking this thing up I got a list that I want to bring to the attention of some of the authorities. Here are four lists, each containing seventy-five names. The highest pay of the able-bodied helpers on these lists is $120 a year. I find some getting $76 a year, and others getting $96 a year—all able-bodied men. Now, the point I am getting at is, what class of men can they be? Why, they are mostly worthless fellows that, though they are able-bodied (they have to be strong, able men), young men mostly, that were very little good to themselves nor anybody else, only to buy drink with every penny that they would get hold of. The consequence is that when they get their $10 a month they go out to the first saloon and drink, and, what is worse, put liquor in their pockets and they are drunk around the buildings. What kind of people are those to handle the poor unfortunate men or women who may be injured. They are not the proper kind. There should be men employed there that would get sufficient wages to induce them to think something of their positions.

I am sure that any of you ladies in hiring a man to do your work, to look after your horses or stable, or anything of that kind, would not hire a worthless loafer for $120 a year. You would pay a man $600 or $700 a year to take care of your horses. These men are not fit to take care of horses or take care of dogs, for that matter, and I am sure they are not proper ones to take care of the poor unfortunates in Bellevue or any other hospital.

It is getting late, and I notice that you want to get away. Now, in relation to welfare work. That can be looked at in different directions. I read in the papers the other day that Mr. Frank Bailey, vice-president of the Title Guarantee and Trust Company, suggested a movement among large money lending institutions whereby a mechanic or working man that is thrifty and has a lot or two somewhere, and wants to start a home, can raise a thousand or two or three thousand dollars. That is something that the money lending institutions never paid any attention to, and that I think would do a great deal of good. It would induce a man that has no other way in the world now of getting a home to start out and try to build up one for himself and his family. Every good mechanic and every good working man that is a good father and good husband has an ambition to start a home. He has an ambition to get away from the tenement house, because a man who has a large family cannot bring up his children as they should be brought up in the City of New York the way it is to-day. If a person has three or four or five or six in the family they can't get a flat—they can't get rooms anywhere. They have to get out and they are driven all around, and finally when they do locate it is in some place that is ill-kept and where a decent mechanic don't care to live. That has been my own case. I have six children, and I lived on Twenty-seventh street. The boys began to grow up and slide down the banister, and I had to move to the Bronx. Afterward I had to move from the Bronx to Yonkers and I am living there now. And I say, God help the poor family that has to live in a tenement house down town. It is a hard proposition, and I hope Mr. Bailey's idea will induce the big money-lending institutions to take up this kind of work.

We have here building and loan and banking associations where the poor men sometimes put in their savings, but what becomes of them? Why, the building loan and banking companies go into the hands of receivers and that is the last of the poor man's savings. Here is a book of a building loan and banking company that went into the hands of a receiver about five years ago. The ower of this book had an ambition to build a little home for himself and family. He was paying in $12.50 a month. In twelve years, then, he would have had a chance of getting a home. He was paying his assessments regularly—at least his wife was—and he went away to the Spanish-American war, and could not afford very well to pay then. But his wife managed to pay them into the building loan by hanging up the rent. Even if she went hungry she paid into the building loan. She paid in and paid in, and finally when he came back he found that it was going under. He went down to draw his money out, and there was $923.22 coming to him. They told him they could not pay him anything and that the institution was going into the hands of a receiver. Out of $923.22 this is all he has got to show for it (exhibiting credit book of the building loan association) and all he ever will have. There were 14,000 stockholders. Many of them were poor women who had two or three children in an institution, and were at work by the day scrubbing and washing to keep paying a few dollars into this building and loan association, hoping that the time would come when they would be able to take the children out, when they would get to be fifteen or sixteen years of age, and they would have these few dollars out of the building company to start up homes. Their few dollars went just the same as the others. And I want to tell you ladies that it was one of the saddest things I ever saw in my life, when the Board of Directors, those scoundrels, called a meeting downtown—to see those poor unfortunate men and women, young and old, crying and pulling their hair, because their few savings that they worked and bled for for years were swept away in one day and all their hopes for the future were blasted.

Then people wonder why is there Socialism and why is there anarchy. Really, I often wonder why we have not more. And I believe that we would have more of it if it was not for the labor organizations and the curb they are keeping upon their people.

I wish that you ladies had an opportunity, and I hope in the near future you will, of visiting the meetings of the trades unions of the laboring men in this city, and to see them as they are; to encourage those men by your presence. I will be glad at any time in my organization to have any of you visit our regular meeting. We meet on Saturday nights. It would be a great encouragement to those men to see that ladies such as yourselves are taking an interest in them.

Now, if this welfare work is going to do any good the employers' wives and the employers' daughters must take an interest in it; must get in touch with the men themselves—the working men. Must see where they are employed; must see where they live and how they live.

It would be a great lesson to you all if you would go down on the lower east and the lower west sides on a hot summer's night and see the mothers out there sitting on the stoop with their babies in their arms, and their poor little tots playing around them gasping with the heat. If you could only see the places where those poor unfortunate people have to live. I have known in the City of New York, and in the outskirts, one house of four rooms where there were two married couples—two men and their wives keeping roomers. It was a foreign settlement section. And how many boarders and roomers do you suppose those two married couples kept, and lived there themselves? They kept seventeen. Seventeen and four are twenty-one people, living in four rooms. That is in the City of New York. They were not American, that's true, but they were here with us. I might say I am not an American born myself, for I was born and raised in Ireland, but when I came to this country I had the advantage, of course, of having the language of the country, and saw something of the ways of living in my old country that I did here. But with those poor unfortunate people brought in here and thrown in such places as that, it's something awful, and it should not be. There are hundreds of other houses almost as bad as the one described, although there is plenty of land in that section and it is up to the people they are employed by, who can well afford to build houses sufficient for them to live in if they want so to do. No, they are not bothering about those people. All they are bothering about is to roll up millions of dollars, as they are doing every year. Their business is a good paying business and they are rolling up that money all right.

Now I want to say, ladies, that the working men of America are not Socialists. The thinking man of America has all the faith in the world in the people that are higher up, as we say. You can look around you and see the men who are associated with the labor leaders and are close to them—such men as Mr. Seth Low, who is close to Mr. Gompers and Mr. Mitchell and the other leaders, and I am glad to say is a friend of mine. Mr. Belmont has worked hand in hand with those men. Dr. Nicholas Murray Butler and other men of high standing in this country have done so, and is there any reason in the world why some more of the men of that class should not get closer, also their wives and daughters, to the working men and the working women of this country?

To-day we have a very peculiar state of affairs. We are threatened in all directions with anarchy. We want to stamp out anarchy, and we want the millionaire and the multi-millionaire, the wives and the daughters and the entire family of those people to assist us. We will be heart and hand with you. We are all American citizens, and let us work together as American citizens to make this country greater and grander than it is—the greatest country in the world—but we can make it greater and grander, especially for the future generations. It is up to you to help us, and I hope you will be with us from now on.

MISS MARBURY made the following request: Mr. Healy, I wonder if you will do us a favor—another favor. We are laboring for good here this afternoon, and I wonder, as long as you are here, if you will go down in our engine room, where we have employes, and see whether the conditions down there are all right, or if there is anything that the ladies of this club can do to make our men more comfortable. I think I am only expressing the feeling of every one here in the club. This building was erected for us, as you know, and we women know nothing about these questions. We took the building as it came from the architects. We believe our men are comfortable, but we do not know, and if you will spare a few moments we shall take you down just to look around and see if the place is all right.

MR. HEALY replied: I will be pleased to do it, Madam. I will be very pleased.

The closing statement, made by THE CHAIRMAN, was: I think that is a splendid idea. Is there anything else we would like to ask Mr. Healy? If not, I suppose the meeting is about ready to adjourn. But I think we cannot do that without expressing our warmest thanks to the speakers. I think those who have spoken this afternoon have given us a wonderful treat, and something which none of us will ever forget. So all those in favor of passing a vote of thanks to them this afternoon will say aye.

(A vote of thanks was unanimously passed.)

NOTE: After inspecting the boiler plant of the Colony Club Mr. Healy reported that "it is a very nice, clean place, and the conditions of the men employed there are first class in every way. Of course the place is small, and the work to be performed is light, as the power to run the plant is taken from outside current. It cannot be compared with large power plants on the outside where one man has to shovel more coal in an hour than a man in the Colony Club would have to shovel in twenty-four hours."

Invitations to attend the meeting of the New York Woman's Committee of the National Civic Federation were extended to:

Mrs. J. Borden Harriman
Miss Anne Morgan
Mrs. Marion Story
Mrs. Harry Payne Whitney
Mrs. John G. Milburn
Mrs. Albert Herter
Mrs. Douglas Robinson
Mrs. Richard Irvin
Miss Florence Rhett
Miss Mabel Choate
Mrs. Otto Kahn
Mrs. V. Everit Macy
Mrs. Frank McN. Bacon
Mrs. Gordon K. Bell
Mrs. C. U. Carpenter
Mrs. D. W. Evans
Mrs. Orrin S. Goan
Mrs. Francis P. Kinnicutt
Mrs. Walter Maynard
Mrs. B. W. Morris
Mrs. William Rand, Jr.
Miss Caroline Shippen
Mrs. Benjamin Stern
Mrs. A. Thursby
Mrs. H. Morton
Miss Elisabeth Marbury
Mrs. Clarence H. Mackay
Mrs. Victor Sorchon
Mrs. Archibald Alexander
Mrs. Ralph Pulitzer.
Miss Mary Parsons
Mrs. F. H. Cabot
Mrs. J. A. Wright
Mrs. James Speyer
Miss C. V. R. Delafield
Miss Virginia Potter
Mrs. Edward Henderson
Mrs. Ernesto Fabbri
Miss Maude Adams
Mrs. Sidney Colgate
Mrs. Joseph Gilder
Mrs. J. M. Ellsworth
Mrs. Cadwalader Jones
Mrs. R. Fulton Cutting
Mrs. Walter James
Mrs. George Brewster
Mrs. Seth Low
Mrs. Wm. Jay Schieffelin
Miss Mary Harriman
Mrs. Malcolm Whitman
Miss Hewitt
Mrs. John Hammond
Mrs. G. LaFarge
Mrs. Arthur Page
Miss F. P. Gilman
Mrs. John Corbin
Mrs. Daniel Frohman
Mrs. Emma Eames Story
Mrs. H. Fairfield Osborn
Mrs. Arthur Dodge
Miss Whitney
Mrs. August Belmont, Jr.
Mrs. Henry C. Potter
Miss Helen Nichols
Mrs. Wm. Fellowes Morgan
Mrs. Julia K. West
Miss Janet Waring
Mrs. Mary Hatch Willard
Miss C. R. Lowell
Mrs. Carl de Gersdorff
Mrs. Charles Tiffany
Mrs. William Sheehan
Mrs. William C. Reick
Mrs. Gustav Schwab
Mrs. Henry Siegel
Mrs. Howard Brokaw
Mrs. Herman Straus
Mrs. Charles Scribner
Mrs. Walter P. Bliss
Mrs. Richard Aldrich
Miss Robb
Miss Viola Allen
Miss Daly
Mrs. C. L. Blair
Mrs. W. Oakman
Mrs. Dean Sage
Mrs. Norman Hapgood
Mrs. Mary Philbrook
Mrs. Paul Morton
Mrs. Langdon Geer
Mrs. George J. Gould
Mrs. Alf Hayman
Mrs. William Rice
Mrs. Charles A. Moore
Mrs. Charles A. Moore, Jr.
Mrs. John S. Huyler
Mrs. Foster Coates
Mrs. B. J. Greenhut
Mrs. Marcus M. Marks
Mrs. W. H. Marshall
Mrs. H. B. Thayer
Mrs. Elbridge Fowler
Mrs. L. C. Penfield
Miss Laurence
Mrs. Lazarus
Mrs. Stuart Duncan
Mrs. Nicholas Murray Butler
Mrs. Clement A. Griscom, Jr.
Mrs. Egerton Winthrop, Jr.

The New York branch divided the work immediately to be undertaken between two committees, which are actively engaged in pursuing their plans.

The Committee on the Needs of Workers in Specific Industries held its first meeting at the residence of the chairman, Mrs. J. Borden Harriman, Friday morning, March 13.

The following sub-committees were appointed, and are making extensive investigations with a view of securing information:

Committee on Conditions of Stationary Firemen and Hotel Employes, including not only hotel attendants and stationary firemen, but also laundry workers and metal (silver) polishers—Mrs. Frank McN. Bacon, chairman; Mrs. Ralph Pulitzer, Jr., Mrs. William Fellowes Morgan.

Committee on Traction Employes—Mrs. Clement Acton Griscom, Jr., chairman; Mrs. Orrin S. Goan, Mrs. James A. Wright.

Committee on Cigar Factories—Miss Caroline Shippen, chairman; Mrs. D. W. Evans, Miss F. P. Gilman.

The Committee on Welfare Work for Government Employes held its initial meeting at the headquarters of the Federation Friday afternoon, March 13, Mrs. Julia K. West, chairman, presiding.

It was decided that there should be the following visiting committees to secure information as to existing conditions:

Federal Employes—Custom House, Miss C. V. R. Delafield, chairman; Navy Yard, Mrs. F. H. Cabot, chairman; Governors Island, Mrs. John Corbin, chairman; Post Offices, Miss Anne Morgan, chairman.

Employes in State Institutions—Prisons, hospitals and charity institutions. Chairmen to be appointed.

Municipal Employes—Public schools, including such employes as firemen, engineers, teachers, janitors and scrubwomen, Miss C. R. Lowell, chairman; charity institutions and hospitals, including such employes as nurses, orderlies and other attendants, Mrs. Mary Hatch Willard, chairman; prisons, police stations, fire department. Chairmen to be appointed.

The members of the Committee on Welfare Work for Government Employes are: Mrs. J. K. West, Miss Anne Morgan, Mrs. F. H. Cabot, Miss Cornelia V. R. Delafield, Miss Lowell, Mrs. John Corbin, Mrs. Ernesto Fabbri, Mrs. E. C. Henderson, Mrs. F. P. Kinnicutt, Mrs. M. H. Willard, Mrs. William Rand, Jr., Mrs. Marcus M. Marks, Mrs. William R. Willcox, Mrs. Edward M. Morgan, Mrs. James S. Clarkson.

AMERICAN TEACHERS TO VISIT EUROPE.

(Continued from page 6.)

classes to the visits of teachers, and accord the latter the fullest opportunity of inspecting the work of the schools. The preliminary schedule includes about 250 different schools and colleges of all classes.

Other schools will be added to it from time to time, and teachers will be notified before sailing of the complete list. In case teachers desire to visit any particular school not mentioned upon the final list, the local committees will be glad to place themselves in communication with the authorities of such schools and secure permission to visit them.

Arrangements will be made by the school authorities to hold frequent conferences during the period of the teachers' visit for the teachers of the different localities. The teachers will be invited to attend these conferences, and will thus have an opportunity of meeting the corps of teachers and becoming familiar with the school problems which are under discussion in the United Kingdom. The visiting teachers will doubtless be expected to give some account of their own schools in the United States at such meetings.

Members of the local committee and other persons of social prominence in the several localities will be at home for afternoon tea, and will give a cordial welcome to the American teachers, who will be introduced through the local committees, and who will thus be afforded a glimpse of the home life of their English hosts.

Through the special arrangement for the transportation of the teachers and for their board while in England, the trip can be made at a very moderate expense to those who take part in it. Without making any allowance whatsoever for purchases while in England, it would appear that the cost from the time of leaving the United States to the time of arrival, calculating a stay of four week in England, can be brought within $110.00 by those who exercise the greatest economy. An allowance of $150.00 would permit the visitor to travel very comfortably, while $200.00 could be deemed a very liberal estimate of the expense. Travel from residence to and from the seaboard must be allowed for in addition to this estimate.

The Boards of Education in the United States through the superintendents of schools, and the boards of control of normal and industrial schools through their principals, have been invited to designate the teachers to whom the advantages offered by the National Civic Federation should be granted. The trip is one of such obvious professional benefit to the teachers that the educational authorities have been asked to continue the salaries of the teachers selected during their proposed absence from their home schools.

The action taken by the Board of Education of New York City is characteristic of the cordial reception whch the plan has generally received. At its session of March 11, 1908, it provided that permission be granted to not more than twenty—later increased to fifty—teachers in the schools of this city to visit the schools of England and the Continent under leave of absence with full pay for a period not to exceed six weeks, all such teachers to be required to file with the City Superintendent of Schools within two weeks after their return written reports of their observations.

Other cities have lengthened the term of absence to two months, recognizing that a shorter absence might in part, at least, defeat the object of the visit by unduly curtailing the time available for the inspection of schools on the other side. This consideration applies with especial force to all inland cities, since allowance must be made for the time necessary to reach the sailing ports and to make final arrangements respecting tickets. Among other cities which have already provided for the payment of teachers' salaries while absent on the visit are Chicago (twenty teachers), Pittsburg (ten), Cleveland (eight), Newark (six), Seattle (five) and Detroit (four), besides many smaller places providing for one or two teachers each. The Boards of Trustees of State Normal Schools are deeply interested and a considerable number of nominations have already been received from them. The hundreds of inquiries from individuals and from school authorities which have been received and the publicity which has been given the matter by the school journals testify to the widespread interest in the movement and guarantee a most successful issue.

The selection of teachers by the Boards of Education and other school authorities will insure the choice of proper persons to take part in the visit and can be made directly beneficial in the solution of local problems, to throw light on modifications of the school work which are under consideration.

Teachers not nominated directly by Boards of Education or boards controlling separate institutions must have the endorsement of their local superintendents or principals.

In case the number designated to take part in the visit should exceed the number of 500 it will be necessary to make an allotment, taking into consideration an equitable geographical distribution and the different types of schools represented.

At the present time, when the whole organization and conduct of our school system is under discussion, the National Civic Federation feels that in organizing this movement it is making an important contribution to the solution of present problems in the educational world.

ANTI-TRUST ACT BE AMENDED?

(Continued from page 5.)

Federal Grand Jury, and procured an indictment against seventy-five of the men who had participated in the council in which that strike was inaugurated; and this, I say, was under the Sherman Anti-Trust law. This case is to be heard in the courts.

Mr. Malby: There was nothing in it but a strike?

Mr. Gompers: That is all.

Mr. Malby: There was no boycott; just simply a strike? There was no picketing?

Mr. Gompers: That was not alleged. I do not think the picketing comes under the Sherman Anti-Trust law. But combination in restraint of trade, that is what it was.

The Chairman: I think the indictment charged a conspiracy in restraint of foreign and interstate trade, these people being engaged in both foreign and interstate trade.

Mr. Gompers: Yes.

Mr. Caulfield: Has not the prosecution of those cases been ordered suspended by the Department of Justice?

Mr. Gompers: I have no knowledge upon that subject. Mr. Keefe, has that been ordered?

Mr. Keefe: Yes; the prosecution was withheld. Those were instructions from the Law Department, I presume.

The Chairman: I do not think that exactly states it right. I have a letter from the Attorney General covering the whole case. There was some question about the validity of the indictment. The Department of Justice is examining into it to ascertain whether the proceedings are regular, and has not issued any affirmative instructions that tend to either impede or promote the progress of the judicial proceedings.

Mr. Keefe: The instructions were to withhold the prosecution of the case.

The Chairman: I do not get that impression from the Attorney General's letter. Of course, you may be right about it, but I see nothing in the letter of the Attorney General to indicate other than that the Department of Justice is considering the matter.

Mr. Gompers: Well, there is no question but what they were indicted. That is the statement I made.

The Chairman: You are correct about that.

Mr. Gompers: As to whether they will be prosecuted, of course none of us can say, but they are liable to prosecution under the indictment unless it is nolle prossed.

The Chairman: I am not advised as to the details. Whether they proceed depends altogether upon the facts that exist and the charge under the indictment.

Mr. Gompers: Addressing myself for a few minutes to the bill itself, let me say, as I have already said, that I give the fullest support I can. I am authorized to say that—for the purpose that the bill has in view, in so far as to corporations owning capital stock and common carriers, but so far as labor organizations are concerned we are averse to the registration of the labor organizations.

The Chairman: May I inquire right there, please. The labor organizations are not incorporated organizations, they are simply voluntary associations?

Mr. Gompers: Yes, sir; voluntary associations. Most of them are unincorporated. Some are incorporated, but most of them are not.

The Chairman: Is your American Federation of Labor an incorporated or voluntary association?

Mr. Gompers: It is a voluntary association of associations.

The Chairman: That is, the most of them are also voluntary associations?

Mr. Gompers: Yes, sir.

The Chairman: And you do not think these associations should be subjected to this provision in relation to registration, as I understand you?

Mr. Gompers: Yes, sir; I think we ought not to be required to register.

The Chairman: That proposition under the bill is to register in order to get what might be termed immunity under the act.

Mr. Gompers: Yes, sir.

The Chairman: And you do not think your associations ought to be required to register in order to get immunity?

Mr. Gompers: I think we ought to be placed in a position at least as the organizations of labor were before the Sherman Anti-Trust law was enacted.

The Chairman: Is it your view that the purpose of the legislation is to relieve the Federation of Labor, for instance, of the embarrassments of the Sherman Anti-Trust law?

Mr. Gompers: Not only the American Federation, but the local associations or organizations.

The Chairman: Is it your idea that is the purpose of the legislation, to relieve the organizations of employes from the operation of the Sherman Anti-Trust law?

Mr. Gompers: I can not tell you, sir; but I have my doubts.

The Chairman: If that is not the purpose, are you in sympathy with it?

Mr. Gompers: I want to explain that if I may?

The Chairman: Certainly.

Mr. Gompers: And say that taking as a basis the amendment to the Sherman Anti-Trust law when it was still in a formative state, and to which I referred earlier in my remarks—the provision that passed the Senate—taking that as a basis, labor has prepared this and wants to offer it as an amendment to the pending bill. First, the provision to eliminate from the bill those parts which refer to organizations and corporations not for profit and without capital stock, and then to have these amendments, and in these two amendments the representative of the farmers' organization or union is by instruction giving us his aid and support.

The Chairman: Who is the head of the farmers?

Mr. Gompers: Mr. Barnett, of the Farmers' American Society of Equity, and Mr. Barrett, of the American Farmers' Union. I can not speak for the Farmers' Union other than that having communicated with them, through their representatives, and giving them a statement of what we apprehended and what we asked, the Secretary sent a telegram stating that our efforts have the hearty approval of his organization and their support in every way.

The Chairman: Are these organizations you speak of differentiated from what we know as the Grange?

Mr. Gompers: They are part of the Grange, most of them.

The Chairman: Are they affiliated with the American Federation of Labor—that is, the two you speak of?

Mr. Gompers: No, sir; except as we may combine on general interests. We exchange fraternal delegates to each other's conventions and mass meetings, and at conferences of all sorts we have either a representative of labor there in theirs, or they have a representative of the farmers in our conferences.

The Chairman: And while in a general way you work in harmony for common purposes, you are not so allied that your Federation exercises any control over them?

Mr. Gompers: No, sir.

The Chairman: What is the address of these two gentlemen, please?

Mr. Gompers: Mr. C. M. Barnett is President of the Farmers' American Society of Equity, and his headquarters are in the Clayton Building, Indianapolis, Ind. I have not Mr. Barrett's address with me; it is somewhere in Georgia. I should say that in reply to the notification to that society of farmers that this hearing was to take place to-day, their Secretary said that Mr. Barnett could not be here, but that Mr. Nelson, a member of their executive board, would be authorized to act as their representative before this committee to-day.

The Chairman: Mr. Nelson is here, I suppose?

Mr. Gompers: I think he is.

The Chairman: What is that organization composed of—practical farmers?

Mr. Gompers: Yes, sir.

The Chairman: Or of people simply interested in agriculture? Is it composed of practical operating farmers or farm laborers?

Mr. Gompers: Operating farmers. If you will permit me to read the further amendment you will observe what they ask, which we have given our adherence to, and they have given theirs to our proposition. It is this:

"That nothing in said act or in this act is intended, nor shall any provision thereof be enforced so as to apply to organizations or associations not for profit or without capital stock; nor to the members of such organizations or associations. That nothing in said act, or in this act, is intended, nor shall any provision thereof hereafter be enforced so as to apply to any arrangements, agreements or combinations among persons engaged in agriculture or horticulture, made with a view of enhancing the price of their own agricultural or horticultural products."

Now, I want to read for information from the British Trades Dispute act. It will not occupy more than two or three minutes. The act was passed by Parliament in December, 1906:

"1. It shall be lawful for any person or persons acting either on their own behalf or on behalf of a trade union or other association of individuals, registered or unregistered, in contemplation of or during the continuance of any trade dispute, to attend for any of the following purposes at or near a house or place where a person resides or works, or carries on his business, or happens to be (1) for the purpose of peacefully obtaining or communicating information; (2) for the purpose of peacefully persuading any person to work or abstain from working.

"2. An agreement or combination by two or more persons to do or procure to be done any act in contemplation or furtherance of a trade dispute shall not be ground for an action, if such act when committed by one person would not be ground for an action.

"3. An action shall not be brought against a trade union or other association aforesaid for the recovery of damages sustained by any person or persons by reason of the action of a member or members of such trade union or other association aforesaid."

The Chairman: Have you the full act?

Mr. Gompers: These are the three sections, and then there is the enacting clause.

The Chairman: What connection does that have with the act of, I think, 1873, passed by Parliament?

Mr. Gompers: The law of 1875, I think it was, was rendered practically nugatory by the Taff-Vale decision which so intensified the feeling of British workmen and the British public generally that it resulted in the Trades Dispute act.

The Chairman: Does this operate to repeal the act of 1875, as you understand it?

Mr. Gompers: It affirmatively takes its place and wipes out the effect of the Taff-Vale decision.

The Chairman: Have you a citation so that we can get the case to which you refer:

Mr. Gompers: You know, Mr. Littlefield, I am not a lawyer.

The Chairman: I thought perhaps you had a citation of the case—where it was reported.

Mr. Gompers: No; but I can get it. Mr. Low has—

The Chairman: Has Mr. Low got it?

Mr. Low: I have a copy of the act.

The Chairman: No; I wanted the citation of the case, so that we could look the case up.

Mr. Gompers: I am of opinion there would be little difficulty in obtaining it. Surely, you have ample facilities to obtain it. The Library of Congress certainly has a compilation of laws upon that subject. I am satisfied it has.

The Chairman: Very well; if you think we can find it without any trouble in such a compilation.

Mr. Gompers: I have here some citations of decisions and opinions in several courts in the matter of strikes which I should like to submit.

The Chairman: And make them a part of your remarks without reading?

Mr. Gompers: Yes, sir.

The Chairman: You may do so.

At this point a number of citations were inserted in the record.

Mr. Gompers: In conclusion, let me say that in my judgment, speaking not only as President of the American Federation of Labor and as a representative of workmen, but as an American citizen, I believe firmly that there is no question before this Congress possibly, nothing equal in importance to this question which can arise in a very long time. It ought not to be deferred until some other time; it ought not to be postponed until a hereafter. The workmen of the country feel that they have been outraged, that their interests have been invaded. I could not interpret to you in words the feeling or reflect their sentiments or views, even if I should attempt to do so, and no matter what time I might take in so doing. The men of labor of this country feel outraged, I repeat; they feel that they have been robbed; they feel that they have been shorn of the only protection that they have—their organization, the right to combine, the right to associate, the right to help each other, the right to help bear each other's responsibilities and burdens; the right to protect themselves from greed, from the rapacious. For in truth we must bear this in mind. We have not any hesitancy in saying that the large majority of employers are fairly inclined, but it is equally to their protection as it is to the protection of the men who labor that we organize and have all the fullest rights of our normal activities as workmen and citizens in order that we may compel the man who is always nibbling at the wages of workmen, that we can protect the fair-minded employers from the nibbling wage cutting policy and niggardliness of the unfair and antagonistic employer.

In the interest of men of labor, the women of labor, of American manhood and womanhood and citizenship, I make this appeal to you gentlemen of the Judiciary Committee, that we can not wait much longer for relief; and if I judge the temper of the American workmen accurately, and I think I do, they are going to hold to a strict accountability the men or parties whoever and whichever they may be who fail to fairly respond to this urgent appeal.

The Chairman: Now, Mr. Gompers, a word. Would this amendment you suggest, if it became a law, authorize the prosecution of such a boycott as was attempted in the Danbury hatters case, which was in violation of the Sherman Anti-Trust law? Is that the purpose?

Mr. Gompers: One of the purposes; yes, sir. That case was brought under the Sherman Anti-Trust law.

The Chairman: Yes. And the purpose of the amendment you have offered is to relieve you from the operation of the Sherman Anti-Trust law as construed by the court in that case?

Mr. Gompers: Yes, sir.

The Chairman: And to authorize that kind of an interstate boycott?

Mr. Gompers: Yes, sir.

The Chairman: Do you, as the representative of organized labor, favor the boycott, both as an interstate and a local proposition?

Mr. Gompers: I do, sir.

The Chairman: And your organization stands for that?

Mr. Gompers: It does, sir.

The Chairman: You filed a petition of intervention in the Danbury hatters case on the ground that it was one of the fundamental purposes of the organization, and for that reason you had a vital——

Mr. Gompers: Your assumption is wrong. It is not the fundamental purpose of the organization. It is only one of the means.

The Chairman: I may be wrong about that. I was simply speaking on the basis of the expressions contained in your petition, which in part reads as follows:

" * * * and that a decision herein in favor of the plaintiff in error would seriously obstruct and hinder the said American Federation of Labor, petitioner, in carrying out the purposes for which it was organized, and destroy, at least to some extent, its usefulness to its members, and would likewise and in like manner injure said members."

* * * * * * *

"First. That the constitution of said American Federation of Labor, petitioner, makes special provision for the prosecution of boycotts, so called, when instituted by a constituent or affiliated organization, as is described in the complaint filed in the District Court by the plaintiff in error herein, through the agency and pursuant to the approval of the executive council of petitioner; but what are alleged in said complaint to be boycotts are in reality legal and proper proceedings set on foot and carried on in order to accomplish lawful ends of your petitioner and the said affiliated or constituent associations."

I suppose that accurately states the attitude of your organization?

Mr. Gompers: Yes, sir; but that is not one of the fundamental principles.

The Chairman: Well, your constitution provides for the prosecution of boycotts, does it not?

Mr. Gompers: No, sir.

The Chairman: But this petition, signed by the American Federation of Labor, Samuel Gompers and Frank Morrison, by T. C. Spelling, attorney, says: "First, That the constitution of said American Federation of Labor, petitioner, makes special provision for the prosecution of boycotts,". I know nothing about it except what I see here.

Mr. Gompers: The constitution makes provision for the selection of a committee on boycotts, and also regulates the manner, or, rather, restricts the number of boycotts which an organization can apply for endorsement, and it also restricts the central bodies from endorsing certain boycotts.

Your questions make it necessary for me to say just a word more, if I may.

The Chairman: Certainly.

Mr. Gompers: You must bear in mind that in the case in point, the hatters, their organization has had a continuous history. There has been a continuous history of the organized hatters for over five hundred years. From the old-time guilds they have their records. There is that esprit de corps, there is that feeling of mutuality, of the old-time chapel, as it was called in the printing trade, which also obtains among the hatters. They have had, and have, agreements with seventy of the largest hat manufacturers in America. They meet every year and agree upon wages, hours and conditions of employment. They got into a dispute with Mr. Loewe; the merits of it I shall not attempt to discuss. But they contended for conditions of employment, conditions of labor, wages, etc., whatever they were, which obtained throughout the trade among the workmen employed in the other factories. To these Mr. Loewe objected. They came to a disagreement. Whatever the merits were or the demerits were, I shall not attempt to discuss, but they came to a disagreement. It was necessary that the men in the trade—the hatters—must fight in order to maintain that scale of wages. Otherwise how could they expect these other seventy manufacturers to pay the scale, to pay decent wages which would give the men an American standard of living? It was a matter of self-defense. They had to fight. They will fight, and I will help them to fight, if I can. Any set of workmen or workwomen in this country who want help in protecting their interests or advancing their rights, I shall, so long as God gives me life, try to help them to the very best of whatever little ability I may have; and whatever that may involve, too. And I want to say that in my fifty-eight years of life I have been a law-abiding citizen. There is no man who can ever point to any act in my whole life that reflects to my discredit as a man and as a citizen. I want to assure you on my word of honor that so long as I live I will never buy a Loewe hat or a Bucks stove or range until these gentlemen come into organized labor and grant us conditions of fairness. Then they will get our support and help. Until then, you may call it by any other name—boycott or no boycott—but I won't buy your hats anyhow.

MR. A. B. GARRETSON, President of the Order of Railway Conductors, made the following statement:

The decisions which have already been made under the Sherman Act have brought men who desire to be law-abiding citizens into a peculiar situation. While we believed for very many years that the terms of that act had no bearing upon men placed as we were, members of labor unions, it has developed of late that it has control of our acts embodied in it as well as the acts of others.

I want to say to you that our organizations believe in the original intent, as they understand it, of the restraining legislation known as the Sherman law. They believe in proper regulation and supervision of combinations of that character, but they do not believe in the unreasonable restriction of the effort on the part of modern men to adjust themselves to modern development whether it be commercial, industrial or otherwise.

We, of the railway service, stand in possibly a little different relation to many of these questions to what the wage workers in other respects do, because we become subject to a class of legislation that does not apply to others. There has grown up now interstate commerce legislation, and we being an integral part in the handling of interstate commerce, it has been made apparent, to the public at least if not to ourselves, that investigation and publicity are a part of our fate, whether we desire it or not. Therefore we are reasonably willing to accept for ourselves precisely the same condition of publicity and of regulation that our employers or other commercial bodies are subjected to under the act. We favor the original act in that it provides for reasonable regulation and for the punishment of illegitimate combination. On the other hand we favor the amendment to the law as here presented in the sense that it makes possible legitimate combination. We are not sticklers over what might or might not be decided to be legitimate object or reasonable restraint of trade. We hold something of the view that it will always depend in a degree upon the tribunal which determines, and upon the character of men forming the tribunal. The idea involved in it is precisely the same, I suppose, as under the old English trial procedure. If you consult Jeffreys and Sir Matthew Hale on what constituted treason you will always find there is greater diversity of opinion among men as to what will constitute reasonable and unreasonable restraint.

Mr. Low: I would like to ask Mr. Garretson if I am not right in believing that among the ranks of labor there is a very great fear as to whether the right to form unions, the right to combine, the right to strike, and the right to make trade agreements is not endangered under the Sherman law as it stands?

Mr. Garretson: That feeling is almost absolutely universal among the men that I represent. Here is a condition that I come in contact with in business circles as well as in labor circles. Our dealings lie altogether with the managing officials of railway companies, men who are as thoroughly masters of their business as any on the continent, men who receive the highest wage on account of such ability that is paid in the country. Those men are as badly at sea as we ourselves as to what does or does not place them in violation of the law, if the law in regard to combinations applies alike to them and to us.

Mr. Garretson cited an instance in which an agreement had recently been reached with the mediation of the Interstate Commerce Commission in regard to wages on railways in the southeastern part of the country. Friendly relations were continued and business was not interrupted, nor was the public confidence destroyed by a great industrial dispute. And yet under the opinion which had been handed down there is no doubt in the minds of many that both the companies and the unions were subject to punishment under the terms of the law in question.

By a line of questions the Chairman endeavored to bring out the fact that if this agreement had not been reached a strike would have occurred, and that if the strike had occurred by virtue of a previous agreement to strike in such a case, that it would be considered a conspiracy or agreement in restraint of trade.

A. B. GARRETTSON.

THEODORE MARBURG.

J. W. JENKS.

Summing up, the Chairman expressed his personal opinion that a strike independent of a preliminary agreement beyond all question is authorized and lawful, but that strike which is the result of a combination or agreement in restraint of interstate trade and commerce is an unlawful strike.

MR. THEODORE MARBURG characterized the bill as one of regulation as against ruin. Around us we find financial institutions ruined, railroads unable to make needed improvements or improve present facilities. We find industry depressed and the laboring man out of employment.

For the cause we must turn in part to the law. The fine imposed on the Standard Oil Company appears largely in the nature of a revenge. The mistaken attitude of the public as expressed through both the Federal Government and the State Governments against the railroads has also contributed. We need better service, not hostile legislation for our railroads. The law which gives the Interstate Commerce Commission the power to actually fix rates has injured the roads. They are no longer profitable. It may be admitted that the Interstate Commerce Commission has been very conservative, but the legislation vesting such wide powers in it has had a baneful effect in stimulating crude and ill-advised legislation by the States. All this has shaken confidence. It was a merit of the Aldrich financial bill that it intended to restore confidence in railway bonds.

This bill provides for the correction of certain evils. It permits pooling among railroads. In so doing it corrects the Interstate Commerce Act.

It goes further. It exempts from the operation of the Sherman Anti-Trust Act, in so far as proceedings by the United States may lie, reasonable combinations, strikes and lockouts. It provides that persons injured by acts coming under the prohibition of the Sherman law shall recover simple instead of triple damages.

Most important is the provision which provides registration. We are getting down now to what we have been talking about for some years. This law prescribes registration as a condition precedent to the enjoyment of the benefits of the present bill. This to my mind is the most valuable feature of this measure. Under this clause the President can investigate the organization of corporations; that is to say, whether it is one corporation or whether it is a combination. He can investigate its financial condition so as to protect the public from losses.

Too much stress cannot be laid upon the advantages which will accrue to the public from the publicity which will result from this measure. Its scope is very wide. Since State lines had been broken down by the telephone, telegraph and the railroad, there are very few big industries existing to-day whose operations are strictly confined to State limits. The problems I have been referring to are problems of interstate commerce. If the investigation could be extended to unfair methods, we could open the door to potential competition. Then potential competition would become real.

At the recent Trust Conference in Chicago, in October, the demand for a revision of the Sherman Anti-Trust law was heard on all sides. I think I am correct in saying that the business sense of this country is in favor of the modification of the Sherman Anti-Trust law. As to what this modification should be was not, it is true, decided by the Conference.

Addressing himself to the provisions of the act referring to employes, etc., Mr. Marburg said this means that the modification relates only to the Sherman Anti-Trust law, that it in no way protects the rights of labor under the common law, nor any other statute law whether Federal or State. It means that men should be permitted to combine and strike or permitted to combine and have trade agreements. Now economists are a unit in feeling that the trade agreement is the most powerful instrument for peace in the industrial world. It anticipates the trouble. There should certainly be nothing in the law to prohibit the trade agreement. We do not say that the present law prohibits trade agreements or prohibits the strike; but we see in the actual indictment of laboring men for striking the probability that it does.

April 6th, Morning Session.

At the opening of the hearing Mr. Low presented a list of the persons who had been consulted in the preparation of the bill, as follows:

Nicholas Murray Butler, Albert Shaw, Talcott Williams, J. W. Jenks, E. H. Gary, Samuel Mather, Marcus M. Marks, Henry L. Higginson, Robert Mather, Isaac N. Seligman, James Speyer, W. A. Clark, August Belmont, Francis Lynde Stetson, Victor Morawetz, J. H. Ralston, Samuel Gompers, John Mitchell, D. J. Keefe, James O'Connell, P. H. Morrissey and D. L. Cease.

He also filed a supplementary statement in regard to the bill, which, for convenience, has already been printed with his principal statement.

PROFESSOR J. W. JENKS, of Cornell University, continued the argument in favor of the bill. After giving some account of the labor expended and the interests consulted in the preparation of the draft, he proceeded to take up the bill section by section, and interpreted it.

He called attention to the fact that the object of the first section is to provide for publicity. The reasons for placing the framing of questions in the hands of the President were two. It was felt that the act would be cumbersome if the specific questions to be asked were enumerated in the act, and it was felt further that under conditions which might arise in the future it might be desirable to introduce new questions not specifically provided in the law itself. These conclusions were reached after efforts had been made to formulate a statement of the information which should be obtained.

The sub-committee desired that the suggestions referred to which had not been incorporated in the act should be discussed in order that the general scope of the provision as understood by the framers of the bill could be placed in clearer light. Before taking up these questions, the Chairman called attention to the fact that the information to be asked for should be such as was related specifically to interstate commerce, and requested that in each case the connection between the information desired and interstate commerce be clearly set forth.

Mr. Jenks: Of course, we have no means of knowing that these questions are just the class which the President would ask. They are those that personally I should be willing to take the responsibility of inserting in the act. They are concerning corporations, as follows:

Its name, State of incorporation (if incorporated), and location of principal office, together with a true copy of its charter or articles of incorporation (if incorporated), or of association, and a true copy of all special or private acts (if any) under which it was organized or constituted or continued, or a reference thereto, as published in the official laws of the State in which any such acts have been passed.

Second—The names of its officers, directors and standing committees, if any, with residences.

Third—A complete copy of its by-laws. It is under the by-laws, of course, that it will commit these offenses or will carry on its business in the proper way.

If such corporation or association shall be one having a capital stock, its statement shall include the following additional data:

The nature of its business—that seems directly pertinent, if it is to be engaged in interstate commerce—a description of the different classes of its stock, if any.

Further, I should say, a description of the different classes of its stock, if any, with respective amounts authorized and outstanding, and the terms, privileges, restrictions and conditions of each class separately, and also a description of its funded debt, and the several issues thereof, and the respective amounts thereof issued and outstanding.

A statement of the amounts of its stock held by other corporations, specifying such corporations, and the amounts held by them respectively.

A statement of the amount of stock in other corporations held by it, stating the names of such corporations and the separate amounts of stock held therein.

A copy of the balance sheets and of the income account, and of all reports to stockholders of the corporation for the two preceding years.

Similar information as to any other corporation more than one-half of whose capital stock is held by it.

The Chairman: How do the preferred stock and the common stock and the bonds have any real or substantial relation to interstate commerce?

Mr. Jenks: The second section of the Sherman Act has to do very strongly with the effort to monopolize and with monopolizing traffic. The power to obtain a monopolistic control of interstate commerce depends very largely upon the size of a corporation, upon the way in which that corporation is organized legally, upon the way in which its stocks and bonds stand relative the one to the other, and upon its relations with the other corporations which are engaged in similar lines of business. And it seems to me that under those circumstances the connection is direct enough so that we are warranted in getting that information in order to enable us to deal directly with the questions of interstate commerce that come up.

The Chairman: On the theory which you have just been stating, how do you get the connection with interstate commerce unless you are able to show relations with other capitalizations?

Mr. Jenks: When you get your complete statement then you have your relation with the interstate commerce.

The Chairman: Do you think a court would compel a corporation to file a return that on its face did not disclose any power of the court to compel it to be done, on the hypothesis that later new conditions might be disclosed that would compel them to file it?

Mr. Jenks: So far as this bill is concerned, there is no thought of bringing any compulsion whatever upon any corporation to register if it does not wish to do so.

Mr. Low: Any corporation doing interstate commerce which has stock of various kinds seeks the money of the public as investors for the purpose of doing interstate commerce. Is it not a perfectly legitimate thing to ask that corporation, if it wants to do interstate commerce on the basis of all sorts of stock and bonds, for the benefit of the investor whose money is to be engaged in interstate commerce, to state the conditions upon which that money is to be used in interstate commerce?

The Chairman: That comes right down to the question as to whether, under our power to regulate commerce, we have any power to protect the investing public as a part of the regulation of commerce. I will ask Professor Jenks to tell us what he thinks about that. Under the power to regulate commerce, have we any power to so regulate corporations as to protect the investing public? And if so, what connection has the security-investing public with interstate commerce?

Mr. Jenks: I am very glad Mr. Low spoke of that. I should say that under the power to regulate commerce the United States Government does have a perfect right to invite corporations that are engaged in interstate commerce to answer any questions that will serve the public welfare.

The Chairman: Oh, but that is not quite it, is it—'invite"?

Mr. Jenks: "Invite"? Certainly.

The Chairman: No; my question is, do we have any power, under the power to regulate commerce, to so regulate it as to protect the security or value of the investing public's investments? Is that a part of our power to regulate commerce?

Mr. Jenks: I should say that it is part of your power to regulate commerce or to make any other law. I think it is entirely within your power, and I think, moreover, it is part of your duty, in passing laws to regulate interstate commerce or to do anything else, to keep in mind distinctly and fully the public welfare. If you can secure that welfare easily and well and legally and properly by suggesting that in their reports they shall furnish certain information that will be of benefit to the investing public and to others, it is perfectly proper and legal and wise for you to do it.

The Chairman: So far as I can judge, the information that you have suggested is everything that a State Legislature could require of a corporation chartered by the State. Is it your conception of the legal situation that Congress has the same power with reference to requiring reports from corporations engaged in interstate commerce that a State has in relation to a State corporation that it charters?

Mr. Jenks: No, I think not; but I think there is this distinction that should be made in connection with what I have just said; and that is that Congress, in my judgment, does have the power to prescribe the conditions. You will remember that this is not a compulsory thing; this is a permissive thing. It simply says: "If you, the corporation, wish to do this interstate commerce"—and they are not restricting it to that, either—"and wish, furthermore, to get special privileges that we are willing to grant under certain conditions, you may have those privileges if you willingly come and give us this information."

Mr. Low called attention to a bill introduced in 1905 by Mr. Littlefield calling for substantially similar information. Commenting upon it Mr. Littlefield said that the time he introduced the bill he had had no doubt of its propriety, but the subsequent decision in the Howard case, which expressly held that you cannot regulate corporations because they are engaged in interstate commerce, but only as to the things which relate to interstate commerce, had modified his views.

Mr. Washburn: Why is it important to inquire into the individual financial condition of each one of the corporations when the only act of theirs on which the Sherman act can operate is the combination itself?

Mr. Jenks: In a great many cases it is not important either one way or the other; but on the other hand it might also be that these corporations are such that by virtue of this agreement they are acquiring a monopolistic power, and under these circumstances it is of extreme importance that the Government should know how they are put together, how they are getting that monopolistic power, and how they are exercising it.

Mr. Sterling: If that be true, can there be any serious question, then, about the Federal Government having power to impose any condition on interstate corporations that will enable it to intelligently regulate the commerce in which they are engaged?

Mr. Jenks: That was the contention that I myself was making, exactly as you are stating it; but it is a little bit different from saying that the Congress has the same power over interstate commerce and over corporations that may be engaged in interstate commerce, that the State Legislatures have over corporations engaged in intra-state commerce; and it was the distinction that I understood the Chairman was making. I myself intended to take, and I thought did take, exactly your position—that Congress could practically impose any conditions it pleased in reference to the regulation of interstate commerce; but not necessarily that it had the same power over corporations engaged in interstate commerce that the State had which itself created those corporations.

Mr. Malby: Professor, there cannot be any question but that in the case of a corporation which is created by a State itself, receiving its corporate existence and receiving all its rights and privileges from the State itself, that State may require from that corporation any kind of a report it pleases?

Mr. Jenks: Certainly.

Mr. Malby: But the distinction between that case and the one in which the corporation is engaged in interstate commerce, where the charter in every case is granted by a statute, is that our inquiry, under the decisions of the Supreme Court, is limited to those acts which go exclusively to the interstate commerce.

Mr. Jenks: Provided you are compelling it. If, on the other hand, you wish to say: "If you will give us this still further information that we perhaps would not have the power to compel you to give, we will grant you certain other immunities and privileges," I conceive that you have the right to accept that.

Mr. Malby: Can we compel by indirection a corporation to furnish information which we could not compel it to furnish by direction?

Mr. Jenks: I believe that Congress does have a right to secure the public welfare, which in this case would be the securing of the information by offering certain privileges to those who wish to accept them. It is a very common and practically universal form of legislation in all the States and under all conditions everywhere.

This is not a compulsory act, it is a permissive act. These are certain things that are in the interest of the public that we would like to have carried out. We say to them, "If you will furnish this information, if you wish to come under this law, we will grant you certain immunities. You take your choice. It is perfectly immaterial."

The Chairman: Should we enact legislation to compel the production of information that is not Federal in its character? I will put it that way. That covers the whole ground. That is, should we, as a matter of policy, enact legislation, Professor, for the purpose of compelling the production of information that is not Federal in its character?

Mr. Jenks: Personally, I should be inclined to say that we ought not to compel the production of information that is not Federal in its character, but there is no compulsion here.

The Chairman: Do we not practically do it if we say that we will give the corporation immunity from crime if it will furnish it?

Mr. Jenks: Certainly; you grant the immunity provided they are willing to do that; and they take their choice. I do not think it is right to call that compulsion.

Mr. Low: Mr. Chairman, I do not think we do grant immunity from crime in the ordinary sense.

The Chairman: Why not?

Mr. Low: What we do say is: "Upon that condition you can ascertain what the attitude of the prosecuting arm of the Government is going to be—whether they are going to attack you for this thing which you have done or want to do, or whether they are not;" and that is all that the bill covers. This bill of ours does not change the legal status of any action done under the Sherman Anti-Trust Act, but it does say——

The Chairman: It does not change the legal status?

Mr. Low: I do not think so, of anything done.

The Chairman: Does it not make combinations reasonable that are now unreasonable under the strict construction of law? And if it does not, what does it accomplish?

Mr. Low: I think it simply gives an opportunity to the executive arm of the Government, represented by the Department of Commerce and Labor, to say whether it is going to attack that combination or not under the Sherman law. That is all it does; and it says that quickly, instead of leaving it uncertain for a long period of time. If, in the brief period that may be fixed by the bill, it does not say that the thing is in unreasonable restraint of trade, it can still attack at any time in the future if it changes its mind, if conditions show that it has been mistaken; but then it can only attack on the ground that the thing is in unreasonable restraint of trade.

April 6th, Afternoon Session.

Mr. Jenks continued his statement, with a consideration of the second part of the section which had to do with the registration of corporations and associations not for profit.

It was not, he said, the purpose of the committee to confine this to incorporated organizations, but that it should apply to all organizations whether incorporated or not.

The Chairman asked whether the power which was vested in the Commissioner of Corporations under the first section was executive or judicial power, and asked further whether it was competent for Congress by legislation to vest in the executive branch of the government any judicial powers.

Mr. Jenks: I am very familiar with the question and also with the difficulty. The difficulty of the answer comes largely on this account, that both those words, executive and judicial, are used with a great variety and number of shades of meaning. If I say yes, you can cite any number of examples where we have separated the powers, and if I say no, you can cite any number of instances where you know perfectly well both powers are exercised by the same body or person.

Speaking on the reasons for not requiring corporations and associations not for profit to file their contracts and agreements, Mr. Jenks said:

The agreements that are made primarily by the trades unions, trade agreements, if you like, between them and their employers, the agreements that they make among themselves, so far as their organization is concerned, are agreements that have to do primarily with them as individuals, with their liberty to act as individuals, and not primarily with property. It seems, therefore, that it is entirely proper and right to make a distinction between organizations that may be attempting, we will say, to monopolize capital, to monopolize the power of capital in many ways, and those that are dealing with their power to work, simply; with their personal power and not with the power to handle capital of others.

One class of corporations is conducted for profit and has capital stock, and the other is not for profit, and it has no capital stock. This second class of corporations or associations comprise various kinds. There are some such examples as the Associated Press, which furnishes a convenient way of handling their business all the way through, and there are others, such as are represented by these gentlemen here to-day, which are organized for carrying into effect objects in which they are interested, which are not for profit, directly. There are others, like the farmers' organizations, for carrying on the work that they think is wise and just, and to promote their legitimate interests, and there are several others, such as I am connected with. All of these are not for profit.

The Chairman: I understood you to say that there is a difference in the kind or effect of the contract. Will you give me an instance of a contract of the kind you mention?

Mr. Jenks: I should say contracts made between employers and employes with reference to conditions of labor and wages of labor, and matters of that kind, even though those contracts do affect, more or less directly—rather less directly than more—interstate commerce, are contracts that are so essentially different in their nature that they should be treated in a different way from those between two or three different railroads or two or three great manufacturing establishments with reference to the limitation that they shall place upon their output, or the way that they shall distribute their goods among the different states.

I wish to take up section 7 with reference to triple damages. I had supposed that when the Sherman act was passed, that provision for triple damages was imposed largely on account of the popular apprehension that there was very grave danger, such as there is in connection with these great corporations, and it was thought that if threefold damages were imposed, it would tend to check the growth of these great corporations. The suggestion was made to remove this provision for triple damages and simply provide for recovery of the damages sustained and the costs of suit, including a reasonable attorney's fee. This takes away punitive damages. Such damages are imposed, of course, under certain circumstances, under the common law; but there is then some case of flagrant or outrageous fraud, or there is some apparent intent on the part of the person who is committing the injury to hurt, beyond a mere matter of money damage, the person that is damaged.

The Chairman: Is it not predicated in the main on the theory that the injury is malicious?

Mr. Jenks: That is it, that the injury is malicious. Now, so far as the provision here is concerned, I will say that generally speaking the imposition of punitive damages under ordinary circumstances where there is no malicious intent would be wrong, and is not good policy. Now, under the Sherman law people may make contracts, usually in their own interests, with no particular thought of hurting anybody else, and at the same time they may hurt other people, and if so they would be mulcted in triple damages. It seems to me they should pay the actual damages, but there is no reason why they should have punitive damages imposed upon them. There might be cases where that is true, but ordinarily not.

The Chairman: Are you in favor of their being allowed to conspire and combine, to secure their rights, to destroy the business of another person?

Mr. Jenks: I am not in favor of their being allowed to conspire. Not to combine, if the word "combine" is to be pushed to the extent of injuring other people wilfully. It is possible that in such a case as the Danbury hat case the primary purpose of the laborers was not a malicious injury of others, but the securing of their own rights, even though the injury was done. With the same frankness, I think that the employers, in the action they take in many cases, are simply endeavoring to obtain their own ends and to secure their own rights, even though there may be irreparable and very great injury done to the laborers. I think we ought to recognize in these disputes between employers and employes that there is often very great feeling. The prime purpose is to secure their own rights, and they are careless of the others. We ought to be rather cautious about imputing malicious intent to either side.

The question was asked as to the reasons for striking out the provision for triple damages. On behalf of the committee, Mr. Jenks expressed the opinion that these triple damages might be an inducement to vexatious litigation. The opponents of the bill felt that without the triple damages private individuals would not be moved to secure the enforcement of the law, because of the costs involved. With the triple damages they had ample margin to pay the considerable costs of litigation in suits of this character. On behalf of the committee it was urged that simple damages were a reversion to the rules of the common law. While it was pointed out that the common law admitted punitive damages, it was contended that such punitive damages were only allowed in exceptional cases not parallel to the case in point.

In explanation of the so-called immunity provisions of the bill, Mr. Jenks said that it was very desirable at the present time to remove from business men the apprehension of attack under this Sherman act for agreements that they might have made or might make, that they thought to be reasonable. So the provision has been made here that no suit or prosecution under the first six sections of the act would be begun under any contract or combination, unless the same be in restraint of trade. We felt that so far as the Federal government itself was concerned, that should take effect immediately, so that unless the suits had been begun the people might feel that any contracts they might have made before, even though they were in restraint of trade, if they were reasonable, should stand. So far as private individuals were concerned, we felt that the situation was quite different. Private individuals may have been injured, and they should have the right to recover damages for an injury. Moreover, it is quite probable that it would be unconstitutional, even if it were desirable to attempt to cut off the right of private individuals from getting damages, now. As I say, it was not considered desirable to do that anyway, and it would have been unconstitutional, probably, if it had been attempted. It was thought the wise thing to do to provide a statute of limitations which might be short, so that there might not be too much apprehension or too long a time for attacks along this line, but at the same time long enough so that all just causes could be brought and pushed through to a conclusion; so that a provision was made that if this act was passed the Federal government should not bring any suits unless they were prepared to prove that the contracts or agreements were unreasonable. So far as private contracts and agreements were concerned, they could bring suit in a year. I think that covers practically all of the points in the bill. We recognize fully that the bill is by no means a perfect bill. A great many of us have been working on it, and we believed that it was the best we could do. We believe that it is a practicable bill, although there may be minor amendments to be made here. We have tried to provide for what is reasonable and practicable, to secure a considerable amount of publicity, the more the better, because we think that is a remedial action, and we do believe that the amendments of this nature to the Sherman act are very sadly needed, and there is perhaps no other action which could be taken by Congress which would so greatly improve business conditions at the present time as this. We think, in addition to that, that it would be a bill that would promote justice among business men and workingmen.

A discussion at some length ensued as to whether under the bill unincorporated bodies which were registered were obliged to file with the Commissioner of Corporations copies of their agreements, thereby submitting to that officer the question of the reasonableness of such agreements. It was pointed out that there was no such obligation. There was a privilege to file such agreements in case the association so desired, in which case they submitted themselves to the rules set forth in the bill. But there is no intention in the bill to create a compulsory record of such agreements.

MR. SAMUEL GOMPERS made a further statement, saying:

I want just to call attention to the fact that as one of the representatives of the labor organizations who have appeared before the committee, I have stated that we desired the clear distinction made as between the organizations that have capital stock and are organized for profit, the organizations of the men who deal in products of labor and the distribution of those products, and the other associations of men and women who own and control no wealth, who are organized not for profit, those associations which have no capital stock, and whose only object in association is the protection of themselves, their lives, their labor power. That distinction should be clearly and distinctively drawn; and I said that our position is that in so far as the bill applies to the corporations and associations and common carriers, the associations and corporations that deal in the products of labor and distribute the products of labor, the bill is necessary. And so far I am in hearty accord with its purpose. In so far as it refers to the labor organizations which you refer to as associations not for profit, and without capital stock, I ask that those features be entirely eliminated from the bill, and the amendments which I submitted to the committee take the place of them throughout.

In so far as the restraints of trade are concerned, if I may answer for myself in regard to that, it may be suitable to the corporations for profit and owning capital stock. It is unsuitable to the labor organizations, for this reason if for no other, that it would immediately establish compulsory arbitration. The decision of the United States Supreme Court held that the labor organizations come under the provisions of the Sherman anti-trust act. If, then, the contracts and agreements and the activities of the labor organizations are subject to the review of either the Commissioner of Corporations or the courts as to the reasonableness or the unreasonableness of an agreement, the matter assumes immediately the position of compulsory arbitration. The Commissioner determines the reasonableness or unreasonableness of an agreement with employers, and finally becomes the arbiter of what the conditions shall be.

I want to present just a thought or two upon the subject of the boycott. May I say that I do not believe that I would intentionally hurt any man or woman, or child, or beast, or reptile, only in self-defense. I say that so that you may understand that I am not one of those men who run amuck, and aim to hurt and injure. I know this, that never in my whole life, my private life, or in connection with the labor movement, has any act of mine been governed and controlled or initiated from motives of malice, nor has personal feeling entered into it. I believe in the boycott. I believe in the right of the boycott.

After all, what is the boycott, not in the sense in which some people construe it, of personal attack, of unlawful threats, of intimidation of a character that is unlawful and improper. But the threat to do a certain thing is perfectly proper to indulge in if the doing of the thing itself is not improper nor unlawful. I hold that no man has any vested right in my patronage or the patronage of any other man, and when I speak of the boycott I speak of it exclusively in the sense of the bestowal or the withholding of patronage. No man has any vested right in the patronage of another.

There are conceptions to-day as to the rights of men that were wholly different in time gone by. The conception of the rights of men will be broader as time goes on. At one time a strike was a criminal act, punishable by imprisonment, by branding, by hanging. A different concept has come over the minds of people as time went on, and it will so continne. The workingmen of to-day are, generally speaking, in the enjoyment of greater rights than they had twenty, fifty or one hundred or more years back. Perhaps the decision of the Supreme Court of the United States has thrown them back; and it undoubtedly has. It has shorn from them rights which we believed were ours. But the Supreme Court decisions have been changed and modified, and I am in hopes; I am optimistic. I not only hope, but I firmly believe, I am firmly persuaded and convinced, that the normal activities of the working people of our country are going to be accorded to them, and to be regarded as absolutely normal and right. There is no purpose in the labor organizations either to destroy industry or commerce, not even of one man. It is a mistake to believe that our purposes are different. If Professor Jenks's construction of the Hepburn bill is correct we shall find it necessary to have introduced in Congress the amendment to the Sherman Anti-Trust law, which I submitted Saturday, as a separate bill.

After arrangements had been made for a further meeting of the committee in order to hear the objectors to the bill, MR. GEORGE F. MONAHAN, of Detroit, made the following statement:

Mr. Chairman and Gentlemen: I desire simply to be recorded as being here representing the National Founders' Association. The organization itself comprises some 500 firms and industries located in the various parts of the United States, and employs in various capacities considerably over a quarter of a million of men. We feel very seriously on the subject of this measure, and although I came prepared with a brief and ready to discuss the legal features of the matter somewhat at length, I believe my mission may be at least partially completed at this time, if further time is not afforded a week from now for further discussion of this matter, by stating in brief the proposition involved. Believing as we do that the Loewe decision, recently rendered by the Supreme Court of the United States, is in consonance with what the law should be, and that the law as it now is, under the Sherman Anti-Trust act, in so far as it relates to labor unions, is just precisely what is necessary, we emphatically protest before this committee against any modification of that law, such as is contemplated in this act. We believe, as do the gentlemen who have spoken in reference to this matter and their desire to still continue the opposition that they feel against the boycott, that their desire was not to diminish the force of this bill, so far as the boycott is concerned. We believe that their opposition in that regard, though not well taken under the verbiage which they have asked, is sincere. We believe, however, that the bill, as it is, is a substantial modification of the law as it is, and that it will afford to labor rights which labor should not have, particularly with reference to the so-called secondary boycott.

The committee then adjourned until Thursday, April 16.

The text of the bill follows:

H. R. 19745
IN THE HOUSE OF REPRESENTATIVES
March 23, 1908.

Mr. Hepburn introduced the following bill, which was referred to the Committee on the Judiciary and ordered to be printed:

A BILL

TO regulate commerce among the several States or with foreign nations, and to amend the act approved July second, eighteen hundred and ninety, entitled "An act to protect trade and commerce against unlawful restraints and monopolies."

Be it enacted by the Senate and House of Representatives of the United States of America in Congress assembled,

That section seven of the act approved July second, eighteen hundred and ninety, entitled "an act to protect trade and commerce against unlawful restraints and monopolies" be, and the same is hereby amended so as to read as follows:

"Sec. 7. That any person who shall be injured in his business or property by any other person or corporation by reason of anything forbidden or declared to be unlawful by this act may sue therefor in any circuit court of the United States in the district in which the defendant resides or is found, without respect to the amount in controversy, and shall recover the damages by him sustained and the costs of suit, including a reasonable attorney's fee."

Sec. 2. That in any suit for damages under section seven of the said act approved July second, eighteen hundred and ninety, based upon a right of action accruing prior to the passage of this act, the plaintiff shall be entitled to recover only the damages by him sustained and the costs of suit, including a reasonable attorney's fee; and no suit for damages under said section seven of the said act, based upon a right of action accruing prior to the passage of this act, shall be maintained unless the same shall be commenced within one year after the passage of this act.

Sec. 3. Nothing in said act approved July second, eighteen hundred and ninety, or in this act, is intended, nor shall any provision thereof hereafter be enforced, so as to interfere with or to restrict any right of employees to strike for any purpose not unlawful at common law, or to combine or to contract with each other or with employers for the purpose of obtaining from employers peaceably or by any means not unlawful at common law satisfactory terms for their labor or satisfactory conditions of employment, or so as to interfere with or to restrict any right of employers for any purpose not unlawful at common law to discharge all or any of their employees or to combine or to contract with each other or with employees for the purpose of obtaining labor on satisfactory terms peaceably or by any means not unlawful at common law.

Sec. 4. That the said act approved July second, eighteen hundred and ninety, is hereby further amended by adding at the end of said act the following sections:

Sec. 9. That any corporation or association which may be subject to this act, but not subject to the act approved February fourth, eighteen hundred and eighty-seven, entitled "An act to regulate commerce," or the acts amendatory thereof or supplemental thereto, shall be entitled to the benefits and immunities in this act hereinafter given, if and when it shall register as herein provided, and shall comply with the requirements of this act, hereinafter set forth, but not otherwise.

"Such registration, by a corporation or association for profit, and having capital stock, may be effected by filing with the Commissioner of Corporations a written application therefor, together with a written statement setting forth such information concerning the organization of such corporation or association, its financial condition, its interstate contracts, and its corporate proceedings, as may be prescribed by general regulations from time to time to be made by the President pursuant to this act; and such registration by a corporation or association not for profit and without capital stock may be effected by filing with the Commissioner of Corporations a written application therefor, together with a written statement setting forth, first, its charter or agreement of association and by-laws; second, the place of its principal office, and, third, the names of its directors or managing officers and standing committees, if any, with their residences.

"Thereupon the Commissioner of Corporations shall register such corporation or association under this act. In case any corporation or association so registered shall refuse or shall fail at any time to file the statements or to give the information required under this act, or to comply with the requirements of this act, or in case information furnished by it shall be false in any material particular, the Commissioner of Corporations shall have power to cancel the registration of such corporation or association after thirty days' notice in writing to such corporation or association. Any corporation or association aggrieved by such action of the Commissioner of Corporations may apply to the Supreme Court of the District of Columbia, in a suit or proceeding in equity, for review of such action and such relief in the premises as may be proper, and said court shall have jurisdiction to hear and determine such application and to affirm, reverse or modify such action of said Commissioner, subject to appeal as in other causes in equity.

"Sec. 10. That the President shall have power to make, alter and revoke, and from time to time, in his discretion, he shall make, alter and revoke, regulations prescribing what facts shall be set forth in the statements to be filed with the Commissioner of Corporations by corporations and associations for profit and having capital stock applying for registration under this act, and what information thereafter shall be furnished by such corporations and associations so registered, and he may prescribe the manner of registration and of cancellation of registration.

"Nothing in this act shall require the filing of contracts or agreements of corporations or associations not for profit or without capital stock, and such corporations and associations while registered hereunder, and the members thereof, shall be entitled to all the benefits and immunities given by this act, excepting such as are given by section eleven and section twelve, without filing such contracts or agreements; but from time to time every such corporation or association shall file with the Commissioner of Corporations, when and as called for by him, a revised statement giving, as of a date specified by him, such information as is required to be given at the time of original registration under section nine of this act.

"Sec. 11. That any corporation or association registered under this act, and any person, not a common carrier under the provisions of said act approved February fourth, eighteen hundred and eighty-seven, or the acts amendatory thereof or supplemental thereto, being a party to a contract or combination hereafter made, other than a contract or combination with a common carrier filed under section twelve of this act, may file with the Commissioner of Corporations a copy thereof, if the same be in writing, or if not in writing, a statement setting forth the terms and conditions thereof, together with a notice that such filing is made for the purpose of obtaining the benefit of the provisions of this section.

No prosecution, suit or proceeding by the United States shall be begun under the first six sections of this act for or on account of any such contract or combination hereafter made of which a copy or written statement shall have been filed as aforesaid, or for or on account of any acts done in performance thereof by or in behalf of such a corporation, association or person, unless such contract or combination shall be in unreasonable restraint of trade or commerce as defined in section three of this act, or shall constitute a conspiracy in violation of section one or of section three of this act, or shall be in violation of section two of this act. If in the opinion of the Commissioner of Corporations any such contract or combination, of which a copy or a written statement shall have been filed as aforesaid shall be in unreasonable restraint of trade or commerce as defined in section three of this act, or shall constitute a conspiracy in violation of section one or of section three of this act, or shall be in violation of section two of this act, said Commissioner shall be authorized and empowered and it shall be his duty to enter an order to that effect, which order shall set forth briefly the grounds upon which it is based. Any such order may be made by the Commissioner upon his own motion and without notice or hearing within thirty days from the date of the filing of such contract or written statement. After the expiration of such thirty days no such order shall be made by the Commissioner except after notice to the party or parties who filed such contract or written statement and after giving such party or parties an opportunity to be heard, and such order shall take effect upon a date therein to be specified not less than ten days after the filing thereof, but any person aggrieved by such action of the Commissioner of Corporations, or the United States in case of his non-action, may apply to the Interstate Commerce Commission for a rehearing of the case, and said Commission (with which the Commissioner of Corporations is hereby authorized to sit for the purpose of such rehearing with the powers and duties of a member) is hereby authorized and directed after due motion to rehear such case and thereupon to enter such order in the case as seems to it proper, subject as in other instances to appeal to the courts as hereinafter provided. If any party or parties to any such contract or combination of which a copy or a written statement shall have been filed as aforesaid shall do any act in performance of such contract or in pursuance of such combination after the Commissioner of Corporations or the Interstate Commerce Commission shall have entered an order as aforesaid, such party or parties, unless such order of the Commissioner on the rehearing hereinbefore provided shall have been replaced by a new order or such order shall have been suspended or set aside by order of the court as herein provided, shall be deemed guilty of a misdemeanor and on conviction thereof shall be punished by fine not exceeding five thousand dollars or by imprisonment not exceeding one year, or both said punishments; and the United States may institute and maintain proceedings in equity under section four of this act to prevent and restrain the performance of such contract and the continuance of such combination and any action pursuant thereto in violation of this act.

No corporation or association authorized to register under section nine of this act shall be entitled to the benefit of this section if it shall have failed so to register or if the registration of such corporation or association shall have been cancelled; and the United States may institute, maintain or prosecute a suit, proceeding or prosecution under the first six sections of said act for or on account of any such contract or combination hereafter made, of which a copy or written statement shall not have been filed as aforesaid, or as to which an order shall have been entered as above provided.

Any party affected by any such order entered by the Commission may institute and maintain a suit to enjoin, set aside, annul or suspend such order in the Supreme Court of the District of Columbia, and jurisdiction is hereby given to such Court to hear and determine such suits and to grant such relief; but no interlocutory order or, decree, enjoining, setting aside, annulling or suspending any such order of the Commission shall be granted except after not less than five days' notice to the Commission. The provisions of "An Act to expedite the hearing and determination of suits in equity, and so forth," approved February eleventh, nineteen hundred and three, shall be, and are hereby, made applicable to all such suits, including the hearing on an application for a preliminary injunction. An appeal my be taken from any interlocutory order or decree granting or continuing an injunction in any suit, but shall lie only to the Supreme Court of the United States: Provided, That the appeal must be taken within thirty days from the entry of such order or decree, and it shall take precedence in the Appellate Court over all other causes, except causes of like character and criminal causes.

No corporation or association for profit or having capital stock, and registered under this Act, that hereafter shall make a combination or consolidation with any other corporation or association, shall be entitled to continue its registration under this Act, unless without delay it shall file with the Commissioner of Corporations, pursuant and subject to the provisions of this section, a statement setting forth the terms and conditions of such combination or consolidation, together with a notice as hereinabove provided.

Sec. 12. That any common carrier under the provisions of the said Act approved February fourth, eighteen hundred and eighty-seven, or the Acts amendatory thereof or supplemental thereto, being a party to a contract or combination in the nature of a traffic agreement, but not including pooling of freight or earnings hereafter made, as provided by Sec. 5 of said Act approved February fourth, eighteen hundred and eighty-seven, or any other party to such contract or combination, may file with the Interstate Commerce Commission a copy thereof, if the same be in writing, or if not in writing, a statement setting forth the terms and conditions thereof, together with a notice that such filing is made for the purpose of obtaining the benefit of the provisions of this section.

No prosecution, suit or proceeding by the United States shall be begun under the first six sections of this Act or on account of any such contract or combination hereafter made of which a copy or written statement shall have been filed as aforesaid, or for or on account of any acts done in performance thereof by or in behalf of such corporation, association or person, unless such contract or combination shall be in unreasonable restraint of trade or commence as defined in section three of this Act, or shall constitute a conspiracy in violation of section one or of section three of this Act, or shall be in violation of section two of this Act. If in the opinion of the Interstate Commerce Commission any such contract or combination of which a copy or a written statement shall have been filed as aforesaid shall be in unreasonable restraint of trade or commerce as defined in section three of this Act, or shall constitute a conspiracy in violation of section one or of section three of this Act, or shall be in violation of section two of this Act, said Commission shall be authorized and empowered and it shall be its duty to enter an order to that effect, which order shall set forth briefly the grounds upon which it is based. Any such order may be made by the Commission, upon its own motion and without notice or hearing, within thirty days from the date of the filing of such contract or written statement. After the expiration of such thirty days no such order shall be made by the Commission except after notice to the party or parties who filed such contract or written statement and after giving such party or parties an opportunity to be heard, and such order shall take effect upon a date therein to be specified not less than ten days after the filing the thereof; but any person aggrieved by such action of the Interstate Commerce Commission, or the United States in case of its non-action, may apply to the Supreme Court of the District of Columbia for review of the case; and said Court is hereby authorized and directed to hear and determine such application and to affirm, reverse or modify such action, or in case of its failure to act to enter such order in the case as seems to it proper, subject as in other instances to the provisions of section eleven and to appeal to the Supreme Court of the United States as herein provided.

If any party or parties to any such contract or combination of which a copy or a written statement shall have been filed as aforesaid shall do any act in performance of such contract or in pursuance of such combination after the Interstate Commerce Commission shall have entered an order as aforesaid, such party or parties, unless such order of the Commission shall have been enjoined, annulled or suspended by a decree or order of a Court as herein provided, shall be deemed guilty of a misdemeanor and on conviction thereof shall be punished by fine not exceeding five thousand dollars or by imprisonment not exceeding one year, or both said punishments in the discretion of the Courts; and the United States may institute and maintain proceedings in equity under section four of this act to prevent and restrain the performance of such contract and the continuance of such combination and any action pursuant thereto in violation of this Act.

No corporation or association authorized to register under section nine of this Act shall be entitled to the benefits of this section if it shall have failed so to register, or if the registration of such corporation or association shall have been cancelled; and the United States may institute, maintain or prosecute a suit, proceeding or prosecution under the first six sections of said Act for or on account of any such contract or combination hereafter made, of which a copy or written statement shall not have been filed as aforesaid, or as to which an order shall have been entered as above provided.

Sec. 5. That no suit or prosecution by the United States under the first six sections of the said Act approved July second, eighteen hundred and ninety, shall hereafter be begun for or on account of any contract or combination made prior to the passage of this Act, or any action thereunder, unless the same be in unreasonable restraint of trade or commerce among the several States or with foreign nations; and no suit or prosecution by the United States under the first six sections of the said Act approved July second, eighteen hundred and ninety, shall be begun after one year from the passage of this Act for or on account of any contract or combination made prior to the passage of this Act, or any action thereunder; but no corporation or association authorized to register under section nine of the said Act approved July second, eighteen hundred and ninety, as amended, shall be entitled to the benefit of the provisions of this section, if it shall have failed so to register, or if the registration of such corporation or association shall have been cancelled before the expiration of one year after such registration, exclusive of period, if any, during which such cancellation shall have been stayed by an order of the Interstate Commerce Commission or an order or decree of court subsequently vacated or set aside. Anything herein contained to the contrary notwithstanding, all actions and proceedings now or heretofore, pending under or by virtue of any provisions of the said Act approved July second, eighteen hundred and ninety, may be prosecuted and may be defended to final effect; and all judgments and decrees heretofore or hereafter made in any such actions or proceedings my be enforced in the same manner as though this Act had not been passed.

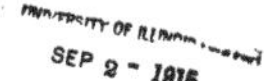

The National Civic Federation Review

II. NEW YORK, MARCH, 1909. No. 6

AN EVENT TRULY AMERICAN IN SPIRIT

NINTH ANNUAL DINNER OF THE NATIONAL CIVIC FEDERATION—NINE HUNDRED GUESTS AT THE HOTEL ASTOR JOIN IN A MANIFESTATION OF CIVIC FRATERNITY

most striking feature of the ninth annual nner of the National Civic Federation, ecember 15th, 1908, was the presence of -elect and Mrs. Taft as the guests of The occasion was one of special interest ration, one long to be remembered by who had the good fortune to be present. undred guests had assembled in the banquet hall when the first bars of "Hail to the Chief," played by the orchestra, announced the entrance of Mr. and Mrs. Taft. There was spontaneous and hearty applause as the man who is to stand at the nation's head during the next four years walked to his place, escorted by Mr. John Hays Hammond, chairman of the Reception Committee. The entire assembly rose and gave hearty greeting, and finally, as a conclusion to its enthusiastic reception of the guests of honor, sang "America," accompanying the music played by the orchestra.

The scene was brilliant with color, light and animation, when, the ovation ended, the guests sat down to the tables which filled the spacious rooms. There was scarcely space for passage between the decorated tables, but the crowding together only

HON. WILLIAM HOWARD TAFT,
irman Public Employes' Committee of the Welfare Department, The National Civic Federation.

MRS. WILLIAM HOWARD TAFT,
Chairman Committee on Welfare Work for Government Employes of the Woman's Department, The National Civic Federation.

its financial condition, its interstate contracts, and its corporate proceedings, as may be prescribed by general regulations from time to time to be made by the President pursuant to this act; and such registration by a corporation or association not for profit and without capital stock may be effected by filing with the Commissioner of Corporations a written application therefor, together with a written statement setting forth, first, its charter or agreement of association and by-laws; second, the place of its principal office, and, third, the names of its directors or managing officers and standing committees, if any, with their residences.

"Thereupon the Commissioner of Corporations shall register such corporation or association under this act. In case any corporation or association so registered shall refuse or shall fail at any time to file the statements or to give the information required under this act, or to comply with the requirements of this act, or in case information furnished by it shall be false in any material particular, the Commissioner of Corporations shall have power to cancel the registration of such corporation or association after thirty days' notice in writing to such corporation or association. Any corporation or association aggrieved by such action of the Commissioner of Corporations may apply to the Supreme Court of the District of Columbia, in a suit or proceeding in equity, for review of such action and such relief in the premises as may be proper, and said court shall have jurisdiction to hear and determine such application and to affirm, reverse or modify such action of said Commissioner, subject to appeal as in other causes in equity.

"Sec. 10. That the President shall have power to make, alter and revoke, and from time to time, in his discretion, he shall make, alter and revoke, regulations prescribing what facts shall be set forth in the statements to be filed with the Commissioner of Corporations by corporations and associations for profit and having capital stock applying for registration under this act, and what information thereafter shall be furnished by such corporations and associations so registered, and he may prescribe the manner of registration and of cancellation of registration.

"Nothing in this act shall require the filing of contracts or agreements of corporations or associations not for profit or without capital stock, and such corporations and associations while registered hereunder, and the members thereof, shall be entitled to all the benefits and immunities given by this act, excepting such as are given by section eleven and section twelve, without filing such contracts or agreements; but from time to time every such corporation or association shall file with the Commissioner of Corporations, when and as called for by him, a revised statement giving, as of a date specified by him, such information as is required to be given at the time of original registration under section nine of this act.

"Sec. 11. That any corporation or association registered under this act, and any person, not a common carrier under the provisions of said act approved February fourth, eighteen hundred and eighty-seven, or the acts amendatory thereof or supplemental thereto, being a party to a contract or combination hereafter made, other than a contract or combination with a common carrier filed under section twelve of this act, may file with the Commissioner of Corporations a copy thereof, if the same be in writing, or if not in writing, a statement setting forth the terms and conditions thereof, together with a notice that such filing is made for the purpose of obtaining the benefit of the provisions of this section.

No prosecution, suit or proceeding by the United States shall be begun under the first six sections of this act for or on account of any such contract or combination hereafter made of which a copy or written statement shall have been filed as aforesaid, or for or on account of any acts done in performance thereof by or in behalf of such a corporation, association or person, unless such contract or combination shall be in unreasonable restraint of trade or commerce as defined in section three of this act, or shall constitute a conspiracy in violation of section one or of section three of this act, or shall be in violation of section two of this act. If in the opinion of the Commissioner of Corporations any such contract or combination, of which a copy or a written statement shall have been filed as aforesaid shall be in unreasonable restraint of trade or commerce as defined in section three of this act, or shall constitute a conspiracy in violation of section one or of section three of this act, or shall be in violation of section two of this act, said Commissioner shall be authorized and empowered and it shall be his duty to enter an order to that effect, which order shall set forth briefly the grounds upon which it is based. Any such order may be made by the Commissioner upon his own motion and without notice or hearing within thirty days from the date of the filing of such contract or written statement. After the expiration of such thirty days no such order shall be made by the Commissioner except after notice to the party or parties who filed such contract or written statement and after giving such party or parties an opportunity to be heard, and such order shall take effect upon a date therein to be specified not less than ten days after the filing thereof, but any person aggrieved by such action of the Commissioner of Corporations, or the United States in case of his non-action, may apply to the Interstate Commerce Commission for a rehearing of the case, and said Commission (with which the Commissioner of Corporations is hereby authorized to sit for the purpose of such rehearing with the powers and duties of a member) is hereby authorized and directed after due motion to rehear such case and thereupon to enter such order in the case as seems to it proper, subject as in other instances to appeal to the courts as hereinafter provided. If any party or parties to any such contract or combination of which a copy or a written statement shall have been filed as aforesaid shall do any act in performance of such contract or in pursuance of such combination after the Commissioner of Corporations or the Interstate Commerce Commission shall have entered an order as aforesaid, such party or parties, unless such order of the Commissioner on the rehearing hereinbefore provided shall have been replaced by a new order or such order shall have been suspended or set aside by order of the court as herein provided, shall be deemed guilty of a misdemeanor and on conviction thereof shall be punished by fine not exceeding five thousand dollars or by imprisonment not exceeding one year, or both said punishments; and the United States may institute and maintain proceedings in equity under section four of this act to prevent and restrain the performance of such contract and the continuance of such combination and any action pursuant thereto in violation of this act.

No corporation or association authorized to register under section nine of this act shall be entitled to the benefit of this section if it shall have failed so to register or if the registration of such corporation or association shall have been cancelled; and the United States may institute, maintain or prosecute a suit, proceeding or prosecution under the first six sections of said act for or on account of any such contract or combination hereafter made, of which a copy or written statement shall not have been filed as aforesaid, or as to which an order shall have been entered as above provided.

Any party affected by any such order entered by the Commission may institute and maintain a suit to enjoin, set aside, annul or suspend such order in the Supreme Court of the District of Columbia, and jurisdiction is hereby given to such Court to hear and determine such suits and to grant such relief; but no interlocutory order or, decree, enjoining, setting aside, annulling or suspending any such order of the Commission shall be granted except after not less than five days' notice to the Commission. The provisions of "An Act to expedite the hearing and determination of suits in equity, and so forth," approved February eleventh, nineteen hundred and three, shall be, and are hereby, made applicable to all such suits, including the hearing on an application for a preliminary injunction. An appeal my be taken from any interlocutory order or decree granting or continuing an injunction in any suit, but shall lie only to the Supreme Court of the United States: Provided, That the appeal must be taken within thirty days from the entry of such order or decree, and it shall take precedence in the Appellate Court over all other causes, except causes of like character and criminal causes.

No corporation or association for profit or having capital stock, and registered under this Act, that hereafter shall make a combination or consolidation with any other corporation or association, shall be entitled to continue its registration under this Act, unless without delay it shall file with the Commissioner of Corporations, pursuant and subject to the provisions of this section, a statement setting forth the terms and conditions of such combination or consolidation, together with a notice as hereinabove provided.

Sec. 12. That any common carrier under the provisions of the said Act approved February fourth, eighteen hundred and eighty-seven, or the Acts amendatory thereof or supplemental thereto, being a party to a contract or combination in the nature of a traffic agreement, but not including pooling of freight or earnings hereafter made, as provided by Sec. 5 of said Act approved February fourth, eighteen hundred and eighty-seven, or any other party to such contract or combination, may file with the Interstate Commerce Commission a copy thereof, if the same be in writing, or if not in writing, a statement setting forth the terms and conditions thereof, together with a notice that such filing is made for the purpose of obtaining the benefit of the provisions of this section.

No prosecution, suit or proceeding by the United States shall be begun under the first six sections of this Act or on account of any such contract or combination hereafter made of which a copy or written statement shall have been filed as aforesaid, or for or on account of any acts done in performance thereof by or in behalf of such corporation, association or person, unless such contract or combination
in unreasonable restraint of trade or comı
defined in section three of this Act, or sha
tute a conspiracy in violation of section
of section three of this Act, or shall be in
of section two of this Act. If in the o
the Interstate Commerce Commission any
tract or combination of which a copy or
statement shall have been filed as aforesaid
in unreasonable restraint of trade or com
defined in section three of this Act, or sha
tute a conspiracy in violation of section
section three of this Act, or shall be in
of section two of this Act, said Co
shall be authorized and empowered and it
its duty to enter an order to that effect, wh
shall set forth briefly the grounds upon wh
based. Any such order may be made by
mission, upon its own motion and without
hearing, within thirty days from the date
ing of such contract or written statement.
expiration of such thirty days no such or
be made by the Commission except after
the party or parties who filed such contrac
ten statement and after giving such party o
an opportunity to be heard, and such order s
effect upon a date therein to be specified
than ten days after the filing the thereof;
person aggrieved by such action of the I
Commerce Commission, or the United State
of its non-action, may apply to the Supreme
the District of Columbia for review of the c
said Court is hereby authorized and directe
and determine such application and to affirm
or modify such action, or in case of its failu
to enter such order in the case as seems to
subject as in other instances to the provisio
tion eleven and to appeal to the Supreme
the United States as herein provided.

If any party or parties to any such co
combination of which a copy or a written s
shall have been filed as aforesaid shall do
in performance of such contract or in purs
such combination after the Interstate C
Commission shall have entered an order as
such party or parties, unless such order of
mission shall have been enjoined, annulled
pended by a decree or order of a Court
provided, shall be deemed guilty of a misd
and on conviction thereof shall be punishe
not exceeding five thousand dollars or by
ment not exceeding one year, or both said
ments in the discretion of the Courts;
United States may institute and maintain
ings in equity under section four of this ac
vent and restrain the performance of such
and the continuance of such combination
action pursuant thereto in violation of this

No corporation or association authorized
ter under section nine of this Act shall be
to the benefits of this section if it shall ha
so to register, or if the registration of such
tion or association shall have been cancel
the United States may institute, maintain
cute a suit, proceeding or prosecution under
six sections of said Act for or on account of
contract or combination hereafter made, of
copy or written statement shall not have b
as aforesaid, or as to which an order shall h
entered as above provided.

Sec. 5. That no suit or prosecution by th
States under the first six sections of the
approved July second, eighteen hundred an
shall hereafter be begun for or on accoun
contract or combination made prior to the p
this Act, or any action thereunder, unless the
in unreasonable restraint of trade or commer
the several States or with foreign nations;
suit or prosecution by the United States unde
six sections of the said Act approved July
eighteen hundred and ninety, shall be begun
year from the passage of this Act for or on
of any contract or combination made prio
passage of this Act, or any action thereun
no corporation or association authorized to
under section nine of the said Act appro
second, eighteen hundred and ninety, as
shall be entitled to the benefit of the prov
this section, if it shall have failed so to regis
the registration of such corporation or as
shall have been cancelled before the expi
one year after such registration, exclusive o
if any, during which such cancellation sh
been stayed by an order of the Interstate C
Commission or an order or decree of cou
quently vacated or set aside. Anything he
tained to the contrary notwithstanding, al
and proceedings now or heretofore, pending
by virtue of any provisions of the said Act
July second, eighteen hundred and ninety,
prosecuted and may be defended to final ef
all judgments and decrees heretofore or
made in any such actions or proceedings m
forced in the same manner as though this
not been passed.

The National
Civic Federation Review

Vol. III. NEW YORK, MARCH, 1909. No. 6

AN EVENT TRULY AMERICAN IN SPIRIT

THE NINTH ANNUAL DINNER OF THE NATIONAL CIVIC FEDERATION—NINE HUNDRED GUESTS AT THE HOTEL ASTOR JOIN IN A MANIFESTATION OF CIVIC FRATERNITY

THE most striking feature of the ninth annual dinner of the National Civic Federation, December 15th, 1908, was the presence of President-elect and Mrs. Taft as the guests of honor. The occasion was one of special interest and inspiration, one long to be remembered by every one who had the good fortune to be present.

Nine hundred guests had assembled in the banquet hall when the first bars of "Hail to the Chief," played by the orchestra, announced the entrance of Mr. and Mrs. Taft. There was spontaneous and hearty applause as the man who is to stand at the nation's head during the next four years walked to his place, escorted by Mr. John Hays Hammond, chairman of the Reception Committee. The entire assembly rose and gave hearty greeting, and finally, as a conclusion to its enthusiastic reception of the guests of honor, sang "America," accompanying the music played by the orchestra.

The scene was brilliant with color, light and animation, when, the ovation ended, the guests sat down to the tables which filled the spacious rooms. There was scarcely space for passage between the decorated tables, but the crowding together only

HON. WILLIAM HOWARD TAFT,
Chairman Public Employes' Committee of the Welfare Department, The National Civic Federation.

MRS. WILLIAM HOWARD TAFT,
Chairman Committee on Welfare Work for Government Employes of the Woman's Department, The National Civic Federation.

made the occasion the more informal, the more interesting to the guests of the Civic Federation.

The New York daily press characterized the dinner as a "love feast between capital and labor," and the idea thus expressed was strongly impressed upon observant people among those present long before the speaking began. There was little to indicate to the eye of a stranger that in this gathering capitalists and masters of finance, women and men of the world of fashion, as well as scholars, writers, journalists, clergymen and other makers of public opinion sat at table with representatives of labor in its organized branches. It looked like any other great public dinner where men and women meet each other on grounds of good-fellowship and understanding, but when one knew the personalities of the guests who talked together around those tables it became far more interesting than any usual social gathering.

At the table presided over by President Low sat William Howard Taft, President-elect of the United States, and among those at the same table were Judge and Mrs. Alton B. Parker, Mr. Samuel Gompers, Mr. August Belmont, Mrs. Andrew Carnegie, Mr. A. B. Garretson, President of the Brotherhood of Railway Conductors, and Hon. Melville E. Ingalls, of the Big Four Railway.

Mr. Andrew Carnegie, Mrs. William Howard Taft, Mr. John Mitchell and Dr. Lyman Abbott formed a notable quartet at another table, where they sat with Mr. and Mrs. John Hays Hammond.

Mr. Herman Ridder, president of the American Newspaper Publishers' Association, and Mr. James M. Lynch, president of the International Typographical Union, with the president of the Paper Makers' Union, were in amiable conversation at one table; Mr. and Mrs. J. Borden Harriman, Mr. and Mrs. Philip Lydig, well-known members of the fashionable world, had with them Mr. James Duncan, general secretary of the Granite Cutters' International Association of America, and Mr. John Golden, president of the United Textile Workers.

Mr. George W. Perkins, a director of the United States Steel Corporation, and Mrs. Perkins were seated at the same table with Mr. P. J. McArdle, president of the Amalgamated Association of Iron, Steel and Tin Workers. While Mr. A. C. Bedford, director of the Standard Oil Company, had Mr. and Mrs. Timothy Healy for neighbors, Mr. Healy being president of the International Brotherhood of Stationary Firemen.

Mr. and Mrs. John D. Rockefeller, Jr., were at a table near that where Mr. and Mrs. Frank B. Kellogg sat with an interesting group of New York labor leaders, including President Coakley, of the Central Federated Union, and Mrs. Coakley, and the veteran labor leader Joseph R. Buchanan and Mrs. Buchanan. Mr. Kellogg had lately been prosecuting the Government's inquiry into the Standard Oil Company.

Mr. Samuel Untermeyer, the corporation lawyer, and his wife found it interesting to talk across the table with Mr. John D. Crimmins, of the Metropolitan Street Railway, and the Rev. Thomas R. Slicer, while Mr. Milo R. Maltbie, of the Public Service Commission, and Mr. Louis B. Gawtry, of the Consolidated Gas Company, were comfortably seated near each other and both were in most amiable state of mind, so far as could be observed.

Another interesting group was that including Mrs. Horace Brock, the newly elected chairman of the Woman's Department; Miss Anne Morgan, Miss Elizabeth Marbury; Mr. Daniel J. Keefe, of the Longshoremen's Union, and Charles A. Coffin, president of the General Electric Company; Mrs. Archibald Alexander, chairman of the New York and New Jersey Section Woman's Department; Mr. Henry W. Taft and Mr. Frank H. Hitchcock.

It was a gathering truly American in the best sense of the word. Representatives of every walk in active, healthful life, of every shade of political opinion were to be found among the men and women in the crowded rooms. The company seemed to enjoy the stimulating effects of the meeting between the ultra-fashionable and the radical, employers and employees, men of wealth and men of wages, social magnates, who touched elbows with the men of labor. Millionaires were in close contact with men who denounce from pulpit and forum the acceptance by religious or educational institutions of "tainted money," and the wives and daughters of the men of this representative company seemed to enjoy the occasion more than any one else.

Every part of the country was represented, and there were guests from across the seas. The presence of a Japanese lady in the full dress of her native country excited general interest. Major and Mrs. A. E. Piorkowski were guests, the Major being the well-known representative of the Krupp Company, of Germany. Another guest was Mr. Ernest Aves, special investigator on behalf of his Britannic Majesty's Government, Board of Trade, London, England.

At one table sat Mr. and Mrs. William H. Crocker and Mr. and Mrs. William H. Bourne, of California, and Mr. and Mrs. Arthur Lee, of West Virginia. From the South were Mr. and Mrs. B. Frank Mebane and Mrs. W. T. Harris, of North Carolina.

Among the guests from the Middle West was Mr. Charles S. Case, president of the Cleveland Chamber of Commerce. From Pennsylvania, Mr. J. W. Kinnear, representing the Pittsburg Chamber of Commerce, and Mr. Mahlon W. Kline, representing the Philadelphia Trades League. Mr. E. A. Filene, of the Boston Merchants' Association, was one of the New England guests.

New York City was represented by men and women of every interest in life—scholars, clergymen, lawyers, men of letters, journalists, men of business and affairs, women of fashion, as well as women thoroughly immersed in earnest, practical work. It was an assemblage unique in its make-up, and one as cordial and hospitable to ideas as could well be gathered together anywhere in the world.

The souvenirs of the occasion called forth much pleased comment. They were ice cream boxes, the covers of which, in raised figures of white upon red, presented a design by Homer Davenport, showing Uncle Sam supported by Labor and Capital.

The Reception Committee was as follows: John Hays Hammond, chairman; William R. Willcox, Benedict J. Greenhut, Marcus M. Marks, V. Everit Macy, John A. Sleicher, J. B. Reynolds, J. H. Stoddard, C. A. Griscom, Jr., E. T. Hargrove, C. U. Carpenter, John H. Stahl, Charles A. Moore, Jr., Rev. James E. Freeman, Orrin S. Goan, M. E. Ingalls, Jr., Rev. Charles Stelzle, Charles R. Towson, Thomas W. Slocum, Sereno S. Pratt, Otto M. Eidlitz, Timothy Healy, Herman Robinson, B. A. Larger, J. P. Archibald, A. J. Boulton, Joseph R. Buchanan, A. MacS. Gaillard, James P. Holland, William A. Coakley, Frank Cramer, E. A. Moffett, Joseph Healy, James Beers, J. J. Jennings, D. L. Cease.

The after-dinner speeches were all extemporaneous, and all were characterized by the utmost good feeling. The audience was quick to appreciate every point raised, receiving with laughter and applause especially the sallies of Mr. Carnegie and Mr. Taft, both of these being at their best in the informality of after-dinner talk, and both evidently feeling themselves to be among congenial and appreciative friends.

Mr. Low started the speech-making by proposing three cheers for Mr. and Mrs. Taft; these were given with a will. After the chairman had finished his address he introduced Mr. John Mitchell, who spoke upon the work of his department of the Federation. Mr. Mitchell was received with great enthusiasm by an assemblage which listened to him with much interest and apparent sympathy for most that he had to say.

Mr. Gompers aroused intense enthusiasm at the beginning of his talk, when he said, with convincing earnestness, "there might be left some impression upon the mind of some one that Mr. Taft is going to be less the President of Samuel Gompers than of any other man. Well, he won't be!" And when Mr. Taft's response to Mr. Gompers came the entire audience applauded vigorously, anticipating the gratifying reception, by the country, of the making of peace between the President-elect and his opponent during the recent campaign. Mr. Taft's words in announcing his attitude toward the labor leaders who had been against his election were cordial and convincing.

"It has been very pleasant," he said, "for me to meet here at this board Mr. Mitchell, Mr. Gompers and other labor leaders. I trust they know, and I know they do know, that whatever may have happened as regards any citizen of this country is all wiped out as far as my conduct as President of the United States is concerned, and I want to thank Mr. Gompers for his statement that I will be as much his President as that of any other man."

Mr. Melville E. Ingalls evoked considerable applause by his onslaught upon the Sherman law, and his expressions upon this subject were of special value because they brought forth an important declaration later, made by Mr. Taft in his address when he touched upon the Sherman law: "Probably it does need amendment," he said, "but even the amendments need not be extensive. It is more important to enforce it than to repeal it."

When Mr. Taft was introduced the entire audience arose and gave him a tremendous ovation. His speech was listened to with great attention and the assembly gave many expressions of pleasure and approval as he progressed, his opinion as to the Sherman law and its value being received with the most earnest applause that was given during the whole evening. He recommended to the Civic Federation the consideration of a National Employers' Liability law, and, as will be seen by those who read his entire speech, which follows, gave cogent reasons for his interest in such legislation. Something not to be overlooked is the opinion of the President-elect of the purpose of the Civic Federation, which he gave as follows:

"The Civic Federation, if I understand its purpose, is to enable those who represent labor and those who represent capital, and those who represent the public and are affected by the operation of both, to come together for the purpose of learning how they differ and where they agree." He continued: "Most of the quarrels, most of the controversies in the world, have arisen because the parties to them did not understand what the other one contended for, exactly; and where they meet on terms of equality for a discussion like this, and step by step can follow through the controversy, they usually find, or they frequently find, that they don't disagree at all, and they usually find that they agree on many points and differ on very few."

A complete report of the speeches of the evening follows:

MR. LOW'S OPENING REMARKS.

THE CHAIRMAN: Ladies and Gentlemen—The good wine at this banquet is going to be kept for the last. The National Civic Federation is greatly honored by the presence here to-night of the President-elect and Mrs. Taft. I propose three cheers for Mr. and Mrs. Taft.

I have never had a speech of mine punctuated by so much music before. The way in which you have greeted our distinguished guests confirms me in the hope that the honor they have conferred upon us this evening will be to every one of us what the touch of the sword is on the shoulder of the newly made knight, filling us with the inspiration of *noblesse oblige* to do more than ever to develop and maintain good relations between capital and labor, and in the whole domain of industry and commerce.

I suppose that there is no other country in the world where such a dinner as this could be held, at which workmen and their wives and capitalists and their wives mingle at every table throughout the room, with the ruler-that-is-to-be of the nation and his wife all meeting on the same democratic footing.

I emphasize this because if the National Civic Federation had done nothing more than this it would have justified its right to be; for, after all, it is in the power of the democratic spirit that the great economic questions of our time and country are to be met and settled; for that spirit, if I interpret it aright, recognizes freely the essential brotherhood of man, and it also believes with all its heart that nothing is ever settled until it is settled right, and that in every just settlement the interests of the weak as well as of the strong, the interests of the strong as well as of the weak must be considered.

The National Civic Federation differs from most organizations in one vital characteristic. Most organizations have a membership that believes not only in the common object, but which has similar interests. The National Civic Federation has a membership with a common object, certainly, but with very different interests, and that is why it can speak with such a unique voice on many of the great questions with which it concerns itself.

We all believe in industrial peace and industrial progress, but sometimes when we come to convert that general belief into the precise act we are reminded of the great Bunsby in "Dombey and Son," who, you will remember, always rounded up his opinions with this statement: "The point of this is in the application." We all agree on the general principles, but we do not always agree on the application of them, because it is clear that in every industrial and commercial enterprise there are three parties concerned—the employers, the workmen and the public; and in these days of vast enterprises, dominated everywhere and always by the spirit of organization, it is easy to understand how it is that each one of these parties is able to perceive its own interests a little more clearly than it can perceive the interests of others. But the National Civic Federation, by uniting in its membership representatives of all these parties, is in a position to do—and I think it does do—a kind of service that no other organization in the country is capable of doing, for it brings together for mutual discussion men of these different interests, so that each is able to see and to recognize the other's point of view.

My observation is that nothing removes prejudice about a man, in most instances, better than meeting him. I think nothing broadens a man's outlook more than hearing the other side presented with great ability; and I am very certain that nothing removes difficulties better than doing away with misunderstanding; and it is the aim of the National Civic Federation to accomplish those results.

We have at our general meetings, at our private conferences, almost in every case, men who are large employers of labor and men who are workmen, and men who, like myself, are neither one nor the other in the technical sense. If you have been to any of our meetings you must have noticed that every question is debated from the point of view of the employers, and also from the point of view of the workmen, and if anybody can be found who is neither one nor the other, from that point of view too.

The Civic Federation aims to bring men together who are tending toward misunderstanding and strife. We never try to impose our own views on anybody. We never try to bring about a conference between employer and employe unless we are asked to do so by one side or the other; and yet just because our membership is what it is we are often able to prevent industrial strife simply because we make it easy for contestants to meet each other.

I think I shall yield to the temptation of giving an illustration on that point, which I have used before, and which some of you may have heard, but it illustrates it so dramatically that I think it will bear repetition even for those who have heard it.

I was at my farm one day, in Westchester County, forty miles north of New York, when the telephone bell rang and I found myself talking with a banker in Philadelphia. He said to me: "Our firm are the Eastern representatives of the street railway system of a certain city on the Mississippi, and we are threatened with a strike; we are afraid the men will go out before anything can be done. Can you not telegraph Mr. Mahon, head of the Street Railway Men's Union, in Detroit, and ask him to delay matters?" I said: "What can I say? Can I say that you will arbitrate?" "Well," the banker replied, "I do not want to commit myself quite so far as that at the very outset." "Well," I said, "may I say that I think we can bring about arbitration?" He said: "Yes, you may say that." I telegraphed thereupon to Mr. Mahon. Being in the country, I called up the office of the Federation by telephone, and dictated a telegram, which was immediately sent to Detroit to Mr. Mahon, reading something like this: "I am very sorry to hear that a strike is probable in such and such a city. Can you not prevent it until the National Civic Federation has had a chance to see what it can do?" By evening I had his reply by telegram: "You may be sure that no strike will take place until the National Civic Federation has had a chance to see what it can do. If arbitration is offered on fair terms it will be accepted." I believe I had said: "I thought we could bring about arbitration." I want you to notice how frank that was—the cards were laid down on the table—"If arbitration is offered on fair terms it will be accepted." The next morning I called up my Philadelphia friend by telephone again, for he had given me his number, and I read him the reply from Detroit; and, after discussing with him, I sent a second dispatch that the people in the East would instruct their representatives in the West to confer with the men and to reach an agreement, if possible. If not, they would offer to arbitrate; and I added: "If you have any more trouble please let me know."

I never heard again from the subject until about two weeks later. I was in the office of the Civic Federation when I found a letter from both sides, thanking us for our good offices and saying that the trouble was entirely adjusted. Now, I think that is a pretty good story up to this point, and it interests me because you notice I never saw anybody. I talked through a "hole in the wall" once or twice, sent a telegram and received a telegram, but no human beings met. In that delicate adjustment it was simply the fact that the Civic Federation, as I said, is what it is—that it was made easy for those two people to get together; for they did not know how to get together, and when they got together the thing was settled. They settled it themselves.

Now, the other day that question came up the second time, and this time from the side of the men. Mr. Mahon telegraphed (we do not see people, I should say, in these modern days). Mr. Mahon telegraphed: "We are in trouble out here. Can you help us out as you did the other time?" I communicated with the banker at once by telegraph, of course, and the matter was adjusted again without the slightest embarrassment to anybody. So that twice in the same city the Civic Federation, simply by being what it is, prevented the disorganization of traffic that follows the tying up of a city railway system.

I shall not stop to-night to discuss the work of the Federation in all its branches. I simply want to emphasize as I close that which I suggested at the beginning—that it is the democratic spirit pervading the organization which finds expression in all its work; the notion that we Americans have that we can trust one another; that belief that is innate in us when we come right down to it that the other man means to be fair; and the sort of sneaking idea that when we do not agree it is because we do not quite understand the other man's point of view. At any rate, it is in that spirit that we attempt our work; and more and more, I should say, as the years go by, we are able to make it effective.

I will now call on a man to speak to you who has recently left the ranks of labor in order to take up the work of the Trade Agreement Department of the National Civic Federation; a man who, having served labor with great efficiency, will serve hereafter both labor and capital equally well, and in serving both will serve our whole country—Mr. John Mitchell.

A GOOD COUNTRY TO LIVE IN.

MR. MITCHELL—When the members of the National Civic Federation and their guests assembled in this hall one year ago the country was in the throes of a financial and industrial panic. In a brief address delivered on that occasion the suggestion was made, and afterward elucidated and emphasized by Mr. Gompers, that a resumption of normal activity would not be accelerated by wage reductions or industrial disturbances. Subsequent events have demonstrated the wisdom of that suggestion, as is evidenced by the fact that we are emerging from the shadow which hung over us at that time.

The experience of the past year seems to indicate that the old theory of wage reductions being a panacea for industrial depressions has given way to the more advanced and eminently more humane idea that the evils and hardships of an industrial recession can best be cured, or their effects minimized, by maintaining, so far as possible, the purchasing and consuming power of the people. However, whatever difference of opinion there may be as to the soundness of this philosophy, the forces of labor and capital are to be congratulated upon their patience and forbearance during this trying period.

It is a matter of general comment that we are recovering our industrial and financial equilibrium more speedily and more rationally than we have after any of the great panics preceding the one through which we have just passed.

And in connection with this subject it may not be amiss to emphasize the oft repeated statement that there is no fundamental antagonism between labor and capital. Capital is, in large measure, the product of labor, and there can be, or at least there should be, no conflict between him who creates and the thing he creates. In the final analysis the problem is in the distribution of wealth; there always has been, and possibly there always will be, a difference of opinion as to the equitable distribution of wealth. But I am optimistic enough to believe that as time goes on the men of both labor and capital will, to a greater and greater extent, adjust their relations amicably and honorably, and without recourse to the strike or lockout, and the thought has been revolving itself in my mind all through this evening that such gatherings as this must make for a better relationship between the forces of labor and capital.

After all, this is a pretty good country in which to live; other countries may have adopted some measures in the interest of labor which are more advantageous than those existing in our own country, but the problem is more difficult here, because of our complex civilization. I have an abiding faith in the humanity and in the business sagacity of the American workman and the American employer, and I am confident that a basis of harmonious co-operation will be established between them. This assemblage to-night, while in some respects a social affair, is nevertheless indicative of that broad spirit of democracy which permeates our American atmosphere, and, while immediate results may not be discernible, such gatherings as this must, in the end, make for a wider view, a broader tolerance, and a closer sympathy between these indispensable elements in the development of our national destiny.

As Mr. Low, the chairman, has said, I have given up my duties in other fields to devote my time to the work of the National Civic Federation. In severing my official connection with the organization of my trade it was with the hope that in this field I might be helpful in straightening out some of the difficulties between workmen and employers. But, my friends, unless time demonstrates that I can be of real usefulness in reconciling some of the differences between labor and capital, I shall go back to the trade whence I came. I do not believe that there is an irreconcilable conflict between labor and capital; I believe that if workmen and capitalists will strive earnestly and conscientiously they can solve this problem.

THE CHAIRMAN: I am now going to have the pleasure of presenting to you as the next speaker a gentleman who used to be a captain of industry. If there be such a thing, I suppose that he would be correctly described now as a captain of peace. I like to quote these lines of James Russell Lowell, when, speaking of the poets, he says: "For I believed the poets; it is they who gather wisdom from the central deep, and, listening to the inner flow of things, speak to the ages out of eternity." In this week, when we have been celebrating the three hundredth anniversary of Milton, we must recall that splendid line in which he wrote: "Peace hath her victories, no less renowned than war." I introduce to you Mr. Andrew Carnegie.

FOR PEACE BETWEEN CAPITAL AND LABOR.

MR. CARNEGIE—Mr. Chairman, President and Mrs. President-elect—they were elected on the same ticket.

I thank you, Mr. Chairman, for pronouncing me a "man of peace," but I want you all to understand that there is no phase of the peace question in which I take a deeper interest than in that peace which is coming between capital and labor.

I see the future clearly. Capital is to employ itself by and by. There will be capitalists and laborers, but every laborer will have a minimum wage, and he will be a shareholder and a participator in the profits. Alas, this is not my text this evening.

My text is a new one—it is "Old Age Pensions," a subject upon which I have never said a word and have thought very little, but I could not help, while in Britain, watching most closely the new measure which has passed Parliament, and I read a good deal about that. Now, speaking about our own country. In my opinion, we are in that happy position that we can postpone that question and give our attention to things of great and immediate importance. I do not think it necessary for the Government to take up the subject. In our land it is much easier for the saving, sober workman to make a competence for old age than it is in the crowded lands of Europe.

There are two systems now in Europe; the German, that is a contributory system, which requires a man himself to contribute in his youth toward the pension he is to receive in his old age. I think that is a most salutary feature. It gives a man that feeling of independence and true manhood that he is doing for himself, and when he has contributed to his pension, and the time comes to get it, it is not another's money he is getting—it is his own. I would not sacrifice the manly, independent spirit of the American for a great deal.

The British system is not contributory. It resembles a charity, given to all without their participation, and I cannot think that it has as stimulating an effect upon the young man as the German.

There is a third plan—because in this country of ours we are never far behind—in which I have been deeply interested, and that is the Massachusetts insurance plan. That is wholly contributory and the State Government has nothing to do with it. The banks and savings banks of Massachusetts are now permitted to issue insurance policies, and these are kept sacred from the banking department under strict supervision of the State, and there is no danger that the man who insures himself will not receive his pension at the time stated. I rather like the American plan, although it is premature to decide upon any plan. We should wait and watch. Another objection to either of the two plans, and one which favors the American in my mind, is this: It is all very well for the little island of Britain to legislate for that island, or for Germany even—which is only as large as one of our larger States—to legislate, but a pension fund requires such supervision, such constant watchfulness over the individual; it must follow him where he goes; it must watch him in his old age; it must know all about him, and in this continent of ours consider this difficulty. Suppose a man born in Massachusetts, or suppose he is so fortunate as to be born in Ohio—some men achieve greatness, some men are born great, and some fortunate men are born in Ohio—take the average life of the American born in the East, he is in Texas in youth trying to do something there, and in the South next, and in the North, anywhere, everywhere. How few of our citizens really live their old age where they were born! These are few, so that one national system would be so difficult that I am inclined to believe that the State and not the general government would be the best organization for taking up the pension system. So that for these reasons, and for others, I move a postponement of the subject for the second term of Mr. Taft.

Now I hope you will permit me to say one word about Mr. Low's speech and about this man Mitchell. Mr. Low is quite right—the Civic Federation is doing a great work, and is continually proving that you only hate those that you do not know. Employer and employed have only to get together and know each other well. I have had some experience with labor, and I'll tell you this: the more I knew of labor the higher my estimate of labor rose. If you are only fair with workingmen and like them you will find the majority of them will like you and be with you without fail in everything that is fair. Now Mr. Mitchell has associated himself with our Federation. He is going to be a great force for peace, because the men he worked with as a workman respect him as a laboring man, and we who have known him for years in the Federation respect him for his manhood, his kindly nature, his brain, his sympathies, his heart. We all have faith in John Mitchell.

I thank you for listening to what I have had to say. Pardon me for straying from my text and believe me when I say, the longer I am connected with the Civic Federation the higher I rate its importance, the more valuable I think its work, and I predict for it a great and beneficent future in hastening the reconciliation and finally the successful co-operation of labor and capital.

THE CHAIRMAN: It is very astonishing what an idea the average American has about Ohio, Mr. Taft. I remember that when I was for the time being the

Mayor of this city I was the guest of the Ohio Society, and the president of the society told me that there were at that time about twenty-five thousand men, born in Ohio, living in the city of New York, and I told him that I felt sure that that was an understatement, because there were forty-five thousand places on the city payroll alone.

It sometimes happens in the Civic Federation that there arises a difference of opinion upon political questions and upon questions involving great measures of public policy. I think I have heard of such differences taking place outside of the Federation in our American life. But in the Federation we do not break apart because of such differences; we rather agree to disagree where we must, in the full belief that just because of our differences our influence is all the greater as to the things upon which we can agree, when we do agree.

Now, it may interest you to know that Mr. Gompers and I have agreed to try to convert each other in the columns of the *American Federationist;* but to-night we are here, side by side, united in the single purpose of doing honor to Mr. and Mrs. Taft, not only as the President-elect, and his wife, of the people of the United States, but also because of the personal service which they have given to this Federation in days gone by, and the interest which they feel and which they acknowledge by being with us this evening.

I take great pleasure in introducing Mr. Gompers, the President of the American Federation of Labor.

MR. TAFT TO BE MR. GOMPERS' PRESIDENT, TOO.

MR. GOMPERS: Ladies and Gentlemen—By the manner in which the President—our honored President of the Civic Federation—introduced me to you, there might be left some impression upon the mind of some one that Mr. Taft is going to be less the President of Samuel Gompers than of any other man. Well, he won't be. I am sure that Mr. Taft has the satisfaction of having differed from me. I want to state just as clearly that I have had the honor of differing from him. The differences have been fought out upon our American plan, and the decision has been reached, and every law-abiding, liberty-loving American citizen yields obedience to the decision rendered. When the matter shall present itself in the field of legislation or administration, I entertain the hope that I may have as my joint contestants for a mental discussion the President-elect, Mr. Taft, and the President of the Civic Federation, Mr. Low. After all, it is one in which we are vitally interested. I would not enter into a contest in which I did not honestly believe. At this meeting—meetings of this character around the festive board—surely we are not looking for points of disagreement and to their discussion. We are here to try, if we can, to find points of contact, points of agreement, and I shall leave any controversial matter for a more appropriate time.

I just want to add this one thought, or rather this one expression, in connection with this particular feature—to say that every sincere American hopes, from the bottom of his heart, that the administration of Mr. Taft may be pre-eminently successful and conduce to the welfare of the people of our common country. And he may rest assured that every effort that the men of organized labor can make to help toward the attainment of that purpose will be cordially and promptly given. If we shall happen to disagree, we shall endeavor to contest our respective grounds in such way that at last the best may be accomplished.

My friend and colleague, Mr. John Mitchell, stole my thunder. Happily we are not, or rather fortunate for him that we are not—stopping at the same hotel, otherwise I might suspect him of having stolen my manuscript, which, by the way, I did not possess. We think largely on parallel lines, and I am really gratified at having heard him present the thought, which is a reminder of a statement made by both him and myself at our last banquet a year ago, which, when uttered, I am sure—I am sure—was not so very cordially received.

But I want to say a word or two upon a feature of constructive, economic, industrial legislation. I sometimes am in doubt whether, after all, there must not occur a readjustment of our ideas in regard to the jurisdiction of our State governments and their relations to the Federal government in dealing with industrial legislation. Last March a gentleman participating in the conference at the White House, when the subject of the conservation of our national resources was discussed, made use of a phrase which has become quite famous, and was quoted a little more than a week ago by no less a gentleman than the honored guest of the evening, Mr. Taft, at the Belasco Theatre, when in presenting the question as to where, between the jurisdiction of our State governments and the jurisdiction of our Federal government—to use another quotation—"the malefactors escape." And I want to use the illustration that in the "twilight zone" of Federal and State jurisdiction it is most difficult to have constructive legislation enforced that shall deal with the industrial affairs of our working people. My experience in appearing before the committees of State legislatures—to urge reformatory or constructive legislation in the interest of the workers—has been to be told that after all this industry or commerce is interstate rather than intra-state, and hence jurisdiction of the Federal government applies, and then in appearing before the committees of Congress upon exactly the same proposition, to be told that these are matters that are not conceded by the States, and hence are under the State jurisdiction, and between the two it is a case of the shuttlecock between the battledoors.

I would not want any man or any woman here to imagine for a moment that I am a Federalist, in the popular conception of that term. I am wedded to no one thing that stands in the way as an obstacle to the progress of our people. Surely, I am not in favor of the concentration of power so recently urged, not even in so good a man as Mr. Taft. May I suggest this one thought, and I shall be done? After all, we realize that upon our material welfare much of our progress will depend, but let us not, I pray, devote our entire thought to material things to the exclusion of fundamental principles. May we not take a retrospective view and take some of the lessons taught by the seers, the forefathers and the patriarchs of the early days of our Republic? May it not be well for us to consider also some of the phases involving the fundamental principles of human justice—the liberty of the people of our country?

I shall not now attempt to dwell upon or discuss the thought that I have in mind, resting content by the mere statement of it. Yesterday, in the meeting of the Civic Federation, I took the opportunity, in a rather more fairly comprehensive manner, of presenting the thought that I have upon that subject, and I also, in the report which I had the honor to submit to the American Federation of Labor at its recent convention in November, presented it in fuller terms and in greater detail. If there be any here who are sufficiently interested in trying to fathom the enigma which I have presented to-night, if they will communicate with me I will send them in print the views I entertain upon this subject.

Now, just this word in regard to the Civic Federation itself. Yesterday I said that I was perhaps the oldest member of the Civic Federation present. I did one gentleman an injustice in that statement, though unintentionally. I refer to the genius of the National Civic Federation, Mr. Ralph M. Easley. I have tried to give him much of what I could to advance the object and the purpose of the Civic Federation.

I have been brought up to have a rather high conception of Americanism, of American ideals, and of American fair play—to fight your battle fair and square, and then, even for a time, but honestly and faithfully, yielding and abiding by the results.

On the rostrum of the National Civic Federation men strongly differ quite frequently, but after a full discussion, though we may not convert each other, we entertain respect for each other and each other's judgment and character. We yield nothing in our Civic Federation other than what our own judgment dictates. It is a magnificent institution, and, as has been well said, could not be duplicated in any other country on earth. It is an honor to be a member; it is an honor to participate in these proceedings; it is an honor to be selected as one to assist our chief, the President of the National Civic Federation, in the effort to make the highest purpose and object a success, and with that hope and that thought, I thank you for your attention to what I have had to say.

THE CHAIRMAN: Mr. Gompers has called your attention to questions that are arising in regard to that "twilight zone" as it affects the laborers of the country; and in the hope that it may help some to think on that line and on kindred lines more deeply, without any reference to the fact of whether we are Federalists or not, I would like to call your attention to three things that have recently come to my own knowledge. There are five federal systems in the world—Switzerland, Germany, Mexico, Brazil and ourselves; and ours is the only one that does not put the entire subject of commerce under the general government. I suppose that that is because our Federation was established before the railroad was thought of. The others, having come into being later, were able to foresee what was likely to take place, and have provided for the solution of commercial questions by putting them all under the general control.

Last Spring I made some effort to ascertain what, in the opinion of competent men, is the proportion at the present time between interstate commerce and State commerce in the United States, and whether I asked men from New Jersey or Illinois or Rhode Island, the answer was uniformly that interstate commerce was from ninety to ninety-five per cent of the whole; and while it is true that our general government can regulate interstate commerce, it cannot regulate the agents that do it, because these are created by the States and are controlled by the States. On the other hand, the States can regulate the agents that do interstate commerce, but they cannot regulate the interstate commerce that is done, because that is under Federal control; the result being that neither the national sovereignty nor the State sovereign can regulate in this country both interstate commerce and the agent that does it.

I do not wonder, under such circumstances, that we have a "twilight zone." Let me illustrate by an incident that came to my knowledge in Indiana when I was campaigning. I found there that there had been some controversy as to demurrage. Some firm, it had been thought, was charged excessive demurrage by a railroad; and the question was whether that would come before the State Railroad Commission, that question, or whether it would be under the Interstate Commerce Commission. Those who claimed the latter said that the demurrage arose on goods shipped from another State; those who claimed the former said that the demurrage arose entirely in the State of Indiana, and that therefore it was a local question. I believe that that question has been definitely before both commissions for many months, and nobody knows yet, as the laws stand, whether that is a State or a national question. I do not wonder that this whole question of the relation of the State to the nation, and of the nation to the State is attracting more and more attention from thoughtful men as the years go by, because the conditions have so changed since our constitution was formed that it may yet be necessary to have constitutional amendments upon that subject before the nation is very many years older. I speak only as a layman, and I do not know much about the law, but I think I have stated correctly the particular points to which I have referred.

I want to introduce to you now a man who has always been active in the work of the Civic Federation. No one has done more for its support than he, and we owe to him almost personally that splendid report on the question of municipal ownership of public utilities that is hailed as a textbook wherever that question is studied—Mr. August Belmont.

CIVIC FEDERATION'S CONFIDENTIAL WORK.

MR. BELMONT: Ladies and Gentlemen—But fifteen minutes ago I understood from our President that I was not going to be called upon, and even had I prepared to say anything to you I could not have well supplemented all that has been said by him and by the other members of the Federation on the subject of its usefulness. No greater honor has fallen to me than when I was the President of the National Civic Federation, and when I resigned the office to my successor I felt that I could have no greater interest in the future than to retain my connection with the Federation and promote its interests to the best of my ability.

It has often occurred to me that we who are here from one year to the other attending to its duties and its meetings alone understand what the real work of the Federation is, and therefore cannot fail to see how important an organization it is and how much it does for the welfare of both capital and labor, and consequently the interests of our common country. However, it is not well understood throughout the country, and I presume the reason is that, differing from all other organizations, it does not indulge in strife, and its contests are not brought to the attention of the public at large. The very relation of its most important work is largely confidential. What the President related to you with reference to a strike occurring in the West, occurs constantly, and the same results have been obtained. You will notice that he did not even give you the name of the corporation or the bankers between whom the difficulty existed, because, as the mediator, it is necessary that this organization should observe secrecy always. It cannot plume itself on what it has done. It cannot appeal for support by relating its accomplishments, as other organizations do; therefore it is a pleasure to see these gatherings grow, and I do hope that the members will disseminate thoroughly and in detail, and widely, the results of these meetings, so that it may be learned what this Federation does, what it claims to receive support upon, for support it must have. It must have means to administer its affairs, and it depends entirely upon the voluntary contributions of those who have promoted its existence.

THE CHAIRMAN: I want now to ask you to listen to a little from the railroad world; and I want to introduce to you a man who, as chairman of the commission, made that most valuable report to which I referred a moment ago on the "Municipal Ownership of Public Utilities." I remember to have read an estimate of that work and of the value of it in the London Times not very long ago, and it spoke of it in terms that did the friends of that commission a great deal of good, which I shall not try to recapitulate, lest I make Mr. Ingalls blush more. I now propose to introduce to you Mr. Melville E. Ingalls.

GLAD TO SEE DIFFERENCES SETTLED.

MR. INGALLS: Ladies and Gentlemen—I think it will be very easy to find a jury in this gathering who would indict Mr. Low for injury. Here is our President-elect waiting. You all came here to hear him, and yet Mr. Low is putting up us muckers, as you might call us, who do not know much about the subject and have no eloquence, and just take up time. I suppose he wants to get you real hungry for the feast!

My text this evening will refer to what some of you who heard or read the Chairman's address yesterday, and also read or listened to Mr. Gompers's speech, will remember—his criticism of "the Sherman law." I am glad to see to-night that the President-elect and Mr. Gompers have settled, because I really expected to see Mr. Gompers behind the bars very soon if he should continue to violate this Sherman law by projecting these combinations among the unions. Really, my friends, I think that the best thing the Civic Federation can do at this time is to take up and urge the repeal of what is known as the Sherman law. Mr. Low undertook to do it three months ago and he invited me down to Washington, but when I looked at his bill I could not support it. Instead of wiping the thing out, he undertook to amend it so that it would not apply to anyone but college professors and ministers of the gospel. Everybody else was exempt.

That law was passed twenty years ago. It was passed in deference to political sentiment and demands, and changes since have altogether altered the situation. It was passed at that time when they thought nobody would enforce it.

There is not a more useless thing for a country to have upon its statute books than a law which cannot be enforced, and which nobody supposes is wanted to be enforced. Therefore I say the time has come to take a new departure and wipe it off and commence over again. I have stated this many times when I have had a chance and I am glad to say that the repeal or the change of it has been approved by almost every one in the land, among others the present President of the United States, who has in several messages and speeches stated it ought to be changed.

It is impossible for a man to be honest and conduct a successful competitive business to-day without landing in the penitentiary if that law is enforced. Now, my friends, let us wipe it out. We do not need it to control the railways. You have your Hepburn bill. Leave it there. Change it if you please. Add to it. Put more power in the hands of the Interstate Commerce Commission. Make them the great body and let them take care of the railroads. Then when you come to the business corporations, the industrial corporations, establish a large Bureau of Commerce and give them the power to turn the limelight on those concerns, and you will have no troubles. Examine the Board of Trade act of Great Britain, and you will find that that great industrial country has found a way to control those corporations without bringing their managers into the criminal courts. Mr. Gompers could then work out his labor union combinations without being indicted and branded as a criminal.

You may think this is all talk, but it is not, and as I said one year ago in this place, and I say it again to-night, I believe that every man who organizes a labor union puts himself in danger of the penitentiary under the Sherman law. If any two men agree on rates from here to Washington, they are liable to go to the penitentiary. If any two men agree on prices in manufacturing, it cannot be done now in this dawn of peace and good will. Let us wipe this off the statute books and put a different law upon the books which shall meet the country's needs.

We are just about to change our President. We have a gentleman here who soon comes into power—a man we all love, Republicans and Democrats alike. There has not been for years such an era of good feeling. It reminds one of the plain old man who came to New York and told his friend Silas that one Bill Wilkins up in the country was dead. "Dead!" says the friend; "what complaint?" "No complaint," was the answer, "every one is satisfied." That is exactly where we are to-day.

Now, my friends, in this era of peace and good will; at this time, when we are recovering from business depression, when we want to enlarge our agreements, and take possession of the commerce of the world, when we want the sails of our steamers and ships on every sea, when we want new business, in God's name do not keep upon your statute books a law which prevents it! Let this Civic Federation start. It is composed of men to whom cannot be attributed a selfish motive. Let them propose that this law shall be wiped out. There is intelligence enough in this country to control the situation.

When Mr. Low spoke of the agricultural interests in his bill, I did not quite understand what he meant, and I must tell you this story to show you how this law works. About that time I went out to California and interviewed in Southern California various gentlemen, and I said: "You seem to be very prosperous out here." They said: "Oh, yes. Since we have organized and control the shipment of these fruits East we have made money and are a happy people." I said: "Don't you know every one of these organizations is against the law and subjects you to imprisonment?" The fellow said: "Oh, yes; but there are not enough men to build jails to hold us!"

You cannot tell me it is for the interest of this great country of ours to keep such a law as that upon its statute books. I said yesterday that this great country would avoid strikes and would avoid all troubles between capital and labor if it would make, as I think Mr. Carnegie said to-night, every man a capitalist and every man a laborer. Start your profit sharing. Possibly Mr. Mitchell and Mr. Gompers may have to change their jobs a little, but they would soon adapt themselves to the new condition of affairs. We would then go on as a hundred million of happy people. But you cannot do it unless you radically change your legislation.

The question has been fought out and we are all satisfied, and now let us start—start with a new ideal. Let us have the proper legislation. Let us take from the experience of our cousins over the water, who are the greatest merchants of the world, who have gone all through this and have worked it out in the last fifty years. Let us favor, so far as we can, profit sharing between our railways and our industries and their employes. Let us wipe out the Sherman law and put in its place something that will strengthen, like the English Board of Trade act, the examination and control of our corporations. Let us strengthen the interstate law. Let us make, as was said in the speech of acceptance of the President-elect, a great body of that commission. Let us give them more power and fill them up with the best men in the land. We will then, indeed, have an industrial business which will make this country the first and foremost country in the land, and enable us to do things which we can in no other way.

THE CHAIRMAN: It seems to me, ladies and gentlemen, that there are few things in the world more touching than the genuine democrat's grief at the present situation. To come to that Sherman act: I do not want to be held responsible for all the things Mr. Ingalls said I did. He proposes to us that we imitate the practice of Great Britain. Now, Great Britain has an omnipotent Parliament, and they pass bills for the whole of it.

I spent two days of nearly ten hours each before the House Judiciary Committee last Spring, when the sole question under consideration was whether the United States Government had the right to ask a corporation created by the State, doing interstate commerce, what its capital was, what its bonds were, and all that. When Mr. Littlefield, the chairman, had proceeded a certain distance I arose, with his consent, and said: "Mr. Chairman, I hold in my hand a bill introduced by a Mr. Littlefield, of Maine, only last year, unanimously reported by the Judiciary Committee of the House, asking those very questions." Mr. Littlefield admitted that it was a fair parliamentary hit, but he said: "I am obliged to say that until last year I thought there was no doubt about Congress having that power, but in view of the most recent decisions of the United States Supreme Court, I have changed my mind. I do not believe it has that power."

Now, I don't know whether Mr. Littlefield is right or wrong. I have no doubt there are others who think Congress has that power, but it brings up again the question of how to deal with such matters as that when the twilight zone between State and Nation is so large, and really so indistinct.

I want to introduce now, as the last speaker but one a gentleman who reminded us yesterday of a conference that was held in Chicago in the early months of 1907, at which there were represented all of the railroad systems west of the Mississippi, except four roads, covering 190,000 miles of track, and of those four three sent word to the conference that they would accept whatever decision was reached. On the other side were representatives of all the railroad employes—the engineers, firemen, conductors and the trainmen. They represented so great a capacity to interrupt trade west of the Mississippi that the railroad men said at once that if they were to go out they would make no effort to fill their places, because they knew it could not be done. With that admitted power in their hands, after listening to the discussion of the questions at issue, the representatives of the Brotherhood made concessions at the suggestion of the Government officials who served under the Erdman act as arbitrators or conciliators, and abandoned things that their Brotherhoods had voted to stand for. In doing so they not only recognized the importance to the country of not paralyzing traffic on that immense scale, but they recognized that their ability to persuade their constituents grew out of the fact that they had trade agreements with the railroads all over the land. Ninety-nine per cent of all the railroads in the country are conducted under trade agreements, and it is because the men who work for the roads by that relationship have learned something of the railroad business on the operating side—that they were able to see not only the justice but the necessity of making concessions in that far-reaching controversy. I have great pleasure in introducing to you one of the men who represented the Brotherhoods there, Mr. A. B. Garretson, President of the Brotherhood of Railway Conductors.

ORGANIZED LABOR INCULCATES CIVIC DUTY.

MR. GARRETSON: Ladies and Gentlemen—I wonder how many of you ever thought of whether or not membership in a labor organization unfits a man for the duties of citizenship. Men who have for years been connected with the labor movement were used to assertions of that kind being made in days gone by, but they are not often reasserted in these later times.

I noticed a statement some time since made before a government commission by a man who occupied a commanding place in the commercial world in the region where his residence and interests were held, which was: "Labor organizations are to-day the greatest menace to the Government that exists inside or outside the pale of our national domain, and their influence for disruption and disorganization of society is far more dangerous than would be the hostile array on our borders of the armies of the entire world combined." I believe that the average citizen would find that a rather difficult statement to subscribe to, especially after attending a conference of the Civic Federation and the events that follow it. The representatives of other interests are surely equally guilty under a law based on such premises as is the average walking delegate under the Sherman act for combining.

When you consider as to the truth or falsity of a statement of this character, it is rather a good plan to make comparisons of that which has been with that which is. It has been written that the only way to judge the present and the future is by the past, and it would be worth a man's careful study to know what tendencies have developed from organization among the individuals of the working class in days gone by. If you go back far enough, you find out that the very essence of effort on the part of those men who endeavored to subvert the liberties of the body of the people lay in the hindering of the members of the community from coming into contact with each other, whereby they could exchange mutual opinions or agree upon any combined action, because it was asserted on their behalf that such association and interchange of ideas stimulated self-respect and self-consciousness, and that the results thereof would be inimical to the interests of those who had in view retaining within their own hands the agencies of government. Therefore, associations of the people were forbidden, banquets of trades and crafts proscribed, gatherings which were not attended by representatives of the tyrants in themselves constituted as serious an offense as two men agreeing what is to be the fare from here to Washington, which has been referred to by a former speaker, because such agreement, if not immoral, was at least illegal, if the interpretation placed upon the Sherman act is correct. I don't believe it is. I am not posing as an unconvicted criminal.

Take the period of the domination of the Roman emperors and you find that the collegia, supposed to have been combinations of tradesmen, were suppressed because they offered a means of inter-communication among the people, and, true to the precepts of the tyrant, Tarquin thus dealt with them, depriving the common people of any opportunity to conspire against his rule. Under Augustus, he who truly set aside the Roman republic and established the domination of the emperors, who did more to subvert the liberties of the Roman people than all who preceded or followed him, the edict went forth from Macænas, favorite minister of the emperor, that no oathbound organization should be allowed to exist wherever the Roman eagles marched. Under Charlemagne, who stood as one of the earliest representatives of universal dominion, membership in an oathbound organization was punishable by death, and during his reign more than three hundred men were executed therefor, but instances multiply wherein men whose avowed object was to gather into their own control all the elements of power studied to deprive men of the common class of the opportunity for an interchange of ideas which it was believed would lead to a community of purpose that would displace the wielder of despotic power and set up instead a government that should be, in greater or lesser degree, by, of and

1—William H. Taft.
2—Mrs. Edwin Warfield.
3—Judge Alton B. Parker.
4—A. B. Garretson.
5—Melville E. Ingalls.
6—Mrs. John Hays Hammond.
7—John Mitchell.
8—Mrs. William H. Taft.
9—Andrew Carnegie.
10—Isaac N. Seligman.
11—Nahum J. Bachelder.
12—John Hays Hammond.
13—James M. Lynch.
14—Ex.-Gov. Edwin Warfield.
16—Jacob Wertheim.
17—Mrs. Jacob Wertheim.
19—Lee Hart.
20—Mrs. Alton B. Parker.
21—Miss Coffin.
22—Henry W. Taft.
23—Miss Anne Morgan.
24—Daniel J. Keefe.
25—Miss Elisabeth Marbury.
26—Mrs. Horace Brock.
27—Frank H. Hitchcock.
28—Gordon Knox Bell.
29—Miss Cornelia V. R. Delafield.
30—F. H. Cabot.
31—Mrs. Gordon Knox Bell.
32—Major A. E. Piorkowski.
33—Mrs. William H. Bourn.
34—Arthur Lee.
35—Mrs. William H. Crocker.
36—William H. Bourn.
37—Mrs. Arthur Lee.
38—William H. Crocker.
39—Mme. A. E. Piorkowski.
40—James O'Connell.
41—Herman Ridder.
42—St. Clair McKelway.
43—Mahlon N. Kline.
44—Mrs. St. Clair McKelway.
45—Mrs. O. H. Rogers.
46—D. P. Kingsley.
47—Mrs. D. P. Kingsley.
48—Charles A. Moore, Jr.
49—Rev. Charles Stelzle.
50—Dr. O. H. Rogers.
51—Mrs. L. D. Alexander.
52—Charles R. Towson.
53—Mrs. V. Everit Macy.
54—P. J. McArdie.
55—F. A. Buckner.
56—Carlton Macy.
57—James Bronson Reynolds.
58—Mrs. Fred'k D. Underwood.
59—Mrs. B. Frank Mebane.
60—Fred'k D. Underwood.
61—V. Everit Macy.
62—Mrs. John D. Rockefeller, Jr.
63—Marcellus Hartley Dodge.
64—J. H. Finley.
65—Rev. Thomas R. Slicer.
66—Louis B. Schram.
67—John D. Rockefeller, Jr.
68—Victor Morawetz.
69—William D. Guthrie.
70—Milo R. Maltbie.
71—Otto M. Eidlitz.
72—Hugh F. Fox.
73—Robert C. Ogden.
74—John D. Crimmins.
75—Theodore Marburg.
76—Robert Mather.
77—Mrs. W. A. Coakley.
78—D. L. Cease.
79—Timothy Healy.
80—Mrs. Timothy Healy.
81—Horace E. Deming.
82—W. C. Brown.
83—Mrs. W. C. Brown.
84—W. G. Lee.

1—Augustus P. Loring.
2—John E. Parsons.
3—J. Borden Harriman.
4—Mrs. Philip Lydig.
5—James Duncan.
6—Prof. Morris Loeb.
7—Mrs. Morris Loeb.
8—Ernesto G. Fabbri.
9—Mrs. Ernesto G. Fabbri.
10—Mrs. F. McNeil Bacon, Jr.
11—Mrs. W. Fellowes Morgan.
12—Mrs. Richard Irvin.
13—William Fellowes Morgan.
15—Mrs. Paul Morton.
17—Mrs. Orrin S. Goan.
18—Orrin S. Goan.
19—Mrs. Eva McDonald Valesh
20—Norman Hapgood.
21—Miss Frances P. Gilman.
22—Harvey Bell.
23—Miss Susan Waring.
24—Miss Janet Waring.
25—Theodore Gilman.
26—Miss Clara Wise.
27—Dr. Lee K. Frankel.
28—W. S. Forbes.
29—Marquise d'Autier de la Rochebriant.
30—Mrs. Edward Lauterbach.
31—Mrs. J. Ellen Foster.
32—Miss Helen Varick Boswell.
34—Mrs. Joseph R. Buchanan.
35—Joseph R. Buchanan.
36—Mrs. Mary Hatch Willard.
37—Miss Ethel Arnold.
38—Miss Florence M. Rhett.
39—Ross Sheinwald.
40—Mrs. Ross Sheinwald.
41—Yejiro Ono.
42—Samuel Adams.
43—John R. Butler.
44—Mrs. Gilbert Colgate.
45—Gilbert Colgate.
46—Mrs. Henry Siegel.
47—Henry Siegel.
48—Major J. G. Schmidlapp.
50—Mrs. James Cushman.
51—Rev. James E. Freeman.
52—John C. Freund.
53—Mrs. John C. Freund.
54—Mrs. Sol. Bloom.
55—Sol. Bloom.
56—Miss Pauline Bancroft.
57—William B. Howland.
58—T. C. Martin.

for the people. Therefore, it is by a man with an ulterior object in view, government, social or commercial, that the associations of working men are viewed with condemnation, and, by the law of opposites, if men who are actuated by improper motives are so bitterly opposed to the existence of combinations among those who, for one of the reasons named, they desire to exploit, this would stand as a reasonable proof that such associations do bring about results that are desirable to the great body, not only of those who toil, but to those who direct their labor.

If you come down to the period of the Middle Ages, the time when might was nearer right than possibly at any other time in the history of the world of which we have an accurate record, when learning was eclipsed and the spirit of equality at its lowest ebb, what do we find? Where was the spirit of liberty maintained? Through the whole Frankish-Germanic region there sprang up the "Fehm Gericht," or Fehmic courts, which for scores of years remained the only barrier to the rapacity of the robber barons and kept alive during the darkness of that period the principle that the humble man was heir to a portion of the fruits of toil and had at least the right to live and love.

In every country that is lauded to-day for its maintenance of the rights of man the association of the humbler sort was either tolerated or encouraged. Every land that cradled the early races that are denominated the Anglo-Saxon recognized in their system of polity the gathering of the people for the purpose of expressing their will in regard to their own local self-government. The Folkmote of the early Saxon is a fair example of what contributed to the after developments of the characteristics that wrenched Magna Charta from the unwilling Norman King, and the continuation and development of that spirit is what has made the Lion of St. George and the Stars and Stripes the emblem of power and freedom wherever they are thrown to the breezes.

Many men have said that the guild was only the precursor of the union, but of this there is no real evidence, but the spirit that created the guild is the same that underlies and accounts for the existence of not only the trades union but of the democratic form of government. I suppose that few men have had more intimate knowledge of the men that compose labor unions than myself, and if I wanted to find men who were ready to sacrifice every interest for the upholding of the flag I would not go into other channels. The thing that makes the man the best citizen is the teaching of the average labor union of the present day.

How many men are there who do not wear upon their breasts the emblem of a labor union who ever have taken the trouble to determine what the actual teachings of a labor union are. The labor union takes a man when he is embarking on the sea of life, at a time when his views are unformed, when he is untrained, inefficient as a citizen, as well as a tradesman whose whole energies heretofore have been concentrated on gaining a knowledge of the craft which he has chosen to pursue, which will render him fit to enter into the race for maintenance for himself and the family that he possesses or hopes to possess. In connection with the development of his craftmanship it is made apparent to him that his best interests would be served by associating himself with others likewise engaged. When he wakes to the fact that membership in a union representing that craft is a thing to be desired, and when such membership is perfected, what does he therein learn? By contact with his fellows he becomes cognizant of those things which he comes to believe are his inherent right. Dwelling upon these questions widens his mind until ideas before non-existent come to him. He advances them among his fellows and, in an effort to defend them and to impress them upon his associates, his horizon is widened and his power to gain a hearing added to. He is taught that which is to be done should be done by himself, and that all responsibility should not be placed upon others. He likewise absorbs the knowledge that rights alone cannot be acquired, but with them go duties and responsibilities. He schools himself, and his associates unconsciously with him, in the principles of government applied at first to the union, but he just as unconsciously applies his methods of thought and training to the duties of citizenship with which he is confronted outside of his union connections, and before it is realized he has been transformed from the unthinking, unlettered unit into the thinking, reasoning citizen. It is true that in a majority of instances this evolution has weakened his party affiliations. He has shaken himself loose from the shackles of party domination, asks neither employer nor associates how he shall vote, but makes up his mind for himself and, when it is made up, votes accordingly.

No other agency abroad in the land to-day exercises so potent an influence in the creation of good citizenship as those organizations, for the simple reason that our methods are upright and the number of men affected is greater than reached through any other channel. Strip the mind of prejudice and judge of this question as you would other matters of like import, and see what conclusions would be reached.

Contrast the status of union labor with its status at the beginning of the period which memory spans. Then membership in a labor union was a reproach. The unionist of that period stood in a similar estimation in the community in which he lived to that in which the suspected criminal does in the present day. He was believed to be one who advocated subversion of the principles of good government. The community regarded him with suspicion; the law with condemnation; the courts with an eye to punishment; and his employers with a certainty of dismissal. To-day he has won his way regardless of the handicap then existing until, in his community, he has the support and the sympathy of a large majority of those around him. From the law he has full recognition; from the courts the right to be heard; from his employers the respect that always comes to him who contends manfully for that which is reasonably conceded to be his right, and this has been brought to him, not from an outside influence or force, but by the effort of himself and his associates alone. These are all questions worthy the investigation of every one who has an interest in the Civic Federation.

I am a believer in the Federation because I believe that its influence militates for good to the country at large. I believe that, regardless of membership in a labor union, I have as much devotion to the flag that flutters over us as has any other man, whatever the position he occupies.

No man ever really knows what the flag means to him until he has passed from under its protection. Let him live and labor abroad, and then he learns something of what the Stars and Stripes are emblematic of. There was a time in my own career when I had an able-bodied belief that I was deficient in patriotism. I don't know whether I had lost it in transit or whether it had never been transmitted, but it was one of the things that I did not have on my inventory, according to my own belief, but a sojourn of a year in a foreign country, when my eyes were never able to greet its heaven-kissed colors, taught me something of what the flag meant to those who had died for its adoption or had lived maimed for its protection when imperiled. Let a man be deprived for a continued period of all those things which the banner represents, let him realize by contrast that which is guaranteed to the man who dwells beneath its divine folds, then is when he knows the sensation which brings the unbidden tear to the eye and denies the ability to speak, and when he will feel, as others have felt upon the return to the land beneath it, that he could kneel and kiss the ground upon which its shadow falls, and, instead of that feeling being lessened by years of membership and training in a labor union, I believe that it is intensified thereby.

THE CHAIRMAN: We want to make public acknowledgment of the organization this year of the Woman's Branch of the Civic Federation, and to express to Mrs. Brock, the president of that branch, our best wishes, and to assure her of the cordial co-operation of The National Civic Federation in every possible way.

I now have the pleasure of telling you that Mr. Taft, the President designate of the United States, will speak to you.

CAMPAIGN DIFFERENCES ALL WIPED OUT.

MR. TAFT: Mr. President, Ladies and Gentlemen —Mr. Andrew Carnegie was introduced as a captain of industry. I did not have the pleasure of knowing him then; therefore I think he belongs to me, or to my class—that of an itinerant preacher. I have spoken with him now twice behind a Methodist pulpit, and this inclosure looks not unlike something ecclesiastic.

It is a great pleasure to be here in this company. Looking about, I see possibly some gentlemen that before the election it would not have been right for me to be closely associated with, but with the mixture that is here the association is entirely safe.

The Civic Federation, if I understand its purpose, is to enable those who represent labor, and those who represent capital, and those who represent the public and are affected by the operation of both, to come together for the purpose of learning how they differ and where they agree.

Most of the quarrels, most of the controversies in the world, have arisen because the parties to them did not understand what the other one contended for exactly; and when they meet on terms of equality for a discussion like this, and step by step can follow through the controversy, they usually, or they frequently, find that they do not disagree at all, and they usually find that they agree on many points and differ on very few. Now, when that association is accompanied by the presence of ladies, and by that flow of souls that accompanies a good dinner, the opportunities and the desire to agree on those points that are not material brings about a condition much to be desired in all dealings between men.

Time was, as the last speaker has most eloquently said, when everybody who employed labor was opposed to the labor union, when it was regarded as a menace. That time, I am glad to say, has largely passed away, and the man to-day who objects to the organization of labor should be relegated to the last century. It has done marvels for labor, and will doubtless do more; and what it will do for labor more is in the very particular pointed out by the last speaker. It will, I doubt not, avoid the reduction to a dead level of all workingmen, whether shiftless or earnest in their work, and will, by the force of public opinion in the union itself, enable the men in the union to feel that there may be inequalities among them, brought about by the difference in energy, by the difference in application to labor, and that it shall not prove to have that effect of levelling down, but shall encourage to level up, and that those who lead in energy may have the leadership.

There was a time, on the other hand, when those who led labor in the interest of labor thought that the introduction of machinery was against the interest of labor, and many a tragedy and many a controversy arose over that, but by careful consideration and discussion that, too, has been eliminated and ceases to be a cause of contention between the two.

And then we have the combination of labor. The trade agreement has sometimes presented an opportunity for controversy, but I believe now that all are agreed that it is wise and makes for industrial peace. The truth is that the time has come when the employer who says, "I deal alone with my own labor, and I do not recognize a general interest in what is done with respect to my labor," is far behind the times and does not recognize what exists—what must exist for the benefit of labor, and what those who are charged with general policies must hope always to encourage, to wit: Organization of labor on the one hand; the recognition that it is for the time being a class to be represented by leaders, and on the other hand, that capitalists, too, may combine in the same way in order that the two powerful elements may meet on a level ground—may meet where they are neither at arm's length and neither at the mercy of the other.

Now, I feel some hesitation and embarrassment in getting up to take up some of the subjects that have been mentioned to-night. I am sworn—or expect to be sworn, if I live—to uphold the constitution of the United States, and I think, in anticipation of that obligation, I ought to rally to the defence of that poor, battered, old instrument under to-night's discussion. I agree that our system of government is a complicated one; I agree that even so great a statesman as Mr. Gladstone, when he came to describe us in his paper, "Kin Across the Sea," gave up any attempt to explain the conflicting jurisdiction of the Federal courts and the State courts in many respects, and yet it was 1776 when we began, and the constitution was adopted and put in force in 1789, and we have gotten along pretty well with that constitution. It is true that we have had at times questions of doubts in reference to its construction, and it is true that some of those questions of doubt led to perhaps the bloodiest civil war ever fought, and yet we have gotten along and we do have an efficient government. It is proper, until it is settled by the Supreme Court of the United States, to refer to a "twilight zone" of jurisdiction, in which there is doubt as to the State or Federal power, but as we look back in the past we can see many problems that at the time seemed quite as difficult of solution as the one with respect to commerce now and the one with respect to the conservation of our resources. Now, I think we can depend upon the acumen, upon the patriotism and upon the general understanding of the Supreme Court of the United States, of Congress, so to construe that constitution as to give the Government of the United States power to carry out within its jurisdiction those reforms that are necessary as the needs of our civilization advance, and to ascribe to the States that power given them by the constitution, which they, in turn, within their jurisdiction, may use to carry out such reforms.

I do not believe that the constitution is to be perverted in its construction, but what I mean is that when you examine that wonderful instrument you will find that the men who made it made it short, made it comprehensive, made it simple in order that it might open to enable us to carry out what the future has in store for this Government, and what they could not foresee except in the most hazy outline.

I am not either quite ready to part with the anti-trust act, the Sherman act. I quite agree that it probably needs amendment; but I venture to think that the amendments need not be extensive, and that it is more important to enforce it than to repeal it. One difficulty in reference to legislation like that is loose statements and sketchy impressionist pictures without a close study of the language of the statute itself, and without understanding the meaning of words and the necessity there is for making definite what is a crime, what is an offense, and what is something to be controlled by the equitable process of the court. It is a work for lawyers with an intimate knowledge of business—of business necessities, and of the evil that every business man must recognize which has come to us, growing out of the combination of capital. I agree that the combinations of capital are absolutely necessary to the progress of the business world, but I also insist that those combinations may be used, or rather may be abused to the detriment of the public, and we must have on the statute books something to prevent and punish those abuses.

Now, as I was telling Judge Parker that at Yale, when a minister comes up there to preach a sermon before the boys, he asks President Hadley how long he can speak, and the president tells him this: that he has full opportunity to speak as long as he chooses, but that there is a tradition in the college, handed down from Abraham Pearson, the first president, that no souls are saved after twenty minutes. And therefore I do not propose to-night to go further into a discussion or a construction of the Sherman anti-trust law, lest I should lose the opportunity for conversion.

But now there is one additional suggestion I should like to make. It has been exceedingly agreeable to me to meet here at this board Mr. Mitchell, Mr. Gompers and other leaders of labor. I trust that they know, but I hope I don't attribute to myself unwarrantedly, that what happened in the campaign before the election, so far as my conduct is concerned with reference to any citizen of the United States, as President of the United States is wiped out as if it never was. And I thank Mr. Gompers for saying that I am his President as much as I am anybody's President.

In the next Congress, and in the Congress that succeeds that, there will doubtless arise, as there ought to arise, suggestions with reference to legislation especially directed to the assistance of labor. I have in my own mind a number of questions that ought to be considered, and might very well be considered in the Civic Federation. One of them is as to an employer's liability act. I cannot stop to-night, but I may say, incidentally, that in my judgment one of the greatest dangers to this Republic is the delays, and therefore the injustices, of our administration of justice, civil and criminal. If, by a reasonable employer's liability act, both in the Federal and in the State government, we could remove from the courts nine-tenths of those suits brought for the recovery of damages and settle a just award under some provision for arbitration and an administrative, but quasi-judicial tribunal, we could not only help the poor laboring men who suffer the accidents to a quick recovery of needed damages—for in such cases the old rule that "he who gives quickly gives twice," applies—if we could do that we not only would confer a great benefit on labor on the one hand, but we would remove from the courts a great burden of litigation that would allow them to carry on other litigation expeditiously, and not be clogged as they now are, so that justice does not fail to be done by reason of wrong decision, but by delay in reaching a right decision.

I want to testify, as Mr. Gompers did, to the efficiency of Mr. Ralph M. Easley. I hope he is as persistent in the good works of this Civic Federation as he is in making those whom he wishes to speak and work in it uncomfortable, and I assume, from what Mr. Gompers says, that he is; certainly he is indispensable to the success of this Federation.

And now, I thank you for your attention. I thank those who were good enough to say something pleasant about the incoming administration for what they have said, for I am glad to get it now. I have heard of the man who went into office with a majority and went out with unanimity.

The Chairman: Good-night.

NINTH ANNUAL MEETING, NATIONAL CIVIC FEDERATION

PRESIDENT LOW'S ANNUAL ADDRESS—BENEFITS OF TRADE AGREEMENTS UNDISPUTED

The National Civic Federation's Trade Agreement Conference took place in the assembly rooms of the Hotel Astor at 2 o'clock Monday, December 14. The meeting was opened by Hon. Seth Low, president of The National Civic Federation, who read his annual address.

At the conclusion of his address Mr. Low introduced Mr. John Mitchell, chairman of the Trade Agreement Department of the Federation. Mr. Mitchell addressed the assembly and then introduced the following speakers in the discussion of the subject of the day, The Trade Agreement:

Louis B. Schram, of New York, chairman Conciliation Committee National Brewers' Association.

James Duncan, of Quincy, Mass., secretary of the Granite Cutters' Association of America.

Otto M. Eidlitz, of New York, Building Trades Employers' Association.

James O'Connell, Washington, D. C., president International Association of Machinists.

G. W. Traer, president of the Illinois Coal Operators' Association.

Melville E. Ingalls, of Cincinnati, Ohio, chairman Board of Directors Big Four Railroad.

A. B. Garretson, of Cedar Rapids, Iowa, president Order of Railway Conductors.

F. A. Acland, of Ottawa, Deputy Minister of Labor of Canada.

August Belmont, of New York, president August Belmont Company.

John Hays Hammond, of Gloucester, Mass., mining engineer.

James M. Lynch, of Indianapolis, president International Typographical Union.

Herman Ridder, of New York, president American Newspaper Publishers' Association.

Samuel Gompers, of Washington, D. C., president American Federation of Labor.

The addresses at the Conference on Trade Agreement will be published in a special report of the annual meeting issued by The National Civic Federation.

MR. LOW ON THE TRADE AGREEMENT.

To the Members of The National Civic Federation:

The year just closed has been an active year for the Federation, and in several directions I have the pleasure to report substantial progress.

It has been our good fortune during the year to associate Mr. John Mitchell with the active work of the Federation, as the Chairman of its Trades Agreement Department. Mr. Mitchell entered upon his duties on August 1, and we have already had many opportunities to perceive the advantage to our work likely to result from his permanent connection with it. Through correspondence with labor unions and with the employers who have trade agreements with labor unions, he is building up an exceedingly strong department, the influence of which ought to be very helpfully felt in furthering the use of the trade agreement as a means for promoting industrial peace and progress.

There are still some, though they are fewer in number than they used to be, who maintain that the relation of the employer to the employe is an individual one, and who therefore will not deal with men as members of an organization in matters relating to their employment. I read in the paper the other day that there are 89,000 stockholders in the Pennsylvania Railroad Company. No one contends that these people organize into a company in order to fight labor. They organize because they have to in order to work together, and, as a result of organizing, they are represented in every use made of their capital by their officers. Can any one seriously contend that these 89,000 stockholders, speaking through their officers, are justified in saying to their 160,000 employes, We insist upon dealing with you, man by man; we will not recognize your organization. Is it not rather clear, that the 160,000 employes, so far as their interests are common, must unite if they are to have anything at all to say as to the conditions upon which they will work, and, if they unite, they must have an organization and they must be represented by their officers?

And is it not further clear that they are justified in organizing along the lines of their trade, it they wish to do so, rather than in groups as they happen to be employed at any given moment? It is sometimes said that labor organizes because capital organizes. That, I think, is a very superficial statement. It is a misleading statement, because it obscures a much more fundamental truth. And it is an unfortunate statement, because it immediately suggests antagonism to capital as the motive behind all organizations of labor. One might as well say that the sun goes around the earth because it seems to do so. But the fact is that the earth goes around the sun because it has to do so. Labor organizes for the same reason that capital does, and for no other; and both organize, because without organization neither can enjoy the benefits that come from combined action. That is the reason why this nation of freemen organizes into political parties, and that is the reason why capital organizes and why labor organizes.

Take another illustration: The United States Steel Corporation employs, in round numbers, 200,000 men. Of this vast army of workmen about 44,000, nearly all of them representatives of organized labor, own stock in the corporation. In their capacity as stockholders, these 44,000 workmen are represented by the officers of the corporation. Can it be contended that they are any the less free, or have any less right, to be represented, in their capacity as workmen, by the chosen representatives of their trade organization? And when the two attributes of holding stock and taking employment are thus united in the same persons, will any one any longer contend that these men, as workmen, organize for the purpose of antagonizing themselves as capitalists?

Now it is out of conditions that have produced a situation like this that the so-called "trade agreement" has sprung. In its simplest statement, a trade agreement is an agreement between organized stockholders and organized workmen, both acting through their chosen representatives, to determine, for the period of the agreement, the general terms of employment of the various classes of workingmen concerned. That each side tries to make the best bargain it can, goes without saying. That conditions favor sometimes one side and sometimes the other is equally true. That each side tends, when it has in its turn the upper hand, to push the other too hard is not improbable. But just as certainly as a pendulum, after swinging from one side to the other, tends to rest in a position of equilibrium, so such trade agreements tend to relieve the trade to which they apply of the extreme swing from conditions favoring capital to conditions favoring labor, and *vice versa*, which so often spells disaster to capital and labor alike. In other words, trade agreements that are revisable from time to time certainly make for industrial peace, and they ought as certainly to make for industrial progress. In the meanwhile they are constantly educating everybody concerned into a realization of the fundamental importance of keeping faith.

But someone will ask, in view of the decision of the United States Supreme Court in the hatters' case, Are not trade agreements forbidden by the Sherman Anti-Trust law? I am not a lawyer, and I claim for my opinion no weight that does not attach to it on the surface. But my opinion is that a trade agreement that does not issue in restraint of inter-State trade lies altogether outside of the Sherman Anti-Trust law. In other words, a trade agreement that is unconnected with any attempt to affect the sale or disposition of merchandise, it would seem to me, must lie as much outside of the scope of the Anti-Trust law, whose sole object is to make restraint of inter-State trade illegal, as manufacturing itself has been decided by the Supreme Court to lie. It is quite conceivable that a trade agreement might concern itself with the use of particular materials, and by so doing it might easily come within the scope of the Sherman Anti-Trust law; but if a trade agreement confines itself to its legitimate object of determining the conditions of employment to prevail in a certain trade or employ, it is not conceivable that such a trade agreement could be condemned under this act. The National Civic Federation believes that the trade agreement is the best method yet devised, in this age of universal organization, for promoting alike industrial peace, industrial well-being and industrial progress. For this reason the Federation proposes to do everything in its power to promote the use of the trade agreement in a constantly widening field.

WELFARE DEPARTMENT.

Hon. William R. Willcox, chairman of the Public Service Commission for the First District of the State of New York, has become Chairman of our Welfare Department, the Hon. William H. Taft being chairman of the Public Employes' Welfare Committee, and Mr. Charles A. Moore, chairman of the Industrial Employes' Welfare Committee.

During the past year inquiries from employers have been most numerous in relation to mutual benefit funds, indicating that industrial insurance is one of the problems pressing for solution.

Many manufacturers have asked for suggestions upon plans for providing pure drinking water, emergency hospitals, employes' periodicals, baths for molders, boarding houses, industrial training, factory lunch places, playgrounds for children of employes, machinery safeguards, prizes to employes for suggestions in running factories or offices, and inventions, and there have been innumerable requests for information in a general way involving all of the phases of welfare work. One of the successes has been the introduction of the visiting nurse in one of

SPEAKERS AT THE NINTH ANNUAL MEETING.

the Southern cotton mill villages. The benefits resulting have stimulated other cotton mill presidents to introduce hospital work. One of our experts has planned a recreation building and boarding house for young women, in connection with a cotton mill in New England, and has earned expressions of gratitude from an employer in Illinois, where a coffee house has been erected and put into operation on a self-supporting basis. Assistance has been rendered by our architect in consultation over plans for a new building, in which every known device for the physical comfort and recreation of employes will be provided by a publishing company in Pennsylvania.

Welfare work has been given further impetus by the distribution of our own illustrated literature, and by the furnishing of material and photographs for magazines, Sunday newspapers and trades union journals.

Lectures upon welfare work have been given in various parts of the country. One, with illustrations, before an employers' association in Kentucky, resulted in the formation of a committee on welfare work, composed of manufacturers, the purpose being to employ an expert, who will investigate the needs of employes of the various companies composing the membership of that organization, and make recommendations. A public service corporation in Massachusetts called in its superintendents and foremen from twenty-five constituent companies, in order to listen to addresses by two of our members, the object being to gain their co-operation in installing the welfare work which the president of the company is about to undertake.

A meeting, attended by many public officials, was held in Washington in May, for the express purpose of stimulating interest in welfare work for public employes. At this time the President received our members, and definitely and emphatically expressed himself in favor of the Government becoming an ideal employer.

At that time there was also organized the woman's branch of the Welfare Department, which has been very active in New York, and is rapidly extending its work throughout the United States.

The ladies interested in this movement have taken hold of their work with great vigor, and have appointed the following National Standing Committees:

Committee on Welfare Work for Industrial Employes.

Committee on Welfare Work for Government Employes.

Committee on Industrial Economics.

The whole country is to be congratulated that, precisely as the President-elect has been the chairman of the Committee on Welfare in its relation to the public service, so Mrs. Taft has been the chairman of the same committee in the Woman's Department. Mrs. Taft's interest has been active and personal, and the example she has set will doubtless be an inspiration to every one connected with this work at any point. The work of the year has been largely that of organization, but it is not too much to hope that future years will record a story of great progress along the lines in which the Woman's Department is interested.

INDUSTRIAL ECONOMICS DEPARTMENT.

One of the significant movements of the year was the visit of American teachers to the schools of the United Kingdom. Through the good offices of President Nicholas Murray Butler, chairman of the Industrial Economics Department, the International Mercantile Marine Company offered very favorable transportation rates to teachers who might be certified by the National Civic Federation.

TEACHERS' VISIT TO EUROPE.

The selection of teachers to participate in the visit was made by those qualified to judge of educational capacity, and no teacher was sent unless nominated or endorsed by the educational authorities where he or she taught. The plan was everywhere received with enthusiasm. Leading educators lent us their aid as an advisory committee. City school boards, in many cases, authorized the payment of salaries of teachers absent on the visit, and in a few cases paid their expenses. Upwards of three hundred teachers have already availed themselves of this opportunity, and more will go in January. Mr. Alfred Mosely, of London, to whom our thanks and the thanks of the teachers are heartily due, has acted as advisor in England, and has established an efficient system for the reception and entertainment of the teachers. Those who have already returned have expressed themselves in most grateful thanks for the opportunities which have been afforded, and have shown a most sincere appreciation of the arrangements made here and abroad for their comfort. There can be little doubt that this visit will be of the highest value to the educational world, and will contribute in a modest way to better understanding, esteem and good feeling between the two great English-speaking peoples.

CONCILIATION COMMITTEE.

The Conciliation Committee of the Federation has been called upon, as usual, to do what it could to avert misunderstandings and strikes in various industries, and, in some cases, it has been successful, and in others not. In a general way, it may be said that the economic conditions prevailing throughout the year have tended to make labor controversies less frequent than usual.

[The continuation of Mr. Low's address, that portion in which he dealt with the Sherman Anti-Trust Act, and the efforts for its amendment, will be found on page 13.]

WELFARE DEPARTMENT ANNUAL MEETING

SUBJECTS DISCUSSED: WAGE-EARNERS' SICK, ACCIDENT AND DEATH INSURANCE, PENSIONS, EMPLOYERS' LIABILITY AND SALARY LOAN EVIL

ON Tuesday, the Welfare Department held two sessions, Mr. William R. Willcox, chairman of the Welfare Department, opening the morning meeting with a brief address and introducing the speakers. In the afternoon, Mr. Samuel Gompers presided, and the meeting was closed by President Seth Low.

SPEAKERS AND SUBJECTS.

Wm. R. Willcox, Chairman, "Insurance for the Wageworker."

Lee K. Frankel, of the Sage Foundation Fund, New York, "Facts in Connection with Workingmen's Insurance in the United States and Europe."

Louis D. Brandeis, attorney at law, Boston, "The Massachusetts Savings Bank Plan for Annuities."

Marcus M. Marks, Chairman New York Merchants' Associated Committee on Postal Affairs, "Postal Savings Banks."

James O'Connell, President International Association of Machinists, "Insurance Fund of the Machinists' Union."

Haley Fiske, Vice-President of the Metropolitan Life Insurance Company, New York, "Industrial Insurance by Private Companies."

Major A. E. Piorkowski, representing the Friedrich Krupp Company, Essen, Germany, "Employes' Mutual Benefit Association of the Krupp Company."

Frederick L. Hoffman, Statistician, the Prudential Insurance Company of America, "Relation Between the Cost and Benefit of Private Insurance."

Dr. Roland P. Falkner, "Retirement Fund for Government Employes," and "Accidents of Industry."

Augustus P. Loring, President Plymouth Cordage Company, Boston, Mass., "Pension Funds of Individual Employers."

J. D. Beck, Commissioner of Labor and Statistics of Wisconsin, "The Burden of Compensation."

William J. Moran, attorney at law, New York, "Unbinding the Eyes of Justice."

John Mitchell, "Shall Industry Bear the Cost of Industrial Accidents?"

F. A. Acland, of the Department of Labor, Ottawa, Canada, "The Labor Laws of Canada."

Frank H. Tucker, of the Provident Loan Society, New York, "Salary Loan Evils."

Benedict J. Greenhut, of Siegel Cooper Co., New York, "Employes' Association Lending Plan."

H. S. Dennison, of Dennison Manufacturing Company, South Framingham, Mass., "Employes' Savings and Loan Fund."

F. C. Lawton, of the Gorham Manufacturing Company, Providence, R. I., "Mutual Loan Association."

Launcelot Packer, attorney at law, Washington, D. C., "The English Compensation Act."

At the close of the sessions the following resolution was passed:

Whereas, Industrial insurance is a matter of serious importance to the wage-workers of the country, and the facts relative to the subject are not readily available in a form by which the various methods may be compared, to the enlightenment of those to be insured;

Be it resolved, That this Conference recommends that a commission be appointed under the auspices of the Welfare Department of The National Civic Federation to investigate and report upon industrial insurance in this country—that is, insurance for the wage-earner—provided principally by:

1. Mutual benefit funds contributed to by employer and employees;
2. Trades Union funds, and fraternal lodges;
3. Liability (indemnity) insurance companies;
4. Private insurance companies, such as the Metropolitan, the Prudential and the John Hancock companies; and
5. The savings bank plan of Massachusetts.

The addresses made at the Welfare Meeting will be published in a special report of the annual meeting issued by the National Civic Federation.

ANNUAL ELECTION—NOMINATIONS.

At the close of the morning session of the National Civic Federation December 15, President Low appointed the following Committee on Nominations of Officers for the Federation during the ensuing year:

Theodore Marburg, of Baltimore, Chairman.

W. D. Ryan, General Secretary of the United Mine Workers' Union.

Marcus M. Marks, of the Clothiers' Association.

James M. Lynch, President of the Typographical Union.

V. Everit Macy, of New York City.

W. G. Lee, President of the Brotherhood of Trainmen.

ELECTION.

At the afternoon session Mr. Theodore Marburg, Chairman of the Committee on Nominations of Officers, presented the following ticket, which was unanimously elected:

Seth Low, President.

Samuel Gompers, Vice-President.

Nahum J. Bachelder, Vice-President.

Ellison A. Smyth, Vice-President.

Benjamin I. Wheeler, Vice-President.

Isaac N. Seligman, Treasurer.

Ralph M. Easley, Chairman Executive Council.

William H. Taft, Chairman Public Employes' Welfare Committee.

William R. Willcox, Chairman Welfare Department.

Charles A. Moore, Chairman Industrial Employes' Welfare Committee.

Nicholas Murray Butler, Chairman Industrial Economics Department.

Melville E. Ingalls, Chairman Public Ownership Commission.

John Mitchell, Chairman Trade Agreement Department.

Seth Low, ex-Officio Chairman Conciliation Committee.

John Hays Hammond, Chairman Committee on Organization.

Franklin MacVeagh, Chairman Immigration Department.

D. L. Cease, Secretary.

MITCHELL ADDRESSES COLONY CLUB.

"The American Federation of Labor" was the subject of John Mitchell's address to a large audience of women in New York City, February 16. The gymnasium of the Colony Club, used as a hall, was filled with interested members of a section of society which is often counted as being devoted exclusively to pleasure and fashion. The description by Mr. Mitchell of the purposes and aims of the great aggregation of national and international trade unions known as the American Federation of Labor was listened to with great attention. At its conclusion the speaker was enthusiastically applauded.

Questions asked, upon Mr. Mitchell's request, by women in the audience, showed intelligent interest in labor unions, and expressions of sympathy with their leading objects were general.

The New York Tribune's comment upon the meeting was as follows:

"John Mitchell, former president of the United Mine Workers, gave a number of wealthy women his views on the subject of trade unionism yesterday at a meeting of the Colony Club, of which Mrs. J. Borden Harriman is president. The members of the Colony Club have taken up industrial and economic questions, and this was one of a series of fifteen lectures on these subjects, which are being given weekly.

"At these meetings it has been arranged that outsiders preside, and August Belmont was the chairman yesterday. Mr. Mitchell gave his usual arguments in favor of the unions, stating that they had always prevented a competition in wages which would often be disastrous to the wage-workers; that they were educational and tended to good citizenship, and that they had come to stay and were part of the inevitable evolution of the industrial system."

THE NATIONAL
Civic Federation Review

Office: 281 Fourth Avenue, New York City
RALPH M. EASLEY, Editor

The Editor alone is Responsible for any unsigned article or unquoted statement published in THE NATIONAL CIVIC FEDERATION REVIEW.

PUBLISHED BY
The National Civic Federation

A PROGRAMME OF GREAT UNDERTAKINGS.

The annual meeting, with its inspiring review of the past year, was the starting point for renewed efforts along the lines laid out for itself by The National Civic Federation.

Probably no better illustration could be gained of the purpose of the Federation "to organize the best brains of the nation in an educational movement toward the solution of some of the great problems related to social and industrial life" than by a glance at a brief summary of its more recent activities.

One of the leading subjects now occupying public attention is the needed amendment of the Sherman Anti-Trust act. The efforts of the National Civic Federation to assist in presenting to Congress such measures as would effect this purpose have been long continued and earnest. The deep interest of the active and controlling elements of our nation in this subject was indicated by the appointment of over a thousand delegates by governors of States and by national organizations of industrial, commercial, agricultural and manufacturing interests to the Trust Conference, held in Chicago, under the auspices of The National Civic Federation. This conference in its resolutions declared that the enforcement of the Sherman act had revealed "the necessity for legislation which shall maintain all that the Sherman act was intended to secure and safeguard interests it was never expected to affect."

The National Civic Federation's effort to secure amendment of the Anti-Trust act followed. The experience of the last two years and the growth of intelligent appreciation of the problems involved promise to assist in the difficult work laid upon the new committee which has been appointed to draft and recommend to Congress such amendments as seem now to be most needed. It is made up of Seth Low (who, at the request of the lawyers on the committee, acts as chairman), Frederick P. Fish, H. W. Taft, Frederick N. Judson and R. D. Silliman.

The organization of the Trade Agreement Department, under the chairmanship of Mr. John Mitchell, is one of the most important and beneficial of the great undertakings of the organization since its inception. The bringing into closer relations of over a thousand employers and employers' organizations and the leaders of the wage-earners, who meet face to face in conference over hours, wages and conditions of employment, is an immense advance in industrial progress.

It is known that Mr. Mitchell accepted the chairmanship of this department at no small sacrifice of high official and pecuniary personal benefits. He was urged by one of the great national parties to accept nomination as Governor of Illinois, and before that offer was made he had been earnestly solicited by the same national party to stand for Vice-President of the United States. Holding the interests of labor above all others, Mr. Mitchell chose the work in which he now exerts his vast influence and his practical powers of application for the benefit of the industrial world.

A new work of far-reaching significance is being initiated by the Federation through its committee, headed by Mr. John Hays Hammond. It is intended to organize State councils of one hundred members each, with the object of making a systematic effort toward securing something approaching uniformity of legislation among the States of the Union. From the point of view of the practical man of affairs who is deeply interested in the material development and well being of his State and local habitation to the larger outlook of the statesman who confronts the affairs of the nation, this attempt to bring order into the confused product of long years of rapid growth in these States is of pronounced value. That it will involve long continued, patient and intelligent endeavor, conservative judgment and courageous perseverance is certain. If in the end it serves its purposes and aids in welding into a more compact, efficient and united whole the States which make the Union, the object of the Federation in projecting and setting the enterprise in motion will have been gained.

The Welfare Department, which is mainly devoted to interesting employers in improving the conditions under which employes in all industries work and live, has organized an Industrial Insurance Commission, with Mr. George W. Perkins as chairman. It will collect information relative to wage-earners' insurance, including accident, sick and death funds, as well as pensions. Especial attention will be given to the subject of compensation in case of accidents, and an examination is to be made by the commission of the various methods employed at home and abroad in connection with the subjects in which it is interested. Ultimately this commission will try to secure uniform legislation throughout the United States to provide for the protection of wage earners.

The Woman's Department, in perfecting and extending its organization and inaugurating its own practical steps in welfare work, is rapidly developing in efficient and influential activity. Its membership is largely drawn from women who are themselves stockholders or who are financially interested in industrial organizations through family relationship, and who therefore naturally should also be interested in the welfare of workers in the enterprises from which they draw their incomes.

In this department Mrs. William Howard Taft, wife of the President-elect, is chairman of the National Committee on Welfare Work for Government Employes. At the annual meeting of the Woman's Department Mrs. Taft aroused great enthusiasm by her attendance and report on a plan of work for the coming year.

The visit of American teachers to the United Kingdom, which was arranged through the Industrial Economics Department, proved to be a very successful affair. Upwards of four hundred teachers availed themselves of the opportunity to visit the schools of England on two months' leave from the American educational authorities. The teachers give enthusiastic accounts of the courteous and friendly assistance and entertainment which they have received on all sides from our kin across the sea. In addition to the facilities extended to them in visiting the schools, many delightful social affairs were arranged, including a reception at Dorchester House by the American Ambassador and Mrs. Whitelaw Reid. A special number of the *Review*, devoted to the reports of the teachers, is now being prepared.

The Industrial Economics Department is making a study of three subjects of vital interest at the present moment.

First—"In its fundamental principle, is our government representative or democratic?"—involving consideration of direct nominations; the initiative and referendum; imperial mandate and recall; direct election of judges and of United States Senators; abolition of the executive power of veto; and the amendment of the Constitution by a majority vote.

Second—"Has any portion of society the right to use its combined purchasing power for its own benefit, and if so, in what manner and to what extent?"—involving consideration of the first and secondary boycott; the white list, the union label; co-operative purchasing, etc., etc.

The third subject—"The menace of Socialism to American institutions."

No more important and useful inquiry will be made by the Civic Federation than the one now under way by its Public Ownership Commission. As will be remembered, that commission, after eighteen months' investigation in this country and Europe of the relative merits of private and public ownership and operation of quasi municipal utilities, recommended regulation rather than operation by the public. The Civic Federation commission will investigate and report on the question, "How far can regulation go without interfering with management?"

Thus the closing of one year is but a mark as to time. No stop is made in the work of the Federation, for it must keep one hand on the plough, even while it looks back over the just turned furrow to mark its line and course.

THE CONTEMPT CASES OF MESSRS. GOMPERS, MITCHELL AND MORRISON.

By SETH LOW, President of The National Civic Federation.

THE National Civic Federation has in its membership both large employers and the leaders of organized labor. In a matter like the injunction proceedings in the Buck's Stove and Range case it seems as if it ought to be possible to make each side realize the other's point of view at least fairly enough to enable both to do justice to each other. This article is an attempt to do this.

In one of the international rifle matches of twenty-five or thirty years ago one of the contestants took careful aim and made a bull's eye; but he failed to score because he hit the wrong target. Something like this is seen in the firing of both sides in this famous controversy. They hit the other side's weak point, but not that of their own. The manufacturers and those who sympathize with them in condemning the boycott that figures in this affair—and that means a very large section of the American people—starting with the idea that such a boycott is obnoxious to fair play as well as unlawful, are inclined to believe that anything which enables the courts to contend successfully against such a boycott is a legitimate weapon to use in such a struggle.

Organized labor, on the other hand, as represented by the American Federation of Labor—starting with the belief that such a boycott is a natural right—sees in the effort to destroy the boycott an attempt to crush organized labor—and identifies its objection to the actual use made of the writ of injunction in this case with a struggle to preserve for all Americans the right of free press and free speech. The claim of organized labor is that every man is entitled to control his purchasing power in his own interest, and that, therefore, an organized body of men should be free to do the same thing. This is the basis of organized labor's belief that the boycott is a natural right.

It does not seem to occur to either party that both may be partly right; that the boycott as illustrated in this case may be the hateful thing that many believe it to be; but that, also, the method adopted for contending against it may involve the use of powers by the court as dangerous as the boycott itself.

When Samuel Johnson was asked why he believed in free will, he replied: "We know we're free, and that's the end on't." It is probable that no one who has not found it to his personal advantage to use the secondary boycott in an industrial controversy ever has looked upon it or ever will look upon it as involving anything but a tyrannical use of the power of the many against the well-being of fellow citizens who have done them no wrong. This is something that the disinterested know by intuition, as Dr. Johnson knew that his will was free. It is significant that in England, neither before nor since the passage of the Trades Disputes Act of 1906, has any such boycott ever been attempted. It is true that in our own Revolutionary days such boycotts were put in force; but this was as a political not as an industrial measure—and led right up to actual war. It is also clear that in the contemplation of the Sherman Anti-Trust Act such boycotts are now not improbably illegal in the United States while that law remains as it is. It should be pointed out, however, that when this Buck's Stove controversy began the decision in the Danbury Hat case had not been rendered by the Supreme Court. It may well be believed that organized labor, as an evidence of its good citizenship, will refrain from such boycotts as have been condemned by the court until, in an orderly way, it can bring about, if it can, a change in the law so that the law will permit what it now forbids. All who believe that organized labor is, in its essential being, law abiding will recognize that such boycotts must be a thing of the past while the law remains as it is.

On the other hand—the contention of organized labor that the effort to down the boycott through publicity, by the use of the injuction, involves in this case, and necessarily, an attempt to control the freedom of the press and the freedom of speech is not to be lightly dismissed. The injunction issued in the Buck's Stove and Range case enjoined in fact many different actions, and it did in terms forbid the use of the press to enforce the boycott, and the use of speech to the same end. This is the particular aspect of the injunction which is called in question.

The exact phraseology of Judge Gould's injunction is that the defendants are enjoined, among other things, "from publishing or otherwise circulating, whether in writing or orally, any statements or notice of any kind or character whatsoever, calling attention of the complainant's customers, or of dealers, or tradesmen, or the public, to any boycott against the complainant," etc.

Messrs. Gompers, Mitchell and Morrison have been adjudged guilty of contempt because they have treated this part of the court's mandate as void because unconstitutional. The injunction was obeyed in the particular command to omit this firm's name from the "We don't patronize list," but the *American Federationist* and these gentlemen continued to discuss the propriety of the injunction. Partly because the case became a "cause celebre" such discussion of the injunction became more effective than the "We don't patronize" list itself in enforcing the boycott, and the court has held that the gentlemen were in contempt because the attempt of the court to shield this firm's business by injunction, against injury by publicity, had been rendered nugatory by them; while, on the other hand, it must be recognized that the action of the court itself in enjoining publicity has resulted in publishing the fact of the boycott more widely than ever.

It was argued as contempt of court, for instance, that the injunction itself was printed in the *American Federationist*. Every other paper and magazine in the land could print the injunction as a matter of news, but, when the *American Federationist* printed it, it became contempt of court. Furthermore, Mr. Gompers was held in contempt because he discussed the case, or for the manner in which he discussed the case, in the political campaign, in a perfectly legitimate effort to bring about, in an orderly way, a change in the policy of the country in respect of such questions.

The determination of the legal questions at issue can safely be left to the Supreme Court of the United States; but it is legitimate to call attention to two aspects of the case which cannot fail to impress a layman. Every other person in the United States, except the persons affected by this injunction, is left free to do what those defendants are forbidden to do; that is, discuss in the press and on the platform all the aspects of this case despite the publicity thereby given to the boycott. Of course, the injunction might be extended to cover others, in case of need. But what would be the effect of the injunction if it were made universal? If this procedure be a proper remedy at all, why may it not be applied to everybody; and if it were to be so applied, would there not be at least one subject in the United States as to which free press and free speech would not exist?

Secondly, in this aspect of the case the injunction was issued to prevent the publicity of the boycott, and it has increased the publicity of the boycott a thousandfold. As a preventive of publicity, therefore, the injunction seems to be a failure entirely irrespective of any violation of it by the defendants. If boycotting by publication is illegal, why not enforce the law against it in the usual way? If it is a crime, why is not somebody indicted, tried and convicted? If it is not a crime, why not sue for threefold damages, as has been done in the hatters' case under the Sherman Anti-Trust Act? But what ground is there for resorting in such a controversy to the exceptional process of an injunction against publicity which can only be made effective by forbidding certain men to do what every other man in the country is left free to do at his pleasure—that is, discuss the action of the court as it bears upon the controversy to which it refers?

To the writer the boycott as practised in this case seems wrong as well as probably illegal, but is the remedy by an injunction upon publicity a proper remedy?

INDUSTRIAL INSURANCE COMMISSION.

Will Make Exhaustive Examinations in This Country and Europe of All Employers' Liability, Old-Age Pension and Industrial Insurance Plans for Aiding the Wage Earners—Geo. W. Perkins Has Accepted the Chairmanship.

PURSUANT to a resolution adopted at the annual meeting of the Welfare Department of The National Civic Federation, the Executive Council of that department has authorized the appointment of a commission to make a thorough study of industrial insurance, including compensation for wage-earners in the form of sick, accident, old age and death benefits. Mr. George W. Perkins has accepted the chairmanship of this commission, the personnel of which will be announced later. The commission, which on being called together will map out the plan and scope for its work, will be composed of experts who have investigated foreign plans, employers especially interested in securing benefits for

GEORGE W. PERKINS.

their employes, and wage-earners and public spirited citizens. It is expected that the commission will collect data, compare various methods now in force in Europe as well as in this country and promote such legislation as may be deemed necessary.

An entire day at the annual meeting of the Welfare Department was given to this subject. It was shown that the United States is far behind European countries in making provision for the protection of this class of the unfortunate. The plans abroad were contrasted with industrial insurance in this country now provided by:

1. Mutual benefit funds contributed to by employer and employes;
2. Trades union funds and fraternal lodges;
3. Liability (indemnity) insurance companies;
4. Private insurance companies, such as the Metropolitan and Prudential;
5. The Savings Bank Annuity Plan in Massachusetts.

Some of these plans are desultory and apply to comparatively few of the mass of wage-earners.

Questions pressing for consideration in the interest of laborers are:

SICK INSURANCE.

How may the wage-earner be protected against the necessity of borrowing from the usurer when he or some member of the family may fall ill?

PENSIONS.

Shall we by Federal or State legislation, as has been proposed, follow the example of England in providing pensions for the superannuated by general taxation?

Can we adopt Germany's plan for compulsory old age insurance, dividing the burden of premiums between the employer and the employe and the State?

WORKMEN'S COMPENSATION.

Is one of the great needs in industrial relations in the United States a radical change in the law respecting the employer's liability?

Should the victims of industrial accidents and their families bear the cost?

Should the industry through trade associations of employers, as in Germany, bear the burden incident to death or bodily injury of employes?

Or, should individual employers, as in England, be held liable?

AMENDING THE SHERMAN ANTI-TRUST LAW

COMMITTEE TO DRAFT BILL—VITAL INTERESTS INVOLVED—PRESIDENT LOW'S VIEWS—MODIFICATIONS MUST APPLY EQUALLY TO LABOR AND CAPITAL

THE Executive Council of the National Civic Federation has appointed a committee to draft proposed amendments to the Sherman Anti-Trust act. By request of the lawyers upon the committee Seth Low will serve as chairman. The other members are Frederick P. Fish, of Boston; Frederick N. Judson, of St. Louis; Reuben D. Silliman, of New York, and Henry W. Taft, of New York.

No attempt will be made to submit anything to the present session of Congress. It is proposed to draft a tentative bill as soon as a careful study of the problems will permit. This will then be submitted for examination and suggestion to various representative bodies in all parts of the country, and with the aid of the comments thus received the final draft of the bill to be submitted will be prepared. The National Civic Federation confidently appeals to all who believe that the public interests require a rational amendment to the Sherman Anti-Trust law for their co-operation in this movement.

President Seth Low in his annual address described the situation as regards the amendment of the Anti-Trust act to the Federation as follows:

SHERMAN ANTI-TRUST LAW.

The most important activity of the Federation, during the year under review, was the effort to obtain at the last session of Congress an amendment of the sweeping provisions of the Sherman Anti-Trust Law. The members of the Federation will recall that in October, 1907, a Conference was held in Chicago under the auspices of the Federation, at which the sentiment appeared to be substantially unanimous that some amendment of this law ought to be had. This Conference adopted certain resolutions, and appointed a Committee to present them to the President and to Congress. When these resolutions were presented to the two Houses, the Conference Committee was asked to submit a definite Bill in legislative form to carry out its proposals. The Conference itself had given no such authority to any Committee; but, in view of the situation as it had developed, the Executive Committee of the Federation took the matter up. The result of its action was the preparation of a Bill, which was submitted in due time to Congress, and which became the subject of numerous hearings before the Judiciary Committees both of the House and of the Senate, but especially of the House. The Bill of last Spring was based upon the belief that at that time, and before the approaching Presidential election, it would be impossible to change the substantive law as embodied in the Sherman Anti-Trust Act. This being taken for granted, it became impossible to do more than propose a method by which, without changing the law, certain restraints of trade, if not disapproved in advance by some government authority, might be assured freedom from prosecution. The hearings before the Congressional Committees made it evident that no relief from the embarrassments caused by the Sherman Anti-Trust Law can be looked for along this line of procedure. Perhaps it ought also to be said that none ought to be looked for, because the situation really calls for a change in the substantive provisions of the law. Let no one imagine, however, that it is an easy thing to say what such changes in the law ought to be. Your Committee last Spring began its work in the hope that it would be able to submit a law which would command very large support, not only from employers but also from organized labor. After working upon the subject for many weeks, the bill which it actually presented commanded no large measure of support from either. The mercantile classes favor amendments to the law which, instead of forbidding all restraints of trade, will forbid only unreasonable restraints of trade; and which will provide amnesty for the past, (1) on the theoretical ground that what has been done has often been done without any realization that it was contrary to the law; and (2) on the practical ground that to attempt to rip up what has already been done will destroy the industry of the country. The representatives of organized labor, on the other hand, ask to be omitted altogether from the provisions of the Sherman Act. It is evident to your Committee that the changes desired by the mercantile classes are going to meet with very serious objection, unless they are combined with some positive legislation which will provide some effective method of assuring to the country, in the future, the power to protect itself in advance from new combinations in the industrial sphere; such as have been made in the past, and which originally created the sentiment which placed the Sherman Anti-Trust Law upon the statute books.

FREDERICK P. FISH.

HENRY W. TAFT.

FREDERICK N. JUDSON.

REUBEN D. SILLIMAN.

In other words, precisely as a city may desire to limit the height of buildings, for the future, without taking down those that are already erected, so many persons believe that the right to make commercial combinations, in the future, should be under some sort of governmental control, even though those already formed be left unmolested; and such persons, also, believe that there is the same inherent right in the body politic to do the one as the other. On the other hand, the demand of organized labor to be exempted altogether from the operations of this Act has been objected to in the past, and is likely to be objected to in the future, as class legislation of a kind that has no place on American soil, because organized labor is believed to be capable of exercising restraint of trade no less than commercial corporations.

These being the terms of the problem, it is apparent, on the face of things, that the effort to amend the Sherman Anti-Trust Law in any effective way is beset by difficulties at every turn. The Anti-Boycott Association objects to the use of the words "reasonable" and "unreasonable" in the law, on the ground that they will make the meaning of the law so indefinite as to destroy the law as a penal statute. Others think that the use of these words will destroy the law for any purpose. The whole subject is made infinitely difficult by the Constitutional limitations upon the power of Congress, which have led the United States Supreme Court to decide, in effect, that Congress can regulate inter-State commerce, but cannot regulate the corporation that does it; because the corporation that does inter-State commerce is a creature of the State and not of the United States. The separate States, on the other hand, can regulate the corporations that do inter-State commerce, because they create them; but the States cannot regulate the inter-State commerce that is done, because under the United States Constitution, inter-State commerce is under National control. It cannot be too clearly apprehended that the effect of this situation is, that neither sovereignty—neither the National sovereignty nor the State sovereignty—can regulate both the agent that does inter-State commerce and the inter-State commerce that is done.

This seems to me personally a situation very nearly intolerable, when it is recognized that, at the present time, according to the best estimates obtainable, perhaps 90 per cent. of all commerce is inter-State commerce, and only 10 per cent. intra-State commerce. As a result of this situation, I look for a constant strengthening of the demand for Federal incorpora-

(Continued on page 15.)

A STRONG MOVEMENT FOR NATIONAL UNITY

EFFORTS TOWARD SECURING MORE UNIFORMITY IN STATE LAWS—DANGERS OF SECTIONALISM—BETTER UNDERSTANDING NEEDED AMONG STATES WIDELY SEPARATED

THE National Civic Federation, through its experience in holding national conferences on such subjects as the trusts, taxation, immigration and election reform—conferences to which the Governors of States sent official representatives—has become impressed with the necessity for a systematic national effort toward securing, within reasonable limits, more uniform legislation in the States of the Union.

There are useful national organizations of farmers, manufacturers, wage-earners, bankers, merchants, lawyers, economists and other organizations which hold national meetings for the discussion of affairs peculiar to their own pursuits and callings. The Civic Federation, however, provides a forum in its annual conference for representatives of all these elements to discuss national problems in which they have a common interest. Heretofore there has been no effort to crystallize into State organizations this representative membership for the accomplishment of concrete aims.

A committee has been appointed to organize a Council of one hundred representative men in each State.

Mr. John Hays Hammond has accepted the chairmanship of this committee, of which the following are also members:

Messrs. Alton B. Parker, New York; Myron T. Herrick, Ohio; David R. Francis, Missouri; Curtis Guild, Jr., Massachusetts; Nahum J. Bachelder, New Hampshire; Edwin Warfield, Maryland; Herman Ridder, New York; C. F. Brooker, Connecticut; Bruce Haldeman, Kentucky; Victor Rosewater, Nebraska; Clark Howell, Georgia; P. I. Bonebrake, Kansas; James Lynch, Indiana; Harry Pratt Judson, Illinois; A. H. Revell, Illinois; John B. Lennon, Illinois; John H. Holliday, Indiana, and Benjamin Ide Wheeler, California.

The continued existence for eighteen years of the Annual Conference of Commissioners on Uniform State Laws, created by the different States at the instance of the American Bar Association, shows that the State Executives and Legislatures are fully alive to the importance of this subject. The last-named organization has been instrumental in securing the passage in thirty-five States of a uniform negotiable instruments law, and is promoting other commercial measures, including a uniform food law to conform to the national law.

This necessity for uniform legislation is further illustrated by the proceedings at the annual meetings of the National Association of the State Attorneys General and of the State Labor Commissioners, Insurance Commissioners, etc., etc.

The development of the nation, and the changes in conditions brought about by that development, have emphasized the harmfulness of the incongruities in the laws, adopted as they have been without any attempt at uniformity in regulating the same subject matter.

Professor Edwin R. A. Seligman, of Columbia University, at the National Civic Federation Conference on Taxation at Buffalo, referred to the injustice resulting from our present lack of uniform laws as follows: "Mississippi is vastly different from Massachusetts. South Dakota is not the same as Pennsylvania. A system of taxation may still work fairly well for an agricultural community and may be entirely unsuited for its industrial neighbor." "Yet," he continued, "even here it must be remembered that in Mississippi and South Dakota, as well as in Massachusetts and Pennsylvania, we find the railroad, the telegraph, the electric light and the bank—*i. e.*, some of the agencies of a complex modern society—in the midst of a new, pioneer, or still primitive economic community. . . . An unequal tax on a farmer in one State may make it difficult for him to sell his product in the world's market; an unjust tax upon the manufacturer or business man may drive him out of the business in that State; an unfair tax upon a corporation may cause it to move to another State. Action by any State is sure to react upon its neighbor. The business of the United States has become national and international."

JOHN HAYS HAMMOND.

Elihu Root, in 1906, when he was Secretary of State, in an address before the Pennsylvania Society, declared, "No State can live unto itself alone," and insisted that it is the duty of each State to frame laws and administer the public business "with reference not only to its own social affairs, but with reference to the effect upon its sister States." And Mr. Root has recently pointed out the need of patriotic and intelligent action in strengthening the efficiency of the State governments.

In his address at Albany, in January, 1909, he said:

"But there are two dangers coming with the development: One is the danger that the National Government will break down in its machinery through the burden which threatens to be cast upon it. This country is too large, its people are too numerous, its interests are too varied, and its activity too great for one central government at Washington to carry the burden of governing all of the country in its local concerns, doing justice to the rights of the individual in every section, because that justice can be done only through intelligent information and consideration.

"And the mass of business that is now pressing upon the legislative and executive and judicial branches of our government in Washington seems to have come about to the limit of their capacity for the transaction of governmental business.

"The other danger is the danger of breaking down the local self-government of the States. After all, the thing that we have government for is ultimately the preservation of our homes and our individual liberty. And we ought to be at liberty to regulate the affairs of our homes in accordance with our own ideas."

Further, the importance of the proposed organization as an agency making for a deeper sense of the unity of the people of the whole country becomes apparent in view of the benefits arising from the coming together of representative men from all parts animated by a broad patriotic spirit.

Washington, in his Farewell Address, warning his countrymen against the spirit of sectionalism, pleaded for the maintenance of the unity of the American people as "the main pillar in the edifice of their real independence." Manifesting his solicitude for the welfare of the entire country, East and West, North and South, "protected by the equal laws of a common government," he set forth the dangers attending "geographical discrimination—Northern and Southern, Atlantic and Western—whence designing men may endeavor to excite a belief that there is a real difference of local interest and views." And, he continued, "one of the expedients of party to acquire influence within particular districts is to misrepresent the opinions and aims of other districts. You cannot shield yourself too much against the jealousies and heartburnings which spring from these misrepresentations; they tend to render alien to each other those who ought to be bound to each other by fraternal affection."

During the century which has passed since Washington spoke his warning the country has expanded far beyond the known territory of that day. It has indeed been bound together from ocean to ocean and from lakes to gulf by the railways, the telegraph and the still stronger invisible bonds of social, commercial and political interests in common. Yet the mischievous effects of sectionalism have been constantly felt and they are still shown. The people of the various sections of the country do not sufficiently know each other. It is confidently expected that the meeting for the common good of men from all the States and the opportunities such meetings will afford for better understanding and appreciation of the people and the institutions of widely separated sections will bring about an increased sense of the unity of the whole people and a deeper and more intelligent love of country.

AMENDING THE SHERMAN ANTI-TRUST LAW

(Continued from page 14.)

tion of all the larger organizations that are carrying on inter-State commerce from Maine to California. Granted Federal incorporation, the United States Government would then be related to federally incorporated enterprises doing inter-State commerce, precisely as it is related now to National banks. It can then provide for a similar supervision of such corporations, and can pass laws, if need be, defining what such corporations can do and what they cannot do. No one, I suppose, desires to have the Federal Government attempt such oversight of all inter-State commerce. The desire for such control is limited to the few very large corporations whose uncontrolled power may make them a source of danger both to the people and to the commonwealth. It is evidently impracticable to determine the corporations that must be federally incorporated by the percentage of business which they do; and any effort to discriminate between inter-State corporations upon the basis of capital, while it offers a more easily applied rule, is, after all, purely arbitrary. It has occurred to me that possibly an effective discrimination could be made by requiring all corporations doing inter-State business to incorporate federally, whose stocks or bonds are either listed upon the exchanges or sold upon the curb. In other words, it is ordinarily only such corporations that attain a magnitude sufficiently great to involve serious questions of public policy. There is no object whatever in interfering with the class of corporations which in the olden time would have been partnerships, but which, in our day, have taken the corporate form for purposes of convenicnee. I recognize that such an outcome, if it is ever to take place, will be the result of a long agitation, and it may involve an amendment of the United States Constitution before anything of this sort can be done. I speak of it here because it seems worth while to point out the radical questions that are involved in any attempt to deal thoroughly with the conditions aimed at by the Sherman Anti-Trust Law. Almost any large interest, by insisting that nothing shall be done until it gets all that it wants, may easily keep this law upon the statute book without any amendment, indefinitely; thus exposing both corporations and labor enterprises to the extreme hazard of having this law enforced without rhyme or reason, like a savage running amuck.

The law as interpreted by the Supreme Court, declares all restraint of interstate trade illegal. United States Judge Lacombe, in the Tobacco Trust case, recently decided in the Circuit Court of New York, uses the illustration, originally used, I think, by Mr. Justice Holmes of the Supreme Court, of two expressmen who combine forces, instead of competing with each other as before; and says that even such a combination, under the law, would be illegal, because competition to that extent would have been lessened. To leave a law on the statute books, unamended, as drastic as this is to invite disaster.

Every one who realizes what an instrument of oppression and destruction this law can be, in the light of recent judicial decisions, ought to be willing to concede something to secure its early modification. One thing goes without saying, whatever modification of the law is made to apply to combinations of capital must apply equally to combinations of labor; and whatever amnesty as to the past is given to capital must be equally given to labor. If all the elements concerned will approach the question in this spirit of adjustment, it is possible that some amendment may be devised which will command sufficient backing to be successful. Except in such a spirit, I apprehend that nothing can be done. The Executive Committee of the Federation has placed the matter once more in the hands of its president to carry forward, if possible, the work already begun. I take this opportunity of asking the co-operation of all of our members in this most necessary and most difficult undertaking.

SOCIALISM'S MENACE TO THE FAMILY

A WARNING FROM "PROBLEMS OF TO-DAY," MR. CARNEGIE'S LATEST BOOK—CITATIONS OF SOCIALIST TEACHINGS AS TO MARRIAGE AND THE HOME

THE most serious objection to Socialism one hesitates to name, but this cannot be avoided. We gladly believe that most of the so-called Socialists of our English-speaking race would repudiate it, and yet it is clear that the system would naturally tend to produce, at least in some degree, the effects feared. We refer to the foremost of civilization's triumphs—the creation of the happy home—the product of man and woman, holily married, with the blessings of children coming to them, to give us here a taste of heaven on earth. Of all that evolution has given man during the long, slow march of ages, from savagery till now, this is the crown. Take this away, and to millions who possess it—the best of the race—life becomes undesirable. The holy of holies is the pure and happy home.

We have been treating of wealth, land, labor. Changes regarding these are unimportant compared with threatened changes in our family relations. That way degradation lies. Here rests the most precious root of all that elevates, refines, and improves human nature.

The writer would gladly have omitted reference to this feature of Socialism, but he felt it could not be ignored. One looks in vain through the booklets, so far published, for a repudiation of the sentiments of Socialistic leaders, both past and present, who admit that family relations must be greatly changed under Socialism.

The writer confesses it was with surprise that he found several modern and well-known writers going so far in the direction of accepting the doctrine that Socialism compelled this change.

The first exponent of modern Socialism, Fourier, is responsible for this taint, although even Owen quarrelled with the accepted views of marriage, so that it is not a recent development.

It appears advisable that the best-known writers among acknowledged Socialists, especially those of our own race occupying eminent positions, should give to this feature prompt attention, and, we trust, public repudiation.

We quote from "The Case against Socialism," pp. 374-398:

We have the admission of the leading English Socialist historian of Socialism, in no less a work than the "Encyclopaedia Britannica," that "In the Marx school, which in Socialism is by far the most important in this as in other countries, there is a tendency to denounce the legally binding contract in marriage."

The connection, however, bases itself upon this, as treated by Lamartine in his celebrated History of the French Revolution of 1848: "Communism of goods leads, as a necessary consequence, to communism of wives, children, and parents, and to the brutalization of the species."

Other historians have arrived at a like conclusion. Not only this, but Socialist leaders have themselves admitted all that Lamartine here asserts, save only his last conclusion. Jager, in his "Socialismus," observes that the possession of land and soil in common, if it arises out of Materialism, leads also to community of wives as being another expression of materialistic Communism.

In his essay treating of 'Socialism and Sex," Professor Karl Pearson, said to be one of the most distinguished of Socialist writers in this country, writes: "With the centuries as the last traces of the patriarchate vanish, as woman obtains rights as an individual, when a new form of possession is coming into existence, is it rational to suppose that history will break its hitherto invariable law, and that a new sex-relationship will not replace the old?"

In a later passage Professor Pearson throws further light upon the nature of this "new sex-relationship."

In his essay he informs us that woman will be the "physical and mental equal" of man "in any sex-partnership they may agree to enter upon.' For such woman I hold that the sex-relationship, both as to form and substance, ought to be a pure question of taste, a simple matter of agreement between the man and her, in which neither Society nor the State would have any need or right to interfere."

This latter conclusion Professor Pearson proceeds to modify in the case where "the sex-relationship does result in children; then," so Professor Pearson emphatically declares, "the State will have a right to interfere . . .;" and, apparently, in the writer's opinion, will be forced to interfere.

One of the greatest of French Socialist writers, M. Gabriel Deville, in advocating the suppression of marriage under Socialism and the substitution of "free love," summarizes the principal reasons which account for the inherent antipathy to the continuance of marriage on the part of Socialism, saying: "Marriage is a regulation of property, a business contract before being a union of persons, and its utility grows out of the economic structure of a society which is based upon individual appropriation. By giving guarantees to the legitimate children, and ensuring to them the paternal capital, it perpetuates the domination of the caste which monopolizes the productive forces. . . . When property is transformed, and only after that transformation, marriage will lose its reason for existence."

Bebel, the great international Socialist leader, in his "Woman and Socialism" (translated into English under the title of "Woman: Her Past, Present, and Future"), expresses much the same views as Deville in the following passage:

"The *bourgeois* marriage is a consequence of *bourgeois* property. This marriage, standing as it does in the most intimate connection to property and the right of inheritance, demands 'legitimate' children as heirs. It is entered into for the purpose of obtaining them, and the pressure exercised by society has enabled the ruling classes to enforce it in the case of those who have nothing to bequeath. But, as in the new community there will be nothing to bequeath . . . compulsory marriage becomes unnecessary from this standpoint, as well as from all others."

"The existing monogamic relation," write two of the foremost leaders of English Socialism—Mr. Belfort Bax and Mr. H. Quelch—concerning marriage, "is simply the outcome of the institution of private or individual property. . . . When private property ceases to be the fulcrum around which the relations between the sexes turn, any attempt at coercion, moral or material, . . . must necessarily become repugnant to the moral sense of the community."

Lecky says: "It is perfectly true that marriage and the family form the tap-root out of which the whole system of hereditary property grows, and that it would be utterly impossible permanently to extirpate heredity unless family stability and family affection were annihilated. . . ."

Mr. Hepworth Dixon, who has devoted special study to the actual working of communistic societies, observes that, "The fact remained, and in time it became known, that Fourier's system could not be reconciled, any more than Owen's system could be reconciled, with the partition of mankind into those special groups called families, in which people live together a life devised by nature, under the close relation of husband and wife, of parent and child."

"The very first conception of a Socialistic State is such a relation of the sexes," again writes Mr. Hepworth Dixon, "as shall prevent men and women from falling into selfish family groups. Family life is eternally at war with social life. When you have a private household you must have personal property to feed it; hence a community of goods—the first idea of a Social State—has been found in every case to imply a community of children and to promote a community of wives. That you cannot have Socialism without introducing Communism is the teaching of all experience, whether the trials have been made on a large scale or on a small scale, in the old world or in the new."

The late Mr. William Morris, in company with Mr. Belfort Bax, has written in denunciation of the present "sham" morality, the aim of which "is the perpetuation of individual property in wealth, in workman, in wife, in child."

. . . .

Professor Karl Pearson writes:

"Such then seems to me the Socialistic solution of the sex problem: complete freedom in the sex-relationship left to the judgment and taste of an economically equal, physically trained, and intellectually developed race of men and women; State interference, if necessary, in the matter of child-bearing, in order to preserve inter-sexual independence on the one hand, and the limit of efficient population on the other."

"The Socialistic movement with its new morality and the movement for sex-equality," writes Professor Pearson in an earlier passage, "must surely and rapidly undermine our current marriage customs and marriage law."

Mr. H. M. Hyndman predicts under Socialism the complete change in all family relations which must issue in a widely extended Communism.

M. Jules Guesde, one of the leaders of International Socialism, writes, "The family was useful and indispensable in the past, but is now only an odious form of property. It must be either transformed or abolished."

There are other quotations in the book named, which we refrain from quoting.

In judging Socialism, we are forced to consider this aspect of the question and see where it leads us. The opinions expressed, we trust, are not accepted by many Socialists of our own race. What concerns us is whether the result of the Socialistic system tends to change or destroy marriage and present family life as it exists to-day.

Socialism, with its equal conditions of life and equal incomes, must tend to evolve the common assembling room, the aggregation of members in one common building, and all the features of the barracks. Mrs. Besant pictures these conditions—"public meal rooms," "large dwellings which are to replace old-fashioned cottages," "one great kitchen," "one dining-hall," and "one pleasant tea-garden."

The result of all this must be to destroy the home as we know it, and tend to substitute the ideal of the Socialist, all people being brethren and members of one family and one home; hereditary wealth and hereditary blood relationships abolished, father and son, wife and mother, sisters and brothers no more to each other than other members of the one great Socialistic household. The ties of kindred, even of father and mother and children, must eventually sink into one common affection for all.

All are to stand upon an equality of relationship, one to the other, under the sway of Socialism, in respect of homes, property, food, dress, and all other things. Even the children are to be taken care of by the State. "But if any provide not for his own, and specially for those of his own house, he hath denied the faith, and is worse than an infidel," becomes obsolete, for the home of Socialism is not to be Individualistic but Communistic. It becomes the Socialist's duty henceforth to provide for all as for his own, they being members of one great household and one family. Such is apparently the final aim of the extreme Socialist. This would mean a second fall of man. Farewell to human happiness in its purest, most elevating, most entrancing form. Destroy our home life as it exists to-day, and we may well lament that—

> "The wine of life is drawn, and the mere lees
> Is left this vault to brag of."

Just as Socialism goes back to the savage past and urges man to return to Communism, so seemingly it contemplates the return of man and woman to barbarism in their holiest relations, if we are compelled to accept literally some of the writers quoted in "The Case against Socialism," as true exponents of the new system.

The laws of Britain compared with those of America are less favorable to woman, and those of continental nations still less so; under American laws she has proper standing, proving the estimation in which she is held by American men in all the relations of life. Socialism being a continental outgrowth, the references made to woman by French and German Socialistic writers, some of which we have ventured to quote, shock our sense of what is due to beings who in their highest development are capable of reaching heights unattainable by men.

It is earnestly to be hoped that the respected leaders of Socialism will deal effectively with this phase of the question by repudiating the sentiments expressed.

A pagan philosopher, weighing the claims of Christ to rank among the great teachers, would probably give first place to what He did for the elevation of woman. Civilized man in his upward march has not only outgrown, he has reversed the Miltonic idea of Adam and Eve.

> "For contemplation he and valor formed.
> For softness she and sweet attractive grace;
> He for God only, she for God in him."

In the happiest and holiest homes of to-day, it is not the man who leads the wife upward, but the infinitely purer and more angelic wife whom the husband reverently follows upon the heavenly path as the highest embodiment of all the virtues that have been revealed to him: he for God in her. Throughout the English-speaking race, as a rule, to-day, it is the wife and mother who sanctifies the home.

If all the dreams of the wildest Socialist were realities purchasable at the cost of the present happy home of Individualism, with wife and children, the sacrifice were too great—the blow to our civilization would be fatal.

EXECUTIVE COUNCIL OF THE NATIONAL CIVIC FEDERATION.

SOCIALISTS ACTIVE IN THE AMERICAN EDUCATIONAL FIELD

GOSPEL OF DESPAIR FOR TEACHERS AND CHILDREN—THE KARL MARX VIEW OF AMERICAN HISTORY—SOCIALIST SONGS AND SCHOOL BOOKS

By ADA C. SWEET.

An active contingent of the Red Flag fighting line is made up of those who aim to reach college men and women. These converts, in their turn, are expected to influence the schools, and so bring the youth of the nation into close touch with Socialism. The proletariat is for the moment ignored by this section of the Socialistic propaganda, as the element to be converted, or it is exploited mainly in the limelight for dramatic purposes.

When the Intercollegiate Socialist Society was formed a few years ago, it was recognized by a few here as an offshoot of the International Society of Socialist Students and Graduates, which holds its congresses regularly in Europe from year to year. This American branch was started by Jack London, J. G. Phelps Stokes, Oscar Lovell Triggs, Upton Sinclair, and other Socialists, and in the colleges and universities of the country it has many sympathizers, and not a few agitators and propagandists among the students, and even in the chairs of professors.

At the January, 1909, dinner of this society, there were present among three hundred guests more than one hundred who registered themselves as from institutions for higher education. While the reports then made by Prof. Scudder of Wellesley, and by a Vassar student, did not show a great number of Socialist converts at those two colleges, there was exhibited in the meeting an enthusiastic interest in the scheme to enlist college students and graduates in the United States.

In New York City the "Inter-High School Socialist League" has been formed, the object being to place before high school pupils the theories of Socialism through a systematic study of books and the hearing of lectures Saturday afternoons.

Another Socialist movement of immediate interest is one whose object is to bring into the ranks of the Red Flag the school teachers of the United States.

The *Progressive Journal of Education* is a new Socialist publication which makes its appeal especially to teachers. The editor, in the third number of the magazine—that for January, 1909—declared that the publication is now firmly established; that "its roots have already taken deep hold, and nothing can keep it from steadily growing but the neglect of its friends."

Garbed in unobstrusive style, the magazine presents the appearance of the ordinary periodical devoted to educational objects, and its price, fifty cents a year, brings it within the means of any teacher or student of pedagogy. To the more ambitious among these such a publication may well seem to promise something worth reading and study, especially as it has among its contributors such an authority as Professor John Dewey of Columbia University, who is well known among private and public school teachers through his educational work and writings. Another Columbia University Professor, William Noyes, of the Teachers' College, is a contributor, while Catherine E. Dopp of the Chicago University presents her views on "The New Education" in the January issue.

In looking through its pages the careless reader would not at first be struck by the Socialistic features of this magazine, as the articles of several contributors are neutral so far as their bearing may be seen at a glance. But one or two subscribers who had not been interested enough in the magazine to read it have lately been led to examine it by the circular which its publishers have sent to its Socialist readers. In some instances this circular was inadvertently mailed to teachers whose Socialistic tendencies were guessed at rather than known, but it is evident that some care was used in selecting the persons who were to be thus appealed to.

Here is the circular as it is printed on the back of a subscription list blank:

"THE SOCIALIST FIGHT OF 1920.

"Socialism is not coming four years from now and perhaps not eight years from now, but it may come twelve years from now if all who are now Socialists will bend every effort during the next twelve years. It takes time, argument and thought to make Socialists.

"THE PROGRESSIVE JOURNAL OF EDUCATION, THE NEW SOCIALIST SCHOOL PERIODICAL, is destined to play an important part in the steady process of conquering capitalism. Already it has begun its work of IMPLANTING SOCIALISM IN THE MINDS OF THE SCHOOL TEACHERS OF AMERICA, thus opening the way to the training of the youth of the land along progressive instead of reactionary lines.

"The value of propaganda among the school teachers of America is two-fold.

"(1) Because of the influence of the teacher on the community. THE TIME IS NOW PASSED WHEN FOR A TEACHER TO BE KNOWN AS A SOCIALIST WILL ENDANGER HIS OR HER JOB; AND, SINCE THE TEACHER, especially in rural districts, is looked up to for superior learning and intelligence, THE KNOWLEDGE THAT HE OR SHE IS A SOCIALIST WILL HAVE GREAT EFFECT.

"(2) Because of the influence of the teacher on the child. Prejudices instilled in the mind of a child are hard to eradicate. AT PRESENT THE CHILD IN THE PUBLIC SCHOOL IS THOROUGHLY STEEPED IN EXAGGERATED PATRIOTISM AND INDIVIDUALISM, SO THAT, AFTER IT GROWS UP, IT IS HARD TO REACH WITH SOCIALISM. SCHOOL TEACHERS WHO ARE SOCIALISTS CAN CHANGE ALL THIS.

"TWELVE YEARS FROM NOW, WHEN SOCIALISM IS FIGHTING ITS DECISIVE BATTLE, THE SCHOOL CHILDREN OF TO-DAY WILL BE FIGHTING AS ADULTS ON ONE SIDE OR THE OTHER.

"During the next twelve years the *Progressive Journal of Education* can be the means, either directly or indirectly, of winning a million votes for Socialism. It all depends on the use which the Socialist makes of it."

After reading this circular one takes up the rather dull looking *Progressive Journal of Education* and examines it with interest.

Two characteristic Socialist articles are found in the January number, both by typical Socialists, and both belonging to series of articles on very important general subjects, namely, "American History and Economics."

An interpretation of history from the Socialist point of view is well worth examining when we consider that it is addressed especially to American teachers. It it remembered by people who are familiar with the Socialistic propaganda in Europe that Prof. Enrico Ferri, of the University of Palermo, addressing the International Congress of Socialist Students and Graduates, once said:

"We should introduce Socialism into the student's mind as a part of science, as a logical and necessary culmination of the biological and sociological science. No need of making a direct propaganda which would frighten many of the listeners. Without pronouncing the word Socialism once a year, I make two-thirds of our students conscious Socialists."

And touching the subject of history, a Socialist paper in indorsing the idea of publishing a teachers' journal, made the following frank and illuminating suggestion: "Let the object be by all means to reach the teachers of history in the public schools and get them to teach THE MATERIALISTIC CONCEPTION OF HISTORY. This can be done without mentioning the word 'socialism,' and in most cases they won't see any connection."

Mr. A. W. Simons began his "New Interpretation of American History" in the December issue with his introduction and a chapter on "Conditions Leading to Discovery." These are followed in January by an article entitled "Why the Colonists Came to America."

This interpretation of history is not new, nor does it follow the tactics of sophistication laid down in the above quotations. Mr. Simons, thorough-going Socialist that he is, takes his text from Karl Marx, giving book, chapter and page with all the precision of a disciple. The gist of Mr. Simons's article, as might have been predicted, is that the colonization of America was but a part of the "revolution which was placing the capitalistic class in power," and Mr. Simons goes out of his way to say that "the Reformation, with its individualism in theology, was as complete a reflex of capitalist interests as was free competition and *laissez-faire* in economics. 'Every one for himself and the devil take the hindmost' became the motto of capitalism in industry, economics, religion and politics."

This inscription will seem to American teachers and students rather unique, when affixed in fancy to the altars of the Reformation and inscribed over the humble doors of the fathers who settled along the shores of the Atlantic in the New World to found what was to become the American Republic!

But Mr. Simons in his introduction has given in brief compass the crass materialism of his conclusions as to the great events of American history. Heroism, devotion to great ideals, sacrifices for love of liberty, individual responsibility or individual virtue, these are allowed no consideration in the Marxian philosophy. Here is a bit of it as expressed by this Socialist interpreter of American history:

"The discovery of America was not due to the appearance on this earth of a more devoted and intrepid navigator than had ever appeared before, but to the industrial and commercial changes which had taken place on the continent of Europe. The 'fathers of our country' will be found to have had a very direct and immediate interest in the revolution and to have been acting strictly in accord with their class interests in furthering that revolution. The Constitutional Convention will be shown to have been but a general committee from the possessors of the commercial, financial, manufacturing and plantation interests. The proceedings of that convention are little more than an attempt to divide power between these interests, and principally to secure the permanent subjection of the farming and laboring portion of the population.

"When the truth is told about the struggle between the North and the South we shall find that the ruling class in each section was pursuing the policy which furthered its own interest. We shall discover that the Civil War was a fight between two divisions of the ruling class, each of which wished to use the national government to further its own interest. The emancipation of the chattel slave (if we call it emancipation to change the form while retaining the substance of slavery) was but an incident in the great military conflict."

The second Socialistic series, begun in January, is that of "Charles F. Dight, M. D., University of Minnesota"—to copy from the magazine its style of presenting its writers. In "The Economic Wrongs of Capitalism" Dr. Dight makes a savage attack upon the entire life, thought and aspiration of to-day, his main argument and conclusion being that whatever is is wrong. This piece of destructive criticism was announced by the publishers as the beginning of a "notable series of articles on economics." An idea of the style can be gathered from the following quotations, the first being employed by Dr. Dight to characterize what he calls "the masters of industry and middlemen attachés":

"Their thought is to get more machines and material, with which to work more men, women and children, to make more profits, in order to get *more* machines, to work *more* men, women and children, to make *more* profits, that they may get *more* machines to work *more* men, women and children, and to make *more* profits, *ad infinitem*."

There follows the usual Socialistic rant about "wage slaves" and "their masters," there being nineteen counts in the indictment of capitalism, duly numbered and paragraphed, and then the unwearied Jeremiah notes that there are "many other objections of a major and specific type besides the nineteen enumerated," and concludes with a grand volley of musketry and artillery directed toward "capitalism, the system to which the whole category of economic wrongs is chargeable."

"These wrongs," says Professor Dight, "are so vast, and so ever with us, that we are blinded to them, as children who grow up accustomed to see their parents kill and eat other human beings do not realize the horrors of cannibalism. Only by pointing it out to them can they be made to see it. Born into capitalism, and having grown up under it, we are ametropic to its outrages, to the economic cannibalism which we practice. The few fatten, the millions emaciate and die. Yet the objectors to Socialism lament that it would limit what they call the 'earning capacity of the capable ones.' Cannibals, likewise, would not have their 'earning capacity' circumvented."

So the fangs of Socialism are snapped in the faces of teachers and students as they read the publication which poses under the grandmotherly guise of "Progressive Education."

That school children of the United States are in danger of having their minds drugged by the deadly materialism and spiritual hopelessness of Socialism is not good news. To teach children that they and their entire country, and indeed the whole world, are in the grasp of influences entirely cruel, strong and pitiless, that there is no hope for any individual under prsent conditions, no matter how he may struggle and labor, is to permanently cripple and make useless for life the boy or girl who really absorbs and accepts such teachings. The worst feature of Socialism as it is now being taught in the United States is the mental and spiritual paralysis which must follow acceptance of its doctrines. In its eagerness to attack the present system of society by destroying the private ownership of property, Socialism weighs down the spirit with such a load of pessimism that only a strong mind is able, when subjected to it, to keep up hope and endeavor for a life of usefulness, happiness and good works for self and others. If the ideas advocated by the *Progressive Journal of Education* could be placed before the children of our public schools, as is contemplated, during the next twelve years, and if the children should become converts in large numbers to those ideas, there would be a nation of cowardly, hopeless and desperate men and women at the beginning of the second quarter of the twentieth century.

There are already in the large American cities many Socialist schools for children. Nearly all of them are Sunday schools; that is, they are in session on Sunday. It is not for teachers in these regular Socialist schools that the *Progressive Journal of Education* is published. That magazine is primarily intended for the public school teachers, who have in their charge the great majority of American children. These teachers the Socialist propagandists hope to convert and influence, so that while using the ordinary school books they will interpret their texts according to Socialistic ideas, especially in the studies of history and economics. Thus is it planned to introduce into the minds of the youth of the country the germs of the Socialistic doctrine, without the authority, consent or sympathy of parents, school boards or school officials.

That the lessons of the Socialist schools are quickly absorbed by some of the mites of humanity to whom they are given seems to be shown by the writings of the children themselves. The Socialist weekly, "The Workers," has published samples of "essays" said to have been written by Socialist Sunday school children on such subjects as "The Cause of Crime," "Social Organism," "The Moral Order," "Class Struggle," etc. Little Lena Rosenbeck, aged thirteen, in her essay on the social organism, says that "the science of Socialism proves that the individual is not a responsible being; first, because he is practically unconscious of the universal ego; and second, even upon becoming class conscious he is powerless to act freely, being the slave of capitalism!"

Another philosopher, aged eleven, wrestling with the subject of the moral order, succumbs to fatalism. "It cannot be different," he says; "people cannot be kind, true or honest under the capitalist system." Of course, these little people have only repeated, parrot-like, what they have been taught. It may be that they and the other children of the Socialist schools will forget their lessons in despair and pessimism as easily as most children forget what they are taught in school. But some things are too easily learned, things which once taken for granted and adopted exert an influence for evil during the entire life of the unfortunate pupil. After all, what lessons are so easy to learn, for children or grown-ups, as those of irresponsibility? What rises so easily to the lips as the excuse, old as Adam, laying blame for failure, delinquency or crime upon others rather than oneself?

For use in the existing Socialist Sunday schools and for Socialist meetings there has been published a pamphlet of Socialist songs, with music. The words of these songs are for the most part set to well-known airs, and the songs themselves are often travesties and solemn parodies of old and popular favorites. The "Marseillaise," of course, appears among these songs; it has been universally favored by the International Socialists as their anthem. But the other songs, like everything else which proceeds from the prevailing Socialistic propaganda, are full of despairing and complaining, but without fire or valorous inspiration, and offer no hope except in the one promise of faraway but approaching relief from all sorrow and distress upon the coming of Socialism, whatever that word may represent.

Here are some specimen verses from a song entitled "A Harvest Hymn":

"There's light upon the cornfield, and yellow grows the grain,
The Summer now is over, and harvest comes again;
The year is crown'd with glory, the vales with corn are glad,
But the reaper's voice is silent, the farmer's heart is sad!

"The lords have now the vintage, the bankers claim the corn,
The produce of the farmer, by craft and guile is torn
From both himself and household, to spend in court and hall
On minions and their masters, who crowd to hunt and ball."

The old drinking song "Down Among the Dead Men" has received a new touch or two to make it apply to the much-berated capitalists. A verse of this is enough:

"There's liquor left, come, let's be kind,
And drink the rich a better mind—
That when we knock upon the door,
They may be off, and say no more,
And he that will this health deny,
Down among the dead men let him lie!
Down, down, down, down,
Down among the dead men let him lie"!

Another song, to the rollicking air of "The Elephant Now Goes Round," deals with "The Long-Haired Kings." From France, where the warrior kings came to grief, the story comes across the water to John D. Rockefeller and predicts the time coming when he, with the other kings of to-day, shall be brought low:

"For the Socialists smile
In their sleeves all the while
For they know what is next to come"!

"The Red Flag" is an international song with a rousing chorus. After appeal to the martyred dead of France, Germany, Moscow and *Chicago*, each verse ends in the chorus:

"Then raise the scarlet standard high;
Within its shade we'll live and die.
Though cowards flinch and traitors sneer,
We'll keep the red flag flying here"!

These songs, if the "Marseillaise" be excepted, are not incendiary or warlike. To the ordinary fighting American they are worse than that; they take the spirit out of the people instead of rousing vivid life. Every one of them contains a draught from the stupefying cup of pessimism.

That existing conditions are perfect no one will argue. There is much to be done to make life worth living for not a few, but for all human beings. But is it possible to prepare young people for the great task of helping to uplift humanity by instilling into their minds hopelessness, and, worst of all, by teaching hatred for any of their fellow men?

The sense of humor compels a smile as one reads some of these songs, but the smile must disappear when it is remembered how easy it is to arouse to violence by the most banal words of abuse people whose minds are unformed, or in some degrees unbalanced, or who are lacking in self-control and moral resolution. The subtle power of mental suggestion is used to advantage in many Socialistic songs. There are usually no open threats, it is true, but none the less the idea of vengeance is introduced.

What happened to the "long-haired kings of France" and what is going to happen to the capitalists need little further exposition after the jingles about them have been sung to a miscellaneous crowd. And the grotesque introduction through the old drinking song refrain of the idea of the fate which should overtake the rich is a clever piece of this jugglery of the mind. Nothing is more certain than that the shafts thus aimed will often hit their mark.

He who teaches hatred is giving preparatory lessons for every form of violence and crime.

Illustrating the clever adaptation of means to an end by which the Socialists teach their doctrines to beginners in reading English, either children or grown-ups, the *Review* prints six fac-simile pages of "The Socialist Primer." This red-covered pamphlet, which is issued by the *Appeal to Reason*, teaches class hatred in words of one syllable in thirty-two easy lessons, and along with the lessons in hatred is pressed the view that by circumstances and conditions alone life is governed, and that without material prosperity no one can prepare for or live a life of usefulness, excellence or happiness. This is the teaching of The Rose, Lesson XXI, and it appears in perhaps less conspicuous form, but quite effectively, in every page of the publication.

It should be remembered that in the large cities of the country are many men and women of foreign birth whose first care in preparing themselves for American life is to learn English. That these people should be taught the lessons of hopelessness inculcated by the Socialist primary school books is nothing less than a calamity to themselves, as well as an injury to society at large.

FIRST LESSONS IN CLASS HATRED.

LESSON XII.

Lots Of Room — Too Much Food — Starve Homes Dies

O, see the Map! It is the *Land* they call the States. Do you live in the States? Does your chum live in the States? Yes, we all live in the States. A few years ago it held no folks too rich or too poor. All had some food to eat and a home in which to live. This was in the days when the west was new and men went west to be free. The States is big and all the men in the world could live in the States. There is land here for all. Do all the men have land? Do all men have homes? The soil is rich, and we can work so that all men will have food. Do all men have good food? Why is it that men have no land? The rich, Fat Man owns it! Why is it that men have no homes of their own? The Rich, Fat Man owns most homes: Why is it that men have no food? The rich, Fat Man owns the right to most of the food. Is this right? No, it is not.

ALL MEN MUST HAVE NICE HOMES. ALL MEN MUST HAVE GOOD FOOD.

LESSON V.

HERE IS A MAN who begs. Why does he not go to work? He would, but he can not get a job. Can he not go to work in a shop? No; for a Fat Man owns the shop. Can he go to work in a mine? No; for a Fat Man owns the Mine. Can he go to work on the Land? No; for a Fat Man owns the Land. IT IS A GREAT SCHEME! When the Thin Man can get work, he must work for the Fat Man. The Thin Man is poor. Is the Fat Man poor? The Thin Man makes the Fat Man rich. Would you like to be the Thin Man?

WHO WORKS FOR THE FAT MAN? WHO IS A SLAVE?

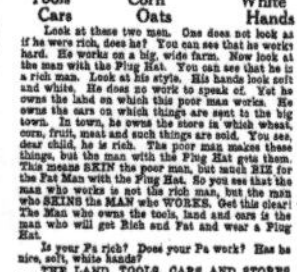

LESSON XV.

Land Tools Cars — Wheat Corn Oats — Soft White Hands

Look at these two men. One does not look as if he were rich, does he? You can see that he works hard. He works on a big, wide farm. Now look at the man with the Plug Hat. You can see that he is a rich man. Look at his style. His hands look soft and white. He does no work to speak of. Yet he owns the land on which this poor man works. He owns the cars on which things are sent to the big town. In town, he owns the store in which wheat, corn, fruit, meat and such things are sold. You see, dear child, he is rich. The poor man makes these things, but the man with the Plug Hat gets them. This means SKIN the poor man, but much BIZ for the Fat Man with the Plug Hat. So you see that the man who works is not the rich man, but the man who SKINS the MAN who WORKS. Get this clear! The Man who owns the tools, land and cars is the man who will get Rich and Fat and wear a Plug Hat.

Is your Pa rich? Does your Pa work? Has he nice, soft, white hands?

THE LAND, TOOLS, CARS AND STORES ARE FOR ALL MEN.

LESSON XXI.

Rose Pot Grow — Air Sun Rain — Men Bad Place

What is this? It is a rose in a pot. Would you like a rose? Yes, all men like a rose. The rose is in a pot. The pot is in a bad place. Can the rose grow if it has no air, sun and rain? No, it can not grow? If you put the rose in a nice place and give it air, rain and sun, will it grow? Why, to be sure it will! Then it will be a nice rose, and smell sweet. It is just so with men, my dears. Put men in a bad house with few good things, no love, joy or good clothes, and they will be bad men. But if you give them all the good things they need to real life, they will be nice, good men, and they will bloom like the nice rose. Do you like good men? Do you want to be a good boy or girl?

DO NOT FIND FAULT WITH THE MAN. CHANGE HIS MODE OF LIFE, AND YOU WILL HAVE A REAL RULE OF GOLD.

LESSON XVI.

Toil Pick Digs — Must Have Chance — Thus Makes Wealth

What do we see here? It is a man at work with a pick. What is his name? We call him TOIL. Will he dig all day? No, he will work eight hours. He will work two hours to make his own wage, and six hours to make his BOSS rich. Is this fair? This poor man keeps his wife and babe poor, while his BOSS is rich and wears silk and drinks wine. This is not fair! This is what we call a wage slave. If you tell this man that he is a wage slave, he will get mad. He wants to think that he is free. Is he? He is not, for the job he has, and the tools that he must use are owned by the rich man. Thus the rich man takes the wealth made by the poor. The poor man must have a chance. He will get a chance when all the men will own all the tools and land that they must have to live. Man must also have rest as well as work.

THAT WHICH GAVE US LIFE, GAVE US THE RIGHT TO BE FREE.

LESSON XIX.

Strike Poor Slave — Law Said Work — Food Keep Store

See the poor Slave! See the man with the whip! Will he strike the Slave? It would be bad to do so. Is he not a bad man to hit the poor slave? But he has this right. He owns the Slave and may do with him as he will. The law said a man may own a slave. No law like that now. It was a bad law for the Slave, was it not? Is it nice to be a slave? No, it is bad to be a slave. The Slave had to work. He got no wage. But he got his food and keep. He got this sure! Does the white slave now get his food and keep? Does he get it sure? I know lots of men who would be glad to work for their food and keep. Right in this town where we are told that we have no slave. Would you like to be a slave? Do you want a slave? Is your Pa a slave? Does he want to be free? The law will wipe out the wage slave.

LET US BE FREE. NO WHIP. NO WAGE SLAVE.

SOCIALISTS PLAN TO UNDERMINE AMERICAN ARMY AND NAVY

MUTINY A VIRTUE—DESERTION HEROIC—AUSTRALIAN SOCIALISTS CONSPIRED TO SAP THE LOYALTY OF SAILORS OF VISITING AMERICAN FLEET

[From a chapter entitled "Anti-Patriotism," by Martha Moore Avery, in a forthcoming volume on Socialism.]

ANTI-PATRIOTISM, the sometimes veiled and sometimes brazen-faced product of Socialism, has long since set up its "battle plan" in every department of industry, philosophy, politics and education. Within trade union lines, as we are told, the work goes on in the shop, at noon hour, at local meetings, at the State and national conventions, but nowhere more freely than in the labor-press does the "insidious propaganda" go on. Year after year there is a perpetual deluge of oratory and of imagery wearing away the virtue and the valor of patriotism.

Its meaning is veiled when it argues that "the Socialists ask no arbitration. They do not recognize that the employer has any rights to arbitrate; (*International Socialist Review*, October, 1904). But it is brazen-faced when it presents its annual resolution at the American Federation of Labor Convention asking for support in demanding the abolition of the militia system of the United States in favor of some other "method of arming in a well organized and orderly fashion *every* sober and reputable citizen in the United States." For while *there is such a thing as mutiny*, it were probably not the "shortest route in the end" to Socialism. At all events, with scientific arms in every *sober* Socialist's hands, there would be a large and constantly increasing contingent in the "armed nation" which "would make it possible to introduce a Socialist Republic gradually, peacefully and without convulsions and revolutions. It might take a little longer—and yet it would have to be the shortest route in the end;" (*Social Democratic Herald*, Dec. 21, 1907. Editorial in defense of the anti-militia resolution which was offered at the American Federation of Labor Convention that year by Victor L. Berger.)

Having, upon the floor of the convention, freely delivered himself of his treasonable intentions toward the country in which he votes, Mr. Berger was stoutly assailed for his lack of patriotism. And although he had openly advised "union men to stay away from the militia," and had argued his scheme in the interest of a "peaceful revolution" by which the United States should lose its life, Mr. Berger had the effrontery to make a great display of self-pity that he should have been so "misrepresented." . . .

Yet the issue is sharply drawn between unionists and Socialists. The *American Federationist*, of August, 1903, states emphatically the loyalty of unionists to the militia. But because Socialists have "no country," membership in the militia is forbidden by their organization.

The official committee of Clinton, Mass., sent to Charles Stevenson a letter which makes this plain. It reads in part as follows: "It is the unanimous opinion of your associates on the Socialist Town Committee that your action in joining the militia is in violation of the spirit and aim of the great worldwide Socialist movement. The present structure of government is the creation of the ruling class. That being so, the militia is part of the equipment of capitalist society. . . . Your membership on the Socialist Town Committee is not desired by the other members thereof, and by vote of the committee your resignation is asked for;" (the *Worker*, Aug. 16, 1903).

The Socialist organization of Waltham, Mass., having refused to recall one of its members who had been elected to public office in the town, for the reason that he was a militiaman, the Massachusetts State Committee intervened to suspend the local. The *Worker*, Dec. 25, 1904, editorially endorsed the suspension in no uncertain words. "When a local so flagrantly violates party discipline in so important a matter as that of the attitude of the party toward the militia," the action of the State Committee should be upheld by all loyal Socialists.

There are, it is true, few such flagrant violations of party discipline, for the obvious reason that patriotism is almost an unknown quantity within the Socialist camp. . . .

Although the means that are now employed are largely intellectual and psychological, there should be no illusion about the quality of that energy which attacks our nation from every quarter of the globe at once—in the guise of science, under the impact of the class-struggle, and in the name of a higher stage of social development. . . .

A gibberish of tongues joins with the old New Englander to pluck up love of country by the roots. North, South, East and West the Socialist Sunday-school children are taught that they have "no country," that their wage earning fathers are slaves, and that their mothers are slaves to slaves. And when, under this instruction, a group of small children tore down and insulted the picture of the President of these United States, it went throughout the English speaking world that this uproar "was an inspiring moment—a pleasure too deep for words;" (the *Socialist*, Seattle, Wash., April 10, 1904.) . . .

"Will They Submit?" is the title of a discussion which has been running for weeks in the *Wage Slave*, as to the probable difficulty Socialism will encounter when it shall be ready to enter upon its course of wholesale robbery. Eugene V. Debs has been all along of the opinion that "they" will not. "The time will come to incite the populace. In the very near future there will be an uprising of the people; Congress will be dispersed and the Supreme Court abolished. When that time comes, you can count upon me. I will be ready to shed the last drop of my blood when that time comes;" (address, St. Louis, August, 1897).

MRS. MARTHA MOORE AVERY.

Because "there is such a thing as mutiny" it has become the satisfactory business of Socialism to foster disobedience to lawful orders. The National Secretary of the Socialist party in the *Call*, Sept. 11, 1908, sounds the keynote on this score. "We find," writes Mr. J. Mahlon Barnes, "immense encouragement" in the fact that several incidents prove that the soldiery, being honeycombed with the idea of Socialism, refuse to obey orders. "All hail to the man who will not shoot against the men of his own class."

The New York *Socialist*, April 18, 1908, reports that the General Committee of that State passed a motion calling upon the National Executive of the Socialist party to send to all its locals in the United States asking them to protest against increasing the army, and making the especial request that individual "comrades" be asked to do all they can to induce trade-union bodies to follow the Socialist lead.

Such is not merely an American policy; as we have seen, it is international, though over the water it is somewhat further advanced in its stage of action. In France five editors are now serving jail sentences for publishing a symposium on "What to Do in Case War Is Declared." *L'Humanite*—Jaures' paper—champions undermining the French army, and defends the editors of *La Voix du Peuple*. Under a commendatory title, the *Call*, New York, Oct. 7, 1908, gives to its American readers the gist of the advice which was given to the new recruits in France, through the columns of *La Voix du Peuple*, in case the mob should take into its own hands the law: "Soldiers, do not fire! You are not under arms to assassinate workmen! And if an order to massacre is given, be executioners of Justice, not assassins. Aim and kill without pity him who gives the murderous command, no matter what epaulets he may wear." There follows the comment that as Aristide Briand, the present Minister of Justice, being a Socialist, holds this advice to be entirely defensible, a prosecution of the paper "can hardly be expected," notwithstanding the "great excitement" which was provoked by the Socialist instructions to the French army.

In her lectures, as reported by the Chicago *Daily Socialist*, July 18, 1907, Mrs. Lena Morrow Lewis makes it an especial point to impress upon her audiences that "there is such as thing as mutiny." Mrs. Lewis's advice to our soldiers is given in the form of suggestion: "If it ever comes to a crisis in this country, they will probably follow the example of German soldiers and refuse to shoot down the working class of their own or any other country." . . .

Evidently thinking that the diversion of the soldiers from their sworn duty to protect their country was their best way to keep their oath of allegiance, three officers, being members of the "camp local," were selected to procure from headquarters bundles of Socialist literature to spread among the 7,000 men of the camp. It would indeed be "safer," in the time of trouble, if the army were "honeycombed" with treason, for officers to remember that "there is such a thing as mutiny." And that in the event of a Socialist triumph at the poles the State shall "die out."

There should be "No Fear of the Army," announces the *Call* of Jan. 6, 1909. Its confidence is grounded in a visit of Eugene V. Debs to Capt. W. E. P. French at his country place on the Hudson. This intimacy is the cause of the *Call's* hope that the army is being subverted by the conversion of its officers to the notion that our country's defense is merely the "big stick" of the capitalist class; and that therefore it shall be fit only for treason and for spoils. . . .

More than two years ago a group of revolutionists of Oakland, Cal., entered upon the publication of a Socialist paper exclusively in the "interest" of the enlisted men of the army and navy of the United States. The circular setting forth the argument for its usefulness to the cause was indorsed by many prominent Socialists, Jack London among them. And the proposal was not "condemned" by a single Socialist. The reasons supporting the venture are that "the United States Government—always incompetent and impotent—will be powerless to stop our propaganda. So long as the army and navy are loyal to the capitalist class, it will be well-nigh impossible to introduce a co-operative commonwealth; but armies are not always loyal to their masters: There is such a thing as mutiny." This circular was printed in the Chicago *Daily Socialist*, Nov. 13, 1906.

Later, the proposal, which "not a single Socialist, so far, has condemned," was realized in the Oakland *World*. Its management has the determination to "deluge" soldiers and sailors with "class conscious literature." And it is predicted that "the results will be astonishing." For "there is such a thing as mutiny."

The Oakland *World* it was that carried the information into every port made by the great cruise that "every battleship of the Pacific fleet carries on it a band of devoted Socialists, who are spreading the propaganda" (the *Call*, Oct. 1, 1908).

The "cheering" information was brought out from an investigation, which was ordered by Secretary of the Navy Metcalf relative to ascertaining if there be any violation of the United States regulation in the formation of Socialist clubs, "there are 100 on one vessel, and that 40 per cent of the enlisted men on the torpedo boat flotilla are Socialists." James Flynn, fireman, a writer of Socialist pamphlets, attached to the cruiser West Virginia, was called before the captain, McCracken, of the vessel, "three times in one day and closely questioned" (Chicago *Daily Socialist*, July 30, 1908). So it is "cheering" news that the navy is being undermined!

On land and on sea the vicious work goes on. The *Tribune*, Seattle, Feb. 3, 1908, reports resolutions from the party organization of Los Angeles in condemnation of the world cruise as a policy "by which always and everywhere the chains are riveted more firmly on the limbs of labor." Continuing, its members are exhorted to do all in their power to induce labor unions to pass resolutions asserting "that the military arm of the Government does not show any friendliness toward organized labor."

To the Chicago *Daily Socialist*, May 28, 1908, a special from Seattle gives the news that thousands of papers and pamphlets were given to the "jackies" who thronged the park, and the literature was taken "aboard." Hundreds of sailors "expressed sympathy" and many declared themselves "full-fledged" Socialists.

When the fleet was in Los Angeles, the editor of the Oakland *World* went on board the Connecticut and distributed literature among the officers. He learned that "on *every* battleship in the fleet which came around the Horn" there was a Socialist group. On board the West Virginia, where seventy-two copies of the *Appeal to Reason* are received each week, there are 100 in the group. Socialists aboard say confidently that the entire army and navy is being "honeycombed with Socialist thought." With more effort put into this line of propaganda "amongst the so-called defenders of the flag it would not be long before the masters of this land would find themselves up against the same conditions which developed in Russia and France." For "there is such a thing as mutiny."

Being international in its principles and in its policies, the Socialists of one country logically take an active part in undermining the *force de resistance* of another. To quote from the *Call*, of Nov. 1, 1908: A correspondent from Australia reports that "a novel reception has been accorded the officers and men of the visiting American fleet by the Melbourne Socialists." Permission being granted, they swarmed aboard distributing Socialist literature, principally a circular of "Socialist welcome." In return for this courtesy from men of another nation, since "leave was granted, hundreds of sailors visited the Socialist hall and signified their approval" of the Australians' efforts in undermining the American navy. To give, in part, the circular:

"SOCIALIST WELCOME TO THE AMERICAN FLEET."

"We greet you in all sincerity. . . . We know, and are fully confident that you also know, that the armies and navies of the world are utterly inimical to the true interests of the workers and exist exclusively in the interests of the dominant plutocracy. .

"Comrades—Great as your navy is, we belong to a far greater fighting body. We are members of the great class-conscious fighting proletariat of the world. . . .

"Brothers of America, our hearts go out to you as men; and our blood thrills with increased animation to know that among you are many straight-out *Socialists*. It was with very great pleasure we learned from the *World*, of Oakland, Cal., that 'every battleship of the Pacific fleet carries on it a band of devoted Socialists, who are spreading the propaganda' . . . 'that agitation is carried on continuously.' . . .

"We are at one with you . . . believing . . . 'the world is my country' . . . therefore we view with exceeding pleasure the rapid march of international Socialism. . . . Do not forget . . . and remember that we, too, are ready . . . when the hour arrives for the workers to throw off their oppressors and establish the Socialist Commonwealth throughout the world.

"Yours for the Social Revolution,

"The Members of the Victorian Socialist Party."

Perhaps no other argument will be deemed necessary to convince the American people that Socialism is a deadly foe to this great nation than the presentation of a treasonable circular which was, by a Socialist paper, sent broadcast throughout the country, and without the whisper of dissent coming from any "revolutionary" quarter.

This paper, the *Appeal to Reason*, claims a paid subscription list of over 300,000, and a bundle circulation that is enormous besides. It has an indefatigable corps of unpaid workers who propagate Socialism not alone by means of the *Appeal*, but by other literature which the management sends out, tons upon tons.

This circular letter to the "Appeal Army" lauds desertion as a new mode of virtue. Money is wanted! So, with a full heart, Mr. J. A. Wayland, the editor, not alone hails the man "comrade" who learned treason from his own columns, but he opens them wide to the some-time soldier—now of "no country" —that he may sow for a multitudinous crop.

It was after more than three years of dutiful service that Mr. C. Hudspeth "fell in with a copy of the *Appeal*, and from that time" he was too much of a Socialist to serve . . . in the organized mob called the army of the United States."

Having turned his face to this *Appeal to Reason*, he fled from duty and honor. Mistaking shame for glory, Mr. Hudspeth tells the tale of his own crime exultingly. He "deserted the armed mob, and after one year they caught" him. Hence his eighteen months in prison. And then the little "piece of yellow paper"—a dishonorable discharge—his badge of shame—of which he seems vastly proud.

His record of infamy proved his passport to the columns of the *Appeal*. And in a series of five articles—"Enlisting," "Drilling," "Fighting," "Deserting," "The United States Military Prisons"—Mr. C. Hudspeth did what he could to "undermine the army."

The circular calls for money to send out the five editions containing the story of how "I was formally and officially tabooed by the plutes;" and that "they gave me a piece of yellow paper to certify that I am no longer worthy to be called a servant of the plutes."

In "bundles of five to every army post in the United States and its foreign possessions," this story should be sent to show "the power of the *Appeal*—and "to a class of men we need to reach." Under his own signature Mr. Wayland informs his readers: "I never received a letter that did my old heart more good" than this one from Deserter Hudspeth. For "it shows the power of the *Appeal*"—to cultivate the virus of treason among "100,000 men who are just as susceptible to our teachings as is the comrade" who was, alas! once an honorable man.

WOMAN'S DEPARTMENT ANNUAL MEETING

REPORTS FOR 1908—PLANS FOR THE ENSUING YEAR—ENERGETIC ORGANIZATION WORK

OFFICERS AND EXECUTIVE COMMITTEE OF THE WOMAN'S DEPARTMENT, 1909.

MRS. WILLIAM H. TAFT, the Honorary Chairman.
MRS. HORACE BROCK, Chairman, Lebanon, Pa.
MRS. J. BORDEN HARRIMAN, First Vice-Chairman, New York City.
MRS. JOSEPH MEDILL, M'CORMICK, Second Vice-Chairman, Chicago, Ill.
MRS. JOHN K. OTTLEY, Third Vice-Chairman, Atlanta, Ga.
MRS. WILLIAM H. CROCKER, Fourth Vice-Chairman, Burlingame, Cal.
MRS. B. FRANK MEBANE, Fifth Vice-Chairman, Spray, N. C.
MRS. EVA M'DONALD VALESH, Sixth Vice-Chairman, Washington, D. C.
MRS. MARY HATCH WILLARD, Treasurer, New York.
MRS. MARCUS M. MARKS, Secretary, New York.
MRS. ARCHIBALD ALEXANDER, Hoboken, N. J.
MRS. S. THRUSTON BALLARD, Louisville, Ky.
MRS. WILLIAM B. BOURN, San Francisco, Cal.
MRS. FRANCIS HIGGINSON CABOT, New York City.
MRS. ANDREW CARNEGIE, New York City.
MRS. W. MURRAY CRANE, Dalton, Mass.
MRS. SARAH S. PLATT DECKER, Denver, Col.
MRS. MICHAEL DREICER, New York.
MRS. MARSHALL FIELD, Chicago, Ill.
MRS. EDWIN FARNHAM GREENE, Boston, Mass.
MRS. CLEMENT ACTON GRISCOM, JR., New York City.
MRS. ARCHIBALD HOPKINS, Washington, D. C.
MRS. OVERTON LEA, Nashville, Tenn.
MRS. ARTHUR LEE, Elkins, W. Va.
MRS. NICHOLAS LONGWORTH, Cincinnati, O.
MRS. FRANK O. LOWDEN, Oregon, Ill.
MRS. V. EVERIT MACY, New York City.
MRS. BOWMAN H. M'CALLA, Santa Barbara, Cal.
MRS. CYRUS HALL M'CORMICK, Chicago, Ill.
MRS. HENRY B. F. MACFARLAND, Washington, D. C.
MRS. A. F. M'KISSICK, Greenwood, S. C.
MRS. CYRUS PITMAN ORR, Birmingham, Ala.
MISS ANNA D. SLOCUM, Boston, Mass.
MRS. SAMUEL SPENCER, Washington, D. C.
MRS. CORNELIUS STEVENSON, Philadelphia, Pa.
MRS. OSCAR S. STRAUS, Washington, D. C.
MISS ADA C. SWEET, New York City.
MRS. WILLIAM H. TAFT, Cincinnati, O.
MRS. EDMUND LEIGHTON TYLER, Anniston, Ala.
MRS. TALCOTT WILLIAMS, Philadelphia, Pa.
MRS. ROGER WOLCOTT, Boston, Mass.
MRS. BENJAMIN IDE WHEELER, Berkeley, Cal.

Chairmen of National Standing Committees

On Welfare Work for Government Employes, MRS. WILLIAM H. TAFT.
On Welfare Work for Industrial Employes, MRS. J. BORDEN HARRIMAN.
On Industrial Economics, MRS. CORNELIUS STEVENSON.
Membership Committee, MRS. CLEMENT ACTON GRISCOM, JR.
Finance Committee, MRS. MICHAEL DREICER.

The annual meeting of the Woman's Department of the National Civic Federation was held at the Hotel Astor, New York City, on December 14 and 15, 1908.

The proceedings were restricted to reports of officers and committees, the adoption of plans for the ensuing year, and the election of officers and appointment of committees.

Mrs. J. Borden Harriman, Vice-Chairman, presided on Monday, the 14th, in the absence of the National Chairman, Mrs. J. Medill McCormick.

The Chairman, in her opening remarks, reported:

"There are at present four organized sections, namely:

"New York and New Jersey, Mrs. Archibald Alexander, Chairman.

"California, Mrs. William H. Crocker, Chairman.

"District of Columbia, Mrs. Samuel Spencer, Chairman.

"Kentucky and Tennessee, Mrs. S. Thruston Ballard, Chairman.

"In addition there have been authorized by the Executive Council:

"New England, the Sectional Chairman to be selected in consultation with Mrs. Roger Wolcott.

"Pennsylvania, Delaware and Maryland, Mrs. Horace Brock, Chairman.

"Virginia and West Virginia, Mrs. W. T. Harris, Chairman.

"North and South Carolina, Mrs. B. Frank Mebane, of North Carolina, Chairman, in consultation with Mrs. A. F. McKissick, of South Carolina, with power to create two sections of this territory if desirable.

"Georgia and Florida, Mrs. J. K. Ottley, Chairman.

"Alabama and Mississippi, Mrs. Cyrus Pitman Orr, Chairman.

"Illinois and Ohio, the Chairman to be selected in consultation with Mrs. Cyrus H. McCormick."

The rules and plan of work for the ensuing year of the following national standing committees were presented by:

Mrs. William Howard Taft, Chairman of the Government Employes' Welfare Committee.

Mrs. J. Borden Harriman, Chairman of the Industrial Employes' Welfare Committee (read by Mrs. Cornelius Stevenson), and Mrs. Horace Brock, Chairman of the Industrial Economics Committee.

These comprehensive reports will be published in the Handbook of the Woman's Department.

Mrs. Archibald Alexander, Chairman of the New York and New Jersey Section, reported:

"The work accomplished by the New York and New Jersey Woman's Department, since the last report was made in Washington in May, might be divided into three parts: The work of organizing and the actual field work of our two committees.

"This section, being the first one formed, has found it necessary to feel its way as the work progressed in order to find a form of organization allowing enough freedom for the committees to do their work unhampered and yet enabling our efforts to tell as a whole and as part of the national work, while also preventing as far as possible mistakes which might prove extremely serious to the large interests involved in our investigations.

"We are also engaged in the task of organizing our office in a business-like way, and we have been fortunate in securing, as our Executive Secretary, Dr. Lucy A. Bannister, who for several years has been in charge of the very successful welfare work of the Westinghouse Lamp Company. It will be the duty of Dr. Bannister to accompany committees on their visits, and she will also have charge of filing reports which in time should prove valuable.

"We are trying a plan of having an office morning, when the chairman and vice-chairman of the department are to be found in the office, so that any one wishing information or suggestions will know when and where to find them.

"The reports of our two working committees are as follows:

"Work that has been done since March 15, 1908, by the Industrial Employes' Welfare Committee has been: Investigations by the Cigar Factories, Garment Trades, Recreation, Stationary Firemen and Traction committees. But we have confined ourselves principally to securing information, addresses being made by persons who could illuminate us along the line of endeavor of our sub-committees.

"We accomplished one result very gratifying as being directly in accordance with the policy of the Woman's Department of the Civic Federation. One of the members of the Committee on Stationary Firemen persuaded her husband, for the first time in the history of his place, to give a two-weeks' vacation to each of the stationary firemen in his buildings. The Stationary Firemen's Committee also cites the Belmont Hotel as an instance of model welfare work.

"The Recreation Committee has found that two sizes of halls are much needed for the working people in New York—one with a capacity of 3,000, for dancing purposes, and a smaller one for meetings of two to three hundred persons."

It was not proposed at present to appoint any new committees. Mrs. Alexander further reported the following suggestions of subjects coming from the Industrial Employes' Welfare Committee, on which the section might be addressed by expert welfare workers: "Provision for Leisure Time;" "The Physician's Place in a Manufacturing Institution;" "The Needs of Women Workers in a Department Store;" "Some Experiences in Connection with the Relief Department of a Local Transportation Company;" "Industrial Training from the Employers' and Employes' Standpoint," and "The Trades Union Movement."

With the Chairman of the Industrial Employes' Welfare Committee, Mrs. J. Borden Harriman, are the following chairmen of sub-committees: Cigar Factories, Miss Caroline Shippen; Garment Trades, Mrs. Marcus M. Marks; Stationary Firemen, Mrs. Frank McNeil Bacon; Traction, Mrs. Clement Acton Griscom, Jr.; Recreation, Mrs. Orrin S. Goan; Printers, Miss Dorothy Whitney; Teamsters, Mrs. D. W. Evans.

Mrs. Alexander also read the report of the Committee on Welfare Work for Government Employes, which was formed in the Spring of 1908. Its duties are to investigate the working conditions of Federal, Municipal and State employes, to ascertain what welfare work has been undertaken for their benefit, and to inquire into the need for improvements.

Through the sub-committee on postal employes an investigation of the Post Office stations in Manhattan was made last Spring. The committee made a recommendation, through Postmaster Edward M. Morgan, who requested suggestions, that the roof of the new Post Office at the Pennsylvania Terminal be used as a swing room for letter carriers between shifts. The committee also sent a letter indorsing the amendment to the Post Office appropriation bill to increase the salaries of postal employes receiving more than $1,000 per annum, and to allow thirty days' vacation to all postal employes.

In April several visits were made to the Brooklyn Navy Yard, which resulted in a proposal to establish a lunch room for the men within the gates of the yard. At times 6,000 mechanics are employed there daily; when work is slack, 3,000. The sub-committee still has this subject in hand.

Owing to the vast scope of its work, and the danger of lacking in thoroughness in attempting to cover such a field, the committee has decided to take up one department at a time. In this way all the members of the committee can concentrate on the work in hand, and the monthly lectures can relate to the work being done at the time.

A new Buildings Committee has been formed to get the plans of proposed new buildings—city, State and Federal—and make suggestions for the welfare of employes before the buildings are put up.

The work of the Government Employes' Committee is mainly that of investigation. This work moves slowly, but it leads to legislation. This committee has the idea that the government may become the best employer in the city, State and nation, and an example to others. For this end its members are striving, meantime training themselves to work more intelligently.

With the Chairman of the Government Employes' Welfare Committee, Mrs. Francis Higginson Cabot, are the following chairmen of sub-committees: Navy Yard, Miss Anne Morgan; New Buildings, Mrs. Mary Hatch Willard; City Hospitals, Mrs. Ernesto G. Fabbri; State Hospitals, Mrs. A. H. Harris.

Mrs. William H. Crocker, Chairman of the California Section, reported that this section was organized at the Fairmont Hotel, in San Francisco, on September 18 last. Previously, however, heads of large industries and department stores had promised not only their own hearty co-operation, but also that of their wives and daughters.

Mr. Benjamin Ide Wheeler, who was a guest of the Section on September 18, addressed the ladies present, explaining the aims of the Civic Federation and especially of the Woman's Department. The following officers were elected on that occasion: Mrs. W. H. Crocker, Chairman; Mrs. John Johns, Secretary; Mrs. John F. Merrill, Mrs. William B. Brown, Mrs. Andrew Davis, Vice-Chairmen; Mrs. Arthur Cornwall, Treasurer; Miss McKinistry, Membership Committee; Mrs. Reginald Knight Smith, Press and Literature; Miss Jessica Peixotto, Programme; Mrs. McCalla (Navy) and Mrs. Maus (Army), Government Employes.

In some notable instances the work of the Civic Federation has been anticipated in California, as in the cases of two large stores, in both of which, employing hundreds of women, rest and lunch rooms and proper toilet facilities are provided.

Mrs. Crocker, in concluding her report, said: "The Southern Pacific Railway and the Santa Fe Railway have done good work in providing for their trainmen clubs at which they find relaxation and shelter from the influence of the saloon. The club at Dunsmuir has been in operation two years and is extremely successful. Others have been located at important points like Tucson, Sparks and Rocklin. This work is under the charge of Mr. Athearn, graduate of the University of California, who is showing ability for this line of work.

'The two fields distinctly Californian are the great ranch and farm enterprises and mines. In some of the great ranches hundreds of men are herded together, and little or nothing is done to relieve their lives from utter sordidness and coarseness. I believe that nothing has been done for the miners. In regard to the Goldfield Consolidated Mines of Nevada, Senator Nixon has already promised his co-operation in installing welfare work whenever we are ready to make suggestions, which will be in February or March of this year."

Mrs. Samuel Spencer, Chairman of the District of Columbia Section, reported that at a meeting at the New Willard Hotel, in Washington, on May 11, 1908, at which Mrs. Archibald Hopkins was chairman, Mrs. McCormick, the National Chairman, made an address to the women assembled. A committee to nominate officers and members of the Executive Committee was thereupon appointed. On the 12th the section was formally organized, and the following, being the nominees of the committee, were unanimously elected: Mrs. Samuel Spencer, Chairman; Mrs. John Boit, Treasurer; Miss Mary Sheridan, Secretary; Miss Alice Lovering, Assistant Secretary. Honorary Vice-Chairmen—Mrs. William H. Taft, Mrs. James R. Garfield, Mrs. George B. Cortelyou, Mrs. Oscar S. Straus. Executive Committee—Mrs. Archibald Hopkins, Miss Mabel Boardman, Miss Maude Wetmore, Miss Georgia Nevins, Mrs. S. W. Woodward, Mrs. Richard Wainright, Mrs. A. Lisner, Mrs. William C. Eustis.

The officers and members of the Executive Committee met a few days later at Mrs. Spencer's residence to plan for the work. They drew up sectional by-laws and appointed the following committees, to be enlarged and added to when the work is thoroughly established: Committee on Welfare Work for Government Employes—Mrs. W. C. Eustis, Mrs. Archibald Hopkins, Miss Maude Wetmore, Mrs. Oscar S. Straus. Committee on Welfare Work for Industrial Employes—Mrs. Charles W. Richardson, Mrs. S. W. Woodward, Mrs. A. Lisner, Mrs. Collins, Mrs. James F. Harlan. Committee on Programme—Mrs. Archibald Hopkins, with four assistants whom she was authorized to select. Committee on Press and Literature—Mrs. Jas. Hobson, with three assistants of her selection. Committee on Membership—Mrs. Richard Wainwright, Mrs. Ward Thoron, Mrs. James F. Harlan.

The chairman of authorized sections made the following recommendations and reports:

Mrs. Roger Wolcott, of Massachusetts, while unable to accept an executive position, expressed a willingness to aid in the initial work by forming a committee in Boston to interest the women of that section in the Federation.

Mrs. B. Frank Mebane, of North Carolina, reported that while her section had not been organized, a great deal of enthusiasm had been created in Richmond, Va., Danville, W. Va., Charlotte and other cities in North Carolina. She stated that there is a great desire to organize and that Mrs. William H. Taft would accompany her to Spray, N. C., where there are 10,000 employes in the cotton mill industry, for the purpose of making an address to women in that vicinity. She said this will give an impetus to the work of organization. She also hoped to have a meeting in Richmond, Va., in January.

Mrs. Cyrus Pitman Orr, Chairman of the Alabama and Mississippi Section, who was detained at the last moment, in offering recommendations, wrote:

"Once districted the work in Alabama, Mississippi and Georgia would naturally go into three channels: department stores, mines and furnaces, and cotton mills. Having few large cities, the department stores problem is not acute. In my own State of Alabama missionary work on the part of the Conciliation Department seems the crying need of the hour in the coal and iron industries, and may precede welfare work. . . .

"The third department, that of the cotton mills, is one that appeals to me—this situation is complicated by no foreign element, or practically none. Here is a place where we do not have to make Americans. We only educate, encourage and sustain them; with all the faults and some of the virtues of the pure American type, they sometimes seem refractory ones, but with the proper flux none yield so fine a return of the pure metal. They are the illiterates of whom we hear so much, at once the menace and the hope of our Southern country. Among them are the men who would make the bed rock of our civilization. Failing them, the gaps in our structure of democracy will affect every part of our great country. This work in cotton mills is along the lines of least resistance. Manufacturers are already doing their work, and will welcome our assistance. We have taken from the East some of their earnest workers, and we have already mills which are garden spots in the counties where they are located. 'Nothing succeeds like success,' and although the success was not ours we can use it."

Mrs. Horace Brock, Chairman of the Committee on Amendment of By-Laws, presented its report, the proposed amendments being discussed and passed upon. The by-laws as amended will be published in the Handbook of the Woman's Department.

Upon the motion of Mrs. Eva McDonald Valesh, seconded by Mrs. Brock, the Chairman appointed the following committee of seven to nominate officers and members of the National Executive Council: Mrs. V. Everit Macy, Chairman; Mrs. Archibald Alexander, Mrs. Arthur Lee, Mrs. B. Frank Mebane, Mrs. Eva McDonald Valesh, Mrs. Marcus M. Marks, Mrs. William B. Bourn.

At the close of the first session, Hon. Seth Low, the President of the National Civic Federation, said:

"Ladies, I feel much gratified that the Ladies' Department has taken up the work with us. There certainly is no more important work to be done in the country in bringing about good relations in the field of industry and commerce than the welfare work in which you are specially concerned. It is one very important and very humane part of the business.

"The last time I had the pleasure of seeing the late German Ambassador von Sternberg, he said to me that he thought the Civic Federation, in its efforts to deal with this question, was doing a work of the utmost importance—not only for our own country, but for all countries, because, as he said, this is the most difficult problem of modern civilization, and it really requires Americans to handle it. In other words, every possible influence that can be brought to bear to make a better understanding all along the line between the employer and the employe is very helpful, and no one knows better than some of you ladies how much there is to be done in making the conditions, under which men and women spend a greater part of their time, such as ought to be provided where men and women have to work. Of course, the men are trying to aid along that line too, but I am fully persuaded that there is a real field for women, in which they can be very helpful. I have little doubt that you will find many things that can be done and that are worth doing.

"I simply want to add, Mrs. President and ladies, that if at any time or in any way, as the chairman of the general organization I can be of service to you in your work, I hope you will feel at liberty to qualify me. Thank you very much for giving me the privilege."

The second session of the Woman's Department, on Tuesday, December 15, was called to order by the Vice-Chairman, Mrs. Cornelius Stevenson.

Mrs. V. Everit Macy, Chairman of the Nominating Committee, reported the nominees for officers and members of the Executive Committee, who were duly elected. The list appears at the beginning of this report.

MRS. TAFT AT SPRAY, NORTH CAROLINA

HER ADDRESS AS HONORARY CHAIRMAN OF THE WOMAN'S DEPARTMENT ON THE OCCASION OF ORGANIZING A NEW SECTION

On December 17, immediately after the annual sessions of The National Civic Federation in New York, a meeting was held in Spray, N. C., at the home of Mr. and Mrs. B. Frank Mebane, under the auspices of the Woman's Department, with a view to organizing a section for that part of the South.

Mrs. William Howard Taft, wife of the President-elect, accompanied Mrs. Mebane from New York to North Carolina, Mr. Mebane meeting them at Danville, W. Va., with a special train.

Mrs. Taft, who was the principal speaker of the occasion, was one of the original members of the Woman's Department. She was last year chairman of the Committee on Welfare Work for Government Employes. While retaining the position for the present year, she was also elected in New York Honorary Chairman of the Department. Her appearance at the first public meeting of the Woman's Department held in the South Atlantic States was regarded by all present as significant and promising.

The proceedings were opened by Mrs. W. T. Harris, of Danville, who presided. Following her preliminary talk in which she explained the purpose of the meeting, Mrs. Harris introduced Mrs. Taft.

There were present about two hundred Southern women who had become interested in the work of The National Civic Federation. Among the members of the Woman's Department were Mrs. A. F. McKissick, of Greenwood, S. C., who, after Mrs. Taft's address, told those in attendance of her work and that of others to promote the welfare of operatives in South Carolina cotton mill towns, especially in Pelzer, her former home, and at Greenwood, where she now lives.

Mrs. Charles D. McIver, of Greensboro, N. C., was one of the speakers. She urged the extension of schools in the country districts of the State.

Another interesting speaker was Mrs. Lindsey Paterson, of Winston-Salem.

Other Southern women present were Miss Jennie English, Atlanta, Ga.; Mrs. J. W. Menefee and Mrs. Tom Meade, Danville, West Va.; Mrs. J. Allison Hodges, Richmond, Va.; Mrs. Ralph Dula, Mrs. A. B. Carrington, Mrs. Henry Vass, of Virginia; Mrs. Robert L. Parrish, Covington, Va.; Mrs. Alma Richardson, Greensboro, N. C., and Mrs. Claude A. Swanson, wife of the Governor of Virginia. The universal enthusiasm in the cause of welfare work was described by one of the women guests as "amazing."

After the assembly had dispersed, Mrs. Taft was conducted through some of the large cotton mills in Spray, a town which has ten thousand operatives. In the evening she returned to Danville, where she joined Mr. Taft on his way South.

Mrs. Taft's address was as follows:

MRS. TAFT'S ADDRESS.

The Woman's Department of The National Civic Federation is the outgrowth of the Federation's efforts to promote Welfare Work. It enlists the ready sympathy of women, and the Woman's Department affords an opportunity for active support. Our main object, as declared in our articles of organization, is "to secure needed improvements in the working and living conditions of women and men wage-earners in the various industries and governmental institutions throughout the United States." There are three reasons why this work should appeal strongly to women: First, they have the opportunities; second, it often concerns their interests closely, and, third, they have a peculiar fitness for it by situation and disposition.

The opportunities of women to influence the economic well-being of the world's workers are greater perhaps than they realize. They are, as stockholders, the too often silent partners in many large industrial enterprises. In one of the great railways alone it is stated that 28,000 stockholders—practically one-half—are women, their holdings amounting to $148,000,000. Besides those who hold stock in their own names there are many others who through family relationship are financially interested in, or dependent upon, industrial agencies, mills, railroads, stores and mines. Some of them are actively concerned for the well-being of the workers in the enterprises from which their incomes are drawn. Some are members of our department, and we feel sure that many others will join in our efforts when they realize the opportunities which they have at hand.

In public affairs the wives and daughters of officials can exert a wide influence in awakening an interest in the conditions of government service. The government itself is one of the largest employers of labor in all parts of the country. In many branches of its service, notably in the Post Office, it may well be worth while to investigate whether all is being done which should be done for the health and comfort of employes.

The country has grown so rapidly in population and developed so enormously in a short time that its public institutions often have helplessly fallen behind the best ideals. In the State and municipal institutions, such as asylums and hospitals, and in the police and fire departments of our cities, much remains to be done before the employes of the public can be said to be respectably, not to say comfortably, cared for. And when we think what interests are confided to them it seems superfluous to insist and argue that they should be well housed, furnished with proper food and given opportunities daily, not only for rest, but recreation and exercise.

That women have a legitimate interest in these matters is apparent, when we stop to think how much of the world's work is done for women and the home. Women's interests are almost commensurate with the whole field of industry. The employes of railways and of mines, the stationary firemen and engineers who work in ill-ventilated basements and sub-basements, the coal passers who toil in all sorts of narrow and crowded quarters, hotel employes, bakers, and the throngs of mill hands in the textile industry, the teamsters of great cities, all these and many others are engaged in work in whose ultimate results women have a personal interest.

INTERIOR COFFEE HOUSE, ALTON, ILL.

NAVAL CLUBHOUSE, MARE ISLAND, CALIFORNIA.
Provided by Admiral and Mrs. Bowman H. McCalla.

But, again, there is a peculiar fitness for women engaging in such work where they can in many respects ameliorate the conditions of their own sex. The old-fashioned family duties have passed in large measure from the home to the factory and workshop. The United States statistics for 1900 show that one out of every three women between the ages of sixteen and twenty is a breadwinner, and that of all women over the age of sixteen years one in five works for wages. Many, it is true, very nearly one-quarter of them, are in domestic service. The remainder are in mills, factories, shops and offices, and nearly one-half of them are under twenty-five years of age. From them will spring many of the new generation. To secure for them healthful, orderly places in which to work, with facilities for innocent recreation, proper exercise and opportunities for social relaxation and educational improvement, is obviously a proper activity for this department.

LIBRARY FOR ENLISTED MEN, MARE ISLAND.

The Woman's Department seeks to accomplish its purpose through committees, of which three are now in existence.

The Committee on Industrial Economics, still in its infancy, will seek to familiarize the women of our department with the larger aspects of the industrial life of the present.

The Industrial and the Government Employes' Welfare Committees will investigate the conditions of such employes in private enterprises and in government institutions to learn what welfare work has been undertaken for their benefit and what improvements, if any, are needed.

That the friendly influence of women may be felt both in private enterprise and in public service may be indicated by two examples.

The glass industry of this country is in special need of arrangements for the comfort of the men and women workers. Probably no other large industry is conducted in such old and dilapidated buildings, with such inadequate provision for either heating or ventilation. Arrangements for the comfort of employes too often reflect these primitive industrial surroundings. Through the efforts of two of our members, who are the daughters of the president of a great glass manufacturing company, the women employes of the works have recently been substantially benefited by the establishment of rest rooms for their special use, and in October of this year a coffee house was opened in the yards for the benefit of the glass blowers, the restaurant being kept open night and day to meet the needs of those who work on eight-hour shifts. The work having begun, other manufacturers are asking for information and examining into the possibilities for improving their own works.

No better example of the co-operation in good work of the wife of a public official can be given than that of Mrs. Bowman H. McCalla. Twelve years ago, when Admiral McCalla was stationed at Mare Island, he and Mrs. McCalla witnessed the pitiful condition of the boys and young men who were carried there on ships to be repaired in the Navy Yard.

The town of Vallejo, opposite the naval station, is a workmen's town of 12,000 inhabitants, with over two hundred saloons. Mrs. McCalla has been working for five years in the interest of the bluejackets and marines, who when she began had no decent place of amusement to visit when on leave from their ships; their uniforms debarred them from respectable places. For the purpose of providing pleasant companionship and amusement for the enlisted men she and her husband undertook to provide a permanent club to be patronized only by that type of government employes; it has bedrooms, bathrooms, a library, a game room, an auditorium, a bowling alley, shooting gallery and restaurant within its four walls, thus securing for the men the enjoyment and recreation of the saloon without its injurious elements. This naval clubhouse was opened in 1904, with an attendance exceeding 50,000 during its first two years. It is reported that in that period over one hundred thousand dollars of the men's pay had been placed by them in the club's bank for safe-keeping, this money having been spent formerly in the saloons or worse places.

The clubhouse is overcrowded, and Admiral McCalla has been informed by the chief of police that arrests diminished in Vallejo seventy per cent during the first two years after the opening of the building.

But the cost of this splendid achievement in welfare work was not, as it should have been, met by the employer—the Government of the United States. A heavy burden of debt was incurred by Mrs. McCalla and a committee of women interested with her, funds having been loaned by private citizens, without interest, and the lot having been purchased, sad to relate, with all of Admiral McCalla's prize money of the Spanish War, so great was his interest in many cases of heart-breaking misery where boys of fifteen going into the navy were hopelessly ruined in body and soul. He and Mrs. McCalla felt impelled to alleviate the conditions of a special temptation assailing the lads who had left home and friends and were thrown upon their own resources in a strange town.

We hope to assist the Public Employes' Committee of The National Civic Federation in having extended the efforts of the government for the benefit of its employes, such as beneficial features instituted in army stations, army posts, and at Panama, that it may be financially responsible and not permit its employes to be dependent upon haphazard contributions of sacrificing and interested citizens.

The establishment of provident funds, including industrial insurance, pensions and safe investments for savings for women as well as men employes, and for government as well as private employes, we consider to be of great importance, and we are planning, as members of The National Civic Federation, to aid in that line of endeavor.

The Woman's Department sees and appreciates great possibilities for usefulness. May it live up to its best and highest ideals, and help to secure and maintain a spirit of good will and fair understanding—the true American spirit.

REST ROOM FOR WOMEN PACKERS,
ILLINOIS GLASS COMPANY, ALTON, ILL.

A GROTESQUE TRAVESTY OF LINCOLN'S SPEECHES

AMERICAN LABOR'S GOOD WHOLE CLOTH CUT UP AND MADE INTO SOCIALISTIC PATCHWORK

By Ada C. Sweet

COLOSSAL impudence is shown by the Socialist press in publishing garbled and mutilated sentences, half-sentences and paragraphs from the speeches and papers of Abraham Lincoln in an attempt to pretend that the great Emancipator held Socialistic opinions. Robert Hunter, commenting upon these maimed and distorted extracts torn from their context and printed in an issue of the *Social Democratic Herald* with his own article, declares that Lincoln "stated powerfully the entire demand of Labor and Socialism." Concerted action among Socialists to appropriate the great name of Lincoln to their own purposes is shown by an article entitled "Lincoln and Labor," by W. J. Ghent, the Socialist leader, published in the *Independent* of February 11, and by the printing of some of the same garbled extracts from Lincoln's speeches as those used by the *Social Democratic Herald* in the programme of the conference on Socialism, held by the friends of the movement in Boston, February 5-7, of this year.

The confusing and indentifying of labor with Socialism is constantly kept up by Socialist speakers and writers, and it is a very useful, though entirely unauthorized, adjunct to their efforts. By this false assumption it is possible to torture into some form of apparent complaisance with Socialistic ideas every utterance of broad charity and justice toward mankind in its struggle which has come from the leaders and the prophets from the time when words were first recorded.

Of course, Abraham Lincoln not only conceded, but urged the just claims of labor. But he did not ignore the just claims of capital, nor of the element of society which neither does manual labor nor draws its maintenance from its own capital, the section to which Lincoln himself belonged during most of his years after he reached maturity.

The method employed by the Socialist enthusiasts in their effort to get something of their dismal gospel into Lincoln's mouth is to quote paragraphs, sometimes unfinished, and sentences and half sentences from his notes and speeches. An example is furnished by the quotation of several passages, mutilated, from Lincoln's message to Congress, December 3, 1861.

Referring to the Civil War, which he called "the insurrection," Lincoln, alluding to the dangers of the situation and the arguments of the Slave Power, is quoted as saying:

"It is not needed or fitting here that a general argument should be made in favor of popular institutions, but there is one point, with its connections, not so hackneyed as most others, to which I ask a brief attention. It is the effort to place capital on an equal footing with, if not above, labor, in the structure of government. It is assumed that labor is available only in connection with capital; that nobody labors unless somebody else, owning capital, somehow, by the use of it, induces them to labor. This assumed, it next considers whether it is best that capital shall hire laborers and thus induce them to work by their own consent." . . .

The conclusion of this last sentence, "or buy them and drive them to it without their own consent," is omitted. This omission was, without doubt, intended to blind present day readers to the fact that Lincoln was speaking in that address of the doctrines of slavery as opposed to those of free labor.

Again, the following is quoted from the same message by the Socialistic publications:

"Labor is prior to and independent of capital. Capital is only the fruit of labor, and could never have existed if labor had not first existed. Labor is the superior of capital, and deserves much the higher consideration." And the immediately following sentences are left out, viz.: **"Capital has its rights which are as worthy of protection as any other rights. Nor is it denied that there is, and probably always will be, a relation between labor and capital producing mutual benefits."**

This omission is at once significant and amusing.

In another instance Lincoln's words are quoted as follows, the fact, however, being that the opening sentences of the paragraph—which we print below the quotation—are left out:

"No men living are more worthy to be trusted than those who toil up from poverty; none less inclined to take or touch aught which they have not honestly earned. Let them beware of surrendering a political power which they already possess, and which, if surrendered, will surely be used to close the door of advancement against such as they, and fix new disabilities and burdens upon them till all of liberty shall be lost."

The omitted beginning of the paragraph is as follows:

"Again, as has already been said, there is not of necessity any such thing as the free hired laborer being fixed to that condition for life. Many independent men everywhere in these States a few years back in their lives were hired laborers. **The prudent, penniless beginner in the world labors for wages awhile, saves a surplus with which to buy tools or land for himself, then labors on his own account another while, and at length hires another new beginner to help him. This is the just and generous and prosperous system which opens the way to all, gives hope to all, and consequent energy and progress and improvement of condition to all."**

The passage from which these fragments were taken by the Socialist publication was included, says the *Social Democratic Herald*, in Lincoln's reply to the Workingmen's Association of New York, March 21, 1864. But this very paper has in it such complete refutation of these absurd Socialistic assertions regarding Lincoln, and withal so much characteristic good sense and strong feeling, that The Review prints the opening and the two closing paragraphs. It will be observed that Lincoln tells what he was contending for in the message of December, 1861, the very document which Socialism is now trying to torture into an attack upon one portion of society, and then use it for the inflammation of class prejudice generally:

REPLY TO A COMMITTEE FROM THE WORKINGMEN'S ASSOCIATION OF NEW YORK.

March 21, 1864.

"Gentlemen of the Committee:

"Honorary membership in your association, as generously tendered, is gratefully accepted. You comprehend, as your address shows, that the existing rebellion means more than the perpetuation of African slavery—that it is, in fact, a war upon the rights of all working people. Partly to show that this view has not escaped my attention, and partly that I cannot better express myself, I read a passage from the message to Congress in December, 1861.

[Here follows the extract from his message.]

"None are so deeply interested to resist the present rebellion as the working people. Let them beware of prejudice and hostility among themselves. The most notable features of a disturbance in your city last Summer was the hanging of some working people by other working people. It should never be so. The strongest bond of human sympathy, outside of the family relation, should be one uniting all working people, of all nations and tongues, and kindreds. Nor should this lead to a war upon property, or the owners of property. **Property is the fruit of labor; property is desirable; is a positive good in the world. That some should be rich shows that others may become rich, and hence is just encouragement to industry and enterprise.**

"Let not him who is houseless pull down the house of another, but let him work diligently and build one for himself, thus by example assuring that his own shall be safe from violence when finished."

FOUR YEARS OF PROGRESS.

New England Civic Federation Executive Committee Hears Reports and Discusses Industrial Situation in Meeting at the Parker House, Boston.

A meeting of the Executive Committee of the Civic Federation of New England was held at the Parker House, Boston, Friday evening, December 4, 1908. The following were present, including the chairman of the Welfare Committee and one of the vice-chairmen, and several members of the Federation at large, who attended by special arrangement in behalf of committee members who were unable to be present:

Henry Abrahams, Secretary Cigarmakers' Union, Boston.

Louis D. Brandeis, vice-president New England Civic Federation.

George W. Brown, treasurer United Shoe Machinery Company, Boston, and Vice-Chairman Welfare Committee.

James R. Crozier, Carriage and Wagon Workers, Boston.

Dennis D. Driscoll, Secretary-Treasurer State Branch American Federation of Labor, Boston.

John Golden, President United Textile Workers of America, Fall River.

Hon. Charles S. Hamlin, Boston.

John Mason Little, Boston.

Augustus P. Loring, President Plymouth Cordage Company, Boston, and Chairman Welfare Committee.

Frank H. McCarthy, Organizer American Federation of Labor, Boston.

Norman E. McPhail, President Typographical Union, Boston.

Wallace L. Pierce, President Walworth Manufacturing Company, Boston.

James L. Richards, President Boston Consolidated Gas Company, Boston.

Hayes Robbins, Secretary New England Civic Federation, Boston.

Gen. Thomas Sherwin, President New England Telephone and Telegraph Company, Boston.

P. H. Sweet, President State Branch American Federation of Labor, Boston.

Lucius Tuttle, President Boston & Maine Railroad, and of the New England Civic Federation, Boston.

Edmond F. Ward, United Brewery Workmen, Boston.

W. C. Winslow, Metropolitan Coal Company, Boston.

Secretary Robbins presented a report on the work of the past year, reviewing also the efforts and results of the movement during the four years since its organization in New England. In the course of this report the secretary announced that on account of impaired health he was obliged to retire from the work, for the present, at least.

Mr. John B. McPherson, of Cambridge, was engaged to conduct the work of the Federation during the absence of Secretary Robbins. Mr. McPherson, who was formerly secretary of the National Association of Wool Manufacturers, took up his new work on January 1.

MISS ADA C. SWEET.

Miss Ada C. Sweet, formerly of Chicago, has taken up her work in the Department of Industrial Economics, at the headquarters of The National Civic Federation, in New York.

Miss Sweet is an active worker in clubs and organizations of a public and semi-public character. She was a member of the Board of the original Civic Federation of Chicago, founded in 1894, and was the first president of the Municipal Order League of Chicago, a society of women whose object was to obtain and maintain for that city public health and cleanliness, order and beauty. In 1895 she was president of the Chicago Woman's Club, an organization of which she has been an active member since 1885, and of which she was recently elected an honorary life member.

Upon the death of her father, the late General B. J. Sweet, President Grant, in 1874, appointed Miss Sweet United States Agent for Paying Pensions, at Chicago, and she was reappointed for the term of four years by President Hayes, and again by President Arthur. After an interval of foreign travel she opened an office as United States Pension Attorney, in Chicago, and continued in that work until 1905.

Miss Sweet is known to many people as a writer, having been connected with the Chicago daily papers, both editorially and writing over her own signature, during the past fifteen years, with occasional ventures into the magazine world.

The National
Civic Federation Review

Vol. III NEW YORK, MARCH 1, 1910 No. 9

A GREAT CONFERENCE ON VITAL PROBLEMS

UNIFORM STATE LAWS DISCUSSED IN WASHINGTON MEETING—NATIONAL AND STATE EXECUTIVES, SCHOLARS AND STATESMEN JOIN THE GREAT ORGANIZATIONS IN VOICING LEGISLATIVE NEEDS

1—MR. JOHN HAYS HAMMOND.
2—HON. ELIHU ROOT.
3—MR. CHARLES A. MOORE.
4—HON. HENRY B. BROWNE.
5—GOV. AUGUSTUS E. WILLSON.
6—HON. ALTON B. PARKER.
7—MR. JOHN MITCHELL.
8—PRESIDENT WILLIAM H. TAFT.
9—MR. ISAAC N. SELIGMAN.
10—HON. SETH LOW.
11—PROF. J. W. JENKS.
12—MR. SAMUEL GOMPERS.
13—HON. H. B. F. MACFARLAND.
14—MR. JAMES SPEYER.
15—HON. WILLIAM R. WILLCOX.

THE National Civic Federation's Conference on Uniform State Legislation at Washington was in its purpose and in its representative character, in its dignity and authority, unexampled among national gatherings. The 750 delegates, representing by appointment of the Governors forty-four States in the Union, or sent by over one hundred civic, commercial, labor, professional, agricultural, financial, manufacturing, economic and other national organizations, gathered in Belasco Theatre Monday morning, January 17th, 1910.

The assembly was a study of unrivaled interest. Many of the Governors, present at the Capitol to attend the Governors' Conference, sat with their State delegations, and members of national associations from the various parts of the country arranged themselves in congenial groups awaiting the opening of the meeting.

The personnel of the gathering in itself was impressive, and when its meaning was thoroughly understood it became doubly significant for its earnest purpose was nothing less than the binding more closely together of the States in harmonious union. The correspondent of the Richmond (Va.) *Times-Dispatch* well expressed the spirit of this assembly and the impression it made in the following special dispatch to his paper:

"Welded together by the common purpose of uplift, the visitors cared not that different points of view are leading them to the goal, nor that geographically they arrived in Washington from the four corners of the Union. The result was little groups of executives from the North and East discussing States' rights and the need of uniform laws with similar representatives of the South and West with as much mutual satisfaction as if there had been no Civil War in the sixties, and no Robert E. Lee statue to threaten the peace of the United States Senate in 1910; those interested in Civic Federation problems cared not a whit whether the person best equipped to illuminate certain phases of the work in hand was a bona-fide voter, a suffragist or a suffragette, and the Forestry Association declared its superiority by entirely ignoring the erstwhile, all-absorbing Ballinger-Pinchot controversy, with its present and future results."

Surely sectionalism, the influence against which Washington so strongly cautioned his countrymen, is no longer a menace. Local pride and national love of home, neighbors, institutions and people, happily remain, but the cruel old spirit of geographical discrimination and intolerance is fast disappearing. The last stand of sectional criticism is perhaps the current discussion as to the elimination, or the over-exploitation in different sections of the country, of the letter "r" or the final letter "g" in the spoken language of our people.

Escorted by President Low, of the National Civic Federation, and Judge Alton B. Parker, the President of the United States came upon the stage. The audience arose, warmly greeting the national Executive and remained standing until he was seated. On either side of President Taft sat Mr. Low, Judge Alton B. Parker, Associate Justice Brown, retired, Samuel Gompers, president of the American Federation of Labor, and John Hays Hammond. There were also upon the stage ex-Senator Dryden, of New Jersey; Senator Root, of New York; Commissioner Macfarland, of the District of Columbia; Governor Willson, of Kentucky; John Mitchell, William R. Willcox, Charles A. Moore, James Speyer, J. W. Jenks, N. J. Bachelder, Isaac N. Seligman and ex-Senator Dryden.

Immediately after the inevitable flash-light photograph, which explodes its harmless batteries upon even the most august public assembly, Mr. Low began his opening address, in which he declared the purpose of the Conference "to give an impulse to the movement for uniform legislation by the States as to matters upon which such legislation is desirable." He expressed appreciation of the presence and assistance of President Taft, and of the Governors of the States, and in urging the standardization of State laws by making them uniform as to matters which affect the interest of all the people in common, he paid a tribute to the patient labors and substantial achievements during the past twenty years of the Commissioners on Uniform Laws.

After closing his address Mr. Low introduced President Taft, and the audience rose and gave the Chief Executive a rousing reception. President Taft was in his happiest mood. Speaking without notes, he easily carried with him the entire assembly in his discussion of such themes as the responsibility and luty of the States, and the problems of marriage and livorce, or condemned the deep wrong of delayed udicial procedure which afflicts the entire nation.

Governor Willson, of Kentucky, made a delightfully nformal speech. In his own behalf and that of the ther Governors he thanked the Civic Federation for s consideration and courtesy extended to them and xpressed himself as strongly in favor of standardiza-ion, or uniformity in the State laws.

Judge Alton B. Parker quite captured the Confer-nce by his opening remarks, in which he good aturedly commented upon President Taft's hit at he Constitutional lawyer as "a gentleman who has one out of the practice of law and into politics." udge Parker's allusion to his own case as a lawyer, nd, for a few months a politician, was received with ughter and applause. The able address with which udge Parker followed his introductory talk was stened to with strict attention and received by the ssembly with many expressions of approval.

The Conference met in the ball-room of the Arling-n Hotel on Monday afternoon, with Judge Parker, ho had been elected as permanent chairman, presid-g. Again there was present a large audience of terested men and women. The delegates were now rouped by States, presenting the usual appearance f a national convention and affording facilities to he onlookers of finding in the delegations this or at celebrity or distinguished visitor to the capital.

Walter George Smith, president of the Conference f Commissioners on Uniform State Laws, addressed he assembly, giving an outline of the work of the ommissioners, describing their methods and the re-ults so far attained. For most of those present the ll scope and significance of the national movement r Uniform State Laws became defined with in-reasing clearness as President Smith proceeded in is speech. In closing, the speaker, in referring to e occasion and the Conference he was addressing, id: "This gathering, representing as it does, al-ost every department of human activity, is perhaps ore representative in character than any which has er assembled in the United States. Its conclusions ust have weight."

One of the most inspiring addresses delivered at e Conference was that of Senator Elihu Root, hose appearance was greeted with great applause. r. Root, originally one of the promoters of the idea the widening and deepening of the movement for niform State Laws, gave a clear-cut review of the esent chaotic conditions affecting the entire people the nation because of legislation which had little [illegible] no co-operative and harmonious activity of thought its initiation in the different States. His speech, d those of Mr. Low, President Taft, Judge Parker, r. Walter George Smith and Governor Willson are inted in full in this issue of the *Review*.

Each session of the Conference was attended not ly by the delegates, but by crowds of interested sitors, the occasion being recognized by the public one of first importance.

In taking leave of the delegates previous to the al adjournment, Judge Parker, the chairman, said: The results of this meeting cannot fail to be far-aching. There have been more than were ever con-mplated by the most enthusiastic among us. Ac-pt my deep appreciation for the service you have ndered your communities by your presence here. d be assured that the work thus begun will be car-ed on by willing hands."

OPENING ADDRESS—PRESIDENT LOW.

MR. PRESIDENT, Ladies and Gentlemen: On behalf of the National Civic Federation, it ves me the utmost pleasure to welcome you to is conference. We appreciate the action of the overnors of so many of the States in appointing legates, and also the action of the many com-ercial and other influential bodies which are here presented. You are all heartily welcome!

In particular, Mr. President, the conference is ghly honored by your presence, not only because u are here, but especially because your presence dicates your active sympathy with the objects the conference.

This conference has been called to give an im-lse to the movement for uniform legislation by e States as to matters upon which such legis-tion is desirable. The National Civic Federation es not pretend to be the originator of this move-ent; but it does hope that, as a result of this nference, the importance of uniform legislation y the States as to many subjects will be more idely understood. The Federation is confident that, recisely in proportion as this is understood, will the strength of the popular demand for such tion by the States.

Laymen though many of us are, we all know that e Federal Government has exclusive control of me subjects; while each State has exclusive con-ol, within its own borders, of other subjects. We so know that there are some subjects as to which oth the Federal Government and the State gov-ernments may each legislate within their respec-tive spheres. This situation has naturally led, in constitutional discussions, to the placing of the emphasis upon the effort to define accurately the limitations of power as between the Federal Gov-ernment and the State governments. In the mean-while, without any regard to such limitations, the people of the whole Union have been growing to-gether in their business relations, and in all the relations of life, without regard either to State lines or to constitutional theories. The result is, that of late years, especially, during which this process of unification of the vital and material interests of the people has been going on with continually increasing rapidity, the conviction has been steadily growing that uniform legislation by the States on many subjects is becoming, if it has not already become, essential to the welfare of the people of each State and of every State. I venture to think that before this conference adjourns, even those who are best informed will be astonished to learn in how many different fields such legislation is al-ready felt to be desirable, not to say necessary. Under most systems of government, the central legislative power, whatever it may be called, would pass the necessary laws, and these would then con-trol from one end of the country to the other; but under our Federal system this is not possible and we can obtain uniformity of statutory law in only one of two ways. We can give, by constitutional amendment, additional and exclusive power to Con-gress; or we must develop the capacity and the habit in the separate States of acting together with reasonable uniformity upon the subjects of common interest that overleap State lines. Thus far in our history as a people we have been content, mainly, to develop only the elements of strength to be found in the Federal Government and in the States, acting separately. Now we want to develop the almost unsuspected resources of the States, acting each one in its own field, but acting together. There are many matters as to which each State's interests are peculiar to itself; and, as to these, each State will naturally act from its own point of view alone. But there are also many matters which concern equally the people of other States, and as to these, it is full time that each State should habitually legislate, to use Senator Root's happy phrase "as one of a family of States."

There are some subjects, like Uniform Bills of Lading, for example, in which the people of all the States are interested and all in the same way. There is no reason why a statute regulating Bills of Lading, which is good for one State, should not be good for all. A statute on this subject, which is the same in all the States, is better for everybody than an ideally more perfect statute that should differ in important particulars in many States. Uniformity means that shipper, receiver, and common carrier, all have the same rights everywhere; while diversity in the law means that everywhere one must make a special study to know his rights and be prepared to make special efforts to maintain them, if they are exposed to differ-ent dangers in different communities.

There are other subjects in which groups of States have such a predominant interest, that common action by the States of this group is all that is essential. Such a subject is the proposed change in the theory of the laws of negligence, which would substitute workmen's compensation for employers' liability. This change has been made in every country of Europe as a result of modern industrial conditions. It is not without importance to all of the States; but it is of vital importance to the group of industrial States. Uniform legislation on this subject by the States of the industrial group would probably make it possible for these States to adopt the more modern system safely, while a single State, moving alone, might incur grave danger to its industries in acting by itself. In other words, uniform legislation does not mean in every instance that every State should act on all subjects. In many cases, action by groups of States will be as effective as action by all. If uni-form action by the States, in groups or as a whole, can become habitual as to matters affecting the com-mon life of the people in whatever State they live, there is no reason why there may not be added to all the other advantages of our federal system this new element of strength, that we may enjoy the ad-vantage of legislation in common such as the common interest may demand, without forfeiting that in-dividuality of legislation as to interests purely local which the federal system aims to preserve.

Uniform legislation is the equivalent in legislation of standardization in mechanical construction. Form-erly, there were broad gauge railroads and railroads with a narrow gauge. Broad gauge railroads and narrow gauge railroads could not connect. At last the gauge of all railroads was standardized, that is to say, made uniform, and now the cars of every railroad can be used on the tracks of every other railroad, and no one would think of going back to the old system. The broad gauge, as a mechanical proposition, had some advantages over the narrow gauge; but these were wholly insignificant compared with the advantages resulting from standardization, that is to say, from uniformity of gauge. Difference in gauge did not make railroading impossible, but the did make it inconvenient, costly, and slow. Similarl differences in laws relating to the common life c the people do not make business impossible; but the do hamper business relations by causing inconven ence, expense, and delay.

The lack of uniformity in the legislation of th States as to the law of Negotiable Instruments, fo example, makes inconvenience, because trade affectin two States with different laws upon this subject i hampered by the necessity of complying with both it makes expense, because the necessity of complyin with different laws makes it necessary to secure leg advice often in two States; and it makes delay, c loss of time, because the different requirements c two States have to be met, instead of the same r quirements in both States. Uniform legislation o such subjects, for this is only a type of many su jects where the common interest altogether outweig the individual point of view, is, in a word, like th standardizing of parts, which is one of the most no able methods by which, under modern manufactur the convenience of the public has been advance This is well illustrated by the standardizing of th size of screws, nails, bolts, and other objects of th sort; so that the size needed can be obtained ever where. It is, in fact, one of the great industrial a vantages which this country enjoys over Europ which is broken up into small countries, that he standardization of parts has taken place on a lar scale, while there it has been possible to adopt only in a limited way.

If the States can be induced to standardize the laws by making them uniform as to matters th affect the interest of all the people in common, one can overestimate the advantages that will accr to the people of each State and of every State. Th standardization of statutes will make intercourse an business transactions easier, in a great many field and will increase such relations indefinitely; and a these advantages can be had, if the States pleas without hazarding a single attribute of sovereignt or limiting, in any way, the right and duty and o portunity of each State to legislate from its own poi of view alone upon subjects that are purely local.

Happily, the instrumentalities are at hand for secu ing uniformity of legislation by the States on great a scale as public opinion will support. Twent years ago, more or less, the American Bar Associ tion called attention to this subject; and, as a resu of the action taken by it, many of the States hav already appointed Commissioners on Uniform Law This movement has, in fact, proceeded so far th Commissioners on Uniform Laws have been appointe by forty-four States, by two Territories, by the Di trict of Columbia, and by the Government of th Philippines. These Commissioners organized them selves into a National Conference on Uniform Legi lation a number of years ago, and last Autumn the held their nineteenth annual conference. In the nineteen years, this conference has perfected five law which it has recommended to all the States for ado tion. These laws are:

1. The Negotiable Instruments Act.
2. The Warehouse Receipts Act.
3. The Sales Act.
4. The Bill of Lading Act.
5. The Stock Certificates Act.

I believe also an act on divorce which was p pared by the National Conference on this subje and which has been approved by the Commissione on Uniform State Laws.

The careful procedure, the systematic confere with all associations that may be interested, the peated study and examination by the best legal min of the country, to which these have been subject will be explained to you more at length during t progress of this conference. It is only necessary, this time to point out that machinery already exi by virtue of the action of almost all of the Sta themselves, for the careful preparation of unifo legislation as to any subject on which such le lation may be generally desired.

Fortunately, during this same week, the confer of Governors which was initiated in 1908, by the vitation of President Roosevelt to the Governors of the States to meet in the White House to consider Conservation of our Natural Resources, is also to m in Washington. By the courtesy of Governor Will of Kentucky, who is the chairman of that con ence, and of the Committee on Program, of w Governor Hughes, of New York, is chairman, an h has been reserved on the afternoons of the first second days of the Governors' conference, that i January 18th and 19th, during which communicat from this conference on Uniform Legislation wi received. It is hoped that our conference will se way clear to recommend to the organizations represented that they urge the passage in all of States of the uniform laws already approved by National Conference of Commissioners appointed the States. If so, it is proposed that a repo this effect be made to the Governors on the afte of Tuesday, January 18th. It will be developed, m over, in our conference, that there are many sub upon which uniform legislation is desirable which are not yet ripe for action, such as railway regulation, corporation regulation, workmen's compensation, pure food, pure drugs, good roads, vital statistics, insurance and many other matters. It is hoped that this conference will take the necessary steps to have these different subjects studied into and submitted for action, in due course, to the State Commissioners on Uniform Laws. Some of these subjects, at least, may well be brought to the attention of the Governors on the afternoon of Wednesday, the 19th inst., with a request that the Governors take such steps as they may deem proper to secure consideration of these subjects by the people and legislatures of their respective States. It is believed that, if this course is followed, public opinion in all of the States will be educated to a better understanding of these subjects, and will be likely to receive proposals for uniform legislation as to them, when they are ready to be made, in a hospitable spirit.

It is hoped that this conference will see its way to do several specific things:

1. To urge upon the States and Territories which have not already appointed Commissioners on Uniform State Laws that they forthwith appoint such Commissioners.

2. To urge upon all the States which have made no appropriations for the conduct of the work of these Commissioners to make a suitable appropriation which will enable the work to be carried forward more expeditiously and more effectively. It is estimated that $500 from each State would be sufficient.

3. To refer to suitable committees the drafting of laws on such subjects as the conference may determine, in suitable form to be passed by all the States; such drafts to be submitted to the National Conference of Commissioners on Uniform Laws for such action as they may see fit to take.

The coincidence in the meeting of these two bodies—the conference of Governors and this conference on Uniform Legislation by the States—is not simply a happy accident. It is due to the sagacious suggestion of the President of the United States, for which I am glad to take this opportunity, on behalf of this conference, to express our sincere thanks. The advantage to the cause, to be derived from the opportunity of placing immediately before the Governors the things that this conference wishes to call to their attention cannot be overestimated; for it means that information upon these subjects will be carried at once into almost every State of the Union by the Governor of the State himself. Public sentiment in all the States, therefore, should be immensely stimulated as a result of these two gatherings.

The President of the United States has consented to be here this morning because of his keen appreciation of the importance of this subject to all of the States and to the people of all the States. He knows by his experience as a lawyer, and upon the bench, the importance of such action in its legal aspects; and from his commanding point of view as the President of the United States, he is better able than any one else to understand its far-reaching possibilities for good. I have now, therefore, the very great pleasure of presenting President Taft, who has kindly consented to address this conference.

PRESIDENT WILLIAM HOWARD TAFT.

IN the first place I am glad to welcome the Civic Federation to Washington. I think the sun shines a little brighter in Washington than it does anywhere else along on the same latitude, and it is a very pleasant place either to live in or to be in; therefore, I congratulate the Civic Federation in having had the good sense to come here. (Applause.)

You are not the only citizens of the United States who look in this direction. I am glad that you came here at the same time that the Governors did, so that your deliberations and theirs in the same direction, and the right direction, as they doubtless will be, will have the weight of two great forces upon not only the National Legislature, but upon the State Legislatures, for from Washington everything radiates to the end of the country.

In the discussion of uniformity of legislation, when you take a man who has gotten out of the practice of the law, so that he does not remember with great exactitude those principles that are applied in actual cases, he cannot help falling back on a discussion of the Constitution. A constitutional lawyer is a gentleman who has gotten out of the practice and who has gone into politics. (Applause.)

Now my friend Senator Root, whom I am delighted to class with me in the same category, some years ago was greatly misunderstood with reference to his view of the Constitution and the trend under the Constitution towards centralization of government. If I understood him, his view was that, unless the States did their duty in the exercise of the functions which it was necessary they should exercise in the interests of good government, there would be a tendency toward the enlargement of the Government at Washington, and he uttered a warning to the States that if they would retain the power given to them under the Constitution in all its integrity, they must see to it that they exercise that power in the interests of the people and in the interests of the country generally. The misunderstanding led to ascribing to him views in favor of centralization that would certainly have been radical, but I am sure he does not have them.

We have a nation, and we have a centralized government, and the reason why we have it is because John Marshall was put at the head of the Supreme Court early, and exercised that power which a good judge always exercises with his colleagues. He did not minimize the power of the Supreme Court to construe that Constitution authoritatively. (Applause). And so construing it, he made this a nation with all the powers incident to a nation. And then when he left the bench, after that long period of useful service, he was succeeded by Chief Justice Taney and his associates, and at that time the trend toward a national power and authority of the party from whom Chief Justice Taney was selected led him right along in the same path that Marshall had marked out until we came to the war. And then, with the war amendments, the same tendency to make this Government a nation as distinguished from a federation continued to the present day. (Applause.)

Now it is said that we have centralized too much. There are jurisdictions that might be asserted under the Constitution that Congress has not asserted, notably in the jurisdiction of the Federal courts. So too in bankruptcy; so too in elections. With respect to the jurisdiction of the Federal courts there is a large measure that Congress does not assert which it might take away from that which the State courts now exercise. And so with respect to bankruptcy, it might be made much more exclusive of State jurisdiction in that regard, and with respect to elections, they have gone back entirely to the States.

There are other matters under the Constitution which I shall not stop to mention which show that all the power conferred upon the National Government has not yet been exercised, but the reason why it seems as if we were becoming a more centralized government is not because of a change in the construction of the Constitution, but a change in the importance of the power which was always given to the National Government under that Constitution, to wit: the Interstate Commerce Law. When the Constitution was framed the State traffic, as distinguished from the Interstate traffic was as 25 to 75, and now instead the Interstate traffic is to the State traffic as 75 to 25—a complete reversal of the amount of Interstate business done as compared with the State business, and that is the reason why the National Government's power seems to have grown so largely, because its power covers more volume than it ever did before. With respect to that, I am inclined to think that it will be found wise after a time to recognize those great organizations, concentrations of wealth, and plant, and capital, that do a country wide business, going into every State, whose business is almost wholly Interstate, to recognize them as instrumentalities of Interstate commerce and to incorporate them in order that we may get them more directly under the control of the National Government.

I admit there are grounds for dispute and I have only recommended this as something that I look forward to in the future, as a means of saving to the public what is valuable, and there is a great deal that is valuable in those trusts, and eliminating permanently that which is vicious and contrary to public policy. (Applause.) But you are not Congress and I did not come here to convince you on that subject. (Laughter). I only mention it in passing.

There has been, during the last ten or fifteen years, an earnest desire on the part of some people to minimize State power altogether. They say—I heard the distinguished Governor of Massachusetts say—the United States Government can better regulate child labor than can the States, so what's the use of talking! Why not put that power into the United States Government? And so with reference to every power, the suggestion is that the central government has more capital, being more centralized, its execution of the laws is more certain and less affected by the local conditions and therefore it is wise in the interest of effective government to put what we can in the central government, and so we invoke the old "general welfare clause." We have got the money in the treasury and we can spend the money, therefore, for anything we choose, because there is no court to prevent it. We cannot issue an injunction against the Secretary of the Treasury, dishonoring an appropriation of Congress, and when it comes to the expenditure of money, the history of the United States is full of appropriations and expenditures that cannot be explained on any ground except that of "old general welfare." (Applause and laughter.) And the way they propose to expend it when there is a particular subject that needs attention, is to organize a bureau and let that bureau occupy an advisory relation and an experimental relation to the States in the exercise of that jurisdiction which is undoubtedly theirs. They have got to a point where, just before I sent in my message, in the list of the bureaus that was asked for was a bureau on earthquakes. (Laughter.) I assume the argument was that as earthquakes did not know any State bounds, neither did the exercise of jurisdiction with respect to them know any State bounds.

Now the lesson that this teaches is that we have a Constitution in which the Government of the United States cannot accomplish all reform and that there is a burden and there is a heavy responsibility, eloquently described by Mr. Root, upon the States with reference to meeting the demands of those who call themselves progressive and who are in favor of the reform to uplift the people and to make the comfort of the individual greater.

In no department of the government, in no reform is this uniformity of legislation going to be more important than in the conservation of our resources. (Applause.) The Federal Government has no power to compel owners of forests to attend to those forests with a view to the welfare of the community of the neighbors who live there, or of those who are affected by the denudation of the land of the trees. That must be done through the State Government if it is done at all, and so with respect to many of the streams. Indeed, if one follows out legal reasoning, it will seem, I think, that there is more to be done by the States in the conservation of resources even than by the Federal Government—large an influence as that Federal Government may have by reason of its ownership of the public domain.

Now there are many other subjects that ought to occupy the States with reference to uniform legislation. If I had been a member of the Constitutional Convention, I would have voted to have included marriage and divorce in the Federal jurisdiction, but it will never get there now.

The theory upon which they put in bankruptcy was that where a man was declared a bankrupt it fixed his status and that status ought not to vary in one State from the status in another. But when a man is married he has established a status and certainly that status ought not to vary between the States, but as it is not possible to secure an amendment to the United States Constitution placing that subject within Federal cognizance, it certainly calls for uniform legislation on the part of the States. (Applause.) I state that because I think everybody will agree with me. Then I am not going on to say what kind of legislation there ought to be, because I am told that in that discussion, as yet, even the Civic Federation has not reached a result.

Then there is another subject upon which there may well be uniformity of legislation after we, in the Federal Government, have adopted a proper system, and that is with respect to judicial procedure. If there is anything in our whole government, State and national, that justifies an attack upon our present system of living, it is the delays in our judicial procedure, (Applause) and the advantage that wealth gives in the struggle in the courts against those who haven't the means to meet the expense that is now imposed on them. (Applause.)

Now, if we can do something in the National Government to introduce the simplicity of the English procedure in equity and in law, perhaps uniting them, that will be a model for State legislatures to adopt a uniform system.

I might go on with respect to other subjects; I have said a great deal more than I intended to, and I have only—so to speak—"shot on the wing," but if you had to write a message a week, perhaps you would only write when you have to.

HON. AUGUSTUS E. WILLSON.

Governor of Kentucky.

THE invitation to me is really extended to the Governors, and not to this particular member of the Governors' body. Almost by accident it fell to me to issue the call for the Governors, and that resulted in some correspondence with the president of the Civic Federation, and that has brought me here to-day. I am not directly authorized to speak for the Governors, but I know from the men who compose that body that they would not wish me to let this greeting pass without their earnest and sincere acknowledgement of the courteous consideration which is extended to them, and so, speaking for them and not assuming any authority, I thank you, Mr. President, sincerely, and I thank the conference, the Federation, for extending this courtesy.

I felt right keenly the President's welcome to Washington and perhaps I might be pardoned even in an open expression of a disappointment when he began a verse, "The Sun Shines Bright," and then ended up "in Washington." We know the sun shines bright, more or less, everywhere, but we don't think it is ever in its full glory anywhere except in the old Kentucky home. (Applause.) When I come to speak of the object of this meeting, I feel very much in the predicament of a pretty grim old Kentucky lawyer who was called upon at a Bar Association banquet to respond to the toast "How to Explain to Your Client How You Lost His Case." He began his remarks by saying very grimly, "I deprecate the idea that I have been assigned to this toast because of any special qualification." (Laughter.)

I deprecate the idea that I have been called upon here from any personal merit, and will only speak very briefly to express my earnest sympathies with this movement for uniform legislation. I have been deeply interested in what the President has so well said to us. I always look upon him as a very thoughtful man and it is a great pleasure to listen to his expressions, so sincere and earnest, and so happily made, without any formal writing or paper of any kind, but just the happy, serious thoughts of a serious minded man. One does not appreciate the wonderful balance, the thoughtfulness and wisdom of those expressions on every occasion, but I have already said more than I intended to say in his presence.

This subject, the condition of our laws in regard to uniform legislation, is almost incredible in the people of our stock, with their determination and their practical common sense and their readiness to meet every consideration, and I cannot get it through my mind how a thousand years have passed without believing that on these subjects, the every day life of the common people all over the world, the rules ought to be the same everywhere, thereby avoiding a multiplicity of rules, and an embarrassment of rights and endless expense. To think that a man hardly is sure of that status that the President speaks of; a man may be married all right in Illinois and may not be so sure of it when he crosses the State line into Indiana; to think that a man anywhere on earth has to consult anything but public tradition as to how to make a will. There ought not to be any difference as to how to make a valid will in any place on the earth; it ought to be the same all over the earth, not merely through the United States, but all over the earth, but I suppose there are forty-six different ways to make a will in the United States, and make it valid—perhaps not that many, but a great many.

Mr. Low has spoken very happily of standardization. All of us lawyers and a great many business men have come to appreciate the good qualities of a standard insurance policy, instead of having one for everybody. The great advantages of standardization of large and important subjects are just as obvious as the advantages of having standard sized bolts and nuts, but it is far easier to take a half bushel of nuts and find one to fit a given sized bolt, than it is to find the status of a contract in forty-six different States. We can all see the great advantage and the time saved by having standard sized nuts to fit given standard sized bolts, and how far greater and more important is it that we should have uniform legislation and standardization of large and all-important subjects with which every State in the union is dealing every day in the year.

I am in most earnest sympathy and in hearty accord with your movement and especially in respect to these more urgent matters and I hope it will not be long before we meet with material progress; in Kentucky, we have progressed somewhat, and I want to say that the meetings of the Governors which we will hold in your city this week will afford an opportunity for us to present these more important features. We, in Kentucky, expect to present a message to our General Assembly, just as the President has presented one to you, and if necessary we will write one as often as the President of the United States says that he is writing one, and ultimately we can, by our action, have a great deal of force to bring a desirable result to pass.

With the most earnest good wishes for an interesting and prosperous meeting, and with the greatest gratitude for your kindness, I thank you.

ADDRESS OF HON. ALTON B. PARKER.

OUR honored and much-beloved President laid down one proposition, I think, in language quite too broad. He said in effect that no lawyer discusses the Constitution until after he has got into politics and out of the law. He cited an instance. (Laughter.) Now I am going to discuss very briefly to-day—at least I am going to refer to the Constitution in a written address which I make to you, and I promise at the beginning that it will be short, and yet, I assume, you do not need any assurance from me that I am still practicing law (Laughter and applause), and certainly you need none to the effect that I am not in politics. (Laughter and applause.) After nineteen years of judicial work I was in politics for a very few months, and then the people effectually put me out (Applause), and I think laymen as well as lawyers should consider the Constitution, and I do not believe it is safe for us to leave that subject entirely to those who have gone into politics. (Laughter.)

In 1787 a convention was held, the declared purpose of which was "to form a more perfect union, establish justice, insure domestic tranquillity * * * promote the general welfare, and secure the blessings of liberty to ourselves and our posterity," and to-day we are in convention, in the hope that we may contribute, be it ever so little, toward the promotion of the aims which induced the creation of the Union. We are met to aid in an undertaking which gives promise of great public usefulness and may prove helpful in maintaining in all its integrity the Union as formed.

Our ancestors were moved by the spirit of freedom aroused by the galling yoke the dominant country would fasten upon them. Many now are not a little moved by the gradual encroachments of the Federal Government beyond the limits which were plainly set to it. Their belief is that because of State indifference to matters in respect to which each State is, and of right ought to be, independent of the central government, and through want of concert of action on the part of the States, Congress has been tempted to invade that sphere, undertaking to prescribe what it conceives to be right or wise and to forbid what it conceives to be wrong or unwise, with such vindicatory sanctions as it chooses to prescribe.

Action and reaction is the law of the universe, the ultimate effect of which, if wisely observed, is to purify the social, moral and political atmosphere. The extreme assertion of the doctrine of State rights reacted in the form of our great Civil War, and now a reaction, let us hope, is beginning against one of its extreme consequences, namely, paternalism or centralization. So much was accomplished by the necessary centralization of power during that fratricidal struggle that we have all but unconsciously come to regard the central power as the panacea for all the evils of diverse State policies and laws. And so it may be accepted in the end, unless there be harmony in respect, at least, to the general principles of legislation in the several States and uniformity in respect to formal matters.

Looking backward to the beginning, is it to be doubted that the Fathers appreciated the history of the republics that have come and gone, when they sat down to construct a government? A government which, so far as might be, should meet the ideal of a government of the people, by the people and for the people? Can we hesitate to believe that they sought understandingly to avoid the rocks upon which preceding republics had drifted to their destruction? Certainly any student of the history of their time must answer in the affirmative, as he must also acknowledge their wisdom when he considers the smoothness of the working for more than a century of the governmental plan formulated by them.

The people wished local government and local courts. The history of their ancestors made them afraid of entrusting the protection and enforcement of their rights and liberties to jurors who were strangers and to officials independent of local public opinion. So they conferred upon the Federal Government abundant power to maintain its dignity abroad, and for public defense, as well as power to regulate interstate commerce and affairs of national concern, but reserved by the very instrument creating the Federal Government all power which they did not grant.

Now this precaution was a vital part of the scheme of the Fathers to protect their cherished rights and liberties from governmental tyranny. To the State government was granted every needed power for local self-government, but not all the powers possessed by a free people by any means. Many powers were and are distinctly reserved from the State government and maintained in the possession of the people themselves—powers that may or may not be later surrendered to either the Federal or the State government as the people may will. The powers of the people, therefore, have been divided by them into three parts. The Federal Government possesses one, the State government another, and the other remains in the people. An attempt by either the Federal Government or the State to acquire by usurpation power withheld is an attempt to seize powers reserved by the people for the protection of precious rights and liberties, won only after centuries of effort. And there have been such attempts in both State and Nation, attempts participated in by both the executive and the legislative departments of government.

Many suggestions there have been of methods by which the citizen may be deprived of the protection of the Constitution and the law, but none more striking, perhaps, than the suggestion of the national executive at Jamestown, June 10, 1907, that a proposed Congressional Employers' Liability Law "should be such that it will be impossible for the railroad to successfully fight it without thereby forfeiting all right to the protection of the Federal Government under any circumstances." In oth words, the proposition is to so penalize the victim Congressional usurpation as will effectually preve him from appealing to the judicial department government for redress.

Mr. Bryce, in his Essay on Obedience, says:

"The greatest peril to self-government is at times to be found in the want of zeal and ener among the citizens. This is a peril which exists democracies as well as in despotisms. Submissi is less frequently due to overwhelming force tha to the apathy of those who find acquiescence easi than resistance."

It is only when some interest is attacked, an directly attacked, which is at the moment deemed vital concern, that the people are aroused to defen their rights. Speaking to this proposition, Mr. Bryc in the same essay says:

"The English people were a people singularly a tached to their ancient political and civil rights, y Charles the First might probably have destroye the liberties of England and would almost certainl have destroyed those of Scotland, if he had left r ligion alone."

One danger, then, is lest, in the absence of dire attack upon any institution deemed of great in portance by the public, our protective measures- which consist in the division of powers between th Federal Government, the State government and th people, and the further division of the powe granted to the Federal and State governments, b tween the executive, the legislative and the judici departments of each—may in the meantime be i sidiously weakened or obliterated.

The long strides that have been taken in th direction have apparently attracted but little pu lic interest. This may be due in part to the reaso assigned by Mr. Bryce, but in the main it is du to the belief that a remedy is needed, and the on proposed is accepted because suggested by one upo whose leadership the people for the time rely.

Latterly complaints have arisen of inefficienc resulting from the division of powers between th Federal and the State governments. It is said, de pending upon the point of view, that some State grant charters which are far too broad, while other go to the opposite extreme. That in some State the law has not been enforced against disobedien corporations and their officers, while in others th tendency is to presume them guilty of a desire t violate all law, written or unwritten.

The public complaint for the present is mor generally that the States have been lax in the en forcement of law, with most disastrous cons quences. The charge of neglect must be admitte by all who appreciate that every one of the co porations now struggling for life was created the face of the law under which they are no prosecuted,—a law which by reason of its deliberat non-enforcement was assumed by the corporatio founders to be "more honored in the breach tha in the observance."

This is not the time to consider whether the on government or the other is the more responsibl for this condition. For the claim is that in an event efficiency is sacrified in the dual form government, and that in the interest of busine prosperity efficiency is of greater importance tha all else.

This brings us to a consideration of the purpose government. What is the object of government? it itself the end and the aim of its existence? If then efficiency is the only criterion. To efficienc all must be sacrificed. There must be, in th language of mechanics, as well no friction as lost motion anywhere in the government machin *A despotism* more nearly approaches that standa than any other form of government, for it excels mere efficiency of administration.

There is no political government on earth so ef cient as the government of the United States Ste Corporation from a purely business standpoin Every step it takes is in obedience to a mast mind. Everyone connected with it must subor nate his ambitions and plans to that of the maste In times of business depression he must learn live more prudently that loss of surplus capital m not affect the efficiency of the corporation. *But may safely be said that no one would be willing have our government thus managed, however mu national wealth might be augmented each year.*

We *are* ambitious, it is true, for wealth and t comfort it brings, *but we have not yet lost* our fai in the proposition that the object of government the greatest good to the greatest number. It is d sirable therefore *now*, as it was in the *beginnin* that we should endure a less efficient form of go ernment *in order to avoid* the greater evils whi would otherwise arise.

But that is not to say that we should not be our energies to make our dual government efficient as may be. On the contrary, those w

(Continued on page 6.)

CONFERENCE OF GOVERNORS AT WASHINGTON

MEET AT CALL OF GOVERNOR WILLSON—OBJECTS OUTLINED BY GOVERNOR HUGHES—INTER-STATE RELATIONS, CONSERVATION OF RESOURCES AND UNIFORM LEGISLATION DISCUSSED—ENTERTAINED BY PRESIDENT TAFT

(Reading from left to right, lower row seated)—GOV. FRANK B. WEEKS, Conn.; GOV. JOHN FRANKLIN FORT, N. J.; GOV. JOSEPH M. BROWN, Ga.; GOV. SIMON S. PENNEWILL, Del.; PRESIDENT TAFT; GOV. AUGUSTUS E. WILLSON, Ky.; GOV. HERBERT S. HADLEY, Mo.; GOV. MARTIN S. ANSEL, S. C.; GOV. BRYANT E. BROOKS, Wyo.; GOV. JOHN E. SHAFROTH, Col. (Reading from left to right, row standing)—GOV. EDWIN L. NORRIS, Mont.; GOV. RICHARD E. SLOAN, Ariz.; GOV. ARAM J. POTHIER, R. I.; GOV. W. W. KITCHIN, N. C.; GOV. WILLIAM E. GLASSCOCK, W. Va.; GOV. JOHN O. DAVIDSON, Wis.; SECRETARY WILSON; GOV. JAMES H. BRADY, Idaho; GOV. JUDSON HARMON, Ohio; GOV. BERYL F. CARROLL, Ia.; GOV. ASHTON C. SHALLENBERGER, Neb.; SECRETARY HITCHCOCK; GOV. ADOLPH O. EBERHART, Minn.; GOV. GEORGE CURRY, N. M.; GOV. R. S. VESSEY, S. D.; GOV. JOHN BURKE, N. D.

THE second Conference of Governors was held in Washington at the same time as The National Civic Federation Conference on Uniform State Laws, January 18, 19 and 20, 1910. It was at the suggestion of President Taft that the two conferences were held simultaneously, and the wisdom of the President's arrangement was demonstrated to the satisfaction of everybody who took part in the two great national meetings.

Although President Roosevelt called his famous Conference of Governors in 1908, the gathering this year was the first meeting of the State Executives as a body, having been called by the chairman of its own committee, appointed in 1908, to provide for future meetings.

Governor Augustus E. Willson, of Kentucky, November 30, 1909, issued an invitation to the Governors of all the States and in the course of his letter he said "The President, on the Deep Waterways Excursion, told the Governors that while the laws prohibit arranging for the meeting at the public expense, the latch-string of the White House would be out, and he cordially wished and hoped for the meeting. * * * The National Civic Federation has changed its meeting to January 17, 18 and 19 to be in touch with the Governors and this will help to make the event one of exceptional interest and importance, probably greater than any meeting of the kind ever held in our country."

The Governors were requested to suggest to Governors Charles E. Hughes, of New York, Judson Harmon, of Ohio, and Thomas Marshall, of Indiana, any subjects which they thought would be useful for the Conference to take up, and the following topics were suggested by Governor Willson, as germane: Inter-State Relations, Taxation, Conservation of Natural Resources, Uniform Legislation, Extradition and the Constitutional Amendment. Governor Hughes, as chairman, and Governors Harmon and Marshall, were named to act as a Committee on Programme and Meeting with The National Civic Federation, and Governors Claude A. Swanson, of Virginia, Austin L. Crothers, of Maryland, and Edwin S. Stuart, of Pennsylvania, were requested to act as a committee on arrangements as to place, hours of meeting, reporting, etc.

The Conference of Governors, after its first session at the White House, was held at the New Willard Hotel.

President Taft welcomed the Governors at the White House Tuesday afternoon, January 18. He expressed his appreciation of the movement for co-operation and conference among the Governors, declaring his regard for it as of the utmost importance.

"I feel," said the President, "that this is the beginning of conferences which are certain to lead, in the end, to an adjustment of State legislation that should make our country capable of doing much more team work for the public good than we ever have before thought possible."

Governor Hughes, in his address, outlined the functions of the regular conferences of the State executives. "When President Roosevelt called a conference of Governors of the States to meet at the White House in May, 1908," said Governor Hughes, "he gave impetus to a movement which could not be confined within its original bounds. By the action of the Governors then present provision was made for a committee with power to arrange for a further conference, and this meeting is the result.

"The present Conference of Governors is held on their own initiative, and is not limited to any one subject. Great as will be the interest attaching to the question of conserving our natural resources, and to the other subjects which may be presented for discussion, the matter of fundamental importance I believe to be the consideration of the potential advantage of these conferences and the best means of securing the full benefit they are able to bestow.

"At the outset the relation and proper limitations of our efforts should be recognized. We are here in our own right as State Executives. We are not here, I assume, to deal with questions which are admitted to be of exclusively National concern. If Congress acts within its power as defined by the Constitution neither its authority nor the wisdom of its acts is the subject of challenge by State officers, as such. If Congress act beyond its authority its action is nugatory and the Supreme Court of the United States may so declare it.

"Whatever view may be taken of the advisability of extending Federal power or of a wider exercise of existing Federal power, it is manifest that the future prosperity of the country must largely depend upon the efficiency of State Governments. National activities inevitably will widen, and if we are to prevent an excessive strain upon national administration, we must develop our local agencies to their maximum efficiency within their proper spheres.

"The scope of these conferences may be deemed to embrace at least three groups of questions: The first relates to uniform laws, the second relates to matters of State comity where, if absolute uniformity may not be expected, causes of friction may be avoided and the general welfare may be promoted by accommodating action; the third relates to matters which, though of local concern, can be better treated in the light of the experience of other States. . . .

"The ancient jealousies that have divided us are now forgotten," Governor Hughes said in conclusion. "The sentiment of national unity has overcome divisive prejudices and the people of this great land, from one ocean to the other, are animated by a common patriotic impulse and intense devotion to the common interest, against which sectionalism will direct its attacks in vain. This sentiment of national unity, which is the outgrowth of an increasing intimacy of relation and facility of communication, should enable us the more easily to maintain and perfect, with wise and harmonious adjustment, the essential instrumentalities of State government, upon which, as well as upon our national activities, the welfare of the people depends."

President Low, of The National Civic Federation, followed Governor Hughes, presenting a report on the drafting of uniform laws, urging uniformity as to negotiable instruments, storehouse receipts, bills of lading, bills of sale, and divorce, and recommending the modeling of pure food and drug legislation after the national laws.

At the session January 19th, the Governors listened to a speech by Ambassador Bryce, the distinguished author of "The American Commonwealth," who said that he believed that the Conference would emphasize the importance of the Governorship, and that the chief executive of each State was coming more and more to be looked upon as the personal representative of the people of his State.

States' rights with especial reference to the conservation of resources and the regulation and supervision of public service corporations was the subject of most of the addresses delivered at this session.

Among the speakers were Governor Quinby, of New Hampshire, who made a plea for the conservation of forests under the direction of the Government. He was followed by Governor Willson, of Kentucky, on the right of the State to have control over water power, and Governor Carroll, of Iowa, who declared himself in sympathy with the movement for uniform laws in all the States. Governor Draper, of Massachusetts, advocated State ownership and control of the water power of streams. Governor Hughes considered the forests among the State's most precious possessions and said the State, so far as it could, should own and preserve them. He also advocated the development and State control of water power.

Governor Brooks, of Wyoming, and Governor

Shafroth, of Colorado, addressed the Conference on the subject of "The Value and Control of Water Power," Governor Shaforth contending that the ownership of land by the Federal Government in a State was a proprietary right and not political or governmental; that the United States holds the land the same as an individual, and that the government of the land rests in the State.

Governor Fort, of New Jersey, advocated State supervision of and regulation of quasi-public enterprises. He said that the authoritative right of the State over its public utilities companies was ample for the protection of the people. Governor Hadley of Missouri, spoke on the subject of railroad rate legislation, saying that the charges for the transportation of persons and property should not be left to the owners of the lines, but that control should be exercised by the Government.

Governor Draper, of Massachusetts, delivered an address on the regulation of automobiles. "The proper basis for automobile regulation is reckless driving," said the Governor. "Were it possible at all times to determine what reckless driving is, I should say speed limits were unnecessary, but in the present development of the industry, I believe it is necessary to have a proper speed limit established as prima facie evidence of law-breaking."

On the last day of their meeting the Governors were addressed by Governor Eberhart, of Minnesota, on the conservation of natural resources in Minnesota; Governor Shallenberger of Nebraska, on "Conservation," Governor Brady, of Idaho, on "Irrigation," and by former United States Senator Dryden, of New Jersey; Governor Carroll, of Iowa, spoke on "Divorce."

Permanent Organization.

A plan for permanent organization was unanimously adopted, the plan having been drafted by a committee headed by Governor Hughes. It provided for annual meetings at a State capital instead of at Washington, the next conference to be held between Thanksgiving and Christmas, 1910. A committee on arrangements was appointed to fix the exact date and place of meeting and provide a programme, the Committee of Three consisting of Governor Willson of Kentucky, Governor Hadley, of Missouri, and Governor Ansel, of South Carolina.

After considerable discussion the Governors decided to adjourn without passing any formal resolutions endorsing the many subjects before them, but the Governors, speaking each for himself, and without any formality, pledged themselves to an effort for uniformity and harmony in State laws for corporations, divorce, negotiable paper, and most of those things for which The National Civic Federation has contended. In planning for continuity of effort by themselves and their successors, the Governors had in mind, apparently, the purpose to compare notes and to take counsel one with another as to the State needs, with the common needs of all their people in view.

Social Events.

The Conference at Washington was marked by distinguished social events.

Mr. and Mrs. John Hays Hammond gave a dinner [Tu]esday evening in honor of the visiting Governors [an]d members of the Executive Committee of the [Na]tional Civic Federation at their home, 1500 Rhode [Isl]and avenue.

The guests were:

Governors Braxton B. Comer, Alabama; Frank B. [We]eks, Connecticut; Simeon S. Pennewill, Delaware; [Ja]mes H. Brady, Idaho; Augustus E. Willson, Ken[tuc]ky; B. M. Fernald, Maine; Eben S. Draper, Massa[chu]setts; Herbert S. Hadley, Missouri; Ashton C. [Sh]allenberger, Nebraska; Henry B. Quinby, New [Ha]mpshire; John F. Fort, New Jersey; Charles E. [Hu]ghes, New York; Martin F. Ansel, South Carolina; [Geo]rge H. Prouty, Vermont; William E. Glasscock, [Wes]t Virginia; Robert S. Vessey, South Dakota; [Rich]ard Sloane, Arizona; William Spry, Utah; John [F.] Shafroth, Colorado; J. O. Davidson, Wisconsin; [Aram] J. Pothier, Rhode Island; Beryl F. Carroll, [Iow]a; Judson Harmon, Ohio; Joseph N. Brown, [Geor]gia; Edwin L. Norris, Montana; George Curry, [New] Mexico; A. O. Eberhardt, Minnesota; John [Burk]e, North Dakota; Walter R. Stubbs, Kansas, and [mem]bers of The National Civic Federation, Seth Low, [Augu]st Belmont, Alton B. Parker, W. R. Willcox, [Ellis]on A. Smyth, James Speyer, I. N. Seligman, [Fran]klin B. MacVeagh, Samuel Gompers, John [Mitch]ell, Timothy Healy, James O'Connell, John M. [...], Marcus Marks, V. E. Macy, R. M. Easley, Rollin [W]oodruff, Walter G. Smith, Lewis Parker, John F. [...]on, Dr. J. A. Holmes, Admiral Chadwick, and [Hay]s Hammond.

At the White House.

Wednesday evening, the 19th, President Taft [ent]ained at dinner at the White House a company [of m]ore than seventy guests, inviting the visiting [Gove]rnors, the members of their families who were with them in Washington, and including the officers of The National Civic Federation and members of their families. The banquet was held in the State dining room, which was beautifully decorated with tropical palms. The table at which the guests were seated, extending from end to end of the stately room, was a-bloom with pink carnations and maiden-hair fern. As Mrs. Taft was ill and unable to be present, her sister, Mrs. Anderson, received with the President. The guests included:

The Secretary of War and Miss Dickinson.
Governor Pennewill, of Delaware, and Miss Burton.
Governor Fort, of New Jersey, and Miss Fort.
Governor Brown, of Georgia, and Mrs. Brown.
Governor Weeks, of Connecticut, and Mrs. Weeks.
Governor Draper, of Massachusetts, and Mrs. Draper.
Governor Ansel, of South Carolina, and Mrs. Ansel.
Governor Quinby, of New Hampshire, and Mrs. Quinby.
Governor Hughes, of New York.
Governor Kitchin, of North Carolina, and Miss Kitchin.
Governor Pothier, of Rhode Island, and Mrs. Pothier.
Governor Prouty, of Vermont, and Mrs. Prouty.
Governor Willson, of Kentucky.
Governor Harmon, of Ohio, and Mrs. Harmon.
Governor Comer, of Alabama.
Governor Fernald, of Maine.
Governor Hadley, of Missouri.
Governor Carroll, of Iowa.
Governor Davidson, of Wisconsin, and Miss Davidson.
Governor Eberhardt, of Minnesota.
Governor Stubbs, of Kansas, and Mrs. Stubbs.
Governor Glasscock, of West Virginia, and Mrs. Glasscock.
Governor Shallenberger, of Nebraska, and Mrs. Shallenberger.
Governor Shafroth, of Colorado,
Governor Burke, of North Dakota.
Governor Vessey, of South Dakota.
Governor Norris, of Montana, and Mrs. Arthur G. Coffee.
Governor Brady, of Idaho, and Miss Grade Dugger.
Governor Brooks, of Wyoming.
Governor Spry, of Utah.
Governor Mills, of New Mexico.
Governor Kibbey, of Arizona.
Hon. Seth Low.
Judge Alton B. Parker and Mrs. Parker.
Mr. and Mrs. John Hays Hammond.
Mr. and Mrs. Isaac N. Seligman.
Mr. Walter George Smith and Miss Smith.
Mr. James Speyer.
Mr. August Belmont.
Hon. George B. Cortelyou.
Mr. John Mitchell.
Mr. Samuel Gompers.
Mr. Ellison A. Smyth.
Mr. Lewis Parker.
Mr. Ralph M. Easley.
Mr. Nahum J. Bachelder.
Mr. William R. Willcox.
Mr. Marcus M. Marks.
Mr. Edwin R. A. Seligman.
Mr. Frank S. Streeter.

ADDRESS OF HON. ALTON B. PARKER.

(*Continued from page 4.*)

revere the wisdom of the Fathers should be most diligent in such effort, to the end that we may surely continue to enjoy the blessings of liberty as well as the advantages of prosperity.

If it be asked what necessary relation has efficiency of government with the perpetuation of the present form of it, *the answer* is that the charge of inefficiency is put forward to justify invasion by the Central government of home rule powers of the States. And such invasion has been apparently welcomed, rather than resisted, when it has related either to matters in which uniform legislation would the better subserve the common welfare, or to official neglect to enforce the law.

Indeed, it has been said by one of our leading statesmen that

"There is but one way in which the States of the Union can maintain their authority and power under the conditions which are now before us, and that is by an awakening on the part of the States to a realization of their own duties to the country at large."

We are in full accord with this admonition to the States of the *value and importance*, and, therefore, of the *duty* of reasonable co-operation. *As one great family* of sovereign States we ought always to work unselfishly together for the general good.

Animated by that spirit, the legal profession representing every State gave birth to what may now be called an institution of our country, the Co[m]missioners on Uniform State Laws. That commis[sion] was conceived by lawyers and brought forth by [the] American Bar Association. The conception was [one] of patriotism, of a genuine love of country,—a [de]sire, absolutely free of selfish notions, to simpl[ify] the problem of life, to discourage legal strife [and] make smoother to the lawyer the pathway of u[se]fulness.

One of the objects of that association, stated [in] its constitution, is "to advance uniformity of leg[is]lation." One of the first reports to that associati[on], made in 1879, the year following its creation, reco[m]mended co-operation to secure uniformity.

A Committee on Uniform State Laws was [ap]pointed in 1889, consisting of one member fr[om] each State. Subsequently it was decided to a[sk] each State to appoint three persons to represe[nt] it in the Commissioners on Uniform Laws. T[he] meeting of the Commissioners was held in Detro[it] in 1895, at which the first step was taken towa[rd] formulating what is now known as the Negotiab[le] Instruments Law, which already adorns the statu[te] books of thirty-six States, two Territories and t[he] District of Columbia.

If time would permit, I would like to speak of t[he] faithful and efficient service rendered by the Co[m]missioners without other reward than the sense [of] duty performed. The work covers other bills no[w] ready for adoption, one of which has already m[et] the approval of fifteen State legislatures.

Let me cite the action taken in preparing t[he] Uniform Sales Act as an illustration merely of t[he] method employed by the Commissioners in all the[ir] work. They secured the services of Professor Wi[l]liston of Harvard to draft the bill. This draft w[as] then considered in conference, section by sectio[n], the author taking part. This draft, with explanator[y] notes and citations of leading cases, was printe[d] and sent throughout the country to legal author[ities], jurists, professors in law schools, judges, leadin[g] lawyers, heads of business associations, and other[s] for criticism. Later final action was taken on th[e] completed draft by a roll call of the States, eac[h] State casting one vote, resulting in unanimous a[p]proval. After all of which it was approved by th[e] American Bar Association, which has each year fo[r] a long time back contributed liberally of its fund[s] to defray expense of drafting, printing and distribu[]tion.

During twenty years members of the bar know[n] for their attainment, their large and varied experi[]ence and high character, have given freely an[d] cheerfully their energies and the best results o[f] their study, observation and patiently acquire[d] knowledge to the end of simplifying and makin[g] common throughout the States of the Union th[e] rules of law that should obtain for the best interest[s] of all in the more important relations, such as are or should be, independent of local conditions; s[o] that the lawyer in Maine may safely advise hi[s] client of how he may deal in matters having thei[r] consummation in Georgia, whether it concerns [a] bill of exchange, a bill of lading, a conveyance o[f] realty, a will, the formation of a corporation, trans[]action in stocks, or investment or transaction o[f] whatever kind; and this without other compensa[]tion than the satisfaction of serving their country. They have not accomplished all these things. On[e] of the most marked characteristics of their labo[r] has been the slowness with which they have mad[e] haste, if I may so speak. They have demonstrate[d] that the plan is feasible, as well as wise, and, there[]fore, worthy of the support which this conventio[n] can give.

We do not aim at absolute uniformity of la[w] throughout the States, but a wise and conservativ[e] uniformity. There is danger in pressing uniformity to extreme lengths. There are diversities of climate of production, of tradition, of heredity, of population of pursuits among the people of our several com[]monwealths which should be generally respected.

Uniformity should be promoted along the line[s] marked out by the Commissioners on Uniform Laws and as much further as the diversities to which [I] have referred will reasonably permit. Other mat[]ters there are which it is most desirable shoul[d] be the subject of uniform legislation, and some o[f] them will be brought to your attention.

MR. WALTER GEORGE SMITH.

President Conference of Commissioners on Uniform State Laws.

I HAVE felt that it was of the utmost importanc[e] at the beginning of your proceedings that yo[u] should have an outline of the history of the confer[]ence of Commissioners on Uniform State Laws. Al[]though very many of you are already Commission[]ers and what I shall say will be a twice-told tale I will ask you, none the less, to bear with me i[n] order that you may know exactly what has bee[n] done. Many of you, perhaps, have never heard o[f] the Commission before and do not know just wha[t] that body is and what it has done and what it will ask you to do.

On the 21st of August, 1878, there assembled at Saratoga Springs a number of representative lawyers from all parts of the United States, in response to a call issued under date of July 1 of the same year and signed by leaders of the Bar from fourteen different States. Thus was founded the American Bar Association, its object as expressed in Article I. of its constitution, being "to advance the science of jurisprudence, promote the administration of justice and uniformity of legislation throughout the United States, uphold the honor of the profession of the law, and encourage cordial intercourse among the members of the American Bar."

Annually since that time meetings of this organization have been held and its roll of membership now includes 3,748 members from all the States and Territories and insular possessions. The living and the dead members of this great organization include the very flower of the American Bar, and the records of their proceedings are filled with the most valuable contributions, not alone on technical legal subjects, but upon those affecting more especially the economic, social and, indirectly, political welfare of both State and nation.

It was not until 1889, however, that a special committee on the subject of uniformity of legislation was appointed. In that year the following preamble and resolution were adopted:

"Recognizing the desirability of uniformity in the laws of the several States, especially those relating to marriage and divorce, descent and distribution of property, acknowledgment of deeds, execution and probate of wills; therefore be it

"Resolved, That the President of this Association appoint a committee, consisting of one from each State, who shall meet in convention at a time and place to be fixed by the President, and compare and consider the laws of the different States relating to these subjects, and prepare and report to this Association such recommendations and measures as will bring about the desired result."

This action of the American Bar Association was followed in 1890 by an Act of the Legislature of New York, authorizing the appointment by the Governor of that State of three commissioners by the name and style of "Commissioners for the Promotion of Uniformity of Legislation in the United States," it being made their duty to examine the subjects of marriage and divorce, insolvency, the form of notarial certificates and other subjects; to ascertain the best means to effect an assimilation and uniformity in the laws of the States, and especially to consider whether it would be wise and practicable for the State of New York to invite the other States of the Union to send representatives to a convention to draft uniform laws to be submitted for the approval and adoption of the several States, and to advise and recommend such other course of action as shall best accomplish the purpose.

When notice of this action was brought to the attention of the American Bar Association, it was resolved to recommend the passage of a similar resolution by each State and by the Congress of the United States for the District of Columbia and the Territories, with the additional subjects for consideration of descent and distribution of property, acknowledgment of deeds, execution and probate of wills. From the impetus thus given to the movement originated by the American Bar Association and formulated by the Legislature of New York has grown the Conference of Commissioners on Uniform State Laws made up at the present time of commissioners representing forty-eight States and Territories, its object as set forth in the constitution being "to promote uniformity of State laws by affording the Commissioners on Uniform State Laws, appointed by the different States of the United States of America, an opportunity of meeting in annual conference for the better accomplishment of the work for which they were appointed."

Fourteen standing committees are authorized, viz.:

1. Executive.
2. Commercial Law.
3. Wills, Descent and Distribution.
4. Marriage and Divorce.
5. Conveyances.
6. Depositions and Proof of Statutes of Other States.
7. Insurance.
8. Congressional Action.
9. Appointment of New Commissioners.
10. Purity of Articles of Commerce.
11. Uniform Incorporation Law.
12. The Torrens System and Registration of Title to Land.
13. Banks and Banking.
14. Publicity.

these being the subjects for the most part susceptible of uniform treatment by the different States.

For nineteen years this Conference has proceeded with its work unostentatiously, but laboriously and effectively, first under the presidency of Hon. S. M. Cutcheon, of Michigan, from 1895-96; then the Hon. Lyman D. Brewster, of Connecticut, from 1896-1901; the Hon. Amasa M. Eaton, of Providence, R. I., from 1901-9.

The formation of the American Bar Association and the Conference of Commissioners on Uniform State Laws, which is, as we have seen, directly attributable to that organization, was in response to a feeling that had been gathering force for more than a generation. As early as 1851 in an address delivered by John William Wallace, for so many years the accomplished reporter of the Supreme Court of the United States, before the Law Academy of Philadelphia, some of the uncertainties, inconveniences and dangers arising from the divergencies of the commercial laws of the different States were pointed out; and as the volume of interstate business increased, these inconveniences became intensified.

Our dual system of government, under which there exist side by side courts of the United States and courts of the States exercising jurisdiction over many identical subjects, led naturally to a diversity of the law as expounded by the courts between the Federal and State jurisdictions in notable instances, while the State Courts of last resort on many subjects of commercial law differed from each other on fundamental principles. Added to these causes of divergency are the differing statutes, where statutes have been enacted.

Obviously, if our system of government is to be preserved, and at the same time the legitimate demands of the business world are to be heeded, there must be one law on those subjects that affect business interests for all of the States, or loss, irritation and serious injury to the prosperity of the country which have already ensued will be continued, and eventually the remedy, probably more fatal than the disease, will come in an all-embracing centralization of power in the Federal Government.

Again and again, in papers and addresses delivered by my distinguished predecessors and other able lawyers, the scope of the work of the Conference of Commissioners has been outlined and the evils that it has sought to overcome have been described.

"Uniformity of laws," says Henry C. Tompkins, of Alabama, in a paper read before the American Bar Association in 1890—"The Necessity for Uniformity in the Laws Governing Commercial Paper,"—"is not needed on all subjects. Though modern invention and discovery have done so much to bring the people of this great country together and make those residing in distant States near neighbors, in the large majority of matters that affect the daily life of the citizen it is not only not necessary that there should be uniformity in the laws of the different States regulating and controlling them, but, on the contrary, such uniformity is undesirable and absolutely impracticable. There is, and will continue to be, a difference in the character and surroundings of the people residing in different portions of the Union that will require a difference in the laws governing them; but, while this is so, it is equally true that the laws governing those matters in which the people of the different States are equally interested—those matters which arise daily in their business intercourse the one with the other—should be uniform, so that the citizen of one State may know the exact character of his act and contract, the full extent of the liability attaching to it, without regard to the locality in which the act is done or the contract made, and, without regard to the tribunal which passes upon it." (13 Rep. Am. Bar Ass'n, p. 247.)

The first efforts of the Conference were confined to matters of importance, but of minor importance as compared with those which subsequently occupied its attention. It was thought that until the movement gathered sufficient strength to be joined in by a majority of the States it would be better to consider the smallest matters and of obvious utility. So brief acts were drafted recommending forms for written instruments of title, a standard of weights and measures, the legalization of foreign wills and the abolition of days of grace.

In 1896 the first ambitious work of the Conference was completed under the title of a general act relating to Negotiable Instruments. This was followed by a Uniform Warehouse Receipts Act, a Uniform Sales Act, a Uniform Stock Transfer Act, a Uniform Bills of Lading Act, and in addition the Conference has adopted the work of the National Divorce Congress as formulated in a Uniform Divorce Act and Acts relating to Marriage and Divorce statistics. Besides this completed work the Conference has now under consideration the draft of a Uniform Act relating to Corporations, a Uniform Act relating to Marriage, a Uniform Act relating to Wife Desertion, and an Act relating to the Execution and Probate of Wills.

It will appear, therefore, that there is now in existence, and has been quietly at work for almost a generation, a body of lawyers endeavoring to attain the end for which this Conference, called under the auspices of The National Civic Federation, has been brought together to encourage. The limits allowed for the many subjects that will engage the attention of this Conference preclude an elaboration of the arguments in favor of attaining the necessary end demanded by modern conditions of business and social life through agreement by the legislatures of the States in the adoption of uniform laws. Excepting to the extreme advocate of a powerful central government such arguments are unnecessary, and even to thinkers of that peculiar school it must be apparent that the difficulty of securing the amendments to the Constitution, preliminary to vesting the general Government with the necessary power, is almost insuperable.

The Conference of Commissioners, therefore, does not concern itself with political questions, but accepting the view of the relations of the National Government to the various States set forth in the Constitution as expounded by the Supreme Court, addresses itself to the task of framing such legislation upon the subjects which it deems appropriate for uniformity as represents the sound, prevailing view of the community. A brief statement of the history and scope of the various bills already adopted may appropriately be presented, and first I take this occasion to say that the Conference has caused a pamphlet to be printed, containing a copy of each of the five commercial acts, with a history of each of the acts, and an annotation after each section which calls for annotation, explaining the reasons, where the statutes differ from the law in certain States. The Conference has adopted the decisions effecting the weight of authority, and in the course of the afternoon these pamphlets will be put in your hands. Those of you who are lawyers will receive them with keen interest, and after you have had opportunity to examine them, I believe in the very great majority of cases you will set the seal of approval upon them, and even where the law of your States has been changed, and where the Commission has been so unfortunate as not to convince you, you will see at least that in no one case have they acted arbitrarily, have they acted hastily, nor have they acted otherwise than with a strong weight of authority back of the conclusions that they have reached. It is hoped that a copy of this pamphlet will be put in the hands of every member of the judiciary committees of the various bodies, who after considering them will report in favor of them. And think, gentlemen, of what an advantage, what an enormous advantage that will be to the business world if there is the same law in Massachusetts and the same law in Oregon, the same in Texas and the same law in New Hampshire, governing these five important subjects.

The Negotiable Instruments Bill.

A full and careful account of the history of this act is given by the late Judge Lyman D. Brewster, for many years President of the Conference of Commissioners, in a paper read before the American Bar Association in 1898 (21 Rep. Am. Bar. Ass'n, p. 315). It appears that in 1878 a digest of the laws relating to bills of exchange was prepared by M. D. Chalmers, an eminent English jurist, who had been Parliamentary Counsel to the Treasury, Judge of County Courts and Law Member of the Viceroy's Counsel in India. In form, it was modeled after the Indian codes and the works of Sir James Stephen on the Law of Evidence, and Frederick Pollock on the Law of Partnership. In preparing his work, Judge Chalmers examined 2,500 cases on the subject, beginning with the first reported case in 1603, and where there was a dearth of authority he had recourse to American decisions, and to inquiry as to the usages among bankers and merchants. Two years later he discussed the subject of codifying the law of Negotiable Instruments before the Institute of Bankers, and, as a consequence, that body and the Associated Chambers of Commerce instructed him to prepare a bill on the subject. The bill was prepared and introduced into Parliament in 1881 by Sir John Lubbock, the President of the Institute. It was then referred to a select committee of merchants, bankers and lawyers, with Lord Herschell as chairman. Lord Herschell reported the bill with some amendments and it passed the House of Commons, and after a few amendments in the House of Lords became the law of England on August 18, 1882.

It was a practical enactment of Judge Chalmers's digest, and was epoch-making because it was the first important enactment of any branch of the common law in England. No material changes were made excepting where necessary to reconcile conflicting cases. It is not alone the law of Great Britain, but of all of her colonies. The whole of the general principles of the laws of bills, notes and checks are contained in a single act of one hundred sections. But few cases have arisen under the act in England, and where, by reason of omission, a new question should arise not covered by the act, it is provided expressly that "the law of merchants shall govern."

After this act had been in operation for thirteen years the Conference of Commissioners employed John J. Crawford, of the New York Bar, to prepare a uniform act to be recommended to all of the States, based upon the English statute, and so well has Mr. Crawford done his work that, after careful revision by the Conference, it has met with acceptance in thirty-eight of the States, Territories and Federal districts. Among the many encomiums upon this monumental work, perhaps that of the late Professor Huffcut, of Cornell, may suffice. He says in his work on Negotiable Instruments, "It presents the best statement available of the results of the English and American judicial decisions."

As a result of the adoption of this law in so many different jurisdictions, merchants whose business extends beyond their own State lines need no longer apprehend the danger arising from divergent decisions and statutes, but have a reasonable certainty that the provisions of the law relating to commercial paper in all its forms are not alone identical in letter but are likely to receive substantially the same interpretation in case of litigation in an overwhelmingly preponderating majority of the American courts.

The next act which has received the largest acceptance, having been adopted in eighteen States since its completion in 1906, is

The Warehouse Receipts Act.

This act was drafted by Professor Samuel Williston, of the Harvard Law School, and Barry Mohun, Esq., of Washington, D. C., the author of a work on the law of Warehouse Receipts. The Commission was urged to draft this act by the American Warehousemen's Asociation, the best judges of the necessity of such legislation. Speaking of this act Professor Williston says:

"Warehouse Receipts and Bills of Lading have become very important commercial documents and merchants have developed a systematic theory in regard to them. This theory is based on the analogy of Bills of Exchange and Promissory Notes, the law of which also had its origin in the custom of merchants. If we examine the history of the law, we find that the courts did not readily adopt the custom of merchants as it extended to Bills of Exchange and Promissory Notes, and the further extension to Warehouse Receipts and Bills of Lading also met with opposition."

But, as he further points out—

"The fundamental doctrines of the mercantile theory, doctrines which are essential for the proper mercantile working of the system, are the complete assignability of the document if it runs to order, and the complete identification of the document with the goods which it represents. Both these doctrines are contrary to ordinary common law principles. As to the first, the common law doctrine is that choses in action are non-assignable. And as to the second, though the common law has recognized constructive delivery to some extent, it has never made much attempt to insure the goods themselves from being dealt with in the hands of the actual possessor directly after constructive delivery had been made by means of the document. Thus the constructive delivery might be deprived of any real value.

"The extent to which courts have adopted the mercantile theory varies. Probably no courts have gone so far as the suggested legislation in regard to Warehouse Receipts, unless a statute has been passed. The courts have to some extent, however, recognized the custom of merchants in regard to documents of title, though not to the full extent. An attempt has been made to meet the difficulty by legislation frequently, and this bill has the precedent of many statutes attempting to confer negotiability on Bills of Lading and Warehouse Receipts. These statutes have to some extent failed in their purpose, because they have failed to define what they mean by negotiability. In the nature of the case, there are some differences between a Bill of Exchange and a Warehouse Receipt."

Perhaps the most radical provision of the act is that section (Section 25) which provides that where goods are in the hands of a warehouseman, or have been put there by an owner, and a negotiable receipt has been issued, they cannot thereafter be attached in the hands of the warehouseman without first the surrender of the receipt to the warehouseman, or its being impounded by the Court. The effect of this will be to give full negotiability to these Warehouse Receipts, excepting that the title will not pass if they fall into the hands of a thief.

How important this act is will appear from a brief study of the statistics of the values of merchandise flowing into customs bonded warehouses. A leaflet prepared by the American Warehousemen's Association shows that in 1906 the average monthly value of such merchandise was nearly $60,000,000. "The grain, hay, sugar, cotton, whiskey, tobacco, rice, coffee, tea, pig iron, machinery and manufactured articles, etc., in other merchandise warehouses for the same period has been variously estimated at from $100,000,000 to $300,000,000. Taking a mean of these two extremes, we find that we have in bonded and general merchandise warehouses a value aggregating in round numbers at least $200,000,000."

It is then shown that the aggregate value of merchandise in cold stores at certain seasons of the year approximates $500,000,000.

"These enormous values are held in warehouses all over the country; in the cotton warehouses of the South; in the grain elevators of the West; in the cold stores of the North; in the customs and free stores of the Atlantic and Pacific Coasts, and in the yards and warehouses of the manufacturing centres of the Middle and Eastern States. Such, however, is the diversity and ambiguity of the legal enactments of the several States governing the use of these values as represented by warehouse receipts, that the larger portion of the investment in them is inert and a gatherer of expense rather than of profit as it should be. Through the Warehouse Receipts Act it is sought to remedy this evil by substituting uniformity and certainty for this diversity and uncertainty; to make the legal government of the warehouse receipt the same in all States and to thus give it the same value in the eyes of all men. By its general enactment it is hoped to make the receipts for goods warehoused in one section of the country good collateral for loans in all other sections. It is also hoped that in time under its influence the use of the warehouse receipt as bankable paper will become so general that manufacturers will be encouraged through it to produce their wares in times when demand is at the ebb as well as when demand is at the flood, thus keeping up a uniformity of output throughout the years at the lowest possible cost by the continuous and consequental economical employment of labor and machinery."

The beneficent effect of this act will be to unlock many millions of capital, because the banks will not hesitate to loan on receipts when the possession of the receipt is tantamount to possession of the goods with a title that cannot be disputed.

The prompt acceptance of this act in such great commercial States as Illinois, Louisiana, Massachusetts, New York, Ohio and Pennsylvania argues well for its passage by all of the States.

The next act of general importance formulated by the Conference is

Uniform Sales Act.

This act is based upon the English Sale of Goods Act, another monument to the industry and ability of Judge Chalmers. In the preface to the first edition of his work on the Sales of Goods Act, Judge Chalmers says of it:

"The bill was originally drafted by me in 1888. I then settled it in consultation with Lord Herschell * * * * In 1893 * * * * it was settled in its present form. * * * * it endeavored to reproduce as exactly as possible the existing law."

The act known as the Sales Act, which has come before the public with the weight of the authority of the Conference of Commissioners, was prepared in 1902-3 by Professor Samuel Williston, and after undergoing criticism until 1906 it was finally adopted in its present form. The arguments in favor of this act are thus summarized by its draftsman:

(1) That it is an advantage for any subject to be reduced to simple rules, as much of the mercantile law can be, and to have it in this form. It is convenient both to business men and to lawyers.

(2) This reason has been sufficient to induce England to pass codes in regard to negotiable instruments, the sale of goods and other matters. In this country the reasons are far stronger because of the peculiar conditions arising from our political system, which are themselves the controlling reason for this whole movement for uniform legislation.

As in the drafts of other acts, there is included in this no change in any principle where a uniform rule of law has been established, but where authority is divided upon a point, the weight of authority has generally been followed.

"If," he says, "a view though supported by fewer courts seemed better to conform to general principles or to commercial convenience, it was adopted. The most noticeable illustration of this is found in the sections relating to documents of title. The mercantile view of the document of title has been fully adopted by the bill, as opposed to what may be called the common law view. If the bill is enacted it will make no radical change in the law of any State. It will, however, make some minor changes probably in the law of every State which passes it, these minor changes being the concession which each State makes to secure uniformity. Probably the most noticeable change from a practicable point of view is that in regard to the Statute of Frauds. * * * *

"Thereby small sales, which are usually oral, will not be affected, but large transactions which by prudent business usage should be in writing, will be covered. It should be noticed that the English limit, ten pounds, which has been translated into fifty dollars in many American States, was fixed at a time when the value of a pound was much greater than it is now."

The provisions relating to negotiable documents of title, beginning at Section 27, have been necessary in order to cover the entire subject. It will be found that there is a close connection between these sections of the act and those of the Warehouse Act. They follow, in some respects, the analogy of bills and notes, with the important distinction that a negotiable receipt may not be negotiated by one who takes by trespass or a finder.

Although so short a time has elapsed since this act was formulated, it has already been adopted in the important States of Connecticut, Massachusetts, New Jersey, Ohio, Rhode Island and the Territory of Arizona.

Uniform Stock Transfer Act.

This act was also drafted by Professor Williston and was considered in committee and in convention of the Conference for two years prior to its final approval in August, 1909. In many of its provisions it is in advance of the existing law, but follows the thought already expressed in the Sales Act and in the Warehouse Receipts Act in the endeavor to make certificates of stock negotiable practically to the same extent as other commercial paper. If adopted, the transfer of the certificate will operate as a transfer of the shares represented thereby, changing the provisions of the common law which make a registry on the books of the company necessary for a complete transfer. The fundamental purpose of the whole act is to make the certificate to the fullest extent possible the representative of the shares of stock. Thus the transfer on the books of a corporation becomes like the record of a deed of real estate under a registry system.

If at first the provisions of this act seem radical, it will be found on examination of the reasons which influenced the Conference to formulate it that they are all based upon a clear, settled and intelligent purpose of protecting the innocent holders of certificates of stock from loss, and making shares of stock in corporations so easily transferable as to facilitate the use of them either as collateral security or as investments.

Uniformity upon this subject is obviously of great importance and the adoption of this act will be a great step towards obtaining uniformity of legislation on all subjects relating to corporations.

Uniform Bills of Lading Act.

This proposed bill comes also from the hands o[illegible] Professor Williston. The first draft was submitted t[illegible] the Conference in 1906. Subsequently it was unde[illegible] consideration at public sessions of the Committee o[illegible] Commercial Law held in Philadelphia and Portlan[illegible] Me., in 1907, and in New York in 1909, and was car[illegible]fully considered, not alone by the committee charge[illegible] with the responsibility of revising Professor Willi[illegible]ton's work, but by representatives of various associ[illegible]tions and corporations, including the American Ban[illegible]ers' Association, the American Warehousemen[illegible] Association, the National Board of Trade, Merchant[illegible] Association of New York City, the Chamber of Co[illegible]merce of Richmond, Va., the National Industri[illegible] Traffic League, the National Manufacturers' Associ[illegible]tion, the Erie Railroad, the Pennsylvania Railroa[illegible] the New York, New Haven & Hartford Railroad, t[illegible] Old Dominion Steamship Company, the Bills of La[illegible]ing Committee of Railroads in Official Territory, re[illegible]resentatives of the Harvard Law School and the La[illegible] Schools of Columbia University and the University [illegible] Pennsylvania.

Four tentative drafts were printed and issued, a[illegible] finally, after the Conference, in accordance with [illegible] custom, had carefully considered the act section [illegible] section it was recommended by them to the Leg[illegible]latures of the various States for passage.

Subsequently at a conference called especially [illegible] consider this subject, held on the 13th of Septemb[illegible] 1909, in the City of Chicago, under the auspices [illegible] the American Bankers' Association (there being pr[illegible]ent representatives of the most important interest[illegible] after a careful explanation of the provisions of [illegible] bill by Francis B. James, Esq., Chairman of the C[illegible]mittee on Commercial Law, the Conference una[illegible]mously endorsed the Uniform Bills of Lading Act.

We come now to a subject which will proba[illegible] present greater difficulties than any of the other a[illegible] to which I have referred, and which may take ye[illegible] of effort before it is perfected in the form that s[illegible] be accepted by all of the States. I refer to a

Uniform Incorporation Law.

A draft of a Uniform Incorporation Law has b[illegible] prepared and is now in the hands of a standing c[illegible]mittee under the chairmanship of John C. Richb[illegible] Esq., of Chicago, which it is hoped will be comple[illegible]

SOME OF THE SPEAKERS AT THE TENTH ANNUAL MEETING, NEW YORK, AND THE UNIFORM STATE LEGISLATION CONFERENCE, WASHINGTON.

the community been more apparent than in this matter of divorce. The fact that, by reason of the divergence of the laws of the different States on the subject of jurisdiction, persons may be held as married in one State and unmarried in another, with the sorrowful consequences affecting the legitimacy of children and the many embarrassments relating to ownership of property, has been one but certainly not the only cause for the widespread dissatisfaction among the best elements of the community with the existing situation. So long as the attitude of a majority of the people favors divorce for any cause, statutes providing for it and regulating proceedings to obtain it will remain upon the books, and, necessarily, there will be much unhappiness and scandal associated with the subject. But there is no good reason why the laws relating to jurisdiction and the effect of decrees when granted should not be made uniform, or why the consensus of the community that divorce should not be granted excepting where intolerable conditions can be avoided in no other way, should not find expression in just and reasonable laws.

The provisions of the Uniform Divorce Act, which bears the stamp of the approval of the National Conference, were reached after careful, conscientious consideration by a body of reasonable men and women fully alive to the importance of the problem they were appointed to solve. These men and women, appointed by the Governors of all the States, the District of Columbia and one of the Territories, with the exception only of the States of Nevada, Mississippi and South Carolina, might well claim to represent the average thought of their various communities.

It has been suggested that the Conference should not attempt the solution of any sociological problem such as divorce, but confine its attention strictly to matters relating to business. It is submitted that this is a narrow view of the functions of the Conference. It has been well said by eminent authority that the family relation and its preservation and sanctity and permanence are of far greater importance than any laws relating to any other subject, no matter what it may be. Besides, the Conference has acted in obedience to one of the purposes for which it was organized in taking up this subject and pressing it for consideration. Perhaps the end will be obtained, however, by partial legislation on various matters included in the whole general subject, such as jurisdiction, the effect of decrees obtained in other States, etc., and it is the purpose of the Committee carefully to consider recommendations leading to that end.

The following general principles, having been approved by the Divorce Congress, are embodied in the uniform law recommended by that body and accepted and recommended by the National Conference:—

All suits for divorce shall be brought only in the State where the plaintiff or the defendant has a *bona fide* residence.

When courts are given cognizance of suits where the plaintiff was domiciled in a foreign jurisdiction at the time the cause of complaint arose, relief should not be given, unless the cause of divorce was recog-

[illegible] as a co-respondent should be given an opportunity to intervene.

Hearings and trials should always be before the court and not before any delegated representative of it, and in all uncontested cases, and in any other where the court may deem it proper, a disinterested attorney should be assigned to defend the case.

A decree should not be granted unless the cause is shown by affirmative proof, aside from any admissions on the part of the respondent.

A decree dissolving the marriage should not become operative until the lapse of a reasonable time after hearing or trial upon the merits of the case.

In no case should the children born during coverture be bastardized, excepting in the case of bigamous marriages or in the usual exception of impossibility of access.

A divorce obtained by an inhabitant of a State, in another State or country to which he has gone for the purpose of obtaining it, or for a cause which would not authorize a divorce by the law of the State of domicile, should have no effect therein.

Fraud or collusion in obtaining or attempting to obtain a divorce should be made statutory crimes by the criminal code.

It will be seen that these resolutions partly relate to matters of substantive law and partly to what has been called adjective law. No one of them is based on theory, but all have been tried practically in some jurisdiction. It is submitted that if divorce is to be tolerated at all, the adoption of a statute which embodies these resolutions will safeguard the trials, so that a minimum of injustice will be done both to the parties themselves and to the community.

The Uniform Divorce Law has been adopted in New Jersey, Delaware and Wisconsin and its essential features are already the law of Illinois, and many of its best provisions are based upon the existing law in other States.

It is too much to hope that the adoption of this law will stop the tide of divorce, but it will at least make it more difficult to obtain divorces which are fraudulent as between the parties and the community, who in theory of law have a right to be represented in every case.

The Uniform Divorce Act differs in structure from the commercial acts. Those commercial acts to which I have made reference are expected to be passed in each of the Districts in which they are represented. Not so with the divorce act. We will be pretty well satisfied if we can embody the principles which are given in the resolutions, and there will be this result: That each of the communities in accordance with the varying standard of average of morality, if you choose, will have its own laws. It is not for Pennsylvania to criticise South Carolina because South Carolina has no divorce law whatsoever, and it is not for South Carolina to criticise California because California has a divorce law, or if they choose to criticise them, not to influence public opinion, as they may by their criticism, but it is the business of each of those States to respond in their divorce laws to the tone of opinion of the subject in those States, and in that way the difficulty, which at first seemed absolutely insuperable, of obtaining uniform laws seems by the Commissioners

from this conference or from any of the constituent elements that it represents.

HON. GIFFORD PINCHOT.

I WANT to say a word or two this afternoon about the first opportunity for legislation in conservation, something about uniform legislation among the States, and something about the situation in Congress and what may be done there. The policies that are now grouped under the name of conservation are various agencies. Some of them, like the policy of forest preservation, have been advocated by Americans for more than one hundred years. Some of them, like the control of power monopoly in the public interests, are younger than the present [illegible] tury; but all of them are to-day of equal impor[illegible] and interest to the general welfare. We con[illegible] last to the point that we have been seeking for [illegible] years; we come at last to the point of action [illegible] we have either got to go ahead or to fall back.

Now this conservation field is a mighty fiel[illegible] uniform action between the States themselves [illegible] between the States and the nation. If I had [illegible] time this afternoon I should like to talk to yo[illegible] the immediate necessity of uniform legislation [illegible] fire protection and for equitable taxation on f[illegible] lands in the States. Fires, like a good many o[illegible] things, pay no attention to State boundaries, an[illegible] operation between the officials under the same [illegible] ditions across State lines is many times of th[illegible] most importance in securing the protection of [illegible] forests from fire. In the same way a uniform [illegible] tude toward the taxation of forest lands between [illegible] States is now one of the absolutely essential [illegible] indispensable conditions of forestry on private la[illegible]

Private owners now control four times as m[illegible] timber land as do the States and the nation put [illegible] gether. Unless the private owner in one State, [illegible] peting with a private owner in another State for [illegible] production of timber, finds himself met and [illegible] trolled by the same system of taxation, compe[illegible] automatically wipes out many times the possi[illegible] of the practice of forestry and makes distribu[illegible] of timber lands impossible to an equal degree [illegible] should like to ask, therefore, that you will be [illegible] enough to consider whether, among the vastly [illegible] portant subjects that meet you at this time, [illegible] form laws on forest fires and forest taxes m[illegible] not fairly come within the purview of this meet[illegible]

The idea of uniform State legislation was lar[illegible] in the minds of the Governors when they met at [illegible] great conference in the White House two years [illegible] last May, looking toward the appointment [illegible] National Conservation Commission and a State [illegible] servation Commission in every State, for the [illegible] purpose of reaching some uniform action betw[illegible] the States of the nation and the nation, and betw[illegible] the different States themselves. Forty-two of [illegible] States have already carried out this recomme[illegible] tion and you have now under your hand, ready [illegible] action, a most powerful weapon, a most powe[illegible] tool in the direction of uniform action between [illegible] States on all questions concerning conservat[illegible] Now, these conservation questions are to-day [illegible] overshadowing problems between the States, for [illegible] benefit of the general public. The manner of their solution, the direction in which we move, will affect every man now alive and every citizen of this country, and no question could be of more vital importance at this time or any other time, than that. The great principles we have been working for, for many years, may now at last, at this time, be enacted into law; an opportunity is before us and we may take advantage of it or the chance may pass. Public sentiment is controlling the way.

For the second time, a President of the United States has embodied in a message to Congress the principles for which the efforts of conservation have been at work for years. Most of those principles contained in the recent message are well-known to the friends of conservation, and well approved of. If it has omissions or passages with which I disagree, I have no concern with that to-day. Specific bills have been prepared embodying the recommendations of the message; when these bills are made public, as they have not yet been, they will be the legitimate subjects for approval, for condemnation, for criticism of various kinds and for careful scrutiny at every stage of their passage through Congress. If there is disagreement or criticism, all that will come at its proper time and in its proper place. To-day, the first consideration is this: That the friends of conservation must not allow themselves to be divided. The issues at stake transcend from no personal issues whatsoever. The plain duty of all the friends of conservation is to sink all their differences, to unite their efforts and agree on essentials, and to demand with a unanimous voice that Congress shall act on the recommendations of the President, act wisely and act at once. The President himself urges that his message be taken up and disposed of promptly without awaiting the result of the investigation which has been determined upon. There can be no reason to await the result of the investigation in order to gain the establishment of these measures; they stand by themselves, whatever the result of that investigation may be.

In the face of this great opportunity, let us go even farther than the President has recommended, and so far as these issues are concerned, let us disregard the controversy altogether in the general effort to attain what every good citizen so earnestly desires. To my mind it is clearly the object to look above the lesser subjects of contention whatever they might be. There are very many of these subjects ready to be acted upon, about which there can be no controversy whatever; for instance, the leasing of coal lands instead of virtually giving them away, the prevention of water power monopoly in the public interest, the conservation of our soils, the maintenance of the national forests, the protection of forests and of the woodlands at the head of navigable streams. All these things are ready, we know them to be ready, and they can be dealt with properly only in the light of the general welfare and for no other interests.

Now is the time for all good men to come to the aid of the conservation movement. Now is the time precisely, that without regard to party, or to prejudice, or to any personal considerations whatsoever, the public good comes first.

JOHN HAYS HAMMOND.

MINING is rated by insurance companies as an extra-hazardous vocation, and, in view of the mortality that obtains in this country in particular, justly so. While there are certain inherent trade risks, the industry in regard to the safety of its employes is susceptible of great improvement; and not only from an humanitarian point of view, which in itself is sufficiently potent, but even from the aspect of commercial advantage it behooves both the engineers and the statesmen of this country to improve the situation by their active co-operation.

The recent disaster at the Cherry coal mine in Illinois has cost the public for relief work upwards of $300,000, in addition to which it is estimated that the coal company's expenses will amount to more than $200,000, making a total cost of over half a million dollars as the direct pecuniary loss sustained in this disaster.

While there are no available statistics to admit of even an approximate estimate of the preventable deaths among the mine workers, I think it would be a conservative statement that the number of fatal accidents could be reduced more than thirty-five per cent by raising the standards of safety. In 1908 there were mined in the United States about five hundred million tons of coal at a cost of 2,450 human lives. There has been a steady increase during the past twenty years in the number of men killed in the coal mines of this country for each thousand men employed, and in 1908 it reached the figure 3.60.

A comparative summary extended over an average of five years, showing the number of men killed for each thousand employed in France, Belgium, Great Britain, Prussia and the United States, respectively, is instructive: France, .91 per thousand; Belgium, 1.00 per thousand; Great Britain, 1.28 per thousand; Prussia, 2.06 per thousand; United States, 3.39 per thousand. There has been, as I have stated, a gradual increase in the mine casualties in this country, whereas in Europe there has been a steady decrease.

Owing to increasing depths in the exploitation of coal mines, the fatality rate tends to increase, especially in those mining districts where fire-damp is prevalent. Therefore, under the conditions of mining obtaining at present, the outlook is extremely discouraging. The decrease in the fatality rate in Europe is obviously due to the introduction of better mining methods. Notwithstanding the greater amount of coal mined per man in the United States, the number of men killed for each million tons of coal produced is 5.57, compared with 4.31, 4.17 and 4.96 in Great Britain, France and Belgium, respectively.

It is a popular belief that the most important cause of the loss of life in coal mines is due to explosion from fire-damp. Such a dreadful catastrophe as that recently at the Cherry mine in Illinois, where three hundred miners were suffocated, serves to create this erroneous impression; but as a matter of fact not over ten per cent of the fatalities are due to gas and dust explosions, while nearly fifty per cent of the fatal casualties are due to the falls or cavings of roofs, etc. In the United States, deaths from falls of roof and coal, per thousand men employed, are about 1.[illegible]; in Germany, .92; in Great Britain, .64; France, .047, and Belgium, .40, less than twenty-five per cent of that in the United States. Accidents coming under this category result in the death of usually not more than two or three miners at a time and, therefore, do not attract the attention which they deserve because of the great number of fatalities in the yearly aggregate.

The same unfavorable, I may say humiliating, comparison exists in the case of fatal accidents due to explosion of fire-damp. Belgium, where fire-damp exists in greater quantities than in any other of the coal mining countries of the world, shows a loss due to mine explosions of but .039 per thousand miners—but little more than ten per cent of that in the United States, where the fatalities due to this cause amount to .37 per thousand. The figures I have given are certainly impressive and should suffice to enlist universal interest in this important subject, and yet I have not presented figures to show the number of casualties of a non-fatal character, nor have I discussed the excessive mortality due to unhygienic conditions. A consideration of these aspects would greatly emphasize the necessity of improving the present mining conditions.

Now, to what causes is this disparity to be ascribed? Certainly not to adverse physical conditions existing in the coal deposits themselves, for here, indeed, the conditions are more favorable for safe mining than in Europe. The plain, unvarnished truth is in the answer that Governmental control and regulation in this country are totally inadequate. In this respect we are far behind European methods in the safeguarding of the lives of the miners.

A case in point is the ruinous competition now pre- the inordinate desire to obtain a maximum output so as to minimize working costs, and human life is consequently one of the sacrifices made for the attainment of that end. Not only is human life sacrificed in the pursuance of such a policy, but in coal mining in particular a great waste of the coal resources of the country results.

A case in point is the ruinous competition now prevailing in some of our important bituminous coal fields, where the operator, in order to mine coal—not to obtain profit, be it understood, but to prevent actual financial loss—is compelled to adopt methods not only dangerous to his employes, but also inevitably entailing an enormous waste of coal. It is estimated that not more than fifty-five per cent of the coal existing in the coal beds is at present being saved, from forty to fifty per cent being irretrievably lost because it cannot be mined at the present low market prices. Dr. Holmes, the chief of the technologic branch of the United States Geological Survey, estimates the yearly loss of coal resulting from such wasteful methods at two hundred fifty million tons.

Belgium has passed through a similar crisis with attending great loss of life and waste of coal. At that time the loss of life and waste of coal under the methods then prevailing were fully as costly as those in our country to-day, but the intervention of the State, whereby the coal operators were encouraged to enter into an arrangement which assured them a reasonable price for their product at the mines and at the same time protected the consumer from unreasonable prices, put a stop to this disastrous policy. The result of the establishment of a price which enables the coal operator to make a reasonable profit has been most gratifying in the introduction of methods which have very greatly decreased the mining casualties and at the same time have prevented a waste of the coal resources to the amount of from thirty to forty per cent. Coal in Europe costs from one and one-half to two and one-half times the cost in this country.

An increase of not more than twenty cents per ton would enable the coal operator to introduce improved methods of mining, thereby raising the standards of safety and at the same time resulting in the adoption of methods affecting an enormous conservation of our coal resources. This added cost would not be any considerable hardship on the consumer, as it represents but a very small percentage of the cost of coal when it reaches him. The added cost of the necessaries of life would be hardly appreciable in the case of the poor, the bulk of the coal being sold to large corporations.

The bulk of the bituminous coal which is sold at the pit's mouth for one dollar per ton, when it reaches the consumer in New England, for example, is sold for from five to seven dollars; therefore the extra cost to the consumer by the additional charge referred to of twenty cents per ton would not exceed from three to four per cent, and this sum should be saved by reduction of the transportation rates and of the profits of the middlemen who handle the coal. The assumption by the present generation of the extra burden of twenty cents per ton would, I believe, save the next generation more than fifty cents per ton in its coal bill. Such a course is dictated by the professed altruism of the great movement for the conservation of our natural resources.

The remedy of these conditions obviously lies in the improvement of the present methods of mining, and it is the function of the State to introduce such innovations. Uniformity in the mining laws of all the States is indispensable. It would obviously be unfair for a State to impose drastic legislation upon its mining industry, adding to the cost of production, where laxity in this respect prevails in neighboring sister States.

Another cogent reason is the fact that miners are more or less migratory and it is costly in life and in money to impose upon them the necessity of learning the new mining laws of the States to which they migrate. But there should be no ill-considered or drastic legislation, for unless the laws are rational they will inevitably be honored rather in the breach than in the observance of them. These laws must appeal to the intelligence of both the coal operators and the miners, for the benefit to be derived will depend upon their hearty co-operation.

There are many foreigners employed in our mines, our coal mines in particular, who have not only had no previous mining experience, but understand and speak English imperfectly. From these circumstances it is imperative that the State laws compel the mining companies to give such men at least an elementary education and training into methods of mining before placing them in any position where their ignorance might cause disaster to their fellow workmen.

But before remedial legislation there should be a thorough investigation into the causes of mine accidents and the proper remedies to be applied, by a corps of impartial and competent experts, such as has been making investigations of this kind under the direction of Dr. Holmes, of the United States Geological Survey. Much time and money could be saved the States by co-operating with the Federal Government in the solution of these important problems, after which the requisite laws should be enacted and a corps of State inspectors appointed to see that these laws are properly administered.

Accordingly, we would recommend that the Governors of the States in which mining constitutes an important industry, select some well-qualified mining expert to confer with the chief of the Technologic Bureau in Washington and to assist him in preparing a draft of a model mining law, to be submitted to the Governors for their recommendation to the legislatures of their respective States. The physical and economic conditions that obtain in the mining districts of the United States present no difficulties in the drafting of a model mining law of universal application.

To-day the supervision exercised in this respect in the States is altogether inadequate. For example, in the State of Illinois, which produces about fifty million tons of coal per annum, where fifty thousand miners are employed and where there are nine hundred mines in operation, there are only ten mine inspectors, who receive the meagre salary of $1,800 each annually. It is manifestly a physical impossibility for one inspector to supervise the operation of ninety mines.

It is most important that inspectors of a superior class be appointed and that a corps be established of the character of that of the United States Geological Survey, without the pale of political influence and composed of men of undoubted integrity and technical ability.

I have omitted discussions of the technical features of this subject, as to the uses of safety lamps, es, etc., as those subjects are now being d by Dr. Holmes, from whom detailed in- :an be obtained, but the committee wishes immediate installation in the mining dis- ıe country of those appliances which have ed effective and indispensable in rescue in work of first aid to the injured.

liscussion of this subject I have referred e coal mines; but in some of the important ng districts of our country the rate of considerably larger than that given as the ate of fatality in the coal fields. For ex- . one of the large iron mining districts of the fatal accidents for one thousand em- ıve reached over a period of several years in many of the other metal mines of the the average is greater than that in coal Compared with the casualties attending the of metals in other countries, similar opera- this country are but little more satisfactory the case of the mining of coal, and the reme- gested in connection with coal mining apply, mutandis, to metal mining.

AUGUST BELMONT.

ie conference held recently in New York by e National Civic Federation on the subject ef department funds of corporations, the the speeches followed generally a description various plans existing among the indus- transportation companies and public service ations providing for the health, safety and te care of employes when injured or inca- ed.

advantages of uniform laws on the subject of lling corporations to make adequate and defi- provision for the same was discussed and a y of methods were advocated.

ery close and well-delivered argument was made ubject of one of the speeches at the banquet ı followed the conference, urging the compul- use by law of insurance to cover liabilities in- d through injuries to employes in discharging duties. Unfortunately, some of the force of recommendations of the speaker was lost upon ıearers from the fact that he was an insurance rt and the earmarks of special pleading were rent, but in the main it struck me as funda- tally sound.

surance has the advantage of distributing the so that the less hazardous vocations may help rotect the more dangerous ones. The burdens ıe end fall upon the consumer through the in- sed cost of production, for the cost will finally there through the inflexible laws of trade. To e each industry bear directly its cost of relief to loyes as a part of the cost of production, as ad- ted by one of the ablest speakers of that even- would make for hardship in many directions. mining, for example, is extra hazardous, but is e part of wisdom to burden a necessity of life, ufacture and transportation with full cost of its lities for injuries, if a system can be devised by h the less hazardous occupations may help bear expense through a well devised application of law of averages?

advocating uniform laws to cover employers' lities through insurance, it must not be forgot- that uniform insurance laws are necessary as

his entire subject is crying loud for solution— bringing about of uniform laws throughout the es. It will take time, but from an economic dpoint this seems to me very clear that the es which have the wisdom to march in the van his movement will enjoy a distinct advantage as abor. Labor will be attracted to the States af- ing them the fairest and safest protection, and employer will hail this, too, as an advantage to self.

nother consideration, and perhaps one of the test, is the impediment to liberal treatment of r employes by corporations in the matter of in- s which unequal laws produce.

have in mind, as an illustration, the National vester Company. Mr. George A. Ranney, of that pany, is quoted as saying:

Any large company doing business in several es could be more liberal in its benefits, provided State laws were uniform and they knew the imum liability they would be called upon to pay any one State."

his conference is affording the opportunity of ussing the greatest question of the day. In it not only the solution of a great and unjust den on labor, but an escape from the dangers overburdening our National Government with du- it could never perform with the same efficiency the several States, once at one in the character their respective laws.

ADDRESS OF HONORABLE ELIHU ROOT.

I HAVE come in to speak a few words this afternoon, rather to show my interest in the subject upon which you are engaged than with the idea that I can contribute anything of substantial value to the deliberations which are being enlightened by the gentlemen who have studied much more thoroughly than I have had the opportunity to do the subjects under discussion.

It seems to me that at this meeting all that you are doing now should be regarded not as the working of the perfected machinery for uniform laws, but rather as a part of the initial process by means of which a permanent and effective system shall be produced. I cannot doubt that what we are engaged in doing now and the many articles that have appeared in the press and the many speeches that have been made on various platforms upon this subject are testimony to a general sentiment among the people of the United States. You do not find conspiring views of people from different environments and differents parts of the country to any such extent as we have seen recently on this subject, unless there is a general sentiment on the part of the people. Every important movement has to pass through a period of incubation. The first proposition of a new departure ordinarily appears to receive but little attention, but it is repeated, it is duplicated, it is reduplicated, it gradually sinks into the minds of men, and after a long, and to a great extent, silent and unnoted process we ultimately find that if the proposition was one of sound merit it has won its way in the minds of the whole people.

Now I think that this meeting is an illustration of the fact that the proposed laws which are being advocated here have already taken their place in the serious consideration and the favorable consideration of our people. It is not necessary for us to discuss questions of jurisdiction under the Constitution as between the national government and the State government. It is quite apparent that there is a wide field of governmental activity which belongs to the States and which does not under any school of construction or upon any contention fall within the powers of the national government, but a field in which a great variety of most important legislation is necessary, affecting not alone the individual State which is legislating, but affecting a great number of the sister States, and it is upon that field that we are now looking for greater efficiency in law making and enforcement, and it is that field that we seek to affect by the propositions which are here made.

When our Constitution was made, of course we had a great number of comparatively separate communities, and the makers of the Constitution put in the hands of the national government a great number of things which occurred to them then as being of general importance concerning the general welfare of the people of this country, but the increase of communication and the bringing together of all those different communities into what is in many respects one great community has developed a great number of other things of general importance which clearly were not vested in the national government, but which rest with the States. How shall we deal with those other things? Is it necessary to revise the Constitution and put them all in the hands of the nation, or, on the other hand, is it necessary to have legislation regarding those subjects carried on as if we were separate and entirely distinct communities, having no regard each for the other, as if we were communities living in the old times, when the people of every other country were regarded as presumptively enemies? Are we shut up to those two alternatives? I think not; plainly not. We have abundant lesson from the method by which the sovereign powers of Europe who have no such intimate bonds of friendship and brotherhood as our States have with each other,—the way in which those countries have met on all matters of common interest. Since the Congress of Vienna in 1815, in which the powers of Europe for the first time undertook to deal with subjects of general interest to them, as distinct from specific situations which were the results of war—up to three years ago there had been over one hundred and twenty congresses or conferences of representatives of a considerable part, practically the whole of the civilized powers of the earth, and those conferences or congresses have accomplished a great variety of things. They have established an international postal union; they have agreed upon and put into force rules for the protection of industrial property, patents, copyrights, and trademarks; they have established rules for sanitation or control and to some degree the prevention of disease, under which each country binds itself to so legislate and so enforce its laws as to prevent its being a nuisance to the other countries with whom it is in conference. That was accomplished first by a series of conferences participated in by the great powers of Europe and by the United States, resulting in a convention at Paris a few years ago, and that was followed by another conference, which included all the American powers, and under a convention signed here in Washington three years ago substantially the same rules were adopted. They have united in measures for the abolition of the slave trade, for the abolition of privateering, for the establishment of agreement upon rules of the private international law, so that private rights depending upon the laws of different countries may be recognized and dealt with under uniform rules; they have in a series of conferences held at Geneva established rules for the enforcement of humane principles in the conduct of war, and by rules, adopted at The Hague, for the enforcement of humane rules in the conduct of war by sea; they have established for the greater part of the world uniform weights and measures; they have agreed upon rules designed for the prevention of the white slave trade; they have, by a series of conferences, agreed in Europe upon a number, as yet a comparatively small number, of provisions for the protection of labor; they have agreed upon rules for telegraphic communication, rules for the protection of ocean cables, rules for the government of wireless telegraphy.

As to certain special matters which have affected the states of Europe, in one congress sixteen powers united in providing for the abolition of the sound dues imposed by Denmark. In another congress seventeen nations united in getting rid, by means of an adequate payment, of the duties imposed by Hanover upon the navigation of the River Elbe. In another congress at Brussels twenty powers united in securing free navigation of the Scheldt. In a long series of congresses European powers united in the adoption of self-denying ordinances in relation to the payment of bounties for the production of sugar. Within the last year there have been deposited by fourteen European powers ratifications of conventions regarding the procedure of the civil courts of all fourteen countries. There has been agreed upon at a conference of all the great maritime powers held in London a series of rules settling long-standing discussions between international lawyers regarding the rights and duties of neutrals in naval warfare There has been a conference including all the powers having any interest in the Far East, a conference held at Pekin, at which resolutions were agree upon for the prevention and cessation of the traff in opium. There has been proclaimed by our Presi dent the sanitary convention establishing rules fo sanitation to twelve American countries, and in th City of Washington there has been agreed upon an promulgated a series of principles, or declaration principles, regarding the conservation of natur resources participated in by the United States, Mexico, Canada and Newfoundland, including th whole of the North American continent north Guatemala. There have been recently the great wor conferences at The Hague, with which we are familiar, dealing with a great variety of matte which are of the utmost importance to civilizati and to every political body within the limits civilization.

Now, it seems quite absurd that a body of forty- States, bound together by the ties of comm patriotism and a common interest, should not be a to do, regarding the matters that are entrus to their individual legislation and not commit to any superior power, the same sort of thing t all the civilized, the widely separated civilized pow of the world have been doing for almost a cent past. Observe that every one of these in national conferences has been attended by a orized delegates—delegates authorized to v as a rule to sign, sometimes absolutely sometimes ad referendum. So that the re of these conferences has been the productio something in black and white; something that agreed upon to be done, and in the great mass of conferences the result which has been agreed has been done, has found effect in the affirm legislation of the different States, of the diffe countries that took part. Observe that in every of them—every country that took part w sovereign country having no superior, just a regard to the particular subjects of legislation I have been talking about, each State would a conference having no superior. Observe th these conferences there is no compulsion wha It is the free action of each State respondi argument, to information, to discussion, to suasion, to enlightenment—but never to compu

Now, there is the model worked out by the pra experience of mankind; worked out by the civ nations, America being a part, and playing a part in a process, and in regard to all these m which are not committed to the national gover but are committed to the States, and in which ent States have a vital interest—an interest goes beyond their own boundaries—I can s reason whatever why the same example shall not be followed.

Observe that there are a number of different kinds of subjects dealt with by these conferences. In the first place, there is a great variety of laws which may perhaps be put in one form or another equally well. Now that is so among our States. Take as an illustration the question whether there should be days of grace on promissory notes. Now it makes no earthly difference to any one whether there are days of grace on a promissory note or not, but it is important to an American business man that he shall know whether in another State with which he is doing business there are days of grace or not, that is, whether there are to be three days added to the period for which the note runs. I say it makes no difference which way you have it, only it ought to be the same as to all. (Applause.)

No two lawyers ever sat down each by himself to draw a paper without drawing the paper in a different form. It is impossible that they shall coincide, and we have a great variety of laws which differ merely because they were drawn by different men, and the differences in which are of no earthly consequence except that they are differences, and that is the first and the simplest body of laws to be dealt with and reduced to conformity, so that these more immaterial, unimportant and unessential differences shall not be a hindrance to our intercourse. As to those laws, the commissions upon uniformity of the laws have been doing most excellent work, and I take it that it is a kind of work which the commissions were expected chiefly to do; that they were not, when they were appointed, expected to deal with large questions of State policy. Their relations to the legislative bodies of the States have not been such that they would consider themselves justified in undertaking, when they get together, to act upon important questions of State policy.

Now, that leads me to a second class of cases, and that is cases in which the policies of the States differ, and intentionally differ, because people of one State have different views about what the law ought to be from the people in another State. That is quite distinct—a distinct class. The people in one State may think that there ought not to be any divorce except for adultery, and the people in another State may think that there ought to be divorce for incompatibility of temper. They differ as to their views, but it does not follow that they always must differ. And there is a great number of subjects covered by our State laws which are nobody's business but the business of the States, as to which a fair presentation of the inconvenience caused to other States by the policy followed by a particular State might lead to a change. If it is worth trying as between separate nations, is it not worth while to try it as between our States, and is it not worth while, instead of trying to get the Constitution of the United States changed so as to take away from the States their power over matters which are really essentially of local concern—is it not worth trying to see if the States cannot agree upon such modifications of their peculiar policies, of their individual policies, as to do the least possible harm and cause the least possible inconvenience to their sister States? (Applause.)

That is a subject which ought to be taken up by men delegated by the States, men of high authority recognized as having commanding ability, men who are forces in the communities in which they live, and delegated for the purpose of doing that thing. These conferences that have been held between separate and independent nations are attended by men of the first order of ability, men whose ability to present the views of their country creates confidence.

Then there is a third class of cases, and that is where there are things that ought to be done which are generally recognized as desirable, but the doing of which does not fall within the province of the national government and cannot be done by any particular State, and can only be done by the conjoint action of a number of States; for instance the preservation of a forest area for the head waters of numerous rivers which water the soil of many States and where no one State has such an extensive ownership as to make it possible for it to do the thing that ought to be done. Clearly that is a case where all the States whose interests are concerned and whose ownership and jurisdiction give power, ought to come together and unite for their accomplishment of the purpose just as time and time and time again the nations of Europe have united for accomplishing such a purpose; just as they united to free the Danish sound; just as they united to free the Elbe and Scheldt from the duties that were imposed upon navigation of those rivers.

Now, all three of these different classes of cases ought to be taken up as between the States. It seems to me that the machinery has yet to be perfected for the doing of these things. The Governors' meeting, I think, must be regarded also as being merely evolutionary, for Governors are not elected by the people of their States up to this time, for the purpose of discharging such functions as have been indicated here. Commissioners to secure conformity of the laws have not been appointed for discharging such wide or important functions as we are now considering. It seems to me that every State ought to appoint men in such way as it sees fit, delegates to an interstate conference which should be held every year, authorized to enter upon the consideration and the discussion of these great interstate questions calling for the formation and the execution of a common purpose and authorized to sign—subject of course to the approval of the legislative authorities of their States—agreement upon the rules or the principles that are to be enforced. Of course, any agreement properly so called, to be binding upon the States would have to have the consent of Congress, but if the process is deliberate and considerate, so that the result is mature and represents the real opinions and desires of the States, I apprehend that there will be but little doubt of the free and cheerful consent of Congress to the great remedial measures that ought to be reached through such a process.

I have high hopes that we are on the threshold of a new departure in more effective legislation for the benefit of our States and the removal of many evils and abuses that undoubtedly do now exist because of the want of that kind of discussion and consideration and concentration of public opinion upon State legislation—including concentration of the public opinion of America upon State legislation that ought to be wiped off the statute books, which we would have through carrying out such a process as I have described. (Loud Applause.)

THE GENERAL PROGRAM.

GIFFORD PINCHOT, "Conservation of Natural Resources."

DR. W. J. McGEE, member of the National Conservation Commission, on "Uniform Laws Relating to the Use of Water."

CHARLES LATHROP PACK, "Conservation and Taxation."

ALLEN W. HOLLIS, "Uniform Taxation of Timber Lands."

J. HORACE McFARLAND, President American Civic Association, "The Protection of Vanishing Forests."

COLONEL J. A. DAPRAY, of the National Drainage Association, "National Drainage and the Interests of the States in that Subject."

GOVERNOR EBERHART, of Minnesota, "Conservation and Development of Resources in Minnesota."

THOMAS E. DRAKE, Chairman Life Insurance Commissioners, "Desirability of Enacting Uniform State Insurance Laws."

JOHN F. DRYDEN, President of Prudential Insurance Company of America, "Uniform Law and Legislation on Life Insurance."

FRANK LOCK, National Board of Fire Underwriters, "Uniformity in Fire Insurance Legislation and in the Interpretation of Fire Insurance Contracts."

GEORGE SEWARD, representing New York Chamber of Commerce, "Federal Supervision of Insurance."

PIERRE JAY, Chairman of the delegation from the National Association of Supervisors of State Banks, "Banking."

LEWIS E. PIERSON, President American Bankers' Association, "Banking Laws."

JOHN C. RICHBERG, Chairman Committee on Corporations, Commissioners on Uniform State Laws, "Harmonious Incorporation Legislation; State and National Aspects of the Problem."

J. E. STERRETT, President of the American Association of Public Accountants, "Legislation for the Control of Corporations."

EDWIN R. A. SELIGMAN, Columbia University, Chairman Department of Taxation of the National Civic Federation, "The Need of Uniformity in Taxation."

ALLEN R. FOOTE, President National Tax Association, "Uniformity and Taxation."

THEODORE MARBURG on "Uniformity."

CHARLES THADDEUS TERRY, General counsel of the American Automobile Association, "Uniform Motor Vehicle Legislation."

N. J. BACHELDER, Grand Master of the National Grange, "Uniformity in Road Legislation."

SAMUEL GOMPERS, President of the American Federation of Labor, "Industrial Accidents."

JOHN MITCHELL, Chairman Trade Agreement Department The National Civic Federation, "Industrial Accident Legislation."

JOHN HAYS HAMMOND, "Mining Accidents in the United States."

AUGUST BELMONT, "Compensation for Industrial Accidents."

GEORGE M. GILLETTE, of the Minnesota Commission on Employers' Liability, "Industrial Accident Legislation."

SENATOR WAINWRIGHT, of New York, "Needed Labor Legislation."

HENRY W. FARNAM, President of the American Association for Labor Legislation, "Uniformity in Labor Legislation."

JOHN WILLIAMS, International Factory Inspectors' Association, "Labor Laws."

SAMUEL McCUNE LINDSAY, "Interstate Competition in Industrial Legislation."

ISAAC N. SELIGMAN, Chairman Finance Committee, National Child Labor Committee, "Uniform State Child Labor Laws."

HOLLIS R. BAILEY, Chairman Child Labor Committee for the Commissioners on Uniform State Laws, "Legislative Work of the National Child Labor Organizations."

JOHN R. HARTLEY, Brotherhood of Stationary Firemen, "Prison Labor."

EDWARD B. PHELPS, of New York, "Conservation of the Human Asset, Child-Bearing Women, in Factories."

ORRIN MILLER, of Missouri, "Child Labor."

MARTIN S. DECKER, President of National Association of Railway Commissioners, "Regulation of Railways and Public Utilities."

CHARLES BIGGS, President of the National Credit Men's Association, "The Relation of the National Association of Credit Men to the Movement for Uniformity in Laws Governing Commercial Transactions."

HARVEY S. CHASE, Delegate from the Commonwealth of Massachusetts, and from the National Municipal League, "Uniform Municipal Accounts."

STEPHEN H. ALLEN, State Delegate from Kansas, "Court Procedure."

DR. CHARLES McCARTHY, Director of the American Legislative Reference Bureau, "The State Legislative Reference Bureau."

CHARLES JEWETT, "Uniformity in the Laws Regulating Marriage and Divorce."

W. H. BALDWIN, of the District of Columbia, "Non-Support Laws."

MRS. R. M. KIRKLAND, of Georgia, "Marriage and Divorce."

WILLIAM J. SCHIEFFELIN, National Wholesale Druggists Association, "Food and Drug Legislation."

W. C. BREED, National Wholesale Grocers' Association, "Food and Drug Regulation.

DR. O. J. DARLING, of Michigan, "Pure Food Law."

GEORGE L. DOUGLASS, the Proprietary Association of America, "Pure Food and Drug Legislation."

A. B. FARQUHAR, "Suggestions for the Conference on Uniform Legislation."

GEORGE M. WHITAKER, "Uniform Dairy Laws."

C. D. CHAMBERLAIN, "Uniformity of Oil Inspection."

PROFESSOR GEORGE M. KOBER, Professor of Hygiene, Georgetown University, representing American Medical Association, American Public Health Association and Committee of One Hundred of the Association for the Advancement of Science, "Uniform Medical Practice Act."

FREDERICK L. HOFFMAN, Statistician Prudential Insurance Company of America, "Uniform Vital Statistics."

R. W. POPE, Secretary American Institute of Electrical Engineers, "Standardization."

RESOLUTIONS PASSED BY THE NATIONAL CONFERENCE ON UNIFORM STATE LEGISLATION.

ENDORSE BILLS PREPARED BY COMMISSIONERS ON UNIFORM STATE LAWS.

"*Resolved*, That this National Conference on Uniform Laws advise the Governors of the States now in session at Washington that it endorses the acts prepared under the direction of and recommended by the Commissioners on Uniform Laws as stated below, and that this body hopes that the States which have not already done so will without delay enact these measures into law, viz.:

The Negotiable Instruments Act.
The Warehouse Receipts Act.
The Sales Act.
The Bill of Lading Act.
The Uniform Divorce Act."

URGE SUITABLE APPROPRIATIONS FOR COMMISSIONERS ON UNIFORM STATE LAWS.

"*Resolved*, That every State and Territory which has made no appropriation for the work of the Commissioners on Uniform State Laws be urged to make suitable appropriations annually for the efficient conduct of that work."

URGE REMAINING STATES TO NAME COMMISSIONERS.

"*Resolved*, That the States and Territories which have not already appointed Commissioners on Uni-

(*Continued on page 18.*)

THE NATIONAL
Civic Federation Review

Office: Metropolitan Building
Fourth Avenue and Twenty-third Street, New York City
RALPH M. EASLEY, Editor

The Editor alone is Responsible for any unsigned article or unquoted statement published in THE NATIONAL CIVIC FEDERATION REVIEW.

PUBLISHED BY
The National Civic Federation

Broadening Work of the National Civic Federation. The far reaching activities of the National Civic Federation are clearly illustrated by this number of The Review. In the report of the annual meeting is shown the vital importance of certain industrial questions which are forcing themselves upon the attention of the entire country. The immense and rapid industrial development of the United States has brought about conditions common to all institutions and affairs when they have outgrown their environment and working facilities, thus becoming subject to problems to be dealt with, not only by those involved personally, but by the public through its legislative machinery.

No longer can it be left to employers and employes to settle between themselves all that belongs to daily work in its surroundings, its machinery of production and the many questions and considerations that arise among workers and the employers of workers. Compensation for industrial accidents is now in the United States a burning question. At the annual meeting interest was shown in this matter surpassing that exhibited in any other connection. Closely connected with it—indeed, inseparable from it—is the subject of measures for safety appliances and all possible devices for the prevention of industrial accidents. It is argued that laws which place the responsibility for accidents and compensation for the same fairly and squarely upon industry itself will be strong influences for the prevention of injuries to workers by furnishing an incentive for a larger use of safety appliances in all mining and manufacturing plants.

The wisdom of the National Civic Federation's initiative for the conference on uniform State laws has been amply certified by the nation-wide interest taken in the great meeting, which included delegates from every section of the Union, representing almost every branch of useful endeavor. This great movement for State efficiency and interstate harmony will mark a new era in the history of the United States.

Through President Taft's suggestion, the conference on uniform laws was held during the same week with the Governors' conference at Washington, and with very beneficial results. According to the resolution passed by this large and truly national gathering, the National Civic Federation will organize in all of the States branches to urge legislative measures drafted by the Commissioners on Uniform Laws. The work of these commissioners will now go on with the prospect of intelligent support in all parts of the country, and as these commissioners, with their special ability and experience, are amply equipped for their task, they should be properly supported by the people of the States.

An important feature of such nation-wide gatherings as the Conference on Uniform Laws—though something aside from the main work and effort of the meeting—should be noted here. In such a conference men of similar activities in business, trade, industries and the learned professions are brought together socially as well as in convention assembled. They meet in committees, and on other occasions of consultation or of recreation and relaxation. Acquaintances and lasting friendships are so made, and inevitably prejudices and false notions, provincial and metropolitan alike, re effectively nipped and discouraged.

In such an immense country as ours it is unusual for people from the widely separated States to meet each other for some days in any save the excited partisan political conventions. Conferences on subjects of common personal, business, professional or occupational interests are especially useful, enlightening and inspiring even when not counting their main objects. The preconceived pictures conjured in the imagination, let us say, of the Connecticut man, as to the man from Texas, or by the Texan of the Yankee, melt away like the first frost before a September sun when the Eastern and Southwestern American of the same pursuits and aims meet in reality. Long harbored notions as to externals are routed, while the freed mind busies itself in marking how much alike, after all, are Americans from any and every quarter within the nation's great boundary lines.

Is the Boycott Legal? A letter from one of our members asks if all boycotts are illegal and, if not, what are legal; also, has an employer the right to refuse to employ union men and has an employe the right to refuse to work with non-union men? All these questions are practically answered in language that a layman can understand by Justice Van Orsdel of the Washington Court of Appeals in the decision handed down in the celebrated Buck's Stove and Range case. Additional interest attaches to his utterance, because it was made in an opinion in which that judge decided against Messrs. Gompers, Mitchell and Morrison.

"The right of laboring men to organize into unions, and the right of these unions to conduct peaceable strikes, is justified because of their inability to compete singlehanded in contests with their employers. In this competition, any peaceable and lawful means may be resorted to, and i is only when the means employed become unlawfu that the courts will interfere. The law recognize the right of both labor and capital to organize.

"The contest between employer and employe i one which courts of equity should recognize a entitled to be fought out upon the basis of equality and the rule applied by the courts to the strike i based, I think, upon that principle. The fundamental principle underlying this contest is, that th employer who employs one thousand workmen is i possession of the same competitive power to forc those workmen to his terms as the one thousan workmen, by the most powerful lawful organization have to force him to a compliance with their terms The contest, therefore, opens with the one on on side and a thousand on the other upon a substantia basis of equality.

"The employer has a property right in his business which he asks the courts to protect, and whic is entitled to protection. It consists, among othe things, in his right to employ whom he pleases That right extends to a discrimination against workmen of a certain class, or to men belonging to labo organizations. He may use in his business suc types of machinery and appliances as he may thin adapted to carry out his work most successfully, s long as they are reasonably safe and sanitary. Th law protects him in these rights, and the court will require others to respect them. On the othe hand, the thousand employes have a property righ in their labor, which is equally sacred with that o the employer. They have a right to engage thei services wherever and to whomsoever they ca secure the largest rewards and the fairest treatment. They have a right to cease working for thei employer, with due regard for their contractual re lations, when, in their judgment, they can bette their condition by so doing.

"They have a right to organize for this purpose and they have a right to advise others to join thei organization, and the law will protect them in th exercise of these rights equally with the rights o the employer. The refusal of the employes to wor for the employer may result in his financial ruin but the loss will be no greater than the damage hi refusal to employ the one thousand laborers ma work in the aggregate upon them and those dependent upon their labor. In this contest between em ployer and employed, it should be remembered tha the one who most strictly recognizes and observe the legal and equitable rights of the other, enter the struggle with tremendous odds in his favor.

Applying the same principle, I conceive it to b the privilege of one man, or a number of men, t individually conclude not to patronize a certain per son or corporation. It is also the right of these me to agree together, and to advise others, not to ex tend such patronage. That advice may be given b direct communication or through the medium of th press, so long as it is neither in the nature o coercion or a threat.

"As long as the actions of this combination of in dividuals are lawful, to this point it is not clea how they can become unlawful because of their sub sequent acts directed against the same perso or corporation. To this point, there is no con spiracy—no boycott. The word 'boycott' is her used as referring to what is usually understood a 'the secondary boycott'; and when used in thi opinion, it is intended to be applied exclusively i that sense. It is, therefore, only when the combina tion becomes a conspiracy to injure by threats an coercion the property rights of another, that th power of the courts can be invoked. This poin must be passed before the unlawful and unwar ranted acts which the courts will punish and r strain are committed."

Important Meeting Executive Committee. President Seth Low has calle the Executive Committee of the Na tional Civic Federation to me March 3 to consider the subject national incorporation of companies doing interstat business and related questions, and to determi what action, if any, shall be taken by the Federatio

---

Organization of State Branches. In accordance with the resoluti of the National Conference on Un form State Legislation held la month in Washington, the Executi Council of The National Civic Federation has unan mously decided to form branches in all the Stat for the purpose of promoting uniform State legisl tion. The plan adopted provides for the work organizing to be conducted simultaneously from fi centres: New York, Chicago, Denver, San Francis and Atlanta. Each State branch will be made up the representatives of agriculture, labor, bankin manufacture, the bar, the colleges, insurance, co merce and transportation.

THE NECESSITY OF NATIONAL INCORPORATION OF COMPANIES DOING INTERSTATE BUSINESS

By SETH LOW.

I AM well aware that in many respects the division of powers under the United States Constitution between the Federal Government and the State Governments has worked exceedingly well, and no one, I suppose, would wish to break the division down and to reduce the States to impotency. I have myself just now returned from Washington, where I attended a conference on uniform State legislation, the whole trend of which was to urge the States to deal with the questions of common interest from the common poin. of view and by so doing to limit the tendency to centralization as far as possible. But this subject of interstate commerce is in a class by itself.

Two years ago, when The National Civic Federation attempted to secure the amendment of the Sherman Anti-Trust Act, I introduced the subject at the first hearing before the Judiciary Committee of the House of Representatives, with the statement that I thought national incorporation of companies doing interstate business was not above the horizon. These hearings continued many weeks and opened up the subject in every direction. At the last hearing, in summing up the impressions made upon me by the discussion, I expressed my belief that national incorporation of such companies was the next thing to be done. The detailed study of the same question by the present Administration at Washington has brought it to the same conclusion, as I think it would bring most people who would go with equal care into the question from all sides. This belief is strengthened by the fact that Mr. John C. Richberg, the chairman of the committee on a uniform incorporation law of the National Conference of Uniform State Law Commissioners, should have said in a recent address, "Congress should pass a national incorporation law for corporations engaged in interstate commerce, and the States adopt a uniform law for local corporations."

It may satisfy the critic to denounce this plan of national incorporation as unconstitutional; but that does nothing to relieve the intolerable situation which the plan is intended to amend. What the country needs is constructive statesmanship in this matter, and the critic should be turned out of court unless he can present a plan as good or better that will give the necessary relief. In case of need, the Constitution must be amended.

The intolerable situation to which I refer is this: That in the United States there is now no Government at all which controls both the company that does interstate business and, at the same time, the interstate business that it does. The State controls the corporation, because the State creates it; and Congress, under the authority of the National Constitution, controls the interstate business that the corporation does. For the purpose of emphasis, I ask again, therefore, that you notice what the real question is. It is not whether the Nation, rather than the State, or the State, rather than the Nation, should exercise this authority. The situation at the moment is, that neither the Nation nor the State does exercise at present such comprehensive authority both over corporations doing interstate business and over the interstate business that they do.

Evidently this is a condition of governmental feebleness that exists as to nothing else. How has it come about? By the growth of artificial persons called corporations, created by the States, since the Constitution was formed; and by the changes in business which have thrown manufacture and interstate commerce altogether, on a vast scale, into the hands of these new State-formed corporations. If manufacture and interstate commerce were now carried on only on a scale such as can be conducted by a partnership and with the private resources of one or two persons, very likely little trouble would have arisen; but the State-made corporation has changed all that, and in changing it has created conditions that were not contemplated when the interstate commerce clause of the Constitution was drafted. The result is the absence of any government at all in the United States, at the present time, with authority to control both interstate commerce and the agent that does it. If a narrow construction is given by the courts to the interstate commerce clause as regards the power of Congress to insist upon national incorporation of companies doing interstate business, no matter what else they do, to that extent the changes of time will have defeated the object of the interstate commerce clause.

If I interpret the National Constitution correctly, the so-called interstate commerce clause is to be considered in connection with the provision of the Constitution which, in effect, forbids one State from levying duties upon the products of another State. This latter clause was clearly the outgrowth of experience under the confederation of the States, which immediately followed the termination of the Revolutionary War. The framers of the Constitution, as I view it, deliberately determined to prevent one State from interfering with the business activity of another State. They embodied this purpose, according to my view, first, in the clause virtually forbidding the States to levy duties on the products of other States. They also perceived, however, that what the States could do directly, they could also accomplish indirectly and, therefore, they embodied the interstate commerce clause in the Constitution with the express purpose of putting under general control all questions relating to commerce between the States.

All the federal systems in the world, except our own, place the entire subject of commerce under the national government. These federal systems are Germany, Switzerland, Brazil, Mexico, Canada and Australia. If an explanation were sought of the reason why the federal system of the United States does not do the same thing, would not the probable reply be that our system was framed much earlier than any of the others and before the railroad and the telegraph had made it clear that commerce is inevitably a thing national in character?

The suggestion has been made that the only adequate relief for the present situation is the repeal of the Sherman Anti-Trust Act. In passing, I want to point out that, even if the Sherman Anti-Trust Act were repealed, such repeal would not provide a remedy for the difficulty which I have just pointed out, and the suggestion further assumes that the country can permanently develop its interstate business without having any government that controls both the corporation doing interstate business and the interstate business that is done. That I do not believe. I think that the reason why public sentiment placed such a drastic law upon the statute book as the Sherman Anti-Trust Act is to be found in the very fact that the national government, as things stand, is helpless in its relation to corporations doing interstate business. Prior to 1890 the people saw trusts, and combinations, and pools springing into existence on every hand and they feared the result; and because Congress was helpless to forbid such acts on the part of corporations formed by the States, the people demanded that Congress should do what Congress could, that is, strike out at the interstate business to be done, in the effort to avoid the effects of abuses that could have been much more easily avoided by preventing the abuses at their source.

But, assuming for the moment that the repeal of the Anti-Trust Act would meet all the requirements of the situation, let us face fairly and squarely the difficulties involved in the suggestion. Does anyone seriously believe that public sentiment would sustain the President in recommending the repeal, or Congress in repealing that act, at a time when the high cost of living is perplexing everyone and when multitudes believe that one factor, at least, in that situation is the arbitrary control of conditions by corporations created by the States, but whose interstate business the States cannot reach? If I am right, the demand for the repeal of the Sherman Anti-Trust Act, under existing conditions, would fall upon deaf ears. When the corporations themselves that do interstate business, are made subject to the same government that controls the interstate business that they do, it may be possible to modify the Congressional attitude, but, until this is done, any attempt to repeal this law or essentially to modify it appears to be idle, for such action, in substance, amounts to a claim that the corporations doing interstate business should be permitted in the future to do, uncontrolled, everything that has created the sentiment which put the Sherman Anti-Trust Act upon the statute book and which keeps it there. I can imagine that Congress may be persuaded to let bygones be bygones, if adequate safeguards are provided for the future. President Roosevelt was willing to do this. But adequate safeguard for the future against old abuses is, I think, a *sine qua non;* and I know of no form in which such safeguards can be so effectively, and at the same time so helpfully given as through national incorporation.

Is not the real problem this? Under modern conditions trade agreements that limit production and more or less affect prices are the only alternative in many kinds of business to ruinous competition. I have been out of business for a great many years; but I have an impression that at the present time there are few, if any, kinds of commercial business that can be conducted without resort to this method. If this be so, then, indeed, the dilemma with which business is confronted while the Sherman Anti-Trust Act remains on the statute book, is a serious one, and the question is highly important, what is the way out of the dilemma? I do not believe that the way lies in the direction of antagonizing the national incorporation of companies engaged in interstate business. I think it is rather to be found in subjecting the agents that do interstate business to national control, so that one law, which shall be the same from Maine to California, can prevent specific abuses on the part of the corporations doing interstate business, as the need arises. The national banks are incorporated under act of Congress. They suffer no inconvenience as a result of that fact; but, on the contrary, through governmental oversight the national banks as a whole are kept within the lines of legitimate business, and enjoy a very large measure of public confidence. You will observe that national control of the banks takes the form of regulation of the banking corporation and not of the business that it does. The national banking law does not prevent large aggregations of capital, but it does prevent the capitalization of wind and water. The national banking law does not pretend to regulate the rates at which money shall be loaned, but it does make unlawful certain practices by which individuals in control of the banks can make improper gains. I am aware that private commercial business differs from national banking in many respects; but these illustrations suffice to show that most of the abuses complained of in interstate commerce are easily reached by the government which creates the corporation without the necessity of touching the legitimate business that is done.

The question arises, why do not the States, which create the corporations that do interstate business, afford this kind of control? The evident answer is, because there are forty-six States and each State is unwilling, not to say afraid, to put itself at a disadvantage in comparison with other States by dealing strictly with such corporations, and because out of the forty-six States there are some States which act as if they do not care. It has been recently suggested that Congress by appropriate legislation can give to the States the same control over interstate commerce as has been recognized in the States in the matter of controlling the interstate sale of liquor, so that each State may defend itself against unwelcome legislation by another State by forbidding the right of entry into the State so legislating of merchandise manufactured or sold by any corporation that is feared. This would appear to me to be an excellent method of destroying interstate commerce; but not of promoting it, nor of regulating it so that it may grow with the country's growth. Upon the surface, it would violate the spirit of the federal Constitution, which deliberately places interstate commerce under national control.

So far as changes in the method of doing business, through corporations instead of by individuals, have tended to magnify the control of the States over interstate commerce and to lessen the national control, the modern development of business tends to nullify the purpose of those who framed the United States Constitution when they undertook to place interstate commerce under national control. These changes, which have substituted State-made corporations for natural persons, affect not only the scale upon which interstate business is done; but they have also often thrown manufacture and commerce into the same hands, with the result that it becomes increasingly difficult, when this is so, to discriminate between them. We, of the United States, may well ask ourselves why we should hesitate now to give to our national government the full control of interstate commerce which, as I have pointed out, every other federal system in the world, formed at a later period than our own, has deliberately lodged with the general government.

The choice must be made between three alternatives.

First—What we have now, with one government controlling the corporation that does interstate business and another government controlling the interstate business that is done, but with no government at all controlling both the agent and the business that it does;

Second—Through the contributory action of Congress to have forty-six States control both the agent doing interstate business and the business that it does, each State looking out for itself against all others;

Third—To have the national government, through the exercise of its power under the interstate commerce clause, incorporate companies to do interstate business, and thus control all over the Union both the agent doing interstate business and the interstate business that it does.

As between these three alternatives, is it not clear that the last represents the dictates of good sense, of our own experience, and of the general practice of commercial nations?

(Continued from page 13.)

form State Laws be urged to appoint such Commissioners as soon as practicable."

UNIFORM AMENDMENTS.

"*Resolved*, That, if any persons or organizations, after studying the laws submitted by the Conference on Uniform State Laws, think that any of them need amendment, such persons and organizations be earnestly urged to try to bring about such amendment through the National Conference of Commissioners on Uniform State Laws, to the end that, even in amendment, uniformity may be preserved."

COMMISSION FOR OTHER THAN TECHNICAL OR LEGAL SUBJECTS.

"*Resolved*, That in the opinion of this Conference it seems advisable that in the matter of a uniform tax law and in that relating to certain labor subjects upon which this Conference favors uniformity and upon other subjects not technically of a legal nature, it is the opinion of this body that the drafting of these laws may well be considered by Commissions specially appointed in the different States, the membership of which shall not be restricted to members of the legal profession, and that this action be communicated to the Governors."

UNIFORMITY BY GROUPS OF STATES.

"*Resolved*, That we commend to the attention of the administration of the various States of the Union, whenever a subject of legislation affects the interests of a group of contiguous States, the possibility of joint and uniform action upon such subjects by Interstate Agreement or Convention to become effective upon ratification by the legislatures of the States involved."

LEGISLATIVE REFERENCE BUREAUS.

"*Resolved*, That we recognize the system of Legislative Reference Bureaus as one of the important agencies to bring about greater uniformity of legislation, and that we urge the States which have established such bureaus to develop them further and those which have not yet done so to forthwith establish them."

UNIFORMITY IN LEGAL PROCEDURE.

"WHEREAS, the system in vogue for the trial of causes in the criminal, equity and law courts of the United States and of the several States is the subject of much current discussion, both lay and professional, and is severely criticised for its technicalities and its useless expense and delay; and

"WHEREAS, the matter of procedural reform is receiving the thoughtful consideration of the American Bar Association through a special committee created for that purpose; therefore be it

"*Resolved*, That this Conference recognizes the need for radical changes in the administration of the law both in criminal and civil action;

"*Resolved*, That a committee of fifteen on Reform in Legal Procedure be created and appointed by the Chairman of the Committee on Uniform Legislation of the National Civic Federation, and that such committee be instructed to co-operate with the Committee of the American Bar Association to suggest remedies and formulate proposed laws to prevent delay and unnecessary cost in litigation, and to use the influence and power of The National Civic Federation to simplify, cheapen and expedite judicial procedure."

PURE FOOD AND DRUG REGULATIONS.

"WHEREAS, Congress in June, 1906, passed the National Food and Drugs Act, which law has since been adopted in all substantial provisions by upwards of twenty-six (26) States,

"*Resolved*, That this Convention recommend the adoption of this model uniform statute by the legislatures of all States which have not already so acted, and urge upon the Governors and Legislatures of all States that they approve and pass only such food and drug laws, or amendments thereto, as are modeled after the provisions of the national law."

CONTROL OF SALES OF NARCOTICS.

"*Resolved*, That all States be urged to enact such uniform laws in regard to controlling the sale of narcotic and habit-forming drugs that the sale of these drugs will be confined to their proper channels and uses."

VITAL STATISTICS.

"*Resolved*, That this Conference recommend uniform State legislation on the subject of gathering and preservation of vital statistics."

REGULATION OF THE PRACTICE OF MEDICINE.

"WHEREAS, uniformity in regulating the practice of medicine is of the utmost importance to the public health of the Nation and to the peoples of the several States,

"*Resolved*, That it is requested of the Committee on Public Health, or other appropriate committee of the Commissioners on Uniform State Laws, that they cause to be prepared a model act for regulating the practice of medicine in the several States."

COMPENSATION FOR INDUSTRIAL ACCIDENTS.

"WHEREAS, the present remedies for compensation for industrial accidents throughout the various States are slow, uncertain, and wasteful, and

"WHEREAS, there is not, and cannot be, any equitable solution thereof, based only on the fault of the employer, and

"WHEREAS, twenty-three of the more progressive commercial nations abroad have bettered, and in some instances solved, the problem on the basis of Workmen's Compensation Acts, and

"WHEREAS, we believe that such acts can be adequately substituted for our present laws and applied to our institutions with equal satisfaction and profit,

"Now, therefore, be it

"*Resolved*, That this Conference recommend to the Governors of the several States now assembled in this city, and to the States, that workmen's compensation acts fair to the employer and employe and just to the State, be uniformly substituted for the present system of Employers' Liability for injuries received in and arising out of the course of employment."

BUREAU OF MINES.

"WHEREAS, the increasing loss of life in American mining operations and the enormous waste of resources essential to both the present and future welfare of the nation, plainly indicate the need of more uniform, rational, and enforceable mining laws and regulations in each of the several mining States; and

"WHEREAS, there is now pending before the Congress of the United States a bill to establish a Bureau of Mines in the Department of the Interior, for inquiry and investigation, to aid in the accomplishment of these purposes,

"*Now, therefore, be it resolved* by the National Conference on Uniform Legislation that we earnestly urge upon the Governors of the several States the importance of co-operating with the Federal Government to procure uniformity upon which intelligent State legislation may be based."

CONSERVATION OF AMERICAN FORESTS.

"*Resolved*, That this Conference endorses the Conservation of American Forests and

"WHEREAS, The effective handling of forest land in private ownership depends mainly upon uniform State laws, providing for right methods of forest taxation and for the effective protection of forests from fire,

"*Resolved*, That this matter be referred to the Commission on Uniform State Laws."

REGULATION OF WATER POWER.

"WHEREAS, the development of water powers is a subject of growing public importance, and the regulation looking to the uniform control of these powers by State and Nation is a matter of public concern.

"*Therefore, be it resolved*, That this Conference recommend to the Commissioners on Uniform State Laws of the respective States the importance of the consideration of this subject, with a view to securing uniformity of State Laws as to the regulation of water power on non-navigable streams, and the necessity of uniformity of State regulations as to water power on navigable streams, with the object of securing proper and uniform co-operation between each State and the Federal Government in the development and control of water power."

TAXATION.

"*Resolved*, That every State ought to have constitutional powers to classify property for taxation and that all the States ought to impose their taxes in conformity with such a system of comity between the States that there shall be no double taxation which shall be unfair or oppressive to any citizen."

UNIFORM INSURANCE CODE.

"*Resolved*, That we favor a Uniform Insurance Code for adoption in the several States."

CHILD LABOR.

"*Resolved*, That this Conference recommend to the Governors the adoption of uniform laws for the protection of children employed in industries."

EXECUTION AND PROBATION OF WILLS.

"*Resolved*, That we recommend to the Governors of the several States and to the Commissioners oh Uniform State Laws—uniform State legislation on the general subjects of the execution and probate of wills and the form of acknowledgments; and the manner of the conveyance of real estate."

UNIFORM GOVERNMENTAL ACCOUNTING.

"WHEREAS, the National Municipal League, the League of American Municipalities, the American Association of Public Accountants, the American Economic Association, the American Statistical Association, the Association of Municipal Comptrollers and Accounting Officers, the Government Accountants' Association and various other national and State bodies have endorsed the principles of uniform governmental accounting and standard governmental reports, and

"WHEREAS, the States of Ohio, New York, Massachusetts, Indiana, Rhode Island, Colorado, West Virginia and Wyoming have recognized this principle and have enacted legislation establishing Uniform Accounting Bureaus or Boards of Control and similar legislation is under consideration in various other States,

"*Therefore, be it resolved*, by this Conference upon Uniform Legislation that the Governors and Legislatures of the several States are hereby urged to enact such measures upon conformitory lines, departing only so far as may be necessary from a standard form which shall thereby tend to become uniform throughout the country."

PUBLIC ACCOUNTANTS.

"WHEREAS, some twenty-one States have enacted laws regulating the profession of public accountancy, all of which seek to attain the same ends but differ in important particulars as to standards and requirements, and

"WHEREAS, the proper regulation of the profession of accountancy is a subject of rapidly growing importance to the business community, therefore be it

"*Resolved*, that this Conference heartily commends the principle of uniformity in certified public accountancy legislation, which should in every case require adequate standards as to education and training for admission and should provide suitable punishment for unprofessional conduct."

WHITE SLAVE TRAFFIC.

"*Resolved*, That this National Conference on Uniform Legislation recommend to the Governors' Conference that efficient and uniform legislation should be adopted to suppress and prevent the procurement of women for immoral purposes—known generally under the name of the White Slave traffic; and that the Commissioners on Uniform State Laws be requested to draft a bill which will carry into effect the foregoing recommendation."

"*Resolved*, That The National Civic Federation be requested to promote State organizations for the advancement of uniform legislation and that it be also requested, if deemed advisable, to arrange for annual national conferences upon the same subject to the end that the work may take more definite and concrete form."

"*Resolved*, That this Conference on Uniform State Legislation offers its thanks to the President of the United States for his deep interest in the objects of this Convention, and to the Governors and commercial and civic organizations who have appointed delegates to this body; and,

"*Resolved*, That this conference offers its thanks to the Conference of Governors now in session in Washington, for their courtesy in giving a place upon their programme for the purpose of receiving reports from this Conference; and,

"*Resolved*, That the thanks of the Conference be also offered to Senator Root, of New York, for his instructive and valuable address."

NOTE—Neither the States nor the organizations represented at the Conference are committed by the action of the Conference; but the action taken does represent the judgment of the Conference itself.

COMMITTEE ON RESOLUTIONS.

Members at Large.

SETH LOW....New York
President The National Civic Federation.
C. A. SEVERANCE....Minnesota
EDWIN D. PAGE....New York
H. E. MILES....Wisconsin
SELDEN P. SPENCER....Missouri
WILLIAM P. BREEN....Indiana
GEORGE B. CORTELYOU....New York
HARRY ST. GEORGE TUCKER....Virginia
WILLIAM E. CHANDLER....New Hampshire
SAMUEL GOMPERS, President American Federation of Labor.
JOSHUA STRANGE....Farmers' National Congress
GEORGE H. SIMMONS..American Medical Association
W. J. SCHIEFFELIN, National Wholesale Druggists' Association.
W. C. BREED, National Wholesale Grocers' Association.
L. E. PIERSON....American Bankers' Association

State Members.

BELTON GILREATH....Alabama
GEORGE TILLES....Arkansas
H. H. TROWBRIDGE....California
JAMES F. CALLBREATH, JR....Colorado
HENRY WADE ROGERS....Connecticut
GEORGE W. MARSHALL....Delaware
FREDERICK L. SIDDONS....District of Columbia
W. I. MACINTYRE....Georgia
FREMONT WOOD....Idaho
JOHN C. RICHBERG....Illinois
EMORY B. SELLERS....Indiana
CHARLES W. SMITH....Kansas
MISS JEAN GORDON....Louisiana
HARVEY S. CHASE....Massachusetts

(Continued on page 26.)

FOR GUARDING LIVES AND SAFETY OF WORKERS

LABOR'S NEEDS CONSIDERED—EMPLOYERS' LIABILITY AND PREVENTION OF ACCIDENT LAWS DEMANDED—BRILLIANT DINNER AT CLOSE OF ANNUAL MEETING OF THE NATIONAL CIVIC FEDERATION

THE tenth annual meeting of the National Civic Federation, held November 22 and 23, 1909, at Hotel Astor, New York, was devoted to the discussion of wage-earners' insurance affecting public as well as private employes.

The official commissions appointed by the Governors of the States of New York, Minnesota and Wisconsin and several voluntary commissions studying the same subject were the special guests of the Federation.

The dominant ideas at the tenth annual meeting were that the present antiquated State Employers' Liability laws must give way to a system of compensation, and that there is immediate necessity of increasing means for preventing industrial accidents.

At this meeting leading employers, with humane inclinations, and national labor leaders, with the needs of their followers in mind, were agreed that a system more in accord with an enlightened policy must be secured. There were clearly brought out what is being done abroad, modern improvements in the United States in the way of initial efforts involving progress in the last five years, and what is lacking to lessen hardships from the hazards of industry. The evils of the present system of employers' liability, its weakness, and the foreign substitutes for it were fully presented, all agreeing that the present system is intolerable. Thus there was furnished information upon which to base efforts toward securing sane and practical means of relief. Progress, at the best, must be slow, but the Federation desires, if possible, to avoid prolonged experiments, which it is hoped this full consideration of the subject may obviate.

The immediate outcome of the annual meeting has been a program of actual work resulting in the appointment by President Low of the following four committees:

Committee on Prevention of Mining Accidents.
MR. JOHN HAYS HAMMOND, Mining Engineer, Chairman.

To investigate the causes of accidents in mining;
To collect information relative to safeguards against mining accidents;
To look into the need of improving State laws and unifying such laws requiring mine owners to introduce all reasonable means for ventilating and otherwise safeguarding the lives of miners;
To investigate means of saving life after accidents have happened and advocate the provision of such apparatus as is now used in Germany and France by rescue crews and the training of such rescue crews;
To publish and widely circulate illustrated literature showing safeguards which may be advocated in mining, and apparatus to safeguard rescue crews; and
To work for the establishment of a Federal Mining Bureau to encourage the introduction of life-saving devices.

Committee on Wage-Earners' Insurance.
MR. GEORGE W. PERKINS, Chairman.

To promote employers' voluntary relief associations; and
To investigate the need for uniform legislation covering such employers' voluntary sick, accident, pension and death benefit associations.

Committee on Compensation for Industrial Accidents and Their Prevention.
MR. AUGUST BELMONT, Chairman.

To inquire into the need of amending State laws on employers' liability, with a view to securing uniform provisions looking toward compensation for industrial accidents; and
To look into means of preventing accidents in all commercial and manufacturing enterprises.

Committee on Pensions for Public Employes.
HON. WILLIAM R. WILLCOX, Chairman.

To investigate existing and proposed plans for old age retirement funds for civil service employes; and
To look into the need for municipal, State or Federal legislation to provide for such public employes.

In this issue of the REVIEW will be found in full or in brief several of the addresses delivered at the annual meeting. Limitation of space prevents the printing here of some of the most important contributions to the discussions of this great gathering.

While the complete addresses of speakers at the annual meeting and annual dinner are to be found in the published report of the proceedings, we give below abstracts from some of these valuable papers. At the opening session, November 22, Hon. Seth Low, president of The National Civic Federation, presided and in the course of his report of the activities of the Federation the past year, said:

"It is a matter of common observation that such a rapid industrial recovery from a great panic has never been witnessed before in the United States. It is also true that after no other panic have employers so uniformly maintained the rates of wages prevailing before the panic. Many have criticized this policy as contrary to sound political economy. The question may well be asked, however, whether the rapid recovery from the industrial depression is not partly due to this change of attitude toward labor. The country has been entirely free from labor troubles incident to an attempt to reduce wages. More men may have been thrown out of employment than had a different policy been pursued, but the purchasing power of the vast body of men that remained in employment was not cut down. I do not know whether this maintenance of wages is related to the rapid industrial improvement, as cause or effect, or whether they coincide only accidentally. One thing, however, is certain, that both capital and labor have been spared the costly losses that result from the prolonged struggles incident to a reduction in wages (I mean, of course, a widespread reduction), and they are now being spared again the losses incident to the prolonged struggles to regain the old standards of wages that usually follow the return of prosperity.

"The National Civic Federation, through its entire membership of employers, workingmen and the general public, is keenly interested in everything that relates to the question of compensating workmen for loss of limb, life or health in the pursuits of modern industry. Several of the States have appointed commissions to study into this subject and to make recommendations. The National Civic Federation is co-operating with all these commissions and I have the pleasure to-day, on behalf of our members, of welcoming them to our annual meeting, which is wholly given up to this subject. The papers and discussions are being prepared along lines suggested, in part, by members of these commissions, and it is hoped that both the papers and the discussions will have practical value, by reason of the presence of these commissioners—even greater than otherwise might follow. It goes without saying that a subject which is of vital interest to the entire industrial community is a subject the importance of which cannot be exaggerated. The opinion is almost universal in well-informed circles that some change of system in the United States is greatly to be desired. The best direction in which to move is the thing to discover. It is greatly to be hoped that the discussions of our present meeting will throw valuable light on many aspects of this question."

In enumerating a few of the important subjects upon which uniformity of State legislation is desired, President Low said:

"The great movement for the conservation of our natural resources inaugurated by President Roosevelt cannot be carried to its perfect consummation until the States adopt, with considerable uniformity, laws upon the subjects of forestry, water power and reclamation of land by irrigation. In the effort to propose suitable amendments to the Sherman Anti-trust Act, our committee was not unmindful of the fact that, if satisfactory amendments were finally made, their effect would be nullified in many important instances unless the anti-trust laws of the various States were made, substantially, to conform. Probably no better illustration could be given than that of railway regulation. The Interstate Commerce Commission, of course, can deal only with interstate, while the States can deal only with intrastate traffic. The confusion and conflict, without uniform action, can readily be imagined. Each State has its own railway commission. These State commissions, slowly learning it was essential to have some uniform principles of regulation, organized the National Association of State Railway Commissioners, inviting first the co-operation of the Interstate Commerce Commission, and, afterward, that of the railway managers' associations and the shippers' organizations. These four elements, which may well be taken to represent everybody, have substantially agreed upon a number of important regulations which, to become effective, will require action by all the State legislatures.

"The National Association of State Bank Supervisors and the American Banking Association have come to agreement on certain propositions upon which they desire uniform State legislation. In the matter of insurance, both life and fire, national associations have been organized, and, in the latter case, are working with the State Supervisors of Insurance in an effort to secure State uniformity. The agricultural organizations, the wholesale grocers, the wholesale druggists and a number of other national organizations are working for uniform pure food laws. The labor organizations want uniform workmen's compensation acts, uniform legislation as to guarding dangerous machinery, factory inspection, convict made products, regulation of the employment of women and children, etc. The American Medical Association desires uniformity on registration and preservation of vital statistics. The National Grange, the American Automobile Association and the American Roadmakers' Association have united in the demand for uniform State legislation on the regulation of motor vehicles and the building of good roads throughout the country.

"The question which has been selected for discussion at this annual meeting is employers' liability, as it is called, an old law of master and of servants, and of negligence in the several States and in the United States. Naturally, we in the United States want to know what has been done in other countries. Our problem is a more complicated one, growing out of our Federal system because, as the annual report, to which you have just listened, has pointed out, to get complete results we must secure co-operation, not only between, at any rate, the industrial states, a good many in number, but also as between the States and the Federal Government. It, therefore, becomes a matter of immense importance, if we are going to change old conditions in any respect, to take whatever step we do take in the right direction. We, very likely, shall have to proceed slowly, but we do not want to retrace our steps after we get under way."

WORK IN THE WELFARE DEPARTMENT.

By HON. WILLIAM R. WILLCOX,
Chairman Public Service Commission.

THE remarkable impetus which has been given to welfare work through the efforts of the Welfare Department is not only indicated by requests for assistance in installing such work, but also by accounts and illustrations of new welfare enterprises which constantly come to us as the result of inquiries. One company in New Hampshire, employing twelve thousand operatives, is now introducing a comprehensive plan for housing and recreation, an improvement upon anything which has yet been undertaken in the United States. The mills of this company are already models of cleanliness and appliances for good ventilation and sanitation.

The Welfare Department, in three ways, has secured unique co-operation by:

(1) Addressing letters of information and inquiry to employers in fifty different industries;

(2) Securing the consent of employers' associations to arrange programmes at their annual meetings on the welfare work in their respective trades; and

(3) Asking trade journals to collect and publish illustrated accounts of welfare work in the industries covered by their periodicals.

In this way, the theory of working along non-aggressive lines with emulation for the spirit of the movement has proven its worth.

The most important undertaking at the present time is to issue small leaflets illustrated twice a month to engineers and architects throughout the country, calling especial attention to welfare devices. It is hoped thus to secure improvements at the time of the erection of new buildings, the cost being very slight then as compared to installing conveniences in old shops. The chairman of the Industrial Employes' Welfare Committee, Mr. Charles A. Moore, has been in a position to influence owners of buildings in process of erection to plan thorough schemes of welfare work for them. This is equally important with reference to public

Up to the time that I took up officially,), utilities instead of public buildings, I | many Government buildings and many ; as postmaster, and I say emphatically 'e yet to see a Government building in ry that is properly constructed for the r which it is used.

:IT OF THE CORPORATION TOWARDS ITS EMPLOYES.

HON. GEORGE B. CORTELYOU.

ent of the Consolidated Gas Company.

onsolidated Gas Company manifests an in- t in its employes in three ways:

y assisting them in maintaining an em- l society;

by providing annuities for superannuated and

oy making allowances for vacations and

vitable tendency of the future is toward d better relations between the corporate and employe, wherein the principle of their y of interest will be recognized and o its full development. If these relations on right lines there will be none of the ling that is engendered by a patronizing y on the one hand and of sullen aloofness her, but there will be a mutual recognition .ct that the welfare of each is bound up, or ill, with that of the other. The employer eive that the highest efficiency of the em- attained only when he is fairly remunerat- is labor, when the conditions under which is performed are sanitary and wholesome, 1 the mind of the employe is freed, as far le, from apprehension as to what will hap- im in case of accident, and as to what will o his family in case of his death. The em- ll perceive that it is his duty to give his the best service of which he is capable romote his interests loyally and faithfully as the employment lasts. When this relation- been fully established, when there is this d sympathetic understanding between em- nd employe, then we shall have not only a improved social order, but we shall have becoming more and more a necessity under ss of modern business competition—a great- ased efficiency of labor.

all very well to offer employes opportunities sement and improvement, as by building and furnishing means for recreation, but system for securing loyalty and efficiency that leaves both the corporation and the with their self-respect intact. And the best is that, too, which secures to employes fair by means of which they can of their own provide properly for themselves and their , both for mere material wants and for eeds.

onduct of a corporation upon this basis in- ne developing of a spirit among its workers ne of which cannot be calculated in dollars its, and furthermore the workers so recog- nd so treated become its best guarantors be- public of the integrity of its management its realization of its duties to its stockhold- to the public.

NSATION FOR VICTIMS OF INDUSTRIAL)ENTS, THE EMPLOYER'S VIEWPOINT.

By GEORGE M. GILLETTE,

Iinneapolis Steel and Machinery Company, esident Minnesota Employers' Association, nesota Employes' Compensation Commission.

necessity of a change in or from our ex- ing system may be assumed as a fact. In State of Minnesota, the State Bar Associa- representative employers and the employes ves, both by organic expression and by the f their leaders, have in equally strong and e manner declared in favor of such a change. bring the existing system before the bar of opinion and charge it with: First, disturbing tions between employer and employe; second, perjury; third, failure to prevent or de- accidents; fourth, uncertainty; fifth, inhu- and, sixth, waste.

o initial legislation by any State which un- s it, I believe it will be necessary to make pensation moderate, to pay no compensation first few days of disability, not to pay for ional diseases, and, even then, in my opinion, t will be such that it will be necessary for ployes to contribute toward the fund out of those compensations are paid. Either this done or the compensation must be adjusted e the cost to the employer not exceed the cost. Personally, I am in favor of a more scale of compensations to the employes than would be possible if the total cost under the competitive conditions between our States was all to be borne by the employer. And why should not the employe bear a part? Not only in the State competition would it safeguard the interests of the employer, but it would make the employe himself interested in safeguarding the cost, in the prevention of malingering. It would forestall all the attempts of agitators at every succeeding session of the legislature from attempting to increase the compensations, as the excess cost would have to be borne in part by the employes themselves.

The result of imposing excessive burdens on the employers of one State as compared with those of another State, I am afraid is not generally appreciated. The necessary legislation must be accomplished by the uniform action of forty-eight different States. Each State is justly jealous of its rights.

The transition to the compensation principle is sufficiently revolutionary in itself, so that in its carrying out, in my opinion, additional revolutionary elements should not unnecessarily be added. It should be an insurable proposition, first for the reason that no foreign act has been successful which was not accompanied by an insurance scheme, and, second, by reason of our commercial and financial system it would be practically impossible for new industries to be established, or those owned by moderate means to be carried on unless these undertakings could be insured against the liabilities of such an act. Insurance is equally essential to safeguard the interests of the injured employe, to make sure that the compensations named in the act will surely be paid to the injured or his dependents, regardless of the ability of the employer to respond in large sums and, further, to insure the employe against the employer's insolvency. What sort of insurance should be provided? In my judgment not the existing kind. It should be provided by existing agencies and existing companies, but not by a plan under which but 25 or 30 per cent of the premiums collected will be paid out in compensation.

I would favor the abolition of our present system and the substitution of one which, conservatively begun, would ultimately develop into a system under which every branch of industrial enterprise should reasonably compensate, care for and protect the victims of such enterprise.

"BUY A HOME WITH RENT MONEY," OR INSURANCE MONEY.

By D. A. TOMPKINS,

Director of the Equitable Assurance Society and of the National Manufacturers' Association.

THE weaknesses of industrial insurance, as at present handled, would seem to be, first, a very high rate of insurance made necessary to carry collection of premiums by canvassing agents, and second, the number of insured who drop out and forfeit their policies. Mr. Paul Morton, of the Equitable Society, conceived the idea of issuing an industrial policy which reduces both these faults to a minimum. If industrial policies should be issued, according to his idea, the amount for which a policy is sold would be loaned in cash on proper security to the insured to build a home. Thus the borrower would have an incentive to pay his premium, voluntarily, without cost of a canvasser to collect it and he would also have an incentive to keep up his payments to the end of the contract. The premium might have to be a little more than those of the regular life, but not approximately as expensive as those of the usual form of the industrial insurance.

Loans would generally be made on a basis of 66 2-3 per cent of the valuation of the entire property. Thus if a man had a lot worth $1,000, the loan to him to build a house would be $2,000, the total value of the house and lot being $3,000. In the case of farmers, the ratio would be entirely different. The mechanic makes his living outside of his house and lot and his trade constitutes an asset independent of his house and lot. The farmer must have his farm to make a living. The farm is the asset which offsets the mechanic's trade. Therefore, the loan to a farmer to build a home should not exceed 20 per cent of the value of the farm. The average borrower would be delighted to pay six per cent interest, and it would be cheap for him to do so. Besides good management of the society's business, a sufficient interest rate to make the borrower always absolutely safe is essential.

The fact of ownership of a home is not all the advantage that the borrower gets. The ownership of the home is a foundation upon which he can build other advantages for himself, material and moral. It stands to reason that the average workingman stands a fair chance of getting his wages bettered, but, without regard to better wages, there are many little betterments and improvements that a family can make about a home that they would not be disposed to make about a rented house.

By selection of term of policy any one may buy a home with rent money and get a life policy thrown in. If the premium and interest for ten years is too much, he can choose a 15-year policy, and if this is still too much, he can still choose a 20-year policy.

Such a plan gives philanthropy without charity. It gives the best economic use of money as a means of home building and its most frequently repeated use for that purpose.

THE BENEFIT PLANS OF THE INTERNATIONAL HARVESTER COMPANY.

By GEORGE W. PERKINS,

Chairman Finance Committee, International Harvester Company.

IN all the inventions and ingenuity that have been brought to bear on business affairs in the last quarter of a century, nothing has been found to take the place of the human mind. Nothing has been found to take the place of individual incentive to accomplish results. Nothing has been found to take the place of a man's ability to do—with a proper incentive behind that ability—and no such substitute ever will be found. It is, therefore, of the utmost importance to American business interests of to-day and to-morrow that every man in any given concern be so associated with that concern that he will give the best there is in him to the performance of the duties assigned to him.

If profit-sharing means anything, if providing for old age means anything, if caring for those who become ill or injured while in the service means anything, it should mean the fostering of the interest of men in their work, whether that work be sweeping out the office, shoveling coal or presiding over a great commercial company. In short, it should mean real co-operation between stockholders, managers and employes.

The management of the International Harvester Company, its subsidiary and affiliated companies, believing in the above theories, set out several years ago to see how nearly it could come to applying them practically to its business. As a result, it has devised and put into effect plans covering the following:

First—Profit sharing.

Second—Insurance covering sickness, accident and death.

Third—Old age pensions.

The company is also doing other welfare work. It is called "welfare work" for lack of a better name. It is as much a business branch of the company as any other division. The important features of this work are protection against injury, sanitation, health, educational work, charities, recreation, etc. The welfare work is controlled by an advisory board composed of the superintendents of all the "works," who, through an executive committee, dictate the welfare activities of the company.

Special attention is given to protection against injury and to sanitation. The accident hazard can never be removed because of the human element—that is beyond the realm of possibility. Therefore, the company is trying to arrive at the point where the occupation is surrounded with every known safeguard and only the man is the hazard. In all parts of its business, at home and abroad, in the office force, in the factories, in the sales department—everywhere, the average interest of the individual in the business is greater than formerly. The saving of the waste here, there and everywhere is noticeable. The employes throughout the organization are vying with one another more and more to improve their respective branches of the business. This means profits for the stockholders, means extra compensation in various ways for the employes—in short, means co-operation that is real, and that is beneficial to one and all.

DOES LIABILITY INSURANCE COMPENSATE EMPLOYES FAIRLY?

By LOUIS B. SCHRAM,

Chairman of the Labor Committee, United States Brewers' Association.

THE workman, under our laws, assumes practically all the risks of his employment. The employer is required to furnish adequate tools, a safe place in which to perform his work and to exercise reasonable care in the selection of those men who direct the workmen in their work; and when he has done that he is absolved from further responsibility. All the risks inherent in the nature of the employment fall upon the workman.

It has been suggested that insurance against accident, and perhaps old age disability as well, could be provided through the existing liability insurance companies. This means that the employes would be insured in liability companies against all accidents, premiums to be paid by the employer, or jointly by the employer and employe. An arrangement of that kind would, in my judgment, prove entirely inadequate and unsatisfactory, the reasons being:

First, its high cost necessitated by the heavy expenses of administration and profit to be paid to the liability companies' stockholders;

Second, the great delay involved in the settlement of claims (long experience warrants us in making this statement), and

Third, the fact that the workman would ultimately receive but a portion, and sometimes a small portion, of the amount awarded to him because of the necessity of employing lawyers to look out for his interests.

If it is true, then, that the present system of liability insurance does not furnish the workman the protection which we all believe ought to be provided; that compensation dependent upon the initiative and volition of the employer can never be adequate, because it would never be universal; and that accident and old age insurance through liability companies would not meet the case, what is left?

Evidently there remains one solution of the question: Compulsory provision by legislation. I maintain that it is entirely feasible and, if worked out by a commission consisting of employers, workmen and public spirited citizens of ability, would result in systematic, practical protection of the workman, and this, in turn, would make for higher efficiency and the eradication of a host of evils that invariably follow where the bread-winner of the family is prematurely disabled.

THE FEDERAL LIABILITY LAW AS APPLIED TO NAVY YARD EMPLOYES.

By Admiral J. B. MURDOCK,
Commandant Brooklyn Navy Yard, New York.

THERE seem, apparently, to be three ways of treating this question of indemnity to employes. The first, and unquestionably the best, has just been dealt with at considerable length. If the work is done by the employers for and in the interest of the workmen, it is certainly more effective than any other method can be. The second seems to be to do nothing at all. That calls for the third, which is regulation by law.

The indemnity law for United States employes has now been in effect since August, 1908. It applies to all mechanics and artisans in the employ of the United States arsenals, navy yards, Panama Canal and in other public works.

The first section provides that payment shall be made in case of injury to men working under these conditions. The payment is to be limited to twelve months and no payment is to be made for a disability extending over a period of less than fifteen days. The only proviso is that there shall have been no negligence or misconduct on the part of the workmen. The Government takes the responsibility in full for all accidents which may occur. This, of course, is very different from some of the laws of the States, in which indemnity is sought which has to be secured by legal process. There is nothing of the kind here. The Government acknowledges responsibility at the very beginning.

The second section of the law provides for beneficiaries in case of death, or in case of a man who dies during the year from the effect of injuries received. This extends to the limit of a year's pay—that is, the pay that the man would have received if he had continued at the work he was doing at the time of the accident. It varies for different men, of course, as their daily wage differs a very great deal. The procedure is very simple for a Government law.

The Civil Service system is, of course, very complex. Our labor organization is something which, occasionally, seems designed to prevent any work being done at all. We are not allowed to do as we wish for fear we shall favor somebody. We are tied up quite rigidly, and under these circumstances it is certainly very pleasant to find that a law can be made for indemnity which is as clean and sharp-cut as this.

PREVENTION VERSUS CURE IN THE INDUSTRIAL WORLD.

By HENRY R. TOWNE.
President Yale & Towne Mfg. Co.

PENSIONS and old age insurance are designed to be a partial remedy for the disabilities and needs of old age. Anything tending to prevent or to delay the advent of these disabilities should certainly be recognized and encouraged. If effective, it not only defers the time when aid may be needed, but prolongs the period of activity and usefulness of the individual.

In considering the pension problem we are sometimes apt to forget or overlook the large expenditures which are being made continually for purposes tending to prolong the period of usefulness of employes and to delay the advent of disability. These expenditures relate to the following:

Heating and ventilating;

Sanitation, drainage and water supply;

Effective lighting, by day and by night;

General cleanliness of premises;

Wholesome drinking water, filtered if necessary and properly cooled;

Comfortable and sanitary lavatories;

Locker rooms, with individual lockers for each employe;

Emergency service; provisions for first aid to injured;

Removal of dust and noxious fumes, where these are incident to manufacturing processes;

Safety appliances on machines, to prevent or minimize danger of accident; and

Libraries, reading rooms and lecture rooms, where these exist.

In considering the broad subject of industrial insurance and pensions, it is pertinent to keep in view the character and influence of the expenditures thus made by the employer, especially in modern plants of the best type, and to recognize the substantial contribution thus made for the benefit of the employe.

In like manner, those who are active in forwarding the movement for industrial insurance and pensions, recognizing these facts, should make it part of their work, when studying individual plants, to note the extent to which welfare work of all of the classes above specified has been carried, to award praise where it is justified and to stimulate improvement where it is needed, especially in plants of the older type and of minor character and in localities where effective inspection and supervision have not yet been undertaken by the State.

NEW DEVELOPMENTS IN INDUSTRIAL LIFE INSURANCE.

By HALEY FISKE,
Vice-President Metropolitan Life Insurance Company.

I AM here to give you an account of one or two new developments in industrial life insurance. The first is what is known as "group insurance." The plan is that if under the law a hundred or more can be gathered together who will take those policies, who will themselves attend to the collection of the premiums and pay them to us in bulk, a new table of benefits will be used, and that table as published—and I won't detain you by reading it—gives benefits from 25 to 33 per cent larger than the benefits given under our ordinary policies. This is a subject which may well interest you as an association composed of employers and employes. We are ready to co-operate with you to procure for the workingman life insurance in small amounts at cheap rates.

I may say that our regular individual insurance policies since your last meeting have been increased ten per cent in amount for the same premium. I pointed out to you last year that we were endeavoring to cut down the expense of industrial insurance. We have succeeded so well that, in July this year, we increased the benefits on the policies ten per cent and then made them retroactive on all policies issued on the plan adopted when the Armstrong Law went into effect, two years and a half before; and we even went back to all death claims that had been paid in the two and a half years, and sent an additional check for ten per cent to all death claims we had previously paid. The amount this cost us was $250,000.

The other subject I am asked to speak to you about is "welfare work." The company which I represent has in its employ about 14,000 people. We have been accustomed for years to take care of those who had been in our service for any length of time and became incapacitated. We find that among our policyholders about eighteen per cent die from tuberculosis. We are trying to help in the work of eradicating that disease. We have had three or four millions—three millions, I think, but it may be more—of pamphlets on tuberculosis delivered to our policyholders; an illustrated treatise showing how to prevent and how to cure it. If we can build a sanatorium, we propose to take care of our tuberculous agents and clerks, of whom there are no doubt hundreds in our employ. It is obvious that the question of taking care of policyholders is a difficult one. We have associated with us in this tuberculosis work various dispensaries throughout the United States, and we invite correspondence with any policyholder who is afflicted, and give him advice, and then refer him to the nearest hospital or dispensary.

In New York, Boston, Baltimore, Washington, St. Louis, Chicago and Cleveland we are trying, experimentally, the system of having bed-ridden policyholders visited by trained nurses. We are trying it as an experiment on the theory that we may help our mortality record and, I may say too, on the ground that a company which has under its care and contributing to its income 7,000,000 of workingmen owes some duty beyond the mere contractual relations which exist between a policyholder and his company.

SHOULD THE INDUSTRY BEAR THE BURDEN INCIDENT TO INDUSTRIAL ACCIDENTS?

By LEWIS W. PARKER.
President Columbia and Victor Mills (S. C.).

THE doctrines which have prevailed, heretofore, in our courts relating to accidents, viz., the doctrines of contributory negligence, of fellow servant and of assumption of risk, are legal principles which were honest, fair and properly applicable in the years in which they were adopted but, in the progress of industry, in the enlargement of industry, the time has come when there must be some change from these principles.

But whilst we may believe this, we must further recognize the fact that it is much more easy to abolish than to establish and that simply to abolish the defences previously recognized, as is constantly sought, simply to declare that the doctrines of fellow servant, of contributory negligence and assumption of risk, should no longer be fair defences, does not meet conditions. We must not only abolish but, in the very act of abolishing, conceive a new principle.

What is that new principle? It is that whilst the burden of the accident is no longer to be cast solely upon the employe, it must be brought home to the employe himself, not only that it is his duty to prevent the accident if it be within his power, but that he will suffer to some extent, at least, if this duty be not carried out, that it is his duty to co-operate with the employer in prevention of accidents and, if he does not exercise that duty, that there is, at least, a limit beyond which he may not go in seeking relief from the employer? The employer must be required to carry insurance in the interest of the employe, but the employe must be required to contribute to the cost of this insurance and permit be granted to the employer to deduct from the wages of the employe a proportionate part of the cost. As a matter of fact, I know that, in the end, the employer will practically pay, in the way of an increased wage to the employe, the amount which is deducted from the employe as a consequence of the cost of insurance, but by the deduction there is brought home to the employe the fact of the cost of the insurance, which must be determined by the number and character of accidents, which vary in reverse proportion to the degree of care that is exercised by the employe himself.

Co-operation between employer and employe is essential to reduce the proportion of accidents which certainly in America is astonishingly large. It matters not how earnest an employer may be in his effort to prevent accidents, this prevention can only occur when the employe is filled with the same desire and is earnest in co-operation with the employer. While the burden of compensation to the employe, if insurance be carried, may not be very great, yet it is to be recognized that this burden would put to disadvantage the industries of one community if the same burden is not to be cast upon like industries in other communities.

It is not sufficient that any one State or community provide for compensation to injured employes. We must bend our energies to seeing that provisions of similar character are made throughout the whole United States.

Other speakers at the annual meeting were:

A. H. GILL, Member of Parliament, of Bolton, England, and Secretary Operative Cotton Spinners' Association—"The Workmen's Compensation Act in England; Is It Just to Labor?"

A. E. PIORKOWSKI, Representing the Friedrich Krupp Company, Essen, Germany—"Workmen's Insurance of the German Empire."

LEE K. FRANKEL, Head Industrial Department, Metropolitan Life Insurance Company, New York City—"Insurance Plans in Foreign Countries Other than Germany and England."

LAUNCELOT PACKER, Attorney at Law, Washington, D. C., retained by Federal Government to Investigate English Compensation Act and Conditions in the United States—"Workmen's Compensation vs. Employers' Liability."

F. W. RAMSEY, Cleveland Foundry Company, Cleveland, Ohio—"Employers' Obligation to Safeguard Machinery and the Compensation Plan of the Cleveland Foundry Company."

W. G. COWLES, Secretary, Liability Department, The Travelers' Insurance Company, Hartford, Conn.—"How to Avoid Accidents More Important Than Compensation."

JOSEPH P. COTTON, Jr., Counsel for the Commission on Employers' Liability and Causes of Industrial Accidents in New York State, New York City—"The Work of the New York State Commission on Employers' Liability."

H. V. MERCER, Chairman of the Minnesota Employers' Compensation Commission, Minneapolis, Minn.—"Practicability of Workmen's Compensation Acts," "Constitutional Phase of Compulsory Compensation for Accidents."

(Continued on Page 22.)

NNUAL MEETING WOMAN'S DEPARTMENT THE NATIONAL CIVIC FEDERATION

THE Woman's Department of The National Civic Federation held its annual meeting at Hotel Astor, New York, November 22, 09, there being two sessions.

MRS. HORACE BROCK, of Philadelphia, the chairman, presided. There were reports from tions and standing committees, and officers for ensuing year were elected.

MRS. SAMUEL SPENCER, of Washington, D. C., chairman of the District of Columbia Section, d of work being done in the Government offices re. She stated that a committee had been per- tted to go over the plans for new buildings and l been able to suggest many improvements in the y of rest, recreation, first aid to the injured and cheon rooms, a roof garden, lighting, sanitation l other matters pertaining to the health and com- t of the employes.

MRS. B. FRANK MEBANE, of Spray, N. C., chairman of the North and South Carolina Section, orted that through the influence of the Spray nmittee the mill owners have established a day rsery for the children of the operatives and a ne for the young women employed in the fac- ies, to supplement other welfare work in opera- n, including a reading room, skating rink and usement hall.

MRS. FRANCIS HIGGINSON CABOT, of New York, chairman of the New York and New sey Section, reported the existence of four stand- committees, namely, Press and Publication, mbership and two working committees, one for Welfare of Industrial Employes and the other the Welfare of Government Employes. She gave omplishments of committees on Cigar Factories, tionary Firemen, Recreation, Garment Trades, w Buildings, Printers and Lithographers, and ction Employes, as well as committees on City spitals, Navy Yard Lunchrooms and New Govern- nt Buildings.

MRS. WILLIAM H. CROCKER, of San Francisco, is chairman of the California and Ne- la Section. The report of that section was sub- ted in the form of a communication by Mrs. John ns, secretary of the section, who reported the d of proper and pleasant homes for working girls, rents and boarding since the fire have increased, l outlined a plan to meet the situation.

MRS. J. BORDEN HARRIMAN, chairman of the National Committee on Welfare Work for In- trial Employes, reported that the members of her nmittee had visited factories and mines in the ghborhoods in which they live and that she had sonally visited, in the preceding six months, nty-one mills in New Hampshire, Massachusetts, ginia and North and South Carolina. Mrs. Harri- n stated that, inspired by the Garment Trades -Committee, the Industrial Employes Welfare nmittee is now engaged in collecting instances ine welfare work in cotton mill villages and min- for illustrated literature, to be circulated among ployers.

(Continued from page 21.)

E. McEWEN, Commissioner of Labor, State of linnesota, and member Minnesota Employes' ompensation Commission, St. Paul, Minn.—"Rea- ons for Changing Existing System of Employers' iability."

LLIAM C. HANSON, State Board of Health, Bos- n, Mass.—"Dusty Trades in Massachusetts."

ORGE A. RANNEY, Chairman Advisory Board n Welfare Work, International Harvester Com- any, Chicago, Ill.—"The Welfare Work of the In- ernational Harvester Company."

EPH A. HOLMES, Expert in Charge Technologic ranch, United States Geological Survey, Wash- gton, D. C.—"Coal Mine Accidents and Their Pre- ention."

B. GARRETSON, President Order of Railway onductors, Cedar Rapids, Iowa—"The Operation the Federal Liability Law—Has the Railroad an Been Adequately Compensated?"

L. CLYNES, M. P., Secretary Gas Workers' and aborers' Union, Oldham, England—"Present Pen- on System in England."

IN WILLIAMS, Commissioner of Labor, State of ew York, Albany, N. Y.—"The Need of Adequate actory Inspection and Trained Inspectors."

DERICK L. HOFFMAN, Statistician, Prudential surance Company of America, Newark, N. J.— What Has Been Done in Foreign Countries to Pre- ent Industrial Accidents."

GUST BELMONT, Chairman Board of Directors, nterborough Rapid Transit Company, New York— The Insurance Plan of the Interborough Rapid ransit Company."

ARTHUR WILLIAMS, New York Edison Company, New York—"Industrial Insurance Fuuds—Do They Adequately Compensate?"

J. G. PANGBORN, Special Representative, Baltimore and Ohio Railroad Company, Baltimore—"Organized Relief."

WALTER S. MAYER, Post Office Inspector in Charge, New York—"Retirement of Superannuated Employes in the Federal Classified Service.

WILLIAM BUTTERWORTH, President Deere & Company, Moline, Ill.—"The Mutual Benefit Plan of Deere & Company."

W. H. MOULTON, Welfare Manager Cleveland-Cliffs Iron Company, Ishpeming, Mich.—"Compensation for Injured Workmen in Discharge of Their Duty."

R. W. CORWIN, M.D., General Manager Sociological Department, Colorado Fuel and Iron Company, Pueblo, Col.—"Prophylactic Suggestions."

J. N. REDFERN, Superintendent Relief and Employment Departments, Chicago, Burlington and Quincy Railroad Company, Chicago.—"Railroad Relief Departments."

EDWARD A. MOSELEY, Secretary Interstate Commerce Commission, Washington, D. C.—"Federal Employers' Liability Law."

W. L. SAUNDERS, President Ingersoll-Rand Company, New York.—"How to Save Human Lives in Mines."

T. P. O'CONNOR, M. P., England—"Free Discussion and Self-Government."

ANNUAL DINNER.

THE annual dinner of The National Civic Federation is an occasion whose opportunities lift commercial, political and economic questions to a broadly human and social plane. There the labor leaders, the financial and industrial captains, the political magnates and the university dons and doctrinaires meet in friendly spirit at the common table. Aloof from the heat and clamor of the daily struggle and grind, after a season of debate and discussion from opposing sides during the preceding meetings, the dinner guests take counsel together and with friendly voice talk over the issues in which they are interested.

The tenth annual dinner was pre-eminently of this type, and it stands alone among public occasions in its thorough representation of every phase of the intelligent life of the American nation. Attended by nine hundred men and women, with all its magnitude as to numbers and the brilliancy of surroundings, in the beautiful new ballroom of Hotel Astor, it was genuinely informal in its spirit and in all of its manifestations. As an indication of the representative nature of the occasion the names of a few of the Federation members and guests are given below.

President Seth Low, in calling the company to order to listen to the speeches, was warmly applauded when he said: "Here are representatives of the great captains of industry, as they have been called; here are representatives of the great legions of American industry who have achieved greater victories than the legions of Rome ever sought, and here, also, are representatives of the public, like myself, that sometimes finds itself ground between the upper and the nether millstones—that public which supports the industries and is supported by them."

Fresh from a two days' discussion of the pressing and insistent problems of industry and labor, and saddened by contemplation of the cruel toll of life and limb and health which is paid year by year by the nation's toilers, sobered and thoughtful after the plans and suggestions and difficulties voiced over ways and means to lift from labor the dangers and the burdens under which its men and women bravely live and work, the members of the Civic Federation sat down with their guests and the themes of the day's speeches—wage-earners' insurance and compensation for injuries—were first the subject of conversation at the tables and then most of the after-dinner addresses.

Mr. Darwin P. Kingsley, President of the New York Life Insurance Company, was intently followed as he spoke upon the moral obligation of employers under modern conditions, and as, commenting with severity upon the life insurance legislation of New York and of other States, he closed by declaring for the placing of interstate life insurance under Federal control.

Mr. Samuel Gompers, in his talk upon his recent trip to Europe, was applauded by the entire assembly when he spoke of the disability under which Europe labors by reason of its everlasting preparation for war, its numerous customs barriers and difference of tongue, and said that the great advantage of America lay in the absence of caste. His earnest manner, as well as his words, again stirred the audience when he said: "I never felt how much I loved America until after my trip to Europe. To me it seemed a home-coming and the song, 'My Country, 'Tis of Thee,' had a new meaning."

Senator Elihu Root was the next speaker after Mr. Gompers. Referring to Mr. Low's suggestion that he speak only five minutes, Mr. Root took the diners into his confidence as he complained that the limitation was in "violation of the Sherman act to restrain" his output. He paid a tribute to The National Civic Federation as affording the very useful means of full and free discussion of difficult problems. Continuing, Mr. Root expressed sympathy with the prevailing opinion in the Federation upon the subjects under discussion. He declared our present system of dealing with those injuries that come to employes in our industrial life to be foolish, wasteful, ineffective and barbarous. "The cost of support," he said, "which is made necessary by the injuries suffered in a business is just as much a part of the cost of the business as the tools that are worn out and the material that is consumed. It ought to be paid for by the business as a part of that cost. * * * It ought to be paid for so that the man who has spent his life and his strength and his limbs as a necessary part of doing the business will feel that he has been paid in a way that preserves his manhood instead of being thrown upon charity in a way that destroys it."

Mr. John Mitchell spoke emphatically in criticism of the present employers' liability law and made a passionate plea for safeguards in all industrial enterprises. His hearers endorsed his appeal when he declared: "It is high time for the American people to stop and think. Is it to their credit that there are more men killed here in industry than in any other country in the world? In my trade not less than twenty men must die to-morrow. Every day from ten to twenty men who go down into the dark and damp of the mines never return home to their wives. This is the problem that cries aloud for solution." In conclusion he urged that some system of workmen's compensation be worked out by which compensation be paid, automatically, immediately after the accident and not from two to five years later.

T. P. O'Connor, M. P.—the well-known "Tay Pay" of the English-speaking world—enlivened the evening by his witty and sympathetic address. After his opening sentences he spoke earnestly and seriously, and, commenting on Senator Root's observations upon The National Civic Federation as a forum for public debate, Mr. O'Connor said: "No other country is like this. I do not know any country in the world where discussion is so free, so tolerant, so good-tempered as in America." As regards Ireland and England, he declared that while there has grown up in the last thirty years a new Ireland, it would not be candid of him not also to say that there has grown up a new England as well. The brilliant Irishman's talk was received with much favor.

Another Member of Parliament, A. H. Gill, one of the labor members of the House of Commons, was the last speaker of the evening. He spoke upon the Workmen's Compensation Act of Great Britain, saying that it applies, practically, to every worker in every occupation in the United Kingdom. This speaker commended the National Civic Federation's efforts to promote co-operation and understanding between employers and employes, and said: "There is no labor leader who is worth his salt who will have a strike if he can possibly avoid it, if he can get a satisfactory settlement by peaceable means. That is the position of our country. I believe that it is the position of all the reasonable men in your country. * * * So far as I can see the meetings of your Civic Federation tend to promote peace in industry. I believe they will tend to promote peace also nationally and internationally."

After this speech from one of our English cousins the chairman declared the dinner adjourned. Thus closed, in attendance, interest, enthusiasm and resolve for future practical effort, one of the greatest of the annual dinners of the National Civic Federation.

IMPRESSIONS GATHERED DURING EUROPEAN TRIP.

By SAMUEL GOMPERS.

THE reference of our honored president to myself in introducing me to you, suggesting that I might relate some of my impressions of the recent trip I made to Europe, caused me to wonder whether possibly he did not have in mind that I might expatriate myself. I have had many impressions abroad. I would prefer to deal, however, if I dared, with circumstances and conditions here; for, after all, that which I may have observed in Europe can have only a relative importance to our own activities at home. Before going further, I might say that I found myself in exceeding good company upon returning within the sight of these shores. I never felt how much I loved America until after my trip to Europe. To me it seemed a home-coming and the song, "My Country, 'Tis of Thee," had a new meaning.

During my journeyings I was carried to Great

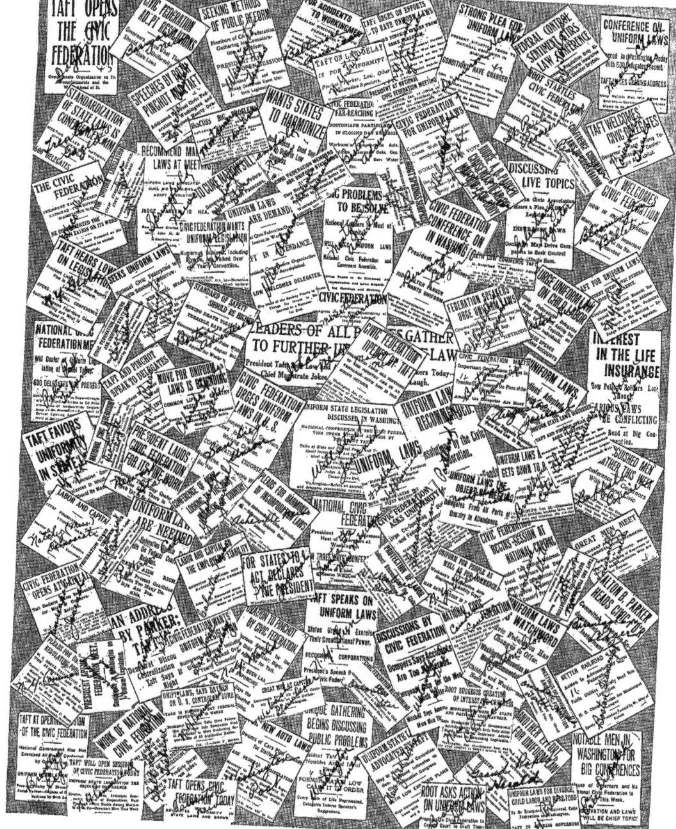
TAFT OPENS THE CIVIC FEDERATION
SEEKING METHODS OF PUBLIC REFORM
FOR ACCIDENTS TO WORKINGMEN
STRONG PLEA FOR UNIFORM LAWS
CONFERENCE ON UNIFORM LAWS
SPEECHES BY BOTH PINCHOT AND TAFT
STANDARDIZATION OF STATE LAWS IS CONSIDERED
WANTS STATES TO HARMONIZE
CIVIC FEDERATION FOR UNIFORM LAWS
ROOT STARTLES CIVIC FEDERATION
TAFT WELCOMES CIVIC DELEGATES
RECOMMEND MANY LAWS AT MEETING
DISCUSSING LIVE TOPICS
THE CIVIC FEDERATION
UNIFORM LAWS ARE DEMANDED
CIVIC FEDERATION WANTS UNIFORM LEGISLATION
BIG PROBLEMS TO BE SOLVED
CIVIC FEDERATION CONFERENCE ON IN WASHINGTON
WELCOMES CIVIC FEDERATION
TAFT HEARS LOW ON LEGISLATION
SEEKS UNIFORM LAWS
CIVIC FEDERATION
TAFT FOR UNIFORM LAWS
NATIONAL CIVIC FEDERATION MEETS
LEADERS OF ALL PARTIES GATHER TO FURTHER UNIFORM LAWS
INTEREST IN THE LIFE INSURANCE
TAFT AND PINCHOT SPEAK TO DELEGATES
MOVE FOR UNIFORM LAWS IS SPREADING
CIVIC FEDERATION URGES UNIFORM LAWS IN U. S.
UNIFORM STATE LEGISLATION DISCUSSED IN WASHINGTON
UNIFORM LAWS RECOMMENDED
TAFT FAVORS UNIFORMITY IN STATE LAWS
PRESIDENT LAUDS CIVIC FEDERATION FOR USEFUL WORK
UNIFORM LAWS
UNIFORM LAWS GETS DOWN TO A
UNIFORM LAWS OBJECT OF MEETING
LABOR AND CAPITAL
UNIFORM LAWS ARE NEEDED
NATIONAL CIVIC FEDERATION
GREAT MEN MEET
FOR STATES TO ACT, DECLARES THE PRESIDENT
CIVIC FEDERATION OPENS AT CAPITAL
AN ADDRESS BY PARKER; TAFT
TAFT SPEAKS ON UNIFORM LAWS
DISCUSSIONS BY CIVIC FEDERATION
UNIFORM LAWS WATCHWORD
ALTON B. PARKER HEADS CIVIC FORUM
UNIQUE GATHERING BEGINS DISCUSSING PUBLIC PROBLEMS
TAFT AT OPENING SESSION OF THE CIVIC FEDERATION
WORK OF NATIONAL CIVIC FEDERATION
TAFT WILL OPEN SESSION OF CIVIC FEDERATION TODAY
TAFT OPENS CIVIC FEDERATION TODAY
NEW AUTO LAWS
NOTABLE MEN IN WASHINGTON FOR BIG CONFERENCES
ROOT ASKS ACTION ON UNIFORM LAWS
UNIFORM LAWS FOR DIVORCE, CHILD LABOR AND PURE FOOD

Ireland, France, Holland, Belgium, Germany, Bohemia, Hungary, Italy and Switzerland. . some of the principal industrial cities of those countries beside attending several es of labor. I had many consultations with esentatives of the wage-earners, and with ; and file, as well as the representatives of ial class, and with the inquiring spirit of our not only looked around, but also tried to see the surface.

tes taken while abroad on that journey have ; on record, but on this occasion it is fitting ation should be made of some of the broad) and lasting impressions made upon me, on king back over those weeks and weeks of traveling.

nited States is, both through fortuitous circes and its civic and industrial development, ad of the world. Indisputably our people do d under the dreaded shadow of war, which ase constantly in the countries having large armies, with aristocracies of officers as- with the classes to whom war might be ly or politically profitable. The incessant ions for war and the ever-present possibili- ar in Europe only result in retarding human . The burden of standing armies especially on the wage-earners.

ave within our borders the largest area of de in the civilized world. The continual iterruptions to commerce by the tariff walls divide Europe—the limitations of tariff sys- ithin the boundaries of cities in the same as well as the boundaries of each country— onsequent detrimental effects upon the pro- of farm and factory, entail national losses rred by us in anything like the same degree. cores of languages spoken on the continent e are obviously a hindrance to economic and intellectual development. Where a commer- in Europe spends years of his youth in the schools, acquiring perhaps three foreign lan- under the delusion that it is education, ener- ung America goes to work, moves about in try, picks up the necessary qualifications for callings, and either as journeyman or in any sition takes his place among the big machines complicated organization of a large industry ps turn out a product the cost of which, in ment and in transportation, is the lowest in ld.

European country are our common schools in their opportunities for education, in their siveness to the pupils, and in their quality as ry of wholesome, manly and womanly senti-

aring the railway systems of Europe with f America, the traveler is obliged to look rd and backward, for in that respect Europe . century behind time.

roduct of the American press, taken in its cope, its magazines, its newspapers and its a marvel to Europeans in output and cheap- price, as well as in richness of interest to all s of society.

e least difference by far lies in the rejection f the idea of caste. We have innumerable rcles, but none are secure in hereditary titles settled exclusive privileges by which they manently take precedence of the people in rcles. We have done with kings and czars les. Our heroes are men and women. In ublic gathering of our citizens the great ma- resent rejoice that the hard work of their ers helped to build up this representative tic Government. It is this democratic senti- at makes our republic possible and progres- d that regards the relation of our people to as equals. We may be unequal in physique, al gifts, in acquirements and character, but stence is among us—I repeat—before the law quals. In Europe the higher orders of caste, nily prerogatives and privileges of property aw, form a power as well as social standing emocracies deny.

erica, also, the full scope of political rights is ed in our fundamental legal principles and ly in their practice. These are the right of y us of lawmakers and administrators, the petition, of assembly, of freedom of thought eligion, of free speech and a free press. Pro- xists for a test under our Constitution of ne of these rights, as they may not yet be ly defined in every aspect of our rapidly de- industrial society.

clash of interests it may become the duty of the standard bearers of certain groups of ons to set out to ascertain the truth with re- what they and their fellow members believe e rights of those groups under the law and stitution, and, if they act under the advice of o in consequence of their legal training, prob. character have won the respect of the Nation, ecially, if they find division of opinion upon the questions at issue among the judges upon the bench, these standard bearers have no choice but to state and to restate their opinions, respectfully, yet firmly and even spiritedly to their fellow citizens, and to carry the issue on to the court of last resort. We protest against the conception that a law is broken until it is finally and fully decided what is the law.

Those who contribute to making the law clear, definite and settled, perform a public service, and in the meantime, if the clamor and misrepresentation of opponents put them in a false position before the general public, they must wait in patience and fortitude until the day when the Nation has spoken the last word, either through the highest judicial tribunal, where bias or prejudice or misconception is not to be expected, or through a change by legislation affecting the points at issue.

In some countries of Europe, and particularly in Germany, a wilful, and I might say a malicious, misrepresentation has been made of the purposes of this Federation. There it is charged that this Civic Federation has been organized to antagonize every effort of the working people of our country for their protection or for the material improvement of their condition. Digressing for a moment, I may say that in Germany there exists an organization known as the Reichsverbund, an imperial band or society, composed of military and naval officers, captains of industries and intellectual opponents to the organized labor movement of that country, and in order to throw odium upon the American labor movement, in order to misrepresent the Civic Federation and the association of labor men with the Civic Federation, the statement has been made that this National Civic Federation is the prototype of the Reichsverbund.

I am sure it is unnecessary and superfluous for me to explain to you who are assembled here to-night how the Civic Federation is organized, that its constituent parts bring together equal representation of employers of labor, of representative workmen and representatives of the general public, and that its primary purpose is, as its first law provides, to try to establish better relations between workmen and their employers. The history of the Civic Federation is its greatest asset, its helpfulness in the endeavor first to avoid rupture and to bring about amicable adjustment of contests which have arisen. Great contests have been prevented and other great conflicts have been brought to an amicable close. So I may say, even here, some selfish employers of labor are thus in exact accord with pretended friends of the toilers in denunciation of what we aim to do.

In The National Civic Federation no one surrenders his convictions. It is a forum where each contends for the principles and the faith and the hope that is within him. Though conflicts may arise among the members of its component parts, it has been helpful to a better judgment in the ennobling purposes of organized labor, and has never in its history done one act which has been or was calculated to be, or might tend to be, detrimental to the rights and the interests of the working people of our country.

In Europe the germ of a great awakening is evident on all hands. Much is going on there among the nations which will contribute to their own and our higher attainment. Industry, commerce, the means of transmitting information and enlightenment, and the intermingling of peoples coming from their country to ours, and moving from one European land to another, are making and will continue to make a broader and deeper fraternity than has ever transpired in the history of man.

As for our own people, the men of labor have always stood for home and country. They have done their share in bearing the burden and doing yeoman service in defense of liberty and justice. In return, they ask for and insist upon that justice, that equality before the law, without which a republican form of government is impossible. Organized labor is in accord with the fundamental principle of the Declaration of Independence—that all men are entitled to life, liberty and the pursuit of happiness.

IMPORTANCE OF SEEKING REFORM THROUGH STATE GOVERNMENTS.

By HON. ELIHU ROOT.

I HAVE a decree by the president of The National Civic Federation limiting my hours of labor on this day to five minutes and a contract in violation of the Sherman Act to restrain my output. I have come here welcoming the opportunity to express my sympathy with the purposes and my belief in the usefulness of this organization. The essential process of free government is free discussion. Discussion confined to people of the same way of thinking, with the same interests, the same purposes and prejudices, tends only to strengthen their common difference from all others and to increase the divergence between different groups of our people, but discussion, information, sincere and earnest attempt to get at each other's minds and to learn as well as to teach among people with different environments, different specific interests and different points of view leads to that common public opinion whose expression in the end comes the nearest to being the voice of God that man has ever attained. The essential quality of that discussion which makes a free people competent to govern itself is self-restraint, respect for the opinions and the wishes, aye, for the prejudices and the mistakes of others, a sincere desire for harmony of view, for reconciliation of difference and for the reaching of the right and just conclusion. As between individuals, as between groups of citizens, as between nations, isolation is the parent of misunderstanding, of hatred and of strife. Conference, mutual knowledge, the softening that comes from meeting our fellow men face to face—that is the process by which good citizenship and sound and rational judgment results.

I wish, also, to express my sympathy with the prevailing opinion that I perceive here upon the specific subject of your recent discussion. It seems to me that our present system of dealing with those injuries that come to the employes in our great industrial life is foolish, wasteful, ineffective and barbarous. To have a great enlightened nation ignoring the fact that in all industries there are accidents and that every crushed foot, every broken arm, every ruined life, is expended in the business, is a part of the cost of doing the business, is discreditable. All accidents, all injuries are subject to the law of average. The cost of support, which is made necessary by the injuries suffered in a business, is just as much a part of the cost of the business as the tools that are worn out and the material that is consumed. It ought to be paid for by the business as a part of that cost and not left to the charity of the Nation at large. It ought to be paid for so that the man who has spent his life and his strength and his limbs as a necessary part of doing the business will feel that he is being paid in a way that preserves his manhood instead of being thrown upon charity in a way that destroys it. I hope we have begun on the pathway that will lead to more reasonable and rational treatment of this subject.

I cannot altogether agree with the view taken by Mr. Kingsley as to throwing the burden of dealing with insurance upon the National Government. I have long thought that in the case of Paul and Virginia, which decided the question to which he referred, the Supreme Court of the United States was right. If, however, there were no other question but the question whether the National Government or the State Government should deal with insurance, it might not be so important and I might feel willing to say, as Mr. Jefferson suggested when he bought Louisiana, that the advocates of his view of constitutional interpretation ought to be willing to suspend their views for a little while for a particular and useful purpose. But you cannot confine the proposal to insurance alone. The framework of our Government aimed to preserve at once the strength and protection of a great national power, and the blessing and the freedom and the personal independence of local self-government. It aimed to do that by preserving in the Constitution the sovereign powers of the separate States. Are we to reform the Constitution? If we do it as to insurance, we must do it as to a hundred and thousand other things. The interdependence of life, wiping out State lines, the passing to and fro of men and merchandise, the intermingling of the people of all sections of our country without regard to State lines, are creating a situation in which from every quarter of the horizon come cries for Federal control of business which is no longer confined within the limits of separate States. Are we to reform our constitutional system so as to put in Federal hands the control of all the business that passes over State lines? If we do, where is our local self-government? If we do, how is the central Government at Washington going to be able to discharge the duties that will be imposed upon it? Already the administration, already the judicial power, already the legislative branches of our Government are driven to the limit of their power to deal intelligently with the subjects that are before them. This country is too great, its population too numerous, its interests too vast and complicated already, to say nothing of the enormous increases that we can see before us in the future, to be governed as to the great range of our daily affairs, from one central power in Washington. After all the ultimate object of all government is the home, the home where our people live and rear their children, with its individual independence, its freedom; and I am not willing, for the sake of facilitating transaction of any kind of business, to overturn limitations that have been set by the Constitution—wisely set—between the powers of the National and State governments. Great is our Nation. Let it exercise its constitutional powers to the fullest limit, but do not let us in our anxiety for efficiency cast away, break down, reject those limits which save to us the control of our homes, of our own domestic affairs and of our own local governments. For there in the last analysis under the protecting power of our great Nation, there must be formed the character of free, independent, liberty-loving citizens upon whom our republic must depend for its perpetuity.

PREVENTION OF INDUSTRIAL ACCIDENTS.

By JOHN MITCHELL.

IF The National Civic Federation had rendered no other service to the people of our country, it would have won a place of distinction because it has brought men and women together holding divergent views upon great public questions and enabled them to present their views and often to reconcile their ideas. For the past two days members of the Civic Federation have been discussing the subject of "Industrial Insurance" and incidentally the subject of "Prevention of Industrial Accidents." I am not at all sure that I am at this time in a frame of mind to discuss impartially and dispassionately the subject of industrial insurance. Within the last ten days a terrible disaster overtook many of my old friends and neighbors—men with whom I worked in the mines—and perhaps, more than others here, I have been shocked at that awful calamity.

There was a time when the criminal law was a matter of private settlement, when a man could relieve himself of responsibility for the murder of his neighbor by making a blood payment of so much money to the kinsmen of the murdered man. Our attitude toward preventable accidents is still much the same. If an employer pays a ludicrously inadequate sum to a workman who has been injured, or to the kinsmen of a workman who has been killed, society assumes that he has discharged his full obligation and that his concern in the matter has ceased. It seems to me that this is an entirely wrong attitude. It seems to me that the first consideration of society should be the protection of the men who are least able to protect themselves. The recent President of the United States—Mr. Roosevelt—in a letter to the Society for the Exposition of Safety Devices and Industrial Hygiene, made this very significant statement: "As modern civilization is constantly creating artificial dangers to life, limb and health, it is imperative upon us to provdide new safeguards against the new perils. In legislation and in our use of safety devices for the protection of workmen, we are far behind European peoples and, in consequence, in the United States the causalities attendant upon peaceful industries exceed those which would happen under great perpetual war. Many, even most of these casualities are preventable and it is not supportable that we should continue a policy under which life and limb are sacrificed, because it is supposed to be cheaper to maim and kill men than to protect them."

And what is probably more important, the deaths that result from violence constitute only a small proportion of the industrial casualties. The slow death that comes from working in a vitiated atmosphere, from breathing the fine, sharp dust of metals, the death that comes from working in constrained and unnatural postures, and the slow death that comes from over-exertion, or from under-nutrition, swell beyond computation the unnumbered victims of a restless progress.

Is it not high time that we should stop and think? Is it not high time that the American people should recognize and assume the responsibility that rests upon them? It is not to our credit that in America, in this country we all love, more men are killed in industry, more men, both in the aggregate and in proportion to the number employed, than in any other country in the world. In my own trade four men are killed for each one killed in other countries. In my trade, to-morrow, not less than twenty men must die. Every day the dawn breaks, from ten to twenty men who enter the darkness of the mine return no more to their wives and loved ones. This is a problem—a living problem that cries aloud for solution, and I am pleased to say that The National Civic Federation, denounced as it is by the extremes of labor and capital, is doing its full share to bring about an intelligent understanding of the requirements of the occasion and the means of prevention.

I am heartily in favor of workmen's compensation. I believe that our laws should be so amended, or that such contracts should be made between employers and workmen, that when a man is injured or a workman is killed, the money needed for the relief of the injured workman or for the relief of the family of a workman who has been killed, should be available at once, not five or ten years after the death or accident occurs. Only a short time ago I was reading in a magazine an article regarding an accident that occurred in Chicago some twenty-one years ago. A cargo of cotton was being taken through the Chicago River and an accident resulted—an explosion occurred in which a large number of sailors were injured and killed—and twenty-one years after the explosion occurred a commission made a preliminary report as to the cause of the accident. That is, of course, an exceptional case, yet every day accidents occur, the settlement for which takes place from two to five years later. A workman's compensation act or a compensation agreement that would work automatically is what we need—one that will give relief immediately when the accident occurs.

A great philosopher once said that a free man was one who lived in a country where there were no slaves and I believe that a happy man is one who lives in a country where there is no avoidable misery. I do not believe that a person has a right to happiness if there is avoidable misery which it is within his power to relieve.

It seems to me that in our mad rush for wealth and power, for idleness and leisure, we are not properly regardful of the interests and the happiness of our neighbors. It seems to me that no country is really and truly great that is not concerned about the welfare of the humblest of its citizens or the least of the little children in the factories.

And, ladies and gentlemen, so far as the men and women of The National Civic Federation are arousing people to the necessities of the occasion, so far as The National Civic Federation is bringing men and women of divergent views together, enabling them to unite on a sane constructive program looking to the betterment of all the people. The National Civic Federation deserves the support and commendation of all right thinking people. I think that among its many achievements the one of which it can be most proud is that it has won the condemnation of the extremes on both sides. When the extremists on the side of capital and the extremists on the side of labor can find nothing to commend in the work of The National Civic Federation, it is a pretty good guarantee that it is doing useful service. It still has much to do. There are great problems to solve; there are great achievements to accomplish; and if The National Civic Federation is supported as it should be and as it has been, there is no doubt in my mind that it will continue to render to our country and to all our people a useful and beneficial service.

"LIFE INSURANCE AND THE MORAL OBLIGATION OF EMPLOYERS TOWARD THEIR WORKINGMEN."

By DARWIN P. KINGSLEY,

President of the New York Life Insurance Company.

THE growth of life insurance and the development of a deep sense of responsibility on the part of employers of labor toward their employes are contemporaneous and kindred phenomena. They represent a better knowledge of the value of human life and a recognition of the increasing demand now fairly made on the controlling forces of society by age and industrial misfortune as well as by infancy, congenital incapacity and weakness. There are sound reasons why corporations should avail themselves in this work of the highly developed system of insurance and annuities presented by the responsible insurance institutions of this and of other States. Any effective system, if established by corporations independently, will be based on the principles and methods used by the insurance companies, and, therefore, the work for obvious reasons is in the end likely to be more effectively and more economically done by men who are experts and specialists than by men who undertake it with no special training and with minds chiefly occupied by the demands of other lines of work.

The energy of life insurance management, in other words, and the obligation which the laboring man feels toward his family, have in their development far outrun the sense of obligation of the employer. We have now reached the point when the employer is beginning to do his part, but as yet he has only made a beginning. That he will do more is certain; that he will do much is almost equally certain. That existing insurance institutions will be utilized is, I believe, a necessity. But if this is to be done there are certain interfering conditions which must be dealt with before any such plan, however desirable, complete and beneficent, can be carried into effect.

First, insurance—and other business, too—must be relieved of the annoyances and burdens which attach to compliance with the behests of forty-six sovereign masters—forty-seven now, since the general government has decided to create a Federal Insurance Bureau for purposes of taxation only. Business is faced by the reactionary effect of having within our own country to deal with forty-six different frontiers, and is being paralyzed by the fact that the individual States are attempting to supervise affairs that comprehend and relate to all the States. In other words, under the plea that States' rights must be preserved, the States are invading the national domain and are enormously retarding national development.

The possibilities of social betterment which lie in a wise joinder of the function of insurance in its various activities on the one hand and the moral obligation of the employer of labor on the other are

State Members.

(*Continued from page 18.*)

. HIGGINS....Maine
)DORE MARBURG ....Maryland
. OLDS....Michigan
M T. STOVALL....Mississippi
RGE M. GILLETTE....Minnesota
DERICK W. LEHMANN....Missouri
PH W. BRECKENRIDGE....Nebraska
NK S. STREETER....New Hampshire
EST R. ACKERMAN....New Jersey
LIAM R. WILLCOX....New York
AMIN FRANKLIN McCANN....Ohio
. REED....Oregon
RGE G. WILSON....Rhode Island
RUE MUNSON....Pennsylvania
IS W. PARKER....South Carolina
I C. HIRSCHY....South Dakota
ACE H. SMITH....Utah
MAS NELSON PAGE....Virginia
7. SANBORN....Wisconsin
ARD F. SNIDER....West Virginia
I C. TODD....Washington

OFFICERS OF THE CONFERENCE.

.ALTON B. PARKER, Chairman.

Secretaries:

OHN M. STAHL, Farmers' National Congress.
ROME JONES, Georgia State Federation of Labor.
NO S. PRATT, Chamber of Commerce of the State of New York.

MITTEE TO PRESENT RESOLUTIONS TO GOVERNORS' CONFERENCE.

I LOW.... New York
President the National Civic Federation.
DERICK W. LEHMANN....Missouri
RLES F. LIBBY....Maine
TER GEORGE SMITH....Pennsylvania
ER W. MELDRIM....Georgia
E G. BROWN....Minnesota
RY WADE ROGERS....Connecticut
N C. RICHBERG....Illinois
SA M. EATON ....Rhode Island

CREDENTIALS COMMITTEE.

CUS M. MARKS....New York
. ROBINSON....Philadelphia
LIAM H. SMILEY ....Colorado
V. FROST....Wisconsin
DAW....West Virginia
IALEN M. GARLAND....Pennsylvania
S B. SCHRAM....New York
T C. BONE....District of Columbia
ON JONES ....Indiana
. H. GAITHER....Pennsylvania
. DUCKWORTH....Georgia
CLARA B. ARTHUR....Michigan

MMITTEE ON ORDER OF BUSINESS AND PROGRAM.

RY B. F. MACFARLAND.....Washington, D. C.
DORE MARBURG ....Maryland
REN S. STONE....Ohio
ARD SAULSBURY ....Delaware
GE S. YERGER....Tennessee
LES W. SMITH....Kansas
IAS H. BETHARD....Illinois
RAINE ....Missouri
ERICK L. HOFFMAN....New Jersey
S O'CONNELL ....Washington
REED SMOOT....Utah
JENKS....New York
GODARD ....Kansas
E C. McCORMICK....Pennsylvania
B. MILLS....Minnesota

[illegible] Association of Supervisors of State Banks.
National Association of Railway Commissioners.
National Association of State Labor Commissioners.
Association State and National Food and Dairy Depts.
American Bar Association.
American Bankers' Association.
American Federation of Labor.
National Grange.
Farmers' National Congress.
Association of Life Insurance Presidents.
National Board of Fire Underwriters.
American Life Convention.
National Association of Credit Men.
American Mining Congress.
National Rivers and Harbors Congress.
Trans-Mississippi Commercial Congress.
National Industrial Traffic League.
American Warehousemen's Association.
American Street and Interurban Ry. Association.
National Association of Clothiers.
National Wholesale Grocers' Association of the U. S.
National Wholesale Druggists' Association.
The Proprietary Association of America.
National Wholesale Lumber Dealers' Association.
National Association of Automobile Manufacturers.
American Automobile Association.
Auto Club of America.
Agricultural Implement and Vehicle Manufacturers
National Hardware Association of the United States.
National Association of Retail Druggists.
National Association of Retail Grocers' of the U. S.
National Lumbermen and Manufacturers' Association.
The National Hay Association.
Southern Supply and Machinery Dealers' Association
American Paper and Pulp Association.
United States Brewers' Association.
National Metal Trades Association.
National Conservation Association.
American Civic Association.
International Tax Association.
New York Tax Reform Association.
National Municipal League.
League of American Municipalities.
National Child Labor Committee.
National Committee on Prison Labor.
International Apple Shippers' Association.
Appalachian National Forestry Association.
National Hickory Association.
American Medical Association.
American Public Health Association.
Committee of One Hundred, National Health.
National Petroleum Association.
American Academy of Political and Social Science.
American Institute of Architects.
National Academy of Sciences.
Affiliated Presidents and Secretaries of Commercial and Trade Organizations.
American Association of Public Accountants.
American Statistical Association.
American Institute of Electrical Engineers.
American Society of Mechanical Engineers.
American Gas Institute.
National Drainage Association.
American Water Works Association.
Ohio State Brotherhood of Railway Clerks.
National Printing Pressmen.
Glass Bottle Blowers' Association.
United Brotherhood of Carpenters and Joiners.
International Brotherhood of Stationary Firemen.
Illinois State Federation of Labor.
Brotherhood of Locomotive Engineers.
International Association of Machinists.
Allied Printing Trades Council.
Order of Railway Conductors of America.
Brotherhood of Railroad Trainmen.
International Typographical Union.
Merchants' Association of New York.
Harrisburg (Pa.) Board of Trade.
New York Board of Trade and Transportation.

W[illegible] Washington women are effectively doing whatever they put their hands to:

Mrs. William H. Taft, mistress of the White House; Mrs. Richard Wainwright, wife of the admiral; Mrs. John Hays Hammond, wife of the mining engineer, who is confidential adviser to President Taft and head of the National League of Republican Clubs.

These ladies are members of the Welfare Committee of the National Civic Federation, for Washington, and more particularly members of the Sanitation Committee. In that capacity they reformed the sanitation in the Government Bureau of Engraving and Printing. The process was simple. They appealed to the director, who said he would be glad to make any improvements necessary, but he didn't have the authority. He got it, almost immediately, from the White House.

Then the committee discovered that the ventilation of the Census Office, where 1,500 men and women are employed, was bad. Again the director agreed with them. Mrs. Taft took the matter up with the President and again the authority came at once. Fans, insuring purer air, will now be put in.

Next, the committee will take up the Treasury Department and it seems probable that conditions in all the bungalows and catacombs called public buildings in Washington will be improved in the course of this administration, if the committee retains its enthusiasm.

Much of the credit for the reforms effected is due Mrs. Wainwright, who, as chairman of the Committee on Sanitation, has been quietly conducting a far-reaching campaign for the betterment of the sanitary conditions surrounding women workers in Washington. She has visited the Government departments, the department stores and private offices in which women are employed.

The project of a lunch room for the women employes of the Washington Navy Yard has been a favorite one with Miss Anne Morgan, daughter of J. Pierpont Morgan, and one of the most enthusiastic workers in the Federation. Miss Morgan believes that Uncle Sam should be a model employer.

The Treasury Department, which employs a larger percentage of women than any other department, will absorb a large share of the attention of these Federation women. Like the work they have accomplished elsewhere, it will be done on the "gumshoe" plan and without any fanfare of trumpets. Feminine diplomacy and tact will have their share in the work and the sympathies of high officials will be enlisted whenever possible.

The Federation is counting much on Mrs. Taft, whose practical common sense and knowledge of Washington conditions is much valued by her associates. During her husband's term as Secretary of War, Mrs. Taft's name was enrolled among those of the founders of the Women's Welfare Committee of the Federation, which numbers among its members Mrs. Hanna, widow of the Senator, who founded the Federation; Mrs. Samuel Spencer, widow of the president of the Southern Railway; Mrs. John B. Henderson, one of the most progressive women of Washington; Mrs. Larz Anderson, Mrs. Archibald Hopkins and other women equally well known throughout the country.

While the work in Washington will be concentrated on the departments, private employers will receive attention. For weeks the committee has been gathering statistics relating to conditions surrounding the women and girls in department stores.

The Federation believes that Washington is an ideal city for this reform work, for the reason that its feminine population outnumbers the masculine by 16,000.

NEW ENGLAND—SETH LOW, FREDERICK P. FISH AND JOHN MITCHELL SPEAK

(From Boston Globe.)

THE annual meeting of the Civic Federation of New England was held in Boston January 26, there being present about 400 members and guests, including some of the most prominent business men and representatives of labor in this section of the country. There were also present in the gallery a number of women.

After the business meeting the question of "Industrial Accidents," which is engaging the attention of the national association and all of the industrial States, was discussed by John Mitchell, ex-president of the United Mine Workers of America; Hon. Seth Low, president of the National Civic Federation, and Frederick P. Fish, ex-president of the American Telegraph and Telephone Company.

All the speakers deplored the present system of laws by which employes recover, or seek to recover, damages for injuries or accidents, because of the time it takes to get a trial and judgment, and the small portion which eventually goes to the victim or the family of the victim. Of the $100,000,000 paid out for accidents in the United States in 1907 only $22,000,000 went to the victims. The balance went into costs of litigation, etc.

President Tuttle, of the Boston & Maine, who is also President of the Federation, presided. Previous to the discussion there was a business meeting, at which officers were elected.

Frederick P. Fish.

Mr. Fish believed that in any solution of the problem care should be taken that the fundamental principles of the present liability law be not materially changed, especially the feature which requires reasonable personal responsibility. During [illegible] speech he said:

"If it is true that we are behind the times in this country in the number of accidents we have, isn't it our first duty to find the cause and then the remedy? I don't know the cause, but I believe that if the Civic Federation will take hold of the matter in a scientific manner, if found it will be corrected. I think the laws regarding employers' liability never go as far as the circumstances demand. If proper attention were given to the making of machinery and conditions of work as safe as possible many accidents would be prevented.

Workmen Careless.

"Workmen themselves are a very careless crowd, and that in a way is very much to their credit. I have little respect for a man who is always looking out for his hide; but on the other hand recklessness is to be deplored. I believe rules should be made and enforced to prevent employes from being careless.

"Something should be done so that money paid in injuries should go to those who are hurt. I think the law of Massachusetts pretty good as it stands, and think some things in it should never be changed. I think no man should be compensated for injury due wholly to his own fault. What we need is a new kind of a scientist who can go into the future from the present and past, analyze facts, go forward to the future and see how to shape the development of known facts for the best interests of the human race.

"Hitting the Wrong Target."

Hon. Seth Low, President of the National Civic Federation, said in part:

"I think the trouble with the employers' liability law, though aimed well, is that it hits the wrong target.

"A few years ago I built a house in the country, and it pleased me to do it by day labor, employing the men myself. I realized that my liability as an employer was very direct under these conditions, so I took out employers' liability policies of different sorts. Happily the only serious accident was the loss of a finger on the left hand by a carpenter. That accident happened about the beginning of September and the work closed the first of November. With great difficulty I persuaded the insurance company to let me keep the man on my payroll as long as my work lasted. I wanted to pay him until he was able to begin his work again in January, but that they absolutely declined; they would not let me pay him without forfeiting my insurance and it cost me a great deal, and that is what led me to say that the policy which I had taken out because of the employer's liability that exists under this law protected me, but it did not go to the fellow that was hurt.

"That is not the conception behind the law in my judgment. I then began to look into the question and I discovered what Mr. Fish said he learned in Washington—that out of a sum of $25,000,000 believed to have been paid in 1907, 20 per cent was paid to brokers, 20 per cent to insurance companies and 20 per cent for litigating claims, leaving 40 per cent for the person hurt. And the general belief is that that is usually divided half and half. So that out of this vast sum, which is already paid out of the business to save the employer from his liability for the workman, only 20 per cent reaches the person who is hurt. That is the reason why I say that the law as it stands to-day hits the wrong target."

John Mitchell.

The German and English systems of compensation for injuries were referred to by several speakers as examples to be studied in seeking a solution of the problem for this country. Mr. John Mitchell also suggested State bureaus of safety devices and hygiene, which should secure drawings of safety devices from all over the world and furnish these to manufacturers and employers generally, thus affording all classes an opportunity to learn about such devices. He said:

"It is all very well for a man to receive $1,000 or $2,000 for the loss of an eye or a leg, but it is much better for the man, as it is for society, that the eye or the leg be not lost.

"It is true, as has been said by Mr. Fish, that many accidents are due to carelessness, but I dare say that if the American workmen were to propose in a formal and definite way to exercise all the precautions exercised by the workmen of other countries the employers of the United States would not be willing to make that sort of contract with them.

"If the American workingmen could have their present wage scale for one-third less work they would be perfectly willing to exercise all the care that is exercised by the workmen of the old world. The American bricklayer lays one-third more bricks than does his brother across the pond. The American miner mines one-third more coal than does the miner of other countries, so that the carelessness which the courts declare has been responsible for the large number of casualties is as a matter of fact carelessness which we cannot control. I have found from investigation I have made and information that has come to me that where workmen are members of trades unions accidents are not so numerous or so serious as where the men are not organized."

Whole Principle to Be Changed.

"I am thoroughly convinced that we must change the whole principle of responsibility for industrial accidents. As has been pointed out by Mr. Fish and Mr. Low, we are wasting 80 per cent of the money now paid by employers.

"I have made some study of the German system and of the English system, and I believe that the English system of compensation would be most practicable in our country. In Germany they have developed the most comprehensive system of workingmen's insurance and compensation that is known in the world. What we ought to adopt is a system which will give us immediate relief, that will place upon employers no greater responsibility and no greater burden than we can help putting upon them; but we ought to place the burden on the industry, that is, place it on society, because when you put it on industry you have in the last analysis put it upon society.

"I believe in connection with your State factory department or your labor department you should establish a bureau of safety devices or industrial hygiene, that you ought in that bureau to collect from every country in the world the drawings of safety appliances, and that these safety drawings and appliances should be sent out to your railroad managers, to your factory managers and to your mill managers in order that they may know what safety appliances have been adopted in other industries and in other countries. If the State would supply that information to every employer it would enable the employer to put on his machines protective devices which he is even now anxious to use if he only knew about them and their value."

Letters from Friends of Cause.

Secretary Henry Abrahams read letters of regret from prominent men that contained matter pertinent to the subject discussed. The first of these was from Charles P. Neill, United States Commissioner of Labor, in which he said: "Our present laws, both Federal and State, are thoroughly unsatisfactory, alike to employers, to wage-earners and to the thinking public. The principle embodied in our statutes dealing with remuneration for industrial accidents is a principle which has been discarded by practically every other industrial country to-day."

W. S. Stone, Grand Chief of the Brotherhood of Locomotive Engineers, in his letter said: "This is something that has not been given the attention it should, and something that the laboring classes must look to in the future for some remedy."

Archbishop's Letter.

In his letter Archbishop Ireland said: "The number of industrial accidents annually occurring in the country is appalling. Something should be done, if America be worthy of its fame as a civilized country, to reduce in number those accidents, and, when accidents do occur despite all reasonable precautons, to alleviate the remediable consequences resulting from them.

"All things considered, the simplest and fairest solution is to place the responsibility of compensation for accidents upon the industry within the sphere of which they have arisen. Those who are impoverished through industries cannot be left to starve, and it is not those who did not profit by the industries who should be called upon to make compensation for damages caused thereby."

Officers Elected.

The officers elected at the business meeting were as follows: President, Lucius Tuttle; Vice-Presidents, Frank H. McCarthy and Louis D. Brandeis; Treasurer, John Mason Little; Recording Secretary, Henry Abrahams; Secretary, John B. [illegible] Executive Committee:

On the part of the public: W. Murray [illegible] ton; Henry L. Higginson, Boston; Bishop William Lawrence, Boston; William J. Tucker, Hanover, N. H.; Louis D. Brandeis, Boston; John Mason Little, Boston; William A. Gaston, Boston; William F. Henney, Hartford, Conn.; Thomas I. Gasson, S. J., Boston; Frederick P. Fish, Boston; W. H. P. Faunce, Providence, R. I.; Charles S. Hamlin, Boston; Alvah W. Sulloway, Franklin, N. H.; Hayes Robbins, North Adams.

On the part of employers: Lucius Tuttle, Boston; William L. Douglas, Brockton; Amory A. Lawrence, Boston; Charles H. Taylor, Jr.; J. L. Richards, Boston; T. E. Byrnes, Boston; C. L. Edgar, Boston; J. H. Hustis, Boston; P. F. Sullivan, Boston; Garrett Schenck, Boston; Arthur T. Lyman, Boston; W. C. Winslow, Boston; James Logan, Worcester.

On the part of wage-earners: Frank H. McCarthy, Boston; John Golden, Fall River; Henry Abrahams, Boston; P. F. McCarthy, Barre, Vt.; Samuel Ross, New Bedford; Francis J. Clarke, Brockton; Dennis D. Driscoll, Boston; Thomas F. Kearney, Providence, R. I.; Edmond F. Ward, Boston; John J. Connolly, Boston; P. F. Sheehan, Brockton; William H. Frazier, Boston; Arthur M. Huddell, Boston; Thomas P. Curtin, Boston.

WELFARE WORK METROPOLITAN LIFE

(Continued from page 28.)

duty ten hours, being relieved for two and one-half hours by fifteen minutes' recess.

The clerks in the home office are provided with little metal lockers in which to keep the towels furnished. They are washed and laundered free of charge. There are automatic soap-holders attached to each marble washbasin, and all the mirrors, marble floors and sanitary arrangements are kept scrupulously clean, matrons always being in attendance. Large metal lockers and showers are provided for the stationary firemen and engineers.

There are also medical rooms furnished, with couches, for the use of sick employes, and competent physicians are in attendance.

All apparatus throughout the building, such as those used for carrying cool air into the boiler room, and for filtering drinking water, are of the most modern type.

WELFARE WORK OF THE METROPOLITAN LIFE INSURANCE COMPANY

[illegible]TARY WORK PLACES, RECREATION, THE SHORT WORK DAY AND CIVIL SERVICE PRO[illegible]MOTION SYSTEM

[illegible]R deliberate consideration and in the firm [illegible]lief that it was in the interest of the com[illegible]ny and of its office staff, The Metropolitan [illegible]rance Company inaugurated a lunch room [illegible]ome office employes, the luncheon being [illegible] all without charge. Formerly the company [illegible] employes the necessary space for a lunch [illegible]d furnished tea and coffee free, requiring [illegible] pay for anything they desired to eat, [illegible] being sold, practi[illegible] cost.

[illegible] a luncheon is served [illegible]e, to over 2,700 em[illegible] More than one-half [illegible]en. The luncheon [illegible]vers 35 minutes. The [illegible]ooms are situated on [illegible] upper floors of the [illegible]ilding, one floor for [illegible] employes and the [illegible]r the women em[illegible] The kitchen, which is [illegible] on the roof, is spa[illegible] well ventilated and [illegible] with all facilities [illegible]r-saving devices. The [illegible] pantries, also, are ex[illegible] equipped, so that this [illegible]mber of employes can [illegible]d in a short time.

[illegible]arge floor space re[illegible]for dining rooms, the [illegible] capacity being about [illegible] admirably light and [illegible]ed, and the best hy[illegible]conditions are main[illegible] The whiteness of the [illegible]en and of the wait[illegible] uniforms afford a [illegible] effect on enter[illegible] There are also [illegible] for [illegible] and executive officers. [illegible] meal which is served [illegible]esome, consisting of [illegible]ith soup or fish sever[illegible] each week, vegeta[illegible]eets, and milk, tea or [illegible] Its nature is best indi[illegible]y the sample menu [illegible]elow:

MENU.

[illegible]rsday, July 15, 1909.

[illegible]nglish Beef Soup
[illegible] of Oxtail and Macaroni
[illegible]oast Leg of Veal
[illegible]otatoes Green Peas
Cold Cuts:
[illegible] Beef Boiled Ham
Salads:
[illegible]umber Lettuce
[illegible] Pudding, Cream Sauce
[illegible] Tea Coffee
[illegible]ilk Buttermilk
[illegible] 7c, 8c, 10c, 13c, 15c, 2[illegible]

[illegible] cost of this meal to [illegible]pany is approximate[illegible]ents each day per in[illegible]. This amount in[illegible] not only the expendi[illegible]or food but the addi[illegible] cost of waitresses, [illegible]ing table linen and [illegible]tal value of the space [illegible]d by the dining rooms. [illegible]tated, no charge is [illegible]or the luncheon. It is [illegible] by the company [illegible]any of its employes [illegible]nly limited earnings and, if they were re[illegible] to economize, it is more than likely that the [illegible]on where the saving would be made would be [illegible] midday meal. To ensure efficiency, the com[illegible]nds it good policy to provide nourishing food [illegible] of its employes. This luncheon is not con[illegible] a gratuity but rather as a supplement to the [illegible] which are as high if not higher than wages [illegible] others in the same line of work. There is on [illegible]arge waiting list of applications for employ[illegible]y the company.

There is a gymnasium for the use of both men and women employes, equipped with all the latest appliances, including lockers and shower baths. A physical instructor attends each afternoon to coach clerks. The men even find sport in having racing and hurdling contests, and many of them have joined the Metropolitan Basket Ball and Baseball Teams. As the office hours are from nine to four-thirty, and nine to one on Saturdays, there is ample time for clerks to take advantage of the gymnasium before or after hours. Certain days in the week are set aside for the men employes and others for the women employes.

The employes are, also, allowed a large portion of the roof for recreation, such as running contests and other athletic diversions.

The assembly hall is used by the women clerks during lunch hour and after office hours for amusement, particularly for dancing. From time to time the newly organized but, already famous Metro[illegible]tan Glee Club, to which all men employes ma[illegible] long without charge, holds its concerts in this [illegible]tiful hall, which seats over one thousand. [illegible] for these concerts are distributed to the office [illegible] without cost. The demand, however, has be[illegible] great that it is frequently necessary to repe[illegible] concerts in order that all the employes may have [illegible] opportunity of attending.

Employes, Metropolitan Life Insurance Company, Exercising on Roof Home Office Building.

The company, for a [illegible]ber of years, has [illegible]tained a staffs' saving [illegible] to which the [illegible] may contribute. The [illegible] thus obtained are in[illegible] by the officers so [illegible] bring the largest return. [illegible] fund is administered [illegible] board of trustees, of [illegible] some of the officers [illegible] part, and some of the [illegible] from the field are member[illegible] The company agrees to [illegible] 50 per cent. to the contribu[illegible]tions of the members of [illegible] staff, either in the field [illegible] the home office. One [illegible] withdraw from the fund [illegible] any time and for any [illegible] If voluntarily retiring, an [illegible]ploye takes out of it all [illegible] money put in, plus all inter[illegible]est accumulations, [illegible] between 5 and 7 per cent. except in the [illegible] of withdrawal, [illegible] per cent. from the last inter[illegible]est day to the date of with[illegible]drawal. Where an employe stays in the entire [illegible] in, contributions, [illegible] earnings, the company's con[illegible]tributions of 50 per cent. [illegible] the interest [illegible] that, are all, in one sum, paid to the widow in case of death or to the disabled person in case of invalidity. According to the last report there were 4,428 members, of whom 1,9[illegible] are agents, 1,061 of the cleri[illegible]cal force and 1,464 superin[illegible]tendents and assistants. The average rate of interest earned has been over 10 per cent. and the fund amounts now to $628,000. As an illus[illegible]tration, there is one employe whose deposits amount to $1,390 (he is a home office clerk), and with the compa[illegible]ny's subscription and interest he now has in the fund $2,282; there is one superin[illegible]tendent who has deposited $1,200, and the additions to that have been $900; there is an assistant who has depo[illegible]ited $802 and he has to his credit $1,395; there is [illegible] agent who has deposite[illegible] $689.81, and with the com[illegible]pany's subscription and in[illegible]terest there is to his credit i[illegible] this fund to-day $1,273. It [illegible] a system by which invalidit[illegible] and physical incapacity ma[illegible] be provided against by th[illegible] clerk or agent or assista[illegible] who is an employe.

Each employe, including th[illegible] stationary firemen and eng[illegible]neers, receives a vacation [illegible] two weeks each Summer at full pay. As the yea[illegible] of service in the company increase, so does th[illegible] duration of the vacation until finally, at the end [illegible] twenty years an employe receives a vacation of o[illegible] month at full pay. Vacations in the shape of [illegible] occasional day off are allowed to the elevator me[illegible] porters and scrubwomen at full pay.

The elevator men work in ten-hour shifts, the fi[illegible] shift starting at 8 in the morning and remaining

(Concluded on page 27.)

The National Civic Federation Review

Vol. III NEW YORK, JULY 1, 1911. No. 11

A BROAD PROGRAM OF CONSTRUCTIVE WORK

LEADERS OF AMERICAN THOUGHT AND ACTION ARE GRAPPLING WITH GREAT PROBLEMS THROUGH THE NATIONAL CIVIC FEDERATION—SCOPE OF ACTIVITIES IS COMPREHENSIVE

THE past year has witnessed a great extension of the influence of The National Civic Federation through the organization of State Councils in twenty-seven States. The meetings held for the purpose of organizing these Councils were, as a rule, held in the State House, the Governors rendering great assistance, and in most instances presiding at the meeting.

The purpose of the State Councils is to urge uniform State legislation on those matters that are intrastate; to work for the coördination of State with Federal legislation where conflict now exists and to aid in securing Federal legislation on interstate matters that are concededly in the interest of public welfare.

The more important subjects which will be considered by the Councils are:

"Regulation of Industrial Corporations;"
"Regulation of Railroads and Municipal Utilities;"
"Banking and Currency;"
"Taxation;"
"Insurance;"
"Reform in Legal Procedure;"
"Pure Food and Drugs;"
"Workmen's Compensation;"
"Industrial Mediation and Arbitration;"
"Good Roads and Automobile Regulation;"
The Commercial Measures Drafted by the Commissioners on Uniform State Laws ("Negotional Notes," "Bills of Lading," etc.)

The importance of this movement to all business and commercial institutions is clearly recognized, when we consider that our larger corporations—such as the railroads, telegraph, insurance, banking and trust companies and, in fact, so far as taxation is concerned, all manufacturing concerns whose plants are in different States—are subject to forty-six masters, each with a mind quite different from that of the others. The "interminable" law's delay, the clashing of the States upon the question of regulation of corporations and combinations, the diversity of State laws on ordinary commercial matters, such as warehouse receipts, bills of lading and negotiable notes, the urgent need for a uniform bill on compensation for industrial accidents, all give emphasis to the seriousness of our present chaotic legislative situation.

Governor Hadley of Missouri well voiced the views of Governor Marshall of Indiana, Governor Davidson of Wisconsin, Governor Deneen of Illinois, Governor Shallenberger of Nebraska, Governor Draper of Massachusetts and Governor Stuart of Pennsylvania when he endorsed the movement in the following language:

> "There is no one topic proposed for discussion by the Federation that has any political bias. They are all of the utmost importance, and should be studied and acted upon from a non-partisan point of view. One reason why the uniformity of laws throughout the States is difficult to secure is because political parties rule them. The question is not what are the merits of the proposition we put forward, but what are the politics of the man who puts this proposition forward. Measures are favored or opposed according to the political complexion of the proponents and of those to whom they are proposed. This is a mischievous system which should be put out of existence in connection with such laws as those contemplated by the uniform law movement, and such a body of representative men from all classes as you have here to-night can, working together, bring about a great reform in this matter. I hope to co-operate with the organization that has been formed here in placing uniform laws on the statute books of Missouri."

REGULATION OF COMBINATIONS.

The regulation of corporations and questions dealing with the limitations of combinations in restraint of trade, whether in manufacturing, finance, labor, agriculture or in other fields, have been considered by the Federation at two national conferences, each of which was attended by over five hundred delegates appointed by the Governors of the various States. At the Chicago conference in 1907 resolutions were unanimously adopted urging a thorough inquiry into the advisability of inaugurating a system of Federal license or incorporation as a condition for the entrance of certain classes of corporations upon interstate commerce, and also into the relation to the public interest of the purchase by one corporation of the franchises or corporate stock of another. The resolutions also recommended that any proposed legislation should include modification of the prohibitions now existing on the following subjects:

1. National and local organizations of labor and their trade agreements with employers relating to wages, hours of labor and conditions of employment.
2. Associations made up of farmers, intended to secure a stable and equitable market for the products of the soil, free from fluctuations due to speculation.
3. Business and industrial agreements or combinations whose objects are in the public interest as distinguished from objects determined to be contrary to the public interest.

No one was in favor of the repeal of the Sherman Act, however drastic its enforcement might seem, and it was declared firmly that "On none of the subjects mentioned must what has been gained be sacrificed until something better appears for enactment."

At the eleventh annual meeting of The National Civic Federation in January, 1911, the subject in all its aspects was again considered, and in pursuance of a resolution adopted, President Low has appointed the following committee to consider the subject of State and Federal regulation, the principles underlying each being practically the same.

Seth Low, Chairman; E. A. Bancroft, Illinois; William Dudley Foulke, Indiana; Frederick P. Fish, Massachusetts; James R. Garfield, Ohio; J. W. Jenks, New York; Charles L. Jewett, Indiana; Frederick N. Judson, Missouri; H. B. F. Macfarland, District of Columbia; Theodore Marburg, Maryland; G. H. Montague, New York; George W. Perkins, New York; John C. Richberg, Illinois; W. Z. Ripley, Massachusetts; Leo S. Rowe, Pennsylvania; C. A. Severance, Minnesota; F. L. Siddons, District of Columbia; Reuben D. Silliman, New York; J. J. Spalding, Georgia; Walter George Smith, Pennsylvania; Frederic J. Stimson, Massachusetts; Henry W. Taft, New York; Frank Trumbull, New York; Samuel Untermyer, New York; A. Leo Weil, Pennsylvania; Talcott Williams, Pennsylvania.

The above committee met in New York April 21, and authorized Chairman Low to name a sub-committee to outline a policy and mode of procedure looking to uniformity in State legislation on the regulation of combinations and trusts; to make a digest of all the trust laws of the States and the decisions on the subject to date for the service of the State Councils of the Federation; and to propose legislation along Federal lines should such action at any time be deemed wise.

NEED FOR UNIFORMITY IN THE REGULATION OF RAILROADS AND MUNICIPAL UTILITIES.

The proper regulation of railroads and municipal utilities is a subject in which The National Civic Federation has been deeply interested since the inquiry made by its commission into the relative merits of private versus public operation of quasi-public utilities in this country and in England.

That commission, presided over by Melville E. Ingalls, former chairman of the Executive Board of the Big Four Railroad, was composed, as will be recalled, of officers of representative public utility corporations, leaders of movements advocating municipal operation of such utilities, and leading publicists and labor officials who were variously described as neutrals.

This commission, after spending many months with engineers, accountants and experts selected by the "Antis" and the "Pros," respectively, unanimously agreed upon a number of recommendations. That referring to regulation follows:

> "First, we wish to emphasize the fact that the public utilities studied are so constituted that it is impossible for them to be regulated by competition. Therefore, they must be controlled and regulated by the Government; or they must be left to do as they please; or they must be operated by the public. There is no other course. None of us is in favor of leaving them to their own will, and the question is whether it is better to regulate or to operate."

The commission then declared for adequate regulation by a competent public authority, with power to require for all public utilities a uniform system of records and accounts, giving all financial data and all information concerning the quality of service and the cost thereof, which data should be published and distributed to the public like other official reports, and also recommended that no stock or bonds for public utilities be issued without the approval of some competent public authority.

While this commission dealt entirely with the regulation of municipal utilities, railroads, telegraph and telephone companies, both interstate and intrastate, are equally concerned in the question: "What is adequate regulation?" or in other words, "How far can regulation go and be efficient without unreasonably interfering with management?" The Interstate Commerce Commission, of course, has only to do with interstate railroads, telegraph, telephone and express companies, but many of the forty-one State railroad commissions regulate both the intrastate railroads, telephone companies, etc., and the municipal utilities in such States. In New York State, the State Commission has more power over the railroads running into New York City than has the Interstate Commerce Commission.

With public sentiment practically unanimous in favor of the proper regulation of all public utilities, whether State or interstate, and with forty-one different State commissions making as many dissimilar rulings, serious conflicts can readily be imagined, not only between the States themselves, but also between the State and the Federal Commissions and courts.

There are many questions which in their consideration involve identical principles, whether in relation to interstate railways or to quasi-public utilities, not the least important of which is the method of valuation of the property as a basis for rate-making or cost of service to the public.

President Low has appointed a national committee, representing all the interests of society affected by such regulation, to study this subject in all its phases and report recommendations. The personnel follows:

FRANKLIN K. LANE....................California
Interstate Commerce Commission.

B. H. MEYER....................Wisconsin
Interstate Commerce Commission.

WILLIAM R. WILLCOX....................New York
New York Public Service Commission.

ARTHUR W. BRADY....................Indiana
President American Electric Railroad Company.

MARTIN S. DECKER....................New York
New York Railway Commission.

F. E. BARKER....................Massachusetts
Chairman Mass. Gas and Electric Light Commission.

CHARLES F. BROOKER....................New York
Director N. Y., N. H. & H. Railroad Company.

EMERSON McMILLIN....................New York
Pres. American Light & Traction Company.

ROBERT R. PRENTIS....................Virginia
Pres. Nat'l Ass'n State Railway Commissioners.

MILO R. MALTBIE....................New York
New York Public Service Commission.

B. A. ECKHART....................Illinois
Chairman Illinois Railway Commission.

JAMES CAMPBELL....................New York
President North American Securities Company.

JOHN C. BELL....................Pennsylvania
Attorney-General of Pennsylvania.

ROLLIN S. WOODRUFF....................Connecticut
Former Governor of Connecticut.

CHARLES R. CRANE....................Illinois
Crane Valve Company, Chicago.

MYRON T. HERRICK....................Ohio
Railroad Director, Banker.

THEODORE N. VAIL....................New York
President American Telephone & Telegraph Co.

DAVID R. FRANCIS....................Missouri
Railroad Director, Banker.

WILLIAM C. BROWN....................New York
President New York Central Lines.

GEORGE B. CORTELYOU....................New York
President Consolidated Gas Company.

GEORGE W. PERKINS....................New York
Railway Director, Banker.

DANIEL WILLARD....................Maryland
President Baltimore & Ohio Railroad Co.

SAMUEL INSULL....................Illinois
President Commonwealth Electric Company.

JAMES SPEYER....................New York
Railway Director, Banker.

ROBERT WINSOR....................Massachusetts
Banker, Director Public Utility Companies.

AUGUST BELMONT....................New York
Chairman Board Directors Interborough Railroad Company.

FRANK TRUMBULL....................New York
Chairman Board Directors Chesapeake & Ohio Railroad Co.

H. M. BYLLESBY....................Illinois
Electrical Engineer (Chicago).

TIMOTHY S. WILLIAMS....................New York
President Brooklyn Rapid Transit Co.

ROBERT MATHER....................New York
President Westinghouse Electric and Manufacturing Company.

DR. ALBERT SHAW....................New York
Editor Review of Reviews.

WARREN S. STONE....................Ohio
Grand Chief International Brotherhood Locomotive Engineers.

V. EVERIT MACY....................New York
Director Queens Borough Gas & Electric Company.

A. B. GARRETSON....................Iowa
President Order of Railway Conductors.

TIMOTHY HEALY....................New York
Pres. Internat'l Brotherhood Stationary Firemen.

W. W. FREEMAN....................New York
Pres. National Electric Light Ass'n.

CHARLES L. EDGAR....................Massachusetts
Chairman Committee on Public Policy, National Electric Lighting Association.

FRED. G. MOFFATT....................Colorado
Banker (David N. Moffatt & Co., Denver).

FRANKLIN Q. BROWN....................New York
Railroad Director, Banker (Redmond & Co.)

BLEWETT LEE....................Illinois
General Solicitor Illinois Central Railroad Co.

W. J. CLARK....................New York
General Electric Company.

W. Z. RIPLEY....................Massachusetts
Professor Political Economy Harvard University.
Railway Expert.

W. W. FINLEY....................Washington, D. C.
Southern Railway Company.

ALLEN B. FORBES....................New York
Banker, Director Public Utility Companies.

JOHN H. GRAY....................Minnesota
Professor Political Economy, University of Minnesota.

H. U. MUDGE....................Illinois
President Chicago, Rock Island & Pacific Railroad.

CHARLES A. STONE....................Massachusetts
Stone & Webster Management Company.

P. H. MORRISSEY....................Illinois
Ex-Grand Master Brotherhood Railroad Trainmen.

LEO S. ROWE....................Pennsylvania
Professor University of Pennsylvania.

JAMES J. STORROW....................Massachusetts
Banker, Director Public Utility Companies.

OSCAR S. STRAUS....................New York
Former Secretary of Commerce and Labor.

GEORGE F. SWAIN....................Massachusetts
Professor Political Economy, Harvard University.

S. C. WOLCOTT....................New York
Banker (W. P. Bonbright & Co.)

C. E. MERRIAM....................Illinois
Professor Political Economy, University of Chicago.

JAMES H. McGRAW....................New York

COMPENSATION FOR INDUSTRIAL ACCIDENTS AND THEIR PREVENTION.

The Federation's Department on Compensation for Industrial Accidents and Their Prevention is composed of employers, representative labor men, members of the ten official State Commissions and the Federal Commission, members of the National Association of Uniform State Law Commissions in thirty-eight States, members of the Compensation Committee of the American Bar Association, attorneys who have specialized upon workmen's compensation, insurance experts, economists, State officials and others concerned about this great problem.

This department drafted a bill for compulsory compensation, with definite rates, as a sketch model and submitted it to the Legislatures of the thirty-three States which met during the past Winter. The principles of this bill have been adopted in a number of States. One important feature is a clause permitting voluntary agreements between employers and employes. The act simply stipulates that such schemes shall not be less favorable to the workman than the plan embodied in it.

The American Federation of Labor sent out to its local unions, throughout the country, with its endorsement, twenty thousand copies of The National Civic Federation's bill on Workmen's Compensation.

The Workmen's Compensation Department of the Federation has sent to the Governor of each State recommendations for improvement in State inspection of factories in the interest of prevention of accidents. Mention of this department's recent activities will be found elsewhere in this issue of the Review.

Pensions for employes is a topic co-related to workmen's compensation in that disabled employes may become pensioners. The Federation's Department on Wage Earners' Insurance encourages employers to start proper voluntary relief associations, which include sick and death benefits as well as pensions for aged employes in commercial enterprises; and the Committee on Pensions for Public Employes has for its purpose the securing of proper legislation for retirement funds in the Federal classified service and for State and Municipal employes.

To become incapacitated and have no earning capacity after years of loyal service, with no means of support, is the dread of every thinking wage worker. The main problem involved in pension plans, especially for public employes, is the question, "Shall employes contribute to retirement funds?" From the public standpoint it is of serious moment that the work of the Government, whether Municipal, State or Federal, should not be hampered by retaining in the service employes incapacitated by age. Until a proper pension plan is worked out, public machinery will be clogged, as no official has the heart to throw out upon the world those who have devoted their lives to the service of the Government. The "common surfman" in the Life-Saving Service, who has an enforced vacation of two months in the year without pay, and makes only $65.00 a month, presents one of the many types in the employ of the National Government appealing for its consideration. To urge legislation on pensions for public employes, fair to the State and to the employe, is the object of the Federation's movement. The entire subject of wage earners' insurance for Government and industrial employes, including accident, sick, death and pension funds, touches the whole social fabric.

NEED FOR REFORM IN LEGAL PROCEDURE.

President Taft said at a recent meeting of The National Civic Federation:

> "The greatest question now before the American public is the improvement of the administration of justice, civil and criminal, both in the matter of its prompt dispatch and the cheapening of its use."

The National Civic Federation has appointed a committee on this subject which is co-operating with a similar committee of the American Bar Association. This joint committee is trying to secure, through Congressional action, a simplified practice act for the Federal courts which can be used by our State Councils as a basis for a reformed practice act in the several States.

This bill passed the House at the last session of Congress, but there was not time for it to be reached in the Senate. It is hoped that public attention will be focalized on this measure sufficiently to secure its enactment into law at the next session of Congress.

The two committees forming the joint committee referred to are:

For the American Bar Association—Everett P. Wheeler, chairman; Roscoe Pound, Chicago; Charles F. Amidon, Fargo, N. D.; J. H. Beale, Jr., Cambridge, Mass.; Prof. Frank Irving, Cornell University; Samuel C. Eastman, Concord, N. H.; H. D. Estabrook, New York City; Charles S. Hamlin, Boston; W. L. January, Detroit; Charles E. Littlefield, New York City; Arthur Steuert, Baltimore; Samuel Scoville, Philadelphia; Edward T. Sanford, Knoxville.

For The National Civic Federation—Ralph W. Breckenridge, Omaha, chairman; Morgan J. O'Brien, New York City; William E. Chandler, Washington; John B. Sanborn, Madison, Wis.; Selden P. Spencer, St. Louis; Stephen H. Allen, Topeka, Kan.; Charles L. Jewett, New Albany, Ind.; Thomas W. Shelton, Norfolk Va.; Stephen S. Gregory, Chicago; Willard Saulsbury, Wilmington, Del.; A. M. Eaton, Providence, R. I.; J. F. Vaile, Denver; W. I. MacIntyre, Thomasville, Ga.; C. La Rue Munson, Williamsport, Pa.; Lawrence Cooper, Huntsville, Ala.

Our people generally do not realize the importance of this subject because it impresses them as something purely academic. The joint committee, however, says:

> "The miscarriage of justice in criminal cases is generally due to the defective administration of the law and the technicalities which arise in criminal trials. *Ninety per cent* of the proverbial 'law's delays' are due to the system under which the law is administered, rather than to the intention of the lawyers interested in delaying suits or the benefit resulting to either side from delays."

The injustice to the workingman in the law's delay is so great that he can scarcely avail himself of the courts to bring a suit in any matter. This is particularly true in cases resulting from injuries through accidents. By the time the injured man receives a verdict, which he does after many delays and reversals for technical reasons, the court costs deprive it of much of its value.

According to the statistics of the American Bar Association, *new trials are granted in forty-six per cent of all the cases in our courts involving a penitentiary offense*. And in sixty per cent of this number the new trial is granted, not because of a question affecting the possible guilt or innocence of the prisoner, but *because of a purely technical point of dispute in the conduct of the case.*

In nearly half of the criminal cases in American courts it requires two or more trials to convict the prisoner. And in sixty per cent of these cases his guilt is plain. He is given a new trial because the higher court holds that there has been an error of "pleading and practice," either on the part of the lawyers or the judge.

Illustrations can be taken from any State. Hugh Weir, giving examples of the technical rulings, practice and abuses in our courts, says:

> "Here are two cases from Alabama and North Carolina which sound almost incredible. Indeed, were they not matters of court record, the average American citizen would dismiss them with a shrug as sensational journalism:
>
> "In the former State, a man charged with murder went free, because the Clerk of Courts, in writing the word 'malice' in the indictment, left out the letter 'i.'
>
> "In North Carolina an enraged citizen shot a neighbor through the breast, inflicting a wound which resulted in the latter's death and his own arrest for murder. A short time later, however, he was released from custody. In the indictment the clerk had spelled breast as 'b-r-e-s-t.' The court held that this misspelled indictment was not legal and freed the prisoner."

NEED FOR UNIFORMITY IN STATE TAXATION.

In scarcely any domain of social life have the difficulties arising from lack of uniformity made themselves more apparent than in the field of taxation. Professor E. R. A. Seligman, Chairman of the Department of Taxation of The National Civic Federation, than whom there is no greater authority in the United States, describes these difficulties in the following language:

> "Laws which were devised for an economic stage which has long since passed away can no

longer work efficiently; a system which was designed to secure justice, and which did roughly attain justice, breeds to-day, under entirely diverse conditions, inequality and injustice. It is this practical injustice of the working out of an antiquated fiscal system which cries for remedy. . . .

"When we deal with personal property we are entering upon a very troublous sea of difficulties. Personal property is of two kinds, tangible and intangible personalty. So far as the personal property is tangible it might be said that the same rule ought to apply as in the case of real estate, and that a man's property ought to be taxed where it is situated. But in modern times, with the moving of individuals from place to place, from State to State, this rule becomes difficult to enforce, and has been largely supplanted by the other principle that movables follow the person. Unfortunately, however, there is no agreement among our tax jurisdictions as to the precise principle to be followed in any particular case. In some places tangible personalty is assessed to the owner; in other places tangible property is assessed where it is situated. The consequence is that on the one hand we have instances of double taxation, where one State taxes the owner and the other State again taxes the property, while in other cases we have a complete exemption of the taxpayer, the one State absolving the taxpayer under the assumption that the property itself is taxed in the second State, while the second State pursues the reverse policy and exempts the property on the assumption that the owner is taxed elsewhere.

"These difficulties connected with tangible personalty are, however, after all, relatively slight when compared to the complexities of the taxation of intangible property. . . . A man lives, let us say, in New York, and owns securities of a corporation whose head office is in Chicago, whose chief tangible property may be in a group of New England States and whose business is carried on or whose products are sold primarily in a group of Southern States. Where shall the man be taxed? Shall he be taxed by New York, where he lives; by Illinois, where the interest and dividends are distributed; in Massachusetts, where the factory is situated, or in Mississippi, where the goods are sold? Or shall he, as sometimes actually happens, be subjected to a quadruple taxation, New York taxing the personal property in the shape of bonds, Illinois taxing the corporation on its capital, Massachusetts taxing the tangible property, and Mississippi levying a license tax on the sales? The situation would not be so bad if the individual knew beforehand exactly what to expect; for one can adjust oneself even to quadruple taxation, provided he knows that every other man is similarly treated. The irony of the situation consists in the fact, however, that scarcely any two States pursue the same policy: that the fortunate corporate investor in one State may go entirely free, as in New York State, where the owner of corporate shares in domestic corporations is exempt, and where the domestic corporation may also be expressly free from the State tax and corporate franchise, and where there is no tax at all on sales. If, however, the investor lives in Massachusetts, he is legally taxable on the securities of a foreign corporation, and it depends entirely upon the chances of the particular case as to whether he is subject to a double, a triple or a quadruple tax. . . .

"The same story would be true of the new item in our list of State and local taxes, namely, the inheritance tax. Whole books have been written on the difficulties and complexities of this newer system. Suppose in the case of a man who has lived all his life in Pennsylvania, and who happens to die in New York; his business interests are in Ohio, and most of his securities are in a safe deposit company in New Jersey. Where shall he be taxed and how? Shall he be taxed by New York, by Pennsylvania, by Ohio, or by New Jersey? Shall he be taxed in part by each? Shall he be taxed in whole by all? Or is it perhaps possible that he has been occupying a Summer villa at Newport, and thus escapes taxation entirely, on the ground that he votes in a State where there is no inheritance tax? All degrees of complications are possible, actually ranging from unjust tax dodging to double, triple and quadruple taxation of more or less unfortunate decedents. . . . We may conclude, therefore, that the situation is one which cries aloud for immediate remedy. It is not so important that any particular theory be adopted and realized in principle, as it is that the theory, no matter what it be, be followed with some degree of uniformity in the various States. Just as a business man desires above all things stability rather than high prices suddenly followed by low prices, so the taxpayer, in his quest of equality, desires above all things uniformity. With every year's progress in the national consolidation of economic interests, the present conflict of tax jurisdictions becomes more and more anomalous and produces greater and greater hardships. . . .

"Let the States look to it that they agree no longer to disagree, and that they effect some working method of uniform and equitable action. Otherwise there is grave danger that what they declare themselves unable to accomplish will be carried through by some form of pressure from above. To those who really have at heart the maintenance of State autonomy, and of independent commonwealth activity, I would say: 'Do your housecleaning yourselves, before some one else steps in to do it for you.' The achievement of a reasonable uniformity in tax legislation is one of the most insistent demands of this housecleaning that cannot much longer be deferred."

The New York *Evening Post* recently gave the following illustration:

"If a resident of New Jersey should die leaving $2,000,000 of bonds of a Wisconsin corporation in a safe deposit vault in New York City, and by his will bequeath this property to his nephew, the New York tax would be nearly $420,000, the New Jersey tax $100,000, the Wisconsin tax nearly $300,000, making a total of over $800,000. Before he had any enjoyment of his property, except the pleasure of paying these taxes, suppose the nephew died and in turn left his property to his nephew; it would be again taxed, so that the estate which the second nephew received would be brought down to about $700,000, the different States having absorbed the balance in the guise of taxation."

In quoting the above illustration, *Life*, a humorous paper, makes the following very pertinent statement:

"'That looks to us like excess of zeal in inheritance tax legislation. The State that has the first right to pick the bones of a decedent must find some means to defend the carcass against the exactions of other State claims."

PURE FOOD AND DRUGS.

There is no subject of greater interest to the American people than that of pure food and pure drugs. The wealthy are able to pay the highest prices and are less liable to be imposed upon by the sellers of impure or adulterated foods and drugs, but the masses have no other protection than that which is granted by the Federal Pure Food and Drug Act and the various States' acts which are to a great extent in conformity with the Federal Law.

While a great improvement has been wrought in the situation since the passage of that act in 1907, yet the administration of the law by the Federal, State and Municipal authorities is greatly hampered by the lack of sufficient inspectors and effective machinery to detect violations and in some cases by corrupt alliances between the officials and the manufacturers and sellers of rotten food stuffs.

The recent exposures in New York, Philadelphia and Chicago indicate the magnitude and far-reaching character of the violation of the food and drug laws. Not only were the poor defrauded by adulterated and impure food, but they were also cheated as to measurements and weights. It is a situation which calls for drastic treatment. The monthly bulletins issued by the United States Department of Agriculture describe hundreds of convictions secured annually by that Department (generally on the confession of guilt by the manufacturers or dealers) which are enough to arouse the indignation of all good citizens.

The whole situation in regard to the enforcement of Pure Food and Drug laws is thus stated in the American Year Book for 1910:

"Many food reformers make the mistake of attacking the national food law, when they mean to attack the departmental interpretation of the law, erroneously believing that the interpretation put upon the law by officials is the law itself. It is also important to note that in many cases brought under the food and drugs act the law has been greatly hampered by the laxity of the courts. In one case in which it was found that milk was adulterated, in that it consisted in whole or in part of a filthy, decomposed, and putrid animal substance, a fine was imposed of $10. Again, an infant soothing syrup, said to contain no morphine, and guaranteed to be perfectly harmless, was found to contain morphine, the label containing false and misleading statements intended to mislead and deceive the purchasing public. In this case the firm was fined $10.

'Where tomato ketchup was found to consist wholly or in part of a filthy, decomposed, and putrid vegetable substance, and to contain a large number of bacteria and molds, which rendered it unfit for food, the fine was $50. In another case of adulterated milk the fine was only $5. A coffee firm found guilty of coating coffee with lead chromate and other poisonous and deleterious substances, which rendered the coffee injurious to health, was fined $10. In short-weight cases the fines have run as low as $1.

"Many cases are on record of the adulteration and misbranding of drugs, headache powders, drug-habit-forming medicines, maple syrups, flavoring extracts, and condiments, for which the penalty was too small to deter the adulterator from continuing his fraud in comparative peace. It should not be overlooked that the law also provides for prison sentence.

"A conscience that would poison a baby's candy, paint it with varnish to make it look like chocolate, pollute the infant's milk with formaldehyde, dope it with chloroform and other opiates, and embalm other products with aniline dyes, salicylic acid, sulphate of copper, and all manner of chemicals, is not going to be troubled over a nominal fine. The national food law, however, is not to blame. It affords adequate punishment if properly enforced.

"There exists, however, a provision that permits of great harm, which is one shortcoming of the national food law. The law permits the sale of imitation and other juggled foods if their manufacturers label them 'imitations,' 'compounds' or 'blends.' The jobber or retailer thus buys them as 'imitations' or counterfeit foods, but, unless they are contained in 'original packages,' they are invariably sold to the consumer as real, genuine foods. Thus bakery products are in large part made of spoiled eggs, shipped in carload lots and deodorized with formaldehyde. Pie fillings are sold in wholesale lots to restaurants and bakeries, which are indescribably nauseous. Tarts, jams and ice creams are made of fictitious foods. In fact, an entire meal was recently prepared in a chemical laboratory without a particle of real food in it—a repast that had all the appearance of wholesome dishes, but was entirely substanceless. Such is the magic power of chemicals!

"The hotel or restaurant proprietor, the bakery owner or the grocer may distinguish the fictitious foods he buys by the words 'imitation,' etc., printed on the label, as required by the law, and also by the low price he pays for them. But the consumer never has a chance to see these labels, and under existing conditions it is difficult for him to tell whether he is eating real or imitation foods. Likewise many things we buy in bulk in grocery stores may be nothing but synthetic, substanceless foods, or worse.

"Thus it is plain that, without the aid of honest and efficient State and city food laws and food officers, the national food law can be greatly crippled. This fact the food adulterator seems to have discovered, and in some directions it now looks as if he had really transformed the national law into a tool to aid him in exploiting, robbing and poisoning the public. If the city and State food officers would do their duty, such conditions would not exist. If they would be as strict as the national authorities, they would see that the 'State' foods are as pure as those that enter into interstate commerce, and that the consumer be permitted to know when he buys 'imitation' foods as well as the grocer or baker. Hence, with State and municipal enforcement, even as efficient as the national enforcement, America's dream of pure foods would be nearly realized."

The press of the country was recently filled with the sensational account of the seizure of carloads of adulterated frozen eggs, the product consisting in part of (to quote from the judgment of the court) "a filthy, decomposed and putrid animal substance absolutely unfit for human consumption."

The New York *World*, during an investigation two months ago, had 300 prescriptions filled by big and little pharmacists in all parts of Manhattan, and then had them analyzed by noted chemists, with the result that, as charged by the *World*, 50 per cent of the preparations were found to be positively harmful or worthless; where some of the remainder were correct in strength and purity, they were short as to weight or measurement.

In connection with this investigation, one of the proprietors of a large pharmacy on Broadway made the following emphatic statement:

"There is no doubt that the lives of the people are greatly jeopardized whenever a prescription is filled, and every possible protection should be afforded.

"I am sorry to say that there are too many unscrupulous men among us in the drug business, men who do not hesitate to substitute one drug for another and take chances they have no right to take.

"There are certain sections in this city where I would not think of having a prescription prepared for a member of my family. I would as soon think of giving them poison."

The Federation will soon have a National Committee on Pure Food and Drugs and a sub-committee on the same subject in each State, the chairmen of the State committees also being members of the national committee.

One of the important features of the work of this committee will be to make evident to employers how their employes are imposed upon in this matter.

The public need only be clearly informed of true conditions to put an end to the sale in this country of impure and deleterious drugs and adulterated and rotten foodstuffs.

INDUSTRIAL CONCILIATION DEPARTMENT.

While the questions discussed above are all legislative, the following paragraphs briefly describe other activities of the Federation:

The Conciliation Department deals entirely with strikes and lockouts. The services of this department have been enlisted in over five hundred cases, involving every conceivable phase of a problem interwoven with or underlying an industrial controversy. Its membership includes representatives of leading organizations of employers, of wage-earners and of the general public.

Wherever it is possible to do so, the Federation co-operates with the State Boards of Mediation, supplementing their efforts by bringing to bear through its members the weight of its influence as a disinterested volunteer force.

This department is urging an amendment to the State arbitration laws which seeks to prevent strikes and lockouts on quasi-public utilities.

INDUSTRIAL ECONOMICS DEPARTMENT.

The Industrial Economics Department, of which Nicholas Murray Butler is Chairman, was formed to promote discussion of practical economic problems. Its mmbership is composed of leading economists, including the heads of the departments of political economy in universities, lecturers and economic and legal authors; editors of the daily press, of politico-social magazines, of trade papers and of labor journals; representatives of the pulpit; large employers and representatives of labor.

Under the auspices of this department there have been discussions by the ablest experts to be procured upon many of the vital and frequently irritating questions that arise in the Conciliation Department in connection with the prevention or settlement of controversies.

These questions include such subjects as: "Government by Injunction," "The Boycott," "The Right to Strike," "The Trade Agreement," "The Union Versus the Non-Union Shop," "The Shorter Work-Day," "Restriction of Output," "The Minimum Wage," "Piece Work Versus Day Work," "Scientific Management."

One session of the recent annual meeting was devoted to a discussion of the last-named topic, the efficiency engineers speaking in favor of "scientific management" and the labor representatives opposing it. As a result of this discussion, a commission will be appointed to make a thorough study of the subject and report to the Federation at a later date.

EMPLOYERS' WELFARE DEPARTMENT.

The Employers' Welfare Deparment of the Federation is composed of 500 leading employers and public officials throughout the United States. Its work is the humanitarian phase of the Federation's activities. The methods employed are educational, the effort being to prove its value by holding up as good examples employers who have successfully introduced Welfare Work for the benefit of their employes.

Some of the subjects involved in Welfare Work are:

Sanitary Work Places: Systems for providing pure drinking water; for ventilation, including the cooling of superheated places, and devices for exhausting dust and removing gases; for lighting work places; and for safeguards against industrial accidents; wash rooms with hot and cold water, towels and soap; shower baths for moulders and stationary firemen; emergency hospitals; locker rooms; seats for women; laundries for men's overalls or women's uniforms; the use of elevators for women, and luncheon rooms.

Recreation: The social hall for dancing parties, concerts, theatricals, billiards, pool or bowling; the gymnasium, athletic field, roof garden, vacations and summer excursions for employes, and rest rooms or trainmen's rest houses.

Educational: Classes for apprentices; in cooking, dressmaking, millinery; first aid to the injured; night classes for technical training; kindergartens and libraries.

Housing: Homes rented or sold to employes, and boarding houses.

Provident Funds: Include employers' plans for savings or lending money in times of stress, as well as all forms of industrial insurance.

WOMAN'S WELFARE DEPARTMENT.

The Woman's Welfare Department is composed largely of women who are themselves stockholders or who, through family relationship, are financially interested in industrial organizations (including railroads, mills, factories, mines, stores and other work places) and who, therefore, should be interested in the welfare of workers in enterprises from which they draw their incomes; there are also, among other influential members, the wives of public officials.

Types of employes whose conditions have been improved through its efforts may be found in Federal and Municipal Departments such as the Treasury, the Bureau of Engraving and Printing, the Census Bureau, the Post Office, the Pension Office, the Interior Department, Navy Yards, City Hospitals, Public Schools, and, in industrial concerns: stationary firemen, hotel employes, wage earners in dangerous and unhealthful industries affected by mercurial poisoning, particularly in the manufacture of felt hats, and employes in cotton mills; and there is a movement for recreation and vacation resources in connection with summer outings.

WORKMEN'S COMPENSATION THE KEYNOTE

ABLE ARGUMENTS FOR CORPORATE REGULATION AND UNIFORMITY IN LAWS—INDUSTRIAL CONCILIATION WORK EXTENDED—A PURPOSEFUL GATHERING OF THE NATION'S LEADING MEN

THE eleventh annual meeting of the The National Civic Federation, which was held at Hotel Astor, New York City, on January 12, 13 and 14, 1911, was characterized by a purpose, fullness, dignity, authority and brilliance that surpassed even previous gatherings of this great representative body of the employer, the wage earner, and the general public.

Probably the dominant note of the meeting was the deep and earnest discussion of the effort to effect in this country a system of just compensation for industrial accidents, a boon to employer and wage-earner alike, and the reports of progress shown in this direction.

Scarcely less impressive was the announcement, by PRESIDENT SETH LOW, of the formation of twenty-four State Councils, including the District of Columbia. The value of these in furthering uniform legislation in the several States, along lines laid out by the Federation, can scarcely be exaggerated by the most optimistic. This is one of the biggest constructive moves ever made by this organization.

The addresses were notable, among other things, by reason of the prominence of the speakers, and further, because they represented all classes.

In the course of the deliberations, the former President of the United States, Theodore Roosevelt, expressed his satisfaction with The National Civic Federation, saying that in it he realized his desire "to see radicalism prosper under conservative leadership."

As verbatim proceedings of the annual meeting are published in pamphlet form, an abstract only will be given in these pages.

First Day—Morning Session.

FEDERAL AND STATE REGULATION OF CORPORATIONS FIRST CONSIDERED.

The first general topic of consideration at the meeting was "Federal and State Regulation of Corporations."

SAMUEL UNTERMYER, Esq., of the New York Bar, who made the opening address on "Combinations and Trusts," discussed the alternative of their extermination or regulation. He announced his opinion that the Supreme Court of the United States, in two pending cases, will emphasize the principle announced by the lower courts so as to hold unlawful "every form of combination the direct purpose and effect of which is to hamper or limit competition." But he declared also his belief that such decisions will have no result beyond possible changes in forms of organization, unless the combinations are attacked under the criminal section of the Federal statute. There is no thought of confiscation; to resolve combinations into their constituent parts appears impossible, as those have lost their identity. Even a decision of these cases for the Government would be an academic victory, and the property of the trust would probably meet such disposition as would enable the same interests to continue the same business, under the protection of a judicial decree.

Mr. Untermyer laid down six propositions, which may be summarized: 1, The attitude of the courts during the first ten years of the Anti-Trust Law, rendering its enforcement then almost impossible, is largely responsible for the development of existing Trusts; 2, the Government having tacitly assented to the legality of the most vicious of them, it would cause now almost financial and industrial chaos to exterminate them, even if that result were possible; 3, The Constitution forbids the destruction or confiscation of property rights; 4, abortive attempts at extermination are of questionable advisability; 5, The present activities of the Government will not imperil the existence of the combinations most inimical to the community, and no attempt has been made at criminal process against individuals.

The only criminal prosecutions of recent years have been directed against pools or trade agreements for regulating prices and production. These were clearly illegal, but resulted mainly from ruinous competition among many small concerns, and touched almost every field of industry. But the most effective price arrangements are known as "gentlemen's agreements," both unlawful and dangerous, but not prosecuted. The Government enjoined sucessfully the Railroad Association from a conspiracy to increase rates, but no person was prosecuted. Uniformity of prices and restriction of production in coal, iron and steel are immune. The action of the Government has caused a feeling that officials are unable to reach the big offenders and try to appease public demand by proceeding against smaller ones. These problems are essentially national and cannot be dealt with by the States. There is little to be expected from them, so that it is fortunate that the subject is beyond their jurisdiction. The only solution is rigid regulation under Federal law, which is practicable where permissive Federal regulation would answer every purpose. It would involve no discrimination. Regulation would preserve such economic benefits as the elimination of destructive competition. The real problem is how to prevent the evils of overproduction and at the same time protect the public against the dangers of combination between competitors. It would be necessary to recognize that tolerated combinations owe duties to the public; that the protective tariff is based upon the theory of home competition; and that combinations impairing home competition must submit to Government supervision. There must be power to prevent summarily the creation of excessive profits through the power to limit prices. The difficulties are more imaginary than real. The judicial power of regulation would be invoked only where a responsible complaint was lodged of undue profits or unfair methods. A tribunal in fixing a maximum price would not go further than to protect the public against extortion. Changes of conditions could be met by reviews of judgments at stated periods. Mr. Untermyer concluded his paper with a review of the laws applicable to the subject in Germany, Austria, France and England.

AN HISTORICAL VIEW.

MR. WILLIAM DUDLEY FOULKE emphasized as one of the radical changes in history the transformation of the industrial system from competition to co-operation and monopoly. He declared that there is now an acknowledged effort to create "an oligarchy in place of a democracy." The peril to free institutions in this tendency he illustrated by the commercial rise of Carthage only to fall before the assault of then sturdy Rome, by the decadence of Rome from the Republic to the Empire, accompanied by the growth of great fortunes and the beggary of the multitude until the ruler of the world became the prey of the hordes of Germany and Scythia by the successive prosperity and ruin of Florence and Venice. "Now our turn has come," declares Mr. Foulke. The wealth of the richest nation on earth is in the hands of the few. There are private fortunes in the United States greater than the world has ever known before, fortunes that control legislation, so that there has become necessary "an insurgency against the thraldom imposed by our political masters." Hence, in his view, the issue is present, whether the Government shall control the power of wealth or organized capital shall rule. The emergency is national and demands national measures. The remedy lies in more thorough Governmental control of corporations. He found in Canadian and German legislation a possible solution of the problem which, he declared, was past the academic stage and demands a practical remedy for "the most threatening evil of our modern institutions."

LABOR AND THE LAW.

Mr. SAMUEL GOMPERS, President of the American Federation of Labor, declared as to the trust question that it made little difference to the wage-earner whether wealth is in the hands of an individual or of a combination of individuals. The corporate or individual position of the employer mattered little. Wages, hours and conditions of labor were the questions confronting the wage earner. The demand to curb evil practices of great corporations found expression in the Sherman anti-trust law of 1890. Leading Senators gave assurance that labor would not come under the operations of that statute. The combinations of wealth have gone on, and it might not be desirable to stop them, since "industry must continue to develop into the highest and best forms and upon the most economical basis and results." But under the Sherman anti-trust law the Supreme Court of the United States has decided that workmen, as individuals or in organizations, may be sued by any one and may be prosecuted criminally. Wage earners are in accord with the proposition that we must have equality without favors. Labor insists upon equality in the law. But is it right that a combination dealing in oil, steel, pork or beef should be placed in the same category legally with an association of shirtwaist workers who strike against sweatshop conditions? Yet, under the law as interpreted by the Supreme Court, labor organizations, engaged in no enterprise in which they own or control products, are classed with those combinations which deal in the products of labor. Mr. Gompers pointed out that in history, when popular assemblage had been denied, the first act of the combinations of wealth that had ruined republics was to attack combinations of the working people. In this country a similar attempt had been made. Through interpretation of the courts there had been constant extension of the jurisdiction and power of the Sherman anti-trust law when applied to the organization of working people. The Canadian act to regulate industrial combines excludes from its operation organizations of workers, and Parliament in 1906 exempted labor organizations from the operation of a similar law. The same exemption American organized workers have asked from Congress in the Wilson bill, urged especially since the decision mulcting hatters in Danbury $222,000 with fees and costs, and since workmen have advised co-operative action in New Orleans to withhold labor in support of strikers, and since shirtwaist workers and their sympathizers have been sued for about $150,000. Such suits are a constant menace. Organized labor will not exist merely at the sufferance of any administration or of any party. In the old days, when courts decreed or tribunals ordered their dissolution, the organizations of working people dissolved. But the labor organizations of America have done so much for the working people, to improve their moral and social and political condition, to bring light into their homes and hope into their hearts, that they would not be driven from existence. "The economic power vested in the hands of the working people is the most potent check to capitalist aggregation." We shall work to the end "that a law shall pass the Congress of the United States that shall not throw in the same category human hearts and men and blood with a ton of coal or a barrel of pork." The production of wealth should go on, with the maintenance of an American standard of life, and "we are contributing in the great struggle, having always before us the ideal of a greater and a better and a more human system of society and government and fellowship."

THE CANADIAN PLAN.

An explanation of the "Combines Investigation Act" of Canada was presented by W. L. MACKENZIE KING, Minister of Labor in the Dominion. The act was passed at the last session of Parliament and its first application, an inquiry into the operations of the United Shoe Machinery Company of Canada, is pending before the Superior Court in Quebec. The legislation was in response to the outcry against the increased cost of living. The Minister held that there were many causes, but this act recognizes that consumers and producers are alike entitled to the fullest protection from the State. The benefits of organization are fully recognized. The purpose is to secure to society at large some measure of the advantages derivable from combination. The remedy for enhancing prices or restricting combination is expressed by investigation, publicity and penalty. To secure an inquiry, application must be made to any High Court Judge by six resident British subjects, who must present to his satisfaction reasonable ground for believing "(1) that a combine exists injurious to trade, or (2) which has operated to the detriment of consumers or producers, and (3) that an investigation would be in the public interest. Expenses are borne by the State. An order for investigation is communicated at once to the Minister of Labor. It is provided that each interested party be represented on the Board of Investigation, of which the third member is chairman, and must be a judge of a court of record and appointed by joint recommendation of the other two members, or by the Minister of Labor. The Board is vested with all the powers of a court of record in civil cases. Such investigation is expected to get at facts and make them public, recognizing the moral sense of the community as a compelling force. But provision is made also for penalties, when required. If it be shown that a combine as to any article is facilitated by customs duties, the Governor in Council may reduce or remit the duty. Where it is established that rights under the Patent Act are used to monopolistic ends, the Exchequer Court may revoke the patent. If a company operating under the Inland Revenue Act attempts to establish a monopoly, the Dominion Government may revoke its license. For similar reason, bounty or subsidy may be withdrawn.

TRUST STATUTES AND THE COURTS.

Legislation and judicial decisions were the methods of regulation of trusts discussed by GILBERT H. MONTAGUE, Esq. Legislation had been in response to the demands of consumers against exorbitant prices and of business men against oppression by rivals.

Anti-trust legislation should determine what acts interfere with competition, and then define those acts. The motive for trade competition is the enjoyment of temporary relief, through success, from its struggle. But defeat of one competitor cannot be extended to all so long as the field is open. The mere largeness of a business does not make it a monopoly. Statutory regulation of public service companies has succeeded because they enjoy powers conferred by the State. They are natural, as well as legal, monopolies. The State can enforce upon them the duty to serve all, adequately, without discrimination and upon reasonable terms. The evil lies in the misuse of the means of competition. The legitimate competitor seeks to excel his rival in efficiency. The illegitimate competitor employs instead threats and other unlawful means. There were suggestions as to definition in the language of court decisions. The effectiveness of definitions would prohibit improper interference with free competition.

First Day—Afternoon Session.

CORPORATIONS AND CIVILIZATION.

In taking the Chair at the afternoon session of Thursday, Hon. OSCAR S. STRAUS emphasized the importance of the topic as one affecting the life of the people in all civilized countries. In such a body as The National Civic Federation the question could be discussed with a freedom of thought and of expression which would instruct public opinion and guide legislation. It was through his association with this organization and through the advantages of its discussions that he had perceived the breadth and the several sides of the subject; and such, he thought, had been the effect upon many minds. Mr. Straus called upon Mr. Edgar A. Bancroft, General Counsel of the International Harvester Company.

SUPERVISION AND PUBLICITY.

The regulations of the Sherman act were analyzed by EDGAR A. BANCROFT, Esq. He considered that the attempt to regulate railroad rates by compulsory competition should be abandoned. Rates should be based, not upon cost of service alone, but upon the character and value of the articles carried. The present need is authority to enter into agreements toward uniformity in classification and rate-making, subject to the approval of the Commission. The need is to prohibit any consolidation having for its purpose issues of new securities rather than increased transportation efficiency, and also against engaging in other business. For industrial and commercial corporations, competition must be preserved. The two points to be secured are fair prices and fair dealing toward competitors. The scope of manufacturing and trading corporations is national. The provisions of the Sherman act are appropriate for constitutional rather than for practical application. It is a masterpiece of prohibition rather than a remedy. He cited the Canadian act as pointing to the need of a Federal incorporation act. Uniformity in State laws as to corporations seems doomed to failure, as local sentiment diverges. Whether incorporation under Federal law should be voluntary or not is debatable. The benefit of Federal supervision is shown by the National banks. Publicity is needed, which should be prompt and automatic. If all other methods prove inefficient, then the State will attempt positive regulation of methods, prices and profits. "There is ground for this assurance: the corporation which conducts its business honestly and fairly, with a scrupulous regard for the moral rights of the public and of competitors, is not in serious danger of destruction or injury, but the ruthless, unfair and oppressive corporation will surely come to grief."

THE ECONOMIC ASPECT.

Professor JEREMIAH W. JENKS, of Cornell University, chose as his topic "The Economic Basis of Corporation Law." He declared that economists, while not questioning the legal learning and patriotic good faith of the Supreme Court in its early decisions under the Sherman Anti-Trust Act, thought it clear that the Court had not recognized the benefits as well as the evils that might come from the business conditions under which great corporations and combinations had grown up. Early decisions of both Federal and State courts had taken as precedents the English common law, precedents of a time when the so-called national monopolies of the present day were non-existent. The principles then laid down would need to be modified when applied to modern conditions. Even under the English common law, contracts in restraint of trade, if clearly in the public interest, were enforceable. It is now recognized that in natural monopolies there can be no competition. Economic conditions as to legislation regarding great corporations are substantially the same throughout the country. Different types of legislation are not needed in different sections. Under the Constitution most of the corporation laws must be those of States. Many of these laws have been made so drastic that in blocking possible evil they have killed certain good, by driving capital, enterprise and some business brains out of the State. More careful study of economic conditions might make it possible to prevent the evil while retaining the good. In other instances, the desire to attract capital has caused States to permit companies to incorporate upon such terms as to injure other States. Congress cannot act to restrain evils in interstate business to the best advantage unless it keeps business conditions always in the foreground. "If there were uniformity of our State laws we could easily control the capitalization of corporations." Promotors of corporations could be controlled in their acts, directors could be held to proper responsibility; the interests of stockholders could be guarded by requiring reports accurate and sufficiently complete; mergers could be regulated or prevented in accordance with public policy; unwise double taxation could be prevented. Under certain circumstances, we should not be afraid even to legalize monopoly, putting it positively under public control. Under other circumstances, by recognizing conditions we shall know how to block monopoly that is injurious. In all cases, conditions must be recognized.

A BUSINESS MAN'S PROGRAM.

"A Business Man's Program of Government Regulation," was the title of a paper by JAMES T. YOUNG, director, Wharton School of Finance and Commerce, in the University of Pennsylvania. He considered that the difficulties warrant the formation of a new group of legislative committees from the business associations, which should agree on fundamental principles for a program. It is necessary for the great industries to educate the people upon the industrial needs and facts of the time. Prices should be fixed by combinations and agreements between producers. That is contrary to present Government policy, but is essential to business progress and stability. Steady prices are more essential than low prices, else fluctuations in cost of production must be increasingly harmful to all business enterprise. But there must be Government supervision and control of prices and combinations. There should be enforced strict rules of credit and protection against fraud.

SCIENTIFIC MANAGEMENT—EFFICIENCY.

"Justice, Common Sense and the Pay Roll," was the subject of Mr. HARRINGTON EMERSON, introduced as an expert upon economy. He proposed a scheme that he claimed would mean higher earnings, lower labor cost, increased output and employment for more workers. He declared that "piece work is so bad in practice that I have yet to see a single good example of it." Piece work speeds men and women beyond endurance, and he had seen girls overwork until vitality was sapped. His scheme involved "time equivalents for all operations," just as dairymen determine the yield and cost of each cow, or a liveryman keeps a separate account for each horse. Promotion should go to workers according to efficiency. One who exceeded the standard fixed by those qualified should be promoted. Thus he would stimulate production by rewards for increased individual effort, a plan which he presented in detail and which was regarded as another plan for "speeding" workers.

WORKING TO CAPACITY.

Mr. H. L. GANTT, industrial expert, presented a paper upon "Industrial Efficiency." He asserted that the unions had increased generally the price of labor without increasing the output. In manufacturing, the plan of Mr. Gantt involved keeping an individual record of each worker. Machines should be arranged so that a foreman could supervise a group and the work of each man. Then he would pay a bonus to each man who did the full task called for in any day, and a bonus to the foreman, or "speed boss," for each man under him that performed the required task. To quote: "If the work is done within the time allowed by the expert, and is up to the standard for quality, the workman receives extra compensation in addition to his day's pay. If it is not done in the time set, or not up to the standard for quality, the workman receives his day's pay only." Still another feature is that a further bonus is paid the foreman if all the men under him make bonus. Thus, to quote again, "A foreman having ten men under him would get 10 cents each, or 90 cents total, if nine of his men made bonuses; but 15 cents each, or $1.50 total, if all ten made bonuses. The additional 60 cents * * * made him devote his energies to those of his men who most needed them." As a result, a superintendent reported, "We have furnished the automatic incentive for men to work up to their capacity." This Mr. Gantt terms "intelligent selfishness." The "task setter" teaches the workman "to do the work in the time and manner specified," otherwise, no bonus for him nor for the workman. An additional bonus for performing the work in less than the given time places before the workman "an incentive to do as much work as possible." The bonus to the foreman "made him devote his energies to those of his men who most needed them."

THE LOCOMOTIVE ENGINEER.

Mr. WARREN S. STONE, Grand Chief of the International Brotherhood of Locomotive Engineers, spoke upon the efficiency system from the point of view of a "graduate of the school of hard knocks," having spent twenty-three years in the cab of a locomotive. He declared that his Brotherhood stood for efficiency, as proved by its record during forty-seven years, a statement that would be corroborated by the management of the railroads throughout the country. The Brotherhood would fight against the bonus system. On a limited passenger train, the piston packing blows out, the engineer is required in a cloud of steam to make time. The trouble was that the machinist who put in that packing was working on a bonus. If he could put it in in twenty minutes, instead of thirty or forty minutes, he would get a premium, but would have slighted the work. The traveling public is interested, because sometimes the engineer who is hurt takes some of the passengers with him. Engineers want the best work possible; they do not want piece work and they do not want some man to be paid a bonus to slight his job. The labor union does not oppose efficiency of the man. In all of these efficiency and bonus systems, one contends with the fact that men are not all alike. There is somewhere a point where men reach the maximum of output. There is no business in the world managed upon so close a margin as that of the American railroads and yet we are told by Mr. Brandeis that they could save a million dollars a day! But he never designed a locomotive. He never shoveled coal into a locomotive, and yet he says that half that coal could be saved. "Who's Who in America" states that Mr. Brandeis is a very able, highly accomplished attorney of Boston, who gives his talents and services free to help the downtrodden and oppressed, but he appeared in Washington as the attorney for the Shippers' Association. Does he think the shippers are oppressed? They are the people who have been reaping the benefits of rebates while they themselves do not pay a dollar of the freight. Any one who comes before the bar of public opinion should come with clean hands. Justice is the cornerstone of the Brotherhood of Locomotive Engineers. It has no strife with the employer and it is opposed to the bonus system.

BONUS PLAN DENOUNCED.

Mr. JOHN MITCHELL expressed his belief that any system claiming the title of "Efficiency" should be presented undisguised. He doubted a theory claiming to increase wages and production at the expense of less work. The purpose of such a system should be frankly stated to be the increase of profits; but the working people would have something to say about an alluring plan that promises less work and more wages. He had read a prediction by Mr. Taylor, the father of this system of efficiency, that the wage-earners would drop the labor union for the plan of a bonus, but he declared this prophecy groundless. The bonus was but another form of the piece-work system. Working people of experience had rejected it. Mr. James Hill, President of the Great Northern Railroad, after experience called the plan "bosh." The attraction of additional pay is an incentive to overwork, but under this system the bonus is divided between foreman and worker, so that it is to the interest of the foreman to drive the worker. But there is a fundamental objection. The worker needs no initiative, no exercise of intelligence. He simply becomes part of the machine. To substitute monotony for pleasure in work makes work drudgery and means deterioration both of worker and of work. The employer may determine for himself the basis, moved by the desire to pay as little wages as he can. The better way is for employers and wage-earners, individually or collectively, to determine mutually the wages, hours and conditions of labor. The best condition of industry is that of agreement by mutual consent and not dictated by one or the other. The assertion that the railroads of the country could save a million dollars a day was as absurd as was the statement that the Government by scientific management could save $300,000,000 in one year, when it was discovered that the Government did not spend that amount in the departments where it was to be saved. "The working people will reserve to themselves the right of having something to say in determining what conditions of industry are good for them; and we suggest that the advantages of the new theory of efficiency be presented not in the name of the wage-earners, but in the name of the manufacturers, because the system is not acceptable to the wage-earners and should not be put forward as their friend."

Second Day—Morning Session.

UNIFORM LEGISLATION.

The sessions of the second day were devoted to "Need for Uniform State Legislation," upon "Taxation," "Banking," "Insurance," "Pure Food and Drugs," "Reform in Legal Procedure," "Regulation of Corporations," and the "Commercial Bills of the Uniform State Law Commissioners." The opening address was made by the Hon. ALTON B. PARKER, who emphasized the common interest that binds together the family of States. There was no reason why the citizens of one State should try to take advantage of the citizens of another. The highest interest of all requires working together for the common good. When the American Bar Association years ago took up the subject of uniformity of law they had in mind, not local questions, but commercial paper, for example, as to which the law should be the same in every State. The first work of these patriotic men was the negotiable instruments law. They succeeded in creating the Commissioners of Uniform Laws, made up to-day of three representatives from each State. The work which they did, in connection with a committee of the American Bar Association, was stupendous and was performed solely with the purpose of doing their duty as citizens. There should be a uniform corporation law in the United States. There is no reason why a few States, for the selfish purpose of local revenue, should be permitted to authorize corporations with charters so broad that the great majority of the States would not think of granting them. This subject was considered at several meetings and it was determined that The National Civic Federation should aid the American Bar Association through the momentum of public attention and interest. One result was the great convention at Washington, where about 600 delegates, representing State and National organizations, held an interesting meeting of three days. Its effect was to arouse interest, not alone in the importance of the questions discussed, but in the practicability of the movement, and there was laid the foundation of accomplishment. After that convention there was devised machinery for effective organization, consisting mainly of State Councils composed of public-spirited men, in thirty-five States, representing every interest; and he predicted that a State Council in every State would make it clear that there would be efficient and generous support of the movement.

REFORM IN LEGAL PROCEDURE.

The next topic of consideration was "Reform in Legal Procedure," and the first speaker was Ralph W. Breckenridge, of Omaha. He reviewed in detail the discussions between the committees of The National Civic Federation and of the American Bar Association in New York City, May 31 and June 1, 1910, and at Chattanooga August 29, 1910, and placed upon record the principles there formulated. He thought that some of these principles might in certain jurisdictions require constitutional amendments. He declared that the proportions of the task should not be underestimated. It encountered both the spirit of conservatism and unwillingness on the part of lawyers to make criticism of a system that might be construed as criticism of the courts. There was no intention to provoke expressions of disrespect for the judiciary, but to magnify the law and to do away with hindrances and embarrassments to its administration, and which themselves provoke popular dissatisfaction with the administration of justice. He considered that when a system of procedure should do away with technicalities of practice and useless appeals, the people will recall with wonder and disgust the chains they wore under the present system.

COMMERCIAL BILLS.

Hon. AMASA M. EATON, of Rhode Island, former Chairman of the Commissioners on Uniform Laws, discussed the project of Commercial Bills, formulated by that Commission. He explained the method of work. The Commissioners meet in conference each year, when the American Bar Association is in session. All are lawyers, but they employ upon each particular subject the most competent expert they can find. Each expert takes years to prepare a draft of a bill, with a study of the law on that subject in each State; a study of decisions under those respective laws; weighing of the principles involved in conflicting decisions and embodying the best of them in an act. Each Summer a draft of the act is submitted in the rough, with annotations. Each section is discussed in committee of the whole. By argument and amendment each section is made more nearly final. The committee of the whole reports each section to the conference and then a vote is taken, usually by States, each State having one vote. Nearly always the final vote is unanimous. During successive years editions are printed and distributed widely among representatives of all interests affected. The acts that have been framed are upon Uniform Negotiable Instruments, which have been adopted in thirty-eight States and Territories and in the District of Columbia; upon Uniform Sales, adopted in eighteen States; upon Uniform Bills of Lading, involving many different and conflicting interests, a subject upon which the Interstate Commerce Commission has arrived at some conclusions, and the act on Partnership, which has been six years in moulding and is not finished yet. Unexpected phases develop and unanticipated difficulties are encountered in the work. During eight years, as President of the Commissioners, Mr. Eaton delivered an annual address, including a summary of decisions in all the States under the Uniform Negotiable Instruments Act. These show the necessity of uniform decisions, for which it is necessary that the judges of the different States must familiarize themselves with the decisions of other States under the same law. This has not been done, particularly in the State of New York. It is necessary that counsel study this law and the decisions, thus aiding the Court to rise to the new jurisdictive conception of uniform legislation. There are cases under this act in which no reference whatever is made to it. In other cases, judges have cited old cases instead of the provision in the statute book before them. There is need that lawyers awaken enthusiasm for this new kind of common law, common to all States.

INTERSTATE INSURANCE.

The topic of "Insurance," and its need for uniformity in legislation, was announced by the Chairman, who introduced ROBERT LYNN COX, President of the National Association of Life Insurance Presidents. Mr. Cox pointed out that every correction of a great evil was of slow growth. The present serious consideration of uniformity in State laws is caused largely by changing social conditions and material surroundings. A man in Chicago may direct branches of his business in Kansas City and in New York. State lines still exist, as they should, technically and for governmental purposes, but from a practical and business standpoint, they should not. To make laws uniform is like opening gateways in a wall, to the obvious advantage of those on both sides. The problem in the insurance business is merely a part of the great problem confronting business activities generally. The highest court of our land has held that insurance is not commerce. Essential to the interest of policy-holders, one-fifth of our population, is that the business extend, limited only by strict State supervision. Insurance should cover many occupations and classes, and a large number of individuals, so as to make an uncertain ratio a certainty. Companies should extend their business to cover many localities and a variety of living conditions. It is important that companies shall be allowed to extend their fields of investment, so that calculations shall not be disturbed by local losses. Large companies can be created only by insuring a larger number of people than can be obtained by one company in one State. Life insurance is interstate business, and life insurance companies are interstate institutions. Economy of administration would be increased by uniform laws. It has been calculated that in one life insurance association compliance with conflicting State laws costs policy-holders more than a million dollars each year.

FACTORY AND LABOR LAWS.

HON. JOHN WILLIAMS, Commissioner of Labor in New York, was introduced to speak upon "Need for Uniformity in Factory and Labor Legislation." He pointed out that legislation affecting labor, when not uniform, might affect unfavorably an industry in one State in competition with the same industry in another State. Thus restriction of hours of labor might impair productivity as compared with the result of less restriction in another State. There should be uniformity in the requirements for safeguarding of life and limb. But statutes requiring the safeguarding of machinery in some States are conspicuously absent in others. Then there are differences in administration and in application. It is essential to make a serious attempt to secure uniformity that shall guarantee equal safety to the operative in every part of the Union, making an equal condition in competition. New York has as good a code of labor laws as can be found in any other State. But they are not perfect; there is no inclination to stop and we hope that The National Civic Federation and kindred bodies will continue to urge upon legislatures uniform enactments.

UNIFORM LAWS ON DRUGS.

Uniform Legislation for the Drug Trade was the subject discussed by WILLIAM J. SCHIEFFELIN, President of the National Wholesale Druggists' Association. The two phases of this topic of interest to the public, he said, are the quality of the drugs sold and the restriction of habit-forming drugs. The use of opium in the United States is as great per capita as in the Chinese Empire. The importation is probably eight times as much as can be used legitimately. Opium and morphine are more prevalent than is cocaine. More stringent regulations as to cocaine are needed. Even five offenders out of 2,200 druggists in New York City can do much harm. When such men learn that they are watched they will import cocaine from other States. To stop this the Foster bill in Congress requires every dealer in morphine, opium or cocaine to take out a license, and that an internal revenue stamp be put upon every package sold and an accurate record kept of every sale and purchaser, so that the drug can be traced. For all this uniform State legislation is needed. The National Wholesale Druggists' Association has for years favored uniform State food and drug laws. These should not vary from the National law, which does not require the weight or measure to be stated on labels on packages of food, but only that if stated they must be plainly and correctly stated. A manufacturer cannot tell where the goods he sells will be eventually retailed. This subject affects the interests, not only of manufacturers and dealers, but also of consumers, since the latter have to pay the cost of conforming with conflicting State laws.

PURE FOOD AND DRUGS.

DR. HENRY H. RUSBY, Dean of the School of Pharmacy, Columbia University, discussed "Some Obstacles to the Purification of Our Food and Drug Supplies." The present condition of these he described as far from satisfactory, but hopeful to the degree of assurance. The objection to an impure food or drug may lie against its being used at all, or only against a particular use. For example, polluted food or a drug that has lost activity or that has acquired an undesired activity should not be used at all. But in a shipment of sugar with 50 per cent of clean sand, it would be morally wrong to waste the sugar. The sand can be removed, a perfect product resulting. To sell the mixture for sugar would be as wrong as to waste it. From belladonna leaves containing only half the percentage of atropine required by the legal formula, the atropine may be extracted, thus preventing the total loss of that crop. But what means is there to determine that the importation will be so used? The fact that an article differs from the standard may be "plainly stated" upon the label, but in language utterly meaningless to the consumer. This may apply to food as well as to drugs. An important contention over this principle is pending in Pennsylvania, where the statute requires that the "plain statement" be fully intelligible to the consumer, while the Federal statute imposes no such requirement. An importer may obligate himself under bond to restrict an article to its proper use. But when the goods are in his possession he may evade in various ways. An importation, once it has reached the State where it is to be consumed, is beyond Federal jurisdiction. The result as to its use will depend upon the local law, which varies and also differs in administration. It is a general, but vital mistake, to assume that physicians are qualified for this work, when, in fact, they know little more about drugs than men in other professions. The study of drugs in medical schools has been practically abandoned. Pharmacy should be accorded a much higher position. Not all pharmacists, however, are unworthy of their trust. Competent pharmacists can be found to co-operate with physicians upon boards of drug control. When fraudulent products, excluded from one State, are dumped into others, the percentage of injury will rise in the latter communities.

UNIFORM COURT DECISIONS.

The reform of pleading and of judicial procedure is a subject that the HON. THOMAS W. SHELTON, of Virginia, considered of interest to the people who are taking the last interest, the business man. The day has passed when one State can be a law unto itself. A man in New York may transact business intimately connected with industries in West Virginia, or Carolina, or Vermont. But any law in one State affecting wages is bound to affect the ultimate cost and output and so becomes a factor in competition. If uniformity of law is important, uniformity of court decisions is of greater importance, since pleading and practice are the vehicles of enforcing law. It is the spigot that determines the quantity and quality of the water drawn from a reservoir, of whatever size and quality. To-day, every representative of human endeavor has left pleading and procedure to the lawyers. It is absolutely unjust to say that lawyers stir strife. But if they are able to gain ground, even through technicalities, it is their sworn duty so to do. The time has come to be fair. The plan suggested here is good, and it is no departure from general principles. Our forefathers adopted the common law of England, and that law has watched over the liberties of America. Procedure in England, modified to this date, is as old as English civilization, and as new as the latest idea. It were better to follow that plan rather than a new code. Let the Court of Appeals prepare this system, or let the Supreme Court of the United States prepare it during the coming Summer.

Second Day—Afternoon Session.

WORKMEN'S COMPENSATION.

The fourth session of the meeting, on Friday afternoon was devoted to compensation of workingmen injured in industrial accidents. The Chairman of the committee delegated to draft a bill upon this subject, for the promotion of uniformity in legislation, opened the program.

RELIEF FOR INDUSTRIAL ACCIDENTS.

P. TECUMSEH SHERMAN, Esq., presented an explanatory statement upon a draft bill reported by the legal committee, the scope of which he defined to be to "provide prompt, certain and just relief to the victims of industrial accidents and their dependents, without unnecessary hardship to employers, and, if possible, to reduce the economic waste and public burden of accident litigation." The problem was to present a practical measure which, if put into effect in the immediate future, "would do the most good with the least incidental harm and serve as a basis for future progress and development." He enumerated as essential to a correct conclusion "the history and principles of our law of master and servant, of the various forms of compensation law and of our constitutional law, the status of public opinion as to the justice and necessity of a change to compensation or insurance, and the industrial conditions upon which the practicability and desirability of each particular form of compensation law depends." In accordance with that analytical outline, Mr. Sherman observed that, stated broadly, the common law involves the rule of the assumption of risks and assumes that wages in hazardous employments are higher in proportion to the hazard, so as to compensate for such risks. But it is now recognized generally that both of these premises are economically false, and consequently that "the assumption of risks rule, along with its corollary the fellow-servant rule, is unjust." To remedy this injustice the common law has been modified by statutes which limit those rules and impose upon the employer uncertain or impossible duties. Their practical effect has been to increase uncertainty and expense to employers, and to waste in legislation the money paid, leaving relief to the injured as slow and uncertain as before. "The law seeks concrete rather than abstract justice * * * and should therefore seek a rule which, however comparatively less just in theory, will result in a higher average degree of concrete justice in practice. That rule is to be found in the basis of the compensation laws of Europe." Mr. Sherman reviewed the form of compensation law, applying only to the most dangerous industries, and in the majority of European countries and in Great Britain and its colonies; discussed compulsory insurance, taking the German system as the best so far devised, but as not feasible in the United States because of its paternalism, which is forbidden by our constitutions. Yet it were well to have in mind an approximation to the German system, as an ideal. But as a practical first step, it is necessary to turn to the simple compensation laws, of which system the English is the best example. The English compensation law has been extended, in the act of 1906, to cover practically all employments, not casual. This action was in response to general public belief; and the extended liability to employers became a subject of insurance. The law has worked satisfactorily, in general, but it has led to discrimination in employment against the aged, infirm and defective and those of unknown health and habits. The better opinion is that the extent of this evil is serious. A doubtful constitutional question, underlying all forms of compensation law, is whether it is "due process of law" to impose upon an employer a predetermined liability for the consequences of an accident beyond his reasonable powers of prevention.

It is a great constitutional risk to make the employer liable presumptively for compensation for all accidents in the employment. But the great constitutional difficulty, about which there is most divergence, is whether it is safer to restrict compensation for injuries to the more dangerous industries. The employer must be made liable only pursuant to some reasonable public necessity. The greater the evil, the more justifiable is the exercise of the police power. But among the objections is that a law limited to the more hazardous industries would be held to offend against the constitutional prohibition of "unreasonable discrimination between persons or classes." Mr. Sherman cited decisions in support of this view, but pronounced the weight of opinion to be "strongly in favor of the proposition that incidental and unavoidable discriminations resulting from a reasonable and correct classification by industries do not constitute *unreasonable* discriminations." It is to be assumed: (1) that those who have studied the subject are generally in favor of some change in existing law in the direction of compensation or insurance; (2) that the general public are not yet familiar with the subject; and (3) that the demand for immediate relief is acute only in the great dangerous industries, there being no pressing demand from such classes of employes as clerks, stenographers, domestic servants, salesmen. To these conditions, the draft bill here submitted is the answer proposed. "The bill contains the outlines and essential provisions of a *simple compensation law*, without compulsory insurance." It applies only to the more dangerous industries enumerated; only to workmen earning less than $1,800 a year; excepts injuries shown to be due to certain moral faults of the injured workmen; provides that for an accident due to the personal fault of the employer the injured workman may either accept compensation or sue the employer for damages at common law. The provision for compensation aims to pay approximately one-half the estimated loss of wages, with limitations dictated by public policy. For fatal injury, dependents are to receive a lump sum equal to four years' wages, but never to exceed $3,000. The payment of one-half wages is not to exceed $10 a week or to continue more than ten years. The employer is required to furnish medical and surgical service as necessary, not to cost more than $100. The employer may attend the physical examination of claimants. In this bill, the English rates of compensation are about doubled. The exclusion of small employers, as in Massachusetts, is objectionable because it has no relation to danger and because it imposes a fact hard to prove. Mr. Sherman summarized the reasons for the procedure. He regarded the best method of accomplishing the purpose to be voluntary benefit associations, established and maintained in whole or in part by the employer or associations of employes. Mr. Sherman specified the principal differences between this bill and the New York Compulsory Compensation Law of 1910. Mr. Sherman explained that no member of the committee was prevented from dissenting from the bill in general or particular. It is offered merely as a sketch model from which to frame a law. Mr. Sherman concluded: "We must make a move toward compensation soon. Otherwise we will continue, with ever-increasing impetus, down the broad way of the Employers' Liability laws, which lead to social destruction."

ANDREW CARNEGIE FOR COMPENSATION.

In response to the request of the Chairman. ANDREW CARNEGIE declared that no proposition could be sounder than that injuries occurring in dangerous pursuits should be considered a part of the cost of production. The lawyers may perfect the details of such a law, but employers should know the practical effect. Insurance against accidents is a step in the right direction in the relations between employer and employed, and it is a proof of progress and of improvement in the relation between capital and labor, of which it is to be said: "The more the employer does for labor, the more profit he makes." The evidence that the employer has a heart and recognizes what he owes to his workmen means that in time of trouble employer and employe are devoted friends. The foundation of nine out of ten strikes is not wages, but that the right man is not in the right place. The employer ought to know his men, or at least their leaders, and when he sits down with them and wants to do the fair thing there is little trouble. When a man knows that he will be cared for in case of accident in the service of an employer, and all the men know the same thing, and the law is there to enforce it, all that is more beneficial for capital than for the working man himself. Employers cannot go too far in this direction, even from the economic standpoint. Uniform legislation is desirable, yet Mr. Carnegie believed that the employer who paid for accidents when others did not is not at a disadvantage, because of his finer relations with the men. Nevertheless, it is well to strive for uniform legislation. He thought that the United States Steel Company, from which he is retired, had acted with great liberality. Of the five millions of dollars that he left to the workmen when he retired, four millions were for pensions for old persons when they had to retire. Recently the company, in accordance with the suggestion of Mr. Carnegie that the idea be extended, had added eight millions of dollars to the fund, so that there are now, at 5 per cent, two thousand dollars a day to pension the old men who have served faithfully and must retire. They have also provided against accidents on a scale that they are not compelled to follow. Any general law upon the subject would of course make it necessary to adjust present arrangements. Mr. Carnegie gave the measure under consideration his hearty approval.

PRESIDENT ROOSEVELT ON AUTOMATIC INDEMNITY FOR INJURY

The former President of the United States, THEODORE ROOSEVELT, upon being presented by Chairman Low, declared that this organization realized his desire "to see radicalism prosper under conservative leadership." He felt it absolutely essential to the welfare of this country that there should be progressive action among the people and government. To stand still is to go backwards; but to go off in a spiral, to one side, is not going forward at all. He would see progress made in the spirit of Abraham Lincoln, who was a radical progressive compared to the schools of Buchanan and Fillmore, but who was denounced as a timid conservative by those who denounced the Constitution and who described Abraham Lincoln as the "slave hound of Illinois." Mr. Roosevelt would have the great movement for betterment go forward so that no step need be retraced. He would see labor legislation undertaken always in consequence of a good understanding between the wise leaders of labor and men who favor what is good for any of the people of our common country. He cited an address upon Conservatism in which Dr. Eliot had said in effect that not only must government in this country do more compared with what is left to be done by the individual than formerly, but it must work more often on a national scale. Increase in collective activity must take place notably in two ways, first in the attitude of the public toward the aggregations of wealth used in business. The man who, in conjunction with others, enlarges his business from that of a retail butcher or grocer so as to deal in railroads or whatever it is on a scale that covers States becomes too big for any one to deal with in his individual capacity. We must ship and travel by his trains. Therefore, we face a situation where the other man has the entire power and yet where our need of dealing with him is absolute. This situation was utterly unknown a century and a quarter ago. There is only one popular artificial entity able to deal on behalf of all of us and that is Uncle Sam. He must have the power to guarantee the corporation against injustice and to exact justice in return. It must be to the interest of the corporation to do business, not merely for its sake, but for ours, and on the other hand we must have power to see that the corporation does justice to us. The use of the collective power of the people through the Government is more necessary than ever in dealing with great corporations, alike from the standpoint of the general public and from the standpoint of the employes of corporations. Changes in modern industrialism are most evident in the relations between employer and employed—first in the power of the employer and in the knowledge that one has of the other; and second, in the connection between the men serving together under the employer. A century and a quarter ago, an employer could not be very harsh, because the employe could easily go elsewhere; he could go and take up a farm for himself. Moreover, there was an intimate personal relationship between the employer and employe which usually made any interference beween them by the law unnecessary. Second, very little analogy can be drawn beween fellow servants under the old system and under the present system, and legal decisions, which follow Eighteenth rather than Twentieth Century precedent, enforcing a line of action which works cruel injustice at the present time. So the misused doctrine of liberty of contract exhausts patience. A wage-earner may face the necessity to work or starve; then it is right that the State shall decline to recognize a liberty that is merely fictitious and to recognize any contract made under such conditions against his welfare. In legislation as to compensation to the injured, America has lagged behind every nation of any size of the industrial type in the world. In industry we face the same certainty of loss of life and limb as in war. The chance of loss of life to the workman in putting up a steel building is greater than it was to any soldier in a battle in the Spanish war. As in war, the burden of injury should not fall wholly upon his wife and children. The whole public should pay and the payment will be distributed if we make the employer responsible for the loss to the man. The right to sue is not just either to the employe, to whose lawyer the chief benefit may go; it is not just to the employer because the jury, through sentiment, may award excessive damages. The workman should receive automatically indemnification for injury, at once, and the business should be able to tell in advance its liability. The loss should be treated as part of the risks of the trade. The Nation should take care of all its employes who are maimed in its work. An alien employed in Panama was crippled for life and was actually shipped to his own country because he had lost the power of self-support. Such an incident must cause indignation. The work on the canal, the way the men have been housed and looked after as to amusement may give us national pride; yet we are powerless to do justice in such a case. Let us then endeavor to secure just workmen's compensation acts, which shall affect all Government employes no less than those in private enterprise."

Second Day—Evening Session.

A SYMPOSIUM AT ANNUAL DINNER.

In opening the discussion following the annual dinner of the Federation, on the evening of January 13, PRESIDENT LOW spoke of the addition of strength resulting from the organization of twenty-four State Councils. The other great movement had been for compensation for injured workmen. He introduced UNITED STATES SENATOR CUMMINS, of Iowa, who spoke upon "The Regulation of Interstate Commerce," basing his discussion largely upon competition as fixing prices and limiting profits. The question was whether some other force for the distribution of profits and wealth should be substituted for competition. If competition is to give way it must be to altruistic co-operation. Nothing could be more naturally selfish than combinations of both corporations and wage-earners. The result of these conditions must be that "in capital, monopoly will become complete," but that will not be so with labor, because of its immediate necessities. It is clear that labor unions are not a menace, because they will never obtain more than their just share of the fruits of toil. Hence he believed that the sole regulation of labor organizations should be to prevent interference with the rights of others, as is recognized by none more completely than by the laboring men themselves. Mr. Cummins summarized the passing of competition as a controlling factor and the arbitrary fixing of prices subject only to the homely idea of not killing the goose that lays the golden egg. But now and in the future the many will not be slaves to the few. "The sooner we recognize the imperative warning that we must have universal competition or that we will have universal co-operation, the more certainly will we avert the disasters which always follow universal discontent." The Anti-Trust law is not to be disparaged. But he favored a direct regulation of those engaged in interstate commerce, which should provide a Federal tribunal with power to limit the capital employed. Thus would be introduced into every field of production and sale the competition which the Anti-Trust law is powerless to preserve.

COMPENSATION AND PREVENTION.

The chairman introduced AUGUST BELMONT, who spoke upon the work of the Department on Compensation for Industrial Accidents and their Prevention. He explained the processes of gathering information in order to formulate recommendations. The work as to Compensation was referred to a Legal Committee, with instructions to draft a tentative bill, and also to a Committee on Statistics and Cost. The question of the Prevention of Industrial Accidents was referred to a third subcommittee, whose work has been primarily in the direction of factory inspection. He emphasized the purpose, as to Compensation, to form a bill likely to meet with favorable attention in State Legislatures. He summarized the reasons for restricting the bill to hazardous industries, and pointed out that it would not interfere with existing agreements, provided they do not prescribe rates less than those of the bill. The measure is not intended to be academic, but purely practical. He pointed out that if the measure should prove invalid, the State would revert automatically to the old liability and common law provisions. The committee offers an entering wedge, subject to the processes of time and further consideration.

LEWIS PARKER, Chairman of the State Council of the Civic Federation in South Carolina, emphasized the absence of sectionalism. He recognized that accidents in industry are inevitable, and he believed in fair compensation and in the exercise of all proper means of prevention. By such a method he had reduced the cost of insurance. Due attention to prevention of accidents would lessen the number of injuries. He believed that every employer having a sense of duty considers what he may do that is best for those of whose welfare he should think. He believed that accidents could be largely reduced by the exercise of proper care. In his own experience, with a pay-roll of over $300,000 per pear, compensation for the injured had never exceeded $1,000 a year. The amount was charged to the account of ordinary costs.

MYRON T. HERRICK, former Governor of Ohio, and Chairman of the Federation's Ohio State Council, expressed his belief that proper compensation of the injured workman is a need more pressing than ever in the history of this country. Mr. Herrick referred with force to the influence that members of The National Civic Federation had had in the past in bringing about a better understanding between capital and labor, and expressed the opinion that the Federation would be equally successful in the present matter of compensation.

SAMUEL GOMPERS, called upon as a representative of labor in The National Civic Federation, declared that there is no other factor so powerful in the discussion of great problems as these regular gatherings. The complete address made by Mr. Gompers appears on page 11.

GEORGE W. PERKINS, of New York, thought it a pity that this audience could not step out and look at itself, for it was an inspiring and representative gathering. He paid a tribute to the memory of Senator Hanna. He thought the relation between labor and capital to be a very live issue, and one that demanded serious consideration. Agitation would lead to popular enlightenment. This is a get-together period throughout the world. Competition has become a deadly game. He believed that the strict application of honesty would make practical the substitution of co-operation for competition. The completion of the Panama Canal will place this country at the center of commercial development. He could not see how unregulated competition could go on. He thought evolution from competition to co-operation would be certain.

PRESIDENT LOW pointed out that the question of co-operation could not be limited to the United States, but involved foreign commercial relations. He called upon CHARLES L. JEWETT, of Indiana, who declared the question of industrial compensation to be urgent. In these days compensation by process of law was awkward and cumbersome. The principle is that who gives limb or life has contributed to production and is entitled to a return upon the investment.

OSCAR S. STRAUS, upon request of the chairman, said that it was simply his function to say the benediction. He thought that this representative gathering, in this banquet hall, showed a spirit of endeavor to bring about a fair understanding between capital and labor. All should look forward to equity, was his parting word.

Third Day—Morning Session.

INDUSTRIAL MEDIATION AND ARBITRATION.

At the opening of the sixth session of the meeting, January 14, PRESIDENT LOW called to the chair FREDERICK KLUMP, of Michigan, and chairman of

(Continued on pages 11 and 12)

R AND THE NATIONAL CIVIC FEDERATION

By SAMUEL GOMPERS

From the March AMERICAN FEDERATIONIST

Cullinan, presented to him by the mine operators.'" . . .

JOHN MITCHELL LIBELED.

The assertion that Vice-President Mitchell received a diamond ring as a present from the mine operators is the sort of statement the Socialist leaders can make without wincing when denouncing trade union representatives. The whole world at all interested in this matter knows that the ring in question was presented to John Mitchell by the members of the Mine Workers' Union as an expression of their appreciation of the great services he has rendered to them, and not by the mine operators. This piece of baseless vilification in Loeb DeLeon's paper is a key to the probable truth in any other assertion that paper has made or may ever make.

Day by day during The Civic Federation sessions, the *New York Call* treated its readers to a wild and whooping war-dance, with the meeting as its subject. The premeditated scream of derision and scorn reached the top note in every issue. Some of the headings in its articles were:

"Everybody Saved by Civic Federation;"
"Wolf and Lamb Lie Down Together;"
"Look Them Over;"
"Stone Defends Bosses;"
"Oh Joy! Labor Puts on its Dress Suit;"
"Andrew Carnegie and Theodore Roosevelt Josh the Noble Workingmen."

In the Call's descriptive matter of the meetings occur such passages as these:

SNEER AT WORKMEN'S COMPENSATION.

"Testimonia's about this compensation specific will be given by the celebrated African traveler, Theodore Roosevelt, who is looked upon as a young man with a future, and is even mentioned in certain circles as a likely incumbent for a certain wide, oh very wide, chair that might be vacated in Washington during the winter of 1912-13.

"Andrew Carnegie, famous in most American libraries, and also famous in certain Pittsburg slums, will also have a word to say in behalf of Dr. Belmont's specific for workingmen who lose a hand or foot, and sometimes their whole blamed life, in factory accidents." . . .

"Haven't you got a picture of Tim Healy and John Mitchell sitting down to a love feast with August Belmont and Marcus Marks?" . . .

"P. Tecumseh Sherman opened the afternoon session with a valiant effort to convince everybody that a workingmen's compensation law, built along the lines of the one which Belmont and John Mitchell had modelled for their guidance, would provide many immediate blessings and open the way for other and more 'progressive laws.'" . . .

"Chairman Straus, of Macy's department store, introduced Mitchell as 'a member of The Civic Federation who graduated from a labor union.' It looked like a big advance to Straus, who probably knows better than the general public all that it entails." . . .

"Marks here let the cat out of the bag by saying that at no time and in no instance have employers found strikebreakers profitable. The fact is, he said, the employers have as much abhorrence for a strikebreaker as the employes, because strikebreakers are expensive. The only way to do away with the strikebreakers, he thought, was mediation whenever a dispute between employers and employes arises."

"President Gompers said he didn't care who owned the trusts so long as they were run in the interest of the workingman—that is, partly in the interest of the workingman—far be it from him to interfere with dividends or anything else which Belmont and Straus are interested in." . . .

But it is the dinner of The Civic Federation which gives the Socialist leaders a toothache. The introduction to the *Call's* two column article of ripping, tearing, slashing, howling sarcasm descriptive of this function is as follows:

"The starving strikers of Tampa and Chicago, the merciless persecution sustained by organized labor in Los Angeles, the crushing of the men on August Belmont's subway five years ago, the thousand battles which labor has fought to wrest from capital a living by which it could maintain even decency were forgotten Friday night when the leading officials in America's biggest labor organization came in evening clot..es, glistening white shirt fronts and silk hats to one of the huge and luxurious dining rooms of the Hotel Astor, there to sit down, laugh and feast with the richest nabobs and capitalists in the world. It was the annual dinner of The National Civic Federation." . . .

And, again:

"But why mention these depressing things? Let us rather think of the splendid Broadway hotels, the fine dinners, the luscious music, the well-groomed men and women, and above all, the truly noble, humanitarian and Christian sentiments flowing as freely as the imported wines."

SOME SOCIALIST CONSISTENCY.

That sort of writing has its uses to an intelligent mind in betraying the estimate entertained by its authors of the grade of intellect and character of the readers to whom it is addressed. It is, in short, contemptible, because insincere and designed to stir up those meanest of passions, envy and the malice arising out of envy. This demagogy is inconsistent. That radicals may sit at the tables of the rich every day in the year is illustrated in the lives of a number of American Socialist leaders, whose incomes from their own labor are of the slenderest description; whose incomes, in fact, so often come from their wives. That Socialists may dine sumptuously while starvation plagues the poor is a spectacle to be seen wherever the Socialists have the price. Here is a touch of description (from the *Literary Digest*) of the concluding scenes at the World Congress of the Socialists at Copenhagen last December:

"At the conclusion, however, all shook hands and held a great reception. 'In short, it was a congress of compromise which ended in a dance.' Mr. Bourdeau thinks there was something droll in the sumptuousness of the supper given by the delegates at the 'magnificent town hall' of Copenhagen. He says the German Socialist paper *Vorwaerts* described 'the Pantagruelic sideboard,' on which figured 'hams and scarlet lobsters, and various choice dainties and delicacies which stood amid long-necked bottles.' 'We saw nothing of the cabbage-soup which Proudhon served out to his guests.' *L'Humanite* (Paris) protests against such luxury. 'To tell the truth,' cries Mr. Jaures in his paper, after sharing the good thing of 'the Pantagruelic sideboard,' 'I was ashamed to indulge in all this fine fare.' The innocent orgy, says this writer, concluded with a dance. To quote his words:

"'To the voluptuous measures of Viennese waltzes and couples joined arms and hands; round and round they whirled, and the god Cupid was one of the party. The congress ended in delight, for the most celebrated Socialists were to be seen and admired circling in the most frantic of farandoles. A fine comment on Bernstein's dictum "congresses are all humbug."'" . . . .

So it is seen that all this Indian war dance, this tomtom beating, these shrieks of horror, these imprecations, this attitudinizing by the Socialist leaders, is a hollow travesty on bad acting. It is the veriest and most transparent demagogical rot. It is politics run mad—untrue, unsound, insincere, contemptibly bad tactics supported by acting execrable to the last degree. What manner of man can be caught by it all?

HANDS CLASPED WITH UNION HATERS.

But why should C. W. Post and the other radicals of the Manufacturers' Association rail at organized labor and The Civic Federation? The Socialists are doing their work in this respect most faithfully. There is a striking similarity in the tone and phraseology in the attacks on the trade unionists and The Civic Federation in Post's advertisements and in the similar attacks of the Socialists. There are the same bitterness, the same baseless assertion, the same unreasonableness of attitude. Post, on inditing his most furious articles against the employers and organized workers who believe in systematized methods in endeavoring to maintain all possible industrial peace, might count with certainty on having them inserted without charge if he were to send them in some Socialist's name to the *Chicago Daily Socialist*, the *New York Call*, the *International Socialist Review*, the *Milwaukee Democratic Herald*, and the *New York Volkszeitung*, or the *New York Vorwaerts*. Post and the Socialists are in this instance the proverbial "strange bedfellows" that are made by politics, for in both these parties the animus of their onslaughts is a base form of politics which includes the weakening, if not the destruction, of the two institutions which stand in the way of their designs, namely, the trade union movement as governed by its present principles and The Civic Federation. It is really a fortunate thing for the trade union men in The Civic Federation that they can point on the one hand to the venomous Post and on the other to the bitter-tongued Socialists and direct the attention of the country to the resemblances between them, which are the reverse of flattering to either.

RADICAL EMPLOYERS' VIEW.

John Kirby, Jr., President of the National Association of Manufacturers, recently denounced The Civic Federation because Samuel Gompers and John Mitchell were "not only participants, but moving spirits in the movement as well as officers in good standing," and because of the "doctrines they preach." Kirby hoped the day was not far distant when The Civic Federation would "clear its literature of the union label." He quoted a manufacturer as telegraphing to him: "I am opposed to our sending delegates to Gompers' convention"—the annual meeting of The Civic Federation—and another as saying: "I agree absolutely with your action in declining to appoint delegates to The National Civic Federation of Gomperism," and another, "There ought to be some way to enlighten the innocent or assumed innocent members of The Civic Federation that they are the tools of organized labor." C. W. Post had the following, August, 1909: "*The Square Deal* has persistently called attention to the fact that The National Civic Federation has almost uniformly lent itself to the support of the 'Labor Trust' in its attacks on the industry of the country and the general welfare of the people. We can recall no instance in which it has failed to obey the wishes and behests of Gompers and Mitchell," etc. *The Square Deal*, the official organ of The National Association of Manufacturers, has this in an editorial, July, 1909:

"Mr. Mitchell, after having held on to his lucrative position as president of the Mine Workers' Union as long as he could, was taken to New York and given a six-thousand-dollar-a-year job with The National Civic Federation. It would not be at all surprising if, through the efforts of The Civic Federation, he were nominated and elected to Congress by one or other of the corrupt rings which control the political parties in New York City."

If either the Socialists or Kirby, Post and Company, were actuated by common sense and sincerity or even by the aim of getting at results equally desirable to both their organizations, they might well agree that one of them should carry on the work of smashing the trade unions and The Civic Federation. Each of them wants to do so, and both are carrying on their attacks with equal rancor. A trouble which both have brought upon themselves, however, is that the big general public clearly sees that both of them cannot be right in their charges at the same time, since the two sets of charges are contradictory in the extreme, and that hence there is but one motive—that of unworthy partisanship—at the bottom of the ravings which render the Socialists and the Post-Kirby combination equally ridiculous.

NO SACRIFICE OF PRINCIPLE.

Now, let us look for a while at The National Civic Federation as an established American institution. It has finished a decade of work in the national field. It is proper—it would seem to be a duty—of the average citizen of honest intentions to review the character of the work performed by that Federation and ask himself questions pertinent to its character as a useful agency in promoting the public welfare. Has it in any case betrayed public confidence or perverted the usefulness of trade unionism? Has it called on any representative of labor to sacrifice any of his principles, even the most radical? Has it made any stipulation to a labor man except that he should represent a bona fide labor organization? Has it or has it not the support of the body of representative labor men who joined it at the beginning? Have its enemies ever been strong enough to bring out a vote against it at any of the annual conventions of the American Federation of Labor? Has it or has it not confined itself in its general character to the work planned for it from the beginning? Has it gone into partisan politics? What has it done not in keeping with the character of a helpful remedial institution, within its proposed sphere of activity? Such questions as these outline the test by which its usefulness is to be measured.

The answer to these questions is to be found in the very columns of the Socialist newspapers reporting The Civic Federation conference. In its news matter, unavoidably interlarded with the screams of contempt and of objurgation injected by the biased Socialist reporters, the *Call* itself was obliged, notwithstanding the bad faith of its descriptions in general, to take notice, even if the briefest possible notice, of the various measures of helpfulness undertaken under the auspices of The Civic Federation.

Let us merely state some of the timely questions of national import and of import to labor, discussed at this January meeting, of which Governor Herbert S. Hadley, of Missouri, truly said: "There is no one topic on that list which has any political bias." Here are the subjects as contained in the circular announcing the meeting this year:

"The State Councils of the Federation, organized the past year in thirty-four States, will be represented by delegations. The importance of these State Councils is indicated by the fact that in nearly every instance the Governor presided over the initial meeting and nominated the members of the Council. At the annual meeting these councils will decide upon the subjects on which they will concentrate their efforts for uniform State legislation and their method of procedure. While at the National Conference on Uniform Legislation, held under the auspices of the Federation, uniformity was urged upon over fifty important subjects, the discussions at these meetings when the State Councils were organized centred largely around ten subjects, to wit: 'Regulation of Combinations and Trusts,' 'Regulation of Public Utilities,' 'Taxation,' 'Insurance,' 'Banking,' 'Compensation for Industrial Accidents,' 'Reform in Legal Procedure,' 'Pure Food and Drugs,' 'Uniformity in Good Roads Building and Automobile Regulations,' and the commercial bills of the Uniform State Law Commissioners." . . .

"The subjects for special consideration at the annual meeting will be 'Compensation for Industrial Accidents,' 'Regulation of Corporations, State and Federal,' 'Industrial Mediation and Arbitration.' "

A SAFEGUARD TO LABOR.

Is there any other national voluntary agency in the United States which has in hand the most difficult and complicated question of compensation for industrial accidents? Could it be possible that the interests in this matter of immediate importance to the working classes could be placed in more faithful and competent hands than those of John Mitchell, a Vice-President of the American Federation of Labor? At a time when there are specious and treacherous efforts being made by agencies inimical to trade unionism to divert compensation from a plane on which the best results may be obtained for all our workers, is it not well to have a man like John Mitchell always on guard to protect the interests of our wage-workers? It is to be kept in mind that the United States is behind all other civilized countries on this question; that an enormous amount of suffering is occasioned every day in America by reason of not having a compensation law. When compensation was up for discussion in Germany, were not the trade unionists as well as the Socialists of that country on hand to guard the interests of the working classes?

The "regulation of corporations, State and Federal," is at present in a state of chaos in this country. It would seem to us that, if Socialist programmes were to be supported intelligently, before the national ownership of monopolistic corporations could be brought about a large amount of work for the purposes of control must in the nature of things precede the wiping out of private ownership—if that is ever to come about. What practical efforts in this direction are the Socialists of this country making? Irrespective of radical reversals of ownership in railroads, is it not well that men representing all phases of opinion should come together and discuss this subject in its present situation? The Civic Federation furnishes the means of such discussion.

But what of The Civic Federation's attitude in the industrial field? Let its own declarations serve as the best answer. They are as follows:

"TO PROMOTE INDUSTRIAL PEACE."

"The scope and province of this department of The Civic Federation shall be to do what may seem best to promote industrial peace; to be helpful in establishing rightful relations between employers and workers; by its good offices to endeavor to obviate and prevent strikes and lockouts; to aid in renewing industrial relations where a rupture has occurred.

"That at all times representatives of employers and workers, organized or unorganized, should confer for the adjustment of differences or disputes before an acute stage is reached and thus avoid or minimize the number of strikes or lockouts.

"That mutual agreements as to conditions under which labor shall be performed should be encouraged and that when agreements are made the terms thereof should be faithfully adhered to, both in letter and in spirit by both parties.

"This department, either as a whole or a subcommittee by it appointed, shall when requested act as a forum to adjust and decide upon questions at issue between workers and their employers, provided in its opinion the subject is one of sufficient importance.

"This department will not consider abstract industrial problems.

"This department assumes no powers of arbitration unless such powers be conferred by both parties to a dispute."

A CHALLENGE TO CRITICS.

These declarations of purpose are submitted to the judgment of thoughtful, sincere trade unionists and others. We challenge the criticism of any one to point out wherein it offends against trade union-given in The Civic Federation to the leading capitalists of the country to show that their professions of square dealing are more than hollow promises, and many of the best known among them have responded to the call. They have taken hold of several of the most pressing wage-workers' questions of the day and are endeavoring through study and conference to reach conclusions regarding them that will help labor to bring the United States in these respects up to the level of other nations, and even to surpass them. The more active among these capitalists in The Civic Federation have now faithfully adhered to their self-imposed task for a time sufficiently long to demonstrate a sustained sincerity. Several of the most prominent including the first President, steadfast to the last in their duty, have died since The Civic Federation was established. The employers and the representatives of the public in the organization bring to the working out of its problems a body of legal and other expert talent, and resources in general, which labor if working alone could not command. Beyond this, the labor representatives participate fully in the work at every stage and defend in each particular the interests of all the wage-workers.

We believe that this is an accurate description of the situation in The Civic Federation of to-day, and it would be cowardly and criminal in us not to stand up for the truth in this respect as it has been evolved in the course of time and trial.

LABOR'S DUTY TO CO-OPERATE.

We deny that there has been any deleterious effect on the trade union movement, or on the general social movement of the workers, through the existence and operations of The Civic Federation. In another part of this issue of the *American Federationist* appears the address delivered by President Gompers before The Civic Federation upon the Sherman Anti-Trust Law and the application of that law by the courts to organized labor. On that occasion the opportunity was seized of bringing to the country the conclusions of organized labor as to the operations of that statute. To the Socialists it may be a matter of utter indifference that the courts have held that the organized effort of the workers comes under the provisions of the Sherman Anti-Trust Law, but to the trade unions it is of vital importance. It is essential for organized labor to obtain relief now from such a legal status. The only way that it can be secured is through Federal legislation. If the representatives of organized labor can gain the assistance of many influential men to arrive at that result, is it the part of wisdom to repudiate association with them? Is it not rather the duty of organized labor's representative men to co-operate to the attainment of that end?

Upon any matter in which the interests of labor conflict with the interests of others in The Civic Federation, there comes the parting of the ways, and upon such differences the men of labor clash with those who are opposed to them, working together with them only upon those measures of policy upon which agreement may be had.

We append the following record of sentiments which we uttered at the dinner at the recent meeting, and challenge critics, Socialists or otherwise, to find in it the flaw that is shown either by the suppression of our convictions or by an exaggeration of the performances of The Civic Federation, or through any blinking of the fact that in radical matters most employers may reject working-class ideals:

STRIFE HAS BEEN AVOIDED.

"The men of labor realize that while in this forum are men who strongly differ on matters of interest, of policy, of philosophy, of principle, and who may all strongly contend for the faith that is in them, no man surrenders his point of view by his association in The National Civic Federation. I imagine that many of you ladies and gentlemen who are here this evening have participated in other meetings and I believe that you will agree with my statement when I say that the representatives of labor have not been mealy-mouthed in the assertion of the faith which they hold, and we are not going to be so to-night. I am ready to acknowledge, and I do gladly acknowledge, that by reason of our coming together much strife has been avoided, and many reconciliations established where the relations between employer and employe have been ruptured. There is now, due to the organized effort of the working people and of our Civic Federation, a better general concept among all the people of this country of the duties we owe to one another. For instance, there is a better understanding and a more ready acquiescence in the thought that the labor of children must be restricted, and we are united in the common effort to so restrict it. And as to the discussion of these past few days, and particularly to-day, of the question of compensation for accidents and their prevention, I ask our hypercritical friends where on earth they can find a body of men in which large employers of labor, great captains of industry, sit in counsel with the representatives, and true representatives, of labor, to try and devise ways and means by which injury and accidents may be prevented and compensation given where accidents are unavoidable.

"I shall not attempt an encomium of The Civic Federation; that is not my function. But may I trespass upon your time for a few moments to say that no one appreciates more than I the good work done and the good work attempted by this organization? I have heard propositions submitted for greater production, for more efficiency in labor, for bonuses and profit-sharing, industrial education, vocational education, welfare work, and kindred matters with much of which I am in entire accord and from some of which I strongly dissent; but let me say this to the advocates of any of these suggestions, that any one of them which undertakes to eliminate the organization of the working people will reckon without its host. We trade unionists stand for the best in all our people; we believe in the joint bargain, in the trade agreement; we believe in working by concerted effort for industrial progress and industrial peace. I want to join in the expression of great appreciation for the splendid address of Senator Cummins. I would like to supplement a thought or two to some of his references to the organizations of labor. Substantially I claim no credit for verbal accuracy. He said that the organizations of labor will never secure for the working people adequate wages. Now the question reverts to what are adequate wages? What were adequate wages a decade ago are inadequate wages to-day, and what may be regarded as adequate wages to-day will be inadequate wages to-morrow. The fact of the matter is, I doubt that so long as there shall be a divergence of interests between employers and employes there ever will be such a thing as adequate wages. The men and the women of labor are somehow constituted like other people, and that is, that inasmuch, as the Senator so well said, as most people are striving for more money, greater possessions—and he said that he did not know that he wanted to be differentiated from those who tried to get more profits, more acquisitions—so with the working people. Whatever they have, poor as it is and fair as it may be, they have this common aspiration for more, and when they secure more the common attribute of their natures will still be in activity, and they will strive for more. And I trust that the time will never come when they will fail to aspire for still more. Surely this fact is self-evident, that if it were not for the labor organizations of our country the aspiration for more through joint effort would die in the laborer's breast.

"I was pleased to hear the Senator speak of the Sherman Anti-Trust Law, and its application as now interpreted by the courts to the labor organizations, and his belief that they should be taken out of the operations of that act. He added that they should be dealt with independently. I will stand here for myself, speaking only for myself, gladly meeting that issue. Let the Congress of the United States differentiate between combinations organized for profit and dealing in the products of labor from the organizations of the working people who are engaged in the effort to promote their own interests by the exercise of their personal activities, not for profit, and we shall meet the subject of independent legislation upon that question.

"Just a word of reference to the right of workmen when non-union, when unorganized, to dispose of their labor as they will. This is a self-evident proposition from which no earnest thinking man can dissent, but in the assertion of that principle it carries with it also this logical conclusion—the right of the union workmen to dispose of their labor as they will.

"I fear I have trespassed beyond the ten minutes allotted to the speakers. I shall not detain you longer—much as some thoughts are pressing upon my mind for expression. I merely want to close with the expression of my hope to be of some service to my fellow-men. This I believe is the mainspring of the best thought of the best men and women, and in that spirit, and in that thought, I close in the hope of success of the great work of our National Civic Federation."

WORKMEN'S COMPENSATION THE KEYNOTE

(Continued from page 8.)

a body of representatives of State Commissioners on Arbitration. Mr. Klump introduced EDWARD W. FROST, of Wisconsin, who compared the wars of industry to those between nations in their waste and suffering. He thought that the Erdman Act should be extended to industrial troubles. A way must be found to lay down the weapons of strike and lockout. Boards of arbitration have power to judge industrial disputes only upon request of both parties. Moreover, they rarely heard of a conflict until it was started. There is needed power to investigate and a method of notifying the State Board of impending trouble. The law should be uniform in those respects. The people should have the right to set in motion the arbitration machinery.

UNIONS A FACTOR FOR PEACE.

HARRIS WEINSTOCK, of San Francisco, discussed the question, "Will Trade Unionism Endure?" which he regarded as worthy of the same answer as "Has Corporate Wealth Come to Stay?" Each is an integral part of modern civilization. Neither can ignore the other. It is the economic interest and corporate wealth shall carry on great industrial and commercial enterprises. Else would labor return to a miserable daily existence on a handful of barley. Such a condition would imperil free government. Man can govern himself successfully only when fairly protected against hunger and suffering. Otherwise he relapses into savagery. Whatever tends to give him more leisure for intellectual development tends to make him more fit for self-government. The Orient to-day shows conditions of workers before the time of corporations. Great combinations have brought blessings to the worker and strengthened civil liberty. But they have brought responsibility that the worker can not meet individually and alone. The world never abandons any power for its betterment, therefore both organized labor and organized capital are here to stay. These two camps can be hostile, or can work together for common good. Wherever employers are organized to fight unionism, there follow loss of millions of wealth and consequent suffering. England prospers because of collective bargaining, with resultant strengthening of industrial peace. The Civic Federation has done much for the promotion of peace by bringing together employe and employer. It has much more work to do and deserves encouragement from labor, capital and the public.

COMPULSORY INVESTIGATION.

CORNELIUS J. DOYLE was introduced as Chairman of the State Board of Arbitration of Illinois. The causes of strikes and lockouts he defined as three: The question of open or closed shop; wages and working conditions. The method of dealing with them should be uniform. During the past year some $50,000,000 has been added to the payroll of the railroads, benefiting more than 300,000 workers, with only two incidental strikes, and those were mistakes. Intelligent administration must have a law to administer. The railways and the railway brotherhoods each deserve credit for regard for the public welfare. He would advocate compulsory investigation, as in Canada. He quoted the Illinois statute as an advanced measure, though imperfect. Investigation and publicity would avert many strikes. Neither corporation nor labor union would fly in the face of enlightened public opinion. It had been shown repeatedly that so to do meant failure. The Erdman Act should be strengthened by making compulsory the investigation of threatened trouble. Both employers and employes hesitate to submit their differences to men looked upon as politicians, even though well qualified for their duties. The main purpose will be attained when in every State there is a Board of Arbitration with the power of investigation under a uniform law.

STATE CONCILIATION BOARDS ADVOCATED.

PRESIDENT SETH LOW said that he was in accord with the suggestion that the next step forward should be based upon publicity, as precedent to uniformity. He called attention to the importance of the work being done in the State of New York under present law and officials. The express strike was the only open breach that had gone beyond their control. He read this letter that he had received from Mayor Gaynor: "I should be glad to attend the dinner of The National Civic Federation, but the plight I am in with my throat prevents me from doing so. I desire to thank the Committee of the Federation for the assistance they gave to the Mayor in settling the express strike some weeks ago." Many agencies contributed to that result, and all of them illustrated the force of public opinion. That opinion should be focused, as were the searchlights of American men-of-war upon the exit from Santiago Harbor. Public opinion in the United States would not accept the provisions of the Canadian Act. The Erdman Act recognized the right of organized labor to be represented officially when a labor dispute comes within Federal jurisdiction. The law of the United States recognizes such a right the very moment a railroad comes under its control through a receivership. He offered an amendment for consideration.

ARBITRATION DELAYED.

The First Vice-President of the American Federation of Labor, JAMES DUNCAN, declared that organized labor had made much advance during the past twenty-five years. When the newspapers gave the movement scant notice. But the press first discovered that organized labor represented a good cause. In time the church awoke and the congregations asked for more representative labor men to address them. In the boot and shoe industry in Massachusetts, the State Board of Arbitration is overworked, and its decisions are delayed. Hence it is agreed that pending the decision of any dispute the status quo shall remain. Mr. Duncan narrated his experience at the house of Oscar Straus, where Mr. Carnegie had called the Massachusetts plan "first class." He thought the whole trend of the discussion pointed toward an enlargement of Federal authority. Such discussion as this shows that evolution is at work. The Briton goes at the subject more directly, upon the proposition that the workman or the employer must be right or wrong. He dwelt upon the impossibility of compulsory arbitration, and urged the extension of the practice of the trade agreement.

JUSTICE, NOT MIGHT.

MARCUS M. MARKS, prominent in the National Association of Clothiers, emphasized the importance of settling industrial disputes upon the basis of justice, not of strength. He would extend the Erdman Act so as to give the right to intercede without the request of either party. Thus would be avoided the interpretation as a confession of weakness of first asking for a conference. The little flame easily becomes a conflagration. He would extend the idea of the Erdman Act to the States. He believed that the principles of the Canadian Act could be applied in the States as to public light upon labor troubles. He quoted some of the results of his inquiries in Quebec. Any man who takes work for a public utility goes into a quasi-agreement not to strike without a statement of grievances. It should be understood that employers do not want strike breakers, who are both expensive and inefficient. In Canada, out of eighty-two boards of arbitration in the last three years, seventy-six agreed in decisions that were accepted.

PRACTICAL WORK FOR PEACE.

W. C. ROGERS, of the New York State Board of Mediation and Arbitration, explained that arbitration is permissive by either the State or a local board. The investigation is prompt. The law is better than the Erdman Act, as an investigation may be made without application by either party. There is in this country a growing sentiment to prevent interruption by strikes and lockouts in public service corporations, but not by compulsory arbitration. A decent regard for the public should require that the reasons for interruption should be presented to the State Board of Mediation early enough to permit an effort at conciliation. Public opinion, rightly informed, will exert a pressure that cannot be overcome.

NEW MEMBERS NATIONAL EXECUTIVE COMMITTEE

ANNUAL MEETING WOMAN'S WELFARE DEPARTMENT

REPORTS OF THE TWO NATIONAL COMMITTEES ON WELFARE WORK FOR INDUSTRIAL AND FOR GOVERNMENT EMPLOYES——WORK OF SECTIONS OUTLINED

ADDRESS OF MRS. HORACE BROCK, THE CHAIRMAN.

THE annual meeting of the Woman's Welfare Department of The National Civic Federation was presided over by the Chairman, MRS. HORACE BROCK, who opened the meeting with an enthusiastic report upon the results thus far attained by "women in the department, whose training, leisure and feminine qualities permit them to do valuable investigation work, and who, by educating themselves as to comparative conditions in the various industries, may encourage employers to improve such conditions where necessary." She stated: "I feel more and more that no work for our country can be of greater importance than that which we have undertaken—the amelioration of the conditions of those who labor and the promotion of better understanding between employer and employe. The work in the Employers' Welfare Department is conducted on a large and general scale, good examples being held up for emulation and the encouragement of others in the same line of industry, and large enterprises apply to it to obtain advice in caring for their employes. Both lines of work are of far-reaching importance and supplement each other without overlapping.

"The seeming indifference of men and women to labor conditions is largely due to ignorance, and not to hardness of heart or conscience. The rush and strain of modern business leave the employer, the head of the corporation, and even his subordinates, little time to look into such conditions, and there is not always a woman in the establishment to bring abuses to his notice. The Woman's Welfare Department seeks to supply that influence by bringing woman to her rightful place as the inspirer and helper of man in his work.

"Reference to a few specific instances of splendid endeavor must include mention of the continued interest of our honorary Chairman, Mrs. William Howard Taft, whose great help on many occasions has especially aided in obtaining improvements for Federal employes."

After commenting on matters of organization and policy and complimenting the Chairman of the Ways and Means Committee, Mrs. Augustus P. Gardner, upon her valiant service, Mrs. Brock called attention to the work in Pennsylvania, where recreation and amusement centres were investigated, particularly in Philadelphia, where it had been possible, through friendly influence, to call the attention of manufacturers in various districts to the need for suitable places of amusement. Mrs. Samuel Spencer was pointed to as the generous and gracious member of the District of Columbia Section, whose beautiful home on two occasions had been the centre for educational meetings. The New York and New Jersey Section, of which Mrs. Francis McNeill Bacon, Jr., is Chairman, was especially congratulated upon its work in connection with new buildings, where provision for the comfort of employes had been ensured before the erection of such structures, and special reference was made to the valuable report on "Dangerous and Unhealthful Industries." Attention was called to the status of the work in other districts, as reported by Mrs. B. Frank Mebane, of North Carolina; Mrs. Roger Wolcott, of the New England Section, and Mrs. John K. Ottley, of the Georgia and Florida Section.

Mrs. Brock stated that "from the cleaning of the windows in the Printing Office at Washington, to save the eyesight of the employes, to the report upon mercurial poisoning in New York seemed a long step, but that both are in the right direction, and that when a woman is once aroused and her sympathies enlisted the difficulty is to make her add knowledge to her zeal and, above all, to cultivate patience and a willingness to wait, essential to accomplishing good work.

"In the extension of this work it is to be kept in mind that conditions vary in different States in response to the nature of the industries, climatic conditions and the character of the population. Moreover, what is useful in a city may not be practicable in a country town, and what is applicable in a large establishment may not always be possible or desirable in a smaller one.

"Such provisions for comfort and pleasure as lunch and reading rooms may not be advisable in all instances, but there is a great general principle which applies everywhere, namely, wholesome conditions of work based upon a living wage and reasonable hours.

"Foundation stones are not showy and are forgotten when the building is erected, but if not well laid the structure, however beautiful, suffers from the neglect. I feel that we have accomplished much in the past year, in that our foundations are well laid. In retiring I feel warranted in the confident hope that the next Chairman will be able to build upon them a noble structure which will be a credit to the American women, a tower of strength and a beacon light for the nation."

Mrs. Bayard Henry, holding the dual office of Secretary and Treasurer, reported upon the routine business of the year.

NATIONAL COMMITTEE ON WELFARE WORK FOR INDUSTRIAL EMPLOYES.

CHAIRMAN, MRS. J. BORDEN HARRIMAN, OF NEW YORK CITY.

The past year's record of the National Committee on Welfare Work for Industrial Employes made by the Chairman, MRS. J. BORDEN HARRIMAN, of New York City, includes announcement of the publication of a pamphlet on "Examples of Welfare Work in the Cotton Industry," which has been distributed among employers in cotton manufacturing. The information was gathered in person by members of the Committee during visits to mill towns in New England and the South. With the purpose of spreading knowledge of welfare work, Mrs. Harriman has delivered addresses by invitation, during the past eight months, in and near New York City and in Long Island, Connecticut and Massachusetts, emphasizing always the importance of women's influence toward educating employers and the preventive nature of welfare work. In detail, the report gives accounts of welfare work in cotton manufacturing towns, and is to be followed by a like investigation of the mining industry and the issuing of literature concerning mining camps. Such pamphlets will not only be informatory to members as to the welfare work expected in factories and mines in which they are financially interested, but also may be used by them to extend interest among employers generally in such improvements.

The members of the committee are:

For the Cotton Industry—

Mrs. Cyrus Pitman Orr, Birmingham, Ala.
Mrs. Lewis W. Parker, Greenville, S. C.
Mrs. Thomas F. Parker, Greenville, S. C.
Mrs. A. F. McKissick, Greenwood, S. C.
Mrs. W. T. Harris, Danville, Va.
Mrs. John K. Ottley, Atlanta, Ga.
Mrs. Frederick A. Flather, Lowell, Mass.
Mrs. Edwin Farnham Greene, Boston, Mass.

For the Mining Industry—

Mrs. R. L. Parrish, Covington, Va.
Mrs. Arthur Lee, Elkins, W. Va.

In her introduction Mrs. Harriman states:

The exercise of care for the welfare of employes is becoming more and more scientifically understood and extensively practised. One of the earliest problems in the development of factory life was that of the housing and of the social environment of the inhabitants of mill towns. Such towns were, at the outset, of artificial creation. Their location was determined by that of the new factory, which was, in turn, dependent upon circumstances of power and transportation. A century ago, therefore, the management of such a mill was confronted with the question of how to build houses for the workers at a cost which would afford a return for the investment while keeping the rent within its proportion of the cost of living of the wage earners. Accompanying this question of housing there was then, as there is now, the necessity of providing for these communities schools for the children, and churches, which should in some measure be the social centres of the towns, in addition to their moral influence and training.

Some of the first efforts in the United States to introduce welfare work were begun by manufacturers of cotton goods. One "corporation boarding house," as it was called, at Lowell, Mass., afforded evidence, not only of the employers' interest in regulating the price of board, but of the necessity of housing in order to secure the necessary operatives.

The growth of the municipality and the introduction of electric rapid transit, making possible homes in the country, have now rendered unnecessary some of these corporation boarding houses. The five corporations that manufacture cotton goods in Lowell still contribute toward the maintenance of a hospital and a technical school. Mrs. Frederick A. Flather, whose husband is treasurer of the Boott Mills, has initiated a rest room for the women operatives, a novel arrangement in that locality.

The Pacific Mills, of Massachusetts, Mr. Edwin Farnham Greene being the treasurer, were pioneers in this field, but gradually their activities, such as a free library, benefit associations, etc., have been taken over by the municipality, or by other organizations in the city of Lawrence.

As the manufacture of cotton goods has extended to the South, mill villages in several notable instances have there been developed along broader lines than in the cotton mill towns of New England. The surroundings of the mills and the houses are beautified, flower seeds are distributed annually, and prizes are awarded for the most attractive and best kept gardens. There are emergency hospitals, kindergartens and classes in domestic science to teach the proper preparation and serving of food, how to buy groceries, the desirability of cleanliness in the home, and how to make comfortable and economical clothing. It goes without saying that a good, wholesome meal will make a more healthful body and that the disappearance of slovenliness from the household will make the fireside an attractive and winning competitor to the saloon when the day's work is over.

The question of recreation also receives consideration, and opportunities for enjoyment, through athletic sports, indoor games, stereopticon lectures, and other methods are opened to the operatives.

Examples of Welfare Work.

Amoskeag Manufacturing Company.

The report in detail first invites attention to the plan for village development—designed by Loring Underwood, landscape architect—for the Amoskeag Manufacturing Company, at Manchester, New Hampshire, where there are 12,000 employes in the cotton mills. The treasurer of the company, who expressed enthusiasm in showing the tract to be devoted to this scheme, is F. C. Dumaine, of Boston. The plan is adaptable to similar applications elsewhere by other manufacturing concerns, and includes radial streets starting from the athletic field. One feature is that no two houses actually face each other, thus affording open views in front and rear. A large depression in the ground, with an adjacent supply of fresh water, provides an inexpensive swimming pool. Water mains and sewer pipes are at the rear of dwellings to prevent the tearing up of streets for house connections. The style of the cottages, as well as the plans for shrubs to conceal back yards and tree planting for the streets and circles, are unique and attractive.

Monaghan Mills.

Among the features described at Monaghan Mills, Greenville, S. C., is the night school, which affords instruction regarding the processes in which the operatives are occupied during the day, and also the opportunity to learn the elementary branches of common school education. The employes' annual fair, held two days in October, is commented upon, the programme for which includes exhibits in cooking, sewing, fancy work, live stock, vegetables and mill products, with the awarding of prizes, and outdoor sports and music.

Dan River Power and Manufacturing Company.

Mrs. W. T. Harris, whose influence and guiding hand are manifested in the village of Schoolfield, situated about two miles from Danville, Va., reports:

"The streets are electrically lighted, the water filtered, schools partly supported by the company and an assembly hall, hospital and day nursery are included in the welfare work.

"The methods here are ideal as to management, embodying the direct interest of the employer in the employe. This interest is manifested personally and enlists specialists under the direct supervision of the employers and their wives. The president and secretary of the mills receive a weekly report, and they know as well how the welfare department is progressing as how much cloth they produce."

Olympia Mills.

The visiting nurse, Miss Clara H. Kenyon, writes concerning activities under her direction: "I began work by getting acquainted with the people, mostly by house to house calling. We have 500 houses, 300 in one village and 200 in the other. The Medical Dispensary contains a large club room, operating

(Continued on page 17)

67
65
64

THE NATIONAL
Civic Federation Review
Office: Metropolitan Building
1 Madison Avenue New York City
RALPH M. EASLEY, Editor

The Editor alone is Responsible for any unsigned article or unquoted statement published in THE NATIONAL CIVIC FEDERATION REVIEW.

PUBLISHED BY
The National Civic Federation

PRACTICAL EFFORTS FOR VITAL REFORMS.

This issue of the REVIEW is devoted to a description of the various activities in which The National Civic Federation is now engaged. We think our readers will agree that these reforms are vital and that the methods pursued in the attempt to secure them are practical and promise to be effective. It would be idle to attempt in this space even to outline the whole work of the Federation, but there are five movements, involving large legislative programs, to which we especially desire to call attention as being typical of the work of all its departments. The two on the Regulation of Combinations and Trusts, and on the Regulation of Railroads and Municipal Utilities, deal with large business problems. The other three, on Compensation for Industrial Accidents and Their Prevention, on Pure Food and Drugs, and on the Reform of Legal Procedure, deal with labor and humanitarian interests. All concern the varied classes of membership in the Federation.

As explained in this issue, the Federation has been for years interested in the effort to secure an effective and practical regulation of industrial corporations, including combinations of manufacturers, agriculturists and workingmen. It has held two national conferences on the subject, to which delegates were sent by Governors and by national organizations of manufacturers, farmers, workingmen, economists, merchants, bankers, lawyers, and other associations. At the last annual meeting of the Federation one day was devoted to this subject and there was adopted a resolution which authorized President Low to appoint a national committee representing the various interests concerned, to consider the question of drafting a proposed model bill for the regulation of such combinations by the States and to propose amendments or substitutes for the Sherman Anti-Trust Act, if deemed desirable, after the decisions of the Supreme Court on the Standard Oil and American Tobacco Company cases were rendered. This committee, as stated elsewhere in the REVIEW, has met and organized sub-committees on both Federal and State lines. The consensus of public opinion, as evinced by the discussions throughout the country since the decisions of the Supreme Court were made, seems to indicate that one of the most important questions now is: "Shall regulation of industrial corporations go to the extent of permitting the Government to fix the prices of commodities?" The statements of the president of the United States Steel Corporation and of the presidents of other large corporations, together with the article of Colonel Roosevelt in "The Outlook," all endorsing the idea of the fixing of prices by the Government, have given great prominence to this phase of the question. To the criticism of that idea, made by its opponents, which is that it would be the height of folly for a central government or for any government to go into the business of price-making for a million or two commodities, as eventually the fixing of prices would become a matter of politics, the answer is made, that that is not what is contemplated by the proposal to have regulation of corporations "similar to that of railroads." The Interstate Commerce Commission does not make the million and a half rates for the railroads. The railroads make their own rates and a hearing is given only when there is complaint, backed by sufficient evidence. Then a decision is rendered as to whether or not such rates are reasonable; if they are adjudged unreasonable, a new rate is named. It is claimed by many that the Canadian Act, regulating Trusts and Combines, points the way. This Act provides that, if any six citizens believe that a corporation is practising extortion, or is a monopoly, they may make complaint before a Supreme Court Judge and, if a *prima facie* case is made, the judge orders the empaneling of a Board, the applicants naming one member, the corporation one and, if they do not agree upon the third, the judge himself appointing him. This Board then makes a thorough investigation of the whole matter and, if it finds the prices unreasonable, fixes them. Those advocating that the Government should fix prices also point out that Germany has found a way to deal with the question, which is illustrated by its action in the Potash Case. In regard to the potash fields, of which the Government owned 10 per cent, the Government made an investigation, and upon finding that the competition was becoming ruinous, called the owners of the other 90 per cent to meet its representatives, and formed with them a syndicate or, as it would be termed in this country, a "pool," allotting to each one his proportion of production and shutting down certain plants. In such instances provision was made for the workmen thus thrown out of employment, either by securing employment for them or by giving them pensions until places could be obtained. This same principle is now being applied in Germany to the electrical industries and to what is known as the "whiskey trust."

This discussion also raises the question squarely: "Shall the policy of this country be to compel competition in industry, or shall it be to permit combinations under proper Government regulation?"

In many respects there is great similarity between the problems that arise in the attempt to regulate railroads and municipal utilities and those in regard to industrial combinations. The work of the Committee on the Regulation of Railroads and Municipal Utilities is described in this issue. The committee has already begun its inquiries into the question: "How far can regulation go to be effective without interfering unduly with management?" Of course, in this field the question of fixing prices does not exist controversially, as in the case of combinations, since there is a recognized difference between quasi-public utilities and private industrial corporations. Congress has settled the question of rate-making, so far as interstate railroads are concerned, and State commissions are rapidly being given power to fix rates for gas, electric lighting and street railway companies, the latter, generally, being through negotiations between the companies and the city governments. Complications, however, arise in this line of endeavor which do not appear in the other field. For instance, there are forty-eight State Railway Commissions, which have authority over intrastate railways, while the Interstate Commerce Commission has control only over the interstate railways. On account of the lack of uniformity of the regulatory laws within the States themselves, conflicts arise between the States, and on account of the lack of co-ordination between the State laws and the Federal laws, conflicts arise between the State and the Federal Commissions. The Public Service Commission of the State of New York has more authority over the New York Central Railroad Company than has the Interstate Commerce Commission. It controls all the terminals, the issuance of stocks and bonds, and hundreds of other matters that, under our present Constitution, must be handled by the States. The crying need is for uniform State legislation and co-ordination between the Federal and State governments.

A department which more directly affects employers and employes is that which is dealing with the subject of a model act for workmen's compensation.

To all employers of labor it is of the highest importance that a fair and equitable compensation law be placed on the statutes of our various industrial States in place of the present liability laws. If this is not done, the workingmen will insist on legislation which will sweep away all the defenses of the employer, leaving him at the mercy of jury decisions in suits pressed by shyster, ambulance-chasing lawyers. The leaders of labor in this country are fair in the matter, and prefer compensation laws with definite awards, enabling workmen to secure all that is legally due them *at the time they need it*, and without risking law suits finally resulting in no compensation, or if decided in their favor, from 30 to 50 per cent of the amount allowed by the verdict.

The Workmen's Compensation Department has had an appreciable effect in moulding sentiment in the several States and in influencing legislation during the past winter through its model bill for compulsory compensation to injured wage earners and through its recommendations for improved State inspection of factories relating to the prevention of accidents. A study of the new laws discloses many evidences of its helpfulness to the Governors, the State Commissions and State Legislative Committees dealing with the subjects.

The constitutional questions being raised in New York State as the result of the adverse decision of the Court of Appeals and in the various States where elective compensation laws have been enacted, are being studied by this department. Francis Lynde Stetson, who is one of the greatest constitutional authorities in the United States, is chairman of the committee authorized to recommend necessary revisions in the Federation's model bill for compulsory compensation, prepared by the best experts in this country who are familiar with practical conditions here and thoroughly informed upon the subject abroad. That bill, which was submitted to the various legislatures in January, will be introduced, with possible changes, in the legislatures convening next winter.

The Department also will press for the enactment of its bill which was introduced in Congress for interstate commerce by one of the Federation's members, Hon. David J. Lewis. The bill at present is before the Federal Liability Commission, the secretary of which, Launcelot Packer, is thoroughly versed upon the subject in European countries as well as in America. He is also secretary of the Federation's department. The report upon this subject will be made to Congress in January, 1912. The enactment of the Federation's bill, if sustained by the United States Supreme Court, would have great weight in influencing uniform State legislation providing for compulsory compensation.

There is no subject of greater interest to the American people than that of pure food and pure drugs. The wealthy are able to pay the highest prices and are less liable to be imposed upon by the sellers of impure or adulterated foods and drugs than the masses, who have only that protection which is granted by the Federal Pure Food and Drug Act and the various States' acts, which are to a great extent in conformity with the Federal law.

President Taft said at a recent meeting of The National Civic Federation: "The greatest question now before the American public is the improvement of the administration of justice, civil and criminal, both in the matter of its prompt dispatch and the cheapening of its use." The National Civic Federation has a Committee on Reform in Legal Procedure which is co-operating with a similar committee of the American Bar Association.

ANNUAL MEETING WOMAN'S WELFARE DEPARTMENT

(*Continued from page 15*)

room, sterilizing room and bath room and two large closets, one being used for the loan closet, which contains articles needed in the sick room for lending to any family in the village. Twice a week we have free clinics, and I keep office hours every day from 11 to 1, except Sunday. I found dental clinics to be greatly needed."

"Recently we kept open house and served tea to more than 150 men, women and children. The dispensary was transformed into a beautiful Japanese tea-garden, with vines, moss, purple wistaria hanging in the corners and over the window seats, and there were small tea tables, Japanese dishes, and the women were dressed in Japanese costume. Outside we had Japanese lanterns and window-bells and the beautiful moss that grows in the trees here. We served tea and rice wafers and had Japanese incense, candy, Japanese toys, tricks, flowers that open in water, and games for entertainment. We gave each guest a small Japanese parasol.

Greenwood and Ninety-six Mills, N. C.

A report of progress in welfare work at Greenwood, S. C., where are the Grendel and Greenwood cotton mills, and at Ninety-Six, S. C., for the Ninety-Six mill, is made by Mrs. A. F. McKissick. She oversees the educational system, carries baskets to the families at the Christmas season and generally guards the welfare of employes and their families in these remarkable sanitary villages, containing well-built, pleasant homes. Mrs. McKissick follows, in her work, the methods inaugurated by her father, Captain Ellison A. Smyth, at Pelzer, S. C., described in Mrs. Harriman's report last year.

NATIONAL COMMITTEE ON WELFARE WORK FOR GOVERNMENT EMPLOYES.

CHAIRMAN, MRS. JOHN HAYS HAMMOND, WASHINGTON, D. C.

In the absence of the Chairman, Mrs. Archibald Hopkins read the report of the "Committee on Welfare Work for Government Employes." In the review of the year's work, while a great deal was of an educational nature which could not bring results for some months, much practical work was accomplished. In the Federal Buildings, under the existing laws and with the small appropriations available, improvements in conditions can only be made slowly.

The Treasury Department.

In the Treasury Department, the hearty and intelligent co-operation of the Secretary and his subordinates has made the building a place where employes now work under better conditions than ever before. Pending further structural changes, the Secretary is causing many improvements to be made, such as better sanitary conditions, improved rest rooms and inspection of tubercular suspects.

The Bureau of Engraving and Printing.

All that could be done in the old building of the Bureau of Engraving and Printing was accomplished. The new building will combine every requisite for the most modern conditions for the health and comfort of more than 4,000 employes, including lunch rooms, rest rooms and adequate and convenient dressing rooms.

The Census Bureau.

The Director of the Census Bureau requested our Committee to assist in placing in proper lodgings the thousand women who temporarily were engaged in the new census work. With the consent of the Secretary of Commerce and Labor, all clerks who applied to us were placed in homes, moral, healthful and within their means. The conditions in the building, which is unfitted for the work and for the number of employes, have been made better as to dressing rooms, installing ventilation pipes and pure drinking water, thanks to the Director and Chief Clerk. Up to the time when we, with the assistance of the Red Cross Society, had rest rooms made possible, there was no spot to put a sick or fainting woman, except on a hard sofa in the toilet room or directly upon the bare floor if that sofa were occupied. Since our help has been made of use, in the rest room of the main Census Building over 2,000 cases have been handled. On one hot day alone of last August 80 persons were treated.

The District Jail.

While this work started in the interest of the employes' welfare in the jail, the committee found conditions so bad for the inmates that it waived the general rules of the Woman's Welfare Department and made no distinction between the employes and inmates. That this work was needed is shown by the following description:.

The first person to visit the District Jail was Mrs. J. Ellen Foster, who was appointed by President Roosevelt to visit other Federal prisons as well, she having reported conditions to him. Nothing, however, was done to remedy the terrible state of affairs in the District Jail until the members of the Woman's Welfare Department personally went to verify the statements made and then reported the same directly to Attorney-General Wickersham. He then went himself to the jail, the only Attorney-General in thirty years who had made a personal visit there.

Under his direction the improvements herein detailed were effected by Warden McKee. In the men's department, a large doorway has been cut between every other cell, and instead of two men living, eating and sleeping in a cell, 8x5 feet, without proper toilet facilities, as was previously the condition, they have the use of two cells, one to live in and the other to sleep in, a toilet has been put in each of these latter. At the extreme end of the long row of cells are the new baths. Before the remodelling, there were two baths for six hundred prisoners; now there will be six shower baths, four tubs and one chemical bath and four dressing rooms, which was something unthought of before. Even the dungeon has received its share in the reconstruction and is now decent and rat-proof, but happily is seldom used, for the present warden rarely needs to resort to that kind of punishment.

In the central building the old cupola has been removed, as it was considered a danger and menace. In the long glass enclosed rooms outside the corridors are reading tables with books and periodicals. The men are allowed the use of these rooms three hours each day for exercise, recreation, smoking and card playing, but no gambling is permitted. Instead of having to eat their meals together, they have now a dining room for white and one for colored men prisoners, and they also have plates, cups, knives and forks to use. When the ladies of the Woman's Welfare Department first visited the jail the prisoners ate their food (which was shoved through the bars of their cells) out of tin basins and with their fingers.

The storeroom is a source of great pride to the warden on account of its wonderful transformation. It was, a short while ago, simply a dungeon under the kitchen; the only way of entrance was by means of a rope down a trap door. The warden has had put in a flight of stairs in one corner of the kitchen, and then had several windows and a door cut in the foundation wall, making a large, light, well-ventilated cellar and storeroom. He next had two immense refrigerators built in the room—and in passing I want to say that all work in connection with these improvements was done by the prisoners. The ventilation is extremely good; there is a flue high up in the wall with a fan inserted to carry off all the impure air that arises, and by holding a handkerchief in this opening you can readily see just what a strong current of air there is. The staple supplies are kept in lockers, and the vegetables are in three bins arranged around the walls.

Even the dispensary has had its share in the general improvements and now the instruments and medicines are supplied from the funds for the jail and not by the visiting physicians.

So taken all in all, if our Woman's Department had only accomplished the improvement of the conditions at the jail the past year it would have been a year well spent.

The Washington Navy Yard.

Bringing about the establishment in the Washington Navy Yard of a restaurant for the workmen, similar to the one successfully run in the Brooklyn Navy Yard, has the sympathy of officials and the hopeful expectation of more than 800 workmen.

Fire Drills.

A fire drill has been suggested for all Government buildings where present conditions in case of fire would menace many lives. Under present conditions there probably would be terrible loss of life, as the old buildings have dark, ill-lighted passages, many elevators and relatively few staircases.

In all the investigations in Federal buildings we have been received with the greatest courtesy and every facility was afforded us. Within the limits of the powers of officials and their appropriations they have endeavored to carry out our suggestions.

THE NEW YORK AND NEW JERSEY SECTION WOMAN'S WELFARE DEPARTMENT.

CHAIRMAN, MRS. FRANCIS M'NEIL BACON, JR.

The report of the New York and New Jersey Section covers the work of six standing committees—on Welfare of Government Employes, on Welfare of Industrial Employes, on New Buildings, on Press and Publications, on Lectures, and on Membership.

Government Employes' Welfare Committee.

City Hospitals.

The city hospitals have been studied from the point of view of the employe, and recommendations have been made to the hospital authorities and Board of Estimate and Apportionment concerning specific changes and urging certain appropriations. Replies show that these recommendations are receiving careful consideration. Discarded books from the Public Library and elsewhere have been obtained for the employes.

Post Office.

The Committee found upon examination, through the courtesy of Postmaster Morgan, that the plans of the new post office at the Pennsylvania Terminal show thought on his part for comforts for employes, including space above ground for the swing-rooms. The Committee recommended a drying apparatus for carrier's uniforms; provision for disinfecting mail bags, and drinking fountains in the building, instead of faucets. These recommendations, the Committee is assured, will be carried out so far as practicable, that for drying clothes being already in the plans. No recent visits have been made to sub-stations, as the Postmaster, who is in sympathy with the establishment of welfare features, states that where conditions are bad modern stations are being substituted as rapidly as possible.

Committee on Schools.

The formation of the Committee on Schools followed the assurance of the president of the Public Education Association that it would be of welcome assistance. Eleven schools have been visited and interviews held with principals and teachers. It is shown that new systems of ventilation have not always proved successful, because of unintelligent janitors. The majority of schools have no satisfactory arrangements for teachers as to restrooms, lunchrooms, toilet rooms and drinking fountains. Changes in plans of new school buildings will be urged.

Brooklyn Navy Yard Lunchroom.

The lunchroom at the Brooklyn Navy Yard has been in operation now over a year and a half. That it is appreciated by the men is proved by the attendance remaining practically the same as to number and personnel. The report of the fiscal year ending December 31, 1910, showed a deficit of $17.58.

Realizing that steady work, reasonable hours and an equitable wage are the first essentials to the welfare of employes, the Committee very carefully looked into the question of living expenses in Brooklyn, and as a result early in December increased the wages of the women employed in the lunchroom to meet their requirements. During the Summer they were given a day's outing at Coney Island, and the day before Christmas there was provided a tree with gifts for all in the lunchroom.

During the year the lunchroom was honored by a visit from the Secretary of the Navy, who, apparently, approved its method of operation. This sign of interest greatly encourages this section in the hope that similar plants may be established in other navy yards in furtherance of the idea uppermost in the minds of the members when this one was installed.

Industrial Employes' Welfare Committee.

The Industrial Employes' Welfare Committee has sub-committees on Stationary Firemen, Hotel Employes, Recreation and Vacation Resources, and Dangerous and Unhealthful Industries.

Stationary Firemen's Committee.

The Stationary Firemen's Committee has discontinued investigations for the present, but it keeps in touch with the president of their organization, who has interesting vacation plans in which the Committee may co-operate.

Hotel Employes' Committee.

A committee was formed, including wives of hotel owners and managers, which is investigating the conditions of living and work among domestic employes in hotels. It is hoped that the hotels where conditions are satisfactory may serve us an example to persuade others that good conditions are the most satisfactory, as well as the most economical.

Committee on Recreation and Vacation Resources.

A Committee on Recreation and Vacation Resources, formed last Spring in co-operation with another organization, has directed more than 500 girls to boarding houses where they spent happy and wholesome vacations. The work for the Winter will include the gathering of information through letters of inquiry to one thousand employers as to what they are doing in regard to giving vacations, with or without pay. The information will be used in promoting a public meeting.

Committee on Dangerous and Unhealthful Industries.

The Committee on Welfare of Industrial Employes, with the sanction of The National Civic Federation, has taken up through a sub-committee the study of dangerous and unhealthful industries. This included a special study of industrial processes involving the use of mercury or its compounds; a published report upon mercurial poisoning in England, where the danger has been reduced to a minimum, and a study of conditions in the local field.

Although the field of Phosphorous Poisoning has been covered, and various Commissions are working on Lead Poisoning, so far as we know, our Section is the first organization to take up the investigation of Mercurial Poisoning in this country.

Permission having been obtained from The National Civic Federation, a preliminary report was sent to the St. Louis Conference of the American Association for Labor Legislation, a portion of which is included in the following:

As neither Labor nor Health Bureaus, State or National, had any data, our investigation had to start with elementals. Processes in some fourteen industries were found to be involved, but the "felt hat" trade was the first taken up.

The search for statistics opened with an examination of the death certificates of Manhattan and Brooklyn. Owing to the fact that classification is not made according to occupations, it was necessary to examine each certificate separately, since Mercury is a toxicant which predisposes to other ailments, such as tuberculosis, gastric and kidney trouble. Its slower and subtler effect is merged in the more conspicuous affliction. This makes Mercurialism especially hard to trace. Hospital records were searched where permission could be obtained, and in connection with these records numerous physicians were interviewed. Professional secrecy debarred many from giving the history of cases without the patient's consent. In many cases it was impossible to obtain such consent, since men growing ill from Mercurialism in many instances leave the trade and move away. Even when located it is often exceedingly hard to get a recital of experiences. The fear of displeasing the "boss," of appearing disaffected to his interests and so of losing the chance to work—this is the living barrier between these victims of industrial disease and those who would, by revealing the true conditions, bring about protective legislation.

But beyond and above these impediments stands the unwillingness of most factory owners to allow any inspection of health conditions among their employes, and our Civic Federation, being unofficial, is dependent largely upon the good will and indulgence of employers. The New York State Labor Bureau, both through its Commissioner and its Medical Inspector—have been loyal and valuable allies. They are willing to assist in collecting data, but until the law (which we are all seeking) directing physicians to report all cases of industrial disease to a central bureau, is passed and gives them authority, they cannot themselves enter the factories to inspect workmen for diseases resulting from their occupation. The Medical Inspector will make, however, for our benefit, some air tests in factories to determine the precentage of mercury vapor in the atmosphere. From these tests we may deduce the degree to which it is getting in its poisonous work.

Every avenue of right and rational approach in this search is seen to be seriously blocked and our advances have been necessarily slow, toilsome and circuitous. The number of cases we shall succeed in tracing will be a very inadequate gauge to the amount of illness incident to the trades concerned. When, however, we can show after three months' work a record more or less complete of sixty cases of Mercury Poisoning, the situation begins to have meaning. In a report which the Chairman prepared upon Mercury Poisoning in English Industries, it is shown that in twelve years the total number of cases reported for all Great Britain is only ninety-four. The relative prevalence of Mercurialism would seem to justify our investigation.

The first action of Mercury Poisoning is mental. The subject becomes melancholy, morose and despondent, and among hatters there is a predisposition to suicide. An early effect on the body is shown in the mouth. The teeth become loosened and blackened and salivation sets in. The digestive tract and the kidneys are invaded and soon partial nerve paralysis shows itself in a tremor of the arm, hand, feet, facial and speech muscles. This tremor or "shake" is the destructive feature of Mercurialism in the hat industry, for as soon as the hands grow unsteady the man, however expert, must leave the most delicate processes, where he tears the soft hat bodies. Often he is docked $2.00 for each hat that he spoils, and the sums deducted, combined with his ever lessening earning capacity, too rapidly force him down. The melancholia and the ever present need for bracing the unsteady nerves unite to bring about a use of stimulants which only aggravates the disease. Notwithstanding this, the very worst cases of Mercurialism upon our list have no alcoholic history.

It is to be regretted that some of the cases cannot be detailed. The human story is often touching. The manful stand of the wage-earner against an onward creeping paralysis, the worry and despondency born of disease and the lowering income, the pressures which force the wife and then the children one by one into the labor market, these are the living, pulsing griefs.

The study of Industrial Mercurialism has thus far been confined to the hat industry, which is only one of the fourteen industries in which this poisoning is developed. That the remaining group are experiencing illness due in some degree to the use of the metal is inevitable, although the effects of Mercurial Poisoning are slower and more insidious than those of Phosphorus and Lead.

Committee on New Buildings.

The Committee on New Buildings, through the courtesy of public officials and private owners, examines plans for proposed buildings and makes suggestions for improvements before erection. The results are more healthful working conditions for innumerable men and women. Both the Government and Industrial Branches of this Committee have been very active in making such examinations, after acquainting themselves with the requirements which constitute a standard for the particular type of buildings to be constructed.

Press Committee.

Notices of meetings, lectures and special items of interest relating to the work are sent by the Press and Publication Committee to the daily papers, thus bringing the work of the Section to the attention of the public.

Lecture Committee.

The Lecture Committee has given each year for the benefit of the Section an instructive course of lectures touching important questions, realizing that our work is largely educational.

Informal talks are given after the regular monthly meetings on subjects relating to some phase of betterment work and the members are thus brought into a closer knowledge of industrial conditions.

Membership Committee.

The activity of the Membership Committee has resulted in tripling the number of members during the year.

DISTRICT OF COLUMBIA SECTION WOMAN'S WELFARE DEPARTMENT.

CHAIRMAN, MRS. SAMUEL SPENCER.

The District of Columbia Section of the Woman's Welfare Department made progress especially in the efforts to aid in improving conditions of Government employes.

Industrial Employes' Welfare.

As we have no large manufacturing plants in Washington, work for industrial employes is of lesser importance. In this connection it has been our policy to act in conjunction with other associations—the Red Cross, the Young Women's Christian Association and the Travelers' Aid Society.

Government Employes' Welfare.

As the report of the National Chairman of Government Employes' Welfare Committee has shown, our efforts lately have been especially directed toward the Census Building, Treasury Building, Winder Building (the headquarters of the Auditor of the Treasury), the Federal Jail, the Pension Office Building and the Interior Department.

Luncheon and Rest Rooms.

The question of inadequate provision for luncheon and rest rooms in the majority of Government buildings is a very serious one. We have accomplished more in the way of suitable rest rooms than in helping toward securing proper luncheon facilities.

The rest room in the Census Building, provided through our efforts, assisted by the Red Cross, has cared for 2,000 persons since its opening. More than eighty were treated in one day alone during August.

Our National Chairman, before leaving Washington last Spring, made special recreation arrangements for those women employes.

Appropriations Needed.

Two large problems always confront us—one is the cry, "We have no appropriation from Congress for this;" the other is, "We are to have a new building before long, so there is no use doing much in this one, which will then be abandoned."

It can well be seen that buildings constructed for the work of a Government of nine millions of people, now used to administer the affairs of ninety millions, are packed beyond endurance. But, by patient perseverance, we are ameliorating conditions as to ventilation, overcrowding and uncleanliness.

City Market.

We are working to secure further improvements in our city markets, the large Center Market being in much better condition than when we began the investigation a year ago; the majority of the residents of Washington being Government employes, it is in their interest that this effort has been made. By interesting the President of the Market Company and the Board of Managers, who had never considered the subject, we have, through the commissioners who had appointed extra inspectors for all markets, secured changes in conditions everywhere—new standards of inspection, new stalls and new galleries overhead to hold the stock and keep it from being packed under the stalls. It is essentially work for employes from the President himself to the lowliest laborer, for all deal at the markets, and the food is now treated in a cleaner, more hygienic way.

Membership.

We have, through our members, direct affiliation with the Cabinet and Congress and can, therefore, frequently accomplish much by personal interviews.

Loan Shark Bill.

Our effort to stop usurious rates of interest, charged to all types of employes who need to borrow money, has been put in the form of a bill introduced in Congress, known as the Loan Shark Bill. The ladies of the Woman's Welfare Department appeared at the hearing of the bill in the District Committee Room, and their position in regard to it was stated to the members of the Committee by our vice-chairman. The bill was passed by the Senate and was favorably reported by the Conference Committee of the House.

Sanitary Inspection Bill.

We are especially urging what is known as the Sanitary Inspection Bill. It provides for the creation of a National Board of Sanitary Inspectors, composed of the Surgeon-General of the Army and Marine Hospital Service, the Chief of the Bureau of Medicine and Surgery of the Navy, and the Supervising Architect of the Treasury. They are to be assisted by retired officers of both branches of the service, who, without extra pay, will inspect all Government buildings *at least once* in three months and report to the Board as to their sanitary and hygienic conditions. The passage of this bill will mean wonderful improvement in the future as to segregating or eliminating tubercular cases in the various Government departments and as to general cleanliness.

ROOF GARDEN, LUNCH AND REST ROOM. GOVERNMENT BUREAU OF ENGRAVING AND PRINTING, WASHINGTON, D. C.

NORTH AND SOUTH CAROLINA SECTION WOMAN'S WELFARE DEPARTMENT.

CHAIRMAN, MRS. B. FRANK MEBANE.

During the past year we feel that quite a gratifying amount of Welfare Work has been accomplished at Spray, N. C.

Club House.

The Spray Civic Association, which is composed of the managers of the mills, has the general welfare of the employes at heart and generously provides the money for putting into execution the ideas of the women forming our local Welfare Committee, in addition to its regular civic duties. During the year just passed the Association voted $20,000 for a club building for men and boys, under the management of the Y. M. C. A., which is most successful. Having more than 500 members, it provides for them bowling alleys, billiard and pool tables, reading rooms, a gymnasium fully and perfectly equipped, and classrooms where night schools are held; also a large assembly hall, used for gatherings of all kinds, suppers every Monday evening and so forth, facilities being provided for serving seventy-five. The members pay the sum of $5.00 a year for men and $1.00 for boys. Possibly more enjoyed than all else are the shower baths, a large number being taken each day. During the months of October, November and December the attendance numbered 2,700. There were 9,800 who participated in the games and 114 in the classes and clubs. There are entertainments for mixed audiences. There is also in the building a medical room, where 288 school children were examined this autumn by the physicians, and there is a specialist for operations on eye, ear, nose and throat, all free of charge.

Dispensary and Emergency Rooms.

Through efforts of the women of the Spray Welfare Committee there has been equipped a dispensary, where the children needing treatment only (no operations) may be cared for by the District Nurse. There has been completed also an emergency room, used in case of accidents in or around the mills, and for operations where the patient has no facilities at home. By means of this emergency room we hope definitely to ascertain the need of a hospital at Spray. At present I am glad to say it looks as if the hospital will be unnecessary and that the emergency room will be adequate since the percentage of accidents is astonishingly low and the surgical cases for hospitals rare, and as it is almost an impossibility to persuade this class of people to go to a hospital for general illness unless it can be clearly proven first that it is a case of life and death.

District Nurse.

The work of the District Nurse has been most satisfactory, the health of the entire village, as well as the appearance of the outside and inside of the cottages, the streets and the gardens having been greatly improved. Keeping the premises in a sanitary condition requires constant and vigilant work. As there have been only fifty cases of fever among the 8,000 inhabitants of Spray since the Nurse began her visits, July 1, by beginning the precautionary measures in March this year we expect to reduce this number materially.

Girls' Home.

The Girls' Home is well established, and is managed by a competent woman. For the sum of $2.50 a week the girls are given nice bedrooms (two girls in a room, separate beds if desired), well-cooked food, three meals each day, a sitting room for receiving their friends, books and magazines for those inclined to literary pursuits, and each week we have an organ recital and club meetings at the Home, cooking and sewing being taught the girls by the matron.

Women's Club Proposed.

In April we expect to put in a petition to the Spray Civic Association for a sum to build, for the girls and women, a clubhouse commensurate with that already built for the men and boys, in which it is planned to have bedrooms, meals also to be furnished.

Day Nursery.

The need for a day nursery was evidenced by the shocking discovery one day of the half-charred body of a little child near one of the open fireplaces commonly used in that part of the country. The nursery, now thoroughly established, is a great success.

SANITARY AND LOAN SHARK BILLS ENDORSED.

It was determined that the Woman's Welfare Department should endorse the action of the District of Columbia Section; that there should be printed and distributed, among the members, cards giving the name and title of each bill, with its purpose and scope, and that the members should be asked to write personal letters to their Congressmen and Senators urging the passage of these bills.

It was voted that the Department should ask every woman's organization to use its influence for the passage of these Sanitary and Loan Shark bills.

The Chair announced as a committee to carry out these ideas: Miss Maude Wetmore, chairman; Mrs. Archibald Hopkins and Miss Anne Morgan.

NEW CHAIRMAN OF DEPARTMENT.

MRS. JOHN HAYS HAMMOND, who was elected National Chairman of the Woman's Welfare Department, is a Southern woman by ancestry. She was born in Vicksburg, Miss., of Virginia Colonial stock, and her people were among the pioneers of Mississippi. Her father, Judge J. W. M. Harris, was a lawyer in Vicksburg of high repute, and was one of the auditors in Richmond under the administration of Jefferson Davis. Her uncle was Brigadier-General Nat. Harris, whose portrait hangs in the gallery in Richmond devoted to Southern generals. Her great-grandmother, Letitia Gibson, after whose family Port Gibson was named, married Nathaniel Harrison at Natchez when that place was a Spanish fort. She was brought to New York by her parents as a child, and at fifteen was sent abroad to study languages and music. She met Mr. Hammond in Dresden, Germany. He was then studying in the Royal School of Mines in the adjacent town of Freiberg. They were married in America.

Her high intellectual ability and great personal charm have won for Mrs. Hammond a world-wide circle of friends. She is the mistress of a beautiful home and enjoys the personal friendship of rulers and men prominent in administrative and legislative circles, and of women engaged in educational activities in the principal capital cities of the world. She has the personal quality of a warm sympathy that manifests itself naturally. With her preparation of experience and natural gift of adaptability, she brings to her activities an enthusiasm that contributes to

MRS. JOHN HAYS HAMMOND.

her effectiveness. She is fortuitously equipped for the field of work to which she is called. Throughout all her experiences she has won the good will and cordial co-operation of both wage-earners and employers. She has been active, for example, in the life of mining camps for the welfare of employes of the companies with which her husband was connected. She is one of the founders of the Woman's Institute in London, which carries on work to improve the condition of women wage-earners in every branch of industry, where they are employed. She has of late devoted increasing attention to improving the conditions of government employes, a field in which she has worked diligently. She has shared with her husband his travels and explorations in examining gold fields in California and Mexico, and when he was Consulting Engineer in San Francisco. Since her part in his career in South Africa, Mrs. Hammond has had the advantage of his continued work of examining mines.

The Woman's Welfare Department, of which Mrs. Hammond is Chairman, is composed largely of women who, as stockholders or through family relationships, are financially interested in industrial organizations, in factories, mines and other places of work. Among other influential members are also the wives of many men in public life, who are interested in bettering the conditions of the employes in government departments.

Mrs. Hammond made prompt response to the call to duty involved in her election. She had just returned from a journey with her husband in Russia, Germany and England, and as an initial step gave a reception at the Colony Club in New York City to meet the officers and members of the New York and New Jersey Section of the Woman's Welfare Department. The reception was voted as brilliantly successful, both socially and in its practical purpose.

In quick succession she turned her attention to organizing in new fields. At Atlanta, Ga., there was next held a reception at the Capital City Club, where she earnestly presented the desire to forward the welfare of industrial and public employes throughout that region. She was assisted by Mrs. John K. Ottley, Miss Jennie English, Miss Isma Dooly, Mrs. Walter Lamar and Mrs. Cyrus Pitman Orr.

There were approached most recently another group of Southern women at a reception given in Mrs. Hammond's honor at the Woman's Club, Richmond, Va. Mrs. J. Allison Hodges, Mrs. B. Frank Mebane and Mrs. W. T. Harris lent their efforts in promoting this endeavor.

Among visiting members of the Woman's Welfare Department of the Federation were: Mrs. Richard Wainwright, Mrs. Samuel Spencer, Mrs. James Pilling and Mrs. Robert S. Chew, National Secretary, of Washington, D. C.; Miss Maude Wetmore, of Newport, R. I.; and from the New York and New Jersey Section: Mrs. Francis McNeil Bacon, Jr.; Miss Maud Rives Borland and Mrs. Walker Smith.

OFFICERS AND EXECUTIVE COMMITTEE WOMAN'S WELFARE DEPARTMENT FOR ENSUING YEAR.

MRS. WILLIAM HOWARD TAFT, The Honorary Chairman.
MRS. JOHN HAYS HAMMOND, Chairman, Washington, D. C.
MRS. J. BORDEN HARRIMAN, First Vice-Chairman and Chairman National Committee on Welfare Work for Industrial Employes, New York City.
MRS. RICHARD WAINWRIGHT, Second Vice-Chairman and Chairman National Committee on Welfare Work for Government Employes, Washington, D. C.
MRS. JOHN K. OTTLEY, Third Vice-Chairman and Chairman Georgia and Florida Section, Atlanta, Ga.
MRS. HORACE BROCK, Fourth Vice-Chairman, Philadelphia, Pa.
MRS. B. FRANK MEBANE, Fifth Vice-Chairman and Chairman North and South Carolina Section, Spray, N. C.
MRS. EVA McDONALD VALESH, Sixth Vice-Chairman, New York City.
MRS. ROBERT S. CHEW, Secretary, Washington, D. C.
MRS. FLORA E. DURNO, Executive Secretary, Washington, D. C.
MISS MAUDE WETMORE, Treasurer, Washington, D. C.
MRS. AUGUSTUS P. GARDNER, Chairman Ways and Means Committee, Hamilton, Mass.
MRS. J. MEDILL McCORMICK, National Chairman Public Hospital Employes' Welfare Committee, Chicago, Ill.
MRS. FRANCIS McNEIL BACON, Jr., Chairman New York and New Jersey Section, New York City.
MRS. ARCHIBALD HOPKINS, Chairman District of Columbia Section, Washington, D. C.
MRS. W. T. HARRIS, Chairman Virginia and West Virginia Section, Danville, Va.
MRS. CYRUS PITMAN ORR, Chairman Alabama and Mississippi Section, Birmingham, Ala.

EXECUTIVE COMMITTEE

MRS. ARCHIBALD ALEXANDER	Hoboken, N. J.
MRS. FRANCIS McNEIL BACON, Jr.	New York City
MRS. AUGUST BELMONT	New York City
MRS. WILLIAM B. BOURN	San Francisco, Cal.
MRS. HORACE BROCK	Philadelphia, Pa.
MRS. ANDREW CARNEGIE	New York City
MRS. ROBERT S. CHEW	Washington, D. C.
MRS. W. MURRAY CRANE	Dalton, Mass.
MRS. WILLIAM H. CROCKER	Burlingame, Cal.
MRS. MICHAEL DREICER	New York City
MRS. WILLIAM CORCORAN EUSTIS	Washington, D. C.
MRS. MARSHALL FIELD	Chicago, Ill.
MRS. AUGUSTUS P. GARDNER	Hamilton, Mass.
MRS. EDWIN FARNHAM GREENE	Boston, Mass.
MRS. CLEMENT ACTON GRISCOM, Jr.	New York City
MRS. JOHN HAYS HAMMOND	Washington, D. C.
MRS. J. BORDEN HARRIMAN	New York City
MRS. W. T. HARRIS	Danville, Va.
MRS. PASCAL ENOS HATCH	Springfield, Ill.
MRS. BAYARD HENRY	Philadelphia, Pa.
MRS. ARCHIBALD HOPKINS	Washington, D. C.
MRS. OVERTON LEA	Nashville, Tenn.
MRS. ARTHUR LEE	Elkins, W. Va.
MRS. NICHOLAS LONGWORTH	Cincinnati, O.
MRS. FRANK O. LOWDEN	Oregon, Ill.
MRS. V. EVERIT MACY	New York City
MRS. MARCUS M. MARKS	New York City
MRS. BOWMAN H. McCALLA	Santa Barbara, Cal.
MRS. CYRUS HALL McCORMICK	Chicago, Ill.
MRS. JOSEPH MEDILL McCORMICK	Chicago, Ill.
MRS. HENRY B. F. MACFARLAND	Washington, D. C.
MRS. A. F. McKISSICK	Greenwood, S. C.
MRS. B. FRANK MEBANE	Spray, N. C.
MRS. PHILIP N. MOORE	St. Louis, Mo.
MISS ANNE MORGAN	New York City
MRS. CYRUS PITMAN ORR	Birmingham, Ala.
MRS. JOHN K. OTTLEY	Atlanta, Ga.
MRS. DOUGLAS ROBINSON	New York City
MISS ANNA D. SLOCUM	Boston, Mass.
MRS. WALKER BREESE SMITH	New York City
MRS. SAMUEL SPENCER	Washington, D. C.
MRS. OSCAR S. STRAUS	New York City
MRS. WILLIAM H. TAFT	Washington, D. C.
MRS. EDMUND LEIGHTON TYLER	Anniston, Ala.
MRS. EVA McDONALD VALESH	New York City
MRS. RICHARD WAINWRIGHT	Washington, D. C.
MISS MAUDE WETMORE	Washington, D. C.
MRS. BENJAMIN IDE WHEELER	Berkeley, Cal.
MRS. MARY HATCH WILLARD	New York City
MRS. TALCOTT WILLIAMS	Philadelphia, Pa.
MRS. ROGER WOLCOTT	Boston, Mass.

BANQUET OF THE DISTRICT OF COLUMBIA SECTION AT WASHINGTON, D. C.

THE FEDERATION'S WORK ENDORSED BY SENATOR HENRY CABOT LODGE AND PRESIDENT TIMOTHY HEALY

THE first speaker at the banquet of the District of Columbia Section of the Woman's Welfare Department, introduced by Mrs. Archibald Hopkins, was the National Chairman, Mrs. JOHN HAYS HAMMOND. She defined the organization, its purpose and its method of work.

UNITED STATES SENATOR HENRY CABOT LODGE, of Massachusetts, attributed the admirable work of The National Civic Federation to the spirit of its members in working together for one end and said that its most valuable feature is that it has interested representative people to do work themselves for the solution of great problems. The tendency to turn to the Government to do everything tends to sap the strength of individuality. But there is now realization that people make governments and laws, not the reverse. Hence the Civic Federation is of very great value, in that it is composed of all sorts of people who have joined in the purpose of making things better. They bring employer and employed together as they should be in a land where there should be no feeling of class.

The President of the International Brotherhood of Stationary Firemen, TIMOTHY HEALY, declared that he was willing to give all that he could of effort and time to The National Civic Federation. The Socialists did not agree with him, nor with themselves. He said: "The Socialist movement is getting stronger, and they are making threats now that they will drive all our trades unions out of The National Civic Federation. Something has to be done to curb the Socialist movement in this country, and I believe that the Civic Federation, working along with the trades union men, is the greatest force that possibly could be brought against it. Washington's Birthday this year was not observed as a holiday in Milwaukee and the Socialist Mayor refused to display the Stars and Stripes on the public buildings. If they should be successful in this country, there would be no Stars and Stripes. The red flag would take their place. I am in The National Civic Federation because it is doing the same work the labor unions have been doing—uplifting humanity. Though the labor unions of this country and the world are often condemned, I never knew of any issue that was put forward that was not for the good of the greatest number. A generation ago, there was scarcely anybody outside the labor unions who had a word to say or bothered his head about how young the child went into the mill or factory and the mine, or how hard it worked there or how many hours it was kept inside. We want decent hours for our men to work. The Civic Federation want the same. They believe that we are right. We want healthful surroundings and living conditions for the workers, not only in the workshops, but in the homes where the wives and children can enjoy good conditions, too. We want sufficient wages to clothe, feed, educate and raise the children as American citizens should be raised. My friends, the wage earners, men and women, have been neglected in the mad rush to build up large fortunes and great enterprises. If the captain of industry had paid as much attention to his employes—of course there are exceptions—as he did to his machinery and his mules we would not have had so much trouble. And you, ladies and gentlemen, of The National Civic Federation, who are taking an interest in the down-trodden, are doing a great deal for humanity and for the future of this great country. The history of The National Civic Federation will never be known, because they act and work quietly, and you would be surprised if you were to know the labor troubles and strikes that have been avoided through its channels in getting employers and employes together. They are doing wonderful work, although they are not dealing with brass bands or getting into the newspapers. I believe that the Men's Department in the near future should establish a movement for systematizing wage scales of Federal employees. These people are not in a position to help themselves and are sorely in need of somebody to look after their interest. Right here in the city of Washington are men who can get no redress for injustice—the class of men that I represent—the stationary firemen. I find that men doing the same class of work are getting $2.25 a day in some departments, while others are getting $2.75, $3 and $3.25, all having the same hours. That is not just. It also is a shame that men doing such laborious work for 365 days in the year should get $720, the same as they worked for twenty or twenty-five years ago, when the cost of living has almost doubled. I believe that this country is rich enough and great enough to give a decent living to every workingman—every man that wants to work. He should have it. The fellow who don't want to work ought to be in jail."

MRS. WILLIAM HOWARD TAFT.

Mrs. JOSEPH MEDILL McCORMICK narrated an experience in the stock yards where she addressed some working girls. One of the girls spoke up, saying: "What good does it do for you to come down here and talk? A great many have come down and talked. We don't want talk, we want something accomplished. Do you own any stock here?" Upon receiving an embarrassed, negative reply, she said, "There is no use in coming down here. If you can interest Mrs. Armour, Mrs. Swift or Mrs. Libby you can help us, but until then you cannot do any good." Mrs. McCormick felt that she was exactly right. This led to a conference with Miss Morgan and Miss Harriman, who were interested in the plans for organizing the Woman's Welfare Department and the determination that women who draw dividends from industrial concerns should know the conditions under which those dividends were earned. Mrs. McCormick said that the work had made such progress among employers that "now we have letters asking us to come and make suggestions."

Mrs. ARCHIBALD HOPKINS spoke of the work of the Washington Section under her predecessor, Mrs. Samuel Spencer, praising the Government officials for their efforts to improve working conditions for their employes. She announced that a lodging house for working girls would be started in Washington by Mrs. J. Medill McCormick, explaining that the Woman's Welfare Section would act as an advisory board. No generation of women has ever had such an opportunity given as the women of the Twentieth Century to help the world on in the battle of life.

SEMI-ANNUAL MEETING WOMAN'S DEPARTMENT

MRS. TAFT'S GARDEN PARTY IN HONOR OF FEDERATION'S MEMBERS

THE most notable event in connection with the recent Washington meeting of the Woman's Welfare Department was Mrs. Taft's first garden party of the season, given in honor of the members of that department of The National Civic Federation. The President and Mrs. Taft received their guests on the White House lawn under the protecting boughs of the great old trees. The Springtime freshness of the verdure surrounding the playing fountain, with the great white columns of the official home for a background and set off by the red uniforms of the Marine Band, afforded a scene of rare beauty.

Mrs. TAFT, the Honorary Chairman of the Woman's Welfare Department, attended the reception at the residence of Mrs. John Hays Hammond the same evening, and, as evidence of her great interest in the work, also lent her presence at the morning meeting when the following addresses were made:

Mrs. JOHN HAYS HAMMOND: Do you realize that every morning an army of 7,000,000 working women march out to meet the day, an industrial army which is contributing its service to increase the material wealth and, in that way, the political importance of our country among the nations on the earth?

What are we doing—we women who are not in the wage-earning class, but who are enriched and benefited by our patient Sisters of Toil? This is a question we cannot ignore. It is your duty and mine, in the name of *humanity* and *patriotism*, to work to ameliorate the condition of the less fortunate of our community so as to remove any just cause of grievance that now exists against the more prosperous of the country. It is our peace mission to bring about a better understanding between wage-earner and employer.

Not more than three years ago The National Civic Federation—a body of influential men of earnest purpose—established a Woman's Welfare Department as an offshoot of their organization to provide a means to enable women to discharge such humane and civic duties.

1. What is the Woman's Welfare Department of The National Civic Federation?

An organization of women interested in the welfare of Government and industrial employes.

2. What is its object?

To establish committees in various sections of the United States for the purpose of furthering welfare work.

3. What is Welfare Work?

It is improving the working and living conditions of the employe by the employer. This includes the safeguarding from unnecessary risks in dangerous and unhealthful industries; the provision of good ventilation, light and sanitation; lunchrooms and restrooms; educational and recreation resources; good housing conditions; savings funds and benefit and loan associations; recognizing always that the first essentials to the welfare of employes are steady work, an equitable wage and reasonable hours of labor.

4. How can Welfare Work be accomplished?

By interesting employers in the special needs of their employes, and thus bringing about a better mutual understanding.

5. How do the methods of The National Civic Federation differ from other organizations engaged in similar work?

By using educational methods to demonstrate to employers what has been accomplished for employes by employers in kindred industries.

6. Is there need of Welfare Work in every community?

There is in every community where there are factories, stores, mines, railroads or public institutions, such as city hospitals, post offices, schools and other Government buildings.

7. What is necessary to start a Section of the Woman's Department of The National Civic Federation in order that Welfare Work may be successfully introduced into a community?

(a) A well-organized working committee composed largely of women, who, as stockholders or through family relationship, are financially interested in industrial organizations, in factories, mines and other places of work, or whose families have official relations with Governmental departments.

(b) A knowledge of conditions under which employes work and of the special needs of such employes; a conservative and non-aggressive method of making tactful and comprehensive suggestions to employers.

(c) A large membership, so that the interest of a great many women in the community may be enlisted.

(d) Lectures and informal talks on social and economic subjects to the non-working members, so that their interest may be kept alive.

Although barely three years old, this Woman's Welfare Department, through the efforts of my predecessors in office and their co-laborers, has achieved most gratifying results. We have already brought good ventilation, restrooms and lunchrooms into many of the obsolete Government buildings of Washington. And, perhaps, more far-reaching in future effect has been the result of our agitation, in that Congress has at last awakened to the realization of its responsibility—has formed committees to inspect these buildings and to report as to their proper sanitation—and will, we hope, shortly pass the bill appointing for all time a regular Board of Sanitary Inspectors. We have established night schools, dispensaries, medical clinics, visiting nurses, kindergartens, lessons in cooking, sewing and household economics in mill towns of the South.

No detail is too small for our care. We have dried the wet garments of the overworked postman—provided reading-rooms, local barber shops, baths, bowling alleys, pool tables, conducted without drinking and disorder; we have concerned ourselves with the grading of streets and lighting of towns by electricity, the planting of domestic gardens, and even the proper pasturing of family cows has been part of our work. In every case the most encouraging feature of our labor has been the ready realization by the employer of the great importance and value of our co-operation.

As I have said, the Woman's Welfare Department is as yet in its infancy; our work has been relatively local. Since I assumed office—a little over two months ago—we have formed a new Section each month—one in Atlanta, Ga., and one in Richmond, Va.—but it is our aim and expectation to extend this organization throughout every State and Territory of the Union. In the North, South, East and West, in every region of our great country where women are employed, there is work for us to do—intelligent, sympathetic aid to be given. We need workers. All of us can contribute in some way, whether by financial assistance or personal service. There is room for every kind of woman—the young women, with their splendid enthusiasm and energy, the middle-aged, experienced veterans of many hard-fought life battles—more tender because of their grim scars. We need wise, quiet council of the women who, from the twilight of their years, can speak rare words.

Will you come and join our ranks,—remembering those beautiful words of Portia?

"The quality of mercy is not strained,
It droppeth as the gentle rain from heaven
Upon the place beneath; it is twice blest,
It blesseth him that gives, and him that takes."

Mrs. Hammond then introduced the Chairman of the District of Columbia Section, Mrs. ARCHIBALD HOPKINS, who presided over the meeting.

ANNUAL COMPETITIVE DRILL, FIRST AID CORPS, PHILADELPHIA AND READING COAL AND IRON COMPANY.—Dr. J. B. Rogers Inspecting Dressings for Rating in Final Contest.

DEPARTMENT ON COMPENSATION FOR INDUSTRIAL ACCIDENTS AND THEIR PREVENTION

By AUGUST BELMONT, Chairman

It is an especial matter of gratification to me to have watched the growth of the Woman's Welfare Department and now contemplate the magnificent future which is before you, because it was during my administration of The National Civic Federation as President that the Woman's movement started, having its inception at a meeting at Mr. Carnegie's, in the Winter of 1907. I congratulate you upon the growth of your numbers, the work you are accomplishing, and, finally, your good fortune in having Mrs. Hammond as your Chairwoman. Her well-known energy and active interest afford a source of great strength to you.

The Department of Compensation for Industrial Accidents and their Prevention has much in the character of its work which dovetails in with what you are and will be doing. Its tentative bill, which was presented for the Federation's consideration and adopted at the annual meeting, was, through various channels, submitted to the legislatures of thirty-three States during the past Winter. The principles of this bill have been adopted in a number of the States. The object of the bill was in the direction of compulsory compensation, based upon the police power of a State, and we believe it to be a reasonable step at the present time, providing for workmen injured under the conditions prevailing in modern industry. It follows the lines of those already pursued by substantially every industrial country of Europe so far as it goes, we having for reasons confined it to hazardous occupations. It abandons the old common law theory—that the employer is liable for injury only on the ground that the employer has done his workman a wrong; and follows a new theory—that under modern conditions industry should bear the charge of the damage caused to persons as it already bears the charge of damage to machinery and equipment. In the State of New York a law was passed last year, involving the principles of compulsory compensation, known as the Wainwright Act, and, so far as the State of New York is concerned, our bill depended upon the outcome of the test case involving the constitutionality of the Wainwright Law. The Court of Appeals declared the Act unconstitutional, but it does not follow that in other States the principle may not be sustained.

In spite of this, the demand for a workable compensation law is so universal that my department has redoubled its energies toward a solution of the question. A legal committee, with the Hon. Francis Lynde Stetson as chairman, has undertaken to redraft the measure to meet the new conditions arising in New York State. The Compensation Committee of the American Bar Association, and a similar committee of the National Association of Commissioners on Uniform Laws have tendered their assistance to Mr. Stetson's committee, as have also the attorneys who conducted the suits which resulted in declaring the Wainwright Act unconstitutional. It is impossible to forecast what the outcome of their labors will be. In New Jersey the constitutional question seemingly has been avoided by what is called an elective act. This provides that both the employe and employer, the first when entering the service of the employer, and the second in engaging his employe, without any written agreement, ipso facto enter into a contract to seek redress for accidents under a definite compulsory compensation law. But in case either one of the two does not wish to avail himself of the same but prefers to seek redress, in case of need, through the common law provisions governing claims for accidents, a definite notice in writing must be given by either one to the other that he will not avail himself of the compensation law. It is yet too early to pronounce upon its value.

To all employers of labor it is of the utmost importance that fair and equitable compensation laws should be placed on the statutes of our various industrial States in place of the present liability laws. If this is not done, the pressure from workingmen must ultimately result in sweeping away many of the defenses which the employer now has, and exposing him to jury decisions pressed by shyster lawyers and a class of harpies known as ambulance-chasers.

The Federation knows that labor leaders in this country are fair in this matter, and prefer compensation laws with definite awards, that the workmen may secure all that is legally due them and, moreover, at a time when they need it, without the risk of lawsuits which either in the end result in no compensation or, if decided in their favor, secure to them only a percentage of the award, sometimes not even 50 per cent., the rest going to their counsel for taking their case on a contingent fee. At the present time our liability laws tend to engender ill feeling between workmen and employers by reason of the character and outcome of much of the litigation. It cannot be hoped that any scheme will be devised nor is there any in existence in any part of the world, providing for full insurance in case of accident. The best that is now provided is one-half pay for certain specified periods.

While this work of the Federation is going on, it is also pressing through another committee for improvement in State Inspection of Factories and compelling the use of safety appliances. This committee is at work upon a model safety act, which, like the Federation's act for compensation, it hopes will form the basis for some uniform State legislation. This committee has done excellent work in the field of comparative study of statistics and statutory requirements as to accidents and their prevention. The report indicates a manifest absence of uniformity of law and of action in the various States and inadequate machinery for carrying into effect statutory requirements for the promotion of health, safety and comfort of wage-earners.

At a recent meeting of our organization in New York, the Hon. CYRUS W. PHILLIPS, a member of our Committee on the Improvement of State Inspection of Factories and Chairman of the Committee on Causes of Industrial Accidents of the New York State Commission on Employers' Liability, made the following statement relative to the Triangle Shirtwaist Factory's fire:

"The recent fire, by reason of the fact that the appalling loss of life occurred at one time and at the same place, aroused public attention to the dangers and hazards of modern industrial life. Yet this loss of life is but a small part of the mortality and bodily injuries due to industrial accidents which go comparatively unnoticed. More than twice as many workers are killed each year in the factories in this State, while the number of railroad men killed in their work in this State, outside of the City of New York, reaches nearly twice the number of those who lost their lives in the fire."

This same ratio, it is fair to presume, would apply to the whole country. What a field is open to us all for the doing of good!

EMPLOYERS' WELFARE DEPARTMENT

By WILLIAM R. WILLCOX, Chairman

SO many ask me the question, "What are you doing through the Employers' Welfare Department?" that I shall, for the benefit of those who are not familiar with its work, open my remarks by stating that our efforts are entirely devoted toward interesting employers, whether public or private, in improving the conditions of employes in all occupations and industries.

The Employers' Welfare Department of the Federation is composed of 500 leading employers and public officials throughout the United States. Its work is the humanitarian phase of the Federation's activities. The methods employed are educational, the effort being to prove the value of Welfare Work by holding up as good examples employers who have successfully introduced such features for the benefit of their employes, as sanitary washrooms, factory lunchrooms, libraries, clubs, classes for technical education, homes rented or sold, and wage-earners' insurance.

To quote the growth of the welfare activities of several of the members of the Employers' Welfare Department is to show the impetus which has been given to Welfare Work through our efforts.

For example, a stereopticon address by one of our lecturers before two hundred manufacturers in a single industry, picturing fine washrooms and baths for men, lunchrooms, ventilation devices, drinking-water fountains, seats for women workers, men's and women's clubrooms and dancing pavilions, roof gardens, emergency hospitals and proper homes for employes resulted in the president of the largest factory in that trade sending to the Welfare Department for advice and expert assistance in providing separate artistic, yet practical, lunchrooms with food at cost for the men and women; and, in two of his villages, he has destroyed old houses rented to the people, after substituting modern sanitary dwellings surrounding social buildings. While this accomplishment was in the woolen industry in New England, a contrasting illustration is the demand upon this Department for information as the result of an address before an association of box manufacturers at its annual convention recently in one of the Central States.

The success of the Welfare Work in one great industrial organization, employing between twenty-five and thirty thousand wage-earners and clerks in its mines and plants in Michigan, Wisconsin, New York, Ohio, Illinois and other States, which was initiated by one of the members of our staff, is exemplified by a conference of more than one hundred welfare workers in its employ held within the last ten days. The fact that this company requires such a large corps of welfare supervisors, such as doctors, nurses, matrons, machinery safety inspectors and clubhouse managers, under the direction of an efficient welfare secretary, indicates the systematic conduct as well as the vastness of its Welfare Work. This company brought its welfare workers together from different States to make tours of inspection through three of its great factories to view safeguards for machinery, hospital arrangements, lunchrooms, clubhouses, ventilation devices and various other schemes for the benefit of employes. After inspecting the Welfare Work in Chicago plants, there was given a dinner at which there was an interchange of experiences, with addresses by the president and other officials of the company.

Another employer in Kentucky has given his men an eight-hour workday in three shifts, with the same pay that they had when on two shifts of twelve hours each. This affords them time to go home for meals, has greatly improved their health and affords opportunity to use their clubrooms in the mills, where they play billiards and other games.

One of the most comprehensive examples is that of one of our members manufacturing shoe machinery in the State of Massachusetts, where there are 4,500 workers, the majority highly skilled and receiving good wages, but the head of the company, who has progressed with us from the beginning of the organization of our Welfare Department, has incorporated in the work of that company all the underlying principles for which we have stood. In addition to a short workday (the hours being fifty per week) and high wages, there has been erected an industrial plant in a beautiful rolling country outside of Boston, the building itself having 75 per cent. of the wall space devoted to windows, and great fans being installed all over the plant to bring down inhalations of fresh air from the skies and send it throughout the workrooms. To quote from the report of an investigation: "Here is an industrial community where fathers, daughters, sisters and brothers are congregated under one great kindly administration; and the spirit of American chivalry, that the woman must be guarded and cared for, is fostered by the officials and perpetuated by the employes. The women begin their work ten minutes later than the men, and leave ten minutes earlier. They have their rest room in charge of the matron. It contains a piano, reading matter and comfortable chairs and couches. There are individual lockers, and adjoining are bath rooms with ample hot and cold water, where the shower baths are among the most popular of the many excellent innovations. 'We assume that they are all in good health when they come to us, and it is our duty to keep them that way,' said one of the officials. For instance, they must leave the atmosphere of the factory during the midday lunch time. They must either go to their homes, if not too far away, to the restaurant, where they may sit at separate tables, or to the restroom. This enforced relaxation keeps them happy and contented. The men also have excellent lockers, bathrooms and lunchroom. There are no annual "house cleanings." Men go about constantly, clearing away dust and litter, and not for an unnecessary minute is a mechanic allowed to leave a piece of machinery or tool lying about. In Massachusetts there are in force, according to the most recent report of the State Savings Bank officials, 2,521 savings bank insurance policies, and of this number about one-sixth, or 402 policies, are held by the thrifty employes at this Beverly plant. The limit allowed to each policy under this form is $500, and as the Beverly employes hold an aggregate of $201,000, it is a simple process of arithmetic to show that the average is over $490. Whenever one of the employes is stricken, he or she is quickly carried to the emergency hospital, one of the best equipped in the country, where prompt professional treatment is administered. The corporation has spent great sums in preventive measures. The dangerous sections are guarded by covers, and powerful fans drive the dust from the grinding machines upward and away from the worker. One of its officials stated, in presenting a clubhouse to the employes, that 'all having learned to work hard, they must now learn to play hard.' The clubhouse, which cost thousands of dollars, is as complete in its appointments as any country club, and is operated on a self-respecting basis. Best of all, perhaps, is provision for the future of the boys who will one day be inventors and trained mechanics. Two groups, each containing thirty-five boys, alternate between the factory and the Beverly High School. The company furnishes all materials and keeps the accounts. The boys are paid one-half the price which would be paid to men performing the same tasks. The other half goes toward the expenses of the schools."

One of the greatest accomplishments of the Employers' Welfare Department has been the result of an investigation of the factories of one company, where there are 10,000 employes distributed in various States from Missouri to Rhode Island. The report with recommendations made by our Department resulted in the appropriation on the part of the company of a fund of $100,000 for important sanitary improvements.

Homely illustrations of particular phases would show, for example, our commissary expert having installed in a Connecticut factory within the last six months an artistic self-supporting lunchroom for men and women employes, where the product manufactured is hotel silverware. Now he has just completed designs for a lunchhouse in a dental factory on Long Island, employing 2,000 men and women, which will be one of the finest in the United States; and at the same time he is installing a lunchroom for women in a cotton mill in New Jersey.

None the less useful has been an annual conference of the heads of Welfare Departments in various factories, stores, mining corporations and railroads, held in January, where, through an interchange of experiences, there was brought to the attention of many employers for the first time the extremely important idea of night ventilation for workrooms. While there were other valuable presentations on proper lighting of workrooms for ensuring of health, emergency hospitals in mines, et cetera, this new theory is worthy of special attention, and I, therefore, quote from the address of Dr. Bannister:

"While night ventilation originated in our medical department, it had to be placed on an economic basis. It occurred to me if the windows could be opened at night, that the girls and all the workers would have the advantage of going into a well-ventilated workroom the next morning. Previously, as soon as work was done, every window was closed. When the watchman made his rounds and found one open, he closed it. So, the question of night cleaning came up from an economic point of view. We have a night force of about ten men in charge of what we call a night foreman. An overseer at night is absolutely necessary. They tried putting two men on each floor with the overseer running around to keep them busy. That didn't work for the reason that we kept the whole factory illuminated, which was an expense, and oft-times the overseer would go around and find one man asleep, because the factory is large, and he had to cover a great deal of ground. Now we take each floor separately, putting all the men there and having it illuminated. We have the overseer on that floor. All the windows are opened, the floor is cleaned and all the dust taken out. Then the windows are left open and

UNITED SHOE MACHINERY COMPANY.

1. Employes' Club House. 3. The Factory. 5. The Gun Club.
4. Interior View. 2. Interior View.

TYPIFYING AMERICAN WOOLEN COMPANY'S METHODS FOR REBUILDING MILL VILLAGES.
1. Three New Tenements in "Long Block" Showing Street Curbing. 2. Old Mill Boarding House with Village Improvements in Process. 3. New Employes' Cottage. 4. Ten Displaced Old Tenements in "Long Block" As They Stood for Fifty Years. 5. New Mill Boarding House and Recreation Hall.

the lights turned down, the force going to the next floor, where the same routine is gone through. We have a system of going through the lavatories, cans are carried out, and so forth, but the main point is all the windows are opened. Early in the morning, at probably 3 or 4 o'clock, the windows are supposed to be closed. Having plenty of windows, certainly we have plenty of fresh air, and the girls and men are better fitted for the day's work than they were before."

The work of the Employers' Welfare Department of The National Civic Federation has practically doubled during the past year, which indicates the widespread interest it has created among employers, many manufacturers having consulted us either by correspondence, through their representatives or personally, and having secured material through our Bureau of Exchange, recommendations from expert investigators, or submitted plans of work for our criticism.

ADDRESS OF PRESIDENT SETH LOW

I shall say a few words about The National Civic Federation as a whole. Someone has likened society to a three-legged stool, one leg being the employer, another leg the employe and the third leg what we now hear called the ultimate consumer. At any rate, whether the illustration will hold or not, that does suggest one of the possible divisions running through society. You could easily perceive that, if one leg of the three is shortened up, the stool is not very comfortable for society as a whole, and when one is seriously injured, there may be a disaster. The peculiar thing about The National Civic Federation, that which is unique in it, not only in our own country but in all countries, is the fact that it consists of large employers of labor, the representatives of organized labor, and of persons, like myself, for example, who are neither one nor the other—representatives of the ultimate consumer.

You can easily perceive that those three different elements do not always run parallel with each other; but we all get the benefit of learning from the others what are their points of view. We get many illuminating illustrations on all sorts of questions in that way. One may interest you. I think I hear labor unions criticised as often because of their attitude toward apprentices as for any other one thing. You hear men say they will not allow the young fellows to be taught any more in their trade. I always used to sympathize with that as a thing that did not admit of dispute until I heard a labor union man say at one of our conferences at the office one day, "The trouble is, an employer in modern industry employs a boy as an apprentice; they set him to work to run a machine or several machines. In a short time he can run those machines as well as a man. At the end of his apprenticeship, or during his apprenticeship of several years, the employer gets a man's work done for a boy's pay, and when that boy becomes a journeyman, he does not know anything more about his trade than when he began. He knows how to run that one machine and that is all." I happened to speak of that at a gathering of large manufacturers in Providence, R. I., very soon after I heard it, and one of them said to me, "That is absolutely a fair indictment of modern industry." The other one said to me that his father and grandfather had conducted a machine shop in Providence ever since 1830 or thereabouts; that they had pursued the old policy always of teaching every apprentice every part of his trade, with the result, he said, that they have never had a strike in seventy or eighty years, and that "You can find our men who have been taught as apprentices in our machine shop in every machine shop in Providence."

I venture to think that no one coming face to face with the industrial questions of our day, from the angle of most of those in this room, any more than I myself, would ever have got that understanding of the motive lying behind the trade union's attitude toward apprentices. This union leader that I speak of remarked that in their business the trade agreement made it a necessary requirement of the apprentice system that every boy taken in should be taught every part of his trade. This union leader said, "If that were the attitude in all trades, you would find the position of the labor unions on the apprenticeship question changed very radically and very quickly."

Now, that serves to illustrate the point that I think is so fundamental in connection with all the work of The National Civic Federation that, whether we can agree or not, we do by meeting, by bringing together these three different elements that are concerned with all industries—the employer, the employe and the ultimate consumer, each one gets the other's point of view, at the very least.

But there are certain things in regard to which we can agree. It may surprise you, but on this question of regulating workmen's compensation, in regard to which Mr. Belmont reported, there was, I think, absolute unanimity of opinion between the employers, the employes and The National Civic Federation on the desirability of that movement, and, so far as they were in New York, they supported the New York law which was pronounced unconstitutional. I think, therefore, you will see that when they do agree, these employers and these employes and the ultimate consumer, that they represent a tremendous power in a democracy like ours, a tremendous power in any country, because every country to-day is governed, whatever be its governmental form, in the last resort by public opinion. But in a country like ours, such a united front can carry almost anything that is desired in any State in the Union, if effort is maintained long enough and intelligently enough.

Perhaps we will hear some man inclined to say, "Why do you have the leaders of organized labor, or a very small fraction of the laboring element of the United States?" The answer is that unorganized labor cannot be represented because they are unorganized. No individual has any authority to speak for the unorganized millions, but organized labor can be heard just because it is organized, and that is the reason why we have organized labor in our councils rather than unorganized labor. One other reason is that I think it is the common or universal belief on the part of those interested in the Federation that organized labor, with all its mistakes—and no one appreciates how many it makes better than its friends—has been a tremendous force in improving the hours of labor, the rate of pay and the conditions under which our industries are carried on and, therefore, we want to work with them. We strive never to hesitate to criticise what we believe should be criticised and, when we cannot agree, as I said before, we can do nothing. But nobody, by joining the Federation, abandons his personality or his individual relation to public questions or industrial questions, or anything else. You may find members and officers of the Civic Federation, as we saw in the last presidential campaign, speaking on every platform and supporting precisely the opposite doctrines; but that does not prevent us from working together, when we can agree, nor from striving to enlighten each other when we do not agree.

I think we live in an age that is full of interest, and if there be any keynote of it that is more significant than any other, I think we should have to say it is an age of combination. I suppose that we all have our own philosophy of the times, and my own is that we have reached in human society just the moment that was reached in the art of printing when each type came to represent a single letter. You remember they used to print from blocks with several words on them and you did not get to the time of limitless combination, as represented by the art of printing, until you individualized your type. Now, precisely so, we do not reach the era of combination on such a scale as we see it to-day in human society until we do individualize our man. The struggle of the ages has been to make every man count for what he was entitled to count, to make every man equal before the law, and the best blood of all the nations throughout all time has been poured out in that cause.

And some men say, just look at it! Here is the individual capitalist disappearing in the corporation and the individual laborer disappearing in the trade union; the corporation is disappearing in the trust and the trade union is disappearing in the Federation of Labor. Of course, if one thinks that individuality is disappearing I should think everything in our day would seem amiss. But, if on the other hand it be true, as it seems to me it is, that we have all of this combination just because we have more successfully individualized each human being than before, then I think there is every reason to be encouraged, just because we see the combination taking on always new forms and acquiring always new power. Of course it is, comparatively speaking, a new force in human society, just as much so as electricity was twenty-five years ago. How have they learned to make electricity our servant instead of its being a source of constant danger? Simply by experiments, and by experiments that have often cost great loss of life and great destruction of property.

Precisely so I think this idea of combination in human society has to be brought out by experience. Capital organizes—I do not like to use the impersonal thing; capital does not do it; it is the men, the stockholders if you please—the stockholders organize in response to the law that I speak of; labor organizes in response to the same law. Neither one nor the other organizes to fight the other. They organize for their own sake now. They feel the new strength at their command. At first they think they can do anything if they try. By and by they find out that although they are organized, they are organized within a society that is greater than any of them. Society places this law upon them, when it knows what it ought to be and says within those limits you can act; outside of those limits you cannot act. I think that is the process that is going on all over the world, in a thousand ways, more conspicuously in industry, perhaps, than in any other field. If that be true, I think you see again why the philosophy of The National Civic Federation is so useful in composing itself of the three elements which together comprehend the whole of human society. At least those of us who throw ourselves into that work will understand better the other's point of view; and useful service is apt to be proportioned directly to the intimate knowledge of the problems to be dealt with.

I trust this meeting will respond perfectly to Mrs. Hammond's hopes. I want to assure her of the heartiest co-operation.

WELFARE WORKERS' FOURTH CONFERENCE

MEMBERS OF PROFESSION MEET UNDER AUSPICES EMPLOYERS' WELFARE DEPARTMENT

A CONFERENCE of the Welfare Workers, under the auspices of the Welfare Department of The National Civic Federation, was held in the Assembly Room of the Metropolitan Building, New York City, on the day preceding the annual meeting.

Morning Session.

Address of Welcome: Hon. William R. Willcox, Chairman, Employers' Welfare Department, New York City.
Opening Address: The Human Machine: M. W. Alexander, General Electric Co., Lynn, Mass.
Ventilation: Dr. Winthrop Talbot, Director, Health and Economics Department, National Electric Lamp Association, Cleveland, Ohio.
Night Ventilation of Factory Workrooms: Dr. Lucy A. Bannister, Welfare Manager, Westinghouse Lamp Co., Bloomfield, N. J.
Light Work Rooms: Arthur A. Ernst, Consulting Engineer of Light and Technical Adviser, New York.
First Aid to the Injured in Anthracite Coal Fields: Dr. J. M. Wainwright, Moses Taylor Hospital, Delaware and Lackawanna R. R. Co., Scranton, Pa.
Our Effort to Prevent Tuberculosis: Miss Mary L. Goss, Welfare Secretary, International Harvester Co., Chicago.

Afternoon Session.

Stereopticon Views on First Aid to Injured Miners: Dr. George H. Halberstadt, Philadelphia and Reading Coal and Iron Co., Pottsville, Pa.
The Work of the Welfare Manager: Miss Anna A. E. Van de Carr, Forbes Lithograph Co., Boston, Mass.
New Developments in Our Industrial Villages: W. E. C. Nazro, Welfare Manager, Plymouth Cordage Co., North Plymouth, Mass., and Welland, Canada.
A Complete Factory Welfare Plan: D. C. Lowles, Sherwin-Williams Co., Cleveland.
Home Work: Mrs. G. H. Furman, R. H. Macy & Co., New York.
The Department Store Problem: Mrs. L. L. Ray, Greenhut-Siegel Cooper Co., New York City.
Sanitation in Mining Villages—the Home, School and Club: W. H. Moulton, Superintendent Welfare Department, Cleveland Cliffs Iron Co., Ishpeming, Mich.
Five o'Clock Tea: At the residence of Mrs. J. Borden Harriman, Chairman of the Industrial Employes' Welfare Committee of the Woman's Department of the Federation, in honor of participants at Conference.

There was an attendance of Welfare Workers and special experts on the subject, including employers and economists from a number of States. An exchange of experiences brought forth new and helpful information. Following the address of the Chairman, HON. WILLIAM R. WILLCOX there was an introductory speech delivered by MR. M. W. ALEXANDER, of the General Electric Company, Lynn, Mass., who presided over the conference.

The opening address of Chairman Willcox follows:

"It gives me great pleasure to welcome members of this comparatively new profession at the Fourth Conference of Welfare Workers, called by the Welfare Department of The National Civic Federation.

"The first meeting was designated a 'Conference of Social Secretaries,' as that title had been given to workers in this field, but when these professional workers came together they refused to accept the term. After considerable deliberation it was decided to accept the proposition of Mr. W. G. Mather, President of the Cleveland-Cliffs Iron Company, and take officially the title of 'Welfare Manager.' That term was adopted by many, while others have taken 'Welfare Director,' 'Welfare Superintendent' or 'Welfare Secretary.'

"The true origin of the term 'Welfare Work' is found in the kindred language of Germany. The machinery of that language is adapted to the liberal expression of thought in the form of a single though comprehensive word. The Germans took advantage of their linguistic convenience by naming the various arrangements which may be devised and which employers may carry into effect for the protection and comfort of wage-earners, *Wohlfahrtseinrichtungen*, which has received the explanatory translation 'Examples of personal care for their workers by employers.' When we began the modification and adaptation of this work to the less paternalistic social and industrial conditions in the United States, we made use of the term 'Welfare Department,' not only as descriptive of the organization of the voluntary efforts that have been made in Germany by the employer for the betterment of the living and working conditions of the employe, but as suitable for use in this country.

RESCUE CORPS WITH DRAEGER HELMET, FINDING MINER OVERCOME BY GAS.
ILLUSTRATING ADDRESS OF DR. J. M. WAINWRIGHT.
COMPLIMENTS OF CAPTAIN W. A. MAY, GENERAL MANAGER, HILLSIDE COAL AND IRON CO., AND PENNSYLVANIA COAL CO., SCRANTON, PA.

"There has been some objection made to this specific application of the term, but the adverse criticism seems not to rest upon a sound basis. Upon the contrary, the objections that have been made to its use imply in some degree the erroneous assumption that the underlying motive of welfare work is charity. The preamble to the Constitution of the United States, in its concise but comprehensive summary of the purposes of that instrument, includes the phrase 'to provide for the common welfare.' This affords historic and distinguished precedent for the use of the word in expressing the purpose of this department. The framers of the fundamental law of this country did not have the word 'charity' in mind, at least in its restricted sense of almsgiving, when they included the 'general welfare' among its vital purposes. The essential reason for the promotion of welfare work is that its true object is the mutual and inter-active benefit of each of the human factors in industrial production, the employer and the employed; a result that includes the great body of consumers grouped in the term the 'general public.' Hence it is that the phrase of the Constitution 'the common welfare' happily and correctly expresses the inclusive purposes of this organization, that gathers and that welcomes its friends here to-day.

"But it is not alone this origin of the term 'welfare work' that it is appropriate to consider. The phrase has proved so attractive as to invite, not the flattery of imitation, but the abuse of misapplication. There have been those who have, whether unconsciously or with appreciative design, taken the term as promising an impetus to movements that have no relation whatever to the promotion by the employer of the welfare of employes, whatever proper and peculiar merits may be claimed for those enterprises.

"Now, welfare work in its practical application has a number of divisions, among these being placed as of first importance, sanitary work-places, to which a list of specified provisions for physical welfare is accounted essential. The use of the word 'welfare' came readily into the vocabulary of those who sought to forward the physical as well as the mental benefit of pupils in the public schools. Again, certain genial persons sought to forward through a dinner a cause that they termed 'municipal welfare,' and again there appeared promoters of a 'child welfare exhibit,' and the attractiveness of the term to the literary mind appeared in the adoption of it in the modified title of a periodical published in the high cause of altruism.

"There is no desire to file a caveat or to apply for a patent in the tribunal of economic literature as to exclusive proprietorship in the application of this term. A serious reason for objecting to its appropriation as a phrase descriptive of efforts foreign to and distinct from those for which it was originally intended is that it has caused confusion in the minds of employers and of some writers, and of others. It is a term precisely descriptive as it is applied to the work of this organization, and no research or ingenuity has discovered one more fit.

"Our work largely is educational, the main point being to interest employers in promoting welfare work as we understand it, namely, improving of the working and living conditions of employes by the employers.

"In promoting the work it is recognized that the first essentials to the welfare of employes are steady work, an equitable wage and reasonable hours of labor, but that the employer has a further obligation.

"It is advocated that the beginning of all welfare work should be directed toward meeting the pressing necessities for the physical well-being of employes in their work-places.

"We have five divisions covered by the phrase 'Welfare Work': 1, Sanitary Work-Places; 2, Recreation; 3, Educational Opportunities; 4, Housing, and 5, Provident Funds.

"We find interchange of experiences as most valuable between employers as well as between those engaged in supervising the activities for the benefit of employes in any enterprise.

M. W. ALEXANDER dwelt upon the fact that the welfare of employes is a highly important factor in industrial production. Every industrial proposition involves the problem of raw materials, for which purchasing agents, chemists and physicists are employed in order to obtain the necessary results; it involves also the problem of machinery to do the work in the shortest time and at the least possible cost. Then, there is the most important of all—the problem of the men which has, perhaps, received the least attention of all. One machine is like another save in small details, but every human being is different from every other one. The competitor may buy raw materials and machinery at equal advantage, but in the personnel of the establishment there arises the question of increasing the efficiency; therein lies an asset of great value and reality. Waste of life and of human energy is to be avoided. The waste of human effort on the part of employers and employes is an impairment to the asset of production. The whole effort of welfare work must result in the lessening of this waste. This problem is now the study of all practical men in welfare work.

Dr. WINTHROP TALBOT, Director of the Health and Economics Department of the National Electric Lamp Association of Cleveland, Ohio, impressed the importance of the comfort and welfare of the worker as an economic feature. He discussed particularly types of ventilation and the value of cross currents. Drafts may be prevented in workrooms and offices by perforated screens. The conditions of air in the Government buildings in Washington and in other cities are so bad as to be abnormal. The speaker liberated some ozone in the hall to illustrate its practical efficiency in sterilizing vitiated atmosphere.

Dr. LUCY A. BANNISTER, Welfare Manager for the Westinghouse Lamp Company, at Bloomfield, N. J., stated that the first problem was to convince employers that comfort of wage-earners reduced expenses. She dwelt particularly upon ventilation of factory rooms at night as a preparation for the next day; at the same time, in cold weather the working rooms must be properly warmed in the morning. She had known foul air to be pumped from one room to another merely to save the expense of heating, but that this was not true economy. She emphasized the statement that welfare work is not philanthropy, but sound investment. It is her experience that there should be a hospital in every factory for emergency cases, or for cases of weariness, for the women workers, because of the better attention that could be so given. She spoke also of lunch rooms and counters and recreation rooms as highly important.

"Light Workrooms" was the topic discussed by ARTHUR A. ERNST, Consulting Engineer of Light and Technical Adviser, New York City. He stated that results had been directly shown of the effect of insufficient or too intense light upon the worker. It would affect the entire system. Every effort was made to utilize free daylight in our modern structures. Proper light promotes safety, reduces fatigue and increases efficiency and output. In artificial light must be considered, first, intensity, which may fatigue the eye and head if the source be not correctly gauged. The results of too bright a light within the field of vision may be very great, causing contraction of the pupils and the admission of insufficient rays; insufficient illumination may cause short-sightedness and headache. A bill is in preparation for the New York Legislature to regulate and standardize the light in factories.

"First Aid to the Injured in the Anthracite Coal Fields" was the topic of Dr. J. M. WAINWRIGHT, of the Moses Taylor Hospital, Scranton, Pa. Conditions proved that First Aid was needed in the stores in New York, upon their streets, and upon railroads, which began to provide operating rooms for the victims of accidents near stations along their lines. The first thing of pressing importance was to check the loss of blood and to prevent infection by the use of sterilized dressing. The first five minutes might affect all subsequent treatment, and might cause a simple injury to become fatal or result in permanent disability, which might have been prevented by the prompt application of a simple piece of gauze. The mines provide packets for first aid, as also do some railroads. The mines also have what is known as a surgical dressing room underground. These rooms are now required by statute in Pennsylvania. There is an ambulance always at hand at the mouth of the mine, and a hospital nearby. The first aid men are taught simply to prevent further injury, and never to undertake further treatment which might cause harm. Their first purpose is to place the patient in condition for transportation from the place where the injury was received. There are prizes for competition between First Aid teams. The corps competing for the prizes are watched by hundreds of spectators. The miners are as proud of their First Aid teams as the college boy is of the work of his football team. The speaker showed photographs of the helmets and other equipment for First Aid workers. Carelessness among miners can be cured only by education and not by punishment. Miners, for example, frequently try to drive a one-inch dynamite cartridge into a seven-eighth inch hole, with, of course, disastrous results. They are being taught, through illustrated literature, "How not to do things."

ANNUAL CONTEST, FIRST AID CORPS, PHILADELPHIA AND READING COAL AND IRON COMPANY, POTTSVILLE, PA.
1. Vice-President, W. J. Richards. 2. President, George F. Baer. 3. Surgeon, George H. Halberstadt.

"Our Effort to Prevent Tuberculosis" was the topic of Miss MARY L. GOSS, Welfare Secretary of the International Harvester Company, Chicago, Ill., who stated that it comprehends all work for better health in the sixteen factories and one hundred offices throughout the United States. Attention is given more and more to light, calsomined walls, clean floors, sprinkling before sweeping, removal of dust and gases, circulation of fresh air, sanitary drinking fountains and sanitary cuspidors, proper wash places and other lines of sanitation in our factories. Great consideration has been given to ventilation in all our works, the removal of fibre and metal dust, and noxious gases. Some effective systems have been installed, and others, which are inadequate, are still being tried. A thorough investigation into the conditions surrounding our industrial family of 40,000 showed home circumstances to be more largely responsible for infection than those in the shops. One stenographer became ill, having indications of lung trouble. Knowing the office to be light and well ventilated, I looked into home conditions and found that she kept late hours, had attended, evenings and Sundays, a friend who died from consumption, and that she slept with an elderly relative in a room with no open window. She died despite our efforts. Among certain types of foreigners, particularly Polish and Austrians, the attempt to improve home conditions is met with stubborn opposition. The doctor's report upon one case is: "Has pulmonary tuberculosis; getting worse every day; lives in one room in basement; surroundings about as bad as possible and cannot get him to better them." Interest is awakened by distributing circulars calling for increased sense of responsibility, urging co-operation with boards of health and tuberculosis associations, and giving lists of health suggestions. Our plan is for foremen to watch their men and send them to the dispensary for advice and treatment if lung trouble is indicated. Some advice given in our literature, posters and cards follows: "How to prevent consumption!" "Don't give it to others." "Don't let them give it to you." "Avoid food from consumptive animals." "Avoid dusty places." "Avoid foul air." "Avoid human jams." "Build up your resistance." "Occasionally look up the source of neighborhood milk supply." "Encourage out-of-door life, recreation and playgrounds." We ask street car companies, railroads, churches and public bodies to help in the fight for health.

W. L. SAUNDERS, President of the Ingersoll-Rand Company, New York City, spoke on the "Practical Methods of Ventilating Offices Without Draughts." He gave credit to the Benefit Association in that establishment for successful welfare work.

At the afternoon session Dr. GEORGE H. HALBERSTADT, of the Philadelphia & Reading Coal & Iron Company, Pottsville, Pa., explained some of the devices for first aid at coal mines, and the teaching of classes of workers. Charts are used for primary instruction in anatomy. There are now one thousand men in the anthracite region so instructed and supplied with first dressings. Applications by the army medical corps of several foreign governments had been made for samples of packets containing these appliances. An outside hospital is at the mouth of every shaft and an ambulance is within call. Some of these hospitals are supported by the State and others by private aid. The territory is divided into two districts and these are competitive, and there are held drills for prizes between representative teams. "Prevent Further Harm" is the motto of these first aid workers. The company has established a laboratory for instruction, including the use of first aid apparatus. This work has led to the study of medicine by several of the pupils. The speaker exhibited stereopticon views of first aid apparatus and of its use at the mines.

Miss ANNA A. E. VAN DE CARR, of the Forbes Lithographing Company, Boston, Mass., spoke upon the "Work of the Welfare Manager." She emphasized the lack of friction in this work as a guarantee of its progress. The absentee list had been large and expensive both to employers and workers. This has been reduced greatly—as much, in fact, as 75 per cent. Men, for example, would lose wages by staying at home to nurse a sick wife, not knowing enough to hire a nurse. There are emergency rooms and a physician is always within call. She described a system of savings conducted by the employers by a deduction agreed upon until the amount had reached $50, when it was deposited in a bank to the credit of the employe.

W. E. C. NAZRO, Welfare Manager of the Plymouth Cordage Company, North Plymouth, Mass., and Welland, Canada, described "New Developments in Our Industrial Villages." He outlined the work done for village improvement and its effect. He traced from the beginning the development of the work to its present proportions, including the installation of books in the free library, the increase of use of baths, the growth of the factory dining room; all showing increased interest among the employes. At Welland, beside other developments, the problem of housing had been of especial importance. He showed photographs of the celebration of Labor Day at Plymouth, which had much influence in promoting good relations between the interests of the factory and the homes.

D. C. LOWLES, of the Sherwin-Williams Company, Cleveland, O., spoke upon "A Complete Factory Welfare Plan." This industry extended from mines in Mexico to the workers in Cleveland, and to shops in Canada and England, and the plan was intended to be applicable to all. Health and safety of the employes were the first problems. Compensation for injuries in work were rated as a part of the operating expenses. A plan for pensioning employes would be put into operation immediately. He explained also a plan for advancing money to employes for proper purposes and in time of need. Industrial education is of special importance to an employer of large numbers of workmen. Recreation is another feature that must come in response to the wishes of the workers, and means to that end should be made to co-operate so far as possible with existing institutions.

In describing the "Home Work" of R. H. Macy & Co., Mrs. Geneva H. Furman gave a number of interesting illustrations. She told how the cause of a girl packer's frequent fainting spells was traced to her attempt to support a sick widowed mother, half starving herself. Food, medical attendance and many other necessities were furnished and the girl was given a better position. Her mother has recovered and they are now happy and comfortable. The weeping of a child bundler led to the discovery of a home where the father had committed suicide because of inability to get

MINING VILLAGE, CLEVELAND CLIFFS IRON COMPANY, GWINN, MICH.
1. CHURCH, HOSPITAL AND CLUB HOUSE. 2. HIGH SCHOOL. 3. FOOT-BRIDGE, ESCANABA RIVER. 4. EMPLOYES' HOMES. 5. STORE BUILDING AND BANK.

work. The man was laid out in the cheapest way on a long bench, covered with a black canopy having a convenient flap to open and show the face. The house was a ramshackle tenement, broken panes being replaced by sacking dancing in the wintery blasts, and the family was destitute. Their immediate wants were supplied and later the mother was given a position, the family now being self-supporting. The prejudice of another girl's mother and friends against operations and hospitals was overcome after four months' effort, and the girl, once badly disfigured by a tumor back of the eye, which would have crowded it from the socket, is now very pretty. A refined young woman in the state of melancholia and about to commit suicide because she had been abandoned and left homeless by her brother-in-law, was given sympathy and money and restored to a normal, happy business woman who makes life worth while for all about her. The men also receive attention. A visit to a porter, recovering from a long illness, showed his two children in bed with scarlet fever, all windows and shutters closed tight, a dispossess notice on the door and a doctor asking excessive charges by threats of no more calls. The rent and the doctor's bills were met. Good food, fresh air, disinfectants and the services of the store physician soon restored the family to health and happiness. A store girls' tuberculosis was traced to the dying father, for whom she was caring before and after working hours. Not only was he put into a hospital and later his funeral expenses paid, but she was sent to a sanitarium and kept there until restored to health. She is now happily married and grateful for the help she had when it was most needed.

MISS HELEN H. SNOW, Secretary of the Welfare Department of the Curtis Publishing Company, said: "Our building will have a glass enclosed roof garden, with outdoor promenade, a dancing space for the girls, with good floor, a library, an adequate lunch room, two emergency hospitals, distilled drinking water, locker rooms, shower baths, the latest heating, lighting and ventilating arrangements, while there will be a fireproof zone for the elevators, stairs, fire escapes, water pipes and electric conduits. All dangerous shafting will be supplanted by motor power."

R. W. CORWIN, M.D., LL.D., General Manager Sociological Department, The Colorado Fuel and Iron Company, Pueblo, Colorado, reported: "In addition to our regular work, we have equipped all of our school houses now with electric lights, which makes it possible to have stereopticon lectures and moving pictures at almost every camp. Much stress has been put, in the last year, upon the installation of safety devices in the mines, looking to the prevention of mine accidents, and a system of prizes has been established among our mine superintendents, based upon the decrease of accidents for the month. Our company is the first in America to have a Mine Rescue Car, equipped and ready at all times, and when the United States Government decided to equip a car, they borrowed our man to demonstrate the rescue helmets. A year ago we employed a man to look after the religious life of the mines where no church organization was at work, and this has proven very successful and will be continued. At Sunrise, Wyoming, the company is erecting a new church building, with the agreement that the Presbyterian Board give us a $1,200 a year man. This method gets rid of the cheap missionary who is going off on a tangent, and who could not be used anywhere else. We are demanding the best men, so that the church services will appeal to the best element in the mining camps. In the boys' work, we have been establishing the Boy Scout movement, with some success, but, of course, have difficulty in getting good leaders."

MRS. J. BORDEN HARRIMAN, Chairman of the Industrial Employes' Welfare Committee of the Woman's Department of The National Civic Federation, opened the addresses at the reception at her home by saying that specialists, meeting in this way, and interchanging experiences, make for progress. Anything that assists in the upbuilding of our institutions should be encouraged. It is helpful to the work of this committee to obtain the counsel of such experienced workers.

MRS. L. L. RAY, Welfare Secretary of the Greenhut-Siegel-Cooper Company, explained the development of the work there, saying:

"Our first step in welfare work was taken when we started the employes' association, and that for a time filled all the needs. This included the doctor's services any day during the year while at the store, all the medicines free and half of their salaries for six weeks in the year. A few years later, Mr. Greenhut started welfare work on a systematic basis, being convinced that it was advisable to have a welfare secretary or manager to do for his employes what he would like to do, but had not time. One can readily see that with 7,000 employes, there is a field for thought and a great deal to be done. Since this step was taken, there have been improvements throughout the store in general. We have a sick room, a restaurant and better dressing rooms, and best of all a lunch room, where food is served to employes for less than cost. The milk is examined and the food inspected, and we are always glad to have others come and test it. Since we have broadened out it has enabled the welfare manager or secretary to come in touch with the home environment, where we can better see the needs of the employes through this personal contact."

W. H. MOULTON, Superintendent of the Welfare Department of the Cleveland Cliffs Iron Company, Ishpeming, Mich., said:

"The Cleveland Cliffs Iron Company is a producer of iron ore in Michigan, Wisconsin and Minnesota, owning a railroad line, charcoal iron furnaces and a steamboat line to the lower lake ports. The work which we have done along welfare lines is for the direct benefit of the men employed. In our mining department we have careful inspection of our mines by a competent committee with the suggestion for remedies in every particular case of a serious accident. The sanitation and ventilation of the mines are carefully looked after. The best of washing facilities, with single washing basins, is provided. The men have individual steel lockers and shower baths. A pension system for old employes is provided and the widows and orphans of men accidentally killed also receive a pension. The families of our men have the services of visiting nurses, who visit the homes and render aid to any one who may be ill or injured and console the wives and children. In the Summer a rest home is provided for the invalids or the mothers of families who are used up from overwork. A new mining town has been built in the last three years at Gwinn, Mich. The business portion of this town is of brick or stone buildings, and all streets are macadamized. In the building of this town, the first thing was the introduction of the water and sewer systems, on account of which there was not during the building a single case of typhoid fever, which is usually prevalent in all this new work. Buildings were both for rent and sale to the employes, and school buildings with the most up-to-date equipment, were erected. The school buildings have bathrooms for the pupils, and are modern in every particular. The clubhouse has been erected by the President, William G. Mather, and thoroughly equipped. It serves as the social centre of all the town festivities."

EMPLOYES' LUNCH HOUSE, PLYMOUTH CORDAGE COMPANY, NORTH PLYMOUTH, MASS.

MISSION LUNCH HOUSE ADDED TO WELFARE WORK AT ALTON, ILL.

AN example that may be inspiring to others, of the application of Welfare Work by women who are interested financially in industrial enterprises is that of Mrs. Pascal Enos Hatch, at the works of the Illinois Glass Co., at Alton, Ill. This establishment is the greatest producer of glass bottles in the world. The Welfare Work there has been progressive and, from the beginning, has been carried out in accordance with the advice of and by experts furnished by the Employers' Welfare Department of The National Civic Federation. The first efforts of Mrs. Hatch were directed toward improvements in sanitary rooms; providing a rest-room for the women packers, furnished with easy chairs and a lounge, and brightened with plants and pictures; and, upon going through the factories and seeing the workmen eating cold lunches, she decided to start a hot lunch place in the yards. The original lunch-house, which was a small brick structure, appropriately called the "coffee station," is now to be converted into an emergency hospital. It was a beginning made in the spirit of efficient helpfulness, simple but nutritious food being served with coffee or milk at a counter at most reasonable prices, and yet making the place self-supporting. Progress has been made to a much larger establishment, 90 by [illegible]0 feet, in mission style of architecture. The concrete floor and wainscoting are chocolate brown, the walls being light tan. The ceiling is exposed sheathing, finished with two coats of oil. The roof is supported by iron trusses. All exposed iron work is painted black. All interior woodwork, and tables and chairs are finished in weathered oak. The outside window and door trim is black, the overhanging cornice and lookouts being finished with two coats of oil. All cement plaster finish is painted with one coat of concrete gray waterproof paint. The roof is imitation tile, painted dark green. There is a concrete walk around the building. It contains not only a long counter with stools for fifty-five customers, but an additional space for one hundred men, equipped with tables, seating four each, and chairs. This restaurant is well lighted and attractive. The character of the food, cooking and service is indicated by the continued attendance of the men as well as by their repeated expressions of appreciation. The building was erected and furnished at the expense of Mrs. Hatch, daughter of the late president of the company, William Eliot Smith, who was a member of the Federation's Welfare Department. The restaurant is open day and night. All the neat china is marked and the knives and forks are triple plated with silver. The kitchen, well lighted and ventilated, is furnished with modern appliances, including steam warming tables, steam coffee urns, bread-slicer, potato-peeler and dish-washer, all three electrically driven. The kitchen utensils are principally of aluminum. The coal-heated oven will bake 150 loaves of "home-made" bread, and there is especial provision for making wholesome pies, sold at 5 cents per quarter. There are urns for milk, cream and ice water. The cooking is done principally by steam. Much credit for these results is due to Miss Emma L. Condon, the efficient manager, who finds economy in buying the best food, and whose combination of good cheer with dignity of manner have proved as important in results as is her business ability. Mrs. Hatch has stipulated that the quality of food be the best and that the portions served be liberal. The prices are: Soup, coffee and milk, 3 cents each; meat sandwiches—beef or ham—with two thick slices of home-made bread—including potatoes, 10 cents; roast veal, 5 cents; hash, 3 cents; mashed potatoes, 3 cents; sauerkraut, 5 cents; and pudding, 5 cents. The restaurant runs day and night, the men working on eight hour shifts and receiving the highest wages paid in any industry excepting "rollers" in steel mills. The company makes annual trade agreements with the Glass Bottle Blowers' Union.

ILLINOIS GLASS WORKS, ALTON, ILL.
1. Interior New Mission Lunch House. 2. Interior—Men Seated at Tables in Rear. 3. Exterior View, New Mission Lunch House for Men. 4. Women Employes' Rest Room in Factory. 5. First Coffee Station, Now Being Used As Emergency Hospital.

SAFETY OF EMPLOYES

ADDRESSES UPON THE REPETITIVE LESSONS OF FATAL FIRES AND OF INDUSTRIAL ACCIDENTS AT A MEETING OF THE NEW YORK STATE EMPLOYERS' WELFARE COMMITTEE

THE program for this meeting, held at the rooms of the New York Board of Trade and Transportation, in New York City, was in charge of the Committee on Improvement of State Inspection of Factories of the Department on Compensation for Industrial Accidents and Their Prevention.

The recent deplorable fire, bringing suffering and death to many employes in the Triangle Shirtwaist Factory, emphasized the importance of securing a widespread introduction of welfare work, including sanitary workrooms, free from debris, fire escapes, fire drills and compulsory workmen's compensation, which would cause employers more to safeguard against such insurance loss by better protecting the workers.

There were addresses upon "The Duty of the Employer," "The Duty of the State," "The Duty of the Municipality" and "The Standpoint of Labor," by W. L. Saunders, president the Ingersoll-Rand Company; John Williams, State Commissioner of Labor; Cyrus W. Phillips, Chairman Committee on Causes of Industrial Accidents, New York State Liability Commission; Edward F. Croker, then Chief of the Fire Department of the City of New York, and J. W. Sullivan, of the Typographical Union. There was made an earnest appeal for more efficient State inspection of factories by Louis B. Schram, Chairman of the Federation's committee on that subject. Other speakers were: Colonel Edward D. Meier, President American Society of Mechanical Engineers, and President the Heine Safety Boiler Company; Senator Howard R. Bayne; Frank B. Gilbreath, a contractor and builder; Professor T. R. Hutton, and James P. Archibald, of the Painters' Union.

In opening the meeting, the Chairman, W. L. Saunders, stated: "It should be the duty of every employer of labor to care for the health, comfort and safety of the workers. He should be held responsible for the employes' welfare and life while at work and in cases where carelessness and neglect are proven, that responsibility should be both civil and criminal."

The principal recommendations made by other speakers follow:

Commissioner JOHN WILLIAMS: "The State Department of Labor has no authority to enforce the provisions of the factory fire escape law in Greater New York, but it has power in every other part of the State. That section of the labor law should be changed to permit the substitution, for the present drop-ladder, of a counterbalanced stair reaching from the lower balcony of the fire escape to the ground, such stair to be inseparably attached to the balcony so as to be available for use at all times and to be of sufficient length to allow a proper slant. Fire escape balcony floors should be erected approximately on the same level as factory floors. Exits from factories to fire escapes should be fitted with doors placed at the extreme ends of the balconies and hung to open outward against the end rail of the balcony. Fireproof balconies, so constructed, should extend the full length of manufacturing buildings and be connected by proper iron stairs. Requirements for new buildings should include fireproof stairs and halls of ample width and thoroughly lighted. Doors leading into hallways should open outward and be hung on the wall side, that they may be pushed back against the wall and give full use of the passage. In existing narrow halls, doors should not open outward, but there should be given authority to require sliding doors. Spring locks, readily turned on the inside, would render exits immediately available. The State also should clothe the Commissioner of Labor with the authority to regulate internal conditions in factories that ample passage ways to stairs and fire escapes may be maintained. Smoking in any factory using inflammable material should be a penal offense. Every owner of a building used for manufacturing should be required to register such building in the State Department. There should be an adequate appropriation by the State to afford a sufficient number of inspectors, there being at present only fifty to cover sixty thousand places in New York State."

J. W. SULLIVAN: "We are here to arraign a system in the employment of labor which results in burning working people alive. All in the community are not to blame. The trades unions have worked unceasingly to better factory laws and compel employers to live up to them. The Typographical Union spent more than five million dollars to get an eight-hour day for printers because of the dangerous nature of the trade due to bad ventilation, overwork and the like. Before these benefits were obtained, affecting at least twenty thousand printers, the deaths from tuberculosis to the total number were 30 to 35 per cent. The Women's Trade Union League had pointed out to employers in the garment industry the very deficiencies of firetraps such as the one just burned. It is for such meetings as this one and such organizations as the one promoting this meeting, to bring to the working people some help in sound thought, some practical step toward better workshop conditions, some designs for efficient factory laws, some reorganization and strengthening of the State Labor Bureau, some additional civilized agencies that will curb the lawless greed of conscienceless employers and, especially, some method for promoting the well-being of the poorest class of wage-earners. Something must be done! It must be done either through the force of extremists preaching destruction or through the painstaking activities of men animated with a desire to be fair to their fellow men who toil and determined to punish that worst of wrong-doing—the exploitation of the poor. The question before New York is whether betterment to its masses is to come through the principle of class consciousness or the principle of human consciousness."

Chief EDWARD F. CROKER: "When the Fire Department arrived at the Triangle Shirtwaist Factory fire, the employes were jumping from the windows on the eighth and ninth floors. When they struck the sidewalk the impact was so great that they broke through the deadlights into the cellar and sub-cellar. It will readily be seen that, as they went through an iron grating, naturally they would have crashed through our canvas nets.

"To prevent a recurrence of such a disaster, I would recommend outside fire escapes on all buildings; standpipes; sprinkling connections with outlets on all floors; buckets filled with water; fire extinguishers; weekly fire drills; automatic fire alarm telegraph communication; and, where possible, outside enclosed fire escapes, known as 'tower fire escapes.' They afford the only means of escape in a bad fire.

"Responsibility should rest upon one department, preferably the Fire Department, which should inspect buildings, serving written notice upon occupants, not owners, that they must comply with its regulations. At the expiration of two weeks to thirty days there should be re-inspection and, if regulations have not been complied with, the buildings should be immediately closed with the following notice placed upon the doors: 'DANGER! Closed by order of the Department.' The buildings should be kept closed until they have complied with the regulations."

CYRUS W. PHILLIPS: "For the year ending September 30 last, 25,390 accidents were reported to the Department of Labor as occurring in factories, mines and quarries. Of these 353 were fatal, *2,410 resulted in permanent injuries*, while *2,476 were reported as serious and probably permanent.* During the same year the reports to the Public Service Commission of the First Department showed 9,424 accidents to employes of common carriers, gas and electric companies, while the reports of the Public Service Commission of the Second District for the same period showed 2,909 accidents to employes of common carriers, *257 of which were fatal.* On September 30 the building trades commenced reporting their accidents under a law passed last Winter, and these reports, *for three months*, showed about *2,500 accidents*, nearly one-half of which occurred in excavation work, and more than one-half occurred in public work, such as the aqueduct and barge canal. It

FRANCIS LYNDE STETSON,
Chairman Committee on Legislative Policy, Workmen's Compensation Department.

is safe to estimate that there are annually 50,000 accidents to industrial workers in New York State. The value of accident prevention is apparent when it is considered that more than 2,000 accidents have occurred in the past four years due to the operation of belting and shafting, and that accidents of this kind are of a serious nature, maiming the victims for life. During the year 1908 twenty-five men were killed by being caught in belting and shafting, according to the reports of the Labor Department. It is a waste of time to pass laws requiring installation of safety devices and the curing of dangerous defects in factories unless a sufficient force of men is provided to enforce such laws.

"If the State were to be divided into districts with a high-class supervising inspector in charge of each, the work of accident prevention by the Labor Department would be more effective. A supervisor could, by consultations and conferences with employers and employes, bring about safer conditions. Many employers have started inspection bureaus and safety committees of their own, but they look more and more to the Labor Department for advice."

LOUIS B. SCHRAM: "Let us hope that this great calamity destroying so many human lives will arouse the public to action. For every life lost in a destructive factory fire, hundreds are sacrificed annually through the use of machinery not adequately protected by safety devices. The toll in lives lost and bodies maimed, bread-winners disabled and families rendered helpless, is almost beyond belief; and, in comparison with it, even so dreadful a calamity as the destruction of life in the Asch Building almost pales into insignificance. The vast majority of these accidents are not only preventable, but can be avoided without the expenditure of much money and without interfering with the usual methods of conducting the business. The remedy is adequate and thorough factory inspection involving the compulsory use of approved safeguards on all machinery the operation of which is attended with danger. The agitation to accomplish this should be nation-wide, and it should not rest content until every State in the Union has adopted a perfect Factory Inspection Law and has placed its enforcement in the hands of a sufficient number of competent inspectors. In this State there are fifty inspectors. There should be eighty-five, if not one hundred. They should be selected with a sole view to fitness and their tenure should be such as to divorce them from the vicissitudes of politics. There should be a Chief Inspector, whose work, outside of being the responsible head of the Inspection Department, should be to provide means for training the inspectors to even greater efficiency. Another provision has been suggested in this connection, and its great value seems apparent—the establishing of State Museums of Safety, preferably with appliances in operation. By this means the fact could most readily be brought home to the manufacturer that it is as easy, and as cheap and vastly more profitable, to run a safe, comfortable and efficient factory than it is to operate a deathtrap. The National Civic Federation, through its Committee on Improved Factory Inspection, has for some time past been engaged in this work. It is now framing a Factory Inspection Law, which it hopes to make as nearly perfect as its ability may permit, such proposed law to be offered for introduction in the Legislatures of all the States. This committee numbers among its members important manufacturers in many lines, many prominent in the ranks of organized labor, who have at heart the welfare of the workmen, and the Labor Commissioners and Factory Inspectors of many States. Its labors are known to many of the Governors, who have expressed their readiness to co-operate. There is one element more that we want to enlist, without whose hearty and earnest co-operation we cannot hope to achieve success. I mean an enlightened, active, persistent public opinion."

COL. EDWARD D. MEIER: "Scaling ladders and safety nets are inadequate for our present skyscrapers. Canvas tubes three feet square applied to the windows in the manner of the knitting needles of our grandmothers are adequate for a height of ten stories. To shoot the people down, perfectly trained firemen are needed, two men at the top and three at the bottom to hold the tube taut. They must throw the people in head first, on their backs, and let them slide down. This principle has been applied in tall buildings by using a spiral slide. The sprinkling system is adaptable to any height where water pressure will reach. It is the most difficult thing in the world to extinguish a fire where the material is filmy. It burns like an explosive. Therefore, smoking and the use of matches, absolutely, should be forbidden where there are cotton goods. There should be a permanent commission, after giving power to the Fire Department, to study facts and figures and devise better means than those yet considered, for with any precaution, and you can't be too drastic, you will simply find that you have not gone far enough."

SENATOR HOWARD R. BAYNE: "We in the Senate and Assembly are extremely cautious about instituting drastic measures, the effect of which we do not understand. You must make practical suggestions to the Legislature to forefend the dangers upon the whole industrial community. You are practical men, know what the industries of the State require and will stand. We need your help and information. Many of us are practical legislators and want to do the wise, prudent thing. Frame your measure and bring it to us! There will be no difficulty about getting it passed as soon as we know that it will not do more harm than good."

FRANK B. GILBREATH: "In the art of putting fires out after they have been started, we have reached a high degree of efficiency. In keeping fires from starting, we are as savages to-day. What is it that burns? It is wood! It can be eliminated, it no longer being necessary in construction."

PROF. T. R. HUTTON: "Experts should be appointed to tell the Legislature what we desire to accomplish."

JAMES P. ARCHIBALD: "The idea of eliminating wood is excellent, but the tower fire escape, in all four corners of every building and in the middle, will make every man and woman perfectly safe, it accessible. Fire drills are important. The enforcement of the laws that affect the poorest class of people is not, as a rule, put into the hands of men of high integrity."

VALMORA INDUSTRIAL SANATORIUM, AT WATROUS, N. M.

Founded by twenty-five Chicago firms and others for the care of employes suffering from tuberculosis in its early stage, or threatened with that disease. It is intended to be self-supporting but without financial profit, the charge for each patient being $10 a week, exclusive of laundry and personal expenses. It is built on the cottage plan and at present accommodates thirty patients. The water supply is from a beautiful spring and is piped directly into each cottage. Milk and cream of superior quality are supplied by their own herd of Jerseys. The altitude is 5,988 feet above sea level; the climate ideal all the year round; the Summer never too hot nor the Winter too cold, there being a clear, bracing atmosphere. For the rank and file sanatoria nearer home have been found more practical.

ANNUAL MEETING, WASHINGTON, D. C., MARCH 5, 6, 7, 1912

The National
Civic Federation Review

Vol. III NEW YORK, FEBRUARY 15, 1912. No. 12

TO PROMOTE INDUSTRIAL PEACE AND PROGRESS

PRESIDENT TAFT WILL OPEN ANNUAL MEETING OF THE CIVIC FEDERATION AT WASHINGTON, CARDINAL GIBBONS PRESIDING—GOVERNORS ENDORSE OBJECT OF MEETING—DELEGATES NAMED

THE NATIONAL CIVIC FEDERATION has so far received from the following Governors of States acceptances of the invitation to send delegates to its Twelfth Annual Meeting, to be held in Washington, D. C., March 5, 6 and 7, 1912, namely: Governor Robert P. Bass, of New Hampshire; Governor W. Hodges Mann, of Virginia; Governor Aram J. Pothier, of Rhode Island; Governor Chester H. Aldrich, of Nebraska; Governor Albert W. Gilchrist, of Florida; Governor W. W. Kitchin, of North Carolina; Governor Emmet O'Neal, of Alabama; Governor John A. Mead, of Vermont; Governor Lee Cruce, of Oklahoma; Governor Chase S. Osborn, of Michigan; Governor Joseph M. Carey, of Wyoming; Governor Eugene N. Foss, of Massachusetts; Governor John Burke, of North Dakota; Governor John A. Dix, of New York; Governor Judson Harmon, of Ohio; Governor Charles S. Deneen, of Illinois; Governor O. B. Colquitt, of Texas; Governor George W. P. Hunt, of Arizona; Governor George A. Donaghey, of Arkansas; Governor John F. Shafroth, of Colorado; Commissioners of the District of Columbia; Governor Adolph O. Eberhart, of Minnesota; Governor Herbert S. Hadley, of Missouri; Governor William J. Mills, of New Mexico; Governor John K. Tener, of Pennsylvania; Governor Robert S. Vessey, of South Dakota; Governor William E. Glasscock, of West Virginia; Governor Francis E. McGovern, of Wisconsin.

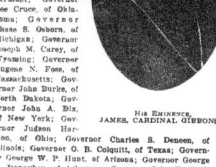

His Eminence,
JAMES, CARDINAL GIBBONS

The general theme for the program of the meeting will be "Industrial Peace and Progress." It will be held in the Peace Hall of the Pan-American Building. His Eminence, Cardinal Gibbons, will preside on March 5, and the opening address will be made by President William Howard Taft. The relation of employer to employe will be considered from three standpoints, viz.:

The private employer to his employes.

The public utility company to its employes.

The Government, Federal, State or Municipal, to its employes.

Copyright by Pach Bros.
THE PRESIDENT

Where Capital Treats With Labor.

There will be discussed the practical operation of the trade agreements between the railway systems of the country and the brotherhoods of engineers, firemen, conductors, trainmen and other employes: the successful operation of the three years' contract between the National Association of Newspaper Publishers and the International Organizations of Printers, Pressmen and Stereotypers; as well as the contracts in many other trades, such as street railways, building trades, coal mining, and brewing. The contract between the publishers and their employes is one of the most remarkable in this country, which is the same as saying "in the world," as nothing in any of the European countries can compare with it. In this industry they have worked out a model plan, which practically amounts, so to speak, to voluntary compulsory arbitration. The contract provides for a local arbitration committee, composed of an equal number of representatives of the local employers' and the employes' organizations concerned, and to this committee must be submitted all grievauces that may arise. If either side is displeased with the award of this local committee an appeal may be made to the National Board, where an odd man can be selected, if necessary. The National Board consists of Charles H. Taylor, Jr., of "The Boston Globe"; George C. Hill, of "The Indianapolis Star," and H. M. Kellogg, Secretary of the American Newspaper Publishers' Association; and for the Typographical Union, James M. Lynch, its President; Hugo Miller, its Second Vice-President, and J. W. Hays, its Secretary and Treasurer.

SETH LOW, President
The National Civic Federation

The feature, however, which is most unique and also most potential in the interest of peace is that should the men in any office, from any cause, violate the agreement and strike, instead of submitting their grievance to the arbitration board, their places will be filled by the union, and not by the employers, who are thus protected from being obliged to enact the role of strike-breaker with all its unpleasant accessories; and the very fact that every member knows that if he violates his contract and strikes, his place will be filled by union men makes him think long and hard before he throws down his tools. This provision, also, is tantamount to an underwriting by the national organization of the contracts made by the men, and being entirely voluntary it is much more satisfactory than any legal methods of incorporation that have been proposed. While the printers have such restraints put upon them, the publishers also e restrained from violations of the contract or at-mpts to interpret it unfairly, because every dispute n be referred to the national body, which is called e Supreme Court in the industry, and as it pro-des for an odd member of the board, there is bound be a decision.

Public Utilities Concerned.

What has been done in private industry, it is aimed, can well be done also in such quasi-public ilities as street railways, electric light and gas mpanies, and there are, in fact, many contracts ' that kind already existing between the street rail-ays and their employes. Street railway strikes in hiladelphia and Columbus, the express strike in ew York City, and the shop men's strike on the nion Pacific and Southern Railway systems empha-ze the need for doing everything possible to reduce a minimum such disturbances.

The need for careful consideration of the relation ' public employes, Federal, State and Municipal, to ieir employers, the people represented by the Gov-nment, is emphasized by the tremendous upheavals hich have occurred in Europe, especially in Paris, here the controversy with the letter carriers and ie employes of the Government railway almost led a revolution. This subject will be discussed at ie annual meeting under the head of:

"How Can Public Employes Secure Redress of Just rievances Without Resorting to a Strike?" In the ederal Government the controversy on this subject ith the Federal employes is becoming acute. Fol-wing the defeat of Congressman Loud, Chairman of ie Appropriations Committee, by the Letter Carriers' ssociation because of his refusal to approve certain new legislation which they demanded, an executive order was issued by President Roosevelt, which has since been re-issued by President Taft. This order reads:

"All officers and employes of the United States, of every description, serving in or under any kind of executive department or independent government establishment, and whether serving in or out of Washington, are hereby forbidden, either directly or indirectly, individually or through associations, to solicit an increase of pay or to influence or attempt to influence in their own interest any legislation whatever, either before Congress or its committees, or in any way save through the heads of the departments or independent government establishments in or under which they serve, on penalty of dismissal from the government service." This order, the employes claim, was a denial of their right to petition and they are now supporting a bill in Congress, introduced by Senator La Follette, which would give them the right to organize and to petition Congress direct on any matter they choose.

Similar questions have been raised in several States, where the school teachers, firemen and policemen have organized campaigns to secure an increase in salary. There are those who justify the action of public employes in organizing and bringing political influence to bear, when necessary, to secure better conditions of employment, but who deny the right of such public servants to use their political power for the purpose of forcing an advance in their salaries, claiming that such action is against public policy. "Is there such a distinction?" is a question which will be discussed.

Public vs. Private Working Conditions.

For, aside from the wage question, it is well known that in many instances public employes work under conditions much worse than those of wage-earners in private establishments. While there are no important instances of school teachers, firemen or policemen striking to better their conditions, strikes of public employes have occurred in many other lines, the most recent instance in New York City being that of the garbage drivers, while last year there was a strike of the firemen on the Municipal ferry boats. Just how such questions have been answered in all the countries of Europe will be presented at this meeting.

Compensation for injuries sustained during employment by public employes and industrial wage-earners will receive a further impetus by devoting a part of the program to its consideration. It is appropriate that that subject should have presentation in the National Capital at this time, as the Congressional Commission is about to report, through the President, to Congress a compensation act for interstate railways. That Commission has adopted the principles of the Federation's model Workmen's Compensation Act. It is hoped, if these are enacted into law and upheld by the Supreme Court, that this action will have great weight in the interest of uniform State legislation for compulsory workmen's compensation, in which the Federation is particularly interested, and it will doubtless take action to assist in the passage of this Federal measure.

ensure compensation to injured Federal employes not now covered by national legislation. For example, letter carriers may receive injury and even though those injuries should occur after years of faithful service, their pay stops the moment incapacitation comes.

Pensions and Retirement Plans.

"Pensions for Federal, State and Municipal Employes" as well as "Retirement Plans for Wage Earners in Private Enterprises" will be urged. Pensions for employes is a topic co-related to workmen's compensation, in that disabled employes may become pensioners.

To become incapacitated after years of loyal service with no means of support, is the dread of every thinking wage-worker, whether in private industry or in public service. The main problem involved in all pension plans is the question, 'Shall employes contribute to retirement funds?" From the public standpoint it is of serious moment that the work of the Government, whether Municipal State or Federal, should not be hampered by retaining in the service employes incapacitated by age. Until a proper pension plan is worked out, public machinery will be clogged, as no official has the heart to throw out upon the world those who have devoted their lives to the service of the Government.

The "common surfman" in the Life-Saving Service, who has an enforced vacation of two months in the year without pay and makes only $65 a month, presents one of the many types in the employ of the National Government appealing for its consideration.

The Superannuation Problem.

There are now more than 250 men in the Government Printing Office over sixty-five years of age. It would be an advantage to the Government to provide for the retirement of men who cannot perform an average day's work.

To urge legislation on pensions for public employes, fair to the State and to the employe, is one of the objects of the Federation.

Regulation of Industrial Corporations.

The Department on Regulation of Industrial Corporations, of which President Seth Low is Chairman, will consider its proposed legislation supplementary to the Sherman Act and also a proposed model bill for the regulation of State Corporations. This Federal Bill, when finally endorsed by the Federation, will be presented to the Senate Committee on Interstate Commerce for its consideration and disposition.

The analysis of the sixteen thousand responses to the Questionnaire sent out by this Department of The National Civic Federation to representative manufacturers, bankers, merchants, lawyers, college presidents, representatives of labor and agricultural organizations, chambers of commerce, etc., will be reported upon in detail and, together with the proposed bill, will furnish the basis for discussion.

Workmen's Compensation and Safety Acts.

The Department on Compensation for Industrial Accidents and Their Prevention, of which August Belmont is Chairman, will discuss and consider the proposed Federal Bill for interstate commerce, to provide compensation for railroad employes; the situation in States which have adopted different types of Compensation Acts applicable to industrial employes, generally; and the Federation's Model Safety Act, designed for uniform State legislation in the interest of accident prevention, and covering safety devices in manufacturing enterprises.

The Congressional Commission, after exhaustive research work and public hearings on all phases of the subject, has adopted the principle of "compulsory" compensation which is the basis of the Federation's Model Workmen's Compensation Act. Its passage by Congress, if later upheld by the United States Supreme Court, will have great weight in influencing uniform State legislation of that character, which is the great purpose of The National Civic Federation. It is, therefore, of paramount importance that the Federation should consider what action it should take in furthering the bill when introduced into Congress.

Control of Public Utilities.

The Department on Regulation of Interstate and Municipal Utilities, of which Emerson McMillin is Chairman, will meet to consider the reports of its Executive Council, which is already beginning an exhaustive inquiry into the question, "What is adequate regulation?" or, in other words, "How far can regulation go and be efficient without unreasonably interfering with management?" Professor John H. Gray, of the University of Minnesota, the Secretary of the Department, with a force of experts to assist him, will devote six months of his time to directing the investigations throughout the country.

The Department on Pure Food and Drugs, of [illegible] Hammond is Chairman, will coordination between the State and Federal laws on this subject are important principles underlying the work of the Department.

Broad Powers for State Food Officials.

It is is also important that State Food Commissioners should be given broad powers for the enforcement of the food laws of their respective Commonwealths, together with the power to adopt regulations, so as to make possible uniform enforcement in the State and National law. To this end, Congress and State Legislatures will naturally be appealed to to make sufficient appropriations, that such food laws may be efficiently enforced.

The Department on Reform in Legal Procedure, of which Alton B. Parker is Chairman, will organize and will outline its work for the coming year. This Department, which has only recently been formed, comprises representative lawyers from every State in the Union.

Representative Women to Speak.

The Woman's Welfare Department, of which Mrs. John Hays Hammand is Chairman, will hold its annual meeting on Thursday, March 7. Its program will consist of a business meeting in the forenoon and addresses from representative women from different parts of the country in the afternoon.

During the annual meeting there will be a conference of the chairmen of the State Councils of the Federation to consider important matters relating to their work.

The Annual Dinner will take place at the New Willard Hotel on the evening of Thursday, March 6, and on Friday evening, March 7, Mr. and Mrs. John Hays Hammond will give a reception at their home in Washington to the delegates and members of the Federation.

STINGING REBUKE FOR SOCIALIST INTRIGUERS

President Timothy Healy, of the Stationary Firemen, Defends American Institutions in Patriotic Speech—Tells of Efforts to Hamper Good Work He is Doing.

TIMOTHY HEALY, President of the International Brotherhood of Stationary Firemen and a member of the Executive Committee of The National Civic Federation, used plain, forceful and patriotic language in accepting again the presidency of his organization at the eleventh biennial meeting at Milwaukee. Mr. Healy was elected unanimously.

The speech was an interesting exposition of the attitude of the Socialists toward American institutions and toward the love of those institutions that is so characteristic of the wage-workers of this country. Mr. Healy also showed the baleful influence exerted by Socialists in the ranks of organized labor, and their constant intriguing against labor officials who decline to subscribe to their disloyal creed. His own words, however, are much more to the point than any paraphrasing of them could possibly be. He said in part:

Defends Flag and Country.

"Attacks have been made upon me for the smallest and most trivial things. I have been attacked because I would not stand for certain things. I would not stand for some things I felt were not proper. If a man who is the official head of this city refuses to have the Stars and Stripes hoisted on the municipal buildings of Milwaukee; if he refuses municipal employes a holiday on Washington's Birthday, and then makes the statement, as we are informed on good authority that he did, that Washington was the biggest liar the country ever produced—I want to ask if that man is fit to open the convention of a labor organization? I say he is not, and with all the power at my command I will at all times raise my voice in protest against any insult to our flag and against any man who will defame the memory of the Father of our Country. The man who will not do that is not an American citizen; he is not entitled to that distinction.

"As trades unionists we must stand by the flag of our country. There may be wrongs committed under it that ought to be righted; there may be injustice done under it; but for all that we should not stand for revolution against it. We stand for American institutions; we stand for the American form of government; we stand for American liberty at all times.

"A Dangerous Institution."

"I have been accused, among other things, of being a member of The National Civic Federation, which some of our friends of the radical type brand as a dangerous institution. That sort of statement is only what we may expect from those people when we con-

WHAT SHALL BE DONE WITH THE SHERMAN ACT?

16,000 REPRESENTATIVE AMERICANS FROM ALL WALKS OF LIFE SAY: "DO NOT REPEAL, BUT AMEND OR SUPPLEMENT IT WITH CONSTRUCTIVE LEGISLATION IN HARMONY WITH THE BUSINESS AND ECONOMIC DEMANDS OF THE DAY"

THE GIST OF THE MATTER.

"The replies indicate little sentiment in favor of the unconditional repeal of the Sherman Act. On the other hand it is shown that there is practically no desire to abolish large combinations. The public have no desire for government ownership, on one side, or unrestricted and unregulated private or corporate control on the other. They will accept large combinations adequately regulated."

MORE than sixteen thousand Americans, representing the learned professions, business in its various branches, the capital, talents and energy employed in our great industries, and the skill and toil which have built up and maintained those industries have answered a series of questions presented by The National Civic Federation on the Sherman Anti-Trust Act.

"Questionnaires" were sent to editors, political economists, lawyers, publicists, statisticians, manufacturers, merchants, bankers and the officers of commercial, labor and other organizations. As introductory to the questions it was pointed out that "the Sherman Anti-Trust Act has now been interpreted by the Supreme Court to mean, as to interstate commerce, that any combination in restraint of trade with the purpose of controlling prices and stifling competition is unlawful."

This questionnaire was prepared and sent out by the Department on Regulation of Industrial Corporations of The National Civic Federation, which is preparing to propose constructive legislation to deal with the business situation as it relates to the Sherman Anti-Trust Act; and in the same connection is considering what State legislation is called for, so far as State legislation is needed, to cover such phases of the subject as Federal law cannot reach.

The Executive Committee of this department, of which President Low is Chairman, consists of the following gentlemen:

Seth Low, Chairman; E. A. Bancroft, Illinois; John B. Clark; William Dudley Foulke, Indiana; Frederick P. Fish, Massachusetts; James R. Garfield, Ohio; J. W. Jenks, New York; Charles L. Jewett, Indiana; Frederick N. Judson, Missouri; H. B. F. Macfarland, District of Columbia; Theodore Marburg, Maryland; G. H. Montague, New York; George W. Perkins, New York; John C. Richberg, Illinois; W. Z. Ripley, Massachusetts; Leo S. Rowe, Pennsylvania; C. A. Severance, Minnesota; F. L. Siddons, District of Columbia; Reuben D. Silliman, New York; J. J. Spalding, Georgia; Walter George Smith, Pennsylvania; Frederic J. Stimson, Massachusetts; Henry W. Taft, New York; Frank Trumbull, New York; Samuel Untermyer, New York; A. Leo Weil, Pennsylvania; Talcott Williams, Pennsylvania.

A sub-committee of the department, consisting of Messrs. Low, Clark, Foulke, Garfield, Severance, Smith, Stimson, Untermyer and Williams, is drafting the proposals relating to Federal legislation, and is also making a digest of the trust laws of the States, with a view to drafting a uniform, model bill for the regulation of intrastate corporations.

The answers leave no doubt that the public is thoroughly aroused to the vital importance of the problems dealt with by the Sherman Act. This condition of the public mind is appreciated just as much by those controlling great combinations of capital as by the business man and the wage-earner.

Charges Against Combinations.

The evils charged against large combinations are well known. These include the power to exploit the producer and consumer by depriving them of a competitive market, thus making the prices of the raw material unduly low, and those of the finished commodity unduly high; the concentration of power, sometimes perilous in a few hands, through holding companies; the ruin of competition in a given locality by selling at prices below the cost of production; the selling of one variety of goods at less than cost for the purpose of driving from the field a rival who produces chiefly that variety; refusing to furnish goods at trade rates to merchants who buy anything from rival producers, or who refuse to maintain list prices, as required by "sellers' agreements;" the use of patents to protect what is not patented; checking improvements in methods of production when monopoly is successfully assured; the exploitation of investors by the manipulation of stocks and securities, and the buying up and suppression of useful inventions to prevent their introduction from diminishing the profits of monopoly.

Certain Advantages Claimed.

Among the advantages claimed are economies in production and distribution, the greater use of by-products; steadier employment of labor, and at better wages; better protection against industrial accidents; more command over international trade; a command of the best ability; assurance of a steady market, and avoidance of those fluctuations which, under old competitive conditions, so often brought disaster alike to employer and employe, and the standardization of products, so that dealer and ultimate consumer know exactly what they are purchasing.

No Unconditional Repeal.

The replies indicate little sentiment in favor of the unconditional repeal of the Sherman Act. On the other hand it is shown that there is practically no desire to abolish large combinations. The public have no desire for government ownership, on one side, or unrestricted and unregulated private or corporate control on the other. They will accept large combinations adequately regulated.

Business Disturbance Felt.

That business conditions are disturbed nearly every reply admits. In the thousands of replies received a large majority assert that business conditions are unsatisfactory. Enforcement of the Sherman Law is most frequently mentioned by business men as a disturbing cause, on the ground that they do not understand the law, and that the uncertainty as to its meaning retards enterprise, makes capital hesitate to enter pon new investments, and prompts those in charge of business undertakings to restrict expenditures to the absolute demands of trade.

What Labor Wants.

It is significant that the leaders of organized labor, representing three millions of wage earners, are practically unanimous in demanding that the Sherman Anti-Trust Act should be either repealed or amended to exempt from its operations organizations of labor and organizations of farmers. Many of them, however, argue for its amendment from the standpoint of the business interests. Their experience and training in organization work and their contact with the employers of the country have led them almost universally to the position that too much competition is the death of trade. Samuel Gompers, John Mitchell, James Duncan, Warren S. Stone, W. S. Carter, W. G. Lee, James M. Lynch and A. B. Garretson all reflect this view.

Some labor organizations took a referendum vote on the questionnaire and their answers were sent in under official seal.

It is interesting to note that the manufacturers, bankers, wholesale and retail merchants and also commercial organizations that took a membership vote are strongly opposed to the repeal of the Sherman Act, but just as strongly want it amended along lines that will permit regulation through an Interstate Industrial Commission of some kind.

ANALYSIS OF THE OPINIONS OF 16,000 PROMINENT AMERICANS ON SHERMAN ANTI-TRUST ACT.

AN overwhelming majority of the answers—eighty-four per cent—pronounce the Sherman Law neither clear nor workable, or workable without being clear; but only some twenty per cent declare in favor of its repeal. Of these latter the larger number add that "if not repealed, it should be amended," etc. Substantially, the usual phraseology of suggestions for amending the Sherman Law is—"make it so that business men can understand it," or "bring it into line with modern business conditions."

Federal License or Incorporation.

Eighty per cent of the replies favor Federal license or incorporation for companies engaged in interstate commerce, about one-third of the eighty taking Federal license as an alternative. Seventy-five per cent are opposed to holding companies, while of the remainder nearly all want holding companies bound by restrictions that would prevent abuses.

Regulation of Capitalization Approved.

Government regulation of capitalization is approved by ninety per cent of those to whom that question was submitted, a few of the minority who disapprove suggesting that over-capitalization is not always an evil, but sometimes brings capital into action that would otherwise remain idle.

Three important advantages claimed for those doing business on a large scale—economies in production, economies in distribution and greater use of by-products—are admitted without dissent by all who answer that query. "Steadier employment of labor and at better wages," and "better protection against industrial accidents" are denied by thirty-five per cent, and "more command of international trade" and "command of the best ability" are doubted by ten per cent of those answering.

Interstate Industrial Commission.

About eighty per cent favor an Interstate Industrial Commission, some qualifying with the condition that it should be composed of business men only, and two labor representatives proposing that the Commission should consist of one member from each State—a sort of Interstate Business Senate.

A comparatively small proportion are in favor of control of prices by an Industrial Commission.

Some Dull Times Diagnoses.

Only ten per cent mention a defective banking and currency system as a primary source of trouble, and several urge the adoption of the Aldrich currency plan. Extravagant living and a reaction from recent prosperity are given among other reasons by sixty per cent of those who answer that question. The tendency to desert the farms for the cities, thereby reducing the number of producers, is mentioned as an unsettling cause in some fifty per cent of the answers. Tariff agitation figures in thirty per cent of the replies—many of these being from business men who have interests protected by the existing tariff. One reason that has probably not suggested itself to the public mind is offered by a considerable number of men in business circles. That reason is the automobile, the use of which, it is declared, has diverted a good many millions of dollars from the ordinary channels of trade to indulgence in that article of usefulness and of luxury. Increased production of gold, poor crops in some localities, sales of "fake" stocks, the approaching Presidential election, the demands of organized labor, emigration to Canada, and unsettled conditions in Europe and Asia are among other causes set forth.

TEXT OF A FEW REPRESENTATIVE EXPRESSIONS THAT "QUESTIONNAIRE" PROVOKED.

THERE is given herewith the text of a few of the many interesting expressions provoked by the "questionnaire." In selecting those to quote it has been attempted both to present opinions that are typical and also such as will give an idea of the wide range of views expressed on the subject:

SAMUEL REA, Vice-President Pennsylvania R.R. Co., Broad St. Station, Philadelphia, Pa.

I believe the Sherman Law, as now interpreted, is not yet clear, but under court interpretation will become workable. I do not consider it feasible to return to what are commonly known as old competitive methods in business, for it means unreasonable and generally ruinous competition. Competition is desirable, and we can have it if the laws of supply and demand are permitted to take their course. I do not favor a repeal of the Sherman Law. I am not prepared to make any reply as to amending the Sherman Law. The matter should first be studied by a commission of wise and experienced men whose findings and recommendations should determine this question. Railroads should be allowed to enter into agreements affecting rates, subject to the approval and regulation of the Interstate Commerce Commission. This necessary privilege should never have been withheld.

Trade unions should not be exempted from the operation of the Sherman Act. No worse violation of the act has been experienced than the abrogation, through force and intimidation, of the free right to labor and the restraint of trade caused by strikes and labor union activities.

President JAMES C. FARGO, of the American Express Company:

I do not favor a repeal of the Sherman Law, though I do not consider that it has been made clear and workable. The Sherman Law should be amended, first, so as to make it intelligible; and, second, not only so that "the concentration of capital essential in the full and efficient development of modern business" be made legitimate, but when so used it must not be left subject to confiscation.

ALBERT A. SPRAGUE, President of Sprague, Warner & Co., wholesale grocers, Chicago, Ill.:

Commercial corporations have been the chief factors in the growth and development of the country, and at the same time, almost without exception, they have reduced costs to the consumer. As such, they should be fostered and encouraged by the same protection, and given the same rights as are granted to the individual or the copartnership in the same kinds of business.

Indiscriminate public antagonism to corporations fostered by an indiscriminate press and self-seeking politicians; uncertainty as to the scope of the Anti-Trust Act; and agitation and uncertainty regarding tariff action and anti-trust legislation on the part of Congress tend to hamper enterprise and to keep business unsettled. The Sherman Law should be amended or supplemented so that an intelligent public can understand it, and know definitely what is a reasonable and what an unreasonable "restraint of trade." Railroads should be allowed to enter into agreements affecting rates. I favor a national incorporation law, if it does not duplicate the expense and is not in conflict with State incorporation. I favor an Interstate Trade Commission with limitations. It would be absurd to give the government the power to fix prices on merchandise.

A. C. BARTLETT, President of Hibbard Spencer, Bartlett & Co., Wholesale Hardware, Chicago, Ill.:

The Sherman Law will never be satisfactorily workable until the necessity for determining the legal status of each individual case by submission to the courts is eliminated. If aggregations of capital to an unlimited extent are to be permitted—as it must be under present conditions—stifling of legitimate competition must be prohibited, but the old competitive methods would prove ruinous to any enterprises not employing immense capital.

I would favor an Interstate Trade Commission with limitations. No trade commission could successfully fix the prices upon all manufactured articles from knitting pins to ocean liners; nor could it intelligently or satisfactorily fix any prices. The present disturbance is due to a combination of past extravagance, doubt regarding the disposition of the Government (Federal and State) toward so-called trusts, the usual dullness which precedes a Presidential election, aggravated at this time by extraordinary political disturbance and a general reaction from an extended period of prosperity.

J. M. LYNCH, President International Typographical Union, Indianapolis, Ind.:

I do not regard the Sherman Law as clear and workable, nor do I consider it feasible to return to what are commonly known as old competitive methods in business. I favor either a repeal of the Sherman Law or amendments that will make its intention (the intention of Congress) clear. The Sherman Law should be amended to make it regulatory of the combinations. Railroads should be allowed to enter into agreements affecting rates subject to the approval and regulation of the Interstate Commerce Commission, and trade unions should be excepted from the operation of the Sherman Act. Combinations of farmers should not come under the Sherman Act. If they or the trade unions must be regulated by law, then it should be by special act. I doubt, however, the necessity for such a law.

I favor a statute for the regulation of big business that will be clear and workable and prevent extortion. But such a statute must recognize that the Trusts, so-called, are an economic development that cannot and should not be legislated out of business. Combinations are inevitable and scientific. But they should benefit in the greatest degree all of the people.

SYLVESTER C. DUNHAM, President Travelers Insurance Company, Hartford, Conn.:

I favor Federal charters for corporations doing an interstate business, including insurance companies. I also favor legislation recognizing the fact that modern business must be transacted by large corporations operating on a large scale. A law amended up to date and sufficiently specific should be enacted. I believe in holding companies under suitable restrictions. The advantage to the public of competition is greatly overestimated. The public pays the penalty for reckless and irresponsible competition, which is worse than unfair competition. I favor laws providing for government regulation and publicity.

In addition to the advantages claimed for those doing big business on a large scale should be added suppression of ruinous and irresponsible competition whereby degraded products are imposed upon the market—such as adulterated foods, shoddy garments and Buddenseik buildings.

The Sherman Law as now interpreted has not yet been made clear and workable. It should not be repealed, but modernized. Railroads should be allowed to enter into agreements affecting rates.

JOHN MITCHELL, former President United Mine Workers of America, Mt. Vernon, N. Y.:

The Sherman Law has not been made clear and workable, and I favor its repeal. I do not consider it feasible to attempt to return to what are commonly known as old competitive methods in business. If the Sherman Law is not repealed, I favor amending it so as to exclude from its operation associations having no capital stock and not organized for profit.

Railroads should be allowed to enter into agreements affecting rates subject to the approval and regulation of the Interstate Commerce Commission. Trade unions and combinations of farmers should be excepted from the Sherman Act.

I favor an Interstate Trade Commission with powers not unlike those now enjoyed by the Interstate Commerce Commission in relation to common carriers.

Disturbed business conditions are due, in my judgment, to uncertainty as to the meaning of the Sherman Law; demand of the people for a greater measure of control and a more direct voice in the administration of legislative and administrative affairs.

I believe that Congress should create a commission composed of representatives of wage-earners, employers, legislators and economists, whose duty it should be to make a study of this entire subject and recommend to Congress such reforms in the legislative, administrative and judicial branches of our government as may seem necessary because of the changes and the development in our industrial and commercial life.

CHARLES A. BOSTON, Hornblower, Miller & Potter, Attorneys-at-Law, New York.

The Sherman Law owes its existence to a spirit which is as old as the English people. Hitherto, that spirit has not been quellable. It was manifested in the Charters of Liberties and of the Forests; in the Statutes of Mortmain and the law against perpetuities; in the deep-rooted objection to the grant of monopolies; in the continual controversies in the American Colonies with the Royal Governors; in the execution of Charles I. and the situation which forced the abdication of James II.; in the Boston Massacre, so-called; in the tea-parties at Annapolis and Boston; in the Acts of Settlement of the English Crown; in the Declaration of Independence; in the Bills of Rights; in the American Revolution and the War of 1812; in the refusal to recharter the Second United States Bank, and in the Civil War. The Sherman Law is a historical, political and economic landmark. It does not oppose big business, because it is business, but because it is dangerous.

W. D. CREWS, Farmer and Editor and Proprietor The Union Farmer, Murphysboro, Ill.

In my judgment, the present disturbed business conditions are caused fundamentally by the evolution of the human race from old and inadequate conditions to better and more progressive conditions: incidentally, too much selfishness and dollar-chasing: also a lack of sufficient progressive spirit on the part of the masses to keep up with the classes.

A tadpole has to change its tail for legs to become a frog. The butterfly must work its way out of the cocoon. A child must experience the pain and inconvenience of teething in order to develop a digestive apparatus sufficient for the needs of an adult. Human progress is somewhat slow and disagreeable, partly because we are not wise enough to lightly adjust ourselves to the great strides of progress from a competitive to a co-operative system of business.

M. WES. TUBBS, Secretary-Treasurer Wisconsin State Union, American Society of Equity, Madison, Wis. (official communication from the union).

We recognize the advantages claimed for those doing business on a large scale when the advantages are properly managed.

The Sherman Law, as now interpreted, is not clear and workable. It should be amended to make it more explicit. Railroads should be allowed to enter into agreements affecting rates, subject to the approval and regulation of the Interstate Commerce Commission. Combinations of farmers to restrict production or to hold a crop for higher prices should be lawful up to the limit of average cost of production, with a reasonable profit added.

We do not consider it feasible to return to old competitive methods. We favor a national incorporation law and an Interstate Trade Commission with powers not unlike those now enjoyed by the Interstate Commerce Commission in relation to common carriers.

E. W. RANKIN, Manager Farmers' Mail and Breeze (agricultural paper), Topeka, Kan.:

The Sherman Law should be amended to make it more specific and to use the undoubted but seldom used power of Congress to prevent the Supreme Court from nullifying it. I am not sure as to whether railroads should be allowed to enter into agreements affecting rates, subject to the approval and regulation of the Interstate Commerce Commission. Trade unions should be excepted from the operation of the Sherman Act.

In my judgment, the causes of the present disturbed business conditions are various; crops under average; increasing number of non-producers; middlemen; political apprehension; too high prices; growing inequality in the distribution of wealth—these may all be regarded as causes of existing unsatisfactory conditions. What we need is more democracy, the making of laws from the point of view of all the people, and not of special classes of the people. For instance, the lumber people should not dictate lumber tariffs, nor the bankers dictate all banking laws.

WALTER G. OAKMAN, President of Hudson Companies, etc., New York:

The Sherman Law is not clear, but perhaps workable, failing other legislation. Unlimited competition would result in survival of the strongest and a recurrence of conditions now deemed requiring regulation. The country would not accept a repeal of the Sherman Law unless substituted by other legislation. Perhaps the best solution would be a control of the amount of the total of any industry by any one corporation. A general control of business by a commission covering the details of each activity would be impossible and destructive.

CHARLES F. COX, Railway Treasurer, Grand Central Terminal, New York:

In general, all laws should be repealed which lead to prosecutions of corporations or individuals because of what they may intend to do, or have the power to do, instead of for specific and material acts they have performed. In regard to advantages claimed for those doing business on a large scale, no one can reasonably believe that the numerous corporations into which the Standard Oil Company is dissolved can serve the public better and more economically than was done by the original corporation.

HENRY R. SEAGER, Professor Political Economy, Columbia University, New York:

In my opinion the trust movement has been in part artificial, due, that is, to opportunities afforded to promoters for large gains. Enforced publicity and fair competition would enable small producers in many lines to hold their own. In some, great monopolistic combinations might prove more efficient, that is, able to produce or sell at lower cost than smaller companies, and for them regulative policy might have to include eventually control over prices. I believe, however, that has yet to be demonstrated.

I prefer Federal incorporation—this might be made optional at first and coupled with certain privileges as well as certain responsibilities, but should, I think, eventually be made obligatory on companies doing interstate commerce. I do not believe in holding companies. We should have an amendment to the Sherman Act specifying practices in reasonable restraint of trade. The German plan of enforced publicity and limitation of capital to actual bona fide investments appeals to me. I favor an Interstate Trade Commission, but do not believe that such a commission should have power to fix prices until need of such power under the new system is clearly demonstrated by experience.

JOSEPH SELIGMAN, J. & W. Seligman, Bankers, New York:

The Sherman Law will not be clear and workable until the courts define more clearly what constitutes "reasonableness." I do not consider it feasible to attempt to return to old competitive methods, but competition is greatly to be preferred to Government interference and inquisition, which has so disturbed conditions of late. I do not favor a repeal of the Sherman Law, but its amendment. It should be amended by enacting more stringent laws against directors and promoters of guilty corporations; the establishment of a Government Corporation Bureau; enforcement of a law compelling all corporations to incorporate under Government statutes.

I decidedly favor a national incorporation law, but it must not entail inquisition into the private affairs of innocent persons constituting the corporation, such as stockholders who are connected with the management. I favor a Federal license law and an Interstate Trade Commission.

In my judgment, the cause of disturbed business conditions is too much Government attempt at remedying all at once the entire corporation "evils" of the country, coming as it did in a time of European and world-wide unrest and financial disturbance.

J. B. WHITE, Lumberman and Farmer, Kansas City, Mo.:

Industrial corporations have proved to be the fortunate opportunity to thousands of men. Look at them in every village and city, especially in the Middle and Eastern States. Hundreds of thousands of men of little means have been enabled to club together and unite their savings in an industrial corporation, where their money and labor are employed, with the result that they have made and are making a financial success, and own their own homes.

I am told that in Jamestown, N. Y., where there are 143 industrial corporations, there are hundreds of small prosperous stockholders, but not a millionaire amongst them. And there are thousands of similar examples. We require competition, but not that kind "with the red tooth and the bloody claw." We want co-operation, and not merciless, unrestrained competition, where only the luckiest or the strongest survive at the expense of the weak and the unfortunate. A living wage should be the first corner stone of every industrial enterprise.

The endeavor to create a condition of enforced and unrestrained competition, causing the over-production of low wages and enforced idleness among the laborers, has caused much trouble. The Sherman Law should be repealed or amended so that manufacturers may be able to legally ascertain the supply and demand and be enabled to avoid committing waste by exceeding the demand and by selling their products under the price of production.

The late JOHN BIGELOW (written just a month before his death):

I know of no other law ever enacted for our Federal Government that I thought more absurd when enacted than the Sherman Law, and I still think the same of it.

As the man shortened the vicious dog's tail by cutting it off close behind his ears, so I would do with the Sherman Law. There is no amending a law that defies common sense.

We will never have a just government, nor be a free people, nor an honest people, until we open every port of the country to the commerce of every nation as freely as the port of New York is open to the commerce of New Jersey or Connecticut.

JAMES DUNCAN, Secretary-Treasurer the Granite Cutters' International Association of America, Quincy, Mass.:

The Sh rman Law, as now interpreted, is not clear and workable. I would favor a repeal of the Sherman Law only to permit the passage of a practical similar act. The Sherman Law should be amended to bring and keep large financial and transportation corporations under governmental supervision and control, preventing corporation monopolies, and the "freezing out" process of small competing concerns should be declared positively criminal. Railroads should be allowed to enter into agreements affecting rates. Trade unions should be excepted from the operation of the Sherman Act. They are not in business, nor are they, nor can they form transportation, interstate or profit-making trusts or corporations; hence are not comprehended in such an "act." As to combinations of farmers, restriction of production should never be "rendered lawful" under the "Sherman" or any other act. Holding crops for higher prices, when done by individuals as such, is not unlawful, but a combination by farmers to do so simply to force higher prices should be "rendered unlawful."

I favor a national incorporation law—one such as would require publicity of the business, purposes, and workings, including profits, of the concern incorporated, and that all large interstate concerns should come under the law. I consider that some such commission as an Interstate Trade Commission with powers not unlike those now enjoyed by the Interstate Commerce Commission in relation to common carriers would be helpful.

M. S. CARTER, President Brotherhood of Locomotive Firemen and Enginemen, Peoria, Ill.:

It seems to me that the present "disturbed business conditions" are largely based upon a doubt as to whether the "common people" will much longer stand for the present high cost of living, which they believe is of artificial creation, and is not a natural economic result of the condition of the country.

In August of 1909 my business called me to Texas, where I was astonished to observe farmers (or fruit growers) shaking their peach trees so that the peaches would fall off and be consumed by their hogs. These peaches were finer than I had ever seen before. I asked many why it was that these peaches were not shipped to the Northern States, where the housewives were paying $2.25 per bushel for an inferior quality. I was told that the farmers could not afford to gather, sort, pack and deliver at the railroad station these peaches for less than sixty cents per bushel, and that they were not offered as much as sixty cents for these peaches. Further investigation showed that a carload of peaches shipped to the city of Chicago in a refrigerator car would cost about thirty-five cents per bushel. That is, if the farmer got sixty cents and the railroads got thirty-five cents for delivering a carload of peaches into Chicago, the cost F. O. B. Chicago would have been ninety-five cents per bushel. Yet, at the same time, peaches of inferior quality could not be secured by the citizens of Illinois for less than $2.25 per bushel. I imagine if it now becomes evident that the people are going to demand "Who got the $1.30?" that there will be "disturbed business conditions" until the people "go to sleep again." I read an article contributed by a leading manufacturer of pianos recently wherein he protested that the manufacture of pianos was not prosperous because the consumer had to pay 100 per cent more for the piano than the manufacturer received for the finished article.

I have been told by those who should know that an automobile that is sold for $2,200 does not net the manufacturer $1,000.

I might go on indefinitely with almost every article of commerce and the story would be the same.

F. W. TAUSSIG, Professor of Political Economy in Harvard University, author of Tariff History of the United States, Wages and Capital, Principles of Economics, and Editor of the Quarterly Journal of Economics.

In addition to the methods of unfair competition mentioned in the circular, there should be adduced the deliberate sale of a product by a large concern or combination at less than cost, for the purpose of driving smaller competitors out of the business. Mention should be made also of the establishment of bogus competitors, in reality controlled by the combination. The whole subject of fair and unfair competition should be newly dealt with by the Legislature. Unfair competition should be more carefully defined and further remedies of a penal sort should be added to the civil remedies which the law now provides.

The holding company system is bad. It lends itself to manipulation and fraudulent management, and above all to concealment. Yet, as matters stand, we must move with caution toward getting rid of it. If an interstate trade commission were established, it could appropriately supervise the holding of securities by great corporations, and require from them a full statement of their holdings, direct and indirect.

Among the advantages on which stress is laid in favor of combinations is the prevention of relentless competition, and thereby of unwholesome alternations of activity and depression. It is not clear how fully an advantage of this sort is attained. Steadier employment of labor, better protection against accident, greater command of international trade, may perhaps all be secured by large scale production, not necessarily by competition; and for this phase of the problem we must still await the outcome of experience.

I favor the creation of an interstate trade commission which might be developed from the existing Bureau of Corporations. For the present its functions should be limited, and should be directed more particularly toward the enrollment and supervision of the great industries which threaten to develop into combinations. In time, it will perhaps prove expedient to enlarge its functions. It is not inconceivable that eventually direct control of prices may be entrusted to it, as control over railroad rates is entrusted to the Interstate Commerce Commission. But regulative legislation of this sort should proceed tentatively, and should begin with the gathering of accurate information.

WHAT IS ADEQUATE REGULATION OF RAILWAYS AND PUBLIC UTILITIES?

CIVIC FEDERATION'S NEW DEPARTMENT WILL ENDEAVOR TO ASCERTAIN HOW FAR PUBLIC CONTROL MAY GO WITHOUT INTERFERING UNDULY WITH MANAGEMENT—ALL INTERESTS REPRESENTED—BROAD SCOPE OF INVESTIGATION

THE Executive Committee of the recently formed Department on Regulation of Interstate and Municipal Utilities, at a meeting held in New York City December 2, appointed seven sub-committees, among which is distributed, among other duties, the work of formulating a model act designed to afford adequate regulation of public utilities. The personnel of these committees is given elsewhere in this article.

This department of The National Civic Federation was organized at a conference of public service officials, officers of public utilities and representatives of organized labor, held in New York City last July. At that meeting a sub-committee of seven was appointed to prepare a report on the plan and scope for an inquiry into the extent to which regulation can go and be effective without interfering unduly with management.

Effective Impetus Given Work.

At subsequent meetings the plan and scope were finally decided on, officers were elected and an Executive Committee and Executive Council appointed, and further steps, noted above, were taken to give effective impetus to the work of the department.

Emerson McMillin, chairman of the Executive Committee of the American Light and Traction Company, heads the newly-formed department. A complete list of officers and committees is given further along.

The work that this department proposes to do is the logical sequence of the investigation of private vs. public operation of public utilities, made by The National Civic Federation in England and this country. The commission which conducted that investigation was composed of those in favor of municipal operation, of private operation, and those classed as "neutrals." This exhaustive study resulted in a practically unanimous agreement that in this country, under the present condition of municipal government, private operation is preferable to public operation, *provided* there be adequate regulation to protect the public in the matter of price and quality of service. The proposed inquiry is to determine, as stated above, what constitutes adequate regulation of public utilities.

Territory to Be Studied.

One of the purposes of this department is to outline a model State or municipal regulation bill. This will involve a careful study of the subject in the United States, England and Canada, the examination in this country being made in such typical States as New York, Massachusetts, Wisconsin, Texas, Kansas, Tennessee and Nebraska.

Some Past History.

The original commission was presided over by Melville E. Ingalls, former chairman of the Executive Board of the Big Four Railroad.

After spending many months with engineers, accountants and experts selected by the "Antis" and the "Pros" respectively it unanimously agreed upon a number of recommendations. That referring to regulation follows:

"First, we wish to emphasize the fact that the public utilities studied are so constituted that it is impossible for them to be regulated by competition. Therefore, they must be controlled and regulated by the Government; or they must be left to do as they please; or they must be operated by the public. There is no other course. None of us is in favor of leaving them to their own will, and the question is whether it is better to regulate or to operate."

The commission then declared for adequate regulation by a competent public authority, with power to require for all public utilities a uniform system of records and accounts, giving all financial data and all information concerning the quality of service and the cost thereof, which data should be published and distributed to the public like other official reports, and also recommended that no stock or bonds for public utilities be issued without the approval of some competent public authority.

Present Scope Broader.

While this commission dealt entirely with the regulation of municipal utilities—railroads, telegraph and telephone companies, both interstate and intrastate, are equally concerned in the question: "What is adequate regulation?" or in other words, "How far can regulation go and be efficient without unreasonably interfering with management?" The Interstate Commerce Commission, of course, has only to do with interstate railroads, telegraph, telephone and express companies, but many of the forty-one State railroad commissions regulate both the intrastate railroads, telephone companies, etc., and the municipal utilities in such States. In New York State, the State Commission has more power over the railroads running into New York City than has the Interstate Commerce Commission.

With public sentiment practically unanimous in favor of the proper regulation of all public utilities, whether State or interstate, and with forty-one different State commissions making as many dissimilar rulings, serious conflicts can readily be imagined, not only between the States themselves, but also between the State and the Federal Commissions and courts.

There are many questions which in their consideration involve identical principles, whether in relation to interstate railways or to quasi-public utilities, not the least important of which is the method of valuation of the property as a basis for rate-making or cost of service to the public.

REPORT OF CONFERENCE AT WHICH DEPARTMENT WAS FORMED.

In opening the conference at which the Department on Regulation of Interstate and Municipal Utilities was formed, PRESIDENT LOW epitomized the problems to be considered in the following words: "I can perfectly understand that dissimilarity of State legislation on this subject may easily be a source of injustice, both to the railroads and other corporations whose limits extend beyond one State. Many States are considering the enactment of public service regulations, and it is quite possible that if a model law could be drafted by men who know what they are dealing with, such a draft might be very beneficial to the legislation of the States which have not yet acted."

All Interests Represented.

PROFESSOR JOHN H. GRAY, of the University of Minnesota, who is now secretary of the Department on Regulation of Interstate and Municipal Utilities, formed as a result of this meeting, was the first speaker called on. He argued strongly that all parties at interest should be represented in the work of formulating a model law for the regulation of interstate and municipal utilities. He called attention to the fact that within the past four years there had been a marvelous growth in the sentiment which favors Government regulation of public monopolies. "That being true," said Professor Gray, "we are confronted with the proposition of what kind of regulation we shall have, to what degree we desire regulation, and, also, what arms of government ought to exercise that regulation."

President Hadley Cited.

The speaker tersely outlined the situation confronting these public utilities in their relation to the public, with the statement that regulation by forty-seven different States is an impossibility, and he endorsed the position of President Hadley, of Yale, that such regulation must come, on the one hand, through the substantial control of such utilities by the Federal Government, as the result of the interprotation of the law; direct control of them by the same authority through the remote contingency of amendment of the Constitution of the United States; or, on the other hand, through public ownership.

Professor Gray thought that the time was ripe, both in view of what The National Civic Federation had already done, and of the tremendous growth during the last few years in public sentiment for adequate regulation to do "a great national public service" by undertaking a thorough investigation of the control of public corporations and of how far such control can be carried without working injustice to business. "It seems to be a very logical outcome of the investigation already undertaken through the instrumentality of The National Civic Federation," said he, "and certainly if the time ever was ripe for some serious consideration of this problem, it is to-day."

Professor Gray broadly outlined the objects of a model law on public utilities as including, first, publicity of accounts; second, the extent to which the State may go in regulating service; third, what profit such utilities should be allowed to make.

On the question of uniformity of legislation, the speaker said, in part: "There is no reason for assuming that we cannot get a very considerable uniformity of State legislation on these matters, therefore I think we can submit a model law, framed not from one point of view, but from the most comprehensive point of view that we can obtain, and I think it is possible to get a law as a sketch, at least, for legislation. If so, that is a great gain."

BLEWETT LEE, general counsel of the Illinois Central Railroad, expressed the opinion that it was very desirable, at the present time, that a model law of some kind should be drafted; and he thought that such a law should be prepared by experts and considered and weighed by persons experienced in the practical working out of such things.

Federation's Great Opportunity.

F. E. BARKER, chairman of the Massachusetts Electric Light and Gas Commission, expressed the opinion that the fundamental principles which ought to prevail in the regulation of the utilities under consideration are very much the same in all those industries, and that there ought not to be any insuperable difficulty in discovering what those fundamental principles are, and perhaps in giving them form. Mr. Barker expressed the opinion that the questions pending to-day indicate a rather more acute state of supervisory activities than has been manifest hitherto, and, in consequence, he thought the importance of some uniform understanding of these principles and of the method of their application had come to be of increasing importance.

Mr. Barker said that his commission would do what it could to help work out such legislation as was under consideration along lines that would be considerate of all interests, both public and private. "I think," said he, "that The National Civic Federation has a great opportunity in respect of this proposition, and we in Massachusetts look to see it take advantage of that opportunity in a way that shall be profitable."

MARTIN S. DECKER, former president of the National Association of State Railway Commissioners and a member of the New York Public Service Commission, expressed the opinion that it might be well indeed after the experience had in some years under the different statutes, which may differ in words, but not greatly in effect, to draft a model law. "There are experiences which the Public Service Commissions of the various States have had," said he, "which indicate that those laws ought to be still further strengthened, and there are some few points, perhaps, wherein they might be weakened." Mr. Decker suggested a careful study of the working, not only of State Commissions, but of State laws, and what part these ought to play in constituting or instituting proper regulation of the great public utilities.

Model Law "Crying Necessity."

JOHN C. BELL, Attorney General of Pennsylvania, gave an interesting account of attempts at regulatory legislation in that State. The problem of regulation, as seen by Mr. Bell, is: "Whether public service corporations shall be let alone to manage their own business; whether there should be public ownership or private ownership; or whether there should be reasonable and proper regulation." The speaker argued strongly for proper regulation, and for uniformity, citing the uniform legislation now on the statute books with regard to negotiable instruments, bills of lading, etc. Mr. Bell thought that there was a "crying necessity" for a uniform public service law. The speaker said that a model law drafted under the auspices of The National Civic Federation with corporate, labor and banking interests all represented, would be "a long step toward a practical solution of the civic evils of the time." He held that a bill so drawn would satisfy legislators at once that it had been well considered and, further, that it would silence opposition from their constituents who would have, in a sense, been represented in the framing of such a statute.

P. H. MORRISSEY, former president of the Brotherhood of Railway Trainmen, said that in his opinion The National Civic Federation is in a peculiarly happy position to give expression on the subject of regulation of utilities. "Your work on municipal ownership was one that was well received," said he, "and I think that your organization can feel complimented on your accomplishments in that direction." Mr. Morrissey made complimentary reference also to the work of The National Civic Federation in the matter of workmen's compensation, and added that these past accomplishments impressed him with a belief that whatever a well-balanced, representative committee on this subject in the name of the Federation might say to the public with regard to railway regulation would have a considerable influence not only with the railways themselves and their employes, but with the public. Mr. Morrissey laid particular stress on the fact that the question of regulation of public utilities is too important to be done by inexperienced hands, that it requires the best thought and most experienced consideration that can be given, and he expressed confidence in good resulting from the method that The National Civic Federation is proposing to use in handling this matter.

Emerson McMillin Relates Some Experiences.

The remarks of EMERSON McMILLIN, the next speaker, are given in full because of the illustration they afford of the attitude of enlightened public service corporations toward adequate regulation in the interest of the public which they serve, and also for the quality of humor which the speaker injected into his subject. Said Mr. McMillin:

"The first attempted regulation that I know anything about occurred in Ohio, where the Legislature had given the city councils the power to regulate the price of gas.

"That was fought by the gas companies bitterly, and they were defeated and thought they were ruined. At that time I was managing gas works in Ohio, and I have been managing gas works and other facilities most of the time since then, having investments in ten to twenty States, and in all of these years Ohio has been the best place in which to have a gas company. There was a time when the companies were being raided everywhere else by new companies springing up. It was assumed they would not go into the business except to be bought out; but when they applied for franchises in Ohio it was said: 'Why should we have two companies in an Ohio city? The city can fix prices!' It was the best State in the Union in which to own gas companies, and in all the years since then I have never known a city council to abuse its privilege save in one instance, and other gas companies were glad of it, because that particular company had been very ugly with the city when it could, and when its contract expired it, as we say, 'got it in the neck.'

Massachusetts' Pioneer Commission.

"I think it was very fortunate that Massachusetts was the first State that brought out a commission, and still more fortunate that they should have got my friend Mr. Barker as president of the Board.

"As a result of my familiarity with the Massachusetts Commission's work, I have, in all the States in which I have been interested, advocated the appointment of commissions. I do not recall an instance where any commission has done anything palpably wrong. That city councils and legislatures will do wrong from our viewpoint is before us every day. I quite agree with the gentleman who said here to-day, that no company would ask the repeal of the commission law. It would know better. That would be the way to make the law stand—to ask for its repeal. But, generally, companies absolutely do not want the commission laws repealed.

Believes in Regulation.

"I believe that the companies ought to be regulated. I believe it because other people favor it, not because of experience. I have in mind now an instance where a gas company was granted a perpetual and exclusive franchise, sustained by the Supreme Court, and it has always sold gas at less than in any other city in the United States. Now two or three years ago the State in which this company is located passed a commission act. The law was about as radical as it could be. Every company that could be put under it was forced there, and the law provided that the property might be appraised for purchase by the city and the courts could not interfere; and one of the worst features, to my mind, was that the cities that had *perpetual and exclusive franchises* were the only places authorized to have opposition gas companies. Where there were no exclusive and perpetual franchises the law provided that there should be no opposition, but where there was the exclusive privilege then the city council was authorized to grant opposition franchises.

"Now, recently, there was advocated a law reducing the price of gas to 60 cents. It was defeated in the Senate by one vote. The average price of the gas had been about 77½ cents. Notwithstanding we were selling gas at 77½ cents, we began late last winter to prepare our figures to reduce the price still further. But, feeling that if the Legislature passed a 60-cent bill, we would want to adhere to the old rate as long as we could during the fight that would follow, we did not make the reduction until we were asked to do so unofficially by a member of the Commission, and thus was saved the State's good name. They knew we had the figures all ready, and the member suggested to us that we make the reduction. We waited, however, until the bill was killed.

The Humorous Side.

"When that Commission was appointed we were sued in another city in the same State, and in that suit all the questions that were ever likely to come up in that State were brought in and thrashed out. The Commission appraised our property a good deal lower than it cost us. It didn't matter at all what it cost; but under the law they appraised it at the figure at which it might be replaced. They also said how much we should make, what percentage, and they fixed the prices which in their opinion would make that percentage.

"The suit lasted two years, and at the end of the first year thereafter we had to go to them and ask permission to reduce the price, as we were making too much money.

"We would not be without commissions, not because we love the commissions more, but because we love the legislatures and city councils less."

Must Preserve Initiative.

The preparation of a general plan without too much detail was advocated by MILO R. MALTBIE, of the New York Public Service Commission. He suggested a thorough investigation of the results of regulation and methods of control of gas and water companies in Great Britain, and particularly pointed to the fact that in some directions at least that country has solved the problem of how to control such utilities without interfering with initiative. Mr. Maltbie thought that any law must offer a reward for initiative. He, too, argued for the employment of trained men in an investigation of the subject under consideration, and among the good results that he thought would follow would be the possibility of accurately drawing a line between State activities on the one hand and national activities on the other.

Following the extended and interesting discussion detailed above, a motion prevailed that the chairman appoint a committee of seven on Plan and Scope, with instructions to report as early as possible, with the understanding that if the plan proposed should meet w.th approval, steps necessary to make it effective would be taken promptly. On taking this action the meeting adjourned.

REPORT OF THE COMMITTEE ON PLAN AND SCOPE.

The report of the Committee on Plan and Scope, together with its personnel, follows:

NEW YORK,
July 28, 1911.

At a meeting of the Department on Regulation of Interstate and Municipal Utilities, held in New York June 23, 1911, the undersigned were appointed a sub-committee to outline a proposed plan and scope for work.

It being taken for granted that Government regulation of some kind and character is essential, your committee starts with this premise. Our recommendations relate solely, therefore, to the general field to be covered and the organization to be provided. We have not attempted to prescribe in detail upon either of these two points, for, as the committee proceeds, new lines of investigation will appear and other opportunities for effective work will develop. It is necessary at this time merely to provide a general groundwork and organization so that these new functions and new matters may be taken up as they arise.

Combined Action Necessary.

This is considered necessary when one considers the importance and scope of the questions connected with the regulation of public utilities. In an undeveloped country each person relies, to a large extent, upon individual action. Each family is a self-contained unit. It protects its own members, instructs the young, administers justice, provides its own conveniences, and seldom comes into contact with the neighbors or unites with them in communal enterprises. With an increase in population and the greater congestion which accompanies such increase, combined action is not only more possible, but more necessary, and out of the common needs have sprung the great public utilities providing transportation and the other services which are now such an essential part of our civilization. An elaborate water system supplants the old well; gas and electric light take the place of the candle and the oil lamp; the telegraph and the telephone supplant the infrequent call and the written communication; the electric street railway and the trans-continental line replace the cumbersome wagon and the stage route. It is utterly impossible to imagine the United States without its steam railroads. Our whole economic, social and political life depends upon them. Even a short and partial paralysis upon an important line produces an immediate effect, often of far-reaching consequences.

Special Obligations Inhere.

These utilities, which now represent investments of millions and millions of dollars throughout the United States, are vital to the growth and development of the country and the well-being of our cities. Various authorities have granted to public service corporations extraordinary and far-reaching powers, powers which the individual does not possess, powers which are entrusted to corporations only because of their public character and the great functions which they perform in the life of communities. The acceptance of these special and important powers carries with it duties and obligations from which the individual and the ordinary corporation are entirely free.

The nature and character of these public services tend to make them monopolistic. Combination and consolidation have gone further in certain localities than in others, but every large city has witnessed the trend towards monopoly. In the smaller cities generally competing companies never got a foothold. Similar utilities in different areas have also been united until free and unrestricted competition has either been curtailed or largely eliminated, and in some cases even competing services have been brought under a single management. Railroad lines which were formerly disconnected units have been bound together into trans-continental lines. Although the corporate organization may change when a State boundary is crossed, one journeys through State after State without realizing such change and without passing from one system to another.

Must Be Adequate Control.

Uncontrolled monopoly not only contains elements of danger to the public, but sometimes leads to stagnation and inefficiency, which, reacting, are harmful to the public and may prevent the development of a community or a nation. A proper system of public regulation should, therefore, not only protect the interests of the public but should provide a means whereby initiative and enterprise may receive proper reward and encouragement while securing to the public upon the other hand proper service at reasonable rates.

"Public Utility" Defined.

While it is difficult to define a public utility with precision, every one has a general idea of the services ordinarily included. These are railroads, street railroads, express lines, gas plants, electric supply plants, water works, telegraphs and telephones. There are many others, however, of a similar character which are important in certain localities, such as pipe lines, steam-heating plants, fire and police signal systems and a long list of other minor utilities which are generally included under the expression "common carriers." Your committee believes that the utilities to be considered by the national committee should include the principal services, namely, transportation—steam and electric—communication, lighting and water. It does not believe, however, that any absolute limit should be fixed, for there have been interesting experiments in the control of other utilities, and it may be found very desirable to have such experiments investigated and considered in the preparation of the final report. Furthermore, if model statutes are to be prepared, one of the important points to be decided will be what utilities should be regulated. This question is one of public policy, and, therefore, not to be passed upon by your sub-committee.

History of Regulatory Laws.

The regulation of steam railroads in the United States, starting with the recommendatory process in Massachusetts and the mandatory and rate-fixing method in Iowa, receiving great impetus from public demand in the so-called Granger States, followed by the original enactment of the Federal "Act to Regulate Commerce," and that scheme in turn, successively, as structural changes of the Federal statute have been made, furnishing the basis for radical amendments of State statutes, has developed into combined general systems of advanced governmental supervision and control, showing, however, many differences in regulating methods and widely varying construction and application of powers. The time seems ripe for full investigation and thorough discussion of these various plans of governmental regulation. All concede that these public agencies must be effectively controlled.

Pitfalls to Be Avoided.

Few conceive as yet that such supervision and control may proceed so far through legislative action and growth of administrative authority along independent lines in each of the States, and as between the States and the Nation, that the results will be not merely incongruous but damaging to the interests of commerce, thus tending to defeat the underlying reason for transportation regulation, and that this can be avoided only by the attainment of general uniformity in statutory provisions and methods of administration. We have before us the problem of securing such uniformity while necessarily recognizing the jurisdictions of the States as against each other and the Nation as a whole and the jurisdiction of the Federal Government as against those of the States, in accordance with the Constitution of the United States, as that supreme law has been interpreted by the court of last resort.

Suggestions for Inquiry.

It is recommended that investigation should be made into the principal methods that have been tried in the United States and Europe, particularly Great Britain. For instance, the laws enacted in New York and Wisconsin within a few years, and the results of the regulation provided for therein, should be considered. Likewise, the experience of Massachusetts, which was the first State to attempt to control in any broad way the public utilities other than railroads. The results of the operation of the Texas law would be interesting and profitable. The recent experience of such States as Virginia, Nebraska and Tennessee would be illuminating.

THE EXECUTIVE COUNCIL.

UPPER ROW (left to right)—EMERSON MCMILLIN, CHAIRMAN; FRANKLIN K. LANE, MARTIN S. DECKER, MILO R. MALTBIE, FRANKLIN Q. BROWN, VICE-CHAIRMAN.
LOWER ROW—BLEWETT LEE, JOHN H. GRAY, SECRETARY; F. C. WALCOTT, TREASURER; P. H. MORRISSEY, LEO S. ROWE.

it is questionable how far foreign experience would helpful, for our conditions are in many ways dif- ent from those obtaining in any European country; t certainly the methods that have been found suc- ssful in Great Britain, particularly as to gas and iter companies, would be of great value, and doubt- s England's experience with railroads would point moral and adorn a tale.

Published Reports a Feature.

These subjects and fields of investigation are sug- sted merely as illustrative. Your committee does t believe that any fixed limit should be imposed at e present, for one of the most valuable features of e work of the committee will be the publication of ports upon the various methods and experiments at have been tried and the results which they have oduced. If thorough and impartial reports are epared by competent investigators, who will can- dly report the facts, such reports will not only be great value to the committee in preparing the commendations it may see fit to make, but will be great use to the entire country and will become recognized source of information and an authorita- ve document upon the subject of public regulation. our committee has not attempted to outline the pre- se fields which should be traversed, but this phase the work is extremely important and it should be arefully and scientifically done.

Skeleton Scheme Suggested.

Your committee also believes that a most useful inction will be the preparation in outline of a tatute providing for public regulation and the or- anization to carry it into effect. We appreciate that ew States have precisely the same conditions. Fur- hermore, constitutional provisions vary from State o State, and judicial decisions have been made which ust be recognized in the framing of any statute. It s believed, however, that a general scheme of regula- ion could be prepared which would not go too far nto detail, but which could be used as a framework r skeleton in the preparation of a law for any State.

Executive Council Proposed.

To carry forward the work, your committee recom- nends the appointment by the President of The Na- ional Civic Federation of an executive council to upervise the various investigations which are to be nade, to determine the precise subjects to be investi- gated, to appoint sub-committees upon the various phases of the subject, to provide the necessary means for the conduct of the work, and to employ and direct all experts and investigators, subject always to the general supervision of the department.

Without intending to limit the functions of the executive council or to determine what that body should do, we consider that at least the following committees should be appointed by the executive council, and that, so far as practicable, members of the council should be chairmen of such sub-com- mittees:

(*a*) Regulation of Rates.
(*b*) Control of Service.
(*c*) Control of Accounts and Reports.
(*d*) Regulation of Financial Matters.
(*e*) Conflicts of Jurisdiction.
(*f*) Control over Labor Questions.
(*g*) Legal and Legislative.
(*h*) Committee on Ways and Means.

Sub-Committees' Functions.

The sub-committee on each one of these subjects would consider the various questions connected there- with. For example, "service" is to be considered as including not merely the number of trains to be oper- ated or the illuminating power of gas, but every point at which the public comes into contact with the cor- poration through the service which it provides, such as the amount and character of cars and other equip- ment to be operated, safety-devices, gas pressure, the purity of water, etc.

The committee on financial matters, for example, would consider to what extent the issuance of stocks, bonds, notes, etc., should be regulated, how such con- trol should be exercised, what conditions should be attached to the approval of securities, the methods of amortizing discounts, the question of issuing stock below par, etc.

The committee on conflicts of jurisdiction has a very broad and difficult field. It would naturally con- sider how far Federal regulation should extend and how far matters should be left to the States; also the delimitation of the jurisdiction of the courts in their control over administrative bodies, the separation of Governmental powers, etc. Respectfully submitted,

SUB-COMMITTEE ON PLAN AND SCOPE.

EMERSON MCMILLIN, FRANKLIN K. LANE,
M. S. DECKER, FRANKLIN Q. BROWN
JOHN H. GRAY, P. H. MORRISSEY,
MILO R. MALTBIE.

EXECUTIVE COUNCIL AND COMMITTEE, OFFICERS AND SUB-COMMITTEES.

Following the approval of the above report, an Executive Committee, whose personnel is representative of all interested in the rightful solution of the problem involved, was appointed to provide for the carrying out of its proposals. This committee follows, together with the Executive Council, which is in immediate charge of the work of the department, and the various sub-committees:

Executive Council.

EMERSON MCMILLIN, Chairman.
FRANKLIN K. LANE Chairman Committee on Rates.
MARTIN S. DECKER, Chairman Committee on Control of Service.
MILO R. MALTBIE, Chairman Committee on Control of Capitalization.
BLEWETT LEE, Chairman Committee on Franchises.
FRANKLIN Q. BROWN, Vice-Chairman.
LEO S. ROWE, Chairman Committee on Accounts and Reports.
P. H. MORRISSEY, Chairman Committee on Safety of Operation.
JOHN H. GRAY, Secretary.
F. C. WALCOTT Treasurer.

Executive Committee.

ALFRED L. BAKER (Bond and Stock Broker), Chicago, Ill.
F. E. BARKER (Massachusetts Gas and Electric Commission), Boston, Mass.
JOHN C. BELL (Attorney General of Pennsylvania), Harrisburg, Pa.
AUGUST BELMONT (Chairman Board Directors Interborough Railroad Company), New York.
UNION N. BETHELL (Vice-President American Telephone and Telegraph Company), New York.
ARTHUR W. BRADY (President American Electric Railroad Company), Anderson Ind.
CHARLES F. BROOKER (Director New York, New Haven and Hartford Railroad Company), Ansonia, Conn.
WILLIAM C. BROWN (President New York Central and Hudson River Railroad Company), New York.
H. M. BYLLESBY (Contractor, H. M. Byllesby & Co.), Chicago, Ill.
JAMES CAMPBELL (President North American Securities Company), New York.
JOHN N. CARLISLE (Former Member New York Railway Commission), Watertown, N. Y.
W. J. CLARK (General Electric Company), New York.
GEORGE B. CORTELYOU (President Consolidated Gas Company), New York.
F. A. DELANO (President Wabash Railroad Company), Chicago, Ill.
B. A. ECKHART (Chairman Illinois Railroad Commission), Chicago, Ill.
CHARLES L. EDGAR (Chairman Committee on Public Policy, National Electric Lighting Association), Boston, Mass.
HALFORD ERICKSON (Railroad Commission of Wisconsin), Madison, Wis.
W. W. FINLEY (President Southern Railway Company), Washington, D. C.
ALLEN P. FORBES (Banker, Director Public Utility Companies, Harris, Forbes & Co.), New York.
DAVID R. FRANCIS (Railroad Director and Banker), St. Louis, Mo.
W. W. FREEMAN (Vice-President and General Manager Edison Electric Illuminating Company), Brooklyn.
A. B. GARRETSON (President Order Railway Conductors), Cedar Rapids, Iowa.
TIMOTHY HEALY (President International Brotherhood of Stationary Firemen), New York.
MYRON T. HERRICK (Railway Director and Banker), Cleveland, Ohio.
ALEXANDER C. HUMPHREYS (President Stevens Institute of Technology), Hoboken, N. J.
SAMUEL INSULL (President Commonwealth Electric Company), Chicago, Ill.
D. O. IVES (Manager Transportation Department, Chamber of Commerce), Boston, Mass.
J. C. LINCOLN (President National Industrial Traffic League), St. Louis, Mo.
THOMAS N. MCCARTER, (President American Street and Interurban Railway Association), Newark, N. J.
JAMES H. MCGRAW (Publisher), New York.
F. J. MCNULTY (Grand President International Brotherhood of Electrical Workers), Springfield, Ill.
V. EVERIT MACY (Director Queensborough Gas and Electric Company), New York.
WILLIAM D. MAHON (President Amalgamated Association of Street Railway Employes), Detroit, Mich.
T. C. MARTIN (Secretary National Electric Light Association), New York.
C. E. MERRIAM (Professor Political Economy, University of Chicago), Chicago, Ill.
B. H. MEYER (Interstate Commerce Commission), Washington, D. C.
H. U. MUDGE (President Chicago, Rock Island and Pacific Railroad Company), Chicago, Ill.
JOSIAH T. NEWCOMB (General Counsel Stone and Webster Company), New York.
H. B. PERHAM (President Order of Railroad Telegraphers), St. Louis, Mo.
ROBERT R. PRENTIS (President National Association of State Railway Commissioners), Richmond, Va.
W. Z. RIPLEY (Professor Political Economy, Harvard University), Cambridge, Mass.
JOHN H. ROEMER (Railroad Commission of Wisconsin), Madison, Wis.
ALBERT SHAW (Editor "Review of Reviews"), New York.
ALFRED H. SMITH (Vice-President and General Manager New York Central and Hudson River Railroad Company), New York.
JAMES SPEYER (Banker), New York.
MASON B. STARRING (President United Railways Investment Company), New York.
CHARLES A. STONE (Stone and Webster Company), Boston, Mass.
WARREN S. STONE (Grand Chief International Brotherhood of Locomotive Engineers), Cleveland, Ohio.
JAMES J. STORROW (Banker and Director of Public Utility Companies), Boston, Mass.
OSCAR S. STRAUS (Former Secretary of Commerce and Labor), New York.
GEORGE F. SWAIN (Professor Civil Engineering, Harvard University), Cambridge, Mass.
FRANK TRUMBULL (Chairman Board Directors Chesapeake and Ohio Railroad Company), New York.
THEODORE N. VAIL (President American Telephone and Telegraph Company), New York.
ARTHUR D. WHEELER (Chairman Board Directors, Chicago Telephone Company), Chicago, Ill.
WILLIAM R. WHEELER (Traffic Manager, Chamber of Commerce), San Francisco, Cal.
JOHN H. WIGMORE (Dean of Law School, Northwestern University), Chicago, Ill.
DANIEL WILLARD (President Baltimore and Ohio Railroad Company), Baltimore, Md.
WILLIAM R. WILLCOX (New York Public Service Commission), New York.
TIMOTHY S. WILLIAMS (President Brooklyn Rapid Transit Company), New York.
ROBERT WINSOR (Banker, Kidder, Peabody & Co.), Boston, Mass.
ROLLIN S. WOODRUFF (Former Governor of Connecticut), New Haven, Conn.

AND THE MEMBERS OF THE EXECUTIVE COUNCIL.

Sub-Committees for Detail Work.

After careful consideration, the Executive Council appointed the following sub-committees, in order to make effective the suggestions contained in the plan and scope of work:

Rates.

Chairman, FRANKLIN K. LANE; F. A. DELANO, HALFORD ERICKSON, J. C. LINCOLN, ALEX. C. HUMPHREYS, THEODORE N. VAIL.

Control of Service.

Chairman, MARTIN S. DECKER; B. A. ECKHART, D. O. IVES, ROBERT R. PRENTIS, UNION N. BETHELL, CHARLES L. EDGAR, ALFRED H. SMITH, WILLIAM R. WHEELER, CHARLES A. STONE.

Control of Capitalization.

Chairman, MILO R. MALTBIE; JAMES SPEYER, GEORGE B. CORTELYOU, B. H. MEYER, TIMOTHY S. WILLIAMS, W. J. CLARK.

Franchises.

Chairman, BLEWETT LEE; MASON B. STARRING, ALFRED L. BAKER, JOHN H. ROEMER, JOHN H. WIGMORE, H. M. BYLLESBY, JOHN N. CARLISLE, SAMUEL INSULL, CHARLES E. MERRIAM, THOMAS N. MCCARTER, JOSIAH T. NEWCOMB, LEO S. ROWE, ARTHUR D. WHEELER.

**Accounts and Reports.*

Chairman, LEO S. ROWE.

**Safety of Operation.*

Chairman, P. H. MORRISSEY.

**Ways and Means.*

Chairman, FRANKLIN Q. BROWN.

Inquiry Actively Begun.

Professor Gray is now in active charge of the work of the Department on Regulation of Interstate and Municipal Utilities as director of the investigation that is being made.

A staff of experts has been recruited, and will be added to from time to time as the work demands. No pains will be spared to make the inquiry as thorough and as authoritative as it is possible for it to be.

Announcement of the creation of this Department and of the work it proposes to do has met with widespread and gratifying commendation from those interested in a rightful solution of the problems involved.

*Personnel of these committees not yet completed.

FEDERATION'S MODEL COMPENSATION ACT FINDS FAVOR

ITS PRINCIPLES ADOPTED BY SPECIAL COMMISSION FOR RECOMMENDATION TO CONGRESS—SAFETY MEASURE IN PREPARATION—INTERESTING WINTER MEETING

A MEETING of the Department on Compensation for Industrial Accidents and Their Prevention was held December 8, at 1 Madison avenue, New York City. The gathering was distinguished by reason of the number and prominence of those who attended, and also because of the scope of the program and the quality of the speeches. The importance of the proceedings is such that they have been published in booklet form. Extended notice will not be given here.

The published proceedings contain a wealth of material which would seem to be almost indispensable to anyone who wishes to keep posted on the developments in workmen's compensation legislation and the prevention of industrial accidents. Compulsory compensation, elective compensation and compulsory State insurance are all discussed at length by speakers of recognized authority.

There are presented herewith, as a summary of the meeting, the speech of the Chairman, August Belmont, which gives a succinct account of the most recent developments in workmen's compensation, and the text of an amendment, proposed by Francis Lynde Stetson, which is designed to remove the constitutional obstacle in the path of effective workmen's compensation in the State of New York.

Mr. Belmont's Address.

"The topics for discussion to-day relating to Workmen's Compensation in themselves indicate the progress which has been made since the adoption of our model Workmen's Compensation Bill and the subjects show the necessity for educational work on our part. They are:

"'Compulsory Compensation vs. State Insurance.'

"'Compulsory Compensation vs. the Elective Plan.'

"'The Situation in New York Concerning Proposed Amendments to the Constitution Permitting the Enactment of a Workmen's Compensation Law.'

"'The Next Step in Workmen's Compensation in New York State.'

"Our model bill was submitted to the States where legislatures were in session last February with the suggestion that it be prepared in form for submission by attorneys familiar with the legislative diction in the several States.

"The adverse decision of the Court of Appeals in New York State upon the Wainwright Act following very quickly made the advocates of Workmen's Compensation hesitate to favor the compulsory principle, and as you know, there have come into existence State insurance laws and the elective plan.

"We find sentiment on the part of some employers and wage-earners in favor of State insurance—both having given the subject casual study, recognizing the advantages, but failing to see the evils which may arise, under a system of State insurance. But as a rule the leading labor men are following the same line that The National Civic Federation has adopted in its model bill.

"The American Federation of Labor sent out to its local unions throughout the country, with its endorsement, twenty thousand copies of the Civic Federation's bill on Workmen's Compensation.

"State Insurance is now operative in the State of Washington, but has not been in existence long enough to furnish a conclusive illustration. In Ohio the State insurance laws, while having passed, are not yet in operation. In Wisconsin the elective method has been sustained by the higher court; in New Jersey only by the lower court; but the indications are that that method will be sustained where adopted. No compulsory law has yet been endorsed by the higher courts.

"A law has been passed in Massachusetts, and its endorsement by the higher court is expected. In other words, it has been submitted to the Supreme Court before being put on its passage.

"The principle is mutual insurance. It is an elective system which, if entered into, gives the employer immunity from other claims under the liability law. I understand from the Massachusetts Commissioners that the insurance companies are somewhat opposed to it.

"The greatest encouragement has been the adoption of the principles of our bill by the Congressional Commission on Employers' Liability and Workmen's Compensation.

"The Chairman, Senator George Sutherland, at a conference with some of our active members recently in New York, gave his reasons for adopting our plan, and asked our assistance in securing the passage of the bill to be recommended for interstate commerce by the Congressional Commission January 1, 1912.

"If this bill is enacted into law by Congress and upheld by the United States Supreme Court it will have great weight in influencing uniform State legislation on Workmen's Compensation, which is the great purpose of The National Civic Federation.

"At the meeting of the Department held May 26, 1911, it was determined to have committees appear before the Congressional Commission at its hearings, and the Department has been represented on three such occasions.

Valuable Briefs Submitted.

"The briefs which were submitted to the Commission have since had a wide circulation and great influence in moulding sentiment. These briefs are:

"First, one submitted at the first hearing of the Congressional Commission in June jointly by four of our legal members—Messrs. Francis Lynde Stetson, P. Tecumseh Sherman, Launcelot Packer and William J. Moran. That brief is an argument for compulsory compensation.

"At the next hearing of the Congressional Commission at Chicago in October, 1911, there was presented a brief by Mr. P. Tecumseh Sherman, Chairman of our Legal Committee, opposing State insurance and a Federal tax.

"At that same hearing Mr. Louis B. Schram, Chairman of our Committee on Improvement of State Inspection of Factories with Special Reference to Safeguarding Machinery, emphasized the desirability of adopting the Lewis Bill based upon the Civic Federation's model act, and also presented arguments in favor of the establishment of Federal and State museums of safety and the adoption of a standard uniform blank for reporting industrial accidents in the interest of accident prevention.

"There were afterward submitted by Mr. Francis Lynde Stetson, Chairman of our Committee on Legislative Policy, an opinion upon the police power of the United States Government, and a brief by Mr. William J. Moran against the elective system of compensation.

"These documents, in addition to the views of our Legal Committee concerning the effect of the decision of the Court of Appeals in New York State, are sought from every point in the Union by men giving consideration to the subject of Workmen's Compensation.

"Upon invitation from the Congressional Commission we arranged to have at its last hearing in Washington, November 6, experts from large corporations having voluntary compensation plans, and representatives of trades unions having relief funds, to offer suggestions upon such matters as the following:

"'The amount which injured men shall receive'; 'The method of ascertaining the truth of their claims, and extent of injuries'; 'The number and degree of independents'; 'Medical examination by employer immediately following accident'; 'A practical scheme for eliminating malingering'; and some plan whereby a concern which has to pay compensation during a long period of time may follow up the recipient, etc., etc.

"We have been co-operating closely with the Workmen's Compensation Committee of the Uniform State Law Commissioners and a like committee from the American Bar Association appointed at our request.

SOME OF THOSE HEARD AT THE MEETING

(1) August Belmont, Chairman; (2) Francis Lynde Stetson, (3) William J. Moran, (4) J. Walter Lord, (5) Timothy Healy, (6) Louis B. Schram, (7) John Calder, (8) Cyrus W. Phillips, (9) James L. Gernon, (10) Marcel A. Viti, (11) Edgar T. Davies.

States Especially Active.

"Our correspondence shows especial activity in the following States: West Virginia, Texas, Colorado, California, Maryland, Michigan, North Dakota, Montana, Connecticut, Rhode Island, Missouri, Indiana and Iowa.

"These have not yet adopted any form of compensation laws with the exception of Montana.

"We recommended last year that compensation commissions be appointed where they do not yet exist, and we should continue that activity by urging again that such commissions be appointed by the twelve legislatures in session this season, and that there be a new commission in New York State to continue the work so ably pursued by the Wainwright Commission.

"You will receive encouraging word from the Committee on Improvement of State Inspection of Factories as to the manner in which its recommendations have been received in the various States, and there will come to you for discussion from that committee a report upon a Model Safety Act. I am sure that its report is going to be not only constructive, but indicative of great progress and usefulness for the future."

Amendment Submitted by Mr. Stetson.

Great interest was shown at the meeting in an amendment to the Constitution of the State of New York that was proposed by Francis Lynde Stetson with a view to making possible the enactment of a Workmen's Compensation Law. The amendment follows:

"The Legislature may require employers, or employers and employes jointly, to make provision for, and to pay reasonable compensation, regardless of fault, to employes on account of injuries suffered by them arising out of and in course of the employment, or to the dependents of any such employe dying from such injury.

"To assure the payment of such compensation the Legislature may prescribe or approve methods of insurance which may or may not include the mutual association of persons responsible

(Continued on Page 24.)

TO AID PURE FOOD AND DRUG CAMPAIGN

NEW DEPARTMENT OF CIVIC FEDERATION—REPRESENTATIVE COMMITTEE ON PLAN AND SCOPE—OPPORTUNITY FOR WORK OUTLINED AT GATHERING OF OFFICIALS, EXPERTS, MANUFACTURERS AND DEALERS AND LABOR LEADERS

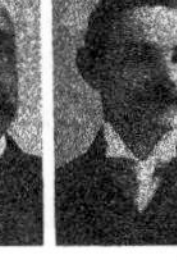

PLAN AND SCOPE COMMITTEE.

UPPER ROW—JOHN HAYS HAMMOND, CHAIRMAN; HARVEY W. WILEY, DR. WILLIAM J. SCHIEFFELIN, SAMUEL GOMPERS, W. C. BREED, MRS. S. S. CROCKETT, LUCIUS P. BROWN.
LOWER ROW—NAHUM J. BACHELDER, JAMES O'CONNELL, W. G. LEE, JOHN GOLDEN, GEORGE M. WHITAKER.

IN accordance with a resolution adopted at a meeting held in New York City on October 2, the following Committee on Plan and Scope has been named by President Low for the Department on Pure Food and Drugs, of The National Civic Federation, which was organized on that occasion:

Committee on Plan and Scope.

JOHN HAYS HAMMOND, Washington, D. C., Chairman.
DR. HARVEY W. WILEY, Chief Food Chemist, Department of Agriculture, Washington, D. C.
LUCIUS P. BROWN, President of the Association of State and National Food and Dairy Departments, Nashville, Tenn.
DR. WILLIAM J. SCHIEFFELIN, former President of the Wholesale Druggists' Association, New York City.
W. C. BREED, Counsel for the National Wholesale Grocers' Association, New York City.
B. L. MURRAY, Chairman American Chemical Society, Rahway, N. J.
GEORGE M. WHITAKER, President Farmers' National Congress, U. S. A., Washington, D. C.
N. J. BACHELDER, former Master of the National Grange, Concord, N. H.
SAMUEL GOMPERS, President of the American Federation of Labor, Washington, D. C.
W. G. LEE, President Brotherhood Railroad Trainmen, Cleveland, Ohio.
JAMES O'CONNELL, International Association of Machinists, Washington, D. C.
JOHN GOLDEN, President United Textile Workers of America, Fall River, Mass.
MRS. S. S. CROCKETT, Chairman Public Health Department, the General Federation of Women's Clubs, Nashville, Tenn.

Other representative women will be added to the committee.

Attendance Was Representative.

The meeting in question was notable for a number of things, among them being the large attendance of leaders in the movement for pure food and drugs in this country; of representatives of labor and of the various associations of manufacturers who work under pure food and drug laws. A word of greeting was also given from a member of the Farmers' National Congress and the National Grange.

The opinion was expressed by several speakers that progress in food regulation had gone further to date than that in drugs, but all agreed that there was great work yet to be done in both lines.

There seemed to be a unanimity of sentiment that The National Civic Federation could play a useful part in furthering the cause of pure food and drugs, and special emphasis was laid by several speakers on the helpful work that they thought the Federation could do in the matter of educating the public in this matter.

Attention was called by some of the speakers to what they declared to be the tendency on the part of some of the States to adopt food and drug standards of their own with great resulting confusion. On this point William C. Breed, of Breed, Abbott & Morgan, attorneys, who is counsel for the National Wholesale Grocers' Association and other trade organizations, voiced the views of these and other food manufacturers as follows:

Conflicting Standards Weighty Question.

"The tendency toward the adoption of conflicting standards is the weightiest question that confronts the manufacturers to-day. Experience certainly leads to the conclusion that if standards for food products are to be formulated for the American people the movement should originate as an amendment to the national act, or at least should arise out of the authority of some national statute. The only intelligent method of handling a subject of this sort is through a commission which should be given the power not only to adopt standards, but to change them.

"The State of Wisconsin has already adopted a standard of its own, and other commonwealths have legislated similarly with regard to vinegar, milk, etc. In Indiana the use of benzoate of soda has been prohibited, although the Federal Government permits it. The matter is now in litigation, and the Supreme Court of the United States will pass upon it.

Great stress was laid on the necessity for uniformity between the States and the Federal Government in legislation on the subject of both food and drugs.

Leaders of organized labor called attention to the fact that the people they represent are probably more frequently the victims of unscrupulous purveyors of food and drugs than any other part of our citizenship. These gentlemen demanded stringent laws and a broad educational policy, and asked that The National Civic Federation exert its influence to the utmost to this end.

Spirit of Fair Play.

A number of those who spoke, while urging that no loophole be left for the unscrupulous dealer, insisted that encouragement be given manufacturers and dealers who are sincerely putting themselves in touch with the great national trend toward purity in food and drugs.

The distinguished and representative character of the attendance, the broad scope of subjects discussed, and the high character of the addresses that were delivered, made the meeting one that will likely be regarded as of more than passing importance in the campaign for pure food and drugs in this country.

Federation Wants Information.

In opening the meeting PRESIDENT LOW, of The National Civic Federation, who presided, said that he would waste no words in an effort to show the importance to the people of good food and good drugs. "The marvelous thing," said Mr. Low, "is that any one can be found who is willing wilfully to offer to the people for their use bad food and bad drugs." The speaker went on to state that The National Civic Federation had determined on creating a Department on Pure Food and Drugs, to consider the subject and to deal with it, "not because the Federation has any theories or any special knowledge, but it wants information, and when it secures that information it wants to sustain the authorities in protecting the interests of the people of the United States."

DR. HARVEY W. WILEY, chief food chemist of the United States Department of Agriculture, the first speaker, argued interestingly and at length for so much of a paternalistic attitude on the part of the Government in conserving the health of citizens as is necessary to bring about that result.

Speaking of the existing Federal law, Doctor Wiley said that he did not claim that this act had had its full fruition, that all knew as a matter of fact that it had not, but the speaker claimed a great step forward had been made, and that there was considerable hope in the near future for the complete realization of the ideas which had been enacted into law in that statute.

"Real Service for the People."

"The National Civic Federation," said Dr. Wiley, "in taking up this subject of the purity of drugs is doing a real service for the people of this country."

Dr. Wiley said that people are still dying by the thousands from preventable diseases because of their absolute indifference to the conditions surrounding them, and added that just as soon as they demanded the same protection of the Government that it now gives the laborer in Panama or the soldier on the Rio Grande, fear of infectious diseases would be practically abolished.

Dr. Wiley closed his speech with the advocacy of a National Board of Health, whose head should have a seat in the President's Cabinet, basing his argument for the establishment of such a board upon the statement that health is our greatest national asset simply measured by its money value, and that if those who look after agriculture, post-offices, our foreign relations, and so forth, have a seat in the Cabinet.

one who is charged with conserving the public health certainly should sit there too. The speaker's concluding words were: "It seems to me that if The National Civic Federation in its wisdom should see fit to promote a movement having to do with the public health, it would perform one of its most useful functions."

Work for the States.

LUCIUS P. BROWN, who followed Dr. Wiley, is president of the Association of State and National Food and Dairy Commissioners. In his opening remarks he expressed pleasure at being present on an occasion when "there is to be begun constructive work in another of the numerous and useful activities of The National Civic Federation for the public welfare." The speaker said that the protection of a food supply naturally assumes two forms, namely, (1) the assurance of the purity of foods as to their ingredients, and (2) the assurance of their freedom from disease-producing contamination. The first division named again divides itself under the heads of adulteration and misbranding. In discussing the protection of food from disease-producing contamination, Mr. Brown pointed to the fact that the Federal Government can aid scarcely at all in this, and that the work must therefore be done by the States.

After a general survey of the field, the speaker advocated certain concrete efforts that in his opinion should be made through organization in furthering the pure food and drug movement in this country. First among these he placed educational measures; second, organized effort was recommended to secure as early as possible an amendment of the National Food and Drugs Act so as to carry out the evident intent of its framers and make such other changes as nearly five years of experience have shown to be desirable; a third line of action recommended was the addition of such provisions to the Federal law as will prevent the misrepresentation of the therapeutic action of drugs. Mr. Brown spoke of the necessity of getting in the several States legislation which shall be uniform in its essentials with a future revised Federal Act, and he argued that the execution of pure food and drug laws should be taken strictly out of politics. He endorsed Dr. Wiley's proposal of a National Board of Health, and stated that one of the crying needs of food control work at this time is co-operation among the States and between the States and the nation.

State Drug Laws Needed.

"I regret to say," said Mr. Brown, "that pure food laws, well administered, are much more abundant than pure drug laws." The speaker expressed the opinion that The National Civic Federation could do no better work than to aid in the passage of pure drug laws in States which do not now possess them.

The question of short weights and measures was touched upon briefly with the statement that this evil is known to be "most flagrant everywhere." The opinion was expressed that a peculiarly favorable time had been chosen to inaugurate this department of The National Civic Federation, and that it could not engage in a work which would redound more to its credit with the masses of the people, nor one by which more could be done to quicken the public conscience or develop public morality.

German Testing and Inspecting.

Prior to the introduction of GEORGE L. FLANDERS, of the Department of Agriculture of New York, Chairman Low referred to a bulletin that had been handed him which showed that there exist in the whole German Empire 174 institutions which are required to test and inspect articles of food. Of these, 27 were founded with government capital, 49 with local community capital, 10 by agricultural boards, and 88 with private means.

Mr. Flanders, the next speaker, expressed agreement with Dr. Wiley that the common law doctrine of, "let him who purchases beware," should be modified in the matter of pure food and drugs with the establishment of certain paternalism, expressing the opinion, however, that care should be taken not to go to the extreme of paternalism, and thus run the risk of getting too far ahead of public sentiment and suffering a setback. Mr. Flanders stated that in New York during the past three years there had been referred to the Attorney-General for prosecution as violations of the food law more than 3,300 cases. Of these he said not ten per cent, and possibly not five, were cases in which a question of health was involved, but rather that it was almost invariably a question of fraud, which he assumed came within the police power.

The speaker laid emphasis on the fact that the law as it now stands is practically that the public cannot be sold any deleterious or harmful products, but that other adulterated goods may be sold if they are shown to be so on the label.

Important to Toilers.

Organized labor was heard from, following Mr. Flanders, in the person of JOHN GOLDEN, president of the Textile Workers of America. Mr. Golden at the outset endorsed Dr. Wiley's advocacy of a National Department of Public Health. He said that the creation of a Department on Pure Food and Drugs by The National Civic Federation was of importance to the toilers, first, because of the fact that this class was an easy prey to the unscrupulous adulterator and manufacturer and the false-weigher, and, secondly, because it could ill afford to stand short weight and short measure, particularly in view of the high price of commodities. Mr. Golden related an interesting experience, and an unfortunate one, it may be added, that a friend had who endeavored to administer honestly the office of sealer of weights and measures.

"I know," said the speaker, "that our people are wide awake with regard to the system of short measures and short weights, but I believe they need a whole lot of education with regard to adulteration of products. I feel there is a wide field for this National Civic Federation in its new department to aid in such education."

Great Public Service Possible.

HUGH FOX, secretary of the United States Brewers' Association, outlined succinctly and interestingly the role that he felt The National Civic Federation could play in the matter under discussion, in the following words:

"Now the mere fact that The National Civic Federation has suggested this new department is a crowning proof of the popularity of the public health movement. We believe that an organization like this, taking hold of this question in a careful manner, can do a very great public service."

Mr. Fox endorsed the proposition of a public health bureau. He said that he thought the day was coming when a man would be proud of the fact that he was a recognized purveyor to the American public and had lived up to the standards that had been set forth.

Resolve to Organize a Department.

Prior to the adjournment of the morning session DR. THOMAS DARLINGTON, former Commissioner of Health of the City of New York, and now secretary of the Welfare Committee of the American Iron and Steel Institute, offered the following resolution:

> RESOLVED, That it is the judgment of this meeting that a Committee of Fifteen be appointed to prepare a plan for a Department on Pure Food and Drugs, of The National Civic Federation, and to define the scope of such a department; and it is further resolved that the President be, and hereby is, authorized to appoint such a committee.

In seconding the above resolution, Herman Metz, former Comptroller of the City of New York, said: "We want a definite law that will mean something. I second that resolution most heartily."

Following the unanimous adoption of Dr. Darlington's resolution the morning session adjourned.

Lucius P. Brown in the Chair.

The afternoon session was called to order by Lucius P. Brown, who introduced Dr. THOMAS DARLINGTON as the first speaker. Dr. Darlington spoke in part as follows:

"Few people realize how great is the problem of furnishing pure and wholesome food to a large community. Inspection of the food supply cannot be made in a single place. It must be watched from its production to the table. Thus, in the inspection of milk, which may be taken as a type, there are six links in the chain:

"1. The care and inspection of the dairy.
"2. Transporting the milk to the creamery or receiving station.
"3. Handling the milk at the creamery.
"4. Shipping the milk on the train.
"5. Receiving and distributing the milk in the city.
"6. Care of the milk in the household.

Dr. Darlington Defines Proper Inspection.

"So there is a chain of links in the inspection of nearly all food. Yet how little of it is done compared with the vast amount of food sold and consumed! The inspection should see that the proper weight is given; that the food is not adulterated or colored, nor has anything in it that purports to make it better than it really is, nor contains deleterious preservatives, and that it is really that which we desire to purchase.

"We sit down to our daily meal and partake of ham from Westphalia, bananas and pineapples from Panama and Central America, olive oil from Italy, wines from France, cheese from Switzerland, sugar from Cuba, cream not yet twenty-four hours old from Canada, coffee from Brazil and tea from China, little mindful that the localities to which we are indebted for the supply of a single meal encircle the globe. Naturally, the assimilating of as great an amount of foods from such separated localities of divers interests affords opportunities for mistakes and frauds. We must admit that at this daily meal our Westphalian ham may come from Chicago, our Italian olive oil from the cottonseed of the South, our French wines from California, our Swiss cheese from New Jersey or New York, and our Java coffee may contain a mixture of chicory, dandelion, legumes, sawdust, date stones, acorns and other articles.

When Food Is Impure.

"Food is to be regarded as impure when sold under any misrepresentation; although it is not necessary that such misrepresentation should be productive of injury to health. Impure food may be divided under four heads: Decomposition, Infection, Substitution and Adulteration. To my mind, decomposed or infected food is the worst. It is that which is infested with bacteria that renders it unfit for human consumption. To illustrate: The way in which decomposed meat acts injuriously is that it contains certain poisons. When an animal is killed and the meat is kept too long or improperly, putrefaction commences. This cannot take place without bacteria. These little workers break up complex substances into those which are less complex, so that ultimately organic substances such as meat become water, carbonic acid and ammonia. But in the process of transition from meat to these substances many chemical products are formed and include what are known as ptomaines. So ptomaines are chemical poisons which are produced in putrefying flesh by the action of germs. They vary in character according to the stage of decomposition and are of various kinds; some crystalline, some liquid, etc. Many of these have been isolated so as to make distinct chemical compounds, and in their action resemble very much the vegetable alkaloids. Some are like nicotine, atropine, etc., covering nearly the whole list of alkaloids. Such ptomaines have been extracted from nearly all kinds of decaying albuminous material, from horseflesh, cheese, milk, etc. Some are not poisonous and others are extremely so. Thus, a few milligrams of neurine are sufficient to kill a cat. These ptomaines are of the most importance to us from the fact that, under certain conditions where the food has not been properly kept, they are found in some of our common articles of consumption, such as sausage, milk, ice cream, etc., and, unfortunately, people have been made ill by them and wholesale poisonings have occurred."

In introducing WILLIAM C. BREED, general counsel of the National Wholesale Grocers' Association, Chairman Brown paid the following compliment to the organization with which the speaker is connected: "Among the associations which are intimately connected with food work is one which has always stood for purity and for the square deal. I mean the National Wholesale Grocers' Association."

Mr. Breed expressed the opinion that the time had now come in the fight for pure food and drugs where a practical discussion of results should be had, together with some real agreement on the principles that must govern future food legislation and administration. The speaker said that it might seem strange to some that many of the trade organizations had been the leaders in the movement for uniform food legislation, and stated that this was in part to be explained by the fact that all business is opposed to chaos and that the picture of a manufacturer whose products are sold throughout the United States trying to follow the provisions of forty-six different statutes, not even mentioning the various interpretations of food commissioners, afforded a good example of the chaotic.

Another matter of concern, the speaker said, to those who are interested in the subject of pure food and drugs is the question of what to do with the various amendments that are continually being suggested under the guise of improvements upon the national law.

Weight and Measure Branding.

Mr. Breed said that organizations such as he represents had come to the belief that the public desires package goods to be branded with weight or measure and that accordingly they had approved a bill amending the national law in that particular. If passed, he said, it would be the first amendment to the national law since that measure was passed by Congress and adopted by a majority of the States. The speaker argued for national initiation of further legislation relating to pure food, showing that in the past legislative year, for instance, thirty-seven weight laws were introduced in the various State legislatures, all of which differed in terms. "Suppose, for example, that one-half of them had passed," said he, "what would have become of this principle of uniformity, which I think all agree is absolutely necessary to the successful handling of this great subject?" Mr. Breed argued strongly against any attempt on the part of any of the forty-six States to adopt a set of standards. "Experience certainly leads to the conclusion," said he, "that if standards for food products are to be formulated for the American people the movement should originate as an amendment to the National Act, or, at least, should arise out of the authority of some national statute. The only intelligent method of handling a subject of this sort is through a commission, which should be given the power not only to adopt standards, but to change them."

Broad Powers for Commissioners.

Argument was made for the giving of broad powers to food commissioners. Particular emphasis was laid on the fact that there are several States that have no specific food laws, and a large number which have no enforcing officer except the district attorney, and it was further stated that in nearly all the States the appropriation for making the statute effective was inadequate.

Mr. Breed spoke of co-operation between those who are interested in improving conditions under which food products are prepared and packed and those who actually do the work. "The committee proposed to be formed by The National Civic Federation," said he, "can do much to bring about the desired condition. It is a great opportunity to become a medium between the consumer, the producer and the official."

A Physician's Views.

In introducing Dr. E. ELIOT HARRIS, chairman of the Committee on Legislation of the New York County Medical Society, the Chairman said: "There is no class which has done more to put the pure food and drug laws upon the books than the physician." Dr. Harris said he hoped that the department which it was proposed to form would consider the value of the private agencies that work in the interest of pure drugs and wholesome food. Druggists, he said, when they hand out the product that is upon their shelves know very little of what it contains, because they buy from the wholesale druggist and have to take their merchandise on faith. "That faith," said the speaker, "under the present incomplete inspection, is not always well placed." He agreed with Mr. Breed that food and drug standards should not be incorporated in the laws of any State, and argued that the standardization of food products should be left with a commission.

HARRY THOMPSON was introduced by the chairman as a member of the Toledo bar who had given to the question of legal procedure in the enforcement of regulatory laws very considerable thought. Mr. Thompson's speech was mainly an arraignment of what he conceived to be the tendency toward paternalism in the regulatory laws of the country. "When Congress," said he, "undertakes under the Food and Drugs Act—when it has undertaken to control the health, pocketbooks and morals of the people—it has distorted and usurped a power never intended to be granted to it by the primeval law of the land."

Labor Asks Protection.

The speech of TIMOTHY HEALY, president of the International Brotherhood of Stationary Firemen, was given close attention. Mr. Healy strikingly outlined the necessity of pure food and drugs to the man who earns his living by manual labor. Said he, in part: "The laboring man is not in a position to protect himself in this matter; therefore I am glad to have an opportunity this afternoon to appeal to the men who are interested in this subject and understand it, and to The National Civic Federation to protect the workers, and to try to do away with the unwholesome and unhealthy food that is going into the bodies and stomachs of the great mass of the people to-day."

The speaker paid a tribute to Dr. Thomas Darlington and called attention to the unusual opportunity for aid to working people that lay within the power of the latter.

The opinion was expressed that The National Civic Federation had assumed one of the most important pieces of work that it had ever attempted, and an appeal was made to the various associations of dealers and manufacturers to lend a helping hand to the Federation in its work. Mr. Healy said that the matter should be viewed from a patriotic standpoint, adding, "If we are to poison the bodies of our children with rotten foods, what manner of men and women will they be?"

Trend in Pharmacy Business.

DONALD McKESSON, of the drug house of McKesson & Robbins, made an effective speech, which was given close attention. Mr. McKesson argued strongly for thorough consideration from every standpoint of any laws that might be proposed. He spoke interestingly of the changes that recent years had wrought in the business of pharmacy, saying that it had become so unremunerative that from it alone the small pharmacist could not make a living.

Force of circumstances, the speaker said, was driving the better class of men out of the business into more lucrative lines. Mr. McKesson expressed the opinion that it would be a good thing for the country if the practice of pharmacy could be restricted to those who are seriously entering it as a profession.

A paper from GEORGE M. WHITAKER, in charge of the Market Milk Section of the United States Department of Agriculture, was presented, Mr. Whitaker being prevented at the last moment from attending the meeting. The writer, as secretary of the Farmers' National Congress, and as a member of the National Grange, presented to the meeting, on behalf of those organizations, the best wishes of the agricultural people of the country.

Reactionary Legislation Menace.

The speaker cited instances in five States where recent legislation of a reactionary nature had been passed with regard to matters affecting food material, and said that such cases pointed to the need of education as being necessary in many instances before there can be a suitable law.

Mr. Whitaker expressed the opinion that the consumer should be shown that differences in quality mean differences in cost, and that a low cost product may be dangerous and expensive in the long run. He counseled against too much reliance upon law to right all that was wrong.

Following the reading of this paper the meeting adjourned.

SEEKS TO PREVENT DELAY IN LEGAL PROCEDURE

Civic Federation Advocating Bill for Federal and State Adoption That Would Cut Litigation Costs, Too—Its Special Department Aiding Bar Association.

The Executive Council of the National Civic Federation is urging the passage of a bill now in Congress (known as Senate No. 3750 and House No. 16461), designed to prevent delay and unnecessary cost in litigation through reversals by higher courts on technicalities.

The text of the bill is as follows:

"No judgment shall be set aside, or reversed, or new trial granted, by any court of the United States in any case, civil or criminal, on the ground of misdirection of the jury or the improper admission or rejection of evidence, or for error as to any matter

Judge ALTON B. PARKER.

of pleading or procedure, unless, in the opinion of the court to which application is made, after an examination of the entire cause, it shall appear that the error complained of has injuriously affected the substantial rights of the parties. The trial judge may in any case submit to the jury the issues of fact arising upon the pleadings, reserving any question of law arising in the case for subsequent argument and decision, and he and any court to which the case shall thereafter be taken on writ of error shall have the power to direct judgment to be entered either upon the verdict or upon the point reserved, if conclusive, as its judgment upon such point reserved may require."

President Low is also addressing letters to the Governors of the States in which Legislatures are now in session, asking them to urge the passage of this bill by their respective Legislatures.

It has already become a law in Kansas, Wisconsin and California, and in Ohio it has been adopted with some modifications.

The National Civic Federation has a Department on the subject of Reform in Legal Procedure, which will meet during the sessions of the Federation's Twelfth Annual Meeting, to be held in Washington, March 5, 6 and 7, 1912. This Department, of which Alton B. Parker is Chairman, is working in conjunction with the American Bar Association. Its Executive Committee includes the following well-known attorneys and deans of university law schools:

Representative Executive Committee.

Alton B. Parker (Chairman), former President American Bar Association, New York.
Stephen H. Allen, Topeka, Kan.
Charles B. Aycock, Goldsboro, N. C.
Charles J. Bonaparte, Baltimore, Md.
Ralph W. Breckenridge, Omaha, Neb.
William P. Breen, Fort Wayne, Ind.
William E. Chandler, Concord, N. H.
Lawrence Cooper, Huntsville, Ala.
Frederick P. Fish, Boston, Mass.
Walter L. Fisher, Chicago, Ill.
Ernst Freund, Chicago, Ill.
Charles Noble Gregory, Iowa City, Iowa.
Stephen S. Gregory, President American Bar Association, Chicago, Ill.
William O. Hart, New Orleans, La.
Frederick N. Judson, St. Louis, Mo.
George W. Kirchwey, New York.
Frederick W. Lehmann, former President American Bar Association, St. Louis, Mo.
Charles F. Libby, Portland, Me.
William Minor Lile, Charlottesville, Va.
Nathan William MacChesney, Chicago, Ill.
Charles F. Manderson, former President American Bar Association, Omaha, Neb.
Lawrence Maxwell, Jr., Cincinnati, Ohio.
John G. Milburn, New York City.
Peter W. Meldrim, Savannah, Ga.
Morgan J. O'Brien, New York.
George R. Peck, former President American Bar Association, Chicago, Ill.
Roscoe Pound, Chicago, Ill.
J. H. Ralston, Washington, D. C.
Henry Wade Rogers, New Haven, Conn.
John Bell Sanborn, Madison, Wis.
Willard Saulsbury, Wilmington, Del.
Thomas W. Shelton, Norfolk, Va.
Charles W. Smith, Stockton, Kan.
Selden P. Spencer, St. Louis, Mo.
Francis Lynde Stetson, New York.
Moorefield Storey, Boston, Mass.
Hannis Taylor, Washington, D. C.
Charles S. Thomas, Denver, Col.
Bradley Martin Thompson, Ann Arbor, Mich.
Henry St. George Tucker, Lexington, Va.
George Turner, Spokane, Wash.
Everett P. Wheeler, New York.
John Henry Wigmore, Chicago, Ill.
Westel W. Willoughby, Baltimore, Md.
Frederic J. Stimson, Boston, Mass.

Injustice to Workingman.

The injustice to the workingman in the law's delay is so great that he can scarcely avail himself of the courts to bring a suit in any matter. This is particularly true in cases resulting from injuries through accidents. By the time the injured man receives a verdict, which he does after many delays and reversals for technical reasons, the court costs deprive it of much of its value.

According to the statistics of the American Bar Association, *new trials are granted in forty-six per cent of all the cases in our courts involving a penitentiary offense.* And in sixty per cent of this number the new trial is granted, not because of a question affecting the possible guilt or innocence of the prisoner, but *because of a purely technical point of dispute in the conduct of the case.*

In nearly half of the criminal cases in American courts it requires two or more trials to convict a prisoner. And in sixty per cent of these cases his guilt is plain. He is given a new trial because the higher court holds that there has been an error of "pleading and practice," either on the part of the lawyers or the judge.

Some Pertinent Illustrations.

Illustrations can be taken from any State. Hugh Weir, giving examples of the technical rulings, practice and abuses in our courts, says:

> "Here are two cases from Alabama and North Carolina which sound almost incredible. Indeed, were they not matters of court record, the average American citizen would dismiss them with a shrug as sensational journalism:
>
> "In the former State, a man charged with murder went free, because the Clerk of Courts, in writing the word 'malice' in the indictment, left out the letter 'i.'
>
> "In North Carolina an enraged citizen shot a neighbor through the breast, inflicting a wound which resulted in the latter's death and his own arrest for murder. A short time later, however, he was released from custody. In the indictment the clerk had spelled breast as 'b-r-e-s-t.' The court held that the misspelled indictment was not legal and freed the prisoner."

SAMUEL GOMPERS—THE FLAG AND McNAMARA INCIDENTS

By RALPH M. EASLEY.

SINCE the confession of the McNamaras in the Los Angeles dynamite cases many letters have been received by me as editor of THE NATIONAL CIVIC FEDERATION REVIEW, both from friends of the Federation and from its critics, asking about the relation of Mr. Samuel Gompers to that matter and to various incidents which have taken place since, including the recent charge that he had "defiantly and contemptuously trampled upon the American flag."

Four Questions Commonly Asked.

Instead of attempting to reply to each of these correspondents, I will group their questions under four heads, to wit:

1. Is Mr. Gompers guilty of defiantly trampling on and insulting the American flag at a Labor Day meeting in San Francisco?
2. Does Mr. Gompers use his influence to prevent members of the unions from joining the State militia?
3. Did Mr. Gompers have criminal knowledge of the crimes of which the McNamaras were guilty, as accessory either before or after the fact?
4. Why does not Mr. Gompers cancel the charter of the International Association of Bridge and Structural Iron Workers until that Association purges itself of its dynamiting members?

---

1. Is Mr. Gompers guilty of defiantly trampling on and insulting the American flag at a Labor Day meeting in San Francisco?

LET us take first the incident of the flag, which seems to be the climax of a virulent campaign of insinuation, innuendo and denunciation against Mr. Gompers, conducted ever since the day of the McNamara confessions. In fact, this recent attempt has been so palpably unfair that it has proved a boomerang, and is giving color to Mr. Gompers' claim that he is being persecuted. This is well voiced by the following editorials from "The New York Sun," "The New York Evening Post" and "The Chicago Tribune":

From THE SUN, January 4, 1912.

"The Labor Leaders and the Flag."

"We have our opinion of Mr. Samuel Gompers and of some of his associates in the misleading of union labor. We do not hesitate to express this opinion plainly whenever it becomes proper to discuss his or their pernicious acts and utterances. But we do not believe that GOMPERS, or any other leader sufficiently astute to get into a controlling position in the vast organization, would be fool enough, even under momentary excitement, to plant foot leather upon the American flag in a spirit of defiance or insult. The yarn from San Francisco will not wash. The man mad enough to do anything of that sort would cease by the very fact to be dangerous as a misleader, for he would be defying and insulting his own American audience."

From THE POST, New York, January 3, 1912.

"Silly Piece of Business."

"The charge that Gompers trampled on the American flag while making a speech in California on Labor Day last year looks like an extremely silly piece of business. Mr. Gompers has many faults, but he is not an imbecile; and, even supposing that his sentiments would incline him to such a performance, no man of sense will believe, without overwhelming evidence, that he was such an ass as to indulge in it upon a public occasion. If the photographs that are being exploited are genuine, then we may be sure there is some simple explanation of the appearance they present, having in it no taint of treason. The dynamiting inquiry presents too much that is serious to give room for such childishness as this flag business; the only result that it is likely to have is to give Gompers ground for the accusation that he is being persecuted. Possibly an industrious search might discover that he, or some other labor leader, has wiped his mouth with a paper napkin having the flag imprinted on it; and there would be just about as much use in following up that scent as in trying to read disloyalty into those Labor Day photographs."

From THE CHICAGO TRIBUNE, January 3, 1912.

"A Vicious Piece of Claptrap."

"The story that President Gompers stood on the flag to show his contempt for it at a radical labor meeting in California will not be believed by any sensible American until it is proved beyond a doubt as to all its circumstances. Mr. Gompers is not a fool. Moreover, Mr. Gompers is yet to be shown to be lacking in patriotism. Both would have to be true if this yarn is true as given out.

"The story, moreover, is especially untimely now. Mr. Gompers has been severely criticized for his course prior to the McNamara trial. The arrest and prosecution and confession of these men have brought about something like a crisis in the history of union labor. Public opinion should keep cool, and sane, and just. It would be an injury to the whole nation if, whatever the outcome of the proceedings initiated against the McNamaras, demagogic passion, class prejudice and reaction should be permitted to turn the public conscience against legitimate union labor and the cause of the wage earner's advancement."

Not a Government Organ.

There are, however, many people who still believe the story which has been sent broadcast over the country, founded on the charges made by the *Army and Navy Register*. This paper is supposed by the general public to be an official organ of the War and Navy Departments, whereas it has no official connection whatever with the Government, and is simply what would be called in the commercial world "a trade journal." Under the heading of "The Enemies of the Army," this paper charges that a systematic attack has been made on the military service on the Pacific Coast; and that there is being conducted "a campaign by means of street harangues and defamatory posters with a view to prejudicing public sentiment against the army and discouraging enlistment."

This journal makes it appear that Mr. Gompers is connected directly with that agitation, which statement the officials of the War Department promptly denounced as untrue, saying that the American Federation of Labor had no part in that agitation, and that it was the work of the Socialist and Anarchist organizations on the Coast.

Referring specifically to the flag episode, the *Army and Navy Register* states that "the War Department is in possession of photographs showing these speakers standing on the American flag and addressing their audience. The photographs are sent officially and are duly authenticated."

A Palpable Fraud.

If anything more is needed to show the fraud perpetrated on Mr. Gompers in this matter than Mr. Gompers' own emphatic denial, which follows, and an explanation of the plates published by the *Army and Navy Register*, it certainly will be furnished by a careful scrutiny of the two pictures on the next page, which have been taken from the *Michigan Tradesman*, an employers' journal, published in Detroit, December 6, 1911. The upper picture is the same as that published by the *Army and Navy Register*, but the second one seems to have been too palpable a fraud to be used in the recent story going the rounds of the press. If the latter picture had been sent out, I am sure most of the journals that I have seen publishing the first picture would have quickly repudiated the whole matter, for the industry of producing composite fake photographs is quite thrifty and is well understood in all newspaper offices. Even President Taft recently has been compelled to have an injunction served on a Washington photographer who has been furnishing to any sitter a photograph showing him shaking hands with the President at a public or private reception, the President taking a walk with him, or the President showing him over the White House, etc.

Mr. Gompers' Statement.

Mr. Gompers' denial, given to the press on January 2, 1912, is as follows:

"Of the two addresses I made in Oakland, Cal., one was on Labor Day, in connection with the San Francisco demonstration and mass meeting, and that was during the day. The other meeting was during the evening, and was some days later, in a hall.

"My recollection of the meeting at Shellmound Park, Oakland, was that it was a park for athletics. There is a grandstand and a large field. A temporary stand was erected in the middle of the grounds, the speakers facing the grand stand, and in this instance there were thousands of men and women standing between the speakers' temporary stand and the grand stand. The crowd was so great that many of them overflowed and stood on the temporary platform, so that the speakers could not have been seen by any one other than those on the temporary speakers' stand. There was a table on this stand, intended for the speakers' notes, and having a pitcher of water and a glass on it. The table was festooned with an American flag. No part of it, except possibly an inch, was overlapping the table, and this simply for the purpose of holding it in position.

"When the meeting was called to order the disadvantageous position of the speakers was observed, and the public officers (School Superintendent, Mayor, Supervisor, etc.), as well as the speakers who addressed the assemblage, were called to by the crowd to ascend the table. The crowd manifested its discontent because it could not see those who were to address them and they shouted their disapproval, and those nearer shouted to us to 'get on the table.' A chair was furnished and we stood on the table. They did not one of them, nor did I, stand upon the American flag. *I would as lief insult the memory of my revered mother as to insult the flag of my country.* But anything and everything is good enough to charge me with and try to bring me into contempt with the American people. But my life of more than sixty-one years has been so straightforward that my good name and the work that I have tried to do in the interest of the people of our country will live long after my traducers will die and their names be coupled with the contempt of the people of the United States."

A "Built-Up" Photograph.

Mr. Gompers also produced correspondence with Mr. Orion T. Thomas, dated Los Angeles, October 24, 1911, stating that the charges had been made before Stanton Post, G. A. R., Los Angeles, and that the Post had adopted resolutions censuring Mr. Gompers for desecrating the American flag. Mr. Gompers immediately telegraphed his denial, embodying the above explanation. In his reply, under date of November 6, 1911, Mr. Thomas made the following statement: "As soon as I saw the photo I was convinced that it was a 'built-up' or 'composite' picture, and stated my opinion and how such photos were made. I also submitted the picture to several of the artists on the *Los Angeles Examiner*, who pronounced it the rankest kind of a 'fake' photograph."

As stated above, the daily press, so far as I have been able to discover, has not published the flag picture in which Mr. Gompers seems to have been jumping all over the table with soles properly inked at intervals. It would seem from that picture that Mr. Gompers must have been very precise in his motions, as at no time did he cross his tracks. Also, the stripes seem to be going the wrong way, according to the other picture. At one time he would have been standing eighteen inches off the table, resting his one hundred and eighty pounds avoirdupois on the salubrious climate of California. There are plenty of other evidences of the picture's having been made to order.

How the Real Picture Looks.

The writer has seen a copy of *The San Francisco Call* of Tuesday, September 5, 1911, the morning following Mr. Gompers' Labor Day speech, and the picture in that paper shows clearly that there is no flag on the table from which he spoke. That picture, published the day after the meeting, agrees entirely with the statement of Mr. Gompers when he says that there was a flag draping the table and the edges of it were turned over, presumably to be tacked down. So, too, do all the circumstances I have narrated above, including the tell-tale footprints. But it will be noted that the tale they tell is one of deception and fraud by the author and finisher of the photograph.

2. Does Mr. Gompers use his influence to prevent members of the unions from joining the State militia?

I HAVE known Mr. Gompers for fifteen years, and, while I have found him to be a vigorous and vehement speaker on many subjects, and have known him to take many positions with which I do not agree, I have never heard any of his utterances or read anything in his writings that had the least taint of disloyalty to the Government. On the contrary, his speeches have been intensely patriotic. It has happened frequently that some local union, controlled by the Socialists or Anarchists, or, for the time being, by radical union men who had had a sanguinary conflict with the State Militia, has passed resolutions refusing to permit members of that union to belong to the State Militia. In one case, I believe, the union expelled a member because he had joined the State Militia. Mr. Gompers' position on that matter is clear and convincing. I quote a letter which he habitually sends in reply to questions on this subject. The particular copy of this letter which I have is addressed to Mr. W. L. Amthor, Dickinson College, Carlisle, Pa. It reads:

Militia Bulwark Against Standing Army.

"Now, as to the matter of members of trade unions joining the State Militia, I beg to say that you have an entirely erroneous idea. As a matter of fact, a man who is a wage-earner and honorably working at his trade or calling to support himself and those dependent upon him has not only the right to become a citizen soldier, but that right must be unquestioned.

"The militia, i. e., the citizen soldiery of the several States in our country, supplies what otherwise might take its place—a large standing army.

"The difference between the citizen soldiery of the United States and the large standing armies of many European countries is the difference between a republic and monarchy—it is the difference between the conceptions of liberty and tyranny.

"While organized labor stands against the arbitrament of international or internal disputes by force of arms, yet we must realize we have not yet reached the millennium; that in the age in which we live we have not the choice between armed force and absolute disarmament, but the alternative of a large standing army and a small one supplemented by a volunteer citizen soldiery——the militia of our several States.

"With this both wisdom and policy, as well as principle, should warrant our trade unions in not taking any cognizance of the matter at all, allowing each member to follow the bent of his own inclinations, insisting only that he shall be a wage-earner, a faithful member of his union, and true to the cause of labor—the cause of humanity.

"In connection with this subject-matter I would also call your attention to the action taken by the recent convention of the American Federation of Labor, held in San Francisco."

Socialists' War on Militia.

That patriotic position is taken by Mr. Gompers and all the representative national leaders of the American Federation of Labor and the Railway Brotherhoods, which organizations include ninety-five per cent. of the organized labor in this country. At one of the meetings of the American Federation of Labor, where a resolution was offered by the Socialists, refusing to members of the State Militia membership in the unions, Mr. Gompers left the chair and made an impassioned speech against the resolution, which resulted in its being tabled by an overwhelming vote. So much for his loyalty to the Government.

3. Did Mr. Gompers have criminal knowledge of the crimes of which the McNamaras were guilty, as accessory either before or after the fact?

IN reply to the above question I will say that, speaking for myself, I do not *know* whether he had or had not, but I do not believe he had. No man can *know* what any other man suspects or what any other man *knows*. It is hard enough for a man to know all the time just what he himself knows and suspects. If there is any evidence that Mr. Gompers did know of these crimes of the McNamaras such evidence should be produced. Mr. Gompers has challenged and defied the world to produce a scintilla of incriminating evidence against himself. On the theory that every man is presumed by the law to be innocent until he is proved guilty, are not those who attack Mr. Gompers making the same kind of mistake that he is criticized for making, except that they are taking for granted guilt when he took for granted innocence?

"Assassins" versus "Martyrs."

I hope also that all other labor men, union or non-union, or their sympathizers, involved in any criminal manner in dynamiting or other lawless outbreaks will be adequately punished.

I have no sympathy with the maudlin sentiment expressed in certain quarters that the McNamaras are martyrs of oppression. They do not belong in the class of martyrs who go to the stake or the guillotine for a principle. The martyr suffers. The hired assassin takes pay. The ruling quotation of the McNamaras was $125 to $250 for a murder or murders, discount for job lot of bridge explosions.

As to the charge that Mr. Gompers had guilty knowledge of the McNamara outrages, the general counsel of the National Erectors' Association, Mr.

Photographic Reproduction from The Michigan Tradesman, December 6, 1911.

Union Labor Leader Desecrates American Flag

Gompers Tramples Under Foot "Old Glory" While Discussing Disrupted Labor Conditions

SAMUEL GOMPERS

President American Federation of Labor, desecrating the American Flag by standing on it, while speaking at Oakland, Cal., September 5, 1911. Will the honest laboring men of this free land approve of such treatment of "Old Glory?"

The American Flag stained with the footprints of Sam Gompers. These stains and the opposition to the Boy Scouts by the American Federation of Labor are enough to cause George Washington and Abraham Lincoln to rise from their graves. Let the American people judge of these insults. "Up with 'Old Glory'—down with the desecrators."

Walter Drew, has publicly announced that that association has no evidence incriminating Mr. Gompers in any way. The appeal from District Attorney Fredericks to Mr. Gompers to unseal the mouths of the McNamaras would of itself imply that he knew of no evidence against Mr. Gompers; otherwise his request would have been stupid. If Mr. Burns had any evidence it might be presumed that either Mr. Fredericks or Mr. Drew had knowledge of it; and yet, of course, this does not follow. It must not be forgotten that the charges of knowledge made against Mr. Gompers come largely from Mr. Burns. Now, Mr. Burns, in addition to being an able detective, is also a very human man, and after Mr. Gompers had so vehemently and, as I think, ill-advisedly, charged that there had been a conspiracy to plant the various dynamite bombs throughout the country for the purpose of injuring organized labor, Mr. Burns naturally wished to get back at him on every possible occasion, and he certainly was in a position to do so when the McNamaras confessed.

In this connection I want to repeat President Low's statement that the American people owe a debt of gratitude to Mr. Burns, to the Erectors' Association and to all who were concerned in securing evidence so incontestable that it forced the confessions of the McNamaras, because only by those confessions was a class war averted on the Pacific Coast.

A Call for Fair Play.

Mr. Gompers, in addition to challenging Mr. Burns to produce in court any evidence against him, has also issued a challenge to Senator Heyburn, who in the United States Senate undertook to prevent the acceptance by that body of a petition from the American Federation of Labor because it was signed by Samuel Gompers. That the Senate did not uphold Senator Heyburn was proved by the fact that his motion was defeated by fifty-seven votes against three. I think every one will agree that the fair thing for the men whom Mr. Gompers has challenged is either to accept his challenge or to admit publicly that they have no evidence against him.

I know that many of the important representative men in this country who are acquainted with Mr. Gompers, and have worked with him, feel from their knowledge of the man that he is not capable of such conduct as is charged against him. This does not mean that there is not criticism of his action in rushing to the rescue of the McNamaras and so sweepingly charging their accusers with fraud and conspiracy. Many of Mr. Gompers' friends think that that was bad judgment, and since the confessions he probably thinks so himself, but bad judgment is not a crime. If it were the jails would not hold us all.

A friend of Mr. Gompers recently compared him to a bear with her cubs, instantly on the defensive, irrespective of conditions or theories. The two millions of members of the unions are Mr. Gompers' cubs, and if they are attacked he is at once on the defensive. This quality is at once his strength and his weakness.

Path Not Strewn with Roses.

Another characterisic of Mr. Gompers which frequently makes enemies for him is his vehement manner of speaking. It has been said that, if he should make the statement to an audience that two and two make four, he would do it with clenched fist and with such force and energy as to arouse immediate hostility and provoke a denial of the proposition. One explanation of this is to be found in the fact that, in the thirty years of struggle to build up what even his enemies will concede is the greatest labor organization in the world, his path has not been strewn with roses. It has been one battle after another, and it may well be surmised that all the combative elements in his nature are well developed and trained for instant action. In this long struggle he has embittered many people, including individual employers and organizations of employers. He also has developed a hostile feeling in a great section of the daily press in the large cities, so that at times it seems almost impossible for him to get a fair showing in many of our important newspapers.

But, while Mr. Gompers has developed this hostility it is more vital to him to feel that he has the affection and confidence of ninety per cent of the American Federation of Labor—the remaining ten per cent being the Socialists, who would destroy him if they could. The more he is unfairly attacked by his critics in or out of the press, the stronger becomes the loyalty of his people. In this respect he is like a Congressman who has his own constituency solidly with him and everybody else against him. It is his own people about whom he cares, and he can afford, politically speaking, to snap his fingers at all the others. The rank and file of the unions read few of the daily newspapers which are the most unfriendly to Mr. Gompers, but when they do read what they believe to be the unfair attacks on him it only makes them grit their teeth and shout all the louder for their President.

The Deadly Headline.

As an instance of the alleged unfairness of many papers toward Mr. Gompers, his followers point to the headlines over the Indianapolis dispatches on January 3, 1912, purporting to give the statement of Ex-Mayor Charles A. Bookwalter, of that city, in reference to the investigation he had once made of dynamite explosions in Indianapolis. Here are three that were brought to my office by two officers of an important union:

"TOLD GOMPERS OF DYNAMITE TWO YEARS AGO."

"AVERS GOMPERS WAS COGNIZANT OF DYNAMITING."

"SAYS GOMPERS KNEW OF McNAMARA'S GUILT."

These dispatches stated that Ex-Mayor Bookwalter, as the result of his investigation, had come to the conclusion that McNamara was responsible for the explosions in his city. In answer to the specific question whether he had told Samuel Gompers, he said: "No, I don't know Mr. Gompers well enough to talk about these things." And when asked if any of the men he had told had reported it to Mr. Gompers, he said: "I don't know whether they told him or not." Then this dialogue occurs:

"Do you think Mr. Gompers knew while these explosions were going on who was responsible for them?"

"Gompers is the general of a great army, and, like a general, he did not inquire when any of his men were engaging in guerilla warfare. But, if this were called to the attention of the General, naturally he would rebuke them."

"Do you think he could have stopped it had he tried?"

"I do not, as the iron workers were only an allied organization to the American Federation of Labor. *John J. McNamara was not the kind of man to take orders from anybody.*"

That was all there was upon which to build the headlines, and yet, unless the readers of these papers read through the entire article, they would certainly think that Mr. Gompers had been told of these crimes.

Vigorous Opponent of Socialism.

There may be a reason for this unfairness other than a common unfriendliness to Mr. Gompers in newspaper circles, which is not generally understood. Mr. Gompers is a most vigorous opponent of Socialism. He has been charged by the Socialists, both here and abroad, with having been responsible for keeping the trade unions of this country from joining the Socialist party. Also, Mr. Gompers and other leaders of the American Federation of Labor at the Annual Convention held in Atlanta, Georgia, last November, completely routed the Socialists, by a vote of three to one, on the proposal to force the labor leaders out of The National Civic Federation. This might naturally be supposed to be a reason why Mr. Gompers should have friends, rather than enemies, on the daily newspapers, whose interests and sympathies are all against revolutionary Socialism.

In this connection the following excerpt from a letter recently received from a prominent labor man in New York may well be worth considering:

* * * * * * *

"Has it occurred to you that much of the venom contained in the attacks by the newspapers generally on Mr. Gompers does not necessarily represent the feeling of the owners and responsible publishers of those papers? It is well known to all readers of Socialist papers that the chief object of their hatred to-day is Samuel Gompers. While they do not love John Mitchell, James Duncan, James O'Connell and the other labor men more, they love Gompers less. Now, the Socialists by their own statements, borne out by what we can see in the daily papers, are pushing their propaganda in nearly all the large newspaper offices in the country. I quote an extract bearing on this subject, taken from an article by George Allen England, a magazine writer, which I think ought to be sent to the proprietors and managers of all daily papers for their information:

Socialists in Editorial Sanctums?

"'In almost every newspaper and magazine office to-day Socialism has its adherents. I am informed by the editor of a great daily that in Chicago the newspaper offices are so full of Socialists, not only in the composing and pressrooms, but also on the editorial staffs, that, should occasion arise, the Socialists, by striking, could instantly put an end to the publication of the papers. . . . Many a plutocratic magazine owner would be horrified if he knew the truth that one or more of his apparently subservient editors were out-and-out Marxian Socialists, dues-paying party members and enthusiastic workers in this field. The moral and intellectual influence exerted by these large numbers of directing spirits scattered throughout the publication offices of this country, even though their work must, perforce, be carried on sub rosa, can hardly be over-estimated. . . .

"'I personally had the privilege, somewhat over a year ago, of helping organize in Philadelphia and in New York City Socialist clubs comprising professional and literary people of national repute, editors, writers, illustrators and the like. The Philadelphia club was holding, and is holding, large banquets, "full-dress" affairs, at fashionable hotels, where, by speeches from prominent Socialists, the new doctrines can be taught to a class of people who would refuse to attend the working class meetings. The membership of the New York club is now close to fifty. It meets once a month to discuss radical topics and consider means of furthering the Socialist propaganda through the printed word.'

"With the newspapers of the country 'honeycombed with Socialists,' and with Samuel Gompers recognized as the greatest enemy of the Socialists, there need be little surprise that a vigorous campaign is being made by the newspapers against him. A Socialist headline-writer on a daily newspaper, understanding as he does the Socialist philosophy and tactics, can do great work for Socialism and against all the enemies of the Socialist party. The managers may be none the wiser, and in this particular case, as they have a dislike for Mr. Gompers on general principles, the headline-writer may get an advance in his salary if he does an exceptionally good job."

* * * * * * *

I will not comment on the above. I do not know how far the statements of the Socialists to whom the writer of the letter refers are true. I am sure, however, that there are some papers which oppose Mr. Gompers that are not influenced by the Socialists.

4. Why does not Mr. Gompers cancel the charter of the International Association of Bridge and Structural Iron Workers until that Association purges itself of its dynamiting members?

IN reply to the question given above, I would say that the answer is perfectly clear to those who understand the organic character of the American Federation of Labor. Unfortunately, and also naturally enough, outside of the labor organizations themselves, very few of the ninety million people in this country do so understand it. The same question has arisen many times with reference to strikes. Why doesn't Mr. Gompers, as President of the American Federation of Labor, do this, or that, or the other thing? The fact is that Mr. Gompers has no more authority to tell the structural ironworkers what they shall do or what they shall not do than has President Taft the power to tell South Carolina what it shall do in the case of the lynching of a negro; nor has Mr. Gompers any more power to cancel the charter of an association of labor men than would the President of the United States have to read South Carolina out of the Union if he did not like its conduct. The American Federation of Labor is a federation composed of delegates elected annually by the one hundred and thirty organizations affiliated with it. While Mr. Gompers is the president of the organization, he does not own it; he is the paid employe of the one hundred and thirty unions.

Authority Is Limited.

His duties and powers are clearly defined by constitution and by-laws. Under these he has not a vestige of authority to interfere with the internal government of any of the constituent organizations. An attempt on his part to do so would be instantly resented, and should he persist, the organization involved would doubtless prefer charges against him at the ensuing annual convention of The American Federation of Labor. If the organization were not sustained by the Federation in convention assembled, the complainant organization would be likely to withdraw from The American Federation of Labor.

A charter can be revoked only by a two-thirds vote of all the delegates elected to an Annual Meeting of The American Federation of Labor. Where charters have been revoked by the Executive Council it has been in cases where the offending organizations have disputed an order given by The American Federation of Labor itself in convention assembled. No set of people are more jealous of their prerogatives and rights than the officials of labor organizations—National, State and local. When one organization is involved in a strike with employers, it is impossible to get labor leaders of other crafts to interfere in any way. They may be willing to give advice if it is requested, but they will not volunteer it. This unwritten law is just as potential with organizations of employers, mercantile associations, and in fact all classes of organizations that have national and affiliated State and local branches, as it is with labor organizations.

Outside Interference Resented.

When the President of the New York Periodical Publishers' Association was engaged in the controversy with the Typographical Union, he would have

(Continued on Page 25.)

THREE PRIME INDUSTRIAL ACCIDENT PREVENTI

Workmen's Compensation Act | Model S

PRACTICAL MEASURES FOR ACCIDENT PREVENTION

THE NATIONAL CIVIC FEDERATION, through its Department on Compensation for Industrial Accidents and Their Prevention, is urging the uniform adoption by the several States and the Federal Government of the following measures, or the principles underlying them, all of which, it is felt, would be potent factors in reducing the loss of life through industrial accidents:

1. A Model Safety Act.
2. Standard Accident Report Blank.
3. Model Workmen's Compensation Act.

Essentials of Accident Prevention.

The essentials of industrial accident prevention seem to lie:

First, in laws providing for the safeguarding of machinery.

Second, in the requirement of reports of industrial accidents of such definiteness as shall afford knowledge of the common causes of those casualties and hence point the way to their removal.

Third, in the education of the wage-earner and the employer as to the dangers of machinery and the inculcation of habits of care and caution in the former; and

Fourth, in the enactment of workmen's compensation laws so designed that the employer has every incentive to prevent accidents in his plant.

Finally, in the establishment of museums of safety, preferably with machinery in motion, similar to those that are to be found in almost every civilized country of Europe.

The Federation's Model Safety Act, drafted by a Special Committee consisting of Cyrus W. Phillips, Chairman; P. Tecumseh Sherman, John Calder, Louis B. Schram, John Williams, Edgar T. Davies, H. W. Forster and Abram I. Elkus, is based upon the principles and theories involved in the following:

Exhibit Arranged by Committee on Improvement c

MEASURES OF THE NATIONAL CIVIC FEDERATION

Act

Uniform Accident Report Blank

Specify Dangerous "Mechanical Elements."

With regard to laws safeguarding machinery, the trend of opinion among those who have given serious study to this question seems to be against the enumeration in any statute of all specific dangerous machines, excepting, of course, elevators and common utilities in structures, in power generation and transmission, and the substitution therefor of a catalogue of the "dangerous mechanical elements" which are found on machinery and appliances, with the requirement that these "elements" be always guarded where found, with certain exceptions that need not be noted here. The great advantage claimed for this method is that these mechanical "elements" are few in number, fixed and unchangeable, and they cover every sort of machine that ever has been devised or ever will be; whereas, it seems to be well agreed, that a specific enumeration of all the dangerous machines is impossible.

Board of Experts Suggested.

Those who argue for this comprehensive and undetailed method of machinery safeguarding suggest as its concomitant a board of expert advisers for the Commissioner of Labor, which shall be clothed with authority to make, amend and abrogate specific rules for safeguarding in accordance with the general and comprehensive authority in that direction that would be contained in a law formulated along the outline given above.

WHAT THE CLIPPINGS TELL

THERE are shown here a few newspaper headlines, setting forth the main features of the industrial accidents that are detailed in the body of the several articles to which they apply. These accidents have been classified in some measure by industries or by their character, chiefly for the purpose of grouping such illustrations as they afford of the importance of prevention. The period covered is restricted to the second half of 1910 and the greater part of 1911, but it should be understood that these are by no means a complete record, nor do they cover the entire country. They are only an indication of similar disasters that it may be assumed received only local record.

"I am convinced, from a lengthy, practical experience, that at least one-third of all our factory injuries can be prevented by legal, administrative and practical measures."—John Calder.

THE NATIONAL
Civic Federation Review

Office: Metropolitan Building
1 Madison Avenue New York City
RALPH M. EASLEY, Editor

The Editor alone is Responsible for any unsigned article or unquoted statement published in THE NATIONAL CIVIC FEDERATION REVIEW.

PUBLISHED BY
The National Civic Federation

The Annual Meeting.

"Industrial Peace and Progress" is the timely theme of the twelfth annual meeting of The National Civic Federation, to begin in Washington on March 5, Cardinal Gibbons presiding and President Taft delivering the opening address. This is an era of the greatest progress the world has known. Already the twentieth century is outstripping the nineteenth; the age of steam is giving way to electricity. Wireless telegraphy, the aeroplane, Niagara harnessed for industrial plants hundreds of miles from the cataract, horses disappearing before the automobile, the telephone talking across the continent—are some of the marvels of a century that has barely entered upon its second decade.

Progress, however, has not had peace for a handmaiden. Industrial unrest is the rule, not in the United States only, but throughout civilization. Within the bounds of order, and of loyalty to civic obligations, this is not an unhealthy sign. Ably and wisely directed, industrial unrest makes for economic and social betterment. The inspiration of good citizenship, of every one who loves his fellowmen, who not merely wishes well to his country and to humanity, but who is willing to do something to make his wishes effective, should be to turn industrial unrest into channels of improvement and advancement, to establish and maintain harmony between capital and labor, to bring about the reign of "Industrial Peace and Progress."

The National Civic Federation has aimed from the first to bring capital and labor together in relations of harmony and mutual respect, of mutual regard for each other's rights, in mutual devotion to our country and to its leadership among nations in industry, in commerce, in all that makes for national greatness and prosperity. Much has already been achieved in that direction; capital and labor have met in friendly handclasp under the auspices of The National Civic Federation; each has learned that the other has good qualities not heretofore suspected, and that the average workingman and the average capitalist are both trying to act fairly, according to their honest understanding of conditions. An appreciable advance has been made toward that industrial peace without which progress is impossible. Obstacles are being overcome, and difficulties, as they arise, are giving way before a calm and temperate presentation of the claims of employer and employed.

Scope of the Federation's Work.

A glance through this number of the "Review" will, we think, convince its readers that the reforms for which the Federation is working and the methods pursued in the attempt to secure them are desirable. The work falls naturally into two divisions—that dealing with humanitarian questions and that dealing with business questions. The mere enumeration of the departments of the national organization that are now active suggests their far-reaching scope and importance, and the personnel of the chairmen is a guarantee of the practical results that may be expected. State councils of the Federation are being organized with sub-committees corresponding to the national departments, the chairman of each sub-committee being a member of the executive committee of the corresponding national department. The national departments, with their respective chairmen, are as follows:

Department on Regulation of Industrial Corporations—Chairman, SETH LOW.

Department on Regulation of Interstate and Municipal Utilities—Chairman, EMERSON McMILLIN.

Department on Reform in Legal Procedure—Chairman, ALTON B. PARKER.

Department on Compensation for Industrial Accidents and Their Prevention—Chairman, AUGUST BELMONT.

Department on Pure Food and Drugs—Chairman, JOHN HAYS HAMMOND.

Department on Taxation—Chairman, EDWIN R. A. SELIGMAN.

Department on Industrial Economics—Chairman, NICHOLAS MURRAY BUTLER.

Employers' Welfare Department—Chairman, WILLIAM R. WILLCOX.

Woman's Welfare Department—Chairman, MRS. JOHN HAYS HAMMOND.

Meetings of these departments will be held in Washington at the time of the annual meeting in March.

The Socialist Repulse at Atlanta.

Organized labor never rose more manfully to a sense of civic duty, of the rights, the obligations and privileges of American citizenship, than in the annual convention of the American Federation of Labor held at Atlanta in November last. By the overwhelming vote of 11,851 to 4,924 the convention rejected the demand of the Socialists that officers and other members of labor unions should retire from membership in The National Civic Federation.

Naturally, the layman will ask, "Why are the Socialists making such demands?" The reply to this question lies deep in the very constitution and organization of The National Civic Federation. This body stands, first of all, for INDUSTRIAL CONCILIATION AND ARBITRATION. It fosters the idea of the best possible relations between capital and labor. Through peaceful agencies, it believes, can be prevented many of the unfortunate strikes and lockouts which harass alike worker, employer and the general public. The Civic Federation upholds and sedulously encourages the principle of COLLECTIVE BARGAINING, which means that organizations of employers and organizations of workingmen shall get together and work out mutual contracts in reference to wages, hours and conditions of employment.

The Socialists are against conciliation and arbitration and collective bargaining. They do not want the settlement of labor disputes and troubles to be made in a peaceful manner. They believe in the "general strike," which is the Socialist plan for tying up all industry, as attempted in France, beginning with the Government employes in Paris.

The essence and the spirit of the utterances in the Atlanta Convention went far beyond The National Civic Federation, far beyond the interests of labor and capital, using those terms in their conventional meaning. They raised the greater issue whether the American people shall endure as one people, whether class shall be arrayed against class, whether the attitude of labor toward capital and, conversely, of capital toward labor, shall be one of inextinguishable hate and extermination, or of mutual tolerance, mutual respect, mutual goodwill and recognition of common citizenship, common humanity, common share in our magnificent heritage.

The result could not have been otherwise. The genius, the intelligence, the keen and broad comprehension of issues affecting his own welfare and that of the nation at large, characteristic of the American workingman, made it inevitable that the decision of the convention would be what it was, that the mission of The National Civic Federation would be approved, and that the representatives of organized labor who are taking part in that mission would be commended instead of condemned.

One of the principal arguments made by the Socialists at that convention was that the labor representatives had no business to associate with employers of labor, because some employers had been unfriendly to their workmen at some time or other. Delegate James M. Lynch, president of the International Typographical Union, punctured this argument when he said: "Ten years ago when we made a contract with the Newspaper Publishers' Association, Otis was a member and opposed any relations with the International Typographical Union. Since then we have increased wages in ninety-five per cent of the cities where we have gone to arbitrate with the newspaper publishers, and Otis is still a member of the Newspaper Publishers' Association. Reasoning the same way as the delegates who have spoken of Carnegie and others, there can be but one conclusion, and that is that the officers of the International Typographical Union, when they took up the negotiations with the Newspaper Publishers' Association, made a mistake—that they have made a mistake in continuing their relations with the Newspaper Publishers' Association, despite the increase made in wages." Mr. Lynch very aptly disposed of this phase of the attack on The National Civic Federation with the remark: "Their argument is fallacious to start with, founded on false reasoning, and not worthy of consideration."

We have no space to repeat the many favorable statements made at the Atlanta Convention of the good results that have come to labor through The National Civic Federation, of clouds cleared away that had overhung and obscured the better feelings of both employers and employed, of wage concessions and labor agreements in the bringing about of which The National Civic Federation has been a potent factor. On another page we give a summary of the speeches made in behalf of The National Civic Federation, and we urge all our readers to read every one of them. The National Civic Federation has things to do and is too busy with its appointed tasks to indulge in recrimination. The record that the Civic Federation has made, and will continue to make, shall be a sufficient rebuke for its enemies and a sufficient defense for its friends.

We express heartfelt thanks to the representatives of continent-wide union labor who voted at Atlanta their faith and trust in The National Civic Federation.

The Trust Question.

In another column will be found an analysis of the sixteen thousand votes taken upon the Questionnaire sent out by the Department on Regulation of Industrial Corporations of The National Civic Federation on the subject of repealing, amending or supplementing the Sherman Anti-Trust Act. A book containing 600 pages is now on the press, giving the gist of the replies made by some fifteen hundred manufacturers, merchants, bankers, lawyers, college presidents, representatives of labor and agricultural organizations, chambers of commerce, boards of trade, etc., etc. These replies have been analyzed for the use of the sub-committee of the department which is now framing a bill proposing supplementary legislation. This bill, when endorsed by the Executive Committee of the Federation, will be presented to the Interstate Commerce Committee of the Senate for its consideration. A day will be devoted to the discussion of the proposed measure at the Federation's annual meeting on March 5, 6 and 7.

SOME NEW FEATURES IN WELFARE WORK

TAKING AEROPLANE FROM SHED, EMPLOYES' COUNTRY CLUB.

CORNER CHILDREN'S PLAYGROUND, COUNTRY CLUB.

BEAUTIFUL COUNTRY CLUB FOR HEADS OF DEPARTMENTS AND THEIR FAMILIES.

NATIONAL CASH REGISTER COMPANY, DAYTON, OHIO.

LEFT—HONOR ROLL, COMPRISING 262 EMPLOYES—Recipients of yearly bonus, $100, paid all faithful, efficient employes, mechanical and manual labor departments, after ten years' service. Three served over 33 years; six over 25 years; thirty-four over 20 years; ninety over 15 years, and 129 over 10 years. The Company appreciates experience. A small army of itself. RIGHT—A FIELD DAY SCENE—TUG OF WAR.

REMINGTON TYPEWRITER COMPANY, ILION, N. Y.

RESTING AFTER LUNCH.

VIEW FROM BRIDGE LEADING TO ROOF GARDEN.

EMPLOYES' ROOF GARDEN LUNCH ROOM.

GIMBEL BROTHERS' DEPARTMENT STORE, PHILADELPHIA, PA.

REAU OF EXCHANGE—EXPERT WELFARE WORK INFORMATION FOR EMPLOYERS

HE increasing number of daily demands that are made on the Employers' Welfare Department of The National Civic Federation, through reau of Exchange, for the loan of exhibits illus- of various phases of welfare work, seems to timely a brief reference to this important h of the depart- 's work.

is well within the ds of conservatism to hat the data on every of welfare work as- led in the Bureau of ange is absolutely e in point of com- ness, arrangement authority of presen- n.

uable Welfare Data.

lfare work was high- oradic in this country crystallized into a na- l movement of prime rtance by this de- ment of The National Federation. From time the effort to as-

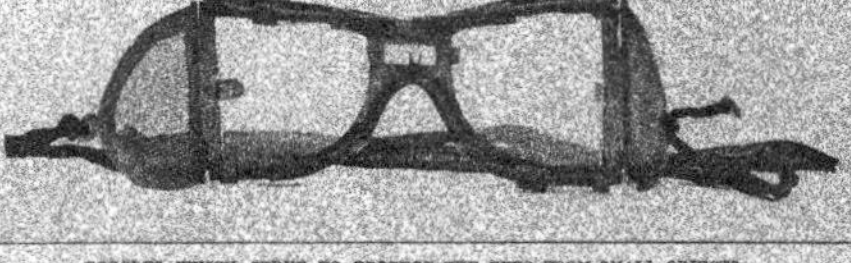

GOGGLES WHICH SERVE TO PROTECT THE EYES FROM SMALL OBJECTS.
They are provided with glass fronts and adjustable side guards. The frame is fitted with small rubber tubes to make it rest easily against the face.

Goggles and Other Forms of Body Protection in Actual Use in Germany

GEORGE GILMOUR,
O DISCOVERED IN GERMANY THE GOGGLES PICTURED ON THIS PAGE.

ble as complete data as possible on every phase the work in question has gone ceaselessly on.

Employers Appreciate Service.

he earnestness of the efforts that have been put h is meeting with what is felt to be deserved gnition by employers who have welfare problems olve. To such as these the Bureau of Exchange nishes as a loan the experience of the leading loyers of the country on any phase of welfare k in contemplation, giving forms applicable to e or small numbers of employes and causes of ure as well as successes in this great branch of anitarian endeavor.

peaking somewhat more specifically, it may be d that this data includes not only literature, but plans and photographs relating to sanitary angements, recreative efforts, industrial educa- , homes for employes and provident funds or ployes' insurance associations.

hat the value of this clearing-house of informa- is appreciated by many employers is evidenced the voluntary testimonials which have been re- ved.

A Typical Inquiry and Answer.

typical inquiry and the manner of handling it is trated by the example given here.

The following letter was received from the presi- t of a steel company making open-hearth steel tings:

"I have at my desk a report of fifty-two accidents occurred in our steel foundry during the month December, 1910. Twenty-nine of the fifty-two, or 56 per cent. of these cases, were caused by being struck in the eye with pieces of flying steel, these eye cases happening chiefly in the roughing and finishing department, where the pieces of steel are caused to fly by clippers when cleaning and finishing castings. Many of these cases result in the loss of eyesight.

"It is quite distressing to us, as we feel deeply on these matters, and for a long time have provided goggles for the men to wear. The goggles seem to be distasteful to the men and they do not wear them, and we are wondering if there is not some way to meet this situation. Have you any suggestions to offer? If you can learn of any concern that is using a goggle not objectionable to the men, we would be glad to send for a sample and see if we cannot supply that kind to our men.

"The other twenty-three cases were chiefly minor ones, being bruises to hands or feet, etc., etc., which would probably result in some temporary physical discomfort, but no serious injury. It is the eye troubles that are bothering us chiefly.

"Greatly appreciating any suggestions that you can offer us and the good work that you are doing, etc., etc."

Types of goggles which men *do use* and other devices for eye protection were loaned for the inspection of the officers of the company making the inquiry, but this account is limited to illustrations furnished by Mr. George Gilmour, a member of the Federation's Committee on State Inspection of Factories, the purpose of which is particularly the prevention of accidents.

Sketch of George Gilmour.

The views show German goggles and other forms of body protection found in actual use by Mr. Gilmour during a visit to Germany for the New York State Employers' Liability Commission. Mr. Gilmour is chief engineer of the Travelers' Insurance Company, being at the head of an inspection department composed of more than 125 experts whose duties are to investigate industrial concerns applying for insurance to determine whether or not the machinery and work places are so protected against accident as to make them safe risks for liability insurance. He is a member of the American Society of Mechanical Engineers, of the Engineers' Club of New York and the Machinery Club of New York and Hartford.

Pupil of Lord Kelvin.

His experience has afforded him unique opportunities, of which, it may be said, he has taken full advantage. His father is Chief Naval Constructor for the Russian Government. Mr. Gilmour, after studying under Sir William Thompson, afterward Lord Kelvin, in Glasgow, and learning his trade with a large contract firm in that city, spent years of service in South America, Panama, Jamaica and New York with great mechanical engineering companies and others. He is therefore competent to speak with authority.

Mr. Gilmour states that "the use of goggles in Germany is compulsory." It is well known that employes have to be educated to use many forms of safeguards, but that when proper devices which do not handicap the employe are afforded, with adequate information, there is little difficulty in that connection.

SHOWS GOGGLES PICTURED ABOVE IN ACTUAL USE BY A WORKER.

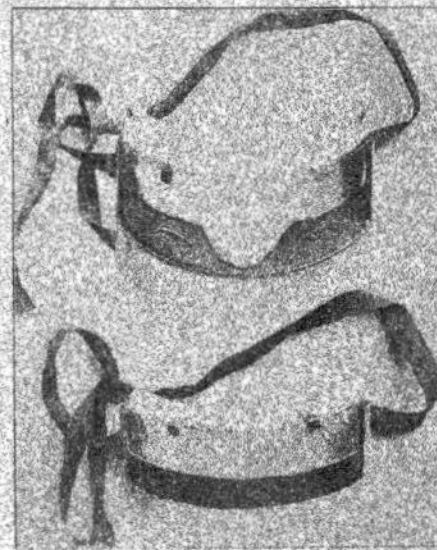

TWO KINDS OF GOGGLES—ONE WITH THE FRAME CUT AWAY TO FIT THE NOSE.

A Plan for Workmen's Compensation and Pensions in the Brewing Industry.

Pioneer work in workmen's compensation in this country is being done, jointly, by the United States Brewers' Association and the International Union of United Brewery Workmen. Nearly two years ago a committee representing these two organizations started work on a scheme for accident compensation and old age pensions which has now been completed and is being sent out to the various local unions and the company members of the Brewers' Association for ratification. The plan that is being submitted is based on an investigation of accidents in brewery work, reports from 15,374 workmen having been gathered by the committee in the course of its investigation.

Recognition is given the fact that accident prevention is the great aim to be sought in any scheme of workmen's compensation and every provision that is possible is made in order to realize this consummation. Not only must employers comply with State regulations which seek to effect safety in factories, but a Board of Directors and Award, which is included in the scheme, may require further safety devices and make all proper rules with regard to sanitation. To make this part of the scheme thoroughly effective, it is stipulated that an employer failing to install any safety appliance that may be required shall be liable to a fine imposed by his fellow employers equal to five per cent of the total compensation awarded the workman who has been injured as a result of the delinquent employer's neglect.

A fund is provided for to which each employer must pay one and five-tenths per cent of the amount of his payroll, and each employe five-tenths per cent of his wages. The pension clause is made applicable to salaricd officials of the union. This provision constitutes a recognition of organized labor as a legitimate business institution, and the broadmindedness that prompts it reflects great credit on the Brewers' Association.

GOGGLES TO PROTECT THE EYES OF THE MEN FROM STRONG LIGHT WHEN WORKING IN FOUNDRIES, GAS WORKS OR IN WELDING.
They consist of bent glass set in aluminum frames and are held to the head by a band. Two kinds of glass are used, the lower part being dark to protect the eyes from strong light and the upper part ordinary glass to give the man a free view. The picture shows the goggles in use during oxygen welding.

The main compensation features may be summarized as follows:

1. First aid is to be provided for all injuries.

2. Workmen are to receive from the fund sixty-five per cent of their wages after the first week, in case of temporary disability, unless the period of disablement lasts longer than four weeks. In that event, compensation will be paid for the first week also.

3. For total disability not resulting in death within two years it is provided that sixty-five per cent of the injured workman's wages shall be paid for a period of five years.

A SUIT OF CLOTHES MADE OF ASBESTOS WITH A WIRE FACE MASK.
This is designed particularly for use by foundry men.

4. In no class of disability is the payment to be more than $20 a week nor less than $5.

5. There is a provision that in case of "uuquestioned" disability a man may be paid a lump sum equal to the total weekly payment for five years.

6. Approximately four years' wages are paid for death resulting from accident within two years from date of injury, but the total is limited to $3,400. In this connection there is a provision for the advancing of funeral expenses. This compensation is to be paid irrespective of any negligence, delinquency of fellow-servant, or other statutory or common law defence.

The pension provisions are as follows:

1. One-half the pensioner's average weekly wage during the six months prior to his retirement is provided for where a workman has been in the service of a member of the Association for twenty-five years and has arrived at the age of sixty years.

2. The same pension as the above will be paid to any man retired on account of incapacity.

3. Certain minor provisions are that twelve months' cessation of work for any cause is not to interfere with a continuous employment record, nor will change of employment from one Association member to another.

The compensation feature of the plan is to go into effect as soon as adopted and the pension provisions on January 1, 1913. The Board of Directors and Award will administer the fund. It is to be composed of three members each, representing employer and employe. Local boards of award are provided for, together with certain rights of appeal.

The plan is to be effective when approved by a majority of the union membership in referendum vote, and by brewery proprietors whose output represents forty per cent of the beer manufactured in the United States. The outlook for final adoption is bright, as the union has already expressed itself as favoring the principle involved in the plan.

STINGING REBUKE FOR SOCIALIST INTRIGUERS

(Continued from Page 2.)

good men and women in high society as well as there are in the most lowly; and I want to say, as a trades unionist, that any man or any woman who is willing to sit down with me and discuss the questions that affect my organization is looked upon by me as a friend to labor and not an enemy.

"The National Civic Federation was organized for noble and good purposes. It was organized for the purpose of bringing all classes of people together, and to wipe out class distinctions. I know of no institution that has better objects in view than that.

"This is a great and powerful country. There are men in this hall to-day who have benefited by the opportunities that were given them through our form of government. These are opportunities we did not have in the old countries. Those who do not appreciate their opportunities ought to go back from whence they came and starve and die, for they are not big enough to appreciate American institutions."

REGULAR HOURS FOR XMAS SEASON.

Those interested in the humanitarian movement to reduce the business hours of retail stores during the Christmas season to a reasonable basis will find encouragement and inspiration in the efforts to that end of Mr. M. F. Schlesinger and the Women's Garment Association of San Francisco and Oakland, of which he is President. Mr. Schlesinger says that he came years ago to the belief that a good retail business can be done up to and including Christmas Eve in the regular hours for business, namely, 9 a. m. to 6 p. m.

AN AUTOMATIC DUST PAN.

W. W. Bird, director of the Washburn Shops of the Worcester Polytechnic Institute, Worcester, Mass., who furnished the illustration of the automatic dust pan installed there, states that it works well.

At convenient intervals there are in the factory these galvanized iron boxes, connected with an exhaust system which carries away the shavings from the machines. The vertical pipes arising from the boxes are provided with dampers, that the exhaust may be turned on or off. This obviates the necessity of conveying rubbish from the workrooms.

"SWEEP BOX," OR AUTOMATIC DUST PAN.
(THE WASHBURN SHOPS, WORCESTER, MASS.)
Shavings and waste are swept in and a damper opened, permitting all sweepings to be carried by an exhaust blower to the boiler room.

BOSTON GIVES SPLENDID WELCOME

MASSACHUSETTS AND RHODE ISLAND SECTION OF WOMAN'S WELFARE DEPARTMENT ORGANIZED AT REPRESENTATIVE GATHERING IN THAT CITY

A MASSACHUSETTS and Rhode Island Section of the Woman's Welfare Department was organized, following the efforts of the National Chairman, Mrs. John Hays Hammond, under the most promising conditions, at a representative gathering held in Boston, November 24.

The meeting closed with the election of a Committee on Organization, which has since announced the election of the following officers:

Chairman, MRS. CHARLES R. HAMLIN.
Treasurer, MRS. MATTHEW BARTLETT.
Secretary, MISS ELIZABETH S. PORTER.
Chairman of Membership Committee, MRS. GEORGE R. AGASSIZ.

The speakers, whose addresses constituted the larger part of the program of the meeting, included manufacturers with wide experience in welfare work, physicians, officers of boards of health, and Mrs. Hammond, Chairman of the Woman's Welfare Department, and Mrs. Francis McNeil Bacon, who is at the head of the New York and New Jersey Section.

Those who spoke were unanimously of the opinion that a field of useful endeavor lay before the new organization, and one which is not within the scope of any other body.

"Plucky and Pioneer Spirit."

In introducing MRS. JOHN HAYS HAMMOND, Mrs. Roger Wolcott, who presided over the meeting, said:

MRS. JOHN HAYS HAMMOND — AUGUSTUS P. LORING — MRS. FRANCIS MCNEIL BACON, JR.

"Mrs. Hammond has shown a plucky and pioneer spirit, which well fits her for this important work. I ask your cordial support and co-operation."

Mrs. Hammond explained at the opening of her speech that the meeting had been called to interest those present, as influential women in Massachusetts and Rhode Island, in the formation of a section of the Woman's Welfare Department and that that department is a branch of The National Civic Federation. After explaining concisely the scope of The National Civic Federation, the speaker addressed herself to the purposes of the Woman's Welfare Department.

"We who are interested in this welfare work," said she, "realize that human beings constitute by far the most important of our natural resources, and therefore the proper preservation of human life and strength is of vital consequence."

Mrs. Hammond explained that the various sections of the Woman's Welfare Department were composed largely of women who, as stockholders or through family relationship, were vitally interested in industrial corporations, and that there were also in their membership wives and relatives of men prominent in public affairs and women desirous of being helpful in all work which tends to improve the condition of the wage-earner.

Recognition was made of the fact that excellent and efficient societies already exist in Massachusetts and Rhode Island that are engaged in work that aims to improve the condition of all wage-earners, but the speaker stated that after a close investigation and after interviewing many of the leaders in the different welfare organizations in Boston the consensus of opinion was that the work which the proposed organization would undertake would in nowise conflict with that of the associations referred to.

Co-operation the Keynote.

Mrs. Hammond called attention to the fact that it was well recognized that intelligent and experienced women can do much to aid industrial progress. "We have this problem to solve," said she, "and, as conscientious women, we should all co-operate. *Co-operation therefore should be our keynote.*"

Reference was made to the fact that social problems in Boston have ever been dealt with discreetly and with intelligence, and a full appreciation of this fact, the speaker said, impelled her all the more to solicit the aid of the city's representative women in the work that had been outlined.

An interesting outline was given of important results accomplished by the various sections of the Woman's Welfare Department, attention being called, among other things, to the fact that Congress, animated by the efforts of the Department, had appointed a committee to inspect buildings and report as to their needs in the way of proper sanitation. The audience was told of the establishment of restaurants and the securing of better ventilation in Government buildings at Washington, and also of important results accomplished in the Treasury, the Census Bureau, the Federal jail and the Bureau of Engraving and Printing.

The New York and New Jersey section and its Chairman, Mrs. Francis McNeil Bacon, Jr., were warmly praised for notable work which has been done, and the audience heard of the establishment in the mill towns of the South of night schools, dispensaries with visiting nurses, medical clinics and kindergartens and of provisions made for lessons in cooking, sewing and household economics.

For Women and Children.

Mrs. Hammond explained that in each State there were individual problems to be met and that an especial effort would be made in Massachusetts and Rhode Island for the improvement of conditions of women and child wage-earners. In support of this policy she quoted from a recent public address of Professor Irving Fisher, of Yale University, to the effect that in spite of all agitation against the employment under improper conditions of women, especially of married women, little practical reform had as yet been accomplished as compared with what was necessary from the standpoint of industrial efficiency.

The speaker stated that one-quarter of the entire number of women in Massachusetts were wage-earners and that in Rhode Island, within the scope of the Factory Acts alone, there were forty-six thousand women at work and three thousand girls under sixteen years of age. Practical and businesslike methods were urged in the prosecution of the work proposed.

In her concluding remarks Mrs. Hammond pointed to the fact that a moral obligation inhered in those on whom she was calling for support not to permit the fathers and mothers of future generations to be overworked and to become victims of insanitary conditions. "What does it profit us," said she, "if the spirit of the home is destroyed? The woman makes the home. A clean, pure home is the solution of our social and economic problems."

Employer Who "Practises What He Preaches."

The next speaker, AUGUSTUS P. LORING, was introduced as an employer who practises what he preaches. Mr. Loring spoke on the theory of Welfare Work.

Problems involved in welfare work, according to the speaker, fall naturally under three principal heads, the first of these having to do with the provision of a suitable place and surroundings for workmen, the second dealing with housing problems and the third with those questions that have to do with financial affairs such as profit-sharing, annuities, retirement schemes, etc. Great stress was placed by the speaker on the necessity of good air in the factory, and the opinion was expressed that this is not by any means recognized as fully as it ought to be.

Emphasis was laid on the great amount of tact needed in that part of welfare work which is done outside the factory. "Anything you do in the factory," said the speaker, "the workman cannot do for himself, but when he gets outside of it he naturally resents anything that seems to him interference or dictation as to his private life." Mr. Loring added that it was his opinion that it is better on the whole for the manufacturer not to undertake anything that the operatives can or will undertake by joint effort or that the public ought to do at the general expense and pay for by taxation.

Citing an instance in which a request had come from certain employes to add bathrooms to tenements owned by his company, coupled with an offer to pay more rent in return for this improvement, the speaker said, "That only shows that when that is done for which there is a demand by the workingmen themselves it is appreciated and they will ask you to do more. To go very far beyond their demand is a mistake." Mr. Loring told an interesting story of the conversion of a threatened failure in interesting those in his employ in gardening into a decided success through the offering of prizes and the institution of exhibits. The speaker ended his address with the following words, which brought forth loud applause: "It seems to me most important that all these things be done, not by compulsion of the law, but by the will of the manufacturer; that it is much better to have them done because noblesse oblige than because the Legislature says so."

No Charity or Philanthropy.

The keynote of sincere welfare work was sounded by LOUIS A. COOLIDGE, Treasurer of the United Shoe Machinery Company, when he said at the opening of his remarks, "I would call welfare work sympathetic and intelligent industrial co-operation, for everything that we have undertaken has been with the help of our employes, and whatever we have done has been with the feeling that while it was doing good to them it was also doing good to us." Mr. Coolidge said that real welfare work should be divorced from charity or philanthropy absolutely.

The importance of light in factory buildings was dwelt on by the speaker, who told of three immense structures in the group of buildings that constitutes the Shoe Machinery Company's plant in which ninety per cent of the wall space is of glass. The speaker evinced a thorough knowledge of and deep interest in safeguarding of machinery against accidents, and also sanitation, ventilation and recreation. He told how systematic work by a Safety Committee in his plant had reduced the proportion of accidents to employes by seventy-three per cent within the space of one year. The results were obtained mostly through the installation of safeguarding appliances.

"Our company," said the speaker, "has never undertaken to give anything to anybody in the factory without some kind of an adequate return," and he told of a relief association within the factory with a membership of twenty-three hundred (this being a little over half of the total number of employes), together with a savings bank insurance in force with $210,000 in policies and 420 policy holders.

The novel industrial school, supported by the United Shoe Machinery Company, was detailed at some length. In this school half of the sixty-eight pupils are in the factory one week while the other half are in the high school at Beverly, Mass., receiving technical training. Space does not permit the giving of details of this successful and highly unique scheme.

Good Work in New York and New Jersey.

MRS. FRANCIS MCNEIL BACON, JR., Chairman of the New York and New Jersey section of the Woman's Welfare Department, was the next speaker. Her subject was the work of that Section, which she has directed with marked success. The speaker outlined a unique course of lectures on the departments of the Federal Government, in which the name of almost every member of President Taft's Cabinet appears as a speaker. The work of the Section's Vacation Committee was detailed at some length. This committee is engaged in an effort to aid working women in securing wholesome and attractive summer boarding houses in which to spend their vacations, and also is endeavoring to stimulate them to save so as to make possible a yearly vacation.

Mrs. Bacon was given close attention, and her remarks showed the possibilities for good of a well-organized branch of the Woman's Welfare Department.

DR. WILLIAM C. HANSON, Assistant Secretary of the Board of Health, of Massachusetts, spoke on the necessity of welfare work in that State. The speaker pointed to the fact that the Woman's Welfare Department of The National Civic Federation is unique in that it considers factory conditions in connection with home conditions, and he expressed the belief that this work rests upon a broad and eminently sane and practical basis. "Your methods," said he, "are persuasive, and you deal directly with manufacturers on behalf of wage-earners and the public. . . . Finally, you do not convey the impression to employes that they are to take no part in bringing about their own welfare."

Dr. Hanson spoke of the immense value to physicians in their work as sanitarians that the effort of the branch about to be organized would be. He requested that a direct effort be put forth to induce manufacturers to adopt protective measures against lead poison, stating that employers and workmen both have been found who were absolutely ignorant of the danger involved in exposure to lead, and that even where such knowledge exists precautions are not often taken.

Great Possibilities in Work.

"You could show the manufacturers," said he, "the wisdom of providng such establishments and such protective devices as to make the expression 'occupational disease' lose what significance it now has." The necessity of teaching the workers in white lead and other compounds of that metal the importance of using respirators was urged. Dr. Hanson asked that the new branch of the Woman's Welfare Department stimulate manufacturers to adopt standards, if anything, far above the legal requirements for safeguarding, sanitation, hygiene, etc. He expressed the opinion that an organized force of visitors to the homes of tenement dwellers could do great good, and he thought that these visitors could co-operate with the manufacturers' staff in such a way as to revolutionize the industrial community from the point of view of the welfare of the manufacturer, the employe and the public.

The speaker outlined succinctly many other things that appealed to him as coming within the scope of activities of the proposed organization, and he asked that help be given the State Board of Health in showing that if the avoidable dangers in cotton manufacture are removed the only menace that will remain, practically, will be the cotton dust that occurs in some of the processes. "When some of our manufacturers," said he, "have cotton mills that are practically beyond reproach, is it not worth while to get others to bring their buildings into the same class? Is it not equally worth while to ask if there is a good reason why women should be kept at work in rooms which require gaslight at 11 o'clock in the morning on a bright day?"

DR. RICHARD C. CABOT emphasized the fact that success in getting anything done for health or morals or anything of like nature depends upon sticking to the idea that the effort constitutes a personal problem, and not a scientific or economic one. Dr. Cabot told of the experience of a health inspector in Massachusetts who found operatives working in a factory under conditions menacing to health, while respirators, which had been provided under the law, were hanging on the wall, with evidence of the fact that they had not been used for a long time. Instances of this sort, the speaker thought, showed strongly the need of personal work with employes. "Shall we ever," said he, "get anything done unless we succeed in bringing about in the employe a state of mind in which he will care enough for life and home and friends to avoid the particular form of death which he faces? Such a change does not come about as the result of handing a circular to a workman, but only following personal influence."

Problem Involves Friendship.

The problem involved in welfare work, as seen by Dr. Cabot, was closely allied with that of friendship and, he added, that there was room enough for all in that field. Continuing, the speaker said that those proposing to engage in welfare work must make it perfectly clear to themselves that they were not trying to make the poor more like the rich. "We want," said Dr. Cabot, "to make the rich or the poor or anybody else better citizens. In my work in the Massachusetts General Hospital I see how this social service idea is utilized and what can be done by reason of getting into close contact with those who need our effort and giving them such personal, friendly, close help that the best results may be obtained. It seems to me that this organization has a good work to do, which will be attained in so far as it sticks to that point of view."

DR. HARVEY W. WILEY, Chief Food Chemist of the Department of Agriculture, made the concluding address. He said that without proper nutrition no betterment of any kind in our scheme of civilization can be accomplished. "In fact," said he, "the food question is an underlying problem of all social reform and is becoming more acute every day."

The speaker expressed the opinion that every city should pass an ordinance prohibiting the building of any new factory within its borders, arguing that this territory is not the place for production, but for exchange only. "Every man who works in a factory," said Dr. Wiley, "should have a garden and plenty of fresh air."

"Less Meat," Says Dr. Wiley.

Dr. Wiley argued for less meat in the dietary of workers of all classes and kinds, and for a well-balanced ration with special emphasis on wheat and milk as perfect foods. He expressed the opinion that this would result in increased efficiency on the part of all workers and, at the same time, effect considerable economy in their living. Dr. Wiley expressed himself as immensely pleased with the story told earlier in the meeting by Mr. Loring about the employes in whom had been stimulated a desire to excel in the raising of vegetables. Said he, "That is the best news I have heard in a long time, because it is the fruition of a theory that I have been preaching for years."

At the conclusion of Dr. Wiley's address a motion prevailed to form a Massachusetts and Rhode Island section of the Woman's Welfare Department of The National Civic Federation, and a Committee on Organization was forthwith elected.

Following this action the meeting was declared adjourned.

MERCURY AS A MENACE TO WORKERS

Interesting Monograph on the Part It Plays in Industrial Processes—Suggestions for Safeguarding—New York and Vicinity the Territory Investigated.

"Mercury Poisoning in the Industries of New York and Vicinity" is the title of a monograph, just published, which constitutes an interesting contribution to the rather meagre bibliography of the part played by poisons in the various industrial processes of this country. The author is Mrs. Lindon W. Bates, Chairman of the Committee Upon Dangerous and Unhealthy Industries of the New York and New Jersey Section, Woman's Welfare Department, The National Civic Federation.

The Executive Committee, under whose authority and co-operation the investigation was carried out, is composed of the following prominent women:

Mrs. Francis McNeil Bacon, Jr., Mrs. William Rand, Jr., Miss Maud Rives Borland, Mrs. George Blumenthal, Mrs. Walker Smith, Mrs. Charles F. Meyer, Miss Gertrude Robinson-Smith, Miss Elizabeth Marbury, Mrs. Archibald Alexander, Mrs. Lindon W. Bates, Mrs. August Belmont, Mrs. Francis Higginson Cabot, Mrs. John Corbin, Miss Cornelia Crooke, Mrs. James S. Cushman, Mrs. Charles Noe Daly, Mrs. Ernesto G. Fabbri, Mrs. M. D. Kalbfleisch, Mrs. V. Everit Macy, Mrs. Marcus M. Marks, Mrs. Gilbert Montague, Miss Anne Morgan, Miss Marie B. Pond, Mrs. Ralph Sanger, Mrs. Alexander Shaw, Miss Caroline Shippen, Mrs. Lyndsay Van Rensselaer, Mrs. Mary Hatch Willard, Mrs. William R. Willcox.

Deals Largely with Hat Making.

The work in question deals largely with the manufacture of felt hats and the preparation of material used in their making, the statement being made that this is almost the only important branch of manufacture in which the use of mercury remains a menace.

The author seems to have approached her task with an open mind, and to have maintained an excellent balance throughout the painstaking investigation which the work in question evidences.

Mercurial poisoning in hat and felt making, we learn, results primarily from the "carrotting" of fur, a process which involves the use of a solution of the poisonous metal. Apparently there is more danger in the handling of the fur after it has been "carrotted" than in the operation itself.

Mercury enters the system through the skin, lungs and digestive tract, principally in the form of vapor or minute dust particles. Mercurial poisoning, the disease, has three stages, viz.:—psychic, tremors, final.

It manifests itself in distressing and sometimes loathsome forms, including tremors, degeneracy, despondency and decay of the will, memory and brain.

Four Impressive Facts.

Four impressive facts, encountered in the course of the investigation, are strongly emphasized by the author as follows:

1. Mercurial poisoning is easily curable until it reaches the stage of tremors, and the risk of contracting the disease can, in large part, be eliminated by simple, prophylactic measures, sanitation being a great aid.

2. The disease is highly insidious, years not infrequently elapsing before decidedly unfavorable symptoms appear, but it early creates a fertile field for the germs of pneumonia, tuberculosis and other maladies, the responsibility for which it is, in the very nature of the case, seldom charged with.

3. The history of practically every case of poisoning is accompanied with a rapid and substantial decline in the earning power of the victim, to say nothing of the intervals in which he is not able to labor at all.

4. Substantial progress cannot be made in this country in reducing mercurial infection without stringent laws designed to effect prophylaxis, and a sufficient number of inspectors to see that those laws are enforced.

Interesting Data Given.

Mrs. Bates has found her material chiefly in the facts obtained in an investigation of 122 cases of mercurial poisoning and dermatitis, nearly all of which were treated in some hospital. A full report of each case investigated is given, and there is, in addition, a tabulation of the salient facts. Other sources of information were physicians and hospitals in hat manufacturing communities, employers, workers and labor organizations.

Divergent and perplexing statements are given from various authorities with regard to the prevalence of mercurial poisoning. These range from practically a denial that it exists at all to the statement of one physician that ninety per cent of those exposed are in some degree affected and that fifty-five per cent ultimately succumb. Much emphasis, however, is given by the author to the statement that workers in three of the numerous divisions of the hat making process are denied protection by insurance companies.

A point strongly emphasized is the need of suitable eating quarters and hygienic provisions, instances being cited where food and drink were daily exposed to mercury-laden dust and mercurial vapor.

Two Interesting Cases.

The following excerpts are taken from two of the 122 cases reported:

Case No. 1.—Mr. S—— had the "shakes" in his arms; his teeth were blackened and he was salivated. His throat and stomach were most seriously affected, and Dr. S—— attributed the tuberculosic throat to chronic sore throat brought on by breathing mercurial vapor. He belonged to the Finishers' Union, to which no benefit association was attached. He had worked as a hatter for seventeen years, eight of which were spent in ——'s factory. He had been married five years, and had one child (a girl of four years). At the time of his illness he was working at ——'s factory, —— avenue, Newark, N. J. He carried no life insurance, but was receiving a sick benefit of $5 a week from the Sons of St. George, of which he was a member. Five dollars was the sole income of the family at the time of the visit.

The dwelling was a tenement flat of three rooms; bedroom off the kitchen in which Mr. S—— was in bed, and a third room off the kitchen, with a cot for mother and child.

Mr. S—— had worked for two years in ——'s hat shop.

Could get no information on factory conditions. Mr. S—— did not chew tobacco. He was able to average $20 a week during the time he had steady employment.

Case No. 2.—P—— C—— was found living in a very neat little flat with his daughter, a rather delicate looking girl, who keeps house for him and his son, aged sixteen, who has just started to work. Mr. C—— is a pleasing-looking man and seemed very willing to give all the information he could.

His symptoms are the usual ones: excessive salivation, discolored teeth, diarrhoea, morbid frame of mind, and has the tremors and shakes in a most exaggerated manner. He has worked with this same company, which has changed hands several times, for thirty-five years. Says Mr. G—— is very wealthy. They have paid his full wages for the six weeks he has been out. Mr. C—— is very much worried as to what is going to become of them all and feels sure he will soon die. His brother F——, aged forty, died on January 15, 1910. Had worked for many years at the same place, and his symptoms were exactly the same.

The brothers worked in a poorly ventilated basement over a boiling combination of mercury, nitric acid and epsom salts, and the fumes were simply frightful. The mouth used to fill with a horrible slime, and they had to cough and gag, and "saving your presence, lady, spit blood sometimes." P—— says the air was not so bad until their plant was surrounded by tall buildings.

There is no special place for them to eat lunch, so they eat in the workrooms. He knew of no other case of mercurial poisoning. Said nobody ever stayed long enough to get it. He had it out six years ago and was out of work for a ile, but apparently recovered and went back. e did not know *why* he went back, except that was the only thing he knew how to do.

In a conversation with the daughter, later, she ied and said she did not know what would beme of them if the firm stopped paying her ther. She said that he had never done anything his life but go to work, come home, get his pper and go to bed, and the next day get up d do the same thing. He never drunk to excess. he said it was very hard to live with a sad erson like that—she had "tried to get Pop to go the moving picture show, but he won't go." he did not know why this trouble had come o them.

t is just to say that Case No. 2 is declared to e been one of the worst discovered.

Conditions in Best Factories.

n the best class of factories Mrs. Bates finds t everything is being done that can be with the gle exception of the education of workers in the ngers of mercurial poisoning through placards, a actice that obtains universally in Great Britain. ith the class of factory in question it seems that thing further, practically, can be done until a bstitute is found for mercury in the process of arrotting."

It should be stated, however, that the number of ctories Mrs. Bates would put in the first class is mparatively small, and that in the case of the hers she would recommend the adoption of the easures contained in the eleven recommendations ven below, accompanied in every instance, of urse, with adequate inspection by the State.

Eleven Recommendations Made.

The recommendations suggested as the result of e investigation are concisely summarized by Mrs. ates as follows:

1st.—Placards announcing the unhealthy nature f the trade should be set up in factories and workhops warning men of the need for precaution.

2nd.—Eating and drinking and the keeping of food hould be forbidden in rooms where mercurial proesses are carried on. Some suitable lunching place hould be provided.

3rd.—Ample washing facilities should be installed.

4th.—Proper drinking water should be supplied.

5th.—Sweeping should be superseded by the vacuum system of suction cleaning.

6th.—Mixing of mercury and acids should be done after work hours.

7th.—Rubber gloves and simple respirators should be supplied.

8th.—The industry should be regulated by special legislation, requiring the elimination from the atmosphere of steam, heat, acid and mercury fumes, fur and dust, at their source of production. THIS IS THE HEART OF THE WHOLE MATTER.

9th.—Regular medical inspection is advisable. This would warn both the men and the management of mercurial attack in its incipiency, and transfer to other processes could give a chance for cure.

10th.—Compensation for disease should be a tax upon the poison-using industry begetting it and profiting from it.

11th.—The industry should supply insurance for men working in processes of such unhealthiness that insurance companies decline the risk.

A LECTURE COURSE OF DISTINCTION

Most of President Taft's Cabinet Will Address New York and New Jersey Section, Woman's Welfare Department — Vacation Committee's Excellent Work.

The New York and New Jersey Section of the Woman's Welfare Department is carrying out a program consisting of a series of ten lectures, explanatory of the working of the various departments of the Federal Government, which has attracted wide attention. The press has commented at length on the scheme.

These lectures are being given on Monday afternoons at 4 o'clock at the Waldorf-Astoria Hotel, New York City. The distinguished lecturers and their subjects are as follows:

December 5, "Government".....PROF. JOHN B. MOORE
December 11, "State"..............SECRETARY KNOX
December 18, "Treasury"......SECRETARY MACVEAGH
January 8, "War"................SECRETARY STIMSON
January 15, "Justice"...ATT'Y-GENERAL WICKERSHAM
January 22, "Interior"............SECRETARY FISHER
January 29, "Post Office"...FORMER SEC'Y CORTELYOU
February 5, "Navy".................SECRETARY MEYER
February 19, "Agriculture"...ASST. SECRETARY HAYS
February 26, "Commerce and Labor"....SEC'Y NAGEL

Miss Marbury in Charge.

Each Cabinet officer will discuss his own department. Miss Elisabeth Marbury is chairman of the Committee on Lectures. The following from the Evening Post, of New York, gives a comprehensive idea of the lecture course:

"Led by Miss Anne Morgan, daughter of J. Pierpont Morgan, the women members of the New York and New Jersey branch of The National Civic Federation have arranged for practically all the members of President Taft's Cabinet to speak in a series of Monday afternoon lectures at the Waldorf-Astoria this winter. The lectures are for the public, and men are cordially invited."

Mrs. Bacon Explains Lecture Scheme.

"Mrs. Francis McNeil Bacon, Jr., chairman of the Executive Committee of the New York and New Jersey Section, explained the undertaking as follows:

"'We wanted to learn something about these various branches of the government, so we went to the men who would surely know all there is to know on the subject. To most of us the government is a sort of invisible automobile that is carrying us along all right, though we don't know a thing about the mechanism. No, we don't expect the "good old wagon to break down," and we are not preparing to volunteer in case it should. But we are interested, and a lot more women would be interested if they had the first idea what politics and political economy and elections were all about. I think there are a good many people voting for President to-day who would not be ashamed to admit that they are pretty hazy on even the fundamental points of our government machinery.

"'If there are, we hope they will come to these lectures and learn. They are open to the public. To teach lessons in democracy—that was Miss Morgan's idea. We want those who are interested to contribute a modest share toward a course that is requiring a big endowment.'"

Working Women's Vacations.

Another interesting phase of the Section's activities is the work of its Vacation Committee, whose personnel is herewith given: Miss Gertrude Robinson-Smith, chairman; Mrs. August Belmont, Mrs. Selden Bacon, Miss Marshall, Miss Anne Morgan, Mrs. Henry B. Binsse, Miss Maud Rives Borland, Mrs. Alfred A. Cook, Miss Rachel Crothers, Mrs. Michael Dreicer, Mrs. M. D. Kalbfleisch, Mrs. William Rand, Jr., Miss Evelyn Smith, Mrs. J. E. Spingarn (representing the Committee on Amusement and Vacation Resources).

This committee exists principally to investigate and recommend to working girls wholesome and attractive vacation boarding houses within easy access of New York City, to sow the "paid vacation" seed in the minds of employers and to stimulate the woman worker to save for her vacations through a fund it has established for that purpose.

Boarding Houses Investigated.

There have been investigated one hundred boarding houses within sixty miles of New York City, and the enthusiastic comments of the young women who patronized the committee's approved list of houses during the past summer leave no doubt of the success of the work that has been done.

During the winter a series of "Vacation Evenings" for working women is being held at the Section headquarters. The social side is emphasized at these gatherings, and they also furnish opportunity to stimulate the idea of saving for next summer's vacation.

The New York and New Jersey Section secured two hundred new members within two weeks recently and has nearly seven hundred enrolled altogether now. Every cent of income and much more is needed to keep its work up to the standard of efficiency which it has always striven to maintain.

FEDERATION'S MODEL COMPENSATION ACT FINDS FAVOR

(Continued from Page 9.)

for, or of persons entitled to such compensation, or both, with or without others. Any employer so insured may be relieved from personal responsibility for such compensation.

"After the enactment of a compensation law no civil proceeding, other than as authorized by such law, shall be maintainable in respect of any accident covered thereby.

"In the exercise of the powers herein conferred the Legislature shall not be affected by antecedent provisions of this constitution requiring trial by jury and forbidding limitation of the amount recoverable in the case of injury resulting in death."

The necessity of some sort of amendment lies in the fact that the Court of Appeals held the Wainwright Compensation Law unconstitutional.

Avoidance of Encumbrances Sought.

The proposal of Mr. Stetson, who is Chairman of the Committee on Legislative Policy of the Department on Workmen's Compensation of The National Civic Federation, is in the nature of a substitute for several amendments that have already been suggested, in all of which he finds objections to the extent that they undertake to do something other than and different from making provision for a suitable workmen's compensation law.

Commenting on the situation with regard to these amendments, Mr. Stetson said:

"We want to get a proper Workmen's Compensation Law, and we want to get it as soon as we can. My belief is that the introduction of ancillary, even though desirable, provisions which are questionable and questioned by many, will lead to a postponement and not to a facilitation of the enactment of a proper workmen's compensation law; and so, having that subject and object near to my heart, I do trust that every friend of wise legislation on the subject of workmen's compensation will be willing to join with all of us in an amendment having that special and single object in view, and that if these other objects are to be sought they shall be sought through a different series of amendments, depending upon their own merits and upon a discussion concerning them."

PROGRAM—WINTER MEETING, DEPARTMENT ON WORKMEN'S COMPENSATION.

OPENING ADDRESS
AUGUST BELMONT, Chairman Department on Compensation for Industrial Accidents and Their Prevention. The National Civic Federation, New York City.

COMPULSORY COMPENSATION VS. STATE INSURANCE
P. TECUMSEH SHERMAN, Chairman Legal Committee, Workmen's Compensation Department, The National Civic Federation, New York City.
J. WALTER LORD, Chairman Maryland Council, The National Civic Federation, Baltimore, Md.
HON. JOHN T. MCDONOUGH, former Secretary of State for New York, of Albany, N. Y.

COMPULSORY COMPENSATION VS. THE ELECTIVE PLAN
WILLIAM J. MORAN, Member Legal Committee, The National Civic Federation, New York City.

RIGHTS OF NON-RESIDENT ALIENS UNDER WORKMEN'S COMPENSATION ACTS
CHEVALIER MARCEL A. VITI, Philadelphia, Pa.

REPORT FROM COMMITTEE ON IMPROVEMENT OF STATE INSPECTION OF FACTORIES
LOUIS B. SCHRAM, Chairman.

REPORT UPON A TENTATIVE BASIS FOR A MODEL SAFETY ACT FOR UNIFORM STATE LEGISLATION.
Presented by JOHN CALDER.

WHAT A MODEL SAFETY ACT SHOULD EMBRACE.
JOHN CALDER, Manager Remington Typewriter Works, Ilion, N. Y.

THE SITUATION IN NEW YORK CONCERNING PROPOSED AMENDMENTS TO THE CONSTITUTION PERMITTING THE ENACTMENT OF A WORKMEN'S COMPENSATION LAW
FRANCIS LYNDE STETSON, Chairman Committee on Legislative Policy, Workmen's Compensation Department, The National Civic Federation, New York City.
PROF. HENRY R. SEAGER, Columbia University, New York City.

LEGAL PHASES OF THE TENTATIVE MODEL SAFETY ACT
ASSEMBLYMAN CYRUS W. PHILLIPS, of Rochester.

HOW LABOR BUREAUS MAY HELP IN THE EFFECTIVE ADMINISTRATION OF SAFETY LAWS
HON. EDGAR T. DAVIES, President International Association of Factory Inspectors.

THE NEXT STEP IN WORKMEN'S COMPENSATION IN NEW YORK STATE
CYRUS W. PHILLIPS, member former New York State Commission on Employers' Liability, Rochester, N. Y.
JAMES L. GERNON, Chairman Committee on Employers' Liability and Compensation, New York State Federation of Labor, New York City.

SAMUEL GOMPERS—THE FLAG AND McNAMARA INCIDENTS

(*Continued from Page 15.*)

resented an attempt of Mr. Baer, of the Anthracite Coal Operators, to influence his conduct just as quickly as would John Mitchell, when he was leading the great strike in the anthracite coal fields, have resented the offering of advice by James M. Lynch, President of the International Typographical Union. And yet, while this simple rule of insisting upon every one's attending to his own business is perfectly understood in all other walks of life, there seems to be an idea that in labor controversies all that the President of The American Federation of Labor has to do is to push a button and every union man in the country is to dance. When it comes to the dancing business, the union men can make Mr. Gompers, their paid President, do the dancing if they are not satisfied with his administration. His position is exactly the same as that of the president of any large railway company or public service corporation. The stockholders and directors are the bosses when it comes to matters of policy or important questions outside of general routine.

Now, in closing, let me ask those who would drive Samuel Gompers from the leadership of the labor movement whom they would put in his place. As the only opposition to Mr Gompers of any importance comes from the revolutionary Socialists, those who would oust Mr. Gompers would have to substitute a Debs or a Haywood. Is that what they want? There are those who would profit by the disintregration of the union movement in this country who will say that Gompers is no better than Debs or Haywood, and that it would make little difference if either of them took his place, but the great mass of thinking people in this country know better.

Socialism vs. Organized Labor.

The importance of a clear discrimination by men of education and affairs between the principles underlying the American Federation of Labor and the Railway Brotherhoods and those underlying the Socialist party in this country cannot be too seriously emphasized at this time. There has just occurred a national referendum election in the Socialist party for the seven members of the National Executive Committee which governs its affairs. One of the candidates for election was William D. Haywood, the leader of what is called the violent or Anarchist branch of the Socialist party, "The Industrial Workers of the World." Some of the members of the Socialist party were so much alarmed over the possibility of Mr. Haywood being elected that they began an attack upon him in the Socialist papers. They quoted extracts from Haywood's book, "Industrial Socialism," in which he states that any worker who understands Socialism

> "retains absolutely no respect for the property rights of the profit-takers. He will use any weapon which will win his fight. He knows that the present laws of property are made by and for the capitalists. Therefore, he does not hesitate to break them. He knows that whatever action advances the interests of the working class is right, because it will save the workers from destruction and death."

Haywood's Anarchistic Principles.

This was declared by Mr. Haywood's opposers to be anarchy. Mr. Haywood came to New York during his fight for election and made a speech at Cooper Union, in which occurred the following clear and ringing declarations for revolutionary Socialism and anarchy:

> "Can you wonder that I despise the law? I understand the class struggle. I am not a law-abiding citizen. More than that, I do not believe you here ought to be law-abiding citizens. Out there they called the troops out after us and one of their mills went up. So much dynamite was under the mill that it went up so high I guess parts of it have never come down yet.
>
> "Let us Socialists be frank. We want to overthrow the capitalist system and establish in its place an industrial democracy. Why then say we are law-abiding?
>
> "I believe in coercion. Every trade union believes in coercion. But I would have this game of coercion played on so large a scale that it would be irresistible instead of sporadic as it is now. I believe in a boycott backed by a hundred street cleaners, who are left alone in their fight because their union brothers who might have supported them are all tied up with contracts and trade agreements.
>
> "Better no organization of any kind than one which makes contracts to lie dead for a year or three years and be out of the struggle. You know if we had this organization we could protect our lives at work, shorten our hours, and finally declare a general lockout, backed up by armed warfare against the capitalists. Try it, fellow workers. You have only your chains to lose and a world to gain."

BUT HAYWOOD WAS OVERWHELMINGLY ELECTED.

Mr. Gompers Denounces Socialism.

In contrast with these Socialistic-Anarchistic utterances of Mr. Haywood, I want to call attention to the well-known and able opposition to Socialism which has always been led by Mr. Gompers, and to close this article by quoting again the same pronouncement that appears on another page in this issue (and it ought to be at the head of every newspaper in this country that believes in American institutions): I refer to what Mr. Gompers said in Faneuil Hall in Boston, in closing his eloquent speech against the proposition of the Socialist party to commit the American Federation of Labor to its propaganda, namely:

> "I want to tell you Socialists that I have studied your philosophy; read your books upon economics, and not the meanest of them; studied your standard works, both in English and German—have not only read, but studied them. I have heard your orators and watched the work of your movement the world over. I have kept close watch upon your doctrines for thirty years; have been closely associated with many of you, and know how you think and what you propose. I know, too, what you have up your sleeve, and I want to say that I am not only at variance with your doctrines, but with your philosophy.
>
> "*Economically, you are unsound; socially, you are wrong; industrially, you are an impossibility.*"

MR. MARKS PROVES EFFICIENT ARBITER

Danbury Hat Makers and Workers Call on Civic Federation to Furnish Umpire Under Clause in Their Agreement.

A HAPPY example of industrial arbitration was afforded recently in the decision of Marcus M. Marks, chairman of the New York Arbitration Committee of The National Civic Federation, in a controversy between the United Hatters of North America and a member of the Danbury and Bethel Hat Manufacturers' Association.

At the termination of trouble, in 1909, between the national organizations of employers and workmen in the hat making industry, an agreement was entered into between the hat manufacturers of Danbury, Conn., and the United Hatters of North America to the effect that all matters in dispute should be arbitrated by a committee on which both sides should have equal representation. In the event agreement could not be had in this way, the selection of a final arbiter was provided for.

MARCUS M. MARKS.

It was, however, a further part of the agreement that if the committee failed to decide upon some one as final arbiter within five days he should be chosen by the chairman of the Conciliation Committee of The National Civic Federation.

Both sides requested President Low to act in accordance with the provision just referred to, and he designated Mr. Marks to act as final arbiter, each party to the controversy having expressed itself as thoroughly satisfied with the choice.

Investigation by Mr. Marks showed that the controversy was not of such a nature as to be susceptible of settlement by conciliation, it being a question of "piece-work" and "task-work." In view of this fact an abitration of the matter was entered into.

Mr. Marks' findings as arbitrator were accepted by each party, and the threatened trouble seems to have been most happily averted.

The decision of Mr. Marks in the case follows:

Decision of the Arbiter.

"TO THE

"UNITED HATTERS OF NORTH AMERICA, 11 Waverly Place, New York City.

"DANBURY AND BETHEL HAT MANUFACTURERS' ASSOCIATION, Danbury, Conn.

"GENTLEMEN: A study of the matter presented to me for arbitration, under the contract existing between the Danbury and Bethel Hat Manufacturers' Association and the United Hatters of North America, reveals the fact that the dispute does not hinge upon the relative satisfaction of the week-work and piece-work systems, as had been intimated, but concerns a complaint against what I should term the system of *task-work* operating for the past three years in the factory of the Delohery Hat Company, member of the Hat Manufacturers' Association. The union demanded a change to the piece-work system, such as exists in all the shops of other members of the Manufacturers' Association, and the adjustment of the piece price to a scale which would give satisfactory earnings to the employes of the department of 'sizing' hats and 'starting on the machine.'

"The bill of prices offered to the men by Mr. Delohery on May 1, 1911, is as follows:

"'PLANK SHOP BILL OF PRICES TO CONTINUE TO APRIL 30, 1912.

> "'Wages for machine sizing to be at the rate of $20 per week of fifty hours' work.
>
> "'Wages for starting on machine to be at the rate of $20 per week of fifty hours' work.
>
> "'Nine hours constitute the time for a day's work.
>
> "'Sixty-four hats agreed on as a fair day's work from a sizer, and twelve dozen agreed on as a fair day's work from a starter.
>
> "'Slow men to be paid in proportion to above bill.'

"It will be seen that while a certain task is expected for the weekly wage designated, a proportionate reduction is stipulated for smaller production. There is, however, no provision for higher pay for higher production. In other words, no steady weekly wage is offered nor any minimum pay stipulated, but a maximum earning power is rigidly set. This, in spirit, is, in my judgment, against the best interests, not only of the workingmen who, in the Delohery bill, are met with a blank wall, limiting their hopes, but it is equally against the interests of the employer. It does not stimulate men to do their best. Extra production does not proportionately increase the overhead charges of the factory and therefore brings an increased net return to employer as well as employe.

"The present task-work system led to increase in the practice, on the part of rapid toilers, of quitting work early in the afternoon, when their stipulated task was completed, and led to a disregard of the terms of the association agreement in force to work nine hours per day for five days and five hours on Saturday.

"An agreement of this kind should mean what it plainly says and be so carried out. Men should work to the full extent of their ability (with due regard for the protection of their health) during those hours, and they should be entitled to full pay for their output in accordance with the ability they show.

"For reasons best known to the hat trade in Danbury and Bethel, the piece-work system has been in vogue in all the factories except the one complained about at this time.

Price List is Fixed.

"Since there is keen dissatisfaction with the operations of the task-system in this one case, and since it has offensive features per se, I see no reason for its continuance, but must decide that, for the good of both parties and to further the uniformity of system among the members of the Manufacturers' Association, the piece-work system be adopted in the 'sizing and starting' departments of the Delohery Hat Company until April 30, 1912. As to fixing a price-list to be operative until April 30, 1912, I must frankly state that I feel the responsibility very keenly. I have studied the price-list of a number of the manufacturers in Danbury, but find that the case is simplified by the fact that there is but one other factory employing the same system of manufacture as that of the Delohery Hat Company. In the shop to which I

(*Continued on Page 28.*)

DOCTRINE OF CLASS HATRED IS SMITTEN HARD

URDY AMERICANISM IN FEDERATION OF LABOR REJECTS SOCIALISTIC PROPOSAL—UNION OFFICIALS MAY CONTINUE TO AID THE CIVIC FEDERATION IN ITS EFFORTS FOR INDUSTRIAL PEACE

TURDY Americanism arose in its might at the recent annual convention of the American Federation of Labor, at Atlanta, Ga., and smote p and thigh "class consciousness" and the various her doctrines by which Socialism tries to sow the eds of hate, malice and envy among the wage-orkers of every country.

The vote was nearly three to one. The oppor-nity to assert its revulsion at these Socialistic octrines came to the delegates to the convention in ıe following way:

Three resolutions condemning the Civic Federa-ion, and either directly or indirectly calling upon ny member or officer of any labor union holding nembership in the Federation to withdraw, were resented.

One of these was offered by a delegate from the llinois State Federation of Labor; another by a epresentative of the United Mine Workers, and a third jointly by representatives of the United Mine Workers and the Michigan State Federation of Labor.

One of these resolutions alleged that the employing class had banded itself into an organized union known as the Civic Federation, "ostensibly for the purpose of averting strife between the workers and the employers, but really for the purpose of blinding the workers as to their true condition;" another alleged the favorite doctrine of Socialism that, "conflict between the employing class and the working class is constantly becoming more intense." The third resolution offered found fault with the Civic Federation because "a number of those who contribute to its financial support are enemies of the labor movement and are working to destroy the labor unions of the country."

REPORT OF THE COMMITTEE WHICH INVESTIGATED ALLEGATIONS MADE IN THE RESOLUTIONS.

To the allegations outlined above, the Committee on Resolutions replied in a report which strongly endorsed the efforts of The National Civic Federation to bring capital and labor into closer relationship and also its efforts to better the working conditions of wage-earners. The report states that, after careful investigation, the allegations made in the resolutions are found to be without foundation. The complete report of the committee follows:

"Your committee in connection with the consideration of these resolutions has endeavored to secure such information relative to The National Civic Federation as could be presented by the delegates introducing them, and in addition such information as could be given by those who as trade-unionists have held membership in that body, or who have in any manner noted the influence of The National Civic Federation upon the safety and progress of the trade-union movement and the principles for which it stands.

"In addition your committee has examined its official records for the purpose of discovering the aims and objects of The National Civic Federation and of assuring itself as to whether there existed any variations between the principles of that organization as laid down in its organic laws and the rules it has adopted, and in its practice.

"Your committee finds that The National Civic Federation was organized in part for the purpose of furthering the adjustment of disputes between employers and their employes through the methods of friendly conference, conciliation or arbitration when mutually acceptable, and the consummation of joint contracts and agreements covering the terms of employment. In addition, to bring together representative men from all groups for the public discussion of the questions affecting the relations between employers and organized workmen. This organization, we find, at the time of its inception, set the official seal of its approval upon the recognition of trade unions by employers, and as endorsing the consummation of formal agreements covering the terms of employment between employers and organized workmen.

"Your committee has had no information placed before it which would indicate that The National Civic Federation has at any time departed from its policy as above outlined, but evidence has been presented which demonstrates that it has extended its original program by creating departments whose entire work has been to give a widespread influence in favor of the peaceful adjustment of all questions arising between employers and organized workmen.

"In evidence of this fact your committee quotes from the official announcement of The National Civic Federation creating the Department of Conciliation, as follows:

"'Declaration of the Purpose of the Conciliation Department.

"'The scope and province of this department shall be to do what may seem best to promote industrial peace and prosperity; to be helpful in establishing rightful relations between employers and workers; by its good offices to endeavor to obviate and prevent strikes and lockouts, and to aid in renewing industrial relations where a rupture has occurred.

"'That at all times representatives of employers and workers, organized or unorganized, should confer for the adjustment of differences or disputes before an acute stage is reached, and thus avoid or minimize the number of strikes or lockouts.

"'That mutual agreements as to conditions under which labor shall be performed should be encouraged, and that when agreements are made, the terms thereof should be faithfully adhered to, both in letter and spirit, by both parties.

"'This department, either as a whole or through a sub-committee by it appointed, shall, when requested by both parties to a dispute, act as a forum to adjust and decide upon questions at issue between workers and their employers, provided in its opinion the subject is one of sufficient importance.

"'This department will not consider abstract industrial problems.

"'This department assumes no powers of arbitration unless such powers be conferred by both parties to a dispute.'

"We have carefully examined such records as were available, to learn whether The National Civic Federation has officially or unofficially committed itself to the assumption that the interests of capital and labor are identical and we have failed to find any evidence that this question has ever been passed upon; we have found, however, in the public statements of the officers of this organization, who were not members of trade unions, and in its official publications, expressions of the conviction that in the profits arising from production, the interests of the employer and the workman were not identical, as both endeavored to secure to themselves as large a share of the value of products as possible.

"From its attitude and official expressions of opinion The National Civic Federation seems to have committed itself to the belief that the primary purpose of trade unions is to secure a larger share of the actual value arising from production, through collective action, than would be possible for their members to acquire through their efforts as individuals, and that the employers frequently associate themselves together that they might be in a better position to retain the largest possible portion of the profits.

A Friendly Influence.

"Your committee has had no evidence presented to it which would indicate that the influence of The National Civic Federation has ever been unfriendly to organized labor or that it has been detrimental either when negotiations were in progress between employers and trade unions or when industrial controversies had led to strikes and lockouts. Officers of national and international unions affiliated with the American Federation of Labor have appeared before your committee and testified that on numerous occasions interviews and conferences were secured with employers who had previously refused to meet any representatives of their organizations, through the kindly offices of The National Civic Federation, and that as a result of these interviews and conferences and the friendly influence of that body, satisfactory adjustments of controversies were effected.

"Your committee is aware of criticisms which have been directed against The National Civic Federation by some members of organized labor, but none of these compares with the vindictive and vicious attacks which have been made against it by every association of employers in America which is organized for the purpose of opposing and antagonizing our trade unions and the principles they are contending for.

"The bitter hostility of the anti-trade union associations has evidently been directed toward The National Civic Federation because that body has emphatically declared its conviction that trade unions are essential to the workmen's welfare, and that as indispensable organizations they should be given full recognition and encouragement.

A Covert Blow at Individuals.

"It appears to your committee that the criticisms which have been made by members of labor organizations are directed more toward certain individuals holding membership in The National Civic Federation than against that body itself.

"It is not to be expected that in an association composed of representatives of trade unions, employers and the general public that every member will be equally acceptable to all of the others because of his views and personal attitude; men differ in their view-point, and these differences become more apparent when representatives of such groups as organized workmen and employers meet upon a common footing to discuss problems affecting both directly. But are we to hold that we shall not meet and discuss the grave problems which affect the wage-earners' standard of civilization with an association whose membership may include some whose vision has not yet been sufficiently broadened?

"These individual members of The National Civic Federation, against whom criticism has been directed, are in many instances active members of the church, of fraternal and of other civic organizations, contributing to their support. Their attitude toward many questions may fail to meet with the approval of their associates, but is this sufficient reason why any member should withdraw his affiliation from such organization or organizations, or that recommendations should be made by this convention that members of organized labor should withdraw from any of them?

"Since the formation of The National Civic Federation there has been in its membership a number of trade-unionists, among these being men who have deservedly earned our full confidence, and who for years have been selected by organized labor in this and their own organization as among the most trusted and capable officers and members. These representative men have had the fullest opportunity of becoming familiar with the policies and the influence of that body upon the welfare and progress of our trade union movement, and we are convinced that if any of them had discovered that the The National Civic Federation was in any manner inimical to the welfare of our movement they would have been the first to sound a note of warning.

"Your committee therefore recommends non-concurrence with the resolutions."

SPEECHES OF LABOR LEADERS OF NATIONAL PROMINENCE IN SUPPORT OF COMMITTEE'S REPORT.

DENNIS A. HAYES, President of the Glass Blowers' Association of the United States and Canada, favored the Committee's report in a strong speech. He said that he was a member of The National Civic Federation as an individual, and not as a representative of his trade, and that no one induced him to join, but that he had done so of his own accord; and he held that in so doing he had exercised the same privilege that he did in becoming a member of a trade union.

Mr. Hayes took the broad position that organized labor should seize every opportunity offered for explaining its humane objects to people who do not thoroughly understand them, and he added that, "we were not brought into this movement to be put in a nursery, or to join some select school of economics where we would hear nothing but that which appealed to our own prejudices and views." He expressed the opinion that labor had gained probably more increases in wages and reductions in hours of work by meeting employers who were at one time bitterly opposed to it than in any other way, and he pointed to the fact that herein lay one of the purposes of The National Civic Federation, namely, to allay prejudice and ill-feeling on the part of representatives of both capital and labor through friendly intercourse.

The speaker claimed that the few labor organizations that had condemned The National Civic Federation had done so without investigation of its purposes. Mr. Hayes, in common with practically all who spoke in favor of the Committee's report, pointed out the fact that if he could be told to leave The National Civic Federation, his religious and political affiliations could similarly be interfered with. He paid his respects to the Socialism animating the resolutions under discussion very concisely with the statement that, "To talk of more democracy, and more liberal conditions of employment, and at the same time foment feeling between the classes seems to me like a contradiction."

John Mitchell Discusses "Chloroform."

The next speaker was JOHN MITCHELL, Vice-President of the American Federation of Labor, formerly President of the United Mine Workers of America. Mr. Mitchell pointed to the fact that he had helped to organize The National Civic Federation, aided in the writing of its laws, and that the President of the American Federation of Labor, and other representative men in the movement, wrote the declaration in support of the trade agreement. He outlined the wonderful growth made by the United Mine Workers of America while he was President, and added, "all this progress and achievement was made while I was supposed to be suffering under the effects of chloroform administered by The National Civic Federation." He pointed to the fact that those behind the movement that led to his voluntary resignation from The National Civic Federation were in reality trying to drive him out of the United Mine Workers of America.

Referring to a few members of The National Civic Federation who had been cited by the opponents of the Committee's report as not in sympathy with the principles of organized labor, Mr. Mitchell said it was all very well to single out such persons, but that he thought it was only common justice that employers of labor who have been in constant agreement with their workmen, year after year making contracts with representatives of organized labor, should be given credit for what they had done.

Mr. Mitchell announced that he would not talk on abstract propositions, nor would he even suggest for the credit of The National Civic Federation, "those numerous settlements made by organized labor as a result of conferences secured through representatives of the Civic Federation." He would, however, he said, refer to some specific instances in which he himself had participated. He thereupon outlined several settlements that had resulted in justice to organized labor and which had come about through the influence of The National Civic Federation.

Mr. Mitchell referred to the fact that in the State of New York a comprehensive factory law, drawn by a commission of which he was a member, had been saved from veto by the earnest representations of August Belmont and other prominent members of The National Civic Federation. "That," said he, "was not an evidence of hostility; on the other hand, it was regarded by those who knew of it as an evidence of friendship. I have here a letter written by a member of the Legislature who introduced the bill extending his thanks to The National Civic Federation because of Mr. Belmont's action."

The speaker declared that the resolution of the Mine Workers of America denouncing The National Civic Federation was "not the expression of a majority of the delegates duly elected at the last annual convention," and charged that a large number of delegates, about fifty from one district alone, sat in that convention with credentials fraudulently given to them, and cast the votes that sent in the resolution in question to the American Federation of Labor. In making this statement, Mr. Mitchell made it plain that no censure of the members of his Union was implied, saying that he had full knowledge that the resolution was passed with the votes of men who had no right to seats as delegates in the Miners' Convention.

A Lack of Evidence.

JAMES O'CONNELL, President of the International Association of Machinists, said that he had hoped that the discussion would have brought out some evidence of the charges contained in the resolutions attacking The National Civic Federation, but that the opponents of that organization had failed to show anything that would warrant the support of the resolution they had presented. Mr. O'Connell stated that while he was not now a member of The National Civic Federation, he had been on its rolls in its early history, and that he was well acquainted with its beginnings, and knew something of the benefit it had been to him and the organization he represented. "The mere fact," said he, "that there may be one or two or a dozen men associated with that body whose records may show unfriendliness toward labor does not indicate by any means that the institution is unfair in any way." The speaker told of the effective use of the good offices of The National Civic Federation in his own

(Continued on Page 28.)

THE PRESS EMPHATICALLY ENDORSES LABOR'S REJECTION OF SOCIALISM

ROCHESTER HERALD, N. Y.—It is fortunate that a majority of the delegates to the convention were wise enough to vote down the resolution. It is a happy augury.

GRAND RAPIDS PRESS, Mich.—When John Mitchell was compelled to resign from The National Civic Federation or be ousted from the miners' organization, The Press expressed the opinion that the unionists responsible for pressing the choice upon him did not really represent organized labor. It is glad to see its good opinion of working men in general confirmed by the refusal of the American Federation of Labor to force the same action on President Gompers and other union leaders.

EVENING POST, New York.—In voting down the resolution * * * the American Federation of Labor puts itself in a distinctly better light than the United Mine Workers, who last Spring forced their ablest member to sever his connection with a body that exists for the sole purpose of fostering good relations between capital and labor in this country.

WHEELING REGISTER, W. Va.—It was a sensible decision * * * when a majority of the delegates * * * voted against the absurd resolution demanding the withdrawal of Gompers, Mitchell and other labor leaders from The National Civic Federation.

ST. PAUL PRESS, Minn.—The work of The National Civic Federation merits the commendation and support of organized labor, and the American Federation of Labor is to be congratulated upon its refusal to follow the Socialists in condemnation of an agency that is doing so much in the way of improving relations between capital and labor.

MILWAUKEE SENTINEL, Wis.—Good for the American Federation of Labor! Its three to one vote at Atlanta against a narrow, asinine and Socialistic resolution * * * was a sensible and salutary performance.

GREAT BARRINGTON COURIER, Mass.—This [the rejection of the Socialist resolution] is creditable to the unions and is an indication of the desire of most of them for fair play.

NEW ORLEANS TIMES-DEMOCRAT, La.—The refusal * * * was, in our opinion, wise and altogether commendable.

GALVESTON NEWS, Tex.—It must be gratifying to every friend of organized labor that the resolution * * * was voted down * * * The National Civic Federation strives to be, and it actually is, a body that considers all public questions from every angle at interest. It differs from nearly all other organizations in that it attempts to consider all civic matters from the standpoint of the national interest rather than from that of any class.

VISALIA DELTA, Cal.—The Civic Federation is providing common ground for an intelligent discussion and investigation of the mutual interests of capital and labor, and it would have been regrettable to allow class prejudice to thwart the good work that the Federation will ultimately accomplish for all the people.

BOSTON ADVERTISER, Mass.—Perhaps the most unpopular thing any group of Socialists have attempted for some time was the effort to stop all conferences between employe and employer. * * * The citizens of this country need, and can profit by, peaceful conferences and arbitration as greatly on commercial and industrial questions as by the same methods on questions involving international policies.

CHICAGO RECORD-HERALD, Ill.—This action reflects credit on the Convention. It is a victory for sense and fair play. The resolution was demagogical, foolish and reactionary. It is highly desirable that representative labor men should confer, associate and co-operate as citizens and students with representative employers and representative "neutrals"—lawyers, economists, educators, etc. The National Civic Federation has never antagonized trade unionism and would not know "class consciousness" if it "met it on the street."

ERIE DISPATCH, Pa.—The fact that so decisive a vote was cast on the side of just feeling and common sense in the labor convention will go a great way towards convincing the country of the fair spirit of the members of the American Federation of Labor.

GRAND RAPIDS NEWS, Mich.—It is a matter for gratulation that, by nearly three to one, the American Federation of Labor * * * defeated the firebrand resolution * * * The Michigan Federation of Labor, which * * * adopted a similar resolution, should make a note of this action by the great international body of which it is only one of many subsidiaries.

OMAHA BEE, Neb.—The decisive vote * * * is at once a severe blow to unreasoning radicalism and a tribute to common sense and fair play.

PATERSON PRESS, N. J.—The resolution was wisely defeated, and Messrs. Gompers and Mitchell will continue their association with a body in which they may, by showing a reasonable and broad-minded spirit, be able to do vastly more good to the cause of labor than they could possibly accomplish in the antagonism to it with which the more intolerant element of the labor unions desire to array them.

INDIANAPOLIS NEWS, Ind.—Those who are deeply interested in the trade union movement and believe in it—and it must be remembered that they are not all members of unions—will be gratified by the overwhelming vote * * * by which organized labor refused to repudiate The National Civic Federation.

UTICA PRESS, N. Y.—The decision reached * * * is wise. It is a manifest mistake to try to array labor against an organization like the Civic Federation, which is seeking the solution of problems of this sort, not in the interest of either side alone, but with the hope of promoting the welfare of all concerned.

BOSTON JOURNAL, Mass.—The Federation of Labor has turned the tables on the United Mine Workers. * * * The status to which labor leaders attain in The Civic Federation should be of great definite advantage in adjusting or arbitrating future difficulties between employers and men.

CHRISTIAN SCIENCE MONTHLY, Boston.—Every member of the labor organization should rejoice because those whom they have given a vote of confidence by electing to office seek to broaden the realm of labor by intercourse with thinkers in other lines. * * * If organized labor does not permit its officers to mingle with men on the other side of the question, the situation resolves itself into this: they either do not wish justice established by learning the other side or they are afraid to trust their officials.

GLOVERSVILLE LEADER, N. Y.—* * * the heavy majority recorded * * * shows very conclusively where the bulk of the level-headed labor element stands on the subject.

WASHINGTON STAR, D. C.—That was a highly creditable performance at Atlanta. * * * The vote was nearly three to one, a most healthy sign in a matter of the first importance.

NEWARK STAR, N. J.—Common sense wins in the American Federation of Labor. If the resolution * * * had gone through it would have discredited the Labor Federation and split it hopelessly.

FORT SMITH TIMES-RECORD, Ark.—If the Federation of Labor had voted to taboo The National Civic Federation that action would have been tantamount to a declaration that organized labor has no interest in common with any other class, that it is an Ishmaelite which has its hand raised against every other interest and expects the raising of the hand of every other interest against it.

DALLAS NEWS, Tex.—It must be gratifying to every friend of organized labor that the resolution * * * was voted down.

CAMDEN COURIER, N. J.—The American Federation of Labor wisely rejected the resolution * * * requesting Federation officials to withdraw from The National Civic Federation.

MILWAUKEE JOURNAL, Wis.—The fight that the Socialists made against the Civic Federation * * * grew out of their desire for destruction, which is the chief policy of Socialism as now practised. Everything that is accomplished toward the betterment of the condition of the manual wage-earners is a blow to Socialism, for hope must give way to despair before Socialism can really thrive.

(Continued from Page 27.)

le in a strike a few years ago in which one of largest railroad systems in this country was in- ed. He showed that a conference with the sident of the railroad in question had been ar- ged through President Seth Low of the Civic eration, and that from that day to this the road question has favored organized labor in every t way. The speaker asked whether the fact t hours have been shortened, wages increased, working conditions improved was evidence of fact that labor members of The National Civic eration have been "chloroformed."

he speaker sensed a real danger in the logic in- ved in the resolutions that had been proposed, said that if these were adopted it would set a fectly valid precedent for demanding that the cers of organized labor should be Catholics or testants, Democrats or Socialists.

V. B. WILSON, a delegate from the United Mine rkers of America, pointed out the fact that The ional Civic Federation, in its conciliation work, two very definite and distinct purposes, one ng to provide a forum from which the view- nts of men representing various opinions may presented to the world; and the other to foster far as possible collective bargaining. In each of se purposes he saw much that was of value to anized labor, and he made the point that every resentative of an international trade organiza- n present on the floor of the convention knew t it was good policy to use every means to get close as possible to the heads of corporations ose conduct labor felt was not friendly to its in- ests. "The National Civic Federation," said he, s given us an opportunity of that kind, and we ght to avail ourselves of it."

Lynch's Logical Argument.

AMES M. LYNCH, President of the International pographical Union, said that when he became a mber of The National Civic Federation his or- nization had 35,000 members, and that it now has 000; "all of this," said he, "despite the 'chloro- m' that has been administered to my organiza- n on account of my affiliation with The National vic Federation." Mr. Lynch referred to the fact at those "responsible for the resolutions denounc- g The National Civic Federation had distinguished mpany in the National Association of Manufac- rers," and quoted from certain correspondence of e Manufacturers' Association in support of his atement as follows:

"In this connection I will express the hope that e day is not far distant when The National Civic ederation will clear its literature of the union bel and will stand squarely before the public com- itted absolutely to the interests of all the people, d freed forever from any alliance with the labor ust and from an affiliation with labor union dema- gues."

The speaker advanced the opinion that the propo- tion that was being debated was not so much op- sition to The National Civic Federation as it was position to the labor leaders associating with rtain men belonging to that organization. "If at is good doctrine as applied to The National vic Federation," said he, "it is good doctrine as plied to other associations. If it is good as ap- ied to the Civic Federation, it is good as applied the Newspaper Publishers' Association." Then r. Lynch went on to tell of the splendid results at had been accomplished through the close rela- ons established between the International Typo- aphical Union and the Newspaper Publishers' As- ciation, and he pointed to the fact that the pub- sher of the Los Angeles Times was then and still a member of the Publishers' Association. Mr. nch said that if the line of reasoning that was oposed were adopted, one must conclude that the ternational Typographical Union is making a eat mistake in continuing its relations with the ewspaper Publishers' Association, despite the man- st betterment that had come to his membership rough that association.

Following Mr. Lynch's speech, it was brought out at one of the largest publishing houses in the untry after bitter resistance to the Typographical nion had been brought into harmonious relations th it through John Mitchell when he was Chair- an of the Trade Agreement Department of The ational Civic Federation.

Mr. Mahon's Story of Subway Strike.

The speech of WILLIAM D. MAHON, President of e Amalgamated Association of Street Railway Em- oyes of America, was of unusual interest, including it did the first public statement from the head of e street railway employes' organization of the ots in the subway strike of a few years ago. Mr. ahon's action was a brave one. He minced no ords in showing that the subway management roughout that trouble had lived up to its part of e contract and that it had been the victim of bad ith. The speaker began his recital of the causes leading up to the subway strike with the statement that before the opening of the subway there was on the elevated system in New York an organization of locomotive engineers composed of some 300 men, which had continued in existence after the steam locomotives had been done away with on that road; and further that there were about 100 firemen who had their organization. Immediately prior to the opening of the subway, Mr. Mahon said, these or- ganizations had made demands on the company with- out effect until an appeal had been made to him, and he, through the Civic Federation, had got in touch with the company, and had been able to work out an amicable settlement. With this brief intro- duction, the next step will be told in Mr. Mahon's words:

"That (the threatened trouble referred to) was in the fall of 1904, I believe. We agreed in the sub- way upon a contract for two years. I wanted our men to remain out of that. Our men insisted that that be part of the subway contract, and they signed it. The contract in the subway was made for two years, dating from August, 1905. The next spring when the subway strike, of which so much is said, took place, our organization on the elevated made demands, outlined a new agreement, sent it to our office and had it approved. It was sent back and given to the company. An arrangement was made that prior to the expiration of the agreement confer- ences would be held and the agreement discussed. In the meantime the engineers for some reason, I know not what, and the firemen became dissatisfied and again got into conference with our men. They decided that they would present an ultimatum to the company repudiating the two years' contract that was made the fall before in the subway. They de- cided to go to the company and lay down an ulti- matum at 2 o'clock in the afternoon and give the company until eleven o'clock that night to sign. They were not to notify the International officers, but the Secretary secretly wired me. I did not know he was simply doing it as an individual.

Protest Against Breach of Faith.

"I went on to New York and met the Secretary at noon with the Vice-President of our organization. He notified me that he was going down town to meet the balance of the committee and that they were going to deliver an ultimatum, which he had read to me. I protested and told him it was ridiculous, that the position they were taking was contrary to all the laws of our organization. I appealed to him and the Vice-President to protest to the committee. They went down, but the committees met and presented the ultimatum. If it was not agreed to by eleven o'clock that night they would enter into a strike. They said they knew it was contrary to our laws and contrary to the Brotherhood laws, but that they ex- pected the strike would be won before we could pro- test."

Mr. Mahon then told of further unavailing efforts to avert trouble and of how the strike was called and speedily lost. Commenting on the breach of faith that had caused the strike, he said:

Endorses Mr. Belmont's Action.

"Mr. Belmont had been assured when represen- tatives of the Engineers called on him a few days before, when he wanted to know their position, as he was going away, that nothing would be done un- til he returned. He said, on the other hand, that the Amalgamated had put in their contract and he knew their policy would be to discuss it and work it out. He left New York feeling that the whole situation was one that would be dealt with accord- ing to the laws of the organization. I will not criti- cise Mr. Belmont for the action he took in that strike; it is the position I would have taken, or that any other man would have taken under simillar cirmumstances."

Continuing, Mr. Mahon said: "Mr. Belmont came into the Civic Federation. I was one who, after getting acquainted with him, persuaded him to come in, and we were able to settle many grievances that came up. I went to him on other railroad af- fairs and got him to assist us. I say this in behalf of the subway strike that the delegates may know that some of the stories that have been circulated around the country are absolutely false. The Civic Federation in these matters has given us assist- ance."

Almost all of Mr. Mahon's speech was taken up with concrete instances of valuable aid rendered his organization by The National Civic Federation in placing him in touch with the heads of large traction corporations with results highly beneficial to the street railway men's union in every instance.

T. W. McCULLOUGH held that the whole ques- tion in dispute was, "Shall we keep in touch with our employers?" Mr. McCulough thought that or- ganized labor should keep in touch. "We are called into existence," he said, "to represent the workers of America, to have their interests in our charge, and to take up matters in contention with employ- ers from time to time. There is not a minute that we are not in contact with the employers on one question or another concerning our employment. The Civic Federation has opened an avenue where the employer and employe can meet on a ground that is as nearly neutral as any that has as yet been suggested. Shall we then close that avenue of opportunity?"

Mr. Healy's Pertinent Observation.

TIMOTHY HEALY, President of the International Brotherhood of Stationary Firemen, expressed the opinion that if the men who were attacking The National Civic Federation had investigated the work it is doing the resolutions that were being debated would never have been presented. "I have thought," said he, "while listening to the discussion here to- day, that if Mr. Parry, Mr. Post, Mr. Kirby and Mr. Walter Drew were here, they would have applauded vociferously some of our orators." Mr. Healy very effectively unmasked the Socialism lurking in the denunciatory resolutions that were being consid- ered, and he advised fledgeling delegates to beware of the Socialist "chloroform."

"No Surrender of Conviction."

PRESIDENT GOMPERS, of the American Federa- tion of Labor, spoke at length in unmasking the mo- tives impelling the Socialists in presenting the reso- lutions under discussion. He said that there was nothing the American Federation of Labor could do to satisfy those gentlemen short of turning the or- ganization over to them.

"There is a sort of reason," said Mr. Gompers, "misnamed a philosophy, upon which all this an- tagonism is based. It is the idea that the working people must get into a condition of abject poverty and misery and by a cataclysm, called a social revo- lution, 'come into their own and take charge of so- ciety and government.' As if an impoverished peo- ple ever really made for constructive revolution! The poorer the people the more abject they become. There may be a revolt, like a riot and a flash in the pan, but the constructive, constant work, day by day, hour by hour, and year after year, is the work in which the trades unionist is engaged."

The speaker said that The National Civic Federa- tion had never adopted a proposition affecting the rights of labor unless the men of labor approved, and that one vote cast against any such proposition by a representative of labor would be sufficient to defeat it. This was in answer to the criticism that organized labor composed only one-third of the Executive Committee of the Federation.

Continuing, Mr. Gompers said: "As a matter of fact, every man who attends these meetings of the Civic Federation knows that we meet there without surrendering one jot of our judgment or our con- victions or our faith in the justice of our cause. When we meet these people we endeavor to drive home the claims of labor. They do not often get this otherwise, and now the proposition is that they shall not get it at all!"

JAMES DUNCAN, President of the Granite Cut- ters' International Association of America, closed the debate in a strong speech in which he called to the attention of the United Mine Workers' organization the fact that he had first heard of the Civic Federa- tion through a good turn it had done that organiza- tion.

The report of the Resolutions Committee reject- ing the proposed criticism of The National Civic Federation was adopted by a vote of 11,851 to 4,924, practically three to one

---

MR. MARKS PROVES EFFICIENT ARBITER

(Continued from Page 25.)

refer the earnings seem to give satisfaction to the workers, and the cost is not objected to by the em- ployer. Allowing for a difference in grade and avoid- ing the technicalities of specific variations in mater- ial, color and weight, I have decided to establish an *average price*, leaving it to the fairness of the Del- ohery Hat Company and their employes to treat equit- ably any exceptional situation that may arise during the next six months, for which this decision estab- lishes the piece-price.

"The uniform piece-price for 'starting' and for 'siz- ing,' which my study of the situation brings me to conclude will be fair in the Delohery shop, is 32 cents per dozen for starting and 80 cents per dozen for siz- ing. This price to be retroactive from October 13, 1911, which is the date when the Manufacturers' Asso- ciation and the union agreed to refer this dispute to an arbitrator selected by The National Civic Federa- tion.

"In the interest of the individual employer and em- ploye herewith concerned, and in the greater interests of the hat industry of Danbury and Bethel, I trust that the men and their employers may work together in the proper spirit, aiming at friendly co-operation, which makes for mutual success. I hope that all per- sonal differences will sink into insignificance in con- sideration of the importance of conserving and de- veloping the greater prestige and prosperity of the cities of Danbury and Bethel. Very sincerely yours,

(Signed) "MARCUS M. MARKS, Arbitrator.

"New York City, November 28, 1911."

SOCIALISM AND THE NATIONAL CIVIC FEDERATION

CORRESPONDENCE BETWEEN MESSRS. MORRIS HILLQUIT AND R. M. EASLEY.

THERE is reproduced herewith some recent correspondence between Mr. Morris Hillquit (member of the National Executive Committee of the Socialist Party and Secretary of the International Socialist Bureau) and Mr. R. M. Easley, (Chairman of the Executive Council of The National Civic Federation) on the attitude of the Socialists toward The National Civic Federation. That attitude is well represented by the following quotation from Mr. Hillquit's letter:

"The game played by the Civic Federation is the shrewdest yet devised by the employers of any country. * * * To the organized labor movement the policy of the Civic Federation is the most subtle and insidious poison. It robs it of its independence, virility and militant enthusiasm; it hypnotizes or corrupts its leaders, weakens its ranks and demoralizes its fights. The Socialist Party is employing all efforts at its command to save American labor from the "benign" influence of The National Civic Federation, hence there is so little love between the two organizations."

MR. HILLQUIT'S LETTER.

320 Broadway, New York, June 16, 1911.

My Dear Mr. Easley—Many thanks for the proof of your pamphlet and the expression of your confidence in my fairness. I have read the outline of the work and plans of your Federation with great interest, particularly those portions which relate to the attitude of your organization toward the labor movement and its problems, and as you rightly predicted, it does not meet with my approval.

It would be difficult to find two other movements so diametrically opposed to each other in principle and methods as are those represented by The National Civic Federation and the Socialist Party. Both movements have their inception in the struggles between capital and labor, but here their similarity ends. The Socialist leaders consider these struggles as inseparably inherent in the present form of industrial organization. They contend that under a system of private and competing industries there is and always must be a conflict of economic interests between the workers and their employers. The smaller the worker's wages, the larger the employer's profits, hence the employer in the natural course of business always strives to secure the utmost labor for the least pay, while the worker as naturally strives to sell his labor for the largest price obtainable. This strife is a chronic social disease, ever present, ever active. The Labor Union and the Employers' Association are its permanent organized forms; the strike and the lockout, the boycott and the blacklist are only the symptoms of its acuter phases. It is a fight to a finish, and one of the two contending sides must ultimately win out. The final victory of capital would mean universal enslavement and national decadence, the triumph of labor would mean social harmony and progress. The Socialists, therefore, frankly and unreservedly ally themselves with the forces of labor in all its struggles against capital. They seek to increase the fighting efficiency of the workers by educating them to a sense of their class solidarity and by organizing them into a compact, independent and class-conscious body, industrially and politically.

Attacks Efforts for Harmony.

The National Civic Federation, on the other hand, regards the struggles between the workers and their employers as purely accidental, as results of deplorable misunderstandings. Its social philosophy is based upon an assumed harmony of interests between the exploiting capitalists and the exploited workers, and its policy is to bring the two classes together, to patch up their differences, to gloss over their struggles. This is the express function of your Industrial Conciliation, Industrial Economics and Employers' Welfare Departments, and the implied purpose of your annual "harmony dinners."

The game played by the Civic Federation is the shrewdest yet devised by the employers of any country. It takes nothing from capital, it gives nothing to labor, and does it all with such an appearance of boundless generosity, that some of the more guileless diplomats in the labor movements are actually overwhelmed by it.

Take your stand on Workmen's Compensation. It is characteristic of your Federation. The pamphlet, of which you have been kind enough to send me the proof, summarizes the subject in the following language: "To all employers of labor it is of the highest importance that a fair and equitable compensation law be placed on the statutes of our various industrial States in place of the present liability laws. *If this is not done, the workingmen will insist on legislation which will sweep away all the defenses of the employer*, leaving him at the mercy of jury decisions in suits pressed by shyster, ambulance-chasing lawyers."

Activities Are "Cheap and Trivial."

What is really meant by this eloquent and touching admonition is about this: The workers of this country have recently begun to show signs of revolt against our barbaric system of law, which practically gives them no redress for injuries sustained in the course of their employment. They are discussing and formulating demands for radical legislative reforms on this subject, and there is danger that this agitation may give rise to a powerful political labor movement along Socialist lines. To forestall this dire possibility, the watchful Civic Federation has drafted a measure of its own, a "Compensation" Act that would not compensate the workers, nor hurt the employers, and now it seeks to divert the movement of the workers into the shallow channels thus created by it. And so it is with all other "reforms" of the Federation. They are cheap and trivial, and their main purpose is to avert the threatening revolt of the workers. To the organized labor movement the policy of the Civic Federation is the most subtle and insidious poison. It robs it of its independence, virility and militant enthusiasm; it hypnotizes or corrupts its leaders, weakens its ranks, and demoralizes its fights. The Socialist Party is employing all efforts at its command to save American labor from the 'benign" influence of The National Civic Federation, hence there is so little love betwen the two organizations.

Very truly yours,
(Signed) Morris Hillquit.

MR. EASLEY'S REPLY.

New York City, July 21, 1911.

My Dear Mr. Hillquit:—I have your letter of June 16, in which you express, frankly and fully, your views in regard to the purpose and work of The National Civic Federation. I had hoped to have replied to it sooner, but absence from the city, necessitating the disposal on my return of much accumulated work, has delayed me until now. Also, as your letter fairly represented much of the general opposition that has been expressed by leading Socialists to the Civic Federation, I felt it my duty to go more fully into the history and scope of the work of the Federation than could have been done in a brief and hasty response.

My first thought on reading your letter was that, were it not an act of discourtesy to you and were my relations with Mr. Kirby, the President of the National Association of Manufacturers, sufficiently intimate to permit, I should like to send it to him. As you probably know, Mr. Kirby is expending a great deal of his surplus time and energy in abusing The National Civic Federation, because, as he says, "it is dominated entirely by and run in the interest of the Gompers-Mitchell Labor Trust, the most infamous of all the trusts." In one issue of an official organ of a manufacturers' organization the declaration was made that "Gompers and Mitchell dictate every policy of the Federation in the interest of the American Federation of Labor and against employers," and the further declaration was made that the writer of this letter is "a paid walking delegate for Gompers." At the annual meeting of the Manufacturers' Association, held a few weeks ago, President Kirby repeated his well-known views on The National Civic Federation, saying, among other things:

President Kirby's, Sentiments.

"My opposition to it [The National Civic Federation] has been relentless, however, and will be relentless, because of its close alignment with the dominating influences of labor unionism. * * * The American Federation of Labor is engaged in an open warfare against Jesus Christ and his cause. Analyze it as you may, you can make nothing else out of it, and those who profess Christ, yet *hobnob with the leaders of that wicked conspiracy and give them encouragement by eating and drinking and smoking and holding social relations with them, cannot segregate themselves from the responsibility that attaches to such affiliation*. On this issue, therefore, I challenge The National Civic Federation to disprove my charges, and if my *conservatism* is denounced as *radicalism*, then my mind goes back to Los Angeles, and I take refuge in the stand of Martin Luther: 'Here I stand; I can do nothing else; God help me!'"

These utterances were applauded by the members of the Manufacturers' Association, who showed their confidence in Mr. Kirby by shortly afterward unanimously re-electing him president; so, it must be inferred that his views on The National Civic Federation, so expressed, were endorsed by the members of the Association, and were not simply the views of President Kirby.

The National Association of Manufacturers not only represents three thousand employers, numbering among them some of the largest employers in the country, but it also includes among its sympathizers other employers who are anti-trade union to the core. Some of the latter denounce The National Civic Federation on the very ground taken by Mr. Kirby, namely, that it is conducted in the interest of organized labor. The president of a very large corporation stated last summer to a member of the Federation that, "had it not been for The National Civic Federation, we (the manufacturers) would have smashed every union in this country two years ago. It (The National Civic Federation) has played up Gompers, Mitchell, Stone, Morrissey and other labor leaders to such an extent at their meetings and banquets that these men now think they are our equals."

From another employer, who received a circular letter, inviting him into membership in The National Civic Federation, a reply was received from which I quote: "No, sir, I will not join The National Civic Federation. I regard it as one of the most insidious schemes ever concocted to promote the damnable practices of the trade unions, including the closed shop, the boycott and the slugging of non-uion men. The very letter you sent me has on it the union label, the badge of slavery. It is an insult to ask any employer to join such an association."

I might go on, my dear Mr. Hillquit, quoting pages of such matter, attacking the Federation because "it is run in the interest of organized labor."

Yet, on the other hand, you charge in your letter that "the game played by the Civic Federation is the shrewdest yet devised by the employers of any country. * * * To the organized labor movement the policy of the Civic Federation is the most subtle and insidious poison. It robs it of its independence, virility and militant enthusiasm; it hypnotizes or corrupts its leaders, weakens its ranks, and demoralizes its fights. The Socialist Party is employing all efforts at its command to save American labor from the 'benign' influence of The National Civic Federation, hence there is so little love between the two organizations."

"Some One Is Mistaken."

Now, it is evident that some one is mistaken. The positions taken by the National Association of Manufacturers, as represented by President Kirby, on the one hand, and by the Socialist Party, as stated by yourself, on the other, are irreconcilable.

Who is right?

The fact is, both are wrong.

If either view is correct, The National Civic Federation ought not to exist; and if either view is correct, men who voluntarily give much time and thought to the work of the Federation—like President Seth Low, for example, who is neither an employer nor a member of a labor union—would no longer wish to be connected with it.

Without undertaking in a letter to discuss all the matters included in your sweeping indictment of The National Civic Federation, there are some points that directly affect the integrity of its work upon which I should like to touch. In doing this, let me say that I am writing to you in my personal capacity and not as an official of The National Civic Federation, as, I take it, you wrote to me in your personal capacity and not officially as a member of the National Executive Commitee of the Socialist Party nor as the Secreary to the International Socialist Bureau.

Let us begin, for instance, with the charge that the Civic Federation was organized as a shrewd game in the interest of the employers. If there were any truth in that allegation, some evidence of it would certainly have been discovered by some of the members of Mr. Kirby's organization, and it would also have been apparent somewhere in the inception of the movement. I am enclosing a printed sheet, containing the original prospectus of The National Civic Federation, which was published in June, 1900, at a time when, I think you will admit, Socialism had not cut much figure in this country and when very few people outside of its limited membership knew anything about it.

Origin of Federation Idea.

The idea of a National Civic Federation grew out a National Conference on Combinations and Trusts, held at Chicago, in September, 1899, under the auspices of the Civic Federation of Chicago, an organization dealing only with municipal reforms. This conference was attended by some five hundred delegates sent by the Governors of the States and by organizations of every description, including Single Taxers, Socialists and Anarchists, Messrs A. M. Simons and Thomas J. Morgan representing the Socialists, and Mrs. Benjamin R. Tucker and George A. Schilling, the Anarchists. The fact that Socialism and Anarchism were little understood at that time is evidenced by the fact of their representatives being invited to participate in this conference.

m the prospectus which I enclose you will ob- that it was the purpose of The National Civic ation:

"To provide for study and discussion of ques- s of national import affecting either the for- ı or domestic policy of the United States, to in the crystallization of the most enlight- d public sentiment of the country in respect reto, and, when desirable, to promote neces- y legislation in accordance therewith."

ı will also observe that the By-Laws provided tanding committees on the following subjects, ı order named: FOREIGN RELATIONS, INSU- AFFAIRS, BANKING AND CURRENCY, IN- RIAL COMBINATIONS, INTERSTATE AND IGN COMMERCE, CONSULAR AND DIPLO- C SERVICE, MILITARY AND NAVAL AF- S, LABOR, EDUCATION, IMMIGRATION, ICIPAL GOVERNMENT, TAXATION, CIVIL ICE, INDIAN AFFAIRS, THE NEGRO QUES-

e Chairman of the Committee on Organization, Franklin H. Head, who was also the first presi- of the Federation, said at the time of the or- zation:

he manufacturers have their national organiza- and meet annually to discuss questions that af- their special interests; the agriculturalists have national grange meetings and farmers' con- ses to discuss their interests; the great labor es of the country have their annual meetings ted to their special questions; also the National cers' Association, American Bar Association, rican Economic and Social Science associations, great church bodies, mercantile, trade and traffic ciations, and many other strictly class organiza- s meet annually or oftener to discuss their ous interests, while the object of The National c Federation, in addition to creating departments tudy national problems, will be to provide a na- al forum, by means of which representatives of these great divisions of society may come to- er and discuss the problems in which all have a mon interest. There are many such to-day, outside olitical questions, in the solution of which such ody may assist in an educational way. The meet- ı will be held annually, or as often as conditions gest, and in different localities. The organiza- will be absolutely non-partisan. That there is eld for such an organization is evidenced by the ı hundred acceptances received on the Advisory ıncil and the hearty endorsement of the plan tained therein."

think that this ought to convince you that The tional Civic Federation was not a "scheme or- ized in the interest of the employers of the coun- ," nor for the purpose of "averting the threatening olt of the workers." In fact, as you will observe, the fifteen subjects to be considered only one re- ed to the Labor question.

How Labor Question Came In.

n order to make clear how the Federation af- ward became so prominently identified with the oor question, allow me to explain that, on a refer- lum vote of the Advisory Council, consisting of ı hundred members, whose names are on the en- sed sheet, it was decided that the first three ques- ns to be taken up should be Taxation, Municipal nership, and Industrial Conciliation and Arbitra- n. The Conciliation question was especially per- ent because of the great coal strike in the Fall of t year. Accordingly, a conference on Industrial nciliation and Arbitration was called, and took ce in December, 1900, at which time the Indus- al Department of The National Civic Federation s organized, with A. C. Bartlett, of Chicago, as airman. The following May a National Confer- e on Taxation was held at Buffalo, to which con- ence three hundred delegates were sent by the vernors of the various States and by commercial, icultural, manufacturing and labor organizations. ter two days' discussion, the Department on Tax- on was organized, with Professor E. R. A. Selig- n as Chairman and Professor John R. Commons Secretary. It was at that time intended to hold October, 1901, a National Conference on Munici- l Ownership, but so much work had developed in ı Industrial Department, through threatened ikes in the anthracite coal industry, a large strike the steel industry, and strikes on street railways several cities, that the time of the Executive icers was taken up, and the Municipal Ownership nference was for the time abandoned. In De- mber, 1901, the first annual meeting of the Indus- al Department was held, and at that time the late nator Hanna was made Chairman. Among the mbers of the Executive Committee of his Depart- nt were Bishop Henry C. Potter and Grover eveland, now deceased, and Charles M. Schwab, muel Gompers and John Mitchell. This meeting turally attracted great attention in the press, and s fact, together with Senator Hanna's strong per- nality, pitched the whole movement, so far as the public was concerned, upon industrial lines. It was not until two years later that the Federation got back to its broader work. The program of work which is described in the proof sent you is different from that announced in the original prospectus of the Federation in 1900, but this is only the difference between theory and practice. We are making prac- tical headway with the questions we are working on to-day, and they better suit the temperament and activities of our members than the original list of subjects. So much by way of history.

Enumeration of "Trivialities."

You say, in speaking of the "reforms" of the Fed- eration, that "they are cheap and trivial," and that their main purpose is "to avert the threatening re- volt of the workers." I cannot think, Mr. Hillquit, that you have read with care the matter sent to you.

Is it "cheap and trivial" to organize a movement to help put a stop to the sale of impure food stuffs and adulterated drugs to the masses of our people, helpless to protect themselves against such fraud? While in the last four years, under the Federal and State Pure Food and Drug Laws, tremendous head- way has been made in accomplishing this purpose, a great deal remains to be done, as stated in the pamphlet (of which you had the proof) herewith sent to you, and only by a determined and or- ganized effort, both Federal and State, can the re- forms be effected.

Is it "cheap and trivial" to work, in conjunction with the American Bar Association, of which I think you are a member, to secure reforms in legal procedure which will enable working people and the poor of all classes to obtain redress of grievances cheaply and expeditiously; and which will assist the laboring classes in suits against employers in the matter of accidents, breach of contract, et cetera?

Is it "cheap and trivial" to work for uniformity among the States on the regulation of combinations and trusts, and for co-ordination between the States and the Federal Government, on matters where there now is conflict, when amending the Sherman Act is regarded as of such great importance to organized labor? Under both Federal and State courts, de- cisions have been rendered, as you know, which organized labor believes strike at the vitals of that movement.

Is it "cheap and trivial" to attempt to get reform in taxation methods in view of the present chaotic conditions and incessant conflict between the States? The relation of the problem of taxation to the con- gestion problem of New York City is too well known by you to make it necessary for me to amplify this point.

Is it "cheap and trivial" to work to secure better regulation of trust companies, loan associations and savings banks? In many States, as you know, the savings of the poor are left with little or no pro- tection, and we have recently had plenty of illustra- tions in this city alone of the lack of proper regula- tion of State banks and trust companies.

Is it "cheap and trivial" to undertake a movement for the purpose of bringing into harmony forty-six States on the many important questions of the day, when, unless such harmonious action can be secured by the States, so many great problems will be thrown upon the central Government that it will, sooner or later, break down? The central Government, you will admit, is already overburdened. So important did this movement appear to the Governors of the various States that, in most instances where State Councils were organized, the Governors themselves presided and the meetings were held at the State Houses. In this matter of uniform State legislation not only are the working men vitally concerned, but also the farmers, the manufacturers, the bankers, the merchants and the lawyers. The working men and women are greatly interested in uniform State legislation in respect to such matters as Child Labor, the Shorter Work Day for Women, Prevention of Accidents in Mines and Factories, Factory Inspec- tion, Workmen's Compensation, and Prison Labor. As a lawyer, if not as a Socialist, I am sure you ap- preciate the great importance of the movement the Federation has initiated for securing uniform State Legislation. The Conference of Commissioners on Uniform State Laws, organized some twenty years ago by the American Bar Association, has testified to the aid it has received from The National Civic Federation in its last annual report, a marked copy of which I send to you. The Commissioners do not think our work is "cheap and trivial" in this matter; neither do I believe that you will do so after glanc- ing through the Uniform State Legislation number of THE NATIONAL CIVIC FEDERATION REVIEW, which I am sending you with this letter.

Some Delay in Socialism's Utopia.

I could continue this interrogatory through all the various subjects with which the Federation is deal- ing, but those I have mentioned are of especial im- port to the working people. You will certainly not deny that the reforms proposed are needed. If you say, "Yes, they are needed, but the Federation is not going to work in the right way," I will ask you to tell me how the Socialist Party proposes to bring about such reforms in our day. I may not be cor- rectly informed but, looking over the Socialist plat- form, the main remedy that I find which that plat- form offers for any of the evils above referred to is the collective ownership and operation by the Government of all means of production and distri- bution and of land. In other words, if we can wait until the Socialist Party has captured the govern- ments of this country, Federal, State and Municipal, and has taken over all the factories, stores, railways, banks, mines and farms, a solution will be furnished of such problems. In fact, many of the leading So- cialist writers put off the day until all the govern- ments of the world shall have been captured. From the cursory reading that I have been able to give to Socialist literature, I gather that the leaders of the party themselves do not expect such a state of af- fairs to be brought about in our time nor in the time of our children, nor even in the time of our children's children. But, my dear Mr. Hillquit, should the peo- ple be obliged to wait until that time for reforms, admitting—which I do not—that such a change would mean reform? The progress that has been made in the last decade alone is so tremendous that every one must feel proud of what has been accomplished. I do not mean to say that there is not much still to be done, a great deal, in fact; but the hundreds and thousands of men and women in this country who have enlisted in the warfare against economic and industrial evils, through the various reform organiza- tions, are a guarantee that the next decade is going to see still further accomplishments and that we shall not need to tear everything up and begin all over again.

I was particularly interested in the paragraph in your letter which you offered as an evidence that the Civic Federation is playing a shrewd game devised by the employers of the country. I quote:

> "Take your stand on the Workmen's Compen- sation. It is characteristic of your Federation. The pamphlet, of which you have been kind enough to send me the proof, summarizes the subject in the following language: 'To all em- ployers of labor it is of the highest importance that a fair and equitable compensation law be placed on the statutes of our various industrial States in place of the present liability laws. *If this is not done, the workingmen will insist on legislation which will sweep away all the de- fenses of the employer,* leaving him at the mercy of jury decisions in suits pressed by shyster, ambulance-chasing lawyers.'"

Now, I might paraphrase your sentence and retort as follows: "Take your *criticism* on our Workmen's Compensation Bill. It is characteristic of much of the *criticism* of the Federation by its enemies." But I won't. I prefer to assume that you did not read our pamphlet carefully, because the very next sen- tence (which you failed to quote) says:

> 'The leaders of labor in this country are fair in the matter and prefer compensation laws with definite awards enabling workmen to secure all that is legally due them *at the time they need it*, and without risking lawsuits, finally resulting in no compensation, or, if decided in their favor, from 30 to 50 per cent of the amount allowed by the verdict."

Labor Endorses Compensation Act.

I think that you will admit that this is a correct statement of the position of the leaders of labor or- ganizations in this country. At any rate, the com- pensation act which you state "would not compen- sate the workers or hurt the employers" was en- dorsed by the Executive Council of the American Federation of Labor and by many other labor bodies. Mr. John Mitchell, who was a member of the New York State Commission on this subject, and who has probably given more careful study to it than any other labor representative in this country, helped to prepare this bill. I hardly think you will contend that such men are not competent to speak for the wants and needs of labor; and, if I am not mistaken, you were on the Joint Labor Conference on Work- men's Compensation of Greater New York, which declared for the adoption of the compensation prin- ciple, and which did not oppose the Wainwright Bill that did not go nearly so far as our bill.

In all events, there is more difficulty in getting employers to see that it is to their interest to sub- stitute compulsory compensation for the liability prin- ciple than there is in getting the intelligent labor leaders to see that it is to their interest. The latter, in fact, saw it long ago and in every civilized coun- try, except our own, organized labor has, as you know, already brought about the change which The National Civic Federation is helping it to effect in this country. The Federation's Department on Com- pensation is made up of six hundred representative employers, wage-earners, political economists, law- yers and publicists who, after a year's study, formulated the model compensation bill which recognizes the principle that industry should bear the burden. It followed the lines of the law drafted at the request of the trades unions of England and I am sure, Mr. Hillquit, that no Socialist, in his most excited moment, will claim that the Civic Federation got in any of its "insidious work" on that law.

Purposeful Welfare Work.

While some of our departments are composed of employers, wage-earners, lawyers, farmers and representatives of all classes, there are two departments whose membership is composed entirely of the employing class, to wit: the Employers' Welfare Department and the Woman's Welfare Department, the latter consisting of the wives, daughters and other relatives of employers, and also women stockholders in industrial plants. The efforts of these two departments are directed toward interesting employers, whether public or private, in improving the conditions under which employes in all industries work and live. In promoting this work, it is clearly recognized that the first essentials to the welfare of employes are steady work, a fair wage and reasonable hours of labor; but that the employer has a further obligation. It is this further obligation that the two Welfare Departments are trying to get employers to discharge. They have nothing to do with the question of unionism or non-unionism, but take up those matters which relate to the physical and social well-being of employes.

Some of the subjects involved in this work are:

Sanitary Work Places: Systems for providing pure drinking water; for ventilation, including the cooling of superheated places, and devices for exhausting dust and removing gases; for lighting work places; and for safeguards against industrial accidents; wash rooms, with hot and cold water, towels and soap; shower baths and racks to dry damp garments for molders and stationary firemen; emergency hospitals; locker rooms; seats for women; laundries for men's overalls or women's uniforms; the use of elevators for women, and luncheon rooms.

Recreation: The social hall for dancing parties, concerts, theatricals, billiards, pool or bowling; the gymnasium, athletic field, roof garden, vacations and summer excursions for employes, and rest rooms or trainmen's rest houses.

Educational: Classes for apprentices; in cooking, dressmaking, millinery; first aid to the injured; night classes for technical training; kindergartens and libraries.

Housing: Homes rented or sold to employes, and boarding houses.

Provident Funds: Include employers' plans for savings or lending money in times of stress, as well as all forms of industrial insurance.

Many union leaders have applied to the Welfare Departments for aid in securing improvements in sanitary conditions. They state that, as their energies are largely devoted to securing changes in wage scales, they welcome outside assistance in obtaining welfare features.

I am sure that, if you could spend a day in this office looking over the work of these departments, you could scarcely withhold from it your commendation. I can hardly believe that you would want to say that men and women wage-earners should continue to work under insanitary conditions, which can be and are being improved daily, until such time as the Socialist Party can bring about its collective ownership and operation of all means of production and distribution and land. At any rate, I think I am safe in saying that 99 per cent of the wage-earners of the country would decide that they would rather have their conditions improved *now*.

The Industrial Economics Department, as its name implies, is one which promotes discussion upon economic questions. It does not attempt to pass resolutions, nor does it attempt to bring people together who can agree, but rather to bring people together who do not agree. At the present time it is arranging for a Commission to make a thorough study of the so-called "Efficiency" proposition which has so captivated the magazines and the press of the country. This department does not accept at one hundred cents on the dollar all the claims that are being made for or against this proposition. The Commission to investigate this subject will include not only employers who advocate the "Taylor System," but employers who have tried it and claim that it is a failure; also members of labor organizations and, last but not least, members of the medical profession who will study the physical and nervous effect produced on the worker by the pace-making part of the scheme. This phase of the subject has been entirely neglected in the discussions in all the popular magazines, whereas it is regarded by many persons as a very important one. A report on the subject by a committee of trade unionists, or manufacturers, or political economists, or doctors, alone, would not be convincing, but a committee made up of all these classes will be pretty apt to bring out all that is good in the plan, as well as to show what is bad in it. This, I am sure, you will not insist is a "cheap and trivial" matter.

Wants "Insidious Poison" Designated.

You say that the Civic Federation, through instilling "subtle and insidious poison," has "robbed the labor movement of its independence, virility and militant enthusiasm." Will you kindly point out in what respect this indictment is true? I invite you to read carefully all the utterances of the labor leaders at the meetings of The National Civic Federation, and I request you to point to one utterance that, by fair interpretation, supports your charge. The Civic Federation is the one place where every member speaks his mind freely, and where a practically unanimous vote is required to make any measure effective. I cannot recall a time when the Executive Committee of The National Civic Federation has ever taken a vote on any matter while in session. Discussion either leads to unanimous agreement or the matter is dropped. Matters are frequently submitted to the Executive Committee by mail, action being taken only when the vote is unanimous. So there is no way for the labor members to be out-voted or duped by the employers or the representatives of the public. The Civic Federation is effective only when it can present a solid front, and there are so many great reforms demanded to-day, upon which all agree, that the questions where differences arise can well be dropped until such time as an agreement can be reached.

If your theory is correct about the hypnotic powers of the capitalists of the Federation, those hypnotic powers certainly were not in good working order when the United States Steel controversy came along. If you can conceive of more things that the American Federation of Labor could have done or tried to do in its fight against the United States Steel Corporation, your imagination is certainly good; and yet the labor members of the Civic Federation are abused by many Socialists for being "hypnotized through hobnobbing and wining and dining with the United States Steel officials." Parenthetically, let me admit that in that same controversy the Federation met one of its great defeats. Its officers, from the President down, including that great ogre of the Socialists, Andrew Carnegie, did everything in their power to bring about a satisfactory settlement, but failed.

Labor's Virile Brand of "Impotency."

I can imagine that the presidents of our great railway systems, "Baron" coal operators, the big builders of the country who deal with thirty-five separate international unions, the publishers of the great dailies and of the weekly and monthly magazines, not to speak of other captains of industry, would smile audibly when told that labor organizations have become impotent. After the Civic Federation had robbed these labor leaders of their "independence, virility and militant enthusiasm" they seem to have retained enough of these virtues to secure a good many millions of dollars in wages and better conditions from the railroad corporations; to secure from the anthracite coal operators alone in 1902 a 10 per cent increase in wages and the sliding scale, which has since netted the miners an additional $30,000,000, in round numbers, to say nothing of a batch of improvements in working conditions too numerous to mention. In the building trade—well—there is an eight-hour day to start with, generally a closed shop and wages that make the bank clerk, the school teacher, the preacher and the average college professor turn green with envy. In the printing world there are the eight-hour day, the closed shop, and an agreement between the publishers of the dailies and the International Typographical Union which has resulted in many wage increases during the past ten years, and the vigorous, successful two-year fight at a cost of $5,000,000 put up by the Typographical Union to secure the eight-hour day in the weekly and monthly publication establishments. And yet in most of those instances officials on both sides of the controversy "hobnobbed and wined and dined together at the Civic Federation's annual meetings and banquets." If the "hypnotic influences" were at work, surely those to do the complaining are not the unions nor the Socialists, but the employers. And may I add a word here in favor of those much-abused "wining and dining" banquets? In the first place, the Federation never had any wine at its banquets, although any guest has been at liberty to order it at his own expense, just as at any other banquet whether a "capitalist," "labor" or "socialist" affair. In the second place, and what is more interesting, some of the most important settlements of labor controversies, which led to improvement in conditions and wages, were initiated at these very banquets, the opposing parties being placed at the same table.

Socialism's "General Strike" Theory.

If by loss of "virility and militant enthusiasm" you mean that the labor organizations are learning to strike less and to resort more and more to methods of conciliation, conference and business negotiations with their employers, then the credit, I must say, is not due to The National Civic Federation, but to the increasing sanity and intelligent business methods adopted by the union organizations and the great railway brotherhoods, which methods experience has shown to be fairly successful. If the Federation has contributed in any degree to this result, it is thankful. It is only the new and raw recruits, plus the revolutionary Socialists within the ranks of the labor movement, who any longer talk about the 'general strike" and the proposal "to tie up all industry" on the slightest provocation.

In regard to your implication that the Civic Federation is concerned about a possible agitation which "may give rise to a powerful political labor movement along Socialist lines" and which the Civic Federation probably is sitting up at night worrying about, I want to say this: If you take the five thousand members, in round numbers, of The National Civic Federation, and subtract the organized labor members and a small percentage of political economists, I think you will find that not many of the remaining members would know what you were talking about. You can take any thousand business men in the United States, and I will make the bold prediction that not more than ten of them have the slightest interest in or conception of what the Socialists are doing and saying. As a rule, they classify the Socialists with the Populists, the Single Taxers, and frequently with the Anarchists. They are infinitely more concerned to-day about the "insurgency" movement, which bears no relation to Socialism, than they are about Socialism.

I do not mean to imply by this that the members of the Federation or the business men of the country generally are ignorant, nor that I share their indifference; but the simple fact is that you haven't got along far enough to attract their attention. They are not scared by the "Milwaukee Revolution," because that seems to imply that Socialism is only another name for municipal reform, and many of those reforms are reforms which have been advocated for years by other people who have no use for the doctrines of Socialism.

Several years ago, I was myself quite excited over Socialism, and wrote some very "able philippics" on the fifty-seven varieties of Socialism, much of which matter I found afterward was not true. Instead of "fifty-seven varieties," I found that there was at that time really only one, the simon-pure Marxian revolutionary Socialism. To-day, I believe the main division is between Karl Marx Marxites and the anti-Karl Marx Marxites; in other words, the "revolutionary Marxites" and the "palliative Marxites," the latter supporting propositions that may eventually enable them to help The National Civic Federation in some of the reforms it is seeking.

The National Civic Federation itself once had a committee to study Socialism in this country. It sent out an appeal for money to make this study. If the Socialists only knew how meagre was the response to that appeal and could see some of the letters received in reply, they would not feel greatly alarmed over an attack from that quarter. In fact, the committee dropped the subject and took up other questions in which the people seemed more interested.

"Corruption" of Labor Leaders.

I doubt if you mean all that your words imply by your statement that the leaders of labor are either hypnotized or corrupted by their association with The National Civic Federation. I quote here your entire sentence:

> "To the organized labor movement the policy of the Civic Federation is the most subtle and insidious poison. It robs it of its independence, virility and militant enthusiasm; it hypnotizes or corrupts its leaders, weakens its ranks and demoralizes its fights."

I know that there are minor branches of the Socialist movement which make sweeping charges against anything or anybody not agreeing with them, but I am amazed that a national officer of the Socialist Party should do this.

The following national labor men are on the Executive Committee of The National Civic Federation:

SAMUEL GOMPERS (President American Federation of Labor), Washington, D. C.

WARREN S. STONE (Grand Chief International Brotherhood of Locomotive Engineers), Cleveland, Ohio.

JAMES M. LYNCH (President International Typographical Union), Indianapolis, Ind.

A. B. GARRETSON (President Order of Railway Conductors), Cedar Rapids, Iowa.

JAMES DUNCAN (General Secretary Granite Cutters' International Association of America), Quincy, Mass.

W. G. LEE (President Brotherhood Railroad Trainmen), Cleveland, Ohio.

WILLIAM D. MAHON (President Amalgamated Association of Street Railway Employes of America), Detroit, Mich.

TIMOTHY HEALY (President International Brotherhood of Stationary Firemen), New York City.

W. S. CARTER (President Brotherhood Locomotive Firemen and Enginemen), Peoria, Ill.

IEL J. TOBIN (President International Brotherhood of Teamsters), Indianapolis, Ind.
. CHASE (Editor "Railway Trainmen's Journal"), Cleveland, Ohio.
N F. TOBIN (General President Boot and Shoe Workers' Union), Boston, Mass.
PH F. VALENTINE (President Iron Molders' Union of North America), Cincinnati, Ohio.
IS A. HAYES (President Glass Bottle Blowers' Association of United States and Canada), Philadelphia, Pa.
LIAM D. HUBER (President United Brotherhood of Carpenters and Joiners of America), Indianapolis, Ind.

› you mean to charge that the men whom I have ed, or any of them, are knaves or fools?
they are corrupt, they are knaves; if they can hypnotized, they are fools.
the great progress made by the labor movement his country is not due to them, their associates their predecessors, then to whom is it due? I k I am sufficiently familiar with the history of trade union movement in this country to assert t to them belongs the credit for securing the rter work day and better working conditions for lions of wage-earners. They have not yet seed for *every* worker an "eight-hour day and a satctory wage," but the great progress which they e made along these lines during the last fifty rs is an achievement without parallel in the an- of industrial history.
think you will agree with me in this statement, ough neither of us is a union man, nor is either n eligible for membership in a union, you being attorney-at-law and I an editor.
ne of the Departments of the Federation whose k is attacked, sometimes viciously, by both the ialists and the non-union employers, is that ch deals with Conciliation, Arbitration and Trade eements. Briefly, the history of the organiza- of that department and its methods is as fol-s: At the Industrial Conference held in Chigo, December, 1900, referred to above, it was animously declared:

"First — That employers and wage-earners should enter into annual or semi-annual agreements or contracts.

"Second — That all industries in the United States should establish boards of conciliation within the several and varied interests, to which boards of conciliation all differences and disputes arising between employer and employe, if not readily adjusted between the immediate interests concerned, might be referred for settlement."

"To Promote Industrial Peace."

At the first annual meeting of that Department, eld in New York, December, 1901, the plan and ope of work for the Department, which was unaniously adopted, contained the following principles:

"The scope and province of this Department shall be to do what may seem best to promote industrial peace and prosperity; to be helpful in establishing rightful relations between employers and workers; by its good offices to endeavor to obviate and prevent strikes and lockouts, and to aid in renewing industrial relations where a rupture has occurred.

"That at all times representatives of employers and workers, organized or unorganized, should confer for the adjustment of differences or disputes before an acute stage is reached, and thus avoid or minimize the number of strikes or lockouts.

"That mutual agreements as to conditions under which labor shall be performed should be encouraged, and that when agreements are made, the terms thereof should be faithfully adhered to, both in letter and spirit, by both parties.

"This Department, either as a whole or through a sub-committee by it appointed, shall, when requested by both parties to a dispute, act as a forum to adjust and decide upon questions at issue between workers and their employers, provided in its opinion the subject is one of sufficient importance.

"This Department will not consider abstract industrial problems.

"This Department assumes no powers of arbitration unless such powers be conferred by both parties to a dispute."

Thus, you will note that the Federation stands learly for conciliation in industrial disputes and for e principle of collective bargaining. Also, you will ote, what our enemies sometimes fail to observe, hat The National Civic Federation is a voluntary ody and has no power to compel people to arbitrate heir disputes. Nor has it power to thrust itself into controversy; State Boards of Arbitration can do hat, but not voluntary boards. Nor is the Federation n arbitrative body. It has no permanent machinery vith which it can arbitrate; but, when called upon, t tries first to bring about a settlement through nediation, asking for arbitration only as a last reort. It adopts this course for the reason that it believes a voluntary agreement is much more satisfactory to both sides than an arbitration, in which an odd man is generally called in to settle the difference, frequently pleasing neither side.

As stated, the Federation believes that the trade agreement is the most advanced and practicable plan by which employers and employes can deal with matters relating to hours, wages and conditions of employment. Certainly, you will not contend that the organized labor movement in this country does not take the same position. In fact, the trade unions had trade agreements twenty-five years before The National Civic Federation was born. That they still believe in them is proven by the fact that every one of the one hundred and thirty-five international trade unions in the American Federation of Labor either has trade agreements with the employers or is seeking to get them. I do not need to call your attention to the collective contracts made between the railway brotherhoods and 99 per cent of the railway systems of the United States, to the collective contracts made between the hundreds of thousands of union men and their employers in the building trades of this country, between the miners and the coal operators, the printers' unions and the publishers' associations, the thousands of street railway employes and the hundreds of street railway companies, the thousands of brewery workers in the United States and the hundreds of brewers, the thousands of members of the musicians' unions and the hundreds of theatrical operators, and so on. If I am not mistaken, you have yourself helped to bring about a very successful trade agreement in this city between the cloak manufacturers and the cloakmakers' union; and I believe you are one of a Board made up of representatives of the unions and the employers, with Mr. Louis D. Brandeis, of Boston, as Chairman. If this a "cheap and trivial" proposal and the Federation is wrong in endorsing it, then the one hundred and thirty-five international trade unions, composing the American Federation of Labor, and the great railway brotherhoods, are wrong in considering vital that which you consider "cheap and trivial." I do not believe, however, that you will insist on that position.

Neither "Assumed Harmony" Nor "Irreconcilable Conflict."

In the work of this Department we do not proceed upon "an assumed harmony of interests between the exploiting capitalists and the exploited workers," as you interpret the Federation's policy, nor upon the idea of an irreconcilable conflict between the employers and the workers, as you represent the Socialist position. We do not contend that the interests of the employers and the employes are always identical, but we do believe that they are generally, at some given moment, reconcilable. As you know, when a committee from an established union—which, as a rule, sends its most intelligent and keenest members—meets with a committee of employers around a table, it gets to be a good deal of a "give-and-take proposition." In these round-table conferences, the procedure runs something like this: First, the men insist upon the "living wage," which means a wage that will give them and their families the necessaries of life. Second, the employers declare that they must have enough to pay their fixed charges, such as rent, interest, taxes, insurance, repairs, provision for wear and tear on machinery, and so forth. These they call their "living wage." After these two "living wages" are established, the two sides spar for a division of the remainder of such business profits as the market conditions permit. The wage-earner wants more provision for his leisure time, the higher education of his children, and, as Mr. Gompers puts it, some of the real "good things of life." The employer also wants some of the "good things of life"—a desire common to our humanity. In arriving at an agreement on all these questions, the union committee shows just as keen an interest in the market conditions as the employer. The men know that if they were to demand a wage that would carry the cost of production to the point where the price of the product would be more than the consumer would pay or where competitive conditions with markets in other countries would interfere, such a course would stop the wheels and they would get nothing. Therefore, while the men want the best possible conditions they can secure, they do not want a wage so high that it will destroy the market. To secure a high wage scale and then have no work to do is not satisfactory to the workmen, as you and I both know. Thus, in the process of arriving at a satisfactory agreement, the interest of both might be called mutual up to the point where the two "living wages" are established. When it comes to dividing the remaining profits, the real clash comes; but it is not an "irreconcilable" one, as evidenced by the thousands of satisfactory trade agreements existing to-day. If you eliminate from the controversy between capital and labor the personality of the laborer, as you seem to have done, then to my mind it would be just as sensible to talk about the irreconcilable differences between the merchants and their customers in the millions of transactions that take place daily. The merchant naturally wants as high a price as he can get for his goods, and the consumer, equally naturally, wants to pay as little as possible, but there is no impending revolution lurking behind those daily transactions. By the natural laws of trade, the differences adjust themselves automatically.

If the public knew the thoroughness with which these questions are gone into in these trade agreement conferences, there would be less hostility on the part of the employer to this method of dealing with wages, hours and conditions of employment. For example, the joint arbitration board formed by the national officers of the American Publishers' Association and the International Typographical Union, in cases where an increase or decrease of wage is involved, goes minutely into every detail of the cost of the business and the cost of living. In a recent case, it even went so far as to have a special report made on the business conditions in the city where the paper is published, to ascertain whether the prospects for the future were good or bad. It found them good and it, therefore, ordered an increase in the wages of the printers.

"Wage-Slavery" Theory vs. Real Benefits.

Now, I am well aware that the real *bona fide* Marxian Socialists will sweep all this away as "tommyrot" in general and "wage-slavery" in particular. They will say that there should not be any wage-system or interest or profits, and assert that, under Socialism, the worker would receive the full product of his labor, etc.; but, as the entire industry of the country to-day is conducted on the other theory, and as there is likely to be no change in this and many succeeding generations, The National Civic Federation stands for helping to smooth the way of the workers on lines that are practical and on lines that are proving fairly successful. One has only to compare the conditions of the working people to-day with those of five hundred, one hundred, fifty, or even twenty-five years ago to note a progress so astounding as to furnish an answer to those who would overturn the present system and launch us, rudderless and compassless, on an unknown and untried sea.

You assert, Mr. Hillquit, that the Socialist Party is employing all efforts at its command to save the American labor movement from the undermining and diverting influence of The National Civic Federation. In this connection, I beg to send you a copy of a pamphlet, entitled "Socialism as an Incubus on the American Labor Movement," by J. W. Sullivan, one of the pioneers of the trade union movement and a recognized leader in all social reforms that affect the wage-earner. It is to his publications on "Direct Legislation" and "The Initiative, Referendum and Recall," which are regarded as standard authorities by all advocates of those measures, that Mr. U'Ren gives the credit for the beginning of the so-called "Oregon Reform Movement." So much for the qualification of Mr. Sullivan to speak on industrial reform matters. Mr. Sullivan's pamphlet, "Socialism as an Incubus on the American Labor Movement," furnishes documentary evidence from the archives of the American Federation of Labor at Washington, dating back many years, showing a persistent effort by the Socialist Party to wreck the trade union movement in this country. He makes it perfectly clear that, in his opinion, nothing in connection with that movement to-day is more vital than the saving of it from the undermining and diverting influence—not of the Civic Federation—but of the Socialist Party. As Mr. Sullivan's views were largely shared by the other labor members of The National Civic Federation, it is not strange that that organization did not take kindly to the Socialist movement.

From Mr. Sullivan's pamphlet (page 74) I make a quotation which seems to be a fitting close to this letter. The statement I quote is made by one who has forgotten more about Socialism than the writer can ever hope to know. I refer to Mr. Samuel Gompers, President of the American Federation of Labor. His statement was made at the annual meeting of that organization, held in Faneuil Hall, Boston, in 1903. Mr. Gompers' declaration, while showing clearly his opposition to the doctrine of Socialism, might also be assumed to indicate that he shared the belief of Mr. Sullivan in regard to the diverting influence of the Socialist Party on the trade union movement. Mr. Gompers said:

"I want to tell you Socialists that I have studied your philosophy; read your works upon economics, and not the meanest of them; studied your standard works, both in English and German—have not only read but studied them. I have heard your orators and watched the work of your movement the world over. I have kept close watch upon your doctrines for thirty years; have been closely associated with many of you, and know how you think and what you propose. I know, too, what you have up your sleeve, and I want to say that I am not only at variance with your doctrines, but with your philosophy.

"Economically, you are unsound; socially, you are wrong; industrially, you are an impossibility."

I am, my dear Mr. Hillquit, very truly yours,

R. M. EASLEY.

The National
Civic Federation Review

NEW YORK, DECEMBER 1 1913 No. 2

...TAL PROBLEMS OF THE HOUR TO BE DISCUSSED

...UAL MEETING OF THE NATIONAL CIVIC FEDERATION WILL CONSIDER PROPOSED AMENDMENTS TO SHERMAN ACT, WORKMEN'S COMPENSATION, FOOD AND DRUG LAWS, REGULATION OF PUBLIC SERVICE UTILITIES, AND INDUSTRIAL ARBITRATION

...Fourteenth Annual Meeting of The National ...ic Federation will be held at the Hotel ...stor, New York City, on Thursday and Fri... ...ember 11 and 12. The program this year ...ds reports from the various departments of ...eration, which reports will call for discussion ... on many important propositions of na... ...that will be presented.

...departments are: the Department on Com... ...for Industrial Accidents and Their Preven... ...Food and Drug Department; the Welfare ...ent; the Woman's Department; the Depart... ...Industrial Mediation Laws; the Department ...ation of Municipal Utilities; the Department ...ation of Industrial Corporations; the Depart... ...Industrial Economics.

...Department on Compensation for Industrial ...s and Their Prevention has a commission of ...who are making a study of the actual results ...rking of the various forms of compensation ...his commission consists of Messrs. Cyrus W. ...J. Walter Lord, Louis B. Schram, Otto M. ...James Duncan and John Mitchell, the two last ...aving been selected by the American Federa... ...abor to represent it in this inquiry. The com... ...has confined its work to the States where the ...ation law has been in effect for at least a ...hich include Massachusetts, New Jersey, ...Ohio, Illinois, Wisconsin, California, Oregon ...ashington. The report of this commission will ...the results of a questionnaire sent to twenty... ...sand employers in these States who have ...ccepted the acts (which are elective) or have refused to do so. The views of the working men themselves, either through their unions or as individuals, will also be included. In the light of the information secured by this commission, the model Workmen's Compensation Bill of The National Civic Federation will be redrafted.

One session at the Annual Meeting will be devoted to the consideration of the food and drug problem. The Federation has an expert committee which will be prepared to propose an outline for work that it is hoped will prove of great assistance to the Department of Agriculture and the forty-eight State and Dairy Commissions which are charged with the administration of the Federal and State laws relating to those subjects. No question can come before this meeting of the Federation of greater importance than the securing for the people of pure food and drugs.

How adequate are the Federal and State laws today? What changes, if any, are proposed? Is the administration of the law effective in protecting the people in these matters?

At a joint conference between the Department of Agriculture and the Commissioners of Food and Drugs of forty-eight States, held in Washington, D. C., November 14 and 15, 1913, an important step was taken by the passing of a resolution of the joint body, asking Congress to amend the National Pure Food Act in the following respects: By adding a clause which will define food as being adulterated that is exposed to filth, flies or other contamination in manufacturing, transportation or serving; by striking out of the law the present guarantee clause on the label of food and drug products, this having been declared to be abused to the extent of its being practically a fraud on the public; by amending Section 8, which provides for the sale of imitations, blends and mixtures under distinctive names. The joint conference further passed two resolutions, one to memorialize Congress to empower the Secretary of Agriculture to promulgate standards of foods, which shall have the force and effect of law, and the other to the effect that, pending such authority being granted by Congress, a committee of nine be appointed, three from the National Association of Food and Drug State Commissioners, three from the Bureau of Chemistry, and three from the Association of Agricultural Chemists, whose duty it shall be to prepare standards of rules of guidance which all will follow. Representatives from these different organizations will take part in the discussion of the food and drug question at the session of December 11 of the Annual Meeting.

The Department on Industrial Mediation Laws, which was so successful in securing the passage of the Newlands Act, providing for arbitration of disputes between interstate railroads and their employees, will report a model State Mediation Bill. If this bill is enacted into law by the various States, it is believed, that it will prove effective in reducing disputes in the industrial world to a minimum. In this measure will be included a special plan for dealing with strikes on public utilities. While the Newlands Act covers interstate railways, it cannot be used in a street railway controversy, because the street railways are under State jurisdiction. A plan

(Continued on page 17.)

...W. ATTERBURY. A. H. SMITH. JOHN H. FINLEY. SETH LOW, Chairman. D. L. CEASE. L. E. SHEPPARD.
(Copyright, Pirie MacDonald, N. Y.)

...ERS OF THE ARBITRATION BOARD IN WAGES CONTROVERSY BETWEEN EASTERN RAILROADS AND THE CONDUCTORS AND TRAINMEN.
(See Page 7.)

ANIEL J. TOBIN (President International Brotherhood of Teamsters), Indianapolis, Ind.
L. CEASE (Editor "Railway Trainmen's Journal"), Cleveland, Ohio.
HN F. TOBIN (General President Boot and Shoe Workers' Union), Boston, Mass.
SEPH F. VALENTINE (President Iron Molders' Union of North America), Cincinnati, Ohio.
NIS A. HAYES (President Glass Bottle Blowers' Association of United States and Canada), Philadelphia, Pa.
ILLIAM D. HUBER (President United Brotherhood of Carpenters and Joiners of America), Indianapolis, Ind.

Do you mean to charge that the men whom I have med, or any of them, are knaves or fools?

If they are corrupt, they are knaves; if they can hypnotized, they are fools.

If the great progress made by the labor movement this country is not due to them, their associates d their predecessors, then to whom is it due? I ink I am sufficiently familiar with the history of e trade union movement in this country to assert at to them belongs the credit for securing the orter work day and better working conditions for illions of wage-earners. They have not yet seired for *every* worker an "eight-hour day and a satfactory wage," but the great progress which they ave made along these lines during the last fifty ars is an achievement without parallel in the anls of industrial history.

I think you will agree with me in this statement, though neither of us is a union man, nor is either ven eligible for membership in a union, you being attorney-at-law and I an editor.

One of the Departments of the Federation whose ork is attacked, sometimes viciously, by both the ocialists and the non-union employers, is that hich deals with Conciliation, Arbitration and Trade greements. Briefly, the history of the organizaon of that department and its methods is as folws: At the Industrial Conference held in Chiago, December, 1900, referred to above, it was nanimously declared:

> "First—That employers and wage-earners should enter into annual or semi-annual agreements or contracts.
>
> "Second—That all industries in the United States should establish boards of conciliation within the several and varied interests, to which boards of conciliation all differences and disputes arising between employer and employe, if not readily adjusted between the immediate interests concerned, might be referred for settlement."

"To Promote Industrial Peace."

At the first annual meeting of that Department, held in New York, December, 1901, the plan and scope of work for the Department, which was unaninously adopted, contained the following principles:

> "The scope and province of this Department shall be to do what may seem best to promote industrial peace and prosperity; to be helpful in establishing rightful relations between employers and workers; by its good offices to endeavor to obviate and prevent strikes and lockouts, and to aid in renewing industrial relations where a rupture has occurred.
>
> "That at all times representatives of employers and workers, organized or unorganized, should confer for the adjustment of differences or disputes before an acute stage is reached, and thus avoid or minimize the number of strikes or lockouts.
>
> "That mutual agreements as to conditions under which labor shall be performed should be encouraged, and that when agreements are made, the terms thereof should be faithfully adhered to, both in letter and spirit, by both parties.
>
> "This Department, either as a whole or through a sub-committee by it appointed, shall, when requested by both parties to a dispute, act as a forum to adjust and decide upon questions at issue between workers and their employers, provided in its opinion the subject is one of sufficient importance.
>
> "This Department will not consider abstract industrial problems.
>
> "This Department assumes no powers of arbitration unless such powers be conferred by both parties to a dispute."

Thus, you will note that the Federation stands clearly for conciliation in industrial disputes and for the principle of collective bargaining. Also, you will note, what our enemies sometimes fail to observe, that The National Civic Federation is a voluntary body and has no power to compel people to arbitrate their disputes. Nor has it power to thrust itself into a controversy; State Boards of Arbitration can do that, but not voluntary boards. Nor is the Federation an arbitrative body. It has no permanent machinery with which it can arbitrate; but, when called upon, it tries first to bring about a settlement through mediation, asking for arbitration only as a last resort. It adopts this course for the reason that it believes a voluntary agreement is much more satisfactory to both sides than an arbitration, in which an odd man is generally called in to settle the difference, frequently pleasing neither side.

As stated, the Federation believes that the trade agreement is the most advanced and practicable plan by which employers and employes can deal with matters relating to hours, wages and conditions of employment. Certainly, you will not contend that the organized labor movement in this country does not take the same position. In fact, the trade unions had trade agreements twenty-five years before The National Civic Federation was born. That they still believe in them is proven by the fact that every one of the one hundred and thirty-five international trade unions in the American Federation of Labor either has trade agreements with the employers or is seeking to get them. I do not need to call your attention to the collective contracts made between the railway brotherhoods and 99 per cent of the railway systems of the United States, to the collective contracts made between the hundreds of thousands of union men and their employers in the building trades of this country, between the miners and the coal operators, the printers' unions and the publishers' associations, the thousands of street railway employes and the hundreds of street railway companies, the thousands of brewery workers in the United States and the hundreds of brewers, the thousands of members of the musicians' unions and the hundreds of theatrical operators, and so on. If I am not mistaken, you have yourself helped to bring about a very successful trade agreement in this city between the cloak manufacturers and the cloakmakers' union; and I believe you are one of a Board made up of representatives of the unions and the employers, with Mr. Louis D. Brandeis, of Boston, as Chairman. If this a "cheap and trivial" proposal and the Federation is wrong in endorsing it, then the one hundred and thirty-five international trade unions, composing the American Federation of Labor, and the great railway brotherhoods, are wrong in considering vital that which you consider "cheap and trivial." I do not believe, however, that you will insist on that position.

Neither "Assumed Harmony" Nor "Irreconcilable Conflict."

In the work of this Department we do not proceed upon "an assumed harmony of interests between the exploiting capitalists and the exploited workers," as you interpret the Federation's policy, nor upon the idea of an irreconcilable conflict between the employers and the workers, as you represent the Socialist position. We do not contend that the interests of the employers and the employes are always identical, but we do believe that they are generally, at some given moment, reconcilable. As you know, when a committee from an established union—which, as a rule, sends its most intelligent and keenest members—meets with a committee of employers around a table, it gets to be a good deal of a "give-and-take proposition." In these round-table conferences, the procedure runs something like this: First, the men insist upon the "living wage," which means a wage that will give them and their families the necessaries of life. Second, the employers declare that they must have enough to pay their fixed charges, such as rent, interest, taxes, insurance, repairs, provision for wear and tear on machinery, and so forth. These they call their "living wage." After these two "living wages" are established, the two sides spar for a division of the remainder of such business profits as the market conditions permit. The wage-earner wants more provision for his leisure time, the higher education of his children, and, as Mr. Gompers puts it, some of the real "good things of life." The employer also wants some of the "good things of life"—a desire common to our humanity. In arriving at an agreement on all these questions, the union committee shows just as keen an interest in the market conditions as the employer. The men know that if they were to demand a wage that would carry the cost of production to the point where the price of the product would be more than the consumer would pay or where competitive conditions with markets in other countries would interfere, such a course would stop the wheels and they would get nothing. Therefore, while the men want the best possible conditions they can secure, they do not want a wage so high that it will destroy the market. To secure a high wage scale and then have no work to do is not satisfactory to the workmen, as you and I both know. Thus, in the process of arriving at a satisfactory agreement, the interest of both might be called mutual up to the point where the two "living wages" are established. When it comes to dividing the remaining profits, the real clash comes; but it is not an "irreconcilable" one, as evidenced by the thousands of satisfactory trade agreements existing to-day. If you eliminate from the controversy between capital and labor the personality of the laborer, as you seem to have done, then to my mind it would be just as sensible to talk about the irreconcilable differences between the merchants and their customers in the millions of transactions that take place daily. The merchant naturally wants as high a price as he can get for his goods, and the consumer, equally naturally, wants to pay as little as possible, but there is no impending revolution lurking behind those daily transactions. By the natural laws of trade, the differences adjust themselves automatically.

If the public knew the thoroughness with which these questions are gone into in these trade agreement conferences, there would be less hostility on the part of the employer to this method of dealing with wages, hours and conditions of employment. For example, the joint arbitration board formed by the national officers of the American Publishers' Association and the International Typographical Union, in cases where an increase or decrease of wage is involved, goes minutely into every detail of the cost of the business and the cost of living. In a recent case, it even went so far as to have a special report made on the business conditions in the city where the paper is published, to ascertain whether the prospects for the future were good or bad. It found them good and it, therefore, ordered an increase in the wages of the printers.

"Wage-Slavery" Theory vs. Real Benefits.

Now, I am well aware that the real *bona fide* Marxian Socialists will sweep all this away as "tommyrot" in general and "wage-slavery" in particular. They will say that there should not be any wage-system or interest or profits, and assert that, under Socialism, the worker would receive the full product of his labor, etc.; but, as the entire industry of the country to-day is conducted on the other theory, and as there is likely to be no change in this and many succeeding generations, The National Civic Federation stands for helping to smooth the way of the workers on lines that are practical and on lines that are proving fairly successful. One has only to compare the conditions of the working people to-day with those of five hundred, one hundred, fifty, or even twenty-five years ago to note a progress so astounding as to furnish an answer to those who would overturn the present system and launch us, rudderless and compassless, on an unknown and untried sea.

You assert, Mr. Hillquit, that the Socialist Party is employing all efforts at its command to save the American labor movement from the undermining and diverting influence of The National Civic Federation. In this connection, I beg to send you a copy of a pamphlet, entitled "Socialism as an Incubus on the American Labor Movement," by J. W. Sullivan, one of the pioneers of the trade union movement and a recognized leader in all social reforms that affect the wage-earner. It is to his publications on "Direct Legislation" and "The Initiative, Referendum and Recall," which are regarded as standard authorities by all advocates of those measures, that Mr. U'Ren gives the credit for the beginning of the so-called "Oregon Reform Movement." So much for the qualification of Mr. Sullivan to speak on industrial reform matters. Mr. Sullivan's pamphlet, "Socialism as an Incubus on the American Labor Movement," furnishes documentary evidence from the archives of the American Federation of Labor at Washington, dating back many years, showing a persistent effort by the Socialist Party to wreck the trade union movement in this country. He makes it perfectly clear that, in his opinion, nothing in connection with that movement to-day is more vital than the saving of it from the undermining and diverting influence—not of the Civic Federation—but of the Socialist Party. As Mr. Sullivan's views were largely shared by the other labor members of The National Civic Federation, it is not strange that that organization did not take kindly to the Socialist movement.

From Mr. Sullivan's pamphlet (page 74) I make a quotation which seems to be a fitting close to this letter. The statement I quote is made by one who has forgotten more about Socialism than the writer can ever hope to know. I refer to Mr. Samuel Gompers, President of the American Federation of Labor. His statement was made at the annual meeting of that organization, held in Faneuil Hall, Boston, in 1903. Mr. Gompers' declaration, while showing clearly his opposition to the doctrine of Socialism, might also be assumed to indicate that he shared the belief of Mr. Sullivan in regard to the diverting influence of the Socialist Party on the trade union movement. Mr. Gompers said:

"I want to tell you Socialists that I have studied your philosophy; read your works upon economics, and not the meanest of them; studied your standard works, both in English and German—have not only read but studied them. I have heard your orators and watched the work of your movement the world over. I have kept close watch upon your doctrines for thirty years; have been closely associated with many of you, and know how you think and what you propose. I know, too, what you have up your sleeve, and I want to say that I am not only at variance with your doctrines, but with your philosophy.

"Economically, you are unsound; socially, you are wrong; industrially, you are an impossibility."

I am, my dear Mr. Hillquit, very truly yours,

R. M. EASLEY.

The National Civic Federation Review

Vol. IV. NEW YORK, DECEMBER 1, 1913 No. 2

VITAL PROBLEMS OF THE HOUR TO BE DISCUSSED

ANNUAL MEETING OF THE NATIONAL CIVIC FEDERATION WILL CONSIDER PROPOSED AMENDMENTS TO SHERMAN ACT, WORKMEN'S COMPENSATION, FOOD AND DRUG LAWS, REGULATION OF PUBLIC SERVICE UTILITIES, AND INDUSTRIAL ARBITRATION

THE Fourteenth Annual Meeting of The National Civic Federation will be held at the Hotel Astor, New York City, on Thursday and Friday, December 11 and 12. The program this year will include reports from the various departments of the Federation, which reports will call for discussion and action on many important propositions of national interest that will be presented.

These departments are: the Department on Compensation for Industrial Accidents and Their Prevention; the Food and Drug Department; the Welfare Department; the Woman's Department; the Department on Industrial Mediation Laws; the Department on Regulation of Municipal Utilities; the Department on Regulation of Industrial Corporations; the Department on Industrial Economics.

The Department on Compensation for Industrial Accidents and Their Prevention has a commission of six men who are making a study of the actual results of the working of the various forms of compensation acts. This commission consists of Messrs. Cyrus W. Phillips, J. Walter Lord, Louis B. Schram, Otto M. Eidlitz, James Duncan and John Mitchell, the two last named having been selected by the American Federation of Labor to represent it in this inquiry. The commission has confined its work to the States where the compensation law has been in effect for at least a year, which include Massachusetts, New Jersey, Michigan, Ohio, Illinois, Wisconsin, California, Oregon and Washington. The report of this commission will contain the results of a questionnaire sent to twenty-five thousand employers in these States who have either accepted the acts (which are elective) or have refused to do so. The views of the working men themselves, either through their unions or as individuals, will also be included. In the light of the information secured by this commission, the model Workmen's Compensation Bill of The National Civic Federation will be redrafted.

One session at the Annual Meeting will be devoted to the consideration of the food and drug problem. The Federation has an expert committee which will be prepared to propose an outline for work that it is hoped will prove of great assistance to the Department of Agriculture and the forty-eight State and Dairy Commissions which are charged with the administration of the Federal and State laws relating to those subjects. No question can come before this meeting of the Federation of greater importance than the securing for the people of pure food and drugs.

How adequate are the Federal and State laws today? What changes, if any, are proposed? Is the administration of the law effective in protecting the people in these matters?

At a joint conference between the Department of Agriculture and the Commissioners of Food and Drugs of forty-eight States, held in Washington, D. C., November 14 and 15, 1912, an important step was taken by the passing of a resolution of the joint body, asking Congress to amend the National Pure Food Act in the following respects: By adding a clause which will define food as being adulterated that is exposed to filth, flies or other contamination in manufacturing, transportation or serving; by striking out of the law the present guarantee clause on the label of food and drug products, this having been declared to be abused to the extent of its being practically a fraud on the public; by amending Section 8, which provides for the sale of imitations, blends and mixtures under distinctive names. The joint conference further passed two resolutions, one to memorialize Congress to empower the Secretary of Agriculture to promulgate standards of foods, which shall have the force and effect of law, and the other to the effect that, pending such authority being granted by Congress, a committee of nine be appointed, three from the National Association of Food and Drug State Commissioners, three from the Bureau of Chemistry, and three from the Association of Agricultural Chemists, whose duty it shall be to prepare standards of rules of guidance which all will follow. Representatives from these different organizations will take part in the discussion of the food and drug question at the session of December 11 of the Annual Meeting.

The Department on Industrial Mediation Laws, which was so successful in securing the passage of the Newlands Act, providing for arbitration of disputes between interstate railroads and their employees, will report a model State Mediation Bill. If this bill is enacted into law by the various States, it is believed that it will prove effective in reducing disputes in the industrial world to a minimum. In this measure will be included a special plan for dealing with strikes on public utilities. While the Newlands Act covers interstate railways, it cannot be used in a street railway controversy, because the street railways are under State jurisdiction. A plan

(Continued on page 17.)

W. W. ATTERBURY. A. H. SMITH. JOHN H. FINLEY. (Copyright, Pirie MacDonald, N. Y.) SETH LOW, Chairman. D. L. CEASE. L. E. SHEPPARD.

MEMBERS OF THE ARBITRATION BOARD IN WAGES CONTROVERSY BETWEEN EASTERN RAILROADS AND THE CONDUCTORS AND TRAINMEN. (See Page 7.)

A NATIONAL STOCK-TAKING OF SOCIAL ASSETS AND LIABILITIES

AN EXAMINATION AND APPRAISAL OF THE RESULTS OF INDUSTRIAL AND SOCIAL PROGRESS TO BE UNDERTAKEN BY THE NATIONAL CIVIC FEDERATION

THE National Civic Federation, through its Industrial Economics Department, is about to undertake a survey of the industrial and social situation of this country, with a view to ascertaining whether recent decades have brought progress or retrogression. Features to be necessarily included in the work will be examining the principles involved in the movement for the abolition of private ownership in the means of production and distribution of wealth and studying the differences in the fundamental aims and methods of the labor movement as conducted by the trade unions, the socialists and the Industrial Workers of the World.

In a recent public statement announcing this great work, long under consideration, President Low said:

"It is believed that there could be no better time than the present to make this national inventory of social assets and liabilities. How far has the general movement of our Republic been toward progress, and what steps can be taken to establish it firmly on the way to further progress? With regard to good or imperfect performance doubtless much will be found on both sides of the ledger, and of a certainty, with a satisfactory knowledge of the assets, Americans will be encouraged to meet their remaining liabilities to the cause of human advancement."

An Advisory Council of representative men and women of all parts of the country are to aid in carrying out the investigation. Included in its membership, which numbers nearly four hundred, are people prominent in labor, agriculture and manufacturing, as well as in finance, law and medicine, and in the press, the church and the college. Many are officials in national organizations having to do with the specific problems covered by the inquiry.

The Committee on Plan and Scope consists of: Talcott Williams, chairman; J. W. Jenks, Charles R. Miller, Charles P. Neill, William D. Baldwin, Samuel McCune Lindsay, James Bronson Reynolds, Ogden L. Mills, Nicholas F. Brady, John Hays Hammond, Samuel Gompers, James W. Sullivan, Walter Laidlaw, E. R. A. Seligman, Charles Stelzle, Frank Trumbull, D. L. Cease, George B. Cortelyou, George W. Perkins and O. D. Skelton.

This committee has already made public a statement of the reasons why, in its judgment, the comprehensive knowledge this inquiry seeks has become of vital moment at just this point in our national development. For, the committee declares, the social and economic situation is disturbing to the public conscience of our Republic. It is sufficiently serious, in the opinion of many who have the welfare of this nation at heart, to make necessary an impartial, dispassionate investigation by experts into the economic changes of the last thirty years with a view to ascertaining both our national successes and failures. The course of the new economic era has been sufficient to render it wise to take an account of our national movement and condition, exactly as "account of stock" is periodically taken in business. The proposed investigation, in order to encompass the facts at issue, good or bad, should include, broadly:

1. The factors concerned in the production of wealth.
2. The methods by which the wealth produced is distributed among the several factors engaged in production.
3. The effect on industrial, social and individual progress.

In other words, let us find out just where we stand. Have we gone forward, gone backward, or are we merely marking time? The evil of the hour or the reform triumph of the day usually absorbs public attention; let us attempt to look at things in a more extended perspective. Have the eventful changes of the last thirty years brought the American people, as a whole, gain or loss? Never have the agencies of intended social improvement been so numerous and so active; school and church and press, trade union and grange, commercial organizations, women's clubs, reform societies without number, enlightened employers, and progressive government have been striving to make life easier and better for the mass of our people. Have they failed or are they succeeding?

The assumption on which the industrial structure of the progressive nations has been based is that the force and initiative of individual enterprise, restrained or instructed, where need be, by State control or by organized public opinion, make most surely for progress and general welfare. Is this assumption justified by study of the facts or must we come to

TALCOTT WILLIAMS, Colum. Univ. School of Journalism.

JEREMIAH W. JENKS, New York University.

CHARLES R. MILLER, Editor "New York Times."

D. L. CEASE, Editor "Ry. Trainmen's Journal."

E. R. A. SELIGMAN, Columbia University.

E. R. L. GOULD, City and Suburban Homes Co.

JAMES BRONSON REYNOLDS, Counsel American Vigilance Ass'n.

J. W. SULLIVAN, Typographical Union.

OGDEN L. MILLS, Lawyer.

WALTER LAIDLAW, Secretary Federation of Churches.

SAMUEL GOMPERS, Pres. Amer. Federation of Labor.

CHARLES P. NEILL, Former U. S. Com. Labor Statistic

VINCENT ASTOR, Capitalist. (Copyright by Marceau, N. Y.)

CHARLES R. TOWSON, Indus. Sec. Int. Com. Y. M. C.

SAMUEL McC. LINDSAY, Columbia University.

FRANK TUCKER, Vice-Pres. Provident Loan Society.

CONDE B. PALLEN, Editor Catholic Encyclopaedia.

F. G. R. GORDON, Immigration Expert.

PLAN AND SCOPE COMMITTEE OF THE NATIONAL SURVEY OF SOCIAL PROGRESS.

agree, in whole or in part, with the revolutionists who find salvation only in overturning our whole political and economic structure?

Is wealth being concentrated in fewer hands? Has the organization of large corporations resulted in a great withdrawal of wealth from the people or a more general distribution of wealth? Has it resulted in the reduction of small establishments? Are the small business men being thrown into the class of propertyless wage-workers?

What of the farmer? Is he holding to the ownership of his farm, or lapsing into tenancy, or sinking under mortgage debt? How does he live to-day compared with thirty years ago, and what changes have occurred in his methods of work? Of what value to him have been the rural delivery and the parcel post?

Have the work of the American Federation of Labor, the railroad brotherhoods and the social reform organizations and the legislation secured by them prohibiting child labor and regulating conditions in factories, mercantile establishments, mines, bakeries, tenement houses and sweat shops really benefited the wageworking men, women and children of this country, or, as alleged by those who are crying out for revolution, have they been merely "a sop thrown by the capitalists to the toilers to blind them to their real condition of wage slavery"?

What special problems with relation to the well-being of the masses have we to solve in consequence of a practically unrestricted immigration?

In particular, these inquiries are pertinent: Have the children of the average American a better opportunity than he himself had? Do they start to work at an earlier or later age than he did? Are their hours of labor longer or shorter? What have been the effects of the changes in these respects upon the physical, mental, material, moral and social well-being of the wage-earning class?

How do the provisions for the wage-earners' health, safety and comfort during working hours compare with those of a generation ago? Are diseases incident to industrial life spreading or being conquered? Are the risks of accident, sickness or unemployment greater or less, and are the means of insurance against those risks adequate? Do statistics show that the American of to-day lives longer than his father, or that the pressure of our speeded-up industry forces him into an earlier grave? Is the demand of the labor organizations for a larger share in the control of the conditions of employment yielding the desired result? How do wages (or salaries) and the length of the working day compare with conditions prevailing thirty years ago? Will the wage-worker's earnings buy more or less to-day? What opportunity for education, recreation and development of his personality does he enjoy as compared with the American of the past generation?

What in general has been the outcome in the United States of the laws framed to give especial recognition to labor, such as those relating to mechanics' liens, the garnisheeing of wages, the protection of tenants in their improvements of agricultural and other holdings, and the Homestead and similar acts?

Where does America stand in the matter of gratifying the more widespread thirst for knowledge? What, in addition to its public and private schools, have been the results of its public libraries and its facilities for technical education for farm and factory?

Housing as well as working conditions should be reviewed. Are city dwellers and country dwellers securing an improved standard of decency and comfort, or light and air, as compared with the mode of living a quarter of a century ago? How about the ownership of homes and the accumulation of savings and the effect of investment through building and loan associations?

How about our political and business ethics? Are our moral standards and our aspirations higher or lower now than at any time in the past? Does the popular concept to-day of the relations to the public of industrial, railway and municipal utility corporations spell progress, as compared with the accepted view twenty years ago? Or is regulation a failure and should the State take the place of private capital? What, if anything, has been gained in the last decade through the demand of the people for publicity in the business methods of banks, insurance companies, trust companies and other private corporations? What, if any, are the gains for purity and cleanliness in politics, through regulation of primaries, publicity of campaign contributions, and other changes in election machinery? Can any qualified citizen have his vote counted as cast if he takes the trouble to cast it? How far is his right of free speech and free assemblage with his fellows protected?

Has the spending of millions of dollars by the Carnegie, Rockefeller and Sage Foundations, by the hundreds of charity societies and reform organizations, and by the churches through their institutional work, been justified by the results? Or should philanthropy be undertaken by the State? What practical value has there been in the industrial and municipal reform work undertaken by the hundreds of Boards of Trade, Chambers of Commerce, etc?

Granted that we have made great progress, what are the admittedly remaining plague spots in our industrial and social life? And are we justified by experience in hoping that we can eventually remove them or are they ineradicable? If the latter, does history give any promise of their removal by overturning the present system of society?

The Twentieth Century, it is clear, is to be devoted to the settlement of these economic issues, just as the close of the Eighteenth and the beginning of the Nineteenth Century were devoted to the solution of political issues.

A new period in the industrial development of our nation began with the formation of the trusts. Early landmarks of this period were the organization of the Sugar Trust in 1885, the enactment of the first Federal Interstate Commerce measure in 1887 and the passing of the Sherman Act in 1890.

The creation of great corporations in this period, the changes in the organization, development and management of industries, the enormous addition to the share and bonded capital of the country, the large immigration drawn from Southern and Southeastern Europe instead of from Northern and Northwestern Europe, the massing of population at centres of industry, the changes in the conditions of life in our large cities, the arrest in the increase of our agricultural population, and the fact that in the last decade for the first time in our history the population has grown twice as fast the food supply—all this has brought profound shiftings in the distribution of wealth, the relations between employer and employed and the circumstances in which people with large and small incomes live. The expenditure of the rich is more visible, and the standards of desires among people of moderate income and in the wage-earning class have risen, emphasizing a disparity in the enjoyment of life and its opportunities. The addition of large populations who have suffered from oppression and wrong in their old homes has multiplied the ranks of those prompt to put the worst construction on the motives of the more fortunate. These causes, together with the improvement in the transmission and the distribution of intelligence, making the acts of the few and their luxuries more known to the many, have brought about, in American political life, parties organized as a challenge to the existing social order and economic system.

At the last Presidential election nearly one million votes were cast in favor of an economic program calling for a revolutionary transformation of society. The party supporting this program, following a sweeping indictment of existing society, proposes the abolition of our present system of wages and private property and the substitution therefor of government ownership and operation of all the instruments of production, distribution and exchange, inclusive of land. In other words, the work of planning, direction and management now done by the farmer, manufacturer, merchant, banker, editor, mine operator, and the manager of trust and insurance companies, newspapers, grain elevators, railroads and other public utilities, Federal, State and municipal, and all other productive enterprises, are to be performed through elected government officials.

Recently an element, within the revolutionary movement referred to, has confronted this country with a yet more radical proposal. This element avowedly aims at the communistic operation of industries, which are to be confiscated through the general strike and then directly operated by the workers themselves. The adherents of this movement refuse to form agreements with employers, they reject arbitration and conciliation and preach sabotage and faithlessness to contracts, while they scout all principles of order and respect for law.

Does either of these programs point the way to progress? Does either embody the promise of a higher civilization, or does the system of liberty and property, as at present established, form a basis, subject to enlightened correction, for the true advance of mankind?

In much of the field thus briefly outlined, the main work will be bringing together the results of official and other investigatons already made. In certain respects further investigation will be required. In other cases, the facts may prove too elusive or the records too incomplete, for a wholly satisfactory report. In the greater part of the work, however, it is possible to reach definite conclusions either by statistical investigation or by authoritative descriptive summary.

On the whole there seems no room for question that it is both desirable and possible, by a thorough and impartial searching out of the facts, to measure broadly the gains and the losses of our changing time, both that we may see the need to face the evils yet to be fought and that we may take fresh heart from the good fights won.

The Plan and Scope Committee is now engaged upon a thorough analysis of the field of the inquiry, as a basis for practical organization of the work.

ADVISORY COUNCIL

OF

THE INDUSTRIAL ECONOMICS DEPARTMENT

As the survey will necessarily inquire into conditions in all sections of the country, so the Advisory Council, now in formation, is composed of representative citizens from every State in the Union. Among those who have already accepted membership are:

ERNEST H. ABBOTT, "The Outlook," New York City.
MISS JANE ADDAMS, Head Resident, Hull House, Chicago, Ill.
JOHN G. AGAR, Lawyer, New Rochelle, N. Y.
STEPHEN H. ALLEN, Attorney-at-law, Topeka, Kansas.
VINCENT ASTOR, Capitalist, New York City.
MRS. FRANCIS MCNEIL BACON, JR., Chairman Metropolitan Section, Woman's Department, The National Civic Federation, New York City.
LIBERTY HYDE BAILEY, Director, College of Agriculture, Cornell University, Ithaca, N. Y.
ALFRED L. BAKER, Banker, Chicago, Ill.
GEORGE F. BAKER, JR., Banker, New York City.
WILLIAM D. BALDWIN, President Otis Elevator Company, New York City.
W. J. BAYERSDORFER, President United States League of Local Building and Loan Associations, Shreveport, La.
AUGUST BELMONT, New York City.
ERNEST P. BICKNELL, National Director, American Red Cross, Washington, D. C.
CORNELIUS N. BLISS, New York City.
MISS HELEN VARICK BOSWELL, Chairman Political Science Committee, General Federation of Women's Clubs, New York City.
NICHOLAS F. BRADY, President New York Edison Company, New York City.
WILLIAM C. BROWN, President New York Central Railroad, New York City.
JAMES M. BUCKLEY, Former Editor "The Christian Advocate," New York City.
MARION L. BURTON, President of Smith College, Northampton, Mass.
KENYON L. BUTTERFIELD, President Massachusetts Agricultural College, Amherst, Mass.
NICHOLAS MURRAY BUTLER, President Columbia University, New York City.
HOMER D. CALL, Secretary-Treasurer Amalgamated Meat Cutters and Butcher Workmen of North America, Syracuse, N. Y.
THOMAS H. CANNON, National President Foresters, Chicago, Ill.
ARTHUR CAPPER, Publisher, "The Topeka Capital," Topeka, Kan.
JOHN N. CARLISLE, New York State Commissioner of Highways, Albany, N. Y.
ANDREW CARNEGIE, New York City.
THOMAS N. CARVER, Director Rural Organization Service, Department of Agriculture, Washington, D. C.
D. L. CEASE, Editor "The Railroad Trainman," Cleveland, Ohio.
JOSEPH H. CHOATE, JR., Attorney-at-law, New York City.
CHARLES HOPKINS CLARK, President and Editor "The Hartford Courant," Hartford, Conn.
JOHN B. CLARK, Professor Political Economy, Columbia University, New York City.
WILLIAM A. COAKLEY, President International Lithographers' Press Feeders' Association, New York City.
REV. HENRY S. COFFIN, Pastor Madison Avenue Presbyterian Church, New York City.
BIRD S. COLER, Banker, New York City.
L. A. COOLIDGE, Treasurer United Shoe Machinery Company, Boston, Mass.
GEORGE B. CORTELYOU, President Consolidated Gas Company, New York City.
JOHN D. CRIMMINS, Builder, New York City.
JAMES W. CROOK, Professor Economics, Amherst College, Amherst, Mass.
MRS. J. HERON CROSMAN, President Patriotic Women of America, New Rochelle, N. Y.
MRS. JAMES S. CUSHMAN, President Young Women's Christian Association, New York City.
R. FULTON CUTTING, President Association for Improving the Condition of the Poor, New York City.
HENRY P. DAVISON, Banker, New York City.
CHARLES I. DENECHAUD, President American Federation of Catholic Societies, New Orleans, La.
REV. PETER E. DIETZ, Secretary Social Service Commission of American Federation of Catholic Societies, Milwaukee, Wis.
JAMES DUNCAN, President Granite Cutters' International Association of America, Quincy, Mass.
SAMUEL O. DUNN, Editor of "Railway Age Gazette," Chicago, Ill.
E. DANA DURAND, Former Director of the Census, Washington, D. C.
R. M. EASLEY, Chairman Executive Council, The National Civic Federation, New York City.
CHARLES L. EDGAR, President The Edison Electric Illuminating Company, Boston, Mass.
OTTO M. EIDLITZ, Building Trades Employers' Association, New York City.
HOWARD ELLIOTT, President New York, New Haven and Hartford Railroad Company, New Haven, Conn.
E. T. FAIRCHILD, President National Education Association, New Hampshire College, Durham, N. H.
HENRY W. FARNAM, Professor of Economics, Yale University, New Haven, Conn.
REV. JAMES M. FARRAR, Pastor of "The Old First Church," Dutch Reformed, Brooklyn, New York City.
W. H. P. FAUNCE, President Brown University, Providence, R. I.
HENRY B. FAVILL, President American Medical Association, Chicago, Ill.
FRANK A. FETTER, President American Economic Association, Princeton, N. J.
JOHN H. FINLEY, President College of the City of New York, New York City.
IRVING FISHER, Professor Political Economy, Yale University, New Haven, Conn.
WALTER L. FISHER, Former Secretary of the Interior, Chicago, Ill.
HENRY FORD, President Ford Motor Car Company, Detroit, Mich.

Hugh F. Fox, Secretary United States Brewers' Association, New York City.
Charles Francis, President Printers' League of America, New York City.
Lee K. Frankel, Vice-President Metropolitan Life Insurance Company, New York City.
Ernst Freund, Professor of Law, University of Chicago, Chicago, Ill.
John C. Freund, Publisher "Music Trades," New York City.
William Gammell, Manufacturer, Providence, R. I.
Harry A. Garfield, President Williams College, Williamstown, Mass.
A. B. Garretson, President Order of Railway Conductors, Cedar Rapids, Iowa.
James Cardinal Gibbons, Baltimore, Md.
John Golden, President United Textile Workers of America, Fall River, Mass.
Samuel Gompers, President American Federation of Labor, Washington, D. C.
F. G. R. Gordon, Immigration Expert, Haverhill, Mass.
Elgin R. L. Gould, President City and Suburban Homes Company, New York City.
John Temple Graves, Editor "New York American," New York City.
John H. Gray, Professor of Economics, University of Minnesota, Minneapolis, Minn.
B. J. Greenhut, Greenhut-Siegel Cooper Co., New York City.
Rt. Rev. David H. Greer, Bishop of New York, New York City.
Charles Noble Gregory, Dean of Law School, George Washington University, Washington, D. C.
John Hays Hammond, Chairman Industrial Economics Department, The National Civic Federation, Gloucester, Mass.
Mrs. John Hays Hammond, Former Chairman Woman's Department, The National Civic Federation, Gloucester, Mass.
Mrs. J. Borden Harriman, Member Federal Commission on Industrial Relations, New York City.
William O. Hart, Attorney-at-law, New Orleans, La.
Colonel George Harvey, Publisher, New York City.
Denis A. Hayes, President Glass Bottle Blowers' Association of United States and Canada, Philadelphia, Pa.
Timothy Healy, President International Brotherhood of Stationary Firemen, New York City.
John Grier Hibben, President Princeton University, Princeton, N. J.
O. D. Hill, Secretary Farmers' National Congress, Kendalia, W. Va.
Charles D. Hilles, New York City.
Rev. Emil G. Hirsch, Rabbi of Sinai Temple, Chicago, Ill.
Frederick L. Hoffman, Statistician, Prudential Insurance Company, Newark, N. J.
Hamilton Holt, Editor "The Independent," New York City.
Lewis R. Hovey, Publisher "The Sunday Record," Haverhill, Mass.
Arthur M. Howe, Managing Editor "The Brooklyn Daily Eagle," New York City.
Clark Howell, Editor "The Atlanta Constitution," Atlanta, Ga.
Woods Hutchinson, Physician, New York City.
Archbishop John Ireland, St. Paul, Minn.
J. W. Jenks, Professor of Government, New York University, New York City.
Hennen Jennings, Mining Engineer, Washington, D. C.
Charles Johnston, Author, New York City.
Frederick N. Judson, Attorney-at-law, St. Louis, Mo.
Mrs. Julius Kahn, San Francisco, Cal.
Frank B. Kellogg, Former President American Bar Association, St. Paul, Minn.
H. N. Kellogg, American Newspaper Publishers' Association, Indianapolis, Ind.
William E. Kelly, President National Association of Letter Carriers, Brooklyn, New York City.
Rev. William J. Kerby, Catholic University, Washington, D. C.
William J. Kerr, President Oregon Agricultural College, Corvallis, Ore.
J. H. Kimble, Secretary Jacob Tome Institute, Port Deposit, Md.
Darwin P. Kingsley, President New York Life Insurance Company, New York City.
Norman G. Kittrell, Judge, Houston, Tex.
Charles W. Knapp, Proprietor "St. Louis Republic," St. Louis, Mo.
Rev. Walter Laidlaw, Secretary New York Federation of Churches, New York City.
Dr. Samuel W. Lambert, Dean College of Physicians and Surgeons, New York City.
William Jett Lauck, Chief Expert, Federal Commission on Industrial Relations, Washington, D. C.
Rt. Rev. William Lawrence, Bishop of Massachusetts, Boston, Mass.
Frederick W. Lehmann, Attorney-at-law, St. Louis, Mo.
W. G. Lee, President Brotherhood of Railroad Trainmen, Cleveland, Ohio.
Adolph Lewisohn, International Smelting and Refining Company, New York City.
Charles F. Libby, Attorney-at-law, Portland, Me.
Samuel McCune Lindsay, Professor of Social Legislation, Columbia University, New York City.
Seth Low, President The National Civic Federation, New York City.
James M. Lynch, former President International Typographical Union, Indianapolis, Ind.
Roswell C. McCrea, Dean of Wharton School of Finance and Commerce, University of Pennsylvania, Philadelphia, Pa.
Mrs. John McLaughlin, Washington, D. C.
Nathan William McChesney, Attorney, Chicago, Ill.
Cyrus H. McCormick, President International Harvester Company, Chicago, Ill.
Rt. Rev. William F. MacDowell, Bishop Methodist Episcopal Church, Evanston, Ill.
Henry B. F. Macfarland, Attorney-at-law, Washington, D. C.
James H. McGraw, President McGraw Publishing Company, New York City.
Andrew W. McKee, President National Association of Civil Service Employees, New York City.
Franklin MacVeagh, Former Secretary of the Treasury, Chicago, Ill.
V. Everit Macy, Publicist, New York City.
W. D. Mahon, President Amalgamated Association of Street Railway Employes of America, Detroit, Mich.
Milo R. Maltbie, Public Service Commission, New York City.
Rev. William T. Manning, Rector Trinity Church, New York City.
Theodore Marburg, Political Economist, Baltimore, Md.
Marcus M. Marks, President-elect Borough of Manhattan, New York City.
Samuel Mather, Picands, Mather & Co., Cleveland, Ohio.
Shailer Mathews, President Federal Council of Churches of Christ in America, Chicago, Ill.
Rev. H. Pereira Mendes, Rabbi Shearith Israel, New York City.
Bradford Merrill, Editor "New York American," New York City.
Mrs. Charles F. Meyer, New York City.
George von L. Meyer, Former Secretary of the Navy, Hamilton, Mass.
Sidney E. Mezes, President The University of Texas, Austin, Texas.
John G. Milburn, Attorney-at-law, New York City.
Charles R. Miller, Editor "The New York Times," New York City.
Ogden L. Mills, Attorney-at-law, New York City.
E. A. Moffett, Former Editor "The Bricklayers' Journal," New York City.
Mrs. Philip North Moore, President General Federation of Women's Clubs, St. Louis, Mo.
J. Edwin Murphy, Managing Editor "The New York Press," New York City.
John J. Murphy, Tenement House Commissioner, New York City.
Charles P. Neill, Former United States Commissioner of Labor, New York City.
Mrs. Truman H. Newberry, President Needlework Guild, Detroit, Mich.
Thomas V. O'Connor, President International Longshoremen's Association, Buffalo, N. Y.
Mrs. Cyrus Pitman Orr, Chairman Alabama Section, Woman's Department, The National Civic Federation, Birmingham, Ala.
Rt. Rev. Wm. Ford Nicholas, Protestant Episcopal Bishop of California, Berkeley, Cal.
Conde Pallen, Editor "The Catholic Encyclopaedia," New York City.
William J. Pape, Editor "The Waterbury Republican," Waterbury, Conn.
Alton B. Parker, Former Chief Justice Court of Appeals, New York City.
Lewis W. Parker, President Parker Cotton Mills Co., Greenville, S. C.
Mrs. Henry A. Peckham, Chairman National Government Employes' Committee, Woman's Department, The National Civic Federation, Washington, D. C.
George W. Perkins, Publicist, New York City.
James Laughlin Phillips, Political Economist, Washington, D. C.
Frank L. Polk, Attorney-at-law, New York City.
Roscoe Pound, Professor Law School, Harvard University, Cambridge, Mass.
John T. Pratt, Attorney-at-law, New York City.
Ralph Pulitzer, Editor "The World," New York City.
J. H. Ralston, Attorney-at-law, Washington, D. C.
William Charles Reick, Editor "The Sun," New York City.
George M. Reynolds, President Continental and Commercial National Bank, Chicago, Ill.
James B. Reynolds, Counsel American Vigilance Association, New York City.
Mrs. George T. Rice, Chairman Massachusetts and Rhode Island Section, Woman's Department, The National Civic Federation, Westwood, Mass.
Herman Ridder, Editor "New Yorker-Staats Zeitung," New York City.
W. M. Riggs, President Clemson Agricultural College, Clemson College, S. C.
Jacob A. Riis, Sociologist, New York City.
Hayes Robbins, Political Economist, Winchester, Mass.
Allan Robinson, Secretary Allied Real Estate Interests, New York City.
Frank T. Rogers, President United National Association of Post Office Clerks of the United States, Chicago, Ill.
Elihu Root, United States Senator, New York City.
Elihu Root, Jr., Attorney-at-law, New York City.
Victor Rosewater, Editor "The Omaha Bee," Omaha, Neb.
Leo S. Rowe, President American Academy of Political and Social Science, Philadelphia, Pa.
Rev. John A. Ryan, St. Paul Seminary, St. Paul, Minn.
William Jay Schieffelin, President American Church Missionary Society, New York City.
J. G. Schmidlapp, President Union Savings Bank and Trust Company, Cincinnati, Ohio.
Mrs. Frederick Schoff, President National Mothers' Congress, Philadelphia, Pa.
Louis B. Schram, Chairman Labor Committee, United States Brewers' Association, New York City.
Jacob Gould Schurman, President Cornell University, Ithaca, N. Y.
Henry R. Seager, Professor Political Science, Columbia University, New York City.
E. R. A. Seligman, Professor Political Economy, Columbia University, New York City.
Isaac N. Seligman, Banker, New York City.
J. G. Shaffer, Proprietor "The Evening Post," Chicago, Ill.
Albert Shaw, Editor "American Review of Reviews," New York City.
Thomas W. Shelton, Attorney-at-law, Norfolk, Va.
Finley J. Shepard, Vice-President Missouri Pacific Railroad Company, New York City.
Rev. Joseph Silverman, Rabbi Temple Emanu-El, New York City.
O. D. Skelton, Professor Queen's University, Kingston, Canada.
Mrs. William Gerry Slade, President National Society United States Daughters of 1812, New York City.
Albion W. Small, Dean Graduate School of Arts and Literature, University of Chicago, Chicago, Ill.
Charles W. Smith, Judge, 34th Judicial District, Stockton, Kan.
George Walter Smith, Attorney-at-law, Philadelphia, Pa.
Selden P. Spencer, Attorney-at-law, St. Louis, Mo.
James Speyer, Banker, New York City.
John M. Stahl, Farmers' National Congress, Chicago, Ill.
Francis Lynde Stetson, Attorney-at-law, New York City.
Henry L. Stimson, Former Secretary of War, New York City.
Henry L. Stoddard, Editor "The Evening Mail," New York City.
Warren S. Stone, Grand Chief International Brotherhood of Locomotive Engineers, Cleveland, Ohio.
Mrs. William Cumming Story, President General National Society Daughters of the American Revolution, New York City.
Willard D. Straight, Banker, New York City.
Percy S. Straus, R. H. Macy & Co., New York City.
James W. Sullivan, Sociological Expert, New York City.
Graham Taylor, President National Conference of Charities, Chicago, Ill.
Hannis Taylor, Attorney-at-law, Washington, D. C.
F. S. Terry, National Lamp Works, General Electric Company, New York City.
Robert Means Thompson, Chairman Executive Committee, Navy League, Washington, D. C.
Daniel J. Tobin, President International Brotherhood of Teamsters, Indianapolis, Ind.
John F. Tobin, General President Boot and Shoe Workers' Union, Boston, Mass.
Charles R. Towson, Industrial Secretary, International Committee Young Men's Christian Associations, New York City.
Frank Trumbull, Chairman Board of Directors Chesapeake and Ohio Railroad Company, New York City.
Frank Tucker, Vice-President Provident Loan Society, New York City.
Henry St. George Tucker, Lawyer, Lexington, Va.
Isaac M. Ullman, President New Haven Chamber of Commerce, New Haven, Conn.
Theodore N. Vail, President American Telephone and Telegraph Company, New York City.
Charles R. Van Hise, President University of Wisconsin, Madison, Wis.
Mrs. Lyndsay Van Rensselaer, New York City.
George Edgar Vincent, President University of Minnesota, Minneapolis, Minn.
F. C. Walcott, Banker, New York City.
Frank P. Walsh, Vice-President Social Centre Movement, Kansas City, Mo.
Frank Julian Warne, Economist, Parkersburg, W. Va.
Booker T. Washington, Principal Tuskegee Normal and Industrial Institute, Tuskegee Institute, Ala.
Miss Maude Wetmore, Chairman Woman's Department, The National Civic Federation, New York City.
Harris Weinstock, Member Federal Commission on Industrial Relations, San Francisco, Cal.
Benjamin Ide Wheeler, President University of California, Berkeley, Cal.
Everett P. Wheeler, Attorney-at-law, New York City.
I. G. White, New York City.
William Allen White, Editor "The Emporia Gazette," Emporia, Kan.
Charles A. Wickersham, President Atlanta & West Point Railroad Company, Atlanta, Ga.
E. W. Wickey, Vice-President and Secretary Farmers' National Life Insurance Company, East Chicago, Ind.
Delos F. Wilcox, Public Utility Expert, New York City.
Harvey W. Wiley, Former United States Chief Food Chemist, Washington, D. C.
Rev. Herbert L. Willett, Church of the Disciples, Chicago, Ill.
Mrs. G. Huntington Williams, Baltimore, Md.
Talcott Williams, Director School of Journalism, Columbia University, New York City.
Mrs. Talcott Williams, New York City.
William F. Willoughby, President American Association for Labor Legislation, Princeton, N. J.
Clinton Rogers Woodruff, Secretary National Municipal League, Philadelphia, Pa.
Rollin S. Woodruff, Merchant, New Haven, Conn.

REPRESENTATIVE PRESS OPINIONS ON THE SOCIAL SURVEY

WIDESPREAD EDITORIAL APPROVAL OF ITS PURPOSES AND POSSIBILITIES FOR PRACTICAL GOOD

THE following selections from the volume of press comments called out by early announcements of the investigation give some idea of the interest the undertaking has aroused in all parts of the country:

Chicago Record-Herald, Ill.—The scientific and non-partisan character of the inquiry is to be taken for granted. The federation represents all schools and shades of opinion, and what it wants is the truth, and nothing but the truth.

Brooklyn Eagle, N. Y.—These are questions upon which the great need of the time is light without heat, and this council of The National Civic Federation is more likely than any other agency to supply it.

New Orleans Times-Democrat, La.—The field to be explored is one that we cannot know too much about, and the knowledge gained by expert and impartial exploration must be a very valuable addition to the national equipment for handling the great questions that already are pressing for satisfactory answers.

Boston Transcript, Mass.—The movement is under direction which commands public confidence. President Low is a man of zeal and experience in such a service. The amendment of the Erdman act at a very critical time was largely the result of his generalship. As this is a volunteer movement, perhaps more interest will attach to it than though it was made through legislation or by executive order one of the formal agencies to investigate the conditions of the period. It will engage in the service, not because a definite duty has been prescribed for it, but because it is anxious to find out as fully as is possible the conditions and the tendencies in the United States of to-day.

Duluth News-Tribune, Minn.—Out of the report will come new ways and means for advancement, new methods of helping people to help themselves, new schemes of betterment and new ways for men of great wealth to spend a goodly part of their fortunes in giving back to the country what the country has so lavishly bestowed upon them.

Philadelphia Inquirer, Pa.—One of the tasks of the investigators should be to enlighten the public regarding the real character and aim of the organizations that pretend to have the interest of the laboring man

(Continued on page 15.)

A NATION-WIDE STUDY OF WORKMEN'S COMPENSATION LAWS

JOINT COMMISSION OF THE NATIONAL CIVIC FEDERATION IS GATHERING INFORMATION OF THE WORKINGS OF ALL STATE LAWS NOW IN EFFECT, AS A BASIS FOR PRACTICAL RECOMMENDATIONS

DURING the last four months a joint commission appointed by the Department on Compensation for Industrial Accidents and Their Prevention, of which Mr. August Belmont is chairman, has been carrying on a thorough investigation of the workings of compensation laws in the several States where such measures have been adopted and are to-day in force. This commission has already visited Massachusetts, New Jersey, Michigan, Ohio, Wisconsin, Illinois, Washington, Oregon and California, and has devoted special attention also to Kansas, Nevada, Minnesota and Rhode Island. The Washington law is of special importance in that it is the only one thus far made compulsory upon all employers and employees. The California elective law of 1911 also becomes compulsory next January, thus setting the Pacific Coast in the vanguard, so far at least as this significant feature is concerned. An amendment to the Ohio law making it compulsory takes effect January 1, 1914.

CYRUS W. PHILLIPS J. WALTER LORD

In addition to close investigation on the ground by conferences and hearings in the several States, the commission has been receiving an immense amount of direct testimony in reply to questionnaires and letters sent to some 25,000 employers and labor organizations in each of the States which have had sufficient experience under compensation laws to warrant the inquiry. The commission has made a careful analysis of the information thus far in hand, and the work when completed will provide for the first time in one body of data a complete and impartial view of the national situation up to date, in respect to the modern application of workmen's compensation.

For several years the Workmen's Compensation Department of The National Civic Federation has been advocating new and enlightened treatment of the entire ineffective and confused employers' liability and accident prevention practice in this country. It has urged legislation providing for automatic compensation in case of accidental injury to workmen and for their families in case of death resulting from such injuries. It has prepared and circulated on two occasions tentative drafts of model acts based upon a study of foreign experience and of American needs and conditions. The first of these, in December, 1910, advocated a compulsory system; the second, prepared last winter, was an elective act to meet changing conditions and the needs of States which are not yet prepared to adopt compulsory measures. Both have been circulated in the interest of uniform State legislation, and twenty-[illegible] State laws have been enacted.

The present purpose is to give to legislators and friends of the compensation movement everywhere the sifted results of the country's total experience upon the subject, in a definite form which it is believed will meet the new problems that have arisen in the workings of the more or less experimental acts now in force. This information will also be of great practical value as a basis for recommendations which may be made for the drafting of a new model workmen's compensation law.

The entire investigation has been carried on under the direction of a Plan and Scope Committee of the Workmen's Compensation Department, headed by Mr. Otto M. Eidlitz, whose enthusiasm and practical grasp of the problems involved have been invaluable to the progress of the inquiry. Other members of this committee are Mr. Louis B. Schram, Mr. Samuel Gompers, Mr. W. H. Marshall, president American Locomotive Company; Mr. Frank V. Whiting, general claims attorney New York Central lines; Mr. Timothy Healy, president International Brotherhood of Stationary Firemen; Mr. E. H. Letchworth, of the Rogers-Brown Iron Co.; Mr. M. F. Westover, secretary General Electric Company; Mr. Raynal C. Bolling, of the United States Steel Corporation.

The members of the joint commission engaged in the actual field work are:

CYRUS W. PHILLIPS, chairman, member of the former New York State Commission on Employers' Liability, and an attorney-at-law, Rochester, N. Y.

J. WALTER LORD, chairman of the Maryland State Commission on Employers' Liability and Workmen's Compensation, recently appointed by the Governor of that State; chairman of the Federation's Maryland State Council, and an attorney-at-law, Baltimore, Md.

OTTO M. EIDLITZ, New York Building Trades' Employers' Association, New York City.

LOUIS B. SCHRAM, chairman Labor Committee, United States Brewers' Association, Brooklyn, N. Y.

JAMES DUNCAN, vice-president American Federation of Labor, Quincy, Mass.

JOHN MITCHELL, vice-president American Federation of Labor, Mount Vernon, N. Y.

Mr. Duncan and Mr. Mitchell were appointed by the American Federation of Labor to co-operate with The National Civic Federation.

Mr. Phillips, in a public statement made during the investigation, describing the progress of workmen's compensation legislation, and the scope of the present inquiry, said:

"In the States so far visited the laws are elective. That is, the employer has his choice either to (1) stay under the old liability law, with the defences of contributory negligence, assumption of risk and fellow servant rule removed; or (2) accept the compensation act under which all employees receive compensation for their injuries according to a fixed schedule, regardless of fault.

"In Massachusetts, Michigan and Wisconsin, at least 75 per cent of the employers and their workmen have elected to come under the compensation act. The original Illinois compensation act was rejected by over 5,000 employers. The amended act of that State, which took effect July 1, 1913, has been rejected by only 500 employers. The Ohio law has been accepted by something like 10 or 15 per cent of the employers. This law has been made compulsory by the new act, which takes effect January 1, 1914. In the States of Massachusetts, Michigan and Wisconsin, litigation involving compensation to employees has practically ceased to exist. To illustrate: During the year that the Michigan law has been in effect, compensation has been paid in over 10,000 cases of disability and only 8 cases have gone into the courts, and these were solely for the purpose of settling some uncertainty in the law.

JAMES DUNCAN. JOHN MITCHELL.

"In these States the law is administered by an industrial accident board, consisting of from three to five members. All settlement agreements for compensation must be adjusted by this board and, in case of dispute, the board acts as arbitrator. The State of Michigan has had 200 arbitrations during the year. These arbitrations do not as a rule, delay the payment of compensation more than two or three weeks. Similar conditions prevail in Massachusetts and Wisconsin.

"It is claimed that the cost of medical attendance in these States has been larger than was originally anticipated and that the amount paid by employers to hospitals and physicians is at least 50 per cent of the amount paid to the injured workmen and their families. A group of employers in Detroit have organized a mutual hospital to which their employees will be sent in case of accident. The subject of medical attendance will be thoroughly inquired into by the commission for the purpose of ascertaining whether the workmen are receiving skilled and effective treatment, the cost of such treatment, and whether it is excessive.

OTTO M. EIDLITZ. LOUIS B. SCHRAM.

"The States visited aim to protect the employee against the insolvency of the employer by requiring some form of insurance. Michigan, Wisconsin and Illinois permit the employer, who can satisfy the board or commission as to his financial ability, to carry his risk without insurance, but require all other employers to take out insurance, either in a mutual or a liability company, or, as in Michigan, the third option of insuring in a State insurance fund is granted. Ohio requires all employers who come under the act to insure in an insurance fund handled by the State. Massachusetts does not permit an employer to carry his own risk, but requires that he take insurance either in a mutual or a liability company."

In New York State the Civic Federation's battle for advanced legislation in this matter has been fought out during the last five years by a special Workmen's Compensation Committee of the New York State Council. Ever since the first compulsory workmen's compensation act in this country on modern lines was enacted by the New York Legislature in 1910, and later declared unconstitutional, the necessary first step in any further progress has been of course to get a constitutional amendment permitting the passage of laws of this nature. The effort to this end was crowned with success last month in the adoption of such an amendment by approximately 250,000 majority. The exact nature of the law to be enacted under it is, of course, the next problem, and may prove a difficult one, but at any rate the stone wall which has until now prevented New York from taking its place in line with other States in this matter has been removed.

The direction of the Federation's part in this splendid result was in the hands of Mr. Louis B. Schram, chairman of the New York State Council's special committee on the subject. The preliminary course of the amendment through the Legislature was ably handled on its first passage by Senator Bayne, and on the second by Senator Griffin, in the Assembly on both occasions by Assemblyman Cyrus W. Phillips, who was in fact its author. The amendment reads as follows:

"§ 19. *Nothing contained in this constitution shall be construed to limit the power of the Legislature to enact laws for the protection of the lives, health, or safety of employees; or for the payment, either by em-*

ployers, or by employers and employees or otherwise, either directly or through a State or other system of insurance or otherwise, of compensation for injuries to employees or for death of employees resulting from such injuries without regard to fault as a cause therof, except where the injury is occasioned by the willful intention of the injured employee to bring about the injury or death of himself or of another, or where the injury results solely from the intoxication of the injured employee while on duty; or for the adjustment, determination and settlement, with or without trial by jury, of issues which may arise under such legislation; or to provide that the right of such compensation, and the remedy therefor shall be exclusive of all other rights and remedies for injuries to employees or for death resulting from such injuries; or to provide that the amount of such compensation for death shall not exceed a fixed or determinable sum; provided that all moneys paid by an employer to his employees or their legal representatives, by reason of the enactment of any of the laws herein authorized, shall be held to be a proper charge in the cost of operating the business of the employer."

During the recent campaign in New York the Federation's State Council, of which Mr. V. Everit Macy is chairman, issued an appeal to voters in behalf of the amendment, in the course of which the following brief statement was given of the case against the old methods of payment for injuries and for the new method of definite and systematic compensation:

"The principle of workmen's compensation, which has long been established in foreign countries and recently inaugurated in some form in twenty-two States in this country, is based upon the theory that a workman injured in the course of his employment is entitled to some remuneration for his physical suffering and financial loss, without regard to fault.

"In Germany, the first country to bring about this proposed social reform, as in this country, employers' liability laws preceded the movement for workmen's compensation legislation; but there, as here, the liability law proved ineffectual, for under that system, if a man suffered by the malice, ignorance or carelessness of another person, only the individual immediately responsible for the disaster—usually a fellow workman or an overseer, could be called to account—not the employer. Therefore, the sufferer or his survivors could rarely obtain a fair compensation, and generally had to go away empty-handed in consequence of the poverty of the responsible party.

"There is little justice meted to workman or employer under the present wasteful, so-called liability system, which falls far short of providing compensation for the injured and their dependents, and which provokes litigation between employee and employer. The mere fact that the employee brings suit against his employer makes for discord where there should [illegible] mutual interest. Occasionally, the wage-earner, who takes a gambler's chance by bringing suit, may be awarded through a sympathetic jury a large amount for damages; but in the majority of instances, if they get anything at all, the workmen receive but a small portion of the amount to which they are entitled—the balance going for attorney's fees and other expenses. It is not always an easy matter to prove the employer at fault. The result is that when the breadwinner is killed, the widow and her children are thrown upon charity and, in the last resort, become a public charge. It is not an uncommon thing to see the case of an industrious, hard-working mechanic, who has suffered the loss of his eyes or some equally horrible affliction, thrown out of court under the present law because of the negligence of a fellow servant. On the other hand, it sometimes happens that a jury may award a verdict that will throw the employer into bankruptcy—which not only means ruin for the business man but takes employment away from the other workmen in his enterprise.

"While there is some difference of opinion as to the form which legislation shall take under the amendment if adopted, the Federation has found unanimous agreement upon the following essential points in the interest of both employer and employee:

"1. That the right to compensation and the amount of it for particular injuries or deaths should be so definite as to leave as little as possible for controversy or difference of opinion as to the amount of compensation to which the injured workman is entitled.

"2. That the workman or his family should be so protected in the making of their settlement after injuries that advantage cannot be taken of them or an unjust or delayed settlement be forced upon them.

"3. That the workman or his dependents should be secured against the insolvency of the employer or other contingency, so that the payment of his compensation will be prompt and certain; and

"4. That there should be no question as to fault, as to contributory negligence, the assumption of risk or the so-called fellow-servant rule.

"The National Civic Federation, composed as it is of men presenting all branches of human activity—employers, employees, professional men, representatives of the church, the bar, the press, economists and social experts—has decided that no adequate compensation act in this State can be secured without a constitutional amendment, and that the interests of all concerned require the adoption of this constitutional amendment. Furthermore, the Federation hopes that its adoption will lead to the enactment of a comprehensive workmen's compensation law which will be of benefit to every citizen in the State, and appeals to all citizens, without regard to their callings, actively to support and vote for the adoption of this amendment to the constitution of the State of New York."

The drafting of this statement was in the hands of a sub-committee consisting of: W. D. Baldwin, president of the Otis Elevator Company; Samuel Gompers, president of the American Federation of Labor; Daniel Harris, president of the New York State Federation of Labor; John Sullivan, president of the Central Federated Union of New York City; and Otto M. Eidlitz, of the New York Building Trades Employers' Association.

It was signed by the following representative business men, labor officials and public-spirited citizens, members of the council, in all parts of the State, typical of the remarkably varied approval the modern idea and program for workmen's compensation commands among all elements in the community:

V. EVERIT MACY, Chairman New York State Council, The National Civic Federation, New York City.
LOUIS B. SCHRAM, Chairman the Federation's New York State Compensation Committee, Brooklyn, N. Y.
SAMUEL GOMPERS, President American Federation of Labor, New York City.
WILLIAM D. BALDWIN, President Otis Elevator Company, New York City.
DANIEL HARRIS, President New York State Federation of Labor, Brooklyn, N. Y.
FRANCIS LYNDE STETSON, Attorney, New York City.
TIMOTHY HEALY, President International Brotherhood of Stationary Firemen, New York City.
A. J. PORTER, President Shredded Wheat Company, Niagara Falls, N. Y.
ROBERT CHAMBERLAIN, Secretary-Treasurer Order of Railway Conductors, New York City.
EDWARD A. BATES, Secretary-Treasurer New York State Federation of Labor, Utica.
J. MAYHEW WAINWRIGHT, Chairman Former Commission on Employers' Liability and Causes of Industrial Accidents in New York State, New York City.
JOHN FITZGIBBONS, Brotherhood of Railroad Trainmen, Oswego, N. Y.
JOHN D. CRIMMINS, Builder, New York City.
JAMES P. HOLLAND, Eccentric Firemen's Union, New York City.
PETER J. BRADY, Secretary Allied Printing Trades Council, New York City.
THOMAS J. CURTIS, International President Tunnel and Subway Contractors' Union, New York City.
OTTO M. EIDLITZ, New York Building Trades Employers' Association, New York City.
THOMAS D. FITZGERALD, Chairman Legislative Committee, New York State Federation of Labor, Albany, N. Y.
CHARLES THADDEUS TERRY, Attorney, New York City.
JOHN J. COLLINS, Representative United Board of Business Agents of the Building Trades of Manhattan and Vicinity, New York City.
JESSE ISIDOR STRAUS, R. H. Macy & Company, New York City.
RICHARD H. CURRAN, Iron Molders' Union, Rochester, N. Y.
HENRY T. NOYES, German-American Button Company, Rochester, N. Y.
DENIS J. CONROY, Molders' Union, Corning, N. Y.
LOUIS WILEY, "New York Times," New York City.
WILLIAM C. WHISH, Chairman Executive Committee, Brotherhood of Locomotive Engineers, Albany, N. Y.
WILLIAM A. COAKLEY, President International Protective Association, Lithographic Press Feeders, United States and Canada, New York City.
CYRUS W. PHILLIPS, Member Former State Commission on Employers' Liability, Rochester, N. Y.
JOHN SULLIVAN, President Central Federated Union (Brewers' Union), New York City.
HALEY FISKE, Vice-President Metropolitan Life Insurance Company, New York City.
FREDERICK T. KELSEY, Chairman Legislative Committee, People's Institute, New York City.
GEORGE H. WRIGHT, President Central Trade and Labor Council, Rochester, N. Y.
JOHN WILLIAMS, Former State Commissioner of Labor, Albany, N. Y.
J. H. WILLIAMS, J. H. Williams Company, Brooklyn, N. Y.
MICHAEL T. NEYLAND, International Association of Machinists, New York City.
E. H. LETCHWORTH, Rogers-Brown Iron Company, Buffalo, N. Y.
EDWARD GOULD, International Brotherhood of Teamsters, Chauffeurs, Stablemen and Helpers, New York City.
F. S. TOMLIN, Secretary Joint Labor Legislative Conference of Greater New York, Brooklyn, N. Y.
E. A. MOFFETT, former Editor "Bricklayers' Journal," New York City.
JOHN HANLEY, Representative United Board of Business Agents of the Building Trades of Manhattan and Vicinity, New York City.
JEREMIAH W. JENKS, Professor of Government, New York University, New York City.
HUGH FRAYNE, Organizer American Federation of Labor, New York City.
H. M. EASLEY, Chairman Executive Council, The National Civic Federation, New York City.
SETH LOW, President The National Civic Federation, New York City.
AUGUST BELMONT, Chairman Department on Compensation for Industrial Accidents and their Prevention, The National Civic Federation, New York City.

With this appeal a campaign of education was carried on all over the State in behalf of the amendment. Copies were sent to every commercial and labor organization urging the passage of resolutions on the subject; to the newspaper press, clergymen and the chairmen of county committees of the three leading political parties, asking co-operation in whatever ways might be found possible. Calls for thousands of copies were received, and other returns from the propaganda show that extensive use was made of the material in all these directions and widespread interest aroused. The amendment adopted, it now remains to work for wisely planned legislation and in this task the forthcoming report of the Federation's Joint Commission should be of invaluable service in New York, and in all the States which have not enacted laws upon the subject.

There never was a time when education on this subject was so much needed. It is believed that this investigation will not only be of benefit to the States which have not yet enacted compensation legislation, but also to those in which laws have been passed, inasmuch as it will bring out the respective merits and demerits of the various laws. It will furnish employers, employees and the public generally a more definite and exact knowledge of the benefits to be derived from this great reform, assist in its further development along just and sound economic lines, tend toward securing uniformity of legislation in the different States, and aid in bringing about a better feeling of co-operation between employer and employee and a clearer understanding of the difficulties involved.

HUMANITARIANISM IN INDUSTRY.

The one-time sporadic efforts to better the working conditions and brighten the lines of wage earners has crystallized into a movement the momentum of which is nowhere more strikingly illustrated than in the growth of the Welfare Department of The National Civic Federation. Its proportions have assumed such magnitude that the demands upon that department have made it necessary to secure additional assistance. Miss Mary G. Potter, who is exceptionally qualified to aid in carrying forward this beneficent phase of the Federation's work, has been appointed secretary, and Miss Gertrude Beeks, who has had charge of the work from its inception, has been made director.

Miss Potter is an experienced business woman, engaged in the practice of law, and has been a probation officer in New York City. Her testimony on the subject of the morality of working girls appeared in the Department Store Number of The National Civic Federation Review, and in the same connection attention was called to her investigations for the Immigration Commissioner of the United States Government in reference to the condition of employment surrounding immigrant working girls and to the importation of immigrant women for immoral purposes. She also was employed by James B. Reynolds, Assistant District Attorney, in connection with the work of the Rockefeller Grand Jury, which led her personally to look into their home conditions and later to organize the tenement house women, with a view to making them realize what they could do to protect their daughters. She found that, owing to the fact that conditions have changed since they were young, they did not realize the temptations which are thrown about girls to-day and their responsibilities as mothers. She organized a group of eight hundred tenement house mothers into the industrial membership of the Woman's Municipal League, living in their district during the first few months of her endeavor. After office hours, she gives personal advice to the members, who go to her with every kind of problem. Her co-operation will be a valuable reinforcement of the rapidly extending work of the Welfare Department.

A JUDICIAL INQUIRY—NOT A COMPROMISE.

"The present proceeding has been in every sense of the word an arbitration. Many proceedings of the kind are, in effect, little more than formal compromises; but in this proceeding the intermediate arbitrators have been obliged to pass upon the merits of every article as proposed. The result is that, in most cases, each article as adopted has been adopted by a vote of four to two, although the majority represents at times the intermediate arbitrators and the representatives of the men, and at other times the intermediate arbitrators and the representatives of the railroads."—*From award of the board in the arbitration between Eastern railroads and conductors and trainmen.*

A GREAT ACHIEVEMENT FOR INDUSTRIAL PEACE

THE CIVIC FEDERATION'S MEDIATION BILL BECOMES LAW IN TIME TO PREVENT DISASTROUS LABOR CONTEST ON THE EASTERN RAILROADS

SETH LOW, Pres. The Nat. Civic Federation. MARTIN A. KNAPP, Chair'n Interstate Commerce Court. DARIUS MILLER, Pres. C. B. & Q. R. R. MARCUS M. MARKS, Chairman N. C. F. Dept. on Mediation Law. W. G. LEE, Pres. Brotherhood R. R. Trainmen. A. B. GARRETSON, Pres. Order Railway Conductors.

SAMUEL REA, Pres. Pennsylvania R. R. W. C. BROWN, Pres. N. Y. Central Lines. CHARLES P. NEILL, Former U. S. Com'r Labor Statistics. RALPH M. EASLEY, Chairman N. C. F. Exec. Council. FRANK TRUMBULL, Chairman Ches. & Ohio Ry. CHARLES A. WICKERSHAM, Pres. Atlanta & West Point R. R.

DANIEL WILLARD, Pres. Balt. & Ohio R. R. W. S. CARTER, Pres. Brotherhood Loco. Firemen. H. B. PERHAM, Pres. Order Ry. Telegraphers.

ROBERT S. LOVETT, Pres. Union Pacific Ry. (Copyright by Gessford.) WARREN S. STONE, Pres. Brotherhood Loco. Engineers.

THE COMMITTEE WHICH WORKED FOR PASSAGE OF THE NEWLANDS MEDIATION ACT.

ONE of the most successful as well as most important achievements of The Civic Federation in the past year has been the work of the Department on Industrial Mediation Law. This department undertook the organization of a committee composed of railroad presidents, presidents of railroad brotherhoods and officials of the United States Government having had experience in enforcing the Erdman Act. The working of that act during the preceding five years had demonstrated that it lacked many essential features for success. This committee was made up as follows:

REPRESENTING THE GOVERNMENT—Martin A. Knapp, Judge, United States Commerce Court; Charles P. Neill, Commissioner, Bureau of Labor Statistics, Department of Labor.

REPRESENTING THE NATIONAL CIVIC FEDERATION—Seth Low, President the National Civic Federation; Ralph M. Easley, Chairman Executive Council; Marcus M. Marks, Chairman Department on Industrial Mediation Law.

REPRESENTING THE RAILROADS—William C. Brown, President New York Central lines; Robert S. Lovett, President Union Pacific Railroad; Darius Miller, President Chicago, Burlington & Quincy R. R.; Samuel Rea, President Pennsylvania Railroad; Frank Trumbull, President Chesapeake & Ohio R. R.; Daniel Willard, President Baltimore & Ohio R. R.; Charles A. Wickersham, President Atlanta & West Point R. R.

REPRESENTING THE RAILWAY BROTHERHOODS—W. S. Carter, President Brotherhood Locomotive Firemen and Enginemen; A. B. Garretson, President Order of Railway Conductors; W. G. Lee, President Brotherhood Railroad Trainmen; H. B. Perham, President Brotherhood Railway Telegraphers; Warren S. Stone, Grand Chief International Brotherhood of Locomotive Engineers.

It began its work at a conference held in February, 1913, in New York City, at which the full committee was in attendance. After several weeks of careful work, a bill was drafted with the unanimous support of all the railroad brotherhoods and the representative railroad presidents just named. Concerning the vital features of this bill President Low said, at the time of its introduction in Congress:

"It is at once a profoundly significant and an encouraging circumstance that the great interests concerned have met together and have agreed with unanimity on a specific measure to be proposed to Congress as a satisfactory means of settling by arbitration all controversies that may arise between them. Like all measures which represent the assent of many minds, the bill as submitted to Congress represents a compromise on certain points. Both the railroads and their employees admit that the arbitration board of three, as provided by the Erdman Act, as it now stands, is too small when the interests affected are the interests of a whole section of the country and not a single railroad. All agree that when a single railroad is concerned a board of three is better than a larger board. When a larger board is desirable the number is fixed in the proposed bill at six—that is to say, two representing the railroads, two representing the employees, and two representing—if you please—the general public. It has been possible to secure the unanimous support for a board of six, and not for any other larger board.

"In the bill just presented to Congress, other deviations from the Erdman Act are proposed as the result of experience under that act. It would be impossible to bring to bear upon this subject greater familiarity with the Erdman Act and its working, than was represented in the preparation of this bill, and both Congress and the country may take it for granted that every deviation from the Erdman Act has been made for some cause growing out of experience with that act. The fact that these proposed deviations have been unanimously accepted by those most directly affected is sufficient to justify their careful consideration, for it may certainly be said that the public interest, as distinguished from the interests of the railroads and their employees, is as carefully protected under this bill as under the Erdman Act in its present form.

"The Erdman Act, broadly speaking, provides for mediation between interstate railroads and their employees at the request of either party by the Chief Justice of the Commerce Court and the Commissioner of Labor. It also provides a method for arbitration under the authority of Federal law. For several years after its enactment no appeal was made to the services of the mediators under the Erdman Act. Of late years, however, it has been increasingly resorted to both by the railroads and by their employees, with the result that as to the mediation features of the law the work has become so continuous and so important that the proposed bill suggests the creation of a Commissioner of Mediation and Conciliation, to be filled by the President, by and with the advice and consent of the Senate, whose time shall be exclusively devoted to this work. With the Commissioner of Mediation and Conciliation is to be associated under the proposed bill an Assistant Commissioner of Mediation and Conciliation.

"The resort to the Erdman Act for purposes of arbitration is of still more recent development. Recent as it is, however, it has grown from the occasional arbitration between one railroad and one branch of its employes into arbitration often involving large groups of railroads and all of their employees. In order to deal effectively with arbitration, the proposed bill, therefore, provides for a Board of Conciliation and Arbitration to be composed of three members; namely, the Commissioner of Mediation and Conciliation and of two other officials of the Government who have been appointed by and with the advice and consent of the Senate, to be designated by the President. The principal function of this board is to name disinterested arbitrators who are to serve in any given arbitration in company with the arbitrators named by the railroads and by their employees respectively, in case the parties to the controversy cannot agree. This being the function of the board, it evidently is not necessary that such a board should sit continuously, and, therefore, the two other officials of the Government who, with the Commissioner of Mediation and Conciliation, constitute the Board of Mediation and Conciliation, may conveniently be designated by the President from other officials of the Government. Under the terms of the proposed bill the only limitation upon the discretion of the President in the designation of these two members of the Board of Mediation and Conciliation is that they shall have been appointed to the offices which they hold by and with the advice and consent of the Senate. This freedom of choice will enable the President to select whatever officials seem to him most available for the discharge of the delicate duties devolved upon this board.

"This proposed bill, like the Erdman Act, relies entirely upon voluntary arbitration. Arbitration which is voluntary has repeatedly proved its value in railroad experience; because, when men arbitrate voluntarily they accept the terms of the award. Compulsory arbitration on the other hand is impracticable, because not even the power of the State can compel men to work under conditions which do not command their assent. When the employers and employes of a great industry, therefore, as in this instance, are simply asking for a law which will give legal sanction to a method of arbitration which both are willing to accept, the argument in favor of such legislation is exceedingly strong."

The bill was introduced into the United States Senate by Senator Francis G. Newlands, and into the House of Representatives by Congressman Henry D. Clayton. A joint hearing before committees of the two houses was held, attended by the members of the Federation Committee.

In the meantime, a threatened strike of 80,000 conductors and trainmen on the Eastern railroads, resulting from their inability to come to an agreement in conference with the managers of the roads, accentuated the urgent necessity for prompt action in order that the law might be available for use in that controversy. There was not a quorum in the House of Representatives when action was first sought on the matter, but through the efforts of Senator Newlands the bill drafted by the Federation was unanimously passed by the Senate. In the House the bill was modified to meet the views of Secretary W. B. Wilson, of the Department of Labor, and its passage secured by Congressman Clayton, chairman of the Judiciary Committee.

By the time this action was taken official representatives of the two brotherhoods involved in the threatened strike had been called together in New York, which made it apparent that if the two houses of Congress could not be brought into agreement at once the conductors and trainmen on all the Eastern railroads would go out. President Low, Marcus M. Marks and Mr. R. M. Easley attended the meeting of the railroad men, and appealed to them, in the name of The National Civic Federation, and on behalf of the public, to delay the call for the strike and to send the presidents of the two brotherhoods involved to a conference at the White House, which had been arranged in the meantime by President Low through Secretary of Labor W. B. Wilson.

At this conference, July 14, all the members of the Civic Federation's committee were present, as well as Senator Newlands, chairman of the Interstate Commerce Committee of the Senate; Congressman Clayton, chairman of the Judiciary Committee of the House; Senator John W. Kern, vice-president of the Senate, and Congressman James R. Mann, leader of the Republican minority in the House. President Low was chosen by the railroads and the brotherhood men alike to speak for them in presenting the situation to the President. The matter was made an emergency measure. An agreement was reached and the bill, as amended, passed both houses within forty-eight hours, and became a law.

After the signing of the law a dispute arose between the railroad managers and the men concerned in the controversy as to the questions to be arbitrated, and President Low again stepped into the breach and brought about a settlement on that point so that the matter in question went to arbitration. Although it is an unwritten law of the Civic Federation that none of its officers shall act as arbitrators, this being the first test of the new law and the Federation having been instrumental in securing its passage, President Low was morally obliged to accede to the requests of both parties and act as chairman of the arbitration board. To this work he has, together with President John H. Finley, given two months of unremitting attention, morning, noon and night.

The members of the board selected by the railroads were A. H. Smith, vice-president New York Central lines, and W. W. Atterbury, vice-president Pennsylvania Railroad; those chosen by the brotherhood men were D. L. Cease, editor Railroad Trainmen's Journal, and L. E. Sheppard, vice-president Order Railway Conductors.

Hearings began on September 11 in New York, and continued until October 10. Another month was occupied by the board in studying the testimony and preparing its report. The award, made public November 10, grants to the men an average increase of 7 per cent in wages, which it is estimated will add about $6,000,000 to the annual expense roll of the railroads. The brotherhood men had asked increases amounting to about 18 per cent, with payment for overtime at time and one-half. On the overtime matter the board fixed certain definite rates, but held that in other lines of industry where time and one-half is paid the determination of whether or not the extra time shall be worked rests with the employer. "In railroading," on the other hand, "it is quite evident that in many cases neither the management nor the trainmen can prevent overtime; and it appears to this board, therefore, that punitive overtime, as it is called, is an unsound principle when applied to the running of trains."

The board estimates the increased cost of living since the last wage adjustment in 1910, at 7 per cent, and therefore recognizes cost of living as a principal factor to be properly considered in the fixing of wage rates. Of equal or greater importance is the treatment the board gives to the matter of freight rates, which it frankly urges may need revision in order to permit the payment of the necessary basic charges and allow for improvements in equipment, for better service and greater safety.

The comments of the board on this subject make a telling statement of the problem which faces transportation companies, under present legal restrictions, all over the country:

"The board has no authority to determine the passenger and freight rates to be paid in the Eastern territory; neither is it in position to determine whether such an increase is justified, as a matter of fact, by all of the circumstances. This board, however, believes that it must make its finding as to what is a proper rate of pay to be awarded to the conductors and trainmen as a result of this arbitration without any reference to the dilemma in which the railroads are evidently placed by the laws which make it impossible for them to increase passenger and freight rates without the authority of the Interstate Commerce Commission, or of the Railroad Commissions of the various States. To take any other view of the question would be to decide that no increase of pay, while the laws remain as they are, can ever be made except voluntarily by the railroads.

"At the present time a ton of freight is moved in the Eastern territory more than three miles for the value of a two-cent postage stamp. This is the cheapest railroad service to the shipper to be found on the face of the globe. In the face of such a fact it would be unjust to say that railroad employees must continue to be satisfied only with what can be paid from freight rates as low as this. The Interstate Commerce Commission, and not this Arbitration Board, has the duty of determining whether the railroads can earn in addition to their other charges, without an increase of freight rates, the rates of pay that this board believes to be due at the present time to the conductors and trainmen."

In respect to the urgent need of improved equipment the board calls the attention of the Interstate Commerce Commission to "the connection between the decrease of hazard, the danger to life and limb, through the installation of safety appliances, by the substitution of steel for wooden cars, by double tracking and by increasing railroad facilities, as railroad business increases.

"Any policy that would make it impossible for the railroads to command this money [for improvements] would be a profound misfortune to the whole nation. Such a policy would be bad enough in its effect upon transportation, because it would reduce the efficiency of the railroads; but it would be criminal, in the sense that it would make the great army of railroad employees, who are numbered by hundreds of thousands, follow their hazardous occupation under conditions more hazardous than are necessary. No American reads the records of railroad accidents in the United States without feeling a sense of reproach. This board wishes to call the attention of the country to its belief that railroad accidents can be reduced almost precisely in proportion to the modernizing of the railroads and the improvement in their equipment."

The wage increases awarded are not based upon the demand of the brotherhood men for standardization of rates throughout the country, nor does the board definitely pass upon the merits of this contention. Here is one of the knottiest problems that has developed in the railroad labor situation in recent years, and the plan the Arbitration Board proposes for meeting it may prove in the long range the most important feature of the entire award. Two of the arbitrators noted the fact that increases on the Eastern roads may be followed by new demands west of Chicago, to equalize the differential which has always been claimed by reason of higher cost of living beyond the Mississippi. This difference, however, has more than once led to requests for a new leveling up on the Eastern roads, based on the theory of equal pay for similar work. On this matter the board says in part:

"Some public authority authorized by the Congress should make an independent inquiry as to whether there is any longer any substantial reason for the maintenance of a wage differential between the West and the East based on territorial conditions. Such an inquiry ought also to result in a recommendation, if it is found that a differential ought to exist, as to what such differential should be. . . . This suggestion does not contemplate that the body making such inquiry should attempt to fix wages; but only that it should make a study of the proper basis for the fixing of wages. Neither is it suggested for a moment that wages, when agreed upon by any process, should become unchangeable. Circumstances change and wage scales must change with circumstances like everything else; but this board does believe that, by the process suggested, some of the artificial embarrassments to the fair and equitable adjustment of railroad wages may be removed. It is possible that the Commission on Industrial Relations recently appointed by President Wilson may be competent to carry out the suggested inquiry. The Interstate Commerce Commission has recently organized a special force to consider the valuation of railroads. Possibly the Industrial Commission may see its way to organize a special force to make the inquiry suggested by this board as to standardization and wage scales between the Eastern and Western territories."

It is probable that public sentiment has been with the transportation companies in this "endless chain" predicament more largely than on any other railroad issue for many years. The cause of arbitration has suffered at the same time from the impression that it might become merely the instrument of a seesaw of Eastern and Western schedules. This, probably without intent on the part of anybody to misuse the method, would of course carry it very far from its original purpose of maintaining industrial peace with justice.

The Arbitration Board proposes a way out of the dilemma which the companies and the men alike should be prompt to accept, working together for a solution of the vexed question once for all. Such an understanding, with or without a government inquiry, would be of course in the public interest but even more in their own. It is far-sighted industrial statesmanship in the midst of a complicated mass of testimony, claims and counterclaims, to put a finger on one of the chief underlying sources of trouble and plan for its future elimination. It is also a vindication of arbitration itself in its larger possibilities, over and above all the practical difficulties which usually surround it.

The entire outcome of this critical situation, upon which the business prosperity and transportation necessities of half the population of the United States depended, is, however, the real justification for the methods so successfully employed. Compared with the enormous losses which would have been entailed by a strike on these lines, the additional costs which will result from the process of judicial inquiry based upon a study of facts instead

(Concluded on page 11.)

THE TRUTH ABOUT WAGES AND VICE

A FEW WORDS WITH CRITICS OF THE RECENT INVESTIGATION OF WORKING CONDITIONS IN NEW YORK DEPARTMENT STORES

WIDESPREAD comment upon the study of department store conditions in New York, published in the last number of the Review reveals almost unanimous approval of the findings as a much-needed clarification of the subject, especially in its bearing upon the alleged relation of the wage scale to the white slave problem.

The results of this inquiry showed a much more encouraging state of affairs for the most part than the public had been led to imagine from much inferential discussion and sensational assertion.

On the other hand, so overwhelming a showing of data and opinion has not, of course, been a welcome contribution in the eyes of those who, for whatever motives, have apparently set their hearts upon proving the department stores a recruiting ground for the white slave traffic. Serious attacks upon the report and its conclusions have been remarkably few, but among these the most explicit appeared in *The Survey* of October 11th in the form of a review by Miss Mary Van Kleeck, secretary of the Russell Sage Foundation's Committee on Women's Work. We are obliged to say of this criticism that by partial quotation of the report and omission of many of its positive recommendations, an entirely wrong impression is given of the investigation as a whole, while some of the very measures advocated therein are in turn advanced by our critic in such a way as to convey the idea that the Federation is opposed to them.

While the agents and investigators who acted on behalf of the Welfare Department do not claim to be infallible, an earnest effort was made to present existing evils and to call attention to the welfare features which have been installed for the benefit of employees by these New York stores. The hours of work, for example, are not, as Miss Van Kleeck remarks, "briefly discussed." Every type of employee is covered; more than 4,000 words are devoted to the subject; an eight-hour standard is recommended, and arguments as strong as we are capable of making are presented for reduction of hours, discontinuing of overtime work, payment therefor when necessary in emergencies; Saturday closing at noon in summer and other changes in the interest of the workers.

Miss Van Kleeck announces as something of a discovery that "the use of the average is dangerous . . . and it is inevitable that their high wage rates should so overbalance the low payments . . . as to give a false impression of the earnings of the majority." This familiar truth, a commonplace of all social investigation, Miss Van Kleeck might have found reaffirmed in the very report in question, as follows: "As averages may mislead and be unfair to low wage groups because a few high salaries considerably increase the wage rate, one special table was prepared to give the **numbers receiving certain definite wages,** and it depicts the condition most impressively."

To support her contention our critic continues: "The use of the average is dangerous when the group of saleswomen in the table quoted includes nineteen earning $30.00 to $39.99; seven, $40.00 to $49.99, and one designated as $60.00 to $69.99." She does not, however, quote this sentence from the report: "The highest wage paid any individual saleswoman (not a buyer or assistant buyer) is $60.00 and the lowest is $3.50."

She fails also to note that the Federation secured the latest figures on high wage rates paid in manufacturing in New York City—i. e., $35.00 under the protocol arrangement in the garment industry, and compared it with $60.00, the highest rate paid to saleswomen—the type of employee for whom the greatest concern is evidenced by the public. She fails to show that the latest Government reports were secured by the Federation with a view to learning whether the conditions had changed materially since the Federation's first investigation was made, and that the median line for factory workers was found to remain somewhere between $6.00 and $6.25 as an average. The exact figures for department stores were an average of $9.31 for saleswomen in the spring of 1912, those for 1909 having been $8.84, as against $6.12 for women in factories, mills and like industries in New York City.

Miss Van Kleeck says: "Even assuming, as seems doubtful, that the duties of the highly paid women were similar to those of the majority behind the counters. . . .'

They were not only similar, but they were absolutely the same—that is, the duties of saleswomen and nothing else, as stated in the report. They do not, however, necessarily "stand behind counters"; they may be in fur departments, where the main work is in open places, or they may be behind counters selling expensive laces, which requires equally expert service and commands high salaries.

This further explanation (in the report) of the use of averages would, we think, have quite removed the point of Miss Van Kleeck's criticism had she seen fit to quote it: "The fairness of the Federation's averages must be emphasized when it is realized that in this inquiry affecting saleswomen the average rate is that of the **full complement** of the sales force in each of seventeen stores, and then of all taken together. In no other way can a correct average be secured. Investigations other than that of the Government into wages of saleswomen made in various parts of the country have not been scientific, for the reason that 'a given number of saleswomen' has been the basis. Under such a plan the full groups selected may all be getting approximately the same salaries and simply represent types from several stores. It would be an easy matter to take a group living in a particular community and to show that their average wage is $6, but in that number there may not be any getting the highest or the lowest salary.'

Miss Van Kleeck informs her readers that it does not appear "that any workers were interviewed in the inquiry into wages in stores." Many were indeed interviewed during the initial steps, and the results were of assistance in pointing to methods to be employed in the wage inquiry, but it is beyond belief that a serious critic could expect the result of such questioning to be taken as definite, dependable statistics, rather than the complete payrolls which were thoroughly examined and verified by public accountants of undoubted integrity.

Almost in the same breath Miss Van Kleeck remarks that no available statistics of value exist, and commends her own "careful study" of the bookbinding trade, which the Federation accepted on the same plane of reliability as the Government statistics which she ridicules. Perhaps they cannot all be unreliable if our critics are "careful." She dismisses the Government inquiry into wages as "of the most casual sort." A reader of these exhaustive reports would find such a statement surprising. The Government figures were, in fact, thoroughly studied by three experts and selected because they were the only ones available which could be interpreted as furnishing a proper basis for comparison.

Miss Van Kleeck's objection on this point is repeated editorially in *The Survey* of November 15, the specific point being that the Federation took from Government data a weekly rate of $6.12 for women workers in factories, and ignored a corresponding wage of $6.07 for store workers, using instead the Government's figures of $8.84 in 1909, and $9.31 in 1911 for saleswomen in department stores only. Our investigators used Government statistics where none more specific were available, and were quite at liberty to compare with these, upon a proper basis, whatever special groups of facts from other sources they might consider reliable and germane to the scope of their particular inquiry. Perhaps in all this discussion the fact has been overlooked that the Federation was not attempting a study of conditions of women workers in all stores, including small retail shops, but expressly limited itself to the typical department stores which have been glaringly pictured as responsible above all others for labor conditions tending to drive their women employees to lives of shame.

To have quoted the Government wage of $6.07 for women workers in miscellaneous stores, instead of discrediting the Federation's conclusions, would merely have added confirmation from another source on this particular point, by showing a much better state of affairs on the whole in the large stores than in the small. Comparing the department store wages with the $6.12 average for women factory workers of all grades was considered proper because of several mutually offsetting items discovered by the accountants who studied both groups of data with great care, and for the further reason that, with the single exception of women garment workers under the new protocol, no such wide variety of occupations and wage rates exists among women factory workers as among store workers; so that it was not believed unreasonable to consider the $6.12 average a fairly representative one for comparison with the department store figures. It is hardly conceivable that the lowness of this rate is due to taking account of any lower groups of wages than may be found at the bottom of the ladder in the wide range of occupations in department stores, all of which were included in the department store averages.

To make allowance for losses in "slack seasons" in averaging store wages, as Miss Van Kleeck proposes, would give us nothing of value, for the simple reason that layoffs are not customary in department stores, except in so far as the temporary force during the holidays is concerned. That is the only time when "irregular employment" needs to be considered, and despite our critic's statement to the contrary, the Federation's report did take that up at length. Its figures were based upon the wage scale for one week in April, when the force is steady, and, therefore only wages of those who are employed throughout the year were considered. They give as accurate an index of the yearly income as it is possible to secure.

In criticising the Federation for using her own statistics on the bookbinding trade, Miss Van Kleeck states that they are taken "by the way, not from the volume on 'Women in the Bookbinding Trade,' but from the publisher's announcement of the book." Does she repudiate the Survey Associates, who published the very interesting leaflet from which, it is true, this statement was taken? Is Miss Van Kleeck willing to say that the following quotation therefrom does not represent her views on wages of bookbinders or that the Survey Associates misrepresented her?

> "Wages Are Low. Allowing for losses in slack season, three-quarters of the women receive less than $400 a year, and the average is $300 a year. This, as Miss Van Kleeck points out, is at the rate of about $6 a week, which is far below the generally accepted minimum of $9 a week on which a woman can support herself in New York."

In the book itself, on pages 220 and 221, Miss Van Kleeck thus emphasizes this estimate of yearly income: "Nearly three-quarters of them receive less than $400 in a year, *in spite of their finding employment in other occupations when they have no work in bookbinding.*" (Italics ours.)

Had this fact of outside employment been noted in the Federation's report it would have increased the disparity between the wages of factory girls and department store girls. Miss Van Kleeck, however, overlooks altogether this statement in the Federation's report: "Although the present average wage in department stores is higher than in factories, that fact does not prove that department store saleswomen get enough, but may rather accentuate the low wage of women in manufacture. It does reduce the cause for criticism leveled at department stores, but not the responsibility for helping to bring about a better condition."

The Federation is fully in accord, in so far as the facts bear out the description, with Miss Van Kleeck's belief that: "To go to work too young; to be used up in hard work which stunts development; to toil long hours and to walk home late at night, unprotected on the deserted streets (while your employer fights every attempt to strengthen the laws protecting women and girl workers) . . . is to be handicapped in a way which statistics can never measure . . . and an industry which makes the young working girls of the community defenceless needs the salutary effect of public discussion."

All employers, however, do not fight humanitarian legislation. It is only too true that many do, and that many fail to observe the laws when enacted. For such there can be no excuse. On the other hand, we must be fair and recognize the fact that many employers have actually assisted in securing legislation in the interest of labor.

Miss Van Kleeck admits that the Federation's report "may have valuable results in a practical way because attention has been called in so detailed a manner to welfare plans in operation in stores"; while elsewhere she ridicules and belittles the social value of welfare work as a proper object of "public suspicion." She is quite correct, however, in stating that to stimulate interest in welfare activities can only be of permanent value when a fair wage scale and a shorter work day are made the first items in any program of improvement. The Federation has, in fact, always insisted upon exactly these points, which are a definite part of its welfare program. The by-laws of the Department affirm that: "In promoting the work, it is recognized that the first essentials to the welfare of employees are steady work, an equitable wage and reasonable hours of labor; but that the employer has a further obligation."

Nothing less than a voice in determining the conditions of their own labor, Miss Van Kleeck sug-

(Continued on page 12.)

THE NATIONAL
Civic Federation Review

Office: Thirty-third Floor, Metropolitan Tower
1 Madison Avenue New York City

RALPH M. EASLEY, Editor

The Editor alone is Responsible for any unsigned article or unquoted statement published in THE NATIONAL CIVIC FEDERATION REVIEW.

PUBLISHED BY

The National Civic Federation

The Annual Meeting Dec. 11 and 12

The topics to be considered at the Fourteenth Annual Meeting of The National Civic Federation make it certain that the occasion will be one of extraordinary interest. No subjects before the public to-day are of more engrossing concern, and none offer more encouraging opportunity for the co-operation of patriotic citizens in promoting their wise treatment, than those on the program for this meeting, notably the proposed amendment to the Sherman Anti-Trust Act, the extension and improvement of workmen's compensation laws, the revision and better enforcement of pure food and drug laws, the problem of labor disputes in the government service and among employees of public service corporations, the proper regulation of street railways, gas and electric light service, and the national inquiry to be undertaken by the Federation into the facts and results of industrial and social progress during the last generation, as well as of the theories and program of the socialist and other revolutionary movements.

Each of these is a problem which should not be a football of party politics, but demands thorough and frank discussion by competent authorities representing all views and interests, to the end that whatever policies are recommended for legislation or for voluntary action shall be genuinely in the public interest and have the largest probability of successful operation.

There will be in addition, as stated in the more detailed announcement of the meeting on the front page of this number of the Review, reports from the Welfare Department and from the Women's Department, with sessions devoted to work in progress and in prospect in each of these important phases of the Federation's work.

The annual dinner has come to be the most broadly representative and impressive gathering of citizens from all parts of the country and all walks of life held anywhere in America, and for that matter in no country to-day probably would anything resembling it be possible. It is a unique focusing of all elements taking an active and helpful part in the civic and industrial life of the republic, and epitomizes the essential democracy of the institutions under which such a gathering is possible. These occasions always tax the capacity of the available seating accommodations, and, in addition to their significance in themselves, are of great practical service in promoting acquaintance and better understanding among men and women needing each others' viewpoints and help in many lines of social and industrial effort.

The National "Stock-Taking."

"First know the facts, then go ahead," is the sound principle out of which the entire plan has developed for a national survey of industrial and social progress, announced elsewhere in this number. That rule is the recognized basis of safe, intelligent action in every line of business and civic effort, but we need to-day to apply it on the national scale. As a nation we do not know how far we have come or where we stand in the really vital matters of social welfare. A comprehensive view of our total situation has become urgently necessary to the wise planning of future policies and focusing of helpful reform work upon the places and conditions most needing it.

The great typical problems confronting us to-day are of nation-wide scope, and have come upon us so fast and with so many complications that we are little more able to judge of their total meaning than a man in the street is able to tell the prevailing drift of the crowds that surround him. This becomes clear, however, from a vantage point high enough to take in the movement as a whole. We need to-day the national vantage point, the ability to see our conditions in the large and in due proportion. To get this it is not necessary that such an inquiry be absolutely exhaustive, on the plan of a government census, but it must be sufficiently far-reaching to discount all margins of error and show conclusively the actual trend of social changes during the last generation, whether in the direction of progress or the reverse, in each subdivision of the field as well as in the general movement.

As stated in the general outline of the survey, in much of the field "the main work will be bringing together the results of official and other investigations already made. In certain respects further investigation will be required. In other cases, the facts may prove too elusive, or the records too incomplete, for a wholly satisfactory report. In the greater part of the work, however, it is possible to reach definite conclusions either by statistical investigation or by authoritative descriptive summary."

Probably no aspect of this undertaking will have greater interest or practical usefulness in the present confusion of social doctrines and revolutionary creeds than the study which is to be made of these theories, both on their merits and in the light of the economic facts the investigation will reveal. To quote again from the announcement of scope and purpose of the inquiry, on another page:

"Features to be necessarily included in the work will be examining the principles involved in the movement for the abolition of private ownership in the means of production and distribution of wealth and studying the differences in the fundamental aims and methods of the labor movement as conducted by the trade unions, the socialists and the Industrial Workers of the World."

Both the Advisory Council and the Executive Committee which will have the practical direction of the work are made up of representative men of the widest variety of interests and viewpoints, a method of supervision which has proved the best possible guarantee of accuracy, impartiality and reliability in all the Federation's studies of special subjects. Included among these, as will be seen from the list printed in connection with the outline of the survey, are large employers of labor, officers of all the leading trade unions connected with the American Federation of Labor, and of the railroad brotherhoods, college presidents and other eminent educators, clergymen, social and charitable workers, lawyers, public officials and officers of agricultural, trade, commercial and civic organizations without number.

The entire purpose of this "stock taking" is not to pile up masses of statistics, but to bring together in one compass the salient features of our national gains and shortcomings in their relation to human welfare. This should afford the most effective possible means of testing the claims upon which current social theories are based. It should prove also a tremendous practical help in locating the actual rather than the imaginary causes of evils and abuses in the social system, as well as in bringing out the features best worth preserving and developing to larger human service.

The Railroad Arbitration.

On another page appears the full story of the remarkable banding together of railroad presidents, brotherhood chiefs and citizens interested from the standpoint of the general community, in a common effort to prevent what might have been a paralysis of transportation throughout the East. Before this could be assured it was necessary at the critical moment to enlist the help of Congress and the President to procure the changes necessary in the Erdman law to make arbitration acceptable to both parties. The railroad managers and brotherhood men could hardly have stood further apart on the wage questions at stake, but in the face of impending disaster they came together as men of one interest in this successful effort to find a better way out. It is a good working illustration of the common stake of labor and capital in the stability of the industrial system, over and above all current questions of division of joint earnings—an economic truth which can neither be harangued nor ridiculed off its foundation.

Nowhere else in the world to-day would it be possible to duplicate on anything like the same scale the industrial good sense and broad-mindedness which made this kind of co-operation possible at just the time when all the direct issues in the case tended to drive the two sides hopelessly apart. Even in England, where organization of labor was something to be reckoned with for half a century before the movement really began in this country, and where the prevalence of trade agreements and collective bargaining is often contrasted with our supposed "crude methods," it has proved impossible to get the heads of the great railroad systems to meet and talk with the official representatives of the men, to say nothing of joint compacts or voluntary arbitration. There is considerable industrial history yet to be made in Great Britain, apparently, before a similar crisis would find these two elements joining hands to get a measure through Parliament enabling them to settle their differences without disturbing the business of the country.

There are serious problems growing out of this arbitration yet to be solved; the board in its award names some of them and suggests ways and means of relief. Nevertheless, had the matter been fought out to the bitter end, as some advisers believed must be done this time "once for all," the same or perhaps ten times greater problems would have remained to harass the future of railroad transportation, and with much poorer prospect of wise remedial action than now is in sight. Even had the railroads won such a battle, at terrific cost, according to all industrial experience the defeated employees would have come up again and again with the postponed issue, which in a matter of wages is far more fundamental than any question of organization or union policies or the leadership of any particular man or men.

There is no short and easy road to escape these periodical readjustments of living costs and earning power, under whatever industrial or social system. The only practical question is whether these inevitable changes shall be handled on the basis of twentieth century intelligence and judicial inquiry, or of mediaeval brute force. The trend of civilization is compelling the sane method as a matter of economic and moral necessity.

A Congress of Labor. Few people not connected with the trade union movement have any idea of the range of topics debated and acted upon at the annual conventions of the American Federation of Labor. How many know or imagine, for instance, that a large proportion of these subjects are not those commonly termed "labor demands" in the specific or class sense, but are literally those of common and similar interest to the great mass of American citizens in all walks of life? Here are some of the matters discussed in the report of the Executive Council at the recent thirty-third annual Convention in Seattle; workmen's compensation, seamen's legislation, immigration, safety appliances, Federal bureau of health, arbitration, child labor, industrial education, old age pensions, the Industrial Relations Commission, minimum wage legislation, proposed welfare amendments, unemployment, the Panama Exposition, occupational disease congress, international peace, the Philippines, farmers' co-operation movement, uniformity of text books, mothers' day, university extension, and conservation of natural resources.

The orderly, businesslike deliberations of this great representative body of American workingmen present a contrast to the typical inflammatory proceedings of socialist and I. W. W. gatherings, professing to represent the "wage-earning masses," which ought not to be lost upon the American public. People who still harbor the notion that any kind of a labor meeting is merely another hatching place for strikes and boycotts might well read this sane, temperate statement from the same report, in connection with the fact that the membership of unions represented in the Federation has passed the two million mark:

"Not only has there been progress made in numbers, but for the increasing numbers there have been increase in wages, shortening of the workday, improvement in sanitary and general conditions under which the work is done, better protection for the life and health of the workers. These are fundamental factors in determining the standard of living prevailing among working people—the greater proportion of all the people. The test of the degree of civilization of any nation is the standard of living generally prevailing. There can be no question of the statement that the general standard of living among Americans has been raised year after year. The things which to-day are held to be necessities were deemed luxuries a decade ago. Furthermore, there can be no question of the statement that the organized labor movement of America has been the most potent force in bringing about this higher standard of living now prevailing among the American workingmen and women and those dependent upon them."

Even more enlightening ought to be the fine spirit of such a declaration as this:

"You who are to transact the affairs of this movement, be fully conscious of the dignity and responsibility devolving upon you—the welfare of the human beings whom you represent. Where so much is at stake, fads, idealistic but impracticable fancy, personal interests, must give way to the larger aspects of all problems. Differences of opinion there must be, for they are inseparable from a growing movement that must adjust to the changing conditions of industry and society. For the success of the cause does not depend upon the elimination of disputes, but upon the spirit in which they are treated."

Any movement which has been able to breed among the workers themselves, mainly with the opposition instead of the help of the rest of the community, a habit of self-control evidenced in sentiments such as these has its place among the useful and necessary factors in American industrial life. Backing up words with deeds, the convention put itself again on record as a bulwark against the revolutionary enemies of society by re-electing Samuel Gompers for the twenty-eighth time, and continuing the main outlines of its trade policies under the opportunities offered by the industrial system of which it is a part.

This great business convention of independent workingmen does not and could not spring from a nation of "wage slaves," of socialist imagination. It is really a congress of the only kind of industrial democracy which has any substantial value or meaning in the productive organization of the community.

An Inside View of I. W. W. Methods. For a really blistering indictment of I. W. W. leaders and policies it is no longer necessary to interview citizens of Paterson or to look up police records. The following lifelike picture of the true inwardness of things appeared on August 23 in a communication signed "L. C. R.," printed in the leading position and with double leads on the editorial page of SOLIDARITY, official organ of the Industrial Workers of the World. There was no accompanying disavowal or criticism, and the article must be taken, therefore, as in accord with the editorial views of the publication. It will relieve the minds of any just-minded citizens who may have imagined that the I. W. W. leaders were a band of zealots painted much blacker than they deserve by the "capitalist press." It brings to light also some of the rocks of dissension upon which this whole movement of industrial anarchy is going to wreck all over the country:

"If the Industrial Workers of the World is going to organize the working class then we will have to make a great change in our attitude toward the labor movement and in the methods that we are now using. At present we are to the labor movement what the high diver is to the circus. A sensation, marvelous and nerve thrilling. We attract the crowds. We give them thrills, we do hair-raising stunts and send the crowd home to wait impatiently for the next sensationalist to come along. As far as making Industrial Unionism fit the everyday life of the workers we have failed miserably. The crowd expects the sensational from our speakers or organizers; the members expect it, and our speakers, if they intend to remain as such, have got to supply them or go out of business. We measure the success or failure of our speakers by the number of spectacular stunts that they are able to pull off. It is child's play to stand in front of some factory and convince the slaves that they have a grievance. Capitalism is generous in that respect. The speaker sheds tears over their misery, he opens the floodgates of sentiment, and, lo, Mr. Speaker becomes a strike leader. With cheap phrases and flowery language the strike leader appeals to the emotions of the crowd, lashing them into a religious frenzy, for he knows well that if he ever allows the strikers to cool down the boasted solidarity will disappear and the men will crawl back into the factory. Take the speaker away from the strike and it will go up in smoke unless the workers or some part of them have been previously organized. Arrest the speaker or strike leader and the crowd will remain firm until another one gets on the job. The new speaker does not have to know anything about the shop conditions to make good. He raves about persecution and the brutality of the police. It is surprising how you can revive the dying enthusiasm of a crowd by a tirade against the police or the army.

'While the crowd is still enthusiastic we take in many members, many of whom would just as soon join the Salvation Army as the Industrial Workers of the World, providing that the S. A. had sense enough to use the same cheap weapons that we are forcing our speakers to use. To stampede a bunch of slaves who are working for $1.62 per day is easy, and spectacular. How often do we hear around our halls a conversation like the following:

"Slim (who has just blown in)—'Gee, this town is dead; we got to start something,' meaning, of course, something sensational. What we really need is less of the sensational and more quiet organization. Organizers that can work and a membership that will allow them to work without a brass band. Had we kept as many organizers in Lawrence after the strike as we had during the strike we would have an organization that could carry on the next battle without the aid of press agents or sensationalists. In Akron it was the same story; the members cried for sensation; Haywood was sent for. He filled the bill, but after the strike was over every organizer was called to other points to supply the thrills called for by the rank and file.

"Not one was left to build up an organization in Akron.

"It is getting to be a habit, and the speakers are catering to it. In Pittsburgh I heard one of our principal speakers give voice to the following: 'Do you think that I am going to come here and talk to 200 people when I can stay in New York and talk to 10,000 people direct and have my speeches carried to thousands more by the capitalistic press?' The poison of sensationalism had entered his veins; his standard of success was the standard of the rank and file who measure the success of an organizer by the noise he is able to make and by the spectacular stunts he is able to pull off. Let the hated capitalistic press give a front page column to the antics of some organizer and he immediately becomes the God of the leaderless rank and file. The cheapest gallery play, idle threat or giant boast is applauded by the members who would disdain to say a kind word for the men who plod along trying to build up a local union that will stand and fulfil its function without the aid of a 'high diver.' If you dare say a word about the efficient work of our present general secretary around a hall, some one will immediately ask, 'What did he ever do?' The hard and thankless routine of organization work means nothing to them. What does it matter to them if he is the ablest man in the movement? He has failed to monopolize the front pages of the daily press, so he is a failure. If he fails to get the necessary funds to keep the sensationalist in the field, we feel as if we had been cheated out of our just due. How we do howl! What does it matter if we have editors who are able and capable of making our papers real propaganda sheets? We want some one who will feed us scandal, gossip, and, above all, sensationalism. We must have it now that we have developed the taste for it. Give it to us or we will elect some one who will. In the choice between ability and sensation, we pick the latter to win.

"Don't think for a minute that because we are growing numerically our present sensational method is right. Oh, no; we are growing in spite of it. The principles of industrial unionism are mighty strong, and even we have not been able to kill the organization. The fault does not lie with the general officers, but with you, the members of the rank and file, who make gods of the 'high divers' and abuse the men who refuse to sacrifice organization for front page articles in the capitalist press. Unless we can organize the workers without doing the spectacular, we are doomed. It is up to you. The organizers and speakers are what you make them. Demand the straight goods and hard work and you will get it. Keep on as you are doing now and don't whine when you get stung."

German Socialists and Militarism. Even among those who would honestly like to know, the difficulty increases of getting at any one statement of socialist doctrine as likely to find acceptance with any other faction as the simon-pure creed. Professor Simkhovitch no sooner tells us that German socialism to-day has practically discarded the Marxian cornerstones of faith, than word comes of socialist support for the Kaiser's expansive military policy. "The German workingman of to-day," according to a statesman of the Fatherland, quoted in the *Literary Digest* from *The Liberte* (Paris), "is convinced that the economic supremacy of Germany, on which his own prosperity is based, depends on the powers of the army, and especially of the navy, whose prestige secures an outlet and a market for national industries. It is this frame of mind that compels the great leaders of the Social Democracy to vote in the Reichstag for the military laws and led the recent Socialist Congress at Jena to take an attitude and pass motions which delighted the Kaiser above every one. . . . Germany is solidly united in aspiring after the creation of a greater Germany. This is the keystone on which all classes are cemented by patriotic enthusiasm whose tendency grows more and more decided toward increased militarism."

Socialist orators have long been in the habit of treating the idea of the brotherhood of man as a private possession, interpreting it to mean not merely the end of militarism, in which they would have many sympathizers not of their cult, but also the wiping out of national barriers and even of "flag patriotism" as an ancient trick of the exploiters to breed strife and divide the world's workers against themselves. If all this is to be painted off the banners in the birthplace and stronghold of the faith, will the leaders of the cause everywhere or anywhere else do likewise and put bayonets into the creed, or give over "pointing with pride" to Germany and German advanced thought? "Every stoic was a stoic," said Emerson, "but in Christendom where is the Christian?" To-day it would take a philosopher indeed to tell us where in socialism to find the correct brand of socialist.

A Great Achievement for Industrial Peace

(*Continued from page 8.*)

of a resort to force are not of decisive moment. They do, however, give new force to the railroads' claim for relief in the direction of a fair and preper readjustment of operating charges in the light of constantly increasing costs of operation. It is a significant fact in this connection that a marked change has come over the attitude even of the commercial and mercantile bodies, most of which have stood determinedly against any change in rates. There is a growing popular appreciation that safety and good service and fair compensation to labor cannot be permanently assured without adequate revenue. This and the question of arriving at a more stable basis for determining wage rates in various sections of the country are the problems next ahead, and they demand the most serious consideration in a spirit of co-operation on the part of the companies, the employees and the public.

THE TRUTH ABOUT WAGES AND VICE

(Continued from page 9.)

gests, "will satisfy the social conscience of a democracy," implying that the report in question recognizes no such need. It does, on the contrary, urge upon the department stores the wisdom of a "Conciliation or Adjustment Board—composed of several heads of departments and several from the rank and file appointed by the firm, or selected in some satisfactory method by the employees." In this, our investigators appear to have gone quite as far as their critic, only in rather more definite and practical terms.

Miss Van Kleeck affirms that the attempt to find a direct "relation between an industry and prostitution in a community is to pursue a 'will-o'-the wisp,' and that the moral effects of any occupation . . . defy statistical treatment." It is indeed difficult to arrive at exact conclusions in any line of social investigation. Nevertheless, in so far as the lumping together of scattered incidents and unproved inferences may be termed "statistics," it is precisely the method employed from the first by the well-meaning people who are endeavoring to show just this direct relation between working conditions and the social evil.

Our critic is disturbed by the published statement of thirty-seven social workers to the effect that: "It is our general belief that low wages of working girls are scarcely ever a direct cause of loss of chastity." She declares reprovingly that: "Social workers should be the first to realize the danger of any final statement on this subject just now, especially if it be negative in character." Nevertheless, the opinions of these unprejudiced authorities, including many of the most representative and practical social workers in the country, upholding the character of working girls and discrediting the idea that any appreciable proportion of them would sell their souls for food and clothing, will enjoy, we are forced to believe, a larger measure of public confidence than Miss Van Kleeck is able to accord them. We take occasion to name again some of the signers of this opinion:

JEREMIAH W. JENKS, Professor of Government, New York University, Former Chairman of Committee of the United States Immigration Commission in charge of investigation of importation of women for immoral purposes.

GRAHAM TAYLOR, President Chicago School of Civics and Philanthropy.

HUBERT WORK, Physician, Medical Superintendent of Woodcroft, a private hospital for the mentally deranged; former President of American Medical Psychological Society, Pueblo, Colorado.

C. R. HENDERSON, Member of the Vice-Commission of Chicago.

GEORGE J. KNEELAND, Director of Investigation, the Vice Commission of Chicago; author of "Commercialized Prostitution in New York City."

SOPHIE C. BARCLAY, Superintendent Margaret J. Bennett Home, Baltimore.

M. EDITH CAMPBELL, Director The Schmidlapp Bureau for Women and Girls, Cincinnati.

KATHERINE BEMENT DAVIS, Superintendent, New York State Reformatory for Women, Bedford Hills, New York.

JAMES BRONSON REYNOLDS, Counsel American Vigilance Association, New York.

MARY M. BARTELME, Assistant Judge of Cook County Juvenile Court, Chicago.

H. W. HERBERT, City Magistrate, Women's Night Court, New York.

ALICE C. SMITH, Probation Officer, New York.

THOMAS ESTILL, Commissioner The Salvation Army, Chicago.

KATE WALLER BARRETT (Mrs. Robert S.), President National Florence Crittenton Mission, Alexandria, Virginia.

ROSE SOMMERFELD, Superintendent Clara de Hirsch Home for Working Girls, New York;

and many others.

"Why will the report tell us so little," inquires Miss Van Kleeck, "about the observance of the State law requiring seats for sales-girls, while merely remarking that 'the problem is a vexing one, from whatever standpoint it is viewed'?" The report, directly to the contrary, does state that seats are provided in all stores, and the subject is referred to more than once. Mention is also made of the fact that zealous buyers (heads) sometimes urge constant activity on the part of the clerks, which prevents them from sitting to any extent; while the policy of other stores is to request employees to be seated when not busy. In some instances, companies are given credit for providing more seats than the law requires, and attention is called to the fact that seats should be provided for bargain tables, though not required by law and not given by any store in New York.

Criticism of the report was contributed to the *New York Evening Post* of August 1 by Miss Elizabeth Dutcher, of the New York Retail Clerks' Union, in comment upon a *Post* editorial on the subject. Miss Dutcher is claimed as a Socialist by *The New York Call*. Several of her objections have already been discussed in connection with Miss Van Kleeck's review, but certain others call for further remark. "We object," said Miss Dutcher, "to welfare work that is a mere device to impress the public." The Civic Federation would equally condemn that type of welfare work wherever found, but it happens that not a single instance of the kind exists in the establishments covered by the report. In only one case has a firm even mentioned its welfare features in the catalog sent to customers, and without approving this exception there is at least to be said in extenuation that the particular work described was so far in advance of anything found in any similar New York institution that a real educational service may be rendered even through this ordinarily undesirable means of spreading information. The welfare work of several of the firms which have actually done the most on this line has been unknown to the public precisely because of their refusal to exploit its details.

Miss Dutcher makes the surprising assertion: "The report has almost nothing to say about long hours," and alludes to what seems to her its "inscrutable reserve" on the overtime question. As already pointed out, the report deals at length with the whole subject of hours, declares in positive terms that the working day is too long and urges that it be shortened in all stores. It recommends further that overtime be abolished entirely, but that when necessary, in emergencies, it be paid for, which would in itself tend, of course, to check the practice on the part of department heads.

Miss Dutcher's observation that lights may be seen burning in different stores after hours is the sort of "evidence" which, had it appeared in the Welfare Department's report, would have immediately occurred to our critics, we fear, as a case of "seeing things at night;" certainly a highly unreliable method of statistical inquiry. Illumination, of course, is needed for janitor work and often for the use of night watchmen, and while it may, in some cases, also indicate overtime work, we submit that inside rather than outside evidence is the proper basis for conclusions on that subject.

Miss Dutcher's statement that eighty-four hours a week "for eight weeks at a stretch is not unusual" seems to imply that the Federation's investigation ignored or denied such a condition, whereas it expressly reports porters and night watchmen found working fourteen hours per day, six nights in the week, and the night watchmen on Sundays, also.

"The store that employs a welfare secretary during the daytime and keeps its employees working until one o'clock in the morning," would be, indeed, as Miss Dutcher remarks, "in an anomalous position." As a matter of fact, we know of but one department store in New York employing a welfare secretary, and here no such 1 A. M. practice exists. The natural inference from the quotation would be, however, that some stores regularly keep their entire force at work until that preposterous hour.

The New York Call, official organ of the Socialist party, naturally condemns the report, as it would any showing of data of optimistic bearing upon an existing condition. "The report neglects to state just what stores it investigated," says the *Call*. Its study of the document must have been expeditious, indeed, since the full list of all stores investigated appears on the front page of the report. The only other specific criticism appears to be that the report includes the wages of the highest-paid saleswomen handling the costly fabrics. We do not know that the *Call's* ready assumption of "whitewashing," based on this discovery, demands any other comment than the fact that the data in question also includes, in the averages obtained, the lowest-paid salesgirls—in fact, the entire selling force—and that tables are presented showing the actual numbers receiving various rates of pay, from the lowest to the highest.

Mrs. Maud Nathan, president of the Consumers' League of the City of New York, writing to the *Evening Post* from the Hague under date of August 19, offers further criticisms of the investigation, based, as she states, upon Miss Dutcher's letter in a previous issue rather than upon the report itself, which at the time she had not seen. Assuming from her source of information that "deceitful" averages characterized the Federation's report, Mrs. Nathan suggests that: "A fairer statement would show how many saleswomen received $6 a week, how many $7, etc." As already noted, the report does show exactly these classified wages, by tables and charts, in great detail.

Mrs. Nathan mentions a wage investigation made by the Consumers' League, showing that of some two hundred and twenty-five saleswomen in New York nearly 60% receive less than $6.50 per week, 33% between $6 and $6.60, and 84% less than $8. Whether this small group was in any way representative of the total body of saleswomen in the various grades of low, medium and high-wage positions does not appear, and we greatly doubt if the League itself, with the best of intentions, could determine the point. The Federation report, on the other hand, is based on the wages of some 5,86[illegible] saleswomen, and includes the entire number of such in the various establishments studied. Reliance upon very narrow premises for broad conclusions is even more deceptive than the all-too-common misuse of averages, and Mrs. Nathan will herself agree, we feel sure, that a statistical pyramid should rest on its base rather than its apex. There can be no quarrel, however, with her statement, after commending the progress of improvements in many New York stores, that the League "cannot in justice to those employees who have real grievances, remain silent in regard to the evils of long hours and low wages in other stores, when those evils exist."

Criticism of an investigation tending to upset a mistaken theory, however sincerely held, is of course to be expected, but the prevailing tone of public comment in this matter was by no means such as the foregoing discussion might imply. It was voiced, on the contrary and in the main, by the editorial opinion of the *Evening Post* already referred to, as follows:

"The thanks of everybody who has been left in a state of confusion and disgust by such 'investigations' as that of Lieutenant Governor O'Hara, of Illinois, are due to The National Civic Federation for its report upon 'Working Conditions in New York Stores.' The report fills the thirty-two pages of the last number of The National Civic Federation Review, and is just what such a document should be. It goes after the main things; it is detailed, but has numerous tables and summaries; it is careful to supply the sources of its information and conclusions; and it is judicial without being colorless. Its presentation of masses of facts and series of inferences constitutes the sort of knowledge upon which, and upon which alone, we ought to base agitation for legislation and individual improvements . . .

"It thus appears that if the department store is responsible to any extent for 'white slavery' it sins in a large company. And this, in the opinion of the Federation's experts, is exactly the impression which it is sought to make. Nothing less than an indictment of our whole industrial system, and with it our whole political system is the aim of those who are raising the alarm. Such persons cannot be expected to fasten their rolling eyes upon so stolid a thing as a fact, still less upon a bit of reasoning. Others, however, and this still means the mass of us, will find something very rational in the comment of an employer who, as a young man, believed rumors of this kind. 'It would be poor business policy,' he remarks, 'for how could a company expect employees to deal honestly with it if those employees were induced by it to lead lives of shame?' The strange thing of these reckless charges is the evident supposition that only a soulless corporation was being attacked, the possible slander upon scores of thousands of girls and women not being even remotely perceived. This phase of the attacks is not absent from the minds of the Civic Federation's investigators, however, and they demolish the whole rotten structure with a completeness that ought almost to convince even the wildest of those who set it up. For, column after column, one impartial authority after another gives testimony to the falsity of any supposition that there is any important connection between occupation and immorality, or even want and immorality, among women.

"The department store is not the last word in industrial organization. Yet it seems to be, not merely no worse than its fellows, but rather better. We have considered only the most damaging of the criticisms that are leveled against it, saying nothing about what it is doing to improve working conditions for its employees. Yet eighteen of the thirty-two pages of the report are upon 'Welfare Work and General Recommendations for Improvements.' These pages bristle with details of what these stores are doing to make life more livable for those dependent upon them, ranging from the distribution of a cooled beverage twice a day in summer to saving and lending arrangements which make mightily for thrift and self-respect. Doubtless no store is doing all it can in this direction. Doubtless every store needs to be under the eye of the fire inspector, and to take heed to what this report has to say, for instance, about long hours. But what was required before all else was more light and less heat, and this the Federation's clear-headed examiners have given us."

W R Willcox

CHAIRMAN WELFARE DEPARTMENT.

TO STUDY CAUSES OF INDUSTRIAL DISCORD

THE NEW FEDERAL COMMISSION WILL ALSO SEEK PRACTICAL MEANS OF PROMOTING BETTER RELATIONS BETWEEN EMPLOYER AND EMPLOYED

FRANK P. WALSH. JOHN R. COMMONS. MRS. J. BORDEN HARRIMAN. FREDERICK A. DELANO. THRUSTON BALLARD. HARRIS WEINSTOCK.

JAMES O'CONNELL. A. B. GARRETSON. JOHN B. LENNON.

THE FEDERAL COMMISSION ON INDUSTRIAL RELATIONS

A LONG step forward toward more intelligent and effective dealing with the causes of discord in the industrial world was made possible when the last Congress authorized the appointment of the Commission on Industrial Relations, which is just now organizing for work. The results of this commission's inquiries promise to be of value not alone in the first-hand problems of organized capital and organized labor, but in the shaping of legislation having to do with a wide variety of working and living conditions.

The make-up of the commission, appointed in June by President Wilson, and confirmed by the Senate in September, gives the best possible guarantee of its fairness, independence and capacity for usefulness. It is interesting to note the widespread acknowledgment of this fact, even among critics of the idea and program of the commission itself.

The chairman, Mr. Frank P. Walsh, of Kansas City, a man better known in the West than as yet in the East, has made a notable record as a fearless, determined fighter for civic reforms and worker for social welfare. Mr. Walsh was a member of the first tenement commission in Kansas City, and originated the idea of the Board of Public Welfare, a sort of municipal directing center of various lines of social service, and he has been its general counsel and moving spirit from the first. He has also, upon occasion, served as arbitrator in industrial disputes, and any man who has filled that most difficult of voluntary judicial positions is presumably equipped with a kind of close-to-the-bone experience which ought to stand him in good stead in such work as lies ahead of the new commission.

Professor John R. Commons, of the University of Wisconsin, is one of the strongest additions that could have been made to such a board, in which the help of a trained economist and social investigator will be, of course, of the first importance. Mrs. J. Borden Harriman, the third member named to represent public interests, and since elected resident commissioner of the board, was one of the leading organizers of the Women's Department of The National Civic Federation, and has for a number of years given most valuable service as chairman of that department's National Committee on Welfare Work for Industrial Employees.

Mr. Harris Weinstock, of San Francisco, the directing head of a number of large department stores; Thruston Ballard, president of the Employers' Association of Louisville, Kentucky, and Frederick A. Delano, of Chicago, receiver and former president of the Wabash Railroad, are the employer members of the commission. Mr. Weinstock was appointed by Governor Gillette, of California, to investigate labor and industrial conditions in Australia and Europe, with special reference to arbitration experience, and was also appointed by Governor Johnson to investigate the I. W. W. "free speech" riots in San Diego. Mr. Weinstock is a member of the Executive Committee of The National Civic Federation, and knows the practical side of social and civic issues from long service as a volunteer in many good causes. Mr. Ballard is a large employer of labor in the milling business, and is a member of the Welfare Department of the National Civic Federation.

The three labor members, Mr. James O'Connell, head of the Metal Trades Department of the American Federation of Labor; Mr. John B. Lennon, treasurer of the American Federation of Labor, and Mr. Austin B. Garretson, president of the Order of Railway Conductors (as well as Mr. Delano, of the employers), were among the nominees originally sent to the Senate by President Taft. Their reappointment by President Wilson gives a genuinely representative balance to the commission, whose duties, it will be remembered, are mapped out in the law establishing it, as follows:

> "The commission shall inquire into the general condition of labor in the principal industries of the United States, including agriculture, and especially in those which are carried on in corporate forms; into existing relations between employers and employes, into the effect of industrial conditions on public welfare and into the rights and powers of the community to deal therewith; into the conditions of sanitation and safety of employes and the provisions for protecting the life, limb and health of the employees; into the growth of associations of employers and of wage earners and the effect of such associations upon the relations between employers and employees; into the extent and results of methods of collective bargaining; into any methods which have been tried in any State or in foreign countries for maintaining mutually satisfactory relations between employees and employers; into methods for avoiding or adjusting labor disputes through peaceful and conciliatory mediation and negotiation; into the scope, method and resources of existing bureaus of labor and into possible ways of increasing their usefulness; into the question of smuggling or other illegal entry of Asiatics into the United States or its insular possessions, and of the methods by which such Asiatics have gained and are gaining such admission, and shall report to Congress as speedily as possible with such recommendation as said commission may think proper to prevent such smuggling and illegal entry. The commission shall seek to discover the underlying causes of dissatisfaction in the industrial situation and report its conclusions thereon."

This is a broad program, and the commission is at present making a preliminary study of the field of inquiry. It has already appointed as general managing expert Professor William J. Lauck, formerly of Washington and Lee University and later connected with the industrial survey of the Immigration Commission. Chairman Walsh, in the course of an interview in the *New York Evening Post* of November 1, outlined the manner in which the commission will approach various subjects, particularly the underlying causes of strikes and lockouts and the relation of judicial decisions to industrial disputes and labor laws.

"We are studying," Mr. Walsh said, "the effects of judicial decisions on industrial questions and how statutes affecting labor are being construed by the courts. We are trying to determine the part common law plays in industrial disputes, and to sift the oft-repeated reports that the courts are unfair to organized labor or are unfair to capital. Any understanding of the influence of the judiciary in these matters involves a survey of all the judicial decisions in injunction cases. Constructively we will try to find out how much friction may be allayed by modifying court rules and procedure, and what changes may be made in the common law. The trend of the courts in sustaining laws for the protection of workers will be looked into, and the practicability of the Government's establishing free legal aid bureaus. . . .

"Our attempt will be to avoid the statistical mill. We will try to get typical situations in various industries by learning the employers' and employees' side of the disagreement, which will be done by sending our investigators out among the men.

> "Another thing which will tend to simplify our labors is our determination not to go into fresh disturbances and current labor disputes with the idea of straightening out local situations, such as have recently existed in Michigan, West Virginia and at Paterson and Lawrence. Of course, we will put our investigators into those fields, but it will be with the purpose of detecting the underlying principles at work. From these, we hope to draw conclusions for our final report. Specific matters are not a part of our province. Our function is more general."

The commission is, of course, getting all manner of advice and prejudgment of its work, not all of it either friendly or fair. Bearing upon this, Mr. Walsh described in *Collier's Weekly* of October 18th what he believes the fair and proper attitude of the commission in its effort to discover facts which shall be of practical service in remedial work, rather than to rake the ashes of old controversies. Referring to the opinions, among others, of W. J. Burns and W. D. Haywood, quoted from *The Survey*, with regard to the commission, Mr. Walsh declared, for instance, that it would be no part of its business to find what, if any, relation organized labor had to the McNamara outrages. "Under no circumstances will the commission consider itself as a sleuth or a prosecuting attorney." Quoting, on the other hand, Haywood's "denunciation of the commission before he knows anything about our hopes and intents," Mr. Walsh continued: "There you have warning of a ominous division. On one side your Haywoods, sullen and distrustful, and on the other your Burnses, eager for pursuits and prosecutions. It is an alignment that must be prevented, if possible, for I can conceive of nothing that will so hamper the work of the commission as being compelled to run the class gauntlet. Some word must be found that will bring a sense of our essential oneness home to every man, woman and child in the country, so that we may have co-operation, not antagonism."

If the work of the commission is carried forward in the spirit manifested by Mr. Walsh and amply assured in the personnel of the entire board, we shall have a right to expect from it a valuable contribution to industrial and social progress in this country.

SENIORITY PROMOTION—WHAT ARE THE FACTS?

FITNESS AND MERIT ARE ALSO IMPERATIVE TESTS ON ALL ROADS—PRECEDENCE BY LENGTH OF SERVICE A COMMON PRACTICE IN OTHER FIELDS

By HAYES ROBBINS

WHEN Governor Foss, of Massachusetts, launched a broadside of condemnation against the locomotive engineers of the New Haven Railroad for their supposed willingness to order a strike on the seniority issue, he probably voiced a widespread feeling that the "limit" had been reached. Almost any settled practice, forced suddenly to the front in the heat of an acute discussion, is pretty sure to bring down a torrent of public criticism which may or may not be justified, but very seldom rests upon a careful, unprejudiced study of the facts. There is not time in two or three days of excited debate either to get at the underlying truth of an unfamiliar situation or to reach safe conclusions.

It developed, for instance, that this particular controversy, later adjusted through negotiation and mutual concessions, did not hang primarily on the seniority question, but grew out of several important changes in the rules made rather unexpectedly in the course of reorganization of the service, all of which the Brotherhood men believed should have been subjects of further conference and agreement. The rule of seniority as a basis for promotion was among these, and in the course of further deliberation between this and other companies and their men it may, of course, undergo other modifications than those already attached to it.

However this may be, and whatever the actual merits and demerits of the rule, it is but common fairness to recognize that widely different opinions may be and are honestly held on this very issue, and that the idea behind it is no more an invention of union labor than the practice itself is confined to the railroad service.

Illustrating the need of a better common understanding of just what the seniority rule implies and how it works, take this typical objection from Governor Foss's letter to the engineers and firemen at New Haven:

> "Promotion and the assignment of duties according to seniority without regard to fitness lower the efficiency of the labor force, make it impossible for the railroad to maintain discipline and impair the ability of the railroad to serve the public. . . . The real issue is not between the railroad and its employees, but between the employees and the people of this Commonwealth; and the question is whether the lives of the people shall be placed in jeopardy by the maintenance of the seniority rule, and whether, in order to enforce this rule, our people must submit to the evils incident to a railroad strike."

In reply to which the Brotherhood men, in the course of a statement signed by Assistant Grand Chief L. L. Griffing, of the engineers, and Vice-President P. J. McNamara, of the firemen, had this to say:

> "Seniority rules have been in effect upon all railroads for many years and have been to the traveling public the greatest possible assurance that only employees of experience and tested ability could be placed in charge of trains. We are of the firm belief that if the traveling public but realized the increased dangers that would exist under operating rules that would permit of favoritism, that is not only possible but probable under the revival of old customs, it would submit to the evils incident to a strike rather than to permit of the revival of the old conditions."

Carrying their defence further, these gentlemen tell the Governor that:

> "No one appreciates more deeply than do those whom we represent that the safety of the traveling public is paramount to all other requirements and it is not a question of 'advantage' with them. It is a question of placing the responsibility for safe operation where it should properly rest."

Here, it must be acknowledged, a fair question is raised. Why should a man have been kept in the service at all if, after a term of years under the watchful eye of the management, he is not believed safe to intrust with larger responsibilities? If the superintendent, when the turn of such a man comes for advancement, does not dare put him in charge, for instance, of a fast express instead of a local accommodation, ought he to have been intrusted with the lives of passengers on any train, slow or fast? It is quite as possible for the engineer of a local as of an express to forget orders or bungle the emergency brakes or overrun signals. In other words, and without championing seniority as an ideal rule of selection, it is still possible to see that a more careful process of weeding out, in the regular course of operating practice, as already provided for in some of the promotion regulations, might bring us to the point where seniority and superior fitness would practically always mean the same thing. That they do already in a large majority of cases, probably most operating officers would themselves readily grant. It is the small but important proportion of exceptions that creates the real problem.

But is the matter after all as bad as it is commonly represented? Is it true that the Brotherhoods rigidly insist upon seniority as the sole determining factor in promotions?

There is no literally uniform rule on this matter, but the following extracts from working agreements actually in force on various roads are typical of the prevailing practice.*

The promotion of railroad trainmen, for instance, is governed by provisions such as these:

Pittsburgh & Lake Erie Railroad—"Rule 22. All trainmen will be considered in line for promotion according to their time of continuous service, *merit, competency and capacity for increased responsibility.* However, to obtain promotion, capacity must be shown for greater responsibility, and *employees must not rely upon mere seniority. The best interests of the company demand that vacancies be filled by men who have shown themselves most worthy of promotion by loyal and faithful service, and intelligent and economical performance.* The limit of promotion will be confined to conductorship as far as seniority is concerned.

"A candidate for promotion to conductorship in the regular line—that is, following the last conductor promoted—will be given ten (10) days' notice to prepare himself. Failing to pass the first examination he will be given thirty (30) days to further prepare himself. If he then passes the examination he will be the senior of any younger employee who may have been promoted in the meantime. Failing to pass the second examination, *he may be dismissed from the service.*"

Norfolk & Western Railway Co.—"Article M, Rule 2. They will be considered in the line of promotion. The oldest in the service shall have preference: First—Fitness for position. Second—Previous record for faithful service. Third—Length of such service."

New York Central & Hudson River R. R.—"Rule 5. Promotion in train service shall be from the oldest eligible freight conductor to extra passenger conductor, and from extra passenger conductor to passenger conductor . . . . . *when they are able to pass proper examinations and are otherwise qualified.* After a man has been appointed a passenger conductor it shall be probationary for one year, *and his continuance as such after that time shall depend wholly upon his efficiency, courteousness and appearance.*"

St. Louis & San Francisco Railroad Co.—"When necessary to increase the number of conductors, the oldest brakeman in service will have preference in line of promotion, *merit and ability being considered.* If it is ruled by a Superintendent, Assistant Superintendent or Trainmaster that a conductor or brakeman lacks the ability for promotion to higher service, the Superintendent, Assistant Superintendent or Trainmaster will notify him, giving the reason for so ruling in writing, if requested."

Nothing very alarming here! In each case severe tests for merit and efficiency go hand in hand with the seniority rule.

How is it with the conductors? The promotion rule, according to President Garretson, of the Order of Railway Conductors, "varies in language on very many roads, but the sense is virtually the same the country over." Mr. Garretson states that the rule considered as fair as any and that recognizes the general position of the conductors on the subject, is that in force on the New York, New Haven & Hartford Railroad, as follows: "Ability, fitness and seniority will entitle a man to promotion when the opportunity offers, provided, in the opinion of the superintendent, he is qualified therefor."

"That rule," says Mr. Garretson in comment, "makes ability the first requirement for promotion and seniority the last. Under the application of that rule on the line the superintendent of the road has the right to object to the man who stands next for promotion, and if he can reasonably demonstrate the grounds of unfitness the man will not receive the promotion, but he is not permitted to set up simply a whim or personal dislike, nor, when he has demonstrated the unfitness of a man can he choose at will some individual whose interests he desires to forward for any one of many reasons, but he must take the next man in seniority unless unfitness is also shown on his part. It is a parallel for the civil service practice that obtains in regard to fitness . . . there is not a place where the evidence of unfitness will not deprive the man of advancement to responsible position."

In the case of engineers, practically the standard rule is that seniority should govern, merit being equal. In other words, where the qualifications of two men are all right, the older in the service has the choice of runs and layovers.

The rule in force on the Atchison, Topeka & Santa Fe Railway (Coast Lines) reads that: "Engineers will be promoted according to seniority *and ability,* in their respective districts."

On the Chicago, Milwaukee & St. Paul Railway, the rule reads: "Promotion of engineers will be made according to their seniority *and ability when found competent and worthy.* When the ability of an engineer in line for promotion is questioned, he may be given an opportunity to prove his competency."

In many of the agreements, the test examinations for promotion are not named in direct connection with the seniority rule, but are elsewhere prescribed and, according to Grand Chief Stone, of the Brotherhood of Locomotive Engineers, "The operating official is the man who decides whether or not the man is qualified, we reserving the right to appeal from his decision if we think any injustice has been done."

In the case of the firemen, the standard rule on forty western roads covered by the Chicago Agreement of 1910, is: "Firemen shall be examined for promotion according to seniority on the firemen's roster; and *those passing the required examination* shall be given certificates of qualification, and when promoted shall hold their same relative standing in the service to which assigned."

This provision, as President Carter, of the Brotherhood states, "in no manner restricts the railroad companies in their educational requirements or severity of examination in order to ascertain the fitness of a fireman before promotion." On the contrary: "Ordinarily, when a fireman fails to pass a satisfactory examination for promotion to position of engineer, he is penalized, the penalty varying on different roads."

On the Missouri Pacific Railway it is provided that: "All hostlers and firemen *shall stand an examination* on machinery and timecard before promotion to position of engineer in switch or road service." Then follow various rules on the nature of the examinations, both mechanical and physical. Another rule states that the senior eligible fireman shall stand first for promotion "provided he first passes the required examinations."

On the Erie Railroad, Rule 41 reads: "In filling the position of hostler, preference will in general be given to firemen according to their age in the service, the company reserving the right to fill such positions otherwise in special cases."

On the Missouri, Kansas & Texas, it is provided in the rules that: "The right to regular engines, to position of switch engineer and hostler, also the right and preference to regular runs will be governed by seniority *and ability* in regular road service on the respective districts to which firemen may be assigned."

The test examinations are no perfunctory affairs. On the contrary, several hundred technical questions must be answered, including a large number requiring a fireman to state what he would do as engineer in various unusual or emergency situations. On one large system, it is reported that more than one thousand technical questions are asked of firemen before promotion, relating to mechanical matters, books of rules, signal systems, etc.

The railroad Brotherhood men urge that in addition to all these exacting tests seniority is of itself a strong evidence of fitness, in that it usually means long service under managers who could at any time have used the power of dismissal for incompetence or neglect of duty. This is, of course, not so simple a matter as may appear on the surface. Railroad managers have insisted that the real trouble comes not so much in the wording of promotion rules as in the practical handling of this or that man's individual case. The difficulty of proving a man unfit,

*Italics in all the regulations quoted are ours.

in whom the superintendent may, nevertheless, lack confidence for various reasons, may be so great that the regular custom is allowed to govern rather than incur the wrangling, bad blood and threats of trouble involved in setting it aside. This is a parallel to the well-known difficulty of getting rid of the occasional man in the civil service who is not equal to the requirements, yet against whom it may be almost impossible to "prove charges."

Any arrangement, however fair on paper, can of course be made narrow and arbitrary in the hands of narrow and arbitrary men. Nevertheless, it must be an exceedingly small number of actually unfit or unreliable men that railroad managers would acknowledge having promoted to responsible positions under compulsion. Unless workingmen are to give up entirely the right of a hearing and appeal in cases of what they believe unjust treatment, it is hard to see how more or less argument and disagreement and perhaps occasional bad feeling can be avoided in any of these practical adjustments of employment relations involving thousands of men under complex conditions. It is a part of the work-a-day experience with human nature all along the line.

Even with the seniority provision entirely abolished, it would still be necessary to decide between rival applicants for the higher positions, perhaps with this man or that backed by some faction among the force, and with the constant likelihood of incurring suspicion of favoritism, whether that motive is actually present or not. There is, at any rate, room for argument whether selections having regard to seniority, after due tests for knowledge and fitness, are any more likely to give us the occasional employee who disobeys orders and invites disaster than would be the case were appointments left solely to a superintendent's estimate of "fitness," an elusive term into which may enter various side issues known only to the official himself, and which the public least of all has any way of checking up or analyzing.

How did the seniority idea get such a foothold in the railroad world, in the first place? Probably the common impression is that the practice was forced upon the companies as the arbitrary whim of a powerful labor aggregation. The powerful labor backing was there, indeed, but very few industrial policies of such scope and importance arise from the "whims" either of individuals or groups. In the main it is true that seniority rules came into being as a measurable escape from evils which tended to grow by what they fed upon.

A generation ago the relations of railroad managers both to the public and to their men were very unlike those of to-day. Commodore Vanderbilt may never have used the famous language credited to him, but the sentiment no doubt was typical of the actual feeling of very many magnates of the rail of that day. Equally arbitrary, to a large extent, was the relation of minor officials to the men further down. Favoritism was a routine commonplace, and the habit still unfortunately common in certain rough occupations of paying for a job or for promotion was not unknown in the railroad world. There were (and may still be) railroad officials who openly favored the seniority idea as one way of stamping out the petty favoritism, parcelling out of jobs to family relatives, and occasional graft, which had become sources of more or less constant ill-will and friction in the service. These facts are recalled as a matter of history.

Every social or industrial arrangement is entitled to be judged, not from the standpoint of what might be under ideal conditions, but in relation to the particular situation it fits, and out of which it has grown. It may not be the wisest device that could be imagined for the purpose, but may still mark a real advance over the practice or custom it replaced. The curse of every known "free hand" system of hiring and promoting employees on a large scale has always been the temptation to give weight to other factors than the good of the service. The only practicable escape from this evil, whether in public or private employment, has been in the direction of some more or less automatic system, with the range of personal choice on the part of appointing officers cut down to definite limits.

Theoretically, the trained, disinterested manager, knowing his men and knowing the work they must do, should be the ideal instrument for building up an ideal force of workingmen. In the smaller, relatively compact and keenly competitive industries, he often is just that. If the same results could be relied upon in the handling of large masses of men, one-man power would remain the best selective method, but the strength of the small enterprise is apt to become the weakness of the large. So many new problems and obligations crowd into the large situation that the managing head is forced to delegate authority, without, however, the power of sub-dividing himself, his own personality, sense of responsibility and singleness of purpose.

The case of industry is much like that in government affairs. The "benevolent despot" may give us efficiency, economy and justice on a plane not often reached under democracy, but we have no way of knowing how long the "benevolent" streak will persist. The next in line may omit it entirely. Therefore, we take our chances with a lower but steadier average of efficiency and equity under popular rule and promptly find that even here the "free hand" of our own elected officials is quite as likely to build up a personal machine as an efficient public service. After government appointments had gone by way of politics, graft and favoritism to the limit of endurance, we resorted to the competitive civil service system, and why? Certainly not because any mechanical scheme of examinations can be trusted to pick the most competent candidate, best fitted by natural ability and general "horse sense" for the work to be done. It did sift out the impossibilities and guarantee a certain average of capacity, and was therefore an improvement on the previous regime of corruption and rank incompetence. Nobody to-day questions the wisdom of the new system; the only argument now is on ways and means of extending it to practically all the remaining unclassified list.

Railroad employment has come to have certain points of likeness to civil service. In fact, the nearer we get to a type of industry operating under fixed rules, hemmed in by many regulations and dividing authority among a hundred and one sub-heads, the "free hand" becomes less and less practicable. Many details of management are reduced to rule and system through the sheer necessity of keeping up uniform standards and guarding against the personal ambitions and trouble-making capacities of men in posts of petty authority. Merit examinations have proved the best available defence against all this in the public service; the seniority rule is one of the attempts, admittedly imperfect, to cope with it in the railroad service. Both have features of rigidity which sometimes give bad results and both are capable, no doubt, of progressive improvement.

In the army and navy promotion has long been a matter of automatic precision, and as it happens on the very basis of seniority, commonly thought of as a labor union invention. The law of October 1, 1890, provides: "That hereafter promotion to every grade in the Army below the rank of brigadier general throughout each arm, corps, or department of the service, shall, subject to the examination hereinafter provided for, be made according to seniority in the next lower grade of that arm, corps, or department."

Congress itself gives us the seniority idea in a form which could hardly be more rigid if a matter of law instead of invariable custom. The ranking members of the House and Senate committees automatically move toward the chairmanship under the force of a tradition which is no more influenced by questions of superior fitness than the rotation of the seasons is affected by the daily advice of the Weather Bureau.

As in nearly all social experience, the psychology of the matter goes far to explain its many outworkings. This should be the case certainly with an idea rooting back into human nature at so many points as does that of seniority as a just ground for preference. Men have always taken for granted a close connection between age, experience and fitness. The oldest male was the head of the patriarchal tribe by common consent. The "elders" of the church are at least in theory what the name implies, and even the college senior enforces the inherited rights of his venerable rank with an iron hand!

All through the ranks of industrial service the feeling crops out that a man who has served long and faithfully ought to stand next in line when vacancies occur higher up. One of the sources of keenest discontent and demoralization of the *morale* among large bodies of employees has been the feeling that tried and trusted service would stand little chance against the sons, nephews or family friends of directors and high officials of the company, not to mention soldiers of fortune with a political "pull." This has been in fact a common cause of attack upon corporations in general by a large part of the same newspaper press which, when a labor organization is concerned, savagely assails the railroad managements for systematically recognizing length of service.

Without this practically certain "reward for faithful service," the cry has been: "What incentive has any man to stand by, year after year, learning patiently all the rounds and duties from the bottom up, in the hope of due recognition by the time he has become fit for nothing else?" Many indignant and touching editorials to this effect could be quoted without doubt from the same columns that have bristled with scorn for the whole "vicious seniority incubus" upon the railroad service.

Whether it is an incubus or not, especially by comparison with any practical alternatives in sight, and considering that fitness tests must also be passed, invariably, would be a hard matter to determine. The problem is receiving new consideration today at the hands of the public as well as of railroad men, and out of the discussion may come some new elements of flexibility in the workings of the rule. Meanwhile, to understand the history and causes of the situation as it stands is the first thing needed, both for intelligent criticism and constructive help in bringing about better conditions.

Representative Press Opinions on the Social Survey

(Concluded from page 8.)

at heart. A true picture of the concern called the Industrial Workers of the World, for instance, should be of value to every man who believes in our form of government, whether he be a workingman or an employer of workingmen.

Boston Herald, Mass.—The far-reaching industrial and social survey which The National Civic Federation, through its Industrial Economics Department, purposes is an attempt to apply for the first time the Grecian philosopher's "know thyself" on a national scale.

New York Herald, N. Y.—By all means give us an official report in many volumes telling us that the country has advanced in thirty years. It may stifle the voices of misrepresentation raised for mischief and in malice.

Boston Globe, Mass.—If The National Civic Federation can find satisfactory answers to its own questions it will deserve a vote of thanks. But somehow they will have to be answered.

Philadelphia Bulletin, Pa.—An accurate comparison of present and past will be healthful, if only it shall serve to stop some of the whining and complaining. Stock taking will not find the world in such bad condition as some of those who would have it put in receivers' hands for the conservation of its remaining moral and social assets would have the rest of us believe it to be.

Houston Chronicle, Tex.—The Chronicle has taken pleasure in calling attention frequently in the recent past to the work of The National Civic Federation, an organization which is doing a wholly unselfish and altruistic work for the public good.

Lynn News, Mass.—The task is a most interesting one, and one which should yield results. If it is well done we shall not be obliged to guess as to conditions—we shall know. And deliverance will be at hand from the misrepresentations of every sensational agitator who for the moment gets the centre of our stage.

New York Telegram, N. Y.—It is a great work, and its value will be greatly enhanced if the facts arrived at are stated so concisely and simply that every one can read and understand them.

Peoria Herald-Transcript, Ill.—The final report on the survey should have a tremendous effect upon the thought of the country.

Concord Patriot, N. H.—May be a season of reforms will follow this period of investigation.

Buffalo Commercial, N. Y.—A national survey of the industrial and social progress made in this country during the last few decades, as proposed by The National Civic Federation, will probably show that such organizations as the I. W. W. increase and fatten on the hordes of uneducated immigrants that swarm to the land of the free.

Christian Science Monitor, Boston, Mass.—The purpose of the Civic Federation's enterprise is to obtain the facts at their sources and to present them, when found, unvarnished and unpolished. This purpose is laudable. We believe that the ascertained facts on every point will support and justify the optimist, but whether they do or not, it is of much greater importance that the truth shall be known than that any individual, group or class shall be pleased.

Chicago Tribune, Ill.—It may be made a great human document that will help the whole nation to practical betterment.

Portland Oregonian, Ore.—If The National Civic Federation's industrial survey of the country is carried out in the spirit of the plan made for it the results can hardly fail to be of the first importance. The federation is a society known to everybody for its impartial catholicity. Among its members are representatives of all classes and parties in our complex social organism. Such men as John Mitchell, who stands for organised labor, Talcott Williams, who speaks for social economics, and Charles Stelzle, who expresses the advanced Christian opinion of the country upon industrial questions, are typical of its membership. Even those who feel most confident that the Civic Federation's survey will bring forth a vindication of society as it is now organized do not expect that it will demonstrate perfection. Far from it. Glaring iniquities will come to light. Injustice will be detected poisoning the springs of social life. Wealth and poverty will be found standing in totally different positions before the courts. Many such facts will be discovered and frankly admitted. But they do not condemn the system as long as they are not irremediable. If the patient is sick, he can still be cured.

AN OBJECT LESSON FROM FRANCE.

"A remarkable decrease in membership has occurred in the French railwaymen's organization. Before their late disastrous strike they had a membership of 60,000. After the battle it had dwindled to 16,000. This strike, which was conducted along the methods advocated by the I. W. W.'s, should prove another valuable object lesson to the workers everywhere. All the I. W. W. theories go to pieces when the acid test is applied. Trade unionism stands for constructive—slow—but sure methods. I. W. W.-ism encourages and practices destruction, wreck and ruin."—*United Mine Workers' Journal.*

A LABOR MAN'S STORY OF THE PATERSON STRIKE

AFTERMATH OF THE I. W. W. REIGN OF VIOLENCE, INTIMIDATION AND GRAFT

By F. G. R. GORDON

FOUR months ago the I. W. W. leaders promised the twenty-four thousand silk workers of Paterson an eight-hour workday; to-day all of the silk factories of that city are being operated on a ten-hour basis. Four months ago the I. W. W. leaders promised the workers of Paterson an increase of 25 per cent in wages; to-day they are working for practically the same wages, with few exceptions, that they received prior to the beginning of this six months' industrial strike. In a few instances manufacturers in certain grades of work gave a slight increase in wages after the strike was practically broken and the workers had returned to the mills.

For several months before the strike the Industrial Workers of the World and the Socialist leaders had discussed the prospect of a gigantic and successful strike, and together they had encouraged the I. W. W. movement to carry on a general propaganda in the city of Paterson for "one big union." They knew there was dissatisfaction on the part of some of the dyers and something like 5 per cent of the weavers, the latter objecting to the three and four loom system, so-called.

At the first meeting of the I. W. W. the leaders promised the workers an eight-hour day and an increase of 25 per cent in wages. As the meeting progressed it grew enthusiastic and violent language was used. Finally, a resolution was passed that when the meeting broke up they should march in a body to the mills and call upon the workers employed to join the strike, and that if they did not come out voluntarily they should be forced out. As Captain McBride of the night watch said, 'This was a direct challenge to the police that violence was to be resorted to in case any one refused to obey the commands of the I. W. W. leaders." Captain McBride and other police officers, Mr. Thomas Morgan, leader of the Textile Union affiliated with the American Federation of Labor; merchants and manufacturers, public-spirited citizens and labor leaders in general all agreed that there were violence and intimidation on the part of the I. W. W. from the commencement of this great strike to its close. Said Mr. Morgan: "There wasn't a day when from ten to fifteen were not beaten up by this mob element." Hundreds of complaints were made to the police as a direct result of the assault. The police were able to protect the workers at the mills and generally upon the streets, but they could not protect them at their homes, nor could they prevent the thousands of threats made by the strikers who sent letters to the homes and often pasted on the doors a threatening notice of bodily harm if the workers dared to go into the mills. There were 1,473 arrests in the Paterson strike.

The public meeting called by the clergy of the city was broken up and free speech absolutely prevented by the howling mob. At the great meeting at the armory, attended by from twelve to fifteen thousand, there was a premeditated and successful attempt for an hour and thirty minutes to prevent free speech. Fifteen hundred I. W. W. men had marched into the armory, taking seats in the front, and the moment the meeting was opened by the American Federation of Labor leaders they set up a howl, a din of shouting, stamping of feet and calling of vile names, absolutely preventing anything resembling free speech until the police reserves were brought into the hall and with their nightsticks moved everybody out into the streets. After this a peaceful meeting was had at which President John Golden and others made speeches.

This strike was started by the I. W. W. leaders in the hope that they could build up a powerful union in all the silk mills throughout the country. The strike began in Henry Doherty's mill, where the employees were against the four-loom system, but only about twenty-five weavers came out of this mill. It was generally stated by the local labor leaders of Paterson that not over 5 per cent. of the silk workers of that city were dissatisfied when this strike began.

Just about a year before, the I. W. W. had attempted a strike in Paterson which resulted in a complete failure.

On March 8 "Big Bill" Hayward at a large meeting of the strikers called upon them to remain out until the eight-hour day was granted, and with wild enthusiasm they voted to follow his advice. The next day, at another large meeting, Hayward scored the Stars and Stripes in a violent speech, saying that the red flag would take its place. This caused the citizens to make a great display of the Stars and Stripes. Seeing the sentiment which Hayward's speech had aroused, the local leaders procured a flag which they raised with the huge inscription: "We live under this flag. We will fight under this flag, but we will not scab under this flag."

By the middle of March many of the strikers were in serious want, and it was their muttered threats of returning to work that caused the first relief store to be opened on the 27th, and this was shortly followed by others. Every one who asked for food was given staple groceries without regard to whether he was a striker or not.

It was in March that Mr. Doherty, in whose plant the strike had begun, offered to take back all of his old workers, giving them the same jobs that they had before the strike on a co-operative basis, practically giving to them everything. This offer seemed to increase the violent demands and to encourage a general strike for the city. Adolph Lessig, the local I. W. W. leader, advocated that they "get out" the workers in the electric plant, the gas plant, power houses, etc., and plunge the city into darkness and create a reign of terror.

Policeman Nathaniel Love just about this time was beaten up by the strikers. Bomb throwing was indulged in, some of these bombs being exploded so near to the police station that the intonations were plainly heard by the officers on duty at the station.

On June 13, at the Sixth Avenue bridge, a large body of the I. W. W. attempted to prevent a number of strikers from returning to work. They showered them with stones and sticks, clubs and everything they could lay their hands to, many of the police being hit by flying missiles. As the strike was prolonged and the strike funds were insufficient to satisfy hundreds of workers who were in want and privation, there was a growing, insistent demand on the part of many for an accounting of the strike funds, and more especially a detailed accounting of the Madison Square show. I. W. W. followers in Paterson who had attended the Madison Square show had reported that there was a packed house and that people were turned away from the doors unable to gain admission. From these reports the strikers were naturally led to believe that there ought to be at least a few thousand dollars profit from that great meeting. Reed, who managed the Madison Square show and its finances, suddenly departed for Europe before any financial report was rendered. When the report was forthcoming, however, it showed a profit of barely $300, and the last report of this big show attempts to prove that there was an actual loss of more than $600. There is still wide dissatisfaction over the outcome of this affair, and hundreds of silk workers who were formerly identified with the I. W. W. swear by all that is good and bad that they are through with this kind of an organization, and through forever.

During the strike Mr. Arthur Price, who employs some fifty hands turning out a special grade of product, offered to take back his former employees, giving them an eight-hour workday and the increase in wages demanded. He was able to do this, or at least thought he was, by reason of the special goods which he produced. His offer was bitterly assailed and opposed by the I. W. W. leaders, and hundreds of threats were made on all sides that violence would result from any attempt of his former workers to return to the mill.

In the early part of the strike the I. W. W. leaders got out a rubber stamp to be placed on a scab notice, which, when filled in, would read something like this: "This informs you that ——— is a scab," the intent of which was to frighten any "scabs" from going to work for fear of a coming vengeance at the hands of the I. W. W. mob.

I said to Tom Morgan, the able, earnest and sincere business agent for the Textile Workers of Paterson, who are affiliated with the American Federation of Labor "What has the I. W. W. accomplished in this six months' strike?" "Absolutely nothing," said Mr. Morgan. "The strikers have lost more than five million dollars in wages. They are back to work under practically the same conditions that prevailed when they came out on strike. Their organization, so far as we can learn, is absolutely destroyed, and, in my judgment, the working people from a legitimate trade union standpoint have received at the hands of the I. W. W. untold misery, and suspicion and distrust of one another and of the labor movement in general."

"What have you got to say, Mr. Morgan, to the charge made by the I. W. W. leaders, the Socialists, the near-Socialists and the uplifters in general, that the American Federation of Labor unions have not attempted to organize the unskilled and low-wage employees?" "That is an absolutely untruthful statement," said Mr. Morgan. "We have literally spent thousands of dollars in the city of Paterson in the effort to organize every branch of the silk industry, and, what is more, we have organized them on several occasions. That they were not organized when this I. W. W. strike broke out is due to the fact that they didn't stick to the unions, just as they have not stuck to the I. W. W."

I asked President John Golden, of the United Textile Workers of America, the same question. In reply Mr. Golden said: "During the past six or eight years we have spent more than ten thousand dollars in the city of Paterson. In 1906 we sent Organizer Mills into Paterson. He spent fourteen months there, and with the help of Business Agents Morgan and Strak and other local leaders we organized 1,100 weavers and several hundred other silk workers.

"I asked Business Agent Morgan about the charge that the American Federation of Labor had such high initiation fees that it discouraged the workers from joining that organization. "Why," said Mr. Morgan, "we have never charged an initiation fee over twenty-five cents, and many times we have offered to the silk workers of Paterson the opportunity to join our union absolutely free. On the other hand, the I. W. W. organization collected thirty-five cents from every member, twenty-five cents to join and ten cents to purchase an I. W. W. button."

The charge made by certain uplifters, Socialistic cranks and other faddists that the American Federation of Labor has not attempted to organize the silk workers is exactly the opposite of the plain truth. Not only have the United Textile Workers of America sent their general organizers into Paterson and other silk towns hundreds of times, but the A. F. of L. organizers have often been engaged in the same work of organizing this industry.

The dyers came out on strike for an eight-hour workday and 25 per cent increase in wages, and are now working ten hours per day for exactly the same wages that prevailed before the strike. In 1902 the dyers were voluntarily granted an increase in wages of $1 per week by the manufacturers. In 1907 the manufacturers gave them an increase of another dollar per week, and in 1912 still another increase of a dollar, making $3 per week increase in wages in this branch of the industry during the past ten years.

Mr. Morgan, the very intelligent labor leader, who keeps thoroughly in touch with wages and conditions throughout the country in the silk industry, informs me that during the past thirty years the wages of the silk workers of Paterson have been increased by something like $8 per week per worker, and he adds that to-day the silk workers of Paterson, taking everything into consideration, receive an average wage 30 per cent higher than any other silk workers in the world, and that it is 35 per cent higher than in many of the silk centres of Pennsylvania and other States.

I asked one of the largest of the local manufacturers what the I. W. W. had accomplished for the workers in Paterson. He made the same reply that Tom Morgan made, "Absolutely nothing." But he added: "They have accomplished something for us. It was the I. W. W. organization, their tactics and their demands, which have resulted in the formation of a solid organization, 'one big union,' if you please, of the silk manufacturers and their allied industry. Up to just recently we had six or eight different organizations in the city, not always in complete harmony and weakened by this division. To-day, however, we are solidly organized in a stronger position than ever to support and defend our interests, and that is the one thing the I. W. W. accomplished in the city of Paterson."

Manufacturers in general expressed themselves as in sympathy with what they called "reasonable demands" of the workers in their industry. They say that whenever business conditions warrant they will increase wages and shorten hours, but they add that they are under a fierce competition from the low-wage silk centres of Pennsylvania and other places.

At the beginning of the strike the Socialist party leaders rushed to the front in the effort to capitalize political prestige and voters on Election Day. They did, perhaps, more than any other organization to raise funds to carry on the struggle, furnishing bonds to many of those who were arrested and assuming an equal partnership with the Industrial Workers of the World in the domination of the strike contest, but to-day there are discord and bitterness on the part of the Socialist leaders. They are denouncing the I. W. W. organization as an "ungrateful gang."

Dr. Maurice Korshet, of Passaic, and Mr. Jacob Panken, of New York, have roundly denounced the I. W. W. leaders in the columns of the Socialist party organ, the *New York Call*. Dr. Korshet, in a two-column article in the *New York Call*, ends his story this way: "If the Socialist party does not proffer enough help the I. W. W. sets up an awful howl. If the party does too much, then it is accused of seeking political notoriety. In either case the help of the Socialist party is never appreciated or acknowledged, and as soon as the I. W. W. wiggles out of trouble it turns upon its Socialist friends with the viciousness of a snake. The Socialists of Passaic have learned their lesson."

The demagogic tactics of the Socialist party leaders have won their just reward, and the I. W. W. leaders, from "Bill" Hayward down, are declaring that never again will they advise political action.

During the strike Assemblyman John L. Matthews, managing editor of the Paterson Daily Press, took a bold and uncompromising attitude, bitterly assailing the policy and principles of the I. W. W. Naturally, he incurred their enmity, and they boasted very loud and very long that this was the end of Mr. Matthews's political career; that they would defeat him at the primary election, or, failing to do that, they would defeat him at the November election. At the primaries, held on September 23, there were seventeen candidates for the Assembly, and Mr. Matthews received the largest vote among all of those candidates. The Socialists and the I. W. W. men charged that Matthews and the *Daily Press* had been subsidized by the manufacturers, and made all sorts of other indecent and violent remarks about that paper and its editor. As a matter of fact, there isn't any question of doubt that the manufacturers of Paterson owe a big debt to Editor Matthews and his paper, but it is a debt that nobody has any idea of paying, and during the six months of this great industrial struggle not a single penny nor any undue influence was offered on the part of the manufacturers or anybody else to Mr. Matthews or to the *Daily Press*. It was simply the fight of a big, patriotic, red-blooded American citizen against a revolutionary gang of pirates who were seeking to not only destroy the city of Paterson from an industrial and political standpoint, but the whole nation as well.

Mr. John Nolan, another Assemblyman, who likewise took a bold and uncompromising attitude, fighting side by side with Mr. Matthews, was also a candidate for renomination at the primaries. His vote was larger than he ever received and very near to the high mark obtained by Mr. Matthews. Mr. Nolan is the business agent of the Bartenders' Union, a staunch union man who had the confidence of the legitimate trade union movement and, knowing the right, dared to take the stand.

The big economic fact about this strike was that with the loss of $240,000 per week in wages the city seemed to keep on an even keel—only a few small business men went to the wall. The big reason for this was explained by an English weaver, who said: "We economized some, of course, and I had a savings bank account and so did most of my neighbors. We simply drew funds from the bank to live on." That tells the story. In the Paterson Institute of Savings on January 1, 1912, there was a total of $12,687,185.12 on deposit, and the total funds of the people held on deposit in Paterson aggregated $34,687,000. This is equal to $265.50 for every man, woman and child in the city. There are few cities in this country that can show a higher record for thrift than this great silk city of New Jersey.

To-day the mills are all running, though some machinery is idle, due to the fact that the trade changed its demand from skein dyeing to piece dyeing during the strike, and also to the fact that there is a shortage of help. There are whole columns of "Help Wanted" in the daily papers, and the manufacturers say that it is impossible to obtain sufficient skilled hands to operate all their machinery. The character of the working population of the city of Paterson has greatly changed in the past twenty years. Up to the early 90's the bulk of the silk workers were Americans, English and French. The French have almost entirely returned to France, and the Americans and English have been largely succeeded by Italians and Russian Jews, these latter constituting nearly 65 per cent of the Paterson workers at the present time.

I was unable to find any evidence from the manufacturers or labor people that sabotage is being practised in Paterson, although this was advocated openly by several of the I. W. W. leaders. Mr. Frederick Boyd advised the strikers, in case they were defeated, to return to the mills with a bottle of vinegar and sprinkle it on the warps. This would rot the silk threads and thus spoil the cloth or yarn. For saying this and other advice along this line Mr. Boyd has just been declared guilty by Judge Klenert and is being sentenced to a jail term, though it is claimed that the case will be carried to a higher court.

The beginning of the I. W. W. troubles took place eight years ago, when the Detroit faction attempted to organize one of the factories. They were defeated by the American Federation of Labor unions, and the organization went to pieces.

The net result of this six months' strike has been the destruction very largely of all organized labor in the city of Paterson, so far as the silk industry is concerned, and possibly has prevented any organization under any banner from being successful for some time. The bombastic I. W. W. leaders inaugurated this strike with a promise to the workers of Paterson of an eight-hour workday and an increase of 25 per cent in wages. They have been squarely defeated, their organization has been broken up, they have neither power nor influence in the city of Paterson, their poor, deluded followers have lost between five and six millions of dollars in wages. This is the organization that boasts of the "victory" in the city of Paterson.

During the past several years, however, the Socialists have been very active in the circulation of literature and general agitation by the party leaders. Thousands of dollars' worth of Socialist papers, books, pamphlets, leaflets, etc., have been placed in the homes of the working class, and almost nothing has been done to combat the misrepresentation so widely circulated. And so, it is not surprising that the Socialist party now boasts of nearly 5,000 votes cast in the recent election.

Coming now to the larger field of trades union effort, I have to cite the fact that during the past ten years the United Garment Workers' Union has expended more than $200,000, directly and indirectly, for organization purposes, and a detailed examination of the expenditures of this vast sum shows that 95 per cent of it has been expended for the purpose of organizing the unskilled low-wage employees of that industry.

Since the organization of the Boot and Shoe Workers' Union, in 1895, more than $600,000 has been expended for organization purposes, largely in the low-wage districts of that industry; 99 per cent of all the people employed in the boot and shoe industry are skilled or semi-skilled.

During the past twelve months, in Greater New York and vicinity, the American Federation of Labor has organized 65,000 people, most of whom are under the head of unskilled low-wage or semi-skilled workers. It is perhaps pertinent to say that during these twelve months twenty-eight strikes took place, of which twenty-five were successful, bringing a reduction of hours which averaged six per week and an increase in wages ranging from 5 to 35 per cent. The three strikes which were lost were due to the fact that the strikers were imbued with I. W. W. principles, and in the conduct of the strike refused to obey the rules of the American Federation of Labor and insisted upon more or less violent tactics.

It is well to cite the experience of the barbers and waiters of Greater New York, who engaged in a gigantic strike contest under the banner of the I. W. W. These two strikes resulted in a disastrous defeat, great loss of wages and loss of employment by more than 2,000 people.

An important item connected with the Paterson strike is the fact that almost 80 per cent of the money which was contributed to aid the strikers in their contest was given by unions affiliated with the American Federation of Labor. In all of the large strikes conducted by the Industrial Workers of the World no real accounting of funds is ever submitted either to the strikers themselves or to the public who contribute the money. Investigations of the many affiliated unions connected with the American Federation of Labor demonstrate the fact that during the past ten years literally millions of dollars have been expended for the purpose of organizing the unskilled and low-wage workers of this country, and during the past twelve months the garment workers alone have expended more money for this purpose than the I. W. W. has expended in all its history, from the foundation of the notorious organization down to the present time.

As in Paterson so in Lawrence, Hopedale, Ipswich, New York, McKees Rocks and wherever the I. W. W. have waged strike contests they have resorted to mob rule, riots, the destruction of property, brutal assaults upon defenceless men, women and children, and a general reign of terror.

No wonder decent people organize vigilance committees, for every thoughtful citizen must recognize that this I. W. W. is not only an organization of traitors to the laws and the Constitution and the flag of the nation, but that they are traitors to their own class—the workers.

As in Paterson so in all their strike contests we find little or no accounting of contributed funds. On the other hand, there almost invariably follow charges of graft and large sums paid to crooked leaders. In the famous Lawrence strike the facts cited by the Master for the Court who investigated the funds contributed show that the sum of $18,695.86 was never used for the purposes for which it was contributed.

In the I. W. W. barbers' strike it is known, and a sworn affidavit is at hand to prove, that one boss barber was given permission to conduct business on payment to a local I. W. W. leader of $5. Wherever the I. W. W. organize and conduct a strike you hear the same story—riot, destruction of property, assaults and grafting by the leaders.

Vital Problems of the Hour to be Discussed

(*Continued from page 1*)

will also be proposed by the Department on Industrial Mediation Laws, providing a method for dealing with strikes of employees of the Government—Federal, State or municipal.

The Department on Regulation of Municipal Utilities will report its proposed model bill for the regulation by the State of street railways, gas, electric light and other municipal utilities. The department has been at work on this question for eighteen months, and it is hoped that the result of its labors, as embodied in this bill, will go far towards answering the question: What is adequate regulation of public utilities? The work of this department is a logical sequel to the report of the commission of twenty-one of The National Civic Federation that studied in this country and Europe the comparative merits of private and public operation of municipal utilities. The committee that has had charge of this work represents all the interests involved and consists of Messrs. Emerson McMillin, Chairman; Franklin Q. Brown, John H. Gray, Franklin K. Lane, Blewett Lee, Milo R. Maltbie, Arthur Williams, Edward M. Bassett, Martin S. Decker, Halford Erickson, Bruce Wyman and F. C. Walcott.

The Department on Regulation of Industrial Corporations, of which President Low is chairman, will present a proposed bill supplementing what is popularly known as "the Sherman Anti-Trust Act." The presentation of this bill will be preceded by a discussion of many of the questions in respect to this subject that are foremost in the public mind to-day.

Some of these questions are: Shall the size of industrial corporations be limited? If so, what shall be the limit? Is there a point at which corporations become so large that they are unwieldly and therefore inefficient? What answer is there to the showing of the Census of 1910 that the output of individually owned concerns and small corporations has been produced at a less cost than that of their competitors, the large corporations? What is the difference between restraint of competition and restraint of trade? Granted that destructive competition is undesirable and uneconomic from the standpoint of the public, how can competition be so regulated as to prevent its reaching that point? Can a regulatory system be devised that will be effective in protecting the public from the evils that flow from a monopoly or a near-monopoly? Should a manufacturer be permitted to fix the price at which a retailer may sell to the consumer? Is the price-cutting of department stores and other mercantile establishments a benefit or an injury to the public? Is the fixing of prices or the limiting of output by farmers, through co-operation or other form of organization, permissible under the Sherman Act? Are agreements between organizations of working men and organizations of employers, fixing rates of wages, hours of labor and conditions of work, in violation of the Sherman Act? If they are illegal to-day, should they be made legal to-morrow? Should there be an Interstate Trade Commission, fashioned somewhat after the Interstate Commerce Commission, which would have power to pass upon trade agreements, whether of labor, agriculture or commerce? Should large corporations be compelled to take out a Federal license, their acts to be supervised by an Interstate Trade Commission?

The Department of Industrial Economics will report upon its plan for making an investigation of the industrial and social progress in this country during the last three decades and an inquiry into the theories and proposals of the different kinds of socialism. This work, which will be one of the largest that The National Civic Federation has ever undertaken, was authorized by the Executive Committee of the Federation last summer.

The Woman's Department, which is a rapidly growing part of the Federation's organization, will report on its various activities in its different branches. A presentation of the work of the New York and New Jersey, the Washington, and the Massachusetts and Rhode Island Sections alone would make an inspiring showing. The department, however, has eight sections and they cover a very large range of country and all are doing useful service.

The developments of the year in Welfare Work, which have been enormous, especially among large corporations, will be a part of the report of the Welfare Department. It will also propose a permanent exhibit to give to employers standards that may be followed, as it has been found that many who are desirous of establishing proper working conditions have small knowledge of successful features now existing in various enterprises.

The Annual Dinner will take place on the evening of Friday, December 12, at the Hotel Astor.

BETTER CONDITIONS FOR WOMEN WORKERS

PROVISIONS FOR HEALTH, COMFORT AND PROTECTION OF WOMEN IN INDUSTRY DISCUSSED AT FIFTH CONFERENCE OF WELFARE WORKERS

THE conferences of workers actually engaged in the management of welfare features in large industrial and mercantile establishments have proved of increasing value, both to those taking part in the discussions and to beginners and special students of the subject. The fifth of these conferences, held in the Assembly Hall of the Metropolitan Building, New York City, was devoted to the topic "The Welfare of the Woman Worker." Those who participated in the morning session were:

Mrs. L. H. Brittin, of The Joseph & Feiss Co., Cleveland, Ohio.

Miss Antoinette Greely, of the Bush Terminal Co., Brooklyn, N. Y.

Miss Mabel Easton, of the General Electric Co., Harrison, N. J.

Miss Frances Ford, of Dunn & McCarthy, Binghamton, N. Y.

Mrs. Laura L. Ray, of the Greenhut-Siegel Cooper Co., New York.

Dr. Lucy A. Bannister, of the Westinghouse Lamp Co., Bloomfield, N. J.

Miss Helen H. Snow, Curtis Publishing Co., Philadelphia, Pa.

Mrs. G. H. Furman, of Gimbel Bros., New York.

Miss Gertrude S. Waters, of the New York Edison Company, New York.

MRS. T. C. CRAVEN.

Miss Ella Phillips Crandall, of the Department of Nursing and Health, Teachers' College, New York.

Miss Florence E. Trigge, of the Western Electric Company, New York.

Miss Diana Hirschler, of R. H. Macy & Co., New York.

Mrs. T. C. Craven, of Gimbel Bros., Philadelphia.

At the afternoon session an interesting lecture was given by Rev. Frank J. Milman, of Newark, N. J., on the "Mining of Anthracite Coal." Mr. Milman was himself once a breaker boy and is, therefore, able to describe conditions from personal knowledge. His remarks were illustrated by 130 colored stereopticon slides, showing mining methods, the problems of light, water and gas, scenes of the miner at work a thousand feet or more under the earth, and incidents connected with his daily toil; the life of the mule and how he lives under the earth, scenes of first aid work and rescue of injured men, and illustrations of the living conditions of the mining population.

The chairman at the afternoon session was Mr. Emerson McMillin, vice-chairman of the Welfare Department, who pointed out the value of conferences of practical workers in that they are able in this way to learn of the successes and failures of others, instead of being obliged to rely entirely upon their own isolated experiences. Mr. McMillin brought out the interesting point that some of the men and women who supervise welfare work began by taking charge of that phase for which their professional training equipped them.

The topic for the morning session was selected at the urgent request of one of the leading men superintendents of welfare work, who believed from his own perplexity in the matter that great good would come of a discussion closing with definite, practical recommendations of steps which might be taken in industrial plants for the comfort of women workers. The suggestion was carried out and more than justified by the interest and profit of the conference, in spite of the fact that only women welfare directors evidenced by their presence interest in the physical environment of working women. Even the welfare superintendent who suggested the topic failed to present himself. Therefore, the scope of the discussions was broadened.

Mrs. L. H. BRITTIN gave her experiences during three years of welfare work in the large garment factory of The Joseph & Feiss Company, Cleveland, explaining that at first she spent her time simply in getting the confidence of the girls. "I discovered troubles which the managers and foremen did not know existed, and that helped secure the friendship of the employees. We established first our rest and sick room. We have a payroll of approximately eight hundred women and two or three hundred men. We find the sick room brings us our greatest personal contact. Men and girls come there for all sorts of ailments, and ask all sorts of questions pertaining to illness at home. Much working time is saved, both for the company and the employees, through the advice and treatment supplied."

A branch of the public library was put in at no expense to the firm except for the services of Mrs. Brittin's secretary, who takes charge of the books. "The only thing we do is to try to supervise the selection of the books, but we very often find that we judge poorly, and that they enjoy books we would not have thought of suggesting to them." A penny bank, established not quite two years, began with the posting of a notice that deposits would be taken from a penny up. In a very short time it was found that besides pennies they brought in nickels and dimes. The depositors get six per cent interest a year on any sum of one dollar or more that has been on deposit three months or more. The interest actually paid has been small, for the reason that the employees save for specific expenditures, so that the money is seldom there long enough to draw interest. Deposits of over one hundred dollars are not accepted. The money is loaned out to employees, "which gives us a great point of personal contact and confidence. A man comes to borrow ten or fifteen dollars before pay-day, and in as tactful a way as possible I inquire into this, and very often find conditions that we are usually able to help—cases of sickness, and troubles of all sorts that we usually investigate. I find they are almost always willing to tell why they want this money. They understand that we want to know simply for the purpose of helping them out. We have loaned from that bank on an average of three hundred dollars a month to our employees, in sums anywhere from fifty cents to fifty dollars, and the only security we have is our personal knowledge of the employee's character. In the two years of the bank's existence we have lost only seven dollars. I have only denied loans in the case of a couple of young men without families, whose salaries were sufficient and who had abused the privilege, coming every week for from five to ten dollars."

The interest charged is a cent on the dollar, all of which goes to the account of the six per cent paid on deposits. It does not go to the firm. In regard to repayment of loans, the employees usually ask the firm to deduct a certain amount from each week's pay. Nearly all the loans, it was found, were asked for legitimate reasons such as doctors' bills or expenses of moving, when salaries were not due on the day needed. When an employee leaves, his pay envelope is made out and, if possible, the sum that has been loaned is deducted.

"In the gymnasium a box of one hundred cigars—'stogies'—was put on the table, and the men were told as they took a cigar to drop a penny in the box. They have used something like 100 boxes, and not a penny has been lost, with absolutely no one in charge of it." A large lunch room accommodates the entire working force at one time, and in the back of the room are tables covered with magazines and newspapers, foreign and English, also dancing space and a piano. Besides the noon dancing and on Friday afternoons at 5, the employees in different departments arrange one or two evening parties each week during the Winter, with suppers provided by themselves.

The first year the penny bank was in existence it reduced the loan sharks' garnishees on the people's wages 58 per cent. It was found also that the noon and Friday afternoon dancing materially reduced the attendance at dance halls in the evening.

There is in summer a very popular baseball league for the men and one for the girls. Once a year a large shop picnic is held. Every one can attend and bring relatives and friends. The only club in existence at the plant is a sewing club of about twenty-five members. "The girls embroider underwear, collars, belts, and clothes for their personal use, and many of them do exquisite drawn work and embroidery. People become interested in the work and give orders for drawn work, tablecloths, sheets and pillowcases, and some of the girls, who spend their evenings in that manner anyway, are glad to get the extra money."

Mrs. Brittin has charge of all the sanitation in the factory, which is scrubbed and cleaned by women during the day and by porters at night. In the dining room, coffee or tea is served with milk and sugar for a cent, which pays the cost of the ma-

MISS FRANCES C. FORD.

terial; milk, a half-pint for two cents; a large bowl of good soup for two cents. The wholesale selling end of the business has also decided to put in lunch equipment, and a large company manufacturing women's clothing in Cleveland has been looking into the welfare question thoroughly and decided to go into it to the very fullest extent, with Mrs. Brittin's co-operation and supervision.

Miss DIANA HIRSCHLER, then in charge of the educational work at R. H. Macy & Company's, said in part:

"We are co-operating with the Vacation Savings Fund in providing the best sort of vacation places at low rates. The Woman's Department of the Metropolitan section of The National Civic Federation originated this excellent idea. Their Vacation Savings Fund issues stamps and the girls save money in small sums for the summer outing. It is a fine idea to help a girl to a good place for the summer; to see that she has a real good, free and jolly time. This means better work for the rest of the year and better health in which to enjoy it.

"We hold that to make the employee more efficient puts him in a position for advancement and promotion. We hold classes during business hours for the sales force and have regular systematic courses of training for better service. You know to give good service in selling means developing the iner woman or the finer man. Every facility that educates and develops a woman, every grace or charm of person makes her a better saleswoman. We have both the men and women in this kind of work.

"Our house protects the morals of our girls. There has been a good deal written by splendid social workers about store life being a source of temptation, about strange men coming in and inviting sales people out. It is utterly and completely false. But the only thing that is never pointed out is the danger that arises among fellow employees. I wish to say that our house dismisses a man if he does not treat the girls properly, no matter what position he occupies; valuable or not valuable, he is literally put out of the house.

"I have been in many stores, I conduct work in other stores throughout the country, by mail, and I know there is a wonderful inside movement among the retail stores to protect their workers from anything that would be insulting or debasing. Good business is back of it, also. A man who will insult a girl will tend to commit other improprieties. We even go out of our way to look after this. Do not believe that the salesgirl has continuously to combat temptations by outsiders and that she is falling often by the way. If you ladies go shopping in those stores and think: 'This is an immoral lot,' does your intuition back you up? Of course, not! You know you are dealing with girls who are just as clean as you or I. There is no more temptation in the retail stores than in other lines of work where the sexes are thrown together, not so much as in a private office or factory or mill.

"In the retail store, the fact that all conduct is open to the public gives small opportunity for a man to introduce himself. To-day, when a man comes in and loiters around a counter, the floorman just comes up and looks at him and he vanishes. I know a store, for instance, that will not permit a fellow workman to put his hand on the shoulder or the arm of a girl worker, even in the elevator. That man is instantly taken care of by a committee for that purpose; and also I know of a store where the girl is protected from the customers, where a girl may go and touch a button, and when the bell rings a member of the committee steps forward and takes charge of the customer."

Miss FRANCES C. FORD told of the very recent beginnings of welfare work in the shoe manufacturing plant of Dunn & McCarthy, Binghamton, N. Y., employing 600 to 700 girls and 800 to 900 men. Of the girls probably not more than one hundred are foreigners. "The firm suddenly awoke to the realizing sense that to keep a steady working organization something must be done besides furnishing the work and the machine." Thus far only a cloak room has been provided, in the way of accommodations, but this is to be followed by a recreation, emergency and lunch room.

"I advise the girls on various things. They come to me with their little troubles, and I try to straighten them out. I have done a good deal of home visiting to get the confidence of the girls. The American factory girl is very suspicious of patronage. They told me afterward that they thought I was going to be the kind who would say, 'Where were you last night, and what were you doing?' And I said: 'It is not any of my business where you are at night, so long as you are decent and respectable; otherwise you can't work here.'

"The first thing I did was to go out and see the people who were staying out half a day or a day at a time. I said, 'We need your work and you need our money, and the two things can only be brought about by your being there.' They stayed away just because they did not feel like coming to work, or did not feel like getting up in time to get there, or because they had to go and buy something. We work nine hours, from seven to five o'clock, and there was no reason why they could not go and buy after five o'clock. If they were really ill, I could excuse them but when the reasons were purely foolish I would say: 'Why, we all have to be there. Each one of you is an important part of that factory. You have a machine to run and if you are not there the girl next to you who takes your work is delayed and then her work is held up, and so on, and before we get through the whole factory is out of gear.' They could see that. Now they try to come and when they cannot they telephone to us. I think it is just because they feel there is something being done for them besides urging them to make shoes."

Miss Ford reported that during the forenoon all operators stop work for a short rest period, while windows are opened, a custom which ought to be far more general than it is in manufacturing plants.

Welfare work for some 5,000 of the employees of the Bush Terminal, in Brooklyn, according to Miss ANTOINETTE GREELY, began with the supplying of drinking water on the beaches. The men had to go half a mile, sometimes, to get a drink of water, and the saloons were nearer. Later a lunch room was provided, serving good food, although the speaker believed there should be a more reasonable scale of prices. The company has two sets of tenements, the model and those that are far from model. The model tenements are not so well occupied as they should be; the construction and arrangement of rooms are not good, and the prices are too high. Rents are being reduced, and the old tenements are to be made a little more livable, but much cannot be done because at any time they may be torn down to make room for factories.

Loaning money to employees, Miss Greely stated, was very much opposed at first, the fact not being appreciated that the only other resort in case of emergency needs was the loan shark. About six hundred dollars have been loaned, and only six dollars lost, this in the case of a man suddenly discharged. Through the Penny Provident Savings Fund the children have saved about $244 in six months, in pennies, practically money which would have gone for candy or moving pictures. "We have a benefit society which the railroad men have run most successfully. About a year ago the firm offered them financial help and it was declined. Since I have been in charge they have come to me and asked if I would see if the firm cared to help them financially. This means we are getting the confidence of the people, without which we can do nothing.

Mrs. T. C. CRAVEN stated that at the time Gimbel Brothers decided to put in welfare work, in the Philadelphia store, she had been five years doing clerical work in the office. Mrs. Craven was in the employment office for a number of years, interviewing applicants for positions, and also for a short time sold goods. It was her belief that any woman taking up welfare work in a department store should know it from the beginning. "Oftentimes, when the salespeople come and say: 'You don't know, you never did it,' I am able to say: 'Ah, but I do know, I have done it.' That, I think, is a very great help to them." As one part of her work at present she gives short lectures each morning on scientific salesmanship, teaching the employees to help themselves as well as the company through more efficient and pleasing methods of dealing with customers.

Two lunch rooms are provided in the Gimbel store, the larger being on the cafeteria plan, which has proved very successful. The employees are quickly served and the menu is quite extensive: "They have shad roe sometimes, creamed chicken, all sorts of delicacies if they wish, vegetables, all kinds of light cakes and drinks, a choice of two ice creams, and tea, coffee and milk—every day a specialty of some kind." In warm weather employees have access to a roof garden equipped with awnings, rocking chairs, swings and hammocks. Luncheon is served there from 11 till 3.

"The employees come to me with their difficulties and trials when they want a little matter straightened out between them and the buyer or the head of the department. Many times the firm will be criticised for things they know nothing about, and I am very glad to say in our store all are made to understand that, if Mrs. Craven says a thing is right, they are to respect that opinion. I have the backing of every member of the firm.

"A girl can lie down and rest if she is sick; in case she is unable to resume her duties I only notify the head of the department that I have sent such and such a person home. We have a visiting nurse and our own physician who prescribes for and treats our people free. Through the work of the visiting nurse untold good has been done.

"We have a wonderful insurance beneficiary association; it is compulsory, which, in my opinion, is the only kind to have. They get each year fourteen weeks of benefits, costing ten cents a week for those getting five dollars or over; under that, five cents a week. There is also a death benefit of $100. We have two beds in the Chestnut Hill Hospital for tuberculosis.

"In connection with the beneficiary association we have a special relief committee. Sometimes we see some one come in in the morning who looks tired; we talk to her and find there is trouble at home—father out of work, several children in the family and she the only one working. We look into the case, and if we find the rent is due, scarcely any coal in the house, and only the salary of the girl or boy for the family support, we pay the rent, put coal in the cellar, put food in the house, and help the man to get a position or employ him, if we can. Last year we helped about seventy people in that way; I myself sent out, through a fund I have charge of, 125 Christmas baskets. Some of the money comes from the beneficiary association, and the firm donates for this purpose."

A "home talent" entertainment is provided every Friday morning, and there is an orchestra, made up of men and boys employed in the store. The salesgirls and other employees all have a chance to attend, although not all on the same Friday. Opportunities for playing baseball are provided in summer and for basketball in winter.

This firm was one of the first to take up the question of getting its employees out of the hands of the loan sharks. Money is now loaned by the firm, but no interest is charged. "We have notices posted saying, 'If you need money, please avoid loan sharks—see Mrs. Craven,' and I take it up for them. I know the people generally; I know about what salaries they are getting, and we always want to know why they want the money. I do not think we have lost a dollar, and I do not think the money has ever been borrowed for a foolish purpose; the people have paid it back in their own way—so much a week, or so much in two weeks. It is taken out of their salary. They say, 'I want to pay so much each week; deduct that.' Then they do not have to bother any more about it."

In respect to moral conditions in the stores, Mrs. Craven wished to emphasize Miss Hirschler's testimony "that the standard of morality in the department stores is far higher than it is generally believed to be. Many people say to me: 'I am so sorry for the poor girls—what temptations they have.' We want to emphasize the fact that the temptations there are not any greater than in social life, nor do I think they are as great. I know whereof I speak, as we have five thousand people, and I have been their welfare manager for a number of years."

"Help the employee to help himself," has always been the motto of the welfare work at the Greenhut-Siegel Cooper store, said Mrs. LAURA L. RAY, the welfare secretary. Mrs. Ray described first the new hospital, perfectly lighted and ventilated, equipped with the most sanitary hospital furniture and every appliance needed for the physician's work. The hospital contains a separate sick room for the men and women, a large bathroom and an X-Ray room.

"We also have a professional nurse. She is most capable and sympathetic and is doing splendid work. It is my duty to visit the sick in their homes; and in hospitals when it is necessary to send them there; to keep in close touch with all sick cases, supplying their immediate need. This gives me an insight into their home conditions; and a wonderful opportunity to do a great deal of good for my firm. I am provided each month with a fund for these very needs." In the well ventilated and cheerful rest room there is a branch of the New York Circulating Library, and a woman is in charge of this room. It is reached by going through the conservatory, giving the girls an opportunity to enjoy the ferns and flowers each day.

Speaking of the moral conditions, Mrs. Ray also corroborated other speakers in respect to the standards maintained in the department store. "I have been doing welfare work in the Greenhut-Siegel Cooper Company's store for seven years, and do not know of a safer place for a young girl or woman to earn her living. Our men respect a good girl, and the management protects them in every way possible. The welfare office is the strongest evidence."

Mrs. Ray has found it absolutely essential to have a list of good boarding places for the girls, especially for those who come to New York from country places. A list of good boarding places at the seashore, mountains and farms for summer vacations is almost equally important, and Mrs. Ray mentioned that she had been wonderfully helped in this matter by the Vacation Savings Fund Committee of the Federation's Woman's Department.

"About 3,600 people, over 2,000 of whom are girls, are employed on the grounds of the General Electric Lamp Works at Harrison, N. J.," said Miss MABEL EASTON. Miss Easton has been managing a little club among the General Electric girls, which met one evening each week in the company's lunch room and the men's clubhouse, and upon taking up the company's welfare work, as secretary of the Y. W. C. A., paid by the company, she at first simply continued and enlarged this work, which for a time many thought was established merely to amuse the girls during off hours. "Little by little, however, the new department is being recognized as something far more vital and has made some advance toward the betterment of working conditions."

A dispensary, with an attendant and a visiting nurse, is provided; also a factory lunch, with a large space in the midst of the plant given over to the girls' club, partitioned off into a reading room, class room, kitchen and big gymnasium. These rooms are open every noon to club members and twice a week to every girl. The two rooms, open to all, are devoted to special programs. These entertainments are most popular and offer almost limitless opportunities for educational purposes.

A factory paper is published, appearing each month, and is distributed free of charge to every employee. It represents all the varied interests of the factory, including the Fire Department, the Salvage Corps, the Men's Club, and the Girls' Club, and aims to be a unifying factor. Social items and health articles are incorporated. It is popular. If a day late in being issued, the employees ask for it.

"One of the ideals of our club organization," said Miss Easton, "is to make the girls work for each other,—in other words, to do welfare work themselves," regarding it as not merely an exclusive affair for a few, but as having a broader outlook and connection with all the welfare work of the plant. "This is an ideal, of course, and I suppose a good many of the girls are not ready for it as yet, but some have glimpsed it and are working along splendid, unselfish lines."

WHAT CAUSES FATIGUE?

By THOMAS DARLINGTON, M.D.

The following interesting and instructive discussion of the causes of bodily fatigue among industrial workers, by Thomas Darlington, M.D., formerly Commissioner of Health of New York City, appeared in the November number of the Medical Times. Dr. Darlington is the secretary of the Welfare Committee of the American Steel and Iron Institute, and a member of the Welfare Department of the National Civic Federation. The article in part is as follows:

In modern industry there is no question of more importance, so far as human activity is concerned, than that of bodily fatigue. To understand fatigue, and the various factors of its causation, we must understand those physiological facts known as metabolism, the building up process being called anabolism, and the breaking down process catabolism.

In some respects the development of energy in the body is analogous to the development of steam in a boiler or the operation of a gas engine. There must be fuel, such as coal, oil or gas; there must be a supply of air containing oxygen, and there are the ashes as waste.

Muscular energy depends largely upon three things:

1. The amount of fuel stored and the ability of the system to bring it into use.
2. The ability of the system to furnish oxygen to burn the fuel.
3. The ability of the system to carry off waste or other toxic substances.

Conversely, fatigue is due primarily to the failure of the system to perform properly one or more of these functions.

Storage of Fuel.

First, fatigue may be caused by anything that interferes with the storage of fuel. This may arise from a lack of fuel. Under this head would come underfeeding, improper feeding, indigestion of food, lack of assimilation of food, and incapacity of the liver and muscles to store sufficient glycogen.

It requires no argument to prove that if fuel is lacking energy must also be lacking. So if one does not have sufficient food he cannot store enough energy. This may also be the case when a large enough quantity is eaten, but not of the proper kind or quality. One has learned much who has learned what food to purchase. For example, cabbage is a very common article of diet, but there is little energy to be derived from it.

To regulate the food according to the demands of the body, to have a properly balanced dietary, comes only as the result of study. Education along these lines in connection with industrial plants is best given in the form of household instruction by trained nurses or domestic educators.

True, since Knoop has shown that the system can change one food into another, an excess of one kind of food is probably converted in the system into others. But physiological tests have shown that a mixed diet is best for the needs of the system. The body is very adaptable, but we should not put upon it unnecessary alimentary burdens.

All of these things relate to the question of the wise selection of food for energy and the needs of the system. An examination of many lunch buckets has indicated to me that sometimes but little thought is given as to the kind of food that goes into them, provided there is quantity. Many times the food in lunch buckets, such as yeast bread, becomes sweated, and milk in the coffee undergoes more or less fermentation. This bears directly upon energy.

After food reaches the stomach there is often much needless waste, particularly of the sugars, due to fermentation in the stomach. The sugars are split into acids before reaching the tissues, and so are partly lost for energy. The fermentation is due to two causes: First, to a lack of gastric juice; and, second, to an excess of bacteria. A lack of gastric juice, and therefore indigestion, is due to an improper selection of food, to a disturbed mental condition (anger, grief, worry) or to reflex disturbances of the gastric nerves from chronic appendicitis, etc. Or there may be an excess of bacteria. This is due either to fermented or putrid foods, or to the addition of bacteria to the food from unclean mouths and bad teeth or dirty hands. Over-eating and rapidity of eating also affect digestion, and therefore promote fatigue.

Lack of Oxygen Causes Fatigue.

Secondly, fatigue is caused by anything that interferes with the carrying of oxygen to the tissues. This may be a diminished amount of oxygen in the atmosphere, diminished carrying power of the blood, diminished lung capacity, or interference with the circulation of the blood.

The two factors which relate especially to diminished amount of oxygen in the atmosphere are bad ventilation and altitude. The main effect of bad ventilation, especially where there are a number of people in a room, is to increase the humidity. The detrimental effect of this humidity, which will be considered at greater length later in this paper, is of more importance than any diminishing of oxygen or increase in carbon dioxide.

From diminished oxygen, altitude produces fatigue.

In industry we are more concerned, however, with the diminished oxygen-carrying power of the blood. Anemia is produced by a variety of causes, among which are deficient light, insufficient iron in the blood, insufficient variety of food, irregularity of the bowels, as the sequel of disease (particularly infectious diseases) and of metal poison, such as lead. So, working at night, or in dark buildings or dark rooms, is injurious to the blood.

Carbon Monoxide.

A matter of particular importance to those in the iron and steel industry is the fact that the oxygen-carrying power of the blood is very much diminished if there is any carbon monoxide in the air breathed by the men. The deleterious effect of this gas is due to its combination with the hemoglobin in the blood, thus injuring the oxygen-carrying function. The affinity of the hemoglobin for carbon monoxide is much greater than its affinity for oxygen, forming a compound with carbon which is a much more stable compound than that formed with oxygen.

Carbon monoxide often produces a fatal effect. So we must guard against poisoning by this gas. This is a product of the furnaces, and is especially dangerous in bad weather, coming down the side of the furnaces. It also occurs in engine rooms from leaky gas engines; and we find it in plants where open fires, such as salamanders, are used for heating purposes in winter, or from blacksmiths' fires. Even though the quantities breathed are small, this gas, breathed constantly, will, in time, produce anemia. So gas engines should be watched. For heating purposes other methods than open fires should be adopted. And blacksmiths' fires should be hooded to carry away gases.

Accumulation of Waste Causes Fatigue.

The third great cause of fatigue is poisoning by accumulated waste in the muscles or poisoning by toxic substances. This accumulation may be due to too rapid formation of the products of waste, or it may be due to the inability of the blood or system to carry away the waste products. If the nerve of a muscle is constantly stimulated, the muscular contractions become smaller in extent and finally cease. The muscle is then said to be fatigued. The sugars and glycogen have been burned, producing energy and leaving as wastes carbon dioxide and lactic acid. Unless eliminated these materials act as poisons.

When a muscle is fatigued there is more, however, to be considered than the local poison. The products of fatigue pass into the blood and poison all parts of the body, including the nervous system.

Drinking of Water Lessens Fatigue.

Perhaps no means of lessening fatigue is of more importance than a proper supply of drinking water. The products of waste, carbon dioxide and lactic acid are taken up by the fluids of the body and carried to the lungs and kidneys for elimination. The accumulation of waste products is often due to insufficient use of drinking water. It has been noticed in the army that the man who falls from heat stroke is the one whose canteen is empty.

Poisons that are very dilute have, as a rule, but little detrimental effect upon the system. The most powerful acids, if sufficiently diluted with water, are no longer caustic. And self-generated poison in the body will, if sufficiently diluted, probably have less effect.

If water is too cold, it is retained for a longer time in the stomach, and its benefits are not so quickly felt. Sometimes if water is too cold it brings on cramps, and sometimes if too large a quantity is taken it is rejected. So the water supply for drinking purposes must not only be pure in quality and ample in quantity, but it must be kept at the proper temperature.

Cold Showers Lessen Fatigue.

Not only internally, but also externally water plays a part in lessening fatigue. So the benefits derived from general bathing should be mentioned. These have been recognized for many centuries, and the therapeutic use of the bath is as old as the art of medicine itself. The public baths of the Greeks and Romans were a prominent feature of their civilization. Recently hydrotherapy has received much study and has become more of a science. The capacity of water for heat makes it valuable for use in extracting heat or in applying heat.

As the skin covers a network of blood vessels and nerves, water can be used to effect a physical reaction.

By means of shower bath the skin is mechanically stimulated by the striking drops. This combined with thermic influence increases the effect of the bath upon the heart and respiration. It also affects metabolism. It increases the production of animal heat. The heart action is increased in force. The secretion of the skin is diminished. It increases th urine and other internal secretions. Examinatio of the blood shows certain changes in the element of the blood itself. Thus water, through the ski affects secretion, excretion and the heat regulatin function.

Shower baths may, therefore, be used to eliminat more rapidly the products of waste, to promote secre tion, to relieve fatigue, to restore the normal fun tions to various organs of the body, to restore th body temperature to the normal, and produce a r distribution of the blood when there is congestion i any one part of the body.

Heat and Humidity Affect Body Temperature.

Every one knows that on a hot, humid day a ma is much less efficient than on a cool, dry day. Th reason for this, however, has only recently bee shown by scientific investigation. Ordinarily bod temperature is maintained at a fixed level with bu little deviation. The control of the production c heat and the regulation of its dissipation rest pr marily in the brain and nervous system. On hot day when there is excessive humidity, the body temper ture rises. Rise of temperature may occur in thre ways: Heat production may increase while heat los remains constant, or heat production may remai constant, while heat loss may be diminished, or hea production may increase while heat loss diminishe There is increase of heat production after the al sorption of a full meal. Muscular work also increase heat production enormously.

By radiation, by conduction, and by the evapora tion of water, there is loss of body heat from th skin. Heat is also lost by the moisture of th breath. When there is much humidity, sufficient t prevent evaporation of sweat and the elimination o the heat which is constantly being produced withi the body, the internal temperature rises and feve results. The elimination of heat by the breath als depends somewhat on humidity. Dr. Denison, o Denver, has shown that fully eight ounces mor water is lost by the breath during twenty-four hour in Denver than in New York. And, according to m own experience and observation in Arizona, thi amount is increased in that drier climate. Con versely, on a humid day we do not eliminate as mucl moisture by the lungs. Heavy clothes preventin evaporation from the skin increase this rise of tem perature.

Observation of those who work in heat and ex cessive humidity shows that they soon pass into condition of fatigue. That is, fever produces a con dition of fatigue. This fatigue which comes from fever is brought about by the energy-forming ma terials in the muscles being burned up rapidly an the poisonous products of such combustion accumu lating within the body. And, what is of great im portance, if there is not a sufficient amount of ca bohydrates for use there is destruction of protei material similar to that found in excessive worl due to the direct action of high temperature. I addition, the blood is drawn to the surface of th body, leaving the brain, the spinal cord, and the i ternal organs correspondingly anemic. This lessen the normal impulses to the muscles, and in itsel will give a tired feeling.

Other poisons besides those generated in th muscles produce fatigue. Fermentations in the i testinal canal produce poisons which have a fatig ing effect. Thus indol, and possibly other substance have been proven to induce fatigue. Indol is foun in the large intestine as the result of bacterial putr faction. It is eliminated in part from the bowels but is in part absorbed in the blood and subsequentl eliminated in the urine, in the form of indican. A indol is produced by the fermentation of certai kinds of albuminous foods, diet is again an importa factor. That the products of waste in the intestin canal should be rapidly excreted is self-evident.

Effect of Lack of Sleep.

Sleep is the period of repair and growth, the tin when the building up process exceeds the breakir down process. During sleep less carbon dioxide eliminated and less oxygen is absorbed. Experimen upon dogs show that if starved even for sever weeks, they will recover, but that they die from lo of sleep in five days. Loss of sleep is much mo damaging than starvation. Loss of sleep is a comm cause of fatigue.

Thus badly ventilated rooms, and over-heate rooms in summer, crowding of rooms, with noise a other discomforts, and the hours of sleep are matte requiring careful consideration by those who empl labor.

Fatigue Lessens Resistance to Disease.

One of the most important results of fatigue that it lessens resistance to disease. It has be shown that after the death of an animal from fatig the body undergoes rapid putrefaction. Clinical e perience and experiments on animals have show that people who are fatigued are much more subje to contagious and infectious diseases. There therefore, a physiological, a chemical and a psycl logical basis of fatigue.

The McConnell Printing Co. 230-242 William Street, N. Y.

THE NATIONAL CIVIC FEDERATION REVIEW

Vol. IV. NEW YORK, MARCH, 1914 No. 3

SOCIAL SURVEY ENLISTS NATION-WIDE SUPPORT

TWENTY-FIVE COMMITTEES OF EXPERTS AND REPRESENTATIVE CITIZENS TAKE UP MAIN DIVISIONS OF INQUIRY, AND THE WORK COMMANDS ENDORSEMENT AND CO-OPERATION THROUGHOUT THE COUNTRY

THE Executive Committee in charge of the national survey of industrial and social progress during the last generation has completed the permanent organisation of this great undertaking, and the work is now in active progress.

At a meeting of the committee held at the headquarters of The National Civic Federation last week, the main divisions of the inquiry were determined and the range of subjects to be studied under each classification was gone over in detail. Announcement was made at the same time that Dr. Roland P. Falkner, the committee's choice for director of the survey, has consented to accept the post and will enter upon its responsible duties immediately. There was also announced the membership of the committees which will have charge of the leading divisions of the investigation. The list of these committees published below demonstrates that the inquiry will have the supervision of the strongest volunteer group of representative authorities and trained experts in every sphere of our national life that has ever been gathered together for a great civic achievement.

In public announcements of this survey, and in the last number of the REVIEW, the reasons were pointed out why it is believed of supreme importance at just this point in our national development that the American people should seriously take "account of stock." Has the social movement of recent years been in the direction of economic justice and a larger human welfare, or the reverse? Upon the answer to this vital question must depend the trend and form of our future public policies, alike with reference to the encouragement of wholesome tendencies, the rooting out of survivals of unfit conditions and the correction of incidental abuses which have grown up amid our new and rapidly changing conditions. As expressed by President Seth Low in a public statement relative to the survey: "Much will be found on both sides of the ledger, and of a certainty, with a satisfactory knowledge of the assets, Americans will be encouraged to meet their remaining liabilities to the cause of human advancement."

Included in the scope of the inquiry, as its natural outgrowth, will be a study of the various economic interpretations and social programs which have grown up alongside the industrial and social changes of the period and require the same test which the survey will apply to the workings of all of our existing institutions—that of verified facts.

In securing the services of Dr. Falkner the committee feels that it has been singularly fortunate in meeting one of the chief conditions of success. Dr. Falkner comes to the task with an exceptional equipment. Trained for statistical work in three German universities, he came into thorough command of the entire field of American and European statistical literature as chief of the division of documents in the Library of Congress. He conducted, as statistician, the colossal investigation into prices by the United States Committee of Finance in 1891. Both in Porto Rico and in Liberia, as well as in other important official positions, he has come in contact with practical administrative problems. As assistant director of the census of 1910 he came into direct contact, as in some of his other work, with the cost of conducting statistical investigations, the limits within which they must be kept and the methods by which efficiency and accuracy can be secured with economy. Those who have conducted such investigations are aware that this indispensable qualification is extremely rare. In Dr. Falkner's case it is united with unusual administrative capacity.

Professor Jeremiah W. Jenks, of New York University, chairman of the Executive Committee of the Industrial Economics Department, presided at the meeting, and Dr. Talcott Williams, chairman of the plan and scope committee, called attention to the large number of letters already received from members of the Advisory Council throughout the country, making suggestions of pertinent topics which should be included in the inquiry and indicating available sources of authentic information. Dr. Williams pointed out that the inquiry requires to only a very limited extent new investigation; rather, it consists almost wholly in bringing together facts already of record, but which have never been co-ordinated.

JOHN HAYS HAMMOND, Chairman Industrial Economics Department.

D. L. CEASE, Vice-Chairman Industrial Economics Department.

ROLAND P. FALKNER, Director of the National Survey.

JEREMIAH W. JENKS, Chairman Executive Committee Industrial Economics Department.

TALCOTT WILLIAMS, Chairman Plan and Scope Committee.

EXECUTIVE COUNCIL.

The members of the Executive Council of the Industrial Economics Department are as follows:

JOHN HAYS HAMMOND, *Chairman.*
JEREMIAH W. JENKS, *Chairman Executive Committee.*
TALCOTT WILLIAMS, *Chairman Committee on Plan and Scope of Social and Industrial Survey.*
ROLAND P. FALKNER, *Director.*
HAYES ROBBINS, *Associate Director.*
JAMES LAUGHLIN PHILLIPS, *Executive Secretary.*
ISAAC N. SELIGMAN, *Treasurer.*
VINCENT ASTOR, *Chairman Committee on Food and Drugs.*

William D. Baldwin, *Chairman Committee on Collective Bargaining and Methods of Mediation and Arbitration.*

George E. Barnett, *Chairman Committee on Industrial Profit Sharing.*

August Belmont, *Chairman Committee on Workmen's Compensation.*

Kenyon L. Butterfield, *Chairman Committee on Agricultural Conditions.*

Paul D. Cravath, *Chairman Committee on Tenement House Conditions.*

Irving Fisher, *Chairman Committee on Public Health.*

Samuel Gompers, *Chairman Committee on Labor Conditions.*

Elgin R. L. Gould, *Chairman Committee on Industrial Loans and Savings.*

Jeremiah W. Jenks, *Chairman Committee on Immigration.*

Adolph Lewisohn, *Chairman Committee on Penal and Correctional Institutions.*

V. Everit Macy, *Chairman Committee on Child Labor.*

W. G. Mather, *Chairman Committee on Employers' Welfare Work.*

Charles R. Miller, *Chairman Committee on Improvement in Political Ethics.*

Ogden L. Mills, *Chairman Committee on Business Ethics.*

William J. Pape, *Chairman Committee on the Theory of Surplus Value.*

Alton B. Parker, *Chairman Committee on Free Speech and Right of Assembly.*

George W. Perkins, *Chairman Committee on Social Insurance.*

A. J. Porter, *Chairman Committee on the Minimum Wage.*

James B. Reynolds, *Chairman Committee on Enforcement of Law and Order.*

E. R. A. Seligman, *Chairman Committee on Distribution of Ownership in Investments.*

O. D. Skelton, *Chairman Committee on Theory of Government Ownership and Operation of Public Utilities and Private Industries.*

William H. Taft, *Chairman Committee on Judicial Procedure.*

Charles R. Towson, *Chairman Committee on Institutional Church Work.*

Frank Tucker, *Chairman Committee on Efficiency of Organized Social Service.*

George E. Vincent, *Chairman Committee on Educational Opportunities.*

Clinton Rogers Woodruff, *Chairman Committee on Municipal Government.*

THE MAIN DIVISIONS OF THE INQUIRY.

Some idea of the far-reaching scope of the survey may be had from the following outline of its general divisions, each of which, of course, requires much more extended space for adequate analysis. In connection with each subject is given the committee which will have its investigation in charge.

LABOR CONDITIONS.

How do wages, hours of labor and the physical conditions of the factory and the home compare with those of thirty years ago? Have the work of the American Federation of Labor, the railway brotherhoods and the social reform organizations and the legislation secured by them prohibiting child labor and regulating conditions in factories, mercantile establishments, mines, bakeries, tenement houses and sweat shops really benefited the wage-working men, women and children of this country?

Committee.

Samuel Gompers, President American Federation of Labor, Washington, D. C.

Warren S. Stone, Grand Chief International Brotherhood of Locomotive Engineers, Cleveland, Ohio.

James M. Lynch, New York State Commissioner of Labor, Albany, N. Y.

T. V. O'Connor, President International Longshoremen's Association, Buffalo, N. Y.

W. L. O'Brien, Kansas State Commissioner of Labor and Industry, Topeka, Kan.

James D. Beck, Member Wisconsin Industrial Commission, Madison, Wis.

W. S. Carter, President Brotherhood Locomotive Firemen and Enginemen, Peoria, Ill.

Fred Lange, Member Ohio Bureau of Labor Statistics, Columbus, Ohio.

Joseph F. Valentine, President International Molders' Union of America, Cincinnati, Ohio.

Charles F. Gettemy, Chief, Mass. Bureau of Labor Statistics, Boston, Mass.

David Ross, Illinois State Commissioner of Labor Statistics, Springfield, Ill.

H. M. Stanley, Georgia State Commissioner of Commerce and Labor, Atlanta, Ga.

James Byrnes, Louisiana State Commissioner of Labor and Industrial Statistics, New Orleans, La.

John Golden, President United Textile Workers of America, Fall River, Mass.

John Williams, President International Association of Factory Inspectors, Albany, N. Y.

James J. Murphy, Factory Inspector for the First District, New York.

EMPLOYERS' WELFARE WORK.

How do the provisions by employers for the wage-earners' health, safety and comfort, recreation, education, housing and insurance compare with those of a generation ago?

Committee.

W. G. Mather, President Cleveland-Cliffs Iron Company, Cleveland, Ohio.

Cyrus H. McCormick, President International Harvester Company, Chicago, Ill.

H. M. Byllesby, H. M. Byllesby & Co., Chicago, Ill.

J. J. Donovan, Bloodel Donovan Lumber Mills, Bellingham, Wash.

Charles L. Edgar, President Edison Electric Illuminating Co., Boston, Mass.

Pierre S. du Pont, E. I. du Pont de Nemours Powder Company, Wilmington, Del.

Paul Feiss, The Joseph & Feiss Company, Cleveland, Ohio.

F. W. Dohrmann, Dohrmann Commercial Company, San Francisco, Cal.

Frederick S. Fish, Chairman Executive Committee, The Studebaker Corporation, South Bend, Ind.

Haley Fiske, The Metropolitan Life Insurance Company, New York.

F. R. Hazard, President The Solvay Process Company, Syracuse, N. Y.

Edwin M. Herr, President Westinghouse Electric and Air Brake Companies, Pittsburgh, Pa.

James T. McCleary, American Iron and Steel Institute, New York.

William C. Muschenheim, President Hotel Astor, New York.

Thomas F. Parker, President Monaghan Mills, Greenville, S. C.

Theodore P. Shonts, President Interborough Rapid Transit Company, New York.

CHILD LABOR.

Has it increased or diminished in recent decades? What has been the effect of State legislation upon age limits, hours worked and opportunity for education?

What is being done by voluntary effort for child welfare, and in what directions is further progress most needed?

Committee.

V. Everit Macy, Publicist, New York.

Hugh Frayne, Organizer American Federation of Labor, New York.

Samuel McCune Lindsay, Professor of Social Legislation, Columbia University, New York.

Ben L. Lindsey, Judge Juvenile Court, Denver, Col.

Mrs. Clarence Burns, President The Little Mothers' Aid Association, New York.

Mrs. John K. Ottley, Woman's Department, The National Civic Federation, Atlanta, Ga.

F. G. R. Gordon, Immigration Expert, Haverhill, Mass.

Rev. Peter E. Dietz, Secretary Social Service Commission, American Federation of Catholic Societies, Milwaukee, Wis.

Joseph A. Hill, Bureau of Census, Washington, D. C.

Ernest H. Abbott, *The Outlook*, New York.

Rev. Charles Stelzle, Consulting Sociologist, New York.

Charles P. Neill, Director, Chairman Labor Committee, American Smelting and Refining Company, New York.

William F. Willoughby, Former President American Association for Labor Legislation, Princeton, N. J.

AGRICULTURAL CONDITIONS.

Is the farmer holding to the ownership of his farm, or lapsing into tenancy, or sinking under mortgage debt? How does he live to-day compared with thirty years ago and what changes have occurred in his methods of work? Of what value to him have been the rural delivery and the parcel post? What is being accomplished by the new movements for betterment of rural life, such as co-operative buying and selling?

Committee.

Kenyon L. Butterfield, President Massachusetts Agricultural College, Amherst, Mass.

L. H. Bailey, Former Dean College of Agriculture, Cornell University, Ithaca, N. Y.

C. F. Sanford, President Farmers' National Congress, London, Ohio.

Oliver Wilson, Master National Grange, Patrons of Husbandry, Peoria, Ill.

Charles S. Barrett, President Farmers' Educational and Co-operative Union of America, Union City, Ga.

John J. Dillon, Editor *The Rural New Yorker*, New York.

Henry Wallace, Editor *The Farmer*, Des Moines, Iowa.

William C. Brown, Former President New York Central Railroad Company, New York.

Edward N. Breitung, Ore Producer, Negaunee, Mich.

J. L. Coulter, United States Department of the Census, Washington, D. C.

Thomas N. Carver, Director Rural Organization Service, Department of Agriculture, Washington, D. C.

F. D. Coburn, Commissioner of Agriculture, Topeka, Kansas.

TENEMENT HOUSE CONDITIONS.

Are city dwellers securing an improved standard of decency and comfort, of light and air, as compared with the mode of living a quarter of a century ago? What has been accomplished and what remains to be done?

Committee.

Paul D. Cravath, Lawyer, New York.

Lawrence Veiller, Director Department for Improvement of Social Conditions of the Charity Organization Society, New York.

John J. Murphy, Tenement House Commissioner of the City of New York, New York.

Alfred T. White, New York.

Jacob A. Riis, Sociologist, New York.

Frederic B. Pratt, New York.

IMMIGRATION.

What special problems with relation to the well-being of the masses have we to solve in consequence of a practically unrestricted immigration?

Committee.

Jeremiah W. Jenks, Professor of Government, New York University, New York.

W. S. Bennet, Lawyer, New York.

Willard D. Straight, Banker, New York.

Edward A. Ross, Professor of Sociology, University of Wisconsin, Madison, Wis.

Cyrus L. Sulzberger, Director Jewish Agricultural and Industrial Aid Society, New York.

Robert M. Thompson, Chairman Executive Committee, Navy League, Washington, D. C.

W. Jett Lauck, Immigration Expert, Washington, D. C.

Thomas N. Carver, Director Rural Organization Service, Department of Agriculture, Washington, D. C.

Samuel Gompers, President American Federation of Labor, Washington, D. C.

Oliver Wilson, Master National Grange, Patrons of Husbandry, Peoria, Ill.

Walter E. Weyl, Economist, New York.

F. G. R. Gordon, Immigration Expert, Haverhill, Mass.

COLLECTIVE BARGAINING, MEDIATION AND ARBITRATION.

What has been the effect of the development of the trade agreement upon industrial discord? To what extent have our industries and the public benefited by the work of voluntary mediation agencies, national and state arbitration bureaus?

Committee.

William D. Baldwin, President Otis Elevator Company, New York.

W. G. Lee, President Brotherhood of Railroad Trainmen, Cleveland, Ohio.

Timothy Healy, President International Brotherhood of Stationary Firemen, New York.

Otto M. Eidlitz, Building Trades Employers' Association, New York.

Marcus M. Marks, President of the Borough of Manhattan, New York.

Herman Ridder, Editor *New-Yorker Staats Zeitung*, New York.

Franklin MacVeagh, Former Secretary of the Treasury, Chicago, Ill.

William D. Mahon, President Amalgamated Association of Street Railway Employees of America, Detroit, Mich.

H. N. Kellogg, Chairman Standing Committee American Newspaper Publishers' Association, Indianapolis, Ind.

Louis B. Schram, Chairman Labor Committee United States Brewers' Association, Brooklyn, N. Y.

EDUCATIONAL OPPORTUNITIES.

Where does America stand in the matter of gratifying the more widespread thirst for knowledge? What, in addition to its public and private schools, have been the results of its public libraries, free lecture courses, correspondence schools, and facilities for technical education for farm and factory?

Committee.

George Edgar Vincent, President University of Minnesota, Minneapolis, Minn.

Jacob Gould Schurman, President Cornell University, Ithaca, N. Y.

Miss Virginia C. Gildersleeve, Dean of Barnard College, Columbia University, New York.

Harry P. Hutchins, President University of Michigan, Ann Arbor, Mich.

Sidney E. Mezes, President University of Texas, Austin, Texas.

Edwin A. Alderman, President University of Virginia, Charlottesville, Va.

Benjamin Ide Wheeler, President University of California, Berkeley, Cal.

Charles R. Van Hise, President University of Wisconsin, Madison, Wis.

EFFICIENCY OF ORGANIZED SOCIAL SERVICE.

Has the spending of millions of dollars by the Carnegie, Rockefeller and Sage Foundations, by the hundreds of charity associations and social settlements,

Finley J. Shepard, Vice-President Missouri Pacific Railroad Company, New York.
Arthur Williams, Chairman Association of Edison Illuminating Companies, New York.
Lyman P. Powell, President Hobart College, Geneva, N. Y.
Charles G. Dawes, President Central Trust Co. of Illinois, Chicago, Ill.
Hennen Jennings, Mining Engineer, Washington, D. C.
William H. Ingersoll, American Fair Trade League, New York.
Alfred L. Baker, Banker, Chicago, Ill.
John H. Wigmore, Dean of the Law School, Northwestern University, Chicago, Ill.
John Grant Dater, Financial Writer, *The Evening Sun*, New York.

POLITICAL ETHICS.

What are the gains for purity and cleanliness in politics through regulation of primaries, publicity of campaign contributions, the secret ballot and the civil service merit system? Are legislative bodies thwarting or responding to popular demands? What is to-day's concept of the relations of government to industry in respect to enforcement of law, restriction of monopolistic and competitive abuses, railroad rebates and passes, etc., compared with standards of a generation ago?

Committee.

Charles R. Miller, Editor *The New York Times*, New York.
Ogden M. Reid, Editor, *New York Tribune*, New York.
Charles W. Knapp, Proprietor *The St. Louis Republic*, St. Louis, Mo.
Clark Howell, Editor *The Atlanta Constitution*, Atlanta, Ga.
John H. Finley, New York State Commissioner of Education, Albany, N. Y.
George B. Cortelyou, President Consolidated Gas Company, New York.
Ogden L. Mills, Lawyer, New York.
John P. Frey, Editor *International Molders' Journal*, Cincinnati, Ohio.
William Allen White, Editor *The Emporia Gazette*, Emporia, Kan.
Arthur Capper, Editor *The Topeka Capital*, Topeka, Kan.

INSTITUTIONAL CHURCH WORK.

To what extent and with what results are the churches engaging in social and civic betterment work as compared with the earlier scope and emphasis of their activities?

Committee.

Charles R. Towson, Secretary Industrial Department, International Committee of Young Men's Christian Associations, New York.
Rev. Walter Laidlaw, Executive Secretary New York Federation of Churches, New York.
Conde B. Pallen, Editor *The Catholic Encyclopaedia*, New York.
Rev. Charles S. MacFarland, Secretary Federal Council of Churches of Christ in America, New York.
Rev. Dr. Hyman G. Enelow, Rabbi Temple Emanu-El, New York.
Right Rev. David H. Greer, Bishop of New York, New York.
John, Cardinal Farley, Archbishop of New York.
Right Rev. John E. Vincent, Bishop Methodist Episcopal Church, Chicago, Ill.
Charles I. Denechaud, President American Federation of Catholic Societies, New Orleans, La.

MUNICIPAL GOVERNMENT.

How far have the efforts of civic reform movements for cleaner and more efficient municipal government yielded substantial results? What of the provision of parks, play-grounds, public baths, the care of streets, etc.?

Committee.

Clinton Rogers Woodruff, Secretary National Municipal League, Philadelphia, Pa.
Harry A. Garfield, President Williams College, Williamstown, Mass.
George Burnham, Jr., Philadelphia, Pa.
H. D. W. English, Chairman Pittsburgh Civic Commission, Pittsburgh, Pa.
Walter L. Fisher, Former Secretary of the Interior, Chicago, Ill.
J. L. Hudson, Detroit, Mich.
John A. Butler, Milwaukee, Wis.
Dwight F. Davis, St. Louis, Mo.
Rev. Charles N. Lathrop, San Francisco, Cal.

JUDICIAL PROCEDURE.

What has been accomplished towards greater simplicity and clarity in legal procedure? What efforts are under way and what can be done to render the administration of justice more prompt and certain for all citizens?

Committee.

William H. Taft, President American Bar Association, New Haven, Conn.
Everett P. Wheeler, Lawyer, New York.
William E. Chandler, Lawyer, Concord, N. H.
Charles Noble Gregory, Dean of Department of Law, George Washington University, Washington, D. C.
William O. Hart, Former President American Bar Association, New Orleans, La.
Frederick W. Lehmann, Former President American Bar Association, St. Louis, Mo.
Lawrence Maxwell, Former Solicitor General, Cincinnati, Ohio.
Roscoe Pound, Professor Law School, Harvard University, Cambridge, Mass.
Thomas W. Shelton, Lawyer, Norfolk, Va.
Hannis Taylor, Professor of Law, George Washington University, Washington, D. C.
Elihu Root, Jr., Lawyer, New York.

PUBLIC HEALTH.

Do statistics show that the American of to-day lives longer than his father or that the pressure of our speeded-up industry forces him into an earlier grave? Are diseases incident to industrial life spreading or being conquered? What of the work of boards of health, hospitals, medical societies and health education movements?

Committee.

Irving Fisher, Professor of Political Economy, Yale University, New Haven, Conn.
W. H. Welsh, Professor of Pathology, Johns Hopkins University, Baltimore, Md.
Hermann M. Biggs, New York State Commissioner of Health, Albany, N. Y.
Henry B. Favill, Former President American Medical Association, Chicago, Ill.
Luther H. Gulick, Director Parks and Playgrounds Association of the City of New York, New York.
William C. Woodward, President American Public Health Association, Washington, D. C.
M. E. Jaffa, Director State Food and Drug Laboratory, University of California, Berkeley, Cal.
Samuel W. Lambert, Dean, College of Physicians and Surgeons, Columbia University, New York.

ENFORCEMENT OF LAW AND ORDER.

Is the security of the citizen in person and property greater or less than thirty years ago? What of our methods of dealing with vagrancy and social vice? What are the effects of changes in penal legislation upon statistics of crime?

Committee.

James Bronson Reynolds, Counsel, American Social Hygiene Association, New York.
Frederick L. Hoffman, Statistician, Prudential Insurance Company of America, Newark, N. J.
Charles C. Nott, Jr., Assistant District Attorney, New York.
Henry de Forest Baldwin, Lawyer, New York.
Charles C. Burlingham, Lawyer, New York.
Arthur P. Hill, Former District Attorney, Boston, Mass.
William H. Wadhams, Lawyer, New York.

PENAL AND CORRECTIONAL INSTITUTIONS.

Are the changes in methods and management of prisons, reformatories and correctional schools in the direction of progress? What lines of further improvement are suggested by experience?

Committee.

Adolph Lewisohn, American Smelting and Refining Company, New York.
Thomas Mott Osborne, Manufacturer, Auburn, N. Y.
E. Stagg Whitin, Chairman Executive Committee, National Committee on Prison Labor, New York.
Nicholas Murray Butler, President Columbia University, New York.
Mrs. August Belmont, Executive Committee, Woman's Department, The National Civic Federation, New York.
Mrs. Francis McNeil Bacon, Jr., Chairman Metropolitan Section, Woman's Department, The National Civic Federation, New York.
Miss Helen Varick Boswell, Chairman Political Science Committee, General Federation of Woman's Clubs, New York.

INDUSTRIAL PROFIT SHARING.

What have been the lines of development both in the theory and the practice of profit-sharing in this country, during the last generation? What are the advantages, the danger points and the future possibilities of the system, as suggested by experience?

Committee.

George E. Barnett, Professor of Political Economy, Johns Hopkins University, Baltimore, Md.
F. R. Hazard, President The Solvay Process Company, Syracuse, N. Y.
James C. Brady, Director American Tobacco Company, New York.
James W. Sullivan, The American Federation of Labor, New York.
Pierre S. du Pont, The E. I. du Pont de Nemours Powder Company, Wilmington, Del.
John T. Pratt, Lawyer, New York.

ERNEST H. ABBOTT, *The Outlook*, New York.
DANIEL J. TOBIN, President International Brotherhood of Teamsters, Indianapolis, Ind.
HARRIS HAMMOND, Gloucester, Mass.
WALTER B. CLARK, Professor of Political Economy, College of the City of New York, New York.
DENIS A. HAYES, President Glass Bottle Blowers' Association of United States and Canada, Philadelphia, Pa.

SOCIAL INSURANCE.

What has been accomplished by way of provision against invalidity, unemployment and old age disability, through savings and provident funds, mutual relief associations, pension systems of industrial and financial corporations, and trade union benefit funds? To what extent and through what means is the wider application of social insurance possible?

Committee.

GEORGE W. PERKINS, New York.
FREDERICK L. HOFFMAN, Statistician, Prudential Life Insurance Co., New York.
A. B. GARRETSON, President Order of Railway Conductors, Cedar Rapids, Iowa.
P. TECUMSEH SHERMAN, Lawyer, New York.
J. N. REDFERN, Superintendent, Relief and Employment Departments, C. B. & Q. R. R., Chicago, Ill.
M. W. ALEXANDER, General Electric Company, Lynn, Mass.
M. G. SCOTT, International Typographical Union, New York.
ARTHUR WILLIAMS, Edison Company, New York.
HENRY ABRAHAMS, Secretary Cigar Makers' Union, Boston, Mass.

WORKMEN'S COMPENSATION.

What is the significance to the wage-worker of the widespread adoption of accident compensation as a charge upon industry, in place of the individual litigation method under liability laws? What further effects may be credited to the new system in respect to equalization of risks and prevention of accidents?

Committee.

AUGUST BELMONT, Chairman Department on Workmen's Compensation, The National Civic Federation, New York.
GEORGE SUTHERLAND, United States Senator from Utah, Washington, D. C.
CYRUS W. PHILLIPS, Chairman Joint Commission on Workmen's Compensation of The National Civic Federation, Rochester, N. Y.
J. WALTER LORD, Chairman Maryland State Commission on Employers' Liability and Workmen's Compensation, Baltimore, Md.
OTTO M. EIDLITZ, New York Building Trades' Employers' Association, New York.
LOUIS B. SCHRAM, Chairman Labor Committee, United States Brewers' Association, Brooklyn, N. Y.
JAMES DUNCAN, Vice-President American Federation of Labor, Quincy, Mass.
H. E. WILLS, Ass't. Grand Chief Brotherhood of Locomotive Engineers, Cleveland, Ohio.

INDUSTRIAL LOANS AND SAVINGS.

What do the records of savings banks and the industrial departments of insurance companies reveal in respect to the accumulation of savings on the part of workingmen and people of small means? What is being done to enable the wage-earner to borrow for legitimate needs without resort to the loan shark?

Committee.

ELGIN R. L. GOULD, President City and Suburban Homes Company, New York.
OSCAR S. STRAUS, Former Ambassador to Turkey, New York.
THEODORE P. SHONTS, President Interborough Rapid Transit Company, New York.
EDWIN S. MARSTON, President Farmers' Loan and Trust Company, New York.
SAM A. LEWISOHN, Adolph Lewisohn & Sons, New York.

FOOD AND DRUGS.

To what extent is the public protected against frauds and impurities in the supply of food products and drugs as compared with earlier decades? What have been the effects of Federal and State legislation and municipal regulations on the subject?

Committee.

VINCENT ASTOR, New York.
DR. CARL L. ALSBERG, Chief Bureau of Chemistry, Department of Agriculture, Washington, D. C.
J. H. WALLIS, President National Association of State Food and Dairy Commissioners, Boise, Idaho.
DR. S. S. GOLDWATER, Commissioner of Health, New York City.
MISS MAUDE WETMORE, Chairman Woman's Department, The National Civic Federation, New York.
MRS. S. R. CROCKETT, Chairman Food and Drug Department, General Federation of Women's Clubs, Nashville, Tenn.
SAMUEL GOMPERS, President American Federation of Labor, Washington, D. C.
JOHN M. STAHL, Farmers' National Congress, Chicago.
EDWARD N. BREITUNG, Ore Producer, Negaunee, Mich.

THE THEORY OF SURPLUS VALUE.

Does the difference between labor cost and selling price represent employer's profit? What changes have taken place in the proportionate return to labor and capital in the gross earnings of industry?

Committee.

WILLIAM J. PAPE, Editor *Waterbury Republican*, Waterbury, Conn.
OSCAR D. SKELTON, Professor of Economics, Queen's University, Kingston, Ontario, Canada.
VLADIMIR G. SIMKHOVITCH, Professor of Economic History, Columbia University, New York.
JOHN B. CLARK, Professor of Political Economy, Columbia University, New York.
JOHN G. AGAR, Lawyer, Mount Vernon, N. Y.
REV. JOHN A. RYAN, St. Paul Seminary, St. Paul, Minn.

THE THEORY OF THE MINIMUM WAGE.

What have been the results of experiments in minimum wage legislation? What of the economic merits of the proposal?

Committee.

A. J. PORTER, President Shredded Wheat Company, Niagara Falls, N. Y.
PERCY S. STRAUS, R. H. Macy & Company, New York.
MRS. H. B. BEALE, Woman's Department, The National Civic Federation, Washington, D. C.
LEE K. FRANKEL, Vice-President Metropolitan Life Insurance Company, New York.
H. J. CONWAY, Secretary-Treasurer Retail Clerks' International Protective Association, Lafayette, Ind.

ACTIVE CO-OPERATION OF THE ADVISORY COUNCIL.

More than one hundred letters have been received from members of the Advisory Council, indicating pertinent lines of inquiry suggested by their experience in many fields, and expressing emphatic approval of the object and general plan of the survey. It is possible to reproduce here only brief excerpts from a few of these communications, but they are typical of the wide range of suggestions offered and indicate the interest the work is developing in all parts of the country.

CHARLES NOBLE GREGORY, Dean of the Department of Law, George Washington University, Washington, D. C.:

"It has seemed to me as if it would be of great value in a time of great discontent to review the immense progress that has been made, not for the rich alone, but for all except those in extreme poverty, and in some respects even for them, in the comforts, conveniences and safeguards of life; for instance, in common supply of pure water delivered under pressure, in good drainage, in common systems of house lighting, in street lighting, in road making, also the great change in cleanliness, in comforts of temperature, and in means of communication, both by sending and receiving goods, by transporting persons and by delivering messages; also the tremendous improvement in the variety and distribution of food.

"My father was a lawyer in good practice at Madison, Wis., with good social station at the capital of Wisconsin. I grew up there in a community where only a very few of the largest houses had baths. Now all except the very humblest are provided. Every one there drew water by bucket from a local well and rainwater from a cistern when I was a boy, and the drainage passed into a cesspool on his own place if any provision were made. Now a fine water system and complete drainage system, with drainage disposal works, are instituted.

"In my youth not a family in the city had soup every day for dinner, and very few persons took a daily bath. Now the daily soup and daily baths are common with all above the rank of laborers, I think.

"When I was a boy tropical fruit was a comparatively rare luxury. Now it is abundant and cheap throughout the year. So I may enumerate in many ways the very great change in the comforts of living, not for the rich alone, but for the great volume of people. When I first knew that city there was not a macadamized or paved street in the city, and the city did not control an acre of park land. She now has many miles of paved streets and macadamized streets and hundreds of acres of fine parks. . . .

"When I was a boy every house in town, substantially, was so cold at night that in Winter water froze all over the house. Now almost all are comfortably heated by night and by day, either by furnaces or by base burning coal stoves. So I might enumerate the tremendous changes which in my own life I have witnessed and which have resulted in a distinct increase of the average duration of life as well as in the comfort of living.

"I think an able, broad and specific representation of these changes and advances and of the benefits thereby conferred either upon all of the people or on the great majority of the people, would be worth while, and there would be no argument for stagnation, but for reasonable contentment with the progress, and it would tend to mitigate the great bitterness sometimes springing up between classes differently situated."

HARRY A. GARFIELD, President of Williams College, Williamstown, Mass.:

"The work which the department is undertaking to do is not only most interesting but, to my mind, vital, and I sincerely trust that the colleges and various organizations represented will each contribute its part."

A. B. GARRETSON, President Order of Railway Conductors, Cedar Rapids, Iowa:

"The high cost of living is charged against the trusts, it is charged against a multitude of other agencies, but I have a belief that the real solution of that difficulty lies in the machinery between the producer and the consumer. If this belief is well founded, intelligent investigation should demonstrate the fact."

WILLIAM GAMMELL, Manufacturer, Providence, R. I.:

"It would seem to me that one part of the proposed survey might include the comparatively recent influx of non-English-speaking foreigners to the population of the manufacturing centers of New England. Some twenty-five years ago nearly all the mill operatives of New England, other than natives, were English, Irish or French Canadians, the majority of whom were easily assimilated with the rest of the population and became, as a rule, useful citizens. At the present time the conditions are very different, especially in the large manufacturing towns. And a continued segregation of this new foreign element, retaining their old standards of living and subject only to leadership from those who speak their languages, would be, in my opinion, a serious menace to the future welfare of New England. An investigation of the tendencies of this new element might be attended with useful results."

MRS. FRANCIS M'NEIL BACON, JR., Chairman Metropolitan Section, Woman's Department, The National Civic Federation:

"In the field of industrial and social progress two problems seem to me of very vital importance, as they lie at the heart of what our future citizenship will be. To put this under two concise headings, I would say trade schools and farm colonies. The former opens the way for the boy or girl toward greater efficiency. The subject is a large one, including as it does vocational, part time and continuation, as well as trade schools. The farm colony idea seems to me to offer the only remedy for that endless returning into society of the unfortunates we punish and corrupt. We must punish, at all events we must protect society, but we should see to it, and without delay, that in so doing we not only do not corrupt, but that we make the best possible use of the human material given into our keeping."

HARRIS WEINSTOCK, Member Federal Commission on Industrial Relations, San Francisco, Cal.:

"The Census shows that, taking the country as a whole, the urban population has increased out of all proportion to the rural population. This tendency carries with it a serious menace to the future of the nation. It is one explanation, doubtless, of the increased cost of living. It means many more city mouths to feed and fewer and fewer country hands to produce the food. It seems to me that it is thoroughly worth the while of your committee to inquire into the causes for this condition and to suggest remedies."

W. O. HART, Former President American Bar Association, New Orleans, La.:

"In my judgment the principal questions before the American people at this time which ought to be studied and considered are, prohibition of child labor or, at least, minimizing it as much as possible; prison reform, to the extent at least of opening the door of hope to the criminal; workingmen's compensation, including perhaps mothers' pensions and old age pensions; and good roads. These, I think, are more important than the tariff, currency reform, anti-trust legislation and the Mexican situation, which all present temporary questions, whereas the others affect the very life of our people."

DANIEL J. TOBIN, President International Brotherhood of Teamsters, Indianapolis, Ind.:

"First, I believe that the immigration question today is one of the most serious confronting our American working men and women. . . . . I attribute a great deal of non-employment to the fact that there are hundreds of thousands of individuals coming to this country who are willing to work for anything and everything under any condition. Second, if employers could be educated to the necessity of dealing with legitimate trade unions and with the men who are at the head of those trade nions, who are honest and sincere, I believe that e industrial revolutions that have occurred to a mall extent in our country within the past few ears, and that have occurred to a large extent in uropean countries, could be prevented in the future.

JOHN B. CLARK, Professor Political Economy, olumbia University, New York:

"What is the social income in its entirety? How uch wealth is annually brought into existence in e United States and how much in each department f industry? No one knows. The inquiries of the ensus were not pushed far enough to determine it, ough they throw a large amount of light on it. It information which it is very difficult to get, but I ave thought that the Civic Federation possessed pecial facilities for obtaining it. My own claim, ased on a study of the census and on some other formation, is that if the capital were nationalized he gain per capita of the working classes would be ery far below the amount expected. . . . I do ot think that any organized body of public-spirited itizens could do another work that would be comarable in value to the work of determining what come exists at present which, under socialism, ould pass over to the working people.

CHARLES R. TOWSON, Industrial Secretary, Inernational Committee, Young Men's Christian Associations, New York:

"Four points in particular have impressed me: irst, the importance of demonstrating the present tatus of our country as to its character standards. econd, the progress in cultural standard. Third, he importance of making the report of the work 'effective,' and the last point is akin to this, viz., the importance of making the results obtained available and pervasive. . . . I trust that in some small measure the Young Men's Christian Association may be helpful in extending the benefits of the knowledge of the facts to be discovered and reported."

HENRY W. FARNAM, Professor of Economics, Yale University, New Haven, Conn.:

"There are a number of elements in our civilization which for a long time have seemed to me sore spots and well worth considering in estimating progress. Among these I should mention crime, divorce, the drug and narcotic habit, changes in the birth and death rate, especially among different social strata, labor disturbances and strikes, etc. On some of these subjects we are much in need of accurate information. I do not suppose that any one can positively say whether crime is or is not increasing. The newspaper accounts lead one to think that it is, and yet we lack definite figures."

MRS. GEORGE T. RICE, Chairman Massachusetts and Rhode Island Section, Woman's Department, The National Civic Federation, Boston, Mass.:

"One of the most growing needs seems to be for a better housing of people in general. I have seen so many instances of where the mills might have the finest possible sanitary conditions, ventilation, modern improvements and machinery, rest rooms and many other advantages; but in going further into the question I find that the homes of the operatives are so often where the seed of disease is spread, and not in the mills. . . . My experience in going about the State is that the employers are most ready to welcome suggestions, and not only to welcome, but also to carry them out."

STEPHEN H. ALLEN, Lawyer, Topeka, Kansas:

"The home may safely be taken as the central point of every inquiry in the survey. It is of the utmost importance to gain a definite knowledge of every condition that unduly retards the building of homes by the young, or that tends to contaminate or disintegrate homes already started. Vice and crime should be studied chiefly with respect to their relation to homes, and home conditions should be studied to gain an understanding of the environments that may produce criminals.

JAMES M. LYNCH, New York State Commissioner of Labor, Albany, N. Y.:

"Has the formation and development of trusts during the last generation rendered employment steadier or otherwise? Can the workers count upon a reasonable amount of employment in the year as a whole? Obviously, accurate determination of the extent of unemployment is difficult, nevertheless some statistical material exists which, because of the importance of the question, should be carefully considered.

"Improvement in the conditions of employment during the last generation is manifest in several directions. An examination would show marked progress toward a shorter workday, greater regard for the safety of workers, both as to accidents and industrial diseases, much done to abolish the exploitation of the labor of children and to suppress or regulate 'sweated' labor. It would be well, also, to trace the growing tendency to accomplish these improvements by collective agreements between the employers and the employees, by conciliation and arbitration, by legislation and by peaceful means generally instead of by resort to the more warlike methods of the strike."

J. G. SCHMIDLAPP, President Union Savings Bank and Trust Company, Cincinnati, Ohio:

"From my own experience, I believe that more can be accomplished by housing than in any other way. . . . This work I want to see carried so far that it will lead to ownership, and as soon as we can get the wage earner in this class it will be difficult for the socialist to enlist him. I draw such a conclusion as this from the peasantry of Germany, where the majority of the farmers own less than five acres, yet the socialists have never been able to make any inroads upon this citizenship."

BOOKER T. WASHINGTON, Principal Tuskegee Normal and Industrial Institute, Tuskegee, Ala.:

"In connection with the investigation which the Federation is making I very much hope that a careful study will be made of the progress which the negroes have made in organized labor, the difficulties met and how they have been overcome in different parts of the country. I call attention to an article which I wrote, 'The Negro and the Labor Unions,' in the *Atlantic Monthly* for June, 1913. I believe you will find in this article a number of points which have direct bearing upon the work which the Federation is trying to do."

DELOS F. WILCOX, Public Utility Expert, New York:

"The continued growth of cities is a phenomenon of first-rate importance in the development of our civilization. What are the essential advantages and disadvantages of urban life in our civilization and what is the relative importance of each? To what extent is the increase in the cost of living due to the increase in the relative proportion of the population which is removed from direct access to the food supplies of the country?"

HENRY B. F. MACFARLAND, Lawyer, Washington, D. C.:

"I should put first the renaissance of conscience in business and politics and the consequent twentieth century view of rights and duties. I should put second the similar awakening in the church using that word in its broadest meaning, and manifestations of that awakening in all their many forms, especially respecting men and boys."

FOR AN INTERSTATE TRADE COMMISSION

PROPOSALS SUBMITTED BY THE NATIONAL CIVIC FEDERATION IN CONNECTION WITH PENDING LEGISLATION

WITHIN the last few months a bill supplementary to the Sherman Act, providing for an Interstate Trade Commission, has been prepared by the Department on Regulation of Industrial Corporations of The National Civic Federation, as the result of the work of a sub-committee consisting of President Seth Low as Chairman, Professor Jeremiah W. Jenks, Professor John B. Clark and Dr. Talcott Williams. The Interstate Trade Commission proposed in the bill would have, among other powers, the right under certain conditions to grant a Federal license to large corporations doing an interstate business.

In view of the fact that the national administration had drafted certain bills designed to cover the questions involved in what is known as the "trust problem," the committee decided not to offer its bill to Congress, but President Low testified at length before the Interstate Commerce Committee and the Judiciary Committee of the House, and submitted the bill with an explanatory memorandum to these committees for such use as they might desire to make of them.

The memorandum is as follows:

It is evident that an Interstate Trade Commission could be created without any reference to a Federal license for interstate trade, and many believe that such a commission would be useful for the administration of the Sherman Law without regard to a Federal license. It is desirable, therefore, to point out, first of all, why this bill proposes to demand a Federal license from very large corporations engaging in interstate trade.

At the present time there is no government at all in the United States which controls both the interstate business that is carried on and the agent that does it. The State which charters the corporation creates the agent, but the State cannot control the interstate business that is done. The Congress, on the other hand, can, and to a great extent does, control the business that is done; but it cannot control the agent that does it. What is fundamentally needed, therefore, is to bring the agents that do interstate business under the control of the Federal government, but only so far as may be necessary, so that the same government which controls the business done shall also be able to control the agents that do it. This result can be accomplished either by requiring Federal incorporation as a condition for the right to do interstate business, or by requiring that State-created corporations, so far as may be necessary, must take out a Federal license if they engage in interstate trade. Through a Federal license the national government can readily accomplish several things which are very greatly in the public interest. It can secure publicity; it can prescribe in advance the essential conditions with which all corporations doing interstate business must comply; and, on the other hand, it can at any time, by means of a license, bring about uniformity of protection for stockholders in all the States by defining the essential features that are necessary in a State charter to entitle a State-created corporation to engage in interstate trade, just as the currency law indicates the conditions upon which State banks may come under the national system. It is a well-known fact that in recent years several of the States have competed with each other in the effort to make charters that would be attractive to promoters and organizers. Such charters, however attractive in such direction, have frequently been made so at the expense of their stockholders by depriving them of the protection to which they are reasonably entitled. If a State wishes to do this sort of thing as to business done within its own borders, that is the affair chiefly of those residing in the State; but if a State launches upon interstate trade a corporation which does not adequately protect its stockholders, and if, as has often happened in the past, the State attempts to give to such a corporation powers that it has no authority to confer, incalculable mischief is done to residents outside of the State that forms the corporation. This sort of thing has been done on a great scale in recent years. Perhaps, for the moment, it is done less now than of late; but what has been done once may be done again, if not in the same form then in some other equally disadvantageous to the public interest. We think that, in this connection, a permanent commission is needed to pass upon and follow up all questions arising under the license, just as the Federal Reserve Board passes upon all questions involving the compliance of the State Banks with the Federal statute.

The proposed bill recognizes that to install a Federal license immediately with reference to all interstate trade would be an undertaking so vast as to be beyond accomplishment. It therefore proposes that such a license be required only for the very large corporations engaged in interstate trade. Such an application of the plan is evidently practicable, and from the operation of it in the course of a few years it would become evident to what extent the system could be and should be enlarged. Any limitation of the application of the system must be arbitrary. This bill proposes a unit which it is believed would limit the application of the law to not fewer than two hundred and not more than five hundred corporations. The size of the unit to be affected by the bill is evidently a matter for discretion; but it is important to point out that every corporation coming within the scope of the bill would be controlled by the terms of the law, should the bill be placed upon the Statute book. The history of the Interstate Commerce Commission in its dealings with the railroads indicates how satisfactorily the system proposed can be administered, year after year. The Sherman Law needs for its administration precisely the same sort of board, for the very reason that its mandates are couched, and must be couched, to a great extent in general language. Only a commission can bring the significance of a general mandate home in detail to the person whom that mandate may affect. The proposed bill, therefore, instead of attempting to define certain practices as forbidden by the Sherman Anti-trust Law, relies upon the general language of the Interstate Commerce Law, which forbids any one to "make or give any undue or unreasonable preference or advantage to any particular person, company, firm, corporation or locality; or to subject any particular person, company,

(Concluded on page 20.)

SHALL THE GOVERNMENT OWN THE RAILROADS?

PRESIDENT LOW DISCUSSES NEW AND CRITICAL PHASES OF THE RAILROAD PROBLEM, AT ANNUAL MEETING OF THE NATIONAL CIVIC FEDERATION.

IN his opening address at the Fourteenth Annual Meeting of The National Civic Federation, President Low devoted his attention chiefly to recent developments in the railroad situation, in their bearing upon national policies and the menace of government ownership.

Referring briefly to the efficient and useful work of the several departments of the Federation, Mr. Low described the preparation and passage of the Newlands Arbitration Law as perhaps the most significant work which has been carried to completion during the past year. The history of the Federation's part in this achievement was given in some detail in the last number of the REVIEW, and with it an account of the first arbitration held under the new law, that between the eastern trunk line roads and the conductors and trainmen. By request of both the railroads and brotherhoods, Mr. Low acted as chairman of this arbitration, which brought under review practically the whole field of operating costs, revenues and conditions of service.

In addition to this adjustment, Mr. Low enumerated twelve other controversies which have been settled or put in the way of settlement, through the United States Board of Mediation and Conciliation during the four months of the new law.

Arbitration is not necessarily a compromise, Mr. Low pointed out, but the fact remains that in the three principal arbitrations in the eastern territory the operating expenses of the roads have been heavily increased, and it is, of course, obvious "that a railroad cannot have its fixed charges indefinitely increased against its will unless it can at some time or another increase the rates which it will charge for service." Mr. Low then entered upon a discussion of these larger aspects of the problem as follows:

"The actual situation of the railroads, at the moment, seems to me so serious that, if this application for an increase of freight rates is declined, I fear the demand for the public ownership and operation of the steam railroads of the country will be inevitably strengthened. In a spirit of despair, men who know better will be apt to say, 'That is the only way'; and out of despair, I need not remind you, wise counsels seldom come. I make no apology, therefore, for pointing out briefly, on this occasion, some of the difficulties attaching to government ownership and operation of railroads in a country like ours, with a Federal government evolved as ours has been, covering half a continent. Such information as I can command leads me to believe that in Germany, France, Australia, Italy and Austria, the earnings of the state-owned railroads in each country barely equal, if they do equal, the sums paid in taxation by the railroads of the United States. The freight rates prevailing in those countries are uniformly higher, I believe, than the freight rates prevailing in the United States. In some cases they are more than double, but it is noticeable that the average passenger rate, disregarding the division by classes obtaining there, is lower in some, and, I think, in all, of those countries than here. This is largely due, no doubt, to the fact that the multitudes there travel third class, and are given accommodations that would not be acceptable here.

"It is needless for my purpose to pursue this comparison into detail. What I wish to point out is, that in our country, by reason of its vast extent and by reason of its Federal government, and its historic evolution, the problem of public ownership, and, not less, the problem of public operation, are surcharged with difficulties that do not exist under different conditions. Leaving out of account altogether the difficulty of securing wise and economic management under the democratic conditions prevailing in the United States, the first point to emphasize is the difficulty of acquiring effective control of the railroads even if desired. Most of the railroads, if not all of them, are incorporated by the different States. This means that every railroad is given the authority by each State to operate within its own borders, and that every such road is equipped with the right of eminent domain to condemn land for railroad purposes within such State. What authority is to compel the States, or rather, what appeal is to induce the people of the various States to permit the railroads to surrender State charters in favor of national ownership; and in addition to grant to the national government authority to equip railroads so chartered with the power of eminent domain in every State of the Union? Without such power of eminent domain it would be impracticable for railroads to be enlarged or for new roads to be constructed. If, on the other hand, each State were to absorb its own railroads, we should have a condition in this country out of which it would be impossible to bring effective unity of action and a railroad service operated for the general good. Imagine, for example, the New York Central Line from New York to Buffalo owned and operated by the State of New York and the Lake Shore & Michigan Southern owned and operated in fragments by the States of Pennsylvania, Ohio, Indiana and Illinois. Who can think for a single moment that the result in public service would be either adequate, economical or satisfactory? Moreover, if the national government, despite every difficulty, were to succeed in absorbing the railroads of the entire Union, every State would lose the control of its intrastate traffic that it now enjoys; and every State would lose all the income which it now collects from the railroads by taxation, because United States property is not subject to taxation in any State. Every State, therefore, in such a case, would be confronted with both an economic and a social problem, born of our Federal system, and the scale upon which these effects would be felt would greatly magnify the embarrassments.

"But, assuming for a moment that this great economic and social change had been sanctioned and actually put into force, try to imagine, if you can, how the conflicting interests of different parts of the United States could be harmonized when the same

SETH LOW,
President of The National Civic Federation.

government is responsible for railroad operation everywhere. The annual bill for the construction of public buildings for the Federal government has acquired the popular name of 'pork-barrel' because it is so universally recognized that appropriations for this purpose are made to gratify local sentiment and to promote the interests of individual congressmen more than upon the merits of the matter, as determined by careful inquiry. What possibility is there that the administration of a system of national railroads would be, or could be, carried on under our democratic government in any other spirit? And in what possible way could the general interest of the people of the United States, in the matter of transportation, be less well served? Furthermore, the political consequences of centering such power in Washington are beyond calculation . . . .

Our privately-owned railroads are themselves largely responsible for the strength of the popular feeling in the United States [in favor of government ownership] . . . No doubt, the rebate system, so long practiced, accounts for most of this feeling. Happily, by virtue of the Interstate Commerce Law and the creation of the Interstate Commerce Commission, that which was a nation-wide abuse has become a rare exception, and it will become more and more rare. In other words, without public ownership, but through public regulation, we have substantially secured equality of treatment at the hands of the railroads for every shipper, large or small, in whatever State he may be. . . .

"It is hard to speak with moderation of the financial abuses connected with railroad management which have done so much to create and to strengthen the demand for the public ownership and operation of railroads. The public has seen railroads loaded with charges for the profit of individuals responsible for the conduct of the roads, charges which add permanently to the cost of transportation. Increases of value, largely created by the public, have been absorbed entirely for private benefit; and all of this has gone on upon so great a scale and for so long a time as to have cost railroad management, to a great extent, but often unjustly, both the respect and the confidence of the people. It is a case where the innocent suffer with and for the guilty. If government regulation can successfully put an end to these evils, no doubt private ownership and operation of railroads may long continue in the United States; but, if government regulation falls short of being as effective in these directions as it has fortunately been in the ending of rebates, the tendency toward government operation, despite all its difficulties and dangers, is not unlikely to grow, unchecked. If the railroads wish to escape public ownership they must consent to the public regulation, for the future, of the issue of stocks and bonds; and it is greatly to be hoped that instead of placing every imaginable difficulty in the way of such legislation, they will cordially co-operate to see that effective and fair legislation to prevent the repetition of the abuses of the past is quickly made a part of the law of the land.

One further observation is legitimate in this connection. If not completely, still very largely, the actual management of railroads in this country has passed, and is constantly passing, out of the hands of financiers and into the hands of practical railroad men who are less and less affiliated with the stock market. It is reasonable, therefore, to hope that we are passing out of the old era into a better order of things. The practical question also arises whether it is not better now to "let the dead past bury its dead" and to turn with united and courageous front towards the better future. An attempt to uncover all of the past, and to try to do ideal justice now for wrongs that were committed long ago, is certain to be very costly to the country as a whole, as well as to the unhappy stockholders, who, without personal fault, find themselves involved in such a predicament. Mr. Evarts used to say that "there are vested wrongs as well as vested rights," which was a wise man's way of saying that some wrongs are so costly to undo that it is better to leave things as they are and turn over a new leaf. . . .

"There is one aspect of public ownership and operation which it seems to me legitimate to point out to the railroad employees who are so largely represented in our membership, and that is its probable effect upon wages. Railroads that are publicly owned have available for wages only such sums as are appropriated by law. In a country of the vast extent of the United States that this difference is substantially certain in wages, as established by law, when they have once been fixed. Working conditions will also then be much more difficult to change than when the railroads are under private management. The cost of living is so different in different parts of the United States that this difference is substantially certain to be reflected in an average wage below that which the railroads can pay under private management. The agricultural interests of the country are enormous, and one of their greatest difficulties comes from the fact that agriculture cannot afford to pay as large wages as transportation and many other occupations pay now. This is, in fact, one great reason for the high cost of food products, that agriculture cannot command the labor that it needs in order to cultivate as it should, and to produce and to harvest larger crops. As long as railroads are privately owned, agriculture must take its chances; but, in this country, if railroads were publicly owned, the granges and other combinations of farmers would certainly be on the job to keep railroad wages as low as possible. They would have to be or they could not work their farms at all. There is a rigidity about law that makes it difficult to change conditions once established; and it is equally hard, under the provisions of law, to take into consideration local qualifying conditions. Such considerations as those satisfy me that railroad employees are not only better off now, under the private administration of railroads, than they would be likely to be under public administration, but also that under existing conditions they can hope for a betterment in pay and rules of service which it would be vastly harder to realize from a Federal government constituted like ours."

CITIZENS AND OFFICIALS UNITE FOR BETTER FOOD REGULATION

THE NATIONAL CIVIC FEDERATION ORGANIZES A COMMISSION TO WORK FOR UNIFORMITY AND EFFICIENCY IN FOOD AND DRUG CONTROL

PRESIDENT SETH LOW of The National Civic Federation has named a Commission to make a study of the operation of the Federal and State food and drug laws. This action was taken in accordance with a resolution adopted at the recent annual meeting of the Federation after a discussion of the subject by experts on all phases of the problem.

The members of the Commission are as follows:

Vincent Astor, Chairman, New York.
Dr. Carl L. Alsberg, Chief, Bureau of Chemistry, Department of Agriculture, Washington, D. C.
J. H. Wallis, President National Association of State Food and Dairy Commissioners, Boise, Idaho.
Dr. S. S. Goldwater, Commissioner of Health of the City of New York.
Miss Maude Wetmore, Chairman Woman's Department, The National Civic Federation, New York.
Mrs. S. R. Crockett, Chairman Food and Drug Department, General Federation of Women's Clubs, Nashville, Tenn.
Samuel Gompers, President American Federation of Labor, Washington, D. C.
John M. Stahl, of the Farmers' National Congress, Chicago, Ill.
Dr. E. K. Dunham, Chairman New York Milk Commission, New York.
Edward N. Breitung, Ore Producer, Negaunee, Mich.

The Federation believes that there is no public duty greater than the securing of pure food and pure drugs for the American people. The wealthy who are able to pay the highest prices are less likely to be imposed upon by purveyors of injurious or adulterated foods and drugs than the masses who have no other protection than that which is accorded by the Federal pure food and drug acts, the various State acts and the ordinances and regulations of municipalities.

While a very great improvement has been wrought in the situation since the passage of the Food and Drug Act in 1906, the administration of this and other laws and regulations by the Federal, State and municipal authorities is greatly hampered by the lack of sufficient inspectors and effective machinery to detect violations, and in some cases, it is alleged, by corrupt alliances between the officials and the manufacturers and sellers of rotten food-stuffs and adulterated drugs.

Recent exposures in different cities in this country indicate the far-reaching character of the violation of the food and drug laws. Not only have the poor been defrauded by adulterated and impure food, but they have been cheated in measurements and weights. The monthly bulletins issued by the United States Department of Agriculture describe hundreds of convictions secured annually by that Department (generally on the confession of guilt by the manufacturers or dealers), which are enough to arouse the indignation of all good citizens, and all the more so because of the utterly inadequate finès imposed by the courts.

The Federation was impelled to take up this question because of representations made to it showing the prevalence of these conditions. The representations came alike from large employors of labor, who had felt it their duty to examine both the dinner pails of their workmen and the stores patronized by them, in order to prevent the employees from being robbed in quality or in weight in their food supplies, and from officials of labor organizations, who had made similar investigations with equally disturbing results. The Commission named by President Low will, as an initial step, make a survey of the situation for the purpose of ascertaining to what extent the people are being imposed upon in these respects.

In addition to studying the extent of misrepresentation the Commission will inquire into the need for additional Federal legislation and consider to what extent there should and can be uniformity between the law of the Federal government and the laws of the various States, as well as between the laws of the States themselves. There are organizations of food and drug manufacturers and of food and drug dealers who represent the best elements in both trades and who have signally assisted the efforts which have resulted in the enactment of better food and drug laws. They can be relied upon to contribute to the success of all legitimate endeavors towards the reform of existing conditions.

Dr. Carl L. Alsberg, in urging The National Civic Federation to appoint a Commission to study this question, said:

"There is one need in food control which is so vastly more important than all others that I propose to urge it alone upon your consideration. It is adequate sanitary and hygienic control of food.

"By the sanitary and hygienic control of foods I mean the prevention of traffic in foods dangerous to health. To prevent this traffic is far more difficult than to prevent mere fraud in food products. Fraud may usually be detected by a chemical analysis. The danger to health that may lurk in a food can easily be detected in this way unless, indeed, the food contain some simple poison like arsenic or lead. If, however, the food be manufactured in unsanitary surroundings, or if it be the bearer of tuberculosis, typhoid, measles, or scarlet fever, this can hardly be detected. Hence, in my opinion, foods such as milk and butter, meat, fish and shell fish, which are capable of this kind of contamination, should receive the greatest attention.

"The only safeguard against these sources of danger is inspection of the place of production and medical supervision of the workmen. It should be impossible, for example, for a dairyman with a case of typhoid in his family to ship milk.

"Obviously the exercise of such control of the sanitary conditions of food production is a task for the individual States. I would, therefore, urge upon you to use every effort to secure such sanitary control of food production in every State. I can conceive of nothing more important.

"If such a sanitary control is to be established, you must clearly understand that to be effective it must rest upon an adequate health service. Outside of our larger cities such a service is most unusual. Most small towns and rural communities are without adequate health protection. The greatest need of the country to-day is an adequate staff of well-trained, well-paid, full-time health officials in every county in every State. With this must go laws that are enforced for the recording of vital statistics of communicable diseases. Until all this is done there can be no adequate sanitary control of foods. Just so long as we do nothing for the health of our country people just so long will typhoid and similar diseases be imported into our city."

Mr. James H. Wallis, President of the National Association of State Food and Dairy Commissioners, in accepting a position on The National Civic Federation's Commission on Food and Drugs, said:

"There is not a food and drug official of experience who does not know that ninety per cent. of the violations of food and drug laws, both State and national, have been caused largely by the ignorance or carelessness of the manufacturer and not with a wilful intent to produce and dispose of adulterated and misbranded articles. Ten per cent, perhaps, of the prosecutions are against manufacturers who deliberately offer debased, deleterious, adulterated and misbranded foods and drugs, and as against this latter class of manufacturers the penalties provided in various laws have been woefully deficient. But how about those manufacturers who have sinned because of ignorance? Have we done our full governmental duty when we say, let the manufacturer beware, let him put out foods and drugs at his peril? Does not such a policy lose sight of the end sought to be attained, which is to secure as quickly as may be possible a pure food and drug supply for the people? Shall we not attain that result more quickly if we educate our manufacturers, show them how to produce pure foods in a cleanly manner, and spread information regarding methods of adulterating drugs, largely perpetrated by the foreign producer upon the American importer who buys in good faith?

"The great majority is honest. It is not right, it is not even politic, to confound the great mass of honest manufacturers with the sordid, dishonest minority. A distinction should be made. Increase the penalties against the dishonest and educate the honest.

"The food and drug control work in the United States is not fifty per cent efficient. This is startling, but it is true. Where is the trouble? How is it possible with a mass of food and drug legislation, with zealous, competent and honest officials attempting to enforce the laws, with generous appropriations, with public opinion strongly behind the work and with a friendly press and helpful judges, that there is not greater efficiency?

"The answer is found in defective organization and utter lack of correlation of several branches of what really is but one subject. The trouble has its root in the laws of the Federal government and in the laws of the States.

"This is where The National Civic Federation can help us food officials. We must secure basic changes in these national and State laws, and this association can help materially."

VINCENT ASTOR.
(Copyright by Marceau, N. Y.)

CARL L. ALSBERG.

SAMUEL GOMPERS.

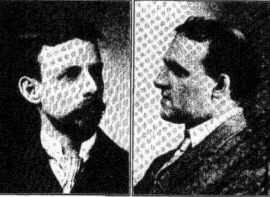

JOHN M. STAHL. S. S. GOLDWATER.

THE ANNUAL DINNER A NOTABLE GATHERING

PROMINENT SPEAKERS EMPHASIZE THE ESSENTIAL DEMOCRACY OF THE NATIONAL CIVIC FEDERATION AS AN OUTGROWTH OF THE AMERICAN SPIRIT

ABOUT 800 members and guests of the Federation attended this notable function at the Hotel Astor on Friday evening, December 12. These gatherings have no counterpart in this or any other country as a democratic intermingling of men and women representing nearly every phase of industrial interest and all manner of civic and political viewpoints.

There was manifest through this unique diversity, as has always been the case upon these occasions, that spirit of unity for the common good in which lies the best possible augury of the safe and progressive development of American institutions.

At the conclusion of the dinner Chairman SETH LOW, in opening the speechmaking, called attention to various interesting aspects of the discussions that had been in progress during the day sessions of the annual meeting. Bearing especially upon the subject of social insurance, which is to be studied by a new department of the Federation, Mr. Low said:

"Mr. P. Tecumseh Sherman, who is one of the best informed men that I know of on the subject of social insurance, has pointed out that the philosophy underlying workmen's compensation requiring the burden of an accident to be borne by the industry, is one thing, while the idea of social insurance against sickness and the ills of life not related to industry in any direct way, is quite a different thing. I am happy to be able to say that Mr. George W. Perkins has accepted the chairmanship of our new Department of Social Insurance, so that the inquiry will be carried on by a man of great ability who is in complete sympathy with all that is best in our industrial life.

"I would like to suggest a single thought on this subject of social insurance. In 1877 and 1878 there was a great agitation in the city of Brooklyn on the subject of outdoor relief—aid given by the city to people living at home who needed assistance. Volunteers were called for to make visits on behalf of the Commissioner of Charities, and I happened to be one of them. In the course of my calls upon applicants for aid I visited a woman who had an apple stand near the ferry. Her room gave every evidence of comfort. It was neat as a pin, and there was no outward indication that she was in any need. I suggested this to her, and, as her eloquence did not seem persuasive, she went to the closet and handed me an apple. I said: 'Madam, if you are rich enough to give me an apple, you are not poor enough to be helped by the county.' Her daughter, who was there, said: 'Mother, he has got you.' Her whole attitude—and she very frankly expressed it—was that if anything was going she wanted her share.

"I quite recognize that social insurance is a very different thing from that, and I think a much better thing than the sort of aid that is given simply because people are poor. I confess that my spirit answers with a great 'amen' to the idea that the whole community act by some system of insurance in which those who are to be insured shall bear their part when they are strong and well; that we do something to preserve the self-respect of such people, and not only preserve their self-respect but make some adequate provision for their hours of sickness and for their old age. But I recognize, as indicated by that experience which I have just related to you, that there are qualities in human nature that are not easily changed, and I think that in our study of social insurance, in all its aspects, if we are to legislate wisely we must remember that human nature does not become strong simply by receiving gifts. It must itself co-operate in the results to be achieved, if the effect upon the individual is to be happy. In this matter, especially, we must not let our hearts run away with our heads."

The chairman's happy introductions of the several speakers and running comments upon incidental points in the discussion kept the great company in most genial mood throughout the evening, apart from the interest of the formal addresses, which are here summarized in brief.

The Future of the Woman's Department.

MISS MAUDE WETMORE, chairman: This is not the first time you have been asked to listen to the achievements of the Woman's Department of The National Civic Federation. The good work continues, and since we last met much that is new has been undertaken and is being carried to successful conclusion. The alleys of Washington, the Vacation Committee, with its 13,000 depositors, the investigation of mills and factories, the completed report on the schools of New York, and the partly finished one on the treadle occupations, all this work speaks for itself and needs no one to boast or brag in its behalf. Full details will as usual be found in our annual report.

What I am now about to ask is your attention to study, for a moment, the future of our Woman's Department. You may think me an enthusiast, but as an actual fact The National Civic Federation offers the women of this country the greatest opportunity for good this land has ever known. Here is an organization which knows no creed or class; any woman joining it can become a factor, no matter what her walk in life may be. The spirit of co-operation is in the air, and through it must succeed much that has failed in the past.

The close relationship which the Woman's Department has always entertained as regards the administration in Washington is a big factor in one part of our work, and its usefulness cannot be easily overestimated. The very real interest which Mrs. Woodrow Wilson has again and again shown us can only be really appreciated by those who for years have striven to make the Woman's Department what it is to-day. Mrs. Wilson, as Mrs. Taft in the past, has lately consented to become its honorary chairman.

[Miss Wetmore described the enlargement of the scope of the Woman's Department during the past year, and among the special phases of new work under way called attention to the prison problem, particularly the evils of contract labor and the lease system. The Woman's Department, in co-operation with the Prison Labor Association, is undertaking a far-reaching work for the reform of those conditions.]

This is a fair sample of national work, and it is in connection with national work that the Woman's Department asks your co-operation. You come from all parts of the country; you would not be here to-night if the solving of problems of this kind did not appeal to you. Have you ever thought what the getting together of organizations, all fighting for the same cause, would mean to a community?

Co-operation for a Larger Industrial Welfare.

FRANK P. WALSH, chairman of the National Commission on Industrial Relations: I consider it a privilege to speak to The National Civic Federation, which, if I catch its spirit, is attempting to perform the same work in its private sphere that our commission has been called upon by the President of the United States to perform in a public way. The thing that has impressed me most is the essential democracy of this organization, the welding together of all manner of views and all manner of men. It seems to me in a most significant manner to be a step in the great onward march of democracy.

The Federal Commission, of which I am a member, is about to enter upon its work with an open mind, coolly, dispassionately, to get the facts, to present them to you, and to your representatives in the State and national legislatures. We are required by the law to inquire into the formation of labor unions, into the construction of employers' associations, and into the relations of such organizations with each other. Of course, under this head come the subjects of collective bargaining, of vocational education, the application of laws affecting combinations in restraint of trade, the question of whether or not this country should adopt anything like the English trades' dispute act. It involves also an intensive study of all of the government agencies at present at work for the amelioration of industrial irritation, the work being done by the State labor bureaus and other organizations of a similar character. Our work, under the law, is to undertake to ascertain the cause of the industrial unrest. This, I take it, makes necessary an investigation of that great mass of unorganized labor engaged in seasonal occupations, an investigation of State employment bureaus, of the migrations of labor, of the militant organization of labor, represented in the syndicalist movement. We have conceived it to be our duty furthermore to investigate the attitude of capital and labor toward the law and the judiciary. Is it true that workmen as such have a contempt for organized society, as expressed through the judiciary? Is it true that those who come in conflict with them have the power of using the law in their own interest? It is the belief of the commission that there is a broad pathway for intelligent and honorable men to take; and our work is to make an investigation of both sides of these questions and a fearless recommendation to Congress of a remedy, if such a thing is possible, based on absolutely ascertained facts.

Justice to Employees in the City Service.

HON. JOHN PURROY MITCHEL, Mayor-elect of the City of New York: In casting about for the reason why I was honored by this invitation this evening, I concluded that perhaps you felt I would be especially sympathetic with the purposes of the Civic Federation because I come to you to-night myself as the result of a species of civic federation in this city—a federation of the forces of honesty and efficiency in government against the forces of corruption and maladministration. We must attack the tremendous task that is now before us with all of the energy we possess, with the firm purpose to carry out the program that we laid before the people in the campaign, and to fulfill to the letter the promises that we made.

Many of the great problems of capital and labor to which this Federation gives its attention are not found in the same form in the city government in which they are presented in private employment. But the fundamental problem common to both is that of giving to the employee a just and fair compensation for his labor, and in securing for the employer full and adequate return for the salaries that are paid. I hope to see New York become a model employer. The work of salary standardization has been more generally misunderstood than any undertaken by the present Board of Estimate. It was generally circulated that the purpose was to make wholesale reductions in the salaries of municipal employees. Quite the contrary. Our object was to establish standards of service and standards of pay that would secure to each municipal servant the assurance of a compensation based on his service and not on political pull, and to the people of the city a full measure of service for the salary paid.

The next administration will try to carry out that purpose by studying the work of each classified service in each department, and then measuring the compensation and adjusting it accurately to the work done. If we do that, the result will be that many a man who has found himself passed by for others who have been advanced over his head, not because of better service rendered, but because they had friends at court, will get in the future compensation that has been denied him in the past. And we shall find, too, that some men whose salaries have been fixed solely because of their friendship with some one influential in politics will be reduced to a sum more accurately related to the kind and character of service that they render.

When that work is done the great body of city employees will find nothing of which to complain, and the taxpayers and citizens will find that they are getting the kind of service to which they are entitled and that the expenses of the city government have been measureably reduced.

Labor's Share in the National Progress.

In presenting Mr. Samuel Gompers as the next speaker the Chairman said:

"The other day in Seattle Mr. Gompers was elected for the thirtieth time the president of the American Federation of Labor, and this year unanimously, the representative of that great body of organized workmen. Let me tell you one other thing about him. 'The last time that I spoke with Speck von Sternberg, the late German Ambassador to this country, he said to me: 'I look upon Mr. Gompers as a really great man. I read everything he says because it seems to me that his discussions of the labor question are truly philosophical,' and he added, 'that is the great question of the day in every civilized country in the world.'"

SAMUEL GOMPERS, president of the American Federation of Labor: It was my pleasure to be at the Seattle convention to which our president referred, and the work of that convention I submit, with my associates, to the judgment and to the conscience of the American people. It was of a constructive, humanitarian and patriotic character. It dealt not only with the every activity of the wage-working masses of America, but with the great questions of political economy, of sociology, of statesmanship, of human rights, of the policies which should be pursued by the States and by the nation. Although we may differ upon some details of the questions with which the convention dealt, I am sure

(Concluded on page 11)

RAPID GROWTH OF THE WOMAN'S DEPARTMENT

ORGANIZATION OF NEW SECTIONS IN CHICAGO, MILWAUKEE AND ST. LOUIS MARKS THE STEADY EXPANSION OF ITS WORK FOR NATIONAL CO-OPERATION OF SOCIAL AGENCIES

THE remarkable showing of growth and broadening activities of the Woman's Department, evidenced in the reports submitted at the annual meeting of the National Civic Federation, is further borne out by the energetic campaign of organization now under way in western cities.

During the month of January the president of the Department, Miss Maude Wetmore, in company with Mrs. Rogers H. Bacon, secretary; Miss Anne Morgan, treasurer, and Mrs. Lyndsay Van Reusselaer, executive secretary of the Woman's Council, met with groups of several hundred of the most representative women prominent in the social and civic life of Chicago, Milwaukee and St. Louis, and presented the work and aims of the Department.

In each case there developed an immediate and enthusiastic response to the central idea of the national co-operation of the many helpful agencies of women's work for social amelioration. It was pointed out that these movements in their several local fields are developing distinctive ideas and methods of social service which might be not only strengthened through larger co-operation, but also given a many-fold multiplied value through the interchange of ideas and experiences possible only by organized association in the national field.

Committees were formed in each of the three cities, and the resident officers are already enlisting a large membership of leading women interested in the program of social welfare which the Department is carrying forward. The motive of bringing to a focus the countless unrelated and often duplicating efforts of women of broad outlook and humanitarian impulse throughout the country—in brief, of making what is found most useful anywhere available everywhere—has been recognized wherever presented as a universal need and one of the most promising opportunities of the hour.

CHICAGO.

The Chicago meeting was called by Miss Jane Addams, whose attitude of working "not for but with people," was emphasized by Miss Morgan as the spirit of the democratic movement the Woman's Department seeks to establish. As the immediate outcome of the meeting, representatives were named from a large number of leading organizations and groups in the city, who in turn took the first steps towards permanent organization by the election of a temporary committee consisting of Mrs. Charles H. Betts as Chairman, Mrs. George Bass Vice-Chairman; Mrs. George A. Soden, Secretary; Mrs. Franklin E. Nelles, Treasurer; Mrs. Frederick C. Bartlett, Chairman of the Membership Committee, and Mrs. Benjamin Carpenter, Chairman of the Vacation Fund Committee.

MILWAUKEE.

In Milwaukee three crowded meetings were held in one day, attended by several hundred leading women of the city and State, and resulting in the formation of a section under the chairmanship of Miss Sherman, Chairman of the Committee of Wage Earning Women in the Central Council of Social Agencies. The work in Wisconsin is to have also the active co-operation of Miss Lundberg, Chief Factory Inspector, which means, of course, to the wide public familiar with Miss Lundberg's work, that the new movement begins with the most promising assurance of fruitful results.

ST. LOUIS.

In St. Louis the meetings for organization were arranged by and held under the auspices of Mrs. Philip N. Moore, former President of the General Federation of Women's Clubs; Mrs. Charles Nagel, wife of the former Secretary of Commerce and Labor, and Mrs. Markham. Some 350 were in attendance and a full working organization for Missouri was perfected, with the following officers:

Chairman, Mrs. Frank V. Hammar; Vice-Chairmen, Mrs. Elliott W. Major, wife of the Governor of Missouri; Mrs. David R. Francis, Mrs. Thomas K. Niedringhaus and Mrs. W. E. Fishel; Treasurer, Mrs. George F. Steedman; Secretary, Miss Florence Haywood; Executive Committee, Mrs. Charles Nagel, Miss Lionberger, Mrs. Henry Scott; Chairman Membership Committee, Mrs. Benoir; Chairman Vacation Committee, Mrs. John Tilden Davis.

Commenting editorially upon the organization of this movement *The New St. Louis Star* said:

"The formation of a Missouri Branch of The National Civic Federation will be looked back upon in after days as one of the big accomplishments of the year 1914. * * * This big work has been successful in the East. It does not use militant methods. * * * The Federation works to bring employers and the women employed closer together for their mutual benefit. Looked upon with some distrust at first, in the States where branches now thrive, employers soon realized that anything which promoted the health and happiness of their employees increased in the same ratio the employees' efficiency. And so, the employers are now the most enthusiastic supporters of The National Civic Federation. * * *

"The splendid body of Missouri women who organized the State branch will see to it that The National Civic Federation in Missouri accomplishes as much if not more than it has in other States. To the employers of women in Missouri, *The New St. Louis Star* commends most heartily the newly organized branch of The National Civic Federation."

WORK IN THE EAST AND SOUTH.

The Woman's Department already has in its working organization sections in New York and New Jersey, Massachusetts and Rhode Island, the District of Columbia, Virginia and West Virginia, North and South Carolina, Georgia and Florida, Alabama and Mississippi. The addition of these principal cities in the middle west is a further step in the plan and intent to make the work truly national in extent as in spirit, affording, as Miss Wetmore declared in her address at the annual dinner of the Federation in December, "the women of this country the greatest opportunity for good this land has ever known."

NEW YORK AND NEW JERSEY.

In connection with the work of the Metropolitan Section (New York and New Jersey) a course of lectures has been given during the month of January, in continuation of similar courses during the past three winters. Miss Elisabeth Marbury is chairman of the committee in charge of these lectures, the first of which was delivered at the residence of Mrs. Reginald de Koven, by Mrs. J. Borden Harriman, of the Federal Commission on Industrial Relations, who described some of the problems the Commission is to investigate. The other lectures of the course were given at the Colony Club, by Miss Ida Tarbell on "Efficiency and Welfare." Mrs. Maud Ballington Booth on "Lights and Shadows of Prison Life," and Miss Jane Addams, of Hull House, Chicago.

The committee in charge of the vacation fund in New York consists of Miss Robinson Smith, Chairman; Mrs. August Belmont, Vice-Chairman; Miss Anne Morgan, Treasurer, and Miss Maud Rives Borland, Secretary. There is also an advisory committee of seven men, of which Mr. Henry W. Taft is Chairman. Under the auspices of the Vacation Committee, a building at No. 38 West Thirty-ninth street, together with two adjoining houses on Thirty-eighth street, has been opened as headquarters for the vacation work and a social center for the evening gatherings, entertainments, clubs, singing classes and other features of this rapidly developing idea. More than 700 people attended the housewarming reception at the new headquarters during the afternoon and evening of New Year's Day. Mrs. Frederick J. Brockway will be the director in charge of the work. As pointed out by Miss Wetmore in her report at the annual meeting of the Federation, the vacation savings fund in the Metropolitan Section has already 120 stations with 14,000 accounts; a total of more than $100,000 has been deposited by working girls in two years since the movement was organized.

DISTRICT OF COLUMBIA.

The work of the District of Columbia Section has been attracting national attention this winter, chiefly by reason of its extremely active campaign in behalf of the improvement of the alleys of Washington, a reform in which it has had the effective personal co-operation of Mrs. Woodrow Wilson, Honorary Chairman of the Woman's Department, and of Miss Margaret Wilson. Other matters which the District of Columbia Section is taking up are an educational campaign with reference to pure foods, and the more thorough supervision of prison management. In connection with the meetings of the District of Columbia Section, lectures or talks are being given, the first two in the series thus far having been delivered by Dr. Carl Alsberg, Chief of the Bureau of Chemistry of the Department of Agriculture, and Mr. E. Stagg Whitin, of New York, who launched the idea of a Federal Bureau of prison management.

Mrs. Archibald Hopkins has been elected Chairman of the District of Columbia Section; Mrs. Theodora North McLaughlin, Vice-Chairman; Mrs. J. W. Pilling, Secretary, and Mrs. J. F. Frazer, Treasurer.

MASSACHUSETTS AND RHODE ISLAND.

The work in Massachusetts and Rhode Island is developing the enthusiastic interest of a large and growing membership. In Boston and Worcester the Vacation Savings Fund is already firmly established. A course of lectures is in progress in Boston, under the auspices of the Lecture Committee, of which Mrs. Malcolm Donald is chairman. The speakers and topics for the course are:

Miss Gertrude Beeks, Director of the Welfare Department of The National Civic Federation, on "Women in Industry and the Social Evil."

Mr. John Graham Brooks, on "The Real Work of The Civic Federation."

Mr. E. A. Hartman, Secretary of the Massachusetts Civic League, on "The Relation of Housing to Industries."

Dr. David L. Edsall, on "Occupational Diseases."

The Executive Council of the Massachusetts and Rhode Island Section is made up as follows:

Mrs. George T. Rice, Chairman; Mrs. Charles S. Hamlin, Vice-Chairman; Mrs. Bradford Norman, Vice-Chairman; Mrs. Matthew Bartlett, Treasurer; Mrs. George R. Agassiz, Miss Mary S. Ames, Mrs. Harold Brown, Mrs. Spencer Borden, Jr., Mrs. W. Murray Crane, Mrs. T. James Bowlker, Mrs. George Crompton, Miss Helena Dudley, Mrs. Walter N. Eldridge, Mrs. L. Carteret Fenno, Mrs. Edwin Farnham Greene, Miss Alice W. Hunt, Miss Louisa Loring, Miss Ida Mason, Miss Elizabeth S. Porter, Mrs. Robert Russell, Mrs. Channing Simmons, Mrs. Eva W. White, Miss Mary C. Wiggin, Mrs. Robert A. Woods, and Mrs. Roger Wolcott.

NATIONAL OFFICERS OF THE DEPARTMENT.

The widening scope and influence of the work of the Woman's Department is further indicated by the list of officers and committee members elected at its annual meeting of December 11 and 12, held simultaneously with that of The National Civic Federation. Among the members of the Department from other States who were present at this meeting were Mrs. George T. Rice, Westwood, Mass.; Mrs. Roger Wolcott, Readville, Mass.; Mrs. Henry L. Higginson and Mrs. W. W. Vaughan, Boston, Mass.; Mrs. A. J. George, Brookline, Mass.; Mrs. Anna C. Bird, East Walpole, Mass.; Mrs. Rodman E. Griscom, Haverford, Pa.; Mrs. Bayard Henry, Philadelphia, Pa.; Mrs. Thomas S. Crago, Waynesburg, Pa.; Mrs. John McLaughlin, Mrs. Henry A. Packham, Mrs. Arthur Willett and Mrs. J. Nota McGill, Washington, D. C.; Mrs. G. Huntington Williams, Baltimore, Md.; Mrs. J. Allison Hodges, Richmond, Va.; Mrs. B. Frank Mebane, Spray, N. C., and Mrs. Albert Thornton, Atlanta, Ga.

The officers and committee members elected at the annual meeting are:

Officers and Executive Council.

Mrs. WOODROW WILSON, Honorary Chairman.

Miss MAUDE WETMORE, Chairman, Rhode Island.

Mrs. ROGERS H. BACON, Secretary, New York City.

Miss ANNE MORGAN, Treasurer, New York City.

Woman's Council.

Mrs. AUGUST BELMONT, New York City.

Mrs. AUGUSTUS P. GARDNER, Hamilton, Mass.

Mrs. MARY HATCH WILLARD, New York City.

Mrs. ROBERT W. LOVETT, First Vice-Chairman. Boston, Mass.

Mrs. CHARLES S. HAMLIN, Second Vice-Chairman, Washington, D. C.

Mrs. ALFRED E. BATES, Third Vice-Chairman, Washington, D. C.

Mrs. BAYARD HENRY, Fourth Vice-Chairman, Philadelphia, Pa.

Miss MAUD RIVES BORLAND, Fifth Vice-Chairman, New York.

Mrs. EVA McDONALD VALESH, Sixth Vice-Chairman, New York.

Mrs. FRANCIS McNEIL-BACON, Jr., Chairman Metropolitan Section for New York and New Jersey, New York.

Irs. ARCHIBALD HOPKINS, Chairman, District of Columbia Section, Washington, D. C.

Mrs. J. ALLISON HODGES, Chairman, Virginia and West Virginia Section, Richmond, Va.

Irs. GEORGE T. RICE, Chairman, Massachusetts and Rhode Island Section, Boston, Mass.

Irs. CYRUS PITTMAN ORR, Chairman, Alabama and Mississippi Section, Birmingham, Ala.

Irs. B. FRANK MEBANE, Chairman, North and South Carolina Section, Spray, N. C.

Irs. JOHN K. OTTLEY, Chairman, Georgia Section, Atlanta, Ga.

Irs. WILLIAM BROOKS YOUNG, Chairman Florida Section, Jacksonville, Fla.

Irs. H. S. B. BEALE, Chairman, National Industrial Employees' Committee, Washington, N. C.

Irs. HENRY K. PECKHAM, Chairman, National Government Employees' Committee, Washington, D. C.

Irs. ROGERS H. BACON, Chairman, National Vacation Committee, New York.

Mrs. LYNDSAY VAN RENSSELAER, Executive Secretary, New York.

Executive Committee.

Mrs. GEORGE R. AGASSIZ, Boston, Mass.; Mrs. RCHIBALD ALEXANDER, Hoboken, N. J; Mrs. UGUST BELMONT, New York City; Mrs. HAR-LD BROWN, Newport, R. I.; Mrs. ORTON B. ROWN, Berlin, N. H.; Mrs. ANDREW CARNEGIE, ew York City; Mrs. E. W. COLE, Nashville, Tenn.; rs. W. MURRAY CRANE, Dalton, Mass.; Mrs. ILLIAM H. CROCKER, Burlingame, Cal.; Mrs. GEORGE, CROMPTON, Worcester, Mass.; Mrs. ARTHUR M. DODGE, New York City; Miss ISMAY DOOLY, Atlanta, Ga.; Mrs. WALTER ELDRIDGE, Newport, R. I.; Mrs. L. CARTERET FENNO, Rowey, Mass.; Mrs. AUGUSTUS P. GARDNER, Hamilon, Mass.; Mrs. EDWIN FARNHAM GREENE, Boson Mass.; Mrs. LINCOLN N. KINNICUTT, Worceser, Mass.; Mrs. OVERTON LEA, Nashville, Tenn.; Irs. ARTHUR LEE, Elkins, W. Va.; Mrs. V. EVERIT IACY, New York City; Miss ELISABETH MAR-BURY, New York City; Mrs. MARCUS M. MARKS, ew York City; Mrs. LAWRENCE MAXWELL, Cinnnati, Ohio; Mrs. CHARLES F. MEYER, New York ity; Mrs. BOWMAN H. McCALLA, Washington, D. .; Mrs. CYRUS H. McCORMICK, Chicago, Ill.; Mrs. MEDILL McCORMICK, Chicago, Ill.; Mrs. J. NOTA McGILL, Washington, D. C.; Mrs. A. F. McKISSICK, Greenwood, S. C.; Mrs. WILLIAM F. McKNIGHT, Grand Rapids, Mich.; Mrs. JOHN McLAUGHLIN, Washington, D. C.; Mrs. GILBERT MONTAGUE, New York City; Mrs. PHILIP N. MOORE, St. Louis, Mo.; Mrs. LINDSAY PATTERSON, Winston-Salem, N. C.; Mrs. SAMUEL SPENCER, Washington, D. C.; Mrs. OSCAR STRAUS, New York City; Mrs. W. WARD THORON, Colorado Springs, Colo.; Mrs. EDMUND LEIGHTON TYLER, Anniston, Ala.; Mrs. RICHARD WAINWRIGHT, Washington, D. C.; Mrs. BENJAMIN I. WHEELER, Berkeley, Cal.; Mrs. ARTHUR WILLERT, Washington, D. C.; Mrs. G. HUNTINGTON WILLIAMS, Baltimore, Md.; Mrs. TALCOTT WILLIAMS, New York City; Mrs. ROGER WOLCOTT, Readville, Mass.

AN INTERNATIONAL CONGRESS ON SOCIAL INSURANCE

THE plans which have been in formation during the past two years for the first meeting in America of the International Congress on Social Insurance have reached the stage of permanent organization. This Congress was established as a result of the legislation in Germany, followed by other countries, establishing insurance of workmen against accidents, sickness, invalidity and the like. It is primarily an official body, composed of delegates of the various governments of the world; but others who are interested in the subject may become members and, subject to such rules as may be adopted, are permitted to take part in discussions.

The International Congress was invited to hold its next meeting in the United States by President Taft, under a special authorization of Congress, which also made an appropriation toward the expenses, which must, however, be provided for chiefly by means of subscriptions.

The Congress will meet in Washington in October, 1915. The Committee on Organization is composed of 120 members selected from different parts of the United States on account of their prominence in connection with matters related to social insurance or on account of their well-known interest in the subject. They are representative of all classes in the community, employers and employed, professional and business men, professors, insurance men, etc., with a view to enlisting as broad an interest as possible. This committee, at a meeting held at the Union League Club, New York, recently, elected the following general officers:

Honorary Chairmen

HON. WM. G. McADOO, Secretary of the Treasury, Washington, D. C.

HON. WM. C. REDFIELD, Secretary of Commerce, Washington, D. C.

HON. WM. B. WILSON, Secretary of Labor, Washington, D. C.

Chairman

HON. FRANKLIN MACVEAGH, Ex-Secretary of the Treasury, Washington, D. C.

Vice-Chairmen

HON. ROYAL MEEKER, Commissioner of Labor Statistics, Washington, D. C.

MISS JANE ADDAMS, Chicago.

SAMUEL GOMPERS, President American Federation of Labor, Washington, D. C.

MISS ANNE MORGAN, Treasurer Woman's Department, The National Civic Federation, New York.

DR. WM. H. TOLMAN, Director American Museum of Safety, New York.

HON. C. H. CROWNHART, Chairman Industrial Commission, Madison, Wis.

HON. A. J. PILLSBURY, Chairman Industrial Accident Commission, Piedmont, Cal.

HON. FLOYD L. DAGGETT, Chairman Industrial Insurance Commission, Olympia, Wash.

HON. WALLACE D. YAPLE, Chairman Industrial Commission, Columbus, Ohio.

Secretary-General

MILES M. DAWSON, Consulting Actuary, New York.

Treasurer

ARTHUR WILLIAMS, Chairman Public Policy Committee, National Electric Light Association, New York.

Executive Committee

EDWARD T. DEVINE, Chairman, Professor of Social Economy, Columbia University, New York.

LOUIS D. BRANDEIS, Attorney-at-Law, Boston, Mass.

ROBERT LYNN COX, President of National Association of Life Insurance Presidents, New York.

MILES M. DAWSON, Consulting Actuary, New York.

RALPH M. EASLEY, Chairman Executive Council, The National Civic Federation, New York.

HENRY W. FARNAM, Professor of Economics, Yale University, New Haven, Conn.

LEE K. FRANKEL, Vice-President Metropolitan Life Insurance Company, New York.

SAMUEL GOMPERS, President American Federation of Labor, Washington, D. C.

FREDERICK L. HOFFMAN, Statistician, Prudential Insurance Company of America, Newark, N. J.

EDWARD M. HOUSE, Publicist, Austin, Texas.

JOHN E. KINNANE, Chairman Industrial Accident Board, Lansing, Mich.

JULIUS KRUTTSCHNITT, Chairman Board of Directors, Southern Pacific Railway Co., San Francisco, Cal.

JAMES A. LOWELL, Chairman State Commission on Compensation for Indust'l Accidents, Boston, Mass.

ROYAL MEEKER, Commissioner of Labor Statistics, Washington, D. C.

JOHN MITCHELL, Former President United Mine Workers of America, Mount Vernon, N. Y.

MISS ANNE MORGAN, Treasurer Woman's Department, The National Civic Federation, New York.

CHARLES P. NEILL, Director and Chairman of Labor Committee, American Smelting and Refining Company, New York.

GEORGE POPE, President National Manufacturers' Association, Hartford, Conn.

W. H. POWERS, President National Fraternal Congress of America, Washington, D. C.

MRS. RAYMOND ROBINS, President National Woman's Trade Union League, Chicago, Ill.

HENRY R. SEAGER, President American Association for Labor Legislation, New York.

WILLIAM H. TOLMAN, Director The American Museum of Safety, New York.

FRANK P. WALSH, Chairman Commission on Industrial Relations, Kansas City, Mo.

ARTHUR WILLIAMS, Chairman Public Policy Committee of the National Electric Light Association, New York.

H. E. WILLS, Assistant Chief, Brotherhood of Locomotive Engineers, Washington, D. C.

Congresses on this subject have been held now for twenty-five years. The International Permanent Committee, with headquarters in Paris, celebrated in October of this year the anniversary of the first meeting held in Paris in 1889. Since then Congresses have been held in Berne, Milan, Brussels, Paris, Dusseldorf, Vienna and Rome, besides conferences at The Hague, Dresden, Zurich and Ghent.

The European membership of the Congress embraces the leading experts upon all phases of the subject in the different countries of Europe. They have conferences annually and are all kept in touch with what is going on through a Quarterly Bulletin published by the International Permanent Committee, of which M. Raymond Poincare was chairman

(Concluded on page 18.)

THE ANNUAL DINNER.

(Concluded from page 9.)

hat it will challenge the best judgment of the best nen and the best women of our country, as being onductive to the welfare of the people as a whole.

In becoming members of this National Civic Federation no one surrenders his right of judgment and of action. It is an effort to try and find a middle ground upon which men and women of all sorts and notions may unite in a common effort for the common good. It has been my pleasure to be associated with its work since its foundation, and with he men who have given it character and purpose. am not given to flattery, but I do want to take advantage of this opportunity of saying that in my udgment no man is better fitted for its leadership han our honored President, Mr. Seth Low. Experience, disposition, character, temperament, all have ombined in making him the ideal president of our Federation.

May I indulge myself with a few words in regard o the question of free assemblage and free speech? Of course we know that if free assemblage is carried o "the limit" it is likely to sometimes inconvenience is, but it is equally true that freedom enjoyed and exercised brings with it a greater degree of concions responsibility, and of responsiveness to the general good. It is better even that we suffer inconvenience sometimes than it is to close down the hrottle and sit on the valve.

It is something not yet fully understood how perectly safe freedom is. This is a republic in which the people are supposed to be sovereigns. Sovereignty implies responsibility, experience, education, knowledge. Without these it is impossible to conduct for any great length of time a government founded upon the consent of the governed. May I express this fervent wish: That this republic of ours may not only be the haven of religious and political liberty, but that it may inaugurate an industrial freedom that shall be in truth a chart and a guide in civilization for the people of the whole world.

The National Civic Federation an Outgrowth of the American Spirit.

TALCOTT WILLIAMS, Director of the School of Journalism, Columbia University: The existence of The National Civic Federation and the fashion in which it has drawn together in this hall those who represent every phase of American life, is possible not because of the Federation, not even because of the reconciling voice and constant labors for the public good of its President, but because the very atmosphere of American institutions brings men and women together, seeing eye to eye, forgetting everything except that they are Americans and have a common country to serve.

Such a Federation comes into being here and does its work without government sanction, because this is the land of initiative and individual opportunity, and every man feels at heart what Lincoln said was the test of democracy: "Not, I am as good as you are, but you are as good as I am."

[Dr. Williams noted briefly the varied activities of the Federation since its inception and the far-reaching results of the service rendered in many fields. Outlining the scope of the national survey of industrial and social progress, to be undertaken by the Federation, he stated some of his own impressions of the conditions a thorough and impartial inquiry of this nature is likely to show.]

I believe it will furnish facts which will end the declaration that the rich are growing richer and the poor growing poorer. I believe it will be shown that the savings of the poor have quadrupled while the population grew one-half; that the increase of the owners of property has gone on at a rate which, in a great corporation like the Steel Trust, makes those who own its shares more numerous than those who labor for it, as is true also of many of our railroads to-day. And I believe the child is living to-day who will see in this nation so universal a distribution of property that, while at present half the families of the United States live in homes that they own, and at least 60 per cent. own property which returns them an income, it will be the exception that a family has not property enough to be secure against the future, and it will come to be literally true that no man or woman who desires to work within the limits of the United States is without the opportunity. I think it will be shown without question that during the last thirty years there has been an advance in the comforts of the home, in the education of the child, in the protection of both women and children, in the diffusion, not alone of the necessities but of the joys of life. These advances have come through the work, not of one, but of the American people as a whole.

THE NATIONAL
Civic Federation Review

Office: Thirty-third Floor, Metropolitan Tower
1 Madison Avenue New York City

RALPH M. EASLEY, Editor

The Editor alone is Responsible for any unsigned article or unquoted statement published in THE NATIONAL CIVIC FEDERATION REVIEW.

PUBLISHED BY
The National Civic Federation

A Great Meeting The Fourteenth Annual Meeting found The National Civic Federation carrying on in many directions work of increasing magnitude and national significance. The bare recital of results achieved in the fields of industrial conciliation, workmen's compensation, trust regulation, control of municipal utilities, welfare work, reform in legal procedure, and in behalf of the many humanitarian causes engaging the attention of the Woman's Department, make a total presentment of social service such as has been possible at no previous annual stocktaking of this character. Very little of this, indeed, could have been foreseen by any of the public-spirited citizens who united fourteen years ago to try the experiment of replacing the narrow and partisan treatment of our common problems by a patriotic co-operation of the best minds and most representative leaders in all our civic and industrial groups. The results are an impressive demonstration that just such an unprecedented grouping was a prime need of American public life at that time, and by the same sign never more so than to-day.

Report of the Compensation Commission The report now in press of the Joint Commission, which has been studying the workings of compensation laws throughout the country, will make a volume of some 200,000 words, dealing with every significant phase of the development of this great movement in theory and in practice. On another page will be found Chairman Phillips' description of the extent and character of this investigation. The net results of the work will have a two-fold value. It will make clear the comparative fruits of our most significant experience in this country on the subject, and in so doing it will also enable public opinion, in quarters where the movement has made little or no headway, to select the most available and successful features of compensation legislation and work for their enactment from the standpoint of knowledge rather than of experiment.

To Study Social Insurance The investigation of the subject of social insurance upon which The National Civic Federation is entering is a logical continuation and expansion of the study it has been giving for several years to the most important phase of this problem, through its Department of Wage Earners' Insurance. The fact that Mr. George W. Perkins, chairman of this department, will have the direction of the work in the broadened field, gives assurance of substantial results. It means, as President Low expressed it in his remarks at the annual dinner, "that the inquiry will be carried on by a man of great ability, who is in complete sympathy with all that is best in our industrial life." It is expected that the investigation will include a study of European experiments in social insurance by a commission of four experts, to go abroad during the coming season for that purpose.

The question of how far and in what manner provision of relief for causes of disability of a general, rather than directly occupational, nature may be afforded under American conditions is fraught with many difficulties, demanding exact knowledge of the workings of foreign experiments, and of the attempts to meet the situation which have been made by many industrial corporations in this country. It will require also for its wise solution the thoughtful judgment of economists and men of affairs, familiar with the temperament as well as the needs and social habits of our own cosmopolitan population. The Federation's inquiry in this field has, by the way, a peculiar timeliness in view of the approaching International Congress of Social Insurance, which is to meet in Washington in October, 1915. By that time it is believed the nature and scope of the problem in this country may be given a much more adequate presentation than has been possible thus far or is possible to-day.

Baseless Charges Refuted. The hard pressed socialist faction in the trade union movement is apparently growing desperate over its continued failure to gain control of the American Federation of Labor. The attempt to make an issue of the alleged personal habits of Samuel Gompers is the latest outbreak of wrath in that quarter, a line of attack everywhere recognized as confession of defeat. So far as concerns the charge itself, made by a delegate to the recent Indianapolis convention of the mine workers, that President Gompers was intoxicated during the A. F. of L. convention last November, the testimony of R. C. McCormick, proprietor of the New Richmond Hotel in Seattle, if indeed any testimony were needed, may be regarded as sufficiently conclusive. Mr. McCormick, in the course of a public statement on the subject, says:

"I know positively that Mr. Gompers never was intoxicated during his stay in Seattle, and I know further that no complaint was made to the night manager that there was unseemly disturbance in his rooms. . . . I consider McDonald's statement malicious in the extreme and probably based on the disagreements that arose here on the convention floor, echoes of which were heard about the hotel during the entire convention."

A Socialist Challenge Squarely Met. The "challenging" habit of some of our socialist friends, especially of the free-lance variety, has apparently received a rude setback in the recent open correspondence between Upton Sinclair and Vincent Astor. As a means of getting publicity for long expositions of socialist ideas it was a line of propaganda that seemed to promise much, on the assumption, of course, that "capital" has no answer to the economic theories of the cult and is debarred by its very position from casting any doubt upon the extraordinary picture of industrial society as it is not, upon which the demand for revolution is based. Least of all have any of these cocksure gentlemen imagined that any conspicuous capitalist himself would come into the open with a frank and broad-minded discussion of the issues.

But in his last "trouble hunting" excursion Mr. Sinclair found that this is precisely what one of them was perfectly ready to do. What is more, for another unforeseen result the Sage of Halcyon Hall emerges from the encounter much the worse for having sought it and roundly scored by other leading lights of socialism for getting outside the breastworks without a safer intellectual equipment. Morris Hillquit, for instance, the recognized head of the Socialist Party in New York, has not only repudiated the Sinclair tale of increasing misery, but frankly acknowledges in the main the improvement in working class conditions shown by the testimony of labor itself, to which Mr. Astor refers in his reply.

In calling upon Mr. Astor to join the socialist movement the zealous Sinclair neglected to furnish any concrete definition of what the movement is or what it actually proposes. This program, however, Mr. Astor says he finds, from his study of socialist literature, boiled down in the following statement by Mr. Hillquit, which comes at least from an authoritative source:

"Stated in more concrete terms, the socialist program requires the public or collective ownership and operation of the principal instruments and agencies for the production and distribution of wealth—the land, mines, railroads, steamboats, telegraph and telephone lines, mills, factories and modern machinery. This is the main program and the ultimate aim of the whole socialist movement and the political creed of all socialists. It is the unfailing test of socialist adherence, and admits of no limitations, extension or variation. Whoever accepts this program is a socialist, whoever does not is not."

It so happens that in common with many thousands—the great majority, in fact—of men of large interests, Mr. Astor is personally interested in various lines of social and civic work, and in some of these has become associated with many of the leaders of the great trade and railroad labor organizations. Not one of these, he tells Mr. Sinclair, "accepts your philosophy as a cure for the evils which we all recognize and deplore." In evidence of this he sends with his reply copies of the American Federationist, the official organ of the American Federation of Labor, for September and October, 1913, and January, 1914, containing the record in great detail of the actual improvement in the various crafts and the gains in National and State legislation during 1912. He calls attention further, as most impressive of all, to the following statement by the Executive Council of the Federation of Labor in its report to the annual convention in Seattle last December:

"Not only has there been progress made in numbers, but for the increasing numbers there have been increase in wages, shortening of the workday, improvement in sanitary and general conditions under which the work is done, better protection for the life and health of the workers. These are fundamental factors in determining the standard of living prevailing. There can be no question of the statement that the general standard of living among Americans has been raised year after year. The things which to-day are held to be necessities were deemed luxuries a decade ago."

"These," Mr. Astor comments, "are the views of men who speak with knowledge and authority for millions of American wage earners"—a right, by the way, which they have yet to confer upon their various volunteer spokesmen of the Sinclair fraternity. Mr. Astor confesses himself unable to see how any one could read such a statement and still assert that we are "moving to-day with the speed of an avalanche into one of the most terrific cataclysms in the history of mankind."

Neither, it is safe to say, could Mr. Upton Sinclair, but for the relative insignificance of facts to the socialist mind.

DOCTOR BABSON AND HIS I. W. W. NIGHTMARE

WE have recently received a letter from a manufacturer in Chicago who seems to be almost scared out of his wits about the terrible things that are going to be done to this country by the Industrial Workers of the World. He enclosed a clipping describing a speech recently made in that city by a university professor, which seems to have been the cause of the gentleman's alarm.

Another recent outbreak on this subject is from Roger W. Babson, a financial writer who has been occupying many pages of valuable space in newspapers and magazines with his voluminous disquisitions, tables and charts. This gentleman, it seems, furnishes financial letters to bankers. In a recent one, after describing the destructive character of the I. W. W. and explaining that their aim is the ultimate ownership of factories, banks, stores and all other industries by the workers themselves, he coolly announces his belief that they are right and will win, and advises the manufacturers and bankers to get in line with the idea that all they have is soon to be confiscated by the workers. He says:

"The great fundamental question between capital and labor will never be settled by arbitration boards nor through the joint control of industries by representatives of labor and capital. One of these two opposing interests must and will ultimately rule. Wise are the bankers, manufacturers and investors who recognize that it will be labor which is to rule. If so, that means that labor must ultimately acquire the industries, as capital will not much longer rest content with present conditions. The Industrial Workers of the World state frankly that ultimately there can be but one head—either capital or labor must rule—and that we are to see a fight to the finish. I regret to admit it," says the learned doctor, "but I nevertheless believe that the I. W. W. theory is the more correct, and many great manufacturers reluctantly agree."

In other words, capitalists are becoming so dissatisfied with their present condition that they are willing to have the syndicalists, anarchists, I. W. W., Babsons, Haywoods and Ettors seize their property and operate it for them. Undoubtedly this would make these capitalists feel considerably relieved, if not entirely so. And yet this gentleman is selling to supposedly hard-headed business men letters containing this advice. It might be remarked that a banker who has no more sense than to pay for such stuff ought to be relieved of his property because he has already been relieved of his common sense.

It might be interesting for Doctor Babson and the sympathetic editors, writers and social workers, as well as our manufacturing correspondent from Chicago, who have become so alarmed over this terrible power, to look inside where "the wheels go round." Just how big is this giant of destruction? Tom Mann, the English syndicalist, who has just completed a twenty-two weeks' visit to this country to study the question, covering the territory from Maine to California, confesses his sad disappointment at finding that there were only 14,000 members in the I. W. W. organization, as shown at the national convention last September, and adds: "Does not the case call for inquiry as to whether the present lines are the right ones?"

Speaking of the delegates to this same convention, who are described as "having arrived in special cars, cattle or box," Ben L. Reitman, the King of the Hobos, himself a delegate, says:

"As I sat in the hot, stuffy, smoky room of the convention hall day after day, and heard the discussions, and saw how little regard the delegates had for grammar and the truth, and realized that most of the delegates knew as much about the real labor movement as they did about psychology, and that they cared little about the broad principles of freedom, and did not have a vision of a new society, where the worker would enjoy the fruit of his labor in freedom and beauty, I marvelled at the big things the I. W. W. have done during their short career. And I said to myself, 'God, is it possible that this bunch of pork-chop philosophers, agitators who have no real, great organizing ability or creative brain power, are able to frighten the capitalistic class more than any other labor movement ever organized in America?' "

But a better statement than that of Tom Mann as to the utter impotency of the I. W. W. as an organization and the causes for such impotency may be found in the following editorial, which appeared in *Solidarity*, the official organ of the I. W. W., about the time that Mr. Babson was sending his lucubrations to his banker subscribers:

"If the Industrial Workers of the World is going to organize the working class then we will have to make a great change in our attitude toward the labor movement and in the methods that we are now using. At present we are to the labor movement what the high diver is to the circus. A sensation, marvelous and nerve thrilling. We attract the crowds. We give them thrills, we do hair-raising stunts and send the crowd home to wait impatiently for the next sensationalist to come along. As far as making Industrial Unionism fit the everyday life of the workers we have failed miserably. The crowd expects the sensational from our speakers or organizers; the members expect it, and our speakers, if they intend to remain as such, have got to supply them or go out of business. We measure the success or failure of our speakers by the number of spectacular stunts that they are able to pull off. It is child's play to stand in front of some factory and convince the slaves that they have a grievance. Capitalism is generous in that respect. The speaker sheds tears over their misery, he opens the floodgates of sentiment, and, lo, Mr. Speaker becomes a strike leader. With cheap phrases and flowery language the strike leader appeals to the emotions of the crowd, lashing them into a religious frenzy, for he knows well that if he ever allows the strikers to cool down the boasted solidarity will disappear and the men will crawl back into the factory. Take the speaker away from the strike and it will go up in smoke unless the workers or some part of them have been previously organized. Arrest the speaker or strike leader and the crowd will remain firm until another one gets on the job. The new speaker does not have to know anything about the shop conditions to make good. He raves about persecution and the brutality of the police. It is surprising how you can revive the dying enthusiasm of a crowd by a tirade against the police or the army.

"While the crowd is still enthusiastic we take in many members, many of whom would just as soon join the Salvation Army as the Industrial Workers of the World, providing that the S. A. had sense enough to use the same cheap weapons that we are forcing our speakers to use. To stampede a bunch of slaves who are working for $1.62 per day is easy, and spectacular. . . .

"Had we kept as many organizers in Lawrence after the strike as we had during the strike we would have an organization that could carry on the next battle without the aid of press agents or sensationalists. In Akron it was the same story; the members cried for sensation; Haywood was sent for. He filled the bill, but after the strike was over every organizer was called to other points to supply the thrills called for by the rank and file.

"Not one was left to build up an organization in Akron. . . .

"It is getting to be a habit, and the speakers are catering to it. In Pittsburgh I heard one of our principal speakers give voice to the following: 'Do you think that I am going to come here and talk to 200 people when I can stay in New York and talk to 10,000 people direct and have my speeches carried to thousands more by the capitalistic press?' The poison of sensationalism had entered his veins. . . . Let the hated capitalistic press give a front page column to the antics of some organizer and he immediately becomes the god of the leaderless rank and file. The cheapest gallery play, idle threat or giant boast is applauded by the members."

This ought to jar the good Dr. Babson's philosophy, and the last paragraph should also furnish the answer to Mr. Ben L. Reitman's question as to why "this bunch of pork-chop philosophers" are able so to frighten the capitalist class. But Dr. Babson is not the only one who has been thus "flim-flammed" by this terrible bogey man. The organ of the charity workers is so pleased with itself for having published so many sympathetic articles on syndicalism that it recently boasted in its columns of having done so; and one of its board of editors, a woman, wrote a ten-page article, sympathetically explaining the sabotage, violence and murder proposals of the Industrial Workers of the World.

A large number of the religious publications of the country have been making it a point to give space to the exploitation of "this great movement for the men lower down, who are shut out from the real labor movement because of its high dues and aristocratic tendencies." It is a favorite allegation of these writers, the falsity of which could easily be ascertained by a most superficial study, that the big labor organizations of the country are devoted to the interests of the high class mechanic. They glibly talk of "industrial unionism," without the slightest suspicion of what it would mean to society if worked out along I. W. W. lines. By "industrial unionism" these people mean "one big union" of all classes of labor in any one establishment. In a printing office, for example, the compositors, stereotypers, pressmen, delivery wagon drivers, scrubwomen, office boys, reporters and editorial writers, all would be thrown together in a single aggregation, with the certainty of endless wrangling among themselves, the magnifying of petty grievances and the paralysis of order and efficiency in the running of the business.

If these writers want to learn the truth about the syndicalist movement they need only study the syndicalist (I. W. W.) newspapers throughout the country—that is, those that are still in existence—and they will find that the organization, instead of becoming an important feature in the industrial life of the country, is already "shot to pieces" and has now become almost a negligible factor in the industrial situation. At the annual convention in Chicago last September, referred to by Ben L. Reitman, the delegates spent two weeks fighting the question of organization *versus* anti-organization, which means that it was a fight between the inside ring, composed of Haywood, Vincent St. John and other officers, and the rank and file, who, being anarchists, wanted to run the machine without any organization.

In other words, the Industrial Workers of the World are going through the same fight that the Socialist Party is going through. The Haywoods and Ettors, who were "fired" out of the socialist organization because of their fight on the machine, now have a machine of their own from which sooner or later they will be fired. The American Federation of Labor and the railway brotherhoods, with their three millions of members, pay absolutely no attention to these wonderful "high divers" and "hair-raising thrillers" who seem to make such a tremendous impression upon Mr. Roger W. Babson and a few impressionable magazine writers who ought to know better.

A SIDELIGHT ON PUBLIC EMPLOYMENT.

At the conference on "Working Conditions of Municipal Employees in New York," during the recent annual meeting of The National Civic Federation, Mr. Solomon Hecht, Associate Editor of the *Civil Service Chronicle*, offered testimony out of his knowledge and observation which ought to be of interest to workingmen with a leaning to the universal State ownership program. "It is a fact," said Mr. Hecht, "that for some reason municipalities are the worst corporations on earth to raise wages. * * * It is like pulling teeth to get a municipal corporation to take a hundred men and raise them one hundred dollars apiece. * * * When making up the budgets at the end of the year the only idea the Board of Estimate has is the tax rate. * * * It does not make any difference how much merit there is in regard to the salary rate. They may believe in it, but the budget is made up four days before election, and they are going to cut it out." For fifty years the New York firemen have been unable to secure any relief from conditions under which "the bravest men in the city of New York are kept on duty twenty and one-half hours a day four days out of five." This has been due in part again to the tax rate obstacle, and in part to general public suspicion of graft or a "loafing job" motive behind the demand for a two-platoon system.

Our socialist prophets would have us believe that there will be no more of this unbrotherly neglect of uninfluential odds and ends in the coming industrial commonwealth. They have not been able to show us in what respect the self-interest of this same general public will be different under "scientific distribution" from the self-interest which already so largely controls its attitude towards appeals from dissatisfied groups of public employees when they happen to be relatively few in number. Every such concession will reduce the fund available for everybody else and furnish the "social whole" with exactly the same ground for suspecting the motives and resisting the claims of minor groups which may not feel disposed to accept their assigned place and portion without protest.

If "the need of one is to become the concern of all," something more radical will have to come into the situation than any change the socialist program effects in the basic relation of the few to the many.

AN INTERNATIONAL CONGRESS ON SOCIAL INSURANCE.

(Concluded from page 11.)

until he was elected to the presidency of the French Republic. The chairman at this time is M. Bourgeois, formerly Premier of France. A large attendance of European experts is expected, and will be arranged for, affording the first and only opportunity on this side of the water for a free comparison of American views and ideas with those which have been born of experience in other countries.

Already in the United States within five years there have been enacted laws in no less than twenty-two States changing the basis of liability of employers from that of negligence to compensation for all industrial accidents; and in a large number of these States provision has also been made for insurance in State funds or in mutual funds under State supervision either as the only method or with choice of companies. By the time the Congress convenes there will be a considerable volume of American experience, which, although new and incomplete, will be valuable for purpose of comparison with the riper results of European experience.

THE "RULE OF REASON" IN TRUST REGULATION

THE PROBLEM OF JUST AND EFFECTIVE CONTROL OF COMBINATION AND COMPETITION DISCUSSED BY SPEAKERS AT CIVIC FEDERATION CONFERENCE

The problem of corporation regulation as affected by recent developments in the industrial and political situation occupied the second day of the Fourteenth Annual Meeting of The National Civic Federation. The conference was opened by President Low Friday morning, December 12, and continued during the greater part of the day. The report here given of this most timely and enlightening discussion is necessarily much condensed, but, as elsewhere stated, certain portions have been published verbatim in pamphlet form.

General Aspects of the Trust Question.

JEREMIAH W. JENKS, Professor of Government, New York University, said that in endeavoring to understand the question at issue we need first of all to free ourselves from the tyranny of words. Competition is not always a public benefit, nor is combination always a curse to the community. When competition results in the cutting of prices in certain localities while they are kept up in others, for the specific purpose of destroying a small rival, it is an evil and should be stopped. It is also true that competition between rivals of equal strength sometimes brings ruin to both and injury to the public. Eventually it is practically sure to lead either to an understanding between the competitors or to a formal combination.

Professor Jenks held also that where there are many small competitors in an industry, even with more or less understanding between them, it is, after all, competition that regulates the price. The opinion was cited of a prominent corporation manager, that the bringing into his combination of each additional member had increased the total efficiency and made it possible both to manufacture and to sell the product more cheaply. The same manager, on the other hand, agreed that the buying up of rivals simply to get control of an industry did not increase efficiency, and it was his belief that the burden should rest upon whoever attempted to form a combination, to show that it would lessen costs and result in public benefit. Professor Jenks considered this a sound test, but in applying it did not favor the fixing of a uniform percentage of output for all industries as the limit within which combination should be permitted. It should depend upon the circumstances in each case, and should stop at the point—whether 25 per cent or 75 per cent—where further increase of size would not add to efficiency.

More than half the industry of the country, the speaker believed, was of a nature such as could never be brought into combination dangerous to the community. This is true especially of industries which are chiefly dependent for success upon individual attention to small matters. Where very large capital is required to get the best results, combination is inevitable. What is needed is some public body through which to regulate injurious competition upon the one hand, and upon the other see that combination does not grow into monopoly, but is permitted wherever and so long as it can show that the public is sharing the benefit of the cheaper production.

"Should a manufacturer be permitted to fix the price at which the retailer may sell to the consumer?"

"Is the price cutting of department stores and other mercantile establishments a benefit or an injury to the public?"

E. W. BLOOMINGDALE, counsel of the New York Retail Dry Goods Association, in opposing the view that a manufacturer should be permitted to fix the price at which the retailer sells, maintained that when a manufacturer sells his goods he parts not only with ownership but with control. The dealer must then assume the entire risk, and if he happens to buy more than the trade will absorb, or if the demand falls off, or the season is unfavorable, what is he to do when his bills fall due and he is prevented from selling his stock for what he can get, under these conditions?

The fact that an article is widely advertised, the speaker urged, does not justify the assumption that it is commercially worth the price it is sought to charge for it. The retailer may properly, if he chooses, put the article on a price quality with other goods of equal merit upon which great sums have not been spent in advertising. His ability to do this, moreover, is a matter for which the manufacturer himself is largely responsible by reason of the discounts to large buyers. Instead of protecting the retail merchant, the fixed price system would in reality enable the manufacturer, after his goods were well introduced, either to raise his price to the merchant or reduce the market selling price and drive the retailer out of existence.

Mr. Bloomingdale pointed out that the large modern store must handle its stock as a whole, with varying profits on different lines of goods and at different times of the year in order that merchandise may be kept moving and the force steadily employed. The public gets the benefit of the special price reductions. These cannot be offset by higher prices on goods of a general nature, because in these days of sharp competition such an expedient would be apparent to the most inexperienced shopper.

Mr. WILLIAM H. INGERSOLL, of the Executive Committee of the American Fair Trade League, took the ground that justice both to the manufacturer and the small dealers demand protection against cutting of prices on proprietary articles. Mr. Ingersoll pointed out the pronounced tendency toward concentration in the retail field, citing especially the cigar and drug trades and the department stores with their later development of chains of stores throughout the country. Some ten thousand of these chain store systems are now doing business in the United States according to Boyd's City Dispatch. Attention was called also to the remarkable growth of mail order houses, and the speaker urged with reference to all these types of large scale business that the time may come when these great new middlemen will be able to dictate what the consumer shall buy and what he must pay for it, and what the manufacturer shall receive for his goods. If the success of these large enterprises is due to unworthy tactics, where dollars overbalance skill and the contest is merely a matter of brute force, then there is no evidence of their superior fitness in an economic sense over the smaller concerns.

This practice of offering standard goods, often below cost, creates the idea that they can be profitably sold at that price, and people are thereafter unwilling to pay their real value. Other dealers who cannot make these reductions and find themselves unable to sell the goods at the standard price cease to handle them. The community is then unable to get the goods conveniently and the market for the manufacturer has been injured.

The speaker held, therefore, that unnatural price cutting is really a restraint of trade. The manufacturer, he believed, should be entrusted with the duty of determining the price at which his goods shall be sold. To have a uniform price on an article of a given brand is no injury to the public so long as the manufacturer has no monopoly of the market. Such monopoly is impossible so long as he must sell his goods in competition with similar articles of other make. In place of dishonest advertising and ruinous price cutting we should have a measure permitting the regulation of prices by those responsible for the goods sold.

EDMOND E. WISE, counsel for R. H. Macy & Co., in the controversy between that firm and the American Book Publishers' Association, discussed the subject from the legal standpoint. The restricted price idea, he said, bears in it the menace that all trade-marked or branded articles will come under the control of combinations of manufacturers who will dictate the price, not by what they think is reasonable, but by what they think the traffic will stand. Mr. Wise did not believe that the great body of retail stores is suffering as had been claimed and pointed out that the trade of the small retailer is mostly in unprotected articles in which there is the utmost free play of competition. The fact was cited as significant that in a copyright case recently decided by the United States Supreme Court, an association of retailers, including 90 per cent of the trade, although parties to the action, refrained from appearing.

The right of price control, Mr. Wise stated, has been condemned as unlawful by four decisions of the United States Supreme Court. The prevailing principle of commerce and of law is that whoever purchases and pays for an article becomes its absolute owner for all purposes.

The speaker regarded as groundless the fear that the public will not be able to buy a useful article because of unrestricted competition in its price. Some one will be ready to supply whatever is in demand, and an article of merit will always find its market. The attempt to establish the first foothold in ultimate price control should meet with determined resistence or it will be followed by combination to establish such control on a wide scale with appalling possibilities of resulting evil.

In the course of further discussion of points involved, Mr. INGERSOLL urged that, as in the case of real estate, a sale may be made with restrictions as to what may be built upon the land, etc., so, he believed it proper that a manufacturer have the right to sell his goods under such agreements as will protect his other customers. He did not recommend price maintenance except with the safeguard that those who exercise it do not have a monopoly and do not favor some buyers over others, but that they shall take goods back if not salable at the price established. He did not believe we should permit the abuse of the names of standard articles of merchandise through wholesale price cutting by large dealers. This puts too great a hardship on those with small resources.

TALCOTT WILLIAMS contended that the right of price control can only be granted if a manufacturer will make his business so public that everybody will be certain that the restriction is not used to increase profits beyond a fair point. There is a fair profit as there is a fair wage and a fair rate for money. Until the manufacturers and the retail stores will open their books and make it clear that only a fair profit is asked, neither can be allowed to restrict prices nor take steps which will lead to monopoly.

In conclusion Mr. INGERSOLL made the point that it is very difficult when a given price is fixed to get more than that price. In other words, in establishing such price it is practically a maximum as well as a minimum. This he regarded as one of the great safeguards to the public.

Should the Sherman Anti-Trust Act Be Amended?

JOHN HAYS HAMMOND, chairman of the Federation's Department on Industrial Economics, characterized large scale production as the genius of modern industry. It places in the hands of captains of industry great power for good and for evil. The power for evil lies in abuses such as the unlawful restraint of trade, stifling of competition and controlling of prices, all tending to monopoly. Because of these abuses the term "trust" has earned much opprobrium, and trust-busting has become a powerful instrument in the hands of unscrupulous demagogues.

Mr. Hammond favored maintaining the basic principle of the Sherman law, but held that it needed further definition and modification. A Federal incorporation law or Federal license, for example, would insure control of one of the chief evils of big business, namely, the over-capitalization of corporations. There would be much less cause for public complaint if government regulation began at the point of incorporation of large concerns, instead of attempting later on to "unscramble the eggs." Another important benefit of Federal incorporation would be the protection of investors in securities and the confidence which would result from publicity.

The speaker acknowledged that there is a point at which large scale production may actually become inefficient and uneconomic, but did not believe that legislation could determine that point. Expansion will be checked by purely business considerations when the limit of economy is reached. Neither should limits be put upon the size of corporations expanding by development within rather than through combinations with other concerns which had been in competition. Corporations should be judged not by their magnitude *per se*, but by their dominant purpose, their methods, and how these affect the public welfare.

Unrestrained competition, the speaker held, often works irreparable injury to industrial communities in the form of lower wages, fluctuations in prices and loss of investments. By way of illustration, conditions in the bituminous coal mining field were cited. On account of the ruinous competition there prevailing, nearly one-half the coal cannot be mined except at loss, and is left in such condition that it can never be recovered. Germany and Belgium, through the Cartel system, have put the coal mining industry on a profitable basis which prevents this waste and has permitted improvements greatly reducing the loss of life.

The regulation of corporations involves problems so complicated and comprehensive that the laws governing them should be left to an Interstate Industrial Commission. Such commission should consist chiefly of business men, experts on economic subjects, and lawyers. The dignity of the commission should be on a parity with that of the Supreme Court, in which case it would appeal to the ambition of men of the highest ability.

The Trend of Proposed Legislation.

GILBERT H. MONTAGUE, of the New York Bar, reviewed at some length the various measures pending in Congress with reference to control of large combinations of capital. These bills, the speaker suggested, might be classified under four heads, following the lines of President Wilson's program of trust legislation outlined in his message to Congress of December 2d last, namely: "Further and more explicit legislation" in the "debatable ground" around the Sherman law; legislation to "clarify" the act; legislation to "facilitate its administration," and legislation to "make it fairer to all concerned."

Under the first head would come the bills dealing with practices not now forbidden under any construction of the Sherman law; besides numerous bills prescribing the organization and powers of corporations engaged in interstate and foreign commerce.

Most of the bills to "clarify" the act, Mr. Montague pointed out, have been drawn upon the assumption that the "rule of reason" established by the Supreme Court in the Standard Oil and Tobacco cases, recognizes two kinds of restraint of trade—reasonable and unreasonable. This assumption, the speaker believed to be inconsistent with much that the court said in these and subsequent cases, but it explains most of the bills designed to "clarify" the act.

Under the recommendation of legislation to "facilitate" administration of the Sherman law belong all the bills establishing trade commissions; and among those which may be classed as attempts to make the law "fairer to all concerned" are the measures exempting certain kinds of corporations. Senator Williams's bill, for instance, proposes to exempt corporations engaged in the business of education, common carrier, banking, insurance and supply of water, light, heat or power; Representative Henry's provides that the law shall not apply to members of organizations not for profit and without capital, nor to agricultural products or live stock in the hands of the producer or raiser.

Attention was called to the investigation about to be made by the Bureau of Corporations under the direction of the President, to determine how far economies have been attained in large scale production, and whether there is a point beyond which increasing organization induces waste instead of economy. Upon these facts, the speaker believed, must depend the whole trend of proposed anti-trust legislation.

The Bituminous Coal Industry and the Sherman Law.

C. M. MODERWELL, of the American Mining Congress, declared that laws or economic systems which result in the waste of our coal supply are wrong in principle and cannot be defended. This great industry, which produces for our factories the cheapest fuel in the world, is suffering because those engaged in it are not allowed to co-operate but must compete. The result is an average return of only 2½ per cent upon an investment of almost a billion dollars.

Because of inability to get a sufficient price, only the easily mined coal is produced, and in many cases 50 per cent is left in the ground and will never be recovered, or, if at all, at tremendous cost. According to the United States Bureau of Mines, 250,000,000 tons of coal were wasted in this manner in 1911.

Admitting the duty of the government to safeguard our coal deposits, ought not co-operation to be permitted under such regulation as will enable the operators to save for future generations the coal now ruthlessly wasted? The speaker showed by concrete illustration the struggling condition of various types of corporate and individual interests engaged in soft coal mining, which could only have the result of crushing the weaker producers out of existence and leaving the survivors with a monopoly of the market.

Agreements which would permit a reasonable return on the investment cannot be made as the law stands. They would not, the speaker believed, result in monopoly, by reason of the vast area of the coal deposits.

Mr. Moderwell advocated an Interstate Trade Commission on the lines of the bills suggested by The National Civic Federation and by the American Mining Congress. Such a commission would have power to inquire into all agreements and contracts to determine whether they unlawfully restrain trade or tend to monopoly. The plan for such a commission is designed to permit business men to conduct their business in accordance with economic principles and yet live within the law.

Are Agreements Between Organizations of Workingmen and Organizations of Employers, Fixing Rates of Wages, Hours of Labor and Conditions of Work, in Violation of the Sherman Act?

A. B. GARRETSON, chief of the Order of Railway Conductors, stated that the idea of bringing labor unions under the provisions of the Sherman act is of later growth than the relation of that act to other interests involved. He did not believe that at the time it was passed it was ever intended to apply to associations of workingmen. He was ready to admit that if such associations indulged in practices against the common good they should be punished, but the issue is, whether the means they employ are of a character that properly bring them under the act. Mr. Garretson believed that if the laboring man, utilizing the only power at his disposition to better his condition—that of combination—comes under this law, then the law is faulty instead of the man. The law applies to the employer only with reference to his products, not his individual ability and experience. The labor of the laborer is to him precisely what the administrative ability, experience and ingenuity of the manufacturer is to him. If the manufacturer wishes to withhold or enter into a combination to withhold his ability from the production of goods, he does not come under the provisions of the act.

If the laborer's one resource is to be counted a marketable commodity, then the Emancipation Proclamation was a mistake. If the combination of a large body of men is a greater sin than combination of a small number, then the railroad men and their employers are undoubtedly guilty in a greater degree than any other industrial class, since the agreements between the railroad companies and the men extend over half a continent and will undoubtedly be continued either until the term "unreasonable" is clarified by law or the courts have declared such agreements illegal.

Whenever it is apparent that laws of this character, instead of protecting the interests of the great body of the people which consists chiefly of laboring men, recoil upon them, they will demand the modification of such enactments. Mr. Garretson believed in government regulation, and considered the exercise of this power more needed in the matter of over-capitalization than in any other direction. With that abuse once removed, two-thirds of the evils now dealt with under trust legislation would disappear. No opportunity was asked for labor men to do illegal or criminal acts, but the right of any man to get the best that he can for his labor should not be made a crime. The speaker alluded to the failure of English legislation through many centuries to control or fix wages of labor, there having been more than 300 such enactments during the period from Henry II. to Henry VIII. There can be no real prosperity, he maintained, unless it affects the body of the people. Any measure that paralyzes the energy and progressive efforts of three-fourths of the people is an influence to destroy rather than upbuild the general prosperity of the nation.

SAMUEL GOMPERS, president of the American Federation of Labor, declared that already one organization of wage earners has been dissolved by order of the courts; that workmen have been indicted in New Orleans for affording co-operation to fellow workmen in another trade where wage reductions were threatened; that in Jacksonville, Florida, workmen have been indicted as conspirators because they withheld their labor from their employers; that President White and other officers of the United Mine workers have been indicted because of endeavoring to protect the interests of the miners in getting a fair wage.

The great coal strike of ten years ago, with all its hardships, brought changes in the material, social and moral wellbeing of the miners and their families that compensated them and compensated the community. In Mr. Gompers's opinion, not even President Baer, their stoutest opponent during that struggle, would now want to go back to the former conditions prevailing among the miners. To-day, nevertheless, all that they have gained is threatened by a combination of mine owners; and because the officers of the union have advised with the miners' representatives and sent them money with which to make the fight of resistance, they are accused of criminal conspiracy under the Sherman act. If put on trial and found guilty they may be imprisoned for a year and fined $5,000, and may be proceeded against civilly, their organization dissolved and their funds confiscated.

The American Federation of Labor and the Bucks Stove & Range Company have been jointly sued by C. W. Post under the Sherman act for the sum of $250,000, claiming $750,000, or three-fold damages, on the ground that the company and the Federation of Labor had come to an agreement, ending a long dispute. About three years ago a number of ladies in Philadelphia who wanted to help the girls in that city who were striking against sweat-shop conditions, were sued for $50,000 and three-fold damages by the shirt manufacturers, and the case is still in court.

The American Federation of Labor, it is true, has gained more than 250,000 in membership during the past year, but it is, nevertheless, true that there is not an organization of labor in the country which does not exist at the sufferance of the Government. Under the interpretations of the Sherman law there has grown up the judicial injunction limiting or prohibiting freedom of assemblage, freedom of speech, freedom of the press, and freedom of association—rights which should be jealously guarded, not only by workingmen but by all the people.

Mr. Gompers predicted that if these rights are denied to the working masses the community will have to contend with other and more dangerous elements. The movement of the working people to protect themselves is essential in this day of concentration of wealth and power in industry, with subdivision and specialization of work. They have no other hope than through this associated effort and collective bargaining to strive against oppression and to secure better conditions for the men and women who toil, better safeguards and opportunities for their children.

"Is the Protocol Between the Manufacturers in the Cloak, Suit and Garment Industry and their Men and Women Employees, which is Designed to Abolish the Sweatshop, Against Public Policy and Illegal Under the Sherman Act?"

JULIUS HENRY COHEN, counsel for the Cloak, Suit and Skirt Manufacturers' Protective Association, of New York, pointed out that many of the decisions against labor unions had been rendered under the common law, irrespective of the Sherman act, and therefore that no amendment of that act excluding unions from its operation would meet the situation.

In the English common law at present there are two diametrically opposite tendencies. Under it men may not combine to fix prices and eliminate competition, but, on the other hand, a group of people interested in improving their condition may combine and fix standards for that purpose. The fact that labor is not a commodity creates the possibility of a distinction between these two principles of the law, but the difficulty lies in the fact that we have developed our legal principles upon an economic philosophy which is now being outgrown. We are recognizing to-day the necessity of collective effort; that a manufacturers' trade association or a trade union can have just as worthy purposes as, for example, The National Civic Federation.

In a case like that of the protocol in the New York garment industry, where a group of manufacturers and a group of workingmen join hands to make conditions decent and establish arbitration, the agreement is attacked by manufacturers and non-union workers who do not wish to become parties to it. It would be a very serious legal question whether a combination could be made that provided for excluding non-union men from an industry, but under the protocol it is agreed merely that the employers will prefer union men, while the union, on the other hand, maintains an open membership.

Mr. Cohen believed that The National Civic Federation should co-operate with the United States Commission on Industrial Relations in its study of this whole problem, with a view to legislation, the end being to harmonize the tendencies of the law so that manufacturers may join to raise the conditions of an industry and working people may unite to raise their own conditions, and the public be protected not only against the danger and cost of strikes, but, as in the clothing trade, for example, against the wearing of unsanitary garments. There must be some clear determination of what the law should be with reference to these joint agreements, rather than an exemption amendment to the Sherman act, which would not cover the case, but would merely furnish opportunity for arousing public opinion. The speaker agreed with Mr. Gompers that serious results would be likely to follow the stifling of the opportunity of business men to organize or of workingmen to raise their standards.

WORKING CONDITIONS OF MUNICIPAL EMPLOYEES IN NEW YORK CITY.

The remainder of the afternoon session was devoted to a discussion of the needs of municipal employees, by Mr. Joseph J. O'Reilly, editor of *The Chief*, and Mr. Solomon Hecht, associate editor of *The Civil Service Chronicle*.

Mr. O'Reilly gave a forceful account of the situation in respect to such matters especially as the appointment of new policemen and firemen, importance of extending the merit system, protection from unjust removal, an equitable retirement law, standardization of equipment, vacations, more definite and certain employment for the large army of per diem men in the irregular service of the city, better wages for patrolmen, street cleaners and firemen, and the two-platoon system for firemen.

Mr. Hecht discussed many of these matters in further detail and urged, in addition, the semimonthly payment of salaries and stricter rules covering the selections for promotion in the civil service. Mr. Hecht pointed out some of the defects in the workings of the firemen's pension system, and made a strong argument for the two-platoon system for firemen, to remedy conditions which are "keeping the bravest men in the city of New York on duty twenty and one-half hours a day, four days out of every five."

CO-OPERATION THE NEED OF THE HOUR IN PURE FOOD CAMPAIGN

EMINENT AUTHORITIES PRESENT THE SITUATION AND URGE THE NEED OF UNIFORMITY AND MORE EFFICIENT REGULATION

During the conference on Pure Food and Drugs at the afternoon session, December 11, 1913, of the fourteenth annual meeting of The National Civic Federation, the following resolution was offered and unanimously adopted:

"Resolved, that in the interest of greater purity, proper labeling and honest advertising of foods and drugs, The National Civic Federation be requested to organize a commission for the study of the subject of foods and drugs, and for the purpose of furthering co-operation between the Federal and State officials, the consumers and the producers."

In accordance with the above resolution The National Civic Federation is now engaged in organizing a commission to work for these important objects, and public announcement of its personnel and plans appears elsewhere in this number.

The chairman of the special session on food and drug control was Mr. Samuel Gompers, President of the American Federation of Labor. The subject was discussed by the following speakers, whose remarks are summarized below:

James H. Wallis, President of the National Association of Food and Dairy Commissioners.

Dr. Harvey W. Wiley, Former Chief of the United States Bureau of Chemistry, Department of Agriculture.

Dr. George Ditewig, Inspector in the Bureau of Animal Industry, United States Department of Agriculture.

Charles Wesley Dunn, Author of Dunn's Pure Food and Drug Legal Manual.

Miss Laura A. Cauble, Bureau of Food Supply, Association for Improving the Condition of the Poor.

Papers which could not be read on account of the lateness of the hour were submitted by:

Louis Runkel, President of the American Specialty Manufacturers' Association, and

Albert Plaut, former President of the National Wholesale Druggists' Association.

James H. Wallis.

The first difficulty in the way of efficient enforcement of food and drug laws has been a lack of effective co-operation among food and drug control officials. We have been deficient also in the quantity and quality of educational work. True, we have sent our bulletins to the consumer, warning him against the frauds and impositions which we have detected in his food supply and in his drugs, and in these same bulletins we have given him the names of those food and drug manufacturers and dealers who have sold him the adulterated and misbranded articles. We have informed him of the dire consequences which the officials of the State have visited upon these manufacturers in the way of fines and other penalties.

This has been good work, but it has not gone far enough. There is not a food and drug official of experience who does not know that ninety per cent of the violations of food and drug laws, both State and national, have been caused largely by the ignorance or carelessness of the manufacturer and not with a wilful intent to produce and dispose of adulterated and misbranded articles. Ten per cent, perhaps, of the prosecutions are against manufacturers who deliberately offer debased, deleterious, adulterated and misbranded foods and drugs, and as against this latter class of manufacturers the penalties provided in various laws have been woefully deficient. But how about those manufacturers who have sinned because of ignorance? Have we done our full governmental duty when we say, let the manufacturer beware, let him put out foods and drugs at his peril? Does not such a policy lose sight of the end sought to be attained, which is to secure as quickly as may be possible a pure food and drug supply for the people? Shall we not attain that result more quickly if we educate our manufacturers, show them how to produce pure foods in a cleanly manner and spread information regarding methods of adulterating drugs, largely perpetrated by the foreign producer upon the American importer who buys in good faith?

The great majority is honest. It is not right, it is not even politic, to confound the great mass of honest manufacturers with the sordid, dishonest minority. A distinction should be made. Increase the penalties against the dishonest and educate the honest. If this be done there will be fewer court cases, because there will be fewer violations of the law.

The food and drug control work in the United States is not fifty per cent efficient. This is startling, but it is true. Where is the trouble? How is it possible with a mass of food and drug legislation, with zealous, competent and honest officials attempting to enforce the laws, with generous appropriations, with public opinion strongly behind the work and with a friendly press and helpful judges, that there is not greater efficiency?

The answer is found in defective organization and utter lack of correlation of several branches of what really is but one subject. This trouble has its root in the laws of the Federal government and in the laws of the States.

This is where The National Civic Federation can help us food officials. We must secure basic changes in these national and State laws, and this association can help materially.

To be efficient we must have all of the activities relating to the protection of the bodily welfare of the citizens combined into one organization. It must be done in the nation and it must be done in each State. I do not care whether we have a national department of health with its head sitting as a cabinet officer. It is not the name and position that count. It is the effective organization which, no matter what it may be called, can group together this widely scattered work and combine under one head and one direction all of these separate forces really working for a common end.

Consider the deplorable condition which exists now. Each activity has its own administrative and executive force, separate clerical and inspecting forces, separate laboratories and experts, separate filing and housing. Think what this means in waste of money and energy, and that is by far the lesser waste. The paralyzing thing is the absence of one broad, far-reaching plan which takes into account all that can be done by each separate line of endeavor and welds the whole into one irresistible engine of progress.

First, we must have national legislation which shall recognize the principle by placing within one organization the various and many health activities of the Federal government. This organization, when created, must be directed to co-operate with the State organizations which will be patterned after it. Every dollar of appropriation for health work must be made to do its work. In cities and towns where government laboratories are located the municipal and State laboratory work should be done in the government laboratory. The Federal government should clothe the State inspectors with all the powers held by Federal inspectors, and the State likewise should make the Federal inspector the agent of the State. The legislation, Federal and State, should be uniform, and if the States are to follow the national law the latter must be progressive and adequate to remedy evils which must be met. When these things are done we shall secure results.

Dr. Harvey W. Wiley.

I want to emphasize first of all my enthusiastic adherence to the program of future work in this great field of ours, which has been outlined by President Wallis. I have for many years been preaching the doctrine that all the health activities of this great government should be centred in one, but there is a very bitter opposition in this country to making any more effective the laws to protect human health. Some of it is religious in its attitude, some of it is academic, some of it is ignorant, and a lot of it is vicious.

The interests which were affected by the passage of the Food and Drug Law were determined in some way to paralyze its effectiveness. They first came to me and said: "You do not intend to carry into effect these doctrines you have been preaching before the committees of Congress? You do not intend to keep preservatives and coloring matters out of foods?" I said: "I am going to do the best I can at it. I have nothing to say about it, except to bring a case, and the Bureau of Chemistry is the only authority in the Federal government that can bring a case. I am going to cite every one of you who continues these practices before the courts." And they said: "That will ruin our business!"

"Yes," I said, "I am going to ruin a business which is striking at the very fundamental principle of human happiness, health and life. You are feeding to the people of the country drugs which they should only use when they are ill and sometimes not then, and giving it to them without their knowledge, and to everybody, young and old, and if I have my way about it you are going to stop it."

I was not simply guessing at it. Many years before this law was enacted I saw the prophecy of it and thought I would be ready for it, so in 1902 I organized that body of young men afterward famous as the "Poison Squad." For five or six years I kept feeding these healthy young men these things which the manufacturers were putting into foods—borax and salicylic acid and sulphate of copper and burning sulphur—and I never failed to find them injurious, sooner or later.

So these people went above me to the Secretary of Agriculture and to the President of the United States. That was in 1907. They told their story in their own way, that if I were not shackled and gagged their business would all be ruined. The President and the Secretary did not know the facts. They listened to these men, who were influential men, business men in high standing. The law said that all questions in regard to adulteration and misbranding should be decided by the Bureau of Chemistry, but they made a new law. It happened often in those days; all you had to do was to sign an executive order. So the President signed an order creating a board to decide the very questions which the law said I, as chief of the Bureau of Chemistry should decide. He took all these things they wanted him to take out of my hands. Borax and salicylic acid they let go, and borax and salicylic acid are unknown to-day in the foods of this country. The Remsen Board was created—men of eminence in their professions. The question of whether or not these things were adulterations and injurious to health was put into the hands of a body of men unknown to the law, and the law was ordered suspended until they should report. They overruled me on benzoic acid and there is not a manufacturer in this country to-day, if he wants to, who cannot shovel all the benzoate of soda he wants into every product he makes. Fortunately the people of this country would not stand for it. Public opinion was so outraged that we refused to eat these benzoated foods, and they are now almost unknown in this country through the force of public opinion.

The whiskey manufacturers wanted a dispensation and they got the Secretary of Agriculture on their side. Then I went straight to the White House, an act of disobedience for which I should have been removed then and there. I saw Mr. Loeb and the President promised that he would not give any decision without first consulting me. Then the delegations came from all over the country—every "rectifier," every man that diluted alcohol, that colored it with calomel, and made ten-year-old whiskey in a minute—they came to the President, urging him to approve this decision of the Secretary of Agriculture. But I got a message, some six weeks after this, to come to the President's office, and he listened to me for two hours and a half. He referred all the briefs and papers to the Attorney-General, whose decision sustained the Bureau of Chemistry in every particular.

Immediately we placed the law in force against the rectifiers. They went to court and tried to get out an injunction to prevent the execution of this order. We had fought that in eight Federal courts and had received an affirmative opinion in every single instance from Baltimore to Peoria. Every one of them appealed it to a higher court, and then there was a change of Presidents. When Mr. Taft came into office he questioned this decision on whiskey and ordered a new hearing before Solicitor-General Bowers; then held a hearing of his own in the White House with the Secretary of Agriculture and Attorney General Wickersham. The decision was absolutely in favor of the rectifier on every point, and orders were issued to change all the old regulations. Appeals were dropped, and to-day whiskey is any kind of old alcohol you want, colored and flavored, as far as official pronouncement is concerned.

There is only one legal interpretation of the food law, and that is what the court says about it, but the only way for the court to act is either through a State official or through the Bureau of Chemistry. Here I was stopped, but a State official carried the benzoate question to the courts. The Department of Agriculture sent the whole referee board to testify in this case against the State of Indiana that benzoate of soda was a perfectly harmless substance.

The Secretary was asked to allow me to testify on the side of the State, and he refused to let me go. They moved the court to Washington, and I was d to appear with the young men whom I had ex- mented on, and we did, and we won the case. It carried to the Circuit Court, and the Circuit rt unanimously affirmed the decision, and now it be carried, I have no doubt, to the Supreme rt.

ttorney-General Wickersham himself, before he office, gave an opinion to the Secretary of Agri- ure that the opinions of the Remsen Board had binding effect on anybody. Yet there are about iteen or twenty of these decisions, legalizing all ls of offenses against the law, and saying they not misbranding or adulteration.

o, through the whole list of concessions, the food has been maimed and paralyzed. Therefore, n we ask our friends, the State officials, to come 1 us and have uniformity of legislation let us have clean hands. The Secretary of Agricul- says he is going to ask Congress to restore the to its pristine vigor and give back to the Bureau Chemistry its rights. Hold the chief of the bureau ponsible (and I think he is a good one) as I ild have been held responsible, and gladly would ave assumed the responsibility for administering great law in the interests of the people of the ted States.

believe from the bottom of my heart that all these ities for the protection of health should be ught under one head, but meanwhile let us do best we can with what we have, and not lie su- sly idle waiting for a better law. Let us get all good we can get out of the present law. We get a of it.

he greatest wealth of this nation is its health. I I think by joining forces with the State officials with the great public opinion we can correct all se evils. We will put the law above the interests- will put it in a position where no mercenary in- ests can touch it, because it will be a law for the fare of the people of this whole country.

Dr. George Ditewig.

'ederal meat inspection is limited to the product establishments that are engaged in interstate or sign commerce. It is estimated that a little more n one-half of the total meat supply of the United tes comes under Federal inspection. Most of the nainder receives no inspection whatever, while a tion is subjected to a limited inspection by State local officers. It is a duty which the State or nicipality owes to its citizens to install and main- n a system of meat inspection that will afford ade- ate protection against diseased and unwholesome ats, so that all meat sold locally which has not sed the Federal inspection will come under the uirements of an efficient local inspection system.

ne effect of the Federal inspection has been to se the owners of diseased or suspicious-looking mals to send them for slaughter to an uninspected ce rather than to an establishment where they ld have to run the gauntlet of strict inspection. these reasons it is certain that the percentage of ease is much higher among animals slaughtered the small local places than among those slaugh- d under Federal inspection.

uninspected slaughter houses, as a rule, have ny features that are not only objectionable but gerous to health. The conditions at some of the ntry slaughter houses are inexpressibly foul and ly. Usually there is no protection to the meat inst rats, flies, other insects and vermin, and this dition is a dangerous source of contamination and ection. Even in some of the large cities there are ter abattoirs which do a purely local business, and which the conditions and methods are exceedingly sanitary, and where a very poor class of live stock slaughtered.

f a system of local inspection is to provide ade- ate protection to the health of the community it ould cover absolutely all meat offered for public e and which has not been subjected to Federal other competent inspection. All places of slaugh- should be subjected to inspection and regulation, d permitted only by license. If the sale of un- pected meat is allowed, or if any slaughtering ce is allowed to remain uninspected, there will be nger to the health of the community.

Dr. Ditewig in conclusion showed a large number stereopticon pictures illustrating the work at ughter houses under Federal inspection as con- sted with the bad conditions at places operated thout inspection.]

Charles Wesley Dunn.

The need for uniform food and drug legislation has n urged continually and earnestly by all who have en any consideration to the subject. In 1904, two rs before the enactment of the Federal Food and ugs act, Dr. Harvey W. Wiley addressed the Com- ssioners on Uniform State Laws, earnestly urg- them to consider the uniformity of food and g laws. Since the enactment of the Federal law the Commissioners have recorded their recommenda- tion each year that the food and drug laws be uni- form. In 1904 and in 1909 the Committee on Purity of Articles of Commerce reported to the same effect. The American Bar Association has concurred in these recommendations.

The National Civic Federation in 1910 called a national conference in Washington to promote uni- formity of commercial legislation, and by resolution strongly urged that the food and drug laws be uni- form. Many other organizations have taken similar action. This general, spontaneous and insistent movement for uniformity through various agencies demands respect and consideration.

There exist in this country three kinds of food and drug regulation—national, State and municipal. And as products are subject to both the special and gen- eral laws (where there is no special law) we have at present a bewildering and rapidly increasing mass of legislation difficult to follow even to those who are somewhat familiar with this class of legislation.

[Mr. Dunn quoted at length from government sta- tistics showing the variations in standard bushels for a large number of the common necessities of life, and in the legal standards for dairy products in the several States and Territories. Differences in the laws of many States were also pointed out with ref- erence to various food products and drugs.]

There should be a national poison law on the statute books, carefully and scientifically framed to safeguard the sale of poisons by labelling or what- ever requirements in particular instances may appear just and equitable. Such a national law would serve as a model, and would stimulate similar State legis- lation. A national narcotic law would serve a simi- lar purpose and a uniform pharmacy law would equally regulate the trade in medicinal and poison- ous preparations.

Standardizing of regulation will establish rules of guidance for the various administrative officials, who, through collaboration, may all be equally pos- sessed of the information necessary for their work. An efficient, fair and just uniform law protecting the consumer and placing no unnecessary or unrea- sonable hardship on the manufacturer and dealer is not a burden to the manufacturer or dealer, as it merely indicates the practice of the honest man.

I am deeply impressed with the magnitude and completeness of this meeting, probably the most im- portant, from many aspects, that has ever been held in the consideration of this subject. It is a matter of the greatest satisfaction and pride to the people of this nation that such an organization as this ex- ists, and is a living vital force, the melting pot of all those interests and influences which are in any way connected with this field, official, commercial or lay, to mold and cast public opinion, as it were, and bring forth the greatest good for the greatest number.

Miss Laura A. Cauble.

Miss Cauble discussed the subject from the stand- point of domestic science. She described briefly the conditions encountered in her work among the poor, on behalf of an association which has for years ex- pended annually about $60,000 in the direct provision of food. Miss Cauble pointed out the need of domes- tic science training adapted to the needs of children in the common school grades. Especially is this im- portant in the poorer districts, where the great ma- jority of the children do not get beyond the first year in the high school, and where the children of parents who cannot speak English become very often the family buyers of food products. Alongside the need of pure and wholesome food products, in other words, is the importance of their better utilization in the home, through education in marketing, in economical use and in proper methods of cooking.

Louis Runkel.

The products manufactured by members of the American Specialty Manufacturers' Association cover almost the whole field of packaged foods and are pro- duced in enormous quantities. I would like to call to your attention the fact that the advent of the branded food has been one of the most potent factors for better foods in this country. A manufacturer who puts out his foods over his own signature, under his own brand, thereby standardizes his products, and their subsequent sale depends entirely upon their merit. Purity, wholesomeness, quality and honest weights or measures, and honest labels, once borne home to the consumer, backed by the reputation so earned, make the manufacturer's name the most val- uable asset in commerce—whose mere mention means the confidence of the consumer.

The American Specialty Manufacturers' Associa- tion originated some five years ago. Our constitu- tion pledges us to co-operate in the enactment and enforcement of just and equitable food laws, and I am proud to state that we have endeavored to live up to our constitution in every way. If our methods may be improved, if our conditions of manufacture may be made more sanitary, if our formulas may be bettered, if any improvement is possible, mechanical or otherwise, we would heartily welcome it.

As in any other calling of life, you will find dis- honest food manufacturers, men who will cheat and defraud, and even, I am sorry to say, injuriously adulterate their products. But I am sure that that class is small and becoming smaller, and that the majority of the food manufacturers of this country are honest, law-abiding and God-fearing manufac- turers and citizens.

Our association is as much against such fraudulent manufacturers and dealers as are the national and State governments, as we realize that, aside from public considerations, a special weakness reflects upon us all to some degree, and we offer you our hearty support against such practices.

Honest weights and measures legislation is a sub- ject in which we have been actively interested. We have always firmly believed that the consumer is entitled to know the quantity he is receiving and thereby assuring full weights and measures. Such a practice is ordinary honesty, and claims no more merit than any proper action should claim. When the question arose of a weights and measures law for New York State, we at once took an active interest in en- couraging and aiding this proposed law, and we did not cease working until the present law was enacted.

One of the greatest difficulties food manufacturers have to contend with is the lack of uniformity in the pure food laws. The legislation in this field is very extensive. We do not object to regulation, no matter how severe, either as to manufacture or labelling, if it is at all reasonable and just and equitable in the final interest of the consumer, but we do ask most earnestly that such a regulation when determined should be uniform throughout the land, so that we may most economically distribute our products, which is to the benefit of the consumer.

On behalf of the American Specialty Manufac- turers' Association I pledge to all who are repre- sented here to-day that our association as a whole and each individual member, will offer you any aid in our power to the end that the pure food laws of this nation shall be more effective, more efficiently ad- ministered and more fully complied with.

Albert Plaut.

I do not agree with the statements which are fre- quently made that notwithstanding the enactment of the Food and Drugs act, adulteration of food and drugs is carried on in a wholesale way and that the public health is thereby endangered. The affairs of the drug business I know intimately, and I deny that there are any evidences of adulteration or miscon- duct coming under the Food and Drugs act which ought to cause alarm to anybody.

Ninety-five per cent of the drugs sold in the United States are supplied in a wholesale way by compara- tively few manufacturers and dealers. These are all large and responsible firms, having staffs of chemists in their employ constantly watching their output, and I am sure that the public is well served as far as its supply of drugs and medicines is concerned.

In substantiation of these statements I need only refer to the small number of convictions that have been obtained under the Food and Drugs act on drug products. I have looked over the notices of judg- ments issued by the United States Department of Agriculture from No. 1500 (June, 1913) to No. 2572 (to date) and among them I have found only 25, surely a very insignificant percentage.

Among these many have been obtained through the desire of government officials, not so much to ameliorate existing conditions, as for the moral and political force of the number of convictions. The casual observer and a goodly number of people who have to be fed on sensationalism will naturally be more impressed by a large number of convictions obtained by the department, showing its diligence, than by an actual betterment of conditions and few convictions.

The lack of standards for food products and those drugs not found in the pharmacopoeia has helped the Department of Agriculture in obtaining a large number of convictions. Manufacturers and dealers will willingly comply with the standards if they are known to them. We have to give Dr. Alsberg credit for promulgating such standards now; if they had been furnished from the beginning, the manufac- turers, the dealers and the public would have bene- fited far more than from convictions obtained for in- fractions of the law caused by the lack of standards.

I am against all amendments of the Pure Food and Drugs act at the present time. It has given the Gov- ernment the necessary authority to control the manu- facture and sale of foods and drugs, and nobody can say that the law is not well administered. In my opinion, it would require quite an effort on the part of any druggist to obtain in the open market any- thing but pure and standardized drugs and drug products, for I for one do not know where any other can be purchased.

LEADERS CONFER ON WORKMEN'S COMPENSATION

REPORT OF THE JOINT COMMISSION AND DISCUSSION UPON THE OPERATION OF STATE LAWS, METHODS OF INSURANCE AND ACCIDENT PREVENTION

The subjects of workmen's compensation and accident prevention occupied the third day, Saturday, December 13, of the Fourteenth Annual Meeting of The National Civic Federation. AUGUST BELMONT, Chairman of the Federation's Department on Workmen's Compensation, in opening the conference, called attention to the fact that during the last six months the Federation's Joint Commission on Workmen's Compensation had made an exhaustive study of compensation legislation in this country. Representatives were present at the conference from several of the States visited by the commission and whose experience under the new acts has been of significant interest.

Work of the Joint Commission.

The members of the Joint Commission, whose report is now in press, are:

Chairman, Cyrus W. Phillips, member of the former New York State Commission on Employers' Liability; Rochester, N. Y.

J. Walter Lord, Chairman of the Maryland State Commission on Employers' Liability and Workmen's Compensation; Chairman of the Federation's Maryland State Council, Baltimore, Md.

Otto M. Eidlitz, of the New York Building Trades Employers' Association, New York City.

Louis B. Schram, Chairman Labor Committee, United States Brewers' Association, Brooklyn, N. Y.

James Duncan, Vice-President American Federation of Labor, Quincy, Mass.

John Mitchell, Vice-President American Federation of Labor, Mount Vernon, N. Y.

Chairman PHILLIPS' report for the Commission recalled the fact that the first real recognition in this country of the principle that the cost of industrial accidents should be charged to the industries causing them was given in the report of the New York Commission on Employers' Liability, created by the Legislature of 1909. Since then, compensation laws have been enacted in twenty-two States, and more than five million men and women have come under their protection. Two million more would be added on January 1 by the new compulsory acts in California and Ohio.

The objections raised by either employers or employees, before the enactment of these acts, said Mr. Phillips, have been mostly removed by experience under them. Employers have freely stated to the Commission that although the new law costs them more they were mistaken in their original opposition and would oppose any effort to repeal it. They are very strong, however, in desiring uniformity of laws. They have often asked, also, in States where the law was elective, that it be made compulsory in order to put all employers on the same competitive basis.

Employers generally prefer that the law cover all their work people in order to avoid uncertainty as to whether an injured employee comes under the compensation act or the liability law. Where the act is limited to hazardous trades, it often happens that employees in a business coming under the act will receive compensation for comparatively slight injuries, while others suffering much more serious injury in a trade not classed as hazardous receive no compensation. Workmen will not understand the reasons for these conditions.

The speaker described the different practices in the several States in regard to medical attention and hospital aid. The charges for this service have often proved excessive, and plans are being considered for regulating and reducing the cost without injury to the workman.

In order to insure prompt payment of the compensation without litigation or expense, industrial accident boards have been created in a number of States. All settlement agreements between the employer or an insurer and the employee must be filed with and approved by these boards. The Commission found that these boards are giving general satisfaction, and, by contrast, that in States where no such safeguard is provided the door for fraudulent imposition upon the workmen is open. The case of New Jersey was cited, where the Commissioner of Labor has no power to investigate and it is evident that only part of the settlements are reported to him. Many of those reported show that the employees do not receive the amounts to which they are entitled, and the Commissioner estimates that nineteen per cent of the New Jersey settlements are contrary to the compensation schedule fixed by law.

The amount of compensation in different States varies from fifty to sixty-six and two-thirds per cent of the wages of the injured employee. Not much complaint has been heard from employers in States paying the higher rates, the important thing appearing to be that the schedules be scientifically drawn and that the terms of the laws be definite and certain, and, as already stated, uniform as between the States.

Upon the difficult problem of protecting injured workmen against insolvency of the employer, the Commission found great diversity of views. There was agreement that the workman was entitled to as full protection in this respect as possible, but at the same time a strong feeling among employers against being restricted in their method of insuring. Many wish to carry their own risk, some want power to create mutual insurance companies, and in most States laws have been passed permitting this. Others prefer to insure in stock companies and some in a State insurance fund created by assessment upon employers. It was generally felt that with industrial accident boards passing upon all settlements, both employer and employee would be protected under any of these three methods and the employer would receive the benefit of the competition between them.

The Situation in Maryland.

J. WALTER LORD, a member of the Joint Commission and Chairman of the Maryland State Commission on Workmen's Compensation, stated that Maryland was the first State to enact a law (in 1902) partaking of the nature of a compensation act, and intending to secure exclusive compensation in case of death in certain extra hazardous industries. In 1910 an act was passed limited to coal and clay mining, under which employers and employees were required to contribute largely to a fund from which the injured man, or his dependents in case of death, were paid compensation. This was a compulsory act and has proved satisfactory, but is limited in scope and inadequate in amount of indemnity.

The Legislature of 1912 considered many compensation bills, but the subject was little understood and no satisfactory measure was passed. Last May the Governor of Maryland appointed a Commission to study the subject and draft a bill for submission to the next Legislature, to meet January 1, 1914. This Commission has given six months of very careful study to the problem and has reported its proposed act, which has been printed and circulated not only in Maryland but outside the State.

The Commission in its report favors a compulsory act applying to all trades, but for constitutional reasons permits employer or employee under certain conditions to elect whether its terms shall apply.

The Commission in preparing this bill was unanimous in the opinion that State insurance would not be the best form of compensation, particularly in the State of Maryland, both on account of the narrow average of risk and the probability that State insurance would not tend to reduce the number of accidents, as does direct compensation.

California's New Compulsory Law.

WILL J. FRENCH, of the Industrial Accident Board of California, explained that the new compulsory compensation act in that State, to go into effect January 1, had three essential features: Compulsory compensation, a State insurance fund and a safety department. The 65 per cent rate of compensation provided in the existing elective law is retained in the new legislation. The California law will have a new feature, so far as this country is concerned, in that it will take into account in case of accidents the nature of the injury or disfigurement, the age and the occupation. The loss of earning power will be considered and a schedule is being prepared for each industry, so that both employer and employee will know the amount that should be awarded in given cases. For instance, Mr. French pointed out, a bookkeeper who might lose a foot would receive less than a structural iron worker for the same accident, not because in the large sense any man can be compensated for such a loss, but because the bookkeeper can still go on with his work, while the iron worker must find some other occupation.

The employer will have the option of insuring with the State against compensation risk, or with one of the regular companies authorized to do business, or with a mutual company, or may carry his own risk. To provide against the contingency that an employer may not be able to pay compensation, the law makes certain provisions which the speaker illustrated in the case of the building trade. I[illegible] sub-contractor is unable to pay compensation, [illegible] principal contractor is held liable, and if nec[illegible] sary the owner of the building, the result of wh[illegible] is that no owner will let a contract and no c[illegible] tractor a sub-contract unless each respectively c[illegible] ries insurance.

The safety department in the California law [illegible] considered very important. Negotiations are n[illegible] under way with a safety engineer to go to C[illegible] fornia from the Middle West. In place of the m[illegible] usual practice of specific safety laws, Califor[illegible] follows the Wisconsin plan of permitting the Ind[illegible] trial Commission to issue rules and regulations a[illegible] hearings at which both employers and employ[illegible] may be present.

Mr. French stated that in California there [illegible] been a marked change in sentiment, which is n[illegible] practically unanimous in the belief that trans[illegible] ence of the burden for industrial accidents [illegible] deaths to the industry is the better way of h[illegible] dling the problem.

State Insurance on Trial in Ohio.

WALLACE D. YAPLE, Chairman of the Ohio Ind[illegible] trial Commission, in discussing the new compuls[illegible] compensation act of 1913 in that State declared t[illegible] in his judgment the most vital question involved [illegible] a compensation law is whether each employer sh[illegible] bear his own burden of insurance, or choose the fo[illegible] of insurance, or be required to adopt some par[illegible] ular form of insurance. The present compuls[illegible] act was made possible by the passage of a con[illegible] tutional amendment in 1912.

The speaker maintained that the people of O[illegible] thought that if it is a proper exercise of the pol[illegible] power of the State to provide workmen's compe[illegible] sation, it is also a proper governmental function [illegible] provide the machinery by and through which [illegible] compensation is paid. It was felt that a law sho[illegible] not only provide for compensation, but should ma[illegible] its receipt certain and definite through the medi[illegible] of a fund administered by the State. Mr. Ya[illegible] presented a comparative table for many different [illegible] dustries, giving the compensation rates now char[illegible] under the Ohio State plan and by private insura[illegible] companies in Michigan and Wisconsin, tending [illegible] show that the rates in Michigan are more th[illegible] three times those under the Ohio system, and [illegible] Wisconsin almost four times.

The law requires employers to contribute to [illegible] State insurance fund unless the Industrial Comm[illegible] sion finds that a given employer making appli[illegible] tion is financially able to pay compensation and [illegible] nish medical attendance direct, in which case [illegible] necessary authority may be given him. An [illegible] ployer who contributes to the State fund is [illegible] liable to damages unless the injury or death of [illegible] employee is caused by the employer's wilful act [illegible] is due to the violation of safety laws, in which c[illegible] the employee may, if he choose, enter a suit in [illegible] courts instead of filing a claim under the compen[illegible] tion act. However, out of more than 15,000 injur[illegible] under the new system thus far the Commission h[illegible] been advised of only five such suits. In connect[illegible] with the State fund there is an organized medi[illegible] and claims department through which awards [illegible] made on an average within nineteen days after [illegible] filing of the claim.

Under the elective act of 1911 more than 3,[illegible] employers, employing nearly 200,000 wage earne[illegible] have become subscribers to the State insura[illegible] fund, contributing thereto nearly $1,000,000. It [illegible] estimated that more than 20,000 employers, hav[illegible] more than 1,000,000 employees, will be affected by [illegible] new compulsory act and that annual contributio[illegible] to the State fund will be not less than $3,500,000.

The speaker made the point that under the O[illegible] system a claim for compensation does not assu[illegible] the nature of a controversy between the emplo[illegible] and employee, since the claim of the latter is agai[illegible] the insurance fund, and every honest employ[illegible] while interested in protecting that fund from [illegible] ploitation, is also interested in seeing his inju[illegible] employee receive the exact amount of compensati[illegible] provided by law.

Another View of the Ohio Experiment.

CLARK B. FIRESTONE, President of the Fi[illegible] stone Bank of Lisbon, Ohio, was unable to appr[illegible] the State monopoly of industrial insurance, which [illegible] characterized as the distinguishing feature of t[illegible] Ohio law. In that respect he considered it t[illegible] worst law in the country, by reason of its den[illegible] of American traditions of free association [illegible] service or profit and its rejection of the benefits mpetition. He had never heard any reason for is feature except the assertion of Governor Cox at the accident and casualty companies of Eng- nd and Holland were trying to rule Ohio. The eaker suggested this "vision of the Dutch peril" d undoubted frauds in the referendum petition as obable reasons for the Governor's refusal to grant e people of the State the right to vote upon the bject.

Mr. Firestone maintained that the figures which d been given by the previous speaker were com- risons, not with what Ohio had proved it could do the line of economic management, but with what hoped to do in the future. He considered any fig- es misleading which are based upon what insur- ce companies pay under employers' liability in mparison with rates under workmen's compensa- n.

'ith the general principle of workmen's compen- ion Mr. Firestone was heartily in accord. Atten- was called to the fact that inequalities in many our laws must be remedied and that an undue or to an injured workman does injustice to the njured, by loading his industry with burdens ch will make it suffer in competition with ers. Mr. Firestone figured that under the Ohio as much as $30,000 might be paid in cases of l disability.

'he Ohio law, he believed, when amended in re- ct to the State fund, would do more than com sate for injury; it would prevent it. It has vi- zed neglected portions of the factory act and led ployers to instal safety appliances and protect nts of danger. The speaker also believed that leaders of labor may be confidently expected to ing home to their followers the necessity for doubling their caution in avoiding accident, lest ey entail upon industry a burden which would mper its ability to pay the living wage.

A Labor Opinion on the Michigan Law.

CLAUDE O. TAYLOR, President of the Michigan ate Federation of Labor, maintained that the im- rtant end to be attained in compensation laws is t the paying of money to the injured employee, but e preventing of accidents in the first place. The chigan law, which he believed the best in the untry, has reduced fatal accidents during its first ar from two a day to less than one and a half, d during the last six months to less than one. n-fatal accidents have been reduced from one ndred a day to less than sixty-five. The Michi- n law is so equitable that it has not caused hard- ip to the employer, who is able to adjust conditions d spread the expense upon the cost of production. e success of the law, in the speaker's opinion, was e to the fact of co-operation both in the planning d the passage of the act. Organized labor met th the large employers and there were two labor en on the Commission appointed by the Governor, ose report was adopted without change by the gislature.

Under the Michigan law an employer may insure mself through State insurance, self insurance, mu- al insurance, or stock company insurance. Mr. Tay- was at first in favor of State insurance, but stated at in Michigan it is practically a farce, for the rea- n that when a case comes to the Industrial Acci- nt Board for appeal, recourse is allowed to the At- rney General's office against the employee as to ether he should receive compensation from the ate fund or not. The mutual companies and the lf-insured employers and stock companies are do- g the chief work for the prevention of accidents, d in Detroit one large corporation pays $5,000 a ar to a safety expert. "Safety first" is also the ob- t of the mutual companies. In Lansing $38,000 has en spent in the last six months for the prevention accidents. Michigan intends to keep an eye on ws passed in other States with a view to possible provements in its own law, but in studying the sults of other acts the significant points would not how much is saved to the employer or the ate, but how much is given to the man for whom e compensation is written; how many accidents e prevented, and how many workmen are saved their families.

stacles to Compensation Legislation in Pennsylvania.

Prof. FRANCIS H. BOHLEN, of the University of nnsylvania, Secretary of the Pennsylvania Indus- al Accidents Commission, regretted that Pennsyl- nia experience at least did not confirm the belief at the principle of workmen's compensation is now cepted everywhere without question. He had found at among the State senators, most of them law- rs of the old school, the idea of responsibility thout fault was repulsive in the last degree. The nnsylvania compensation act failed in the last gislature, and the line-up in the Senate seemed be largely that of city against country, the sup- rt coming mainly from the cities. Prof. Bohlen l not, however, consider that this was due to the clusion of agricultural employees in the act. Personally he could not see why agriculture and domestic service should be excluded. The decisive opposition came from a class of employers who had been for years practically free from legal responsibility in respect to accidents. The Pennsylvania Commission is still in existence, however. A compensation bill would be introduced in the next session of the legislature and the speaker had confidence that it would pass.

The Weak Point in the New Jersey Law.

LEWIS T. BRYANT, Commissioner of Labor of the State of New Jersey, declared the compensation law in that State to be one of the most practical and workable in the country, but greatly limited in effectiveness by the fact that employers and employees may enter into settlements at variance with the compensation schedules in the law. Settlements are constantly being made for amounts less than the law provides that an injured workman shall receive. In illustration of this, Commissioner Bryant cited cases in which $425 was due and $250 paid; $168 due and $151 paid; $282 due and $257 paid; $114.25 due and $41.50 offered, of which $14 was to be returned to the employer; $1,500 due a family for death of a workman and $380 paid; $1,500 due and $650 paid. Of the settlements actually reported to the department, nineteen per cent are found contrary to the legal schedules. Mr. Bryant maintained that some proper authority should have supervision and power of approval of all such settlements in order that injured employees may be protected in their rights.

PREVENTION OF INDUSTRIAL ACCIDENTS.

LOUIS B. SCHRAM, Chairman of the Compensation Department's Committee on Improvement of State Inspection of Factories with Special Reference to Safeguarding Machinery, opened the second division of the day's program. Mr. Schram pointed out that the work of The National Civic Federation in connection with accident prevention had taken on several phases. For one thing, the accumulation of accident statistics had been advocated for a long time in the belief that the work of prevention would be effectively aided by systematic recording of accidents and study of their causes.

Mr. Schram believed that the mutual insurance feature provided for in the new compensation law in New York would do much not only to solve the question of workmen's compensation, but to bring about more effective prevention of accidents. Opportunity would be given for grading premiums according to the safety of various plants, and an employer would soon find that the fewer his accidents the lower would be his premium rate.

The National Civic Federation also has advocated the establishment of museums of safety. State museums such as exist in many European countries are an important factor in showing employers the best ways and means of avoiding accidents. These exhibits tend to remove the wrong impression many employers have that safeguarding machinery means expenditure of large sums of money.

In speaking of the model safety act which had been prepared by the Federation, Mr. Schram explained that it was not to be regarded as a perfect measure, but that it is the result of the best available thought and practice as a pattern for legislation in the several States.

Safety Management Must Accompany Safety Devices.

JOHN CALDER, former President of the International Motor Car Company, of New York, and former inspector of factories in Scotland, said that at one time it was thought a sufficient protection against accidents merely to provide physical safeguards. The speaker knew from his experience as manager of large establishments employing from 3,000 to 8,000 men that seventy per cent of the accidents have nothing to do with unprotected machinery. After the physical safeguards are provided there must be safety management. If the foremen are careless or neglectful, accidents will continue. The foreign laborer especially does not know the risk; the things men will do from sheer ignorance are almost unbelievable. That can be removed by good supervision. With the machinery once protected the greatest hope for accident prevention is the permeation of our industrial plants and their managers with a sense of social responsibility; that they have not discharged their duties unless they have delivered the product to the consumer and the man to his home.

Mutual Compensation Insurance in Massachusetts.

DAVID S. BEYER, of the Massachusetts Employees' Insurance Association, said that any employer in the State may become a member of the association, but retains the option of insuring with one of the authorized liability companies, or of staying outside the provisions of the act entirely and relying upon his common law rights.

The membership of the association has more than doubled within a year, and it now numbers more than 900 subscribers, employing about 130,000 working people, or about one-fifth of all the employees in manufacturing industries in the State. Only one of the twenty commercial liability companies writing workmen's compensation insurance in the State on an equal basis of rates exceeded the volume of business handled by the new association during its first six months, although it was working on a purely competitive basis without State aid of any sort.

The Employees' Insurance Association has made safety of employees its first consideration. It has nine trained safety engineers, each insured plant is inspected from two to five times during the year, 7,660 specific safety recommendations have been submitted to subscribers, covering more than 20,000 danger points, and more than 97 per cent of these have been adopted by the members. This indicates first that the recommendations were practical, and second, that the members were quick to realize the advantage of carrying them out and thus cutting down accident loss.

State insurance, the speaker held, arouses suspicion on the part of business men from the danger of inefficient management and political influence. With a mutual company the subscribers themselves have complete supervision of the management, and it is clear to the members that every accident prevented means a direct saving to them in the form of increased dividends.

Settlements have been upon a liberal basis, and in more than 90 per cent of the cases the regular compensation payment has been made promptly the first of each succeeding week. In only 43 cases out of about 15,000, or 99.78 per cent, has it been necessary to call upon the Industrial Accident Board for a decision. In all others the association has made settlements automatically under the act. This is in striking contrast to the long delays, costly litigation and incidental injustice and discontent prevalent before the act was passed.

The rates first put into effect have been reduced, but dividends of 20 to 30 per cent have been paid to subscribers on all expiring policies. Liberal reserve allowances have also been made. The association has a system of merit rating which gives a plant the benefit of reduction in premium for specified safety conditions, and this system has since been adopted practically in all details by nineteen of the leading stock liability companies for use in Massachusetts.

Safety and Health Promotion.

DUDLEY M. HOLMAN, of the Massachusetts Industrial Accident Board, was called away during the conference, but submitted a copy of his address. It is estimated by those who have made a study of the subject, Mr. Holman states, that 50 per cent or more of industrial accidents are preventable; that 25 per cent can be avoided by adoption of safety devices, and 25 to 40 per cent eliminated by educational work.

In Massachusetts during the year ending June 30, 1913, there were 476 deaths from industrial accidents, and 89,694 accidents reported to the Industrial Accident Board. If one-half these accidents were preventable, nearly 250 lives might have been saved, and an army of employees would have been kept at work. Under the compensation act practically $1,677,380.82 was paid out during the first year for compensation and medical attendance. The cost of insurance under the act during the same period is estimated at $4,000,000. If compensation and medical treatment alone could have been reduced 50 per cent $838,690.41 would have been saved to Massachusetts employers.

The Massachusetts legislature has empowered the Board of Labor and Industries and the Industrial Accident Board, jointly, to order the installation of safety devices and to make rules and regulations covering occupational diseases. In carrying out this work the Board has decided to establish a museum of safety as a clearing house of information for employers and employees. Among other educational means for promoting industrial safety stereopticon lectures, moving picture slides and education in the schools are considered of great value. Safety experts agree that the mere installing of safety devices will not suffice without the hearty co-operation of superintendents, foremen and the employees and their shop committees.

Mr. Holman favors the requirement that machinery manufacturers shall put on proper safety appliances before the machines leave the factory, as already provided by law in some States. There should also be insistence on fire drill, both in schools and business places, and upon the equipment of buildings with fire escapes and automatic fire prevention sprinklers.

The obligation to provide proper safeguards in respect to sanitation and industrial hygiene, as well as machinery, should rest upon the employers and machinery makers, and not upon the inspectors, who can only be occasional visitors. Special bulletins of various trade risks and practical remedies, such as are already being sent out by The National Civic Federation, the National Association of Manufacturers and other agencies, should form a part of our educational task.

DEPARTMENT STORE REPORT SUPPORTED BY CRITICAL ANALYSIS

PRESIDENT LOW REVIEWS THE OBJECTIONS RAISED BY THE CONSUMERS' LEAGUE, AND STATISTICIAN JOSEPH A. HILL SUSTAINS THE ACCURACY OF THE REPORT AT EVERY POINT.

SINCE the publication of the last number of the REVIEW, some of the criticisms upon the report of the Welfare Department on working conditions in New York department stores, discussed in that issue by Mr. W. R. Willcox, chairman of the Department, have been repeated by Mrs. Frederick Nathan, president of the Consumers' League of New York, in a letter sent to members of the Executive Committee of the National Civic Federation. Under date of December 29, President Low replied to Mrs. Nathan's communication, enclosing a statement from Mr. Joseph A. Hill, head of the Division of Statistics in the Bureau of the Census, Washington, to whom the department store report and the criticisms upon it had been submitted for critical analysis and opinion. Mr. Hill is recognized as one of the most competent experts in his profession in the country.

PRESIDENT LOW'S REPLY.

The principal portions of President's Low's reply to Mrs. Nathan's letter are as follows:

December 29, 1913.

"Your letter of December 10, addressed to me and to many other members of The National Civic Federation, has been referred to me for reply. In view of your most unusual course in communicating with the Federation otherwise than through its president, I must ask you to let me have a list of those to whom your letter was sent, so that my reply may surely fall into the hands of those who have received your unfavorable comments upon the report of the Welfare Department of The National Civic Federation with reference to department stores.

"Let me observe, in the first place, that the Welfare Department does not claim for its report any other weight than that to which it is entitled upon its merits. The Department has been scrupulously careful to inform the public that the expenses of the investigation were met by the department stores themselves; it has given the names of the public accountants who are responsible for the figures as regards wages; and it has also given the name of every expert employed or consulted in connection with the investigation. The public, therefore, by the action of the Welfare Department itself, is perfectly equipped to form its own opinion upon the merits of the report.

"So far as I am informed, neither you nor any other critic has questioned the accuracy of a single fact stated in the report. If any inaccuracy is pointed out the Welfare Department will be glad to admit its mistake; for the Welfare Department is anxious, above everything else, to have this question considered by the public in the light of facts rather than of theories.

"In view of the criticism of the Department's report made by Miss Van Kleeck, the secretary of the Committee on Women's Work of the Russell Sage Foundation, the Department's report and Miss Van Kleeck's criticism and the various *Survey* articles were sent to Mr. Joseph A. Hill, head of the Division of Statistics in the Bureau of the Census, Washington, with a request that he examine both the report and the criticism and give to the Federation the benefit of his opinion. I have the pleasure of handing you herewith Mr. Hill's reply, which I have been authorized to use in this way. Mr. Hill was turned to as a competent and presumably unbiased judge of the statistical questions involved in Miss Van Kleeck's criticism and the various *Survey* articles tains the assumptions and the arguments of the Welfare Department upon every point raised by Miss Van Kleeck; and he makes clear that, upon every point discussed in the Welfare Department's report, which has also been covered by governmental inquiry, the conclusions reached by the Department on the basis of this investigation coincide with the conclusions of the governmental investigators.

"In response to your observation that it is undesirable to have any part of the expenses of such an inquiry as was made by the Welfare Department met by the firms under investigation, let me point out that in making the fact public the Department relieved itself of any just criticism that might otherwise attach to this course. Your comment must mean then, either that the public accountants would be swayed from their duty because they were paid by the Federation with money received from the Dry Goods Association; or else, that the Department itself could not be impartial in its conclusions because the investigation was made possible in this way. So far as the accountants are concerned, the examinations of banks and insurance companies in the State of New York are, by law, paid for by the companies examined. The reputation of an accounting firm is at stake in each investigation it makes. So far as the Welfare Department is concerned, you have failed to notice, I think, that the Department, in undertaking to make the investigation upon these terms, specifically pledged itself to report what it found, whether its findings helped or hurt. I regret that any of our fellow workers in the field of social uplift should attempt to discredit the report of the Welfare Department under those conditions on this ground. The fact that the conclusions reached by the Welfare Department on the basis of this investigation coincide so closely with the conclusions of the United States investigators, carried on from time to time under the authority of the Government, should, however, serve to set your mind at rest in this particular instance.

"You protest that any report on the general conditions of wage earners which does not go more thoroughly into the subject of overtime, and puts, on the other hand, so much emphasis on welfare work, is of necessity misleading in its general conclusions. I am greatly interested to know whether this statement is based upon exact information in your possession on the subject of overtime, or whether it is a mere impression. The Welfare Department frankly stated that the information secured as to overtime did not cover all the stores examined. The report, however, distinctly recommends that overtime work be discontinued except in cases of emergency; and that overtime be paid for on the basis of time and a half for evening work and double time for holidays and Sundays. If you have facts in your possession which justify a different conclusion, I shall be greatly obliged if you will furnish them to me so that the Federation may make such a study of them as the importance of the subject deserves; but if the facts are not at command, how is it possible for you, or any one else, to say, with authority, that the report of the Welfare Department is misleading in this particular?

"You suggest that 'such subjects as ventilation and sanitation should not be regarded as welfare work but as basic requirements in all establishments, and that to refer to them as welfare work gives a false impression to employers and the public.' I agree with you in thinking that ventilation and sanitation are basic requirements; but I think you are mistaken in assuming that the effort to improve sanitation and ventilation is not properly described as welfare work. George William Curtis used to say that 'the only way in which a man could be as good as his father was to be better than his father;' by which he meant, I suppose, that the standards of each generation ought to be higher than the standards of the generation before. It is evident that buildings which may have met reasonably well the standards of five, ten, fifteen or twenty years ago do not come up to the standards of our own time. It seems to me, therefore, that it is welfare work of the most usefu character to encourage improvement in ventilatio and sanitation in all existing buildings, and to er courage the provision of the most desirable arrang ments in all new buildings; so that each new buildin constructed may carry the standard of actual prac tice upward and forward as far as possible. I thin you are mistaken in believing that to call efforts suc as these welfare work gives a false impression t either employers or the public.

"It is scarcely necessary for me to add anythin to Mr. Hill's comment upon the headlines of the We fare Department's report. Yet it seems desirable t point out that there is a school of thought whic believes that every social ill is traceable to a economic cause. Writers of this school have nc hesitated, very recently, to place a stigma upon th many thousands of women working in departmen stores in the effort to induce the public to accep the correctness of their theories. At least, I ca imagine no other explanation of many of the article and items which have appeared recently in some c the magazines and in our newspapers. If, therefor you think that the headlines of the Welfare Depar ment's report are scarcely consistent with a seriou and scientific study, I submit that they are at lea very human and well calculated to help to dispel a opinion which is cruelly unjust to every good woma employed in a department store.

"What you call 'the inaccuracies and misinterpret tion of the data of this report, which have bee pointed out in detail by Miss Van Kleeck,' are show by Mr. Hill to be, on the contrary, inaccuracies an misinterpretation of the report itself on the part c Miss Van Kleeck.

"While I have attempted to show that the u favorable comments of the Consumers' League upc the report of the Welfare Department of the N tional Civic Federation are not well founded, I wis to assure you, for myself and for my colleagues in th Federation, that we have the highest possible appr ciation of the aims and purposes of the Consumer League; and we regret that the League and the Fe eration do not see eye to eye in this particular."

MR. HILL'S STATISTICAL ANALYSIS.

The report by Mr. Joseph A. Hill, enclosed wi President Low's letter, is a study in close detail the several features of the report called in questic by Miss Van Kleeck, including the use of average the comparisons between wages in department stor and in factory occupations, and the facts and expe testimony upon which the Federation based its co clusion that the department stores are not a recru ing ground for white slavery. By reason of lack space, it is not possible to present Mr. Hill's stat ment in full, nor is it practicable to give in abstra an adequate impression of its exhaustive and co vincing character. It is perhaps sufficient to no that as the net result of his examination, Mr. H reaches the following conclusion:

"In the report of the Civic Federation the prese tation of wage rates for the women employed in t department stores in the City of New York appea to be reliable, complete and scientific. The sourc of data are frankly stated. The stores included a given by name so that any one may have an oppc tunity to judge whether the results may be accept as typical. The wage earners are classified acco ing to kind of work done, and then according to ra of pay, with percentages to show what proporti of the total falls within each pay group. Averag are presented for the totals of all establishmen combined and also for each individual establishme I can see no indication either in text or tables of a attempt to mislead the reader or disguise the fact

AN INTERSTATE TRADE COMMISSION.

(Concluded from page 5.)

firm, corporation or locality to any undue or unreasonable prejudice or disadvantage in any respect whatsoever."

This general phraseology has enabled the Interstate Commerce Commission to put an end to every unfair practice in railroading as any such practice is brought to the notice of the Commission. A hearing is had, the actual thing complained of is passed upon, as to whether it is fair or unfair, lawful or unlawful, and then the defendant is told what he must do, as to the particular thing complained of, in order to bring his action within the law. There is nothing uncertain about it; there is nothing arbitrary about it. On the contrary, the general phrase is given a specific meaning, the significance of which no one can misunderstand. There is, of course, an appeal to the courts from the determination of the Commission; but the appeals that are taken are few in comparison with the number of objectionable practices that have been abated by virtue of this authority. It is believed that an Interstate Trade Commission, acting under general authority such as this, could put an end to one unfair practice after another, existing in actual business, as such practices were brought to its attention either through its own discoveries or upon complaint. It is submitted that language such as this, which has been repeatedly interpreted by the Supreme Court of the United States, is both more searching and more comprehensive than any specific definitions could be, and that this plan is desirable in continuation of the work so well begun by the Attorney-General, in addition any specific definitions concerning what is unlaw under the Sherman Law, if such definitions a made.

There appears to be no way except through t agency of an Interstate Trade Commission to secu uniformity of interpretation of the Sherman Act a uniformity in its application to business through series of administrations. The proposed law, the fore, so far from being an agency for the arbitra control of business, is to be an agency to help bu ness men to determine whether what they are doi or proposing to do, is probably lawful or unlawf and we believe it to be of not less importance to t consuming public. For to them it would afford agency, always accessible, for the full and pub consideration of serious complaints.

A REMARKABLE YEAR OF PROGRESS

MMARY OF REPORTS OF DEPARTMENT CHAIRMEN PRESENTED AT THE FOURTEENTH ANNUAL MEETING OF THE NATIONAL CIVIC FEDERATION

HE following annual reports of the chairmen of departments of The National Civic Federation were presented during the Thursday morning ion (Dec. 11) of the Thirteenth Annual Meeting, he Hotel Astor, New York. President SETH V occupied the chair.

WOMAN'S DEPARTMENT.

ISS MAUDE WETMORE, chairman: The work the chairman of the Woman's Department of e National Civic Federation has to report is one reorganization. Ten and a half months have psed since The National Civic Federation held its nual meeting here in New York. Since then the oman's Welfare Department has become the oman's Department, and is of equal standing with e other departments of The National Civic Fed- ation. Permission has been granted it to deal with dustrial economics as affecting women and chil- en; including the question of wages and hours; king up as well legislative work, but with the un- rstanding and assurance that the Woman's Depart- nt would never act on legislative questions inde- ndently of, or conflicting with, The National Civic deration.

This larger scope of work has enabled our de- rtment to respond to the offers of co-operation ich have now naturally come from other organi- tions. No report can be made as regards this work it is still in the early stage of construction.

Mr. Low has appointed Mrs. Harriet Blaine Beale d Miss Thalia Brown representatives of the oman's Department on the Committee of Plan d Scope, for an inquiry in relation to the "mini- um wage." Mr. Low also appointed twenty-five omen of our department on the Advisory Council the Industrial Economics Department, to help in e reorganization of this department of The National vic Federation.

On October the 15th the chairman, accompanied Mrs. Archibald Hopkins, Mrs. Francis McNeil acon, Jr., Miss Robinson Smith and Miss Elizabeth orter, went to Knoxville, at the invitation of Mrs. orace Van Derventer, the president of the Woman's epartment of the National Conservation Exposition, explain the object of our work. The day was nown as "The National Civic Federation Day," and e outcome of this visit will be the formation in e very near future of a Tennessee section.

Five delegates of the Woman's Department were nt to the National Conservation Congress which met Washington, D. C., on November 17, 1913. Al- ough the chairman has to report the discontinuance the Congressional Section, it is gratifying to know at our membership has increased from 1,436 to 779, and that Mrs. Woodrow Wilson has followed hat we hope will now become a tradition of the hite House, that the wife of the President of the nited States be always the honorary chairman of e Woman's Department.

The chairman of the Government Employees Com- ittee reports the formation of a National Committee n Prison Reform, but the work is practically only now eing organized. The Assistant Secretary of the reasury is considering the plan of asking the Presi- ent to extend the executive order issued by the st Administration and place under the Bureau of ublic Health all government buildings in the United tates. It is also gratifying to know that this sug- estion did not come from the Woman's Department, ut because of the work the department has ac- omplished in Washington. The extension of the xecutive order means that where an officer of public ealth is stationed the Woman's Department would ork in co-operation with him as it does with Sur- eon-General Blue in Washington.

The National Vacation Committee is gradually es- ablishing branches and mailing-in stations in differ- nt parts of the country.

The Metropolitan Section for New York and New ersey has much of interest to report, but lack of pace permits of but a few words to be said con- erning the most important committees.

Navy Yard Committee.—At the Brooklyn Navy ard the Men's Co-operative Association has run the estaurant most successfully, showing a profit on une 30 of $505, thus allowing the Association to eclare a 10 per cent dividend. The month of Octo- er, 1913, showed a profit of nearly $100.

The School Committee, after a careful investiga- on from a selected list of over sixty-seven schools, arried to a successful issue its campaign for a sufficient number of perfectly equipped retiring rooms, suitable for lunch purposes for teachers in each public school. The findings of this committee, endorsed by different educational organizations, local school boards and teachers' associations, were presented to and passed on by the Board of Education. On September 27 the section was notified that the superintendent of school buildings had been authorized to purchase the necessary equipment with money already on hand for the schools of Manhattan and Brooklyn. Those of the Bronx, Queens and Richmond were laid over until 1914, when more funds will be available.

The growth of the Vacation Committee's work in the Metropolitan Section speaks for itself:

Stations existing to-day in New York........	120
Girls opening accounts with the Vacation Savings Fund	14,000
Deposited by working girls in the two years of the Vacation Savings Fund's existence..	$101,000

The Society for the Prevention of Useless Giving was founded. It has enabled thousands of girls to continue saving their earnings at Christmas time, which earnings, until very recently, the "collective giving" and the "exchange system" had during that period pretty well eliminated.

The Committee on Occupational Diseases is at present investigating the effect of treadle work on women. An expert investigator is gathering the information, but her report will not be finished before the first of the year.

The District of Columbia Section continues its wonderful work in the Federal buildings of Washington. The new building of the Bureau of Engraving and Printing, soon to be opened, will be a model factory. Tumbling machines for the cleaning and disinfecting of mail bags in the General Post Office are being installed. The matter was brought before the proper authorities, and the acceptance of our suggestions means probably a far-reaching reform throughout the United States. The death rate in this division alone has run as high as 32 per cent.

The housing problem has been thoroughly studied, and a bill bearing the President's stamp of approval is shortly to be introduced in Congress. It provides that in ten years' time the alleys of Washington will be entirely done away with. Many of them are to be converted into minor streets, and in the meanwhile no new dwelling houses are permitted to be erected.

The question of making use of schools as social centres is one which has long been agitated by many organizations in Washington. Recently, under the auspices of the Woman's Department, a meeting was called at the White House by Miss Margaret Wilson, chairman of the Recreation Committee, and every society interested in this work was invited to a conference. The Woman's Department, acting as a "clearing house," encouraged a general and concerted action. Two bills, approved of by over a hundred organizations, are the result of this meeting and their enactment into laws is almost assured.

The Massachusetts and Rhode Island Section is ever busy with its factory and mill inspection. The Vacation Committee has taken a firm hold in Boston, and is gradually increasing its membership. With the consent of Governor Pothier of Rhode Island, the State institutions are being visited and the hope is entertained of ultimately improving conditions which to-day fall far below our modern standards.

A system of drinking water along the lines suggested by the Federation is being installed in one of the large textile plants. The management furnished our committee with specifications and the cost of installation. This system is being offered to other manufacturers, with the result that the mill community is discussing the problem and four manufacturers are considering its introduction.

Statistics from hitherto unavailable sources covering infant mortality in a large textile city have been compiled and verified, comparing the mortality of the children whose mothers had worked in mills with that of the children whose mothers had not.

The chairman of the North and South Carolina Section reports no new work undertaken, but a general broadening on the old lines at Spray. Four trained nurses, where formerly one only was employed, are busy caring for the sick and teaching the well how to live and make their homes comfortable and attractive. A resident physician is always on hand, and a dispensary has been established.

The Virginia and West Virginia Section reports growing interest in welfare work throughout these States, but no increase of membership, as the advantages derived from a national organization are not yet understood.

The Georgia Section in the past year has prepared, published and distributed through factory neighborhoods series of "Health and Right Living" bulletins.

In the spring of 1913 the Southern Sociological Congress met in Atlanta. An important place was provided for the work of the Woman's Department upon the crowded program of this busy gathering. The new work of inspecting jails and prisons has been largely covered by the Georgia Section, and a report will be made in the near future.

The Florida Section is investigating, for possible improvements, all jails, the county prison farm, the county hospital and State reform school.

Half holidays in business establishments have been suggested, and a change in the hours of opening and closing for the benefit of the employees.

The Woman's Department has a right to be proud of what it has accomplished in 1913. Its broader scope of work enables it to take its proper stand among the national organizations of women in this country. We are keen to occupy the same relative position among women that the Civic Federation does among men. We are a "clearing house," working for unselfish, universal co-operation. We gladly extend the hand of fellowship; our dearest wish is to have it cordially grasped.

DEPARTMENT ON WORKMEN'S COMPENSATION.

AUGUST BELMONT, Chairman: We have been working in this Department since 1908; first, to create, through public discussion, an interest in the subject of workmen's compensation for industrial injury arising out of and in the course of employment; and, second, to provide a model compensation act for uniform State legislation.

The National Civic Federation gave the first impetus in this country to the agitation for workmen's compensation, by its discussion at the annual meeting of 1908, preceding the appointment of the first State Commission—that of New York. This Commission had for its purpose a study of the subject of employers' liability and work accidents. It completed its work by recommending legislation, which was subsequently enacted.

The principle of workmen's compensation is, first, that industry in general should bear the burden of accidents rather than the particular person who happens to be its victim; and, secondly, that this can only be accomplished through the agency of the employer, who, in computing costs and fixing the price of his finished product, can and shall include in it the resultant losses. Human shortcomings that affect industrial operations being broadly considered, the question of direct fault is not material. The fact that loss of bodily faculty and regular wages occurs entitles the victim to compensation, unless his injuries have been received with willful intention. This is to-day's concept of a social obligation. It is interesting to note how it has worked out in the various States now under compensation laws.

[Mr. Belmont here traced the history of the Federation's efforts in behalf of uniform State legislation upon the subject, including the special campaign carried on in New York, culminating in the adoption last November of a constitutional amendment under which the legislature has already enacted a compensation law. Mr. Belmont also described the work of the Civic Federation's Joint Commission of six, appointed last July, which has been collecting data and visiting various States, from Massachusetts to California, in which compensation laws are in operation. Each of these phases of the Federation's work in connection with the subject was treated at length in the December issue of THE NATIONAL CIVIC FEDERATION REVIEW, and further particulars appear in the report of the Workmen's Compensation session at the recent annual meeting, published elsewhere in this number.]

As may readily be understood, our commission has gathered a larger amount of testimony bearing on every point of the compensation question than has been possible to any other agency. Whereas study of the question hitherto has been for specific, and at times self-interested, purposes on the part of attorneys or insurance companies, or has been conducted by official commissions having in view the conditions of industry in their own States, the Federation's commission has covered sufficient area to represent in effect all interests in the entire country. While a general summary of its findings may be given in brief space, the full report warranted by the large collection of facts will necessarily make a good-sized volume.

The present purpose of the investigation is to give to legislators and friends of the compensation movement everywhere the sifted results of the country's total experience upon the subject. It will be in a definite form which it is believed will meet the new problems that have arisen in the workings of the more or less experimental acts now in force. The information will also be of great practical value as a basis for recommendations which may be made for the drafting of a new model workmen's compensation law by the Federation. * * *

A large advance demand for the report of our commission has developed from citizens and organizations interested in proposed legislation in the various States having the matter under active consideration. * * *

There has been a great demand for the Federation's Model Safety Act. Its principles were the basis for the reforms in the labor laws of New York State last year which were of great moment.

The original draft of this proposed safety act has been improved through criticisms and suggestions from commissioners of labor, factory inspectors, members of safety boards in manufacturing concerns, labor representatives and other experts, and may be said to represent the best thought on the subject.

Employers in States where compensation acts are

AUGUST BELMONT,
Chairman Workmen's Compensation Department.

in existence have applied to us for our uniform accident reporting blank, and this we consider very encouraging, since it is practically impossible to draw conclusions from statistics existing to-day, because of the varied methods of recording and tabulating. * * *

The differentiations between workmen's compensation and various forms of social insurance are bewildering to the lay mind. As we are just beginning in this country to consider seriously the problem of caring for wage-earners in times of sickness and invalidity through accident and old age, it is right that at the outset we should discriminate and plan for each condition of disability upon correct lines, if possible, in order to avoid the pitfall of increasing pauperism, as seems to have been the result in Germany.

The correlation between accident compensation, sickness and invalidity insurance and old age pensions in Germany has brought this subject of social insurance before our Legal Compensation Committee, of which Mr. P. Tecumseh Sherman is chairman. The information so carefully collected by that committee, in connection with its special line of inquiry, will prove of especial and immediate value to our Welfare Department, which is already doing practical constructive work in the field of social insurance. Through its Committee on Wage Earners' Insurance, of which Mr. George W. Perkins is chairman, it has been and is devoting itself to the encouragement of employers' and employees' voluntary relief associations. It has for its further object an investigation of the need for uniform legislation covering sickness and accident relief, pensions and death benefit associations.

It seems to be the common assumption on the part of public speakers and magazine writers that there are great systems of social insurance in vogue in Europe, which if in effect here would prevent nearly all the suffering and distress from sickness among our poor. While that seems to us now to be misleading, in view of Mr. Sherman's investigation, it is apparent from the questions arising that the subject should have the most careful study. * * *

A number of vitally pertinent questions, which we can here merely indicate, suggest themselves in the light of Mr. Sherman's careful study of these experiences. What, for instance, can be done wisely and helpfully for the better protection of working people against misfortunes not covered by accident compensation? Do we see a solution in any of the various voluntary systems of workmen's insurance in vogue in this country, such as the trade union benefit features, the establishment funds and social societies? Would the foreign methods of sickness and invalidity insurance prove practical in a country having an immigration population so large as ours, or where so considerable a proportion of the working people frequently move from place to place and change occupations as opportunity may present? If voluntary methods of providing this class of insurance would prove inadequate, can we apply it through any workable compulsory scheme, under American conditions? If made a compulsory charge upon employers, for instance, would it be transferred by them to labor in the form of wage reductions, as some predict, or would the expense be added to prices and thus borne by the consuming public at large, or would the employers find themselves obliged to make good this added cost through new economies and better organization of industry?

We shall have to ask ourselves further, in facing this whole question of sickness and invalidity insurance, what is the meaning of the fact that the volume of poor relief in Germany has not diminished, nor has the cost of treatment, nor the average term of sickness? Is it true, then, as Price Collier has put it, that "the people are sick by being paid for it," and why is it that the neighboring wage-earners of France, thrifty by nature, obstinately oppose the adoption in their country of the German invalidity and old age insurance?

They insist that they can make this provision better for themselves.

We find in this connection that the voluntary system in France, whereby sickness insurace is carried in workingmen's self-managed mutual associations, with moderate government subsides and employers' contributions, secured through an attractive system of honorary membership, is yielding most significant results. The number of insured has increased from less than 2,000,000 in 1898 to about 6,000,000 at the end of 1912, while the showing of maintenance expenses is much more favorable than under the German method.

May not this French system prove, from the standpoint of our conditions, one of the most promising experiments in this perplexing and tremendously far-reaching field of social insurance? It demands at least our careful consideration, once we recognize the obligation resting upon us to at least move in this matter beyond our present practice of unregulated, unsystematized and unaided individual endeavor.

Merely to describe these manifold phases of the general problem of workmen's compensation and industrial insurance is to indicate the broad scope and complicated nature of a subject demanding the most complete information obtainable and much more thorough study than has yet been devoted to it in our American experience. It indicates further both the opportunity and the necessity for extensive work by the several departments of the Federation having different phases of the topic under consideration, to the end of assisting in the formation of sound public opinion and the framing of wise legislation in behalf of this great humanitarian cause. Mr. George W. Perkins is to promote this branch of work under a separate department, and no one can be found better equipped for such a task.

DEPARTMENT ON REGULATION OF INTERSTATE AND MUNICIPAL UTILITIES.

EMERSON McMILLIN, Chairman: At the last annual meeting of the Federation the chairman of this department reported the progress that had been made in the investigation of public utility regulation and the methods that had been employed. At that time the work of gathering, compiling and analyzing the material used in the investigation was about completed, and with a single exception the investigating staff was disbanded shortly thereafter. The statutory material gathered by the department has been published in a volume entitled "Commission Regulation of Public Utilities." This is a comprehensive compilation and analysis of existing public utility laws of all the States as at the end of 1912. * * *

The Executive Council has held many impor[illegible] meetings during the year. At these meetings, [illegible] bill for the regulation of public utilities has be[illegible] scrutinized with the greatest care and a wide ran[illegible] of suggestions and criticisms has been ca[illegible]vassed. * * *

As a result of its two and a half years' activit[illegible] the Council has prepared a bill for the regulatio[illegible] of public utilities. This bill is now presented to [illegible] National Civic Federation—a copy thereof acco[illegible]panying this report. The Council of the Departme[illegible] expresses the hope through its chairman that [illegible] bill so prepared may meet with the approval of yo[illegible] body.

That the regulation of public utilities is necessa[illegible] is no longer a debatable question. The busine[illegible] which they conduct is closely related to the publ[illegible] welfare. The best interests of the public will [illegible] conserved ordinarily by the conduct of such bu[illegible]ness only as a monopoly. Managers of public uti[illegible]ties no less than other members of the public re[illegible]ize that without recognition of the common intere[illegible] in the conduct of such business conditions mig[illegible] eventually become intolerable; in fact, it has co[illegible] to be generally believed that regulation of publ[illegible] utilities is the alternative to public ownership an[illegible] operation. No one of the important public utiliti[illegible] has reached a point where in the interests of t[illegible] public it can dispense with the initiative, zeal, ente[illegible]prise and courage which in the past have characte[illegible]ized American business methods.

Accordingly the bill which we have prepared is [illegible] endorsement of the principle of State regulation [illegible] public utilities. It stands squarely for the publ[illegible]

EMERSON McMILLIN,
Chairman Department on Regulation of Interstate [illegible] Municipal Utilities.

interest in these matters. Unhesitatingly and wi[illegible]out equivocation it gives to a public commissio[illegible] powers of the greatest importance to the well-bei[illegible] and prosperity of the companies. The commissio[illegible] may investigate and fix absolute rates. It may p[illegible]scribe absolute standards of service and require a[illegible]herence thereto. It is required to provide unifo[illegible] accounting and statistical methods, and compani[illegible] are obliged to make such reports to it as the co[illegible]mission may desire. It is charged with the [illegible]sponsibility of approving issues of stocks and bon[illegible] and the transfer of property and franchises from o[illegible] company to another. These powers and others a[illegible] conferred on the commission in the firm belief th[illegible] their exercise is required under a system of adequa[illegible] regulation, but also with the belief that their abu[illegible] will be as destructive, ultimately, to the public i[illegible]terest as it may be immediately to the private i[illegible]terests of the companies regulated.

The bill provides for a single State commissio[illegible] to undertake the regulation of all utilities with[illegible] the State. This plan is believed to be eminentl[illegible] preferable to any scheme of divided jurisdicti[illegible] whether on territorial lines or on business lin[illegible] Municipal regulation of local utilities must nec[illegible]sarily be expensive and probably inefficient. Uti[illegible]ties no longer are confined to the limits of munic[illegible]palities. Of even greater concern, however, is t[illegible] difficulty, if not impossibility, in a majority of ca[illegible] of obtaining through a municipal regulating bod[illegible] degree of scientific accuracy and judicial impartiali[illegible] and fairness which is necessary to a proper soluti[illegible] of public problems.

The bill throws about existing investments t[illegible] protection from competition offered by the requi[illegible]ment that a certificate of public convenience a[illegible] necessity issue from the commission before a n[illegible] erprise is begun in competition with an old one. is provision summarizes the experience of a num- of States. Competition in a field which lends if naturally to a monopoly is economically and lly wasteful. The rule applies as well whether proposed competitor is a private company or a nicipality. So long as an existing agency is fur- ing adequate service at just and reasonable rates respects in compliance with the provisions of public utilities law there can be no justification the introduction of competing agencies.

he bill strikes a blow at another abuse which cost the people of this country humiliation, itical disease and the propagation of graft, which ults from the short-term franchise requiring re- als at periodical intervals. A modification of Massachusetts plan with respect to new fran- ses granted after the passage of the act, and ditty less extreme than the Wisconsin plan with pect to franchises existing when the act takes ct—the bill takes a long step in the direction of ity in the adjustment of the important franchise ationship.

n important feature of the indeterminate fran- se principle is the provision made for the termi- ion of franchises by municipal purchase. Full ortunity is afforded municipalities to purchase property of utilities operating under indetermi- e grants for a price and on reasonable terms and ditions determined by the commission. Munici- ities are authorized either to operate public util- es so acquired or to contract with private com- nies for their operation. Every municipality that ns a public utility is required to keep uniform

W. R. WILLCOX,
Chairman Welfare Department.

ounts prescribed by the commission and to re- t to the commission as private companies are uired to do.

he model bill as submitted to you is the result rduous and long drawn-out investigation and con- eration. It is of necessity a compromise produc- . Each and every member of the Council objects some feature of the bill; but, as a whole, it has received the vote of the entire Council, with single exception.

WELFARE DEPARTMENT.

WILLIAM R. WILLCOX, Chairman: Our depart- ment has to its credit this year, as its larg- single achievement, the completion of the most ustive study ever made in this city, or probably where else, of working conditions in the great tail department stores. This inquiry, carried on a group of expert investigators, with the single tive of learning the exact truth, went into the es of wages, hours and all the surrounding con- ons of employment in some twenty-two establish- nts in New York City, having a total of 39,000 em- yees, of whom 22,000 are women.

he report, which has been published in full in Department Store Number of THE NATIONAL ic FEDERATION REVIEW, is exhaustive, containing 000 words and numerous illustrations of interest- welfare features.

We have encouraging signs of a new impulse in ne quarters to remedy conditions found by our estigators in need of improvement. Just so far such results follow, the chief motive of the Wel- e Department in undertaking this large inquiry l be accomplished.

We found that the heads of some of these stores were not able to interpret the recommendations made to them, since they had not actually seen or studied welfare features in operation. We were disappointed, furthermore, to find that these same managers apparently do not as yet grasp the importance of establishing grievance boards and organized welfare departments, in the interest of harmony and of good relations with the working forces.

The inability of many employers in all lines of industry to realize these advantages has led our department to make plans for a permanent Welfare Exhibit. A vast store of material, photographs, models, descriptions and detailed data of successful work is in our possession; but at present it can be made available only by sending to inquiring employers selected portions suited to their needs. Once opened up, classified and properly displayed, as a permanent exhibit, where it could be studied at any time and consultation had with welfare experts, this fund of working knowledge upon welfare work—called "bumfare work" in the socialist papers—would become many times more useful to the industrial community and furnish the one opportunity most needed to-day for the wider adoption of welfare work.

The employer who adopts welfare work on any considerable scale is going to need trained help; and with this fact in view a course of study for welfare workers has been provided at the New York University School of Commerce, Accounts and Finance, under the immediate direction of our Welfare Department. No such attempt has ever before been made to give this special training in a thorough and scientific way. It means that welfare management is rapidly passing out of the field of experiment and becoming a trained profession.

The lectures were delivered by prominent welfare workers, leading economists, specialists, practical business men and one national labor leader. All phases of welfare work to be found in an industrial village or a city building were covered. An effort was made to bring before the students the pitfalls to be avoided, by explaining thoroughly the first principles in welfare work.

The economic phase of welfare work was presented by Dean Joseph French Johnson, while its origin was covered by the chairman of this department. Its full scope was described by Miss Beeks, with stereopticon illustrations of practical features and contrasting views.

The new welfare worker needs to be shown how to make inspections, especially upon going into a plant which previously has had no welfare work, in order to determine what are essential to the comfort of the wage earners, and this was taken up by H. W. Forster, mechanical engineer, who also covered the subject of "Industrial Accidents and How to Safeguard Against Them."

Other lecturers at the school were:

Robert D. Kohn, F. A. I. A., "Safe and Sanitary Factory Buildings."

Timothy Healy, President International Brotherhood of Stationary Firemen, "Trade Agreements."

Dr. W. G. Hudson (du Pont Powder Co.), "Industrial Poisons and Health Precautions."

Wm. R. Scott, Superintendent John Wanamaker Commercial Institute, "Commercial Training in Relation to Industrial Efficiency."

S. T. Simmonds (The Celluloid Co.), "Employees' Savings and Lending Plan."

John H. Derby, Consulting Engineer, "Fire Prevention, Extinguishment and Protection."

W. E. C. Nazro, Manager Welfare Department, Plymouth Cordage Co., "A Model Industrial Village" (Stereopticon illustrations.)

Miss Laura L. Ray, Secretary Welfare Department, Greenhut-Siegel Cooper Co., "The Work of the Welfare Secretary in a Department Store."

Frank J. Milman, upon working and living conditions in the coal mining regions.

Miss Maud E. Wyckoff, in charge of welfare work, American Woolen Co., "Comfort of Employees in a New Office Building." Trip through the structure.

Christoph D. Roehr, Commissary Department, Metropolitan Life Insurance Company, "Operation of Factory Lunch Rooms."

C. L. Close, Chairman, The Welfare Board for Safety, Sanitation and Relief, of the U. S. Steel Corporation, "The Organization of First Importance." (Students' inspection of safety exhibit.)

Miss Helen Howard Snow, Welfare Manager, Curtis Publishing Co., "Welfare Work for Clerks and Mechanics in a Large City." (Stereopticon illustrations.)

Miss Elizabeth F. Briscoe, Welfare Manager, Joseph Bancroft & Sons Co., "Factory and Home Conditions of Employees."

Dr. Thomas Darlington, Secretary Welfare Committee, American Steel & Iron Institute, "Factory Village Sanitation." (Stereopticon illustrations.)

Dr. Lee Galloway, upon "Business Organization."

Dr. R. W. Corwin, General Manager of the Sociological Department, Colorado Fuel & Iron Company, upon "Surgery in Welfare Work," with stereopticon illustrations.

M. I. Berger, Director of the Welfare Department, Chicago Wholesale Clothiers' Association, upon "Trade Recreation Centres and Other Efforts."

Anson T. Berry, Superintendent of the Relief Department, Interborough Rapid Transit Company, upon "Voluntary Relief Funds."

Dr. F. W. Loughran, Director of the Laboratory of Industrial Hygiene and Sanitation, upon "Medical Departments in Factories."

Some of our notable and unique efforts the past year can be here merely outlined:

An appeal came to us from the Synagogue and Labor Committee of the Conference of American Rabbis for assistance in conducting an investigation of the conditions of employees in the factories and other work places of Jewish employers. This determination on their part to look into their own labor conditions, with a view to bringing them up to par, is most encouraging. There was provided for them a detailed inquiry blank to be used by the investigators personally and to be mailed to Hebrew employers. It was so formulated that it could be understood by each individual, although quite unfamiliar with welfare work.

Another new scheme of welfare work is the one started by Mr. Robert Garrett in Baltimore, to provide especially for the employees of the tenants in his new building. He had our advice when erecting the building, and secured a welfare worker to take charge of the activities.

ALTON B. PARKER,
Chairman Department on Reform in Legal Procedure.

In two instances we have been called upon to formulate a comprehensive plan for a welfare organization; one in a large factory in New England, having thousands of employees, and another for this hotel, the Astor. The welfare worker in charge a year here has been encouraged by the proprietors to the utmost. They have gone even so far as to dismiss, when it was found that a certain set of the employees would not help to care for their co-workers properly, the entire crew responsible for providing food for them. There has been brought about co-operation between the public school system and the Welfare Department, through the establishment of maids' training classes with school teachers furnished by the City of New York at its expense, the hotel itself furnishing the school room, books and equipment in general.

We were appealed to by the welfare worker of one of our members in New Jersey having a large plant, to assist her in making her employers understand the inadequacy of their welfare features. Odd enough was it to find that an employer who would go so far as to employ a welfare worker would not even provide a proper hospital and lunch room. The miserable, dark emergency room called by the company "the fit room" was indeed unworthy of the effort of such an advanced corporation. This young woman spent a couple of weeks going about to view high standards of welfare work, with the result that there has been a complete reformation, with great plans ahead for new activities.

There are many inspections under our auspices to give standards which may be followed, and, fortunately, we have our headquarters in a building which is itself the highest example of welfare work for employees in city industrial establishments. We thus have practical illustrations of many phases which can readily be shown to visitors from other cities, including devices for mechanics in the building across the street.

We are still having demands for information upon profit-sharing plans, and have an elaborate amount of data which is furnished with the statement that as yet we know of no plan operating successfully. One large employer having an enormous plant came to us only last week with his altruistic plan to make his men so well satisfied through a profit-sharing scheme that there never could be a strike. We hastened to inform him that he was following a "will o' the wisp," but he writes to us as follows:

"It may be that I am Quixotic in persisting with my plan, but if it can be worked out it will undoubtedly produce very large results and would work very much to the benefit of the men, for when the company makes profits they are large." We can only hope that he may devise and develop one which will add materially to the wages of his men and touch what it is intended to do—the rank and file.

One of our members applied to us for the experience of others upon the prevention of lead poisoning. We, therefore, instituted an inquiry, as there were no available data on the subject, and found that some of our leading members were able to furnish invaluable data for their use.

We are called upon to assist various employers to such a degree that we are now obliged, owing to our limited force, to diminish the amount of missionary work that we have done in the past and to make definite charges for the time of our experts.

Not the least important of our undertakings has been the advice, at their solicitation, to the New York factory investigating commission.

Specifically, we have suggested that there could be nothing more important than an inquiry into the hours and wages of the vast number of attendants in apartment buildings, apartment hotels and office buildings. The usual thing for elevator boys, for example, is a twelve-hour day, with the exception of those in some of our big office buildings, where there are some special arrangements for relief. A twelve-hour day means a fourteen or sixteen hour day really for those who live at a distance, and owing to their low wages they are burdened with the heavy carfare expense. These elevator boys who carry human freight are expected to be alert and keen and yet they have not sufficient time for rest nor wages to provide wholesome food and other comforts.

Another type needing relief is the night watchman who guards against fire in our great buildings and generally works seven nights in the week the year around. We can scarcely know what it would mean to these men to have one night off a week, and the same consideration should be allowed to the stationary firemen. There is urgent need also of better ventilation of the firemen's quarters. The insanitary conditions in tenement factories on the East Side demand attention. Here the employers are mostly foreigners and have no standards in the matter of sanitation. Something should be done for their better education on this line through illustrated lectures and instruction in cleanliness.

Other conditions which ought not to be tolerated are the crowding of young women operating typewriters into one room, as is the case in many offices. Many break down from nerve strain. Telephone operators working in unventilated or poorly ventilated booths give us another illustration of neglect. In few places is there a rest room for use at the noon hour, and if a girl is ill or faints there is no way to give proper attention; in fact, few employers as yet adequately comprehend the needs of women in business.

The Young Men's Christian Association has developed its work in industrial villages in the South and in logging camps in a most useful way. The secretary for the Southern States, during a recent visit at our office, stated that we had paved the way for them to go out and do the work and that before we popularized it they were scarcely able to get interviews with employers who now seek their help.

Half a dozen years ago we asked trade journals and employers' associations to inquire into the welfare work in their specific lines and publish the results. That has developed to such an extent that now we are able to secure much literature from them. All of this points to the splendid work of various companies and assists in calling it to the attention of others.

Several State Legislatures have appointed industrial welfare commissions to guard the health of the employees in those States.

DEPARTMENT ON REFORM IN LEGAL PROCEDURE.

ALTON B. PARKER, Chairman: During the year which closes with this month one significant and important step has been taken toward the simplification and modernization of legal procedure.

This movement toward the desired goal was the first conference, in connection with the meeting of the American Bar Association, of the judges of our Federal and State courts.

It is widely conceded that there can be no simplicity or uniformity nor indeed much common sense in our legal procedure until the legislative department of government in dealing with the courts be confined to its proper function of the definition and prescription of jurisdictional and fundamental matters, and the details of procedure be left completely to the regulation of the courts.

This is the basis upon which earnest effort is being made to repeal the act of Congress regulating procedure on the law side of the Federal courts to the United States Supreme Court, which attained a result so eminently satisfactory in its reformation of the equity rules of the Federal courts.

With the procedure all under the direction of the courts it needs no sign posts to lead us to an appreciation of the wisdom of an annual convocation of all our jurists. Reformation would follow discussion, and the experience of each court which had accomplished some simplification of procedure would inspire emulation.

The year has accomplished many changes for the better in countless jurisdictions. It would be impossible, of course, to catalogue these in a report even if it were possible to obtain a record of all the changes.

Even the omniscient press is not cognizant of all these reforms effected. One newspaper complained recently of the verbosity of criminal indictments, only to be promptly informed by James C. Cropsey, the District Attorney of Kings County, that even the time-honored phraseology of the Grand Jury indictment had, in that jurisdiction at least, been whittled down by common sense to the essential statements of allegations.

He submitted first an old form of indictment for murder which was in part as follows:

"The Grand Jury of the County of Kings, by this indictment, accuse John Johnson of the crime of murder in the first degree, committed as follows:

"The said John Johnson, late of the Borough of Brooklyn, of the City of New York, in the County aforesaid, on the 15th day of October, in the year of our Lord one thousand nine hundred and nine, at the borough, city and county aforesaid, with force and arms, in and upon one Peter Smith, wilfully, designedly, premeditatedly, feloniously, and from a deliberate and premeditated design to effect the death of said Peter Smith, did make an assault. And the said John Johnson, a certain pistol then and there charged and loaded with gunpowder and one leaden bullet, which said pistol he, the said John Johnson, in his right hand then and there had and held, then and there wilfully, deliberately, premeditatedly, feloniously and from a deliberate and premeditated design to effect the death of said Peter Smith, did discharge and shoot off, to, at, against and upon the said Peter Smith, and the said John Johnson, with the leaden bullet aforesaid out of the pistol aforesaid, then and there by the force of the gunpowder aforesaid, by the said John Johnson, shot off and discharged as aforesaid, then and there wilfully, deliberately, premeditately, feloniously and from a deliberate and premeditated design to effect the death of said Peter Smith, did strike, penetrate and wound him, the said Peter Smith, in and upon the side, chest, lungs, body and vital parts of him, the said Peter Smith . . ."

He then submitted the form of indictment for murder which is now used in Kings County. The new and abbreviated and simpler form ran:

"The Grand Jury of the County of Kings by this indictment accuse the defendant of the crime of, murder in the first degree committed as follows:

"The defendant on Oct. 15, 1909, in the County of Kings, wilfully, feloniously and of malice aforethought, shot Peter Smith with a revolver, thereby inflicting injuries of which he died on Oct. 18, 1909.",

This is but another evidence of how a little leaven leavens the whole loaf.

A few recognized leaders of thought, a few great organizations like this Federation, the American Bar Association, and State, city and county associations of the Bar, direct the attention of the public, and direct it persistently to a matter that demands attention and in addition to the organized effort that results, individual thought and effort are directed to the accomplishment of reformation at the point it is needed and the great work goes on and advancement is made in mass and in detail without the possibility that a full record of the enormous good accomplished shall be kept anywhere but in the "great ledger of the recording angel."

Emerson tells us "every reform was once a private opinion." The private opinions which become reforms are those accepted by the people. The idea of one man becomes the task of the masses laboring individually and through organization. Inevitably many of the details of accomplishment ar sight of. But history shows the extension of tory to which every effort expended has ma material contribution. That is the story of t of all great reforms. And the evidence of its ity is the deep interest shown by individual great organizations like this Federation.

PLAN AND SCOPE COMMITTEE SURVEY OF SOCIAL AND INDUS TRIAL PROGRESS.

TALCOTT WILLIAMS, Chairman: "The Na Civic Federation has been carrying on for ly half a generation the work of bringing labc capital into closer and more harmonious rel For a generation, since 1885, the organizati both these factors in production has been in pr through the trades unions and the trusts. Th general organization of labor in the United bringing the trades together, came a little thirty years ago. The first trust, in the m sense, was organized twenty-eight years ago. ing nearly one-half of this period the National Federation has been adjusting labor differ preventing strikes by mediation, urging arbit and seeking at manifold points the betterm labor conditions, the enactment of new legis public education in the interest of both labc capital, and public knowledge of the most imp facts of American social conditions, the creat a feeling among those who direct capital and who lead labor, that there is no difference be them which cannot be adjusted by mutual con tion and settled upon a basis of justice.

While all this has been going on here aft American fashion, by the action of individuals doing his own personal duty, there has grown this country, first, a protest and next a viole position to the whole economic and social s Whether it be the Socialist Party, polling or lion votes, as opposed to sixteen times this n accepting the present social system and upc whole satisfied with it, or syndicalism, deridir socialistic movement and urging violence as a remedy, both offer the challenge that the e organization of society has worked injustice a social and economic exploitation of the ma the few. All this demands that a national ind survey help us decide whether these asserti true or false. The Federal government, every many corporate inquiries and investigations stitutions of learning have brought together a reservoir of information which can solve this

First, the basis and plea of this social a needs to be met and answered. Second, the in tion already accessible in regard to the shor of hours, the improvement of labor conditior increase in wages, the advance in the stand living, the betterment of housing, the widen education, the opening of opportunity an growth of the savings of the many, need to be visible. Much of this will be done by the unions, which have entered heartily into this tigation. The rapid increase in the distribut wealth, so that to-day nearly one-half the fa in the United States own the houses in whic live, and at least two-thirds of the familie something, needs to be examined, and put in where all can know it. We have in Ameri day that miracle the world has never seen be the wage earner's house which has both a bat and a piano. To make that sort of thing vis the object of this survey. What is needed simply to show what exists now, but to demo that what exists now has come about by a s continuous improvement.

For six months The National Civic Federati been preparing to attack this problem. It h ganized what may fairly be said to be one of th strongest committees of over four hundred bers ever brought together to take up a great It has received the assurance and desire to erate, so far as existing appropriations permit every government agency that has been appro including the Interstate Commerce Commissic Federal Bureau of Labor, and corporations, a as other agencies, Federal and State. The l of the American Federation of Labor are as ested in this great task as are the managers great corporations in production, manufacture, portation and distribution.

This work is now reaching the point of e organization and of the actual collection great mass of facts, most of which need only co-ordinated in order to complete the task. that a year from now, at the next annual m of The National Civic Federation, we shall b to lay an abstract of this investigation befo that it will be in process of publication, an this work will become a great arsenal of nated fact and of national record for thos desire to aid the progress of society.

The McConnell Printing Co. 230-242 William Street, N. Y.

THE NATIONAL
CIVIC FEDERATION REVIEW

ATIONAL AUTHORITIES DISCUSS RURAL PROBLEMS

HE NATIONAL CIVIC FEDERATION RESPONDS TO WIDESPREAD CALL IN CONSIDERING THE FORMATION OF A DEPARTMENT TO CO-OPERATE WITH RURAL LEADERS FOR THE IMPROVEMENT OF AGRICULTURAL CONDITIONS

MEETING OF THE EXECUTIVE COMMITTEE OF THE NATIONAL CIVIC FEDERATION TO CONSIDER THE ESTABLISHMENT OF A DEPARTMENT ON AGRICULTURAL CONDITIONS. *(See next page.)*

DISCUSSION ON PROBLEMS OF AGRICULTURE AND RURAL LIFE

WHAT promises to be one of the largest and most useful lines of public service ever undertaken by The National Civic Federation was inaugurated at a meeting of the Executive Committee at Hotel Astor, New York, March 23d. It was an occasion of remarkable interest and enthusiasm, bringing together, in addition to members of the committee, a representative group of national authorities on agricultural conditions and problems of rural life.

The service the Federation has been able to render during the last fourteen years, from the public standpoint, in the fields of manufacture and commerce, transportation, and labor relations, has naturally suggested the extension of similar efforts to this great remaining field, representing the largest single producing group in the nation, and the basic industry essential to the life of all the others.

The call to this undertaking has been under consideration for some time. Recently, out of the rapidly growing interest in the subject and the multiplicity of suggestions and plans for rural betterment, it has become manifest that one of the greatest needs is intelligent co-operation with and extension of the movements developing among the farmers and citizens of rural communities themselves, thus approaching the subject from the first-hand standpoint of working with and through the people who themselves know best the really vital needs and the true nature of their own problems. Out of a forward movement starting at this point ought to come, naturally, improvement in the entire relation of rural interests to those of the rest of the community.

This was the point of view and attitude emphasized at the meeting of March 23d as the first essential in determining the character of the work in prospect. The tone of all the addresses might be epitomized in the language of a telegram received from Dr. T. N. Carver, director of the Rural Organization Service of the Department of Agriculture, that in entering this field "The Civic Federation has a great opportunity."

Mr. Carnegie's description of the work for a better educational system, which has already been undertaken with marked success in the State of Vermont under the auspices of the Carnegie Foundation, proved particularly interesting as an illustration of what can be done and is being done in a practical and not merely theoretical way.

The formation of the department was foreshadowed by the unanimous adoption of the following resolution, offered by Dr. Albert Shaw:

> "RESOLVED, That it is the sense of the Executive Committee of The National Civic Federation that a department on agricultural conditions and rural betterment be organized, and that President Low is hereby authorized to appoint a committee on plan and scope, which shall be representative of the various interests concerned, and of which he shall be the chairman."

President Low presided at the meeting, and after the luncheon outlined briefly the importance of careful consideration of the proposal in hand and the need of suggestions and frank discussion. The speakers of the afternoon were:

SHEFFIELD INGALLS (Lieutenant-Governor of Kansas), Topeka, Kansas.
ANDREW CARNEGIE, New York.
CHARLES McCARTHY (Expert on Co-operative Marketing, Dairies and Elevators), Madison, Wis.
DR. GRACE KIRKLAND (Farmers' Educational and Co-operative Union), Atlanta, Ga.
LEONARD G. ROBINSON (General Manager of the Jewish Agricultural and Industrial Aid Society), New York.
JOHN M. STAHL (Farmers' National Congress), Chicago, Ill.
ALBERT SHAW (Editor *The American Review of Reviews*), New York.
JOHN LEE COULTER (Secretary of the Commission to Investigate and Study Rural Credits), Washington, D. C.
Dr. LILIAN W. JOHNSON (Rural Organization Service, Department of Agriculture), Washington, D. C.
FREDERICK H. ALLEN (Delegate to the Permanent American Commission), New York.
MRS. HAVILAND H. LUND (Chairman Executive Committee of the National Forward to the Land League), Chicago, Ill.
MRS. THOMAS M. OWEN (President-General of the Women's Auxiliary, Southern Commercial Congress), Montgomery, Ala.
A. P. BOURLAND (Secretary Southern Education Board), Washington, D. C.
WILMER ATKINSON (Editor *The Farm Journal*), Philadelphia.

The following cablogram, telegrams and letters were read:

From Hon. Myron T. Herrick, American Ambassador to France:

"Letter with invitation received. Good luck to you. Agriculture is a subject now occupying the attention of the best minds in Europe. National and international conventions have been held annually during recent years. It is a topic at social gatherings, as well as in financial and business circles, and newspapers and periodicals are full of it.

"The coming generation will witness a development in agriculture as great as that witnessed by the present generation in trade, commerce and industry. All agree in Europe that the best way to advance agriculture is to extend the practice of co-operation. The most successful farming communities are those where the farmers have organized co-operative societies for banking and also for buying supplies and marketing their produce.

"The propaganda and even organization work in the co-operative movement is conducted by altruistic bodies like The National Civic Federation in many instances. There is a great new field of activities for the Federation. I congratulate you upon deciding to bring the matter of opening up an agricultural department before the Executive Committee on the 23d."

From Professor T. N. Carver, Director of the Rural Organization Service, Department of Agriculture, Washington, D. C. (telegram):

"Civic Federation has great opportunity. Farmers will produce more whenever they can market more profitably, purchase raw materials of production more economically and improve their credit facilities. All these things call for organization."

In a letter following the telegram Dr. Carver said:

"There are two things above all others which need to be done. The rewards of labor, abstinence and enterprise in the country must be still further increased, and more of the adornments and embellishments of life must be made available for country people. In order to increase the farmers' income we must spread scientific information more effectively; we must have better methods of marketing, of purchasing farm supplies and of financing the farmers' business enterprises. In order to increase the adornments and embellishments of life in the country, we must have better schools, better sanitation, better recreation and more general beautification of the countryside. These are all essential parts of a constructive rural program. Every item in that program calls for organization."

From Hon. E. R. Bathrick, Member of Congress from Ohio (telegram):

"I commend in the highest terms your effort to establish a farm department of the Federation. Great sociological and economic problems demand relief of city congestion and repopulation of the farm. All efforts to accomplish this will fail of necessary expedition without low-cost money. Every leading nation on earth but ours lends low-cost money to farmers. Aside from cordial co-operation of your Farm Bureau with leaders of prominent farmer organizations, I suggest advocacy of material government aid, and that men of great fortunes and sincere beneficence divert their contributions from universities and libraries and employ their money to the establishment of low interest rate banks for labor and agriculture. Much precedent exists for these suggestions in the practice of the world. Should opportunity arise again I would deem it a pleasure to elaborate facts and conclusions respecting these suggestions."

From Arthur Capper, editor "The Topeka Capital," and proprietor of a group of agricultural papers:

"In my judgment The National Civic Federation does well to consider the organization of a department on Agricultural Conditions and Betterment. The Country Life Commission did a work of great and lasting value. I myself felt that this commission should have been made permanent. The Country Life Department of The National Civic Federation can do the kind of work for the farmer and for the country which a permanent Country Life Commission could have done. The National Civic Federation cannot better serve the country than by the application to farm conditions of the same unselfish effort it has employed in the attempt to adjust satisfactorily the relations between capital, labor and the public at large."

From T. C. Atkeson, Master of the West Virgini[a] State Grange, Morgantown, W. Va.:

"I heartily endorse and am in full accord with the idea of the organization of a Rural Betterment Department in The National Civic Federation, and will do what I can to promote its work."

From Clarence Poe, Proprietor of "The Progressi[ve] Farmer," leading agricultural weekly in the Sout[h], Raleigh, N. C.:

"I am very glad to know that The National Civic Federation is to undertake the work mentioned in your note of March 12th, and only regret that other engagements prevent me from being with you. I hope you will get the movement started, and shall be glad to co-operate with you in any way I can."

From Henry Wallace, Editor of "Wallace's Farmer, Des Moines, Iowa:

"I do think there should be a Department on Rural Betterment. Any betterment in rural conditions must come through the farmers themselves; and about the only thing that can be done is to inspire them with a desire to benefit themselves and to show them how, as well as an outsider can. I am sorry I cannot be with you, but will be glad to help in any way that I can in this work."

From Harris Weinstock, Member Federal Commission on Industrial Relations, Washington, D. C.:

"One of the weak spots in American rural life is, as was shown by our last census, that farm tenancy is increasing in this country out of all proportion to farm ownership, and that unless heroic steps are taken to check this tendency we are likely to become more and more a land of farm tenants, with absentee landlords, which in due time will bring with it all the ills to which Ireland was a victim for so many generations. No better way to check this ill suggests itself than some plan whereby the farm hand or the farm tenant who has accumulated a small capital can become a farm owner. A system of rural credits embracing the plan of a small payment down and small installment payments for the balance, spread over a period of thirty or more years at the lowest rate of interest, will do this effectively. As you perhaps are aware, there is now a bill before Congress, known as the Moss bill, presented by the United States Commission, which has this end in view. While to my mind it is not the best conceivable bill, it may be the best possible bill, and one that is at least worthy of the serious consideration of your executive council."

In opening the meeting Chairman Low said, i[n] part:

"The National Civic Federation is fully conscious of the importance of the group of questions which we are here to consider in their national and in their State aspects.

"The questions which those who are responsible for the policy of the Federation are confronted with, briefly, are these: Can the Civic Federation do anything for these great questions that is not already being well done by some other agency? And if so, what is that thing, and how should we go to work to do it?"

The chairman read the following letter from Ho[n.] David F. Houston, Secretary of Agriculture:

"DEPARTMENT OF AGRICULTURE,
"Washington, D. C., March 18, 1914.

"My Dear Mr. Low:

"I regret very much that pressure of business here will make it impossible for me to visit New York in the near future. I especially regret that I cannot be at your meeting on Monday, March 23d.

"It is somewhat difficult for me to answer your question whether it is desirable for The National Civic Federation to establish a Department on Agricultural Conditions and Rural Betterment. There is a good deal of enthusiasm for rural improvement at this time. The danger is not so much that nothing will be done as that many half-baked schemes will be urged and that attempts may be made to put some of them into operation. Of course, I know that The National Civic Federation would make a most careful inquiry about any plan or proposal before lending it support and aid. Having this conviction, I naturally feel that the Federation could probably render a service by establishing the department suggested. The main function of the department, as I conceive it, would be to examine plans and proposals for rural betterment and to commend and support meritorious plans and to condemn unwise and futile ones.

"The plans proposed for rural betterment are numerous. There are plans for rural organization, for co-operative enterprises specifically for the marketing of farm products and for rural credits, for rural sanitation, for improvement of the social and intellectual side of country life, for good roads, etc. Unquestionably there should be improvement in all these directions. The question is mainly one of agency and method. I should be able, of course, to form and express a much more useful opinion after hearing your discussion Monday. I shall be very much interested in knowing what conclusion you reach.

"With best wishes, sincerely yours,

"D. F. HOUSTON, Secretary."

The chairman then presented Lieutenant-Governor Sheffield Ingalls, of Kansas, whose remarks, as well as those of the other speakers, are here reproduced as fully as space permits:

Sheffield Ingalls.

This great organization has justified its existence on so many previous occasions that I do not feel it can undertake a work of vaster importance to the world at large than this agricultural question.

There is no good reason why every intelligent farmer in America shoud not be using modern methods. America should be in the van instead of merely keeping up with the procession in agriculture. Since the passage of the Morrill act, in Lincoln's Administration, the United States has spent more money in establishing State and national departments or boards of agriculture and in founding agricultural schools and colleges than has any other nation. The technical knowledge thus acquired has made this country a recognized expert so far as theories are concerned. But some other nations have passed us by in the practical application of those theories. As a result, we have to go to Europe to learn how to use the ideas and things that we have thought out or devised in many instances.

Comparing farming by standards set for other business, I would say that the troubles of American agriculture are due largely to waste or needless expense in production; to the lack of organized systems for the purchase of supplies and the distribution and sale of farm products, to a failure to utilize credit facilities and the farmers' own financial resources in a judicious way, and last, but not least, the isolation which makes country life lonely and monotonous, especially to the women folks.

Can these troubles be removed? I believe that most of them are unnecessary evils and would disappear if associated action were applied to agriculture with the spirit of mutual self-help and fraternity which is gradually manifesting itself in all other industries.

Agriculture cannot be industrialized unless it be adequately financed. A man who wishes to become a farmer or a farmer who wishes to improve or enlarge his farm must have money; else he must have credit, and that means character. The credit value of American farmers is difficult to determine by reason of their isolation and distance from the money centers. This explains, in my opinion, the complaint that they are discriminated against by the banks and other money lenders. There is no question as to their sterling worth nor as to the safety of the security which they can offer. The easiest way to make this known and to utilize the security available is through the establishment of co-operative credit societies, to be owned and managed by the farmers themselves for their mutual benefit.

Andrew Carnegie.

One reason that gives me confidence that we shall determine this question rightly, whether the Civic Federation shall adopt this new addition to its labors, is that we have such a president to guide us in our decision.

It is a great gratification to me to see that this important question—this one department in which we are more behind than in almost any others, as compared with the leading nations—has been taken up by this Federation. We shall make no mistake. We have decided wisely, and we shall maintain the reputation that this Civic Federation has made.

Agriculture is a department with which heretofore I have had very little to do, except that as the owner of a large agricultural property I have had to learn something of farming, and of the Scottish, system. They are good farmers, the Scotch, and they have a system of banking from which we are taking lessons. There is not a poor farmer in Scotland who does not get a loan upon his property at the same rate of interest paid by the greatest banker in London getting money from the Bank of England. The rate is uniform throughout the country. But the model country is little Denmark. The State of New York is more than three times larger than the whole of Denmark, but just listen to what that little country does. Last year she exported to Britain alone butter to the value of fifty-two and a half millions of dollars, eggs to the value of over ten million dollars and bacon to the value of thirty-three and a half millions of dollars.

We have made great progress in the West, especially in California, in the one thing needful in farming—that is, co-operation. You drive through the orange groves and the great orchards of all kinds and you find that each little piece of ground sold carries with it a right to so much water, and this is part of the property; it cannot be sold separately. They bring their products to one warehouse, and they sell wholesale, and at the end of the season when accounts are made up each owner of a farm receives payment upon the same scale as his brother farmer.

Now, this is what we need. This will do more to meet the conditions of the farmer than anything else possibly can.

One of the Carnegie Foundations, I am happy to say, has taken up this subject. It was asked to investigate the education system of Vermont and has made its report. So pleased were the legislators of Vermont that they adopted it, and the recommendations are now being accepted. My friend, Sir Horace Plunkett, who has done so much for Ireland in aiding the small crofter to become owner of his farm, before sailing for the other side recently, left with me a report showing how he benefited those farmers and his mode of working, and our organization therefore has resolved to say to Vermont that we would be willing, on a small scale, to employ the proper men and to have them individually plant the Irish system or the Danish system in Vermont. I think that we show our modesty in choosing so small a State. We would not like to risk undertaking Kansas or Virginia.

I did not know, at the time I gave my consent to that plan, that this institution was to be asked to consider this subject, but I assure you you have only to take charge of it, when we shall be only too glad to be at your service and act under your orders, thinking the best will come.

Charles McCarthy.

Some people say that you cannot organize Americans; that they are too individualistic. There are no people in the world that organize like the American people when they get at it. The trouble is that we have organized so rapidly in the past, and we have not known what we were doing. It is a question now of showing our organizations which already exist how to do things.

The agricultural colleges have been very deficient in this matter. In the past we have thought it sufficient to tell the men how to get the right kind of potato seed and put it into the ground and put some particular matter on the bugs when they come along, and then sell the crop at auction afterward. We have not told them the rest of the story. The agricultural schools must pay just as much attention to the marketing of produce in a scientific way as they are now paying to the raising of the product itself. That is not a hard thing to do. All the agricultural colleges have to do is to send men to the countries where they have worked out these things, and then have teachers in the colleges to instruct from these examples.

In Wisconsin we have organized our people to standardize the potato, so that the railroads can take them by the hundred thousand bushels. That means the same kind of seed planting and the same kind of care. You get your potatoes to the market on those standards, and the middleman does not have to come in. So it should be with all products. I am now working on the question of standardizing cheese, and hope soon to have the first State brand on cheese, which will guarantee to you in New York that cheese under that Wisconsin brand will be of first-class quality and produced in sanitary factories.

Denmark has a standard for butter, establishing purity, quality, etc., and every one whose product comes up to that standard can have a certain brand. In order to maintain such a standard you must have a certain kind of inspection; to know the kind of cow, the kind of food given to the cow, etc. Hogs are another example. Most of the hogs in Denmark are killed at two hundred pounds; all the same breed, all fed in the same manner, and all this is represented in the brand. That is what we are going to do with our products in Wisconsin. But we are bound up by trust laws which forbid many of these things.

This is the work, and if your philanthropists and the people working with you go at it rightly it will be only a short time before the American colleges take it up. Mr. Carnegie is right. It is a question of self-help. The Government cannot do it. The men must do it themselves. When you bring the Government into it and make it paternalistic, it won't work. You have to work it out through hard-headed knowledge. Some of these so-called credit bills you must be mighty careful about. I have not seen any that I would favor.

I saw a plan this morning by Secretary Burleson, of the Post Office Department, by which he is going to have the post offices take parcels from the farmers and bring them into the city. I want to say that he had better study that problem carefully before he goes into it. What about the standardization of that produce? If you write to a farmer through the parcel post and you don't know the standards of butter and eggs, the first you get from him may be fine, but the next stuff may be poor. He will write you that he has something to-day, and to-morrow he will not have it. There is no way of pro-rating the orders to those who have the produce. You must deal through organization.

We cannot do this all at once. The fundamental thing is education, and your Civic Federation can do a tremendous service for this country.

Dr. Grace Kirkland.

There is but one way by which the farmers of this country can or will in any way be helped, and that is through themselves, through the leadership developed from their own ranks, leaders in whom they have confidence. The helping to train that leadership is one great work in which the Civic Federation could assist.

As has been made very clear, the Federation has no fixed plan at this date. It has looked over the field, seen a great deal that is being done by a great many other organizations—a great deal that is being attempted would be a better word. Every day we have new schemes, new systems and ideas presented, and there is no fault to find with almost any plan, except the fundamental one that it won't work. If we could only understand that handling commodities, handling of business generally, is not handling people! We can take butter or milk or bacon or flour as such and standardize them, but in a co-operative concern we must deal with the human beings who are producing these things.

The problem is to get the independent-spirited American to hang to the co-operative enterprise. In order to do that you must have him appreciate that those who urge upon him for his own good to do certain things are persons in whom he can confide. There comes again the great thing—the individual leadership of those the farmer knows and trusts.

The outsider can help if he stays modestly a little on the outside, but not by going into the organization itself and attempting to show the farmer what he should do. It simply is against human nature. The way by which the farmer can be really helped is by helping those among the farmers' own organizations whom the great mass of farmers both in the organization and out have the willingness, patiently and earnestly, to follow.

Leonard G. Robinson.

The Jewish Agricultural and Industrial Aid Society was organized in 1900. To-day there are sixty-four local Jewish Farmers' Associations in the United States. These are federated into a central organization—the Federation of Jewish Farmers of America. A number of co-operative enterprises were launched as a result. A co-operative purchasing bureau was established in 1910. The co-operative credit unions were founded in 1911. There is also co-operative fire insurance, a co-operative creamery, co-operative livestock insurance, co-operative marketing, and a mutual benefit fund. There is scarcely an angle in the many complex rural problems that the Society has overlooked.

While grappling with our own problems, I have often wondered why American philanthropy has overlooked so vast and so fruitful a field for constructive endeavor. Our rural problems are vital human problems. They will not be solved by the self-seeker or the visionary. What is needed is an organization of such unquestionable sponsorship and predominance as to command general confidence. I cannot think of any organization so eminently qualified to assume that commanding position as the National Civic Federation. If the new Agricultural Department of the Civic Federation accomplishes nothing more than the elimination of the visionary, the self-seeker, the irresponsible, from the agricultural field, it will perform a signal public service and fully justify its creation.

Albert Shaw.

I am going to say a little about the interesting work that the General Education Board, in connection with the Department of Agriculture, has been carrying on principally in southern States.

The Board, desiring to promote better rural education, soon found that country schools, to be supported, must have local taxation. But as the soil was not yielding enough to give the farmers who cultivated it more than the barest margin, they could not pay taxes. The consequence was, cabins for schoolhouses, very slightly educated teachers and the principal schools running no longer than three or four or five months in the year. The Education Board began to see that it was more important to teach those neighbors what they could do with their soil, how they could get a better living, have something to tax, than it was merely to see if we could establish a better kind of school house, and by degrees lengthen a little bit the school term. The Board began to co-operate with the Agricultural Department's demonstration service, and thousands of small farm demonstrations are going on in the South under the direction of the Department with the cooperation of the General Education Board.

I farm rather a large piece of Virginia soil, and the things I have been trying to learn about the conditions of the country in general, through editing, are the things that I find myself dealing with in the concrete. I could tell you why we in the East may go all the way to Wisconsin if we have Guernsey or Holstein calves to sell—we sell them to Wisconsin, and go there and buy them back! We have no other way to do, because in Wisconsin they have learned the business of producing dairy cattle. Organization is worth millions to Wisconsin. The single county of Waukesha shipped out several hundred thousand dollars' worth of surplus dairy cattle in carload lots, their surplus stock. They still maintain their herds to the full extent of the grazing possibility.

Heretofore we have not been farming in the United States, we have been pioneering. We have pioneered the country from one edge to the other, and we have wasted and spoiled the soil in doing it. Now we have got to learn to farm. We plowed up the prairies in a period when we had thirty or forty million people in this country, and now we have nearly one hundred million in just the same expanse of territory. That explains a great deal of the situation.

Under the laws of the Northwestern States we did get our wheat standardized—officially graded—and with regulated elevator service all along the railroads the farmer is now fairly well protected. In the South the cotton is graded, but just as the South is ripping up all the old yellow pine lands as fast as it can for the purpose of planting cotton, it is discovered that other parts of the world can raise cotton. Until this year our South raised a good deal more than half of the whole cotton crop of the world, but this year the rest of the world has raised a good deal more than half. The opium fields of China, which now by international arrangement, have had to be diverted to some other use, have suddenly begun producing cotton. The cotton crop of China last year was about four times as large as it was two years ago.

These international phases of the problem are very important. They mean for the South that they must farm rather than raise cotton. The South has learned that it can raise grasses. If we can only bring about the business methods that Dr. McCarthy and our other speakers have explained, we can produce dairy products through the South, and we can develop both in the East and the South all sorts of diversification in farming, instead of doing those single things that belong to the plantation man and the wheat speculator. It is simply a matter of learning how to farm, and that involves as well the problems of association, standardization and neighborhood life.

John Lee Coulter.

In the first place, I think it would be worth while for a department of The National Civic Federation to make a brief survey of the question of productiveness of American farms as compared with European farms. The average American acre of land produces only about one-half to one-third as much as the average European acre, and I think it would be found that the low yield in America is not due to poorer soil, worse climate, or any other defect in nature, but due to the extensive methods of agriculture in this country. This brings us to the question, "Why do we not cultivate more intensively if it would yield so much more produce?" This is merely an illustration of the problems which might well be considered.

A department of The National Civic Federation might well ask for the facts with reference to ownership of farm property. Reference to public documents would show that 37 per cent., let us say, of all farms are operated by tenants, the other farms being operated by owners, and that in the last ten years the farms operated by owners increased only 8 per cent., while farms operated by tenants increased 16 per cent. The department might well investigate the causes of this tendency, and if the investigation showed that the country was drifting into an unfortunate condition, it would seem reasonable for the department to make a study of preventive measures, and probably suggest necessary legislation.

Naturally other questions arising would be such as the problem of supply, demand, wages and living conditions of farm labor. Reference to official reports will show that over 3,000,000 farmers in the United States each year employ more or less labor for wages. Labor bureaus have not been established having in mind the bringing of laborers to the farm operators when their work is needed. It might be that the department of The National Civic Federation could work out some recommendations with reference to employment agencies which would make possible quite a material improvement in this general field.

An inspection of the facts at hand would show that only one-half of the land in the United States is now in farms, and only one-half of the land in farms is improved. According to the latest reports, only 17 acres out of every 100 in the United States are actually in crops, cultivated regularly. It is possible that an investigation would show that our whole system is at fault, inasmuch as we have given little or no thought to the big problem of agricultural development.

Dr. Lilian W. Johnson.

It has been well said that co-operation must come from the people themselves; that self-help must be the motto. But I feel, too, that if the rural organization and betterment are to come it must be not by the organization of a class but by the organization of a community; that if the farmers attempt to organize in co-operative enterprises for their own economic good, irrespective of the good of the community, they will fail. We must have not only betterment in agriculture, but we must have betterment in education, in health, in the home, in the public utilities, such as good roads, telephone, and water power; in social, in moral and in religious life.

What we want is to secure leaders from the people themselves, and we must do this through the organized agencies. No more admirable way could be suggested than that which Mr. Carnegie has spoken of in the State of Vermont, to go to the organized agencies of education, agriculture and health in the State, and say to them, "We will help you to reach into each little community, to give to every county its county collaborator in agriculture, to give the health officer in that county a corps of nurses, and, if necessary, a sanitary engineer; to get the leaders for the improving of the public roads, the water power, etc.; to get also leaders for the social and moral and the religious side of life." I can tell you of a church aid society, where a woman started out to help lift the church out of debt, and the women at first gave the eggs that were laid on Sunday as their part of the contribution, and now from that they have standardized on butter and eggs, and are shipping eggs and butter from St. Louis to Montgomery, simply because a woman from town told them of a home bulletin of the United States Department of Agriculture.

The thing is to get the people started. Go to our great teachers' colleges, like Columbia, the University of Chicago, and the one at Nashville, and say to them: "You must organize to train the leaders, and we will stand behind you in what you do."

Frederick H. Allen.

It is as important to consider the city consumer as it is to consider the farmer. The National Civic Federation could do no better work than by approaching this matter and employing its activities in bettering the consumer's position. When one considers that among most of the people of the City of New York, or any other great city, forty-five to sixty per cent. of the family income is spent upon food, it can be readily seen what an important benefit could be brought about by securing less expensive distribution of food products, once they have reached the city. The wastes of distribution in our cities are enormous, and the tolls enacted by the wholesale jobber and retailer add unduly to the cost of food. An investigation which was made in the city of Rochester, N. Y., showed that the duplication of milk deliveries brought about an excess cost of over 2 cents a quart, and that $500,000 a year could be saved in the cost of milk alone to the citizens of Rochester by stopping this waste. The city of Turin was divided into quadrants, the farmers in each quadrant delivering their milk to certain depots in the city, each depot serving its own district, and milk was sold at these depots in the city of Turin for 4 cents a quart. If Rochester wastes $500,000 on the delivering of milk alone, probably New York City, with its 5,000,000, wastes ten times as much.

An immense work for the benefit of the wage-earners and the poorer classes of the city lies before such a body as the Civic Federation, whose energies are directed, as I understand it, toward the benefit of the wage-earner and the toiler.

Mrs. Haviland H. Lund.

We should here take stock of the national situation, find out all who are ready to do the work, the means at their disposal, and so plan that there will not be three men in one county endeavoring to do the same work, and other counties with no workers. Agricultural instruction, public health, farm labor both for men and women, marketing, credit and rural recreation, together with vocational training in the rural schools are vital parts of this huge problem. We need to tap the unused reservoirs of information that have been gathered at such great expense by the State and Federal Governments, and get it into the hands of the masses. There must be a proper distribution of information. This information must be made attractive to those who need it. This work is too heavy for any one body of laborers, however energetic. It is too great even for The National Civic Federation. The business of the department under consideration should not be to pull the train but to lay the rails. I am especially gratified to know that the great rural organizations of the United States so enthusiastically welcome the creation of this department by the Civic Federation.

It has been said by many: "Get the real farmer into this." We cannot get hold of the unorganized farmer, however much we wish, but the organized farmers can help and should lead. They are the first to be called to assist in working out the plan and scope of such a department.

We cannot expect people to be enthusiastic about living in the rural community as it is to-day. The death rate in the country is higher than in New York City. The boys and girls from the country flock to the town with evil results to both country and town. And all this while the moving picture and mechanical music have made wholesale amusement so inexpensive that it will be easy to transform every school house into a social centre. The very development which renders rural life what it should be to those now there also renders it attractive to the man in the city who longs for a home on the land, providing it does not rob his children of social and educational advantages.

One of the first things, it seems to me, this department should consider, is mapping out a course of instruction for instructors. The call for rural organizers, those who can teach the farmer co-operation, already far exceeds the supply. Our universities should give instruction to these organizers. The wrong people in the field doing this work will set us back years. Where we do anything we should see that it is done right.

Mrs. Thomas M. Owen.

The farmer down in our part of the country buys his grain and meat from the West. I went through a wholesale house in Montgomery the other day. They had a quarter of a million dollars' worth of stock on hand, meat, grain, flour, milk, and everything that we could grow and raise ourselves, and our farmers were coming in there with their cotton and carrying back those supplies from other parts of the country.

We certainly ought to change those conditions in some way, if it is possible to be done. We have such inefficient teachers and such poor leaders. Years ago the politicians would take charge of the Farmers' Union and use the men so to their own interest that they lost interest. They have undertaken co-operation and have at times failed in it, and been discouraged, but I think it is a great thing and I hope we shall succeed in getting the propaganda properly before the people.

I know the women of the country are very anxious to help. I succeeded in interesting women in sixteen of the southern States to the extent that they had an attendance of 250 at the convention in Mobile. The main things we talked about there were those we have talked about here: How we can better the home, how to improve the roads, how the canning club can help, how our women are not conserving the products of the farm or the garden as they should be taught to do, and all manner of country problems. We are working on these lines, and I think the South will try to do her part in this new movement.

Wilmer Atkinson.

It is well that The National Civic Federation should institute a department for rural betterment, and when instituted it will be the part of wisdom for the Federation to learn from rural people themselves what they stand in need of.

There are three primary requirements for rural uplift:

First, the power to borrow money on the part of the young men on the farm at a low rate of interest for a long period, so they may become land owners. Second, farmers must get a fair return for the produce they raise for market, which now they do not. Third, agricultural laborers on the farm and in the home must be adequately housed, which now they are not.

Given these three essentials and rural communities will uplift themselves.

Less costly money would enable young men with a desire to follow the honorable occupation to which they are brought up, to secure homes at the time in life when they have the most zest and therefore the greater likelihood of working out of debt and sooner becoming independent.

ANDREW CARNEGIE

ALBERT SHAW

CHARLES McCARTHY

SHEFFIELD INGALLS

FREDERICK H. ALLEN

JOHN M. STAHL

DR. GRACE KIRKLAND

DR. LILIAN W. JOHNSON

MRS. THOMAS M. OWEN

MRS. HAVILAND H. LUND

WILMER ATKINSON

A. P. BOURLAND

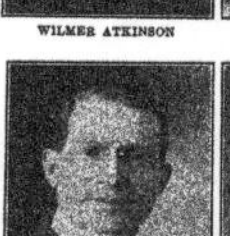

LEONARD G. ROBINSON

JOHN LEE COULTER

SPEAKERS AT THE MEETING ON AGRICULTURAL CONDITIONS AND RURAL LIFE

But it is also essential for the farmer's well-being that he should get more than 30 or 50 cents out of every dollar's worth which he produces. Sporadic efforts have been made at widely divergent points to bring the producer and the consumer together for their mutual advantage, but these efforts being unrelated and lacking coördination, have been for the most part ineffective. The recent extension of the parcel post, and the lowering of express rates, give promise of some relief to farmers, but no general concerted efforts have been made to bring consumers in touch with producers through these instrumentalities. The times cry loudly for some sort of concert that will reach the entire farming community and effect a solidarity that will insure to the farmer a just return for his labor and risk, both of which are now out of all proportion to his meager gains.

If conditions are hard at the barn and in the field they are much less tolerable in the kitchen and the dining room. What the housewife's situation demands is a tenant house where the farm help may be fed and sheltered, so that she may be relieved of the hard drudgery of cooking three meals a day, and of washing stacks of dishes; and that the family privacy and sanctity may be maintained both for the comfort of the wife and the welfare of her children.

Better schools are needed in the country; these will be provided if farmers prosper; more interest in the rural church will be shown if farmers prosper; the feathered friends of the farmer will be protected, as they should be, but are not, if farmers prosper; good roads will be built without mortgaging the future, if farmers are not too poor to build them; there will be better sanitation, better health, nurses to care for the sick and more pleasant and uplifting social intercourse if farmers become prosperous land owners; communities will be contented and happy if farmers have a fair chance to prosper.

To seek rural uplift in any other way then as here pointed out will prove a delusion and a waste of time and effort. There ought to be collective wisdom enough among the public spirited men who are genuinely anxious for rural betterment to help solve the problems above indicated. Any earnest well-planned effort that this Federation shall make in behalf of rural betterment will be gratefully appreciated by the objects of its solicitude.

John M. Stahl.

The National Civic Federation has done so many things so very well that we are justified in believing that it can have a department devoted to farm problems that will be a real help to farmers and a real benefit to agricultural interests and at the same time be of service to other classes. The live question is not whether there should be such a department, but how it shall work and what it shall do.

Farming has two parts of almost equal importance—the productive and the distributive. Literally, a thousand organized agencies, beginning with the national Department of Agriculture have been and are giving consideration to the productive part. If the farmer does not produce to the best advantage it is not because he is not taught how. The new department of The National Civic Federation need not concern itself about the productive part of farming, but it may well concern itself about the distributive part. Quite frequently the price paid by the city consumer for such staple products as potatoes or apples is three and even four times the price received by the farmer one hundred miles away. I believe that first of all the farm department of The National Civic Federation should concern itself with the problems growing out of the relations between the farmer and the man in the town. These problems are many. They cannot well be dealt with by the ordinary agricultural organization, nor by the ordinary city organization. In fact, The National Civic Federation is the only organization I can think of that can deal with these problems in the right way to obtain valuable results.

To give just one further illustration—in almost every State there is, in political conventions and in the Legislature, a decided feeling of distrust and hostility between the people from the town and those from the country. This is used by the lower class of politicians and office seekers to their benefit and to the hurt of the public. The town cannot get the legislation that it needs because of the opposition of country members of the legislature, and the country cannot get the legislation that it needs because of the opposition of town members of the legislature. The organization that has so often succeeded in getting hostile elements to confer, and has found that conference alone is needed to smooth out difficulties, is the organization best fitted of all to bring town and country people to a right understanding and to realize that at the bottom their interests are so nearly identical that there should be no distrust and hostility between their representatives.

In accordance with the resolution adopted by the Executive Committee, the Chairman has named the following Committee on Plan and Scope, which will outline the character and specific objects of the work to be undertaken, and plan of organization:

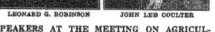

SETH LOW, Chairman, President of The National Civic Federation, New York.
FREDERICK H. ALLEN (The Permanent American Commission), New York.
THOMAS C. ATKESON (Master, West Virginia State Grange), Morgantown, West Virginia.
WILMER ATKINSON (Editor, *The Farm Journal*), Philadelphia, Pa.
CHARLES S. BARRETT (President, Farmers' Educational and Co-operative Union of America), Union City, Ga.
EDWARD N. BREITUNG (Ore Producer), Negaunee, Michigan, and New York.
CHARLES W. BURKETT (Editor, *American Agriculturist*), New York.
KENYON L. BUTTERFIELD (President, Massachusetts Agricultural College), Amherst, Mass.
WALLACE BUTTRICK (Secretary, General Education Board), New York.
ARTHUR CAPPER (Editor, *The Topeka Capital*), Topeka, Kansas.
ANDREW CARNEGIE (Capitalist), New York.
THOMAS N. CARVER (Director, Rural Organization Service, Department of Agriculture), Washington, D. C.
PHILANDER P. CLAXTON (Commissioner of Education, Department of the Interior), Washington, D. C.
JOHN LEE COULTER (In Charge Division of Agriculture, Bureau of the Census), Washington, D. C.
JOHN J. DILLON (Editor, *Rural New Yorker*), New York.
MYRON T. HERRICK (United States Ambassador to France), Paris, France.
CHARLES W. HOLMAN (University of Wisconsin), Madison, Wisconsin.
RALPH INGALLS (Writer on Farm Problems), New York.
Dr. LILIAN W. JOHNSON (Rural Organization Service, Department of Agriculture), Washington, D. C.
Dr. GRACE KIRKLAND (Editor, *The National Field*, official organ of Farmers' Educational and Co-operative Union of America), Atlanta, Ga.
Mrs. HAVILAND H. LUND (Chairman Exec. Comm., National Forward to the Land League), Chicago, Ill.
D. O. MAHONEY (President, American Society of Equity), Viroqua, Wisconsin.
CHARLES McCARTHY (Expert on Co-operative Marketing, Dairies and Elevators), Madison, Wisconsin.
Mrs. THOMAS M. OWEN (President, General Women's Auxiliary, Southern Commercial Congress), Montgomery, Alabama.
G. HAROLD POWELL (President, Fruit Growers' Association), Los Angeles, Cal.
LEONARD G. ROBINSON (General Manager, Jewish Agricultural and Industrial Aid Society), New York.
ALBERT SHAW (Editor, *The American Review of Reviews*), New York.
JOHN M. STAHL (Legislative Agent, Farmers' National Congress), Chicago, Illinois.
HENRY WALLACE (Editor, *Wallace's Farmer*), Des Moines, Iowa.
Miss MAUDE WETMORE (Chairman, Woman's Department, National Civic Federation), New York.
OLIVER WILSON (Master, National Grange, Patrons of Husbandry), Peoria, Illinois.

PROGRESS OF THE NATIONAL SOCIAL AND INDUSTRIAL SURVEY

MANY COMMITTEES ORGANIZE UNDER STRONG LEADERSHIP FOR STUDY OF COMPARATIVE CONDITIONS, PROMISING RESULTS OF REMARKABLE INTEREST AND VALUE

THE past month has seen the active organization of a considerable part of the work of the National Survey of Social and Industrial Progress, which is being carried on under the direction of the Industrial Economics Department of The National Civic Federation.

Many of the committees in charge of sub-divisions of the inquiry have held meetings to determine the scope and limits of the respective subjects, and to develop all available sources of pertinent data. At each of the committee meetings, attended by representative men and experts in close relation with each subject, there have been discussions of remarkable interest and value. Out of these have come suggestions and unforeseen sources of information such as rarely, if ever, lend themselves to the usual courses of government investigation, and when taken upon a broad scale with full verification afford a graphic illustration of changing conditions not possible to get from bare columns of official statistics.

The unique and distinctive feature of the survey, which is attracting so much interest and voluntary co-operation, is the fact that it is to show not merely the broad sweep of conditions as they are to-day, but side by side with this the corresponding conditions of a generation ago. This is the central idea of the entire inquiry, and the one in which it differs from any other ever undertaken in this country or elsewhere, except on single topics or in local fields.

Committee meetings which have been held thus far are:

February 16—*Social Insurance.* Chairman of Committee, George W. Perkins, New York.

March 11—*Division of National Income.* Chairman of Committee, William J. Pape, editor Waterbury Republican, Waterbury, Conn.

March 16 and April 15—*Business Ethics.* Chairman of Committee, J. G. Schmidlapp, President Union Savings Bank and Trust Company, Cincinnati, Ohio.

March 20—*Immigration.* Chairman of Committee, Professor Jeremiah W. Jenks, New York University, New York.

March 20—*Immigration.* Chairman of Committee, Vincent Astor, New York.

March 24—*Free Speech and Public Assembly.* Chairman of Committee, Alton B. Parker, New York.

March 25—*The Church's Influence on Social and Economic Progress.* Chairman of Committee, Charles R. Towson, International Committee of Young Men's Christian Associations, New York.

March 28—*Workmen's Compensation.* Chairman of Committee, August Belmont, New York.

March 31—*Penal and Correctional Institutions.* Chairman of Committee, Adolph Lewisohn, American Smelting and Refining Company, New York.

March 31—*Enforcement of Law and Order.* Chairman of Committee, James Bronson Reynolds, Counsel American Social Hygiene Association, New York.

April 8—*Factors Affecting Children.* Chairman of Committee, V. Everit Macy, New York.

April 9—*Tenement House Conditions.* Chairman of Committee, Paul D. Cravath, New York.

April 17—*Municipal Government.* Chairman of Committee, Clinton Rogers Woodruff, Secretary National Municipal League, Philadelphia, Pa.

April 29—*Distribution of Ownership in Investments.* Chairman of Committee, E. R. A. Seligman, Columbia University, New York.

Other meetings are being held each week and plans of work put into operation.

The preliminary discussion of the subjects and the means of investigating them show that for many of the topics authoritative material already exists in abundance but in scattered form, while in others it is comparatively rare. It appears advisable to supplement existing material in many cases, and in others to bring material to light by a direct appeal for information to the persons immediately concerned. For example, the subject of employers' welfare work, and that of labor conditions, lend themselves very conveniently to this form of investigation.

EMPLOYERS' WELFARE WORK.

The subject of Employers' Welfare Work is to be studied, in connection with the national survey, by a committee of which Mr. W. G. Mather, President of the Cleveland Cliffs Iron Company, is the Chairman. At the request of this committee, the Welfare Department of The National Civic Federation is preparing a thorough inquiry among employers with respect to this phase of the subject. The inquiry is confined to welfare work, i. e., the improvement by employers of the working and living conditions of employees in stores, factories, mines, upon railroads and in public institutions. The committee will advise its correspondents that the Federation seeks to learn what is being done for the physical well-being of wage earners; to provide for leisure time; to assist in the education of their children or increase their own efficiency; to provide comfortable, sanitary homes at reasonable prices—rented or sold; and last to insure them against misfortune resulting from industrial diseases or accidents, old age or family sickness, through voluntary provident funds.

It is proposed to send letters of inquiry concerning these matters to 25,000 employers in various lines of business. In order that no essential points may be overlooked the letter will be accompanied by a schedule of subjects pertinent to such a study. In the case of each one of these special topics the employer will be asked for information relating not only to the present time, but to thirty years ago, or as far back as the information may be had, within that period, in order that a study may be made of the changes which have occurred. Photographs will be requested, illustrating actual and comparative conditions. This outline, which gives a very useful summary of the scope of welfare efforts, here follows:

Length of Work-Day.
- Total number of hours constituting work-day.
- Length of lunch time.
- Seasonal work.
- Length of lay-off.
- Extended period of overtime work.

Method of Discipline.
- Fines for errors or lateness.
- Docking for absence.

Type of Work Place.
- Structural material.
- Method of heating and cooling.

Sanitation.

Drinking Water.
- Drinking water analyzed at definite periods to determine changing quality.
- Source of supply.
- Sewerage system to prevent contamination of wells by proximity to privy vaults.
- Bubble drinking fountains having high flow of water.
- Location of drinking stations.
- Paper drinking cups or other means of avoiding common drinking cup.
- Method of cooling drinking water.

Ventilation.
- Cross-current natural ventilation.
- Forced ventilation.
- Exhaust fans for cooling super-heated places.
- Devices for exhausting dust or noxious gases.

Light.
- Percentage of window space.
- Artificial system, especially where dangerous machinery is in operation, and for accountants.

Wash Rooms.
- Method of ventilation.
- Individual wash bowls.
- Number of bowls for given number of employees.
- Soap furnished—Liquid, powdered or cake.
- Towels furnished. Paper. Linen, and when changed.
- Hot water supplied for types of employees having unclean work.

Toilet Rooms.
- Accessibility to work places.
- Outside exposure.
- Method of flushing closets.
- When cleaned.
- Method of cleansing.
- Separate entrances for men and women.
- Number of closets for given number of employees.

Shower Baths.
- Furnished for stationary firemen, molders, painters, miners or powder workers.
- Where located and how heated.

Locker Rooms.
- Separate dressing roms for men and women.
- Individual metal or wood lockers.
- Drying racks for wet garments.

Lunch Rooms.
- Prices charged for food.
- Type of service.
- Style of equipment.
- Attractive decorations and furniture.
- Separate rooms for men and women.

Fire Protection.
- Fire brigade.
- Fire drills of employees.
- Sprinkler system of extinguishment.
- Automatic electric fire alarm signals.
- Enclosed stairways.
- Fire escape tower.
- Exit doors opening outward.
- Chemical engines, type approved by fire underwriters.

Seats for Women.
- Adjustable backs or foot-rests.

Uniforms.
- Furnished to women.

Laundry.
- Men's overalls, Women's uniforms, Towels, Lunch room linen. } Laundered.

Elevator Service.
- Separate employees' elevators.
- Escalator.
- Freight elevators used by women.
- Method of safeguarding elevators.

Janitor Service.
- Dustless or dry sweeping.
- Method of maintaining cleanliness.
- Sanitary corps.

Emergency Hospitals.
- Location and equipment.
- Physician, chiropodist, dentist, trained nurse or visiting nurse.
- Attendance charge.
- Medical examination of new employees.
- Care of tuberculous employees.
- Occupational disease—its prevention or treatment.

Accidents and Safeguards.
- "Safety First" organization.
- Methods employed to safeguard machinery and dangerous work places.

Recreation.
- Club house or social hall—a separate building or in industrial establishment.
- Type of entertainments—concerts, theatricals, billiards, pool or bowling.
- Club Canteen—
  - Control of liquor selling.
  - What factors have entered into reduction of intoxication.
  - Relation of recreation to liquor problem.
- Gymnasium—athletic field.
- Fresh air exercise.
- Roof garden.
- Play-grounds for employees' children.
- Women's rest or silence room.
- Railroad trainmen's rest houses.
- Men's smoking room.
- Attention to the aesthetic—artistic colorings and decorations.
- Vacations with pay.
  - Types of employees so recognized.
  - Length of vacation.
- Legal holidays recognized.
- Additional time given when legal holiday falls on Friday.

Educational.
- Instruction classes for beginners.
- Meetings of heads of departments.
- Suggestion system.
- Employees' periodicals.
- Charge made—free distribution.
- Kindergartens for children of employees.
- Manual training or gardening for sons of workmen.
- Cooking, dressmaking or millinery classes for women employees or daughters of workmen.
- Employees' classes in "first aid to the injured."
- Health lectures.
- Company contribution toward public schools.
- Assistance by State or Local Board of Education in technical class work, night classes or kindergartens.
- Library—in industrial concern or separate building.

Housing.
- Industrial villages.
- Homes rented or sold to employees; types and prices charged.
- Window screens.
- Garbage disposal.
- Sewerage system.
- Swamp drainage—elimination of the mosquito.

(Continued on page 11.)

THE NEXT STEPS IN WORKMEN'S COMPENSATION LEGISLATION

EXECUTIVE COMMITTEE OF THE WORKMEN'S COMPENSATION DEPARTMENT DISCUSSES THE RESULTS OF EXISTING STATUTES AND THE PROBLEMS YET TO BE SOLVED

AUGUST BELMONT, Chairman Workmen's Compensation Department.

EXECUTIVE COMMITTEE MEETING OF WORKMEN'S COMPENSATION DEPARTMENT

GEORGE SUTHERLAND, United States Senator from Utah.

AUGUST BELMONT, Chairman of the Workmen's Compensation Department of The National Civic Federation, who presided at a luncheon given by the Executive Committee of that Department, Saturday, March 28, 1914, in the Metropolitan Tower, New York City, said in opening the meeting:

"We have come together to confer over the next step to be taken by The National Civic Federation in its Workmen's Compensation Department.

"Great emphasis was put upon the need for uniformity of State legislation by the Joint Commission of The National Civic Federation and the American Federation of Labor, which made a thorough study of the operation of existing State laws and reported exhaustively in a volume published as Senate Document No. 419, which you all doubtless have received.

"This report shows that in States where there are workmen's compensation acts, the principle of workmen's compensation is well established and the benefits of such legislation are fully conceded. In those twenty-two States, the problem for the future is to make the compensation acts equitable, scientific and as nearly uniform as possible.

"One important feature in developing legislation is the adjustment of the schedule in such way as to make it fit various injuries, and to give consideration to the probable decrease in a workman's earnings. An injury to a particular member in one trade may incapacitate a young man for following his occupation for life, while in another trade the same injury may not lessen his ability to perform his work after he has recovered from the immediate effect of the accident. A proper schedule, which must necessarily be complex in its application, is an intricate problem to solve.

"To determine upon what shall be adequate compensation to the workman (which is the first object of such legislation) and what shall be the cost to the employer, is essential to the ultimate success of this legislation.

"Here, as in the work of our Committee on the Prevention of Accidents, we find also the importance of uniformity of action with relation to the method of gathering statistics. This refers particularly to accident prevention. These statistics are needed to inform us where the majority of accidents occur and where safeguarding is most urgently required. For example, a chart recently issued by an important company in Illinois shows 35 per cent of its accidents in a given period to have been injuries to the eyes of the workmen. Then again, through the recent report of the Massachusetts Board, we learn that a comparatively small percentage of the fatal accidents were due to machinery—the great majority coming through hand labor. The Chairman of our Commission suggests that discipline is a large element in the prevention of accidents, and I hope he will enlarge upon the foregoing points during the discussion this afternoon.

LOUIS B. SCHRAM. CYRUS W. PHILLIPS JOHN MITCHELL.

MEMBERS OF THE COMMISSION WHO WERE PRESENT AND SPOKE AT THE MEETING

"The unprecedented demand for the report of our Commission on the operation of State workmen's compensation laws has indicated the value of the Federation's educational work in this connection. It has been sought in large quantities by the State Boards and by employers, who regard it as a convenient publication for the purpose of informing heads of departments, superintendents and foremen not familiar with this new type of legislation and their responsibility under it.

"A still greater need for education is indicated by letters received from States which have undertaken to secure laws this year. They indicate that the public, as well as State commissioners and legislators, are seeking knowledge concerning the subject.

"Hostility toward writing in the statutes the principle of workmen's compensation, on the part of legislatures which met this year, was due largely to the fact that either the lawmakers or the employers or workmen concerned were not prepared to deal with the subject, as it was too new to them."

Among the letters read by Mr. Belmont from governors, commissioners and members, was one from James Duncan, First Vice-President of the American Federation of Labor and a member of the Joint Commission of The National Civic Federation and the American Federation of Labor, who wrote expressing regret that he was unable to be present and said:

"I have received copies of the report of the Joint Commission to study the operation of the State laws, of which I had the honor of being a member, and I think the report puts us in a position of being of great assistance to all the interested parties in furthering the practical work incidental to legislating and practically putting into use the principles and purpose of workmen's compensation. I know that the discussion of plans to make effective the report of our Commission is one of the very important phases of the main question."

FEDERAL BILL AND STATE UNIFORMITY.

Hon. GEORGE SUTHERLAND, United States Senator from Utah, who was the author of the Federal Workmen's Compensation Act applying to railroad employees in interstate commerce, now pending before Congress, opened his remarks by expressing the desirability of having uniformity in State legislation, especially upon the subject of workmen's compensation, although exceedingly difficult to secure, and commented upon the practical character of the report of the Joint Commission, written in plain English so that every man can understand it, adding that it should aid materially in bringing about uniform legislation. He expressed regret that some of the States were adopting the principle of State insurance which has weaknesses that are not developed at once; that the amount of compensation that is to be paid during the early years will be comparatively little, but that as the years go on they will accumulate and difficulties will develop. He feared that State administrative boards would be cultivated by the employer to have the tax upon him made as low as possible, and by the employee to get just as much compensation as possible—both tendencies being to deplete the fund, which will ultimately become insufficient, necessitating a resort to State taxation. The State board cannot settle a case without investigating it as the employer can, for he is dealing with his own money.

He said further: "I believe thoroughly in the English system of direct payments, although there must be some method of guaranteeing payments on the part of small employers. The system of direct payments is an incentive upon the individual employer to cut down the number of accidents. The best managed manufacturing establishment is penalized for the benefit of the worst managed, when the latter is not required to pay more in the form of a tax than the former."

Mr. Sutherland urged the exclusive remedy and a compulsory law, and said: "A law is supposed to be a rule of conduct demanding what is right and prohibiting what is wrong, but the so-called elective law does neither. It lays down a set of rules and says, 'You may accept these principles or not, as you please.' It is good advice, but not law, because the very idea of a law implies compulsion. If you give the employee the option of suing at common law or accepting the provisions of the compensation law, you continue one of the evils which it is intended to prevent—that is, the element of waste. To say that the employer should continue to respond, at the option of the employee, to the sometimes extravagant verdicts rendered by jurors, and at the same time be liable in every case for certain definite compensation is not justice. Furthermore, by preserving the two systems, it is not possible to pay the employee as large compensation. The injured wage-earners and their dependents should be given as large compensation as the employer can be burdened with and the whole compensation should go to the victims of industrial accidents." He illustrated this point by stating that the Federal Commission, before preparing its legislation, collected statistics from the railroads representing 57 per cent of the payrolls of the country, for the three years 1908, 1909 and 1910. It was learned that the aggregate amount paid out for personal injuries from 1908 to 1910 was approximately $10,085,000 per annum, of which amount nearly, if not quite one-half, was wasted in going from the railroad companies to the beneficiaries. Under the Federal Workmen's Compensation Act now pending, railroads would pay $18,000,000 annually for exactly the same number of injuries and the same character of injuries that occurred during those three years—approximately $18,000,000, as against $10,000,000 under the liability law. If the optional system were imposed, the cost would be beyond $18,000,000; but whatever it is, let it be imposed upon them so that the whole amount will go to the employees. Even though the cost to the railroads under workmen's compensation legislation would be increased, I believe they would be better off, as it would make for certainty in cost and they would not be compelled to maintain expensive legal and claims departments.

He urged the importance of treating the men as a class and distributing the $18,000,000 annually rather than to continue the present system under which nearly half the amount is wasted in going from the treasury to the pockets of the employees, the greatest amount going to attorneys. We should get rid of the system which makes the contingent fee a necessity and put into operation the one single system of compensation for every injury, irrespective of the negligence of the employer. No matter how much care is taken, modern industry is so huge and complex that a certain number of accidents are inevitable. The doctrine of averages has taken the place of the law of chance. We can predict by the use of statistics with a reasonable degree of certainty. Upon the railroads of this country there are approximately 4,000 men killed and 60,000 injured every year out of the total payroll of 1,700,000. He said that while a certain percentage of the accidents are due to the negligence of the employer and a certain percentage to the negligence of the employee and some to nobody's negligence, about one-half are due to the inherent risk of the industry, and it is not fair that that great mass of humanity should go without compensation or be a burden upon the community. He explained further that a fair compensation law takes away from the wage-earner his gambling chance of securing damages through litigation under a liability law and gives him instead, certainty of insurance, irrespective of negligence.

It will be difficult to get uniformity of action upon the schedule of compensation, as people differ so about details. His judgment is that it is better to extend the time over which payments are made to the injured than to extend the amount which shall be received for a shorter length of time. A man must be given a reasonable sum during the period of his disability, but it should not be fixed so high as to constitute an inducement to him to remain idle after he is able to work or to simulate injury which really does not exist. Men should not be paid more than they could earn year in and year out.

In speaking upon the status of the Federal compensation bill, Senator Sutherland said:

"When not as generous in its terms as it is now, it passed by a large majority in both the Senate and House, the latter adopting amendments too late to be ratified by the Senate because of the opposition. The present situation is irritating. The pending act would be of the greatest benefit to the railway employees. It is more generous than any law in any country in the world, and yet we find these employees meeting and passing resolutions against it, notwithstanding the fact that the heads of their organizations, who have studied the question thoroughly, have committed themselves in favor of the law with one exception. I am told that the opposition is due to the attitude of personal injury lawyers. I do not complain of the contingent fee lawyer, but of the system of which he is a part. We have only half a dozen men in Washington sufficiently familiar with the details of the act to push it, while in every community where railroad men live there are several dozen lawyers who depend upon the perpetuation of the present system. A lawyer goes to one of them and says, 'This law proposes to take from you your right to bring suit against your employer if he has been guilty of negligence. Do you want that?' He says no. The lawyer doesn't say to him, 'This law proposes to take from you your gambling chance for the future to maintain a successful action against your employer, and gives you in place of it a policy of insurance.' He does not put it to him in that way. He says to him, 'I had a case for Jim Smith, a brakeman, who lost an arm, and I got $10,000 for Jim Smith.' At once the employee thinks that is the standard; that if he loses an arm he is entitled to $10,000. What the lawyer neglects to say is that Jim Smith got this after two or three years of litigation, starving years for him and his family; that, when the judgment was paid, Jim Smith, of the $10,000, got $5,000 and the lawyer got $5,000. Tom Jones and Harry Robinson, two others similarly injured, got nothing. It seems to me if he had said to this man, that this proposed workmen's compensation law will take $15,000, instead of $10,000, and give it to the three men, or to the three families, in case of their death, instead of giving the whole $10,000 partly to the lawyer who has not been injured and partly to the employee who has been injured, that he would have been stating the case fairly. There are two engineers in a head-on collision. One is guilty of negligence, the other is not. Both are killed; both leave families, a wife and three children in each case. Those families must be taken care of by somebody. Isn't it better, in the interest of humanity, in everybody's interest, that each of those families should receive $10,000 than that one should receive $12,000 and the other nothing at all? That is the philosophy at the foundation of this legislation, as I understand it."

CYRUS W. PHILLIPS, of Rochester, N. Y., Chairman of the Joint Commission, said that uniformity will come by evolution and the knowledge of the growth of the subject in the different States, and that it can come about only through some central organization like The National Civic Federation that brings together the experience of the States. They are provincial, and each is apt to think that it has the best law. It is necessary that the experience of the different States shall be carried from one to another. In the beginning, workmen were slow to give up their rights, but the majority of the States now have the exclusive remedy. There is a tendency to increase the waiting period and toward a uniformity with regard to insurance. It is generally accepted that the workman is entitled to have his compensation guaranteed and that the employer should have the option as to the method of insurance.

The danger ahead is in the schedule, and we need to gather statistics and work out carefully that problem. The tax is indirect and falls on the consumers, who do not realize that they are paying it, and are, therefore, indifferent as to how much money is spent. Statistics, doubtless, would show that the workman will pay a larger proportion of the tax than a man with a greater income. The manufacturer who is making a ten-dollar suit of clothing is going to pay just as much for compensation as the manufacturer who is making a twenty-five-dollar or twenty-dollar suit. The result is that the man who buys a ten-dollar suit is paying just as much of a tax on compensation as a man buying a twenty-dollar one. The man who buys clothing from a custom tailor will probably pay a still smaller proportion of that tax. The workmen are most seriously affected—this tax would largely come out of them as consumers, and for that reason it is necessary to have thorough statistics and the whole subject of this cost brought home to the people.

California is trying to work out a schedule based on the nature of a man's occupation, so that he gets a larger compensation if his injury affects him to a greater extent in his particular occupation. The Massachusetts Commission has recommended to the legislature that that plan be adopted there. There will be difficulties in working out the plan. But you can only get at the right solution by attacking the subject and studying it thoroughly.

In New York State there is fear that our death benefits are going to run high. The reason is that a young widow will draw thirty dollars a month the rest of her life, if the man was getting a hundred dollars, which may run fifty or sixty years, and the children get their proportion until they are eighteen. We must have statistics on that; find out what proportion of widows are young and what proportion remain unmarried after widowhood, and the length of life afterwards. Then there has been another suggestion that in a good many cases the decedent may have been a man of advanced years, whose earning power had been nearly exhausted, and that for that reason his widow did not suffer any great financial loss. You will undoubtedly find by statistics that that will occur less often among working people than other classes. Very few elderly men, working at workman's wages, and whose working power is exhausted, will marry young women. So that that probably is a phase that will not affect the situation to any great extent. But yet, in order to ascertain these facts and demonstrate them, we must gather thorough statistics. Those statistics should be uniform throughout the country, with an idea of working out all these different questions. That can only be done by some central body like this, that will adopt a proper schedule for a proper table of statistics and present them to the different commissions.

Those are the principal questions confronting us, and also the practice of fraud, if any exist, in the making of payments. It comes back to the workman who is paying a large part of this tax, and it is to his interest that all malingering and fraud be cut out. If that tax was a direct one on the workmen, they would realize it, and it would encourage them to start safety committees among themselves. It being an indirect tax, they are slower to do so, as we are all slow in matters of that kind. The question of discipline among the men must be taken up, an affirmative action upon their part to prevent accident, as well as on the part of the employer, superintendents and foremen. It seems as though the statistics, schedule of compensation, and the prevention of accidents and then the active participation of the workmen themselves, are the essential things for the future upon this subject.

There is danger that a State working alone without co-operating with other States will gather only the statistics that are deemed necessary for the purpose of administering the particular law in force at that time; when, as a matter of fact, the statistics ought to be broader than the existing requirements in the particular State, as they will not only be of use in administering the laws of other States, but will also be available in case the State involved subsequently desires to change its law. While I will not at this time attempt to make a comprehensive suggestion as to the kind of statistics that are essential, it will occur to us at once that we need to know the number of employees injured in each industry, the cause of their injuries, the nature of their injuries, the average wages paid not only in the industry but to the employees receiving particular types of injuries. Of those receiving total permanent disabilities, it is desirable to know the average age at the time of injury and the average duration of life after injury. For those receiving fatal injuries we must know the proportion leaving dependents in each industry, the number of widows, the age of widows, their duration of life during widowhood, the percentage of subsequent marriages, the number of children, the age of children, the cost of medical attention. Many other subjects upon which statistics are necessary will occur to you.

It will be necessary to call the attention of the different State governments to the absolute necessity for gathering statistics in the hope that they will make sufficient appropriations to enable the industrial accident boards and commissions properly to carry on their work. In determining upon a plan of uniform statistics, the co-operation of the different State boards and commissions will be necessary.

SOME BACKWARD STATES.

ROYAL S. MARSTON, Chairman of the Maine Legislative Committee, of Skowhegan, said in part:

"We attempted to pass a bill in Maine, but no one understood what it meant. We exempted the farmers n order to make possible the passage of the bill. A ·anufacturer, opposed to that provision, said there ·as no more reason why farmers should be exempted ·han small saw-mill men. Then the legislator who ·ad made the best popular speech in favor of the bill, aid: 'Of course, small saw-mill men are exempted. · am a small saw-mill man myself.' We wound up ·ith a sort of compromise by appointing a committee o draw up a bill for presentation at the next session. Ve need all the information possible, and I want to hank you and the Federation for its report, which ave us more valuable information than we had from ny other documents or literature."

JOHN MITCHELL, of Mount Vernon, N. Y., one f the two delegates from the American Federation f Labor who assisted the Civic Federation in its tudy of the State acts, expressed the belief that the 'ederation could render the greatest service by placing ıe emphasis upon the desirability of workmen's compensation legislation—that is, to continue actively to ecure the passage of compensation laws by States ·hich have not as yet acted. He said so many of the tates have enacted laws giving the workmen from 0 to 66⅔ per cent of their wages, and that they would ot willingly have this amount reduced to secure uniormity in schedules. The sentiment is growing among ·orking men, employers and others that the payment or those permanently and totally disabled should coninue for a longer period than was originally offered › the legislatures in this country. Instead of comensating them for eight or ten years, some provision hould be made, perhaps on a reduced scale, for the ntire period of disability.

If working men are to accept compensation as their xclusive remedy, they will insist vigorously that they hall be paid more than 50 per cent of their wages. I m in favor of an exclusive remedy, provided the compensation is reasonably high. If not, I think the working man should retain the right to sue for full damges in case the accident is due to the gross negligence f the employer or to the violation of the factory law n the part of the employer.

There is no longer any question about compensation ecoming the established process for the settlement of uestions affecting injuries to workmen in all the tates, but the absence of information in some maniests itself every day in letters received by The National Civic Federation from men active in the work. mployers and working men and others want information upon the character of the laws they should enact. n States not largely industrial, laws may be acceptble which are not quite as liberal as in those where ıe industrial population is numerous.

In referring to the Federal act, he said: "I hope · will be revised, if necessary, to enable the members f Congress to pass it, since compensation, with its utomatic settlements, is preferable to litigation ·ith all its chances."

DAVID A. REED, of Pittsburgh, Chairman of the ennsylvania Industrial Accidents Commission, stated ıat the problem confronting them in his State was ıe passage of a law, and not uniformity of that law ·ith those in other States. One has been urged with ıcreasing success at three legislatures. He said: We have had the unqualified support of organized ıbor and all the larger employers outside of the soft ·al mining companies. Under the Pennsylvania Liaility Law, the superintendent, mine foremen and all ·erating officers around the mine are fellow servants ·ith the miners; the result is that recovery by an inıred miner is seldom found. One of the largest soft ·al mining companies in a recent year had forty-six ıtalities, which cost them an average of less than $25 ıch—less than would be awarded by any workmen's ·mpensation law. It is easy to understand why emloyers in such a peculiarly favored position would ·sist the enactment of a workmen's compensation law.

"Such a law in Pennsylvania will have to be elective ·cause of the constitutional restrictions; but it is inended to have it an exclusive law, with the election as ı New Jersey, bringing every employer, who does nothıg, under its terms. While in Michigan and Massaıusetts the exercise of the election is signified by the ıking of insurance, not so large a percentage signify ·eir acceptance. The Pennsylvania Commission, however, believes the proper solution to be a compulsory ıw, compelling the employer to insure or signify his ·bility to carry his own risk. It is urging at present ırect payments, leaving it optional with the employer › insure or not. By placing the burden directly on ıe employer, we believe the result will be to make it ·ore to his interest to prevent accidents, than if the ·urden were to fall on the insurance fund, in which is interest is rather remote.

"We found it impossible to get through a law proiding a maximum of 500 weeks in cases of total perıanent disability, and we shall be obliged to accept ıe 400-week limitation and trust to the future to reıove it.

"We have adhered to the idea that disputes were to · adjudicated by the courts and not by a commission. 'e dread the tendency of a commission to administer ıe fund, dealing with each case as a charity rather ıan a matter of justice. We do not like to have a ublic official's position depend upon the favor of the class for which he is constantly making decisions, and we believe that there is greater chance of justice under the courts. While your Commission's report indicates that where the remedy is left to be enforced in the courts, the employee will receive less than the amount provided by the compensation law, it seems to us that eventually these cases will diminish to the vanishing point, as the law becomes known. It hardly seems wise to establish the injured workmen as the peculiar wards of the State. We think it best to leave the assertion of their rights to the men themselves or their dependents, and the enforcement to the courts.

"We think that this year we shall have a legislature composed of men who are in favor of the law, which was not the case at the last session."

MR. WILLIAM A. COAKLEY, of New York, General President of the International Protective Association of Lithographic Press Feeders of the United States and Canada, said:

"There is brought out the question as to the desirability of having awards made by an elected commission. I would raise a question—are not the courts also elective? That being the case, the same principle applies to both methods of administration."

MR. E. K. WOODWORTH, of Concord, N. H., representing the New Hampshire Manufacturers' Association, said:

"It is the desire of my organization to bring about the enactment of a proper compensation act which will put an end to litigation between the employer and the employee. I have come to detest thoroughly an economic condition which makes it possible or necessary for the employer and the employee to assume a position of hostility the moment an accident has happened. The economic waste seems almost criminal. The money paid to lawyers on both sides should go to the relief of the suffering, and go there promptly.

"The law in New Hampshire is the worst in the United States dignified by the name of a workmen's compensation act. It represents an effort to draft a law which would stand a constitutional test in fulfillment of a platform pledge. Section 1 is a drastic employers' liability law which the employer can get rid of only by electing in advance to be governed by the compensation features of the bill, while the employee is left to bring suit. The liability companies established rates very much higher for the employer who accepted the option of compensation than for the one who did not. The result is that very few employers have accepted the compensation option and litigation is more rampant than ever—in fact, well-nigh intolerable.

"At the last session of our legislature, the labor men introduced the bill of the Pennsylvania Commission. We supposed there was unanimity between employers and employees in regard to the establishing of the principle. We were surprised to find the labor interests not represented at our hearings by their attorney who had introduced the bill, but by attorneys who were engaged in bringing suits for plaintiffs, who persuaded the State Federation of Labor that they did not want a compensation law, but a wide-open employers' liability law. The result was no legislation. It was with the definite hope that I might find out the attitude of labor leaders who favor the principle of workmen's compensation that I came here, and I trust that we shall be able to get together. The employers are almost entirely in favor of workmen's compensation legislation in New Hampshire—just the reverse of the situation as given by Mr. Reed for Pennsylvania."

MR. HOLLIS R. BAILEY, of Boston, Mass., Chairman of the Workmen's Compensation Committee of the Uniform State Law Commissioners, explained the activities of that organization in this connection, and stated that several years ago The National Civic Federation suggested that his body should appoint a committee to help work out this problem, which was done. Successively the committee determined upon the exclusive remedy, a compulsory law, the administration by a new kind of tribunal not hampered by the existing rules of the court in their rigidity, and an alternative elective act for States having constitutional restrictions. He said:

"The Commission is considering the matter of compulsory insurance to safeguard the wage-earners' payments, believing that the employer should have an option to insure in mutual companies. The constitutional question arises, can you compel insurance? It seems to be a safe provision.

"Our schedule has been merely suggestive. When you say that a young workman of 21 permanently disabled is to receive 60 or 66 per cent of his wages for the rest of his life, the figures become so large that they frighten one; and the same is true where a young workman is killed and leaves a young wife who may live forty or fifty years, and the amount may run up to $40,000 or $50,000 for one person. Of course, it is possible to award 60 per cent, and then in fine print state that it shall not exceed a total of $6,000.

"I wish to add my word of praise for the work of the Civic Federation's Commission. Its report is of great practical value all over the country and to my committee. It is the latest word, and I hope the gentleman from Pennsylvania, before going to the legislature again, will consider whether the industrial accident board, after all, is not something better than going to the courts. If the experience in this country indicates that we are a little bit old-fashioned, we should stop and see if there is not something better.

"I think the Civic Federation may well have a committee of experts to work out a scientific schedule. Our Commissioners get only $100 or $200 from each legislature and have practically no money, but we have been successful in getting uniform laws when we have had the support of organizations like this. There has been great harmony and co-operation between my committee and the officers of the Civic Federation. By working together, we can accomplish more than by going singly in undertaking to get uniformity of legislation on this subject."

The following resolution, introduced by Senator Sutherland, was adopted:

"*Whereas*, It is important that there should be developed as great a degree of uniformity as is possible in workmen's compensation legislation, be it

"*Resolved*, That the Chairman of the Workmen's Compensation Department of The National Civic Federation be authorized to appoint a Committee on Uniform State Legislation to prepare, in co-operation with the Uniform State Law Commissioners, a memorandum of suggestions upon main provisions requisite to adequate workmen's compensation laws, taking into consideration the best features of existing laws, to be used as an educational document in the interest of such State uniformity of legislation; and

"That the Chairman be authorized to invite each State Board and Workmen's Compensation Commission to appoint a member to serve upon this committee, and that in any States where there are no administrative boards or commissions to study such legislation, the Governors be asked to co-operate by appointing a proper representative from their States; and

"That this committee be instructed to report at a meeting of this Department to be held not later than Ocober 10, that an outline for such educational work may be determined upon in ample time for use among the large number of legislatures to be in session next year."

MR. LOUIS B. SCHRAM, Chairman of the Labor Committee of the United States Brewers' Association, spoke for his large and important group of employers, especially upon the percentage of wages which should form a basis for compensation. He said:

"I have never objected to the 66⅔ per cent of wages as the basis of compensation for several reasons. The additional burden which is cast upon the employer by reason of compensation laws will be calculated in the cost of his product, and will be borne ultimately by the consumer, and therefore the question is not so much what burden it imposes on the employer, but is it just and equitable? From my view, and I think that is the generally accepted view, the theory of compensation instead of liability is that the industry shall bear the burden of industrial accidents. The industry consists of the workman and of the employer, and when the workman gives up one-third of his earnings he is contributing vastly more toward the burden, toward carrying this burden, than the employer does. And, therefore, it does seem that a dispassionate consideration of this subject would indicate that this yielding up of one-third of his entire earning power is going a great step and doing a great deal by the working man toward carrying his share of the burden which is cast on the industry. But there is one feature of this branch of legislation which I think has been incorrectly solved by the New York law, and that is the definition of the average weekly wage of the workman. The New York law entirely ignores the fact that the working man does not work three hundred days in the year. A bricklayer in New York receives six dollars a day for his wages, but it is never contemplated, either by the employer or by the bricklayer himself, that he earns eighteen hundred dollars a year. It is well known that he works probably less than three-quarters of the year, as Mr. Sutherland has indicated. Under the New York law, the average weekly earnings of that bricklayer would be figured at the rate of six dollars a day, and not upon his annual earnings. The basis of 66⅔ per cent would be figured upon the annual earnings and not upon his daily or weekly compensation. In order to promote uniform legislation, the most essential point is that we should have as complete a knowledge as possible of everything that is incident to this subject, and that can only be gained, as Mr. Phillips has clearly stated, by a systematic and complete set of statistics, and in order that we may acquire as complete knowledge on that point as possible, and build up a system of statistics, I offer the following resolution:

"*Whereas*, It is vital that there should be some uniform method of collecting statistics that there may be a common basis from which comparisons may be made upon amounts paid to injured workmen, the cost of insurance to employers and types of accidents most prevalent, therefore be it

"*Resolved*, That the Committee on Accident Prevention of The National Civic Federation be authorized

(Continued on page 23.)

OFFICIALS AND EXPERTS UNITE FOR GENUINE PRISON REFORM

WOMAN'S DEPARTMENT OF THE NATIONAL CIVIC FEDERATION INAUGURATES FAR-REACHING MOVEMENT FOR IMPROVEMENT IN CONDITIONS AND METHODS

FOR the first time in American experience the idea of organized co-operation is to be applied to the treatment of the prison problem. Through the efforts of the Woman's Department of The National Civic Federation a Joint Committee has been formed during the past month of officers of a number of organizations interested in the subject, public officials and practical workers in the field. The object of this important action was, first, to agree upon certain central principles deemed to be vital; next, to bring the result of the united experience and influence of the members of the committee to bear in behalf of sound legislative and administrative reforms.

This Joint Committee, consisting of eighteen members, has already formulated a "platform" of principles and a comprehensive program of practical educational work which is to be carried forward in New York State during the coming season.

The plan for such a movement has taken form very rapidly. Undertaken first under the auspices of the Section for New York and New Jersey of the Woman's Department, it almost immediately aroused widespread interest and enthusiasm as a vital idea of much more than local significance. If important reforms can be brought about in one quarter through this means, standards are thereby established and methods tried out which ought to prove of great service in other States, under modifications suited to local conditions.

A two days' conference on the subject was arranged and held at Hotel Astor, New York, on Friday and Saturday, March 6th and 7th, with a mass meeting at Carnegie Hall on Friday evening. The presiding officer at both the Friday and Saturday sessions was Mrs. Francis McNiel Bacon, Chairman of the New York and New Jersey Section of the Woman's Department of The National Civic Federation. Mrs. Bacon introduced the Hon. William Church Osborn as chairman of the first part of the program at the day session on the 6th, at which the general subject of "Prison Systems and Correctional Institutions" was discussed by Mrs. Martha P. Falconer, Superintendent Women's Farm Colony, Darlington, Pa., and the Hon. John B. Riley, Superintendent of Prisons, New York. Dr. Katherine B. Davis, Commissioner of Corrections, New York City, was introduced as chairman of the second part of the program, which included two topics, viz., "County Jails" and the "Co-ordination of Boards and Commissions." Dr. O. F. Lewis, General Secretary Prison Association of New York, who exhibited a number of screen views of State and County institutions, spoke on the former topic, and Dr. E. Stagg Whitin, of the National Committee on Prison Labor, on the latter.

The Saturday session was devoted largely to the question of "Substitution of Outdoor Life for the Cell System." This fruitful idea was treated from several angles by Dr. Lewis, Dr. Whitin, Thomas Mott Osborne, Chairman of the New York Commission on Prison Reform; Harry B. Winters, Deputy Commissioner of Agriculture, New York; Dr. J. T. Gilmour, Warden of the Central Prison Farm, Guelph, Canada; Brother Barnabas, of the Lincolndale School, and Governor Oswald West, of Oregon, who emphasized particularly the industrial aspect of the prison problem and advocated a central board of control for all prisons of the State.

The Carnegie Hall mass meeting of Friday evening was a remarkable demonstration of the popular demand for a real forward movement in prison reform. At the same time it was evidence of public appreciation that in the co-operative idea a way had been found of real promise of tangible results.

The Governor of New York, Hon. Martin H. Glynn, presided at the meeting and gave most emphatic endorsement to the plan proposed by the Woman's Department for a general committee to bring about more effective treatment of the subject. "I am with you, heart and soul," said the Governor. "I believe that more criminals become so by accident than by intent. Society must not become the enemy of accidental criminals. Correction is far better than punishment, and crime should not be committed to punish crime." The other speakers of the evening, all of whom voiced the need of united action for the accomplishment of real progress, were:

Hon. Oswald West, Governor of Oregon.

Dr. J. T. Gilmour, Warden of the Central Prison Farm, Guelph, Canada.

Dr. Frank Moore, Superintendent State Reformatory, Rahway, N. J.

Mr. John J. Manning (United Garment Workers of America), New York.

Hon. Thomas Mott Osborne, Chairman, New York Commission on Prison Reform, Auburn, N. Y.

At the closing session of the conference, March 7th, the following resolution was unanimously adopted:

> "That the Chairman appoint as promptly as possible a committee consisting of representatives of all organizations participating in these two days' conferences and members of the Woman's Department of The National Civic Federation. This committee to develop a constructive legislative program and campaign of education on prison reform through the State."

In pursuance of this resolution, the New York and New Jersey Section of the Woman's Department promptly called a meeting of representatives of various organizations interested in prison reform, officials and experts on the subject, for the purpose of organizing for action. Substantially everybody invited to participate in the movement responded to the call, and a sub-committee was named to outline the plan and scope of the work in prospect. A second meeting of the Joint Committee, held on April 9, considered this report and agreed upon the program summarized below. The full committee, which is to work for the objects therein set forth, is made up as follows:

MRS. FRANCIS McNIEL BACON, Jr., Chairman.
THOMAS MOTT OSBORNE, Vice-Chairman.
ALEXANDER CLELAND, Secretary.
JOHN J. MANNING (United Garment Workers of America), New York.
HARRY B. WINTERS (Deputy Commissioner of Agriculture), Albany, N. Y.
COMMODORE A. V. WADHAMS (Member of Commission on New Prisons), New York.
O. F. LEWIS (General Secretary, Prison Association of New York).
MRS. WILLIAM EMERSON (First Director of the Women's Prison Association and Isaac Hooper Home), New York.
E. STAGG WHITIN (Member of the Executive Committee of the National Committee on Prison Labor), Columbia University, New York.
FRANKLIN H. BRIGGS (Superintendent, New York State Training School for Boys), New York.
FRANCIS C. HUNTINGTON (Vice-President, State Commission of Prisons), New York.
KATHERINE B. DAVIS (Commissioner of Correction, New York City).
SETH LOW (ex-officio—President The National Civic Federation), New York.
ADOLPH LEWISOHN (Chairman Penal and Correctional Institutions Committee of The National Civic Federation), New York.
MISS MAUDE WETMORE (ex-officio—Chairman Woman's Department, The National Civic Federation), New York.
MRS. AUGUST BELMONT (Member New York and New Jersey Section, Woman's Department, The National Civic Federation), New York.
MISS EMILY CROSS (Member New York and New Jersey Section, Woman's Department, The National Civic Federation), New York.
MRS. GILBERT MONTAGUE (Member New York and New Jersey Section, Woman's Department, The National Civic Federation), New York.
MRS. CAROLINE B. ALEXANDER (Member New York and New Jersey Section, Woman's Department, The National Civic Federation), Hoboken, N. J.

Mr. Alexander Cleland, in whose hands will lie the immediate direction of much of the educational program of the Joint Committee, was Investigator for Governor Hughes's Commission on Immigration, in New York State, and more recently Secretary of the New Jersey State Commission on Immigration. By reason of his experience in these and other fields of social and civic work, and his special studies of the prison problem in connection with the preliminary plans for the present undertaking, he comes to the large task in hand with a particularly strong equipment.

The Committee takes its stand definitely upon the following general principles:

"The Joint Committee on Prison Reform regard the propositions embodied in the following statement as basic in any plan for improvements in administration, methods, and surroundings in the care and treatment of persons confined in correctional institutions:

"GENERAL

"1. The elimination of politics from the management of correctional institutions.

"2. The development of character and self-control in the prisoner through the honor system, and a larger degree of self-government within correctional institutions.

"3. The study and further development of the principle of the indeterminate sentence.

"4. The development of farm industrial prisons and other modern correctional institutions.

"5. The development of the State-use system of prison labor throughout the country in order to develop the best that is in the prisoner and at the same time conserve the interest of the State.

"6. Co-operation to secure Federal legislation which will make possible an effective State-use system in every State.

"7. The application of proper rules regarding just compensation of prisoners in all correctional institutions, with a view to creating an interest in the prisoner in his work and sense of responsibility for the support of himself and his family, and ability to provide such support.

"8. The establishment and improvement of prison schools for instruction in elementary subjects in correlation with industrial education.

"9. Specialized treatment of tramps, vagrants, inebriates, feeble-minded, and youthful misdemeanants.

"STATE.

"1. Improvement in administration.

(Note)—In New York State to-day improvement in management is far more vital than improvement in material appliances. And that does not mean that the latter is not also important.

The most perfectly constructed prison that modern science can invent will not reform the criminal unless it is run by a warden who has high executive ability and has also a heart and a personality that can win the confidence both of the guards and the prisoners.

"2. The State management of all County Penitentiaries.

(Note)—The five county penitentiaries in this State are an anomaly. Each one serves not only its own county, but many surrounding counties, and performs a State function. The penitentiaries should be taken over and managed by the State.

"3. The State care of all persons convicted of crime. County jails to be used only as places of detention.

(Note)—The present county management is, in general, deplorable. Prisoners are usually kept in idleness and herded together without adequate supervision, and for the greater part of the day with none.

The county jail should be used only as a place of detention for persons accused of crime. Convicted prisoners should be in State institutions.

"4. The development of the State farm for women at Valatie; the acquisition of a farm for the prisoners at Auburn; the development of the prison farm at Clinton; the extension of road and reforestation work and other outdoor employment for prisoners; the completion of the State Industrial Farm Colony for tramps and vagrants, of the Yorktown State Training School for Boys, the State Reformatory for Misdemeanants, and the establishment of a custodial asylum for the feeble-minded delinquents.

(Note)—*State Farm for Women.*

Two buildings to house women have been built at Valatie. This institution should be finished. It awaits appropriations. It is much needed. (Laws of 1908, Chapter 467.)

State Industrial Colony for Tramps and Vagrants

Established by the Legislature of 1911. This also needs appropriations, and should be finished at once.

Reformatory for Male Misdemeanants.

This was established by the Legislature of

1912, but no appropriations have been made since. This institution is much needed.

"5. An amendment to the Constitution allowing a bond issue for the completion of necessary State correctional institutions.

"6. Amalgamation as far as practicable by constitutional amendment of the various boards and commissions and other bodies having control over prisoners.

"7. The development of a court of parole for State prisons and of adequate parole boards for other correctional institutions. Also the development of adequate systems of probation and parole investigation and supervision.

(Note)—The probation and parole systems have grown up in a most haphazard way. Each has great good in it, but is open to grave abuse.

The work of a probation officer and of a parole officer is very similar. The ward of each is a convicted criminal. If he is put on probation it is immediately on his conviction, and without being sent to prison. If he is put on parole, it is after he has served a part of his sentence in prison. In each case he is convicted, and needs the same sort of supervision. The case of convicts on probation and convicts on parole should, therefore, be under one set of officers, covering the whole State, since personal contact between the officer and the convict is the essential thing, and a given number of officers dividing the territory between them will each have less territory to cover than if the whole body of officers is first divided into two divisions and each division tries to cover the whole territory. The officers also need more systematic supervision. The present system, by which a convict is turned over to a probation officer or a parole officer is very much like turning over a convict to a keeper in a prison with no warden to look after the keeper. Both systems should be thoroughly studied and plans worked out in detail.

"8. The establishment of a separate building, apart from the main prison, for incarceration of prisoners under sentence of death, and a separate building for executions.

(Note)—As all executions in the State are to take place at Sing Sing, it is desirable that a building separate and distinct from the main prison be established to avoid the present method which upsets the whole prison routine when an execution occurs.

"9. The study and survey of the Sing Sing problem, involving (among other things) the following possibilities:
(a) Renovation of Sing Sing as a permanent prison.
(b) Renovation of Sing Sing as a temporary reception prison and laboratory.
(c) Abolition of Sing Sing, as permanent prison, and establishment of a farm industrial prison on wide acreage."

The methods of work to be followed in the effort to translate these ideas into positive accomplishments are these:

"*Educational.*

A Prison Exhibit to be used throughout New York State during 1914-1915.

Conferences in New York City, and elsewhere in the State, Winter of 1914-1915.

Lectures, addresses, after-dinner talks.

Publicity campaign during Fall and Winter of 1914-1915, for unanimously endorsed legislation.

Press publicity.

"*Legislation.*

Conference in Fall of 1914 on proposed legislation.

Survey of legislation in other States."

PROGRESS OF THE NATIONAL SOCIAL SURVEY

(Continued from page 6.)

Location of closets.
Manchester system of cleaning.
Sanitary regulations.
Milk supply tested.
Co-operation with Board of Health.
Churches built or supported by firm.
Boarding houses or portable camps for men or women. Prices charged.

Additions to Wages.

Profit Sharing.

(Profit sharing is understood to involve an agreement between an employer and his work people, under which the latter receive, in addition to their full current district wages, a share, *fixed beforehand*, in the profits of the undertaking. Copartnership plans enable the worker to accumulate his share of profit in the capital of the business, with the possibility of leading to share in the management.)

(a) Periodical division of percentage of profits based on wages or length of service.
(b) Firm's stock sold to employees at special prices or on installment plan.

(a and b) {
Limited to superintendents and foremen.
Rank and file included.
Success of plan.
Method of inducing employees to retain stock, to promote continued interest and loyalty.

(c) Employees' preference for higher set wages.
(d) Bonuses or commissions on extra amount of production or sales.
(e) Meritorious rewards for prompt attendance or efficient work.
Or for refraining from use of tobacco or liquor.
(f) Cash bonus at Christmas.
(g) Premiums on life insurance policies paid by firm.
Based on term of service or efficiency.
(h) High rates of interest paid on employees' savings, or for home building.
(i) Plan for lending to employees without interest or at nominal rate.
(j) Discounts on househould goods or necessities sold to employees.
(k) Christmas or Thankgiving remembrances.
(l) Prizes for suggestions and gardens.

Provident Funds. (May be additions to wages or may be only half wages when ill.)

Relief or insurance association.
Sickness insurance.
Death benefits.
Pension fund.
Industrial accident insurance.
Company contribution toward fund.
Employees' contribution toward fund.
Voluntary or compulsory membership.

Supervision of Welfare Work.

Conducted by a systematically organized Welfare Department on same basis as any other business department.
Person in charge.
Number of assistants.
Supervisory Board composed of leading executives.

LABOR CONDITIONS.

The Committee on Labor Conditions proposes as a part of its work to utilize a similar procedure, and has prepared in the form of questions a series of inquiries covering a wide scope, the answers to which promise to throw a broad light upon labor conditions past and present. These inquiries will be addressed to the heads of wage workers' organizations throughout the country. The questions are given below in illustration of the careful effort which is being made to bring out adequately the real situation, both today and at the earlier point of comparison.

SCHEDULE OF QUESTIONS FOR OFFICIALS OF WAGE-WORKERS' ORGANIZATIONS.

(In cases where figures cannot be given for the periods named, i. e., the present date and twenty-five years ago, please give the closest that can be obtained.)

1. *Paid-up membership:*
What has been the increase in the last twenty-five years?

2. *Wages:*
(a) What has been the increase or decrease in the last twenty-five years?
(b) Have there been additions of extra pay?
(c) Has pay for holidays been added?
(d) Have there been any other forms of wage increase?

3. *Hours of the workday:*
What have been the changes in the last twenty-five years?

4. *Percentage of your trade organized:*
(a) What percentage in cities or industrial centres?
(b) In the country otherwise?

5. *Forms in organization:*
(a) Has the tendency been toward concentration? or
(b) Has the tendency been toward lesser autonomous groups?

6. *Changes in working conditions:*
(a) Is there greater freedom from injustices of the management?
(b) Is there greater freedom from blacklisting?
(c) Is there greater freedom from fines, suspensions, discharge without cause assigned, etc?
(d) Is there fairer apportionment of work among employees? If so, was it suggested by employers or by fellow workers?
(e) Are appeals permitted to the management?
(f) Are there betterments in workshop or while at work outside?
(g) Are there betterments in sanitation?
(h) Are there betterments in comfort in general brought about by organization or by employers?
(i) Has there been abolition of the company store system?
(j) Is there compulsory patronage (other than the company store) or tenantry of workmen and their families?

7. *Living conditions:*
(a) Is there better housing?
(b) Is there better transportation to and from work?
(c) Are there better amusement facilities?
(d) Are there better educational facilities (libraries, etc.)?

8. *Cost of living:*
What have been the changes in cost of: (a) Food? (b) Rent? (c) Clothing? (d) Fuel? (e) Light? (f) Furniture and house equipment?

9. *Insurance:*
(I) What have been the changes in your occupation as to compensation for accidents?
(II) Have there been any improvements in forms of insurance not connected with labor organizations?
(III) Have new forms of union mutual benefit funds been introduced?
(IV) What are they: (a) Burial? (b) Accident? (c) Sickness? (d) Out-of-work? (e) Old age (or special easy work)? (f) "Home" or other institution for invalid or indigent members? (g) Tool? (h) Kit?

10. *Technical, trade or vocational education:*
(a) Has any come through the union? or
(b) Through the employer? or
(c) for women, in the matter of home economics, civic rights and duties?

11. *Changes in status as between employers and employed:*
(a) In trade agreements?
(b) In welfare work?

12. *Organized labor and governmental agencies and representatives:*
(a) New laws passed advocated by labor?
(b) Especially, laws protecting women and children?
(c) Are organized labor's present political demands in general practical?
(d) In what particular have you suggestions to offer?
(e) Is the attitude of the courts toward labor improving?
(f) What suggestions have you to make for any improvements?
(g) Are the radical political parties asking any improvements possible to labor at present which the unions have neglected advocating? If so, please state them.

13. *Organized labor and public opinion:*
(a) Attitude of employers or the professional classes?
(b) Attitude of church organizations?
(c) Attitude of other organizations?

14. *Unemployment:*
How is unemployment managed in your organizations, as compared with twenty-five years ago?

15. *Unity of organization:*
(a) In working for immediately obtainable ends, how far do the Central Labor Unions, the State Federations and the American Federation of Labor, with its several departments, accomplish every effective point in all desired "solidarity"?
(b) In the railroad brotherhoods, how far is the situation the same?
(c) In appealing for legislation, how far is there a general co-operation between the American Federation of Labor organizations and the railroad brotherhoods?

16. *Organization of the unskilled:*
(a) Is the lack of organization among your unskilled due to their own ignorance of or indifference to the American economic labor movement?
(b) What have been the efforts of your union to organize the unskilled?
(c) What is the proportion of the native-born whites in the unskilled of your industry?

17. *Age of beginning work:*
(a) To the best of your knowledge, at what age did the children of the workers in your occupation leave school to go to work twenty-five years ago?
(b) At what age now?

THE NATIONAL Civic Federation Review

Office: Thirty-third Floor, Metropolitan Tower
1 Madison Avenue New York City

RALPH M. EASLEY, Editor

The Editor alone is Responsible for any unsigned article or unquoted statement published in THE NATIONAL CIVIC FEDERATION REVIEW.

PUBLISHED BY

The National Civic Federation

EXECUTIVE COUNCIL.

SETH LOW, President.
SAMUEL GOMPERS, Vice-President.
BENJAMIN IDE WHEELER, Vice-President.
ISAAC N. SELIGMAN, Treasurer.
RALPH M. EASLEY, Chairman Executive Council.
JOHN HAYS HAMMOND, Chairman Industrial Economics Department.
WILLIAM R. WILLCOX, Chairman Welfare Department.
MISS MAUDE WETMORE, Chairman Woman's Department.
AUGUST BELMONT, Chairman Workmen's Compensation Department.
EMERSON McMILLIN, Chairman Department Interstate and Municipal Utilities.
GEORGE W. PERKINS, Chairman Department on Social Insurance.
VINCENT ASTOR, Chairman Food and Drugs Department.
ALTON B. PARKER, Chairman Department on Reform in Legal Procedure.
SETH LOW, Chairman Department on Regulation of Industrial Corporations.
MARCUS M. MARKS, Chairman Department on Industrial Mediation Law.
E. R. A. SELIGMAN, Chairman Taxation Department.
D. L. CEASE, Secretary.

EXECUTIVE COMMITTEE.

On the Part of the Public:

WILLIAM HOWARD TAFT (President American Bar Association), New Haven, Conn.
FRANKLIN MacVEAGH (former Secretary of the Treasury), Washington, D. C.
ELIHU ROOT (United States Senator), New York City.
ANDREW CARNEGIE (Philanthropist), New York City.
JAMES SPEYER (Speyer & Co.), New York City.
FRANCIS LYNDE STETSON (Attorney), New York City.
ROBERT M. THOMPSON (Chairman Executive Committee Navy League), Washington, D. C.
V. EVERIT MACY (Capitalist), New York City.
WALTER GEORGE SMITH (former President Conference of Commissioners on Uniform State Laws), Philadelphia, Pa.
ALBERT SHAW (Editor "Review of Reviews"), New York City.
THEODORE MARBURG (Political Economist), Baltimore, Md.
JEREMIAH W. JENKS (Professor of Government, New York University), New York City.
TALCOTT WILLIAMS (Director of the School of Journalism, Columbia University), New York City.

On the Part of Employers:

WILLIAM D. BALDWIN (President Otis Elevator Co.), New York City.
WILLIAM C. BROWN (former President New York Central Lines), New York City.
GEORGE B. CORTELYOU (President Consolidated Gas Co.), New York City.
OTTO M. EIDLITZ (Building Trades Employers' Association), New York City.
ADOLPH LEWISOHN (International Smelting and Refining Co.), New York City.
SAMUEL MATHER (Pickands, Mather & Co.), Cleveland, Ohio.
OGDEN L. MILLS (Director International Paper Co.), New York City.
LEWIS W. PARKER (President The Parker Cotton Mills Co.), Greenville, S. C.
GEORGE M. REYNOLDS (President Continental and Commercial National Bank), Chicago, Ill.
HERMAN RIDDER (President New York Staats Zeitung Corporation), New York City.
J. G. SCHMIDLAPP (Banker), Cincinnati, Ohio.
LOUIS B. SCHRAM (Chairman Labor Committee, United States Brewers' Association), New York City.
FRANK TRUMBULL (Chairman Board of Directors, Chesapeake & Ohio Railway), New York City.
THEODORE N. VAIL (President American Telephone and Telegraph Co.), New York City.
HARRIS WEINSTOCK (Weinstock-Nichols Co.), San Francisco, Cal.

On the Part of Wage Earners:

SAMUEL GOMPERS (President American Federation of Labor), Washington, D. C.
WARREN S. STONE (Grand Chief International Brotherhood of Locomotive Engineers), Cleveland, Ohio.
JAMES DUNCAN (President Granite Cutters' International Association of America), Quincy, Mass.
JAMES M. LYNCH (former President International Typographical Union), Indianapolis, Ind.
A. B. GARRETSON (President Order of Railway Conductors), Cedar Rapids, Iowa.
W. G. LEE (President Brotherhood Railroad Trainmen), Cleveland, Ohio.
WILLIAM D. MAHON (President Amalgamated Association of Street Railway Employees of America), Detroit, Mich.
TIMOTHY HEALY (President International Brotherhood of Stationary Firemen), New York City.
W. S. CARTER (President Brotherhood Locomotive Firemen and Enginemen), Peoria, Ill.
JOHN GOLDEN (President United Textile Workers of America), Fall River, Mass.
WILLIAM A. COAKLEY (President International Lithographic Press Feeders' Protective Association), New York City.
DANIEL J. TOBIN (President International Brotherhood of Teamsters), Indianapolis, Ind.
JOHN F. TOBIN (General President Boot and Shoe Workers' Union), Boston, Mass.
JOSEPH F. VALENTINE (President International Molders' Union of North America), Cincinnati, Ohio.
DENIS A. HAYES (President Glass Bottle Blowers' Association of United States and Canada), Philadelphia, Pa.
T. V. O'CONNOR, President International Longshoremen's Association, Buffalo, N. Y.

AND MEMBERS OF EXECUTIVE COUNCIL.

A National Campaign for Pure Food and Drugs. The questionnaire on the subject of pure food and drugs published on another page indicates in part, but only in part, the detailed and exact nature of the inquiry under way by the new Food and Drugs Department of the Federation. It is definitely the end and aim of the Department not merely to learn just where we stand in this matter, but to bring about on the broadest scale an aggressive movement for the securing of pure food and drug products, correct labeling and honest advertising. In some cases this may mean new laws or amendments of present statutes; in others, better enforcement of existing regulations; while for all the purposes of this reform it will require a better and more efficient co-operation of responsible authorities, Federal, State and Municipal.

Back of all this there must be, of course, a working together of many voluntary agencies, representing both producers and consumers, for the strengthening of public sentiment in support of the maintenance of proper standards. The study of such standards, and agreement upon the requirements which should be considered essential, will form a further part of the plan the new Department of the Federation has in view. That this large problem is in the hands of public-spirited citizens, competent experts and officials of the highest standing, is the best assurance that we are to have at last a national forward movement for the conservation of our greatest natural resource—the health of the people.

To Study Agricultural Conditions. The proposal to create a department to study agricultural conditions marks a further rounding out of the idea in the minds of the founders of The National Civic Federation. To bring to bear for the solution of our common problems the experiences and views of the best industrial and civic leadership of the country is a working theory of unofficial democracy which has proved its immense value in every field to which it has been applied. It has been the underlying plan alike of the Federation's national conferences, investigations and permanent departments for the constructive treatment of problems associated with manufacturing industry, transportation, public service utilities and the manifold phases of the labor situation.

But in all this, thus far, the interest of the farmer has been represented only indirectly. The chief difficulty in approaching this subject has been the very great range and variety of the problems involved, and the uncertainty as to which of these were fundamental. There has been the utmost confusion as to the line or lines along which useful service could best be rendered. Something of a key to this complex situation has been provided, however, in the growing activity and definiteness of various movements organized by, of and for the farmers themselves. Among these, the emphasis has been centering on the really pressing needs as known from their own experience—that of better rural credit facilities, for example, more direct relations between producer and consumer, co-operative marketing and buying, and the improving of rural community and farm life conditions.

The importance of wider knowledge of what is already being done successfully, of the methods employed, of the ways and means of correlating many of these efforts so as to secure larger effectiveness, and of strengthening the arm of the local association working on lines of larger possibilities—all this has been gaining clearness and points the way to the opportunities for helpful co-operation with local leadership. Details of the intended work of the new department are in the hands of the Committee on Plan and Scope, appointed by President Low, and it is expected will take definite form in the near future.

A Permanent Welfare Exhibit. Definite assurance may now be given of the opening in the near future of a permanent Welfare Exhibit in charge of the Welfare Department of The National Civic Federation. The exhibit will occupy the entire Thirty-Fifth Floor in the Metropolitan Tower, above the offices of the Federation. The plan for such an exhibit has been long under consideration, and the collections of many years already in hand, with those immediately available as soon as proper facilities for display are ready, will make it in effect a museum of enlightened industrialism of national scope and service. Chairman William R. Willcox, in his last annual report for the Welfare Department, outlining the need for this new development, said:

"A vast store of material, photographs, models, descriptions and detailed data of successful work is in our possession; but at present it can be made available only by sending to inquiring employers selected portions suited to their needs. Once opened up, classified and properly displayed, as a permanent exhibit, where it could be studied at any time and consultation had with welfare experts, this fund of working knowledge upon welfare work would become many times more useful to the industrial community and furnish the one opportunity most needed to-day for the wider adoption of welfare work."

This is the need which the Welfare Department is now in a position to meet in a way and to an extent never before possible. Other recent achievements of the Department are of a similarly gratifying character, marking the steady expansion both of its practical work and of the idea for which it stands. Especially notable is the movement under way for the provision of modern welfare features for employees in all departments of the New York City Government. Particulars of this and other matters of interest in the industrial welfare field appear in another part of the REVIEW.

New Achievements of the Woman's Department. It is a really remarkable record record that the Woman's Department of the The National Civic Federation is making from month to month, in many States and in many fields of useful effort. All along the line there is rapid growth in numbers and enthusiasm, and even more in the credit account of good work carried through to tangible results. Here, as in all parts of the working organization of the Federation, experience is confirming the strength and possibilities of its central idea—the co-operation of the best intelligence of the country, in all industrial, social and political groups, for the just and helpful treatment of our common civic problems.

In this number of the REVIEW may be found a detailed account of the work of the several sections of the Woman's Department, now in progress, and notable recent achievements in many directions. There is also a description of the spacious and attractive headquarters lately opened on Thirty-ninth street, New York City, to take care of the large and remarkably successful work of the Vacation Savings Fund. An account of still another large undertaking, the formation of a New York State Joint Committee on Prison Reform, composed of officers of several prominent associations interested in the subject, experts and public officials, is given in this number, together with a full statement of the principles and program of work agreed upon by the new committee as the basis of the campaign to be carried on in behalf of much needed reforms.

The total record is indeed a wonderful showing of what can be done for genuine social progress, with the aid of an inspiring idea plus businesslike organization, strong leadership and downright hard work.

A National and International Meeting Ground. The exceptional position of The National Civic Federation as a common meeting ground of representative leaders in American civic and industrial life has enabled it to serve a similar purpose upon many occasions of international interest. The commissions of experts which have been sent abroad, in connection with certain investigations carried on from time to time by the Federation, and the co-operation with and assistance to similar commissions from other countries engaged in studies of American conditions, have firmly established this enlarged scope of the Federation's service.

Many interesting exchanges to similar purpose occur in the course of its regular activities. One such to be noted is a conference, held within a few days in New York City, apropos a visit to the Federation's headquarters of Sir Newton Moore, former Premier of Western Australia, for the purpose, as he put it, of "learning something more about one of the institutions of America." The former Premier found much to interest him in the varied activities of the Federation, and in the principle of voluntary co-operation for public service upon which it is founded. Within a few hours an informal gathering was arranged at a downtown lunch club of men interested in learning at first hand the present status of industrial conditions and social experiments in Australasia, and in a position at the same time to give the foreign guest a direct insight into the corresponding situations in this country and the lines upon which we are attempting the solution of more or less similar problems. In attendance at this meeting besides Sir Newton Moore and his associate, Mr. Wittenoom, were President Seth Low, of The National Civic Federation; Ogden L. Mills, Esq.; Isaac N. Seligman; W. L. Saunders; Louis B. Schram; Henry Bruère, City Chamberlain; James W. Sullivan, of the Typographical Union; Dr. Talcott Williams; John Mitchell; G. B. Woodward, and Miss Gertrude Beeks, Director of the Welfare Department of The National Civic Federation. Such issues as government ownership of railroads, the minimum wage and compulsory arbitration were among those discussed, and the interchange of experience and ideas proved of extraordinary interest to all participating.

In much the same way the possibilities of the com- uon meeting ground were illustrated a few days ago t a conference arranged during a visit to the city of Charles S. Barrett, President of the Farmers' Educa- ional and Co-operative Union of America, an associa- ion of more than two and a half million members. The remarks of Mr. Barrett and of Samuel Gompers, epresenting respectively the largest organizations of armers and of wage-earners in the world, were typical f the possibilities of these gatherings, many times erified, in bringing the special problems and needs f great organized groups into better understood rela- ion with those of the whole community. There were resent, besides Mr. Barrett, Seth Low, President of The National Civic Federation; Andrew Carnegie, Samuel Gompers, John Hays Hammond, Alton B. Par- er, Albert Shaw, John Mitchell, William R. Willcox, Haley Fiske, Leonard Robinson, James W. Sullivan, I. D. Estabrook and Ralph M. Easley.

This co-operation of men directly representing forces f such magnitude in our national life, in a common urpose to further not merely class interests but the eneral welfare, is the most promising civic method vailable in the present confusion of economic and ocial issues. It is the particular method The National Civic Federation was designed to establish nd the object to which, in one form or another, its ntire public service has been devoted.

A NATIONAL ASSOCIATION OF WORKMEN'S COMPENSATION BOARDS AND OFFICIALS.

The Workmen's Compensation Department has met rith great success in its appeal for co-operation in the nterest of uniform State legislation made to the Gov- rnors of States having no workmen's compensation aws, to the commissions in such States now studying he subject with a view to formulating legislation, nd to the chairmen of industrial accident boards ad- ainistering workmen's compensation laws.

They were requested to appoint representative citi- ens or representatives of their boards or commissions, a) one familiar with the legal phases of the question o serve upon the Federation's Committee on Uniform tate Legislation upon Workmen's Compensation; and b) another interested in statistical methods to act pon the Committee on Accident Prevention which has een authorized to extend its work to promote uni- ormity in methods of collecting statistics upon the ost of insurance to employers and amounts awarded or given injuries, types of accidents most prevalent nd their causes. The officials in many States have lready made their appointments. Hon. George Suth- rland, Chairman of the Federal Workmen's Compen- ation Commission, has accepted the chairmanship of he Federation's Committee on Uniformity of State egislation on Workmen's Compensation, and Cyrus V. Phillips has been appointed Chairman of the ommittee on Statistics and Cost.

Sub-committees are preparing plans for consideration y correspondence on the two topics involved before alling the committees together in the early fall to ase upon definite outlines which may be circulated mong the forty legislatures convening next winter.

There will be close co-operation in this work not nly with the uniform State law commissioners, as dicated by the remarks of Hollis R. Bailey, Chair- an of its Workmen's Compensation Committee, ap- earing elsewhere in this number of the *Review*, but lso with the new national organization of State In- ustrial Accident Boards and Compensation Commis- ions, formed at a meeting called by the Industrial ccident Board of the State of Michigan, held at ansing, April 14-15, 1914, at which The National ivic Federation was represented under an invitation xtended to Mr. August Belmont, the Chairman of the Vorkmen's Compensation Department.

The object of the conference was especially to con- der administrative and legislative features in con- ection with existing laws. There were addresses by peakers from different States upon "Relation of Com- ensation to Safety," "Accident Prevention by Insur- nce Companies," "Uniform Practice in Dealing with ernia Cases," "Rates and Reserves Under a Com- ensation Law," "The Value of Compulsory Work- en's Compensation Laws," "State Insurance Experi- ce in Ohio," "Lump Sum Settlements" and "The ational Civic Federation and Uniformity," which was resented by Hon. Cyrus W. Phillips, authorized to peak for the Workmen's Compensation Department f that organization.

The Workmen's Compensation Department of The National Civic Federation was elected to membership the new organization. This recognition of its work connection with the enactment of compensation acts the different States was highly complimentary, as was the only civic body elected to membership, the ther members being the various official boards and ommissions charged with the administration of the w. This organization of the different boards and commissions will be of great public benefit and will materially help in perfecting the various laws, especially the administrative features.

The officers of the National Association elected were: President, John E. Kinnane, of Michigan; Vice-President, Dudley M. Holman, of Massachusetts; Secretary, Richard L. Drake, of Michigan.

FOOD AND DRUGS INVESTIGATION BEGUN BY CIVIC FEDERATION COMMITTEE

A STUDY OF THE NATIONAL SITUATION TO BE UNDERTAKEN AS A BASIS FOR UNITED ACTION IN BEHALF OF PURE AND CLEAN PRODUCTS, RIGHT LABELING AND HONEST ADVERTISING

THE newly organized Food and Drugs Department of The National Civic Federation is actively entering upon its work in behalf of purity in the manufacture and honesty in the marketing of food and drug products. The Department has been established in accordance with action taken at the recent annual meeting of the Federation, as the outcome of a special conference on this question, second to none in vital consequence to every man, woman and child in the country. Some of the best known authorities in direct practical relation with the problem in the national field took part in the conference, and the Federation was urged to take the initiative in bringing about co-operation between Federal and State officials, the consumers and the producers, "in the interest of greater purity, proper labeling and honest advertising of foods and drugs." A resolution to this effect was unanimously adopted.

The Committee on Plan and Scope, appointed to outline the work of the new Department, has decided as a first step to make a national survey of the situation with the aid of expert investigators, and by means also of a questionnaire. This, the committee feels, will best develop the exact lines upon which the Federation can be most helpful in the work of securing pure food and drugs for the American people.

The questionnaire will be sent to the Federal and State food, drug and dairy commissioners, the State health officials, the municipal health officials in 5,000 cities and towns, the agricultural chemists, the professors of chemistry in the universities and colleges, members of the associations of food and drug manufacturers, representative wholesale and retail dealers in food and drugs in the particular cities of the United States, and organizations and experts dealing with any phase of the problem.

The committee in charge of the work is as follows:

VINCENT ASTOR (Chairman), New York City.

DR. CARL A. ALSBERG (Chief, Bureau of Chemistry, Department of Agriculture), Washington, D. C.

J. H. WALLIS (President, Association of American Dairy, Food and Drug Officials), Boise, Idaho.

DR. S. S. GOLDWATER (Commissioner of Health), New York City.

MISS MAUDE WETMORE (Chairman Woman's Department, The National Civic Federation), New York.

SAMUEL GOMPERS (President, American Federation of Labor), Washington, D. C.

JOHN M. STAHL (Farmers' National Congress), Chicago, Ill.

EDWARD N. BREITUNG (Ore Producer), Negaunee, Mich., and New York City.

The questionnaire to be sent to the Federal, State and Municipal officials will include such questions as the following:

Meat.

To what extent is the meat bought today in the average market from diseased animals? Putrid and decomposed and restored by the use of chemicals? Filthy because of unsanitary surroundings? To what extent is bobveal offered and sold?

Poultry.

In the average market, what proportion is represented as fresh, when it is in fact cold storage? To what extent has the cold storage poultry and fish deteriorated because of such storage and to what extent is such deterioration injurious?

Milk.

What is a clean milk? Is a really clean milk found in the average supplies of our cities? What is the significance of a high bacterial count arising from uncleanliness?—from age? To what extent is such milk responsible for disease in the average family?

To what extent is the average milk supply a source of infectious disease, such as tuberculosis, typhoid, scarlet fever, diphtheria, tonsilitis and similar conditions?

Eggs.

To what extent are eggs misrepresented as to whether fresh or storage? To what extent are storage eggs found in the average market of a good quality? To what extent is there deterioration from poor quality when entering storage, from too long storage, from keeping too long after leaving storage? To what extent are any or all of those conditions injurious to health?

Pastry.

What is the quality of the ingredients in the average baker's product? To what extent are such products unfit for food because of uncleanliness? To what extent because of poor quality of butter and eggs?

Are the dried and frozen eggs of bakers of good quality and healthful?

Drugs.

To what extent are the drugs of the average pharmacist true to standard? To what extent have they deteriorated from age? To what extent is substitution practised, either by regular dealers or peddlers, and what classes of drugs are the subject of such substitution? To what extent is it harmful or mere fraud?

To what extent have proprietary remedies advertised to the public a real therapeutic value? To what extent are the claims for such remedies fraudulent? To what extent do physicians prescribe such remedies?

Is the present method of establishing official standards of drugs satisfactory? Do you favor government control of the pharmacopoeia instead of through a convention of several hundred delegates, selected by custom from institutions, etc.?

To what extent are restraints needed in the sale of habit-forming drugs?

Stock Feed, Fertilizers and Seeds.

To what extent are food-stuffs for stock, fertilizers and seeds misbranded and adulterated?

Weights and Measures.

To what extent are our present weight and measure regulations efficient?

General Inquiry.

To what extent do the conditions noted in each of these respects result from incompetent or dishonest administration of efficient laws; from inefficient laws; from conflict of interstate and intrastate laws; or from lack of uniformity of laws?

On each of these points of inquiry as well as the all important matters of misbranding and adulteration, the information will be sought with specific reference to a classified list of the principal food and drug products. For example, in addition to those already named this will include butter, cheese, cereals, baking powders and other chemicals, vegetables, flavoring extracts, spices, sugar, molasses, etc., lard, wines, liquors and non-alcoholic beverages, tea, coffee, cocoa, etc., and all manner of official and non-official drug products, crude and prepared, proprietary and non-proprietary remedies and cattle foods.

In addition to securing this information, it has been decided to appoint a sub-committee to draft a model health and sanitary code for use in the smaller towns and rural villages. The theory is, that, while all the larger towns have some kind of restrictive regulation on this subject, the smaller communities very frequently have practically none.

A special committee will be named to draft a schedule of instructions to housewives on the question of how to select wholesome food in the market and how to protect such food from deterioration after it reaches the home.

The Uniform State Law Commissioners will hold their annual conference October 12, and for that reason the Federation's Uniform State Legislation Committee on Workmen's Compensation has been instructed to report, not later than October 10, an outline to be circulated among the large number of legislatures to be in session next year.

WHAT ARE THE ESSENTIALS IN FEDERAL TRUST REGULATION?

VIEWS OF THE CIVIC FEDERATION COMMITTEE PRESENTED BY PRESIDENT SETH LOW AND PROFESSOR JOHN BATES CLARK AT CONGRESSIONAL HEARINGS ON PENDING BILLS

DURING the recent hearings before committees of Congress on the several bills to amend and amplify the Sherman Act, President Seth Low of The National Civic Federation and Professor John B. Clark of Columbia University appeared by invitation before the Committee on Judiciary of the House of Representatives and discussed the questions particularly of prevention of abuses without destruction of legitimate enterprise, and the relation of proposed legislation to labor and agricultural associations. President Low also addressed the House Committee on Interstate and Foreign Commerce, on the bill for an Interstate Trade Commission.

During the last two years a committee of the Federation, consisting of President Low, Professor Jeremiah W. Jenks, Professor John B. Clark and Dr. Talcott Williams, has been engaged in a thorough examination of the field of Federal trust legislation and the scope and character of the changes or new provisions demanded in the light of experience and of new conditions which have arisen. This committee drafted certain bills embodying the results of its consideration of the problem, but, as pointed out in the last number of the REVIEW, it was decided not to offer any specific measures to Congress, but to submit their principal features for the consideration of the Congressional committees having in charge certain bills designed to carry out the recommendations made by the President in his message of December 2. The text of the memorandum filed by the Federation committee with the two House committees referred it was also published in the March REVIEW.

It is particularly gratifying that the Trade Commission bill, as reported to the House by the Committee on Interstate and Foreign Commerce, proves to be in its most important particulars in accord with the conclusions reached by the Civic Federation Committee as set forth in the testimony of Mr. Low and Professor Clark.

In fact, the proposal in itself for the creation of such a Commission, with powers of investigation for the purpose of aiding in determining the status of business enterprises under the law, formed the central feature in the plan developed by the Federation committee for more scientific and effective regulation of industrial corporations.

The safeguarding of the publicity provisions was advocated by Mr. Low before the committee as of urgent consequence. The original proposal, under which all information of whatever name or nature gathered by the Commission would become virtually a public record, open to the inspection of anyone, it is believed would have opened the door to grave abuses by enabling business rivals to gain knowledge of each other's secret processes or trade connections. The bill as reported provides that information obtained in investigations carried on to determine whether a corporation is violating acts relating to restraint of trade, for the purpose of recommending readjustments to bring the conduct of its business within the law, may be made public only in the discretion of the Commission; further, that information obtained concerning any unfair practice not in violation of the law shall be reported to the President to aid him in recommending new legislation, and be made public only by his direction. Penalties are provided for the unauthorized publication of any information obtained by the Commission.

Still another matter favored by Mr. Low in the testimony at the hearing was that of uniformity in the system of reports to be required by the Commission. Obviously such a provision would greatly simplify the analysis and comparison of data and tend to forestall wrong conclusions which might be drawn from statistics compiled with no reference to a common standard. The pending bill provides that the Commission may prescribe, in so far as practicable, such a system of uniform reports.

The important provisions in the trust regulation bill reported by the Committee on the Judiciary, defining the status of labor and agricultural associations under the law, are also in substantial accord with the general principles advocated by Mr. Low with respect to this particular phase of the problem.

Apart from its immediate and significant relation to pending legislation, the testimony of Mr. Low and Professor Clark, based upon the careful and disinterested study given by the Federation committee to this problem during so long a period, is in itself of exceptional interest and value in its clear statement of fundamental principles. The more important portions of the discussion at the two hearings are here summarized, necessarily in condensed form.

Before the Committee on the Judiciary, Hon. Henry D. Clayton, Chairman:

STATEMENT OF HON. SETH LOW.

Mr. Low—Mr. Chairman and gentlemen of the committee: I am here in response to the invitation that has been given to discuss tentative bill No. 2, a bill—

> to include within the meaning of every contract, combination in the form of trust or otherwise, conspiracy in restraint of trade or commerce among the several States or with foreign nations, and within the meaning of the word "monopolize," certain definite offenses, and to prohibit the same.

I confess, Mr. Chairman, a certain feeling that it is not altogether wise to attempt to add definitions to the Sherman law; partly for the reason that because of the many litigations under it its meaning has become pretty definite already; and partly because we in the Civic Federation, who have been studying this matter for a good while, have come to exactly the same conclusion which was reached in Congress when the Sherman law was passed, that it is very difficult to define, and that it is better to leave the language of the law in general phrases.

Professor Clark and myself are members of a committee of the National Civic Federation which has been studying this question for a year or two. We kept certain definitions in our draft bill for a year or more, but finally took them out in order to substitute for definitions the language of the Interstate Commerce law, which, as you remember, forbids the railroads from making or giving—

> any undue or unreasonable preference or advantage to any particular person, company, firm, corporation, or locality in any respect whatsoever.

Or subjecting—

> any particular person, company, firm, corporation, or locality to any undue or unreasonable prejudice or disadvantage in any respect whatsoever.

We think that under the clause a great many unfair practices have been obliterated from railroad practice. Perhaps you recall the report of the Interstate Commerce Commission in regard to the use of sidings and tracks belonging to industrial organizations. They said that they thought these practices amounted to rebating, but whether they did or not, they certainly were an undue or unreasonable preference or advantage in favor of these concerns as against all others. In other words, this practice, which could not have been in mind when the Interstate Commerce law was passed, is in the process of being brought to an end under that general language. Therefore, it seems to me that if more is needed than the Sherman law now contains, that is the form in which to embody it in any new bill. I think that if an interstate trade commission is created, and given authority to administer that clause, it would be able to put an end to one unfair practice after another in general business.

That leads me to the fourth paragraph of the bill concerning which I am speaking. I think it hits the wrong target. It is penalizing or forbidding combinations instead of forbidding unfair practices. This fourth section is so broadly worded that agreements entirely innocent in themselves, and which, perhaps, have never been in the minds of the framers of this bill, would be forbidden.

I would like to illustrate that proposition along the three lines with which I have had some little intimacy. First, from the point of view of the railroads; second, from the point of view of labor unions; and third, from the point of view of farmers.

The Interstate Commerce Commission passes upon railroad rates. Railroads no longer make rates in combination, but they do confer in advance in regard to rates before they are published and submitted to the Interstate Commerce Commission for consideration. They fear that that would be impossible under this paragraph, and that it would be impossible to conduct the railroads' business in any other way. They do not want to enter into agreements with each other which are forbidden by the Sherman law; but they want the privilege of discussing in advance the rate from New York to Chicago, for example, so that the different lines that are competing with each other may publish tariffs that the Interstate Commerce Commission can pass upon readily. I only refer to that as opening up a line of inquiry to your committee which is quite important, and I am quite sure the railroads themselves will develop it amply.

When it comes to the effect of this definition upon labor unions I think you are confronted with a situation of the utmost consequence to the welfare of our people. Let me read that fourth proviso:

> Fourth. To make any agreement, enter into any arrangement, or arrive at any understanding by which they, directly or indirectly, undertake to prevent a free and unrestricted competition among themselves or among any purchasers or consumers in the sale, production, or transportation of any product, article or commodity.

Now, how does that bear upon the policy of collective bargaining on behalf of labor unions? That certainly is an agreement to prevent free and unrestricted competition among themselves on the subject of wages, and that is reflected directly in the price of the article that is produced; and I should think that definition, if it stands, would make it absolutely unlawful for organized labor to protect its interests by uniting together in the matter of securing better wages and better hours of work. It seems to me that in considering the relation of labor unions to the Sherman law there is a very broad distinction which must be recognized, unless we are to drift into a situation that will be full of embarrassment to the country.

I favor absolutely taking out from the law—if it is there—any doubt whatever as to the right of laboring men to combine for the sake of shortening hours, improving wages, and the conditions of labor; for collective bargaining as to these things, if you please. But if labors enters into the field of boycotting, as it sometimes does, or has done in the past, which is a direct interference with interstate trade, then I think the law forbidding restraint of trade should apply. If you recall, the Anthracite Mine Commission discussed that question of the boycott and differentiated between what they called the direct boycott and the secondary boycott. They said that it probably was legitimate, in their judgment, for the members of a union to decline to buy of anybody that they were dissatisfied with; that they could do it themselves as members of a union as properly as they might do it as individuals; but that when it came to the secondary boycott and they pursued the merchandise beyond the limits of the original quarrel, they were entering a field that was not only improper but unlawful.

I look upon a corporation as a union of stockholders, and that they form the corporation for the purpose of collective bargaining through officials of their own choice. I do not see why labor should not have the same privilege of combining for collective bargaining that the stockholders of a corporation have. But that very right is in question under the Sherman law at the present time.

Some of you have heard of the so-called protocol in New York City. It was an arrangement made at the end of a long strike between the shirt-waist manufacturers, or cloak manufacturers, and their employees, providing for arbitration between the employers and shirt makers, and as a part of the arrangement there is a board of appeals. Under that protocol for two years or more industrial peace has been maintained in a trade that before was constantly in trouble; and not only industrial peace has been maintained, but the conditions of pay for these women workers and the conditions under which they labor have been greatly improved. Yet an independent manufacturer, who is not a party to the arrangement, has begun a suit under the Sherman Anti-Trust law as it stands to-day to test the legality of the protocol under that law. It would be, in my judgment, and, I think, in the judgment of almost everybody in New York City who knows anything about it, a most profound misfortune if that sort of an agreement were to be declared unlawful.

Now, if I may, I would like to take up the farm side of the proposition. The fundamental problem of the farmer, certainly in the eastern part of the country, and I suspect more or less all over the Union, is this: That he buys at retail and sells at wholesale. I submit to the committee that there is not another business in the country that can do that. Imagine what would happen to any manufacturer, or any railroad, if they had to pay retail prices for coal and everything that they purchased, and then had to sell their product at the wholesale price of the day. That was the problem that confronted Denmark and all the European countries. In Europe, where the pressure has been greater, they have solved it through co-operative societies which have two objects. In the first place, they want to buy together, so as to get things at wholesale rates instead of at retail rates; then they want to sell together, so that they can get the benefit of businesslike care in the handling of their products.

England is especially notable for these co-operative associations of consumers. They were founded in Rochdale fifty or sixty years ago, and they have become enormous. Those people do not combine—neither the consumers or the farmers—for the purpose of monopoly. Not a single co-operative association aims at monopoly; it aims at something very different. What it wants to do is to enable the small farmer to buy his plow, his fertilizer, and his seed at prices that a man with capital has to pay and at no higher prices. The members agree to give all of their business to the co-operative association, otherwise that association does not know on what scale it can operate nor what expense it can carry. As I see it, under this section 4, that would be absolutely impossible.

Then these co-operative associations perform another function for the farmers. It is not so hard for a farmer to get the science he must have, nor to get the art that he must have; but to add to these the business qualifications that lead to success is an immensely difficult thing, and that is one very great reason why farmers get such small incomes. But the co-operative association carries on the business side of his affairs. Take the co-operative associations for eggs in Denmark, for instance. The farmers give all of their eggs to this association, and the first thing the association does is to create a standard. It says to the farmer, "We will not take any old eggs you have; we want eggs that will candle free from defects." After a week or two the farmer understands that, and only good eggs are sent to that association.

The scale upon which they operate is so great that they can employ the most skilled expert in the disposition of eggs that Denmark can command. They grade their eggs; they keep in contact with wholesale markets everywhere, and they sell on a great scale. The result has been that Denmark has risen, within fifty years, from a country that was on the brink of despair into the most prosperous country of farmers to be found on the face of the globe. They have actually captured the London market for many things; and now Ireland by the same process is doing the same thing. I assure you, gentlemen, that if you want the greatest possible agricultural production kept up in this country, you have got to make it possible for our farmers to learn how to do that thing and to permit them to do it with the utmost possible freedom. The State of New York only last year passed a law especially authorizing co-operative associations; but this paragraph would make it absolutely impossible; that law would be a dead letter on the statute books. I do not think you at all realize the injury that would be done to the country if these definitions make such things impossible.

Mr. MORGAN—What is your view as to whether or not some governmental board or authority should be permitted to approve certain trade agreements before they are entered into or become valid? What do you think about the importance of that to the business interests of the country?

Mr. LOW—I think it is very important. In connection with natural products, like coal and timber, it is not only desirable, but is of the utmost consequence. In two addresses made at the last annual meeting of The National Civic Federation it was pointed out that in the coal mines only 40 per cent of the coal in the seam is taken out under existing conditions, because the operators are unable to agree as to the price of coal at the pit's mouth, and therefore the prices are much lower than they ought to be in order to permit a payment to the miners of a large enough sum to justify them in working on coal that is difficult to get out. Europe has been all through that. It was exactly the same in Belgium, France and Germany. A few years ago a large portion of their coal was not being mined, and for the same reason the protection of life and limb was very inadequate. They have since adopted a policy of permitting trade agreements under Government regulation, and the result is that they now get out all the coal in the mine and have fewer accidents to the miners. I think that is a thing we ought to do, and do as quickly as public opinion can be brought to sustain it. I think that in the matter of coal mining and in the matter of forestry we are pursuing a policy that makes low prices to-day at the expense of the people who are to come after us; they will have to pay much more than they ought to pay.

This forest question is a vital one. Some years ago I remember a public man saying to me that he had been asked by a great body of owners, men who owned contiguous stretches of forest land, about the conduct of their business. They said, "We want to conduct our forests in harmony with the most practical methods of modern forestry; none of us can do it alone; together we can do a great deal. Are we at liberty to enter into an agreement to do that together? Under the Sherman law can we do it?" My friend said to them, "I cannot tell you, and no other living man can tell you." This was years ago, before there had been so many decisions. He said, "You must do it at your own risk; but ten years from now you may be put in jail for making a mistake as to the meaning of the law."

(Supplementary Statement, with reference to the Bartlett bill proposing to exempt labor unions, agricultural and horticultural associations from the operation of the Sherman law.)

Mr. LOW—I have looked over this bill of Mr. Bartlett's very hurriedly, Mr. Chairman, and I am perfectly in sympathy with the first six lines: "That it shall not be unlawful for persons employed or seeking employment to enter into any arrangement, agreements, or combinations with the view of lessening the hours of labor or of increasing the wages or of bettering their condition." I think that ought to be the law of the land.

Do you not want to make it lawful for employers to enter into such arrangements with employees? Under the strict meaning of the definitions that I was discussing earlier, laborers might have the right to make such agreements, but employers might find themselves deprived of that right.

Mr. CARLIN—I think that is a valid criticism.

Mr. LOW—So I think you must make it apply to both sides.

I am personally in sympathy with the phraseology of this act from lines 15 to 21, where it says:

> In construing this act the right to enter into the relation of employer and employee, to change that relation, and to assume and create a new relation of employer and employee, and to perform and carry on business in such relation with any person in any place or do work and labor as an employee shall be held and construed to be a personal and not a property right.

I think it ought to be a personal right; I do not think it is a property right at all.

In regard to horticultural and agricultural combinations, it seems to me you would accomplish what is intended by saying in the law that nothing shall prevent the formation of co-operative associations on the part of farmers for the purpose of buying more cheaply and of selling their products to better advantage. I think in that way you would avoid a sort of criticism which I have seen aimed at this bill—that it is class legislation. I do not think anybody can say it is class legislation to say that laboring men can have the same right to combine for collective bargaining as stockholders have. Neither is it class legislation to say that farmers and consumers can combine for the sake of buying more cheaply or selling to greater advantage. That is not class legislation; everybody ought to have that right. I think you can leave the abuses to the general phraseology. If those associations when formed become offenders against the Sherman law, they can be brought to book under the Sherman law.

STATEMENT OF PROF. JOHN BATES CLARK.

Prof. CLARK—Mr. Chairman and gentlemen of the committee:

There are two ways in which the problem of dealing with trusts in the making may be approached, and both are legitimate; but one is enormously more important than the other.

The more important one consists in identifying monopolistic acts and putting an end to them; the other is dealing with combination as such without special reference to the means by which it is brought about.

History has something to say as to attacking combinations as such. At the time when manufacturing business was conducted in guilds and in very small shops with a master workman, a journeyman, an apprentice or two and now and then two or three hired workmen there were laws which forbade partnership, on the ground that it extinguished competition between those who formed the partnerships and without reference to the question whether any essential harm was done by it. It was discovered at once that if the partnerships competed vigorously with other partnerships no essential harm was done, and that the public was adequately protected. In many instances the competition which took place between the larger units was more vigorous and afforded a better type of protection for the public than did the competition which existed between the master workmen. The real distinction which the law needed to draw was between that amount of partnership building which would sacrifice the interests of the public by extinguishing competition outside of the partnership; and that which left competition in full vigor. The laws became a dead letter. They have stood on the statute books for centuries without having any effect or any attention paid to them.

There are, among others, two very familiar and well-known ways in which trusts can grow to the proportions of monopoly. One is local competition—cutthroat competition in a limited territory, where a rival is working, accompanied by a sustaining of prices elsewhere; the other is what used to be known as the factor's agreement; that is, an agreement not to sell a product to anybody who will buy a similar product from any one else. Suppose there is a manufacturing concern operating in about three States; there is a trust producing a similar product operating all over the country and in foreign countries. In addition to having a larger area of operation it has a larger variety of products. The small competitor has only one kind of product and the trust has twenty kinds of products. It could almost afford, if necessary, to give away the one kind on a large scale to carry out its purpose and acquire a complete monopoly. Now, under those conditions, the trust has two possible ways of easily crushing the local competitor. One is to enter his territory with cutthroat competition and make it impossible for him to sell his product at a rate that will pay the cost; the other is to refuse to sell any of the trust-made products to the rival's customers and so bring about a boycott of the independent producer by the merchants who have been handling his products.

Let us suppose it does the latter. Suppose it sends its agents to the customers of the independent producer and gives them notice that if they buy any more from the local producer they cannot have any of the trust-made products, which they need to have in order to conduct a successful mercantile business. That plan will produce a more immediate effect on the local producer and will be done with even less cost to the combination than the former method of cutthroat competition. It is cheaper and quicker in some cases. In somo cases it is not as sure as the other, and the other has to be resorted to. I should not have a particle of objection, from an economic point of view, to the making of independent definitions of those things and forbidding them, provided I was satisfied it would not be necessary to bring suits in order to secure an interpretation of the language of the new statute.

The problem I would like to raise is whether the Sherman law as it stands, and under the construction that is now put upon it by the courts, would be sufficient to enable that man easily to bring an action that would at once restrain the trust from doing what it was doing, and so give him adequate protection and enable him to go on in safety in his business. If it would, that is all that is needed; and it is a lawyer's question whether it would or not; but unless something in the law will accomplish exactly that result and enable a person who is confronted with such a condition as the one described to get redress quickly and cheaply, and not be forced to wait for a complete monopoly to grow up before taking action, we shall have very troublous times.

Mr. NELSON—I would like to ask you this question: The Sherman law prohibits every restraint of trade. The Supreme Court has read into that the words undue or unreasonable. When a judge interprets the law in order to discover whether some alleged violation is undue or unreasonable, what will he have to draw upon, his legal knowledge or his economic views?

Professor CLARK—I should say that, with a background of legal knowledge which would be a very essential thing, he would here use his economic knowledge.

There is many a line which it is perfectly possible to draw clearly in theory, but it will take a good deal of skill and judgment to draw such lines in practice. That I conceive to be the situation here. I do not think there is any haziness whatever in the scientific delimitation of the reasonable conduct, but I do see that conditions shade each other by such imperceptible degrees that any court would be liable to more or less of error in applying the principles. I do not see how it is possible absolutely to avoid this, and yet I do not think it will be possible to have a tolerable condition unless the law brings the action of corporations into line with what is described as the rule of reason.

I would like to add that the sole objection which I have urged against any part of the series of tentative bills under consideration applies to a phrase in Bill No. 2. Four general purposes of combination are specified as bringing a combination under the condemnation of the proposed law. The fourth of these would seem to prohibit any combination or partnership between independent producers, even though competition were not less effective after they had combined than it was before. Competition has been rendered comparatively ineffective in some part of the market for the goods produced; a natural economic law fixes the prices of them and protects the public from extortion. After A has ceased to compete with B, and C has ceased to compete with D, A and B in partnership may compete so vigorously with C and D in partnership as to afford an undiminished

(Concluded on page 18.)

OPENING OF THE VACATION HEADQUARTERS

A DEMOCRATIC SOCIAL CENTER FOR SELF-SUPPORTING GIRLS AND WOMEN IN THE HEART OF INDUSTRIAL NEW YORK

RECEPTION ROOM IN THE VACATION LODGING HOUSE, VACATION HEADQUARTERS.

THE RESTAURANT.

THE new Headquarters of the Vacation Savings Fund at 38 West Thirty-ninth street, New York City, was formally opened on Wednesday, April 1. The occasion marked a long forward step in the development of the work of the Vacation Committee—the largest and one of the most interesting and successful undertakings of the Woman's Department of The National Civic Federation.

In two years the work of the Vacation Savings Fund, and the larger possibilities growing out of the idea, developed to such an extent that the provision of a definite centre for its many activities became a real necessity. A large house on Thirty-ninth Street and two immediately adjoining in the rear on Thirty-eighth Street were taken for the purpose, connected, remodeled and equipped throughout with thoughtful attention to every detail of comfort, attractiveness and a homelike atmosphere. The controlling idea in the planning of all the arrangements was to meet the actual needs and desires expressed by the depositaries of the fund themselves. Indeed, the entire plan has in view a practically self-sustaining and self-governing home center and social gathering place for all the 15,000 or more members of the Vacation Savings Fund who may choose to become "taxpayers" to the extent of one dollar per year towards the maintenance expenditures of the Headquarters.

There are no restrictive "club" conditions of membership, and no rules other than the common obligation of the mutual observance of mutual rights. Included in the facilities of the two buildings are an attractive lunch room, a large and airy recreation hall, a lounging room, writing room, dressing room with private baths and dressing compartments, local secretaries' living room, juniors' room, reception room for men and women, and a considerable number of bedrooms, most attractively decorated and furnished, for rent upon reasonable terms to girls entitled to the privileges of the building.

The Executive Committee of the Vacation Savings Fund, under whose auspices the new Headquarters has been established, consists of Miss Robinson Smith, chairman; Mrs. August Belmont, vice-chairman; Mrs. Montague Flagg, secretary; Miss Anne Morgan, treasurer; Mrs. Rogers H. Bacon, Mrs. C. H. Hill, Mrs. A. W. Porter, Miss S. F. Robbins, Miss M. Sullivan and Miss Caroline Shippen.

The story of the Savings Fund work, merging into the enlarged activities of the new Headquarters, is best told by Miss Robinson Smith, chairman of the committee, to whom the original idea of the fund and much of the successful direction of its spontaneous growth are due. In The Bulletin of the Woman's Department, Miss Smith, in response to requests for a history of the undertaking, traces its origin to the forming of a committee in 1910 to bring about co-operation between the New York and New Jersey Section of the Woman's Department, and the Committee on Amusements and Vacation Resources, which had been engaged in investigating country boarding houses for the benefit particularly of women employees of industrial and mercantile establishments.

In the course of the work of this committee the fact developed that a great many girls could not avail themselves of the lists of approved boarding places, because no vacation money had been saved. Vacations with salaries are very far from universal, and many who do receive salaries while absent have other obligations to meet.

"A number of years ago," says Miss Smith, "I was very much interested in a girls' club, and the first Summer of its existence we found that our girls did not leave the city during the hot months. In the Fall I asked a number of them about this, and they all said it was because they had not had the money to go away. I then suggested the perfectly obvious plan that they should put aside a definite amount each week for their Summer vacation, and in order to make it more interesting to them we organized a Vacation Club. A great number of girls took advantage of it, and the following Summer about fifty of them had enough saved to go away. The plan worked so admirably and suggested so many possibilities that it made me feel that it could be done on a larger scale; therefore, when we were confronted with the same 'lack of saving' problem in the Vacation Committee I wrote in August, 1911, to the chairman of the Section, Mrs. Francis McNeil

Bacon, and outlined the present system of the Vacation Savings Fund as a means of overcoming the difficulty. The question was presented to Mr. Low, president of The National Civic Federation, who approved of the idea. A mass meeting was called of the girls who had used the lists of investigated Summer boarding houses, and, after an informal discussion, they requested the Committee to work out some plan. As a result the Vacation Savings Fund was organized in December, 1911, with forty-three girls, who deposited $26.70.

"The stamp system was adopted, stamps serving as receipts for money deposited. These stamps are pasted on a card until the amount of $2.00 is reached, when the amount is transferred to a pass book, as the Committee assumes responsibility only for the pass book. No interest is paid to depositors, every one withdrawing cent for cent what she has deposited. In order to facilitate depositing by saving time and carfare we decided to seek the co-operation of the various employers in the city with a view to enlisting their interest so that they would arrange the time for one of their women employees to act as local secretary and permit a local station to be opened in their factory or shop. The local secretary must be in sympathetic touch with the girls, and the success of any station depends on the way she presents the plan to them. The employers' interest was immediate and sustained. To-day one hundred and fifty local stations have been opened, and over sixteen thousand girls have deposited $125,000, of which $98,000 has been withdrawn principally for vacations.

"To advertise the Vacation Savings Fund among the self-supporting women and girls of the city we hold vacation evenings every month; they also serve the purpose of bringing together informally the girls, the local secretaries and the members of the Committee. These evenings have been really illuminating, as they show the wonderful spirit of good fellowship which has been developed between the members of the Committee and the girls. The sympathetic interest which gave them birth was genuine and continues to increase in depth and potential possibilities. The meeting is opened by the girls singing the "Star Spangled Banner"; a monthly report is then made by the chairman, and is followed by an open discussion as to the ways and means of developing the work. The entertainments on these occasions are varied; music, fancy dancing, vaudeville skits, moving pictures (both educational and entertaining), have been included in the program, with talks on topics of interest by prominent speakers. Dancing and refreshments always close the evening. Three halls have been outgrown, the attendance increasing from one hundred and twenty at the first in December, 1911, to fourteen hundred at one time, when we were obliged to turn away five hundred girls. Since that time we have issued cards of admission for depositors.

"The success of this work largely depends upon the interest and co-operation of the local secretaries, who for the past year have been represented on the Executive Committee of the Vacation Committee. This group of women have become so essentially helpful that we suggested they should form a committee of local secretaries, and elect their own officers and representatives on our Executive Committee; in this way, all questions of importance are discussed by their committee, as well as by the depositors at the Vacation Evenings, before they are finally passed upon by the Vacation Committee. We try to make the work as nearly self-supporting as possible, though at present we are not entirely successful. The depositors help to defray expenses by their annual ball at the Grand Central Palace, in conjunction with which an entertainment is usually given, in which depositors take part. Last year the ball netted $3,000, and this, with the interest from the girls' money, represented their share of the expense of the Committee.

"Last Spring it was decided to further enlarge the work by renting a house for the use of depositors. This house, known as the Vacation Headquarters, was opened on January 1, 1914. There is a restaurant where girls may lunch and dine, and where they may bring their men friends for dinner. In the Assembly Hall there are weekly 'hops,' moving pictures, social evenings, Sunday afternoon concerts and classes in dancing, dramatics and singing. A special feature is a room where they may at any time receive their men friends. We feel that this is particularly important, as it prevents girls from meeting men in public places or on street corners. On the upper floors there are dressing rooms and baths and rooms where the girls may rest quietly, read or write. In the two adjoining houses we have bedrooms for rent. Any depositor wishing to have the full privileges of the Headquarters must become a taxpayer. This she may do upon payment of $1.00 a year. The taxpayers govern the policy of the Headquarters, and in time we hope they, too, will form a committee with their own officers, and so take more complete charge of the work. We try to keep the organization as elastic as possible in all its developments, so that at any time we can undertake anything new that presents itself. As, for instance, in the case of the SPUGS, which was an outgrowth of the Vacation Savings Fund.

"In the Fall of 1912 one of the local secretaries came into the office and told us that there was no need of sending our collectors to her station again before Christmas. When we questioned this she said that the girls would not be saving their money on account of the Christmas presents which they would have to give the girls in the shops, and the contributions that they would be obliged to make for the collective presents to the

BUSINESS OFFICE OF THE VACATION FUND.

THE ASSEMBLY ROOM.

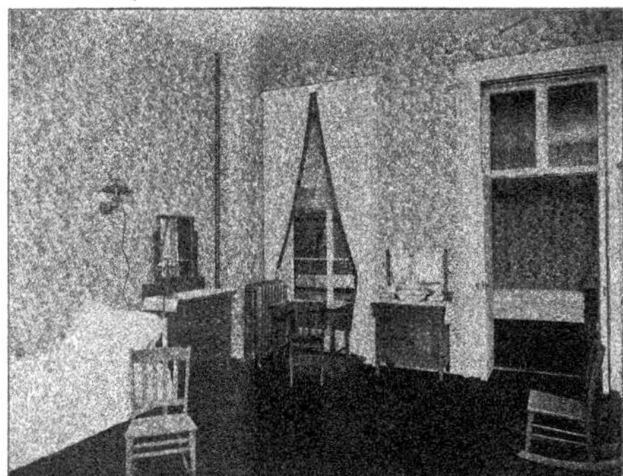

ONE OF THE BEDROOMS IN THE VACATION LODGING HOUSE, VACATION HEADQUARTERS.

'man higher up.' We immediately started an investigation, and found that this evil was even more serious than we had at first been led to believe. The consequence was that Mrs. August Belmont made a splendidly stirring address at one of the vacation evenings, with the result that the Society for the Prevention of Useless Giving was organized, and, as you know, has been taken up all over the country. The first year we gave a SPUG Christmas party in our office, to which over one hundred and sixty people came. The success of this party made us feel that we wanted to do it on a larger scale this year, and so on Christmas Day the Grand Central Palace was thrown open to any lonely man, woman and child who had nowhere else to go. We had a beautifully lighted tree, which was given by the State of Maine, and a lunch counter from which coffee and sandwiches were served. A friend gave a band, so that there was dancing and great joy throughout the afternoon and evening for over five thousand people."

As we go to press, arrangements are in progress for the third annual entertainment and ball at the Grand Central Palace, on Thursday evening, April 30. This is, perhaps, the crowning event of the year in the varied activities of the Vacation Fund and Headquarters, serving to bring together, as is possible on no other one occasion, a very large proportion of the entire membership. Judging from the experience of previous years, the attendance will be upwards of ten thousand.

The Vacation Fund has been the most conspicuous feature, also, of the work thus far undertaken by the Massachusetts and Rhode Island section of the Woman's Department. More than two thousand depositors have been registered there during twenty-two months, with a total account of upwards of $18,000. The Vacation Fund idea proved to be one, furthermore, which developed the most immediate interest and enthusiasm in the recent formation of a new section of the department in Chicago, where the organization of the work is now in successful progress.

ESSENTIALS IN TRUST REGULATION

(Continued from page 15.)

guaranty of fair prices. An economist must distinguish between the combination which reduces the total amount and efficiency of competition and that which does not, and the law will need to take account of that same distinction.

Before the Committee on Interstate and Foreign Commerce, Hon. William C. Adamson, Chairman.

STATEMENT OF HON. SETH LOW.

Mr. LOW—I welcome very heartily, Mr. Chairman and gentlemen, the development of the Bureau of Corporations into an Interstate Trade Commission, because I think that the Commission will prove itself a very useful agency for the advantage and benefit of business in the United States.

Section 3 of this bill gives the proposed Commission the widest possible rights of search, which I suppose to be a natural function of government for the enforcement of law. However, when you reach Section 4 the bill says that the information so obtained "shall be public records," and the Commission shall, from time to time, "make public such information in such form and such extent as it may deem necessary." It seems to me that the result of publicity is eminently good within the proper limits of publicity. I do not suppose that Congress would willingly take the ground that it could go into the private affairs of every individual practicing business, that is, carrying on interstate business in the United States, and make such affairs public records. Do we not find the basis for publicity, in the sense contemplated by this bill, in the fact of incorporation? In other words, when men are carrying on business at the hazard of their entire fortunes, they are entitled to a quality of privacy, if you please, that is not reasonable for anyone when he asks from the government the authority to carry on business with limited liability.

Mr. F. C. STEVENS—Are there not two other reasons upon which Congress has the perfect right to demand the publicity of private affairs; first, whenever it is needed for the purpose of legislation; second, for the purpose of administering justice?

Mr. LOW—Precisely. But have you the right under the first clause to send agents into private houses and inquire as to the details and secrets of business? All that I am contending for is that the Section 4 ought to be protected as Section 9 is protected, and as the Bureau of Corporations was protected. If you turn to Section 9, at the close, you find the permit in these words:

> "Said findings shall become a public record of the Commission, as provided in Section 4, only upon the direction of the Attorney-General or the President."

It seems to me that that restriction ought to be placed in Section 4 of this act. I should also be afraid of Section 3, unless it is very carefully administered; lest there would be built up a great army of "grafters," to use the phrase that is so common in the public life of the country, because of what they may thus learn. If the Commission keeps close track of all the inquiries that it makes through authorized agents, perhaps that fear is an unnecessary one.

Mr. SIMS—I should like to ask if you think it could possibly be to the public interest for rivals in the same business to have access to each other's books to the end that they might use them against each other, rather than to benefit or improve their own business? If they were ordinary public records, like the registry of deeds, they would be subject to anybody's inspection, and rivals in the same business would have access to them just the same as anyone else. Would it not be injurious to the public as a whole? Would it not promote controversy between rivals, rather than promote the public interest?

Mr. LOW—I think that would be the distinct effect. The suggestion that this bill should be further amended so as to provide for uniform accounting I think is a perfectly legitimate object for the Congress to try to bring about. Especially, now that the income tax has become part of the fiscal system of the country, it is almost incumbent upon Congress to have the accounts of these great industrial corporations kept in a similar manner, just as the railroads now account in a uniform way, so that they can be sure that the basis upon which the income tax is paid is the same in all cases. In its relation to the tariff question, also, we never shall know how much these corporations are making, at any rate comparatively, unless we have the same sort of accounting from them all. Of course, you could not compel uniform accounting of industrial corporations that were essentially unlike; yet I think it has been of very good service in connection with public utilities of every kind. I should like to see this Commission equipped to consider that problem.

Mr. ESCH—Do you believe that the Trade Commission should have the right even to investigate through its agents the secret processes or formulae?

Mr. LOW—I do not think it should. But I think that under Section 3 it could.

Mr. ESCH—I agree with you. I think that is very embracing language.

Mr. LOW—It seems to me that the two legitimate objects of inquiry on the part of the government are, first of all, to learn whether any law is being broken. If there is anything that it is necessary to inquire into to determine that, I should think the government could properly do it. The other thing is, so much publicity as to the financial methods and standing of a corporation as will justify the limited liability under which it operates. It seems to me that as long as men carry on their business with their whole fortunes at stake, it is a very novel proposition, to an American, at any rate, that the government can inquire into everything they do, when they are not charged in any way with wrongdoing.

What we see at the present time is that the Attorney-General of the United States, by agreement with different corporations which he thinks are violating the Sherman law, arranges with one and another a basis which will bring them in his opinion within the law. As a temporary procedure I am inclined to think that plan is serving very well, but as a permanent method of administering the law I do not think I have been trained in a way to think that it would work well. In the first place, Attorneys-General do not remain always in the office, and one Attorney-General may succeed another whose views are entirely different. Consequently you may have the law interpreted one way during one Presidential term, and in another way during another Presidential term, and instead of having a uniform law you have a law that is changeable. It may mean one thing during four years and another thing during another four years. I had supposed that this bill was intended to do away with that danger, and to supplant the possible variations of opinion of different Attorneys-General by creating a permanent Trade Commission whose membership changes slowly, and whose administration of the law, in time, would become pretty uniform and well established, so that the business of the country would have the benefit of uniform law.

Mr. ESCH—If a corporation dominates the field to the extent of monopoly, would you advocate giving this Trade Commission power to order it to stop or to reduce its size?

Mr. LOW—I do not think we gave any such power to the Commission in the bill the Civic Federation drafted. The sub-committee, which prepared the draft, kept certain definitions in its bill for a year and a half, and the more we inquired into the matter the less possible we found it to make definitions which would accomplish only what we wanted them to accomplish. We could not forsee the multitude of effects that general definitions would have.

MANY-SIDED ACTIVITIES OF THE WOMAN'S DEPARTMENT

.EPORTS OF WORK IN PROGRESS FROM NEW ENGLAND TO FLORIDA SHOW GROWING ENTHUSIASM AND A LONG RECORD OF PRACTICAL RESULTS

THAT the Woman's Department of The National Civic Federation is rapidly becoming one of the most effective of our present-day agencies direct social amelioration is clear from the survey re given of the vigor and success with which it is king hold of great opportunities, as well as neg-cted corners, in many departments of industrial d civic life.

NEW YORK AND NEW JERSEY.

An account of the efforts of the New York and ew Jersey Section in behalf of prison reform, cul-inating in the formation of a State-wide Joint Com-ittee of eighteen members, is given on another ge.

The opening of the new center on Thirty-ninth reet, New York, for the accommodation of the fast owing and varied activities of the Vacation Savings und, is also described elsewhere in this number.

Simultaneously, the New York and New Jersey ection has been carrying forward aggressively the ork of its several committees engaged in special ases of social service.

Workhouse Committee. Mrs. F. H. Cabot, Chairman. his committee is actively co-operating with the ew York Prison Association in its efforts to co-rdinate and systematize the work of various agen-es already in the field. The improvement in condi-ons at the Workhouse since Commissioner Katherine . Davis took office has been marked. Physical and ental examinations are now being made, enabling e matrons to make suitable segregation of the omen and transfers to the proper institutions for ose mentally defective.

Hotel Employees Committee. Mrs. Marcus M. arks, Chairman. The work of this committee has een the amplifying on broader lines of the inves-gation of last year. A special investigator has isited 100 hotels to date, finding the need of social orkers, and a right type of woman for housekeeper, be everywhere apparent.

Occupational Diseases Committee. Mrs. William and, Jr., Chairman. A comprehensive study of the ect of treadle occupations upon women workers s undertaken, in charge of Dr. Ebba Almgren derer, of Cornell University. So persistent has en the impression that treadle work is injurious at exceptional care is being taken to trace all ses, and forestall any charge of inadequate inves-gation before the final report is printed.

School Committee. Mrs. Chauncey Marshall, Chair-an. In October, 1913, the Board of Education in-rmed this committee that appropriations had been ade of sufficient moneys to properly equip the achers' retiring rooms, according to our standard commendation, in the schools of Manhattan and ooklyn. The committee has been actively rein-stigating, to be assured of the proper carrying out the recommendations.

New Buildings Committee. Miss M. B. Cross, hairman. The New Buildings Committee has been pecially active, and many plans of hospitals, rses' training schools, factories and stores have en examined, and various suggestions for possible provements made.

Industrial Welfare Committee. Mrs. Magee Ells-orth, Chairman. This committee was recently rmed, to co-operate with the other committees nd to follow up any suggestions from them re-arding conditions observed and needing investiga-ion. The scope of this committee is to be greatly nlarged, as it has been asked for advice and co-peration by a number of managers of large office uildings.

MASSACHUSETTS AND RHODE ISLAND.

The annual report of the Massachusetts and hode Island Section of the Woman's Department, ust issued, is a splendid record of widening efforts nd solid results achieved. The following portions f the report prepared by the Chairman of the Sec-ion, Mrs. George T. Rice, give an illuminating ac-ount of the progress of the work in hand. With pecial reference to the work of the Industrial Com-ittee, the report says:

"Under this committee, Mrs. Roger Wolcott, Chairman, sub-committees on Building, Housing and Occupational Hygiene have been formed. Since the last Annual Report more than 100 interviews have been obtained with officials, and 161 visits have been made to manufacturing and mercantile establishments in 43 cities and towns.

"Typewritten recommendations forwarded to the manufacturers following visits have been well received. Inspections have been undertaken of the Stations in the Boston Postal District, and have been completed at the main office, North and South Postal Stations, and Essex Street."

"The Prison Committee," says Mrs. Rice, "with Mrs. Francis Gray as chairman, is now in process of formation. This committee, with the approval of and in conjunction with various authorities, intends to undertake the care of women for at least one year after their discharge from penal institutions, each member taking an interest in one ex-prisoner.

"Upon the request of the Governor of Rhode Island, visits were made to State and county institutions, including jails, House of Correction, Alms House, Prison, Reception Hospital, State Hospital for the Insane, and Industrial Schools for Boys and Girls. Reports of inspection, together with recommendations for the new buildings for which an appropriation has been made, have been submitted to the Governor.".

Attention is elsewhere called in this number to the growth of the Vacation Savings Fund in Massachusetts, represented chiefly by the stations in Boston and Worcester. Miss Elizabeth S. Porter is chairman of this committee, which "has registered in its Stamp Savings Fund over 2,000 depositors, with a total deposit, since the beginning of the work twenty-two months ago, of more than $18,000. * * * A list of investigated summer boarding-houses, both country and seashore, has been prepared for the past two years, and distributed, gratis, to depositors."

The report calls attention to the lectures given during the past winter under the auspices of the Lecture Committee. Mrs. Malcolm Donald, Chairman, and states that it is expected to continue these lectures next winter, with a longer course.

DISTRICT OF COLUMBIA.

Similarly inspiring is the report recently made public by the District of Columbia Section of the Department, covering the work of the last three months. Mrs. Archibald Hopkins, Chairman of the Section, thus summarizes in part the recent activities in progress:

"The Government Employees' Welfare Committee, Mrs. McLaughlin, Chairman, reports that in the Sixth Auditor's Office of the Treasury a recommendation has been made by Surgeon-General Blue of the Public Health Service, that the punching machines used in that office should be worked by electricity instead of by women, as it is a most injurious form of work. There is every reason to think that this recommendation will be carried out in the near future.

"The Public Printer, Mr. Cornelius Ford, has promised to install much needed rest and lunch rooms in the Government Printing Office, where 4,000 employees work day and night. * * * The Department of Commerce has promised to install lunch and rest rooms in their new building to which an addition is being built for the use of the permanent Census Office.

"A dispute between employer and employees in a large business firm has been settled to the absolute satisfaction of both sides. The personal thanks of the heads of the concern have been received. This is felt to be the best piece of work d.ne by the District of Columbia Section.

"The lunch room at the Navy Yard, started by this Section and now managed by a committee of three men, is self-supporting and is feeding 800 men daily, with good food. * * * The Tuberculosis Hospital is under the management of a committee, whose chairman is Mrs. McGill, and her committee is working with the approbation and full consent of the Board of Charities. The hospital is quite equal to any similar one in the country and the dietary is above the average, and practically on a level with that of any family of ordinary means.

"The Section, in connection with the Monday Evening Club, the Associated Charities and other civic and charitable organizations, over 200 in number, have united in presenting and pressing a bill for opening the schools as civic centers. This work is under the chairmanship of Miss Margaret Woodrow Wilson.

"In connection with other civic organizations the Section is urging the passage by Congress of three items in the District Appropriation bill. The first is for a new Municipal Hospital, the conditions of the present one being absolutely impossible. The appropriation for a new municipal lodging house is being urged, as the existing one is a disgrace. Again the Section, in connection with all other associations, is urging a bill for a place where feeble-minded of both sexes and both races can be sent.

"The Alley bills for converting the alleys, in the course of the next ten years, into minor streets, playgrounds, garages and stable alleys, have been introduced by Senator Smith and Hon. Ben Johnson, Chairman of the District Committees in the Senate and House, and are now being carefully considered by the sub-committees to which they have been referred. Should these bills pass, it is felt in them alone, the existence of the District of Columbia Section will have been justified, as they will change the living conditions of over eleven thousand people who until now have been living under unbearable conditions.

"With a view to the passage of these bills, a tremendous effort is being made to provide sanitary dwellings for the thousands to be evicted, and to that end the Section has been the means of turning $15,500 into the treasury of the Sanitary Housing Company, an organization which furnishes sanitary houses from $7.50 to $13.50, and pays 5 per cent to subscribers, with a reserve of 4 per cent. This company placed nearly a year ago 214 of its apartments in the hands of the Housing Committee of the Section, Mrs. Ernest P. Bicknell, Chairman, for management. With the aid of a trained social worker, success has been very great, and it is planned at the end of the year to hand the property back to the company, to be continued, it is hoped, under the management of the same worker, and to try to get other houses and to bring them up to the same standard.

"The membership runs an average of about 350. The semi-monthly lectures on topics of interest are largely attended and create a great deal of interest. Mrs. Wilson honors us almost invariably by her presence, and her influence and help are of the greatest possible value.

"Mrs. Archibald Hopkins, Chairman of the District of Columbia Section, has been appointed by the President of the United States as Government visitor to the Hospital for the Insane."

A further extension of the work of the District of Columbia Section is the recent formation of a Teachers' Section, which is interesting itself chiefly in the subject of vocational guidance in connection with the public school system. A meeting of this committee, of which Miss Elizabeth V. Brown is Chairman, was held at the public library in Washington, and addressed by Mr. Meyer Bloomfield, director of the Vocation Bureau of Boston.

PROGRESS IN OTHER SECTIONS.

Efforts along similar lines to those in Washington for the improvement of alley and housing conditions are under way in Baltimore and Richmond. A recent meeting of the District of Columbia Section, devoted to a discussion of the co-related work in these two cities, was addressed by Miss Harlean James, of Baltimore, and Mr. Gustavus A. Weber, of Richmond. Mrs. Hopkins, presiding at the meeting, urged the co-operation of Washington with Baltimore and Richmond for the solution of these and other civic problems common to the three cities.

Mrs. John K. Ottley, Chairman of the *Georgia Section*, reports that improved conditions for employees are being provided by employers with increasing interest. Some of the most important work being carried on by the Georgia and Florida Sections has been that of prison inspections, followed by recommendations of needed changes.

Mrs. William Brooks Young, Chairman of the *Florida Section*, states that deplorable conditions were found at the State Reform School at Marianna, and reported to the Governor. The Florida Federation of Women's Clubs was asked to take up the matter. "This year," said Mrs. Young, "the Legislature gave an increased appropriation, changed the name of the institution, and appointed a much more efficient board of managers. While much remains to be done, public opinion in the State has been aroused."

Among the various other useful labors of the Florida Section, Mrs. Young notes that owners and lessors of large buildings under construction have been visited and asked that especial attention be given to retiring rooms for women employees. These

(Continued on page 24.)

PRACTICAL WORK OF THE WELFARE DEPARTMENT

SOME of the most significant and interesting among the recent activities of the Welfare Department have been the services rendered in connection with the following new undertakings:

(1) Establishment by the Sinking Fund Commission of the City of New York of a restaurant and rest room for the five hundred women employees in the new Municipal Building; followed by a conference of the Mayor, the Comptroller, the City Chamberlain and the presidents of five boroughs of the city to consider the introduction of welfare work for municipal employees in all departments of the city administration.

(2) Installation of extensive welfare features at the Shelton Looms, Derby, Conn.

(3) Provision of a rest room, including emergency hospital equipment, for the use of women employees of tenants of the offices in the new Garrett Buil[ding,] Baltimore.

(4) Exhibit of welfare work at Hotel Astor d[uring] the recent annual meeting of The National C[ivic] Federation.

Particulars of two of these matters are given be[low] and a description of the other two will appear in [a] number of the REVIEW. Each furnishes, from diffe[rent] angles, illustrations of the modern spirit in indus[try.]

Conference of New York City Officials, upon Invitation of Haley Fiske, member of the Welfare Department of The National Civic Federation

To conside[r] the Introductio[n] of Welfare W[ork] for Employe[es] in all City Departme[nts]

1. HALEY FISKE
2. JOHN PURROY MITCHEL, Mayor of New York
3. GEORGE McANENY
4. HENRY BRUÈRE
5. WILLIAM A. PRENDERGAST
6. MARCUS M. MARKS
7. LEWIS K. POUNDS
8. MAURICE E. CONNOLLY
9. DOUGLAS MATHEWSON
10. C. J. McCORMACK
11. C. L. CLOSE
12. F. J. H. KRACKE
13. WILLIAM R. WILLCOX
14. DR. LEE K. FRANKEL
15. RALPH M. EASLEY
16. Miss GERTRUDE BE[EKS]
17. Miss MARY G. POTTE[R]
18. Miss CARRIE B. OSG[OOD]

WELFARE WORK FOR NEW YORK CITY EMPLOYEES

Welfare work for municipal employees in New York City has been launched in a big way by the new administration. The initiative was taken by the City Chamberlain, Hon. Henry Bruère, who wrote to the Welfare Department of The National Civic Federation at the end of February, stating: "We are to have about 500 women in our new Municipal Building and I am very anxious that we should make proper provision for their comfort by way of rest rooms, lunch rooms, et cetera." His request for an interview with the Director of the Welfare Department resulted in an appeal on her part for a general scheme to cover all Departments of the city, with the result that the entire Board of Estimate enthusiastically accepted an invitation extended by Mr. Haley Fiske, a member of the Executive Committee of the Welfare Department, to attend a luncheon on Friday, March 27, 1914, to consider the matter and to learn what has been done in private enterprises which might be regarded as good examples to be followed. The luncheon was held in the Executive Dining Room of the Metropolitan Life Insurance Company for the reason that it has provided model welfare arrangements for its employees in that building worthy of emulation in an exceptional degree, and applicable in most respects to conditions under which large numbers of men and women are employed in the service of the city.

Those who were present, in addition to the Mayor, John Purroy Mitchel; the President of the Board of Aldermen, George McAneny; the City Chamberlain, Henry Bruère; and the Comptroller, William A. Prendergast, were: The Borough Presidents, Marcus M. Marks, Douglas Mathewson, Lewis K. Pounds, Maurice E. Connolly, C. J. McCormack, and the Commissioner of Bridges, F. J. H. Kracke; and John R. Hegeman, President of The Metropolitan Life Insurance Company; C. L. Close, Chairman Welfare Bureau, The United States Steel Corporation; William R. Willcox, Chairman Welfare Department, and R. M. Easley, Chairman Executive Council, The National Civic Federation; Dr. Lee K. Frankel, Sixth Vice-President, The Metropolitan Life Insurance Company; Miss Gertrude Beeks, Director, and Miss Mary G. Potter, Secretary, respectively, of the Welfare Department of The National Civic Federation.

Mr. HALEY FISKE, Vice-President of the Metropolitan Life Insurance Company, who was the host on this occasion, in extending a cordial welcome to the city officials, stated that the Chairman of the Welfare Department, William R. Willcox, had long been of the opinion that the municipality ought to be the leader in welfare work for its employees. He explained that the bundles of literature at the guests' plates contained, in each instance, accounts of beneficial arrangements of twelve corporations and that, during luncheon, there would be thrown upon the screen stereopticon views of features in the plant of The Curtis Publishing Company at Philadelphia and of like conveniences in the Metropolitan Building in New York, applicable to the various buildings of the city, as well as others indicating some of the developments and large expenditures in this connection by employers throughout the country.

Upon request, Mr. Fiske outlined the activities of his company. He stated, among other things:

"We have 12,000 men in the field and 4,000 employees in our home office. We spend $300,000 a year in pensions, treating each case according to its needs—a man with a dozen children receiving more than a bachelor.

"We have something over $2,000,000 in our staff savings fund and nearly 9,000 depositors. The company contributes 50% of the deposits made by the employees each year. An employee cannot draw out the company's contribution until laid aside by sickness, but his own may b[e] drawn at any time. Employees receive abo[ut] 9% on their savings.

"We built a sanitarium at Mt. McGregor, cos[t]ing about $2,000,000, for the care of tubercul[ous] employees. It will, when completed, accomm[o]date 200 patients. At present there are 2[..] men and women there. It is being made [a] scientific centre for the study of diseases.

"Our clerical force numbers about 3,800, 2,0[00] being women. The men average $20 a we[ek] in pay; their length of service 9 years a[nd] their age about 30. The women average $1[.] in pay, 7 years in service and 27 years in a[ge.] The women receive $300 in cash at the end [of] five years, $500 at the end of nine years a[nd] $200 extra per year thereafter. The minimu[m] wage for women clerks is $9 and for stenogra[]phers $11.

"Lunches without expense to them and [re]garded as a supplement to wages are given [to] all men and women clerks and to elevator me[n,] porters, stationary firemen, mechanics in th[e] printing building, and to heads of departments, amounting to more than 4,000 every day and costing last year $166,982. The menu to-day is: Clam chowder, Spanish mackerel, corned be[ef] hash, potatoes, cup custard or ice cream, and tea, coffee or milk. This is, in the case of man[y] women, the most substantial meal of the day.

"Wedding lunches are permitted in the youn[g] ladies' lunch room. We had 27 weddings last year.

"There is a gymnasium, both interior and out[]door, upon the roof. We have a large and beau[]tifully decorated assembly room for recrea[]tion thirty-five minutes after luncheon and to be used by the Choral Society, the Men's Gl[ee] Club, and for dancing. There is an athle[tic] association.

"The hospital is attended by trained nurs[es] and physicians, among these being eye, nos[e] and ear specialists. Ten thousand cases we[re] cared for last year in the emergency hospital.

A nurse visits the sick in their homes. About [illegible] of the patients are women. The head nurse, Miss Robbins, makes friends with all the girls, inquires into their circumstances and home surroundings and performs every type of service from 'burying the baby to arranging a European trip.'

"At present, we are especially concerned as to our hygienic conditions. Five hundred cubic feet of air is allotted to each person, the ceilings being 12½ feet high. We are now analyzing the air, looking into the means of ingress and egress and looking generally into the physical efficiency of the plant.

"Sanitary arrangements are of the best type. Shower baths are provided in the gymnasium and for the stationary firemen in their quarters. There is a locker for each employee; 2,000 umbrellas are maintained to be loaned; individual towels are furnished and laundered free, each employee having a small individual towel locker with key.

"The men and women use different elevators. They work from 9 a. m. to 4:30 p. m., except on Saturdays, when they stop at 1 p. m. Employees are rewarded for punctuality and fined for absence without leave.

"Two weeks' vacation are allowed with the right of the superior officer to grant four with pay. After that, the matter is taken up by the Finance Committee. In case of serious illness, there is no time limit. Such contingencies are guarded against by having physical examination of new employees. In spite of this, they sometimes break down after a few months in our employ but, once in, we always take care of them when ill.

"There is also a civil service examination in writing, arithmetic and other fundamentals. Our examination papers are equivalent to the Eighth grade of the public school. The applicant passes on an average of 80% and is placed on the available list, generally numbering about 1,500 or 2,000, from which we make selections.

"We have a library for the employees containing from six to seven thousand volumes, and also have a branch of the New York Public Library.

"Our employees are given instruction in stenography, English, French, German, business letter writing, and so forth. The classes are held after 4:30 o'clock."

Chairman WILLIAM R. WILLCOX said that there as been a great step forward among employers in ndustrial enterprises in the way of providing welare accommodations, but that much had not been one in this connection by the governments of the tates or cities. He also said that the large sum of 6,000,000 expended annually by the United States teel Corporation for its 200,000 employees is inicative of what might be undertaken by a city ke New York and that, in his experience as a ublic official, he had not known of a government uilding properly arranged for the purpose for hich it was intended. Particularly did he find his to be true in post-offices, where two-thirds of e force was sorting letters by artificial light and entilation was poor.

It may be laid down as a principle that the workan is entitled to good light and air and should ot be required to be without the ordinary comforts f life in basement work rooms, or health endanered by contact with insanitary mail-bags. He tated that, of course, it is not possible to rebuild ll municipal structures, but that a great deal can e done to improve conditions; that rest and rering rooms might be provided and welfare work radually widened along the line of the great merantile establishments and insurance companies. e said that we all realize that it is impossible r the city to give free lunches and some other ings which a company like Mr. Fiske's might find profitable to do. He advocated the establishment f a Welfare Board to look into conditions of emloyment in the various departments, believing that ere is a great field for effort. He closed by thankg the city officials for giving the time from their usy lives to give thought to the subject as applied city employees.

The officials were given for consideration a prooosed plan for a Welfare Board which follows:

ROPOSED WELFARE BOARD FOR NEW YORK CITY.

It is especially desirable to have a Welfare Board composed of a representative of each Borough, appointed by the Borough President, and a representative of each Department, selected by the proper authority.

This Board would meet periodically—perhaps monthly.

While the conditions of the departmental employees vary greatly, as their duties are different, there are many principles in common, and policies could be worked out jointly—and this would be particularly helpful in the matter of preventing overlapping.

The Welfare Board could have the conditions of different classes of employees investigated and reported upon, and then make recommendations for carrying out suggested plans for improvements.

Periodical inspections of working conditions could be made and reported upon by sanitation, medical or other experts, who would gradually come into the welfare organization.

Such a Welfare Board would tend to harmonize sub-officials who are jealous of their prerogatives, as a recognition through special committees in the departments would gradually come.

Such Welfare Boards exist now in companies manufacturing steel, agricultural implements, twine, garments, cotton goods, etc., and in a hotel.

Mr. C. L. CLOSE, Chairman of the Welfare Board of Safety, Sanitation and Relief of the United States Steel Corporation, in support of the idea, said:

"I think that if you are seriously considering taking up the work, a proper organization should be formed. I will recite to you our welfare organization. First, we have the Steel Corporation Committee; it is made up of representatives from our different subsidiary companies; we get together periodically and discuss all these problems. We have in each subsidiary company a committee made up of representatives of different plants, mines or railroads. Then we have committees of individual plants made up of the different departments—representatives of each, and last, department committees composed of the workmen themselves. We feel that it is a very good thing to take the workmen into consideration in this connection and find out their ideas. We give them as much time as they need to make a thorough investigation of the property and recommend what should be done to improve conditions. By the process of elimination these suggestions go from the plant committee to the committee of the subsidiary company and thence to the Steel Corporation Committee, if necessary.

"We had last year 4,678 men on that work. We take a workman, a foreigner who cannot speak English, put him on a committee, leave him on a month or two and then take him off. He understands that he is then an ex-officio member—our idea being that in time every employee will be a part of our organization. They are appointed by the superintendent or foreman. In one or two cases, they are elected by the workmen. At a recent election of this kind, 97% of the men voted, showing the great interest in the matter. This is all new; we are trying it out. We have so many localities, different places, different conditions under which we work, and different classes of labor that the problem is quite complex. We try to put the burden upon the subsidiary company itself to do this work. They are responsible for the costs and the product, and we maintain that they are also responsible for the welfare of the workmen. We assist them through our committees and bureau, by disseminating information regarding work done by the subsidiary companies. We started it on accident prevention, and as it proved successful, its scope was widened. If one company had an accident and they devised some means of preventing such an accident thereafter, the information was sent to my office and disseminated from there to all the companies. We have over 11,000 men to our credit that we have saved from serious injury through safety prevention measures."

In illustrating methods employed, Mr. Close said:

"For instance, if the question comes up about putting a swimming pool in a mining town—whether it would be a good thing for the men, etc., we pass upon it and also upon such questions as those referring to sanitary drinking fountains and the like. We recommend to all companies that they abolish the common drinking cup and the common roller towel. We pass upon sanitary regulations—the number of lockers, shower baths, wash basins per employee, etc. All the companies understand that what we recommend is in a sense law. It is not hard to keep up interest, because every one has a feeling for humanity—almost every one is willing to do something for some one else. The president of one company said to me lately, 'I have the greatest trouble now to keep down this expense. They all want to go further than they should.' So it is not hard after you get the thing going in the right way. The all-important point is to have the organization with some one at the head of it full of practical ideas and wholesome enthusiasm with ability to impart the enthusiasm to others. In 1912 we spent over $6,000,000 in our welfare work—this covering pensions, accident relief, etc."

The City officials asked many questions both of Mr. Fiske and Mr. Close to draw out information which would assist in solving the problems surrounding city employees.

The Mayor, JOHN PURROY MITCHEL, among other things, said:

"That the Board of Estimate is anxious to make a beginning is shown by the determination to establish a rest room in the Municipal Building. How far we can carry the work is difficult to say owing to the limitations of the law.

"Yesterday, I established a Review Board for police cases, which is practically a grievance board. One of its functions is to consider cases of men dismissed by the Commissioner, and it will report to the Mayor with recommendations that he may determine whether or not a rehearing shall be granted. There has been some discussion as to whether or not something approximating that should be established in all the Departments and how to solve these questions without interfering with discipline while we are trying to establish ameliorative measures.

"We shall try to secure the co-operation of city officials by making them understand that what we are trying to do is in their interest. It seems to me that the things shown here suggest the possibility of carrying matters further than we have in mind. Possibly the Committee on Welfare Work would be best adapted to assist our Board of Estimate in this connection.

"We had planned only to have a nurse in attendance in the rest room in the Municipal Building, but here we find not only nurses but physicians in the Metropolitan Building. It seems to me possible for us to have a physician. The matter is worthy of serious consideration. There are 5,000 men and 500 women to be housed in the Municipal Building."

Comptroller WILLIAM A. PRENDERGAST said that a physician would be especially useful as the Departments had always lacked medical care. To illustrate this point, he said that for many years there was a physician in the Department of Finance who, up to four years ago, had nothing to do except testify in cases of personal injury in the city's interest. Since that time, he has been used as a departmental physician to examine the physical condition of employees, and has been very helpful. Employees asking for vacation on the ground of illness are examined. In one instance, the physician reported: "Two weeks will not help this man at all. What he needs is three months. In several such instances, where I have sent a man away, he has come back entirely recovered."

The President of the Board of Aldermen, Mr. GEORGE McANENY, in commenting upon the medical examinations of the United States Steel Corporation, which Mr. Close stated had revealed the necessity of coping with trachoma, said:

"I think the degree to which we can use a physician ought to depend upon our courage in the matter of going the whole length."

The Mayor called attention to the fact that the present estimate for pensions for employees in New York City is $10,000,000 a year, and said that the figure of the United States Steel Corporation of $6,000,000 annual expenditure for all its welfare work, including insurance and pensions, made a sharp contrast.

The President of the Borough of Manhattan, Mr. MARCUS M. MARKS, introduced the idea of having the city as a model to all employers and evidenced his willingness to co-operate in forming a welfare board.

The City Chamberlain, Mr. HENRY BRUERE, advocated the necessity for the officials to take the employees into their confidence and make every effort to obtain from them the co-operation and support needed. He said:

"I think we would get along more quickly if the employees could be made to understand that they will have the opportunity, in a measure, to determine the policy, by getting them to make suggestions."

The Comptroller brought out the difficulties due to the short tenure of service on the part of public officials.

Attention was called to the fact that the Welfare Board was advocated partly because of the lack of continuity in office for the reason that a system is likely to continue from one administration to another, whereas the policy of any individual head of a department may not.

The officials have taken a deep interest in furthering the work so auspiciously started at the luncheon above described. The City Chamberlain and Commissioner of Bridges have taken up the details of the Municipal Building with three experts of The National Civic Federation. Information as to the methods employed in conducting the lunch rooms in the Navy Yard, Bureau of Engraving, Census Department, Treasury Building and Pension Building at Washington, D. C., as well as the

WELFARE EXHIBIT AT HOTEL ASTOR, NEW YORK, DURING ANNUAL MEETING OF THE NATIONAL CIVIC FEDERATION.

An exhibit of typical welfare arrangements was made at the annual meeting of The National Civic Federation, by the Welfare Department. Although comprehensive and elaborate, it was designed merely to be illustrative of the vast store of material, photographs, models, descriptions and detailed data of successful welfare work already in its possession and which it is intended to classify and display as a permanent exhibit. Arrangements have just been completed for the early installation of this exhibit, which is to occupy the entire thirty-fifth floor of the Metropolitan Tower, New York City.

The inability of many employers, who have not had experience or have not observed model welfare institutions, to appreciate their advantage has led to this undertaking to provide standards applicable to different industries which may be studied at any time, both by employers beginning such endeavors and those desiring to extend lines already established. Such examples of welfare work, it has been proven thoroughly by the past endeavors of the Welfare Department, encourage the wider adoption of such arrangements when graphically illustrated either to employers individually or in groups in separate trades.

Industrial villages, large factories, small factories, big department stores, small retail stores, railroads, mines and public institutions—Federal, State and Municipal—showing what may be done for the comfort and social well-being of all types of employees in large and small enterprises, had their part in the exhibit at the annual meeting. There were shown model homes, lunch rooms, wash rooms, changing houses for miners, rest houses for railroad men, first-aid devices, ventilation schemes, club houses and other recreative arrangements, and other features to alleviate conditions of employment—not the least being thrift and money-lending plans, as well as schemes for insurance against sickness, accident and death.

The exhibit was in charge of Miss Anna C. Phillips, one of the twenty-nine students graduated from the first welfare training class under the direction of the Welfare Department of The National Civic Federation, held a year ago at New York University. She was assisted by Miss Ruth Schram, daughter of one of our leading employer members, and by Miss Clara H. Kenyon, an experienced welfare worker. A number of the students in the course in welfare work acted as a reception committee to explain the exhibit to members and guests of the Federation. Among these were: Mr. Everett Dominick, Miss Faith Habberton, Mr. J. P. Jacobson, Miss M. C. Hyatt, Mr. W. P. Gallatin and Miss Genoveva Petit.

A stereomotograph was in constant operation, showing stereopticon slides of the very remarkable arrangements in the new building of the Curtis Publishing Company, of Philadelphia, and two hundred other typical views—running the gamut from sanitary work-places, educational opportunities for employees, recreation, and homes and boarding houses, to the picture of the old pensioner, eighty years of age. Photographs of the welfare work of more than one hundred companies were mounted upon fifty placards of uniform size in neat frames and spread about the assembly room. Books outlining the thorough and practical work of the Cadbury Company, an English corporation, were distributed through the courtesy of Mr. John H. Patterson. Other foreign books showing extraordinary developments, with architectural drawings, portrayed activities of the Kanegafuchi Spinning Company of Japan, the Krupp Steel Works, the Arbeiter Rolonde (Gwinderedorf) and the Badische Company, of Germany. Among other companies or associations of employers whose welfare work was exhibited were: The Edison Electric Illuminating Company, of Massachusetts; John Wanamaker, of Philadelphia; American Iron and Steel Institute, Colorado Fuel and Iron Company, International Harvester Company, Plymouth Cordage Company, Sears, Roebuck & Co., National Cash Register Company, Delaware, Lackawanna & Western Railroad Company, National Food Company, Pennsylvania Railroad Company, National Cloak and Suit Company, General Electric Company, Morgan Machine Company, United Gas Improvement Company, Westchester Lighting Company, Draper Company, Ballard & Ballard, Avery Company, American Woolen Company, Westinghouse Air Brake Company, Parker Cotton Mills Company, Ludlow Manufacturing Associates, Eagle and Phoenix Mills, American Waltham Watch Company, Enterprise Manufacturing Company, Cleveland-Cliffs Iron Company, Elgin National Watch Company, American Locomotive Company, Gorham Company, Solvay Process Company, H. J. Heinz Company, Sidney Blumenthal Company, Edward V. Price Company; The Emporium of San Francisco, John A. Roebling's Sons Company, Lowney Chocolate Company, and such department stores as McCreery's, Altman's, Lord & Taylor's, Macy's, Greenhut's, Gimbel Brothers' and Bloomingdales'.

What may be done in a rural community in a large way was shown by the very elaborate and handsome exhibit of the United Shoe Machinery Company, in charge of Mr. J. M. Van Heusen and Mr. Towle, of Boston. Equally convincing model arrangements for employees in a great city were indicated by literature, photographs and charts of the Metropolitan Life Insurance Company and the American Telephone and Telegraph Company. A screen, put up by the United States Steel Corporation, called especial attention to what has been done to improve sanitation in mining villages.

Navy Yard in Brooklyn, has been furnished for their guidance, together with statements as to the amount of space provided for lunch rooms, rest rooms, and hospitals by the Federal government in those places. Attention was called to the fact that employers, except in banks where the clerks are needed at noon time, generally charge nominal prices for lunches. After outlining the plans of the Federal government lunch rooms, the Welfare Department recommended the following one for the Municipal Building in New York.

SUGGESTED PLAN FOR LUNCH ROOM—MUNICIPAL BUILDING.

Board of Trustees to be appointed by the proper city official.

This Board to have charge of fund for operating expenses and the lunch room manager to be responsible for it.

After the lunch room is in operation, it would be possible to raise a fund for operating expenses by having a lunch club and charging dues. It would be much better to be able to demonstrate before undertaking to organize such a club than to appeal to the imagination in advance of the opening of the lunch room.

In the event that the City should not find it practicable to appropriate the fund, several citizens might be interested to subscribe the amount for operating expenses, and it could be refunded within a reasonable time after the club is organized.

The Board of Trustees should continue to be responsible for the operation of the lunch room in the event that a manager is employed by the club. This course is the best, as a better quality of food and larger portions will be ensured than by contracting out the privilege.

The foregoing is based upon the supposition that the City will furnish the space without rental charge and will supply the equipment.

In determining this plan, there were analysed answers to the following questions sent to public officials in Federal Departments having lunch rooms:

(1) Do you serve warm food cooked in the building to your employees?

(2) Do you charge rental space against the operating expenses?

(3) Did the Government furnish the money to purchase the equipment?

(4) Do you contract out the privilege?

(5) If not, have you a committee appointed, to whom the lunch room manager is responsible, or do you take the responsibility?

(6) Have you a lunch club? If so, what are your dues?

(7) How did you secure the initial operating expenses?

In the Bureau of Engraving at Washington, D. C., at present, lunch is supplied by a woman caterer, the Government furnishing without charge the necessary space and cooking utensils. It is intended, however, that a co-operative association now being formed by employees will operate the lunch room—the initial funds being obtained by men members contributing one dollar and women members fifty cents, the number of employees at this time being about twenty-five hundred. Plans are not yet completed, but the general proposition is that an experienced manager not an employee will be engaged. The Government will have no financial responsibility in them thereafter, and will simply have general supervision.

At the Navy Yard in Washington warm food is served; the Government makes no rental charge against the lunch room and furnished the equipment. There is a committee of officers and employees to supervise the contractors and the Government allotted the initial operating expenses. At the Brooklyn Navy Yard, where 7,000 square feet were set aside by the Government for a lunch room which seats 500 men at one time, the Brooklyn Navy Yard Committee of the Metropolitan Section of the Woman's Department of The National Civic Federation purchased and gave the equipment to the Government and it is now thoroughly in operation. The Commandant of the Navy Yard is virtually in charge, but there is a stockholders' co-operative association of 1,000 employees, the shares being $1 each, and there is a waiting list, there being 3,300 men in the shops there. The manager of the lunch room is held entirely responsible by the elected board, but has absolute freedom in purchasing and managing the lunch room, the latter fact being the secret of its success. The books are audited by the directors. There is a good dinner with roast beef, including dessert, coffee and bread and butter, for 25 cents. Roast beef, potatoes and one vegetable are given for 15 cents. A dividend of 20% was declared during the past year.

The Municipal Building has been inspected by the Federation's experts with reference to possibilities in arranging lunch rooms, and the City has been commended upon the fine sanitary rooms therein. Particularly has it been fortunate in having them placed on alternate floors and not too remote from work places. An advanced step has been taken by having a retiring room, which will be equipped with a couch, adjacent to each sanitary room. Too much cannot be said in praise of these conveniences.

THE NEXT STEPS IN WORKMEN'S COMPENSATION LEGISLATION

(Continued from Page 9.)

to extend its work, which heretofore has been confined to uniform accident reporting blanks, by extending its personnel to bring into co-operation representatives of the various States having workmen's compensation laws and which are now collecting statistics, that their methods may be compared with a view to uniformity." (Adopted after some discussion as to the magnitude and large cost of such an undertaking.)

BUREAU OF INVESTIGATION AND STATISTICS.

Dr. Lee K. Frankel, sixth Vice-President of the Metropolitan Life Insurance Company, while deeming that uniformity is a desideratum to be worked for, expressed the belief that at the present moment we need to tabulate the experience in the respective States. Insurance companies, life and fire, have gotten beyond the doctrine of chance, due to the tabulation of their experience. He said: "The most important department of any insurance company is its actuarial or statistical department.

"After twenty-five years' experience in Europe there is no such thing as uniform legislation. It is conceded that the system in England is not applicable in Germany, because of the peculiar conditions. It is likely in the United States the law in New Jersey could not be maintained in Colorado where we have comparatively little industrial development, and the development is mining and agriculture. It may be more desirable to have a variety of laws than uniformity of laws. Whether or not that is true, with the limited experience we have in the United States—I think now practically all of our legislation is less than five years old—we are not in position to know which method of settlement or law is better, which amount of benefits should be maintained, and what the premium should be, whether it should be taken care of by the State, whether it should permit accident and other companies to come in. All of these questions we must determine by actual experience.

"It seems to me that the opportunity here is given to The National Civic Federation to do a rather remarkable piece of work. The government cannot do it. Commissions cannot do it because they are apt to be prejudiced. Insurance companies cannot do it for the same reason. Here is the Civic Federation, an altogether impartial body that could undertake, in the fashion not possible to any other organization, to definitely tabulate the experience that is being gathered in every State in the Union and by the Federal Government.

"I should like to go even further than the resolution offered by Mr. Schram. It seems to me what the Civic Federation ought to have is a permanent investigation bureau with a paid official at its head, with a staff sufficiently large to constantly make inquiries and to get the co-operation, as recommended in this resolution, of commissioners in every State, and of departments in every State, definitely tabulate the experience and eventually present to the people of the United States the data and results thus ascertained. When we once have that, we are in position to say which law is better, which we ought to vote for and strive for, as uniform legislation."

Mr. W. A. Coakley, in furthering the idea of Dr. Frankel, said: "Statistics on the cost of workmen's compensation are especially important to the interests of labor when increases in wages are asked, because workmen's compensation is a charge upon the industry and employers will claim that their expense item in that connection is so high that they cannot afford such increase in wages. In every arbitration case, it is the operating cost which is brought to us in argument against our demand."

COMPENSATION REPORT A PUBLIC DOCUMENT

THE UNITED STATES SENATE ORDERS PRINTED FOR DISTRIBUTION THE EXHAUSTIVE STUDY OF THE OPERATION OF STATE LAWS, MADE BY THE NATIONAL CIVIC FEDERATION AND THE AMERICAN FEDERATION OF LABOR

THE report of the Commission created last July by The National Civic Federation to investigate the operation of State laws on workmen's compensation has been published and is now available for distribution. This Commission was appointed by the Workmen's Compensation Department, of which Mr. August Belmont is chairman, and was composed of employers, legal experts and representatives of the American Federation of Labor.

The extraordinary value of the report is attested by the fact that the United States Senate ordered it printed as a public document.

Both the Federation's edition of the report and that printed by the Government were almost immediately exhausted by demands from all over the country, as well as from abroad. There is under consideration the issuing of a further edition.

In advocating the passage of the original resolution calling for the printing of the report with an additional edition for distribution, Senator Sutherland, of Utah, said in part:

"Mr. President, that document is an exceedingly valuable one and one which will have a very wide circulation. * * * The investigation made by the Joint Committee of the Civic Federation and the Federation of Labor was a very thorough one.

"The great value of the report which has been presented by the committee is that it takes up these various laws and enters into a discussion of their operation in the various States; and the great usefulness of it will be that it will have a tendency to bring about a uniformity of legislation upon this subject which is very sadly wanting at present. There are almost as many different kinds of workmen's compensation laws in this country as there are States that have passed upon the subject. One deals with it from the standpoint of State taxation and State adjustment, as in Washington and Ohio; other States, as New York, from an entirely different standpoint; Michigan from another standpoint, and so on. It is comparatively a new subject in this country. It is one which we are concerned in. I mean by 'we' Congress itself. It is exceedingly important that we should have all the light we can upon this subject. * * * There can not be the slightest doubt about there being an exceptionally large demand for this document. It is a subject that is engaging the attention of nearly every State of the Union. Commissions are at work, and there are hundreds of people who are investigating it in its various phases."

The volume is practically a working handbook of 200,000 words. The workings of the various compensation laws in States having had any important experience are reviewed and analyzed in a way to bring out distinctly the strong and weak provisions.

The findings are based upon personal conferences and hearings in different sections of the country all the way from the Atlantic to the Pacific Coast, and upon replies to thousands of letters of inquiry and questionnaires, the answers representing a payroll of $358,640,383. The labor viewpoint as to the benefits derived from workmen's compensation laws was sought and opinions were secured from employers, public officials and insurance men.

Some of the subjects covered are: "Degrees of satisfaction given by compensation as against liability laws;" "The value of elective versus compulsory compensation laws;" "Reasons for accepting or rejecting elective acts;" "The amount of compensation;" "Contributions by employees;" "Methods of insuring;" "Cost of compensation;" "Exclusiveness of compensation remedy;" "Employers' defenses abrogated under elective acts;" "Employments covered;" "Injuries covered;" "Who are dependents;" "Non-resident alien dependents;" "Contractors' liability to employees of sub-contractors;" "Length of waiting period;" "Medical and surgical aid;" "Effect on prevention of accidents;" "Litigation under compensation acts;" "Methods of administration;" "Effect upon relations of employer and workmen," and "Suggestions for amendments to State laws."

Other provisions of the report are: A topical digest of the principal provisions of statutes in force January 1, 1914; rules and forms used by State boards to facilitate the administration of the laws, and valuable statistics furnished by them.

PLAN AND SCOPE COMMITTEE.

The Committee on Plan and Scope, which outlined the inquiry, appears below:

Chairman, Otto M. Eidlitz, New York Building Trades Employers' Association, New York City.

Samuel Gompers, President American Federation of Labor, Washington, D. C.

Louis B. Schram, Chairman Labor Committee, United States Brewers' Association, Brooklyn, N. Y.

W. H. Marshall, President American Locomotive Co., New York City.

Frank V. Whiting, General Claims Attorney, N. Y. C. & H. R. R. R., New York City.

Timothy Healy, President International Brotherhood of Stationary Firemen, New York City.

E. H. Letchworth, Rogers-Brown Iron Co., Buffalo, N. Y.

M. F. Westover, Secretary General Electric Co., Schnectady, N. Y.

Raynal C. Bolling, United States Steel Corporation, New York City.

THE JOINT COMMISSION.

The Commission, which gave six arduous months to this investigation, was made up as follows:

Chairman, Cyrus W. Phillips, member of the former New York State Commission on Employers' Liability, Rochester, N. Y.

J. Walter Lord, Chairman of the Maryland State Commission on Employers' Liability and Workmen's Compensation, Baltimore, Md.

Otto M. Eidlitz, of the New York Building Trades Employers' Association, New York City.

Louis B. Schram, Chairman Labor Committee, United States Brewers' Association, Brooklyn, N. Y.

James Duncan, Vice-President American Federation of Labor, Quincy, Mass.

John Mitchell, Vice-President American Federation of Labor, Mount Vernon, N. Y.

Mr. Duncan and Mr. Mitchell were appointed by the American Federation of Labor to co-operate with The National Civic Federation.

FIVE MILLION WORKMEN UNDER COMPENSATION LAWS.

The Commission found that not only are more than 5,000,000 workmen now under the operation of compensation laws, but that laws going into effect during the coming year will bring several million more workmen under this system. Even elective acts have been so generally accepted by employers and employees in States where they are in force that in

(Continued on next page.)

those instances a vast majority of industrial accidents are covered.

The employer who complains of the law because it requires him to pay compensation for an accident in which he is clearly not to blame, or which possibly may be due to the fault of the injured person, will get a broader view of the law when later he is relieved from a liability suit with full damages in a case in which he has been wholly at fault. Likewise, the employee who receives no compensation, for the reason that his injury incapacitates him for a time shorter than the legal waiting period, will get a different and a better idea of the law later when he or some fellow-worker meets with a permanent injury and receives compensation promptly without controversy.

While at the outset the compensation acts were not exclusive, but were given in addition to the workmen's common law right of action for negligence, the tendency to make the compensation remedy the exclusive one has grown until now the majority of the statutes furnish an exclusive remedy, and it can be well said that the principle of making the remedy exclusive, provided the compensation is adequate, is now accepted by both employers and workmen as the proper method.

In the absence of compensation laws, undoubtedly there would have been a further expansion of the employers' liability, with their defenses removed and the adoption of strict safety requirements. This is indicated by the recent decision of the United States Supreme Court in reference to the Federal Safety Appliance Act, under which the railroad company is even held liable to an injured employee for failure to keep safety appliances in order. But it is recognized that under the best liability law a large percentage of workmen must be without protection, as many accidents cannot be traced to legal fault on the part of the employer and may occur where safeguarding appliances cannot be installed.

The Commission found a growing satisfaction with compensation laws among both employers and workmen. All suggestions for changes related to the compensation law, no one seriously thinking of repealing it or going back to the old liability system. Persons attended the conferences who had originally opposed the compensation plan, but who, after experience under it, expressed their warm approval of its principles. Among these, beside both large and small employers, were workmen.

RELATIONS BETWEEN EMPLOYER AND WORKMEN IMPROVED.

The workmen's compensation laws have improved the relations existing between the employer and workmen; they have had a marked effect upon accident prevention by calling attention to the subject and exciting interest in safeguarding machinery and in the organization of safety committees, and they have created a general campaign for accident prevention. The difficulties feared by some employers and some workmen have not, to any great extent, materialized under the actual operation of the laws; while the Commission heard some statements to the effect that the laws lead to fraud, deception and malingering on the part of employees, and discrimination by employers against certain classes of workmen, these complaints have generally come from those who have had little or no experience under such a law, or have had so few accidents in their establishments that their opinion can hardly be considered against those of men at the head of establishments who have had a large and active experience even in the short time that the laws have been in effect. The latter class of employers generally stated that they have found little, if any, malingering or deception; that that can be avoided, and that the laws are easy in administration and fair in their operation. However, it is claimed by some that there has not been sufficient experience, during the short time that the statutes have been in force in the United States, for these troubles to develop; that they do exist in European countries, and that they will develop here unless the administration of the laws is safeguarded in these respects.

ADMINISTRATION FAIR UNDER STATE BOARDS.

In the States where there are Industrial Accident Boards, having power to pass upon settlement agreements; to make rules and regulations; to require the filing of receipts showing the actual payments of compensation to the men; and having arbitrations and hearings before them in cases of dispute, the law is being fairly administered, and employees are receiving promptly their full compensation under the law. It is evident that danger of fraud and deception can be prevented only when the law is administered through a board or officials charged with powers and duties similar to those of the existing State Boards. For instance, in New Jersey, where there is no duly constituted authority, not over 60 per cent of the amounts payable under the statute are received by the workmen.

It is the general opinion both of employers and workmen in the States covered by this inquiry that all employments, with the possible exception of farm labor, domestic servants and casual employments, should be included, and that any restricted classification is not only unjust but leads to confusion and uncertainty.

MEDICAL ATTENTION.

The subject of medical attention to injured employees is one of utmost importance. With a few exceptions, the States require that the employer, in addition to the compensation, shall pay the medical bills of the injured workmen, with certain restrictions. Outside of the State of Washington, the Commission found no sentiment opposed to this requirement, it being generally conceded that the workman is not only entitled to medical treatment in addition to his compensation but that it is to the interest of the employer and society to see that he receives it, thereby to minimize the extent of the disability. There has been a great deal of discussion, however, with regard to the cost of medical service. Various methods have been suggested and are now being worked out in different States for the purpose of reducing this cost, which amounts to a sum equal to 40 to 50 per cent of the amount of compensation received by the workmen.

AMOUNT PAID WORKMEN.

The amount of compensation has aroused considerable discussion, and it varies from 50 to 66 2-3 per cent of the wages of the injured employee with minimum and maximum weekly amounts varying in different States, to be paid during the period of his incapacity, or, as in some States, limited to specified periods, with definite allowances for amputations and certain enumerated injuries. While employers, in States paying only 50 per cent of the injured workmen's wages, feel that their schedules are fair and are fearful of the effects of increasing the percentage, there is not much complaint from employers in States having a higher rate of compensation. Definiteness in provisions relating to awards for particular injuries is desired by both employers and workmen.

Uniformity of cost is an element of vital interest to employers. For this reason they have frequently asked, first, that the elective acts of their States be made compulsory, so that all employers may compete on the same basis; and secondly, that there be uniformity in cost under the acts of the various States. Among workingmen the sentiment for compulsory compensation laws is practically uniform, and the tendency of legislation is in the direction of compulsory enactments. This is evidenced by the recent change in Ohio and California from elective to compulsory acts, and by the adoption in New York State of a compulsory act.

LITIGATION ELIMINATED.

Litigation, so far as accidents to workmen are concerned, has been practically eliminated in the States in which compensation acts have been generally accepted by employers. About 2 per cent only of the compensation cases are disputed so as to require arbitration; not more than ten cases out of 10,000 compensation cases have gone into the courts. The payments of compensation to employees are prompt and usually commence at the end of the second or third week, and where arbitration is had, the payments are not delayed on an average more than three or four weeks.

PROTECTION AGAINST EMPLOYERS' INSOLVENCY.

One of the most difficult problems, and one that has caused more diversity of views than any other, is that of protecting the injured workman against the insolvency of his employer. As the payments are not usually made in lump sum but extend in some cases through a long series of years this is important from the standpoint of the workman and his family. The Commission found it generally accepted by employers that the workman was entitled to as full protection in this respect as possible, but a strong feeling existed among employers against being restricted in their method of insuring. Many wanted to carry their own risks without insurance, provided they could show that their financial condition would warrant it, claiming that in that way they could better carry on their safety plans. Some wanted power to create mutual insurance companies, and, in most States, laws have been passed permitting this; others desired permission to insure in stock companies, while others wanted the State to create an insurance fund by assessment upon employers. In States in which either of these methods, or all of them, were in operation, there was little, if any, complaint as to the methods of making settlements or payments. It was generally felt that, with an industrial accident board passing upon all settlements and determining all differences and with such other restrictions and regulations as might be necessary, both employer and employee were protected under these three methods of insurance, and that the employer received the benefit of the resulting competition. The mutual companies have undoubtedly, by their competition, aided in the reduction of rates to a larger extent than the amount of their business would indicate, as they furnish a field to which employers can go in case they feel that the rates of stock companies are too high. This is also true of the State insurance funds, except that they have been organized to a less extent and have done a smaller business than the mutual companies.

COMPENSATION PRINCIPLE ESTABLISHED.

Mr. Belmont said, in announcing the publication of the report:

"It is apparent that the principle of workmen's compensation is well established, i. e., that the industry rather than the victim shall bear the financial burden resulting from accidents incident to it. The experiments with different theories in the first stages of legislation upon the subject have developed workable features worthy of perpetuation, but now we have reached the melting-pot period.

"Education never was more needed upon the subject than now, and we propose not only to give to legislators, citizens and organizations interested in the movement this sifted result of the country's total experience, but also to utilize the report in drafting a new model workmen's compensation act to be used as a guide. To Legislatures convening this year and workmen's compensation commissions in twelve States studying the subject, the report has been made immediately available.

"The report bears every evidence of a conscientious effort to present the facts impartially, with no attempt to offer theories or to make recommendations. It is believed that it will be of benefit not only to States which have not yet enacted workmen's compensation legislation, but also to those proposing to amend their laws, and especially in promoting uniformity among the twenty-two States having such laws."

ACCIDENT PREVENTION.

In commenting upon accident prevention, Mr. Belmont said:

"Two documents, also available *gratis*, in the interest of accident prevention, are the Civic Federation's model safety act and uniform accident reporting blank.

"The safety act, now reflected particularly in the factory laws of New York, New Jersey and Illinois, not only enables State officials to place the responsibility directly upon employers, but, at the same time, gives the latter information as to their obligations in the matter of accident prevention.

"Adequate safeguarding cannot be had without statistics showing the causes of accidents, and where they occur in the greatest number. Accuracy in drawing conclusions from such statistics depends upon uniformity in collecting them."

ACTIVITIES OF THE WOMAN'S DEPARTMENT.

(Continued from page 10.)

requests, so far, have been given the required consideration. A canvass of all business establishments was made with a view of ascertaining how many gave a weekly half holiday. The largest retail establishment in the city decided, at the Chairman's suggestion, to change its hours of opening and closing for the benefit of its employees. The regulation of dance halls, investigation of State and county institutions and wonderful improvement in the County Hospital, the County Jail and the City Prison Farm can be reported.

The *Virginia and West Virginia Section*, of which Mrs. J. Allison Hodges is Chairman, is doing excellent work, chiefly in the nature of co-operation with other bodies engaged in improving economic conditions of women and children. Owners of tobacco factories and cotton mills, particularly, are beginning to realize the importance of the work. Mrs. Hodges mentions that the Riverside and the Dan River cotton mills of Danville are examples of the finest type of welfare and efficiency.

The year 1914 promises to be a busy one for the *North and South Carolina Section*, in the opinion of the Chairman, Mrs. B. Frank Mebane. Speaking particularly of the welfare work at Spray, N. C., Mrs. Mebane says:

"Sand and building bought for a hospital, the building being a large house which will be equipped with everything necessary for a modern up-to-date hospital. Work on it is going ahead rapidly and it is a cause for much rejoicing, since it is something that is much needed. In addition land has been purchased by the mill owners for a school building of generous dimensions and work will be commenced on that at once; the old school building is not large enough to accommodate all of the scholars. We hope to equip it for a girls' club—girls and married women—a modest beginning, which may later develop into a large Y. W. C. A., or, at any rate, into a place of rest and recreation for tired girls and worn-out mothers."

The McConnell Printing Co. 230-242 William St., N. Y.

The National Civic Federation Review

IV. NEW YORK, DECEMBER 5, 1918 No. 5

SAMUEL GOMPERS' GREAT MESSAGE

[E]FFORTS OF DISLOYALISTS TO DIVIDE LABOR FROM ALLIED GOVERNMENTS DEFEATED, BUT FIGHT AGAINST ANARCHY MUST CONTINUE TO SAFEGUARD A JUST AND VICTORIOUS PEACE

By CHESTER M. WRIGHT

(Of the American Alliance for Labor and Democracy)

[S]AMUEL GOMPERS returned from his remarkable tour of Europe bringing warn[ing]s of these things: Bolshevism, [pac]ifism, Pro-Germanism, and [so]cialism. And for the most part [he] wraps all of these things up [in] one package and puts a com[mon] label on the mess.

Mr. Gompers went to Europe [as] chairman of an American Fed[er]ation of Labor mission, and [pur]suant to instructions of the [Fe]deration given him by the St. [Pa]ul convention last June. There [wa]s no pussyfooting about the [Go]mpers mission, if reports [br]ought back by him and his fel[low] members tell the story. It [wa]s a fighting mission.

President Gompers made his [firs]t address upon his return on [No]vember 8, in the Chicago Audi[tor]ium, at a national mass meet[ing] arranged by the American [Al]liance for Labor and Democ[rac]y. Men and women from all [pa]rts of the country and of all [wa]lks of life were present. In [Mr]. Gompers' stirring address [the]re was this clarion note:

"The principles of democracy [are] not flash in the air; they are [no]t fanciful, they are not theo[re]tical. If they are thought of in [tha]t connection they lose their [pot]ency and virility and effect. [De]mocracy must be practiced and [tes]ted every day of our lives to [be] true."

In its day to day work the [Am]erican labor movement exem[pli]fies this teaching. It practices [de]mocracy by dealing in the most [fu]ndamentally democratic fashion [wi]th the employers of labor. [Or]ganized labor meets and bargains, collectively, [dem]ocratically, with employers of labor. Democ[rac]y is bedded deep in the structure and life of [the] labor movement. There could be no labor [movement] without democracy.

In his Chicago address, Mr. Gompers paid a [hi]gh tribute to the fidelity and integrity of Premier Lloyd George, Premier Clemenceau, and the principal guiding spirits of the war in each of the Allied nations. He found that the great masses of the people in all these countries had appreciated the worth of their true leaders and that there had been a generous, intelligent and unflinching loyalty on the part of all except a small minority of noisy pacifists and pro-German propagandists.

SAMUEL GOMPERS

Of these it seemed evident that the mission found the most pronounced brand in Italy, where every possible effort was made to undo the work of the mission. But in every case where Bolshevism was encountered the overwhelming mass of people turned to the mission with such accord as to prove beyond doubt the status of the disloyalists in point of numbers.

Mr. Gompers did not mention Arthur Henderson in his speech. He made no mention of pacifism in England. But this was learned from other members of the mission:

MISSION ENCOUNTERED "STOCKHOLMISM" AND BOLSHEVISM.

The London Inter-Allied Labor Conference appointed a sub-committee of two from each nation. A meeting of this committee was arranged to be held in Paris on the return of the American mission to that city from Italy. Mr. Gompers did not remain for the meeting, owing to the death of his daughter, but two members of the mission did stay. The meeting was not held. When Mr. Henderson, with Camille Huysmans, secretary of the one-time Socialist International, went to the dock at a British port to board a channel steamer events transpired which prevented the sailing. As the two proceeded to board the ship, the crew declared that if Henderson and Huysmans came aboard the crew would go ashore. Thereupon the two did not go aboard. Henderson thereupon went to the commander of a destroyer flotilla and demanded passage. The commander said that if the channel steamer would not carry him the destroyers could not undertake to do so. The next appeal was to the commander of a sea-plane squadron. The sea-plane commander declined to go over the head of the destroyer commander.

Henderson and Huysmans then picked up their luggage and loaded it into a cab, into which they also climbed. A crowd of soldiers and civilians acquainted the cabbie with the identity of his passengers, whereupon he immediately ordered them to get out. The two picked up their bags and walked to their hotel, jeered on the way by the assembled crowd. Thus has the glory of Stockholmism faded.

But the spirit that was in Stockholmism is not dead entirely, either in France, England, or Italy, according to the mission. And the fact that there is in this spirit the essentials of Bolshevism is proved by the fact that when one object of its attacks is removed as an issue by the passing of events it immediately seizes upon another. Stockholmism has ceased to be an issue. But the spirit that was in it fights on against those who stand for the protection of human liberty by armed force when necessary, and for the development of human life through the orderly processes of democracy. It may safely be drawn from the utterances of President Gompers and his mission that the fight must be made in the days to come, as in the days just passed.

President Gompers did not go exhaustively into the work of his mission in his Chicago speech. But he did indicate the general trend and the general result, which was one of victory for sanity, solidarity and orderly progress. For the first time since war began unity among all the democratic nations was secured on a program of fundamental principles. The conference endorsed the fourteen points laid down by President Wilson and long since approved by the American labor movement.

AMERICA'S IDEALS.

From President Gompers' Chicago speech are taken the following paragraphs revealing the trend of his thought on that wonderful homecoming night:

"It was a great mission entrusted to my associates and myself—a mission to convey the message of fraternity and good-will and cooperation and sacrifice, that the opportunity to live the lives of free men and women shall not be crushed from the face of the earth; the message that America had arisen to the stature of her greatness and thrown herself across the path of the conquering Hun; a message that if need be our America would sacrifice and die rather than live the ignominy of cowardice.

"America is more than a country. America is more than a continent. America is more than a name. America is an ideal. America is the apotheosis of all that is right.

"Where a great principle is involved and men fail to defend it, where a great principle is involved and men refuse to make a sacrifice to preserve it, there is no hope for them or for those who come after them. Fight for the right and even though you are defeated, the spark is still in the heart and the brain, handed down from father to son, from mother to daughter and to the generations after that until finally that spark bursts into flame and the torch of liberty is again alight.

"In the work of our American Federation of Labor Mission to England, to France and Belgium, our conferences with our men there, our public discussions with the men of labor and of other affairs there, we predicated our position upon the declared basis of the American labor movement, and we put forth our position not only upon the righteousness of our cause and our stand, but upon the further fact that we had two million of our own American boys over there.

AMERICAN LABOR DECLARATION AT LONDON.

"Before the United States entered into the war it might have been regarded as gratuitous for us to even suggest anything to any of the democratic nations involved in the struggle, but now that we are in the war up to the hilt, well, nothing could be done by Kings or Cabinets or men of labor without the full consent of the representatives of our Republic. And it was with no mealy mouths that the American Labor Mission expressed their firm convictions.

"I call your attention to part of the declaration adopted by the conference of America's workers at Washington on March 12, 1917, to which the Executive Council had summoned representative labor men. American labor, American workers stood one hundred per cent behind the Government and the President of the United States. I am quite confident that as time goes on the utterances in this declaration will become more and more important. I refrain from reading it because it is too lengthy. I will not even read the declaration made by the London Inter-Allied Labor Conference of September. I wish merely to call your attention to the fact that *the American labor mission proposed and the conference adopted*, not in the same words, but in the same sense and purpose and meaning, *the declaration of organized labor of America of more than a year and a half before.*

"That conference which in secrecy had declared its pacifism, and some other things, was held in executive or secret session; but at the demand and at the proposal of our mission, that conference in which we participated was had with the searchlight of public opinion right upon every delegate present. We held that we could not be consistent in denouncing secret diplomacy and at the same time hold executive, secret sessions ourselves. Whether they liked it or not, they voted for open sessions. From that time we knew that America's position was right and would be endorsed. Men can't help being a little more decent in public than they may be in secret and private.

FOES OF REAL DEMOCRACY ABROAD.

"The condition which we found to exist in our Allied countries was something to give us all concern. Every attempt that we made was combatted by the pro-Germans, by the propagandists, by the pacifists and by the French and Italian Bolsheviki. The Socialist Bolsheviki press of those countries endeavored to forestall every movement we made or were about to make. In Italy, for instance, we were represented by this press as fakes and frauds, as not representing American labor. We answered that the difficulty with these people is that whatever labor movement exists is usually dominated by some professor, some failure in professional life, who had got his fangs into the labor movement there and usually poisoned and destroyed it; that the American labor movement was composed of working men and working women, and that the men in the official positions of our movement were men who had been taken from the mine, from the shop, from the building, and we said: 'Now, you don't build any more, you don't mine coal any more, you don't make brick any more; we want you to be our spokesman, our defender, our advocate.' And that doesn't sit well in the crop of the so-called intellectuals of England, France or Italy, or even in the United States.

"I shall not pay too great a tribute to my associates nor make any claim for myself. All I think I should say, and what I am justified in saying, is that we did try and succeeded to some degree in putting some stiffening into the backbone of the people of the countries which we visited to stand behind their countries at least until after the war was won. We have come back to our country more thoroughly American than ever; more thoroughly convinced that our people and our government stand out as a wonderful object lesson to the peoples of the whole world.

ilding Labor Adjustment Board

V. EVERIT MACY

has adopted the policy of making its districts co-terminous with those established by the Emergency Fleet Corporation.

The present districts are as follows:

(1) New England District
(2) North Atlantic District
(3) Delaware River District
(4) Middle Atlantic District
(5) South Atlantic District
(6) Gulf District
(7) Great Lakes District
(8) South Pacific District
(9) North Pacific District

In each one of these districts there is a chief examiner who has the authority of the Board within his district in settling disputes and adjusting grievances, but subject always to appeal to the Board.

In addition to their duties as examiner, these men are also District Representatives of the Industrial Relations Division of the Emergency Fleet Corporation and in their dual capacity are responsible for all labor matters in the shipyards under their jurisdiction.

The Board early discovered not only that its decisions must apply to neighboring shipyards as well as to the yards actually involved in a dispute, but that the district for which uniform wage rates were established must be made larger and larger to prevent the wasteful shifting of employees from yard to yard, consequence on difference in rates of pay for similar work. In the decision issued on October 24, 1918, not only are the shipyards of the country divided into two districts for wage adjustment purposes but the rates of wages for most of the shipyard occupations are made identical in the two districts. The only important exception is the rates for labor were made higher for the Pacific coast than for the Atlantic coast and Great Lakes and that a lower rate was authorized for common labor in the South Atlantic and Gulf corresponding to local conditions.

Next to the adjustment of wages, the most important work of the Board has been the establishment of standards with reference to hours and working conditions. The Board has made standard in all shipyards the eight hour day, with time and a half for overtime in connection with new work and double time for overtime in connection with repair work and on the stated holidays.

A third matter to which the Board has given much thought has been the establishment of shop committees in shipyards which had not already adopted the policy of dealing collectively with their employees through their regularly constituted labor organizations. In the development of such shop committees the Board has attempted to insure that every employee shall be given the privilege of voting for a shop committee of three to represent his craft. The Chairmen of these shop committees constitute a joint shop committee through which grievances affecting more than one craft are handled. Both types of committees have the privilege in case they cannot adjust a dispute without outside aid of calling in an adviser to take up issues with the higher officials of the plant. Only after the attempt to adjust the grievances through the shop committees has failed or when the issue is of such a nature that it must be referred to the representatives of the Board which the examiner brought in. Only when the examiner cannot make a decision that is satisfactory to both sides is the issue brought to the attention of the Board for settlement.

The most striking difference between this shop committee plan and the plans worked out by several employers is that it respects the predilection of employees to handle disputes along craft lines rather than through a general plant committee which can only deal with grievances along industrial lines. This is due to the conviction of the Board that organization along craft lines is in conformity with a sound principle which should be encouraged. Moreover, it reconciles the international unions who have been parties to the creation of the Board to the activities of shop committees which they might otherwise deem inimical to the interest of organized labor.

Although organized to meet the war emergency, there is nothing in the constitution of the Board or the machinery which it has created which would not seem to be equally well adapted to peace conditions, particularly in connection with an industry which is largely carried on for the benefit and at the expense of the government. Steps have been taken to insure the continuance of the Board for at least a year after the peace treaty has been signed and it is gratifying that this extension appears to have the approval of all of the parties interested.

The principal achievement of the Board has been the maintenance of industrial peace in the shipyards during the past year. Shortly after its organization serious strikes occurred in the shipyards in San Francisco, Seattle and Portland. The first work of the Board was to visit the Pacific coast and adjust wages there. All the strikes were settled through its efforts and efforts of local representatives of the government. The decision it rendered in November, 1917, has regulated wages and working conditions in the Pacific coast shipyards, except as modified by subsequent rulings, and until it was superseded by the wage decision issued on October 24th, 1918. There have, of course, been stoppages of work in different yards on the part of groups of employees, but during the entire period there has been no stoppage affecting all the employees of the yard and no interruption has continued for more than a few hours until the machinery for the adjustment of grievances could be brought into effective operation. In view of the fact that in this period the employees in shipyards under the jurisdiction of the Board have increased from 50,000 to 400,000, this is a remarkable demonstration of the essential soundness of the underlying policy upon which the Board rests.

War Activities of The National Civic Federation

CO-OPERATION WITH COMMITTEE ON LABOR, ADVISORY COMMISSION, COUNCIL OF NATIONAL DEFENSE—CONSERVATION AND WELFARE OF WORKERS—EDUCATIONAL CAMPAIGN EXPOSING GERMAN PROPAGANDA—ORGANIZATION OF LEAGUE FOR NATIONAL UNITY

NOW that the war is over, it is proper that the general membership of The National Civic Federation should be made acquainted with the activities of the organization since our entrance into the international struggle.

Recognizing in February, 1917, that our participation in the war was impending, an official pronouncement of the organization was issued and telegraphed to President Wilson. It follows:

> "At this crucial hour, which may well mark a turning-point in our nation's history, The National Civic Federation, composed of representative wage earners, employers, and the general public, sends you our pledge of hearty support in the continuance of peace, if possible, and in prosecuting war if that is necessary. We wish that our country's honor be upheld, its citizens be protected and that it play a fitting part as the leading neutral nation to promote the permanent welfare of mankind. On you rests the responsibility of leadership—on us the burden of action in loyal service. Call upon us in whatever way the service will be greatest."

When there was authorized by Congress the Committee on Labor of the Council of National Defense, having for its Chairman Samuel Gompers, President of the American Federation of Labor and Vice-President of The National Civic Federation from its inception, Mr. Gompers recognized the peculiar adaptability and utilized the machinery of the Civic Federation in promoting the work of his Committee. The first among its officers and members to become especially active was President Macy who accepted the chairmanship of Mr. Gompers' National Mediation Committee and afterward, because of his practical experience in dealing with labor problems, was appointed by President Wilson Chairman of the Labor Adjustment Commission of the United States Shipping Board. Various other departments of the Federation, in addition to the one on Mediation, lent themselves as readily to the development of the work of the Committee on Labor, to which Mr. Gompers added "including Conservation and Welfare of Workers." For example, Louis A. Coolidge, Chairman of the Federation's Welfare Department, became the Chairman of the Labor Committee on Welfare Work under which H. E. Miles, as Chairman of the Section on Industrial Training for the War Emergency, actively developed it for 18 months and later was appointed Chief of Training in the Division on Dilution and Training of the United States Department of Labor. Philip Hiss, Chairman of the Federation's Industrial Housing Committee, became Chairman of the Section on Housing. In the fruition of this effort, Otto M. Eidlitz, a member of the Federation's Executive Committee, successively became Chairman of the Committee on Housing of the Council of National Defense, and Director of the Bureau of Housing and Transportation of the United States Department of Labor. Other members of the Federation served upon the Labor Committee's Executive Committee—namely, Louis B. Schram and Dr. Lee K. Frankel; while Dr. Frederick L. Hoffman took the Chairmanship of the Committee on Information and Statistics.

The following members of The National Civic Federation also participated in the work of the Committee on Labor: Percy S. Straus, Chairman Executive Committee, Section on Industrial Training for the War Emergency; Dr. Thomas Darlington, Chn. Division on Industrial Fatigue; Dr. W. G. Hudson, Chn. Division on Industrial Diseases and Poisons; Robert D. Kohn, Chn. Division on Structural Safety; M. A. Dow, Chn. Division on Accident Prevention; Lewis T. Bryant, Chn. Division on Dust and Fumes; Dr. Alvah H. Doty, Chn. Section on Public Education in Health Matters; and A. Parker Nevin, Chn. Section on Standard Guides for Employers.

Some additional experts who were brought into the activities through the Welfare Department of the Federation are: L. R. Palmer, Chn. Industrial Safety Section; Ira H. Woolson, Chn. Fire Prevention Division; Dr. William A. Evans, Chn. Sanitation Section; L. B. Marks, Chn. Lighting Division; Werner Nygren, Chn. Heating and Ventilation Division; Albert L. Webster, Chn. Drinking Water Division; Dr. George M. Kober, Chn. Village and Public Sanitation Division; and Dr. George J. Fisher, of the Young Men's Christian Association, Chn. Recreation Section.

COMPENSATION FOR ENLISTED MEN.

Compensation for soldiers and sailors and their dependents was the first vital effort initiated and furthered by the Committee on Labor. In June, 1917, the Council of National Defense authorized the Committee on Labor, in accordance with its earlier recommendation that the Government should assume full responsibility for the care of the men in the Service, and for their relatives, to draft legislation covering the questions of separation allowances, compensation for injured soldiers and sailors and death benefits for their dependents. To this there was added the opportunity to secure insurance, at low rates, in amounts from $1,000 to $10,000. To carry into effect that portion of his plan of work (proposed April 2, 1917, and adopted April 6), Mr. Gompers called into conference on the 8th of July, 1917, at the headquarters of the Workmen's Compensation Department of The National Civic Federation, New York City, leading experts who were affiliated with it in the study or development of workmen's compensation, social insurance, pensions and foreign systems for separation allowances, to advise with him and Judge Julian W. Mack, Chairman of his Section on Compensation for Soldiers and Sailors and Their Dependents, one of the activities of the National Sub-committee on Welfare Work of the Committee on Labor.

Among those participating in this advisory conference, in addition to Judge Mack, who presented exhaustively the different phases of the subject, were: August Belmont, Chairman of the Federation's Workmen's Compensation Department; Warren S. Stone, Grand Chief International Brotherhood of Locomotive Engineers; P. Tecumseh Sherman, Social Insurance Expert and Attorney-at-Law; Dudley M. Holman, President International Association Industrial Accident Boards; V. Everit Macy, President The National Civic Federation; Dr. Lee K. Frankel, Third Vice President, Metropolitan Life Insurance Company; Frank V. Whiting, General Claims Attorney, New York Central Lines; D. L. Cease, Editor *The Railway Trainman;* Captain S. Herbert Wolfe, Consulting Actuary; Charles Thaddeus Terry, Chairman Committee on Uniform State Laws, American Bar Association; Prof. F. Spencer Baldwin, Member Former Massachusetts Commission on Pensions, Annuities and Insurance, and Manager State Fund, New York Industrial Board; Ralph M. Easley, Chairman Executive Council, The National Civic Federation; Hugh Frayne, Labor Member, War Industries Board, and General Organizer, American Federation of Labor; Dr. Frederick L. Hoffman, Statistician Prudential Insurance Company; William J. Moran, Attorney, Travelers Insurance Company; John Golden, President United Textile Workers; A. Parker Nevin, Counsel, National Association of Manufacturers; Leon S. Senior, Secretary New York Compensation Inspection Rating Board; J. W. Sullivan, of the Typographical Union, and Assistant to Samuel Gompers as Member Advisory Commission, Council of National Defense; E. E. Rittenhouse, Public Service and Conservation Commissioner, Equitable Life Assurance Society; John Mitchell, Chairman New York State Industrial Board; Timothy Healy, President International Brotherhood of Stationary Firemen; and Miss Gertrude Beeks, Secretary Executive Committee, Committee on Labor.

The result was the appointment by Mr. Gompers of a committee to draft the proposed legislation. The members of the Drafting Committee were: P. Tecumseh Sherman, Chairman; D. L. Cease, Secretary; Frank V. Whiting, Prof. F. Spencer Baldwin, Captain S. Herbert Wolfe, and J. W. Sullivan. It held several sessions in New York and at Washington in conference with Judge Mack and the Chairman, P. Tecumseh Sherman, in the light of the discussions performed the invaluable service of drafting the bill. For this purpose, with Judge Mack, he also studied the necessary administrative requirements in the Treasury Department, through which it would have to function when enacted by Congress.

The bill was adopted by the Committee on Labor on the 20th of July, 1917, soon thereafter sent by Secretary McAdoo to the President, approved by him and introduced in the House on August 10. With some amendments, it was enacted into law and signed by President Wilson on the 6th of October, 1917. It is considered the greatest humanitarian measure ever devised along insurance lines and an improvement upon Civil War pensions dependent upon annual Congressional appropriations.

INDUSTRIAL TRAINING FOR THE WAR EMERGENCY.

H. E. Miles, a practical manufacturer of long experience in mechanical training and Chairman of the Industrial Training Committee of the National Association of Manufacturers, was drawn from the Federation's Welfare Department to take charge of this Section of the Committee on Labor. It advocated the installation of vestibule schools by the manufacturers, and actually installed or was influential in starting a large number in aeroplane, heavy ordnance, light arms, textile and other plants, both government and privately owned. It has thereby helped to increase production all the way from 10 to 40 per cent in those places. The plan followed has been to adapt and instruct skilled mechanics from idle trades, such as the building line; and to train unskilled men and women, under the scheme of "dilution" used in England and France.

(Inc.), with Mr. Eidlitz as president, to which was referred the program of the Bureau of Industrial Housing and Transportation of the Department of Labor, and which has vast developments under way.

The three big welfare activities, above described, were inaugurated and effectively engineered by experts, the leaders in America in their respective lines, furnished by the Civic Federation. All gladly gave their services and paid their own expense.

MEDICAL EXAMINATIONS.

Medical examination of applicants as one of the functions of government labor recruiting agencies was recommended by Chairman Gompers to Secretary William B. Wilson, as the result of a conference held at headquarters of the N. C. F., July 15, 1918. A resolution, favoring the proposition designed to help maintain the health of our industrial army, embodies the consensus of opinion of experts, industrial physicians, public health workers, representatives of labor, and employers. The purpose is health conservation, essential to maximum production—a war necessity—and not to eliminate but to adapt the employee to work for which he is physically fitted, and also to permit follow-up or curative efforts. A standard examination card, dealing with such subjects as previous occupations, laboratory diagnosis, general appearance relating to deformities, malnutrition and glands, diseases of eyes, ears, nose, mouth and throat, lungs, heart, nervous system, extremities, and such general matters as hernia, hemorrhoids, and evidence of actual venereal disease, was adopted as the result.

HEALTH CONSERVATION REPORTS.

Reports upon subjects important to physical comfort and health of workers were rendered promptly by committees whose chairmen and members largely were experts from the Welfare Department of the Federation.

MUNITION WORKERS.

A guide to employers in providing healthful conditions for workers in the manufacture and loading of high explosives—to prevent industrial diseases and poisons—and indicating the fixtures requisite for toilet arrangements, eating facilities, and dust prevention, also proper medical supervision and other essentials, was one of the first adopted. Representative of employers in that trade previously were drawn into conference and agreed to adopt these standards as the practice of their shops. Thousands of copies were circulated upon application from employers in the poisonous trades and from many others since the standards are applicable to other lines of manufacture.

LIGHTING CODES.

Similarly, lighting codes have been prepared and distributed, in cooperation with state authorities, in the various states where war products are being made. Four states have adopted these codes. The National Lighting Committee, with a representative in each state, has inaugurated instructional conferences for the special guidance of factory inspectors. They consist of a series of talks by specialists, together with laboratory demonstrations of practical lighting, its technique and measurement. The effort is to improve industrial lighting which it has been proven results in saving eyesight, in the increase in quantity and quality of output, and lessened spoilage and waste.

INDUSTRIAL FATIGUE.

The best means of preventing industrial fatigue and the safe conditions under which maximum output may be obtained, have been indicated in a pamphlet widely circulated among employers. It deals not only with the means of detecting fatigue but the introduction of rest periods, providing adjustable seats, omitting unnecessary motions, proper ventilation of workrooms, adjusting the hours of work, avoiding overtime, omitting Sunday work, and sanitary conditions outside of factories.

VENTILATION.

A report upon requirements and standards for heating and ventilation, comprehensible to the layman, gives practical advice on what may be accomplished through natural and mechanical means without inordinate expense and with increased working efficiency. It refers both to home and shop conditions.

VILLAGE SANITATION.

Another report, with special reference to new industrial villages and construction camps, deals with rural sanitation. It takes up all phases of the subject in detail and is a vertiable text book for executives in welfare work.

INDUSTRIAL SAFETY.

The Section on Industrial Safety prepared codes for educational purposes upon (a) structural safety, (b) fire prevention and (c) accident prevention. There were incorporated in these recommendations only such codes as the modern employer would naturally have in his plant and therefore no hardship, or possible interference with quick war production, would be entailed by their adoption. It is intended to use them in drafting safety standards, the Bureau of Standards of the Interior Department, the Division on War Labor Service of the Department of Labor and the Section on Industrial Safety of the Committee on Labor of the Council of National Defense cooperating.

RECREATION.

This Section confined its efforts to shipbuilding, aeroplane and munition centers. It made surveys of conditions and afterward drew up recommendations upon minimum standards for entertainment and athletic features of social life, together with proper municipal or state regulations. This complete program of recreation, deemed especially necessary in view of the tension of war work, covers separately industrial plant and industrial community requirements. It was prepared by experienced social workers after conferring with representatives of federal departments concerned.

WELFARE EXHIBIT.

The Welfare and Safety Exhibit loaned by the Welfare Department of The National Civic Federation has been installed in the rooms of the Committee on Labor, Council of National Defense Building, at Washington, for the period of the war. It includes illuminated views, literature, posters and photographs illustrating the best practices to provide healthful work places, a pleasant social environment, and comfortable homes initiated voluntarily by employers.

STAFF PARTICIPATION.

By action of the Executive Council of The National Civic Federation, the services of its Chairman, Ralph M. Easley, and of the Director of its Welfare Department, Gertrude Beeks Easley, were tendered to the Committee on Labor and they became respectively Assistant to Mr. Gompers and Secretary of his Executive Committee. They have spent an average of three days a week in Washington, their expenses being borne by the Federation.

APPRECIATION EXPRESSED.

The estimate of the value of the Federation's cooperation was given by Mr. Gompers in his first report to the Council of National Defense for Congress, as follows:

> "The Committee on Labor could not have accomplished what it has done, had not The

National Civic Federation been in existence and extended patriotic service through its Welfare, Compensation, Mediation and other departments. Officials of The National Civic Federation have given their time since the first of April, 1917, and are continuing to do so. It also donated a clerical staff, paying its living and traveling expenses for the months pending the organization of the official clerical force."

GERMAN PROPAGANDA INTERPRETED.

So much for the concrete services rendered the Committee on Labor, but prior to our entrance into the war the Federation had contributed much material looking to the formation of a right, public sentiment. Decisive analyses of events and of agitation by anti-American movements, and adequate presentation to the people of such findings pointing to the ulterior purposes of active destructive forces, naturally became lines of endeavor of The National Civic Federation during the world war and at no time was its influence greater.

Primarily, the organization is an educational institution. The public service which it has been able to render, particularly since the United States entered the war, largely because its membership brings into close range all the elements of national life, has been demonstrated by the effect upon the common mind of its educational pronouncements persistently set forth in the press.

To furnish a proper interpretation and understanding of the bewildering efforts to undermine the morale of the people, various brochures have been circulated, completely exposing attempts to unsettle industrial, political and economic conditions.

The utilization of the Federation's years of experience with industrial subjects in conjunction with problems growing out of the war almost immediately made it one of the strongest defense forces in combating the insistent fire of the enemy aimed, through various destructive agencies, at our industrial institutions and movements.

The issuance of articles exposing the pro-German use of the pacifist, I. W. W. and socialist traitors, has been as continuous as have been the constant efforts of German agents thus to weaken the fortification of our national liberty.

One of the first publications of the Federation, a pamphlet on "Socialism and War," clearly explained the intrigues of the Socialist Party and showed that its opposition to the war was not on humanitarian grounds but for revolutionary purposes: that is, the socialists opposed armament because they do not want to have that obstacle to overcome when undertaking to confiscate the property of the world and take over the governments. This presentment was convincing to the most skeptical, because it was a collation of statements of purpose made by socialist organs and authorities, and was therefore incontrovertible.

No other agency than the Civic Federation was equipped to bring such facts to public attention. This setting forth of their anti-war attitude, which carried with it the explanation that the socialists welcomed the efforts of the belligerents to "bleed each other to exhaustion so that the coming social revolution may have an easier job," led the war series of educational bulletins which have helped to mould sound public opinion.

Others, equally valuable, dealt with and exploded the proposals of the Karl Marxian socialists for the "government ownership of all means of production, distribution and land"; and the oft-repeated assertion that in the "division of the products of modern industry, the lion's share goes to capital." One exposed the traitorous socialist effort to strengthen the German peace offensive through the much vaunted Stockholm International Socialist Conference. Another laid bare the relation of the German war party and German Exchequer to the various peace movements in the United States and to food riots in a number of our large cities during the unemployment period of the war. It brought out Germany's methods of bolstering certain enfeebled newspapers and magazines; indicated how the Kaiser's agents had stimulated Bolshevism and used I. W. W. and anarchist movements to foment internal dissension here; and disclosed the scheme to launch by pacifist-socialists, through certain "intellectual" channels, the so-called British labor program—i. e. state socialism. The Federation showed, by the use of German original documents, the deception practiced concerning welfare conditions of the workers, which gave the general impression that Germany was a social paradise, while the real situation showed an underpaid, overworked body of wage earners, extreme poverty, miserable slums and congested tenements such as are unknown in America, utterly inadequate social insurance benefits, a farcical farm loan system, an unwarranted claim to leadership in world invention and a backwardness in art and literature, her achievements being based on the robbery of the inventions and discoveries of other nations.

All these statements of facts concerning Germany's conduct of the propaganda portion of her military program and her misrepresentation as to supreme beneficial social amenities served to strengthen our national conviction relative to Teuton trickery.

Articles were published showing the loyal position of labor as represented by the American Federation of Labor and the railway brotherhoods, and dispelling the idea that the socialist and I. W. W. movements, numerically speaking, were sufficiently large to be indicative of the attitude of this country's workers in relation to the war.

The National Civic Federation is a recognized obstacle to the culmination of the plans of the Socialist Party in the United States. In fact, the danger threatened the socialist cause by the employer and employee combination of the Federation is recognized beyond the boundary lines of our own country. In fact, six years ago, at the International Socialist Congress in Vienna, the Federation was frequently attacked and an effort was made to bar out delegates from the American Federation of Labor because they were members of the "hated capitalistic combination, The National Civic Federation." After a two days' battle on the matter, the French delegates outvoted the Germans and the A. F. of L. delegates were seated.

In furthering its educational work, questions having a critical bearing upon national action were discussed at open meetings. "What is adequate preparedness for national defense?" was taken up, and when resident enemy aliens became a menace there was considered "What, if any, should be the changes in our policy and legislation to meet the new immigration conditions at the close of the war?" This is still a vital matter.

EFFORT TO DISRUPT LABOR.

Special sources of information revealed to the Civic Federation early in the world conflict, effort to stir up industrial strife on the docks, in ordnance and light arms factories and other munition-making centers. The mechanism of the Federation and particularly the composition of its Executive Committee, with one-third labor, made it possible to make effective use of this information. President Gompers of the American Federation of Labor left no stone unturned to assist in bringing to the attention of the Federal authorities those efforts to interfere with our neutral rights in the manufacture of war supplies for the Allies' governments. by discrediting and disrupting the labor movement in the United States. He and the leaders of the international and national unions, especially concerned in the manufacture of war products, have courageously met this effort to purchase and corrupt labor. Also, their voices have been lifted in protest to correct erroneous interpretation of propaganda designed to confuse the general public.

The four labor delegates sent to the United States by Premier Lloyd George at the request of Samuel Gompers, Chairman of the Committee on Labor of the Council of National Defense in May, 1917, that we might have the benefit of their experience under war conditions, and the munitions expert of the Balfour Commission were conducted to various large cities under the auspices of the American Federation of Labor and The National Civic Federation, the latter arranging for their entertainment and public appearance in all instances, exclusive of labor gatherings. These gentlemen—Right Hon. C. W. Bowerman, of the British House of Commons and British Trade Union Congress; Hon. James H. Thomas, Member of Parliament and of the Union of Railwaymen; Joseph Davies Secretariat of the Prime Minister, and H. W. Garrod of the Ministry of Munitions, as well as Judge Maurice Sheldon Amos — materially assisted in indicating why we are fighting and the effort which America would have to make to preserve her liberty.

Other foreign labor officials have been brought before the public in a similar way. A second Commission, composed of Messrs. Charles Duncan, M.P., Secretary General Workers' Union; W. A. Appleton, Secretary General Federated Trades Union; Joshua Butterworth, Member Associated Shipwrights' Society; William Mosses, Member Pattern Makers' Union, and Crawford Vaughan, former Premier South Australia, which toured the country under the auspices of the American Federation of Labor, was given a farewell luncheon by The National Civic Federation, March 16, 1918.

At this luncheon there was made a complete expose of the schemes undertaken in this country by the so-called group of intellectuals and sentimentalists who were trying to defeat the program of the American Labor movement through advocacy of a so-called British labor program, which is in fact, as before pointed out, nothing more nor less than Karl Marx socialism. A resolution was adopted, calling for the formation, in the countries of the Allies, of organizations of employers and employees to cooperate with The National Civic Federation in promoting collective bargaining and other recognized propositions that are accepted by both sides as practical methods for reducing industrial strife to a minimum.

THE LEAGUE FOR NATIONAL UNITY.

The League for National Unity was organized in Washington, D. C., September 12, 1917, by The National Civic Federation, as a special branch to take up war policies. It is composed of representatives of the various elements that make up American national life—labor, agriculture, manufacturing, commerce, banking, the church, the bar, women's and teachers' organizations, and the respective heads of the Democratic and Republican National Committees. The formation of the new organization was welcomed by President Wilson in an address delivered at the White House October 8, 1917, to the executive committee, in which he emphasized the need of team play by the forces of American thought and opinion and endorsed the specific work which the League proposed to undertake.

The purpose of the League, as stated in its by-laws, is "to create a medium through which loyal Americans of all classes, sections, creeds and parties can give expression to the fundamental purpose of the United States to carry on to a successful conclusion this new war for the

(Continued on page 15)

adow Huns and Others

By T. EVERETT HARRÉ

an advertisement, published on November 25, 1918, soliciting three-months' subscriptions at $1 per. In the New York daily newspapers of November 1, while the Supreme War Council was in session at Versailles, it appealed to readers to subscribe "in order that you may clearly understand the President's policies." It would be assumed that a magazine asking for public confidence on the ground that it occupied the peculiar and favored position of semi-officially interpreting the Administration would not misrepresent the President or misinterpret his statements, that above all things it would not be party to playing any German game, that, being edited by gentlemen, it would not present the President in the embarrassing role of being compelled, in dealing with the heads of the Allied governments, to deal with crooks and knaves. In the first year of the war Germany sought to eliminate France from the conflict through an inside propaganda designed to estrange the French from the British. In this advertisement for subscribers at the time the armistice terms were being formulated at Versailles, the *New Republic* published the following:

"Soon or late, the peace conference will gather. * * * What spirit will wield the gavel there? Will it be the high idealism in which the war began for us? Or will it be the old and sinister philosophy which for generations has patched the peace of Europe and never made it secure? If the diplomats should begin once more their ancient game of chess with peoples as pawns, the game of military supremacies, selfish alliances, balances of power, strategic frontiers and economic barriers—it would be the supreme tragedy of history." The advertisement went on to say it was for "American civilian opinion" to "say whether the President's program shall prevail." This brings up the pertinent question as to who in the Allied councils, in the opinion of the *New Republic*, would have been opposed to Mr. Wilson's program? What parties at the peace conference were accused by implication of possibly forcing "the old and sinister philosophy"?

With a peace of victory now assured, with the United States and the Allies unanimously agreed upon such a program as will guarantee security from future German militarism, light upon the purport of this singular announcement may be afforded by reference to the *New Republic's* pronouncements in the past. This organ of Bolshevism, in its issue of August 10, declared, "the President's Siberian policy gives evidence of divided counsels." With its usual air of authority, commenting on intervention in Russia, which it had opposed, it announced that "the President has been subjected to tremendous pressure not only from partisans of intervention at home but from the Governments of our Allies." In other words, the President against his better judgment was forced to comply to the desires of self-seeking Allied statesmen.

CONCERN FOR GERMANY.

Just as it was solicitous about leaving the German-subsidized Bolshevik autocracy in absolute power in Russia, the *New Republic* was frankly concerned about the sort of peace terms which the victorious Allies might impose upon Germany. This solicitude was shared by Mr. O. G. Villard's *Nation*, a weekly sublimated version of the New York *Dail Call*. The *New Republic*, like *The Nation*, staunchly supported the Russian Bolsheviki, and the British Labor Party in its program for peace discussions—over and above the head of the Allied Governments—with radical laborites from the Central Powers. To the American public this organ sought to picture labor in England—represented by Arthur Henderson—as being opposed to the British Government in its war aims. "Any tendency to 'defeatism' which exists in the British and French labor parties," declared the *New Republic* of August 10, "arises from a fear that some of the Allied Governments will prolong the war unnecessarily and make impossible a desirable peace by insisting on excessively drastic terms or by subordinating political to military victory." The *New Republic* implied the hope that an unconciliatory peace policy, such as might be adopted by the Allied governments, would be rejected by the labor parties of England and France. In the same issue it interpreted a speech by Mr. Lloyd George as indicating "a genuine diversity of outlook between Mr. Lloyd George and Mr. Wilson." While "nursing" the idea of Allied disunity, the *New Republic* showed a contrasting concern for Germany. "With the right kind of peace, Germany ought to get her share, but not more than her share" of raw materials after the war. "A purely punitive policy, designed to treat Germany the more harshly the more completely she is forced to acknowledge military defeat would encounter in America not perhaps active opposition, but all the doubts and delays that characterize the negative side of American policy."

The *New Republic*, of August 17, volunteered the opinion that "a German peace offensive is still possible, and even probable this fall." It predicted that the answer "will not consist, as so many Americans seem to think, in refusing all parleys until the Allied armies cross the Rhine." However, there followed the familiar suggestion of disunity among the Allies:

ALLIED "ECONOMIC PRETENSIONS."

"It is notorious that they are still very far from being politically united." And something like a veiled threat followed: "Germany may not be able to take advantage of their latent disunion during the coming fall, but she will be able to do so sooner or later." For, when the military advantage passed to the armies of the Allies, it was up to them satisfactorily "to give a joint political definition of the victory for which they are continuing to fight. The refusal to do so would offer the Germans their best remaining chance of cashing in a considerable measure of ultimate success." In view of the *New Republic's* announcement as to what might be expected of the labor groups of England and France, did it intend to intimate that labor in those countries would revolt against their governments for refusing to give to Germany an obliging peace?

President Wilson's speech in the Metropolitan Opera House in New York, on the night of Sept. 27, was interpreted by the *New Republic*, of October 5, as "a warning to the statesmen both in friendly and in enemy countries." The sort of peace conference which Mr. Wilson proposed, according to the *New Republic*, "will not work to collect damages and divide territories." Did a vast gulf, therefore, exist between Mr. Wilson and the men at the helm of the Allied governments?

"Practically all the regular European and American statesmen, with rare exceptions such as Lord Grey, while they may not be opposed to the formation of an international league, measure the value of the coming settlement, not in terms of a permanent international structure built purposely to provide a habitation for the spirit of justice and fair play, but in terms of the satisfaction of specific territorial and economic pretensions or grievances.''

''Specific territorial and economic pretensions or grievances'' referred, no doubt, to the alleged imperialistic aims of the Allied Governments. It would be interesting to know where, in the opinion of the *New Republic*, the demand for ''compensation by Germany for all damage done to the civilian population of the Allies and their property by the aggression of Germany by land, by sea and from the air'' become ''terms of the satisfaction of specific territorial and economic pretensions or grievances.'' The *New Republic* dwelt upon the phrase, ''if the Allies insist upon a dictated peace.'' ''Now they have gained 'the assurance of complete victory,' they (the Allies) are bound to declare by what agencies and acts they propose to translate the victory of power into the victory of justice,'' said the *New Republic*. Was justice extraneous to the cause of the Allies, a foreign quality which had been brought into their councils and policies by outside agencies? Why was it necessary to ''translate'' their victory into a different kind?

HAILING THE HUNS.

The *New Republic* cordially greeted the various German and Austrian peace bids and advocated peace by negotiation. Admitting that an armistice could be granted only on condition of ''the evacuation of all occupied territory and such further military precautions as would prevent the Germans in the event of a rupture of negotiations from improving their military position in the meantime, it declared that the part of the bid offering negotiations on the basis of Mr. Wilson's fourteen points could not ''be so summarily dismissed.'' ''It would be a mistake,'' the *New Republic* of October 12th went on to say, ''to reject it without discussion. * * * If discussion is rejected, the Germans will be united upon resistance to the end and the Allies will be divided by disaffection on part of the labor groups of France and Great Britain.'' Was this a warning of active treason on part of British and French labor in the interest of a peace invited and desired by Germany? Did the *New Republic* view any such possible treason with disfavor? Emphasizing by implication that the undemocratic war aims of the Allies might hinder peace, the *New Republic* contrastingly presented the concessions of the Central Powers as removing ''many of the obstacles to an agreement which hitherto have been properly considered most formidable. * * * American public opinion should recognize how many and how formidable are the obstacles to a satisfactory peace, which the present attitude of the Central Powers has removed.'' Mr. Wilson was represented by the *New Republic* as having attempted ''to democratize the Allied war aims.'' A refusal on part of the Allies to discuss peace would cause the Germans to ''screw themselves to resist until the end, and their resistance will be prolonged and intensified by the knowledge that their enemies, while they proclaim the principles which should determine a just settlement, refuse to discuss or act on their own principles.'' The *New Republic* in a previous issue had accused the men at the helm of the Allied Governments of entertaining a peace settlement ''in terms of the satisfaction of specific territorial and economic pretensions or grievances.''

The *New Republic* evidently had not looked forward to such a military victory over Germany as would remove the menace of her future power to make war. The Allies had supposedly done their worst, or their best; the war, presumably, had ended in a final tie. ''Nothing can be done to Germany as the result of still more complete victory which will absolutely prevent her from coming back, and upon the treatment which she receives hereafter depends whether she will come back as a disturber of the peace or as one of its guarantors.''

Is there not something familiar about the argument that Germany was so strong as to be invincible, and that she could not be finally crushed?

THE HARD-HEARTED ALLIES.

''The Allies have an opportunity of obtaining from their victory a Germany with which they can live or a Germany with which they cannot live. The way to get a Germany with which they can live is to strengthen the better element in Germany by treating it with more consideration than they do the worse element.'' One seeks for an equal concern that ''consideration'' be secured toward martyred Belgium, Serbia and France. But, then, was France not fighting for ''revenge''?

''The German nation has stripped itself of all its pride and in effect prostrated itself on the ground before its conquerors. * * * Its rulers are submitting to these voluntary humiliations in the expectation either of obtaining a tolerable peace or, failing that, of securing an intense and universal popular determination among the German people to fight until the end in order to save their nation from being exterminated.'' What did the *New Republic* or the German rulers consider a ''tolerable peace''? What were the ''voluntary humiliations'' of Germany? The offer to get out of Belgium?

The terms of peace agreed upon by the Supreme War Council at Versailles, as a matter of fact, were interpreted by the *New Republic* as a ''triumph'' of President Wilson's principles over the would-be policy of the Allies. ''The immense body of punitive sentiment throughout the Allied world,'' said this sheet of November 9, ''has been held in check by President Wilson's diplomacy.'' Commenting on this misrepresentation of the President and the heads of the Allied Governments, the New York *Globe* said: ''It is implied that the President forced an unwelcome dose down the throat of Lloyd George and Clemenceau. This is, of course, highly insulting and is calculated to destroy the mutual confidence which must exist if there are to be institutions of peace. Dishonor,'' said the *Globe*, ''was attributed to President Wilson by those who pretend to speak in his name.''

While the *New Republic* wilfully sought to make it appear that the Allied powers were forced practically against their will to agree to peace terms more just than they were inclined themselves to give, the *Nation*, edited by Oswald Garrison Villard, apparently did not see in the terms any ''defeat'' of the ''imperialistic aims'' which have been chronically ascribed to the Allies by the *New Republic*, the *Nation*, the *American Review of Reviews*, the New York *Evening Post*, the New York *Daily Call*, Max Eastman's *Liberator* and George Sylvester Viereck's scrubby *Fatherland*. The prospect of a complete victory over Germany obviously did not thrill Mr. Villard's pulse.

A GAME OF GRAB, SAYS VILLARD.

''Now that the war is nearly over,'' Mr. Villard fretted in the *Nation* of November 9, ''and the Allied statesmen see victory within grasp, they are largely ceasing to talk about ideals, and are getting down to the practical business of remaking the map. The indications are that most of them want to remake it on the old basis of seizing all that they can get, and letting their confederates have what is necessary to pacify them. * * * Doubtless it is necessary to be 'practical,' but if the war has been fought for this sort of thing, we ought to cease here and now to talk humbug like self-determination, the rights of small nations, no annexations, no punitive indemnities, and all the other principles which, originating in Russia, have yet come to be identified with the name of President Wilson; for a settlement of this sort would make them plain humbug, no more, no less.''

Mr. Villard, who attributes all the high principles enumerated to those German agents, Lenine and Trotzky, has distinguished himself as a pacifist. Mr. Villard didn't approve of America's going to war. A review of the New York *Evening Post*, under Mr. Villard's management, and of the *Nation* reveals a very curious anxiety regarding the peace that should be imposed upon Germany. Was it possible Mr. Villard was more solicitous about getting ''magnanimous'' terms for Germany than about securing reparation from Germany for wrongs committed? This might not be surprising on the part of a man who told the New York public months ago, in answer to a question, that he would not resist the invasion of America, and who, when asked if he ''would resist the violation of American women,'' declined to answer ''because the meeting was breaking up and it would take a good deal of time to go into it fully.'' Mr. Villard's methods of helping to preserve national unity during the period that America was at war were very unlike those employed by the majority of American editors. Mr. Villard disparaged the aims of the Allies and extolled the Bolsheviki who had surrendered Russia to Germany. Mr. Villard, like the *New Republic*, hailed every Teutonic peace offensive and advocated peace by negotiation and compromise. He implied that if peace was delayed it would be delayed by the greed of England.

"DIPLOMATS AND SPOILS."

Mr. Villard has pretended to a very lofty, condescending intellectualism, an exalted impartialism far removed from the passions of the crowd. On part of less intellects this pose merely indicates a neuter mentality, anaemia of the blood and soul. It represents generally a type of mind of which neither apostles nor heroes are made. It was among cold-blooded academic ''intellectuals'' that Germany found her chief defenders and tools—college pundits, caponized ''uplifters,'' radical sophomores, pacifist clergymen, ''the weak sister'' class. Many were the kind who probably would not have resisted the violation of American women, and who saw no reason for our going to war over the killing by German submarines of helpless women and children. Naturally, it has been this spiritless breed who of late have been whining about showing mercy and magnanimity to Germany.

Mr. Villard, like the mental adolescents of the *New Republic*, construed President Wilson's Liberty Loan speech as revealing differences between himself and the Allied statesmen. Mr. Villard read into the speech ''a warning to the Allied imperialists as to the enemy.'' In one breath Mr. Villard classed Sonnino, Lord Milner, Mr. Balfour and Lord Northcliffe with the Prussian and Austrian Junkers. He averred that Mr. Wilson's speech came ''at the very moment that diplomats of the old type are beginning to parcel out the spoils.'' To Mr. Villard the speech gave ''the Germans assurance that their fate is to be settled not by revenge but by justice.''

And what, pray, was this declaration in essence? That the wicked Allies were not bent upon justice? So far as the whole war was concerned, Mr. Villard, in commenting on Mr. Wilson's speech, confessed: ''Not that we can agree with him that the war is now or ever was a people's war.'' With American boys fighting and dying, what kind of war was it?

OLD-FASHIONED GERMAN HONESTY.

While he impugned the sincerity and honesty of the motives of the Allied Governments, Mr. Villard right off accepted Germany's words on their face value. Despite the scrapping and ruthless breaking of solemn covenants, despite the Brest-Litovsk treaty, Mr. Villard clung to the legend of German honesty. He considered the German reply of October 20th as ''unusually clear-cut and straightforward." That reply, he wrote in the *Nation* of October 26th, "seems as complete, as straightforward, and as final as any one who desires to be fair could possibly ask." With Germany manfully and squarely accepting Mr. Wilson's terms, Mr. Villard declared "peace is plainly within our grasp." If, however, we did not jump at the noble German assurances and make peace, "the war," he said, "will degenerate into one of revenge, and the German people, conscious of having made truly reasonable replies to the demands of President Wilson will be fortified to a determined resistance upon their own boundaries."

"On to Berlin" was a popular slogan in the Liberty Loan campaigns. The idea seemed to appeal to all virile Americans. But not so with Mr. Villard. "Must we batter our way to Berlin at frightful cost if Berlin comes to us, and upon its knees?" he wrote. "Shall we recklessly cast aside the opportunity to do the work of healing * * * and all for the sake of taking a bloody revenge on a people misled and mistaught by their militaristic rulers?" Did Mr. Villard forget that the "good German people" gave themselves up to a holiday of rejoicing over the sinking of the Lusitania? The *Outlook*, in a recent issue, recalled Mr. Villard's own opinion of the sinking of that ill-fated vessel. In the New York *Evening Post*, of May 10, 1915, of which Mr. Villard was at the time the controlling owner, there appeared on the first page a despatch from Washington regarding the destruction of the Lusitania, signed by Mr. Villard himself. In that despatch he made the statement:

"Had the submarine given thirty minutes' warning to the crew and passengers of the Cunarder, the exploit would have gone down in history as one of the most brilliant in the annals of naval warfare."

Upon which the *Outlook* commented: "Every man who did not spring to his feet in protest against the unwarned and cruel drowning of the women and children on the Lusitania was at heart pro-German and cannot complain if he is forever suspect."

U. S. AS BAD AS GERMANY?

Mr. Villard went to grave lengths in championing peace such as Germany was willing to make. He went so far, indeed, as to charge that the arbitrary power which may plunge a country into war, which President Wilson demanded be taken from the German autocracy, has been exercised by the President of the United States himself. In the *Nation* of October 19th, Mr. Villard confessed his "disappointment at the lack of generosity and of definiteness" in President Wilson's second reply to Germany. Commenting on the President's demands regarding the autocratic German Government, Mr. Villard said: "What does this mean? * * * How much of an interference in the inner concerns of Germany is actually intended? * * * As to arbitrary power which may plunge a country into war. That power exists in every nation. Mr. Wilson used it at Vera Cruz; England has seen it exercised on numerous occasions."

With this tense anxiety about "interference in the inner concerns of Germany," with all this nervous apprehension as to what the Allies might demand of Germany, Mr. Villard pleaded for "magnanimity and generosity." Is the governing mind of the *Nation* so negative as not to remember the "magnanimity and generosity" displayed by the Huns in Belgium, northern France and Serbia?

"It is now plain," wrote Mr. Villard in his paper of October 12th, in regard to the German peace offer, "that the President can have peace the moment he wishes it. * * * To us it seems as if the hour had come for the United States and the Allies to lay down the precise conditions, lest the Entente be placed in a false position and the cause of democracy within Germany—a cause which has taken an amazing step forward in a week—be hindered and not aided." Mr. Villard's implied suspicion of the Allies was in marked contrast to his spontaneous confidence in Germany. Mr. Wilson's statement that we could not come to terms with the German rulers was, according to Mr. Villard, "out of line with earlier assurances that we do not wish to interfere in the domestic concerns of the Central Powers." And he pleaded:

"It is unthinkable to us that, with an honorable, just and wise peace so clearly at hand, the noble cause of the Allies should be allowed to degenerate into a war merely of revenge."

Germany, you see, had offered to make "an honorable, just and wise peace." Her word was beyond question, her penitence beyond doubt, her political regeneration beyond suspicion! Therefore, if peace was not made it would have been because the Allies were bent upon revenge.

A SWEET SOUL SNEERS.

A citizen and patriot of such high standing in the community as Mr. Villard would not, of course, hold up to derision and ridicule the institutions of his own country. The pacific Mr. Villard—note his solicitous attitude regarding Germany—has been all sweetness and gentleness. However, how shall we explain what seems like a bitter sneer, like a pen-knife jab of sarcasm, in the following in the *Nation* of November 2:

"The news from Germany that there is henceforth to be a responsible Ministry in the Reichstag will make many Americans feel a keen sense of envy. We may not come to that for a long while, if ever."

The *Nation* of November 16 will remain a curiosity in American journalism, a sort of unconscious pathological record, a disquieting thing when examined as an American editorial expression on the outcome of the war. Austria and Germany had accepted the Allies' armistice terms. The Huns were to be bereft of military power, with necessary safeguards set up against possible Hun treachery. In this complete victory, the fulfillment of the hopes of a suffering world, the peoples of the Allied nations rejoiced. Oswald Garrison Villard seemed to bewail "the drastic terms of the armistice—drastic enough to take the wind out of the sails of the unconditional-surrender shouters, howling for a march to Berlin." Mr. Villard interpolates a "dark side" to the past year of military achievements. "The dark sides has to do with the illiberal forces in the Government, and lately, its Russian policy." He goes on to say:

"Undoubtedly the most sinister feature of the armistice terms granted to Austria-Hungary is that giving to the Allies the right to conduct the government of any portions of the Dual Monarchy in which their troops may find themselves."

TWO HEARTS THAT BEAT AS ONE.

Why is this feature "sinister?" Are the Allies not to be trusted? Are they liars and hypocrites who sneakingly betrayed Austria into a trap which would enable them to make their predatory way into that country and subjugate it by setting up an alien government? Mr. Villard is concerned lest the Allies put down revolutionary movements. "This, of course," he complains, "runs entirely counter to Mr. Wilson's principle of self-determination and his avowals that we are not in Europe to interfere in the domestic concerns of any country."

Rose Pastor Stokes, the rampant pro-Bolshevik who is under sentence for violating the espionage act, declaring that she had lost faith in President Wilson, in a speech in New York, called the terms of the armistice "infamous terms of interference with the free peoples of Germany."

Mr. Villard quotes an editorial from the New York *Evening Sun*, in which it is said:

"Obviously it is not to the interest of the world at large that the reconstruction of the German State and the substitution of democratic rule for autocracy should be permitted to degenerate into a reign of terror and a regime of ruin. There may remain no choice to the Allies save to pacify the country and turn it over to a sobered and stable popular government inspired by the judgment of the citizens, not by the passions of the mob."

This suggestion of helping to establish real democracy in Germany, in case anarchy was unleashed, provoked Mr. Villard to the pronouncement:

"Nothing could be worse for Germany or civilization than any such course as is herein suggested."

Is the peaceful Mr. Villard a disciple of Judge Lynch? Does he infer that wild mob riot would be best for Germany and for civilization? The pacifist paradoxically welcomes revolution.

"It may turn out after all we owe to Trotzky and Lenine and their propaganda a large share of the credit of pulling the German Colossus to earth. In our minds the probability of extreme revolutionary movements has loomed large for months past—not only in Germany, but in Austria and Italy as well. The world is surely in for a cycle of extreme radicalism."

"PRUSSIANISM IN WASHINGTON."

The abdication of the Kaiser and the surrender by Germany of its autocracy was not due, we learn from the *Nation*, to the Allies' victory. "The infectious example of Russia, close at hand, told. So we see the almost incredible spectacle of the Kaiser unhorsed, not by fiat of the Allies, but by the most despised of his political parties, the Socialists." Was Mr. Villard so unacquainted with current history as not to know the German Socialists supported the war until even the German autocracy realized their cause was lost?

America and the Allies had defeated and brought to terms the haughty military autocracy which had abrogated treaties, devastated Belgium and wrought the killing of more than ten million human beings. The Kaiser had abdicated. Was it a victory of right over wrong? Had the ideals which many of us cherished achieved final and complete triumph in the crushing of Prussian militarism? "The Kaiser is but the vilest flower of a system, and it is the system and the spirit which underlie it that must go. The battle against Prussian militarism is not yet won. Its first bloody phase is, thank God, at an end. But if this war has proved anything, it is that the spirit of Prussianism exists everywhere, in Paris, in London, in Rome—very strongly—and in Washington. Only in Moscow is it wholly crushed to earth."

Therefore, we engaged in this war as a nation of either hypocrites or deluded and deceived helots. We sent our soldier boys to die in combatting an evil which flourished right within our midst — yea, which was seated high in Washington. Englishmen, Frenchmen, Italians bled for four years in fighting a bogie, under the direction of masters as baleful as the German masters, indeed, themselves defending a system as aggressive and oppressive as the German system which had precipitated the war. Heroes and martyrs? We were Pharisees. We saw the mote in the Germans' eyes, and not in our own eyes. The whole war, then, this so-called fight to make the world safe for democracy was a burlesque; the agony, the shedding of blood a comedy that might have been staged in hell. And as for our victory over Germany, when Germany signed "a humiliating armistice on the enemy's terms"—what was it? In what did the world rejoice? For what did the glad bells of every city and hamlet ring on November 11? A

(Continued on page 19)

THE NATIONAL
Civic Federation Review

Office: Thirty-third Floor, Metropolitan Tower
1 Madison Avenue New York City

RALPH M. EASLEY, Editor

Published Twice a Month Two Dollars a Year

The Editor alone is Responsible for any unsigned article or unquoted statement published in THE NATIONAL CIVIC FEDERATION REVIEW.

NOTICE

THE NATIONAL CIVIC FEDERATION REVIEW *will deal with the issues of paramount importance arising in the period of reconstruction, and seeks to bring to the solution of these great problems the co-operation of the constructive and humanitarian forces of the nation. It will also throw light upon the sinister forces seeking to undermine our institutions.*

Non-members receiving this and subsequent SAMPLE *copies of the* REVIEW *are assured that no bill will be rendered therefor.*

The Blessings and Dangers of Peace. The President of the United States will soon take a seat at that historic council table at which will be settled the momentous terms for reestablishing peace. The world has gone through the trial of the most terrible war in the history of the race—a war unparalleled in scientific savagery, in bloodshed and agony. Yet out of the mortal suffering, to all who have made sacrifices for the ideals of freedom at stake, to the whole earth, should come commensurate blessings. The long oppressed spirit of many races and nations is already glowing. Humanity, through suffering, has undergone a spiritual purging. To the dealings of men with men, as of nation with nation, will be brought a keener spirit of justice, of conciliation and amity, of fraternal understanding and loving-kindness.

In America the great mass of people, regardless of condition, putting aside personal advantage, joined as one in the supreme task of winning the war. Leaders of industry, finance and commerce forsook their callings and gave their services to the Government. American labor, organized and unorganized, putting aside minor differences and agreeing to the settlement of disputes by arbitration, by and large took a stand loyally to back the war to the end. In the free-hearted, spontaneous subscriptions to the Liberty Loans and the giving to works of amelioration and healing, we beheld such an outburst of eager self sacrifice and warm generosity as lighted the common way through the dark days of war. The rich man gave his thousands and the widow her mite. It was an unloosing of purse strings and the springs of the human heart.

On the other side, in the trenches, our men faced death with a glory in their eyes. Fighting together for the ideal of equality, freedom and fraternity, class distinctions based on the mere possession of money, of birth or of education, gave way to the real democracy which attests the worth of men by their humanity, their love of their fellows, their willingness to die for a cause that is just. Our boys were baptized in the fire of that Americanism which holds our great heritage more precious than life, and when they come back they will still be ready to fight on, if fighting be needed, that "government of the people, by the people, for the people shall not perish from the earth."

With the war over, grave problems of readjustment, of repairing the ruin of war, challenge us. Shall not the spirit which was born out of the self-sacrifice and travail of the war be translated into a practical humanitarianism, a co-operative working together permanently to the common weal? It will be, and the world will be a better world, unless the sinister foes of peace and of good will are allowed to triumph.

They are at work now, here and abroad, seeking to undo all that has been won. They have come out clamorously in the open, preaching doctrines of hate and discord; they are at work in secret, plotting assassination, sabotage and revolution. They are taking advantage of the very problems which the war has produced—problems which only peaceful co-operation can solve—to foment social unrest. They threaten that the whirlwind which wrecked Russia will sweep the world.

In the surrender of Germany, America and the Allies won a victory over organized military might, over the most formidable autocratic power the world has ever seen. As that tyranny went down, another tyranny has arisen. It is the tyranny of ignorance and inhumanity, prejudice and persecution, of mob malice and savagery, of the worst human passions incited and played upon for their own advantage by artful demagogues. Shall the terrible struggle of the war against armed autocracy end only in universal mob chaos? Shall we have given our best blood to dethrone one Caesar only to let bigoted and brutish despots, such as Trotzky and Lenine, extend a bloody rule over us? Shall we have peace or social war? Shall we have good will among men, or a reign of hate? Shall the dark forces of disintegration and anarchy be permitted to undo all that was achieved out of the agony of the war and turn into dead sea fruit the very blessings of peace?

Or shall we not, quickened through the war to higher concepts of duty, work so together for the general good that these evil winds will die away? Shall we not continue in such a spirit of conciliatory cooperation, such unity of purpose and ideals in the work of readjustment and reconstruction as will render inert forces which would take advantage of the difficulties of these disturbed and unsettled times? The task of the readjustment of industry, of labor and of society to the normal conditions of peace are formidable —yet the task will be done as the work of war was done, and we shall have made steps ahead. Of the future, not ignoring present dangers, we have hope. For, as never before, the world rises with a new spirit to meet the problems and trials of a new day.

"The War after the War." "All Socialists," announced Victor Berger at a meeting of the Chicago branches of the Socialist Party, on November 17, 1918, "are pro-Bolshevists today." This is the same Berger who as long ago as 1909, in his organ, the *Social Democratic Herald,* declared in favor of "a violent and bloody revolution" and advised each of the Socialist voters and workingmen to provide themselves with "a good rifle and the necessary rounds of ammunition in his home and be prepared to back up his ballot with bullets if necessary." It is the same Berger that is under four indictments for seditious propaganda, and boasts of them. Is it a coincidence that the very Socialist party leaders who were of aid and comfort to Germany during the war should now simultaneously in many places here come forward as the promoters of Bolshevism?

The great pretense upon which the Bolsheviki agitated and shot their way into power was that they would give Russia "bread and peace." No sooner were they in control of governmental force than they quickly revealed that it was not peace they wanted but a world-wide war of ass against class. To buy immunity for their ar of extermination in Russia itself, they made shameful peace with the Germans who, in fact, ere their backers. Then their campaign of rrorization and slaughter of what they called ie Russian "bourgeoisie" started and has since rown in bitter intensity.

Uninformed people in America and other ountries may fondly imagine that these events far-away Russia do not threaten their safety nd institutions. A greater mistake could not made.

Having achieved what they consider success Russia the Bolsheviki and their organs (no pposition newspapers being allowed) began reatening that they "would carry the class war to every country in the world." This notifi- ation should have been taken seriously, but it as not. For years Socialists and the I. W. W. ave been preaching the class war. They had e design but lacked the means. The Bolshe- iki have the financial resources, and the Social- t Party spokesmen and their followers in the nited States are now boldly avowing them- lves Bolshevists.

How many of our people here know that the olsheviki have control of 800,000,000 rubles in old which is part of what they found in the ussian treasury as a reserve when they seized ower? But this is by no means all. They ound also 800,000,000 francs in gold which had een transferred from Rumania before the Rev- ution. In addition, they have confiscated im- ense sums in private funds and have appro- riated great quantities of jewels and other aluables.

This constitutes a campaign fund for instigat- g the class war wherever they can. They are sing it effectively. "Lenine is flooding the candinavian countries with propaganda oney," cables Bassett Digby, the Stockholm orrespondent of the *New York Globe* and the *hicago Daily News.* "The Bolsheviki have eir own printing works near Berne and 10,- 00,000 rubles are admitted to have been placed the Swiss Bank to the credit of their propa- anda," cables Julian Grande, the Berne cor- espondent of the *New York Times.* In Eng- nd, Italy, France and other countries the olshevik movement has suddenly sprung into idespread activity and shows signs of being ell financed. "We are feverishly awaiting the ve of the Western European Revolution," re- ently exulted *The Red Army,* a Bolshevist Mos- ow daily newspaper.

What of America? Many of the Bolshevist aders—and the most powerful—are men who ent back from here to Russia in 1917. No ob- ervant person can have failed to notice the sys- ematic outbreak of Bolshevist agitation here. xpensively manufactured magazines have sud- enly made their appearance. *The Class Strug- le,* published in Brooklyn, every line of which a Bolshevist incitement or distortion, is an istance. Book after book is being run off the resses. "We know," says *The Red Army,* "the ord democracy is associated with the word re- ublic only to cheat the people." The book riters promptly take their cue. "There is a *ar beneath the war,*" insists Walter E. Weyl his recently issued book, "The End of the Var," in concluding which he says: "It will a wider conflict than that which now rages the great world war], and the alignment will be y classes and interests rather than by nations."

From Montreal comes this Associated Press espatch: "Lumber camps in Canada are ver- able hotbeds of Bolshevik and I. W. W. propa- anda, according to the Rev. Thomas Joplin, eld secretary of the Shanteymen's Christian ssociation, who has just returned from a tour f the camps. He declares thousands of inflam- atory pamphlets have been distributed in the amps urging the workers, most of them for- gners, to resist all authority, 'by dynamite if ecessary.'"

"We have sent out in all directions the call of the international workers' revolution," triumphantly announces Lenine in a signed statement.

These are only a few signs of a brewing menace. All of the forces of civilization that do not want an unleashing of armed anarchy will do well to reflect upon their meaning and hasten to act.

Bolo Pasha Diplomacy. It is a common practice of advertisers in general to exaggerate, misrepresent and deliberately "fake" when describing their wares. If these wares consist of stoves, corsets or chewing gum, little harm is done, because the public has learned to discount such statements. In the case of newspapers, magazines and other periodicals, however, which seek to shape public opinion, such misrepresentation presents a different aspect. An illustration of the latter is found in the case of a pretentious weekly journal which is just now making an appeal for an increased circulation. Among the inducements presented as to why the benighted public should send in $5 subscriptions, is the following:

> For four years it (this paper) has developed and consistently advocated the principles for which we finally entered the war. It was one of the first journals in America to urge that we go in for the sake of these principles, and it insisted that the war must go on until Germany was defeated and a League of Nations made possible.

If there were even a semblance of truth in this statement, that would be something; but when one reads such analyses of this journal's editorial course—or various courses, rather—as that published by William English Walling, under the title "Highbrow Hearstism", and that by T. Everett Harré, in this issue of the REVIEW, the claim made by the paper becomes farcical in the extreme. In fact, if it were a matter of any moment, it might be characterized as an attempt to obtain money under false pretenses.

One editorial alone taken from the columns of this journal, which is claiming to have so "consistently advocated the principles for which we finally entered the war * * * and insisted that the war must go on until Germany was defeated and a League of Nations made possible," will serve to illustrate the above statement. This editorial appeared in the issue of May 19, 1917, just six weeks after we entered the war—and reads as follows (the italics are ours):

> If Russia is not prevented from drifting out, a military decision becomes impossible except on one condition. There can be no victory over Germany except as a consequence of as complete an organization of the fighting power of the United States as that which has taken place in France and Great Britain. Germany could then leave a mere retaining force in the East and concentrate all reserves of guns, ammunition and men on the Western line. The result for this summer and the next would at best be a hideously expensive stalemate. The deadlock could be broken only by the dispatch of a huge American army to Europe—*one so large that it could not be recruited, equipped and trained until the summer of 1919. Even then it might be impossible to transport it to Europe.* In that case, instead of preparing to enlist and discipline a million conscripts, we ought to be planning a draft of all able-bodied men between twenty and forty, and training camps for at least four million soldiers. Instead of providing for financing a two years' war, and levying $1,750,000,000 in taxation, we ought to look forward to three or four years of fighting, to casualties of several millions, to a revenue from taxation of $4,000,000,000 a year, to an ultimate national debt of not far from $40,000,000,000, and to a general condition of extreme famine in all the basic supplies of food and materials. *It is an appalling outlook, and it will go ill with the men responsible for the government which brings consequences of this kind upon the American people. The result would almost certainly be a revolution in America far more bloody and drastic than the revolution in Russia. A war conducted until 1920 on the scale required by a military decision might bring peace with victory, but it would also bring victory with suicide.*
>
> As long as Russia continues in its existing state of mind, the war certainly cannot be won by armies and now that the United States is going to exert all its resources in ship-building, it almost certainly cannot be won by submarines. *The final victory must be won by diplomacy.*

The difference between the spirit and purpose of this editorial and the defeatist propaganda for which Bolo Pacha was shot is not discernible to the naked eye.

It might also be of interest to note that the writer of this defeatist editorial and the advocate of "victory by diplomacy," is at present in France, representing the government of the United States in this work of "diplomacy."

Real Labor Speaks. The recent Pan-American Labor Conference at Laredo, Texas, was a notable achievement for the American Federation of Labor, which organized and brought it together. The United States, Mexico and five Central American Republics were represented. Samuel Gompers declared that it is the aim of the American labor movement to bring about the best possible fraternal, cooperative and sympathetic agreement of the working people of all American countries. Plans were developed for the formation of a Pan-American Federation of Labor.

The resolutions show what the American labor movement considers as fundamental to the vital importance of all wage earners. They are:

> "That in law and in practice the principle shall be recognized that the labor of a human being is not a commodity or article of commerce.
>
> "Industrial servitude shall not exist except as a punishment for crime, whereof the party shall have been duly convicted.
>
> "The right of free association, free assemblage, free speech and free press shall not be abridged, that the seamen of the merchant marine shall be guaranteed the right of leaving their vessels when the same are in safe harbor.
>
> "No article or commodity shall be shipped or delivered in international commerce in the production of which children under the age of 16 years have been employed or permitted to work.
>
> "It shall be declared that the basic work day in industry and commerce shall not exceed eight hours a day.
>
> "Trial by jury should be established."

This is a sterling constructive policy. It is in marked contrast to the destructive Bolshevist theories that highbrow and lowbrow publications are trying to make popular—theories which have already produced such bloody chaos in Russia. It is a relief to turn from the airy speculations of the professionalist leaders of the so-called British Labor Party to the sane, practical program of the American Federation of Labor.

Seeds of Suspicion. Is there no significance in the fact that the journals which promulgated "defeatism," by implying that Germany was invincible, and which advocated a peace by negotiation and compromise, more recently have concentrated their efforts toward sowing seeds of suspicion and distrust regarding the war aims of the Allied governments? Why the attempt to implant in the minds of the American people a belief that the aims of Lloyd George and Clemenceau were opposed to the peace principles enunciated by President Wilson? Why the insidious and persistent suggestion that "divided counsels" exist? What purpose was back of the propaganda which pictured America as alone being guided by unselfish motives and high ideals and which presented our associates in the Allied governments as being far from above suspicion?

Leaders in the Fight Against the Enemy Within

HON. JOHN LORD O'BRIAN

HON. JOHN LORD O'BRIAN.

WHEN the United States entered the war the Government was confronted by a problem such as it had never been required to deal with before—the problem of rooting out and defeating the complicated and intrenched system of German espionage and propaganda.

Germany's spy system was an efficient instrument even before the Franco-Prussian war. During more than forty years afterwards the most cunning and subtle brains of Germany, experts in psychology and highly trained specialists, were devoted to the perfection of a spy system whose ramifications were universal, and to a baffling system of propaganda extending into every country of the globe. When America entered the war we had to combat not only the armies of the foe abroad, but an army of foes at home. Germany had intensively developed during nearly three years agencies for insidious propaganda and an organization of spies for purposes of espionage and destruction. We confronted an internal situation of the gravest danger, such as none of the Allied nations had to deal with when they were forced to war. Not the least difficult of our problems was that of dealing with a vast population of alien enemies and of citizens whose sympathies, because of birth or racial extraction, had been with the Central powers.

What happened in the United States is an answer to the Teuton argument about the inefficiency of democracies. During the period that we have been at war, better order has been preserved in this country than in any nation at war. At the beginning, naturally, there were fears of widespread outrages and sabotage on the part of German agents and sympathizers. Yet within a few months after the declaration of war, the United States established laws and agencies which have been so effective that German plots and German espionage came to almost nothing. German propaganda was practically exterminated.

For a large part of what has been accomplished recognition is due to John Lord O'Brian who, in October, 1917, was asked by Attorney General Gregory to take charge of the war work of the Department of Justice. What Mr. O'Brian has done is not generally appreciated, for he has worked quietly and has avoided publicity. It is not known to the country at large that the whole scheme for the registration and internment of enemy aliens was devised by Mr. O'Brian. Whenever an enemy alien was proved dangerous to the country and to the successful prosecution of the law, he has without fear or favor recommended his internment. On the other hand, he has consistently refused to intern Germans or Austrians who he believed would abide conscientiously by the law. Under these regulations thousands of German and Austrian aliens have been so subjected to Federal control that the sum total of anti-American activities has been surprisingly small. Mr. O'Brian helped to prepare the Sabotage Act and Passport Act, and to him, perhaps more than to anyone, credit is due for the system of protecting the sea coast, water fronts and army and naval bases.

Mr. O'Brian's policy toward free speech has been liberal; yet whenever he found that free speech was used merely as subterfuge for wilful attempts to interfere with the conduct of the war, he has recommended that action be taken. The Department of Justice has never prosecuted organizations nor taken the stand that membership in organizations implied disloyalty.

German propaganda aiming to nullify our part in the war was most rife in December, 1917, and January, 1918. It took the form of interpreting the war as a capitalistic war and sought to foment resistance to the draft. That was effectively and vigorously suppressed. As in the cases of the *Masses*, of Victor Berger and Rose Pastor Stokes, prosecutions were conducted under Mr. O'Brian's jurisdiction. Religious pacifism came next. The Italian Government complained that Pastor Russell's pacifist literature was being sent into Italy from Greece and that an anti-war sermon by John Haynes Holmes was dropped by Austrian aviators into the ranks of the Italian armies. Mr. O'Brian took charge of the prosecution of the "Russellites," with the result that Rutherford, the leader, and others were convicted. Mr. O'Brian found an insidious form of propaganda conducted among the negroes of New York and the far south. The suppression of this, as well as the more familiar anti-British propaganda, was under Mr. O'Brian's supervision. Part of Mr. O'Brian's work was the enforcement of the provision of the draft act and the routing out and detection of slackers. This is a military act which depends upon the civil branch of the government for its enforcement. The efficiency of the act was mainly due to the intense activities of the Department of Justice.

Mr. O'Brian has been a life-long Republican. He began the practice of law in Buffalo, and soon won distinction because of his extraordinary powers and keen intellect. After serving several terms in the State Assembly he was appointed United States District Attorney by President Roosevelt. In this capacity he won many legal triumphs, notably in the prosecution of the railroad companies and the Standard Oil Company for violating the Anti-Rebate law. Mr. O'Brian's incumbency of the office of United States Attorney did not come to an end until some time after the commencement of President Wilson's first administration in 1913. Attorney General Gregory thus came to entertain a high regard for his ability as a prosecutor and retained him as special counsel to prosecute the "Coal Trust," and later as special counsel for the government in the prosecution of Franz von Rintelen, the German agent and spy.

ALFRED L. BECKER

ALFRED L. BECKER.

To deal with the problem of German esp[illegible] age and propaganda the State Legislature [illegible] New York on May 21, 1917, passed the P[illegible] and Safety act, under which the State At[illegible] ney General enjoys the unusual powers of be[illegible] able to subpoena witnesses and compel them [illegible] give testimony under oath. This is a pow[illegible] not possessed by any branch of the Federal [illegible] ernment charged with investigating espiona[illegible] and propaganda.

Under this law Attorney General Lewis [illegible] his Deputy in immediate charge of the admi[illegible] tration of the peace and safety act, Alfred [illegible] Becker, obtained the proofs necessary to [illegible] vict Bolo Pasha in France, and bring about [illegible] execution as a traitor. The steps of Joseph Ca[illegible] laux, former Premier of France, through Bra[illegible] and Argentine were retraced and the swo[illegible] story of his machinations with Count von L[illegible] burg, German Minister to the Argentine, [illegible] furnished to the French Government. The pr[illegible] of how the representatives of Germany for[illegible] a pro-Ally subject of the Sultan of Turkey, [illegible] lih Gourdji, out of Constantinople becaus[illegible] sought to tell the truth through a news age[illegible] which he controlled, was made a matter of re[illegible] ord. The secret methods of the German prop[illegible] ganda office in the Wilhelmstrasse have be[illegible] laid bare in a deposition showing how [illegible] Kaiser's chief censor, Roediger, spread thro[illegible] the United States, more than a year before it [illegible] tually happened, the report that the Kaiser w[illegible] about to be overthrown, with the intent of p[illegible] alyzing America's military effort. The sord[illegible] story of how the representative of the Germ[illegible] Red Cross, Dr. Bernhard Dernburg, organi[illegible] the forces which attempted to corrupt pub[illegible] opinion in the United States and keep our co[illegible] try out of the war, was set forth in sworn [illegible] positions published for the education of [illegible] American people in the ways of the Teuto[illegible] mind.

To no one belongs so much recognition [illegible] these noteworthy achievements as to Deputy [illegible] torney General Alfred L. Becker, who was pla[illegible] in charge of investigations under the peace [illegible] safety act. Mr. Becker has said that the cor[illegible] principle of investigation of German plots i[illegible] "follow the money trail." The discovery [illegible]

Leaders in the Fight Against the Enemy Within

the sources of the 10,000,000 francs with which Bolo Pasha bought a controlling interest in the Paris *Journal* for the purposes of defeatist propaganda is an illustration of the application of this principle of investigation.

Having determined to help to expose so far as might be possible the whole series of plots of Ambassador von Bernstorff and his associates, Mr. Becker obtained from the banks where the German embassy had accounts every available record showing the recipients of embassy funds. One of the first fruits of this investigation was the proof that the New York *Evening Mail* had been bought with money furnished by the German government. For more than a year the Department of Justice had suspected that Edward A. Rumely bought the *Mail*, late in May, 1915, with German money, but the proof was lacking. Within a day after Mr. Becker obtained the records of the New York banks, he had traced $1,700,000 from the bank accounts of the embassy through intermediaries to Edward A. Rumely. The arrest and indictment of Rumely and his attorney soon followed.

Through Mr. Becker's investigation of German embassy expenditures he obtained conclusive evidence of the plot of Dr. Albert, the Commercial Agent of the Embassy, and William Wilke of Buffalo, to corner the stoneware market of America so as to cripple the manufacture of explosives, in mixing which such pottery must be used. He found the proof of the enormous expenditures through Dr. Hugo Schweitzer for buying up nearly all the carbolic acid in the country with a similar motive. He discovered Dr. Albert's plan, partly carried out, of monopolizing all the available shipping space for several months after the end of the war so that Germany would be able to dictate the conditions upon which she would buy foodstuffs in the United States. He showed how George Sylvester Viereck, one of the most slippery of German propagandists, received $100,000 and more from the embassy for issuing a propaganda weekly, *The Fatherland*, and publishing a whole series of books cunningly written so as to set forth in disguise the German argument. Mr. Becker uncovered the activities of Dr. William Bayard Hale, and exposed him as the secret director of Hun propaganda. The whole ugly nest of German agents was routed out and rendered incapable of future harm by fearless nation-wide publicity.

Only a part of Mr. Becker's discoveries have been published. With a grasp of the situation gained from nearly two years of study, Mr. Becker is continuing investigations, which, now that the war is won, may do much toward preventing Germany from winning the commercial war that is to come.

SOLICITOR WILLIAM H. LAMAR.

SOLICITOR WM. H. LAMAR

DURING the first days of the war the mails of the country were flooded with tons of propaganda matter, books, newspapers, magazines, pamphlets and circulars, the purpose of which was to create in every way obstruction to the prosecution of the war. It was a comparatively easy matter to apprehend demagogues who openly preached resistance to the war and otherwise violated the espionage act. But it was a difficult problem to detect and clear the mails of printed matter, much of it adroitly handled and subtly disguised by the writers in an attempt to evade criminal liability.

At the very beginning of the war it was evident that there existed an organized effort to create anti-war sentiment, and that this widespread campaign was but the outgrowth of the German propaganda begun here in 1914. The stamping out of disloyalty and sedition, as it worked through the channels of the Post Office, was in charge of William H. Lamar, Solicitor of the Department.

The Post Office Department did not at first have an organization capable of coping with the problem. But after the declaration of war Solicitor Lamar, working in close touch with the Postmaster General, promptly recruited corps of attorneys, translators and readers, and took measures to secure the full cooperation of the entire Post Office Department, including officials, postmasters, clerks and carriers. They were made fully acquainted with the provisions of the statutes, and were instructed to examine matter deposited in the mails for objectionable material. Whenever such matter was found clearly to be in violation of the law, it was at once ruled out of the mails. But whenever there was doubt the matter was held and submitted to the Solicitor for instructions.

Solicitor Lamar was confronted with the problem of detecting pro-German propaganda under many disguises. Opposition to the war was based in some quarters on specious religious ground. Socialists opposed the war as a capitalistic war. To the ultra-Irish it was made to appear that America was fighting for the British King; to the ultra-Protestant the assertion was made that we fought for Italian Catholicism; other religious groups were told that we were helping in a fight against all religion by assisting French atheism. Anti-Japanese propaganda, which took the form of a demand that the white races stop bleeding themselves to death lest the yellow races dominate the earth, formed no inconsiderable part of the insidious campaign. After the passage of the Espionage Act and the Trading with the Enemy Act action was taken against various publications, and in every case brought before the courts the Government was sustained. Among the papers which Solicitor Lamar found had violated the Espionage Act was Tom Watson's paper in Georgia and Victor Berger's *Milwaukee Leader*. William Voss Lloyd, a candidate on the Socialist ticket in Chicago, had put out literature endorsing the St. Louis platform of the Socialist Party. The Post Office declared this matter unmailable, and the Socialists went before Judge Landis to secure an injunction to prevent the Postmaster from holding the mail. Judge Landis decreed in favor of the Government.

Whenever they got into trouble the noisy Socialists made a great clamor about the Constitution guaranteeing freedom of speech, and contended that it was unconstitutional for Congress to pass any act limiting the expression of honest convictions. Solicitor Lamar's answer, which has been sustained by the courts, is that the use of the mails is a privilege, and not a right, and that Congress had absolute right to determine what should, or should not, be carried through the mails.

Those who sought to obstruct the war employed various devious and deceptive methods. The I. W. W. and International Socialists sent literature through the mails opposing the war, and some defended their infractions with the argument that they only consistently pursued policies advocated long before the war. Solicitor Lamar replied that this is a question for debate, but not for consideration in applying the law. "A Mormon," he said, "cannot continue the practice of polygamy on the ground that it was recognized and permitted as a religious custom or tenet for many years before it was outlawed." When the statute was applied, these efforts were found to work along the well-defined plan of playing the German game.

Under the Trading With the Enemy Act, which tended to reinforce the Espionage Act, foreign language newspapers were compelled to file translations of all matter bearing on the war or the governments engaged in war against Germany with the Post Office Department before or at the time of publication. Where papers were of such a character that they might be freed of the requirements, permits subject to revocation were given. As the plan of handling the foreign language press worked out, disloyal papers lost advertising and subscribers and a number went out of business.

Today the amount of disloyal literature going through the mails is negligible. Solicitor Lamar, to whom this great achievement is principally due, entered the Postal Department in 1894 and served in various capacities until 1906, when he became an Assistant Attorney in the Department of Justice assigned to the defense of suits against the United States in the Court of Claims. On the incoming of the first Wilson Administration he was appointed Assistant Attorney General for the Post Office Department, the title of which office has been changed to Solicitor.

ANNOUNCEMENT.

In the next issue of THE NATIONAL CIVIC FEDERATION REVIEW will appear:

"Bolshevik 'Industrial Government,'" by Gustavus Myers, which shows how Bolshevism worked out in practice, as told by men who saw the demoralization of industry and terrorization by wholesale massacres in Russia first hand.

"Shadow Huns and Others," by T. Everett Harré, a continuation of the article begun in this number.

"Works of the War Labor Board"—a study of the Governmental agencies dealing with relations of employers and employees under war conditions, showing phases which it would be valuable to continue in times of peace.

"Social Insurance"—an article dealing with the present status of the efforts in this country to secure compulsory State health insurance and labor's attitude toward it. Is it practical and desirable?

"The Pan-American Labor Conference," by Chester M. Wright, an account of the notable conference held at Laredo, Texas.

The British Labor Party's Program

A SCHEME FOR REVOLUTIONARY SOCIALISM PROMOTED UNDER THE GUISE OF SOCIAL REFORM

By RALPH M. EASLEY

After reading the proposed British Labor Program, one is possessed of two dominant ideas: First, that it is a very cleverly written political document designed to replace the Conservative and Liberal Parties of England with a Socialistic Party, and therefore deals principally with British questions, having little if any bearing upon problems in the United States. It contains much criticism of the "lack" of sufficient industrial legislation in England and where they have satisfactory legislation, of a "lack" of its proper administration. There is also much space devoted to a discussion of democratic self-government in the "Britannic Alliance" and the proposed "Imperial Federation."

The second outstanding idea is that its constructive proposals are largely a rehash of the resolutions adopted at international socialist congresses, the various socialist platforms and the pronouncements of the socialist leaders of all countries during the past twenty years.

By a barrage of glittering generalities, its authors seek to disguise the fact that its program is state socialism, pure and simple. But a little scrutiny soon discloses scattered through the document such tell-tale phrases as these:

> "The individualist system of capitalist production, based on the private ownership and competitive administration of land and capital * * * will receive its death-blow. And the Labor Party refuses absolutely to believe that the British people will permanently tolerate any reconstruction * * * involved in the abandonment of British industry to * * * separate private employers. * * * What the Labor Party looks to is a genuinely scientific reorganization of the nation's industry * * * on the basis of the common ownership of the means of production; the equitable sharing of the proceeds among all who participate in any capacity and only among these, and the adoption, in particular services and occupations, of those systems and methods of administration and control that may be found, in practice, best to promote the public interest."

Then it goes on:

> "The Labor Party stands not merely for the principle of the common ownership of the nation's land, to be applied as suitable opportunities occur, but also, specifically, for the immediate nationalization of railways, mines and the production of electrical power."

In other words, the state is to take over and operate all the farms, factories, mills, mines, stores, banks, street railways, steam railways, mercantile marine, gas and electric light utilities —in fact, all the productive industries and means of distribution, which is Marxian socialism without any disguises. The definition of socialism, which many loose writers like to say consists of fifty-seven varieties, was officially defined by Morris Hillquit, before the Industrial Relations Commission, in the following concise language:

> "Stated in more concrete terms, the socialist program requires the public or collective ownership and operation of the principal instruments and agencies for the production and distribution of wealth — the land, mines, railroads, steamboats, telegraph and telephone lines, mills, factories and modern machinery.
>
> "This is the main program, and the ultimate aim of the whole socialist movement and the political creed of all socialists. It is the unfailing test of socialist adherence, and admits of no limitation, extension or variation. Whover accepts this program is a socialist; whoever does not, is not."

This socialist British labor program is headed "Labor and a New Social Order" and the opening paragraph is under the title of "The End of a Civilization." The latter phrase is based upon an alleged utterance of Count Okuma, of Japan, at the darkest hour of the war—to wit: "Watching the present conflict from the other side of the globe, it is nothing less than the death of European civilization."

The report goes on to state: "We of the Labor Party can so far agree in this estimate as to recognize, in the present world catastrophe, if not the death, in Europe, of civilization itself, at any rate the culmination and collapse of a distinctive industrial civilization, which the workers will not seek to reconstruct." In other words, industrially speaking, whatever is, is wrong, and the present industrial system, under which such tremendous progress has been made during the last fifty or one hundred years, is to be scrap-heaped and we are to begin all over again with a new dream, which is exactly what they are now trying out in Russia. They have overturned all of their institutions and have begun at the bottom, and seem to be going lower. That is to say, the drafters of this report, the "three tailors of Tooley Street," Messrs. Webb, Henderson and MacDonald, the latter being the Morris Hillquit of England, assume that civilization has already passed away and that it is up to them to create a new world. This appalling task, however, does not feaze them and they go ahead and construct it overnight with a paste-pot and a pair of scissors from the political-socialist libraries.

The report deals with many stock industrial subjects over which there has been much controversy for decades, such as a national minimum wage, compulsory unemployment insurance, compulsory housing reform, health insurance, labor exchanges, etc., and to which there is contributed not a single new idea. There is also discussion of what is to happen at the close of the war when the millions of men and women in the factories are demobilized and the millions of boys return from the front.

This part of their report is interesting but it contains not an idea that has not been discussed in this country almost since our entry into the war. They have come to a conclusion, however, on the matter, and that is that the government must see that every soldier gets back his job or gets another one just as good, and that at the same time every woman who has taken a soldier's job must keep hers or get another one just as good—some task!

On the unemployment proposition, they have nothing but the old socialist program of the government's building of residences, public buildings, roads, afforestation, the reclamation of lands, building of "light railways," "unification and reorganization of railway and canal systems" and the "development and better equipment of our ports and harbors," etc., etc.

All of the foregoing questions, and many others, were made the subject of careful study by all the experts in this country, at the beginning of the war in 1914, when the panic of that winter threw millions out of work. Not to go into these questions in detail but to refer to one—that of unemployment—it was soon discovered that wars and panics do not come on schedule time, giving a year's notice. Therefore, Governments—Federal, State or Municipal—could not have the money ready, the plans ready, or the material ready to do all the building that is proposed by these dreamers, until long after the emergency had passed. It was pointed out, for instance, that the several million needle trade workers of New York, Chicago, Boston and Cleveland would not make much headway in building houses or railroads. These Russian Jews, which most of them are, with their women and their children, are not carpenters nor bricklayers nor trench-diggers, nor could they become such overnight. Neither would they get very far with "afforestation". True, that is a high-sounding word; but when we realize that it would mean that the men and women in these industrial centers throughout the country who are thrown out of work during a depression would have to be transported to localities somewhere in the South or West, where they would have to build homes, pull out the stumps, clear up the debris and make over the soil before they could cultivate even a garden, let alone a farm—when we realize this, the seductiveness of the enterprise, as well as its practicability as an emergency employment relief measure, vanishes.

Again, it was found that the establishing of employment exchanges, which proposition bulks large in all socialist programs, did not meet the situation, for they could not produce the only thing wanted,—jobs. With five men for every job, no employer needed an agency to provide him with workers—they were at the gates. While in good times no skilled workers would apply to agencies for jobs.

Another of the proposed panaceas in the Henderson, Webb, MacDonald program is the "democratic control of industry." They slide along very gently and avoid defining just what they mean, for the reason that for the time being, democratic control of industry is going a little lame, in view of the Lenine and Trotzky experiments. Democratization of Industry means that the workers in a given plant shall themselves take over and run it, under an indefinite number of committees, sub-committes and sub-sub-committees. This certainly would be democratization of industry as well as its complete destruction.

This same idea of democratic control of a shop that has proven so destructive in Russia finds its counterpart in England in a scheme called the Shop Steward System, which means that in every shop, as in Russia, there shall be committees of the workers who shall undertake to deal with the employers on all matters pertaining to the production and distribution of the work of the factory. This system in England has worked out so badly that it is finally being denounced for what it is—Bolshevism, pure and simple. Upon his return from Europe, Charles Edward Russell, a loyal socialist, in an interview published in the *New York Times* of Sunday, September 29, said in regard to this movement:

> "Very much akin to syndicalism, the shop steward movement takes its name from the fact that, in many of the industries in England, men engaged in various lines of industries form themselves into shop units, and elect a chairman known as the shop steward, who tells the manager what shall be done for the workers and determines the conditions of labor in his particular shop. Thus, in a munition factory, the men engaged

> in making the noses of shells would organize in their particular shop, elect a shop steward, and leave him to act as their intermediary in all demands upon their employers. The various shop stewards in a factory also assemble and form a council of shop stewards for that particular factory, which also has its chairman, and which devotes itself to the task of seeing that the manager or employers afford the workingmen the desired conditions of employment.
>
> "Curiously enough, the shop steward movement pays no attention to trade union affiliations, even though the great majority of the workers are members of trade unions. It is a development entirely independent of trade unions and marks a new epoch in English industrialism. The shop steward movement in England makes it appear that in certain contingencies after the war, or even before the end of the war, the allied countries may have a form of Bolshevism to deal with. As yet the shop steward movement in England has acquired no political flavor. The British Labor Party is more or less afraid to touch it. It is generally feared that once the shop stewards are brought into the party they will soon take dominant control of the whole organization."

In a recent number of the *Survey*, the unofficial organ of the charity workers in this country, which, strange to say, has largely degenerated into a socialist-Bolshevist publication, there was published a supplement on the subject of shop control, written by one C. G. Renold, an "English employer"; this article, when examined, shows that by this system it is proposed, practically, that the employees shall vote on everything that is done in the factory, from top to bottom. Of course, Mr. Renold admits that he has not tried it in his own shop. Evidently he wants his competitors to take it up and smash themselves on the various wheels that his program would set in motion. This idea is "democracy run mad" and means, as before stated, the dislocation and destruction of all industry. Mrs. Pankhurst stated recently that when she was in Russia, she found that the Bolsheviki had even applied the "democratic principle" to the hospitals, whereby the patients would vote upon whether or not they would obey the orders of the doctors, adopting from the army the idea of having the soldiers decide when they would obey orders from their officers.

That the socialists understand what is involved in all of these schemes clearly appears in the speeches made by Scott Nearing in his campaign for Congress at the recent election in New York City. He would say to his audiences: "Yes, you people have political democracy. You are allowed a voice in the election of the President, the Congress and all officials. But industrial democracy you have not. Who selects the foreman in the shop? The autocratic employer. Until you select your own shop boss you have no industrial democracy."

When one goes over carefully this program of the Socialist Labor Party in Great Britain, one wonders why anybody in this country with a thimbleful of brains should take it seriously. But when one considers still further, the conclusion might be reached that it is just that type of person who have been taking it seriously—the highbrow editors of pacifist-socialist magazines, I. W. W. admirers and their backers, and the preachers and college professors who were appealing for $50,000 to keep Haywood and his band of outlaws out of jail.

Under the title of "A Revolution in National Finance," an elaborate scheme of taxation is proposed, by which, among other things, all the wealth of the country is to be conscripted at the close of the war to pay the entire debt, wrecking every industry in the country. This certainly is sufficiently revolutionary to warm the cockles of even that pair of precious hearts carried around by Lenine and Trotzky; and it also bears striking resemblance to the ebullitions of the Amos Pinchots, Max Eastman & Co., Ltd., and others of similar calibre in this country.

Another nice revolutionary proposal is the confiscation "for the benefit of all" of every income beyond a reasonable "standard of life", which reasonable standard would, of course, be what is considered reasonable by the proletariat political committees that would run the government under this interesting scheme—and, of course, what they might consider reasonable would be a little bit more than they were in the habit of getting, themselves. To most of them, twenty-five hundred dollars would be a great income.

A campaign is being launched in this country by the *New York Daily Call*, by its weekly edition, the *New Republic*, by the *New Republic's* evening edition, the *New York Evening Post* (under the Oswald Villard management), and by all the other socialist and Bolshevist papers in the country, in support of this British Labor Program. Recently, the National Economic League, which has branches in some twenty-five cities, sent to all its members copies of the supplement to the *New Republic* containing the program, and, strangely enough, some me who might be supposed to be immune from such teachings indicated a friendly attitude toward it. Upon inquiry, however, it was found that these gentlemen in most cases had not read the report but had heard it interpreted by socialist sympathizers.

The labor movement of America has a program but it is not based upon state socialism because the practical hard-headed leaders of the American Labor movement know that Utopias are only for the millennium, and they want some of the good things of life while they and their children are on earth. They do not want the State to take over the factories, the mills, the mines and the farms, because that would take from them all initiative and independence and make them government employees to be ruled by political bureaucracies. They much prefer to have their industries in the hands of private owners, where their economic power will enable them to deal directly on matters of wages, hours and working conditions. They do not want any profit-sharing nor any partnership schemes. They do not want to share in the responsibility of running the business, despite the claims of many "broad humanitarians" who are trying to "bridge the industrial chasm" by superficial schemes to give the workers "a compelling voice in conducting the industry." They know that if they once accept a share in conducting the business, they must also share in the responsibilities for failures and hence will be expected voluntarily to reduce their wages. They are willing for the employers to own the plants and to earn sufficient profits to pay interest, rent, overhead charges, taxes and to pay them a just wage for reasonable hours of labor with proper shop conditions—and a just wage means one that will give not only the necessities of life but a share in the luxuries and sufficient leisure to enjoy them. In order to secure the just wage and reasonable hours and conditions of labor referred to, they demand the right of collective bargaining, which right has been granted to them through an agreement jointly worked out in the National War Labor Board by representatives of the employers of the country and organized labor, and covering unorganized workers as well as organized labor. The provisions of that agreement, officially promulgated by President Wilson, were heralded as the Magna Charta of American industry; but our intellectual promoters of the British Labor program, as well as the Bolsheviki of all shades and degrees, will have none of this sane and practical method of dealing with the questions arising between employers and employees. It is the moon for them!

War Activities of The National Civic Federation

(*Continued from page 6*)

independence of America, the preservation of Democratic institutions and the vindication of the basic principles of humanity."

The League is presided over by Theodore N. Vail. The Honorary Chairmen are: James Gibbons, Cardinal, and Frank Mason North, D.D., President Federal Council, Churches of Christ in America. Other officers are: Vice Chairman, Samuel Gompers, President American Federation of Labor, and Charles S. Barrett, President Farmers' Educational and Cooperative Union of America; Chairman Literary Bureau, Talcott Williams, Director School of Journalism, Columbia University; Chairman Next of Kin Division, Wheeler P. Bloodgood, Member Executive Council, Wisconsin Loyalty Legion; Treasurer, Otto H. Kahn; Director, Ralph M. Easley, Chairman Executive Council, The National Civic Federation; and Secretary, D. L. Cease, Editor *The Railroad Trainman.*

One of the first efforts of the League was the issuing of an Appeal to the Voters of the United States to Support the Government by electing a War-Till-Victory Congress in November, 1918. It originated the slogan "A Congress 100 Per Cent American" and called attention to the difficulties encountered by President Lincoln in 1862 when fourteen out of eighteen Congressmen in Ohio were elected on an anti-war platform, and it showed that President Wilson would be obliged to combat the pacifists, socialists and pro-Germans just as bitterly as Lincoln had to fight the Copperheads.

A suggested test for loyalty was widely distributed. It follows:

> "That candidate, in or out of Congress, or that citizen can be regarded as loyal who since the declaration of war has by word and act unreservedly supported and will support the Government in the vigorous prosecution of the war to a complete and decisive victory, and who has not attempted to destroy allied unity and effort by attacks upon nations fighting with us against a common enemy."

It issued a declaration signed by its officers and executive committee condemning a premature peace and pledging its support of continued war until a military victory is achieved and the autocratic power of the Imperial German Government is broken.

One of its functions has been to spread accurate information on questions arising from the war and to correct misleading statements and erroneous impressions calculated, whether intentionally or not, to disturb that united purpose and harmonious cooperation between all loyal Americans which, while eminently desirable at all times, are absolutely necessary in war times.

The Next of Kin Division, composed of relatives of boys in the military and naval service, was organized to supplement efforts of the government and civilian agencies. The intense patriotism of fathers and mothers organized into a virile force is one of the agencies helping to stamp out disloyal elements in various communities.

What significance is there in the fact that the same journals which defended the Bolshevik leaders who surrendered Russia to Germany have advocated Bolshevism here? Is it more than coincidence that while they sought to create discord and division between America and the Allies they engaged at the same time in seeking to foment internal social discord and strife?

The Forces of Disorder

By RALPH M. EASLEY

THE visit of Mr. Gompers and his associates to Great Britain, France and Italy last September was for the announced purpose of attempting to harmonize the war policy differences between the labor movement of those countries and the America labor movement—which differences, while directly political and economic, indirectly affects the military status.

Not the least difficulty in the situation arose from the fact that in Italy and France the socialists dominate the labor movement almost wholly, whereas in England, while the real trade union movement, like the labor movement in this country, is thoroughly anti-socialist, it is handicapped by a noisy lot of professional political socialists, who, up to the present time, through a heterogeneous federation of the so-called "hand and brain workers," have assumed to speak for labor. Through the "brain workers'" clause, the Bernard Shaws, the Sidney Webbs, the Philip Snowdens, and the Ramsey MacDonalds are allowed a controlling voice, although Sidney Webb and Bernard Shaw represent the Fabian Society, which has only 2,000 members, and Ramsey MacDonald, the Morris Hillquit of England, represents the Independent Labor Party, which is the real Socialist Party, and has only 50,000 members.

In this country, thanks to the virility and sanity of the American labor movement, the political socialists and the "brain workers"—that is, the Hillquits, the Bergers, the editors of *Solidarity, The New Republic, The New York Daily Call, The Masses, The Survey, The Blast, The Public, The Nation* and other organs of pacifism, pro-Germanism, socialism, I. W. W.'ism and all other unwholesome "isms" have not been permitted to participate in the slightest degree in the control of the American movement. Hence, the leaders of the American Federation of Labor are *anathema;* also they are "reactionary"; and "old fogy"; Samuel Gompers* is "intellectually and spiritually decrepit"; "the leaders have no vision": they want "only better wages, hours and living conditions"; they do not stand for revolution—the overturning of everything that is and the substitution of everything that isn't, *a la* Lenine and Trotzky, Arthur Ransome, Raymond Robbins, the editors of *Novy Mir*, the *Volks Zeitung* and some others who were publically advocating the recognition of the Soviet Government in Russia until the President gave them a smashing blow in the face through his Russian proclamation. Since that event they have been singing their little songs only at dinner tables and private parties and encouraging underground Soviet propaganda.

The group of "brain-working" socialists who do not like the way in which the labor movement is conducted in this country and whose only relation to it, in so far as it has any relation, is that of an incubus, never did a day's work in their lives, other than that performed by "their jaws and their pens." Some of them edit papers and all are skilled in the gentle art of extracting dollars from the idle and brainless rich of both sexes, who think that in "giving up" to these professional "panhandlers," they are really helping the "under dog,"** when, in fact, they are only helping the fleas which infest the "under dog." For instance, these rich sentimentalists give freely of their money to help the I. W. W. in its attempt to accomplish its boasted purpose of disrupting the American labor movement—the American Federation of Labor and the Railway Brotherhoods. In time of strikes, such of those of the Silk Workers in Paterson, the Textile Workers in Lawrence and the Garment Workers in New York, it is nothing for these people to contribute thousands of dollars to the I. W. W. leaders—of course, incidentally getting their names and pictures into the papers. Some of the "professionals" referred to are young statesmen, nearly all of whom came within the first draft age period, but none of whom apparently went nearer to the front than certain "bomb-proof jobs" in Washington.

Now, while these fomenters of Bolshevism in this country are numerically unimportant, their vociferousness, as well as their persistence and cunning, make it incumbent upon those who believe in the ideals and policies of the trade union movement, and in the determination to fight the war to a victorious conclusion, to be on the alert.

But the rich sentimentalists have no monopoly in this surrender to socialist blanishments, as is shown by the equal facility with which they have gone among the business and professional classes and, to use their own slang, "made monkeys" of them. For instance, socialists can be found tucked away on many of the editorial and reportorial staffs of the important newspapers of the country, and also well represented on the contributing staffs of our magazines.***

In the colleges they are running rampant; they are not tucked away but are standing out in the open. The president of one of the largest universities in the country told the writer within the last few weeks that they were openly teaching Bolshevism in the class-rooms and that the trustees were powerless to stop it. For them to expel such a professor would be to make him a martyr, thanks to the success of the spurious socialist propaganda in favor of "academic freedom of speech." One university finally did expel a couple of them, and so outraged was a third, who should have been kicked out at the same time, that he resigned, expecting the public clamor to force him back; but the public clamor at that particular moment was not in the mood for functioning in that direction, and the trustees accepted his resignation with thanks and without any signs of offense on the part of the public. For years this particular professor had been publicly declaring that the framers of our Constitution, the signers of the Declaration of Independence—in fact, all the great names of that period which the masses had been taught to revere—were practically grafters and governed in their public actions by none but mercenary motives. He now holds a much better paid job as the head of a reform organization, his salary coming from supposedly hard-headed business men.

One of the most arrant frauds "put over" under the name of education is the so-called Intercollegiate Socialist Society which, under the guise of "promoting intelligent interest in socialism among college men and women" is nothing but a straight out socialist propaganda organization. Every member of its executive committee is a socialist and in a list of some fifty

---

*Mr. Gompers at a recent meeting, referring to his position on socialism, made the following clear statement, which certainly does not have the ring of "intellectual and spiritual decrepitude":

"I want to make my position clearly understood. I don't want any man or woman to believe that I am unwilling to go to the full limit of the ideals of democracy and justice. The only limit to my activities is the practical application of the highest ideals, and if the high ideals do not and cannot conform to practical application, to that degree I will either discard them or wait for a better time. My intense desire—and I think I interpret the American labor movement accurately when I say this—my intense desire is to establish the very best possible conditions for the masses of our country and the masses of every other country on the face of the globe. We realize that its achievement is a matter of development and not of cataclysmic eruption, and we must not imagine that a transaction from infancy to full-grown manhood, from peasantry and slavery, can be transformed overnight into a full-fledged co-operative commonwealth. And, in passing, I don't want any one to infer for a moment that I am committed to a co-operative commonwealth. I believe in democracy, in justice, in fair dealing and opportunity for the development of the best that is in the human, and to make for a social conscience and for social justice and the attainment of the best conditions consistent with the intellectual development of the people of our country. I offer that thought to Russia as well. To think that Russia from her condition of impoverished peasantry, with little industry, can be transformed from a subjugated people into a condition where the highest concepts, the highest ideals of human justice, of human relations, can be established by mere proclamation, is idle—is impotent—must be impotent and ineffective. Just as Germany, with her imperialist Government, undertook to prepare the military arm of her Government for world conquest, she suborned and she propagated this idea among the German workers as represented by the socialists of that country, that internationalism, international brotherhood, should be the dominating cries and watchwords of the world's affairs; and while Germany and German socialism undertook to chloroform the people of the other countries of the world in perverting the ideals of internationalism and of human brotherhood in all the countries of the world, the idea of nationalism and of Germanism was impregnated in the minds of the people of Germany—so much so that many of us were infected with this beautiful thought and ideal of internationalism and many of them carried along with them until long after the time when that ideal had been dispelled."

**At a recent meeting Mrs. Pankhurst, referring to the Bolshevist situation in England and this country, said:

"We have Bolshevism in England, we have it in Great Britain, and we have it in France, and in every one of the European allied countries, and because some of us are quite conscious of that fact and have been working against it since 1914 on the whole front, as we call it—because I believe that is going to be the last attack of the Germans—because we are working against it in Great Britain, I came here hoping to be able to confer with the people who realize the dangers of this Bolshevism. I have been here since June, and that has been long enough to find that Bolshevism is at work here, and I think the most dangerous place where it is working—perhaps there are two dangerous places: It is hard at work among sentimental sympathizers with labor, people who had no experience with labor, who never worked themselves, who have discovered labor during this war. They did not know it existed. And these are often very rich people, very kind people, very honest people, and they are giving their money to promote and help Bolshevism in the press and in organizations everywhere. That is one thing. The other danger: It is among the workers—Bolshevism in the factories and workshops, and the coming in of untrained, untried, unorganized people into industry."

***J. G. Phelps Stokes, in an article in the *New York Times*, commented on this strange situation as follows:

"Only yesterday," he said, "I was told by a prominent New York editor that he had among his personal friends as many as twenty socialistic editors of daily and weekly magazines, whose publications are not socialistic but whose personal opinions are unqualifiedly so. It is easy to observe the influence of their opinions on the matter which they publish. Many of our leading magazines, especially, are advocating socialism in a veiled way. Nearly all the literature of criticism, of so-called 'exposure', is really socialistic in degree.

"It is true of journalistic leaders elsewhere in the country. They are not all socialists, but more and more they are expressing socialistic sympathies to socialists and doing what they can to admit socialistic articles and arguments into their columns. And the most successful magazines are those which oftenest print analyses of modern conditions by men who are, in fact, true socialists. The most widely read medical journal in America is edited by socialists."

the American people. While here and there they have a member or two in a city council, their relative importance is absolutely nil. In certain communities filled with foreign-born socialists, they have frequently elected an entire city council, but the incumbents so mismanaged affairs that they were kicked out at the next election.***

But if these people amount to so little, how is it that there is so much made of them? In the first place, a noisy minority can always get a hearing, because they invariably denounce somebody or something, and that gets headlines. John Spargo, in an article in the *New York Tribune* of August 22, 1918, referring to the greater noise made by minorities, said, in speaking of the pacifists in the ranks of the British workers:

> "Of course, there are some pacifists among the British workers. It would be foolish to deny that fact. They are, however, not very numerous. As is the custom with aggressive minorities, they make a great deal of noise, out of all proportion to their numerical strength or importance, and the noise misleads a good many people on both sides of the Atlantic. England is a land where such minority groups have always been able to play this game with particular success. I know, because I have played the game!"

But another reason why they get such attention is explained in the statement previously made—that they are "tucked away" in all the newspaper offices. Men who have left the Socialist Party since the United States entered the war and men who are still in the party but are against the German-socialist organizations, have referred to this very situation and have asked why it was that the daily papers throughout the country would allow these socialists thus to work their schemes. These men are always looking for an opportunity to "slip something over" for the socialists; as Mr. Stokes says, they make headlines for them; they get in interviews with them, and so forth. But there is no use in bewailing the fact that, as advertisers, they have succeeded in making themselves a factor to be dealt with. It was from the so-called "intellectual socialists" that sprang the forces which finally debauched and destroyed Russia, seized Italy and France by the throat a year ago, started a campaign in England, and are now at work in the United States. We not only have to meet them today, but, as the days go on, the various German peace offensives will reveal themselves through these elements.****

But now the war is over and with all the intriguing of the German agents in this country and in the countries of the Allies, and some of these agents are in high places, an armistice was forced which meant unconditional surrender for Germany. But, does that end the matter and are we free to relax our efforts in thwarting the treasonable schemes of the innumerable groups of pacifists, socialists and Huns, set to going by Bernstorff and his disreputable gang?

Mr. George Creel, than whom no man has been more loyal to American ideals and who is better equipped to know the inside of the German game than any other individual, said in a speech Saturday night, November 16:

> "Never at any time since the outbreak of the European war has German propaganda been busier in the United States than it is at the present moment. The German propagandists, women as well as men, are working overtime in an effort to create for themselves an undeserved sympathy in America." (He referred to the message to Mrs. Wilson a few days ago as an example of the kind of propaganda the wireless from Nauen is now flashing across the Atlantic into the United States.)
>
> "Even the women of Germany have joined in the propaganda which is set in motion for our benefit," said Mr. Creel, "and these women, who never grieved for a single moment when the Lusitania with her innocent men, women, and children was torpedoed, who never lifted their voice in protest when the babies of Belgium were slaughtered at the breasts of their mothers, who had no word of pity for poor, outraged Serbia, or the horribly mistreated people of northern France, are now flashing their cry to America for sympathy and for help, while the male propagandists are holding out their hands dripping with blood and begging for mercy. Think of it, a nation protesting against an armistice the purpose of which is to keep them from fighting, and protesting at a time when their pockets are full of stolen property. The damnable cant of Germany is trying to poison the mind of the world at this late day."

The "damnable cant" is showing itself on every side. The pacifists, the pro-German socialists and the Huns of every type are, as Mr. Kahn says, "sneaking out" with suggestions not only looking to the creation of sympathy for women and children in Germany but also with suggestions provocative of friction between our Government and those of our Allies. And, as they become bolder, they will again begin suggesting that "broadly speaking" there are many things we must settle also with England; and that in some instances, Germany was more sinned against than sinning; and even the famous or infamous "Two Thousand Questions" may again be put into circulation.

What is being done to cope with this new situation? First, the government agencies are all alert. John Lord O'Brian, special assistant to United States Attorney General Gregory, in charge of the war activities of the Department of Justice, has just issued a warning against relaxation of vigilance against enemy aliens and pro-Germans generally. "There is still

---

***With almost unlimited money for use in the Congressional campaign just closed, every socialist candidate was overwhelmingly beaten, except in the case of Berger of Wisconsin who was openly supported by the Kaiserite Germans in a district which could well be dubbed "Little Germany." He is under indictment for seditious utterances and doubtless will be "playing checkers with his nose" about the time the next Congress convenes; if not, it is inconceivable that any American Congress will seat such a shameless and notorious representative of Potsdam.

****Mr. Otto H. Kahn, who recently returned from Paris, in referring to the pacifist-German propaganda that would confront us this winter, said:

"I was in Paris during the two weeks which were probably the darkest weeks of the war, the week beginning May 27th, when the Germans broke through at Chemin Des Dames, when there were twelve aeroplane bombardments in fourteen days, and thirteen long-range bombardments in thirteen days, when it seemed, at the time when the Germans had come within forty miles of Paris, that they might, and it was feared they would, reach Paris, or at least come within bombarding distance of Paris, and when the people of Paris, high and low, asked, and asked in great anxiety, 'What is going to happen if the Germans do get to Paris?' Will the French people stand it? Can they stand it? Can flesh and blood stand it? It is their very heart. It is much more to them than the capital of other countries is to their people. Incidentally it is their railroad center, and it is the greatest center for their war industries. What will happen? And during those two weeks, when true Frenchmen were in doubt and grief and anxiety, you could see and you could feel Bolshevism slink out of its holes and corners everywhere, and how it grew and fed upon the fear that this war might not be won, and if it was not to be won, hadn't we better do this and this now. You could see and feel it. It was everywhere. And you could see again, when this marvelous thing happened, when fifty thousand Americans were thrown in at Chateau-Thierry and rushed forwards through the retreating French, without battle order, without system, without any particular command, rushed forward, rushing like wild Indians, shouting, 'Where are the damn demons! Get them and stop them!' and turned the tide, and the French turned around and fought with them and beat the Germans to a standstill and saved Paris. I saw again how Bolshevism slunk back into its hole and corner, and it has not been heard of since."

danger," he said, "from this quarter, for the defeat of Germany in the field does not mean that the malevolent minds of Teuton sympathizers here have necessarily changed."

But what can the loyal Americans do to help the Government at this time? Many of these pro-German agents work their sinister programs in ways that cannot be reached by governmental bureaus. As a concrete method for assisting in counteracting the propaganda and other schemes of the Huns, Mr. Wheeler P. Bloodgood, Chairman of the Next of Kin Legion, has proposed the following resolution for adoption by his organization and it is now under consideration.

> "Resolved, That it is the duty of the fathers and mothers of sons in the military or naval service of the United States to use every possible effort to discover and have removed from positions of authority or importance in this country every pacifist, every anti-war socialist and every Hun, whether in governmental departments, in the pulpit, the colleges, the public schools, the press, the charity organizations, or any civilian body supported by public subscription; and not to contribute to the payment of the salary of any man or woman who comes within this category."

Mr. Bloodgood explains: "In connection with this proposed resolution, the word 'pacifist' is not meant to refer to those members of peace societies who, prior to 1914, were seeking to prevent future wars. Various elements, however, now posing as pacifists were then most vociferous in preaching war. True, it was a class war they urged, but war it was nevertheless, and meant all the indescribable horrors and bloody massacres that we are now seeing enacted in Petrograd and Moscow. But the pacifist of today is the man or woman who treacherously intrigued to bring about a 'negotiated peace,' or who speaks of the war as a 'capitalistic war,' or 'an imperialistic war,' or 'an unrighteous war,' or who in governmental positions, social settlements or churches, or in any place, continually emphasizes the terrible loss of life and the horrible aspects of the war, without explicit reference to Germany's responsibility therefor."

According to Mr. Bloodgood's explanation, by "anti-war socialist" is meant a member of the Socialist Party in the United States, which is under the domination of Germany, and their German appendages, the I. W. W.'s, the defenders of Bolshevism, and the anarchists. From the Socialist Party many leading American socialists have withdrawn and are patriotically standing for the prosecution of the war to a victorious conclusion.

By the word "Huns" is meant pro-German Germans and Austrians, anti-English Irish, and the pro-Germans in our midst coming from neutral countries, as well as all Germans and Austrians here, naturalized or unnaturalized, who, before our entrance into the war, lent themselves to the Bernstorff intrigues against the honor and integrity of this country. These include lawyers, bankers, college professors, preachers and editors. They are the people, in high positions, whose insidious influence during the coming months must be vigorously combatted. They are the ones who will come "sneaking out of corners with suggestions" of consideration for peace terms favorable to Germany that will reach us in every possible form. It is just as important to have these disloyal Germans catalogued for our information after the war as it was during the war, for having entered into traitorous relations with representatives of the German Government during the war they can never be trusted afterwards and should be sent out of the country on the declaration of peace. The men and women in high places who cooperated with the Bernstorffs, the Erich von Zwiedinecks, the von Papens, the Boy-Eds, the Dr. Alberts, the Pavenstadts, the Hans Tauschers, von Rintelens

(Continued on page 19)

Future Relations of United States and Poland

CHARLES MAYER

In the era of peace before us, among the great rewards for the sacrifices and bloodshed of the war, will be the fulfillment of the aspirations and ideals of long oppressed and subjected peoples. Kings have fallen from their thrones, and great and small nations which have groaned under the yoke of autocracy will be made free. In the new world Poland, long misruled and exploited by Austria, Germany and Russia, will occupy a notable place among the nations. For many years this dream of an independent Poland, which seemed to many an impossible dream, was cherished in the heart of one of the world's greatest artists, who will figure in the pages of history as one of the world's greatest patriots—Mr. Ignace J. Paderewski. Devoting his thoughts and his wealth to this cause Mr. Paderewski's dreams are now to be realized.

The consummation of any ideal—and at that the ideal of a whole people—is an inspiring thing. And it is cause for heart-glowing that America, which entered the war for ideals, was able so powerfully to help the Poles. Toward the success of this cause no individual American did more than Mr. Charles Mayer, of Washington, D. C. At a time when the Polish movement encountered all sorts of difficulties, he associated himself with Mr. Paderewski and helped to promote the movement which resulted in the raising of more than $10,000,000 in America. Mr. Mayer's enthusiasm for what many people long considered a "lost cause," antedated the outbreak of the European war.

During the Russo-Japanese war Mr. Mayer was called to Russia to act in an advisory capacity to the Russian government in the rehabilitation of State-controlled industries in the empire. The program included not only the development of manufactures and construction, but the building of the Trans-Siberian railroad with the purpose of making Russia independent of other nations in exporting her products.

In the course of his mission, Mr. Mayer visited Poland in order to make recommendations toward the bringing about of a more liberal treatment of the inhabitants of Russian Poland, and toward the establishing of industries. At that time he came in contact with, and came to love, the Poles. He found them to be a people of extraordinary industriousness and high qualities of character. The Russian program for the development of Poland was, however, interfered with by the mild revolution which broke out at that time in Russia and which ended in the battering down of the barricade of Moscow.

Later Mr. Mayer made several visits to Russia and Poland. The last occasion was a visit to the Prime Minister of Russia in 1914, before the outbreak of the war, when he was struck by the tremendous progress which the Poles had made. Manufacture, at some places on a vast scale, had developed everywhere. More than ever was he impressed by the enormous resources and economic possibilities of Poland—of the possible greatness of a Polish nation could the people be freed from foreign rule.

Mr. Mayer months ago urged that the Allies give financial and military support to the organization of a Polish army toward the re-establishment of an Eastern front. He was active also, in urging the recognition by the American government of the informal Polish National Council.

At a luncheon given in honor of Mr. and Mrs. Paderewski by The National Civic Federation early in October, Mr. Mayer told of the struggles of the Poles to raise an effective national army in Russia.

"The movement toward the formation of a Polish Army was started by the Polish Supreme Military Committee in June, 1917," he said, "and despite the strongest opposition of German interests in Russia and the lack of support by the Kerensky government, the Poles succeeded in forming a corps of about 80,000 under the leadership of General Dowbor Musnicki. Two other forces were formed, one in Ukrainia under General Michaelis and another in Bessarabia under General Stankiewicz. Polish soldiers scattered in various regiments through European and Asiatic Russia, partly armed and unarmed, were prepared to join their national army at the first opportunity. At the end of 1917 the Polish Military organization outside the army of General Musnicki comprised over 200,000 soldiers. General Musnicki's army was betrayed to the Germans by the Bolsheviki and was surrounded and forced to surrender and disarm. Part of the forces under General Michaelis and General Stankiewicz retreated to the East, where they are now fighting the Bolsheviki, side by side with the Czecho-Slovaks.

"The Polish element in Russia has been of the greatest importance to the Allies because of its numerical force and fighting spirit. The Poles are anti-German, and have realized there can be no independent Poland without an absolute Allied victory. The Poles once paid dearly for the experiment of forming an army without the financial and military support of the Allies. In response to a cablegram sent by Mr. Paderewski to the Poles in Siberia, urging them to begin preliminary activities, the Poles immediately began to organize an army and offered to cooperate with the Allies in operating the Siberian Railway, which is of vital importance to the conduct of military operations. The Poles form a big percentage of the railway employees in Siberia, and the presence of a Polish National Army would raise their spirit by giving them the certitude that they are working for and serving their motherland."

With their hopes fulfilled and the future of a free Poland now assured, Mr. Mayer looks forward to a renaissance that will astonish and inspire the world. In the development of industries and trade expansion the Polish leaders have invited the cooperation of the United States. To America Poland will offer an opportunity for the establishment of new and desirable markets. Between the re-arisen republic which gave ideals of democracy to the world and which was the first country, in 1413, to adopt the form of a united states government, and our great nation, which entered the war to make democracy secure, there will be relations of extraordinary intimacy and cordiality.

Forces of Disorder

(Continued from page 18)

and the Hugo Schmidts, or had knowledge of their infamous schemes to undermine the Government of the United States with the ultimate object of placing this country under the domination of Germany in case "the Beast of Berlin" should subdue France and England, should not be permitted to remain in this country, much less to retain any positions of honor or trust here; and no settlement at the peace table should grant immunity for one moment to these creatures.

Of itself it means nothing that a German had taken out citizenship papers, or was the purchaser of United States Government bonds or a leader in the Red Cross, the Y. M. C. A. or other patriotic activities; a great many of the men now interned at Fort Oglethorpe were doing just these things; a disloyal German would seek to cover up his disloyalty by exactly that kind of action. The test is, what is the feeling he exhibited in his home and in his German circles when he read the headlines that have been appearing in the newspapers here since July 18? Was it one of elation or one of depression? That is the acid test.

Mr. Bloodgood concludes:

"But, while it is true that every effort should be made to rid this country of all treasonable Germans, great care should also be taken that full credit be given to the large majority of Germans whose loyalty and patriotism to the United States has been of the highest order, whose sons gave their lives on the battle fronts as freely as any other Americans, and whose chagrin at the conduct of disloyal German-Americans has led them to make even greater sacrifices at home than, in many cases, they are really able to bear. All honor to them! But all dishonor and suitable punishment to the other type of Germans and pro-Germans in our midst!"

Those who think the above resolution, with its explanatory clauses, a little drastic now that peace has come, are asked to re-read the words quoted above from Mr. George Creel.

So far as the need is concerned for "digging out" and "tagging" the exponents of socialism, the breeder of pacifism and Bolshevism, who are tucked away in positions of importance in official and unofficial life, I will ask the reader to re-read the quotation from Mr. Samuel Gompers used above in this article, in which he shows that socialism is entirely of German origin and intended by the Germans to undermine all civilizations except their own.

The reason the United States is not today in the hands of the Bolsheviki and socialists is not because of any concerted intelligent effort on the part of representative educated citizens to combat them. On the contrary, there are supposedly intelligent, hard-headed business men who, instead of opposing socialism, have by coddling its advocates flattered themselves that by pretending to sympathize with it they were pursuing a "far-sighted policy" that would tend to neutralize it. Nothing more puerile could be done. Every socialist who has a "capitalist friend" is making use of him to the limit and telling his audiences that capitalism is about to surrender and therefore encourages them to go on. Warming an adder in the bosom only to be stung by it is simple in comparison.

It is the American labor movement that is entitled to all the credit today for our freedom from Bolshevism, anarchy and revolution in this country. While fighting socialism, the American labor movement at the same time had to fight unfair employers, some of whom were even backing, financially, papers and magazines which advocated socialist policies and furnishing the money for movements undoubtedly under the control of those revolutionists who never miss a chance to take a whack at Samuel Gompers and the trade union movement.

Whether Mr. Bloodgood's resolution is finally adopted by the Next of Kin Legion or not, it certainly rings with the right spirit and points out the dangers that confront us. The two million boys who went to the front with our army and navy and the other two million who were preparing to go when the armistice was declared, with their relatives, friends and sympathizers, including the thirty-five million subscribers to the Liberty Loans and War Savings Stamps, as well as to the war funds of the Red Cross, the Y. M. C. A., the Knights of Columbus and kindred societies, constitute 90 per cent of the American people, and any principles, platforms, dogmas or individuals of which they disapprove will have short shrift in this country.

Shadow Huns and Others

(Continued from page 9)

mockery! A triumph that was grotesquely sham.

"LIVES THERE A MAN WITH SOUL SO DEAD?"

Of the "extraordinary outburst of popular emotion" which broke forth at the first report of Germany's surrender, the *Nation*, in seeking to interpret the reason, asked: "Is it possible that the war was not so popular after all with the rank and file? We confess to being completely baffled in our effort to analyze something in which fervor, excitement and suddenness could surely never be surpassed."

Is it hard to understand the inability of the editorial mind of the *Nation* to become elated over the Allies' complete victory, and to comprehend the simple human joy at the end of the killing, the spontaneous gladness that at last victory had come? To the negative academic mind, itself incapable of devotion to any high cause, simple human emotions as well as simple human virtues are incomprehensible. "Academic neutrals," incapable of allegiance and devotion to any cause or any master, have figured all down in the world's history—in the New Testament story, in our own revolutionary war, and in this war. They have not figured as exemplars of loyalty, chivalry or patriotism.

At the very time that Mr. Villard confesses his incapacity for understanding the joy of November 11, he ruefully "thinks of all the great things that Germany has accomplished for the world, its contributions to art, literature, music and science." And he shrinks as ever from what the Allies might consider justice in dealing with Germany. He inveighs against President Wilson: "He has seemed of late so infirm of purpose. To the inexcusable blundering invasion of Russia he yielded; one by one in response to foreign pressure he yields on his fourteen peace terms, last week in the matter of punitive indemnities and freedom of the seas." Was the mere demand by the Allies for reparation of material damage done by Germany "punitive"?

It was obviously considered a wrong to ask Germany to give up anything. But what about the Allies? Mr. Villard would "desire no end to revolution abroad until custom houses everywhere have gone by the board * * * until all the makers of secret treaties are cast out. * * * We would have England retire from Egypt and Persia, the Italians from Tripoli, and Japan from Kiao-Chou, France from Cochin-China and Madagascar, and Belgium from the blood-stained Congo, while the United States sets the example by retiring from the Philippines, Haiti, San Domingo, and Nicaragua." Had Germany, alas! not been compelled to give in to "humiliating" terms, such a Quixotic course of voluntary getting-out would have been most accommodating toward the speedy achievement of her stepping into her "place in the sun."

DR. HALE PLUS DR. SHAW.

In regard to the war there were others who were neither flesh, fowl nor good red herring. Dr. Albert Shaw, the gifted editor of the "American" *Review of Reviews*, "saw both sides of the question." Dr. William Bayard Hale, while in the Kaiser's pay, sought to prevent America from going to war with Germany over the submarine issue; Hale, for a wage, sought to foment American public sentiment against Great Britain's maritime policy. Hale opposed the war as a war forced by the capitalistic plutocracy. Dr. Shaw gratuitously did the same things that Hale did. Dr. Shaw asserted that the U-boat issue was not an adequate reason for our making armed resistance against Germany. He implied that the American Government had discriminated against Germany and in favor of Great Britain. He urged action against England because of her interference with neutral shipping, and advocated compromise with Germany over the U-boat issue. Like Dr. Hale and Scott Nearing, Dr. Shaw interpreted the war as having been accelerated by Wall Street plutocrats. "The tremendous effort," said he, "to bring the United States completely into the war had its origin in the chief centres of business and finance." In common with Scott Nearing, he impugned the motives of the Allies and accused them of "imperialistic programs." Scott Nearing was indicted; Dr. Hale has been exposed. Shaw, some time ago, was invited to become one of a party of patriotic and loyal American editors to visit Great Britain and France. Perhaps the British never read his "American" review. But here is part of Dr. Shaw's war record:

At the time the controversy with Germany over unrestricted U-boat warfare was reaching its climax, in the issue of the *Review of Reviews* of March, 1917, Dr. Shaw, referring doubtless to President Wilson's handling of the crucial issue, said:

"It would be shocking, indeed, if a democratic people were to acquiesce in the novel idea that the issues of war and peace should depend upon the processes of a single mind. * * * War as an expression of extreme disapproval in a given case may be neither practically expedient nor morally requisite. * * * Our expressions herewith are made in the hope that war may be averted."

Of the German announcement of the resumption of ruthless U-boat warfare, Dr. Shaw in the same issue said:

"In London and other capitals of the Entente Powers it was received with more jubilation than dismay, on the ground that it would result in bringing the United States into action against Germany and thus help the Allies end the war on their own terms."

MR. VIERECK PLUS DR. SHAW.

What were the Allied "terms," in Dr. Shaw's opinion? In the *Review* of March, 1918—issued after America had been in the war for a year—Dr. Shaw said:

"The Allies were involved in the meshes and toils of many secret pacts among themselves." In common with the *New Republic*, the *Nation*, the *Masses*, the literature of the notorious People's Council, the New York *Call* and Viereck's *Fatherland*, Dr. Shaw interpreted the Allied terms as "a patchwork program of spoils and conquests."

The Allies' reply to Mr. Wilson's peace note, made in January, 1917, according to the oblique intellect of the *Review of Reviews*, "made it clear that the Allies were determined to mutilate Austria first and then dismember her; and that their purposes for Turkey were nothing short of complete annihilation with a parcelling out of her territories and peoples. Bulgaria, in like manner, was to be reduced in size, deprived of outlets, and made permanently defenseless.

(Continued on last page)

German Evacuation of Russia urged by League for National Unity

The League for National Unity has issued a statement urging that the absolute evacuation of Russia by Germany be made part of the terms of peace.

The signers of the statement include the Executive Council of the League, who are as follows:

Honorary Cha en, James Gibbons, Cardinal, Baltimore, Md., a Frank Mason North, D. D., President Federa Council, Churches of Christ in America, New ork; Chairman, Theodore N. Vail, President American Telephone and Telegraph Company, New York; Vice Chairmen, Samuel Gompers, President American Federation of Labor, Washington, D. C., and Charles S. Barrett, President Farmers' Educational and Cooperative Union of America, Union City, Ga.; Chairman Literary Bureau, Talcott Williams, Director School of Journalism, Columbia University, New York; Chairman Next of Kin Division, Wheeler P. Blcodgood, Member Executive Council, Wisconsin Loyalty Legion, Milwaukee, Wis.; Treasurer, Otto H. Kahn, New York; Director, Ralph M. Easley, Chairman Executive Council, The National Civic Federation, New York; and Secretary, D. L. Cease, Editor "The Railroad Trainman," Cleveland, O.

Also the Executive Committee of the League, which includes:

John G. Agar, Treasurer New York Catholic War Fund, New York; Mrs. Carrie Chapman Catt, President National American Woman's Suffrage Association, Washington, D. C.; John Hays Hammond, President National League of Republican Clubs, Washington, D. C.; Frederick N. Judson, Attorney, St. Louis, Mo.; V. Everit Macy, President The National Civic Federation, New York; Alfred E. Marling, Chairman International Committee of Y. M. C. A.'s, New York; Mrs. Philip N. Moore, President National Council of Women, St. Louis, Mo.; Frank Morrison, Secretary American Federation of Labor, Washington, D. C.; Andrew Parker Nevin, of the National Association of Manufacturers, New York; George Wharton Pepper, Chairman National Committee of Patriotic and Defense Societies, Philadelphia, Pa.; Walter George Smith, President American Bar Association, Philadelphia, Pa.; Warren S. Stone, Grand Chief International Brotherhood of Locomotive Engineers, Cleveland, O.; Mrs. James Wadsworth, Jr., President National Association Opposed to Woman Suffrage, Washington, D. C.; William English Walling, Economist and Author, Greenwich, Conn.; Miss Maude Wetmore, Chairman National League for Woman's Service, New York; and Rabbi Stephen S. Wise, Free Synagogue, New York.

The statement follows:

President Wilson has over and over again pledged the Russian people the sympathy and substantial support of the American nation—and no declaration that he has made since the war have received such general and enthusiastic approval.

Nothing is more important than that Russia shall receive the very fullest consideration in connection with any proposal for an armistice, as well as in peace negotiations of any kind whatsoever. Russia is invaded territory as much as Belgium, Northern France or Serbia. Neither the United States, nor any of the Allies, has ever recognized the shameful treaty of Brest-Litovsk. The Western Front has always been of supreme importance with respect to a military decision, but it is in the East that the fundamental questions relating to world peace will be decided.

Russia was impoverished and economically backward before the war. The actions of the Kaiser and his Russian allies have put her back a generation, reducing tens of millions to the verge of actual starvation, and destroying a large part of her industrial and transport system. They have divided the country into a dozen fighting geographical sections, and the internal chaos they have introduced into each

THEODORE N. VAIL
Chairman, League for National Unity

of these sections is not the civil or class war known to history, but an endless series of class conflicts in which every man's hand is against his neighbor.

Germany's allies are slaughtering not merely the privileged classes of the old regime, not merely the bourgeois plutocracy, but also the middle classes, the small peasant owners who have achieved even a miserable beginning of prosperity, and even the skilled and intelligent workingmen who protest against these murderous and diabolical acts. The persons slaughtered are chiefly the leaders of the Socialist and Democratic parties who propose resistance to Germany and Germany's Russian allies.

The practice of "mass terrorism" or wholesale massacre of the educated and possessing classes in Russia has already called forth the solemn protest of all civilized mankind except those nations within the immediate reach of the German armies. But since President Wilson called for this protest, these massacres—which are aimed exclusively at the enemies of Germany—have reached the point where it can be said that the brain of Russia is being slaughtered in order that the masses of the population may the more easily fall under German domination. Nicolai Lenine has recently written over his own signature that what Russia needs is German intelligence, discipline and organization—in a word, German Kultur.

The American and Entente armies in Russia are met either by forces composed in part of German and Hungarian prisoners or by mixed forces largely non-Russian, led by German officers or military advisers and deceived by the most monstrous lies—largely of German origin—portraying imaginary American and Entente defeats, brutalities and purposes to conquer and exploit Russia.

In both cases, these armies are chiefly composed of mercenaries and represent no large proportion of the Russian population. They are controlled absolutely by a handful of political desperadoes in open alliance with Germany and—in addition—in relations with the German Government which they dare not disclose even to their crazed and ignorant followers.

In the Ukraine, the Caucasus, and other vast Russian territories, the armies of Germany, Austria and Turkey are obliged to maintain their brutal and bloody rule with little or no assistance from native allies.

But the most dangerous and difficult element of the situation remains to be mentioned. Germany maintains not one army in Russia but three. Besides all her many forms of military force, she maintains an army of agents and an army of spies—each of which is probably more numerous and more powerful than her armed forces. Her commercial army acts largely in the open. Germany took possession of a large part of the economic resources of Russia by the supplementary treaties following the surrender of Russian territory at Brest-Litovsk. Her hundreds of thousands of agents, taking advantage of the plundering and murdering by Germany's Russian Allies have purchased for a song nearly everything of value that remained, and protected from harm by the Kaiser's strong arm, are firmly installed in possession of the chief remaining resources of the country.

Even more dangerous than the military and economic armies is the great political army, composed in part of volunteers and in part of paid secret agents. Even before the war Russia swarmed with Russian-born Germans who owed political and economic allegiance to the Fatherland; Baltic barons and traders, German speaking and thinking agriculturists and citizens of the border districts, and officials, police and spies in the supposed service of the Czar. To these have been added not only hundreds of thousands of former German prisoners now in Russian civil life, but many thousands of Russian speaking emissaries who have been sent from Germany since Brest-Litovsk.

A well-known American correspondent now in Siberia has correctly stated the probable effect of an early peace and military evacuation of Russia under these conditions:

> "Germany is more anxious than ever to make peace now with the Western Powers. She could even afford to promise to evacuate Russia, knowing all the time that with her present organization here it would be years, if not decades, before the Allies or the Russians themselves could interfere with her Russian booty."

This correspondent quotes the American General in command at Vladivostock as saying:

> "Peace with Germany now would turn Russia entirely over to Germany, perhaps preventing the Allies forever from making headway in this country."

In the case of Russia, there should be an evacuation by Germany's political and economic armies as well as her military force.

Germany apparently is beginning to make real and not merely deceptive concessions to the Entente. She will make further concessions as her armies meet further defeats. But this is the very last concession she will make. Yet the war must not cease until every form of German intervention in Russia—since her political and economic intervention in the last analysis also rests upon past military coercion, is brought to an end.

For unless this war frees Russia, Germany will have gained a substantial victory. Not only will America have broken her pledge to the Russian people, but Germany will gain all the vast resources of Russia—and after having organized Russia's hundred and fifty millions into military and industrial dependents, she will be in a position to bring under her influence the hundreds of millions of India and China. Compared to this prospect, the Belgian ports and iron mines of Lorraine and the "Berlin to Bagdad" scheme are utterly insignificant. The one great question left by the war is Russia. And even less than any other of the great questions of human liberty involved is it subject to "any sort of compromise."

Shadow Huns and Others

(Continued from page 19)

Germany was to lose her entire Colonial Empire permanently to Great Britain, and was to be stripped for the benefit of France, not only of Alsace Lorraine, but also (by a secret agreement between France and Russia) of a further portion of her territory adjacent to the Rhine."

The Allied nations, in the opinion of Dr. Shaw, "were suffering and dying for the sins of their diplomats" and not in defense against the Hun onslaught for world dominion. In fact, according to Shaw, Germany did not precipitate the war with any aim of world conquest. It was the Allies and not Germany, who brought the squalid lust for territory and loot into the war. Dr. Shaw declared: "The vital point is that the concrete imperialistic programs of Russia, England, France and Italy hardened the German program of European domination into a definite reality, whereas it had previously been rather more a dream than a practical project." In other words, the Allies, instead of defending themselves, were forcing the war to continue in order to impose terms of extortion and revenge; the evil motives of the Allies were responsible for the "crystalization" of Germany's rather idealistic dreams of mere European domination into reality.

(Mr. Harré, who gave valuable assistance to various Governmental departments in their investigations into German propaganda and intrigue, will tell in the next number of further activities on part of American writers which were calculated to work to the advantage of Germany.)

The National
Civic Federation Review

NEW YORK, DECEMBER 20, 1918 No. 6

INDUSTRIAL RECONSTRUCTION

TER WAR IMMIGRATION POLICY—GOVERNMENT OWNERSHIP OR CONTROL OF PUBLIC UTILITIES AND BASIC INDUSTRIES—FUTURE OF LABOR MEDIATION—COMMISSIONS TO STUDY RELATIONS OF EMPLOYERS AND EMPLOYEES AND ECONOMIC ADJUSTMENTS AT HOME AND ABROAD.

NDUSTRIAL relations during and after the war; immigration and its effect upon unemployment and wage standards under re- ıstruction conditions; government ownership control of public utilities and basic indus- es; federal labor adjustment methods; and ıer current social and economic problems were ısidered at a meeting of the Reconstruction mmittee of The National Civic Federation ld at 1 Madison Avenue, New York, Monday, ecember 2, 1918.

The outstanding result of the discussions was ction authorizing the appointment by Presi- ent V. Everit Macy of two Commissions, one study the relations of employers and employees nd war emergency measures in England, rance and Italy, and one to make similar in- uiry in the United States.

INDUSTRIAL RELATIONS.

V. Everit Macy, President of The National ivic Federation, who presided at the confer- nce, made the following opening statement:

"During the past eighteen months, few meet- ıgs of The National Civic Federation have been eld. Many of its members have been engaged ı Government work. The Executive Committee elt that it was a time for action rather than for onference as there was only one great goal be- ore the nation, namely, the winning of the war, nd that the most effective way to accomplish is end was to cooperate without question with ll Government agencies.

"While peace has not yet been officially at- ained, it now seems an appropriate moment to iscuss our war experience and to decide whether any of the administrative war machin- ry should be retained, either as now constituted r in some modified form.

"A greater centralization of control in Fed- ral agencies than any of us had ever dreamed f was required for the successful prosecution f the war. To let this highly concentrated ma- hine disintegrate now without any definite lans for a transitional period seems most dan- erous. Such procedure would seem to lead to he greatest confusion.

"At the present time conferences are being alled on all subjects directly or remotely re- ated to the war. It seems wise, therefore, to onfine this conference to the subject of indus- rial relations during and after the war.

"It has been said that a successful man is one who is right 51 per cent of the time. If we apply this same standard to the Government method of dealing with the problem of employer and employee during the war, we must confess that it has been most successful as practically no interruption of industry of any magnitude has occurred during the past year and a half. All friction has not been avoided and here and there an occasional stoppage of production has occurred but, thanks to the far-sighted policy adopted by the Government, to the patriotic response of the employers and men, and especially to the statesman-like leadership of our Vice-President Mr. Gompers, the nation was spared any domestic strife while fighting an enemy without. When one considers the tremendous changes in industry necessitated by the war, the peaceful adjustments made were no small accomplishment.

"The National Civic Federation should take much satisfaction in the fact that the methods employed to prevent strife and interruption of production were the same methods that have been employed by the Federation for many years, namely the submission of all disputes to appropriate boards composed of representatives of employers, representatives of organized labor and representatives of the Government or the public. Unfortunately, these various boards were established only when a crisis arose in a particular industry or in the work of a particular department. They were, consequently, created upon varying foundations and with varying powers. This naturally resulted in the rendering of somewhat conflicting decisions and a total lack of related action.

"For instance, the agreement creating the Shipbuilding Labor Adjustment Board provided for the districting of the country and, in so far as practical, in fixing uniform conditions and wages within each district, the Board was also to be guided by the increased cost of living. On the other hand, the Cantonment Adjustment Board was compelled to render its decisions in accordance with established local conditions. This frequently resulted in the two Government boards setting different wages for the same craft in the same locality. The Shipbuilding Labor Adjustment Board and the National Adjustment Commission dealing with harbor crafts and longshoremen could only take jurisdiction after disputes occurred. In other words, if the employers and their employees agreed on a wage scale or on any condition of employment, the respective boards had no power to set aside such scales or conditions.

"In peace times, it is probably perfectly safe to permit employers and their employees to agree on any points that they can but it is a most dangerous and disrupting influence in war time, for during a war the Government is virtually the sole employer and it makes little difference to the manufacturer what wage is agreed to, as long as he can attract the labor to his plant for the Government directly or indirectly foots the bill.

"A few days before the signing of the Armistice, a plan had been worked out for a better coordination of the work of the various adjustment boards which would have been the beginning of a national labor policy. Since the signing of the Armistice, all is changed and there is a pronounced tendency for all boards to relinquish whatever control they have exerted.

"It is safe to say that if these various boards had not been established, there would have been constant interruption of production, an immensely increased labor turn over, much higher wages and a tremendously reduced output.

"If voluntary agreements to submit all questions in dispute to labor adjustment boards have proved of value in time of war, why should not similar boards be useful to industry in times of peace? We must not lose the benefit of the splendid spirit of cooperation to work for a common end that has been shown by both employer and employee during the war and which has produced such fine results.

"The only way, however, that this cooperative spirit can find effective expression in normal times is by better organization of employers and better organization of employees. I use the word 'better' in its broadest sense; it means more complete, it means more disciplined, it means more intelligent and broader minded action upon the part of members of the organization and their leaders, a greater loyalty to the organization and the substitution of a national for a purely local or trade point of view. Nothing can be accomplished in industry without cooperation and organization. It is not the organization of large business or of unions that we should combat but only the organization of narrow minded selfishness.

"The National Civic Federation in the past has advocated trade agreements. As the result of our war experience, can we not in the future develop voluntary labor adjustment boards to

RESOLUTIONS ADOPTED AT MEETING OF THE RECONSTRUCTION COMMITTEE OF THE NATIONAL CIVIC FEDERATION.

ENGLAND, FRANCE AND ITALY FIELD FOR INQUIRY.

RESOLVED, That the President of The National Civic Federation be empowered to name a commission of suitable size and representative character, of which he shall be chairman, to visit England, France and Italy for the purpose of reporting:

(1) On the methods employed in those countries with regard to the relations of employers and employees, especial inquiry to be made into the subjects of collective bargaining, mediation and arbitration, the shop steward system, the Whitley Committee program, profit sharing, bonus and co-partnership, social insurance, and employment exchanges;

(2) On the after-the-war policy of the governments of those countries with respect to continuing, amending or abolishing Government ownership and operation of public utilities and basic industries, as well as regulating price-fixing affecting the essentials in production; and

(3) On the methods in operation or under consideration for providing homes or cultivable lands either for the men released from war service or for citizens in general.

STUDY OF HOME WAR EMERGENCY MEASURES.

RESOLVED, That the President of The National Civic Federation name a committee of suitable size and representative character to inquire into and report upon the operation of the various war emergency measures adopted to secure cooperative relations between employers and employees, and likewise to report upon the effectiveness of the Government operation of public utilities and basic industries, as well as of the regulations fixing the prices of essentials in the United States.

which all disputes will be submitted without the interruption of industry or inconvenience to the public? These boards could be composed of representatives of the employers' organizations and the unions involved, with perhaps one or more representatives of the public. One of the difficulties that the labor adjustment boards had to meet during the war was the lack of any tradition or prevailing practice within any given industry, craft or even single plant. Such boards as have been suggested would, by their successive decisions, tend gradually to develop a code of minimum good practice in an industry and thus help to systematize the industry. A wide scope still would be left for individual initiative since we find that among the shipyards having the same wage scale and the same conditions of employment, the cost per ton of shipping produced will vary at least two hundred per cent. Such a plan cannot be successful without well disciplined organizations on both sides. This brings us to another point that we are destined to hear much discussed—that of raising or lowering of wages. The real question that should determine the wage scale is that of the cost of production per ton or per unit. It is too often assumed that high wages mean high cost and that low wages mean low cost. The manufacturer must realize that no industry should survive that cannot pay a living wage. The employees must realize that no industry can survive where there is not a living profit. Cost cannot be reduced except through good management and an honest day's labor, nor can high wages and reasonable profits be obtained, except by the same means. Competition and equipment are other factors that cannot be ignored if an industry is to be successful and most important of all is a cooperative spirit between the management and the men employed.

"In the past, little thought seems to have been given to the human equation in industry. Employers have paid large salaries to general managers and various experts but they have left all contact with their employees in the hands of foremen and sub-foremen, men often of limited opportunity, experience and understanding. On the other hand, the unions have placed too much power in the hands of local officials who are frequently also men of equally limited capacity. Some way should be found whereby the many causes of irritation could be handled by well paid representatives of the employer and by responsible representatives of the national unions. Petty foremen and small minded local representatives of unions are the greatest source of discord.

"Do not let us be deceived by the frequent statements that the end of the war is to usher in a new world. No miracle has happened. What is this 'new spirit' and these new conditions we hear so much about? Take for instance the English Labor program. It is nothing new; it is our 'old friend' Socialism. The name is all that is new.

"The Bolsheviki theory is a perfectly familiar one; it is merely anarchy and I. W. W.ism under a new name. Even our idealists are merely trying to find a new name for the centuries old Golden rule. Even the League of Nations is not a new idea for it is merely an extension of the idea of the Hague Tribunal for the settlement of International disputes.

"If nations can agree to arbitrate all differences and if the League of Nations is to prevent future wars, is it too much to expect that industrial disputes may be settled by means of arbitration or by labor adjustment boards and so prevent future industrial warfare?"

AFTER WAR IMMIGRATION POLICY.

Frank Morrison, Secretary of the American Federation of Labor, in presenting his views as to what steps should be taken to prevent the nations from dumping undesirables on our shores, said in part:

"The labor organizations are intensely interested in what is going on at the present moment. As a result of the abrupt ending of the war, thousands of men and women are thrown out of employment. They are in cities where they volunteered to go to do the war work. It is impossible for them to secure employment in those cities. Every day of idleness is so much loss of product to the nation. If the nation needs the product of its workers continuously, it must devise means to secure employment for them. The Government should transport the industrial volunteers to places where they can secure employment, pay their expenses, and more, it should pay those volunteers during their unemployment. That is a huge proposition but the country needs the produ
and if a billion dolla
were spent, it woul
mean peace in thi
country. Unrest come
from lack of employ
ment, and by dumpin
forty, sixty, a hundre
two hundred thousan
workers out of the fa
tories as at presen
there will be unrest i
this country as i
Russia, Germany an
Austria. England ha
already arranged t
pay a specified amoun
per week to the ma
to the woman, and t
the children of th
workers, first child s
much, and second chil
so much, so that we, a
least, have a preceden
to follow in urgin
Congressional appro
priation to pay rai
road fare and unen
ployment wages.

"Congress shoul
enact a law stoppin
immigration entirel
for the period of ad
justment, until th
workers who have bee
working in munitior
factories have secure
employment, and unt
every soldier has bee
returned and has se
cured employmen
After that readjus
ment, we can open ou
doors to our brothe
across the seas.

"If the large em
ployers had been edu
cated to the belief that low wages and lo
standards are not a benefit to the country suc
legislation might not be necessary, but the
will be an effort to bring into this country add
tional labor. It has been the practice of larg
employers always to have an ample supply
labor. It has not worried them to have two me
for every job. It is for the organizations th
have an interest and the welfare of all the cit
zens at heart to bring about a condition whe
every man, woman and child will be able
have employment and live in reasonable con
fort.

"The period now is critical. At Rock Islan
there are 12,500 people working. Prior to th
war there were 2,500. Ten thousand must fin
employment some place else. The governme
cut off a thousand men who expected the wa
to last probably until spring. They put co
in their cellars and took their families there an
employment is not in sight. They must be take
care of now and there is no other force th
can do it outside of the Government of th
United States, through its employement servic
which can secure information as to where wo
is to be secured—but there must be an appr
priation sufficient to transport those men an
to take care of them until they secure emplo
ment. I hope that a strong resolution will
adopted by this body urging protection for th
men that went from their homes to other par
to assist in manufacturing munitions to assi
our soldiers to win the war, and also urgi
proper care of our soldiers who are returnin
I understand that it is proposed to bring ba
a million soldiers at the rate of three hundr
thousand a month. We must take care of th
million. It is a big project for the Governme
but it is able to handle it. It has the mon

power than would soon become a beaurocracy sufficient in size to operate no more than those public utilities which are now temporarily in the hands of the government? As for the operatives, themselves, of these public utilities, they are being urged to make permanent their transfer from employer to master, to a master to whom they must surrender their political independence, and by whom already they have been commanded no longer to exercise their civil rights by taking part in the political life of their communities, of the nation—a command which means, if interpreted after the political habit of the times, that they shall not oppose, but support, the party in power.

"And what shall these citizens receive in exchange for their civil rights, for their political independence, for their freedom of political initiative? An easier berth, a sheltered life, an opportunity to render less service for higher pay. They, like the consumer of goods and services, are to sell their liberties for cash. But in exchange for them the public servants are to receive more money for less service, whereas the consumer will expect to receive more service for less money. Both cannot be paid their price. If the consumer obtains his consideration, the public servant will be defrauded. If the public servant receives his, the consumer will be defrauded. If justice between them be done and a fair division be had, then neither will be better off than under individual ownership, while both will have lost for good traditional rights of enormous economic, moral and political worth, and our government will have been sent on its way to become an oligarchy.

"What is this spirit, that would pull from beneath us the very foundations of the individualistic democracy of the Anglo-Saxon? Professing to be idealistic, it invites us to part with our ideals of freedom in exchange for material benefits, and insolently does so in the very hour that has found us investing our every possession, our flesh and blood, in the preservation of the very liberties it now bids us sell for ready money. However it disguise itself, this spirit is not idealistic; it is sordid. It is not uplifting; it is debasing. It is not constructive; it is destructive. It is not native; it is alien. It is not friendly; it is hostile. It is not *for* the Anglo-Saxon; it is *against* him. Already its searching and inquisitive fingers are touching his vitals, will be gripping them shortly, and then will be tearing them out, as it tore out the vitals of Russia."

PROBLEMS OF GOVERNMENT CONTROL

Jeremiah W. Jenks, after referring to the foregoing stimulating, impassioned appeal against public ownership and management, and in favor of private ownership and management, made the following address:

"In the two very sane, suggestive statements that have been made before, it had impressed me that there was an underlying question that was not answered, as to how far we should go in peace times in the direction of government ownership and management; just where we should stop in that direction, how far we should go backwards toward the conditions that existed before the war.

"I suppose you were all very much impressed, as I was, with the fact that when Secretary McAdoo was made Director-General of the railways, his very first order was to permit universal pooling of the railroads. That is to say, under the powers that were given him, and in these extraordinary war times, he did exactly what all of the railroad managers, all of the economists, who had studied the subject, and the Interstate Commerce Commission itself from its very first organization on to the present time, had recommended. The bitterest discussions, at the time the Interstate Commerce Act was passed in 1887, were over the anti-pooling section of the Act. The railroads favored pooling under Government supervision. But Congress put into the law the anti-pooling clause, and in spite of the fact that the first Interstate Commerce Commission, under the wise leadership of Judge Cooley, and many of the succeeding Interstate Commerce Commissions, have recommended that that anti-pooling clause be repealed and pooling under Government supervision be permitted, the political feeling of the country has been against it; and it was not until we were under the stress of war that the advantages of centralized action could be secured. Now we have had some experience under a centralized action and it is very doubtful in my mind whether we want to give up the advantages. On the other hand, with the advantages of centralized action most people who are familiar with the administration of business find combined many things that are not so favorable. I presume that most of us have been in doubt as to how far some of the difficulties that we have felt as consumers and patrons of the railroads have come from Government management, the management of those who were not trained and experienced, and how far they have come from the exigencies of the war. The same thing applies to the administration of the telegraph and the telephone, and so on. Many things have not been going very well.

"Before we entered the war I attempted to see if I could test this question a little. It was at the time that our very active and energetic Postmaster General decided to increase considerably the work of the Government in connection with the parcels post. I sent out a thousand letters to a thousand shippers of small packages, picked out at random, all over the country, and in all different lines of business, with a detailed series of questions intended by a brief answer of yes or no to indicate whether the parcels post was more advantageous to the public than the express companies, or the contrary. Out of 220 odd replies that came which were complete enough so that they could be tabulated, I gathered these facts: That a very large majority of all of the shippers thought that the costs were less,—that is, the charges of the Post Office Department were less than those of the express companies; but on the other questions that were asked, as to speed of collection and delivery, as to care taken in handling the packages, as to the number of packages lost, as to the packages destroyed in transit, as to collections, the entire range of business, the very large majority of all of the shippers said the express companies were better than the Post Office Department. I then sent an expert investigator to talk with the auditor of the Post Office Department as to the system of cost accounting that he was using. I wanted to see who it was that paid this cheaper cost of service—the shippers, the railroads, the public? Who bore the burden? And certainly the Post Office Department ought to be able to tell. The auditor, in reply to the question as to his system of cost accounting, simply laughed and said, 'Cost accounting in the Post Office Department? There is no such thing! I can't tell.'

"We know that there are great advantages in many cases from centralized control, centralized management, pooling on a universal scale, but there are also certain disadvantages that come from Government ownership and management.

"A body organized, as is The National Civic Federation, to discuss and investigate and study these important public questions, should attempt, as soon as possible, to have the facts collected impartially to show us how far we should retain this Government control and management along various lines that could be suggested, and how far we should go back to the system of private control and ownership and management that we had before. I do not expect to see us get back on the same basis we were before. I don't expect to see the present conditions remain but we should know the facts better than any of us know them now."

LABOR'S PART IN SOLVING WAR PLOBLEMS

Wheeler P. Bloodgood, Chairman Next of Kin Division, League for National Unity, opened his remarks by stating we are now dealing with two extremes, one element being represented by certain commercial organizations and one on the other side by such leaders as Mr. Berger in Wisconsin and Mr. Hilquitt in New York. He proceeded with the following remarks:

"It has seemed to me that the important thing in relation to the after-the-war problems was that we should work together as we have in meeting the war god. I don't think there is any difference in any community. Possibly we may think that in Wisconsin we face more difficult problems than you face in certain other jurisdictions. It is a fact that of our two and a half million of population, probably not to exceed seven hundred thousand are what you would term Americans—that is, Americans coming down from a number of generations. In spite of that, and in spite of the extreme represented by the socialists who, in St. Louis attacked the war, the President and Congress on the ground that the war had been brought about by the criminal conduct of the President and Congress, and who have sent throughout this country circulars and propaganda to the effect that the war was for the benefit only of the profiteers, and would be continued so long as there was profit in it—now, in spite of that, and due to the fact that men and women of every walk of life have gotten together in war agencies and worked around the table, and have heard every side of the question, just as it has been and is the purpose of the Civic Federation to hear every side of the question—they have gotten the result in Wisconsin not only in men and volunteers, but in money and materials way beyond the quota of that State.

"Now, what do we find? Just as soon as it appears that the war is over, these two extremes want to eliminate the agencies of good will that have grown up during the war. I think the vital questions, leaving out all questions of detail, are as to whether we agree on what changes should be made in the immigration laws; as to whether Government ownership is wise or unwise; as to whether we should do what England proposes to do, provide that no man shall be demobilized from the army until he has a job; and whether we should carry out some phases of the English labor program. It will not make any difference what the determination is. If we can in our respective communities work in a spirit of good will and good fellowship with all classes of society represented and having a hearing, we are going to come out of this period of reconstruction with great honor and with great credit.

"On the other hand, if we are going to sit supinely by and see the extremes, both of whom think today that they have in their hands the power of victory—if we are going to see them tear this country apart, we ought to be ashamed of ourselves. We should look facts in the face. Frankly, and I am ashamed to say it, prior to this war I was in about the same position that thousands of other men are. I had looked at but one side of this proposition. I had the impression, until I learned better, that Mr. Gompers and the American Federation of Labor, which he so ably represents, were a menace. I had been taught that. Today I find men of great force in this nation who, now that this war is over, talk about a surplus of labor, and that now is the opportunity for capital to reassert itself because labor has prospered way beyond its share because of the war. Now, that is not the spirit in which we should meet these reconstruction problems. If we go at it in that spirit, we are going to have trouble. Why, when I think of what has gone on in the past year, I realize that the men from whom we have had the real vision, the men who have had the real courage, have been representatives of labor. They have not hesitated to do those things which involved great sacrifice on their part. Now, are we going to forget all these things?

"I think we should in this meeting and in all other meetings endeavor to bring forth the feeling which will result in an expression of public sentiment throughout the United States, that will keep together these great forces that have met in solving the problems of the war so they can work together in meeting the problems of reconstruction."

MAINTAIN AMERICAN STANDARDS.

Samuel Gompers, the Civic Federation's vice-president, introduced by President Macy with the statement that "next to President Wilson, it is safe to assume that no one has done more to mobilize labor behind the war, not only in this country but among the Allies", spoke upon the grave dangers confronting our American people and of problems greater than mobilizing the good will and activities of our citizens. He said:

"To get the men to respond to the call to arms in defense of our Republic and our institutions required much effort but it was not difficult of accomplishment. To persuade our civilian population to do service behind and for the men at the fighting front, was difficult, but not so difficult, as are the problems before us today.

"I am not one who believes that the wisest and best condition of the people is what is generally understood by contentment. Contentment, in my way of thinking, is stagnation. A healthy discontent is the awakening of the aspiration for better things. It is essential today that the people of our country shall be alert to all that is transpiring and all that is impending. Thus far we have lived our lives alone and worked out our own destinies along the line of the policies we believed to be the best for us. Today, after either winning the war or helping to win the war, we are to have our representatives around a table where a treaty of peace is to be formulated. The representatives of no one government can have the controlling voice. Optimist as I am, I never fail to look upon the other side of the shield. Hoping for the best always, and striving as best I can to accomplish the right, or to help accomplish the right, I know the game played by the opponents of right. The democratic legislation enacted by the Congress of the United States, by the several states of our Union, by our municipalities, granting greater freedom of thought and action of a voluntary character, the understanding of what here we mean by sovereignty of citizenship and of the man and of the woman, a conception not held by any other country on the face of the globe—I appealed to the American people, without regard to their station in life, to see to it, to supervise, to be vigilant, lest around the peace table there are purloined from us, right under our very noses, many of the liberties and the freedom of our people.

"The treaty made by the United States with any other country or group of countries, that treaty being ratified by the Senate of the United States, becomes the supreme law of the land, and any law upon the statute books that is in conflict with the terms of that treaty becomes inoperative and ineffective and nil. We don't want to have made in vain all the sacrifices of our boys. We don't want to have that flesh of our flesh and blood of our blood given, and all the treasure given, and all the sacrifice made, in vain, and to have to make the fight all over again for the American people in their homes. While our boys were fighting and our men and women were working here to maintain freedom and democracy abroad, we ought to be alert now to see to it that we are not going to lose our liberty and democracy at home.

"I am impressed particularly with the appeal to the conscience, to the judgment, to the ideals, to the Americanism of our people for united action. You cannot get freedom, nor practice freedom, on empty stomachs. The hungry men may engage in a riot, may engage in a revolt, but their course is never of a constructive character. Hungry stomachs do not make reasoning brains. It is necessary to maintain the standards of life of the American working people that they may have sound bodies, and the opportunity for reasonable thinking, with aspirations of such a character they will build up the institutions of this Republic. Enlightened discontent, the higher and better aspirations of the masses of the people furnish the greatest impetus to progress and civilization. The discontent of hungry people leads to nowhere except chaos, confusion, and reaction.

"During the early months of the war, a phrase was applied to the industrial conditions then in the course of development. It was this: 'During this period, don't rock the boat.' I want to apply that same phrase to the present situation. There are too many circumstances and conditions of turbulent waves of an unruly sea to attempt to rock the boat now."

INDUSTRIAL FEUDALISM PASSED

A. Parker Nevin, formerly General Counsel for the National Association of Manufacturers, made the basis for the consideration of these complex problems the attitude of mind with which we approach them, and said:

"Before we discuss the merits of the great issues with which this country is confronted, let us get ourselves in the proper mental attitude. If we are going to raise discussions before we understand issues, we shall not get very far. And I propose violating the very thing which I have just said and take this opportunity of protesting violently against the utterance of the president of the manufacturers' association (National Founders Association) two weeks ago which provoked and invoked a controversy not very creditable to the manufacturing interests of this country.

"I hope the war will teach all of us a great many things. If it does not, the war, so far as we are concerned, will be a partial failure. I hope it will teach certain employers that the last vestige of feudalism has departed from this country. Feudalism and democracy cannot obtain in the same commonwealth, and unless we get into the consciousness of certain individuals and certain groups that we won't tolerate feudal acts or feudal thoughts, we shall have serious times in this country. Either the American point of view is distinct and stands for separate ideals, or else our strivings for a great commonwealth of democracy for the last hundred and forty-four years have been undertaken unsuccessfully. Either we must reduce the group consciousness in this country, or we shall have to reappraise everything. We cannot run this country on narrow group consciousness. The reason we won the war or contributed to the winning of the war was that all the people subordinated their group consciousness and concentrated on one single objective.

"We have a curious population—all nations, creeds, ideals, lack of ideals, reactionaries, progressives, aggressives, all kinds of groups. But with the exception of the anarchist and the socialist of a certain type, we saw the phenomenon of approximately one hundred and five real work of the Welfare Department in Washington was under the direction of Mrs. Easley and I cannot let this opportunity pass without paying a tribute to her unselfish, indefatigable patriotism. I don't know of anyone connected with the work of the Government in the prosecution of this war who encountered greater problems than she did, and I don't know of any other man or woman who would not have become utterly discouraged by the difficulties with which she was confronted. And yet the result has been that some of the very finest accomplishments in the war were due to her initiative and her inspiration. The questions of housing, industrial training, Soldiers' and Sailors' compensation, factory conditions, ventilation—all questions which have been a part of the work of the Welfare Department for a good many years—found in her and through her an opportunity for real development. What was done there through the war is bound to develop now that the war is over. We are going through a period of waiting and deliberation, adjustment of labor, the change of locality,—and in that transformation there is going to be a magnificent opportunity for the application of the principles of welfare work, which the Civic Federation, to my mind, has done so much to further.''

H. C. Wright, Secretary State Charities Aid Association, urged action concerning adjustments after the war looking toward effort to harmonize opinions and to that end offered a resolution which was referred to the Federation's Executive Council. It follows:

''Resolved, That this Association, through appropriate means, endeavor to bring together representatives of group opinion, with the purpose that all efforts toward civic and social betterment may be directed, so far as possible, to one end, namely, a fuller and completer democracy.''

ADJUSTMENT OF LABOR DISPUTES

Matthew Woll, President International Photo Engravers' Union and Assistant to Samuel Gompers, Chairman Committee on Labor, Council of National Defense, in speaking upon the War Labor Board, and what the future may have in store for it or similar boards, said:

''The War Labor Board has accomplished a wonderful task. It has proven one of the most helpful agencies, not only in stimulating production during the period of the war but it has also made for a better understanding between the employers and the employees. As to the future work, that depends largely upon the attitude of mind that is going to be taken by the employing interest of this country. If it is going to be one of co-operation, one of helpfulness, and one of seeking to approach the problems in the spirit of solving them to do justice to all concerned, then I think the Board will prove of great value in composing the differences of opinion, and in reaching conclusions that will make for harmony and for protection in the future. If, however, the attitude of mind is going to be one of seeking to retard rather than to advance human happiness, then, under our system of government, I feel sure the board will fail; because the decisions of the War Labor Board depend entirely upon voluntary acquiescence and not upon governmental decree. Its future depends upon the fairness of the decisions and awards and, as I stated before, the attitude of mind with which we approach the problems submitted to it.

''At present, the War Labor Board has approximately five hundred cases on its docket of which approximately one hundred and fifty have had joint submission,—that is where both employer and employee have agreed that the War Labor Board should be the determining factor, should be the judge as to what conditions of employment should prevail. In those one hundred and fifty cases, the War Labor Board is in honor bound to bring about a settlement of the disputes. In those cases it acts in the capacity of an arbitrator, and should the employers and employees on that Board fail to come to an understanding, then an umpire is selected, first by their own choice, if that is possible, and if not, then by the President of the United States, that umpire's decision finally to become the decision of the War Labor Board, and to guide those who submit their differences to it. In the other cases, however, a more unfortunate condition exists. The other three hundred and fifty cases, were submitted in the main by an ex parte procedure at the request either of the Department of Labor or upon that of labor officials urging their members to cease to strike, and the employers on the other hand refusing to consent to the War Labor Board making a decision.

''Under the formation of the War Labor Board, it may proceed and hear both sides to the controversy, though one of the parties may not have assented to it. After having a hearing, if the Board can unanimously come to an agreement, then a finding will be rendered which is in the nature of a recommendation—nothing compulsory, and it need not be accepted. If, however, a unanimous decision is not reached, then of course no finding can be had and no ultimate arbitration will result. That situation is unfortunate and it will, I think, lead to a great deal of difficulty unless we can use influence and power to impress all who have controversies before the War Labor Board to acquiesce and accept its findings because in a number of instances men and women who are paid a wage too low under conditions far too onerous, have given up their power to refuse to give service and have foregone the advantage that the war period brought to them and, in answer to the patriotic appeals of the labor officials, have continued at work in the hope that the War Labor Board might secure justice for them. If, since that stress has passed, the War Labor Board ceases to function, or any of its representatives fails to respond, now peace is in sight, as he would have while the war was in progress, then I think a most grave injustice will have been done both to the men and women workers and to the citizens as a whole. I urge all who have the best interests of their country at heart to use whatever power and influence that they may possess to see that that will not be the outcome.

''Reference has been made to the remarks made by the president of the manufacturers' association (National Founders' Association) and to the unfortunate controversy which has resulted as an immediate consequence. I know of no greater danger to the future welfare and cooperative relation between employers and employees than to have the War Labor Board cease to function, at this period, in that same spirit, with that same ideal of justice, that it did during the period of the war. May I also say the War Labor Board realizes that with the termination of the war and the early stating of peace terms, its duty may be ended. A letter was sent to Secretary of Labor Wilson asking for his viewpoint on this subject, suggesting that the War Labor Board might cease to function after clearing its docket of cases. The matter was submitted to President Wilson, as we are informed, and it is the desire and wish both of President Wilson and of Secretary of Labor Wilson that the War Labor Board should continue in its work so well established in the war-time period. What, of course, the future of the War Labor Board is going to be, I cannot prophesy. It has accomplished a great deal of good. It has a place in the readjustment period of our time, and I hope that ultimately some organization of that kind will be estab-

(Continued on Page 17.)

Works of The National War L

SINCE its inception in April, 1918, the National War Labor Board has made awards and otherwise disposed of 358 industrial disputes between employers and employees in war industries and industries directly essential to war production. On Nov. 1, 1918, there were 315 cases awaiting settlement.

That 600 controversies should have come under the jurisdiction of the Board within the seven months of its existence, reveal the necessity out of which this Board was created. A modern war imposes on a nation the tremendous burden of maximum production. Maximum production can not obtain if industry suffers ante-bellum interruptions and slackenings. Strikes, lock-outs, dissatisfaction that in any way tend toward a lesser output, *must* be provided against.

After eight months of fighting Germany, it became apparent that in the interests of maximum production a special, an extraordinary, a hitherto non-existing government agency must be created for the settlement of labor controversies.

As a court to maintain industrial peace during the period of war, and for this purpose alone, the National War Labor Board came into existence. The Board is a step taken by this government in an emergency, to create for a "common cause", an unprecedented alliance between labor and capital. The following resolutions, adopted by the Board on July 31, 1918, clearly indicate the situation.

> This war is not only a war of arms, but also a war of workshops; a competition in the quantitative production and distribution of munitions and war supplies; a contest in industrial resourcefulness and energy.
>
> The period of the war is not a normal period of industrial expansion from which the employer should expect unusual profit and the employees abnormal wages; it is an interregnum in which industry is pursued only for a common cause and common ends.
>
> Whatever have been the accomplishment and effect of the Board must be considered an outcome of this working thesis. With its focus on production, it could show favor to no class, or privileged individual, or to any economic theory. It has been a practical experiment, adjusted to a definite situation, and its single disinterested nature is apparent in every fact in its history and its operation.

FUNCTIONS AND POWERS.

Take for example the steps which led to its establishment. In January, 1918, Secretary of Labor Wilson appointed a War Labor Conference Board, whose members were nominated on the one hand by the American Federation of Labor, representing 4,000,000 organized workingmen of America, and on the other by the President of the National Industrial Conference Board, representing a large body of manufacturers. The avowed purpose of this Board was to devise a method of labor adjustment which would be acceptable to both employers and employees.

On March 29, 1918, this Conference Board recommended to the Secretary of Labor the formation of a National War Labor Board, whose functions and powers should be:

> 1. To bring about a settlement, by mediation and conciliation, of every controversy arising between employers and workers in the field of production necessary for the effective conduct of the war.
>
> 2. To do the same thing in similar controversies in other fields of national activity, delays and obstructions in which might, in the opinion of the National Board, affect detrimentally such production.
>
> 3. To provide such machinery by direct appointment, or otherwise, for the selection of committees or Boards to sit in various parts of the country where controversies arise, to secure settlement by local mediation and conciliation.
>
> 4. To summon the parties to the controversy for hearing and action by the National Board in case of failure to secure settlement by local mediation and conciliation.

Acting on the recommendation of this Conference Board, the Secretary created the War Labor Board, appointing as members an equal number to represent capital and labor and an alternate for each member, who acts and votes for him in his absence.

The complete membership of the Board is as follows:

> William Howard Taft, joint chairman; Frederick N. Judson, alternate and vice joint chairman; Frank P. Walsh, joint chairman; William Harman Black, alternate and vice joint chairman.
>
> Representatives of Employers: Loyall A. Osborne, Vice Pres. of the Westinghouse Electric and Manufacturing Co.; (Alternate not yet chosen); C. E. Michael, Pres. of the Virginia Bridge and Iron Company; Alternate, J. W. Marsh, President of Standard Underground Cable Co.; W. H. VanDervoort, President of the Root and VanDervoort Engineering Co.; Alternate, H. H. Rice, Vice President, General Motors Co.; B. L. Worden, President of Lackawanna Bridge Co. and General Manager, Submarine Boat Corporation; Alternate, C. A. Crocker, President, Crocker-McElwain Co.; Fred. C. Hood, President, Hood Rubber Co.; Alternate, John F. Perkins, Vice President, Calumet & Hecla Mining Co.
>
> Representatives of Employees: Frank J. Hayes, President United Mine Workers of America; Alternate, Adam Wilkinson, member Executive Board, M. W. of A.; W. L. Hutcheson, President, Brotherhood of Carpenters and Joiners; Alternate, T. M. Guerin, member Executive Board, Brotherhood of Carpenters and Joiners; *Thomas J. Savage, member Executive Board, International Association of Machinists; Alternate, William H. Johnston, President, I. A. of M.; Victor A. Olander, Vice-President, International Seamen's Union; Alternate, Matthew Woll, President, International Photo-Engravers Union of N. A.; T. A. Rickert, President, United Garment Workers Union; Alternate, John J. Manning, member Executive Board, United Garment Workers.

Together with the nomination of these men, the War Labor Conference Board submitted a set of principles and policies to govern relations between workers and employers in war industries for the duration of the war. This was adopted as the constitution of the War Labor Board, and is as follows:

Right to Organize:

> The right of workers to organize in trade-unions and to bargain collectively through chosen representatives is recognized and af-

*Mr. Savage died Oct. 9, and was succeeded by his alternate.

ping Board, the Railroad Administration, or in all other Government agencies. The draft boards would be instructed to reject any claim of exemption based on alleged usefulness in war production. The strikers returned to work.

Up to November 1, the Board had rendered 69 decisions, 54 involving wage increases, 14 the right to organize, 9 equal pay for women as for men, 17 the basic eight-hour day, 14 collective bargaining, and 33 involving miscellaneous issues.

JUSTICE OF AWARDS.

Wage increases have been awarded, in practically every case on the basis of cost of living investigations made by the government. The rates of course vary according to locality. For example, twenty-two railway awards were made on July 31, and the extremes are represented by a minimum of 38 cents an hour to a maximum of 42 cents an hour for Galesburg, and a minimum of 43 cents an hour to a maximum of 48 cents an hour for Detroit. In the Waynesboro controversy, a minimum of 40 cents an hour was granted, although the men asked for less. When the Board came to investigate this case, the cost of living could not be computed on a lower scale, and the award was made in accordance. In Bridgeport, a minimum hourly rate for male workers of 42 cents and for female workers of 32 cents was established, to apply to nearly every factory worker in the town.

The Board, preserving its policy of fairness, in nearly every street railway decision has made the following recommendation for an increase in fares:

> We have recommended to the President that special congressional legislation be enacted to enable some executive agency of the Federal Government to consider the very perilous financial condition of this and other electric street railways of the country and raise fares in each case in which the circumstances require it. We believe it to be a war necessity justifying Federal interference. Should this be deemed unwise, however, we urge upon the local authorities and the people of the locality the pressing need for such an increase adequate to meet the added cost of operation.
>
> The credit of these companies in floating bonds is gone. Their ability to borrow on short notes is most limited. In face of added expenses which this and other awards of needed and fair compensation to their employees will involve such credit will completely disappear. Bankruptcy, receiverships, and demoralization, with failure of service, must be the result. Hence our urgent recommendation of this head.

Also, in the News Print Paper Manufacturers' Controversy, the Board prefaced its award in the following manner:

> The National War Labor Board, in rendering its decision relative to working conditions and additional compensation to be paid by the news-print paper manufacturers to their employees, which said decision will measurably increase the cost of production of news-print paper, feels constrained, in simple justice to the parties in interest, to most respectfully request that the case involving the fixing of the selling price of news-print paper recently decided by your honorable commission be reopened, and that your honorable commission reconsider your finding in said case with a view to determine whether our award in this submission should require amendment of your finding.

The Board has invariably ruled against both discrimination against organizations and discrimination in favor of their recognition. Examples of the first instance are the cases of the Western Union Telegraph Co. and the Smith-Wesson which, like the Western Union, was taken over by the Government because of its refusal, at the Board's recommendation, to reinstate union men. Where, as in the case of the Herculaneum, St. Joseph Lead Co., the employer has not been previously committed to recognition of organizations, such recognition can not be granted to the employees by the Board's decision.

Collective bargaining, irrespective of unions, has been granted as the right of every group of workmen. Where no provision existed in the status quo, the Board has taken steps toward this end. Examiners administering awards of the Board in several cases are now establishing the machinery for collective bargaining by employees.

COLLECTIVE BARGAINING.

The general procedure of the Board has been to institute shop committees. Under the direction of an administrative examiner, a trained man sent by the Board after an award has been made, elections are held by the employees, every employee, having, under the protection of the examiner, the right to vote. The representatives of the men meet in committee with an equal or less number of employers to decide certain matters, often left undetermined in the award, and with the provision that all future controversy be considered by them.

The Board has had occasion to institute, besides, certain local committees, which act as central boards of mediation for a whole industrial community. This was the ease in Bridgeport, where practically every plant in the city was engaged in one kind of manufacture, and the grievances of 60,000 employees involved were much alike. The local committee in this case was composed of six members, three chosen by workers of the city and three by employers. The function of the general committee is to settle by agreement those questions which affect the whole community, and which cannot be solved by shop committees.

The importance of this step taken by the War Labor Board, cannot be over emphasized. The principle of collective bargaining has not only been upheld by the government of the United States, but steps have actually been taken under Federal guidance for its institution.

One other great principle has received the support from the War Labor Board—that of the basic eight hour day. The Board has never declared itself for the basic eight-hour day, and as with the question of a living wage, awards shorter hours according to the particular controversy. But wherever it has been proved that government necessity, the health and welfare of the workers, or the custom of the locality require it, the Board has granted a basic eight-hour day.

The awards of the Board have established a nation-wide precedent for the stabilization of industry as it is affected by labor unrest. Many employers, realizing both the wisdom and the power of the Board, have settled with their employees before such disputes as existed between them could come under its jurisdiction. Workers, aware of their rights as defined under the Board's constitution and by its practice, have adjusted their grievances with the employers, or have agreed to bide their time, peacefully at work, until their cases could be heard for arbitration.

This Board is perhaps the first effort of the government to establish, for any period of time, an agency to promote industrial peace on a nation-wide scale.

To guide itself over troubled waters, it was necessary for the government to define temporarily at least some unified industrial policy. The constitution and the practice of the Board are interesting in that they indicate steps which were inevitably taken for the stabilization of industry which the unusual situation of the war imperiled.

M. L.

Bolshevik "Industrial Gover

Prepared for the League for National Unity.

By GUSTAVUS MYERS.

Chapter I.

ORIGIN OF BOLSHEVISM.

"I HAVE noticed that the men who write most abundantly about Russia and with the greatest assurance are those who have just arrived," was the comment embodied in a report written from Petrograd not long ago by Frederick M. Corse, General Manager in Russia of the New York Life Insurance Company, and an American who had lived there for seventeen years.

Of a certain well-identified class of professional writers this observation is unquestionably true. An especially notorious example is found in a book published in New York early this year. Full of theorizing and a priori conclusions, the volume purported to present the Bolsheviki as the great regenerators of a decayed society. The writer of the introduction was an American magazine writer, who, by dint of long self-advertising, had contrived to gain national prominenee. What was the extent of his experience in Russia? He had been there, it is privately said, just *eighteen days*. Returning to America, he at once posed as a noted authority on Russia under Bolshevik power. In his speeches to various groups, designed to influence popular opinion, he glorified the wondrous new industrial civilization that the Bolsheviki were establishing.

This is a characteristic, not an exceptional instance. Already book after book, magazine article after article on Russia has been run hot off the presses. Their authorship and views are various, but their substance is much alike. They rehash the story of recent successive revolutions in Russia, "playing up" the dramatic features and filling in the rest of their padded space with trite political generalizations, with an injection of what their authors think is real Russian atmosphere—the latter for the sake of "coloring."

HOW HAS BOLSHEVISM WORKED OUT?

Inquiring people, however, do not want repetitions of the story of political events in Russia. These they have been able to glean sufficiently from the newspaper despatches at the time of their happening. The Bolshevik movement has proclaimed itself as an epochal industrial revolution. It seorns being called political. Behind it and actuating its leaders is an elaborate set of transplanted theories. How have these worked out? What are the actual results of their application?

This is what the world most wants to know, and this is the information it has not obtained. Some of these popular writers have not lacked the understanding that a theoretical industrial experiment was being attempted on a large scale in Russia. But they could not forego their unfortunate habit of feverishly rushing out books. To wait until a movement has sufficiently developed its character and then painstakingly assemble the facts takes time and patience and a particular ability.

Hence from these published works we learn nothing or almost nothing of the specific facts that we would most like to know. Of the results of Bolshevik theories applied to land, railroads, finance, industry and to life in general hardly an informative word. Even when some sparse data are given their source is suspiciously of partisan origin. The author of one of the few books that does give some consideration to the economic aspects of what is heralded as a mighty industrial revolution was piloted around Petrograd by another American who was an adroit Bolshevik emissary. This visitor saw only what he was allowed to see.

All of these classes of writers can, however, say that they were contemporaneously in Russia. This is more than can be said by other groups of writers here in the United States who have been busily occupied in either creating Bolshevik sentiment or something akin to it. Their not having been in Russia could be passed over if, like President Wilson, they had tried to get information from reliable persons coming from there.

But this special coterie of writers have studiously avoided doing this. From the outset they have welcomed the Bolshevik movement as a great innovation, apparently convinced in advance that the results fitted in with the theories. Numbers of these writers are of that precious circle popularly dubbed as "highbrows." They call themselves "liberal intellectuals" or vice versa. Their imposing command of rhetoric gives a ponderous air of solidity to their writings. Others of this general group here, although personally distinct from it, are certain Socialist Party writers and leaders. With extreme bitterness did they not so long ago denounce and oppose Bolshevik theories. But once the Bolshevik movement attained ruling power they, like the parlor intellectuals, hailed it as the rising order. The very movement that was disreputable out of power became endowed with extraordinary attributes when in power. This power, as is well established, was obtained in Russia by means of German aid and backing.

It may be asked how these groups could formerly have opposed Bolshevism when, as matter of fact, the Bolshevik regime has been in power only a year.

I. W. W. GENESIS OF BOLSHEVISM.

Bolshevism was preached in the United States years ago but under other names. It was called either Syndicalism or I. W. W. propaganda, which were more or less synonymous. The I. W. W. took its doctrines from Syndicalism, which in turn was, to a considerable degree, of anarchistic origin. In a pamphlet on Syndicalism, written in 1913 by Emma Goldman, this definition is given (page 7): "Syndicalism is, in essence, the economic expression of Anarchism." Originally, the industrial union movement in the United States was not connected with anarchist ideas, but later—about 1910—it came distinctly under anarchist influence. The I. W. W. advocated "direct action," which meant sabotage. It insisted upon the general strike and control of industries by workingmen's committees. It fiercely assailed what it termed "bourgeois morality," and demanded the overthrow and extermination of the "bourgeoisie." This particular philosophy was based upon two main premises. One premise was that any means, however underhand, violent or bloody, was justifiable in overthrowing existing society. The other premise was that every man (or woman) was born with equal ability, and that committees of workmen could at once step successfully into the technical and administrative work of running industries.

It was from this movement in the United States that many of those who are now Bolshevik needing the greatest possible intelligence and practical methods of development, that the Bolsheviki set out to try their theories and compel their acceptance.

Chapter II.

LAND, FACTORIES AND BANKS.

The first application of the "committee method" was to the Russian army. There it was that the theoretical scheme of selection by mass elective vote was put into operation in company or regimental meetings. Case after case actually occurred where a regimental commander of the rank of Colonel would be "elected" cook, scavenger or to some other menial post. Burly, mouthy self-pushers, knowing nothing whatever of military art, would be elected Colonels.

"Discipline," wrote Lieutenant Boris Schumanski, a Russian journalist and soldier, in the *New York Tribune*, March 31, 1918, "was supposed to be maintained by committees made up of the soldiers themselves. Every order given by an officer appointed by the committee, could be made the subject of an appeal from the soldier to the committee, and of a political campaign in the company. Politics ran rife through the army. Men became generals because they were orators. . . . . . The new illiterate generals forced many [of the real officers] to do menial work in and around the barracks. . . . The result was hundreds of suicides of real officers in Petrograd."

No doubt much of this practise was encouraged by the Germans with the object of completely demoralizing the Russian army. But as for the basic doctrine of the "committee system" itself it far preceded the war. It was nothing more nor less than I. W. W. doctrine, as everyone familiar with the I. W. W. in this country knows.

BLOODY VILLAGE CONFLICTS OVER LAND.

With the Russian army demobilized and demoralized, the soldiers—mostly peasants—gradually found their way back to the villages, after many of them had stayed in the cities to loot. They carried back rifles, machine guns, batteries and munitions which they claimed as their private property. Regiments in the Russian army, it should be explained, were formed of men from the same or contiguous villages. What has happened since their return? Decrees of the Central Soviet, headed by Lenine and Trotsky, give the impression that the land has been equitably distributed in an orderly way. But these are merely paper decrees. Lenine and Trotsky have little or no power outside of Petrograd and Moscow to which their armed force is mainly confined. Villages have quarreled over which should have possession of land, and have been turning machine guns on one another to settle the dispute by force.

Under the agitation and decrees of the Bolsheviks there set in a universal passion in Russia for unions and committees. According to Samuel Lovich, a Columbia graduate who returned to New York early this year from a trip through Russia for a syndicate of New York exporters: "There is a union of housemaids, a union of janitors, a union of assistant janitors, a union of porters. In each apartment house the tenants form a union against the landlord and strike when he raises the rent. When I say the union of janitors, I should qualify it by saying that in Odessa, where this union went on a strike, one of the demands which they obtained was that they should no longer be called 'janitors' but 'inspectors of homes'."

Fantastic as part of this account may seem it is an understatement of what has actually been happening wherever the Bolsheviki have been temporarily or continuously in control. A well-informed Russian Socialist, a university graduate, who was in Petrograd at the time and recently arrived here, narrates a typical instance of "committee control."

SCRUBMAN ELECTED HOSPITAL CHIEF DOCTOR.

Number 6 Union of Towns Hospital is one of the largest hospitals in Petrograd. It contained 3,000 beds. When the Bolsheviki forced their way into power, this hospital was one of the many institutions where self-constituted committees were immediately formed. In this particular hospital the committee was composed of waiters, janitors, nurses, scrubmen and yardmen. It at once deposed the Chief Doctor, making him a scrubman, and it elected a scrubman Chief Doctor. Later there arrived a trainload of soldiers sick with scurvy. When they were taken to the hospital, the scrubman "Chief Doctor" tried to treat them but finally had to admit he couldn't. He thereupon called the deposed Chief Doctor, and ordered him to attend them. "Oh! No," replied the real Chief Doctor, "you've made me scrubman and that's all that I'll do. I'm scrubman now." Indignant at this tragical farce, a number of the patients rose from their beds, seized their crutches and slew the Bolshevik committee.

When, upon seizing power and by machine guns and bayonets preventing the Constituent Assembly from meeting, Lenine and other Bolshevik leaders denounced parliamentary government as "a deception upon the working class" that was but repeating the I. W. W. slogan long current in this country. The Bolshevik repudiation of Russia's national debt was a doctrine taken from the I. W. W. which long preached repudiation of all contracts. The Bolshevik demand for a bitter, sanguinary class conflict was taken, also, from the I. W. W. which had taken its class conflict program essentially from the Socialist Party. But where the Socialist Party avowed belief in political action, the I. W. W. and their pupils, the Bolsheviki, demanded one kind of control and one only. That was direct control of all economic and governing functions by workingmen and their committees.

This theory they have applied to railroads, street car systems, banks and factories. With what results?

Professor Ludovic H. Grondys, a Socialist, gives much first-hand information gathered during a long tour of Russia recently. At the outbreak of the war he was Professor of Physics and Mathematics in the Technical Institute of Dordrecht, Holland, and also one of the editors of the University Review of Philosophy, Holland. He is now correspondent for *L'Illustration* and *Le Temps*. En route to Siberia, he was in New York in October, 1918, and there gave me ample details of the Bolshevik experiment.

CRIMINALS LARGELY IN CONTROL.

"Almost all the Bolshevik leaders," he said, "are people who have returned from America. These were supplemented by an immense swarm of criminals released from Siberia, as also liberated criminals from the prisons in Moscow, Petrograd and other places. A certain number of those exiled to Siberia under the old regime were political prisoners but a far greater number were actual criminals.

"The first thing that these did after getting back to Russia was to burn courts and police courts. They thus destroyed records and Rogues' Galleries. With the records of their criminality destroyed, they could safely pose as political martyrs. With great assurance they did so. This explains why so many criminals became Presidents of Soviets, and this helps to explain also the bloody conflicts between villages, and why so many criminals are in control. Every town and village has the right to have a Revolutionary Tribunal, and can decree anything it pleases. All laws have been abolished. Only those having certificates of being thoroughgoing Bolsheviki can be elected to Soviets or Revolutionary Tribunals. The principle (!) prevails everywhere that 'Anybody who has been in Siberia and has suffered from the law ought to know something about it.'"

While on the subject of the criminals running Russia, it is well here to advert to a description of some of them given by General A. Dobrajanksky who recently arrived in New York City as the representative of a group of united Russians. General Dobrajansky says:

"As an instance of the calibre of men composing the various Soviets, (self-elected representatives of the Workmen's and Soldiers' Committee,) let me cite a few names of the members of the Soviet of Blagowestchensk. We have the President, Tobelson, a German spy, ex-jailbird and robber; Mochin of the Executive Committee, a deserter from the Russian Army, a counterfeiter and ex-jailbird; his assistant, Tchatkovsky, also an ex-jailbird; Commissioner of Prisons Emilianoff, ex-jailbird and robber; his assistant, Nakileff, previously condemned to jail for robbery; the Commissioner of Food, who was convicted for misappropriation of funds; Korovin, Commissioner of Schools, an ex-jailbird; Tillick, convicted for robbery, now Commissioner of Finance; Mithin, Commissioner of Militia, an ex-jailbird, and finally, we have as Commissioner of Health an illiterate peasant. And these are the men who are at the head of affairs in Russia today!"

To return now to Professor Grondy's statement:

"Does the Soviet system represent the people's will? you ask. It does not. It is forced on the people. There are no real elections. The Bolsheviki use the Red Guards to pack assemblies and force their candidates. Voters are exclusively Bolsheviki, and only Bolsheviki or those having no property can be eligible to office. This claim of Bolsheviki being propertyless is not true. Many of them have amassed money. In all my tour I met only a few of them who were honest. School-masters are not eligible for Bolshevik village Soviets. They are too intelligent, and are regarded as intellectuals."

ARMED ANARCHY IN FACTORIES.

"Soviets have been the great craze. Every great apartment house has a Soviet. Every factory was put under the domination of a so-called Council of Workmen. I personally saw the application of the theory to many factories. For example, Koopp's agricultural machine factory employing 500 men at Alexandroffsky, near Rostoff. The Council of Workmen in this factory voted to make Koopp an employe at 500 roubles a month, and made one of the loudest talking workmen (who was also President of the Soviet) Director of the factory. They voted themselves salary increases of from 800 to 1,000 per cent.

"Every day the workmen held meetings, sometimes lasting several hours, in the factory. There they discussed their rights and privileges but the words duties and obligations were unknown to them. They also voted themselves the right 'as an intellectual necessity' to read newspapers during supposed working hours. Nominally they 'worked' eight hours, but literally not more than four and a half a day. But they paid themselves for all time spent in meetings, reading newspapers and loafing. The funds they obtained by rifling the factory vaults, and when they were empty, they went to Koopp's house and to the banks where he kept his private account, and under threat of using arms, took away what money remained. In all, they seized about 1,000,000 roubles. Many of his workmen were members of the Red Guard. If one of these Red Guards stayed at the factory twelve hours a day with his rifle he would put in a claim for overtime and had to be paid from the factory funds. Workmen brought in their girls to the

(*Continued on Page* 18.)

THE NATIONAL
Civic Federation Review

Office: Thirty-third Floor, Metropolitan Tower
1 Madison Avenue New York City

RALPH M. EASLEY, Editor

Published Twice a Month **Two Dollars a Year**

The Editor alone is Responsible for any unsigned article or unquoted statement published in THE NATIONAL CIVIC FEDERATION REVIEW.

CLOSER UNITY OF LABOR AND CAPITAL. The outstanding result of the war in the industrial field is the greatly increased recognition by both employers and employees of an integral community of interest. That the harmony maintained during the war is not only to be continued but augmented is shown by the recent utterances of Samuel Gompers and a number of large labor organizations on the one hand, and by various preeminent leaders of industry and powerful commercial bodies on the other. This unity of purpose was all the more emphasized when, about a month ago, the president of a large manufacturers' association declared that wages would have to be reduced. Representing labor, Mr. Gompers served notice that organized labor would resist such an attempt to the full extent of its power.

From many quarters there has since come the most gratifying proof that the announcement made by the head of that manufacturers' association was representative of himself only. Many employers throughout the country have declared their opposition to summary wage-cutting, pointing out the injustice of such a course to labor while the cost of living remains at its present high standard.

The attitude of large employers, as shown by a succession of happenings within the last two weeks, goes, however, much further than a declaration of dissent to wage reduction. It has evinced the most sincere aim toward establishing broader and juster relations with employees, and laying further foundations for the mutual recognition by so-called capital and labor of the rights of each other. Convincing evidence of this sentiment is embodied in the program submitted to the United States Chamber of Commerce by its Industrial Committee at the meeting at Atlantic City, by resolutions adopted by the New York Chamber of Commerce, by statements made at the dinner of the Academy of Political Science by Charles M. Schwab and F. A. Vanderlip, and by addresses by John D. Rockefeller, Jr., and other captains of industry throughout the country. It is immaterial that in these resolutions, proposals and speeches there are all kinds of ideas, some practical, some impractical, others vague about how to produce this better state. The essential point is that they are all committed to an attempt to work for a bettering of our industrial conditions.

Carrying out the position of the American Federation of Labor that labor is not a commodity, but that all wage-earners should be treated as human beings, the Committee on Industrial Relations of the New York State Chamber of Commerce, which represents the richest and most powerful industrial and financial district in the world, has presented a report, declaring:

"Wage-earners as a class must be given an opportunity to count as men and women in the vital management of their industries in whatever position they may be qualified to count. This is the more necessary at this moment, since so many wage-earners will be returning from our active campaigns against the enemy, where men have counted as never before in the history of warfare."

Judge Gary in an address before one hundred and forty leading steel manufacturers of the country, members of the American Iron and Steel Institute, after predicting that "the next five years in this country will be the most progressive, prosperous and successful in our history," came out unreservedly in favor of a reduction of prices of their commodities, beginning January 1, 1919, and against a reduction in wages. On the wage question he said:

"For one, I believe we have not been paying more than was proper and just. The necessary costs of living have been growing and unless and until they are reduced it would seem that on the average the present wages are reasonable.

"Judging from the past, all of us believe we should not commence to make reductions at the point of wage rates; sacrifices must previously be made by employers. Our employees must continue to be treated liberally with respect to their compensation and general welfare. We will continue to show them that it is our intention to consider their merits, and to treat them as associates and valuable assistants in our work. We should give no cause for reasonable complaint or unfavorable criticism."

When E. H. Gary, president of the corporation which is the largest employer of labor in this country, John D. Rockefeller, Jr., the next largest employer, Charles M. Schwab, one of the largest employers, and Samuel Gompers president of the largest body of workers, all announce during the same week the same general broad views, there is certainly excellent ground for optimistic feeling as to our industrial future.

NURSING THE VIPER. In a recent statement of his policies, Premier Lloyd George declared:

"After what has happened in the last four or five years it is impossible to entertain in our midst a population of which a considerable portion abused our hospitality. This has been demonstrated by evidence impossible to ignore. They spied and plotted and assisted Germany in forming plans for the destruction of a country which offered them hospitality. They thus have forfeited any claim to remain."

There are detained at Fort Oglethorpe a small army of alien enemies—men who sought to serve the Kaiser and aid the German cause by every species of treachery, espionage and outrage. Before America entered the war they had already begun conducting warfare against us within our midst. After we entered the conflict, and as long as it was possible for them to do so, they sought in every way to negative our part in the struggle. They destroyed munition plants, factories, trains, storage warehouses and other property, incurring the loss of American lives. They fomented strikes. They promoted and secretly financed pacifist movements and encouraged resistance to the draft. They spied upon us, and plotted for our undoing. What shall be done with these treacherous underhand foes?

Already movements have begun agitating for the release of this host of enemy aliens—some of them bankers representing great German interests, others merely dynamiting henchmen and common spies. The Germans in this country have begun a spectacular display of crocodile tears, and with maudlin blubberings have joined the chorus of the "uplift fraternity" for mercy and pardon for all war prisoners. The foe has been beaten; therefore let him be forgiven. The intrigues of the plotters within proved fruitless; therefore let them be released instanter from prison. Why persecute with punishment an unsuccessful, repentant foe? Thus the appeals to cheap sentimentality go on.

Many citizens believe that entirely too much lenience was shown the men who were as actual enemies of the United States as the Huns in the trenches. Shall these interned aliens, when peace is declared, be permitted to go their own sweet way? America suffered more from the reptile Huns who violated our hospitality than did Great Britain. If Great Britain has reason to exclude them, America has a thousand-fold more cogent reasons. From the creatures of Bernstorff and von Papen this country can never expect any good.

Germany, though beaten, is not repentant. Only the other day Premier Ebert, addressing the Prussian Guard upon its arrival in Berlin, declared: "Your deeds and sacrifices are unexampled. No enemy overcame you." Daily reports come that the Germans do not admit defeat and claim virtual victory. The *Kolnische Volks-Zeitung*, protesting against the exclusion of Germany from a League of Nations and the boys after the signing of the armistice, many declared that upon the conclusion of peace they intended to emigrate to America. Since then further reports from Germany tell of a concerted and growing movement to emigrate to our shores. Many of these Germans have relatives here who would assist them to emigrate, and will perhaps urge them to do so. One dominating motive will doubtless be a desire to escape the crushing burden of taxation and evade their share in paying the enormous war indemnities which will be levied. Germany will be in want of raw materials, wages will be low, food scarce and the cost high. Inevitably, the Huns, shirking payment of the just penalty for their crimes, will look abroad for more prosperous employment and more congenial, comfortable and well-fed conditions of living.

Shall we permit an invasion of Huns, of the men who shed American blood, when peace is declared? Shall we permit the race which rejoiced in the sinking of the Lusitania to come here to usurp the jobs which belong to the American boys who went to fight? Shall we suffer demoralization of industry, with lower wages, because of an influx of immigrant "square-heads" willing to work for any wage? Shall we permit the bestial hordes who ravished Belgium women and bayonetted little children to make their homes where American womanhood is held sacred and where innocent childhood is loved? Shall we take the enemy to our bosom, only to be stabbed in the back?

Will it not be the course of wisdom and self-preservation, upon the making of peace, to deport every interned Hun in America and forever forbid his return? Likewise, will it not be wise immediately to enact such laws as will prohibit for all time the landing upon American shores of all who have borne arms against the United States?

BOLSHEVISM IN ACTION. The article entitled "The Bolshevik Experiment In 'Industrial Government'" begun in this issue of THE NATIONAL CIVIC FEDERATION REVIEW is addressed to every thinking person, whatever his or her status in society, who cherishes liberty and values constructive social development.

It will contain nothing of interest to the Bolshevik propagandist because it contains only facts. Facts are utterly unimportant to that class of sociological adventurers who make a profitable business exploiting theories and panaceas.

The facts contained in this article are attested by men whose knowledge of conditions is first-hand. But that will not recommend the conclusions to be logically drawn to the attention of our wordy band of "intellectual" theorists. Their test of the truth or falsity of any statement is simple. Does the fact coincide with their theory? If it does not, the fact cannot be a fact, it is "an invention of the reactionary opposition."

Every evidence that has come from any responsible source proves more and more that the unutterable calamity which has come upon the Russian people has completely disorganized their social and industrial life, desolated their country and holds them under a bloody tyranny far surpassing the worst tyrannies the world has heretofore known.

Do these uncontroverted facts make any impression upon our pro-Bolshevik propagandists? They do not.

Among the supporters of Bolshevism in the United States we discern three more or less clearly defined types. One of these is a conglomeration of individuals of destructive tendencies instinctively scenting a longed-for opportunity to rush up and demolish existing restraints. The second is a scattering of weaklings who, in their wish for better conditions, eagerly grasp at anything without stopping to learn whether it is high explosive or not. The other group—and the most dangerous of all—is that which makes a self-aggrandizing cult of the "social uplift" enterprise. Though small in numbers it is, in general, the mouthpiece for the other two groups. These literary radicals are not risking anything in their support of Bolshevism. Their assurance and audacity would bring them sinecures in a Bolshevik regime, but the moment they thought Bolshevism had become a stigma and reproach in this country they would boldly disclaim their participation and seek some more congenial theory to exploit.

The difficult question to answer is—how much of this propaganda is made by fools and how much by knaves? In the face of such a horror as has resulted in Russia from the combination of German incitement and anarchist fanaticism, books, articles and pamphlets are being turned out here glorifying Bolshevism in its theoretical aspect and completely ignoring its actual results. Does this seeming determination to misinform the American people arise spontaneously?

The first essential of a conscientious social attitude is to understand well the nature of the thing we recommend. Not to do this is deliberately to mislead others, and perhaps involve them in disaster. With a complete disregard of the merest elementals of this principle, these self-styled "intellectual" liberals have been shouting Bolshevism without having the least idea of what it practically is, or without showing the slightest indication that they themselves know.

This article throws some light on the practical aspects of Bolshevism.

DANGEROUS CHURCH "ENTERTAINMENT." "And then, as far as organization is concerned, the average Russian workingman always is so vastly superior to the American workingman in discussing any sort of a problem. . . . I believe the average workingman of Russia reads more serious sociological, economic articles every day, than the average business and professional man reads here in a month." Such is a specimen gem taken from the twaddle of one, Albert Rhys Williams, who after a brief stay in Russia returned to the United States on the evident mission of trying to create a favorable public opinion of the Bolsheviki. Williams boasts of having made speeches from the same platform as Lenine and Trotzky in Petrograd, and describes himself as "an authorized messenger to the American people from Lenine and the Soviet Government." What does it matter to this driveling poseur that the Russian Official Statistics for 1917 showed that 65 to 68 per cent. of the entire population of Russia was illiterate? That only 4 per cent. of the people had been to public schools, and that of every 10,000 soldiers 6,110 were illiterate? That small part of the Russian workers able to read belong to the Menshiviki party which not only bitterly opposes the Bolsheviki but is being killed off by the Bolsheviki and is striking back whenever it gets a chance. Like all the rest of his shoddy tribe who boast of their "vision", Williams is incompetent to understand facts.

If these were merely hallucinations reserved for his own delectation, nobody would object to the weird contents lodged within Williams' cranium. But presenting such balderdash in churches to unsophisticated flocks is quite another matter. Recently, after Williams spoke at the Church of the Ascension in New York City, emotionally reeling out a tissue of assertions similar to the one quoted above, a resolution was passed favoring the recognition of the Soviets. On the strength of his airs and assurance Williams is getting access to other church congregations. The kind of entertainment supplied by the Williams type is of a brand that the authorities should note and take action on.

The Pan-American Labor Confere

By CHESTER M. WRIGHT.

There war seen a great deal of the story of the past, the beginning of what will be part of the story of the future. Here were gathered representatives of the working people of two races—races which are not only possessed of different characteristics in themselves, but which, as typified in this gathering, come out of differing stages of social and industrial development.

Laredo, Texaxs, nestling on the American bank of the Rio Grande, was the scene of the gathering, which convened on November 13 and remained in session four whole days.

There are reported to be 100,000 organized workers in Mexico. This is 1.5 per cent of the population. And, considering Mexico as it has been and as it largely is today, the working population outside this 1.5 per cent has little if any effective voice in determining its conditions of life and culture. International relations of any kind cannot be considered properly without knowledge of and allowance for these facts.

In Laredo the Mexican workers were represented by about twenty five delegates. These men were workingmen, but they were not untutored workingmen. They were men of ability. Some of them were possessed of conspicuous ability. Oratory and the language of oratory were theirs in abundance. Cotton work shirts were no hindrance to fluency of tongue.These men represented the movement in which Mexico has its greatest hope. And yet, even these, presumably the boldest spirits, were clearly men feeling their way into liberty, spinning words in the devious ways of those who speak to be understood by friend and misunderstood by foe at the same time. Often they avoided directness of statement, often they spoke as men fearing some power at their back. Most of them probably stood for the first time in their lives on soil where they could feel sure of perfect freedom of utterance. But when all has been said, when the whole page of debits has been added up, the Mexican delegation was a remarkable delegation. It did magnificent work, it took its stand with American labor and it linked arms in permanency with the one force in the United States that can be of most service because it has no selfish motive.

Latin American workers got in Laredo a first hand impression of the benefits of organization as we know it. In future meetings of the same kind this impression is bound to be deepened. It must be remembered that at Laredo a permanent Pan-American Federation of Labor was organized. Conventions of this new international federation will be held yearly, the first being set for next July in the Republic of Panama.

Nearly all Latin American labor has been inclined towards Syndicalism—some of it very strongly inclined in that direction. The benefits derived from extreme radicalism in labor organization are extremely vague and doubtful. This has been especially true of Mexico, but strangely enough the tide has already set strongly in Mexico toward a more reasonable and solid type of labor organization. When the Carranza revolution was at its height, the great labor organization of Mexico was the Casa del Obrero Mundial (House of the workers of the world). This organization was strongly syndicalistic. It joined forces with the revolution and went so far as to secure a signed contract with the Carranza provisional government recognizing mutuality of aims and pledging support to the revolution because of that. This support it gave in the fullest degree, enlisting whole unions in the revolutionary army.

However, success of the revolution did not bring growth to the organization. It has steadily dwindled in size and strength until now the Mexican Federation of Labor is the great and dominant organization of labor in Mexico. This decided trend toward the right is one of the hopeful features in Mexico. It was the Mexican Federation of Labor which sent the majority of Mexican delegates to the Laredo conference.

Contact with the American Federation of Labor in successive conventions seem certain to result in a growing tendency toward adoption of sane and sound principles, toward a sound scheme of collective bargaining and toward a policy of education and stability among the membership of Mexican unions. Lack of stability has been a good deal of a characteristic in the past.

The Laredo conference adopted some rather striking resolutions. Two or three provide for joint action by American and Mexican labor in solving labor problems, one calls for the establishment of an organizing and educational center in New York. The most important bears on the coming peace and it follows in full:

"Whereas, We, the delegates to the First Pan-American Federation of Labor Conference, meeting at such a critical time in the world's history, realizing that the problems now confronting humanity in the building of an enduring peace are no less acute than the problems of the war, and being deeply and fervently desirous that in the reshaping of the world's affairs the most critical consideration be given those principles that make for an enduring peace and create equality of opportunity for the people of all the nations, and,

"Whereas, The time has arrived when the organized labor movement, with full understanding of its rights, its power and resources, its value and contributions to society, must bring forward its most profound, constructive thought, calculated to establish and insure the principles of true democracy, therefore be it

"Resolved, That we declare that the following essential fundamental principles must underlie the Peace Treaty as well as the principles of all civilized nations:

"A league of the free peoples of the world in a common covenant for genuine and practical co-operation to secure justice and therefore peace in relations between nations;

"No political or economic restrictions meant simply to benefit some nations and to cripple others;

"No reprisals based upon vindictive purposes, or deliberate desire to injure, but to right manifest wrongs;

"Recognition of the rights of small nations and of the principle 'No peace must be forced under a sovereignty under which it does not wish to live;

"No territorial changes or adjustment of power except in furtherance of the welfare of the peoples affected and in furtherance of world peace.

"And be it further

"Resolved, That in addition to these basic principles there should be incorporated in the Treaty which shall constitute the guide of nations in the new period and conditions into which we are entering, the foll wing declarations fundamental to the best interests of all nations and of vital importance to wage earners:

"That in law and in practice the principle shall be recognized that the labor of a human being is not a commodity or article of commerce;

"Industrial servitude shall not exist except as a punishment for crime whereof the party shall have been duly convicted;

"The right of free association, free assemblage, free speech and free press shall not be abridged;

"That the seamen of the merchant marine shall be guaranteed the right of leaving their vessels when the same are in safe harbor;

"No article or commodity shall be shipped or delivered in international commerce in the production of which children under the age of sixteen years have been employed or permitted to work;

"It shall be declared that the basic workday in

Shadow Huns and Others

By T. EVERETT HARRE

(In the previous issue, Mr. Harre analyzed the record of the "New Republic, "The Nation" and showed that Albert Shaw, in the "Review of Reviews" had accused the Allies of forcing the war to continue out of motives of extortion and revenge. Dr. Shaw actually asserted: The concrete imperialistic programs of Russia, England, France and Italy hardened the German program of European domination into a definite reality, whereas it had previously been rather more a dream than a practical project.")

It was because of the Allies' confidence of winning and imposing the terms he has stated, that "Germany," according to Dr. Shaw, "felt herself forced to desperate measures"—the resumption of ruthless submarine warfare.

Referring to the *Review of Reviews* of March, 1917, issued a month before the declaration of war, one finds that Dr. Shaw condoned Germany's abrogation of her solemn agreement thus:

"Taking the view—as they must on both sides—that their very existence is at stake, they cannot forego any measure that would help to insure peace with victory." The submarine was the final "measure" to which Germany had been driven.

There followed this totally astonishing assertion regarding Germany's first appalling "measure" of the war:

"Germany had not the slightest desire or intention of inflicting harm on Belgium. She expected, afterwards, to pay damages for having violated Belgium's neutral rights."

Dr. Shaw accused the United States of not having been fair to Germany, and of having discriminated in favor of Great Britain. To Dr. Shaw, Germany's submarine policy was merely an "inconvenience." It was "far more inconvenient to Sweden and her allies—Norway and Denmark—and especially to Holland, than it is inconvenient to us," said he. The casual interpretation of the murdering of women and children on the high seas as an "inconvenience" is novel.

"We could have afforded well enough at the start," Shaw continued, "to make protests against all illegal acts, while warning American ships and American citizens to keep out of the danger zones that belligerents on both sides were unlawfully creating in waters contiguous to the shores of their enemies." Was Dr. Shaw endorsing the Bernstorff warning published as an advertisement before the sailing of the Lusitania, as well as the proposition embodied in the McLemore resolution? Germany was forced to resume unrestricted U-boat warfare as a reprisal for the British blockade. What was our own part and responsibility in forcing desperate Germany to this measure? According to Shaw:

U. S. DUPED CONFIDING TEUTONS.

"We told England * * * that we were going to be impartial and stand for neutral rights against both sides." The British "practices continued, and our Government did nothing more." And Shaw reiterated: "It is true that the British practices have led to the German submarine reprisals. * * * Here then, is the situation: The United States denounces as illegal certain practices, and declares itself the champion of neutral rights thus violated, solemnly stating that it will not submit to them. The British Government persists in these practices. * * * Germany is entirely familiar with our statements to Great Britain, and waits for many months in the hope that we may take some action to support our words." In other words: The United States made a bluff so far as England was concerned in the matter of protecting neutral rights. We gave Germany to believe we would insist that England abandon the practices which finally forced Germany to submarine reprisals. We did not live up to our word, we deceived Germany, and permitted England to continue her practices; yet when Germany was driven to desperation we demanded, in fact, that she too submit to British aggression and desist from the use of her ultimate weapon. We were not neutral, and why? Dr. Shaw said:

"The banking interests were all committed to the Allied governments as agents for floating their loans or as concerned with contracts for supplies. THE PROSPERITY BOOM HAD ECLIPSED NEUTRALITY."

"We had gone far to conciliate England. * * * England had sea power and was using it illegally. Germany proposed to use a still more illegal form of reprisal. * * * England could have avoided this new submarine campaign * * * if she had chosen to pursue technically legal courses in her relation to neutral trade." Germany, therefore, was the injured party and England was responsible for the submarine measures which threatened to bring America into the war!

Dr. Shaw explained that the object of his resume was "to persuade our readers that for America to assume the status of belligerency just now would probably not serve the highest ends in the best way." For Germany and Austria "had ceased months ago to fight for victory, and their fight now is for terms of peace that will not be too intolerable."

NO AFFRONT MEANT IN SINKING LUSITANIA!

According to Dr. Shaw, America had "no avowed grievance against Germany except that she has created certain zones of terror in the seas." * * * "It would be useless to try to make the American people believe that an affront to us was intended, inasmuch as everyone knows that this is not the case."

Was the murdering of women and children on the high seas something less than an affront to us? Was Dr. Shaw unaware of the war which Germany was conducting against us on our own shores—in the dynamiting of bridges and railroads, the destruction of munition factories and ships, the fomenting of strikes, and the insidious underground work of an army of spies? Had he not read the papers of Dr. Albert, or the exposures of activities of Bernstorff and von Papen?

"Both sides in this war have created illegal zones in the high seas," Shaw continued, "have planted mines and have ordered neutrals to keep out of the way." * * * "We should have no clear reason for using the instrument of war, unless war should enable us effectively and at once to remedy that particular evil."

Inasmuch as he asserted the "particular evil" was committed by "both sides," did Dr. Shaw mean to imply that, if we could have ended it, we should have gone to war with both England and Germany? However, in Shaw's opinion, war would have been hopeless. "We have no soldiers to send against Germany's armies in Europe, nor has Germany any way of sending soldiers to fight on our soil." While, according to Shaw, we should have been helpless in war against Germany, "Germany could, however, immediately declare a danger zone along our Atlantic and Gulf seaboards from Halifax to Mexico, and could send twenty or a hundred submarines over to intercept commerce. It was not so many weeks ago that she sent the U-53 over to make a morning call of courtesy at Newport and to spend an afternoon sinking British ships outside the three mile limit."

Was this intended as a warning not to invoke the displeasure of the Hun overlords? Apparently, we had no course but to submit to the Huns' inhumane and barbarous decree.

AMERICA'S MEAN MOTIVES.

Was it because of Germany's aggressions on the high sea, because of the killing of women and children, that we went to war? Were we inspired by any high ideals in going to war?

Dr. Shaw admitted in the *Review of Reviews* of April, 1917, that Germany's violation of neutral rights on the seas had not in his opinion "supplied in itself a necessary reason" for our having gone to war. In fact, we used the sinking of passenger ships merely as a technical pretext to "throw off the pretense of neutrality."

Dr. Shaw said:

"Dominating forces and influences had determined that the United States should enter the European war as an Ally of the British Empire and France. From the standpoint of these powerful influences Germany's new submarine blockade of February merely afforded the occasion. * * * Presupposing our desire to enter the war, the submarine blockade could, of course, give us ample opportunity for inflaming the public mind by means of a great newspaper campaign, while affording in full measure those legal justifications that the official mind in Washington seems to regard as important. * * * The tremendous effort that was made in the month of February, and in the early part of March, to bring the United States completely into the war had its origin in the chief centres of business and finance."

It is there in black and white—in a magazine of wide circulation, reaching into American homes: the same familiar trite propaganda that Wall Street plunged the country into war, that the Allies were bent upon a program of loot, that Germany was forced by the illegal British blockade to the desperate employment of the submarine weapon. Just what was it that Rose Pastor Stokes and Eugene V. Debs said along similar lines that brought them ten and fifteen years' sentences?

HAD VIERECK, BILL HAYWOOD AND SHAW CARRIED THE DAY.

Today the world rejoices in such a victory as will guarantee all free peoples a secure and just future peace. What would have happened had Dr. Shaw been able to impose his ideas upon the American government in the crucial days when we had either to resist or submit to German aggression? What amity would there have been between America and the Allies had the *New Republic* idea of "divided counsels" prevailed—had we surrendered ourselves to insidious doubts and unworthy suspicions? What sort of peace would have come had the Allied councils been influenced by the views of the non-resistant Mr. Villard? Had Dr. Hale, Viereck, Jeremiah O'Leary, La Follette, Dr. Shaw, Bill Haywood, Victor Berger, Morris Hillquit and others had their way, Germany in all probability would not have been compelled to sue for peace. America would have kept out of the war in shameful submission to Germany, and the Kaiser in all probability would not today be a fugitive in Holland.

Sometime ago a book published by the Review

of Reviews Company, "Two Thousand Questions and Answers About the War," was exposed as a piece of subtle Hun propaganda. This volume interpreted the war a "fifty-fifty" affair, and ascribed the causes to historic wrongs — chiefly against Germany. It accused Great Britain of monopolizing the earth. The interesting thing about the discredited volume is that the line of pro-German argument parallels the point of view expressed editorially by Dr. Shaw in his "American" *Review of Reviews.*

At the time Dr. Dernburg was conducting his propaganda in America, M. B. Claussen, head of the German Information Service, secured a thirty-day option for the purchase of the controlling interest in the American Press Association. This enterprise, which supplies boiler plate matter chiefly to country newspapers, was available to the Germans for $900,000. The purpose of the German agents was to use the concern to fill American papers with propaganda designed to deflect the blame for starting the world war from Germany to England, to agitate for an embargo on the shipment of arms and munitions to the Allies as reprisal for the British blockade, to create anti-British sentiment and to keep America from going to war with Germany because of her submarine outrages. The deal did not go through, for a bigger possibility in the shape of a news service loomed in sight. The printing of propaganda matter for the German Information Service, however, was awarded the American Press Association. Mr. Courtland Smith, president and holder of the controlling majority of stock of the American Press Association, is a brother-in-law of Arthur Brisbane, and Dr. Albert Shaw is one of the directors of the concern. At least, despite the exposure of this proposition by the publication of the Dr. Albert papers in the *New York World* in 1915, Dr. Shaw, according to the 1918 Directory of Directors, did not resign.

The Class War Propaganda

Part II.

WHEN the great war broke out in August, 1914, the issues were immediately and distinctly clear to most right-thinking and intelligent people all over the globe. The neutrality of Belgium had been violated, France and Russia were assailed; imperial Germany, after forty years of preparation, had taken advantage of the Serajevo murder as a pretext to launch her long-nurtured onslaught for universal dominion. The Allied nations rose in self-defense to preserve their soil from invasion, to protect their women, to resist the yoke of a conscienceless oppressor. As one, they joined in a struggle to defend their sovereignty, their heritage of freedom, and to make democracy secure for the whole world. Germany's subsequent outrages but rendered past dispute what was foreseen when she first broke her solemn covenant by the invasion of Belgium. That struggle was bitter and at times seemed well-nigh hopeless and unending. England, France, Belgium, Italy and Serbia poured forth their blood. America, entering the war only after insolent and challenging attacks had been repeatedly made upon us, brought about the turning of the tide. Today German militarism is crushed; the haughty German autocracy is dethroned; the Teutonic dream of world empire has vanished as the smoke of battles.

Yet at this very hour there are still those among us who would turn this sorely-earned victory into defeat; who, in lieu of Teutonic world dominion, would shackle the free peoples with a tyrannous anarchic "internationalism," who, with the haughty German autocracy overthrown, would erect an autocracy of furious fanatics and bigoted zealots employing a life-and-death power derived from a cunning and artful demagogue play upon the passions and prejudices of the masses; who, with German militarism crushed, would plunge the nations into a reign of terror with mob-riot and mob-violence unleashed. These men speak in terms of social justice and reform—which is to be achieved through social chaos and disorder; they talk about making the future peace of the word secure—through revolution and red-handed wholesale murder. Their propaganda has now concentrated upon the so-called "war after the war," the class-struggle, in which the unskilled workingman will be at the throat of his employer, the illiterate roughling at the neck of every man educated in a profession, in which all the vicious, debauched and lawless elements of society will seek indiscriminately to destroy with knives, guns and bludgeons people of gentle breeding, of intellect and learning, of kindly culture. In America, as in every country on the face of the earth, they would precipitate what has happened in Russia.

THE SOPHISTRY OF THE SCRIBES

It is, of course, not surprising that these very hatchers of anarchy and revolution could not see those issues of the war which were vividly revealed to many of us in August, 1914; that they could not in any way hold Germany especially culpable; that in the sacrifice and agony of the Allied nations they could see only a squalid struggle for territories and revenge. Themselves knowing no country, no faith, no cause, they evaded taking any part, or making any sacrifice, in the great struggle. They were variously pacifists, conscientious objectors, and "internationalists." Preaching a class war to come after the war, they of course sought to evade service when the country in which they claim technical citizenship joined in the fight against Germany. Not only were they noticeably lacking in patriotism and devotion, but their work—at a time when it might have done so—was calculated directly to aid the cause of the world's supreme foe. Disloyalty they veiled in a maze of verbiage. Arguments and pleadings calculated to destroy national unity and morale, to dampen our enthusiasm in the war, to create doubts and suspicions of our Allies and to bring about a spirit of lenience, compromise and "magnanimity" toward Germany, were camouflaged in a high-flown intellectualism, a wordy sophomoric sophistry designed to impress the intellectually adolescent and amateur and professional "uplift" fraternity. This clique of sedition-mongers and scribes without a country did not harangue "in the market place"; they sought to reach college graduates, social workers, pacifist clergymen and fossilized college professors, not to speak of fledgling diplomats, academic and provincial government employees, advisers, etc., through ponderous, solemn and rhetorically involved writings in books and expensively printed magazines.

Germany has been beaten. Yet many who carried on Germany's work, consciously or unconsciously, paid or unpaid, are still actively at large. No direct service can be rendered the cause of the Huns; but service can be and is given the baleful cause which was inspired and promoted by imperial Germany in Russia. The little literary Lenines and Trotzkys are not without power and influence. Since the surrender of Germany they have become more insidiously active and brazenly outspoken than ever; they enjoy the ears of certain men in high places in Washington; some, indeed, have wormed their way into influential positions in the Government.

THE PROPAGANDA OF CIVIL WAR

Walter E. Weyl, as a writer, would not call for any particular consideration. He has never marked himself by any special brilliance or originality of thought, and as for his literary style—one might say he writes English like a German. His last book, however, "The End of the War," published by the Macmillan Company, is worth analysis because, through an involved subtlety and play upon stereotyped idealistic phrases, it expresses the whole philosophy, if such it could be called, of the *New Republic*, *Nation* and *Masses* school of thought. Between the covers you find embodied the whole propaganda of social ferment and revolution, Bolshevism, pro-German pacifism and "internationalism"—the identical propaganda imperial Germany itself fostered. The information has been volunteered that this book has influenced men in greater or less position in affairs of state, and various high-brow radicals have admitted it constitutes a sort of complete catechism in the program which aims at upsetting all existing social order. Dr. Weyl, who absorbed his ideas of political economy at the universities of Berlin and Halle, is an editor on the staff of the *New Republic* and spends much of his time holding forth in Washington.

Dr. Weyl's book was advertised on the paper jacket as "an appeal to America to assume leadership" in "the diplomacy that leads to peace," "to eliminate imperialistic elements from the demands of our Allies." The book is recommended by no less an authority than that distinguished exponent of true Americanism, Prof. Charles A. Beard, who in a book interpreted the birth of American independence as an attempt by George Washington and other Colonial plutocrats to enrich themselves. According to Prof. Beard: "Mr. Weyl draws swiftly under review . . . the plans of French, Russian, English and Italian imperialists for spoiling the enemy, Italy's ambitions, the war of new Russia against capitalistic imperialism, the faint hope of German liberalism, the inconclusiveness of a bitter-end peace, the sham of most of the 'guaranties' demanded by statesmen of the old school." Dr. Weyl is one of those best-unclassified self-pushers who have assiduously and slyly tried to propagate the idea that the great war was devoid of any ideals until they were injected by the entry of the United States. Yet, according to Prof. Beard, "he (Dr. Weyl) doubts not that mundane considerations have actuated America as well as Russia and Italy. Mr. Weyl wishes that President Wilson had imposed upon the Entente Allies certain democratic conditions as the price of America's cooperation. That, he is well aware, is crying over spilt milk. . . . Mr. Weyl begs us to listen to the voice of democratic moderation. To beat Germany to earth and then impose terms that will only lead to a new balance of power and renewed slaughter on a grander scale does not seem to him to be the task for which America has girded her loins."

In other words, here we find the doctrine that complete victory over Germany will somehow, in some way, at some future time lead to an even more frightful war than the war which German militarism produced.

UNCONSCIOUS BUFFOONERY

Dr. Weyl, as an exemplar of Christian meekness as well as other Christian virtues, must find himself in congenial company on the *New Republic*, which so modestly in full page advertisements—which must cost considerable money—announces itself as a semi-official interpreter of President Wilson's administration. Dr. Weyl, according to his own admission, wrote his book and "criticised certain actions of the Allied statesmen . . . in order to help bring a just international policy out of the present chaos of indecision." In this self-assumed and considerable role, Dr. Weyl says: "I am standing, I believe, 'behind the President.'" After examining Dr. Weyl's book one is impressed more than we should immediately have accepted, if not that exact formula, at least one that breathed the same spirit, and should have insisted upon its acceptance by the Allies.'' Did Dr. Weyl actually advocate that we connive at forcing our Allies into the same ghastly predicament that the Bolshevik envoys found themselves in at Brest Litovsk? Or was he intrigued by a naive predisposition to believe that the good bluff Germans were more to be trusted than the machiaevelian, insincere, grasping, cold-hearted men at the head of the Allied governments? America's chief trouble, apparently, was not with perfidious, treacherous Germany—not at all; our troubles lay in an alliance with nations that could not be trusted. ''We have been silenced by what we were assured was the superior wisdom and the older experience of European statecraft,'' says Dr. Weyl. ''In so doing we have involved ourselves in a grave and general error. We have forced ourselves to believe that we could fight for democracy and maintain the integrity of the Alliance despite secret arrangements violating the principles for which we fight. *We have believed that we could trust to selfishness, enlightened and unenlightened, to overcome the brutal militaristic spirit of Germany.*''

WAGGING THEIR HEADS AND SCOFFING

''We believed that we could trust to selfishness, enlightened and unenlightened!'' This is a conjuring phrase, an unwitting admission, a self-betrayal in words of idealism that is worth dwelling upon. Among all the nations which for four years valiantly ''carried on'' in that dire struggle, among the peoples who nobly labored with dry eyes and aching hearts to do their share, among the armies which braved the poison gases and fire of a fiendish foe, in all the tribulation, the bloody sweat, the agony and dying, the immortal sacrifice of fathers, mothers and sons, what was there?—*''Selfishness, enlightened and unenlightened.''* This bald, sneering, cynical characterization of all those who resisted autocratic Germany is an ignoble calumny of the men who lie buried in the blood-stained sacred soil of France and Belgium, of Italy and Serbia, a jibe at the very ideals cherished in the hearts of our own boys who went forth to take up that fight. The marvel is that, in this day, one wagging his head could dare thus to revile and scoff at the spirit of humanity sacrificing itself upon the Calvary of that long war. The Huns in their furious onslaught in Belgium destroyed churches and defiled the sacraments. There are men who would likewise desecrate and deny in scornful derision the divine gleamings in the human heart. These are men whose laughter is bitter, the foam of whose mouth is rabid, who approach their fellow men only with a sneer behind their smile. Cynics contemptuous of men, disbelieving in any noble human virtues, in lieu of human kindness their hearts are filled with gall. Their nostrils quiver with an eager scent for human meanness. Behind all unselfish endeavors and self-sacrifice for ideals, they seek only for mean and sordid personal—or national—motives. Incapable of national loyalty and devotion, like unnatural men incapable of love for father and mother, they are strangers in the human family—intellectual pariahs and scavengers battening upon hatred, suspicion, strife and discord. To consider a thinking creature of our species as summing up the epic heroism of France, the giving by England of a million men upon that altar, as ''selfishness, enlightened and unenlightened,'' is appalling. Yet it is valuable—as sometimes odious things are—in revealing a certain stripe of mind, in stripping bare the character of a breed of intellectual strangelings and spiritual aliens that have come up demanding a hearing, and seeking to deceive by subtlety, in our midst.

IS THIS BOLO-PASHAISM?

To pursue the self-revealment of the *New Republic* mind nursed and milked at Berlin and Halle: ''We have fought fire with fire and been burned in the process,'' Weyl goes on in words of a high-brow specious idealism: ''We have kept our own skirts clean and not considered whether those of our Allies were clean or filthy. We have believed that an alliance could be half-moral and half-immoral.''

Again and again, with gyrations and repetitions, Dr. Weyl evinces the twistings of a gnarled mind. He accuses America and the Allies—and not Lenine and Trotzky—of ''having handed over Russia to the Germans.'' And he continues with the familiar defeatist stuff that long ago was inflicted upon France. ''We have allowed the military supremacy to pass temporarily to the enemy. . . . We have created conditions where time no longer fights decisively in our favor and where the pressure of war begins to bear as heavily upon our associates as upon our enemies. We have robbed ourselves of the solace and unifying power of a great ideal, and have made it possible, both in the countries of our Allies and in those of our enemies, for the worst elements in the population to gain control.''

Dr. Weyl, like ''Dr.'' Walter Lippmann, his predecessor on the *New Republic*, was not at all optimistic about a complete military victory over Germany. In fact, did he consider such a victory desirable? Let Dr. Weyl answer: ''Today we are again exhorted to shut our eyes, to offer no negotiated peace and accept none, to make no distinction among Germans, all of whom are equally brutal and hypocritical, and not to think of peace until the enemy is prostrate, starved, shattered, beaten to a pulp. . . . We shall accomplish nothing even if after unparalleled sacrifices we gain the supreme military victory and our khaki-clad soldiers march in triumph down the silent *Unter den Linden*.''

It is seen that Dr. Weyl shared the unique and anxious concern of Mr. O. G. Villard, Dr. Albert Shaw and others regarding the terms which the wicked Allies, if victorious, might impose upon a beaten, prostrate Germany. ''If we and our Allies fight this war as we have fought it for almost four years, for Dalmatia, Constantinople and various Turkish islands, if we fight for a peace at which we at our own will and pleasure are to determine German and Austrian boundaries as Germany now determines those of Russia, the war is lost . . . then we have an ignoble peace, and the war for democracy is a failure and our high pretensions are a mockery.''

THE AGONY OF THE WAR A MERE "INCIDENT"

Despite Dr. Weyl's self-delegated and labored efforts to bring ''a just international policy out of the chaos of indecision,'' Germany accepted the terms of surrender unanimously agreed upon and offered by the Supreme War Council at Versailles, and the world enjoys free breathing. Nor is it likely that the final peace terms to be decided upon at the Peace Conference will be in any degree influenced by Dr. Weyl's busy friend and literary associate, Walter Lippmann, who, despite ''defeatist'' statements in the *New Republic* that might well be investigated by the Department of Justice, managed to crawl into the Government employ and get sent abroad on a diplomatic mission.

However, whatever terms of peace are agreed upon, Dr. Weyl optimistically and with almost unconcealed malignance and glee predicts that harmony and concord among peoples will not be for long.

''The present war is but an incident, disastrous and ghastly, in a larger development, in a struggle between two principles: the principle, of autocracy, militarism and nationalistic imperialism, and the principle of democracy.''

The war against Germany, then, was not in itself a war for democracy, as against autocracy, militarism and nationalistic imperialism; in the victory over Germany, therefore, there has been no complete and adequate victory over the forces opposed to democracy. This terrible, unprecedented war, which counts its dead at more than ten millions, is but an "incident." Inevitably the suggestion arises that if Bolshevism did sweep the world, that if the crew of malcontents and sedition mongers could carry out their program, the world would experience a bloody reign of terror compared to which, in truth, the slaughter in Europe would be a trivial affair. Dr. Weyl frankly wants this other war, the world war of class against class, to go on. The bloodthirsty revengeful program is veiled in the verbiage of humanitarianism and idealism. Weyl plays upon the appealing if cant phrase about the "poor and disinherited." He pleaded for a compromise peace with Germany, yet in this world war, this precipitation of internal strife and social chaos in every nation, he would not leave a stone upon a stone. He would have desolation upon desolation compass the world. It seems this fellow gloats upon the prospect. "The moment the war ends the struggle will change its form, though not its character. . . . Not only the autocracy of Germany, but the English, French and Italian rulers as well, have revealed crassly egoistic class motives concealed under pious phrases. The wage earners of the world and the hundreds of millions who make up the poor and disinherited will have long years in which to reflect upon the lessons of this conflict. . . . They will see the war beneath the war, and will realize that whatever the immediate issue, the victory is to the group in the community that is most conscious of its interests and most insistent upon its rights. . . . There will remain after the war the same clash within the nations as before."

AMERICAN BOYS SENT TO ENGAGE IN "A SENSELESS SLAUGHTER"

The war which has ended with the surrender of Germany is fruitless, and worse than fruitless, farcial. It is now easy to understand why so many intellectual pacifists, "conscientious objectors," possessing this point of view, could see no reason why they should risk their precious carcasses in a purely "incidental" affair. Among the peculiar stripe who read, and subscribe to the views of, the *New Republic* and the *Liberator* were many who failed to enlist, "slackers," evaders of the draft—little young men who preferred to write or to talk instead of taking a manly part in the great struggle. Some, like Roger Baldwin, were sentenced to prison for evading service in the army. Like Dr. Walter Weyl, many of these molly-coddle "world-reformers" found it more to their taste to impugn the ideals and purposes of those who were fighting and dying than to engage in any useful work. To the virile men who did enter military service, who did take up their obligations, Dr. Weyl, like the others, had merely the message to give that the war opened "up the vista of an endless prolongation of a senseless slaughter . . . the persistent hope of a victory that is always to be and never is." *A senseless slaughter! A victory that will never be!* Didn't Germany endeavor to tell the brave soldiers of France, through her sinister agents, that theirs was the "hope of a victory that is always to be and never is?" "To the common run of unmartial people," Weyl goes on, "the war has become odious." The run of "unmartial" people to whom the war, so long as it had to be fought, was odious is, I venture to say, severely limited—and among men of fibre and light, of courage and ideals, these would not be in congenial company. Was the struggle which America entered, and in which American boys went forth to fight and to suffer and die, in any sense or aspect for a noble cause, for high ideals? The associate editor of the *New Republic* says: "It is no 'merry war,' but a desperate, unhonorable conflict, a war of money, deceit, bribery, murder and ruthlessness both against neutrals and enemies." That, mark you, is the interpretation given by Weyl of what they engaged in with such high hopes and self-surrender to the American boys who are coming home maimed and wounded. That is the interpretation to fathers and mothers of the cause for which their sons made the greatest sacrifice, in the giving of their lives. That is the summing up of the mortal struggle and agony of many nations, by a man who would render the whole struggle futile by promoting "the class war after the war"—ergo, international Bolshevism.

"DANGERS OF AN ALLIED VICTORY"

In the "Postcript" to his book, Weyl condemned the Allies' "policy of fighting imperialism with imperialism" and accused them of forcing the war to continue when "in Germany itself a democratic movement was in full swing." On page 23 Weyl describes a group to which he had presumably qualified himself for admission: "Many idealists among the Allies expected that in a few months—in a year at most—they would overturn the Imperial German Government and confer upon the unhated German people the blessings which they themselves enjoyed. Better still, the Germans, perceiving the abyss toward which their dynasts were leading them, would themselves revolt." Dr. Weyl then makes an illuminating and startling admission: "None of all this has happened; on the contrary the Germans have made common cause with their rulers, and believe quite sincerely, that they, and they alone, are fighting for the right." Did Dr. Weyl enjoy this realization when he rose in his might and railed at the Allies for their wicked intentions toward the enemy which had "made common cause with their rulers?" Dr. Weyl plunges into a jeremiad:

"We have tried to hammer the enemy into a confession of sin and into a state of grace, not realizing that for this purpose machine guns and asphyxiating gas are no adequate instruments. Though we cannot win this war without arms, we cannot win it by arms alone."

While in one breath he admits "the Germans have made common cause with their rulers," Weyl in the next paradoxically declares: "In Germany many millions now perceive that they were enrolled in this conflict by a conscription of lies and that the real objects of their exalted rulers were different from those avowed." But Dr. Weyl hastens to add: "Similarly, though in a lesser degree, the Allied peoples are beginning to dread too complete a victory. . . . Divide all conquered territories according to the clashing desires of the flushed Allies and you have a state of Europe and the world of the world, no better than that from which men sought to escape in the insane venture of 1914."

Dr. Walter E. Weyl, student of political economy at the universities of Berlin and Halle and associate editor of the *New Republic*, must today be in an exceedingly depressed state of mind. Is his advocacy of the "war-after-the-war," of the class-struggle, of universal Bolshevism, urged as an escape from the distasteful and irksome conditions which American and Allied victory over Germany means?

AMERICA'S IDEALS—SORDID GAIN?

"It is a discouraging outlook," says Weyl, "a vista of ever new dangers, a dread that the world will escape from the consuming fire of this war only to fall into hotter conflagrations." (Certainly this is a prospect of what Weyl and his half-baked crew are doing their utmost to plunge us into.) "A real victory, a victory of peace, eludes us," he says. "And when we enquire why it eludes us we see that we, the Allied nations, carry into the conflict something of that evil principle against which we fight." The most patent, transparent and consequently futile phase of the official Teuton propaganda instituted by Dernburg was that which sought to besmirch the Allies, especially England, with their own Teutonic tar. Weyl, talking from the he said, with a machiavellian sneer, "Will these gentlemen and noblemen be guided by the unique desire to 'make the world safe for democracy?' . . . Will there be friction and cross lines of interests between allies and a furious scrambling for spoils?"

The peace conference, judging by Weyl's analysis, will be made up of diplomatic bandits, international second-story men, experts in the game of stratagems and spoils. The methods calculated to create distrust of the representatives of the Allied powers have been rendered familiar to the general public through the recent page advertisements of the *New Republic* in the daily press.

What purpose has there been in the sedulous and insidious attempt to create in the American public mind doubt of our Allies, of their war aims, to impose upon the American public the conviction that Mr. Wilson, in going to Europe, has gone to combat the sinister plots and intrigues of international pickpockets, liars and knaves?

Perhaps Dr. Weyl himself gives a reason in the extraordinary and illuminating suggestion:

"If at the Peace Congress Germany could detach Italy, France, or any other powerful opponent, she might, by a threat to throw over the whole proceedings and return to a war status, force great concessions from all her former antagonists. She could play off one against the other."

GERMANY'S SOLE CHANCE

As stated in my previous article, Germany's one hope of obtaining a fairly satisfactory peace lay in estranging the United States from the Allies, in destroying full cooperation, confidence and international morale. She tried to do that in France so far as France and England were concerned, in the early days of the war. It was with this purpose she gave nearly two million dollars to Bolo Pasha, whose proposed propaganda strikingly parallels the defeatist propaganda carried on in the United States by sundry Bolshevik intellectuals. Any attempt to sow seeds of distrust regarding our Allies was in its essence, whether intentional or not, part of the German game. Were these little people and pretentious weekly periodicals merely unwitting instruments in the great Teuton intrigue? Or did they simply function, as their instincts and nature impelled them, toward an end in which their amorphous and dubious sympathies lay?

There is no danger of such division among the Allies as might play into some secret, cunning German game. The efforts to alienate the people of America from the cause for which England, France and Belgium fought and bled have been fruitless. But efforts to negative the great victory achieved through unprecedented sacrifice continue.

"The final war . . . will begin after the war," concludes Herr Weyl. "It will be a wider conflict than that which now rages and the alignment will be by classes and interests rather than by nations. It will be a war which will be waged until separate interests within each nation are completely extinguished." Thus the 100,000-word volume ends, with a gloatingly triumphant blood-thirsty prediction of mob chaos, civil war, wholesale class murder. It is not inapropos in this connection, to recall that the whole program of "separation movements and civil war" throughout the world originated in Berlin; that as Marxian Socialism, which would make man fight and work for his belly instead of his soul, was born in Germany, so was the Bolshevist plot conceived and promoted, to the ruin of Russia, in the land of the Huns.

In a circular letter, dated February 23, 1915, sent by the Director of the Press at the Ministry of Foreign Affairs in Berlin, all German ambassadors were instructed: *"The propaganda will have for its object the inception of social movements, accompanied by strikes, revolutionary explosions, separation movements and civil war, as well as an agitation in favor of disarmament."* That program went through in Russia.

The great question now up to the American people is to what extent we shall allow the reptile brood hatched out in Germany, when German imperialism was at the apex of its power, to continue to spawn and drool their venom in our midst.

(To be Continued)

Industrial Reconstruction

(Continued from page 5)

lished whereby employers and employees may adjust in a friendly way those differences of opinion which are bound to exist."

In response to a question as to the percentage of cases of joint submission and those placed before the War Labor Board ex parte, Mr. Woll said:

"I think the greater number of applications have been on the part of the employees, and the reason for that is that whenever unrest existed, the Department of Labor immediately would send its investigators and conciliators into those localities to avoid industrial disturbance and friction. In almost every instance the appeal of the Department of Labor was heeded and the men and women refrained from using their right to strike, in order that production might continue, and feeling that justice would be done them through that impartial Board. I should say the greater percentage was on the part of strong organizations of labor. Had they exercised their right to strike, there is no question but that they would have been successful. So that it was a real, true, loyal, patriotism that induced them to submit their questions to the War Labor Board. The same is true with some of the employers. There were instances where employers, as you might say, had the upper hand and who, rather than use the upper hand on the employees, submitted their controversies to this impartial Board for adjustment."

President Macy emphasized the points brought out by Mr. Woll by stating that as to the cases referred to the War Labor Board and their decisions—it was all a voluntary matter; and that it was so in regard to all the war labor adjustment boards in Washington. They were all established by agreement. There was no legislation enacted creating any of them. They were established through agreements between the American Federation of Labor and different departments, or between organizations of the employers and the American Federation of Labor. Their representatives were appointed by each side. But there was no statutory compulsion and notwithstanding the fact that it was a free cooperative movement, he said the violations of the agreements on either side could be counted on one hand, and they were of short duration. When pressure was brought to bear on them, when they were brought fully to realize that their action was a violation of any agreement, they rescinded it and abided by the agreement in all cases. "So," he said, "we have a hopeful outlook for the future. I believe that where large numbers are involved in our industrial life, if they can voluntarily and logically settle their difficulties without any statutory measures, we can look to the future with great confidence; with that same spirit of cooperation in peace that has been pursued in war, the same results should follow."

Bolshevik Industrial Government.

Continued from page 9)

factory at night, and voted themselves pay for this 'overtime.' After the Germans took Rostoff, Koopp's factory was returned to him.

"This is a typical instance of what has happened everywhere in Russia under Bolshevik power. Many of the technical staff of the factories were killed on the charge of their being 'bourgeoisie.' Many other administrators, experts, foremen and others fled. Still others of the technical staff who escaped death were ordered to go to the factories, and if they refused were shot on the spot. Hundreds upon hundreds, yes, thousands have been shot without trial. Naturally, in these conditions, the machinery spoiled and grew worse, and everywhere, except where the Germans have come in, factories have had to stop. Nearly all of the factories are discontinued.

"To the outside world the decrees issued by Lenine and Trotzky may seem to represent something. They don't. The workmen don't recognize Lenine and Trotzky unless they want to. They are not sure of Lenine and Trotzky. They recognize only their Soviet, and if they don't like it they set up another. It is armed anarchy.

"There is less freedom of speech than under the Czar. Only Bolshevik papers are allowed. There is no freedom of assemblage whatever. Merely suspicion brings death at once."

THE "COMMITTEE SYSTEM" IN OPERATION.

Of the results of Bolshevik control in the large industrial plants in Petrograd and Moscow, Lieutenant Boris Brasol, of the Russian Army, and now connected with the U. S. War Trade Board at New York City, gave me these facts:

"The Oboukhovsky Steel Works near Petrograd were owned by the Russian Government, and run by the Navy Department. This plant manufactured guns, armor and munitions, and covered about 500 acres. Before the war it employed 7,000 men. After the war started, the number increased to 12,000, and later to 15,000 and 16,000. During 1914-16 the average mechanic's wages were from 700 to 800 rubles a month for an 8 to 8½ hour day. With few exceptions the members of the technical staff were paid lower salaries than the average mechanic's wages. And as for professional pay in general compared with that of manual labor, it was only about 500 rubles a month. Professors in colleges never received more than this amount.

"After the Revolution headed by Kerensky broke out, in April, 1917, the scheme of Workmen's Committees or Councils of Workmen's Delegates was started on the initiative of a member of the Kerensky Government. This personage was not a Bolshevik—in fact is now an exile from Russia—but in this respect he allowed himself to be influenced by Bolshevik doctrines which were being agitated forcibly.

"WORKMEN'S DELEGATES."

"In the Oboukhovsky Steel plant each of about 20 shops elected their own delegates. There was no system at all about it. Representation was not based upon the number of men in each shop. A small shop would have a larger representation than a large shop, and elections were disorderly. Only in exceptional cases were actual workingmen elected. The workmen in the shops elected (for the most part) outside professionals who had a command of oratory and who flattered them. These Bolshevik shop committees are totally unlike the regular British trade unions or the Belgian co-operatives. They are anarchistic.

"The whole group of works elected about 75 delegates, most of whom were outside agitators. About three-fourths of the entire working force in this particular plant knew how to read and write, but only the merest rudiments. So far as real education is concerned, about 95 per cent in this plant as in other plants were uneducated. They were able only to read a few pamphlets, written in crude style, calling upon them to rob the bourgeoisie.

"The first stand taken by the 75 delegates of the Oboukhovsky Steel plant was that the worst enemies of labor was the technical staff. 'Agitators made speeches like this: 'You laborers are working eight and nine hours a day. These fat men of the technical staff are working only three or four hours. But it is the manual labor that turns out the product. The technical staff are ruling you. They belong to the bourgeoisie. Look at their wives! See how well dressed they are! Manual labor must control the technical staff.'

"The immediate result was that when the technical staff gave instructions as to how to produce the best steel or pointed out how some other improvement could be made, the workmen replied that they would hold a meeting and decide as to whether the instructions as to the method of work were right. If the technical engineer pointed out that by holding meetings in work hours the workmen were delaying output, they would exclaim, 'Look how he is agitating against us' At once work would be abandoned and a noisy meeting begun. After a long discussion the meeting would decide that the orders given by the technical staff didn't agree with the interests of the workers and should be refused. The same thing happened in every shop.

INCESSANT MEETINGS—TALK, NOT WORK.

"In the Oboukhovsky Steel Plant the laborers voted to reduce their work hours usually to three and four, and in some cases to six. Every day they held meetings. Some of these were from 20 to 25 minutes, others two to three hours. For this time they insisted upon being paid.

"Frequently, during working hours, some one would suddenly rush in and announce: 'Comrades, a very important procession is going on in Nevsky Prospekt. Let us join.' The men didn't know what it was all about. But, dropping tools, they would form in processions, carrying banners, flags and armed with rifles on the six mile walk to the city. They called these 'Liberty Strikes.' They were paid for them, too. Nobody dared question it.

"Within four months the workers in the Oboukhovsky plant alone had received, under different titles, from the Navy Department an increase in their pay of 90,000,000 rubles. During these same four months their efficiency was, at a very conservative estimate, cut down 80 per cent. Their endless discussions, meetings and processions were partly one cause. Drunkenness was another, for notwithstanding the prohibition of vodka, that fiery liquor is being privately manufactured, and is all the more effective because of the scarcity of food. And, of course, by refusing to follow the instructions of the technical staff the machinery fast went to pieces.

SLAUGHTER OF INDUSTRIAL EXPERTS.

"Since November, 1917, a large number of the technical staffs of all factories have been imprisoned or murdered. Others fled. Thousands upon thousands were put in prison or slain. On the one day that the Bolsheviki had possession of Kieff the Bolsheviki murdered 3,500 'intellectuals,' many of whom were members of industrial technical staffs. In December, 1917, all operations at the Oboukhovsky Steel Works were discontinued. But the Bolshevik Government still kept paying the workmen's wages, and it has supplied them with foodstuffs. The men refused to work on the ground that the war was a 'capitalist quarrel.' Other causes of the shut down were impairment or destruction of machinery. It has been not merely usual but an everyday incident for workmen to carry away products, tools or parts of machinery and sell them for their own profit. Still other causes of the shut down have been lack of fuel and raw material. The same conditions spread everywhere. Miners

"Many of the chief Bolshevik propagandists were bums. One of these bums—an average skilled laborer—was employed in my factory. Addressing some people coming out of a church in a village near Moscow, he denounced them for going to church services and said, 'Don't you know that when the Czar was overthrown, God was abolished too?'

"The Bolsheviki have killed a large number of the technical staffs in industrial centers. These included a great many of the more intelligent, experienced technical engineers, foremen and administrators. Others of the technical staffs have fled. However plausibly the decrees of Lenine and Trotzky may read, the Central Soviet led by them has practically no authority outside of Petrograd and Moscow. Lenine is credited with having some months ago declared in favor of employing technical staffs and paying them higher wages than manual workers. Such a decree means nothing. It is only a paper decree. What is actually happening may be judged from a recent report from Petrograd that at the Poutiloff Works,—a locomotive, car and artillery plant,—100 members of the technical staff were killed in one batch.

"The so-called Bolshevik rule is really a mutiny of slaves and criminals. In the very act of slaughtering what they call the bourgeoisie they themselves are becoming a new bourgeoisie. Many of them have enriched themselves. There was a report that the notorious Commissioner of the Interior, Moses Uritsky, who on August 30, 1918, was assassinated by a Socialist, had salted away 4,000,000 rubles. Paper money is so common that every laborer has plenty.

"The chaos of conditions in Bolshevik Russia is such that we haven't been able to get any advices from our Russian representatives since February, 1918. What has become of the Russian Singer Company's plant since then we don't know."

RUTHLESSLY SHOOTING WORKINGMEN.

"The Bolsheviki," declared Colonel Vladimir I. Lebedov, "are shooting down the workingmen far more ruthlessly than under the old regime. They have been shooting them by the thousands in frequent massacres."

Colonel Lebedov was an officer in the Russo-Japanese war. The oppressions of the Czar's regime made him a revolutionist. He joined the Socialist Revolutionary party and the Union of Revolutionary Officers. In 1907 he led a revolution in the Sebastopol Army. He was forced to flee, living in subsequent years in Belgium, France and Italy. When the war broke out in 1914 he formed a detachment of Russian Socialist refugees and joined the French Army as a private in the Foreign Legion. He was wounded several times, and was named lieutenant and decorated. Returning to Russia after the Revolution, he was Secretary of the Navy under Lvov and Kerensky, but left the Kerensky Cabinet because of failure to take strong measures against the Bolsheviki. He now holds the office of Associate of the Secretary of War of the Russian Omsk Government in behalf of which he visited the United States recently. In New York City, on December 2, 1918, he gave many details of the Bolshevik regime.

"In normal times," he said, "there were about 400,000 workingmen in Petrograd. Early in the war there was a great influx of peasants who went to Petrograd to work. After the Bolsheviki seized power, hundreds of thousands of workers, mostly unskilled, left Petrograd for the country districts. By May, 1918, there were only 132,000 workingmen left in Petrograd, but these were the best kind of skilled labor. They had always lived in Petrograd and had nowhere else to go.

"In May, 1918, they began to revolt against the Bolsheviki. They held several enormous mass meetings which, because of the great numbers present,—more than 100,000 in all—the Bolsheviki were afraid to molest. They elected representatives and drew up resolutions denouncing the Brest-Litovsk treaty as a shameful peace which they didn't recognize, and declaring that instead of peace the Bolsheviki brought internal wars and instead of bread they brought famine. The resolutions further asserted that instead of liberty the Bolsheviki had established a reaction to such an extent as never had existed in Russia. The workmen demanded the resignation of the Bolshevik Government, and the election of a Constituent Assembly. They sent delegates secretly to all Russian cities. In Moscow the workingmen adopted similar resolutions. Here, too, the Bolsheviki were afraid to take action. But in the provincial cities, where the meetings were smaller, the Bolsheviki imprisoned or shot thousands of workingmen in cold blood.

"As for the delegates elected by the workingmen of Petrograd and other cities to the Soviets, the Bolshevik Government would not allow them in those bodies. The Bolsheviki would not permit any Socialist, trade-unionist or laborite in the Soviets. They ordered the Red Guard to shoot them, and this was always done."

AN ARMY OF MERCENARIES.

"What is the Red Guard composed of?" I asked.

"Mostly," Colonel Lebedov replied, "of Hungarians. There is also a conglomeration of Germans, Letts, Chinese, and a few Russians consisting of hooligans and criminals. The Red Army now numbers about 250,000, and is held together by the pay per man of 1,000 rubles a month, plenty of clothing and food, and full license to plunder and commit rape. It is absolutely a mercenary army, and does whatever it is directed.

"All through the summer of 1918 revolts continued. There were several Cossack revolts, and many revolts of industrial workers. For example, at the Izjorsky Metal Works near the City of Perm, a plant employing 40,000 workingmen, a revolt of the workers broke out in July, 1918. For three months the workingmen there fought the Bolsheviki. By October, 1918, the revolts throughout Russia had assumed such proportions that Lenine's position became increasingly difficult as the People's Army became strong in numbers.

"Thereupon Lenine resorted to a trick. In the latter part of September he announced that he had declared war on Germany. He called 15,000 officers to Petrograd and Moscow, and other batches of officers to other cities, and they joyfully responded believing that Russia would again war on Germany. Once the officers had got to the cities he had them all arrested and held as hostages. Many were shot. This was intended to intimidate revolters and deprive the People's Army of officers.

SECRET PACT WITH KAISER REVEALED.

"Then in October, 1918, Lenine made a secret treaty with Germany by which in return for the removal of Bolshevik forces from the German front, the Kaiser ordered all German prisoners to join the Bolshevik Red Army. It was this order that increased the Red Guard from 150,000 to 250,000. With this accession of strength the Red Guard was able to suppress the various revolts, especially as the Allies failed to keep their promise to supply the People's Army with guns, ammunition and other vital supplies. In the suppression of these revolts thousands upon thousands of workingmen were shot down.

"Counting lives lost by massacre, hunger and disease, Russia has lost more lives under the Bolshevik regime than were lost during the time she was in the war."

(To be continued)

Woman's Departmen

NATIONAL CONFERENCE PLANS

A series of weekly conferences, to deal with problems arising during the period of reconstruction, has been announced by the Woman's Department of the National Civic Federation. Miss Maude Wetmore, the National Chairman, in outlining the scope of this new endeavor, stated that:

"At no time in the world's history has it been more essential that women of the Nation should be prepared to understand and take an intelligent part in the discussion and solving of the problems on which the future well-being of our country depends. The signing of the Armistice and the calling of the Peace Conference have suddenly brought to the consciousness of the American people the knowledge that we are, to a very great extent, ignorant regarding the questions fundamental at this critical time. These conferences will be addressed by men and women who are expert and in active touch with movements allied to the topics selected for consideration which have been recommended to all Sections of the Woman's Department and which are given below:

1. PUBLIC EMPLOYMENT SERVICE:
   Plans and Methods; Community Labor Boards; Public Exchanges. How does the service function in your Section?

2. HOUSING:
   Governmental; Private owned. What has been accomplished in your Section? What are the needs?

3. FOOD PRODUCTION AND CONSERVATION:
   What is the demand, and what agencies are meeting the necessity, including concrete demonstrations in conservation?

4. RESPONSIBILITIES OF CITIZENSHIP:
   Alien Group; Citizen Group; Propaganda. Including Information Centres, Community Experiments and Literature. Where may the force of the Woman's Department be expended with the greatest usefulness?

5. PUBLIC HEALTH:
   Federal and Local Laws and Agencies. Wherein do they fail to meet the situation, as for instance, venereal disease, child welfare, etc.

6. PRISON REFORM:
   The situation and the needs.

7. SHOP AND FACTORY WELFARE:
   Developments and necessities. To what extent is welfare work inaugurated in your Section?

8. LEGISLATION:
   Intelligent survey of pending legislation dealing with matters relating to social and economic reconstruction.

VACATION ASSOCIATION, INC.

The purposes and some of the achievements of the Vacation Association, an incorporated committee of the Woman's Department of The National Civic Federation, were set forth in a glowing tribute by Louis K. Anspacher at a luncheon on December 4, at the McAlpin Hotel, New York. The President of the Association, Miss Gertrude Robinson Smith presided.

The following quotations from the address of Mr. Anspacher, who watched the development of the movement from its inception, indicate the usefulness of its activities. In the course of his remarks he said:

"The creed of the Vacation Association states: 'We believe that no one group in a community is self-sufficient'—in other words, we realize that we are our brothers' keepers. 'We believe that true Democracy rests on a mutual sympathy and a mutual understanding between different environments; we believe above all that joy and happiness can be the greatest constructive force in the world.' This last needs no interpretative comment. It is American, pragmatic, optimistic, and it has demonstrated its success. It was organized in 1910.

"Its purpose was to investigate country boarding houses where self-supporting women and girls could safely go for their holiday. During the first year approximately 1000 boarding houses within 75 mile radius of New York were investigated and only 300 met the requirements.

"Many girls used this list and found it very helpful. On the other hand, it was found that great numbers of girls had no vacation. A meeting was therefore called in November, 1911, to ascertain the cause for this. Several reasons were given. First that the girls received no paid vacations; secondly, that if girls took a vacation at their own expense they often lost their positions; and third, that the girls had no money with which to pay for their vacations.

"A survey was made among 3000 employers The astonishing fact developed that the large majority of employers gave no paid vacations, though many of them, especially in the seasonal trades, were willing that their employees should take several weeks holiday at their own expense. Among the girls it was found out that many contributed to the family budget and that often when they received a paid vacation they were unable to go away because of this family obligation. A savings fund by which any self-supporting woman or girl could lay aside each week the small amounts that ordinarily go for the unnecessary things of life was organized. Many employers became interested, and gave it their hearty approval, and further in all concerns where the Vacation Savings Fund was established, they appointed one of their representative women to act as Local Secretary.

"In 1912 it developed that a very unfortunate habit existed of collective giving at Christmas among the employees of all large concerns. Also the custom of giving exchange presents among the employees. After carefully investigating this question, a meeting was held and the movement known as the SPUGS was launched.

"Three years after the work was inaugurated, three buildings were rented; two were turned into lodging houses where the members could have at the nominal rate of $5.00 a week, and a restaurant was opened where approximately 500 girls ate each day. Besides these two activities, there were clubrooms especially arranged for the members and classes in languages, dancing, gymnastic, dramatics, etc., were arranged at a nominal cost. All depositors who wished to take advantage of the opportunities offered them at the Vacation Headquarters paid $1.00 a year for these privileges and became taxpayers. After the first year it was decided to organize the Taxpayers Committee and to make it self-governing.

"In 1915 the Penny Provident Fund felt that we were filling the need that they had heretofore filled and asked us to absorb them. This we gladly did as far as the girls were concerned but we were unable to take care of their boys.

"In 1914 when the war broke out the Vacation Committee organized the Vacation War Relief Committee for the purpose of helping its members, who had lost their positions because of war conditions, to get other jobs. It also opened

The National
Civic Federation Review

Vol. IV. NEW YORK, JANUARY 10, 1919 No. 7

CAN ALL WARS BE PREVENTED?

PROBLEMS ENTERING INTO THE FORMATION OF A LEAGUE OF NATIONS—QUESTIONS FOR THE SERIOUS CONSIDERATION OF THE AMERICAN PEOPLE

ONE of the great questions to be dealt with at the Peace Conference and, on account of the stress laid upon it by President Wilson, the greatest question for this country to consider, is what manner of machinery can be provided to reduce to a minimum the possibility of future wars. The National Civic Federation Review opens with this number a discussion of various programs that have been proposed, beginning with that of the League to Enforce Peace. Its proposals being definite and concrete, it has naturally invited criticism from many writers and speakers, the gist of which is well contained in a speech made by former Senator Albert J. Beveridge last Memorial Day, at Indianapolis, and in a speech by Senator Henry Cabot Lodge in the United States Senate, December 21, 1918.

Dr. Talcott Williams, a member of the Executive Committee of the League to Enforce Peace and one of the sub-committee of five that has had much to do with changes from time to time in the program of the League, was invited to reply to those speeches and to give specific answers to the criticisms made.

EDITOR.

NATIONALISM VS. THE LEAGUE

(Extract from Memorial Day Address to the Veterans of the Grand Army of the Republic, May, 1918)

By HON. A. J. BEVERIDGE

AMERICANS are firmly and unbreakably united for this war upon the solid ground that we went into it because we were attacked. Upon that there is absolute and universal agreement. Some go further; but all go that far. While the war lasts the discussion of all war purposes that will divide us ought to have been avoided. But instead of this an old project, not of American origin, has been and is being urged upon us with all the power and persistence of a highly organized propaganda, although with the highest and most patriotic of motives. Its leading advocates actually state that the establishment of an international league to enforce peace is one of the principal objects for which the American nation is sending into the hell of conflict our conscripted youth and burdening the people with a debt that a century of toil and sacrifice will be required to pay.

SHALL WE ABROGATE THE CONSTITUTION?

If that is so, then Congress stated inadequately, if not untruly, the reason for America's martial declaration; and conscription was adopted by Congress and accepted by the people under a misapprehension.

Since, in the very midst of war, advocates of the League to Enforce Peace press their scheme upon the country, even asserting that the adoption of it is one great purpose for which we are fighting, we are forced to examine it. France has aroused the imperishable admiration of the world, not only by her heroism but also and equally by her intelligence; and it is important for us to note that France has not welcomed with fervent enthusiasm the plan of the League to Enforce Peace and its denationalizing doctrines. If we are to accept them, let us at least do so with our eyes open to the certain results. Two or three obvious consequences of this ancient and foreign proposition will be enough perhaps to put the American people on inquiry as to the wisdom or folly of the whole plan.

To become a member of the league we shall have to destroy one of the most vital parts of the American Constitution—that which gives to Congress the sole power to declare war. This is admitted; and an amendment changing the nation's fundamental law was actually introduced in the Senate. Thus, the mighty question of going to war would be permanently taken further from the people—indeed, neither the people nor their representatives would have the least thing to say about going to war or keeping out of war. If the league should fail to impose its will on the world, we as a member of it would be bound, for all the future, to take part in any war wherever waged, that the majority of the league decided upon.

COMPLICATIONS OF LEAGUE PRINCIPLES

As to small and weak nations, we, as a member of the league, would have had to go to war with various powers several times during the last fifty years—either this or the league would have had to sanction historic aggressions in Asia, Africa and Europe, or the nations making them would have had to keep hands off the little countries absorbed, something which every student knows none of those great powers would have done.

In our own history we would have been forcibly prevented from waging war with Mexico, and California, Arizona, New Mexico, Utah, Nevada and half of Colorado would have been kept under the Mexican flag and would not today be the vital part of the American nation that they now are.

A league to enforce peace would have forcibly restrained us from making war with Spain; and Porto Rico, now ours, and Cuba, over which we have the most absolute suzerainty ever written on paper in the history of the world, would this moment still be Spanish. Yet they command the gateway to the gulf, are indispensable to our safety, belong to us geographically, and the possession of them has been our historic purpose and aspiration since long before the revolution.

FOREIGN NATIONS WOULD DECIDE AMERICAN QUESTIONS

Apply the plan to our present and future purely American questions; these would be decided, not by the American people, but by the votes of foreign nations. Take, for instance, the problem of Mexico. It is adjacent to us and the control of it profoundly concerns the Gulf, our canal, the near Pacific and 2,000 miles of our southern boundary. Legitimate American interests are and always will be greater in Mexico than those of all other nations combined. For years Mexico has been in a state of anarchy; American men and women have been killed and outraged, American property destroyed, the American flag literally trampled in the dust; and the dispatches advise us that the situation again grows alarming.

Yet, as a member of the League to Enforce Peace, the American nation would have no more to say about Mexico than would Holland or Servia, Siam or Germany, Italy or Roumania, Great Britain or Uruguay, Peru or Costa Rica, the Argentine or Bulgaria or Japan. American interests, rights and honor, as affected in Mexico, would be at the mercy of a majority vote of every nation, little and big, near and remote, friendly and hostile, that is a member of the league.

Or take the Monroe Doctrine. Under the regime of the League to Enforce Peace every European and Asiatic government would have as much authority over that fundamental American policy as would the American nation itself.

The control of our canal, built through our territory, by our money and essential to our well-being and safety, would be taken even more completely out of our hands than it already has been. Every question that affects other nations, especially our tariff and immigration laws, would be subject to possible interference by this international super-state, which the propagandists of the League to Enforce Peace proposes to erect for the regulation of the world. Indeed, certain foreign advocates of this international scheme advance universal free trade as one of the necessary results of it.

WOULD DESTROY AMERICAN NATIONAL INDEPENDENCE

Not only would we be involved in every European, African, South American and Asiatic embroilment, bound to expend unestimated amounts of American money and numbers of American lives if necessary to enforce the ukases of the league, but it should be repeated again and again that we would have to surrender American problems, the solution of which vitally affect our economic and political life, to the mercy of those European, South American and Asiatic nations. Unless human nature has been repealed, what, under such an arrangement, would become of the interests, rights and honor of the American people, the richest, most fortunately situated and therefore the most envied nation on the globe?

It all comes to this:

If the League would prevent foreign wars, still it would take out of our hands the settlement of vital American questions and put the disposition of them in the hands of foreign nations. If the League would not prevent foreign war, then, as a member of it, we would be bound to take part in those wars; and also our purely American problems would be dealt with by other governments than our own. In either case America is sure to be the loser, however much certain foreign interests might be the gainer by our loss.

DIFFICULTIES OF ADJUSTMENTS

(From Address to the Senate, Dec. 21, 1918)

By HON. HENRY CABOT LODGE

The words "the league of nations" are captivating and attractive. Everybody would like to bring about a world condition in which wars would be impossible. But we ought to be extremely careful that in our efforts to reach the millennium of universal and eternal peace we do not create a system which will breed dissensions and wars. It is difficult to discuss it at this time because no definite plan of any kind has yet been put forward by any responsible person. Intelligent discussion becomes difficult when the advocates of the league of nations drape themselves in trailing clouds of glory and omit to tell us the conditions to which they propose to bind the nations.

If, however, there is to be a League of Nations in order to enforce peace, one thing is clear. It must be either a mere assemblage of words, an exposition of vague ideals and encouraging hopes, or it must be a practical system. If such a league is to be practical and effective, it cannot possibly be either unless it has authority to issue decrees and force to sustain them.

What nations are to be members of the league? Is Germany to be one of the members? If so, when? How are these nations thus joined in a league to vote in determining the operations of the league? Theoretically, in international law every independent sovereign nation is the equal of any other nation. Are the small nations to have an equal vote with the great nations in the league, a vote equal to that of the United States or England or France? I saw that there occurred in New York a few days ago a meeting of representatives, so called, of some small nations who demanded this equality of voting power. If this were agreed to, the small nations could determine the action of the league, and if the league had an international force behind it they could order that force where they pleased and put it under any command they pleased, which might give rise to complications.

If nations are to vote in the league on a democratic basis, then their voting power must be determined by population. Here, too, some curious possibilities arise, not without a certain intricacy. The population of China is, roughly, four times that of the United States, and this system would give China four times the vote of the United States in the league. If England is to have the right to cast the vote of her possessions, India alone would give her from three to four times as many votes as the United States and ten times the vote of France.

JUSTICIABLE QUESTIONS?

All the plans which have been put forward tentatively for a League of Nations, so far as I know, involve the creation of a court. We must remember that we have carried voluntary arbitration as far as it can practically go. Assuming that there is a distinction between justiciable and non-justiciable questions, who is to decide whether a question is justiciable or not? Is it to be done by the league, voting in some manner hitherto undefined, or is each nation to decide for itself whether a question affecting its own interest is or is not justiciable?

Let me give an example to make my meaning clearer. We have recently purchased the Virgin Islands. Suppose that that purchase had not been effected, and that Denmark undertook to sell those islands to Germany or some other great power. Is that a justiciable question? If it is and it went before a court there can be no doubt that any court would be obliged to hold that Denmark had the right to sell those islands to whom she pleased. In the past the United States would never have permitted those islands to pass out of Denmark's hands into any other hands, because we consider their possession of vital importance to our safety and to the protection of the Panama routes.

The same will be true in regard to Magdalena Bay—a case in which the Senate passed a resolution, with unanimity, I think, stating that on the plain doctrine of self-preservation we could not allow Magdalena Bay, or any other similar position of advantage, to be turned into a naval base or military post by another power. Would that be justiciable? And if not justiciable, then is the League of Nations to compel, nevertheless, its submission?

Let us be honest with ourselves. It is easy to talk about a league of nations and the beauty and the necessity of peace, but the hard, practical demand is: Are you ready to put your soldiers and your sailors at the disposition of other nations? If you are not, there will be no power of enforcing the decrees of the international court or the international legislature or the international executive, or whatever may be established.

WHY A LEAGUE IS INEVITABLE

By DR. TALCOTT WILLIAMS

When a deed is done for Freedom, through the broad earth's aching breast
Runs a thrill of joy prophetic, trembling on from east to west.
Nation wildly looks at nation, standing with mute lips apart,
And glad Truth's yet mightier man-child leaps beneath the Future's heart.
For mankind are one in spirit, and an instinct bears along,
Round the earth's electric circle, the swift flash of right and wrong;
Whether conscious or unconscious, yet Humanity's vast frame,
Through its ocean-sundered fibres feels the gust of joy or shame;
In the gain or loss of one race all the rest have equal claim.
Once to every man and nation comes the moment to decide,
In the strife of Truth with Falsehood, for the good or evil side:
Some great cause, God's new Messiah, offering each the bloom or blight.

"The Present Crisis." Lowell, 1848.

What Lowell published in 1848 is as true today as it was seventy years ago. Read it. Every word fits the hour and pulses to the thrill of the moment. Beveridge, Lodge and all the rest of the Senators are where Webster was in his speech for the Fugitive Slave Bill on the Seventh of March, 1850. "God help her, Massachusetts kneeling with the rest." But not for long. The Senator elected last November carried the State and defeated Senator Lodge's colleague on the issue of a League of Nations. If Senator Lodge has any doubt, he had better poll the State. Let Beveridge start something in Indiana, where great meetings have covered the State and every County is organized for the League to Enforce Peace.

Lodge and Beveridge talk like Patrick Henry in 1787. He was chosen by the Virginia Legislature for the Convention which drew the Federal Constitution. He was not willing to go to Philadelphia and Independence Hall (where, by the way, the League to Enforce Peace was organized in 1915) to sit in the Convention between Washington and Madison. Men like him pointed out to Virginia that the Declaration of Independence made it a "free, independent and sovereign State." It was for that the War of the Revolution was fought. He predicted sudden evils and the loss of liberty if Virginia made a union with twelve other States. He was more eloquent over the perils of that day than Lodge, Beveridge and all can possibly be, for reasons too obvious to mention.

It is a piece of small petty pleading and crass iginorance of history when these men, Beveridge leading, insist that we did not go into the war for a League of Nations. No nation ever finds out for what it went into a war until the war is fought. We went into the Revolution on a tax and we came out a Nation. We fought for Articles of Confederation and we adopted a Federal Union. God bless it and keep it! You could paper a room with editorials in Democratic papers from 1861 to 1865, yes to December 18, 1865, when the Thirteenth Amendment to the Constitution was adopted, that the war was fought to save the Union and not to free the slave; that Lincoln's Emancipation Proclamation was a breach of faith. Beveridge took his seat in the Senate in March, 1899, a fortnight or so after hot debates in the Senate that we went into the Spanish war to "free Cuba" and we must not on any account take the Philippines, and the Senate ratified our treaty of peace with Spain, 55 to 27. One vote would have defeated the treaty. Are the twenty-seven proud of their vote then? Not much! They are forgotten, except by men like a leading Democratic lawyer of Philadelphia, who told me that the Battle of Manila was won "at the loss of one man and all our institutions." Does any one today regret that the United States became a world power or that the Republic has again planted victorious feet beyond the seas?

Now, as always, in all our history, in the debates over the Federal Constitution, over the Jay treaty, over the treaty of peace with Mexico, which gave us an imperial domain on the Pacific, Sumner over the Alabama Arbitration treaty, in the treaty that closed the Spanish War, those who oppose each great step forward, are full of perils and pitfalls, risks and rattraps in which a great nation is to be ensnared. But the change comes in the great march of events and the event brings the wisdom to meet it.

So now. The speech of Mr. Beveridge is only six months old and most of its arguments are as extinct as the Dodo and for the same reason. He wants the American eagle to waddle like a duck and lose the might of its wings for lack of courage to rise to new heights and know the upper air of liberty, justice and a League of Nations, where the world can be seen as a whole and the duty of a Nation not alone to itself but will have been in vain; and the American flag, as the emblem of a free and independent nation, will lose its meaning and its glory.

conquest in Russia or in the East, and that the Slavic populations, which she has mercilessly used in her wars, can never be so used by her again.

We cannot leave Russia lying helpless and breathing out infection on the world. We must help to bring her back to health and sanity and wellbeing. Some proper settlement of the Russian question is absolutely vital to the modern civilization of which we are a part. We cannot disregard it or stand by as idle spectators without making any effort to aid Russia to rid herself of the poison which is now eating out her life and once more resume her place among the great nations of the world.

If the ex-Senator was right in May, how are we going to do all that Mr. Lodge wants? If we set out to do all that the Senator from Massachusetts wants us to do now, to all of which he would vehemently have objected five years ago and tear his senatorial toga to tatters before he would vote for it, how can we get along without a League? Are we going to do the job alone? Are we going to settle the reorganization of ten million square miles and three hundred millions of human beings (put in China, as Lodge does, and it is nineteen million square miles and six hundred million of population) as "nationalists—American nationalists," as Beveridge wants us to be, on our own lonesome?

The American people is opposed to war, dislikes war, abhors needless conflict, and endeavored for the first time in history to put the control over a declaration of war in the hands of an assembly representing the people by requiring Congress to declare war. In England the King could declare war. This constitutional privilege, this protection, Mr. Beveridge declares, would be lost if a League were organized. But this would make no change in the practice of the United States now. Those who drew the Constitution were familiar with international law. They provided for those hostile operations which are necessary if a nation is carrying out a policy, broad, far-reaching and effective, by making the President, Commander in Chief of the Army and Navy, a direct constitutional grant, over which Congress has no control. He is authorized to use the army and navy to carry out any settled policy, but Congress can check his action by refusing to vote appropriations for the army or by legislation.

Through all our national existence, a sharp line has been drawn between mere hostilities not war and war formally declared with all its changes of status as to trading with enemy citizens, communication with the enemy, control of aliens, and espionage laws. Hostile operations arise on a different basis. Under a treaty with Colombia (1846) we had the right to preserve order at the Isthmus. We landed troops there in almost every year from the time the treaty was negotiated until the Canal strip was acquired. Polk sent Taylor into disputed territory. We shared in occupying Alexandria in 1881, and kept order in the town for weeks. We shared in the expedition to Pekin in 1900, took the city by storm and governed a part of it for months. Under the Monroe Doctrine in Rio Janeiro our fleet, with approval from Washington, took charge of the harbor and opened it to trade. Four years ago we occupied Vera Cruz. Not one of these things required a declaration of war or was "war." As a matter of history, in the two centuries from 1700 to 1900 hostile operations went on for weeks and months in more than one hundred cases. Sometimes these brought on war and its status, and sometimes they did not. The territory which England occupied in Egypt in 1881 under an international mandate was held but England never issued a declaration of war. Mr. Beveridge is a good lawyer, he knows all these things; he is familiar with them; he trusts to the ignorance of the people in declaring that if a League of Peace is adopted we shall be making war without a Congress declaring war. This is already the case, with a policy followed, adopted and established. It is necessary in the nature of things that a power should be able to use its military force to accomplish results without a declaration of war. This has been the habit of the United States, whenever its policy required or reprisals were necessary.

The League of Nations would do its chief work in preventing war by the use of military force to prevent hostilities by acting without a declaration of war, avoiding disturbance to trade, to international intercourse, and to credits.

Senator Lodge proposes that the Peace treaty shall provide for his program for the re-arrangements of a great area—the largest population with which any peace treaty has endeavored to deal, and he wants to postpone a League of Nations until this treaty has been ratified. This is to make the treaty nugatory. If the United States is to have the power to do this work with other nations, the treaty must provide some way in which it can act. It is not possible in operations which will extend over years, which will require constant vigilance, perpetual willingness and a capacity to use adequate military force to protect small nations and prevent attack upon them, to act without a settled plan of action. This plan of action in the nature of things will be a league of the nations concerned. To divide a treaty which creates these obligations from the steps by which such obligations will be discharged is to put all out at a stroke. Is it possible that Mr. Lodge thinks that it would be better to have this done by a Republican President and Congress? Is it for this purpose that he is willing to leave this large program open? Would the American people be willing to enter on this job without some steps toward disarmament? Would it be willing to assume the attitude of the old order and leave it possible for any nation to arm at will and to use its powers to suppress revolution and disorder?

The United States could have refused to enter the war, and defended itself at home. If it chooses, having defeated Germany it can stop, withdraw its troops, cease to trouble about Europe, and make peace with Germany alone. But to agree to keep Europe in peace and these small nations unprotected, to take no steps to reduce armaments, provide for no permanent peace, arrange no League to prevent an attack by a strong nation on a weak, as Austria attacked Serbia, increasing all the perils of the past and making no new provision against them. This the country would not accept.

If Senator Lodge is right in feeling the result of the war will be thrown away unless we enter on the problem of the old order, it is as plain as the sun in the heavens that a world authority must exist in order to discharge a world task. Such authority implies a League of Nations to preserve peace. It requires it. Mr. Lodge may wish to postpone action upon it in order to secure partizanship advantage, but this does not make his advice more sound, more safe, or more effective.

A League is inevitable. It must come. It exists already for war. Why fear it for peace? Mr. Lodge assumes that all nations must come in and on equal rates and powers or on some elaborate plan to be arranged now. Why? The League does not propose one. In its meeting at Philadelphia, the League carefully avoided discussing details because details divide. A common cause, a common end, a common determination, these unite. President Wilson is wisely leaving the League to develop.

There are twenty-three nations at war with Germany. Five of them today manage the whole war by land and by sea. No one gainsays them. The League proposes to continue the present plan of action, the big powers doing the work needed to keep the world at peace and the lesser powers sharing in the work. This is to take the five great powers as the Executive Committee of the world. Has Senator Lodge any better authority or agency to offer? None. There is none. Let the Hague Court stand, all nations in it. Enforce its decisions as they come. Provide some agency, the Five Great Powers are again the best, to act as permanent mediators in conflicts between countries, stopping war and insisting on arbitration. If a country is in hopeless disorder, as Russia is, let these powers act, to use President Wilson's happy phrase, as an "international agency" to keep the peace, educate and prepare for self-rule and final independence.

Senator Lodge proposes in the treaty of peace to pledge ourselves to the reform of the world but proposes no way, no method, no League by which to do it. His list is nearer forty than the President's fourteen. When his points are all in the treaty and we are bound by them, how can we meet these vast new obligations unless we are part of a League of Great Nations, using the lesser powers as we can? He proposes some twenty new States, their peoples hating each other, no single boundary that suits both sides, each suspicious, none used to self-government, all illiterate (not over one in ten adults can read) and apparently expects these gigantic changes over an area from forty to fifty times as large as the Balkans and with a population from twenty to thirty times as large, to run in peace with no wars, when once set up, when the Balkans alone have caused five wars in forty years, the last the greatest of all.

This is ridiculous. It is insane. I am not a Senator like Mr. Lodge, or an ex-Senator like Mr. Beveridge; but I happen to have been born in the East. I know those lands. Their tongues and their natures are not unfamiliar to me. There is scarcely a week in the past forty years in which I have not written and spoken on these peoples. My first contact with the Russian nature came in a Russian playmate sixty years ago. He was very affectionate and very uncertain. All that Senator Lodge proposes I have for years felt should be done. It is twenty-five years since, in a course of lectures in Philadelphia, I predicted that America must play its part in the Near and the Far East. Even I would have hesitated in a single speech to redraw the map for a third or more of the human race.

But if this be our duty, can aught be better done than to continue the practical League that now exists? Mr. Lodge's friend and college mate, Theodore Roosevelt, who once saved him from defeat in Massachusetts, urges a hard and fast alliance. If the Five Powers that have saved Liberty, go on to create a new peace and enforce that peace, is not this not only wise but inevitable? If we do as he proposes, can we embark on stormy seas to make over all the world between the Rhine and the Amur, the Vosges and the Thien Shah, can we do this and leave it open to England at any moment to cut off our army by its sea-power; if we disagree? When in peril, trust was possible; but suppose India flames and has to be set right, or Ireland rises, are we to be powerless to advise and urge at least as much justice as we propose between the Adriatic and the Ural? Is one nation to dominate the sea alone? Are we going to spend billions and keep a great army abroad to bring peace for Pole and Slovak, Roumanian and Serb, Croat and Ruthenian and twenty more peoples and do nothing to make a peace so dearly bought for them, permanent for us? Is each of these new nations to begin arming to the teeth as has Poland? Are both navalism and militarism to run a race again? Is there to be no effort by "open covenants of peace openly arrived at" to prevent another conflagration? Does Senator Lodge propose a secret treaty like the "Treaty of London," in which the allies and Italy left Jugo-Slavs feeling they are unjustly treated?

These questions answer themselves. What Senator Lodge proposes assures a League of Nations. Unless all he plans is to tumble into hideous and world-embracing ruin, there must be a League of the Five Great Powers—with a share proportioned to their responsibility for lesser lands—a world court, a world authority, world mediation and a recognition of world reform by a world league, of great powers and small, each doing its share.

If Mr. Lodge, who fears not to overturn, fears to build a secure peace, I return to Mr. Lowell for my answer in closing:—

"New occasions teach new duties; Time makes ancient good uncouth:
They must upward still, and onward, who would keep abreast of Truth;
Lo, before us gleam her camp-fires! We ourselves must Pilgrims be,
Launch our Mayflower, and steer boldly through the desperate winter sea,
Nor attempt the Future's portal with the Past's blood-rusted key."

PEACE BY "AGREEMENT OF MIND"

By RALPH M. EASLEY

THE words of Lowell, quoted by Dr. Williams, are certainly inspiring, if not illuminating, but, if Lowell had gone through all the vexatious experiences that Dr. Williams and many other workers for international peace have passed through during the last three years in trying to work out a plan that would prevent war in the future, he might have contributed more toward a solution of the problem. It may be "a piece of small, petty pleading and crass ignorance of history where these men, Beveridge leading, insist that we did not go into the war for a League of Nations," but is it not true, nevertheless? We went to war for the very good and sufficient reason that had we not done so the Central Powers would have been victorious, and we should then have had Germany to fight on our own shores and alone, instead of on the battle lines in France with the aid of the Allies. This was not altruism in every sense but enlightened self-interest and far-seeing worldly wisdom. As we get away from April 6, 1917, we are too prone to forget events and sentimentalize on the real causes back of our entrance into the war. It is a too common expression now, that we had "nothing to gain by going into the war," that "our whole conduct has been based upon the highest altruism" and that we are "going to the Peace Table with purely unselfish motives." It is a fact that we go to the Peace Table with clean hands and with no selfish demands in the way of compensation for our great loss in blood and treasure, but we did not go into the war for unselfish purposes nor to secure a League to Enforce Peace. Harry Lauder, to my mind, expressed it exactly last June when he said to a group of our men just before they sailed: "Boys, you are not going over to save France nor to save England nor to 'make the world safe for Democracy.' Get that out of your heads! You are going over there, by God, to save your own skins, your own homes, your own wives and children, and you know it and we know it. So, cut out all the gush. The Allies have their backs against the wall. If they go down, you are the next in line and that's why you are going over." I believe that the two million boys who went to France will agree with Harry Lauder.

ram, the League stopped at making "recommendations." Still more teeth for the new rogram!

In the new program, Clauses Three and Four rovide for "an administrative organization for he conduct of affairs of common interest," etc., nd "a representative Congress to formulate nd codify rules of international law," etc.; hen "An Executive Body able to speak with uthority in the name of the nations," etc. And et Dr. Williams says the new plan has dropped he "cumbersome" platform of the old one, hich provided for none of this detailed machinery, and emphasizes the point that "the eague carefully avoided discussing details beause details divide."

DIFFICULTIES OF PROBLEM

The powers contained in the third section of he old program, it will be noted, are incorporaed in the "representation of the different naions" and the "resort to force by any nation" lauses of the new one, the latter referring rathr childishly to "solemn agreements," as if the vord "solemn" added any weight to an nternational agreement! In other words, the nly alterations made in the new program were o change it from a compulsory investigation rogram to one of possible compulsory arbitraion, and to add the provision for complicated dministrative and legislative machinery, as well s the provision for an "executive committee," presumably given all the power of the League to act "in case the peace of the World is in danger."

In the old program, the separation of justiciable from non-justiciable questions or, in other words, the determining whether questions are of minor importance or whether they are of vital import, was left to the same tribunal which passed upon justiciable questions which no nation would be likely to permit an outside body of "disinterested statesmen" to decide for it.

In the new program, this weakness is avoided by no provision being made for the determination of that delicate, and also very vital, difference, the matter ostensibly being left for each nation itself to determine what questions it will submit. This is even weaker, because no nation then would ever submit any matter of importance, on the plea that it is non-justiciable because it is of "vital import" or affects "national honor."

That this is an almost unsolvable problem is well indicated by the fact that the Second Hague Conference spent weeks upon an attempt to agree upon a list of justiciable questions and gave up the problem in despair.

As, in some form, we are sure to have brought before the American people, sooner or later, some sort of a League of Nations program, there cannot be too much discussion of the various questions and responsibilities involved in the acceptance of such a program.

Much of the criticism, so far, has revolved around such questions as:

How is the League itself to be formed? Are all nations to be included? If not, who is to draw the line and where is it to be drawn? Is Germany to be included? If only a selected few, are they to have equal representation? Shall the Allies and the United States form the first League of Nations, which would be simply another name for an alliance of the "Big Four?" Shall all vital questions be submitted and shall this Government turn its army and navy over to any outside combination of powers?

These and other questions require great study, care and wisdom before rightful conclusions can be reached, but there are other questions, about which little has been said, in which labor has especial concern. The reason for this concern is that the principles finally accepted in dealing with international disputes will probably have a bearing in this country on the policy adopted in dealing with industrial disputes.

Furthermore, Lord Robert Cecil, the British representative in charge of all questions affecting the proposed League of Nations at the Peace Conference, in a letter to J. H. Thomas, Secretary of the National Union of Railwaymen in England, stated that a League, when once organized, in addition to dealing with international questions, would, doubtless, deal with labor questions.

In one of the pamphlets sent out by the League to Enforce Peace, entitled "Labor's Interest in the League to Enforce Peace," written by Samuel Gompers, there appears the following paragraph:

> The League's program wisely recognizes the danger of creating a League of Nations that would undertake to enforce the *decisions* of an International Court, and contents itself with enforcing the *submission to* an International Court of all disputes for examination. Until democracy is more clearly universal, until democracy becomes a social and industrial fact as well as a political catchword, a League with power to enforce decisions would almost certainly become the repressive tool of the reactionary and privileged forces of the world.

COMPULSORY ARBITRATION A FAILURE

In this comment Mr. Gompers was referring to the 1915 program, and not to the revised draft adopted in November, 1918.

When Mr. Gompers congratulated the League on not having attempted compulsion, he voiced the almost unanimous view of organized labor, and I may say of organized employers and of all classes of persons who have had any practical experience with industrial arbitration. Those who will examine the matter will find a close parallelism between the principles that underlie industrial and international peace measures. Former President Taft, now President of the League to Enforce Peace, referred to this similarity between nations and people when he said:

> We have no right to assume that we have passed beyond the period in history when nations are affected by the same frailties and the same temptations to cupidity, cruelty and injustice as men.

Compulsory arbitration in industrial disputes has proved a failure in every country where it has been tried. Likewise, compulsory *investigation*, which was all that was involved in the original program of the League to Enforce Peace, has been tried out industrially in Canada and found to be a failure. As it is generally claimed that no nation will agree to arbitrate its vital questions—those affecting its national existence or its honor—so there are questions in the industrial field which cannot be arbitrated. It is a popular belief that there are no questions that wage-earners or employers should not be willing to leave to "high-minded," "disinterested" citizens to pass upon, or that there are no questions between nations that should not be left to a tribunal of "high-minded," "disinterested" statesmen to settle. But red-blooded union labor men would never agree to arbitrate their right to belong to a union; neither would employers agree to arbitrate the demand of a union that they should discharge their non-union men and give the places to members of the union; nor, again, would wage-earners who had the eight-hour day arbitrate the question of going back to nine or ten hours, because experience has shown too often that leaving matters to these "high-minded" representative citizens too frequently means not justice but injustice, in some cases guess-work and, in many, sheer confusion. In fact, so unsatisfactory has been the experience of calling in outside arbitrators that many of the most important organizations of labor and employers, both here and in England, provide in their contracts, in case of a threatened controversy, against any odd man being brought in and provide only that there shall be an equal number of arbitrators on each side, with no umpire. The late Seth Low, after sitting for four months in a great railroad arbitration case, in which he and John H. Finley, as the neutral arbitrators, wrote the decision, when called upon to interpret it, admitted he could not do so. He afterwards declared that he would never again favor outside parties as arbitrators in large industrial matters.

Does any one contend that this country would have arbitrated the questions that led up to the Spanish-American war? And would any one in this country consider arbitrating whether we should give back to Spain Porto Rico and the Philippines and surrender our suzerainty over Cuba? Would the United States have considered a proposition to arbitrate the questions leading to our declaration of war against Germany?

GAMBLE OF THE "ODD MAN"

It is true that we are already bound in the so-called "Bryan treaties," made with nearly all countries excepting Germany and Austria, to arbitrate *all* questions, which would include the questions just referred to, as well as the admission of Asiatics and the Monroe Doctrine, and, for that reason, as asserted by former President Roosevelt, those treaties ought to be annulled, because this country would never pay any attention to them if called upon to submit such questions to arbitration.

The reason the United States would never submit such propositions to arbitration is the same reason that the labor people would never submit their vital questions to arbitration and that is, that, when once submitted, the risk of defeat is always taken and no nation and no labor organization would place in jeopardy its right to live.

The method provided for the selection of arbitrators under the Bryan treaties (and it is the common method provided in all arbitration matters, whether international or industrial) is that each side shall select an even number and that they shall agree upon the odd member. This always means that the odd member is to decide the questions, because, assuming that the vital questions are submitted to it—the Monroe Doctrine, for instance—the representatives of the respective sides would be nothing more than attorneys for their principals. This makes the securing of the odd man the securing of the victory, and it can well be understood what kind of a scramble such a situation would create.

The League to Enforce Peace, in its latest program, proposes for non-justiciable questions a Council of Conciliation which shall hear, consider, and make recommendations and, if the parties fail to acquiesce, the League shall determine what action, if any, shall be taken. This, as before stated, might mean the attempt to enforce compliance by the combined naval and military forces. The implication is that this Council of Conciliation is to be a permanent body. To such a body, of course, no nation would submit a vital question but would, at least, insist on selecting its own representatives, taking a gamble on the odd man, if it should ever agree to submit.

But, if the League did not attempt to enforce a decision and merely handed down a recommendation, it is asked, "What harm could be done?" The proponents of the League point out that it would give time for public discussion and "to cool off," which might prevent a break. This is the great argument that was made in favor of the Canadian Compulsory Investigation Act. What generally happened was that, during the time required for the Government to get its machinery ready and to hear and hand down a decision, the employers were getting ready for the strike, in the event the decision was against them, securing strike-breakers, putting up barracks, etc. This weak spot the State of Massachusetts undertook to meet in a compulsory investigation bill by providing that the *status quo* should be maintained. But it was soon pointed out that, in the case of a street railway company, for instance, threatened with a strike of its employees, while the company could not openly make a contract for strike breakers, strike breakers' agencies could prepare and be ready on an hour's notice to fill the places of the strikers, and there was no way by which to prevent such an advantage being taken.

In case of wars between nations, identically the same situation would arise. There is no way by which to preserve a *status quo*. If the United States should happen to have a controversy with a country less honorable than itself, it would keep its word and not make preparations for war, whereas the other country could prepare—not openly, of course, but finding opportunities to arrange its finances, make secret alliances, provide for obtaining guns, munitions, equipment, etc. In fact, there would be plenty of dealers in those materials doing just what the strike breakers would do for the street railway management—getting all ready for them. As in the case of a union, the nation that finds it necessary to fight, has the right to strike at the most propitious moment; and that moment, despite all questions of ethics, or morals, or philosophies, is when the opponent is the least prepared and the aggressor stands the best chance of more quickly scoring a victory.

HOW EXERCISE INJUNCTIVE POWER?

Take a concrete case within the memory of all. If the United States and Mexico had been in the League to Enforce Peace, before President Wilson could have sent General Pershing after the raiders of Columbus, or, to be exact, invaded Mexico, he would have had to wait until the matter had first been submitted to the judicial tribunal for hearing and judgment, to ascertain whether it was a justiciable or non-justiciable matter. If the latter, it would then go to a Council of Conciliation for "hearing, consideration and recommendation," supposing that such a council could ever have been agreed upon by Mexico and the United States. This board would have had to determine, among other things, such simple questions as—whether Villa had made his raid at the behest of certain Carranzaists, in which case our invasion would have been justified; at the behest of certain American mine owners, in which case this country would have been responsible; or on his own fiendish initiative, in which case Villa would have been morally responsible, but the Carranza government would have been held legally responsible—a proceeding that would require several months' patient inquiry. And, while these interesting proceedings were being conducted, Villa could have been making his way on to Chicago, and we should have been helpless because under the proposals of the League all the battle ships and armies of the world, including our own, would have been staying the hands of the President.

If Germany had accepted the Bryan treaties, as did England, Russia and France, the "Lusitania" and "Sussex" matters would have gone before a board, for the formation of which six months were allowed, were it ever possible to agree on the odd man in so crucial a matter. During all this time Germany could have gone on torpedoing passenger ships without let or hindrance, so far as the treaty was concerned, because the only clause in it covering such a contingency says: "In case the cause of a dispute should consist of certain acts already committed or about to be committed, the Commission shall, as soon as possible, indicate measures to preserve the rights of each party that ought, in its opinion, to be taken provisionally and pending the delivery of its report." That is, restraining action is to be taken by a commission that, in the nature of things, it may never be possible to form. The League to Enforce Peace has no provision covering such a contingency.

When Senator Borah asked what action the United States would take in case Mexico proposed to lease Magdalena Bay to Japan and put the question: "Would the United States submit that question to a tribunal where it has but one vote and one voice and permit its entire future to be disposed of by a court where it has but a single representative?" he was answered by Mr. Theodore Marburg, a member of the executive committee of the League. Mr. Marburg said he agreed with the Senator that the United States could not permit Mexico to make such a lease, but added that there could be no harm in submitting the question to the Board of Conciliation, because the United States would not be bound by the decree and could go ahead and take any action it might choose to take. This was, of course, under the Philadelphia program of the League.

But, under the new program, the League, after hearing the matter, might determine to enforce its decision with the armies and navies of the world, including our own. Mr. Marburg further stated, to meet the weakness referred to in the Bryan treaty: "Pending the inquiry, Japan would be stopped by injunction from proceeding with the objectionable act of taking possession of and possibly fortifying Magdalena Bay." Mr. Marburg was assuming that there would be such an injunctive power. There was no provision for it in the League's program, either the old or the new, and the attempt to draft such a provision would open up endless difficulties.

It may be answered that a League of Nations would and could thresh out and furnish satisfactory answers for all such questions but the United States Senate will not be likely to be satisfied with assurances, but will want to see the program in detail. It will demand this because, in the end, the matter has to come down to a question of whether or not this country is willing to submit its questions of vital interest to a decision by representatives of European governments and the turning over of its army and navy to a league necessarily composed of representatives of a large majority of nations who do not sympathize with our conception of national rights and duties and who, if they did sympathize today, by a change in their own internal politics, might be against us tomorrow. Last October we wanted Liebknecht to develop a revolution that would overthrow the military party in Germany. Now, we are afraid he will succeed. Could we depend on Germany's voice in a League of Nations being sympathetic with the United States, or Russia, or Italy, or France, if the Bolsheviki get control, as many fear?

PRESIDENT WILSON AND LEAGUE COMING TOGETHER

The first paragraph of the new program of the League states:

> The war now happily brought to a close has been above all a war to end war, but in order to insure the fruits of victory and to prevent the recurrence of such a catastrophe there should be formed a League of Free Nations, as universal as possible, based upon treaty and pledged that the security of each state shall rest upon the strength of the whole. *The initiating nucleus of the membership of the League should be the nations associated as belligerents in winning the war.*

This declaration is on all fours with the views of President Wilson, who said before the Sorbonne:

> My conception of the League of Nations is just this—*that it shall operate as the organized moral force of men throughout the World and*

Bolshevism Convicted Out of Its Own Mouth

Prepared for the League for National Unity

By WILLIAM ENGLISH WALLING

I

HE PRO-BOLSHEVIK PROPAGANDA

It would be possible to print volumes of evi-ence as to the Bolshevik regime in Russia. his evidence comes from every possible source. ithout exception the diplomatic representa-ves and the commercial agents of America, rance and Great Britain have told the same ory. With one or two exceptions, the large rps of correspondents stationed in Russia for any years and familiar with the language of e country substantiate the story. Thousands American citizens, tens of thousands of other reigners who have lived in Russia for many ears, have, upon their return to America or eir native lands, given an account which is lentical in every important particular.

But unfortunately the extreme liberality of e American press and the fair-mindedness of e American public has resulted in an almost qually wide publication of utterly baseless pro-olshevik statements. These statements have ad a certain success because the Bolshevik cen-rship, beginning in August, has very much ecreased direct communications with Russia.

This pro-Bolshevik propaganda resembles in very way the pro-German propaganda. It be-ins by denying absolutely the mass of existing vidence, including even the original documents ut forth by the American Government with e direct authorization of President Wilson. ll the vast masses of material gathered directly r indirectly through any governmental sources re rejected on the entirely false assumption hat it is all official or governmental. The daily apers and correspondents with the exception f a few pro-Bolshevik writers are repudiated s being capitalistic. The same is said of all oreign witnesses. The immense amount of tes-imony gathered from other political parties in ussia is rejected as being either "bourgeois" r "partisan."

Having thus gotten rid of all existing testi-ony, the pro-Bolshevik propagandists then roceed to build up an entirely new and im-ginary structure of their own.

The pro-Bolshevik agitation has had little or o success in accomplishing its main object. It as produced few Bolshevists in this country nd not many pro-Bolshevists. But it has suc-eeded in confusing the public mind. For four onths there has been comparatively little new aterial from Russia. During this period the ro-Bolshevists have succeeded in getting before he public many of their imaginative produc-ions. What is the origin of these stories? A ew newspaper correspondents and writers have ecome the official mouthpieces of Bolshevism. or example, the *New York Times* and other ewspapers for many months published the rticles of Arthur Ransome as coming from heir own official correspondent. At the end f this period *The Times* on several occa-ions printed a notice to the effect that Ransome vas the official mouthpiece of Lenine and rotzky. There were several other similar ases. The second group of pro-Bolshevist ropagandists is composed of correspondents or 'social workers" who knowing nothing of the ussian language, Russian politics, Russian eography or the Russian people, went to etrograd or Moscow and spent a few weeks or few months in the country under the chaotic onditions of the revolution. Even in times of peace Russia is difficult to understand because of its huge size and complicated conditions—even by persons who have spent many years in that country. During the revolutionary turmoil, communication has been so bad that it would take months to gather evidence which might be secured in a day in ordinary times. The evidence of these fleeting visitors, most of them entirely without any qualification whatever for such difficult investigation, is all but worthless.

Fortunately there is a method by which the whole situation can easily be cleared up. It is not necessary to consider either the so-called testimony of the pro-Bolshevist propaganda or the vast mass of evidence gathered from hundreds of other sources. The avowed position of the Bolsheviki themselves, their own utterances and actions which they do not deny are quite sufficient for all practical purposes.

This article therefore concerns itself almost entirely with the Bolshevists' own declarations and acts which they themselves do not deny, but, on the contrary, boastfully avow. In order to acquaint the reader with the nature of some of the evidence which comes from non-Bolshevik sources, some of it is referred to only briefly; but most of our space is given to the Bolshevists' own statements.

II

THE BOLSHEVIK PROGRAM

Like the German propaganda, the pro-Bolshevik agitation makes very grave blunders—even from the standpoint of its own interests. The pro-Bolshevists, for example, are making claims on behalf of the Bolsheviki, which the latter themselves deny!

In America, the Russian Bolshevists are represented as being democrats; in Russia, Lenine and his followers lose no occasion to repudiate democracy, both in word and in deed. Our quotations will show that the very basis of Bolshevism consists in the repudiation of democracy!

In America, the Bolsheviki are represented as having given land to a landless peasantry; in Russia, the Bolsheviki attribute nearly all of their troubles to the fact that there has been very little land (not in peasant hands before the revolution) to give—a fact which will also be demonstrated later by quotations from the Bolsheviki themselves.

In America, the Bolsheviki are represented as being pacifists; Lenine and Trotzky have neglected no opportunity to denounce bourgeois pacifism and to assert that they are in favor of a holy war against any and all non-Bolshevik governments wherever such a war has a chance of success.

In America, the Bolsheviki are represented as favoring individual liberty; in Russia, the Bolsheviki absolutely repudiate such regard for personal liberty as being a "bourgeois doctrine and practice."

In America, Lenine is presented as being a hundred per cent Socialist; in Russia, Lenine presents himself as being one hundred per cent anti-Socialist, that is, a "communist," opposed to the Socialist International.

In May, 1917, the first or non-Bolshevik revolution was already sufficiently developed to enable Lenine to define the application of his doctrine to the new political situation in which Russia found itself. From the *New International* (April, 1918), an American Bolshevik publication, we quote the following paragraph of a long article by Lenine:

> The word democracy cannot be scientifically applied to the Communist Party. Since March, 1917, the word democracy is simply a shackle fastened upon the revolutionary nation and preventing it from establishing boldly, freely and regardless of all obstacles, a new form of power; the council of Workmen's, Soldiers' and Peasants'. Deputies, harbinger of the abolition of every form of authority.

Shortly after the Bolsheviki came into power, Lenine defined the new "dictatorship" of the proletariat as follows:

> Just as 150,000 lordly landowners under Tsarism dominated the 130,000,000 of Russian peasants, so 200,000 members of the Bolshevik Party are imposing their proletarian will on the mass, but this time in the interest of the latter.

In order to understand thoroughly the extent and precise grounds of Lenine's repudiation of democracy, let us quote his denunciation of the rival faction of the Social Democratic or Workingmen's Party, namely, the Mensheviki:

> In its class composition this party is not Socialist at all. It does not represent the toiling masses. It represents fairly prosperous peasants and workingmen, petty traders, many small and some even fairly large capitalists, and a certain number of real but gullible proletarians who have been caught in the bourgeois net.

We are progressing into the Lenine psychology. Even "a fairly prosperous" workingman is not a "proletarian."

In a political catechism prepared in the summer of 1917 Lenine asks the question, Is it necessary to convoke the Constituent Assembly, and answers, "Yes, and as soon as possible." This demonstrates that the Bolsheviki did not dare to oppose the idea of a democratic Constituent Assembly and did not intend to oppose it if they could gain control of it. It was only because they found the overwhelming majority of the peasants and a large part of the working people against them that they dispersed the Constituent Assembly and established the "Soviet" doctrine. What this doctrine is we may see from an examination of the Soviet constitution adopted at the fifth Pan-Russian Congress of Soviets.

In the preamble, the Soviets state that they propose "to put an end to every ill that oppresses humanity." The Soviets necessarily proceed to a very extreme policy to carry such a program into effect, declaring for "a dictatorship of the proletariat and the poorest peasantry."

Here the cat is out of the bag. Not even "the poor peasantry" can be relied on. Only a very vaguely defined class of "the poorest peasantry" is trusted to support the dictatorship of the city working classes, which in Russia do not represent more than ten or twelve per cent of the population.

Furthermore, a very large proportion of this working class, as we shall show below is anti-Bolshevik.

The utter impossibility of defining the "poorest peasantry" leads the Soviet Congress to adopt another anti-democratic expedient for preventing the Russian people from controlling Russia—for disfranchising the peasantry representing eighty-four per cent of the population. This expedient is very simple. Each Bolshevik workingman (the non-Bolsheviki being excluded by methods described below) is given the same vote as five peasants! The following is Article One of Section 8 of the Soviet Constitution:

> The Pan-Russian Congress of Soviets consists of representatives of the urban Soviets (one delegate for each 25,000 votes) and representatives of the government congresses (one delegate for each 125,000 voters).

No discussion of the Soviet program will be complete without stating its position on international affairs. The Soviet proposes a world-wide war against all non-Soviet governments, whenever and wherever such a war promises success—and the wars they have actually waged show what they will do if they get the chance.

III

BOLSHEVISM IN PRACTICE

We have given sufficient Bolshevik evidence on the Bolshevik program. Let us now turn to the practical working out of the program, which is a far different thing.

Certain new converts to Bolshevism have been circulating the entire Bolshevik program, together with their plans for the transformation of industry, government, education, literature, music and art as if the mere publication of Lenine's ukases were equivalent to the complete accomplishment of the stupendous changes proposed! We have already quoted expressions of Lenine's showing the breakdown of his program in its most fundamental point, namely, the effort to secure the support of the peasantry. We shall now quote Trotzky and Gorky as to the failure of Bolshevism in other directions.

Gorky is undoubtedly the greatest literary figure among the Bolsheviki. It is true that his paper was forbidden for a long period and that he was for a time practically out of that movement. But he has re-entered it recently and has been given an important position by the Bolsheviki. They not only accept him once more as one of their leaders, but are boasting about his return to the fold. The motives for this return we do not know. Possibly Gorky desired to stay in Russia and to keep his head on his shoulders. Possibly he was influenced by the considerable power given him in matters pertaining to literature and education.

It needs the pen of a master writer like Gorky to describe the practical workings of Bolshevism. And he has done a good job! We shall now reproduce quotations from Gorky's principal articles about the Bolsheviki—with the minimum of editorial comment necessary to bring out the importance of the points raised.

Nikolai Lenine is the Kaiser, the Pope and the Karl Marx of the Bolshevik movement. His doctrines and ukases are absolute. No instance is on record where his doctrines or authority have been impugned. In his works Lenine defends not only a dictatorship of the proletariat, but a highly centralized revolutionary movement with one man at the top. Gorky's description of Lenine therefore becomes extremely important. We see him from the point of the great Russian Bolshevik writer as a sort of Calvin or Loyola, a fanatic, a man who is willing to put his theories into effect regardless of the cost in human life and regardless of the opposition of the overwhelming majority of the population.

GORKY ON LENINE

> Lenine is one of the most remarkable men of the Socialist "International." He is very intelligent, and possesses all the qualities of a "chief," including the absolute moral indifference which is often necessary for such a part. On occasions he does not lack a certain sentimentalism, but, at the same time, he has no pity for the mass of the people. And he believes that he has the right to make this terrible experiment on the Russian people. Weary of the war, and very unhappy, this people has already paid for Lenine's "experience" with thousands and thousands of lives. It will still cost it tens of thousands more. But this atrocious tragedy never makes Lenine hesitate, for he is the slave of dogma, and his partisans are his slaves.
>
> Lenine does not know the people. But he does know—from his books—how to arouse the masses and how to excite their worst instincts. The working classes are to Lenine what minerals are to the metallurgist. Can a Socialist-Nationalist state be made of this mineral? Indeed no, and Lenine doubts it. But why not try? What does Lenine risk if the attempt does not come off? Nothing much.

This description of Gorky's is all the more important because he himself shares a very large part of the Bolshevik theories—he opposes only the violent and autocratic methods of Lenine. In another article in his paper, the *Novoya Zhism*, Gorky resumes his analysis of Lenine's cruel and despotic actions. Let us note that Gorky realizes fully that Bolshevism and the Soviets have become identical. This is important, for the pro-Bolshevists of the *New Republic* and other similar American publications have endeavored to secure the recognition of the Bolsheviki by the round-about method of demanding the recognition of the Soviets—insisting that they are still two separate and distinct things! Gorky says:

> Here begins the line of sharp division between myself and the chaotic, topsy-turvy activities of the Soviets. I regard intellectual Bolshevism to be of great value to the aspiring Russian soul. This intellectual Bolshevism or Bolshevism of ideas could train the Russian soul to boldly demand its own, stir it to readiness for struggle and activity, awaken this indolent spirit to the sense of initiative, and especially give it form and life.
>
> But the practical Bolshevism of the anarchistic-communalistic visionaries which emanates from the Smolny Institute is injurious to Russia, and, above all, to the laboring class. The Soviets regard Russia as so much material for experiments. The Russian people is to them like the horse to the bacteriologist who injects the animal with the bacillus of typhus in order to produce the antitoxin. *It is with this kind of brutality and this form of disregard of consequences that the Soviets treat the Russian people, without giving the least thought to the possibility that the tortured and half-starved creature may die in the process.*
>
> *The social revolution that is planned can never be realized under the present conditions of life in Russia, for the reason that it is not possible to turn overnight into Soviets 85 per cent of the population of the country, which consists of peasants, living together with about twenty million of nomads from alien races.*
>
> My own opinion is that the Soviets are undermining and destroying the working class of Russia. They are setting up formidable towers of fearful and senseless complications that will stand in the path of the working class. Deaf to the voice of reason, they are bringing into existence unheard of insurmountable difficulties for the whole of the future course of the proletarians in their efforts to advance the progress of the war.

THE BOLSHEVIK PROGRAM "WRITTEN ON WATER"

Gorky says that there is practically no relation whatever between Bolshevik professions and Bolshevik practice. The professions are themselves sufficient to arouse the last degree of hostility on the part of every democrat—as we have shown above in quoting the Bolshevik's own statements. The practice is infinitely worse. As Gorky says, the Bolshevik actuality can have no relation whatever with any sort of idealism—not even with the perverted, reactionary and anti-democratic idealism of the Bolsheviki themselves. Gorky says:

> The proletarian is the bearer of a new culture. In these words were incorporated the beautiful dream concerning the triumph of righteousness, reason and love, the dream of the triumph of man over the beast. In the struggle for the realization of this dream thousands of men of all classes gave up their lives. Now the proletarian is at the helm, he has secured the coveted freedom to labor and create freely.

taken to pieces the buildings, the peasants are now preparing for war against one another for the division of the spoil. To this is added the calamity of famine. In some districts the population has long ago consumed all the available stocks of corn, including seed-corn; while in others the peasants, having had a good harvest, are hiding corn and even burying it in order not to share it with their starving neighbors. *All this must lead, and in some places has already led, to a war of all against all, and to the most senseless chaos and universal destruction and murder.*

n a bitter passage, terrible in its irony, Gor- concludes:

> Yes, the process of self-discipline among the masses is proceeding with gigantic strides. The revolutionary army garrison at Sebastopol has already undertaken the last final struggle with the bourgeoisie. Without much ado they decided simply to massacre all the bourgeoisie who lived within their reach. They decided and did it. At first they massacred the inhabitants of the two most bourgeois streets in Sebastopol; then the same operation, in spite of the resistance of the local Soviet, was extended to Simferopol, and then the turn came of Eupatoria.
>
> Apparently similar radical methods of class-war will soon be applied to Greater Russia, for we have already Mr. Bleichmann (the leader of the anarchists) energetically carrying on an agitation within the walls of the Petrograd Soviet in this sense.
>
> In Russia conscience is dead. The Russian people, in fact, have lost all sense of right and wrong. "Pillage whatever there is to pillage." Such is the motto of the two groups of Bolsheviki. The Red Guards, constituted to attack the counter-revolutionaries, shoot without trial any one whom they suspect. Pillage in all its forms is the only thing which is organized. In Petrograd every Bolshevik citizen may share in the spoil. The churches, museums, shops and stores are robbed.
>
> In the provinces still more tragic events are taking place. Almost incredible demands are made upon the population at a few hours' notice. The Crimea is undoubtedly the province which has suffered most. The sailors of the Black Sea Fleet brutally murdered several hundreds of their officers, and repeated these barbarous outrages in several towns, where they also murdered political prisoners. The scenes were such as to cause several cases of insanity among the terrorized population. The slaughter continues, and shooting is rife in the towns.

TROTZKY AND THE PROFESSIONAL BOLSHEVIKI

When the Bolsheviki secured control of the ussian Government by the aid of bayonets and large supply of money, the source of which is till a matter of dispute, the party had from one undred to two hundred thousand members acording to statements of Lenine. These are the rofessional Bolshevists—and it is with them lone that the real power rests. After the Bolheviki had been in power for seven or eight ionths, Trotzky made the following frank tatement of the character of the Russian labor rganizations which compose the Bolshevik ıovement:

> Let us be honest. Who are the leaders of the labor organizations today? Partly worthy self-sacrificing and convinced people who therefore have learned nothing and are scarcely able to read and write, but partly all sorts of adventurers and swindlers who take advantage of every great chance to make a position for themselves.

Trotzky proceeds to explain that the educated lasses (which the Bolsheviki have been proseuting in such a frightful manner) refuse to urnish them the experts and administrators bsolutely indispensable in every department of fe today.

EVIDENCE OF A PRO-BOLSHEVIK PRIME MINISTER OF FINLAND

Oscar Tokoi, first constitutionally elected 'rime Minister of Finland, who has just spent everal months in Russia as an ally of the Bolheviki, an alliance which he has since repudiatd, sums up the situation as follows:

> In comparison with the entire population only a small minority supports the Government, and, what is worse, to the supporters of the Government are rallying all the hooligans, robbers, and others to whom this period of confusion promises a good chance of individual action.
>
> Even a great part of those who from the beginning could stay with the Government and who still are sincere social democrats, having seen all this chaos, begin to step aside, or to ally themselves with those openly opposing the Government. Naturally, as time goes by, there remains only the worst and the most demoralized element. Terror, arbitrary rule, and open brigandage become more and more usual and the Government is not able to prevent it.
>
> Naturally only a small part of the people will remain backing such an order.
>
> A Socialistic society cannot be brought about by the force of arms and cannot be supported by the force of arms, but that a Socialist order must be founded on a conscious and living will of an overwhelming majority of the nation which is able to realize its will without the help of arms.
>
> I do not believe that at this time there is in Russia any social force which would be able to organize the conditions in the country. For that reason, to my mind, we should to begin with, frankly and honestly rely on the help of the allied powers.
>
> The democratic traditions of these countries are some surety that the social order established by them will be a democratic one.
>
> We must destroy the originator and the cause of the war, militarism, by its own arms, and on its ruins we must build, in harmony and in peace—not by force, as the Russian Bolsheviki want—a new and a better social order under the guardianship of which the people may develop peacefully and securely.

IV

SOVIET "ELECTIONS"

The ukases fixing the electoral qualifications for the Soviets are issued from time to time by Lenine and are countermanded or modified when results are not satisfactory. In the middle of last June at Lenine's orders, the Central Executive Council of the Russian Soviets "decided to expel those of its members representing the social revolutionists of the Right and the Center and the Mensheviki. All local councils are asked to expel representatives of the same parties." This is a wireless message of the official Russian Bolshevik agency.

But all Socialist proletarians and even extreme revolutionists who did not agree with the Bolsheviki are now being defranchised. The above mentioned groups are more or less moderate Socialists. Lenine, the official Bolshevik organ tells us, has now proceeded to disfranchise even the extreme Social Revolutionaries of the Left.

> Kazan, July 26.—As the important offices in the Soviet were occupied by Socialist Revolutionaries of the Left, the Extraordinary Commission has dissolved the Provincial Soviet. The Governmental power is now represented by a Revolutionary Committee.—Izvestya, July 28.

The most extraordinary Soviet elections were perhaps those of Petrograd at the end of the month of June.

Maxim Gorky's newspaper, the *Novoya Zhism*, which furnishes the report probably most nearly correct, shows that the Petrograd proletariat was absolutely governed by Bolsheviki:

> The Bolsheviki, it was indicated, won through the votes of the unemployed, the red guards, artificially created government organizations and alleged unions. The Soviets, at the point of the bayonet, arrested opposition leaders, stopped meetings, suspended newspapers and closed factories and workingmen's clubs.
>
> In all the Obuchovsky and Nevsky districts martial law was proclaimed. Many workmen were arrested. Patrols and armored automobiles still fill the districts. The workmen are extremely resentful and a serious outbreak is expected.
>
> A special conference of Petrograd workers decided on a day's strike as a protest. They will demand abolition of capital punishment, which has been one of the methods by which the Bolsheviki retains its power.

The one day general strike was carried out by the labor unions of Petrograd, but without effect. The unions had to content themselves with the issuing of the following manifesto, which, of course, led to their dissolution by the Bolsheviki:

> According to a resolution adopted by the Petrograd shop stewards committees, day and night, in the streets and in houses, murders occur, carried out not only by criminals but also by responsible agents of the Soviet Government.
>
> Murders are committed in the guise of fighting the counter revolution, and the victims belong not only to the enemies of the people but very frequently to the most peaceful class of citizens, workers, students, peasants and soldiers.
>
> Murders are committed without any inquiry or trial, deliberately and coldly, and in the name of the revolutionary proletariat.
>
> We, the representatiives of the Petrograd working class, before the entire people of Russia, proclaim that these murders are polluting the honor of the revolution, of democracy and socialism. We repudiate with indignation all responsibility for these sanguinuary deeds, which form a stain upon our socialist banner.
>
> We call upon all workers and upon all honest citizens to join us in our protest and demand a public trial of the authors of these bestialities and murders.

V

THE GERMAN SOCIALIST VIEW OF BOLSHEVIKI

It is unnecessary to point out that the German Socialists have been deeply interested in the Bolshevik movement from the beginning and have followed it from day to day. We shall not quote the opinion of any of the moderate Socialist wing which is obviously anti-Bolshevik. We shall confine ourselves to quotations from the Independent or Minority Socialists, the group led by Haase, Kautsky and Bernstein.

Karl Kautsky, who is the world's leading Socialist authority and who belongs to the radical wing of the movement, is now Foreign Prime Minister of Germany. In a recent article on the Bolsheviki he says:

"The Socialists must defend democracy, as Socialism without democracy is impossible." He cites Karl Marx to prove that Socialism is attainable peacefully in democratic countries and gives a series of citations from Marx to prove that Bolshevism is false to his principles.

Kautsky says a dictatorship by the lower classes leads to a dictatorship by the sword, and he sharply criticises the Russian Soviet Government, which has taken the power from the masses and created a dictatorship by one party of the proletariat, outlawing opposition.

He says the Bolsheviki are going to lose completely in Russia, as when they lose their power they will be unable to continue as a minority. He says the Bolsheviki know it, and are therefore trying by all means, clean or dirty, to hold power.

In the early stages of the Bolshevik movement, Kautsky gave a lengthy analysis showing how from the Socialist standpoint Bolshevism was an impossibility. His principal expressions were as follows:

> The population of Russia is still three-fourths agrarian and the greater part is illiterate; agriculture is technically backward and the means of communication extraordinarily deficient . . . . *from this it results that the revolution, because of the general character of the country can only be bourgeois and not Socialistic.*
>
> *The dictatorship of the proletariat* meant the discontinuance of the capitalistic production, which would be impossible under the proletariat

(*Continued on page 18*)

THE NATIONAL
Civic Federation Review

Office: Thirty-third Floor, Metropolitan Tower
1 Madison Avenue New York City

RALPH M. EASLEY, Editor

Published Twice a Month **Two Dollars a Year**

The Editor alone is Responsible for any unsigned article or unquoted statement published in THE NATIONAL CIVIC FEDERATION REVIEW.

THE SOVIET PROPAGANDA For six months the pro-Bolshevist propaganda in this country has taken a new form. Very few persons are willing to be labelled pro-Bolshevik, but the propaganda initiated by Lenine and Trotzky has been brilliantly successful in securing sympathy for the "Soviets." The Americans are a hard-headed race; not many have been caught by this superficial scheme, but it cannot be denied that sympathizers with "the Soviet form of government" may now be found in all directions. It is true that most of these sympathizers were formerly among the friends of Germany and advocates of a "peace without victory." Every day some new voice is heard employing the term "Soviet" as representing a desirable, practical and democratic form of government.

It is safe to say that not one out of one hundred persons so glibly using this new word, could give a clear and satisfactory description of the Russian Soviets and the way they work.

What is the Soviet? It is impossible to define within a few words—for the simple reason that the whole institution has changed from day to day to suit the needs and purposes of the Bolsheviki and their dictator, Lenine. The essence of it can be briefly stated. The Russian Communists, as the Bolsheviki call themselves, are violently anti-democratic. They are equally opposed to majority rule in the nation, in the province, in the city and even in the parish. The Soviets, it is true, are elected bodies, but so was the Council of the Empire in Germany and the Kaiser's own pet parliament in Prussia.

While Lenine's ukases, changing the electoral bases of the Soviets, have varied from month to month, the fact that the overwhelming majority of the Russian people are against him has obliged him to settle down to a definite and permanent basis. The one body upon which Lenine can absolutely rely is the Red Guard. Like every Lenine institution, this body is called "proletarian"; but the members of the Red Guard are personally chosen by Lenine and the executive committee of which he is head. This Red Guard is therefore literally a Pretorian Guard or body of Janizaries; nothing like it has been known since Wallenstein's mercenary army, which depopulated large parts of Central Europe during the Thirty Years' War. There is no pretense that the Red Guard is formed on patriotic grounds; exceptionally high pay is offered and a double ration of food (more valuable than gold in Russia today), besides exceptional privileges of loot.

The constitution of the Soviets announced by Lenine has made the Red Guard the foundation of the Soviet power!

The representation in the local Soviets, according to the paper program of Lenine, is as follows: Each one thousand working men to have one delegate and each one hundred and twenty-five Red Guards to have one delegate! That is, one Red Guard is worth eight working men.

But this is only the beginning of Lenine's hierarchy, which goes under the name "Soviet." He established for the provincial Soviets a law by which 125,000 peasants shall have the same representation as 25,000 workmen. That is, one workman is worth five peasants. Now certain changes are proposed in this Soviet constitution, but the sacred proportion which makes one Red Guard mercenary equal to forty peaceful and hard-working peasants is apparently to be maintained. It is now proposed that each five working men shall have the same voice as each two Red Guards and, on the basis of this lordly beneficence, Lenine expects the Mensheviki and social revolutionists to be tempted back into the fold. Fortunately, the democratic or anti-Soviet socialists have not swallowed the bait. But while the working men are possibly to be given a slightly less insulting treatment, the peasants have now been still further humiliated in comparison with the workmen, and in the New York *Nation*, of December 28, the provincial Soviet organization is described as follows: Every one hundred workmen are to have a delegate, whereas each volost, or group of villages, is to have only two delegates. The Russian volost varies greatly in population but it usually consists of from half a dozen to a dozen villages, each ranging in population from 500 to 5000 persons! Thus the volost with anywhere from 1000 to 20,000 families, is to have the same number of delegates in the provincial Soviet as a factory of two hundred working men! That is to say, one working man has the same vote as from ten to two hundred peasants.

This is not in the least surprising to anybody who knows the Bolshevist doctrine and practice. They have not only been suspicious towards the peasant population, which constitutes 85 per cent of the Russian nation, but hostile to it. In all their writings they convict themselves of being anti-democratic, which is the very meaning of the term "dictatorship" of the proletarians—that is, the rule of the manual laborers of the towns.

However, the preference of the Red Guard already referred to shows that Lenine has not even established a dictatorship of this proletariat, but of the Red Guard. According to the figures above given, the 300,000 members of the Red Guard have a vote in the provincial Soviets outnumbering the entire one hundred million peasants. But Lenine takes no chances. He also relies upon the support of the working class element in the Soviet, after having arrested, terrorized, expelled or starved to death the anti-Bolshevist elements, however revolutionary and socialistic they may be.

All the essential parts of the Soviet constitution, as above described, have been laid before the public again and again in the pro-Bolshevist statements of the socialist high-brow intellectuals. The ukases by which the anti-Bolsheviki are to be slowly starved to death, have been boasted of as being the most clever of their methods. What excuse is there then for educated and presumably well-informed persons to pretend that they do not know that the Soviets represent the extreme of anti-democratic violence to be found among any of the nations of the world today?

"HEROES" OF THE SLACKER BATTALION. The heroes of the great war are not represented, good readers, by the brave men who gave their lives in battle with the Huns, by the armless and legless lads who have begun to return to their homes, by the millions who self-sacrificingly and devotedly left their loved ones to fight for democracy and freedom. There were other heroes in this war—that is, if we accept the oleaginous enconiums of *Survey*, *Nation* and *New Republic* writers of the doughty fellows who heroically defied the laws of the land in refusing, or in trying to evade, service under the Selective Service Act. These men, if we are inclined to accept the interpretation of their champions, are the "idealists" of the war. In the *Survey* they are called "war's heretics." "They are not cowards," declares one Norman Thomas, vice chairman of the National Civil Liberties Bureau in the *Survey*. "Indeed, cowardice cannot justly be alleged against any objectors. . . . Only a firm and lofty courage will lead these men to jail."

mincing words declared for a peace of justice, in which Germany would have to pay for wrongs done. Did the British Labor Party carry England, as was predicted by our parlor Bolshevists? Mr. Lloyd George, who has been assailed as one of the arch-plotters against a peace of magnanimity to Germany, won out with a clear majority of 235 over any combination of other parties. The pacifists and Bolshevists were utterly routed. Exit Mr. Henderson, who advocated the Stockholm conference; Mr. Philip Snowden, the pacifist; Mr. Ramsay MacDonald, the Morris Hillquit of England.

Great Britain has given her answer to the pro-German sympathizers, Bolsheviki and foes of internal order. In endeavoring to explain the enormous landslide for Mr. Lloyd George, George Nicoll Barnes, Labor member of the War Cabinet, expressed the opinion that the Labor Party had lost by truckling to the pacifists and Bolshevists. The *Manchester Guardian*, the organ of "liberalism," alleged the Premier had won by "exploiting" the strong popular feeling regarding the punishment of Germany. One thing is certain: The British people have expressed themselves as unalterably opposed to what the *New York Times* has characterized as "a gentle truce with Germany until the next war," or the peace which the *New Republic*, the *Daily Call*, the *Nation*, the *Masses* and *Survey* have advocated.

Premier Clemenceau, addressing the Chamber of Deputies, received an overwhelming vote of confidence. That was the voice of France speaking.

No doubt there will be whimperings and whinings among the shadow Huns here as the Peace Conference progresses. But there has been observable in this country a change in the temper of the people. With American boys returning home wounded, legless, armless, blind, suffering from the gases of a fiendish foe, there has been a noticeable decrease in patient toleration of subtle disloyalty and insidious pro-Germanism.

ENGLAND'S NAVAL SUPREMACY

(From Bulletin Sent to the German-Language Press Under the Above Heading By the American Friends of German Democracy, Franz Sigel, President)

In a German-language paper published in the United States we recently read an article bitterly condemning England's claim to supremacy on the seas. The article which was thoroughly anti-British, culminated in the threat that the American people would even take upon themselves the burden of conscription so as to make it plain to the British that they were not in the mood to be dictated to by any foreigner and to recognize any foreign supremacy, on land or sea.

Similar articles have appeared in other German-language papers of the United States. They are absolutely mischievous, in bad taste, and seem to indicate a desire to embroil the people of the United States with the people of Great Britain. This anti-British feeling has of course nothing in common with the anti-British prejudice which was formerly so prevalent in the United States. The new anti-British feeling is merely an echo of the propaganda conducted in the United States by the late Imperial German Government before we entered the war. Americans of German origin who have felt the baneful effects of this propaganda should be on their guard and not allow themselves to be deceived by catchwords and idle rumors which in the end will hurt them as much as they will hurt the United States.

There is no truth in the assertion that Great Britain will have nothing to do with the proposed League of Nations. The truth is that in Great Britain as well as in France, Italy and the United States, there are reactionary cliques who do not want a peace as outlined by President Wilson. The people of Great Britain, from what we know of them, are heartily in favor of a League of Nations and the British Government has delegated Lord Robert Cecil to the Peace Conference for the special purpose of conducting the negotiations for a formation of a League of Nations.

It is true that Great Britain insists upon naval supremacy, and under the present circumstances no fairminded person can say that such a claim is unjustified. As long as there is no League of Nations to guarantee the peace of the world Great Britain is absolutely at the mercy of a stronger naval power.

The position of Great Britain is unparalleled in human history. There is no other country in the world which could be brought to its knees so quickly by a superior naval force. Naval power alone could never have vanquished Germany. The greatest naval power could accomplish little against the self-supporting United States. France could not be conquered by naval power. But Great Britain which for its food stuffs depends almost entirely on foreign imports brought to the Island across the sea, could be reduced to utter impotence by a superior sea power within six months. The case for British naval supremacy would have an entirely different aspect if the British Isles produced the bulk of the food consumed by their teeming populations. If that were the case it might be fairly argued that the claim of Great Britain for naval supremacy sprang from a desire for world domination and was not the fundamental principle of British national defense.

These facts are too little understood by most people, but in England they are fully appreciated by everyone, even by the pacifists. For the masses of the British people naval supremacy is a question of bread and butter. Even the least intelligent among the British people fully understand that if under present world conditions naval supremacy passed out of the hands of Great Britain, the people could be starved out in a very short time. . . . As long as the present economic structure of Great Britain lasts and especially as long as there is no League of Nations to provide better security against wars, the British people will undoubtedly insist upon having the strongest sea power.

This claim does not indicate a desire to dominate and bully the world, but is merely the result of the natural wish to maintain national security and independence. If President Wilson succeeds in carrying out the American policy of bringing into life a League of Nations it is as sure as anything can be that the apprehensions felt by the British people will disappear and that Great Britain will become one of the stoutest pillars of world peace. Let us remember that it was not Great Britain that willed the Great War. Prince Lichnowsky, in his famous memorandum, clearly pointed out that Great Britain tried to avoid the war in 1914 by all the means in her power. Great Britain, with her vast mercantile marine, had not the remotest interest in a world conflagration. Moreover, a government of pacifists was actually in power in Great Britain when the war broke out. In no other country had the idea of world peace so many adherents as in England.

An American newspaper which attempts to sow suspicion against Great Britain at this time does the greatest disservice to the United States. Mutual recriminations will certainly not advance the success of American policies. A League of Nations must be based upon international trust and confidence. Let us abandon national hatreds and prejudices. The world has had enough of that poison, and if there is one group of the American nation which should set its face sternly against the propaganda of national or race hatreds, it is surely the Americans of German extraction who have suffered so much from the evil passions let loose by the war.

Shadow Huns and Oth

By T. EVERETT HARRÉ

Part III

GENESIS OF "PARLOR BOLSHEVISM"

IN times of peace, when life goes on along the lines of orderly and constructive process, these people who have identified themselves with the motley phases of disguised pro-German and other sinister forms of propaganda would call for little if any notice; in fact, it is only by reason of the unusual times and their extraordinary conduct that they have succeeded in attracting attention. It is only because of their power to work harm, when the world is in turmoil and men's opinions are unsettled, that their work calls for sober and impartial analysis.

To gain an understanding of their untoward activities it is helpful if one appreciates the character of this breed and gauges their motives. Here is a tribe of individuals, divided into several specific groups, who, first of all, opposed our going to war with Germany, who did all in their power to obstruct the country in effectively carrying on the war against Germany, who opposed the draft, sought by every means to destroy the confidence of the people in the Allies, and who to the end waged a campaign against military victory over the foe and pleaded for mercy to the Huns. Some have figured in every pacifist movement that came along. They came out strong in defense of the yclept "conscientious objectors" and tried to raise a defense fund when a hundred or more I. W. W. leaders were on trial in Chicago for seditious conspiracy. They have in every case been arrayed with the forces of disintegration and destruction, and never with the forces of social construction and amelioration. Having done their utmost to prevent the collapse and surrender of Germany, they are now found to be setting themselves forth as exponents of a program which shall bring about an over-night millennium—by the abrogation of all laws and existing social order, by the destruction of representative democratic government, the turning topsy-turvy of civilization and the erection upon the ruins of society of a so-called rule of the proletariat. It is certainly not out of a fine, sincere and sterling desire to help humanity constructively that they have become the mouthpieces of Bolshevism and "internationalism," but out of a very obvious desire to get into the lime-light.

THE "UPLIFTERS'" PROGRESS

Considering their colossal pretensions, these folk fall below mere mediocrities. Utterly unoriginal, lacking any depth, or grace of style, not one could possibly hope to make any mark in the legitimate lines of human endeavor, in art or literature, in politics or philosophy. Consciously or subconsciously realizing their insignificance and pitiful ineptitude, the meagreness of their mental gifts, they have consequently sought to attract attention and get their names into print by attaching themselves to the outré, the fantastic, the supposedly ultra-modern, and as a final recourse to the disloyal, pro-German, anarchistic and disreputable. Snobs and egotists, they are able to flatter and delude themselves with the idea of being above the ordinary when, as they believe, they step out of the common run of humdrum people. Actually these "advanced" thinkers and ultra-modern "liberals" are extremely sixth-rate. Their trumpet calls to humanity to follow is as ringingly clarion as a ten-penny whistle. The role of the leader and prophet fails to hide the shoddy, vulgar and ill-mannered mountebank.

Before the war gave them an opportunity for being unique by being pro-German, these same individuals were found affiliated with every bizarre and freak movement that came along. They originally commercialized and egotized "muckrakeism," and thence drifted on to liberal-clubism, "hereticism," etc. They lined up with Cubism and impressionism in art, *vers libre* in literature; they were on the crest of the wavelets of Socialism, I. W. W.ism, anarchism and Greenwich-villageism. From pragmatism they gravitated easily to tangoism. They were strong for "free verse," "free love," and free grub. Over their table d'hotes and wine in the cigarette-reeking cafés of Greenwich village they ventilated vapid inanities about affinityism and Freudism. Often misled women, past the first bloom of youth, believing they were being introduced into a real Bohemia of advanced art and high thinking, paid for the dinners, the wine and the cigarettes. This crowd advocated "birth control," and every kind of control excepting self control. They were for "social reform," dress reform, and every sort of reform except moral reform. The women took to bobbed hair and going without corsets. The males took to long hair and a mincing gait. Their stock-in-trade included the preaching that marriage is legalized prostitution, yet when it came for them to marry into a house or a flat, with three square meals assured per day, they didn't hesitate at ensnaring other people's husbands and wives. They let off considerable "steam" about wage slavery, the crimes of organized wealth, etcetera, yet did they mix and mingle with their pet proletariat? Did they stick to the East Side? With all their affected emancipation, they craved for respectability, sought entre to the homes of the refined, toadied to possible capitalistic benefactors and wealthy ladies inclined to uplift the lowly, and noisily thronged the forums of fashionable churches. They schemed in every way to waylay and marry wealth, and did so in many cases. Rich adolescents who went in for settlement work, and impressionable heiresses on high-brow slumming expeditions who were taken off their feet by what they thought were Hall Caine and Mrs. Humphrey Ward radical heroes, found themselves married to professional viragoes and social scolds whose main personal ambition was to "live easy." Few of these people, either as laborers or journalists, could have earned their living by an honest day's work. Instead, they exploited theories which they carefully failed to practice. Many, alas, were notoriously deficient in ordinary human decency. A certain woman who was duped and preyed upon by a number of these trousered parasites was sued by her husband, a merely everyday business man, for divorce. The husband got the divorce on the strength of testimony which he secured from the lofty-thinking Greenwich village co-respondents.

VOCIFERATION AND VICTUALS

While they railed at capitalistic imperialism, by every sort of flattery many courted the patronage of the wealthy whom they pretended to despise, and it was only by pursuing the intellectual mendicant game that they succeeded in financing their books, pamphlets and magazines. This tin-cup social uplift, reform-the-world-overnight confidence game goes on. The subsidized pensioneer periodicals come regularly like the old call in the market place please to help the blind.

Before they succeeded in fastening themselves,

e—and you had their word for it—free! y announced that they believed in the theory forth by Bernard Shaw—that the female of species pursues the man. Many did. Some he men in this group who were going to over- society, were, so far as appearance went, et and gentle souls, and they uttered the most idful things in the softest and most persua- tone of voice. The slummers from uptown e thrilled to their toes by the things they rd—it was like listening in on some frightful rchist conspiracy, some plot to commit whole- murder.

'here was, in this group, a large amazonian son, who had left her youth long in the au- nal past, with the features of a gorgon ved in stone, whose gaze was a threat. She e tailor-made suits, with short skirts, affect- a mannish gait and a coarse masculine tone voice. This sibyl of the social revolution spe- ized in expounding to the unwary feminine phytes of Socialism of tender age the philoso- that marriage as sanctioned by those insti- ions of capitalism—the church and state—is alized slavery; a doctrine Trotzky adhered to en he recently established by decree a "free e bureau" in Russia and declared "children o are the issues of these unions are to become property of the Bolshevist state."

)ne summer this advocate of freedom rented cottage on the sea coast, and thence took h her a number of possible disciples of the r sex, one of whom, however, was unmoved the teachings and remained, beause she loved husband, a loyal, faithful and devoted wife. is young woman precipitately departed from summer retreat because she "couldn't stand " She described the evenings, when the anti- trimonial famished fanatic, wrapped in a amer blanket, sat close to a wood fire expound- g Freudism and discussing with savory relish e erotic vagaries of humankind. It was upon r return to New York that the unexpected ppened, that Greenwich Village was taken its ears by the news that this foe of the arriage institution had taken unto herself legally wedded spouse. And that spouse! -meek, mild, with a tender seedlet-sprouting of mind, of the male species a clinging vine. He ore khaki-colored bloomers, which matched his olasses-colored Van Dyke beard. Wandering and down Fifth Avenue, book in hand, he ever wore a hat, not wishing to conceal the ffy locks grown in imitation of Anton Lang, e actor of Ober Ammergau.

"GENIUS" STILL UNHEARD OF

There came nightly to these dens a young et from New Jersey, whose ambition aspired the lofty heights of assisting in the social eak-up and of writing book reviews at thirty llars per for the *New Republic*. He wrote uching verses about Emma Goldman's red wn, incense and choir boys. There was a etty, flashing-eyed, neurotic Russian Jewess, hose chief claim to notoriety was that she d assisted in making bombs in a garret in . Petersburg, and who has lately made a ecialty of writing magazine articles about enine and Trotzky and the women of the Bol- evik revolution. Of course, these recent arti- es extolling the Bolsheviki have basis in such side knowledge of Russia as is gained in Green- ich Village, the ardent girl not having been Russia since 1905. Being in need of ready sh at one time, this daughter of delirium un- rtook to write for a capitalistic publishing ncern a life of Abraham Lincoln. The result as interesting, as she knew nothing of Ameri- n history and was incapable of understanding merican psychology. Today the charming per- n, having never been in England, is anti-Eng- h; having no country of her own to love and r which to fight, is a pacifist, and, not hav- g seen their bloody marauds in Russia, is a uculent and rampageous Bolshevik.

There was a large, soft-muscled, puffy creature, with a putty face, the suave caressive movements of whose hands gave one the "creeps." He is today one of the soap box apostles of the "reds," and at that time was hailed as the novelist of the coming revolution. He was terrible in his arraignment of the wicked capitalist system, and if the hard-hearted plutocrats had known what he said about them over his red wine they would probably have been unable to sleep. In one respect only was this advocate of the general strike and revolution, Christian—he took no thought of the morrow, of what he should eat or what he should drink. There was no need. A fund was raised to finance him while writing the great novel of anarchism—which, needless to say, was never written.

A near-poet, who beceame a paid German agent after the European war broke out, was original in announcing as his most admired and inspiring heroes, Judas, Nero and a poet of unfortunate memory. Over his food this fellow would read to his companions love letters written to him by women who should have known better. He had a face which reminded one of a rat and a gait which called to mind a hopping sparrow. He, too, managed to live by getting donations from certain rich women on the fringe of demi-society who were willing to pay to have a literary flavor given their meretricious, gilded and vulgar drawing rooms by the presence of pseudo-writers and near-poets. A friend of this parasite was a Jew who posed as a Frenchman and assumed a French name. At that time he eked out his bread and butter by writing very bad books which a certain lady with a purse and without position published as her own—at her own expense—in order to enhance her non-existent social standing by a smack of the literary. Of late, this fellow has lectured on syndicalism and Bolshevism and now draws contributions from women who were formerly openly pro-German and whose only outlet for their repressed feelings is to encourage loose talk about Allied imperialism and social revolt.

In those days preceding German propaganda and Bolshevism, one young man busied himself collecting contributions in order to publish thin volumes of thinner verse. His lack of ability was made up by an irrepressible loquacity concerning the greatness of his own Gaelic genius. He gave out visiting cards on which he ingenuously labelled himself, "Poet, Prophet, Patriot." Even among the Greenwich Villagers he was regarded with good-natured pity, being as impecunious of pocket as he was of grey matter. Through the good influences of a Tammany politician he got a job as a sort of office boy *de luxe* in the Senate at Washington, where, after the war broke out, he acted as messenger, for a paltry pittance, for German agents. He boasted of having himself written a bill designed to keep American citizens from traveling on ships carrying munitions. Whether this was so or not, he was the author of an anoymous novel attacking Great Britain which the German agents published in a disreputable pro-German weekly. Any desired effect of this piece of fiction was, of course, negatived by its amateurishness and puerile absurdity. This unconscious scaramouch took part in a burlesque celebration at which the independence of Ireland was declared in 1915 by a half-dozen hare-brained freaks. After America entered the war, and the Department of Justice showed an interest in certain Sinn Fein activities this young "poet and patriot" of the Irish revolution found it healthful to "fade" from assemblages of the Poetry Society and the purlieus of Washington Square. Another member of this group was a leader in the Rand school, and has since become a pacifist. Singular, isn't it, how the whole crew who plied their pens and mouthed so mightily about fighting for humanity, individually and as a body retired when it came to fighting German autocracy!

"HEROES" OF THE REVOLUTION

There is a certain woman who has figured in the past few years in the public prints as an agitator of the social revolution. Before the war, she specialized in woman suffrage. During the war she became affiliated with a string of pacifist organizations, from which incidentally she has drawn large salaries. After America entered the war a group of well-meaning Quakers, possessed of considerable wealth, were induced to subsidize a society which proposed to fight militarism, conscription, etcetera. This woman, as the directing brains of the pacifist organization, drew a salary of something like a hundred dollars a week and expenses, and out of the funds subscribed by the Quakers paid to a particular "gentleman friend," it was said, a salary of $125 per week. Both the lady and the "gent" were against war with Germany, and were strong for the Bolsheviki. A small riot was created in the Washington offices of the pacifist society when the $125 a week revolutionary beheld a mouse mousing among the refuse of waste paper on the floor. Beholding this formidable monster, the gallant knight of the pen, always so eager to take up that trusty weapon in defense of the exploited classes, took refuge upon the height of an office chair, whence, striking frantically with his cane and waving his Derby hat, he called loudly for help from the staff of female stenographers. Of such stuff are the heroes of the revolution made!

Amid the crowd who congregated in the stale atmosphere of the basement regaling places there was one who was regarded by his confreres with an esteem not unmixed with envy. This writer, of little actual literary ability but considerable professional shrewdness and cunning, had chanced upon muckraking when muckraking was in the initial stages of its popularity. He had undertaken to expose the wickedness of politics in the great cities, and his articles, published in a magazine representative of the capitalistic press, had brought him no little revenue and a certain notoriety. He had never done anything of note before the publication of this series —which, by the way, was widely quoted and reprinted in Germany with the purpose of showing the German people how rotten American politics were and how superior the Teuton system of Government was—and he has done nothing since. Except one thing. Having revealed America's political rottenness to the debased American public, as well as to the gratified Teuton public, this gentleman espoused what he called "early Christianity." He commercialized, and lectured upon at so much per lecture, the philosophy of primitive brotherhood. When the war came on he became a pacifist, and after the Bolsheviki surrendered Russia to Germany he put himself forward as an interpreter of Bolshevism and a messiah of the world revolution. In keeping with this role he affected a messianic beard trimmed after the style of beards worn by characters in the religious paintings of the German artist Hoffman. He became theatrically solemn, grave-eyed and quavering voiced. Whenever he addressed well-fed lunchers and convocations of evening eaters he reminded one of an amateur rehearsing for the role of a Charles Rann Kennedy semi-religious sociological play. For some months now he has been engaged in enlightening the ignorant of the American public upon the Russian revolution, how it happened and what it all means. He has particularized upon emphasizing the perfidy of the Allies and in exposing the text, context and significance of their "secret treaties." He tells about the Bolshevik revolution as one who saw it first hand. He was, it is true, in Russia. His personal investigations and profound observations, it is reported, embraced the lengthy period of seventeen days.

To the fell activities of this sentimentalist may be to a large measure ascribed the catas-

(*Continued on page 18*)

Bolshevik "Industrial Government"

Prepared for the League for National Unity

By GUSTAVUS MYERS

(Continued from previous issue)

FORTY BILLION RUBLES DEFICIT A YEAR

Cornelius J. Callahan, manager of the Russian-American Company for International Trade, gave me a further graphic description of conditions in Russia. The company represented by Mr. Callahan did a business of $28,000,000 during three years in Russia. Mr. Callahan was in that country three and a half years, leaving Moscow on August 26, 1918, and Petrograd five days later.

"Industrial conditions in Russia have completely broken down," he said. "Only a few factories have recently been in operation. Such technical experts as have survived or remained have been forced by the threat of utter starvation to go back to work. Their salaries in some cases are lower than the wages of many laborers. The factories are run by workingmen's committees or their agents. But where these have been what the workers considered too strict in their orders, they have been ousted by the men under them. Any of the executives—and they are selected by the men themselves—who try to get a fair amount of work a day from the men at once become unpopular and are summarily removed. The workmen demand executives who will allow them to have their own way. The workday is supposed to be eight hours, but the time spent in meetings is deducted. Sometimes there is more than one meeting a day, and often these meetings of the workingmen last for hours.

"Under such impossible conditions production is pitiful compared to costs, and such factories as have been running have piled up large deficits. There, for example, is the Kolomna Steel Works, sixty miles south of Moscow. This plant, which makes steel and locomotives, is one of the largest in Russia. It employs about 10,000 men, and the average pay is 700 rubles a month. The men are supposed to work eight hours, but they hold daily meetings, and even when they apparently work, they idle much of the time. Probably they don't do more than three or four hours a day efficient work. In March, 1918, this factory produced less than 1,000,000 rubles worth of material, but the pay roll for that month was 7,000,000 rubles. This 7,000,000 rubles of outlay did not, of course, include the cost of raw material.

"I don't suppose production in all plants is ten per cent of what it formerly was. In one of the Government workshops it cost, in August, 1918, the sum of 84,000 rubles to repair a motor truck. The same kind of motor truck could be manufactured in America and landed in Moscow for one half the price the repairing there cost.

"The Bolshevik Government is plunging ahead on a deficit, even growing vaster. This deficit can now be conservatively estimated at forty billions of rubles a year. How is this deficit met? By the printing of prodigious issues of paper money. This avalanche of paper is added to by counterfeiting which is being done on a large scale. Counterfeiting is the only flourishing industry in Russia. When the Bolshevik Government finds a good counterfeiting plant, it puts the counterfeiter to death, and if his press turns out a good product it takes it over and uses it itself—so it is reported.

"The present scale of wages is ten times more than the pre-war scale. But the workmen cannot get an existence. The average monthly pay of 700 rubles will buy only 70 pounds of bread, or 20 pounds of butter or one pair of shoes.

"All of the workmen, both skilled and unskilled, are now opposed to the Bolsheviki. About sixty per cent of these workers, especially those with families, would be pleased to see some strong, stable, rational government established so that there would be some relation between wages and a liveable existence. About twenty per cent of the workmen are neutral, not knowing themselves what they want, excepting that they would like security. The remainder of the workingmen are opposed to the Bolsheviki because they object to any organized power that compels them to work.

"As for the women they are almost unanimously against the Bolsheviki, and they are much more courageous in expressing themselves than the men. Full ninety per cent of the women of all classes would relish any government—no matter what—that would restore the old peaceful conditions.

MILLIONS OF UNEMPLOYED

"Millions of workmen are unemployed. Many came originally from villages, and have gone back there where they have a bit of land or relatives on whose land they can work. About seventy-five per cent of the total population—which several years ago swelled to the abnormal figure of three millions—have left Petrograd, and at least forty per cent of Moscow's skilled and unskilled workmen and intelligencia have quit that city.

"To give you an idea of the temper of the workmen, let me tell you of an incident last July in the Michelson factory at Moscow. The facts were related to me by a person present, Lenine and Trotzky came there to harangue a meeting of the workers. Trotzky started to denounce the bourgeoisie, demanding further severities against them. A workingman interrupted him. 'We've taken their factories from them,' declared the workingman, 'but what have we got? They've got nothing and we've got nothing.' There was a great uproar. Then Lenine came forward to speak. A workingman bitterly shouted: 'We haven't had bread for two days. Now, Mr. Lenine, are we going to get bread tomorrow? If so, you can speak; if not, don't speak!' Lenine promised bread, and was allowed to go on. The workmen in the factory got their bread the next day.

"The machinery in factories has largely been ruined through misuse and improper handling. The textile factories have all gone to pieces. Many factories will need replacing.

"It was rumored in Moscow last June that Lenine wanted to surrender governing functions and work thereafter by underhand propaganda. He and some other of the Bolshevik leaders decided that the experiment had gone far enough, but the extreme elements of the extremists would not agree, and their will prevailed."

THE INTERNATIONAL HARVESTER PLANT

Authentic information reveals that, at least up to some months ago, the International Harvester Company works at Moscow was the only plant that survived Bolshevik methods. When the Bolshevik movement first came into power, the company at once adopted a comprehensive policy of feeding its employes, even going to the extent of having grain made into flour. This and other practical welfare work greatly helped to assure good feeling. When Bolshevik committees that were formed in the plant asked to take over the plant and operate it themselves, the company's representative agreed to turn over the physical plant to them, but firmly declined to transfer the company's funds to them. By its welfare wo[rk] the company had kept open its plant long enou[gh] for its workers to see the ruinous results of B[ol]shevik confiscatory methods in other plants, [a]ll or nearly all, of which had gone to pieces. Th[ey] therefore, realized that unless they abando[ned] these claims, the International Harvester pla[nt] would have to be discontinued, too. At latest [ac]counts the International Harvester works w[as] one of the few plants that escaped the gene[ral] industrial wreckage.

Another American, one who has had extra[or]dinary special facilities for getting informati[on] on events in Russia and who is an influential f[ig]ure in an organization to aid the Russian peop[le] says:

ENSLAVING THE MASS OF WORKERS

"The workmen in Russia are divided into t[wo] classes: first, those who are real Bolshevists, a[nd] second, the real Russian workers. The first cla[ss] is satisfied with anything maintaining their dom[i]nation of the proletariat. The Bolsheviki ha[ve] to have a machine to maintain their power. Th[ey] must maintain themselves by providing for [a] considerable section of the workers. Most e[x]penses are paid by the Bolshevik Government.

"The second class are workmen who are n[ot] Bolsheviki, but who to preserve their lives a[nd] the lives of their families and to get food, si[de] with the Bolsheviki and are willing to work u[n]der existing Bolshevik conditions.

"These workmen see that they are being us[ed] only as pawns for Bolshevik power, and that [as] things are going destruction is ahead. They a[re], therefore, making every effort to get away fro[m] industrial centers and place themselves in t[he] country districts and live away from the terro[r] of Bolshevik power.

"In other words, the great mass of Russia[n] workers—eighty per cent at least—are anti-Bo[l]shevik.

"They see that the present conditions are on[ly] temporary. But they are afraid to run count[er] to the Bolshevik leaders who control the arm[y] and food.

"We have absolute statements from men ov[er] there and who know, that in factories under Bo[l]shevik control the men take away the manufa[c]tured goods which they themselves make. The[se] goods they sell for their private profit. The Bo[l]shevik Government runs the factories, pays t[he] men, and the men in turn privately and for the[ir] own profit sell the goods.

"For example: There is, or was, a big tool fa[c]tory at Moscow. The Bolshevik Governme[nt] supplied the raw materials and ran it. Th[e] workmen took away the manufactured produc[ts] and sold them outside for whatever prices the[y] could get.

"There have been many similar example[s]. There is an absolute condition of industrial cha[os] in sections under Bolshevik control."

BUYING MASS SUPPORT

A. J. Sack, head of the Russian Informatio[n] Bureau in the United States thus epitomizes t[he] industrial situation under Bolshevik power:

"In the directing of factories ability was n[ot] considered. The Bolshevik Government also ha[d] to create jobs for its followers to get mass su[p]port. Men who had no technical knowledge wha[t]ever were put in charge. In many instances t[he] factory force would sell the raw material, shorte[n] the work hours, and raise wages above the capa[c]ity of that industry to pay. Workingmen, urge[d] on by criminals, would ruin the machinery. Th[e] consequence has been that all factories have ha shut down excepting those where the bosses ·e graft to the Bolsheviki. In turn these ses were allowed to charge all they wanted, l to exploit the workers as much as they ıld. There are only a few factories being op- ted, and these but three or four hours a day."

Not to confine this account to sources that Bol- vik advocates might say were prejudiced or agonistic, I went to a Bolshevist headquarters New York City, asking them for their side of story. They handed out a typewritten copy a stenographically reported speech made on ne 11, 1918, by Professor George V. Lomono- f at Madison Square Garden, New York City. though professing not to be a Bolshevik, Pro- sor Lomonosoff spoke under the auspices of e Russian Soviet Recognition League, plead- g for the recognition of the Bolshevik Govern- nt. These are some extracts from his speech:

PRO-BOLSHEVIK ADMISSIONS

"Is it not a fact that the power in Russia rests t in the Bolsheviki as such but in the Soviets? day the majority in the Soviets may be of the lsheviki. Tomorrow, it may be of the social volutionists or even of the Black Hundred..

"According to information from different urces the land at the present time is being di- led among the peasants, and whatever cannot physically divided, as for example, libraries, oductions of art, 'bourgeoise' breeding cattle, d even agricultural implements are being de- royed."

Professor Lomonosoff's argument was that, vertheless and notwithstanding all these ex- sses, "Russia must be helped, regardless of the mposition of the Government and the popula- on. Shoes, locomotives, agricultural imple- ents are a necessity to the Bolsheviki, as well as e Menshiviki, to the Cadets and even to the lack Hundred. Help is needed by the whole ussian people."

Neither he nor the Bolsheviki considered the oint that if, as he admitted, the Bolsheviks were stroying on so widespread a scale such material they had, why should America go to the ex- ense and trouble of sending material to em? If they could not take care of what ey had on the spot, could they take greater care material and supplies shipped thousands of iles to them? Furthermore, Professor Lomono- ff admitted that the Bolsheviki were extermi- ating the intellectuals who in Russia com- rise all the educated classes, including teachers, octors, dentists, technical staffs, etc. The sup- lies sent would be seized, therefore, and held y the Bolsheviki and used to intrench them- lves further in power. No part of them would allowed to reach that great part of the Rus- an people opposed to the Bolsheviki.

THE TYRANNY OF ANARCHY

To a *London Chronicle* representative, a mem- r of a well-known London business house who ad been in Moscow about a year gave on Octo- r 3, 1918, a graphic account of conditions in ussia. He was the head of a party of 76 British gitives from Russia reaching London.

Part of the interview follows:

"What Bolshevist rule means in that land of assacres it is difficult for people at home to lly realize. Banks are, in my opinion, gone; vestments in goods are confiscated; current ac- unts are taken, safes opened, nothing is left. ou cannot close your business on the ground at it doesn't pay, lest the officials hand it over your employes to keep going. If you discharge employe you have to give three months' no- ce and pay three months' money to the Un- nployed Fund.

"There is no law or reason in the taxes. hey may tell you to pay what you did before, d repeat the demand a month later. You can- ot speak in the streets without the risk of ouble. There is no free press. All the papers ave been taken over by the government and confiscated, as has been trade after trade. Houses and flats are requisitioned on various pretexts or none at all. Especially have educated people been victimized. Though there are hundreds of flats empty in Moscow, expensive furniture is dumped in the main streets and left there because the owners have nowhere to take it.

"Women are in a pitiable plight. Thousands whose husbands have been shot in the war or are away on service are stranded, with their war pensions stopped, their investments confiscated, their jewelry confiscated or taxed beyond endurance, and even their stored furs appropriated for the working people. Hundreds of educated and refined women have asked me for work for a mere pittance.

"The government workers had their pay raised 100 per cent, and they get preferential treatment in the use of bread cards. The educated man, such as the doctor, is bottom dog and gets nothing."

Chapter III

PUBLIC UTILITIES

According to information received by well-informed members of the American-Russian League the same conditions of anarchy prevail on such street car lines as are being run. The well-informed person of the American-Russian League heretofore quoted says this reliable information has reached him:

"Tramcars in such sections as are controlled by the Bolsheviki are operated by Government money, and the proceeds—that is to say, the fares—are divided between the workers who run the cars and the Government which needs the money. Apparently the men who operate the power houses and keep the system going are paid out of the Government funds. They don't share in the proceeds graft. The 'system' is one of everything going out and nothing coming in.

"The hours of work are determined in different localities by the local Soviets. Everything is in a chaotic state. Cars are run on a crazy system. Nobody knows when cars will run. This is not the case, however, in sections where the control has been taken over by the Germans."

FOOD AT FAMINE PRICES

In an interview published in the *New York Times*, Sept. 27, 1918, Dr. Angus Campbell who left Moscow early in September and arrived at New York September 26, stated:

"The conditions existing in Russia at the present time are so bad that they cannot be imagined, except by those who have been there. The Bolsheviki hold full sway and are a band of adventurers assembled from all parts of the world. I did not see Trotzky, but I often met Lenine and heard him address meetings. He is a fanatic out and out and very dangerous.

"One thing certain is that the Bolsheviki are pro-German. At first they were passive, but gradually they became bolder and bolder, until they openly acknowledged their partisanship with the Central Powers.

"In Moscow food is at famine prices. When I left there at the beginning of this month bread cost 18 rubles [$9] a pound, butter 32 rubles [$16] and sugar 30 rubles [$15] a pound. Green apples, which gave the people who ate them cholera morbus, cost 3 rubles [$1.50] each.

"The Bolsheviki divided the inhabitants of Moscow into four classes: first, the workmen, who were given what food could be obtained in the city; secondly, the women, who came next in order for the rations; then the clerks, who got what was left; and lastly, the unfortunate wealthy class who were allowed three herrings a day and no bread.

"There are a few street cars running in Moscow but no cabs. The hotels have all been commandeered by the Bolsheviki and I had to go to them to get a room. There are no courts of justice and no regular police. Guards stand at the street corners with loaded rifles ready to shoot on the slightest provocation. They will hold a foreigner up and take his money from him, and may kill him if he has none. It depends upon how the particular guard feels that day.

"Other Bolshevist agents in uniform often stop foreigners in the street in Moscow and take away their papers and money under the pretence that it is for official examination. They tell the victim to call at the police station next morning, but that is the last he will see of any of his property."

CHAOTIC RAILROAD CONDITIONS

One hardly needs to be told, so general is the knowledge in Europe and America of the chaotic condition of Russian railroads.

"The Bolshevik Government," says Mr. Corse, "is a go-as-you-please regime. As a rule the railroad men are a higher class of workmen than the industrial workers. They, too, have their committees. There has been a great deal of friction between them and the ordinary workers and the soldiers. Frequently the Railroad Labor Committees have refused to obey the orders of the Central Soviet. Trains are run on no schedule but on caprice. Often the soldiers take control, override all instructions of train despatchers, with frequent fatal consequences. There have been many bad accidents."

On October 17, 1918, Mr. Corse received a letter dated Stockholm, September 13, 1918, from a personal friend who had arrived there from Russia.

"Believe me," it read in part, "the last few months in Russia have not been far short of hell. A reign of terror existed, and probably exists now, that those outside of Russia cannot imagine. Wholesale arrests have been made among the English and French, and of course rumors of all sorts were flying about concerning what the Bolsheviki had in store for Americans. * * * We left Moscow on Monday, August 26, and arrived at Petrograd, Finnish station, the following day, where we were held up until Saturday. I went into town several times, but toward the end it was too risky, as people were being arrested on all sides by the Red Guard."

Samuel Lovich testifies to the fact that "the employees of a locomotive repair shop struck because they no longer wanted to repair locomotives whose only function, as they saw it, was to facilitate the travelings of the bourgeoisie." Since that incident took place there has been a wholesale slaughter of the so-called bourgeoisie, and such as have survived are being deliberately starved to death.

A cable despatch February 24, 1918, from Amsterdam told of the chaos in Russia as described by an eye-witness in the *Tageszeitung*. Passengers on trains were frozen to death because of lack of glass in the car windows. There were in Petrograd only two locomotives, one of which could only be run ten miles an hour. Repairs formerly costing 30,000 rubles ($15,000 in normal times) now cost 500,000 rubles ($250,000). The riveting of a boiler cost 70,000 rubles ($35,000), "which is not surprising, as the riveter gets 40 rubles ($20) for a day's work of 3 or 4 hours." There were then 500,000 unemployed in Petrograd, and the industrial production of Russia had sunk to 5 per cent of the normal. In some districts most of the blast furnaces had been extinguished. Sugar production last year had been reduced from 1,800,000 tons to 720,000 tons, and this year would not reach 180,000 tons.

The account went on to describe some of the Bolshevik department heads: "The chief of the Finance Ministry is a college student. The fifth army chief is a former actor. The chief of telegraphs is a clerk. The government reporter of the financial commission at Brest Litovsk was a clerk who hadn't the faintest notion of the simplest exchange problems."

"YOU WANT MONEY? ROB THE BANKS!"

In an article in the *New York Tribune*, April 7, 1918, Lieutenant Boris Schumanski wrote:

"The telegraph is nearly abolished in Russia; not that the wires are damaged or the apparatus out of order, but simply because the telegraph operators are so busy with political meetings and discussions that the telegrams arrive at a speed of first and second class mail.

"The mail service is still worse. Letters from Petrograd to Gatchina, which in normal times arrived the same day, take now about a week to deliver, and from Petrograd to Minsk, which is only a two days' journey, letters travel now three weeks and more owing to the scarcity of trains." Lieutenant Schumanski further narrated this incident: "A group of railroad employes came to Foreign Minister Trotzky and complained that they had no money to carry on their work of transportation. 'Why, go to the bank and take it,' he replied."

Trustworthy recent information leaves no doubt of the fact that the railroads are now in a still worse condition. Rolling stock has been destroyed. Quantities of food have rotted because of lack of transportation. The result has been starvation. Even the very few factories that have operated could not obtain enough fuel and raw material. In some places the railroads have stopped altogether. Where railroad trains do run they are overcrowded and there are long delays. Normally the schedule from Moscow to Petrograd was twelve hours. The train on which Dr. Angus Campbell traveled from Moscow was forty-eight hours in reaching Petrograd.

CITIES STARVING; TRANSPORTATION NIL

An exceptionally well-informed observer who had been in Russia six years, leaving Moscow on September 27, 1918, and arriving in the United States on November 10 following, wrote a long special article on conditions in that part of Russia under Bolshevik domination. This article was published in the *Christian Science Monitor*, November 16, 1918. Some extracts are as follows:

"Class hatred, envy, revenge are aflame. The result was inevitable. Although aimed primarily only at the bourgeoisie, anarchy has destroyed anything that resembles normal life. Factory and shop are standing still, or are closing one after the other. The peasant refuses to sell his stores of hidden grain, for in return he cannot receive the much-needed clothing, and even if he would, the railroads are in such a chaotic stage that they could not transport it to the starving centers of population.

"Today, you know your friend alive, tomorrow he might be shot down like a dog without accusation, without trial. Probably some one pointed him out to the secret police as a foe to Bolshevism, nothing more. Your own experience is the experience of hundreds and of thousands of the best families in Russia. The official press of the Bolsheviki printed the account of how 500 political prisoners were selected by lot, and shot down as a reprisal for the killing of Commissary Uritzky in Petrograd. When there was made an attempt to kill Ulianoff (Lenine), the same measures were taken, and reports were pouring into the press that the different commissaries in the province were trying to outdo the capitals in the 'red terror.' Red guards drop into your houses, search you and all you possess, take away the last pound of bread or flour and leave you without redress if you happen to belong to the unfortunate bourgeoisie."

The breakdown of railroads is further pointed out by M. Rosoff, member of the Jewish Central Committee in Russia for Relief of Refugees. He recently arrived in London from Russia on his way to Palestine. At the Zionist Headquarters in London he gave out a long statement, part of which read:

"It is hoped that much assistance can be sent by America by way of Vladivostok. As long as the Bolsheviki are in power, any money sent from Europe will be seized by them. The transport difficulties, owing to the stoppage of railways for lack of coal, is the factor of all others which render the next six months critical in European Russia. With the Volga frozen over there remains no channel of communication for the carrying of foodstuffs."

"Conditions in Russia are very bad," cabled A. R. Decker from Berlin to the *New York Globe*, on December 16, 1918. "The Bolsheviki hold the railroads and factories, but are unable to operate them. The mines produce no metal and peasants refuse to deliver grain where there is little metal remaining. The Bolsheviki fill a few cars and bring them to the cities.

"The residents are divided into four classes: Workmen, who receive 200 grams (7 ounces) of bread daily; light workers, who get 100 grams (3.5 ounces); Bolsheviki office employees, who get 50 grams (1.75 ounces), and bourgeois, who get no bread, but only two herrings. The bourgeois are allowed a few rooms according to the size of the family and in the extra rooms they must lodge the workmen, furnishing heat and light and paying the rent, while they are allowed to collect only a small part of the income."

Mr. Decker further says that the Bolshevik officials are receiving enormous salaries; that local governors are receiving 18,000 rubles a month.

Chapter IV
THE TERROR AND THE NEW BOURGEOISIE

The Bolshevik regime, it would conclusively appear from many reliable sources, has been signalized by an increasingly ferocious persecution of the educated classes. Professor Lomonosoff in disapproving of these imprisonments and executions thus seeks to explain the motive:—

"And what sort of bourgeois is the village teacher? It is a matter of unconscious revenge of the enraged people at everybody who was in a privileged position under the old regime. And since education was the privilege of the idle, the people look upon the educated as belonging to the privileged class."

Other defenders of the Bolsheviki say that the hunting down and disposing of the educated are confined only to those who are counter-revolutionists, and that the Bolshevik movement is one directed against bourgeoisie and church enemies of the Russian people.

Such are the extenuations advanced. What are the facts?

The confidential report made to the American-Russian League of a mechanical engineer recently returned from Russia points out:

TERRORIZING DECENT WORKMEN

"About 3,000,000 of the so-called workingmen of Russia and now considered as being members of the Soviet or Workingmen's Party, and including the industrial centers of European Russia, are made up as follows: One-third or about one million who are really Bolsheviks, including the Red Guard. Their principal object in life being their 20 to 80 rubles a day and privilege to rob. They are made up of pro-German sailors, old regime followers, criminals, idealists, the bad class of Jews and pro-Germans. The remaining two-third of these workingmen can be classed as good men; many of them being exceptional in the skilled labor class. They include some Socialists, some dreamers and good workingmen who are anxious for the return of any substantial government which will enable them to work for an honest living for themselves and their families. The Bolsheviki hold 2,000,000 good workingmen only through fear and the control of bread." He added that about 100,000 intelligent men, centering around Petrograd, and composed of bankers, manufacturers, Germans, the streets. This is a German policy. It kills brains of the nation.''

Iere the fact may be interjected that it is ch more than a German policy. It antedates war. Years ago the I. W. W. in this country re preaching hatred of the professionals. In t I. W. W. branches excluded professionals, l expelled some of their own chief agitators the charge that they had become infected with rofessionalism''. The I. W. W. did not have power to do anything more than exclude or el. In Russia, where their disciples have the ver, professionals are murdered.

'Schools,'' Lieutenant Brasol continued, ave been absolutely discontinued by the Bol-viki. Not only universities, academies and h schools but primary schools. They have n closed on the ground that education is a italist invention. In the Don region near vocherask, the Bolsheviki, in February, 1918, lered that teaching in the grammar school be pped. Nevertheless teachers and scholars nt to school. They were immediately shot wn, teachers and pupils. Most of the scholars re only twelve to sixteen years old.

''At least 70 per cent—perhaps more—of all ıssian workers and peasants are illiterate or n scarcely sign their names. Yet the Bol-eviki have been murdering the very people who uld educate. Hundreds of thousands of peo-e have been shot down in cold blood. There e no laws or trials. Courts have been discon-ıued. There is the most enormous raping of omen. Marriage and the family have been or-red abolished, and every woman over seventeen compelled to give herself up at the first re-ıest. Nobody takes care of the children. ully ninety of every one hundred born die im-ediately.''

REPRISALS AGAINST THE EDUCATED

Pro-Bolshevik organs in England and here are ow making it appear that the Bolshevik leaders have found that the production of factories annot be maintained without the recognition nd co-operation of the technical staffs.'' 'heorists like Lenine and Trotzky may have ound this out after the application of their heories had such bloody and futile results. If ıey have found it out, then their former theories re in the discard. But their followers don't now it and don't want to know it, and they have ontrol.

Thus, in detailing the extremities to which the :ussian intellectuals have been systematically ıbjected by the Bolshevist regime and how the rain workers are in a far worse position than ither the manual laborers or the real capitalists, he Moscow correspondent of the *Berliner Zei-ung am Mittag* says in that paper's issue of Oct. 1, 1918:

''In the long run it is a matter of life or death or the Bolshevist Government to succeed in ffecting an agreement with the intellectuals hich will enable the latter to co-operate with t. The methods of intimidation, the red terror, he requisition of houses and clothing, the forced abor, which compels the brain workers to do ıenial labor such as cleaning the streets, &c., re hardly adapted to reconcile the intellectuals vith the prevailing regime. And the number of he members of the intellectual groups who have lready been shot by the 'Extraordinary Com-nission' as 'counter-revolutionaries,' or hostages, uns into hundreds.''

The whole world recalls President Wilson's re-ent telegram asking joint action on the part of ıll neutral countries in protesting against the 'openly avowed campaign of mass terrorism'' in Russia where ''thousands of persons have been shot without even a form of trial; ill-adminis-ered prisons are filled beyond capacity; and very night scores of Russian citizens are reck-essly put to death; and irresponsible bands are venting their brutal passions in the daily mas-sacre of untold innocents.''

A LEADING BOLSHEVIK ON BOLSHEVISM

The most remarkable summary of Bolshevik rule is that written by Oscar Tokoi, who was no less a personage than Bolshevik Prime Minister of Finland. It was published in full in the *New York Call*, of October 16, 1918, and was sent from Archangel, Russia. These extracts show what a leading Bolshevik found were the results of Bolshevism:

''The workers, liberated from the czarism and rule of the knout, who for the most part are illiterate and ignorant about all social questions, have lost all foundations of reality. Their efficiency and even their willingness to work have altogether disappeared.

''When a law was issued decreeing that if an industrial establishment is shut down, the workers must receive six weeks' or even six months' wages in advance, the result was that the workers of almost all factories decided to close the factories, and every one took his respective wages in advance and became a peddler. The mass of speculators, against whom the government on one hand is fighting, has already, because of this reason, grown tenfold and makes a struggle altogether hopeless.

''A frightfully big number of workers thus have joined the ranks of speculators and opponents to the government. One part of the unemployed who are not sufficiently intelligent to become speculators, remain unemployed because the government is distributing unemployment relief. They are supporters of the government, of course, *but as time goes by they become so heavy* a burden to the government as to become a factor which alone is able to put down any government. And then, lastly, that minutely small group, which still is working, is working with such intensity that the whole production is becoming altogether disrupted and sooner or later will reach complete bankruptcy. * * * *

HOOLIGANS AND ROBBERS

''It is already clear that, in the face of such economic conditions, the whole social order has been upset. Naturally, only a small part of the people will remain backing such an order. The whole propertied class belongs to the opponents of the government, including the petty bourgeoisie, the craftsmen, the small merchants and profiteers. The whole intellectual class and a great part of the workers are also opposing the government.

''In comparison with the entire population only a small minority supports the government, and to the supporters of the government are rallying all the hooligans, robbers and others, to whom this period of confusion promises a good chance of individual action. It is also clear that such a regime cannot stay but with the help of a stern terror. But, on the other hand, the longer the terror continues, the more disagreeable and hated it becomes. Even a great part of those who from the beginning could stay with the government, and who are still sincere social democrats, having seen all this chaos, begin to step aside, or to ally themselves with those openly opposing the government. Naturally, as time goes by, there remains only the worst and the most demoralized element. Terror, arbitrary rule and open brigandage become more and more usual, and the government is not able at all to prevent it. And the outcome is clearly to be foreseen—the unavoidable failure of all this magnificently planned system.''

For daring to tell the truth, Tokoi was recently condemned to death by the Bolshevik government on the ground that he had asked the intervention of the Allies. He, however, contrived to escape to England.

THE BOLSHEVIKI'S HUGE FUND

A cable from Russia, October 21, 1918, stated that the Bolshevist Control Committee's official bulletin, containing a signed Treasury statement, shows a deficit in the first six months of 1918 amounting to 14,740,000,000 rubles (nominally $7,370,000,000). The amount here stated is an underestimate. The actual deficit has been about three and a half billion rubles a month. This is not surprising. With all or nearly all the factories closed, mines shut down, and railroad and street car lines in chaos, productive power has ceased. Nevertheless the Bolshevik Government, so-called, is paying out vast sums ostensibly as wages to great numbers of workers who don't work. These sums are nothing more or less than subsidies to assure the Bolshevik leaders the support of the ignorant mass.

Where do they get these immense sums? The fact is that when the Bolsheviki captured control of the Government they found 1,600,000,000 rubles in gold which had been kept as a reserve in the Russian treasury. They also obtained control of 800,000,000 francs in gold, which the Rumanians had transferred to Petrograd just before the Russian Revolution. Recently, however, the Anti-Bolshevik All-Russian Government, the headquarters of which at present is at Omsk, managed to seize 800,000,000 rubles in gold which the Bolshevik Government had sent to Kazan, not, of course, anticipating that it would be captured. This sum was half of the total of 1,600,000,000 rubles of Russian treasury gold that the Bolsheviki had found upon their assumption of power. The vast quantity of paper money issues that the Bolsheviki have issued are not based upon this gold supply. This paper money is simply fiat money, and is not even numbered and registered. Moreover, they do not contain any signature except in the case of 250 and 1,000 ruble notes.

What, then, has become of the immense supply of gold coin as also of the further huge sums of gold, silver, jewels, securities, stocks, paper rubles, and other valuables that the Bolsheviki have seized from banks, private safe deposit boxes, churches, former crown possessions, stores, homes, factories and other plundered places, the aggregate amounting to a truly colossal sum?

BUYING UP FOREIGN PAPERS

Some hints of their further disposition are given in the statement of Dr. David Soskice, formerly Kerensky's secretary. This statement cabled from London and published in the *New York Sun*, November 19, 1918, said:

''Bolshevik leaders in Russia are packing up. For a long time Bolshevik couriers have been going abroad with their portmanteaux packed with millions of rubles.

''These rubles, stolen from the Russian nation, they exchanged at any price they could obtain for foreign money and placed in neutral banks. When the Central Powers were arranging for an entrance into Russia in the expectation of carrying away grain and merchandise they began to buy rubles, which they believed would enable them to acquire goods.

''They were mistaken, because peasants refused to part with their grain for paper rubles, but it was an immense help to the Bolshevists. Ruble exchange in Sweden, instead of dropping hopelessly on the advent of Bolshevism, has risen rapidly. The Bolshevik agents thus were enabled to deposit immense sums in banks in neutral countries.

''The money thus accumulated was used lavishly in acquiring the influence of the democratic press and especially that of the labor press. A great number of labor papers with strong Bolshevik tendencies appeared in neutral countries. The Swedish Government long allowed the Bolshevists to accumulate financial power and to use it in undermining the social order of the State. Lately they have begun to realize the danger. A couple of months ago Gukovsky, former Minister of Finance in Lenine's Government, arrived in Sweden with 50,000,000 rubles and a cargo of platinum, which he tried to sell in Sweden for foreign money. This time the Swedish Government interfered. In Switzerland tens of millions of rubles likewise have been exchanged and deposited in the banks.''

Shadow Huns and Others

(*Continued from page 13*)

trophe which swept over Russia, took Russia out of the war, and which threatens the civilized world. When Trotzky left America with the purpose of wrecking Russia, he was taken off the ship and held by British officials at Halifax. This American muckraker at once began agitating for Trotzky's release, and actually succeeded in inducing the Department of State to request the Kerensky government to ask Great Britain to let Trotzky proceed on his way. The Kerensky government acquiesced to the representations of the American State Department, as did England to Kerensky's request, with results that have spelled bloodshed and disaster to Russia and calamity to all the world.

One might go on with pen pictures of these pretentious petty folk ad infinitum, and you would find the same intellectual amateurs and dilletante who dabbled in Socialism, syndicalism, pragmatism, Freudism and other isms in the past are now lined up with Bolshevism and "internationalism." To these more recent isms they bring to bear the same sincerity, same quality of mentality, same reasoning ability and clarity of understanding that marked them in the past. These folk, with clairvoyant vision, saw all the evils of society; but they were stricken with blindness when it came to taking up their portion in the struggle against German military aggression. The majority, it is true, "cut little ice," as the saying goes, but certain ones who hail from the intellectual slums, or the purlieus thereof, by reason of a dull persistence, or by racial aggression, or by accident, or by a rich marriage, have gotten books published and have gotten magazines started. The intellectual confidence game has not been entirely unsuccessful. In fact, the more prosperous exponents of Bolshevism and the class war-after-the-war no longer seek congenial harbor in the dingy basement eating hovels about Washington Square, but belong to well appointed clubs, receive in editorial sanctums furnished with impressive antiques, and make regular trips to Washington where, so they aver, they are cordially received by the young intellegenzia who are temporarily lending their powerful intellects to the conduct of affairs of state.

A CERTAIN BRIGHT YOUNG MAN

There was a certain young man who took prizes at school and won a fellowship in college, yet who was never able to advance beyond his first precocity. His was the sort of mind that is fitted for the "nursery" of human life. Yet instead of confining himself within his limitations, instead of, for example, conducting a second-hand bookshop and personally enjoying whimsical fantasies written for children, he with others of his tribe assumed the pose of being a diplomat and statesman of the new school and undertook to write about national and international subjects, about politics and philosophy, about the war and peace—subjects certainly which only the most acute, fine and discerning minds are fitted to handle. Self-satisfied with a vicarious learning painfully absorbed from fossilized Teuton professors, he essayed an impressive and heavy profundity of style and wrote tediously as though he combined the wisdom of Solon and Socrates. Incapable of profound and original thought, his mind warped by cheap cynicism, this young man devoted himself to phrase making, the delight of juggling words; yet his concocted cleverness was patently laborious, his most careful phrases lumbered. The stock arguments of Socialism and internationalism were put forth impressively as ex cathedra facts; the stale slogans of Bolshevism were advanced as a new message for the world.

Another tribesman and friend of this young man, somewhat more clever, more cunning, but no less shallow, was wont to take up his stage-prop quill and write in such wise as to imply that he had inherited the mantle of Plato. Arrogant to those from whom he could expect nothing, servile, flattering and a toady to those in power, a defeatist, having virtually predicted that the war against Germany could not be won, this beguiling-voiced charlatan managed to crawl his way into important positions where his "defeatist" principles were not wholsesome, to put it mildly. To that extent was effrontery and chicanery crowned with success.

THE AFFINITY OF MEDIOCRITIES

Mediocrities generally confederate and band together by reason of the law of attraction and an instinct of self preservation. A mutual admiration crowd, they can help one another along by log rolling and reciprocal boosting; likewise, in their professional conduct they seek to disparage and damage men of genuine talent whose accomplishments they envy and whom they fear as men able to see through them. Enjoying some subsidized organ, printed on good paper, they self-constitute themselves as a tribune to pass upon the products of creative Americans and even to advise, criticise and assail the statesmen of the world. Despite all the astounding pharisaical pretense of intellectuality and ideals, they advance nothing positive, nothing original, nothing concrete. Able to read the work of others and perhaps write glibly, they scavenge for intellectual garbage which, as literary delicatessen dealers, they dress up and palm off as fresh products. The fact that any of their books attract attention is no more proof of substance than the fact that Montgomery's volume of verse ran into eleven editions proved it was poetry. Macaulay took up that volume and point by point showed it had been plagiarized from Byron and other poets. Today Montgomery is a "dead one." No one ever hears his name.

It is not improbable that most if not all of these folk take themselves with genuine seriousness. The indefatigable, undiscouraged, dull perseverence of their efforts week by week, and their total lack of any sense of humor in regard to their muddled, involved and contradictory lucubrations about the great affairs of the world, indicate that. Were their methods of trying to attract public attention less sinister, they might be simply pathetic. One may always feel a spontaneously human commiseration for the poor mountebank who suffers from the obsession that he is supreme in the role of Hamlet. What is certainly astonishing, if not inexplicable, about the whole thing is that these humbugs of radicalism and "Bottoms" of intellectualism have been actually able to get themselves taken at their own preposterous rating by a small number of people whose brains are supposed to function. The phenomenon of such a clique of shallow poseurs actually getting their journalistic enterprises financed, and even getting themselves mentioned in the wills of certain rich men for sums running into the hundreds of thousands of dollars, would be titillating to one's risibilities except for the fact that an actual realization of truth in P. T. Barnum's cynical characterization of humanity conduces to melancholy. I have never forgotten an experience, both pathetic and comic, last winter in Washington. There I had the pleasure of meeting a lady of most extraordinary charm and bewitching presence. Enjoying a unique social position, she had, since America entered the war, given herself unreservedly to a branch of war work and had accomplished results richly abounding to her credit. She had been to Europe, had visited the battle front, and personally in a social way knew most of the Allied statesmen, from whom certainly she could have gained a clear understanding of the ideals and issues of the war. To my surprise, in the course of conversation, I found that she considered Arthur Henderson a more representative leader of the British than Mr. Lloyd George. She was quite convinced that the British Labor Party was "going to run England," and that even America "great changes were going to co after the war." She also entertained the opini that the British war aims did not coincide wi Mr. Wilson's war aims. And then, to my amaz ment, she casually opined: "Of course, it isn right to talk about crushing Germany. Aft all, the German people are human, and if t Allies carried on a war of revenge and le them prostrate we'd simply be sowing seeds future wars."

Naturally, I wondered where she got su "liberal" opinions—was it from the Alli statesmen, the generals of the armies, or t diplomats resident in Washington? Pursui the conversation discreetly, we branched up Bolshevism, the Stockholm conference, the pro osition for a negotiated peace with the Centr powers, and I touched upon certain Americ journals advocating these propositions. A su picion was born that perhaps, unlike the peop of her class, she might be secretly addicted reading Mr. Hearst's editorials. Turning su denly upon me, however, the lady enthusiasti ally exclaimed:

"I *do* hope you read the *New Republic*— gives one such an open-minded view of thing Of couse, it is hard for an ordinary person understand at times—it is so *deep!* Oh, I thin those boys who run it are *perfectly* wonderful!

(*To be continued.*)

Bolshevism Convicted Out of Its Own Mout

(*Continued from page 9*)

government. Has Russia advanced to the poi where Socialistic production is possible? Mor over, the proletariat of Russia is not politicall strong enough or sufficiently developed to tak over the whole machinery of government an adapt that machinery to its needs. *The dange was that the proletariat government would wor in the direction of destroying the governmen instead of taking possession of it and transform ing it.* And another danger arose, that the back ward sections of the country which felt tha they were oppressed (under this new system would protect themselves by declaring for th complete independence of provinces, yes, even o villages, as the Bakunin anarchists did in th early seventies in Spain. *Under the condition existing in Russia the dictatorship of the pro letariat threatened to bring about the politica and social disintegration of the country an to lead in this way to chaos and to the mora bankruptcy of the revolution.*

Bernstein is the Finance Minister of Germany Theoretically he is in opposition to the ortho dox Marxism of Kautsky and is almost as wel known to the entire Socialist world. But he i a member of the Independent Party and agree with Kautsky about the Bolsheviki. In a lon article he declares that the Brest-Litovsk Treat was a calamity both for the Russian and Ger man Socialists, and that the Russian Bolshe viki must be considered as responsible for tha treaty. He says that they pretended to bas their conclusion to sign it on the fact that a German revolution was impending. But he doe not accept this excuse, for he points out tha both these men were fully informed as to Ger man conditions and must have known that the German revolution was still far away. The German revolution, according to all the best observers, awaited the defeat of the German armies and the facts have proven these observers to be correct.

Bernstein also says that the appeal of the Bolsheviki for immediate revolutions throughout Western Europe was equally inexcusable as they must have known that things were not ripe for a revolution in those countries either. The signing of the treaty was therefore nothing more nor less than an alliance with German imperialism.

Among the new figures brought to light by the German revolution has been Kurt Eisner, Prime Minister of Bavaria, an exceptionally radical Socialist. Along with Barth, Dittmann and others of this group—who were in accord ı Liebknecht until the latter went over to :hevism—Eisner totally repudiates the new sian despotism. He says:

> Ours is a bloodless revolution. I was always opp-sed to Bolshevism and shall continue to be so. We don't want chaos and terrr in Germany.
> What about a dictatorship of the proletariat? I believe somewhat in dictators, but they must be nominated by the people and not imposed upon them.

n contrast with this, let us take the view the German Imperialists who recognize the shevik Government and aided it to get into :er by every conceivable means.

)f course, the German Imperialists deeply ›reciate the immense service done for them Trotzky and Lenine. This appreciation has ›here been better expressed than in a recent icle by one of the leading publicists of Gerny, Paul Rohrbach. Rohrbach is not a fire-›r, but one of the most level-headed of the ·man Imperialists. He is even called a beral" and "democrat." No doubt the ultraremists are even more gratified with the 'sheviki and would express themselves even re cynically Rohrbach's "liberal" views more interesting, however, as undoubtedly ›resenting the standpoint of the attitude of · vast majority of the German nation on Bol-:vism. Rohrbach writes:

> The Bolsheviki are gradually getting into trouble. What is our attitude? For the present there is for us no greater interest in the East than the interest of maintaining Bolshevism. Many people have the curious idea of wanting to conclude a commercial treaty with Bolshevism. If anybody expects any benefit from it, by all means let him talk to the Bolsheviki about commercial treaties or similar things; it will do no harm, but what the Bolsheviki are doing for us is something much greater than that.
> They are ruining Great Russia; they are destroying absolutely the very roots of any possible danger from Russia in the future. They have already relieved us of most of the anxiety which we could feel about Great Russia, and we ought to do everything in order that they may continue, as long as possible, activities which are so very profitable for us. If they offer armed help against the Czechs at Samara and Omsk, we should consider the offer very seriously. We should also prevent the Cossacks from going too far against Great Russia, and from seriously disturbing the Bolsheviki. The Bolsheviki themselves believe that they are the salvation, not only of Russia, but of the world. That is the very best creed that we can want—provided that it remains confined to Great Russia. Great Russia for the Bolsheviki and the Bolsheviki for Great Russia! Let us preserve that situation, and we shall earn at the same time gratitude of the Bolsheviki and the profits for Germany.

VI

HE BOLSHEVIK DOCUMENTS PUBLISHED BY THE UNITED STATES GOVERNMENT

The criticisms passed by a handful of persons f the documents published under the direction f President Wilson have been utterly refuted. hese criticisms were so contradictory that they ad little effect on anyone who took the time › study the documents or who was familiar ·ith Russian affairs. What were these critiisms?

1. In an appendix to the documents Mr. Creel ıw fit to print a few *copies* of additional docuıents, the original of which he did not have in is possession. He stated that he did not have ıe originals but at the same time gave grounds, ased upon the other documents, for believing hat these *copies* also were substantially correct. Iearly all the attacks made from Socialist and ro-Bolshevik quarters were based upon this apendix.

2. Two or three professors could not undertand why the Russian-German spies and agents 'ho issued the documents used Russian dates instead of German dates. Has not the connection between the Russian and German secret police always been intimate? This is really no problem at all. Each individual instance of such dates has been thoroughly explained by Mr. Creel.

Based upon these absurd criticisms there has arisen a campaign of suspicion of Mr. Wilson and the whole American Administration, which, after the utmost deliberation, gave the full weight of their support to these extremely important documents. They are just about as firmly established as the Declaration of Independence.

The writer is personally acquainted with one of the individuals chiefly responsible for gathering these documents. This man is not an official of the American Government. He is an American author and Socialist. He has spent years of his life in Russia, and is thoroughly familiar with the Russian Socialist movement, having been for many years in more or less sympathy with that movement, including the Bolsheviki, with whose leaders he is personally and thoroughly acquainted. This man, in cooperation with many Americans and Russians, gathered these documents together from many different quarters.

Mr. Sisson, who was the organizer of the campaign to bring these documents together, is also a man of established reputation. There is, therefore, no ground whatever to suspect the origin of the documents. But the photographic reproductions themselves furnish evidence that has been absolutely satisfactory to every unbiased person who has seen them. Furthermore, they are now reproduced by the government in pamphlet form and have been circulated by the thousands so that every American is able to examine them for himself.

Let us remind the reader of the chief conclusions demonstrated by these documents. We are no longer interested in the relation of the Bolsheviki to the war. But it is important to note that their relations with the German Government were kept secret by Lenine and Trotzky from the Bolsheviki themselves.

It is also important to remember that the German Government named a list of men who were to be elected to the Bolshevik Central Committee, and that these men were elected.

It is important to know that before the Brest-Litovsk Treaty was signed, the Bolsheviki deliberately betrayed Russia by appointing a German-named commander to "defend" Petrograd.

It is interesting and important that the identical arguments used by the German propaganda for two years were employed by the Bolsheviki to demoralize the Russian armies and to overthrow Kerensky.

What are we to conclude from facts of this sort? Were the Bolsheviki German agents? In one sense they were, in another sense they were not. They were never *mere* German agents. *But they were secret allies of Germany.*

These Bolsheviki allies proceeded not only to turn over half of Russia to cruel enslavement by the German armies, but attempted by the means of spies and agents to extend the territory under German control.

Nor did the secret allies stop here. The German General Staff and the Bolsheviki sent agents to bring about revolutionary movements in all the great democratic countries. It is true that Lenine doubtless wished these revolutions for the sake of Bolshevism alone. It is also true that he was willing to run the risk that these revolutions would result in nothing whatever but the victory of German Imperialism and the enslavement of the world. In other words, in order to obtain a chance, however remote, of imposing Bolshevism on the rest of the world through the victory of German arms, he was willing to compel the rest of the world to run the risk of being conquered by German Imperialism.

THE RED RAG AND THE BULL

By ELIZABETH MARBURY

President Women's National Committee, American Defense Society

Representing the National Committee of Women of the American Defense Society, I ask every law abiding citizen to stand sternly and unflinchingly with us in our protest against the public display, the obnoxious and unwarranted flaunting of the Red Flag of Anarchy in these United States, which at this time is naught but a new form of German propaganda and of German effort directed against the spirit of our national unity.

Today duty is grey and grim.
Today education supplants emotion.
Today restraint supersedes rebellion.

We are realizing every hour that normal evolution has given woman her place as an economic producer and that it has demonstrated her right to form a police reserve as well as a battalion of death.

Thus at the dawn of a new era of Peace the women of this country must patrol the streets of our cities and must set the sign posts along the highways of our states. It is the women as well as the men who demand that their mayors and local rulers shall take the same stand as has Mayor Hylan in forbidding the exhibiting of the emblem of resistance to all authority. They must insist that there is only room in our midst for flags that mean law and order and that our beloved Old Glory shall not hang side by side with the flag of lawlessness and of disorder.

The Red Flag does not stand for liberty, but for every crime that has been committed in the name of liberty since the history of the world began.

The Red Flag marches at the head of riot and rebellion. The pretended reconstruction which it proclaims is based upon *unequal* rights, not *equal* rights.

Rapine and robbery cannot dictate the terms of trade agreements.

The Federation of Labor is a better tribunal than are the ash barrel and the soap box.

As a people we have a large store of common sense and our equilibrium cannot be lightly disturbed.

The grip of discontent is undesirable baggage to most of us.

We do not welcome imported grievances.

We fling open our gates to those prospective citizens coming from abroad who seek honest opportunity for honest work. They have their labor to sell, and nowhere in the world will they be paid as high for it as here. The grinding oppressor is no longer a familiar figure in our country. In this connection it might be pertinent to note that with us the sporadic enemy of labor is rarely "made in America".

There should be neither display nor glorifying of the Red Flag in this country where it is no more indigenous to our soil than is the poisonous cobra. The Red Flag cannot be safely waved before the wide open eyes of the American Bull. He will not stand for it.

The sooner the Red Flag is cut into stripes, towards the making of the only flag which we Americans propose to keep floating undisturbed over our land, the more sensible its present advocates will be.

We will then welcome your red as part of our whole, united as it then will be to blue, the color of vision; to white, the emblem of purity, and canopied by the stars which are our inheritance and our pride.

Be loyal Americans with us, not disgruntled aliens against us. Learn to believe in America for Americans even as we do.

Look up and not down, and soon you will find our stars the antidote to the mud of injustice and of oppression upon which you and your fathers have turned your beaten backs.

National Work of the Woman's Department

By MRS. COFFIN VAN RENSSELAER

MRS. FRANCIS McNEIL BACON
Chairman, New York and New Jersey Section, Woman's Department

MISS MAUD WETMORE
Chairman, Woman's Department

MISS ANNE MORGAN
Treasurer, Woman's Department

MRS. FREDERICK S. MEAD
Chairman, New England Section, Woman's Department

The abrupt termination of the war has brought the Nation to the realization that it is face to face with a new era—a new era of infinite possibilities, of greater responsibilities, mutual understandings, and a broader brotherhood.

As a people, united and unified with our great allies, we have carried our share of the fight for democratic principles to a triumphant conclusion. But Victory, in the last analysis, only spells Opportunity, and the fruition of the victory—the crystallization of the opportunity—lies in the hands of the people. They can make or mar this new era. More than ever in the history of the world, women have taken their part in the nation's life, in all phases of endeavor during war time. Politically, professionally, industrially, socially, women met the test of citizenship and have contributed in no small part to the successful termination of the four years' agony. But the greater test is yet to come. Women must, of necessity, take a larger and larger share in public affairs, and the first essential should be an adequate understanding of the problems to be solved, combined with a spirit of real sympathy and a desire to be of real service.

The Woman's Department of The National Civic Federation faces a definite responsibility. The Department was organized in Washington in May, 1908, interesting itself primarily in the welfare of government and industrial employees. As the Department developed it was found necessary to enlarge its scope, and since 1912, it has concerned itself with questions relating to social, economic, and industrial life, as affecting women and children. Its functions are investigation, survey, and constructive experimentation leading to legislation for the improvement of conditions. As a department of The National Civic Federation, it conforms with all principles laid down by the Executive Council.

The Woman's Department is organized under Sections, of which there are eight, comprising fifteen states:

New York and New Jersey Section, Mrs. Francis McNeil Bacon, Chairman.

District of Columbia Section, Mrs. Archibald Hopkins, Chairman.

Virginia and West Virginia Section, Mrs. J. Allison Hodges, Chairman.

New England Section, Mrs. Frederick S. Mead, Chairman.

North and South Carolina Section, Mrs. William N. Reynolds, Chairman.

Alabama Section, Mrs. Cyrus Pitman Orr, Chairman.

Missouri Section, Mrs. J. F. Binnie, Chairman.

Ohio Section, Mrs. Lawrence Maxwell, Chairman.

These Sections are autonomous, working in accord with the ideals of the Civic Federation—the cooperation, mutual understanding and sympathy of the employer, employee, and public. The Department has, as well, a membership-at-large of women interested in its work, and who do not live in parts of the country organized into Sections.

When war was declared the entire womanhood of the nation turned to the obvious and immediate relief work which was so distinctly its province. Its purpose being clearly defined and its functions definite, the Woman's Department advised its Sections to cooperate most closely with the organizations formed for relief alone and not to duplicate effort by introducing a program completely at odds with the object of the organization. That this was wise has been amply proved. It is interesting to know that in almost every State where the Woman's Department was organized, its members were appointed upon the Woman's Committee of the local Council of Defense. Miss Maude Wetmore, Chairman of the Woman's Department of The National Civic Federation, is a member of the National Woman's Committee of the Council of National Defense.

The Sections, during the past two years, have done excellent service, not only in their cooperative efforts, but along the line of their own program. The war brought vividly to our consciousness the housing situation, and in the North and South Carolina Section some interesting experiments were carried through. The rapid development of welfare work through this Section is most encouraging. In all Sections, food production and food conservation have been a vital part of war work. Agricultural experiments were undertaken in cooperation with the State universities and colleges, intensive gardening encouraged, and the Home Economics Section took a very prominent part in developing a conservation programme. In Boston, un[illegible] the New England Section, a Demonstration C[illegible] tre has been run with great success; a special [illegible] was sent throughout the Section, showing [illegible] use of available substitutes; and menus w[illegible] carefully and scientifically prepared at the [illegible] quest of other organizations. In cooperati[illegible] with existing agencies, Emergency Canteens, [illegible] Community Kitchens, are being formed throu[illegible] out the State. In New York active cooperati[illegible] with the Federal and State Food Commissio[illegible] proved of great value.

In the Liberty Loan and War Savings ca[illegible] paigns, the organization as a whole has tak[illegible] an active part, as in all other definite calls [illegible] Government agencies. It has placed its Sectio[illegible] at the disposal of the Federal Public Emplo[illegible] ment Service, to aid in the working out of t[illegible] comprehensive plan outlined by the Departme[illegible] of Labor, through its Community Labor Boar[illegible] and Public Exchanges. As the emergencies [illegible] veloped the Sections have responded to t[illegible] varied calls for service in separate localities [illegible] meet the varied needs. For instance, in N[illegible] York City, at the request of the War Camp Co[illegible] munity Service, a Home Club for Soldiers, Sa[illegible] ors and Marines has been successfully run f[illegible] over a year. But during all this period the r[illegible] purpose of the organization has remained [illegible] guiding principle, and its Committees on Ame[illegible] icanization, Prison Reform, Industrial Relatio[illegible] Shop and Factory Welfare, etc., with th[illegible] supplemental subjects, have been continui[illegible] their work, preparing for the time when t[illegible] fundamentals should again take their essenti[illegible] place; when, happily, the necessity for the i[illegible] mediate relief should have passed.

The Department faces the new era with ho[illegible] and confidence. Its members have been dra[illegible] together through a vital interest, and a desi[illegible] to be of service, with an intelligent understan[illegible] ing of the paramount issues at stake; and whe[illegible] ever the opportunity arises to use such unde[illegible] standing to aid in the betterment of conditio[illegible] the readjustments which must arise, the develo[illegible] ing of the great things whch have come out of t[illegible] war, into a firm and solid foundation for t[illegible] future. Complete reports of the programs [illegible] the various Sections may be had upon applic[illegible] tion to its office, 105 West 40th Street, Ne[illegible] York.

Tyrrel Print. New York.

The National Civic Federation Review

Vol. IV. NEW YORK, JANUARY 25, 1919 No. 8

PROBLEMS OF SECURING PEACE

COMPOSE LEAGUE OF NATIONS OF THOSE THAT WON THIS WAR—ADMIT OTHERS AS THEY PROVE TRUSTWORTHY—WILL NOT INTERFERE WITH NATIONAL SOVEREIGNTY

By A. LAWRENCE LOWELL

PRESIDENT OF THE LEAGUE TO ENFORCE PEACE

WHEN a great war has come to an end and the right has triumphed, the victors are very apt to believe that the millennium is here, or at least that the world is sure to be better than it was before. But this is not always so, unless we look out very carefully. Perhaps there was never a war fought for a higher purpose than our Civil War, but the Civil War was followed by the horrors of reconstruction in the South—blunders which no one now ventures to defend; and just here in New York City it was followed by the Tweed Ring. It is not always true that when one evil spirit goes out of a man, seven do not come back. That story was a parable, but very true. Most wars have been followed by periods of moral relaxation.

Let us look, for one moment, at the condition of Europe before this war and now. Before this war the western part of Europe was in a state of political contentment. It contained two or three large countries—three large countries, you might say,—England, France and Italy. It contained a number of small ones. These small countries, in the first place, were contented, at least passively; they had no desire to fight with one another. They had each of them an entirely separate race, or, as in Switzerland, the races agreed to live happily together. The large countries, it is true, had some differences; France wanted Alsace-Lorraine; Italy the Irridenta; but those things, alone, would not have brought war.

A. LAWRENCE LOWELL

There was, however, in the southeast of Europe, a place which was very far from being contented. In fact, as soon as the Christians had thrown off the domination of the Turk, they proceeded to quarrel among themselves. Everybody had known that that was a black spot; everybody had known it was a collection of explosives which were liable to take fire at any time. All the powers of Europe had got together more than once and tried to settle the affairs of the Balkans, and never did. Why? Because those peoples were infiltrated more or less by one another. They each of them claimed a piece of the other one's territory, because it was inhabited by people of their own race. And it was the occasion of a war in more than one instance.

Of course, the cause of this war was that Germany chose to make a war, but her excuse was the Serbian incident. We believe, more than anything else, that she went to war to carry out the Berlin to Bagdad plan. But do you suppose that if the Balkans had not been in that condition of restlessnses and strife it would have been possible? I do not. It was the condition of the Balkans that made that scheme possible.

What is the state of central Europe at the present day? There are a large number of nationalities there which are bitterly hostile to one another, infiltrated in just the same way. I can give you an example of this strained feeling which came under my own observation. There was in Prague a German student, who subsequently came to Harvard. He went to a concert of the Boston Symphony Orchestra and said that he was very much pleased that he had heard the symphony of a Czech composer which was often played in Prague, but which he had never heard there because it would not do for him, a German, to be seen in a Czech theater in Prague.

Of course, that whole region is in a state of war. An explosion may take place at any moment.

There is not any single race there that is going to be satisfied with any delimination of territory that can possibly be made for it. It is a case of children, each of whom wants the piece of cake and seven of them want it. That is the situation at present, and it runs through the greater part of Central Europe. Besides which, you have the fact that Russia and Germany are in a state of anarchy, which never conduces to a general peace. There is liable to be a fire started at any minute which would spread over all Europe. You have a more dangerous condition than you ever had before, and that will last until those people have been brought under a condition that they recognize as permanent and just.

Now, what should be done about it? Why, it is perfectly clear that there is only one thing to do about it; and that is that some of the great powers must see that justice is done and maintained, and that we do not allow Central Europe to be like packs of wolves, fighting one another and setting the whole world at odds!

Let me point out another matter. What was the occasion of this war? Well, it was Serbian pigs. The exports of Serbia were mostly pigs. Her way of getting out to the markets of the world was through Austria-Hungary. She could not go through Turkey, because Turkey had not railroads and ports sufficient to handle her commerce. Austria formerly kept her in order, because whenever there were open agitations, in Serbia, the Serbian pigs became "diseased" and could not be allowed to come into Austria; and that had a very strong restraining effect upon the people of Serbia as well as upon the pigs.

As soon as Serbia, after the second Balkan war got Sentari and Greece got Saloniki, and there was a railroad from Belgrade to the sea, Scutari cared comparatively little about her relations with Austria. Then additional Serbian agitations took place, the final result of which was the murder of the crown prince at Sarajevo, as a result of which Germany declared war. I do not mean that that was the cause of the war; it was the occasion which Germany took to make war. But Germany was always looking for a disturbance at that spot, as the thing which might start a conflagration.

I think, in such a condition of things, it is pretty clear that it is worth while for the people of Europe to get together and see that that inflammable territory does not start another fire.

And what have we to do about it? We have much to do about it. It is all very well to talk about our glorious isolation and our disinterestedness in the political questions of Europe. Our glorious isolation in this war has not saved the lives of our citizens. Why? For the simple reason that when a war takes place between any two great maritime powers, they are bound to interfere with neutral countries; they are bound to try to check neutral ships from trading with the enemy; they are bound to quarrel with neutrals. We found that out one hundred years ago, when it was perfectly evident that we had to fight either England or France when they were at war with one another. And ultimately we fought England. But one or the other of those two countries we had to fight during the wars of Napoleon.

Why did we go into this war? Oh, we fought this war to make the world safe for Democracy; we fought it to put an end to barbarism; we fought the war for the sake of humanity. But that was not the real reason. We went into this war because we could not, with self-respect, stay out. And that will be true of every war that comes in the future. Therefore in self-protection we must see that fires do not start. It is all very well to say, "My neighbor's house does not interest me. Let him set it on fire if he pleases, and I will sleep comfortably." That depends on how far off your neighbor's house is. Mind you, we saw in the paper the other day that it took to fly from, I think it was, Mesopotamia, to Bombay, 3,000 miles, but 41 hours. That is the distance across the ocean. How far are we from Europe? Is the Atlantic an ocean, a lake or a river? How near are future inventions to bring us together? How far can we keep away?

But I dislike to put the duty of the United States wholly on a selfish basis. It seems to me in justice a man owes some duties to his fellow-man, a nation owes some duties to its fellow-na- of a thousand years hence would point back to this country and say, "Oh, yes, some people called them the country of the Almighty Dollar; but that country not only contributed to civilization through her inventions, but she took her place in the perilous days of the world and helped to organize things so that she was one of the great nations which tended to the uplift of civilization for all time."

There are one or two difficulties, however, which confront us when we consider the formation of a league of nations. People say, "Of what nations shall such a league consist." The organization to which I have belonged for three and one-half years has taken very great pains not to answer that question, believing that the answer would depend largely upon the issue of this war; and I believe that this war has settled that issue. A perfect league of nations in a perfect world, would undoubtedly be one where all mankind was organized into free nations and all were bound together in a great league of humanity. But one does not begin with perfection. One begins with the existing things, and it is surely perfectly obvious today that the only nations that can initiate a league of nations are the nations that have won this war. They may let in others whenever they prove themselves trustworthy, and we hope that many nations will prove themselves trustworthy, but it is not necessary to go too far at once.

I want to take up two or three objections very commonly suggested to a league of nations. One is that Washington never did so in his day. Now, when I was a little boy it was the fashion to make little boys read Casabianca, presumably because it had a good moral influence and raised high moral standards for the little boy. I never got that impression from Casabianca. I never admired the boy upon the burning deck. I never thought that he paid very much respect to the intelligence of his father, who, if he had been present on the burning deck when the boy called to him would have said, "Get off this deck just as quick as you can."

Now, what did George Washington do in his day? He tried to prevent war for, mind you, before the adoption of the constitution we were very close to war between many of the states, and doubtless war would have come. He tried to prevent war by welding those states together in such a way that they would not fight with one another. That was as far as it was wise for him to go. But look at it. Do you realize that at that time New Hampshire was farther from South Carolina in terms of travel and methods of communication and distance and time for covering that distance than we are from Germany. New Hampshire was less likely, if we had been separate states, to be drawn into a war between South and North Carolina than we are to be drawn into a war between Russia and Germany today.

This has happened. We were drawn into a war which began between Russia and Germany. And there is no part of the world now so remote as the two ends of those thirteen colonies were then. Let me say this: Washington was a great man, because he looked the facts of his day in the face, and we are only worthy to be his descendants if we look the facts of our day in the face.

The second objection which is raised is this: "It will interefere with our sovereignty." It has nothing whatever to do with our sovcignty. People say Congress has the power to declare war or not to. But the power of Congress is not in any way affected. We simply agree that in certain conditions we will declare war, but Congress is not bound to do it. The agreement does not interfere with Congress in the least. It does morally bind Congress to declare war, yes, certainly; every treaty morally binds the country to do something. A great change that has come from the Middle Ages, is the change from status to contract, from the time when the relation of things was fixed by the accident of birth to the time when man regulates his relations to neighbors by contract. Contract means limiting your freedom of action in consideration of someone else limiting his freedom of action. And it is in consequence or by reason of contracts that the world is able to advance. More treaties, each of them binding the country to do or not to do certain things, have been made in the last fifty years than in all the history of the world before. Why? Because countries have found it was worth while to bind themselves if others were so bound also.

Now, there is a third objection that I want to take up which is always brought forward. "How about the big and little nations?" Does anyone seriously suppose that anyone is going to allow small nations in a league of nations—to allow nations like Guatemala, for instance,—to have the same votes as the United States? It is easy enough, in a consideration like that, to say it is absurd and throw it down. But no sensible person would believe for one moment that was to be done.

We are told again that our men will have to go and fight in every broil in Europe. But surely the object of the league of nations is to prevent broils in Europe. If the league of nations will not prevent broils in Europe then it is a failure. But does anyone doubt that a league made of the great nations of the earth can stop any broils in Europe? Why, I remember a man coming to my office one day—it amused me very much, and it seems to me it is somewhat similar to this situation. He said to me: "Don't you want to insure your life?" I said: "No; there are so many risks in life that I do not want to increase them by that method." And he replied to that: "Why, this is insurance against risk." And that is the situation here. The object is to prevent war. Of course, if the league will not prevent war, then it is a failure. But it will.

Let me ask you this: if you went to live among barbarous people,—or, let us say in a mining frontier town in the olden days, with its undesirable characters and everyone carrying a gun, what would you do? You would have a pistol and learn to use it quick. And then, a vigilance committee comes, and if you are a good citizen you join that vigilance committee, and it gets to work and puts down that sort of thing, and you lay your pistol away, put it in the bureau drawer and so does everybody else. Are you a bad man because you have to carry that pistol? Not at all. You had to. In other words, a man cannot be an orderly citizen in a disorderly community.

The trouble with us in the present day is that certain nations are trying to be orderly and decent in a disorderly condition of the world. The nations of the world are in just the same situation that you would have been in, in a frontier town of the olden days, when it was necessary for you to carry a pistol. There is only one way to stop it, and that is to make the world an orderly one.

And I want to ask you, are the resources of civilization exhausted? Is this sort of thing bound to repeat itself every little while? Are the most civilized races in the world going to try to exterminate each other with ever increasing ferocity and ever increasing ingenuity of weapons? Is the manhood of the next century to be devoted to seeing how much more wicked we can be? Are we to develop the one horror that did not take place in this war, but was talked of, and that is dropping poison bombs from aeroplanes on undefended cities?

Or, is it possible, is it conceivable, that the world can be brought to a state of peace and orderliness in which scraps between the nations occur no more than scraps among the inhabitants of the town of New York? Is such a hope merely an idle dream? And if that can take place shall America stand by and say: "Civilize the world if you can, but don't trouble us?"

he Real Poland—A Land of Possibilities and Opportunities

By JOHN F. SMULSKI

(EDITOR'S NOTE.—*John F. Smulski, the thor of the following article, is President of Northwestern Trust & Savings Bank of icago, and was formerly State Treasurer of linois and Municipal Attorney of the City of icago. During the absence of Mr. Paderewski road he is the recognized representative in the ited States of the new Polish Government. is also the President of the National Polish partment, which is the chief executive and ministrative body representing the interests four and one-half millions of Poles within the ited States.*)

ALTHOUGH the American business man is still far removed from an appreciation of the importance of the Polish problem in rearrangement of the map of Middle Eu pe, he has a vital interest in the disposal of s issue at the Paris Peace Conference. If the lied Powers in fulfillment of their pledges eate a Poland of large area which will include indisputably Polish populations, with Dant- as a Polish seaport, and with full power of f-government, a positive step will be taken words assuring the real world peace for which are all striving.

If, on the other hand, the spirit of the Vienna ngress of 1815 should prevail and a Poland small area—a new Congress Kingdom as it re—is created, it will be well for the world prepare for wars because the Polish country so rich in mineral resources, so rich in labor, rich agriculturally, that it will be a land given er to the exploitation of the neighboring wers, no matter what their form of govern- ent.

Poland, it must be remembered, is the bridge to Russia. Through Warsaw pours the trade t only into Russia but Siberia and the far st. With a real Poland that bridge will be open way across which the trade of the rld will be free to pour and American busi- ss men will have their entry with all others. small Poland would mean primarily a Ger- an Poland, and the bridge would become a idge-head with German manufacturers taking ll and even blocking the entrance to the Rus- an markets.

This is not my vision alone. The thought ich I have attempted to express has been ex- essed with greater clearness by the statesmen the world. Lloyd George declared that the eation of a United and Independent Poland s necessary for the stability of Europe. esident Wilson a year earlier, but with equal fectiveness, declared that statesmen every- here were agreed that there must be a Polish ate. Pichon, Clemenceau, and Poincaire in ance have been equally insistent and direct, d from the Italian Government officials have me positive pledges. Dr. E. J. Dillon, of ngland, who is regarded as one of the greatest perts on Near Eastern affairs, has gone even rther and declared that but for the mis-hand- ng of the Polish question at the Congress of ienna, the world war just closed would never ve taken place, because a real Poland would ve made the German foray of frightfulness possible.

Now, while these several declarations are sed in part on an appreciation of the suffer- gs of the Polish people and the nobility of eir struggle for statehood during a century d a quarter, it must be admitted that the lied statesmen have also been obliged to re- rd conditions in a materialistic way. Wars ll for suffering and for sacrifice, and a merely ntimental appreciation of the pleas of a peo-

JOHN F. SMULSKI

ple hardly justifies the deliberate creation of conditions which may provoke new wars. The enthusiasm of the Allied governments for a new Poland is not only because the leaders believe that the Poles deserve freedom and have the ability to defend it, but because of their under- standing that a small Poland means a close cor- poration dominated by German influence and with new wars, while a large Poland will mean a real nation standing equal with the other nations throughout the world and peace assured. It is not only for Poland, but for themselves they are standing. Yet from the beginning the vision of the peoples of Europe as well as America with regard to Polish affairs and pros- pects has been seriously clouded by clever Ger- man propaganda. At the Congress of Vienna, the German leaders appeared with an exact and complete understanding of Polish resources and possibilities, for they had made an intensive study of the country, but the French and English statesmen had so little knowledge of the land that they were easily cajoled into an a ceptance if not full approval of the German program. The German plans for the disposal of the Polish problem were so complete that the English and the French felt the matter did not require independent study. Germany thus gained by the ignorance of those sent to trade, and the fostering of this ignorance of Poland among the western European peoples, and lately the American people, has been for some time one of the chief aims of the German politicians.

Within the United States, it must be ad- mitted, German propaganda methods have de- veloped a haziness as to Poland, which has worked to the advantage of the German politicians. The heart of America has been touched by the sufferings of the Poles, and aid has been given because of their need, and the problem has been regarded as a sociological rather than a political one, which has imposed a double burden on those who have been advanc- ing the national claims of the Polish people.

Even today, as in 1815, German statesmen are hoping at the Paris Peace Congress to win by the tongue what they lost through the sword. They are planning today, as over a hundred years ago, to profit in the discussion of the Polish question by the ignorance of the outside world and by their exact knowledge of condi- tions. For four years they have been studying and traversing Poland; the German Chambers of Commerce have established national branches in Warsaw, Lodz and in other cities for some years, with selling agencies in active operation. The Germans have full information as to the coal, iron and oil resources; they have studied the fertility of the soil, the totals of the standing timber, the number of looms in the factories, blast and other furnaces in the iron districts. Knowing these facts they are in an ideal posi- tion to manipulate them according to their own advantage. Only a tithe of this information is in the possession of the Allied Powers, though the Polish Information Bureau in Switzerland, and the Polish offices in London and Washing- ton have for some time been assembling and compiling information which it is hoped will aid in making the real country known.

German propaganda agents have with con- siderable skill succeeded in creating the general impression that Poland at the best is only a small nation which may perhaps have wrongs, but which on the whole has hardly a population sufficient in size to be considered as worthy of special attention. Even within the United States this opinion has taken root and in public discussions and even in formal written articles reference is continually made to Poland as a member of the family of small nations. Poles in America anxious for any comfort or recogni- tion of their claims have themselves at times participated in the gatherings of small and op- pressed nationalities and thus unwittingly have advanced the understanding, which is most un- fortunate.

Poland, the new Poland, will be the fourth nation in population on the European Conti- nent. With 35,000,000 population it ranks close behind Italy. Its population equals the total continental populations of Norway, Sweden, Denmark, Belgium and Serbia, and it will have an area second to that of Germany. But area and even population will not make a great or a free state, and the Polish statesmen have no thought that prosperity can be founded on these mere attributes. The confidence in the future of Poland is based on the homogeneity of the people, the prevalence of one language, one form of thought, one great ambition for union and liberty. And back of that, the economic future is viewed with satisfaction because of the diversity of the industries and the many lines of activity prevalent. For this population is diversified in its employment, having substan- tial numbers of its people employed in mining, in manufacturing, in agricultural pursuits, as well as in distinctly commercial undertakings. It is a population which with freedom will in- crease its needs, its scale of living, and its busi- ness ambitions. It is a population, as evidenced by the Polish immigration in the United States, which is scrupulously exact in its use of credit, its payment of obligations and its thrift. This statement will, it is hoped, dissipate once for all the German fiction that Poland is a small nation.

The new Poland will not only be strong enough to care for its own interests, but it will be able to serve as a barrier state between Ger- many and Russia and thus protect the Russian people against German aggression while they work out their own salvation. It can also lend a helping hand to the Czecho-Slovak state. In- deed while a self-sustaining and competent Poland is wholly feasible of itself, the safety of the Czecho-Slovak nation is dependent absolutely on Poland's being made free.

But the American doubter may say, granting that you will have large area, and a large population diversely employed, what has Poland to offer for the sustaining of these people? We are willing to extend a helping hand to Poland, but will our obligations only involve a loan later to be met from Polish credits, or will we be obliged to advance not only a temporary helping hand but a protecting arm? In short, will Poland be an asset or a liability in a League of Nations?

It will be an asset, and a most valuable one, and in proof of my contention I again will break through German misrepresentations. Poland, it must be remembered, stands forth in the world in the production of wheat per hectare and third in the production of corn. It is producing over 1,000,000 metric tons of beet sugar per year, and with freedom this amount can be materially increased. It has enormous areas of standing timber which even German efficiency was unable to destroy; it has grazing lands for the raising of beef, and the manufacture of dairy products; it has coal mines, iron mines, and oil wells; it has opportunities for the development of hydro-electric activities. Its textile development in Lodz has given to that city the title of the second Manchester of Middle Europe. It has a flexible banking system which makes easy credits for land and plant improvement and it has in process of development an extraordinary system of co-operative stores. In addition, it must be remembered the people are western in their culture. Polish universities and technical schools rank among the best in the world and Polish exploits in chemistry and the applied sciences are known to the civilized world.

Agriculture has from the beginning been the traditional occupation of the Poles. They came to Poland as a grazing and agricultural people and covered the great plains with their flocks and their farming activities. Their warlike attributes were a latter development, made necessary after they had opened the doors to visitors who turned out to be marauders. Although the profession of arms thus developed because of the necessity of defense, it must be acknowledged that they have materially improved since those early days.

But even the arts of the husbandman has aroused the cupidity of their German and Russian neighbors and what progress has been made has only been accomplished despite differential railroad tariffs, custom frontiers, and the lack of a free port, so that even when surplus crops have been accumulated, the Poles have been obliged to let them rot because of lack of means of communication for distribution through Poland and lack of a port by which to sell their products abroad. The farmers have developed considerable technical skill. The land requires intensive cultivation and yet by reason of their willingness to indulge in steady labor, they have reached high production rates per hectare in standard crops. It is figured by those who have studied the situation, that with an elimination of the disadvantages enumerated with the creation of a Polish state, in short, the growth of grain in Russian Poland can easily be increased from 40 to 50 per cent. The potato crop can also easily be developed with an assured water egress to a large export figure. It is also hoped to reintroduce cattle grazing, which formerly was an extensive industry but failed by reason of prohibitive veterinary measures forced by the Prussians and by the feeding of Warsaw and Lodz with cheap Russian beef.

In an independent Poland, there will be great possibilities for the development of cattle raising. In the absence of Russian competition the price for meat and dairy products should reach a high level in the local market which would be in proper relation to the cost of production. Since the Polish government will no doubt create strict veterinary supervision and construct refrigerator plants, it will be able to export considerable quantities of meat and live stock.

The new Poland will have mineral wealth which will assure prosperity of a most substantial nature. It possesses coal, iron, and oil resources sufficient for its own needs and for sale in the markets of the world. Although industrial Poland develops to the degree to which the Polish people aspire, there will be sufficient of these natural resources to meet all demands. The great mineral wealth of Poland is found on the northern slopes of the Carpathians and principally on the western corner near the sources of the Vistula, Nida and Varta.

The centre of the Polish coal-fields is exactly placed under the small town of Myslowice, called the Three Empires' point, because here, before the war, the three frontiers of the Austrian, German and the Russian Empires met together.

The coal-fields occupy an area of 2,048 square miles and are situated in Dombrowa, Krakow and the Silesian basin. The deposits of coal in this area are estimated at 94.33 milliard metric tons. This coal is of good quality and produces little ash, but only the coal of Upper and Austrian Silesia can be transformed into coke. The strata are of considerable thickness and are generally found not far from the surface.

The total production of coal in the different basins amounted in 1911 to 52,168,800 metric tons. The annual production of the three coal-fields enumerated, which is over 50,000,000 tons, represents only 0.055 per cent. of the estimated total deposit of coal.

The Polish oil wells are situated at the foot of the Carpathians, the easternmost being those of Sloboda, Hungurska and Kosmacz, while the most westerly are those of Klenczany. Between these two extreme points, lying almost 240 miles apart, are numerous oil fields. In 1912 the normal average output of crude oil amounted to 1,168,371 tons. While many reservoirs have been built and new appliances added, the development of these fields on an efficient basis has not yet been accomplished and there are opportunities for the further development which under proper governmental regulation should make largely for the prosperity of the country. A fourth or even a fifth part of the output will satisfy Polish needs, which will leave close to 75 per cent. available for export trade. The number of wells before the war numbered 1,825, of which 269 were in process of drilling. German military and economic authorities have since increased this total as they were so firmly satisfied that they would win the war and hold the territory.

The salt industry is important. There are two mportant government mines near Krakow. The Wieliczna mine is one of the greatest in the world and contains approximately 21,000,000 metric tons.

The iron ore production in Poland before the war totaled 510,600 metric tons. Again, there are great possibilities of development. The Silesian ore situation is only moderate. In Galicia thereare four varieties of iron ore and in Congress Poland there are some 29 iron mines which were developed, then allowed to wane, and then redeveloped according to the political orientations of the masters in control.

In addition to the agricultural and mining developments in Poland, there is also a substantial manufacturing phase of life which has escaped attention. Unfortunately for the Poles, their manufactured goods from Posen have been marked as German, and those from Russian Poland have been marked as of Russian production, but in the new and happier era the full volume of a "Made in Poland" label will be well advertised to the world.

I wonder how many Americans appreciate that in Russian Poland alone there are 10,953 industrial establishments employing over half

Czecho-Slovak Republic

By DR. J. F. SMETANKA

HON. CHARLES PERGLER
High Commissioner in the United States of the Czecho-Slovak Republic

the white and red badges, and the overthrow was complete.

No revolution in history has lacked so completely all elements of violence as this thoroughgoing revolution of Prague. No lives were lost, and the only incident savoring of force occurred when an Austrian officer would not take off the imperial badge from his cap and was knocked down. To describe the exalted feelings of the people would require the pen of a poet. The day was a holiday in all Prague. All business ceased; street car rides were free, crowds paraded through the principal streets, enthusiastic speeches were made by leaders of the National Committee, the Allies were cheered, the people wept when the names of Wilson and Masaryk were pronounced. The evening papers on the same day printed the official reports of the Allied chief commands under the heading of "Our Allies," while the German and Austrian general staff reports were inserted under the heading of "Enemy Official Reports." The people were exalted with joy over being free at last, and they were proud that they could range themselves openly on the side of their Allies.

To describe the progress of the revolution throughout Bohemia, Moravia and Silesia would be simply to repeat the story of Prague. The day following the breaking out of the revolution in the capital every Czech city and every Czech district threw off the Austrian rule, and the Czecho-Slovak State sprang into being, complete in every detail, with a perfectly functioning government and the willing allegiance of the entire nation.

The new government had several difficult problems to deal with. Of these, two demanded immediate attention—namely, the problem of the German minorities in Bohemia, Moravia and Silesia, and the occupation of that part of the new state formerly included in Hungary and known as Slovakia.

It is well known that the Czechs have fought the Germans during the entire period of their national existence, for the Czechs constitute an advance guard of the Slavs thrust into German territory. In the course of the thousand-year struggle the Germans succeeded in occupying certain portions of the Bohemian lands, and thus the Czecho-Slovak State had to face a considerable German minority. If that minority held certain well defined territory, they could go their own way; the Czecho-Slovaks desire nothing better than to be rid of the Germans for good. But the problem is not so simple.

Bohemia is a geographical and historical entity. It is surrounded by mountains on all sides; these mountains have been both historical and natural boundaries of the country; it would be impossible to draw new boundaries which would give the German neighbors of Bohemia the crest of the mountain ranges, as well as the slope on both sides. But in addition to that, the two races are so intricately mixed that it would tax the ingenuity of any international commission to separate them. Here and there along the boundaries of Germany are small districts where the population is altogether German. As to these, the Czechs stand ready to trade them for other districts in Prussian Silesia and Lower Austria, where the population is Czech. But for the most part territory in Bohemia, Moravia and Silesia, claimed by Germans, is settled by both Germans and Czechs. According to Austrian statistics the Germans have the majority in large sections of northern Bohemia, bordering on Saxony and Prussia, as well as along some sections of the southern frontier bordering on Upper and Lower Austria. But to accept Austrian statistics as accurate would be erroneous, for they shamelessly favor German claims. In this disputed territory there are in addition to genuine Germans, hundreds of thousands of people of Czech origin who were Germanized by force of circumstances, but who would revert swiftly to Czech nationality if conditions were reversed. There are hundreds of thousands who are undoubtedly Czech, but who were forced by their employers, by the German municipal authorities, by the fact that they were state officials or by other compelling circumstances, to allow the census-taker to inscribe them as people with the German "conversation tongue." The Jews in Bohemia who have heretofore classed themselves as Germans are now aligning themselves with the Czechs.

All this is already exemplified in the case of certain German islands in Czech territory. Some of the cities in Bohemia, and particularly in Moravia and Silesia, were in the hands of the Germans, because the antiquated municipal franchise allowed large taxpayers to outvote the common people; and all the great influence of the city hall was used in cities like Brno, Budweis, and Alomouc to create the appearance that the entire city was German. Czech children were forced to attend the German schools, streets had only German names, policemen spoke only German, and at the decennial census Czechs who did not assert themselves sufficiently were inscribed in the census as Germans. But when the great overthrow occurred in Prague, everyone of these German bastions in Czech territory fell without a struggle. The German mayors and councils submitted without even a protest to being ousted from their offices; in their places commissions were appointed on which the German element of the population received a minority representation, and a clear demonstration was made thereby of how feeble was the vaunted strength of the "state-forming" German element.

With regard to the long and sinuous zone of German preponderance stretching on the outside of Czech territory all the way from Vienna along the Austrian, Bavarian, Saxon and Prussian boundaries, there grew up in November a peculiar, sometimes almost comical, situation.

German deputies to the Vienna Parliament from all this territory followed promptly the example of the Czechs and constituted themselves into a National Council of German Bohemia with headquarters at Liberae (Reichenberg). This is a city of some 35,000 people in northern Bohemia close to the Saxon line. It is an industrial city, with a strong Czech minority which is sure to be turned into a majority when the German pressure is removed. The extemporized National Council declared all the territory in which Germans according to the last Austrian census were in the majority to be a new province under the German Bohemia, as part of the new state of German Austria. The difficulty was that the Reichenberg council did not have its own people back of it. Under its very eyes the population of Reichenberg rioted and plundered army stores of clothing and food. The Council issued orders and proclamations, but no one would obey them. Important state officials in cities as German as Teplitz and Komotau announced that they would obey orders from Prague and not from Reichenberg; the unfortunate council of German Bohemia declared them deposed and entrusted the execution of the orders to local committees of German patriots. That meant that the orders remained unexecuted.

The Czech National Committee observed a waiting attitude, for it knew that events were working in its favor. It made a formal demand upon all the district officials in Bohemian lands to accept the authority of the new Czech government in place of the old Austrian government, but where obedience was refused by German officials in territory with a German majority, the Czech statesmen did not employ force, even though they had it at their disposal. Slowly the opposition of the Germans crumbled. First the German dailies of Prague climbed on the band wagon and exhorted their brothers in Bohemia to make their peace with the new Czech Government and get good terms before it was too late. Then, one by one, the so-called German cities gave up struggling against the firm government of Prague. Some thought of all kinds of impossible expedients; the city of Karlsbad declared itself an independent republic, under American protection, but the Czech troops a few days later occupied the city and the new Karlsbad republic ended its brief life.

The logic of facts was too strong for the Germans of Bohemia. To remain united to German-Austria was out of the question, since they were separated from it by millions of Czechs. To join Germany was not a course that appealed to any hard-headed man, for the employers and the workingmen in the important industries of northern Bohemia realized that they must be protected from German industry by tariff walls; and the German farmers are attached to Bohemia and dislike the German Reich. Only the professional politicians of German Bohemia played the same kind of a game which has made everything German abhorrent to all mankind in the past four years. On November 10 the Provincial Government of German Bohemia endorsed an effort by the German-Austrian State Council to join Germany, expressing "the confident hope that the present political happenings would lead to a firm political union of Germandom in Europe." The same body sent a despatch to President Wilson, through the Swedish Legation, in which they protested against the occupation by Czecho-Slovak troops of cities to which the German Council made a claim. Even more futile were acts of the State Council of German-Austria in which Reichenberg politicians took part. This council prepared a State Declaration on November 14 in which they claimed for German-Austria all parts of the Czecho-Slovak lands which showed, according to the biased census, a bare majority of people with German as their "conversational tongue;" the council claimed also all cities with German municipal administration, even though they were surrounded by Czech territory and had already voluntarily submitted to the authority of the Czecho-Slovak Government. This Vienna Council even dared to lay claim to a partnership in the rule of the industrial district of Moravska Ostrava, although it is overwhelmingly Czech with a German and Polish minority. But nothing was said of the rights of the Czech minorities in the German territory, although in Vienna alone there are half a million Czecho-Slovaks.

If it were not for the Vienna Government of the German-Austrian State, an agreement would already have been reached between the Czecho-Slovak Government and the German speaking inhabitants of Bohemia. Even as it is, a majority of these Germans has by this time recognized the authority of the Prague Government, and in a short while even the outlying portions of the Bohemian lands will accept the changed conditions without compulsion. But Vienna is still making trouble for Prague in the approved manner of German propaganda, hoping to create discord among the Allies and set some of them at least against the Czechs. For weeks the despatches from Vienna were full of complaints about the heartless behavior of the new Czech authorities who would not permit food and coal from their territory to reach Vienna. The fact is that as to food Dr. Kramar, Czecho-Slovak premier, took care to provide for his own people first; all through the war the fertile fields of Czecho-Slovakia had to raise crops to feed the Austrian army and the Austrian capital, while the cities of Bohemia suffered more from hunger than almost any other part of the empire. Now the products of Bohemia go to feed the people of Bohemia first. That may be hard on Vienna, but the Czechs can hardly be blamed for looking first after themselves and not after their enemies.

The outcry made by Vienna about the lack of coal is equally ill-founded. There is not enough coal mined in Bohemia for the needs of Bohemian industry and for the domestic supply; in fact, the excellent sugar beet crop of 1918 is going to waste, because coal cannot be got to run the sugar mills. The Czech authorities agreed to give Vienna a certain quantity of coal, enough to prevent suffering from cold, but naturally not enough for all the manifold needs of the great city. But while the Czechs were faithfully performing their engagement in this respect, the German-Austrian government was sending arms from the Vienna arsenal through Bavaria and Saxony into northern Bohemia and Silesia and was stirring up the German population of these districts to attack the Czecho-Slovaks and occupy the coal mines. The city of Opava, in Austrian Silesia, received 500 rifles and five cannon from Vienna for the specific purpose of making war on the Czechs.

It will take some time before the German masters of Vienna will reconcile themselves to their new lot. They still imagine that being Germans, they are entitled to lord it over the Czechs and that they will induce the Allies to reëstablish in some form or another their ancient rule over the Slavs of the former Austrian Empire. They strive for this the more desperately because failure would mean personal bankruptcy for most of them. Without the Czecho-Slovak lands Vienna will fall from the rank of a great capital to the status of a small provincial city of a state of 6,000,000 people without agriculture and without important industries. It cannot be said that the Czechs contemplate Vienna's prospects with regrets. For three hundred years everything evil that afflicted Bohemia came from Vienna. Now Vienna will no longer live on Czech wealth and Czech industry; she must stand on her own feet.

A second great problem which had to be faced by the Czecho-Slovak Republic at once was the relation of the new state towards the Magyars. Slovakia, measuring more than one-third of the

Shadow Huns and Others

By T. EVERETT HARRÉ

Part IV

ENESIS OF HUN PROPAGANDA

BOUT the middle of June, 1914, various professors, scientists, public officials and other persons throughout Germany were visited by agents directly representing Bethmann Hollweg, the German Imperial ncellor. These men were asked if they ld be ready to answer the call of their gov- nent for foreign service in the event of war. question filled them with amazement, with gled emotions. Europe was tranquil; the in- ational horizon was clear. Could *Der Tag* t hand? Trained to obey their rulers with- question, with tacit submission, their hearts ing high, these servants of the Kaiser an- ·ed to one man that they were ready. Within weeks, on June 28, 1914, the Archduke ıcis Ferdinand of Austria was assassinated erajevo. On July 10, 130 selected German 'essors, scientists, public officials and others e assembled at the Foreign Office in Berlin instructions to act as directors of propa- da in North and South America, in China Japan. Three weeks later they sailed from enhagen for New York in charge of Dr. nrich Albert. Thirty-two members of this :y were destined for propaganda work in the ted States. Among these was Prof. M. J. n, a man of extraordinary suavity and cun- , whose especial mission was to round up erican college professors, educators and pub- ts who might be induced to abet the Ger- s in their sinister efforts to poison American lic opinion.

'acts concerning the inauguration of this spe- propaganda campaign, planned in Germany n before the Serajevo murder, were embod- in a confession made to the American Gov- ment by a German official sent over as one the propagandists and who is now interned. ›tain George G. Lester, of the Military In- igence Division of the General Staff of the ny, testifying on December 13, 1918, before Senate Committee investigating propaganda the United States, declared:

'Many of them (referring to the 130 German nts) were experts and had been working for propaganda in Germany, of which Pan- manism is an example, for fifteen or more rs. I might add that since 1894 Pan-German paganda has been systematically distributed m Germany in every country in the world. exchange professorship idea, for instance, German propaganda, and we got our share :hat."

GERMANY'S "PEACEFUL OFFENSIVE"

Vhile Germany, for a quarter of a century, preparing her armies and manufacturing nitions for her intended onslaught upon ilization, she engaged at the same time in a eaceful offensive" abroad which was designed camouflage her baleful purposes and win for self such esteem and admiration as would ıtralize and disarm the indignation of neu- ls when the time for her blow came. German :nts and propagandists for more than a quar- of a century carried on a world-wide propa- ıda campaign exploiting Germany as su- :me in social progress, industry, inventions l beneficent science. According to this propa- ıda, the German working class enjoyed higher ges and shorter hours of labor than existed ewhere in the world; they were afforded ideal- superior living conditions, picturesque homes, ap food, and recreation; by means of the social insurance schemes, they were solicitously cared for in sickness and old age. There was no poverty in Germany; slums had ceased to exist. The Imperial Government was represented as a benignant paternal institution which had only the well-being of its beloved subjects at heart. The good German Kaiser lived only to serve his people, and the good German people devotedly loved their Kaiser. German justice was a thing to marvel at; German officials being gifted with unexampled virtues of impartiality, integrity and incorruptible rectitude. Political corruption was unknown in Germany! By the comparison, Americans were made to blush for our ballot box frauds, municipal scandals and graft on part of our officials. While Germany's secret agents and abettors glorified the Fatherland and exalted Teuton "efficiency" as something to be desired by all other inferior peoples, subtly, insidiously and cunningly they at the same time sought to belittle American achievements and hold our own institutions, our own Government, our own history in contempt. America was scornfully presented as a land of dollars, of wicked capitalists engaged in ruthlessly exploiting the working classes, of new-rich vulgarity, a country without art, science, literature, without traditions, or national morals. Our own early struggles for freedom were ridiculed; the making of the American Constitution was sordidly interpreted as an effort on part of Colonial plutocrats, including George Washington, to enrich themselves.

By comparison with Germany, all other nations similarly suffered. France was represented as degenerate and backward, and possessed of a maniac obsession for revenge upon Germany. Great Britain, controlled by an effete land-owning aristocracy, was retrograding and falling behind in commerce; the empire was threatened with dissolution. Beset, also, with an insane jealousy of the superior Germans, England, seeking to thwart legitimate German expansion, had conspired to ring Germany about with a combination of envious and hostile powers. Russia, "the land of pogroms," in alliance with France and England, was preparing to launch a war of Slavic aggression. Yet despite this combination of hostile powers, despite every wicked conspiracy, Germany, having only the good of humanity at heart, preserved the peace of Europe for forty years. So we were told.

THE "SECRET KEY" OF GERMAN PROPAGANDA

In this pre-war propaganda, as in the propaganda launched by Dr. Bernhard Dernburg after the outbreak of war, Germany was aided by many American college professors, editors, publicists, professional social "uplifters," and every breed of radical writers. The pro-German activities of not a few Americans—who, whether consciously or unconsciously, intentionally or unintentionally, have until recently been engaged in efforts calculated to aid and comfort the Huns—began long before the European war.

That phase of pro-German propaganda which has today taken the form of fostering distrust and suspicion of the Allies, especially of Great Britain, was actually launched in this country at the conclusion of the Spanish-American war. At the time Prince Henry of Prussia visited the United States, in 1902, the anti-British propaganda was under way. Prince Henry came to America primarily to consolidate American citizens of German birth or extraction into a body which should work in the United States for the interest of their Fatherland, and coincident with his visit there was organized throughout the country the organization of Old German Warriors, who were to train Germans in the use of guns. One of the purposes of this amalgamation of an alien citizenry in our body politic was to prevent our ever going to war against Germany by the threat of an uprising and revolution against us within our midst on the part of the "one-third" of our "German-American" population. Had these plans carried, as expressed by Emil Witte, "any war between the United States and Germany would be in the nature of a civil war."

Emil Witte, at the time of the visit of Prince Henry, was attached to the German Embassy at Washington as secret "Press Attaché." The plans of Germany to influence and control American newspapers and news agencies, and to alienate England and America, were disclosed in a book written by Witte, entitled "Revelations of a German Attaché," published in Leipsig in 1907. In this book, written for Germans, Witte says he drew his "income from the secret disposition fund in Berlin," and frankly went on to say:

"In entering upon my duties, I received general instructions to make every effort to make the papers keep silence which were antagonistic to Germany and to perform the miracle of turning them from bitter opponents to friends and admirers of the Emperor, *as well as also to make it appear that the real enemy of the United States was not Germany but England.*

"As it was absolutely necessary for the success of my mission that the nature of my relations to the Embassy should remain a profound secret, I was enrolled by the Ambassador as a special correspondent of the *Norddeutschen Allgemeinen Zeitung*, and in this character I associated with American journalists, whose acquaintance I made use of for the service of the Ambassador.

"The secret key for the German diplomacy in America at this time, after the Spanish American war, was animosity and envy against England."

INNOCENT "VICTIMS" OF THE GERMAN EVIL EYE!

Was this German propaganda whose inception antedated the war by more than fifteen years at all successful? Were any American writers or editors reached and influenced by the maladroit and furtive activities of such apostles of Teuton "kultur" as Herr Witte? How many Americans, perhaps without consciously realizing it, were subtly converted to the Teutonic point of view, to the belief that the Germans were a superior race, that Teuton militarism was justified, and that Teuton "kultur" was destined by rights to conquer the world? How many were poisoned against Great Britain and led to believe that the real enemy of democracy was not Germany but England? How many were seduced into the belief that the Prussian military autocracy constituted a splendid "representative and responsible" form of government, and that the progressive German nation was menaced by a combination of spiteful, jealous, degenerating, backward powers? How many American writers—men who would not knowingly sell themselves, who could not be corrupted or bribed—were duped and victimized through this propaganda scientifically carried on for many years? May not such conversion explain the extraordinary conduct and point of view of certain American editors who, since we entered the war, have opened themselves to censure if not grave suspicion? May this not make clear the policies of certain journals which have perplexed and vexed all right-minded and loyal Americans?

If it were found, for instance, that certain men whose attitude in regard to the war has been, to put it mildly, inexplicable, had long before the war lent themselves to what was essentially pro-German propaganda, who had in writing subscribed to the German policy of "blood and iron" and had justified Germany's wars of aggression, would there be any significance to that fact?

If it were found that certain editors, who have impugned the motives of the Allies and are at present seeking to stimulate popular suspicion and distrust of England and France, had before the war aided in the glorification of military Germany and in disparaging England and France, would that be at all significant?

If it were found that certain editors, who persistently advocated a peace of compromise with the Central Powers and who, since the armistice, have pleaded for magnanimity to the beaten Huns, had before the war exalted Germany over all other European nations and had preached that the European war, when it came, should be fought to a decisive result, would there be any significance to that?

If it were found that certain editors, now advocating internationalism, disarmament, freedom of the seas, the giving to Germany of foodstuffs and raw materials, and admission of Germany to a League of Nations, had before the war—and when Germany had most in prospect to gain from a successful war—preached that disarmament in Europe was undesirable and that war to a finish might be "a useful and justifiable engine of national policy," would there be any significance to that?

Would there be any significance to the fact that a point of view favorable to Germany when she was unbeaten changed so that it was favorable to Germany when she was beaten?

Would an editorial policy favoring a compromise peace with Germany when she had most to gain from a compromise peace, which championed the Bolsheviki when they played into the hands of Germany, which defended "conscientious objectors" and the I. W. W. leaders who had seditiously conspired to hinder the country in its war work, be at all explained by a pro-German point of view and an obvious pro-German inclination of sympathies before the war?

PUNISH ALLIED ATROCITIES BEFORE WE PUNISH KAISER, PLEADS THE *NEW REPUBLIC!*

Now, certain journals, conspicuous by reason of the very few number of their kind, have ever since the signing of the armistice harped upon the alleged "imperialistic" motives of the Allies. While they have sought in effect artificially to promote widespread distrust of the Allies and have slandered the leaders of the nations associated with us in the war, they have with unwonted zeal campaigned against the levying of any indemnities upon Germany, against any punishment being inflicted upon the Huns. Strangely reticent concerning the atrocities committed by those bestial and besotted Hun hordes, concerning the devastation of Belgium, northern France and Serbia, and the enslavement of Belgian women, silent concerning the conscienceless brutality and inflexible mercilessness of armies schooled for rapine and slaughter, these journals have lately risen up in moral indignation to protest against the "overwhelming body of punitive sentiment in the Allied world."

That weekly sheet of sentimental sophomoric sophism, the *New Republic*, especially, has been stirred to the depth of its cerebral shallows at the thought of punishment being inflicted upon the Kaiser and German leaders. Before punishing the Germans, who have been guilty of atrocities in the war, let the Allies even more severely seek out and punish those on their side who inflicted atrocities upon the Germans, pleads the *New Republic!* "If there have been criminal acts on our side, we ought to insist upon justice being meted out to their perpetrators, rather more strictly, perhaps, than to the enemy criminals." Otherwise, "the punishment will be vengeance, not justice." Could such saccharine-souled sentiments—of which the "contrite and repentant" Huns must gustily approve—possibly be inspired by any possible secret pro-Germanism?

In advocating a peace of compromise by negotiation with the Central Powers, in championing every Hun peace drive, in preaching the invincibility of Germany and the impossibility and undesirability of a decisive Allied victory, in espousing and championing Bolshevism, in defending disloyalists and opponents of the war, in efforts calculated to destroy our national morale and disrupt the harmony and confidence existing between us and the Allies, could it have been possible that the *New Republic's* course was dictated by a Teutonic process of mind? Could any editor of this "up-stage" organ of intellectualism possibly be classed among the "Shadows" of the Huns? Certainly not! The *New Republic* itself is authority for the rejection of so simple and casual an explanation. As a matter of fact, may it not be more than probable that the editors of the *New Republic* do not themselves know what is the matter with them? Merely pro-German? The explanation is a matter of deeper and more obscure psychology.

"INTERNATIONAL" PRO-AMERICANISM

The *New Republic*, which has for months "advertised" the alleged imperialistic and ulterior designs of the Allies, recently defended its course by declaring:

"The policy of the *New Republic* has always been pro-American in the sense of ardent loyalty to the ideals of international security and justice which have usually been the formative influence in American foreign policy."

Why did the *New Republic* champion the early German peace drives and urge peace by negotiation—in other words, a peace of compromise by submission to the Huns?

Why, don't you see, because of its extraordinary pro-Americanism "in the sense of ardent loyalty to the ideals of international security and justice."

It isn't clear to you? You can't just see it? Well, it was all very simple. America might help the Allies to the degree that they could not be routed, beaten, utterly crushed; but America, whatever she might do, could not help the Allies to the degree that they could beat Germany. Germany was invincible; therefore, was not the continued shedding of blood useless? Was it not the logical thing for the Allies to give in? Wasn't it better to truckle to the Huns than persist in a hopeless fight? Wasn't it the bravest and finest sort of pro-Americanism to urge that we give up in order to save our skins? Of course, from one point of view, Bolo Pasha, in undertaking to save the French by exploiting the hopelessness of their cause, was a patriot. Alas! Noble motives are too often misunderstood!

Just six weeks after America entered the war, in its issue of May 19, 1917, the *New Republic* undertook the "patriotic" service of telling Americans how hopeless their cause was. That was before the whole nation was roused to back the war, when seeds of discouragement and discontent found fertile ground. The *New Republic* declared that if Russia were not prevented from drifting out of the war there "*would at best be a hideously expensive stalemate,*" "*a deadlock*" which "*could be broken only by the despatch of a huge American army to Europe—one so large that it could not be recruited, equipped and trained until the summer of 1919.*

really great achievement is possible,'' declared Mr. Herbert Croly, ''and if Frenchmen persist in erecting the virtue of thrift and the demand for safety into the predominant national characteristic, they are merely beginning a process of national corruption and dissolution.'')

Third—That "the Prussian monarchy . . . . has created a national representative body; but it has not followed the English example and allowed such a body to tie its hands; and it has remained, consequently, the most completely responsible and representative monarchy in Europe."

Having indicated the undemocratic and demoralizing influences at work within England and France, Mr. Herbert Croly plunged into an impassionedly frank attempt to justify the course of the military Empire which had readily adopted Nietsche's plan to ''live angerously, to take these risks without which no really great achievement is possible.'' In this volume, published in 1909, the present editor of the *New Republic* asserted that Germany was justified in making war upon France in 1870, and that that German aggression, despite the abuse of victory, was legitimate. Moreover, the present editor of the pacifist *New Republic*—which urged a peace of compromise by negotiation with Germany, advocated disarmament, which has discouraged any unifying nationalism and has preached a demoralizing internationalism—in 1909 declared pontifically:

''The democrats who disparaged efficient national organization are at bottom merely seeking to exorcise the power of physical force in human affairs by the use of pious incantations and heavenly words. That they will never do. The Christian warrior must accomplish the evangelist; and Christians are not by any means angels.''

WEATHER VANES "OF OPINION" AND ILL WINDS

Was it that ''pious incantations and heavenly words''—such as the *New Republic* has edified us with ever since America entered the war—became increasingly efficacious as it became more certain that Germany would lose the war?

Was it that ''peace by diplomacy,'' ''an enduring settlement forged by negotiation,'' became only more desirably practical as the prospects of an Allied victory over Germany became more certain?

The *New Republic* has employed considerable printers' ink, and expensive newspaper advertising space, in endeavoring to exploit the League of Free Nations' program, the alleged purpose of which is to make future wars impossible. With the promotion of the League of Free Nations the *New Republic* has propagandized for ''consideration'' to Germany. ''Nothing can be done to Germany as the result of still more complete victory which will absolutely prevent her from coming back, and upon the treatment which she receives hereafter depends whether she will come back as a disturber of the peace or as one of its guarantors.'' ''The German nation has stripped itself of all its pride and in effect prostrated itself before its conquerors.'' . . . Now that Germany is beaten, now that she may be made to pay for her crimes, in agitating against the alleged ''undemocratic aims of the Allies,'' the *New Republic* expresses a feverish anxiety lest the Allies plant seeds of future wars.

But in 1909, while Germany was preparing for her intended onslaught for world dominion, Mr. Herbert Croly, the pacifist editor of the *New Republic*, said with calm assurance:

"War may be and has been a useful and justifiable engine of national policy."

Why, with Germany beaten, with the menace of German military aggression removed, has Mr. Herbert Croly and his youthful associates on the staff of the *New Republic* so radically changed their point of view?

The editor of this magazine which, like a dog vexed by the moon, has yelped at the victorious Allies and has whined against ''justice . . . at the expense of Germany,'' in 1909, declared as his conviction:

''It (war) was, I believe, justifiable in the case of the two wars which preceded the formation of the modern German empire. These wars may, indeed, be considered as decisive instances. Prussia did not drift into them, as we drifted into the Civil War. They were deliberately provoked by Bismarck at a favorable moment because they were necessary to the unification of the German people under Prussian leadership; and I do not hesitate to say that he can be justified in the assumption of this enormous responsibility. The German national organization means increased security, happiness, and opportunity of development for the whole German people; and inasmuch as the selfish interests of Austria and France blocked the path, BISMARCK HAD HIS SUFFICIENT WARRANT FOR A DELIBERATELY PLANNED ATTACK. No doubt such an attack and its results injured France and the French people just as it has benefitted Germany; but France had to suffer that injury as a penalty for the part she had as a matter of policy played in German affairs. . . . It was inevitable, as Bismarck foresaw in 1848, that French opposition must be forcibly removed, and some of the fruits of French aggression be reclaimed. THAT THE RESTITUTION DEMANDED WENT FARTHER THAN WAS NECESSARY I FULLY BELIEVE, BUT THE PARTIAL ABUSE OF VICTORY DOES NOT DIMINISH THE LEGITIMACY OF THE GERMAN AGGRESSION.''

NEW REPUBLIC EDITOR AND SCHRECKLICHKEIT

If Mr. Herbert Croly, in 1908 and 1909, considered German aggression which ''went farther than was necessary'' legitimate, why, in 1918 and 1919, is he so vehement in his denunciation of the so-called ''selfish aspirations'' of the Allied ''politicians clamoring for the satisfaction of nationalistic and partisan and class aspirations?'' Why should Premier Clemenceau's ''peace settlement that will inflict exemplary punishment'' upon the nation which plotted and began this war, be illegitimate?

Mr. Herbert Croly, in December, 1918, aligned himself in opposition to the party which he said ''would impose a punitive peace, to be perpetuated by a formal or informal combination of the chief Allied Powers, with their frontiers strengthened by strategic annexations and the Central Powers kept under control by dismemberment, by naval and military restrictions and by economic burdens and discriminations.''

In 1909, Mr. Croly, after a glowing tribute to Bismarck for forcing two wars, declared:

"A war waged for an excellent purpose contributes more to human amelioration than a merely artificial peace."

Was this not the identical teaching of the Prussian Junkers and militarists who for years taught the virtues and ennobling effect of war?

But, even in other respects, Mr. Herbert Croly and the Germans were alike in their arguments, harmoniously agreed in their point of view. How, and when, was Mr. Croly converted? It is, indeed, surprising to find in Mr. Croly's volume certain identical arguments which were employed by Dr. Dernburg and his associate propagandists in 1914. It is, in fact, startling to find that the present editor of the *New Republic* antedated Dr. Dernburg by more than five years.

Having established to his satisfaction that the Prussian autocracy was ''the most completely responsible and representative monarchy in Europe,'' Mr. Croly went on to say:

''The modern German nation has been at bot-

(Continued on page 15)

THE NATIONAL
Civic Federation Review

Office: Thirty-third Floor, Metropolitan Tower
1 Madison Avenue New York City

RALPH M. EASLEY, Editor

Published Twice a Month **Two Dollars a Year**

The Editor alone is Responsible for any unsigned article or unquoted statement published in THE NATIONAL CIVIC FEDERATION REVIEW.

PRACTICAL vs. VISIONARY LABOR PROGRAM

In this number of the *Review* will be found the Reconstruction program advocated by the American Federation of Labor. This program was prepared by five of the most representative men in the labor movement—John P. Frey, Editor *International Molders' Journal;* B. M. Jewell, President Railroad Department, American Federation of Labor; John Moore, President of District 6 (Ohio) United Mine Workers of America; G. W. Perkins, International President, Cigar Workers' International Union; and Matthew Woll, President International Photo Engravers' Union. It was unanimously endorsed by the Executive Council of the American Federation of Labor, the official voice of three million organized wage-earners.

In view of the efforts exerted by the intellectual Bolshevists of the United States to exploit the program of the Labor Party of Great Britain, we bespeak for the American program a careful reading. While it is sufficiently radical to please the real progressive minds of our country, its radicalism relates to concrete things and not to abstractions. There is nothing in it about the socialization of all means of production, distribution and of land. It does not declare for "government ownership and operation" of railroads, but says that the railroads should be owned, operated or regulated by the government. It does not declare for that much overworked, illusive proposal for the "industrial democratization of industry." In fact, it talks about those things that the labor men believe will help to make conditions better *now* for the wage earner and his family in the United States, leaving for the millennium most of those things descanted upon by the "high priest" of Fabianism, Mr. Sidney Webb, in his proposed British scheme. One finds in the American program none of the following phrases which are so frequent in the British plan:

"The individualist system of capitalist production, based on the private ownership and competitive administration of land and capital . . . will receive its deathblow. And the Labor Party refuses absolutely to believe that the British people will permanently tolerate any reconstruction . . . involved in the abandonment of British industry to . . . separate private employers. . . . What the Labor Party looks to is a genuinely scientific reorganization of the nation's industry . . . on the basis of the common ownership of the means of production; the equitable sharing of the proceeds among all who participate in any capacity and only among these, and the adoption, in particular services and occupations, of those systems and methods of administration and control that may be found, in practice, best to promote the public interest."

At the recent election in Great Britain, the people passed upon this "Heaven-born" program drafted by the three Socialists, Webb, McDonald and Henderson, and also upon McDonald and Henderson, and they did not leave enough of them to supply material for a decent burial. One reason why the British program never had any standing with the people in England is that the wage earners never had anything to do with drafting it. It was purely the product of the "parlor" Socialist mind. Mr. G. D. H. Cole, the English labor writer, in a recent article in the *Dial*, throws light upon this point as follows, and at the same time correctly characterizes the program itself:

"Labor and the New Social Order is not, in any real sense, the policy of British Labor. It is a program which has received, indeed, the official endorsement of the Labor Party Conference; but it is essentially something accepted by Labor and not something devised and believed in by Labor. It is in effect a series of resolutions drafted and proposed by Mr. Webb, and accepted in default of an alternative program. But such an acceptance does not go deep; and it is safe to say that, even to the majority of Labor candidates, Mr. Webb's Memorandum means and counts for very little.

"It is not a statement of a new program to fit the new conditions, material and spiritual; it is a clear and well-expressed re-phrasing of an old policy—the policy of the Fabian Society and of Mr. Sidney Webb. Eminently practical in its proposals, it is nevertheless vitiated by the fact that it turns for help always to the State, and ignores or under-estimates the vital forces of economic organization which exist and act, in the main, independently of the State."

The American Federation of Labor in its program gives strong reasons why it opposes an American Labor Party. Such a party has always failed in this country—and now it can be added that it has also failed in England. The objection of the trade unionists is based upon purely practical grounds. By helping their friends and opposing their enemies in the two parties, the labor movement of America has made great progress—whereas, as an independent party, it would have had only a few friends in Congress, if any, because its hand would have been against all the other party members; and if it had ever secured sufficient membership to become significant, the other two parties would have united against it, as they do now, when necessary, against the Socialists.

Following closely upon the overwhelming defeat of Henderson and his revolutionary program, the American Federation of Labor Commission, with Mr. Gompers at its head, arrives in London and begins arranging for an international meeting of trade unionists, which will convene at Paris and will work in close affiliation with the Peace Council. The Henderson Socialists and all the other socialists and "brain workers" of Europe will hold so-called "labor meeting" at Lausanne; but the trade union movement of England, Australia and Canada, as well as of France and Italy, has joined with the American labor movement—and as between the two schools of thought, the practical and evolutionary and the visionary and revolutionary, it is not hard to imagine which group will be listened to at the Peace Table.

AMERICAN LABOR MISSION

Five members of the Executive Council, American Federation of Labor, took passage Wednesday, January 8, on the Cunard steamship Campania, with the purpose, first, of attending a conference with representatives of British trade unionism in London, and later of acting in concert with trade union delegations of various countries in Paris during the sessions of the Peace Congress, a primary object being representation to the Congress of the economic principles and purposes of trade unionism in contradistinction to the political aims of the various partisans of Socialism in its many guises and under its confusion of party titles. The composition of this American mission from labor to labor is undeniable evidence that it really represents the labor which works, which is organized, and which is alive to the present practical interests of all labor. On these points the names and official positions of the five delegates are convincing: Samuel Gompers, President of the American Federation of Labor, also Vice-President of the Inter-

· of the Russian Socialists as was proved
the Kerensky government came into power.
eans of German aid and backing and by
ses of bread and peace to the demoralized
an people the Bolshevik minority ousted
erensky government by force and usurped
. The entire Russian Socialist following,
ling both moderates and communistic ex-
sts, was only an insignificant fraction of
hole Russian people. Just before the Bol-
ci came into power the Russian people had
d a Constituent Assembly, the first real
mentary body ever elected in Russia. This
olshevik regime refused to allow to meet,
rsing it by bayonets and machine guns.

ese are the grim facts, yet despite them Mr.
an and others like him persist in spread-
he impression that the Bolsheviki are a
ity. It is not the first time in history that
e minority by violence and terroristic meth-
has succeeded in imposing itself upon a
try the overwhelming majority of which
posed to it.

e Bolsheviki of Germany, called the Sparti-
, used violence because of the very self-
tted fact that they were a paltry minority.
ll informed Socialist made this statement in
New York Call, of January 14, 1919: "The
argument of the Liebnecht group is that the
tariat shall socialize industry before the
ion for the National Assembly. The ground
nced for this is that it will be in the in-
ts of the majority of all the workers, al-
gh but a minority are willing to fight for
Just as the Liebnecht group were a mere
rity in the German Socialist party, so, ac-
ng to this Socialist writer, is the whole
an Socialist party a minority of the entire
age of Germany—Socialists, he says, those
prising "only from 30 to 35 per cent of the
l electorate." In other words, a minority
minority deliberately set out to force itself
its theories by violence upon the great ma-
ty. This is exactly what the Bolsheviki suc-
led in doing in disorganized Russia when
overthrew the timorous Kerensky.

Ir. Cochran can well afford to say that he is
afraid of Bolshevism. He is safely in Ameri-
where law and order obtain and where the
hinery of society is adequately functioning.
Russia—or at least those parts controlled by
Bolsheviki—the utmost chaos prevails. In-
try has completely broken down, massacres
continuous, all except Bolshevik supporters
been disqualified from voting or being
d for, Soviets are run by terrorists and
inals, freedom of speech and of the press
been absolutely abolished, all property con-
ted, and a mercenary army of Red Guards
mployed to shoot down ruthlessly all who
test. The other day the cables reported that
Red Guard fired from rifles and machine
s into a procession of 10,000 starving people
etrograd. So appalling is the disintegration
anarchy in Russia that the Bolsheviki can-
even provide bread—they can only provide
ets which they use mercilessly on any and
ccasions.

this is "the love of justice" which Mr.
hran so lightly eulogizes, the masses of real
sians have shown what they think of it by
ng to get as far away from it as they could.
once populous city of Petrograd, containing
0,000 population several years ago, has been
ced to 500,000 people, and other cities un-
Bolsheviki rule have fared similarly. Great
ses of workmen have fled to the country dis-
ts with the one object of putting as great a
ance as possible between themselves and the
hevik seats of power.

iscerning philanthropy can perform a real
ice to America by engaging a ship and giving
passage to Russia for all who prefer to live
er the peculiar delights of Bolshevism.

NOT A NEW COMPLAINT In a discourse on Americanization *The Public* emits this sneer: "So long as a foreigner is merely another bit of fuel to feed our industrial furnaces, securing no consideration and a very attenuated justice, we shall not make of him a fellow citizen."

This is as malicious as it is untrue. In every decade in American history somebody or other has made the charge that because of this or that defect in our laws or institutions America could not assimilate foreigners. Yet somehow America has been singularly successful in creating a solid body of citizenship from people who were of foreign birth. And this continued despite every advertised deterrent. Until the formation of our Republic freedom of religion was generally unknown in this country. Suffrage based upon property qualification was the law of the day. So was imprisonment for debt. Labor unions were once adjudged criminal conspiracies and so were strikes. The twelve-hour workday was common. Labor was regarded in practice and law as merely a commodity. Chattel slavery was a fixed institution. Naturalization laws were extremely onerous.

All of these and other conditions long since became obsolete. Yet even while they existed, great numbers of foreigners settling here became Americans. Similarly, the same process goes on now whatever other deficiencies may prevail. As the ancient injustices were done away with, so will the modern ones be rectified also. The Clayton Anti-Trust Law, passed by Congress in 1912, made absolutely no distinction between citizens and foreigners when it established the principle in law that labor was not a commodity, that it had definite rights as human beings.

PROPOSED IMMIGRATION RESTRICTIONS At a meeting of the Reconstruction Committee of The National Civic Federation, held in New York on December 2, 1918, a sub-committee was appointed to consider various resolutions regarding the restriction of immigration to the United States. As a substitute for the various resolutions, the following report is made to the Executive Council of The National Civic Federation for further action:

1. The standards of living of the American workman should be maintained.

2. During the period of demobilization of our armies it seems probable that there will be an ample supply of labor in this country without further increase from immigration. Efforts should be made, not so much to increase the number of our working people as to see that those now here are employed on the kinds of work for which they are specially adapted. Through the government employment bureaus and other means special care should be taken to secure this adjustment of working men to the jobs so that there will be the added efficiency with the consequence of added earnings that comes from all men and women being so placed that their productivity is highest. In this way can standards be best maintained and improved.

3. In addition to the present restrictions on immigration in our immigration laws it is suggested that a plan be adopted through appropriate legislation by which the maximum annual immigration permissible from any people shall be a fixed per cent from that people who have already become naturalized citizens, together with the American-born children of that same people.

The percentage permitted should under present conditions be so low that there would be a decided additional restriction.

In order, however, that the needs of increased industry or the special needs of any industry requiring a particular type of laborers not now obtainable here in sufficient numbers may be supplied, provision should be made for a special commission with authority to raise or lower the percentage figure by executive action in order to meet such needs. This same commission should have the right to admit specific numbers of workmen in any special trade or profession when sufficient numbers cannot, in their judgment, be obtained here.

Such a commission should presumably be an ex-officio commission consisting probably of the Secretary of Labor, the Secretary of Commerce, and the Secretary of the Treasury, or some commission similarly constituted.

BRITISH LABOR REPUDIATES PACIFIST REVOLUTIONISTS

By A. M. SIMONS
(of the American Alliance for Labor and Democracy)

British labor is the first to speak since the great war began.

The election result carries encouragement and hope of a free world using its freedom intelligently.

Every pacifist intellectual, every swivel chair revolutionist was defeated.

Those Socialists and labor members who refused to betray the cause of democracy at the bidding of phrase-mongers, who saw in the war a real contest between antagonistic systems and not a doctrinaire discussion of imperialism were elected.

At the same time labor representation in Parliament was doubled and labor becomes officially the opposition party.

Never has labor been so carefully discriminatory in a great election. By its millions of votes British labor said that it wished a new society, that it endorsed the economic program of the Labor Party, that it desired the pressing of the program of housing and conciliation and education that is already revolutionizing British society.

But it refused to trust the carrying out of that program to the men and women who had betrayed the cause of labor and democracy in its greatest crisis.

The result is especially gratifying to American labor.

It was boasted by one of the would-be leaders of British pacifist laborism that the American labor and Socialist delegations had no effect in Great Britain. That statement has been widely spread by the Bolshevist pacifists in this country. At the election that would-be leader was retired to private life after many years in parliament. With him went nearly every person who agreed with him in opposition to the position taken by the American delegations.

At the same time nearly all those members of the Labor Party who stood with the American missions have been re-elected.

While I was in Great Britain last summer Henderson, MacDonald, Lansbury and their followers told me over and over again that the war would end in a draw, that the United States could not bring sufficient force to change the result and that British labor was standing solidly behind them in a demand that peace negotiations be begun. Like our own Socialist Party politicians they were always wrong.

The instinct of labor was right. It has rebuked those who wished their leadership upon labor.

The Independent Labor Party, with its membership of less than 50,000, has long been the tail that wagged the great trade union dog with 5,000,000 members. Today the dog has taken charge of the tail, and apparently has performed an amputation.

Many of these men and women have done valuable service for labor in the past. They are persons of ability and courage. But in the time of greatest test the world has known they failed. There are great lessons in this vote for all the world to read.

The Bourbons may learn from the fate of the reactionary opponents of Lloyd-George, who were practically wiped out, that there is to be no going back. His strength lay in that revolutionary reconstruction program to which he pledged support. The world is going forward.

But it is not going to leap into the air nor into an abyss. The group of editorial Bolsheviks who have sought consciously and avowedly to imitate the British Independent Labor Party and lead American labor into pathless forests of political phrases may now look upon the forecast of their fate.

American Labor's Reconstruction Program

DRAFTED BY THE COMMITTEE ON RECONSTRUCTION OF THE AMERICAN FEDERATION OF LABOR

THE world war has forced all free peoples to a fuller and deeper realization of the menace to civilization contained in autocratic control of the activities and destinies of mankind.

It has caused a world-wide determination to overthrow and eradicate all autocratic institutions, so that a full measure of freedom and justice can be established between man and man and nation and nation.

It has awakened more fully the consciousness that the principles of democracy should regulate the relationship of men in all their activities.

It has opened the doors of opportunity through which more sound and progressive policies may enter.

New conceptions of human liberty, justice and opportunity are to be applied.

The American Federation of Labor, the one organization representing Labor in America, conscious that its responsibilities are now greater than before, presents a program for the guidance of Labor, based upon experience and formulated with a full consciousness of the principles and policies which have successfully guided American trade unionism in the past.

DEMOCRACY IN INDUSTRY

Two codes of rules and regulations affect the workers; the law upon the statute books, and the rules within industry.

The first determines their relationship as citizens to all other citizens and to property.

The second largely determines the relationship of employer and employee, the terms of employment, the conditions of labor, and the rules and regulations affecting the workers as employes. The first is secured through the application of the methods of democracy in the enactment of legislation, and is based upon the principle that the laws which govern a free people should exist only with their consent.

The second, except where effective trade unionism exists, is established by the arbitrary or autocratic whim, desire or opinion of the employer and is based upon the principle that industry and commerce can not be successfully conducted unless the employer exercises the unquestioned right to establish such rules, regulations and provisions affecting the employes as self-interest prompts.

Both forms of law vitally affect the workers' opportunities in life and determine their standard of living. The rules, regulations and conditions within industry in many instances affect them more than legislative enactments. It is, therefore, essential that the workers should have a voice in determining the laws within industry and commerce which affect them, equivalent to the voice which they have as citizens in determining the legislative enactments which shall govern them.

It is as inconceivable that the workers as free citizens should remain under autocratically made law within industry and commerce as it is that the nation could remain a democracy while certain individuals or groups exercise autocratic powers.

It is, therefore, essential that the workers everywhere should insist upon their right to organize into trade unions, and that effective legislation should be enacted which would make it a criminal offense for any employer to interfere with or hamper the exercise of this right or to interfere with the legitimate activities of trade unions.

UNEMPLOYMENT

Political economy of the old school, conceived by doctrinaires, was based upon unsound and false doctrines, and has since been used to blindfold, deceive and defeat the workers' demands for adequate wages, better living and working conditions, and a just share of the fruits of their labor.

We hold strictly to the trade union philosophy and its developed political economy based upon demonstrated facts.

Unemployment is due to underconsumption. Underconsumption is caused by low or insufficient wages.

Just wages will prevent industrial stagnation and lessen periodical unemployment.

Give the workers just wages and their consuming capacity is correspondingly increased. A man's ability to consume is controlled by the wages received. Just wages will create a market at home which will far surpass any market that may exist elsewhere and will lessen unemployment.

The employment of idle workmen on public work will not permanently remove the cause of unemployment. It is an expedient at best.

There is no basis in fact for the claim that the so-called law of supply and demand is natural in its operations and impossible of control or regulation.

The trade union movement has maintained standard wages, hours and life in periods of industrial depression and idleness. These in themselves are a refutation of the declared immutability of the law of supply and demand.

There is in fact no such condition as an iron law of wages based upon a natural law of supply and demand. Conditions in commerce and industry, methods of production, storing of commodities, regulation of the volume of production, banking systems, the flow and direction of enterprise influenced by combinations and trusts have effectively destroyed the theory of a natural law of supply and demand as had been formulated by doctrinaire economists.

WAGES

There are no means whereby the workers can obtain and maintain fair wages except through trade union effort. Therefore, economic organization is paramount to all their other activities.

Organization of the workers leads to better wages, fewer working hours, improved working conditions; it develops independence, manhood and character; it fosters tolerance and real justice and makes for a constantly growing better economic, social and political life for the burden-bearing masses.

In countries where wages are best, the greatest progress has been made in economic, social and political advancement, in science, art, literature, education, and in the wealth of the people generally. All low wage-paying countries contrasted with America is proof for this statement.

The American standard of life must be maintained and improved. The value of wages is determined by the purchasing power of the dollar. There is no such thing as good wages when the cost of living in decency and comfort equals or exceeds the wages received. There must be no reduction in wages; in many instances wages must be increased.

The workers of the nation demand a living wage for all wage-earners, skilled or unskilled—a wage which will enable the worker and his family to live in health and comfort, provide a competence for illness and old age, and afford to all the opportunity of cultivating the best that is within mankind.

HOURS OF LABOR

Reasonable hours of labor promote the economic and social well-being of the toiling masses. Their attainment should be one of Labor's pri cipal and essential activities. The shorter wor day and a shorter work week make for a co stantly growing, higher and better standard productivity, health, longevity, morals and ci zenship.

The right of Labor to fix its hours of wo must not be abrogated, abridged or interfer with.

The day's working time should be limited not more than eight hours, with overtime pı hibited, except under the most extraordina emergencies. The week's working time shou be limited to not more than five and one-ha days.

WOMEN AS WAGE-EARNERS

Women should receive the same pay as m for equal work performed. Women worke must not be permitted to perform tasks dispı portionate to their physical strength or whi tend to impair their potential motherhood aı prevent the continuation of a nation of stron healthy, sturdy and intelligent men and wome

CHILD LABOR

The children constitute the nation's most val able asset. The full responsibility of the gover ment should be recognized by such measures will protect the health of every child at bir and during its immature years.

It must be one of the chief functions of tl nation through effective legislation to put an iı mediate end to the exploitation of children und sixteen years of age.

State legislatures should protect children immature years by prohibiting their emplo ment, for gain, under sixteen years of age aı restricting the employment of children of le than eighteen years of age to not more tha twenty hours within any one week and with n less than twenty hours at school during the san period.

Exploitation of child life for private ga must not be permitted.

STATUS OF PUBLIC EMPLOYES

The fixing of wages, hours and conditions labor for public employes by legislation hampe the necessary exercise of organization and co lective bargaining.

Public employes must not be denied the rig of organization, free activities and collecti bargaining and must not be limited in the exe cise of their rights as citizens.

CO-OPERATION

To attain the greatest possible development civilization, it is essential, among other thing that the people should never delegate to othe those activities and responsibilities which the are capable of assuming for themselves. D mocracy can function best with the least inte ference by the state compatible with due prote tion to the rights of all citizens.

There are many problems arising from pr duction, transportation and distribution, whic would be readily solved by applying the metho of co-operation. Unnecessary middlemen wh exact a tax from the community without rende ing any useful service can be eliminated.

The farmers through co-operative dairies, ca neries, packing houses, grain elevators, distribu ing houses, and other cooperative enterprise can secure higher prices for their products an yet place these in the consumer's hands at lowe prices than would otherwise be paid. There i an almost limitless field for the consumers i which to establish cooperative buying and sel ing, and in this most necessary development, th ade unionists should take an immediate and tive part.

Trade unions secure fair wages. Co-operation otects the wage-earner from the profiteer.

Participation in these cooperative agencies ust of necessity prepare the mass of the people participate more effectively in the solution of e industrial, commercial, social and political oblems which continually arise.

THE PEOPLE'S FINAL VOICE IN LEGISLATION

It is manifestly evident that a people are not lf-governing unless they enjoy the unquesoned power to determine the form and subance of the laws which shall govern them. elf-government can not adequately function if ere exists within the nation a superior power authority which can finally determine what gislation enacted by the people, or their duly lected representatives, shall be placed upon e statute books and what shall be declared null nd void.

An insuperable obstacle to self-government in he United States exists in the power which has een gradually assumed by the Supreme Courts f the Federal and State governments, to delare legislation null and void upon the ground hat, in the court's opinion, it is unconstituional.

It is essential that the people, acting directly r through Congress or state legislatures, should ave final authority in determining which laws hall be enacted. Adequate steps must be taken, herefore, which will provide that in the event f a supreme court declaring an act of Congress r of a state legislature unconstitutional and the eople acting directly or through Congress or a tate legislature should re-enact the measure, it hall then become the law without being subject o annulment by any court.

POLITICAL POLICY

In the political efforts, arising from the workers' necessity to secure legislation covering those conditions and provisions of life not subject to collective bargaining with employers, organized labor has followed two methods; one by organizing political parties, the other by the determination to place in public office representatives from their ranks; to elect those who favor and champion the legislation desired and to defeat those whose policy is opposed to Labor's legislative demands, regardless of partisan politics.

The disastrous experience of organized labor in America with political parties of its own, amply justified the American Federation of Labor's non-partisan political policy. The results secured by labor parties in other countries never have been such as to warrant any deviation from this position. The rules and regulations of trade unionism should not be extended so that the action of a majority could force a minority to vote for or give financial support to any political candidate or party to whom they are opposed. Trade union activities can not receive the undivided attention of members and officers if the exigencies, burdens and responsibilities of a political party are bound up with their economic and industrial organizations.

The experiences and results attained through the non-partisan political policy of the American Federation of Labor cover a generation. They indicate that through its application the workers of America have secured a much larger measure of fundamental legislation, establishing their rights, safeguarding their interests, protecting their welfare and opening the doors of opportunity than have been secured by the workers of any other country.

The vital legislation now required can be more readily secured through education of the public mind and the appeal to its conscience, supplemented by energetic independent political activity on the part of trade unionists, than by any other method. This is and will continue to be the political policy of the American Federation of Labor if the lessons which Labor has learned in the bitter but practical school of experience are to be respected and applied.

It is, therefore, most essential that the officers of the American Federation of Labor, the officers of the affiliated organizations, state federations and central labor bodies and the entire membership of the trade union movement should give the most vigorous application possible to the political policy of the A. F. of L. so that Labor's friends and opponents may be more widely known, and the legislation most required readily secured. This phase of our movement is still in its infancy. It should be continued and developed to its logical conclusion.

GOVERNMENT OWNERSHIP

Public and semi-public utilities should be owned, operated or regulated by the government in the interest of the public.

Whatever final disposition shall be made of the railways of the country in ownership, management or regulation, we insist upon the right of the workers to organize for their common and mutual protection and the full exercise of the normal activities which come with organization. Any attempt at the denial by governmental authority of the rights of the workers to organize, to petition, to representation and to collective bargaining, or the denial of the exercise of their political rights is repugnant to the fundamental principles of free citizenship in a republic and is destructive of their best interest and welfare.

The government should own and operate all wharves and docks connected with public harbors which are used for commerce or transportation.

The American Merchant Marine should be encouraged and developed under governmental control and so manned as to insure successful operation and protect in full the beneficent laws now on the statute books for the rights and welfare of seamen. The seamen must be accorded the same rights and privileges rightfully exercised by the workers in all other employments, public and private.

WATER WAYS AND WATER POWER

The lack of a practical development of our waterways and the inadequate extension of canals have seriously handicapped water traffic and created unnecessarily high cost for transportation. In many instances it has established artificial restrictions which have worked to the serious injury of communities, owing to the schemes of those controlling a monopoly of land transportation. Our navigable rivers and our great inland lakes should be connected with the sea by an adequate system of canals, so that inland production can be more effectively fostered, the costs of transportation reduced, the private monopoly of transportation overcome and imports and exports shipped at lower costs.

The nation is possessed of enormous water power. Legislation should be enacted providing that the governments, federal and state, should own, develop and operate all water power over which they have jurisdiction. The power thus generated should be supplied to all citizens at rates based upon cost. The water power of the nation, created by nature, must not be permitted to pass into private hands for private exploitation.

REGULATION OF LAND OWNERSHIP

Agriculture and stock-raising are essential to national safety and well-being. The history of all countries, at all times, indicates that the conditions which create a tenant class of agriculturists work increasing injury to the tillers of the soil. While increasing the price of the product to the consumer these conditions at the same time develop a class of large land owners who contribute little, if anything, to the welfare of the community but who exact a continually increasing share of the wealth produced by the tenant. The private ownership of large tracts of usable land is not conducive to the best interests of a democratic people.

Legislation should be enacted placing a graduated tax upon all usable lands above the acreage which is cultivated by the owner. This should include provisions through which the tenant farmer, or others, may purchase land upon the lowest rate of interest and most favorable terms consistent with safety, and so safeguarded by governmental supervision and regulation as to give the fullest and freest opportunity for the development of land-owning agriculturists.

Special assistance should be given in the direction of allotments of lands and the establishment of homes on the public domain.

Establishment of government experimental farms, measures for stock raising instruction, the irrigation of arid lands and reclamation of swamp and cut-over lands should be undertaken upon a larger scale under direction of the Federal government.

Municipalities and states should be empowered to acquire lands for cultivation or the erection of residential buildings which they may use or dispose of under equitable terms.

FEDERAL AND STATE REGULATION OF CORPORATIONS

The creation by legislative enactment of corporations, without sufficient definition of the powers and scope of activities conferred upon them and without provisions for their adequate supervision, regulation and control by the creative body, has led to the development of far-reaching abuses which have seriously affected commerce, industry and the masses of the people through their influence upon social, industrial, commercial and political development. Legislation is required which will so limit, define and regulate the powers, privileges and activities of corporations that their methods can not become detrimental to the welfare of the people. It is, therefore, essential that legislation should provide for the federal licensing of all corporations organized for profit. Furthermore, federal supervision and control should include the increasing of capital stock and the incurring of bonded indebtedness with the provision that the books of all corporations shall be open at all times to federal examiners.

FREEDOM OF EXPRESSION AND ASSOCIATION

The very life and perpetuity of free and democratic institutions are dependent upon freedom of speech, of the press and of assemblage and association. We insist that all restrictions of freedom of speech, press, public assembly, association and travel be completely removed, individuals and groups being responsible for their utterances. These fundamental rights must be set out with clearness and must not be denied or abridged in any manner.

WORKMEN'S COMPENSATION

Workmen's Compensation laws should be amended to provide more adequately for those incapacitated by industrial accidents or occupational diseases. To assure that the insurance fund derived from commerce and industry will be paid in full to injured workers state insurance must supplant, and prohibit the existence of, employers' liability insurance operated for profit.

IMMIGRATION

Americanization of those coming from foreign lands, as well as our standards of education and living, are vitally affected by the volume and character of the immigration.

It is essential that additional legislation regulating immigration should be enacted based upon two fundamental propositions, namely, that the flow of immigration must not at any time exceed the nation's ability to assimilate and Americanize the foreigners coming to our shores, and that at no time shall immigration be permitted when there exists an abnormal degree of unemployment.

By reason of existing conditions we urge that immigration into the United States should be prohibited for a period of at least two years after peace has been declared.

TAXATION

One of the nation's most valuable assets is the initiative, energetic, constructive and inventive genius of its people. These qualities when properly applied should be fostered and protected instead of being hampered by legislation, for they constitute an invaluable element of progress and material development. Taxation should, therefore, rest as lightly as possible upon constructive enterprise. Taxation should provide for full contribution from wealth by a tax upon profits which will not discourage industrial or commercial enterprise. There should be provided a progressive increase in taxes upon incomes, inheritance, and upon land values of such a nature as to render it unprofitable to hold land without putting it to use, to afford a transition to greater economic quality and to supply means of liquidating the national indebtedness growing out of the war.

EDUCATION

It is impossible to estimate the influence of education upon the world's civilization. Education must not stifle thought and inquiry, but must awaken the mind concerning the application of natural laws and to a conception of independence and progress.

Education must not be for a few but for all our people. While there is an advanced form of public education in many states, there still remains a lack of adequate educational facilities in several states and communities. The welfare of the republic demands that public education should be elevated to the highest degree possible. The government should exercise advisory supervision over public education and where necessary maintain adequate public education through subsidies without giving to the government power to hamper or interfere with the free development of public education by the several states. It is essential that our system of public education should offer the wave-earners' children the opportunity for the fullest possible development. To attain this end state colleges and universities should be developed.

It is also important that the industrial education which is being fostered and developed should have for its purpose not so much training for efficiency in industry as training for life in an industrial society. A full understanding must be had of those principles and activities that are the foundation of all productive efforts. Children should not only become familiar with tools and materials, but they should also receive a thorough knowledge of the principles of human control, of force and matter underlying our industrial relations and sciences. The danger that certain commercial and industrial interests may dominate the character of education must be averted by insisting that the workers shall have equal representation on all boards of education or committees having control over vocational studies and training.

To elevate and advance the interests of the teaching profession and to promote popular and democratic education, the right of the teachers to organize and to affiliate with the movement of the organized workers must be recognized.

PRIVATE EMPLOYMENT AGENCIES

Essentials in industry and commerce are employes and employer, labor and capital. No one questions the right of organized capital to supply capital to employers. No one should question the right of organized labor to furnish workers. Private employment agencies abridge this right of organized labor.

Where federal, state and municipal employment agencies are maintained they should operate under the supervision of joint committees of trade unionists and employers, equally represented.

Private employment agencies operated for profit should not be permitted to exist.

HOUSING

Child life, the workers' physical condition and public health demand that the wage-earner and his family shall be given a full opportunity to live under wholesome conditions. It is not only necessary that there shall be sanitary and appropriate houses to live in but that a sufficient number of dwellings shall be available to free the people from high rents and overcrowding.

The ownership of homes, free from the grasp of exploiting and speculative interests, will make for more efficient workers, more contented families, and better citizens. The government should, therefore, inaugurate a plan to build model homes and establish a system of credits whereby the workers may borrow money at a low rate of interest and under favorable terms to build their own homes. Credit should also be extended to voluntary non-profit making housing and joint tenancy associations. States and municipalities should be freed from the restrictions preventing their undertaking proper housing projects and should be permitted to engage in other necessary enterprises relating thereto. The erection and maintenance of dwellings where migratory workers may find lodging and nourishing food during periods of unemployment should be encouraged and supported by municipalities.

If need should arise to expend public funds to relieve unemployment the building of wholesome houses would best serve the public interests.

MILITARISM

The trade union movement is unalterably and emphatically opposed to "militarism" or a large standing army. "Militarism" is a system fostered and developed by tyrants in the hope of supporting their arbitrary authority. It is utilized by those whose selfish ambitions for power and worldly glory lead them to invade and subdue other peoples and nations, to destroy their liberties, to acquire their wealth and to fasten the yoke of bondage upon them. The trade union movement is convinced by the experience of mankind that "militarism" brutalizes those influenced by the spirit of the institution. The finer elements of humanity are strangled. Under "militarism" a deceptive patriotism is established in the peoples' minds, where men believe that there is nobility of spirit and heroism in dying for the glory of a dynasty or the maintenance of institutions which are inimical to human progress and democracy. "Militarism" is the application of arbitrary and irresponsible forces as opposed to reason and justice. Resistance to injustice and tyranny is that virile quality which has given purpose and effect to ennobling causes in all countries and at all times. The free institutions of our country and the liberties won by its founders would have been impossible had they been unwilling to take arms and if necessary die in the defense of their liberties. Only a people willing to maintain their rights and defend their liberties are guaranteed free institutions.

Conditions foreign to the institutions of our country have prevented the entire abolition of organized bodies of men trained to carry arms. A voluntary citizen soldiery supplies what would otherwise take its place, a large standing army. To the latter we are unalterably opposed as tending to establish the evils of "militarism." Large standing armies threaten the existence of civil liberty. The history of every nation demonstrates that as standing armies are enlarged the rule of democracy is lessened or extinguished. Our experience has been that even this citizen soldiery, the militia of our states, has given cause at times for grave apprehension. Their ranks have not always been free from undesirable elements, particularly the tools of corporations involved in industrial disputes. During industrial disputes the militia has at times been called upon to support the authority of those who through selfish interests desired to enforce martial law while the courts were open and the civil authorities competent to maintain supremacy of civil law. We insist that the militia of our several states should be wholly organized and controlled by democratic principles so that this voluntary force of soldiery may never be diverted from its true purpose and used to jeopardize or infringe upon the rights and liberties of our people. The right to bear arms is a fundamental principle of our government, a principle accepted at all times by free people as essential to the maintenance of their liberties and institutions. We demand that this right shall remain inviolate.

SOLDIERS AND SAILORS

Soldiers and sailors, those who entered the service in the nation's defense, are entitled to the generous reward of a grateful republic.

The necessities of war called upon millions of workmen to leave their positions in industry and commerce to defend, upon the battle fields, the nation's safety and its free institutions. These defenders are now returning. It is advisable that they should be discharged from military service at the earliest possible moment; that as civilians they may return to their respective homes and families and take up their peace-time pursuits. The nation stands morally obligated to assist them in securing employment.

Industry has undergone great changes due to the dislocation caused by war production and transportation. Further readjustments in industry and commerce must follow the rehabilitation of business under peaceful conditions. Many positions which our citizen soldiers and sailors filled previous to enlistment do not exist today.

It would be manifestly unjust for the government after having removed the worker from his position in industry and placed him in military service to discharge him from the army or navy without having made adequate provision to assist him in procuring employment and providing sustenance until employment has been secured. The returned citizen soldier or sailor should not be forced by the bitter urgent necessity of securing food and clothing to place himself at a disadvantage when seeking employment.

Upon their discharge, transportation and meals should be supplied to their places of residence. The monthly salary previously paid should be continued for a period not to exceed twelve months if employment is not secured within that period.

The federal and state employment bureaus should be directed to cooperate with trade union agencies in securing employment for discharged soldiers and sailors. In assisting the discharged soldier and sailor to secure employment, government agencies should not expect them to accept employment for less than the prevailing rate of wages being paid in the industry. Neither should any government agency request or require such discharged men to accept employment where a trade dispute exists or is threatened. Nor should the refusal on the part of any of these discharged soldiers or sailors to accept employment where trade disputes exist or are threatened or when less than the prevailing wage rate is offered, deprive them of a continuance of their monthly pay.

(Continued on page 18)

Shadow Huns and Others

(*Continued from page 9*)

the work of admirable leadership on the of officially responsible leaders; and among e leaders the man who planned most effect- · and accomplished the greatest results was von Bismarck.'' Bismarck was ''a patriotic ssian, who was exclusively, intelligently and rupulously devoted to the welfare (as he eived it) of his country and his king.'' (By same test, could Mr. Croly other than ap- e of the ''intelligent and unscrupulous iotism'' of von Hindenburg, Ludendorf, von ıstorff, von Papen, Boy-Ed and the captain he submarine which sank the Lusitania?)

Little by little the fertile seed of Bismarck's ssian patriotism grew into a German semi- ocratic nationalism, and it achieved this ısformation without any essential sacrifice ts own integrity,'' pursued Mr. Croly.

GIVING THE PROP TO PROPAGANDA

n an encomium, which rings with surpris- ly virile enthusiasm on the part of a *New ublic* editor, Mr. Croly told how Germany an creating a navy, how railroads were ght by the government and managed, not for benefit of stockholders, but for the benefit of people; how the government spread im- ved methods of farming, and promoted in- trial efficiency. ''In every direction German ivity was organized and was placed under led professional leadership, while at the same e each of these special lines of work was ordinated to its particular place in a com- hensive scheme of national economy. This ternalism' has, moreover, accomplished its rpose. German industrial expansion sur- sses in some respects that of the United States, d has left every European nation far behind.''

There may seem in this a familiar ring. It is actly what the whole crew of propagandists, ıat Dernburg, Viereck, and others, have said only Mr. Croly had the pleasure of saying it fore them. Mr. Croly, born aloft on his Teu- nic Pegasus, paened:

''*THE PRUSSIAN MONARCHY . . . AS REMAINED . . . THE MOST COM- LETELY RESPONSIBLE AND REPRE- ENTATIVE MONARCHY IN EUROPE. . . . Germany alone among the modern Eu- pean nations is, in spite of the temporary em- rrassment of Imperial finance, carrying the st of modern military preparation easily, and oks forward confidently to greater successes in e future. She is at the present time a very riking example of what can be accomplished r the popular welfare by a fearless acceptance ı the part of the official leaders of economic as ell as political responsibility, and by the ef- ient and intelligent use of all available means that end.''*

Dr. Bernhard Dernburg, upon his advent in ıe United States in 1914, five years later, as- rted:

''The Reichstag is a body elected on the most beral ballot law that exists anywhere, more beral even than the ballot law of the United tates for the election of the President. THE ERMAN PEOPLE ARE REPRESENTED S DIRECTLY AND DEMOCRATICALLY N THE GOVERNMENT AS THE AMERI- AN PEOPLE ARE IN THEIRS.''

Dr. Dernburg merely re-echoed his Kaiser hen he declared in 1914:

''Germany holds the record for keeping peace ithin and outside of Europe for the last forty- ur years.''

Mr. Herbert Croly probably considered him- lf an original thinker when he asserted in 909:

''Her (Germany's) official foreign policy nce 1872 has undoubtedly been determined by ıe desire to maintain the peace of Europe un- er effective guarantees.''

When the time came for Germany to destroy the peace which she claimed to have preserved, she sought, like a coward and criminal, to shift from herself all blame. She sought to deceive the world by hypocrisy and lying. To this end she expended millions of dollars.

Dr. Bernhard Dernburg, in the course of his official defense, merely re-echoed his Kaiser when he declared that Germany ''never coveted its neighbors' territory,'' that ''the German military, as well as its naval force, have been created on purely defensive lines''; that ''the sword was forced into Germany's hands,'' and that the war had been precipitated by the criminal and hostile alliance of Russia, England and France. England, explained Dr. Dernburg, was jealous of Germany's economic expansion; France was possessed by a passion for revenge.

"THE WICKED ALLIES" BEFORE THE WAR

Mr. Herbert Croly, having exonerated Germany of all blame for forcing the earlier war against Austria and that against France in 1870, as long ago as 1909 expressed the very arguments which Germany later used in trying to exonerate herself of any blame for starting the war in 1914.

''France,'' wrote Mr. Croly in his book, ''has gradually built up a series of understandings with other Powers, more or less inimical to Germany. (Page 251.)

''Some Frenchmen still cherish plans of revenge for 1870; but candid French opinion is beginning to admit that the constantly increasing resources of Germany in men and money make any deliberate policy of that kind almost suicidal. France would lose much more by a defeat than she could gain from a victory, and the fruits of victory could not be permanently held.

''Russia still looks longingly toward Constantinople.

''The gradual growth of a better understanding between France, Great Britain and Russia is largely due to an instinctive coalition of these powers who would be most injured by an increase of the German influence and dominion; and the sense that Europe is becoming united against them makes German statesmen more than ever on their guard and more than ever impatient of an embarrassing domestic opposition. (Page 253.)

''She (Germany) is partly surrounded by actual and possible enemies, against whom she can make headway only by means of continuous vigilance and efficient leadership.'' (Page 252.)

The cue of the whole German propaganda launched in 1914 was that Germany had been compelled to take up arms in self-defense against these combined powers. Russia had lighted the fuse; England and France had connived against Germany. Russia represented the menace of Slav aggression which meant the break-up of Austria Hungary. ''It was,'' said Dr. Dernburg, ''the Pan-Slavic tendency that got the better of saner views of the Russian Czar that started the ball rolling. . . . The Pan-Slavic theory . . . is threatening to break up Austria and even wipe it off the European slate. . . . The national existence of Austria can never be arbitrated upon. The breaking-up of Austria-Hungary cannot be tolerated by Germany. Austria is the only aid that Germany has for the purpose of defense which can be relied upon. The breaking up of the Dual Monarchy and the absolute isolation of Germany would have made her an easy prey to her neighbors whenever they chose to attack her. . . . It was a necessity for Germany . . . to come to the help of Austria and protect her from destruction and dismemberment.''

Mr. Herbert Croly, in 1909, gave voice to what became the cue of the official German apology in 1914. Said Mr. Croly:

''It is, as we have seen, the international situation and the national ambitions of Russia and Germany which constitute the chief threat to European peace. *Germany's existing position in Europe depends upon its alliance with Austria-Hungary. . . . The German, the Austrian, and the Hungarian interests all demand the perpetuation of the Hapsburg dominion.* . . . Whether the German, Austrian and Hungarian interest does or does not prevail, the fundamental national interests, which are compromised by the precarious stability of Austria-Hungary, are alone sufficient to make disarmament impossible. Disarmament means the preservation of Europe in its existing condition; and such a policy, enforced by means of international guarantees, would be almost as inimical to the foundation of a permanent and satisfactory international system now as it was in 1820. *The fact has to be recognized that the ultimate object of a peaceable and stable European international situation cannot in all probability be reached without many additional wars; and the essential point is that* ***these wars, when they come, should,*** *like the wars between Austria or France and Prussia, or like our Civil* ***war, be fought to accomplish a desirable purpose and should be decisive in result.***''

"A DESIRABLE PURPOSE"—GERMAN GAIN

If, in 1909, Mr. Croly considered the preservation of Europe in its then existing condition ''inimical,'' why, in 1918, when the Germans were frantically eager to get peace on those terms, did he consider a return to the *status quo ante* condition of Europe so highly desirable?

In 1909, Mr. Croly recognized that "**The German Empire is the European power which has most to gain in Europe from a successful war.**"

Was it that, when Germany had most to gain from a prospective war, ''the preservation of Europe in its existing condition'' was ''inimical.'' Germany, we know, was plotting to dominate Europe, to absorb Turkey, extend her empire into Asia—the world is familiar with the story of the Bagdad Railway. At the time when Germany indubitably had ''most to gain in a successful war,'' Mr. Herbert Croly advocated, as we have seen, that European wars when they come ''*should . . . be fought to accomplish a desirable purpose and be decisive in result.*''

If, in 1909, when the Germans had most to gain from a successful war, Mr. Croly believed such a war should be ''decisive in result,'' why, in 1917 and 1918, when the German prospects of victory waned, did Mr. Croly oppose the continuation of war against Germany until allied victory was ''decisive in result?'' Was ''peace with victory'' not the accomplishment of ''a desirable purpose?''

Mr. Croly's *New Republic*, in May, 1917, asserted that ''peace with victory would be peace with suicide.'' It threatened that if the American Government forced the war to continue against Germany until a military decision was reached, there would be a bloody revolution in America. The *New Republic*, which now advertises itself as having ''insisted that the war must go on until Germany was beaten,'' repeatedly told the American people that Germany could not be beaten; that at best there would be a ''hideously expensive stalemate.'' Was this, by any chance, ''defeatism?'' Mr. Croly's ''journal of opinion,'' in August, 1917, at the time of the German offensive against Russia, asserted that America ''is not capable of assuring a military decision to the Allies.'' What was it that Germany paid Bolo nearly $2,000,000 to tell the people of France?

METHINKS 'TIS A SMELL OF RATS

In 1909 Mr. Herbert Croly jeered at the efficacy of ''kind words and noble sentiments,'' of the settlement of disputes by ''congresses and amicable resolutions.'' In 1918, when the Germans, routed by the successful Allies, were in panic retreat, when the imperial Government made its last frantic play for a "peace by negotiation," Mr. Croly's *New Republic* threatened the Allies, in case they rejected discussion, with treasonable "disaffection on part of the labor groups of France and Great Britain." Why, one asks again, was this violent opposition to waging the war to a "decisive result" in military victory over Germany?

After the Germans, beaten decisively, had agreed to the armistice terms offered by Marshall Foch, after a glorious "military decision" had been obtained by the Allies, the *New Republic* brought forth its peculiar hatching—the League of Free Nations proposition. It began furiously to advocate internationalism, limitation of national sovereignty, freedom of the seas, internationalization of waterways, equality of economic opportunities—by all of which abortive propositions Germany might benefit.

With a peace of victory secured and without "suicide" Mr. Croly's *New Republic* launched a widespread campaign urging final settlement by "kind words and noble sentiments," "by congresses and amicable resolutions," with a policy "for durable peace" to be "enforced by means of international guarantees"—all of which program Mr. Croly sternly repudiated in 1909, but which—being now heartily endorsed by the Germans and operating in their favor—he stoutly champions today. As alleged foes of this program, Mr. Croly's journal has carried on a campaign of abuse by implication against the leaders of the Allies. It carried this campaign into the daily newspapers, where, in full page advertisements, the American people were warned about the old-fashioned machiavellian statesmen who were possibly about to play their old game of power politics with nations as pawns. Why, in the hour of victory, is there a campaign of extraordinary scope and publicity which is obviously designed to antagonize the American people against the Allied statesmen, to create doubt, distrust, division between this country and the nations associated with us in the war? Why especially such a sneering and bitter impugning of the motives of Premier Clemenceau of France and Mr. Lloyd George of England? Does all this not smell strangely of the very "secret keynote" of German propaganda described by Emil Witte which was launched in Washington after the Spanish-American war?

NOISE FROM THE INTELLECTUAL BARNYARD

It is extremely doubtful if this mawkish, mealy-mouthed sentimental twaddle about "liberality," "magnanimity" and "mercy" to beaten Germany has had the effect intended upon men of fibre. It is doubtful, indeed, if Lloyd George, Clemenceau and Sonnino have taken a place even in the popular imagination with Ali Baba and his forty thieves, because they may not entertain such cooing-dove sentiments concerning Germany as the editors of the *New Republic*. One is inclined to suspect that the vast sums of money spent by the *New Republic* to "advertise the differences" of war aims between America and the Allies may have been more profitably expended—say for the relief of the widows and orphans of captains of German submarines. The *New Republic* may cherish the belief that it has "seen itself taken into the counsels of statesmen at home and abroad." But how seriously? How seriously, in all actuality, has the country been infected with this turn-the-other-cheek, beware-of-the-wicked-Allies, be-kind-to-the-good-Germans, pro-Bolshevik, class-revolutionary "pacifism?"

The crowing of capons is a very funny sound.

It is curious, however, *en passant*, to note that the editor of this sheet which opposed war to a finish and which now preaches tenderness and gentle consideration to the Huns, back in 1909—when be implied that France was threatened with "a process of national corruption and dissolution," and when, if that were true, Germany certainly had most to gain from a successful war—declared:

"A nation or an individual who wishes to accomplish great things must be ready, in Nietzsche's phrase, 'to live angerously'—to take those risks without which no really great achievement is possible."

That was the doctrine of the German Junkers and militarists. That was the doctrine of Treitschke and Bernhardi. That was the doctrine of von Hindenburg and von Ludendorf. That was the doctrine of those who condemned Edith Cavel. That doctrine was practiced by the captain of the submarine which sank the Lusitania. "To live angerously"—what that means in warfare we saw illustrated in ravished Belgium. That doctrine was spoken when the Hun Kaiser, in order to win the war speedily by "terrorizing the degenerate French," ordered the cutting of the throats of French women and children.

SERMONS FROM STONES OR "IVORY DOMES"

Miss Jane Addams has described the *New Republic* as "that wonderful journal, from which so many preachers are taking their sermons instead of the New Testament."

Are any Christian congregations compelled, by any chance, to hear sermons extolling the Russian Bolsheviki and condoning the crimes of the I. W. W.? Are any religious pulpits given to preaching the gospel of social discord and revolution? Are any churches being infiltrated with pro-German pacifism? Are the sentimentalities of any Christian congregations being played upon in the interest of poor, beaten, starving Germany? How many clergymen are re-echoing calumnies regarding the integrity and honesty of motives of the Allied statesmen?

American boys are returning home wounded—blind, legless, armless, suffering from the poison gasses of a diabolic foe; a foe that knew no "consideration," no mercy. These boys will be inclined very gravely to question the "pro-Americanism" which merely camouflages revolutionary Socialism. These boys will be inclined to look askance at editors who before the war and when "Germany had most to gain," considered disarmament undesirable, who then urged that wars be carried to a decisive result, but who, after we entered the war, have advocated pacifism and opposed war to a military victory over Germany. They will ask the reason why. These boys will dissect the species of "pro-American internationalism" which justified Germany's brutal war against France in 1870, which declared her aggressions legitimate, but which today spends itself in ignoble interpretations of the motives of the Allies. These boys will have a serious concern in the journals and persons who seek to negative the fruits of their hard earned victory by destroying internal order and social concord by the promotion of revolution in our midst.

Mr. Herbert Croly's associate editor on the *New Republic*, Mr. Walter Weyl, asserted in his book, "The End of the War:"

"The final war . . . will begin after the war. It will be a wider conflict than that which now rages and the alignment will be by classes and interests rather than by nations."

WHO PAID FOR THE "ADS"?

The *New Republic* took up the cause of the Bolsheviki and their shibboleth of "peace without annexations and indemnities" at the time the Bolsheviki traitorously sold out Russia to Germany. The *New Republic*, while it propagandized for an indecisive ending of the fight with Germany, at the same time preached Bolshevism and the Bolshevik peace terms here. The *New Republic* viciously attacked the American Federation of Labor, which loyally took a stand back of the war; it championed the disloyal labor elements which were for parleys with the Huns.

Since the defeat of Germany, Mr. Herbert Croly's *New Republic* has militated against any "new balance of power." It has frankly expressed its apprehension of "the machinations of Tories, the imperialists and the exponents of an international order founded on power instead of justice and good faith." It has advertised the coined phrase—"a return to that same sinister system of Power Politics which has bred every war in Europe for centuries," which refers to the machinations of the Allied nations. Directly, and by covert inference, it carried on a campaign—in full page newspaper advertisements, and within its own pages—impugning the motives of the leaders of the nations at war against Germany. "Soon or late the peace conference will gather," ran an advertisement, "What spirit will wield the gavel there? . . . Will it be the old and sinister philosophy which for generations has patched the peace of Europe and never made it secure?" Those who read the *New Republic* have become familiar with the slur about "diplomats" playing "their ancient game of chess with peoples as pawns, the game of military supremacies, selfish alliances, balances of power, strategic frontiers and economic barriers." Mr. Herbert Croly's *New Republic* openly accused the Allied statesmen of "measuring the value of the coming settlement, not in terms of a permanent international structure built purposely to provide a habitation for the spirit of justice and fair play, but in terms of the satisfaction of specific territorial and economic pretensions and grievances."

Why, when Germany is beaten, is a peace demanding reparation for wrongs done lacking in "the spirit of justice and fair play?" Why, when the Allies are victorious, are their demands "terms of the satisfaction of specific territorial and economic pretensions of grievances?"

Mr. Herbert Croly's mushroom "League of Free Nations Association" program differs, he says, from the old program of the League to Enforce Peace "in that it seeks rather to do away with the causes of war than to arbitrate controversies among nations after they arise." Such a League as Mr. Croly desires would not allow *"the victors to profit from the impotence of the vanquished."* In the *New Republic* of January 18, 1919, it is declared: "If the Red Terror did not hover in the background as a genuine alternative, there would be small chance of a liberal and democratic settlement of the war."

AS 'TWAS 'TIS NOT NOW—NEGOTIATION

At the time when beaten Germany has all to gain from any quixotic surrender of national rights on part of the Allies, by "equality of economic opportunity," by the internationalization of rivers, canals, straits and railroads, by freedom of the seas, demobilization of armies, by readmission into a League in which she shall have her a share of decision, Mr. Herbert Croly is for all these things. He is strong for all kinds of NEGOTIATION.

"The same people who formerly declared that if a decisive and humiliating defeat were inflicted on Germany the insuperable obstacle to a peace of righteousness would disappear, now insist upon the futility in this respect of Allied victory to accomplish the desirable political result. According to Clemenceau and his like," sneers the *New Republic* of January 18, "it is just as necessary to provide against future wars with Germany as if the war had ended inconclusively instead of with a decisive victory. . . . We agree with them as to the inability of force to accomplish positive and enduring political results. A triumphant army can be used by statesmen to dictate boundaries, indemnities and the like, but it cannot be used to dictate a stable peace unless the peace itself is composed of the stuff of the political righteousmess. An enduring

ent must be forged BY NEGOTIA-."

t is January 18, 1919. There you have it. Ir. Herbert Croly, in 1909—when he cond disarmament undesirable, the preservaf Europe in its then existing condition as iical," when he admitted that Germany most to gain in Europe from a successful and was of the belief that the European when they came should "be fought to aclish a desirable purpose and should be dein result"—delivered this opinion as to ettlement of "existing rivalries and enmiimong European states" BY NEGOTIA-':

iese rivalries and enmities will not be disl by kind words and noble sentiments. The ation of Europe, like the unification of any, will never be brought about by con-es and amicable resolutions. It can be ted only by the same old means of blood iron."

"kind words and noble sentiments" were e at a time when Germany had most to gain a prospective war, why should Mr. Croly cate "kind words and noble sentiments," gresses and amicable resolutions" as effecand all desirable now when Germany, havnade an *unsuccessful* war, having employed old means of blood and iron," at a of ten million lives, the devastation of lands, and agony immitigable, faces the lty of her crimes?

'MACHINE GUNS AND FRIGHTFULNESS"

1909, Mr. Herbert Croly, in common with Bernhardis and Prussian Junkers, preached virtues and justification of war, and, in on with the German militarists, urged that should be decisive in result.

1919, in common with Dr. Dernburg and lachrymose "kamerad chorus" wailing for don *und etwas zum essen* (or is it *fressen?*) Herbert Croly preaches the virtues of the den Rule.

Ie laments, in the *New Republic* of Janu-11, that President Wilson "has a poor nce of getting the peace he wants," that "he its the Golden Rule substituted for the Lex ionis, and there is no overpowering disposii on the continent of Europe to give him it he wants. . . . *The victorious states-s . . . are callously resuming the old ie of appropriating everything that an en-ed respect for the opinion of mankind will mit, and of justifying the appropriation by ds about rights, justice and civilization.*

For the first time in political history," Mr. ly declares, "the issue is being clearly drawn *veen the friends and the enemies of interional socialization.*"

s "international socialization" Bolshevism? iternational Socialism" means merely politaction. Of "international socialization" Croly says: "The victorious march of these is will be costly, perhaps almost as costly the great war."

s this a bloody prediction of revolutions, l war, wholesale killings—as happened under Bolsheviki in Russia? Is this, by any ins, a threat? Mr. Croly pursues the *New ublic's* unashamed favorite pastime of iming that its policies are the policies of Presit Wilson:

The gospel according to Woodrow Wilson probably have to employ the same rough hods to overcome its enemies as did the pel according to Jean Jacque Rosseau . . . the gospel according to Woodrow Wilson apable of being propagated by the machine and by frightfulness as by the typewriter."

s it not going far and beyond the bounds decency brazenly to ascribe to the Presit of the nation the policies of ghoulish rchy forced upon Russia by those brutal despots, Lenine and Trotzky? Is it not going to dangerous lengths to make a point, to interpret President Wilson as challenging and attempting to force down the throats of the Peace congress a program of "international socialization" which will be "perhaps almost as costly as the great war?" Audacity or madness has reached the limit of tolerance when it openly expresses the threat of using "the machine gun and frightfulness."

And, reading between Mr. Croly's lines, is it not indicated that "the machine gun and frightfulness" will be the alternative unless the Allies handle Germany with kid gloves? Did not the Imperial German Government, in the early days of the war, direct its agents abroad to "foment strikes," promote "separation movements and civil war?" Have we forgotten the s cret documents made public by Secretary Lansing? Can Germany possibly now be up to her old game in order to force the Allies by threat of internal revolutions, of widespread Bolshevism, to give her an easy peace? Is it impossible that some of the "innocent victims" of the earlier wily Svengalis of German propaganda are responding automatically to the masters of their souls?

Mr. Herbert Croly is self-confessedly a "victim" of the theory that the war was a "50-50 affair," and it seems, indeed, that he would not be averse to seeing Germany rehabilitated in the eyes of the world. He says:

"The former ruling classes of Russia and Germany were the chief culprits, but until Englishmen, Frenchmen, Italians and even Americans admit or are forced to admit their share of responsibility for the ruin of Europe there can be no stable reconstruction."

In other words, the former defender of Bismarckism and Prussian militarism today would shift upon the Allies—who rose and shed their blood as water, in defense—the blame for the despoilation of fair Belgium, the razing of beateous cities, the raping of Belgian women, the outraging and murder of little children, the enslavement of a guiltless people, for all the bloodshed, the horror, the bestiality, the utter ignobility, the causing of agony immitigable! *"Their share of the responsibility for the ruin of Europe!"* If this is not the mental callousness, the brutish logic of the Hun, the peculiar Hunnish inability to see right from wrong, then certainly reason and justice have departed from the realm of mankind.

Mr. Herbert Croly devotes a number of pages of his magazine of January 4, 1919, to an article entitled "Justice to the Devil," by an obscure professor of history in Middlebury College. The purport of this screed is obvious. The disloyal purpose is self-defeated by reason of an unconquerable sneering bitterness which betrays the animosity of a curdled spirit toward the victorious Allies. There is in this outburst of petty spleen the same protest expressed by Mr. Croly against "injustices" being inflicted upon Germany.

"Not that we wish to perpetrate any injustice upon our fallen foe," jeers Mr. Croly's contributor, "but, forsooth, he cannot be trusted to share decently the benefits of a just peace. We must hedge him about with iniquitous safeguards, lest he again seek to triumph over our just cause.

"The multitude of lies provided for the nourishment of public opinion in the United States, *seems to indicate* that the German Realpolitik included a lawless lust for Empire," continues the writer. "The Allies, and later the United States, professed and no doubt felt, a holy horror. That horror was somewhat tempered, to be sure, by the conspicuous lack of holiness in the nations who professed it."

Had an enemy-alien indulged publicly in such remarks there is little doubt as to what would have been his fate. Yet the *New Republic,* professing a unique brand of "patriotism," lends it pages to such propaganda as this:

"The great mass of American public opinion seems actually to be unaware that our side has in any important respect abandoned the principles of justice in dealing with our enemy. . . . *The aims and methods of Allied, and even American, propaganda and censorship, have not differed widely from the German.* . . . The task of enlightening American patriotism has been not only thankless but, since the passage of the Espionage act, unlawful. In our somewhat hysterical effort to secure unity of thought and action, we have made it probable that our abandonment of justice will outlast the period of the war.

"First by partisan groups and latterly by the government itself, the belief has been built up that this is a war of Huns against the Saints. . . . If our definition of Hunnishness include lust for empire, unscrupulous diplomacy and frightfulness, we can readily find a good deal more than fifty-six hundredths of one per cent of Hunnishness among the Saints." The writer infers that "it will be extremely difficult . . . to determine what the relative distribution of this deviltry has been in the recent war." "All evidences of like iniquities on our side" have been carefully suppressed, he says, and the result has been "a distortion of truth, an annihilation of perspective," merely the inspiring of soldiers and the general public with a "killing hate."

U. S. "NO LESS UNJUST TO RUSSIA THAN TO GERMANY!"

In an effort, about which no concealment is made, to clear the Germans of extraordinary atrocities, the *New Republic* contributor conjures up the atrocities committed in the Revolutionary War, the war of 1812 and the Civil War. "Frightfulness at least is a new invention of the Hun? Alas, no!" . . . he mocks. "Atrocities may readily be found without going outside the family. . . ."

After this astonishing attempt to befoul our own country and history by the implication that we had anticipated the unspeakable Hun in atrocities, the *New Republic* contributor asserts ambiguously:

"Evidence is rapidly accumulating that we have been no less unjust to Russia than to Germany."

In what were we "unjust to Russia?" By the sending of troops into Siberia? The *New Republic* has protested against that as outrageous injustice. In what have we been likewise "unjust to Germany?" By the sending troops to France to fight the Germans? Obviously!

Can the *New Republic* possibly be pro-German? Can it possibly be anti-Ally in its sentiments?

Or is its patriotism merely different from the commonly accepted variety, perhaps a unique, superior "international socialization" brand? The *New Republic* is constantly approvingly quoted by, and its articles reprinted in, the *New York Daily Call* and Viereck's so-called *"American Weekly."*

SHALL NATIONAL BOUNDARIES RESTRAIN THE MEETING OF CONGENIAL MINDS?

It may, of course, be mere coincidence that the point of view of the *New Republic* has strikingly altered, swerved and drifted in its course along lines similar to the trend of German and pro-German opinion. It may have been mere coincidence that, writing presumably in 1908 or early in 1909, when German agents were subtly at work disseminating the same ideas, Mr. Herbert Croly expressed such a strikingly Teutonic process of mind and point of view. Those German agents were insidious, cunningly beguiling, unsuspectingly subtle. May it not be that Mr. Croly, like other naive but sincere Americans—professors, social uplifters, radicals, et cetera—was reached without his knowing it; that, like many other innocent converts, he was merely an unsuspecting victim? There may be only mere coincidence in the fact that certain arguments used by Dr. Dernburg and other official and paid German propagandists in 1914 and 1915 were similar to arguments for the German policy used by Mr. Croly in his book published in 1909. It may be only coincidence that arguments employed in Mr. Croly's *New Republic* at the present time for a League of Free Nations, for freedom of the seas, for generosity to Germany in the matter of supplying raw materials, as well as arguments against punitive indemnities and attacks upon the "unscrupulous purposes of the Allies" parallel sentiments expressed recently by Dr. Dernburg and Count von Bernstoff.

Count von Bernstorff, who once believed the war should "be fought to accomplish a desirable result and should be decisive in result" for Germany, in an interview with the Amsterdam correspondent of the London *Daily Express*, the other day declared he "endorsed" the plan for a League of Nations" and considered it "practical." Count von Bernstorff also declared that in the program of the League he saw "the only way to prevent war by a limitation of armaments."

Dr. von Bethmann-Hollweg, German Chancellor at the outbreak of the war, approving of a League of Nations, declared: "If the victor exploits the distressed conditions of the conquered, violates his body, compels him to employ his forces of blood and property in enslaved service, he can then boast his power, but justice will veil her head."

Mr. Herbert Croly's *New Republic*, in August, 1918, declared that "with the right kind of peace *Germany ought to get her share*, but not more than her share" *of raw materials after the war.* "A merely punitive policy, designed to treat Germany the more harshly the more completely she is forced to acknowledge military defeat would encounter in America not perhaps active opposition, but all the doubts and delays that characterize the negative side of American policy."

Dr. Bernhard Dernburg, writing in the *Vienna Neuwe Frie Presse* recently, said:

"*Germany needs raw materials* for the revival of her industries, *she needs credit* to cover her obligations, she needs a market for her products in order to pay off this credit and to create deposits abroad. Neither France nor England will or wishes to give it, for both are debtors, and a great part of the reason why they demand a war indemnity from us is that they have to free themselves from the United States. . . . The Allies in victory are at least as unscrupulous as Germany was charged with being in the war."

Mr. Herbert Croly's *New Republic*, of November 30, 1918, under the heading, "How is Germany to Pay," began ironically:

"Germany must make good the physical destruction she has wrought—that is the determination of multitudes in the Allied world. Germany must not find the road to rehabilitation easy. She must encounter difficulties in supplying herself with materials and in marketing her products. Indeed, if it can be compassed, she shall find no markets at all. That is, also, the determination of multitudes. And it is curious to note that those who would punish Germany by throttling her trade are almost to a man advocates of the heaviest possible indemnities. Everyone has smiled over the outraged plaintiff in a divorce case who not only insists upon a generous and reliable flow of alimony, but would like to ruin the business of her sinning husband besides.

THE WORLD IS THEIR OYSTER

"If Germany is to make reparation," continued the *New Republic*, "she must obviously transfer values to the countries she has wronged. What form shall the transfer of values assume? . . . We may dismiss gold as unimportant. . . . There is not in all Germany one-tenth enough gold for the purposes of reparation.

"If Germany is to make reparation it must be *through cash or through credits* translatable into cash or goods. Neither cash nor credits can possibly be had except as a result of export operations."

Dr. Bernhard Dernburg has just said:

"The Germans turn their eyes in expectation toward America and feel sure their expectations will not come to grief. . . . It is quite possible that America will transfer English and French debts to Germany in order to get her money, for America wants not destruction but justice. . . . A clever American policy can, and I think will, secure sympathy for us, thereby providing economic help for our German country now in collapse."

Dr. Dernburg clairvoyantly divined:

"In the question of the freedom of the seas there is a deep gulf. English and French aspirations cannot be reconciled with President Wilson's points."

"Did any divergence actually exist between the political objects for which President Wilson had pledged his countrymen to fight, and the political objects which the British, French or Italian governments planned to achieve in the event of victory?" asked the *New Republic*, and replied by saying that if divergences did exist "it was a patriotic service to advertise them."

"The forces which have opposed President Wilson's peace policy are the more formidable because they are international. . . . Yet," said the *New Republic* of November 9, "they have been conclusively defeated."

In its issue of January 18, 1919, Mr. Croly's sheet evinces a change of mind:

"The best existing chance of a stabilizing treaty depends upon the wearing down of the opposition of the Sonninos and the Clemenceaus. . . . Americans who are hoping for a peace which will act as a future bulwark against power politics, should . . . allow the President, if necessary, to wear out the opposition."

If, by "advertising" the divergences between President Wilson's points and the English, French and Italian aspirations the *New Republic* was performing "a patriotic service," was Dr. Dernburg not performing a laudable and patriotic service likewise?

May it not be that, in a sense, Count von Bernstorff, Captains Boy-Ed and von Papen, Dr. Rumely and Dr. Hale, Viereck and Major J. J. Dickenson, the $30-a-week informer, not to speak of poor Bolo, were "pro-American in the sense of ardent loyalty to the ideals of international security and justice?" That, in a sense, they were "friends of international socialization?"

(*To Be Continued*)

The Real Poland

(*Continued from page 4*)

which to support its purchases. The temperament of the people is such that there need be no fear of losses.

Apart from food, Poland today is in need of moral rather than material support. With insurrectionary Germany to the west, working in combination with Bolshevik Russia on the east, Poland is in danger of beng crushed between two giant forces. It is now serving a double purpose as a barrier to German aggression in Russia and a Bolshevik assault upon Europe, but there is a limit to its endurance. What is needed with all possible haste is a visible demonstration of the sympathy and the support of the Allies.

The United States Employment Service

ITS FUNCTIONS AS A WAR EMERGENCY MEASURE AND ITS FUTURE OPPORTUNITIES

By NATHAN A. SMYTH
ASSISTANT DIRECTOR GENERAL

the first in the series of weekly confer- upon subjects related to post-war social stment problems, under the auspices of deration's Woman's Department, held on y 8, 1919, *and at which Mrs. Coffin Van ller presided, Mr. Nathan A. Smyth made dress which follows.)*

HE war has not been altogether an instrument of destruction. Out of the process of welding a great fighting, ctive machine, we have developed in respects a new spirit, a new vision, ertain new instiutions. One of the onceptions was a realization that not oes the individual and social welfare of the s of the country but also the efficiency of tion as a whole, depend upon the devel- t of a wide-spread and efficient system of ic employment service or what the English o as a labor exchange service. Prior to r, the idea had made faint beginnings in untry. Some States had their State Em- ent Service. We had something here in ork. Ohio had developed rather a good Wisconsin, Illinois, and about ten or a other States had certain systems of public ment offices. None of them operated in ction with others and none were operat- ith any very great success, except in one special instances. The United States Gov- nt itself, back in about 1907 I think, had taken in a small way to find employment mmigrants and aliens, who were out of jobs, gh a subordinate part of the immigration e. That had developed rather gradually to about 1914, when the great war had d. They tried to put a little more life in- at service at that time, and for a year o they worked out certain cooperative ar- ments with State services, and opened a nore Federal offices; there were relatively throughout the country. They were not good and were rather looked down upon erybody concerned.

situation during the early months of 1918 ht the country to a realization of the fact we could not have national industrial effi- essential to the creation of a potent ng machine unless the Government itself took to bring the worker and the oppor- y together. The competition for labor had wages go skyrocketing; employers were ng labor one from another; the turnover p to 100 per cent a week in some places; estlessness, the inefficiency, were some of vils created by leaving the matter to the rdinated efforts of employers.

had before us the experience in Eng- but in that respect, as in others, we did follow the lessons that might have been ed from other countries as rapidly as, in spect, one might have wished. In Wash- n all through the early part of the year until the Fall of that year, there were and efforts to make a real Federal employ- service. An appropriation of $250,000 was to create a Federal employment service. you realize that the pay roll of the pres- mployment service, about a year from that is pretty nearly $5,000,000, you will see nadequate the $250,000 was even to make a ning. Nevertheless the Department set out money in hand, feeling a new service had started separate from the old Immigration au and the thing to do was to start.

e President came along in 1917 with an allotment from his Presidential Emergency Fund, so that it came up to about $1,000,000, and that gave enough to go on until July 1, 1918, the beginning of the present fiscal year. During the year 1917 the coordinated State offices and the federal offices had been doing considerable business, so much in fact that it is quite remarkable that the necessity of it had not been more appreciated before, but nothing more had been done about it. They had had an average of a million applicants a year during that period.

In the Spring of 1918, the work of extending the employment service went on rapidly. It was realized that cooperative arrangements with State systems had to be made. There had to be a federal director in charge in every State, and offices opened in each if this service were to function in time to be of value during the war. Of course, as always happens where an organization must be built over night—a great deal of inefficient material crept in. Real employment service work, to be done rightly, is almost a profession, and should be entered into with something of that spirit. There was no body of trained employment service men in this country in 1918. A few had been trained in the State service, and only a few were of the right calibre even for administrative offices.

After the War Labor Policies Board was organized, it was agreed that all recruiting of unskilled labor for war work should be done through the United States Service. That program inaugurated by a Presidential pronouncement, took effect the first of August. A very rapid development was requisite in June and July to get ready to carry out that great undertaking. With that situation in mind, the Senate first waked up to the necessity of financing such a proposition and an appropriation of five and a half million dollars was given for that current fiscal year, with the understanding that if more were needed, there would be hope of getting it. And we do need more.

When the employment service took over the great task of finding the unskilled workers for war industries, incidentally supplying skilled workers for many, and furnishing almost all the ship yard workers in Boston and at the Hog Island Plant, it realized it would have to make an extension of its organization. The Government had gone ahead so fast in letting contracts, projecting plants, ships and every other thing that could make for a great war instrument two or three years from now, that it overran the available man power. A survey revealed a shortage the first of August of about a million common laborers, more serious shortage of skilled labor, and a great many plants not reported upon. The situation, when the armistice was signed, was serious. Almost every big government project was being held back. Believing there was enough man and woman power in the country if we could bring it all to bear on war work, we started to organize community labor boards of five members each, with a man and a woman, selected by the employers, usually the Chamber of Commerce or manufacturing association of the community; a man and a woman selected by the organized labor of the community; and a chairman selected by the United States Employment Service. Their purpose was to bring pressure to bear in the various communities upon the non-war and lesser industries to get more men; and to get women into all forms of work from which men might be released. The armistice came before full fruition. The women on the boards were to see locally that the conditions of work for women were proper. The Government could set general standards for women's work, but there had to be some machinery to see that they were carried out. We intended to have an assistant to the Federal Director in every State.

Apart from supplying men and women to war industries, the Employment Service carried on the task of helping the person who was out of a job to get one. It took under its wing an institution, the Boys' Working Reserve. The purpose of it was to induce boys to train and go out and work on the farms. Those boys were watched and in many places did magnificent work. That organization will be continued next year. It has proved a fine training for the boy himself.

During the Summer we developed the great farm labor movement. A great army of men was moved all up through the wheat field, starting south and moving along so that practically there was no loss from lack of labor for the crops.

The great problem with regard to women in war industries was not so much to get the women as to find proper jobs and fitting conditions. It was a subject of great delicacy in its relationship to men and organized labor and it was difficult to find out where extensions for women in industry might be made. The great national women's organizations, the National League for Women's Service, The Federation of Women's Clubs, and others were going to give us assistance and had all pledged their full cooperation.

When the armistice came the whole situation changed over night. We no longer had to provide labor for war work. We had to wait several weeks to learn the army plan of demobilization. Canceling contracts, however, began within a few days. Mr. Crowell fortunately stopped this and developed a policy under which contracts for war material would not be cancelled except under a plan jointly adopted and supervised by the War Industries Board and the Department of Labor. It was very necessary to cancel contracts in some form. For example, it is bad economics to go on making tanks at the present time. It is even worse to go on making poison gas. Many destructive implements that have no peace time use should not be manufactured after the war is over. Generally speaking the policy of contract cancellations has been rather wise, so far as possible, in view of the speed with which it had to be done. It was thought the kind of a concern that might shift from war to peace industry should have its cancellations so graduated that shifts would be made gradually and without release of employees. On the other hand, the munition plants, very much overgrown from any peace time proposition, with nothing that they could do inside of a great many years to take the place of the war work, had to be closed down, and generally speaking their cancellations were so ordered that the company could go on with the work it had in process, gradually easing off so that at the end of December in some cases and the end of January in other cases they would come to an end, the theory being the employees would go gradually.

We started in about one hundred and twenty-five characteristic communities to obtain weekly reports of conditions, to get a barometer of what might be happening as a result of these contract cancellations. At the beginning practically all of these cities were short of labor. That situation has changed so fast that last week's report had forty-five or forty-six reporting unemployment. Nevertheless, the unemployment taken by itself would not be very much greater than unemployment usually; not anything so serious as we have passed through many times in the last twenty years. It is nothing to worry about unless it gets worse before the Winter is over, the trend being so rapid.

Industry has not been very rapid in starting up this year. Manufacturers do not seem to be getting orders. Retailers are buying carefully and orders are not coming across. These are factors which make for considerable concern but as yet nothing alarming has developed. Then, to complicate that situation, we have the very rapid process of demobilizing the soldiers. I think either the process of contract cancellations or the process of demobilization could go on by itself all right but when they come together we face the real problem. The army decided to discharge the soldiers without reference to industrial conditions, and as to whether or not they had positions waiting for them. They are sent out with not much money in their pockets, no advance pay, and perhaps a lot of back pay yet to come, and their fare home. The army informed the Department of Labor that it might have a representative in each camp to endeavor to assist these boys in finding jobs. Like most orders from the General Staff, the general order was capable of a very narrow construction, and in one or two places was construed narrowly. The Department of Labor's representative in Camp Meade, for instance, is entitled to tell the Colonel what he knows about the industrial situation and the man who wants a job can come in and find out from the Colonel what he knows about it. In Camp Devins there was a liberal construction. Up to about two weeks ago, the labor representatives there, working with the finest spirit of cooperation from the camp officers, had gone over the whole situation with some eleven thousand men. They found about six thousand of them did not need assistance at all. They helped about five hundred men get their jobs back. They placed about one thousand in new jobs, and about another two thousand they sent off with cards to their agencies at home. It became necessary to devise means of taking care of the men after they left the camps. We had about eight hundred offices throughout the country. We had the labor boards in about sixteen hundred communities. We organized in different States on a different basis. In New York they are given a large territorial jurisdiction in one community labor board. It has always been our policy to let local matters be worked out by local authorities as far as possible. In other states they made more minute sub-divisions. Even those did not cover the country well enough to take care of the soldiers in all the places to which they might come back. We asked the Council of National Defense to come to our assistance with its separate branches numbering about one hundred and eighty thousand. Then for assistance we called on the Red Cross, Y. M. C. A., Y. W. C. A., the Hebrew Association, the Catholic Association, and several others. We organized a central cooperating committee and started a plan for a bureau for returned soldiers and sailors in every community of any size. In some communities, the bureau may be in the hat of the Postmaster; in large communities it must be elaborate; the idea being to get the jobs back for the boys as they come home. It is necessary to pool all the information as to positions that are open. There are a great many men who are being sent from one community to another and it was necessary to have the underlying network of the United States Employment Service offices, who transmit information as to local conditions first to State Directors and then through them to Washington, so that the resources of one community may be available to other communities in finding jobs. That work is well under way. Up to date, except for the largest cities, we don't seem to be encountering any difficulty with the returning soldiers. The influx of men in New York, for instance, who don't belong here, and who are looking for jobs here, instead of finding them back home presents the greatest problem. Just how long that rapid process of demobilization can go on without making for unemployment among soldiers I don't know. We are making every possible effort to make sure that knowledge concerning such jobs as are open to soldiers shall be so concentrated that they can find them. No employment service can actually create work.

With the transition from war to peace comes up the peculiar problem of woman, and woman's work. We struck it first in Washington, with stenographers and clerks there. We have been able to do a great deal in helping them get back positions at home. We find it with women let out of war jobs. That has caused serious disquietude.

Up to the first of November reports of the Employment Service showed that during the year something over two and a half million men and women had found places, a large proportion the latter half of the year, and for the last three or four months the average number of persons who applied at employment service offices, or offices of state services cooperating with us, and all part of the same system, has run up to one hundred and thirty-five or one hundred and forty thousand a week. Generally in employment service work an average of about seventy to seventy-five per cent. of reported placements has been found to be the normal average, and that has been about the average of our figures. In other words, something over one hundred thousand men and women a week have been finding positions through the branches of the United States Employment Service. An average, I should say, of about fifteen per cent. of those are women.

We drew the facilities of the employment service not merely to the skilled artisan and the common laborer but to those with highly professional training. Through this branch of public service reserve in the early stages of the war, a large number of trained engineers were located in army positions and secured commissions, and a lot of those officers are coming back now asking assistance. Early in 1917 we had learned that associations of college alumnae and others had organized offices for placing women. We have been making cooperative agreements with those offices, taking them over, making them free offices rather than fee-charging. So, we have been organizing a professional section, in cooperation with the Teachers' Bureau in the Department of the Interior and engineering societies and others of trained workers. At 42nd Street over one hundred professional persons a day in the last five or six days, have come in and we are actually beginning to get opportunities for them. It is a new line of work. It must be done for the officers. The American Training Camps Association, which secured so many officers for the army, will help to find positions for them. It is all work that had to be thrown together hastily. We are working hard with it and I think it is going to perform a very useful function. So far as the women are concerned, it is not particularly a demobilization problem although there are many trained women, who have had war jobs, to whom it is necessary to give assistance.

We are organizing handicap divisions in Boston and Chicago and in New York, chiefly for men from forty-five to sixty-five; some twenty-three thousand such men were placed in positions where they were able to earn a living. Special work can be done with the employer to get him out of the idea that there are no good men

The National
Civic Federation Review

IV. NEW YORK, FEBRUARY 15, 1919 No. 9

WAR LESSONS IN LABOR PROBLEMS

UE CO-OPERATION BETWEEN EMPLOYER AND EMPLOYEE, COLLECTIVE ACTION WITH ADJUSTMENT BOARD AS FINAL COURT, WILL BRING PEACEFUL SETTLEMENTS IN INDUSTRY

(Speech Delivered at Eighth Annual Convention of the National Retail Dry Goods Association, New York City, February 12, 1919)

By V. EVERIT MACY
PRESIDENT OF THE NATIONAL CIVIC FEDERATION

T is appropriate, while repre- sentatives of the various na- tions of the world are uniting levelop methods for the elimi- on of war between nations, employers should be giving h thought to improving the tions between themselves and r employees. Americans have only surprised themselves but e astonished the world by the er and effectiveness they de- ped during the past eighteen nths. They have shown not latent military ability but nendous dormant industrial acity.

What has been accomplished owing to the fact that each vidual held firmly the same , the same purpose, namely, to the war. All personal desires e secondary to this one great ught. This unity of purpose ded the nation together and ryone co-operated with his hbor for the common welfare. this common aim and co-opera- spirit lies the secret of our in- trial as well as our military cess. Only through a real de- for peace and this same co- rative spirit can the Peace ference at Paris attain its end. nations can find a peaceable way ettle their differences, certainly prevention of strikes and lock- s is not beyond the reach of in- try. It cannot be accomplished, ever, without a sincere and nest determination to maintain ce upon the part of all con- ned. This includes a belief in good faith of both sides.

The war taught us many lessons. particular point which I wish mphasize is that we could not have made our mon aim and co-operative spirit effective ing the war without organization. The vernment had to know on what supplies it ld depend and when and where they could obtained. This was comparatively easy in se industries where there were manufactur-

V. EVERIT MACY

ers' associations; where there were none, com- mittees had to be appointed to speak for the industry. It was also necessary for the Govern- ment to know that there would be no interrup- tion of industry through labor disputes, so it turned to organized labor for aid in stabilizing conditions, and Labor Adjustment Boards were established for the settlement of all disputes. It would have been im- possible to have negotiated with each individual manufacturer and each manual worker. These agree- ments made by the Government with associations of manufacturers and with organized labor resulted in a greater industrial output than any one had believed possible. Or- ganization is the foundation of modern civilization and is propor- tionate to the degree of civilization attained by a people.

There is such a thing as "labor capital" just as there is "cash capital." There is the difference between the two, however, in that "labor capital" cannot be sepa- rated from the individual possess- ing it. When those having cash capital began to organize into cor- porations and demonstrate the value of such co-operative action, it was natural that "labor capital" should seek to benefit in the same way by the formation of trade unions. It is just as absurd for employers to say they will not deal with trade unions as it would be for the workers to say they will not deal with corporations. Both forms of organization can be of great good or of great harm. It is not organization, no matter how large, that we wish to destroy, but merely the predatory use of the power gained through organiza- tion. In the past, too many em- ployers' associations and too many unions have been organized as purely fighting machines. They have been like two standing armies facing each other, each waiting to resent an aggression by the other. The result has been what one might expect, i. e., the aggressive act has in time been made. Each side has often acted without thought of the welfare of the industry as a whole and rarely of the welfare of the nation.

The world moves on without regard to per- sonal preferences and those who stand in the way of any well defined development, instead of trying to direct its course are sure to be left behind in the race or are crushed out. Democracy means the collective action of the citizens. Why should we expect such collective action to be limited to political questions only? Conditions of industry affect as vitally the lives of our people as does their political status. One cannot therefore, with impunity, deny the right of collective bargaining to the workers. While the stability of a democracy depends upon the average intelligence of its citizens, its progress is much influenced by the wisdom of its leaders. We talk too much these days about our rights and think too little about our obligation. We cannot separate "rights" or privileges from obligations and responsibilities. They are the two halves that make the complete whole.

National labor leaders must take the responsibility of leadership and see to it that the local organizations accept the policies laid down by the national body, and abide by the agreements made by their national officers. Let me say here that every National Trade Union having an agreement with the Government during the war carried out that agreement to the letter, and that where, in a few instances, local bodies under unwise and radical leadership attempted to violate an agreement, the National officers invariably ordered their members back to work and when necessary, threatened to take away the local charters. There must not be the benefits from organization unless there is a willingness to accept its responsibilities. Local unions have had too much local automony and local officials have been allowed too much power.

On the other hand, the employers have been slow to realize that the wise handling of the human problem in labor is more difficult than the technical problems of manufacture and have left such matters to subordinates. Many foremen seem to think it more important to maintain their authority than to increase output. Few seem to realize that it does not require much suspicion of unfair treatment or unrest among their workmen to cut down the output of the individual workman and thus, where large numbers are employed, to change a profit into a loss. To get the best out of human beings is much more diffcult than getting the best out of material supplies. The detail application of labor policies should not be left to subordinates, but should be in charge of a member of the firm or one of the highest paid and best trained officials of the company.

At least half the hours a person is awake are spent in the shop. The conditions under which he spends these hours have a vital effect upon the welfare of himself and family and it is only natural that he should demand the right to be consulted as to matters of so much importance to him.

A method that we found most serviceable in the shipyards during the war was provided through a general shop committee made up of the chairmen of the various craft committees in each yard. Each skilled craft within the shipyard elected a craft committee of three members. In this way a dispute that concerned only one craft was kept withih that craft for settlement and only such matters as concerned more than one craft came to the general shop committee. The craft committeemen were elected by secret ballot and every worker was guaranteed the right to vote without regard to his membership in a union. Naturally, however, those elected were, in a great majority of cases, union members, business agents and employers. No one having the right to hire or discharge, or who had a pecuniary interest in the work of the men under his direction was allowed to vote for craft committees. The best results were obtained where these craft committees were given responsibilities and dignity by the management. Where they were given a room and definite hours for meetings and where they were not only allowed but expected to handle such questions, as tardiness, slacking, etc.

Through such committees the management can place before the individual workmen some of the problems of the industry and show them their relation to such problems. The men can often thus be made to see that all decisions are not purely arbitrary but are related to and dependent upon larger questions, often outside the control of the particular firm. Shipyard owners as well as their employees often came to Washington to protest against rulings of the S. L. A. B., but after thoroughly discussing the rulings with them and showing them the conditions in the industry outside of their particular plant, and also the relation of their industry to other war work, they were generally fairly well satisfied. Frequently we would immediately acknowledge that a particular ruling was a hardship upon them and would, after having shown them the National problem, ask for their solution of the problem. In many cases they could offer no better ruling and under such circumstances went away perfectly satisfied to accept the particular hardship.

Every employer, no matter how smoothly his own business may run, is vitally affected by the acts of his competitors. This is as true of his labor situation as it is of his other business relations. It is therefore necessary, not only to have organized dealings with his own employees but to organize these relations throughout the industry, or at least within his competitive district. For this purpose it is essential for the employers to have a well disciplined association that will enter into agreements with the National officials of the labor unions. These agreements should fix the minimum wages and hours and conditions of employment for all members of the association or district. Such matters should not be left for individual plant settlement if industry is to be stabilized, but employers should be left free to employ individuals at rates above the minimum for special proficiency or special work.

By such district agreements industry can be stabilized as to wages and hours and the labor "turn-over" reduced. Fair-minded employers would be relieved of the competition of those willing to "sweat" their workers, for with wages and hours standardized, success will depend upon the efficiency of management and equipment. Real skill in management would then have the broadest opportunity to display its ability freed from unfair competition.

One of the greatest causes of the excessive labor "turn-over" during the war was the indiscriminate bidding of employers for labor. Until a uniform wage scale was put into effect in all shipyards on the Atlantic and Gulf coasts and Great Lakes, the constant shifting of labor back and forth between yards was destructive of all efficiency.

I wish to repeat that the shop committees must not be regarded as a substitute for the union. The employers, through their associations should agree with the National Unions on the larger questions, such as wages and hours. Outside of these general questions there are many local difficulties that can be cared for by the committee system, especially the detailed application of any agreement to a particular establishment. If the prevailing spirit of unrest is to be kept within safe limits, it must be given an opportunity of expression under sane, conservative leadership, such as is afforded through the inter-national leaders of the trade unions. The industrial disturbances that are now taking place in England are due to the fact that the strikers have taken matters into their own hands and in opposition to their national leaders, but at the instigation of the shop committees or local leaders. The same is true in Seattle where there are thirty thousand men on strike in the shipyards. Nothing but discord and anarchy results from the independent action of shop committees or local unions. The National Unions like the National Association of Employers, can view policies from a National standpoint. They have greater responsibilities and therefore give all questions more careful thought before acting. Local organizations cannot long survive if they act without the approval of the National bodies. It is therefore of the utmost importance to strengthen the hands of the responsible Trade Union officials. Otherwise we will have disorganization which will be taken advantage of by self-seeking radicals.

There are two points I wish to emphasize to a body of employers such as this: First, to urge upon you the necessity of taking an active interest in your association and not to leave the formulation of policies to the men who are the most aggressive and most persistent. Do not say "I had nothing to do with formulating a particular policy; I do not believe in it and therefore will do as I please." Take a real part in your organization. My second point is to be loyal to your fellow members and earnestly try to interpret in a fair spirit all agreements made with organized labor. I have talked with many employers, members of different associations and almost invariably their complaint is that their fellow members do not abide by the spirit of the agreements made. By some technical interpretation, they seek to obtain special advantages for themselves. The greatest difficulties the Ship Building Labor Adjustment Board has had to meet, have been where employers have paid more than the scale provided in order to attract men from other yards, or with the employer who tried to place as many as possible in the lowest paid class. If the members of the employers' associations were as loyal to their organizations as the men are to the trade unions, there would be a much better chance of stabilizing industry. The present situation in Seattle is 60% the fault of the selfish employers who violated all orders of the S. L. A. B. and the Emergency Fleet Corporation by paying wages far in excess of the scale authorized, and 40% the fault of radical local leaders who thought themselves strong enough to defy the national officials of their unions.

Both employers and workers must give more thought to the unit cost of production. Low wages do not necessarily mean low costs. Low unit cost is more a question of efficient management than the wage scale. Given the same wage scale in all shipyards, the cost per ton of ships produced varied as much as 200%. The best guarantee of low cost production is the right spirit among your workers. No one can do his best if he feels he is being taken advantage of. One of the greatest benefits derived from the shop committee method of handling labor questions, is that it affords a prompt means of settling petty grievances, for delay only results in the difficulty being magnified. An imaginary grievance needs just as prompt and careful attention as a real one. We have all seen the trouble an imaginary illness can create and the same is true of an imaginary grievance.

Finally an adjustment Board should be provided by agreement between the respective organizations to which all questions not settled by the shop committees and management could be referred for final adjudication, and no strikes or lockouts permitted until the adjustment board has acted or failed in agreement.

With properly organized shop committees, for the handling of plant questions, with agreements between well organized employers' associations and national trade unions as to wages, hours and conditions of employment, and with an adjustment board, to act as a final court, an orderly method will be provided for the removal of much of the friction in industry and the peaceful settlement of all questions. The smoothness with which any plan will work will depend on the sincerity of the parties involved and the extent to which a real co-operative spirit is displayed.

a League of Nations—What?

***By* OSCAR S. STRAUS**

OSCAR S. STRAUS

Nations would conflict with and abrogate our traditional policies as laid down by the Fathers of the Republic, embodied in Washington's Farewell Address, against entangling alliances, and by Jefferson, Madison and Monroe, respecting our continental policy as enunciated in the Monroe Doctrine.

If this were true, it would be unfortunate, but it is not true. Besides, each generation in a progressive nation, if it would escape the fate of China, must face the problems that confront it with the same wisdom and vision that the Fathers confronted the problems of their day.

For America to enter into such a grouping of Powers as referred to by Clemenceau and share in reconstructing the system of "balance of power," would constitute an entangling alliance, but to unite with the free and constitutionally governed nations, and with other nations as may hereafter qualify as such, for the adjustment of international differences on a basis of Justice and Law, as distinguished from a basis of militarism and war, is not an entangling alliance, but a concert of civilization against the rebarbarization of the world.

Washington viewing the conditions of the world in his day and the physical remoteness between this Continent and Europe, stated in his Farewell Address, that Europe had "a set of primary interests which to us have none, or a very remote relation."

He could not have foreseen that a war should break out on the Continent of Europe which would have for us a most vital interest, which involved America's right to the freedom of the seas, more than that, which involved her constitutional rights as a free nation.

Had Washington lived, who doubts but that he would have approved our entering the war and associating our might and power, money and men with the Allies in winning the war for liberty and democracy throughout the world no less than in America? That being true, is it not fair to assume he would approve our entering into a League of Nations to perpetuate that victory in making more secure the peace of the future?

As to the Monroe Doctrine, the President said: "I am proposing as it were that the nations should with one accord adopt the doctrine of President Monroe as the doctrine of the world; that no nation shall seek to extend its policy over any other nation or people, but that every nation should be left free to determine its own policy."

The objectors such as Senator Reed of Missouri, say: "What, do we propose to let the nations determine for us, our Asiatic immigration policy, our tariff, and other like policies?" The answer is, certainly not, no internal policy except the question of a reasonable reduction of armaments comes within the purview of a League of Nations which will seek to safeguard, and not weaken the right of self-determination of the separate national units constituting the membership of the League.

In the old world plan the relationship of nations was anarchistic as modified by entente alliances which in no way elevated the moral standard of that relationship; on the contrary they served to consolidate the baneful influence of anarchistic areas instead of creating a righteous concert among the nations.

THE CAUSE OF WAR

The motives underlying the causes of war divide themselves into two classes, defense and aggression. They are sometimes united, and often purposely beclouded.

It was Bismarck's expressed method always to harry a prospective enemy against whom Germany had planned to make war, so as to compel that enemy to be the aggressor. By such means Germany invariably claimed to be fighting a defensive war, and waived other nations aside. All her aggressions since 1864, and ending with the conquest and annexation of Alsace-Lorraine, were accomplished under this plan.

In the furtherance of this method under Germany's guidance Austria attempted the same tactics in her war upon Serbia. When Germany was appealed to to use her influence with Austria to adjust her differences with Serbia by peaceful methods, she waived aside the request, saying that it was an affair exclusively between Austria and Serbia.

I refer to these well-known facts which everybody is familiar with, to illustrate a condition that lies at the root of the evil.

The relationship of nations, especially in the launching of war between any two of them, should be put on the basis of criminal law, as distinguished from civil or municipal. In the civil law when two parties have a controversy in regard to their rights they go to the court or adjust it in their own way. On the other hand, if a person commits a criminal offence the crime is considered by all civilized states as a crime against the state, and the people of the State in their collective capacity try the criminal and inflict the punishment.

The policy that will control the world under a League of Nations will rest on the basis of the

(Continued on Page 9)

Why Russia Is a Vital World Issue

By HERBERT L. CARPENTER

(*Mr. Carpenter is Chairman of the Executive Committee of the American-Russian League, a national body representing labor, farming, business, educational and social forces of the country, including several prominent members of the Senate and Congress. The League has co-operated with the government and Russian groups in dealing with the Russian situation.*)

AS the Peace Conferences of the Allied Nations in Paris develop, the whole world is beginning to appreciate the significance of the great unsolved problems in Russia, and the need of learning some of the real facts about the causes and developments involved in Russia's invaluable contribution to the Allied Cause and in the struggle of her people for real freedom.

Why has Russia been brought to her present terrible condition? Why is there no precedent in history to guide the friends of Russia in their efforts to help her, or to indicate the probable outcome of the great struggle now going on throughout that land? What has brought about almost complete chaos in the life and government of that nation and a continued and constantly changing conflict between Russians of the various political groups and districts of Russia and Siberia, as well as with their foreign friends and foes? Why, after years of international interest and effort in behalf of Russia is there today a general and almost unreconcilable difference of opinion as to the justice and propriety of our past and present efforts to help the Russians help themselves establish an ordered, representative Government, and rehabiliate their economic life and save and educate their people.

Prussianism in Russia and German propoganda and money throughout the world against a free Russia were and are still the greatest enemies of the Russian people.

Up to this time the perplexing and complex situation involving Russia has been the subject of world-wide political intrigue and it would seem as though every disintegrating and destructive force known to man has had a hand in bringing about the present terrible chaos and starvation in Russia.

The time has arrived when the success of the world principles of justice and freedom, for which this country and the other Allied Nations entered the War, will largely depend upon a prompt and definite world understanding of the facts about Russia and upon united and effective action to save her people. Before an enduring world peace can be arrived at, the facts must be known and faced; the true developments of the past few years must be known; the real enemies of Russia must be driven from that land by the Russians themselves, and the destructive influences of Germany and her agents in Russia and throughout the world must be overcome through the combined efforts of all the Allies. The same world-wide, German-inspired propaganda is still desperately at work to befog the true issues at stake in Russia, and to prevent the 180,000,000 peasants, workers and other people of Russia from gaining their permanent and untrammelled freedom.

When War was declared by Russia against Germany, Austria and Turkey, she entered the conflict on a basis the magnitude of which was far beyond her financial, food and economic resources. Partly through misjudgment and largely through enemy intrigue, millions of vitally needed workers were mobilized into the Army beyond the demands of war or Russia's ability to maintain them, with the result that from the very outset Russia became crippled in her economic and productive strength.

HERBERT L. CARPENTER

For many years prior to the War, Germany and German agents had penetrated the Government and economic life of Russia and were well advanced in a scientific plan of intrigue to weaken and destroy the power of Russia in order that Germany might more readily get control of the great man-power and resources of all Russia, and turn them to her purpose of world domination.

With these conditions to face, with strong armies approaching from the West and South and already seriously undermined by her enemy from within, Russia fought one of the greatest struggles in all history against terrible odds. During the years of 1914, 1915 and 1916 Russia suffered unprecedented losses and sacrifices in the Allied Cause, which extended into almost every family throughout that great land. The noble struggles of the inadequately equipped and trained Russian Armies against the Germans and Austrians cost Russia greater losses than any other nation has sustained throughout the great War. She saved France and the Allied Cause untold losses and sufferings, and this, if for no other reason, must command for her people the help of the world at a time when she is weakened beyond self-preservation and as long as she remains the victim of the powerful, scientific, political and economic intrigue of the hundreds of thousands of German agents still striking at the vitals of Russian life and freedom.

The Russian Revolution of March, 1917, probably the greatest and most important in the history of the world, the delay of the Provisional Government to call the Constituent Assembly for the creating of a representative Government, the disorganization of the Russian Army, the Bolshevik Revolution of November, 1917, and the almost complete breakdown of the food supply, transportation and distributing systems, industries and all branches of the Government, have left the entire country in a condition of chaos and suffering and opened the door even wider to the sinister plans of Germany to force complete dissention and anarchy to a point where the Russian people will be compelled to turn to her German enemies for help, if the United States and the other Allies do not send it quickly. It is evident that the German psychology did not anticipate the Prussian Military defeat in their plans in Russia, but it is equally evident that the control of the people and resources of Russia was and is Germany's most coveted prize and will be the last influence which the remaining power of Germany will relinquish. Recent developments indicate that the political, scientific and economic forces of Germany are still desperately at work to save the future of their country, through the carrying out of their plans for the control of Russia.

Much has been said of the Bolshevik activities in Russia and there seems to be much difference of opinion as to their policies and activities over the past months. Regardless of any differences of opinion as to what Bolshevism in Russia stands for or represents as a popular force, there is no question of the official facts concerning the acts of terrorism and mass-murder and the destructive political intrigue of many of the Bolshevik leaders and their German associates. In addition to any question of these acts of terrorism, the official avowed declarations and orders of these leaders indicate that they do not want peace, but declare war throughout Russia and the world against any non-Bolshevik powers, as long as such war may have any probability of success. Such German-inspired leadership is a menace to the peace and freedom of Russia and of the world. Any general condemnation of the millions of peasants and workers of Russia who may have been forced to submit to the terrorism of a few leaders through their control of food and arms, or the failure to send help to such people would be most unfortunate. As the detrimental influences of the Germans are driven out of Russia and an opportunity is given to her people to select a representative Government to suit their own needs, and as relief in food, materials, and friendly protection from their enemies are sent to them, conditions in Russia will soon change for the better. Germany has been beaten in the West and on the Sea, but the cruelly unjust and yet intelligent and efficient efforts of the Germans in Russia have not yet been defeated. The machinations of the Prussians in Russia will go down as one of the greatest unpardonable crimes in modern history and the Great War will not be fully won until these crimes in Russia and their influence have been permanently destroyed.

The framers of the Armistice of November, 1918, realized the danger and character of the present German influences in Russia and provided in that armistice for the withdrawal of German troops and agents in the territories of Russia, Roumania and Turkey; it provided for the abandonment of the treaties of Bucharest and Brest-Litovsk and of the supplementary treaties, the restitution of the Russian and Roumanian gold yielded to the Germans or taken by that power, to be delivered to the Allies in trust until the signature of peace; the surrender of the Black Sea Fleets and access to the Baltic Sea, Danzig and the Vistula River, into Poland and Western Russia.

The carrying out of the terms of the armistice in Russia is vital to Russia, as well as to the Allies, and seems a pre-requisite to any effective relief to Russia by the Allies. Substantial progress has already been made and with the co-operation of all of the Allies and the Russians themselves to that end a great step will have been accomplished towards the solution of the Russian question.

(*Continued on Page 8*)

Compulsory Health Insurance Legislation

ITS PRESENT STATUS SURVEYED AND LABOR'S POSITION OUTLINED

By WARREN S. STONE

GRAND CHIEF, INTERNATIONAL BROTHERHOOD OF LOCOMOTIVE ENGINEERS
CHAIRMAN SOCIAL INSURANCE DEPARTMENT THE NATIONAL CIVIC FEDERATION

HILE President Wilson is endeavoring to secure freedom and individual liberty to the peoples of the world a all group at home is striving to do away with se rights and privileges which have made nerica the haven of the down-trodden, opessed races. In the endeavor to have enacted mpulsory health legislation, misrepresentation the attitude and desires of labor has been e of the tools employed. During the past two nters it took the form of bills for uniform te legislation introduced wherever legislatures re in session. Comment upon those two bills d the one now offered for adoption in New rk State therefore covers the situation in so : as the efforts to put through these destruce measures are concerned.

The first nation-wide effort in 1917 was anered by the Social Insurance Department of e National Civic Federation in three ways:

(1) A memorandum was prepared by its Legislative Committee composed of Dr. Lee K. Frankel, Chairman; A. Parker Nevin (National Association of Manufacturers); and Hugh Frayne (American Federation of Labor), showing the weaknesses, shortcomings and dangers in the proposed legislation as represented in the New York Senate Bill No. 69, introduced by Mr. Mills, January 15, 1917. This critical analysis was distributed in all states where similar bills were introduced; where state constitutional amendments were under consideration; and where state commissions were studying the question.

(2) There was incorporated in the foregoing document the following resolution:

(*Offered By Timothy Healy*, President International Stationary Firemen's Union.)

WHEREAS, a nation-wide propaganda is at present being carried on in favor of Compulsory Health Insurance by the several states and the Federal Government; and

WHEREAS, the project is made to rest largely upon mere assertions and broad allegations regarding the unsatisfactory economic and health conditions of the country, which assertions and allegations are false and seriously misleading in essential matters of vital concern to all wage earners and the nation at large; and

WHEREAS, in support of this propaganda it is asserted and alleged that the social and sanitary progress of Germany and other European countries which have adopted compulsory health insurance has been far in advance of the corresponding progress of the United States, which is wholly false and seriously misleading, since, as a matter of fact, more pronounced progress in these directions has been made in the United States during the last quarter-century, and the social and physical condition of American wage earners is unquestionably superior to that of the corresponding labor element of European nations, as best indicated by the recent announcement of the United States Census Office that during the year 1915 our general death rate was the lowest on record, which may safely be accepted as the equivalent of a minimum rate of serious sickness prevailing among our wage earners at the present time; and

WHEREAS, such a system of compulsory health insurance would impose needless economic and other burdens and duties upon employers, employees and the general tax-paying public; bring about an entirely unnecessary enlargement of the police powers of the states; establish new and inquisitorial health functions to the serious disadvantage of the future progress of preventive medicine and the practice of medicine as a healing art; and

WHEREAS, voluntary agencies serving social insurance purposes, such as sick benefit funds of trade unions, or establishment benefit funds, or fraternal insurance societies, or group insurance, or other related forms of voluntary thrift, offer adequate facilities for further development in the future; and

WHEREAS, compulsory health insurance is strongly opposed by organized labor, which rightfully considers such a measure to be a menace to its economic interests and a needless interference with its personal freedom;

RESOLVED, That the Social Insurance Department of The National Civic Federation, composed of representatives of organized labor, organized industry and the interests of the general public, emphatically declares itself opposed to the contemplated legislation with reference to compulsory health insurance, as inimical to the best interests, present and future, of the workers of the nation.

(3) There also was circulated a full report of the proceedings of the January 22, 1917, Social Insurance Session of the Annual Meeting of The National Civic Federation, giving the attitude of organized labor and employers—the two elements principally concerned—against such "class legislation."

Despite the efforts to bewilder legislators and the public by claims to the contrary and by local efforts to dissuade labor, there has been no substantial change in its attitude of opposition.

While space does not permit publication of the various resolutions adopted by the American Federation of Labor year by year and reaffirmed at its last annual convention the attitude of its official mouthpiece, President Samuel Gompers, as set forth so recently as the January, 1919, *Federationist*, the organ of the A. F. of L., appears in the following statement made by him to the members of a committee appointed by that body to investigate social insurance. He said in part:

> There are many of our people, including workmen, who look to the Government of our country to do the things which seem so easy for the Government to do and which they imagine should be done by the Government. They do not recognize the pitfalls and the dangers which are entailed by conferring upon the Government the function of doing these things. To my mind, it is a grave danger to place in the hands of the Government the powers which would necessarily result from governmental compulsory health insurance with all the powers vested in the Government incidental to and in the enforcement of health insurance.

It may be of interest here to state that my own organization, the Brotherhood of Locomotive Engineers, at its last convention in May, 1918, unanimously adopted the report of its committee on compulsory health insurance, given below:

We, the Committee appointed to investigate the case of State compulsory health insurance, after giving all correspondence pertaining to this case due consideration, report the following:

First—We do not approve of any legislation that would compel our members to take out health insurance.

Second—We recommend that the Grand Body go on record as opposing any State legislation compelling our members to take out any such insurance, and that our State Representatives be notified to this effect.

We believe that if such compulsory legislation were enacted it would be injurious to our Organization.

(Signed) J. W. Gladden, Chairman Div. 160; H. E. Cowles, Chairman Div. 155; E. S. Pritchard, Chairman Div. 159; Chas. P. Miller, Chairman Div. 251; Chas. Hankins, Chairman Div. 784.

Advocates of pending compulsory insurance legislation link health insurance (no mention of "compulsory") with workmen's compensation as its "twin brother", confusing the layman who is earnestly desirous of aiding labor by helping to ameliorate conditions. Far more misleading was the published statement of a well-informed workmen's compensation state official in a recent issue of the Sunday *New York Tribune* when, in advocating compulsory health insurance, he stated that "most employers opposed the enactment of compensation laws" and argued that employers' opposition to "health insurance" is equally unmeritorious. But "most employers" did *not* oppose the enactment of compensation laws. In New York, for instance, employers generally favored the original Wainwright-Phillips bills. All that employers opposed was the movement in favor of state insurance monopolies. This aspersion upon employers is not warranted nor in accord with facts as shown by records of the Workmen's Compensation Department of The National Civic Federation where employers and representatives of labor, beginning in 1908, worked together always favoring some equitable form of compulsory workmen's compensation, holding the industry liable. An employer, Mr. August Belmont, was and is chairman of that department.

The trickery of the group of social reformers who are attempting to foist upon labor a pernicious system of compulsory health insurance was evidenced when effort was made to convey to the public the impression that Mr. Samuel Gompers had changed his position. This was done during his absence in Europe where he was rendering patriotic service last August. They revamped an address of Mr. Gompers published in the Official Bulletin of the Committee on Public Information and issued it as a press *statement of their own organization. This "made over" speech, originally addressed officially to members of the Committee on Labor, Advisory Commission, Council of National Defense, contained the inserted deduction that "this was regarded as the opening way for the early adoption of social health insurance" (again no mention of "compulsory" which that organization, the American Association for Labor Legislation, advocates). This was quite evidently a sinister, deliberate effort to mislead. Fortunately, a good trade unionist was at hand to protect the position of Mr. Gompers. His assistant in the Committee on Labor, Mr. Matthew Woll, President of the International Photo Engravers' Union, promptly issued a denial.

All admit that there is need for further development of voluntary forms of social insurance and improvements in methods and in state regulations, but such schemes should be in con-

*A photograph copy is in our possession.

formity with the principles of our Government and the spirit of our people. Labor will not welcome an undigested millennium cure-all.

The argument that compulsory health insurance will prevent sickness is offset by evidence to the contrary and by pleas for sanitary working conditions and prevention of illness through better health regulations and public health education.

As persistently as were efforts made throughout the country to secure the adoption of compulsory health legislation did the Social Insurance Department of The National Civic Federation circulate facts as to its true meaning. The general situation today in the main is encouraging.

In California, the referendum submitted to the people, for a constitutional amendment permitting such legislation, was defeated by a large majority vote.

In Massachusetts, several attempts to incorporate provisions for compulsory insurance at the recent Constitutional convention failed. Also the Commissions appointed to investigate the subject reported adversely.

In Illinois, the Sickness Insurance Commission, appointed a year ago, has not yet made its report. A campaign by the proponents is being waged at present in that state.

In Connecticut, a commission has held public hearings and it is understood will report against the proposition at this session of the legislature.

The Wisconsin Legislature has just defeated a bill providing for compulsory health insurance and has gone on record as willing to strengthen the existing health agencies.

The Ohio Commission which only began its work seriously in the late fall has presented a majority report recommending some form of compulsory insurance.

An analysis of the Davenport bill, now before the New York State legislature, has been made by P. Tecumseh Sherman, attorney and social insurance expert. His honesty and ability are recognized and honored by all elements. Mr. Sherman was a member of the committee having as the representative of the wage-earners, J. W. Sullivan, its Chairman; and as the representative of employers, Arthur Williams, which studied the national health insurance system of Great Britain in 1914, before the outbreak of the world war, reporting against it for the United States.

P. TECUMSEH SHERMAN CRITICISES NEW YORK BILL

Upon the pending legislation in New York, Mr. Sherman says:

"New York Senate Bill, Int. No. 73, 1919, introduced by Mr. Davenport, 'To Conserve the Human Resources of the State by Establishing a System of Mutual Health Insurance Funds under the Supervision of the Industrial Commission,' which is almost identical with Senate Bill, Int. No. 496, 1918, by Mr. Nicoll, is better than the Mills Bill of 1917, which was criticised and opposed by The National Civic Federation, in that it is free from the taint of poor-relief which characterized that earlier measure and emphasizes medical care more and pecuniary benefits less. Nevertheless, in my opinion, it is altogether objectionable and should be strenuously opposed.

"The objections to this measure are so multitudinous and fundamental or technical that it is difficult to present them with brevity. And this difficulty is augmented by the fact that the bill merely outlines a plan, leaving many of the most essential working details unformulated. But I will try to indicate some of the objections to it as briefly as possible.

"Briefly summarized, this bill would empower and direct the New York Industrial Commission to divide the State into numerous districts, none to contain fewer than 5000 insured employees, to organize a local sickness insurance fund and, in its discretion, any number of trade funds in each district, and to *compel* all 'employees' (except casual, domestic, and some public employees) and their employers to join the local or appropriate trade fund, subject, however, to the exception that membership in an approved establishment fund would be permissible as an alternative. Each local and trade fund, to be composed of the employees assigned thereto and their employers, would then organize, elect a board of directors, and, subject indefinitely to the approval, direction and control of the Commission, would adopt a constitution and raise contributions from its members sufficient to provide the benefits promised in the bill. The contributions would be payable one half by the employers and one half by the insured employees (except that for the most lowly paid employees the employers would pay two-thirds or all), and would be levied at rates sufficient to provide the benefits, the expenses of managing the funds, some reserves and a common guaranty fund. It is provided that the rate of contributions may be varied according to the sickness hazard of a trade or establishment, *but not according to the physical condition of the insured.* Within each establishment the contribution for each insured employee would be in proportion to his wages; but as a basis for contributions wages may not be considered to exceed $12 per week.

"The benefits promised are: (a) Medical benefits, consisting of medical and surgical treatment, and nursing attendance, when and as needed by an insured employee or any dependent member of his family, but for not to exceed 26 weeks in any one year in case of disability; and also all necessary medicines, medical and surgical supplies approved by the medical officer of the fund. (b) Hospital treatment for an insured employee, when approved by the medical officer of his fund, plus pecuniary relief to dependent members of his family while he is in the hospital. (c) Ordinary dental treatment for an insured employee. (d) Appropriate medical and surgical care during and after childbirth for insured women and the wives of insured men, plus pecuniary relief to insured women during eight weeks of confinement. (e) A cash benefit of two-thirds of wages (but not less than $5 nor more than $8 per week) payable to an insured employee, if disabled, beginning on the fourth day of disability and continuing during disability but for not to exceed 26 weeks in any one year. (f) A funeral benefit of $100 upon the death of an insured employee.

"As will be seen from the foregoing this bill provides for *compulsory* sickness insurance for practically all 'employees'. It will be well, therefore, to run through the elementary objections to compulsory insurance.

"(1). *The danger from an increase in bureaucracy.* This bill would add about a thousand political 'jobs' to those already existing, and would give the Industrial Commission unprecedented power and authority over the disposition of the incomes and earnings of employees and employers.

"(2). *The danger of communism.* If the state may thus decide how much of his income an individual shall set aside for sickness, place that amount in a common fund and then distribute the proceeds of the fund among the contributors in accordance with needs, there is no reason in principle why it should not provide in the same way for invalidity and old age, for widows and orphans, and for the food, clothing and housing of the people generally. In other words, this bill would be a step towards complete communism.

"(3). *The danger of personal tyranny.* Under this bill every employer *must* act as collection agent and accountant for and under the orders of one or more insurance funds, and *must* submit his payrolls to their inspection; and every employee *must* submit to have his wages 'docked' as may be decided by others for use in ways he may most heartily dislike. If measures like this should be multiplied we would all become helots of a political bureaucracy.

"(4). *The danger of weakening individual initiative and individual and family responsibility.* Clearly, if the State is to see to it that every person in need is to be well provided for individuals will have little motive to exert themselves for the purpose of making provision for themselves and their families. It is absurd to contend that there is not a serious social danger involved in thus shifting natural responsibilities.

"(5). *The economic danger from impositions.* Compulsory insurance herds into the same insurance funds along with the 'good risks' not only the bad physical risks but also the bad moral risks, from whom malingering and impositions are to be expected, and gives them legal rights to benefits on the same terms and conditions as the good risks. The inevitable consequence is that sick funds are burdened with the support of a class of parasites who prefer insurance benefits to work and wages. That is a demoralizing burden to impose upon the thrifty and industrious working people.

"(6). *The medical danger.* Compulsory sickness insurance brings the practice of medicine into politics and the effect on its quality certainly is not good.

"Compulsory insurance, therefore, is a dangerous medicine, to be resorted to, if at all, with reluctance and even then to be restricted in scope to those classes only by whom it is positively needed. Even an autocratic German authority—von Posadowsky—admits that to apply it generally would 'paralyze individual providence and the ability to care for one's self. Nothing could exercise a more harmful influence upon the character of a people.' And the same German authority holds that it should be restricted to apply only to 'the working people who are not self-sufficient, who work for others and feel incapable of caring for themselves.' In Germany nearly all wage-earners are in that low class. But certainly all 'employees' in New York are not. Therefore, even from the viewpoint of those favoring compulsory insurance, this bill is objectionable in applying compulsion to classes able and fit to care for themselves, instead of restricting its application to the submerged.

LIBERTY OF CHOICE DENIED

"But this bill goes far beyond mere compulsory insurance. It contemplates that the employee shall be compelled to insure in the particular sick fund prescribed to him by state officials. That would involve the suppression of all liberty of choice by the working people, a political monopoly of the insurance to the exclusion of all competition, the sacrifice of nearly all existing means of sickness insurance for the classes covered, and a serious risk of a collapse of the experiment, resulting in conditions far worse than they are now.

"Obviously a safer course would be to sacrifice no existing means of insurance but to allow a choice between all existing insurance carriers, regulating them as may be proper, allow other voluntary associations to be formed, and establish politically only such new organizations as may be necessary to fill gaps. Such is the program favored by the majority of the partisans of compulsory insurance at recent social insurance conferences and congresses. Why, for instance, should trade union funds and mutual benefit societies be barred from this line of insurance without a trial?

"This bill, therefore, is objectionable, not only because it resorts to compulsion and to compulsion in too broad a scope, but also because it would plunge headlong into the most radical, bureaucratic and least favored form of compulsory insurance.

cost of administering the insurance. In addition there would be the cost of supervision by the State, and the cost of collecting the contributions—which latter would fall principally upon employers. Speaking of the cost of collection, Sidney Webb, referring more particularly to the British law, says:

> Regarded as a means of raising revenue, compulsory insurance of all the wage earning population, with its elaborate paraphernalia of weekly deductions, its array of cards and stamps, its gigantic membership catalogue, its inevitable machinery of identification and protection against fraud, involving not only a vast and perpetual trouble for each employer but also the appointment of an extraordinarily expensive civil service staff, is, compared with all other taxes, almost ludicrously expensive to all concerned.

"And he goes on to estimate that the expense of collection would probably amount to between 20% and 25% of the revenue raised.

"It is true that this bill does not propose the card and stamps method of collecting contributions; but the cash remittance method it proposes would be equally if not more expensive. *Consequently the total expense of administering this plan of insurance may be estimated at somewhere between 35% and 45% of the contributions—although probably only 15% to 20% would be payable out of the contributions.*

BENEFITS QUESTIONED

"Moreover, the value of the medical service would be extremely low in proportion to its cost. The doctors would be heavily burdened with paper work, which would swell their charges far beyond what they would be merely for medical services. They would be more occupied with certifying to disability than with caring for health. And, as British experience demonstrates, the tendency would be for the panel physicians, working on contract and paid per capita or per visit, to restrict their true medical services to the most perfunctory consultations, to prescriptions and to the most ordinary treatments, leaving all special treatments, surgical operations, scientific diagnoses, etc., to be paid for extra or gone without. *That such a medical service would result in any net improvement in the public health is most improbable.*

"There is a point to be noted here in connection with the medical service, although it may appear somewhat out of place. There are those who believe that it would be of great social benefit if the people were subjected to medical discipline, somewhat as are soldiers in the army; and many of the public are led to believe that compulsory sickness insurance would be a step in that direction. But what is proposed in this bill would not. This bill does not require the insured to submit to medical examinations. It permits each insured to select his own physician and does not require him to follow even that physician's advice or directions. As British experience demonstrates, it would permit the continuance of vicious habits, without forfeiting the right to full insurance benefits during sickness due to such habits. It is true that the sick funds—if the Industrial Commission should permit—might make rules to the contrary. But no machinery is provided for enforcing any such rules. Nor could it be provided without increasing the cost of administration far above the level hereinbefore indicated.

"By the foregoing I do not mean to imply an opinion in favor of a medical despotism but merely to point out that the alleged advantages of such a despotism cannot rationally be claimed for the scheme of sickness insurance outlined in this bill.

QUASI-PAUPER MEDICAL SERVICE

"Now as to the amount of the contributions that would be required to carry out this scheme, in other words, the cost thereof exclusive of the expenses of collection falling on employers and the expenses of supervision falling on the State. There is no basis from which to make any reliable estimate of such cost, for the reason that there is no precedent of sickness insurance with any such liberal nursing, hospital, funeral and family medical benefits. From crude comparisons with foreign experience it seems possible that the cost might be kept down nearly to $35 per insured per annum (at present prices), if hospital and sanatorium cases and cases requiring surgical operations or treatment by specialists should be left to the care of free public and charity hospitals and clinics (as in Great Britain), if scientific diagnoses should be gone without or furnished free by a public health service, if home visits by the doctors should be limited to rare cases of extreme necessity, if the promised nursing service and provision of medical and surgical supplies should be cut to the bone, if isolated and itinerant workmen and those residing outside the districts of their respective funds, etc., should be largely neglected, and if a hard bargain should be driven with the doctors. On the other hand, if all the classes interested should be given what they would be led to expect and if the funds should truly pay their own way, the cost might reach as high as $150 per insured per annum. In practice it is probable that some sort of a compromise between these two extremes would be made, arriving at an average cost of somewhere about $45 per insured. But that would provide only a quasi-pauper medical service, far below the standards to which a large proportion of American employees are now accustomed, and with which service, consequently, they would never be satisfied.

"Almost nobody would be satisfied; and the membership of the funds would be split up into those demanding a better medical service at an approximately level rate of contributions per capita, into those demanding a better service but with contributions scaled in proportion to earnings, and into those demanding a reduction of the service in order to reduce the charge. Between these factions there would be continual contentions, supplemented by frequent appeals to the Legislature to amend the law as to the distribution of the cost and—as British experience indicates—for public grants in aid of this, that or another class of the insured not getting the promised benefits.

WOULD PROMOTE DISSENSION

"Another subject of contention would be the question whether the rate of contribution should be varied according to the special hazards of each trade or large establishment. Obviously those employed in the more healthful trades and establishments would be interested to favor such discrimination, whereas others would be opposed, and the issue would divide the members of each sick fund into warring factions.

"The foregoing do not by any means exhaust the causes of contention that would be created by this bill. Although it is proposed that the insured may each choose his own physician from a panel, yet specialists, surgeons, nursing associations, hospitals, etc., would have to be picked by the administrative authorities, leaving little if any choice to the insured individually. Improper influences would often enter into such selections and minorities would often have reason for profound dissatisfaction. German experience shows that one of the most bitter causes of dissension is the apparently innocent matter of choosing the hospitals.

"It is true that in voluntary associations great diversities of interests are generally reconciled and seldom interfere with harmony. But that is because in voluntary associations the members are selected and bound together by some common ideals; whereas here it is proposed generally to herd together all or nearly all the wage earners within each district, of different standards of living, trades, races, religions and political ideals, regardless of the probabilities of agreement or disagreement. In the whole bill there is not even a suggestion of a safeguard for minority rights or interests.

STRIKES AND LOCKOUTS INEVITABLE RESULT

"Not only within but also without the insurance associations would this bill create novel causes of social dissension. There are various methods for the remission of and accounting for contributions by employers, some of which would be grievously burdensome to employers but easy for the insurance carriers, whereas others would be just the reverse. Surely there would be struggles and discontent on one side or the other over the choice. But the great cause of trouble would be the adjustment of the rate of charges by the panel doctors. The fixing of that rate would be a matter of collective bargaining between practically all employees in the State, their dependents and employers, on the one hand, and the doctors, banded and organized, on the other hand. If only the lowly paid wage earners were to be covered, it would be reasonable to expect the doctors to agree to some very low rate of charges. But with even the highest paid employees covered—i.e. nearly all the financially responsible patients except the capitalist and professional classes—the doctors would reasonably insist upon a fairly high average rate. But there would never be any mutually satisfactory voluntary agreement as to what should be such fair average rate; and continual disputes and frequent strikes and lockouts would be the rule, often necessitating coercive interference by the State in favor of one side or the other. Consequently, the rate of the doctors' charges would eventually become a matter to be fixed by the Government and fought over in general elections. In Great Britain, by catching the Government unprepared, the doctors won the first bout, imposing a rate of charges one-fifth greater than had been anticipated as the maximum, in return for a service so limited that it would be dear at any price. In Germany, on the other hand, the doctors have been ground down and kept perpetually discontented by hard bargains.

"It is difficult to believe that the practice of medicine would not be debased and deteriorated by such a condition, and that it would not be infinitely safer, socially, to keep the employment of physicians and their charges, as now, generally matters for individual rather than collective bargaining or agreement.

BILL INCOMPLETE

"I have said above that a multitude of details essential to the proposed plan of insurance are unformulated in this bill. Space and time forbid a presentation of them all, so I will content myself with three illustrations.

"It is provided that all 'employees'—with the exceptions hereinabove specified—shall be compelled to insure. But what is meant by an "employee"? Are high salaried railroad officials meant to be included? Probably not. But if so where and how is the line to be drawn with the statute silent on the point? On farms and in shops sons, daughters and other relatives often work for the proprietors, more or less regularly or intermittently, under all sorts of arrangements as to remuneration. Under what circumstances would such persons be deemed employees or not employees respectively? And what formula would he used to determine their rates of wages as the basis for contributions and sick pay? The bill is silent on these points. And yet these points would all have to be determined pretty definitely—by law and not by tentative rulings by the Industrial Commission—before the scheme proposed in this bill could begin to function anywise decently.

"It is provided that the proposed local and trade funds shall be corporations, each subject to a constitution to be adopted by its members, *but which constitution and every amendment thereto 'shall contain such provisions as the Industrial Commission may direct.'* It is being represented that this bill provides for democratically home-ruled insurance carriers; and such may be the intention. But the provision above italicized would empower the Industrial Commission to reserve all direction to itself, converting the local funds into more agencies and thereby creating an intolerable political despotism. If it really be desired to reserve any rights of self-government to the funds and to limit the supervisory and regulative powers of the Commission, such rights and the limitations upon such powers should be formulated specifically.

"It is provided that each employee must belong to a local or trade fund within the district within which he *works*. But thousands of those who work in our cities reside with their families in other districts or outside the State. How are they to be provided with medical care? The bill leaves that for the Industrial Commission to determine later as it may choose. And how about trainmen, etc., who work in many districts, and those other persons—e.g. contractors' workmen and summer hotel servants—who work part of the year in one district and part in another? The bill makes no provision for itinerants' medical care or for transfer cards. In other words, all these large classes are to pay contributions from the start, but the difficult problem of how to provide them a medical benefit in return has not even been considered.

BURDEN ON WAGE EARNERS

"The provisions in the bill for compulsory contributions to the insurance by employers are the feature that probably appeals to the working people. In my opinion, however, such contributions would profit them little. In first instance the employers' contributions to the insurance would have the effect of an addition to wages; but in subsequent adjustments of wages such contributions would generally have the effect of holding down the wage rate *pro tanto*. For this and other economic reasons I believe that both the employees' and employers' contributions would in effect come out of the pockets of the employees, and that the proposed scheme of insurance should be weighed and adjudged by the working people upon that theory. If they accept a plan of insurance, otherwise unsatisfactory, upon the supposition that they will profit from a provision for employers' contributions, in all probability they will be grievously disappointed."

When Mr. Sherman's points are considered by the workers of New York State and they realize among other things that individuals traveling about will not receive insurance, even Germany with her methods not having worked this out, that trade union funds will be interfered with and that contributions, necessary to pay current cost, may be levied monthly without limit, they are not likely to support any such proposed legislation. A representative commission to investigate the entire subject for New York State should have unanimous approval.

Why Russia is a Vital World Issue

(Continued from Page 4)

Public opinion in all the allied countries seems now to be against any military or political intervention in Russia, whether directed against the Bolsheviki or any other form of Government, but public opinion in the

or Situation In Great Britain

(FROM OUR LONDON CORRESPONDENT)

on January 5, in the British press that indicates a spirit of unrest that had not been believed serious before. Perhaps it is not serious now, but it is worth thinking about. Some 10,000 soldiers were gathered at Folkestone to be returned to France for service. These men wanted to be demobilized—or a great many of them did—and they were not satisfied with government progress. They held a great mass meeting in the streets at Folkestone and decided that they didn't want to go back to France. Many of them were absent without leave. They named a committee of nine to deal with the command and this committee was actually met by the commander and a compromise effected through which the leave period was extended seven days, with a promise of dismissal for all who could prove that civilian jobs waited them. The port of Folkestone was closed for a day or two and an official statement to that effect issued by the war office.

There is no ground to conclude, however, that Britain is heading for the rocks of rough house, for that is not in evidence at all. What is going to happen, so far as I can judge, is that there will be a radical curbing of the Powers of Have, as they are called, with an all-around better deal for the working population. J. R. Clynes, one of the conservative labor men in parliament, declares that more people must be better off and a few rich people less rich. That looks very much like a sane middle course. I say "sane" advisedly, for any attempt to maintain the industrial *status quo* would invite trouble that might be really serious. Britain needs the full productive capacity of her industrial machinery and she must have it if she can get it on any reasonable basis. She must have it for the very simple reason that she must create wealth to pour into the vast and yawning chasm made by four years of war and its accompanying destruction of useful and useable commodities.

It is no secret—or at least it is an open secret—that British manufacturers are worried with one worry that tops all others. That worry is about the possibility of getting maximum production. The great labor organizations have officially pledged themselves to maximum production and they are undoubtedly sincere, for the leaders are good enough economists to know that the national basket cannot be filled unless all chip in to help fill it. And the national basket is so big and so empty that it will require the full effort of all to do a proper job of filling.

British character is a pretty stable thing, however, and there is great store set upon that prime asset. As much as anything else it is that strong national character that guarantees sanity for the future. There may be here and there an outburst of hysterics, but it must never be forgotten that this old island has gone through four years of terrific war—four years in which the red hot iron has burned into the very soul, not only of the social structure, but of the individual.

One excellent indication of the British worker's feeling toward the problems of the future is found in the recent election. That election lends itself to all manner of speculative analysis, but one thing stands out clear and sharp. The pacifists and all who were tinged with pacifism or even remotely associated with it went down to glorious defeat. Liberalism was not defeated—pacifism was. Not a pacifist escaped. Henderson, with all his protestations of support for the war—and he has made them from start to finish—went down because of the company he has kept. They have a whole list of Ramsay MacDonald jokes on the vaudeville stage. Pacifism doesn't go in Britain. But that section of labor—and it is by far the greater section—which stands for progress and patriotism came romping home with double the former number of seats.

To be sure, only a fraction of the soldier vote was polled. Some say the percentage polled was as low as 27 per cent. But it does not seem possible to deny that what was polled constituted an indication of what the whole sentiment is, so far as the distinction between pacifists and bolsheviks and patriotic and progressive candidates is concerned.

What the future is going to develop is by no means certain. There may be eruptions. These may be large or small. No one can say. Much may depend upon how much muddling the British government does. But it is a good bet that the mind of the British people is bent upon getting back to normal life in an orderly fashion to build up what has been destroyed and lost and that whatever there may be that looks like impatience or disorder is in reality impatience over delay in resuming the normal and orderly course of human life—on an improved and more comfortable basis, but normal nevertheless.

Those who are Bolshevists pure and simple and would welcome an abrupt and complete overturn are just as small a minority as ever they were. The mind of the great body politic is sane and sound—absolutely British. There is a pretty fixed idea among the people about where they want to arrive at and while they may "muddle through" to a peace basis, just as they did a good deal of "muddling through" in the early stages of the war, they will arrive just the same in their own good time. And there is no use in trying to compare Britain with America, either, as our own home saviours are so fond of doing. British conditions and institutions are British and ours are American, and that's all the difference in the world. "Let them alone and they'll come home, wagging their tails behind them."

London, February 5, 1919—

If Not a League—What?

(*Continued from Page 3*)

criminal law, and the state that refuses to seek peaceful methods for the adjustment of its grievances and begins war, will be regarded as a criminal against the peace of the world, to be dealt with by the League of Nations under the provisions of their mutual agreement.

No plan that can be humanly devised will under all circumstances prevent war. The power of any nation to make war can no more be taken away from a free nation than the power to commit murder can be taken away from a free man, but the opportunities to make war and the occasions that bring about war can be immeasurably lessened, by enlarging the instrumentalities for the peaceful adjustment of international differences, by restraining the spirit of aggression by protecting the smaller nations in their national rights, and preventing them from being absorbed through the covetousness of their stronger neighbors. As Lloyd George pointed out, this will become the more imperative after this war because of the ten or twelve new nations in mid-Europe and in the Ottoman empire formerly under the yoke of the autocratic Powers and to whom must be given their independent rights as free nations.

THE NATIONAL
Civic Federation Review

Office: Thirty-third Floor, Metropolitan Tower
1 Madison Avenue New York City

RALPH M. EASLEY, Editor

Published Twice a Month **Two Dollars a Year**

The Editor alone is Responsible for any unsigned article or unquoted statement published in THE NATIONAL CIVIC FEDERATION REVIEW.

SANITY OF REAL FARM ORGANIZATIONS

An unusually important conference was held in Washington, February 10 and 11, which seems entirely to have escaped notice in the daily press. It was the meeting of the National Board of Farm Organizations which association consists of nineteen national farm organizations, including The Farmers' Educational and Co-operative Union, The National Grange, The Society of Equity, and The National Dairymen's Association. There were 300 delegates, representing over 6,000,000 members and the discussion showed them to be practical, hard-headed men with their feet entirely on the ground. There were no ranting populists among them.

It is unfortunate that the press did not carry a comprehensive account of their proceedings because last November another body met in Washington, calling itself The Farmers' National Conference on Reconstruction in America and International Reconstruction, and its proceeding, which were of the most radical, Non-Partisan League type, were largely published, giving the impression that such wild demands were those of the real farm organizations. In fact, the November farmers' meeting bears about the same relation to the February one that an I. W. W. meeting bears to an American Federation of Labor convention.

The February meeting, or the meeting of the National Board of Farm Organizations, voted to send Mr. Charles S. Barrett to the Peace Conference at Paris to present the demands for recognition of agriculture. President Barrett sailed on the 15th and will meet in Paris representative agricultural leaders from other countries and it is expected that a joint presentation will be made on matters vital to the greatest of all industries—farming.

In sharp contrast to the radical demands of the Farmers' National Reconstruction Conference, i. e., government ownership of practically everything the farmers have to do with, the National Board of Farm Organizations did not call for government ownership of anything, not even the railroads. In fact, at a meeting in January, the National Board of Farm Organizations, after discussion, voted to "wait and see", while in the February meeting they rescinded even that action.

With this representative body of farmers feeling that way about it, and the American Federation of Labor in its reconstruction program recently issued, calling for government ownership or operation or regulation of railroads, it does not seem as though the American people were disposed to rush pell mell into anything very radical or revolutionary at this time.

Referring to Mr. Barrett's mission to the Peace Conference, it is worthy of note that in the proposed constitution of the League of Nations, while generous and proper recognition is given to the problems of labor, not one reference is made to agriculture notwithstanding the fact that 40 per cent of our population is on the farms. This oversight is all the more remarkable because even President Wilson in his comments on the draft, while speaking feelingly of the "people who go to bed tired and wake up without the stimulation of lively hope", who are to be served by the Bureau of Labor which it is contemplated that the League shall set up, entirely overlooks the farmer. The National Board of Farm Organizations, through President Barrett, will help to remedy that oversight and get proper recognition for this, the most fundamental of all industries.

BLESSING IN DISGUISE

The outbreak of Bolshevism throughout the country following the Mooney meeting in Chicago has proven a boomerang to the Reds and at the same time a cementer of the sane forces of capital and labor.

First, there was the magnificent squelching by Ole Hanson of the impudent attempt to turn Seattle over to a Soviet government by the I. W. W. forces. Then there followed in quick succession the turning upon the Reds by the trade unions in Lawrence, Mass., Paterson, N. J., Bisbee, Arizona, and other cities where strikes had been forced by Bolshevist mobs. In all these places the American Federation of Labor organization at once saw that not only was the good name of labor at stake but even the life of the unions, while the employing classes as quickly perceived that their interests were closely allied with those of the unions, because it was evident that if the union leaders lost control of the trade union organization only chaos could result.

Exactly the same situation developed in the recent strikes in England and Ireland. For a time it looked there as if, through the functioning of the Shop Steward system, an incipient Bolshevism, the rank and file in the union world would repudiate their national offices. This same danger was threatened in Seattle and the other cities in this country, but the madness of the hour passed and the atmosphere is now all the clearer.

An illustration of the wholesome reaction from this Bolshevist uprising is contained in a dispatch from Chicago, dated February 13, 1919:

> A joint appeal by silk manufacturers and labor leaders of 40,000 striking textile workers in the East, calling on the National War Labor Board to standardize the hours of work in the silk industry and expressing a common purpose to counteract the activities of the I. W. W. and other radical elements was made at today's session of the War board.
>
> The appeal was regarded as epoch-making, in that it is the first instance of employers and striking union men combining in a move to oppose the ultra radical elements by having a governmental body fix standard hours for work.
>
> The board was asked to give immediately a basis for temporary resumption of work so that the strike may be ended pending a final decision of the board. A temporary work week of from 40 to 44 hours was suggested.

Also from Springfield, Ill., comes news that Governor Lowden has just held a conference at the capital between officials of the Illinois State Federation of Labor and officials of the Illinois Manufacturers' Association, looking to the making of a joint program for bettering industrial conditions, while the New York Chamber of Commerce and the New York State Federation are forming a Joint Committee on industrial relations, all of which may mean, that, so far as this country is concerned, the attempt to precipitate Bolshevism may prove a blessing in disguise.

A NEW KIND OF EXPLOITATION

While Bolshevik agitators are vehemently denouncing what they term capitalist exploitation, Herr Richter, police president of Berlin, and a noted Socialist, comes forward to declare that society is menaced by a new kind of exploitation. "We have progressed," he recently said, "from exploitation by the capitalists to exploitation by the proletariat, with the distinction that the capitalists were accustomed to reckon more than six weeks ahead."

Kurt Eisner, the Socialist premier of Bavaria, likewise says: "The Bolshevist idea is to replace the present régime by the dictatorship of the proletariat, which is much worse than capitalism."

This is the first time such acknowledgment have ever openly been made by Socialist leader Yet no sect has more consciously and deliberately practised exploitation than professional Socialist theorists and politicians. An organization representing real labor like the American Federation of Labor has devoted its efforts, and successfully, to lessening injustices and promoting better conditions along lines of practical accomplishments.

This policy aroused the keenest antagonism of Socialist professional theorists. Insisting that misery was increasing, they were self-interested in seeing it increase in order to justify their se theory and augment their following and vote As the Socialist party represented itself, although fictitiously so, as a proletarian party this was a particularly cruel form of exploitation of the very working class for which it professed to stand. The leaders of that party sought to aggrandize themselves in the exploiting of the vast mass of workers by ridiculing or deterring immediate measures for improvement of the workers' conditions. Thus they hoped to enlarge the area of discontent, accentuate dissatisfaction, and profit politically in consequence.

But since the rise of Bolshevism, concept have very much changed. Sobered by the terrific perils to all of the productive and decent elements of society of the anarchism underlying Bolshevism, many Socialists have seen a larg new light. This, of course, does not apply to the fossilized variety or to Socialist party leaders like Berger and others who have long regarded the Socialist party as their proprietary possession, and who, fresh from their pro-German activities, have veered to Bolshevism. Having completely lost the respect of all Socialists of principle once aligned with them, these demagogues now appeal to the dregs of society, expecting from those purlieus a new and more pliable following that will make up in quantity for the loss of the quality that quit their party in disgust.

But on the conscientious, rational Socialists Bolshevism has made a profound impression here as well as in Europe. It has caused them to revise many of their former theories and tactics, and influenced them to a willingness to work with the moderate and conservative forces of society. The widespread slaughter, famine and chaos inflicted on Russia by Bolshevism have proved an ineradicable lesson. They now lucidly see how a mere violent faction, usurping the name of the proletariat, have brutally, remorselessly, tyrannically exploited all classes, including the great body of real workers. This has been the result in Russia where Lenine and Trotzky's armed slum barbarians have destroyed all industry, treated Russia like a conquered country and have pitilessly shot down or starved professionals, skilled workers and peasants alike. A more ghastly exploitation was never known. The horrible mockery of it all is that it has been done under the pretense that it was necessary to efface capitalist exploitation. The Bolsheviki pretend to be an industrial proletarian government, although there are virtually no industries left or craftsmen to operate them. Great numbers of people have been butchered and greater numbers have died from starvation. And what actually is the Bolsheviki regime? A political autocracy headed by a voluble group of power-mad theorists who never did a day's manual work or any other kind of work except mouth work. Even the German Socialists, accustomed as they have been to autocracy and exploitation, refused to have these kinds introduced and used summary methods in disposing of those who tried to establish them.

"PACIFIST" INSTIGATORS OF CLASS WAR

To those carefully observing the course of the general run of pacifists the effrontery and fraud of their pose have long been self-evident. But to the body of the people who have not closely followed their careers and serpentine activities, these have not been so clear. Even in ordinary times successive affairs so engage public attention that the memory of previous happenings gradually fade into haziness. During the great war, with its big events fast crowding upon one another, this tendency was even more marked.

No intelligent patriotic American has forgotten that there were sinister groups of self-styled pacifists who sought to frustrate our preparations and hold us back from fighting for humanity. But as time recedes, the personnel of those groups and their evil ramifications are more or less lost sight of. This is a species of public forgetfulness that these careerists calculate upon.

Before the war many of these identical "pacifists" were preaching war and the necessity of war. They spouted it not merely occasionally but incessantly. True, the war they urged was not an international war. It was, however, a far more destructive kind of war, without any of the salutary results that have followed such an international war as that against German autocracy. The kind of war that these individuals preached and promoted was class war, the deadly onslaught of one class against another. Theoretically the class war that they urged was a war at the ballot. But practically, as they well knew, a systematic stirring up of hatred and the inflaming of every malevolent prejudice and passion, was certain, unless sufficiently counteracted, to provoke sanguinary explosions of violence. Has not this been the culmination in Russia with its consequent dreadful slaughter and chaos? In Germany, too, class war teachings have resulted in pitched battles in the streets. The whole class war theory is inextricably bound up with violence. This fact was well recognized by the I. W. W., which acting on that theory and dropping all pretenses, boldly declared their contempt for the ballot and their determination to gain mastery of society by force.

For years such leading propagandists as Morris Hillquit, Victor Berger, Eugene V. Debs, Kate Richards O'Hare, James H. Maurer, Rose Pastor Stokes, Bill Haywood, Scott Nearing, and many other leaders or near leaders of the Socialist Party, were working overtime agitating the class war. So were Elizabeth Gurley Flynn and other leaders of the I. W. W. This particular aggregation was out in the open, pursuing their course with directness. But there were other groups that were spreading the class-war appeal by methods not quite so conspicuously direct but by no means so indirect as not to make their efforts notorious. There were pastors of churches like the Rev. John Haynes Holmes, Rev. Norman M. Thomas, and the Rev. Irwin St. John Tucker; members of college faculties like Jessie W. Hughan, Harry A. Overstreet and Vida D. Scudder, and a number of self-styled "intellectuals" who, in addition to their magazine effusions, turned out with the most mechanical regularity books in which they deftly pushed the class war propaganda.

When, however, the United States was confronted by the critical alternative of seeing democracy perish or going to war, all, or nearly all of these groups, and their motley trail of followers, suddenly discovered that they were "pacifists." To them the fomenting of a class war sundering society into implacably hostile divisions was a justifiable and highly proper "social" duty. But a war to preserve and extend civilization and free oppressed peoples was denounced by them as "a conspiracy of profiteers" and proclaimed by them to be "anti-social". For one class to fight another was, according to their creed, a proof of superior, militant "class consciousness." But for all classes to unite in an unavoidable international conflict was a wicked use of force which interfered with "the orderly processes of evolutionary development." One upon the heels of another they came with their tremolos on the iniquities of war. Always presenting themselves as benign lovers of peace and good will, the whole purport of their outcry showed that they were interested in promoting in this country the very kind of war that Germany was intriguing to bring about here—a class war which would disrupt our unity and paralyze our strength.

A number of members of these groups are in prison or on the way there following conviction for sedition or violation of the espionage law. But there are others who although skirting close to sedition, contrived to avoid its penalties. Among this latter band are leaders who, while goading addled followers to committing outright sedition, had a very careful eye to their own security.

Now that the war is over, these self-same groups, reinforced by other so-called pacifists, have boldly laid aside the mask that they wore, and are more virulently than ever preaching the class war, either openly or by sympathetic interpretation. No longer, now that the need for dissimulation has passed, do they pass themselves as exponents of peace. The class war is their aim and goal. Who can forget the sanctimonious garb of benevolent pacifism with which Oswald Garrison Villard enwrapped himself during the war? There, among other organizations to which he belonged, was the "Fellowship of Reconciliation",—a conjuring name indeed! And what has Villard's periodical *The Nation* been doing recently? Extenuating Bolshevism to make it palatable to Americans, concealing its horrors, and on the whole, stopping just short of the point of actually recommending it. The Bolshevism which has rent and ruined Russia becomes in the pages of *The Nation* a fine and wonderful movement. The very crew that immediately before or during the war formed such organizations as the "American Union Against Militarism", and "Collegiate Anti-Militarism League", the "Liberty Defense Union" and other puerilities, are now, in general, the same who are extolling the Bolshevik Red Guard Army and the mandates of Lenine and Trotzky decreeing mass conscription and iron discipline. Conscription was an indefensible "invasion of rights" when ordered by the American Government, but it becomes highly commendable when the terroristic Bolshevik autocrats of Russia decree it. In this country refusal to do military service was hailed by the aforesaid crowd as "conscientious objection", but the summary shooting down of all who decline to be soldiers for the Russian Bolsheviki is represented as a justifiable disposal of "counter-revolutionists".

With rare exceptions, the chief characters now overtly or slyly inciting armed revolution have revealed themselves craven. Glorifying "martyrdom" in prison, they have themselves tried in every possible way to squirm out of occupying a cell. They adroitly make declarations that tend to provoke others to violence, but are the very first to disclaim responsibility for it and its consequences. They invidiously write and circulate a line of propaganda that may well lead to mob excesses, but would fly with celerity from any scene of personal danger to themselves. And when any cause that they have espoused comes under the weight of popular odium or is permanently registered as an infamy, they are quick to assert most indignantly that their implication has been "misunderstood." Safety first is their inflexible motto.

Shadow Huns and Oth

By T. EVERETT HARRÉ

Part V
THE PLAGUE OF PROFESSORS

TOWARD the close of that great novel of the war, "The Four Horsemen of the Apocalypse," by the foremost living novelist of Spain, Vincente Blasco Ibanez, there is a picture of more than ordinarily poignant significance. Don Marcello Desnoyers, the aged father of a soldier who has given his life for France, views in silent sorrow the burial fields where, under crosses and faded flags, lie buried the brave men who had fallen, and where, too, in deep trenches marked off by fences of wooden strips, had been interred the carcasses of countless Huns. Standing there under the colorless sky of a winter morning, the bereaved father meditates upon the war, and upon the monstrous Teuton philosophy which underlay and inspired Germany's treacherous attack upon the world.

His eyes resting upon those plots where the Huns were buried, the old man muses thus:

> They were the soldiers who carried books in their knapsacks, and after the fusillade of a lot of country folk, or the sacking and burning of a hamlet, devoted themselves to reading the poets and philosophers by the glare of the blaze which they had kindled. They were bloated with science as with the puffiness of a toad, proud of their pedantic and all-sufficient intellectuality. Sons of sophistry and grandsons of cant, they had considered themselves capable of proving the greatest absurdities by the mental capers to which they had accustomed their acrobatic intellects. . . What a shame that there were not here, too, all the *Herr Professors* of the German universities—those wise men so unquestionably skillful in altering the trademarks of intellectual products and changing the terminology of things! Those men with flowing beards and gold-rimmed spectacles, pacific rabbits of the laboratory and the professor's chair that had been preparing the ground for the present war with their sophistries and their unblushing effrontery! Their guilt was far greater than that of the *Herr Lieutenant* of the tight corset and the gleaming monocle, who in his thirst for strife and slaughter was simply and logically working out the professorial charts. While the German soldier of the lower classes was plundering what he could and drunkenly shooting whatever crossed his path, the warrior student was reading by the camp glow, Hegel and Nietzsche. . . He, with the professors, was rousing all the bad instincts of the Teutonic beast and giving them a varnish of scientific justification. . . The *Herr Professors* had proved to their countrymen that such sacking incursions were indispensable to the highest civilization, and that the German was marching onward with the enthusiasm of a good father sacrificing himself in order to secure bread for his family.

What Vincente Blasco Ibanez discerned is, as the world today knows, absolutely true. It was the *Herr professors*, the spectacled savants of the great Hun institutions of learning, who prepared the way for those bestial, blood-besotted hosts which for a time threatened to sweep Europe and menaced the free nations of the world.

PHARISAICISM AND PEDANTRY

While Imperial Germany during forty years was preparing her military machine, manufacturing cannon and training soldiers, the *Herr professors* were engaged in preparing the minds of the German people by preaching the necessity and nobility of war, by justifying utter ruthlessness and conscienceless cruelty in war, and in making the German people united under their masters by an especial appeal to their racial fat-headed vanity. It was the *Herr professors* who filled the mind of Germany with a bloated, bigoted conceit, who led the stolid, beer-driking, bully-spirited Huns to believe that they were superior to all other peoples and were destined to rule the world. It was the *Herr professors* who intoxicated the mind of this heavy-fleshed, obese-brained race with the belief that they were the chosen people of modern times, whose Kaiser, their Moses, was in alliance with their tribal god, and for whose delectation was destined the promised land—domination over all the nations of the earth. It was the *Herr professors* who schooled this people, natively lacking in fine sensibilities, to such barbarity and pig-hearted cruelties as have shocked and sickened the world. Before these people became murderers in fact, the *Herr professors* of Germany made them brutes, egotists and murderers at heart.

Nor was the baleful work of the *Herr professors* in preparation for the intended war, confined to Germany. What Ibanez so vividly analyzed is more than ordinarily significant to us in America.

While Germany within prepared her armies for war, she engaged at the same time in propaganda adroitly designed to prepare the ground among the peoples whom she intended to assail. She sought, as I have pointed out in a preceding article, to win for herself such admiration and friendship among neutral nations as would paralyze their indignation when the time for her intended blow came. For twenty-five years her agents carried on propaganda picturing Germany as supreme in science, commerce, industry, art, and social progress. And while these agents magnified the advancement and humanitarian achievements of Germany, they sought at the same time to disparage the social and industrial conditions, as well as belittle the institutions and achievements, of other nations. Nowhere in the world was this propaganda carried on with such intensity as in the United States. American writers, many perhaps innocently, were intrigued into abetting this ulterior propaganda, and wrote books in which they extolled the progress of the Fatherland. And other American writers, as well, abetted the even more inimical, more insidious and subtly dangerous propaganda which was calculated to undermine confidence in our own institutions and the loyalty and allegiance of our own people to our Government. In all this propaganda Germany enjoyed the aid of a large and obliging portion of the *Herr professor* fraternity.*

THE INVASION OF AMERICAN EDUCATION

The German propaganda was essentially scientific. There is no use trying to blind ourselves to the fact that it was extraordinarily able, shrewd and astoundingly effective. In mapping out propaganda to be carried on among other nations, the best brains of Germany were devoted to a careful study of the psychology of the peoples they intended to reach. They sought to learn exactly through what mediums, by what methods, and by what appeals, different peoples might be influenced. They sought, in order to play upon them, to understand national and racial partialities and prejudices. In the United States, for instance, believing there existed a latent, anti-British sentiment which had carried down from the war of the Revolution, they made

* The intelligent patriotism of the majority of professors in our colleges and universities, and their splendid work during the war, serves by its fair contrast to bring into unenviable relief the activities of those who, both before and after our entry into the war, failed to live up to the highest ideals of Americanism and of American educational institutions. No class of citizens have more indignantly resented the pro-Germanism and tepid "loyalty" of the class characterized as "*Herr professors*" than the great body of 100 per cent. loyal American educators themselves.—T. E. H.

es designed to force an embargo on all ıry supplies to the Allies—did these Ameri- *Ierr professors.*

ey justified the sinking of the Lusitania unrestricted submarine warfare and re- d parrot-wise all the German arguments ying the use of the submarine as reprisal he "illegal" British blockade—did these ican *Herr professors.*

ey opposed our going to war with Ger- over the unrestricted use of the submarine on and lent themselves to various German, ıan-financed pacifist agitations—did these ican *Herr professors.*

ıd even after America entered the war what nany do?

ey engaged in various activities calculated ender us impotent in the conduct of war ıst Germany. They sought to convince le that we should have nothing to do "mere matters of European politics." endeavored to prove that the draft was ıstitutional, and defended the so-called scientious objectors." They enlisted in the nd defense of the I. W. W., when leaders at organization were on trial for seditious piracy. They arrayed themselves on the of the Russian Bolsheviki and endeavored courage and promote Bolshevism, anarchy revolution—which are one and the same —in our midst. They have aligned them- s with the forces which aim at national tegration.

ey have been notorious pacifists.

WEASELS OF THE WORLD

ıce the signing of the armistice, many of American *Herr professors* have side-tracked selves into another propaganda which was eived in and promoted from Berlin—that h brought about the ruin of Russia and that which Germany even now would destroy y nation on the face of the globe. This try are now Bolshevists, internationalists, olutionary radicals, pacifist Socialists, teach- of radical "social research," et cetera. ifists so far as fighting Germany was erned, they are now advocates of that ıss war" which, Mr. Herbert Croly s, may be as bloody as the war which has closed. Friends of Germany from the days edating the war, they are today active foes he institutions upon which American peace security depend. The most extraordinary g about this whole business is that, after erica entered the war, many of these anti- erican pro-German pundits managed to crawl jobs and other important positions in the eral and State Governments. Just as, after erica entered the war, there was an exodus Greenwich village freaks to Washington so there an influx into Government depart- ıts of many *Herr professors.*

efore—and since—the great war, the activi- of many of these scholastic "stuffed shirts" e peculiarly insidious. Much of their propa- da was not outright pro-German. Even more ctive than open German propaganda so far he German interests were concerned, was which undermined the foundations of erican national life, American morale, Amer- ideals, American belief in the principles which our democracy is built.

o the world German agents before the war ured England as being in decline, ruled by effete aristocracy, threatened with revolution disaffection in her colonies; France as being euerate, effete, dilletante and dissolute. ewise, did German agents picture the United tes as the land of dollars, a country without ıls, where the working classes were exploited capitalists and where the Government was he hands of corrupt grafting politicians. So as the people of England were not con- ed that the day of England was over, so as the people of France were not debauched with the conviction of their own degeneracy, no especial harm was wrought. But what about ourselves? Did we escape all harm from propaganda designed to destroy our self respect, our confidence in American institutions, our belief in American ideals and American integrity, our veneration for our heritage of liberty?

PROPAGANDA OF THE DESTRUCTION OF FAITH

It has been said that men need not fear those who seek to destroy the body so much as those who seek to destroy the soul. That is one of the eternal truths. And what Imperial Germany, the arch-betrayer of civilization, sought chiefly to accomplish toward the carrying out of her purposes was the destruction of the soul of the nations of the world.

No such wrong can be wrought against any man as the destruction of that man's faith in what is moral, right and just.

No such theft can be committed against any man as the theft of that man's ethical beliefs. Destroy a man's convictions in all national and religious ideals, in all humanitarian and spiritual principles; take away all his moorings by confusing his mind with theories about motley forms of "liberalism" camouflaged in deceiving idealistic phrases; reduce all life to this man as absolutely materialistic; interpret all human motives as selfish, all historical movements as economic; arouse and foster in him all the meaner passions, envy, discontent, a desire for gain; put him in conflict with his fellows, destroy his idea of good, and you will have made that man worse than a helot, a weakling swayed by his lowest passions, an agent of social disagreement and strife, the helpless prey and unknowing tool of any unscrupulous force seeking to seize national power through anarchy and international power through national disintegration and collapse.

Had imperial Germany been able to destroy in the spirit of the American people those national ideals which they have cherished, their belief in the principles out of which our democracy was conceived, or had her agents imposed upon us the gross materialistic philosophy of self-interest and "economic determination," Germany need never have feared America as a foe. The Germans, in fact, believed their propaganda had been successful and, as von Papen expressed in a letter to his government, they believed that the United States, dominated by money-greed and lacking all chivalrous ideals, would surrender shamefully to Germany over the submarine issue rather than go to war and risk the loss of dollars. The Germans, and their still active agents as well, have failed to understand American psychology or to gauge the temper of the American spirit. What marked American troops abroad was a dauntless spirit, an intrepid courage, a heroism whose flame was fed by no selfish "economic" interests, no lust for material conquest—it was, in fact, that spirit of knightly chivalry, of spiritual zeal for a cause that is right which has illumined the brightest pages of the world's history from the beginning. Theirs was the inspiration of crusaders who fight for a sacred faith. The informing spirit of this country in the world war will make America a shining name forever.

It is that spirit of the nation which Germany and her agents sought to break before the war. It is that spirit which certain sinister forces, having no visible connection or interests with Germany, are seeking today to destroy.

SAPPING THE SOURCES OF MORAL RESISTANCE

In a book entitled, "The German Conspiracy in American Education," by Capt. Gustavus Ohlinger, of the United States Army, just issued by George H. Doran Co.,* the author says:

"Just as Germany planned her own educational system with reference to her military power, so she sought, as a part of her higher strategy, to enhance her superiority by insinuating herself into the moral and intellectual life of foreign countries. If she could introduce her agents into the native education, there disseminate doubt as to the validity of native traditions and with regard to the adequacy of established institutions, replace national spirit by a shallow cosmopolitanism, and foster an admiration of Kultur to the disparagement of national achievements—then she could sap the very sources of moral resistance."

The Senate Committee which is investigating German propaganda in the United States, on January 24, 1919, made public a "Who's Who" of pacifists and radical intellectuals alleged by the Military Intelligence to have led in organizations opposing the war. The list contains sixty-two names, including many of the professional uplift clan, and twenty-six educators. This list is illumining. There are a number of names of educators which it might well have contained, but among those mentioned was:

> BEARD, Prof. Charles A., formerly of Columbia University; member Intercollegeiate Socialist Society, lecturer Rand School of Social Science, New York.

Prof. Beard indignantly protested to Chairman Overman of the Senate Committee against the inclusion of his name, and, declared:

"I am not and never have been a pacifist. . . . When Nicholas Murray Butler, Assistant Secretary of War Keppel, and Elihu Root were manipulating the Carnegie peace millions issuing pacifist pamphlets by the thousands, organizing pacifist societies in our colleges . . . *I was teaching the truth that war has been one of the most tremendous factors in the origin of the State and the progress of mankind.*"

The doctrine that "war has been one of the most tremendous factors in the origin of the State and the progress of mankind" is simon-pure Hun doctrine.

If, at the time that Dr. Butler and other distinguished and loyal Americans were "pacifists"—ergo, the time before Germany dealt her treacherous blow to civilization, and when no normal men dreamed that there could possibly occur such slaughter as the German General Staff had scientifically planned—Prof. Beard was teaching that "war is one of the most tremendous factors in the origin of the State," etcetera, he was teaching in America what Bernhardi and Treitschke had taught in Germany.

BELLIGERENCY BEFORE, AND PACIFISM AFTER, THE WAR

Save for the blood-thirsty, the Hun-hearted, the sinister preachers of sedition and social disintegration, all of us before August, 1914, were pacifists. Many of us believed that in our day such a war as Germany unloosed was impossible. There is a difference between men who were pacifists before German aggression struck at the core of American rights and American honor, and that mongrel breed who justified war so long as Germany had all to gain from war and who became pacifists only as our controversy with Germany approached the climax. Is it not markedly significant that the German apologists, German sympathizers, Socialists, radical intellectuals and preachers of the class-war became pacifists and anti-conscriptionists only when the United States launched its full force against the Huns? If Prof. Beard so staunchly believed in war, why—in a text book for use in public schools—did he so bitterly assail the "hypocritical Allies" for forcing the war to continue?

Prof. Beard, in 1913, through the Macmillan Company, New York, published a volume entitled "An Economic Interpretation of the Constitution of the United States." According to

*This book will be reviewed, in connection with a further expose of the pro-German activities of American educators, in the next issue of THE NATIONAL CIVIC FEDERATION REVIEW.

educators with whom I have talked, this volume by Prof. Beard has exercised a considerable and widespread influence upon American students and teachers.

If Prof. Beard's doctrines have exercised any considerable influence upon American students and teachers, has that influence been healthful? Has it been calculated to make better citizens of American students and teachers? Has it afforded them the highest conception of the moral inspiration of the Federal Constitution, of the idealistic principles upon which American Democracy is founded?

THE GOSPEL ACCORDING TO MARX

There are two schools of philosophic, of religious or ethical, thought in the world. The one is spiritual, the other materialistic. The one teaches that as a man thinks, so he is; that the only reward of value is the spiritual reward; that to contemplate the commission of wrong constitutes guilt; that men shall strive toward the true, the beautiful and good; that the soul of man is immortal and that a divine power governs the universe. The other teaches that man is a beast, actuated solely by passions and gross desires; that motives of gain alone inspire the action of men and nations; that actions alone count; that as men will inevitably exploit one another it is justifiable for races superior in craft to use any means to a desired end; that might is right; that the "kingdom of heaven," so called, is of the earth. Nearly all of the religions of the world, of the earliest, were based essentially upon the instinctive desire of mankind to approach nearer to God; with all their dross of superstitions, they sincerely essayed to make clearer to man the mystery of God, the way to his heart's desire. Confucius, Buddha, Plato, Marcus Aurelius sought to understand and interpret—and thus inspire and guide man onward in his struggle toward his attainment of—the Ultimate Good. And all that the ancient religions, the teachers and prophets, sought to divine, found its supreme expression in the teachings of One who taught that men shall love one another irrespective of race and creed, and that the pure of heart alone shall inherit the heavenly kingdom which is within them. It was this philosophy which has guided humanity toward a greater realization of righteousness, of true liberty and justice, the highest achievements which have been of joy and benefit to the world. As it applies to individual conduct, so there is in this philosophy the ultimate keynote for constructive social progress, for lasting peace among nations.

Side by side with this philosophy, there carried on the other, crassly materialistic, wholly unhumanitarian, inimical to the general good of mankind, which, often in terms of idealism, has tried to lure men to anarchic revolt, to social disintegration, that those who possess its arcana might gain power and profit. That philosophy was imposed upon the people of Germany, and it was the philosophy which underlay Germany's purposes in the world war. That philosophy found expression, in greater or less degree, in the manifesto of Karl Marx. It has been the *vade mecum* of the Bolsheviki in their betrayal of Russia. It is the destructive seed which is being sown in this country through various extreme and subtly camouflaged forms of liberalism and radicalism today.

ICONOCLASM OF IDEALS

Prof. Charles A. Beard, in opening his volume, "An Economic Interpretation of the Constitution of the United States," flatfootedly rejects that school of historical interpretation, represented by Bancroft, which recognizes a "higher power operating in human affairs." He repudiates Bancroft's belief that in the struggle for the Constitution there was "the movement of divine power which gives unity to the universe, and order and connection to events." Shall we say Prof. Beard jeers at Bancroft for saying: "However great may be the number of those who persuade themselves that there is in man nothing superior to himself, history interposes with evidence that tyranny and wrong lead inevitably to decay; that freedom and right, however hard may be the struggle, always prove resistless."

Prof. Beard, like the German Socialists and the Russion Bolsheviki, is an admitted materialist.

Had the German Government scientifically and deliberately sought to undermine the belief of Americans in the ideals and moral principles governing the framing of the Constitution, in the intrinsic principles of liberty and justice inspiring the makers of that document, had it sought to destroy in Americans all reverence for the fathers of the country and hold them and the foundation of our history in disrepute it could not have planned a more scientific and deliberate method than that embodied in this book by Prof. Charles A. Beard, formerly professor of Columbia University, at present lecturer for the Rand School of Social Science and director of the Bureau of Municipal Research.

Were the framers of the American Constitution, as we have believed, inspired by lofty ideals? Is the American Constitution a document based upon moral principles?

"Every fundamental appeal in it," declares this fellow Beard, *"is to some material and substantial interest."*

The school children of America have been taught to venerate George Washington. What sort of interpretation of George Washington would school teachers influenced by Beard give to the children of the land?

George Washington, as one of the members of the Constitutional Convention, according to Charles A. Beard, was not "disinterested."

George Washington, says Beard, was one of "the land speculators and promoters" of his day.

George Washington, in other words, was a Colonial plutocrat, one of those who helped to frame the Constitution for their own profit, who were actuated by self interest, a member of that class which exploits "the poor and disinherited." George Washington not "disinterested"!

The document embodying the principles of American freedom, according to Beard, was inspired by the desire of money-grubbing, unidealistic Colonial plutocrats to enrich themselves.

JUSTICE—"ABSTRACT STUFF"

Prof. Beard manifestly is inclined affectionately to regard that "school of historical interpretation which . . . may be called the Teutonic, because it ascribes the wonderful achievements of the English speaking peoples to the peculiar political genius of the Germanic race." Prof. Beard describes the thesis of this school thus:

"The Teutonic peoples were originally endowed with singular political talents and aptitudes; Teutonic tribes invaded England and destroyed the last vestiges of the older Roman and British culture; they then set an example to the world in the development of 'free' government. Descendants of this specially gifted race settled America and fashioned their institutions after old English models. The full fruition of their political genius was reached in the creation of the Federal Constitution."

Prof. Beard apparently classes himself in an even more modern, more advanced and untrammelled "school of historical research not to be characterized by any phrase."

After an examination of this pretentious pedant's work, it certainly could not be characterized as idealistic or patriotic.

The various promoters of camouflaged German, pacifist, and revolutionary propaganda have all, at some time or another, inadvertently self betrayed themselves, and, once you hit upon the secret keynote of their activities and bring a small wee revealing light of understanding to bear into the recesses of their crafty, subtle and pharisaical minds, much becomes clear. Commenting upon a summing-up by J. C. Carter of the analysis of legal evolution, Prof. Beard naïvely drops this revealing phrase:

"Law is made out of some abstract stuff known as 'justice'."

Any mind that would designate justice as "made out of some abstract stuff" certainly is not the sort likely to appreciate the finest moral ideals. Imperial Germany, planning for ruthless world subjugation, giving itself to the most bestial and terrifying program of scientific atrocities, was certainly of the mind that "justice" is merely abstract stuff.

The Germans believed, of course, in "economic determinism."

So does the guiding spirit of "The New School for Social Research."

"It will be admitted without controversy," says Prof. Beard in his volume, "that the Constitution was the creation of a certain number of men, and it was opposed by a certain number of men. . . . Suppose," he continues, "that substantially all of the merchants, money lenders, security holders, manufacturers, shippers, capitalists, and financiers and their professional associates are to be found on one side in support of the Constitution and that substantially all or the major portion of the opposition came from the non-slaveholding farmers and debtors—would it not be pretty conclusively demonstrated that our fundamental law was not the product of an abstraction known as 'the whole people,' but of a group of economic interests which must have expected beneficial results from its adoption?"

COLONIAL CAPITALISTS AND THE CONSTITUTION

Prof. Beard with Machiavellian suggestion asks:

"Did the men who formulated the fundamental law of the land possess the kinds of property which were immediately and directly increased in value or made more secure by the results of their labors at Philadelphia? Did they have money at interest? Did they own public securities? Did they hold western lands for appreciation? Were they interested in shipping and manufactures?"

Prof. Beard answers:

"Washington, of Virginia, was probably the richest man in the United States of his time, and his financial ability was not surpassed among his countrymen anywhere. He possessed, in addition to his great estate on the Potomac, a large amount of fluid capital which he judiciously invested in western lands, from which he could reasonably expect a large appreciation with the establishment of stable government and the advance of the frontier."

As if no higher motives inspired George Washington than an expectation of material profit when he lent his aid to the making of the Constitution!

In other words, Prof. Beard cannot conceive of men as being inspired by any other motives than the sordidly selfish. Prof. Beard cannot conceive of nations being moved by high ideals, of wars being waged for great causes of human liberty and justice. Man is a debased physical brute, impelled by gross carnal cravings, without high principles or unselfish ideals! Prof. Beard, subscribing to the Marxian doctrine of the "economic interpretation of history," must seek, as an explanation of every human action, for some ignoble selfish motive. Prof. Beard has occupied positions of confidence and trust, and has asked for recognition and a hearing as educator representing the highest American-n. Is Prof. Beard's interpretation of history d the actions of mankind exalted? Is it ilized, in the highest sense? Is it Christian? Is it possible that American history and the litical and social phenomena of our day are ing interpreted to young America by rank aterialists, atheistic and unchristian bigots, en whose only message to their kind, to the owing mind, is subtly disguised Marxian revo-tionary doctrine—the religion of the belly-d?

GEORGE WASHINGTON A "GRAFTER"

Allan L. Benson, former Socialist candidate r the presidency, wrote a book called "Our ishonest Constitution," in which he declared at the Federal Constitution was the work of what today would be called grafters."

Former-Socialist candidate Benson admits at Prof. Beard's book constituted a chief urce of authority for his unpraiseworthy at-cks upon the fathers of the country. When harles A. Beard was quizzed by the New York tate Bar Association, he shiftily evaded a direct swer, declaring that he had not tried to read enson's notorious volume and that he could not undertake to give any attention at all to hat use other people make" of his own book.

Did Prof. Beard, albeit in more euphonious d less courageous language, not also imply, did Benson, that "the sacred document was rawn up in part by a group of grafters?"

Of George Washington, Beard went on to say:

"Washington was also a considerable money-nder and suffered from the paper money perations of the Virginia legislature. . . . e held $6,246 of United States securities."

"It seems safe to hazard a guess," continues rof. Beard, "that at least $40,000,000 gain ame to the holders of securities through the doption of the Constitution."

Alexander Hamilton, says Beard, "had little art in the formation of the Constitution, but was his organizing ability that made it a real strument bottomed on all the substantial in-rests of the time."

Prof. Beard says "the land speculators and romoters . . . embraced all the leading men f the time—Washington, Franklin, Robert Mor-is, James Wilson, William Blount."

Robert Morris "was an effective representa-ive of the land operators, the holders of securi-ies, the dealers in public paper, and the mer-antile groups seeking protection for manufac-ures. Before and after the adoption of the Constitution, he was busy interesting his col-eagues in every kind of enterprise that prom-sed to be profitable."

Prof. Beard dogmatizes:

"It may be shown that the 'general good' is he ostensible object of any particular act; but he general good is a passive force, and unless ve know who are the several individuals that enefit in its name, it has no meaning. When t is so analyzed, immediate and remote bene-ficiaries are discovered."

Doubtless Prof. Beard, with his peculiar ualities of mind, would interpret the Christian Gospels according to this rule.

FRAMERS "NOT DISINTERESTED"

Of the framers of the Constitution, he goes on o say:

"The overwhelming majority of members, at east five-sixths, were immediately directly and personally interested in the outcome of their abors at Philadelphia, and were to a greater or less extent economic beneficiaries from the adop-tion of the Constitution."

Prof. Beard asserts of the framers:

"Personalty invested in lands for speculation was represented by at least fourteen members, . . . personalty in the form of money loaned at interest was represented by at least twenty-four members; . . . personalty in mercantile, manufacturing and shipping lines was represented by at least eleven members; . . . personalty in slaves was represented by at least fifteen members."

Prof. Beard concludes:

"It cannot be said, therefore, that the members of the Convention were 'disinterested.' On the contrary, we are forced to the profoundly significant conclusion that they knew through their personal experiences in economic affairs the precise results which the new government that they were setting up was designed to attain."

The Constitution, asserts Prof. Beard, "was an economic document drawn with superb skill by men whose property interests were immediately at stake; and as such it appealed directly and unerringly to identical interests in the country at large. . . .

"The rich and wealthy worked for the Constitution to prevent the loss of their debts.

"There were no such immediate personal gains to be made through the defeat of the Constitution as were to be made by the security holders on the other side. . . .

"It seems safe to hazard a guess, therefor, that at least $40,000,000 gain came to the holders of securities through the adoption of the Constitution and the sound financial system which made it possible. . . .

"It appears, nevertheless, that the Constitution was not 'an expression of the clear and deliberate will of the whole people,' nor of a majority of the adult males, nor at the outside of one-fifth of them. . . .

"Every fundamental appeal in it is to some material and substantial interest."

The state conventions acting upon the ratification, declares Beard, "do not seem to have been more 'disinterested' than the Philadelphia convention; but in fact the leading champions of the new government appear to have been, for the most part, men of the same practical type, with actual economic advantages at stake.

"The movement for the Constitution of the United States was originated and carried through principally by four groups of personalty interests which had been adversely affected under the Articles of Confederation: money, public securities, manufactures, and trade and shipping.

"The first firm steps toward the formation of the Constitution were taken by a small and active group of men immediately interested through their personal possessions in the outcome of their labors.

"The Constitution was not created by 'the whole people' as the jurists have said; neither was it created by 'the states' as Southern nullifiers long contended; but it was the work of a consolidated group whose interests knew no state boundaries and were truly national in their scope."

In other words, the Constitution of the United States was born out of a capitalistic cabal, a conspiracy of the "aristocrats" against "the poor and disinherited."

Says Beard: "The revolutionary nature of the work of the Philadelphia Convention is correctly characterized by Prof. John W. Burgess when he states that had such acts been performed by Julius Caesar or Napoleon, they would have been pronounced coups d'etat."

This Prof. John W. Burgess, quoted approvingly by Prof. Beard, studied history, public law and political science at Gottingen, Leipsic and Berlin. He was the first American exchange professor to go to Berlin, where he was colossally honored by the presence of the Kaiser at a lecture and decorated by the Hun Emperor with the Order of the Prussian Crown.

In a report on Benson's and Beard's books made by a committee of the New York State Bar Association in 1916, this opinion was given:

BEARD SCORED BY BAR ASSOCIATION

"Prof. Beard's condemnation of citizens, either of the ten bankless states, or else of the three States which had but one small bank apiece, as not 'disinterested', because they invested part of their savings in declining public securities, is as unwarranted as treating as unworthy or unethical a savings banks or trustee who successfully invested below par in three and one-half per cent or four per cent New York City bonds or other gilt edged three and one-half or four per cent bonds during a bond market depression. No European investor will be condemned in history as unpatriotic because he invested at market rates in the war debt or neutrality debt of his nation during the present war or else later during the financial depression inevitably following the treaty of peace."

On the same grounds on which he sought to disparage the makers of the Constitution, Prof. Beard might assail every American citizen as "not disinterested" in desiring to win the war over Germany because they had invested in Liberty bonds!

Whether it was so intended or not, Prof. Charles A. Beard's book was identically in line with that propaganda whereby Germany planned to undermine the morale and spirit of the nations she planned ultimately to challenge and whose rights she intended to assail. Germany sought to conquer nations not only through her armies, but by breaking their spirit. Charles A. Beard has given himself to nothing less than an effort to destroy his own country's soul.

Is Charles A. Beard, therefore, a man who should be permitted to teach students in social research, to influence teachers who in turn will form the minds of American childhood?

In 1915, while the German propaganda instituted by Dr. Dernburg was in full swing, I was told by one of the directors of the propaganda bureau at 1123 Broadway, that it was Germany's intentions to continue her propaganda after the close of the war and to secure absolute control of American public opinion.

"It is our purpose and intention," said this man in effect, "first of all, to secure control, so far as we can, of concerns publishing text books for use in public schools, and likewise to mobilize and influence all writers of school text books. We propose especially to control the preparation of school histories, so that American children will not be taught that Germany began this war, or was guilty of unwarranted atrocities in this war. We shall see to it that American children are instructed so that the blame for this war will be placed where it belongs." My informant smiled narrowly. "The Americans do not love the British," he went on, "and they are inclined to like the Germans. By controlling the preparation of school histories, we can begin to make Americans from the time they are children see the German point of view. We want the friendship of America, and that friendship will be necessary in our plans for commercial recuperation which will have to be done through the economic elimination of England."

BEARD TEXTBOOK THROWN OUT OF SCHOOLS

Just how far did the German agents go in "influencing" the writers of text books for use in the American schools? To what extent was the propaganda of Prof. M. J. Bonn, who had held the Jacob H. Schiff professorship at Cornell, and that of the German University League successful? How many of our *Herr professors* obligingly lent their pens to the German cause?

Prof. Charles A. Beard, in collaboration with Prof. James Harvey Robinson, wrote a school text book, published by Ginn & Company, entitled "Outlines of European History."

Part II of this volume last September was thrown out of the public schools of Seattle, Washington, because, according to the Text Book

Committee of the Seattle School Board, it was filled with flagrant pro-German propaganda. Ginn & Co., through their agent, Albert E. Shumate, admitted in a letter to Superintendent Cooper of the Seattle Public Schools, that the company "set about revising all of their text books, so as to remove anything that might be construed as 'pro-German propaganda'", and that, even before they had learned of the agitation in Seattle against Beard and Robinson's book, they had withdrawn the objectionable volume. They promised an "'expurgated' edition so revised that no reasonable person will accuse them of being in any way pro-German or un-American."

In this precious volume, insidiously sent broadcast as a text book for the instruction of American children, the two American *Herr professors* declared:

"Whoever might have been responsible for beginning the war, Germany has been the first to propose to end it. *The Kaiser could say exultantly that the Allies had at last cast off the mask of hypocrisy and plainly revealed their lust of conquest.*"

Commenting on this deplorable volume by Professors Beard and Robinson, Judge Thomas Burke, of the Text Book Committee of the Seattle School Board declared:

"Entirely apart from the School Book Committee and acting solely on my own responsibility as a citizen deeply interested in the welfare of the Public Schools, I can not let this occasion pass without calling attention to the danger of underestimating the influence for good or evil of the school history according to its character.

THE ENEMY IN AMERICAN SCHOOLS

"Next to the home, the school room is the place where love of our country and its noble ideals, admiration and reverence for its illustrions founders and preservers who wrought so disinterestedly and successfully in the cause of justice and liberty, take deepest root and make the most lasting impressions on the hearts and minds of the youth of the land. Hearts and minds thus imbued in early years will constitute in years to come at once the glory and the real defense of the country. The public school is the Ark of the Covenant of the Republic.

"It is little wonder, then that for some years, even before the German war, the common enemy sought and secured an entrance there. He knew that if, unobserved, he could, from the vantage ground of the school room, direct the education and form the ideals of young America, that sooner or later the country would be at his mercy. And so it came to pass that German propaganda in text book and teaching became rife and rank from the Atlantic to the Pacific.

"To be forewarned is to be forearmed. We know now what the enemy has been up to in secret for many years. It is our duty to the children of the land to seek out this enemy's hiding places and drive him hence and to see to it that he never enters there again. The danger arising out of the situation created in this school district by the attempt to introduce Robinson and Beard's 'Outlines of European History, Part II,' has been removed for the present by the withdrawal of the books for revision and expurgation."

Remarking upon the complaisant readiness, nay alacrity, with which the obliging authors went about "expurgating and revising" their volume after its pro-Germanism had been detected and exposed, Judge Burke said:

"The authors seem to be ready to change their views on historic subjects, holding themselves in readiness to rewrite their book to meet the market. This is one of the surprising results of the criticism of the work here and elsewhere. It reminds one of the case of a school teacher who applied to a country school board for a place as teacher in the district school. In the course of the examination the directors said: 'Now some people think the world is flat; other people say the world is round. What is your view?' To which the versatile candidate replied: 'I am prepared to teach either view, flat or round, to suit the District.'

"It is needless to say that this is not the spirit in which a school history worthy of the name should be written."

Professor Charles A. Beard while at Columbia University defended those so-called "conscientious objectors," Professors Cottell and Dana, who were under fire. Prof. Beard found it convenient to resign from that institution.

(*Continued on page 18*)

AN IDEAL COLLECTIVE CONTRACT

Many commercial organizations have passed resolutions and many large capitalists have publicly declared that labor and capital should come together in joint conference to work out practicable methods for dealing with each other, but the Bethlehem Shipbuilding Corporation went beyond the talkfest stage and put the proposition into actual operation.

Early this year, as the result of many conferences between the officers of that corporation and the Metal Trades Department of the American Federation of Labor, the following agreement was reached:

AGREEMENT made this Seventh day of January, 1919, between the Bethlehem Shipbuilding Corporation, Ltd., a Delaware Corporation (hereinafter called the Company) and the Metal Trades Department of the American Federation of Labor (hereinafter called the Department).

WITNESSETH:

That whereas, the Department is an organization composed of National and International Unions (hereinafter called the Unions) affiliated with the American Federation of Labor, many of the members of the said unions being in the employ of the Company in its various plants, and

Whereas, the Company recognizes the said Unions collectively as a suitable agency to represent its employees in questions arising as to wages, hours of labor and general working conditions, and

Whereas, the Department is authorized by the express consent of each Union which is a member of the Department to enter into an agreement with the Company providing for the relations of the Unions with the Company—

Now, therefore, it is agreed as follows:

(1) The Unions shall select a committee of five members (hereinafter called the Internationals' Committee) which shall represent the Unions in questions arising between the Unions and the Company.

(2) The members of the Internationals' Committee shall be selected in such manner, for such terms, and with such provisions for alternates as the Unions may from time to time determine.

(3) The Internationals' Committee may appoint agents, delegates or officers who shall have such authority in dealing with the separate managements of the plants of the Company, or with Employees' Committees in such plants, or on behalf of such Employees' Committees, as shall be expressly conferred by the Internationals' Committee.

(4) The Internationals' Committee, or any member thereof, or any person expressly authorized by said Committee shall have access to any plant of the Company on the business of the Internationals' Committee, in accordance with rules and regulations agreed to by the Internationals' Committee and the Company's Committee.

(5) The relations of the Unions with the Company and with the separate managements of its plants, (including in the term *Unions* all departments, councils, federations, central, local or other organizations affiliated with the American Federation of Labor, and all agents or officers thereof) in matters affecting wages, hours of labor or working conditions are to be carried on exclusively through the Internationals' Committee, or in accordance with the rules of said Committee from time to time established, and not otherwise.

(6) It is understood that the employees will select local or plant committees that will function in the same manner as provided for in the Shipbuilding Labor Adjustment Board awards subject to such changes or modifications as may from time to time be agreed upon by the Internationals' Committee and the Company's Committee.

(7) The Company shall appoint a committee of five members (hereinafter called the Company's Committee) to meet with the Internationals' Committee at regular intervals and otherwise subject to the joint call of the Chairmen. The members of the Company's Committee shall be appointed in such manner, for such term and with such provisions for alternates as the Company may from time to time determine.

(8) The Internationals' Committee and the Company's Committee shall jointly hear or consider all grievances or other questions affecting wages, hours of labor or working conditions which have failed of adjustment, and any other matters as to which such joint consideration will tend to avoid misunderstandings, or will improve the condition of the industry and of its employees. Any officer representing a Union shall have the right to be present at a hearing in the subject of which the interests of his organization are specially concerned, or to confer with the Committee, sitting jointly, on any question which in his judgment requires consideration or adjustment.

(9) The Internationals' Committee shall pay the compensation and expenses of its own officers, agents or delegates, but the Company will pay the reasonable compensation and expenses of its employees for time actually spent in service on craft or other Committees in accordance with provisions and rules from time to time made and agreed upon by the Internationals' Committee and the Company's Committee.

(10) A National or International Union, any of the members of which are employees of the Company, and which is not a member of the Department, may become a party to this agreement by notice to the Department and to the Company of its intention to conform to the provisions hereof. Any such union may withdraw from the agreement upon notice to the Department and the Company. Either the Department or the Company may terminate this agreement at any time by giving thirty days' notice in writing.

IN WITNESS WHEREOF, Bethlehem Shipbuilding Corporation, Ltd., has caused these presents to be signed and its corporate seal to be hereto affixed by Eugene G. Grace, its President, and Joseph W. Powell, a Vice-President, and the Metal Trades Department of the American Federation of Labor has caused these presents to be signed by James O'Connell, its President, and A. J. Berres, its Secretary, all on the day and year first above written.

BETHLEHEM SHIPBUILDING CORPORATION, LTD.
by E. G. Grace, President.
J. W. Powell, Vice-President.

METAL TRADES DEPARTMENT
by Jas. O'Connell, President.
A. J. Berres, Secy. Treasurer.

Reign of Ruin In Russia

variable rule in such a case is to rule against the complainant on the ground that he had more possessions than the other man, and on that ground alone.

"Indeed," M. Titoff declared, "with industry at a standstill, the state bankrupt, the land unsown, the urban population starving, none but the rabble and the heavily paid horde of Bolshevist officials and soldiery now adhere to, or stand to profit by, the Bolshevist régime.

"And the rabble and the Bolshevist mercenaries are for all practical purposes synonymous terms, for the bulk of the latter are drawn from the lowest class of society.

"Except in the case of this class, which naturally is the only one that can derive any profit from such a state of affairs, the Bolsheviki maintain their hold on the population merely by virtue of force of circumstances, or by the alternate use of bribery or coercion. Thus, in case of the bourgeoisie, many of them have had to take service under the Bolsheviki merely to save themselves from utter starvation, to which the bourgeois class has been deliberately doomed by the Bolshevist administration.

"Again, another favorite device employed by the Moscow Government is to seize upon relatives of its political opponents, and to hold them as hostages.

"Many a strong man is thus prevented from lifting a finger against the established order, or is even compelled to take office under it lest his family should pay the penalty for his refusal with their lives or worse.

A DISILLUSIONED WORKING CLASS

"This, for instance, is the case with many officers in the Red army, whose lot, even apart from this fact, is as unenviable as it well can be. Each officer, namely, has attached to his person a Bolshevist commissary, armed to the teeth, and who, being liable to be shot himself for any offense committed by his charge, is by no means slow to use his revolver on the slightest pretext. The working class population, meanwhile, has become disillusioned by the manifest gigantic failure of Bolshevist economics, and the almost universal misery they have brought in their train.

"Like the bourgeoisie, however, the workers have had to take refuge in the Bolshevist ranks from the starvation that prevails without, while others of their number are kept quiet by dint of the liberal use of paper money, which the government prints in huge quantities.

"The government, for instance, frequently subsidizes such industrial enterprises as are still struggling along, while the work people discharged from those that have already closed down are paid their wages several months in advance from the government funds."

As for the peasantry, M. Titoff reports that the initial hold which the Bolsheviki secured over it by their distribution of the land, has now been effectually undermined. In the first place, the peasant's one idea, now that he has the land, is to keep it, and the Bolshevist régime fails to come up to the standards of order and stability necessary to secure that end.

In the second place, the Bolsheviki, in the country as in the towns, have systematically exalted the lowest class at the expense of those above them, so that the small farmer class now frequently finds itself at the mercy of the laborers and is alienated from the government in consequence.

"Finally," continues M. Titoff, "the dreams entertained by the peasantry of the new era of prosperity have been rudely shaken by the arbitrary fixing of corn prices, and a system of forced sales and confiscation. The result is that the peasant is concealing what stocks he can, while also refusing, in view of the general uncertainty, to sow his fields afresh—a fact of sinister significance, not only to Russia, but to a considerable part of Europe also, and therefore, in the present circumstances, to the world at large."

TERRORISM AND FORCE TO INSURE SUBMISSION

Asked how it was that, in such circumstances, the Bolsheviki are still able to maintain themselves in power, M. Titoff declared that, just as Czarist Russia was kept in a state of perpetual torpor by the sale of vodka, so now Bolshevist Russia is kept under the spell of the reign of terrorism and force.

In Central Russia, it is physically impossible for any section of the community to take action, for the Bolsheviki are the only element in possession of arms and equipment of any kind, thanks mainly to German solicitude on their behalf. This summer alone, for instance, Germany supplied some 800,000 rifles to the Bolshevist troops. Moreover, the mainstay of the Bolsheviki's power is the horde of Letts and Chinese enrolled under their banner. Every regiment of the Red army has incorporated in it a battalion of these men, who need only a word of command to shoot down without further ado any who show the slightest sign of revolt.

Similar alien detachments are posted throughout the provinces ready to strike down without hesitation any who would attempt to move against the established order.

It is these Chinese and Letts, too, who carry out the wholesale executions of all and sundry who come under the Bolshevist ban, and who in fact terrorize the whole population into submission. It is only in southern and northern Russia and in Siberia where the Bolsheviki have never succeeded in thus consolidating their power, that it has been possible to organize any kind of resistance, and those efforts have been hampered hitherto by lack of arms and equipment, from which the population of central Russia has suffered, and from the difficulty of coordinating the steps taken in each region.

SYSTEMATIC STARVATION OF HATED CLASSES

How the Bolsheviki have been deliberately, systematically underfeeding or starving all but their following of manual laborers and Red Guards is shown by the facts given in the Bolshevik official organ, the *Prodovolstvie Severa*. The official decree of the Food Commissariat, there published, gave orders to the effect that in Petrograd from October 15 "until further alteration" the daily ration of bread will be as follows: Class I, three-eighths pound; Class II, one-eighth pound; Class III, one-sixteenth pound, and Class IV, none. Potato rations (per week): Class I, four pounds; Class II, three pounds; Class III, one pound; Class IV, one-half pound.

"The classification of rations according to classes is a specimen of Bolshevist justice," says Ariadna Tyrkova, in the second of a series of special articles on Russia which were forwarded from London to the *Christian Science Monitor*. "The first class includes persons engaged in manual labor. The second includes employees, board and public school teachers, etc. The third category is composed of engineers, lawyers, doctors, professors, and members of the liberal professions in general. The fourth category includes persons living on income derived from property (it is hardly likely that there are any now) and shopkeepers. The last two categories are condemned to go constantly hungry, as it is scarcely possible that anyone can subsist on one-half pound of potatoes a week. However, when the Red army manages to requisition some corn from the peasants somewhere or other, then occasionally even the fourth category get one-sixteenth pound of bread.

"It goes without saying that all who can are escaping from Petrograd. The *Prodovolstvie Severa* for the 19th of October says that in January, 1918, Petrograd had 2,693,000 inhabitants, and by August only 1,513,000 were left. The population is steadily diminishing and by September there was a further decrease of 16 per cent., this diminution varying to a considerable extent according to the class. The first class shows no decrease. The second shows a decrease of 24 per cent., the third of 47 per cent., and the fourth has almost disappeared, the decrease amounting to 85 per cent.

"But it is a mistake to use the word 'escape.' It is no easy matter to leave Petrograd. There are permits to obtain from the committee, money is necessary, and no small amount, as without bribery it is difficult to stir, and it is far more probable that the bulk of persons represented by these statistical data have simply perished of starvation. But the official paper is evasive in mentioning their disappearance, merely saying that 'there is a decrease of so many.' This expression assumes still more significance when it is stated that 'the decrease in the number of young children is very perceptible, amounting to as much as 73 per cent.' Apparently that decrease took place between June and September. But even before that, from January to August, of the 130,000 children under three years of age, only 35,000 remained, while of the 328,000 children under 12, only 191,000 were left. It is to be hoped that even half of these 'children' were got out of Petrograd by their parents. The other half have undoubtedly perished."

In the same Bolshevik organ there was an order of the Bolshevik Government to get ready grain for shipment to Germany. This order called upon all Bolshevik officials "to get ready to render energetic military and alimentary assistance to the working classes of Germany and Austria-Hungary." That was in October, before the Allied nations had agreed to an armistice with Germany. Since then the famine in Petrograd and other Russian cities has reached far more horrible proportions, vast numbers dying from starvation. These victims include Americans and other nationalities as well as Russians. Only a few days ago the Joint Centenary Committee of the Methodist Episcopal Church issued a statement in New York City that it had received information that W. D. Childs, an American, and for many years chief representative of the Western Union Telegraph Company in Russia, had died of starvation in Petrograd.

ONLY DESTRUCTION; NO CONSTRUCTION

"The Bolsheviki are destroyers," said Madame Catherine Breshkowsky, "the mother of the Russian Revolution," who is now in the United States, after having fled from Russia, where the Bolshevik régime threatened her with death. "Ruination is their motto. There has been no construction. Russia has 180,000,000 people and 80,000,000 are illiterate. They never knew the relations of their own country. They never knew there was a Little Russia, a Siberia, or any other of the various parts of their own country where they did not live. They were never permitted to take any part in the government. How can such people proceed to such liberties as they strived for?

"I believe our future depends on the inclination of organizations and their conceptions of democracy. Russia needs a good system of education. There are 2,000,000 orphans in Russia. Another 2,000,000 children are fatherless. It is my business and that of my heart and my conscience to devote my life work in aiding them.

"There are no factories, no mines or mills left. There is no iron for blacksmiths to forge horseshoes. The price of a spool of thread is 20 rubles (normally $10) and it cannot be obtained even at that price, for there is no thread. There is no paper on which to print an alphabet for their children. I pray that in America I may find the money whereby these 4,000,000 children may be supplied with alphabets. They will have to be printed in America.

"Russia is in need of good teachers and good craftsmen, good carpenters and machinists, in fact good men in every craft. Before we have good industry we must learn, and it is to this country that we are looking."

AN AMERICAN RADICAL'S DISGUST

A disillusioned former Bolshevik sympathizer who has just come out of Russia is Robert Minor, a well-known American cartoonist and illustrator. Mr. Minor was for many years a strong socialist adherent in New York, and more latterly has been a believer in the I. W. W. theories. The *New York World*, on February 3, and succeeding days published a series of articles signed by him and cabled from Berlin. Inasmuch as Mr. Minor was admitted to have an interview with Lenine, which interview Lenine knew was to be published in other countries, the question occurs whether Lenine was not cleverly using the occasion to create abroad an impression that he calculated would be to the advantage of his régime. Russia under Bolshevik misrule is in such a chaotic state, lacking goods of any kind, that to sustain their régime, Lenine and Trotzky must furnish essential commodities which can only be obtained from other countries. These will not do business with a country run by a régime based on murder, pillage and repudiation of debts. It is now to the paramount interest of Lenine and Trotzky to try to spread the idea in other countries that their régime is not at all the dangerous affair that it has been represented. Their aims would be advanced if they could have other peoples believe that the Russian business men are actually, although not nominally, in charge of industry. They could thus present themselves as an orderly government, with whom it is safe to do business.

These comments are in order without questioning Mr. Minor's good faith in the premises.

While Messrs. Williams, Reed, Nuorteva and Company have been regaling meetings here with imaginative yarns about how the proletariat had dispensed with the "bourgeoisie" and were effectively running Russia, a very different state of affairs has developed there, according to Mr. Minor. Lenine and Trotzky have now had to go to that very "bourgeoisie"—or what has been left of it—for the necessary ability to restore the factories wrecked by the incapacity or despoiling of Lenine and Trotzky's proletariat. Says Mr. Minor:

FEARED MORE THAN THE CZAR

"As Lenine talked to me he kept hitching his chair nearer to mine until his knees touched mine, and his finger waved under my nose. I really felt submerged by his personality, which seemed to fill the room.

"The tiptoeing stenographers and the sentries about him are seemingly treated as his equals, but it struck me they held him in greater awe than they had ever felt toward the Czar.

"The interview was in the Kremlin, ancient seat of the Czars. As I came away two smart limousines drew up and deposited several we dressed men of the business type. This clas had been lying very low only a few months ag They are of the type the Bolshevik creed d nounces as 'bloodthirsty minions of predator capital.'

"There is a difference now. The busines types ride in fine automobiles as before, live i fine mansions, and are again managing the ol industries, with more authority than ever be fore. Now they are 'People's Commissaries'— servants of the proletariat—and the iron dis cipline of the army under red flags has been de veloped in order to protect them against all an noyance. A rose smells as sweetly to them un der any other name.

"The Bolsheviki won the support of the low est-paid laborers by declaring for equal pay fo all work. As soon as they felt sufficiently stron they contrived devices for raising the incomes o those 'doing unusually important work.'"

Mr. Minor added that the "inflammator Revolutionary language" which the Bolshevi leaders have been using to other nations, is sim ply intended for home consumption. Lenin and his associates have already abandoned man of their theories, including that of repudiatio of debts on foreign loans. They really, Mr Minor says, want to come to terms with othe nations. He declares that instead of havin established the communism and industrial "dic tatorship of the proletariat," which they woul have revolutionists in other nations believe the have effected, the Bolshevik régime has now come to what is in fact actually governmen ownership. Mr. Minor's articles exposed th pretensions, tricks, cant and humbuggery by which Lenine, Trotzky and associates have de ceived their rabble following. They have estab lished what they all along so vehemently de nounced as a "capitalist product," namely, a political state. It is of the most despotic orde of centralization, with themselves as autocrat This arbitrary political power, Mr. Minor let it be understood, they have determined to main tain at all costs.

Shadow Huns and Others

(Continued from Page 16)

Prof. Charles A. Beard came to the defense of the teachers of the DeWitt Clinton High School, New York City, who were accused of unpatriotic teaching, and were subsequently dismissed. At a meeting held in the school on December 15, 1917, a letter from Prof. Beard in defense of the accused teachers was read. In this letter Beard attempted to project into the matter the question of racial prejudice, actually making the charge that the disloyal teachers had been suspended because they were Russian Jews.

Prof. Charles A. Beard's name was mentioned some time ago in a list of people who were to be sent to Europe by the Young Men's Christian Association "to give instruction in citizenship and municipal government to soldiers in order to return to America imbued with high civic standards and better equipped for participation in government." Is the man who so grossly "interpreted" the founders of the Republic and the authors of the fundamental principles of American Democracy likely to be able to imbue American soldier boys "with high civic standards?" Could those lads, who fought the brutal Hun with a glory in their eyes, who were baptized in a fire of real patriotism, learn aught of ideals from a man who villified the Allies, accusing them of "hypocrisy" and "lust of conquest?"

Shall the children of America receive the purest and loftiest interpretation of the history

(Continued on page 19)

f Hyphenism

Friends of German Democracy)

those who still speak of the "glorious old fatherland" with exaggerated pathos, who surround it with a halo of sentiment which has no shadows, but who, when speaking of their new fatherland, do so in words that express "only just enough of love". Insulted by those, who bought Liberty bonds, it is true, but at no loss to themselves, for it was no sacrifice for the well to do, who served their country only when the law demanded it. Insulted by such people were those who gave everything, and who sought no other return than that which true love of country brings.

What happened in Rochester is by no means an isolated case. Exactly like such gentlemen as Herr Hos the "old leaders" are raising their voice, and are coming out of their hiding places in New York, in Chicago, in Buffalo, in Pittsburgh, in Detroit and everywhere. Blind as they were up to April, 1917, they continue, and imagine in their ignorance that with the armistice everything will slide back into the old rut. They seem unable to grasp the fact that American public opinion today, and for years to come will keep a sharp lookout for those who formerly were wont to talk of the duty of the German-American to unite the "glorious old fatherland" with the new, by means of the hyphen. They remind us strongly of the old leaders in Germany, the Bethmann Hollwegs, the Bernstorffs, the Zimmermanns, who are already eager to resume control in the new Germany as well.

German societies, if they wish to maintain themselves further, will have to purify themselves, will have to take the standpoint of one hundred percent Americanism—or disappear. Least of all, are they to assume the right of branding those who, during the last two years, have supported unceasingly, without any mental reservations whatsoever, the American war and peace aims. In the future it shall be one of *our* tasks to expose mercilessly all those who dare to raise again the old banner of the one time German-American National Alliance. In this we appeal to the public opinion of Rochester, through its press, not to permit men to be insulted who are 100 percent American, and who have proven that for them there exists no "glorious old fatherland" or a "new fatherland", but only the one—America.

BERNSTORFF NOT PERSONA GRATA

(*From Bulletin issued by the American Friends of German Democracy, Franz Sigel, Pres.*)

Count Johann Bernstorff will *not* be a member of the German Peace Commission in Paris. That seems, according to the latest reports, to be certain now; and that may be regarded as a proof that the Peace Commissioners will represent the *new* era and that only.

Anything else, a compromise in which a Bernstorff would have played a prominent part, would by all means have been disastrous to the new Germany. It is only surprising that it is still possible today to consider a Bernstorff seriously at all. The leaders of the present Germany could not possibly be so blind as not to know what an impression the pliant tool of the branded German propaganda in America would make on the Allies and especially on the representatives of the United States if this Count would appear in Paris and, wearing an innocent mask and wrapped in garments of spotless white, with his polite smile would address the Conference: "Here I am again. My name is still Bernstorff, but today I no longer serve the 'most gracious sovereign', the Kaiser,—during the night from the 11th to the 12th of November I became a republican. To Hell with the Kaiser! Your humble servant! . . ."

Bernstorff is quite capable of it. With an arrogance which is unique he has had a great deal to say in Berlin in the past weeks and, like his former companions Bethmann-Hollweg and Dr. Zimmermann, has granted interviews about everything under the sun, has wished the Kaiser would go to the devil and has actually imagined that the world, which has already pronounced him guilty of a share in the great crime, will be deceived by his smooth manners, will forget what he once was and will accept his love for democracy at its face value.

It will not be fully believed that Germany has shed her skin, that she has purged herself and become converted until she has relentlessly relegated to permanent oblivion the men who led her astray.

With what false conceptions of America Germany and German-Austria still deceive themselves about the true situation is proven by a notice taken from the "Wiener Arbeiterzeitung," according to which the "Vienna Bulletin", a publication which is intended for the English and the American press, announces that "in Viennese liberal (!) circles it is intended to induce German-Americans, who play an important role in political life, to hold lectures in Vienna about the republican form of government, republican institutions, etc." Invitations would be extended to the "'Republican' member of Congress William Sulzer (!) and the Democratic Congressman Richard Bartholdt!"

Aside from the fact that neither of these two men still are members of Congress, that the latter is not a Democrat and the former not a Republican, could the "liberal circles" not have hit upon anyone else besides Sulzer, who was forced to leave political life in the most ignominious manner, or Bartholdt, who was dragged into the abyss by the German propaganda of the defunct German-American Alliance and who brought the statue of Steuben to Potsdam and to the Kaiser in exchange for the statue of Frederick the Great?

The "Arbeiter-Zeitung" which calls the whole thing a "swindle and gossip of the coffeehouses" is correctly informed. If Americans of German descent are to inform the Germans on the other side on the principles of democracy it will be neither the Bernstorffs nor the Bartholdts or Sulzers, but men who for years past, when the others were still adherents of the Kaiser or greedy politicians, stood in the front ranks of the opponents of Prussian autocracy.

Shadow Huns and Others

(*Continued from page 18*)

of their country, or shall they be corrupted with the "Teutonic" interpretation of "economic determination?"

Prof. Charles A. Beard is one of the moving spirits of "The New School for Social Research," which is being advertised in the New York papers and which announces it has already acquired ownership of a building in which it is starting. Among the lecturers announced are Prof. James Harvey Robinson, Prof. Thorstein Veblen and Robert Bruere, who were all involved in an effort to raise $50,000 in June, 1918, for the defense of the I. W. W. leaders on trial in Chicago for seditious conspiracy.

Are people who defended the "conscientious objectors" and the criminal I. W. W. who sought to hinder the country in its conduct of the war against Germany, desirable instructors for the youth of America in efficient democracy, social research and economic readjustment?

Prof. Charles A. Beard still holds his job as Director of the Bureau of Municipal Research and Public Training, New York.

(*To be continued*)

The French Socialists and the Bolsheviki

(EDITORIAL FROM THE JANUARY, 1919, "AMERICAN FEDERATIONIST")

By SAMUEL GOMPERS

THE political party which claims to represent French labor has indorsed Bolshevism; strong influences are at work within the Confédération Générale du Travail working in the same direction. The French anti-war fanatics and pro-Bolshevists practically obtained control of the French Socialist party at the end of last July. At that time and up until the very day of German defeat, the slogan was "Peace Without Victory" and a compromise with German Kaiserism and militarism. At the National Congress of the party in October their control was re-affirmed and the official party organ passed from the hands of the so-called pro-war politician Renaudel, into the hands of the anti-war politician, Longuet, the grandson of Karl Marx.

In spite of all that the French Socialist party could do to prevent it, the war was continued until the German defeat which brought with it the German revolution. Did the socialists then confess their tremendous blunder or wrong? Not in the least. On the contrary, they claimed that Germany was not defeated by the valiant and heroic armies of the world's democracies, but by an impending German revolution due to the Soviet agitation in that country. They took the armistice as a sign of the failure of democratic internationalism and the victory of Soviet internationalism!

The armistice had not been signed three days when the executive committee of the French Socialist party met and passed the following amazing resolutions:

> The French Socialist party welcomes the German Republic and the taking over of the power in Prussia and the Confederated States by the working class.
>
> As in the Russia of the Soviets, Socialism has appeared in all Central Europe as the proper liquidator of the political and social situation left by the war.
>
> The party thus sees justified the confidence which it has always had in the action of peoples.
>
> Considering that certain of the conditions of the armistice leave the sharply defined fear that the Allied Governments have the intention of further extending the criminal military intervention against revolutionary Russia, the party declares that it will appeal to all the forces of the French proletariat to prevent the Socialism which is being born in Russia, as well as in Germany and Austria, from being crushed by coalitions of foreign capitalisms.
>
> The party urges the French working people most rigorously to rally to the support of their unions and Socialist groups, to sustain their class journals, and to keep themselves ready to make Socialism triumph in France as it has in the other countries of Europe.

This resolution which betrays not only France, but also the democratic League of Nations now in process of formation at Versailles, is as remarkable for what it says as what it omits to say. The only revolution it recognizes in Russia is the counter revolution by which the Bolsheviks overthrew the democratic government of Kerensky and by force of arms dissolved the constitutional assembly. It is assumed that the new government of Germany will be of a similar character and it is demanded that the Socialist minority, representing less than twenty-five per cent of the French people, should bring about a Soviet revolution in France!

All the achievements of the democratic revolutions of the past in France, America and England are ignored or perverted. It is held that there is precisely the same need for revolutions in those countries as there was in Russia and in Germany when the Czar and Kaiser were thrown out! There never was such a thing as a Declaration of Independence, or a French declaration of the rights of man. The universal suffrage of France, England and the United States is ignored as if it had never existed. The growing power of Labor in America, as well as in France and England, is implicitly denied. The assumption is that Labor and the masses generally are in the same position in the world's great democracies today as they were under the Kaiser and the Czar.

If this is not treason to democracy and treason to internationalism, then we would better take the word "treason" out of the dictionary.

Since the Peace Conference is being held in France, the French situation has a new importance, and deserves close attention. While the Longuet faction controls the party there is a strong opposition and the party is split down the middle, but unforunately politicians are almost as common in the so-called pro-war opposition as they are in the controlling pacifist element. It is especially unfortunate that even the most able and honorable Socialist leader, Albert Thomas, formerly Minister of Munitions, signed the Renaudel resolution. Cachin, formerly a strong pro-war man, has now become the editor of "L'Humanité," under the thumb of Longuet. Other leaders of the pro-war faction like Sambat, formerly a member of the war cabinet, are still less reliable. Even the group of forty, composed of Socialist members of the Chamber of Deputies who opposed the war under the leadership of Varenne and Compere-Morel, are apparently tied hard and fast to the principle of "party unity."

It is under this banner of party unity that the politicians have flourished. The party is obviously divided not into two, but into many groups of politicians who change their position from day to day. But it is always possible to justify any position whatever under the pretext of party unity—"my party, right or wrong," and party unity implies absolutely blind and unthinking support of the Socialist International.

Thus, loyalty to this "International" replaces loyalty to Labor.

The last hope of the French working class is with the Confédération Générale du Travail. Jouhaux, the Secretary of the Confédération, who partly followed Longuet against the American Federation of Labor at the Inter-Allied Conference of London, in September, now shows some signs of suffering from an over-dose of this Bolshevism. He has recently issued a scathing denunciation of revolutionary phrases, appealing for a positive program of reconstruction.

Further evidence of a return of wholesome common sense and of a sound labor instinct is given by a proclamation issued jointly by the Confédération Générale du Travail and the Socialist party during the armistice negotiations. This proclamation originated with the pro-war wing of the Socialist party and the Confédération Générale du Travail. It was adopted by the whole party, however, and then by another important political organization called the Union Républicaine.

Here is the importance of this resolution. It developed for the first time in several months a co-operation between labor organizations and other honest and radical democratic elements. But an even greater significance arises from the fact that merely because the Union Républicaine—a non-Socialist organization—signed the manifesto, the Socialist party met and the pacifist wing obliged it to pass a resolution attempting to withdraw the proclamation. However, the Confédération Générale du Travail refused to join in the withdrawal and the manifesto was posted all throughout France. This proclamation has a high value as showing the attitude of the Confédération Générale du Travail on peace terms. We, therefore, reproduce some of its important statements:

> The organizations which represent the most active forces of labor and democracy declare their entire agreement with the fundamentals formulated two years ago and the acts accomplished in the last fortnight by President Wilson. To employ the expression of the Confédération Générale du Travail, we declare that he has formulated the guarantees necessary to bring to the allied countries "the certainty that the injuries which have been done shall be repaired, that the peoples at present subject to the law of force shall be liberated, that the possibilities of a fresh war shall be definitely eliminated."
>
> This conception, common to our democracy (which has arisen from the French Revolution) and to President Wilson, excludes all ideas of conquest and annexation as it rejects any peace by the abandonment of justice.

The pro-Bolshevik element in control of the Socialist party wished to withdraw this proclamation. They have never dared to make open attack on President Wilson or to repudiate him in any important feature. They profess, hypocritically, to follow him. But at the same time they conduct a ceaseless agitation in favor of the Russian Soviets and of a Soviet revolution in France! They are fully aware that Mr. Wilson has personally vouched for the documents showing the secret alliance between the Bolshevik of Russia and the Kaiser and they know that he has successfully appealed to all civilized governments to repudiate the same Soviets. But they still profess to follow the leadership of President Wilson.

Longuet's daily organ, "Le Populaire," contains almost daily columns of defense of the Soviets and of all of their deeds and policies! Of course, about once a month Longuet writes a pro-Bolshevik article in which he is careful to state he does not indorse absolutely everything the Soviets do, but he is well aware that his paper daily gives the opposite impression, namely, of an indorsement which is not only unqualified but fanatically enthusiastic.

It is evident that these French Bolsheviki are in earnest as to their proposed insurrection. Nobody can doubt that they will take the first favorable opportunity—if any opportunity occurs—to attempt it.

The next few weeks will show whether the sane and loyally democratic elements in the French Federation of Labor will be able to resist this mischievous movement. At the beginning of the war the French Confédération Générale du Travail not only supported this war for democracy by an overwhelming majority but agreed to an International Labor Conference at the end of the war from which all politicians, whether socialist or non-socialist, shall be excluded. The French Socialist party has never secured any indorsement of the French Federation of Labor as having the sole and exclusive right to represent the working people politically. If the French Federation is true to its own highly creditable past of the last quarter century and especially to its splendid record during the first three years of the war, it will yet be able to foil this mad movement which can only result in putting back French labor for many years and possibly in wrecking the League of Nations which President Wilson is striving so desperately to bring into being.

Tyrrel Print, New York.

The National
Civic Federation Review

IV.   NEW YORK, MARCH 5, 1919   No. 10

BOLSHEVISM PROBED BY SENATE

MMARY OF THE TESTIMONY ADDUCED BY THE OVERMAN COMMITTEE SHOWS CONDITIONS WORSE THAN ANARCHY EXISTING IN RUSSIA AND THAT THOSE IN CONTROL INTEND TO IMPOSE THE RULE OF FORCE ON THE WORLD

AT the hearings before the Senate Committee investigating Bolshevism, which occupied most of February, e was unfolded the story of betrayal and ruin of Russia by Bolsheviki, under Lenine and tzky. It was an appalling re-al—that testimony of witnesses, luding United States Govern-nt representatives, clergymen, kers, educators, Americans and ssians, who had observed the gn of crime and mass murder in ssia first hand. That story of destruction of a great nation, a people utterly betrayed and lone by a small group of furious atics, is unparalleled in human tory. As bloody despots, Lenine l Trotzky stand unique among the brutal oppressors of man-d.

Just what happened in Russia s accounted by a number of eye-nesses, including the venerable randmother," Catherine Bresh-skaya herself, and each of om gave his own observations, individual report of Russia's gedy. Except for a few wit-sses—and those chiefly self-con-sed paid employees of the Bol-viki—the witnesses confirmed another. The corroborative dence proved irrefutable. It s clear "the truth about ssia" was at last being made own. In a spirit of impartial-, the Senate Committee called chief defenders and press nts of the Bolsheviki, includ-; Jorn Reed and Albert Rhys lliams. Mr. Williams, in his timony, freely admitted that olesale horrors had occurred, l, under cross examination, acknowledged t he could not disprove the testimony of those o had preceded him and who had beheld, der the rule of the Bolshevik, such terrorism l oppression as had not existed under the rule the Czar.

Where the Bolsheviki control, according to the nesses, government has ceased to exist in ssia. Even Socialism, as we interpret the rd, is opposed as bitterly as so-called capitalism. The Bolshevist rulers maintain their autocratic sway by means of armed criminals to whom they give unlimited license to prey on the people, and by a well-armed, well-fed aggregation of Letts and Chinese who once served in the Russian army.

All social laws have been broken down by this tyrannical force. Conditions beggaring description prevail. No man's life, no woman's virtue, is safe beyond the whim of the Red Guard. Trial by courts is a mockery. Starvation is rife. Murder is so common it passes unnoticed. Religion is banned, and the so-called "levelling of intelligence" idea fast is depopulating the country of those who might hope to save it.

That the Bolshevists are endeavoring to destroy the governments of other countries was brought out by the Overman Committee. Millions of rubles are being printed and scattered broadcast in this effort. Seizure of the great Russian gold reserve, of the crown jewels and works of art, and of the Rumanian gold reserve sent from Jassy for safekeeping, forms the basis of this paper currency even at a heavy discount, and finances the propaganda work in other countries.

No man possibly can foresee the outcome. In the early days of Bolshevism the nobility and landed proprietors lost everything. Now the armed criminal minority is attacking the working classes, the small business men and the thrifty peasants. The Senate hearings brought out the fact that less than ten per cent of the population favor Bolshevism, yet because of their terrorist tactics the Bolsheviki are able to dominate the other ninety per cent of the people.

David R. Francis, Ambassador to Russia, who returned on the George Washington with President Wilson, in a statement made in Washington on February 26, said:

"Bolshevism succeeded because it came just at the time that the soldiers were being demobilized and when the people were wearied with war. It could not have succeeded at any other time in my opinion. It gained headway because it promised the end of war, also land and bread, and now the people are realizing that these promises have failed to materialize. It is difficult to distinguish between the various brands of socialism in Russia. There are so many slight differences.

"Lenine is the brains of the Bolsheviki. Trotzky is not such a power. He just plays to

CATHERINE BRESHKOVSKAYA

the circumstances, and again and again lands on his feet."

Ambassador Francis said there could be no doubt that German money was used to enable the present Bolshevist Government to gain control.

"They used their money to corrupt Russia just as they would have used money to overthrow the governments of America, of France, or of England," he said. "They are opposed to everything that is of the nature of an organized government. They call all governments capitalistic."

He was convinced that the Bolsheviki were sending money and propagandists into all countries. They were coining rubles without any thought of the value or consequence and were selling them to the best advantage. This money was finding its way into other countries.

"Until there is a solution for that problem," continued Mr. Francis, "I do not see how there can be any peace for the world. If something is not done to save Russia, the Germans are certain to gain control of the country and its people and Germany with her soldiers and the soldiers of Austria would become a powerful force again. Something must be done to save Russia."

BABUSHKA'S TALE OF HORROR

Catherine Breshkovskaya, "the little Grandmother of the Russian revolution," and familiarly known as Babushka, furnished heartrending word pictures of her native land. She was forced to leave Russia by the Bolshevik régime and is in this country to enlist aid for the restoration of order and adequate relief of the suffering women and children. Among other things she testified:

"Our greatest, deepest, most immediate need is the creation of conditions under which the Russian people will be able to convoke an All-Russian Constituent Assembly. Russia will never be quiet and satisfied until her representatives, freely chosen by the entire population, will establish a Constitution for the State, will lay the foundation for a stable, democratic government, insuring laws that accord with the will and desires of the Russian people. The demand for a Constituent Assembly was one of the main aspirations of the Russian revolution. It was on the eve of its realization when the Bolshevist revolt, in November, 1917, tore out of the hands of the people the beautiful possibility to make laws for themselves, to trace the path for their future, to construct a new life in accordance with the interests of the masses, to strengthen peace and insure the common welfare. The Constituent Assembly, elected by the entire Russian people on the basis of universal, direct, equal, and secret suffrage, was dispersed by the Bolsheviki with bayonets.

"The opportunity was lost, and our masses, simple-minded, naïve, and credulous, tired out by their past misfortunes, became a prey to the base and rapacious instincts of selfish, ambitious and merciless people. Under the circumstances, Russia faces a long and cruel struggle with all the evil which has entered her life. She has to suffer all the pains inevitable in the conditions of a people clearing its way to a better future. Many opposing forces bar this way; they check the normal course of events and make the people suffer and suffer more in their struggle to get the right issue out of the insurmountable chaos.

"Flooded with tears and blood, Russia moans and cries out to the world. She is a living body, and her tortures cannot be looked upon cold-bloodedly as an extraordinary, never-before-witnessed experiment in social evolution. She is alive, and every pore of her body is shedding blood."

Frightful pictures of Russian conditions were drawn by Dr. W. C. Huntington, who was the commercial attaché of the American Embassy

WILLIAM C. HUNTINGTON

in Petrograd in 1916. He was especially careful not to cumber the committee's record with hearsay evidence, and offered many documents in substantiation of his assertions.

Here are some of the things Dr. Huntington showed conclusively.

He produced a copy of an order addressed in September to all Soviets in Russia which called for the slaughter "en masse" of all persons who failed to support the Bolshevist régime. He said that executions were as a rule carried out at night and in darkened places like cellars, the firing squads using Maxim silencers.

Three letters were read into the record by him, all of them from a person of the highest standing, who is still in Russia and whose name for that reason was not disclosed for publication. These letters painted a terrible picture of conditions in the Russian capital.

Dr. Huntington said that at the present time not more than 8 per cent. of the Russian people were in favor of the Bolsheviki. They were held in submission, he added, by terroristic means and by a mercenary force of soldiers made up principally of Letts and Chinese. He said that he left Moscow on August 16 last, accompanied by officials of other allied nations, in each instance the nation concerned leaving one official behind to care for its affairs and nationals. In the case of the United States, the official left behind was Consul General Poole.

"I was ordered to Russia in 1916 by the United States Government," said Dr. Huntington, "as the Commercial Attaché of the American Embassy. My mission was to aid, as far as I could, in the development of Russo-American trade relations. I took up my quarters in the American Embassy at Petrograd and was in constant touch with Ambassador Francis and his staff, and so had unusual opportunities for observation."

Dr. Huntington was present during the entire time of the transition of Government from the control of Kerensky's faction to the Trotzky-Lenine group of agitators.

LEADERS HATE AMERICA

"Is it not true," asked Senator King of Utah, "that the Bolshevist leaders who led the treason against the Allies hate America as much as they hate any of the other Allies?"

"Yes, that is true," was the answer. "It is also true that the Bolshevist group accepted German money to use for propaganda purposes. They were, of course, ready to handle Germany in their own way just as Germany was ready to use them to the best advantage. It was a case of two crooks, each using the other to gain an end."

"Why did they hate us so?" asked Senator Overman.

"For two principal reasons. First, because we are not a Soviet Government, and, secondly, because we went into the war," Dr. Huntington replied.

In answer to a question Dr. Huntington told of the executions of persons who met the displeasure of the Soviets.

"It is an absolute reign of terror, is it not?" Senator Overman asked.

"Yes, and the Bolsheviki do not attempt to deny that such is the case," was the answer. "They admit it and then try to justify the actions taken."

"Is there any freedom of the press in Russia?"

"Absolutely none. The only papers that are permitted to be published in Russia are Bolshevist papers. All others are suppressed.

"At the present only those who are listed as among the proletariat are permitted to vote. The children of the others, it is stated, may be permitted to vote when they become of age provided they take the Bolshevist viewpoint."

"What about the nationalization of industries, of the factories?" was asked.

"In nearly every instance," Dr. Huntington replied, "these factories have come to grief. When the decree of nationalization was issued the factories were placed in charge of committees of workmen. Then came factions and friction and quarrels between them. One would have supplies, another would not, and the result is that few if any factories are running now.

"The principal industry left in Russia now is printing paper money. I have seen the complete overthrow in Russia of all that we know in human life as it exists here at home. I have seen a condition of absolute chaos in all human relations develop in Russia. I have seen conditions attained that amount to nothing less than a reign of absolute terrorism.

"Those in authority take any measures they see fit no matter how unscrupulous. Men and women are held as hostages. Their army is made up principally of Lettish mercenaries and Chinese. They are also using some Austro-Hungarians. To the so-called army have been added other citizens who are forced to serve through threats against their wives and little children.

"The armies they are reported to have are not fired by loyalty to a great cause but are to a large extent made up of men whose condition is such that they have joined in order to be clothed and fed."

Dr. Huntington said that 85 per cent. of the Russian population was of the peasant class and that 7 per cent. of the population were workmen. This 92 per cent., he said, no longer sympathized with the revolution and was held in check by the terrorist machine.

WHAT MR. SIMMONS SAW

Probably the most detailed report of the horrors of the Lenine-Trotzky régime was given by R. E. Simmons, an agent of the Department of Commerce. He was a victim of Bolshevist methods; saw things first hand, and was able to get reports from many parts of the country. Mr. Simmons also succeeded in bringing out valuable Soviet documents that prove the object of the whole movement is a breakdown of all existing law in favor of a small armed minority.

Fragmentary press reports of Bolshevist terrorism and the testimony of other witnesses to the same end were verified absolutely by Mr. Simmons. He left Archangel last November. It took the committee two days to hear all he wished to say.

Even he, accredited to the American Embassy, was cast into prison for two weeks and was liberated only through the intervention of the Swedish Consul General as the American matic officers were helpless. Most of Mr. ons' narrative to the committee is worthy being reprinted and scattered broadcast as icating just what Bolshevism means.

Among other things he said:

'The Bolshevist revolution has as its object putting into power of a few over the many. e worst feature of their program, and this ature is always emphasized, is that of the rit of class hatred. In every corner of Rus- these people are preaching the religion of ss hatred.

ATTACKING MIDDLE CLASS

"In Petrograd I witnessed on one occasion undressing of a refined woman by several diers of the Red Guard. It was in the Nevsky ospekt at about 6:30 p. m. I heard the eam of the woman, who had been taken into side street, and saw the soldiers steal the thes from off her body. The forcible disrob- g was accompanied on the part of the soldiers th insulting language. This was just one case d most of the women subjected to these in- gnities were women not of the aristocracy, but the middle class.

"Bolshevism is directed against every decent an, woman and child who will not bow down the dictates of Trotzky and Lenine. In other ords, they are now fighting the very class that the beginning they said they were struggling put on top and in control. They are fighting y and night now to put on top not the pro- tariat as we know it but the very scum of manity.

"And they are working with all the devil- ness they have to spread their doctrines roughout the world. As late as November 8 last Lenine said in Moscow, and I have a opy of the statement with me, that they had ympathizers with great organizations behind hem in Scandinavia, in Germany, in England, nd in France. He also named this country as ne of the targets they were aiming at.

LENINE THREATENS TO CRUSH U. S.

"'The power that has crushed Germany,' he aid, 'is also the power that will in the end rush England and the United States.'

"On another occasion and within the last few eeks, Lenine said that this year will decide hether or not Bolshevism is to triumph in ther parts of the world.

"And I have the information, given to me in etrograd, that already the agents of Trotzky nd Lenine have been sent to this country, and hat they have in operation a central bureau of ropaganda somewhere in this country. This ropaganda is false and at the same time in- idious. I have been astounded at some of the eople who are willing to take it seriously. nly a few days ago I was at the La Salle Hotel n Chicago, and a Major of the United States rmy told me that they had found a great mass f this treasonable stuff in a camp where large umbers of American soldiers are being de- mobilized."

"Do you know of any agents who have been ent here by the Bolshevist Government?" asked enator Wolcott.

"I heard in Petrograd that a man known as lbert Rhys Williams was one of them. I heard im speak in the shadow of the Capitol a few ights ago, in which speech he lauded the Bol- heviki. This man, I was informed, was em- loyed by the Bolshevist Government and was ent here to organize their propaganda bureau. f I gave my authority it would mean the death f certain persons in Russia. It was of the ighest. I know of agents who were sent to enmark, Sweden and other European coun- ries.

"In the first prison I was in I came in con- act with a great many people and I talked with hem and got their stories. I had expected to ind that most of the prisoners were of the nobility or else were men of considerable means. Such, however, was not the case. They were for the most part of the middle class, mechanics, printers, shopkeepers, peasant farmers, loyal soldiers, merchants, etc. I talked with them all and fully 80 per cent. of them did not know why they were in prison. They had simply been arrested and no reasons given.

"The head of the committee that condemned these men was a Lett named Peters. He had lived in England at one time and, with a man named Eiduk of Vologda, is considered the most bloodthirsty monster in Russia. The Italian Consul General in Moscow told me that on one occasion he saw Peters sign the death warrants of seventy-one men without even taking the trouble to see what their names were or to find out what they were charged with.

"While I was in jail twenty-three men were taken out of the cell in order, it was said, to make room for twenty-six other men who had just been arrested. The twenty-three were never heard of again.

WOMEN FORCED TO DIG GRAVES

"I wish to state that it is through the use of arms that men and women are compelled to work at any labor that the Bolshevist authorities assign them to do. Great numbers of these people are old or frail, persons utterly unfit for such work as they are forced to do at the point of bayonets or guns. They are lawyers, office men, and other persons whose work in normal time was of what we may term a mental nature. The women suffer the same fate. They are forced into the heaviest sort of manual labor. Many are used to dig graves, and I have heard of many who were forced to dig the graves of their own relatives and friends who met the displeasure of the Bolsheviki.

"In Petrograd one day I saw one of these gangs at work in the street breaking with pickaxes the frozen snow. In this gang was a young woman of evident gentle breeding and of frail physique. I offered to help her, but she declined to be an object of charity. She told me everything her family possessed had been appropriated by the Bolsheviki and she had to dig ice out of the streets or perish. It was the only kind of work that the Bolsheviki would permit her to do. This is the case of great numbers of others of the same class."

In answer to a question by Senator Overman, Mr. Simmons told of the hunger conditions in Petrograd, of people dying in the streets. He corroborated the testimony of previous witnesses regarding this phase of Russian horror.

"A few words more regarding the Red Guards," he continued. "The ages for service in the Red Army are from 16 to 52 years. As I have stated, it is a force organized by force and at the point of bayonets.

"Another phase of Bolshevism and one not hitherto referred to at this hearing is what the Bolsheviki call the 'Levelling of Intelligence.' This forms one of the most ghastly effects of the system. Persons, under the regulation, who are considered to have more intelligence than is considered healthy for the cause of Lenine and Trotzky are arrested, thrown into prison, and I am certain in great numbers of instances put to death simply because they were considered of higher intelligence than the leaders approve of. This one phase should indicate to any thinking man or woman in America what Bolshevism is and what its spread means to the civilized world."

REVOLTING TREATMENT OF WOMEN

Of most intense human interest, no doubt, is the Bolshevist attitude toward women, and here Mr. Simmons offered most conclusive evidence of the attempts to break down all moral and religious law. He furnished the committee copies of two Soviet decrees.

The first decree read by Mr. Simmons was dated March 15, 1918, and was issued by the Anarchist Soviet, which was charged by Lenine and Trotzky with the Government of the City of Saratov.

The second decree, read by Mr. Simmons, was issued by the Soviet of the City of Vladimir.

A similar "project of provisional rights in connection with the socialization of women in the City of Hvelinsk and vicinity" has been published in the Local Gazette of the Workers' and Soldiers' Deputies, Mr. Simmons said.

"Gentlemen," added Mr. Simmons, as he finished reading the Vladimir decree, "these documents speak for themselves. God and morality are unknown to the Bolsheviki, and everything that makes life decent and worth living is in jeopardy if this thing is permitted to go ahead."

TELLS OF THE HUN'S SHARE

Germany's connection with the Bolsheviki was placed squarely by Mr. Simmons in his testimony when he said:

"All of the terrorism that reigns in Russia, I believe to have been instigated officially in Germany. I am convinced that Lenine and Trotzky were put in power by Germany. The fact that I am now to disclose I am certain has never appeared in the public prints. My informant is the man who acted for von Bethmann-Hollweg the former Imperial Chancellor. His story was told under oath in the office of the American Consul General in Moscow.

"In 1914, when the war started, this man was in Germany. He is a Russian and a Socialist. The Germans would not permit him to leave the country. He is a conservative Socialist, one who advocates evolution instead of revolution. He swears that one day when in Berlin, he was approached by an agent of the German Government, who told him that the Imperial Chancellor desired to see him.

"When he saw the Chancellor he was informed that the Imperial Government was desirous that he go to Switzerland and make a study of and later report to the Chancellor regarding the various Socialist groups then making their headquarters in that country. The German Government, he was informed, particularly desired reliable information regarding the most radical of those groups. He was told that Germany stood ready to place 5,000,000 marks to the credit of the proper group, which group was to send its agents into Russia for propaganda work.

LENINE EFFECTED GERMAN PLANS

"The Russian selected for the mission to Switzerland, before accepting the proposition, consulted with an American who was in Hamburg and was advised to accept. So he went to Switzerland and mixed with all the various groups and subsequently made a 300-page report to the Chancellor. In that report he stated that the group led by Lenine was by far the most radical, but recommended that it should not be selected because, he said, he was certain that chaos and anarchy would follow in Russia if they gained the upper hand.

"This man was commended by the German Government for his report, and was himself permitted then to return to Russia, where he affiliated himself with the Kerensky faction. Subsequently Lenine left Switzerland, and, under German protection, crossed Germany and entered Russian territory.

"Whether or not Lenine actually entered into an understanding with the Germans I am not in a position to say. He did, however, do the very things that Germany at that time desired to be done. In subsequent writings I think that Lenine almost acknowledges that there was an understanding. I also think that the facts go far toward proving the truth of the Sisson papers. I have also been informed on the highest authority that proof exists that the Bol-

(Continued on page 19)

Housing of Workers in a Manufacturing City

EFFORT TO SOLVE PROBLEM ON LASTING BASIS—LIQUID HOME INVESTMENTS—LOCATION—SURROUNDINGS—SIZE—STYLE—EQUIPMENT—MAINTENANCE AND COST

(Aime Dupont.)

PHILIP HISS,
Chairman Housing Section, Committee on Labor, Advisory Commission, Council of National Defense.

(When Mr. Samuel Gompers, Chairman of the Committee on Labor, Advisory Commission, Council of National Defense, inaugurated the movement to relieve congestion in munition making and shipbuilding centers due to the advent of large numbers of new workmen, soon after we entered the war and authorized an investigation of conditions to be made by Mr. Philip Hiss, Chairman of his Section on Housing, Bridgeport naturally received especial consideration because of the vast number of contracts placed by the Government in that important manufacturing city. The majority of the employers were associated together, in the Bridgeport Housing Company, in a joint effort to improve conditions for the wage earners. When Mr. Hiss reported that local capital would be unable to meet the cost of housing under abnormal war conditions, Mr. Ham and other members of his company, including representatives of banking and manufacturing, were several times called upon to testify, both before the Advisory Commission, and the Housing Committee of the Council of National Defense of which Mr. Otto M. Eidlitz was chairman. At the first hearing, held at the request of Mr. Gompers, Mr. Daniel Willard, Chairman of the Advisory Commission, asked: "Why does not the manufacturer house the workers himself from motives of economy?" It was shown that in placing contracts, government officials had only one concern,—an agreement on the part of the producer to deliver at the stipulated time, that, as usual, the responsibility of housing was left with the employer, and that one reason why he had not given greater attention in the past to making comfortable homes available was the vast amount of capital necessary to start even a modest development. How to finance such undertakings and the disposition of the government houses erected as the result of the efforts above-mentioned are serious problems for future solution. Mr. Ham especially emphasized the former at a recent conference on post-war social readjustment problems held under the auspices of the Woman's Department of The National Civic Federation, the chairman of the program for the day being Miss Gertrude Robinson Smith. Additional articles on the subject of housing will follow. The necessity of giving consideration to improved housing conditions is receiving world-wide attention as evidenced by a recent address made by Mr. Bonar Law at Glasgow when he said, in expressing his faith in the ability of the people of Scotland successfully to combat the Bolshevist element: "The only danger of anything approaching revolution in Great Britain was if the conditions of life became intolerable and whatever the risk from a financial standpoint, the housing problem had to be dealt with."—Editor).

HOME OWNERSHIP AND LABOR MOBILITY

By PHILIP HISS

BROADLY speaking, a building program allowing the industrial worker to purchase his house on terms slightly above the renting price, extending over a period of thirty to fifty years, as in England, is a safe method of financing home building in this country. It is necessary to construct a house that will last from fifty to sixty years without excessive repairs, and care must be taken to choose a locality which will remain fit for habitation during a similar period.

A man should not be tied to a given plant by the purchase of a home. To give the worker the full benefit of ownership in a community so that he can exercise all civic rights, and his wife and children may enjoy socially what only a fairly permanent residence can afford, and yet permit him to be free and not a "slave" as has been suggested, I believe he could purchase shares in a homes company, to be formed on terms just both to the seller and the purchaser, and yet the stock could be disposed of as easily as stocks on the Exchange and be just as liquid. The worker need not own his house. It is his while he is in it; but he may own shares in the homes company and when he wants to move the company can take back the shares for which he has paid. I do not mean the company which employs him.

It is my opinion that the Federal Government should be placed in position, by proper legislation, to advance money to communities, companies or individuals for the stimulation of home building for the industrial communities. In facing the housing of employees, it is necessary for the employer to consider a cost almost as great as that of the plant itself. For example, a manufacturer with a factory costing $2,500,000 and employing 1,000 workers, could not provide for proper housing for less than the cost of the plant. It is not always convenient to capitalize such a housing development. Therefore the Federal bill, embodying the foregoing ideas, which has been presented to the House of Representatives, should receive favorable consideration. Precedence for such legislation can be found in the Federal Farm Loan Act and the Good Roads Bill of the Department of Agriculture, where similar advances were made to communities or individuals. The problem of the disposition of the government-owned houses may result in the prolongation of the Bureau of Industrial Housing another year, carrying it through a period during which peace housing legislation may be enacted.

The urgent necessity of a great housing program as the first thing to be considered was advanced by David Lloyd George at the inception of the campaign in connection with the recent general election in England.

W. H. HAM,
Manager Bridgeport Housing Company.

HOUSING—DEMOCRACY'S BALANCE WHEEL

By W. H. HAM

THE need of a new method of handling homes for workingmen is very apparent and the modus operandi should be thoroughly considered by careful thinkers along the line of proper financing. My somewhat new theory of ownership in securities, I hope may contribute something toward the solution of the problem in a permanent way for several generations. It is not worth studying if it is hopelessly left for each generation to take up anew.

SAFE INSTALMENT LIQUID HOME INVESTMENTS

To have a permanent investment in homes, amortized by the slow process of the continual drop-wearing-away-the-stone variety, would be ideal. If the investment is permanent, safe and natural, it will be liquid.

Loans on homes are sometimes paid and sometimes not, and still we consider home investment problems as most important in our progress toward Americanizing our new people. We must standardize loans and payments. We must relate the money part of the workingman's home to some better form of payment plan than is now common.

If we are to try seriously to solve the home problem fairly for him who invests and who lives in the home, we must probe deep into these attributes of home—location, size, style, surroundings, materials, equipment, maintenance and cost.

LOCATION

Where shall the man getting forty cents an hour live? When this same man gets fifty cents an hour, will he demand a different location for his home? Is the location any handicap to the ambitious worker in his effort to advance? When he ceases to be a wage earner in the sense that John Mitchell defines "wage earner", will he be obliged to move anyway?

Is society of such a form that the man and woman and boy and girl are stamped with the locality or not? Why do the nice young women, who come to rent our small houses, tell us that

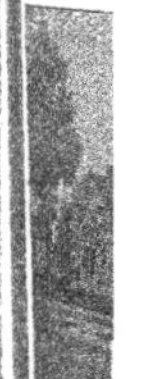

ey like the house very much and it certainly pretty, but "you know I don't want to live on e east side, my friends are all on the west le. Why don't you build one just like it on ch and such a street?" and I have been promng them all along that I would, and now by e help of the United States Government I ve done so.

Now that part of it seems to be settled in idgeport and we have houses in all parts of e town and I believe it is fairly well determined that friendship consideration is necesry in regard to location, but can the man ho earns forty cents an hour live next door to e man who earns sixty cents an hour if the rroundings are studied properly? Can their ildren play together?

Suppose we have built the pretty little home n the west side of town, how long will a nice ttle place on the west side be a nice little ome? Will the transfer of business change all is part of town? We must ask ourselves first all this question: "How can we fix a part town so that it will stay fixed for a period 10, 20, 30, 40 or 50 years?" If we are to ake a permanent investment, we must do this om the standpoint not only of the protection values but from that of continuity of sentient surrounding the home.

ZONING RECOMMENDED

I see no alternative for a successful conclusion of a proper housing movement except to ne our cities. We must call in the doctor who n zone us right or we shall make a mess of it. ow many zone doctors do you know? Is it the chitect, the town planner, the engineer, the ty alderman, the politician, the committee om the Chamber of Commerce, or a lot of emen who fix things, who are to be called to cate successfully the man and his family by s fireside which can remain where it was originlly until the elms grow to full size in the yard?

SIZE

How big is a house to be—just to fit the bride nd groom who have both worked in the chain actory? Will the same size, which is necessary ow, fit the same couple when their grandchilren come to visit grandma for Thanksgiving inner? In my boyhood home a family with mbitions solved this problem by adding an ell the house for each child and the house adanced from the cottage which it was 30 years go to a possession of more than seven gables. Shall we require the same treatment with ur permanent homes? Must the house change size or shall we move the family to a house hat fits in the same locality and surroundings? We have studied this with the result that it is he "house of eight children," additions havng been added when needed.

STYLE

What style house will last and be in good taste for 100 years? Will the mansard or the Mid-Victorian or the Queen Anne satisfy those who dictate styles in houses and also satisfy those to whom styles of houses are dictated? I remember all three of these styles and their abandonment since I was a boy. Is there anything in your father's house that is just right for you, or did your grandfather have better judgment? How about your great-grandfather? Or shall we build a "bungle" house? Shall we follow some magazine until the permanent American style sets in? Have we an architect style doctor who will wager his last dollar on a single type of house which will suit himself for thirty years and at the same time maintain its value in the mind of others? Why did the wealthy man in the last of the eighteenth century, about 1780, change the style of house from that of his grandfather, which had been built several hundred years and by everybody of his acquaintance, to that of the grandfather of Achilles, formerly of Athens. I mean, why did the heavy Doric building of the Greek Revival period spread like measles in the United States among the home builders?

It was the effort of a young architect of Paris to convince the older architects of a mistake they had made which caused a new form of building, exterior and interior, for the wealthy man's home in most of our cities. This student at the Ecole des Beaux Arts was granted leave of absence with funds to visit Greece and measure some of the excavated columns of the old temples on the Acropolis. On his return he made the startling statement that the Greek had no measured enthesis to his column, but that the line drawn by the Greek was a free-hand line independent of mathematics. This was contrary to the belief of architects, and a second student of ability was sent to check the measurements. His findings confirmed the position of the first student, and as a result of the controversy there was published a popular book on the orders of Greek Architecture. This reached America and found our carpenter architect ready for the new line of models and decorations for his buildings, and the important change from the house of the old English and American Colonies to the temple of the Greek God was made. The small house was copied from the big house as is always done, and the working man's home thereafter followed the order of the Greek temple for a period of thirty to forty years. It is pretty hard to say what we are going to have in buildings. The brownstone fronts of 1850 were considered just right in New York and marked social position. However, when Oscar Wilde said they were inartistic, you stopped building them.

We are treading on explosive ground when we establish in our minds anything in the form of a permanent style, but we have certainly this problem as a part of the housing movement in connection with a permanent investment.

Roofs of houses are their hats and umbrellas. Philadelphia, New York, Boston and many other cities just frankly left off the hat and used an umbrella only. Boston had a hard time getting over the hat or roof idea and put on a sort of visor for a cap. Why did we stop building roofs, anyway? New York would answer that she was building so high that a roof was not seen from the ground and, therefore, was of no use, but for the small houses which we are discussing, are we going to have roofs or not? Philadelphia has omitted them frankly.

MATERIALS

Materials for construction are troublesome. The newly discovered processes of building are innumerable. If you observe carefully in New England, every town, you will find, has one octagonal house, usually built of stone. All the others are either stone, brick or wood. But an inventor brought out a machine which would make metal lath so fast that they had to sell it some way and then some architect, who could not resist his client, put it on the outside of a house and we had a near-stone house, called stucco. The first fellow who did this was honest and galvanized the lath and got his final pay on the contract before the lath began to rust, but the painting member of the building trade had been injured because he had lost the right to paint the exterior once in three to five years and, therefore, he invented the method of painting the lath and that used up paint and kept the lath from rusting, at least while it was in transit, and the bars were all down for the building of stucco houses cheap and they are built that way.

Edison told us how to build a house in twenty-four hours, by casting the walls, floors and the doors and the windows, beds, etc., all in a form that was used across the street for a neighbor's house, *i. e.*, uniform. The wild fire of tangled thought on housebuilding by bond salesmen who had not made good and other promoters has hardly been quenched by the sane builders. Some concrete houses have been built, about 90 per cent. too many. However, we must lay a wager on the proper materials with which to build five billion dollars' worth of homes in the next two or three years. I am not ready for the monolithic house.

INTERIORS

Let the material man and the inventor scrap about the walls, roof and partitions. It is what is in the house that makes a home. The little bride, who had an electric chafing dish given her, must have the socket under the table on her

Two-family houses under construction. United States Government housing.

Connecticut Development. Built around children's playground. Also used by men and boys for small games and soccer football. Cut shows front view group dwellings, 2, 3, 4 and 5 rooms each. Occupied by 140 families. Central heating plant. Workmen walk home to lunch.

Rear view. Connecticut Development. Rear pia popular. Yards divided by hedges.

side, the pretty green cord cross the rug to save cutting a hole in it, and it must be arranged so as not to trip her up; she asks us why we don't make such things without a string to them anyway, and the answer is: "They will do it before long." She also wants to know: "Why does my light in the front hall get dim when I use my washing machine? How can I get the grease out of the sink? The electric door opener won't work when it rains? The furnace heats the cellar too hot and when the wind is in the East, I can't heat the dining-room, if I have the draft shut the way my husband makes me run the furnace. I wish you would take the old thing out, anyway, and let me heat with electricity."

PLUMBING

Equipment in a house is a big job with all the new things. When I went to college we had no plumber north of Manchester, N. H. Society demanded bathing thirty years ago, and think of all the trouble in home building since! Seventy-five per cent. of the houses in the United States have no plumbing and no hope of getting any until the manufacturers can catch up making fixtures for the other 25 per cent. Be that as it may, the new house, which is the working man's home, will have all the plumbing it will hold.

SURROUNDINGS

"Let's go out in the garden, that is the only way to enjoy our home," says the young bride. Shall we go and see what was unbelievable five years ago by half of the English-speaking people? That is a kitchen garden on a city lot with enough vegetables to last all winter, by proper canning and drying, thanks to the women's part in the War Saving program. "Oh, yes," she says, "my architect was all right, but you know he didn't plan the garden, the ground planner did that; he found the soil good and by making a curved street let the sun in. It is very nice and the lady across the street is just as fortunate as I am."

COSTS

My feelings would dictate that the bride be left with her house and garden and with no thought of repairs and no bills to pay but the problem, which hits 90 per cent. of us, is one that is connected very closely with money and payments. Does all of this cost so much that we cannot afford it? This question spoils lots of home dreams. What can we afford for home life in America?

BRIDGEPORT'S METHOD

Can we make up our minds to build a home that will last until it is paid for or until the elms grow to full size in the yard? If so, we have to choose, as I did in Bridgeport, Conn., in connection with the building of 1,000 homes for workingmen, materials, style of architecture, and location. I use brick for the exterior because the brick house that was built in Portsmouth, N. H., 100 years ago is in good condition today and salable at 100 cents on the dollar and brick has been used since Babylon was small. If you will let the mason alone and not mix him up with curtain patterns he will lay it just right if you get the brick just as soon as it comes from the kiln. It costs about $150 more per family for brick than wood—about $125 more for a good slate roof than for wood shingle. Let us have a roof. Cost is the only reason that we avoid one and the only questions that are fair to ask are whether we need one and can afford one. We are building in Bridgeport 750 homes with roofs and 332 without. These 332 are in apartments three stories high.

Let us locate in various parts of town and be careful to surround ourselves with such natural barriers that we have proper restrictions and enough people to see the kind of houses we are building and by and by copy them. We may have a new style like our great grandfather would have built before he ran away from the historic house of the colonies to follow the Greek Temple.

FINANCIAL PLAN

Let us sell a piece of land and put it in the deed that this land shall be thus and so for 50 years, and build a house to cost about $5,000. If we figure out that someone must have 4½ per cent. on his money during 50 years and make up our minds to put a sinking fund aside in some savings institution at a proper interest rate, it will pay off the indebtedness incurred in 50 years. Home bonds at 4½ per cent. interest, with a sinking fund, ought to be on the market in every city if a home can be built that will stay put long enough to have the advantage of the sinking fund method of retiring the money.

Let us build a brick house, with a slate roof, follow the style of our colonial ancestors and lay a 50-year wager that it will remain by having it in the deed, and put the burden of proving that we were wrong up to the next generation with the statement that it suited us and let the fellow, who works in the chain factory making automobile tire chains, and his wife who did, too, until the baby came, live in that house and pay the cost of interest and repair charges, taxes and other reasonable expenses and buy the investment. If he makes a success and finds it necessary to make a change to increase his earning capacity and wishes to his investment, another man will come along buy it.

This kind of an arrangement will allow us start the young married couples in a smal number of rooms in group houses with three bath for the first two or three years, and t have four rooms and later five or six; if family demands a more open method of livi on account of children, the bonds can be tur in toward equity in a separate house.

I want to quote from Dr. Tucker, Presid for a long time of Dartmouth College, in very careful thesis on the mind of the w earner. He says: "Mobility is, in the ear stages of the development of the wage earn the source of his strength. He can eas change to his interest. No advantage can taken of his fixity. He can put himself, wi out loss, into the open market. He can av himself at once of the highest market price, p vided his change of place does not affect juriously his fellow workers in the union, exception of growing concern. But in the m advanced stages of labor, the wage earner ga the privilege of localizing himself, and in doing he takes a long step in the direction full and free citizenship. A good deposit in savings bank adds to his social value but t value is greatly enhanced by exchanging it a good house."

LIQUID HOME INVESTMENTS

The purchase of the home too large for ea occupancy and the demand of added inco from some source to support the investme should be studied in such a way as to allow t worker to find himself before tying him do with a hard bargain on a house, and it is f this reason that I have emphasized strongly t liquid character of the home investment. T time has come, in my opinion, to offer to t new investor a share in ownership of proper on a basis which will be easy to acquire, starti with $10. We can stimulate saving quicker b offering an attractive investment in liquid for and it will be liquid if it is worthy of a marke The advantage of salability must be made clea

PAY ROLL AND DIVIDEND OBLIGATIONS

In Bridgeport we have apartments, re houses, independent houses. Playgrounds f every apartment group and proper surround ings for the homes are arranged so that both t front and rear of the houses are made livab inside and out, with every window letting sunlight. We may be able to show the new in vestor, the wage earner, an opportunity to bu

(*Continued on page 18*)

Shadow Huns and Others

By T. EVERETT HARRÉ

Part VI

M GERMANISM TO BOLSHEVISM

OVERNOR W. L. HARDING, of Iowa, was recently appealed to by a combination of patriotic bodies of his state to ider his intention of disbanding the Iowa Council of Defense, because, according to s in the war saving stamp and war relief ttee movements, pro-Germanism had ıg up in various sections since the signing e armistice. From other States have come ar reports. So flagrant has been the propaa designed to estrange the United States Great Britain that the American Friends erman Democracy, an organization com1 of loyal citizens of German birth or exion, undertook a campaign against these ious efforts.

his book, "The German Conspiracy in rican Education,"* Captain Gustavus ıger, formerly of the Military Intelligence he United States Army, pertinently des:

et us not delude ourselves into thinking German propaganda has been extirpated. re the hot blast of public indignation it t under cover, merely to await its opporty. That opportunity has now come. With signing of the armistice the strain of war been relaxed, and public opinion, until rely concentrated upon obtaining an overlming victory, is again disintegrating. The on followed unquestioningly the leadership he President in the prosecution of the war inst Germany. Now that hostilities have a suspended, the terms of peace are slipping , the arena of public debate and into the l of practical politics. The pro-German ator, the German agent, the spy, the radical alist, the Bolshevist and others who use ouflaged theories only to mask their true poses, are again lifting their heads. Again ticians are placating the German vote for vate gain. Unless the nation maintains its lance and is as single-minded in its peace s as in the prosecution of the war, the sacri3 of the last four years may prove to be ely the introduction to an even greater gedy in the future."

KULTUR IN AMERICAN EDUCATION

aptain Ohlinger's volume is, one of the most quate and illumining exposes of the German paganda, especially as it concerned the cortion of the founts of learning in the United tes, published, and his sound warning of the gers which confront us in the future is ed upon first-hand information of German igue. The German conspiracies which inved the destruction of factories, bridges, railds and ships, the warfare which Germany le against us within the confines of our own res, are not considered by Captain Ohlinger dangerous as the effort which Germany le through nearly a quarter of a century to lermine American morale by the Germaniz- of American education. "Bridges, canals, tories and ships are mere physical proper-, easily replaced," says Captain Ohlinger. ur public education, on the other hand, repents infinitely higher values. In a very prae1 sense our schools are the citadel of our ional strength."

In understanding of Germany's scientific paganda program, antedating the war by nty years, is valuable in that it makes more ır insidious activities calculated to create social disintegration which are carrying on at the present time. In these activities, as in the others, certain American professors are playing no inconsiderable part.

In 1881 Germany engaged in her first organized effort for the spread of Kulturpolitik when there was formed "The General School Alliance for the Preservation of Germanism in Foreign Lands." The declared purpose, according to Captain Ohlinger, was "the preservation and promotion of Germanism among the thirty million people of German blood dwelling outside the boundaries of the Empire. The School Alliance established schools and libraries in foreign lands, kept in touch with those already in existence, and, where necessary, rendered financial aid. It maintained a teachers' bureau for the purpose of supplying German-trained educators wherever needed."

The Society was a few years ago merged into the "Society for Germanism in Foreign Lands," and the Imperial Government contributed annually one million marks toward its support. In 1910 there were in foreign lands 5,240 German schools, of which 491 were in the United States. In Southern Brazil—a country which Germany had marked for future aggression—there were more than 600. Captain Ohlinger quotes a German propagandist, occupying a high position in an American university, as saying:

"The spirit of German Kultur must finally seize upon the entire educational system of America. We must practice Kulturpolitik in the highest and noblest sense."

"Not only North America, but the whole of South America must become the bulwark of Germanic Kultur," declared a Pan-German in 1906.

"The war between Germany and the United States began nominally on April 6, 1917," comments Captain Ohlinger. "In reality Germany had begun her scheme of subjugation at least twenty years ago."

"For forty years," declares President William W. Guth of Goucher College, "Germany has so influenced our own scholars and given many of them such a twist mentally, that they have been unable to see how favorable they have been to ideas and opinions purely German."

THE KAISER'S "EXCHANGE PROFESSORSHIPS"

Prince Henry visited the United States in 1902. In 1904, in line with their purpose of "converting" American professors, the Kaiser shrewdly established what was known as the "exchange professorship system," whereby Teuton professors visited America and American professors were invited to Germany. American professors who visited Germany found themselves overwhelmed with ovations and honors. They were flattered, kow-towed to, and taken to the bosom of the Hun savants. They were most graciously received by his majesty, the Kaiser, and decorated with decorations. They were allowed to lecture in the venerable ivy-grown Hun institutions of learning. Their plain brown-sparrow wives were thrilled to suffocation by receptions and overpressing social excitements in Hun university towns. After they came back to America these *Herr professors* were never the same. After the intoxication of an exchange professorship the American *Herr professors* wrote books, many books, exalting Germany and German progress. They wrote articles, multitudinous articles, and lectured. They preached Hun propaganda in their courses at college; their gratitude was indefatigable, colossal!

After the great war broke out not a few responded, as Imperial Germany calculated they would, and took part in propaganda justifying Germany of any wrong and in trying to exonerate Germany of every atrocity.

There was John W. Burgess, for instance, Prof. Burgess had fared innocently forth to the Fatherland as the first exchange professor. Imagine, if you can, the professor's gratification, his totally inebriating joy, at finding that his Majesty the Emperor had condescended to come to listen to a lecture. Former Ambassador Gerard informs us that the Emperor was manifestly bored during Prof. Burgess' talk, that his Imperial Majesty fidgeted and shuffled uneasily in his chair, and that he was visibly distrait, inattentive, during the visiting American's long discourse. Prof. Burgess, however, was probably unaware of any disinterest on part of his gracious Majesty. At any rate, his lecture could not have been altogether unpleasing or unacceptable, for lo and behold, the modest professor found himself decorated with the Order of the Prussian Crown! It was remarked by associates that after his return to the States Prof. Burgess was never quite the same man. He had acquired a dignity, an atmosphere, something that put him above and apart from those envious petty professors who had never been decorated by the Kaiser with the Order of the Prussian Crown.

ORIGINALITY IN PRO-GERMANISM

After Germany started the war Prof. Burgess wrote books trying to justify Germany. In these books he employed the familiar secret "keynote" of German propaganda by attacking Great Britain. Why was America pro-Ally? Prof. Burgess' explanation was naive and novel. It was, for a professor, freshly and indutiably original. For a professor, it showed an actually new viewpoint, which in itself was refreshing. As the offspring of such a seasoned brain it was infantilely young—a conception as unswaddled as a bouncing hour-old babe. Into British society given "in its decline" to "idleness, fox-hunting, horse-racing, gambling, drinking, cheating, debt-making, mendacity, cant, hypocrisy, unchastity, unfaithfulness" had married the "daughters of American parvenus." So wrote exchange-*Herr-professor* Burgess. These daughters of American parvenu millionairedom "became the prey of a broken-down, impecunious, title-bearing aristocracy, both in Great Britain and France." By the beginning of the twentieth century, according to *Herr Professor* Burgess, "an American smart set had been organized on the British and French models, especially upon the British model. It bought its clothes in Paris. It did its shooting on the moors of Scotland. It drank and gambled in London. It brought this sport life with all its extravagance over to Puritan America." Prof. Burgess, exalted in all the glory and prestige of a decoration accorded by the noble ruler of that superior, moral, non-drinking people, the Germans, went on to declare: "It (the American smart set) has become a power in the land and it wields its power mercilessly. . . . It regards this great war as its own. It denounces anyone who is not pro-British or pro-French as pro-German. It waxes wroth over Prussian militarism, Belgian neutrality, and Hun atrocities. It has never yet manifested the slightest consciousness of the deep underlying causes of the war nor of the great purposes the war may be intended to subserve." So, you see, debauched pro-Ally American smart society and "the pro-British American press" accounted for the prejudice against the superior Germans! It is interesting to note, apropos of Burgess' ex-

* Published by George H. Doran Co., New York.

traordinary explanation, that Count von Bernstorff also accounted for anti-German sentiment on the ground that American smart society was pro-British. Prof. Burgess, however, is but one example of this mothy-brained clan who were either too spiritually blind or so effectually Teutonized that they could not see the clear issues and ideals of the war.

Soon after the establishment of the first exchange professorships between Harvard and the Berlin University, according to Captain Ohlinger, "the Kaiser offered to extend the scope of the agreement to other universities in America and Germany. Columbia took advantage of the offer in 1905. James Speyer endowed still another exchange professorship at the University of Berlin. In 1912 Jacob H. Schiff presented the German Department at Cornell University with one hundred thousand dollars as a foundation for the promotion of German Kultur in America. In 1911 Wisconsin citizens of German descent raised a fund of thirty thousand dollars and gave it in trust to the regents of the state university 'for the maintenance of a professor's chair, to be known as the Carl Schurz Memorial Professorship.' The University of Chicago also instituted an informal exchange of lecturers."

"It is more than doubtful," comments Capt. Ohlinger, "that the exchange professorships contributed in any way to scholarship. . . . But they did aid German purposes."

"YELLOW TICKETS" FROM THE HUNS

But there were American professors who had never been honored by an exchange professorship who were just as grovellingly and servilely tools of the Huns. Of course, many of these had studied in the superior German universities, where their trembling virgin minds had been ravished by colossal German learning. There, too, they were kindly given Ph.D's., L.L.D's., and other degrees. After this intellectual debauchment, yellow-ticketed with Hun degrees, what could they see that was worth while in their own barbarian country, what that was admirable in unimperialistic American institutions! These pro-Germanized pundits naturally could regard American history, the American struggle for freedom, the American government, all American ideals and institutions only with a lofty supercilious, superior scorn.

They were probably sincere in what they wrote and said—maybe. Let us at least credit them with that. Masterly hypocrisy and cunning was above their mental calibre. One would not even accuse them of having been bought and paid conscious propagandists. They were, however, only the more effective so far as German interests and German plans were concerned, by reason of their perverted zealotry, their oblique academic sincerity.

In order to mobilize the *Herr professor* fraternity in the United States, Germany organized in America the German University League, the head of which, Otto J. Merkle, was arrested at the point of a revolver and subsequently interned. The purpose of this League was to carry on a scientific propaganda through the colleges and universities of the country, to keep in touch with American educators who were sympathetic with Germany, and to be able quickly to pull the strings when any especial propaganda stunt was to be pulled off in the interest of Germany through available instructors of American youth. The membership list of this organization affords a valuable index to the exponents of Germanism in American institutions of learning and reveals the startlingly widespread ramifications of the sinister Hun intrigue in our midst.*

The German University League sought to create the impression, says Capt. Ohlinger, that it represented, more truly than the administration, the American people, and thus sought "to turn the sharp edge of our diplomacy." After the American Government, on April 18, 1916, had sent a note denouncing the torpedoeing of the Sussex and Germany's submarine warfare, this League sought to neutralize the effect of the American note by sending a wireless message to the rector of the Friederich Wilhelm University of Berlin, in which it was implied that the American people would not stand for war against Germany over the submarine issue. The League deluged the educational institutions of the country with pamphlets defending Germany's course in the war. Through various persons, and under various aliases, it sent letters to the correspondents' columns of the daily press. It organized meetings and lectures.

* This list has been put in our possession.

PRAYS THAT AMERICA BE FORGIVEN FOR HOSTILITY TO HUNS

At one of these meetings an American historian in a speech eulogizing everything German, said he would have felt himself "a traitor to the University of Berlin," had he ignored the invitation to talk and, incidentally, boost Hun Kultur. During a nine-months' visit to Germany, ending immediately before the outbreak of the war, he said that almost everything he saw had struck him more than favorably. About Germany there was nothing to criticise. He was inspired to an almost unprofessorially enthusiastic description of superior German education. What struck him most "was the care and devotion with which the least ray of childish intelligence is hunted down and fostered." He paid his tribute to Germany's "deathless devotion to duty, real interest in the welfare of all the people."

"When I think of what our country could gain by a clear comprehension, by a frank and generous recognition of all that Germany has done for civilization, by a fervent study of her methods and a proper adaptation of them to our needs, instead of by a blind unreasoning hostility as bitter as that of the Jacobins to the aristocrats in the French revolution, I feel like going on my knees and praying to God: 'Father, forgive them, for they know not what they do.'"

That was said after the Lusitania had been sunk, and the American speaker was Ernest Flagg Henderson, a Ph. D. of the University of Berlin.

A professor from Columbia declared that: "As a professor of history I felt that, since the facts underlying this war had not yet been sufficiently ascertained, it would be wise to suspend one's judgment." Speaking presumably for the *Herr professor* fraternity, he said: "We have long since recognized the great debt that we of this country and many others owe to the German fatherland." He spoke of the exchange professors as "intellectual ambassadors." He went on: "We have two great nations in the world: The United States of America and the United States of Germany."

This professor holds a job of considerable importance at Columbia University. After the outbreak of the war, he presided and talked at meetings in the defense of Germany, and, indeed, was almost as busy as Prof. M. J. Bonn himself. This ubiquitous Dryasdust's very amiable and really charming wife lent herself to various Hun pacifist intrigues, and even went so far as to offer to act as go-between for the passing of money from German agents to professional pacifists. What were the motives? By ingratiating themselves with Imperial Germany, through mean and ignoble activities against the Allies, the lady, so she once confided, believed that her spouse would make himself acceptable as ambassador from the United States to Germany when the war should be over!

GERMANISM IN SCHOOL BOOKS

"The most insidious of all forms of German propaganda was that conducted through text books used in the public schools and the fact that much of this propaganda was produced unconsciously and innocently by American born scholars is convincing evidence of ou shortcomings in not insisting upon educatio in political and institutional history," declare Capt. Ohlinger. A reading book for beginner in German produced by a native America teacher in a Chicago high school was found to b filled with glorifications of Germany. In an other school reader was found a tribute to th Kaiser which could hardly have been surpassed by the most zealous Pan-German. In a tex book prepared by a Cornell professor man pages were devoted to enconiums of William II. There was this typical paragraph:

"Although the German Emperor is a soldie through and through, it would be a mistake t consider him a monarch anxious for war. . . ."

German militarism was defended. "In orde to maintain its position, Germany dare not giv up this army, and it stands now at the beginning of the twentieth century as the first military power of Europe."

Of course, German education was presented as superior in every way. "The instruction a the American universities is based largely or German investigation and a large part of the professors at many of our colleges have spen at least one semester at a German university."

The writer evinced no reservations whatever as to Hun greatness. "Germany still maintains its leading place in the field of art and science."

In an English speller, used in the fourth, fifth, sixth, seventh and eighth grades of the Chicago public schools, was a tribute to the Kaiser, in which an episode of his boyhood was related, with the following comment:

"One may say unhesitatingly that a boy capable of such an action has the root of a fine character in him, possesses that chivalrous sense of fair play which is the nearest thing to religion that may be looked for at that age, hates meanness and favoritism, and will, whenever possible, expose them. There is in him a fundamental bent toward what is clean, manly and aboveboard."

Pursuing her underground propaganda work systematically, scientifically, for nearly a quarter of a century, Germany, as Capt. Ohlinger shows, made unsuspected inroads into American education—into grade schools, high schools and institutions of higher learning.

Upon the conclusion of peace, Germany will be confronted by the problem of recuperation, of rebuilding her commerce and finding markets for her goods. Before she faced military defeat, in 1915 and 1916, Germany planned a tremendous after-the-war propaganda, especially aimed at destroying friendship toward England in the United States, South America and other countries to the end that Germany might usurp British trade. At present German propaganda is carried on intensively. That propaganda seeks to create antagonism toward England and to sow seeds of dissension among the Allies. When peace is concluded what form will Hun propaganda take?

BOLSHEVISM INVADES SCHOOLS

Germany, after the conclusion of peace, will profit by the creation of social unrest, or the precipitation of revolution, in any country so long as she herself remains intact. Disturbances of the normal economic conditions of countries, strikes affecting production, will inevitably accrue to Germany's benefit. Germany has not, as we know, been touched by the war; her industries are intact. While France and Belgium are engaged in rebuilding, Germany can plunge into manufacture on a vast scale. Her propaganda organization has not been destroyed; its ramifications still extend into China, Japan, South America, Asia. Nor have all of her secret agents in the United States been interned. Can Germany be depended upon, when peace is made, to desist from secret, under-

(Continued on page 9)

Why the American Socialists Shunned the Berne Conference

e American Alliance for Labor and De- acy has sent out the following statement, ved from its correspondent in Paris, giving easons for the refusal of loyal, patriotic rican Socialists to participate in the Inter- nal Socialist Conference held at Berne, erland:

he Workers and Fundamental Democrats of the Allied and Neutral Countries:

ere has been summoned for Berne, Switzer- beginning February 3, a so-called interna- l conference of Socialists and labor dele- . We have refused to attend this con- ce and we desire to warn you to give no tenance or support, for the following rea- :

e believe it to be fraudulent and dishonest nception and unrepresentative in make-up. was originally proposed as a conference of ens of the Allied countries. By a device we cannot approve, this purpose was covert- tered so as to include subjects of the nations which our countries are still at war. le, therefore, the Interallied Peace Con- nce is yet in session and before it has ad- ed to any conversation any representative he Teutonic powers, it is proposed that we l sit side by side and face to face with such esentatives, call them comrades, and in this lic way condone the hideous and unfor- able crimes against humanity and democracy mitted by their governments; condone them re there has been the least indication of re- or any fixed purpose not to repeat them. his we decline to do.

Ve observe that among the principal movers this conference are persons that while the was actively carried on, opposed the partici- ion in it of Great Britain and the United tes, gave to the autocracies arrayed against democracies their moral aid and support and ght to bring about a peace at times when peace would have ensured the triumph around the world of autocratic imperialism and the suppression of the democratic principle. We say that persons of this record cannot arrange a conference that we will attend.

We observe also among the promoters of this conference gentlemen whose records and recent experiences suggest that the occasion is deemed opportune for fresh adventures on the political field and the regaining of lost constituencies. We have no interest in furthering personal ambitions or political expedients.

We observe that some of the British delegates, though recently repudiated by working class constituencies at the polls pretend to speak for British labor, though the General Federation of Trade Unions of Great Britain, with nearly a million members, has no representation, and we are for this and other reasons obliged to think that the pretense of speaking at this conference for the British working people is unfounded.

We observe that the Italian Socialist Reform Party, which under the leadership of Bissolati, is making such a valiant fight against Italian imperialism, is not represented in this gathering. We observe that the Belgian Socialist Party and Labor Union, by an almost unanimous vote, decided to have no connection with it. We observe that the great American Federation of Labor, the sole voice of organized labor in America, with more than 3,000,000 members, has repudiated this meeting. Plainly, therefore, it is in no way the voice of labor and the democratic reform movement in these countries, and to call it international or deem it significant is an error.

We observe further that the forty Socialist delegates in the French Chamber who loyally supported the cause of Democracy throughout the war have only under protest allowed certain of their members to attend the conference, and these pledge themselves to repudiate it unless the Scheidemann group from Germany is excluded.

We observe that approximately one-third of the membership of this conference is recognized by the Bolshevik chief of Russia as Bolsheviks in good standing. We hold that the cause of democracy and labor reform should not be compromised by mixing it with Bolshevism or with Germanism.

We are quite well aware that at all previous Internationals of this pretension the voting has been so managed by a scandalous misuse of power as to put the entire control practically in the hands of the German delegates, their lackeys and allies. We have every reason to believe that this is a meeting designed to redeem by diplomacy and secret propaganda the defeat Germany suffered on the battlefield. That its real purpose is to hamper and obstruct the Peace Conference. That it is designed to enable Germany to avoid the payment of the indemnity she justly owes to Belgium and France for the ravages she has caused. That it is designed to turn away from her the scorn and condemnation she has earned from mankind by putting forward the insidious plea that this was a capitalistic war for which all nations were equally to blame, in the face of the demonstrated fact that it was a war brought upon the world by German militarism and German lust for domination.

With such a conference we can have no part, and the loyal and thinking peoples of all these countries should be on their guard against its proceedings and outgivings.

For the Social Democratic League of America

By Charles Edward Russell, President;
William English Walling, Secretary.

Justness of French Claims

he New Republic, which editorially attacked claims of France to the Saare Valley, has as yet seen fit to publish the following letter ch was sent to its editor by Mr. Charles Rob- n Smith, under date of January 20, 1919:

he Editor of the *New Republic*:

ear Sir—You probably did not intend it, but your orial paragraph of the 18th on the Saare Valley alculated to seem offensive to our French allies. ou say that the French claim to this valley is d on "pure sophistry", that the Saare was Ger- territory in 1815, when the Prussians took it that it had been "German territory since time emorial"; and then you seem to feel that you given this claim its coup de grace when you "The real reason why France wants the terri- is because it contains coal mines, etc."

assume you wish to be fair, Mr. Editor, espe- y to our friends the French. So will you not at the facts more closely?

he greater part of the Saare Valley in question been an integral part of Lorraine from "time emorial"; and Lorraine had been linguistically nch from "time immemorial." Lorraine had r in any but the most technical sense been Ger- . Prior to 1761 when it came peaceably by ty and inheritance to France it had had its own rs—the dukes of Lorraine. These dukes for e centuries had been held by a loose tie of alage to that loose aggregation known as the Roman Empire—which some call German. This ire was said to have been neither holy, nor an, nor even an empire—so perhaps it is proper all it German. But so loose were ties of vassalage in earlier years and for centuries these same es of Lorraine were also vassals of the dukes of mpagne, who in turn were vassals of the kings rance.

hat part of Lorraine which included Verdun, Toul Metz fell to France in about 1557. The rest, including the Saare Valley, had to wait until 1761. The French had spent the best part of six centuries in redeeming French provinces, one after another, from foreign or local rule and in the making of a great nation out of French speaking people. Lorraine was thus among the last of these French provinces to join the French State.

In 1815 the Saare Valley in Lorraine was wrenched by the Prussians from Lorraine and from France avowedly for strategic purposes, because it contained the fortress of Saarlouis, as well as for commercial purposes.

And so, if after 140 years we are to restore Prussian Poland to the Poles—why in the name of justice should we not after only 100 years restore to Lorraine and to France a part of her territory that had belonged to Lorraine from "time immemorial"?

Shall we refuse now this restoration merely because the Saare Valley contains valuable coal mines? Rather this fact seems to furnish one more powerful reason for such restitution. The Germans have deliberately and wantonly destroyed most of the coal mines of France—and the cession of the Saare Valley will thus not merely effect a restitution of stolen goods but a reparation in kind. Had the Saare Valley never belonged to France—the claim of France to its coal fields could now be justified on grounds of reparation alone.

For four years this war has been fought to secure restitution and reparation as two of the essentials of a permanent peace.

Most of us desire equally with the *New Republic*, the adoption of conditions essential to a permanent peace with as little occasion for rankling left over as possible—but we must be on our guard, lest in our anxiety to spare the finer feelings of the Germans, we do something to hurt the feelings and the interests of Germany's victims, our friends.

Yours very truly,

(Signed) Charles Robinson Smith.

New York, Jan. 20, 1919.

Shadow Huns and Others

(*Continued from page 8*)

hand aggression; from underground efforts to destroy the internal peace of rival nations?

By what we know of Germany's activities in the past, we should be on guard in the future. Is there any significance to the fact that Socialist teachings have been insidiously introduced into our public schools? That public school lecture rooms have been used for the propagation of various insidious forms of radicalism? Is there any significance to the fact that American educators who formerly glorified Germany and defended her in war, have now become preachers of social revolt camouflaged in velvet phrases? Is there any significance to the fact that the former pro-German professors and other propagandists are now internationalists, that the former pacificists are now Bolshevists?

Dr. John L. Tildsley, Assistant Superintendent of Schools of New York, recently declared that the Bolshevik propaganda had invaded the public schools, and that the Board of Education intended a campaign to counteract this insidious influence.

"We are thoroughly alarmed at the situation that has developed," said Dr. Tildsley. "It would be folly to deny its gravity.

"For some time we have been aware that agencies outside the schools have been systematically training schoolboys in Bolshevik doctrines. However, the school authorities have no right or power to dictate what pupils shall do, where they shall go, what they shall read or think outside of school hours.

"What we can do, though, is to present them with a truly American view during school hours of precisely the problems which the Bolsheviki now distort in order to influence these immature minds."

(*To Be Continued.*)

THE NATIONAL
Civic Federation Review

Office: Thirty-third Floor, Metropolitan Tower
1 Madison Avenue New York City

RALPH M. EASLEY, Editor

Published Twice a Month **Two Dollars a Year**

The Editor alone is Responsible for any unsigned article or unquoted statement published in THE NATIONAL CIVIC FEDERATION REVIEW.

THE NEW YORK HARBOR STRIKE

In another part of this issue of the Review will be found the award in the so-called "New York Harbor Strike" made by V. Everit Macy, the arbitrator selected by the War Labor Board. At the time of this writing it is very clear that the award will not be accepted by the men and that they will again go on strike, while it is also evident that the employers are not satisfied with the decision, although they would doubtless accept under protest. This is a good illustration of the impossibility of finding any method or machinery that will absolutely prevent strikes.

The War Labor Board, composed of six employers, selected by the National Industrial Conference Board, an organization consisting of eighteen manufacturing associations, and six representatives of labor, selected by the American Federation of Labor, was completed by two neutral members, one selected by each side represented. The employer group selected William H. Taft as their neutral representative and the labor group selected Frank P. Walsh.

When the Harbor strike occurred in January President Wilson, after all efforts at mediation had failed, cabled from Paris, urging the men to submit the question to the War Labor Board and return to work. This appeal was complied with. The War Labor Board held an exhaustive hearing but could not agree upon an award. Thereupon, as provided by the rules of that Board in such a contingency, the names of ten arbitrators suggested by President Wilson were placed in a hat and the name of V. Everit Macy was the one drawn to be the arbitrator in this controversy.

The reading of Mr. Macy's award will show with what painstaking care he dealt with the subject and to the layman not accurately informed about the practical working of the industry, it sounds very reasonable.

In this particular case arbitration is likely to prove a failure and, if so, it will doubtless be cited as a conspicuous example of the failure of arbitration in general, of collective bargaining and especially of the operation of the War Labor Board. But the fact is that the War Labor Board has dealt successfully with nine-tenths of the controversies that have been referred to it—and there were hundreds of them. This the Board did through mediation, however, and not through arbitration. Those who are familiar with arbitration believe in making use of it only as a last resort. It is better than a strike, the weakness being that it is almost impossible for an arbitrator to render a decision that will satisfy both sides. In the case of mediation, when both sides agree to a proposition, even if it is not all that they want, they will stand by it because they made it themselves.

The history of industrial arbitration parallels the history of international arbitration. As there is no form of industrial arbitration that will absolutely prevent strikes, so there is no form of international arbitration that will absolutely prevent war. Senator Knox greatly stressed this point in his attack upon the League of Nations; but neither he nor any one living can or has been able to devise a scheme whereby all wars or all strikes can be absolutely prevented. They can only reduce them to a minimum and that result is worth all the cost and all the effort that the friends of conciliation and mediation are putting forth both in the industrial and in the international field.

REPEAL OF WAR EMERGENCY LEGISLATION

Mr. Clarence S. Darrow, in an article prepared for the American Alliance of Labor and Democracy which is published in this issue of The National Civic Federation Review, contends that all war emergency legislation should be repealed. With the general argument advanced by Mr. Darrow as to the repeal of emergency legislation most sensible Americans will presumably agree. These war acts were passed to meet situations arising in critical times, when the fate of the nation, at war with an unscrupulous foe, was at stake. With Germany beaten, therefore, shall not all legislation aiming at the suppression of individuals and movements engaged in activities calculated to aid that foe, be categorically repealed?

Unfortunately that intrigue which imperial Germany herself sponsored for the defeat of Russia, and ultimately the distintegration of all other nations, was not ended with Hun defeat. We are not today menaced through any opposition to the selective draft enforcement or efforts designed to weaken the military operations of the United States. Legislation aiming at the arrest and imprisonment of opponents of the draft is therefore obsolete. Acts providing for the incarceration of pacifists who opposed the continuance of war against Germany are likewise out of date. However, the Bolshevik propaganda which Germany financed with the purpose of eliminating Russia from the war, persists, and most of the leading exponents of the propaganda of social separation movements and civil war are the very people who opposed the enforcement of the draft and the waging of war to a military victory over Germany.

Mr. Darrow's analysis of the justness of war emergency legislation contrasts strikingly with the biased logic of the hare-brained ultra radicals who contended that any restriction upon their loose-tongued disloyalty violated constitutional rights. Mr. Darrow pertinently points out that self preservation is the first law of individuals and of nations. If, for the preservation of the nation, it was necessary to apprehend those whose activities, if successful, would have meant German victory, is it not just as urgent now that means be taken to render inert the forces which aim at the overthrow of constituted government and the disintegration of society?

There is a widespread feeling that German propaganda collapsed with the military defeat of Germany. The scientifically organized machine perfected under von Bernstorff has, it is true, been wrecked. But is German propaganda ended? Have we nothing further to fear from the machinations of the Huns? Will it be safe for the nation to rest on its oars? Mr. Harré, in an article in this issue of the Review, quotes Capt. Gustavus Ohlinger, formerly of the Military Intelligence of the United States Army, as declaring that since the signing of the armistice German propaganda has again raised its head; and that the nation must be vigilant against the new intrigue which now especially aims at the promotion of social or class war within the nations which have vanquished Germany and whose true purposes are marked in camouflaged theories. If for the purposes of winning the war, it was necessary to curb pacifists, pro-Germans, and opponents of the draft, is it not now just as expedient, for the preservation of the life of the nation and the weal of society, to enact such measures as will adequately dispose of those who preach class hatred and who would precipitate class war?

Mr. Darrow pleads for free discussion. He argues against the smothering of opinion. Free discussion is the right of free men. The arbitrary suppression of public opinion would be intolerable. No one will contend, however, that the right of free speech permits a man to advocate the murder of specific individuals in a soap box speech. It would be just as extreme to include in rightful free discussion the fanatic who preach class war, which means class murder. By what has happened in Russia we know what Mr. Walter E. Weyl implies when he writes of the "final war" which "will begin after the war . . . which will be waged until separate interests within each nation are completely extinguished" and which Mr. Herbert Croly sanguinarily predicts may "be costly, perhaps almost as costly, as the great war."

With Mr. Darrow we believe that emergency legislation designed to prevent "danger threatened from a foreign foe" should be repealed when that danger is removed and when all purposes have been served. But what about self protection from the danger of internal foes? Compared to the underground secret organization which is today industriously working toward the disintegration of society, which directs the insidious Bolshevik propaganda, the German propaganda of Bernstorff, Dernburg and von Papen was comparatively simple. Relaxed from the terrible tension of the war, luxuriating in grateful relief because of the end of the bloodshed and the killing, shall we laxly permit the forces which wrought the ruin of Russia to have free play in our midst? Repeal purely war measures as their usefulness has ended by all means. But a new emergency has arisen, and self preservation is at stake. A salutary movement was begun when the authorities recently undertook to deport alien I. W. W.'s, anarchists and sundry Bolshevik. That movement will have an adequate conclusion only when such legislation is passed as will denaturalize and expel from our midst all persons seeking the forcible overthrow of our government and the abrogation of the Constitution.

FACT VERSUS SELF-INDORSEMENT

One of the strangest manifestations of human credulity is the ease with which some people gullibly accept representations at their face value. This applies to politico-economic experiments as well as to dubious stock issues. Just as many people have been blithely exchanging their Liberty Bonds for spurious stocks about which they did not even take the trouble to inquire, so others are parting with their common sense for political prospectuses that have no more relation to reality than bogus stock has to tangible property.

A pamphlet entitled "Soviets At Work" by Premier Lenine of the Bolshevik Government is being assiduously circulated in this country and enthusiastically glorified by Bolshevists as proof of the success of the Bolshevik regime. It is characteristic of the self endorsing propaganda enterprise of Lenine and Trotzky that hardly has their experiment started when they already talk and write books about its success.

Other founders of governmental systems in the past, such as the American Republic, for instance, had all they could do to get their undertakings in working order, without having the time to write books about it. They also had the ability and honesty to know that any experiment whether in the field of politics, economics or science had to be given a convincing test before its creators could claim it to be successful.

Lenine and Trotzky, however, differ from all other founders of systems in that they continually prove themselves more concerned with their doctrines than with the results of those doctrines. To them the mere holding of a theory is sufficient, results are immaterial.

Lenine's "Soviets At Work" is reminiscent of another book published some years ago entitled "Socialists At Work." There a most beauteous picture was drawn of the Socialists of Europe and especially of Germany who were depicted as standing as a bulwark against despotism, war and reaction, and the air of cer-

spy system here. But there come to mind handily the names of some of the more notorious offenders, every one of whom should be ousted from the country forthwith. There is Dr. Karl Muck, for instance, former leader of the Boston Symphony orchestra, whose part in the Hun conspiracy was so vile as to be unprintable; and there is Kuhnhardt, another musician, from Cincinnati. Then there are Adolph Pavenstadt, Hugo Schmidt and Carl Heynen, financial representatives of Germany; and Paul Koenig, chief of German spies in America. Frederico Stallforth, associate of Rintelen who plotted to stop munitions shipments by blowing up ships, is trying now to gain his release on the ground that he is a Mexican citizen. He too should be assisted across the border never to return.

Certain legislators seem to think the so-called Burnett bill providing for deportation, gives too much power to the Secretary of Labor. Senator Hardwick of Georgia, and member of the Senate's Immigration Committee, wants a jury trial to decide the fate of the interned. A careful reading of the bill shows that it applies only to those aliens interned or convicted in wartime. With such limitations, the Secretary could do no injustice even if he deported all, and he could rid the country of many dangerous rascals with little red tape and at slight expense.

PLOT TO DISRUPT A. F. OF L.

An important side light on the recent attempt to "Sovietize" Seattle is contained in a private letter that was sent to a number of the leaders of the Mooney conference held in Chicago in January last. This conference, while pretending to be only a movement to work for the release of Mooney, was really an ambitious scheme designed to break up the American Federation of Labor. The discovery of the plot prevented the attempt, which, although it could not have succeeded, shows clearly what is in the minds of the radical element of the labor movement in the West.

The letter follows:

"We will have representation at Chicago of about 3,000 delegates from the American Federation of Labor. I understand from the best authority that Samuel Gompers will instruct the Eastern delegates to stay away from Chicago. This will play right into our hands. The convention will be composed of and controlled by the ultra radical element of the A. F. of L. that will vote for the adoption of the new preamble endorsed by the Washington Federation of Labor.

We will be able to show that the two factions of the A. F. of L. are irreconcilable, and therefore we can slide through a motion to withdraw from the A. F. of L. In so doing, every radical faction west of the Mississippi will join us. We will be able to pull every organization west of Chicago, which will represent over 1,000,000 members of the A. F. of L.

The I. W. W., the Socialist and non-partisans and the Bolshevists will endorse our preamble and we will be able to control the entire West, and we are able to keep the conservatives away from the Chicago Convention.

See Duncan and Green, who have been written to, and I think a slate can be arranged that will win. Long live the Washington Federation for adopting the radical step that will give us complete control of the West. Seattle has always revealed a fine spirit, and we can expect to be the majority party in industrial circles of the West in the next six months.

Further, industrial freedom is rapidly materializing. It has been a hard uphill struggle, but in a few weeks the battle will all be over but the shouting.

Wire me, or if you think that dangerous, write me a letter addressed to Holler, and tell me just what opposition Warren is giving in distribution of literature. It is not against any law, and we will make him live up to the law, or know the reason why. I will write again in two days."

BOLSHEVISM VS. DEMOCRACY

(From Speech Delivered at the Luncheon of the United Waist League, Hotel McAlpin, Monday, January 27, 1919)

By NICHOLAS MURRAY BUTLER

The war has brought several new and strange words to the English language. One of the newest and most strange is Bolshevism. This word came into use as a Russian word about 1905, and was applied to the policy or teachings of those Russian revolutionaries who wished to overthrow, not only the autocracy of the Czar, but the whole modern social and political order. It denoted the maximum program not only of political but of social revolution.

Bolshevism was in the hands of cunning and determined men who saw their opportunity when, following the overthrow of the Czar, Russia was feeling its way toward a new and popular form of government. The great masses of the Russian people are illiterate, easily swayed, and widely spread over a vast territory. When, a few months ago, I asked the famous Mme. Botchkareva to tell me what the Russian people were really thinking, she made this striking answer: "Everybody in Russia is so busy talking that nobody is thinking about anything."

While others talked about what ought to be done, the Bolshevists acted. By forcibly seizing a few strategic points in the scheme of government, they were able, though a pitiful minority of the whole people, to paralyze opposition to their authority and to put themselves in positions of official responsibility. That the result has been a horrible orgy of murder, violation, theft, arson and destruction, no one who is in possession of accurate news from Russia can doubt for a moment.

Bolshevism is at war with civilization, and in particular with democratic civilization. It is now the chief enemy of democracy left in the world. It teaches dominance and control by a group or class. It proscribes capacity, training, thrift and service, and it denies any such thing as citizenship with its equality of opportunity and its equality before the law. Bolshevism bears precisely the same relation to democracy that chaos does to order. Each is the antithesis of the other. In the United States, to their everlasting credit be it said, the great labor organizations have stood like a rock against Bolshevism and its teachings. Americans owe a very great debt to Mr. Samuel Gompers and those who have been associated with him in the conduct of the American Federation of Labor for their clear vision and keen understanding of what Bolshevism is and means. Neither the man who works or the man who has saved can expect any quarter from Bolshevism unless he accepts its degrading and anarchistic doctrine that might makes right, and that the least competent shall organize government and set the pace for the state. In this country we are blessed—or otherwise—with a few parlor, editorial and academic Bolshevists, who, without in the least comprehending the significance of what they are saying or writing, and with the safety of their own skins and incomes guaranteed by other people, profess sympathy with the teachings and aims of these mad and murderous autocrats. But the heart of the American people is clear.

In Russia Bolshevism is the counter-revolution. So long as it continues to distress that unhappy country the Russian people will be prevented from securing the untold benefits of a stable, just and republican form of government in succession to the hateful despotism of the Romanoffs, now happily gone forever.

Russia Seen By British Trade Unionist

CLASS HATRED AND SOCIAL DEGRADATION PUNISHMENT FOR DISPLEASING SOVIETS—ENTIRE TRAD UNIONS BOYCOTTED FOR SLIGHT OFFENSES

A PICTURE of conditions in Russia, by an English workingman, who was in Russia from the time of the outbreak of the revolution until last January, is given in the *Westminister Gazette* in an interview, entitled "The Truth About Russia." As the *Westminster Gazette* generally is regarded as a paper with a strong leaning toward pacifism and as its informant is a trades unionist, only just arrived from Russia, the interview is attracting great attention. The article was cabled to the *Philadelphia Public Ledger* and is reprinted herewith by special permission. The *Westminster Gazette* says:

"There has lately arrived in England a witness of the internal condition of Russia whose testimony is, we believe, more veracious and impartial and likely to have more weight with the mass of the people than any official account given by middle class Russians who have escaped from the country. This is H. V. Keeling, who alone probably of all Englishmen has seen the Bolshevist movement from within and can report of his own knowledge what the Russian working class thinks.

"Mr. Keeling went to Russia five years ago to teach the workmen of a Russian firm which had acquired British patents of certain new processes of the lithographic and printing trades. For twenty years previously hé had been a member of the British Trade Union. He was admitted to membership in the Russian Printing Trade Union and thus spent all his time as a workman among workmen.

BECAME USEFUL TO SOVIETS

"In 1918 he went about the country opening workshops for repairing all sorts of things. In this way he made himself so useful, not to say indispensable, that the Soviets insisted on his remaining in the country. In October last he was appointed to the position of chief photographer of the committee on public education, presided over by Lunacharski, whom he describes as an amiable visionary with his eyes shut to the realities of the Bolshevist régime. How Keeling finally got out of Russia and the extraordinary adventures and hairbreadth escapes he had at the frontier of Finland cannot be told yet. The main fact is that he was in Russia for the whole period of the revolution until January 9 this year.

"Mr. Keeling is still a young man and, although his experiences have bitten deep into him, he has been carried through by his remarkable vitality and intelligence. He speaks with singular impartiality of what he has seen and heard.

"'The population,' says Mr. Keeling, 'was originally divided by the Bolshevists into four categories which exactly turn upside down the social classes of other countries. These are first, manual laborers; second, clerical workers, provided they employ nobody; third, every body who has employed anybody from a small householder employing one servant to a manufacturer employing a thousand hands; fourth, all former idle rich, princes, aristocrats, landowners and courtiers of every description.

DEGRADATION IS THE PENALTY

"'The penalty for failing to please the Bolshevists is to be degraded from the class in which you get some food to the class in which you get scarcely any. In the last few months there has not been anything like enough for the first class and scarcely anything for the others. Class IV, the former rich, I should say, has disappeared. They have either got out of the country or been starved to death or shot or have turned themselves into workmen in order to get food.

"'I cannot tell you more, for nobody knows. Other classes are those that get some food and those that get hardly any officially. To get food you must be in with the Bolshevists, and then they put you into the first class. It is very difficult to get there and very easy to get out. They degrade you for slight reasons which you cannot discover and then you starve. Whole trade unions have been degraded because they opposed the Bolshevists or offended them somehow.

"'One has cards and coupons,' says Mr. Keeling, 'but all private trading is forbidden and nearly all the shops in Petrograd are shut.' There are a few hundred municipal shops, and you are supposed to receive half a pound of bread a day; potatoes, butter, meat and sugar are fixed at reasonable prices; but as a matter of fact for a long time past nothing has been sold but bread, and even that failed for seven days in December.

SIX DAYS WITHOUT BREAD

"'I have been six days without bread, three days without anything to eat except the so-called public dinner, which consisted of watery soup, a small piece of salt fish and one-eighth of a pound of bread. Sometimes they offered me oats, as if I were a horse, when there was no bread. All children are in the first class, for the Bolshevist idea is that all children should be charges of the state while their parents go to work, but the children are starving in great numbers.

"'If you are not in the first class or are degraded from it you have to prowl about and try to get food secretly; but this is a punishable offence, for which sometimes people may even be shot. People go to the country, taking anything they think the peasants will take in exchange for food and get a bag of flour or a few potatoes. But it is illegal to go out of town without a permit or to buy anything when you get there, so the Red Guard stop them and search them as they come back, and if they find anything confiscate it and often arrest the people and carry them off.

"'I saw a woman who had gone to the country and got thirty pounds of flour from her own native place for her children, who were starving. She was seized by the Guard at the station when she was trying to get back, and they took it from her, although she fell on her knees and implored them with sobs to let her keep only a few pounds.

"'Then when she found it was no use she threw herself under a train and was killed.

WORKMEN'S PAY $500 MONTHLY

"'It makes it worse that you have quantities of money in your pocket but can buy nothing, I have had rubles worth £600 ($3,000) in my pocket and have not been able to buy a piece bread. You don't trouble about money. You pay 5 shillings ($1.25) a lump for sugar if you can get it. A workman's wages are £100 ($500) a month at the old values, but though he can still buy a watch for £5 ($25) he cannot buy a roll of bread for £50 ($250). People who have food will not sell it for rubles because they are worth nothing and there is nothing to buy with them, so the Bolshevists cannot get food though they are trying to and having fights with t peasants in consequence.

"'I believe myself there is enough food Russia to keep every one alive for the last ha vest was good, but it cannot be got and it all being hoarded and concealed.

"'Nine-tenths of the people who keep in wi the Bolshevists have to pretend to like them a would do anything to get rid them if they kne how, but you have to remember the Bolshevis are clever, feeding the people who are likely fight. Every man who joins the Red Army sure of his own food, also gets food for his wi and children. The army is fed before any o else and out of all proportion to the other class Even workmen get nothing until the army h had enough, so large numbers of men join t army for the sake of getting food and then ha to keep at it for fear of losing their food. B sides if they try any tricks they not only a punished and shot themselves but their wive families and parents are starved.

MANY SPIES EMPLOYED

"'A man will stand almost anything rath than see his wife, children and parents starv to death and the use they make of this ki of coercion is devilish. Soldiers have to be ca ful for there are lots of spies among them. Th besides the regular Red Army there is a speci picked army which gets everything it want food or anything else, and all these men kn if they don't fight they will starve, so they fig to save their own food and to prevent the wives and children from starving. That is the way of keeping alive.'

"'How can men at the top, Lenine, Trotzl and the rest rest?—Lenine at all events is su posed to have some intelligence and humanity- sit there and let this go on? Are they devils maniacs?' Keeling was asked.

"'Suppose you would say they are qui sane according to our notions, but as things a they cannot help themselves and could not st it if they choose. They have made monst areas helpless. Bolshevism is, in fact, become vested interest for its privileged class, a Lenine and Trotzky are obliged to go on feedi a few, starving the many and shooting obje tors.'

"Asked how men could be found who wou go on day after day administering this di bolical system with this spectacle of helple misery under their eyes Mr. Keeling said:

"'Most of them are quite young, some noto ous bad characters, many mere boys whom should call hooligans. One boy of 17 I kne was a commissary with the power of life a death over forty villages. He goes about with pistol, and one day thrust it in my face, threa ening to shoot me on the spot. I knew how deal with him, but the Russian peasants do n As seen, such lads are terrorizing whole di tricts.'

"Keeling admits frankly that he was tracted by the Bolshevist idea, and hoped at o time it might be good for Russia if not t world in general. He was asked what has ha pened to the Russian people?

"'Is Bolshevism as black as it is painte and if it is, how can the whole nation subm to it?' He said in answer: "The Russian peop are starving, and when you are starving you not think about other atrocities; you think abo nothing except just food to keep yourself aliv You do not trouble much whether you are goi to be shot yourself or whether other people a being shot. You are collecting food like

. I left Russia six weeks ago, but even : cannot get over the habit of thinking my food, and every day I find myself ring where the next meal is to come from.'

eeling expanded on this idea. And on the de millions of people too absorbed with vening thought how to get food for them- their wives and children to think of any- beyond the moment, too exhausted to re- n the other hand, a favored few relatively ed persons prepared for any violence or y to save themselves from losing their ege and slipping into the vortex of famine. whatever may be in the original idea of evism, as Keeling explained, it is simply t confers upon some and denies to others rivilege of eating and that all its other of violence and cruelty are as nothing he supreme cruelty of withholding Keeling went on to explain the sys- lescribing it without color or emotion, as ng in that world he had come to take its :s for granted.

The peasants have got rid of their land- and sat down and divided the land,' con- Keeling. 'They have quarrelled a good out on the whole did it sensibly, each tak- bit of the best land, then another a bit of and so on, but while there was plenty d for one village, there was nothing like enough in another, so the distribution was very unequal and there was great discontent. Instead of having the splendid time they hoped for, they find there is nothing to buy and they are always being worried and threatened by the Bolshevists. They have no tea, no vodka, no tobacco; they feel the loss of tobacco especially, and seem to walk about in a dazed condition, like men used to drugs, who had suddenly to go without. Peasants have implored me to give them tobacco.

"'Peasants work only just as much as they must to keep themselves alive. The next harvest is likely to be very bad and then famine, which now exists in the towns, will begin to spread over the country, and one dare not think what will happen then.

"'My own belief is they, Lenine and Trotzky, know the game is up, but do not know how to get out of it or what to do. The slightest sign of weakening and they are done. So they simply go ahead, grinding out everybody they think dangerous. Even the advanced Socialists are beginning to speak of Czardom as the good old times. No one is safe. It used to be thought they did not shoot Jews, for so many of them are Jews themselves, but two acquaintances of mine, both Jews, were shot a short time before I came away, and they had done nothing except to try a little private trading.

"'It is terrible to live in Russia these times. As you walk in Petrograd you never see any one laugh or smile; men and women are like shadows; little children are so wasted they seem to be all eyes. All the time people are disappearing; nobody knows what becomes of them. Five years ago Petrograd had a population of 2,400,000; now there are scarcely 700,000.

"'I have no personal animosity against the Bolshevists. They treated me as well as they could, but I am a working man, a trade unionist and I don't like to hear British working men talking as if Bolshevism was a great and splendid experiment to be copied by other countries, or as if they were helping the working people of Russia by saying no to all proposals now before the Allies for dealing with it. I want to convince them it is not a question of politics or theory, but just a question of humanity on which we have got to do our duty and help. There is enormous suffering and misery which we ought to stop if we can.

"'I want to say also that it won't do the Socialists any good to mix up with the Bolshevism and make people think that if socialism is tried it must end in wholesale murder and starving millions of people to death, but that is what will happen if the working people confuse socialism with Bolshevism and suppose that socialism must support the Bolshevists.'"

Repeal of War Emergency Legislation

By CLARENCE S. DARROW

(From the Bulletin of the American Alliance for Labor and Democracy)

HE prosecution of the war called forth a large amount of legislation. In the main, these laws were such as are y passed in times of war. The rules for are not the same as the rules of peace and er with or without the war is the conduct ople the same.

ıen a country is engaged in war, there is me to doubt or argue. The great mass of le are ordinarily with the government and they are fighting foreign enemies, they not allow enemies at home to annoy or s them, or otherwise obstruct such action necessary for the protection of the coun- If the mass of people believe in the policy ar they are always intolerant of propa- a by words or writing that is calculated to the enemy or divide their own ranks.

the law takes no notice of it, the people will ent seditious language without law. This lone repeatedly during the War of the Re- n. It was common during the War of the lution when the sympathizers with Eng- were mobbed, hanged and forcibly driven the country. In the removal of Vallan- ıam from the North, as wise and human a dent as Lincoln set the example for this of action. The first law of individuals of nations is self-preservation, and every s will be taken to accomplish this result.

ıch legislation has been passed since our began which seriously interferes with the om of speech and the press. Many men ow in jail, some under long sentences, who been convicted of violating these laws. No t a large number of these men were con- tious and honestly did not believe in the but an individual who is attacked, defends elf without regard to the question of her his attacker is conscientious or not. ıay be insane, but this furnishes no reason ermitting him to take life. A country like- in a state of war is not able to ask ques- as to whether a man conscientiously ob- to a course of policy, or whether he sym- ızes with the enemy. He is necessarily ed by his words and acts, for the first effort e government is to preserve itself.

ere can be little quarrel either in logic or in law with this proposition. It is done by all people, whether they be monarchists, republicans or Bolsheviki. In its last analysis it is the law of self-preservation and nothing else.

It is perfectly obvious that laws that are meant for the prosecution of war may be the most mischievous in times of peace. This country was formed on the idea of broad religious and political tolerance and a wide freedom of speech and the press. A large part of our progress and welfare in the past is due to this freedom and toleration. If laws passed during the war are to be applied to times of peace, the governing power will be able to make freedom of speech a mockery.

Nothing is perfect, and no thinking person would claim that our constitution, our laws or our institutions should not be changed and modified as time goes on. It is of the first importance to progress that there shall be free discussion of all political and social schemes that might result in change. To say that we should take institutions as they are, put on the lid and refuse open discussion, would, of course, mean that the present is good enough and the future should be no better. If it were wise to do it now, it would have been equally wise in the middle ages or any period of the world's history. Persecution and witchcraft and despotism would then be as common as in the dark ages.

When peace is finally declared the first and most important act of Congress should be to take off the lid, remove the restriction of free speech and a free press.

The policy of organized labor has always been to allow the widest freedom of debate. Organized labor is always looking toward the future. Its effort is to improve the conditions of those who need it most, change laws and institutions wherever needful that the common lot may be easier. This cannot be done except by free debate. Of all the people in the world, the trade unions are the last ones that can permit any permanent abridgment of the freedom of speech and the press. Organized labor has always made itself clearly understood upon this issue, which is of the first importance to the development of individuals.

Our present laws, if enforced against labor organizations and those who desire social change, would result either in sending most of the leaders to jail or in revolution. Of course, they were never meant for any such purpose. They were meant for the war and the war only and the danger is that people may forget their purpose and let them linger to obstruct the world after the need is gone.

If under free open discussion, the majority of the people in this country want something, they ought to have it. If the world cannot stand up against Bolshevism and meet it by free speech and a free press, then Bolshevism has the right to rule. It would then be time to try it out and see if it can succeed.

To smother any opinion is at once a confession that it may be true and that it cannot be met by open discussion and fair argument. Our institutions have cost too much to permit them to be destroyed on account of the war. It will not do to make a war fought for democracy result in autocracy. There can be no danger from this if the question is understood and the people act promptly to repeal war legislation when the war is done.

If it is right to repeal war legislation, it is also equally just and pressing that a general amnesty should be given to all of those who are now suffering under this sort of legislation. Everyone knows that large numbers of these men are conscientious and it is intolerable to think that men are in jail on account of their conscience, when there is no longer need that they should stay.

The labor unions did their part in this war. Without them it would not have been possible to bring the United States Government to that solid support that made victory possible. As they were patriotic in times of war, it is equally certain they will be patriotic in times of peace, and from the nature of things they are the ones who first of all should demand the repeal of this legislation and that amnesty be given to all these prisoners. This does not mean that the laws were wrong, or that it was not necessary to send conscientious men to prison during the war, but it does mean that the purpose of the war has been served and there was no thought or feeling of vengeance in any of these prosecutions, but only the purpose to protect the country when danger threatened it from a foreign foe.

Award In New York Boatmen's Case

MARINE WORKERS AFFILIATION OF NEW YORK HARBOR *VS.* THE RAILROAD ADMINISTRATION, SHI PING BOARD, UNITED STATES NAVY, WAR DEPARTMENT, AND RED STAR TOWING AND TRANSPORTATION COMPANY, V. EVERIT MACY, ARBITER

THE questions submitted to me, acting as arbiter for the War Labor Board in the case of the "Marine Workers Affiliation of New York Harbor *vs.* The Railroad Administration, Shipping Board, United States Navy, War Department, and Red Star Towing and Transportation Company, may be divided as follows:

A—Was the War Labor Board, in hearing this case, acting in place of the former New York Harbor Board, and therefore limited as to what matters it could consider by an award of the New York Harbor Board, dated July 12, 1918?

B—Request for the eight-hour day,

C—Increase of wages, and changes in classifications,

D—Changes in conditions of employment,

E—The question as to whether the findings should be retroactive in application.

LIMITATION OF QUESTIONS TO BE ARBITRATED

In the President's telegram of January 11, 1919, requesting the Board to "Take up the case" and to "Proceed to a finding" no limitation as to what the Board was to consider was made. (Exhibit A.) The various Departments of the Government, in a letter dated January 11, 1919, asked the War Labor Board to act and stated "We desire to assure you that we will gladly submit *any* interests which we may have in this controversy to your Board and will abide by such decision as you make." (Exhibit B.) The Marine Workers Affiliation fixed no limitations to the questions to be placed before the War Labor Board.

It is obvious, therefore, that none of the interested parties considered that the War Labor Board was acting as a substitute for the New York Harbor Board, and they apparently had no intention of limiting its jurisdiction. On the other hand, the War Labor Board was specifically authorized to consider "*any* interests in the controversy."

In the last paragraph of the award of the New York Harbor Board, dated July 12, 1918, the following paragraph occurs:

"This award shall be effective as of June 1, 1918, and shall be in full force until May 31, 1919, unless in the judgment of the Board conditions warrant a change prior to the date thus fixed for expiration."

Some of the members of the War Labor Board contend that nothing has happened since June first, 1918, to "warrant a change" in the award of July 12, 1918. With this opinion I cannot agree. The effect of the armistice on the industrial and commercial life of the country is too obvious to require further demonstration. At the time the award was made the nation was at the height of a period of rising prices, necessitating increased wage scales, and a serious shortage of labor existed which required for the national safety the working of long hours. Since the signing of the armistice the entire situation has been reversed. Pending necessary readjustment of our National life to a peace basis we are passing through a period of falling prices, over supply of labor and there is no longer a need for excessive hours if an industry can be readjusted to a shorter workday.

In addition, the employers of the Port of New York, with one exception, who were parties to the award of July 12, 1918 and who control 60% of the harbor craft, refuse to allow the functioning of the Board as provided in the award. Had the New York Harbor Board functioned as provided in the award and had they decided that nothing had occurred warranting a change, then all parties would naturally be bound to have accepted such a decision. As the New York Harbor Board failed to act as provided in the award and as the War Labor Board was not asked by the two parties submitting the case to interpret the award of July 12, 1918, but to consider the entire situation,

I therefore find that the question of wages and hours of the members of the Marine Workers Affiliation of the Port of New York who are employed by the Railroad Administration, the Navy, the Army, the Shipping Board, and the Red Star Towing and Transportation Company are properly before me, acting as arbiter for the War Labor Board, and that acting in that capacity I am not limited by the award of July 12, 1918.

REQUEST FOR AN EIGHT HOUR DAY

The desirability of limiting the working day to eight hours has been recognized by Congressional enactment for all Government Departments and on all direct Government contracts, by most State Legislatures and Municipalities, by the Railroad Administration, and is the prevailing custom in many of our largest industries. Such a general acceptance of the principle of an eight-hour workday has not been obtained merely through sentiment. The nation has come to realize that its security demands that its citizens have a reasonable opportunity for family life, a reasonable amount of leisure and a proper standard of maintenance. In view of this recognition the nation has the right to demand of its able-bodied citizens eight hours' service, for six days in the week, in some useful effort. Good citizenship requires that this service be rendered either voluntarily or for pay, according to the financial needs of the individual. The right to an eight-hour day carries with it the obligation upon the part of the individual to render better service during the fewer hours for no right can be obtained without its corresponding obligation.

Some industries in their operation have inherent disadvantages, such as unusual danger to life and limb. In such industries it is recognized that the workers should be compensated for this risk and therefore a higher rate of wage is paid than obtains in less hazardous occupations requiring the same degree of skill. In such cases the danger is regarded as part of the expense of conducting the industry and is passed on to the consumer in the price of the service rendered or the article produced. In some business the fire hazard is greater and the rate of insurance is high; this is also an expense of production and is consequently paid indirectly by the consumer. Excessive hours are as dangerous to good citizenship as are noxious fumes to the health of workers. There may be certain occupations in which the straight eight-hour day is inherently impossible, if so the basic eight-hour day should be the standard and to pay for overtime regarded as a legitimate expense and a just charge to be borne by the public. It would seem, therefore, that the burden of proof that an eight-hour day is impossible in an industry lies on those who deny its practicability as well as upon those who request its installation. The workers in a dangerous occupation or in one requiring undue hours should not be compelled to carry the b den alone.

The New York Harbor Board has divi the harbor craft into the following classes:

Ferry boats,
Tugs, other towing vessels, and ste lighters,
Lighters, covered barges, and hoisters,
Coal and grain boats, scows and dum
(For the purpose of this award same classification is followed).

FERRY BOATS—The ferry service is a c tinuous service throughout the twenty-f hours with no very serious variation in the nu ber of boats in use for the sixteen hours tween 5 A. M. to 9 P. M. The boats alw leave and return to the same point on fi schedules. An eight-hour work day is con quently practical in this service.

I therefore find that all workers employed ferry boats, operated by the owners appeari in this case, shall be employed for eight ho a day only for six days in the week, and unusual circumstances when required to w beyond eight hours they shall receive time a one-half for all extra time worked.

TUG BOATS, OTHER TOWING VESSE AND STEAM LIGHTERS—The evidence p sented showed that many of these boats w engaged on long hauls requiring more th eight hours for the round trip, or were in c tinuous service during the twenty-four hou that they already employed two crews; and t as a rule they were operated on a more or l regular schedule. It is reasonably practi therefore, for the crews on these boats to employed on a forty-eight-hour week. The th crew remaining on shore when off duty.

I therefore find that all tug boats and oth towing vessels, and steam lighters under jurisdiction of this award, now using two cre shall employ these crews on the basis of a for eight-hour week, no crew to work more tha double shift in any twenty-four hours, and t for all hours worked in excess of forty-ei hours in one week, the crews shall be paid the rate of time and one-half. If the boat engaged in continuous service an additio crew shall be employed to form a third shift.

SINGLE CREW BOATS—The several th sand pages of testimony and the many exhib presented at the hearings before the War La Board and before me as arbiter give little ex information as to the effect a change in hours of employment would have on the co merce of New York Harbor or on the earni capacity of the crews on the harbor crafts. T evidence submitted is largely composed of wl seem to be exceptional cases. It is almost who based on the abnormal conditions that have p vailed in the port of New York since the ginning of the war, in 1914. Both sides h contented themselves with general statemen One side claimed that 75 per cent. of the m could be placed on an eight-hour day with difficulty and that there would be no shortage skilled workers, but gave no suggestions as how this could be accomplished, other than the case of ferry boats and boats employi two crews, nor the number of skilled work available. The other side made a general den of these statements and produced certain figu showing that a shortening of the hours wou result in increased costs. No facts were p justice, in order to force all industry, under a single rule of employment. Justice to all parties, including the public, so far as it is possible of accomplishment should be the only universal rule.

Because twelve hours has been the custom is no reason why, with careful investigation of the facts, that a lesser number of hours might not be discovered to be advantageous, and desirable. Any industry that requires a working day of ten and twelve hours must show affirmatively the necessity for the continuance of such hours.

The commerce of the port of New York is too important to the city and nation to warrant any arbiter in hastily reducing the working day from ten to twelve to eight hours without having before him the full facts as to the probable result of such a change. As above stated, the necessary information is, at present, entirely lacking. I find, therefore, that the working hours for the tugs, towing vessels, steam lighters, lighters, covered barges, and hoisters, under the jurisdiction of this award and at present operating with only one crew, should remain unchanged until the first of July. In the meantime I would recommend that all interested parties in the harbor cooperate with each other in establishing a commission, not exceeding ten in number, to carefully study the above problems and, if possible, for them to recommend what changes in the work day are advisable, how such changes can be made and the probable effect on the port of New York. This will require the detailed study of the daily logs of hundreds of boats.

This commission should be composed approximately as follows: Two representatives of the Government Departments, including the Railroad Administration; three private employers and five representatives of the Affiliated Marine Workers. If they fail to agree, on or before June first, as to the facts or upon recommendations, then each side shall report their findings to the War Labor Board for a final decision. Such an investigation can best be made by the voluntary cooperation of the parties concerned. If such cooperation is not obtainable the welfare of the city and nation cannot be sacrificed by stoppage of work in the harbors and an independent commission must therefore undertake this task. I find that if such a commission is not voluntarily organized, as suggested above, and an investigation begun by the first of April, then the War Labor Board shall itself name a commission to make the investigation and report, and such commission shall report back to the War Labor Board by June 1, 1919, in order that the War Labor Board may then take final action before July 1, 1919.

REQUEST FOR INCREASED WAGES

Just as the armistice has resulted in a condition favorable to the reduction of the working day to eight hours, it has also created a condition unfavorable to an increase in wage. The representatives of the men explained that they did not present to the New York Harbor Board, in June 1918, a request for an eight hour day for patriotic reasons, because they realized that the war necessitated their working regularly long hours. There is nothing in the record, however, that shows that at the time they presented their demands for increased wages in June, they did not ask for the full wage desired. If there is any change in the cost of living between July 12, 1918, and the present time, it is probably in favor of the men, although there is no authentic data on which to base an accurate opinion. Owing to the different season of the year certain commodities may be higher and others lower than on July 12, 1918, but as the seasons change these variations adjust themselves.

It is a fair assumption that the unanimous opinion of the Harbor Board, as expressed in its award of July 12, 1918, and the unanimous opinion of the Railroad Administration Board, fixing the wages of certain harbor workers, effective September 1, 1918, represented a proper wage scale considering all conditions at that time. Representatives of the men were parties to both of these unanimous decisions. It is certainly, therefore, necessary for those asking an increase now to show convincing proof that the desired increase is justified. In order for industry to revive on a peace basis it must be stabilized. This cannot be accomplished during the next few months if wages are to be radically changed, either up or down. Constant readjustment only delays the return of normal conditions.

It must also be remembered that if the employees receive the same wage for eight hours' work as they did for twelve hours, that while they receive no increased income the labor cost to the industry is increased fifty per cent. The only offset to this higher labor cost is greater production per hour than previously prevailed. The records do not show how the efficiency of the harbor crafts can be increased by shortening the work day. An increase of thirty-five per cent. in the labor charge, due to reduced hours of work in operating the harbor crafts would in itself be a heavy burden to carry and precludes granting an increased wage at the same time.

INCOME NOT OUT OF PROPORTION

The annual income of the marine workers is not out of proportion with the annual income of workers in other occupations, requiring equal skill and intelligence. A fact to be considered in comparing the wages of the marine workers with other trades is that these men are usually employed on a monthly basis, the year round, and consequently there is little or no lost time. In addition, many of them receive an allowance of seventy-five cents per day for board and lodging, while others receive free rent.

There is little, or no evidence in the records as to the wages now being paid in other ports for similar services. We cannot assume that the cost of moving freight in the port of New York has no relation to the cost in other ports and an unwarranted cost might easily result in diverting freight, thus reacting unfavorably on the marine workers of New York. This subject should also be studied by the above suggested commission.

No convincing proof was presented for changing the classifications of the occupations as shown in the award of the New York Harbor Board of July 12, 1918. Little evidence was presented by the men to justify the reclassification, as shown in their requests. It is fair to assume the unanimous award of July 12, all parties familiar with the details of the tasks having a voice in that award, represents a better classification and a fairer differentiation between occupations than an arbiter unfamiliar with the details could possibly work out from the unrelated requests by the various crafts.

HERE IS THE FINDING

I therefore find that no wage increase should be granted and that the wage scales in the award of the New York Harbor Board, dated July 12, 1918, and those in the award of the Railroad Administration Board, dated September 1, 1918, shall remain in effect during the life of this award. That those employees whose working day is herein reduced from twelve hours to eight hours shall receive the same monthly wage for the eight hours as they formerly did for twelve hours. Also that the employees whose week has been reduced to forty-eight hours shall receive the same monthly salary as previously. No findings are herein made for occupations not mentioned in the New York Harbor Board award of July 12, 1918, or for occupations not contained in the order of the Railroad Administration Board of September 1, 1918, as practically no evidence was submitted relative to these additional classifications.

WORKING CONDITIONS

TUG BOATS AND OTHER TOWING VESSELS AND STEAM LIGHTERS:

A—Twelve hours shall constitute a day's work where one crew is now employed.

B—Six days, or forty-eight hours for boats having more than one crew, shall constitute a week's work. The day off to be determined by the employer.

C—Work on week days in excess of twelve hours a day, or six days a week, for boats with one crew, or 48 hours a week for boats with more than one crew shall be considered overtime and paid for at the rate of one and one-half times the regular rate.

D—Double time shall be paid for work on the following holidays—New Year's Day, Fourth of July, Labor Day, Thanksgiving Day, and Christmas Day.

E—Double time shall be paid for work on Sundays unless the employee has already had one day's rest in seven, or will have one such day in the current swing of his shift.

F—Crews are entitled to pay on Sundays and holidays for only the actual number of hours that they are on duty.

G—In order to determine the hourly rate for men on a monthly wage multiply the number of hours in the working day by three hundred and thirteen, and divide this product into the monthly wage multiplied by twelve.

H—In the case of those men who, owing to the shorter work day, need no longer be boarded by the company, or who may be boarded only part of the week as may occur in the case of those working on a forty-eight-hour week, seventy-five cents a day shall be added for each day they are not so boarded, or twenty-five cents for each meal not provided by the company in cases where shifts are changed between meals. This provision does not apply to the crews of ferry boats, tugs, and steam lighters now receiving the hourly rates contained in the order of the Railroad Administration Board, effective September 1, 1918, as hourly rate received by these men provides for them to board themselves. This provision applies only for six days a week, unless the employee works an extra seventh day.

I—One week's vacation with pay shall be allowed each employee who has been in the service of the company for a period of one year or more.

J—Carfare is to be paid by the employer when boats change crews at other than designated points.

FERRY BOATS:

A—Eight hours shall constitute a day's work.

B—Six days shall constitute a week's work.

C—All overtime on week days shall be paid for at the rate of time and one-half.

D—Double time shall be paid for work on the following holidays—New Year's Day, Fourth of July, Labor Day, Thanksgiving Day, and Christmas Day.

E—Double time shall be paid for work on Sundays unless the employee has already had one day's rest in seven, or will have one such day in the current swing of his shift.

F—Crews are entitled to pay on Sundays and holidays for only the actual number of hours that they are on duty.

G—In order to determine the hourly rate of pay for men on a monthly wage, multiply three hundred and thirteen by eight and divide the product into the monthly wage multiplied by twelve.

H—One week's vacation with pay shall be allowed each employee who has been in the service of the company for a period of one year or more.

LIGHTERS, COVERED BARGES, AND HOISTERS:

A—Ten hours shall constitute a day's work.

B—Six days shall constitute a week's work.

C—All overtime on week days shall be paid for at the rate of time and one-half.

D—Double time shall be paid for work on the following holidays—New Year's Day, Fourth of July, Labor Day, Thanksgiving Day, and Christmas Day.

E—Double time shall be paid for work on Sundays unless the employee has already had one day's rest in seven, or will have one such day in the current swing of his shift.

F—Crews are entitled to pay on Sundays and holidays for only the actual number of hours that they are on duty.

G—In order to determine the hourly rate of pay for men on a monthly wage, multiply three hundred and thirteen by ten and divide the product into the monthly wage multiplied by twelve.

H—One week's vacation with pay shall be allowed each employee who has been in the service of the company for a period of one year or more.

I—All carfares in excess of ten cents to be paid by the employer to men living within the Metropolitan district, and all carfares to be paid by the employer when the men are on the company's business.

J—The Captain shall receive one dollar and fifty cents for each night he is required to be on his boat for the purpose of watching or towing.

SCOWS, DUMPERS, COAL BOATS, AND GRAIN BOATS:

The Captain of these boats shall receive one dollar and fifty cents for each night that he is required to be active for at least one hour after six P. M. in the loading or discharging of cargo.

RETROACTIVE REQUEST

Throughout the hearings before the War Labor Board and also at the hearings before the arbiter, the representatives of the Marine Workers Affiliation emphasized the fact that the request for shorter hours was not to be taken as an indirect method of raising wages. It is impossible to return the hours that have already passed by any award and as no increases in the wage scales are granted there is nothing to be gained by making a retroactive date for the findings here made. It will require a few days to secure the additional men necessary to man the ferries and other boats for the crews of which an eight-hour day is provided. In order not to inconvenience the public the findings contained in this award shall not become effective until March 1st, 1919, and shall remain in force until peace is declared or otherwise until July 1, 1919. During the month of June the commission or the War Labor Board can prepare a carefully adjusted scale of wages and a comprehensive regulation of hours and conditions of employment for all marine workers in the port of New York.

I recommend that the War Labor Board will follow its usual methods for settling any disputes that may arise in putting this award in operation.

(Signed) V. Everit Macy.

ism and Shop Stewardism

By A. M. SIMONS.

stewards are the petty officers of the union, whose only function is to see that the provisions of union contracts are observed and that any complaints are transmitted to the union headquarters. When the war came union officials in England made agreements limiting the power of members to strike during the war. Thereupon the shop stewards took it upon themselves to incite the members to violate such agreements. The shop stewards formed an organization of their own within the unions, controlled by boys under draft age, slackers, conscientious objectors and various exempt classes. The rank and file was composed of persons new to unionism, of women, children and old men—people who knew nothing of union tactics.

This shop stewards' organization was responsible for a large percentage of the strikes during the war. The membership of the unions flouted the authority of their own elected officials; they felt no responsibility for, nor obligation to keep the contracts made by these officials and became an easy prey to every sort of fad.

So far the movement had not become definitely Bolshevist. It was only irresponsible, erratic and incapable of understanding the powers and limitations of union democracy. It still needed the Bohemian faddist and intellectual element. This was furnished by the leaders of what is known as "guild Socialism". This, again, is but one of numerous sprouts from the old anarchist root. It proposes an organization of industry along the lines of the old guild groups. The resemblance to the Soviet scheme is not hard to detect.

This Guild Socialist movement is supported almost entirely by "intellectuals". It has more "literature" than experience. Like every ready-made social scheme it catches the support of those who have never helped to build the slowly growing structure of democracy. When Russian Bolshevism made its appearance, this class in England, as in nearly all allied nations, was captured by its specious Utopianism and fine-sounding phrases. The Guild Socialists were largely pacifists. They had espoused pacifism along with other fads. In the shop stewards' movement they saw an opportunity, for the first time, to hitch all their schemes to a real labor movement.

There were times during the war when the activity of this movement threatened the success of the Allied arms. It is difficult to give figures concerning its strength. Those that are commonly given are contradictory and indefinite. A better estimate of its dangerous power is afforded by the fact that during the last year of the war there was scarcely a moment during which some strike for which it was responsible was not in progress. The followers of these tactics assured me that a majority of the organized workers of Great Britain were behind the shop stewards and ready to revolt against union officials and organized society. It is only certain that the strength of the movement was sufficient seriously to interfere with the prosecution of the war, to disintegrate some of the unions and to threaten chaos in case of an industrial crisis.

The same tendencies are found in Italy. They have gathered around the *delegates des ateliers* in France. The philosophy of Bolshevism has obtained a large following among pseudo-intellectuals in the United States. Each of these piffling players with industrial problems seems to fancy himself in the position of dictator, wielding the power of an ignorant, aroused and desperate proletariat.

The ending of the war brought about a sudden spread of the movement. The seizure of a multitude of industrial cities, of great factories, of ships in the German fleet, and the exclusion of a whole section of the population from any voice in the new government, speak far louder than any formal disavowal of the extent to which Bolshevism has captured Germany. If it attains power it will only bring about utter confusion and famine, which is already at the door.

Finland, where the attempt of labor forces to form an orderly government, ruled by labor, was crushed out in a bloody massacre by German autocracy, aided and abetted by German Socialists, is turning also to Bolshevism now that the defeat of Germany has removed the terrorism of the White Guard. Sweden, so long under German influence, whose Socialists, with the exception of Branting and his followers, flirted with German autocracy and condoned the treaty of Brest-Litovsk, is now threatened with a Bolshevik outbreak.

Switzerland was threatened with an outbreak of Bolshevism last August. Geneva was in the throes of a general strike, in which the regular unions were largely disregarded and Socialist officials were flouted.

Austria seems to be swept by Bolshevism. At a time when its failure is becoming more and more evident in Russia, it has found favor in half the world among the desperate and the ignorant upon the one hand and the cleverly ambitious would-be dictators upon the other.

Up to the present time it has obtained small hold among actual workers in the United States. The existence of a powerful trade union movement steadily gaining power and privileges for its members is the first bulwark against Bolshevism. The second is the existence of broad democratic institutions that permit social progress to advance as fast as the majority wills. A third obstacle is the mental attitude arising from a knowledge of the possibilities of democracy and the practice of its privileges.

Bolshevism, like other fine-spun theories, flourishes among those who know least of democracy. In Italy Bolshevism was rampant among those who were most inexperienced in industrial management. It was entirely absent in the great productive cooperatives, which the defenders of Bolshevism instanced as examples of the successful application of one phase of their theories.

If the nations of the world, and the powerful industries within the nations, disregard the provisions made for the distribution of the essentials of industry which have been created during the war, and enter into a mad scramble for steel, copper, rubber and the comparatively scarce metals necessary for alloys and high-speed tools, then, when prices have sky-rocketed and again fallen, we may expect a panic. An industrial crisis, with demobilization of military forces to add to the problem of the unemployed, would breed Bolshevism as slums breed tuberculosis.

If to such a condition we add the effort to smash the organized labor movement during the war, we can rest assured that angry, unorganized labor, led by hair-brained, would-be Trotzkys, will cry out that the time has come to "strike upon the job," stay in the factory and drive out the boss.

On the other hand, if we realize that this war has brought us through the hardest part of the social revolution that lies before the modern world; if we continue the conscious organization of society through which we mobilized for war; if we retain the machinery for industrial adjustment which has grown up in the midst of war and which nations like Great Britain are adopting, then we can progress steadily and democratically into whatever social changes the majority of the people shall decide are desirable.

Housing of Workers
In a Manufacturing City

(Continued from page 6)

a share in this real property and acquire it by slow steps for Bridgeport's manufacturers are awakening to the fact that every dollar earned from dividend owes some share of that dollar to some plan for home building. Most of the wide-awake manufacturers have indicated their willingness to put into our building program some share of each dividend. It is true that every dollar earned in every payroll has a certain number of cents' obligation to the financial plan that relates to the home and the amount of this from the payroll earned by a man with a family is about 20 per cent. for each dollar. The amount from the dividend is not definite, depending upon the number of men employed and other factors. Let these two forms of return from labor and capital be combined and produce houses as fast as they are needed and 20 per cent. of the payroll be put into the ownership of homes. Every dollar earned from dividend has an obligation to support Americanization and, as far as our knowledge goes, no better way can be found to invest money in this direction than in some added effort toward homes for the working class, assisting a new investor to own his home. The high wage of today and tomorrow and from now on will give the worker not only the opportunity that comes with the increased income but also the duties and obligations that follow closely. If the great cities are to be the homes of the industries, then this idea can be realized in only a partial degree through suburban homes. But if the industries are to seek out or establish smaller centers, then the wage earner has the opportunity to become more distinctly and more conspicuously a citizen. There are in a town like Bridgeport two sources of capital wealth only—the first the payroll and the second dividend. If we find the right proportion of each to apply to the home problem as an investment, automatically we shall have a sufficient number of homes.

CONSTRUCTION SCHEMES

We find in our closely developed sections of Bridgeport—and it is true of many of the small cities—a large amount of wood construction in areas densely populated and in what is known as the three-decker type. The cost of land affects the density of population. If three families are housed on a lot 50 x 100 feet, there will be little light on the side of the house except in the top story and little advantage from the backyard. We have developed a new type of 3-story home with a density double that of the old three-decker and have so arranged the grouping that there is double the light and air space. This is done by using the two-room deep arrangement and by facing the building units on courts and play grounds.

Heating the house is a very serious difficulty and we have undertaken to prove the advantage of central heating. It can't be safely said that this is the cheapest form of heating the average family in the working class today because the average family does not occupy the whole of the house and therefore does not heat it all. Unless a heating system is very elastic, it is difficult to allow people to live in a partially heated house supplied by a central station. The time will come when heat will be sold by the slot meter the same as gas. We have been successful in heating a group of 86 families with a central plant through the severe test of last winter and are building two additions.

Our introduction of a row house with access to the street from the kitchen may very well apply to all forms of houses in a concentrated part of a city where alleys have never been installed. We offer our development, known as Seaside Village, as a challenge to the architects of America. If the house can be built of brick with a slate roof and the family can have a yard in front and a garden in the rear and we can curve the street so as to let the sunlight in and avoid the monotony of the continuous rows of houses by a few changes here and there, then we can maintain our style of architecture given to us by our forefathers and can make the home surroundings attractive. We are testing our apartment development. Both schemes are needed in a growing city.

THE SOCIAL VALUE

May we not look into the home of the Greek and the Hungarian, or the Slav or our artistic Pole, after he has moved into one of our villages, and hope to find neatness and pride and love of America growing just a bit faster than when he lived on Turkey Hill, a settlement of 1,000 houses built by the inhabitants with lumber "borrowed, begged or stolen," some decent in appearance, but tuberculosis rampant and Bolshevism growing rapidly? As long as the woman wears a shawl on her head it is all right, but as soon as the children enter school they become ashamed of Turkey Hill. They pass my house every day going to the dump to gather things from the ashes. I heard one boy say about us at the bottom of the hill: "We are down among the rich people now and must be careful." We have been housing all nationalities—140 of them—for a year and a half now, and know how vast is the response to the at- tractive home life. We must break up our ne- of nationalities and mix them and let them a- vance. Let us deal fairly with these new pe- ples and get away from pushing off to the d- alley those who have been taught to live on ... We shall find it good business to see to it ... he who advises the new American is not look- for a double profit.

Can Bridgeport offer a better introducti- into our city, to the man and his wife with ... English and no antagonism to us when he ar- rives, than a three-room flat in Seaside Villa- and let him learn that to go forward he mu- speak English and be American?

I am a builder by training and I love mas- ery, but the pleasure in building is greatly en- hanced by knowing that when I have finish- the structure and planted the hedge and ... flowers, the little lace curtain of home will ha- in the pretty window. *The home of the workin- man is the balance wheel of Democracy.*

HIGHER STANDARDS SET

To sum up the work in Bridgeport: The- have been built by the Remington Compan- about 700 houses, designed by an archite- These are all of durable construction, bri- walls and slate roofs with very few exceptio- and are Philadelphia style with flat roofs. Th- Bridgeport Housing Company has built a- proximately 250 homes independently and ... now assisting the Government to build 850 a- ditional home units. Variation in room nu- bers is from two to eight and the feeling wh- is prevalent in Bridgeport is that a new ord- of things has begun. This will go much farth- than the housing of the middle working cla- for the lower paid worker will of necessity ... allowed to take the old house abandoned by ... higher paid brother worker when the new hou- are occupied and the opportunity will be ... hand to revamp and better the unproducti- dark tenements for the use of the lower pai- worker. Our rented home units will se- standard of fairness in the matter of relatio- of landlord to tenant which will reach far b- yond the 2,000 home units which I have ... scribed. The effort of the housing moveme- has brought about another startling result wh- will affect the future of the appearance of ... town very largely. One of the biggest savin- banks in Bridgeport has issued among its ru- that no loan shall be made upon any new ho- unless the same is designed by an architect. ... this rule becomes general in our savings ba- we shall certainly have different appear- cities ten years from now.

At left—Entrance Apartment Building designed for the newly married. Near park. Room arrangement permits plaintiful supply light and air. Doors and window- screened. Roof garden. At right—7-Room Brick Cottage. Original Cottage 5 rooms, 2 added. 8 Children.

Bolshevism Probed by Senate

(Continued from page 3)

entered into an alliance with the Ger to fight the Allies in the north and the slovaks in the west, and in that same ment Germany agreed not to interfere with ork of the Soviets.

one occasion after Lenine and Trotzky into power, Bruhchevich, the secretary of e, made the statement that German ar and German soldiers had passed 'around grad on their way north.'"

BOLSHEVIK SAME AS I. W. W.

George A. Simons, superintendent of ethodist Episcopal Mission to Russia since was another witness thoroughly familiar the country and in a position to learn first hand. His sensational testimony d comment all over America, especially portion in which he told of the leading parts played by Russians who once had been in ountry, in the Bolshevist horrors.

was absolutely impossible, he said, for any o understand what was going on in Russia s he saw it with his own eyes. He told of wholesale murder of innocent civilians, the ging of young girls by the Red Guard, the e without legal process of all property, the together of helpless people and throwing into a river to drown, the absolute sup ion of free speech and a free press, the l starving of those who do not indorse evist teachings and programs, and the ng of huge sums into other countries to stir sorder.

plying to a question, Dr. Simons said that essentials the aims of the I. W. W. and the eviki were the same.

ssia, so far as civilization is concerned, pictured as a dead land. Dr. Simons point t that at the time of the revolution Petro was a magnificent city of 2,300,000 popula Today it is a city under the spell of with a population estimated, he said, at han 800,000.

at the Bolshevist group in Russia is spend millions of dollars in propaganda in other ries was again asserted. In this connection Lowry Humes, the Judge Advocate in e of the examination of witnesses, pro an official translation of a Bolshevist rnment order appropriating 2,000,000 s for propaganda purposes in enemy, dly, and neutral countries.

Simons said that the Bolsheviki were y anti-Ally, though attempting to disguise fact so as to have a refuge in the United s when their régime fell. "They have a affection for Germany," he testified, "as een proved time and again."

Simons here told of his visits, disguised workman, to the meeting places of the eviki. He said that in conversation with gnorant masses of the movement he found few of them had any idea what Bolshevism y was.

told of the haranguing of these people by tors who traveled about the city in trucks. y of these agitators, he added, he recognized ew York East siders he had met in Petrograd ho had been pointed out to him.

To what was due more than to anything the success of these Bolsheviki?" asked tor King.

To the cleverly worked-out program of ter m and to the advocacy of the slaughter of they call the capitalist class. The whole tion might be summed up in their slogan: security of the proletarian cause lies in ng a gun in the hands of the workmen.'"

Simons told of witnessing the murder o young men in front of his office in Petro the killing taking place a few minutes

REV. GEORGE A. SIMONS

before Ambassador Francis, who was his dinner guest that night, arrived at his home.

Asked to estimate the number of persons who had been murdered by the Bolsheviki, Dr. Simons replied that it was in the thousands, but that no man could at this time even approximate the number of the victims.

"The Bolsheviki never investigate. They kill on the spot, as a rule," he added.

BOLSHEVIK PROPAGANDA ABROAD

"You have heard," said Senator King, "of the I. W. W. here in America. I will ask you if you see any difference between that organization and the Bolshevist organization in Russia?"

"I am strongly convinced that in all main essentials the aims of the Bolsheviks and of the I. W. W. are identical. Minister of Posts and Telegraphs Zorin, who lived eight years on the east side, told me once that they expected to get Germany after Russia, and after Germany they would tackle the United States."

"That's a big job," remarked Senator Nelson.

"Do you know the extent of their appropriation for propaganda in other countries?" asked Senator Overman.

"I do not know the total, but we know that millions of rubles were appropriated for that work, a great deal of it for the work in India and China. They are also very active in England."

"Can you tell us anything of the treatment accorded the so-called bourgeoisie or middle classes?" Senator Nelson asked.

"Thousands upon thousands of them have been starved to death," Dr. Simons answered. "I have seen the walking shadows of these dying human beings in the streets of Petrograd. Thousands have dropped dead in their tracks. I have seen them myself. I have seen some of the finest men of the old days standing starving in the streets and with outstretched hands begging a few kopecks. I have been in the homes of the best people of Petrograd, in which there has been no bread for weeks. When I say the better class, I mean the people who believe in a clean handkerchief and a white shirt."

William W. Welsh, of the Petrograd branch of the National City Bank, painted a gloomy picture of Russia under the Bolsheviki in his testimony before the Overman committee. His was the first testimony to connect directly agitators from this country with the existing reign of terror. Mr. Welsh said that in Petrograd he met many of the agitators who went to Russia from this country and who gained power in the Bolshevist Government.

"A great many of these men," he said, "came into the bank to get their American money exchanged for Russian money. I talked with them and I never met one who would admit that he was a naturalized American citizen. Most of them had been in the United States anywhere from three to ten or twelve years. They had no use for the United States. They said there was no freedom over here and that they had come back to Russia to be free. Don't confuse these men with our laboring men, for the honest laboring man, who owns or rents a decent home, who owns a piano, a phonograph, and has good clothes and furniture in Russia would be placed in the bourgeoisie class. Over there, as things are going now, the man who wears a clean shirt or the woman who wears a hat is a bourgeoisie. I have been on street cars in Petrograd and have heard Bolsheviki taunt other women passengers because they happened to be wearing a presentable hat. They sneer at them as 'you women who wear hats.' There are in this country at this moment great numbers of persons who say they sympathize with Bolshevism, who, if they were in Russia, would be placed among the enemies of the Bolsheviki and marked for starvation."

"Did the crowd of agitators from the New York east side and other parts of the United States become officials in Russia?" asked Senator Nelson.

"Yes, practically all of them, except such as were real sincere revolutionists. They were later labeled bourgeoisie."

Ralph M. Dennis of Chicago, and Robert F. Leonard of Minneapolis, were two witnesses who further verified the stories of atrocities by the Red Guards. Each had seen many persons murdered and each was thoroughly familiar with conditions over a wide area of Russia. They agreed that strenuous efforts were being made by Lenine and Trotzky to spread the Bolshevist idea to the United States. In this they were borne out by Professor Russell Storey of the University of Illinois, who asserted that the Bolsheviki were frankly anti-Ally and were openly aiming at world domination.

BOLSHEVIK AGENTS ADMIT HORRORS

Open advocates of Bolshevism heard by the committee convicted the cause they advocated by their own testimony. Among these were John Reed, "Bolshevist Consul General in New York," who told of meeting former New Yorkers, now Bolshevist officials who had changed their names in Russia; of how he hoped to open a propaganda bureau here financed "by wealthy women who had more money than they knew what to do with," and how 2,000,000 rubles had been appropriated for international propaganda work. He also said he helped edit five Bolshevist papers with an aggregate circulation of almost two million daily.

Williams was on the stand for two days. At first the committee permitted him to tell his story in his own way, asking few questions. When he was re-called, however, he was pinned down to facts and it was then that his admissions convicted the Bolsheviks of horrors. At first Williams told the committee that the number killed in Russia totalled fewer than 50,000. In revising his testimony, he admitted that up to last May, when he left, this number must be at least 150,000.

He admitted that the atrocities of the Red Guard were frightful and told the committee that the stories of other witnesses doubtless were true. Williams left Russia months before the others who testified. Moreover, from his testimony it was made clear that Williams' first-hand observations in Russia were exceedingly limited.

From Readers of The National Civic Federation Review

From the beginning of the re-issue of the REVIEW, on December 5, 1918, stacks of congratulatory letters from all parts of the country and from all classes of the community have been received by the editor, the publication of which would require a volume. These letters, while referring to many topics treated by the REVIEW, speak specifically of the wonderful series of articles by T. Everett Harré on "Shadow Huns and Others," of the informing papers by Gustavus Myers and William English Walling on the Bolsheviki, and of the general anti-socialist trend of the discussions on industrial affairs.

Some of these letters were addressed to Mr. Harré personally and many of them seem such good propaganda matter that we are publishing a few in this number of the REVIEW, omitting signature where permission to use them has not been [illegible]d.

Los Angeles, Calif., February 6, 1919.

Mr. T. Everett Harré,
The National Civic Federation Review,
1 Madison Avenue, New York, N. Y.

Dear Sir:

I am reading with great in[illegible] and [illegible]reciation your series of articles on "Sha[illegible] Huns and Others" in THE NATIONAL CIVIC FEDERATION REVIEW. I am a socialist, and doubtless I differ with you profoundly on all sorts of questions. But I recognize the immense importance and value of what you are doing in combating national and social defeatism, Bolshevism and all-round diabolism, as voiced in the *New Republic*, the *Nation*, the *Dial* and the *Survey*. I hope that your articles will be assembled and printed in convenient form as a low-priced pamphlet, and that they may gain the widest possible circulation.

When I say that I am a socialist I must explain the statement by the notation that I have no connection with the Socialist Party of America. From the beginning of the great European conflict I recognized the prevalent pro-Germanism of the party leaders and strove against it. Considerations, however, of loyalty to a movement to which I had given so much of my life, as well as the futile hope that the party would right itself, prevailed upon me to retain my membership until the evidence became overwhelming that the party was irrevocably committed to national defeatism. Then I quit.

Your article in the issue of January 25th is an especially strong presentation of the defeatism and diabolism of the *New Republic* and its editor, and ought to prove convincing even to that friend of the editor's who protested against your previous articles. Probably, however, it will not convince such a mind; for one who can swallow with gusto the mass of untruths, distortions and pretensions with which that periodical constantly feeds its followers, and strain at a statement of fact, is not to be helped by any cogency of reasoning or marshalling of evidence.

I hope you will go on with this work. I wonder that more writers and more journals in the East do not set themselves to the task of taking up and answering, one by one, the outrageous statements, arguments and insinuations that regularly appear in the four periodicals I have named. The neglect to do so has given a certain vogue to this kind of stuff; and increasing numbers of persons are brought under its influence. It wins its way among both softheads and rough-necks; and since, apart from your series of articles there is little that serves for a correction, the plague becomes menacing. You are meeting it in a forceful and telling way, and I congratulate you.

Sincerely yours,
W. J. GHENT.

The following letter is from one of the most distinguished scholars and historians in America:

I have I confess a contempt for a goodly fraction of our so-called "Parlor-Socialists" which takes me to the very limits of Christian charity. They understand only one very minor fraction of America,—*i. e.*, the Yiddish "Near-Soviet" of the East Side, and they are perfectly willing to play with fire, no matter how close they come to the powder magazine, so long as the sparks are bright, and the whole thing is amusing. I have much more respect personally for your real radical, who is struggling against undoubted physical wrongs (however unfortunate his remedies for those wrongs) than for well groomed ladies and gentlemen who love to dabble in social devilitry and stir up discontent, well assured that so doing will not probably cut into *their* particular incomes, and that a certain reputation for being very "advanced" brings them much highly desired advertising.

The *New Republic* is today engaged to use another simile in the alluring but not altogether safe amusement of trying to see how far it can paddle down the Niagara rapids and not get caught in the current and hurried over the falls of unabashed "red revolution"—an accident which would of course destroy all its prestige, circulation and influence and leave it the organ merely of a crude narrow propaganda, carrying no weight except among its own particular "comrades", and too "high brow" to be really useful to them. The *Nation* I think has got well into the rapids already. The *Dial* will also have great difficulty in getting back up stream, in fact its case is practically hopeless.

Inasmuch as the editors of these organs seem determined on a policy that makes them better reading in Great Russia than in America, I think a public service is being rendered in hoisting the proper colors over them as soon as possible that all may know where they belong. I can forgive many things, but I cannot forgive readily a scientifically trained American (often with a long academic record) who deliberately commits himself to the propagation of the most un-American thing in the world—*a gospel of class hatred.*

The following letter, dated Cambridge, Mass., was received by Mr. Harré:

I desire to express to you my great appreciation of the excellent articles you have contributed to THE NATIONAL CIVIC FEDERATION REVIEW on the work of German agents and near-agents.

There is a matter which I hope you may have an opportunity to touch upon in the course of your investigations—if, indeed, you have not already done so. The radical-socialistic journals are at present smoothing the way in this country for inculcation of the virtues of Bolshevism. It is characteristic of this sort of propaganda that it relies almost wholly upon rhetoric rather than definite facts and information. I was recently told by the editor of such a journal (one which is very well known to you) that he was guided in his editorial policy by information brought over by certain Red Cross workers; but he significantly added that he was unable to quote them because they had been asked to keep their knowledge secret 'for the present.' I wonder what authorities have imposed this censorship; It looks very much as if the Bolshevik-mongers were imposing this conspiracy of silence themselves in order to prevent people from realizing just how incomplete, biassed, and untrustworthy the information they claim to possess really is. The sooner the American public is given a complete and authenticated account of the Russian situation the better will be our protection against this irresponsible propaganda.

An interesting analysis of the appeal of destructive radicalism is given in the following communication from Connecticut:

Is it asking too much to request you to send marked copies of the latest issue of THE NATIONAL CIVIC FEDERATION REVIEW to some few citizens of this burg? I think they *need* it.

This instalment of the "Shadow Huns" article is *magnificent, tremendous, splendid.*

I am carried away with admiration and approval. Mr. Harré has done a wonderful piece of work, which ought to be in the hands of everybody.

The *New Republic* has a wide number of pious, sentimental adherents hereabouts, and I presume everywhere, who excuse what "Pro-Germanism" they can "detect" by its evident air of "intellectualism" and emotional morality.

I hope to see all these vicious publications analyzed and laid bare as this has been done. It is the most sinister work that has ever been perpetrated in any country—this defiling the minds of innocent people. And it is astounding to see how guileless people fall for it.

I think the secret of its success with the "educated" and Puritanical classes of the country lies in its essential *conservative* and *reactionary* mental bias, in total contradiction to its pretended radicalism. That is, it flatters its readers' self-love by pretending to present a progressive viewpoint, while at heart it is retrogressive and backward. It plays upon the old passion for mythical, mystical religious conceptions—the love of crusade for a remote sublimated *Ideal*, as opposed to the vigorous, virile, practical religion of the day founded upon *facts*, and marching hand in hand with *science.*

The pious women and the well-meaning fanatics whom you find voicing these high-flown vagaries are invariably of that dreamer type. They don't wa[illegible] a red-blooded religion of everyday life and *truth*— but a vague something that lures them on to [illegible] fanatical crusade which is not abated or modifie[d] by the discovery of facts and recognition of alread[y] accomplished social changes. Their "brain pattern[s]" are formed and cannot be changed.

That is why I say these are essentially the co[n]-*servatives*—the dyed-in-the-wool "stand-patters", wh[o] cannot take in a new idea or recognize a new co[n]-ception of morality founded on *fact* and *knowledg[e]* of mankind and what he will do under certain co[n]-ditions. Their minds are unadaptable—truly con-servative.

This may be far-fetched as a psychological analysi[s] but I thought it might be a suggestion of some us[e] to you if you contemplate a show-up of the *victim[s]* of this propaganda. And to make Mr. Harré's stor[y] complete, that should be an epilogue.

Why, even the school-children here are bringin[g] home this bunk about "sweetness and light" fro[m] Germany! Miss Addams is perfectly right in say-ing that ministers are taking texts from the *New Republic* (I hear 'em, myself!) and I even saw [a] soldier (Young Men's Christian Association room!) devouring one the other day!

The following is a letter from a Presbyteria[n] clergyman:

I have just received and read with interest cop[y] of THE NATIONAL CIVIC FEDERATION REVIEW. I wan[t] to thank you for sending it to me. Your editoria[ls] and articles and article by T. Everett Harré arouse [a] deal of apprehension, and I am glad your paper i[s] presenting the perils that are to be met.

It has occurred to me that we need not only such [a] printed page, but even more—speakers with abilit[y] to bring to the people the same message of warning. I have thought of it in connection with a group o[f] men in my church to whom I would like to hav[e] such an informing address made. We meet ever[y] Monday evening for supper, and a conference follow-ing, for discussion of the problems of the Reconstruc-tion Period. We have about 150 men present. Ca[n] you tell me of a man who could be secured for som[e] Monday evening in January or February, and wh[o] could bring such a strong message as is contained i[n] your articles, or the paper of Mr. Harré? Perhap[s] you or Mr. Harré might come. I am anxious tha[t] the men in this typical American community, an[d] one of the greatest industrial centers, should know the facts outlined.

Will you please let me know what chance ther[e] is of securing a speaker for this purpose, and upo[n] what terms? I thought it might be possible that th[e] Civic Federation has a bureau of speakers. Such [a] plan would certainly not be of less value than t[o] publish the REVIEW.

The following letter, addressed to Mr. Harré, came from a distinguished church historian:

Though a stranger to you, I must write to tel[l] you that I have had much pleasure and satisfactio[n] in reading your articles on Shadow Huns. You ar[e] doing a valuable service in exposing this crew. Specially am I delighted with your attention to th[e] *New Republic.* That nefarious sheet has long neede[d] sharp following up, such as you are giving it. I think it has been clear for some time that it is a pro-German organ; but your treatment of Croly's book and of the parallelism with German propaganda makes this unanswerably certain. Please continue, and treat 'em rough.

You have not yet spoken of another connection between Germany and The *New Republic* of which doubtless you are aware. In your article in THE NATIONAL CIVIC FEDERATION REVIEW of Jan. 25 you mention Prof. M. J. Bonn as having been one of the propagandists sent to these shores in 1914. This German agent wrote more than one article in The *New Republic*, as the index will show.

I feel that I must write you and commend the December 20 number of THE NATIONAL CIVIC FEDERATION REVIEW, especially the articles on Russia, Dr. Shaw, Walter Weyl, and *The New Republic.*

As I have pointed out in the Boston papers, the conservative and intelligent elements here are doing very little to combat the social revolutionary movement, while the radicals are at it all the time. At the last meeting of the Economic Club of Boston, three out of four speakers, including Rhys Williams, Olgin and Thomas Proctor, of New York, (Red Cross), all endorsed the Bolshevik point of view. The radicals here are working to make the League of Nations an instrument of social revolution; and claim that any other use of it means that it will be an instrument of capitalism.

Tyrrel Print, New York.

The National Civic Federation Review

IV. NEW YORK, MARCH 25, 1919 No. 11

EUROPE'S WAR LABOR EXPERIENCE

E NATIONAL CIVIC FEDERATION'S COMMISSION ON INDUSTRIAL INQUIRY STUDYING IT TO APPLY TO CONDITIONS HERE—FAREWELL LUNCHEON TO A. F. BEMIS AND A. PARKER NEVIN

BRING to us Europe's experience in industrial and labor problems," was the keynote sounded at the luncheon given early in the month at the City Midday h to A. F. Bemis and A. Parker Nevin, last he delegates to start abroad to join The Naal Civic Federation's Commission on Indusl Inquiry. Already Charles Mayer, Charles Barrett, Grant Forbes, James W. Sullivan l E. A. Quarles have begun the work. At the ewell luncheon given Messrs. Bemis and vin, the speakers expressed forcefully the need fullest information on industrial conditions l of the steps taken abroad, particularly in itain, to meet reconstruction problems.

When in England, the Federation's Commisn will be aided by the National Alliance of ployers and Employed of which the Rt. Hon. derick Huth Jackson is chairman and W. A. pleton is secretary. The British organization l aid The National Civic Federation's Comsion in mapping its itinerary and in other ys. Simultaneously, the American branch of Commission will conduct an inquiry here. s branch is composed of: V. Everit Macy, L. Cease, George Emmons, Mrs. Sara A. Con-, Albert Russel Erskine, Hugh Frayne, R. J. more, H. H. S. Handy, H. E. Miles, Miss na K. Bowen and Matthew Woll.

Dr. Talcott Williams presided at the luncheon and first called upon Ralph M. Easley, Chairman, executive council, of The National Civic Federation, to outline the purpose of sending the Commission abroad.

"The outstanding feature resulting from the war," said Mr. Easley, "industrially speaking, is the broader and juster attitude taken by the large employing classes toward their employees. Within the last two months there has been a general acclaim demanding that in future so-called 'capital and labor' shall strive to maintain better relations, each recognizing the rights of the other.

"Concrete evidence of this sentiment has been shown by the program submitted to the United States Chamber of Commerce by its industrial committee at the meeting in Atlantic City; by resolutions adopted by the New York Chamber of Commerce; by public statements made by Charles M. Schwab, F. A. Vanderlip, John D. Rockefeller, Jr., and other captains of industry throughout the country. It matters not that in these resolutions, proposals and speeches there are all kinds of ideas, some practical, some impractical, about how to produce this better state of feeling. The essential thing is that they are all committed to an attempt to work out a bettering of our industrial conditions.

"It is the program of The National Civic Federation to try to translate these high ideals into a practical program by making a study, both in this country and in Europe, of the results of the experience in dealing with the 'capital and labor program during the war.'

"For instance: What has England learned during the war in respect to methods dealing with capital and labor problems that can be of benefit to us in the United States? What is the truth about the 'Whitley system' which is held up to us as 'the last word' on the subject? What does 'shop stewardism' stand for? And does it make for peace or chaos? What of the proposed schemes whereby employees are to be given a voice in the management of the business? What is meant by 'democratization of industry?'

"While the 'Whitley system' is much discussed as a new discovery, is it in fact anything more than what already exists in this country in such industries as coal mining, the printing and building trades, the boot and shoe, the textile and other industries where collective bargaining with its various committees has long obtained, the general principles of which have formed the basis for the program of the War Labor Board?

"Is not 'shop stewardism' another name for I. W. W.'ism? And if permitted to function,

HUGH FRAYNE

CHARLES MAYER

MAJOR AUGUST BELMONT

Copyright F. C. Bangs.
A. PARKER NEVIN

CHARLES S. BARRETT

ALBERT F. BEMIS

will it not destroy in this country not only the American Federation of Labor and the Railway Brotherhoods, but private ownership of industry as well? How far have profit-sharing, bonus systems or stock participation schemes proven a satisfactory antidote for industrial unrest? How far is State control of industry—that is, regulation of the functions of both employers and employees—made necessary by war emergency, desirable as a permanent policy?

"These are some of the questions that the foreign section of The National Civic Federation's Industrial Commission is expected to inquire into and it goes to England at a moment when England itself is inquiring into the same questions. While the Labor Congress in Paris is considering only questions of international application, the Joint Industrial Conference in London, now in session, is dealing with the specific questions that concern England and which concern the United States as well.

"It is important to note that both in Paris and London all the programs provided for joint considerations by employers and employees, while at the recent conference in Berne only the interests of socialists and workers were considered. This is the reason why the American Federation of Labor Commission, headed by Samuel Gompers, refused to attend that conference. All employers, whether or not they approve of all the methods of the American trade union movement, will agree that today they are faced with the alternative of joining hands with that movement to put down the anarchy of Bolshevism or of both being forced to succumb to Bolshevism."

STARTS WITH OPEN MIND

Mr. Bemis, answering the toastmaster's question: "What do you expect to do?" said:

"I feel very much in starting off on this mission that I should have the spirit of the open mind. It seems to me we should go without convictions, without opinions—that is, as to what those various things that have occurred over there during the war, those industrial matters really signify and really mean, particularly as applied to conditions in this country. It is perfectly clear, however, that no matter how isolated we may have been in the past, hereafter in this country we must be more cosmopolitan, so to speak. We cannot ignore the conditions of industry in the other principal nations of the world and shut ourselves up in a box in this country and paddle our own canoe without reference to them.

"So that, if there is a specific object that I have as an individual in accepting the kindness

JAMES W. SULLIVAN

of The National Civic Federation or the honor I should say—it is simply to study those particular things to which your chairman has just called attention with a view to determining in what respect any of those things may be adopted in this country which will make of us a greater world power industrially, and which will bring into greater harmony those great forces in industry and society as a whole. These we must recognize—whether or not the Bolshevists do—namely, that we are all workers and that those who act simply as life trustees for capital and are called perhaps capitalists or managers, do, nevertheless, represent a fundamental and essential part of industry.

"We must cooperate, and we must recognize the different elements which constitute our social and industrial life and bring them into as great harmony as possible for the good of society as a whole."

"I have not in many months, or even in years," said Dr. Williams, when Mr. Bemis had ended, "heard a happier phrase than that Mr. Bemis just has given us, that of 'life trustees for the good of society.' If we can succeed in getting on the other side the view that labor are the trustees for the benefit of society, we will be able to reach a solution. Directly opposite me sits one who has been through his career a trustee of society—Major Belmont who succeeded in adjusting a dispute which seemed impossible to adjust in regard to compensation for the injuries to labor, and who will be one of the leaders in the adjustment of this question."

"I have had no warning of this," said Major Belmont. "I would feel much more confidence in what I might have to say had I prepared myself on a subject of this kind, because it is so broad and carries with it so much. I do not feel that even in a lengthy talk I could cover it properly.

USING BORROWED CAPITAL

"I will touch upon but one feature of the situation. It was suggested to my mind by one of the most striking things that has been said on the subject abroad. Mr. J. H. Thomas, M.P., General Secretary of the British Railway Men's Union said,—'for four years the industrial life of the country has been conducted on borrowed capital, which has created an atmosphere fatal to sound economic progress. You will have to do what the nation must do;—retrench and build up your losses as soon as possible.'

"That is the most comprehensive thing that has been uttered on British industrial conditions since the war ceased. In this country we are suffering from much the same thing, but in a greater degree than in England because the English Government took the matter of regulating her industries in hand at an early stage of the war and there was developed a direct understanding with both the employer and the employed. Labor promised it would forego many of its rules and regulations throughout the duration of the war. Employers likewise promised to resume pre-war understandings with labor as soon as the war would be over.

DEPARTED FROM ECONOMIC BASIS

"Here, it has been done in a different way. But the fact remains that as Mr. Thomas correctly said of England, our entire industrial life too has departed from an economic basis because the borrowed money of the government has been running and patronizing industry with but one idea in view,—production without regard to cost. We cannot have any restoration of proper conditions of industry and permanent return for labor and for capital without going back to a sound economic footing; one which will permit of a continuous life for both. If labor demands too much, it must necessarily in the end exhaust capital, and capital exhausted cannot respond to the demands of labor. This is fundamental.

"Here in America, when we entered the war,

(Continued on Page 14)

Radicals Mislead Churches About Labor

AL RECONSTRUCTION PROGRAMS PUT FORTH BY CATHOLICS AND PROTESTENTS ALIKE, BASED ON VIEWS OF NEAR-BOLSHEVIKI, NOT ON IDEAS OF RESPONSIBLE ORGANIZED LABOR

By RALPH M. EASLEY

HE Committee on Special War Activities of the National Catholic War Council has issued a pamphlet on Social Recon- n. The Chairman of the Administrative ttee of the Council is the Rt. Rev. Peter ldon, Bishop of Rockford, and the Rt. seph Schrembs, Bishop of Toledo, the Rt. atrick J. Hayes, Bishop of Tagaste (re appointed to succeed the late Cardinal as head of the Archdiocese of New York) Rt. Rev. William T. Russell, Bishop of ston, are members. This pamphlet has at- considerable attention outside of Catho- les not only because of the distinguished s whose names are attached to its fore- but because of its method of treatment of f our social problems of the day.

pamphlet is also exciting comment from t that it comes from a committee of Catho- For this reason it has been seized upon *New York Call* as evidence that the e Church, the always great bulwark Socialism, is shifting its base. *The Call* ch 8 comments as follows:

> his body of conservatives has reached a point re pious moralizing is less conspicuous and terial measures of a "socialistic" character recommended. It is an advance from which ther advances can be made, if the coming rs show that capitalism is doomed. From the re advanced positions a complete reconcilia- with a socialist society can be made without bling the conscience too much.

same interpretation is being placed upon mphlet by the radical press in general. A g of it shows that, while it contains many ents squinting, as the *Call* says, towards a l socialization of industry, there are other aphs that squint very much in the op- direction.

iew of the prodigious amount of propa- that has been put out in this country and gland in the interest of the British Labour s program, it is not at all surprising that tinguished committee responsible for this ent should have been affected by it. But t be remembered that this is not the view Catholic Church. It is only the expression opinion of the gentlemen signing the docu- nd has no official sanction. But it is not atholic Committee alone that is giving ocialistic utterances. Many of the clergy Protestant Church, also, are lining up he radical forces. The Rt. Rev. Charles Bishop of Oxford, when in this country ll, had uch to say in favor of the British r Party's program and stated that the ishop of Canterbury's Committee on In- al Problems was about to publish a report ning a program almost identical with that British Labour Party.

this country the campaign among the in- uals has been led by *The New Republic, Survey, The Dial, The Nation* and *The* , whose combined clientele includes many men, political economists and social ts.

the "Bibliography and Digest of Recon- ion Programs" put out by the Joint Com- n on Social Service of the Protestant pal Church, practically all the authorities are connected with the aforesaid radical ations, whose industrial campaign is de- entirely to the exploitation of the socialist programs of Europe, as against the trade labor programs of America. An elaborate ntitled "The Study Outline in the Prob- of the Reconstruction Period" has been prepared and published by a committee made up from members of the Social Service Commissions of the Methodist Episcopal, Baptist, Presbyterian, Protestant Episcopal and Congregational Churches. Among the three members of the committee who, it is announced, made the final revision, is Harry F. Ward, of the Union Theological Seminary. Mr. Ward is also secretary of the Methodist Federation for Social Service and has recently issued a bulletin to the Methodist papers, analyzing, apologizing for and, seemingly, defending Bolshevism.* The New York *Nation* speaks of him as "a worthy successor to Walter Rauschenbusch." Other members of the main committee included socialists like John Spargo; Walter Rauschenbusch (since deceased), a pro-German, who for ten years preached German socialism in this country under the guise of Christian Socialism; and Owen R. Lovejoy, who is out with a two-column letter in *The New York Daily Call*, in criticism of the Supreme Court's action in dealing with Eugene Debs.

A glance through this "Study Outline" reveals that all that the members of the Study classes are recommended to read on such subjects as "National Control of Employment," "Employment Guaranteed for All," "Social Insurance Against Unemployment," etc., are the works of Arthur Henderson, the English Socialist, and John Spargo, the American Socialist; The New Republic's Supplement, containing the Report on Reconstruction by the Sub-Committee of the British Labour Party, (which the Committee says is "the most constructive program yet issued,") and the Defense of the I. W. W. by Carlton H. Parker (now deceased), referring to which the Committee boils down his views of this murderous Bolshevist crowd by saying:

"The I. W. W. can be profitably viewed only as a psychological by-product of the neglected childhood of industrial America."

On the question of "Democracy in Industry" —How the Control of Industry may be Shared by the Workers, Representation in Management and on Boards of Directors, etc., the students are referred to such distinguished and practical employers and labor leaders as the Rev. Percy Stickney Grant, Rector of the Church of the Ascension, New York City; our old socialist friend, H. H. Lusk, of New Zealand; radicals and pacifists of the Survey Publishing Company;** and Sidney Webb, the Fabian Socialist author of the British Labour Party's program.

Another scheme that is furnishing great sport for certain of our intellectuals is Guild Socialism, which, while based on an old, exploded idea, has been resurrected and dressed up in a lot of new, fantastic furbelows. It proposes to abolish the wage system and establish self-government in industry, working in conjunction with the State. It will, of course, wipe out the trade unions and equally of course, will "wipe in" the Bolshevists. Father Paul Bull, C. R., an English churchman, in an article published in *The Churchman*, the chief organ of the Protestant Episcopal Church in this country, says of national guilds:

> Various schemes of reconstruction in England fail to satisfy us because they aim only at the improvement of the old capitalist system, while we feel that God is calling us to a new venture which will eradicate the root of our social disease. The National Guilds find that root in wage slavery.

He then makes an elaborate attack on the wage system, which might well have been quoted from any socialist pamphlet.

So much for the Industrial Reconstruction programs of the Protestant churches.

Now, it meant nothing to any of these committees, Protestant or Catholic, that the British Labour Party's Program is not, as stated by the Catholic Committee, "the most comprehensive and coherent program that has yet appeared on the industrial phase of reconstruction," and is not, as stated by Bishop Brent, "the one great religious utterance of the war," but, so far as its constructive proposals are concerned, is largely a rehash of resolutions adopted at International Socialist Congresses, the various socialist platforms and the pronouncements of socialist leaders of all countries during the last twenty years.

By a barrage of glittering generalities, its authors sought to disguise the fact that its program is State Socialism, pure and simple. But a little scrutiny soon discloses scattered through the document such tell-tale phrases as these:

> The individualistic system of capitalist production, based on the private ownership and competitive administration of land and capital . . . will receive its death blow. And the Labour Party refuses absolutely to believe that the British people will permanently tolerate any reconstruction . . . involved in the abandonment of British industry to . . . separate private employers. . . . What the Labour Party looks to is a genuinely scientific reorganization of the nation's industry . . . on the basis of the common ownership of the means of production; the equitable sharing of the proceeds among all who participate in any capacity and only among these, and the adoption, in particular services and occupations, of those systems and methods of administration and control that may be found, in practice, best to promote the public interest.

Then it goes on:

> The Labour Party stands not merely for the principle of the common ownership of the nation's land, to be applied as suitable opportunities occur, but also, specifically, for the immediate nationalization of railways, mines and the production of electrical power.

In other words, the State is to take over and operate all the farms, factories, mines, stores, banks, street railways, steam railways, mercantile marine, gas and electric light utilities,—in fact, all the productive industries and means of distribution, which is Marxian socialism without any disguises.

And this British Labour Party's program, which was, as previously stated, drafted not by workingmen but by a Fabian socialist, Sidney Webb, had so little support from the workingmen of England that practically every man having anything to do with it, who ran for Parliament at the last election, was defeated by an overwhelming vote.

Referring specifically to the "Social Reconstruction" pamphlet of the National Catholic War Council, without entering into any critical analysis, one is struck on reading it by many omissions and inconsistencies. Under the head-

* Dr. Ward's Bolshevist pamphlet has been vigorously attacked by *The Christian Advocate*, the leading publication of the Methodist Episcopal Church. In addition to criticizing the Bolshevist tendencies of Dr. Ward, it criticizes the socialistic flavor of his whole social program. The editorial referred to will be found in full on page 7. Dr. Ward is professor of Christian ethics in Union Theological Seminary.

** In one of the pamphlets they advertise *The Survey* at so much per year and urge all their readers to take it.

ing, "Program of American Labor," it is amazing to note that this distinguished committee makes no allusion to the well known policies of the American Federation of Labor and the Railway Brotherhoods, representing over four millions of wage earners, but refers only to the action of two State Federations of Labor and to the Chicago Labor Party, recently organized for a mayoralty campaign. The American Federation of Labor at its next annual convention will cast over 15,000 votes, based upon its dues-paying membership of three and a quarter millions; and of those 15,000 votes, the California State Federation of Labor and the Ohio State Federation of Labor—the two bodies referred to in "Social Reconstruction"—have one vote each; while the Chicago Labor Party, being a political party, will not even be present. In the complete and exhaustive reports of the Executive Council of the American Federation of Labor to the annual conventions of that body, the discussions and action thereon are available to all these church committees, and they should not only have known but have stated that in those conventions the American Federation of Labor has generally opposed by large majorities the propositions put forth by what are called in "Social Reconstruction" these "three prominent labor bodies."

It is also worthy of note that in the programs put out by the Social Service Commissions of the Protestant Churches, as well as by the Catholic Church, especially one by the Joint Commission on Social Service of the Protestant Episcopal Church, there is not a single reference to the American Federation of Labor or the Railway Brotherhoods or any of their leaders. If this omission had been intentional, it would be misleading and dishonest, not to say contemptible, for it is an insult to the organized labor movement of America to assume that it is represented by socialists, socialistic economists and I. W. W.'ists. Its views are not represented by such publications as *The New Republic, The Survey, The Dial, The Nation,* or by the organ of the Single Taxers—*The Public.* It would have been just as fair to quote *The Call, The Masses* (now *The Liberator,*) or *Solidarity*, the I. W. W. official organ, as any of these "higher-brow" publications referred to. Now, I do not mean to imply for one moment that representative men in the Catholic and Protestant Churches have intentionally done this thing but the work has been intentionally done just the same by the socialists or near-socialists in their ranks. It can be generally stated that the officials of all social welfare commissions are either straight-out socialists or so near to them in thought that the difference is not discernible with the naked eye.

The reconstruction program of the American Federation of Labor, put out officially and signed by the eleven members of the Executive Council, contained practically none of the recommendations found in the programs of the three local bodies referred to in the Social Reconstruction pamphlet. For instance, take the legal minimum wage, which is so stressed by the Catholic Committee: the American Federation of Labor has opposed it for all men and has accepted it for women only under protest. And yet the Catholic Committee says: "There is no longer any serious objection urged by impartial persons against the legal minimum wage." Certainly, the wage earners may be regarded as not "impartial persons", but can they not be regarded as the most intelligent witnesses that can be examined on this question?

Take the question of compulsory sickness insurance, also advocated by the Catholic Committee. The American Federation of Labor is on record as opposed to it by a striking majority. It does not obtain in any state. In California last fall, by a referendum vote, it was defeated by an overwhelming majority. At the recent Massachusetts Constitutional Convention, it was defeated by a large majority, while the Wisconsin legislature has just defeated a bill on that subject. In the various states where commissions have been looking into it, only one has reported in favor of it, but it has yet to run the gauntlet of the legislature. President Gompers, of the American Federation of Labor, in the *American Federationist*, the official organ of that organization, January, 1919, referring to that subject, said in part:

> There are many of our people, including workmen, who look to the government of our country to do the things which seem so easy f r the government to do and which they imagine should be done by the government. They do not recognize the pitfalls and the dangers which are entailed by conferring upon the government the function of doing these things. To my mind, it is a grave danger to place in the hands of the government the powers which would necessarily result from governmental compulsory health insurance with all the powers vested in the government incidental to and in the enforcement of health insurance.

The Brotherhood of Locomotive Engineers, at its last convention in May, 1918, unanimously adopted the report of its committee on compulsory health insurance, stating:

> First—We do not approve of any legislation that would compel our members to take out health insurance.
>
> Second—We recommend that the Grand Body go on record as opposing any State legislation compelling our members to take out any such insurance, and that our State Representatives be notified to this effect.

Speaking before a Committee that was inquiring into compulsory sickness insurance, as well as compulsory unemployment insurance, which is also advocated by the various Church committees, Mr. Gompers made the following declaration against all compulsory propositions relating to the wage-earner:

> But this particular feature I want to present to your minds, you gentlemen of the Committee on Social Insurance, that even the insurance feature of the soldiers, sailors and dependents' compensation bill is voluntary. It is not forced upon the soldier or the sailor; he has the right to decline to be insured, but he has the privilege and the opportunity to be insured.
>
> There is one thing that I want to say to the Committee on Social Insurance. Place in the hands of the government the right to determine who is or who is not entitled to government insurance; to determine regulations and conduct of every man insured, then it means that the government has the power with all the force at the command of the government to enforce the decrees of regulation.
>
> And that applies, too, to unemployment compulsory insurance. The government will determine then what will constitute justifiable reasons for unemployment. It might decide that when men and women are unemployed they are entitled to this insurance. Well, what is the cause of unemployment? Suppose it is a disagreement with employers. The government will decide as to whether the cause of unemployment is justifiable or is attributable to the workmen or to the employers. It is not necessary, then, for me to mention the fact of what that would mean to the work, the policy and the constructive movement of organized labor. The labor movement would lose its voluntary character and its effectiveness, and there would be brought about a condition of affairs in our country whereby the toilers would be rendered ineffective in their work for the protecton and promotion of their rights and interests.

Great emphasis is laid in the Catholic Social Reconstruction pamphlet, under the head "Labor Participation in Industrial Management," on the recommendations of an "English group of Quaker employers," who have proposed a scheme for giving the employees a voice in the management of the industry. The committee adds: "There can be no doubt that a frank adoption of these means and ends by employers would not only promote the welfare of the workers, but vastly improve the relations between them and their employers, and increase the efficiency and productiveness of each establishment."

Irrespective of what a handful of English

w Bolsheviki and Others

By T. EVERETT HARRÉ

. . . by . . . Colonel . . . Raymond . . . Robins.''

Perhaps you may have encountered Shadow Bolshevik propaganda—whispered hints that the United States government was responsible for the signing of the Brest Litovsk treaty because, when Russia appealed for help, America had not responded; that the truth about Russia, about Messrs. Lenine and Trotzky, has been suppressed by the wicked Allied governments and that the reported atrocities are the fabrications of agents of conspiring capitalists. You may have had it, upon certain unknown authorities, that the documents published by the Committee on Public Information, which purported to prove that Lenine and Trotzky were paid German agents, are forgeries. You may have read all the plausible arguments against intervention in such standard-bearers of loyalty, intelligence and patriotism, as the *New Republic*, the *Dial*, the *Nation* and the *Survey*. You may have read the article, ''Aunt Emmy Wants to Know,'' in Mr. Hearst's *Good Housekeeping*, and have come to the conclusion that God was in his heaven and that all was right in Russia—even if it wasn't in our own benighted country. And despite all your previous doubts, you may have been impetuously swept off your feet with conviction concerning the superior virtues and social achievements of Bolshevism, when you learned that one of the chief sources of *Good Housekeeping's* information was no less a person than Colonel Raymond Robins, unfailingly advertised as head of the American Red Cross in Russia.

During the investigation into Bolshevism by the Sub-Committee of Committee on Judiciary of the United States Senate, men appeared who had been in Russia. They told of mass murders, of executions without trial, of a bloody autocracy preserved by the terrorism of the Red Guards, of an oppression infinitely more terrible than the oppression of the Czar. Each time a new witness appeared, each time the Red Reign of Trotzky and Lenine was arraigned, —as each witness drew fire—there screamed out from the quarters of the Bolshevists, pro-Bolshevists, internationalists, conscientious objectors and pacifists, the defiant cry: ''Why—don't —they — call — Raymond — Robins?''

Somehow there was built up by implication the impression that a gigantic conspiracy was afoot to keep the real truth, the comprehensive, absolute truth, about Russia from being known; that in this conspiracy the Government was involved and the Senate Committee was involved; that the Allied governments, all the forces of the capitalistic dynasties, were moving heaven and earth to keep Colonel Raymond Robin's mouth shut. All of this had the inevitable effect of imparting to Colonel Raymond Robins something of actual importance.

ROBINS HAILED AS AMERICAN REPRESENTATIVE

We read in the testimony of Miss Louise Bryant of Colonel Robin's intimate and cordial relationship with Lenine and Trotzky. We were told that by the Bolsheviki he was regarded as ''the mouthpiece of America.'' Just as the former Rev. William Bayard Hale had been received in Germany as a super-ambassador from the American people to the German people, likewise, so were we informed, had Colonel Raymond Robins attained a similarly unique position in Bolshevik Russia. ''In their propaganda papers,'' declared the Rev. Mr. Simons, ''the Bolsheviki described Robins as a man of the people, a former workman, and in contrast pictured Governor Francis, as a typical representative of the capitalistic class. Time and again the suggestion was made that Robins should be made Ambassador.''

Miss Louise Bryant—whose husband, John Reed, had hired himself as a propagandist to the Bolsheviki—said:

''They (the Bolsheviki) did not feel that Mr. Francis represented America. They felt that Mr. Robins was the real representative of this country.''

''Mr. Robins,'' declared Miss Bryant, ''was anxious to be called before this committee.'' Why was he not called? Miss Bryant demanded that Colonel Raymond Robins be called.

Albert Rhys Williams, one of the most notorious champions of Bolshevism and self-admitted paid agent of the Bolsheviki in Russia, averred that Colonel Raymond Robins shared his own views about the Bolsheviki. Mr. Williams, too, demanded that Colonel Raymond Robins be called to testify.

Subscribing presumably to the view that everything derogatory to the Bolsheviki was all invention and that the American public was being bamboozled and hoodwinked by capitalistic agents, that everyone who came out of Russia and failed to say sweet things about Lenine and Trotzky were false witnesses, deceivers and liars, a group of choice folk in New York sometime ago formed what was called ''The Truth About Russia Committee.'' They announced they wanted to get ''the truth about Russia.'' A group, composed largely of members of this initial ''Truth About Russia Committee,'' on February 22 presented to Chairman Overman of the Senate Committee a demand that the committee alter its policy in choosing witnesses and call the men who were best informed about Russia.

PRO-BOLSHEVISTS CALL FOR ROBINS

''A certain group of witnesses have been given every opportunity to state their views,'' the demand read. ''The growing impression throughout the country, however, is that an accurate and impartial picture of the Russian revolution is not being drawn. It is felt that the net result of the investigation, if it is to be continued along the lines so far laid down, will be greatly to intensify the misconception of the Russian revolutionary situation which the general public in America now holds.''

Among the signers of this appeal were Paul U. Kellogg, editor of the *Survey*, who just prior to the war tried his puny best to stir up pacifism and avert our taking sides with the Allies against Germany; James Harvey Robinson, co-author of a text book which was ignominiously thrown out of the Seattle Public Schools because it embodied subtle pro-German propaganda; Albert J. Nock, associate editor of the pro-Bolshevist, pacifist, be-kind-to-the-Germans *Nation;* Harold Stearns, associate editor of the pro-Bolshevik *Dial;* Lincoln Colcord, pro-Bolshevist and secretary to the New Republic's League of Free Nations Association; and Dr. Harry S. Ward, who was recently summoned to answer to the Methodist clergy for attempting to exploit and justify Bolshevism through the Methodist Church.

And all of these sterling American folk, in their appeal to Chairman Overman, demanded vociferously that Colonel Raymond Robins be heard.

There may, or may not, be significance to the fact that it has been chiefly pacifists, conscientious objectors, pro-Germans, pro-Bolshevists and Bolshevist agents who cried aloud to heaven that Colonel Raymond Robins be permitted to speak. Whether this clamor became so irresistible that they were bullied and cornered into acquiescence and had no other escape, or whether they were just mildly curious, modestly desirous of being fair and impartial, at all events the Senate Committee finally did call Colonel Raymond Robins. And on a certain historic morning—it was March 6—Colonel Robins emerged from the innocuous desuetude of private life to tell, as he proclaimed, "the truth about Russia."

MR. ROBINS ESTIMATES HIMSELF

Mr. Robins, it is true, proved eloquent in self-assertions. Mr. Raymond Robins at least succeeded in convincing people of his own conviction of his own self-importance. Mr. Robins declared in so many words that he knew more about Russia than any of the Allied representatives who had been in Russia. Mr. Robins presented himself, in so many words, as "front page news." With sublime unconsciousness, he talked down to the investigating senators from the height of one who had gained and bottled-up a monopoly of special knowledge. The Allied representatives in Russia had only "indoor knowledge"—the opinions of "the seven per-cent." representing the old Czar regime. Mr. Raymond Robins had reserved for himself the "outdoor" point of view. Mr. Robins had "windows" all over Russia. He saw in, he saw out. He saw over plains, plateaus, mountains, valleys, rivers. He saw the panorama of the revolution. He beheld "company after company crumble" after Kerensky's fall. He beheld the division of land under the Bolsheviki, and saw the peasants "cultivate the soil for a year, for one season" and eat "the fruit of their labors from land that they now call their own." His vision encompassed the hitherto unreported atrocities of the Czecho-Slovak troops. But concerning the Bolsheviki, he "saw no organized terror. . . . . happened to see nobody stood up and shot." He never saw, only heard of, Bolshevik atrocities. Investigations proved these reports false. Mr. Robins implied the possession of a bird-eye view of what happened in Russia, something surpassing clairvoyance. He avowed that he "knew the situation." There could be no doubt, taking him as a man of his word, that Mr. Robins' exploring vision—his insight and outsight—was unique, peculiar. For he saw much that others did not see. Likewise he did not see, to an infinitely greater degree, what others saw.

Boiled down from the congested mass of circumlocution, digression, profuse verbiage and involved rhetoric, certain facts in Mr. Robins' testimony stand out. Mr. Robins, according to his own statement under oath, arrived in Russia in July, 1917, and "had six months of Bolshevik rule." He left Vladvostock June 1st, 1918, ten months ago. Mr. Robins told the Senate Committee that he had "percolated pretty well all over" Russia. Cross-examined specifically as to his movements, he admitted that he had not been in Kiev, or at Samara, or at Perm, that he had not gone down the Volga, or the Dneiper, or the Dneister. He had not been in Little Russia. Asked by Senator Nelson as to whether he had not confined most of his work and operations to the big cities, Petrograd and Moscow, Mr. Robins answered:

"Yes."

"And you get your impressions from that?" asked Senator Nelson.

"To a very considerable degree," acquiesced Mr. Robins, "but I went twice all over Russia."

"Did you go to the country and interview the peasants in their mirs?" asked Senator Nelson.

"I went into the country and interviewed them in their groups," answered the ubiquitous Mr. Robins.

SERVING THE BOSHEVIST GOVERNMENT

In the light of Mr. Robins' geographical and encyclopaediacal pretensions, there was something almost miraculous in the rapidity and universality of his movements. During six months of Bolshevik rule he worked in the cities, performed monumental labors for the relief of the suffering masses, distributed 400,000 cans of milk to babies; he walked or motored up to Smolney to interview Lenine or Trotzky at least every twenty-four hours; he was acting faithfully as the unofficial representative of the American Government, was endeavoring to hold the Russian armies along the Eastern front; he was simultaneously establishing "windows" all over Russia and getting an "outdoor" point of view as against the point of view entertained by Allied representatives who listened to the indoor Czarist seven percent. During this active period, in his own words: "I was trying to keep my feet on the ground and see facts, and not to be stampeded by rumor or the unfounded opinions of others."

"I tried to serve the Allied governments and the Russian government, from day to day," said Mr. Robins, apparently placing the Allied governments and the Bolshevik government on a par, "and I am ready to meet the day of judgment on what I did."

While he was performing feats in the cities, Mr. Robins was also out in the rural districts talking to the rustics, probing their class consciousness, and inquiring generally about the conditions of crops. From this he "developed a conviction" that he communicated to his superiors "that there was ample food in Russia to feed the people, and that the whole question was one of assembling and distribution." Doubtless in the course of these peregrinations and the holding of intimate conversazioni with "the eighty-four percent of Russian peasantry" it was that Mr. Robins ascertained that the mass of peasantry desired above any other thing in Russia a distribution of land and that the aspirations and social class consciousness of this peasantry found a perfect incarnation in Lenine and Trotzky.

"Do you speak Russian?" asked Major Humes, in the course of the examination.

"No, sir, only very poorly," confessed this champion of truth, this gatherer of facts, this depository of omniscience.

"Then," asked Major Humes, "the information you got, and the conversations which you had at various times with Russians and those who could not speak English was through an interpreter?"

"Yes," softly conceded the oracle of the Bolshevik "All-Russian" Soviet.

ROBIN'S INVESTIGATOR SECRETARY TO LENINE

From the point of view that the prime qualification for ascertaining an impartial and thorough knowledge of any subject is not to know anything about that subject, from the standpoint of the Robins' "outdoor" psychology, his ignorance of the Russian language was manifestly an advantage. It is plain the use of an interpreter afforded Mr. Robins a lead over other witnesses who had appeared before the Senate Committee, who had lived in Russia many years, who left after Mr. Robins, and who were thoroughly acquainted with the Russian language. It was brought out that Mr. Robins' choice of secretary and interpreter fell upon Alexander Gumberg, a selection in which Mr. Robins was singularly fortunate. For Gumberg's brother, who had adopted the Russianized name of "Sergius Zorin," was a member of the Lenine-Trotzky Bolshevik crew and occupied the position in the

America no Place for Bolshevism

(From The Christian Advocate of February 20, 1919)

s one thing to oppose the use of American
ıyonets against the Bolshevists in Russia
ıd quite another to come out in defense of
ıat party. In view of all our history it is
lt to justify the use of American armed
in Russia, a state with which we are
ally at peace, though circumstances are
vable which would warrant intervention
name of humanity, just as Christendom
have saved the Armenian from the Turk.
must come to equilibrium in her own time
her own way. The Western world sat by
enough and let the Romanoffs go on shoot-
sending into exile those who resisted their
ity, and now that the shoe is on the other
he reasons for the former policy hold good.
Socialist state is what Russia wants, it is
to see why the American republic should
ır nay, unless the brutality of the process
onstruction should pass the limits of hu-
orbearance.

this willingness to let Russia settle her
nternal affairs should delude no American
defense of the monstrous work of Bolshe-
Whatever its aim, there is no lack of first-
uncensored, and presumably unprejudiced
ıce that its methods have been cruel and
y beyond all other revolutions in history.
ession, robbery, starvation, violence, and
er have been commonly used by the Bolshe-
viki to gain their ends. Professing the loftiest aims, and setting up a goal of absolute justice and equality, it is clear that these radical and rabid communists are practicing upon the propertied classes the extreme of injustice, with the apparent purpose of exterminating them. Preaching the common good of all, they practice suspicion and hatred. Some of their American defenders plead that they are putting into effect the social principles of Jesus Christ. But their own spokesmen make no such claim. The government has expressly repudiated the religion of Jesus, and established atheism as the cult to be taught to the young in the place of any other doctrine, it being made unlawful to teach religion in any school, public or private, where instruction is given in any other subject.

The danger of such conclusions as Dr. Harry F. Ward makes public in the name of the Methodist Federation for Social Service is that many people who read them, and are desirous of forming a fair judgment, are liable to be misled into believing that Bolshevism is something very different from what it has shown itself to be. For this reason we have supplemented the Ward statement with a rather full report of the testimony given by Dr. George A. Simns, of Petrograd (Methodist missionary), before the committee of the United States Senate in Washington last week. His knowledge was gained at first hand. No prejudice can be alleged in his case. No public policy had to be supported by his remarks. Certainly his own interests as a resident of Russia would not be served by discrediting the powers that be. We must assume that he told the truth. If this is so, then it is a fact that Bolshevism as revealed in action is contrary to every principle on which American civilization is based. Self-preservation demands that it shall win no foothold here. Dr. Ward's statement is, unfortunately, so framed as to recommend it to favorable consideration. It asks indulgence for the detestable crew which has overthrown the Russian democracy and set up a class tyranny of terror worse than that of the Czars. To accept these conclusions without challenge would be to help on the subtle propaganda which is being diligently spread throughout all lands, partly by the authorized representatives of Bolshevism and partly, as perhaps in this case, by those whose sympathies in the class-struggle disqualify them from giving impartial counsel to others.

VACATION ASSOCIATION CONCERT

THE Vacation Association, Miss Robinson
Smith, president of the Board of Directors, has returned to its objective activities after devoting its time, force and
of its financial resources to war relief
and bond sales. Its most notable sched-
event of the season will be the gala con-
ıt the Metropolitan Opera House, Tuesday
ng, April 8, when Geraldine Farrar, the
ican prima donna, will make her first con-
ıppearance of the season. Still more inter-
; is the first appearance at an evening con-
in this city for the present season of the
delphia Orchestra, Leopold Stokowski, con-
r. The Vacation Association has the dis-
on of giving the only post season concert
e organization and offering them at their
evening performance. Sergei Rachman-
the Russian pianist and composer, com-
s the programme.

aders of THE REVIEW will be especially in-
ed in the concert because the Vacation As-
ion is a branch of the Woman's Depart-
of The National Civic Federation, or as
Smith expressed it: "The Federation's
child."

e return to its former activities of the Va-
ı Association means much to the 8,000 self-
orting women of the department stores,
ess offices and other places where women in
numbers are engaged. It has done such
ive work in its war service as to win high
oval from the committees having charge of
Liberty Loan and War Savings Stamp
s. The list of purchasers among members
e association itself has been unusually large,
a feature has been the fact that purchases
on the instalment plan have been main-
d with fidelity, a tribute to the spirit of
t inculcated by the association.

ats for the concert are on sale at the Vaca-
Association, 38 West 39th Street, the box
of the Metropolitan Opera House and the
ng theatre ticket agencies. They are ex-
from war tax.

Radicals Mislead Churches

(Continued from page 4)

taken by itself, could not be objected to but in its setting in that paragraph it sounds as if the committee were somewhat regretful that we are not more ready for revolutionary changes.

While much of the discussion on industrial matters contained in this pamphlet is of the radical or academic type, the following paragraph from "Ultimate and Fundamental Reforms" indicates clearly that socialism was not in the minds of the distinguished signatories and that *The Daily Call* is reckoning without its host when it thinks the Catholic Church is coming its way:

> It seems clear that the present industrial system is destined to last for a long time in its main outlines. That is to say, private ownership of capital is not likely to be supplanted by a collectivist organization of industry at a date sufficiently near to justify any present action based on the hypothesis of its arrival. This forecast we recognize as not only extremely probable, but as highly desirable; for, other objections apart, Socialism would mean bureaucracy, political tyranny, the helplessness of the individual as a factor in the ordering of his own life, and in general social inefficiency and decadence.

Also, in the following paragraph our friends are on solid ground:

> Nevertheless, the present system stands in grievous need of considerable modifications and improvement. Its main defects are three: Enormous inefficiency and waste in the production and distribution of commodities; insufficient incomes for the great majority of wage-earners and unnecessarily large incomes for a small minority of privileged capitalists.

In other words, it might be said that the diagnosis of our social ills contained in the preceding paragraph is correct, but the cure suggested I believe to be utterly inadequate, if not unsound. But the Catholic Committee is only advocating measures which the Protestant Churches also are advocating. This raises the question, Why are the churches, whether those of wealthy and aristocratic congregations, those of the middle class or those made up largely from the working class, all alike advocating the same radical measures to aid the working classes, which these same working classes themselves do not want?

This is indeed a very grave question. The churches of our country, as a whole, include a large majority of the people of all classes, the bankers, merchants, lawyers, farmers, laborers, college presidents, etc. These churches all are controlled by boards of trustees, made up largely of business men and yet we see that the whole influence today of these millions of people, who believe thoroughly in the rights of private property and the orderly development of society, are represented in the industrial field at this crucial moment in our history by the radical element and in many cases by those who, if their programs were carried out to a logical conclusion, would overthrow our present institutions and inaugurate a reign of chaos. In using this language I am not, of course, referring in any way to the very able and distinguished Bishops whose names are signed to the Foreword of the Social Reconstruction pamphlet. Not one of them would come under such a head. I am speaking of the Church as it is presented to us as a whole today. There must be some answer to this question. We hope in succeeding numbers to present some views of clergy and laity on this subject.

CHESTERTON'S SUMMARY

Gilbert K. Chesterton, the brilliant English essayist, summarizing the Bolshevik movement in his weekly letter to *The Illustrated London News* on January 25, aptly puts the situation thus:

"It is mere robbery. The robbers may call themselves expropriators, though I shall have much more sympathy with them if they call themselves robbers. But, since modern sectarianism has allowed men to be conscientious traitors and conscientious cowards, I am not altogether surprised that it has occurred to other men to be conscientious burglars and conscientious pick-pockets. But it is quite obvious that no society, Socialist or Distributist or anything else, can allow its subjects to expropriate on their own account in this style. And the society will find it simpler not to call it anarchism, and not even to call it anarchy—but merely to call it crime.

"Thus we find that the word Bolshevism really covers three distinct and contrary things—in the country a quite human hunger for land; in the towns a rather inhuman theory of collectivism, and a still more inhuman practice of crime. It looks as if these contraries had come into collision. And the moral is that we must support the one revolutionary element, which will also be conservative, against the other revolutionary elements which can only be destructive. If we do not disappoint the peasants, we can defy both the theorists and the thieves."

Heating and Ventilating Problems

REQUIREMENTS AND STANDARDS FOR INDUSTRIAL ESTABLISHMENTS AND DWELLINGS—GOVERNMI RESEARCH BUREAU ADVOCATED—UNHYGIENIC ATMOSPHERE HEALTH MENACE

By WERNER NYGREN

(*Among the divisional committees, appointed by Samuel Gompers, Chairman of the Committee on Labor—including Conservation and Welfare of Workers—to recommend means of protection under war conditions, was one to deal with the subject of Requirements and Standards upon Heating and Ventilation. It was made a part of the National Committee on Welfare Work, the Chairman being Louis A. Coolidge, who is also chairman of the Welfare Department of The National Civic Federation of which Mr. Gompers is Vice-President. The Sanitation Section, with Dr. William A. Evans as Chairman, gave attention to precautionary measures involving lighting codes, standards for washrooms in munition making or poisonous trades, how to prevent industrial fatigue, rural and camp sanitation and other physical comfort and health matters. Werner Nygren, consulting engineer and Chairman of the Divisional Committee upon Heating and Ventilation, had associated with him Dr. Rudolph Hering in the preparation of recommendations upon that subject. Essential arguments and proposed standards, contained in the report of that committee, are set forth in Mr. Nygren's article in this issue of the Review.—Editor.*)

ASIDE from the aspect of humanity and justice, the securing of healthful conditions for the country's man-power will add to the national strength and production which must be greater than ever to maintain our lead in the world's work. Because a well and satisfied population is foremost among our national resources, it is important to correct all working and living conditions which undermine health. To do this effectively, it is as necessary to guard against concealed menaces as those which are obvious. Many unsuspected tributaries flow into that river which leads to an early grave. Living and working in an unhygienic atmosphere is one and will so remain until it is more universally recognized that a prolonged confinement in vitiated air is injurious.

Broadly speaking, ventilation means cleanliness of the air we inhale and come in contact with, just as cleanliness of the body, more readily apparent, is provided by bathing. Positive standards as to clean atmospheric conditions would considerably simplify the problem of good ventilation, but since our senses do not reliably inform us of air contaminations it is necessary to resort to analysis to determine the degree of uncleanliness.

The complexity of the problem makes ventilation somewhat difficult to understand and introduce universally. When the mere physical function of providing comfort is accomplished by maintaining proper temperature and humidity, ventilation is readily appreciated though the amount of fresh air supplied may be insufficient for the biological and chemical functions necessary to health. Yet, when quite sufficient in all of these respects, it may still be considered insufficient because of "closeness" or "stuffiness" which, although disagreeable, is not necessarily unhealthful. In other words, good indoor air may still be "stuffy" or even ill-smelling and offensive to the senses.

To the layman, this confusion is increased by the diverse theories and controversies of scientists as to whether the physical or chemical functions to be performed by ventilation are the more important; whether the air naturally introduced through the windows or artificially by mechanical means is the healthier, etcetera.

PRODUCTION INCREASED

There is a general lack of understanding of the purely commercial advantages to be gained by effective ventilation of working spaces. No apprehension need be felt that inordinate expenses will be involved, since proper provisions of this kind usually pay for themselves.

A persistent educational campaign should be inaugurated. Articles on ventilation in simple language should be issued explaining the benefits derived from proper ventilation to be followed by statistics upon health standards obtained from striking instances of well-ventilated and poorly ventilated establishments.

In *maintaining and improving the working and living conditions of the industrial and public employees*, the definition of Welfare Work formulated by Samuel Gompers for the Committee on Labor's war work, so far as the surrounding air is concerned, all set notions or problematic theories must be discarded.

Good ventilation means a sufficiently active dilution of the indoor atmosphere to maintain comfort and health. It is necessary when considering the requirements to determine the minimum limits of ventilation to avoid needless expense of installation and operation, and unreasonable structural demands to accommodate the ventilating apparatus. The problem, in every individual case, resolves itself into satisfying the requirements of those physical and other functions which make the greater demand. Usually the greatest amount of air is required to carry away heat and moisture. A human being, laboring or resting, can not possibly be surrounded by air that is too fresh, provided there are no objectionable drafts.

Laws, with established standards for ventilation and heating, have been enacted in various States. Predetermined standards are valuable for ordinary and simple conditions. For exceptional conditions, which usually are the most difficult, set standards are not possible. The laws are therefore mostly inefficient. They are further deficient in that they sometimes establish standards on the basis of *quantity* without stipulating the minimum *quality* results, the latter fixing a better test and capable of a broader application to varying problems.

CHEMICAL ANALYSES

By measuring the properties of the atmosphere, the same as is done for heating, cooling, humidifying, and dehumidifying, it should be possible to determine whether or not quarters for working men are healthy, and this should be the deciding test for all doubtful cases. The formerly much used carbon-dioxide test gives only an indication of the dilution of the room atmosphere and is of no value for ascertaining the presence of bacteria, injurious gases, and other unhealthful ingredients. There is no reason why the quality of atmospheric conditions in working quarters and elsewhere should not be a matter worthy of Government control. Consideration should be given to the establishment of such a bureau to supervise and control all matters pertaining to ventilation, to gather
tabulate statistics of the respective health
tions, and to include a laboratory for res
and testing work, in charge of a competen
wellpaid personnel, to inspire confidence
creation would be appreciated by every h
board and health association in the countr

In heating and ventilating we are confr
with the two problems of meeting the req
ments in new and in old buildings often
utilized for purposes for which they were
originally constructed.

For new buildings, except that they can
be equally definite, laws can be enacted to
heating and ventilating along lines simil
those controlling building construction
plumbing. Existing building laws, with fe
ceptions, can be enforced almost lite
Ninety per cent. of the work can be carried
in strict accordance with predetermined s
ards, leaving 10 per cent. to the judgmen
officials, whereas in heating and ventilating
greater percentage of work has to be don
accordance with judgment of special condit

WINDOW VENTILATION

The limitation of ventilating by opening
dows is mainly responsible for the develop
of mechanical methods. In crowded estal
ments the windows can not, under unfavo
weather conditions, be kept open sufficient
accomplish the necessary air dilution wit
harmful and disagreeable drafts and chi
effects, and there are not always winds to
in the required amount when open windows
be tolerated. In other words, window ventil
can not be depended upon nor effectively
trolled. It usually, though not always, req
reenforcement with positive and reliable de
which will work when natural agencies fa
are insufficient. The old theory that the ope
of windows destroys the effect of mecha
ventilation is not supported. Opening of
dows is often sufficient for small offices and
vate rooms where the occupants are at liber
manipulate them to suit their own com
Proper allowance should be made for una
able air leakage which secures some ventil
even when windows are closed and for the st
izing effect obtained by sunlight. Rooms ha
no windows or skylights, particularly if
happen to be underground and interior
without any wall exposure, require spec
good ventilation by mechanical means.

POINTS OF SPECIAL IMPORTANCE

First—All air supplied for ventilating
poses should be free from dust, pathoge
bacteria, and other contamination.

Second—A sufficient amount of air, prop
tempered and distributed, requires to be
plied per person to satisfy both the biolo
and physical functions of the human orga
and the governing factor determining
amount required must be that function w
makes the greater demands.

Third—Ample allowance must be made
the combustion of gas and oil burnt for ill
nation and other purposes, as this vitiates
air and adds undesirable heat, and additi
ventilation must be provided fully to offset
effects.

Fourth—The room temperature should
kept as constant and agreeable for the
pants as possible, overheating being as objec
able as underheating.

where they are generated. If this is not done and such heat and substances are permitted to mingle with the air, unhealthful conditions will be produced which can not be entirely eliminated by air dilution, even if the same is increased far beyond that given in the standards.

STANDARDS

Minimum requirements to maintain acceptable conditions in all classes of factories, rooms, and spaces devoted to industries follow: Included are offices, stock, sorting, shipping, wash, dressing, locker, and toilet rooms.

Two hundred and fifty cubic feet of space is the minimum for each occupant, the workroom being 12½ feet or less in height. If the height exceeds 12½ feet there should be at least 20 square feet of floor space per occupant.

Rooms having windows whose area is equal to or in excess of 21 square feet per occupant and which open directly outdoors, do not require mechanical means for ventilation except when injurious substances are released or undue heat is generated.

Interior rooms and those having less window area than 21 square feet per occupant require apparatus for mechanical ventilation, to be operated whenever occupied except when external temperature permits keeping windows wide open, provided the total window area is not less than 5 square feet per occupant. A positive supply of outdoor air from an uncontaminated source should be supplied to each room in this class, the amount being stipulated later, and distributed so as to maintain the stipulated temperature without harmful drafts. Sufficient means should also be provided for each room for exit of air corresponding in volume to the amount of fresh air supplied. The exit openings should be so arranged that the movement of the air will be given a direction whereby it will come into maximum contact with occupants, and should, when necessary, be provided with mechanical or other positive means for exhausting it. Rooms having a total area of windows opening directly outdoors amounting to less than 21 square feet per occupant require fresh air in the quantity of not less than 100 cubic feet per occupant per hour for each square foot of window area lacking, excepting that when mechanical ventilation becomes necessary the minimum amount supplied should be not less than 600 cubic feet of air per person per hour.

Rooms above the ground level having wall or ceiling exposure but no windows require 2,100 cubic feet per occupant per hour.

Interior rooms having neither exposure nor windows opening directly outdoors require a quantity of air per hour equal to five times their cubic contents, plus 1,200 cubic feet per hour for each and every occupant.

Underground rooms having neither exposure nor windows opening directly outdoors require a quantity of air per hour equal to six times their cubic contents plus 900 cubic feet per hour for each and every occupant.

Toilet, coat, and locker rooms require mechanical ventilation capable of exhausting air from such rooms in the following amounts:

Toilets, at least 10 complete air changes per hour, plus 1,500 cubic feet per hour for each water-closet and urinal fixture.

Locker and coat rooms, at least six complete air changes per hour, plus 600 cubic feet per hour for each locker or each person's wearing apparel.

Sufficient air inlets for inflow of air to replace the air exhausted should also be provided.

Areas of doors and skylights which can be freely opened may be considered equivalent to window area.

REMOVAL OF INJURIOUS SUBSTANCES

Where dust, fumes, gases, vapors, odors, fibers, or other impurities are created or released in the course of manufacturing, tending to discomfort and injury of health, there should be provided special mechanical or other positive means for removing such substances as fast as created or released.

In case of inability completely to collect and remove injurious substances such additional ventilation is required for dilution of the atmosphere beyond the standards given above as is required to maintain its purity. The percentage of injurious substances permissible should be determined by chemical analyses by medical authorities. This provision should cover all gas burned for illuminating or other purposes from which the products of combustion are released to the indoor atmosphere, and the allowance for such contamination by gas, etc., must be not less than 1,800 cubic feet of fresh air per hour for each cubic foot of gas burned within the room.

When, in the opinion of the proper authorities, the fresh air supplied for ventilating purposes is dust-laden to the extent of being unhealthful and unsuitable, it should be filtered or washed by suitable appliances capable of removing dust and other mechanical impurities.

EXCESSIVE TEMPERATURE AND HUMIDITY

Excessive heat generated by manufacturing processes should either be confined by application of non-conducting material or be collected and carried off in the same manner as described for injurious substances.

Excessive heat or humidity or a combination of the two when sufficiently high to be injurious must be counteracted or reduced so that the relative humidity will not exceed 65 per cent. when the temperature exceeds 75° F., except when outdoor weather conditions prevent or when the working quarters are used for special purposes which, in the opinion of the proper authorities, require or make advisable other degrees of humidity.

The minimum relative humidity for the stipulated temperatures should be not less than 20 per cent. and suitable air moistening appliances, controllable either by hand or automatically, should be provided in the rooms or in connection with the ventilating apparatus.

HEATING REQUIREMENTS

The temperatures in all factories, mercantile establishments, mills, and workshops should be maintained at a uniform degree consistent with reasonable requirements of the manufacturing processes, ranging from 62° F., the minimum for rooms in which manual labor is performed, to 72° F., the maximum for rooms in which clerical or mental work is performed.

Heating apparatus must be of a type to cause no contamination. All direct heating surfaces should be so arranged that the heat radiation will not cause discomfort or injury.

When warm air is used as a heating medium it must be so introduced and distributed as not to cause discomfort and must not be supplied at a temperature higher than 130° F.

Open salamanders must not be used under any circumstances.

Gas or oil heating appliances, discharging their products of combustion into rooms, must not be used unless a sufficient amount of fresh air is supplied to compensate for the vitiation. Gas heating appliances can be used without additional air supply if the products of the combustion are completely collected at the points where generated and carried off.

SUGGESTIONS FOR DWELLINGS

While it is as important to maintain pure atmospheric conditions in the homes as in the working quarters, it is neither reasonable to advocate nor practicable to install mechanical appliances for ventilation. Living and sleeping rooms, even of the dormitory kind, can be effectively ventilated by opening windows liberally if

(*Continued on Page 11*)

THE NATIONAL
Civic Federation Review

Office: Thirty-third Floor, Metropolitan Tower
1 Madison Avenue New York City

RALPH M. EASLEY, Editor

Published Twice a Month **Two Dollars a Year**

The Editor alone is Responsible for any unsigned article or unquoted statement published in THE NATIONAL CIVIC FEDERATION REVIEW.

DEBATE OVER THE LEAGUE OF NATIONS

As this issue of the REVIEW goes to press, the country from Maine to California is engaged in a stirring debate over the questions: "Shall we have a League of Nations, and, if so, does the Paris protocol furnish the best possible program?" The debate began in the Senate of the last Congress and it will continue until the Senate of the next Congress is convened, and after.

Speaking by and large, it can be said that the enlightened public sentiment of the country is gradually becoming unified on certain important features of the so-called "Wilson League." First, it is now known that it is not a "Wilson League"—that the covenant presented by the President is not at all his own draft but a compromise which he had to accept. Therefore, the arguments of those who oppose it because it is the President's creation lose much of their force. Second, the covenant, being only the first draft of a sub-committee's report, is subject to revision, at least so for as its phraseology is concerned. Its most conspicuous opponents and advocates alike agree that changes should be made to clarify many of its passages. So far as fundamental principles are concerned, however, conditions may be such that few, if any, changes can be made. It is in the light of this contingency that those who want to see the possibility of all wars reduced to a minimum must consider this issue now before the American people.

Certain points made clear by the debate so far are:

In regard to most of the provisions, such as limitations of armament and the right to declare war, so fiercely attacked by those who would not listen to any proposal curtailing the sovereignty of the United States through the formation of an international committee in which our Government would have only one voice out of nine, an important discovery was made. These assailants found, upon a closer reading, that none of those things could happen. In other words, it became clear that such an international committee, in which the United States Government had but one voice out of nine, would have only the right to make recommendations to the several governments. In our case, this would mean that Congress would have to pass upon a recommendation before it amounted to anything—a perfectly innocuous proceeding, rendering it immaterial, so far as this feature of the covenant is concerned, whether we had one voice out of nine, or eight or none.

Another serious question raised in the Senate debate is still doing service, although, so far as any committal of our Government by the covenant is concerned, it is answered completely by the discovery referred to above. It revolves around the words of Washington in his farewell address, in which he declared against America's becoming involved in "the entangling alliances and politics of Europe." "Why," it is asked, "should our great and independent country, three thousand miles from Europe, become embroiled in inter-nation conflicts among the Rumanians, Turks, Poles, Czecho-Slavs, Jugo-Slavs and so forth?" That would have been a perfectly good question for George Washington to ask, but it is too late for Woodrow Wilson to ask it and he does not ask it. We are already involved and committed clear up to our necks in all those controversies. And, to be perfectly frank, Woodrow Wilson is not to be blamed for having led us into that "mess"; most of us complained because he did not lead us in earlier. It was not that we, as a nation, felt at that time anything more than an academic concern about the troubles of those countries—and in this we can, in a broad sense, include also the larger troubles of France, England and Italy; but we did have a very vital concern as to whether we could get over there in time to help England, France and Italy beat down the "Beast of Berlin." Our consuming fear was that if we did not get there in time, and that horde of bestial barbarians should vanquish those powers, they would then make a bee-line for the United States of America, knowing full well that in these United States of America they had waiting to assist them anywhere from five hundred thousand to a million well-trained and armed reservists. That is why we went three thousand miles to mix into the European turmoil—and if George Washington had been alive, he would have led our army. Also, when by every possible intrigue that we could devise, we helped to stir up trouble between the Czecho-Slavs, Poles and Jugo-Slavs and Austro-Hungary, it was not because, academically speaking, we cared particularly for those peoples at that time, but it was because we wanted to weaken Austria and then Germany—all with the same great, vital purpose of keeping the Hun from the shores of our beloved America. So now we are there! And it would be dishonorable, immoral and contemptible if we tried to run away.

This situation recalls a tense moment in a debate at Saratoga, August 19, 1898, at a conference called by The National Civic Federation to discuss the future foreign policy of the United States. It was just at the close of the Spanish-American War, but before the peace treaty had been signed in Paris. The issue on which the American people were stirred up then was expansion and anti-expansion. Carl Schurz, who led the anti-expansionist forces in the conference, had just finished an impassioned speech, based largely upon the Washington farewell address and practically all the other arguments which are being used today against our entering into "entangling alliances" and so forth, and which the anti-expansionists had been using for a year past. William Dudley Foulke, who led the expansionist side, arose and leveling his finger at Mr. Schurz, his voice shaking with dramatic fervor, exclaimed: "Mr. Schurz, you are too late! What you have just said would have been pertinent six months ago! Since then, however, we have taken Hawaii and Porto Rico, our battleships have destroyed the Spanish fleet off Cavité and the Peace Conference has been called in Paris to determine whether we should return the Philippines to Spain, leave them alone without any government having destroyed the one they had, turn them over to some other power, or undertake their government ourselves. Mr. Schurz again I say, you are too late! We have already expanded! The question now is not whether we shall expand, but what are we to do with the problems now confronting us, for the solution of which we have become responsible and which we cannot shirk if we are to hold up our heads in the society of nations!"

Likewise, it is now too late to talk about withdrawing from "the embroilments of Europe."

Another inconsistency that looms up in most of the discussions is seen in the criticism of the covenant by certain men on the ground that it does not have "teeth"; that if it does only what some of its friends say, it amounts to nothing and will not prevent war. Now, most of these very critics would be the first to object if it had the "teeth" that the League to Enforce Peace advocated. To mention two points:

First, the League to Enforce Peace and all the organizations in Europe formed to promote peace provided for an international army to be

What are the "new weapons" furnished the German people? Opportunity of an alliance, a close working pact, with Lenine and Trotzky? Have we forgotten the orders issued by the Imperial Government early in the war, instructing Hun ambassadors in neutral and Allied countries to foment "social separation movements and civil war?" Certain American journals, themselves devoted to the fomenting of class hatred and social discontent, have clearly implied that Germany will be forced to this very thing if she is not accorded an easy peace. Is it to be taken for granted that this is an idle threat?

The German armies have been beaten. In the field Germany has been utterly vanquished. But is she incapable of still working any effective harm to the world? Have her fangs been utterly drawn? From South America comes news of the activities of German propagandists. German and Bolshevist agents have inspired strikes in Argentine. From Mexico comes word of the reappearance of German agents and spies. From Spain is cabled the news that German propaganda is again under way. With her armies beaten and her commerce destroyed, Germany's quickest chance of recuperation would be in the economic paralysis of the nations that have vanquished her. Wherever a country could be torn with civil strife, with industry stopped by widespread strikes, it would react to German advantage. Is it impossible for Germany still to utilize the hordes of agents and spies who are still at large?

Is there no significance to the fact that throughout this country scores of pro-Germans are now allied, secretly or openly, with revolutionary radical movements? Whereas they contributed to German war loans before we entered the war, they now contribute to the Socialist Party. Whereas they previously aided Hun intrigues, their support is now given to organizations and propaganda teaching internationalism and Bolshevism.

The New Republic last December advanced "the conception which alone can convert the present association among the victors over Germany from an alliance for the purpose of imposing retribution. . . . It requires," said this sheet, "first of all renunciation on the part of the victorious nations of all ambitious claims. . . . . There are an increasing number of people in Europe who understand the critical need of abandoning these particularist national ambitions. . . . If they (the Allies) do not, they themselves will eventually be engulfed in the anarchy and ruin which is now threatening Europe.

"Ninety millions of international peons in Central Europe would represent a charge of high explosives quite sufficient to rock the planet and shake to pieces whatever civilization adheres to it. Allied statecraft is surely not so short-sighted as to lay such a mine as this. . . . No indemnities is not a counsel of mercy to Germany. It is a counsel of safety to the world."

Walter Lippman, returning without conspicuous honors from Paris, in an article issued as supplement to *The New Republic* of March 22, says the Versailles Congress "cannot damn the German people for all time, desirable as that might be, because German mothers bear German children. They cannot consign them to the hell they deserve, because the location of that hell will be the center of Europe.

"Bolshevism," says the former "diplomat of the new school," "in both Russia and Germany would soon eat the heart out of Poland, Rumania and Hungary where social conditions are already desperate. Now, anyone who supposes that the populations of France and Great Britain will endure the human and economic cost of such an occupation is suffering from a severe case of reading nothing but censored news."

All of which is strikingly along the line of expression of the Berlin *Vorwaerts*. The significant thing is that what the German press is now openly threatening was expressed by *The New Republic* long before they dared articulate it in Germany.

THE HARVESTER INDUSTRIAL COUNCIL In another part of the REVIEW will be found the text of the Harvester Industrial Council, a plan of cooperation between the International Harvester Company and its 30,000 employees on questions of policy relating to working conditions, now in operation.

We publish it in full because it is the most recent one put into operation by a large corporation and can well be said to represent the honest endeavor of broad-minded employers to provide a practical method whereby matters relating to working conditions can be jointly considered in a frank and just manner. Within the last year many large corporations have been moved to give greater consideration to the wishes and welfare of their workers. Such plans have been adopted chiefly in plants not having collective contracts with trade unions. It is largely in those establishments that such machinery is needed because in union plants it is already provided for in the terms of the trade agreements.

The plan removes one of the greatest obstacles to industrial peace by providing an opportunity for the employees to be heard and by omitting from the machinery foremen and sub-foremen who most frequently are the cause of grievances. A real point of contact is secured between the management and the workers, thus ensuring closer relations between the company and its employees. The execution by the company of all accepted recommendations is a proper arrangement.

The International Harvester plan, it will be noted, clearly defines the questions that are to be dealt with by the Council. The second paragraph in Article I states that the representation is to be equal and the questions to be dealt with relate to "working conditions, health, safety, hours of labor, wages, recreation, education, and other similar matters of mutual interest." This does not include matters concerning the management of the corporation.

Much is being said today by newspaper and magazine writers about "democracy in industry"; that "the day of autocracy has gone out and the day of democracy has come in;" that "the worker is now to have a voice not only as to the condition in which he works, but in the management of the business as well." Some of these writers picture the representatives of the wage earners sitting at the board of directors' table, passing with them upon the great questions of markets, prices, finance, and all others related to the business end of the concern. None of these things is to be found in the Harvester program nor in the program of any other corporation so far as we have been able to discover. It is magnanimous and perfectly praiseworthy for a large employer to feel that he would like to have one or two of his employees represented on the board of directors of the corporation, so that the real conditions could be observed. In case, for instance, demands were made for an increase in wages or a shortening of hours, and the financial situation were such that the concern could not afford to grant the concessions, it is the theory of such employers that the men's representatives would understand and could explain the reason to the men. As stated, such an idea is entirely commendable but experience has shown it to be impracticable. The standing of those two employees who would have to go back to the other 5,000 employees and tell them that they could not have the raise they had demanded, would not be a "wholesome" one, to say the least. In fact, they might have to dodge brickbats. At any rate, they would have to meet charges of having been bribed by the employers. There is nothing of this kind in the International Harvester plan.

A criticism of the provisions for arbitration in the Harvester project doubtless will be made by those who contend that all questions should be arbitrated. The principle involved in this proposal is identical with that underlying the discussion over arbitrable and non-arbitrable questions now going on in the League of Nations controversy. In the Harvester scheme, it requires mutual agreement to submit a question to arbitration: either side may block it. Were it otherwise, a critical situation might well arise. Suppose, for instance, the men should become sufficiently Bolshevized to propose that they should have a majority on the company's board of directors. Would the International Harvester Company or any other corporation submit such a question to arbitration? Suppose a corporation, on the other hand, should propose to men who wanted to join a union that they should arbitrate that question. The men would justly claim that that was a legal and natural right and would refuse to submit it to arbitration because whenever anything is submitted to arbitration, a risk is taken; each side must be prepared to lose.

The large employers of the country will watch closely the result of this new venture, as they are also watching those already put into operation by the Colorado Fuel and Iron Company, the Standard Oil Company of New Jersey, the General Electric Company and others.

Problems in Heating and Ventilating

(*Continued from Page 9*)

ample room is allotted per person. Interior and underground rooms, without windows opening directly outdoors, should not be permitted to be used for living and sleeping quarters under any conditions.

Ample provision should be made so that each and every room used for living and sleeping purposes can be heated to a comfortable temperature in the most severe weather. Sleeping rooms, which may usually be kept at somewhat lower temperatures, still require ample provisions for warming in cases of illness. The recognized average standard for living quarters is 70° F., and it would be well to adhere to this standard, so as to have a certain surplus that will permit windows to be kept partly open.

Hot water, steam, furnace, and open fireplace heating, and even stoves, can be considered satisfactory when ample in capacity and properly installed. Individual control of the heating for each room is very important, so that the heat can be distributed in accordance with requirements. Gas radiators and oil stoves, which release products of combustion should be prohibited for permanent heating of living and sleeping rooms, as they produce disagreeable and injurious gases.

Overheating is a prevalent evil. For ordinary rooms, an average temperature of 68° F. is, from the standpoint of health, preferable, except where there are aged people who require a slightly higher temperature. For sleeping rooms, a much lower temperature will suffice, except in cases of illness.

These standards will answer until the suggested bureau of research is created when additional and more definite ones can be made and measuring methods be devised for the establishing of *quality* standards to supersede the present *quantity* standards.

Special provisions for ventilating public halls, schoolrooms, etcetera, are not contested with the antagonism formerly manifested. The war has furnished a striking illustration of what can be accomplished by proper sanitation. Employers and owners of industrial establishments should cooperate with proper authorities to develop the best means of heating and ventilating.

New York State Probe of Bolshevism Asked

UNION LEAGUE CLUB COMMITTEE DECLARES FACTS WARRANT FULL INQUIRY, ESPECIALLY AS TO THOSE WHO SEEK TO STIR NEGROES—ULTRA RADICALS BACK NEW UNION

Valuable work is being done by the Union League Club of New York City in fighting Bolshevism. Its special committee on the subject has gathered many important facts regarding the propaganda in this country, the way in which it is received and who is putting it forth. Archibald E. Stevenson and Robert C. Morris constitute the committee and recently presented their second report, with a recommendation that the club urge a legislative investigation.

Messrs. Stevenson and Morris lay special stress on the efforts being made to spread Bolshevik ideas among negro workers. Elsewhere in this issue of THE REVIEW *will be found* The Messenger *article to which they refer in full. As will be seen, the so-called leaders of the negro and white I. W. W., include such persons as Morris Hillquit who talks socialism when not too busy clipping coupons or acting as corporation attorney; Abraham Shiplacoff, one time Assemblyman, now of the Jewish* Forward; *Rose Schneiderman who wants (as do the I. W. W.) a worldwide union of every worker and who has gone to Paris as President Wilson's appointee to represent women in post-war plans devised by the Peace Conference, and Charles W. Ervin, editor of* The Call.

Following is Messrs. Stevenson's and Morris's second and latest report to the Union League Club:

IN its preliminary report the committee on the study of Bolshevism endeavored to indicate the forces now at play on public opinion in the United States, to define the purposes and objects of the three main currents of radical thought, namely: Anarchism, Syndicalism, and Socialism, and to show that the advocates of these three theories of social order have united upon the common platform of internationalism and the solidarity of the working classes. The propaganda spread by these radicals is calculated to develop sympathy with the movement to establish in this country a socialistic state patterned after the model set up by the Bolsheviki in Russia.

The Rebel Worker, an organ of the Industrial Workers of the World, in the issue for February 15, 1919, says:

> The war has pretty nearly made the world safe for Bolshevism—something not at all in the original program. Russia, Germany, Austria, Holland—even Japan, though to a lesser degree—give evidence of a revolution that has already outrun both capitalist imperialism and Bourgeois liberalism.

The idea presented here challenges attention.

While the Conference at Paris is discussing peace, civil war rages throughout Eastern and Central Europe. The struggle between the radical Spartacus group in Germany and the more conservative Socialists represented by the Ebert government continues to increase. It is impossible at the present time to determine which of these parties will be successful. The Spartacus group, like the Bolsheviki of Russia, is committed to internationalism and the dictatorship of the proletariat. It also spreads throughout the world its appeals for the cooperation of the workers in other lands, as illustrated by the manifesto signed by the late Karl Liebknecht, Rosa Luxemburg, and others, a copy of which appears in the issue of March 8, 1919, of *The Nation*. The manifesto is addressed:

> To the men and women workers of all countries—Comrades, the revolution has reached Germany . . . . . Workers of all countries! If we summon you now to make common cause with us, it is not in the interests of the German capitalists, who, under the banner of the "German Nation" are trying to escape the consequences of their own crime. No! We summon you to make common cause with us in your own interest. Face the facts. Your victorious capitalists are ready to repress in a bloody manner the revolution in Germany because they fear it will reach them. You, yourselves, are not enjoying greater liberty because of the "victory". The "victory" has reenforced your slavery . . . . . That is why we cry aloud: Arise and face the struggle! Arise and act!

The remarkable progress of revolutionary Socialism in Europe may occasion surprise. Prior to the outbreak of the war in 1914, the majority of the Socialists had been converted from the earlier militant form of Marxian doctrines and won to the principles of parliamentarian action, no cooperation existed between them and the Anarchists and only such Syndicalists as were agreeable to parliamentarian action were admitted to the International.

With the coming of the war in 1914, the International collapsed and for a time Socialism seemed to have received its death-blow. Had the war been brief and decisive this might have been the case. However, the length of the war, the unlimited demands made upon the resources of the nations engaged in it, the unparalleled sacrifices imposed upon the peoples of Europe, the shortage of food and the consequent economic and social distress combined to create in the minds of the masses of European peoples a disposition favorable to the development of Socialist doctrines. The progress of the war has been marked by a revival of revolutionary Socialism, which is today stronger, more militant and more dangerous to democratic governments than at any other period in history.

Reference is made to the conditions existing in Europe because the Committee feels that those conditions must inevitably have a reflex action upon the people of the United States. So long as the Bolsheviki are in control of the masses in Russia and remain a force to be reckoned with in the territories which were the Central Powers, so long will they continue to be a menace to the institutions of the United States. To emphasize this, reference is made to the influence which the Jacobin clubs of the French revolution had upon malcontents in the United States in the latter part of the 18th Century. The Whiskey Rebellion of western Pennsylvania was the outgrowth of agitation carried on by Democratic societies going under the garb of protectors of civil liberties and which received their inspiration from the French revolutionary societies. The power of these American agitators continued to grow until Robespierre was guillotined and the political power of the revolutionary clubs of France was destroyed. John Marshall, in his "Life of Washington", published at Philadelphia in 1832, page 353, says:

> Not more than certain is it that the boldest streams must disappear, if the fountains which fed them be emptied than was the dissolution of the democratic societies of America, when the Jacobin clubs were denounced by France.

This interesting reference to past experience carries with it a lesson for today. Repressive methods and even education in this country cannot overcome the pernicious influence of the Bolsheviki propaganda so long as it exercises a dominating influence upon the aspirations, cupidity and avarice of the millions of disorganized Europe. Before the government and people of the United States can safely ignore the agitation of radicals in our midst, order and the rule of law must be established in Russia and in Central Europe.

The purposes of the radical agitators in the United States are similar to those of their European comrades. The object sought to be attained is the establishment of democracy in industry and what is generally termed the Industrial Republic. It is pointed out in radical literature that in the evolution of human society, political democracy was but an initial step; that the demand of the people to select the persons to rule over them was as revolutionary when made as the claim that the workmen today shall have the right to select and control the management of industry. In other words, the claim is made that the first step in social evolution was the establishment of government of the people, for the people and by the people, and that the second step must necessarily be a government in industry of the workers, for the workers and by the workers.

This is the Industrial Republic which the radicals of the United States seek to establish, and this is the government which has already been established in Russia. It is recognized that in order to establish such a republic, a dictatorship of the proletariat is necessary. In a pamphlet entitled "Soviets at Work", Lenine says: "It would be the greatest stupidity and the most absurd opportunism to suppose that the transition from capitalism to socialism is possible without compulsion and dictatorship."

Referring to the Russian revolution, in the same pamphlet, Lenine says:

> We are now in the third stage. Our gains, our decrees, our laws, our plans must be secured by the solid forms of *every-day labor discipline*. This is the most difficult, but also the most promising problem, for only its solution will give us Socialism. We must learn to combine the stormy, energetic breaking of all restraint on the part of the toiling masses, with *iron discipline during work*, with *absolute submission* to the will of one person, the Soviet director, *during work*.

This is the liberty to which the workers seem to aspire.

The propaganda of these radicals in the United States is increasing. Every cause of complaint in any part of American society is used to increase the numbers of the radical forces.

An attempt is being made to arouse the latent discontent in the Negro population in this country by circulating among them Bolsheviki doctrines. An excellent illustration of the character of this propaganda is *The Messenger*, a Negro paper which has been widely distributed among Negroes of New York City and elsewhere. Two quotations from the February number of this magazine will be sufficient to indicate its nature. On page 6 there appears an article entitled "The Soviet", which closes with the following:

> As for the Negro, neither property, life, liberty nor the pursuit of happiness, which, by the way, is only possible by the possession of the former, is secure in the Southern section of these United States.
>
> The *Messenger* denies the right to every capitalist hypocrite in Christendom to speak to the motion of order on the Soviet of Russia. Long live the Soviet.

In another article entitled "We Want More Bolshevik Patriotism", we find the following:

> We want a patriotism represented by a flag so

> red that it symbolizes truly the oneness of blood running through each one of our veins.
>
> We want more patriotism which surges with turbulent unrest while men, black or white, are lynched in this land. . . . We want no black or white patriotism which demands separate camps, separate ships and separate oceans to travel on. What we want is a patriotism of liberty, justice and joy. That is Bolshevik patriotism, and we want more of that brand in the United States.

In order to stimulate an interest in Socialist activities, an association has been formed which is known as "The National Association for the Promotion of Labor Unionism among Negroes", with headquarters at 2305 Seventh Avenue, New York City. The significance of this movement may be gathered from an examination of the names upon its advisory board.

Among these appear Charles W. Ervin, editor of *The New York Call*, a Socialist organ; Julius Gerber, secretary of The New York Socialist Local and a member of the Metal Workers' Union; Morris Hillquit, the well-known Socialist; Harold C. Keys, of The Brotherhood of Railway Trainmen, recently identified with a radical organization known as Young Democracy; Jacob Panken, Socialist Judge in the Municipal Court; James H. Maurer, president of the Pennsylvania State Federation of Labor; Max Pine, organizer of the United Hebrew Trades; Joseph Schlossberg, secretary of the Amalgamated Clothing Workers of America; Abraham Shiplacoff of the Jewish Forward, and Rose Schneiderman.

The president of the association is Chandler Owen, a Negro and one of the editors of the radical paper from which we have been quoting.

The propaganda carried on by the radical groups reaches all parts of the nation, but finds a particularly receptive mind in industrial centers, where large groups of aliens are present. Agitators have been particularly active among the Jewish, Italian, Hungarian, Finnish, and Slavic elements of our population.

In America the fundamental danger comes from social unrest rather than from the special form of socialism instituted by the Russian Communist Party, and known as Bolshevism. The success of propagandists and agitators in enlisting the interest, support or sympathy of a vast number of our population is an indication of how widespread has become the social unrest of our country. Any one familiar with the working conditions in many of our factories and industrial centers, and in the crowded and congested districts of our great cities must recognize the reasons for this unrest. There is a lack of understanding between the employing and working class as a whole.

The educated and employing class has in general been so engrossed in their own affairs as to ignore the thoughts, aspirations and conditions of people of less favored circumstances. The very people whom nature has endowed with the privilege of leadership, and upon whom our form of society has imposed the duty of constructive statesmanship, have in the main exerted their energies and talents in private life toward amassing wealth and power, and in public affairs have played to strengthen their position.

The leaders of radical opinion have in most instances been close to the mass of the people; have seen and sometimes shared the burdens they carry, and have advanced solutions for existing conditions which the workers are taught to believe intolerable. Nevertheless, the solutions offered by these radicals are impractical, unjust, and if put into effect are destined to increase the misery they are designed to cure.

It is, therefore, clear that the duty of the people of means, culture and education is to familiarize themselves with facts as they are; to become acquainted with the forces at play upon the working class, and to recognize that some constructive program must be substituted for the schemes of social reform which are now catching the ear of the masses. As was pointed out in the preliminary report of this Committee, the present radical agitation is as much a revolt against organized labor as it is against capital and the State. This is emphasized by an interesting manifesto which has recently been issued by "The Communist League of New Jersey". It is directed principally against the American Federation of Labor. We quote in part as follows:

> We must reverse the historic attitude of the Socialist Party towards the American Federation of Labor. Since its formation in 1898, the Socialist Party has pursued a policy of friendship and alliance with the A. F. of L. Our members have gone into the craft unions and have struggled to "bore from within". After twenty years we may read the result. Our efforts have collapsed in a heartbreaking failure.
>
> The A. F. of L. has ceased to be a labor union. It has allied itself with the master-class. . . . It has invoked the aid of the capitalist government to exterminate the revolutionary minorities within its unions.

This attack upon the American Federation of Labor, and the numerous other illustrations of the same kind which might be given, suggest lines of reflection. To continue the conflict between capital and labor, and to forget that the interests of employer and employee are identical, is to encourage a state of affairs which cannot but lead to an undermining of the institutions of our country. It should be emphasized that the radical elements are fast weakening organized labor and that if the process continues the power of the American Federation of Labor will be diverted to radical ends.

The obvious conclusion is that a greater cooperation should exist between employers and organized labor and interest should be taken in the experiments now being conducted in England looking towards that end. However, the Committee feels that before any recommendations for dealing with the radical movement in America are made, a more thorough knowledge of the nature, extent and purposes of the movement should be had.

The Overman Committee of the Senate at Washington, investigating Bolshevism, has devoted itself largely to ascertaining conditions existing in Russia and has brought out much valuable information for the enlightenment of the people in this country as to the theories and practices of the Bolshevist regimé. This is important as an object lesson as what the Bolsheviki would do if their ambitions were achieved here, but little accurate information has been obtained as to the exact extent of radical activities in this country.

We believe, therefore, that Bolshevism as it may exist in the United States, and particularly in New York, should be subject to an immediate investigation of a most thorough and painstaking character, and that the testimony heard at such an investigation should be supported by legal evidence only.

The State of New York during the war, through its then Attorney-General, Merton E. Lewis, vigorously applied a statute of which he was the author, known as the "Peace and Safety Law", and demonstrated its ability to curb activities against our government. This was practical war work. The State should now demonstrate its ability to handle in a practical manner the after-war menace of the Bolshevik and other revolutionary agents. Local action in matters of this character is always the most effective, as witness the splendid work of Ole Hanson, Mayor of Seattle.

RECOMMENDATION

We recommend, therefore, that The Union League Club at once request the Legislature of the State of New York, now in session, to appoint a joint legislative committee to investigate the Bolshevik and revolutionary movement. Such a committee could summon before it the real leaders of Bolshevik and revolutionary activities and other persons possessed of actual knowledge concerning these movements within the confines of the State. The actual leaders of this movement should be brought before such an investigating body and compelled to testify.

The full knowledge of conditions in this State which would be gained from such an investigation would enable the preparation of suitable legislation and the taking of such steps as may be necessary to cope with the situation. We do not make this recommendation because we believe that alarm should be felt at the present time, but solely because the Committee is convinced that revolutionary activities exist, and it feels that it is the duty of the people of New York to ascertain, immediately, the extent thereof. We, therefore, offer the following resolution for adoption by the club:

> RESOLVED, That the Committee on the Study of Bolshevism be and it hereby is directed to present to the Senate and Assembly of the State of New York, the recommendation of The Union League Club that a joint legislative committee should be appointed, with all necessary powers to investigate the tendencies, ramifications and activities of the Bolshevik or revolutionary movement in this State with a view to the enactment of such legislation as may be necessary to protect the government of the State and to insure the maintenance of the constitutional rights of its citizens.

(Sgd.) ARCHIBALD E. STEVENSON, *Chairman.*
ROBERT C. MORRIS.

March 13th, 1919.

FOMENTING DISCORD AMONG NEGROES

The insidious propaganda carried on by those who seek to promote widespread class and race antagonism and discontent is indicated in the following article from the negro magazine THE MESSENGER *of February,* 1919, *which was quoted in Messrs. Stevenson's and Morris's report to the Union League Club*:

FIRST, as workers, black and white, we all have one common interest, viz., the getting of more wages, shorter hours, and better working conditions. Black and white workers should combine for no other reason than that for which individual workers should combine, viz., to increase their bargaining power, which will enable them to get their demands.

Second, the history of the labor movement in America proves that the employing class recognizes no race lines. They will exploit a white man as readily as a black man. They will exploit women as readily as men. They will even go to the extent of coining the labor, blood and suffering of children into dollars. The introduction of women and children into the factories proves that capitalists are only concerned with

(*Continued on Page* 20)

Europe's War Labor Experience

(*Continued from Page 2*)

we developed two features abnormally influencing the relations of capital and labor; the one in which the government went into the market as an insistent consumer on borrowed capital and with the unusual right of fixing prices, the other where it went into direct manufacturing with its borrowed capital with no concern regarding profit or the future.

"The vital demands of the war compelled absolute neglect of the economic law of supply and demand, with the result that capital in most directions, and labor in all directions, were placed above the economic level on which they both must finally rest to live fairly in their respective spheres. Capital's position is easily ascertained. Its books and its returns are kept and recorded. It can, if necessary, be regulated by law as to a fair compensation.

LABORER MUST LIVE

"Capital can die for want of a fair economic life. The laborer cannot. He has to continue. He lives anyway. After all, he is really the fundamental element in the situation. Labor as a wage earner or as an individual producer will continue to exist well or badly supplied, but exist he will. Capital cannot if labor unreasonably deprives it of sustenance; that is, a living profit. I mean by that, a margin over and above the cost of labor and material sufficient to reasonably compensate it.

"To be an employer capable of paying high wages and maintaining its labor in a happy, healthy and efficient way it must make money. It cannot attain its best condition in this respect without efficient and contented labor. This reduces the whole question to a mutuality of interests compelling co-operation between the two. Both must reach an understanding on the basis of complete interdependence.

"The economic side of these questions is not understood as it should be. I was speaking to a manufacturer the other day. He found a very curious state of mind among legislators in Washington when appearing before a committee of inquiry. He told me, for instance, of their incorrect conception of the industrial meaning of raw material; treating it with a sweeping definition for price fixing. It is a term if properly applied, given to the basic articles required for transforming the same in various industries into widely diversified products. These products even may again, in certain cases, constitute raw material for some other industry. Consequently, raw material is something starting from nature with capital applied to it in a greater or lesser degree and must be treated from a sound economic standpoint in each case based upon a proper understanding of what it is made up of.

MANY COSTS ADDED

"For example; if I have a factory in the East and I require ingot copper for my finished product, that copper is really not a primary raw material in itself. There enters into it not only the cost of producing it from the ore through the mining of it to the finished ingot, but the cost of transportation must be added with again all its elements of labor and capital involved in the construction and operation of the railroad carrying it to its destination.

"Labor has pyramided itself one wage on top of another until the cost of all articles to labor—itself being the chief consumer—finally lands it in high cost of living. This high cost is capable of reduction largely through concessions from its own present high standard of pay. Coincident with this, capital can and must make its concession.

"Quite naturally on the one side, capital wishes to put as much of the burden on the reduction of wages as it can. Labor wants to put as much of the burden on capital as it can, too often forgetting how far the workmen are consumers themselves. Therefore, I hope this commission will bring back something which will materially contribute to this important question, reporting how far in England they have succeeded in composing their differences so as to go down to a lower level and thus cheapen the cost of living.

"When reconstruction is considered, that fundamental idea will have to be the basis for an intelligent discussion of the subject. There are so many other features, to avoid touching upon them is difficult. One peculiar thing has struck me from the very beginning in the general comment on reconstruction. It is this; that people are thinking of reconstruction as requiring some sort of intricate formula, a formula that is going to bring about a solution, whereas a great part of the solution will be reached by the simple one of real and everyday work.

"The tendency today is shorter hours, more pay, less to do, and with it all to expect a better condition of life. That cannot be done without work. We now must set about to rebuild greatly impaired values. The preachment should be,—everybody work as much as possible, instead of everybody shortening hours and doing as little as they can for as much money as they can get."

Hugh Frayne, one of the members of the American section and the representative of the American Federation of Labor on the War Industries Board, said:

"This question of reconstruction and the after-the-war preparations to meet it is one that is going to take the best effort of every person who believes the country not only ought to be restored to a safe and sound basis, but that it ought to be restored upon a better and higher basis. Things that were not right in pre-war times should be made right in reconstruction times.

WAGES NOT GOING DOWN

"The time is too short to go into detail. It is sufficient to say that wages are not going down where they were in pre-war times. Wages were too low, generally speaking, before the war. Profits in some directions are not going to be—at least many things that were obtainable at a price before the war will not be so obtainable again. There is going to be a new level established, but I hope that in establishing the new condition, the work of economy and curtailment won't begin by reducing wages of the workers.

"If there is going to be cooperation between capital and labor it must be a real, sincere cooperation. Labor must not be asked to do all the cooperating and then he parcelled out anything that the employer may feel that they ought to get and no more.

"I believe that real, sincere cooperation between capital and labor is more necessary now than ever before because of the spirit of unrest that we have among us and that has shown itself in the other countries. That spirit of unrest would show itself more here were it not for the restraining influence of the people. Capital must begin to recognize the distinction between the real, bona fide, labor movement as typified by the American Federation of Labor and deal with it honestly and fairly in the way of cooperation.

"If they are not ready to do that, then they will have to select the other—the I. W. W. element, the Bolsheviki, that sort of labor which will not recognize and does not desire to have any relations with employers, and does not believe, in cooperation or in anything else.

"Whether it agrees with you or not, I know that it is a fact, and I make this statement that had it not been for the active work and the position of the American Federation of Labor, even prior to the entrance of this country into the war, and the influence of labor together with employers and many civic organizations—including The National Civic Federation—had it not been for that influence not only in the industrial field so far as it applied to war industries, but in every field where there was danger of interference with the government in winning the war, I dare say we would have had a much harder time in winning the war. And I doubt whether we could have terminated it at the period at which it ceased to go on.

"That influence proved what is possible to do by honest cooperation. Personally I want to see it. I don't want to see the old order of things under the new reconstruction. I hope that more value will be placed on labor; that sort of labor that is willing not only to work to give service to help build up the institutions of our country, but that labor that is willing to give its all in defense of the country.

TELLS OF WAGE CUT

"Mr. Belmont mentioned a moment ago about copper. The copper producers promised us they would not reduce wages, and the first thing they did, notwithstanding only two per cent production of copper has been going on since the armistice was signed, they reduced the pay of miners one dollar a day. That only amounts to something like ten per cent of the actual cost of the production of copper. But it was the only cost they could control and there was the same old idea of reducing wages in order to economize.

"Coal, coke, oil, machinery and transportation all are excessively high and can stand a reduction much better than can the wages of the working men and working women of this country. Every time there is a wage reduction it means reduction in efficiency as well as in the determination of the working man to give the best that is in him for his industry and the development of the country.

"You cannot develop a high standard of efficiency with a low standard of living among any class of people. So I am for full co-operation between capital and labor. We must not forget that we are standing on a volcano that may show itself in eruption through the influences of those who have come here and who would tear down the very foundations of our government. They do not care whether there is a free institution in this country; whether we have the Stars and Stripes; whether we have a Congress or Senate—it makes no difference to them.

"They want to have the right to go out and take, kill if necessary to take things they never had any part in producing. They have no respect for law and order. I say that unless the employers want to deal with that element, the standards of the American working man should be brought up. That will mean that industry will be brought up proportionately. The wage of the wage earner ought to be such that will properly provide for him and his family. There is no danger that a well returned profit will not go to the manufacturer.

"I do fear that the breach between the employers and the labor movement as we know it will widen so that the other fellow will come between and then substitute that insane idea of government they have in other countries today. That sort of government we don't want. We must unite to prevent it coming in. As a representative of labor I feel safe in saying we stand ready to cooperate with any movement that will stop its growth, even to the extent of driving it from our country entirely."

MR. BELMONT REPLIES

"I have an engagement and should have gone," said Major Belmont when Mr. Frayne finished, "but I remained because I see clearly I must have conveyed a wrong impression in what I said. I would like to correct it. It will take just a moment. I did not intend to convey the idea in speaking of labor as being a fundamental question, that I advocated the reduction of wages; but rather the study of the question, cause I think that capital not only will, but ght to do its share of concession.

"I believe in every word that has been said the last speaker. I believe that I have always en considered to have stood for the principle cooperation, but labor is really the funda- ental question to be dealt with, admittedly, th fairness, for it is properly entitled to erything it can get.

"With that in view, however, the whole onomic subject must be studied, because you nnot put labor upon an improved basis such you hope for unless you have secured indus- y on a sound footing; that is to say, that pital shall have reasonable prosperity so as to able to continue to be an employer.

"When I used the illustration of copper, it as to show that raw material is not to be inter- eted in the sense of a product whose cost is othing as far as labor is concerned. It was to ustrate that. You understand. I thought at I had conveyed a wrong impression, be- ause I cannot and do not wish to be considered s advocating the reduction of wages as a pre- minary to reconstruction."

MAINTAINED AFTER WAR

Dr. Williams here pointed out that after all reat wars wages never had gone to the pre-war evels. "In the period after the Treaty of erlin," he said, "England facilitated the or- anization of labor and I will ask Mr. Burton, Pomeroy Burton, Director of the 'London Daily fail',) in which direction England is facing to- ay in the solution of this labor question."

"Make no mistake about the extent and seri- usness of this worldwide industrial movement," aid Mr. Burton. "It is not merely a show of trength on the part of labor against capital; ot merely a matter of hours and wages. There nderlies this great movement a determination o better the human conditions of labor throughout the world.

"That determination grows directly out of the war, for the war has made men think—men in all grades and conditions of life. The great nations are just now moved by a single impulse—they are uniting their strongest efforts to make war extremely difficult and unprofitable, if not impossible, and that means that their aim is a safe and better state of things for all the world's peoples.

"The work people of the world are the heart and soul and body of that movement. If they did not feel the call and have the vision and share in full measure the aspirations toward a better state of things, then that movement never would have been born, much less have gone so far toward realization. The people are content to leave to the higher statesmen the task of framing the international machinery to make war impossible, but they are by no means content to any longer leave to these statesmen the handling of those problems which rule the details of their work, their homes, their daily lives. In short, labor is out for a complete readjustment of its position.

DETERMINED IDEAS EXIST

"There is a determined feeling among the extremist leaders of many of the workmen's movements that the whole force of tradesunionism should be exerted now to gain for the workers shorter hours, more leisure, higher pay, greater freedom of opportunity, a larger share in the profits of capital and a larger life generally than they have enjoyed in the past, completely ignoring the vital fact that only upon an economically sound basis of production can the workers hope to prosper and progress toward the ends they have in view.

"On an economically sound basis of wages and production, there is work enough and more than enough for everybody. Until this shortage is made up, high prices are bound to continue. It is important to understand the relation of money in circulation and the supply of available goods. If the output of goods diminishes and the volume of money in circulation increases, then the buying power of money declines. That is the great secret of the high cost of living.

"During the war the supply of money has been greatly increased through vast issues of currency and securities based on government credit while the quantity of goods produced has been far below normal. There is today too much money and too few of the essential things people require; the balance is all wrong and this must be righted before the proper buying power of money can be restored.

"Higher wages and shorter hours can only be secured on the sound basis of cost reduction and increased volume of output. Otherwise, though wages, as we have seen during the war, may be doubled, the purchasing power of wages is bound to be still further reduced.

"Wages cannot be permanently raised without a corresponding rise in the standard of production; any wage that is not economically earned is unsound and reactive. Thorough public enlightenment, so that all men may understand these things, is clearly the most urgent need of the hour. All should be brought to a quick and full realization that *industrial warfare on any large scale now would paralyze trade and abruptly stop the process of restoration on which the welfare of all alike depends.*

NEED FOR PUBLICITY

"There is a great need in both England and the United States for a strongly directed governmental publicity bureau to make the people understand every phase of this whole industrial situation. Its work should be supplemented by intensive educational activity by all non-political public spirited bodies throughout the land. The public is in a receptive frame of mind. At heart the average man is reasonable and fair. He would welcome the facts, but up to now he has heard little other than false and misleading arguments so far as industrial conditions are concerned.

"The thing most needed today is the intelligent application of widespread, commonsense publicity, for after all sensible publicity is the one and only antidote to Bolshevism."

Emerson McMillin said:

"For twenty-five years I have had the idea in my head that it was possible for employer and employees to work together so that you could not draw the line between the two. I had hoped to live to see this done. I begin to have some grave doubts about living that long. It is absolutely possible to so organize industries that you could not draw the line between the employer and the workmen, but I am not going to tell you how I would go about it. There is not time.

"We have a case now in one of my own companies where the contract with labor expires in the coming April. The contract was made a year ago and is one that was perfectly satisfactory to the men, but in the end was not fair to them. The cost of living went up during the year. They lived up to their part of the contract, but we voluntarily increased pay in some instances. The contract expires April 1 and when our manager said to the men:

"'You know we are not making any money' (this is a public utility and that is enough to show you there is no money in it for the company) 'you know we are not making fixed charges to-day, so how can we increase wages April 1?'

"The men put up an argument we had not heard before, saying:

"'Within the last year you have been told by the oil men that you had to pay 50 per cent more and by the railways that you had to pay 25 per cent more for freight, and you paid the increase in each case. But when we ask you to increase wages 25 per cent, you say you can't do it. You can do it for everybody but the workman.'

"That is practically true of all industries. We expect the workman always to save us when adjusting profits and losses. They cannot always do it. I think we will have to increase the fares on our street railway and that question is now in the United States court.

"For about twenty-five or thirty years, with nearly all the companies I have controlled in a managerial way, we have made it the custom to pay our men the same rate of dividends and at the same time that we pay dividends to our stockholders. In the case of the stockholder we figure on the amount of stock he has, and with the workman on the money he earns. We have had one strike, I believe, in 35 years and this, too, with ten to fifteen companies in operation.

"It is therefore plain that to have that mode of dividing is an improvement over the ordinary way of compensating labor. But it is only a step; it is not near what ought to be done. It would take a long time of course, to bring ideal conditions about, but it must come. The workmen must share more of the responsibilities and the employers must share more of the profits with the workmen. It would not help workmen much to share profits with public utilities today, but they will not always be as bad as they are now."

H. E. Miles, of the commission, spoke of the need of bringing labor to the highest standards of efficiency through cooperation of the government and employers.

OTHER HONOR GUEST SPEAKS

A. Parker Nevin, the other guest of honor, was the final speaker. He said:

"As you listened to Mr. Easley recite the things the Commission should do in England, France and Italy, it must have occurred to you as to how we are going to spend our spare time. The problems he has outlined are men's jobs. As Mr. Bemis said, we will go over with open minds. It is a great honor to go in this capacity and a great privilege. My whole thought is that we must bring back something to this Association and to the workers and employers of America, some helpful and valuable contribution, not perhaps to any particular specific issue because there is no formula, but some contribution to what I might call the statesmanship of industry.

"If we can do that and shed some helpful light on the problems in this country, our mission will have been justified. I know from the personnel of your delegates that we will do the best we can and my conviction is that what we will bring back to you may be helpful to the great issues affecting industry. I have thought for a good many years that there is only one real burning issue in this country and that is the question of labor. And I use that synonymously almost, with industry—I mean the industrial problem.

"Certainly our country and its institutions and history justify us in believing that the American type of industry, its relation of employee to capital, has a helpful and hopeful future. And if, in this great complicated social, political, economic, industrial, financial problem, those of us you have selected to serve you abroad can in any way help you in your deliberations, we should be most honored and grateful for the opportunity. I thank you."

Those attending the luncheon, in addition to the honor guests and speakers were: James Bertram, Nicholas F. Brady, Timothy E. Byrnes, Mrs. Ralph M. Easley, Haley Fiske, H. H. S. Handy, T. Everett Harré, J. W. Jenks, Capt. Francis Mayer, William Fellowes Morgan, William Jay Schieffelin, Louis B. Schram, Mrs. Coffin Van Rensselaer, Miss Maude Wetmore, Louis A. Coolidge and Matthew Woll.

Shadow Bolsheviki and Others

(Continued from page 6)

clared, moreover, that he told the truth. Asked concerning the reported killing of men without trial, Mr. Robins replied:

"I heard that, Senator Sterling, and in every instance where I investigated it, it proved to be false."

Mr. Robins said that in his judgment the Germans had absolutely nothing to do with the Red Guard, that the Bolsheviki were not officered by German officers, as many witnesses had stated. In fact, the Red Guard, said Mr. Robins, "was composed of men who knew how to die, and the one thing that I found in Russia the only ones who knew how to die were the Red Guards."

"I knew they killed some people," he admitted, casually.

"But you think they were rather moderate in this—is that your view?" asked Senator Nelson.

"At the risk of great misjudgment, may I say this," replied Mr. Robins, "that up to the time I left Russia the thing that was constantly in my mind, again and again, was the lack of vindictiveness, was the lack of actual destruction of life, under the circumstances. If it had been in America, if it had been in any other land I know of, where a mob had taken power like that and had the rifles back of them, I should have expected vastly more of destruction."

HOW DID MR. ROBINS "SHARE" IN THE 'TREMENDOUS HOUR?"

Mr. Robins, by describing firing that was going on, admitted, however, that everything was not as blissfully tranquil as he previously implied. This background of peril may have been romantically necessary, however, for the staging of the melodramatic piece in which Mr. Robins played the heroic role. Mr. Robins had asked members of his Red Cross mission if they would voluntarily stay with him "to play this hand through."

"They stayed," said he, in drawing a descriptive word picture which reminds one of the thrilling episodes of Edmund Dantes' career in the "The Count of Monte Cristo."

"The hour came when it was very perilous in the opinion of many," orated Mr. Robins. "I remember one time when it looked as if we were through with the play quickly. I said to them, coming into the room where they were, when the machine gun fire was going on in the streets: 'I hope we will all get killed.' And they looked at me as if I was crazy. I said: "I mean it. Fellows, we have had the greatest privilege ever given, almost, to men, to see this tremendous hour, to share in it, and not only to share in it but to deal with it; not to believe the lies and slanders and stuff, and not to be buncoed by it, either, but to do our level best day by day. If we ever get out of Russia alive and go to living an ordinary humdrum life in America, it will be so infernal dull we will wish we had been killed.' "

In an eloquent tribute to his precious interpreter, Alexander Gumberg, brother of Bolshevik Minister of Posts and Telegraphs "Zorin", Mr. Robins thrillingly recounted that on a certain occasion "machine gun shots went into the wall above us and all around us."

Despite their almost peaceful revolution—a revolution less destructive than if it had occurred in America!—despite all the felicities enjoyed by the peasants, Mr. Robins undertook emphatically to deny that he favored the unpopular Bolshevik cause.

Of course, having once established an alibi, having impressed folk with a stand of absolute non-partisanship, of a lofty intellectual detachment from the prejudices and passions of the crowd, of an exalted desire only to be fair and to expound the truth, any special pleading becomes therefore all the stronger. The defense of any accused cause has the greater weight.

It could not be said that Mr. Robins is not a tactician. He admitted he knows something of politics. Moreover, since his return to America Mr. Robins, fully appreciating the publicity value of a certain line of conduct, probably also as fully realized that Bolshevism here isn't popular, that it isn't altogether fashionable. So, for one if not another reason, if, for instance, Mr. Robins had political ambitions, if he was looking forward to a high place in the councils of one of the great political parties, what could have been more opportune than a public repudiation of the principles of Bolshevism? Mr. Robins' condemnation of the Bolsheviki, with whom he was so friendly, and whom he absolved, so far as he knew, of crime and murder, is worth reproducing as it shows that in one respect at least he was not in total disagreement with the previous witnesses before the Overman Committee.

"Is there a menace in Russian Bolshevism?" said Mr. Robins. "A fundamental menace, gentlemen, in my judgment—a menace so much more far-reaching, going so much deeper than has sometimes been suggested by its bitterest opponents, that I think it well that we should take high ground and really know the thing we deal with. For the first time in the history of the human race there has been a definite economic revolution, a Socialist class, materialistic, social control by force.

"I regard the Soviet program as economically impossible and morally wrong. I regard it as carrying formulas beyond the range that formulas will produce.

"If you get the menace of the Russian revolution on the basis of German agents, theft and murder, and all that sort of thing, you get a wholly unsound view of the actual scope and power and menace that there is in it. I believe that its decree of workmen's control will destroy production in Russia. I believe that its class theory makes in the end for the class terror and the destruction of life and people without regard to right. I believe that its materialist program challenges the Christian conscience of the world.

"They believe in the use of force, and one of the reasons why a people who believe in settling questions by the ballot are opposed to the Bolsheviki is because the Bolsheviki believe in force."

"They would be willing to send troops into England or France or into our country for the purpose of aiding—" asked Senator King.

"For the purpose of aiding a revolutionary group in any of those countries," supplemented Mr. Robins.

BOLSHEVISM WANTED BY MAJORITY!

To an analytical reader of Mr. Robins' testimony it is difficult to reconcile his viewpoint as to the dangers of Bolshevism and the advantages to be gained by giving economic aid to a movement that aimed to destroy its very benefactor. In one breath Mr. Robins implied that in Bolshevism the Russian people got what they wanted, and in another that they would be cured of Bolshevism by giving them food—which, by the way, in another breath, Mr. Robins said they did not need.

"Do you not believe that if that system of government should prevail in Russia, with their gospel and their creed and mode of operation, that they would attempt to spread it over the world—to internationalize it?" asked Senator Nelson.

"Largely, I think they would," agreed Mr. Robins.

"Would you not regard that as a menace to other civilizations, to our country and to England and to other civilized countries? Would you not regard it as a menace?"

"I tried to make plain yesterday that I regard the formulas, the challenge, of the Bolshevik program as the first challenge and menace to all political democratic governments of the world."

"Now then," said Senator Nelson, "why do you want to nurse it in Russia?"

"I am not wanting to nurse it in Russia," replied the daily visitor to Lenine and Trotzky. "I would like to tell the truth about it."

Mr. Robins continued:

"I am perfectly willing that the Russian people should have the kind of government that the majority of the Russian people want whether it suits me or whether it is in accord with my principles."

"I thought so," said Senator Nelson, "and your idea is that the Russian people, if they want a Bolshevik government full-fledged—"

"Yes—"

"As it is today, ought to have it?"

Said "the mouthpiece of America" to the Bolsheviki, the man who "knew more about Russia than any of the Allied representatives":

"Absolutely."

"So that, boiled down, your mission here is, your first intention is, that the Russian people, if they want a Bolshevik government ought to have it. . . And your next point is, you believe that the Russian people want that kind of a government?"

"At the time I left Russia I believed that the majority of the people were for that government."

"And you consider it one of the greatest menaces to government and law and order and civilization?"

"Absolutely, Senator."

SENATORS SCORE ROBINS

"And yet you want to see it work its way out in Russia," commented Senator Sterling. "Just let me add this—instead of excusing the acts of the government as your testimony seems to do, would it not be better, and would it not be more in accord with patriotism and with good government and real love of order and humanity, to discourage it rather than to say: 'Here, this is a government which has its foundation in certain great abuses; let it go on, just let it go on,' knowing it would be a menace to the rest of the world by its establishment in Russia. It seems to me there is an inconsistency in the position you take—first condemning it and treating it as a menace and so regarding it, and then trying to find excuses for its existence."

"You leave the impression upon my mind," said Senator Nelson, "from your whole statement, that your mission here is to have our government keep its hands off from the Bolsheviki over there and let them have their own sweet will about everything. Is not that what you are here for, and what your mission is?"

"I have not any definite mission of that sort," protested Mr. Robins.

"Is not that the drift of your evidence and of your conduct?" asked Senator Nelson.

"You can judge the drift of it," retorted Mr. Robins. "I am against the use of American arms and American men in Russia against the Russian revolutionary government on a false judgment of the facts in the case."

"It seems to me," dryly remarked Senator Sterling, "that you either do not know the facts in regard to some atrocities of the Bolshevist government, or else you are diligent, a little, in trying to excuse it."

"I understood you to think that Bolshevism is not only a menace to this country, but a menace to the world?" said Senator Overman a little later.

"I do, sir. I think it is the first challenge of the age to our order."

Asked whether he would "be in favor of this country recognizing a government that is such a menace to the world," Mr. Robins evaded a direct answer by saying the thing he would be opposed to "was to blind ourselves to the actual in Russia, not to deal with the actual facts, o inquire into them, but to prejudge the and deal with it on a basis that does not ''

i Mr. Raymond Robins mean to imply that ad blinded ourselves to the actual facts in :a? That we had prejudiced the case of the eviki? That we had dealt with it on a that did not exist?

NS SAYS "OLD GRANDMOTHER" WAS MOVED BY "PERSONAL PIQUE!"

. Robins, queried about statements made to :ommittee, avoided a direct answer by as- ıg that he had not read this testimony.

submit that there is more behind Soviet and the revolutionary government,'' the ess contested, ''than has been suggested in eat deal of the testimony before the commit- '

ow was Mr. Robins in a position to know if he had not read the ''testimony before :ommittee''?

r. Robins was asked if he thought the com- ee could have had a better witness than erine Breshkovskaya.

: would say that one of the most pathetic ʒs in the world to my mind at this moment,'' ıred Mr. Robins, ''is that this splendid old an, with her great record of revolutionary ice, by reason of personal pique, by reason very terrible situation and discouragement, turned so that she can unconsciously be used inst the revolutionary movement in her own l that she helped to create, which seems to to be the fact of the hour.''

f Madam Breshkovskaya's repudiation of a ›lution which aimed—as he admitted—at the :ruction of every civilized government in the ld, was due to ''personal pique,'' to what Mr. Robins' own repudiation of that very g due? Did Mr. Robins reproach the vener- e grandmother for a stand which, certainly · reasons known to himself, he himself person- y assumed to take? Why, if he could deplore lshevism, was it ''pathetic'' for ''Babushka'' do so?

At this point Senator Overman referred to ı testimony of Dr. Huntington, Rev. Dr. nons, American officials, officers of the tional City Bank, officers of the Harvester mpany, all of whom, asserted Senator Over- n, having come from Russia, had corroborated ıdam Breshkovsky as to the ''starvation and l-handed murder'' that prevailed under the lsheviki in Russia

'Are they to be believed?'' asked Senator erman.

''I have not read the testimony, Senator,'' lged Mr. Robins.

Mr. Robins was under oath. Only a few mo- nts before he had asserted: ''I submit there more behind Soviet rule and the revolutionary vernment than has been suggested in a great al of the testimony before the committee.'' If :. Robins had not read the testimony, how was in a position to assume that that testimony s inadequate?

GED U. S. SUPPORT OF GANG OUT TO DESTROY OUR OWN GOVERNMENT

''As I understand,'' asked Major Humes, he avowed purpose of the Bolsheviki is not ly to rule Russia, but to overthrow by revolu- nary means this government as well as all ıer governments?''

''Every government in the world.''

''And do I not understand you to favor the rmal recognition of the Bolshevik govern- ent?''

''Correct,'' admitted the extraordinary Mr. bins.

''You favor economic support?''

''I do.''

''In other words,'' continued Major Humes, hrough economic support you would sanction and encourage and support a further development and strengthening of a government whose avowed purpose is the overthrow of our government. Is that correct?''

Major Humes went on:

''Is it not a fact that the economic strengthening of the Bolshevik government, the building up of that government, the furnishing it with more raw materials, with more material things, would make it possible for them, financially and otherwise, to carry on a stronger propaganda and a stronger agitation and a stronger warfare against our government than they could carry on if they did not have the economic support that you favor?''

Mr. Robins said politely that he did not agree with the question at all and that he did not think it a statement of sound fact. Then it was he gave utterance to what the world so long awaited. Said he: *''The best answer to Bolshevism is food.''*

Mr. Robins had analyzed the Soviet program as doing away altogether with property, a program under which no peasant could call a foot of land his own, yet which, he staunchly asserted, satisfied 93 per cent. of Russia. He declared that Lenine and Trotzky ruled by reason of the support of the overwhelming majority of Russians; that the Russians wanted their system and were satisfied with it. He gave this as his own opinion, based on first-hand—or as he liked to call it ''outdoor''—knowledge, of Russia and the revolution. Despite the glowing satisfaction of the Russians with their lot, Mr. Robins, who is said to be currying favor with Republican party leaders, in reply to Major Humes came forward with this excuse for his having championed an economic alliance on part of the American government with the murderous Bolsheviki:

PROPERTY INTEREST WOULD BREAK BOLSHEVISM!

''I believe that the reorganization of Russian life economically, the beginning to give substantial hope here and there, *beginning to recreate the property interest, and the stake in life, would begin at once to disorganize Bolshevik* power and the adherence to the formulas. Wherever there was a little situation, an oasis as it were, separated from the general situation, where they were getting along fairly well, and people BEGAN TO HAVE A PROPERTY INTEREST IN LIFE, a hope in life, the formulas had less power.''

It was at this juncture that Major Humes happily recalled Mr. Robins' previous testimony describing enthusiastically the land distribution and the popularity and success of the measure. Mr. Robins had said:

''Senators, they have cultivated the soil for a year, for one season, and they have eaten the fruit of their own labors, from land that they now call their own; that is, from land which they had the right to cultivate without paying any landlord rent.''

Mr. Robins, from the advantage of his ''outdoor'' experience, thus testified to the success of the land distribution, to the success of the crops, to the enjoyment by the peasants of ''the fruit of their own labors.'' Previously, telling of his earlier observations in Russia, he had said: ''There was ample food in Russia to feed the people; . . . the whole question was one of assembling and distribution, from surface to centre, from centre to circumference; that task was greatly interfered with by the failure of the general economic and transportation system in Russia to function under revolutionary control.''

CONSISTENCY IN CONTRADICTION

''You have kept track of Russia since you left?'' asked Senator Nelson, sometime later. ''Do you not think that if they had the means of distribution by boat, water and rail, that there would be enough bread, enough wheat, in the whole country to supply themselves with, if they could distribute it and divide it up?''

''Surely, Senator,'' responded Mr. Robins.

''There is no need of importing anything there?'' continued Senator Nelson. ''What they need is transportation?''

''Transportation and manufactured products,'' acquiesced Mr. Robins. Mr. Robins averred that the Allied troops sent into Siberia had prevented the Russians from getting anything from that section.

However, before Allied intervention and while Mr. Robins was himself in Russia, at the very time that, according to his own testimony, ample food was available, he was urging that the United States give material aid to the Russians.

And when he was forced to face the issue, to explain his activities, to explain his opposition to intervention, he came back weakly with the plea and excuse:

''The best answer to Bolshevism is food.''

''On the assumption that there is this need for food, that conclusion might necessarily follow,'' pertinently commented Major Humes upon this assertion. ''But you a few moments ago made the statement that the peasants, who represent some 84 per cent of the people of Russia, by reason of the productiveness of the soil and their having acquired ownership of the land, had enjoyed the fruits of a new era during the last year, and that therefore this want and this starvation that you refer to did not exist. . . . Your statement today has been that 84 per cent of the people are living in a new era; that they are satisfied with the fruits of their first year of possession of the land. If that is true, and that degree of contentment and joy exists among 84 per cent of the people, I do not see that the same necessity for the economic answer to Bolshevism presents itself.''

''Well, I am sorry that I have made myself so unintelligible to you,'' lamely replied the gentleman who knew more about Russia than any other Allied representative!

From Mr. Robins' statements, it was clearly to be implied that the signing of the Brest-Litovsk treaty and the surrender of Russia to Germany was due to the failure of the American and Allied governments to respond to the Lenine-Trotzky overtures.

Of course, the word of Lenine and Trotzky was to be taken at its face value. Despite the fact—as Lenine himself admitted in a statement quoted by Mr. Robins—that the Bolsheviki intended ultimately to destroy the Government of the United States, it was to be taken for granted that in return for material help the Bolshevik would have co-operated with the Allies in fighting Germany.

To some people there may seem something refreshingly naive about Mr. Raymond Robins' mind. But then, unlike the majority of folk who witnessed Bolshevik rule in Russia, Mr. Robins apparently had absolute faith in the high character and integrity of Messrs. Lenine and Trotzky. For one thing Mr. Robins refused to believe that Lenine and Trotzky were conscious German agents. ''Lenine,'' said Mr. Robins, ''is patient, steady, proven.'' Trotzky, in Mr. Robins' words, is ''a thoroughly educated man.''

"90 PER CENT OF RUSSIA REVOLUTIONARY"

Prodded by Senator Overman as to whether he would be in favor of America recognizing a government which he had admitted was a menace to the world, Mr. Robins answered:

''As I understand that the question of recognition of a government does not rest upon the character of the government. If the government is really the government of a people, that is all that any foreign government has a right to inquire into.''

In other words, despite his monotonous urging that we ascertain the facts and learn the truth, he was of the opinion that the American government had no right to question the Bolshevik government and that as it represented the people of Russia the American government should have recognized this autocracy of bloody-handed murderers and plunderers.

Mr. Robins stoutly maintained that the great majority of the Russian people were back of Bolshevism. He said:

"Ninety per cent of the Russian people, the proletariat, are educated in the formulas of revolutionary ideas. They are in the cities. Forty per cent of that ninety per cent goes back twice a year to the villages, at planting time and harvest time. They are the persons who have been away, who have had experience. They go back to the village, . . . and their talk is of the revolution, of the good time that is coming. Their talk is in the terms of the formula, and for that reason there was this widespread agreement in the formula through Russian life; the revolutionary formula and it has a real power and a tremendous significance at this hour, at this time, as it has in our country and the world."

LENINE AND TROTZKY RULE BY WILL OF MAJORITY!

"There is this Soviet form which the Russian mass, the peasants and workmen, have adopted as a framework," Mr. Robins continued. "'All power to the Soviet,' was the cry on which Lenine and Trotzky took possession of the government in Russia. . . They really, discreetly—or rather cunningly—with real political judgment saw that the people liked their self-governing Soviets. . . I think we found, in course of time, in Russia that there was this definite framework that had grown up out of their historic past, that the clever political minds of the Bolshevik leaders fell upon as the way to get into power; so I think there is really something there in structure as well as the actual Bolshevik domination."

"Is there any way possible for the people of Russia to get rid of Lenine and Trotzky without a revolution?" asked Senator Overman.

"I should say so, absolutely, sir. I should say that the moment any considerable mass in Russia wants to get rid of Lenine and Trotzky they can do it," replied Mr. Robins.

In other words, according to Mr. Robins, Lenine and Trotzky rule by will of the majority and not by Red Guard terrorism, and in the Soviet system, controlled by the Bolshevik autocrats, the majority of Russians have what they want.

"The reason that their power has held," pursued Mr. Robins, speaking of Lenine and Trotzky, "has been that for the time they expressed as between the old experience of the past and the new experience, a larger expectation of hope and opportunity for the mass of the peasants and workers of Russia than they had before, and as long as that expectation holds they will support Lenine."

"I gather from your whole statement," said Senator Nelson, "that you are rather of the opinion that Lenine and Trotzky are the men of the hour for the Russian people at this time?"

"The question you asked, Senator," replied Mr. Robins, "might involve the assumption that I thought that they were right in their program. I do not think so. If what you inquired was—did I think that they represented the revolutionary mind in Russia and were the best interpreters of that revolutionary class conscience, socialistic revolutionary, I can say yes, absolutely, that they are the incarnation of it."

Major Humes asked Colonel Robins if the slogan of the Bolshevik government, the appeal to class, was not the appeal of 5 to 10 per cent. only, whether "the rest of the people that acquiesce in the Bolshevik rule are acquiescing simply because of the terrorism, and because of fear?"

To which Mr. Robins firmly replied:

"I do not think that any of the supposititious statements of fact in that series of questions are true."

According to Mr. Robins' assertions Lenine and Trotzky represented 93 per cent. of the population of Russia. However, during the cross examination, the following was brought out:

5 OR 6 OF 84 PERCENT ONLY CONSCIOUSLY REVOLUTIONARIES

"You have, on repeated occasions, referred to the 7 per cent. and the 93 per cent," asked Major Humes. "Are we to understand by that that it is your impression that the Bolsheviki are 93 per cent. of the people of Russia, or is the line between the 7 per cent. and the 93 per cent. simply a line between the great mass of the people and those who were connected with the former government of the Czar's regimé?

"Rather the later, Mr. Humes, but with this effort to clarify. Men have said to me: 'Robins, you do not pretend to say for a moment that the mass of the peasants care about those formulas or are for them—that they have any real articulation in mind about them?' I said: 'No, I would not say that. I would say that of the peasant amount of 84 per cent. there was not more than 5 or 6 per cent. that were conscious at all of the formulas. Those are the leaders of the masses. What I would mean is this—that in Russia there was practically 93 per cent. who would either work with the Bolsheviki and their program or would not work against it; that they were inert when they were not actively with it, and that the leaders believed in the formula and carried the mass of the people with them. . . . About 5 or 6 per cent. of the 84 per cent. who are peasants were conscious, with the formula in their minds, and that 5 per cent. were the leaders of the groups in the Soviets who carried the masses with them. Of the 9 per cent. of the workers, there are perhaps 90 per cent. of that 9 per cent. who are formula men, that are conscious."

Elsewhere in his testimony, Mr. Robins, as before quoted, declared:

"Ninety per cent. of the Russian people, the proletariat, are educated in the formulas of revolutionary ideas."

If only 5 or 6 per cent. of the 84 per cent. of the peasants, and 90 per cent. of the 9 per cent. of workers, consciously stood for the Soviet formula, as Mr. Robins declared, how was it possible, as he elsewhere stated under oath, for Lenine and Trotzky to be "the incarnation" and "best interpreters" of the Russian revolutionary class conscience?

If only 5 or 6 per cent. of the 84 per cent. of the peasants were conscious of the formula of land distribution, of the whole Soviet scheme, how was it possible for Mr. Robins honestly to declare that Lenine and Trotzky held power by the will of the majority and that they "expressed" the expectation of "the mass of peasants"?

If only 5 or 6 per cent. were conscious, and if these were the leaders "who carried the mass with them," how could Mr. Robins decently assume to present the two archleaders, the two brutish and bloody despots at the head of that reign of crime and chaos as representative of the majority of the Russian people?

Ambassador Francis, in his testimony before the Senate Committee, told a good deal about Mr. Robins' activities. Mr. Francis stated that the Bolshevik looked upon Robins as their friend, and told of Mr. Robins' efforts to secure the recognition of the Bolshevik government. On May 15, 1917, at the railroad station at Vologda, on his way out of Russia, Mr. Robins, said Ambassador Francis, "told an Associated Press man there, and a man named Groves, one of my employees, that if he could get one hour with the President he could persuade the President to recognize the Soviet government." According to Ambassador Francis, Mr. Robins was said to have acted as a courier from the Bolshevik government and to have carried communications addressed to the American government over the head of the Ambassador. Whether these were ever presented or not, Mr. Francis did not know.

Mr. Robins, in the course of his testimony, had considerable to say about the appalling atrocities committed by the Czecho-Slovak troops in Russia. Mr. Robins complained: "I find that the atrocities of the Bolsheviki, terrible and wrong and to be opposed by all intelligent and honest men, create more excitement and interest than the atrocities of the Czecho-Slovaks, when they take Bolshevik villages and stand up and shoot the Bolsheviki without trial."

Did Colonel Raymond Robins, out of his telescopic vision, actually witness Bolsheviki villages being taken and Bolsheviki shot without trial? He has testified that he found most of the charges against the Bolsheviki to be false. In fact, if the Bolsheviki had committed atrocities Mr. Raymond Robins, according to his own words, failed to see them.

THE LIE GIVEN TO ROBINS

Mr. Raymond Robins had testified that the movement of Czecho-Slovak troops on their way through Russia had not been interfered with by the Trotzky and Lenine government at the instigation of Germany. In this Ambassador Francis said he thought Mr. Robins was mistaken. Colonel Hurban, who testified before the Committee, was present at the signing of the treaty between the Czecho-Slovak troops and the Bolsheviki. The Bolsheviki, according to both Ambassador Francis and Colonel Hurban, broke the treaty, took the arms from the Czecho-Slovaks and attacked them.

Colonel Raymond Robins' charges against the Czecho-Slovak troops are utterly refuted by Captain Selby James Day and Captain Clifford S. Wheeler, two Americans who have recently returned to this country from service with the Czecho-Slovak army in Siberia. In the *New York Times*, of March 16, Captain Day said of the alleged Czecho-Slovak atrocities:

"It is absolutely untrue and, in my mind, the work of propagandists. Let us lay these atrocities at the hands of the Bolsheviki, for I myself have seen recaptured Czecho-Slovak prisoners of the Bolsheviki who have returned to us in indescribable condition."

Madam Breshkovskaya—who, said Raymond Robins, had turned against the Revolution because of pique—was in Tumen, occupied by the Bolsheviki, when the Czecho-Slovaks were approaching that trading center. "In Tumen," said the "old Grandmother," "there was a Bolshevist inspector of the prison, a ferocious monster, who tortured the prisoners arrested by the Bolsheviki so incessantly that some went absolutely mad, some died from their tortures, and some were buried under the stones and rocks before they were dead."

Finally the Czecho-Slovaks arrived. "It was a thanksgiving day," declared Babushka. "While Colonel Robins tells his stories about the Czecho-Slovak 'atrocities,' I have never heard any complaint against them, never a derogatory remark, even by those who envied their valor. . . It is natural that such excellent people, such examples of bravery and honor, are hated by the Bolsheviki and their supporters.

"I will say that if a man, called as a witness, can slander a whole people and a whole army, known well to all the Russian people as the model of honor and humanity, what credit can be given to all the assertions made by him at second hand, or even, as he says, from his personal knowledge?"

Harvester Industrial Council Plan

NAGEMENT OFFERS EMPLOYEES EQUAL VOICE AND VOTE IN MATTERS OF MUTUAL INTEREST—TO PROMOTE CONTENTMENT AND WELL BEING OF ALL

HE plan of the International Harvester Company for an Industrial Council, given in full below, which was voted upon by its thirty thousand employes on ıesday, March 12, 1919, was adopted by a :ity of the workers at seventeen plants in nited States and Canada. While it was re-
1 in three others, soon after bulletins were d giving the results, employees circulated ions for a re-submission which, under the pany's announcement, could only occur request by them. In submitting the Coun- roposition to the employees, the company's dent, Harold F. McCormick, wrote:

Chicago, Ill., March 10, 1919.

the Employees:—The directors and officers of ompany have for some time been working out a to establish closer relations between the em- es and the management. To this end they now the following Harvester Industrial Council plan he consideration of the employees, hoping that it meet with their approval.

e plan provides for a "Works Council" in which :sentatives elected by the employees shall have l voice and vote with the management in the ideration of matters of mutual interest.

guarantees to every employee the right to pre- any suggestion, request, or complaint and to it promptly considered and fairly decided. Pro- n is also made for impartial arbitration.

ould this plan be adopted by vote of the em- :es, the officers pledge their best efforts to carry t in letter and spirit.

is my hope and belief that the plan, if adopted, materially strengthen our relations in the work have in common, and will make for the greater :entment and well-being of us all.

rticle I. Purpose: The Employees and the Man- nent of the International Harvester Company and subsidiary companies undertake by the adoption :his plan of an Industrial Council to establish e relations upon a definite and durable basis of ual understanding and confidence.

ɔ this end the Employees and the Management l have equal representation in the consideration .ll questions of policy relating to working condi- s, health, safety, hours of labor, wages, recreation, :ation, and other similar matters of mutual in st.

rticle II. Works Council: As the principal .ns of carrying this plan into effect there shall be ınized, at each Works adopting this Plan, a :ks Council composed of Representatives of the ployees, and Representatives of the Management. Employee Representatives shall be elected by Employees. The Management Representatives l be appointed by the management, and shall not :ed the Employee Representatives in number. Both l at all times have an equal voice and voting :er in considering matters coming before the ncil.

hrough these Councils any employee or group of ıloyees, or the management, may at any time sent suggestions, requests or complaints with the ainty of a full and fair hearing. Matters which not be thus disposed of may, by mutual consent, submitted to impartial arbitration as hereinafter vided.

rticle III. Department of Industrial Relations: aid in carrying out this plan the Company has .blished a Department of Industrial Relations ch is charged with the duty of giving special ntion to all matters pertaining to labor policies the well-being of the employees.

rticle IV. Voting Divisions: The basis of repre- tation shall generally be one Employee Repre- tative for each two hundred to three hundred em- rees, but in no case shall there be less than five ployee Representatives in the Works Council.

ı order that the different departments and crafts r be fairly represented, each Works shall be di- :d into Voting Divisions, and each Division shall assigned its proper number of Representatives, :d upon the average number of persons employed rein during the month of December preceding the :tion.

he Works Council may change the Voting Di- ons whenever necessary to secure complete and representation.

rticle V. Qualifications of Employee Representa- :s: 1. To be eligible for nomination as Employee Representative from any Voting Division, the Employee must be employed therein.

2. Foremen, assistant foremen, and other employees having the power of employment or discharge, shall not be eligible for nomination.

3. Only employees who are citizens of the United States, twenty-one years old or over, and have been continuously in the Works' service for one year immediately prior to nomination, as shown on the records of the Employment Department, shall be eligible for nomination as Employee Representatives.

Article VI. Nomination and Election of Employee Representatives: 1. Nomination and election of Employee Representatives shall be by secret ballot. The first nomination and election shall be held as soon as practicable after the adoption of this plan, at which time the full number of Employee Representatives shall be elected.

2. At the first meeting of the Works Council the Employee Representatives shall be divided by lot into two classes, one-half with terms expiring on January 1, 1920, and the other half with terms expiring on July 1, 1920. Thereafter the election of Employee Representatives of the first class shall be held in December and of the second class in June. Except as above provided, all Employee Representatives shall hold office for one year and until their successors are duly elected.

3. Notice of the time appointed for nominations and elections shall be given by bulletins posted publicly in the Works at least two days before the date set for the nominating ballot.

4. All employees, both men and women, shall be entitled to vote, except foremen, assistant foremen, and other employees having the power of employment or discharge.

5. Nominations shall be made in the following manner: Not more than four days before the date fixed for the election a nominating vote shall be taken. A blank ballot stating the number of Representatives to be nominated from his Voting Division will be offered to each employee present at work on the date of the nomination, including all workers on the night turn, if any.

6. On this ballot the employee will write (or he may have a fellow employee write for him) the name of the person he desires to nominate. If his Voting Division is to elect one Representative then one name shall be written on the ballot, if his Voting Division is to elect two Representatives then two names, and so on.

7. Any ballot containing more names than the number of Representatives to be elected from that Voting Division shall not be counted.

8. Employees will deposit their ballots in a locked box carried by a teller representing the employees, who shall be accompanied by a timekeeper.

9. When all who desire have voted, the timekeeper and two employee watchers shall open the ballot box and count and record the votes, in the presence of the Works Auditor, or person designated by him.

10. In Voting Divisions from which *one* Representative is to be elected, the *two* persons receiving the highest number of votes shall be declared nominated. If any Voting Division is to elect *two* Representatives, then the *four* persons receiving the highest number of votes shall be declared nominated, and so on.

11. If any person nominated is disqualified under the provisions of Article V, then the properly qualified candidate receiving the next highest number of votes shall be declared the nominee.

12. The results of the balloting and the names of the nominees shall be posted in the Works as soon as the votes have been counted and the nominations declared.

13. Not more than four days after the nominations are posted, the election by secret ballot shall be held in the same manner as for nominations, except that at the election only the names of the persons who have been duly nominated shall appear on the ballots, and these persons alone can be voted for.

14. The name of the nominee receiving the highest number of votes shall be placed first upon the election ballot; the name of the nominee receiving the next highest number shall be placed next on the election ballot, and so on.

15. At the election the candidate or candidates receiving the highest number of votes in his or their Voting Division shall be declared elected members of the Works Council.

Article VII. Appointment of Management Representatives: Upon the election of the Employee Representatives the management will announce the appointment of the Management Representatives in the Works Council, whose number shall in no case exceed the number of elected Employee Representatives.

Article VIII. Vacancies in the Works Council: 1. If any Employee Representative leaves the service of the Works, or becomes ineligible for any of the reasons stated in V, or is recalled, as provided in Article IX, or is absent from more than four consecutive meetings of the Works Council without such absence being excused by the Council, his membership therein shall immediately cease.

2. All vacancies among the Employee Representatives shall be promptly filled by special nomination and election, conducted under the direction of the Works Council in the same manner as regular nominations and elections. Vacancies among the Management Representatives shall be filled by appointment by the Management.

Article IX. Recall of Employee Representatives: 1. If the services of any Employee Representative become unsatisfactory to the Employees of the Voting Division from which he was elected, they may recall him in the manner herein provided.

2. Whenever a petition is filed with the Chairman of the Works Council, signed by not less than one-third of the Employees of a Voting Division, asking for the recall of their Representative, a special election by secret ballot shall be held in that Voting Division under the direction of the Works Council, to decide whether such Representative shall be recalled or continued in office.

3. If at such election a majority of the employees in the Voting Division vote in favor of recalling their Representative, then his term of office shall immediately cease; otherwise he shall continue in office.

4. Any vacancy so created shall be immediately filled by a special election, as provided in Article VIII.

Article X. Organization and Meetings of the Works Council: 1. The Manager of the Department of Industrial Relations or someone designated by him, shall act as Chairman of the Works Council. A Secretary shall be appointed by the Superintendent of the Works. Neither the Chairman nor Secretary shall have a vote.

2. A majority of the Employee Representatives, together with a majority of the Management Representatives, shall constitute a quorum, and no business shall be transacted at any meeting where less than a quorum is present.

3. The Works Council may appoint such sub-committees as it deems desirable for efficient conduct of its business. On all such sub-committees both the employees and the management shall be represented, and each group of Representatives shall have equal voting power.

4. The Works Council shall hold regular monthly meetings at times fixed by the Council. Special meetings may be called on three days' written notice by the Chairman, Secretary, or any three members of the Council. Sub-committees shall meet whenever necessary.

5. The Company shall provide at its expense suitable places for meetings of the Works Council and its sub-committees and the Employee Representatives thereon.

6. Employees serving as members of the Works Council shall receive their regular pay from the Company during such absence from work as this service actually requires, except that if the Employee Representatives so desire, they shall be at liberty to arrange for compensation to be paid by pro rata assessment among the employees.

7. Employees attending any meeting at the request of the Works Council or any sub-committee, shall receive their regular pay from the Company for such time as they are actually and necessarily absent from work on this account.

8. The Works Council may prepare and distribute to the employees reports of its proceedings, and the expense thereof shall be borne by the Company.

Article XI. Duties and Powers of the Works Council: 1. The Works Council may consider and make recommendations on all questions relating to working conditions, protection of health, safety, wages, hours of labor, recreation, education, and other similar matters of mutual interest to the employees and the management. It shall afford full opportunity for the presentation and discussion of these matters.

2. The Works Council may on its own motion investigate matters of mutual interest and make recommendations thereon to the Works Management, and the management also may refer matters to the Works Council for investigation and report.

3. The Works Council may confer with the Superintendent or other person designated by him in regard to all matters of mutual interest, and shall receive from the management regular reports in re-

gard to accident prevention, sanitation, restaurants, medical service, employment, educational programs and recreational activities, including information as to the cost, efficiency and results obtained.

4. The Works Council shall be concerned solely with shaping the policies of the Company relating to the matters heretofore mentioned. When the policy of the Company as to any of these matters has been settled, its execution shall remain with the management, but the manner of that execution may at any time be a subject for the consideration of the Works Council.

Article XII. Procedure of Works Councils: 1. Employees desiring to bring any matters before the Works Council may present these to the Secretary of the Council either in person or through their Representatives. It shall be the Secretary's duty first to ascertain whether the matter has been properly presented through the regular channels to the Superintendent, and if not he shall see that this is promptly done.

2. If the matter is not satisfactorily disposed of in this manner, the Secretary shall submit a written statement of the matter to each member of the Works Council at least three days before the next regular meeting.

3. Any employee or group of employees thus referring a matter to the Works Council shall have an opportunity to appear before it and present the case. Any such group of employees shall select not more than three spokesmen from their own number to appear before the Council.

4. The Works Council may call any employee before it to give information regarding any matter under consideration. The Works Council, or any sub-committees apponted by it for that purpose, may go in a body to any par. of the plant to make investigations.

5. After complete investigation and full discussion of any matter under consideration by the Works Council, the Chairman shall call for a vote which shall be secret, unless otherwise ordered by the Council. The Employee Representatives and the Management Representatives shall vote separately. The vote of a majority of the Employee Representatives shall be taken as the vote of all and recorded as their unit vote. Similarly, the vote of a majority of the Management Representatives shall be taken as the vote of all and recorded as their unit vote.

6. Both the Employee Representatives and the Management Representatives shall have the right to withdraw temporarily from any meeting of the Works Council for private discussion of any matter under consideration.

7. When the Works Council reaches an agreement on any matter, its recommendation shall be referred to the Superintendent for execution, except that if the Superintendent considers it of such importance as to require the attention of the general officers, he shall immediately refer it to the President of the International Harvester Company, who may either approve the recommendation of the Works Council and order its immediate execution by the Superintendent, or proceed with further consideration of the matter in accordance with Article XIII.

8. In case of a tie vote in the Works Council, it shall be in order to reopen the discussion, to offer a substitute or compromise recommendation, on which the votes shall be taken in the same manner as above provided.

Article XIII. Reference to the President: 1. If after further consideration, the vote in the Works Council remains a tie, then the matter shall, at the request of either the Employee Representatives or the Management Representatives, be referred to the President of the International Harvester Company.

2. The President, or his specially appointed representative, may confer with the Works Council as a whole, or any sub-committee thereof, or any group of Employee Representatives, at such time and place and in such manner as in his opinion will best serve to bring out all the facts of the case.

3. Within ten days after the matter has been referred to him, the President shall either

(a) propose a settlement thereof; or

(b) refer the matter directly to a General Council to be formed as provided in Article XIV.

4. If the settlement proposed by the President is not satisfactory to a majority of the Employee Representatives, and if after a further period of five days no agreement has been reached, then the President may, if he deems it advisable, refer the matter to a General Council to be formed as provided in Article XIV.

5. If the President decides not to refer the matter to a General Council, or if the vote of the General Council is a tie, then the matter may, by mutual agreement of the President and a majority of the Employee Representatives, be submitted to arbitration, as provided in Article XV.

Article XIV. General Council: 1. Whenever in the opinion of the President any matter coming before any Works Council affects other Works of the Company, or whenever he desires to refer any matter as provided in Article XIII, he may call a General Council to consider such matter, and thereafter the Works Council shall take no further action thereon.

2. The General Council shall be formed in the following manner: The President shall issue a notice designating the several Works which he deems jointly interested. Thereupon the Employee Representatives in the Works Council at each of the Works designated shall select two or more of their own number to act as members of the General Council. There shall be one such member of the General Council for each 1000 employees or major fraction thereof, except that no Works shall have less than two Representatives in the General Council.

3. The Management Representatives in the General Council shall be appointed by the President and shall not exceed the number of Employee Representatives.

4. The President or some person designated by him shall act as Chairman of the General Council, without vote.

5. The first meeting of the General Council shall be held within ten days after the President's notice calling such Council.

6. The General Council shall, when necessary, take recesses in order to allow Employee Representatives therein to confer with other members of their Works Councils. For this purpose special meetings of the Works Councils as a whole, or of the Employee Representatives alone, shall (at the request of the Employee Representatives serving on the General Council) be convened at the respective Works, and full opportunity shall be given for conference and discussion with such Representatives regarding their attitude and action on the pending matter.

7. Reasonable traveling expenses, including hotel bills of Employee and Management Representatives serving on a General Council, shall be paid by the Company.

8. The procedure in the General Council with reference to the consideration of matters coming before it and the manner of voting shall be the same as that prescribed for the Works Council.

9. If the General Council is unable to reach an agreement as to any matter, it may, by mutual agreement of a majority of both the Employee Representatives and the Management Representatives, be submitted to arbitration.

Article XV. Arbitration: 1. Whenever the President and a majority of the Employee Representatives in the General Council, or the Works Council, as the case may be, have mutually agreed to submit a matter to arbitration, they shall proceed to select an impartial and disinterested arbitrator. If they cannot agree upon an arbitrator, then the Employee Representatives shall choose one such arbitrator and the President shall choose another, and if these two agree, their decision shall be final. If they do not agreé, then they shall select and call in a third arbitrator, and a decision of a majority of these three shall be final.

2. The arbitrator or arbitrators shall be furnished all the information and testimony they deem necessary regarding the matter in arbitration.

Article XVI. Decisions of General Council or by Arbitration: All decisions of any General Council or of any arbitrator or arbitrators shall be binding upon all the Works originally designated by the President as being jointly interested. Any such decision may be made retroactive.

Article XVII. Guaranty of Independence of Action: Every Representative serving on any Works or General Council shall be wholly free in the performance of his duties as such, and shall not be discriminated against on account of any action taken by him in good faith in his representative capacity. To guarantee to each Representative his independence, he shall have the right to appeal directly to the President for relief from any alleged discrimination against him, and if the decision of the President is not satisfactory to him, then to have the question settled by an arbitrator selected by mutual agreement.

Article XVIII. No Discrimination: There shall be no discrimination under this plan against any employee because of race, sex, political or religious affiliation or membership in any labor or other organization.

Article XIX. Decisions Affecting Wages: Decisions affecting wages made by any Works Council or General Council or by arbitration shall be subject to revision whenever changed conditions justify, but not oftener than at intervals of six months.

Article XX. Amendment or Termination of Plan: 1. This plan may be amended by the Works Council of any Works by a majority vote of all the duly elected Employee Representatives together with a majority vote of all the Management Representatives. Amendments must be proposed in writing at a regular meeting, and no vote shall be taken thereon until the regular meeting following such presentation. No amendment shall be adopted that will destroy or limit the equal voting power of the Employee Representatives and Management Representatives in the Works Council and General Council.

2. If in the judgment of the President any proposed amendment affects other Works, than he shall call a General Council to consider such amendment. The adoption or rejection of an amendment shall not be the subject of arbitration.

The National
Civic Federation Review

Vol. IV. NEW YORK, APRIL 10, 1919 No. 12

BRITISH CAPITAL AND LABOR UNITE

ANALOGY BETWEEN LABOR PROBLEMS IN GREAT BRITAIN AND UNITED STATES—BRITISH WORKERS OPPOSED TO RADICAL, REVOLUTIONARY CHANGES IN INDUSTRY

THE commission of employers sent by the Department of Labor to study industrial conditions in England and France has just returned. It was headed by E. T. Gundlach, of Chicago, and the other members were William H. Ingersoll, of New York; George E. McElwain, of Boston; Dorr E. Felt, of Chicago; F. R. Otis, of Atlanta, and R. J. Caldwell, of New York. In an interview published in the press, Chairman Gundlach gives the following review of the situation as it appeared when the commission left England:

"The air in England is full of talk about revolution, but when we come to analyze this talk in conversation with the workmen we find what they mean by revolution is a great change in the methods of the Government. The British workman also talks a great deal about overthrowing the Government. We must remember that overthrowing the Government in England means a change of administration. Of course there is a radical wave that really wants something akin to a revolution, but I recall particular talks with groups of ultra-radical workmen who talked loud and long about the fact that they were tired of waiting and wanted a complete change in the social structure now. On two occasions I pinned these men down by asking what they meant by 'now,' and it turned out that they merely wanted to start now, and proceed gradually.

"Everywhere we found the working classes aroused and alert. They are seriously attempting to grasp fundamentals of the problems facing them. At Manchester we found that workmen are, in a large degree, spending their free time in school studying economics instead of at sports. The whole air is full of the new era, and every workman thinks he is going to have something to say in this new era, but even those who are theoretical Marxians, I found, are by temperament wholly opposed to any violent change. They have been too long controlled by a Parliamentarian system.

"Unquestionably they are strongly organized. The leaders of the so-called Triple Alliance, composed of the three big unions of coal miners, railway men, and transportation men, have got so much power that if they went on a strike it seems as if the whole of England would have to submit. However, it was pointed out that this would be dictation by a small minority, and, as a violation of the principle of democracy, harmful to their interests in the long run. The coal hearings began just before we left, and there appeared to be no difference of opinion on the point that the coal miners had made out an excellent case for better living conditions. Whether the final outcome will be the beginning of another social order forced through the nationalization of the coal mines or whether this present trouble will be settled by simply giving the miners higher wages and shorter hours remains as a problem."

"There is no great fear of anything resembling Bolshevism in England, provided the great majority of workmen can be kept employed. How far the workers will go in their demand for more and more of the national products, and more and more shares in the national industries remains to be seen. However, with a very small minority which is opposed to harmony and constitutional methods nothing more is needed than a large army of unemployed, or partly employed, labor to create very serious danger—something one might describe as a Bolshevist menace. Again and again, radical labor leaders with whom we talked emphasized the point that they were expressing, consciously or subconsciously, the desires of the multitude. They recognize that they have not the majority of the workingmen supporting them in their present radicalism, but they count upon some upheaval of the industries to bring out their desires.

"In order to avoid the danger of an army of unemployed rising to follow these radicals, employers and labor leaders who believe in orderly procedure are agreed that the greatest attention must be paid to the subject of employment. There is a movement on foot now among business men to keep up manufacturing, even to the extent of stocking up on goods, and every effort is being made to stimulate non-war production trade in order to keep men employed. In the office of Sir Stephen Kent, one of the very wealthy men in the Government service, who, as Director of Demobilization, has charge of employment, we saw tables of figures showing how men are being systematically demobilized by industries. In the engineering trade a great many men are already out of work, so men in that trade were not being demobilized at the time of our interview with Sir Stephen. Employment offices are being greatly enlarged.

"Why did the commission spend practically all its time in Great Britain? Because industrial history shows some analogy between Great Britain and the United States. American development in many instances has followed the British, not because they know better, but because they have had longer experience. This similarity was particularly emphasized recently, because during the war events moved very fast. Great Britain had four years of war, while we had a year and a half. They began to get their shop committees after six or eight months of war, while we began to get our shop committees after we had been in the war for the same time. They had certain types of labor troubles, and we had certain types of labor troubles. It is reasonable to suppose that the events now taking place in Great Britain will take place here also in a more or less degree.

"The question we shall have to meet is that we must get along with these labor people. We cannot get along by trying to smash the workmen's organizations. The employers in England realize that this battle has been fought, and that kind of opposition has been abandoned. They now believe in the conservative organization of labor as one protection against chaos, and they know that the whole organization of labor, as at present constituted, is at stake, and that business, as owned and conducted by individuals, that is, the employers, is at stake.

"One of the big things which we could not very well touch in our report, which will be made public next week, is the very marked feeling among the British that their foreign trade is at stake if this labor unrest cannot be settled, and labor men themselves feel that. And I was greatly surprised to find that the employers and even members of the Great Britain Federation of Industries are talking with considerable favor of international agreements between labor, hoping that labor organizations in various countries will get together—the very thing they looked upon a year ago as anarchy. Of course, this can be accomplished only by national organizations of labor, not by employers. Employers are done with making war upon labor organizations as we have known them in the past, because they fear a more formidable foe.

"We have Bolshevist elements in this country, and if we don't look out and cultivate harmony between employers and conservative employees, and, most of all, see to it that the unemployment problem does not spread to large proportions, we shall have troubles on our hands, with Bolshevist outbreaks aiming at labor's taking control of industry. We must have readjustments, better conditions for the average worker than formerly existed. I think the danger here is that employers are not waking up in outlining programs for closer cooperation with their employees, whereas in Great Britain nearly all employers have waked up. That, I think, is where our greatest danger of protracted labor disturbance lies."

Industrial Training A Way Out

LOW PRODUCTION COST, GOOD WAGES AND FAIR PROFITS—A TRIPARTITE ADJUSTMENT

By H. E. MILES

CHAIRMAN SECTION ON INDUSTRIAL TRAINING FOR THE WAR EMERGENCY, COMMITTEE ON LABOR, ADVISORY COMMISSION, COUNCIL OF NATIONAL DEFENSE—CHIEF OF TRAINING, U. S. DEPARTMENT OF LABOR

EARLY in the war, a machinist said to his foreman in a munition factory upon which both our country and the Allies were largely depending: "Come over and help me a little." Said the foreman: "Weren't you hired as an all-round toolmaker?" "Yes." "Then, —— you, bore that gun or get out!" The man quit, saying later: "I am an all-round toolmaker, but I never saw a 75 M/M gun before in my life, and I did not propose to spoil the first one." This factory had employed in the preceding six months 15,000 workers at an average cost of $50 each in order to maintain a force of only 4,500 men. About a fourth of its machines were broken or out of repair and the repair force was too small to put them in order. A factory making airplane motors, needing sensitive drill operators, brought a man to New Jersey from Vermont who declared he had run a drill successfully for eight years. It developed later that the drill he had operated was in a marble quarry. A barber in Connecticut with a machinist's kit of tools is said to have secured a machinist's job in a small arms factory and held it for several days before being found out.

The country was calling four million men to the colors, many of them skilled machinists for maintenance and repair work at the front. A million new workers were required in the factories, including tens of thousands of women who were either wholly inexperienced in factory work or had done only simple unskilled tasks.

It may have been in anticipation of conditions like these that Mr. Samuel Gompers, as chairman of the Committee on Labor of the Council of National Defense, appointed the Sectional Committee on Industrial Training for the War Emergency, its purpose being to devise and recommend to employers in essential war production, methods of intensively training their host of new workers each for perfection production as nearly as might be in the narrow field in which he was to operate.

The first meeting of the committee was on the 15th of June, 1917, in a tower room of the Metropolitan Building, New York, in the offices of The National Civic Federation, the Federation and the director of its Welfare Department, Mrs. R. M. Easley, being then and since a well-spring of inspiration and assistance, without which little might have been done. Labor men were there thoroughly versed in all the bearings of vocational education as applied to labor; vocational teachers from trade and apprentice schools; women qualified in the subjects; and representative manufacturers. The committee consisted of about equal numbers of representatives of wage earners, employers and experts in training. The harmonious and effective work of the committee illustrates the long-time insistance of the chairman that there are many fields of extreme and common concern to wage earners and their employers in which they should aggressively cooperate, and that such cooperation will bring returns so great as to lessen distrust and antagonisms in other fields where interests are obscure or apparently in conflict.

(Samuel Gompers, Chairman of the Committee on Labor, chose Mr. Miles as chairman of his Section on Industrial Training for the War Emergency because of his successful experience as a practical manufacturer and in industrial training as chairman of The National Manufacturers Association's Committee on that subject. Initial plans were based upon principles agreed upon by Hugh Frayne, chairman of the Industrial Training Committee of the American Federation of Labor. The section's executive committee was composed of John Golden, President of the United Textile Workers' Union; Percy S. Straus, of R. H. Macy & Co.; C. R. Dooley, of the Westinghouse Electric & Manufacturing Co., and Mr. Miles. In all the manufacturing centres of the Middle West and East—Chicago, St. Louis, Milwaukee, Detroit, Cincinnati, Cleveland, Buffalo, Rochester, Philadelphia, New York, Bridgeport, New Haven, Worcester—the idea was spread by visits of the chairman to large factories and by addresses before groups of employers, superintendents and foremen.—Editor.)

Copyright, Harris & Ewing

H. E. MILES

The purpose was not education for its general value but only for the making of munitions in the overwhelming quantity essential to victory. It was agreed that it is possible intensively to develop skill in workers in an incredibly short time by training. Some who worked successfully in factories on war contracts had three days' training, some three weeks, some eight weeks, according to their ability and the nature of their tasks. They were never all-round machinists after such training but each could do well the task assigned.

It was in the natural course that workers from idle trades were to be trained to their new tasks first, and later new comers outside of industry, and that operatives in the trade itself were to be up-graded to higher positions rather than outsiders. It was evident that millions could not be suddenly trained in school houses with little or no equipment. They must be trained in the factories directly upon the work they were to do.

"Vestibule school" such a factory training place was called and, in such vestibules or entrances, thousands of workers the country over were prepared for the particular part they were to play in the great war drama. And thanks to such training of more and yet more workers the piles of war goods at the railway stations and harbor warehouses were many times higher than otherwise would have been. Machinery for the making of air motors, airplanes, micrometers, time fuses, gauges and fine instruments, gun carriages, guns and pneumatic tools for ship riveting—factories for all these things swollen with war contracts and suffering for skilled workers and too much labor turnover—in them were developed these special training departments upon advice of the Section on Industrial Training and often by experts provided by the Section.

In some cases, blocks of machines upon the factory floor were set apart for this training but wherever feasible, machines of each type were set apart in a separate room for training and the worker was there instructed by persons especially fit both in machine operations and in the imparting of information. Every factory has its toolroom in which the material instruments of production are kept sharp and fit. These training departments are Human Toolrooms in which the employees are especially fitted for their work. The success of the plan is illustrated by the following: A war factory with a labor turnover of 9,000 workers a year was spending at the rate of $40 per operative simply to get a new man on the payroll and then spending $50 or more "breaking him in" in the old way and

Machinists' Class, Norton Companies, Worcester, Mass., where eight weeks' intensive training is given.

Women inspecting pistons and valves for airplane motors, Lincoln Motor Co.

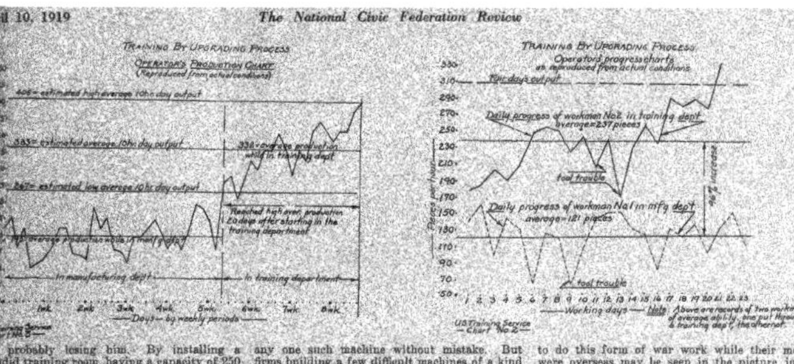

en probably losing him. By installing a lendid training room, having a capacity of 250 rsons, it trained new comers in from 4 to 8 ys to do special tasks better than they had er done anything before. It is an interesting ychological fact that what a man or woman n do well, he likes to do. So these newly ained workers, doing their tasks to the admira- on of all about them were themselves satisfied, d stuck! The turnover was one percent per onth among these workers as against 12% nong workers employed in the old way. It unnecessary to state that the general work- g conditions and welfare of the employees ere considered.

The important principle that wage earners om idle trades must be given preference in aining and employment is illustrated by the cture on the opposite page (at left). This ma- inists' class in training is made of some ocer's clerks, a painter, a musician, a man who rried boxes for a department store, a man who djusted glasses in an optician's office, a corset esigner, a laborer, a butcher, etc. The firm hich maintained this training class built, nong other things, machines used in other fac- ries for grinding crank shafts for airmotors. very such machine built and delivered meant ne more airmotor every two hours. It is easy see why this firm was greedy for machinists nd why when they could not find them ready ade, they trained their own.

The manufacture of rifles and revolvers is so rfected with jigs and stops that two or three ers' good training enabled workers to handle any one such machine without mistake. But firms building a few difficult machines of a kind and frequently shifting from one kind to another had to train their workers from two to eight weeks. They were, however, trained upon regu- lar production and were, therefore, given good wages while in training without loss to the em- ployer who profited equally with the trainee from the skill acquired.

The old man shown at the right hand, once a shoemaker, came to this tool works in June, 1918, and by late July was so far advanced that he was put on the difficult work of assembling. In the view here shown he is putting together a caliper device to be used for fine measurements on parts being surface ground.

Women proved particularly clever in tasks where accuracy was essential. In the making of time fuses, or the adjustment machinery of gun carriages, fine measuring instruments, or the lenses for gun sights, the allowable limits for divergence from absolutely true are .0005 in. or sometimes .0002 or .0001 in. The careful- ness and patience of women, as well as a delicate sense of touch, made it possible for them, after training, to achieve this accuracy in metal hand- ling, even when they had never worked before in any factory. In the picture on the page op- posite at the right, a group of new trainees is shown in a factory where women work on fine instruments to limits of practically no tolerance.

A company in Detroit making airmotors ad- vertised for 300 women, preferably with rela- tives at the front, and received 1,600 answers. The various types of women who were interested to do this form of war work while their men were overseas may be seen in the picture just mentioned.

But the best of this story is yet to come. It was demonstrated, by the time the Armistice was signed, in some 200 vestibule training depart- ments in war factories of all types and sizes, that the skill, happiness, loyalty and accomplish- ment of the 10,000,000 workers in American fac- tories is, and ever will be, what the employers are wise enough to make it, equally in their own interest and the interest of the workers and the country. Proverbially American mechanics have had to "steal" their trades and have been utterly neglected in respect to special training for their occupations. Foremen have been too busy to train and the men have had to bluff their way. Our factory workers are brothers and sisters of the men who went to the Front and like the latter, respond instantly to training, and with the same success as did our new-made soldiers. Women, after proving their perfect equality, are no longer entering the factories. More training departments are being installed now than in war times. Every great national as- sociation of employers is coming to participate in the up-grading of the millions of skilled and semi-skilled workers. The Section on Industrial Training worked without compensation and dis- closed the national need. Congress recognized the need and, upon recommendation of the Secre- tary of Labor acting as War Labor Administra- tor, granted the Secretary $150,000. for the con- tinuance of the work which he then organized

(*Continued on Page 19*)

Woman accurately cutting thread on test screw 26½" long. Blanchard Machine Co.

Man, 63 years of age, shoemaker by trade, doing delicate work of assembling caliper device after brief training.

"Who's Who" in "The New School"

DID THE "NEW CLASS OF LEADERS" SPECIALIZING IN "THE REFORM OF SOCIAL EVILS" EVER EN IN SHADOW HUN, SHADOW BOLSHEVIST OR OTHER UNAMERICAN PROPAGANDA?

"Our hypocrisy is too deep and impulsive for us to detect."—James Harvey Robinson, in the *Atlantic Monthly*, December, 1917.

By T. EVERETT HARRÉ

IN January there appeared in the *New York Evening Post*, and in such organs of outré intellectualism as the *New Republic* and the *Nation*, an advertisement announcing the opening of what was called "The New School for Social Research," which, according to the advertisement, "offers lectures on pressing problems of modern life with opportunity for their practical investigation. Its object is to prepare students who show promise of becoming high-class journalists, original teachers, public administrators, or capacity for dealing with problems of labor, industry and government."

Preliminary to the opening of the New School "with an enlarged staff and a full program in October," were announced courses of lectures extending from February until May. In view of the publicity given the enterprise, including generous space in the columns of the *New York Tribune*, it was only natural that people should ask what purposes lay behind the inauguration of "the New School," what it proposed to teach, who constituted the faculty and who were its backers.

At a time when many people are alive to the workings of insidious forces aiming at social distintegration, the undermining of American ideals and of our national integrity, it is inevitable that any new educational enterprise should escape vigilant precautionary scrutiny. Is a school, thus launched, in the hands of men of proven loyalty and patriotism? Is the school's program designed for "promising students" according to the highest constructive ideals of Christian civilization and the principles of the soundest Americanism?

After the amazing revelations of the extent to which Germanism had invaded American universities and schools during a quarter of a century, the extent to which the minds of American professors had been tainted by the Teutonic virus, it is only natural that Americans should be more than ever alert against baleful influenees still being exerted upon the young of the land from the very seats of learning. Moreover, realizing as we do, that what was German propaganda has simply been converted into another yet no less definite and inimical form, the propaganda of social discontent, revolution and civil strife, which seeks to devitiate and destroy the nations through a cunning, deceptive and destructive "internationalism," it is urgently all-vital at this crucial and unsettled time that Americans be guardedly watchful lest a foe, no less defined, no less materially definite than the armed Huns, defeat the very victory won in the war by furtive and treacherous undermining of national integrity and social peace from within.

Any new school seeking students, especially if it advertises any unique line of teaching or investigation, will expect, of course, a discerning and thoroughly impartial examination of its personnel, and analysis of its purposes.

Who are the organizers of The New School for Social Research?

Who constitute the faculty?

Who are the lecturers?

Among those comprising the Organization Committee are Mr. Herbert Croly, Mr. Alvin Johnson, Mr. Charles A. Beard, and Mr. James Harvey Robinson.

MR. HERBERT CROLY is editor of the *New Republic*, and the author of "The Promise of American Life," published in 1909, a volume in which the now pacifist Mr. Croly exalted imperial Germany, attempted to justify Germany's wars of aggression, and advocated that war should be carried on to decisive results in military victory. Mr. Croly's *New Republic* advocated a peace of compromise with Germany, preached flagrant "defeatism," assailed the motives of the Allies, defended the Bolshevik and has promulgated "internationalism." This sheet is constantly and approvingly quoted by the *New York Call* and Viereck's erstwhile *Fatherland*.

> *"It is our purpose and intention to secure control as far as we can of concerns publishing text books for use in public schools, and likewise to mobilize and influence all writers of school text books. We propose especially to control the preparation of school histories."*
>
> —Statement made to Mr. Harré in 1915 by Dr. Karl Mechlenburg, chief of the Translation Bureau of the Official German Propaganda Organization, at 1123 Broadway, New York.
>
> *"The Public School is the Ark of the Covenant of the Republic. It is little wonder, then, that for some years even before the German war, the common enemy sought and secured an entrance there. . . . To be forewarned is to be forearmed. We know now what the enemy has been up to in secret for many years. It is our duty to the children of the land to seek out this enemy's hiding places and drive him hence and to see to it that he never enters there again."*
>
> —Statement of Judge Thomas Burke, of the Text Book Committee of the Seattle, Wash., School Board, concerning "Outlines of European History, Part II.," by Professor Chas. A. Beard and James Harvey Robinson, which was thrown out of the Seattle Schools because the Board charged that it contained flagrant pro-Hun propaganda.
>
> THEODORE ROOSEVELT, in a letter condemning Prof. James Harvey Robinson's school text-book, "Mediaeval and Modern Times," said:
>
> "THE CHAPTER CALLED, 'THE ORIGIN OF THE WAR OF 1914' . . . IS AN OUTRAGEOUS PIECE OF GERMAN PROPAGANDA AND BECAUSE OF ITS OMISSIONS IT IS A SHAMEFUL PERVERSION OF HISTORIC TRUTH. THIS ONE CHAPTER MAKES THE BOOK UTTERLY UNFIT FOR USE IN AMERICAN SCHOOLS."

MR. ALVIN JOHNSON is an associate editor of the *New Republic* and the author of articles fervently defending various school teachers put on trial for disloyalty and seditious teaching.

VISIONS OF THE GUILLOTINE?

PROF. CHARLES A. BEARD, one of the chief organizers and leaders of the New School, is co-author with Prof. James Harvey Robinson of "Outlines of European History, Part II," which was thrown out of the Seattle public schools because it was declared to contain pro-German propaganda. Beard was one of those named in the list of pacifists given the Overman Committee by Archibald Stevenson, of the Military Intelligence. He has been advertised as a lecturer of the Socialist Rand School. Beard found it convenient to resign from Columbia University after championing the "conscientious" objectors who were under fire, and has of late campaigned for the release of "political prisoners whose offense"—as he puts it—"was to retain Mr. Wilson's pacifist views after he abandoned them" and also for the release of "American citizens held in the interest of foreign governments for interpreting Mr. Wilson's 'liberty, self-government and undictated development' to mean a curtailment of British dominion in some parts of the earth." In his appeal for the release of "political prisoners," distributed in leaflet form at lectures given in th York public schools, Beard concluded cantly: "All this will be in the interest o persons of commonsense and property *wh to keep their money in their purses an heads on their shoulders.*"* Was this so of a veiled threat?

Beard has defended the Russian Bol and—despite the revelations that Leni Trotzky were financed by imperial Ger asserted in the *New Republic* of July 14 "To say that the Russians, in declarin unwillingness to spill more blood for the righting historic wrongs and in announcin readiness for peace without annexations demnities, are tools of the Kaiser, paid p man propagandists, advance agents of G ism, is utter folly." Prof. Beard is the of "An Economic Interpretation of th stitution of the United States," reviewe previous article, "in which," says the *Ne Times*, "he sought to show that the foun this Republic and the authors of its Cc tion, were a ring of land speculators stowed upon the country a body of orga drawn up chiefly in the interest of the pockets. . . . It was a book that did bia much harm," continued the *Times'* ed "just as the two professors who were r dropped for seditious utterances did t versity much harm. It was the fruit school of thought and teaching again bo from Germany, which denied to man larger actions the capacity of noble st and self sacrifice for ideals, that seeks al the prompting motive either the animal d get more to eat or the hope of filli pockets."

PROF. JAMES HARVEY ROBINSON, with one of the chief moving spirits of the New and also one of the lecturers, is a Ph. Freiburg, Germany. He is the author of German Bundesrath," "Mediaeval and Times," and co-author with Prof. Cha Beard of the pro-German "Outlines of pean History, Part II." Prof. Robinson of the signers of the appeal to raise $50, the defense of the I. W. W. leaders whe were on trial in Chicago for seditious cons He was one of a committee, including P Kellogg, which sent a demand to the O Committee investigating Bolshevism th Raymond Robins and certain Bolshevi pathizers be heard and in which the co was made that the witnesses who had Bolshevik crime and misrule had not giv accurate and impartial picture of the Revolution."

"A NEW CLASS OF LEADERS"

In its prospectus, explaining "why" should be a New School, it is asserted:

"An established university, on account diverse obligations, is necessarily hampe investigating and teaching subjects of suc temporary interest as are involved in soc lations. . . . Its form of governme tends to discourage independence, since t ministration is responsible to trustees, \ turn represent the chief sources of i . . . The threatening cleavages in . throughout the world are causing me women of all persuasions to feel uncei about the future. Opinions everywhe crystalizing about certain dogmas and ex

* Italicization employed in quotations in this are my own.—AUTHOR.

of action, and the prospect of orderly ess is correspondingly decreased.''

ie school will not be so radical as the So- s nor so conservative as the established sities,''. Prof. Iobinson was quoted by ew York *Tribune* as saying. ''It will be matic in all its teachings. . . . A of instructors has been selected who ize the pressing necessity of collecting ac- information about political, social and in- ial conditions. . . . *The school will turn new class of leaders.''*

is to be gathered, from Prof. Robinson's nent, that the New School will therefor not radical, not quite so raw in its revolution- reachments, as the Rand School, which is ted by the American Socialist Society, the ration which was recently sentenced to fine of $3,000 for publishing Scott Near- book, ''The Great Madness.'' But was it inferred, nevertheless, that the school will least mildly radical? No specific informa- vas volunteered as to whether the program e New School aims at the dissemination of ed Socialism, camouflaged Bolshevism, or coated ''internationalism.'' Prof. Robin- lid not say whether young and unsophisti- students would be taught along lines of mic determinism, after the doctrine that is a beast spurred to endeavor only by and the urge of his belly, and that they d be trained to view all life, history, all l phenomena, from that basic standpoint egation of all spiritual faith, moral princi- and national ideals which is Marxian ma- lism.

addition to Professors Robinson and Beard, preliminary lecturers announced by the New ol include:

orstein Veblen, Ph. D.
orace M. Kallen
arold J. Laski, B. A.
rdway Tead
obert Bruere

OBERT BRUERE, a student of the University of lin, with Prof. James Harvey Robinson and Walter E. Weyl, was involved in the effort aise $50,000 in June, 1918, for the defense he indicted I. W. W. leaders. Bruere is a tee of the notorious Rand School of Social nce.

HORSTEIN VEBLEN, a Socialist professor of the versity of Missouri, was one of the contribu- to a remarkable pamphlet, ''The Truth it the I. W. W.,'' prepared as a whitewash he I. W. W.'s on trial in Chicago, and issued he National Civil Liberties Bureau, which is e up of such intellectual ''heavies'' and nota- patriots as Paul U. Kellogg, Rabbi Judah L. nes, Scott Nearing, Oswald Garrison Villard Roger N. Baldwin, who on October 30, 3, was sentenced in the Federal Court in New k to serve one year in prison for violation he Selective Service Law.

ORACE MEYER KALLEN, born at Berenstadt, sia, Germany, professor of philosophy at the versity of Wisconsin, speaking at the Tenth ual Convention of the Intercollegiate So- ist Society, presumably classified himself n he declared that the ''difference'' between and Mr. Scott Nearing ''was that the latter essentially religious!'' Aside from differ- s of ''religion,'' Mr. Kallen, according to his words, must therefore be in accord with Mr. ring, teacher of Bolshevism, internationalism class hatred, and author of ''The Great Mad- ,'' which declared ''the entrance of the ted States into the World War on April 6, 7, was the greatest victory that the Ameri- plutocracy has won over the American ocracy.'' Dr. Horace Meyer Kallen is a ile contributor to the pro-Bolshevist *Dial.* is a lecturer at the New School on ''The Evo- on of the International Mind.'' Judging by two volumes, ''The Structure of Lasting Peace'' and ''The League of Nations,'' he is an exponent of that subtle, ambiguous yet esoteri- cally definite stripe of ''internationalism'' which also runs in the blood of such Simon-pure examples of Americanism as Dr. Walter Lipp- mann and Dr. Walter Weyl, both associate editors of the *New Republic.*

Have these chief lecturers of the New School for Social Research qualified themselves by their past record, by their published works, or by their spoken utterances, as unimpeachably sound and safe teachers for American young men and women? Have they proven themselves, in the test of past experience, as loyal, one-hundred percent Americans, exponents of the highest American ideals and ethical principles?

When the war came, when Germany assaulted civilization, were all these ''prominent and pro- gressive teachers'' aligned on the side of de- mocracy? While certain of their colleagues en- gaged in shameless Hun propaganda, did the present instructors of the New School come forth to denounce the imperial Government for its perfidy? Did they condemn Germany for the invasion of Belgium, the sinking of the Lusi- tania, for her policy of frightfulness? Did they see, with clear vision, the Hun intentions which struck at the core of liberty throughout the world? Did they help expose the grisly threat to all free peoples in Hun ''kultur?'' Did they lend themselves to uncovering the sham back of Germany's advertised and vaunted social prog- ress?

And after America had belatedly entered the conflict, did all these ''advanced'' teachers line up to back the Government in its intention to carry on the war until German militarism was crushed? Did they seek to expose and crush those insidious forces which opposed the war, which sought to stir up opposition to the war and to the enforcement of the draft, and which conspired to hinder the nation in its war activi- ties? Did they all loyally and whole-heartedly bring their power and influence to bear against the teachers of sedition, the fomentors of strikes and discord, the opponents of the draft and ad- vocates of pacifism and a peace of compromise with the foe? Presumably, it is by meeting such a test that the staff of the New School for Social Research, or the teachers of any school, would qualify as teachers of the sons and daughters of Americans who unreservedly gave of their blood and substance toward ultimate and abso- lute victory over Germany, who believe faith- fully in American ideals, and who are un- swervingly determined that American institu- tions and American national integrity shall be preserved.

Prof. James Harvey Robinson, one of the organizers, is delivering at the New School a series of twelve lectures on ''The Relation of Education to Social Progress,'' the object of which course, according to the prospectus, ''is to consider the present deficiencies of education as a means of promoting social readjustment.'' ''An attempt will be made,'' it was announced, ''to determine the ways in which education should be readjusted so as to forward the reform of existing evils.''

What qualifications signally mark Prof. James Harvey Robinson as one uniquely fitted to ''de- termine the ways in which education should be readjusted so as to forward the reform of exist- ing evils?''

What is the underlying basic philosophy of Prof. James Harvey Robinson which would color his expounding of American ideals and his suggestions for the readjustment of education and reform of social evils?

NOT GERMANY, BUT "NATIONALITY," CAUSED WAR!

One cannot be more fair to anyone than to let him speak for himself. Mr. Robinson has ex- pressed himself. Mr. Robinson contributed to the *Century Magazine,* of November, 1916, an illumining article entitled, ''What is National Spirit?'' To some people—perhaps old- fashioned people—love of country and love of home has been beautiful and wholesome, a source of strength rather than decadence, a praiseworthy rather than a discreditable and reprehensible thing. Patriotism to these people has not been merely a blind national fetish wor- ship, a stupid apotheosis by the ignorant of their own insular virtues, a bigoted national or racial prejudice and intolerance of others. Pa- triotism has been the family spirit of love, trust and devotion, of cooperative pulling together for the best well being of one's self and one's immediate kin, broadened out to include a larger sphere. It is the spirit that enables men to pull together, constructively and pro- ductively, whether in small social groups such as in factories, or in the larger family group known as the state. That a man's home, where he was born and where he knew the tenderness of a mother, should be sweet to him, has from time immemorial been considered normally human and natural. That a man's native land should be loved, that its ideals should be cherished, has not been regarded as wicked or ugly. That man's belief in the purest ideals of religion, his faith in God, his love and loyalty for his country have wrought chiefly evil through the long evolutionary struggle toward higher civil- ization has probably never been contended even by the most bitter unchristian scoffers, en- venomed cynics and bigoted atheists.

James Harvey Robinson—Ph. D. of Freiburg and champion of the I. W. W. leaders accused of seditious conspiracy to obstruct the country in its conduct of the war against Germany— writing in the *Century Magazine,* said that ''*suddenly, in August,* 1914,'' *the word national- ity ''assumed a terrible significance.''* ''Previ- ously the spirit of nationality had been accepted as on the whole a noble thing, although, like other noble things, it appeared to be a nuisance at times; but *when all the chief states of Europe rushed at one another's throats in the name of nationality,* all thoughtful outsiders began to wonder whether the current favorable estimate of the emotion could be right when it gave rise to such unprecedented woes.''

According to this ''thoughtful outsider,'' pre- sumably Belgium rushed at Germany's throat ''in the name of nationality;'' France rushed at Germany's throat ''in the name of nationality;'' England rushed at Germany's throat ''in the name of nationality;'' Serbia rushed at Austria's throat ''in the name of nationality.'' Therefore, when Belgium, France, England, Serbia and Russia combined ''rushed at'' the throats of Germany and Austria it was ''nationality'' that ''gave rise to such unprecedented woes;'' it was an ignoble and criminal thing known as ''na- tionality,'' and not the imperialistic ambitions of perfidious Germany, that was responsible for the war.

PATRIOTISM, LIKE RELIGION, BREEDS MORE EVIL THAN GOOD!

Prof. James Harvey Robinson manifestly is still not clear as to Germany's guilt in precipi- tating the world catastrophe, for in a pamphlet issued recently by Ginn and Company, entitled ''The Last Decade of European History and the Great War,'' it is stated: ''The exact causes of the Great European War are still questions of dispute.'' Discussing ''the policies which led to it''—the war—Prof. Robinson reviews France's ''imperialistic policies in Africa,'' the ''alliance of England and Japan,'' ''the entente with Russia,'' and notes, as with significant em- phasis, that ''one great power had been rather noticeably left out of this circle of friends— Germany.''

This pamphlet was ''copyright, 1918, by James Harvey Robinson,'' so it must express comparatively recent views entertained by one

(Continued on Page 16)

Smoking Out Hun Propaganda Nests

WONDERFUL WORK OF THE ALIEN PROPERTY CUSTODIAN IN COMBATTING THE SPY SYSTEM, SEIZURE OF ALMOST A BILLION, AND IN TRACING COMMERCIAL RAMIFICATIONS

EVERY American should become familiar with the work of the Alien Property Custodian, A. Mitchell Palmer, and his successor, Francis P. Garvan, in tracing and seizing German property in the United States and in exposing the spy system maintained by Hun commercial houses here. In sixteen months this new department of the government took over almost $700,000,000 worth of enemy-owned property, converted essential industries into channels useful to us in war, and exposed the most gigantic commercial plot ever engineered by a nation. It did some of its most important work in linking individuals with plots against the United States and hundreds of dangerous aliens were interned as a result.

Up to February 15 last reports had been made on 35,400 pieces of enemy property at an administration cost of about $1,000,000, but this cost really was offset by $1,604,539 in unreported, concealed income and excess profit taxes collected as a result of the investigations. In addition, the Custodian seized vast quantities of enemy-owned commodities vital for war work, such as nickel, medicines, surgical instruments, lenses, coffee, rice, etc., etc. Innumerable fraudulent transfers of German-owned stocks to Americans or to neutrals also were exposed, full effect of which will be felt for many years after peace is declared.

To round out his work and make it of lasting value to the nation, the Custodian organized a company to take over hundreds of patents obtained by the Huns here to throttle American trade and the secrets of these processes are being made available for American business men at a nominal price. In handling enemy alien property, Messrs. Palmer and Garvan divide it into two classes—the small investments of individuals and the greater ones made by the great German trusts so interwoven with political and governmental affairs as to be almost officially imperial. The first-named class was treated purely as a trust, and administered as such. Of the second class, Mr. Palmer reported to the President:

> They constituted Germany's great industrial army on American soil. They were the far-flung lines of advance for her kultur and so great had they become with the opening of the world war that it has now become perfectly plain that Germany lived in high hopes of the assistance which would come to her from the organization built up on this side of the Atlantic. These investments were largely in industries which, while accepting the hospitality of American laws to become American corporations, were never in fact Americanized. In many cases the factories, warehouses and offices of these enemy-owned concerns were mere spy centers before America entered the world war and would have been nests of sedition if the Alien Property Custodian had not acted promptly in their seizure. The purpose of Germany in maintaining them here was such as to justify their complete eradication as German enterprises and their thorough naturalization into an American character.

In ferreting out these concerns, invaluable aid was furnished by the British secret service, as well as by our own, and an analysis of the famous British blacklists of 1916 that caused so much furore in this country, shows that in many cases they were fully justified. For instance, in one list of fifty-six concerns named by Great Britain, fifteen were seized and sold by the Alien Property Custodian within a few weeks after we entered the war. Full credit for this aid is given by Mr. Palmer in his report and unofficially it may be said that many blacklisted concerns that escaped seizure did so only because they were wholly owned by Americans, and as soon as we entered the war stopped their pro-German activities.

Copyright, S. V. Buck

A. MITCHELL PALMER

Americanization of the former enemy concerns is bound to result advantageously to the United States, for while foreign capital may be welcomed, foreign labor standards and anti-Americanism are not. "Their first love was for the fatherland," remarks Mr. Palmer, "and all their efforts were in its interest. They spread the German propaganda before America was awake. They hoped to make it powerful enough to be effective when 'the day' should come."

Smashing of the German commercial machine in America doubtless had a strong moral effect on the war, how great it is impossible to estimate. Elimination of the Huns' strangle hold on the dye industry; in textiles, metals, chemicals, electrical and other industries must have been a body-blow and cost them the "war after the war" before it even had begun. Mr. Palmer's industrial offensive was a fitting complement to the British blockade and Marshal Foch's military drive.

No such history of the chemical industry ever was compiled as is contained in the Custodian's report. Tracing the ramifications from the very beginning, he shows how the octopus had grown with government aid until its capital exceeded $400,000,000. He says:

> It cannot be doubted that this enormous engine of commercial warfare has been created expressly for the expected war after the war and that it is intended to undertake still more efficiently and on a larger scale the methods by which German attacks on all competition were carried on. . . . With the aid of patents, especially the product patents, they could, and did, exclude all importations of competing dyes. As if the legitimate advantages of the German industry, supplemented by the ruthless, if legal, tactics of dumping and destructive underselling were not enough, the methods of the great German houses in carrying on their business in this country were from the first honeycombed with corruption.
>
> Bribery of dyers was carried on almost universally and on a large scale. The head dyers of mills were subsidized in many direct and indirect ways. If any one of them wished to have his superiors cease using the dye of one manufacturer and buy the dye made by some other company, nothing was easier than to produce wretched results and by the exercise of a little care with the favored dye have satisfactory results. So extensive was this corruption that I came across only one American consumer who had escaped its ill effects.

Mr. Palmer's report fairly bristles with the names of Hun spies and propagandists as he goes on to analyze the chemical industry. One of the first nests his bureau of investigation smoked out was the by-product plant of the Lehigh Coke Co.

"Every ounce of toluol and nezol which was produced," he says, "was sold under contracts binding the purchaser not to use or permit the use of the product for the manufacture of explosives or for the benefit of the Allies. An examination of the correspondence between Hugo Schmidt, the agent of the Deutsche Bank in this country and the bank, shows that the entire undertaking was a direct effort of the German government to prevent the making of these valuable materials for explosive manufacture in the United States." Mr. Palmer goes on:

> A still more striking instance uncovered by Mr. Garvan was that of the "Chemical Exchange Association." The effect of this enterprise was to corner for a time the supply of phenol in the United States, and to prevent its use in making T.N.T. This undertaking was apparently initiated by Dr. Albert, the financial adviser of the German government in this country, in direct collaboration with von Bernstorff. Dr. Albert carried out the scheme through Dr. Hugo Schweitzer, the chemist and leading spirit of Bayer & Co. (Inc.).

The Chemical Exchange Association even took over the surplus product of phenol from the Edison Selling Company, once the great inventor began its manufacture for his phonographic record business. Through another concern, also German-owned, the phenol was converted into salicylic acid and harmless flavoring extracts, at great profit. Schweitzer's share of those profits went direct to the German government.

"The success of the venture was celebrated in the latter part of 1916," says Mr. Palmer, "by a dinner given by Schweitzer and Kny at the Hotel Astor in honor of Dr. Albert. Among other guests were George Simon, F. A. Borgemeister, Norvin R. Lindheim, and Captain Wolf von Igel of the German Embassy. Striking examples of the same sort could be cited by the score.

"Dr. Isaac Strauss, organizer of the Chromos Chemical Co., arrived in September, 1914, apparently with a direct mandate from the German government for propaganda among the Jews, and established the *American Jewish Chronicle*. Funds to the amount of $85,00[illegible] were supplied for his activities by Dr. Albert and $15,000 by von Bernstorff, and his chemical company, profiting by the enormous war demand and prices, rapidly began to supply further sinews of war. Shortly after the United States entered the war his conduct attracted the attention of the military authorities and the ensuing investigation led to his internment, whereupon his Chromos Chemical Co. and the *American Jewish Chronicle* were taken over by me."

Almost as interesting as the chemical industry investigations and their many resultant seizures were the Custodian's inquiries into the metals situation.

It was in this phase of investigation that the British blacklist played a part, for among the very first firms barred in 1916 several were quickly seized as soon as the Alien Property Custodian began work. Among these were Beer, Sondheimer & Co., one of three firms seeking to control the metal markets of the world.

Another firm was the American Metal Co., dominated by German interests to a large extent. The Custodian seized 49 per cent. of the stock this concern and named five of the board of teen directors to Americanize it. The Ameri-n Metal Co. was organized in 1887 with 00,000 capital. In 1917 this had increased to ,500,000, and in that year was made $7,000,000. the 70,000 shares, 46,624 were held by etallgesellschaft and Henry R. Merton & Co. London, the German controlling influences. he Custodian is seeking to obtain control of the erton shares through the British government.

Ten mining and smelting companies in the nited States and two in South America were ned or controlled by the American Metal Co. addition to interests in other metal concerns. he 1917-18 edition of "The Directory of irectors" shows these officers: Chairman of the oard, Berthold Hochschild; president, C. M. eeb; vice-presidents, Otto Sussman, Henry ygere, Julius Loeb, Harold K. Hochschild; cretary, Julius Goldman; treasurer, Julian B. eaty. All these were directors, as were Henry Putzel, S. Roos and M. Schott.

The five directors named by Mr. Palmer to lly Americanize the American Metal Co. were enry Morgenthau, Andrew W. Mellon, George cAneny, Lewis L. Clarke and F. C. Converse.

"These outposts of German aggression having ained a foothold in the United States, were radually spreading into Mexico and South merica," says the report. . . . With un-mited resources at their command they bought p mines, financed and built smelters and re-neries, controlled their own transportation and ven invaded the oil industry. With the con-rolling power of these great organizations cen-ered in the hands of the Germans—knowing hat we now know about Germany and Germans —who will deny that they have been a menace to he country?"

Summarizing his work in the metal business, r. Palmer says:

> Finding German interests and influences centered in three well defined corporations, American in name but all controlled by the German metal triumvirate, doing a business which ran annually into hundreds of millions of dollars, we have succeeded in thoroughly Americanizing two of these concerns and in liquidating the third, thereby eliminating German influence in our metal markets and our metal industry.
>
> The German metal octopus has spread his tentacles across the ocean and over the United States into Mexico and South America, but for the present surely, and for all time it is hoped, he has been driven back and a wall of Americanism erected which, it is hoped, he will never be able to scale again.

Were any proof needed that Germany planned he great war long ago, Mr. Palmer's chapter on is seizure of the wireless companies would urnish it.

> The farsightedness of the German wireless policy was evident at the outbreak of the war. The vast expenditure on Sayville and Tuckerton and on the ship-to-shore stations was immediately justified. These instruments of warfare on the Allies functioned efficienctly. . . . Germany was able to begin at once the effort to influence American opinion.
>
> The German Ambassador was kept in touch with the war office at Berlin constantly and Dr. Albert and Hugo Schmidt and Richard Timmerscheidt were in receipt through Sayville of detailed orders governing their acts for the German government and German banks respectively. The file of radiograms kept by the Navy officials furnished a perfect mine of information to the government and to my office especially.
>
> Other departments of the government have learned that through the wireless propaganda and sabotage instructions were forwarded to German agents and spies; millions of German war loans were sold and the funds transmitted, and American opinion for a long time was influenced. It is asserted that the instructions to destroy the interned German ships were thus conveyed. As an instrument of politics and war the wireless stood out pre-eminent.
>
> The effect of the work of my department is that Germany has been wholly excluded from the wireless field in America, has been substantially hampered in communication by wireless to the South; and can only after a long effort and at great expense and by the development of a new system recover (if she can recover at all) an independent position in the Western Hemisphere, our government, in turn, is free from the domination of any privately-owned system.

FRANCIS P. GARVAN

Mr. Palmer tells entertainingly of how he eliminated the German interests in the electrical industry, especially in the Bosch Magneto Co., which refused to sell its vital product for airplanes or automobiles that might be used against Germany. Also he tells of how control of the fur industry was taken from the Germans and centered in this country—to stay.

No fiction could be more sensational than the history of the Bridgeport Projectile Co. This is the story of a far-reaching and nefarious plot to prevent the manufacture of arms and ammunition for the Allies during the trying days of 1915 and so extensive were the German government's holdings that when the Alien Property Custodian acted, he seized 19,990 of the 20,000 shares of the concern. Propaganda and crime having failed to prevent shipments of munitions to the Allies, the Huns conceived the idea of using an apparently loyal American corporation to attain their ends.

The plan had the backing of von Bernstorff, Dr. Albert, Dr. Dernburg, Captain von Papen and others. It was planned that the Bridgeport Projectile Co. should buy up all available supplies of powder, antimony, hydraulic presses and other essentials for munitions and that the concern should take arms contracts from the Allies, but never fulfill them. In all, it was expected that $10,000,000 would be spent. The funds were furnished by the Deutsche Bank through Hugo Schmidt and Dr. Albert. In addition to those named, Mr. Palmer says in his report that Carl Heynen, once an American Consul in Mexico, and Hans Tauscher, husband of Mme. Gadski, the singer, and George W. Hoadley, an American, all were closely concerned in the enterprise.

Things went as planned until the exposure of Dr. Albert in August, 1915, when banks and manufacturers refused to deal with the company and then the business went from bad to worse. Finally, the German government withdrew its support and Hoadley organized the Liberty Ordnance Co., which took over the Bridgeport Projectile Co. When we went to war the Ordnance Department commandeered the plant and it soon was busy turning out munitions to beat the Hun.

Particular stress is laid by Mr. Palmer on the acquisition of the Hoboken docks from the North German Lloyd and Hamburg American Co., and the taking over of the latter company's plant after we bought the Danish West Indies, a strategic point close to the Panama Canal. The full effects of these seizures, he points out, will be felt for years after peace is declared.

One of the most dangerous Hun nests uncovered by the Custodian was the Transatlantic Trust Co., a prosperous concern under the presidency of Julius Pirnitzer of Buda-Pest. Not only were its advertisements in the foreign language press wholly anti-American, but it pushed the sale of war bonds for the Central Powers, carried accounts for von Bernstorff and Dumba, and harbored the notorious von Rintelen. Pirnitzer was interned for his activities and the trust company was liquidated as far as is possible until peace permits a balancing of accounts with the parent concern abroad. At the time Mr. Palmer seized the concern, it had a corps of 1,000 agents in Austro-Hungarian communities, many of them pastors of churches.

Another story from the Custodian's report that reads like a romance is the history of the German-American Lumber Co. Starting twenty-five years ago—another proof of the far-reaching plan of Germany to dominate the world—this company acquired St. Andrew's Bay on the west coast of Florida with 150,000 acres surrounding it. This harbor is one of the few really good ones close to the Panama Canal. Little development was done, however, though the several presidents drew large amounts for "expenses," and paid little attention to the lumber business.

"When H. G. Kulenkampf, president of the company, and E. Lutz, former president, were arrested," Mr. Palmer reports, "the government agents found great masses of evidence tending to show that they were more propagandists than commercial agents. In Kulenkampf's house evidence was found which resulted in the internment of two of his kinsmen of the same name, besides masses of pamphlets, thirty or forty kinds, of the sort sent broadcast over the world soon after Germany started the war."

The Emergency Fleet Corporation took over the property and began building ships there to offset the U-boat menace, and Mr. Palmer says: "I believe one of the most important and dangerous links of the German commercial and military propaganda in this country has been wiped out, never again to be in the hands of German agents."

On the first British blacklist appeared the firm K. & E. Neumond of New Orleans, a large grain house. This concern sent large quantities of foodstuffs into Scandinavia and toward the end of 1916 sought to camouflage its German connections. Karl Neumond, the American partner, eventually wound up in the internment camp at Fort Oglethorpe and the illegal shipments were stopped. Other blacklisted firms on the British list that the Alien Property Custodian took over included: Philip Bauer, Brasch & Rotherstein, Maclaren & Gentles, International Hide and Skin Co., Muller, Schall & Co., Schuchardt & Schutte, Orenstein & Keppel Co., Carlowitz & Co., and the Roessler & Hasslacher Chemical Co.

Thus is may be readily seen that much of the stir in this country that followed the issuance of the list was hardly justified.

One could go on indefinitely reciting how the German influence in all sorts of commercial houses was rooted out by the Custodian's keen hunt and how strikes and sabotage plans were foiled in vital industries. Shipbuilding firms, newspapers, food concerns, and even seed houses, all were affected by the insidious and dangerous plots of the Hun. Nest after nest of spies were broken up and the internment camps crowded by those arrested in connection therewith.

Democracy's battle against autocracy truly may be said to have had one of its most valuable aids in the Alien Property Custodian and his hardworking staff that ferreted out the nests of sedition that were a far greater menace from within than the general public ever could realize.

Secret Hyphenated Propa

UNDERGROUND EFFORTS IN FOREIGN LANGUAGE PRESS TO SPLIT GAIN IN THE LONG RUN

DOES a "German-American" problem involving a certain danger to the unity of the American people still exist? Or is it a fact, as claimed by some, that two years of actual warfare against Germany, that the downfall of Kaiserism and autocracy, and the revelations as to the guilt of Germany made by Germans themselves as soon as they were able to discover the truth and dared to speak out, has brought a real and lasting change, blotting out every vestige of divided loyalty and hyphenism?

Looking merely at the surface, one may arrive at the conclusion that such a problem exists no longer. Americans of German descent, they say, have given the authorities comparatively little trouble during the war. The number of actually interned aliens amounted to only six thousand out of several millions; arrests of German-Americans who committed an overt act of disloyalty were few. They have liberally subscribed to the different war loans. Their sons were among the most faithful and valiant fighters. The fathers did not resist the draft; they complied with the food laws and every other war law, and made great sacrifices, perhaps with bleeding hearts, but with smiling lips.

It is certainly true that a good many of those of German blood who had thought up to the outbreak of the war that they owed a measure of loyalty to the land of their birth or their fathers have become true and 100 per cent. Americans. They are thoroughly ashamed that they allowed themselves to be fooled by German propagandists for many years. They honestly rejoiced over the downfall of Kaiserism, and are watching with anxious hearts the struggles of the German democracy, fearing that the machinations of the ex-Kaiser's faithful will eventually wreck the young Republic. These converts to democracy and to Americanism number many, especially among those who have never enjoyed the favor of kings and noblemen, and who today are comparing their happy lot with that of their brethren in Germany. They have come to appreciate America fully. From those we have nothing to fear for the future. They are welcoming every movement of Americanization.

But there is another class. Not large in numbers perhaps. But backed by a portion of the foreign language press, by wealth which has been linked to the "big interests" of Germany; by a certain kind of politicians who still chase the "German vote" (and get away with it as shown in the last national election in several Western states), this class is still in the position to do mischief and disrupt the unity of our people. They have changed somewhat their methods, for they have learned to fear public opinion. But have they experienced a change of heart?

If you hear them in public, they will loudly boast of the amount of Liberty Bonds they have bought, knowing as well as anybody else that a Liberty Bond is a splendid investment, and for a man of some means not a particularly great sacrifice. They will tell you at the slightest provocation of the number of "men of German blood" who fought in the American army. These same people used to count every one bearing a German-sounding name as one of "their own" whenever they wished to convince the Kaiser and his agents that America "with 16 or 25 million German-Americans" could be depended upon. They now coolly appropriate every fighter whose name sounds German as "their own," and from the valor of these fighting American, they deduce their right to be adjudged loyal.

BY AN AMERICAN OF GERMAN BIRTH

A certain portion of the German-language press is to blame for this condition. One who has studied the German-language press carefully during the last year must admit that a number of these papers are honestly striving to educate their readers to look upon things and events only from the standpoint of an American. This portion of the German-language press is careful to avoid the fostering of the old spirit of segregation and of German superiority that formerly pervaded every column of every German-American newspaper.

But there are others, who scrupulously refrain from condemning the old leaders and the old methods of Germany, who dare not denounce the guilt of a Ludendorff or a Tirpitz for fear of losing subscribers. Who, on the other hand, cry out in righteous indignation whenever a German-American is unjustly persecuted, but who are painfully silent when a crime against the American spirit is perpetrated. That is the portion of the German-language press which today is no more in favor of a real democracy than they were when everything German, especially imperial German, was holy to them, and when everybody who doubted the efficiency and superiority of everything German was put down as an enemy.

This group of German-language newspapers, some of them dailies, others weeklies, or religious, or farmers, papers, is in full accord with the old-time leaders of old-time German-Americanism, some of them men of wealth, who only recently have emerged from the cyclone cellar, and are boldly assuming again the role they had played for years. How eager they are for every scrap of news which can be construed as a "sure sign" of a coming conflict between the United States and Great Britain!

When Bernard Shaw, in one of his recent articles published by a New York newspaper of a decidedly anti-British tendency, divided the responsibility for the war equally between Germany and England, that portion of the German-language press responded eagerly and reproduced the Shaw articles, while the same papers had refrained from giving equal prominence to the revelations made by Kurt Eisner, who proved from the archives of the German chancellery clearly the guilt of imperial Germany.

One could hear in the favorite gathering places of this class of German-Americans the great Shaw quoted as the only true prophet, while to them Eisner was—the "contemptible Jew". They invariably prophecy some coming conflict between the United States and Great Britain, for they still "love" England dearly. One can find nearly every one of these old-time German leaders in the ranks of the opponents of the League of Nations, and their following is told that Great Britain dictated the covenant for her own benefit.

Next to Great Britain, Japan furnishes the *casus belli* of the future. When a few days ago it was reported that at Tientsin United States troops and Japanese had clashed, the mischief-makers smiled knowingly to each other and when among themselves drank to the toast "Der Tag". The conviction that because America entered the war against Germany and brought about the final defeat of the German armies we are destined to be involved in war with Great Britain or Japan sooner or later is carefully nursed among these simpletons, who, as of yore, follow blindly the old-time leaders.

All that would not in itself mean a great

The New Tragedy of the War

OLSHEVIST CLASS WAR, HAVING SWEPT RUSSIA, THREATENS TO INVADE OTHER NATIONS AND MENACES SECURITY OF WORLD, SAYS J. G. PHELPS STOKES

lress made at a dinner of the Social Democratic League at which Catherine Breshkovskaya, Nicolas Avksentieff, Andre Argunoff, Vladimir Zenzinoff and Eugene Rogowsky were honor guests)

HE greatest tragedy of Bolshevism, as I see it, lies not in the demoralization and chaos nor even in the hideous suffering that it has brought to Russia or to the sian people, appalling and heartrending ıgh the tragedy within Russia is, but rather he reaction that Bolshevism has produced in Democratic movement throughout the world.

rior to the Bolshevik revolution, I was one of e optimistic people who believed that the se of Democracy was advancing everywhere. ıew that the hearts of men and women the ld over were increasingly thrilled with the spect that Democracy would emerge from the ld war more virile, and more efficient in the se of mankind, than ever before; and with prospect that the spirit of Democracy would ceforth prevail so widely that armaments ld soon be in the main dispensed with, and t the persuasions of right and fair dealing, ked by moderate police powers, would suffice regulate the relations of men and governıts in international as well as in national irs.

ike so many others who, a year ago, saw tocracy tottering and about to fall, I thought w Democracy arising and receiving in ever ater measure the acclaim and confidence and giance of all the peoples of the earth. And hought, as did so many, that civilized peoples erywhere would soon cast aside outgrown and tworn Autocracies, and all other forms of oitrary rule, and accept joyfully the methods Democracy for their own self-government.

I had hoped, as had so many, that the new d the old democratic nations would soon ther around common council tables, and ided by the principles of reason and fairplay, ild a world-wide structure of Democracy, and perfect its machinery that disputes between tions as well as within nations would usually adjusted by parliamentary and judicial thods without resort to arms.

An era of peace and good-will seemed near hand in which large armies and navies might dispensed with and the machineries of war converted to serve the industries of peace. ıd then of a sudden arose Bolshevism, with all hideous fury. Great masses of people, armed Democracy's enemies, and inflamed by ugliest ssions, debased the name of Liberty, using it their shield for the maddest incursions upon liberties of others and for grossest self-inlgence, in contemptuous disregard of all save at they conceived to be the needs of their mediate groups and their group desires to minate and rule the world. A huge nation s soon immersed in chaos, murder became mpant; plunder universal; production ceased; rvation became the hideous portion of all but plunderers, and even they enjoyed wealth ly until their plunder was consumed.

The Class War, they said, was on. None ght have a voice in government save those who d nothing else. The world and all it conned, they said, would henceforth be owned d controlled exclusively by those who had ver before owned or controlled anything. Few e might eat or vote, or find protection from mad excesses of those made drunk by the w-found "liberty". The propagandists of new terror traveled rapidly throughout rope and came even to America. They call w upon the propertyless workers everywhere to arise and overthrow Democracy as they overthrew the new democracy of Russia; and to establish in its place a Proletarian Dictatorship. The Bolshevik appeal for revolution against Democracy, must, and will of course, be met and resisted by all who believe that Democracy is essential to justice and to the highest welfare of mankind.

The greatest tragedy of the present situation lies in the fact that the ending of the war has not ended the need for the maintenance of armed forces everywhere. On the contrary, the democratic peoples everywhere must still look to their defenses, and in proportion as the foes of Democracy multiply, must postpone disarmament and prepare for whatever further sacrifices may be required to meet the new menace and overcome it. Those who love Democracy will not permit Democracy to be overthrown! They will not permit tyranny to supplant it. In Russia, the friends of Democracy were caught ununited and unprepared and have suffered a hideous, though temporary, defeat. The American people, on the other hand, are forewarned. Democracy will not be defeated here! Armaments are no longer required to thwart the lawless ambitions of kaisers and kings, but they appear to be still required to defend democratic governments from determined and dangerous foes within their borders.

It is tragic indeed that this new need for the defense of Democracy against foes within will give the reactionaries in every walk of life the opportunities they crave for demanding further curtailment of the liberties of the people. Herein lies the heart of the new tragedy that now confronts us. Reactionaries now have new and persuasive reasons not only with which to support excessive demands for continued armaments, but also—and this is still more to be deplored—for demanding the continuance of wartime restrictions upon the primary liberties of speech and assemblage and press. It is not going too far to say that the Bolsheviki have given the reactionaries the best arguments the latter ever had.

If the foes of Democracy within the United States or in any nation insist upon revolution for the overthrow of Democratic government; if they insist, as they do in their revolutionary journals that they are "unwilling to wait to be voted into power by parliamentary means;" if they continue to call, as they now do in this country, for "deeds of iron," and "revolutionary mass action of the proletariat" to establish the dictatorship they desire, there will be few friends of Democracy who will refuse their sanction to defensive measures that they would otherwise oppose with all the strength at their command.

It is unimaginable that those who believe in Democracy would idly tolerate its overthrow and the establishment of tyranny in its stead, whether that tyranny be one of wealth or of poverty, of czar, demagogue, mob, or proletariat. If challenged to a test of power, the friends of Democracy will accept the challenge, and, if required, meet force with force. If the unexpected happen, and the menace become so great that "dictatorship" of any kind is temporarily required, the temporary concentration of power must be in the hands of those who are determined to established equality of opportunity and of justice by lawful and democratic means, rather than in the hands of those who demand that propertyless proletarians, or any other class, be privileged to rule the world.

Bolshevism is a tragedy not merely because of the devastation it works among the people under its sway, but because in proportion to its strength in countries that have never known Democracy, it stimulates reaction and for a time lessens liberty, in countries where Democracy is most advanced.

Democracy must and will be preserved at all hazard, and at whatever cost. Here in America we shall endeavor to distinguish between those honest idealists who cry out that the millennium is not yet attained, but who aid their fellows to progress by all fair means towards it, and those fanatics, on the other hand, who because the institutions of men are not yet perfected, would wreck them all in the hope of being able to build in a day a millennium from the ruins of a world. If the attempt be made to create a Bolshevist revolution in this country, those who love Democracy will stand together, liberals and true Socialists alike. Personally, I shall be among those who will take up arms, if need be, in cooperation with all those believers in Democracy who are determined that no form of tyranny shall arise here.

Secret Hyphenated Propaganda

(Continued from Page 8)

merely the English language and American customs. Americanization in this case means the much more difficult task of eradicating a carefully fostered sentiment of sullenness and resentment against America.

It is very well to ridicule this fear by saying that these disgruntled persons are too closely watched to escape the eyes of the law. It is not a question of assaults upon the law. These people do not commit any overt act of disloyalty or treason, for the most part they do not even belong to the proletariat. In a good many instances they are men and women of moderate means, belonging to churches, considering themselves law-abiding citizens. The danger lies in the fact that they are led to breed unrest and dissatisfaction, and a desire to see Democracy which triumphed over their idol weakened and shattered.

Is there a remedy? I know of only one agency largely composed of Americans of German descent which has fully grasped the situation as far as this portion of our population is concerned and has kept an intelligent constant watch over it, fearlessly exposing every attempt, no matter how subtle, which has for its aim the return to the old order of things.

This organization, or some one similar should be maintained and supported by all who view the situation with alarm. Only those who are in constant touch with this element, who know how to read them and read their newspapers and who have worked with the great mass of loyal Americans of German descent, often against open or secret hostility on the part of the old-time leaders, can meet this danger successfully. It must be met—if for no other reason but to protect those who have been loyal Americans and intend to remain so, but who are constantly confronted by the vicious tactics of that small group which tries to kill their faith in America and in Democracy.

THE NATIONAL
Civic Federation Review

Office: Thirty-third Floor, Metropolitan Tower
1 Madison Avenue New York City

RALPH M. EASLEY, Editor

Published Twice a Month Two Dollars a Year

The Editor alone is Responsible for any unsigned article or unquoted statement published in THE NATIONAL CIVIC FEDERATION REVIEW.

THE GOSPEL ACCORDING TO HERR MARX

Those clergymen who have gone in for radicalism, both of the diluted and extreme varieties, and who have opened their churches to forums where Bolshevism is defended and expounded, and whose sermons ring more of the gospel of Karl Marx than of the New Testament, are doubtless in the majority well-meaning and sincere. They have been troubled, as all of us have been troubled, about the ills of the world, and they have been anxiously eager, as all normal and intelligent human beings must be eager, to help right the wrongs and end injustices that have prevailed. Throwing to the winds the eternal fact that man's progress is evolutionary and that the millenium cannot come in a day, these truly humanitarian and well-meaning men have cast in their lot with professional malcontents, Socialists and other radicals who pretend to have hit upon the panacea which will produce in its ultimate perfection and in a lightning-flash what all the teachings of Moses, Plato, the Hebrew prophets, moral philosophers and Christian apostles have only partially brought about during the course of several thousand years.

Can the doctrine of Karl Marx miraculously achieve in its perfect realization what the Sermon on the Mount has only to a degree effected in the relations among men during the running of twenty centuries? Those clergymen who have turned their churches over to Socialist teachings are probably appealed to by those cunning Socialist shibboleths about the "brotherhood of man." They are probably beguiled into the conviction that Socialism is merely concentrated Christianity and that the Marxian philosophy is merely the Christian philosophy taken out of the realm of theological speculation so that it can be put into living practice.

What these clergymen are totally in ignorance of, are the essential principles of Socialism. What they know as little about as a month's old babe, are the basic fundamentals of the Marxian scheme. What they believe in is their own idealization of Socialism, which is as opposite to real Socialism as are the two poles, and they confuse social reform, in which all of us believe, with Socialism.

Professional Socialists are not unaware of the sentimental susceptibility of many clergymen, nor are they blind to the value of churches as a vehicle for the dissemination of their doctrines. They have, therefore, deliberately sought to reach the Christian clergy through a very cunning and adroitly prepared propaganda, in the form of pamphlets and books, in which Socialism is sugar-coated with religious phraseology and the Marxian doctrines are camouflaged in theological terms. This, of course, to some degree may explain the phenomenon of clergymen turning over their pulpits for the promulgation of what is integrally the antithisis of all spiritual ideals, and all religious faith.

Clergymen reading the statement made by Prof. James Harvey Robinson, quoted in this issue of the REVIEW by Mr. Harré, to the effect that patriotism, religion and love have wrought more evil than good in the world, may be offended and shocked, and naturally so. Yet Prof. Robinson is only one of the group of mild or "diplomatic" radicals. What radically inclined clergymen perhaps do not realize is that the "advanced thinkers" to whom they turn over their pulpits entertain even a more extreme contempt for all religious belief than that indicated by Prof. Robinson. Can these clergymen see no significance in the prohibition in Russia by the Bolsheviki of religious practices, the sacking and defiling of churches and sacristies, the assassination of hundreds of Russian priests, the burying alive of Russian bishops, the violation of nuns and the turning of machine guns upon religious processions? Can they read no message in the letter recently addressed to the Archbishop of Canterbury by the Archbishop of Omsk, in which the Russian prelate declared:

"Wherever the Bolshevists are in power the Christian Church is persecuted with even greater ferocity than in the first three centuries of the Christian era."

"Bolshevism, the modern 'scourge of God,'" says David Goldstein, in *The Columbiad*, "is only another name for Socialism—Socialism applied.'"

The Bolsheviki are simply the Left or revolutionary wing, of the Socialists. They are merely putting into hideous practice the Communist Manifesto of Marx. They are anti-Christian because Marxian Socialism is anti-Christian. The Marxian philosophy is fundamentally a materialistic philosophy, which would make men's social and industrial life, their ethical beliefs and intellectual ideals conform to the doctrine of economic determinism—the doctrine that man is a beast actuated only by the desires of his body. The Socialist creed is an absolute denial of the belief that a divine force moves the universe and that man possesses a living soul. The gospel of Marx is the gospel of materialism and atheism.

Many clergymen have probably received the special propaganda pamphlets distributed by the Rand School designed for clerical consumption. How many, however, have undertaken to cover the entire line of propaganda distributed by this organization? In one pamphlet sold at the Rand School, for instance, appears the statement that "Compared with . . . the great martyrs of Russia, with the Chicago anarchists, Francesco Ferrer, and innumerable others, Christ cuts a poor figure indeed . . . Jesus is a veritable nonentity."

The Christian as all true religious philosophies is based upon the truth that the only reform, the only revolution which can effect good in the world, must take place in the human heart. How, therefore, can clergymen espouse any movement which, relegating man to the level of the beast, asserts it can miraculously redeem the world through wholesale murder and terrorism, by crime and violence, when in theory and practice it is a denial and violation of the eternal verity that human progress, human betterment, human good can be brought about only by that regeneration which takes place in the inner hearts of men?

ROBINS' SONG A SWAN SONG?

Colonel Raymond Robins, testifying before the Senate Committee investigating Bolshevism, expressed his amazement at the pacific character of the Bolshevik revolution, declaring that "in every instance" where he investigated the reported killing of men without trial "it proved to be false." Having paid his tribute to the heroic virtues of the Red Guard, the Colonel went on to say:

"Up to the time I left Russia the thing that was constantly in my mind, again and again, was the lack of vindictiveness, was the lack of actual destruction of life." The Colonel averred that if the revolution "had been in America, if it had been in any other land I know of, where a mob had taken power like that and had the rifles back of them, I should have expected vastly more of destruction."

Mr. Robins told of the arrival in Russia of Mr. Bruce Lockhart, the British High Commissioner, to whom Mr. Robins revealed what he knew about Russia, and to use his own words, he knew "more about it than any other Allied representative." "I took him (Mr. Lockhart) to my office and we opened up everything I had of a documentary nature." After giving him this fund of information, Mr. Robins suggested that Mr. Lockhart go out and get the opinions of the Czarist seven per cent.

"He (Mr. Lockhart) came back," testified Mr. Robins. "And he said: 'You told the truth. They sing a different song, just as opposite as it is possible to be; but I believe your song.'"

The Senate Committee and sundry aggregations of radical lunchers have recently heard Mr. Robins sing.

The Senate was told by Mr. Robins that "From that time in January, until I left Russia the British High Commissioner and myself were in absolute agreement on every move. We ate breakfast every morning."

Mr. Lockhart may have appreciated the rare opportunities of the breakfast hour for getting psychological if not political information. That Mr. Lockhart was of an enquiring turn of mind, and that he is not in agreement with Mr. Robins, is revealed in a report made by him and embodied in a White paper laid on the table of the House of Commons on April 5. In his despatch, sent on November 10, 1918, Mr. Lockhart stated that the Bolsheviki had established a rule of force and oppression unequaled in the history of any autocracy and classified some of the charges against them under the following heads:

> First, themselves the fiercest upholders of free speech, they suppressed every newspaper which does not approve their policy. In this respect the Socialist press suffered most of all.
>
> Second, the right of holding public meetings had been abolished, the vote had been taken away from every one except workmen in the factories and the poorer servants, and even among the workmen those who dared to vote against the Bolsheviki were marked down by Bolshevist secret police as counter-revolutionaries.
>
> Third, the worst crimes of the Bolsheviki have been against their Socialist opponents. Of countless executions which the Bolsheviki have carried out a large percentage has fallen on the heads of Socialists who had waged a lifelong struggle against the old regime, but who are now denounced as counter-revolutionaries merely because they disapprove of the manner in which the Bolsheviki have discredited Socialism.
>
> Fourth, the Bolsheviki have abolished even the most primitive forms of justice. Thousands of men and women have been shot without even the mockery of a trial, and thousands more are left to rot in prisons under conditions that to find a parallel to which one must turn to the darkest annals of Indian or Chinese history.
>
> Fifth, the Bolsheviki have restored the barbarous methods of torture.
>
> Sixth, the Bolsheviki have established the odious practice of taking hostages; still worse, they have struck at their political opponents through their women folk.

This prosaic declaration jars discordantly with the beguiling paean rendered by the star soloist of the so-called "Truth About Russia" chorus. Inasmuch as Mr. Lockhart's serious and convincing indictment comes long after Mr. Robins left Russia, Mr. Robins' pourings forth, as they apply to more recent developments and conditions, may be taken as being just as apropos as the chirruping "of the birds that sing in the spring, tra-la."

GERMANISM AND VILLARDRY

"Conspicuous among the novelties of present day doctrine is the threat to go Bolshevist," recently remarked the *New York Tribune*. "If Germany is asked to pay for a fraction of the damage she has done, she responds: 'Well, then, I'll go Bolshevist.'"

Among the high-pitched chorus of wailing that has of late come out of Germany, there now sobs the voice of Mr. Oswald Garrison Villard, editor of the *Nation*, who has been to Germany, who has seen the horrors due to the Allied blockade and who foresees what will happen if the wicked Allies force an unjust peace upon the beaten

Dial says it was because of the blunderings of the Allied nations and their "unwillingness to subscribe to the tenets of a real democratic peace." A Brest-Litovsk peace presumably might satisfy "The Editors." To them America is also a mere presumptuous upstart: "Russians regard us as well as many others in Western nations as political infants." This of Russia where about 68 percent of the people can neither read nor write, and where they have not had an iota of political experience except the tragic imposition of the Bolsheviki. What of the atrocities committed by the Bolsheviki? "Notoriously false" say "The Editors" of *The Dial*, and a contributor signing himself "S. M." It happens, however, that apart from the many other accounts from responsible sources, Professor George V. Lomonosoff, when pleading in New York City last June for recognition of the Bolsheviki Government, admitted that "crying atrocities" had been committed under it.

To intimidate civilized nations from rescuing Russia, *The Dial* holds out the threat that "before the foreign enemy domestic difficulties vanish," and that Trotzky stated "that he could afford to pay 100,000 rubles for every Japanese soldier landed on Russian soil."

The effect produced on all intelligent minds by such stuff is the very reverse of that intended. It is the thoughtless that may be deceived. All having good memories can never forget the cowardly submission of Lenine and Trotzky to the German invaders, and the shameful peace they signed. To "The Editors" of *The Dial* the German invasion of Russia was apparently acceptable; they reserve their indignation wholly for the intervention of the Allies. One of the things of which *The Dial* complains loudest is the suppression of news from Russia. Well, the Bolsheviki have very effectively suppressed news, as for instance, as told here recently by Colonel Vladimir I. Lebedev, a leading Russian Socialist Revolutionist, of the revolts of hundreds of thousands of workingmen against the Bolsheviki—revolts that failed only because the Bolsheviki possessed all the available arms and munitions, and a mercenary army composed largely of Germans, Hungarians, and Chinese to use against the real Russian workers.

While on the subject of "true information" we suggest that public policy demands a goodly supply of it as to the mainsprings of the present activities of *The Dial* and similar publications.

INTERNATIONAL AGRICULTURAL PROGRAM

The National Board of Farm Organizations, consisting of nineteen national farm organizations, delegated Mr. Charles S. Barrett, President of the Farmers' Educational and Co-Operative Union, to appear for it at the Peace Conference in Paris. Mr. Barrett has just returned to this country and had a most successful trip. He not only appeared before the American delegation to the Peace Conference, but conferred with M. Clemenceau, Mr. Lloyd George, Baron Sonnino, and other representatives of the various foreign governments. He found in each case a sympathetic and enthusiastic listener, because the representatives of the foreign governments were only too glad to do honor to a representative of those classes who had made sacrifices to furnish food for the soldiers and civilians among our allies.

It will interest our readers to know just what President Barrett presented as representing the desires of the great organizations of farmers in the United States. The international program proposed by Mr. Barrett was as follows:

a. Extension and improvement of the International Agricultural Institute at Rome.

b. Adoption, so far as practicable, of uniform systems of crop estimating and publishing reports on manufactures throughout the world.

c. Inclusion in the League of Nations of a special body having the international interests of agriculture directly in charge.

d. Adoption as a part of the constitution of the League of Nations of the principle of conservation of natural resources throughout the world and especially in all lands held under the jurisdiction of the League, whether such resources be found on the farm or elsewhere.

e. Provision for cooperative investigation of the relation of weather to crops in all parts of the world.

f. Endorsement of a set of International Agricultural principles, including:

1. Equality of pay, opportunity, and social reward for equal skill and equal work in agriculture as compared with other occupations.
2. Universal free education for farm children universally accessible.
3. Extension of the benefits of modern civilization to the open country, in spite of the added cost, part of which should be borne by general taxation.
4. Universal recognition of the right of farmers to bargain collectively through cooperative and other associations no less than other workers.
5. Adoption of the principle of gradual abolition of farm tenancy, on the theory that no land should be held permanently for renting.
6. Recognition of the right of each nation to withhold from export supplies essential to agriculture which are limited in quantity, subject to withholding such supplies only when so limited.
7. Recognition of the principle that the depression of agriculture constitutes the central danger to civilization, and that the demand for cheap food at the expense of a decent standard of living on the farm leads to agricultural disintegration and general decay.
8. Recognition of the principles that the compensation of agricultural producers on the basis of cost of production plus a reasonable profit is vital to the maintenance of a permanent agriculture, and therefore of a permanent civilization; and that provision should be made for maintaining this principle throughout the world by means of the regulation of international trade.

REMARKS OF MR. EMERSON McMILLIN AT DINNER GIVEN TO MR. CHARLES LATHROP PACK, UNION LEAGUE CLUB, MARCH 20TH, 1919

During the recent war, there were a few Americans—outside of the Army and Navy circles—who made themselves conspicuous by the magnitude and character of the work they performed. In a list of names of men of great deeds—men who have so distinguished themselves—President Wilson must be placed at the head. He has been the greatest and the most conspicuous, necessarily, because of his opportunities. Whether we Americans all believe in the efficiency of his work or not, it is evident to all that he has had the European world at his feet for the last two years.

Second on the list of men who accomplished great things, I would place Mr. Samuel Gompers. His work was great, but less conspicuous than some of the others. His influence in America was of infinite value. It enabled him to guide Labor and keep it in line; to combat the I. W. W.'s and Bolshevism. But his *greatest* work was done abroad. His thorough control of the situation in this country made it possible for him to deal comprehensively and effectively with like elements on the other side. While the press said but little regarding his wonderful achievements abroad, yet—to his influence, and to his intelligent and strikingly efficient work—was due the adherence of LABOR to the Allied Cause—both in England and in France. Without this loyalty on the part of Labor, success was not possible.

Sapping the Foundations of Society

HOW FAR HAVE REVOLUTIONARIES SUCCEEDED BY COVERT AND INSIDIOUS METHODS IN INVADING CHURCHES, THE PRESS, COLLEGES AND SCHOOLS

By RALPH M. EASLEY

What is the explanation for the invasion of churches, the press, colleges and schools by revolutionary Socialist propaganda?

Why is it that many clergymen, educators, writers, social workers and others have been "taken in" by propaganda whose ultimate purpose is the destruction of all religious belief, spiritual ideals, constructive social progress and beneficent institutions of modern civilization?

Do these sincere and well meaning men and women understand the basic crass essentials of the Marxian program? Or have they not been insidiously deceived into accepting Socialism as meaning social reform? Industrial and social progress must be achieved by constructive effort. No one would deny that evils exist and that much remains to be achieved. But to what extent have many people been led away from the consideration of actual evils and their sane remedy to exaggerated evils? To what extent has discontent been deliberately manufactured?

In THE NATIONAL CIVIC FEDERATION REVIEW OF *March 25, in an article published under the title, "Radicals Mislead Churches About Labor," I raised the question:*

"Why are the churches, whether those of wealthy and aristocratic congregations, those of the middle class, or those made up largely from the working class, all advocating the same radical measures to aid the working classes, which these same working classes themselves do not want?"

The fact that the churches of our country, as a whole, include a large majority of the people of all classes—bankers, merchants, lawyers, farmers, laborers, college presidents, etc.—and that these churches are all controlled by boards of trustees made up largely of business men, makes that, I think, a very pertinent inquiry. This situation has not been developed over-night, so to speak, but is the result of a situation long in the making. That our churches, Protestant and Roman Catholic alike, should—as shown in the article referred to—have fallen under the spell of the revolutionary rather than the evolutionary and sane labor movement is not surprising in the light of the situation that has been developing in this country in the last fifteen years.

In 1914, I attempted to describe conditions then existing as they related to industry, in a statement prepared to be given as testimony before the Industrial Relations Commission, before which I had been subpoenaed to appear. I was, however, never called to the stand and this report has, therefore, not been used. As it seems to the writer to present one of the answers to the question above, it will now be published in full.

If the picture presented by that proposed testimony was true at that time—and I think no one will dispute its accuracy, since it was based almost entirely upon statements of the radicals themselves, rather than upon opinions of the writer—no one should be surprised at conditions today. The latter are the logical outcome of the former. In fact, the situation today is the same, only a little more so. What will it be tomorrow if not checked?

In this testimony will be found quotations from several socialists who at that time were extremely radical but who, during the war, repudiated the Socialist Party on account of its disloyalty to our nation. No offense to these sincere, high-minded and loyal men is therefore intended in using quotations which represented views entertained at that time but not today.

This testimony covered a variety of subjects, but the part that came under the head of "Present Day Unrest," one of the subjects appointed to be considered under the act creating the Industrial Relations Commission, is the only one that is used in this connection and only one-half of that will be published in this issue of the REVIEW. *The remainder will appear in the succeeding issue. The topics treated in this number are:*

I. Legitimate Unrest.
II. Manufactured Unrest:
Socialist Propaganda in the Trade Unions;
Socialism in the Press;
Socialism in Social Reform Organizations;
Socialism in Schools and Colleges.
Those topics treated in the next number will be:
Socialism Among the East Side Immigrants;
Socialism in the Churches;
Socialism and Free Speech;
Socialism and Patriotism.
III. Is Wall Street or Socialism Gaining Control of Sources of Public Opinion?
IV. Socialism Versus Industrial and Social Progress.

The enquiry of the Industrial Relations Commission in 1914 sought to learn the causes of unrest. In my report, the publication of which begins herewith, I divided unrest into two classes—normal and manufactured.

NORMAL UNREST

A NORMAL unrest we have had since time began and it is wholesome and essential. Without it there would be no progress and society would die of dry rot. There never has been an age when unrest did not exist or when it was not exploited both for good and bad purposes. There is an industrial unrest today which comes from the education we had yesterday, and the broader education we have today will bring the unrest of tomorrow. Wage-earners of the present era know more about their rights and their needs than did those of an earlier period. They used to be content with the bare necessities of life. Now they, rightly, demand some of the luxuries. They have higher aspirations; and is this to be wondered at when the children of the wage-earners of today are receiving twelve times as much education as did their grandparents?

Unrest? Yes. But instead of charging it primarily to industrial conditions, we must credit most of it to education—the universal popular education of the schools and the even more far-reaching and stimulating education of daily contact and experience with the wonderful achievements of modern civilization.

There are, of course, other causes of normal unrest to which we cannot and should not shut our eyes. There are many black spots in our industrial conditions, as this Commission, in common with other students of the situation, well knows. There are still too many greedy and inhumane employers paying pitifully low wages to both men and women, and working them long hours under grievously bad conditions. There have been revelations in the domain of "high finance", instances of brutal defiance of public sentiment on the part of individual capitalists, arbitrary practices by various large corporations in the early days of their growth, discoveries of "business graft" in unsuspected places and of corrupt alliances between big business and political "bosses"—all of which have played their part in breeding in the public mind a certain amount of distrust of the soundness of our institutions and have thereby contributed to "social unrest".

But we must not forget that it is only an essentially sound body politic that relentlessly turns the light on its own faults and takes stern measures to correct them. The increasing determination of public opinion to know what is going on and to make the way of the transgressor hard is one of the surest signs that we are advancing towards higher civic standards. Our very success in locating and curbing, if not destroying, many of these evils which have existed in one form or another in all times and countries, demonstrates the integrity of the system under which it is possible to accomplish these reforms. We simply refuse to tolerate what earlier generations either ignored or accepted as unavoidable; and we do this because we have come up to a higher level of civilization. At the worst, such instances of industrial and financial misdoing are no more typical of the total situation than our jails and reformatories are typical of the general moral standards of the people. There is not one of the problems of bad working conditions chargeable to greedy or ignorant employers which has not been successfully met by other employers through just and humane treatment, and the proportion of employers of this latter type, to the credit of American industry, is rapidly growing.

The disaster which we constantly see overtaking corrupt practices and frauds, speculative "corners" and unfair business policies, means that the natural laws of business itself, for its own self-preservation and under the spur of a keener public conscience than the world has ever seen before under any state of civilization, work towards the elimination of dishonesty and will not permit anybody to succeed permanently except on the basis of square dealing. There is, therefore, no need for discouragement, but solid ground for confidence that we are working not against but with the tide in our efforts to solve our special industrial and social problems as they arise.

MANUFACTURED UNREST

But the wholesome discontent which attacks these problems with a view to the further bettering of the system under which we have advanced thus far is the very opposite of an artificial, manufactured discontent based upon a philosophy which of necessity denies all progress and the possibility of improvement along these tried and tested lines. Such a discontent or unrest can only be met after its instigated causes are clearly defined and their fallacies exposed.

This illegitimate or manufactured unrest has been deliberately stimulated, especially during the last fifteen years, by a persistent group of people holding to the Marxian economic philosophy and represented in this country by the Socialist Party and its off-shoot, the Industrial Workers of the World. I think this Commission could perform no greater service than to inquire into and report upon the proportion of present-day unrest chargeable to this factitious source.

As I understand it, the group of people who are promoting this artificial discontent asserts in brief that the competitive or "capitalistic" tem is producing a condition of increasing ery which is leading to an inevitable aclysm; that the farms, the mills, the facies and all productive industries are rapidly ng concentrated in the hands of the few, reting in "wage slavery" with all its attendant rors; that the wage-earner is being robbed four-fifths of all he produces; that between a and the employer there can be nothing in amon except a condition of perpetual class r; and that the only remedy for such a state affairs is the overturning of the whole comitive regime and the substitution of "the corative commonwealth"—in other words, a olution.

Accepting this program, these socialists conently attempt to prove that under the present ime everything that is is bad. They admit progress, because to do so would upset their ory. They, therefore, necessarily grossly represent our social conditions. They are ustomed to distort figures and pervert or press facts as may suit the exigencies of their ument. Every working man or woman is a age-slave", "overworked", "underfed" and ays "cowed down". Children of any age der twenty-five are always "little", pinched", "pale", "emaciated" and "anaec". The employer, always "a bloated capital-", is "cold-blooded" and "a slave-driver" d generally "a scoundrel". The picture they int of American industry is a nightmare and longs in the "chamber of horrors". While asting of their "scientific methods" the solists are in reality notoriously unscientific in at they unceasingly try to make the facts fit eir special theory. Their statements are no s partisan than those of the paid attorney of corporation because they see only the things at help their side of the case. It means nothg to the great body of the Socialist Party that me of their most intellectual leaders have reudiated practically all of the Marxian theories ecause of their absurdity in the light of the own facts of today.

While numerically the Socialist Party has ever had more than 125,000 members (now reuced to 75,000), their vote has run as high as 00,000 in 1912. In the 1914 elections the rerns show that they lost from 25 to 40 per cent. every state except Oklahoma, where their vote creased 25 per cent. But a compact organizaon of 75,000 persistent, active people in all arts of the United States, plus hundreds of apers, magazines and millions of pamphlets, l preaching the gospel of despair and class atred, in season and out of season, with a naticism which would be magnificent were it nployed in a better cause, cannot be regarded a negligible factor.

Let me give some illustrations of the character their propaganda in the trade unions, among nmigrants, in the colleges, the press, the pulpit, ad social organizations generally; and ask what e may expect the natural effect to be on the ten illion foreigners who have come into this couny during the last ten years, as well as on the norant and shallow of all classes of our cosmoolitan population; and then ask what part does l this play in manufacturing unrest.

SOCIALIST PROPAGANDA IN THE TRADE UNIONS

As the main proposal of the Socialist Party to better conditions for the working classes, at party naturally makes its strongest appeal the organized wage-earners. The activities of e socialists in this field are frankly and clearly escribed by Jack London, at one time president the Intercollegiate Socialist Society, in the llowing paragraphs:

> *With the control of the police, the army, the navy, and the courts, they will confiscate, with or without remuneration, all the possessions of the capitalist class* which are used in the production and distribution of the luxuries and necessities of life. They mean to apply the law of eminent domain to the land and to extend the law of eminent domain until it embraces the mines, the factories, the railroads and the ocean carriers.
>
> The socialists turned their energies upon the trade-union movement. To win the trade unions was well-nigh to win the victory.
>
> Instead of antagonizing the unions, the socialists proceeded to conciliate the unions. "Let every good socialist join the union of his trade! Bore from within and capture the trade-union movement."
>
> Today the great labor unions are honeycombed with socialists. At work and at play, at business meeting and council, *their insidious propaganda goes on.* Night and day, tireless and unrelenting as a mortgage, they labor at their self-imposed task of undermining society.

So far the socialists have made little headway in capturing the trade unions as a whole. While they have, as stated, in round numbers 75,000 dues-paying members and the Industrial Workers of the World 14,000 dues-paying members, the American Federation of Labor, the railroad brotherhoods and other non-socialist labor organizations have something like 3,000,000 dues-paying members; so that, if the entire 89,000 membership of the Socialist Party and the Industrial Workers of the World combined were members of the trade unions, it would be but an unappreciable percentage, but probably not more than one-half of the members of the Socialist Party are trade unionists.

There are, however, individual crafts where the socialists have captured the machinery of the organization, the most important instance being that of The United Mine Workers of America. This they did at the twenty-third annual convention of that body, held at Indianapolis, Ind., January 17, 1912, when it resolved: "That this convention go on record favoring government ownership of all industries."

This did not mean that the five hundred thousand members of the organization had become conscious socialists, but that the political propagandists of the Socialist Party had been the more active in securing delegates to the convention. On a straight-cut issue socialism would probably now be defeated in that organization by ten to one, but until that resolution is rescinded the United Mine Workers of America stand committed to revolutionary socialism with all that that means.

Ninety per cent. of the leaders of the whole movement of organized labor are *non-socialist.* They have had to resist the socialist attempt to capture the American Federation of Labor by "boring from within" and that has made them thoroughly acquainted not only with the doctrines of the socialists but with their "insidious propaganda", as Jack London puts it. The measure of the full strength of the socialist contingent in any American Federation of Labor convention is shown by their annual unsuccessful attempt to defeat Samuel Gompers for re-election as president. At the last convention, held in Philadelphia, November, 1914, the socialists were so anxious to hide their weakness that they did not even put up a candidate. The antagonism to Mr. Gompers is because of his rooted opposition to the doctrines of socialism, his estimate of which is contained in the following extract from a speech in Faneuil Hall, Boston:

> I want to tell you, socialists, that I have studied your philosophy; read your works upon economics, and not the meanest of them; studied your standard works, both in English and German—have not only read but studied them. I have heard your orators and watched the work of your movement the world over. I have kept close watch upon your doctrines for thirty years; have been closely associated with many of you, and know how you think and what you propose. I know, too, what you have up your sleeve, and I want to say that I am entirely at variance with your philosophy. I declare it to you, I am not only at variance with your doctrines, but with your philosophy. Economically, you are unsound; socially, you are wrong; industrially, you are an impossibility.

That much bitterness is injected into strikes where the socialists have any appreciable hold should be no surprise when we consider the revolutionary character of the matter contained in the literature which they distribute so voluminously among the ranks of the men. This literature is well calculated to undermine the faith of its readers in American institutions and the hope of progress under them.

Just what effect such articles as the following from *The Appeal to Reason*, which has a circulation of 500,000, would have on men who were facing trouble with their employers or on employers who were asked to make collective bargains with men holding such views, it is not hard to imagine:

> We make no apology for advocating the confiscation of the nation's industries as soon as we have the power to confiscate them.
>
> The rebels of '76 confiscated the colonial possessions and drove out King George and his vassals who held the legal title to them.
>
> The Lincoln administration confiscated the slave property of the Southern slave holders and this constitutes its crowning glory.
>
> The railroads of this nation have plundered the people without mercy ever since the first of them was chartered. The people have paid for them over and over again and now when the people come to take possession of these railroads, which they built, and which in very truth belong to them, they would be nothing less than idiotic to turn over the public treasury to the private capitalists whose claim to them would not bear for one instant the searchlight of honest inquiry.
>
> So with the telegraph and the telephone. So with the steel mills and the coal mines; so with the oil refineries and the cotton mills. . . . . .
>
> We would have no one under any mistaken impression so far as our position on confiscation is concerned. We want the capitalists themselves to know that we are organizing to take from them the right and power they have had since the beginning of capitalism to take from us the proceeds of our toil.
>
> *The Appeal to Reason* unfurls the flag of confiscation and appeals to all the toilers of the nation, in the mills and mines, on the railroads and the farms, to rally beneath its folds and hasten the day of their deliverance.

SOCIALISM IN THE PRESS

While the socialists have their own press and literary bureaus, they boast of the great success with which they are making themselves felt not only in the reportorial, literary and art departments but in the editorial rooms of the great daily newspapers.

Mr. J. G. Phelps Stokes, in an interview published in *New York Times,* was so sure of his ground that he made the following frank statement:

> Only yesterday I was told by a prominent New York editor that he had among his personal friends as many as twenty socialistic editors of daily and weekly magazines, whose publications are not socialistic but whose personal opinions are unqualifiedly so. It is easy to observe the influence of their opinions on the matter which they publish. Many of our leading magazines, especially, are advocating socialism in a veiled way. Nearly all the literature of criticism, of so-called "exposure", is really socialistic in degree.
>
> It is true of journalistic leaders elsewhere in the country. They are not all socialists, but more and more they are expressing socialistic sympathies to socialists and doing what they can to admit socialistic articles and arguments into their columns. And the most successful magazines are those which oftenest present analyses of modern conditions by men who are, in fact, true socialists. The most widely read medical journal in America is edited by socialists.

Mr. George Allan England, a magazine writer, makes the following interesting statement:

> Many a plutocratic magazine owner would be horrified if he knew the truth, that one or more of his apparently subservient editors were out-

> and-out Marxian socialists, dues-paying members and enthusiastic workers in this field. The moral and intellectual influence exerted by these large numbers of directing spirits, scattered throughout the publication offices of this country, even though their work must, perforce, be carried on *sub rosa*, can hardly be overestimated.

Hutchins Hapgood, writing in *The New York Call,* explains in the following paragraphs just how he "put the thing over" on the plutocratic owners of papers:

> I have had a good deal of experience as a reporter, critic and editorial writer on the conservative daily newspapers of New York and Chicago, and I am writing, at the present time, editorials for one of New York's daily papers.
>
> Radicalism, when deeply and broadly assimilated and felt, applies to everything in life. A newspaper might be a great exponent of radicalism, a great revolutionary influence, merely by the way in which the news was treated in its columns. A man who wrote what he saw, without undue reference to tradition or countries, who told a news story as if it had never been told before, would be a radical and *his story would very subtly and also deeply disturb the viewpoint of his readers.*
>
> *If you visualize the news, if you deepen the meaning of every item that goes into your papers, you are making a* radical paper, even if the word "socialism" is very rare.

In *The New York Call* of February 7, 1915, the editor in describing with great enthusiasm his achievement in organizing a new socialist press bureau throughout the country, makes the following interesting statement:

> Perhaps one of the most surprising features of the entire situation is that in almost every large city where *The Call* now has a bureau or a correspondent, the representative is a trained newspaper man of ample experience. It is probable that but few have any adequate idea of the number of newspaper writers in active service on capitalist papers who are socialists in active connection with the party.

So successful have these propagandists been in impressing editors with the importance of their views that two magazines in New York have come out openly for socialism, although the support of one of these magazines is largely from advertisers who, if the Socialist Party should succeed in its efforts to overthrow the competitive system and take over their property, would be placed in a grotesque situation to say the least.

Another magazine has been founded during the last year, which is financially backed by a Wall Street business man. This magazine is edited by three gentlemen who together can be regarded as a hotch-potch of progressivism, populism, socialism and syndicalism. One of these editors is exploited by friends of this paper as a "great statesman" and "profound thinker", and he certainly has a right to those titles for he has been on earth for nearly a quarter of a century. This magazine, while containing much high grade matter on current events, nearly always has, sneaking away in some corner or between the lines on all its matter on industrial subjects, its particular syndicalist or socialist philosophy.

A little over a year ago a revolutionary change took place in one of the oldest weekly publications in New York, which in one leap went from ultra conservatism to ultra radicalism, its financial backers under the new management being wealthy manufacturers, two of them in high standing in national politics. In announcing its policy, one of the statements made by this paper was that it aspired to be the organ of "the Feminists"—that bunch of crazy, impossible women whom the backers of the paper would certainly not care to entertain in their own homes. It was also announced that in its art department it would follow closely the path blazed for it by those "brilliant, naughty rebels" who were publishing an anarchist sheet which just keeps itself within the line that permits it to go through the United States mails. That anarchist sheet is not backed by capitalists but by cartoonists, painters, sculptors and writers on the various capitalist newspapers and magazines, who boast of their rebellion against the present order.

An ingenious method which the socialists employ to manufacture sentiment is frankly announced by George Bernard Shaw, the English socialist and playwright, in Fabian Tract No. 41, as follows:

> It only cost us (the Fabian Society of London) twenty-eight post cards, written by twenty-eight members, to convince the newly-born *Star* newspaper that London was aflame with Fabian socialism.
>
> Before the year was out, we had the assistant editor . . . writing as extreme articles as Hyndman had ever written in *Justice*. Before the capitalist proprietors woke up to our game and cleared us out, the competition of the *Star*, which was immensely popular under what I may call the Fabian regime, had encouraged a morning daily, the *Chronicle*, to take up the running; and the *Star*, when it tried to go back, found that it could not do so further than to Gladstonize its party politics. On other questions it remained and remains far more advanced than the wildest socialist three years before ever hoped to see a capitalist paper.

It seems clear from these quotations that there is a well-defined, organized attempt to control the utterances and the policies of the press in the interest of the revolutionary propaganda. May it not be of the highest importance to ascertain to what extent this attempt is successful? The American people do not want editorials or news tainted by revolutionary socialists any more than they want their editorials or news tainted by the capitalists, who alone, so far as I have been able to see, have been charged with insidiously corrupting the sources of our public information.

SOCIAL SETTLEMENTS

Social settlements and the charity organizations form another great field for socialist exploitation. Settlement and charity workers are dealing constantly with poverty. The settlements themselves are located, designedly and properly in places where the greatest amount of squalor and misery are to be found. Necessarily the workers are brought into contact with all the human frailties at their worst, and, like the doctors who are constantly in attendance at clinics, they see only the abnormal. I do not mean to imply that all our social workers and charity experts who make radical utterances become conscious socialists. They see great misery and, to their credit, they resolve to do all that is within their power to remedy such evils. They may become practical social reformers, between whom and socialists there is an unbridgeable gulf. But the workers in these movements are constantly in danger of losing their perspective, imagining that what they see is typical, and concluding that, if the conditions which come to their notice are the product of present-day institutions, the more quickly these institutions are overturned the better, because nothing that could take their place could be worse.

Referring to one of the large charity organizations in New York City, I was told that the superintendent of a certain district spent the time when he was supposed to be instructing the workers in their daily duties in wild denunciations of the capitalist system. My informant said that, after listening to his speeches, she felt more disposed to go out and throw bombs than to dispense alms. Some of the charity workers who are more thoroughly steeped in the socialist philosophy have been heard to say, referring to the poor: "Let them starve. The sooner they starve, the sooner will come the revolution."*

The ingenious way in which the socialists distort and exaggerate is well understood by all students of the literature of rebellion and has already been referred to. A headline in a socialist paper a year ago read: "Women Making Knee Pants at 4 Cents a Dozen. They Earn Only a Pittance of 50 Cents a Day." This statement soon got into the "capitalist" papers and is still going the round. An inquiry into the matter revealed that these women did not make a whole pair of pants, as the headline would imply, but performed only a single operation on them in handsewing; that they worked on the knee pants in their homes between the performance of their household duties; and that, even so, they made from 90 cents to $1.25 a day. These facts were made public but received no attention.

The most fruitful field for this kind of exaggeration is that in which children are concerned, where "social investigators" have reported the finding of children of the ages of "four and five years" at work in cotton mills, canneries and various other industries. As a matter of fact, in such cases the mothers were doing work in the factory and the children playing around. In the campaign against the evils of child labor it is always a popular statement that there are from two to four million "little children wage-slaves" under fourteen years of age working in the factories, mills and mines of this country. It makes no difference that the inaccuracy of these figures has been exposed over and over again. They are still doing duty at the same old socialist stand. It is easy to puncture these statements, because they are admittedly based on the Census of 1900. The probability is that those who make them have never studied the Census reports but have taken the figures from some ranter who started the story. The Census of 1900, to which they refer, showed that two-thirds of these two million children were not employed in factories, mines or mills, but in agriculture, out on the farms where they ought to be, and that three-fourths of the remainder were over fourteen years of age. In other words, in the United States in 1900, instead of there being two or four million children under fourteen years of age working in factories, mines and mills, there were just 186,000, and, according to the Census of 1910, the number so employed in that year had been reduced to 95,000. By the present time that number has been very largely, if not entirely, taken out of industry.

An officer of the National Child Labor Committee, a society which, while devoted to the work of fighting the evils of child labor, has itself been guilty of using these exaggerated figures, became so much disturbed over the injurious effect of these ridiculous statements that, in an article in the *New York Independent*, he referred to it in the following language:

> We doubt the efficiency of pity to solve the problem of child labor. A certain value is derived from pictures of the bent shoulders, the contracted lungs, the tired limbs, the sallow faces, the vacant eyes and the dwarfed intellects of those we are banishing from home, playground and schoolroom to the weary tread of our sweatshops, factories and mines. But not all child laborers are "slaves". Those who denounce the evils of child labor in such generalizations as that "two million little, wan and dwarfed child toilers march in the wage-slave ranks of America's industrial army" are a menace to this reform. Intelligent people, seeing many of these two million children who are not "wan" or "dwarfed", and who bear no other visible marks of slavery, discount the whole cry against child labor as sentiment. Many of the two million working children of America are between fifteen and sixteen years of age and are in occupations and laboring under conditions not injurious to themselves or to society. Not all glass houses employ little boys at night. Not all coal breakers are dense with clouds of dry dust. Not all telegraph offices employ little children to carry messages at midnight to houses of vice. Not all children in Southern cotton mills work through a twelve-hour night. Some one tells of seeing a little girl in a Southern cotton mill rudely awakened at night by a dash of cold water in her face. Homilies on child labor followed this incident, abounding in graphic descriptions of

* One of these same charity workers during the war, although holding a Government position, is charged with having boasted of being disloyal.

numberless little girls cruelly awakened night after night by splashes of cold water.

Nothing is gained by exaggeration; much is lost. It is enough that some of the two million are toiling all night in glass houses; that some coal breakers compel little boys of ten years to work in clouds of dust so dense as to completely hide the light and fill the lungs; that some little girls of eight years toil through a twelve-hour night in Southern cotton mills; that some of the little children of New York are crushed in body and soul in the slavery of sweatshop labor. The truth is bad enough. Let the picture be drawn with simple accuracy, and we may hope to arouse, instead of sentiments of pity, the sense of social justice; an appreciation of the relation of this system to our social institutions. A demonstration of the loss to society, the injustice to the laborer, and the dwarfing of the progenitors of our coming generation, will be more effective than specific pictures of little children who suffer from the wrong.

Owen R. Lovejoy,
Assistant Secretary of the National Child Labor Committee.

SOCIALISM IN SCHOOLS AND COLLEGES

In the colleges revolutionary socialism is being endorsed by many professors and by more pupils. The sixth annual convention of the Intercollegiate Socialist Society, held in New York, December 29-31, 1914, was attended by delegates from local organizations in over fifty of our principal colleges. While this society pretends to be a non-partisan body to study socialism, it is simply an organization to promote socialist propaganda. It was founded by socialists and every officer in it is a member of the Socialist Party. The boys and girls, however, who join the Intercollegiate Socialist Society do not know this and many of them are led into radical socialism through it. A mother told me with tears in her eyes that her son, by imbibing this doctrine of despair through the socialists in this organization, had become so embittered towards society that she feared that his whole life would be wrecked.

In the report of the secretary of the Intercollegiate Socialist Society, Mr. Harry W. Laidler, which was presented at the convention referred to above, occur the following interesting paragraphs:

(The italics are mine.)

> The year 1914-15 is chiefly noteworthy by virtue of the fact that the I. S. S. has, in a greater degree than heretofore, been able to present its message in scores of colleges, before whole college bodies, before economics and sociology classes and before many long-established organizations of undergraduates. In November and December of this year, for instance, the Organizing Secretary addressed twenty-seven economics, sociology and logic classes in twenty colleges of New York and New England, and spoke before college chapels, Y. M. C. A.'s and I. S. S. Chapters, reaching a total of 3,000 students and several hundred of the general public.
>
> . . . . . .
>
> Increasing sympathy toward Socialism is being shown by economics professors. In the sixteen New York and New England colleges in which the views of members of the economics department were obtained, *one professor was found to be a dues-paying member of the Socialist Party; four definitely stated that they believed Socialism to be the next system in economic development*, while a similar number tacitly admitted this fact. Two said that they *strongly suspected* that Socialism would be the next system in economic development, while nine or ten believed the tendency was in that direction, although they were not willing to commit themselves to the whole Socialist program. *One* called himself a "Societyist" and *prided himself on having made Socialists of a number of his students.*"
>
> . . . . . .
>
> Another indication of the increasing interest in Socialism is found in the topics for debates. Colgate, Western Reserve, Ohio Wesleyan, Rochester and other colleges are debating specifically on the subject of Socialism, while many more are arguing the question of collective ownership of railways, etc. Still another promising feature of the year's work is the organization of the New England Sectional Committee, Walter M. Hinkle, Williams, 1914, and a prominent debater, has been secured as organizer, and Ordway Tead, Amherst, 1914, as chairman. Both are doing excellent work in strengthening undergraduate Chapters in New England.
>
> The Intercollegiate Socialist Society has *this year approximately sixty undergraduate and a dozen alumni Chapters*, the same number as at the last Convention.
>
> . . . . . .
>
> Among the most active and largest Chapters this year is *Union Theological Seminary, whose membership comprises about one-fourth of the college body.*

Two years ago the head of one of the most fashionable schools for girls in New York declared herself, at one of the meetings of the Intercollegiate Socialist Society, as a member of the Socialist Party. When asked how it came about that the rich people of New York were sending their daughters to a school conducted by such a prominent socialist, she replied: "Oh, they don't know anything about it, and if they did I doubt if they would care, because they don't know what socialism is. At any rate, these daughters of the rich turn to socialism as the flowers turn to the morning sun."

But the Intercollegiate Socialist Society has as good "running mates" the American Economic Association and the American Sociological Society, composed not of students but entirely of professors of economics and sociology in all the colleges of the United States. If the wealthy founders and patrons of those colleges had any sinister purpose in mind, as is so generally charged by the revolutionists, they certainly have fallen far short of the mark if the public utterances of the leaders of those organizations are any criterion. At the last annual meeting of those two societies held in Princeton, N. J., December 28-30, 1914, the annual address of the president of the American Economic Association was practically a declaration for socialism, while the annual address of the president of the American Sociological Society could be classed with the I. W. W. literature of the day.

I said to a member, whom I knew to be anti-socialist: "Why do you people stand for this kind of stuff? Why don't you hiss some of these declarations?" He replied: "The radicals have captured both of these organizations, and while there are a few of us who are opposed to such doctrines, there are not enough of us to stem the tide." I do not know how nearly correct was this professor's analysis, but if I were to judge alone from the friendly reception these addresses had I should say he was right.

Nor do the socialists confine themselves to the colleges. They are organizing locals among the teachers and pupils in the public schools, and throughout the country there are many important schools in which a socialist teacher or a boy or girl pupil is quietly spreading the socialist doctrines. For it must not be forgotten that the boys and girls of socialist parents are every one of them trained to be Marxian socialists from the age at which they are able to understand the outlines of that philosophy. In the circular issued to the socialists, urging them to organize the teachers, it is particularly pointed out that it is important, in every instance, to secure the teacher of history, as such teacher could interpret historical events discriminately, so as to fit the socialist doctrine of economic determinism.

The easy manner in which a teacher can make his pupils socialists is explained by Professor Enrico Ferri, of the University of Palermo. In addressing the International Congress of Socialist Students and Graduates on one occasion, he said:

> "We should introduce socialism into the student's mind as a part of science, as a logical and necessary culmination of the biological and sociological science. No need of making a direct propaganda which would frighten many of the listeners. Without pronouncing the ord 'socialism' once a year. I make two-thirds of our students class-conscious socialists."

It would be interesting to know just how many Enrico Ferris, avowed or "surreptitious", there are in American universities and colleges today, working, as Jack London says, "at their self-imposed task of undermining society." I have been asked by parents to recommend colleges to which they could send their sons where they would not be made socialists or anarchists. I could not give advice on this subject because while there are in every university some avowed socialists and even syndicalists against whom a parent can protect himself, there are also in every university many more who come under the head of "surreptitious" socialists, and these, from the standpoint of such parents, are, obviously, much more dangerous.

I think this Commission would perform a useful service if it were to "dig them out" and "label" them. A college professor has, of course, a right to be a socialist, a syndicalist, an anarchist, or even a Mormon; but he should be made to declare himself openly as such, in order that the parents who abhor such a philosophy may know how to protect their boys and girls from what they believe to be insidious and dangerous teaching. It would be interesting to trace the influence, which is thought by many to be an evil influence, of the young men and women who have been made socialists in college and are today writing books, articles for magazines and editorials in the newspapers, preaching the "gospel of despair" in the pulpits, manipulating the social reform organizations and, in some instances, occupying important positions of trust in corporations or municipal, state and federal government offices.

Take, for instance, the history of the movement which resulted in the passage of the law creating this very Commission. It originated in the minds of a group of radical people, consisting of charity and social workers and ministers, all of them college graduates. They were over-impressed by the McNamara dynamiting incidents in California and thought that civilization was about to go to pieces. Some of them probably hoped that it would do so. They began a campaign to secure the enactment of a law creating a commission to study the underlying causes of the "great unrest" that was indicated not only by the McNamara incidents but by the Lawrence, Paterson and other eruptions caused by the Industrial Workers of the World. After securing the passage of the law, they tried to get the President to name as members of the Commission the persons whom they recommended, which included a number of themselves. None of the promoters, however, were placed on the Commission, but they had breathed their fears and their spirit into the law to such an extent as to handicap and circumscribe the work that it was to do. The law placed such an emphasis upon the study of unrest that the Commission felt obligated to do the same thing. It would, to my mind, have been much better if the Commission had been instructed, in addition to looking for unrest, normal and induced, to include in its investigation an inquiry into the progress which this country has made, industrially and socially, within the last few decades.

(To be Continued)

"Who's Who in "The New School"

(Continued from Page 5)

of the chief organizers of The New School for Social Research.

Less advanced thinkers than Prof. Robinson have for a very long time, indeed, had no vague uncertainties as to the "exact causes" of the war, as to where the guilt for this world agony lay, and to them it may seem exceedingly strange that any man of American birth—albeit a Ph.D. of Freiburg—can at this late hour regard those "exact causes" as "questions of dispute."

It was apparent from Prof. Robinson's *Century* article that in his opinion the "nationality" of the European states was responsible for the world catastrophe rather than German militarism—a view, of course, with which Dernburg's crew of propagandists were not unsympathetic. "*If nationality causes war,*" argued the "thoughtful outsiders" put forward by Prof. Robinson, "*then nationality must be a wicked thing, which should be got rid of altogether, or so far modified as to lose its ugly traits.*"

Prof. Robinson was painfully reticent, obstrusively shy, about making any direct allusion as to the guilt of German "nationality" in causing the war.

"The national spirit is only patriotism in its modern form," continued the co-author of the pro-German school text book so scathingly pilloried by the Seattle School Board, "and we have been taught from infancy that no sentiment can more safely be encouraged, since none is worthier of man or more pleasing to God than love of country. All national anthems," ironically remarked the cynic of Columbia University, "substantiate this."

"Nationality, in our meaning of the term, is a concomitant of another mystical entity, democracy."

"There is, however, nothing exceptional in this case of a cherished emotion which produces fearful disasters. PATRIOTISM RESEMBLES RELIGION AND LOVE IN THIS RESPECT. TO THE CANDID HISTORICAL STUDENT THE EVIL WORKINGS OF RELIGION ARE, TO SAY THE LEAST, FAR MORE CONSPICUOUS AND FAR MORE READILY DEMONSTRATED THAN ITS GOOD RESULTS."

"AN ALIEN ABSTRACTION CALLED THE STATE"

James Harvey Robinson, unable to place any special blame upon Germany for loosing the scourge of war upon the world, could apparently see in the "workings" of the teaching of the Man who was crucified on Calvary more evil than good results. This strutting sophist, insensible to all its spiritual mellowings, would apparently place upon Christianity the blame of all the persecutions, massacres and crimes actuated by human bigotry, just as, relieving the Huns of direct culpability, he would put the guilt of the war upon "nationality."

"As for love," said Robinson, "St. Paul's eulogy in 1 Corinthians, 13, might fairly and squarely be reversed." Is a man whose soul is utterly callous to the spiritual regeneration worked upon the world by the Christian teaching, a man who could divert the moral guilt for starting the war from Germany by ascribing it to "nationality," who, by perversion of reason or by hypocrisy, can assert that patriotism, religion and love work more evil than good, such a man as might be trusted to mould the thought of young men and women? One's mind goes back to the saying of a courageous Man—hated and ultimately slain by a breed similar to those who today counsel in secret and pack halls where class war is incited—concerning those who scandalize the young and lead young minds astray. And one marvels exceedingly, and is sorely amazed, when the New York School of Philanthropy—Porter R. Lee, director—should select as the Kennedy lecturer for 1919, one who ribaldly wags his head and scoffs at patriotism, religion and love.

"Patriotism," said this champion of the I. W. W., "is made up of two quite different things, love of one's country and dislike and depreciation of foreign peoples. Unhappily the latter is the more vivid and unreasoning sentiment when once aroused." Prof. Robinson aptly said: "The first records of emotions which may properly be called national are to be found in the Old Testament."

German patriotism may have combined with love of country "dislike and depreciation of foreign peoples." But it is a question whether truly Christian civilizations have been "more vivid and unreasoning" in their hate, and the fact that America and other nations accepted Germany as she professed herself to be, that we accepted her at her own valuation and gave generous credit to her flamboyant boasts of superior achievements, is proof of that. Germany alone—and Prof. Robinson ignores this—wallowed in hymns of hate in this war. Prof. Robinson, in making his points, quotes such a distinguished authority as Max Eastman, editor of the *Masses* and *Liberator,* with whose views he seems to be in accord. He quotes the editor of the *Masses* as saying: "The disposition of European people, grouped in nations, to wage war when their nation was threatened, and to believe it threatened upon a very light excuse, seems to be fixed in the nervous tissue, like self-preservation itself. Men who would not contribute a peaceable eight cents to the public weal, drop their cash, credit and commercial prospects and go toss in their lives like a song at the bidding of an alien abstraction called the state."

By this could it be implied that Belgium, France and England considered themselves "threatened upon a very light excuse"? Was that national sovereignty, integrity and liberty which Germany sought to destroy merely "an alien abstraction?"

PATRIOTISM "TOUCHY AND UGLY"

One may have wondered what would be the reaction in such a "progressive mind" as that of Robinson's at the spectacle of America going to war, of millions of boys going bravely forth to fight, of people giving their money unstintedly to war loans and war charities, of the whole nation uniting unselfishly and heroically toward the great task of winning the war.

Here in the face of that spectacle a puny Zoilus sneers and snivels.

"A man who exhibited no public spirit and consistently dodged his taxes in times of peace might find himself hurrying off to the trenches at the bugle's sound, urged on by an innate property of his nature of which he himself had not suspected the existence. The war-dance is in our blood."

That for "Star Spangled Banner stuff"!

"To most of our fellow men," he sourly sniggers, "patriotism is a word that still falls most sweetly on the ear. . . ."

He goes on:

"The chief quarrel with patriotism is its innate tendency to precipitate war with other groups upon the most trivial pretenses. It is, in short, touchy and ugly in its most constant and characteristic manifestation."

Did Belgium rush at Germany's throat upon a "trivial pretense?" Did France? Did England? Did America? Were the invasion of Belgium and the killing of helpless women and children by the submarines "trivial pretenses" upon which to quarrel with Germany?

Was the inspiring spirit of this country throughout the war "touchy and ugly?"

Says the pundit who has risen above the merely human quality of patriotism:

"I AM INCLINED, HOWEVER, TO THINK THAT ANYONE WHO REALLY ACKNOWLEDGED AND BELIEVED IN THE BOTTOM OF HIS HEART ALL THE THINGS WHICH I HAVE BEEN RECALLING WOULD SCARCELY BE SWEPT OFF HIS FEET BY A WAVE OF NATIONAL EMOTION. IF THAT BE TRUE, THEN MUCH CAN BE ACCOMPLISHED THROUGH EDUCATION."

Is it on the basis of this belief—the belief that those accepting as truth what he preached—that Prof. Robinson predicts the New School for Social Research "will turn out a new class of leaders?" Is this—this emasculation of all vital and heroic national virtues—what Prof. Robinson hopes to accomplish through his particular form of "new" education?

Do the people of America want "a new class of leaders" who "would scarcely be swept off their feet by a wave of national emotion?"

One is irresistably inclined to ask whether Prof. Robinson was incapable of "a wave of national emotion" when the Lusitania was torpedoed and helpless American women and children were sent to their death? Was he unmoved by "any wave of emotion" when imperial Germany, breaking her solemn word, announced the resumption of ruthless and indiscriminate killing upon the high seas? Was he unstirred when America went into the war, when American boys first braved that ordeal of steel and fire?

ROBINSON AND THE I. W. W.

Through the tense days of that war, when American blood was spilled that the world's heritage of freedom might be preserved, in the long dark hours of that Gethsemane, was this little professor impervious to the emotions that swayed the crowds? Was he, exalted in some lofty and detached angle of intellectual neutrality, alien to the rising and ebbing despairs, sorrows and enthusiasms of the herd? Scorning nationality, scoffing at patriotism, cold-bloodedly aloof in some superior philosophical dimension of "internationalism," did he fail to share in the warm-blooded hope of "the majority" that our boys rout the bestial Huns and that the Allies break and crush Hun militarism finally and forever?

Or, after America had entered the war, was it not true that this advanced thinker did succumb to a purely human heart glow when American boys in khaki marched down Fifth Avenue? And when he read, in his well-warmed and comfortable library, of their feats at Chateau Thierry, did his pulses not involuntarily thrill to a genuine emotion of patriotism? Was he not inspired to do his "bit" in combatting pacifists, opponents of the draft, the advocates of a peace of compromise, the disloyalists, internationalists and secret abettors of the foe? Despite his academic theories, teachings and speculations, when it came to practice, was Mr. Robinson not "right" after all?

Prof. Robinson, as before stated, lent himself to the effort to raise a $50,000 fund in June, 1918, for the defense of I. W. W. leaders on trial for seditious conspiracy to obstruct the country in its conduct of the war. The majority of those I. W. W.'s were later found guilty of the crimes charged against them and sentenced to long terms of imprisonment.

By those engaged in defending the criminal I. W. W. leaders at that time it was implied that the Government would not give the accused a fair trial. Just as, in more or less the same manner that Prof. Robinson endeavored in effect to deflect the blame for starting the world war from Germany to "nationality," so the defenders of this lawless organization at that time sought to shift the blame for their crimes to "social conditions." Conspicuously among the defenders of the I. W. W. was the *New Republic,* whose editor, Mr. Herbert Croly, is one of the organizers of Prof. Robinson's New School for Social Research. The *New Republic* alleged that the I. W. W. were not on trial for seditious conspiracy—of which they were actually found uilty—but "for revolting against the intolerble by-products of timber mining and crass peculation in public lands." The committee igning the appeal for a defense fund, of which rof. James Harvey Robinson was a member, complained that the indicted I. W. W. leaders "are at least entitled to a fair trial and an open-minded public hearing," implying, obviously, that the Department of Justice would not accord what it was "for American liberals" to make possible.

EMOTION FOR THE HYPHENATES?

When various radical, revolutionary and Socialist magazines were suppressed by the postal authorities for publishing unpatriotic and seditious articles, for opposing the draft and otherwise seeking to hinder the country in its war work, a wail at once went up about the suppression of the constitutional rights of free speech. Among those who sniffled and scolded about the violation of individual rights were the same revolutionary radicals, pacifists, pro-Germans, and others who had defended the I. W. W. and who later became apologists for the Russian Bolsheviki. The most vehement champions of "the constitutional rights of free speech" proved chiefly to be those who were opposed to our waging the war against Germany until a decisive victory was achieved, who urged a peace of compromise and who, since the signing of the armistice, have assailed the Allies and pleaded for mercy and magnanimity to the beaten foe. Of this kidney were the *Nation* and the *New Republic* crew.

Prof. James Harvey Robinson published in the *Atlantic Monthly* of December, 1917, an article entitled "The Threatened Eclipse of Free Speech."

"I cannot share the flushed indignation of those who denounce as traitors all who take a different view of our national policy and of the choice we have made," declared the intellect which has transcended so vulgar a thing as "a wave of national emotion."

"If we can honestly agree with the mass of our countrymen on the wisdom of joining the war, we should be devoutly thankful, for we are lucky in escaping the disgrace and danger of dissent and suspected loyalty."

Prof. Robinson confessedly managed to be one of those "thankful" ones, for he said: *"Some of us who* NOW *warmly support the war cannot find it in our hearts to contemn all so-called pacifists, or even those who are torn by conflicting allegiances."* Thankful that he at least had escaped "disgrace" and "suspected loyalty" by achieving a warm approval of the war, Prof. Robinson did not find it necessary to strain the quality of his mercy toward those dissenters who "appear to be quite as noble as we," whose "ideals are no less lofty than ours," who are "disloyal only in the sense of failing eagerly to co-operate with the majority in a crisis."

"When we see khaki uniforms all about us; . . . when coal runs low in the cellar and sugar in the kitchen; . . . when we . . . are suspected of being a scoundrel if we do not invest in government bonds, the mind is quickened as never before. We would seem to have a right to suspect that many things must have been fundamentally wrong in the old and revered notions of the State, of national honor, even of patriotism, since they seem at least partially responsible for bringing the world to the pass in which it now finds itself."

Some minds that were quickened by the sight of khaki uniforms did not fail clearly to see the responsibility of imperial Germany "for bringing the world to the pass" in which it found itself. Some persons, "saying good-bye to relatives and friends departing for French trenches," failed to see, as did this odd scribe at least a "partial responsibility" for the world agony in our "old and revered notions . . . of national honor, even of patriotism."

NATIONAL FLATTERY AND SELF DELUSION

"Just at this critical juncture," continued the befriender of the I. W. W., ". . . come reports of government censorship, exclusions from the mails, the breaking up of public meetings, and expulsion of teachers from our schools and colleges for expressing opinions adjudged disloyal, seditious, or treasonable . . ."

"We have," complained the man who declared religion, love and patriotism to have worked more evil than good, "furthermore been taught from childhood to sing of our country as a land of liberty and to flatter ourselves that freedom of speech is an indubitable element of 'Americanism.' The Constitution of the United States precludes Congress from passing any law abridging freedom of speech, or of the press, or the right of the people peacefully to assemble and to petition the government for a redress of grievances."

However, the ideals of the Constitution are a snare and a pitfall, for, "according to those very laws which proclaim freedom of speech, 'every individual is to be held responsible for the abuse of the same.' This means that . . . if anyone says anything at a public meeting which is deemed immoral, indecent, inflammatory, or treasonable by the policeman or plain clothes men present, he may be arrested, and mayhap imprisoned or fined." "The courts," bewailed Prof. Robinson with characteristic irony, "have decided that the United States post-office has precisely the same right to refuse to carry the *Masses* that it has to exclude sulphuric acid and dynamite from the mails. So it comes about that the rights of public discussion are always really limited, and that they may readily be impaired by narrow, ignorant and prudish interference."

For the "new vigilance" exercised over meetings and public speeches by "plain clothes men and police officials, our district attorneys, juries and judges" during the war, Prof. Robinson implied that mere "excuses," and not valid, legitimate reasons, were given. *"The excuses for this," said he, "are the activities of German agents and sympathizers."* Did Prof. Robinson not know of these activities, of the plots and pacifist propaganda of Hun agents and sympathizers? Or were the exposures of these Hun conspiracies mere fabrications, subterfuges with which to gag the radical press and shut "advanced" pamphleteering from the mails?

America decided to enter the war, admitted Prof. Robinson, "with the general sanction of the nation." "The minority, who are still unreconciled with this decision or are not yet fully persuaded, must, it is urged, yield to the majority and keep their mouths shut. For them to continue their protests when the boys are in the trenches is giving aid and comfort to the enemy," sarcastically continued the man who abetted the effort to raise $50,000 to defend those I. W. W.'s who, as a jury decided, had given aid and comfort to the enemy. "It is essentially disloyal, if not downright treasonable. . . . When we start out to kill enemies abroad on a gigantic scale," cynically animadverted this superior thinker, "we are not likely to hesitate to gag those at home who seem directly or indirectly to sympathize with the foe. But just here we may well stop and make a couple of distinctions. In the first place difference of opinion is not necessarily disloyalty."

COMFORT TO SHADOW HUNS AND OTHERS

There is, one must admit, in Prof. Robinson's style a gleam now and then of something akin to the fine touch of machiavellian subtlety. Or maybe, it is just "plain clumsy."

"Some people in the United States wish Germany to be victorious. To express this wish *publicly* . . . would certainly be disloyal, not to say treasonable."

Would an expression of the wish privately, in camera, say in one's bedchamber or over a seidel of lager, not have been disloyal, not to say treasonable?

"Those, however, who continue to say that they wish we had not entered the war; that some other less horrible policy might have been selected; that war has never yet begotten lasting peace but only new war; that some men loathe shooting their fellow men under government auspices in the same sickening way that they would loathe private murder—such persons are in no way treasonable, and disloyal only in the sense of failing eagerly to co-operate with the majority in a crisis."

"It is this confusion between real traitors, on one hand," said Robinson, "and on the other hand *those persons whose human sympathy and idealism outrun the common bounds*, that fills many of us with dismay."

Were the I. W. W.'s, who opposed the war and preached resistance to the draft, were Victor Berger and Rose Pastor Stokes, persons "whose human sympathy and idealism outrun the common bounds" of "the majority" who were loyally willing to sacrifice their blood and the blood of their dearest in order to vanquish the brutish Huns?

Prof. Robinson, obviously appreciating with fine discernment, the unwisdom and embarrassment of too rash or too emotional public expressions, did not fail to hold out hope of freedom and relief to those likely "to attract the attention of the postal authorities and guardians of the public purity." In fact, he pointed a way of "safety."

"The censor is commonly slow-footed and heavy-eyed," remarked the sapient Mr. Robinson. *"It is not hard to elude him; one need only avoid a few phrases which he has learned to recognize as wicked or dangerous, and express one's self with a little freshness, or resort to irony, or a scientific phraseology, in order to be quite safe."*

This, presumably, was given as the wisdom that comes from experience. It came with the weight of authority. The suggestion had in itself a quality of freshness, a delightful touch of irony. And the suggestion was given generously to those who might run and read with a prodigality rare among those misers who hoard nothing but their own conceit.

And in this gentle hint, this outburst of kindly magnanimous feeling toward the suppressed, was there not perhaps a suggestion which may have filled the hearts of German well-wishers, sympathizers and agents with a due feeling of gratitude and elation?

DENIAL OF GOD A "PRIVILEGE"

Prof. Robinson, chafing against the rude efforts to restrict freedom of expression by the "slow-footed and heavy-eyed" censor, warmed genially as he discovered and pointed out a loophole for free, unrestricted and loose talk. He thawed and expanded thus:

"At present, all things may be said and printed if only time and circumstance be somewhat carefully considered. One may reject every vestige, not only of Christianity but of all religious belief, even the existence of God and the life to come—and there are many occasions on which this privilege can be exercised."

Having, therefore, given the cue to pacifists, conscientious objectors, the great "unreconciled"—and perhaps inadvertently to German agents and sympathizers—as to how they might all continue to give vent to their painfully repressed emotions without danger of suppression or arrest, Prof. Robinson remarked, as it were, facetiously: "Indeed, except for blasphemy, which is a sort of breach of good order, no arrests, or exclusions from the mails are likely to take place, unless one's negations are accompanied by seditious or otherwise shocking remarks." Those desiring to "exercise" the "privilege" of denying God, of rejecting Christianity, of discrediting as archaic and evil loyalty to country and national ideals, therefore require only that felicitously scientific phraseology, that freshness of cynicism, that delightful spirit of ironic mockery, that velvet suavity and *savoir faire* which have distinguished the author of "Mediaeval and Modern Times" and co-author of "Outlines of European History, Part II."

To the advanced thinker who solicits students for his courses at the New School for Social Research, the Kennedy lecturer for 1919 at the New York School of Philanthropy, was the discovery of an opportune way of rejecting every vestige of Christianity and belief in God a cause for personal exultation? To the man who found in the workings of religion, patriotism and love more evil than good, was it a cause for gratification that, by considering time and circumstance, or by scientific phraseology, or by irony, there are many occasions on which the "privilege" of rejecting Christianity and belief in God can be exercised? Are the two hours in his lecture courses at the New School for Social Research such rare occasions?

Prof. Robinson, at last moved by a wave of emotion, of challenging exultant triumph, went on to boast in the *Atlantic Monthly*:

"ONE CAN ALWAYS CRITICISE AND ATTACK THE POLICY OF ALL GOVERNMENT OFFICIALS, FROM THE PRESIDENT OF THE UNITED STATES DOWN TO THE LOCAL CORONER; THEY CAN SAFELY BE DENOUNCED AS KNAVES, FOOLS, AND LATTERLY, EVEN AS TRAITORS. ONE CAN PICK FLAWS IN OUR CONSTITUTION AND THE COURTS WHICH INTERPRET IT; ONE CAN EVEN QUESTION THE EXPEDIENCY OF THE STATE ITSELF, AS NOW UNDERSTOOD; BUT ONE WOULD BETTER NOT BE ASSOCIATING WITH SUPPOSED ANARCHISTS WHEN SO DOING."

Was that why Prof. Robinson took pains to announce that the New School for Social Research "will not be so radical as the Socialists"?

Prof. Robinson's friend and collaborator, Charles Beard, did "pick flaws" in the framing of the Constitution and, now that it has been pointed out, it seems that he, while so doing, did seek out and assiduously cultivate respectable company.

"SAVAGE TERM SACRED"

Prof. Robinson's somewhat vainglorious admission betrays real acuteness and wordly wisdom, and to many of his colleagues at Columbia may answer their oft-repeated question to how "he gets away with it." To some, however—viewing it from Prof. Robinson's own standpoint—this oracular delivery, one of the truly wisest bits Robinson ever dropped, may seem a self-asserted triumph which carries with it its own defeat, for it "lets the cat out of the bag;" gives away the trick, and ergo, when the secret of the charm is known the charm ceases to work.

Prof. Robinson and his New School colleagues would probably repudiate, with indignation, any suggestion that they intend to teach or encourage Bolshevism or social revolution. But supposing they so wished, according to Prof. Robinson they could do even that by avoiding phrases which people might "recognize as wicked or dangerous," by resorting to "irony" or "scientific phraseology." According to this "secret key," they could teach anything and be quite "safe," provided they did not associate with notorious "supposed anarchists while so doing."

It is declared in the prospectus of the New School for Social Research:

"Everyone who watches public affairs sees that we must now deal with social difficulties of the most complex and dangerous sort, and that we have neither sufficient applied knowledge nor sufficient trained personnel to cope with them." Therefore: "The New School will exist frankly and solely for social research. Its founders are aware of the necessity for disinterested study of the problems of modern society. . . ."

"ABOVE GOOD AND EVIL"

Is that "disinterested" point of view which shall govern the study of the New School indicated by Robinson's definition: "Such a stage of intellectual emancipation that he exempts nothing from scrutiny . . . when that ancient, savage term 'sacred' disappears from our thought and speech?" Which suggests a stage of "intellectual emancipation" so morally neuter that one cannot tell right from wrong.

For, never mentioning Germany so much as in a whispered hint, the emancipated intellect of Mr. Robinson out of much travail delivered this:

"It might be shown that the horrors of the present war are largely due to the perpetuation of outworn institutions, of discredited ambitions, and of illicit national aspirations."

Were the "outward institutions" German? Were the "discredited ambitions" those of his Majesty William II? Were those "illicit national aspirations" the aspirations of Germany for world dominion?

Of Mr. Robinson's writings, prior to the time that Boards of Education began to show a lively and painful interest in them, and he began the revision of text-books indignantly kicked out of public schools, it might be said that at least there was little in them to which the Kaiser could have taken exception.

Professor Robinson gives us his word that: "In the free expansion of friendly conversation, I, at least, can deal damnation round in a way fully to justify my claim to be a patriot." Being, therefore, a patriot, on the strength of dealing out damnation in words, Prof. Robinson could not, of course, have openly implied that the horrors of the war were largely due to the outworn institutions, discredited ambitions and illicit national aspirations of Russia, England and France. Prof. Robinson surely was not pro-German. Intellectually emancipated, possibly; academically neutral, perhaps; morally neuter, maybe. But certainly not pro-Hun.

The very fact that Professor Robinson, after his long, laborious, lonely pilgrimage over the stony road of academic learning, arrived at such a rarefied intellectual altitude where he could impassionately look down upon and contemplate the coarse mobs swayed by vulgar human passions, swept off their feet by "waves of national emotion," moved by such evil working forces as religious beliefs, faith in God, confidence in a life hereafter—whence with impartial because remote vision he could see "the chief states of Europe rushing at one another's throats in the name of nationality"—the very fact that he attained exalted heights where he was lifted above purely national emotions, national prejudices, would in itself preclude any possibility of Prof. Robinson's having any partiality, any biased sympathy, any predilection, any grovelling adoration for Germany. The man who had risen above national emotion so far as the land of his own birth was concerned certainly could not entertain a "soft spot" for the Huns.

PROPAGANDA PLANS OF HUNS

The official German propaganda was scientific. It was subtle. It was, to a surprising degree, able. To create hostile sentiment toward the Allies and favorable sentiment toward Germany, the Imperial representatives sought as their most effective agents men of American birth and of reputable standing. The history of Hun propaganda shows that they did not fail altogether in their enlisting of "distinguished" aides. As has been shown in a previous article in this series, that form of German propaganda which aimed at the creation of anti-British feeling was inaugurated shortly after the Spanish-American war, while the propaganda which aimed to poison the fonts of American learning began twenty-five years before the outbreak of the European war. Anticipating success in her war against the Allies, imperial Germany proposed to carry on her insidious efforts toward ultimate world dominion and commercial supremacy, and toward this end laid out a propaganda campaign which was to continue in the United States and other countries after the conclusion of peace. The imperial government planned an international wireless news service, to compete with the established agencies, which was to be launched as an American affair, and the directorship of which was promised to William Bayard Hale, secret director of Hun propaganda in the United States. News distribution agencies, news syndicates and newspapers were also to be secretly purchased or subsidized by the imperial government. The imperial government proposed thus to secure control of American public opinion. In this propaganda American colleges and schools were not to be neglected by the crafty Huns.

This information was accorded me by no less a person than one of the chief directors of Hun propaganda in the United States.

My informant was Dr. Karl A. Mechlenburg, chief of the Translation Bureau of the official German propaganda organization located at 1123 Broadway, New York.

"Our propaganda in America," said Dr. Mechlenburg, genially expanding one day in 1915 after the report of German victories, "will continue and even widen on a bigger scale after the war. It is our purpose and intention to secure control, as far as we can, of concerns publishing text-books for use in public schools, and likewise to mobilize and influence all writers of school text-books. We propose especially to control the preparation of school histories, so that American children will not be taught that Germany began this war, or was guilty of unwarranted atrocities in this war. . . . By controlling the preparation of school histories we can begin to make Americans from the time they are children see the German point of view."

In these school text-books, according to the German plan, Germany was to be glorified and the Allied nations disparaged; by creating admiration for her supremacy and achievements friendship and partiality toward Germany were to be fostered while hostility and antagonism toward the Allies, especially England, was to be stimulated; the causes of the war were either to be beclouded or laid at the doors of the Allies, and Germany was to be exculpated of all original blame for precipitating the world catastrophe.

[In my next article, I shall endeavor to give an adequate analysis of the amazing propaganda put into American public schools under the guise of a text book, and show how Dr. Robinson, in 1918 and after school boards throughout the country had suddenly evinced a lively and uncomfortable interest in his works, undertook a task of surgically drastic and heroic expurgation and revision such as finds no literary parallel even in the feat of rendering the "Arabian Nights" innocuous reading for children. The spectacle of this dignified historian qualifying impromptu as an intellectual "lightning-change artist" will probably cause a sensation, if not consternation, in the jealously competitive circles of vaudeville. Dr. Robinson's sleight-of-hand, turn-about conversion, under the exigencies of a changed and painfully exacting market, affords an illuminating commentary upon the intellectual integrity and philosophic sincerity of the eminent historian who now presents himself to the American audience as one of the "advanced leaders" of "The New School for Social Research."]

(To be Continued)

Training Department, J. & T. Cousins Co., Brooklyn. Soldiers after intensive training make good shoes.

Regular production going on while training, Independent Pneumatic Tool Co., Aurora, Ill.

Industrial Training

(Continued from page 8)

as the U. S. Training Service, a division of the Department of Labor, which took over and continued the work. The U. S. Training Service has an adequate field force and, with a part of this force, is cooperating with the national organizations in each major trade in developing the best possible method for present and future training. In its Bulletin No. 8, the Training Service declares that careful analysis seems to justify the judgment that more than half of the 10,000,000 factory workers are producing less than one-half of a fair day's output, mostly for reasons that can be corrected by training. It is also found that training is as much needed in the simpler trades as in the more difficult, though more quickly given in the former. In the latter, great numbers of workers have been admitted who lacked the peculiar aptitudes required for success therein. There is a place in which any worker may succeed. Society owes each assistance in finding that place, whether it is in making rubber shoes, cotton cloth, candy, boots and shoes, paper boxes, machinery, fine instruments, silverware, or clerking in a store. This is now being recognized and acted upon by employers in each of these trades.

The only altogether precious possession of any nation is the spirit, brain and muscle of its people. In the United States this is worth today in terms of mere money, about $350,000,000,000. This equals the entire tangible wealth of the nation and is five times more than all our other natural resources combined, and yet our little minds have been worrying about coal and iron and water powers, utterly negligent until now of the supreme possession.

It is known now that by a little training of the right kind almost any employer can get from 20 to 40 per cent. more from his present workers to their increased satisfaction and comfort, for wage earners, like others, hate to do what they do poorly and enjoy doing what they do well.

If training increases per capita output only 20 per cent. it will give $1,000,000,000. more labor return from the present payrolls, with an equal saving in overhead, being a total of $2,000,000,000. annually with which to make the tripartite adjustment for which the country waits in agony; a lowering of the cost of living by reduced prices to the consumer, the continuance of high wages and the safeguarding of profits. As consumers pay at least twice the shop cost, the $2,000,000,000 shop saving here contemplated would be at least $4,000,000,000 to consumers. Said Secretary Wilson, "the employer terest in securing the greatest amount of producand employee have a mutual—not identical—intion from a given amount of labor." With the new margins coming from increased per capita production, we may hear less of profit sharing and isms, for the wage will be high and a just capitalization (as it always has been theoretically) of the worker's share in profits.

As this is written, a representative of the U. S. Employment Service, says—"Last week there were 9,000 idle mechanics in a small New England district. The railroads wanted 800 locomotive repair men but we could recommend for their consideration only 210 out of the 9,000. The roads wanted hundreds of boiler makers, but only one in ten of the boiler makers who applied was good enough." Of all these men said he, "Thousands are *almost* good enough, they just miss it." A nation that leaves vast numbers of its employed or unemployed wage earners, "almost good enough" when they can easily be made plenty good enough, should pray for mercy on bended knees.

How poor workers can quickly be made excellent is shown by two charts elsewhere. In the first, a worker is shown at his accustomed place in the shop producing for five weeks 195 pieces per hour. He was transferred to the training room and in one week reached 300 pieces, and in three more weeks 405 pieces, thereby doubling his income. The company is as happy as the man as its saving in overhead equals the worker's increase in wage. In the second chart an experiment was made with two men who were thought to be alike in all respects. The one represented by the dotted line was left in the shop and averaged 121 pieces without improvement for 28 days. The other was taken into the training department and in one week reached 250 pieces, and by the end of the 23 days 330. Each had tool trouble. Little was made of this in the shop but the training room is a laboratory for all things and the study of the tool trouble there brought an improvement to the whole shop. All places of employment now promise to become also places of education. Workers will learn while they earn.

Lest it may seem that educators have been spoken of inconsiderately, the following quotation is given from *one of the most distinguished of them:

> "Is not the plan of vocational education here suggested the only one that will assist our workers in modern highly specialized productive enterprises.
>
> . . . . Given opportunities of the kind here suggested, we are justified in assuming that the more ambitious and gifted boys will push on from level to level. As they reach twenty-two to thirty years of age some of them will become aware of their possession of natural powers of leadership. They will see possibilities of becoming foremen, inspectors, managers, inventors, technical specialists. They will attend special upgrading schools, correspondence schools, or else take a year or two off to go to a technical school or college in the field of their special interest."

The U. S. Training Service solicits correspondence from any who may be helped through its service. This Service will possibly be discontinued with other war activities of the Government at the end of the present fiscal year, June 30. It is thought by many to be of such great consequence in the following twelve months of reconstruction as to make its continuance for one more year by Congress highly desirable.

*Dr. David Snedden, Prof. of the Psychology of Education, Teacher's College, Columbia University and President of The Nat'l Society for Vocational Education,—SCHOOL & SOCIETY, Dec. 28, 1918.

Classroom in Training Department, General Electric Co., Fort Wayne, Ind.—Upgrading promising employees in shop arithmetic, blue print reading, safety, health, shop economics, etc. Also in the machine training room.

A Model Training Department—Several returned soldiers being trained as operators on engine lathes, milling machines, shapers, drill presses and hand automatic screw machines. Also upgrading old employees.

The Red Glow of Bolshevism

A NEW "SCOURGE OF GOD" MAKES MORALITY IMMORALITY; WOULD ABOLISH EVERY PHASE OF SOCIAL STRUCTURE; MARXISM APPLIED IN DICTATORSHIP OF PROLETARIAT

By DAVID GOLDSTEIN, in the Current Issue of "The Columbiad"

SO lurid is the red glow in the sky of Russia that the eyes of the whole world are centered on the land of the Czars. There is fear in every country that Bolshevism will over-run the world as the "Scourge of God" with his hordes over-ran the center of civilization some fifteen centuries ago.

The nickname, Bolshevism, given to the modern "Scourge of God," has somewhat obscured its identity. Yet, to those who know, Bolshevism is only another name for Socialism—Socialism applied. It is carrying out the doctrine of Marx and Engels as set forth in "The Communist Manifesto," "Das Kapital," "Anti-Duhring" and the other authoritative writings of these fathers of modern Socialism. It is the self-same Socialism that Pope Leo XIII condemned so long ago as 1878, when from his watchtower at the center of the moral world he warned civilized peoples, Catholic and non-Catholic alike, of the movement that was gathering its force for a vital assault upon religion, the family, private property, and the commonwealth.

A REVOLT AGAINST A REVOLT

It took a Leo to drive back the fifth century "Scourge of God," and it will take the teachings and the practices set forth by the Thirteenth Leo to overcome the Scourge of Bolshevism: "When they shall have recognized that the Church of Christ is possessed of a power to stave off the pest of Socialism, too mighty to be found in human enactments or in the strong hand of the civil power or in military force, let them re-establish that Church in the condition and liberty needed in order to be able to exercise her most salutary influence for the good of society in general" (Leo XIII "Concerning Modern Errors" December 28, 1878).

What then is this mighty power of which the nations may well be afraid? It is a well nigh universal reaction against political tyranny, economic extortion, social iniquity. It is a blind attempt to remedy these evils by a proletarian domination of society. It seeks by its programme the confiscation of private capital, the abolition of civil and religious authority in marriage; the absolute, compulsory secularization of education; and by a promise of more of this world's goods and greater leisure it seeks to unite the power of the working class under a dictatorship of its own.

In Russia Bolshevism found a most fertile field for manifesting itself upon a national scale. It was in Russia, where despotic rule had not been shorn of any of its power by a parliament, that the proletariat did not have to pass through the stage of parliamentarism on its journey from Capitalism to Socialism. The advantage was this, the Bolsheviki had not been tamed down, as were their comrades across the border in the Reichstag by their long fight within a parliamentary body where discussion, personal contact with representatives of other parties, passing upon specific measures, appointments, appropriations, and the other realities of legislative life lead to reform rather than to revolution. No, the red glow of Bolshevism had not lost what the Russian Premier calls its "almost exclusively agitation habits" as had their comrades, in some more favored political lands. Ah! but the Russians knew their Marx.

Just a glance at the speed with which "the dictatorship of the proletariat" sprung into power will show how well the Bolsheviki know their Marx. When the Czar was overthrown and the Constituent Assembly was organized the Marxians found themselves in the minority. They knew that to meet on equal terms with the representatives of other classes of their countrymen would inevitably lead to compromise on specific legislative statutes. "No Compromise, No Political Trading," was their made-in-Germany shibboleth. It had not been carried out by the majority of the German Socialists, but the Russians would carry it to its logical end—a real Socialist revolution. So with bayonets and machine guns the determined Bolsheviki—a minority—broke up the democratic Constituent Assembly, of which they were a part, declaring parliamentary government to be "a deception upon the working class." Then was their proletarian mission entered upon. They set up Soviets, councils made up of delegates representing shop workers, peasants, and soldiers. What then to do?

David Goldstein (in car) and Sergeant Corbett (on ground) about to leave San Francisco on their 13,000 mile speaking trip.

SEEK CLASS-LESS SOCIETY

To a proper understanding of the Bolsheviki, it is necessary to know, first of all, that the Socialist aim is a "class-less society." It is to classes that Socialists attribute all the evils of society; the very "evil" existence of the State itself; the subjugation and exploitation of the workers; the domination of the workers by capitalism. Socialists hold that but one class can justly claim the right to exist at all, namely, the working class, whose historic mission is to wrest control of government from the hands of the property owning class and thus to "expropriate the expropriators." To this end, says Nikolai Lenine, Premier of the Russian Soviet Republic, "we must adhere to the brief, sharp, exact and vivid formula of Marx, *the dictatorship of the proletariat.*"

So it was that Russia reacted immediately from the tyranny of one despotism to the tyranny of another.

Since "no other class has any right," upon gaining control of the government at Petrograd Lenine and his followers established, forthwith, a "Council of the People's Commissaries." One of its divisions, "The Supreme Council of National Economy," was given authority to execute the will of the proletariat—to "confiscate, requisition, sequestrate, and syndicate different branches of industry and commerce." Complete expropriation has not yet been carried out.

A stroke of genius was revealed in the make-up of the delegate body of Soviets. One delegate is elected to represent each thousand workmen, and one delegate to represent each one hundred and twenty-five Red Guards; thus the vote of a Red Guard equals the vote of eight workmen. The *provincial* Soviet representation is so arranged that the vote of less than half a million of the Red Guards equals that of a hundred millions or more of peasants living in the Russian "volosts"—groups of villages. Thus the dictatorship of the proletariat is amply safeguarded in what Eugene V. Debs is pleased to call "the first real attempt at actual democratic administration in the history of the world."

Some interesting experiences in *freedom* have been made by the Bolsheviki that led to the discovery "that behind the screen of liberty lurks, in fact, freedom—to poison and bring confusion into the minds of the masses." Therefore the utter abolition of free press became necessary to the liberty of the proletariat, by the proletariat. Great is confusion confounded!

Likewise morality has become immorality. Religious institutions are forbidden to own property, or to "enjoy any prerogative or subsidy whatsoever." The teaching of religion is forbidden in any private or public school.

Surely the attack upon every department of organic society is complete. What then shall we see in devastated Russia but the lurid glow of red ripe Socialism, running its blind course to chaos. To Catholics the call comes to advocate the principles and to promote the practices set forth by Pope Leo XIII. Only so shall our well beloved America be safe from the "Scourge of God."

Tyrrel Print, New York.

The National
Civic Federation Review

.IV. NEW YORK, APRIL 25, 1919 No. 13

AMERICAN LABOR MISSION RETURNS

AMUEL GOMPERS DESCRIBES AT NATIONAL CIVIC FEDERATION LUNCHEON WHAT WAS ACCOMPLISHED ABROAD AND MENACE OF BOLSHEVISM—TAFT LAUDS WORK

LOVE and respect, keen interest and en-usiasm, marked the ception and luncheon given on April 12 st, at the Holland ouse, New York ty, to Samuel Gomrs and his fellow legates of the American Federation of bor's foreign mison, on their return om the Paris Conrence. More than ree hundred men d women, including illiam Howard aft, former President of the United ates, assembled at e invitation of The ational Civic Federation, to do honor the veteran labor ader and his assoates and to hear at st hand of the wonerful work done road for internaonal industrial ace.

Whole-hearted apause and cheers punctuated the speeches made V. Everit Macy, president of the Federation, o presided at the luncheon; President Taft; mes Duncan, president of the Granite Cutters' ternational Association, one of the mission, the masterly address of Mr. Gompers. United endorsement was given by those present the expressed sentiments in favor of the ague of Nations, the recital of what had been complished toward improving labor conditions throughout the world and the denunciation Bolshevism. All three topics commanded the sest attention.

At the guest table, in addition to the speaks, were: Mme. Catherine Breshkovskaya, "the tle grandmother of the Russian revolution"; illiam Green, secretary-treasurer, United Mine orkers of America, (mission member); Frank ffy, secretary Brotherhood of Carpenters and ners, (mission member); Major August Belont; Miss Maude Wetmore; Mrs. F. Lothrop es, Boston; Otto H. Kahn. Also present was Major G. H. Berry, president, International Printing Pressmen, who had been associated with the labor mission, though not a member. John R. Alpine, general president, United Association of Plumbers and Steam Fitters, one of the labor mission, was not present at the luncheon, having returned before the other delegates and having gone on to his headquarters in Chicago.

LUNCHEON OF WELCOME TO SAMUEL GOMPERS AND THE FOREIGN COMMISSION OF THE AMERICAN FEDERATION OF LABOR, GIVEN IN THE HOLLAND HOUSE, NEW YORK, APRIL 12, 1919, BY THE NATIONAL CIVIC FEDERATION. THE HONOR GUESTS ARE IN THE BACKGROUND, STANDING.

"Whatever inconvenience you have suffered to-day," said Mr. Macy in introducing President Taft, the first speaker, "I hope you will excuse, for we have had less than twenty-four hours to prepare to welcome our returning delegates owing to the fact that the wireless on Mr. Gompers's steamer broke down. Some weeks ago the whole city turned out to welcome our returning soldiers. And I am sure, had we had the time, we would have had almost as large a celebration in welcoming Mr. Gompers and the other delegates, for their work has supplemented that of our military men in a most important way. Their endeavors in Europe as delegates to the International Conference on Labor have been an effort to make a permanent peace, and a peace that can be permanent only because it does justice to all nations. Therefore their work was as important, looking to the future as that of any of our military forces.

"There is no one in our country who is doing more at present to show us what relation and what burdens or what sacrifice and what spirit the American nation must have to maintain and help establish peace throughout the world, and there is no one who has done more to maintain a just peace in industry throughout the country as a whole than our well known and beloved citizen, President Taft."

MR. TAFT'S SPEECH

"Mr. Chairman, Mr. Gompers, gentlemen of the Commission, and members of the Civic Federation: It is the good nature of the Chairman and of Mr. Gompers, our chief guest, that enables me now to speak in an order that I am not entitled to have followed," said President Taft, "but, as you know, this was a hastily gotten up meeting and I am a bird of passage, a kind of a rotatory, gyratory animal, and Mr. Easley, with all that energy that he has frequently displayed, caught me on the wing. I could only come here with the condition that I should stay but a few minutes, but I was glad to come in order that I might bear witness to what I think is the debt of gratitude owing to Mr. Gompers and his associates in these labor commissions which have been to Europe during the war and who are now returning from their labors.

"It does not need any examination of history to know that Mr. Gompers and I have often been on opposite sides. My favorite form of addressing Mr. Gompers when we fall into correspondence is 'My dear Old Antagonist.' Nevertheless, I am sure we have mutual respect for each other and the arguments and the reasons and the bases of our positions on each side. And when I find myself with him, it is a gratification for me to say so.

"We have been through a great war, and it is a fact that with the resiliency of the American people, we are able to ignore or forget, and are able to minimize the lessons that we had to have from the war, and the experiences of other nations. There is nothing that this war has developed so much as the complete dependence of a nation in modern war upon labor. If labor deserts the cause, the country is gone. The war is fought not only in the trenches with the brave boys who are there, but in the fields of agriculture and especially in the manufactories and in the preparation of raw materials in the mine, which are so essential to carry on modern war, that we are all hoping may now disappear from the world. Therefore, it was of the utmost importance that in order to win this war for the benefit of world liberty and world independence, the laboring men should realize what the real issues were before them, and should stand up to those issues, and not be led away by the insidious propaganda which had been put out by a country that had been studying for half a century to make that propaganda effective.

"Few people realize how much we are indebted to Mr. Gompers and those associated with him in the American Federation of Labor for holding our own ranks of labor. And I fancy that there are few who understand what the commissions sent abroad, the labor commissions, have done and did do during the war in preserving the morale of the laboring men in France and Italy and England. Had that morale yielded to the influences that were wearing it out, nobody knows what the result of the war would have been. And it was through the encouragement that they received by the labor commissions that were sent over there and discussed with them and steered them properly and eliminated the vicious evil elements that were struggling for mastery among them, that we were able, with other factors of course—we were able to win the war as we did. I feel a debt of gratitude to those men who went over and maintained the patriotic and the conservative view that they advocated and put through, and feel a gratitude that I am delighted to come here and testify to.

"I have been the representative of the public appointed by a committee of national industrial manufacturers to sit on a National War Labor Board in which we attempted so far as we could, to maintain maximum production and avoid halts due to strikes and lockouts. So I have come again into association with both sides. I have had the privilege of hearing each side tell the truth to the other side, or, at least, what it conceived to be the truth, with a candor that left nothing to be desired certainly in openness of statement and eloquence of invective.

"But it shows the advantage of clearing away the bile in the body social and the body politic, and finally we got down to principles and induced twelve men to sign a statement of principles that when we began three weeks before, anybody but an optimist of the most ideal character would say was impossible. And we have attempted to do what we could in reaching the object of that National War Labor Board. The ranks of labor have by reason of this war become a much more important element in the community than they had been before. They have been convinced of their power, and it is of the highest importance that they should exercise such power as they believe to have with moderation and restraint, with a view to playing a part and playing their part right in the conduct of the government and the maintenance of society.

"I conceive it to be the duty of those who occupy a somewhat adverse position in that they are to divide the joint product of labor and capital, to realize the change from the old times, and that we must all, capitalists and laborites and the people between, welcome and encourage that part of labor which has a sense of responsibility for the entire government and for the country. And that is to be found in the ranks of organized labor and their present leaders.

"Now, this is not to say that I wish to express an agreement with my friend Gompers in respect to platforms and constructive views of very many kinds. As to those we doubtless differ. But there are certain things upon which I am sure we stand together, and one of them is that it is the duty of the employers to seek every means possible in adopting the rules, the terms, the wages and the environment in which working men are to work, to follow the rule that the workmen shall have the fullest opportunity for the freest consultation and expression of their opinions through men whom they select to represent them, because the great amount of industry is carried on with such great bodies of working men that it is impossible to have that personal contact that used to exist, and that personal confidence that used to exist where there were only ten or a dozen laborers and only one employer and perhaps the employer worked along with the laborers.

"That time has passed, and now the question is for the creation of a machinery by which the men engaged in the work shall have the full and freest opportunity to appoint their representatives and then to have those representatives consulted with respect to everything that is done. That is called industrial democracy.

"What does that mean? Does it mean that necessarily the laborers with their committees are to prevail simply by a vote of the laborer? No. That is not it. That has got to be reached by adjustment between the employer and the employee, and if it cannot, then there is a halt, then there is a waiting, then there is the exercise of what is called in our Board 'economic pressure.' But what we believe is—those of us who have had experience in this National War Labor Board—that in that industrial democracy so-called is meant that men who are to be affected by a change in conditions or by existing conditions in respect to which they ask a change, or in respect to which the employer contemplates a change, shall have an opportunity fully to bargain with him and fully to bring before him what those conditions are and what their views of those conditions are.

"And I verily believe that while that is not going to end controversies, because between people of adverse interests we must expect a controversy only to be settled by a sense of responsibility on both sides, what is referred to as collective bargaining makes greatly for advance in that direction. That I believe to be the position of Mr. Gompers and organized labor, or the American Federation of Labor. My experience in the National War Labor Board leads me fully to approve that principle, as we did approve it when the manufacturers and the working men signed that agreement through their representatives before this War Labor Board came on.

"I want to say personally for Mr. Gompers that I read his statements in respect to the war with profound admiration and gratitude, because there never came from him any doubtful word as to what must be done with reference to carrying through this war. No pro-German was ever able to gather from what he said any consolation in respect to the policy that this government was to pursue in fighting the war

The National Civic Federation Commission in London

(*From the London Daily Telegraph, March* 26, 1919)

T a period like the present, when Labour problems are giving rise to general unrest, the activities of the National Alliance of Employers and Employed will less command the attention of all interested industries of the country. The organiza- ame into existence three years ago with the fold object of promoting cordial cooperation all questions affecting labour and employ- the welfare of the workers generally, and :ating the reinstatement in civil occupations n who have been demobilized. In further- of its purpose, the alliance has rendered ent service. It embraces eleven employers' ations, representing between 8,000 and 9,- rms, and fifteen trade unions, aggregating ,000 workers. A commission from The Na- Civic Federation of America—an organ- n which has been engaged in similar work United States for many years—arrived in on a few days ago, and are to visit various of the country in order to inquire into trial matters. A hearty welcome was ex- d to the delegates last evening at a dinner was given in their honour by the alliance e Holborn Restaurant, under the chair- iip of the Right Hon. F. Huth Jackson. nembers of the commission who attended

. C. S. Barrett (vice-president of The Na- Civic Federation and chairman of the ers' Union, U. S. A.), Mr. Albert Farwell is, Mr. A. Parker Nevin, Mr. James W. van, M. E. A. Quarles, and Mr. Grant es. Among the general company were: Mr. utler Wright, Mr. F. L. Mayer, Mr. W. S. ell, and Mr. C. C. Williams, members of the rican Embassy, Colonel D. Carnegie, Sir rnon Firth, Bt., Mr. J. T. Clatworthy, and H. F. Dawtry.

fter the toasts of "The King" and "The ident of the United States" had been ured,

ne CHAIRMAN, in proposing "The National c Federation of America," mentioned that body had nearly completed twenty years of rm of social service which in its main fea- s had remained without change. It aimed arily at bringing "the best brains of rica" to the task of maintaining industrial e so far as possible by means of conferences een employers and wage earners. He ght the alliance might look forward to the re with much more confidence when they knew and realized the great work which had been done on similar lines in America by The National Civic Federation. (Hear, hear.) He regretted the absence of Mr. Samuel Gompers, who would have been present had he not been detained in Paris. The war had brought together all the nations which had fought for the cause of civilization and humanity, but none had been brought into closer brotherhood than England and America. (Hear, hear.) Now that peace was within sight it was for the citizens of both countries to see that this bond, created by the war, did not relax, and he could not conceive anything more calculated to perpetuate this spirit of comradeship than an affiliation on a definite and constitutional basis between such bodies as The National Civic Federation of America and the National Alliance of Employers and Employed. (Hear, hear.) The commission were to visit the great industrial centres of Swansea, Manchester, Liverpool, Glasgow, and Dundee. He trusted there would be in the future the spirit of real cooperation between Capital and Labour on an equitable basis for the general benefit of the whole community.

MR. JAMES W. SULLIVAN, who replied, said the primary principle of The National Civic Federation was prevention of waste in the relations between wage-payers and wage-receivers. In seeking membership among employers and employed the Federation in effect had said: "Why waste time in long-distance sparring? Why keep up misunderstandings? Why fight through the Press or any third parties? Be sensible; be a little democratic; get together; get your legs under the same conference table—(laughter); look each other in the eye, and see how and where you can begin. You are urged to do this systematically, for good business of course, but what is more, for the immediate peace of society, and possibly for some ultimate assistance to a higher civilization." (Cheers.) An undoubted benefit through the Federation had been the promotion of acquaintanceship among people of various interests and social ideals, and especially among the more active men on the opposite sides of the wage question. The Federation had sent three commissions to Europe. The first came to study municipal as compared with private ownership, and the operation of public utilities. The second investigated social insurance, and the third was inquiring into British methods of reconstruction.

MR. ANDREW PARKER NEVIN, who next replied, said he had always believed that public opinion was sovereign and the keystone of life in Great Britain. He had been profoundly impressed by the scholarly, constructive, and sincere utterances of the newspapers here regarding the Labour issues. The new spirit of industry was not constructed geographically. It was sympathetic and reciprocal. Industry in America and England could never again harbour narrowness and prejudice, but must be broad, liberal, and enlightened. (Hear, hear.) Men and women workers were human and divine, and must be treated as such. Personally, he had not the slightest doubt that the genius of Great Britain would work out her present problems of commerce, labour, and industry. They in America were watching with great interest and real sympathy. They would never forget what the men of Britain and her Fleet did from 1914, which made it possible for them to discuss the reconstruction of industry and gave the right to men and women to live peaceful lives and to work out their own destiny. (Cheers.)

MR. A. FARWELL BEMIS also returned thanks.

In the absence of the Hon. C. Mayer, the toast of "The National Alliance of Employers and Employed" was submitted by Mr. E. A. QUARLES (secretary of the commission).

MR. W. A. APPLETON, in responding, said their American friends had come to this country at at time when we were troubled by much confused thought and utterance. We were hearing much of rights, without men seeming to comprehend the fact that all rights were circumscribed by other rights, and that these could never be satisfied except the spirit of compromise entered into our arrangements. If ever compromise was to be effective it must be organised and lead to legal control. The alliance recognised this, and endeavoured to promote understanding. It had had opposition, due sometimes to misunderstanding, sometimes to animosity. It was overcoming this because the mass of men understood the need for production. Our troubles were to-day no worse than those which assailed Britain in the seventeenth century. We came out of that, and we shall come out of this. (Hear, hear.) The problem was a world-problem, and the Anglo-Saxon-speaking peoples were under an obligation to collaborate. If they did so the world would overcome the difficulties and dangers which faced it. (Hear, hear.)

The toast of "The Chairman" brought the proceedings to a close.

Sapping the Foundations of Society

By RALPH M. EASLEY

PART II

the last number of THE NATIONAL CIVIC ERATION REVIEW *there was published the half of a statement prepared for the Indus- Relations Commission of 1914 on conditions existing as related to industry. "The situa- today is the same, only a little more so," I in introducing Part I.*

the first instalment I discussed "Legitimate est," and began the analysis of "Manufac- d Unrest." In this Part II. I complete the nd topic and give the additional chapters: Wall Street or Socialism Gaining Control of Sources of Public Opinion?" and "Socialism ndustrial and Social Progress."

SOCIALISM AMONG EAST SIDE IMMIGRANTS

WHAT may fairly be assumed to be the effect upon the immigrants arriving here from Russia, Poland, Hungary, y and other countries of Europe, when they are met at Ellis Island by socialists and the Industrial Workers of the World and told that they have gone from bad to worse in coming to America? These preachers of the gospel of despair inform the newcomers to our shores that conditions for working men and women in the United States are infinitely worse than in any of the monarchical countries which they have left; that these "wage-slaves" receive starvation wages and are worked night and day, under the lash; that there is no such thing as justice for the working man in the courts and no freedom of speech; and that capitalism controls everything.

A man who worked for years among the socialists on the East Side in New York wrote me that at one time he had thought there was no higher ideal for one to strive for than a socialist commonwealth and no more sacred work to devote one's life to than converting people to the socialist ideas. He said that after many years of work in the socialist movement on the East Side he became sceptical in regard to the idea of a socialist commonwealth and the propaganda in its behalf. He had become convinced that it was a disgrace for the East Side and a misfortune to the young immigrants from whose ranks "the cause" recruited the greatest part of its following. He pointed out that in Russia, the country supplying the greater part of the East Side population, to be a socialist means the jeopardizing of one's liberty and quite often of one's life. A socialist, therefore, in Russia is looked upon as a hero and a martyr. The immigrants, having that idea of a socialist, naturally accepted as gospel everything they heard in this country from the socialist speakers or that they read in the socialist newspapers. He added: "The socialist propaganda all over means discontent and class hatred. In order to make the workingman dissatisfied with his lot the socialist agitator draws a gloomy, disheartening picture of the life of the toiler, and in order to enrage him against the employers the capitalist is pictured as a terrible monster, a vampire sucking the blood of thousands of working men and spending his long hours of leisure in wild bacchanalian revels.''

SOCIALISM IN THE CHURCHES

In the church field, also, we find socialists and syndicalists, both open and ''surreptitious''. While the Socialist Party itself has little or no use for the ''Christian Socialists,'' as they style themselves, the latter are just as loyal to the socialist program as is Eugene Debs, whom they supported for President, and their statements about industrial conditions are just as reckless as those which appear in the most radical socialist publications.

During the last few years several of the Protestant denominations have organized social service departments, some of them very largely dominated by the socialist contingent within these bodies. The secretary of one such department, at a convention of the religious denomination to which he belonged, made an address in which he paid the following tribute to Haywood and the other sabotage and violence preaching leaders of the Industrial Workers of the World:

> Syndicalism, as every investigation has shown, finds a field only in our industrial centres where immigrants are herded. Without a vote, strange, bewildered, 'put upon,' deserted by the Church, the labor union, and the socialists, it was syndicalism which went to them in their distress and gave them courage and hope. All honor to the I. W. W. leaders that they were found at the hottest point of the industrial conflict!

Another feature at this convention was a radical socialist speech by a western bishop who was then president of what is known as the Christian Socialist league. This bishop was killed in an automobile accident and his successor in office, before his consecration, proudly announced that he had been taken into membership by the socialist local in his home town.

An illustration of the recklessness of speech of practically all clergymen who espouse socialism is the following extract from a sermon by the Rt. Rev. Theodore I. Reese, Bishop of Southern Ohio, published in *The American Socialist* of January 23, 1915. In this sermon, which was preached in the Cathedral of Sts. Peter and Paul, Chicago, described by *The American Socialist* as being ''in the heart of the slum district'' of that city, Bishop Reese said:

> Conditions today are almost exactly similar to those immediately preceding the French Revolution. There is the same thoughtless gayety among the upper classes, the same widespread misery among the lower; and today as then, there is a great deal of superficial interest taken in the investigation of conditions by the upper classes.
>
> Marie Antoinette and her court at Versailles dressed themselves as shepherdesses, and thought that they were solving the problem of life. And today 'slumming' and dabbling in social economics are fashionable among the rich.
>
> I am not saying that another French Revolution is sure to follow; I am saying that the conditions are similar.

That a man of education in a post of large responsibility and influence could permit himself to declare from the pulpit that conditions in this country today are like those in France prior to the French Revolution is unaccountable except as testimony to the curious effect of the socialist mental attitude upon the power to see correctly or state dispassionately the facts either of history or of present conditions. The absurdity of this particular parallel has rarely been shown more effectively than in a review of Brooks Adams's ''Theory of Social Revolution'', in *The New York Times Review of Books*, December 7, 1913; and it is quite likely that the bishop had read this book by the brilliant but erratic Brooks Adams. That review, while it answers the allusions of Bishop Reese to the French Revolution, refutes so many other false views held by clergymen of socialistic tendencies that I quote it in full:

> Mr. Adams's narrative of the French Revolution is thrilling, and its interpretation is instructive. But only those with whom the wish is father of the thought can go with him in applying the French precedent to our case. The differences lie on the surface, and the parallel is obscure and forced. In the French Revolution the poor ate grass, and slept on mud floors. Their poverty was not their fault, for their substance was exhausted by taxes which went to feed the luxury of incompetent and corrupt rulers. The wealthy could purchase nobility and the nobles were exempt from taxation. The church owned a third of the lands and took most of what the tax collectors left. The landlord and the cultivator divided equally a mere third of the produce of the land. This was the regime which the courts upheld, and which the Royalists were too dull to see must be reformed. It was despair which drove the wretched peasants to revolt. How can it be held that there is any likeness to our conditions? In our happy land the taxes are just what the electorate makes them. Over six million individual farmers hold over 800,000,000 acres of land and levy their tribute upon consumers. Of privilege before the law there is no trace, and the free people have just destroyed the industrial privilege which they created. In France conditions were about the worst the world ever knew. Our conditions challenge the best to surpass them. Our poor enjoy comforts or even luxuries which Kings of old might envy them.
>
> If this picture is thought too glowing it should be remembered that while the Frenchmen of the time of Louis were oppressed, and helpless without violence, our affairs are entirely in the hands of those who are complaining. The Frenchmen could not use the ballot to remedy their conditions. Their wrongs were part of the system which the courts defended. Our wrongs are the creation of those who have voted for what exists, or who have not used the ballot to destroy it. The laws are made by elective lawmakers. It is the fault of the electorate if incapable legislators pass laws whose interpretation baffles ingenuity and brings the courts into disrepute. Mr. Adams ventures to say that the courts defend the capitalists, when it is notorious that capitalist organizations are prostrate before the law, and that if a shred of them survive it is because there is not ingenuity to destroy them without doing greater damage. On the other hand, while the railway trusts, and the industrial trusts, are forbidden and dissolved by the law the statutes make exceptions in favor of the working class. The President signs a law preventing their prosecution, and laws are proposed to make their offendings no crime, without even taking the verdict of a jury upon it. The industrial system which Mr. Adams arraigns as capitalistic is such because all are capitalists, or may be. Mr. Carnegie had forty millionaire partners. The billion dollar trust which succeeded him has twice forty thousand stockholders, including thousands of workers in the trust's shops. One eighth of the entire railway capitalization is held by insurance companies, of which there are 20,000,000 policy holders. Nine million depositors in savings banks own four billions' worth of securities unknown at the French Revolution. If the existing industrial system were abolished the world could not feed nor clothe its present population. There are multitudes alive who would not have come into being but for the system of organizing and financing industry which is represented as an outrage on the poor.

There are socialist Sunday schools, with no suggestion of religious training, entirely devoted to teaching the children of working people class hatred, through systematic ''lessons'', songs, pictures and violent attacks upon all owners of capital and the system which guarantees the right of private property. At the spring festival of socialist Sunday schools, held in Carnegie Hall, Sunday, May 4, 1913, there were over seven hundred children of all nationalities present in gala dress, affording no aspect of poverty or of being the underfed, anaemic or crippled products of capitalist greed. The psychology of the gathering is well shown by the following report in *The World* of May 5, 1913:

> "How many good rebels are there?" cried Prof. Kendrick Shedd of Rochester, turning to the seven hundred children of the socialist Sunday schools of New York, who yesterday after-

Menace of Recognizing the Russian Soviets

ON LEAGUE CLUB'S COMMITTEE ON STUDY OF BOLSHEVISM WARNS AGAINST MOVE ABROAD AND WORK OF MISSION HERE

er alert and patriotic, the Union League of New York City sounds a warning to the n and the authorities at Washington against roposed recognition of the Russian Soviet of government. Through its Committee on tudy of Bolshevism, the chairman of which chibald E. Stevenson, formerly of the Mili- Intelligence, the Club has forwarded a re- on conditions to our diplomatic representa- at the Paris Peace Conference, the Attor- eneral, and to every Senator and Repre- ive.

s report, in addition to being signed by tevenson, is signed by Robert C. Morris heodore F. Sanxay. Its text and the ac- mying resolutions follow:

HE Committee on the Study of Bolshevism feels that it is necessary to report certain international phases of the sub- committed to it, which should engage the ghtful consideration of the members of this . Evidence is daily accumulating which ates that the representatives of the Ameri- people at Paris are considering more and favorably the question of giving recogni- to the Russian Soviet Republic. This ques- is brought forcibly to our attention by a item which appears in the issue of the *New Times* for April 8th, 1919, from which we the following:

> Ludwig C. A. K. Martens, the Bolshevist envoy ho hopes to be Ambassador to the United States, established permanent offices in the Tower Building, at 110 West Fortieth Street, yesterday. The offices are to be known officially as The Russian Soviet Bureau in the United States.

he article further states that one of the pur- s of the Bureau is "to re-establish trade ions between the United States and Russia, prepare the way for ultimate recognition." nswer to the question, "Have Mr. Martens's entials been acknowledged by the State De- ment?" Mr. Nuorteva is quoted as saying, t yet. I imagine that the State Depart- t, before acting in the matter, must first nunicate with Paris."

appears, therefore, that an unofficial diplo- c mission has been established in New York by the Russian Soviet Republic. It is ap- ntly well supplied with funds, for the Bu- has taken an entire floor in the office-build- referred to. Its commercial department is ed by Mr. A. A. Heller; the legal depart- t is in charge of Morris Hillquit; the Chan- ry is under the direction of Gregory Wein- , who was formerly editor of the *Novy Mir;* ailway department is in charge of Professor V. Lomonosoff, and the diplomatic depart- t is in charge of Santeri Nuorteva, who erto has conducted the Bolshevik propa- la in the United States.

e desire to call your attention to the Official hevik communique received from Moscow on same day, which is reprinted in the *Evening* for April 8th, 1919, as follows:

> On the Archangel front fighting occurred near Tcheriserskoe, the statement said. In the region of Peliatsek we advanced twelve miles, capturing several fortified enemy positions. West of Obozerskoe, enemy attacks against Ozerki were frustrated.

ur troops are the enemy referred to in this munique.

hese two items of news show that a condition s in the foreign relations of this country h is unique in its history. Never before has vernment with which the armed forces of the United States have been engaged in battle, openly established a mission within our borders for the purpose of carrying on propaganda looking towards its recognition.

The American representatives at Paris have chosen to send a diplomatic mission to Russia, the exact purpose of which has not been officially disclosed, consisting, according to report, of William C. Bullitt, Lincoln Steffens and Walter E. Weyl. This commission has recently returned to Paris and is reported to have expressed itself in favor of a recognition of the Russian Soviet Republic. Your Committee believes, therefore, that the question of the recognition of the present de facto government of Russia deserves the thoughtful consideration of every citizen who holds in esteem the institutions of the United States. We therefore direct your attention to the nature of the government which seeks recognition.

As has been pointed out in the previous reports submitted to the Club by this Committee, the present Russian Government is a class government. It is in no sense representative of the people of Russia. It was created and maintained by the armed forces of the Russian Communist Party, which dispersed at the point of the bayonet the constituent assembly elected through the suffrage of the whole Russian people. It is committed to the proposition of the expropriation of all capitalists and the permanent destruction of the Bourgeoisie. The government set up by Nikolai Lenine and his followers, is a Socialistic State founded upon the principles of the first Internatinale, and dedicated to the proposition that class rule shall maintain throughout the world.

The international policies of the Soviet Republic are written into its constitution. That document sets forth the rights and duties of the workers as follows:

> To keep in mind always and everywhere the sacred duty of liberating labor from the domination of capital, and to strive for the establishment of a world-embracing fraternal league of working people.
>
> In proclaiming these rights and duties the Russian Socialist Republic of the Soviets calls upon the working classes of the entire world to accomplish their task to the very end, and in the faith that the Socialist ideal will soon be achieved, to write upon their flags the old battle cry of the working people. PROLETARIANS OF ALL LANDS UNITE! LONG LIVE THE SOCIALIST WORLD REVOLUTION!

The document further states that it is the duty of the workers,

> To fight everywhere and without sparing their strength for the complete power of the working classes, and to stamp out all attempts to restore the dominion of the despoilers and oppressors.

The purpose of this government is made still clearer in the preamble of the same document, as follows:

> In order to put an end to every ill that oppresses humanity and in order to secure to labor all the rights belonging to it, we recognize that it is necessary to destroy the existing social structure, which rests upon private property in the soil and the means of production, in the spoliation and oppression of the laboring masses, and to substitute for it a Socialist structure. Then the whole earth, its surface and its depths, and all the means and instruments of production, created by the toil of the laboring classes, will belong by right of common property to the whole people, who are united in a fraternal association of laborers.

The international character of the Russian Soviet Republic is further emphasized by the following provision of its constitution:

> In its efforts to create a league—free and voluntary, and for that reason all the more complete and secure—of the working classes of all the peoples of Russia, the Soviet Republic declared itself a federal republic and offered to the laborers and peasants of every nation the opportunity to enter as members with equal rights into the fraternal family of the Republic of Soviets (through action taken) independently in the plenipotentiary sessions of their Soviets, to any extent and in whatever form they might wish.

It was for this reason that the Congress of Soviets of the United States held in New York City during the month of January of this year was called the Pan Colonial Congress of Soviets. This provision of the Russian constitution purports to give the right to American citizens to organize Soviets within our own boundaries and by their independent action to become citizens of the Russian Soviet Republic.

We are thus brought face to face with the proposition of admitting to the society of nations by recognition, a de facto government which has written into its constitution the duty of stimulating, encouraging and assisting revolutions in all countries of the world. The mere statement of such a proposition would of itself seem sufficient to render the recognition of the Russian Soviet Republic impossible. However, many forces have been set at work to accomplish this purpose. The fear of the spread of Bolshevism through Central Europe has clouded the judgment of many statesmen. It has been argued that should the present Russian Government be recognized, it would discontinue the world-wide propaganda of revolution which it has set in motion. But such a hope cannot be entertained because it would involve a violation of its fundamental law. Your Committee therefore suggests the necessity of considering what effect the recognition of the Russian Soviet Republic would have upon the people and the Government of the United States:

Agents of the Soviet Republic would of necessity be received officially in this country and be protected in their activities by diplomatic custom and international law. The use of the diplomatic service by the Imperial German Government in working against the interests of the United States at a time when it was supposedly a friendly power, is an indication of what may be expected from a representative of a Government which is committed to the policy of stimulating revolution in the country to which he is accredited.

The experience of the United States with one representative of a revolutionary government should be sufficient to teach her statesmen not to repeat the same error. We refer to the reception by the United States of Edmond C. Genet, Minister Plenipotentiary of the Revolutionaries of France. This Minister of the French Revolutionary Government, immediately upon his arrival in the United States on the 8th of April, 1793, began a campaign for the violation of the neutrality of the United States in the war then existing between France and Great Britain and her then allies, and to appeal to the people of the United States over the protest of President Washington, to justify his acts, which almost involved this country in a war with Great Britain.

It would require but little imagination to believe that the representatives of the Bolshevik Government of Russia, who in the past have advocated revolution in the United States, would continue such activity while representing officially a Government which is committed to that proposition. Diplomatic and Consular agents could unquestionably form centers for agitation for proletarian revolution, and investigating bodies of this Government would be powerless under diplomatic usage to investigate the accounts and the disposition made of Russian funds for unlawful purposes here. The red flag of world revolution would become the flag of a friendly nation and might be used on all occasions by those elements of our population who show a desire to emulate the Russian Proletariat.

Your Committee feels that the consequences of recognition of the Russian Soviet Republic by this country would be to add fuel to the flame of internal disorder within our boundaries.

In the second report of this Committee it was pointed out that the influence of the Jacobin Clubs of the French Revolution upon the malcontents in the United States in the latter part of the 18th Century, was sufficient to stimulate and inspire the organization of Democratic societies which sought to disturb and overthrow the administration of justice by our constituted authorities. We attempted to point out that the experience of the French Revolution should teach us that so long as the Bolsheviki continue to exercise a dominating influence upon the millions of disorganized Europe, so long would they continue a menace to the institutions of the United States. The recognition of the Russian Soviet Republic would necessarily increase that menace.

The period through which we are now passing is analogous to that period of doubt and indecision which preceded the declaration of war upon Germany. The issues are confused in the public mind. Certain individuals in this country have publicly given their approval to the proposition of a recognition of the Lenine Government. It is obvious, however, that they have not understood the consequences of the position which they have assumed.

The presence in this country of the mission heretofore referred to, makes us inquire whether it is possible that the Russian Soviet Republic can have received encouragement with respect of recognition, which has warranted their establishing a bureau here. It is hardly conceivable that such a mission would have been sent unless such encouragement had been received.

When by reason of revolution a Government is overthrown, it has long been the custom for civilized nations to withhold recognition from the new authorities, in order that they may pass through a period of probation before being admitted to the society of nations. The object of this "is to enable other States to judge of the probable stability of the new 'Government' before entering into relations with it." (Pitt Cobbett. Cases and Opinions on International Law. Part I, p. 82.)

While the power to recognize a new government appears to be vested in the Executive branch of our government, a doubt has been present in the minds of our Presidents as to the safety of relying upon their own judgment in recognizing a new State when the consequences of such an act involve delicate international questions. In the case of the recognition by the United States of the Spanish-American Republics, of Texas, Hayti and Liberia, the then Presidents before recognizing the new States, invoked the judgment and cooperation of Congress.

In his special message of December 21, 1836, President Jackson observed that a resolution, which had been introduced in the House of Representatives, "distinctly intimated that the expediency of recognizing the independence of Texas should be left to the decision of Congress. In this view, on the ground of expediency, I am," said President Jackson, "disposed to concur, and do not, therefore, consider it necessary to express any opinion as to the strict constitutional right of the Executive, either apart from or in conjunction with the Senate, over the subject."

W. J. Ghent Makes Critical Analysis

We are glad to give space to the following letter from William J. Ghent to Henry R. Mussey. Mr. Ghent is well known as one of the ablest socialist writers in this country and in Europe, but, because of his true Americanism, he left the Socialist Party when it became the mouthpiece for the German propaganda in the United States.

Henry R. Mussey is the editor of "The Nation," which journal has already been described in these columns.

In 1908 the editor of the Review *took occasion to protest to the Y. M. C. A. for permitting Professor Mussey, then of the University of Pennsylvania, to give before its organization in Philadelphia a series of lectures on socialism, which, while pretending to be an honest and dispassionate discussion of the subject, was in fact nothing more or less than veiled socialist propaganda. About that time Mussey had come to Barnard College, and a Columbia professor who was largely responsible for having brought him there, took up the cudgels in his behalf, stating among other things that Mussey had told him that "it would be impossible for him ever to be a socialist."*

The reply made to that was that whatever Mr. Mussey might think about it, he was in fact a socialist just the same, and that an analysis of his addresses, made by five different men who were competent to pass judgment in such matters, unanimously pronounced him such.

Mr. Ghent, ten years later, adds this closing chapter on the subject:

627 Belmont Ave.,
Los Angeles, California,
March 15, 1919.

My dear Mr. Mussey:

Your letter of February 27th was delayed in reaching me, owing to the fact that it was addressed to a non-existent "Vilmont" avenue instead of to Belmont avenue. It was not delivered to me till the 12th. I assure you that I was glad to receive it, since it gives me an opportunity to speak a few things that I have had in mind for some time.

Let me say first that I note well your reference to the upsetting of so many persons' judgments these recent years, and that on this point I join my testimony with yours. I, too, have met with abundant proof of the wide range and unexpected incidence of this malady. If the reference is intended as the mere statement of a striking fact, I willingly subscribe my agreement with you. If it is intended with some measure of reproach, I reply that I hold myself blameless in the matter, since I have done what lay in my power to check the malady, while I think *The Nation* has done very much to foster its spread. And if, as I greatly fear, the reference is intended to express a serene complacency as to the equilibrium of your own judgment and a doubt to the equilibrium of mine, then I reply: Read this letter; you may be right, but I have something to say to the contrary.

All the information I had about the organization of the Truth About Russia Committee was contained in the dispatch carried by the Associated Press. Of course I did not know that the announcement was unauthorized, and that upon the publication of this announcement the three representatives of *The Nation*, as well as Mr. Kellogg, at once withdrew. But these matters are immaterial. Your letter says that "the suggestion of the formation of this committee was made absolutely and solely with the purpose of giving publicity to any authentic information that could be got from Russia, no rse-thieves might draw up a constitution ining many altruistic and high-sounding rations. But the publication of such a con-ion would give only a very misleading a of that organization or its workings. the world is entitled to know is not only the horse-thieves have to say about them-, but what the people feloniously divested eir horse-flesh have to say about the thieves. all that you print about Russia I find only rossest partisanship: in the testimony, only which favors the Lenine-Trotzky regime, in the editorial comment the assumption no other testimony is of the slightest value. do, indeed, occasionally print a sentence aiming support of the Bolshevik regime; on two recent occasions (December 21 and h 1) you generously permitted two corre-lents, in letters to the editor, to enter mild urrers to the Bolshevik claims. But aside these, all that you print on the subject is ·iously pro-Bolshevik matter.

hat you think of the adverse testimony is ips best summed up in an editorial declara-in the issue of February 1:

he emigrant Russian princes and prin-s, ex-ambassadors of the Czar and Kerensky, secret agents who, safely in exile in Europe merica and abundantly supplied with money ι mysterious sources, have been filling the ı of both continents with denunciations of Soviet government or the Bolsheviki . . . who in the meantime have been carrying on npudent and insidious propaganda."

ou here link together revolutionist and re-nary, democrat and imperialist, the life-servant of the Russian people with the site who has lived upon them, in one com-mass of discredited adventurers; and you ıot see, such is the blind violence with which have written this sweeping sentence, that in use of the little phrase *safely in exile* you e perpetrated a ghastly joke on your own rtions of the mildness and justness of shevik rule.

/hat you think of this adverse testimony is her shown (issue of February 22) in an orial on the Overman committee, in which say: "The committee . . . went on to : out a series of witnesses who would heap se on the present government of Russia. *have no space to deal with individual wit-es or their specific testimony.* Suffice it to that it is mostly the same sort of wild hear-with which our press has been filled for ths; little of it would stand for five minutes ny court of justice."

ATROCIOUS LIBEL ON THE COMMITTEE

he first sentence is an atrocious libel on the mittee which took testimony from all sides. second sentence is true enough, but not ıtly to the credit of a periodical which pro-es to "utilize absolutely every source of in-ıation concerning Russia that it can get." third sentence is more atrociously false than first; for these witnesses included Catherine shkovsky (February 14), for whom you onally profess so reverent a love; Roger E. mons (February 15), William C. Hunting-(February 12), the Rev. G. A. Simons bruary 13) and Prof. Ralph Dennis (Febru-14), all of whom gave accounts of matters ı which they were intimately acquainted.

ou pretend to know more about what is pening in Russia than do these people. Do ? I say rather that in this rejection of this mony and the insulting reference to these ıesses you are merely revealing a working ıula of your office: "Pro-Bolshevist testi-y is necessarily believable testimony; anti-hevist testimony is necessarily the reverse."

o refresh my memory and to re-examine the s of my criticism, I have read through a file our periodical from November 16 to March ıclusive. I must say that the case, thus re-documented, now appears to me a much clearer one than it did when I wrote my letter to the *Times*. I was prepared to find that I had over-looked something in your defense; that the cumulative impression made on me from reading these issues week by week might be in some measure an erroneous one. But I find my view confirmed by overwhelming evidence.

I say now that you cannot point to a single line in these fifteen issues that gives to an open-minded reader the slightest indication of a wish to treat the Russian situation fairly. You may have wished to treat it fairly; you may have thought you were treating it fairly; but the evidence that you have not so treated it is here in unmistakable black and white. There is one side, and one only, presented. The honored leaders in the long history of the Russian revo-lution are for the most part ignored, or they are mentioned only to be dismissed as of no conse-quence. To Babushka "the Drifter" (Febru-ary 8) pays a personal tribute. But of the volumes of testimony given by her in interviews, in speeches, in her examination before the Over-man committee and in her formal message to the American people, there is not here or else-where a syllable. There is, indeed, the statement that "her viewpoint of affairs Russian and in-ternational differs widely from the *Nation's*"; but this is presented as though it settled the matter by reducing the value of her testimony to zero. Tschaikowsky, well known and well loved in America, is mentioned twice (December 21 and February 8) and pushed aside. Of his frequent detailed statements regarding Bolshe-vist rule, you print not a line. I find no men-tion of Kropotkin, Bourtseff, Axelrod, Savin-koff, Avksentie or Plechanoff (now deceased), and yet the testimony of every one of these, some part of which appeared during these fifteen weeks, is still an enduring indictment of the Bolshevist regime.

MUCH MATTER IGNORED

A great deal of reputable anti-Bolshevist testi-mony from many other sources appeared during these fifteen weeks; and a great deal more, which appeared somewhat earlier, is available and still forms a part of the documentation of this case. But no part of it, not even a refer-ence to it, except the admission (December 21) that "the partisans of the Kerensky regime, or of any regime at all save the present one, go on denouncing the Bolsheviki and clamoring for military action," is to be found in your journal. During those fifteen weeks appeared, among a great mass of contributions to the general sub-ject, the following:

A remarkable series of papers (a part of which was published earlier) by Ariadna Tyrkova, in the *Christian Science Monitor*.

An article by George Kennan in the *New York Times*, January 23.

Several formal statements by Dr. David Soskice.

A protest against Bolshevism addressed to J. Ramsay MacDonald (December 7), by a delega-tion representing the Esthonian republic.

A formal statement (published in the *Christian Science Monitor*, January 22) by Mr. Titoff, mod-erate Socialist and member of an anti-Bolshevist delegation from Russia.

A statement (published in London in Decem-ber and sent here by Associated Press corre-spondence dated January 1) signed by five repre-sentatives of Russian political organizations.

The official dispatches of O. Wardrop, British consul-general at Moscow.

An address to President Wilson, presented to him on his visit to London, signed by 100 prom-inent members of the Russian colony of that city.

Several statements by G. A. Martuchin, former secretary of finance in the government of North-ern Russia.

Various translations from *Pravda* and *Izvestya*, Bolshevik organs, confirming the truth of anti-Bolshevist charges.

Against your preposterous statement that you have been "utilizing absolutely every source of information concerning Russia" that you could get, I set down the plain and indisputable fact that you utilized in print, during the period named, nothing of the slightest consequence from any anti-Bolshevist statement.

This sweeping indictment I must, on again examining my material, qualify to the extent of one instance. Under the heading, "The Siberian Duma," among the fine-print notes in the issue of November 16, you print a summary of a speech by M. Vologotsky, then president of the council of ministers of the Omsk government. The speech as a whole is a resume of what the Omsk government has done and is at least im-pliedly a criticism of the Bolshevist government, and it contains at least two sentences in which the Bolsheviki are plainly denounced.

In another instance my statement may be qualified or not, accordingly as one views the matter. In the introduction, headed "A Bol-shevist Outbreak," to a letter by E. Odier, Swiss Ambassador to Russia, and a reply by G. W. Tschitscherin, people's commissary for foreign affairs, in the same issue, occurs the sentence: "It will be observed that the fact of the out-rages against which the neutral diplomats com-plained is not denied." This curious sentence may have been inserted either to show the culpability of the Bolshevik government or to show your approval of its contemptuous resist-ance to the impudent demands of the Allies. Since you have taken the trouble to italicize all the most arrogant and calumnious assertions of Tschitscherin, thus giving them an editorial ap-proval, I cannot think there is much doubt about your intention. But if the former inter-pretation is to be made, my statement is obviously to that extent qualified; if the latter, my statement is not affected.

The article, "Who Shall Inherit the Power in Russia?" by Vladimir Grossman, translated from the *Morganavisen*, a conservative journal of Bergen, Norway, does indubitably contain many hard words about the Bolsheviki. But the motive for printing it is easily enough revealed in the argument of the writer, which is, that if Bolshevism goes down, Czarism is apt to come up. To have excised the denunciations of the Bolsheviki would have completely destroyed the point which you sought to make; and so faced with the alternative, you could do no less than admit these passages to your columns.

WHY THE INDICTMENT STANDS

Otherwise my indictment stands. You had special articles by Albert Rhys Williams (November 16), Michael S. Farbman (Novem-ber 30 and February 8), George V. Lomonosoff (March 1), "Christian" (December 21)—the last-named a woozy melange of mysticism and flapdoodle—and John Rickman (January 11). With the exception of Rickman's article, which is nebulous in the extreme, these are all, in greater or less degree, pro-Bolshevist contribu-tions. The article by "Christian" is fanatically so. The first of Farbmau's might seem to a considerable number of persons the adulatory tribute of a hired man to his employer. I do not, however, press this matter, though I am sure that had the same kind of stuff been written by Dr. David Soskice in praise of Kerensky you would have so treated it, with an outburst of scornful rhetoric. My point is that as a set-off against these articles you can point to nothing whatever for the other side.

Your failure to print anything explanatory of the Socialist and democratic opposition to Bolshevism might possibly be attributed to chance, though he would be a bold man who would so contend. But your distortion of par-ticular episodes cannot, even by the widest stretch of charity, be so explained. You treated, with characteristic denunciation, as a lie out of the whole cloth, the press story of an intended

(Continued on page 15)

THE NATIONAL
Civic Federation Review

Office: Thirty-third Floor, Metropolitan Tower
1 Madison Avenue New York City

RALPH M. EASLEY, Editor

Published Twice a Month Two Dollars a Year

The Editor alone is Responsible for any unsigned article or unquoted statement published in THE NATIONAL CIVIC FEDERATION REVIEW.

HOW CAN THE "PEOPLE" BE REPRESENTED

A correspondent has written the editor of the REVIEW, asking "What on earth is the meaning of all this talk about having the people rather than the governments represented in the League of Nations, just as though the representatives of our Government, for instance, were not representatives of the people?" Also he inquires: "What is the significance of the proportional representation idea that they talk about?"

These questions are quite natural, because of the various references to these subjects by so-called "liberals" of all countries, who, by the way, are today nothing but radicals and revolutionaries. There was a time when the word "liberal" meant something. Today it means principally that to be a "liberal" is to be more or less a Bolshevist, or at any rate a socialist. But to answer the questions of our correspondent:

When the socialists at Berne demanded that the League of Nations should not be constituted of representatives of the governments, they meant that they wanted them to be selected by the various parliaments or legislative bodies, instead of being named by the executive heads of the several governments. Their reason for wanting proportional representation was that in practically all the governments in Europe the revolutionaries had representation—and in some countries, both in Europe and South America, the minority representation is very large and may at any time become majority representation. This would let the socialists and even the anarchists secure membership in the League of Nations, enabling them to hold up every measure squinting in the direction of sanity. Also, this possibility of the revolutionaries capturing a majority of the governments of the world explains why originally some of their more radical groups so enthusiastically supported the League of Nations' idea. They hoped to work the thing around to the point where all the nations of the earth would be admitted on equal terms. Then they would capture the League of Nations, and, with the armies and navies of the world in their hands, the future, for them at least, was quite rosy, if not carmine-hued.

The left wing of the Berne conference, however, not satisfied with having the legislatures select the delegates for the League of Nations, insisted on having the people do it directly, and this absurd idea has been taken up by the revolutionaries and freaks of this country, the reason being that if Congress selected our League of Nations representatives, it would not enable them to have any voice in that body, because, thanks to the good sense of the American people, none of them are allowed to enter our national legislative body. Proportional representation would therefore do them no good. It would simply mean that the representation would be made up of democrats and republicans.

Just how these ghost-dancers of the League of Free Nations propose to have the American people get together and select representatives "proportionally" is, of course, not stated. Probably they propose to call the hundred million people of the country to meet in some nice, quiet spot and "thresh it out" at a town meeting. Or if that would seem a little bulky, they might decide to divide it up and have a few million people called together in each state. If, after the deep thinkers thought some more and found that such a crowd would also be a little unwieldy, they might consider that it would be well to reduce it to county mass meetings of a few hundred thousand people and finally get back to towns and wards and election districts, just as we do it now, in which case they would again find that the American people have too much sense to select any of the R's and F's to represent them anywhere except in institutions for the feeble-minded.

On the "representation by the people" propositiou, President Wilson, in his explanation of the League of Nations program to the Peace Conference, greatly stressed the idea of having met this demand. But when the covenant was examined it was found that all it meant was that he would name three representatives instead of one, and of course if he wanted to appoint one of these revolutionaries or freaks he would have that pleasure; but, also, the Senate would express its views on the matter before they reached the peace table.

The proportional representation idea, generally speaking, is a dishonest proposition to emphasize artificially the importance of a minority, which frequently amounts to a handful of men holding the balance of power between the two great parties, enabling them to blackmail one side or the other into supporting measures to which they are opposed. A weekly journal of high standing, but with socialistic leanings, bemoaned the fact that in the 1916 Congressional elections, the ten or twelve socialist candidates running had not been elected so as to act as a "balancing force" in Congress. One can readily imagine what would have happened where there were only three votes between the republicans and democrats, to have the disloyal Berger and the pacifist, and worse, Hillquit leading the ten socialists. They would have practically dictated much of the legislation and policy of that body by playing the democrats against the republicans, and where they could not have dictated, they would have blocked.

Therefore, proportional representation not only permits a minority to prevent the majority from expressing the will of the people, but, as it frequently works out, is an immoral proposition.

It is well to note that it is only where the "liberals" are in the minority that they want proportional representation. Where they are in the majority, as in Petrograd and Moscow, Professors Lenine and Trotzky, those princes of "liberals", are not bothering about giving the *bourgeoisie* any minority voice except when they face the firing squads, and then they are allowed to scream.

JUSTICE DEMANDED FOR THE NEGRO

A call for a National Conference on Lynching, to be held in New York, May 5 and 6, 1919, has just been issued by a committee of citizens, of which Moorfield Story, of Boston, is chairman and John R. Shillady, of New York, secretary. It is certainly an anomaly, to say the least, that there should be need in the United States at this time for such a convention. Well may the enemies of our country point to this burning disgrace to our American civilization.

The call for delegates to this convention says:

> The prevalence in many states of the spirit which tolerates lynching, accompanied too often with inhuman cruelty, and the inability or unwillingness of the public authorities to punish the persons who are guilty of this crime, threaten very seriously the future peace of the nation. Not only is lynching a denial of the right secured by law to every man of a fair trial before an established court in case he is charged with crime, not only does it brutalize the communities which suffer it by breeding a spirit of lawlessness and cruelty in the young people who see barbarities unpunished and uncondemned, not only does it terrorize important bodies of our citizens, but it inevitably leads the people whose rights are

Socialism Versus Industrial and Social Progress.

principal merit of this matter, if any be, consists in the quotations from socialist yndicalist authorities. If the description of conditions in 1914 was even approxiy correct, there should be little surprise at onditions we face today. This burrowing een going on insidiously and insistently since 1914, just as Jack London boasted t would, and it will continue to go on unless ıne forces of our nation are aroused and rly organized to combat it.

will be a shock to social reformers to read ear-cut statements contained in the quotafrom socialist writers, who frankly declare hey do not want to bring about better cons in the present state of society but want r it up by the roots and begin all over again. eir pronouncements to that effect, it will be ved that five years ago they used language olent as that employed by Lenine and ky today.

answer to the socialist stock claims that alists, through their great wealth, are conlly plotting to thwart and suppress liberalnd radicalism is given in this issue of the w. In a word, it shows that just the reis true. Apparently, the larger the capitalhe more willing a victim is he to the blandents of the smooth-tongued and hypocritical utionaries who are masquerading as "social mers."

NOTE TO READERS

ing to the temporary illness of T. Everett, the second instalment of "Who's Who in ew School", scheduled for this issue, will ar in the next number of the REVIEW.

O'GRADY TAKES EXCEPTION TO CRITICISM OF THE CATHOLIC SOCIAL RECONSTRUCTION PAMPHLET

THE NATIONAL CATHOLIC WAR COUNCIL.
932 14th Street, N. W.,
Washington, D. C., April 9, 1919.

Ralph M. Easley,
ATIONAL CIVIC FEDERATION REVIEW,
New York City.

ear Sir—An article in the issue of your EW for March 25th, entitled "Radicals Mis- Churches About Labor," contains some ping criticisms of the National Catholic Council's reconstruction program.

e have no desire to engage in a controversy the merits of the program. It speaks for f and justifies itself. We want, however, to ect a few misconceptions. You say that the gram "is only the expression of the opinion he gentlemen signing the document and has official sanction.". That is not true. The ops signed it, not as individuals, but as the inistrative Committee of the National olic War Council. As such, they are the orized representatives of the Catholic rarchy.

ou find fault with the program for not mening the reconstruction proposals of the rican Federation of Labor and of the Indus- Conference Board, but neither of these had eared when the Bishops' program was writ-

You intimate that the general policies of American Federation of Labor are well wn and should have been noticed. But the ops were not discussing the general policies ny organization. They deal with the opin- of others only in so far as these had found ression in formal programs of reconstruction, the only documents of this sort that had issued by labor in the United States up to time that they wrote were the declarations of the state and city federations which they cited. In the same way they noted the declaration of the National Chamber of Commerce because that was the only reconstruction statement then available from employers, and there are more employers in the National Chamber of Commerce than in any other organization in America.

You complain that the Bishops have made recommendations which are at variance with the policies of the American Federation of Labor. Well, the Bishops were stating their own views and program. While sympathizing with and endorsing the fundamental aims and views of labor, they were no more obliged to adopt all its opinions than those of organized capital.

The heading of your article is not exactly complimentary to the Bishops. They have sufficient intelligence and sufficient knowledge of social thought and conditions to protect themselves against being "misled by radicals."

Your statement that a certain sentence in the program "sounds as if the Committee were somewhat regretful that we were not more ready for revolutionary changes," is an entirely gratuitous bit of interpretation.

In your concluding paragraph you say that "the churches are all controlled by boards of trustees, made up largely of business men." In the Catholic church the control is in the hands of the Pope and the Bishops.

Very truly yours,
(Signed) JOHN O'GRADY,
Secretary, Committee on Reconstruction.

REPLY BY RALPH M. EASLEY

Dr. O'Grady takes exception first to the statement that the bishops, who as members of the Administrative Committee of the National Catholic War Council signed the foreword to the pamphlet on "Social Reconstruction", had no official sanction for so doing. It would be presumptuous for the writer to discuss that question with so eminent an authority. However, it is only fair to remark that the idea was not gathered from the clouds. The pamphlet came to the writer, in the first place, through a Catholic, who was shocked at what seemed to him the socialistic trend of its contents and it was a Catholic labor man who called attention to the editorial which appeared in *The New York Daily Call*, and said: "I never expected to see the time when the policy of my Church could be approved by that revolutionary sheet which is not only the organ of the socialists but is rapidly becoming the organ of the 'Left Wing', which means Bolshevism."

In regard to the authority of the National Catholic War Council's Administrative Committee to pass upon economic matters, certain Catholics were consulted who are regarded as being versed in Catholic procedure. Their composite opinion is contained in the following paragraphs:

"The hierarchy of the United States addresses its communications to the Catholics of this country ordinarily when assembled in Plenary Council. Not more than three such councils have been held, and never has the hierarchy, out of Council, addressed a joint official communication to clergy or laity.

"The National Catholic War Council consists of the Archbishops, represented by an Administrative Committee of four bishops. The bishops of the country take no active part in the War Council, nor, so far as is known, a consultative part.

"The War Council is authorized to act only in War Work proper and it is to cease its activities just as soon as it will have expended its present funds in War Work. Its Administrative Committee and Committee on Special Activities will then cease.

"The War Council is not considered by the bishops generally to act in other than war matters, such as Social Reconstruction is considered to be.

"If the bulletin on Social Reconstruction were an official hierarchial statement it would have been issued as such and signed by the members of the hierarchy or by representative bishops specially designated for this.

"Catholics generally do not recognize it as an official statement of the heirarchy, but only of the Administrative Committee of the War Council.

"There was a meeting of the bishops at Cardinal Gibbons's Jubilee in Washington. This meeting did not endorse or take action in the matter of this statement."

These views are not published for the purpose of disputing Dr. O'Grady's statement, but simply to give some justification for the assertion on the matter of authority contained in the REVIEW article.

The reason given by Dr. O'Grady for the ignoring of the well-known policies of the organized American labor movement by the Catholic War Council's committee is, in the writer's opinion, not at all adequate. He says:

"The bishops were not discussing the general policies of any organization." Well, they did more than merely discuss the British Labour Party's Program, for they pronounced judgment upon it, declaring that it was "unquestionably the most comprehensive and coherent program that has yet appeared on the industrial phase of reconstruction," although admitting that "This program may properly be described as one of immediate radical reforms, involving a rapid approach towards complete Socialism."

Concerning the report, the REVIEW article stated that "On reading it, one is struck by many omissions and inconsistencies." A Catholic critic adds that it is also "a superficial treatment of the capital and labor problem, and more or less a 'hotch-potch', something like the first draft of the League of Nations covenant, which was made up by throwing together parts of various drafts by many different individuals."

To discuss the labor question in the United States and omit any reference to the policies and work of the American Federation of Labor or the Railway Brotherhoods is almost inexcusable. In the opinion of the writer, those responsible for the pamphlet should either have gone into the matter thoroughly or they should not have touched upon it at all.

To make a positive declaration that "The State should make comprehensive provision for insurance against illness, invalidity, unemployment and old age," is to attempt to place the great Roman Catholic Church behind a group of socialistic ventures that neither the wage-earners nor the employers want. The reason is that they have learned that in foreign countries such schemes have not accomplished what is claimed for them by the socialists here. Take the genesis of the movement for compulsory social insurance in the United States. It will be something of a shock to those interested in constructive efforts to learn that the self-styled "first advocate", the socialist Dr. Isaac M. Rubinow, in an article entitled "A Socialist Remedy for Unemployment," published in *The New Review*, November 15, 1915, frankly states:

> "Twelve years ago, when I began to preach social insurance, I was a man with a new idea in this country. . . . After all, social ills, like bodily ills, have only one true remedy, though it is not always known in time, and if we socialists are at all right, these remedies must be in line with our philosophy."

This same socialist, Dr. Isaac M. Rubinow, in an article in *The New Republic*, July 27, 1918, lets in a little more light upon the peculiar origin

(*Continued on page 16*)

WILLIAM GREEN

FRANK DUFFY

JOHN R. ALPINE

American Labor Mission Returns

(Continued from page 2)

go to Berne, Switzerland, to attend the so-called international meeting there. The principal reason we had for not going was that, as representatives of the organized labor movement of America, we had no need to go to a neutral country to debate the question. What we had to say and do, could, and should, be said and done in an allied country. We were not prepared, since peace was not signed, to go and meet delegates of organized labor from Germany, Austria and Bulgaria, thereby appearing to give them an advantage which their countries had lost through their own choice of the arbitrament of war."

Marked applause greeted Mr. Duncan's definition of organized labor's position in this matter and he roused further enthusiasm by telling of labor's stand on the League of Nations and on reconstruction.

"We have learned that democracy means self discipline," said Mr. Macy, "and it does not mean license. It does not mean a dictatorship of the proletariat, whatever that means, the dictatorship of religious sects, or the dictatorship of any part of the community. But it does mean the cooperation of all in the community to work toward a common end. Wherever there has been oppression in this country, wherever a body has signified a desire for better democracy, we have been long accustomed to seeing Mr. Gompers, our honored guest, in the front of that fight.

"While he has always been one of the strongest advocates of peace, he has been one of the most persistent fighters all his life for justice to the greatest number. He is now regarded as the champion throughout the world of these same rights of democracy and order and constructive progress. We have been most fortunate in having Mr. Gompers in Paris at this critical time in the world's history where he has been able to add his statesmanship to that of the other delegates to the Peace Conference.

"Notwithstanding our pleasure at having him there, and our pride, I am sure we are still more glad to have him back home with us. We feel more comfortable when he is here where we can advise with him constantly. Mr. Gompers."

As one man, the gathering rose to greet the venerable leader of the American Federation of Labor and it was some minutes before he was permitted to speak because of the prolonged applause. Then he said:

"Perhaps one of the greatest difficulties with which a man has to deal is to speak when a great tribute has been paid him. I want you, Mr. Chairman, my fellow countrymen and country women, to accept my assurance of a deep, deep sense of gratitude that I owe to you and to all my fellow Americans for the kindly thoughts that they have had for my associates and myself, and the efforts which we have made to be helpful to our own country and to the common cause of justice and humanity.

JAMES DUNCAN

"I do not care to add much to what has been said as to the efforts made by the men and women of the American Labor movement to stabilize the good opinion and loyalty and devotion to the cause which America represents.

"Let me relate one incident that may be of more than passing interest. In February, 1918, there was held in London a conference of the representatives of labor and of socialists, and after several days' meeting, a declaration was made by that body calling upon their respective governments to bring about peace with Germany and Austria by negotiation. In September, 1918, another conference was held representative of the same bodies which I have mentioned, but in addition there was a delegation representing the American Federation of Labor.

"At that conference, made up of the same peoples, aye, of the same personnel except that the American Labor movement was represented, that September conference declared the unflinching support to the governments of the United States and of our allied countries until victory has been won and the enemy driven from the invaded countries.

"There were only five delegates from America and there were about 88 representing the other countries. And we thought that that was rather a declaration that would help to stabilize the conscience and the conduct of men who have been trimming and trimming and trimming with the common enemy.

"We had no votes to ask. We had no support to appeal for other than having had our country assailed and invaded and our innocent men and women and children murdered in cold blood, and we had the right to say that we were going to fight until at least some reparation shall be made to common humanity for the most monumental crimes ever committed by any people or any nation. And it has come about. The war has practically come to an end and the greatest military power on the face of the globe has been humbled into the dust.

"And now, my friends, let me say this, that the propaganda now being conducted, and conducted since the armistice has been signed, is just as vigorous and just as—perhaps more—insidious than at any time before, during or since, the war.

"It is the same junker crowd there in control in Germany as it was under the Kaiser. The propaganda now going on and having been carried on is the propaganda to win by diplomacy and agitation what Germany has lost on the battlefield.

"It is during these trying times of peace that it is necessary for every man and every woman to be on the alert lest the whole victory shall be turned into defeat. With my associates we had the great privilege of meeting in conference with our great President, the spokesman and practical leader and humanitarian, who speaks for the world of justice and of right. It has been our privilege to meet with our other commissioners and to place before them our views of the situation and what should be done. We simply tried to make our contribution to the world in the remaking. Here during those times and while over in France, the President made another American and myself a commission to represent our country in an international commission for Labor Legislation. The commission did me the great honor of making me its presiding officer. It may sound humorous to you, for while great tributes were paid to me and to the years of long continued service that I had given to the cause of right and freedom, I found myself nine times out of ten in a lonesome minority.

"It was a hard fight. It was a great struggle, and the best that was in me was given toward trying to reach some conclusion of a beneficial character to the world. And I may say that after thirty-five sessions lasting each of them from three to seven hours, a conclusion was reached. A covenant was created. It was a great problem and in all likelihood the dual ster of our government was one of the est problems that we had to meet.

But the problem was solved—it is too long ry to try to tell it or explain it—and then were but two questions with which we had al. One was relative to interstate com- and the other, foreign commerce. We guarded the instrument and our govern- al rights and integrity by a declaration a protocol of the covenant, that no state untry shall be asked or required to en- conditions which are lower or less than in the country or state. And so a great nization has been perfected.

The news published in this morning's pa- shows that at the meeting of the peace missioners yesterday that covenant has been ted by the unanimous vote of the commis- And the instrument has been referred to has come to be known as the 'Big Four', ecide whether this covenant creating an in- tional labor conference each year to be and a governing body to have adminis- ve functions and powers during the in- n—and the question was whether this in- ment should be made a separate treaty or me a part of the treaty of peace.

In addition to this convention or covenant, hat it may be called, the International Com- sion adopted recommendations and placed n before the peace commissioners, asking that be made part of the treaty of peace, and all read them to you.

But lest it shall slip my memory, I want to e one observation now. That is, that in that nization created by the representatives of allied countries and of the United States, e is not one thing that, when Germany and tria shall have signed the treaty of peace— e is not one of its conditions or terms that react to the injury of the working people Germany or Austria. It is to make for a better life and a better standard, and hope more independence and less regard for dictatorship of a Kaiser.

The clauses proposed for insertion in the aty of Peace are:

The high contracting parties declare their ac- ceptance of the following principles and engage to take all necessary steps to secure their realiza- tion in accordance with the recommendations to be made by the International Labor Conference as to their practical application:

1. In right and in fact the labor of a human being should not be treated as merchandise or an article of commerce.

2. Employers and workers should be allowed the right of association for all lawful purposes.

3. No child should be permitted to be em- ployed in industry or commerce before the age of fourteen years, in order that every child may be insured reasonable opportunities for mental and physical education. Between the years of fourteen and eighteen, young persons of either sex may only be employed on work which is not harmful to their physical development and on condition that the continuation of their technical or general education is insured.

4. Every worker has a right to a wage ade- quate to maintain a reasonable standard of life, having regard to the civilization of his age, time and country.

5. Equal pay should be given to women and to men for work of equal value in quantity and quality.

6. A weekly rest, including Sunday or its equivalent, for all workers.

7. Limitation of the hours of work in indus- try on the basis of an eight-hour day or forty- eight-hour week, subject to an exception for countries in which climatic conditions, imperfect industrial development or industrial organiza- tions, or other special circumstances render the industrial efficiency of the workers substantially different. The International Labor Conference will recommend a basis approximately equivalent to the above for adoption in such countries.

8. In all matters concerning their status as workers and social insurance, foreign workmen, lawfully admitted to a country, and their families should be insured the same treatment as the nationals of that country.

9. All states should institute a system of in- spection in which women should take part, in order to insure the enforcement of the laws and regulations for the protection of the workers.

SAMUEL GOMPERS

You who know me or who have heard of me, have heard me express myself, or have seen the expression of my absolute opposi- tion to Bolshevism either in theory or in fact. In theory it is a mental impossi- bility. In fact, if it were put in operation, or could be, it would mean the decadence and perversion of the civilization of our time. To me, the story of the destruction of Samson when he pulled down the tem- ple upon his head is an example of what is meant by Bolshevism. I am unwilling that the service that I have tried to give my fellows to bring a little light into their lives shall be destroyed because of mad- dening desperation—Samuel Gompers at The National Civic Federation's luncheon of welcome.

"I count it as one of the great privileges to have had the opportunity to help in the con- struction of this great scheme that shall make for the world's betterment.

"You who know me or have heard of me, have heard me express myself, or have seen the ex- pression of my absolute opposition to Bolshe- vism either in theory or in fact. In theory it is a mental impossibility. In fact, if it were put into operation, or could be, it would mean the decadence and the perversion of the civili- zation of our time. To me, the story of the destruction of Samson when he pulled the tem- ple down upon his head is an example of what is meant by Bolshevism.

"I am unwilling that the service that I have tried to give to my fellows to bring a little light into their lives shall be destroyed because of maddening desperation. I might say this to you also—that it is well for us to see that our own house is kept in order. There is another element in our life which needs scrutiny. Bol- shevism is not the only danger confronting our institutions. The 'stand-patter' and the profi- teer are equally a menace to our civilization.

"Since our coming ashore—not more than a day past—I find the situation right here where men entrusted with great industrial transit in- terests of our community have said to the work- ing people in their employ, 'You cannot talk to us and you cannot labor for us, with the griev- ances or the complaints that you claim you have.' The industrial autocrat who thinks that he is master of all he surveys is the incentive and motive power for all the resentment that you can find in people.

"I was very much interested in what was said, not only by my associate, Brother Duncan, with which, of course, I am in entire agreement always, but particularly with the statement by the Honorable William Howard Taft, when he spoke of the collective bargaining, and of the right of the workers to sit in council with their employers and talk over the industry and com- merce and production and cost, and to try and reach an adjustment.

"Of course it is not a solution. There is no such thing as a solution, because there is no such thing as an end. Not even death. There is no such thing as a solution, but it is the com- mon sense way of trying to get along with the least possible friction to the attainment of the very best possible conditions. No man in this day and time can stand up and say that he is the master of all he surveys. He must be will- ing to yield some. If he does not, he has not learned anything of the lesson of this war. I am pleading for a clean life for our people. I want to see America, my America, not only the foremost democracy of the world; I want to see it true to history, true to its birth, true to its conception and ideals, and that we shall not only be the great industrial and agricultural and commercial country of the world, but also that we shall stand foremost like a beacon light to the whole world, and say justice and right and freedom must prevail in every relation of life.

"In these reconstruction times, it must cause us to pause, and be alert and active, and to give devoted service now. Now! Now, men and women, is the time that is trying our very souls and the institutions under which we are living.

"I want to say a word in regard to the cove- nant for the establishment of a League of Na- tions, and using in essence the words of our President when he laid the covenant before the High Commissioners, it is not only a League of Nations but a league of free peoples of the nations of the world. It may be true that the covenant, as it was tentatively adopted by the Commission and which the President of the United States brought with him to our coun- try—it may be true that it is not a perfect instrument. It may be true, as it is true, that it will require some change and modification or strengthening. We must be safeguarded in America against those who might wish to men- ace this Republic of ours.

"It may need amendment, but, my friends, in principle it is right.

"Whoever heard of a written instrument that in its first conception and publication did not require time to make some changes? The Con- stitution of the United States—who would say that that Constitution is of no value to the people of our country and of the world? And you know how often we have amended it. I do not know—I may say that I don't know that we have always amended wisely. And per- haps the last amendment was the silliest of them all. But in the language of Kipling, that is another story.

"As Mr. Taft said, there are some people who will not learn, and because of it they may successfully oppose the ratification and adop- tion of this covenant for the free peoples of the world in a league to conduct a police force, if you please, in order to make some people be- have themselves.

"War with all its untold miseries and suffer- ings, its pangs and its horrors, its nightmares— all, all, all—we must, if we can, endeavor to prevent such a holocaust coming upon the peo- ples of the world again. If that be in our pow- er, we should do it. At least, it demands from every one of us to give the best that is in us,

(Continued on page 14)

Sapping the Foundations of Society

(Continued from page 4)

and secretary respectively of the Free Speech League, which had the fight in charge, in which these officials of the League stated:

> Most of the I. W. W. organizers who came to San Diego to speak used language upon the street corners such as would not be tolerated in any civilized community. They were foul mouthed and vile. . . . As a result, they inflamed the people and the police and the restricted district ordinance was passed. . . . The I. W. W. kept on sending men from the entire Pacific Coast to San Diego. Many of these men came simply in order to be supported.

Confirmatory of the above statement that money-raising was one of the prime objects of these various free speech propaganda, is the following extract from an appeal for money published in *Solidarity*, the official organ of the Industrial Workers of the World, during the controversy at Little Falls, N. Y.:

> In the meantime it is necessary that demands be made all the time on Governor Sulzer, Albany, N. Y., for an immediate grand jury investigation of the Little Falls authorities. BE SURE TO SEND ME A COPY, so I can get it into the local papers; that will help some here. *I might add that a public meeting for such resolutions consists of a chairman, secretary and audience. So, you see, three persons can be a meeting. A tip to the wise should be sufficient for a lot of action along these lines. Be sure and use all of the hack-worn expressions, etc., that you can think of. Paper is cheap and may do a little good in this instance.*
>
> But the most needed here are funds. DON'T FORGET THIS.

This was signed by J. S. Biscay, the organizer in charge of that particular campaign.

SOCIALISM AND PATRIOTISM

One of the persistent efforts of the socialists and Industrial Workers of the World is to stifle the patriotic impulse of the people. Love of country, or what they term "nationalism", is, they say, unethical. Books and pamphlets dealing with this question have been specially prepared for different classes of people, school teachers and children as well as for soldiers and policemen. In fact, the very word "patriotism" is anathema to the socialists. In *The Young Socialist Magazine* for April, 1912, is a good illustration of this feeling in the form of an acrostic, which also indicates the kind of teaching which the children of the socialists and of their sympathizers are receiving:

"WHAT IT SPELLS".

"P owder
A sininity
T rouble
R
I
O
T
I dioey
S uffering
M urder."

The socialists have a number of text books for children, by means of which they develop in the mind of the student a hatred for all employers

LESSON XI.

We See Ape — He Gets Nuts — Babe No Starve

What have we here? Where did you see an Ape? Does the Ape live in the woods? The Ape lives on Nuts. Does one Ape own the woods? No; all the Apes get nuts. The Apes must have nuts to live on. They would not let one big Ape own the woods and trees. If they did the small Apes could get no nuts that the big fat Apes did not want them to get. The small Apes would be the slaves of the big fat Apes. Did you ever see an Ape beg? No; not so long as there were nuts in the woods. Is one Ape the slave of the big, fat Ape? No, they are all free Apes. Does the Babe of the Ape work? Does the Babe of the Ape starve so long as there are nuts in the woods?

THE BABES OF THE APE DO NOT STARVE.

LESSON XII.

Lots Of Room — Too Much Food — Starve Homes Dies

O, see the Map! It is the Land they call the States. Do you live in the States? Does your chum live in the States? Yes, we all live in the States. A few years ago it held no folks too rich or too poor. All had some food to eat and a home in which to live. This was in the days when the west was new and men went west to be free. The States is big and all the men in the world could live in the States. There is land here for all. Do all the men have land? Do all men have homes? The soil is rich, and we can work so that all men will have food. Do all men have good food? Why is it that men have no land? The rich, Fat Man owns it! Why is it that men have no homes of their own? The Rich, Fat Man owns most homes. Why is it that men have no food? The rich, Fat Man owns the right to most of the food. Is this right? No, it is not.

ALL MEN MUST HAVE NICE HOMES. ALL MEN MUST HAVE GOOD FOOD.

LESSON XVI.

Toil Pick Digs — Must Have Chance — Thus Makes Wealth

What do we see here? It is a man at work with a pick. What is his name? We call him TOIL. Will he dig all day? No, he will work eight hours. He will work two hours to make his own wage, and six hours to make his BOSS rich. Is this fair? This poor man keeps his wife and babe poor, while his BOSS is rich and wears silk and drinks wine. This is not fair! This is what we call a wage slave. If you tell this man that he is a wage slave, he will get mad. He wants to think that he is free. Is he? He is not, for the job he has, and the tools that he must use are owned by the rich man. Thus the rich man takes the wealth made by the poor. The poor man must have a chance. He will get a chance when all the men will own all the tools and land that they must have to live. Man must also have rest as well as work. as work.

THAT WHICH GAVE US LIFE, GAVE US THE RIGHT TO BE FREE.

LESSON XVII.

Child Works Shop — Wheels Big Near — Love Hate Wrong

O, see the shop! The child is in the shop. See the big wheels! They are near the child. The child works hard. The child should be in the school, and not in the shop. You don't want to go to the shop to work all day? You like play; and you like a good time as well as you like the school. Can the child in the shop play? It must work. Why must such a small child work? Are there no men who want to work? A child works cheap. The Big, Fat Man owns the shop. This is a crime. The child is a slave. Men are out of work. Men beg. The child dies. The time will come when there will be no child in the shop. Men will not be out of work. They will not need to beg. "CHILD SLAVE" will be no words in use, for we will have no slave. All will be free. That will be nice for all. Joy and love will take the place of hate and wrong.

THE CHILD NEEDS PLAY. ALL MEN WILL WORK.

LESSON XIX.

Strike Poor Slave — Law Said Work — Food Keep Sure

See the poor Slave! See the man with the whip! Will he strike the Slave? It would be bad to do so. Is he not a bad man to hit the poor slave? But he has this right. He owns the Slave and may do with him as he will. The law said a man may own a slave. No law like that now. It was a bad law for the Slave, was it not? Is it nice to be a slave? No, it is bad to be a slave. The Slave had to work. He got no wage. But he got his food and keep. He got this sure! Does the white slave now get his food and keep? Does he get it sure? I know lots of men who would be glad to work for their food and keep. Right in this town where we are told that we have no slave. Would you like to be a slave? Do you want a slave? Is your Pa a slave? Does he want to be free? The law will wipe out the wage slave.

LET US BE FREE. NO WHIP. NO WAGE SLAVE.

LESSON XXVI.

This, my dear child, is what is meant by the term "Class War." One class of men work and make our food, clothes and homes. While one class of men do no real work, but live on the hard work and the sweat of the first class. Who works? What do we call the class that does the real work? Is your Pa in this class? The Big, Fat man does no real work. Yet he eats. The big Fat Man is the Boss of the earth. He can give, or not give, your Pa and Ma work. The big, Fat Man owns the shops, mills, mines and the land. He can tell your Pa and Ma to "Get off the earth." You see he is the Boss. Did he make the earth? Did he make the shops? Did he make the mines? Did he make the mills? No, my dear child, these things are here for all, and not for the few big, Fat Men. Some day each man will be his own Boss. These things will be for all. Then the big, Fat Man will have to work just like the Thin man. We will all have lots of joy, time to play, and no Boss. Would you like to see this time? I would!

HE WHO WILL NOT WORK SHALL NOT EAT. WE WANT NO CLASS WAR.

FACSIMILE PAGES FROM "THE SOCIALIST PRIMER."

be produced a thousand quotations of the :haracter.

909 Victor Berger made the following pre- in *The Social-Democratic Herald*:

> In view of the plutocratic law-making of the esent day, it is easy to predict that the safety d hope of this country will finally lie *in one rection only—that of a violent and bloody colution.*
>
> Therefore, I say, each of the 500,000 socialist ters, and of the two million workingmen who stinctively incline our way, should, besides do- g much reading and still more thinking, also ve a good rifle and *the necessary rounds of imunition in his home and be prepared to back his ballot with his bullets if necessary.*

n Spargo said:

> . . . When the slaves answer the challenge socialism with a united war-cry for justice d economic freedom, *all who resist them will swept away as chaff, before the fury of the le. And that, I believe will be the result.* ie despoiled and disinherited, urged by the ighty passion of socialism, will rise and enter to full possession of their own, hurling into e dust of oblivion false and unjust religions, ate crafts, and political economies.

my article in a daily paper referred to I stated that there was no excuse for the societies not knowing just what the so- t position was and I predicted that the ists themselves would thank me for writing rticle. My prediction was verified. The r of *The Call* the day following its publica- acknowledged the debt and said:

> *The Call* is much indebted to Mr. Easley for is assistance in putting us right before the ipitalistic minded public. We will take the iance of his doing us any harm.
>
> There has always been some difficulty in etting our propaganda clearly understood, and iough we always insist upon accentuating the evolutionary character of socialism, there are lways great numbers who will persist in rank- g us with reformers and futile mollycoddles f that species and its numorous variations.

WALL STREET OR SOCIALISM GAINING CONTROL OF THE SOURCES OF PUBLIC OPINIONS?

iere is undoubtedly today a widespread feel- that in some subterranean way the hand of tal is directing the principal agencies of pub- pinion and education.

have given a few typical instances, out of hundreds that could be cited, of the easy is these preachers of social hatred seem to to the editorial columns of the so-called itocratic press," the pulpits of wealthy ches, the lecture halls and student clubs of colleges and universities, and the working s of privately endowed philanthropic bodies social settlements, and, astonishing as it seem, even in some of the great foundations is an active socialist contingent and influ- working in and through them. Instead of organizations being used to promote the h capitalistic interests of their founders, as iarged, my observation is that just the re- is true. The foundations are more often inated in some of their most important de- ments, if not in their entire attitude, by so- sts and radicals of various types than by igning emissaries of capitalism." Many of creators of great fortunes which are now de- l to the furtherance of social reform move- ts would turn in their graves if they knew to t an extent their money was being used today romote socialism and other revolutionary rams.

ie simple truth is that there is no mysteri- underground way through which these great ochs of capitalism are continually plotting conspiring against the people. Their every is not invested with a deadly and sinister ition to strike a blow at our democratic in- tions.

It is an erroneous assumption that, because a man has been successful in business he has great ability and shrewdness in everything else to which he turns his hand. Dense ignorance of economic and social questions, not to say personal animosities, would alone prevent philanthropists from agreeing upon any plan of action which could have a sinister or baneful effect upon our institutions, even should they so desire. The danger, as I have stated, is entirely the other way. They are more likely to be used by promoters of revolutionary cults to the detriment of these very institutions. The capitalists knew how to organize trusts and combinations in the days when such things were tolerated by law and public sentiment, but today, when they strike the economic and industrial field, they are helpless and become "easy marks" for the "ghost dancers" and "dealers in gold bricks". One might almost say of them, as Haywood did of the judge who tried him in Paterson, that they "don't know the difference between anarchy and arnica," much less the difference between the trade unionists, the socialists and the Industrial Workers of the World.

When the movement to have Ettor and Giovannitti released from the prison in Lawrence, Massachusetts, was worked up, one of the prominent leaders was an important man in a big foundation and the Industrial Workers of the World made great capital out of the fact that this man was helping them, which showed, as they alleged, that the "infamous treatment" that Giovannitti and Ettor had received was such that even this capitalist felt it his duty to take up the cudgels for them. They suppressed the fact that this man was a socialist and a personal sympathizer with and admirer of Haywood and the whole industrial Workers of the World movement. For years one of the vice-presidents of a large insurance company has been a member of the Socialist Party and his bank account was always at the disposal of that party. This man's socialist utterances were used as coming from "a prominent Wall Street capitalist". The socialists themselves knew that he was one of the party members but the people whom they were trying to impress did not suspect that fact, which made great capital for the socialists.

In the offices of many industrial corporations there may be found revolutionary socialists. In one of the largest industrial corporations of the country, the highest priced expert, commonly called "the one hundred thousand dollar man", is a radical socialist and his writings and speeches are used throughout the country by the socialists, giving his full title in this big manufacturing establishment, without any objection, so far as I have heard, from the capitalist owners of that great plant.

In a large casualty insurance company the expert is an out-and-out socialist, who prefaces his books on social insurance problems with a statement frankly warning the reader of his possible bias. If socialism should be achieved, of course that insurance company would go out of business. The financial editor of a large daily paper is affectionately known in socialist circles as "the Wall Street Red". He makes no attempt to conceal his straight-out Karl Marxian views and he doubtless has the "Open Sesame" to "Broad and Wall" and the other big financial institutions, which fact alone ought either to acquit the Wall Street powers of any well-defined intention to "put anything over" on the people or else to convict them of dense stupidity.

One of the prolific sources of socialist propaganda has, strangely enough, come through commercial organizations which, ignorantly or indifferently, have permitted socialists to make social and industrial surveys for them in different cities. One in Chicago that dealt with conditions in the stockyards was made by a member of the Socialist Party who is now a socialist alderman in that District. It is easy to imagine what his report was; and yet this was paid for by good, hard-headed business men who probably swallowed the stuff that was turned in to them. Of course it was indigestible and therefore valueless.

A leading charity publication, which has among its directors and patrons some of the prominent capitalists of the country and whose president is a large New York corporation lawyer, is completely dominated by the revolutionary forces. Some time ago it boasted in its editorial columns of having been so magnanimous to the syndicalists as to have run four articles from the pens of those fomenters of disorder. It printed one article of six pages by a woman member of its regular staff, which was designed to explain sympathetically the sabotage, violence and murder proposals of the Industrial Workers of the World.

As I have already pointed out, there are churches in all the large cities with socialist preachers, although the trustees of these churches include leading bankers and other business men. The preachers are teaching socialism right under their noses and they do not seem to know it. In one conspicuous instance in New York City the church is noted not only for the almost anarchistic utterances of the preacher but for his activity in organizing movements for no other purpose than to promote the socialist propaganda. This church last winter took up the unemployment situation in New York City and, as the chairman of the committee which made the report was a radical socialist leader, his report naturally represented that practically everybody in the city was out of employment. And yet the trustees of this church include some of the most wealthy of the manufacturers and "predatory rich." Either they do not know or do not care, indicating at any rate that they are not searching for means to despoil the common people of their rights.

A financial writer who maintains a bureau for the dissemination of so-called "facts and statistics", which he sells to the bankers of the country, in one of the letters (for which the bankers are paying) after describing the labor situation and the destructive character of the Industrial Workers of the World, and stating that "the aim of the workers is the ultimate ownership of factories, banks, stores, and all other industries by the workers themselves", coolly announces his belief that the theory of the Industrial Workers of the World is right and advises the manufacturers and bankers to get into line with the idea that all that they have is soon to be confiscated by the workers. He says, "Capital will not much longer rest content with present conditions." In other words, capitalists are becoming so dissatisfied with the present conditions under which they own their own property that they are willing to have the socialists, anarchists and Industrial Workers of the World seize it and operate it for them! And yet this gentleman is selling letters containing this advice to supposedly hard-headed business men, who are accused by the radicals of eternally plotting and scheming to despoil the people. It might be remarked that a banker who has no more sense than to pay for such stuff ought to be relieved of his property, because he has already been relieved of his commonsense.

One of the richest men in the United States for some years assisted a campaign conducted by one of the most radical socialists in the country to prove that low wages were the cause of vice. This socialist announced publicly his views when he started in on this work, as follows:

> I believe that so-called "white slavery" is a disease of the social body; that it cannot be cured by treating the symptoms; that it can be cured only by eradicating the cause. I believe that the cause is economic—that the cause is poverty. I therefore believe that the only way to cure white slavery is to cure poverty. And

> I know of no cure for poverty save the erection of an industrial system whereunder a living wage shall be guaranteed to all workers, whereunder all persons capable of working shall be forced to work, whereunder private property shall be abolished, and the entire means of production and distribution, now owned by the few for the enrichment of the few, shall be owned and operated by the many for the benefit of all. In a word, I know of no cure but socialism.
>
> All suggested cures are and must be futile save the cure that socialism alone can supply.

The wealthy man referred to, who is attacked as one of the chief of malefactors, was pointed to by the socialists as having accepted their doctrine, when as a matter of fact practically every expert on the social evil would declare this theory of white slavery entirely groundless as well as a libel upon the working girls of this country, and this wealthy "malefactor" himself would not accept such a theory.

There is a journal of high-brow pretensions, recently started in this city by a combination of populists, socialists, syndicalists and all-round freaks. This publication is backed by a rich young man, who is making good its deficits. Its editors are generally twenty-five-year old statesmen, superficial and reckless. They boast of their ultra radicalism and at the present time are making a specialty of feminism and birth control. And yet rich men, with high business connections, are "putting up the money."

I give this picture of the socialist inroads into capitalism to show the utter absurdity and screaming farcicalness of the cry that capital is very alert and vigorous in its efforts to protect its own selfish interests. These illustrations could be continued indefinitely but I have given sufficient to show that whatever crimes may be charged against the capitalists they cannot be convicted of sitting up at night to devise ways and means for destroying American ideals and American institutions. Rather should they be charged with the gravest negligence in not interesting themselves in the intelligent and patriotic defence of these ideals and institutions from the onslaughts of those who would destroy them in the interests of a philosophy subversive of individual liberty and industrial progress.

While the cumulative effect of the enumeration of the activities of the socialists in all fields might seem alarming to some, I do not want to give the impression that I share that feeling. It is true that socialism is gnawing at the vitals of all that most people hold dear but I think it contains within itself the seeds of its own destruction. Education is showing that its philosophy is false, its indictments of society absurd and its methods utterly impossible.

SOCIALISM VS. INDUSTRIAL AND SOCIAL PROGRESS

The socialists, if we grant their philosophy, are of course perfectly consistent in ridiculing and opposing definite social reforms. If the evils incident to modern industry should be abolished—and many of them are being abolished—they would have nothing upon which to base the demand for revolution, and it is revolution they are working for, and not reform.

The lack of a clear perception of this important distinction has confused many good people. All right-minded persons are heartily in favor of practical social reform, but the real party socialists, who are the only socialists having a right to speak for the party, are not reformers at all but revolutionists. It is true that in the socialist platform there is a long list of what are termed "immediate demands," which include every conceivable change in social conditions that anyone has ever suggested, without any relation to socialism; but it is made perfectly apparent that this is only done for campaign purposes as the platform always closes with this clearly understandable paragraph:

> Such measures of relief as we may be able to force from capitalism are but a preparation of the workers to seize the whole powers of government in order that they may thereby lay hold of the whole system of socialized industry and thus come to their rightful inheritance.

That the Socialist Party has no use for social reform was well stated by Keir Hardie at an annual conference of the Independent Labour Party of England (the title of the Socialist Party in that country) when he declared:

> The Independent Labour Party is not a reform organization. It is revolutionary in the fullest sense of the word. The party does not exist to patch up the existing order of society and make it a little more tolerable, but to overthrow the existing order and build up a Socialist State.

The Progressive Party at its convention in 1912, held in Chicago, struck the double-dealing political policy of the socialists like a Kansas tornado, and the wreckage was to be found in the editorial pages of all their papers. They were in a veritable panic. With the Progressive Party declaring for many of the immediate reforms which the socialists had pretended that they stood for, the latter had to come out in the open and either ADMIT that they were not sincere in demanding these measures or else support Colonel Roosevelt in that campaign.

That they decided to throw off all pretence for reform and come out boldly for revolution was well shown by Charles Edward Russell, then socialist candidate for Governor of New York, in a political speech made on Saturday evening, September 7, 1912. Referring to the social reforms included in the platform of the Progressive Party, he said he wished it to be distinctly understood that the socialists had no interest in them. He added:

> Some gentlemen in this campaign believe that two or three fragments of the socialist program, with a few worn out remedial laws, will spike the socialist guns.
>
> They have jimmied the back door of the socialist house, have stolen half a dozen silver-plated spoons and think they have shut down the house, and they forget that the Socialist Party is not a party of reform but of revolution.

To a reporter on *The Evening Sun*, who asked Mr. Russell if there were not socialist ideas in the Progressive platform, he replied:

> Not a single one. Those who say that there are don't know what the word "socialistic" means. The Progressive Party is just as far from socialism as it is from democracy. Their planks are mere palliatives and nostrums, idle as the wind—not worth talking about.

Mr. Russell's criticisms of the Progressive platform would, of course, apply with equal force to the social reforms proposed in both the Republican and Democratic platforms.

A later and probably more official statement to the same effect is the following extract from *The New York Call* of March 17, 1915:

> No doubt there are many people attracted to the socialist party by impressions they have received—not from it—that it is a party of reform. Some of these stay, even when they discover that their first impressions were untrue, and that they have joined a party whose central object, purpose and idea is social revolution and the abolition of the present established system of capitalism. They gradually comprehend and accept its revolutionary object. Others again get out as soon as possible when they discover their mistake; and others again, unconsciously obsessed with the reform virus in every cell of their intellectual being, and at the same time complacently satisfied with their intellectual superiority, stay in and make trouble or at least strive to make it.

. Ghent Makes Critical Analysis of "The Nation"

(Continued from page 7)

re on November 11th. Yet it was not nd of an untruth; it was a report that plausible basis. Even *The Liberator* usually shows an entire absence of fair- rgot itself for the moment and explained, January issue, the origin of the story. ıreat of a general massacre, admits *The tor,* was actually made, "in a heated ," by Zinovieff, then president of the rad Soviet. It is unlikely that you are nt of what appears in *The Liberator.* have since passed, but you have made no n of Zinovieff.

December 14 you indulged in some rather ntine humor over the charge that Bolshe- nds were being used to foment revolution many. On January 18 you granted your- other indulgence in the same pleasantry. othing is more certain than that these were so used. The fact has been admitted Bolshevists Joffe and Radek, and by cer- f the Independent Socialists, particularly and Haase. Joffe says that up to Decem- 3d altogether 24,000,000 rubles had been at the disposal of the German revolu- ies. The matter has been widely discussed German press and has been further de- in the national assembly at Weimar. That part of the funds may have been intended e relief of Russian prisoners may or may true; but no reasonable person now denies sential truth of the original story. Never- s, though weeks have since passed, you have no admission of the unfair treatment you o this episode.

have shown a like unfairness in the ent of Kerensky's testimony. During the d I have named, the former head of the ian republic, in a number of speeches and views, gave voluminous accounts of condi- in Russia. You may say that they were san and therefore to be distrusted; but no scrupulosity guided you when you pub- l Tschitscherin's infamous paper and care- emphasized by italics the most impudent ges. This matter, however, is neither here here. What I wish to point out is that you shed not one line of Kerensky's testimony. ter, however, when Kerensky became em- red by his realization of the fact that he not to be restored to power, and assailed the s, you suddenly shifted your attitude rd him and eagerly accepted him as a com- nt witness. You say (December 21st) that sinister interpretation is put upon the ian policy of the Allies by Kerensky in his ed Press interview of December 11th," and quote some of his utterances. So long, fore, as Kerensky was denouncing Lenine Trotzky his testimony was negligible; the ent he turned to denouncing the Allies his nony acquired a sterling worth.

t your treatment of the testimony of Col. imir I. Lebedeff is perhaps the most striking ration of the fraud which you persistently tice upon your readers. Lebedeff, in his al statement, issued by the Russian In- ation Bureau, relates conditions in Russia e knows them. No reasonable being who his statement can doubt this man's sincer- r his competency as a witness. Yet in spite our professed determination to "utilize utely every source of information concern- Russia that you can get," you ignore every- g he says about the Bolsheviki. No one d ever have known from your journal that a person as Lebedeff existed had you not ed upon a paragraph in his account in h you think you discover something to the edit of the Allies. This you exultantly ish.

There are many other similar instances which I could mention; but for the present these will do. You suppress one kind of testimony, and you disseminate the opposite kind. But your distortion and suppression are not limited to the mere matter of the juggling of testimony. In your editorial comment you carry the work further. You constantly assume as facts what the most reputable witnesses assert to be untrue. You constantly declare or imply that all the opponents of the Bolsheviki are reactionaries, in spite of the fact that most of the noblest and the best of the Russian progressive elements have opposed these usurpers. You repeatedly pay out praise to yourself for your alleged practice of truth-telling, although no other journal so uniformly distorts the truth; and you repeatedly harp upon the alleged "lying" of other journals, although these journals have printed the most dependable testimony that has come out of Russia. And you never fail to pour out upon those persons, no matter how upright, who oppose your position, a stream of objurgatory epithets.

Of course, this editorial manner is a traditional one in your office, and perhaps there is no escape from it. It comes down from the days of E. L. Godkin. There is, however, a difference. Godkin scattered the largess of his odium in cynical disdain; you people do the thing in riotous frenzy. Your journal has long been the particular organ of the college professors and detached intellectuals, and this manner is after their hearts' desire. These cloistered savants are, in the main, a timid folk who do not ordinarily venture far from their sheltered retreats. But what they lack in contact with actual life they make up in imaginative adventure. Just as shopgirls and serving maids find escape from the trammels of everyday life in the glowing pages of Bertha M. Clay and Laura Jean Libbey, identifying themselves with the heroines of these romances and listening to the ardent wooing of princelings, lordlings and rich manufacturers' sons, so these *faineant* intellectuals ride to glorious adventure on the wings of your denunciatory rhetoric. Your battles become their battles; and they see themselves the doughty victors on a thousand fields.

Now, strangely enough, you have taken on a new clientele—one of pro-Bolshevists, anarchists and I. W. W.'s. I find them out here the eager purchasers and hungry readers of your journal. These folk are not necessarily timid folk like the intellectuals; indeed, some of them sometimes give examples of what is called "rough-house" that might make even Trotzky envious; but since their wonted activities are more and more restrained by the brutal hand of the police and the secret service, there rises in them also this upwelling of suppressed desires, and they, too, must find imaginative adventure along the torrent of your denunciation.

Now I find nothing in the character of your journal which gives warrant for this arrogant assumption of the right to pour out a constant stream of convictions and sentences against persons who disagree with you, and in addition to shower upon them, like a "hanging judge," a rain of vituperation. If your habit was impartially to give the facts of an episode or a situation; if you revealed in your editorial policy a consistent fairness of treatment; and if, furthermore, you held to a consistent social philosophy of any kind, no matter what, which gave to your expressed judgments a character of uniformity and dignity, then you might fairly claim some of this Rhadamanthine prerogative.

I have already shown that to the first two of these virtues you can lay no claim whatever; and I say further that you are equally lacking in the third. I say that anyone who reads your editorial comment and understands what he is reading, will inevitably find three wholly different strains of social theory. Sometimes they are separated by paragraphs or articles, and sometimes they are inextricably wound together. The first is the *laissez-faire* of the Godkinian tradition; the second is state collectivism, or, if you prefer, state capitalism; and the third is that amorphous thing, borrowed from the philosophers of the *New Republic*, unnamed as yet, but which I propose to call, after the terminology of that school, the "federationism of experimental allegiances." You thus give the spectacle of yourselves not knowing what you are after, of having no fixed social belief, and yet as of one pretending to know all things, dealing out Olympian judgments.

As for your journal's distortion of the truth, there is, of course, this to be said in mitigation of my criticism. All radical and so-called liberal journals habitually do this thing. The capitalist journal appeals to the general mass of readers, and no matter what its disposition may be, it must in some measure restrain the temptation to juggle and suppress. No such restraint is obligatory upon the radical or so-called "liberal" journal. Its business is to furnish a particular bias to a group of particularly biassed minds. For the "greater glory of the cause" it stretches and warps and makes over what it uses and ignores what it finds inconvenient.

If, then, the reader must scan with caution what he finds in a capitalist journal, he must scan with a far more careful scrutiny what he finds in the journals of professed enlightenment. My complaint against *The Nation* is that it carries this distortion to a greater extreme than do other journals of its class, that at the same time, more loudly and more persistently than they, it professes the highest virtue, and that with greater frequency and more passionate vehemence than they it shouts "liar" and "knave" at its opponents.

You tell me that I should not question motives. Perhaps I should not; but this is strange counsel from the office of your journal, which exceeds all other journals with which I am acquainted in the outrageousness with which it does this very thing. Of course, in the explanation of your policy there is an alternative interpretation, and that is the fanaticism of self-deception.

Let me say, however, that I have been in the radical movement all my life and that I have met with fanaticisms of a wide range and degree, but never with one which could compass so wide a chasm as that between the professions and the practices of your journal.

At any rate I have given the facts; they are notorious, indisputable, and of a nature that calls for some remedial action. I marvel at the stupidity of the capitalist press in New York that it lets your journal go on, week after week, virtually unrebuked. It seems to me that a three months' campaign by any daily newspaper could force your journal to a shriving of past sins, to the making of new resolutions and the adoption of a new policy.

Maybe the opinion prevails that it is best to let *The Nation* shout itself out in vain and impotent diatribes. If that is the case, I fear that not much is to be done, for I see no evidence of an inclination toward reform from the inside.

Very truly yours,

W. J. GHENT.

(*Quotation from Letter from W. J. Ghent, dated April 17, 1919.*)

"I had a reply from Mussey. It was very tame. The only thing he could find to say in confutation was that he had not himself italicized the most offensive passages in the Tschitscherin letter, but had used them as he found them. I can't think that much of a point. Whether he did the italicizing himself or adopted another's work, the effect was to show editorial approval, as I had said. The fact is that Mussey knew I had the goods on him, and there was nothing to say."

Dr. O'Grady Takes Exception to Criticism of Pamphlet

(*Continued from page 9*)

of the social insurance movement in this country, when he says: "Within less than five years, originating with a small committee in New York, it has gained so much headway that nine states have appointed government commissions for its investigation, with a total appropriation of considerably over $100,000." He might have added that this "small committee in New York" was made up entirely of doctrinaires, not one employer nor one representative wage-earner being admitted into that incubating conference. He might also have stated that all this money spent on commissions has availed little, because there is not today a compulsory health insurance law on the statute book of any of the forty-eight states; that in California, although the commission which employed Dr. Rubinow as actuary favored the proposition, the people turned it down by more than two to one majority, on a referendum vote; that in Massachusetts, the constitutional convention voted it down by a large majority; that in New York the Legislature refused to enact such a law; and that the commissions in Wisconsin and Connecticut have reported against it.

It may be true, as Dr. O'Grady asserts, that there are more employers in the Chamber of Commerce of the United States than in any other organization in America; the figures are not available to the writer. But the statement criticised was: "The Chamber of Commerce of the United States is not a body representative of manufacturers or producers. It is largely representative of what may be called the commercial or 'middleman' class." True, merchants are employers; so are bankers, stockbrokers and professional men who have stenographers and clerks; and so are farmers who have hired help. But they are not the employers, such as manufacturers and mine owners, who deal directly with large labor problems. When the National War Labor Board was formed by President Wilson, he did not call upon the Chamber of Commerce of the United States to furnish the employer group, but upon the National Industrial Conference Board.

It is not desirable to resume a detailed discussion of the reconstruction program. However, as one of the many expressions of opinion received by the writer from Catholics since the publication of the article referred to has gone rather fully into certain phases of the report, it is given in part below:

"The pamphlet entitled "Social Reconstruction", being No. 1 of the "Reconstruction Pamphlets" of the Committee on Special War Activities of the National Catholic War Council and dated January, 1919, contains a "Foreword," subscribed by four eminent Catholic Bishops, which exhorts American Catholics to be zealous in the solution of the great social problems which now face us and in a general way approves the program for social reform advocated in what follows. That is to be construed as an endorsement of the general ends and purposes of the measures advocated in the pamphlet and of the strictly moral features of such measures; but it does not carry with it an authentication of all allegations of fact to be found in the pamphlet and much less enjoin upon Catholics the support of the particular political measures advocated. However, that Foreword is liable popularly to be given a broader construction. Consequently, this pamphlet looks like a case of inadvertent ecclesiastical approval of propaganda of social discontent.

"For, the opening matter in this pamphlet, which purports to present the reconstruction program of labor and capital in Great Britain and America, is partial, misinforming and misleading. And the program of social reform that follows is replete with doubtful assertions of fact, calculated to convey a false and exaggeratedly pessimistic impression of social conditions in this country, and presents as certain means for the economic betterment of the masses a series of political measures of doubtful practical expediency and involving grave social risks. For examples:

> It is stated (p. 14) that the average rate of pay of American wage-earners has not increased faster than the cost of living. To say the least, that is an assertion to be doubted.
>
> It is stated (p. 14), on the authority of Lauck and Sydenstricker, that in 1915 four-fifths of heads of American families obtained less than $800. Certainly much that is implied in that statement is both disputable and vigorously disputed.
>
> It is stated (p. 22) that the incomes for the great majority of American wage-earners are "insufficient"—this statement, in conjunction with the context, conveying the impression that such incomes are insufficient for a decent livelihood. Without denying that on the average the wage-earners deserve a greater share in the products of industry, this assertion may rightly be characterized as a gross and rash exaggeration.
>
> It is stated (p. 22) that in the present industrial system there is enormous inefficiency and waste in the production and distribution of commodities. Inevitably in all human operations there is some inefficiency and waste. But that enormous inefficiency characterizes production and distribution in America is a bald assertion that merits indignant denial. And the allegation of waste, because general and undiscriminating, deserves like condemnation.

"Such is the character of the premises upon which is based the program of reform advocated in the pamphlet. Certainly they grossly and inexcusably exaggerate the grounds for social discontent.

"Turning now to the particular measures advocated:

> It is stated (p. 15) that the great cities "ought to" take up and continue the National Government's work of housing. But surely, as a practical question, it is doubtful whether a city, like New York, which cannot build a court house in ten years and without wasting some millions of dollars in the preliminary operations, ought to embark upon any such project as here urged.
>
> It is stated (p. 16) that the means of avoiding the toll taken from industry by various classes of middlemen is "the operation of retail and wholesale mercantile concerns under the ownership and management of consumers." But those who have studied actual experiments in this line certainly have ground for a reasonable belief that the remedy here advocated is not only far from being a generally applicable panacea, but, on the contrary, that it is a dangerous one for ordinary consumers to experiment with.
>
> It is stated (p. 22) that the full possibilities of increased production will only be reached when the majority of the workers become owners, at least in part, of the instruments of production, which stage can be reached through cooperative productive societies or copartnership arrangements. But certainly the average person of experience cannot be expected to believe that cooperative ownership and management of "grand industries" by the workers would be otherwise than destructive. Practical experience indicates that the Bolsheviki are wrong not only morally but also practically.
>
> It is stated (p. 23) that excessive gains by privileged capitalists may be prevented by heavy taxation of incomes and inheritances. That may be true; and yet it is admissible to believe that the waste and extravagance incident to taxation concentrated upon only one class of the people will make the remedy worse than the disease.
>
> It is stated (p. 18) that "the State should make comprehensive provision for insurance against illness, invalidity, unemployment and old age." But closely following it is further stated that "any insurance scheme" "that tends to separate the workers into distinct or dependent classes, that offends against their domestic privacy and independence or that threatens individual self-reliance and self-respect, should not be tolerated." Although these propositions are really very indefinite, they are undoubtedly intended to convey the impression that the State ought to provide a system of compulsory social insurance for wage-workers generally and that it will be practicable to do so without violating the conditions

The National
Civic Federation Review

Vol. IV. NEW YORK, MAY 15, 1919 No. 14

MR. TAFT ENDORSES THE COVENANT

HE SAYS VALID OBJECTIONS ARE MET BY CHANGES IN PHRASEOLOGY ADOPTED BY THE PARIS CONFERENCE AND THAT AMENDMENTS STRENGTHEN IT

By WILLIAM HOWARD TAFT

(Copyright, 1919, by Public Ledger Company)

THE amendments to the covenant of the league of nations adopted in Paris on Monday (April 28) will bear careful study, and perhaps it is unwise hastily to express a confident opinion. But several readings suggest the following comment:

In the first place, the language and arrangement of the articles have been greatly improved. The use of different terms to mean the same thing, which tended to prevent an easy reading of the document, has been largely avoided. Provisions having immediate relation to one another have been assembled where they belong, avoiding application of them to subjects or countries which they were not intended to affect. Then names, misleading or clumsy, have been changed. The executive council, which was and is not executive but advisory, has become the council. The body of delegates has become the assembly, a much more suitable term.

Second, rules of construction that ought to have obtained in interpreting the original covenant are now made express and relieve the real doubts of friends and supporters of the league. The most important of these, perhaps, is the privilege specifically reserved to any member of the league to withdraw from it after two years' notice and after a compliance with its obligation under international law and the league covenant incurred before withdrawal. This gives any nation an opportunity to test the operation of the league and its usefulness and to avoid undue and unreasonable danger or burden in the future which actual trial may develop. Moreover, taken with the power of amendment which can be effected by a unanimous vote of the nine countries whose representatives compose the council and by a majority of the members of the league, there is ample opportunity for such a country as the United States to secure a revision of the covenant and a re-examination of the status of the states composing the league after peace has stabilized conditions and has shown where changes should be made. We are so important a member of an effective world league, and so indispensable to its successful working, because of our impartial position and world power, that an announcement of our purpose to withdraw unless amendments were made would be most persuasive. In this view Mr. Root's suggestion that it would be well to re-examine treaty provisions made just after the war in the light of the test of five years or more of peace can be carried out.

Copyright, Underwood & Underwood

WILLIAM HOWARD TAFT

The second change of the same character is the provision that, except where otherwise specifically provided, the action of the council or the assembly shall be by unanimous vote. The original covenant, properly interpreted, meant this, but it is of great importance to remove objections of those who did not think so. There are some who believe that such required unanimity will make the league ineffective and that a majority would have sufficed. But progress toward complete international cooperation in a new field like this must be gradual, and must, for the present, leave safeguards to nations against abuse of joint power which, experience may show, can be dispensed with. The required unanimity in the action of the council is very important in the answer it gives to the claim that under Article X and Article XVI the United States may be required to send expeditionary forces into distant parts of the world to defend the integrity and independence of a country with which we have no relation of interest or to suppress remote wars not affecting us. Such expeditions are to be planned and recommended by the council, and the plan is to be accepted in the discretion of the countries to whom the recommendation is addressed. The plan would certainly mark the limit of the obligation of the nations to whom it is presented. The United States will have a representative on the council, whose vote must approve the plan before its presentation. Is it likely, then, that the plan will be unreasonable in proposing an undue share of the league's work to the United States? May we not be sure that what is to be done will be apportioned according to the convenience and natural interest of the members of the league, because it must in effect be by mutual agreement?

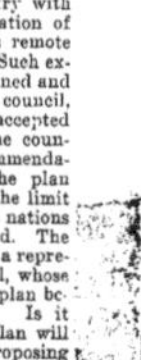

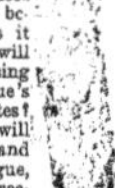

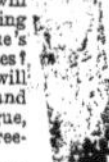

It is now made clear that under Article VIII the limit of armament for each country, under a general plan of reduction proposed by the council, is only to be adopted and made binding as a covenant for each member of the league after its full examination and agreement. Moreover, there is to be a re-examination of the plan and the limits every ten years, and meantime a specific limit may be increased by consent of the council. Thus we are to stop forever the race of armaments, the truculence and bullying they engender, their temptation to war and their cruel and enormous destructiveness when war ensues. Unless we have this league of nations, this race of armament must go on with the dreary round of events—first, burdensome taxation and consumption and waste of producing capacity, then war, then world suicide. These are the only alternatives to a league.

It is now made an express provision that only nations who choose to accept the duty may be made mandatories of the league. This removes another objection that was strongly pressed. We don't have to take charge of Constantinople or Armenia unless we choose to do so.

ARBITRATION MADE DEFINITE

One important change made by addition is the result of Mr. Root's constructive criticism. Mr. Root thought, and all who supported the plan of the League to Enforce Peace agreed with him, that the provision for arbitration ought to have required arbitration in justiciable issues, and he defined what he thought was clearly within the meaning of that term. By the present Article XIII the members agree to submit to arbitration any dispute which they recognize as suitable for arbitration. The covenant then declares disputes of the character described by Mr. Root, and, as the writer recollects, in Mr. Root's language, to be suitable for arbitration. Disputes as to interpretations of treaties, as to international law, as to facts upon which its application turns and damages for its breach are all declared to be arbitrable, or, in other words, justiciable. This imposes on members of the league having a dispute the duty of recognizing such disputes to be arbitrable and to submit them to arbitration. Can this duty be enforced under the league? Practically yes. If a nation declines to arbitrate such an issue, it goes to the council or assembly, with interested members excluded. Such body will at once recommend arbitration or will refer the issue to an international court of the league, as it may, to determine whether the issue is arbitrable under the obligations of the league and will doubtless follow the judicial advice thus given. As this machinery thus works out indirectly the result sought for in the plan of the League to Enforce Peace, an amendment to substitute a court of the league to take up and decide such questions directly will doubtless approve itself to the nations.

Mr. Root was anxious that, in addition to the declaration in the preamble, there should be practical recognition of international law as a guiding star of the league, its tribunals and its action. In the addition to Article XIII, which we have been discussing, we find such a recognition in the present Article XIV providing for a permanent *international court of justice* which is competent to hear and determine any dispute of international character submitted to it and to give an advisory opinion upon any dispute or question referred to it by the council or assembly.

The provision for mediation and recommendation of settlement in the first report of the covenant, which met Mr. Root's unqualified approval, has not been changed, except that the unanimity required for an effective recommendation by the body of delegates is now made unanimity by countries represented in the council and a majority of the assembly, a change which makes for effectiveness. Another important change is the addition of Article XXI, as follows:

> Nothing in this covenant shall be deemed to affect the validity of international engagements, such as treaties of arbitration or regional understandings like the Monroe Doctrine, for securing the maintenance of peace.

This meets two of Mr. Root's criticisms in full. First, it removes all doubt that all present arbitration treaties are to stand and bind the parties to them whether members of the league or not, and relieves those who were concerned lest progress toward peace by arbitration already made might be lost.

Second, it not only enables the United States to maintain the Monroe Doctrine, which was all that friends of that doctrine asked, but it recognizes it as a regional understanding for the securing of international peace. Never before in our history has the world set its approval upon the doctrine as in this covenant. It is really a great triumph for the supporters of the doctrine. It is not only a reservation in favor of the United States asserting it, but it is an affirmative declaration of its conventional character and of its value in securing international peace.

DOMESTIC QUESTIONS EXCLUDED

The exclusion of immigration and tariff and other internal and domestic questions is secured by the following:

> If the dispute between the parties is claimed by one of them and is found by the council to arise out of a matter which by international law is solely within the jurisdiction of that party, the council shall so report and shall make no recommendation as to its settlement.

If anything is clearly settled in international law, it is that except where a nation limits its rights by treaty, it may impose whatever condition it chooses upon the admission of persons or things into its territory. Those who express alarm lest the council should reach a different conclusion, in spite of international law, can hardly be aware how jealous all countries must and will be as to their method of raising taxes and protecting their industries, and how acutely many of the nations will insist on the right to exclude persons not desirable as permanent residents. Indeed, Japan has not urged the view that immigration was anything but a domestic question in this conference, but only pressed for an express recognition of racial equality of treatment of foreign persons resident in each country, and even this the conference did not deem it wise to grant.

Finally, we come to Article X, by which the members of the league undertake to respect and preserve against external aggression the territorial integrity and political independence of every member of the league. Mr. Root, as the writer understands, strongly favors this article; but he thinks there should be a re-examination of the arrangements made under the influence of the recent war, after conditions have become stabilized by peace, to remedy the possible mistakes made and to avoid too great rigidity. How this can be brought about indirectly through powers of amendment and withdrawal has already been pointed out.

The arguments against Article X which have been most pressed are those directed to showing that under its obligations the United States can be forced into many wars and to burdensome expeditionary forces to protect countries in which it has no legitimate interest. This objection will not bear examination. If Germany were to organize another conspiracy of militarism against the world, or if she and her old allies, together with Russia, were to organize a militant campaign for Bolshevism against the world, we should wish to do our share in fighting her, and in doing so quickly. If a stronger nation were to attack a weaker nation, a member of the league, our immediate and selfish interest in the matter would be determined by the question whether it would develop into a world war, inevitably dragging us in. But we are interested as a member of the family of nations in maintaining international justice in the interest of international peace everywhere, and we should do our share in maintaining it. It was a mixture of all these motives which carried us into this war and we accepted as a slogan the cry: "The world must be made safe for democracy. We make this war to secure the liberty and independence of nations against the doctrine that 'might makes right.'" This is all that Article X proposes. It is an answer to Germany's assertion of her right of conquest. It organizes the powers of the world to maintain the international commandment, "Thou shalt not steal by force."

FACES WITHERING ISOLATION

How much will it involve us in war? Little, if any. In the first place, the universal boycott, first to be applied, will impose upon most nations such a withering isolation and starvation that in most cases it will be effective. In the second place, we'll not be drawn into any war in which it will not be reasonable and convenient for us to render efficient aid, because the plan of the council must be approved by our representative, as already explained.

In the third place, the threat of the universal boycott and the union of overwhelming forces of the members of the league, if need be, will hold every nation from violating Article X and Articles XII, XIII and XV, unless there is a world conspiracy, as in this war, in which case the earlier we get into the war the better.

The warning effect of such a threat from a combination of nations, like those in the league, is shown conclusively in the maintenance of our Monroe Doctrine. The doctrine was announced in 1823. Its declaration was deprecated by American statesmen because it would involve us in a continual friction and war. It was directed against most powerful European nations. Yet we have maintained it inviolate without firing a shot or losing a soldier for now near a century. Article X merely extends the same protection to the weaker nations of the world which we gave to the weaker nations of this hemisphere against the greed of non-American nations. If our declaration accomplished this much, how much more can we count upon the effectiveness of the declaration of a powerful league of world nations as a restraint upon a would-be bully and robber of a small nation?

Labor and the Golden Rule

(Extracts from an Address before Carnegie Institute, Pittsburgh, April 24, 1919)

By OTTO H. KAHN

THE principle on which we should deal with the labor question is very simple. It is the principle of the Golden Rule.

I think the formula should be that, first of all, labor is entitled to a living wage. After that, capital is entitled to a living wage. What is left over belongs to both capital and labor, in such proportion as fairness and equity and reason shall determine in all cases.

The application of that formula is, of course, complex and difficult, because there are so many different kinds of labor, there are so many different kinds of capital. Not infrequently the laborer and capitalist overlap and merge into one. You have skilled labor and unskilled labor and casual labor; you have the small employer, the large individual employer, the corporate employer, the inventor, the prospector, etc. And then, circumstances and conditions vary greatly, of course, in different parts of the country and in different industries. It is impossible to measure by the same yardstick everywhere, but the principle of fairness can be stated, the desire can be stated to do everything possible to bring about good feeling and good understanding between labor and capital, and willingly and freely to cooperate so that labor shall receive its fair share in the fruits of industry, not only by way of a wage return, but of a larger return in comfort, in joy, in the happiness of life.

It seems to me that, in the main, right-thinking men of capital and of labor would concur in the following points:

(1.) The workman is neither a machine nor a commodity. He is a partner with capital. He must be given a full voice in determining the conditions under which he works either through organization in each factory or other unit, or through labor unions, or through both. Everything practicable must be done to infuse interest and conscious purpose into his work, and to diminish the sense of drudgery and monotony of his daily task.

The closest possible contact must be maintained between employer and employee. Machinery for the adjustment of grievances must be provided which will work smoothly and instantaneously. Every feasible opportunity must be given to the workman to be informed as to the conduct of the business of which he forms a part. He must not be deprived of his employment without valid cause. Wherever it is practicable and really desired by the workmen themselves to have representation on the Board of Direction, I think that, too, should be conceded. It would give them a better notion of the problems, complexities and cares which the employer has to face. It would tend to allay the suspicions and to remove the misconceptions which, so frequently, are the primary cause of trouble. The workman would come to realize that capitalists are not, perhaps, quite as wise and deep as they are given credit for, but on the other hand, a good deal less grasping and selfish than they are frequently believed to be, a good deal more decent and well meaning, and made of the same human stuff as the worker, without the addition of either horns or claws or hoofs.

(2.) The worker's living conditions must be made dignified and attractive to himself and his family. Nothing is of greater importance. To provide proper homes for the workers is one of the most urgent and elementary duties of the employer, or, if he has not the necessary means, then of the State.

OTTO H. KAHN

(3.) The worker must be relieved of the dread of sickness, unemployment and old age. It is utterly inadmissable that because industry slackens, or illness or old age befalls a worker, he and his family should therefore be condemned to suffering or to the dread of suffering. The community must find ways and means of seeing to it, by public works or otherwise, that any man honestly desirous to do an honest day's work shall have an opportunity to earn a living. Those unable to work must be honorably protected. The only ones on whom a civilized community has a right to turn its back are those unwilling to work.

(4.) The worker must receive a wage which not only permits him to keep body and soul together, but to lay something by for a rainy day to take care of his wife and children, and to have his due share of the comforts, joys and recreations of life.

(5.) Labor, on the other hand, must realize that high wages can only be maintained if high production is maintained.

The restriction of production is a sinister and harmful fallacy, most of all in its effect on labor. The primary cause of poverty is under-production. Furthermore, lessened production naturally makes for high costs. High wages accompanied by proportionately high cost of the essentials of living don't do the worker any good. And they do the rest of the community a great deal of harm. The welfare of the so-called middle-classes, i. e., the men and women living on moderate incomes, the small shopkeeper, the professional man, the farmer, is just as important to the community as the welfare of the wage-earner. If through undue exactions, through unfair use of his power, through inadequate output, the workman brings about a condition in which the pressure of high prices becomes intolerable to the middle classes, he will create a class animosity against himself which is bound to be of infinite harm to his legitimate aspirations.

It must be admitted, unfortunately, that for a long period in the past, society failed to give labor a square deal or to do anything like its duty by labor. But in their rightful resentment against exploitation and in their determination for the redress of just grievances, labor should not permit itself to be misled by plausible fallacies or self-seeking agitators. It must not give credence, for instance, to the absurd preachment that practically all wealth other than that produced by the farmer, is the product of the exertions of the working men. There are, of course, many other factors that enter into the creation of wealth. Thus, the "directive faculty," the quality of leadership in thought and action is not only one absolutely needful in all organized undertakings, great or small, but it becomes increasingly rare and, consequently, increasingly more valuable as the object to which it addresses itself increases in size, complexity and difficulty.

Let us take as an example the case of Mr. Henry Ford. Through the organizing genius and enterprise of a self-made man, Mr. Henry Ford (not by monopoly, but in keen competition with other manufacturers), the automobile, instead of being a luxury of the few, has been brought within the reach of those of modest means.

The cost of the product has been vastly cheapened. The margin of profit on each automobile sold has been greatly diminished. Wages have been very largely increased, the living conditions of employees greatly improved. Work has been found for a great many more men than were employed before.

In other words, every single human factor concerned in either production or consumption has been advantaged. New wealth has been created at the expense of no one. It cannot be said that it was created by the workingman, except in the physical sense. It was not created by either monopoly or privilege. It was created mainly out of Mr. Ford's brain and at his risk.

By far the largest percentage of this new wealth goes to pay the wages of workingmen and other expenses of the business, but out of what is left, Mr. Ford's share is, by common report, in excess of $1,000,000 a year.

1. Did Mr. Ford *earn* $1,000,000 in one year? If not, how much did he *earn*? By what scale would you measure the proportion due to him of the new wealth created mainly by his faculties?

2. If he had not been allowed to earn the large sums which he did earn, how and where could he have found the means to enlarge and improve his factory, so as to make possible an enterprise which immensely cheapened the product to the consumer and largely increased the wages to the workingman and the opportunity for employment? Is there any instance where communistic or even merely cooperative undertakings have produced similar results? Is there any instance where governmental management has produced similar results?

In a recently published, very able, pamphlet on "Reconstruction," Miss Christabel Pankhurst, the well-known English leader in the fight for woman suffrage, says:

> Certain people, who ought to know better, have falsely taught that the poverty or semi-poverty of the many is due to the luxurious living of the prosperous sections of the community. This is not the truth, and if through all the years of preachings of agitators the result of each year's industrial effort had been divided equally among the members of the community, there would have been no appreciable increase of prosperity for any, and there would have been one dead level of poverty [illegible]

The way to progress is no[illegible] down to a common level of [illegible] means ultimately a common level of [illegible]ness, but to help everybody up.

It is not material success which should [illegible]

abolished. it is poverty and justified discontent which should be abolished.

We cannot abolish poverty by division, but only by multiplication.

It is not by the spoliation of some, but by creating larger assets and broader opportunity for all that national well-being can and must be enhanced.

I wonder how many people realize that, if all incomes above $10,000 were taken and distributed among those earning less than $10,000, the result, as near as it is possible to figure out, would be that the income of those receiving that distribution would be increased barely ten per cent.

And the result of any such division would be an immense loss in national productivity by turning a powerful and fructifying stream into a mass of rivulets many of which would simply lose themselves in the sand.

I wonder how many people know that the frequent and loud assertion that the great bulk of the wealth of the nation is held by a small number of rich men, is wholly false; and that the fact is, on the contrary, that seven-eighths of our national income goes to those with incomes of $5,000 or less, and but one-eighth to those with incomes above $5,000.

We have heard it said frequently recently—it has become rather the fashion to say it—that the rulership of the world will henceforth belong to labor. I yield to no one in my respect and sympathy for labor, or in my cordial and sincere support of its just claims. The structure of our institutions cannot stand unless the masses of workmen, farmers, indeed all large strata of society, feel that under and by these institutions they are being given a square deal within the limits, not of Utopia, but of what is sane, right and practicable.

But I venture to say that this prediction that the world will belong to labor will not and ought not to come true, for the rulership of the world will and ought to belong to no one class. It will and ought to belong neither to labor nor to capital, nor to any other class. It will, of right and in fact, belong to those of all classes who acquire title to it by talent, hard work, self-discipline, character and service.

He is no genuine friend or sound counselor of the people nor a true patriot who recklessly, calculatingly or ignorantly raises or encourages expectations which cannot or which ought not to be fulfilled.

We must deal with all these things with common sense, mutual trust, with respect for all, and with the aim of guiding our conduct by the standard of liberty, justice and human sympathy. But we must rightly understand liberty. We must resolutely oppose those who in their impatient grasping for unattainable perfection would make of liberty a raging and destructive torrent instead of a majestic and fertilizing stream.

Liberty is not fool-proof. For its beneficent working it demands self-restraint, a sane and clear recognition of the reality of things, of the practical and attainable, and a realization of the fact that there are laws of nature and of economics which are immutable and beyond our power to change.

Nothing in history is more pathetic than the record of the instances when one or the other of the peoples of the world rejoicingly followed a new lead which it was promised and fondly believed would bring it to freedom and happiness, and then suddenly found itself, instead, on the old and only too well-trodden lane which goes through suff[illegible] and turmoil to disillusionment and [illegible]

[illegible] of us when we were twenty [illegible]-cut to the millennium and were

Now that we are older, though we know that our eyes will not behold the millennium, we should still like the nearest possible approach to it, but we have learned that no short-cut leads there and that anybody who claims to have found one is either an impostor or self-deceived.

Among those wandering sign-posts to Utopia we find and recognize certain recurrent types:

There are those who in the fervor of their world-improving mission discover and proclaim certain cure-alls for the ills of humanity, which they fondly and honestly believe to be newly discovered and unfailing remedies but which, as a matter of fact, are hoary with age, having been tried on this old globe of ours at one time or another, in one of its parts or another, long ago—tried and found wanting and discarded after sad disillusionment.

There are the spokesmen of sophomorism rampant, strutting about in the cloak of superior knowledge, mischievously and noisily, to the disturbance of quiet and orderly mental processes and sane progress.

There are the sentimental, unseasoned, intolerant and cocksure "advance thinkers" claiming leave to set the world by the ears and with their strident and ceaseless voices to drown the views of those who are too busy doing to indulge in much talking.

There are the self-seeking demagogues and various related types, and finally there are the preachers and devotees of liberty run amuck who in fanatical obsession would place a visionary and narrow class interest and a sloppy internationalism above patriotism, and with whom class hatred and envy have become a ruling passion. They are perniciously, ceaselessly and vociferously active, though constituting but a small minority of the people, and though every election and other test has proved, fortunately, that they are not representative of labor, either organized or unorganized.

Among these agitators and disturbers who dare clamorously to assail the majestic and beneficent structure of American traditions, doctrines and institutions there are some, far too many indeed—I say it with deep regret, being myself of foreign birth—who are of foreign parentage or descent. With many hundreds of thousands they or their parents came to our free shores from lands of oppression and persecution. The great republic generously gave them asylum and opened wide to them the portals of her freedom and her opportunities.

The great bulk of these newcomers have become loyal and enthusiastic Americans. Most of them have proved themselves useful and valuable elements in our manyrooted population. Some of them have accomplished eminent achievements in science, industry and the arts.

When the great test of the war came, the overwhelming majority of them rang wholly and finely true. The casualty lists are eloquent testimony to the patriotic devotion of "the children of the crucible," doubly eloquent because many of them fought against their own kith and kin.

But some there are who have been blinded by the glare of liberty as a man is blinded who after long confinement in darkness, comes suddenly into the strong sunlight. Blinded, they dare to aspire to force their guidance upon Americans who for generations have walked in the light of liberty.

They have become drunk with the strong wine of freedom, these men who until they landed on America's coasts had tasted little but the bitter water of tyranny. Drunk, they presume to impose their reeling gait upon Americans to whom freedom has been a pure and refreshing fountain for a century and a half.

Brooding in the gloom of age-long oppression, they have evolved a fantastic and distorted im-

Admitted in generous trust to the hospitali of America, they grossly violate not only t dictates of common gratitude, but of those e mentary rules of respect and consideration whi immemorial custom imposes upon the newcom or guest. They seek, indeed, to uproot t foundations of the very house which gave the shelter.

We will not have it so, we who are America by birth or by adoption. We reject these imp dent pretentions. By all means, let us move fo ward and upward, but let us proceed by t chart of reason, experience and tested Americ principles and doctrines, and let us not entru our ship to demagogues, visionaries or shallo sentimentalists who most assuredly would ste it on the rocks.

The strident voices of the fomentors of u rest do not cause me any serious apprehensio but we must not sit silently by, we must n look on inactively. Where there are grievanc to redress, where there are wrongs existing, v must all aid in trying to right them to the be of our ability.

To the extent that social and economic inst tutions, however deep and ancient their root may be found to stand in the way of the highe achievable level of social justice and the wide attainable extension of opportunity, welfare an contentment, they will have to submit to chang And the less obstructive and stubborn, the mo broadminded, cooperative and disinterested tho who pre-eminently prospered under the old co ditions will prove themselves in meeting th spirit of the new day and the reforms which may justly call for, the better it will be both fo them and for the community at large.

But to the false teaching and the variou pernicious "isms" with which un-American 50 percent Americans or anti-Americans ar flooding the country, we must give battle throug an organized campaign of education, of informa tion, of sane and sound doctrine, both spoke and written. The masses of the American pe ple want what is right and fair and just, bu they also want progress. They do not mea to stand still. They have no use for the stand patter and reactionary. They want to be show They will not simply take our word for it tha because a thing is so and has always been s therefore it should remain so.

Even before the war, a great stirring an ferment was going on in the land. The peopl were groping, seeking for a new and bette condition of things. The war has intensified the movement. It has torn great fissures in th ancient structure of our civilization. To re store it will require the cooperation of all patr otic men of sane and temperate views, what ever may be their occupation or calling or po litical affiliations.

It cannot be restored just as it was befor The building must be rendered more habitabl and attractive to those whose claim for adequat houseroom cannot be left unheeded, either justl or safely. Some changes, essential change must be made. I have no fear of the outcom and of the readjustment which must come. have no fear of the forces of freedom unless the be ignored, repressed or falsely and selfishly le

Changes the American people will make a their needs become apparent, improvements the welcome, the greatest attainable wellbeing fo all those under our national rooftree is thei aim; they will strive to realize what formerl were considered unattainable ideals, but the will do all that in the American way of san and orderly progress—and in no other. What ever betide in European countries, this natio will not be torn from its ancient moorings Against foes within, no less than against ene mies without, the American people will eve know how to preserve and protect the splendi

Is America Worth Saving?

A PROGRESSIVE REPUBLIC—OR FALSE INTERNATIONALISM AND A SOCIALIST AUTOCRACY?

By NICHOLAS MURRAY BUTLER

(Address Delivered Before the Commercial Club of Cincinnati, Ohio, April 19, 1919)

THOSE whose eyes are turned toward a state built not upon the civil liberty of the individual but upon the plenary power of organized government, are designated in a general way as Socialists. The words Socialism and Socialist, though less than a century old, have lately become very common among us and are so loosely and so variously used as to make it difficult to think clearly regarding the ideas for which they stand. Socialism, in the large, general and vague sense of the word, means simply social reform. In that sense, every intelligent and forward-stepping man or woman is a socialist.

All of us who are in our right minds are anxious to improve social conditions, to better the public health, to decrease the hours and the severity of labor, to increase the rewards and to add to the satisfactions of those who do the hard manual work of the world, to increase and make secure provision against illness, unemployment and indigent old age, to use the power of public taxation to build roads, to multiply schoolhouses, to aid with information and guidance those who farm and those who mine, to bring together collections of books, of objects of beauty and of art for the information and the pleasure of the great body of the people, to improve the conditions of housing in large cities, and to see to it that such essentials of life as water, light, and transportation are furnished of the best quality and at the lowest practicable cost.

If by Socialism be meant that the individual must not live for himself alone, but must use his powers, his capacities, and his gains for the benefit of his community and his fellows, then every American and every Christian is a socialist, for these are fundamental to American life and to Christian teaching. All this, however, is social reform, not Socialism.

THE FALSE ASSUMPTIONS OF SOCIALISM

Socialism, in the strict and scientific sense of the word, is, however, something quite different from this. Socialism involves not social reform but political and social revolution. It is the name for a definite public policy which rests upon certain historical and economic assumptions, all of which have been proved to be false, and it proceeds to very drastic and far-reaching conclusions, all of which are in flat contradiction to American policy and American faith. The assumptions of socialism are these:

First, that all of man's efforts, both past and present, are to be interpreted and explained in terms of his desire for wealth and of the processes which lead to the satisfaction of that desire. This assumption excludes at once all moral, religious, and unselfish considerations from history and from life, and makes of man nothing but a gain-seeking animal preying upon his kind wherever he can lay hands upon him. There have been, and there doubtless are, many individuals of this type; but to suppose that the whole human race can be brought under such a description is an outrageous travesty on history, on morals, and on religion. This assumption would reduce all human history to the product of blind gain-seeking forces and would exclude from it both moral effort and moral purpose. Under such a theory, no man would make any sacrifice for liberty or for love, but only for gain. All human experience contradicts so cruel and so heartless an assumption.

DR. NICHOLAS MURRAY BUTLER

Second, that in the struggle for wealth men are divided into permanent classes—those who employ and those who labor—and that between these classes there is and should be a class struggle or class war to be carried on to the bitter end until those who labor not only conquer those who employ, but exclude them from any place in the community.

This doctrine of class struggle is the savage teaching of Karl Marx, a man whose consuming passion was hate. It has been well said of Marx that

> He was without religion, having been conveyed from Judaism to Protestantism by his father at the age of six, and having abandoned Protestantism for aggressive Atheism when he grew to manhood. He was a man embittered by persecution, enraged by antagonism, soured by adversity, exasperated by suffering. . . . His inspiring and dominant passion was the passion of hate—hate in its virulent and peculiarly Germanic form. . . . It was hate that goaded him to his enormous literary labors; it was hate that determined his selection and rejection of historical facts for his distorted description of industrial England; it was hate that fixed his economic principles, that twisted all his arguments, that vitiated all his conclusions. . . . *Das Kapital* (1867) is the enduring testament of Marxian animosity. . . . It is a work of dogmatic mythology, the formula of a new religion of repulsion, the Koran of the class war.*

It is the extreme form of the doctrines of Karl Marx which Lenine and Trotzky have been applying in Russia for a year and a half past with such terrible results. In consequence, that once great country of boundless possibilities is now as helpless as a child, and it lies, for the moment, in social, economic, and moral ruin, and is relapsing into barbarism. Its reorganized schools now devote part of each day to instruction in atheism and to removing any lingering traces of what used to be proudly called civilization. Russia has lost, happily, the cruel and tyrannous Tsar who ruled over it, but unhappily it has gained in his stead a small group of violent and equally cruel autocrats whose operations make those of the Tsar seem like child's play. For the first time in history, on a stage which the whole world can witness, and on an immense scale, the doctrines and theories of Karl Marx are being put to the test of practical application.

*Hearnshaw, *Democracy at the Crossways* (London, 1918), pp. 209-210.

No one not himself blinded by hate or by ignorance can be in any doubt as to the lesson which the world has quickly learned from the untold sufferings of Russia.

This doctrine of permanent economic classes and of a class struggle is the absolute contradiction of democracy. It denies a common citizenship and an equality of rights and privileges in order to set up a privileged and an exploiting class by sheer force and terrorism. Here in America we know full well that there are no permanent and conflicting economic classes, for the wage-worker of today is the employer of a few years hence. With us the son of the farmer may be the leader of a learned profession in a distant city, and he who begins self-support as signalman or telegraph operator may easily find himself in a few short years the directing head of a great railway system. Not long ago public attention was called to the fact that no fewer than nineteen of the men who then directed the great transportation systems of the United States had in every case begun their careers as wage-workers in the service of one or another of the railway companies.

We know, too, that the fundamental doctrine of American citizenship absolutely excludes the notion that men gain or lose anything by reason of their occupation. Here every man and woman stands on a level of political equality, and the vote of the man of wealth is no more potent than the vote of the man who at the moment may be seeking employment. In the socialistic state, permanent economic classes with differing and opposing rights and privileges are fundamental. From the democratic state, on the other hand, they are excluded. Robert Burns was a true poet of democracy when he sang "A man's a man for a' that."

Third, that in the course of economic development, the rich are getting steadily richer and steadily fewer, while the poor are getting steadily poorer and steadily more numerous. This assumption is easily disposed of by the facts, which show that as applied to America, these two statements are absolutely false.

Ours is a land in which more than twenty millions of men, women, and children have just now subscribed to Liberty Bonds.

It is a land with more than 18,000,000 dwellings occupied by about 21,000,000 families.

It is a land in which fully 6,000,000 families own their own homes without incumbrance, while 3,000,000 own their homes subject to mortgage.

It is a land in which more than 12,000,000 persons are depositors in mutual, stock, or postal-savings banks, with total deposits amounting to more than $6,500,000,000.

It is a land in which there are nearly 6,500,000 farms having a value, including their buildings and equipment, of more than $41,000,000,000, and yielding an annual product of a value of more than $8,500,000,000.

It is a land with more than 266,000 miles of railway in operation, carrying in a year more than 1,000,000,000 individual passengers and more than 2,225,000,000 tons of freight.

It is a land in which sch[illegible] people are maintained at a total ex[illegible] $650,000,000, with an attend[illegible] 20,000,000 children.

It is a land in which there are more than [illegible] public libraries, having on their shelves more than 75,000,000 volumes for the instruction and inspiration of the people.

It is a land whose total wealth is now not less than $225,000,000,000 and in which the distribution of that wealth is steady becoming more equitable and more satisfactory under the operation of the forces and principles that have guided American life so long and so well.

Who is it that has the temerity to wish to undermine the foundations of so noble and so inviting a political and social structure as this!

Forty years ago and more, when the doctrine of Socialism was systematically put forward by Karl Marx, it was quickly seized upon by those in Germany and in every other European land who were discontented with existing forms of government and of social organization, and was converted by them into a political program. That program, which was to all intents and purposes made in Germany, although written in London, contradicts Americanism and democracy at every point. It calls, not for any program of social reform in accordance with American principles and American ideals, but for a program of collective control over the individual life, the individual occupation, and the individual reward that would destroy America absolutely. It would erect upon the ruins of our democracy an autocratic state in which the tyranny of a temporary or class majority would take the place once held by the tyranny of an hereditary monarch or an hereditary ruling class. Its most extreme exponents have not hesitated to announce themselves, as did Bakunin fifty years ago, as apostles of universal destruction.

THE SOCIALIST PROGRAM IN AMERICA

As yet the number of formal adherents of the Socialist Party in the United States is not large, but the theories and teachings of socialism are being eagerly and systematically spread among us. Many schools and colleges and many pulpits are either unconscious or willing agents in this work. In the election of 1916 the Socialist Party of the United States obtained almost exactly 3.3 per cent. of the total vote. It is probable that by formally adopting the international policy of the Russian Bolshevists, the Socialist Party has alienated enough of its former supporters to reduce its probable vote today to less than 2 per cent. of the total. Small as this number is, it represents organization and activity out of all proportion to its size.

There should be no mistake about its program. It openly calls our Constitution dishonest. It denounces the fathers of our country as grafters, as crooks, as men of mediocre intelligence, and as attorneys of the capitalist class. In the making and building of America the socialist can see nothing of idealism, nothing of sacrifice, nothing of high principle, nothing of love of liberty, nothing of aspiration for a finer and a freer manhood. The Socialist Party Platform of 1912 explicitly demanded not only the usual collectivist and communist policies, but also the abolition of the United States Senate and of the veto power of the President; the abolition of all federal courts, except the United States Supreme Court and the election of all judges for short terms; the abolition of the power of the Supreme Court of the United States to pass upon the constitutionality of legislative acts; and a revision of the Constitution of the United States.

The Socialist Party is in particular antagonism to the courts, and the reason is easy to state. Under our American system the courts are established to protect civil liberty from passion, from mob control, and from improper assumption of power by public authorities and public agents. All [illegible] is hateful to the orthodox social[illegible] lay the hand of force upon [illegible] to destroy it for a despotism of [illegible] making. The courts of justice are an [illegible]cle in his way.

The sinister fact, never to be forgotten, about his party and its program is that they are in essence and of necessity unpatriotic and un-American. Republicans and Democrats differ sharply as to public policy, but they both accept the principles of the Constitution and endeavor to apply and improve them each in their own way. Neither Republicans nor Democrats would change the form of government under which we live. The Socialist Party, on the other hand, openly declares its purpose to wreck the present form of government, to undo all the work that has been accomplished for a hundred and fifty years, and to bring to an end the greatest experiment in republicanism and the greatest achievement in social and political organization that the world has ever seen. Let there be no mistake about the definiteness of this issue. America's existence is challenged.

SOCIALISM AND INTERNATIONALISM

Orthodox socialists are internationalists of a special kind. They are really not internationalists at all, but rather anti-nationalists. They are not in favor of closer, more kindly, and more constructive international relations as a means toward justice and the security of the world, but they desire that sort of internationalism which shall extend class consciousness, class cooperation, and the class struggle beyond the boundaries of existing nations, and so assist in breaking down those boundaries. This is why the logical orthodox socialist is of necessity unpatriotic. He does not believe in patriotism, because he regards it as an obstacle to the farther extension of the successful class struggle and of class rule. Happily, we have seen in our recent experience that men may be sincere believers in many of the tenets of Socialism and yet remain patriotic and loyal Americans. Such men as Russell, Walling, Spargo, and Montague have illustrated this fact. Unfortunately, these men have been but a small minority in the Socialist party or group, and they have seceded from it. Orthodox Socialists as a body cannot be loyal and devoted Americans, for the simple reason that American institutions and American ideals lie straight across the path which they would like to pursue.

This distinction between a true and a false internationalism is to be taken into account and clearly reckoned with in shaping the policies of the world. Just as the family relation enriches and strengthens the individual, and just as the community relation enriches and strengthens the family, and just as the State relation enriches and strengthens the community, and just as the national relation enriches and strengthens the State, so will a true international relationship enrich and strengthen every nation that enters into it. Any plan for a Society of Nations that would destroy national initiative, national responsibility and national pride, would be merely a strait-jacket upon human progress. The true and wise Society of Nations will be one built out of nations that are stronger, more resourceful, and more patriotic because of their new association and their new opportunities for world service.

Signs are not wanting that the advocates of Socialism think it will be easier and quicker to gain ground in the United States by the indirect method of involving us in a false international policy than by the direct method of attempting to secure control of the machinery of government through the suffrage. This explains why Socialists and those who at heart sympathize with them without openly assuming their name, are so anxious that Lenine and Trotzky shall be formally recognized as heads of a government with which civilized and honorable men may have relations, and that the German people should, so far as possible, be saved from the consequences of their public crime and their

"Intellectuals" Invading Labor Field

TACK IN "THE NATION" ON SAMUEL GOMPERS, WHEN ANALYZED, SHOWS EFFORT OF OUTSIDERS TO SET AMERICAN FEDERATION'S POLICY

T is a well known practice of stagedom to let go with a great blare of trumpets while the proud hero is brought down ge for the inspection of the assembled multi- le. Stagedom probably got the idea from such timers as Nero and the Ptolemies. Where l Hohenzollern got the idea isn't quite clear, ; he used it regularly.

Jeorge P. West has just been brought to the tlights to a similar accompaniment in order it proper attention may be focused upon him ile he hurls his javelin against Samuel mpers.

The Nation, which is a weekly publication ving its home in New York and which is blished by Oswald Garrison Villard, is agency which selected Mr. West to undo r. Gompers. A fanfare of advertising pre- ded publication of Mr. West's article. In this vertising *The Nation* asked in large type hether the "Gompers rule" in the American ederation of Labor could survive the Atlantic ity convention, after which it proclaimed that eorge P. West would supply the answer in the sue then forthcoming. The issue is before us. 'e read what Mr. West has written. And we arvel—or we do not—according to our frame mind.

George P. West, I concede at the outset, is acere in his own mind. He believes he is set- ng the story down accurately and he believes is doing a service in letting the great public on the hidden truth.

MATTER OF SALESMANSHIP

Somehow or other the story that Mr. West ells is always set forth by the uplift writers as hidden truth about a grave menace, but this s mostly salesmanship on their part, for there s nothing new in the whole story.

This year, however, there seems to be a some- hat concerted attack of similar nature, deliv- red from a number of sources at the American 'ederation of Labor. This concert of attack eems to come from allied or semi-allied sources nd to have a common object. It is not quite as t has been in other years, though no year has assed out of the last dozen or more, without its ttack on Samuel Gompers and what is called he "Gompers machine."

Let us see something about what Mr. West as to say and then let us indulge ourselves in bit of study of Mr. West himself and his fel- ow uplifters and regenerators of the human ace.

Mr. West asks in the title of his article, "Will abor Lead?" The title is not a good one. It oesn't express what Mr. West has in mind. What he means, if he would but say it in plain English is, "Will they defeat Samuel Gompers or re-election?" As a matter of fact, that is hat most of the labor movement destroyers nean, but they refrain from saying it directly, referring the more scholarly method of indi- ection.

Setting down in their order the points Mr. West makes in his article we find these:

1. The Atlantic City convention ought to approve a policy of independent labor political action. If it doesn't "these movements for the time being . . . sporadic and unrelated . . . . must eventually form in the national field an orientation that will be the end of Gompersism."

2. The labor program, which it has been announced President Wilson would lay before Congress upon his return, will have the effect only of "strengthening Mr. Gompers' position and the weakening of the demand for a national labor party," the insinuation being that this is a

By CHESTER M. WRIGHT

(Of the American Alliance for Labor and Democracy.)

political trick probably framed up by Mr. Gompers and President Wilson with the double object of keeping Mr. Gompers and Mr. Wilson in their present offices.

3. ". . . it may well be that the labor party movement is chiefly an unconscious and instinctive expedient for circumventing the control of Mr. Gompers and establishing a new agency of expression."

4. Today "the most important industrial movements" are "entirely out of the hands of Mr. Gompers and his lieutenants," and are "in the hands, significantly enough, of the very men whose excursion into politics Mr. Gompers denounces on the ground that it will divert the movement from 'economic' action," and this largely, we are instructed, because of the alleged fact that Mr. Gompers and his associates have been negligent of the industrial interests of the workers and have had to be "dragooned" into such activities as the organization of the steel workers.

5. Mr. Gompers opposes secession movements and stands against allowing the labor movement to be wrecked by that insidious process.

6. If this be a point, Mr. West concludes that "it is not too much to say that already the leadership of the American labor movement, so far as it has any leadership, has passed from Mr. Gompers and his little group of ultra-conservatives at Washington."

It has not been easy to isolate these points. They are so shrouded in a haze of what may be termed Mr. West's constitutional and mental attitude that they are brought into outline by themselves only after a painstaking process of dissection.

However, now that the points—we will call them points for want of a more accurate term—have been isolated, as the medical men say when speaking of germs, let us go behind the points and see what may be there to be seen.

TILTED AT MR. GOMPERS OFTEN

George P. West has been tilting at Samuel Gompers, as was his right, ever since the demise of the United States Commission on Industrial Relations, of which Frank P. Walsh was chairman and of which Mr. West was a publicity representative. Coming down the trail since that time, Mr. West has left among a great many of those who have followed him an impression that he belongs to what W. J. Ghent so well describes as "an indescribable assortment of the fitful and fretful worshippers of the Cult of Something Else."

I do not know from whence the inspiration came, or whether there was an inspiration, or whether it is coincidence, but it is an interesting fact that a number of young men whose recent arc of travel has been almost identical have come to engage in the same present pursuit—that same being the "fitful, fretful" business of attacking Samuel Gompers and his monstrous "bossism." It is a highly important sidelight that none of this "little group of serious thinkers" has any real connection with the labor movement or has had the benefit of any of its training. Neither have they borne any of the strain of its hard labor nor the suffering of its times of trial. They stand on hill tops and throw rocks into the valley where work is done.

In Russia this type is known as the "intelligentsia," which means the little over-educated group that tells the great mass where to get off at. Recently the Russia "intelligentsia" has come into power in such a manner as to cause the balance of the world to stand aghast in contemplation of what high-power brains can do in the way of complete and thorough going destruction.

In France and England this type is grouped under the general heading of "intellectuals", which means that small group which comes from the outside in effervescent enthusiasm and holy devotion to tell the working people how to be saved. They always tell the working people how to *be* saved—not how to save themselves. Of course if working people understand how to save themselves, then the "intellectual" becomes a by-product of little value.

In Germany this type belongs to the professorial group, of which the German labor movement has had such a load to carry that at the real crisis of its career it broke under the strain. However, the Herr Professor was a man who had to be listened to. Didn't the Herr Professor say so himself? He did, and the German mind understood that to be enough, sufficient, and plenty. The Herr Professor was listened to.

Down in Mexico they used to have a class called "scientificos", because they always pretended that they were scientific. They told the people that since they were scientific they were right and that in them resided all truth and in them alone. They had a monopoly of the supply of truth in Mexico. And thus glorified by science they scientifically robbed the Mexican workers, fooled them, led them to the slaughter and played a sort of Jack-at-all-trades Judas game with them for several generations under the kindly and doubtless scientific and scholarly patronage of the well known Porfirio Diaz.

STRANGE LIBELS ON EDUCATION

Strange are the libels perpetrated upon the good name of education. Wondrous are the slanders of which true intellect is made the innocent victim.

I have not just come from "seventeen weeks in Russia", but I have just come from France and England and I have for some years kept somewhat of a close check on what is being done in those countries. Mexico and the story of Mexican workers has been something like a hobby. I do not know of any labor movement in the world that has been able to demonstrate the success of "intellectual", "intelligentsia", "professorial" or "scientifico" leadership. That, however, is what Mr. West desires to wish on the American labor movement and regardless of words and their infinite shading of meaning and their infinite capacity for getting away from the naked facts, that is what his whole complaint is about and with which his whole philippic is concerned.

Let us look for a moment at an interesting phase of the European labor situation, where Mr. West's idea prevails largely.

Russia has no labor movement—no industrial movement of workers joined in unions; only an "intelligentsia" dominating a helpless mass.

France presents the spectacle of a labor movement that is next to voiceless. If you want to know about labor in France you don't go to Jouhaux, secretary of the Confederation Generale du Travail; you go to some one of the various Socialist party spokesmen, selecting that one which comes nearest to holding the views that you wish to hear expressed. You may go to Renaudel, to Thomas, to Longuet, to Compere-Morel—but seldom would you go to Jouhaux, because you would understand thoroughly that while his views might be sound they would not be the views of the highest authority. The movement is one of politics and the game of politics is largely one of personal ambition. This is so in the Socialist party, as it is elsewhere. That accounts for the large number of newspapers, which are not news papers, but opinion papers. If you are an "intellectual" and wish to be a leader you start a newspaper.

In England there is much the same situation. When I wanted to find out about the plans of labor in connection with the Berne conference I was directed to Labor party headquarters. From the temple of politics came the voice of authority. The executive council of the British Trade Union Congress is not so called; it is called the Parliamentary Committee, in clear acknowledgment of the idea that politics is supreme. Mere industrial activity runs second.

In Italy the condition is the same, only hopelessly more so. Labor opinion is not expressed by a movement having to do with work. It is expressed by a movement having to do with politics.

And the "intellectual" domination of the European labor movement, to which Mr. West and his fellow delvers into deep stuff point with so much pride and satisfaction—what about that?

First, the name is in a way a misnomer. The name has been given to that class which comes from without the labor movement with a ready-cut plan of salvation which it seeks to foist upon the labor movement. The uplifters, the quick-service salvation people, the "follow me" persons, the enthusiastic young students who have seen a great light about which they must rush to tell the populace—these are the "intellectuals". They come with the fruit of their bursting brains and upon this fruit they seek to diet the labor movement in order that it may crawl through the eye of the needle into a promised land beyond—a promised land all a-glitter and a-glow with good things and fun! They are called "intellectuals", though not by way of indicating that they have real intellectual strength and poise.

Second, it must be said in connection with the "intellectuals" that labor does not spurn intellect, does not get frightened and run away from scholarly ability, does not shy at a learned man and roughly tell him to go to blazes. What labor balks at is the attempt of persons outside of the labor movement to dominate the movement. Labor resents the claim that outsiders, "intellectuals" though they be, can know more about what ought to be the policy and tactics of labor than labor itself knows. That is what American labor resents. If European labor finds it more to its liking, or even to its benefit because of possible local conditions, to submit to this extraneous domination and to the parliamentary tactics that are so largely followed in Europe, that is the affair of European labor. European labor may do as it sees fit, but American labor reserves unto itself the unqualified right to do the same. And in pursuance of doing what it has seen fit and right and wise to do, American labor has built a policy and a tactical program to suit what American labor conceives to be the needs of American labor.

ENTHRALLED BY OVERSEAS IDEA

Certain critics of the American labor movement look across the sea and they behold there something different—what Ghent calls "Something Else"—and they are enthralled. Formulae that fit into resounding sentences, programs that look nice in print, tactics that offer niches for various persons to fit themselves into, these have a strange attraction for the "intelligentsia" of America. And furthermore, it is quite the probability that the American "intelligentsia", looking across the sea and beholding its European counterpart in a position of authority and power in the world of labor, contemplates the situa[illegible] seriousness and concludes that [illegible] "intelligentsia" has put something [illegible]merican brethren which is neither [illegible]dit nor the profit of the American contingent of the International Brotherhood of Superior Brains.

This survey of the situation almost constitutes in itself an answer to all that Mr. West has written, for every point that he makes is rooted in the old, old plaint that American labor will not submit to the outside dictation of the "intellectuals" and that it does not go in for the great game of partisan politics. There is in America a considerable class that has a constitutional grouch against the trade union movement of our country on just that account. The socialists have always baited the trade unionists because of it. Latterly they have been joined by the comparatively recent growth of non-socialist "radicals" of "intellectual" type who understand it to be their mission in life to drag labor up out of its sluggish course into the more spectacular, if shallower, stream that makes up for depth by voluminous splashing over the rocks.

However, it is well that we give some attention to the detailed propositions that we have been able to extract from the depths of Mr. West's scolding as it appears in Mr. Villard's publication, *The Nation*. Let us take them as they come!

First, the Atlantic City convention ought to approve a program of independent political action; if it doesn't "Gompersism" is going to be ended.

To begin with, Mr. West implies that the present non-partisan political policy of the Federation is "Gompersism". The fact is that this policy is the policy of the American Federation of Labor, made so by the Federation and repeatedly sustained in convention after convention. If this policy should be changed it would mean nothing more than the simple fact that the Federation has changed its policy. If the tried policy is continued, it will mean that the American Federation of Labor has deliberated and decided to continue a policy that it has tested and found good.

If the movements, "for the time being sporadic and unrelated" actually are movements of the membership of the American Federation of Labor and as such do eventually "form in the national field an orientation" they may, by action in the Federation change the policy to suit the new conviction—and that will end nothing but a policy.

The mistake made by a great many critics is in thinking that the Federation is something bossed from above, by Samuel Gompers "and his little group". The fact is that there is no more democratic institution in American life than the organized trade union movement. Nothing that we know about functions more nearly in accord with the desires of the component parts. Of course, what most of the critics want is something that *is* bossed from above—from up where they themselves wish to be.

At a meeting of the Executive Council of the Federation in New York City on Dec. 28, 1918, the question of political policy was opened for consideration and it was there determined that the council found the old policy wise and once more declared against independent partisan labor politics. The council also made it plain that local central labor bodies may engage in partisan politics if they deem it wise, and in so doing violate none of the rules of the Federation, but that to enter the national field would constitute a violation.

WISDOM PLAINLY APPARENT

This policy of American labor has grown up with the Federation through years of experience and observation. I take it that the world labor situation today is to any fair critic an ample justification of the wisdom of that policy. Not in any nation anywhere is labor so favorably positioned as in these United States. There are no exceptions. American labor claims the right to continue master of its own policy in order that it may bring to the workers of America the greatest progress.

Second in Mr. West's list is a question scarcely worth discussing further. President Wilson has announced that he is coming home with a number of proposals to lay before Congress in relation to labor. If the President does offer suggestions for legislation of benefit to labor Mr. West ought to be pleased. Arguing for politics, he yet sees intrigue and scheming in politics the moment the President proposes to suggest labor legislation. I am confident that American labor does not yet know what the President has in mind and I know it will be less precipitate than Mr. West. It will reserve its judgment until it does know. Labor, being bound by no partisan ties, has not hesitated when need arose to oppose President Wilson with its full strength and if there should be need of such a course again that course will be adopted. But labor waits until it knows before it enters the lists for or against. Therein it functions as a responsible entity, a restraint and balance which offers but little resistance to the fitful plunging of a number of its hill-top critics.

Third, we find that perhaps the labor party movement "is chiefly an unconscious and instinctive expedient for circumventing the control of Mr. Gompers and establishing a new agency of expression." This looks like a handful grabbed right out of the red hot cosmic nebula. First, the assumption that there is such a thing as a Gompers "control" is a false assumption. Usually when an argument is built upon a false premise destruction of the premise lets the whole thing fall. There is no Gompers control. Mr. Gompers is president of the Federation. He is a leader and he is the foremost leader. He leads by virtue of a mandate—a command made known by votes freely cast from year to year. He wields no magic autocratic influence. He cannot maintain himself in the presidency any longer than the voters wish to have him there. The "Gompers machine" is one of the great myths of the Cult of Something Else. I tried to find it myself once—and I found democracy.

Neither is there any "unconscious and instinctive" groping for some new kind of expression. That is the sheerest tommyrot. The New York labor party venture has not revealed any great urge, conscious or unconscious. The contrary is true. The lack of it will be apparent at once to any person who will trouble himself to inquire about the membership figures. The Chicago election showed no great urge, the total labor party and socialist vote having been about what the socialists would have been expected to poll alone had there been no labor party. This idea does not urge nearly as much from within as it is urged from without.

"CONTROL" MYTH IS TIRESOME

Four in the category brings us to a repetition of that "Gompers control" myth. It is a tiresome thing. The most important industrial movements are "entirely out of the hands of Mr. Gompers and his lieutenants." That Mr. Gompers ever had these movements "in his hands" would doubtless be surprising news to him.

But there is a meaner charge than this concealed in specification No. 4. It is that Mr. Gompers is losing this control because he has been negligent of the economic interests of these great organizations. Mr. Gompers had to be "dragooned" into the work of organizing the steel workers. He didn't organize the packing house workers.

True history relates that Mr. Gompers, as president of the American Federation of Labor, has been not only energetically in the forefront of every organization movement, but that he has been a very real leader in this sense. Far from having had to be "dragooned" into the

(Continued on page 17)

Compulsory Health Legislation Opposed by Labor

(From the Christian Science Monitor of April 22, 1919.)

THE Brotherhood of Locomotive Engineers, representing about 82,000 railroad engineers of the United States and Canada, are vigorously combating various legislative measures for compulsory health insurance now pending before the legislatures of Ohio, New York and other states.

Warren S. Stone, Grand Chief of this Organization and Chairman of the Social Insurance Department of The National Civic Federation, talking over the subject with a representative of the Western News Office very recently, set forth some of the many reasons why this organization of locomotive engineers is opposing all forms of compulsory medical examinations and medical insurance under State or Federal authorization.

"We do not want any such form of insurance," Mr. Stone declared. "There are many objections to those widespread efforts to secure legislative power for compulsory service by them for which the public must pay."

"Our organization has for years been fighting this form of medical autocracy," added Mr. Stone. "I do not want any man sent to my house with power to enter and examine me or any of my friends. Under some of these proposed laws, and all of them I think, the individual cannot in any way choose his physician, even if he wants one. Some doctor is selected to look over promiscuously some five hundred individuals who must submit to this encroachment on their personal rights without question. The whole thing is un-American to my sense of things, autocratic and useless.

"We are sending out just now to our members large numbers of the address delivered in New York last December before the International Association of Casualty and Surety Underwriters by Dr. George E. Tucker, formerly associated with the National Industrial Conference Board as its chief medical investigator. Dr. Tucker declared that 'social insurance is an integral part of Germanism, an adjunct of that militarism that leads directly to social slavery along the well-trodden paths of paternalism, registration, inspectorships, and the whole mechanism of docketing and discipline.' Furthermore, he said that 'the professional social reformer and the "for revenue only" human uplifter groping blindly for some new panacea upon which to focus public attention gladly accept and enthusiastically welcome any proposal which, for the time being, offers opportunity for publicity and incidentally for replenishment of an always too uncertain financial income.'

WARREN S. STONE

"Dr. Tucker has stated, and we agree with him, that 'compulsory health insurance, as revealed by the evidence, has already been a signal failure in Great Britain because of the lack of fundamental knowledge of the public health problem, and because the principle upon which it is established lacks the element essential to a scheme seeking to be considered an insurance proposal; and that the essential difficulties requiring solution in connection with the public welfare from a health standpoint would not be met and in the main their prevention would be entirely ignored. Also, facts show that the cost is always out of all proportion to the benefits to be derived, and finally that neither we nor any of the allied countries would be justified in copying any German plan which is known to have been conceived in iniquity, enforced through militarism and aimed to destroy individualism and democracy.'

"Again, the California Research Society of Social Economics has declared that the bill will destroy medical freedom, compel the workman to buy and pay for sickness insurance whether he wants it or not and make his home subject to invasion by inquisitive political 'inspectors' and 'investigators'. Finally, it says that sixty per cent of illness is preventable. Why, then, should those workmen be called upon to pay out millions for misfortunes that may be prevented by other means? These are some of the reasons why the International Brotherhood of Locomotive Engineers is opposed to all forms of compulsory health insurance."

Matthew Woll on the "One-Big-Union" Idea

(From the Christian Science Monitor of April 26, 1919.)

VIEWING the broad field of organized Labor in the United States from the vantage point of a national leader at Washington, Matthew Woll told a representative of *The Christian Science Monitor* recently that two big and serious problems had arisen within the American Federation of Labor and were being pressed from various points. The One-Big-Union propaganda was the first; second, Labor's going into politics. The One-Big-Union scheme would fail, because in actual operation it had been found impracticable, Mr. Woll testified from his own experience. The formation of a national Labor party he could not regard as anything but disastrous to the economic ends for which Labor organized.

Mr. Woll's home is in Chicago, but for the last 18 months he has been in Washington, serving since last June as assistant to Mr. Gompers as chairman of the committee on labor of the Council of National Defense, and editing the *American Federationist*, official organ of the American Federation of Labor, in Mr. Gompers' absence in Europe. Mr. Woll is president of the International Allied Printing Trades Association and also of the International Photo-Engravers Union.

Mr. Woll noted that a determined attempt is being made to tear down the international form of organization of the trades unions. He said the American Federation of Labor did not favor the Mooney strike.

The federation has not taken any action on the "no beer, no work" movement, but it does not countenance strikes of any kind which have not first met with the approval of the international unions, Mr. Woll said. To his knowledge no international union has taken action on this proposition.

MATTHEW WOLL

On One-Big-Unionism, Mr. Woll said he spoke from experience. He had belonged to just that form of organization. It had existed in the printing trades. They were all in the one Labor union together—compositors, pressmen, stereotypers, photo-engravers, and the others. Compositors outnumbered everybody else. When anything affecting the compositors came up, it got attention; but when an important question affecting, for instance, the photo-engravers arose, the compositors were likely to regard it as a minor difference. As a consequence, the photo-engravers of the country were poorly organized and their wages low. Finally they got tired, as Mr. Woll said, of being used chiefly to pull chestnuts out of the fire for the bigger groups of the union, and they organized their own union. This was characterized by Mr. Woll, its president, as the strongest in the printing trades, and the photo-engraver, he said, got the highest wages of any man in these trades.

Now the various trades in the printing industry have come together in a common organization, called the International Allied Printing Trades Association, Mr. Woll pointed out, each preserving therein its individual craft identity. This is unification within the industry which the American Federation of Labor encourages.

Mr. Woll declared that the A. F. of L. has consistently and for some years been developing this getting together within the industry along craft lines, but that the proponents of the One-Big-Union idea have ignored this tendency. Mr. Woll called attention to the building trades department of the A. F. of L., which purposes to remove jurisdictional disputes between the organizations and to deal collectively for the conditions which should prevail in the building industry of the country without destroying the identity of the individual trade organizations.

"Thus," concluded the trade union leader, "there is evidence that the American Federation of Labor has been fully responsive to the need of coordinating the activities of trade organizations within the same industry and has been doing it in a way which would not destroy that form of organization which experience has demonstrated as absolutely essential to deal with economic questions in a fair and efficient manner."

THE NATIONAL
Civic Federation Review

Office: Thirty-third Floor, Metropolitan Tower
1 Madison Avenue New York City
RALPH M. EASLEY, Editor
Published Twice a Month Two Dollars a Year

The Editor alone is Responsible for any unsigned article or unquoted statement published in THE NATIONAL CIVIC FEDERATION REVIEW.

ENEMIES OF THE TERMS OF PEACE

Germany, through her representatives, came to Versailles seeking peace, yet in that same hour there began the renewal of hostilities held in check since the signing of the armistice and which in America had abated since our entry into the war—hostilities now directed against the terms of the settlement for peace which Germany had presumably come to seek. There began, with the delivery of the terms, a war not of guns, but of propaganda—a campaign whose aim and purpose is to neutralize or render inert the very conditions of the treaty. What she failed to achieve through victory in the field, Germany now seeks to achieve through world propaganda and international intrigue. And the forces which of old aided Germany, which directly and indirectly abetted the imperial establishment, which for a time were driven to cover, have now come forth assailing and seeking to undo the terms of the treaty.

Unrepentant, unregenerate, defiant, Germany speaks for herself. "We are not a defeated people," declares Matthias Erzbergér. "We agreed to the armistice because President Wilson laid down fourteen points upon which the Allies would base peace. If the peace submitted to us now is not a Wilson peace, but an imperialistic peace aiming at annexations, indemnities and the total annihilation of the German future, it will not be signed."

Philip Scheidemann, Chancellor of the new German Government, referred to the treaty as "this document of hatred and madness." Frederich Stampfer, editor of the Majority Socialist organ *Vorwaerts*, spoke of it as "the undefinable instrument of pressure which * * * is no instrument of peace." Declaring that Germany will not sign, he said: "The enemy will attempt to occupy parts of Germany and to force the rest to surrender by hunger." And he added, with sinister significance, "we shall then see how long his inner and outer unity prevails."

While Germany, with wailing and gnashing of teeth, raises her voice against paying, if only in part, what is the just penalty of her crimes, there rises also throughout the world, in America and the Allied countries, a singular and significant echo of protest against the terms of the treaty. And from whom come these protests that Germany pay for the wrongs committed?

Meeting to consider the terms imposed upon Germany, the National Executive Committee of the British Labor Party issued a manifesto declaring that the treaty in some essential particulars was "opposed to the declarations of President Wilson, of the Inter-Allied Labor Conference and the Berne Conference, and very defective from the standpoint of world peace." It went on to say:

"It bears evidence of a compromise by capitalism and imperialism, which still dominate European states." It criticised the failure to give Germany representation on the reparations commission, and the omission of provisions for a prog[illegible] limitation of armaments. It pro-[illegible] the separation of the Saar Basin [illegible] countries and Central Powers, and which also promoted the Stockholm conference.

The Independent Labor Party, of England, in a manifesto, declared:

"We strongly denounce the document as a misnamed treaty. The terms violate the conditions of the armistice and are opposed to every public statement of Allied aims * * * The treaty does not end militarism."

The International Socialists, meeting in Paris on May 12, issued a statement declaring that the covenant seems to be the instrument of a victorious coalition dominated by five great powers rather than an organ of international justice and attacked the disposition of the German colonies as "imperialism satisfying itself with the spoils of war." The statement was signed by the following Socialists, who were appointed by the Berne Labor Socialist Conference to make a study of the covenant and the treaty: Hjalmar Branting, Sweden; Camille Huysmans, Belgium; Arthur Henderson, J. Ramsay Macdonald and G. H. Stuart Bunning of Great Britain, and Pierre Renaudel and Jean Longuet of France.

The statement concluded:

"This peace is not our peace. The nations are still menaced by the policy of the victors in sharing the spoils without thought of the inevitable consequences."

In France, the only voice of protest against the treaty came from the Socialist press. One Socialist paper, under the headline, "A Peace of Oppression and Injustice," said: "The capitalist and imperialist world as it exists could only produce a capitalist and imperialist peace, which prepares the way for another war. Between President Wilson's 'fourteen points' and certain stipulations communicated to Count von Brockdorff-Rantzau there are hiatuses and contrasts which are too striking."

Mr. J. L. Garvin, the editor of the radical *Sunday Observer*, of London, declared:

"These terms give no fundamental solution to any European problem. They revolve in the vicious virulence of the old diplomacy, they repeat the fatal precedents which have always led back to war."

The *Herald*, the British Labor organ, complained:

"There is no honor left for any of us * * * It is a patched-up peace and simply makes the world safe for plutocracy."

The *New York Daily Call* comments:

"Germany now knows, from the point of view of the underdog, the feel of a Brest-Litovsk peace . . . 'It is a good peace,' said Clemenceau. For the victorious diplomats, we suppose every peace has been a good peace . . . To the victorious diplomat that peace is good which gives him his day of glory."

The Non-Partisan League, through its official newspaper, the *Fargo Courier News*, the editorial policy of which is directed by A. C. Townley, president of the League, attacks the treaty thus:

"The peace treaty they have drawn is a ghastly mockery of democracy . . . It is written with the primary purpose of safeguarding capitalism in France . . . The European governments, flushed with victory, were greedy with lust for revenge and plunder."

The Russian Soviet Bureau, of which Ludwig C. A. K. Martens is the head, and which constitutes the Bolshevist headquarters in America, issued a propaganda sheet denouncing the treaty terms.

George Sylvester Viereck, one of the most s[illegible] did and notorious Hun propagandists and edit[illegible] of the former "Fatherland," said:

"Judging from a cursory study of peace co[illegible] ditions, I should say they are in flat contradi[illegible] tion to Mr. Wilson's fourteen points. In fa[illegible] they turn our fourteen pledges into fourte[illegible] scraps of paper."

The *New Republic*, which propagandized f[illegible] a peace of compromise with Germany, says ed[illegible] torially:

"A peace will be signed. It will not be in [illegible] the essentials the kind of peace which was pro[illegible] ised to the world while the exaltation of the w[illegible] was at its height. There is small evidence [illegible] Paris of any profound conviction that a ne[illegible] order of international affairs has been inaug[illegible] rated."

To create public sentiment against and [illegible] undo the treaty, the German propaganda m[illegible] chine, in Germany and without, has unleashe[illegible] its forces with frenzy and fury unsurpasse[illegible] since the early days of the Great War. And a[illegible] the forces which in America opposed our goin[illegible] to war with Germany, which fostered pacifis[illegible] which defended resisters of the draft, whic[illegible] campaigned for a premature peace of compr[illegible] mise with Germany, the same forces which abe[illegible] ted the propaganda of the British Labor Part[illegible] for a Stockholm conference, which defended th[illegible] Bolsheviki and preached Bolshevism, as well a[illegible] all the pro-Germans, pacifists, anti-English Iris[illegible] Socialists, "internationalists" and motley radi[illegible] cals are now enlisted in assailing the terms of th[illegible] treaty offered to Germany.

In the consideration of the treaty, the Leagu[illegible] of Nations covenant, and the proposal of Presi[illegible] dent Wilson to ask the United States Senate t[illegible] guarantee protection to France should she b[illegible] again assailed by Germany, the character o[illegible] those forces making the attacks will doubtles[illegible] have due weight.

POISONING THE FONTS OF LEARNING

It is, of course, quite natura[illegible] that the propaganda methods o[illegible] both the Socialists and the Ger[illegible] mans should be in many respect[illegible] strikingly identical. Marxian Socialism—th[illegible] application of which finds an object lesson i[illegible] present-day Russia—was "made in Germany." Like the German propaganda, its methods o[illegible] dissemination and fertility in hypocrisy an[illegible] deception, are strikingly Teutonic. The Ger[illegible] man propaganda, as has been shown in article[illegible] published in this magazine, sought to undermin[illegible] American national integrity and moral re[illegible] sistance by an invasion, years before the wa[illegible] began, of our schools and colleges. Socialism likewise, has sought to poison the fonts of Ameri can learning.

A wholesome movement to safeguard pupils i[illegible] our public schools from camouflaged Socialis[illegible] teachings was announced recently by Dr. Joh[illegible] L. Tildsley, associate superintendent of school[illegible] of New York. Dr. Tildsley will recommend t[illegible] the New York Board of Education that th[illegible] economic views of all prospective teachers b[illegible] examined to the end that no teachers shall b[illegible] licensed who are revolutionary Socialists. "W[illegible] all believe in freedom of speech," said Dr. Tildsley, "but we are not talking about freedom o[illegible] speech—we're talking about teachers. I don't want to keep these Marxian Socialists from talking—no one has to listen to them unless he desires to—but I object to their impressing revolutionary views upon a girl or boy of fourteen to eighteen years who is forced by law to attend school."

What Dr. Tildsley has proposed to do in New York might well be followed by the directors of public education in other cities. The promul[illegible] have sacrificed this country to the Hun is a letter addressed to Debs by Owen R. Lovejoy, General Secretary of the National Child Labor Committee.

This letter was seized upon by *The New York Call* as being so much in line with its campaign of personal appeal that it was displayed in double column measure and large, black type on the *Call's* editorial page. In full, the Lovejoy letter reads:

"Good Night, Comrade—and Good Morning". (This letter was sent by Owen R. Lovejoy, one of the world's greatest fighters against the iniquity of child labor, to Eugene Victor Debs. We are proud of the privilege of printing it). From *The New York Call*.

My Dear 'Gene:—You are the first of my own personal friends to be put behind the bars of a penitentiary. Your going fills me with a new; strange emotion, and I cannot see how you can be so calm about it. To think of you who love so to roam the fields and woods and look across broad plains—confined to a prison cell; to think that the faces and handclasps of the little children who have flocked around you on the streets of your own city—henceforth shut out from your view; to realize that those eager multitudes who have thronged to hear your cheering message of human freedom and just government are to hear your voice no more; that while we whose natures are less ardent, whose sense of duty is less keen, whose vision is less clear, whose hearts are not so warm and tender, and whose love of God is less intense—to think that we are to be at liberty while you are confined, that we may speak while you are silent, that we may enjoy sunshine and flowers and the contact of friends, while you are confined within the narrow dungeon walls:—what outrage cloaked in technicalities could so clearly prove the bankruptcy of the present social order!

You are convicted of hating war. I think you are guilty. I recall how your voice has always been against any violence, even when you saw your own beloved fellow workers crushed under the oppressor's heel. I remember how you used to denounce Prussian militarism in the old days before the war, while presidents and congressmen and judges and diplomats were consorting with the Kaiser, and our accredited ambassadors were kissing his mailed fist. They say you are a pacifist; that you have long protested against war. Of this I believe you are also guilty. You are sent to prison for saying last year what all the representatives of all the governments at the Paris Peace Table are saying today—that WAR MUST CEASE. You have looked forward as Victor Hugo looked toward a day "when a cannon will be exhibited in public museums, just as an instrument of torture is now, and people will be astonished to think such a thing could have been." You looked for the day when the seas would no longer be crowded with battleships or infested with mines and submarines, but when nations would extend the hand of fellowship across the ocean. You were not afraid to give voice to your belief—and for this confession we cage you as a wild beast and a menace to society. You have openly defied the law of the jungle and brazenly conducted a vendetta of universal brotherhood.

I will tell you the trouble with you, 'Gene—you came on earth too soon. We aren't ready for you yet. You are as premature as Lincoln was, or Huss, or Wycliffe, or Jesus. Well might you say as you pass us in the shadows of your Gethsemane—"Sleep on now and take your rest; behold, the hour is at hand."

We shall awaken by and by. Henceforth liberty will seem less precious to us, now that you may not share it. Prison walls will partake of the glow of the walls of the Holy City, now that we know your radiant soul is within. Thousands of little children who today shrink from a "convict" as an unclean thing will begin to look deeper into his face to discover whether, after all, he may not be a saviour wearing the robes of derision and crowned with thorns. I am pouring out only the poor tribute of my personal love in this letter, yet I believe I voice the thought of many thousands to whom you have been a help and inspiration in turning your own beautiful words back upon yourself—that while you are of the lower class, we also are of it; while you are branded a criminal, we also are criminals; while you are in prison we are not free.

Good Night, Comrade—and Good Morning.

Distinct relief from the nauseating bathos of Lovejoy's "letter", and telling just what crimes Debs committed to cause the prison sentence, is the plain statement of fact made by A. Mitchell Palmer, Attorney General of the United States, when he refused to ask executive clemency for Debs. Said Mr. Palmer:

"Debs was convicted, not because of his political or economic views, but because he plainly violated the laws of the land. On June 18, 1918, during the most critical period of the war, Debs made a public speech at Canton, Ohio, in which he urged that wage-earners refrain from giving any aid to the American Nation in the war, asserting that the war was brought on and conducted solely in the interest of capitalists; told his audience that they needed to know that 'they were fit for something better than slavery and cannon fodder,' held up to admiration as martyrs to the cause of labor a number of persons who had been convicted for violating the Draft Act, and urged wage-earners to stand together as a class to prevent the success of our country in the war.

"In his address to the jury Debs said: 'I have been accused of obstructing the war. I admit it. Gentlemen, I abhor war. I would oppose the war if I stood alone.'

"He was given a fair trial by jury. The charge of the trial judge was eminently fair, and, on appeal to the Supreme Court of the United States, that court, by a unanimous decision, affirmed the judgment of conviction.

"Both prior and subsequent to the delivery of the speech mentioned Debs had on numerous occasions publicly urged wage-earners to adhere to the so-called St. Louis program of the Socialist Party adopted in April, 1917. This document asserted that participation of the United States in the war against Germany could not be justified, branded the declaration of war by the American Government as a crime against the people of the United States, declared that in all modern history there has been no war more unjustifiable, and urged 'continuous, active, and public opposition to the war.'

"Following the action of the Supreme Court the defendant has indulged in violent public criticism of the American courts of justice and practically defied the power of Government to administer the law against him. In a public speech made at Cleveland, March 12, he said: 'With every drop in my veins I despise their law and I defy them.' A few days ago he declared that if an attempt is made to imprison him he will have a general strike called in support of his attitude.

"In this situation my duty is clear. Respect for the law and our institutions is the basis upon which every application for executive clemency must rest. Open defiance of the law and threat of force to obstruct its orderly administration call for only one answer. The law must be respected and obeyed. To make sure of that, it must be enforced. I would be doing a grievous wrong to the country and striking a blow at law enforcement if I adopted any course which would interfere with the normal administration of justice in this case."

Efforts to Revive German Music

INSIDIOUS PROPAGANDA UNDER GUISE OF ART RESUMED WITH ALL ITS PRE-WAR ACTIVITY

By AN AMERICAN OF GERMAN BIRTH

GERMAN music, which for so many years has been synonymous with German propaganda, is in our midst again, not that there has been a cessation, but there was a perceptible lull which has now disappeared, and we find German artists, singing societies, quartettes, etc., again rampant. It seems of little importance to many that peace negotiations have not been concluded, unless perhaps, the musicians, as well as the general public, have accepted the armistice as a final peace, or an excuse upon which to re-establish German music and its insidious propaganda. We are having entire programs of German music jammed down our throats, a notable example being the first concert of the Society of Friends of Music given at the Ritz-Carlton a short time ago.

German agents who have striven to build here a stronghold of Teuton music are more active than ever, and their propaganda is not only greater in volume, but it appears in a more subtle and enticing form. The idea of saying that music is either international or supernational in order to camouflage attempts to bring German music and its powerful propaganda back again is a trick—a bandying of words. Music is not international—it is eclectic, selective, and those who attempt to revive German music are simply helping one of the greatest sources of German propaganda.

Music as propaganda originated with the now fallen (but still unpunished) Wilhelm Hohenzollern, whose spirit imbued the German people not only with militarism, but with war, hatred, rape, murder. He recognized the value of musical propaganda as one of the most powerful and advantageous means of bringing the German people, the educated ones especially, into the hearts and homes of the American people. Did he not arrange farsightedly to place a German at the head of nearly every great orchestra in the United States? Many were especially released by royal order to go to America for the sole purpose of furthering German Kultur.

Because of our German population, which numbers over 22,000,000, America has always been a fertile ground for propaganda, and although the people only hear of the well-known cases—such as the dastardly work of Dr. Carl Muck, erstwhile conductor of the Boston Symphony Orchestra—there are many others who were associates and coworkers of the famous orchestra leader, who were untiring and successful in their work. The Kaiser figured that if the beauty of much of the German music was made to create a deep and lasting impression that some of the people of the United States, especially those far from the battlefield and the scenes of wanton destruction, would doubt the enormity of the German crimes, saying that minds capable of producing such beauty could not be capable of the debasing outrages recorded.

This theory has been propounded even by patriotic Americans through sheer ignorance. Now is the time for enlightenment! The people must be told about the subtle, cunning ways used by the Monster Mind of Germany, the thing upon which it thrived and flourished for many years. One of the things we in this country must insist upon is the utter abolition of all things German—music as well! At least until we have destroyed the propaganda system which was the foundation of that which made it possible for Germany to bring on this dreadful catastrophe, for which she alone is responsible.

The restoration of German opera must not come to our stage until mental and physical conditions have so changed that the works of the German composers can no longer be regarded as reflecting the deceit, conceit, pretence and arrogance of Germany of today. To quote our esteemed critic, Mr. W. J. Henderson of the *New York Sun*, April 13th, 1919: "When they do come back (referring to grand operas) to our stage, they should be sung in English. The language of the damned is not fit for decent ears."

What has Germany ever done toward the upbuilding of music of other nationalities that we should put ourselves in a position to say: "Well, it is art for art's sake?" The hideous fact remains that in the name of Kultur she put the torch to, or destroyed, the finest historical monuments, the most precious treasures of science and art. She has not only destroyed humble homes, but the noblest edifices within the power of man to construct. For years, yes for half a century, she prepared the greatest inventions for human debasement the world has ever known—all under the guise of a supremacy of "intellectuality and Kultur."

The Hun was not only content to wage warfare in a material way, with cannon, ships and explosives, but he waged war through the mind, the heart, the soul, the spirit, the senses, sparing neither the flesh of his people nor the science of his doctors or theologians. Anything and everything was a justified means to an end, and his propaganda was most deadly, from the spreading of disease germs to the application of music.

Even the music plates from the great Russian publishing houses, stored in Germany, were melted and turned into shells, bullets, and other instruments of torture. All of which means, that little, if any, of the new and beautiful Russian music will be available, and it is the Russian school that has been the most flourishing in the last generation.

There is a strong nationalism in music, and as the world war created both a social and political catastrophe, it could not help affecting the cause of music and other artistic expression. If we have been warring against Germany socially, politically and commercially, why not artistically, and through music, the particular branch of art which helped her most in establishing her spies and in spreading propaganda?

Within her own boundaries, as well as without, she used music as a medium to incite her people to crime and atrocities, and yet despite this, there are some who would permit it in America. Here are one or two examples. The "German Song-book" voices the hellish spirit that led Germany to start her long-cherished, well-prepared war, in the concluding verse of the "Christmas Hymn of Hate":

> Sons of Germany in arms,
> Hurl down, strike with thunder, break in pieces!
> Rush forth, overthrow, transfix, devastate,
> Burn, kill, kill, kill!
> Such is the life of Glory.

A verse of the infamous, favorite German soldier-song, a song of murder, fire and rape, "Deutschland Uber Alles," goes:

> Make roar whatever is able to roar, in towering light and flames!
> Germans, everyone of you, stand fast together for the Fatherland!
> We, all of us, will today redden the sword with blood,—
> With the blood of hangmen and Frenchmen.
> Sweet day of vengeance! That sounds fine to all Germans.
> That is a glorious cause!

Despite these quotations, the music optim
the musical idealist, the "art for art's sal
person, will tell us that there is no such th
as "enemy music." But it does exist, just
same as the national anthem, war songs
patriotic songs are enemy music when the co
try from which they spring makes war upon
"Die Wacht Am Rhine," "Deutschland U
Alles," and all the traditional German songs
of the German people and are just as much
enemy in the field of music as the sword is
the hands of the German soldier on the field
battle.

It was very pleasant to note that Ru
Christians was foiled in his attempt, for reas
of German propaganda, to force German op
on the New York public early in March, and
think how far Christians was able to go with
plans. He had the cooperation necessary
bring the performance up to the very min
of its proposed presentation. He, the tolera
citizen of an enemy country, such as Germ
is and will be in our hearts and minds for ye
to come, dared to bring not only something wh
savored of the German language, but a comp
production representing the language, mu
art, and artists of his people!

And of such a people! A people not o
whose government but whose ideals are the m
barbaric, uncultured, and degenerate the wo
has ever known. Think of the presumption
Christians in attempting to force German op
down our throats while we are still in a state
war, if not actually engaged in spilling blo
He proposed German opera, German sing
German conductors! The armistice has
been fully complied with, and no peace tre
has been signed, to say nothing of the fact t
our casualty lists are still a noticeable feat
of the daily news—lists of names of the flower
our country, our brave and gallant youths v
gave of their life's blood so that right
righteousness should live and triumph over
criminal Germany of today. And yet Christi
proposed that our music critics write resur
of opera given in the language of, and by
very men who sent our boys to their death.
is incredible!

Every musician and everyone who has
power in directing musical activities should ra
against Christians and his ilk, and fight Germ
music, for the present at least, while the wou
of the flesh are still fresh and the heart s
bleeding for the dear ones lost in battle.

The way German music has crept back
many of our programs since the armistice
signed is typical of the German propagan
who was so powerful before and during the
in this country. This must be stopped and
mediately! The people over here do not real
the use to which German music has been pu
only seeing its musical value. German music
one of the greatest known forms of propagar
to Germanize the United States. Back in 1
Bismarck is quoted as saying, in answer to
question as to what he considered the great
disaster in the world—that he considered
fact that the North American continent was
English-speaking country! His idea and
who followed in his footsteps was to German
America—not only through emigration, but la
when their colonists got here, through the m
successful of all sources—education.

The German language, and we can say
same of German music, was, prior to the w
the chief modern foreign language studied
our schools and universities. This was due

In answer to this, the *Courier* says:

> The sentimental bit about German singers and actors facing actual starvation in America today leaves us cold. American artists took pains to learn how to perform in German before they sought employment in that country, and the German artist can learn English if he wants work in America. How many of them would like to be enabled to return to their native land at tne present moment? They may be "facing" starvation here—although we doubt it in the case of most of them—but with their native land behaving as it is today, they would be apt to have a nearer acquaintance with starvation than a face-to-face one.
>
> The whole Viereck article is rank German propaganda of the sort which we hoped and believed had been effectually stamped out here—but evidently that is not the case. We Americans are too lenient, as we have found and will continue to find to our cost. What a misnomer is that title "The *American Monthly!*"

In addition to what the *Musical Courier* has already commented upon in referring to Viereck's statement that "German actors and musicians are facing starvation in the United States," it might be well to say they all seem well supplied with money. Lectures, recitals, concerts, and other entertainments are being given to raise money for them, and this they appear to be doing successfully.

Dr. Glogau, president of the Social Scientific Society of New York, as the so-called German intellectual clique has seen fit to call itself, is active in his endeavors to raise money. A concert scheduled by him was to have taken place at the Hotel McAlpin Wednesday, March 19, but the manager of the hotel objected to the concert, and it was cancelled. Margaret Ober, Johannes Sembach, Hermann Weil, Carl Braun, and Otto Goritz, former Metropolitan Opera stars released on account of their nationality in November, 1917, were to have been the artists; Arthur Arndt, husband of Margaret Ober, was scheduled as pianist and accompanist. The concert was to have been a testimonial in honor of Margaret Ober and the Madrigal Quartet, as the others were known. Dr. Glogau says that there are about 170 members in his society and asserts that all are American citizens, but only 10 per cent. were born in this country.

Although the concert did not take place, the Social Scientific Society is giving private concerts, such as the Reicher lecture recitals, and is raising money from German sympathizers and German-Americans, of which New York City alone harbors more than eight hundred and fifty thousand.

The following letter tells of the Reicher lecture cycle:

> The undersigned invite you and your friend to take part at the second Emanuel Reicher Lecture-Cycle. The short presentation of the first meeting was a dazzling artistic and also social success. There are six evening lectures at intervals of two weeks; the first will take place February 8th, 1919, at 8:45 P. M. in the house of Dr. Otto Glogau. The price of the cycle will be $5.00. The names of new people will be taken by the secretary of the Society, Mr. S. R. Bursch, 416 Broadway:
>
> The Reicher evenings are always, above all, interesting. After the pre-eminent literary treat given by the prime movers of the modern German stage and their sensitive interpreters, a very spirited tea will take place, and the superlative men and women artists will lend their musical talents. We expect, therefore, a very great attendance.
>
> FRIEDRICH MICHEL.
>
> Dr. Otto Glogau,
> 64 East 91st Street.

Letters, editorials, and articles have appeared recommending Wagnerian productions for the coming season. Among others, Henry T. Finck recommends giving this music at the Metropolitan Opera House, and some time ago W. H. Humiston wrote a detailed letter to one of the dailies, telling of excellent translations which would make "Tristan and Isolde" ready for immediate production.

The many reasons offered for giving the Wagner operas are all excellent and no attempt is made to criticise anything said FOR these productions. But what may be said is AGAINST them. The arguments advanced have not been errors of commission, but of omission.

It is all very true that Wagner was not on German soil when he wrote the famous "Tristan and Isolde," being an exile due to some truthful and unpleasant criticisms which he permitted himself to utter against the Prussian government. It is also true that the plot of "Tristan" does not have its action on German territory, which applies also to "Parsifal," "Rienzi," and "The Flying Dutchman." And it is also true, as several of the Wagnerian enthusiasts have told us, that we have many English translations at hand, namely, by Corder, Jamieson, Forman, Le Gallienne, and last, but not least, the late Henry Chapman.

Again it is true, as Mr. Finck said in the *Evening Post* of July 27th, that American artists are now easily available to make up excellent casts. In speaking of the Wagner performances given in England, he said: "How much better we could do in New York, with such singers as Geraldine Farrar (whose greatest role is *Elizabeth* in 'Tannhauser'), Olive Fremstad, Frieda Hempel, Louise Homer, Riccardo Martin, Clarence Whitehill, Florence Easton?" But what guarantee have we that Americans will be put in the casts and that any one of our excellent American conductors will be awarded the baton?

If the German or Austrian-born artists were to be put in the casts under direction of one of our enemy or "friendly enemy" conductors, we would be reinstating one of the greatest German propaganda movements in this country. Even if we had a guarantee that the operas would be cast entirely with Americans, we would still be encouraging German influence and would be catering to the German population still in this country. They would be attending the performances in droves and would not only be satisfying their desires in hearing their native music, but, what is infinitely worse, they would be provided with added places in which to meet.

Under present conditions most people will agree that it is hardly wise to make it possible for our enemies (which they are still) to congregate, even in places of amusement or education. The military authorities would take this attitude, at least until the peace treaty is signed, and Germany herself has forced us to consider military authority first.

Here is another phase: Wouldn't it be absurd to follow our usual custom at the Metropolitan by opening a Wagnerian performance with "The Star Spangled Banner?" The idea of playing our national anthem at an opera written by a composer belonging to an enemy race would not only be ridiculous but sacrilegious!

Some people have called attention to the fact that England is giving Wagnerian performances. But England has not the huge German or hyphenated population that we have, nor has she German conductors or German-born singers. It would be decidedly unpleasant to hear these German singers with a pronounced German accent endeavor to give us an American version in English of what Wagner meant to convey in German, a lá Hohenzollern.

Recent interviews with various American artists indicate that they are not only willing, but anxious, to express their opinions against German music, and they should be heard, for after all, it is the artist who in expressing public opinion and public demand, is most potent. If our American musicians and musical audiences cannot see that music is not international, let

(*Continued on Page* 15)

Problem of the Finns in A

By HERMAN MONTAGU DONNER

TIME was, say twenty or even fifteen years ago, when the Finn was universally regarded in America as the type of immigrant the country had every reason to welcome with open arms. He was generally acknowledged to possess the personal attributes which go toward making the most desirable class of citizenship, particularly in a land largely in the formative stage. Unlimited capacity for work, thrift, veneration for law and order, frugality, temperance, a deep sense of religion, and, what singled him out from all other immigrants, a singleness of mind and an indomitable perseverance that enabled him to triumph over difficulties that appeared insuperable to men of other nationalities—these were the qualities that won for the Finn the admiration and esteem of the people of the United States.

Unfortunately this high regard for the Finnish-immigrant has not remained unimpaired. It has, in fact, suffered a considerable decline, within the last decade especially. A lecture tour in northern Michigan in 1911 first brought within my personal ken the extent to which the Finn in America has declined in the estimation of his New World neighbors and revealed something of the causes that had contributed to bring about the comparative disfavor into which he had fallen. American business men and employers with whom I then conversed, deplored the socialistic tendencies developed by the Finn and many expressed a positive antipathy to the latest comers from Finland as, if not downright Anarchists, at any rate belonging to the class of demagogues and agitators that contributed so greatly to labor unrest and disturbances more or less grave.

I am free to admit that in the eight years that have elapsed, American opinion so far as it has interested itself in the Finn at all, instead from veering from this viewpoint, has tended rather to become even more antagonistic. To be sure, this attitude does not show itself justified when we come to examine the facts closely, but we have to deal with facts as they are and not as we would wish them to be, meanwhile endeavoring first to explain this misconception about the Finn, and then to correct it.

In the first place, it is not to be denied that a great number, perhaps a majority, of the Finns who have emigrated to the United States during the last decade, either have belonged to the Social-Democrat party in the home land or have been induced to join the Socialist party—and that means, unfortunately, the extreme wing of it dominated by Morris Hillquit and men of his stripe—after their arrival here. And like the immigrants of other nationalities in similar case, these men are not brought into contact with the right influences that would bring them into touch with the real spirit of Americanism; indeed, they are from the start weaned away from such. Unhappily, this is brought about not merely through coming into contact with the more undesirable elements of our over-vaunted civilization, in the way of petty tyranny and graft, municipal corruption, and exploitation by sharpers of foreign as well as native extraction, always on the look-out for new and easy victims among the unsophisticated freshly landed. No, it is a deliberate procedure shrewdly engineered by the Socialists of New York and other seaboard cities to draw the newcomers into their ranks while yet mentally unformed and ignorant of true conditions in the land of their pilgrimage.

Not only is this done through propaganda directed toward them even before they leave their native shores, and increasingly pressed upon their minds after arrival, but through a practical organization which offers the immigrant certain associations, comforts and recreation. No other agency, least of all the U. S. Government which should be the first in the larger and saner view of its own interests to endeavor to attract the foreign visitor, so far has shown itself to possess the studied inclination or the means to provide for its prospective citizens.

Right here we strike the fundamental weakness of the whole American government policy towards its polyglot wards. Instead of actively interesting itself in their welfare from the moment of landing and seeing to it that every possible legitimate inducement shall be held out to them to familiarize themselves with the country of their adoption and the customs of its inhabitants, our government acts on the assumption that it has done its full duty in affording the immigrant a safe haven from the poverty or oppression from which he has fled. It forthwith washes its hands of him and leaves him to his own devices and the machinations of those who are eager to prey upon him in his mental confusion and helplessness in a strange land. Such a policy of aloofness is especially prejudicial to America as well as to the immigrant, in the case of a national as reserved in temperament and retiring in disposition as the Finn.

In the case of the Finn, the resultant loss is the more serious because of the many excellent qualities which he has to bring to the upbuilding of any State of which he becomes an inherent part. For of no nationality can it be said with greater truth that he has the defects of his virtues. The very steadfastness and perseverance of the Finn which enable him to triumph as a land settler and a farmer over obstacles which dismay the native American as well as other foreigners as evidenced in the abandoned farms of the Eastern states and the swampy and rocky terrain of Wyoming, degenerate into a stubbornness and obstinacy which make the Finn an element far more formidable and difficult to deal with in the ranks of the I. W. W. than any other nationality from which the Reds gain recruits. He will hold out to the bitter end against every threat and every manifestation of what he has been led to believe is tyranny or exploitation in any form.

This characteristic of tenacity so predominant in the Finn has its roots in centuries of conflict with the elements and a none too generous soil in his native land, intensified by the unmerited, but unremitting, oppression which he has had to undergo for the last quarter of a century at the hands of the Czar and the Russian bureaucracy. This oppression the Bolsheviki under Lenine and Trotzky have endeavored to intensify, a blind and suicidal policy which has also had the effect of increasing the Finn's native suspiciousness and distrust, with the natural result of making his lot as an immigrant still harder among an optimistic and easy-going people like ours.

On the other hand, this marked quality of the Finn makes strongly for the good of any community among which his lot may cast him, not alone in the reclamation of waste areas, but in the domain of citizenship where it blossoms naturally into loyalty to a cause or an ideal, to a government or an employer, once the immigrant has become convinced that fair dealing is to be expected from those holding relationship with him in an administrative or commercial or social capacity.

Such being the case, it can easily be seen that a grave responsibility rests upon us of the New World to see that the legitimate expectations of the Finn are promptly realized, especially in

An American View of the Industrial Unrest

By J. W. SULLIVAN

(Published in "The Organizer", Organ of The National Alliance of Employers and Employees, March, 1919)

the United States there is at present no ·neral profound social unrest. There is deed more surface clamor for radical than usual. There is continual news- comment on the uncertainties of employ- on demobilization. There are strikes, of the largest being demonstrations of ity in view of post-war adjustments. is alarm in the finance columns of the especially over railroad problems. There ie customary wild outcries from the W., from the unorganized migratory :s, from the Socialist soap-boxers. There e pessimistic views for the present and ight prophecies for the future, through et schemes of legislation, coming, as regu- from the parlor and college panacea work- There are projects by politicians for new parties. There are groups of farmers call- r long lists of good things, for themselves e got through law, combination, and what all cooperation. But to infer from these iusual phenomena that the hundred mil- ire worked up to painful anxiety over a ile social crisis would be misleading.

e it certainly is that more than ever the y is considering the welfare of the wage- rs, the rights of the plain people, and the ds of the farmer, who, it is to be kept in is in general a land owner having in respects his own particular interests.

w the highest welfare of the wage-worker be reached is the point on which counsels f course, divided. The lesser anti-conserva- groups—I. W. W.'s, syndicalists, anarchists, ocialists—being picturesque and offering at thrill news stuff, obtain space in the press oportionate to the possible outcome of their tion. Their principal common character- is profitless disturbance. But the socialists point to no permanent economic or civic vements as results of their occasional suc- s in gaining control of municipal govern- s. Their maximum membership in legisla- runs from next to none at all in most of the s to an uninfluential half-dozen in two or of the Industrial States amid a hundred ore of the two old party representatives. In Federal House, one lone Socialist has for ast decade been present to testify to his 's stagnation. The split of the Socialists e war has deprived them of the best of their rican leadership. The loyal wing, while ig itself Socialist, would in France be ified as Socialist-Reformist and not Social- evolutionist. The fact that the voter in the ed States may exercise democratic rights r the laws as they stand deprives the Ameri- Socialist party of much of the reason for existence of social democracy in backward opean countries. Face to face with economic lems, the American Socialist is baffled. He no immediate practical project peculiar to party. He has no ideal at once realizable. has no revolutionary scheme workable. e the great public cannot be moved by his als.

ie cause for the comparative abatement of asoning or violent social unrest in America at during the last four years immigration been at a standstill. The riotous mobs of strial centres, the supporters of the red s, the orators and audiences of the type of ic meetings which pass resolutions protest- at the wrongs of members of the interna- il brotherhood suffering under far-distant otisms—these in America are largely com- d of non-English-speaking foreigners. At the Socialist national headquarters in Chicago most of the literary staff are translators of the proceedings and finance-books of numerous branches in which business is conducted in the languages of continental Europe.

In the last four years the mass of un-Americanized foreigners has diminished sensibly. It has not been fed annually, as had been the case, by more than half a million newcomers. It has learned English words and American ideas. Moreover, it has become possessed of that blight on revolution—lucre.

One vexatious vice, from the viewpoint of the revolutionist, is characteristic of the poor immigrants to America. They work. They have saved. A chapter of the war-times has been that the savings banks of New York and New England, indices for the entire country, have touched the highest level of deposits in their history, that small property holders have shown no evidences of panic by selling out, and that the sales of war bonds have with each issue surprised the Treasury officials by the unexpected multitude of buyers in small amounts. In these respects the new immigrants, in many cases the majority in munition works, have come up to the mark with the Americans. Before the war, that is, before the cessation of immigration, the stories of desperate poverty in America applied for the most part to the immigrants, ignorant of the country's language, friendless, and in the ranks of unskilled and ill-requited labor. In those circumstances were seen causes for a fierce social unrest, not entirely non-existent now, but much diminished.

The Americanization of the foreigner transforms him as a citizen. He may be none the less a social idealist, but he learns to await opportunity and to labor for his ends by orderly means. First of all he becomes a real American. An egregious error of Germany's rulers was the assumption that the children of German emigrants to America must be Germans in spirit, thought, hopes, intentions or kultur. But, if one looks over the list of casualties in the American army in the great war, he will note the numerous German names of unhyphened Americans, bravely performing their duty for a land and a government they love to call their own. The American fights for his country in war, and he pursues legitimate methods for its betterment in peace. As the foreigner is assimilated, he follows American example.

Remedies for unrest? They are suggested in the foregoing lines. Let America remain American, or let it welcome only people prepared for its citizenship. That's the first desideratum. Improvements in the wage-workers' lot are now freely and continuously operative, especially through the American Federation of Labor. The Federation has gained whatever good has been possible to the masses through either economic or political means. No other reform agency has equaled it in these respects. It decides, by democratic processes, what legislative measures are helpful to the working people, as well as practicable, and persistently advocates them. It has seen the rise and fall of many other organizations while in every decade for nearly forty years it has doubled or even quadrupled in strength. It holds back where necessary, and is derided as conservative; it pushes forward where possible, and is charged with reckless radicalism. But, on the whole, it has assisted in giving to the workers higher wages, shorter hours, better working conditions, a needed mass discipline, a clearly defined field of economic operation, and an honorable record in citizenship. It has gradually gained the respect of the general public and the confidence of a great body of the employers. It has justified its members and supporters in replying, when asked for social remedies, that industrial peace is promoted, on behalf of the wage-workers, by its methods more than by any other yet tried.

Significant, indeed, is the fact that throughout the war, and since, the American Federation of Labor has been unswervingly loyal to our country and the Allies.

Granted, the purposes of American tradeunionism do not immediately look to the last word and the final measure in the field of economics. All the thoughtful world is contemplating less drudgery for the overworked, greater rewards to labor, a nearer approach to the profits problem, the projects of national ef- equality in opportunity for the sons of men. The land question is, in the minds of the just, ficiency and the highest production in every industry. But, in those respects, who, or what party, has all the sure, the positive, the directly effectual "remedies"?

Efforts to Revive German Music

(Continued from Page 13)

one example show what the Germans recognize in it.

Max Merz, who, with Reinhold Warlich is doing all in his power to bring German music in our midst again and who on April 8 had twenty-one German and Swiss German dialect out of twenty-one songs on his program at Cooper Union, tells us in concrete form in the foreword of the program dated January 21:

> In the folksong, the poetic and musical peculiarities of the various nations have found their fullest and richest expression. Race and origin, thoughts and feeling, the meaning and destiny of a people, its joys and sorrows and all that is involved in the process of national evolution, live forever in these songs. Not only the soul and the story of a people live in its songs, but these songs also reflect the entire physical character of a country—its climate, the wealth or poverty of its soil, its mountains and valleys, its winds and waters, and its manners and customs. Dethroned and forgotten gods and heroes live again under new guises, memories of the past and prophecies of the future are to be found here.

Could anything be more definite? Mr. Merz tells us openly, in print, what the Germans think and feel about music.

Every truly American musician feels a strong antipathy against German music, particularly Wagner. They feel that the sentiment "you-can't-make-war-on-music" is a thing of the past. German idols lie shattered in the mud. Even the very finest of Wagner's music serves only to remind us of the bloody atrocities committed, of Zeppelin raids and of the untimely deaths of the brave Americans and their Allied brothers who fought, bled, and died on the "Wotan" line, the "Brunhilde" line, and the "Siegfried" line.

Do not imply for a single minute that Wagner, had he been alive, would have sanctioned any such use of the characters from his operas, but Wagnerian music is part of the German people, yes, part of their very souls.

Those who have striven to establish German music in this country are now more active than ever, and true blue 100 per cent. American musicians (not those who prate about their Americanism, but who live it) should do everything in their power to beat down all propaganda, especially the branch they are most capable of handling, which in this instance is music.

Bolshevism in the United

THREE VARIETIES EXIST, ALL OF THEM INT

By W. J. GHENT

Article I.

BOLSHEVISM in Russia, for all its tyranny, violence and enforced starvation, is at least understandable as a historical consequence—as an outgrowth of czarism. The American article has, of course, no such genesis and background. It is a compound of many diverse factors, and it appears in many guises with varying degrees of intensity. It has three main varieties, easily enough distinguishable in typical cases. But not all of the individuals of the species run true to type; and some of them—perhaps many—are a complex of all three varieties. The grouping is as follows:

I. The Bolshevism of the I. W. W.'s.
II. The Bolshevism of the Defeatists.
III. The Bolshevism of the Romanticists.

THE INDUSTRIAL WORKERS VARIETY

The Bolshevism of the I. W. W.'s, menacing as it is to order and welfare, has at least the merit of being real and sincere. It is no pale reflex of the Russian article, but a native growth, with a dozen years of history before Lenine came to power. It is plainly a program of overthrow and destruction. It cares nothing about democracy. It rejects political action. To the democratic counsel to achieve social gains by a strike at the ballot-box, it replies with the anarchistic slogan, "Strike at the ballot-box with an ax!" It aims at dictatorship, and this dictatorship is not even that of the proletariat as a class, but merely of a small group of extremists themselves.

Its leaders were quick to see a kinship in the Lenine-Trotzky movement, and hailed with acclaim its victory. Subsequent developments, it is true, have not been wholly to their liking. A member of the hated rival, I. W. W. (the Detroit faction), making his way from America to Russia, was received into the inner councils of the duumvirate and has remained there; moreover, the working out of the soviet rule has not proceeded strictly according to program, and a disillusioned intellectual of the I. W. W. leanings, for some time a sojourner in Russia, has recently returned to tell the story of Lenine's humiliating compromises with the despised bourgeoisie.

But Bolshevism in Russia may flame or fade with small consequence to the I. W. W.'s. They have their own system to impose upon the unwilling, and this they are confident they will, when occasion ripens, establish and enforce with an utter disdain for compromise.

BOLSHEVISM OF THE DEFEATISTS

The Bolshevism of the defeatists is more complex. It is, moreover, plentifully tinctured with insincerity. Of course, the I. W. W. were and are themselves defeatists; but the defeatist variety of American Bolshevism flows through a wide range of individuals wholly apart from the I. W. W. The thing which is primarily defeatist (and not primarily I. W. W.) is a development of the war, and in its present state is a "hang-over" from that tremendous conflict. All the persons who were once active in attempting to obstruct the war against German aggression are now equally active in chanting the praises of Lenine and Trotzky. This particular variety of Bolshevism began in pro-Germanism, or ultra pacifism, or anti-nationalism, or any one of a number of other aberrations, or in some cases all of them together, and it shaped itself, more or less consciously, according to the progress of events.

When Bolshevism first appeared in Russia it seemed to promise a crushing defeat for the Allies and a victory for the Central Powers. Naturally enough, defeatism in the allied countries, and especially in America, associated itself with Bolshevism, and persons who a few years before would have looked with horror upon the practices of the Bolsheviki now professed to find in these extremists the hope and promise of a regenerated world.

Had there been no European war—had the Russian revolution broken out in time of world peace and yet followed exactly the course which it has taken—there would have been very little of this particular type of Bolshevism in America.

Take, for instance, the party Socialists. Leninism is an utter negation of almost everything for which the American Socialist party stood up to the time of the war. What we now know as Bolshevism was in effect condemned by a two-thirds vote in the national convention of 1912. This verdict was confirmed, also by a two-thirds vote, in the referendum which followed; and it was again confirmed, by an even larger majority, in the early part of the next year, in the referendum which unseated William D. Haywood from the national executive committee.

Yet the party Socialists, out of their insincere pacifism and their more or less sincere pro-Germanism, have now become the most violent partisans of the Bolsheviki. The testimony regarding Russia which before the war would have been accepted by Socialists as conclusive—the testimony of the Plechanoffs, the Axelrods, the Tschaikowskys, the Bourtzevs—that testimony they now reject and suppress, and instead they accept and disseminate that only which unqualifiedly supports the Lenine-Trotzky regime. They cannot be wholly blind to what in normal times they declared Socialism to be; they cannot be blind to the complete reversal of attitude they have taken, nor to the factors that led them to this reversal. Since August, 1914, they have been playing an insincere part, and every shift in the course of events has forced upon them some fresh insincerity.

By the same process all the other heterogeneous elements in the army of defeatism have been led to a more or less rapturous support of Bolshevism. In nine out of ten cases the change is, as in the case of the Socialists, a reversal of the pre-war attitude. The "radical democrat" of a certain kind finds now no difficulty in identifying democracy with a regime which dissolves a constituent assembly at the point of the bayonet, which excludes large elements from a share in government and which punishes with a firing squad the expression of a heterodox opinion.

The "conscientious objector" and the ultra pacifist apparently find nothing inconsistent with their views in compulsory service in the Red army. Presumably, if the thing is called "conscription" and is practiced in America, it is a very bad thing; but if it is called "revolutionary discipline" and is practiced in Russia, it is a thing most praiseworthy. The "humanitarian" of a certain sort is none the less a Lenine though he knows that infinite cruelties have been practiced upon Russians not favorable to the regime; and every furtive opponent of America and the Allies finds easy adjustment of his social principles with the violation of those principles in Russia.

The Bolshevism of the defeatists is a malevolent thing; and it is also, in considerable degree, an insincere thing.

encouraged, for among these persons there are held a variety of reasons for wishing to have the Federation disrupted and made powerless as a factor for bettering the lives of the American working people. Identities doubtless will occur readily to those who know the industrial situation.

Sixth, we have a regular blanket charge, typical of the blanket variety—a straight out assertion that the whole thing is wrong and hopelessly on the toboggan and due for the grand smash. Mr. Gompers has lost his leadership and that is all there is to it. This is truly a ponderous package. Thus, by fiat, does Mr. West settle the whole question of whether Mr. Gompers is the leader of the American labor movement. Argument is useless, fact futile. He who has to be "dragooned" into action for labor doubtless is no longer a leader. The only trouble with this is that Mr. Gompers was not dragooned, nor is his position of leadership different than it has been.

This alleged loss of leadership, we are told, is more true in the political field than in the industrial field. It is in the political realm, we are further instructed, "where labor's broader aspirations must be fulfilled." Not only has Mr. Gompers failed in this "broader" field, but Mr. Wilson has failed also, the implication being that these two men have failed *together*. Thus we see what marvelous information may be had by reading the writings of the truly studious in the great journals of "light and leading".

Of course Mr. West believes that something must be done about it. The workers have a great doubt—a regular capital D doubt—about President Wilson and Mr. Gompers. "It will take more than the pardoning of Eugene Debs or the urging of a liberal programme on a hostile Congress to remove this doubt." So. Look what we have in the house! It must be here, because Mr. West says it is here. And everything is going to crash in a grand smash. Mr. West has it on his schedule for Atlantic City, June 9. It is nice to be able to schedule things that way. It makes for a reputation for order and scholarly precision.

Mr. West, however, is careful enough to leave a back door open, and this he does at the opening of his article, possibly because of a notion that it may be forgotten by the time the conclusion is reached. "It is not a question of the sentiment of the rank and file", we are informed. "It is a question of organizing that sentiment and then breaking through the obstacles that prevent its free expression." Since the convention "is always boss ridden" Mr. West foresees difficulties.

FREE FORUM OFFERED

It may be rude to say to this that the American Federation of Labor in convention offers a forum than which there is no freer in America. It is this very freedom that has shattered the dream of so many disruptionists and placed the tombstone carefully over so many chimerical notions. Ideas go into that convention to get hammered all around the ring. If they come out sound and proven they get a place. If they break under the strain, then the Federation knows that it has avoided something that ought to be avoided. This is fact and not opinion. Proof is written all through the record and may be had by any one who cares to attend a convention and watch with both eyes.

Atlantic City will be like other conventions. Ideas will go into the ring and they will get hammered around. Ideas that stand the test will be sifted from ideas that do not. Beyond that there is nothing to be said. There is no dark secret, no deep and ugly plot.

Just one more fact remains to be chronicled. Among those who seek the destruction of the American Federation of Labor by means of attacks on President Gompers, such as the one Mr. West has made, there is a strange mixture of pacifism, Bolshevism and I. W. W.ism.

When *The Nation* wished to report the Pan-American labor conference at Laredo, Texas, Nov. 13, 1918, it sent a writer who at once proclaimed his pacifist views and who left the constructive gathering there in progress after having spent but one restless day in the vicinity. *The Nation*, in common with some other publications of that type, and in common with Mr. West, has long been possessed of a desire to worship at the shrine of Something Else whenever the American Federation of Labor was concerned. The I. W. W., Bolshevism, pacificism—anything except an ordered, constructive progress toward greater things for mankind—so it goes with the fitful, fretful ones.

But the American Federation of Labor IS a constructive organization. It DOES know where it is going. And it is not going the destructive, fruitless route, even though that route may be urged by the most "intellectual" and scientific critics. American labor prefers getting somewhere to vague experimenting along doctrinaire lines. It prefers arrival to derailment. It is likely to continue firm in the conviction that arrival is the thing to be desired, the "intelligentsia" to the contrary notwithstanding.

Is America Worth Saving?

(*Continued from page 6*)

ness to make use of the teachings of past experience, or to read the lessons of history and apply them to the problems of today. The real reactionary, who is always an egoist, insists that his own feelings, his own desires, his own ambitions, take precedence over anything that all the rest of mankind may have said or done or recorded. He wishes to start life all over again in a Garden of Eden of his own, with a private serpent and a private apple. The true progressive, on the other hand, is he who carefully reads history and carefully examines the experience of mankind in order to see what lessons have already been learned, what mistakes need no be repeated, and what principles of organization and conduct have established themselves as sound and beneficent. Upon all this the progressive builds a new and consistent structure to meet the needs of today in the light of the experience of yesterday. He does not find it necessary to burn his own fingers in order to ascertain whether fire is hot.

America will be saved, not by those who have only contempt and despite for her founders and her history, but by those who look with respect and reverence upon the great series of happenings extending from the voyage of the Mayflower to the achievements of the American armies on the soil of France, and upon that long succession of statesmen, orators, men of letters, and men of affairs who have themselves been both the product and the highest promise of American life and American opportunity. The Declaration of Independence rings as true today as it did in 1776. The Constitution remains the surest and safest foundation for a free government that the wit of man has yet devised. Faithful adherence to these strong and enduring foundations and a high purpose to apply the fundamental principles of American life with sympathy and open-mindedness to each new problem that presents itself, will give us a people increasingly prosperous, increasingly happy, and increasingly secure.

Just so soon as the American people, with their quick intelligence and alert apprehension, understand the difference between social reform and political Socialism, and the distinction between an internationalism that is false and destructive of patriotism, and an internationalism that is true and full of appeal to every patriot, they will stamp political Socialism, together with all its subtle and half-conscious approximations and imitations, under foot as something abhorrent to our free American life. They will prefer to save America.

The Failure of Public Ownership

SOCIALIZED INDUSTRY THROUGHOUT THE WORLD A FAILURE—WORST OF ALL IN DEMOCRACIES

By F. G. R. GORDON

MR. HARRY W. LAIDLER, a state socialist, is the author of a booklet of forty-eight pages entitled "Public Ownership Throughout The World." It would be difficult to pack more misinformation in forty-eight pages. Mr. Laidler says that governments have urged public ownership as a means of raising revenue and to increase economic and military efficiency. Governments may have attempted this, but they have always failed miserably. Governments everywhere require from two to three men and from two to three dollars to accomplish the same result that private ownership accomplishes with one man and one dollar. And this I propose to prove absolutely.

In the first place Government ownership—or to be more correct, State and Municipal Socialism—is characterized everywhere by poor service, low wages, high rates and large annual deficits. This is true because what is everybody's business is nobody's business and, therefore, the only business of any government official in the conduct of industry is to draw as much pay and perform as little work as possible. Thus we find that in a democracy like New Zealand, or the Australian states, it requires three men to perform one man's labor, and this has resulted in the highest debts and the highest cost for government in all the world. Let us take a few items that Dr. Laidler makes prominent:

MAIL SERVICE

Socialists generally point to the United States mail service as a fine illustration of the "success" of socialized industry. Our Post Office is the worst managed big business in this nation. It has a billion complaints a year, and not the slightest attention is paid to most of them. The "know-it-all" clerk you will find in the post office and not in the private-owned railway, telegraph or telephone companies. From 1865 to 1915 our socialistic post office lost more than $700,000,000 directly and indirectly, or an average of $14,000,000 a year. But from 1900 to 1915 the losses averaged more than $18,000,000 a year.

Recent government reports from Australia show that the post office, telephone and telegraph are all going from bad to worse and that the deficits are increasing while the service is degenerating.

In connection with our own post office, it may be well to mention the fact that it pays nothing for the space it occupies in the public buildings, nor does it pay the salary of the Postmaster General and his staff, or the auditor and his staff, hundreds of highly paid officials who draw their salaries from the Treasury Department. Thus we see that the Post Office Department *grafts* upon the Treasury Department more THAN A MILLION DOLLARS A MONTH. By ignoring these facts and the other overhead costs, the state socialists make it appear that the post office pays. *It never paid and it never will pay under government operation.*

TELEPHONES

Every one who uses the telephone or the telegraph in Europe, Australia, or elsewhere, complains of the "wretched service." And yet there is not a great government telephone system in all the world that is able to make both ends meet. Under normal conditions the British telephone system has from $3,000,000 to $4,000,000 annual deficits. For many years Germany has owned and operated the telephone. She invested $700,000,000 in the system. Wages there have averaged only one-third of what they are in America. The service has always been very poor. Germany, before the war, had an operating income of $28,000,000. But she had to pay $24,000,000 annual interest charges; she lost $12,000,000 a year from displacement of taxes and other overhead charges made an annual loss of $5,000,000 and more.

France is not much better off. She loses several millions each year, gives execrable service and the rates are actually higher than in this country. Wages on the socialized telephones of Europe average from $2.60 per week in Belgium to $5.20 in Switzerland, and every socialized telephone in Europe is losing money. Before the war the Paris rate was $77.20 a year. More than 90 per cent. of the telephone users in the United States pay less than the average Paris rate, yet wages in this country, in 1914, averaged a little more than 400 per cent. higher than the rate in France.

This nation has three-fourths of all the telephones in the world. Chicago has more telephones than all of France. Even in Japan, where wages average $76 a year, the cost for telephone service under the blight of public ownership is higher than in Massachusetts. Great Britain and Ireland have only 650,000 telephones, but we are increasing the number of telephones in this country by 700,000 a year!

TELEGRAPH

The United Kingdom socialized its telegraph system in 1870 and from that date to the beginning of the Great War, lost more than $200,000,000. It is not the masses in any nation that use the telegraph, for we find that 96 per cent. of all the messages that go over the wires of Great Britain are sent by only four per cent. of the people.

While the wages of the telegraphers in Europe average only one-third that of American operators, the telegraph rates are practically the same. In America we have excellent service. In Europe it takes on the average four times as long to send a telegraph or a telephone message as in this country, and if time is worth anything, our rates are less than half the rates in Europe. New Zealand lost before the war an average of $313,000 a year on its wire system and Australia lost almost $800,000 annually. Since the war the losses have increased enormously.

RAILROADS

Mr. Laidler makes a general statement as to the railways, and it is most unfortunate for him that he picks the Italian railways as an illustration of "going over" to socialism. In 1905 the Italian government socialized 8,386 miles of railroads. Under private ownership these lines paid small dividends; paid millions in taxes to help support the government and gave good service. Under public ownership the government, up to the breaking out of the war, had added 50,188 hands to the pay-roll without adding a single mile of new line. The railways have become politicalized from end to end.

While the wages average about one dollar a day, the freight rate is twice as high as in this country, and the annual average losses from 1905 to 1914 were from $35,000,000 to $42,000,000, to say nothing of the $10,000,000 or $12,000,000 lost in taxes. Since the war the losses have increased tremendously and the government had to vote $360,000,000 recently to rehabilitate the whole system. The Italian railways under government ownership are capitalized at more than $198,000 a mile, as compared with only $66,000 in this country, yet our socialists are yel about "watered stocks"!!

The Austrian railroads are even worse t those of Italy and the losses are greater. . freight rates on the socialized railroads of rope average from 90 to 300 per cent. hig than in this country, though the wages are than half those paid here.

PRIVATE OWNERSHIP

Under private ownership we enjoyed cheapest freight rates in the world, and the service. We obtain nearly $160,000,000 a in railroad taxes. In 1914 our privately-ow railways carried a ton of freight one mile .72 cents. The rate in Germany was 1.37 ce in France, 1.33 cents; in Denmark, 2.33 cents more than three times as high as our rate, on 1,216 miles of state-owned railways, Denm lost, in 1914, about $1,300,000. In Austria socialistic rate is 1.50, or more than twice high as here and those socialized railways more than $50,000,000 a year before the Today they are bankrupt.

AUSTRALIAN SOCIALISM

Australia and New Zealand have plunged state socialism more extensively than any o nations, and as a result they have become champion debt-ridden states of the world. January 1, 1914, the public state and fed debts of those countries amounted to $1,936,0 000. On that date the combined debt of ou states and of the Federal Government amour to $1,313,000,000, round numbers. This was average debt of $65 for every family in Amer but in New Zealand and Australia it was average debt of $1,555 or *twenty-four ti greater than in this nation.*

For the year ending June 30, 1914, New land, with 1,152,000 population, actually rai and expended for the year $57,550,000. New York State has nine times the populat of New Zealand she would have expen $517,000,000 for one year's expenses had plunged into state socialism to the same ext that New Zealand has! Like that prospect?

Australia, with less than half the populat of New York, taxes the farmers' land $19,000, a year. Imagine the farmers of New York p ing $36,000,000 a year just for a land tax. entire expenses of Australia in a year for s government averages more than £43,000,000, over $200,000,000, with one-half the populat of New York.

And this is what state socialism has done the most democratic countries on earth.

MUNICIPAL OWNERSHIP

Mr. Laidler brags about the fact that th are 1,562 socialized electric lighting plants the United States. The privately-owned pl numbered 3,659, and they had an output of k watt hours according to the United States cen of 1912 of 10,995,436,276; while the sociali plants had only 537,526,730. The census shows that the gross revenue per kilowatt h was: Private plants, 2.54 cents; sociali plants, 4.32 cents.

This shows that the municipal-owned pl charged *70 per cent.* higher rates than the vate plants. And the private plants *pay ta* while the municipal plants escape all taxat

Mr. Laidler refers to Germany as a nat that has "gone over" to socialistic things. sure has. In 1914 we find that the munici debts of the great German cities were the hi est in the world based upon wages and gen income. For instance: Dusseldorf had a deb per family as against one of $140 per y in Chicago, and the true measure would ,500 in that German city as against only in Chicago and $90 in Detroit. In Munich ebt on the same basis was $1,250, and in kfort $1,400 per family, against $140 in Chicago and Milwaukee.

d yet, in spite of the vast socialistic es of the German cities we find that the for the poor was increasing at the rate of per cent. for each ten-year period since . So, with all of their boasted municipal lism the cost for paupers in every nation in pe increases twice as rapidly as in this n with little socialism compared with pe.

U. S. RAILWAYS

Laidler seems to glorify the government gement of our railways, and he boasts of ischarge of the $5,000 to $20,000 managers. *and because of this the cost of operating railways has increased enormously.* Under nment operation we had our passenger ce reduced by 30 per cent. and were forced ut up with vastly inferior service. Passen- rates also were increased 50 per cent. and ht rates 25 per cent. (25% in addition to 15% allowed the roads before they were n over).

hen Congress created a revolving fund of ,000,000. They rightly called this a revolv- fund for it quickly revolved itself out of ! Now Congress will have to vote another lving fund of $750,000,000 and it will take t six months for that to disappear. Our sportation bill for 1918 was *$1,500,000,000 than it was for 1917 under private owner- and management.* And on top of this we have to pay $212,000,000 in direct losses. should be an object lesson to every sane rican to steer clear of socialistic ownership operation of anything.

HY WE SHOULD FIGHT SOCIALIZATION OF INDUSTRY

we socialized the American railways within years we would add 500,000 men to the pay- without adding a mile of extension. We ld also add 80,000 to 100,000 officials who ld politicalize the lines. Within ten years would double the cost of operation. Who the wealth producers of the nation would for this added burden? A bureaucracy is r efficient, never economical, never progres- It is always wasteful, always extravagant, always becomes politicalized.

is the high cost of government that makes high cost of living. Every family in Amer- this year will pay $1.66 a day just for the of being governed. How would you like to two or three times as much? You will pay or three times as much if you begin socializ- industry.

his nation and its people are not much dif- nt from any other people, especially those Canada and Australia, and in the two latter ntries, through socialization of railways, tele- phs, telephones, meat industry in Australia ome extent, also coal mines, sugar industry, etc., they have piled up national debts that from ten to twenty-five times higher than are in this country with corresponding cost annual interest charges. Mr. Laidler and rest of the state and municipal socialists t us to travel the road that leads straight to ional and municipal bankruptcy; that bur- s the people with enormous costs and if per- ed in leads to industrial stagnation and ay.

The question is naturally asked why are the rges and the cost of operation so much higher ler socialistic management as compared with vate management and ownership?

Now take the simple matter of supplying water to the citizens of a great city. Most people naturally suppose that the business is so simple that a city ought and should supply water at a cost much less than a company that wishes to make a profit. Facts, however, show that the cost of administration has always increased after the municipality has taken over the plant.

The great Metropolitan Water Board of London actually exceeded the combined cost of the eight companies which it replaced. And it is a well known fact that the cost for pumping water in our American cities has increased 25 per cent after socialization.

When Switzerland acquired the five railway companies and consolidated the staff into one administration, the State Socialists shouted with glee at the supposed economy. But the official reports show that the staff now, under the blight of bureaucracy, is much larger and far more expensive than the five combined staffs under private ownership. And what I say of Switzerland is true of every railway, telegraph and telephone that has been socialized throughout Europe and the Australian states.

Under government ownership the effort always is being made to "pass the buck" to some other department. Socialization always reduces the ambitions of young men who enter the government service, for public ownership always discourages initiative and independent judgment, and the civil service of bureaucracy actually works for incompetency in any and every great business enterprise that government attempts to operate.

These very evils are reduced in an autocracy. Thus we find that on the socialized railways of Japan there is a large degree of efficiency because there is no democracy whatever. The railway workers of Japan are not permitted to join a union or any organization. However, the people of Japan paid .90 cents per ton per mile for the transportation of freight as against .72 cents in this nation in 1914, though the wages on those socialized railways are only $115 a year as against $810 in America (1914).

The blight of a socialized industry will arrest progress, and in time abolish it entirely. And the blight of a bureaucracy is always far worse in a democracy than in an autocracy; and it is far more dangerous too, because in the former it will lead straight to the *dictatorship of the proletariat.*

SOCIALIZED TROLLEY SYSTEMS

The proposition of the socialists and public ownership advocates to socialize the street railways, due to the fact that the War Labor Board has increased wages of street railway employees from 25 to 60 per cent, and other costs have increased from 50 to 125 per cent, and the corporations are asking for increased fares, calls for serious consideration.

The socialistic elements tell us that the interests of owners and public are diametrically opposed. If that statement be true, then it is none the less a "fact" that the interests of the owners of the shoe factories, are likewise opposed to the interests of those who wear shoes, simply because one party sells and the other buys.

It is claimed that private ownership seeks to congest the people in our cities. Just the opposite is the truth. Congested working people do *not* ride, they walk, whereas men and women who live in the suburban districts *do ride.*

In Europe however, with the zone system which prevails on all the socialized systems, congestion is a mighty evil, made so by the very zone socialistic system. I say socialistic system because it was brought about by municipal socialists.

EXTENT OF SOCIALIZATION IN EUROPE

One would think to read the publications of the Rand School or the National Public Ownership League, that all the street railways of Europe were already socialized. Here are the facts:

Out of 85 cities in Germany having a population of 50,000 or more, only 36 own and operate their street railways, and out of these 36 only nine have ever been able to make both ends meet. In other words, 75 per cent of the socialized street railways of Germany were a financial failure before the war; and to-day they are practically bankrupt. These German socialized street railways charged two and a half cents fare with no transfers and the two and a half cents in Germany before the war was equal to an *eight* cent fare in any city in America, yet, the wages on those socialized lines were barely one-third of the rate, here in 1914.

Very few street railways in Italy, Denmark, Sweden and Norway are socialized and those that are have proved a miserable failure.

British street railways seem to be the ideal of all the socialists and half-baked socialists everywhere. In the United Kingdom 136 street railway systems were socialized and operated before the war.

The municipalities had invested $226,000,000 in these lines. Twenty-seven of them were actually losing money, that is, they were unable to make both ends meet and had the overhead costs as a direct loss. In 1913, the socialized street railways of London lost $750,000 without reckoning displacement of taxes. Since the war, they have been losing more than a million dollars a year. They are in debt for more than $49,000,000 (1913). And it is reported that the present debt is nearly $60,000,000. The zone system prevails in all the cities and as a result you pay an average of twice the cost to ride in this country.

In 1913 the city of Glasgow received only $67,000 in taxes while the city of Boston, serving about the same number of people received $1,394,611. And in addition to this they expended nearly $300,000 in paving, cleaning snow from the streets, etc., and paid $677,900 for rentals for subways.

Labor receives out of each fare in the United Kingdom less than one cent, while in this country, in 1914, labor received 2.05 cents. (It is not far from two and a half cents at present in this country and a little less than one cent in the United Kingdom.)

SOCIALISM IN AMERICA

Seattle has for some years owned and operated thirteen miles of street railway and she has lost $75,000 a year. The service is poor, compared with the private lines and the fare is the same.

In San Francisco there is a socialized street railway but no one knows what the actual losses are, for municipal book-keeping never keeps books. But by ignoring $5,000,000 of capital and other costs, the municipal socialists try to make out a success for this socialistic line.

The failure of state and municipal socialism throughout France has placed a damper on any further socialization of industry and so we find that Paris and other large cities are dealing with private corporations for their transportation problems.

The socialization of a street railway anywhere in this country will transform a great industry from the domain of business to that of politicalization and this will mean here, as it has meant everywhere, poor service and large annual deficits.

Four years ago President William Mahon and the great street railways union in the city of Detroit successfully fought municipal ownership of the Detroit Street Railway lines and I may mention the fact that President Samuel Gompers told me in Portland, Maine, in 1916, that he was absolutely opposed to the socialization of industry whether it be street railways or anything else.

By EUGENE DOANE

NO more striking epitome of the Young Men's Christian Association's war work with the American Expeditionary Force could be had than George W. Perkins's pregnant words: "The Y. sought service, not fame." Those six words aptly summarize the report of a special committee of the War Work Council sent to Europe in December, 1918, to study the work "and do everything possible to further its efficiency." Mr. Perkins was aided in this task by Mortimer L. Schiff, F. S. Brockman and John R. Hall.

Only the Y. M. C. A. work in France, England, Germany and Italy was considered. No account was taken of the problems tackled at the camps in this country; for the Navy; for the prisoners of war, nor the accomplishments among our men with the Allied forces in other parts of Europe. The report should be a source of gratification to every one who contributed to the Y. M. C. A. war chest and it indicates, though in not so many words, that much was done toward winning the war by sustaining the morale of our fighting men.

No great business—except that of making war itself—ever met and solved so many perplexing problems as did the Y. M. C. A. From more than 150,000 candidates, 11,229 were selected for service overseas and last month 8,350 of these (5,693 men and 2,657 women) still were in Europe caring for our boys on duty there, lightening their leisure hours and conducting athletic and educational campaigns of unparalleled magnitude.

"That the workers as a whole were brave and unselfish is shown by the fact that 14 Y. M. C. A. secretaries were killed and 126 others were wounded while engaged in their work," says one part of the report.

Analyzing the greatest problem of all, that of obtaining supplies, Mr. Perkins says:

> There was a time when the war was at its height, that it cost the Y. M. C. A. almost as much to get an automobile from the United States to France as the automobile itself cost in the United States. The same was true of canteen supplies. One day the Y. M. C. A. could get supplies sent on a Government boat without freight charges. The next day the only way to send them was to pay almost as much in freight as the goods cost. It will be readily seen that it was almost impossible to arrive at anything like an average cost price at which to sell these goods.
>
> The Y. M. C. A. never solicited money for the purpose of giving away its canteen supplies. The constant policy of the Y. M. C. A. was to sell canteen supplies as nearly as possible at cost, and to bend every effort, when fighting was in progress, to furnish the men at the front with supplies free of charge where it was at all possible to get the goods to them.
>
> Some have criticized the Y. M. C. A. for not giving away more articles, such as cigarettes, chocolate, etc. Its policy has been not to give away generally but only in special and needy cases.
>
> From June, 1918, to April, 1919, the Y. M. C. A. handled in France alone upwards of 2,000,000,000 cigarettes, 32,000,000 bars of chocolate, 18,000,000 cans of smoking tobacco, 50,000,000 cigars, 60,000,000 cans of jam, 29,000,000 packages of chewing-gum, and 10,000,000 packages of candy. These are only a few of the items handled, but the size of these figures should convince anyone that it would be financially impossible for the Y. M. C. A. to give its supplies away generally.
>
> Furthermore, the army does not favor any such policy. It thinks that it is far better for the men to spend their money on such articles as these, than to spend it in other ways. For the most part the men hold the same view.

Transportation of supplies, entertainers, workers from the base depots was another tremendous problem and with only 700 motor

GEORGE W. PERKINS

trucks at its disposal, the wonder is that so much was done. From June, 1918, to February, 1919, the railroads handled 9,554 carloads of Y. M. C. A. material and in October alone, with the final drive clogging all arteries of supply, there were sent forward 765 carloads of general supplies, 86 cars of flour, 148 cars of sugar, 150 cars of tobacco, 59 cars of chocolate, 63 cars of raw material for the Y. M. C. A. factories and 144 cars of lumber and hut materials.

Speaking of the Y. M. C. A. factories, the report says:

> Early in the war, because of its inability to get certain supplies from the United States or elsewhere, the Y. M. C. A., through the courtesy and with the assistance of the French Government, succeeded in reopening a number of factories, the Y. M. C. A. supplying the raw materials, supervising its manufacture, and taking the entire product. The 20 biscuit factories, 13 chocolate factories, 3 candy factories and 8 jam factories operated in this fashion, when working at their maximum, produced monthly:
>
> 10,160,000 packages of biscuits.
> 7,400,000 tablets of drinking-chocolate.
> 3,500,000 bars of sweet chocolate.
> 1,000,000 bars of milk chocolate.
> 3,800,000 bars of chocolate cream.
> 1,500,000 nut-covered chocolate rolls.
> 3,100,000 cartons of caramels.
> 2,000,000 tins of jam.
>
> For the manufacture of chocolate, the Y. M. C. A. had to transport cocoa beans and wooden material for the cases, as well as the paper in which it was wrapped. For the manufacture of biscuits, it had to transport flour, sugar, bicarbonate of soda, almonds, peanuts, figs, etc., as well as material for cases.
>
> For the manufacture of paper and envelopes, it was necessary at times to transport the pulp of which the paper was made, the machinery for its manufacture, lampblack for the printing-ink, gum arabic for the mucilage on the envelopes, and talc with which to surface the paper.
>
> For example, it employed the paper factories in Tolosa, Spain, to manufacture paper. One hundred million sheets were made there. This employed practically the entire town, men, women and children. And yet the output was only one-third of the total amount of writing paper manufactured in France by the Y. M. C. A., while large additional supplies were sent from New York. In all, over 400,000,000 sheets of writing paper, with the necessary envelopes, and 16,[illegible] postal cards were distributed to the soldiers.

Still another tremendous business problem was the supply of buildings, yet in France alone on

The National Civic Federation Review

Vol. IV NEW YORK, JUNE 5, 1919 No. 13

IF NOT COMPULSORY INSURANCE—WHAT

VOLUNTARY SOCIAL INSURANCE AND HEALTH CONSERVATION EFFORTS URGED—COMMITTEE REPRESENTING ALL INTERESTS APPOINTED TO PREPARE CONSTRUCTIVE PLAN

IF not compulsory sickness insurance through legislative enactment, then what in the way of a constructive program should be adopted? was the question considered at a meeting of the Social Insurance Department of the National Civic Federation, held Monday, May 19, at headquarters, 33rd floor Metropolitan Tower, New York. The conference was presided over by the chairman of that Department, Warren S. Stone, Grand Chief of the International Brotherhood of Locomotive Engineers, who outlined the vehement opposition on the part of the working people to compulsory health insurance with the espionage that accompanies it, compulsory medical examination and lack of freedom in choosing physicians. He expressed the belief that it would destroy the initiative of the industrial worker necessary to our development as a nation. Agitation for compulsory sickness insurance legislation in the United States has to date failed of achievement.

Among the various suggestions for consideration made at the conference were:

(1) The prevention of unnecessary illness through education of the public concerning health matters, at present inadequate, the vast majority of the working people being uninformed in regard to means of prevention of disease. It was urged that ministers should spread facts from authoritative sources; that employers, government agencies and public health nurses should be utilized and that there should be resort to moving pictures.

(2) The necessity of securing an actual record of absenteeism due to sickness, at present unknown, to permit correct estimates upon cost of health insurance and to indicate requisite health conservation work.

(3) Some means of providing the fundamental necessity, payment of wages when ill or financial benefit during the period of illness; better medical care, and greater efficiency in state health departments.

(4) The importance of improving, regulating, and developing all voluntary methods of insurance, including trade union funds, fraternals, employers' establishment funds and those of industrial insurance companies; and

(5) The creation of health schools throughout the Union whereby health officers and others might receive instruction upon public health matters.

WARREN S. STONE

Attention was called to the failure of the systems of compulsory insurance in England and Germany. The Federation was urged to send a second commission to England, representative of all American elements concerned, to bring back facts for the information of legislators, employers and wage earners now confused by misleading propaganda disseminated by that group of social reformers which has undertaken to promote compulsory health legislation.

Exception was taken to the statement, widely circulated, that sickness is the cause of poverty. It was urged that the problem is economic and that the workman should be put upon his own feet and permitted to purchase his medical attendance in his own American way. In support of this contention, while agreeing with the idea that the period of illness is the one when the worker needs the most and receives the least financially, the result of a first hand investigation in England was cited to show the utter fallacy of collective or group medical service and the necessity of keeping in this country individual relations between the doctor and the patient.

It was pointed out that the campaign for health insurance in New York State, Ohio and elsewhere is built upon gross misstatements of fact and delusions; also that to put compulsory sickness insurance and practically pauper medical service upon the American working man would cause universal dissatisfaction and injure the public health. Labor men emphatically claimed that the only way is to have sickness insurance voluntary in every respect and that no workman should be forced into such an association.

CONSTRUCTIVE PROGRAM PLANNED

What may be a practical substitute for propositions now advocated to protect the worker in time of idleness through illness and to prevent unnecessary disease will be developed by a special committee charged with the duty of presenting a definite constructive program. The following committee, which was appointed by Chairman Stone to carry out this purpose, held its first meeting on Monday, May 26, and will hold a second session June 19, its work already being well under way:

Dr. Alvah H. Doty, (Chairman), Medical Director, Western Union Telegraph Company, New York;
M. W. Alexander, Managing Director, National Industrial Conference Board, Boston, Mass.;
Mrs. F. Lothrop Ames, Chairman Industrial Committee, Women's Department, New England Section, The National Civic Federation, Boston, Mass.;
Mark A. Daly, General Secretary, Associated Manufacturers and Merchants of New York State, Buffalo, N. Y.;
Dr. Lee K. Frankel, President American Public Health Association, Third Vice President, Metropolitan Life Insurance Company, New York;
Hugh Frayne, General Organizer, American Federation of Labor;
Dr. Frederick L. Hoffman, Third Vice President and Chief Statistician, Prudential Insurance Co., Newark, N. J.;
A. C. McLean, President National Fraternal Congress of America, Sharon, Pa.;
John Roach, Chief Bureau of Hygiene and Sanitation, Department of Labor, State of New Jersey (Formerly Leather Workers' Union), Newark, N. J.;
P. Tecumseh Sherman, Attorney and Social Insurance Specialist, New York; and
Miss Margaret Loomis Stecker, National Industrial Conference Board, Boston, Mass.

In opening the meeting, the chairman, Warren S. Stone, Grand Chief, International Brotherhood of Locomotive Engineers, of Cleveland, Ohio, said:

"It seems to me that the whole plan of health insurance or social insurance, from the standpoint of the workers at least, is altogether wrong. If we have accomplished anything as a nation, it has been due to the fact that the men and women of the country have been allowed to work out some of these problems. I do not take much stock in paternalism; I do not believe in a government that tucks you in bed at night, and if some plan of health insurance is adopted, worked out and finally made a law, I fear its effect on our country; I fear it will be the beginning of the end. I do not believe any nation can prosper when the government does everything for the industrial worker. It destroys initiative and makes him a dependent upon the bounty of his government. I understand that a somewhat different plan is to be presented this afternoon and I think the meeting should bring out something valuable in the way of constructive suggestions.

"Senator Davenport, who introduced the Social Insurance bill in the New York State legislature, still insists that we must have social insurance of some kind and I gathered from our short talk today that he believes it must be compulsory. But I want to say to you frankly as a representative of labor that there is not going to be any compulsory health insurance if we can help it. When you say to the American working people that they must do this or that thing, every drop of red blood in them resents it. I think it is summed up in a homely phrase, 'You can push all you like but you mustn't shove'."

PUBLIC HEALTH MENACED

An abstract of the discussion and recommendations made during the meeting follows:

Dr. Alvah H. Doty, Medical Director, of the Western Union Telegraph Company, New York:

"The plan I have to suggest is rather an old one. The idea is simply to educate the public concerning health matters. There has been an attempt to do it but it has never reached the element we are after; that is, the laboring classes. I think there is a belief that they do not care to get this education, that they do not respond. That is not so. Two years ago we had an investigation made by sixty nurses, covering about a thousand families. The nurses went to the homes and asked what their idea was in regard to the means by which disease was transmitted, whether they were willing to help and why. The replies were about the same as those which would have been received in the Middle Ages; they showed that these people knew absolutely nothing about the subject; they held all sorts of theories. Almost all of them spoke vehemently about doing their part; when asked why, they said they desired to help preserve the life and health of their children. So there was a motive.

"Then the rather important question was asked: Have you ever received any education of any kind along these lines and in what way—any bulletins or anything of that sort? Not one stated that any real, first-class information had been received. Some had received bulletins which were thrown down at their doors, but many of them could not read; some of them were foreigners. So we found the situation to be the same as it is today; we have absolutely no concerted means by which the public in general is receiving information concerning public health or the prevention of disease. It is true, the municipal and state health departments have ordinances but they do not fill the bill.

"The result has been that we are surfeited with health ordinances but there is no co-ordination between the states, and that is the feature, I believe, that calls for present action on the part of practical sanitarians. How can we educate the people of every class? That has not been done and we find constant indications of the need of it. I believe the critical point is how to educate the public and there is no question but that it can be done.

"We have not utilized all existing means. For instance, the ministers of the country have a strong influence with their people; they deal with public matters and they could devote a certain portion of a Sunday or even a few minutes to studying certain facts, not their own theories, but things given to them by authoritative sources; work could also be done by presidents of associations and nurses; through moving pictures, etc., but I do not believe the government could do it. It must be undertaken by some national association and there is small cost attached to it. There should be cooperation throughout the country. It could be done the moment such an organization was effected."

ABSENTEEISM AND COST

Mark A. Daly, General Secretary of the Associated Manufacturers and Merchants of New York State, whose headquarters are at Buffalo, stated that:

"The Davenport compulsory health insurance bill, introduced in the New York legislature, which passed in the senate, was defeated through the efforts of Speaker Sweet and the Republican Assemblymen. He said that at the least calculation it would have cost each employer $20 per employee every year and that as originally drawn, had the bill become law, the cost would have been $40 per employee.

"Our Association, at a meeting of its board of directors last week, decided that it would go to work on an educational campaign and also a campaign of investigation. What we ran up against at the last session of the legislature was the intolerable ignorance of the employer members as to what health insurance meant and that ignorance extended down the line to the employee. As a matter of fact, in New York state we found, upon investigation, that possibly 5 per cent of the people, who would be directly affected by it, knew the terms of the bill that they were discussing and, when it came to the fundamental principles, the remaining 95 per cent knew nothing at all about the subject.

"Our association, for instance, is going to take up the matter of cost. There are several est mates as to cost in New York State. The supe intendent of insurance made one, our actuarie made another and someone else another and, think, there was a little matter of $25,000,000 c $30,000,000 difference between them. In orde to get accurate data, which I do not believe eve the insurance companies have, as to the numbe of cases of illness, the duration of illness on th basis of the Davenport bill after a period c three days, etc., we have prepared a plan throug which it is hoped that accurate and practic facts, concerning absenteeism and illness workers in factories, may be obtained which w enable the association and individual membe to deal intelligently with the problem.

"The outline of the plan contemplates its i stallation in plants employing 2,000 or mo persons. To get an experience that will be wor anything we must have, as a minimum, 200,0 employees covered. If we could get 300,000 e ployees it would, of course, increase the wor of the experience. The record must be accura enough so that it can be sworn to. This w mean that a clerk or investigator of intelligen must be employed to devote his entire time the work in the larger plants. The general pri ciple is good for all plants and may be put in operation where the number of employees is t small to warrant the employment of individu investigators by several joining together. T experience to be developed will cover six mont beginning the first of July."

Percy S. Straus, of R. H. Macy & Compan New York, described the establishment fu of that firm, stating that:

"Possibly our method which has been in e istence some years and which is somewhat the basis of the Davenport law might be of i terest. Under this plan, the employees enga doctors and nurses; the contributions are ma by the employees and the firm. Any employ who is sick reports by postal card (which is su plied) that he is sick and the cause of his a sence. He is then visited by a doctor or nur and I think that would serve to check up. If employee chooses to stay away for fishing, et his freedom is in no way affected. That do not come in under a health insurance syste he is not insured against lack of work or ba ball or fishing. But, on the whole, the plan l worked out successfully. One thing acco plished is that the employee knows that the d tor will give him the sort of treatment to whi he is entitled and that the nurse will come a report on the illness. It guarantees the e ployee who is actually sick, from suspicion, a if an employee is sick, it insures his position ing kept open. The only compulsion is tl they shall have medical attendance when nec sary. The cost per employee is comparative small. The service to the employee is distin ly helpful because it largely serves to keep h out of the hands of doctors, of whom the city filled, who are absolutely incompetent."

Mr. Stone: In your company, all the e ployees are required to belong, whether th want to or not?

Mr. Straus: Yes, they are told about it wh they are employed. Of course, they do not ha to work for us.

Mr. Stone: We have the same thing in o railroads. Your remark that they can wo elsewhere is applicable when work is plenty b when it is scarce as it is at present—for examp in Cleveland where we now have 49,000 une ployed, 28,000 being skilled workmen—the e ployee has to get what he can. You say t majority of the employees select the docto How can they pass on the qualifications of doctor in a great plant like Macy & Co.? Is not largely a matter of guesswork?

(Continued on Page 16)

Do the Co-Operatives Offer A Solution?

HIGH COST OF LIVING ALLEGED TO BE LARGELY DUE TO UNSCIENTIFIC DISTRIBUTION DESPITE VARIED EXPEDIENTS DESIGNED TO REDUCE CHARGES

By WILLIAM H. INGERSOLL

WILLIAM H. INGERSOLL

Eighteen years' experience in operating a large mail order business, running a chain of retail stores, doing jobbing and manufacturing on a large scale, and personal investigation here and abroad, fit William H. Ingersoll, writer of the following article, to an unusual degree as an expert on distribution costs. Incidentally, his training as an electrical engineer gives him an angle on the subject from the scientific point of view, while as an officer of sales and advertising organizations he has solved many cost problems from the practical side. Finding customers for 20,000 watches daily is another task that fitted Mr. Ingersoll especially for his work as a commission member studying cooperative sales and producing systems in Great Britain.

WE are all dissatisfied with the cost of things, especially with that part of the cost own as middleman's profits, e part absorbed in the distri tion of merchandise as dis guished from its cost of ysical production.

There is reason aplenty for e deep unrest over the waste. l inefficient system of distrib ing goods from farm and tory to user. And yet there no other important phase of r economic life in which such se and footless reasoning is dulged in or such baseless hope relief held out.

An English laboring man, a rker in a shoe factory, put the oposition effectively to me on recent tour of investigation in urope, when he asked why his mily and the workers in other ctories should have to pay enty shillings per pair for oes on which he worked and hich he knew cost only seven illings to make. It is approxi ately the same on the bulk all we buy in this coun y. The farmer gets hardly third of what we pay for our otatoes. Two-thirds of what e pay for our clothing and rnishings goes for distribution d only one-third for the goods. nd we can't eat or wear the stribution!

There is no doubt that the borer is exploited far worse as consumer when he comes to ex ange the proceeds of his work r the products of the work of thers than he is as a producer receiving the short end of hat he makes.

So much for the indictment! here has been argument both y academicians and practition s and attempted demonstra ons for years, during which e cost of living has gone eadily higher.

MUST REACH THE CAUSE

Now, it sounds unreasonable, at it should cost twice as much sell a thing as to make it, if is a useful thing and the price air. It is unreasonable, but it won't be reme ied by abusing the middlemen or by attempting mprovements which don't reach the *cause* of e waste. The familiar hope is to "eliminate e middleman" either in part or in whole. arious devices have been used to accomplish is. Briefly, we may set them down as:

1) The department store which aims and claims to eliminate the wholesaler or jobber by buying in quantities from the manufacturer;

2) The multiple system of chain stores which have the same hope of economy as the department store;

(3) The mail order house which has the same objective economies as the department store and also goes more extensively into manufacturing its own goods in some lines;

(4) The manufacturer of specialty merchandise such as branded shoes or candy, who sets up his own retail stores and "eliminates" the independent wholesaler and retailer;

(5) The cooperative factory which is owned by the workers in the enterprise, eliminating the monopolistic capitalist owner;

(6) The cooperative store, factory, and plantation in which the consumers own the local retail distributing stores, the wholesale distributing warehouses which supply the retail stores and the factories and sources of raw materials and have as their paid employees the producers in the factory and on the farms. This system "eliminates" all middlemen and the manufacturer and theoretically makes the consumer his own producer and middleman.

Various combinations of these devices are found in actual practice in numerous lines of trade. Some department stores own manufacturing shops where they make for themselves the goods for some of their most important departments. The chain store and mail order concerns often do some of their own manufacturing. Specialty manufacturers frequently eliminate the wholesaler by selling direct to the retailers throughout the country or partially do so by selling in the larger towns, leaving jobbers to cover the country villages. Retail stores sometimes join in subscribing funds to operate their own factories to make some of their more important merchandise requirements.

Cooperative enterprises exist in all stages of development. Other economies are claimed by all of the institutions described above besides that of eliminating one or more links in the chain, but elimination of the middleman and his "unnecessary" profit or tax is quite generally the starting point in the attempt to reduce the cost of things, especially in the reasoning of the non-commercial consumer and the economist.

Only three avenues of hope lie before us in effecting a lower cost in the things we buy, if we except as outside of our present study, the cost of production. These three avenues may be described as:

(a) Eliminating unnecessary *labor* in the customary method of distribution;

(b) Eliminating unreasonable or unearned *profit* customarily exacted in the processes of distribution;

(c) Increasing the *efficiency* of the distributors.

We may apply these tests to these various forms of modified distribution under trial and we may examine their workings and the actual values they deliver, compared to the values contemporaneously delivered by the ordinary methods to see if the supposed economies are realized.

As to the first of our tests we can't fairly judge of the successful elimination of middlemen, held to be superfluous or parasitic, unless we are familiar with the net minimum of work to be done in distribution and the functions and organization necessary to discharge it.

To distribute goods produced in quantities in

a factory or on a farm at one point so that they may be accessible to multitudes of individual consumers scattered over a continent, involves several inevitable steps or stages as will be shown, and all efforts to reduce the number result merely in a change of form without intrinsic gain or in the substitution of less direct and more expensive means.

Let the sketch represent a large, typical area of the United States. A simple and direct statement of the problem is, *what are the steps or processes by which the factory represented in the lower left-hand corner, can most economically distribute its goods to the consumers represented by the smallest dots and scattered all over the territory?*

THE CONDITIONS TO BE MET AND EXISTING TRADE ROUTES

Each of the lettered squares may be considered a large commercial point—called a jobbing center in trade parlance,—the hub of a zone, at which supplies are collected and from which they are disseminated to the tributary territory surrounding it. Such centers are typified by such cities as Boston, Baltimore, Atlanta, Buffalo, Pittsburg, Cleveland, Cincinnati, Toledo, Chicago, St. Louis, Minneapolis, Duluth, Denver, Seattle, San Francisco, Los Angeles, Dallas and also by smaller points like Portland, Me., Trenton, Binghampton, Erie, Akron and Des Moines.

The circles represent all other communities not great enough commercially to be business junction points, trade marts or wholesale centers, but composed of few or many households of consumers. Everything from suburban towns to rural villages and including the bulk of the towns of less than 50,000 population and many larger, are represented by these circles. No hard and fast lines separate jobbing centers from tributary towns. Relatively small points do a jobbing trade in groceries and other necessities, while only large points in wholesale jewelry, so that one town may easily be a jobbing point in one line and not in another. But here in the places represented by these circles we have groups or bunches of consumer population to be served as indicated by the dots around the circles.

But about half the people of the United States do not live in communities at all. They are rural dwellers—people on farms. This is crudely reflected by the dots scattered between the towns.

To serve these rural residents there are over a hundred thousand cross-roads stores, ordinarily called general stores but dealing largely in "convenience supplies" which the country people buy at frequent intervals and in volume not worth waiting to go or send to town for,—tobacco, soda crackers, tea and coffee and sugar, etc., as well as needles, sox and collars.

The "X" marks will serve to remind us of these country stores.

STUDY OF NECESSARY MOTIONS

Now for a study of the minimum number of motions by which the product of the factory can be made readily available to all the people in the area shown by the sketch.

Let us assume that the factory makes shoes of a popular grade and of general utility, both for men and for women.

We will view the problem first from the standpoint of the consumers and then from that of the producer—the factory.

Suppose that a school teacher in one of the small towns up north of the jobbing center "B" wants a pair of shoes. She wants a good looking, well made, durable pair, soft, black and high cut. They must fit her and be comfortable. And she wants the best value in the market for her money.

She does not know shoes or the best leather for her purpose; nor can she tell an oak tanned sole when she sees it. She is uninformed as to what constitutes good sewing and good workmanship. She does not know all the factories there are making shoes nor their location—nor which makes women's shoes or which makes the best or what different styles each makes. She knows nothing as to which is the most efficient, economical manufacturer and marketer of shoes, or which is most reliable.

In short, she is a specialist in one vocation, giving her expert services for the benefit of others and consequently she cannot be informed on shoes, and clothes and jewelry and drugs and hardware and househould furnishings and groceries and all the other branches of trade and industry.

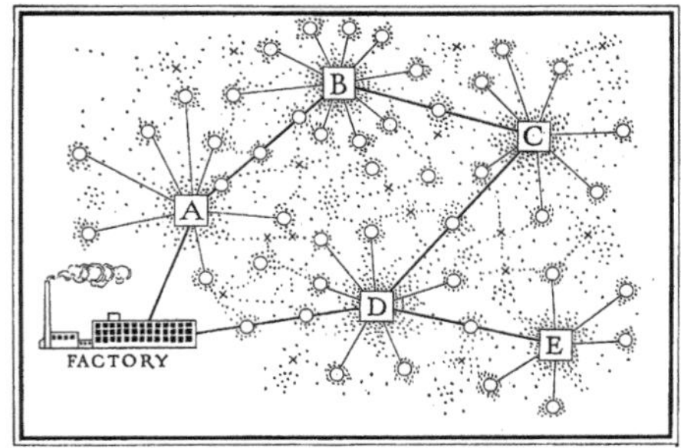

The squares show population zones comprising towns and villages of secondary importance. The circles indicate local communities in the trading zones. The crosses show general, or cross roads stores for rural dwellers, and the dots designate the individual households of consumers comprising the local communities.

# of Their Own Mouths

By T. EVERETT HARRÉ

To some of their less sophisticated and less discerning readers, the course of these journals must have been perturbing, perplexing, difficult of understanding. It surely was not possible that these organs of aloof high-browism could be anti-Ally or pro-German! Both addressed their readers from a high and lofty standard of Americanism, a peerless liberalism, a moral integrity beyond reproach. The mere implication that the sweet souls guiding the editorial policies of these sheets could be tenderly inclined toward the Huns was by themselves repudiated with indignation. What they wanted, they reiterated, and their siren protestations went forth beguilingly, was a new world order, a peace or justice that would endure. Singularly, with a new world order and an enduring peace of justice in view, they zealously championed radical, pacifist, Socialist and revolutionary movements, defended and befriended the murderous Bolshevist regime in Russia, railed against Allied intervention in stricken Russia, defended and befriended the I. W. W. leaders who had engaged in a conspiracy to thwart and obstruct the country in its war against Germany, defended and befriended as well as the "conscientious objectors;" likewise, they opposed a peace of victory by fighting until a military decision was obtained over Germany—the one and only peace which would disarm the German power and make democracy secure—and advocated instead such a peace as would have left the German power unimpaired and German Imperialism intact.

"LIKE, BUT OH HOW DIFFERENT!"

These two eccentrically distinguished journals are the *New Republic* and the *Nation*. The *New Republic* is a comparative parvenu compared to the *Nation*, which still travels on a prestige dating from the time of the Civil War. The editor of the *New Republic* is Mr. Herbert Croly. The now pacifist Mr. Croly published, in 1909, a book, "The Promise of American Life," in which, indicating the undemocratic and demoralizing influences at work in England and France, he glorified military Germany, justified Germany in her wars of aggression, and advocated that war should be carried on to decisive results in military victory. An associate editor of the *New Republic* is Mr. Walter E. Weyl, who published a book, "The End of the War," in which, to use the words of Charles A. Beard (himself the author of a book impugning the Fathers of the country and the Constitution): "Mr. Weyl draws swiftly under review . . . the plans of French, Russian, English and Italian imperialists for spoiling the enemy, Italy's ambitions, the war of new Russia against capitalistic imperialism, the faint hope of German liberalism, the inconclusiveness of a bitter-end peace," and in which he (Weyl) predicted that "the final war for democracy will begin after the war. It will be a wider conflict than that which now rages and the alignment will be by classes and interests rather than by nations. It will be a war which will be waged until separate interests within each nation are completely extinguished." Another associate editor is Mr. Walter Lippmann, formerly but no longer connected with Colonel House's peace commission, author of the assertion "The Congress of Versailles is not the Last Judgment. . . . They cannot damn the German people for all time, desirable as that might be, because German mothers bear German children." The editor of the other strangeling-sheet, the *Nation*, is Oswald Garrison Villard, whose father, Heinrich Hillgard, was born in Speyer, Germany, and who is the author of "Germany Embattled," published in 1915, in which he asserted of German frightfulness in Belgium: "Few of these stories of atrocities can be supported," and in which he maintained that "Men of light and leading are protesting that Germany must not be degraded" and that much in Hun Kultur "must be preserved."

Considering these magazines as ranking among loyal and patriotic journals and their editors as ranking among sterling, 100 per cent American editors, there was that in their editorials and editorial policy which was, to say the least, ambiguous, dubious, confusing, open to question. While all loyal, true-blooded journals sought to fortify and fuse the spirit of the country in a selfless enthusiasm, a confident conviction that right must win, the *New Republic*, for instance, just six weeks after America entered the war in its issue of May 19, 1917, devoted its columns to a most discouraging example of defeatism. Implying the almost absolute hopelessness of Allied Military victory, it declared that the despatch of such an American army to Europe as would break the stalemate which would at best result in case Russia drifted out of the war, "could not be recruited, equipped and trained until the summer of 1919" and that even then it might be impossible to transport it to Europe. The *New Republic*—which has since had the effrontery and unconsciousness to declare in advertisements that "it insisted that the war must go on until Germany was beaten"—presented "an appalling outlook," in the continued waging of war against Germany, and it said: "The result would almost certainly be a revolution in America far more bloody and drastic than the revolution in Russia.* A war conducted until 1920 on the scale required by a military decision might bring peace with victory, but it would also bring victory with suicide."

Doubtless weight was given by some people to what the *New Republic* published, if only because of the implication adroitly given that it represented unofficially the point of view of the Administration and that it had "seen itself taken into the counsels of statesmen at home and abroad." In an advertisement published November 25, 1918, the *New Republic* made an appeal that people subscribe "in order that you may clearly understand the President's policies." New readers accepting this sheet, upon this pointed suggestion, as an articulate echo of the point of view entertained in Washington were doubtless confused, doubtless troubled, by its persistent advocacy of peace through negotiation with Germany, by the policy adopted, when German military defeat became certain, of assailing the Allied leaders and charging them with a program of revenge and plunder. Having preached defeatism, the hopelessness of Allied military victory, immediately after our entry into the war, the *New Republic* during the period that Germany was still undefeated, chronically advocated entering into peace negotiations with Germany and bringing the war to a close by "a peace by diplomacy." This sheet was a perfervent champion of the proposed Stockholm conference. Upon the routing of the Hun armies by Foch, upon Germany's catastrophic defeat and the signing of the armistice, the *New Republic* then charted a slightly new course in which it specialized in a policy of impugning the motives of the Allies, the purposes of the Allied leaders, and by which it sought to sow seeds of suspicion and distrust of the nations associated with us in the war. It

* That the imposition by the Allies of strong terms for peace upon Germany would make Germany go Bolshevik and cause revolutions in the Allied countries, has been the familiar argument of German propagandists and of such American pacifists as Mr. O. G. Villard.

went so far in its impassioned exploitation of Allied dishonesty and intended brigandage as to carry its campaign against the "wicked Allied statesmen" into large newspaper advertisements. "If the diplomats should begin once more their ancient game of chess with peoples as pawns, the game of military supremacies, selfish alliances, balances of power, strategic frontiers and economic barriers—it would be the supreme tragedy of history." So ran one of its costly newspaper "ads."

It may, of course, be mere coincidence that so long as Germany had all to gain and nothing to lose by the creation of disagreement between America and the Allies, by the creation of hostile American opinion against the Allied leaders with whom Mr. Wilson had to deal, by the destruction of amity, confidence and concord, that so long as Germany gambled for advantage upon this very possibility of differences and dissension, the *New Republic* strained its caponized powers in presenting President Wilson as opposed to the Allied statesmen and their purposes, in interpreting the war on part of the Allies as having been lacking in all ideals until ideals had been interjected by the foreign hand of Mr. Wilson, in picturing Mr. Wilson and Clemenceau especially as being at bitter odds, in representing Mr. Wilson as standing heroically alone for the principles of humanity and justice against a gang of unscrupulous cut-throat statesmen fully as bad as the Prussian Junkers. It may be mere coincidence that the *New Republic* pursued a policy which, so far as German purposes and German advantage were concerned, was strikingly in accord with the most discreet and subtle form of pro-German policy—a policy which, had it succeeded, would have estranged America from the Allies, have torn the Allies themselves with dissension, rivalries, animosities and antagonisms, and would consequently have resulted in "a liberal peace" what Mr. Villard called a "magnanimous" peace—ergo, a pro-German peace.

"THEIR OWN DREAMS AT LENGTH DECEIVE 'EM, AND OFT REPEATING, THEY BELIEVE 'EM."

So long as it was not publicly repudiated by the "leading statesmen at home and abroad" by whom it claimed to be taken as counsel; so long as Mr. Herbert Croly had the free entree to the Washington offices of Mr. Felix Frankfurter, known to be high in the confidence of the Administration; so long as Mr. Walter Lippmann was in a position to "assist" Colonel House's commission by his help and advice; so long as Mr. Walter Weyl had the full run of the Hotel de Crillon in Paris; so long as the Steffenses and Bullitts seemed to be given confidence as unbiased reporters on the Russian situation, if not world affairs, the *New Republic* may perchance have flattered itself that it was in the singular position of enabling its readers to "clearly understand the President's policies." But was it? And what, in essence, was the sort of peace which the pretentious *New Republic* championed? Was the peace it advocated, the peace after its heart, an Allied peace—or the peace Germany wanted? Was it a peace which indemnified so far as possible and made secure from future aggression the wronged and invaded nations—or a peace "without annexations and indemnities," which "let Germany down easy," which would treat her as though she had not been the aggressor, but one of the wronged parties in the war? If the *New Republic* was heart and soul on the side of America and the Allies, fighting a war of defense against German aggression, why did it so enthusiastically espouse the German peace proposals and endeavor to further the German peace manoeuvers aiming at an indecisive ending of the war at a time when the Allied governments were united in rejecting any consideration? Why did this sheet support the proposed notorious pro-German, German-engineered Stockholm conference? Why did it endorse the pacifist stand of the British Labor Party? Why, once Allied victory and Hun collapse were certain, did it intensify a policy of defamation of the Allied statesmen?

It is conceivable that many sensitive humane people, shocked and sickened by the prolonged killing, believing possibly that Germany could not be broken, longed for peace, even if by compromise with the foe, in order to prevent the further shedding of blood. Sincerely in sympathy with the cause of the Allies, opposed to Germany and Germany's plan of world subjugation, these people could not but have rejoiced when at last the Hun debacle occurred and the victorious Allies pursued the fleeing hordes through France and Belgium. Once the Hindenburg stronghold was smashed and German collapse was sure, these people would not at that late hour have listened to any suggestion for compromise. And once Germany had virtually surrendered, once the Allied council had agreed to the terms of peace, these people could only have exulted in a victory that had been beyond their expectation, a triumph almost past belief. Anyone not at heart pro-German, not at heart disloyal, not at heart antagonistic to the Allies, could not but have found full satisfaction in the glorious consummation. Presumably it is by their joy or their rage over German defeat, by their support or opposition to the terms of the Allied treaty, that it can be ascertained on which side people's sympathies lie. In their reaction to the Versailles treaty—and this applies especially to pacifists, the faint-hearted, the doubtful—is the final test.

What was perhaps not clear to some people in an editorial policy certainly not in conformity with the policy of the loyal American press, may be made clear now by the reaction to the peace treaty experienced by the *New Republic*. Ardently supporting President Wilson previously, indeed, pretending to be a sort of unofficial interpreter of his views, the *New Republic*, upon the publication of the terms drawn up at Versailles, turned immediately and furiously upon the President as having betrayed, in agreeing to the treaty, the "liberal opinion of the world." Cautious and camouflageous in its course before, ambiguous, studiedly subtle, cold-bloodedly academic, carefully restrained, the *New Republic*, upon the publication of the digest of the proposed treaty, as if goaded to a rage beyond restraint, roiled with a frothing despair and chagrin, like a frantic termagent, abandoned itself to a scolding fury in which all caution, all restraint, all diplomacy were thrown to the winds. It may be that at last, perhaps, this organ spills the beans; that inadvertently perhaps, it discloses its hand; in not so much a slip of the pen as a slip of the spleen, as if suffering from a species of mental rabies, it turns upon the Versailles treaty as if to rend it to shreds. Repudiated in its previous advertised pretensions, its self-assumed, self-advertised role, the *New Republic* finds itself in the embarrassing position of being provenly preposterous and quite ridiculous. Of course, to the most obtuse intelligence it is uncomfortable to be made funny. Campaigning for subscribers and for public confidence on the implied claim that it was able to make clear Mr. Wilson's policies, this sheet of *jejune* intellectualism now finds itself utterly discredited.

And in the light of its almost involuntary reaction to the peace terms to be imposed upon Germany, the *New Republic* itself perhaps answers the question as to whether it was at all pro-German, as to whether the peace it proposed and fostered was a peace of advantage and security to the Allies or a peace of advantage and recuperation to Germany. Bearing somewhat upon its vicious turning against Mr. Wilson, upon its virago outburst against the treaty, may be the fact that its associate editor, Mr. Walter Lippmann found it congenial to return from Paris, that the scheme for recognizing the Bolsheviki as advocated by the pro-Bolshevist Stef-

ilroad Brotherhood An Object Lesson in Labor Progress

ORGANIZATION OPPOSED TO RADICAL MOVEMENTS THAT BRING MISERY AND RUIN

(Speech Delivered at Convention of Brotherhood of Railroad Trainmen, Columbus, Ohio, May 16, 1919)

By W. G. LEE

PRESIDENT OF THE BROTHERHOOD OF RAILROAD TRAINMEN

WHATEVER promises for the welfare of the Brotherhood of Railroad Trainmen promises to be equally beneficial to society at large. Sometimes, in con ng the effects of economic changes as they from increased wages and changed con of employment, we might be led to believe, accepted seriously all of the statements re made, that railroad employees are not a f the public. Unfortunately there has been sition in the past two years to array pub timent against the railroad organizations the pretense that whatever was secured in ay of wage and service betterments would to be made good by the consumer. The ent is absolutely true and there is no dis on on the part of these organizations to way from it, but the statement also in all ss should have accompanied the effort to dice the public mind against railway em s to the effect that all economic betterments hieved only by the ultimate consumer pay e entire cost of the achievement. It is not prejudice the public mind against the rail organizations by making it believe, even h it should know better, that railroad oper only comes out of the public pocket book. have said, every advance in wages in every occupation must receive its proper share of ocket books of the railroad employees, and make this contribution without any prejudi eferences about having to meet the extra f whatever advantages come to their associ orkers. They had to meet the cost out of wn pockets and did not attempt to retard rogress of their fellows by any prejudiced ption that they alone will have to meet the ased costs attached thereto.

e railway organization employees, of whom Brotherhood of Railroad Trainmen repre the largest single class, are a most im nt part of the public. Their entire sym es are for every public betterment, regard f the effect it may have upon them as it es to their cost of living. They have long ed that any betterment that comes to any cular portion of society is only gained at xpense of all society, but it is an evolution process which with each successive better affects its particular class of society and e end benefits all society.

ere is nothing in our economic life that is understood as the labor organization. The er part of this misunderstanding arises from atural prejudice that attaches to anything presumes to arrange terms of employment. employer has always made himself believe it was his absolute right to hire whom he ed and for what wage he pleased. In tak his position he did so without any regard e rights and welfare of society and these organizations have taken it upon them s to protect their own interests and in so have protected the interests of the general unity.

e Brothochood has tried to be fair to the c, the employer and to itself. It has ac d its responsibilities and consistently stood that it agreed to do, although there have many times when taking that position ght down upon it the most bitter censure those who have yet to learn that a labor or ation to be successful must be a business or ation that holds its word as sacred as its

W. G. LEE

Our organization is a business organization. Its purpose is to protect the general welfare of its members and in so doing does not confine itself to its own men employed in any given occupation, but covers both wage rates and service rules for every man employed in that service. This feature of the Brotherhood is responsible for whatever has come to the service in the way of improved conditions and wages. It has been accomplished in a progressive and orderly manner, and we know that what has been done is going to stand the test of time.

I do not mean to convey the impression that service conditions are ideal, that wages have reached the point beyond which they cannot go, for that is far from the fact. The progress of the world has been due to the honest discontent of labor, a discontent that expresses itself in terms of better living, which can only be secured by progressive wages and service conditions that always will assure a fair standard of living with all of the opportunities we understand attach to that standard.

We are progressive American citizens in every sense. We have no more use for the purely contented man than we have for the unreasonably discontented man. We believe in good government, we believe in law and order and we know the only way to perpetuate government, good citizenship, and enforcement of law and order is by guaranteeing our population a fair day's pay for a fair day's work and decent treatment with every service condition.

The Brotherhood also conducts an insurance department, which we think is one of the best in the world, more liberal in the payment of its obligations and more generally helpful than associations of the kind usually are. We paid approximately $35,000,000 in death and disability claims to 45,000 claimants in the past 35 years. This of itself is a wonderful record of what insurance properly managed and carefully directed can accomplish in a very few years, and it is insurance that would never have been paid had it not been provided by this organization. The hazard of the service has barred our men from participating in other insurance by its prohibitive cost.

I stated that we were a business organization. In this connection I desire to clinch my statement by saying that in the past year this organization has been called on to make extra payments approximating $3,000,000 due to demands made by war and pestilence, and I am proud to say that the Brotherhood of Railroad Trainmen has met every claim promptly. It has paid every demand made upon its insurance department without having to levy a special assessment or cause one minute's delay. I think the statement of what the protective feature of the Brotherhood and the Brotherhood insurance have done will be amply sufficient to verify the assertion made that the Brotherhood of Railroad Trainmen is a business organization.

In a legislative way the Brotherhood has very many honorable results to show for its efforts. There are times when organization effort is unable to secure general results and in such event legislation is the only way left us to accomplish our purposes. The Brotherhood is largely responsible for the enactment of Federal and State legislation. Among its achievements can be counted the Safety Appliance, the Federal Employers Liability, Standardization of Equipment, the Federal Arbitration, Federal Hours of Service, and the Eight Hour Day Law, and in addition to this record, it has made another of State legislation achievement, in which can be taken considerable satisfaction and pardonable pride. This has been only a part of the work of the Brotherhood of Railroad Trainmen, and not alone in the interests of railway employees, but in the interest of the general public, for we take the position that whatever affects the organization, in its turn affects society generally.

There are labor organizations that are such in every sense, and there are other organizations that seek refuge under the banner of labor unionism that properly have no right to claim affiliation with labor organization, and in proof of this is their readiness to raise the red flag of anarchy and declare for the revolution at every opportunity. I want to assure you that the Brotherhood of Railroad Trainmen has neither part nor purpose in any scheme that proposes to destroy this government or take from any citizen either privilege or property that properly belongs to him; we have no sympathy with any plan that finds its basic purposes in the destruction of government or the organized forms of law and order; we do not subscribe to any propaganda that proposes a policy of destruction to find in a common basis of misery its expected hopes for reconstruction; we have not lost faith in our government nor in our fellow men; we know that we have in our keeping the continuity of our government, the perpetuation of our own common welfare, and we believe that it is not necessary to transplant anarchy, or an autocratic government by a few self-selected rulers to preside over the destinies of a nation of free born American people. The very assumption of power or autocracy established by those who have superseded former governments give truth to the assertion that in whatever changes of this kind have been made one autocracy has succeeded in which the last condition of the people was worse than the first and the very fact that a few assume to control the welfare and the destinies of the many, sets at naught all of their pretenses to a common rule, by the common people, for the common people.

We have no part or sympathy in any of the plans that pretend the hope of the world is only to be found in its destruction. This organization is 100% American. Its representatives come from the two great democratic governments, the United States and Canada. We believe in the orderly processes of law that have brought our respective governments to the first place among the nations of the world. We place our dependence on a continuity of these same processes of order to bring the level of the lowest to the level of the highest. We do not subscribe to any theory that proposes to throw everybody into one common slough of despond for the purpose of experimenting in the hope that out of this general mental and physical misery an average may come that will bring about a general better condition of affairs for a majority of the people. We stand for no such doctrine of destruction or ruin; we believe in the government of our representative nations, and stand as 100% Americans ready to defend our principles and our faith.

In proof of our Americanism and our readiness to defend it are the 16,000 men of this organization who took their places willingly in the ranks of our armies, who were ready to assume all the responsibilities for protecting the government, who were ready to make the supreme sacrifice if necessary in defense of our government, our homes and our firesides, and almost 200 of them are resting today in the sacred soil of France in proof of their loyalty and devotion to the land they called their own.

We propose in the future to go ahead with our work as an organization along the same lines that we followed in the past. We believe in our government, we believe in the expressions of our President and all the other authorities of the government who have declared emphatically their belief that the American workman is entitled to a wage that will insure a reasonably decent standard of living. We propose to direct our energies toward getting that decent standard of living and we propose to do it along orderly and legal lines, wholly within our rights as American citizens and in keeping with our belief that the workman is worthy of his hire.

To sum up the status of the Brotherhood of Railroad Trainmen is to say that it is one of the conservative representative organizations that stands foremost in the ranks of labor. Through its work, the financial, moral and intellectual standing of the men and their families have been greatly improved, and we propose to continue our work in this general direction. It never will be finished. The honest discontent of free American labor will always find expression by its demand for participation in the direction of the business by which it is employed, and a fair share of the revenues it creates for its employer.

Frank Morrison's Award in the Printing Case

ONE of the most important wage rulings of the year has just been made by Frank Morrison, arbitrator of the questions at issue between the Publishers' Association of the City of New York and Typographical Union No. 6, familiarly known as "Big Six." Under the findings and award by Mr. Morrison, the printers gain practically every point, the most tangible being an increase in wages of $9 a week. The award is made retroactive as of April 1 last and the agreement will expire March 31 next.

The printers also asked for double time for overtime, instead of time and one-half, but Mr. Morrison ruled against them, saying:

The evidence submitted indicated a desire of both parties to eliminate overtime wherever possible. Under ordinary circumstances your Arbitrator believes that overtime should be penalized to the point of prohibition, except in cases of emergency, but because of the expressed opposition of both parties to this practice and the contentions of the Publishers that much of the overtime was due to unavoidable conditions, your Arbitrator decides against the demand of the Printers for an increase from price and one-half to double time.

Radical changes in the working hours were asked by the publishers, most noteworthy of which was the extension of the work day from seven and one-half to eight hours. The printers opposed the abandonment of the present rule which had been in force for many years. On this subject Mr. Morrison ruled:

Your Arbitrator is of the opinion that to lengthen the work day in any calling, and especially in this intensified industry, would be in opposition to the world-wide agitation for a betterment of the workers' conditions, and for physical reasons alone it cannot be justified.

Even were your Arbitrator to ignore these facts, it is neither wise nor practical to take from workers long-established conditions.

It is therefore ordered that no change be made in the hours constituting a work day, or work night.

The publishers also asked that the time in which work should be performed be changed to have day work from 6 A. M. to 6 P. M., instead of 8 A. M. to 6 P. M., and night work from 6 P. M. to 6 A. M., instead of 6 P. M. to 3 A. M., with the "third shift" from 3 A. M. to 10 A. M. eliminated. This point they lost too, Mr. Morrison holding that the custom of 28 years should not be upset, and saying "it would be a most regrettable decision because of the resultant upheaval of the workers' social life." The publishers, however, retain their old right to call the printers to the office for any unforeseen reason or emergency before the hours specified in the limitations.

Naturally a large part of Mr. Morrison's findings is devoted to the wage increase question. Of this he says in part:

FRANK MORRISON.

In supporting their demands for the wage increase, the Printers submit that they have never received a wage commensurate with the intelligence and skill required of them; that since 1914 the cost of living has increased more than 79 per cent, and during that period their wages have been advanced about 15 per cent; that this increase of 15 per cent is much less than the increase granted other newspaper workers; that it is small in comparison with the increases received by the skilled and unskilled workers employed in other callings throughout the country; that the newspapers of New York were never so prosperous; that advertising has increased, notwithstanding the increase in rates, and that some of the newspapers have been compelled to refuse many columns of advertising each day; that until recently the newspaper printer was the highest paid in the printing trades and that the long period of apprenticeship and the mental and physical strain under which the work of the newspaper printer must be performed are all factors which justify this wage increase.

Tables showing the increases in other trades ranging from 11 per cent for electrotypers to 105 per cent for Delaware River shipyard blacksmiths and the advances in retail prices for 1915, 1916, 1917 and 1918, are made part of Mr. Morrison's findings.

Concerning the publishers' side of the wage question, it is said:

The Publishers submit that they have raised wages $4.50 a week since January 1, 1918; that the present wage "is a fair wage that compares most favorably with wages paid printers' crafts in newspapers all over the country"; that there is "a probability of a steadily decreased cost of living in view of the ending of the war"; that the "Publishers are not now opposing the demand of the Typographical Union on any ground except that it is exorbitant and unwarranted by either business conditions confronting the Publishers or by necessities confronting the Typographical Union Members."

In the Publishers' brief they suggest that in the event that the Arbitrator "feels that the members of the Typographical Union are entitled to any relief at all in the matter of wages," that the Arbitrator change certain working conditions which "might in a measure mitigate the charge against the Publishers." (*Changes in work days as mentioned above.*)

In his final ruling on this wage question, Mr. Morrison says:

It would be fruitless at this time for your Arbitrator to enter into a discussion on the causes of increased living costs now confronting the worker. The question offers no escape by theorizing.

What interests us is the fact that the high living cost exists, and if the processes of arbitration are to be used with purpose and effect rather than as a vehicle to allay a remedial unrest, we must attempt to re-establish the living standards of the plaintiffs in this case.

* * * To ask the Printers to continue to accept a standard of living lower than the Publishers themselves agreed to when they accepted pre-war rates is no more equitable than to ask the Publishers to reduce their living standards to meet the increased production cost. While this proposition is unusual it can be justified on moral ground and elementary justice, if the theory of mutuality between Capital and Labor is not merely a shibboleth.

The point is made to emphasize your Arbitrator's belief that there is an unescapable obligation on the New York newspaper industry to maintain the living standards of Printers employed therein. * *

Your Arbitrator, therefore, sustains the Printers on this question and orders an advance in wages to the full amount of $9 a week.

Mr. Morrison also made some minor changes in the several sections of the working agreement to make his ruling and the new wage scale effective equitably for all the workers. He also pointed out that even with the increase, New York's scale still was behind Portland, Ore., and Seattle, Wash., where living costs had not advanced as sharply as in New York.

One important point on which Mr. Morrison sustained the printers concerned the hiring of "extras". The workers made the charge that foremen generally were not distributing extra work in an equitable manner. The publishers claimed that the present rule debarred the office from the services of "very competent extras." They also asserted that as the foremen are union members they were subject to its discipline. Mr. Morrison held the extras are an essential class in the newspaper trade and that their rights should be as carefully safeguarded as the rights of regular members. He therefore sustained the old rule under which they were hired, a rule that limited work to three consecutive days or nights in any one week under certain conditions.

Suppressed Facts About Bolshevism

WHAT ALBERT RHYS WILLIAMS FAILED TO TELL ABOUT THE SOVIETS AND RED RULE SUMMARIZED BY HENRY L. SLOBODIN

ERIFIED facts about Russia's red terror existing under the régime of Lenine and Trotzky have been condensed in most readable form by Henry L. Slobodin in mphlet just published, entitled: "Questions he Bolsheviks and the Soviets which Albert s Williams failed to answer and The An-s." Every angle of the misrule in Mus- is taken up and analyzed. Authorities for y statement are given. Words are not ed, and the composite result is an arraign-it of the Bolsheviki that is so sweeping, so n and so convincing that the veriest tyro in rnational affairs is impressed with the truth. n a separate chapter under the heading, "A shevik Propagandist," Mr. Slobodin analy- Albert Rhys Williams, the ex-clergyman, in uncertain terms. He says:

r. Albert Rhys Williams visited Bolshevik Rus-armed with a sympathetic heart, enormous gul-ity and absolute innocence of any knowledge of shevism, Socialism, Russian language, history, litions or anything at all that would help him ppraise critically and to form a correct judg-t of people and events in Russia. The Russian ronment reacted in Mr. Williams' emotions in culiar way. Evidently Mr. Williams landed right he midst of indescribable commotion and noise—ple were running to and fro, gesticulating, yelling, Williams did not know what; everywhere speak-were exhorting crowds, Mr. Williams did not w what about; everywhere people were shooting er people, Mr. Williams did not know what for. he well known mass psychology, or as some call nob spirit, seized upon Mr. Williams' very recep-emotions. He cast aside the old Williams. A w Williams was born. He ran with others to and ; he gesticulated and yelled as others did, only body understood him. * * *

He plunged head foremost into this whirlpool of ning, scorching words and blazing phrases. Words d phrases became the only reality. Things, facts, ditions became unreal, non-existent. Thunder- pronunciamentos proclaimed the Industrial Re-blic. Promptly to Mr. Williams' emotions the In-strial Republic became a fact. Russia is an In-strial Republic, he declared. He was deaf, dumb d blind to the fact that not one of the factors essary for the establishment of an Industrial Re-blic was under the control of the Bolsheviks, or the program of the Bolsheviks. There was no vanced industrial development. There was no in-strial autonomy, nor was it on the Bolshevik pro-am. On the contrary, Lenine proposed, not only a itical, but an industrial dictatorship as well; "an conditional and most severe subordination of the l of thousands to the will of one." Finally, the rkers had no experience, traditions or intelligence furnish a basis for an Industrial Republic. What s going on in Bolshevik Russia was a chaos that ggared description and defied definition. But the rase was there. That was enough for Mr. Wil-ms. He reported in America that he saw the In-strial Republic in Russia.

Likewise with the Soviets. How should Mr. Wil-ms know that the Soviets were organized by So-lists while the Bolsheviks opposed their organi-ion? How should he know that the Bolsheviks re actually destroying the Soviets as representa-e bodies? It is true all this might have hap-ned right before Mr. Williams' eyes. But evident- Mr. Williams' senses and mind were not function- normally at the time. He bid farewell to sense d reason and gave free rein to emotion.

Mr. Williams saw a proclamation decreeing rotherhood of the Toilers of the World." At least, was told that such was its import. At once, he w it as a fact. There it was—the Brotherhood a blaze of glory. And he tells the story in nerica.

Mr. Williams endowed the world with the reaction his emotions in Russia in a pamphlet entitled he Bolsheviks and the Soviets." If Mr. Williams ed sincerely although ignorantly in Russia, in heat of a revolutionary environment, it is quite vious that his motive has undergone a tremen-us change since his return to America. In Rus-, Mr. Williams was a neophyte, then a zealot. America he became a propagandist. And Mr. lliams' propaganda takes as little account of facts d reality as the Bolshevik faith does. Everything mes out of Mr. Williams' mind distorted by his new psychology. Nothing that he says of Russia is so. But do not jump to a hasty conclusion that Mr. Williams lies. He is only telling a Bolshevik truth. Fact, reality, reason must give way before this higher truth. Hegel asserted that only that was real which was reasonable. The Bolsheviks assert that only that is true which is unreasonable. It is this unreason that stares at you from every statement of Mr. Williams.

So he discourses grandiloquently of the Bolsheviks and the Soviets as if they belonged to each other, entirely ignoring the fact that the very first thing the Bolshevik government did when it came into power was to disperse the All-Russian Soviet of Workmen and Soldiers' Delegates and also the All-Russian Soviet of Peasants' Delegates. The Bolsheviks were astute enough to retain the name for business and propaganda purposes.

And Mr. Williams loyally adheres to the Bolshevik methods in his propaganda in America.

Mr. Williams tells us that the delegates to the Soviets "are elected in the shops and unions," and that "at present 95 per cent in Russia can vote." Since over 80 per cent of the Russians are peasants, how they can vote in shops and unions Mr. Williams fails to disclose. Thirty-six million votes were cast for delegates to the Constituent Assembly. Since then, the Bolsheviks refused to permit a general election. Nor was any local election permitted except in Bolshevik shops and among the red guards. Why does Mr. Williams say that "95 per cent in Russia can vote" when not even one per cent were allowed to vote, except the Bolsheviks? The answer is, Mr. Williams is totally irresponsible for any statements he makes before any forum of reason or truth. He is a propagandist possessed with a fixed idea. Mr. Williams is dangerous to the over-emotional and weakminded. Unfortunately of these, there are many among us. They should be protected from the insidious unreason and untruths of Mr. Williams.

Mr. Slobodin quotes from M. C. Eroshkin, chairman of the Perm Socialist Revolutionary party and a Kerensky official; from *Izvestia*, the official Bolshevik organ; Maxim Gorky; Lenine's own letters; Gen. K. M. Oberouchev who organized the first Soviets in the Ukraine; many Russian newspapers, both Bolshevik and anti-Bolshevik, and numerous Russian writers of all shades of opinion. In his first chapter, "The Present Government in Russia," he describes the form as "a militaristic terrorism organized by the Bolsheviks, a Socialist sect, whose hatred of all other Socialists is their chief characteristic."

The real control, Mr. Slobodin points out, rests in Commissars appointed by the Executive Committee over which only Lenine and Trotzky have control. "The Bolshevik profession of 'proletarian dictatorship' is merely a dogma," he says, "for no proletarian holds power. In fact, Lenine says that a dictatorship of the proletariat does not mean a working class government, but just the opposite. Lenine's methods are simplicity itself: first, he declares every one but the Bolsheviks 'bourgeois' and then he deprives them of all rights, after which they may be murdered, pillaged or raped *ad libitum*."

In Chapter II., comparing the Bolshevik Revolution with other upsets of government, Mr. Slobodin says:

The French overthrew an autocratic government. The Bolsheviks overthrew the greatest democracy in the world—a Constituent Assembly elected by 36,000,000 votes. The French faced a world in arms in defence of their fatherland. The Bolsheviks betrayed their country to the enemies. The Americans fought for independence. The Bolsheviks sought to make Russia a vassal or colony of Germany. The Americans established a most advanced democracy. The Bolsheviks established the most barbarous tyranny.

Also proved in this chapter is the conspiracy of the Bolsheviks and minions of the ex-Czar to kill the Russian democracy, Mr. Slobodin naming no fewer than seven Bolshevik leaders who formerly were spies or agents of the old Russian autocracy. He also shows how the so-called nationalization of factories resulted in greatly curtailed production, ruin in many cases, and Lenine's plan for compulsory labor in an effort to hold power.

Chapter III. tells how "Russia Repudiates Bolshevism," Mr. Slobodin analyzing the early socialist definitions of proletariat rule and the facts as existing in Russia. He shows that with the collapse of Russian industry, workmen in the cities starved to death, went into the villages hunting food or joined the red guard. Hundreds of peasants refused to cultivate the land, burying and destroying food rather than feed the Bolsheviks, "The so-called proletarian dictatorship in fact deproletariarized Russia," he adds.

Many prominent socialists in other lands, he says, are anti-Bolshevik and he quotes the recent Berne Conference as condemning the Bolshevik movement, by a vote of four to one, as "anti-democratic, anti-Socialist and counter revolutionary," with the Bolsheviks "branded as traitors to everything they once professed." Coming to America, Mr. Slobodin answers the question: "Who are the Bolsheviks in America?"

With few exceptions they were noted for their pro-Germanism or pacifism during the war. Victor Berger of Milwaukee is a type. He gloried in the German devastation of Serbia. He advocated war with Mexico, Japan, anyone to help Germany. Now he is a pro-Bolshevik.

Many of the quondam pacifists are now in ecstasies over Bolshevik bloodletting. They are living in a world of romance. Bolshevik pillage and murder is the manifestation of a great elemental force. Bolshevik bloody hands are baby pink. Nothing is real. They think the Soviet is a new form of advanced democracy. And they think Russia is governed by Soviets. Both propositions are false. The Soviets were originally central labor bodies. Now Russia is governed not by Soviets, but by Commissars. The Soviets serve as a mask.

Ghastly details are given in Chapter IV., "Bolshevik Black Terror," all of them quotations from Bolshevik organs, Lenine's decrees or orders of the Commissars. Gen. Oberouchev's observations also are freely used in this chapter, the whole forming a terrible word picture of wholesale slaughter and terrorism unequalled in the world's history.

There is a brighter side to the Russian situation in Chapter V., "The Kerensky Government," for here Mr. Slobodin tells what the real program for democratic Russia includes, reforms worthy of the most enlightened of countries. This chapter also holds out the hope that the Kerensky program eventually may prove effective, for it quotes workingmen's appeals against the Bolsheviks and the opinions of leading Russian reformers. Those appeals and opinions show that the great mass of the Russian people are fully alive to the dangers that beset the nation and the disaster bound to follow continuance of the Bolshevik rule.

Workmen, Socialists, peasants and intelligentsia all are quoted by Mr. Slobodin and their manifestos promise concerted action against the Bolshevik dictators.

Before closing his brochure, Mr. Slobodin reprints the statement to the Foreign Office of R. H. Bruce-Lockhart, British High Commissioner, that refutes absolutely Raymond Robins' statement to the Overman committee that the Commissioner concurred with him that the Bolshevik government really represented the mass of Russians. Mr. Bruce-Lockhart's report is so utterly at variance with Robins' excuses for the Bolshevik rule that were it not so tragic a subject the contrast would be laughable.

THE NATIONAL
Civic Federation Review

Office: Thirty-third Floor, Metropolitan Tower
1 Madison Avenue New York City

RALPH M. EASLEY, Editor

Published Twice a Month Two Dollars a Year

The Editor alone is Responsible for any unsigned article or unquoted statement published in THE NATIONAL CIVIC FEDERATION REVIEW.

EUROPEAN INDUSTRIAL INQUIRY COMMISSION TO REPORT

By the time this issue of the REVIEW reaches its readers, the commission sent by THE NATIONAL CIVIC FEDERATION to England and France to study the industrial situation, will have sailed for home. The purpose of that inquiry was to learn what of value the experience, under the various bureaus and commission plans for dealing with socalled labor and capital problems in those countries, had to offer to the wage earners and employers of the United States. Especially was the commission charged to study the operation of the Whitley system, the shop steward, shop committee and democratic control of industry programs; the operation of bonus and profit sharing schemes, the effect of compulsory sickness and unemployment insurance legislation as well as other matters relating to the general betterment of the conditions of workers.

While this commission has been working abroad, another has been studying the operation of our various Federal war emergency plans dealing with industrial matters.

It is intended to have a joint meeting of these two commissions late in June—the time and place to be announced later. Employers and representative wage earners, other than members of the commissions, will be invited to attend and there will be a general discussion of the situation here with a view to proposing an industrial charter for the guidance of American industries.

DISINTEGRATION OF ORGANIZED DISLOYALTY. Every time our Government has undertaken to deal vigorously with the I. W. W., Bolshevists, revolutionary socialists or any of the other "impossible" classes of people, loud cries have gone up from all the "intellectual" friends of those forces of disorder that the Government was persecuting these "misunderstood" people; that these governmental attacks would only result in making these lawless forces more lawless, more numerous, and therefore more powerful; and that a much more effective policy than prosecuting them would be to arouse society to the needs for industrial reform and to remove the causes that produce these distempers.

Especially vociferous was this clamor when the Department of Justice swooped down upon upwards of one hundred revolutionary and disloyal I. W. W.'ites who, through sabotage, terrorism and murder, were deliberately interfering with the draft and the Government's preparations for war. This particular move of the Government called forth an appeal, signed by some preachers, college professors, and others, in an attempt to raise a fund of $50,000. to defend these indicted I. W. W. leaders. Fortunately, the Federal Government had the courage and ability to "finish the job", which it did by convicting the I. W. W. leaders and locking them up in penitentiaries.

The verdict was no sooner rendered than there was started a series of so-called "mass meetings" in all industrial centres, at which protests were issued and threats made that on the day that the prison doors closed on "Big Bill" Haywood a general strike would occur which would paralyze industry. Sinister suggestions were also made of "popular removals" of important men. At these alarming manifestations of "popular sentiment" against the Government's methods of dealing with "industrial slaves," certain editors, preachers and college professors gleefully pointed out that this was only what they had predicted: "You see what is happening; it is just what we told you would be the result," and so forth and so forth, *ad nauseum.*

Well, "Big Bill" went to jail. The sun rose as usual the following morning and not a man or woman or kiddie struck.

And now, to cap the climax, this I. W. W. terror, which was to grow into an overpowering force, has recently held its annual convention in Chicago, where there were present just sixty-one delegates, representing the total membership of the I. W. W., which their official reports showed had dropped from 275,000 to fewer than 25,000 members. So much for the moral effect of locking up "Big Bill" Haywood and his scoundrelly co-adjutors.

But this is not all. At this I. W. W. convention of sixty-one delegates, so effectively had that organization learned the lesson taught by Uncle Sam, that they kicked out "Big Bill" Haywood as president and, further, provided unanimously for amending the constitution and by-laws to prevent anyone under indictment or out on bond from holding an elective office.

The Christian Science Monitor, in reporting the convention, makes the significant comment: "The I. W. W. make no secret of what has happened to their organization in the last year and a half. The government had it helpless." This is the answer to the high-brow writers, professors and preachers who upbraided the Government for enforcing the law instead of attempting to produce the millennium, when there would be no cause for unrest.

So much for the passing of the I. W. W. bugaboo. Coincident with its passing is the passing of another bugaboo—the Socialist Party of the United States. As an organized force, it has been going down for the last four years. All its loyal members deserted it when we entered the war. From a boasted membership at one time of 900,000, it has for the last two years had less than 75,000, and nearly half that membership—Russian, Lithuanians, Ukrainians and Letts—to the number of 30,000, were expelled from the party at the meeting of the executive committee in Chicago during the past week. The reason for the expulsion of these foreign groups was that they had organized a Left Wing, or Bolshevist division, of the Socialist Party and would soon have overthrown the organization. That the party is on its last legs is plainly shown by Morris Hillquit in a three-column address to the Socialist Party published in the *Call* of May 21, in which he describes "The Socialist Task and Outlook." In this he clearly recognizes the growing strength of the Left Wing. His closing sentence, which is here quoted, shows the hopelessness of the situation:

> But the performance is too sad to be amusing. It seems perfectly clear that, so long as this movement persists in the party, the latter's activity will be wholly taken up by mutual quarrels and recriminations. Neither "wing" will have any time for the propaganda of Socialism. There is, as far as I can see, but one remedy. It would be futile to preach reconciliation and union where antagonism runs so high. Let the Comrades on both sides do the next best thing. Let them separate, honestly, freely and without rancor. Let each side organize and work in its own way, and make such contribution to the Socialist movement in America as it can. Better a hundred times to have two numerically small Socialist organizations, each homogeneous and harmonious within itself, than to have one big party torn by dissensions and squabbles, an impotent colossus on feet of clay. The time for action is near. Let us clear the decks.

In other words, the party is hopelessly split and the thing to do is to "clear the decks" for action and "go at" demolishing each other. This is not exactly what Mr. Hillquit proposes but it is what will happen.

So, as far as these two organized forces of destruction are concerned, the public need give them little further thought. The people with whom it has to deal now, those who will carry on the undermining propaganda of those organizations, are of two types. One is to be found in the sanctums of certain newspapers and magazines, in the pulpits and forums of certain churches and in the professorial chairs of certain colleges and universities. Happily, these men are becoming pretty well "tagged" and the American people will sooner or later see that they are well taken care of. The other type consists of the criminal Bolshevist and scattering revolutionary groups that are openly preaching the overthrow of our form of government and the substitution of a proletariat dictatorship. These groups are being secretly supported by the pro-German Germans and other contingents in this country unfriendly to the Government. They also will be satisfactorily dealt with by the American people.

A most dangerous propaganda at the present time is that put out by the pacifists, who are appealing to "humanitarianism" to "save the world." "The war is over," they say, "and hatred should be replaced by love for all mankind." Under cover of this the un-American forces in our midst are plotting and intriguing for the overthrow of our Government just as infamously as they were while we were at war.

This is no time for "pussy-footing" but for red-blooded Americanism.

TWO NOTABLE UTTERANCES FROM TWO STATESMEN. Much of the criticism of President Wilson when he sailed for Europe last December was that he was "an idealist," "a theorist," "an academician"; that he was "proposing an impossibility"; that he was "pursuing an *ignis fatuus*"; that his dream of a League of Nations, whereby all disputes arising out of racial, religious or territorial differences would be happily composed, was "an absurdity,"etc. In fact, the unfriendly cartoonists portrayed him with haloes and wings and sent him forth as an apostle of peace a la Ford and Company.

One reason for this attitude of criticism was that he could not, or would not, answer the questions: "How do you propose to do it? What is your plan? Let us see the mechanism." Instead of giving a concrete answer, he chose to deal in glittering generalities. In his famous Guildhall speech he made this beautiful but idyllic statement:

> And back of us is that imperative yearning of the world to have all disturbing questions quieted, to have all threats against peace silenced, to have just men everywhere come together for a common object. The peoples of the world want peace, and they want it now, not merely by conquest of arms but by agreemen. of mind.

It is entirely conceivable that the President dealt in these glittering generalities simply because he had no plan, and he had no plan because neither he nor anyone else could work out one that would accomplish all that was promised by the friends of the League of Peace idea in all countries. But the President talking at the Guildhall in Christmas week, and the President talking to the Paris International Law Society at the end of May, were two very different men.

ıe Paris address we have a most illuminat- intelligent and splendid statement from a who was not then "an idealist," "a theo- ' or "an academician," but one of the most rienced and practical men in all the coun- represented at the Peace Conference, be- › he had had six months of the most intensive ing, bumping up against all the great minds urope, as well as the selfish minds, the com- ial minds and all the other minds that go ake up the statesmanship of all the nations e world. In the six months he has been in ıpe, President Wilson has jumped from the hman class to the Senior Class, and in the wing sentences it is the Senior and not the hman who is speaking:

› of the things that disturbed me most in recent hs is the unqualified hope men entertained where of immediate emancipation from the s that hampered and oppressed them. You can- n human experience rush into the light. You to go through twilight into the broadening day e noon comes and the full sun shines upon the ıcape. We must set out to see that those who aren't disappointed by showing them the proc- of law, the processes of slow disentanglement many things that bound us in the past. You ot throw off the habits of the individual imme- ly. They must be slowly got rid of, or, rather, must be slowly altered. They must be slowly ted. They must be slowly shaped to new ends vhich we would use them.

ıe supreme fact that all great changes come ly, that civilization has been thousands of s in reaching its present stage of advance- t, is just as true in industrial affairs as in national affairs, and it is this supreme fact h the so-called "radical" and "progressive" strial elements, equally with the interna- ıl radicals and progressives, cannot grasp. discover an evil today and they want it shed by tomorrow. If that is not done, they unce our society, our institutions, as being cient, capitalistic and autocratic. Such ele- ıts have in Petrograd and Moscow a living mple of how such "over-night" perform- es do not work.

ıs a companion piece to President Wilson's esmanlike utterance in Paris, here is another erance by another president—not of a nation, ıough of an important part of a nation— uel Gompers, president of the American leration of Labor. In answer to the socialists › criticized the methods of the American Fed- tion of Labor as being too slow, too archaic, uel Gompers said:

he difficulty is, my friends, that there are some ple who won't understand the real facts of life, that it isn't declarations which count, but the rcise of normal activities. I want the stars in heavens. My aspirations know no limit for my ɔw men, but I am vain enough to believe that ıve some common sense and understanding of the rations of the human mind. I am not going to › up voluntarily the labor movement with its ievements of today to look for the chimerical orrow. I think the greatest, the most radical, most idealistic and the most fantastical declara- which any body of men has made has been by Bolsheviki of Russia. And they have lost, not the meat from the bone but the bone itself, and e not even the shadow. They went out for the imum for the masses, for land, bread and peace, they haven't their land or bread or peace. We 'er to go on in this normal way of trying to make conditions of life and labor better today than were yesterday; and better tomorrow and to- row and tomorrow's tomorrow than each day has gone before.

President Wilson and President Gompers are v in the same class. They are "reactionaries," y "have no vision," but, fortunately, they e brains, and their plans, if not designed to ng a millenium overnight, are practical, con- ıctive, and the vital thing is, they work.

E ISSUE IN E BERGER ЭE Concerning the action of Congress in regard to the investigation of Victor Berger, the *New York Call* comments:

'Now that the initial antagonism engendered ıinst Berger in Congress by the capitalist press, from which the members obtained their sole information relative to the Berger case, has subsided, it is freely admitted the case is the most important that has ever come before Congress. It is not Berger's personality that is in question. . . . This question brings up squarely the fundamental principle of representative government."

The Berger case is, indeed, important in that it is up to Congress to decide whether it shall permit to sit among the representatives of the people a man who sought to defeat the cause of America in its conflict with a foreign foe and who advocated the cause of an autocracy that threatened the democracy of the whole world. In its statement that Congress obtained its information from the capitalist press the *New York Call* simply pursues that familiar line of hypocrisy and dishonesty with which the professional Socialist malcontent seeks to deceive his gullible proletarian audience. The facts of the Berger case are to be found in the editorial pages of Berger's *Milwaukee Leader*, just as facts about Mr. Hillquit, Mr. Debs, Bill Haywood, or the late Kaiser, are to be found in their own writings and speeches.

Berger himself, ignoring the charges of which he was convicted, threatened that "if the capitalist class will abolish the free press and curtail free speech for the working class and imprison its spokesmen, . . . then the workers may be in favor of proletarian soviets that will abolish capitalist jails and capitalist courts with the capitalist laws."

Can Mr. Berger with a straight face pretend that when he opposed our going to war and championed Germany, when he engaged in disloyal activities in violation of the espionage act, he was functioning as a "spokesman" of the working classes of America?

According to the jury that convicted him, Berger, in his paper, the *Milwaukee Leader* sought to hinder the nation in its conduct of the war against Germany. In his untoward activities, Berger, himself of the Teutonic race, was neither better nor worse than a majority of leaders of the Socialist party. Eugene Debs was sent to prison because of his efforts to obstruct the draft, and Debs is not a German. Morris Hillquit campaigned for the office of mayor of New York on the Bolshevist platform of a separate peace by negotiation with Germany. Such a peace—and for such a peace all the radicals united—would have left Germany victorious and the Allies defeated. Instead of "a peace without annexations and indemnities", the Allies and the United States would have had to submit to another Brest-Litovsk betrayal by the undefeated Huns. Was it possible these leaders of the Socialist party actually wanted Germany to win?

The stand is taken by Berger's Socialist friends that he was elected by the voters of the Fifth Wisconsin district by a plurality over his nearest opponent of more than 5,000 votes, and that he, therefore, is entitled under the Constitution as the representative of that majority to take his seat in Congress. This raises the pertinent question as to whether any preponderating body of citizens of German birth or extraction in a district, shall be permitted to use the polls to elect to Congress a man more representative of Berlin than of American public opinion, and whose record and acts are more in accord with the sinister forces who would destroy internal peace and promote strife and civil war in our midst than with the majority of loyal Americans who believe in order and the principles of the Constitution. The Socialists, in contending that Berger represents the majority of voters in his district, have raised the question as to whether such a body of voters supporting a candidate such as Berger, should not themselves be disfranchised.

The inevitable whine about persecution by capitalists and the suppression of free speech is characteristically crawling and cowardly. If the heroic and doughty leaders of the social revolution were ordinarily honest and sincere even with themselves, they would be men enough to stand by their published utterances and stated principles. Caught with the goods, this breed can only squeal.

PACIFISTS AGAIN ABET THE HUNS Immediately upon the publication of the terms, there broke forth a wailing and gnashing of teeth, not only in Germany itself, but from those identical forces and personalities in this country who had long ago opposed our taking up arms against Germany and who, after the declaration of war, campaigned for a peace of compromise. As if some invisible master had pulled the strings, the Socialists, internationalists, pacifists and radicals of various stripes joined in a wailing chorus of protest. The gentle Mr. Villard rent the air with lamentations of bitter chagrin and rage. The *New Republic*, exasperated beyond restraint, gave way to a self-betraying species of mental rabies. Young Bullit, who with Lincoln Steffens was sent to Russia, offered his resignation as a member of the American Peace Commission, on the grounds, according to reports, of dissatisfaction with the terms. The Central Committee of the International Labor and Socialist Conference at Berne assailed the treaty, and the Women's International Conference at Zurich sent in hot haste to the Peace Conference a protest in which it declared;

"By guaranteeing the fruits of secret treaties to the conquerors, the terms of peace have tacitly sanctioned secret diplomacy, denied the principle of self-determination, recognized the rights of the victors to the spoils and created all over Europe discords and animosities which can only lead to future wars."

The Congress decided, according to despatches, to organize in each country meetings of protest against the terms of the treaty, and voted unanimously at its concluding session to call a world-wide strike of women in the event of another war, even though that war be sanctioned by the League of Nations.

The member presenting this proposal was Fraulein Hertzka, a delegate from Vienna.

The American delegation to the Congress included Miss Jane Addams, Mrs. Florence Kelley and Miss Lillian Wald. Mrs. Florence Kelley has distinguished herself as a pacifist. Miss Jane Addams and Miss Lillian D. Wald were mentioned in the "Who's Who" given to the Overman Committee by Mr. Archibald Stevenson. According to this list, Miss Addams has been chairman of the Woman's Peace Party; vice chairman of the American Neutrality Conference Committee, member of the executive committee of the American Union Against Militarism, a member of the Council of Fellowship of Reconciliation and the American League to Limit Armaments. Miss Addams actively figured in the promotion of the Ford Peace expedition, originally engineered by Madam Rosiska Schwimmer, the German-Austrian agent. According to Mr. Stevenson's list Miss Wald, of the Henry Street settlement, has been a member of the American Neutral Conference Committee, American Union Against Militarism, the National Civil Liberties Bureau, the American League to Limit Armaments and the Women's Peace Party of New York.

Certain respect and esteem are due these women for their humanitarian work. But where the future peace and well-being of the free nations of the world are at stake, such sentimentality as may mislead otherwise tender-hearted and fine women into becoming unconscious instruments of a propaganda inimical to the best interests of America and

(Continued on page 19)

Bolshevist Bolsterings

ATTEMPT TO EXPLOIT RAYMOND ROBINS IN ROOSEVELT MANTLE

OF BOLSHEVISM as it attacks and appropriates private property we have heard a great deal from eye-witnesses and people who have suffered thereby. Just how Bolshevist methods may work out when applied to reputations, by infringing upon a truly great man's prestige and fame in the exploitation for personal advantage of another, is instanced in the June number of the *Metropolitan Magazine*.

The *Metropolitan Magazine* achieved a unique and enviable distinction by publishing each month an article by the late Colonel Theodore Roosevelt, that splendid, heroic and sterling American, and champion of the highest and noblest Americanism. In the June issue of the *Metropolitan Magazine*, appealing to the same audience which Colonel Roosevelt had won to that journal, appears the first of a series of articles entitled ''Bolshevist Russia—Raymond Robins' Story, told to William Hard.'' Mr. Raymond Robins, we presumed, had fully told his story. He has told it industriously and repeatedly to various bodies throughout the country. He has expended much in mileage to tell that story. He told it in extenso to the Senate Investigating Committee. Bolshevist friends and sympathizers quoting Mr. Robins as their supreme authority, have given further currency to repetitions of that story. Indeed, it seemed there could be nothing more to tell.

Mr. Robins admitted to the Senate Committee that he favored the recognition of the Bolshevist government, that he favored our giving economic support to the Bolshevist government — a regime whose destructive doctrines, he acknowledged, constitute in his own words ''the first challenge of the age to our order.'' Despite the contrary testimony of many men who have come recently from Russia, Raymond Robins represented the Bolshevist regime of Lenine and Trotzky as being supported by the majority of the Russian population—a claim in which Mr. Robins involved himself in ambiguities and contradictions, and which has been thoroughly exploded as inaccurate and untrue.

KNOW-IT-ALL-ISM AND ITS PROPHET

Mr. Robins boldly presented himself to the Senate Committee as knowing more about Bolshevism than any Allied representative in Russia. Mr. Robins said so himself. In the *Metropolitan Magazine* of June, and to the audience of readers attracted to that journal by Mr. Roosevelt's articles, with an impudence that is as shameless as it is unconscious, Raymond Robins is presented by his personal friend Mr. William Hard, a regular contributor to the *New Republic*, as one who has inherited the mantle, and who speaks with the approval, of that man of gigantic spiritual stature, that heroic American, the late Colonel Theodore Roosevelt. Raymond Robins is represented as having gone to Russia at the urging of Mr. Roosevelt. Raymond Robins is represented as having brought back from Russia reports and conclusions concerning the Bolsheviki to which Mr. Roosevelt ''gave the deepest consideration and respect.'' Confidence in Raymond Robins' Russian story — a story in conflict with the testimony of innumerable men who have come from Russia, a story which, as told to the Senate Committee, included egregious charges of brutality against the brave Czecho-Slovak troops and which cast unworthy reflections upon that bravest of brave women, Catherine Breshkovskaya—is sought on the ground that it had impressed, if not influenced, the views of Colonel Roosevelt himself. Nor is this all. In what is presumably Mr. Hard's own introduction, the statement is made that Raymond Robins is ''welcome'' to the columns of the magazine, which was distinguished and honored by Mr. Roosevelt's monthly contributions, ''not only because of himself and because of his narrative, which we believe to be of the greatest immediate world-importance in the present world-encounter with Bolshevism, but also because of his intimate association with Colonel Roosevelt.'' Adequate comment upon the ''immediate world importance'' of Mr. Robins' oft-told and now rather stale narrative may be found in the fact that the American Government did not see fit to follow Mr. Robins' suggestions, if not urgings, that the *de facto* government of those red murderers, Lenine and Trotzky, be recognized and given economic aid, in the fact that the Council of Four is considering recognizing any non-Bolshevik government in Russia which agrees to convene a national assembly and respect certain decisions of the League of Nations.

Mr. Hard brazenly launches the very man who is most quoted as an authority by Bolshevist sympathizers and supporters, with this totally astonishing declaration:

''*Colonel Robins is one of the men who will most effectively carry on the Roosevelt tradition in this country.*''

ROBINS' PHOTO PLACED IN PARALLEL WITH MR. ROOSEVELT'S

Parallel to a photograph of Theodore Roosevelt, among the greatest of all great Americans, famed and greatly loved, is published a photograph of Raymond Robins, in the uniform of a Red Cross Colonel, whose claim to public attention of late is due mainly to a story which tends in its effect chiefly to exonerate the Bolshevist arch-criminals of the wholesale killings and terrorization charged by reputable witnesses against them.

Were it not for its transparence and utter ridiculousness this effort at exploitation by the use of Mr. Roosevelt's great name and great fame would be akin to profanation. Even as it is, to all who revere Mr. Roosevelt's name this example of fulsome boosting becomes nauseous if only by reason of its lack of mere ordinary human good taste.

Introducing Robins' story, Mr. Hard refers in a brief stroke to the Red Cross Colonel's activities in politics in 1912, and quotes in abbreviated form, a letter from Colonel Roosevelt to Robins just as the latter was setting out for Russia in June, 1917. ''My dear fellow, you will do a great work. I cannot say how glad I am you are going over,'' runs the quotation. Mr. Hard then says:

''When Colonel Robins returned from Russia, he went, of course, to Oyster Bay and laid his final views of Russia before Colonel Roosevelt in person. He also presented them to him in written form. We highly value the response Colonel Roosevelt made, as evidence of the impression produced upon his experienced mind by the national and international facts and by the suggestions of national and international policy which Colonel Robins had brought before him and which he now brings before our readers. This response was:

'' 'Dear Raymond Robins: I value your letter. I shall use some of what you say; and, as far as I possibly can, I shall adopt the spirit of what you say in what I am writing as to the lesson of Russia for us.' ''

That letter was dated September 3, 1918. That letter was written soon after Robins' return and before he became so prominent in the role, which he assumed, of knowing more about Russia than any Allied representative who had been there. To the casual reader it might appear that Colonel Roosevelt had accepted almost in toto Robins' views on the Russian situation. But Mr. Hard, the chronicler, does not venture to let this assumption by deduction stand without qualification, for he immediately adds:

''We do not mean to say that Colonel Roosevelt concurred in all the conclusions and in all the suggestions made by Colonel Robins regarding Russia and regarding American policy toward Russia. Nor do we know, on the other hand, that he dissented from them, at any practical point, in questions of action by our Government, when he had learned the facts which Colonel Robins had reported. What is important to us is simply that Colonel Roosevelt, with his knowledge of public men and with his knowledge of public affairs, national and international, gave weight—and great weight—to the findings and opinions of Raymond Robins, and gave confidence—and great confidence—to Raymond Robins himself.''

What Robins reported to Colonel Roosevelt does not appear. Presumably that report could not have differed very materially from his testimony before Senator Overman's committee that investigated Bolshevism. There, Robins, of course, was sworn to ''tell the truth, the whole truth, and nothing but the truth.'' And so he could hardly have told Colonel Roosevelt anything contrary to what he told the committee, and therefore his testimony in Washington may be taken as a summary of that private report sent to Oyster Bay.

MR. ROOSEVELT'S OPINIONS *VS.* ROBINS'

Robins testified before the Overman committee that he personally found reports of Bolshevist assassinations to be untrue; that the Germans had absolutely nothing to do with the Red Guard, and that German officers did not command the Guard.

''*Up to the time I left Russia,*'' testified Robins, ''*the thing that was constantly in my mind, again and again, was the lack of vindictiveness, was the lack of actual destruction of life under the circumstances. If it had been in America, if it had been in any other land I know of, where a mob had taken power like that and had the rifles back of them, I should have expected vastly more destruction.*''

Just how, in fact, was Colonel Roosevelt ''impressed'' by reports of such a pacific revolution, by that tale about ''the lack of vindictiveness, the lack of actual destruction of life'' in the Bolshevist overthrow of all order?

Writing in the December number of the *Metropolitan*, after, of course, he had received Robins' report in August, Colonel Roosevelt said:

''Before our eyes the unfortunate Russian nation furnishes an example on a gigantic scale of what to avoid in oscillating between extremes. The autocratic and bureaucratic despotism of the Romanoffs combined extreme tyranny with extreme inefficiency; and the Bolshevists have turned the Revolution into a veritable Witches' Sabbath of anarchy, plunder, murder, utterly faithless treachery and inefficiency carried to the verge of complete disintegration.''

In the same article Colonel Roosevelt diametrically opposed Robins' report as to Germany not having aided Bolshevism, when he said:

''Russia would have been saved from the abyss

which she had fallen, for in her inevitable ɔlution the Bolshevists would not have had German support which has enabled them to nch loose the very foundations of their ɔtry.''

efore the Overman committee Robins ad-ted that he advocated that the Bolshevist gov-ment should be recognized and be given economic support of the United States, de-te the fact that, as he had previously ad-tted, Lenine and Trotzky purposed to over-ow by revolution the American Government well as all other governments.

What Colonel Roosevelt thought about recog-ing the Bolshevists was plainly shown in his icle on the League of Nations in the *Metro-litan Magazine* of January, in which he said:

''Russia's action during the last year would ıke any international guarantee of action on r part worth precisely nothing as a warrant : promise or action on our part.''

And previously, in the December *Metropoli-*ı, he brought this out strongly when he de-red:

'Since the Bolshevists rose to power, Russia s betrayed her own honor, and the cause of rld democracy, and the liberties of the well haved minorities within her own borders, and e right to liberty and self government of small ell behaved nations everywhere.''

·APITALIZES ACQUAINTANCE WITH REVERED DEAD

Yet in the face of the published expressions this courageous and sound American, in the ce of his stern repudiation of Bolshevism, Mr. 'illiam Hard, writing in the *Metropolitan*, seeks impress the very readers who gave loving nfidence to the great dead, with the assertion:

''Colonel Roosevelt * * * gave weight— d great weight—to the findings and opinions Raymond Robins, and gave confidence—and reat confidence—to Raymond Robins himself.''

To capitalize one's acquaintance with the dis-inguished dead may, to many people, seem a ıatter of very questionable taste. To seek to 'in confidence in Mr. Raymond Robins and his tussian story on the grounds that Theodore toosevelt ''urged Colonel Robins to go to Rus-ia'' and ''gave weight to the findings and opin-ɔns of Raymond Robins'' may seem like going eyond the lines of decent press agency, es-ecially if facts do not support so bald a pre-ension. Prodded by Senator Overman as to hether he would be in favor of America recog-ıizing a government which he had admitted was menace to the world, Mr. Robins at the Senate earings answered:

''As I understand that the question of recog-ıition of a government does not rest upon the haracter of the government. If the govern-ıent is really the government of a people, that s all that any foreign government has a right o inquire into.''

''There is this Soviet form which the Russian ıass, the peasants and workmen, have adopted s a framework,'' Mr. Robins continued. '' 'All ɔower to the Soviet,' was the cry on which Le-ıine and Trotzky took possession of the govern-ıent in Russia * * * They really, discreetly —or rather cunningly—with real political judg-ıent saw that the people liked their self-govern-ng Soviets. * * * I think we found, in ourse of time, in Russia that there was this lefinite framework that had grown up out of heir historic past, that the clever political minds ɔf the Bolshevik leaders fell upon as the way to get into power; so I think there is really some-hing there in structure as well as the actual Bolshevik domination.''

''Is there any way possible for the people of Russia to get rid of Lenine and Trotzky without a revolution?'' asked Senator Overman.

''I should say so, absolutely, sir. I should say that the moment any considerable mass in Russia wants to get rid of Lenine and Trotzky they can do it,'' replied Mr. Robins.

In other words, according to Mr. Robins, Lenine and Trotzky rule by will of the majority and not by Red Guard terrorism, and in the Soviet system, controlled by the Bolshevik autocrats, the majority of Russians have what they want.

''The reason that their power has held,'' pursued Mr. Robins, speaking of Lenine and Trotzky, ''has been that for the time they expressed as between the old experience of the past and the new experience, a larger expectation of hope and opportunity for the mass of the peasants and workers of Russia than they had before, and as long as that expectation holds they will support Lenine.''

In the December *Metropolitan* article, before quoted, Colonel Roosevelt said:

''There are no worse enemies of America than the American Bolshevists and the crew of politicians who pander to them. We ought therefore clearly to understand what the Bolsheviki attempted in Russia and what after a year of power they have done for, or rather to, Russia. *They utterly repudiated the idea of a democracy where every man is guaranteed his rights and is limited in his power to do wrong.* Their effort was to create a Marxian socialistic state, based on the class conscious purpose of the proletariat to destroy and rob every other class. *They oppressed and plundered impartially all former oppressors and wrongdoers and all former champions of fair dealing and liberty. They attacked the erstwhile corrupt bureaucrat or wealthy landowner who had neglected all his duties not a whit more venomously than they attacked the small shopkeepeer or skilled mechanic or industrious farmer or thrifty workingman who, because he had saved some money and had begun to live decently, they denounced as having adopted 'bourgeois standards.'* They definitely sought to realize the stark formulas of Marxian socialism; and therefore they have made a genuine contribution for warning and prevention against destructive adventure of a similar character in our own land. The followers of Trotzky and Lenine, like the followers of Robespierre and Marat, have just one lesson to teach the American people: what to avoid.''

ROOSEVELT DENOUNCED LENINE'S AGENTS

And as evidence that Colonel Roosevelt was not influenced by Robins's assertion that the Germans did not aid the Bolsheviki, the article went on:

''In the peace treaty of last March the Russian Bolshevists and the German autocracy joined against the free nations. Anarchy and despotism joined against liberty. The representatives of the privilege of a proletarian mob and the representatives of the privilege of a plutocratic oligarchy struck hands against the men who believe in no privilege. Germany recognizes that anarchy destroys freedom; therefore Germany encourages anarchy in every land to which she cannot apply her iron despotism, for she wishes to destroy every nation she cannot enslave. The Bolshevist leaders—it matters not whether they were sinister visionaries or the corrupted agents of Germany—played Germany's game.''

These ''sinister visionaries or corrupted agents of Germany'' were the men Robins boasted he visited at least three times a week at the Smolny Institute and under whose auspices he spoke in parts of Russia as ''Comrade Robins.''

Whether he gleaned it from reading Robins' ideas on Bolshevism, since expressed publicly in speeches and before the Overman committee, or not, Colonel Roosevelt had no illusions as to the menace of the insidious propaganda put forth in America by friends or agents of Lenine and Trotzky. In the December *Metropolitan* he said:

''Prominent, though not always powerful, among the various exponents of American Bolshevism are the professional intellectuals who vary from the softhanded, noisily selfassertive frequenters of frowsy restaurants to the sissy socialists, the pink tea and parlor Bolshevists who support what they regard as 'advanced' papers, and aspire to notoriety as make believe 'reds.' I call these persons 'intellectuals' in deference to the terminology of European politics, for they ape the silly, half educated people and the educated able people with a moral or mental twist, who in almost every European country have found notoriety and excitement in fomenting revolutionary movements they were utterly powerless to direct or control. Unless the term intellectual is to be construed as excluding either character or common sense, it can be applied to them only in irony.

''In our own vernacular they have been styled the exponents of Highbrow Hearstism or Bolshevism.''

MR. HARD'S STORY A REHASH

Mr. William Hard's story is little more than a rehash and reassembling of the testimony advanced by Robins before the Senate investigating committee, except that it is dressed and garnished after Mr. Hard's best style and that it presents the Red Cross Colonel in a heroic role such as he could hardly, with good grace, have assumed himself. Mr. Hard is manifestly a sincere admirer of the Red Cross Colonel. We have had it from Mr. Hard that they were friends long ago in Chicago. Were it not that Mr. Hard, led away by his enthusiasm, ''lays it on too thick,'' his article as a piece of press agency work might be fairly effective. But hero-worship, except when a Carlyle does it, is dangerously prone to become mawkish. Picturing the contrast between his doughty American hero and an assemblage of Russians, Mr. Hard draws this sketch of his friend who is advanced for the role of ''one of the men who will most effectively carry on the Roosevelt tradition'':

''He is among the Americans on whom the American climate and environment have perhaps already had a physical effect. His complexion is quite dark, with not a little in it, I should say, of a coppery coloring; and his black hair has an Indian straightness; and his eyes have the searchingness of the forest and the prairie; and the contours of his face have a weathered suggestion of the modelling done by America on the faces of those who preceded us in our present hunting grounds.''

And more in the same tone—very much, is it not, like the rousing oratory of the election spell-binder campaigning for a candidate?

Colonel Robins preceded his eulogist in eulogy when he presented himself before the Senate Committee as having gotten an ''outdoor point of view'' in Russia. Mr. Hard further pictures him as ''knocking his shins'' against the Soviet ''when diplomats were only hearing about it.''

''The Indoor Mind,'' writes Mr. Hard, ''goes to a country like Russia, where seven per cent of the population had been masters of everything. It finds the seven per cent swept out of mastery and the ninety-three per cent in full control.''

Mr. Robins, with the ''Outdoor Mind,'' is represented as getting in touch with the ninety-three per cent, and the modest Mr. Robins by his Boswell is made to say:

''If I do not know more about the opinions of the common soldiers and of the common workmen who made the Bolshevik revolution of 1917 than any other foreign representative then in Russia, it is because my intelligence was not equal to my opportunities.''

Mr. Hard's version of Mr. Robins' ubiquitous activities is equal only to Mr. Robins' own account. Telling of his success as a busy platform orator in Russia, Hard writes:

"His hearers would listen attentively. Robins would speak for thirty minutes, and would then answer questions for two hours. After testing audiences in many parts of the world, Robins has come to the conclusion that a Russian audience can stand more punishment than any other audience living. The peasants and workmen who listened to him in armories and arsenals and barracks were willing to listen, and also to talk, to the end."

In the course of cross examination at the Senate investigation, Mr. Robins was asked by Major Humes:

"Do you speak Russian?"

"No, sir, only very poorly," admitted the Red Cross Colonel.

"Then," said Major Humes, "the information you got, and the conversations which you had at various times with Russians and those who could not speak English was through an interpreter?"

The rousing orator to the common soldiers and common workmen of Russia, who held his audiences spellbound and answered their questions for hours, conceded this was so.

ROBINS' INVESTIGATOR NOW SECRETARY TO LENINE

It was brought out at the Senate hearings that Mr. Robins' choice of secretary and interpreter fell upon Alexander Gumberg, a selection in which Mr. Robins showed singular judgment. For Gumberg's brother, who had adopted the Russianized name of "Sergius Zorin," was a member of the Lenine-Trotzky Bolshevik crew and occupied the position in the Bolshevist government of Minister of Posts and Telegraphs. Another person who worked for Mr. Robins in Russia—one of his "windows" presumably—according to the testimony of Louise Bryant, was Boris Reinstein, a Russian Jew, who had lived in Buffalo, a Socialist writer, who later became secretary to Lenine. Among Mr. Robins' choice and selected staff of "investigators"—according to Miss Bryant—in addition to Gumberg and Reinstein, were Reed and Williams, both in the service of the Bolsheviki, and Miss Bryant herself. Rhys Williams, John Reed and Boris Reinstein were all members of the Bolshevist Propaganda Bureau in Petrograd. It was thus made clear that Mr. Robins enjoyed extraordinarily close connections with headquarters, and it will be seen just what unique facilities Mr. Robins enjoyed for getting his much self-advertised "Outdoor" point of view.

Ambassador Francis, in his testimony before the Senate Committee, told a good deal about Mr. Robins' activities in Russia. Mr. Francis stated that the Bolshevik looked upon Robins as their friend, and told of Mr. Robins' efforts to secure the recognition of the Bolshevik government. On May 15, 1918, at the railroad station at Vologda, on his way out of Russia, Mr. Robins, said Ambassador Francis, "told an Associated Press man there, and a man named Groves, one of my employees, that if he could get one hour with the President he could persuade the President to recognize the Soviet government." According to Ambassador Francis, Mr. Robins was said to have acted as a courier from the Bolshevik government and to have carried communications addressed to the American government over the head of the Ambassador. Whether these were ever presented or not, Mr. Francis did not know.

MR. ROOSEVELT'S WARNING

One of the first speeches delivered by Colonel Roosevelt after the presumable receipt of Robins' report late last August was his address at the dinner of the National League for Women's Service, presided over by Miss Maude Wetmore. The ideas of the Red Cross Colonel must have been fresh in the real Colonel's mind and any "*weight*" or "*confidence*" he might have had in Robins might reasonably be expected to be manifest in this speech. Yet hardly a fortnight after getting Robins' report, Colonel Roosevelt, as recorded in the *New York Sun*, of September 19, 1918, said:

"I take little interest in the discussion as to whether when the Bolsheviki rip Russia asunder they do it because they are corrupt or because they are incompetent fools. What I am concerned in is the results of what they did. They have, according to their capacity, done all the damage possible to the free nations of the earth, and they have done it in the name of theories which foolish dreamers in this country would have us believe as desirable to follow."

Mr. Hard should have remembered that speech before he wrote, in touting Robins' story in the *Metropolitan*:

"Nor do we know, on the other hand, that he (Col. Roosevelt) dissented from the suggestions made by Colonel Robins regarding Russia."

The record stands for itself.

Colonel Roosevelt went on record in opposition to the Robins' conclusions as to the Bolshevist government, when on October 6, 1918, barely a month after receiving the Red Cross Colonel's ideas about the United States recognizing Lenine and Trotzky, he made a Liberty Loan address at Billings, Montana. In that speech, Colonel Roosevelt handled the Non-Partisan League and its Bolshevist doctrines without gloves, in its own stronghold.

Again, in a ringing speech at the Illinois Centennial, at Springfield, on August 26, 1918, Colonel Roosevelt defined in no uncertain terms his opinion of the Bolsheviki—of the Russian and American "intellectual" variety. As reported in the *New York Sun* the next day, he said:

"The pacifists are the American Romanoffs and Bolsheviki. For the moment the pacifists and internationalists and pro-Germans dare not be noisy. But let our people beware of them as soon as peace negotiations come and from that time forth. They have worked together in the past and they will work together in the future, the pro-Germans furnishing the most powerful and sinister element of the combination, while the pacifists and internationalists prance in the foreground and furnish the rhetoric."

It is probable that Colonel Roosevelt had studied Robins' written report at that time. At any rate, he had received the Red Cross Colonel's verbal opinion of the Bolsheviki. Yet for Colonel Roosevelt to class the very people who have been making such ado about Robins' reports and their importance, for Colonel Roosevelt to class the very people who have of late hailed Raymond Robins as their prophet with "pacifists and internationalists and pro-Germans" may tend to indicate just what "weight—and great weight—and what confidence—and great confidence—" Colonel Roosevelt gave to Robin's opinions and to Raymond Robins himself.

T. EVERETT HARRÉ.

Out of Their Own Mouths

(Continued from Page 6)

Commenting on the disposition of the Saar valley:

"There is no excuse in law or in morals for raising the question of sovereignty in the valley," says this organ of the Crolys, Weyls and Lippmanns. "It is a German valley * * * The Saar will furnish an embittered Germany not only a real reason for discontent, but a symbol with all the necessary moral attributes for cultivating a policy of revenge.

"The injustice will rankle and fester, and into it will be injected the poison of another injustice. Germany will point out that the principle of nationality has been applied only when it injures her and never when it might favor her."

The prohibition of union with German Austria, continued the *New Republic*, is a violation of Mr. Wilson's principles. "The drastic Polish cessions" are "a terrible blow to Germany." Doubtless, early in the war Germany had not the faintest anticipation as to this outcome! How well the *New Republic* interprets and expresses the German mind!

"It looks as if millions of Germans would have to emigrate or blow up," pursued the *New Republic*. "The Germans, in our opinion, will quit. A government may sign this peace, but it will never be altogether executed. For the trouble with the treaty is that it gives the Germans too many good reasons for feeling themselves thoroughly abused."

One might gather, from all this, that in the war Germany was one of the injured parties, that she had committed no crimes deserving of punishment, that in bringing her to account the Allies had betrayed the hopes and future of the world.

"The world which will result from the document can by no stretch of language be made to agree with the picture which the President had in mind when he went to Paris, or when he spoke in the days of his glory of what was to be accomplished. * * * By the standards of which he himself was the most eloquent spokesman he has failed."

In its issue of May 24, the *New Republic* referred to the treaty as "this inhuman monster," hatched by European politicians "with American complicity." "Their handwork will breed cynicism, hypocrisy or vindictiveness in the minds of future generations."

"CANTS WHICH ARE CANTED"

The authors of the Versailles treaty, in the opinion of the *New Republic*, "do this thing because they themselves are the unconscious servants of the cupidity and the vindictiveness which infect the psychology of an inhumane and complacent capitalist society. They crave at any cost the emotional triumph of imposing on the German nation the ultimate humiliation of solemnly consenting to its own abdication as a self governing and self respecting community."

"In our opinion the treaty of Versailles subjects all liberalism and particularly that kind of liberalism which breathes the Christian spirit to a decisive test. * * * It is essential that the ratification should not take place with the connivance of the sincerely liberal and Christian forces in public opinion.

"The Treaty of Versailles is damned because it does nothing to moralize the future exercise of political and economic power. * * * What it treats with utter ignorance is the Christian doctrine of atonement and redemption. At a crisis in the history of civilization, the rulers of the victorious Christian states conclusively demonstrate their own contemptuous disbelief in the practical value of Christian moral economy."

In this prating about "the Christian spirit" and "the Christian doctrine of atonement and redemption" by a magazine edited by Messrs. Walter Weyl and Walter Lippmann, which is read as their gospel by the intellectual "yellows," and which carries on the propaganda of that covert and esoteric "internationalism" by which the spiritual alienry would undermine all nationality and disintegrate the Christian civilization of the world, there is something unconsciously and grotesquely ironic. It would seem this tribe of "intelligentzia" are sublimely "dark" to the fact that some people in this world see through them thoroughly and realize exactly what they are up to, and that these appreciate fully that the whole program of Bolshevism and species of internationalism insidiously preached by their "journal of opinion" is in its essence and at its base sinister—anti-Christian.

"It seems an unavoidable conclusion that the presence of America in Europe and the promise of her continued participation has aggravated the national claims of every one of the Allied peoples," says the *New Republic* of May 31, continuing its assault upon the treaty. "America gave them a sense of security which they have used in order to press to the limit demands they would not have dared to make under other circumstances."

Does the *New Republic* imply that if America had not been present in Europe, if America had not sent troops to Europe and participated in the war, that it would have been Germany, and not the Allies, who would have "pressed" demands under the "other circumstances"? Or that, at least, in case of a stalemate, which it predicted, with a peace through compromise, which it had urged, the Allies would not have been in a position to dare press demands for adequate reparation from Germany? Would such a peace have been more acceptable to the editors of the *New Republic*, more desirable; in their novel opinion, more just?

"The effect of Mr. Wilson's popularity," pursues this organ, "has been not to democratize the settlement, but to prevent the democracies from influencing it. They gave him their trust and affection. They believed he would fight their battle in the secret meetings. They held their tongues so as not to embarrass him, and the result of his failure was that they were neutralized. They expected America to do for them what after all they could do only for themselves, and the result is a peace which no government in Europe would have dared to propose to its people were it not temporarily painted up with the fading glory of Wilson the democrat. Mr. Wilson's presence in Paris has been mischievous for Europe just because he drained to himself practically all the reason and sense and humanity in Europe, and then surrendered them."

"THAT MEN SHOULD PUT AN ENEMY IN THEIR MOUTHS TO STEAL AWAY THEIR BRAINS!"

Had the Allied nations been so exhausted that they would have been obliged to compromise with Germany at the very time that the *New Republic* and the *Nation* were urging peace by negotiation, would the terms that Germany would have proposed have constituted the terms of a just peace, a humane peace, a stable peace? Would the Kaiser's presence at the dictating council not have been "mischievous"? So unsatisfactory does the *New Republic* find the treaty that it now proposes boldly that the American Senate pass a resolution repudiating any commitment by the United States to support by its economic resources, its military forces or its foreign policy "to intervene in the territorial or economic arrangements of Europe or Africa." The *New Republic's* suggested resolution would leave "the execution of the treaty to the European powers concerned." In other words, we withdraw—and let Germany foil the Allies as best she may.

Having failed, first, in its policy of defeatism, second, in bringing about a *compromise* peace, third, in estranging America from the Allies and the securing a treaty that would have let Germany off easy, this sheet openly advocates that the United States withdraw its support from the enforcement of the treaty which the Allies have been able to dictate. In whose interest?

In whose interest was the *New Republic's* propaganda of defeatism?

In whose interest was the *New Republic's* efforts to bring America and the Allies to talk peace with Germany at a time German imperialism was unsentimed and German militarism undefeated?

In whose interest was the *New Republic's* campaign of slander against the Allied statesmen?

In whose interest are its frantic and enraged efforts now to undo the terms of the treaty?

After its despairing rage over the terms of the terms of the treaty, a new note of opthnism, of faintly glowing hope is heard in the *New Republic of June 7*. This optimism concerning "a peace that will last" is founded not on the basis of the Versailles treaty and its enforcement, but is inspired by "Germany's Counter Proposals."

"It is," says the *New Republic*, "possible to build up an enforcible peace on the foundation of the German offer."

"The Germans propose an indemnity up to twenty-five billions. That sum is probably more than sufficient to cover all the items of damage specified in the armistice agreement."

Having long championed a compromise peace, a patched-up peace, a peace of negotiation with Germany, a peace presumably in which the Allies were not absolute dictators, the *New Republic*, flushed, sanguine, inspiritedly declares:

"The Peace Conference can now take advantage of the leverage they have gained to make a peace that can last. It is hard to believe that the conference will act on the assumption that all its earlier determinations, however impractical and disturbing to the peace, must stand."

In whose interest is this "peace that can last" which it is possible to build "on the foundation of the German offer?" In whose interest will be concessions to the German plenipotentiaries, deference to the German objections, abdication by the Allies of their terms?

Campaigning for subscribers by means of a postcard just sent broadcast, the *New Republic* asks: "Do you long for the truth and nothing but the truth?" And it proceeds:

"What you are suffering from is an urgent need for a publication that is not 'lined up' with any party, class or creed—that is nobody's organ."

So far as that great body of Americans who backed the war to a military decision in victory over Germany is concerned, "nobody's organ" is right! As for not being "lined up," a comparison of the frothing-mouthed expressions of German leaders and the German press with the expressions of the *New Republic* regarding the treaty may adequately dispose of that claim. How many American fathers and mothers who gave their own blood in the struggle for victory, how many valiant American boys who have come back after having braved a fiendish foe, will desire, after reading this sheet's final assault upon an American and Allied peace, to take a "special acquaintance subscription for only $1 * * * and defy the press agents of the world" it is not difficult to hazard. However, it is not improbable this sheet will at least find an enthusiastic and sympathetic response among Hun sympathizers, "intellectual neutrals," the "internationalist" tribe who own no country and no country's cause, unfrocked clergymen, dismissed college professors, the soft-handed, the fish-hearted "pacifists," "conscientious objectors," "warm slaves as had as lieve hear the devil as a drum, such as fear the report of a claiver worse than a struck fowl or a hurt wild goose, . . . with hearts in their bellies no bigger than pins' heads, . . . the cankers of a calm world." Among such, doubtless, will be many inspired to "pin a dollar bill or check" to the post-card.

"BUT WOE AWAITS A COUNTRY WHEN SHE SEES THE TEARS OF BEARDED MEN!"

Mr. Oswald Garrison Villard's *Nation* pursued a policy very similar to that of the *New Republic*. After the signing of the armistice Mr. Villard himself visited Germany, the land of his forefathers, and sent back harrowing accounts of the starvation brought about in Germany of the cruel Allied blockade. Despite the contrary testimony of American troops in Germany he pictured German babies as perishing from lack of milk; he drew heart-rending pictures of the tragedy of the empty, aching German belly. Upon the publication of the terms of the treaty, Mr. Villard, in common with the *New Republic*, entirely lost his head, his poise, his well-bred restraint.

The world, he cried out, was prepared "for a rigorous peace. * * * But it was not prepared for a peace of undisguised vengeance, for a peace which openly flouts some of the plainest dictates of reason and humanity, repudiates every generous word that Mr. Wilson has ever uttered regarding Germany, flies in the face of accepted principles of law and economics, and makes the *very name of democracy a reproach*."

It was this same pacific Mr. Villard who commented thus in the *New York Evening Post* of May 10, 1915, of the sinking of the Lusitania:

"Had the submarine given thirty minutes' warning to the crew and passengers of the Cunarder, the exploit would have gone down in history as one of the most brilliant in the annals of warfare."

And now this same gentle soul, which could regard the sinking of the Lusitania in the light of a possible brilliant naval exploit, is rent with tearful anguish over the cruel and heartless terms of the treaty. Perhaps Mr. Villard's manly grief and noble indignation, finding such sympathetic echo in Germany itself, may help to interpret the singularly "independent" course of his journal during the progress of the war. He bewails out of the bitterness of his soul:

"The German people, who, it was repeatedly affirmed, had had no part in bringing on the war, and who at the worst were the helpless instruments of its prosecution, were to be freed from tyranny and given a chance to take their place among the peoples who love liberty and practice righteousness. * * * Germany and the German people are virtually to be destroyed. * * * As the treaty stands, Germany is to be stripped of its means of defense as well as of offense, while its conquerors hover about it fully armed. * * *"

And with ever higher key, Mr. Villard's lamentations rise:

"The heinousness of its offending, the calculating harshness of its demands and impositions, the gross repudiation of moral obligations and good faith which it involves, its gross injustice to the Allied people themselves and to their moral standing, become only the more apparent as its terms are studied. It is a peace of vengeance, not of justice. * * *"

Upon that wicked tribunal which indicted Germany and held her to account, as a modern Portia accusing the wicked Allies of insisting upon their pound of flesh, Mr. Villard points a finger of annihilating accusation:

"There has been enthroned at Versailles an arrogant and self-sufficient autocracy of five Great Powers, two of which are practically at the mercy of the other three: an autocracy owning no authority save its own will, deliberating in secret, parcelling out privileges and territory as best serves its own interests. * * * It is this Versailles autocracy which, in crushing Germany as a world Power, has itself assumed the role of world dictator. * * *

"How Mr. Wilson has repaid the confidence which the peoples gave him, all the world now knows," Mr. Villard woefully vituperates. "The one-time idol of democracy stands today discredited and condemned. * * * The camouflage of ethical precept and political philosophizing which for long blinded the eyes of all but the most observing has been stripped away, and the peoples of the world see revealed, not a friend faithful to the last, but an arrogant autocrat and a compromising politician."

BY THEIR OWN WORDS

Imperial Germany fostered and financed Bolshevism in Russia. Imperial Germany launched a world-wide propaganda the purpose of which

(*Continued on page 19*)

What — If Not Compulsory Insurance

(Continued from Page 2)

Mr. Straus: No, but they have a committee that looks into the qualifications as thoroughly as such a thing can be done.

Dr. Lee K. Frankel, President American Public Health Association and Third Vice President Metropolitan Life Insurance Co., New York, said in part:

"It seems to me that there are certain fundamental things to be considered in this connection. We do know that practically the greatest amount of poverty we find today in the United States is due to illness. The records of practically all the charitable societies and relief organizations show that from fifty to seventy-five per cent of the families under their care have been reduced to their present condition by illness. On the other hand, is it not clear that a considerable part of this sickness is not caused by industry? Much of the illness is due to lapses and shortcomings in the way of health administration.

"Of course, the primary purpose of sickness legislation is to replace the financial losses the individual suffers during his period of illness. If you are not going to do that through an insurance scheme, then is it not a fit matter for us to study to determine whether it can be done otherwise? I think one of the interesting developments recently with us is the fact that industry is realizing the value to it from a utilitarian standpoint of paying wages to responsible honest workpeople during illness, as a purely voluntary matter on the part of the industry. Large commercial plants are assuming that payment of wages during illness to individuals in their employ who are honest and upright is something to which they are entitled,—simply as a matter of good faith and good will between employer and employee.

"It seems to me that an opportunity is offered for a committee of this type to study other substitutes that might be suggested in lieu of what apparently is contrary to the belief of many here—a scheme of compulsory insurance with the machinery that that entails, complicated as it is in the nature of espionage and conducted under our political conditions—and one that has been reverted to by The National Civic Federation before. I happened to be the chairman of the Federation's committee which criticized the original bill presented in the New York legislature.

NEED OF ADEQUATE MEDICAL CARE

"Another matter we must consider is the question of giving the employee adequate medical care. First, we must cover the need of wage payments and then comes the matter of prevention of disease. Here comes the matter of the question of adequate preparation by the state for the conduct of health departments—state and particularly local—so they may have the machinery at their disposal for the reduction of what are today known to be preventable diseases.

"What are the possibilities of development of group practice in medicine applicable to large groups of employees and in particular to small groups? The difficulty has been that the large plants are able to do these things. But how about the employer with 5 to 15 employees? He is not able to make provision along this line. What about the casual, the unskilled and the periodical workers? They require provision just as much as the others.

"These are the things I believe a committee of this kind can sit down and study out; they require careful consideration and deliberation:

1. Provide financial benefits during the period of illness.
2. Give better medical care than is feasible today under any contract plan yet devised either in a plant or under any bill.
3. How to encourage the State to do the one thing the State is thoroughly justified in doing, employ and equip its health departments so as to reduce disease and possibly make provision for adequate medical supervision, inspection and care of the workpeople in the state."

Dr. Charles P. Neill, of the Southeastern Railways, Washington, D. C.:

"I should like to second the suggestion along the same line. The discussion so far seems to have been that the present trend of legislation is unwise. There is no question about that. On the other hand, we are facing a proposition—there is a large and important movement in this country as well as others for handling sickness on a group basis. It will keep on growing. This committee should analyze the defects and the merits.

"In connection with Dr. Frankel's suggestion, when you have taken care of all the plants, there are 49,000 men in Cleveland who have no employment and they are going to get sick, probably more frequently than if they were working. Who is going to take care of them? They are probably going to cheap physicians. We may have to come to some sort of state insurance; you can call it anything you want to. The state takes care of them now, with these two radical defects—one, they do not get decent treatment and two, the tax for the burden they are compelled to carry is levied on the basis of the tender-heartedness of the men who pay for it. This, of course, is rotten. In the third place, the thought of charity breaks down the self-respect of a man and the better class do not want it. The question is whether we are going to adopt an intelligent sane method or let the old scheme continue. We have got to change. It seems to me we should work out some plan and be in the position to say we are going to recommend certain other constructive proposals that will eliminate present defects. I do not believe anyone will say we do not need anything. We all know the need for relief."

Miss Margaret Loomis Stecker, of the National Industrial Conference Board, Boston:

"As this is a sickness problem, the National Industrial Conference Board has gone into it from that point of view. Is the sickness problem the first question? Of course, the answer is Yes. And is health insurance the best way to meet it? The conclusion we have come to is that in advocating insurance for sickness you are putting the cart before the horse, because it is foolish to offer insurance to meet a problem a large part of which can be prevented entirely by the elaboration of machinery existing at the present time. I think that is the main contribution that the Conference Board has to make. There will be sickness and there will be people brought to poverty because of sickness.

"I am not so sure as Dr. Frankel that sickness is the cause of poverty so directly. It seems to me that the two are closely related—one of those vicious circles so to speak in which it is very difficult to find the beginning; but the position of the Board is that preventive activities should be engaged in and tried out under the best conditions and that the public health work especially should be improved. After this machinery has been tried out, there may still be a need for other things. Before that, however, there should be worked out an organization of the agencies for preventing sickness rather than paying compensation for loss of wages through sickness, a large proportion of which might be prevented if ill health and the conditions leading to ill health were taken in hand.

RECORDS SOON TO BE AVAILABLE

"The Conference Board is now analyzing the hundreds of sickness records kept by many representative plants over a representative number of months last year, showing causes of absence. The results of that investigation should bear directly on this problem. The results are not yet available but it is anticipated that they will be soon."

Miss Mary Wood, Chairman Legislative Committee, Federation of Women's Clubs:

"All sane and sensible people are taking notice of the great change in conditions and we cannot close our eyes to the revolutionary methods that are coming to us. Personally, I used to be very much opposed to this question of health insurance; I felt that it was rather socialistic. I felt that there were great objections to the Workmen's Compensation law—and whatever way you put it, the public always pays. Now, the question is, How is it to be paid? In regard to the health insurance bill recently introduced in Albany, the women interested in it—the clubwomen—felt that it was not perfect, but they did go on record as favoring the principle of some sort of insurance by which working people could be possibly compelled—the chairman does not like that word but we are all compelled to be obedient—to set aside a certain sum which would relieve them from the feeling that they were accepting charity, where they had contributed in connection with the employer to a fund which would take care of them during illness. We shall come to it sooner or later. I am glad that this is a real committee to work out some sensible plan and one that will not be objectionable to anybody."

H. E. Miles, President Racine Sattley Co., Racine, Wis.:

"I am not afraid of this word 'compulsion.' Society rests upon compulsion. Law is compulsion. In my state a law was passed to compel the release of every child after 8 hours' work a day. That was compulsion; but the minute the law was passed, every employer was delighted. They said 'If John and Jim are doing it, we are all for it. It should have gone into effect 20 years ago.' We have a definition, too, as to socialism which we apply in considering all legislative proposals. It is this: Does this weaken the personal initiative? If it does, however that law is worded, it is socialistic. Does it stiffen the back of the worker, does it energize his will? If so, no matter how it is worded, it is not socialistic. It is unendurable that 51 per cent of the population can control 49 per cent, but I think there is a type of social insurance which is something like the education of the young. We all know we should do it so we express a common judgment in terms of agreement which is, in a word, compulsion. Compulsion is nothing but a common judgment expressed in terms of agreement. In many of our states they know that the boys should be trained and made worth while but not one starts this work because Jim is waiting for John. Through compulsion employers insure against accidents. I was against it at first; I thought it would weaken the employees. However, no one puts his finger voluntarily into a saw. We can go by the road toward compulsion if we have the intelligence for it."

Dr. Frederick L. Hoffman, Third Vice President and Statistician Prudential Life Insurance Co., Newark, N. J.:

"I think it very false and illogical to draw from statistics concerning poor derelicts on the scrap heap, conclusions supposed to be applicable to the health of millions of wage earners who work honestly for a living. These derelicts are in poverty, always have been in poverty, and that condition is congenital in many of them. They are ignorant or imbecile in many cases—not competent. First, as to the how or why of social insurance, we must get that from only ountry in the world. The evidence from any is overwhelmingly against it, showing be a wrongful practice as indicated by all ts during the past six or seven years. These iow that malingering has enormously in- d. The only country we care about is ind. If the evidence available from Eng- in 1911 showed that it was a success, they have had it here—the American Associa- for Labor Legislation. They would have rom a thousand and one medical officers, leaders, and so forth, overwhelming evi- proving its success. Here is a book by am Brend entitled 'Health and the State.' in indictment so condemning that it simply nothing for the English system and shows it leads to ruin of the independent laboring nt of that country.

BRITISH INVESTIGATION PROPOSED

think we should make a fair and impartial tigation in England of their system and find whether we should be for or against Their material is not in any foreign lan- e and the laboring people there are very like our own. On the other hand, I think eed a more constructive health program. n no country having health insurance has been any lower death rate than we have without it. The moment you hand out a y inducement to be sick and to stay sick, urse you hinder all other agencies to remedy conditions making people sick. Now, this ther so or it is not so, and we want to find he truth. The people who have gone abroad udy the question have been loaded up with ents by government officials. They have d the great praise of the German system and shouldn't they? The German Government ted out 30 years ago to make other govern- ts follow their example and it has been back very movement along this line. Why has Canada adopted it if it is so wonderful? y has not Japan, Argentine or Brazil, if it uch a wonderful panacea as claimed?

Would it not be a fine thing to establish a r class in this country such as these college fessors talk about? They seem to have this he brain. We have no labor class. We have bor element but no class in which anyone is a and stays as in England and Germany. moment you establish social insurance reby a class can get free doctors from the e you will have a class different from the free independent American we now know.

The National Civic Federation has done at service in the study of social insurance. 1914 it sent a commission abroad consisting Mr. P. T. Sherman, Mr. J. W. Sullivan and Arthur Williams, and their report was of at value. It was the only document in Eng- that was available at that time. Of great ie also are the proceedings of the conference social insurance called by The National Civic leration in 1914. These publications have a profound influence on the thought of im- tial statesmen and others instrumental in s far defeating the plans and purposes of se who have been making propaganda for com- sory health insurance."

s Helen Varick Boswell, Chairman Industrial Committee, Federation of Women's Clubs, New York:

'I am for education and against compulsion. ave not yet heard of the thing to take the ce of compulsion which I should like to r."

n Roach, Chief, Bureau of Hygiene and Sanitation, New Jersey Department of Labor (Leather Workers' Union), Newark:

'Social insurance is a scheme of doubtful ue. The problem confronting us all is an nomic one and we are trying to apply a medical cure. What you want to do is to try to put the workman on his feet so he can buy his own medicine in his own way. I doubt very much whether the amiable and well-disposed people as well as the uplifters who have taken a deep interest in those matters—I doubt whether they want to see social justice done to the workers. You are not rendering social justice to the man or woman who is selling his or her labor—you are not giving social justice simply because you send a doctor to them. Go into a bank or counting house and talk with a three or four thousand dollar a year man and he will tell you about the outrageous demands the average worker is making in the sale of his labor. In Newark the ship-workers are making $50 a week. Why shouldn't they make more than the bank clerk? Very likely it takes more training and it is a lot more disagreeable. But the trend of opinion seems to be that the men and women who are trying to get social justice are doing some wrong to society and that we ought to devise some scheme that will satisfy them, but in my opinion it should not be less than actual social justice. Social insurance does not hit the mark.

"This question of spreading education is good. There are lots of things the employer can do. One thing he should not be made to do is to bear any burden for health insurance. But employers of labor are doing some mighty good things.

"Local boards of health have not measured up to their responsibilities. In the larger industrial communities, what have we? Sometimes a few clinics but none where an average man for a small sum can get good medical attendance. If he has not a cent and applies to charity he can get good treatment. I think present machinery should be utilized before more complex machinery is demanded."

P. Tecumsch Sherman, Attorney and Social Insurance Specialist, New York:

"The important feature about this intense movement for health insurance in this country, as it strikes me, is that it is not for complete health insurance but merely for sickness insurance. That is, for short sicknesses. Health insurance must cover also long sicknesses, infirmities, permanent disability or invalidity. I have searched Europe pretty thoroughly and I have found no form of compulsory *short* sickness insurance that does not injure the public health. I was in England in 1914 at the outbreak of the war, at which time unfortunately our investigations were stopped. But I met Mr. Sullivan in London and the first sentiment we agreed on was that this health insurance scheme is opposed to the public health. I think Dr. Brend's book will explain why. But everyone in England who has investigated the subject knows that if you go out and hire doctors to give public contract medical service, that medical service will be a sham, a danger and a disgrace. I have gone from Glasgow all the way to London looking into this matter, in factories, hotels, private dwellings, etc., inquiring into the experience of the insured. You all have an idea that the English worker is now insured—that is, that he is sure of medical attendance, and so on. But he isn't. Suppose he gets sick; he goes to a doctor —to a sort of corner grocery arrangement—and sits on a bench. When his turn comes the doctor sees him, gives him a certificate of disability and a prescription or directions to go to the hospital. He may be dying, but the doctor may not help him any further than that. He goes to a hospital and can't get in. The prescription may not be filled at the drug store because the last year's bills have not been paid—for the reason that the drug fund would not go around. I tell you this to show the foolishness of the whole thing. That is how things were when the war broke out.

PUBLIC HEALTH MENACED

"Now, I do not say that that same thing would necessarily happen here—only that is what compulsory insurance has actually amounted to. If you do have compulsory insurance, let the men choose their associations, then let those associations choose the doctors. I think then probably they would get a very much better medical service; but it would be very hard on the doctors.

"I do not believe in a general collective medical service. I do not believe in thousands of men contracting collectively with doctors to give them a common service. I believe the proper relations between doctor and patient are the individual relations we now have; and I think a large proportion of the American working men want to be in a position where they can employ doctors of their own choice and have the present personal relations with them. I think to force compulsory insurance, with a practically pauper medical service, upon the self sufficient class of our working people would injure the public health and cause universal dissatisfaction.

"Another point against compulsory sickness insurance is that involved in insuring money benefits—sick pay—for a short time illness. I do not know of any way in which you can insure men money for being sick; that is, offer them money to be sick and not go to work, without increasing lost time by a certain class at the expense of the other classes of the insured.

"I have heard that the sickness societies in France, which are voluntary, select their members, are small, organized generally on trade union lines, and insuring only small benefits, succeed in holding down impositions. I understand that the general opinion there is that there is not ten per cent of fraud on the benefits. I was going over to investigate that question when the war broke out. But certainly such is not the fact in Germany nor in England. When I say benefits are imposed upon, do not get the idea that the industrious people are imposing. It is the parasite, the down-and-outer who, by compulsory insurance, is forced in on an equality with the best class, and entitled to the same rights. I have never seen any form of money benefit insurance for sickness *like that*, that would succeed. I have heard it said over in England that sickness is not an insurable risk, that is, *short* sickness. You cannot insure a man 66 2-3 per cent of his wages for all disabling sickness, because there is no criterion of such sickness. Am I too sick to go to work today? I can get a doctor's certificate that I am. Therefore, would an insurance company pay me two-thirds of my earnings? No. There is no criterion of such sickness. It depends upon the doctor you have.

"I am talking very strongly against one line of social insurance. I am not such a bigot against compulsion when it comes to the real insurable subjects. I am against socialism *prima facie;* but there might be times and conditions when it might be expedient for the state to compel men to insure against old age and invalidity.

"The campaign for health insurance in this country is built up upon a tissue of gross, deadly lies, lies, lies! Simply a system of lies emanating from the father of lies. It is false in every particular. They are trying to delude the people; and what I am afraid of now is, they have deluded the people. This is what they did at one hearing—they represented that an employer and his workman could each put in $7, and the workman get back benefits that couldn't be provided for $150. In course of amendments to the Davenport bill they cut the benefits to two-thirds and still promised more than they could give for the money. All along they have been telling fairy tales, until a great many intelligent, studious people are thinking you can put a penny in here and get $10 back. You cannot do it. God save America!"

Do the Co-operatives Offer a Solution?

(Continued from page 4)

manufacturer, carries stocks to serve a more or less extended zone or district, and has an organization suitable for selling not to individual consumers, but in quantities to fit community needs as bought by dealers.

In this form distribution has worked itself out the world around. From olden times to the present and from New York to Shanghai, either way around the earth, this constitutes the backbone of the system by which the bulk of commodities is transferred from maker to user.

TENDENCY IS TO SPECIALIZE

It represents the natural endency of man to specialize. Production, distribution and consumption are three separate and distinct economic phases. They are utterly different in nature and requirements. Combining them under a single ownership does not eliminate the functions to be performed or the labor of fulfilling them. This existing division accommodates itself not only to man's nature, but to his geographical distribution in cities, towns, villages and on farms scattered across the land.

Before attempting to see how the several endeavors in the way of chain store systems, cooperative schemes, manufacturers' stores, etc., to eliminate the middlemen compare with the ordinary system we have just examined, let us consider the problem from the producer's viewpoint for a moment.

Take the manufacturer in the sketch for example, situated adjacent to a large territorial area in which are millions of people, all of whom wear shoes and most of whom presumably could under favorable circumstances be induced to use his products.

But how can the individuals of a nation scattered over a great area be approached individually by the manufacturer? He does not know who they are or where they are. He cannot write to them all. He is in one place, they are in thousands of other places; the cost of sending traveling representatives to serve these individual consumers would be prohibitive.

Even if he could find some way of getting them to order by mail without seeing or trying on his shoes, how would the matter stand? Supposing the school teacher had by chance had a pair of his shoes which were exactly right and knew the current price and sent him the money by mail for a duplicate pair. This order for a single pair would entail about the same work as a wholesaler's order for a thousand pair;—the letter must be opened, read, the money counted and compared with the price list, records entered in cash books, etc., the particular style and size of shoe picked out in the stock room, special packing and wrapping and individual addressing of the package, provided besides records and receipts for reference in case the teacher complains that the shoes never reached her. And then commences another series of labors in transporting and delivering this pair of shoes disproportionately great as compared with the same work on a case shipment or carload of shoes. This parcel must be called for or delivered to the express company or post office. The address must be examined and classified and the package routed. This must be done over and over again, involving the use of expensive human time and attention at each new stage of the journey. Two pairs could go about as cheaply as one,—a dozen as two.

It is not the weight of the package so much as the care necessary to be bestowed in the handling and re-handling of each individual consignment whether large or small.

WHERE EXPENSE MULTIPLIES

Retail operations should be confined to the local retail store. To require the manufacturer and the transportation systems to perform these unescapable retail operations is to multiply expense.

The manufacturer is a specialist engrossed in the operations of production—contracting for raw materials, providing plant, equipment, machinery, organizing for its upkeep and operation, dealing with labor and administration. In the nature of things he is not organized to handle retail orders at the factory.

And as to transportation, it is an elementary economic principle that goods should be transported in bulk to as near the point of consumption as possible. Therefore, the factory will ship in great consignments, the needs of a whole zone to the zone centers A, B, C, etc. There the goods are subdivided and shipped in community lots to the towns surrounding the centers. There in retail stores the retail operations of filling individual consumers' needs can best be performed. This discloses the falsity of most of the appeals to "buy direct from the maker and save middlemen's expenses."

Now let us see whether the chain stores, the department stores, the mail order houses, the manufacturer's own stores or any cooperation plans really succeed in eliminating either the wholesaler or the retailer. The producer and consumer we know are principals who cannot be eliminated.

The department store aims to eliminate the jobber (wholesaler). Does it do it?

In principle the department store is a collection of stores in different lines of business under one roof. At the head of each sub-store or department is a buyer and manager, a paid employee who takes the place of the proprietor of the ordinary specialty store, so that there is a change of form but not of essence in this regard. Some of the departments of the larger department stores in the greatest centers do buy direct from manufacturers, thus appearing to eliminate the wholesaler (jobber). But generally speaking they do not buy in genuine jobbing quantities or accept deliveries of stock in advance of seasons or carry stocks ahead as do the jobbers. This has necessitated that manufacturers who cater to this department store trade establish their own branch warerooms in the leading centers for the convenience of these customers so that in place of the independent jobber we have the manufacturer setting up what amounts to a jobbing business with his own capital—a change of form but not of substance. Nothing has been eliminated. No labor has been saved—merely the producer assumes what was previously the jobber's job.

But several other associated facts should be borne in mind. Most department stores buy largely from jobbers. Some lines of goods they buy "direct" but still as a department store carrying full assortments, not a one could exist without the service of the jobber with his ready stocks to supply their "fill-in" orders between seasons and the incidental convenience items that they only buy in small lots. Therefore, to the extent that they do buy direct and cause the establishment of manufacturers' warerooms for their convenience, they are superimposing these new substitute-jobbers upon the already existing system of jobbing establishments which must be continued for the service of ordinary stores and even for their own use on goods they cannot buy direct. Therefore, instead of eliminating they have added to the complexity of the distributing machinery and somewhat to the expense. It may not be without significance that even before the world war the most striking advances in the cost of living were concurrent with the great development of the various methods calculated to eliminate and save middlemen. It cannot, however, be implied that they were alone responsible for it. Again as to department stores, it must be remembered that those really falling under this head are to be found only in our very largest cities. They are adapted to serve o in congested centers of population and that e in these centers they are so far from the ho of the residents that smaller neighborhood sto and specialty stores do many times the volu of trade of all the department stores of a c put together. They are therefore an insign cant factor in the whole system of distributi of a nation.

WHAT THE CHAIN STORE ATTEMPTS

Next take the chain stores. Chain stor in contrast to the department store, may be scribed as a multiple system of establishme under one ownership and in one line of bu ness under different roofs. They are found the grocery, drug, hardware, hat, shoe, clothir haberdashery, candy, cigar and other lines. So combinations operate over a thousand stores a stretch from coast to coast. Obviously they not eliminate the retail store because they a essentially local retail stores themselves. Do th eliminate the jobber?

Take a typical chain store concern doing bu ness in the Eastern states. Its headquarters a in New York. Here it buys for a hundred stor It orders in genuine jobbing quantities just does the ordinary jobber who sells to sever hundred stores. At its headquarters it has large staff of buyers and a warehouse at whi it receives its goods from the manufacture But how do these goods reach its branch store They must be stored, held in stock, orders r ceived from branches, the goods packed, bille shipped and accounted for exactly as in a jobbing concern. Assume that it has one two stores in Portland, Me. Numerous sma shipments must go from New York to Portlan The ordinary small independent store in Por land, however, can buy from jobbers in Por land who carry stocks bought for dozens of r tail dealers in and around Portland and brough there direct from the factory in great bulk. Ha there been intrinsic gain or loss in this attem to eliminate the wholesaler? I submit that amounts only to a change of form with gener disadvantage in the change.

We need not go on through the list to disse the operation of each of the other methods a tempted in the hope of "eliminating the middl man". We may content ourselves with an e amination of the manufacturer who sets up hi own stores and the purest cooperative systems o consumer-owned systems. If the same old mid dlemen continue to bob up in some form or othe we may accept them as inevitable and see wher hope really remains.

TAKES UP THE JOBBER'S WORK

Chains of manufacturer-owned shoe stores ar among the commonest of this type. The produce deals "direct" with the consumer. True, th company which owns the stores where the con sumers buy, makes the shoes. But there is n marked difference between the stores and thos of independent retail shoe dealers. They per form the same functions in about the same meth ods and a paid manager takes the place of th customary proprietor on the principle of th absentee landlord in agriculture. It may also b noted that whereas the independent local deale represents the consumer, the local manager o the chain store represents the manufacturer an is restricted to the products of one company in stead of choosing among many.

The place of the jobber is taken by the manu facturers' own warehouses set up in centra points from which the goods are distributed t the local stores of the company. As a matte of fact chain shoe stores are generally confine to large and medium sized cities and in th smaller towns local shoe dealers act as agent for these same companies buying "direct" fron the manufacturer, but receiving their stock through the same branch warehouses whic the stores of the companies. It is a com- ary upon the economy involved in the sys- to note that the independent "agent" deal- re sold on terms that enable them to sell to imers at the same prices as the company- d stores. Nothing has been eliminated; the ch warehouses of the factory are merely sub- te jobbers. Invariably the functions of esaler and retailer must be performed and nly change is in the name of the machinery doing it.

inally, how do consumer-owned cooperative rprises function on this proposition of elimi- on?

air examples are found in the great coopera- societies of England and Scotland.

he customary process in the formation of e enterprises is for the people of a com- ity to join together and each to subscribe the valent of about $5 or $10 towards the capi- for setting up a local retail cooperative store ch sells both to the subscribing members and he general public, but dividends based upon profits of the store are paid to the subscrib- not in proportion to their stock holdings, to their purchases at the store.

hey start out then by *not* eliminating the re- store but by establishing a new one in the nmunity and owning it themselves.

"COOPS" GO TO THE SOURCE

Although many of these "coop" stores buy in t or mainly from ordinary jobbers, the ma- ity have joined in setting up their own co- rative wholesale societies. Thus the con- ers own the retail stores and the retail stores n their own jobbers. Single ones of these olesale "societies" do a business of several idred million dollars a year, selling exclusive- to the cooperative retail stores. So great are ir operations that they also own several fac- ies and on foreign continents own their own ntations and warehouses. Most of the wheat ported from Canada to Scotland is for the ills of the Scottish Cooperative Wholesale So- ety. The actual producers are the employees the consumers in this enterprise.

But in these very facts of the way in which ese consumer-owned institutions organize to rform their functions, is the strongest demon- ation that the wholesale and retail middlemen nnot be eliminated. They may be owned, their ofits may be turned back to the consumers or rt of the consumers, but it is futile to start to ouy direct" or to cut out the jobber or re- iler. And the wastes and losses also must be rne by the consumer and it must not be over- oked that these "coop" stores often fail or n into losses.

It remains to be considered whether in spite the non-elimination of middlemen the coopera- re society and the other recent types of dis- ibutors merit the measure of success they en- y or whether they are psychological rather an economic phenomena, temporary and pass- g.

As to the cooperative store system it may be lmitted that there is no saving in the machinery distribution. Even to the matter of travel- g salesmen representing the wholesale socie- es and calling upon the very retail stores which vn them, all of the paraphernalia of the or- nary jobbing and retail system is duplicated. he wholesale societies find that it is necessary explain their wares, answer questions and ob- ctions and stimulate the managers of the re- il stores to order more and new goods and ey maintain a large staff of travelers to ac- omplish these and other purposes. Advertis- g is similarly employed.

If they do all of the work of the conventional stributing system and eliminate none, where ay they be expected to make savings for their onsumers?

The second of our tests referred to saving unearned or unreasonable profits taken under the existing distributing system. Can the cooperative or other large retail institutions maintain themselves more efficiently and cheaply and thus make savings and earnings to the ultimate users of commodities?

ON A KEEN COMPETITIVE BASIS

Or do the ordinary wholesalers and retailers extort exorbitant profits offering a chance to puncture inflated prices on that account? They are on a keenly competitive basis. They compete with each other and also with the chain stores, manufacturers' stores and department stores. If there were any general, willful overcharging, it would seem as though it would immediately react to drive trade from those who indulged in it. Yet the vitality and persistence of the stores and jobbers of the old order baffle and annoy those who look for and seek their early removal. On the other hand, the growth of department stores, chain stores and especially of the great "coop" systems of Europe and the popular impression in some quarters that they can and do undersell the small stores which obtain their goods through customary channels has caused them to be sometimes hailed as deliverers from the burdens of the high living costs which have grown so persistently higher and their commercial success is accepted as proof of fitness.

Yet if all the work of the old system remains to be done under the new, one must wonder whether it is because a hired manager of a store which he does not own is necessarily more capable or interested or efficient than the owner-proprietor whom he is intended to replace. Do people ordinarily work better for others than for themselves? Do they watch the small economies, have they the incentives for hard work, close supervision and skillful management when others take the profits or stand the losses? Will the managers, foremen and laborers work harder, produce more or take less wages in a factory owned by absent consumers than in one of the ordinary variety?

We are back upon old questions here and argument will lead nowhere.

But in a briefer concluding article under the title "Dissecting the Consumer's $" in the next issue of this publication, we will examine the facts obtainable as to the comparative operating costs and methods of the newer distributors beside the old. We will take the consumer's Dollar apart and see how much of it goes for the production of the goods, how much for the maker's expenses and profits, how much to the wholesaler and what toll and profit the retailer takes.

Costs should be lower. There is a way of saving even though we cannot eliminate any of the links in the distributing chain. It is not to discourage effort by showing what cannot be done that this article is written, but to save misdirected effort and divert it into fruitful channels. This the subsequent article will also attempt.

Pacifists Abet the Huns

(Continued from page 11)

the Allies cannot but call for severest censure. The greater their eminence in sociological and welfare work, so much the greater becomes the effectiveness of the service—undoubtedly unintentionally—performed by these people in the interests of the Huns. There is no escaping what is unpleasantly obvious. The action of the Women's International Conference merely supplements the propaganda against the treaty which is being intensively carried on in Germany and is furthered by German agents and sympathizers in America and the Allied countries under the specious guise of promoting justice and securing peace.

Commenting upon the proposal made by a British delegate that women be represented in the League of Nations and that she be appointed a member of the council, Miss Addams is quoted as saying: "Such a scheme cannot be realized, for in America at the present day none is more detested than the pacifist."

"Detested," beyond peradventure of doubt, are all those pacifists who opposed America's entry into the war, who campaigned for an indecisive premature peace by negotiation, and who, in now agitating against the terms of the treaty and the so-called "crushing" of Germany, whether they know it or not, are engaged in no less a task than the effort to make futile the hard-won victory of America and the Allies and make of the peace merely a period of recuperation and easy rehabilitation for Germany —a resting and a breathing space for preparations for a conflict again to come.

Out of Their Own Mouths

(Continued from page 15)

was to stimulate social discontent, civil war and revolution in every country on the globe. Mr. Villard's *Nation* took up and championed the Bolshevist cause after Germany had launched it in Russia. And now Mr. Villard, apoplectic in his rage and despair, vengefully prophesies "the great revolution to whose support the friends of freedom must now rally everywhere." He declares: "Versailles has forced men into two main camps, the radicals and the reactionaries. * * * With Germany crushed and autocracy enthroned, with the strong hand of power at the throat of liberty, the battle opens which is to make men free." And he says, as't were piously: "Heaven grant that the revolution may be peaceful, and that it may destroy only to rebuild."

Did not Germany naively threaten, in case the Allies imposed drastic terms, to go Bolshevist and with the aid of Russia, to drag the other nations with her into chaos? Did the official German organs, in order to intimidate the Allied council, not threaten to make an alliance with the Russian Bolsheviki and precipitate world revolution? Did not the *New Republic* and Mr. Walter Lippmann draw dire pictures of what would happen if the Allies prevented "a contented population in Germany" and the Central Powers were "forced" by excessive demands into Bolshevism? Does not the gentle Mr. Villard simply reecho the Hun's attempt at intimidation?

In much that appeared in the *New Republic* and the *Nation* during the past few years there was a strangely, if not pleasantly, familiar ring. And what is now being said in plain words in these sheets could not better serve the Hun interests, or more accurately articulate the Hun point of view. Hun rage and resentment over the treaty, if it were written in Berlin. There is undoubted sincerity in these impassioned, vituperative jeremiads against the treaty — indeed, there is manifest such deep stirring of feeling as becomes reckless of discretion and restraint. At last it is evident the gentlemen of the staffs of these journals write frankly and outspokenly, just as they feel; at last the tepid insipidity and drakish dullness of these sheets give way to a real enthusiasm albeit more shrewish than virile. And, as often happens, truth is blurted out in hysteria and fury just as it oft comes out in wine. By their own words, by their honest rage and rebellion, by this final chapter of their war record writ by themselves without hypocrisy or dissimulation, and which at last exposes the keynote and makes transparently clear all that was camouflaged in a maze of academic verbiage and ambiguous idealism before, the *New Republic* and the *Nation* stand self-interpreted, finally, adequately and unmistakably self-revealed.

Recognize the Omsk Government

APPEAL TO THE AMERICAN AND ALLIED NATIONS FOR A PERMANENT PEACE IN RUSSIA

By LIEUTENANT BORIS BRASOL

VICE CHAIRMAN OF THE VOLUNTARY ASSOCIATION OF THE RUSSIAN ARMY AND NAVY OFFICERS IN THE UNITED STATES

UNDER the heavy blows of Admiral Kolchak's forces, the Bolsheviki defense lines are crumbling along the entire Eastern Front. The Great Russian artery, the Volga, is on the verge of being captured by the anti-Bolshevist forces led by the Omsk Government. General Denikine's troops in the south of Russia are threatening the existence of the soviets in the Little Russian regions. The Finnish and Esthonian troops, under command of General Judenich, are at the very gates of Petrograd. The Polish drive against the Bolsheviki, under General Pilsudski, is menacing the Bolshevist rule from the West. The gallant Rumanian army is battling against the Red Army along the entire Bessarabian border. Finally, in the far North, the Allied troops, reinforced by loyal Russian units, have succeeded in driving the red gangs back to the South, and thus the Bolsheviki, after a year and a half of tyrannical rule, find themselves encircled from the North and South, from the East and West, and the hour of their downfall is rapidly approaching.

The time for action has come. Hesitation is no longer justified, therefore it is no longer possible. All the anti-Bolshevist forces in Russia, with minor exceptions, are under the supreme authority of Admiral Kolchak. Both General Denikine and General Judenich have pledged their support to Admiral Kolchak, and their military operations are fully coordinated with those of the Siberian forces. Within a short period of time Admiral Kolchak has succeeded in suppressing the Bolshevist movement throughout Siberia, in establishing law and order in the regions controlled by him, in regenerating the national spirit among the soldiers of the young and brave Siberian army, and finally in setting up a stable government with strong administrative branches all through Siberia and in the Seven River region. Notwithstanding tremendous difficulties which Admiral Kolchak had to overcome, notwithstanding the chaos which reigned in Siberia at the time when he made his first step to overthrow the red rule, he succeeded in conquering the sympathies of the Siberian population at large. It was not by means of sentimental phrases that Admiral Kolchak won his success; it was due to the iron will of this man who fears nothing, who is cool-headed both in success and danger, and whose chivalrous bravery is well known throughout Russia that a constructive policy could be started in the Far East.

It is not only the right, it is, certainly, the supreme duty of the American people to give their open support to the Omsk Government.

It is no longer possible to cling to a policy of "no policy" toward Russia. It is no longer possible to display a selfish indifference towards the unspeakable sufferings of a great nation which is struggling for its liberty, for its very existence; nor is it longer possible to reject Admiral Kolchak's authority on the basis of the theory that he is a "dictator," that he was not chosen by the people through regular parliamentary methods. *Anarchy is a brutal force; anarchy can be combatted by force only;* under the prevailing conditions bayonets must precede electional campaigns. Admiral Kolchak has stated quite distinctly and on various occasions that he is going to lead the Russian people to the convocation of a National Assembly; he took an oath, and as a man of honor he will uphold it, that he would merely consider himself as a

LIEUT. BORIS BRASOL

temporary ruler, and that he would lead the nation to the polls. Parliamentary life, however, is practically impossible in a country where utmost ruin is the basis of economic conditions and where wholesale starvation is a feature of national life. Anarchy must be crushed in order to give the people the opportunity to work out a national policy of their own and such a political status which would best fit their historical traditions and national aspirations.

There are moments in history when a dictatorship is the only path to liberty, and this is exactly what has been proclaimed by the Omsk Government: "*To liberty—through dictatorship.*" There is no other choice: Russia will either remain Bolshevist, which would constitute a menace to the civilization of the whole world, or she will become free and a "fit partner" of the civilized world, provided she succeeds in breaking the Bolshevist chains and eliminating the very memory of Trotzky's disgraceful rule from the minds of the Russian people.

There are two practical ways of helping the Omsk Government: (a) The United States Government, as well as the governments of the Allied nations, ought to recognize immediately the Omsk Government as a *de facto All-Russian Provisional Government;* (b) the American people should render practical assistance to the Omsk Government by means of equipping Admiral Kolchak's forces with ammunition which is no longer needed by the United States Army. The recognition of the Omsk Government will automatically weaken the Bolshevist cause not only throughout Russia but throughout the world, and at the same time will strengthen the anti-Bolshevist cause as such, and the political situation of Admiral Kolchak. This will also stop the insidious pro-German propaganda throughout Siberia, whose aim it is to sow discord among the Allies and to raise a feeling of hatred towards the latter on the part of the Russian people.

Mere phrases will never compel the Russians to believe that the people over here are in sympathy with their national future. This must be proven; this can be proved by means of recognition of the Omsk Government as an organized endeavor to free Russia from the bloody tyranny of the Lenines and Trotzkys. Moreover, the recognition of the Omsk Government as an All-Russian Provisional Government will give a legal title and moral impetus to the activities of Admiral Kolchak and his associates. However successful will be the military operations of Admiral Kolchak, there will always remain a shadow of doubt in the minds of the Russian people as to the legal authority of the Omsk Government as long as the latter remains unrecognized by the Allied nations. It is more support that we ask and that we expect to get from the American people; it is a word of encouragement to the loyal Russian forces that we hope to hear from those who are themselves loyal to the best American traditions and to the highest American ideals.

It must be clearly understood that a partial solution of the Russian problem, namely, the recognition of the Omsk Government as a local Siberian Government, would inevitably weaken its position and would encourage factional differences among the loyal Russians themselves. On the contrary, the recognition of the Omsk Government as an All-Russian Provisional Government would induce the loyal Russian factions to pledge their entire support to Admiral Kolchak and his administration. *Furthermore, a clear Russian policy towards the Entente Powers is as vital as a clear policy on the part of the Entente Powers toward Russia.* A national policy can be worked out only by a national government; therefore it is to the advantage of this country, as well as of the Allied nations, to see Russia as soon as possible guided by one government responsible to the people.

The Peace Treaty, which is going to outline a new map for Europe, may prove to be a failure unless a loyal Russian government will approve by its responsible signature the new order established by the World Conference. It should be borne in mind that the Central European question, the dominant problem of the Peace Conference, can not and will not be settled without a solution of the Russian problem. Invisible links are tying up the fate of the Middle European peoples with that of Russia's future. The loyal Russian Government, if recognized by the Allies, will be duty bound to support the decisions of the Parisian Peace Conference. On the contrary, should the Allies neglect to recognize the Omsk Government before the Treaty has been signed, they cannot expect the Omsk Government to follow and support the decisions outlined by the Entente Powers. This would lead to a series of grave political disturbances immediately after the treaty is signed; this would inevitably convert Europe into the "Balkans of the world."

The League of Nations itself would prove to be a failure were the greatest European power—the Russian link—left out of its chain. Therefore, the recognition of the Omsk Government is not a matter of political taste, but a matter of political wisdom. The sooner a formal recognition of the Omsk Government, as above outlined, is brought about, the more chance there is that the actual unfortunate political situation throughout Europe will be solved in a way which will enable the Entente Powers to affirm that they have really won the greatest war and that they have achieved a lasting peace.

History has taught the civilized world that peace without victory over Germany cannot be maintained. Let us not forget that victory without peace in Russia is but an imaginary victory which can be easily converted into an overwhelming defeat of the sublime principles of Civilization and Justice.

Tyrrel Print, New York.

The National
Civic Federation Review

Vol. IV. NEW YORK, JUNE 30, 1919 No. 16

LABOR VOICES ITS PATRIOTISM

AMERICAN FEDERATION'S CONVENTION AT ATLANTIC CITY MAKES SPLENDID RECORD ON GREAT DOMESTIC AND INTERNATIONAL QUESTIONS

By CHESTER M. WRIGHT

AMERICAN Labor has just closed its most important convention. Not even the great war time conventions in Buffalo and St. Paul recorded so much of vital and lasting interest to the American nation, for the convention just closed was important to the whole people of America. Questions of fundamental citizenship were discussed and acted upon in Atlantic City, as well as questions of interest only to the workers.

There are two main thoughts that indicate the drive of opinion as it found expression in the convention.

> 1—Whatever tends to undermine the institutions of the American democracy or to disintegrate the machinery of the American trade union movement must be contested at every step and defeated.
>
> 2—Autocratic rule, where it still obtains in industry, must be overcome in order that there may be an orderly and steady improvement in the condition of all life through legitimate trade union activity.

There is not anything particularly new about the strong development of feeling upon these two lines, but there was a new emphasis placed upon them, due primarily to new conditions, and to new factors in the life of the nation.

It is impossible to get a view of the convention by a process of vivisection. The sessions formed a cumulative process in which threads of various kinds were woven into one fabric.

SAMUEL GOMPERS

There was the action of the convention on the question of Bolshevism. The convention came down flat-footed and with the utmost vigor in denying support to Bolshevism, but the entire feeling of Labor on the question of Bolshevism is not apparent until other declarations of the convention are considered, nor until the whole spirit of the convention is taken into account.

There were three resolutions dealing directly with the question of Russia, all of which involved the issue of Bolshevism in one form or another. The Resolutions Committee offered as a substitute the following, which was adopted unanimously:

> Resolved, that this convention express its well-considered conviction that the United States Government should withdraw all American troops from Russian soil at the earliest possible moment, and be it further
>
> Resolved, that this convention refuse its endorsement of the Soviet Government of Russia or any other form of government in that country until the peoples of Russia, through a constituent or other form of national assembly shall have established a truly democratic form of government.

Without making the application direct, however, the convention went more deeply into the question of Bolshevism and struck nearer to fundamental principles in adopting the report of the committee on Executive Council's report declaring that American Labor believes that every element in society has the right to a voice in society. This, of course, means absolute condemnation of Bolshevism everywhere as well as of any other form of dictatorship.

The voice of the convention was emphatic in denying the request for an all-inclusive amnesty. The convention felt that the Government had acted wisely and properly in committing to prison enemies who had actually attempted the undoing of the country while at war and it clearly felt that to release such prisoners at this time would be a mistake from which no good could come. Clear emphasis, however, was laid upon that portion of the declaration calling for a repeal of wartime legislation affecting the freedom of expression and assembly.

One of the most important declarations of the convention in this work of clearing away obstacles to freedom of action and to democratic progress, was a strong declaration adopted on the question of judicial construction of law. This question was so important and was so strongly emphasized by the convention itself that expression of the determination of the trade union movement was widely read and noted.

Branching out in the two directions I have specified and acting with equal vigor and determination in both directions, the whole spirit of the convention was probably best expressed in a paragraph from the opening address delivered by President Gompers in which he said:

"The workers of the world are determined that this new concept of the relation between man and man and this new concept of the right of the workers to have a voice in the determination of the conditions of their labor and their lives shall be recognized."

It may be well by way of amplification, and to make the meaning more clear, to give just three or four additional sentences from that opening address:

"The principles for which this labor movement has been contending from its very inception must come to full fruition," said Mr. Gompers, "we are making no unjust or unwarranted demands upon employers or upon society as such, but for the service which the men and women of labor give to society—the service without which civilization itself would perish—for that service we insist upon a return that would give us the opportunity to live a full, rounded life and to make of this country of ours and this world of ours, a place worthy of the civilization of our time."

SUMMARY OF CONVENTION'S WORK

It was in that spirit and in furtherance of the dominant desire to clear the road of autocratic obstacles to progress and to keep it free from the contaminating and destroying influence of Bolshevism that the convention acted upon the most important questions in the manner indicated in the following partial summary:

1—Endorsed the League of Nations covenant and Labor's Bill of Rights as contained in the Treaty of Peace, urging the workers of America to support the Treaty.

2—Denounced in detailed bill of particulars the "company union" plan of labor organization.

3—Demanded the removal of the Postmaster General from office.

4—Denounced the proposed strike for Thomas J. Mooney and declared that he should have a fair trial.

5—Enacted a provision to prevent central bodies or outside organizations from taking a strike vote of the membership of international organizations.

6—Adopted a strong resolution in furtherance of a campaign to organize the iron and steel workers. (An organizing committee for this purpose held two enthusiastic meetings during the convention and laid plans for an energetic continuance of the campaign. President Gompers resigned the chairmanship to which John Fitzpatrick of Chicago was unanimously elected.)

7—Declined to alter the established political action policy of the Federation because of unlimited proof of the success and superiority of the policy as stood.

8—Adopted the report of the special committee on Reconstruction with the following explanatory comment submitted by the Committee: "Your committee recommends approval of this program not because it believes it all-comprehensive, but fundamental; not because of its novelty, but because it is founded on experience and justice."

9—Declared in favor of prohibition of immigration for a fixed number of years and especially during the period of readjustment.

10—Adopted a program for guidance in educational work consisting of 25 numbered clauses and having no relation to the report of a special committee appointed by the Executive Council under direction of the St. Paul Convention, to investigate and report upon the workings of schools operated by labor organizations or by cooperation between labor organizations and public school authorities.

By far the most strenuous debate of the convention raged around the treaty of peace, though the vote for approval, 29,909 to 1,860, indicates the sweeping and conclusive character of the endorsement. Andrew Furuseth, president of the Seamen's Union, made a determined attack on the treaty, specifically on the covenant of the League of Nations and on the section known as "Labor's Bill of Rights." This brought out the heaviest fighting equipment of the pro-treaty forces and caused President Gompers to deliver what many consider one of the greatest speeches of his life.

Treating the whole broad subject of the coming peace, the committee's report contained also this constructive proclamation of democracy's purpose as opposed to the philosophy of despair and the tactics of desperation which Bolshevism seeks to implant in our national life:

The past has gone forever. Autocracy and militarism, we hope, are buried with it. The future is our immediate concern. Ignoring what has gone before except so far as the lessons taught, we shall build along the lines of reason, judgment and the experiences gained.

Typifying democracy and its true spirit, the labor movements the world over, if they be true to themselves and to the best interests of the masses for which they speak, must recognize that democracy in its truest sense, and act on the fundamental principles of equality, justice and humanity.

All elements of society are necessary for the highest development and greater progress in civilization, economically, socially and politically.

The world's war brought to a triumphant conclusion has prepared the world for democracy on the political field. The mere ending of the war, however, has not insured democracy and justice for the workers on the industrial field. It has not materially changed working and living conditions, but it has aroused fresh hope and quickened aspirations and labor's ambitions. It has created the opportunity whereby the workers regardless of abode can, if functioning through trade unions, more readily, more freely and more effectively carry forward the work of securing justice and safeguarding for labor a fuller measure of democracy in industry. It is the first duty of our own trade union movement, and in our judgment it ought to be that of the movement of other countries, to see to it that this opportunity is not destroyed by diverting the minds of the workers or by delving into the alluring realms of unproven speculative theories which judged by experiences are false and destructive in their nature.

In every phase of its effort the convention marked itself out sharp and clear as the fighting exponent of true Americanism, levelling its guns at the destroyers of democracy in whatever guise they may appear, within or without, and clinging fast only to those agencies and methods that are clearly constructive in purpose and method and democratic in operation.

How clearly this thought runs through the mind of the committee is shown in the Executive Council's report submitted to the convention and which was adopted by unanimous vote:

A careful review and unbiased observation of all the activities and accomplishments of the American Labor Movement, as related in the report of the Executive Council demonstrates

> conclusively that our movement is the peer of all organized efforts to protect and defend the rights of man and to bring into being a better life, greater happiness and a larger degree of justice and democracy.
>
> The trade-union movement, as exemplified in the report of the Executive Council, in its broadest terms is the effort of men to live the lives of men. It is the systematic struggle of the masses to attain more leisure and larger economic resources. It is the conceived movement for self and others directed against oppression in every form. It is a constant recognition of the fact that men and women of the mine, the shop, the mill, the factory, are men and women—not cattle or articles of commerce. It is a movement of protest against all conditions that tend toward the degradation of humanity.

Practical application of the expressions contained in that declaration were not wanting. It was had in the Mooney strike case and again with great emphasis in connection with the proposal emanating from Basil Manly and W. Jett Lauck of the War Labor Board for a conference of labor and employers under government auspices for discussion and action on labor problems. Under this plan Frank P. Walsh was suggested as labor's leading representative by sponsors of the plan.

When the matter was brought before the convention the result was almost unlooked for. Labor's declaration came clear and sharp and quick that it considered itself confident to select its own representatives and that in addition it had no desire for more commissions. Radicals who stood against the majority on most other questions came to the front saying that on the integrity of the labor movement as involved in this issue there could be but one front and one cause.

Immediately a telegram was sent to Senator Poindexter by President Gompers, asking him to defer action on a bill introduced embodying the Manly-Lauck plan. What the convention meant in this and in the Mooney case was that organizations not a part of the labor movement cannot come in to direct the work of the movement. Help and counsel will be accepted. Dictation will be rejected at every turn.

Not less emphatic was the convention in its analysis of the company union idea and its condemnation of that plan of organization. This declaration came to the convention in the form of a resolution introduced at the request of the National Committee for Organizing the Iron and Steel Workers. This committee later submitted a resolution to the convention designed to assist organization work. The committee also, in a meeting apart from the convention, outlined the opposition to organization in Western Pennsylvania and expressed determination to establish there the right to organize. Twenty-four national and international presidents volunteered to go into that territory, if necessary, to speak in public where the authorities have denied the organization the right to hold public meetings.

A BILL OF PARTICULARS

The resolutions that accompanied the "company union" action pointed out in their preamble the main objections to the plan. "The employers," it was stated, "are actively enforcing a series of vicious practices that hamstring such organizatons and render them useless to their employees." These practices were said to be "Unfair Elections and Representation;" "No Democratic Organization Permitted;" "Intimidation of Committeemen;" "Expert Assistance Prohibited;" "Company Union Devoid of Power;" and "Company Diverts Aim." Then the resolutions read:

> WHEREAS, In view of the foregoing facts, it is evident that company unions are unqualified to represent the interests of the workers, and that they are a delusion and a snare set up by the companies for the express purpose of deluding the workers into the belief that they have some protection and thus have no need for trade union organization; therefore, be it
>
> RESOLVED, That we heartily condemn all such company unions and advise our membership to have nothing to do with them; and, be it further
>
> RESOLVED, That we demand the right to bargain collectively through the only kind of organization fitted for this purpose, the trade union, and that we stand loyally together until this right is conceded us.

Possibly as important as almost anything that took place within the convention was an agreement that developed in the meeting of the Building Trades Department just prior to the convention. In this agreement, the building trades unions join with the American Institute of Architects, the Engineering Council, the Associated General Contractors of America, the National Association of Builders' Exchanges and the National Building Trades Employers' Association in a program for the elimination of jurisdictional strikes.

A tribunal known as the National Board of Jurisdictional Awards in the Building Industry is set up with eight members, three of which are selected by the unions and one each by the other organizations associated in the plan. The Board has power to investigate disputes and to hand down awards upon its findings. Headquarters of the board will be in Washington, but hearings may be held elsewhere when necessary. It is the hope that under the new plan disputes will not only be settled quickly, but that they will be prevented from arising by settling jurisdiction before specifications are made in cases likely to create disputes.

Fourteen negro delegates sat in the convention. They came asking a separate charter for negro workers. This desire grew out of conditions, of course, but when the four or five resolutions bearing on the question of negro organization came up it was made clear that the internationals have an eye on the situation and are striving to do their best to bring to the negro workers the full benefit of organization. The Federation declared, naturally, against issuing a charter for a separate negro organization, but the committee report, which was adopted, contained this clause:

"We further recommend that the Executive Council give particular attention to the organizing of colored workers everywhere, and to assign organizers for that purpose wherever possible."

Where internationals refuse admission to colored workers they will be organized under charter direct from the Federation. Statements by delegates on the convention floor show that at least forty-six organizations admit negro mem-

DELEGATES TO THE AMERICAN FEDERATION OF LABOR CONVENTION

bers. The negro workers found assurance in the convention that the concern of black men is likewise the concern of white men.

It had been expected that health insurance would take up some of the time of the convention, but it was disposed of quickly. The matter was re-referred to the executive council with instructions that the conclusions reached by it are to be reported to the next convention. In the case of political action and the minimum wage by law, disposition was accomplished with equal dispatch. Action in both cases was adverse to the proposal.

World affairs occupied a position of importance in the convention. Delegates were elected to the international trade union congress to be held in Amsterdam July 25; to the Pan American Federation of Labor convention in New York July 7; to the British Trade Union Congress and the Canadian Trades and Labor Assembly. The convention also expressed the hope that it might be possible to send a delegation to Japan. President Gompers will be one of the delegates to the Amsterdam congress and to the Pan American convention.

In addition to these elections, there were the lengthy reports of various missions sent abroad during the year. Never has any Federation convention dealt with such a volume of business in connection with world problems.

Prominent among the delegates was Mrs. Sara A. Conboy, International Secretary-Treasurer, United Textile Workers of America, who holds this important post in a union composed of 60 per cent of men and 40 per cent of women. Mrs. Conboy is the leading woman trade unionist in America and she exemplifies the attitude taken by the chief trade union women who prefer to work collectively and connectedly with men trade unionists in their craft organizations rather than in separate existing women's associations which have been formed to represent the interests of trade union women.

Mrs. Conboy was secretary of the committee on organization at the convention, and some of the big problems with which that committee had to deal included the organization of the steel workers and those in the oil fields.

She was also chosen by Samuel Gompers to christen the Afol, named after the American Federation of Labor. The United States Shipping Board, taking the initials of that body named the ship Afol and Mrs. Conboy will christen it.

An unexpected, but well-received, contribution to the record of the convention was the program brought in by the committee on education, of which Prof. Charles Stillman, president of the Teachers' Union, was secretary. John B. Lennon characterized the report as second in importance only to the winning of the war. The new educational program thus adopted contains twenty-five clauses.

Thus did the convention act on the greater issues before it. In addition to these things, many other things were done. There were more than 215 resolutions and in addition to these the reports of special committees and missions to Europe. There were fewer of the typical "red" resolutions than usual, though they were by no means altogether absent. Borrowing from Europe's mad career, one delegate introduced a resolution for election of shop foreman as a companion piece, perhaps, to the resolution asking a referendum on recognition of the soviet so-called government.

MRS. SARA A. CONBOY

Anything that came in with a tinge of cardinal was promptly thrown off the pier into the ocean. So tightly was the line drawn against any "red" incursion that the casual onlooker might have thought bigotry held sway or prejudice ruled. That was far from the truth. The truth was that every issue brought up in the convention has long been studied and that a flash was enough to determine whether it was in accord with the practices that American labor has proved sound. It was mature judgment and ripe experience on the job, not bigotry or prejudice.

No convention has had to grapple with so many mighty problems. None has had to assume responsibility so great. And none has handled with more ease and confidence the business before it than this largest of all American Labor conventions.

The convention met determined, builded carefully and soundly for the good of all America, and went home to work patiently, but diligently along the lines laid down in Atlantic City for the betterment of mankind through justice.

The forty-four week endorsement was one of the big things of the convention, even though it came on the closing day. The Federation went on record for the forty-four hour week, but did not fix that as a hard and fast figure, leaving the door open to any organization to go after a lower figure if conditions in the industry made it advisable. The convention was emphatic on the point that overtime is not wanted, but that what really is wanted is reduced working time for the sake of the benefits that go with normal effort accompanied by time for rest, recreation and education.

One of the most dramatic moments of the two weeks' gathering came when a resolution to increase the salary of the president to $10,000 and the salary of the secretary to $7,500, came

DELEGATES TO THE AMERICAN FEDERATION OF LABOR CONVENTION

before the house. President Gompers took the floor and made an earnest appeal to the delegates to vote against raising his salary. He declared that such an act would be misunderstood here and abroad. He said that he had found prejudice in Europe because of the salary he already was receiving, which was $7,500. He said that in France and Italy the workers thought that a fabulous sum and that in some sections in America it was thought he got too much.

"And another thing," he said, "I do not want it said in my last years that I am a money seeker. The salary that you are paying me is enough and I do not want more."

President Gompers never made a more insistent appeal than this against an increase in his salary, but the delegates voted him down with a roar and thrust upon him money that he emphatically did not want.

(The four large pictures accompanying this article, printed on pages 2, 3, 4 and 5 are the four sections of one picture of the American Federation of Labor Convention delegates posed as a group on the boardwalk at Atlantic City.)

Dissecting the Consumer's $

THE ONLY ROAD TO A LOWER COST OF LIVING—NO ROYAL ROAD TO LESSENED COSTS OF DISTRIBUTING GOODS

By WILLIAM H. INGERSOLL

SOCIAL unrest and the dissatisfaction of workers is due largely to the meagre comfort with which people's earnings can be made to provide them. Labor wants a change in its status and in its participation in what is produced, but the most immediate desideratum is a better standard of living. This a true reduction in living costs would accomplish and so it will be understood that when we refer to the cost of living herein we do not merely have in mind prices *per se*, but rather the cost of the essentials of wholesome living in relation to current wage scales, for it has been amply demonstrated since 1914 (if it needed demonstration) that wages themselves mean nothing except as measured in purchasing power to satisfy needs. And though we may have the wage earner primarily in mind in seeking to reduce living costs, the demand is equally strong from all elements of society and the consuming public at large would benefit by a change in the direction sought.

In a preceding article ("Do the Cooperatives Offer a Solution?" in the issue of June 5, 1919) it was pointed out that roughly two-thirds of the cost of the things that we buy are absorbed in the processes of distributing those things after they are made, and that only approximately one-third went into the original cost of physical production.

Granting that costs are too high and that particularly it costs too much to distribute our goods, we then proceeded to examine the aims and efforts of those who would accomplish a reduction through the elimination of the middleman.

We studied the operations of those great retail institutions, the department store and the chain store, which aim and claim to eliminate the wholesaler. We found that instead of eliminating him they substituted a new one. The department store requires the establishment of wholesale warerooms by the manufacturer as well as a continuation of the regular wholesaler, while the chain stores set up their own central wholesale establishment where goods are received from the factories and sub-divided and distributed among their stores, precisely in the manner followed by the customary wholesale house to its retail customers, involving all the labor of receiving goods in bulk, opening, sub-dividing, repacking, forwarding and accounting, with resulting disadvantage and expense rather than gain.

In each chain store we found a substitute proprietor in the person of a hired manager, requiring additional safeguards and expense against dishonesty, indifference and inefficiency.

Similarly, when the manufacturer essayed to establish his own retail stores and eliminate the retailer and wholesaler, we found that the retail stores still existed and that he had to have intermediate warerooms of his own to replace the wholesaler, involving all of the functions, operations and labor of the ordinary distributing system.

Again, when we examined the great cooperative societies of Great Britain, we found the same distributing elements, and we were forced to the conclusion that in the nature of the consumer's needs and his geographical distribution over wide areas, the machinery of distribution require three indispensable elements—namely: the producer, the wholesaler, and the retailer, and that no effort to eliminate any of these units had succeeded in reducing the amount of labor to be performed, or in doing more than to change the name of the functionary performing it.

The mail order system was found to be a retail institution combined with wholesale warerooms, and in some instances factories, and to save no labor, but rather to violate an elementary principle of transportation in that it involves the carrying of retail packages over long distances instead of carrying goods in bulk to the community where they are to be consumed and there opening the factory cases and sub-dividing and delivering through a retail establishment to the consumer individuals.

It was left to us to inquire, therefore, in view of the fact that elimination of the middlemen could not be achieved, whether any of these methods of distribution succeeded in performing the inevitable labors at a lower expense or in relieving the consumer of paying exorbitant or unearned profits, and whether in the event that these hopes failed there was any other direction in which we might look for relief from the high costs which are admitted to be greater than they should be.

In our preceding article it was set forth that three and only three possible ways of saving on distributing costs lay before us—viz., (a) eliminating useless *labor;* (b) eliminating unreasonable or unearned *profit;* (c) increasing the efficiency of our distributors.

There is no opportunity for saving in the motions, processes or labor of the producer-wholesaler-retailer system without substituting more expensive methods. If further demonstration of this were needed, it might be found in the relative prices of articles sold and delivered by the manufacturers, through direct factory agents as in the case of typewriters, adding machines, cash registers, sewing machines, and a host of other things sold by the manufacturers' organizations without the intervention of the wholesaler or retailer in the ordinary form and the prices of which to the consumer are approximately five times the cost of production instead of the customary three. One other observation is in order here, *i. e.*, that when we discuss the question of eliminating middlemen we have in mind that the numerous speculators and non-productive meddlers in some lines of trade have not entered into our consideration and are not to be recognized as performing the legitimate, necessary functions of the wholesaler and retailer, though in some trades it is sometimes permissible to subdivide the functions of these latter and add a link.

It is commonly supposed that large businesses operate more economically than small ones, and there is a popular impression therefore that the large department stores, the chain stores, the mail order houses and the great cooperative enterprises of Europe make savings which they can pass on to consumers, or that they work on a smaller margin of profit and give better values.

As to operating costs in point of fact, it is found that the large stores are under greater proportionate expense than small ones, as will be shown in a moment.

The assumption to the contrary is a natural one until a fundamental distinction in the character of the functions of distribution as contrasted with those of manufacturing, is recognized.

It is true that within certain limits, production can be more economically conducted on a large scale than on a small one.

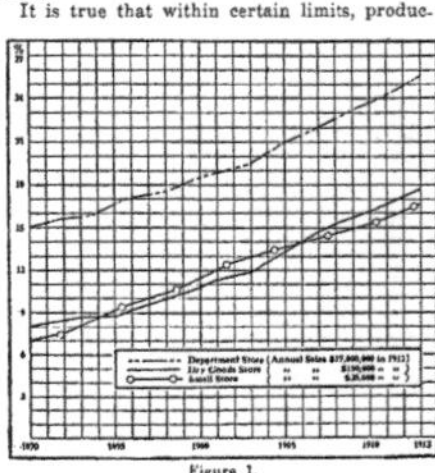

Figure 1.

MUST DEAL WITH HUMAN NATURE

But manufacture is a matter of materials, machinery, labor organization and management concentrated in one unit under a single control. It is done in one place. When we come to distribute the manufactured product, we deal not with metals, machinery and organization, but with the variable quantity, human nature. We must inform, educate and persuade thousands or millions of people of different temperament, experience, purchasing power, viewpoint, and needs, scattered across a continent to adopt our new invention, to discard their old habits, to drop their prejudices, to accept our product instead of some other. We must deliver the individual's retail requirements, not the factory's wholesale output.

This can best be done by widely separated efforts distributed over each small area as the population is grouped. Thus it tends to keep stores small and situated close to the consumers. The retailer, the neighborhood store, knowing intimately the local needs and peculiarities, selects suitable goods with greater precision, has access to the people of the vicinity more often and can get into closer touch with the consumer and show the new products, explain them and make sales with less expenditure for advertising, delivery systems, etc., than the large store further away. His show window is a constant medium of communication. He buys closer according to the local preferences, carries smaller stocks and suffers smaller losses through left-over and mark-down merchandise. Hence, the undiscriminating supposition that because large industrial units are economical, the same will be true of merchandising establishments, is unwarranted and is disproved by an examination of their ratio of operating expenses.

This explains the tenacity with which smaller stores hold out and do the bulk of the country's business, both in the great cities and smaller towns. They are capable of rendering service both from the standpoint of convenience and values. Many other factors enter into the situation, such as the expertness of the specialist who devotes himself closely to one line of business and one community instead of striving to master many with the help of employees, as does the department store; and it has not the "overhead" expense of a co-ordinating organization to keep track of many departments, protect against shoplifting, dishonest clerks, managers, buyers, etc.

It is not to be inferred that the department store does not serve a useful purpose in its own sphere. We are considering only its ability to reduce living costs as indicated by its operating expenses compared with those of the smaller store. Since it does not save *work,* we are striving to find out if it can save in the *performance* of the work.

GETTING DOWN TO FIGURES

Let us now refer to figures.

While it had long been common knowledge among business men that the cost of doing business of the large stores was heavier than that of the small ones, as evidenced by their buyers who argued among other reasons that they must have lower prices on their purchases because their expenses demanded it, there are available the results of several extensive researches into the subject.

On account of the abnormal conditions obtaining since the beginning of the European war in 1914, we will confine our attention to figures gathered before that time.

In his book, "Keeping Up With Rising Costs," Walter Sammons, of *System Magazine,* publishes extensive findings covering the years 1890 to 1913. Typical of general conditions are those pertaining to three stores of different sizes.

One is a large department store doing a business of $17,000,000 a year. Another is an ordinary dry goods store with sales of $150,000 and the third a small store selling only $25,000 a year.

The chart, Figure 1, is reproduced from page 13 of Mr. Sammons' book and shows that throughout the period, the operations of the department store cost about 10% more of the money it took in than did those of the two smaller stores based upon theirs.

That these are not exceptional circumstances is shown by Figure 2, reproduced from page 33 of the same book. The figures represented by this diagram are a composite result obtained by a study of nearly a thousand stores in all sections. It shows that the percentage of the operating expenses in proportion to the business done is higher in the large department store than in any other retail store, save only the jewelry store dealing in luxuries, which is about the same as the department store. The jewelry department in the latter, however, would be found to be about 10% higher still.

Chain stores are not considered in this diagram, but it is generally recognized in business circles that their expenses are higher than those of the department store.

MAIL ORDER COSTS, AN ERROR

The mail order expenses which are shown in the diagram to be the lowest of all, are admittedly in error, the explanation, I understand, being that they were based upon insufficient data. Dr. Paul H. Nystrom of the University of Wisconsin, in an investigation carried on about the same time, found the mail order expenses to be about 22%, to which must be added the cost of transportation of the goods to the consumer to make them comparable to the figures of the retail store which delivers the goods locally. This would make the expense of the mail order business 10% or more higher than shown in the diagram, or about 25%. Dr. Nystrom's research in other particulars generally confirmed that of Mr. Sammons, and his book "The Economics of Retailing" throws other lights on the subject.

Another country-wide investigation is that of Mr. C. C. Parlin of the Curtis Publishing Company, and his findings are partly published in his book, "Advertising as a Business Force." They substantially agree with those of Mr. Sammons.

To offset the higher cost of doing business of the large retail institutions, it must be borne in mind that they buy at lower prices than the smaller stores by about 15% based on their cost prices. This about balances their higher operating expenses, which are figured on their selling prices and permits them to compete in values. Whether they rightfully earn the price advantage they enjoy is beside the question before us.

To those to whom the proof of the pudding is

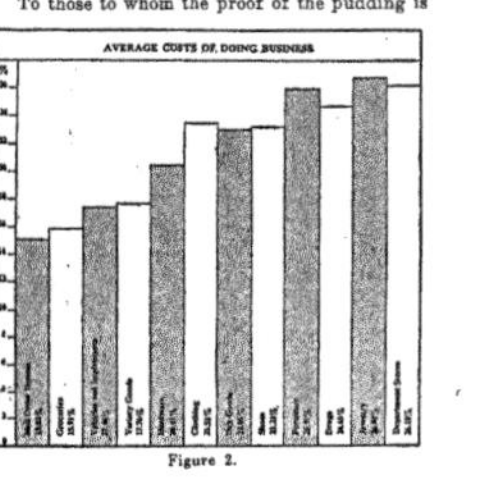

Figure 2.

the eating and who have experienced unde- ıble bargains from the big stores, it should explained that frequently they pick up large s of goods at genuine savings. This is part their service to manufacturers, wholesalers d the public. Also they have more "left ers" to be sacrificed. Again, some of them asionally sell well-known articles at an ac- l loss in order to draw trade, but in the long ı they must make money and they must re- ıp themselves for their sacrifices and cover eir losses on the ordinary run of their mer- andise, which on account of their high ex- nses must be sold proportionately high.

In a long series of purchases extending over period of years and made from big stores and tle stores in the same vicinity at the same ne, for the purpose of examining comparative lues on identical or nearly identical goods, conclusive advantage was found on either le. Sometimes and on some classes of goods e larger stores appeared the cheaper. On oth- s the small stores had the advantage. Gener- y speaking, country stores were cheaper than ; city stores. The same holds true for the ain store and mail order tests. In range of riety the large stores excel and likewise in le merchandise they have the later fashions. t in the same goods for equal quality in other spects they are higher priced. The small store cels in convenience of location, in personal rvice, in promptness of delivery and extension sound credit.

From all of the foregoing, we may conclude at bigness does not mean economy and that ither in the attempt to eliminate labor or per- rm the labor at lower operating expense do e large distributing institutions achieve re- lts.

As to cooperative stores, there are no large ccesses in the United States and my data re- rding those in Europe so far as their expenses e concerned, is at present too meagre and in- onclusive to mean much. Having visited them, owever, and having made comparative pur- hases from them and from neighboring inde- endent stores without apparent differences in alues, and knowing that they save no labor nd do not appear to be more capably managed nd that they suffer several material disadvan- ages in comparison with the independent stores, am forced to conclude that they accomplish o more in economy of operating expense than o the other efforts at "eliminating the middle- ıan".

This brings us to a consideration of whether here is a prospect of saving unearned or ex- rbitant profits, since the saving of labor and xpense has disappeared. To judge of this we ıust have before us some approximation of the rofits absorbed in the existing system of dis- ribution from maker to wholesaler, wholesaler o retailer and retailer to consumer.

While expenses and profits vary in the dif- erent lines of trade and different sections of he country and in different stores in the same ind of business and in the same store from eason to season, it is possible to approximate he general percentages over yearly periods and ıake a composite covering principal lines of usiness.

ALL SORTS OF COSTS TRACED

Figure 3 represents diagrammatically the re- ults of an inquiry made in the early part of 916. The products of 40 typical factories pro- lucing foods, drugs, hardware supplies, fuel, ıousefurnishings, clothing, jewelry, shoes, dry oods, notions, automobile supplies and several ther lines, were traced from maker to user hrough large and small stores widely scattered. The observations were reduced to composite verages and are exhibited in the chart before ıs. The effects of the European war in the orm of increased operating costs are shown in he figures, yet there is not a wide discrepancy between the retailers' expense of doing business at this time and at the time of Mr. Sammons' investigation. The consumer's dollar thus dissected reveals unreasonably heavy *expenses* in distribution, but the *profits* of the middlemen are not an unreasonably heavy burden upon the consumer.

The retailing profit of 6 cents remaining after the operating expense of 28 cents is deducted from the gross profit of 34 cents out of each dollar taken in, would pay a return of $1,800 a year on the ordinary store's volume of $30,000 sales. This is slightly less than $35 per week and considering a usual investment of from $5,000 to $10,000 in the business and the risks taken, it is a modest reward for the services to the community and with interest on investment subtracted amounts really to less than $30 per week, which is less than the skilled laborer frequently receives for shorter hours, less anxiety and without risking his own money in the enterprise.

For purposes of simplification in the diagram, fractions of cents were discarded and the nearest whole number taken. Thus the wholesaler's profit shown as 3 cents really figured to be only a trifle over 2½ cents. But taking it at 3 cents and adding the retailers' 6 cents, we have the total profit of those two middlemen as 9 cents out of the consumer's dollar.

The most then that any scheme of saving middlemen's profits could hope to attain would be to save a *part* of this 9 cents. Interest on investment and salaries of managers in place of the proprietor's profits would necessarily reduce the amount that could be saved. Only a narrow saving could possibly be looked for.

But in order to hope for *any* saving, it would be necessary to conduct the distributing operations as expertly as they are now performed and without increase of operating expenses. If the ambition contemplated benefits to any large proportion of the people, it would require that the present proprietors be induced to work for others for a smaller remuneration than they now receive as owners or to supply a new school of managers to take their places. Neither of these alternatives is immediately probable.

If for a moment we indulge in a consideration of a vast scheme of collective ownership by consumers, including retailing in all lines of business, wholesaling, manufacturing, growing and mining, we are confronted with problems of organization and management greater than those of government.

NOT EVEN A RIPPLE IN TRADE

The cooperative movements of Great Britain, great as they are and involving hundreds of millions of business annually, are not large enough to have made a ripple on the surface of Britain's trade. The ordinary retailer and wholesaler still do business without concern.

Successful as the "coops" are generally regarded, they have made no general change in conditions and it is seriously to be doubted whether they have conveyed any real economic benefits. Side by side the older wholesale and retail houses successfully compete with them for trade, smaller though they are and without the psychological advantage of having the consumers as "members" or shareholders with all the prejudice that men hold in favor of things to which they "belong" and which belong to them.

To extend the cooperative system to a point where it became a material factor in the situa-

(*Continued on page 18.*)

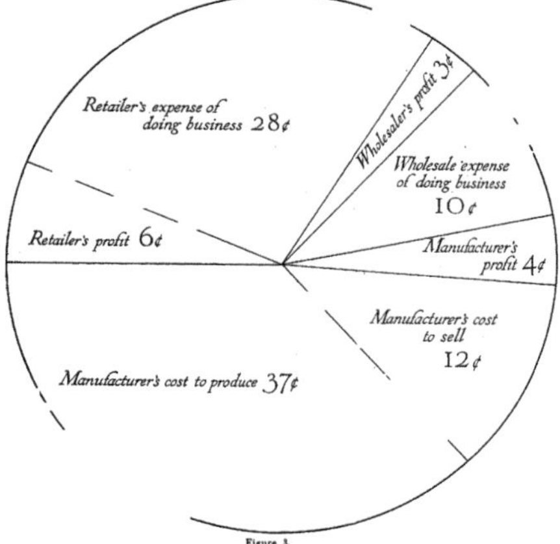

Figure 3.

Where the Consumer's Dollar goes, as shown by an inquiry following through to the consumer the products of 40 staple and specialty manufacturers in various leading branches of trade.

Undermining the Foundations of National Morale

A FOREWARNING OF THE NEW GERMAN PROPAGANDA OF SOCIAL DISCONTENT AND CIVIL STRIFE—POISONING THE FONTS OF LEARNING—A LESSON FROM THE PAST

By T. EVERETT HARRÉ

PART I

GERMANY'S war against democracy and for dominion over the free nations of the world did not begin on August 1, 1914, nor had Germany become the enemy of America only when she struck her first blow at American sovereignty and rights by the sinking of neutral ships and the murder of American women and children peacefully traversing the high seas. Germany's war began when, scientifically laying out her plans for world subjugation, she first inaugurated her campaign of "peaceful" invasion by propaganda, the purpose of which was the destruction of national integrity and the undermining of national morale. Germany had launched her warfare against democracy in America when, immediately after the Spanish-American war, she began propaganda to stimulate hostility in this country against Great Britain, and when, after the visit of Prince Henry she instituted a vast campaign the purpose of which was to debauch and poison American public opinion in favor of Germany. She assaulted American sovereignty when she invaded the schools and colleges of America by the winning over or subsidizing of American educators, by the pro-Germanizing of text books for the use of American school children, by poisoning the fonts of learning at their source.

Nor will Germany's war against democracy, against the peace and welfare of the free nations of the world, end with the signing of the treaty and the formal conclusion of military hostilities. G rmany, unregenerate and unrepentant of heart, will, upon the technical conclusion of the war, seek to obtain by "peaceful means" what she failed to achieve through military victory. The new German propaganda, which has already been carefully worked out, with adroitness and far-seeing cunning, will be carried on with an intensiveness, a subtlety, a calculatingly shrewd mastery of conditions and events, as find no precedents in the past. And in this propaganda Germany will have gained from her experience, by her failures; she will put to profit those lessons which are learned only from defeat.

"THE WAR AFTER THE WAR"

Ideals are the vital things back of all human movements, back of any war. There is no victory, there can be no victory, unless the spirit of the thing against which you fight admits its surrender or is utterly crushed. Germany, indignantly repudiating her guilt in causing this war, refusing to admit her unparalleled crimes, has neither been defeated in spirit nor eliminated as a potential foe to the security and peace of the world. The war of armies, it is true, has ended; but a greater war, a moral war, a war of intellectual deceit and cunning, a war of spiritual treachery, has begun.

Germany will seek, immediately upon the signing of the treaty, to recuperate economically and financially. With her land uninvaded and her factories intact, with the vast resources of machinery looted in the lands invaded, with tremendous stocks of manufactured products to sell, she will seek to flood the markets of the world with merchandise and regain the commerce lost during the war. To this end, the German propaganda will seek to create hostile feeling toward her rivals in the countries whose trade she covets. Wherever it serves her ends, Germany will endeavor to stir up quarrels among political and commercial rivals, fan racial and national differences into active animosities, turn nations one against another, as well as promote social and labor unrest, strikes, revolutionary movements and civil war within the countries whom she seeks to damage.

Germany, protesting that she accepts peace conditions by force, signs the treaty with her tongue in her cheek, and a dagger hid in the folds of the sackcloth of submission. Germany, having signed the treaty, will indubitably scheme to evade fulfillment of the terms of the treaty, and she secretly plans to evade payment by the stimulation of division and disagreement among the Allies and between the United States and the Allies so, that thus estranged, they will not act in concert when Germany fails to fulfill her pledges. That Germany has changed no more than the proverbial wolf in sheep's camouflage is indicated by the fact that, while she made a show of repudiating the figurehead Kaiser and becoming a republic, she maintained in the background as advisers and directors of her affairs the same old gang with whose malfeasances the world has become sadly familiar—the unspeakable Count von Bernstorff, who, while Ambassador to America, directed the slimy intrigues of the Huns, infested the country with spies and ordered the dynamiting of railroads, factories and ships, inflicting a loss of property and life; Dr. Bernhard Dernburg, head of the Hun propaganda, who was forced to leave American shores because of his notorious defense of the sinking of the Lusitania; Dr. Heinrich Albert, Hun propaganda paymaster in America; those bankers with international affiliations who acted as financial go-betweens for the promotion and financing of the Bolshevik revolution in Russia, as well as the vast crew of trained propagandist chiefs, agents and spies. That Germany, whose affairs are still conducted by the same old trickstering gang, will continue her propaganda into the era of peace, was indicated by the far-reaching propaganda campaign scientifically laid out even before America took up arms against her.

THE HAND OF THE HUNS

Germany planned, at that time, to continue her world propaganda after the war, with the purchase or subsidizing of great daily newspapers, of news agencies, the establishment of a cable and wireless news service covering the globe, to the end that she debauch and secure control of politics and public opinion in all the great countries of the world. That Germany has never had any intention of giving up her old game is further shown by the fact that the chiefs of her propaganda bureau in the United States, after their return with von Bernstorff to Germany, simply moved their headquarters to Geneva where they continued their labors. Recently, according to reports, an insidious propaganda of world-scope has been directed from Breslau. Scheming to retain what she gained in Russia and to have free access for the exploitation of the resources of Russia, the German propaganda seeks to hinder if not frustrate the setting up of a free and united Poland, and to this end has flooded the world with anti-Polish propaganda. This has taken the form of lurid reports of pogroms against the Jews—reports which, according to the American Minister, Hugh Gibson, are grossly exaggerated. This propaganda has been instigated and backed by certain German financial groups which desire free access for the exploitation of Russia, and at least one of which figured as fiscal agent for the Huns in financing the Bolshevist revolution. The purpose is to destroy confidence and sympathy for the new Polish Republic, to arouse such racial antagonism and powerfully hostile influence as will paralyze the development of the new nation, discredit Poland to such a degree as will make the floating of a foreign loan of the Polish Republic an impossibility in the world markets. According to Chairman Porter, of the House Committee on Foreign Affairs, many reports of pogroms appearing in the United States are sent out by a German-owned newspaper at Copenhagen "for the purpose of impressing the world with the idea that Poland is not capable of self-government." That this German-inspired racial propaganda has not been without tremendous effect is shown by the pulling off of huge mass meetings, parades of protest and fanatic agitations in every great city in America. It is very probable that, on account of its adroitness and furtiveness, this propaganda has been innocently abetted by many people who would be opposed to any new hyphenism and any effort to turn Poland over to Germany and German international bankers.

Minister Gibson in his report very aptly declared: "Violent agitation abroad based on unwarranted reports of conditions cannot help the Jews, but has exactly the opposite effect," and he asserts that the American Department of State "can render a service to the Jews of Poland by discouraging agitation based upon exaggerated or unfounded reports." Chairman Porter declared it struck him as "quite significant that there was no protest over the killing of the Jews in the Bolshevist country, Russia," where, according to his information, "there are 300 Jews killed in Russia to one in Poland, and probably 500."

THE NEW PROPAGANDA OF SOCIAL DISINTEGRATION

The new propaganda will not appear on the surface as German propaganda. That phase which sought to render countries subservient under German aggression by the creation of an excessive admiration for German achievements and German *Kultur*, and which sought after the outbreak of the war to swing public sentiment in favor of Germany, has ended. The new phase will have for its supreme and ultimate object the promotion, in countries whom Germany seeks to destroy, of such movements as that by which she successfully brought about the surrender of Russia. Germany will not cease to strive for world advantage, for dominion in the politics and markets of other nations, but her armies will not be the goose-stepping soldiers—they will be comprised of the Socialists, anarchists, revolutionaries, I. W. W.s and various breeds of agitating malcontents. And zealously aiding and abetting Germany in her insidious underground onslaught against the security, integrity and peace of the nations, will be that whole tribe of intellectual pariahs, parlor Bolshevists and editor-statesmen of the "new school" who, glibly mouthing their disloyalty and sophistries in terms of idealism and liberalism, have played the German game from the beginning to the end of the terrible war. Unconsciously serving to the best of their power as Germany's agents and tools, will be the whole pusilanimous chicken-hearted flock of pacifists, international-

(*Continued on page 14.*)

Studying Industrial Reconstruction in Great Britain and France

By E. A. QUARLES

SECRETARY COMMISSION ON INDUSTRIAL INQUIRY OF THE NATIONAL CIVIC FEDERATION

LAST February there set sail for Liverpool one of the most important commissions The National Civic Federation has ever sent abroad. Its general instructions were to make a study of and report on the various phases of the industrial reconstruction problems that the world war has brought to the fore. The field of operations designated was Great Britain and France. The personnel of the Commission, which was representative of Capital, Labor and the Public, follows:

Charles Mayer, Chairman; Charles S. Barrett, Albert F. Bemis, J. Grant Forbes, James W. Sullivan, A. Parker Nevin, E. A. Quarles, Secretary.

The determination to send the Commission abroad was reached at a conference held in this city in December at which a resolution was adopted providing that the Commission should, in general, ascertain what England had learned during the war in respect of methods of dealing with capital and labor problems that can be of benefit to us in the United States, and especially requiring it to investigate the following subjects:

The Whitley Councils in Great Britain.
The shop steward, shop committee and democratic control of industry programs.
Operation of bonus and profit-sharing schemes.
Compulsory sickness and unemployment insurance legislation.
The housing problem.

Shortly after arriving in London, where headquarters and offices were established in the First Avenue Hotel, a splendid formal welcome was given the Commission under the auspices of the National Alliance of Employers and Employed of Great Britain, an organization similar to The National Civic Federation. This took place at a large dinner on the evening of March 25 at the Holborn Restaurant, presided over by the Honorable E. Huth Jackson, Chairman of the Alliance. Representatives of practically every important labor and manufacturers' organization in Great Britain were present, and nothing could have served better to inspire the visitors to their best efforts or to make them more certain of the cordial welcome that the employers and workmen of the United Kingdom wished to extend.

Busy days, filled to the full with absorbing interviews with leaders in the British labor and manufacturing world followed. The investigators set no limit to their activities and every phase of opinion was sought in the British industrial world from the most conservative to the ultra-radical.

WENT AT A VITAL TIME

No better time could have been chosen for the Commission's visit, for Great Britain was in the throes of industrial unrest due to the upheaval of the war, its unexpected termination, and the wholesale release of thousands of soldiers, jobless, upon the community. For several weeks it seemed possible that all means of transportation might be cut off at any minute and the insistent demands of the Miners' Union at the same time promised the shutting down of all industry at almost any moment. Surely few moments in the industrial history of the world have been more pregnant with awful possibilities than these few weeks during the early part of 1919.

Sound statesmanship and patriotic action on the part of leaders in British industry averted the threatened catastrophe, and there had been set up in Great Britain before the Commission departed, machinery for the working out of the problems that have to be faced that gives promise of success.

Part of the Commission and its hosts on the trip through Great Britain's industrial centers as guests of the National Alliance of Employers and Employed. Left to right: James W. Sullivan, American Federation of Labor; Lieut. General Sir Edward Bethune, Chief Organizer of the Alliance; E. A. Quarles, Secretary of The National Civic Federation's Commission; Arthur H. Patterson, Secretary of the National Alliance; Albert F. Bemis, one of the employers' representatives on the Commission.

One of the most important accomplishments of the stay in England was a visit to the principal industrial centers of the United Kingdom, which included Manchester, Swansea, Liverpool, Glasgow and Dundee. This was taken under the auspices of the National Alliance of Employers and Employed, and the Commission was the guest of that organization throughout the journey.

At every place visited a formal welcome was given by the Mayor and city officials, following which the most intensive work was immediately resorted to. Thanks to the excellent arrangements of our hosts, we were able at each place to get immediately into contact with the men principally concerned in working out the labor problem. The Commission particularly requested that it be permitted to interview those representing every shade of opinion and endeavored to make it clear that it was seeking only the facts. All were impressed with the frankness of expression of both employers and employees and even more so with the spirit of give and take that was manifested and the ardent desire to work out Great Britain's industrial destiny in a harmonious manner.

All who took this trip feel especially grateful to those members of the staff of the National Alliance whose work made possible its success. Mr. A. H. Patterson, Secretary of the Alliance; Lieutenant General Sir Edward Bethune, General Organizer; Captain A. F. Wornum, his Assistant; Mr. T. A. Jackson, Labor Adviser, and Mr. Harry Dewberry, Labor Organizer.

Shortly after the completion of this journey, the Commission took train for Paris for a brief study of the industrial situation in France. On arriving there, its work was greatly expedited by Dr. E. J. Dillon, the famous journalist, who placed it in touch with many of the most prominent French labor leaders. Dr. Dillon also entertained the Commission handsomely and contributed greatly to the pleasure of its stay.

While there are unions in France fairly like those in this country, the great majority are composed of men whose leaders, at least, are frankly revolutionists. It is not too much to say that they are heartily in sympathy with Bolshevism. France, however, is largely an agricultural country and it is the hardworking, land-owning French peasant who dominates the country. While Michel has little regard for the capitalist, he has even less for the syndicalist (the revolutionary labor leader) and it would seem that he presents a formidable barrier to the spread of Bolshevism westward.

In France the days seemed all too short with the vast amount of conferences with labor people, employers, economists and Government officials that constituted the daily program.

FRENCH SITUATION UNIQUE

Taken as a whole France does not seem to be so alive to the industrial problems created by the war's upheaval as does Great Britain, but evidence was found that in some industries, notably the metal trades, efforts are being made by employers to bring about closer relations with employees. As the principal French unions are avowedly revolutionary and openly state that they are working for the downfall of the capi-

(*Continued on page 19.*)

THE NATIONAL
Civic Federation Review

Office: Thirty-third Floor, Metropolitan Tower
1 Madison Avenue New York City

RALPH M. EASLEY, Editor

Published Twice a Month Two Dollars a Year

The Editor alone is Responsible for any unsigned article or unquoted statement published in THE NATIONAL CIVIC FEDERATION REVIEW.

A. F. OF. L. VOICES POLICY OF CONSTRUCTIVE PROGRESS

The thirty-seventh annual convention of the American Federation of Labor, which has just concluded its sessions at Atlantic City, was the most noteworthy ever held by that remarkable body of representative working men and women. To describe, even by title, all the constructive and useful measures adopted would cover more space in our editorial columns than can be allotted to the purpose. Mr. Chester M. Wright has performed that service in a special article in the REVIEW and we bespeak for it a careful perusal.

It is not too much to say that at the very moment in the history of our country when such qualities were most needed the American organized labor movement displayed its greatest Americanism, loyalty, sanity and courage. The declarations of this convention will serve as a crushing answer to the defeatists, revolutionaries and so-called liberals of Europe who have been confidently whispering in public places, in the last two months that America would "hear something drop" at Atlantic City.

Before the convention assembled, as before all other of its conventions, there were prophecies of "the disintegration of the A. F. of L.," of its capture by the radicals, of the elimination of "Gompersism," and of all the dire disaster wished on it by its ancient enemies, but this particular convention had the distinction of having those sure prophecies more numerous and the forces back of them better organized than ever before. The usual elements of disorder bent on the destruction of the American Federation of Labor were this year reinforced by a definite cabal of revolutionary "intellectuals," running the gamut all the way from *The New Republic, The Dial, The Nation, The Public*, and *The Survey*, to *The New York Call, The Rebel Worker, New Solidarity* and *The Liberator*. Even the revolutionary preachers in certain fashionable churches joined the cabal and directed splenetic soap-box sermons at the head of Samuel Gompers for so persistently and ably defying their anathemas and vanquishing the forces of revolution. One weekly, *The Nation*, was so wrought up over the matter that it published a special article predicting the downfall of Gompers and his reactionary cohorts, and it advertised its own imbecility in this respect in the daily press throughout the country. The fact that the opposition to President Gompers in the convention was so weak that only one out of the handful of its fire-eaters had the temerity to vote against him, is a fitting answer and rebuke to the motley group of anarchists, I. W. W.ites, socialists, pseudo-intellectuals, editors, preachers and college professors ranged against him. In other words, it was a vote of thirty thousand to one—a fairly safe majority.

But, aside from their discomfiture in the attempt to unhorse the Grand Old Man of Labor, the revolutionary forces met overwhelming defeat along the whole line of battle. The only time they dared stand up and be counted was on a proposition to substitute on the Executive Council an official of one of the numerous needle trade unions (the Balkans of American industry) for Thomas A. Rickert, President of the United Garment Workers, an organization anti-socialist and thoroughly American. When one reads of "mass meetings" of the needle workers (most of them "Russians") in Madison Square Garden or in any of the other hundred-and-one halls in New York City, Boston, Cleveland, Philadelphia or Chicago, where they assemble by the thousands, the impression is received that there are millions of them, but when they stood up to be counted at Atlantic City their relative importance in the labor movement showed for just what it was worth. Mr. Rickert received, in round numbers, 29,000 votes, and the revolutionary candidate 2,600.

Most of the other radical propositions — the recognition of Soviet Russia, the indorsement of the I. W. W., the "one big union" scheme of organization, the release of the conscientious objectors and the violators of the Espionage Act, and a dozen other proposals tainted with un-Americanism—were defeated by a vote ranging from 20 to 1 to 30 to 1.

No one witnessing the proceedings at this Atlantic City convention could have any difficulty in discerning the fundamental difference between the labor movement in America and the labor movement in other countries. There is in Italy practically no trade union movement at all; what there is in France is made up chiefly of syndicalists and anarchists and variegated socialists, with only in spots a real trade unionist. In England the trade unionists, a minority force, are submerged in a mixed-up political socialist movement. In America the organized labor movement is anti-socialist, in Great Britain it is fundamentally socialist. Between those two positions there can be no compromise.

The labor reconstruction programs of the two countries stand in contrast. The British asks that the State shall eventually take over all industries; the American calls on the State to keep out of everything possible. The British Labor Party would have State interference in all the affairs of daily life; the American labor movement would not tolerate the State's interference with the citizen except wherein it should be absolutely necessary. With reason, during the war emergency the American organized labor group, as well as all divisions of our people, surrendered individual rights to the State. Decisions had to be made quickly, right or wrong, and the cost of service, and even its quality, was not to be considered; the first requirement was rapid service. Now that peace has come, the American labor movement says: "Stop!" The British Labor Party says: "Go on!" It has had a taste of parental pap and likes it. The people do not want to have to do their own thinking; the State is to do it for them. It believes living on half rations without working at all, under the Unemployment Donation Act, is a good Socialist plan.

Some much-quoted writers and speakers who have returned from England in the last six months fail to perceive the fundamental difference between the labor movements of the two worlds. They applaud things in England that lie entirely on the surface. They make much of the fact that Lloyd George could bring together in general conference four hundred employers and four hundred labor representatives, resulting in the appointment of a sub-committee of sixty—thirty from each side—which unanimously agreed upon a proposed charter of industry. This points the way for this country, say these importers of foreign-made reform stuffs, and some ardently enthusiastic but rather shallow people are urging speedy imitation here. But these innovators do not tell us the whole story. They do not tell us that the conference was called at a crucial moment in the history of England—one that may never recur—when labor of various classes was threatening to tie up everything and everybody, leading to paralysis of industry and possibly to revolution, the fond hope of the Lenines and Trotzkys of Great Britain. As designed, the direct effect of the conference was to relieve the nation's tension, and on that score alone it was justified; but of nothing else connected with the affair could American people approve. The program of the committee of sixty provided that in their respective groups the various organizations of manufacturers and employers should establish rules and regulations and fix prices, to be enforced uniformly by parliamentary law. For labor, standards for rules, regulations and wage rates were to be established by the unions and by law imposed upon all the workers of the respective crafts. In other words, the practical effect is to compel every manufacturer by law to join the organization of his industry and to compel every wage earner by law to join the union of his craft. It is hardly believable that such legislation would ever be enacted by the Congress of the United States, and, for that matter, it is worth while noting that it has not yet been enacted by the British Parliament and may never be. But this is the wonderful outcome of that most wonderful conference of employers and labor leaders in London.

Nor do our importers of sociological novelties tell us that this untried economic medicine was to be taken "for only the time being" by British labor in pain. The labor committee unanimously sent in a supplementary report, restating the radical demands of the British Labor Party's program, which prescribe that the state shall take over and operate all factories, mines, mills, banks, stores, farms, elevators and railroads—in fact, cover all productive industry with its protective paternal hand.

After reading the industrial program of the British Labor Party, it is refreshing to turn to the reconstruction program of the American Federation of Labor and the proceedings of that organization's Atlantic City Convention just closed. We wish every reader of the REVIEW could have attended that Convention and seen our sturdy, brainy men of Labor in action.

PEACE—BUT IS GOOD WILL AMONG MEN SECURE?

By the time this issue of the REVIEW goes to press the peace treaty will probably have been signed. There will have formally ended the most terrible of all wars, a war unexampled for fiendish cruelty and scientific savagery on part of a people seeking without compassion or scruple to obtain dominion over the nations of the world. In this consummation of the struggle, with victory over the world's foe purchased at so precious a price, civilization will rejoice. And after the long travail, the unstinted sacrifices, the unutterable heartache, the nations which have fought and defeated Germany look up to a new era—an era which, if all the bloodshed is not to be in vain, shall be richer in good will among mankind, in a living Christian love among men and nations.

Germany has been defeated in the field; her frightsome engines of destruction have been stilled; she cannot now impose upon the world a dominion and system of kultur by force, by "blood and iron." Physically she is conquered—but has she been conquered in spirit? Does the treaty which Germany signs make the peace of the world secure? In fighting Germany the nations arrayed against her fought ideas no less real, no less tangible than the brutish armies wreaking fire and bloodshed in Belgium and France. Those armies have been routed—but have the ideas so deeply embedded in the heart of the German nature been uprooted and destroyed? Can Germany be trusted? Will she keep her solemn pledges? Does she seek readmittance among the nations with a penitent and regenerate heart?

There is not one of us but in his better self desires to forgive those who trespass against us, not one of us but would forgive the German le if, conscious of the evil had done, they manfully honestly admitted their t.

reat as must be the joy of world that peace has come, ould be worse than folly, ould be a betrayal of all for which the nations have , to blind our vision to the menace that confronts us he era of peace.

the very act of suing for e, Germany defiantly re- liated her guilt and denied manifest and monstrous ues. In the very act of ing to alter the terms of treaty, Germany sought to tect from being held to ac- nt those former rulers who plotted and deliberately de the world war. Upon very threshold of signing treaty, German sailors sunk fleet which had been sur- dered to the Allies and a sive hate-inspired German burned those sacred flags en in 1870 from France and ich Germany was pledged to urn. In the very note in ich they agreed to sign the aty, the German plenipo- tiaries insolently character- d the terms as "unbearably sh" and asserted that the rman Government "yields force." Protesting against territorial terms, with azing effrontery or uncon- ousness the German repre- tatives declared: "The rman Government, there- e, finds itself compelled to line all responsibility for difficulty which may result m the resistance of the in- bitants against their separa- n from Germany." "No of violence can touch the nor of the German people. . . . Yielding to superior ce, and without renouncing the meantime its own view the unheardof injustice of peace conditions, the gov- nment of the German repub- declares that it is ready to ept the peace conditions im- sed."

Was this not tantamount to ing official warning and pub- notice that, while she may ept the terms, those terms would not be filled?

The French press accurately gauged the spirit which Germany agrees to the treaty when it lared that Germany will observe the terms y with a sword at her throat. That sword st be the united moral force, united armed wer, the concerted vigilance, the perfect con- d, the indivisible alliance of America and the ied powers. When the nations which fought rmany are estranged and turned one against ther with rivalries, enmities and antagonisms, en they are within themselves torn by social rest and civil strife, when the whole world thes with a ferment secretly stimulated by rmany, then, and only then, can Germany de- lt in her obligations, repudiate the terms of treaty, and obtain through the social disin- ration and moral collapse of other peoples what she failed to achieve through military means.

That day must never come. And that this day shall never come, that the treaty which has been signed shall be a living document, the nations of the world cannot afford to trust Germany, to relax in their watchfulness, or let suspicion and division destroy that union and concord which has been sealed with precious blood. Unless backed by the united and formidable moral and material force of America and the Allies, the treaty just signed will be, as the Berlin *Vorwaerts* declares, merely another scrap of paper. It was this same paper, the Socialist *Vorwaerts*, which last March boldly spoke of the "new weapons" which Bolshevism offered Germany for defeating the victory and evading fulfillment of the peace terms of America and the Allies.

It required vision and strength, vigilance and the spirit of sacrifice to win this war. It will require vision and strength, vigilance and a spirit of live patriotism that will not compromise nor grow faint to maintain that the war has gained. Lest, after peace, good will among men be destroyed, let not the sentinels of the nations sleep on the watch-towers of the spirit.

ALTON B. PARKER

Alton B. Parker has been elected President of The National Civic Federation by the Executive Council and has accepted the position, filling the unexpired term of Mr. V. Everit Macy. On account of a serious operation, Mr. Macy has been ordered by his physicians to withdraw for the time being from all positions of responsibility. He will retain his membership on the Executive Council and will enter once more into the active work of the Federation when his health is completely restored.

Judge Parker needs no introduction to the members of The National Civic Federation or, for that matter, to the American people. He has shown his sympathy for the wage earner not only as Chief Judge of the Court of Appeals of New York State, but as an eminent member of the Bar. Employers and wage earners alike respect and trust his impartial judgment. He is the fifth president in the nineteen years of the Federation's history, the other four being: Marcus A. Hanna, August Belmont, Seth Low, and V. Everit Macy.

TO PROBE PROPAGANDA IN SCHOOL TEXT BOOKS

Impressed by the extent to which pro-German and un-American propaganda had invaded American public schools and colleges, and had influenced the writers of school text books, as has been revealed by various, if somewhat sporadic, investigations during the progress of the war, a committee is being organized by The National Civic Federation to undertake a systematic and comprehensive examination of various text books used in public schools in order to detect and report upon the inclusion of pro-German, un-American, pro-Socialist and otherwise radical propaganda insidiously put forth in text books on history, civics and political economy. What is put into the public schools will come out in the public opinion and the public action of the land. As school books are today, so will public opinion be tomorrow. True of primary and grammar schools, this is still more true of the high school—the people's college. There, history, economics and political science are taught. There American institutions are presented, their workings studied, their effect on the wage-earning life of men and women described and comparisons made between European conditions and our own.

These studies are vital to the Republic. Only fourteen out of every thousand students who begin in public schools complete a college course, sixteen years later. Even out of every thousand pupils who enter the high schools only fifty-five complete a college course. The training of the vast mass in the field of citizenship is public school and high school training, and public school and high school training almost alone.

The books for these and for all public school studies are selected by school boards on the advice of superintendents, teachers and publishers. No one before the war thought of inquiring into possible non-American, un-American or anti-American teaching in the studies that deal with the duties, the responsibilities and the actions of the citizen. War came, and through the aroused spirit of vigilance and inquiry of the nation, it was found that among the text books which its sons and daughters were studying, were German reading books which praised the Kaiser and exalted German Kultur, books on political

(Continued on Page 16)

Timely Points in Pope Leo's XIII's Labor Letter

ENCYCLICAL PROMULGATED IN 1891 SETS FORTH DUTY OF EMPLOYERS AND EMPLOYEES AND DEFINES PROBLEMS THE WORLD FACES TODAY

Because of the widespread interest throughout the country in the problems of labor and re-adjustment, as well as because of the discussion interjected into churches of Bolshevism and other radical programs, many readers of THE NATIONAL CIVIC FEDERATION REVIEW *have suggested the reprinting of Pope Leo XIII's famous Encyclical Letter on The Condition of Labor. That extraordinary document, the product of a mind of profound sanity and vision, was promulgated in May,* 1891, *and as it bears so cogently upon conditions and problems confronting the world today, its re-reading will be an inspiration to all constructive Americans,—Roman Catholics, Protestants and Jews alike.*

IT is not surprising that the spirit of revolutionary change, which has long been predominant in the nations of the world, should have passed beyond politics and made its influence felt in the cognate field of practical economy. The elements of a conflict are unmistakable: the growth of industry, and the surprising discoveries of science; the changed relations of masters and workmen; the enormous fortunes of individuals and the poverty of the masses; the increased self-reliance and the closer mutual combination of the working population; and, finally, a general moral deterioration. The momentous seriousness of the present state of things just now fills every mind with painful apprehension; wise men discuss it; practical men propose schemes; popular meetings, legislatures, and sovereign princes, all are occupied with it—and there is nothing which has a deeper hold on public attention.

Therefore, Venerable Brethren, as on former occasions, when it seemed opportune to refute false teaching, We have addressed you in the interests of the Church and of the common weal, and have issued Letters on Political Power, on Human Liberty, on the Christian Constitution of the State, and on similar subjects, so now We have thought it useful to speak on

THE CONDITION OF LABOR

It is a matter on which we have touched once or twice already. But in this Letter the responsibility of the Apostolic office urges Us to treat the question expressly and at length, in order that there may be no mistake as to the principles which truth and justice dictate for its settlement. The discussion is not easy, nor is it free from danger. It is not easy to define the relative rights and the mutual duties of the wealthy and of the poor, of capital and of labor. And the danger lies in this, that crafty agitators constantly make use of these disputes to pervert men's judgments and to stir up the people to sedition.

But all agree, and there can be no question whatever, that some remedy must be found, and quickly found, for the misery and wretchedness which press so heavily at this moment on the large majority of the very poor. The ancient workmen's Guilds were destroyed in the last century, and no other organization took their place. Public institutions and the laws have repudiated the ancient religion. Hence by degrees it has come to pass that Working Men have been given over, isolated and defenceless, to the callousness of employers and the greed of unrestrained competition. The evil has been increased by rapacious Usury, which, although more than once condemned by the Church, is nevertheless, under a different form but with the same guilt, still practiced by avaricious and grasping men. And to this must be added the custom of working by contract, and the concentration of so many branches of trade in the hands of a few individuals, so that a small number of very rich men have been able to lay upon the masses of the poor a yoke little better than slavery itself.

SOCIALISTS AND PRIVATE PROPERTY

To remedy these evils the *Socialists,* working on the poor man's envy of the rich, endeavor to destroy private property, and maintain that individual possessions should become the common property of all, to be administered by the State or by municipal bodies. They hold that, by thus transferring property from private persons to the community, the present evil state of things will be set to rights, because each citizen will then have his equal share of whatever there is to enjoy. But their proposals are so clearly futile for all practical purposes, that if they were carried out the working man himself would be among the first to suffer. Moreover they are emphatically unjust, because they would rob the lawful possessor, bring the State into a sphere that is not its own, and cause complete confusion in the community.

It is surely undeniable that, when a man engages in remunerative labor, the very reason and motive of his work is to obtain property, and to hold it as his own private possession. If one man hires out to another his strength or his industry, he does this for the purpose of receiving in return what is necessary for food and living; he thereby expressly proposes to acquire a full and real right, not only to the remuneration, but also to the disposal of that remuneration as he pleases. Thus, if he lives sparingly, saves money, and invests his savings, for greater security, in land, the land in such a case is only his wages in another form; and, consequently, a working man's little estate thus purchased should be as completely at his own disposal as the wages he receives for his labor. But it is precisely in this power of disposal that ownership consists, whether the property be land or movable goods. The *Socialists,* therefore, in endeavoring to transfer the possessions of individuals to the community, strike at the interests of every wage earner, for they deprive him of the liberty of disposing of his wages, and thus of all hope and possibility of increasing his stock and of bettering his condition in life.

MAN'S NATURAL RIGHT TO PRIVATE PROPERTY

What is of still greater importance, however, is that the remedy they propose is manifestly against justice. For every man has by nature the right to possess property as his own. This is one of the chief points of distinction between man and the animal creation. For the brute has no power of self-direction, but is governed by two chief instincts, which keep his powers alert, move him to use his strength, and determine him to action without the power of choice. These instincts are self-preservation and the propagation of the species. Both can attain their purpose by means of things which are close at hand; beyond their surroundings the brute creation cannot go, for they are moved to action by sensibility alone, and by the things which sense perceives. But with man it is different indeed. He possesses, on the one hand, the full perfection of animal nature, and therefore he enjoys, at least, as much as the rest of the animal race, the fruition of the things of the body. But animality, however perfect, is far from being the whole of humanity, and is indeed humanity's humble handmaid, made to serve and obey. It is the mind, or the reason, which is the chief thing in us who are human beings; it is this which makes a human being human, and distinguishes him essentially and completely from the brute. And on this account—viz., that man alone among animals possesses reason—it must be within his right to have things not merely for temporary and momentary use, as other living beings have them, but in stable and permanent possession; he must have not only things which perish in the using, but also those which, though used, remain for use in the future.

This becomes still more clearly evident if we consider man's nature a little more deeply. For man, comprehending by the power of his reason things innumerable, and joining the future with the present—being, moreover, the master of his own acts—governs himself by the foresight of his counsel, under the eternal law and the power of God, Whose Providence governs all things. Wherefore it is in his power to exercise his choice not only on things which regard his present welfare, but also on those which will be for his advantage in time to come. Hence man not only can possess the fruits of the earth, but also the earth itself; for of the products of the earth he can make provision for the future. Man's needs do not die out, but recur; satisfied to-day, they demand new supplies to-morrow. Nature, therefore, owes to man a storehouse that shall never fail, the daily supply of his daily wants. And this he finds only in the inexhaustible fertility of the earth.

Nor must we, at this stage, have recourse to the State.

MAN IS OLDER THAN THE STATE

And he holds the right of providing for the life of his body prior to the formation of any State. And to say that God has given the earth to the use and enjoyment of the universal human race is not to deny that there can be private property. For God has granted the earth to mankind in general; not in the sense that all without distinction can deal with it as they please, but rather that no part of it has been assigned to any one in particular, and that the limits of private possession have been left to be fixed by man's own industry and the laws of individual peoples. Moreover, the earth, though divided among private owners, ceases not thereby to minister to the needs of all; for there is no one who does not live on what the land brings forth. Those who do not possess the soil, contribute their labor; so that it may be truly said that all human subsistence is derived either from labor on one's own land, or from some laborious industry which is paid for either in the produce of the land itself or in that which is exchanged for what the land brings forth.

Here, again, we have another proof that private ownership is according to nature's law. For that which is required for the preservation of life and for life's well-being, is produced in great abundance by the earth, but not until man has brought it into cultivation and lavished upon it his care and skill. Now, when man thus spends the industry of his mind and the strength of his body in procuring the fruits of nature, by that act he makes his own that portion of nature's field which he cultivates—that portion on which he leaves, as it were, the impress of his own personality; and it cannot but be just that he should possess that portion as his own, and should have a right to keep it without molestation.

e arguments are so strong and convinc-
at it seems surprising that certain obso-
inions should now be revived in opposi-
what is here laid down. We are told
is right for private persons to have the
the soil and the fruits of their land, but
is unjust for anyone to possess as owner
the land on which he has built or the
which he has cultivated. But those who
this do not perceive that they are robbing
f what his own labor has produced. For
il which is tilled and cultivated with toil
ill utterly changes its condition; it was
efore, it is now fruitful; it was barren,
ow it brings forth in abundance. That
has thus altered and improved it becomes
y part of itself as to be in a great measure
nguishable and inseparable from it. Is
that the fruit of a man's sweat and labor
be enjoyed by another? As effects fol-
eir cause, so it is just and right that the
of labor should belong to him who has
d.

h reason, therefore, the common opinion
ikind, little affected by the few dissentients
have maintained the opposite view, has
in the study of nature, and in the law
ure herself, the foundations of the division
perty, and has consecrated by the practice
ages the principle of private ownership,
ing preeminently in conformity with hu-
nature, and as conducing in the most un-
kable manner to the peace and tranquility
man life. The same principle is confirmed
nforced by the civil laws—laws which, as
as they are just, derive their binding force
the law of nature. The authority of the
e Law adds its sanction, forbidding us in
ravest terms even to covet that which is
er's:—*Thou shalt not covet thy neighbor's
nor his house, nor his field, nor his man-
nt, nor his maid-servant, nor his ox, nor
ss, nor anything which is his.**

'S NATURAL RIGHT AND HIS SOCIAL AND DOMESTIC DUTIES

e rights here spoken of, belonging to each
idual man, are seen in a much stronger
if they are considered in relation to man's
l and domestic obligations.

choosing a state of life, it is indisputable
all are at full liberty either to follow the
sel of Jesus Christ as to virginity, or to
into the bonds of marriage. No human
can abolish the natural and primitive right
arriage, or in any way limit the chief and
cipal purpose of marriage, ordained by
's authority from the beginning. *Increase
multiply.*† Thus we have the Family; the
iety" of a man's own household; a society
ed indeed in numbers, but a true "society,"
rior to every kind of State or nation, with
ts and duties of its own, totally independent
e commonwealth.

hat right of property, therefore, which has
proved to belong naturally to individual
ons, must also belong to a man in his ca-
ty of head of a family; nay, such a person
t possess this right so much the more clearly
proportion as his position multiplies his
es. For it is a most sacred law of nature
a father must provide food and all neces-
s for those whom he has begotten; and,
larly, nature dictates that a man's children,
carry on, as it were, and continue his own
onality, should be provided by him with all
is needful to enable them honorably to
themselves from want and misery in the
rtainties of this moral life. Now, in no
r way can a father effect this except by the
ership of profitable property, which he can
smit to his children by inheritance. A
ily, no less than a State, is, as we have said,
ue society, governed by a power within it-

euteronomy v. 21. †Genesis i. 28.

self, that is to say, by the father. Wherefore, provided the limits be not transgressed which are prescribed by the very purposes for which it exists, the Family has, at least, equal rights with the State in the choice and pursuit of those things which are needful to its preservation and its just liberty.

We say, at least equal rights; for since the domestic household is anterior both in idea and in fact to the gathering of men into a commonwealth, the former must necessarily have rights and duties which are prior to those of the latter, and which rest more immediately on nature. If the citizens of a State—that is to say, the Families—on entering into association and fellowship, experienced at the hands of the State hindrance instead of help, and found their rights attacked instead of being protected, such association were rather to be repudiated than sought after.

THE STATE MAY NOT ABOLISH NOR ABSORB FRATERNAL RIGHTS

The idea, then, that the civil government should, at its own discretion, penetrate and pervade the family and the household, is a great and pernicious mistake. True, if a family finds itself in great difficulty, utterly friendless, and without prospect of help, it is right that extreme necessity be met by public aid; for each family is a part of the commonwealth. In like manner, if within the walls of the household there occur grave disturbance of mutual rights, the public power must interfere to force each party to give the other what is due; for this is not to rob citizens of their rights, but justly and properly to safeguard and strengthen them. But the rulers of the State must go no further: nature bids them stop here. Paternal authority can neither be abolished by the State nor absorbed; for it has the same source as human life itself; "the child belongs to the father," and is, as it were, the continuation of the father's personality; and, to speak with strictness, the child takes its place in civil society not in its own right, but in its quality as a member of the family in which it is begotten. And it is for the very reason that "the child belongs to the father," that, as St. Thomas of Aquin says, "before it attains the use of free-will, it is in the power and care of its parents."* The Socialists, therefore, in setting aside the parent and introducing the providence of the State, act *against natural justice,* and threaten the very existence of family life.

And such interference is not only unjust, but is quite certain to harass and disturb all classes of citizens, and to subject them to odious and intolerable slavery. It would open the door to envy, to evil speaking, and to quarrelling; the sources of wealth would themselves run dry, for no one would have any interest in exerting his talents or his industry; and that ideal equality of which so much is said would, in reality, be the leveling down of all to the same condition of misery and dishonor.

Thus it is clear that the main tenet of *Socialism,* the community of goods, must be utterly rejected; for it would injure those whom it is intended to benefit, it would be contrary to the natural rights of mankind, and it would introduce confusion and disorder into the commonwealth. Our first and most fundamental principle, therefore, when we undertake to alleviate the condition of the masses, must be the inviolability of private property. This laid down, We go on to show where we must find the remedy that we seek.

THE CHURCH ALONE CAN SOLVE THE SOCIAL PROBLEM

We approach the subject with confidence, and in the exercise of the rights which belong to Us. For no practical solution of this question will

*St. Thomas, *Summa Theologica* 2a 2æ Q. x. Art. 12.

ever be found without the assistance of Religion and of the Church. It is We who are the chief guardian of Religion, and the chief dispenser of what belongs to the Church, and we must not by silence neglect the duty which lies upon Us. Doubtless this most serious question demands the attention and the efforts of others besides Ourselves—of the rulers of States, of employers of labor, of the wealthy, and of the working population themselves for whom We plead. But We affirm without hesitation that all the striving of men will be vain if they leave out the Church. It is the Church that proclaims from the Gospel those teachings by which the conflict can be put an end to, or at least made far less bitter; the Church uses its efforts not only to enlighten the mind, but to direct by its precepts the life and conduct of men; the Church improves and ameliorates the condition of the working man by numerous useful organizations; does its best to enlist the services of all ranks in discussing and endeavoring to meet, in the most practical way, the claims of the working classes; and acts on the decided view that for these purposes recourse should be had, in due measure and degree, to the help of the law and of State authority.

Let it be laid down, in the first place, that humanity must remain as it is. It is impossible to reduce human society to a level. The *Socialists* may do their utmost, but all striving against nature is vain. There naturally exists among mankind innumerable differences of the most important kind; people differ in capability, in diligence, in health, and in strength; and unequal fortune is a necessary result of inequality in condition. Such inequality is far from being disadvantageous either to individuals or to the community; social and public life can only go on by the help of various kinds of capacity and the playing of many parts, and each man, as a rule, chooses the part which peculiarly suits his case. As regards bodily labor, even had man never fallen from *the state of innocence,* he would not have been wholly unoccupied; but that which would then have been his free choice, his delight, became afterwards compulsory, and the painful expiation of his sin. *Cursed be the earth in thy work; in thy labor thou shalt eat of it all the days of thy life.** In like manner, the other pains and hardships of life will have no end or cessation on this earth; for the consequences of sin are bitter and hard to bear, and they must be with man as long as life lasts. To suffer and to endure, therefore, is the lot of humanity; let men try as they may, no strength and no artifice will ever succeed in banishing from human life the ills and troubles which beset it. If any there are who pretend differently—who hold out to a hard-pressed people freedom from pain and trouble, undisturbed repose, and constant enjoyment—they cheat the people and impose upon them, and their lying promises will only make the evil worse than before. There is nothing more useful than to look at the world as it really is—and at the same time look elsewhere for a remedy to its troubles.

THE CHRISTIAN INTERDEPENDENCE OF CAPITAL AND LABOR

The great mistake that is made in the matter now under consideration, is to possess oneself of the idea that class is naturally hostile to class; that rich and poor are intended by nature to live at war with one another. So irrational and so false is this view, that the exact contrary is the truth. Just as the symmetry of the human body is the result of the disposition of the members of the body, so in a State it is ordained by nature that these two classes should exist in harmony and agreement, and should, as it were, fit into one another, so as to maintain the equilibrium of the body politic. Each requires

(*Continued on page 19.*)

*Genesis iii. 17.

Undermining the Foundations of the National Morale

(Continued from page 8.)

ists and liberals who, instead of rejoicing over Allied victory in the field, have of late been bawling over the heartlessness of the Allies to poor, afflicted, stricken Germany and have been vociferously whining protests against the terms of the Allied treaty. Aiding and abetting Germany, consciously and boldly, will be all those Huns and Shadow Huns who were prevented by the espionage laws from outright disloyalty and acts of treason during the war, and who of late have been flocking to the congenial ranks of the Socialists and revolutionary radicals. Aiding and abetting the Huns in their "pacific" warfare will likewise be all those who preach a class war after the war, "the final war" which, to use the words of Mr. Walter E. Weyl, associate editor of the *New Republic,* "will be a wider conflict than that which now rages and the alignment will be by classes and interests rather than by nations . . . . which will be waged until separate interests within each nation are completely extinguished."

GERMANY'S "NEW WEAPONS"

To the promotion of this class war—which, after succeeding in Russia, Germany and German agents sought to promote in France, in England, in Italy, and now in the United States—will be devoted the major efforts of Hun propaganda of the future.

This propaganda of social disintegration and the undermining of national integrity and morale is not new with Germany, and, in fact, the plan long antedated its being carried into effect in Russia. So long ago as February 23, 1915, a circular letter was sent by the Director of the Press at the Ministry of Foreign Affairs in Berlin to all German ambassadors, ministers and consuls, stating:

> THERE HAVE BEEN ESTABLISHED WITHIN THE TERRITORY OF THE COUNTRY WHERE YOU ARE SPECIAL BUREAUS FOR THE ORGANIZATION OF PROPAGANDA IN THE COUNTRIES THAT ARE IN THE WAR COALITION AGAINST GERMANY. THE PROPAGANDA WILL HAVE FOR ITS OBJECT THE INCEPTION OF SOCIAL MOVEMENTS, ACCOMPANIED BY STRIKES, REVOLUTIONARY EXPLOSIONS, SEPARATION MOVEMENTS AND CIVIL WAR.

What she failed to accomplish by force of arms, Germany succeeded in accomplishing through Lenine, Trotzky and their gang, including imported East Siders, in Russia. What she has failed to achieve by military triumph, Germany in the days of her defeat will seek to accomplish in other countries through the same identical forces employed successfully in Russia. The workings of the crafty Hun mind, and its ulterior intentions, were indicated by an article in the Berlin *Vorwaerts,* reputed to voice semi-officially the opinions of the "reformed government," last March, at the time Germany sought to intimidate the Allied council by threats of going Bolshevik. Of course, the leaders of Germany never had any serious thought of "going Bolshevik." But as for helping to make other nations "go Bolshevik," that is another matter. The *Vorwaerts* declared that, "Until now Germany deliberately has opposed the Russian method of instigating a world revolution," when as a matter of historical fact Germany herself brought about that revolution in Russia. After this hypocritical declaration, the *Vorwaerts* threateningly went on to say: "But if Germany is forced to refuse to sign the peace treaty it could not fail to affect a great change in her policy. She would center her hope on achieving similar far-reaching changes to the Western countries and concentrate her revolutionary energies and resources to the task. . . . *Germany may be forced to choose the harder fate of resisting the Entente's coercion, not with arms in hand, but by new weapons which recent developments furnished the German people.*"

So authoritative an oracle of matters revolutionary and subtly pro-German as the *New Republic* as long ago as last December predicted that if the Allies did not abandon "particularist national ambitions" "they themselves will eventually be engulfed in the anarchy and ruin which is now threatening Europe." There could hardly perhaps have been a more clairvoyantly articulated interpretation of the process going on in the Hun mind than the statement, made in a supplement to the *New Republic* of March 22, by Mr. Walter Lippmann: "Bolshevism in both Russia and Germany would soon eat the heart out of Poland, Rumania and Hungary where social conditions are already desperate. Now, anyone who supposes that the populations of France and Great Britain will endure the human and economic cost of such an occupation is suffering from a severe case of reading nothing but censored news." And lately, in a diatribe against the Allied council because of the peace terms asked of Germany, that mildly-shining minor star of pacifism, that turn-the-other cheek apostle of a compromise, patched-up peace, O. G. Villard, in the *Nation* asserts:

"With Germany crushed and autocracy enthroned, with the strong hand of power at the throat of liberty, the battle opens which is to make men free. . . . Heaven grant that the revolution may be peaceful, and that it may destroy only to rebuild."

AUXILIARIES OF THE HUNS

To be forewarned is to be forearmed. Germany, and her friends, adept in strategy and trained in guile, calculate to take advantage of the relaxation, the laxity, the resting on their oars of the peoples over-weary from war. And lest the enemy obtain advantage because of this lack of vigilance, it is all vitally important to understand and ever bear in mind the workings of the foe in the past, to apprehend the scope of what was planned, to comprehend what was actually accomplished. By this, may be gauged what lines the German propaganda will pursue in the campaign to frustrate the Allied treaty, and secure political and commercial supremacy by distintegrating rival nations by an undermining process from within.

Germany will use, as she has used in the past and is now using, all the various radical movements, the Socialists, the I. W. W., pacifists, internationalists and anarchists. She will foster and give support to all movements seeking to promote civil war, "direct action" by the workers, the overthrow of government and existing order. Secretly and cunningly she will artificially stimulate social discontent, labor unrest, inflame religious, political and racial prejudices, and take advantage of all differences and conditions of discontent wherever they arise. She will seek to break the organized labor movement. She will attack the foundations of our national life, and seek to undermine and destroy national feeling, the spirit of patriotism, loyalty, belief in the nation's ideals, confidence in our institutions and social order, that national solidarity and morale which alone give strength and resistance against treacherous and subtle foes. Her propaganda, as before, will be scientific, shrewdly far-seeing, brainy and ruthless. She will endeavor, in her effort to undermine the spirit of nationality, to make her attack at the very sources where national ideals and the national spirit are supposed to be fostered and nurtured. She will seek to poison the minds of children, to destroy the moral fibre of the coming generation, in schools, the fonts of learning. It was the theory of Imperial Germany, in her propaganda extending into schools, that if you color the mind of a child at the f[illegible] mative period, your work is accomplished. [illegible] survey of what Germany actually succeeded [illegible] doing before the Great War may indicate wh[illegible] potentially grave dangers menace us in t[illegible] future.

In the propaganda of Socialists, I. W. W[illegible] and so-called liberals, in their tons of pamph[illegible] teering, in all the revolutionary harangues [illegible] fanatic reds, there is not so much danger as l[illegible] in the subtle propaganda which aims at destro[illegible] ing in the minds of children love of countr[illegible] patriotism, reverence for the principles out [illegible] which our nation was born, belief in spiritu[illegible] ideals, a living Christian faith, and which woul[illegible] instead, render cynical, hard and sterile t[illegible] minds of the young with irreligion, unbelief, i[illegible] reverence for the nation's ideals and for i[illegible] past—a philosophy of gross unidealistic mat[illegible] rialism. Were it covertly, insidiously insin[illegible] ated into the minds of children that our gover[illegible] ment was based upon an entirely wrong and ev[illegible] system of economics, that the framers of the Co[illegible] stitution wrote that document primarily to en[illegible] rich their pockets, that patriotism, love and r[illegible] ligion work more evil than good, that in all hu[illegible] man movements not ideals but economics motiv[illegible] mankind, that man is an animal urged by ca[illegible] nal desires and not spiritual faith, the gener[illegible] tion thus poisoned would be ready prey fo[illegible] those malcontents and internationalists whom Germany has already used to such advantag[illegible] in betrayed and stricken Russia.

SOCIALIST PROGRAM TO DEBAUCH CHILDRE[illegible]

In a series of remarkable and illuminating ar[illegible] ticles recently published, Rheta Childe Dorr tel[illegible] of the Socialist program of proselytizatio[illegible] among school children:

> There is one certain or almost certain metho[illegible] of holding young radicals through life. Th[illegible] method is being employed in Socialist locals, i[illegible] centers like the Rand School all over the coun[illegible] try. It consists in destroying all ideals of mod[illegible] esty, reticence, reverence for parents, respect fo[illegible] women or faith in any ultimate spiritual good[illegible] As a substitute for these ideals, without whic[illegible] the world would never have advanced beyond bar[illegible] barism, the reds preach the most unbridled l[illegible] cense in speech and behavior. They make an[illegible] kind of religion, or even intellectual agnost[illegible] cism, a possession to be ashamed of. Atheism of the most blatant kind is preached. Grosses[illegible] materialism is substituted for the ideals an[illegible] dreams which are instinctive in the minds of al[illegible] normal girls and boys. . . .
>
> So far as I know, as far as my reading o[illegible] history has revealed, the first human beings wh[illegible] ever deliberately undertook a whole campaig[illegible] to debauch the minds of their youth, the firs[illegible] ones who ever preached sex excesses as a duty are the revolutionary socialists at work in th[illegible] United States of America to-day.
>
> A teacher in the English department of on[illegible] of our schools prepared a bibliography of con[illegible] temporary literature which he recommended t[illegible] his young students. This bibliography in th[illegible] form of a small booklet, he caused to be place[illegible] on sale in the school store and to be advertise[illegible] in the school paper. Included in this bibliog[illegible] raphy were books which the public library for[illegible] bids even adults to read except in a privat[illegible] room under the eye of an attendant. . . .
>
> A standard work on anarchism, from the ex[illegible] treme anarchist point of view, was included, an[illegible] for regular reading, periodicals later suppresse[illegible] by the government. . . .
>
> The principal of the school knew that thi[illegible] bibliography had been prepared, but he did no[illegible] know that it was on sale in his school until th[illegible] head of the English department so informe[illegible] him. The teacher was brought up on charge[illegible] and dismissed from the school system. But hi[illegible] dismissal was a mere incident in the campaig[illegible] to instill materialistic poison into the minds o[illegible] youth. . . .
>
> To indecent books add indecent pictures. Jus[illegible] now the New York Yipsels, the Young People' Socialist Leagues, are wallowing in what the[illegible] call psycho-analysis, but which is really littl[illegible] more than education in sex license.

MORAL CORRUPTION OF YOUNG IN RUSSIA

Just how the extreme Socialist program i[illegible] practice reaches out to corrupt and debauch th[illegible] famed the framers of the Constitution and derogated that document now be tolerated in any public school within the confines of our land? Should text books written by any man who jeered at patriotism, who held that patriotism, like religion and love, has worked more evil than good in the world, be given to an innocent American child? Shall men notoriously known to sympathize with the Socialist movement, who have lent their aid to the defense of the criminal I. W. W., who have defended the red-handed Bolshevik despots and championed "conscientious objectors," be allowed to write the text books which shall form the point of view of the coming generation? Can such men be trusted in the future?

If the people of America are not to forfeit what they have gained at so costly a sacrifice, it will be their public duty to safeguard the nation at the very well-springs of national life. "The Public School is the Ark of the Covenant of the Republic," declared Judge Thomas Burke, of the Text Book Committee of the Seattle, Washington, School Board, commenting upon "Outlines of European History, Part II," by Professors James Harvey Robinson and Charles A. Beard, which was withdrawn from the Seattle schools under charges that it contained pro-German propaganda. "It is little wonder, then, that for some years even before the German war, the common enemy sought and secured an entrance there. . . . We know now what the enemy has been up to in secret for many years. It is our duty to the children of the land to seek out this enemy's hiding places and drive him hence and to see to it that he never enters there again."

In the new Hun propaganda, which will seek to undermine the foundations of national morale and sap the very sources of moral resistance, Germany will endeavor, as before, to invade the schools and colleges of the land, so as to poison and corrupt the minds of the coming generation at the formative and impressionable age of immaturity. What precautions can be taken against this new invasion by the enemy of democracy and civilization? Can those distinguished college professors who lent themselves to the dissemination of Hun propaganda be trusted to have aught to do with the education of young men and women in our higher institutions of learning? Can those professional compilers of school text-books, who adroitly sandwiched pro-German propaganda in their pages, be trusted to have aught further to do in the preparation of school histories and text books on citizenship and economics?

SCHOOLS REPOSITORIES OF NATIONAL SPIRIT

It is beyond question to the public interest to know to what extent German propaganda had succeeded in invading American schools and colleges prior to the outbreak of the war in 1914, and to appreciate by what subtle and covert methods flagrant pro-Hun propaganda found its way into public schools even after the invasion of Belgium and the tragic sinking of the Lusitania. An approximation of what was accomplished by subtlety or stealth may afford loyal and patriotic Americans a sense of what measure of vigilance will be necessary so as to thwart the propaganda of the future.

Captain Gustavus Ohlinger, who was in charge of investigations into German propaganda for the Military Intelligence, declares in a book recently issued:

"The rivalries among the liberated Nationalities of Europe, the possible misunderstanding and differences among the people who have fought the war for freedom, will undoubtedly, in the future, furnish fresh opportunities for German propaganda. Against this propaganda, and its resulting disintegration and dissentation we must still stand guard."

Citing various outrages, dynamite plots, the fomenting of strikes, and the destruction of factories by German agents in this country while the United States was at peace with Germany, Captain Ohlinger very pertinently declares that these plots "recede into the background when viewed in relation to the far more dangerous and insidious conspiracy which Germany, through her agents, sympathizers and dupes, has prosecuted against American education."

Captain Ohlinger continues:

> Bridges, canals, factories and ships are mere physical properties, easily replaced. Our public education, on the other hand, represents infinitely higher values.* In our schools are transmitted the traditions of the past; there are generated those moral forces which bind us together and vitalize us as a nation. They are the repositories of our national spirit, and national spirit cannot be made to order. It is born of the travail of history, of the sacrifices of countless thousands in the past, of the work of those rare geniuses that flash upon a nation's horizon as infrequently and mysteriously as comets from an unknown stellar system. Once perverted or destroyed, it cannot be restored. With it, there succumbs the nation, and the nation's institutions and achievements pass into history. The plots engineered by Kaltschmidt, Koenig, von Igel, Consul General Bopp, von Papen, Boy-Ed, Ambassador Bernstorff and their retinue of lesser malefactors have furnished the press frequent opportunities for sensational headlines. But the activities of these men are insignificant when compared with the insidious and far-reaching conspiracy against our education.
>
> Just as Germany planned her own educational system with reference to her military power, so she sought, as a part of her higher strategy, to enhance her superiority by insinuating herself into the morale and intellectual life of foreign countries. German schools and churches abroad she set down as important outposts of her power. If, in addition to supporting these institutions, she could introduce her agents into the native education, there disseminate doubt as to the validity of native traditions and with regard to the adequacy of established institutions, replace national spirit by a shallow cosmopolitanism, and foster an admiration of *KULTUR* to the disparagement of national achievements,—then she could sap the very sources of moral resistance. It would be an easy matter to fit the people with a coat of *KULTUR* cut to her own measure and according to her own patterns. This accomplished, political domination would come in due course, either through voluntary submission, or after a short war in which every moral and material advantage was with the aggressor.
>
> The evidences of this programme, a definite part of Germany's higher strategy, are writ large over the parochial schools, the public schools and the colleges and universities of America—they are as unmistakable as the gun emplacements which Germany built within the territory of her friendly neighbors. The purpose of both was the same—military conquest and political domination.

THE INVASION OF KULTUR

In his book, "The German Conspiracy in American Education," published by Geo. H. Doran Co., New York, Captain Ohlinger briefly sketches the history of the German invasion of American schools and higher institutions of learning. In 1881 there was formed in Germany the General School Alliance for the Preservation of Germanism in Foreign Lands, which established schools and libraries in foreign countries and maintained a teachers' bureau which supplied German-trained educators. The alliance was a few years ago merged into the Society for Germanism in Foreign Lands, which was given an annual subvention by the German government of a million marks.

---

* The far-seeing designs of Germany to secure industrial control of the United States were revealed in the report made by A. Mitchell Palmer, formerly Alien Property Custodian. Just as Germany schemed to obtain the industrial conquest of the continent, she sought at the same time to undermine American morale through schools and higher universities of learning. As Capt. Ohlinger indicates, what Germany sought to destroy through our public education represents infinitely higher values than the mere material domination aimed at in industry.

"Nowhere did the *Verein* operate so actively and so successfully as in the United States," says Captain Ohlinger. "For years it maintained its secret agents in our midst, working in favor of German language schools and pulling wires for a German political party."

In a review of its work made in 1909 the society declared with gratification that, "had this annual meeting brought nothing more to the *Verein* than the inspiring report of Germanism in North America, the expressions of common interests and the promises for future cooperation, those things alone would have been of immense significance for our cause."

In order to gather together and use in German propaganda those American educators who had studied in Germany and had received degrees at German institutions of learning, there was organized at a banquet given in honor of Prince Henry, on the occasion of his visit in 1902, by four hundred former students of German universities the Union of Old German Students. Carol Beck, the first president of the Union, declared: "These Americans who have attended German Universities are permanently inoculated with the German virus. They have only good things to tell of Germany. Even for German immoralities they have words of extenuation—yes, they go so far in their courtesies as even to imitate our faults."

In 1904 there was established the Exchange Professorships, by which American and German professors exchanged visits. The Kaiser was personally interested in this further scheme to pro-Germanize American professors. A striking example of Germany's success in "capturing" visiting professors is found in John W. Burgess, the first exchange professor, who after the outbreak of the war, became one of the most notoriously flagrant champions of Hun *Kultur*.

Later there came into being the German University League, of New York, whose membership included not only native Germans but also native Americans, the purpose of which was to mobilize, direct and command American educators in the organized pro-German propaganda instituted after the war.

NATIONAL GERMAN ALLIANCE

On October 6, 1901, The National German-American Alliance" was permanently organized. The sinister and inimical activities of this federation were exposed after America entered the war against Germany. To the powerful influence and pressure exercised by this organization, which was more devoted to serving the interests of Imperial Germany than those of the United States, was largely due the amazing invasion of American schools by Hun propaganda in text books and the astonishing compliance of publishers of school text books in specializing in books in which Germany was exalted and glorified and in which Germany's rivals, such as England, were derogated and disparaged. The National German-American Alliance entered into relations with the Pan-German League and the General School Alliance of Germany, and, says Captain Ohlinger, "became the mouthpiece of Pan-German ideas in America. The propaganda of world dominion in Germany boasted of the superiority of their Kultur, denounced the Latin races as suffering in the last stages of decadence, described the British as hopelessly addicted to sport and besotted through wealth and luxury; the Germans were the one race singled out by Providence to rescue Civilization. In the same way the leaders of the National German-American Alliance extolled the superiority of the German element. . . ." They taught that Great Britain was filled with commercial jealousy of Germany and France obsessed by the *revanche*.*

By 1916 the National German-Alliance had an organization in every State and in the territory of Hawaii, and it claimed a membership of two and a half million and a control of the same number of votes.

"DIRECT ACTION" ON PUBLIC SCHOOL SYSTEM

Captain Ohlinger says:

"They undertook to operate directly upon the Public School system. 'Strict control of the public schools is necessary,' they declared, and early in the career of the Alliance, the following program was laid down:

"1. The teaching of the German language in all elementary schools, beginning, preferably, with the first grade; such teaching, moreover, to be given in such a manner 'as to produce familiarity with Germany and with the German race in America';

"2. 'A dignified place in the curriculum for German history';

"3. 'The rewriting of American history so that not only descendants of the Anglo-Saxon race, but those also of the German and of other races who have contributed to the civilization of the United States may come into their rights, and so that contemptuous expressions, such for instance as those applied to the Hessian mercenaries, may be eliminated from school text books';

"4. 'Instruction in the geography of Germany.'"

The National German-American Alliance, working in conjunction with the German American Teacher's Alliance, conducted an organized nation-wide campaign to force the introduction of German into public schools. Intimidation was used when intimidation became necessary. "In those communities where the introduction of German was left to the Local School Board," declares Captain Ohlinger, "the procedure was to send questionnaires to candidates for the Board, ascertain their attitude, and then to actively campaign for those who gave satisfactory answers. This was done in Chicago in 1916. . . . In Detroit, even after the break in diplomatic relations, the city alliance interrogated candidates and prepared to enter the local campaign. In Indianapolis they succeeded in electing one of their own officers, the first Vice President of the national organization, to the school board and he later became its president. This worthy was at the same time the paid propagandist and organizer of the brewers and liquor dealers of America. . . . In Milwaukee, another Vice President of the National Alliance was made assistant superintendent of schools. . . : In Cincinnati, according to its records, the local alliance had the situation well in hand. . . .

"Where State Legislation was necessary to facilitate the introduction of German the alliance was equally active. Questionnaires on the proposed measures were sent to all candidates. This was done in Ohio in the election of 1912. In this manner the state alliance of Nebraska secured the passage of the Mockett Law, requiring the teaching of a foreign language beginning with the fourth grade—the foreign language being of course German—whenever the parents of fifty children in attendance upon the school requested it. . . .

"Of course the propaganda never revealed its real purpose when presented to the state legislators or school boards. It always came before them in plausible pedagogical disguises. It was said that the study of German improved the student's mastery of English."

ALLIANCE USED BOYCOTT

Captain Ohlinger points out that the leaders of the German movement always contended that historical text books used in American public schools were replete with falsifications, showed astounding omissions, slighted the part which the German element had played in American history and unjustly omitted German history. To bring about the desired Germanization of historical text books there was incorporated in 1901 the German American Historical Society, the purposes of which were encouraged and accelerated by the National Alliance. Captain Ohlinger goes on to say:

In those districts where Germans were in the majority the text books could be controlled through the election of the members of the school boards. But this would not accomplish the result principally desired—the enlightenment of Americans in the districts where the Americans were numerically stronger.

The school committee therefore hit upon an original idea. "To reach an American one must get at his pocket book," the chairman reported. The Alliance could best accomplish its purpose by allying itself with some energetic publishing house that had put out a book most nearly approaching the German point of view. The Alliance could endorse such a book, and through its numerous branches advertise it, bring it to the attention of school boards, and secure its adoption. Requests for the insertion of other desirable matter could then be made of the publishers from time to time. Such a course was actually pursued in the case of Bourne and Benton's "School History of the United States." . . . The book was endorsed by a number of state alliances and an active propaganda was undertaken in its behalf.

At the same time a covert threat was exercised upon all publishers of text books through the request that they submit copies of their publications. They were made to appreciate the financial loss they would incur if they ignored Germanism in the presentation of history. Professor Samuel B. Harding, of the University of Indiana, relates an interesting incident in this connection. Early in 19[illegible] he prepared a chapter on the present war for use in a text book. He read it before the historical society of the University. Within two weeks there were forwarded to him by his publishers letters which they had received demanding that the chapter be omitted from the book, and practically threatening a boycott, not only of that particular book, but also of the firm as well.

The most insidious of all forms of German propaganda was that conducted through text books used in the public schools and the fact much of this propaganda was produced unconsciously and innocently by American born scholars is convincing evidence of our shortcomings in not insisting upon education in political and institutional history.

(*To be Continued*)

Probe Propaganda In School Books

(*Continued from Page* 11)

science which hymned the advantage of autocracy and a "strong" government; historical text books in which praise was lavished on city administration in Central Europe under which the few profited and only the outside of the platter was made clean, while the children of the poor had a heavy death-rate and forty percent of the families in Berlin lived in one room and a kitchenette. History was rewritten along materialistic, so-called "modern" lines, no longer with approval of the faith that endured persecution in the struggle for liberty and the sacrifices of patriotism; instead these things were marshalled as the causes of bloodshed and the fruits of mistaken and ignorant superstition alike in freedom and in faith.

With peace gained at so costly a sacrifice in a war waged by America and the Allies for the purest ideals, this sort of thing must stop. So the whole country is resolved. Facts a[illegible]

* This Hun propaganda was aided and abetted with an amazing degree of audacity or unconsciousness by certain American citizens. Roger W. Babson, the presiding genius of the Babson Statistical Bureau, for instance, wrote a series of fifty-one articles for the German-bought New York *Evening Mail*, for which, it is said, Babson was paid $5,100. Babson, in these articles, declared: "I want my sister Susie to sew no socks for any sick soldiers." He averred that if England and France had not gobbled up the colonies of the Earth the war might not have taken place, and he asked: "May not some of Germany's rich neighbors be as guilty as Germany?" Babson asserted that "as a nation England needs somebody to keep her where she belongs." In his little books Babson further extolled the superiority of Hun Kultur. It is known this adviser of investors breakfasted genially with Hugo Schmidt, representative of the Deutsches Bank and Hun paymaster in the United States. If Germany so readily found aides in her propaganda in 1914-1915, will she find it difficult to align in her new propaganda men who have, consciously or unconsciously, served her in the past?

ted. A close examination of the books which ı the basis of American education is deded. Neither fear nor favor can be pered to influence the decision. The National c Federation Committee proposes to take up examine various text books and lay the facts verdict before the school boards, members ·hich are public servants, who select school :s in the city, country and state boards.

he job will not be easy. It is not pleasant. ill arouse wide opposition and perhaps some ats. But the work must be done. It is a lic duty. In peace, any man is at liberty to any opinion before the American people who not incite to violence in support of that ion. The American people wishes to hear y side of every question. This is lawful, and just, and tends to public safety.

ur schools are supported by taxation; they established by law; their support is provided by every State Constitution, and they teach erican history, American principles and erican practice to American citizens. The erican people has decided through its Constiou what are the principles and practices by ch the nation is to be governed. Any man a right to propose a change, and in its be- go before the voters of the land who can both sides, provided he does not advocate use of force. If he can get enough votes, an make the changes he urges. But no man a legal or moral right to go before the chiln of the State, who can hear but one side, teach what he pleases, subverting the prines and practice ordained and ordered by the erican people. No school board has a right ouy books that do this. No teacher should them. And no teacher who does not subbe to the principles of the Constitution ald be granted a license to teach in our ools. Public education must teach, preach support the public aims and principles for ose support the American people has estabned the schools.

As a first step, it is proposed to take up textoks on history and read them in the light of tles which our sons have won to establish perpetual security the Constitution of Washgton, and to destroy the Constitution of Bisrck. Books and authors that support the mer Constitution should be used. Books and thors that have championed the latter should proscribed. We shall judge these books by at they say about the institutions of Washgton and of Lincoln and about the institutions of Bismarck and of the ex-Kaiser. The terion by which these books shall be judged ll be the ideals and principles of Washingn, of Lincoln and of the American nation. The nmittee will work to the end that only such oks as pass this test shall be used in our pub- schools until the American people itself anges its estimate of these men and their intutions. May the living spirit of American erty and freedom—which in three centuries s made of a little flock in the wilderness, a eat nation, mighty for liberty through law er all the earth—forbid that this land pert any to tamper through its schools with the undations of the temple of its constitutions, stitutions and laws.

ROF. J. HARVEY ROBINSON TAKES EXCEPTION TO T. EVERETT HARRÉ'S ARTICLE

New York, June 12, 1919.

THE EDITOR OF THE
NATIONAL CIVIC FEDERATION REVIEW:

r:

An article entitled "Who's Who in the New School" hich appeared in your issue of April 10th, accuses considerable number of well known liberal writers an illicit passion for Germany and a tendency to rward "bolshevism" in our country. Anyone who ll take the trouble to acquaint himself with the aracter of the promoters and the aims of the New hool for Social Research and with the instructors and courses of study announced for the coming year will find no basis whatsoever for the allegations in the article. I deem it, therefore, superfluous to discuss them. Nor do I think that any fairly intelligent reader of my articles in the Century Magazine and in the Atlantic Monthly on nationalism and freedom of speech, to which your writer alludes, would be able to detect any tendency to shield Germany. Indeed it was the cruel workings of inordinate German nationalism and of Prussian suppression that led me to write the articles. I wish, however, to say a word about the charge that in my textbooks I have sought to conceal the guilt of the German government in precipitating the war and endeavored to minimize its responsibility for the unheard of atrocities that have ensued.

The facts are these: Before the outbreak of the war, historical students treated the modern development of Germany in exactly the same spirit that they dealt with France, England or Italy. They were intent on telling what seemed to them at once true and important without regard to European animosities. Portraits of Bismarck and the Hohenzollern rulers seemed quite as much in place as those of Cavour or Gambetta or of Queen Victoria. During the first two years of the war there came a natural demand that school histories be brought up to date. Our country was in peaceful relations with all the belligerents; we had been enjoined by the President of the United States to maintain an attitude of strict neutrality and school authorities in view of the divided sentiment of the period recognized the expediency of this. It was at this juncture that new editions of two of the school books with which my name is associated appeared with an added chapter on the origin of the war. This was highly praised at the time as at once clear and impartial.

When the United States entered the war I was asked by the publishers to prepare a supplementary chapter on the recent course of events in which I took real satisfaction in exposing what we now know to be the true nature of the German program. I also revised earlier portions of the books with a view of satisfying the reader's natural curiosity as to the nature and development of German militarism. I could hardly expect to satisfy everyone, for all text book writers who have to touch upon living and controversial issues find it almost impossible to maintain the high standards of historical truth, as it appears to the scholar, and at the same time meet the demands of those critics whose knowledge is derived mainly from the daily newspaper and who allow themselves to be swayed by the impressions of the moment.

There was nothing in my treatment which could offend the most ardent patriot who reckoned with the great change that had overtaken public opinion. But the competition among the agents of rival textbooks is keen and at times unscrupulous, as any school superintendent or member of a board of education can testify. An attempt was made to discredit my books on the ground that I had not dealt with German matters in the same way before our entry into the war as I did after. This was equally true of all historical text books for reasons I have described, although none of their authors, so far as I am aware, were pro-German in sentiment. As it happens, I am descended from a long line of New England ancestors and while I studied in Germany many years ago I have never been partial to that country, or ever desired to visit it again.

Not content with charging that I was a friend of Germany, the writer of the article in question, accuses me of adhering to the I. W. W. The only basis for this is the fact that I signed a petition approving the raising of a fund to enable certain persons arrested on the charge of illegal conduct in connection with the I. W. W. to engage counsel. This was no reflection on our courts, nor did it indicate any approval whatsoever of the I. W. W. or their violent methods which I abhor as much as any other peace loving citizen but merely a precaution to insure justice in a time of great popular indignation. I suppose that it was a certain Anglo-Saxon love of fair play that led me to lend my name to the request for funds and I was too simple minded to anticipate how completely "interested parties" could distort my motives.

I should hardly have taken the trouble to defend myself against the attacks made upon me were it not for the fact that I believe that the public interested in education should be aware of the difficult situation in which not only I, but all writers on recent history, are placed.

(signed) JAMES HARVEY ROBINSON.

We gladly give space to the above letter from Mr. James Harvey Robinson, which is an answer to observations made upon certain of Mr. Robinson's writings by T. Everett Harré, of the staff of THE NATIONAL CIVIC FEDERATION REVIEW. This letter refers specifically to the article in the REVIEW of April 10, which we hope all our readers will re-read in the light of the statements made above by Mr. Robinson.

Mr. Robinson does not complain that any of the quotations used by Mr. Harré are incorrect, but makes the assertion that he thinks "no intelligent reader" of his articles in *The Century Magazine* or *The Atlantic Monthly* "would be able to detect any tendency to shelter Germany." Mr. Harré made no attempt to imply that Mr. Robinson's articles tended "to shelter Germany." That deduction is Mr. Robinson's. Reference to Mr. Harré's article discloses the fact that it was mainly devoted to an analysis of Mr. Robinson's article in *The Century Magazine*, of November, 1916, on "What is National Spirit?" and his article in *The Atlantic Monthly*, of December, 1917, on "Free Speech." Mr. Harré sought to interpret Mr. Robinson's attitude toward national spirit, toward the national virtue of patriotism, as well as his attitude concerning the limitations placed upon free speech by the operation of the espionage laws. As to whether or not Mr. Harré's interpretation of the undisputed quotations is justified, "intelligent readers" will decide.

The text books, "Medieval and Modern Times" and "Outlines of European History, Part II.", were not dealt with in the article of April 10; but a second article, then in preparation, was announced, which was to be devoted to an analysis of Mr. Robinson's history, in which statements in the 1916 edition, published before we entered the war, were to be compared with statements in the edition of 1918. The publication of the second article was deferred for the reason that Mr. Harré, the writer, had to undergo a hospital operation. Otherwise, the article would have appeared in the succeeding number, as announced.

During this period of delay, however, complaint was made to the editor of the REVIEW by friends of Professor Robinson that a great injustice had been done, because the 1916 edition of "Medieval and Modern Times" had been withdrawn and a revised edition of the book brought out at great expense to the publishers. This edition, it was shown, was officially passed by the Military Censor's Bureau of the War Department and is therefore unobjectionable so far as German propaganda is concerned.

Furthermore, the friends of Professor Robinson pointed out that many of the histories written prior to the entry of the United States into the war were colored by the pro-German point of view. To the question put by these gentlemen, "Why should Robinson's history alone be singled out for attack?", there was but one answer, and the assurance was given to them that the publication of the second chapter of Mr. Harré's article would be postponed until after a thorough study had been made of the other histories, and that when the publication of these articles was resumed all histories found to contain objectionable matter would be discussed. It was stated to these friends of Mr. Robinson that if the information as to the pro-German character of other histories was correct, it made the situation only so much the more serious, because it raised the question as to how far the charge that German propaganda had invaded American schools and colleges and school text books had any basis in fact. For that reason, and after consideration by officials of The National Civic Federation, as stated elsewhere editorially, it was decided to appoint a committee of experts to look into all the histories that have been used in our public schools and colleges, and not only the histories but text books on political economy, political science and civics, and that this committee would deal with the entire situation.

As the committee referred to is going to deal with this whole subject, we will not at this time enter into a discussion of the various statements made in the letter printed above.

THE EDITOR.

Dissecting the Customer's $

(Continued from page 7.)

tion would bring such complication in organization and management that men could hardly cope efficiently with them. We would have business on a scale analogous to that which governments have had to carry on during war time in making, buying and distributing munitions and clothing and food supplies. The limitations of human capacity would be felt, waste, lost motion, high costs, politics, favoritism, indolence, jealousy, bureaucracy, if not graft, would creep in. Is it not better to divide the job up into small lots and leave it to men according to their initiative and ability to handle it on their own responsibility under competitive conditions and within limits that they can comprehend and grapple with, instead of lumping it into so great a task that the magnitude surpasses even imagination?

The socialist will answer one way, the democrat the other. But I submit that we have seen that bigness has resulted so far in increased operating expense and that except for inside prices of doubtful validity, it could not compete. Why then extend it? I further submit that so long as human nature remains as it is, and so long as we employ the principle of private property and capital at all, that moderate sized units closely and competently managed under the customary incentives of the profits of the competitive system, will excel larger units in economy of operation if artificial advantages to the latter are withheld. And the limits of size in the field of distribution are much sooner reached than in the industrial field.

We have found no way of eliminating the labor of distribution. Our experiments in new forms of distributors have not disclosed economies in the performance of the work. We have not discovered an exorbitant profit, absorbed by the "grasping middleman." Personally, we know the dealer to be much like other men, we know him as a neighbor and citizen, and we know that usually he works hard without getting rich.

THE REAL WAY OUT

Have we followed this long reasoning then only to end in discouragement? No! There is a way,—not a royal, easy road to lower living costs, not a simple change of form and names and ownership in the elements of the distributing chain to bring a wondrous reformation, but a reasonable way to secure benefits in return for patient, intelligent effort toward our goal.

Let us give democracy a real trial.

Let us improve the system that we have, instead of looking at the green fields far away. How?

The one unreasonable condition that our analysis has disclosed is the *expense* of distribution, not the multiplicity of unproductive functionaries that may easily be eliminated, nor the burdensome profits so often suspected. But our distributors do spend too much to do the job.

Figure 3 indicates that 50 cents out of each dollar goes for the manufacturers and middlemen's selling expense.

Our next suspicion might be that while we cannot dispense with the wholesaler or retailer, that there may be too many of one or both to be supported economically in the field. While I believe that there would be a small net gain if the number were reduced by half or two-thirds with sturdier size for the remainder, there has not been an advantage with size or concentration of trade to warrant hope on this ground alone.

But a saving of expense could be realized by greater skill and efficiency on the part of the distributors. We suffer from too great an investment in stagnant stocks.

Supposing for simple illustration, that a dealer carries a stock worth $30,000 at selling prices and that this allows him a gross profit of 33 1/3% of his sales, thus making the cost of his stock $20,000. Supposing further that he sells out his stock once a year, i. e., he does a business of $30,000 at a gross profit of 33 1/3% or $10,000. Assume that his expenses are 28% or $8,400. He would then make a net profit of 5 1/3% on his sales or $1,600. This based upon his investment in stock would be 8% on his capital employed. On this basis he could not safely do business on less than 33 1/3% gross profit, which means 50% added to what he pays for his goods as the consumer's price. Indeed, on this basis he would be better off to invest his money in Liberty Bonds and hire out to work on a salary without risk to himself. Yet this would be a great burden on the consumer. To have his goods marked up 50% on the last distributing operation alone is "too, too hard."

Supposing now that a new dealer buys out this store and by more capable handling, without investing any more in stock, is able to sell out three times a year. Figure the results. Allowing for the moment that his expenses remain the same, he would have $90,000 of sales at 33 1/3% gross profit or $30,000 and his net profit would be $4,800 or 24% on his capital invested. Again, if he could sell out 6 times a year on the same investment in stock, he would net 48% on capital invested. On this basis even though his selling expense remained at 28%, he could somewhat reduce his prices to consumers with safety.

But let us see if his expense percentage reasonably need remain at 28%. If we analyze his expenses, we find that they fall into two classes, one depending upon the length of *time* his goods remain in stock and the other depending upon the *labor* expense of handling and selling. The first then relates to the rate of selling out,—in trade parlance called "turn over." It applies to such items as rent. The longer the goods remain in stock, the longer the dealer must charge them with rent expense for shelf-room. The second relates to the amount of goods handled irrespective of the time occupied in the process, though there need not be a direct variation of labor expense in proportion to volume. It applies to such items as advertising and wages paid to clerks.

Taking the one turnover a year if we examine the dealer's expenses they would be found to be somewhat like this:

ONE TURNOVER

	Percent	
Time Expenses:		
Rent	6	
Interest	6	
Heat, light and insurance, etc.	2	14
Labor Expenses:		
Buying and traveling	1	
Clerk hire	8	
Advertising	2	
Expressage, delivery and supplies	1	
Breakage, loss, obsolescence, miscellaneous	2	14
		28

Suppose now, that we see what results from speeding up the turnover so that the same store with the same stock investment sells out 6 times instead of once. Its time expenses amounting to half its total expense are immediately divided by six. As long as the stock is held down there will be no more rent or other "time" expenses, so that an operating charge of 14% is at once reduced to 2 1/3%.

As to labor expenses, the *amounts* will surely increase with more goods to be handled, but the *percentages* should not increase, but on the other hand should tend to show a reduction. It should not for instance, require six times as many be able to recommend goods of appropriate size, design, form and color, according to the individual need of the purchaser.

When our merchants are more thoroughly qualified in the fundamental principles of merchandising; when they understand statistical accounting, cost keeping, stock keeping, buying, practical psychology, organization, the elements of art, and the other subjects, a mastery of which would qualify them in their work, a large part of the waste in distribution will disappear. The day is coming when a man will be no more permitted to set up in the profession of distribution without first demonstrating his qualifications to society, than the druggist is now permitted to dispense drugs, the doctor to practice medicine, the lawyer to practice law, or the engineer to put "M. E." after his name.

In the meantime, governmental and other agencies can do much toward spreading some rudimentary knowledge of value in this coming profession among those already in it, just as our agricultural schools have helped the present generation of farmers. Better business record keeping can be spread. Until such a time as a more capable school of distributors is available, it will accomplish nothing to rail at the middleman, who is doing the best that he can under the conditions that society has provided, or through cooperative or other movements to set up new stores under the charge, as usually happens, of those who are even less experienced and less qualified than the present distributors. And when the same principles of improvement are applied not only to the retailer, but to the wholesaler as well, and to the marketing departments of the manufacturers, a truly great economy will be found possible.

I submit, therefore, that this is the only road to lower costs; that we cannot eliminate the middle man; that high prices are not due to his extravagant profits, but to the undeveloped standards of operation, and that no device save that of education will overcome this fundamental deficiency.

Pope Leo's Labor Letter

(*Continued from Page* 13)

the other; capital cannot do without labor, nor labor without capital. Mutual agreement results in pleasantness and good order; perpetual conflict necessarily produces confusion and outrage. Now, in preventing such strife as this, and in making it impossible, the efficacy of Christianity is marvelous and manifold. First of all, there is nothing more powerful than Religion (of which the Church is the interpreter and guardian) in drawing rich and poor together, by reminding each class of its duties to the other, and especially of the duties of justice. Thus Religion teaches the laboring man and the workman to carry out honestly and well all equitable agreements freely made, never to injure capital, nor to outrage the person of an employer; never to employ violence in representing his own cause, nor to engage in riot and disorder; and to have nothing to do with men of evil principles, who work upon the people with artful promises, and raise foolish hopes which usually end in disaster and in repentance when too late. Religion teaches the rich man and the employer that their work people are not their slaves; that they must respect in every man his dignity as a man and as a Christian; that labor is nothing to be ashamed of, if we listen to right reason and to Christian philosophy, but is an honorable employment, enabling a man to sustain his life in an upright and creditable way; and that it is shameful and inhuman to treat men like chattels to make money by, or to look upon them merely as so much muscle or physical power. Thus, again, Religion teaches that, as among the workmen's concerns are Religion herself, and things spiritual and mental, the employer is bound to see that he has time for the duties of piety; that he be not exposed to corrupting influences and dangerous occasions; and that he be not led away to neglect his home and family or to squander his wages. Then, again, the employer must never tax his work-people beyond their strength, nor employ them in work unsuited to their sex or age. His great and principal obligation is to give to every one that which is just. Doubtless before we can decide whether wages are adequate many things have to be considered; but rich men and masters should remember this—that to exercise pressure for the sake of gain, upon the indigent and destitute, and to make one's profit out of the need of another, is condemned by all laws, human and divine. To defraud any one of wages that are his due is a crime which cries to the avenging anger of Heaven. *Behold, the hire of the laborers * * * which by fraud has been kept back by you, crieth; and the cry of them hath entered the ears of the Lord of the Sabaoth.** Finally, the rich must religiously refrain from cutting down the workman's earnings, either by force, fraud, or by usurious dealing; and with the more reason because the poor man is weak and unprotected, and because his slender means should be sacred in proportion to their scantiness.

Studying Industry Abroad

(*Continued from Page* 9)

talistic system, it can be seen that the French employer faces a situation radically different from that of his British neighbors.

The French Government does not seem as alive to the demands of the industrial reconstruction period as the British, though a national eight-hour law has recently been passed and Government officials are by no means blind to the situation that must be faced.

After three tense weeks in Italy, part of the Commission returned to England to take up the loose ends of a number of matters that it had been impossible to bring to a conclusion before the departure for Paris. Shortly before our departure we had the pleasure of entertaining our friends of the National Alliance of Employers and Employed at an informal dinner, and there cemented friendships which we are sure will always endure. There is a good prospect of a visit from these British friends this fall and the Civic Federation is doing all in its power to make this possible. If the British Commission comes, it will make a special study of housing.

Just before sailing, the Commission waited on Ambassador Davis, at his request, and made a verbal report on the information it had gathered, with which he expressed himself as being well pleased.

No account of the trip would be complete without an acknowledgment of the contribution made to its success by the Chairman, Mr. Charles Mayer, who, despite a serious illness while abroad, and heavy responsibilities as Counsel for the National Farmers Union at the Peace Conference and Adviser to the Polish Government, nevertheless never failed to respond when needed and, through his large acquaintance abroad, was able to get the Commission into instant touch with individuals and organizations that were important to its work.

Certainly everyone who went abroad feels that he witnessed a wonderful time in the world's industrial history and none who went can ever forget the splendid hospitality that was met with wherever the Commission went.

The Commission is now hard at work on its report, which should be of great value to American industry.

*St. James v. 4.

Freedom of Teaching in the Schools

SOCIALISTS BELIEVING IN COMMUNIST MANIFESTO HAVE NO PLACE IN PUBLIC SCHOOL SYSTEM

By JOHN L. TILDSLEY
ASSOCIATE SUPERINTENDENT, DEPARTMENT OF EDUCATION, NEW YORK CITY

(From a speech before the Public Education Association, New York City, April 26, 1919)

THE most important portion of to-day's discussion is the question of freedom of expression. One teacher of the De Witt Clinton High School was disciplined for certain things that he said. Another one was disciplined for certain things that he said and also for recommending a list of books to pupils in his class through the medium of a pamphlet that he put in the bookstore. These two cases bring the question flatly before us.

I do not want to have a teacher in a public school system who wears a muzzle or who even wears a bridle. But there are certain kinds of people that I believe have no place in a school system. I believe that any teacher who needs to be muzzled in order to keep him decent or who needs to be bridled in order that he may not run amuck among the morals of the students, is not the kind of person who ought to be in our school system at all. The remedy is not to limit freedom of speech, but it is to limit the kind of teacher that you have in your school system.

I think the time has come frankly for us to recognize that there are certain undesirable types of people who are applying for admission to the teaching ranks, and who ought not to be in the teaching ranks. It is not an accident that this trouble has arisen only within the past two years. When I came into this school system twenty-one years ago, we did not have troubles of the kind we have been discu[illegible]g, not because we were any less intelligent [illegible] the young men who are coming today, not b[illegible]se we were any less ambitious, not because we were any the less interested in the welfare of our pupils, but because in those days the men [illegible]d women who came into our school system ha[illegible] een brought up in an American environmen[illegible]

THE OLD-T[illegible] TRAINING

We had been trained to believe that progress is a matter of slow development; that experience is a most valuable asset in life, and that we go on improving our day and generation by taking advantage of that which is past. For the last few years we have had coming into our school system some people who have never had the advantage of that experience; they have never had the benefit of these ideas; and they have come in not steeped in those Anglo-Saxon ideas, or more liberally those Western European ideas of which our President is so conspicuous an exponent.

But they have come in with the idea that all that is old is useless; that that which has stood the test of time in matters of government, in matters of thought, is not worthy of their notice; that to believe in that which has stood the test of experience is to be old fashioned, whether it be in matters of government, in matters of the conduct of business, in matters of morals, or in matters of taste. Consequently our trouble arises at the present time not because our Board of Education is drawing a tight rein, but because we have in our school system teachers who have not the feeling that the first business of a teacher is to be decent.

I realize that this is a strong statement, but I am prepared to defend it. For example, in a pamphlet entitled—"Toward the New Democracy" (page 84) we find: "Modern psychology teaches that books in themselves cannot be objectionable; it is rather the subjective state of the contemplative mind that determines the objection. 'To the pure, all things are pure.' Consequently, you can take any book no matter how sensuous, no matter how lascivious, and put it into the hands of a boy or girl of fourteen years of age, and no harm will come.

Now I do not wish to put limitation on the right of the teacher holding such views to speak. I say that man has no right to be in the school system. We won't muzzle him! We won't have him in the school system at all!

I was quoted today as having said a few years ago that a man who was a socialist has no place in the school system. I do not know whether I said it or not. But I will say today, speaking only for myself, and not for the Board of Education or the Board of Superintendents, that men and women who are Marxian Socialists, who believe in the communist manifesto, have no right in the school system because such teachers believe in the overturn by force of those elements on which our civilization is based. They are opposed to the rights of property; they are opposed to the family as at present constituted; they are opposed to the very thing for which Lowell pleads—the right of every man to his chance in a democracy and to know that he has a chance.

For under a Marxian democracy, so-called, under a Marxian dictatorship of the proletariat, there would be no chance for the development of the individual. In a public school system under a democratic government such as ours, there is no place for the Marxian revolutionary socialist. To prove that I am not tilting against windmills allow me to read quotations from a letter in *The New York Call* signed by thirteen persons, three of whom have been teachers in our schools:

> We believe that the Socialist party must teach solely and agitate exclusively for the overthrow of capitalism and the establishment of an industrial democracy. A political party cannot organize all workers in the economic field; but we believe that the party should assist this program of organization by a propaganda of *revolutionary* unionism. . . .
>
> We believe that the Socialist party should send delegates to participate in an international congress to be attended by representatives of the *revolutionary* socialist parties of all countries, but that the party should refuse to participate in any conference called by moderate Socialists or social patriots.

Another provision calls for the abolition from the party platform of all plans for social reform. This "party of the Left" stands for the absolute overthrow of all movement for the development of society by orderly progress and this letter is signed not only by Scott Nearing, Louis Lochner and others, but also by David P. Berenberg, who until one year ago was a teacher of English in the Boys' High School, by Benjamin Glassberg, of whom you have heard today as one of the martyrs of the autocratic Board of Education, and by Jacob Lawn, a teacher in the elementary schools.

We are, then, face to face with the question of the day. We all agree that the idea of freedom of speech, freedom of thought; but, unfortunately we are confounding two ideas. Nobody desires to interfere with your freedom of thought as a person. You can think as you see fit. But what we are discussing today is the qualification of teachers in a public school. The term "inquisition" was used today and I was criticized because I called in some teachers of the De Witt Clinton High School and asked them certain questions about their views. It has been said that a man's views should not enter into t[illegible] question of his qualifications as a teacher. B[illegible] I believe that far more important than a man conduct or what he says, are his views; f[illegible] what a man thinks, that he is. Every teach[illegible] will inevitably teach that which he is. Ther[illegible]fore all remedies seeking to solve the question [illegible] what limits to set to freedom of speech will fa[illegible]

The only remedy is to devise some syste[illegible] by which the teachers who enter a school syste[illegible] shall be the teachers who will take our boys an[illegible] girls and make of them the kind of citizens th[illegible] the majority of the people of this country d[illegible]sire them to be. I believe that the majority [illegible] the people of this country today, that the m[illegible]jority of the people of the City of New York, [illegible] not wish their children trained to believe th[illegible] the best way to bring in the better day is by [illegible] overthrow of our present established institution[illegible]

FUTURE RESTS WITH TEACHERS

I believe in constant change. I believe th[illegible] you all believe in constant change. I belie[illegible] that we all think that tomorrow ought to be be[illegible]ter than today and I agree that upon the teac[illegible]ers of this city rests the future of the city. T[illegible] make that city worthy of the city's past is o[illegible] task, and we ought to realize that it is our tas[illegible]

If we are not in sympathy with the belief [illegible] the aspirations of the majority of the people [illegible] this country, we do not have to remain teacher[illegible] It is always within our power to resign, to g[illegible] out where we can think as we please and spea[illegible] as we please. The unfortunate thing is that w[illegible] as teachers, think too much of our own individu[illegible] welfare. The schools do not exist for our benef[illegible]

I, for one, cannot see why it is that the insta[illegible] we find that a teacher is advocating a poli[illegible] which is destructive of our American instit[illegible]tions, that any other teacher should feel calle[illegible] upon to come to his defence and to insist th[illegible] such a man be retained in our school system. [illegible] do not believe that you do. I think those wh[illegible] do are very few in number.

Allow me one closing word—I have been [illegible] member of the public school system of the Cit[illegible] of New York for twenty-one years; as a teache[illegible] of history; as principal of a high school, an[illegible] now as superintendent. I have always been fre[illegible] to think as I saw fit, to teach by any metho[illegible] that I saw fit; to teach any content I saw f[illegible]

As superintendent in charge of high school[illegible] at the present time I am not hampered by th[illegible] Board of Education or the Board of Superi[illegible]tendents. They cooperate with me in every wa[illegible] possible to carry out the policies which hav[illegible] been decided upon in the high schools. A[illegible]though our system has its defects, I do not b[illegible]lieve the person who is energetic, who is though[illegible]ful, who is willing to plan, is seriously hampere[illegible] If, because he suffers a rebuff, he stands in [illegible] corner and sulks, then he cannot accomplish r[illegible]sults. But I see about me everywhere person[illegible] who have thought their own thoughts, worke[illegible] in their own way, and who have accomplishe[illegible] great things for the city.

I believe that autocracy in the school syste[illegible] does exist, but that it can be overcome by an[illegible] teacher who, instead of nursing his grievance and thinking only of his own advancement, wi[illegible] devote himself to the development of the boy[illegible] and girls committed to his care and to makin[illegible] smooth and effective the working of the grea[illegible] organism of which we are all a part.

Tyrrel Print, New York.

The National
Civic Federation Review

Vol. IV. NEW YORK, JULY 30, 1919 No. 17

PLOT TO OVERTHROW GOVERNMENT

N. Y. LEGISLATIVE PROBE EXPOSES RADICAL GROUPS UNITED TO ESTABLISH "DICTATORSHIP OF PROLETARIAT" IN AMERICA—RAND SCHOOL HOTBED OF SEDITION

WITH the well-defined, specific and deliberate purpose of overthrowing the existing government of the United States and establishing a "dictatorship of the proletariat," such as exists under Lenine and Trotzky in Russia, the radical organizations of the country—divided into three principal groups, anarchists, syndicalists and socialists—have united and are now working together on a common platform. That platform is the platform of the Russian Communist party, known as the Bolsheviki, which overturned the democratic Kerensky government by armed force and which has prevailed in Russia through the exercise of arbitrary armed might.

By T. EVERETT HARRÉ

That the Socialists, including both the Right and Left, or revolutionary, wings, the syndicalists, including the I. W. W.'s, and the anarchists have combined in a nation-wide propaganda designed to convert every class of workers to the theories of Trotzky and Lenine, the ultimate purpose of which is to precipitate in America a revolution such as has made of Russia a bloody shambles, has been definitely and conclusively proven by evidence produced during the investigations of the New York State Legislative Committee, of which Senator Clayton R. Lusk is chairman, into seditious and disloyal activities in the State of New York.

So alarming have been the revelations already made of the nature and extent of inflammatory agitation seeking to promote mass revolution for the overthrow of the government and the destruction of all existing order, that the Hon. Alfred E. Smith, Governor of New York, has called a special term of the Supreme Court to begin August 11, for the purpose of investigating criminal anarchy and all other criminal activities directed against organized government in the state and nation. Aroused by the widespread activities of Bolshevist agents, a number of states in the Middle West have notified Senator Lusk of their intention of be-

LEGISLATIVE COMMITTEE INVESTIGATING BOLSHEVISM

Standing, left to right: Assemblyman W. W. Pellett, Assemblyman Frederick S. Burr, Attorney General Charles D. Newton and Assemblyman Peter P. McElligott.
Seated, left to right: Senator J. J. Boylan, Senator J. H. Walters, Senator Clayton R. Lusk, chairman; Senator D. Carroll and Assemblyman Louis M. Martin.

ginning investigations, asking that any information developed in the New York inquiry which bears on their states be afforded. Already the State authorities of Ohio and Illinois have sent representatives to New York to confer with the Lusk Committee, with this purpose.

New York City, as it was the center and hotbed of German propaganda, has been likewise the center and hotbed of the propaganda of the "reds." When the proposal was made that the New York Legislature appoint a special committee to undertake an inquiry into seditious and disloyal propaganda and intrigues, it was believed that by uncovering the chief centers of revolutionary activities in New York the ramifications of their organizations, agents and propaganda throughout the country would also be exposed. By reason of a special espionage act passed shortly after America entered the war, the Attorney General of the State of New York enjoys unique powers enabling him to subpoena witnesses and to compel them to testify under oath. Attorney General Newton is acting as chief counsel to the Lusk Committee, and has assigned one of his deputies, with full powers, to cooperate in the investigations. The probe of the Lusk Committee, to be supplemented by a special Grand Jury investigation, is the most important of its kind ever undertaken, and the evidence already produced establishes the gravity of the situation and the great and real menace confronting the country in the plots and propaganda of the enemies of peace and order. As a result of the investigations, it is proposed by the members of the Committee that the legislature of New York State—and it is hoped the legislatures of other states as well—will pass drastic measures to curb disloyal and un-American agitation and to suppress absolutely the activities of all those who advocate the overthrow of government by force.

AMERICAN RADICALS ABET LENINE'S AGENT

Sensational as have been the disclosures already made by the Lusk Committee, it is declared by members that the investigation so far has only scratched the surface of revolutionary radical propaganda. The evidence already produced clearly proves the connection between American Socialists and official representatives of Lenine and Trotzky. This evidence has established the fact that the Soviet Bureau located at 110 West Fortieth Street, New York, of which L. C. A. K. Martens is head, has been working in conjunction and in close cooperation with Socialist organizations, especially the Rand School of Social Science.

Preliminary to the hearings of the Lusk Committee, and acting upon search warrants issued by Magistrate William McAdoo, raids were made of the headquarters of Ludwig C. A. K. Martens, "representative in the United States of the Russian Socialist Soviet Republic," and of the Rand School of Social Science, 7 East Fifteenth Street, New York. From the documents and correspondence seized, it was revealed that the Soviet Bureau, while pretending to be purely commercial, spent no money whatever for commercial purposes; that the daily credit bank balance of the bureau varied from $5,000 to $9,000; that deposits were made in cash by Martens; that "large sums" of money had been received for propaganda purposes from Russia, and that the Soviet organization maintained a bureau for the defense of men charged with crimes against the Government of the United States. It was shown that the Rand School of Social Science was a hotbed of seditious activities and a clearing house for the dissemination of Bolshevist revolutionary propaganda urging the taking over of the State and the establishment of a dictatorship of the proletariat by mass action. It was shown that the Rand School booked as lecturers men who had been convicted and sentenced for crimes against the Government of the United States.

HUGH FRAYNE

Whose Testimony Showed All Groups of Radicals United on Bolshevist Program.

A form letter sent out by the correspondence department of the Rand School, of which David P. Berenberg is director, declared: "What are you going to do when the State robs you and your union and so make you helpless to strike? There is only one thing to do: Take over the State. Are the members of your local prepared to take over and conduct wisely and well the affairs of your town and country? Are you ready to meet the militia when the powers of the state and courts are against you?"

Among the papers seized at the Rand School was a copy of the *New York Communist*, of June 14, 1919, of which John Reed is editor, in which it was declared: "The Left Wing hopes that the proletariat will conquer its enemy, the capitalist class, with as little bloodshed as possible." Among papers seized in the offices of the so-called "ambassador" from the Lenine-Trotzky government was a letter addressed to the workers of Europe and America by Nicholas Lenine, in which he advocated the "overthrow of the bourgeoise and the annihilation of bourgeoise parliaments, ... soviet rule and proletarian dictatorship." The tremendous scope of the Socialist, revolutionary, Bolshevist propaganda, through newspapers, monthlies, books and pamphlets, as well as lecture itineraries covering the entire country, in which the Soviet ambassadorial bureau and the Socialists cooperated, was demonstrated by the seized documents.

An illuminating sidelight upon the profits enjoyed by the professional "emancipators of the disinherited and downtrodden," the spell-binders of the proletarian revolution, was afforded by an examination of the bank books of the Rand School. Scott Nearing, who had been dismissed from the University of Pennsylvania, would, according to the Committee, have probably earned a maximum of $200 a month by teaching. According to the accounts of the Rand School, Mr. Nearing, as a "silver-tongued" monger of sedition and social discontent, a "champion of the oppressed and exploited," earned in one month a total of $555, which with "extras" added, amounted to $610. Just how the "poor and disinherited" are gulled for contributions running into the thousands was revealed by correspondence of members of the Rand School, one letter telling that $25,000 had been raised toward a fund of $40,000.

NAMES HEARD BEFORE

Of especially significant interest were lists of names—"evidently," according to Archibald E. Stevenson, associate counsel to the Committee, "a specially prepared mailing list"—found in the headquarters of the "official ambassador" from Lenine. This list included the names of a number of persons who had been mentioned in the "Who's Who" of radicals and pacifists given to the Overman Committee in its investigation of German propaganda. It included the names of people who have been notoriously active in pacifist and anti-war propaganda, who had opposed our going to war with Germany, who had advocated a premature, compromise, patched-up peace with Germany, who more recently have rabidly frothed at the mouth over the terms asked of Germany in the Versailles treaty, who have defended the I. W. W. and conscientious objectors, who have defended and befriended the Russian Bolsheviki, and who have openly or covertly sympathized with or abetted various revolutionary, radical and un-American movements. On the list were also the names of men who, having held government positions, would not, it would be supposed, be in sympathy with a movement which meant the overthrow of the existing government and the abrogation of the Constitution of the United States.

Among the names on the list were: Leonard Abbott, according to Mr. Stevenson, "connected with the Ferrer association of anarchists in New Jersey"; Robert Bruere, a writer; B. W. Huebsch, pacifist, and publisher of "a large number of books on anti-war subjects"; John Lovejoy Elliot, "active on the Board of Directors of the National Civil Liberties Bureau"; Carleton Hayes, an associate professor at Columbia, signer to an appeal made in June, 1918, to raise a defense fund of $50,000 for the I. W. W. leaders on trial in Chicago for seditious conspiracy to obstruct the Government in its conduct of the war, and until lately associated with the Military Intelligence division engaged in the investigation of seditious and disloyal activities; Morris Hillquit, leader of the Socialist Party, who campaigned for the office of mayor of New York in 1917 on a platform advocating a separate peace with Germany and now legal counsel for the Soviet Bureau; Paul U. Kellogg, editor of the *Survey*, who did his midget best to keep America from going to war with Germany and later advocated the British Labor Party plan for peace by negotiation with the Central Powers; George W. Kirchwey, federal director of the United States Employment Service; Louis Lochner, secretary of the Ford Peace expedition and since active in the People's Council; Rabbi Judah L. Magnes, who has impugned the loyalty of his own race by boasting of the leadership of Jews in revolutionary movements and who was mentioned in an aerogram, "No. 381," of Count von Bernstorff to his government as "belonging to circles very friendly to us"; Max Pine, of the United Hebrew Trades; H. Overstreet, a professor at City College; Gilbert Roe, legal counsel for various radicals; Norman Thomas, agitator for "conscientious objectors"; Walter E. Weyl, associate editor of the *New Republic*, author of "The End of the War," in which the Allies were contemptibly assailed and peace by compromise with Germany was urged; Amos Pinchot; Thomas D. Thatcher, of the Y. M. C. A., who has in lectures exonerated the Bolsheviki of crimes charged against them; Lillian D. Wald, head of the Henry Street Settlement, member of pacifist organizations and American delegate to the recent International Women's Congress at Zurich which attacked the terms of the Versailles treaty; Scott Nearing; John Reed and Albert Rhys Williams, both formerly engaged by the Bolshevist publicity bureau in Petrograd; and the famous and dashing Raymond Robins, Red Cross Colonel, exploited in the *Metropolitan Magazine* as having inherited the mantle of Theodore Roosevelt, and who is the most popular and most-quoted authority of Bolshevist advocates, agents and sympathizers. Testifying before the Senate Committee investigating Bolshevism, this same Robins

JAMES P. HOLLAND
Declared A. F. of L. Invulnerable to Radical Assaults

it to be a center of Bolshevist propaganda and to a large extent of Left Wing Socialist and I. W. W. propaganda as well, Attorney General Charles Newton began proceedings for the annulment of the charter of the American Socialist Society, the corporate title of the organization operating the Rand School of Social Science. There immediately rushed to the defense of the Rand School all those organs which had made a unique record for themselves by opposing our going to war with Germany, by advocating a premature compromise peace through negotiation with the Central Powers, by defending and championing the German-subsidized Bolsheviki, and which of late have howled execrations against the terms of peace exacted by America and the Allies from the Huns. Loud in their denunciation of the raids made upon the headquarters of the Bolshevik agent, Martens, and of the Rand School were the *New Republic* and the *Nation*, which now adds to its inglorious and un-American record the crowning dishonor of publishing a confidential communication from the United States Department of State to Col. House in Paris, which, with other confidential documents, it is reported, were, according to evidence in possession of the Government, stolen in Paris by certain radicals who had gained entrée to the headquarters of the American Peace delegation.

To the defense of the Rand School have rushed, with two or three exceptions and with two or three new sympathizers, the same old crowd of radicals, so-called liberals, pacifists, pro-Germans and others, who are mouthing the same old trite and hypocritical protests about the violation of constitutional rights and of the rights of liberty and free discussion.

Vociferous in their stock, stereotyped rantings about the violations of the "fundamental rights of freedom," the persecution and jailing of "thousands whose only crime consists in voicing their protest against economic junkerdom in America" and who "languish in jail because they dare to think," the Socialists on July 21 launched at the People's House in New York, the headquarters of the Rand School, a campaign to raise $100,000 for the nation-wide dissemination of propaganda and to fight the Lusk Committee and other official bodies engaged in attempting to prevent the spread of radicalism. Upon the launching of this campaign, the People's House became a center of feverish activity; a special corps of stenographers and typists engaged in sending out thousands of letters asking for contributions, in which appeal the recent raid on the Rand School by agents of the Lusk Committee was called a "Cossack invasion" and our national and state administrations were denounced as the obedient tools of Capitalism. It was announced that more than $3,500 had been collected at the meeting at which the drive was formally launched, and that the radical defense fund had been enriched by a single contribution of $2,000, sent with a letter in which the Lusk Committee agents were characterized as "raiders and safe crackers." Out of the money contributed to the fund, the radicals propose to distribute 50,000,000 pamphlets throughout the country. After referring to the appropriation by Congress of $2,000,000 to probe and suppress revolutionary activities, the Socialist appeal declared: "We are being confronted by an enemy with millions at his disposal. Will we at least respond with thousands to carry on the conflict?" At six open air meetings held simultaneously on July 21, in New York City by Socialists to protest against the actions of the Lusk Committee and the attitude of the United States toward the Bolshevik régimes in Russia and Hungary, resolutions were adopted demanding the immediate withdrawal of American troops from Russia and the lifting of the blockade against Soviet Russia and Soviet Hungary.

A so-called "non-Socialist" protest against the action to revoke the Rand School charter, issued through the National Civil Liberties Bureau—which has engaged in the defense of the criminal I. W. W. leaders, "conscientious objectors" and persons convicted of violation of the espionage laws—was signed by Stanley Bowmar, John A. Fitch, J. A. H. Hopkins, Rev. John Howard Melish, Allen McCurdy, Don Seitz, George Foster Peabody, Paul U. Kellog, editor of the *Survey*, Walter Lippmann and Walter E. Weyl. Walters Lippmann and Weyl are associate editors of the *New Republic*, whose record in the war has been fully analyzed and exposed. Weyl is the author of a book assailing the Allies, advocating a compromise peace by negotiation and prophesying a "final war after the war," a class war, such as Bolshevik-agent Martens, the Socialists and other radical organizations, including the Rand School, according to the record of the Lusk Committee investigation, have been engaged in promoting.

RADICALS MOSTLY ALIENS

Among the representatives of organized labor who have testified before the Legislative Committee, and who have proven of invaluable help in exposing the character and activities of the enemies of orderly and constructive social progress, were Mr. Hugh Frayne, General Organizer of the American Federation of Labor in charge of the New York office, and Mr. James P. Holland, president of the New York State Federation of Labor.

The American Federation of Labor, declared Mr. Holland, has proven itself proof against the radicals, who, since the socialistic element completely wrecked one of the strongest labor organizations in the country in 1889, have made mighty efforts to win over members of conservative organizations and disrupt the Federation. At the last convention in Atlantic City the radical element met with an overwhelming defeat when they attempted to put through a resolution favoring the soviet form of government. Of a total membership of 900,000 union members in the state of New York, not more than 60,000 or 70,000 are radical, and of these only 25,000 have been converted by the radicals in the last three years. The radicals, said Mr. Holland, had not succeeded in getting into the building trades, longshoremen's and other organizations, but had met their greatest success among the garment workers, furriers, boot and shoe manufacturers, machinists and hotel and restaurant employees. "At least 85 per cent of them," said Mr. Holland, "are people who are not citizens and do not intend to become citizens." While ninety per cent of the American Federation of Labor members are citizens, less than thirty per cent of the radical organizations are American citizens, and some of these are citi-

(*Continued on Page 12*)

Striking Contrasts Between U. S. an

FUNDAMENTAL DIFFERENCES OF UNDERLYING PRINCIPLES SHOWN AMERICAN OBSERVERS RETURNING FROM ABROAD AND

By RALPH M. EASLEY

THE members of the commission sent by The National Civic Federation to study industrial conditions in England, France and Italy have returned and are now at work formulating their report. While many of the questions which they will discuss will be of general interest to the readers of the REVIEW, some of them will be of especial interest to employers and wage earners. The Federation's commission is the only one sent from this country to Europe since the signing of the armistice, which has been composed of representatives of the three groups—employers, wage earners and the public, and therefore its conclusions, where unanimous, ought to be of great value at this time.

On every returning steamer for the last three months there have been business men who, since the signing of the armistice, have been studying commercial and financial propositions in Europe, either in behalf of the Government or of private interests. Naturally, these men have something to say about the labor question, because no one could go to Europe now without hearing the labor question discussed on every street corner, in every meeting place, club and parliament. Out of this chorus of clashing views, the public emerges bewildered. British, French and Italian labor politics baffle the most expert students of international labor affairs. Even labor men themselves sometimes throw up their hands in despair. So these business men could hardly be expected in a few short weeks to grasp all the intricacies of that complicated situation. Some of them make a comparison between the British and American labor movements, to the disadvantage of the latter. Many vigorously assert that labor is going to be the ruling force in all governments and some of them fear that the United States will soon be in the hands of Lenine, Trotzky, Bela Kun and Company. This article is written in the hope that it will throw a few side lights, however feeble, on the situation, with the consciousness that there are those who will doubtless say that it only adds to the confusion.

One of the puzzling questions upon which it is hoped The National Civic Federation's commission will throw light is: "What is meant by 'democratization of industry?'" Or, to state it in another way: "What part of the management of industry is demanded by Labor?" So generally have writers and speakers voiced the feeling that labor is to have a larger, if not a dominating, share in the management of the plants, that employers and labor representatives are alike using those phrases, although they do not mean the same thing when they do.

When trade union men talk of "democratization of industry," they mean collective bargaining, through which agency they can negotiate on equal terms with employers on their wages, hours and working conditions. Employers using the term are generally non-union employers and when they do so they usually refer to the method of dealing with those same questions, not through the unions but by means of shop or "grievance" committees, organized along many different lines but with that general idea in view. Others mean by "democracy in industry" profit sharing, stock participation and other schemes of that character. When the socialists use the term they mean the state taking over the industry and running it. The I. W. W., the Left Wing Socialists and the Bolshevists, which are all about the same thing, mean by "democracy in industry" the taking over of the plant and the operating of it by the workers themselves.

A recent statement that has attracted wide attention is that of Mr. Bernard M. Baruch, who represented our Government at Paris in a financial capacity almost from the beginning of the Peace Conference. This statement comes to this country as an interview given by Mr. Baruch to a correspondent of *The New York Times* in Paris:

> Labor never again will be satisfied with the old conditions. A proprietary share in what he produces must be given to the workingman and he has got to be taken into the management of the corporations by which he is employed. The workingmen must sit on the boards of directors. These conditions are here and must be promptly recognized. Capital, instead of hanging back and passively resisting, should run to meet the advancing conditions, or else labor may not be satisfied merely with what it is entitled to, and may demand more than its share.

What does Mr. Baruch mean by "a proprietary share?" Does he mean profit sharing or stock participation or the bonus system? If so, he can easily ascertain by inquiry that not a single trade union organization in the United States or, for that matter, in any part of the world, demands or even believes in profit sharing or any other substitute for "just wages." As organized labor is growing by leaps and bounds, no employer can be satisfied that a scheme he works out satisfactorily with his non-union men today will not be overturned tomorrow by the advent into his plant of the union agent. Therefore the voice of organized labor, whether one agrees with it or not, cannot be ignored in dealing with this subject.

Unfortunately, the history of profit sharing does not point to profit sharing as the great panacea. If it did, England, the home of profit sharing, would have approved it. The British government in 1912 published an analysis of every attempt at profit sharing made in the United Kingdom during one hundred and twenty-five years. It showed that there had been 299 such ventures, 133 of which had gone by the board. In the remaining 166 there were only 106,000 employees involved, out of a possible 15,000,000, and of that number three-fourths were in public utility plants, where there was practically always a profit to distribute. Here and there in this country, as in England, there are to be found a few corporations which seem to have made it work, but there are particular reasons for it in those instances. As a general proposition, it has failed.

Again, what does Mr. Baruch mean when he says: "The workingman has got to be taken into the management of the corporations by which he is employed?" Or, is that answered by his next declaration: "The workingman must sit on the boards of directors"? There is a vast difference between one or two workingmen sitting on a board of directors with twenty-five capitalists, and their being "taken into the management of the corporation." Of course, "taken in" might be used in a facetious sense, but Mr. Baruch did not mean it that way. If the workingman is going to sit on a board of directors as a stockholder, it will be necessary for him to own stock. But in a billion-dollár or a hundred million-dollar or even a million-dollar corporation, how much voice would a workingman be likely to secure by the shares of stock he is able to buy? If the purpose is merely to have him present at board meetings, so that he can explain back to his brother workers why market conditions, for instance, would not permit of socialism. The following extracts from it have the familiar ring of the Marxianists, also of the Trotzkyists.

> The individualist system of capitalist production, based on the private ownership and competitive administration of land and capital—may, we hope, indeed have received a deathblow. . . . And the Labor Party refuses absolutely to believe that the British people will permanently tolerate any reconstruction . . . involved in the abandonment of British industry to . . . separate private employers. . . . What the Labor Party looks to is a genuinely scientific reorganization of the nation's industry . . . on the basis of the common ownership of the means of production; the equitable sharing of the proceeds among all who participate in any capacity and only among these, and the adoption in particular services and occupations, of those systems and methods of administration and control that may be found, in practice, best to promote the public interest.
>
> The Labor Party stands not merely for the principle of the common ownership of the nation's land, to be applied, as suitable opportunities occur, but also, specifically, for the immediate nationalization of railways, mines and the production of electrical power.

So much for the "fear disarming" program of the British Labor Party. But fully as much to the point is the special report of the labor members of the Provisional Joint Committee of the British Industrial Conference. Notwithstanding the radical agreement reached and signed by both the employer and labor members of that committee, the labor members felt called upon to add a memorandum, in the nature of a minority report, based entirely upon the British Labor Party's program, from the "Conclusions" of which we quote the following familiar socialist phrases, the italics being the Committee's:

> The fundamental causes of Labor unrest are to be found rather in the growing determination of Labor to challenge the whole existing structure of capitalist industry than in any of the more special and smaller grievances which come to the surface at any particular time.
>
> These root causes are twofold—the breakdown of the existing capitalist system of industrial organization, in the sense that the mass of the working class is now firmly convinced that *production for private profit is not an equitable basis on which to build*, and that a vast extension of public ownership and democratic control of industry is urgently necessary.
>
> * * * * * * * * *
>
> It is not enough merely to tinker with particular grievances or to endeavor to reconstruct the old system by slight adjustments to meet the new demands of Labor. It is essential to question the whole basis on which our industry has been conducted in the past and to endeavor to find, *in substitution for the motive of private gain*, some other motive which will serve better as the foundation of a democratic system. . . .
>
> This cannot be done so long as industry continues to be conducted for private profit, and the widest possible extension of public ownership and democratic control of industry is therefore the first necessary condition of the removal of industrial unrest.

It is not strange that anyone meeting the British labor leaders in the way that Mr. Vanderlip, or any other business man going to Europe to ascertain conditions, would meet them, should form a splendid impression of them and be strongly influenced by their views. These labor men are plausible, able and always genteel. They have such an air of sincerity and apparent wisdom when they announce with dogmatic fervor their "fundamental economics" that it is easier to go along with them than to combat them. But when Mr. Vanderlip made the following statement in his celebrated speech at the dinner of the Economic Club in New York, he forgot for the moment his own knowledge of economics and laid aside his own wide experience in detecting fallacies. He said:

> It is not altogether hunger and want, because you find the present order of society questioned and questioned by a considerable minority in England. There has come to be a suspicion of the efficacy of higher wages in the minds of a great many workers. They organize, they strike, they get advances, and they find they have no more comfort than they had before. The cost of living has risen in many cases more rapidly than even the rapidly rising wages, and there is a grave suspicion in the minds of a great body of workers that there is some legerdemain, there is something by which you can apparently hand them higher wages but so manipulate the value of what they pay the wages in that they are worth no more to the man who earns them; and, with that suspicion in the minds of men, there is always inflammable material.

On this *The New York Call* makes the following comment:

> Such statements are not calculated to confirm the faith of the masses in the permanence or the desirability of modern capitalism.

The Call is right; and Mr. Vanderlip is wrong in his statements. He is only repeating what socialist writers and speakers have been saying for the last twenty years and what they will continue to say for twenty, forty or a hundred years to come.

The Rt. Hon. James H. Thomas, M. P., already referred to in this article, has just been paying a second visit to America. At a number of private meetings of employers, where he was a guest, he made statements which many desired to combat but the character of the occasions forbade anything of a controversial nature. However, the *New York Tribune*, on July 6, published a full page interview with him, in which he repeated some of the statements he had previously made privately, thus releasing them for public discussion. One of these statements was to the effect that a Labor government would soon succeed the present Coalition government in Great Britain and he then went on to say:

> There seems to be far more apprehension in this country than at home of the probable results of a labor government in Great Britain. I suppose the explanation is that the British people know us best. We are neither bandits nor robbers, anxious to confiscate property and pull down the old bases of society. Our party is made up of men trained to face responsibilities, who recognize that justice is an essential feature of any political programme. No party can exist unless actuated by and influenced in all its decisions by the high moral principle of justice and equity to all.

A question which many persons wanted to ask Mr. Thomas was: "Just what people in England is it who are feeling so complacent, secure and happy over the prospect of having these 'trained and responsible' men of labor take over the government of Great Britain?" Does anyone in England have such a feeling of trust in the British Labor Party and its fantastic program of State Socialism, outside of the members of that party? There are, of course, Lord Leverhulmes in every country and there are always the "intellectuals" with their wagons hitched to the stars. They will follow the Bernard Shaws, the Sidney Webbs, the Ramsey MacDonalds and the Arthur Hendersons; but the great middle class, the agriculturists, the real trade unionists and the hard-headed employers are not so trustful and so simple-minded as Mr. Thomas would have us believe. They realize that the British Labor Party's program is a plan for the state to take over all the mines, mills, factories, farms, stores, warehouses, banks, railroads, steamship companies, etc.; in other words, all means of production and distribution, and operate them, which, by and large, is about what Lenine and Trotzky are trying to do in Russia.

The Tribune, in its interview, said:

> Mr. Thomas remarked that, in so far as labor suffers any disadvantages in the United States, it was largely attributable to its failure to wield its inherent political power through the formation of a separate party. He said the attempt to

(*Continued on Page* 15)

The Milk Problem—A Practical Program

By IRWIN G. JENNINGS
ASSISTANT SECRETARY METROPOLITAN TRUST COMPANY

IN September, 1916, the receipt of the daily milk supply of New York City was seriously jeopardized. For more than a week, the producers, under the leadership of their "association," had been on a strike demanding increased prices from the New York dealers. Much good milk in the possession of those seeking to deliver it to shipping stations was destroyed by the striking producers. A large part of the milk received during this period was not of a sanitary character. A deadlock was reached. The Mayor of the city intervened and tried to settle the dispute, but he made no progress whatever. The dealers were proceeding on the theory that the public would not stand for a rise in the price of milk, and their profits were so small that a very slight advance in the cost of milk to them, if they were compelled to sell at the then retail prices, would drive practically all of the small companies out of business.

The producers were conscious that the price they were receiving from the dealers did not cover the cost of production and so were determined at all events to see the strike through. Beyond the interest taken by the Mayor, there was no authoritative assertion of the right of the New York public to receive its daily supply. The controversy was finally settled, but the public paid the bill. From this time on, the price of milk to the consumer was progressively higher until in November, 1917, but little more than a year from the time of the first strike, grade B milk rose from 9 cents to 15 cents, an advance of 66 2/3% over its former price.

In the fall of 1917, controversy again arose. Public authorities began to take cognizance of the situation and the District Attorney even threatened to indict the leaders of the producers who were making what seemed to him to be exorbitant demands. It was reported that if the District Attorney should carry out his threat against one or more of the members of the Producers' Association, the cows would be killed and the milk destroyed. Again the New York milk supply was jeopardized and again the controversy was settled by the New York public's paying the bill.

Something more than a year has passed. In the meantime, the Federal Food Commission which had adjusted the price between the producer and the distributor during the war, after the armistice discontinued its efforts along that line. Under the Commission, the policy followed was that the dealers should charge their patrons just as much more for their milk as the commission permitted the producers to add to the existing price. Thus both the dealers and the farmers got along very nicely at the expense of the consumer. But, in January, 1919, the first month that these two interests in the industry were left to themselves, on account of their inability to agree, a milk strike resulted. There were three conflicting factors in this strike, the dairymen's league, the milk dealers' pool and the New York public.

The strike was finally settled by the dealers and the producers agreeing upon prices for a period of three months, after which time the question of future prices might potentially arise any month with new possibilities of disagreement.

NECESSITY FOR A STEADY MILK SUPPLY

Greater New York is today a city of more than five million people and growing rapidly. In it there are estimated by the Board of Health to be 130,000 babies under one year of age and 126,000 babies between one and two years of age. The health, welfare, and probably the lives, of the greater percentage of these babies are dependent upon an uninterrupted, sanitary milk supply. Besides this, there are a number of convalescing invalids, some of them wounded soldiers, who must have milk.

IRWIN G. JENNINGS

THE PLAN.

1. *The formation of a central association composed of both milk dealers and producers for the purpose of building constructively the milk industry as a whole and stimulating the increased sale and use of dairy products, especially fluid milk.*
2. *The administration of the affairs of such an association in general, by a Board of Directors with representation thereon of both producers and dealers and possibly the public and in detail, by a capable and responsible director who would give his entire time to the work.*
3. *The organization of local units or business units participated in by both dealers and producers for the purpose of stimulating cooperation, efficiency, business methods and good will among its members.*
4. *The establishment of one or more thoroughly equipped laboratories, ably manned, for the purpose of making a systematic study of milk as a food, its most healthful and wholesome form and the most sanitary and marketable method of its handling and distribution.*
5. *The maintenance by the central association of a clearing house of information and industrial facts for the purpose first, of stimulating the standardization of sanitary methods, grading, supervision and reporting, so that results throughout the country can be competently compared and intelligently interpreted; second, the promotion of cooperation throughout the industry; third, a provision for the economic study of the industry, especially matters relating to markets.*
6. *The maintenance of a method of disseminating the information obtained in the laboratory and under the supervision of the director, to both dealers and producers in or out of the local units.*
7. *A campaign of publicity to which both dealers and producers shall contribute which shall use both the best established and new methods for acquainting the public with the facts obtained, thereby stimulating the demand for and use of more milk.*
8. *The provision by the director through educational and experimental means, of a stimulus, looking to the more efficient production, distribution and sanitary control of milk on a large scale in order that increased demands for the product may be met.*

Milk is a vital necessity. There are no satisfactory substitutes for it. The milk supply cannot with impunity be tampered with. To do so may mean death to many human beings. To be the direct or indirect cause of a single death means more than fines or jail to the guilty persons. The New York public's right to life and health is fundamental. There are some things about which the interests may quarrel, but their quarrels should not be allowed to imperil the lives of the people. A milk strike in the hot summer months would be disastrous. Those months are now upon us.

Both the dairymen's organization and that of the producers, whatever may have been the theory of their original organization, of necessity have become fighting machines for the purpose of preserving what seems to each of them to be its rights in the industry. It may still be necessary for them to maintain these organizations and to continue a fight for their rights, but the question may well be asked whether the time is not at hand for a more constructive program.

No interest in the milk industry has in the past sufficiently appreciated the dignity, importance and responsibility of the functions it has been performing. To this fact is due most of the disrepute into which the industry has fallen. The public attitude and that of the press toward the industry have been wrong. The milk distributor, instead of being looked upon as a business man performing a public service function and entitled to credit for work well done, has been universally regarded with suspicion. The presumption has been against him. No morsel of news has been so luscious in the eyes of the ordinary reporter as a front page account of adulteration or dirty containers, or of responsibility for disease traced to a milk dealer's door. It has been a popular pastime for the social reformer to attack the milk dealer and to charge him with fraud, dishonesty and uncleanliness, and the latter has had well-defined reasons for taking a position calling for the least possible publicity.

The good will of a milk business is its main asset. The milk plants, the machinery, the wagons and the cans of a concern that is not going are worth little. To preserve the good will is most important. The most effective menace to this good will is unfavorable newspaper notoriety. To keep his cases out of the general courts has been considered by the milk dealer essential in order to escape such publicity. To plead guilty and to take reprimands in the minor courts accomplished this purpose. On the other hand the greatest insurance of good will in the industry would be a program of constructive publicity based upon a firm foundation of facts scientifically ascertained.

A SUGGESTED PROGRAM

What is to be done in the matter? The present situation is precarious to the public and destructive to the industry. Two facts are apparent: first, the health and welfare of the New York public must not be periodically placed in peril by lack of cooperation among the various interests of the milk industry; second, some program must be devised that will protect the public, give it a greater interest in, and knowledge of, the industry, insure a better product and better service, and which will constructively build, rather than persistently destroy, one of the greatest industries of the country. The following suggestions are practicable and might be carried out profitably under proper leadership, developed either in the industry or out of it:

(*Continued on Page* 17)

Spargo's Camouflaged Socialist Propaganda

RADICAL MARXIAN THEORIES EXPLOITED UNDER ADROIT GUISE OF DENOUNCING BOLSHEVISM

By DAVID GOLDSTEIN

EING the first in the field, John Spargo's "Bolshevism" hit the American purse just when everybody was asking "what is Bolshevism?" The book was sent forth "a plain and easily understandable outline the origin, history and meaning of Bolshevism . . . a fair and reliable statement of the ilosophy, program, and policies of the Russian lsheviki." It is no such thing! It is, as an derstandable reading will show, an astute ce of Socialist propaganda. Professedly, it s hurriedly written in fulfillment of a promise "dear Will," so that the author is "very scious of the imperfections of the book as it nds." One may indeed wonder what would 'e been its contents if the author had at leisure ised to realize the lack of common sense rea- ing that he has, on paper, convicted himself

The book *as it stands* is a very clever and, must admit, a too successful attempt to turn anti-Bolshevist sentiment of our country to advantage of Socialism; for the truth of the tter is that when put into practice Socialism hat is, today, nicknamed Bolshevism.

)ne-half of the book is taken up with an :resting re-write-up of the struggle of the ssian people against an autocratic dictator-), especially the fight of recent years. It tains not a few reprints of documents and eches giving somewhat in detail the forces t overthrew the Czar and established a Con- :uent Assembly. Passing on from the Con- :uent Assembly that was to govern Russia)n a democratic basis, the book deals with *coup d'etat* of Lenine-Trotzky *et al.* and setting up of the Russian Socialist Federated viet Republic.

From thence on to the end, the text assumes inconsistency between Bolshevism and Social- n that is wholly unwarranted by the facts in e case past or present; since Bolshevism is but e ripest fruit yet plucked from off that poison- s tree planted by Marx and Engels and as- luously cultivated ever since by Socialists of iatsoever brand—"Utopian or Scientific." As e psychology is rather forceful to the man hav- g neither the time, ability nor inclination to idy those radical forces that have hammered the foundations of civil society, since the days ien the Communist Manifesto was sent forth tell the world that "the Communists [Social- s] ends can be attained only by the forcible erthrow of all existing social conditions," he ll lay down the book with a false impression. is spirit will be aroused against Lenine-Trotzky *al.*, but not against Bolshevism in its essential inciples—namely, Socialism in action.

ALIGNED WITH SOCIALIST SET

The uncritical mind will hold in view the Bol- eviki five thousand miles away in Russia, not e Bolsheviki here in our own dear homeland. he should become completely psychologized ith the Spargonian camouflage he will find mself lined up with one set of Socialists ;ainst another set of Socialists, the only differ- ice between them being one of temperament. here are those who wait for society to evolve mechanical fashion and those who have the ish to "leap from the kingdom of necessity to e kingdom of freedom" *a la* the Paris Com- une and Soviet Russia. Yet since society is)t evolving their way and as the "leap to free-)m" is a jump into tyranny and chaos, a ague rests on both their houses.

The reader is deftly disarmed: the preface lls him that the author's "aim" is "to make a eliberate and scientific study" of Bolshevism, it once he gets into the body of the book the ithor's aim is seen to be to "remove from thé great international Socialist movement a shameful reproach" (p. 214) that Lenine and Trotzky have put upon it. It were candid in the author to say that his aim is to win public sympathy for the Mensheviki as against the Bolsheviki. Even so, from the basic point of view one is as bad as the other; and it is Spargo's assertion that both are "Socialists of the school of Marx" (p. 59).

This issue may be put easily to the touchstone, since the industrial development in Russia is still in a primitive state the vital issue falls upon the question of land ownership. Granted, freely, that the peasants have rightly complained of the injustice under which they have been compelled to toil, the question is pertinent: What difference is there between the Bolsheviki whom Spargo condemns and the Mensheviki whom he upholds? None whatsoever, since both accept the pronouncement of the Communist Manifesto in favor of complete proletarian monopoly of land. Indeed, both groups go Marx one better, their abolition of private property in land, without compensation, shall stay even the hand of changing phenomena as well as those principles writ in the Decalogue. With an assumption of omnipotent power they call a halt to evolution,—never more shall it evolute, for private property in land shall be abolished FOREVER.

Bolsheviki	*Mensheviki*
"The landlord's property in all land is herewith abolished without compensation."	"The right to privately owned land within the boundaries of the Russian Republic is hereby abolished forever."
"The right of private ownership in land is abolished forever; land can neither be sold, nor bought, nor leased, nor mortgaged, nor appropriated in any other way. The whole of the land of the State, of the appanages of the Crown, of the monasteries, of the churches, as well as majorats, lands in conditional possession, or endowed to persons, or concerns, privately owned land and land belonging to public bodies, and to peasants, and so on, is herewith expropriated without any compensation whatever, and it becomes the property of the whole people and is transferred for use to all who till it."	"All land, mines, forests, waters, at present owned by and otherwise in the possession of individuals, associations, and institutions, are confiscated without compensation for the loss incurred."

The abnormal vision of the Bolsheviki and the Mensheviki in Russia, just as that of the Debs and the Spargos in America, fails to grasp the fact that the *right* to own property in land is a natural right that even the majority upon the principle of might, though they have the power, have not the right to abolish. Again, that it is the duty of the State to maintain the inviolability of this natural right and to its advantage to increase the number of owners of land rather than to centralize the ownership of it into the hands of the State or of a favored few.

Nothing sounder as against the unjust proposal of the Socialists has been said than this from Pope Leo XIII:

> "The right to possess private property is from nature, not from man; and the State has only the right to regulate its use in the interests of the public good, but by no means to abolish it altogether."

Again Leo XIII said—and this was in 1891—the

> "great labour question cannot be solved except by assuming as a principle that private ownership must be held sacred and inviolable. The law, therefore, should favor ownership, and its policy should be to induce as many people as possible to become owners."

Very clever, or very dull, in its double meaning is the sub-title of Mr. Spargo's "Bolshevism"— "The Enemy of Political and Industrial Democracy"—for the implication is direct that the author takes his stand against the enemy of political and industrial democracy. Thus while denouncing the enemy of Americanism Mr. Spargo deftly advances Socialism in public favor as he has ever done since the day he landed in New York City. If, indeed, the author is blinded to the fact that Bolshevism in Russia is merely American Socialism rotten ripe he is neither a sound reasoner nor a safe guide of public opinion. We shall leave him to take either horn of his sad dilemma and come to the rescue of common-sense.

Again, in the text there is a dual personality that in the interest of right, reason and love of country should be understood. Mr. Spargo assumes that democracy, in its etymological and its historical sense, is entirely incompatible with the soviet form of government in Russia (p. 162). This we shall gladly grant—that this government of Commissaries is in reality a despotism of the very few over the vast majority. Precisely, "democracy has always meant absence of class rule; proletarian dictatorship is class rule." But when Mr. Spargo says the "Bolshevists are not Marxians" (pp. 238, 266) because they did not await the predicted time when the proletarians would be in the majority before setting up the "dictatorship," which Marx did declare for, we are aware that a hair-splitting Talmudic discussion is entered upon which essays to save Socialism in theory from Socialism, we may not say practical, but rather, impractical operation. The indisputable fact is that Marx coined the term "dictatorship of the proletariat," and it is fair to say that it means that a dictator shall rule in the interest of the proletariat during the period of transition from "Capitalism to Socialism." But since a "classless society," a one class society, contemplated by the Marxians, is absurd it is fair to say that this goal shall never be reached under Bolshevism or any other Socialist title. The soviet form of government as it lay in the imagination of Trotzky (p. 161)—a "true unadulterated democracy"—is precisely what Engels called for—"a government of things"—another absurdity since things are not governed, they are used or misused by men. Here is the crux of the whole matter, because of their materialistic philosophy Socialists are unable to grasp the fact that we have a government not of men, but of laws carried out by men. A dictatorship, whether proletarian or otherwise, is a despotism which it is not in the nature of free men to tolerate, since it is human power to which they are subjected, not the force of right principles that never change.

Even though a government were made up exclusively of representatives of the several industries, rather than of representatives of territorial divisions, as wards, towns, cities, counties or states, as Socialists propose, it would be class government—working class government—and it is true that class government is etymologically and historically incompatible with democracy. If then Spargo would have democracy he must quit Marxism both in the green wood as in its fruit, deadly ripe. He cannot, logically, condemn his cause and advocate his cause in one and the same book as he has in "Bolshevism."

The naivete with which Mr. Spargo expresses surprise that a radical like Max Eastman gives his benediction to the Bolshevist suffrage system (p. 281) shows a fine skill at making black white. For after all this is quite Marxian, there never was a time in the history of his cause that any means to the end was out of vogue. Indeed the autocratic manipulation of the suffrage, that is supposed to be free and equal, gave to Marx the control of the International Socialist Congress by the misuse of blank credentials and by keeping Bakunin out of the Congress. This was innocently done by calling the assembly in a place inaccessible to exiled Bakunin. It is interesting to note that base tactics are not out of date in the Socialist movement of Spargo's adopted country. Just now comes the news that the inner powers that be in the Socialist Party have expelled 40,000 members without the semblance of a trial to make sure of controlling the party here in America. Evidently Max Eastman believes in Bolshevist tactics to carry out Bolshevist ideals, so, too, does John Spargo believe in Bolshevist ideals and in the self-same tactics, differently applied, in order to "remove from the great international Socialist movement a shameful reproach" (p. 214).

Again (pp. 216-217), the moral irresponsibility that the father of Modern Socialism bequeathed to his numerous followers finds a star exemplar in Spargo. He vehemently condemns the "inconsistencies" of the Bolshevists in Russia and vehemently approves inconsistencies in himself. Mr. Spargo is a patriot! so he is. An international patriot—God save the mark!—is a man who loves no country; for Socialism calls upon workingmen of all countries to unite, since they have nothing to lose but their chains and a world to win. Oh it were pitiful!—"The red flag was borne by debauched and drunken mobs. What a fate for the symbol of universal freedom and human brotherhood!" (p. 199). The "shameful reproach" against the anti-patriotism of the movement must be *removed*, so it must! But marvel of marvels the anti-patriotism of Socialism must be removed while Socialism itself—the very essence of treason—must be advanced in order to bring about the world *Revolution* incidentally trailing Old Glory in the dust while running up the red flag over the Capitol at Washington. Don't doubt it! Spargo himself has said so, he is a Social Democrat and an International Socialist (preface) all because he believes in Americanism with all his undivided heart—a heart that loves two absolutely opposite things, treason and patriotism, with a wholesale fervor.

Blandly, the author of "Bolshevism" asks: "Is there any logical sense in the average radical's mind?" (p. 217) Surely, the correct answer is—*No*. However, it is not the "average radical" who sets himself down illogically between covers, so we cite Spargo's "Bolshevism" as a complete vindication of the sane opinion that at least one distinguished radical has by far outstripped the average radical in the lack of "any logical sense."

Of course, a logical process of thinking, resting upon a reasonable premise will lead to a common sense conclusion. But since a rational basis is not to be found for Socialism in any one of its phases, it goes without saying that however logical their process, their aim is all wrong since their foundation is all wrong. Take their aim "the expropriation of the expropriators," in other words that of taking from private owners the land and capital in their just possession and making these means of production the property of the working class—"the only class that has any right to exist"—is logical enough if one accepts the utterly unsound premise that the one and only source of modern capital is the unpaid wages of the working class in the years that are passed. Placed upon such an absurd foundation what aim is too ridiculous, tyrannical or treasonable? And what means, to such an end, is too unreasonable, illogical or contradictory? It is or it isn't the thing to do not because it is right or because it is wrong, but because at a specific time and place it is or it is not thought to be good propaganda by those who man the steam roller. To illustrate, when the advocacy of sabotage threatened to retard their propaganda the majority of the convention of the Socialist Party (1912) made its repudiation a prerequisite of membership; but when this threatening danger from within was thought to be passed the convention of 1917 of which Spargo was a prominent member unanimously rescinded the action of the former convention.

QUESTIONS FOR MR. SPARGO

To promote the understanding of the Socialist mind we note the position taken by John Spargo. Was he opposed to the wanton destruction of property and the possible loss of life that results from the practices of sabotage because *per se* it is immoral? Perish the thought, what should a Marxian have to do with morality or immorality—there is no such thing in their philosophy. We quote Spargo's "Syndicalism, Industrial Unionism, and Socialism" (pp. 172-3):

> I am not opposed to sabotage because of any love of "law and order," or because of any regard for the "rights of property." None of these things is particularly sacred to me, none of them is one thousandth part as dear to me as the emancipation of my class. If the class to which I belong could be set free from exploitation by violation of the laws made by the master class, by open rebellion, by seizing the property of the rich, by setting the torch to a few buildings, or by the summary execution of a few members of the possessing class, I hope that the courage to share in the work should be mine. I should pray for the courage and the hardness of heart necessary. It is not, then, because of a lack of revolutionary will that I oppose sabotage and the appeal to other violent methods, but because I believe that they can only leave my class more hopelessly enslaved than ever. It is not that I would be careful not to harm the masters of bread and life and to preserve their property, but because I would not destroy the *morale* of my class as a fighting force.

Does the Lenine-Trotzky regimé rest upon any better ground or upon any worse ground than this reason—that is not reason—given by Spargo in defending his own conduct? True, moral irresponsibility may take on a multitude of forms but it is all of one substance—rebellion against the authority of Almighty God and treason to one's country.

Again, ardently patriotic for the nonce as a good Socialist tactician may be, Lenine is condemned (p. 91) for his advocacy of "revolt among the soldiers regardless of the fact that it would mean Russia's defeat and Germany's triumph"! Really, how splendid! Lenine carries forward his cause of destruction and Spargo carries forward his cause of destruction, one with deeds and the other with words, and both are consistent with the ugly premise of International Revolution.

Ferrer tried to do the deed in Barcelona while Spain was at war in Morocco that was done with words at Stuttgart (1907) and at Basle (1912). Both these International Socialist Congresses declared that advantage should be taken of war in every country to overthrow the capitalist system of society.

Lenine has unhappily carried out his words with deeds. Together with Rosa Luxemburg, Lenine presented the proposal to the Stuttgart Congress. Happily Spargo's power resides merely in words, yet words have a far-reaching effect. Surely the set of resolutions presented by Spargo to the 1912 Socialist Party Convention calling for a propaganda in our army and navy may have prompted others to do the ugly deeds.

Adroitly Spargo argues that "the Bolsheviki are not Socialists because they adopted the name Communist Party when they quit the Social

Early Closing Helps Efficiency of Workers

By MAY L. MANNING

HE world is seething with discontent. Profiteers are grumbling at a tax of 87 per cent. on their profits. All others wish they had profits to be taxed. Labor st is crystallizing into the threat of a great l upheaval under the leadership of that t spawn of the devil—Bolshevism—unless th is more equally distributed. Idealism ls by bewildered.

tween the two extremes Americanism tries idge the gulf of diverse opinions to save the try from the threatened clash of class :d. In this process of education, thinkers a steady head in analyzing those local dis- :nts, which are contributory causes of the spread of this Bolshevist infection among especting workers, who would be 100 per good citizen if they could, lest the issue be ised.

is too true that one-half the world does not how the other half lives, and these literal pictures taken at random from the lives of next-door neighbors may arouse interest, even prompt, practical constructive help for : who stand in need of it. The "one touch ature (sympathy) which makes the whole d kin" may prove to be the antidote to this ness when it is expressed in terms of man-to- and woman-to-woman cooperation in light- g the worker's burden. Only that touch of on humanity will convince him of the utter ıness of Bolshevism, and that even multi- ›naires are helpless in the grip of world tions. Arbitrary customs enslave us all the top dog to the under one. But the er dog carries the heaviest chains.

SYDNEY, AUSTRALIA, 1863

umanity in terms of practical plans to ease worker's burden, has always been the sub- scious handmaid of Australia's industrial social development. Away in the early ties", Sydney—the first spot inhabited by te men in Australia, and not yet 75 years —began to show consciousness of class re- ısibility in various ways, resulting among :r reforms in the eight-hour day and the y closing of shops to give the workers time lawful recreation. This last contribution to health and contentment of a valuable ele- ıt of the community was, in its first incep- ı, the outcome of a voluntary decision on the t of society women not to shop after 1 p. m. Saturdays. That was the hour when govern- ıt, professional, and business men closed their :es for the day, and their wives argued that ıt was good for mental workers must be ally good for manual workers. They noticed effect of long hours in the pallid faces of p assistants, and it set them thinking of their ı responsibility towards them. They called :tings of their friends and talked after this hion:

'Shops keep open as long as they think they get custom. We control that situation, for nen are the chief shoppers. If we systematize marketing and shopping on Saturdays so t it can be all done by 1 p. m., we can go to proprietors where we deal and say: 'We ık your employees are as much deserving of ,alf holiday as our husbands, so we have de- ed not to shop on Saturday afternoons, and will keep our word.' "

Those society women kept their word, and by ;5 all the better class shops in Sydney had ›pted the rule of closing at 1 p. m. on Satur- ', because, after their busy morning, there ı not enough afternoon custom to make it rth while keeping open. From that time on :ry shop of any standing has closed *all the ır round on Saturday afternoons.* Naturally the custom became an unwritten law in the younger colonies as they developed.

The little seed of sympathy prompted by a sense of *noblesse oblige* in that handful of gentle-women way back in the early "sixties", has grown into a mighty tree since then, though it was 35 years before the Early Closing Act was inscribed on the statute book of New South Wales, and not till 1912 did it become a law of the last of the six States under the Factories Act, and shop employees were universally given time from their labors to "find themselves" and enjoy some home life. The final act of legislation was the direct effect of an Employees' Association, who brought before the legislators the evidence of doctors to prove the devitalizing effects of long hours in a deoxygenated atmosphere on the health of the men and women who were to carry on the race, and clinched their arguments for a nine-hour day for five days, one late night a week, and a full half holiday by asserting that housekeepers need only be asked to methodize their shopping and marketing in the name of the health of the nation to bring about a reform that would benefit all and harm none.

On January 1, 1900, the law first came into operation, with two late nights and a half-holiday on a day suitable to local conditions, and, like all reforms, worked hardship on a few, such as the lone widow depending for custom on the improvident housewife, who rushed out at the last moment for supplies. But that was a small matter in comparison with the benefit to a big class of the community which is now a valuable bulwark of law and order, instead of a disintegrating mass of discontent. Certain shops are exempt to meet public needs, but the rights of employees in them are safeguarded.

LONDON, 1905

Early in October, 1905, two women were driving across London about 6:30 p. m. They had landed at Tilbury that afternoon, the one from Australia, the other from a visit to India. The Australian's eyes were popping out of her head in the excitement of recognizing streets, parks, and historic buildings she had heard of all her life, but now saw for the first time. All at once it struck her that though the clock hands pointed to 6:45 p. m., shops were open and workmen were busy building.

"Look at the people shopping, and the men working at this hour," she exclaimed. "You don't mean to say people have to work so late?"

"Of course. Shops don't close as long as people want to buy, and houses must be built before the winter," replied the Englishwoman.

"But what about the shop people and the workmen? Don't fathers get home in time to see their children before their bedtime? Is there no early closing law in London?"

"Of course not! Whoever heard of such a thing?"

"We have one in Australia and it works all right for everybody," protested the Australian.

"How do you manage when you get home and find there is no butter in the house?" asked the friend sceptically.

"Go without if we are such bad housekeepers as to neglect our business. We often had to in the first days of Early Closing, we forgot lots of things because we had the bad habit of expecting shops to be open to suit our convenience, never considering the unfortunates cooped up inside till all hours."

"Oh! well, they're accustomed to it," came the indifferent reply.

"Do you suppose they like it any better for that? Do you think they should be enslaved in this way? Their health affected, their minds embittered, and the welfare of the nation menaced through them just because women, who are the shoppers of the world, are too indifferent to the wrongs they do to systematize their shopping and do it in reasonable hours? Thoughtless selfishness is what it amounts to!"

"To tell you the truth I never thought about the matter before?" the Englishwoman admitted apologetically.

"But you *have* remarked on the improvidence of the poor. Did you never think that it was their obsession of eternal work which causes a sort of mental inertia, and paralyzes the sense of proportions? Women had better wake up to their responsibilities and help workers to help themselves to better conditions if they have the good of dear old England at heart. . . . Besides, it's much better for their pockets to shop by daylight. You know how difficult it is to judge of quality in materials by artificial light."

"Oh! as to that, we have to do it in London for six months of the year. Wait till you see our fogs."

"All the more reason why the worker should have a chance of being in the sunshine when the sun *does* shine! You should see our workers going off with their families early Saturday afternoon for outings or picnics around Sydney Harbour! It just does one's heart good to see them streaming across Circular Quay to the ferry boats, with their baskets and billies to have a good time together under the gum trees or on the beaches."

"But where can they find places for picnics near such a big city as Sydney?"

"Very easily. The Harbour is big, and has over 100 miles of foreshore, and much of that foreshore on the northern side is reserved as a public recreation ground for all time, and ferry or excursion boats carry you to fascinating picnicking grounds, where the Government has built rough fireplaces for people to make a small fire to boil the billy for tea. Sometimes if you are first on the spot you may find a small pile of wood thoughtfully put ready for you by the forest-ranger, but mostly you skirmish round for your own fuel, or economize with what some other party has left from their put-out fire.

"Then there are large shelter pavilions with trestle tables and benches where big parties feast, and dance to band music. Moonlight picnics are very popular in summer, and people linger in the coolth till there is only time to catch the last boat or trolley by the skin of their teeth. Life is well worth living in Australia, especially for the worker, I can tell you!"

"It certainly sounds like a workman's paradise, and you've got your work cut out if you are going to start reforms of that sort here in the cradle of conservative tradition," laughed the Englishwoman.

"I'd like nothing better, only a self-supporting woman is handicapped, but I'll talk."

NEW YORK, 1919

In the intervening years the Australian woman has gained wide experiences of the old world's traditions and the new world's customs. Passing from a purely British environment where one language is spoken and one point of view is held, to the purely cosmopolitan one of New York, she realizes the peculiar difficulties of dealing with a huge amorphous mass of foreigners, representing forty different races, speaking as many languages, and understanding none but their own properly. Full of hereditary antagonisms, and set in their ways, yet held in the invisible grip of American hustle, these

(*Continued on Page 19*)

THE NATIONAL
Civic Federation Review

Office: Thirty-third Floor, Metropolitan Tower
1 Madison Avenue New York City

RALPH M. EASLEY, Editor

Published Twice a Month Two Dollars a Year

The Editor alone is Responsible for any unsigned article or unquoted statement published in THE NATIONAL CIVIC FEDERATION REVIEW.

WHAT SHALL BE OUR ATTITUDE TOWARD GERMANY WHEN PEACE IS CONCLUDED?

Upon the ratification of the peace treaty by the United States Senate peace will have been formally concluded with Germany. Ambassadors will be appointed, commercial and financial relations will be resumed, we shall be again on a friendly basis with the people who sought to impose their dominion on the world by force and whose record for crime and outlawry has been unparalleled in the history of mankind. With the reestablishment of friendly relations some exceedingly serious questions arise.

Every loyal American would desire to be chivalrously generous toward Germany if she showed some signs of recognizing her own guilt and if, beyond doubt, she had been rendered impotent to do further harm. But is that the situation which confronts America and the Allied nations? As it is, we can be generous only to the degree within which positive safety lies. America and the Allies have gone through an experience in dealing with barbarous cruelty, monstrous lawlessness, unscrupulous treachery and deceit, which it would be sheer madness for them to forget; they have learned a lesson which has been paid in treasure incalculable and bloodshed and suffering immeasurable.

Are we to forgive, to forget, to give full confidence and trust, simply because Germany, confronting inevitable defeat, found it expedient to capitulate and get out of the war as best she could?—When German leaders themselves designate the treaty as merely another "scrap of paper," when they have openly declared *Der Tag* has only been postponed?—When even now, after the German assembly has ratified the treaty, Minister of Defense Noske boldly announces the terms are impossible of fulfillment, that he gives Germany's victors warning that she will not be able to carry out the terms accepted, and that her delegates signed the document with reservations regarding certain articles, among them that concerning the admission of her guilt?

Count von Bernstorff, in a recent statement, urges Germany to cultivate friendship with the United States, and for what purpose? That by winning the friendship of America, there could be most easily brought about modifications or abrogations of certain of the treaty terms. Can Germany be trusted?—When members of the new government openly avow their intention of seeking to nullify the treaty and default in their solemn agreements? When the German press openly discusses a war of revenge in the future? When the *Berlin Vorwaerts* has threatened, if Germany was compelled to sign the treaty, that she would retaliate upon her victors, by creating world-wide social chaos and revolution, through "the instruments offered by Bolshevism."

That is the admitted Hun intention. That is the deliberate Hun plan. There is already every sign that Germany will ally herself with the Bolshevist regime in Russia, and already a commission has gone from Berlin to Moscow to make a study of, and work out a plan for, the exploitation of the resources of Russia. Under such an arrangement Germany would have access to such vast resources of raw materials as would make her economic recuperation extraordinarily rapid; with the Red Guard under her dominion, and officered by Germans, she would have free access for the speedy dominion of Asia. While restoring herself economically, she would meanwhile undertake to destroy the industry and trade, as well as political and social peace, of her rivals. "Through the weapons offered by Bolshevism," with the machinery of Lenine and Trotzky in her hands, she would seek to spread industrial and social unrest everywhere, foment labor disturbances, "strikes, revolutionary explosions, separation movements and civil war." That was her plan, as revealed in a circular letter dated February 23, 1915, sent by the Director of the Press of the Ministry of Foreign Affairs in Berlin to all German ambassadors, ministers and consuls, concerning the "countries that are in the war coalition against Germany." That is her plan today concerning the nations who will soon resume friendly relations and receive her ambassadors, ministers and consuls. Can we, therefore, afford to trust Germany without reservations, to give implicit confidence and unhampered freedom in their activities to the army of agents, official, financial, commercial and others, who will presently arrive on our shores? What shall be the attitude of 100-percent loyal Americans toward the hundreds of thousands of citizens, of German birth or extraction, who did all in their power to keep America subservient under Hun aggression, who were against America in their hearts, who intrigued and plotted to obstruct the country in its war activities, and who, through all sorts of secret organizations, went to the extreme length at a time when this country was neutral of organizing Germans in this country for military training so that they might be ready for action against us on our own shores should Germany win on the western front?

Every American wishes to give full credit to those citizens of German birth or extraction who opposed Germany because of her guilt in the war, who gave not only of their treasure but of their blood, and whose sacrifices were in sooth greater than those of native Americans, because they were called upon to fight the land of their birth, with which they were connected by blood and heart ties. It is from information afforded by loyal German-American sources that we know that various Kriegebunds, and other "bunds," "fests" and "vereins"—which had operated as species of military organizations before America went to war with Germany and whose harmless names have camouflaged the activities of enemies within our midst—are renewing their propaganda and can be counted upon in the future to be against the interests of this country and on the side of the interests of Germany.

At a meeting held on July 24 at the Deutscher Liederkranz, New York, to organize a Central Committee for the Relief of Distress in Germany and Austria, six hundred German-American men and women amid the wildest excitement cheered declarations that "the German spirit is not dead and will never die," that "Germany lives on, though wounded sorely," and that propaganda was needed "to bring the German spirit, German education and German kultur to the American people and to the world."

Already that notoriously disloyal and defunct organization, the German-American Alliance, has been supplanted by a new organization, "The German-American Citizens League of America," which comprises over seventy organizations, and which flooded Congress early in June with an appeal urging the rejection of the treaty. The appeal brazenly declared "the starving German people" had been "deceived" by President Wilson, that because of the treaty "the American people appear before the world as hypocrites," and that the treaty is "barbarian." This new organization first became active in the Chicago elections last April when it supported William Hale Thompson for mayor. It frankly avows its purpose of taking political action. Can the meaning of this be mistaken? Is there any mistaking the meaning of the influx of Germans into the Socialist organization and the financial support given of late to socialist and revolutionary radical propaganda?

Realizing the treachery and underhand acts committed against us by the German Ambassador when the American Government and the American people were trying to be absolutely neutral; recalling that, through Von Bernstorff and Von Zwiedinck, Austrian Charge d'Affaires, there was organized a system of spies, of from 20,000 to 30,000, ranging from bankers, lawyers, editors, college professors, society women, agents in the musical world to tools among anarchists and professional dynamiters;

ANNOUNCEMENT

THE Commission sent by The National Civic Federation to study industrial conditions in England, France and Italy, the personnel of which includes representatives of employers, wage earners and the public, has just returned. The purpose of this study was to discover any information which the commission might deem helpful in promoting better relations between employers and wage earners in this country.

The drafting of the commission's report, which will soon be made public, has been entrusted to Mr. James W. Sullivan, representing the labor group; Mr. Albert Farwell Bemis, president of Bemis Bro. Bag Company, Boston, Mass.; and Mr. A. Parker Nevin, attorney-at-law, representing the public.

Mr. Sullivan's chapters will discuss: "The Shop Steward Movement;" "The Democratization of Industry;" "British Labor and Politics;" and "Factors for Economic Change in Great Britain." Mr. Bemis, in addition to setting forth the situation from the employer's standpoint, will make a special report on the subject of housing. Mr. Nevin will summarize his conclusions from the point of view of the public.

Another commission was charged with the duty of studying and reporting upon the operation and results of the various governmental bureaus and commissions created under the war emergency to deal with labor conditions in the United States, such as the National War Labor Board and the War Labor Policies Board, with a view to recommending what, if any, of the activities of those bodies could effectively be adapted to peace conditions. A report on this matter will be made by the Domestic Commission at a meeting to be held in New York City on September 8 and 9, at which time there will be considered a number of important problems bearing on the relations of capital and labor in the United States.

Four questions that are of especial significance now, when so many employers are seeking to find ways and means for establishing better relations with their employees, are:

1. How far do profit sharing, stock participation and bonus plans meet the demand of the wage earner for "a larger share in the product of his labor?"
2. How much, if any, *control* do the wage earners demand on the business side of industry?
3. Is there a fundamental and necessary conflict between trade unions and the so-called "employers' unions?"
4. What methods can be adopted that will more generally promote collective bargaining?

It is the purpose of the committee in charge of the forthcoming meeting in September to arrange for a thorough discussion of the above questions by representatives of employers, commercial organizations and national trade unions.

''coercion of minority opinion'' was shown sometime ago, after the Lusk Committee had made its raid on the Rand School and the headquarters of Bolshevist-agent Ludwig Martens, when a group of New York clergymen issued a statement urging ''that fair hearings and just trials be given to men, irrespective of their political or economic opinions, so that it may be truly said that in America no man's case, be he an I. W. W. or a Bolshevist or the most reactionary conservative, is prejudged by an appeal to popular feeling,'' and ''that the attempt be abandoned to coerce minority opinion so long as it does not promote disorder.'' It is hardly necessary to say that by employing this very species of verbiage those well-meaning persons were all simply furthering and giving importance to the stereotyped propaganda of radicals and disloyalists to the effect that fair hearings and just trials are not given and that minority opinion is ''coerced''. Are hearings and trials not fair? Is such action as has been taken against the Rand School ''coercion of minority opinion.''

The radicals and others who sought to raise a fund of $50,000 to defend the I. W. W. leaders on trial last year in Chicago for seditious conspiracy obviously had little if any faith that the Department of Justice would permit a ''fair trial'' and that it was therefore up to ''American liberals'' to afford this. In the matter of the Rand School, the *Nation* is of the opinion that the evidence against the Rand School ''is so weak and flimsy that the whole proceeding must be regarded as a peculiarly vicious and vindictive piece of railroading.'' Mr. Paul U. Kellogg, of the *Survey*, and Messrs. Walter Lippmann and Walter Weyl, of the *New Republic*, subscribe to the point of view that the action against the Rand School is ''coercion of minority opinion.''

Were the actions of the Lusk Committee in raiding the Rand School and the headquarters of Martens, and of the Attorney General in seeking to obtain an annulment of the Rand School charter, nothing more than efforts to ''coerce'' and suppress ''minority opinion?'' Or have not the Lusk Committee and the Attorney General taken a genuinely urgent and vitally necessary action to discover, root out and exterminate activities gravely endangering the public welfare, the peace and security of the country, and which aim at the ultimate overthrow of the government itself? Is the exposure of a conspiracy between direct agents of Lenine and Trotzky and Socialist organizations in America, aiming at the establishment of a ''dictatorship of the proletariat,'' ''vicious,'' a ''coercion of minority opinion?'' While Germany was murdering American citizens on the high seas there were many who urged that we remain supine and submissive under Hun aggression. When official Bolshevist agents, receiving funds from Russia, have set up headquarters in this country and seek, through propaganda and lecturers, to convert American workers to the theories of Trotzky and Lenine, and when they are aided and abetted by American Socialists and Socialist organizations in propaganda openly advocating world revolution, are we to remain supine and submissive, ''to permit them to be heard and observed?'' Is the effort to protect American institutions a departure ''from traditional American liberty?''

The evidence produced at the hearings of the Lusk Committee, and quoted in part by Mr. Harré in his report of the hearings in this issue of the Review, adequately demonstrates the incitement made by radicals to ''violence and revolution'' and the relations existing between the Rand School and the direct official agents of those arch-enemies of civilization, Trotzky and Lenine. Like their blood-brothers, the Huns, these enemies of peace and order depend on getting defenders and support among those well-meaning, over-sentimental and soft-hearted people who are only too easily gulled and duped by specious appeals to liberal ideals and humanitarian sentiment. As with the Germans, so it is with those forces who constitute today Germany's chief instrumentality for working harm, through the promotion of internal discord and civil strife, to the nations which have won the war. Intelligent vigilance, and when necessary drastic action, alone constitute the price of safety.

MORE VARLETRY AND VILLARDRY To its unenviable record achieved during the war and during the peace negotiations with Germany, the *Nation*, which in bygone years enjoyed a certain unique prestige as being loyal, honorable and reputable, adds the crowning baseness of publishing confidential correspondence sent through the United States Department of State to Colonel House and which was presumably stolen. This is the second time that a confidential governmental communication, obtained through some ''leak,'' has been made public. The first message, addressed to Secretary of State Lansing in Paris by Mr. Polk, was read by Max Eastman at a meeting held in Madison Square Garden on June 20 to protest against the raiding of the offices of Ludwig C. A. K. Martens, Lenine's representative in the United States, by agents of the Lusk Committee. Both Eastman and Villard have protested they do not know the sources of the information and that the messages came to them anonymously.

To receive and use for one's benefit stolen goods is a common crime. To betray confidence has generally been regarded as an act of mean men, without honor. To betray, and give publication to, confidential documents belonging to a department or representatives of one's own government, will, to most people, appear as hardly less than moral treachery and moral treason.

The Department of Justice has begun an investigation as to how the State Department document sent to Mr. Lansing and the document forwarded to Colonel House through the State Department were obtained. The National Civic Federation Review on a number of occasions expressed grave concern regarding the measure of confidence given by officials high in the Government to certain young men notoriously known for their radical and un-American opinions, regarding the way in which certain young ''editor-statesmen'' whose forebears came from Germany managed to worm their way into positions high in the Administration, regarding important missions entrusted to pro-Bolshevist radicals, one of whom was hardly past the age of adolescence, and regarding the free entrée enjoyed at the Hotel de Crillon, the headquarters of the American Peace Delegation in Paris, by certain writers who had qualified themselves as being anything but 100-percent loyal and American. At least two of these worthies, after being given special favor and confidence, were so roiled and upset over the terms asked of Germany in the Versailles treaty that they turned upon President Wilson in opprobrious public denunciation.

According to the *New York Times*, ''the evidence now in the possession of the Government clearly indicates that the cable messages which were stolen in their decoded form or by someone who had possession of a State Department code were obtained in Paris, probably by two men, both of them well known in the radical world.'' The New York *Tribune*, commenting upon the act of the *Nation*, says it ''does what may well be regarded as a public service.'' Not only may this publication, as the *Tribune* says, reveal the ''misinformation and misadvice'' concerning Russia which was received by the Department of State from ''fanatical social theorists,'' such as Arthur Bullard, who in his message attacked Kolchak, but it serves further to demonstrate the dishonesty, disloyalty and moral turpitude of those who are more concerned about the vindication and success of Bolshevism than about the security and well-being of their own country.

Plot to Overthrow Government

(Continued from Page 3)

zens only by naturalization. Mr. Holland said the majority of radicals are Italians, Spaniards and other aliens, with Russian Jews predominating.

In organizing the garment workers, the Socialists, declared Mr. Holland, employed as their agent Jacob Panken, now a municipal court justice in New York. The garment workers, said Mr. Holland, "do not believe in the Government; they preach this today behind closed doors, and some in the open. There isn't a place where one of their speakers goes that he doesn't ridicule the form of government of the United States." This organization has 70,000 members in the United States and Canada.

Of 750 labor organizations in New York state, only 25, according to Mr. Holland, are radical. Mr. Holland mentioned Local 23 of the International Pressmen's Union as being such and declared that the president, James J. Bagley, "preached on the floor of the Central Federated Union not alone to break up the Government, but to smash up the printing presses. We were amazed that the Government permitted him to get away with it. This can be found in the records of the Central Federated Union." Mr. Holland asserted that in the Central Federated Union radicals who agitated for war with Mexico opposed our going to war with Germany. According to Mr. Holland, the I. W. W., the W. I. I. U., the Socialists and Socialist Labor Party make it a practice to send out agitators to the big industrial centres, and especially try to break in whenever a legitimate strike occurs. These agitators are seldom labor men; the leaders of the radicals are so called "intellectuals," and of eleven Socialist Assemblymen recently elected in New York only one carried a union card.

The Women's Trade Union League was characterized by Mr. Holland as having been for the last year or two "a tail to the Socialist kite." Miss Maud Schwartz is president and Miss Rose Schneiderman is secretary. In going to Europe as a "representative" at the Peace Conference of American working women, Mr. Holland declared Miss Schneiderman did not go "with the consent of American laboring men or women." He said her organization "adopted resolutions in favor of the Russian Soviet Government," and named as financial backers of the organization Mrs. J. Sergeant Cram, Miss Mary Dreier and Mrs. Raymond Robins. Mrs. Cram has been affiliated with various pacifist organizations. Miss Mary Dreier and Mrs. Raymond Robins are sisters of Miss Katherine S. Dreier, who was chairman of a group of signers to a suffrage appeal in 1916, in which it was declared: *"The Teuton ideals have always stood for Freedom and Equality."* Mrs. Raymond Robins, according to evidence produced by the Committee, as before stated, paid part of a bill rendered S. Nuorteva, a representative of the Russian Bolshevist Government, by the Rand School of Social Science for copies of Lenine's "Soviets at Work."

That all the radical groups of the country, formerly divided by differences in philosophy and programs, have united on a common platform—that the platform of the Russian Bolshevists—and that they are cooperating toward the ultimate and common object of overthrowing the existing government and present order of society with the purpose of establishing a "dictatorship of the proletariat" in the United States, was brought out in the testimony of Mr. Hugh Frayne. Mr. Frayne's testimony, which has served as a basis and groundwork for the investigation of the Lusk Committee into seditious activities, consisted mostly of evidence drawn from the official statements and publications of these radical groups themselves. Mr. Frayne interpreted them out of their own mouths. He showed where these groups had formerly differed and how of late, in rallying to the Lenine-Trotzky program, they had come together.

"A study of the radical literature issued here," said Mr. Frayne, "and the radical organizations which have been formed in this country for the past few years, indicates that they divide themselves into three principal currents of radical opinions—namely, anarchism, syndicalism, and socialism. An examination of the current literature and of the speeches made by leaders of these groups indicates that under the inspiration furnished by the Russian Communist party, otherwise known as the Bolsheviki, the leaders of these groups have found a common platform upon which they may cooperate for the establishment of a dictatorship of the proletariat in this country."

SOURCE OF PROPAGANDA FUNDS

Testifying under oath before the Lusk Committee in executive session, Ludwig C. A. K. Martens, so-called official ambassador from the Lenine-Trotzky Bolshevist Russian Government to the United States, and A. A. Heller, head of the so-called Commercial Department of the Soviet Bureau in New York City, according to the record, declared that their activities were purely commercial. Much of the evidence found in the papers seized during the raid upon the Soviet headquarters was presented at the hearings of the Lusk Committee. "A careful search of the files was made," testified Mr. Stevenson, "and there is no indication that any commercial transaction was entered into at all."

In a letter written to Mr. Henry Ford asking for an appointment—and to which a favorable reply in the form of a telegram from Mr. Ford's assistant secretary was received—the "Soviet Ambassador" said: "Writing to you, I have, however, in my mind something else than the purely commercial interests your firm may have in Russian trade. We would like very much to discuss with you the social aspect of the regeneration of Russia."

According to evidence seized in the raid on Martens' bureau, "large sums" had been received from Russia, while other funds sent by the Soviet Government had been intercepted. It was brought out from the seized bank accounts that the daily credit balance of the bureau varied from $5,000 to $9,000. "This was replenished from time to time," explained Mr. Stevenson, "and the curious feature of that is that all the substantial sums were deposited by L. Martens, meaning Ludwig Martens, and examination of the bank book so far shows that these deposits were made in currency by Mr. Martens, and gives no evidence as to the source of these funds."

"In connection with the financial situation," said Chairman Lusk, "I want to call the attention of the members of the committee . . . that it appeared in the evidence of Mr. Martens and Mr. Heller that they have not paid out any money in any commercial transactions. So, whatever money they used must necessarily have been used for something besides commercial purposes."

That the Soviet Bureau was not regarded as a purely commercial agency by Socialists and other radical organizations was proven by innumerable communications sent to Lenine's representatives by Socialists and other radical organizations all over the country, and which were offered in evidence. In these communications various Socialist committees and locals greeted Martens as the "first official representative of the Russian Socialist Federal Soviet Republic in the United States," wished him "rapid success in your activities for the benefit of the Russian Republic" and pledged their support to "the world revolution and brotherhood." A letter addressed to Martens from the Socialist party, Sixth Assembly District, New York, dated April 3, 1919, and signed by Charles Grossman, organizer, declared:

"The revolutionary Socialists of the Great East Side are, it goes without saying, behind Soviet Russia."

Another communication, from the Eighth Assembly District, of the Local New York Branch of the Socialist party of America, signed by Rebecca Bouhay, secretary, declared:

"The members . . . pledge our cooperation in establishing the first representative of the workers' government of Russia in America. We also pledge ourselves to work unceasingly for the propagation of those principles and policies and tactics that will end directly in the establishment of a Socialist Federated Soviet Republic in America."

"We are ready to meet and battle for the future," ran a communication to Martens from the Young People's Socialist League, Circle Six, Manhattan, which was signed by David Levison, organizer.

According to a letter from the National Office of the Socialist party, Chicago, Illinois, dated February 15, 1919, and signed by Adolph Guerner, executive secretary, Santeri Nuorteva, the chief associate of Martens in the Soviet Bureau, was "nominated as a delegate to the International congress." Mr. Stevenson said he offered this in evidence "as showing the extremely close relations between Mr. Nuroteva and the Socialist party of America."

HILLQUIT SOVIET "CHANCELLOR" IN U. S.

Morris Hillquit, one of the national leaders of the Socialist party, is the legal counsel of the Soviet Bureau, which, as the evidence proved, has maintained a department—to use Mr. Lusk's words—"for the defense of men charged with crimes against the United States." Among the twenty-eight employees of the Russian Soviet Bureau, according to the testimony, were two, Theodor Fedotoff and Anton Taitsen, who had been convicted under the sedition law in New Jersey, and who are out under $5,000 bail, pending an appeal. Mr. Hillquit's status in the Lenine-Trotzky organization in the United States was presumably better defined in a bulletin issued by Nuorteva. "Mr. Morris Hillquit," ran the announcement, "has accepted the post of Chancellor of the Russian Soviet Bureau in the United States . . . Mr. Hillquit has been in close touch with Mr. Martens and his bureau from the very day of Mr. Martens' appointment."

Correspondence between Nuorteva and Eugene Debs, sent to prison for violation of the Espionage Act, (who has been appointed by Lenine as "Proletarian Dictator" of the United States upon the successful culmination of the proposed revolution) proved the extremely cordial relations and spirit of harmonious concord existing between these two.

Innumerable invitations to address meetings were sent by Socialist organizations all over the country to both Martens and Nuorteva. According to the evidence, Nuorteva appeared to be the chief speaker for the Soviet Bureau, and was filling speaking engagements throughout a large part of the United States. Several hundred letters in the seized files relating to his engagements proved that this Bolshevist arch-agent was being booked through Socialist party locals. One of the communications, relating to a meeting at which he was invited to speak, was announced as being "only for discharged soldiers, sailors and marines." A paragraph in the announcement of this meeting read: "If you want to rebuild society, there is only one way to do it, join with the rest of the workers in one big union. It is useless to try to buck the system alone. Bosses are too strongly entrenched. You might as well try to capture a fort single-handed. If the workers get together and stick together there is nothing they cannot accomplish. Di-they are helpless. United they are in-le. The world is theirs. The only way to reedom is to TAKE it.''

ıile Mr. Martens professed to be engaged e establishment of purely commercial rela- between the United States and Soviet a, the evidence secured in the raid upon eadquarters demonstrated that he was en- l in disseminating, and in promoting the nination of, propaganda material exploit- he theories of Lenine and Trotzky in the d States. A weekly bulletin, issued by oviet Bureau, according to Mr. Stevenson, subscribed to by various branches of the list party, each of which took from twenty- to one hundred and more copies weekly. rding to the testimony, at the Soviet Bureau found a letter addressed to the workers urope and America by Nicholas Lenine, an appeal by Lenine, asking American ing-men for their cooperation, in which xpressed ''confidence'' and ''conviction'' the American working class ''will go with ainst the bourgeoisie.'' The Soviet Bureau ıformation distributed an approved list of ications giving favorable information con- ng Bolshevism and Bolshevist Russia. ng publications whose articles were endorsed he official representatives of Lenine and zky in the list, which was offered as evi- e, were the *Dial*, Mr. Oswald Garrison rd's *Nation*, and the *Survey*, of which Mr. l U. Kellogg is editor. There were also mmended the following books: ''Russia in eaval'', by E. A. Ross; ''The Red Heart of sia'', by Bessie Beatty; ''Six Red Months in sia'', by Louise Bryant, and ''Ten Days that ɔk the World,'' by John Reed. There were mmended also pamphlets published by the alist Publication Society, of Brooklyn, New k, the People's Institute, San Francisco, fornia, and the Rand School of Social nce.

RAND SCHOOL HOTBED OF SEDITION

ınswering an inquiry as to ''what literature he best to put out to the people in regard to true situation in Russia,'' Ludwig Martens, German-born official agent of Lenine and tzky in the United States, referred an in- rer—one, S. C. Haskin, of South Bend, iana,—to the Rand School of Social Science, here,'' said Martens, ''you can obtain all in- mation desirable.'' That the Rand School Social Science directly cooperated with the ial agents of Lenine and Trotzky; that it ked lecturers who spoke ''aggressively in or of the Bolsheviks;'' that it engaged in the ribution of Bolshevist propaganda, including writings of Lenine openly advocating the rthrow of organized governments, suppression the right of private ownership of property, e by the mob and the destruction of the sent forms of government in the United tes and European countries; that it dissem- ted translations of the Bolshevik constitution l governmental regulations; that in its cor- pondence courses it promoted the theories of soviet form of government, that in its letters correspondents it advocated preparedness resist'' and the taking over of the State; that listributed and freely sold inflammatory mat- advocating ''a political revolution by force,'' brought out by correspondence, documents l propaganda material seized in the raid on Rand School premises.

ılgernon Lee, educational director of the Rand ıool and Socialist member of the Board of lermen, acted as chairman of a meeting held Madison Square Garden on June 17, 1919. the stenographic report of a speech delivered Lee at this meeting, and which was presented evidence at the Lusk hearings, was the declara- n:

'The cause of Soviet Russia is identified with the cause of labor and liberty here in the United States and the world over.''

One, David P. Berenberg, is director of the correspondence department of the Rand School. From the letter-files seized there, evidence was produced showing the kind of propaganda conducted through Berenberg's department. In a carbon copy of a letter to Harry L. Perkins, of San Diego, Cal., dated June 7, 1916, the statement was made:

''When we read of 'preparedness' that is in full force in the camps of the capitalists we realize that unless we organize and fit ourselves to resist, and to take over the government, we will one day find ourselves where our French and German brothers are today, dead or maimed in the fray.''

''In other words,'' commented Chairman Lusk, ''for over two years this Rand School has been advocating armed preparedness to take over the government.''

A letter—obviously after a form letter sent to correspondents generally—dated October 3, 1916, addressed to M. E. Rabb, Xenia, Ohio, offered as evidence, contained the following:

''WHAT ARE YOU DOING WHEN THE STATE ROBS YOU AND YOUR UNION AND SO MAKES YOU HELPLESS TO STRIKE? THERE IS ONLY ONE THING TO DO: TAKE OVER THE STATE.

''ARE THE MEMBERS OF YOUR LOCAL PREPARED TO TAKE OVER AND CONDUCT WISELY AND WELL THE AFFAIRS OF YOUR TOWN AND COUNTY? ARE YOU PREPARED TO MEET THE MILITIA WHEN THE POWERS OF THE STATE AND COURTS ARE AGAINST YOU? ARE YOU ARMING YOURSELF WITH THE KNOWLEDGE OF THE FOUNDATIONS OF OUR SOCIETY SO THAT WHEN THESE CRISES COME TO YOU, YOU WILL HAVE AN ORGANIZATION STRONG ENOUGH TO HAVE FORESEEN AND FORESTALLED THEM? ARE YOU TRAINING YOUR MEMBERS IN SCIENTIFIC SOCIALISM?''

This same adroitly phrased incitement was found in other correspondence.

A letter written by David Berenberg, dated April 16, 1919, and addressed to ''Dear Helen'', informed his correspondent of a proposed ''cross-country trip to establish connections with the radical movement throughout the rest of the country'', and stated, ''If I can possibly put St. Joseph on my program I shall be glad to visit your town again.'' An interesting part of the letter were the following comments upon the draft as it touched Mr. Berenberg and upon the Versailles Congress:

''I should be very glad to hear from you or in fact from anyone in the family. Let's at least know what's going on. Was Emanuel drafted? If so, did he serve? If so, what happened to him? It seems to me you might at least have kept us posted. Everyone of us here lived through the war; none of us were touched, and the danger did not come because I was liable to be drafted, but for other reasons which I will not go into now.

''I don't know how much you are interested in the developments of things in Europe. In fact, I don't know how much of the real news of things—which doesn't get into the newspapers—penetrates into the Wild West. I do know that we are due in this country for a reaction which will make us for a period of some five or six years, the most backward country in the world.

''Isn't it amusing to see Wilson, Lloyd George and Clemenceau tearing each other to pieces over the question of who should own this or that piece of territory? *It strikes me the whole thing is much ado about nothing anyway, since the Bolsheviki will get them before long.*''

Further discussing his proposed visit to St. Joseph, Berenberg's letter went on to say:

''Tell Uncle Dave to leave off his uniform when I come out; otherwise, it might be his duty to lock me up as an enemy, and with all the jails in the country to choose from, I do not know why I should pick out the jail in St. Joseph as my stopping place.''

In a reply, dated May 13, 1919, addressed to ''Dear Dave'' and signed ''Helen'', it was brought out that the ''Uncle Dave'' referred to was engaged in detective work in St. Joseph.

RAND SCHOOL SOCIALISTS GOT "SICK OVER" BEING DRAFTED

Interesting light upon the attitude of certain of Mr. Berenberg's associates in the Rand School regarding the draft was afforded by a carbon copy of a letter dated July 26, 1917, addressed to ''Dear Jenny'', found in the Rand School files, which was offered in evidence, in which the following appeared:

''You ask about the draft. Only a few of our boys are caught by the draft, so far. Most of their numbers are so high that we are quite sure they will be safe. Schurter and Benj. Gordon and Grant are caught, but will probably go to jail instead of into the army, Sonabend also. I hear that many of the union men will go to jail, but that is rather indefinite information. We are awaiting developments somewhat anxiously, as there must be others we know not of that will be caught. Schurter is just about sick over it, and we for him.''

The declaration that the Rand School ''boys'' would probably go to jail rather than fight Germany, the satisfaction expressed that the majority would be ''safe,'' certainly indicates the attitude of the Rand School crowd toward the war. And indubitably it ''places'' this crowd, composed mostly of unassimilable alienry, so far as loyalty and Americanism are concerned. Enjoying American opportunities and yet enemies of American institutions and the American Government, their first whine, when they are detected in disloyalty, is about their rights to freedom and their rights to free speech. The spectacle of this gang of shirkers and cowardly crawlers advancing themselves as deliverers of humanity, as the apostles of a new order, would be simply grotesquely comic were it not for the fact that, as has been proved by the Lusk Committee exposures, they do constitute a serious and very real menace as a force in our national life inciting to discontent and disorder.

In the Rand School files, with the above mentioned correspondence, was found a letter addressed to ''Dear Comrade Mailly''—presumably Bertha M. Mailly, executive secretary of the Rand School—and signed ''Jennie Matyos.'' From the correspondence it was shown that ''Jennie'' lived in Chicago. In the above quoted letter, commenting upon the draft as it affected the ''comrades'', the following—which gives some insight into the fund-raising activities of these ''champions of the poor and exploited''—appeared:

''The school building fund is growing beautifully, better than we could have dreamed. What we must do now is to keep up the pace already set and all will go well. Forty Thousand is no small amount to raise, you know. $25,000 is already subscribed, but the last will go more slowly, I presume, because the first half includes several large contributions, one of five thousand. But isn't this a fine beginning?''

In another letter written from the Rand School to ''Jennie,'' the statement was made: ''We have paid ten thousand dollars on the new building.''

That the Rand School—whose ''boys'' got ''sick over'' being drafted and who preferred to go to jail rather than fight Germany—got single contributions of $5,000 is not, of course, any more surprising than that William Bayard Hale, paid secret director of Hun propaganda in the United States, should, in the autumn of 1917, have joined the Socialist Party in support of Hillquit and his program of a Bolshevist separate peace with the Huns. It would not, naturally, be surprising if now—when the radical movement offers to the Huns the most convenient and effective vehicle whereby to damage their victors by the promotion of social discontent and civil strife—that the vast funds left by Bernstorff in South America and elsewhere should be made liberally available to the foes of peace and order in the United States and the Allied countries as well. Nor is it surprising that all varieties of these foes of peace and order should find a common meeting ground in the platform of the Bolshevists, whose propaganda was first inspired and promoted by Germany.

"IDEALS WHICH TODAY INSPIRE LENINE" IDEALS OF RAND SCHOOL

That the Socialist Party and the Rand School of Social Science teach nothing less than the economic theories which the Bolsheviki are endeavoring to carry out through terrorism, mass murder and armed force in Russia appears to be the fact from "Lesson XII" of the Correspondence Department of the Rand School, entitled "The Human Element in Economics," offered in evidence. In this lesson sent out in the correspondence course, was the following:

"The workers of Russia adopted a constitution in July, 1918, which represents and attempts to put into practice some of the principles of industrial democracy. . . The second chapter of the Declaration of Rights provides for 'the abolition of exploitation of men by men, the entire abolition of the division of the people into classes, the suppression of exploiters, the establishment of a Socialist society, and the victory of socialism in all lands. . . Furthermore, all workers are to be armed and all members of the property class are to be disarmed.' . . .

"The application of the principles embodied in this Soviet Constitution, whether made in Russia or elsewhere, means inevitably the overthrow of capitalist and class government and the establishment of an industrial democracy. . . The struggle between plutocracy and democracy is a struggle for life and death. One must survive, the other must be destroyed."

"This is typical of the correspondence instruction given by the Rand School in its correspondence course," explained Mr. Stevenson, "and I think shows conclusively a real sympathy for the Soviet form of government."

Illustrating the product of a course of training in the Rand School of Social Science, Mr. Stevenson presented to the Committee a copy of a valedictory speech by Oscar Edelman, apparently made at the time of Edelman's graduation. In this speech the young graduate said:

"For us as students, Socialists and Labor Unionists, our work is laid out. We must help educate the workers of America so that their slogan, 'a fair day's wage for a fair day's work' be replaced by the revolutionary slogan, 'abolition of the wage system.' . . In the great world-wide struggle which is taking place today, we must take active part. . . The ideals which today inspire Debs and Lenine are the ideals which inspire us."

An instance of the very close relationship existing between the heads of the Bolshevist Bureau in New York and the leaders of the Rand School of Social Science, was found in a letter sent to A. A. Heller, Director of the Soviet Commercial Bureau, by David P. Berenberg, recommending Gertrude Pignol for a possible position in the Soviet Bureau. Gertrude Pignol was one of the teachers dismissed from the New York Public Schools because of her views regarding the war. Other correspondence seized in the files of the Rand School proved the cooperation between the lecture bureau of the Rand School and the Left, or revolutionary, Wing of the Socialist Party. It also revealed that the Rand School, as late as April 3, 1919, was booking Joseph M. Coldwell to lecture. According to the record, Coldwell, formerly state organizer of the Socialist Party of Rhode Island, was convicted of violating the Espionage Law, was sentenced to three years imprisonment in Atlanta, and while the Rand School was booking him he was out under $25,000 bail.

ANSWER "CANNON WITH CANNON"

Nicholas I. Hourwich, a son of one of the Rand School instructors, and a contributing editor of *The New York Communist*, the organ of the Left Wing of the Socialist Party, according to information afforded Mr. Stevenson by the office of the District Attorney of Lackawanna County, Pennsylvania, was arrested in Scranton on July 6, 1919, under the Pennsylvania anti-sedition law. According to District Attorney George W. Maxey, Hourwich, at a meeting held in Scranton, made the following remarks:

"Russia is ruled by communists, that is, Bolsheviks. Who are the Bolsheviks? We, the working classes, who now rule in Russia. In Germany and in Austria we have quite a hold, and here in America the American Communist Party is strong for the cause, the same cause that has succeeded in Russia after many years of strife. Men, kneel down on your knees and pray for a leader who is proletarian, a dictator of the working class. All in favor of proletariat communism hold up their right hands. Do we believe in force? Most assuredly we do believe in force. It would be folly for us to go out with bare hands and oppose the trained armies of the capitalistic government. We must answer their cannon with our cannon."

When the raid was made on the headquarters of the Rand School there was found freely on sale in the book store, together with seditious literature issued by the Left, or revolutionary, Socialist Wing, literature of the I. W. W., including the *One Big Union Monthly*, a periodical published in Chicago by the I. W. W. In the May, 1919, issue, a copy of which was taken from the Rand School library, was an editorial entitled, "The Onward Sweep of Bolshevism," in which the following statements were made:

"The tide of Bolshevism is still rising to our immense satisfaction. . . Bolshevism is a great popular uprising against the upper class of the old world. Its first point of attack in every country is directed against the existing government, and the first thing the victorious Bolsheviks do, they take possession of the government buildings and the institutions of the state. They capture the government by force and put Bolsheviks into office in place of the officials of the old regime. The typical Bolshevik revolution is A POLITICAL REVOLUTION BY FORCE."

Among the papers found freely on sale at the Rand School book store and offered as evidence, were copies of the *New York Communist* of Saturday, June 14, 1919, in which was an article beginning: "Do we hold that the revolution must come by violence? To answer this question by yes or no would be asinine. It may; again, it may not. The Left Wing, all the protests of the Right Wing to the contrary notwithstanding repudiate Socialism by assassination. The Left Wing hopes that the proletariat will conquer its enemy, the capitalist class, with as little bloodshed as possible."

Among the seizures at the Rand School, and which appear in the record of the Lusk Committee, were amazing documents relating to seditious and revolutionary propaganda among the negroes of the country. In a letter addressed to Francis J. Peregrino, 4 Fernando St., Pittsburgh, Pa., dated May 16, 1919, who had written for information concerning a correspondence course which would equip him for doing "missionary work" among negroes, David Berenberg made the following remark:

king Contrasts Between U. S. and British Labor

(Continued from Page 5)

eparate the industrial sphere from the political vas a mistake, tending to make trade unionists 'lobbyists" when they came into contact with the egislative bodies.

"I perceive," said Mr. Thomas, "a fast growing entiment in favor of an independent labor party n this country."

r. Thomas, so the promoters of the American or Party claim, expected, when he landed , to make a number of speeches in different s of the country in the interest of that movet. In fact, his only public appearance in country was before a New York group of small faction in the American Labor movet that is trying to promote an independent tical labor party, thereby disintegrating the erican Federation of Labor and turning the r movement of this country over to the Bolist and other disruptive forces. There is space to discuss here the merits of this ques. Suffice it to say that that proposition ed so little strength at the Annual Conven of the American Federation of Labor at antic City that its proponents tried to keep rom coming before that body to prevent its kness being revealed. And yet Mr. Thomas rceives a fast growing sentiment in favor n independent labor party in this country." ı easy to conclude with what labor people he ciated while here. It is a matter of record he did not attend the Atlantic City Conven and, for some reason, apparently kept aloof n the recognized trade union leaders.

he merits of the British and American labor cies will be illuminatingly discussed by Mr. W. Sullivan, the Labor member of the comsion sent to Europe by The National Civic eration. Comparing accomplishments, which what counts, the American labor movement, h its feet always on the ground, is getting ults, while the British Labor movement has ne up into the clouds and does not know how get down. Results to it mean nothing; politijobs mean everything.

While Mr. Baruch and Mr. Vanderlip, quot above, are financiers and therefore do not etend to speak from actual experience, aner gentleman who was a member of a comssion of employers, appointed to study indusal conditions in England from the standpoint an employer, has just returned and is putting a good deal of printed matter, giving his own ws of the situation. This employer is not so ll known as are Messrs. Baruch and Vander and does not bear the same relation to emyers that those two gentlemen do to the bank fraternity. He does, however, speak as an ployer. We refer to R. J. Caldwell, who in *e New York Times*, of June 22, in a threeumn article, discusses the remedy for labor rest. Mr. Caldwell does not fail to use the ck argument about democratic government. says:

> I have merely come to the inescapable conclusion that we must apply to industry the principles of democracy which we are enjoying politically, and that our mills and factories must be governed with the consent of the governed.

What was said in reference to this point in earlier part of this article applies equally to r. Caldwell. But he has discovered other ings besides the fact that the "factories must governed with the consent of the governed." e says: "We must abolish the Three Big Terrs of labor: the fear of disemployment, of illalth, and of old age in a poorhouse."

Of course, this simply means that Mr. Caldell is looking at the situation through the ectacles of the socialistic British Labor Party. e doubtless has accepted at par value all the claims made by the defenders of English paternalism. Mr. Caldwell, considering the matter entirely from a commercial point of view, has figured out that compulsory health, unemployment, old age and invalidity insurance could all be provided for without taxing the employer more than five per cent on his pay roll. He entirely ignores the point of view of American labor, which is that it should not be done at all, whether it involves five, ten or only one per cent. Their objection is based upon a fundamentally greater and more important proposition than that of dollars and cents. They say, we do not want to reduce the American working people to the condition that is bound to follow such paternalistic legislation. The disintegrating effect upon the moral fibre of the English working men and women who are applicants for unemployment insurance, the loss of independence of character and the pauperizing of the individual, would require a volume to discuss, as shown by preliminary reports from investigators now on the ground.

Mr. Caldwell, unlike most employers who have visited England since the war, says on his return: "We cannot do better than to profit by the example of England which is much further advanced than this country or any other in the matter of meeting labor problems." He then tells how for thirty years in the cotton industry of England they have had joint committees made up of representatives of employers and wage earners working together—as if England had anything to teach us along that line! In our mining, building, printing, boot and shoe, stove manufacturing and forty other industries, such agreements have been in vogue for anywhere from twenty to forty years. But stranger still, Mr. Caldwell says it is inconceivable that progressive America should fail to "profit by the experience of Great Britain and Australia in their methods of settling labor disputes." He adds: "It would be un-American to require twenty years of embittered and costly strife to apply to our industry the benefits derived by Great Britain."

Mr. Caldwell should forget Great Britain and Australia for a few months and devote himself to a careful study of what has been done in the United States along all those lines. Australia and New Zealand made complete failures of all their compulsory arbitration schemes, as everybody knows who has given any study to the question, and there is nothing in the labor governments of those two countries that American labor, much less the employers, would think for a moment of wanting to copy. Even the minimum wage which Mr. Caldwell puts out as one of the demands of labor was voted down by an overwhelming majority at the American Federation of Labor Convention at Atlantic City in June and much of the objection to it comes from the knowledge of the failure of its operation in the countries Mr. Caldwell is so anxious to have us imitate.

On the objections to compulsory sickness and unemployment insurance, we will quote two of the most representative labor leaders in this country, Mr. Warren S. Stone, Grand Chief of the International Brotherhood of Locomotive Engineers, and Mr. Samuel Gompers, President of the American Federation of Labor. At a recent meeting to discuss compulsory social insurance held at the headquarters of The National Civic Federation, Mr. Stone said:

> It seems to me that the whole plan of health insurance or social insurance, from the standpoint of the workers at least, is altogether wrong. If we have accomplished anything as a nation, it has been due to the fact that the men and women of the country have been allowed to work out some of these problems. I do not take much stock in paternalism; I do not believe in a government that tucks you in bed at night, and if some plan of health insurance is adopted, worked out and finally made a law, I fear its effect on our country; I fear it will be the beginning of the end. I do not believe any nation can prosper when the government does everything for the industrial worker. It destroys initiative and makes him a dependent upon the bounty of his government.
>
> But I want to say to you frankly as a representative of labor that there is not going to be any compulsory health insurance if we can help it. When you say to the American working people that they must do this or that thing, every drop of red blood in them resents it. I think it is summed up in a homely phrase, "You can push all you like but you musn't shove."

In the January, 1919, number of *The American Federationist*, an editorial by Samuel Gompers said on "Political Labor Party—Reconstruction—Social Insurance":

> There are so many of our people, including workmen, who look to the government of our country to do the things which seem so easy for the government to do, and which they imagine should be done by the government. They do not recognize the pit-falls and the dangers which are entailed by conferring upon the government the function of doing these things. To my mind, it is a grave danger to place into the hands of the government the powers which would necessarily result from government compulsory health insurance with all the powers vested in the government incidental to and in the enforcement of health insurance.
>
> There is one thing that I want to say to the Committee on Social Insurance. Place in the hands of the government the right to determine who is or who is not entitled to governmental insurance; to determine regulations and conduct of every man insured, then it means that the government has the power with all the force at the command of the government to enforce the decrees or regulations.
>
> And that applies, too, to unemployment compulsory insurance. The government will determine then what will constitute justifiable reasons for unemployment. It might decide that when men and women are unemployed they are entitled to this insurance. Well, what is the cause of unemployment? Suppose it is a disagreement with employers. The government will decide as to whether the cause of unemployment is justifiable or is attributable to the workmen or to the employers. It is not necessary, then, for me to mention the fact of what that would mean to the work, the policy and the constructive movement of organized labor. The labor movement would lose its voluntary character and its effectiveness, and there would be brought about a condition of affairs in our country whereby the toilers would be rendered ineffective in their work for the protection and promotion of their rights and interests.

When the English socialists, the Hendersons, Thomases, *et al.*, can capture the American labor movement, then all these paternalistic propositions will be tried here, but not before. In the meantime, it is safe to predict that those employers of this country who have their feet on the ground, and that is 95% of them, will on these questions prefer to follow the lead of the representatives of the American labor movement, such as Samuel Gompers, Warren S. Stone, James Duncan, W. G. Lee, Joseph F. Valentine, Matthew Woll, John P. Frey, William D. Mahon, John A. Voll, Daniel J. Tobin, John Golden, T. V. O'Connor, George W. Perkins, Frank J. McNulty, and a thousand other big and brainy American labor men, rather than the lead of the Hendersons, Thomases, Smillies and Williamses of the British Labor Party. Our sane employers here know that, when it comes to a comparison between the labor leaders of America and those of Great Britain, those of America are not only more brainy, more statesmanlike and more farseeing, but have also proved their loyalty to their country during the war. They have refused to follow in the footsteps of the defeatist, pacifist British labor leaders, who played into the hands of Germany in 1918 by trying to force "a negotiated peace" with the enemy and are now endeavoring to coerce their government in its international policies. They said, in effect, to the British Government at Southport in June, 1919, "Take the troops out of Russia; lift the embargo on Russia; lift the embargo on Germany; release the conscientious objectors; reject the Peace Treaty because of its severity to Germany; reject the League of Nations covenant because it is not democratic—*i. e.*, because it is not so framed as to give the socialists, bolshevists and anarchists of Europe control! Do these things,'' say Robert Smillie, of the Mine Workers, and Robert Williams, of the Dock Workers, ''or we will call a general strike and tie up the industries of the nation. Not only that; we will get Italy and France to join with us.''

And this is what those sane and conservative labor leaders of Great Britain, with Arthur Henderson at their head, are now trying to accomplish. The only reason that the Rt. Hon. James H. Thomas, general secretary and head of the National Union of Railwaymen and treasurer of the Triple Alliance (of railwaymen, transport workers and miners) and a Member of Parliament, was not mentioned in the reports of this Southport meeting as joining in the resolutions, along with Henderson, Smillie and Williams, was that he was in the United States at the time, telling the American employers how safe it would be for the affairs of Great Britain to be turned over to the Labor Party.

Contrast this situation at Southport with the Annual Convention of the American Federation of Labor which was held at Atlantic City a week earlier. On every proposition that convention stood with our Government and for Americanism and against Socialism and Bolshevism with all their accessories. They refused to endorse the Soviets of Russia, they refused to condemn the League of Nations, they refused to ask for the release of the conscientious objectors, they refused to endorse the general strike to help Mooney, they refused to favor a Labor Party on the lines of the British movement. In fact, they refused to endorse almost all the things which the British Labor Party was demanding should be done. And yet we have employers in this country who are expressing the wish that the leadership of the American labor movement might be placed in the hands of men like Thomas, Henderson and Smillie, instead of being in the hands of men like Gompers, Duncan and Stone; and they applaud Mr. Thomas when he says: ''Our party is made up of men trained to face responsibilities, who recognize that justice is an essential feature of any political programme and the British people, knowing this, have no apprehension for the future should the Labor Party come into power'' just as if he were to be taken seriously.

To all such employers we commend a careful consideration of the following extract from *The New York Daily Call*, the leading socialist organ, commenting upon the Atlantic City Convention, and a statement made to the United Press by Jean Longuet, Socialist Deputy and the leading spirit in the international proletariat alliance of French, British and Italian workers.

The Call says:

> Atlantic City, June 18.—The high tide of reaction in the affairs of the American Federation of Labor was reached here yesterday when the Gompers machine crushed all proposals of the radicals and progressive elements of the trade unionists of this country.
>
> Practically every expectation that this convention of the American Federation of Labor would condemn every progressive idea as outlined in the *Call* by your correspondent has been borne out by the developments here.
>
> There will be no strike to save Tom Mooney; the Soviet government has been denounced; the millions of starving Russians blockaded by the Allied governments are to be left to their fate; the Labor Party idea has been smashed and, as for industrial unionism, the A. F. of L. intends to go on its old way. This is the grist of two days' grinding in the Gompers mill.
>
> It was a field day for Gompers, for every parliamentary trick that might be employed to shut off debate was used by him.
>
> The convention has shown opposition to a joint termination of contracts, is opposed to the democratization of industry to the exent of refusing to recommend the election of foremen on jobs by the workers, refuses to assist in the formation of 'soldiers' councils that would be helpful to labor, sets its face against any letting down of the craft bars or aiding industrial organization and finally has defeated a recommendation to the international unions to adopt an initiative and referendum clause in their constitutions.

Mr. Longuet's statement is:

> French and Italian workers are already bound closely together, while English laboring men are lining up more and more closely with us. We have already succeeded in establishing an alliance of workers which does not recognize European national boundaries.
>
> But at the present time we have gained but little support from America. This fact is chiefly due to the opposition of Samuel Gompers and other conservative leaders who control the destinies of the American Federation of Labor and who have complete power over labor organizations. Also, the fact that numerous workers own their homes breeds conservatism.

But, to bring the matter home more concretely, it is announced by Mr. John O. Jones, an organizer of the British Labor Party, who say
accompanied Mr. Thomas to New York, that
representatives of the Triple Alliance of G
Britain, Messrs. George Smillie and George
liams, are coming to America to organize
railway workers, the miners and the dock w
ers of this country into a Triple Alliance
America. These are the same men who h
just ordered a referendum which, if carried
will authorize them by direct action to tie
the three industries referred to at any time.
quote Mr. Jones:

> The plan in America is to win the rail
> workers, the harbor workers, and the mine w
> ers to the general strike movement. A strik
> the three would mean a walkout of 3,000,000 n
> it is said, and would paralyze any effort to m
> troops.

So our employers who seem so greatly
amored of the British Labor leadership n
have a taste of it a little sooner than they
pected.

Mr. American Employer, were this situat
not so serious, it would be ludicrous.

British Official Reports Indict Bolsheviki

HORRORS of Bolshevik misrule in Russia, described before the Overman Committee of the United States Senate last Winter, are fully confirmed by official British reports recently presented to Parliament. Chaos in the stricken country is spreading rapidly and steadily in the vast districts still controlled by the Reds. Testimony before the Overman committee only related to conditions existent up to September, 1918; the British reports cover the period up to February 15 of the present year.

Every sensational story of cruelty, oppression and misgovernment brought from Russia since Lenine and Trotzky attained power practically is confirmed by the British reports. No hope is held out in any one of them that the dictatorship established after Kerensky's fall ever will result in anything except armed mob rule. Even anarchy does not prevail, the great mass of the population being held under a sway of terror by a small minority backed by the meagre food supplies of the nation and the guns of criminals, forced soldiers and non-Russian mercenaries.

Even the hope that the great middle class and the peasants might rise against Lenine and Trotzky and reestablish something like the idealized republic of Kerensky's time no longer is held out. The populace, long starved and cowed by innumerable murders, no longer has hope of a successful rebellion. Disease, grief and privations have so weakened the spirit of the many that the few well armed and well fed Reds rule practically with impunity. Only the advent of armed forces working for law and order can redeem Russia, is the inevitable conclusion drawn from the many, varied pictures of conditions there. Those pictures come from sources so reliable that the British government has accepted them fully and has incorporated them in its official documents.

Shocking as are the conditions of the civil population under the mob rule, their counterpart in industry is unprecedented in any time in the world's history. Food production almost is at a standstill. Factory work is so scarce that it excites comment. Living costs have risen to such heights that even the favored Bolshevik supporters resort to robbery of their fellows once they trace the smallest food supplies. Banking virtually is abolished and the wholesale printing of paper money—much of it deliberately counterfeit—has gone on to such an extent that the nation's finances are in even greater chaos than the civil administration.

Most interesting and significant are those pa
of the British report that deal with Socialis
Lenine and Trotzky, it will be remembered, r
to power largely through their promise to est
lish a socialist state modelled after the teachin
of Marx and Engels. Once they had gain
control, the dictators turned on the very o
who had helped them to power. Forming th
Red Guard from the criminal classes and by e
listing at high money and food pay of Chine
Letts and German and Austrian prisoners, th
proceeded to oust all Socialists from the sovi
and to put in their stead the Bolshevik riff-r
that had joined their army only to loot the hel
less middle class. Any who protested again
the mob rule thus established, whether he we
Socialist, bourgeoise or of the landed class, w
at once denounced as a traitor to the proletari
Thousands of such starved to death in the pr
ons. Other thousands were tortured and kille
Other thousands escaped from Russia. Tho
who escaped those fates now lead the existen
of animals, hunting their food where they m
dodging the Red Guard daily and in immine
danger of summary execution if caught.

Nationalization of the industries—the Marxi
dream—has worked out most disastrously. Wh
Lenine and Trotzky took control of the factori
no compensation, not even the depreciated pap
currency, was given to the owners. In less th
six months after the commandeering of the fa
tories, an English business man reports that t
important metal trades were at a standstill. T
linen industry soon dwindled to less than 40 p
cent of normal. The wool and cotton manufa
tures fell off more than 60 per cent. The on
enormous industry in making silk has disa
peared. Paper and coal production, at the la
report, only were at 60 per cent of the norm
while agriculture alone showed an increase.

A ''Mr. G.'' who was in Petrograd as late
last November, made the following comment
Russian industrial conditions:

> It is an extremely curious feature of the Ru
> sian revolution that a movement which h
> proclaimed itself as social and democratic h
> achieved in the first instance total destructi
> of those social groups on which a social dem
> cratic organization is mainly based—the cla
> of the industrial workmen. All factories, wi
> a few exceptions of those engaged on munitio
> work, are stopped, and the industrial workme

(*Continued on Page* 17)

The Milk Problem—A Practical Program

(*Continued from Page 6*)

First, a systematic study should be made of the value of milk as a food, its most healthful and wholesome form, its most sanitary and marketable method of handling and distribution.

Second, a plan of publicity devised that will acquaint the public with these facts.

Third, a stimulus provided looking to the more efficient production, distribution and sanitary control of milk.

While milk is admittedly indispensable to certain classes of our population the general public does not know nor appreciate to what extent it is a desirable and virtually necessary article of diet for everybody, nor its relative importance and economy as a food. Great progress has been made, however, in the past few years in scientific studies conducted to ascertain the nutritive qualities of milk. But this is only the beginning. There are questions as to the effect of pasteurization upon the food value of milk, the relative nutritive value of the butter and the salts in milk, the real facts as to certain types of bacteria, the value of milk in its sweet and sour form, which have not been definitely settled. Then again, the relationship between pasteurization, safety, and marketability, and the determination of the best packages and containers, are all matters of vital interest.

While studies of these matters would be interesting and useful from a scientific standpoint, their real value would be determined by just how far they became matters of general public information. If the facts were known, the public would both appreciate and buy, thereby increasing the demand for milk in its best and most wholesome form, and automatically creating the greatest natural stimulus to its efficient production and distribution.

Let us suppose that the dealers and producers of the country would unite upon a program of this kind by establishing one or more laboratories manned by the best experts obtainable for the purpose, whose object it would be to study constructively every phase of milk production and handling. Let the results of these laboratories be checked up and modified by experiments made on an industrial scale under the same competent supervision. In other words, instead of the industry being led by the findings of health boards and private laboratories with only a general interest in milk, the industry itself would thus anticipate and lead in the progressive movements for milk betterment, and to this extent would be a step in advance of the findings of either public or private health agencies. This fact alone would dignify the industry and invest the men engaged in it with something of the prestige and dignity that always accompanies public service endeavor.

GIVING PRACTICAL EFFECT TO SCIENCE

The next step would be to establish a publicity organization which would intelligently bring before the public all the facts of a constructive nature determined by the laboratory experiments. A tremendous amount of good could thus be accomplished. Such an organization could revolutionize the annual conventions of the industry from associations for the mere purpose of discussing technical papers and indulging in industrial politics, to great vital factors in the movement for industrial growth.

Further, no better news material could be devised than the reports of the laboratory put into popular form and distributed by means of magazine articles and the pages of newspapers devoted to the interests of women, children and public health. Such publicity would be very economical for the industry and most valuable in news interest to the periodical handling it.

Again, by pooling the contributions of both dealers and producers a national campaign of direct advertising could be carried out which would be economical and comprehensive in its nature and wonderful in its results. It is obvious that an advertising campaign directed by the whole industry would carry more weight and bring better results than if conducted separately by the producers or dealers.

The whole theory of the above organization would be to sell more milk and to make clear the reasons why it should be sold. It would become a gigantic sales agency for the whole industry, and at the same time serve as a protection against unfair discrimination in legislation, railroad rates or any other of the manifold obstructions which might from time to time beset its path.

The selling price of milk would react to the regulating efforts of such an organization. As the matter now stands, there is no scientific rule that governs the price to be charged in the future for milk except that dealers would be expected to charge the public high enough to insure a profit over the cost of the milk to them. It will be logical to expect that the higher the price charged by the producers, the greater the percentage of profit to the dealers. Such a process will constitute a price to the consumer tending to discourage the public in its use of milk and leading it to seek cheaper substitutes, all of which would be most regrettable to those engaged in the bigger movement.

SOMETHING TO THINK ABOUT

It will be presumed that many of the dealers and producers represented in the newer organization would also be members of the existing separate organizations of dealers and producers. The point of view of these men in their work in the new organization would undergo a revision, causing them to see the danger of overcharging and likewise do much to assure a more sympathetic relationship between the original organizations, in place of their old mutual bitterness. An organization such as we are planning, in addition to creating an increased demand for milk, will also be in a position to recommend the best manner in which that demand can be supplied.

To create a sufficient supply in itself would become a stimulus to more efficient production and distribution. Better sanitary control of the product would be guaranteed since the very foundations of the new organization would be laid in the laboratory experiment, and industrial analysis. By such constructive processes public interest in the industry would be increased. The importance of the producers and dealers as public service agents would be more fully and readily recognized. The business would so thrive in private hands and under private management that all thought of public ownership and undue public regulation would virtually disappear.

Under a leadership that both could respect, the distributor and the producer would be encouraged to work together. Each country creamery could be made an educational dairy center where the best interests of the producer, distributor and consumer would be freely discussed. The distributor could become the business agent of the industry, taking the initiative in the cooperative buying of feed, not on the basis of profit to himself, but on that of saving to his patrons. Cow testing associations could be provided for and encouraged, thus enabling the producers to learn their poor cows and to substitute better cows for them. All such educational enterprises would naturally fall within the scope of the functions of the laboratory and publicity organization.

The question of prices for the milk in the city would be discussed not only from the viewpoint of profit to those engaged in the industry, and rightly so, but also with the great end in view of building increased sales of milk to the point of diminishing returns, thus carrying out the purposes of the organization. Conversely, matters of distribution would not be left exclusively to the judgment of the dealers alone, but would necessarily have to be considered from the standpoint of the progress of the whole industry. Obviously, the more efficient the method of distribution the greater saving in the basic cost of milk, and the greater demand for milk.

Both production and distribution are distinct functions of the milk industry, each dependent on the other, and with the consumer entitled to efficiency in both. Production or distribution alone is a big enough job for any one man, and these two functions should be kept separate. But efficiency in performing these functions properly becomes the common interest of producer, distributor and consumer. An organization made up of both distributors and producers keeping always in mind the interests of the public will be best equipped to reconcile factors of quality, price and efficiency.

The chief interest of the producer is not production alone, but a healthy industry throughout.

The real consideration of the distributor is not distribution alone, but a healthy industry throughout.

Certainly the best interests of the consumer lie in encouraging an intelligent industrial policy and increasing its consumption of this most valuable of all food products.

The great demand of the present is for all American industries to consider their problems from the four corners, comprehensively and constructively. In no other way will those petty differences tending to destroy be relegated to the background. There is no better time nor place in which to begin these considerations than now, in the milk industry. In no other field will the public enjoy greater benefits.

British Official Reports Indict Bolsheviki

(*Continued from Page 16*)

have to return to their villages with which they had lost ties, or enlist in the Red Guard. The younger men, nineteen to twenty-six, to a great extent have chosen the latter alternative and it is they who form the nucleus of the Bolshevik army.

To speak of the growing success of the management of industrial concerns under soviet rule is an absolute misrepresentation. It would be sufficient to disprove this statement only to cite the instances of the factories of Petrograd, Moscow and Nishny, where formerly many thousands were employed and where now only a few hundred are working.

The British reports show that the greatest factor in cutting down the factory output is the need of food. Workmen, though theoretically paid the highest wages in Bolshevik paper money, find it impossible to get enough to eat, hence have to forage for food or join the Red Guard. The wages paid fail to meet in any degree the prices fixed by the soviets and cannot even touch prevailing food prices. An idea of the chaotic financial condition of Russia may be had when conservative estimates state that there is outstanding in paper more than 100 times the amount of the country's gold reserve. That fact helps explain the following scale of food prices by the pound obtaining in Moscow in February, 1919:

Black bread	$3.00 to $3.50
Wheat flour	5.00 to 6.00
Potatoes (rotten)	1.00 to 1.25
Sugar	25.00
Butter	25.00 to 30.00
Beef	7.50

(*Continued on Page 20*)

WELFARE WORK

Edited by Gertrude Beeks Easley, Director Welfare Department, The National Civic Federation

The purpose of this department of the Federation is to secure improvements by employers in working and living conditions of employees, especially in mines, railroads, factories, stores, and public institutions. Articles will appear continuously in The Review, *dealing with existing activities or recommendations upon sanitation and safety, recreation, industrial and domestic science training and other educational opportunities, homes for workers, voluntary social insurance, provident funds, pensions, workmen's compensation, and profit sharing.*

Standards for Factory Wash Room Facilities

CONSERVATION of the health of workers engaged in making munitions and supplies as well as ships in which to transport them, was one of the primary war efforts of the Welfare Division of the Committee on Labor, a part of the Advisory Commission of the Council of National Defense. As a part of the educational program, Samuel Gompers, Chairman of the Labor Committee, circulated standards for employees' washrooms and other sanitary devices. Louis A. Coolidge, himself an employer, was chairman of the Welfare Division whose Section on Sanitation developed this code especially designed for high explosive plants and to guard the workers against industrial poisons. After several conferences, representatives of the industry especially concerned agreed to adopt the rules and regulations as the practice for their various plants.

The cordial feeling of employers toward the endeavors of the Committee on Labor and its relation to the war emergency are indicated by the following statement by Dr. William A. Evans, under whose Sanitation Section the Divisional Committee on Industrial Diseases and Poisons operated. He said when recommending the committee's report for acceptance:

"In most states it will be impossible to secure the requirements for the conservation of health of labor that will be necessary in those industries that are speeded up by purposes of war. Legislatures meet at long intervals and the securing of laws is a slow procedure. The only possibility that we can see of getting action immediate enough to be of service is through the agreement of the interested parties to adopt the rules laid down. The conferences were attended by more than one hundred representatives of manufacturers of high explosives, those loading high explosives and making war material."

The standards, which are given below, are applicable to factories in general. Installations of this character will not bring undue hardship to the employer whose working conditions are not equivalent to such regulations. They are a little better than the requirements of any state law. Among the expert members of the committee who assisted in their development were: Dr. W. G. Hudson, Chairman, Wilmington, Del.; Dr. R. P. Albaugh, Columbus, O.; Dr. George Apfelbach, Chicago, Ill.; Dr. Lewis Booker, New Castle, Del.; Col. Lewis T. Bryant, New Jersey State Commissioner of Labor, Trenton, N. J.; Dr. E. R. Hayhurst, Columbus, O.; Dr. F. D. Patterson, Department of Labor and Industry, Harrisburg, Pa.; Dr. J. W. Schereschewsky, U. S. Public Health Service, Pittsburgh, Pa.; Dr. W. Gilman Thompson, New York City; Dr. Alice Hamilton, Bureau of Labor, Washington; Dr. B. S. Warren, Public Health Service, Treasury Department, Washington, D. C.

WASHING FACILITIES

There should be provided by the employer without expense to the employee one (1) wash basin for every five (5) persons up to one hundred (100) on a shift; one (1) wash basin for every eight (8) persons between one hundred (100) and five hundred (500) on a shift and where there are over five hundred (500) persons on a shift, the wash basins should be one (1) for every ten (10) persons on a shift.

Or, there should be two (2) feet of trough for every five (5) persons up to one hundred (100) on a shift; two (2) feet of trough for every eight (8) persons up to five hundred (500) on a shift and where there are over five hundred (500) persons on a shift there should be two (2) feet of trough for every ten (10) persons. Where double-sided troughs are used, half the above trough space should apply.

It is recognized that where the trough is used, there should be flowing water and no stoppers. It is the part of wisdom to provide one faucet for every five persons. In practice it has been found that shower baths may be substituted in part for such faucets.

Continuing, the standards also provide that:

Where there are ninety (90) persons or less on a shift, there should be one (1) shower for every fifteen (15) persons; ninety (90) to five hundred (500) persons on a shift, there should be one (1) shower for every twenty (20) persons; five hundred (500) to one thousand (1,000) persons on a shift there should be one (1) shower for every twenty-five (25) persons; and when there are one thousand (1,000) to five thousand (5,000) persons on a shift there should be one (1) shower for every thirty (30) persons.

There should be provided hot and cold water, soap and fabric or paper towels.

TOILET ARRANGEMENTS

1. General Provision: Toilet facilities should be provided in accordance with the following standards:

2. Apartments:

(a) *Location*: All toilet facilities should be located conveniently to and easily accessible from all places where persons are employed.

(b) *Separation*: Toilet rooms for each sex should be maintained separate and apart from each other and from all workrooms and passageways. Such rooms should be marked so as to designate plainly and distinctly the sex for whose use they are intended.

(c) *Screening*: If the water closet is not located within a separate screened compartment in the toilet room, the entrance to all toilet rooms should be provided with a screen to insure privacy. This screen should be at least six (6) feet in height, and extend to within at least four (4) inches of the floor, and, if the space permits, should be not less than two (2) feet wider than the door leading into such toilet room.

(d) *Distance*: All toilet rooms not having sewer connection and maintained outside of buildings where people are employed should, on new installations, be at least twenty-five (25) feet from such buildings and in all factories where the workers are exposed to excessive heat, humidity, or fatigue from physical exertion, there should be a covered passageway connecting said building with toilet or toilets.

(e) *Construction*: The outside partitions of all toilet rooms should be of solid construction and may be opaque or translucent, but not transparent, and should extend from floor to ceiling, or such rooms should be independently ceiled over. All partitions separating toilet rooms provided for the different sexes, should be at least two (2) inches in thickness and constructed of such materials as are not transparent or translucent, and they should be sound proof, and no openings in such partitions should be permitted.

(f) *Floors*: The floors of all toilet rooms should be tight, smooth and constructed of a substance that should be impervious to moisture.

(g) *Walls*: The walls of all toilet rooms should be tight and of a substance that can be readily cleaned and kept clean.

(h) *Ceilings*: In those toilet rooms which have ceilings, the ceilings should be tight and of such substance that they can be readily cleaned and kept clean.

(i) *Light*: All toilet rooms and water-closet compartments should be adequately illumined by natural or artificial light.

(j) *Ventilation*: All toilet rooms not lighted by windows that open easily should be adequately ventilated to the outside air by artificial means. Similar methods should be employed for every water-closet compartment entirely separated from the remainder of the toilet room by partitions extending from the floor to the ceiling, and not provided with a window opening easily.

On new installations, every toilet room or every water-closet or urinal compartment should have a window opening directly to the outdoor air. No such window should be less than one (1) foot wide, nor have an area of less than six (6) square feet, measured between stopheads, for one water-closet or urinal. For every additional such fixture, the area of such window should be increased at least one (1) square foot. A skylight should be deemed the equivalent of a window, provided that it has fixed or movable louvres with openings of the net openable area prescribed for such window.

Every such window should open upon a street or upon a yard or open space, uncovered at the top, which in its least horizontal dimension, should be at least one-tenth (1-10) the height of the highest abutting wall but in no case less than six (6) feet.

(k) *Heating*: All toilet rooms and wherever practicable, water-closet compartments, should be adequately heated at all times.

(l) *Cleanliness*: The occupier should be responsible for the maintenance of all toilet rooms or water-closet compartments in a clean and sanitary condition.

(m) *Entrances*: All toilet facilities should be adequately protected to prevent the entrance and breeding of flies, as far as practicable.

FIXTURES

(a) *Kind*: The use of any form of trough water-closet or latrine, or school sink should be prohibited—individual closets should be provided. The bowls of the water-closets shall be of smooth, impervious material. Pan, plunger, washout, faucet and long hopper closets should not be permissible. The seat should be finished with a smooth, impervious waterproof substance. Types of chemical closets, or other closets which are approved by the properly constituted authorities should be permitted.

(b) *Connections*: The disposal of all contents of toilets and urinals should be in accordance with the laws, rules and regulations of the properly constituted authorities of the locality in which they exist. Provision should be made for the adequate flushing of every water-closet.

Privies should be permitted only in cases outside of the sewer zone, and where cesspool, septic tank, or chemical closets or other closets which are approved by the properly constituted authorities, are not practicable. Privies not connected with the sewerage system should be built in accordance with the standards recommended by the properly constituted authorities.

(*Continued on Page 19*)

rly Closing Helps Efficiency of Workers

(*Continued from Page* 9)

ners suffer exploitation through their ınce, but they also exploit through their .on to the enslaving customs of their native

competition of this servile spirit has its ɔn in a financial vassalage of a most subtle armful sort on the entire body of workers; ore so since it is never tyrannical enough ive its victims to the eruptive point, but them in a state of nervous irritability st conditions of life, when they confuse and cause in blaming the apparently care- :lasses above them for hardships resulting of them from iron-bound custom. . . . It y to see the mote in the other fellow's eye, ıever to suspect the beam in one's own! us Bolshevism is accepted as a disease of -trodden peoples, and not likely to spread under conditions of life said to be the best e world for the worker, therefore the re- ve state will be found wanting. The same have been said of the influenza plague; yet ne and exacted an enormous toll in spite of erally high standard of health and medical ıutions.

dustrial unrest in any class is a contributory s of Bolshevism, and there are countless in- :es where this discontent is justified by diable conditions.

ɔr example: Take the lot of the small store- er on the East and West sides of New York. is even more heavily enslaved by arbitrary om than his confrère in London, because day trading eats into his one day of rest till half of it is left. Admittedly it is very con- ent for the housewife to feel there is always ore open every day of the week at any hour, ɛpt perhaps between midnight and 6 a. m. what of the mental and physical reaction on obliging shop people who rarely feel the rays ɔeneficient sunshine, or breathe the compara- ly pure air of the streets? Ask them.

aid a prosperous East Side storekeeper to :

This is a life of slavery. I am at work from) in the morning till 10 at night, and on Sun- morning till 10 o'clock. I would willingly ɛrve chain store hours, but if my neighbors p open I must do the same, for I cannot afford ose a customer."

Why not get your neighbors to close too? ıy can't get enough custom half the time to for their gas?"

That's true. We did try closing on Sundays, l as long as the police stood round it was all ɔt. But as soon as they moved off one man ned, and then another, till we all had to open in in self-defense."

'Well, why not stop competing with each er by becoming cooperative traders when you compete with chain stores on equal terms, ich you can't do now? Sooner or later they'll ve you out of business anyhow."

'I don't know anything about cooperative ding except that it has not been successful ɛn tried here."

'That is not the fault of the cooperative sys- ı, but of the people who have misused its vers for their own profit. In every country the world, except the U. S. A., it has been salvation of the struggling man. Read up ɔut it."

'I have no time for reading; if I get a look at headlines of the paper it's as much as I can in the day. . . . 'Girlie' (calling to his ıghter, who was his cashier), 'would you like read up about the cooperative movement for ?'"

A slim pretty girl of about 18 came out of office, and it was easy to see she was the father's treasure. Her fair skin was already sallowing and her wavy hair was fading from its natural gold to a drab hue.

"I have no time, father, for reading. You know I am here always," she replied with gentle reproach in her voice.

It was cruel to see how her birthright of joyous youth had been suppressed and stultified by long hours of solitary work, under unnatural conditions till she was just a meek ghost of exuberant youth. Her natural destiny was to be the mother of future citizens. What sort of fighting heritage could she give them?

"Why do you submit to such long hours? Why don't you young ones form an Employees' Union and agitate for Early Closing?" I asked impatiently.

"But what could *I* do?" she exclaimed in amazement.

"Do? Why get together all your friends who are working in stores, organize yourselves into unions in community blocks, and agitate! What others have done, you can do. In my country Early Closing has been a law for many years. But it might never have come about for all stores if shop assistants had not agitated to help themselves. It is all as simple as a, b, c. You only have to show the public how the national health is being sapped through selfish custom, and tell women if they did their shopping and marketing in reasonable hours they would give you a chance of living like a decent American, and of being a credit to your country. . . . You have the vote now. What is it for but to improve your conditions? Use it for early closing, and you'll win out. . . . Think what it would be to have five free evenings, a free Sunday and a half holiday of daylight and sunshine each week. Why life would be worth living again!"

The girl looked like a soul awakened, and with a gospel of hope put into her hands which quickened the blood in her veins, sending a faint flush to her cheeks. Both father and daughter wanted to be 100 per cent. American, but the wearing monotony of endless work was sapping patriotism and preparing their minds for any mischievous doctrine of pretended salvation that came by.

"If only the laws that exist were enforced," remarked the storekeeper, "we might have a chance. But they are not, and what hope is there that fresh ones will have any better luck?"

The yearning of these two for a day's work of normal length, and time for natural recreation in which to find themselves, together with their lack of initiative in fighting for better conditions, seems typical of would-be good citizens under the acid test of arbitrary custom.

In a drug store nearby was a tall anaemic young man, son of the proprietor. Nature had intended him to be a fine strapping young fellow, but the long hours of indoor life had made him sappy and reedy. Despondency was his keynote.

"I have no time for reading, I am here all day from early morning till late at night, always on tap," he remarked in a weary toneless voice.

How could he be 100 per cent. American when already initiative and energy were killed? For him there was no joy in living, no incentive to ambition. A paternal government had insisted on his having a free education which would stimulate desire for rational pleasure, while arbitrary custom had tied him to a treadmill just when his pulses were beating fastest and life should be most alluring. Worse still, he was already in the grip of hopelessness and incapable of a fight for better conditions. Could there be more fertile soil for subtle Bolshevism?

Into a garage I went for some gasoline. A young, respectable foreman measured out the quantity, remarking apologetically that it would be 3 cents more to me than the marked-up price. That was all right, but prompted the question: "Why is gasoline double the old price, and still going up?"

"Why?" he replied with intense bitterness, "because every time Rockefeller gives a million dollars in charity he puts up the price a penny, and we pay for his generosity."

This led to a discussion on the tyranny of trusts in boosting prices at will, and of Bolshevism as Lenine's cure, when the man said in accents of intense scorn of himself and his class:

"The only difference between those people in Russia and us is that *they have backbone and we haven't.*" The contempt of himself and his class, the antagonism to capital, the denunciation of trusts, breathed in his every word, indicated a dangerous mental perspective. Yet there was that about him which convinced me he would willingly be 100 per cent. American if the conditions of life were less harsh for him.

I looked at the bloodless face, at the thin, nervous body, at all the hall marks of unnatural repression, and walked away reflecting on the menace of such opinions to the well-being of the nation, when just a little easing of the worker's financial burden would make the scales fall from his eyes, and he would judge of Bolshevism at its true worth as "mere robbery without extenuating circumstances."

This placing of the responsibility of poverty on the shoulder of capital seems to me to mask an inarticulate cry for fair play, for sympathy, for brotherhood, expressed in a practical constructive plan to ease the worker's burden, and bring about a juster distribution of the world's wealth than exists now.

Man is a selfish animal, and what he gets he keeps. But woe to the profiteer if Bolshevism rises to a flood tide in this country!

Welfare Work

Standards for Factory Wash Room Facilities

(*Continued from Page* 18)

(c) *Number and Ratio*: When there are one hundred (100) or less persons on a shift there should be one (1) toilet (closet) for every twenty (20) persons (in practice it has been found advantageous to provide one closet for every fifteen persons); when there are one hundred (100) to five hundred (500) persons on a shift, there should be one (1) toilet for every thirty (30) persons; when there are five hundred (500) to one thousand (1,000) persons on a shift, there should be one (1) toilet for every thirty-five (35) persons, and when there are one thousand (1,000) to five thousand (5,000) persons on a shift there should be one toilet for every forty (40) persons.

URINALS

(a) *Kind*: Urinals should be either individual or slab. At least two (2) feet of slab should be considered the equivalent of one (1) individual.

(b) *Construction*: All urinals should be composed of smooth material, impervious to moisture.

(c) *Connections*: All urinals should be connected by means of waste pipes to sewers or cesspools, which sewers or cesspools should be constructed in accordance with the laws, rules and regulations of the properly constituted authorities of the locality in which they exist.

Unless water runs continuously over the walls of a urinal, each urinal should be provided wherever practicable, with an adequate water flush. When individual tanks are used, the flushing should be accomplished by pedal action, or if water flush is impracticable, then with other proper means for cleanliness and safety.

(d) *Number and Ratio*: One (1) urinal, or its equivalent should be provided for every fifty (50) men on a shift.

(e) *Entrances*: All urinals should be adequately protected to prevent the entrance and breeding of flies, as far as practicable.

In practice it is recognized that separate urinals should be arranged throughout the work places convenient to the points where the men work.

Bolshevist Buncombe Regarding Germany's Defeat

By W. J. GHENT

OVER and over again, from pro-Bolshevist sources in America, one hears, or reads the statement that the war was brought to an end by means of Bolshevist propaganda in Germany. Not the hammer strokes of Foch, Haig and Pershing brought Germany to its knees, but the demoralization of the army and navy subtly influenced by Lenine and Trotzky, with perhaps some assistance from Karl Liebknecht and Rosa Luxemburg.

No proof is offered to support this amazing assertion. It is merely repeated, in various forms, as though repetition could take the place of evidence. It was first made, apparently, in an article by John Reed, in the January *Liberator*. This article told of the propaganda sown by Bolshevist agents in foreign countries, particularly Germany, and it made a great number of wild and sweeping statements about the influence exerted. "Soviet Russia," it declared, "Conquered Imperial Germany." Reed was for a time an employee of the Bolshevist Bureau of International Revolutionary Propaganda, as were also Albert Rhys Williams and Boris Reinstein, and it is only natural that he should feel a sense of the immense importance of his activities. But he presents not a scintilla of real evidence to support his boasts.

NO CONFIRMATION FROM GERMANY

The testimony of the Germans themselves refutes the assertion. In the Weimar assembly Ebert declared that revolution in the rear had had nothing to do with the collapse of the German military power, and his declaration was received with applause. The testimony of the military chiefs is to the same effect. There was no revolution, nor anything that looked like a revolution, until after Germany had sued for peace. Nine months earlier there had been a number of strikes in the industrial centers, but they appear, in the first place, to have been easily suppressed, and in the second place, to have had no relation to Bolshevist propaganda.

The German offer of peace was made on Oct. 6, 1918. Six days earlier (Sept. 30) Bulgaria had formally surrendered, and a day earlier (Oct. 5) Austria-Hungary had made a most abject plea for peace, while Turkey had already made her first move for an armistice. The German army and navy were at that time intact.

Four days later (Oct. 10) the *Munich Post*, the leading official paper of the Bavarian Social Democracy, published an article (quoted by Karl Dannenberg, in the *Radical Review* for January-March) by its Berlin correspondent which discussed the question, "Who is responsible for Germany's latest and most all-embracing offer of peace?" The answer named several factors, but it entirely excluded the Socialists, revolutionists and Bolsheviki as one of them. "The change," it says, "is not at all to be attributed to the Socialists—it came from the very opposite direction. That is, it came solely from the higher-ups, who knew that the army had been vanquished and was daily becoming weaker."

SOCIALISTS AND ARMY CHIEFS AGREE

This is contemporary Socialist testimony; and though the Bavarian Social Democrats were not on good terms with the majority Social Democrats of Berlin, neither the *Post* nor its correspondent could well have ignored the fact of a revolutionary factor in the change had there been one.

Ludendorff, in his recent book, says that as early as Aug. 8 the Germans had lost hope of a military victory, and that at a meeting of the crown council, on Aug. 14-16, he had declared that a victory was impossible. On Sept. 8, in a talk with Hindenburg and Hintze, he had said: "The western front may at any time have to withdraw further, and the worse our military situation becomes, the harder will be the conditions."

Hindenburg was apparently slower in reaching the same conclusion. A letter of his, dated Oct. 30 and published in March by the Wolff Bureau, declares that the "Macedonian disaster" a month earlier, with its attendant weakening of reserves of the west front, made the imposing of peace on the allies impossible. He accordingly advised: "It is imperative that we cease the struggle in order to save the German people and our allies from unnecessary sacrifices."

NO EVIDENCE OF BOLSHEVIST INFLUENCE

What was the situation behind the front? Of evidence of Bolshevist influence there is none. As for the Spartacan agitation, Karl Liebknecht could not have been a factor before Oct. 24, when he was released from prison. But Germany had already, on the 20th, committed herself to the acceptance of the proposal for an evacuation of occupied territories and had made request for the arrangement of an armistice. Though there were anti-war demonstrations on the streets of Berlin on the 25th, there is no evidence of any demoralization in the army other than the demoralization resulting from constant defeat.

The German note of Oct. 27 was generally regarded as a note of surrender, since it gave tacit consent to the principle laid down in the President's note of Oct. 23 that the armistice must be on terms which would preclude Germany from renewing hostilities. When, therefore, the mutiny in the fleet broke out on Oct. 31, Germany as a power was already finished, and was merely awaiting supinely the drastic terms then being drawn up by the Supreme War Council in Paris.

REVOLUTION FOLLOWED THE COLLAPSE

The mutiny was not a revolution, but a strike against putting out to sea on a suicidal adventure. The formal demands made by the sailors upon the authorities had to do with conditions and disclipine, but were not a revolutionary ultimatum. Though revolutionary sentiment was at work in Berlin and other centers, there is nothing to show that it was other than a home-made product. It was an inevitable reaction from the realization of the overwhelming defeat of the army and the impending abject surrender. Even so it was without force until the Majority Socialists, seeing their opportunity of taking over the government, joined hands with the Independents. This shift came only at the last moment. A manifesto of the national executive committee of the Majority Socialists, issued on Nov. 6, says nothing about revolution but warns the people to avoid riots and demagogues. During all the previous month the negotiations for the armistice were going on, and the allies were smashing their way forward. By the 8th, when the Majority Socialists had swung over to revolution, the Kaiser's delegates were standing before Marshal Foch and hearing the terms which reduced Imperial Germany to impotence. The part which Lenine, Trotzky and Reed played in the great drama is nowhere visible.

British Official Reports Indict Bolsheviki

(*Continued from Page* 17)

Pork	10.00	
Lard and Bacon	20.00	
Horseflesh	3.00	to 4.00
Dog flesh	1.00	to 1.75
Cat flesh	1.50	each.

One of the greatest pities of the foregoing table and the fact that thousands are starving, is the fact reported by many of the British observers that in parts of Bolshevist Russia there is food in plenty. The reason for the pressing shortage and the high prices elsewhere is the fact [illegible] the trans[illegible]tation system has broken down [illegible]ly. A[illegible] t[illegible] this the[illegible] great deal [illegible]ng and [illegible]g by the peasants. Unles[illegible] is fort[illegible] [illegible]ough to have real coin it is [illegible]lt to b[illegible]d from the peasants, so distrus[illegible] [illegible]ave they become of the depreciated paper tok[illegible] [illegible]n circulation.

Many of th[illegible] British agents reporting the facts in Russia are [illegible]dden under initials, but among the signed reports are some from Sir M. Findlay, at Christiania; Sir E. Howard, at Stockholm; and Sir R. Paget, at Copenhagen. All their reports relate to murders of British subjects by the Red Guard, or the arrest of British officials and consuls. There is also a report from R. H. Bruce Lockhart, a British diplomat widely and favorably known in the United States. Lord Kilmarnock at Copenhagen, Colonel Wade at Warsaw, Sir H. Rumbold at Berne and Sir C. Eliot at Vladivostock also contributed details of the Bolshevist rule, so it may be readily seen that the pictures of conditions drawn could not be exaggerated.

No story of the happenings in Russia under Lenine and Trotzky would be complete without the recital of wholesale killings and tortures of innocent persons. The British reports are honeycombed with the bald facts of such incidents and almost everything printed heretofore is verified by these official observers. Men and women frequently are compelled to dig large graves and then, standing on the brink, are shot down without mercy. Officers of the former Russian army have their shoulder straps nailed to the shoulder when caught and the most menial tasks—and worse—are the fates suffered by the educated women and girls seized as hostages by the Bolshevik leaders.

Not less important than these verified details of atrocities are the excerpts from the Red press forwarded by the British agents. The Red organs by the score record with apparent glee the excesses to which the cultured classes have been subjected. Others incite the armed mob to further killing by bloody appeals far worse than those that filled the German press in the early days of the Great War. The press extracts are incorporated in an appendix to the report and fully confirm the stories of terrorism rife ever since Lenine and Trotzky took full control.

One of the most striking press quotations comes from the Krasnaya *Gazette*, which said on September 1 last: "Without mercy, without sparing, we will kill our enemies in scores of hundreds. Let them be thousands; let them drown in their own blood. For the blood of Lenine and Uritski, Zinovief and Volodarski, let there be floods of the blood of the bourgeoisie—more blood, as much as possible."

And the flood of blood thus demanded for the attempts on Lenine's life still is apparently flowing unchecked throughout the Red-stricken land.

Tyrrel Print, New York.

The National

Civic Federation Review

Vol. IV. NEW YORK, AUGUST 30, 1919 No. 18

GREAT FARMERS' ORGANIZATION

WILL BUILD TEMPLE OF AGRICULTURE AT WASHINGTON — AT CONFERENCE IN SEPTEMBER WILL START CAMPAIGN TO PROTECT NATIONWIDE INTERESTS

FARMERS of the nation have awakened. Perfection of a great national organization is being rapidly attained. Plans are being worked out for a Temple of Agriculture costing $1,250,000 at Washington. Subscriptions are being asked for an endowment of more than $6,000,000 more. It is planned to use building and endowment for the centering of the complex interests of the farmers so that the organization may rank with the Chamber of Commerce of the United States, the American Federation of Labor and similar combinations.

The National Board of Farm Organizations, Charles S. Barrett, chairman, has the project in charge. Fourteen leading farmers' unions, with more than 2,000,000 active members, are thus united. Many of them are national or interstate in scope. Mr. Barrett, chairman of the National Board, long has been head of the National Farmers' Union and represented the interests of the American farmer before the Peace Conference in Paris. His work there brought international recognition of farm interests never attained before in the world's history. M. Clemenceau and David Lloyd George consulted with Mr. Barrett immediately on his arrival abroad, but his sailing times and President Wilson's crossed and they passed one another in mid-ocean.

CHARLES S. BARRETT
President Farmers' Educational Cooperative Union of America and Chairman of the National Board of Farm Organizations

Already the National Board of Farm Organizations has a home in Washington, having bought the old mansion at 1731 I Street, N. W., not far from the White House. In this mansion, on September 16 and 17, will be held the fifth semi-annual conference, a meeting that bids fair to be momentous for the farming interests of the nation. Hundreds of delegates from the great farmers' organizations—grange masters, officers of grain, livestock, cotton and milk producing associations, will attend. Needless to say, the occasion will reveal to all the imperative need of the Temple of Agriculture and its endowment for protecting the agriculturist.

Few realize what has been accomplished by the National Board of Farm Organizations since its foundation in 1917. Its three representatives on the food price fixing committee were largely instrumental in obtaining the guaranteed price of wheat. They presented to President Wilson vital facts concerning the nation's position on the all-important food question. Modifications of the draft law as it applied to farmers and their helpers enabled the country to continue its output of foodstuffs at the one time they most were needed. An Agricultural Advisory Committee was formed by President Wilson and two of the board's members—Mr. Barrett and Milo D. Campbell, president of the National Milk Producers' Federation—were made members.

In furtherance of its campaign for the strongest kind of organization of farmers, the National Board just has finished a series of meetings throughout the West. The speakers were Senator Thomas P. Gore, Dr. W. J. Spillman, Milo D. Campbell, Charles S. Barrett, John A. McSparran and A. A. Elmore. The trip was most successful and the building fund was increased by a six figure amount in consequence.

At the Spokane conference, more than 4,000 farmers attended and their response to the fund appeal was a contribution of $20,000. Other places visited were Lexington, Kentucky; Salt Lake City; Modesto and San Jose, California; Bozeman, Montana; Bismarck and Fargo, North Dakota, and Mitchell, South Dakota. Wide publicity was given each of these meetings and some of them extended over several days. Thousands of farmers were made to realize the need of a strong national organization and their belief in the plan was expressed in cold dollars—the most striking medium of endorsement.

John A. McSparran, who is treasurer of the fund, is the master of the Pennsylvania State Grange. The Keystone state is one of the largest agricultural states in the union, despite the great industrial developments that overshadow its farming activities in the public eye. His speeches on the tour were forceful explanations of the need of federation in the right way. In showing how the farmers should get together, he cited the instance of $2.26 wheat for which three men stood steadfastly for weeks and won. One of them was Charles S. Barrett, a cotton planter who never raised wheat, but who plainly saw that the guaranteed price was necessary if the world were to be fed.

A. A. Elmore, chairman of the Temple of Agriculture Committee, is president of the Washington Farmers' Union. He brought out clearly that the National Board was wholly nonpartisan, non-sectarian and purely economic. He said that it was certain that the problems of the farmer could only be met by fullest cooperation, something that the National Board of Farm Organizations furnished.

All of the speakers on the tour told the farmers of the many important measures pending in Congress. It was shown that efforts were being made to blame the farmers for the hight cost of living; that there were certain influences at work to put the onus of everything on the farmer. They told of the efforts to get cheaper potash and of the opposition to the bill to regulate the sale and shipment of fertilizers. The imperative need of trained economists, field men and lawyers to represent the farming interests properly was shown to be greater than ever and it was declared that the only way to get this vital protection was to perfect the National Board of Farm Organizations at once. Emphasis was laid on the fact that the feed men, the fertilizer men, the canners, the packers and the millers, were all strongly organized and working for legislation to aid their businesses, while the farmers—the basis of all the other industries—were without adequate representation.

In addition to Messrs. Campbell, Elmore, McSparran and Barrett, other members of the Temple of Agriculture Committee are:

J. H. Mills, president Georgia State Farmers' Union;
Joe Niccolls, representative Iowa Farmers' Union;
Gifford Pinchot, president Pennsylvania Rural Progress Association;
Maurice McAuliffe, president Kansas Farmers' Union;
S. J. Lowell, Master New York State Grange.'

In working out the plan for the Temple of Agriculture and its accompanying endowment, it is also proposed that each state shall raise $150,000, interest of which would serve to maintain a representative of farm organizations within the state in addition to the representative of the National Board of Farm Organizations.

As showing how fast the National Board is growing, it might be said that at the conference in August, 1918, thirty-seven states were represented and that eighteen organizations (in addition to the fourteen in the Board) sent delegates.

HOME OF THE NATIONAL BOARD OF FARM ORGANIZATIONS, 1731 I STREET, N. W., WASHINGTON, D. C.

NATIONAL BOARD DEMANDS "COLLECTIVE BARGAINING"

The National Board of Farm Organizations at a recent meeting at its headquarters in the Woodward Building, Washington, issued an appeal to farmers of the country to protest by petition, ballot, or other lawful or orderly means against the unfair and un-American methods being used against farm organizations engaged in the collective sale of their farm products. The immediate cause for this appeal was the arrest on August 9 of seven prominent farmers in Ohio who were acting as representatives of the Ohio Farmers' Cooperative Milk Company in the sale of the farmers' milk to the dealers of Cleveland. These men were arrested at their farm homes in the night and thrown into an overcrowded vermin-infested room of the city jail. In the appeal, congress and legislatures are asked to take early action to clarify a situation which the Farm Board asserts is widening the gulf between the city and the country. The statement of the National Board follows:

"On the 9th day of August, 1919, seven farmers who were acting as officers of the Ohio Farmers Cooperative Milk Company were indicted by a Grand Jury in the City of Cleveland, Ohio, for having acted as representatives of the farmers who were selling milk to the dealers of that city.

"The price charged was below the cost of production by the farmer, as found by all investigations, and was lower than in most of the other cities of like class in the country. The offense consisted of 'collective bargaining' and was not inordinate profits. The men indicted were among the most prominent and respected farmers of the state, several of them being township and county officials.

"In order to make their humiliation or intimidation more pronounced and public, these men were arrested at their farm homes in the night, taken to the city of Cleveland and there thrown into jail without opportunity to secure bail until the next day. The jail itself was full of vermin and the treatment accorded these men was barbarous and extreme.

"The National Board of Farm Organizations, standing at all times for law and order and asking no immunity for violators of the same, nevertheless, records its vigorous protest against the use of our criminal laws for the personal advancement of ambitious city politicians and for the benefit of profiteering combinations operating between the farmer and the consumer.

"The National Board of Farm Organizations calls attention to the fact that if farmers shall be denied the right to do collective bargaining in the sale of their products; if they are to be branded as criminals for doing openly what all business is permitted to do unmolested, that such class distinction will not always be borne with patience by the farmers of the country.

"The National Board of Farm Organizations recalls that in almost every large city of the United States within the last two years, farmers from outside such cities have been caught within their boundaries and branded as felons for daring to confer with their neighbors or for joining with them in the sale of their milk or other common products; that some of these indictments are still pending, others are being threatened and all without regard to the farmers' increased cost of production.

"The National Board of Farm Organizations believes that organization and collective bargaining in the marketing of farm produce is essential if profiteering and unnecessary expense shall be eliminated between producer and consumer. These indictments by cities against milk producers whose industry cannot survive without this right, are being justly construed as indictments against all farmers whether they be named or not in the indictments themselves. We view this widening breach between city and country with fear and alarm.

"The National Board of Farm Organizations confidently asks:

"1. That every farmer through petition, by the ballot, or by other lawful or orderly means makes his protest known against the unfair and un-American methods so being used again t him.

"2. That Congress and Legislatures by early action make clear the original purpose of our anti-trust laws that are now being misinterpreted and misdirected so that by unmistakable terms farmers shall have the right to do collective bargaining in accord with the original intent of the law."

The Senate Committee on Agriculture and Forestry recently issued a statement on the agricultural situation which emphatically asserts the need of changing wheat grading rules and discounts, which, it is claimed, if unchanged may rob wheat growers of from fifty to seventy-five cents a bushel on millions of bushels of wheat. The senators and farm organization representatives say that the wheat, although shriveled owing to the unusual heat of the summer, is of the highest milling value and will enter in large measure into the production of the high priced patent flours and be sold to the consuming public at prices based on "Number One" wheat, so that producers will be defrauded and consumers receive no benefit. The statement has the endorsement of the entire committee and has received the unqualified support of the National Board of Farm Organizations and the National Grange, which have a combined membership of approximately three million producing farmers.

The Labor Situation Abroad Following the War

Part of the report of the Commission sent by The National Civic Federation to England, France and Italy to study industrial conditions has been completed, and the chapters by James W. Sullivan, the labor member of the Commission, which cover "The Passing of the British Shop Steward Movement," "The 'Democratization of Industry,'" "Chaotic British Labor Politics" and "Great Britain's Triple Alliance," are here published in abridged form.

Few men are better known in the labor world than Mr. Sullivan, and this applies to the other side of the Atlantic as well as to this. For more than a quarter of a century he has been in active touch with labor organizations and leaders of Great Britain and the continent, having been sent abroad as a delegate of the American Federation of Labor on several occasions.

During the war he was Assistant to Mr. Gompers on the Advisory Commission, Council of National Defense, and, concurrently, head of the Division of Labor and Consumers' interests in the United States Food Administration.

The Chairman of The National Civic Federation Commission was Charles Mayer, chairman of the Board of the France & Canada Steamship Corporation. Other members were Albert Farwell Bemis, President of Bemis Bro. Bag Co., Boston, Mass., who represented employers, and Andrew Parker Nevin, a well known New York attorney, who represented the interests of the American public. The reports by Mr. Bemis and Mr. Nevin will be published in the next issue of THE NATIONAL CIVIC FEDERATION REVIEW.

The Commission's full report, comprising a careful analysis of industrial conditions on the other side of the Atlantic, will soon be printed in book form.—EDITOR.

THE PASSING OF THE BRITISH SHOP STEWARD MOVEMENT

I

AMONG the many unusual developments in the course of the abnormal conditions which characterized the industrial situation in Great Britain during the war, few were viewed with greater interest than the so-called "shop stewards movement." It was mainly in its beginnings a war-time schism from regular trade unionism, and later a thrust toward nationalizing and democratizing industry. Following its rise and rapid growth, most extravagant claims were made for it in various radical publications in the United States. How unsubstantial these claims were is, I think, conclusively shown in the history of the shop stewards movement which follows, for it evidences on how slight foundations utopias may be built by impatient social perfectionists, and also how widely the British and American trade union systems differ in organization, practice and effectiveness.

SHOP SPOKESMEN LONG A FEATURE

In various British industries, shop spokesmen chosen by their fellow wage-workers have long been a necessary feature of works operation.

In Britain, with the war, came hastily assembled working forces in large new munitions works and other manufactories. In these establishments, department representatives of the workers were usually recognized as a necessity by the employers, and, prompt decisions regarding working conditions for all the departments being frequently required, the various representatives on presenting themselves for conference were recognized as a general shop committee.

In the non-union shops these committees could directly adjust differences, to the extent of the powers conceded them by the employers and their fellow workers. But in the union shops a first and serious obstacle to speedy decision existed in the unit organization of certain trade unions, especially that of the machinists (in England, "engineers").

MEMBERSHIP BY LIVING AREAS

In a British branch union of engineers, the membership is by living areas and not by working areas. Hence the branch may be made up of members at jobs in various other living areas, and contrariwise a shop force may be made up of members of different branch unions. British trade unionists account for this form of unit organization by the fact that usually the "branch" combines trade union with "friendly society" features. Workmen's organization benefits are better administered by neighbors,

JAMES W. SULLIVAN

it is argued, than by shopmates living far apart, some of them casual workers.

Previous to the war, by the practice of the engineering trade union, which for at least half a century had authorized shop committees, a "convener of committee" was appointed in case of trouble, but there was no trade union official present regularly as deputy to carry out affairs of the general union. In American trade unions the confusion of this situation is obviated by making the workshop, or the shops of a given locality, the unit for the branch union, with its chairman representing the general union in local administration.

LACK OF UNITY IN ORGANIZATION

It was in this lack of shop unity of organization, and consequently of direct executive union action, that during the war troubles through shop stewards, both independent and union, clogged the work.

This gap in efficiency characterized some of the largest British trade unions having members engaged in war work. Continuous operation necessary, the shop stewards, union and unorganized, learned to take on authority for themselves. Consequently, union stewards drifted away from control by their headquarters; stewards for the unorganized, new-blood "labor leaders," became powerful men of the day. With the dilution of skilled labor came relaxed union organization together with distrust of the higher trade union officials because of their impotence in sudden crises.

Here was opportunity for the modern youthful agitator—energetic, unafraid, unencumbered, chafing under restraint from his elders in union positions. When fired by socialistic faith, the steward standing for the unorganized recked little of immediate consequences could he but promote the cause. He was in office for that purpose.

CHURCHILL RECOGNIZES STEWARDS

It was at this stage that a deputation from the stewards of the Woolwich Arsenal was assured by Winston Churchill as Minister of Munitions that they should be the body consulted concerning work in that important government establishment, thus ignoring the regular union officials. Similar recognition was soon extended to other large industrial centers.

District committees, seeing shop stewards recognized and setting aside union laws, ventured to follow suit, and in turn were suspended. In many parts of the country local, unofficial shop or craft spokesmen practically dominated in dealings with perplexed employers, uncertain whether agreements were to be observed.

Differing from the United States, there was no authorized central executive standing for a general wage-workers' organization, covering all occupations for the entire country, with which employers, singly or in bodies, might treat.

AMERICAN FEDERATIONS PROVED EFFICIENCY

The capability of the American Federation of Labor to come to a working understanding with our government on its entering the war, and to offer to employers a complete union mechanism applicable to every industry throughout the country, with models of rules, regulations and organization for the rapidly forming unorganized working forces, even to having an authorized union agent in every considerable workshop, is a matter of very recent history.

Everyone of the one hundred and eleven general ("national" or "international") unions covers comprehensively as to its own trade and exclusively of all other trades the whole of the United States. A traveling member of any local union is thus entitled to free, direct, unobstructed membership in every other local union of his occupation throughout the country. The workshop local unions uniformly represent, not living but working districts; in this respect certain building trades allowing latitude. No union man is under constraint to support any political party.

The Secretary of the American Federation of Labor reported in 1919, before the accession of the Brotherhoods, that the membership was 3,260,068, regular dues for the previous year of exactly that number having been paid into the treasury. Exempted members not being paid for—the sick, the unemployed, the idle by lockout or strike, an average year by year of approximately 10 per cent—the true membership was then 3,600,000. Today the grand total, with the Brotherhoods, ranges from 4,200,000 to 4,500,000.

FOUR "NATIONAL" BRITISH UNIONS

The British labor movement, differing fundamentally from that of America is politico-economic in character. It has four separate organizations, varying in type and purpose:

(1) The Trade Union Congress, meeting an-

nually to decide principally upon the several measures to be asked of Parliament and to elect its "Parliamentary Committee," whose mandate is "to watch all legislation affecting labor." The Secretary's report of the 1918 meeting gives the total membership as 4,532,085; the number of delegates 881, representing 262 societies.

(2) The "General Federation of Trade Unions," described by its Secretary as "the largest purely trade union organization outside of the United States," and as having March 31, 1,215,107 members.

(3) The Co-operative Union, its fraternal delegate to the Congress reporting a membership of 3,500,000, the great bulk trade-unionists; associated since 1917 in the Labor Party.

(4) The British Labor Party, its membership composed of wage-workers and other citizens, mixed, polling a vote equal to somewhat more than half the total membership claimed for the trade unions in the Congress and represented in Parliament by 59 out of 707 members.

MEMBERSHIP FIGURES DISCONCERTING

While 4,532,085 was recorded as the membership represented at the British Trade Union Congress of 1918 at Derby, these figures stand for the total number for which entrance fees were paid by the delegates at their option at the rate of ten shillings or less per 1,000. Between the membership of the unions reported, separately or in total, nearly all in round numbers, in this way in the Congress proceedings, and those given officially in detail in other union or government publications, there is wide divergence.

In comparatively few cases are the 262 organizations participating in the British Trade Union Congress of 1918 national in the sense of representing either England or the kingdom. In the "National Federation of General Workers," for instance, are nine organizations (four of them having "National" in their titles), all separately represented in the Congress, each with its own headquarters and independent administrative machinery, and mostly with special fields of operation, local or regional, the total membership claimed being 961,466. Similar instances might be cited almost ad infinitum.

BRITISH TRIBUTE TO FEDERATION

Commenting on the business-like completeness, unity and efficiency of the American Federation of Labor, a British trade unionist, for years high in the councils of the movement, said: "I believe that the superiority in organization of the American Federation of Labor is due largely to the fact that among its originators were Englishmen who, having had experience with the shortcomings of British organization, suggested correct forms for America." Cole, an indefatigable "intellectual" writer on labor matters, suggests, as to the local union: "Let the general principle be that of the works branch (instead of the residence branch)." British union and non-union employers alike frequently express the desirability of facing representatives of all their employees directly without loss of time.

In 1918 the British Parliamentary Committee's income was, in round numbers, $45,000, and its expenditures $35,000. It neither owns the building in which its offices are located nor issues a periodical. It does not employ organizers. The American Federation's income last year was more than $650,000; its expenditures nearly $590,000. In its new headquarters building in Washington it has invested $200,000. It paid for printing and publishing the *American Federationist* $122,000. It employed 112 paid organizers, fifty of them on full time, at an expense of $165,000, besides directing a corps of more than a thousand volunteer organizers and maintaining office communication with the numerous paid organizers of the separate national and local unions.

Abundant confirmation of the statements made previously in this article is found in writings of numerous leaders in the various branches of the British labor movement. For instance, Arthur Henderson, Secretary of the Labor Party, wrote in the *Daily News* of March 27 that "the pressing need of organized labor was fewer trade unions and more trade unionists." J. H. Thomas, Secretary of the National Union of Railwaymen, is quoted in the Manchester *Evening Chronicle* as saying, "The gravest danger now is not between the Government and the railwaymen, but between the unions themselves."

However, crude and clumsy as it is, British trade unionism possessed sufficient resisting power to throw off the shop steward fever, after the armistice came. From that time the stewards never won a strike and the mass of the wage-workers in the engineering trade repudiated both irregular leadership and insurrectional tactics. Product of the war emergency, with which British trade unionism was incapable of coping, the stewards' growth and power passed away with the cessation of war materials.

In the United States, as a social reformer, the shop steward never had a footing with its workers. To American trade unionists, accustomed to their own complete organization mechanism, as a workshop official supplementary to the union representatives he would have been classed with the proverbial fifth wheel to a wagon.

THE "DEMOCRATIZATION OF INDUSTRY"

II

IN the article immediately preceding I endeavored to show how shop stewardism had been born in Great Britain as the result of abnormal conditions combined with inefficient functioning of the British trade unions. It was also shown that this movement, hailed at one time by the radical American press as the dawning of a new era in world industry, quickly died when the exceptional conditions that gave it birth had passed.

It is hard to discourage our utopians, however, and we have been hearing a great deal lately about the "democratization of industry," "workers' control," "a voice in management," "an economic democracy," "labor to head the business," "wage workers at the directors' table" and similar verbal coinages which are in favorite use among a group of stampeders after economic will-o'-the-wisps. They are a busy tribe not regarded too seriously by American trade unionists accustomed to deal with grimy and untheoretical fact.

Behind these phrases is screened a big idea—a compound of syndicalism, socialism, and the new-fangled Guildism. One of the good sentimentalists promoting the new doctrine declares: "The application of the principle of workers' control (self-government in industry) is the greatest functional advance for democracy since the state extended its operations beyond police power and became an administrator of public services." And he goes on: "Workers' control is an elastic term. It means, first, a little control in the workshop in regard to welfare and general workshop conditions; then more control in relation to discipline, sanitation; and so on, up to full participation in control over the whole industrial process inside the shop and *in the industry as a whole*. The degree of control will be set by the capacity of the workers for exercising control."

DESCRIPTION IS ALLURING

The kindly apostle of "self-government in industry" who indited that scenario expresses his opinion that the wage-workers of Great Britain have already paved much of the way to the goal of his vision, first, through having their spokesmen in the workshop; secondly, through the "enlightened self-abnegation of autocratic control" by certain employers; and third, through government action on the Whitley Committee Report.

Have the wage-workers of Great Britain, or of any other country, for that matter, really paved much of the way to the goal seen in the vision of the writer quoted above? This can best be answered by considering somewhat in detail just what is involved in the management of the average business. First, it must be set up, which requires among other things the marketing of shares, determining the form of incorporation, and multitudinous other things that will suggest themselves at once to the average reader. Next comes the purely physical side, which means that a site must be selected and a building erected, following which machinery must be installed. There are of course many other features involved in the development of this phase of management. The plant to be run must have efficient operating and sales forces. Then there are evident financial questions, such as the buying of supplies and raw materials, meeting the methods of competitors, action in crises such as fire, flood and disaster, and many other things too numerous to mention, which require long experience, sound education and good judgment. There are also such questions as the fixing of the percentage of depreciation, employment of attorneys, choosing forms of charity, and other similar questions which are certainly far removed from the province of labor as we know it in any country at the present time.

The whole matter comes down to the fact that workmen sharing control in any industrial establishment must have either personal training or expert advice as to the points enumerated above, coupled with sufficient general education and brain power to cope continually with keen-minded competitors. They must also be able to rise to the self-discipline necessary to secure united action in a board of directors representing both capital and labor. Furthermore, placed in such a position, labor would necessarily be compelled to accept all the consequences of control, including, when necessary, the passing of dividends, sharing of losses, reducing of wage scales, dismissing surplus employees, abolishing the minimum wage, sacrificing certainty of income, and incurring various forms of liability.

The promoters of the recently discovered route to a reign of democracy in industry begin their argument by calling attention to the "control" by shop spokesmen under agreements with employers. The degree to which that control goes, or whether in fact it should be called control, merits consideration.

SHOP REPRESENTATIVES' TRUE FUNCTIONS

The functions of shop labor representatives are usually defined in the contracts made between employers and trade unionists. They commonly name as matters of negotiation wages, hours, shop facilities, superintendence, regulations, with the many ramifications of each.

The second stage toward "self-government in industry" is achieved, by the new theory, when the workers absorb functions turned over to them, in part, through the "self-abnegation of autocratic control by far-sighted employers." The most conspicuous illustration submitted of this alleged transmission of directive powers to the workers is the Renold factories at Manchester. It may legitimately be examined as a test of the theory.

In a memorandum on the subject, Mr. Renold himself submits a list of subjects which he regards as matters susceptible to negotiation between employers and employees, and he includes in this list all of the subjects mentioned above,

(Continued on page 13)

Andrew Carnegie—the Friend of Labor

ANDREW CARNEGIE, one of the greatest constructive forces in the development of American industry and one of the most magnanimous philanthropists of the world, has passed away. With his gigantic accomplishments in business, his benefactions exceeding $350,000,000, his labors during a quarter of a century to secure universal peace, most people are familiar. His rise in life from a poor boy who came to America at the age of twelve to one of the dominating figures in the nation, whose wealth was estimated at possibly $500,000,000, is one of the romances of the age, a story that is well known, an inspiration to all who are filled with ambition for notable accomplishment. One phase of Mr. Carnegie's character has, however, escaped publicity and yet it is doubtful if this deep interest of his heart was even exceeded by his interest in world peace. That was his deep concern regarding the welfare of workers, the betterment of working and living conditions, the amicable adjustment of disputes between labor and capital.

Various revolutionary radicals, seeking to foment discontent and class hatred, have pictured the genial Scotsman—who was one of the most loyal, ardent and exemplary Americans—as one of the heartless exploiters and oppressors of the working classes; anarchists and socialists have pointed to him as an enemy of labor. Yet during all the time that Mr. Carnegie was in business only one single clash with labor occurred. That was the Homestead strike in 1892, for which his detractors held him responsible. And yet the truth is that for this single clash with labor Mr. Carnegie was not himself and in no degree whatever responsible. He was away in Scotland at the time, and as soon as word reached him of the trouble he immediately cabled orders urging a conference for a speedy and amicable settlement with the men.

The facts of the Homestead strike were gathered and presented by Edward W. Bemis, formerly Professor of Political Economy in the University of Chicago, whose report was quoted in THE NATIONAL CIVIC FEDERATION REVIEW of March, 1905. As the strike has been so generally misunderstood and the facts misrepresented by anarchists, socialists and the enemies of organized labor, and as these facts absolutely absolve Mr. Carnegie of any responsibility for the unfortunate happenings, Prof. Bemis' report is important in any presentation of Mr. Carnegie's notable career.

After the arrival of the militia in Homestead, Mr. Hugh O'Donnell, upon the request of two of the labor leaders, approached Mr. Whitelaw Reid, then candidate for the vice-presidency on the Republican ticket, and asked him to get in touch with Mr. Carnegie and urge him to order Mr. Frick to reopen conferences with the men. Mr. O'Donnell, as well as President Weihe of the strikers' organization, stated that there was no disposition on part of the employees to stand upon a question of scale, of wages, of hours, or of anything else, but requested that the Carnegie Company "recognize the Amalgamated Association by reopening the conference doors." Mr. O'Donnell had been charged by the Carnegie officials with murder in connection with the events of July 6, and was released under $10,000 bail. After receiving his appeal, Mr. Reid endeavored to secure Mr. Carnegie's address from Mr. Frick. Upon Mr. Frick's refusal to give the address, Mr. Reid secured it from the American Consul General in London, John C. New. Mr. Reid then cabled Mr. Carnegie and Mr. Carnegie immediately replied. In his reply Mr. Carnegie accepted the terms proposed by Mr. O'Donnell for the workers and urged that Mr. Frick be seen at once with a view to effecting a settlement. In the meantime Alexander Berkman, the anarchist, who had no relation with the strikers, had attempted to assassinate Mr. Frick, and when the gentlemen who undertook the mission of reconciliation reached him with the message from Mr. Carnegie, they found him confined to bed.

Addressing a meeting of The National Civic Federation some years ago, Mr. Carnegie told a story which is illustrative of his attitude toward his men. Burgess McLuckie, one of the Homestead strikers, disappeared after the riots to avoid arrest. Sometime afterward Professor van Dyke, of Rutgers College, told Mr. Carnegie he had found McLuckie working as a laborer in a mine at Sonora, Mexico. Mr. Carnegie asked Professor van Dyke, upon his return to the West, to offer McLuckie any help he might need. "You don't know," said Professor van Dyke

(Continued on page 8)

NOTABLE CONFERENCE, INCLUDING 200 LABOR REPRESENTATIVES, HELD IN MR. CARNEGIE'S NEW YORK HOME IN 1907 UNDER THE AUSPICES OF THE NATIONAL CIVIC FEDERATION

Great Leaders of the Union Labor Movement

By W. C. ROBERTS

COMPILER OF THE AMERICAN FEDERATION OF LABOR HISTORY, ENCYCLOPEDIA AND REFERENCE BOOK

MANY men have left the impress of their personality on the labor movement of America. Any one who will read, as I did, the thirty-nine annual proceedings of the American Federation of Labor will find that the names of a score or more of delegates stand out like stars in the labor firmament. They have stood side by side with Samuel Gompers in every critical situation and have led the trade union movement along a path in which it has been protected from its natural enemies as well as from foes within.

These men are of strong character. They did not always agree with Mr. Gompers, or he with them. But with all of them the battle was for the good of the organized labor movement, and in their discussions they always sought to find the best way to obtain better conditions.

Few people realize that the big work in the American Federation of Labor conventions is in committees. The committees must scan every word of the resolutions presented in order to prevent the adoption of some subtle and dangerous proposition. Resolutions are sometimes clothed in beautiful language, but hidden within them are "jokers" that, if adopted, would endanger the very life of the organization or at least make it the laughing stock of its critics.

In the thirty-nine years since the American Federation of Labor was organized it has been the custom for President Gompers to be the spokesman for labor. Those who have aided him and worked in harmony with him in advancing the fundamental principals of trade unionism sat silent willingly, for their only desire was to obtain results, not personal prestige. They thought only of the cause of labor, not their own advancement.

But it is a great cause they were part of and in which they were selected to lead. And they knew whatever President Gompers had to say was what they would say. It is this frame of mind of the builders of the American labor movement that has made the American Federation of Labor the most remarkable organization that ever existed. No other organization ever met as many formidable obstacles and overcame them. No other body of men and women has been attacked so insidiously and viciously by those who would make it impotent, and who lure it into paths leading to disaster.

The struggles of the American Federation of Labor for a higher standard of living for the people of the nation, its battles for remedial laws that would benefit all the people, its loyal stand when the freedom of our country was threatened by a resourceful and dangerous enemy, constitute a most interesting history.

Through all these crucial struggles were many men who stood as the Rock of Gibraltar against diverting the trade union movement into channels that would make it detrimental to not only its members but all the people. History will remember these men's persistency in fighting for the right, their unprecedented sacrifices and their unswerving principles. The purpose of this article is to present some of these big, brainy, energetic statesmen of labor—men who, had they been public officials, would have made a record unsurpassed by any who have served their country in public office.

They made history not only as officials of international unions, but as members of committees which analyzed and passed upon all propositions presented in American Federation of Labor conventions. Their unceasing work has been of incalculable value. Their advice has been shown to be right, while the principles they have advocated, which the conventions indorsed, have proved enduring.

It is impossible to refer to all chairmen, secretaries and members of committees who served since the formation of the American Federation of Labor. But the Atlantic City convention emphasized the value of those who know the labor movement thoroughly, for they had a tremendous task to perform. The following are a few of the great men of labor who served as chairmen or secretaries at that convention and whose knowledge and ability gave them a discerning insight into the resolutions presented:

JAMES DUNCAN

President Granite Cutters' International Union and First Vice-President of the American Federation of Labor

JAMES DUNCAN, familiarly referred to by his friends as "our Jim," has been one of the bulwarks of the labor movement. Strong in character, a splendid orator and a firm believer in his convictions, Duncan has been an imposing figure in the struggles of the labor movement for recognition. His sledge-hammer verbal blows against all labor heresies have many times killed the propaganda of those who would destroy the labor movement for partisan political purposes. His courage is phenomenal, as he never sits silent when an attempt is made to endanger the labor movement.

Duncan is a granite cutter. He joined the International Granite Cutters' Union in 1881. In 1895 he became its general president, and has held that office continuously since. Next to President Gompers he has the longest record of representing his union as a delegate in American Federation of Labor conventions. His first convention was in 1886. In that session he established himself as a leader of men. Almost his first act was to present a resolution favoring compulsory education, a principle he has vigorously supported ever since.

In 1894 at Denver he was elected second vice-president and in 1900 was made first vice-president, a position he has held since continuously. One of the dangers recognized in the early days was the attempt on the part of certain men to betray the labor movement into chimerical schemes that would interfere with trade union activity.

Early in the history of the American Federation of Labor, Duncan won distinction by his cleverness in debate, his logical reasoning and his efforts to prevent what were termed "ghost dancers" getting a stranglehold on the organized labor movement.

Duncan's ability was recognized by President Gompers in 1887, when he was appointed on the constitution committee. But his splendid ability to analyze propositions presented for consideration by conventions soon made him chairman of the resolution committee. After making a report on a resolution written for an ulterior purpose and the resolution committee had reported adversely, it was his duty to explain the reason. Those who have attended conventions in the last twenty years could not fail to observe that after Duncan had made the explanation for the defeat of a proposition he invariably was upheld.

During the New Orleans convention, when it was feared the socialists would capture the convention by a trick resolution, Duncan made a remarkable speech in opposition which resulted in its defeat. He spoke for three hours and mentioned every labor movement in history that, after gaining its ends, had been sacrificed by ambitious leaders on the altar of partisan politics.

Probably the Atlantic City convention proved the most strenuous to the resolution committee. There were 277 resolutions presented, many of them favoring every impractical idea conceived by the radical delegates during the unsettled period of the war. The committee held continuous day and night sessions for more than a week. But out of the mass of good and bad resolutions a masterful report was made that, when adopted, showed the labor movement of America has no desire to change its policies for some of those now endangering the labor movements of Europe.

When the Great War was looming up before the people of the United States, Duncan was one of the men who prepared the famous declaration that while the labor movement was against war they would, if war was declared, offer their "services to our country in every field of activity to defend, safeguard and preserve the republic of the United States of America against its enemies."

Duncan has had a part in the world labor movement. In 1898 he was fraternal delegate to the British Trade Union Congress. In 1911 he represented the American Federation of Labor in the convention of the International Secretariat at Budapest, Hungary. In 1913 he was selected a member of the United States Commission on Workmen's Compensation, and in 1917 he was appointed by President Wilson, with five other public citizens, as envoy extraordinary to Russia.

While wielding a powerful influence on the adoption of principles to benefit the work of the American Federation of Labor, he has been editor of the *Granite Cutter's Journal* since 1895. His writings have been quoted from coast to coast and have been of great good in presenting the hopes and ambitions of the labor movement.

Early this year Duncan, John R. Alpine, Frank Duffy and William Green, with President Gompers, were selected by the executive council as a commission to attend a labor conference in Paris while the Peace Conference was in session. The mission was authorized by the Buffalo and St. Paul conventions to protect the interests of the American working people. While in Paris, President Gompers was chosen a member of the Commission on International Labor Legislation by President Wilson, and the commission made him chairman. The other members of the American labor commission acted as advisers to President Gompers in his difficult task of securing the adoption of principles acceptable to the labor movement of this country.

JOSEPH F. VALENTINE

President Iron Molders' International Union and Second Vice President American Federation of Labor

Education has constituted one of the most important subjects studied in American Federation of Labor Conventions. In fact, the committee on education has had a difficult work to perform, as no question requires deeper thought or more careful findings. For years it has had as chairman Joseph F. Valentine, who has submitted most far-reaching and adequate reports of methods to increase knowledge and to eliminate illiteracy.

Valentine as president of the Iron Molders' International Union has had an exceptional experience. No harder worker for his fellowmen can be found anywhere. It is not generally known that he is so enthusiastic over the problems he has to solve for the molders that he gives his entire time to their interests. Night and day he can be found at work in his office, in his home, or on the train while traveling.

The Iron Moulders secured the first trade agreement in this country and their gains have been secured through business-like methods. Mr. Valentine's record has been marked by a calm confidence and decisiveness of thought and action.

Early in his labor experience Valentine discovered that the children of workingmen were not obtaining the education they should have. Owing to small wages, fathers were compelled to place their children in industry. This disturbed Valentine, who set out to seek a remedy for the evil. He bombarded legislatures and other legislative bodies to bring about greater education. This experience he brought to the committee on education of the American Federation of Labor, and it is by most of this that he has been able to advance so many practical plans for both elementary and industrial education.

WILLIAM D. MAHON

President Amalgamated Association of Street and Electric Railway Employees and Fifth Vice President of the American Federation of Labor

Nearly thirty years ago a driver of a horse car in Columbus, Ohio, shook the snow from his clothing and the icicles from his mustache and declared he never would return to his job until the street railway employees of the land were treated like human beings.

For the next year he traveled from town to town to organize the carmen. Sometimes he rode in a Pullman side-door sleeper, on the rods, or in an uncomfortable seat just behind the engine. But he persevered, and now W. D. Mahon is president of an association of nearly 100,000 members, who are receiving something approaching a proper wage.

Bringing the organization up to its present standing was not accomplished without the most difficult kind of agitation. Mr. Mahon was fighting the most resourceful opponents who made it exceedingly disagreeable for him for many years. Gradually his opponents began to recognize in Mahon a spirit that would not give up. They saw he was determined to win his struggle for better conditions, and gradually they began to deal with him in arranging wages and hours of employment for the carmen in the various cities.

Mr. Mahon is one of the men who year after year has helped make the labor movement better and better. As a member of some committee or its chairman, he has striven to give the best that is in him for the benefit of those who need helpful advice and assistance.

Mahon is of a jovial disposition, one of the best story tellers known, and the life of any party. In times of trouble he meets all obstacles without flinching. He is considered a most clever press agent for his cause during a strike. He does not know what the word "fail" means. No matter how bitter a fight may be, he never loses his good humor or his head. He is regarded as a marvel by the big men he has opposed in the financial field. As a clever manipulator of peculiar situations he cannot be equaled.

Mr. Mahon has proved an exemplary administrator, intelligent, courageous, persevering, and in his own organization is fearless in enforcing discipline.

During many years of trials and heartaches—and he must have sometimes thought he might never succeed in his object—Mahon learned many lessons. These taught him what was best for the labor movement, what should be done to protect it from its enemies and what should be the treatment of a traitor from within.

MATTHEW WOLL

President Photo-Engravers' International Union and Eighth Vice President of the American Federation of Labor

Many young men grow up in the labor movement almost unnoticed until some great issue brought them and their talents to the front. In the labor movement we have been accustomed to see only those who have been with us for many years, who have led the struggle against wrong and who became so well known that newcomers by contrast stand in the background.

Such may be said to be the case of Matthew Woll. When he attended his first convention he was placed on the adjustment committee and soon became secretary. He demonstrated so much ability that he was appointed secretary of the committee on executive council's report and also on the committee on international labor relations. Many subjects that bear upon the fundamental principles of the American Federation of Labor are referred to this committee and

the utmost care is necessary to separate the wheat from the chaff. As secretary of the committee on executive council's report in 1916 he wrote this declaration, which was adopted by the convention:

"It seems to be the settled purpose of interests antagonistic to the freedom of men and women who labor to persuade and then use the judiciary to misconstrue constitutional guarantees and thereby nullify legislative enactments so as to leave but one remedy. We therefore recommend that any injunctions dealing with the relationship of employer and employee, and based upon the dictum 'Labor is property,' be wholly and absolutely treated as usurpation and disregarded, let the consequences be what they may."

In the 1919 convention at Atlantic City, all the shrewdness coming from years of analyzing resolutions stood Woll in good stead. The committee on executive council's report was overloaded with vague ideas presented by delegates, and in their consideration and preparing of decisions thereon Woll made an extraordinary record.

In the trying times of the war the untiring ability of Woll was given greater opportunity to function. While President Gompers was in Europe this year, Woll acted as editor of the *American Federationist*, a difficult and most trying position. He also represented President Gompers on the National Council of Defense, and when Victor A. Olander became stricken with illness he took his place on the War Labor Board.

Recently Woll took part in a conference on War Risk Insurance, in which some of the most able men in the country participated. His suggestions were carefully considered and adopted.

Since then he has furnished several strong articles on war risk insurance that have attracted the attention of many public men who are looking for the right way to conduct that most meritorious institution.

While performing all these tasks Woll has not neglected his international duties. The photo-engravers have advanced rapidly because of his persistence for their welfare. As editor of *The Photo-Engraver* he has been able to advance many propositions of a national character. As editor of the *American Federationist*, a position he is still filling, he has pointed out many defects in the labor policies followed by irresponsible members and in the advice given by self-appointed regulators of the organized labor movement.

Being ingrained with the policy that has made the American Federation of Labor so great, he was a most acceptable candidate as fraternal delegate to the British Trade Union Congress in 1916. When he returned he was more determined than ever in his support of the fundamental principles of the American Federation of Labor.

During the war he was a bitter critic of the pacifists and all those who would hamper the government in prosecuting the crusade for world freedom. His editorials have been widely copied. In fact, so well known has he become that every moment of his time that he can get away from his special duties is occupied in conferences and speechmaking to widen the influence of the trade union movement.

Woll is still a young man, has studied law and is in a position to do wonderful work for the labor movement. As older men pass away there must always be someone to take their place. It was fortunate for the movement that such a resourceful character as Mr. Woll has dedicated his life to the cause of labor.

DANIEL J. TOBIN

President International Brotherhood of Teamsters and Treasurer of the American Federation of Labor

After the great panic of 1893-6 the failure of employers to increase wages as their prosperity improved caused a wave of labor organization to sweep over the United States, especially in the great industrial centers. Early in the 1890's the boom was tremendous. In cities like Chicago workers in every kind of occupation organized so they might make demands for a proper wage. While there had been unions of teamsters they were not organized on the right plan. Owners of teams were admitted. The Chicago teamsters started union after union, but finally in 1901 had nearly 30,000 members. They then spread over the entire country like wildfire.

In 1905 a great strike was called in Chicago, which lasted one hundred and five days. It was a drawn battle. Both sides had carried a chip on their shoulders before the strike. This changed afterward and from that time on few strikes have occurred. But the teamsters of the United States after that strike found a new leader who sent them forth on the right path and in a few years built up one of the most remarkable organizations in the country.

The leader who has done so much for the teamsters by his generalship is Daniel J. Tobin. He is a common-sense fighter for not only his own fellow workers but for all others. He has been of great support to the policies preached and followed by the American Federation of Labor.

When the executive council met to select a fellow delegate to go with President Gompers to the Amsterdam conference, Tobin was chosen. He proved a worthy champion of all that the American labor movement stands for. When the German delegates sought to show that the war was in the interest of commercialism, his voice was raised in protest and it was heard on this side of the water.

Because of his knowledge of the necessary rules governing labor organizations, Tobin has been made chairman of the committee on law of the American Federation of Labor conventions. His reports have sought to add only that which would be good to the constitution.

(To be continued)

Andrew Carnegie—the Friend of Labor

(Continued from page 5)

to McLuckie afterwards, "whose money I was told to help you with." He did not. When he was told, McLuckie in a slow, earnest voice said; "Well, that was damned white of Andy." "When I heard this," said Mr. Carnegie in recalling the story, "I suggested to my friend van Dyke that it wouldn't be a bad epitaph to grace one's tombstone."

Mr. Carnegie's disposition, whenever labor difficulties came up, was to work for an agreement rather than call in new men to replace others. In an article published in the *Forum*, in 1886, he declared himself thus:

"To expect that one dependent on his daily wage for the necessaries of life will stand by peaceably and see a new man employed in his stead, is to expect much. . . . In the case of railways, and a few other employments, it is, of course, essential, for the public wants that no interruptions occur, and in such case substitutes must be employed; but the employer of labor will find it much more to his interest, wherever possible, to allow his works to remain idle, and await the result of a dispute, than to employ the class of men that can be induced to take the place of other men who have stopped work. Neither the best men as men, nor the best men as workers, are thus to be obtained. There is an unwritten law among the best workmen, 'Thou shalt not take thy neighbor's job.' No wise employer will lightly lose his old employees. Length of service counts for much in many ways. Calling upon strange men should be the last resort."

One of the most notable gatherings of representative employers, labor leaders, professional men, educators and publicists was held in Mr. Carnegie's home, in New York City, in the summer of 1907. The purpose of this gathering, which was held under the auspices of The National Civic Federation and which was attended by over two hundred labor representatives, was to discuss means of improving conditions of labor, the relations between employers and employees, to ascertain means of lessening industrial strife and to promote industrial world peace. That gathering was an inspiring one and no one showed himself more interested in the welfare of workers throughout the world than Mr. Carnegie himself. The speakers of that evening included Mr. August Belmont, then president of The National Civic Federation; Archbishop Farley, Dr. Nicholas Murray Butler, president of Columbia University; Doctor Lyman Abbott, the Hon. Seth Low and Mr. Carnegie. Among the representatives of labor present at the meeting was "Big Bill" Weihe, who had led the Homestead strike. Mr. Weihe came to New York to attend the meeting in response to a special invitation and his meeting with Mr. Carnegie was a thrilling moment. It was the first time they had met since they had seen each other in Pittsburg before the Homestead strike. "Big Bill" Weihe, brawny-muscled and fully six feet tall, grasped the hand of Mr. Carnegie, who seemed little of stature beside him. The eyes of both lighted with affection, and the hand-shake was long and hearty. Both Mr. Carnegie and "Big Bill" Weihe had a good time that night talking of old days.

What Mr. Carnegie had to say in his brief speech of welcome concerning industrial peace was characteristic of his great vision and true wisdom. "It is a fundamental point in law that no man shall sit as judge in his own cause," declared Mr. Carnegie. "So it should be with trades unions and employers. Neither the men nor the employers should assume to sit in judgment on their own case, because neither sees both sides of the question. It is very rarely, indeed, in my experience, that one party is entirely right and the other party wholly wrong. You must get a disinterested party to judge between them, and all will be well.

"That same principle applies to nations. Nations should no longer be allowed to disturb the general peace of the world, because all nations are now interdependent and much concerned, materially as well as morally, in the preservation of peace.

"So it is in the industrial system. No branch of employers should be allowed to sit in judgment upon their own case and disturb the operations of the community in which all are interested. And the man or the nation that refuses to submit his judgment to disinterested parties is prima facie in the wrong. The man says: 'What, my honor! Shall I allow a man to insult me and not strike back?' No man ever insulted, dishonored, another in the world. No nation can dishonor another. All dishonors from which we suffer are self-inflicted. The principle of arbitration is what laborers should stand for; is what employers should stand for.

"It gives me a special pleasure to meet the representatives of labor. When I look back I think how much pleasure I have experienced with my interviews with workingmen. I could tell you many stories about strikes, and I wish to say this word: It is not wages, as a rule, that cause strikes—no, it is the lack of recognition on the part of the employer for his men. I remember a serious point when we had a committee of sixteen and a committee of thirty-four, and we presented a sliding scale, and they wanted to see me. I was at Pittsburg. Billy Edwards rose. 'Mr. Carnegie, that scale upon the whole we don't object to; that is a fair scale, but what we object to is that it is not rightly divided. Now, Mr. Carnegie, you take my job.' I said, 'No, Mr. Edwards, Mr. Carnegie takes no man's job.' They began to laugh, and

(Continued on page 12)

If Bolshevism Came to America

RUSSIA'S MONSTROUS OBJECT LESSON IN APPLYING PROGRAM ADVOCATED IN UNITED STATES BY SOCIALISTS AND OTHER RADICALS DESCRIBED BY FORMER U. S. CONSUL TO RUSSIA

By T. EVERETT HARRÉ

IT was a cloudy, penetratingly chill, dour day in April of the present year, the twenty-third. Accompanied by Judge Paul Blumenthal, presiding judge of the Bellebei court under the Kerensky government, and several newspaper correspondents, John A. Embry, United States Consul at Omsk, Siberia, on his way back to the United States through Russia, visited the town of Bellebei and its environs, in Western Russia, to hear accounts from eye-witnesses and victims, and to see himself the aftermath, of Bolsheviki atrocities and outrages. Bellebei, a town of 12,000 inhabitants, had been captured by the Bolsheviki in December, 1918, and had been delivered from the grip of Lenine's Reds by Kolchak's Siberian armies only eight days before Mr. Embry's arrival. Leaving a church, where the Bolsheviki had broken the sacred icons, desecrated the pictures of Christ and the Madonna, and where they had installed a free motion picture show for the benefit of the vicious and criminal Red Guards, playing obscene tunes on a gramophone, Mr. Embry and his companions saw a crowd going into a wood some half mile distant. They were told, in response to an inquiry, that in a pit in the woods there had been discovered that morning a large number of victims of the Bolsheviki who had been murdered without trial, and whose bodies were uncovered by the melting snow.

Copyright, Underwood & Underwood.

JOHN A. EMBRY, FORMER U. S. CONSUL AT OMSK, SIBERIA, AND MRS. EMBRY. SHE WAS MLLE. NADEJDA DOBROVELEKI, DAUGHTER OF GEN. MICHAEL DOBROVELSKI, AND SUFFERED MUCH UNDER THE RED RULE.

Called recently to testify before the New York Legislative Committee investigating disloyal and seditious activities, Mr. Embry, who had just arrived from Russia, recounted what he had heard and what he had witnessed—a story revealing Bolshevism in its stark and grisly workings, and graphically demonstrating, through that hideous and appalling object lesson, just what it is which Socialists, revolutionary radicals and various pseudo-intellectuals are at the present time advocating through propaganda in the United States.

On that dismal day in last April, standing with his companions on the verge of the pit, Mr. Embry beheld—fully revealed through the melting snow, their bodies still perfectly preserved by the cold—the bodies of twenty men and women. They looked as if they had been slain only a few hours before. Describing that awful spectacle, Mr. Embry said: "The men for the most part had their skulls crushed, smashed, and the brains were lying on the snow. The faces were mutilated by gun shots at close range. On the larger pile of dead bodies the topmost figure was that of a young girl, seventeen or eighteen years of age. Although her face was not mutilated, there was an ugly gunshot wound in her left breast which was uncovered and exposed to the gaze of the crowd. Her left hand was folded across her breast, and the third finger was amputated at the second joint, and the ring which doubtless she had worn was not to be seen." Mr. Embry admitted that the spectacle brought tears to his eyes.

Before turning away he hastily took a photograph of the pit, a copy of which was given as evidence to the Lusk Committee. That picture, he said, had been offered to various newspapers as proof of what was commonly and everywhere done where the Bolsheviki had power, but American newspapers refused to print the picture. It was too horrible.

MAIN OBJECTS TO LOOT AND KILL

In Bellebei, when they gained possession of the town, the Bolsheviki, according to Mr. Embry, made a criminal, whom they released with all other convicts from prison, one of their commissionaires. They looted the city, seized private property, ejected people from their houses and apartments, in which the unsavory Red leaders were luxuriously installed. In the parlor of the president or head commissionair of the so-called Bolshevik Council of Domestic Economy, whose chief function was to loot, were found three pianos which had been stolen from other people's homes. Upon the setting up of the Bolshevik Executive Committee, which as everywhere else assumed autocratic absolute power, the president, Belt by name, had brought from a hospital in an invalid chair the president of the former local government. Helpless, unable to move, this invalid was heartlessly shot by Belt himself in the public square. A so-called Extraordinary Investigating Committee was set up which had the absolute power of executing without trial any man, woman or child charged with being counter-revolutionary. Its special function was the imprisonment and killing of all suspected of being opposed to Bolshevik rule. Two objects, said Mr. Embry, were pursued by the Bolsheviki wherever they gained power with mad, fanatic, indefatigable zeal. These two prime objects were the seizing and looting of property and the wholesale assassination of people, especially the educated and intellectual, whom the malignant, envenomed forces of "internationalism" had reason to fear or hate. "In no case," testified Mr. Embry, "did I hear of any execution by the Bolsheviki which had any just cause, except in the few cases where a Bolshevik Committee or a Bolshevik organization of some kind would get after another Bolshevik organization because there were conflicts of interests, and sometimes they actually executed their own members because two conflicting parties would have a battle for power in the organization, and whichever one was the stronger would have the opponents put to death. They fought for the spoils in just the way that a pack of wolves fight for a corpse."

Recounting the outrages described to him by eyewitnesses in Bellebei, Mr. Embry continued:

"One of the most striking was that of sixteen hostages brought from Ufa, a city of 75,000, about 150 miles east of Bellebei. Among them was a high school girl of about 17 years of age. These sixteen hostages, according to the statement of the judges (residents of Bellebei who were among Mr. Embry's informants), were placed in the county jail. Nobody knew why they were in jail. Nobody knew what the charges were. They were held in jail until the jail became overcrowded. One day the Bolsheviki of Bellebei decided to make room in their jail. These sixteen helpless victims were brought out into the pubic square and shot.

(Continued on page 16)

THE NATIONAL
Civic Federation Review

Office: Thirty-third Floor, Metropolitan Tower
1 Madison Avenue New York City

RALPH M. EASLEY, Editor

Published Twice a Month Two Dollars a Year

The Editor alone is Responsible for any unsigned article or unquoted statement published in THE NATIONAL CIVIC FEDERATION REVIEW.

IMPORTANT PROBLEMS TO BE DISCUSSED SEPTEMBER 11 AND 12.

Granted that the public has a paramount interest in the continuous operation of our great Federal steam railway systems and our municipal traction, gas and electric light systems, is there any way by which that public can protect those interests? This is one of the outstanding questions confronting every citizen today. The nation faces this question through the possible tie-up of all the steam railway systems which may occur at any time that the demands of the employees are refused, while in New York, Brooklyn, Boston, Chicago and other large cities, the question has concretely presented itself through the temporary paralysis of the street railway systems.

It is easy to declare that it is a blot upon our civilization to permit these injustices, not to say crimes against humanity, to continue.

But this is not a new question.

Since the Debs railway strike in 1893, the street railway strikes in Columbus and St. Louis in 1898 and the Interborough strike in New York in 1903, the press, the pulpit, the platform orator and the statesman have been declaring that this intolerable thing must be stopped. Yet the strikes go on just the same, and, owing to the abnormal situation arising out of the war, there are a great many more of them now than before.

There is, at this time, another situation in which all agree that paramountcy of the public interests should be recognized, and that is involved in the question: "How far can the public safety permit the organization of its police, its firemen and other municipal employees to form striking unions?"

With this last should also go the companion question: "What methods has the public provided for its employees, federal, state or municipal, to redress just grievances in any way other than through the organization of a union?" The recent strikes of the firemen in Pittsburg, the municipal employees in Chicago and the threatened strike of the police in New York and in many American cities, as well as the actual strike of the police in London, all serve to bring this matter to the front for serious consideration.

In the case of quasi-public, as well as industrial employees, the compulsory principle has been tried and found wanting. The experience of Australia and New Zealand with compulsory arbitration and that of Canada with compulsory investigation in connection with municipal utilities, show that the answer does not lie in that direction.

One of the important questions that will be considered at the meeting of The National Civic Federation, September 11 and 12 next, is: "Can any new voluntary machinery be created which, even though it may not prevent all strikes and lockouts, will reduce them to a minimum?" In connection with this general topic, there will be discussed the question: "How can collective bargaining be most effectively promoted in this country?" It is conceded that in the United States and Great Britain, the two countries where employees and employers are best organized, despite disappointments and certain weaknesses, collective bargaining has been found to offer the most hopeful line along which progress can be made.

Many employers, in an effort to deal with the great unrest among their workers, have inaugurated plans with a view to granting them a voice in the determination of questions relating to hours, wages and general working conditions. These include all kinds of shop committee and joint council programs, one providing for organization on the Federal system of a lower house, a senate and a cabinet. Others, to meet this situation, rely upon profit sharing, bonus systems and stock participation plans. All these schemes have been coupled in the public mind with the general proposition for a greater democratization of industry.

Other employers criticise such plans on the ground that the organization of the men for such purposes is only a stepping-stone to their eventually becoming affiliated with the real trade union movement—that once the employees begin acting together in any kind of an organization, Mr. Gompers "will get them" sooner or later.

But the American Federation of Labor, at its recent annual convention in Atlantic City, passed a series of resolutions denouncing all such programs as employers' schemes promoted for the purpose of preventing the organization of their men into trade unions. The headings of the "Whereases" are: "Unfair Elections and Representation;" "No Democratic Organization Permitted;" "Intimidation of Committeemen;" "Expert Assistance Prohibited;" and "Company Union Lacks Power."

Which is right?

Employers and workers will discuss all phases of this subject at the Federation's meeting.

In dealing with the profit sharing and public utility subjects, the recent proposal for a participation in the management and a share in the profits by the railway brotherhoods, and other plans proposed for giving the employees a voice in the management of the railway systems, will be discussed.

How long can the present program of raising wages and shortening hours go on before it results in the utter collapse of production? The management committee of the British General Federation of Trades Unions declares that "November, 1919 to May, 1920 will be fateful months" and that "unless sanity returns and production increases, they will be tragic months." Is that warning not equally applicable to the industrial situation in the United States?

In addition to the discussion of the domestic problems referred to above, the Commission sent to Europe by The National Civic Federation to study industrial conditions will present at the meeting its report describing the relations between employers and wage earners in England and France.

THE HIGH COST OF LIVING

According to the Bureau of Statistics of the Department of Labor, the advance in the cost of food and clothing from December, 1914, to June of the present year in various cities was as follows: New York, 151 per cent; Philadelphia, 135 per cent; Boston, 137 per cent; Cleveland and Detroit, 125 per cent; Chicago, 157.67 per cent, and San Francisco, 134 per cent. The highest advance was in clothing and house-furnishings, and food came third. Throughout the nation people have become gravely concerned over the advance in price of the necessities of life; following the war the high cost of living has become one of the most acute and most vital problems of the time. With the Government considering legislative action to control prices, with the Department of Justice engaged in a nation-wide crusade against food hoarding and profiteering, with the Fair Price Committee working after a plan outlined by Attorney General A. Mitchell Palmer to employ pitiless publicity to keep prices from soaring, everywhere, in the largest cities and smallest communities, people are asking the question—What is the solution?

What is the solution? Is there any magical key which will at once, entirely and ultimately offer a solution to the problem? Or does the solution not lie in a scientific study of the causes of high prices and the application of constructive methods to restore life to a normal basis such as existed before the war was unleashed upon the world? There are many who say the world will not, and can not, be the same as it was before August, 1914, and they are right. Never was the world so shaken, so unsettled from its base, so fundamentally disturbed as it was by the catastrophe precipitated by Imperial Germany; never was there such a cataclysmic upheaval in all history, economical, social, spiritual. With the war over, a readjustment will come, a new co-ordination, an equalization in the economical, social and spiritual phases of life which were all utterly deranged during the long period of a devastating war. But as the war utterly ravelled the social life of the nations and upset life at its vitals, the swinging to a balance cannot take place in a moment, in a day, in a year. The process of recovery, of world healing, must come as do all processes of nature. No one save the idiotic, the fantastically idealistic, the hare-brained, save mountebanks and deceiving demagogues, will pretend to have the open sesame to the new order, the abacadabra which will restore a chaotic world to a millennium over night. That is, however, the blatantly proclaimed pretense of the revolutionaries, by which they seek to lead to still further disaster the long suffering masses of the world. That is the Mumbo Jumbo of the Bolsheviki, the fee-faw-fum propaganda of the Socialists. But intelligent people, and the sane majority of the working people of America, will not be beguiled by any promises of a miracle. They have seen too unmistakably what has been produced by Lenine and Trotzky's Aladdin's lamp in unhappy Russia. They know that the world will not be restored by any incantation, be it Bolshevist, Socialist or otherwise.

But we have problems, among them the high cost of living, with which we have to deal, a constructive solution of which we have earnestly to seek. That is the present task of the nations of the world, a task perhaps no less great, no less grave than was the winning of the war over the nation which sought to destroy the democracies of the world and the freedom of man's spirit.

Whatever affects that upon which physical life depends, whatever makes for the ease and happiness or for the difficulty and hardship of the home-life of men, is of the most vital importance as a matter of social peace or of social unrest. If the cost of living exceeds the earning capacity of a man he naturally becomes a prey to legitimate discontent. To any discerning mind there is no single cause for the high cost of living, and therefore there can be no simple single remedy. The causes are various. As pointed out by George W. Perkins in the *New York Times* of August 17, the inadequacy of, and lack of co-ordination in, the transportation of supplies and the utter lack of any system of centralization for storage and distribution in the great cities, constitute a great factor in keeping up the price of food. Mr. Perkins urges Federal control and legislation to bring about legalized and publicly controlled co-operation. The point of view of the farmers was expressed in a statement issued in Washington by T. C. Atkeson, of the National Grange, in which it is pointed out that the guaranteed price of wheat put on by the Government has kept prices down and not up, and that, because of a shrinkage of crops throughout the world, a removal of restrictions would bring about "such a sky-rocketing of prices as to wreck the financial and economic fabric of the world. The price of subsistence is high," declare the farmers, "because the price of work is high. The way to cure this shevism and inspired to riots was demonstrated recently in Washington and Chicago.

According to a statement made by Attorney General A. Mitchell Palmer, the Department of Justice has possession of evidence showing that Bolshevik propaganda has been conducted among negroes of the South. According to evidence gathered by the Lusk Legislative Committee, agitators are being sent among negroes by direct orders from Trotzky, and much of this propaganda has been financed with money sent from Russia. I. W. W. demagogues were sent to Chicago from New York more than a month ago, and all these agitators have sought especially to antagonize the negroes against the American Federation of Labor. A negro magazine, published in New York City, and which is supposed to be devoted to educational and welfare work among the negroes, has of late given itself to teaching subtle forms of radicalism. Another negro monthly, now making a drive to raise $50,000 and which announces a circulation of 33,000 copies, has openly urged the negroes to revolt, and in a recent issue declared: "The red tide of Socialism sweeps on in America. . . . Soviet government proceeds apace. It bids fair to sweep over the whole world. The sooner the better. On with the dance." In this same magazine was an editorial "Break Up the A. F. of L."

According to a report in the *New York Tribune*, William Monroe Trotter, the negro editor of the *Boston Guardian* and leader of the Colored National Equal Rights League, declared at a meeting of 2,000 negroes that unless white Americans behave themselves they will find out that when they taught the colored boys to fight they started something they will not be able to stop. The inculcation of such a spirit among the negroes, or among any class for that matter, is fraught with serious menace, and if it is allowed to continue the Chicago and Washington riots may be only the beginning of greater troubles.

THE FORTY-EIGHT MILLENNIAL MIRACLE WORKERS AGAIN ON THE JOB

The editor of THE NATIONAL CIVIC FEDERATION REVIEW has received a circular letter from a so-called Committee of Forty-Eight, asking if he agrees that "The time has come for the people to meet together and discuss the real facts of American life, the issues which vitally affect the welfare of individual citizens, and decide on some line of action which will meet the sitnation."

The reason for this meeting to "discuss" and "decide" things is that, to quote from the circular:

> We have come to be one of the worst ruled, one of the most completely controlled and dominated governments in the world—no longer a government by conviction and the vote of the majority, but a government by the opinion and duress of a small group of dominant men.
>
> This control and dominance of the few has increased. Two years of ruthless censorship has added to its strength. The American press has not only refrained from printing the truth but has wilfully misinformed the American people. A small group of dominant men who control credit dictate the decisions of both political parties, and either directly or indirectly censor and inspire the news.

Enclosed with the circular is a pamphlet giving the purpose of and the reasons for the Committee of Forty-Eight. Its indictment of society, the Government and everybody and everything in general is made up of stock diatribes so familiar in the pacifist, socialist and pro-German literature, and even harks back to the old days of Populism. It greatly stresses the ills of the "laborer" and the "farmer," stating in one paragraph:

> The very classes whose labors in factory and field are the basis and substance of our economic power, find no effective political medium through which to express their economic demand, but by deceptive diversions of our party-system are denied their proper representation in the law-making bodies of the nation.

This great solicitude for the factory and field worker is readily explained when one notes the many sturdy and brawny farmers and mechanics on the General Committee—given on the letterhead as follows:

ROBERT W. BRUÈRE	ROBERT MORSS LOVETT
LINCOLN COLCORD	ALLEN MCCURDY
OTTO CULLMANN	DUDLEY FIELD MALONE
WILL DURANT	GEORGE NASMYTH
WILLIAM P. EVERTS	MARY PATTISON
GILSON GARDNER	GILBERT E. ROE
JOHN HAYNES HOLMES	MARY K. SIMKHOVITCH
J. A. H. HOPKINS	GEORGE P. WEST
MARY H. INGHAM	ARTHUR G. WRAY
HORACE M. KALLEN	CHARLES ZUEBLIN
OSWALD W. KNAUTH	WILLIAM F. COCHRAN, Treasurer

There is also in the pamphlet a list of some 225 signers of this call for "Saving the Nation," which incidentally furnishes salaries for certain brain workers out of jobs. It is unfortunate that there is not sufficient available space in the REVIEW columns to allow for the complete list, as it is a gem and ought to be filed among the "Who's Who" of those ardent and industrious folk who never get anywhere. Like the General Committee, its membership shows an utter lack of men who labor with their hands, in the field, or the shop. Their work is done mostly with their pens and their jaws. While the committee includes a few high-minded and loyal Americans who have no business in such a menagerie, it is composed largely of pacifists, socialists, Single Taxers, Bolshevists, England-hating Irish and Germany-loving Germans.

When the Committee of Forty-Eight declare that ours is "no longer a government by conviction and the vote of the majority," that "a small group of dominant men who control credit dictate the decisions of both political parties," and that "our country is menaced by the growing power of an autocratic and reactionary minority," it states what is baldly and absolutely false. With the direct primary and the Australian ballot system of voting, all the men and the majority of the women citizens of the United States have the privilege and the duty of participating in the selection of those who fill the positions of government provided by our federal and state constitutions, and if they do not avail themselves of this opportunity it is entirely their own fault. The truth is, however, that the American people do avail themselves of this privilege, but they do not see fit to place in positions of honor and trust any of the class of individuals who are so largely represented in the Committee of Forty-Eight. Will these political ghost dancers tell the American people what new methods they propose for enabling the voters of the United States to select their representatives in Congress, the legislatures and the municipal councils (the only places where legislation can be enacted) other than the direct primary or the convention and election under the protection of the Australian ballot laws?

Also, will the promoters of this "Happy Thought" movement, who are so strong for democratic methods and who are appealing for our "time, enthusiasm, advice and money," tell the public just how it was organized? Was a mass meeting called at Cooper Union in New York, for instance, and in the other large centers of population in the country, to select, democratically, this General Committee that is to "decide on a line of action" and manipulate the machinery of a so-called New Party? Or w s it created by a self-appointed clique in some purple Greenwich Village tea-room or in a back office of the *New Republic*, the *Nation* or the *Dial*? Come out, gentlemen, and give us some pitiless publicity as to the origin of this great, democratic, anti-autocratic, anti-government-by-minority, anti-ring, anti-everything movement!

"I'd Fight for America," says Stokes to Sinclair

J. G. PHELPS STOKES, who left the Socialist party to support the American cause in the war and who has come to be known as one of the ablest exponents of democracy in every phase of the contest against autocracy during the war and since, just has made public through the American Alliance for Labor and Democracy, his reply to a hypothetical question propounded to him by Upton Sinclair, California socialist and one of the editors of the *Appeal to Reason*, in the columns of which he asked the question which Stokes has answered.

Mr. Stokes informs Sinclair that if Sinclair wishes to continue the debate he will be happy to oblige the Californian.

This is the question put by Sinclair, which Stokes answers:

> Imagine, just for the sake of argument, that the American workers were to accomplish a revolution of physical force and set up a dictatorship of the proletariat, and then imagine that the capitalist governments of Great Britain and Italy and France and Japan were to say to the American working-class government: We demand that you shall abdicate and restore the old-time capitalist democracy to America. We will block your coast, we will invade your country from all sides and seize it, and set up American capitalist governments wherever we can, and meantime we will take your lumber and your coal and your iron to pay interest on the debts you owe to our capitalists—do I have to hesitate very long to decide what I would answer to the capitalist governments of England, Italy, France, and Japan? I wonder what my friend, J. G. Phelps Stokes, would answer under the circumstances?

Elsewhere in addressing Stokes, Sinclair says: "I admit that America has a democracy of a sort," though he thinks there might be much discussion about how complete it is. "We have, of course," he says, "never had a real democracy in America," adding, however, that he believes "America does sincerely believe in and intend a great deal more democracy than it actually carries into practice from hour to hour."

REPLY OF MR. STOKES

Stokes' reply to Sinclair follows in full:

Mr. Upton Sinclair,
Pasadena, Calif.

Dear Upton:

Thank you very much for sending me copy of the highly compounded hypothetical question which you addressed to me publicly in last week's *Appeal*. I received it this morning and am very glad indeed to answer at once, but since no single answer could possibly fit all the ingredients of so complex a question, I shall have to answer its several parts seriatim.

You assume for sake of argument that several things happen: 1st, that the workers of America set up a dictatorship of the proletariat; 2nd, that such dictatorship would really be a "working class government"; 3rd, that Great Britain and other powers demand the restoration of "old time capitalist democracy"; 4th, that these aggressive foreign powers "invade our country from all sides and seize it," and restore the type of government now existing; 5th, that meanwhile they "take" our American lumber and coal and iron to pay interest on our alleged debts to them. You ask what your friend, myself, "would answer under the circumstances."—Would I line up with the dictators or their opponents? You intimate very plainly that you would line up with the dictators.

I answer unhesitatingly as follows:

"1st The majority of the workers in America are not proletarians, and never were proletarians and never will be proletarians unless such preachments as yours bring about complete chaos and ruination for the workers here, like that which prevails now in Bolshevik Russia. In that event everybody would of course be proletarians, unless perhaps the dictators and their henchmen. The workers of America cannot conceivably become fools enough, in my opinion, to be guided by such preachments, or to subject themselves to the dictatorship of any group whatever.

"2nd Your assumption that the Bolshevik style of dictatorship is really a working class government, is, I am convinced, very far removed from the truth. And when I say 'I am convinced,' I do not speak idly. I do not believe there are many Americans who have followed the Russian situation more closely than I have.

"Let me cite one or two examples out of many: When the *Workmen's International*, official organ of the Left Wing Mensheviki, declared on August 7th of last year that the Bolsheviki were 'attempting to bribe the proletariat,' and that they were 'driving the peasantry into the arms of the counter-revolution,' it must have been at least their opinion that neither the proletariat nor the peasantry were supporting the Bolshevist 'government,' very enthusiastically at that time; and when Zinovieff, Chairman of the Petrograd Soviet, declared shortly afterward, 'We must win over to our side 90 millions of the 100 millions of the population of Russia,' he must have meant that that task was still to be accomplished. (Zinovieff's statement as above appeared in the *Northern Commune*, official organ of the Petrograd Soviet, in its issue of September 19th, last.)

"The Bolsheviki may, of course, have won a good many adherents since last September, but they have lost a good many, too; not through 'invasion' by Great Britain or other powers, but through the revolts of workingmen in almost every part of Russia. Vladimir Bourtzeff recently sent to friends in this country a list of seventy-five Russian districts where notable revolts of the workers occurred last year. The Bolsheviki have in fact lost since last September about one-third of the Russian territory that they controlled at that time, and they have lost nearly all of this at the hands of Russian workingmen, notably those in the armies of the native Russian leaders Kolchak, Denikine and Petlura. As General Vatsetis, Commander-in-chief of the Soviet armies, declared in his recent proclamation as published in the Left Wing organ here (*The Revolutionary Age*, of May 31, 1919), 'The numerous bands of White Guards and traitors [not foreigners], like hungry jackals, attack us on all sides and the struggle against them [not against the foreigners] gradually becoming more intense, has become a struggle of life and death.'

"3rd I thoroughly approve of the workers of all lands responding to the very tragic appeals made over and over again by the democratic workers of Russia for aid in their desperate struggle to overthrow their dictators and to establish democracy in their government. If, when they have secured democracy, the Russian workers should voluntarily give all power to Lenine and Trotzky, or to some other dictatorial group, I should very greatly regret it, but should say 'Hands off! Let them work out their own salvation in whatever way they choose.' Until, however, the Russian workers have created the democratic machinery through which their will, whatever it may be, may be freely expressed and made effective, I say 'Hands off!' not to their friends who help them from other lands, but to their dictators.

"4th If aggressive foreign powers should 'invade America and seize it,' I should of course do everything in my little power to oust them, and most gladly give my life, if need be, to aid in effecting that object. But if the foes of democracy in America should enter into a compact with some autocratic foreign power, as the Bolshevik dictators did, and with the aid of that foreign power arm 60 thousand Chinese laborers in this country and 100 thousand unemployed and all the inmates of the prisons, and thus seize or attempt to seize New York and Washington (as the Bolsheviki with German aid armed 60 thousand Chinese laborers who had been employed on the Murmansk Railway and all the unemployed and prisoners they could persuade to fight for pay, and with their aid seized Petrograd and Moscow), then I should certainly accept service, gladly, as a common soldier in the army of democracy and fight to the limit to overthrow such tyranny and to re-establish and maintain 'old time democracy'—capitalistic democracy if no better form were to be had—until such time as the workers of America could be brought to a realization that Democratic Socialism would be preferable, and until they would vote to put Democratic Socialists and their system of government in power.

"5th If foreign powers or any other powers should attempt to seize or hold the natural resources of America, I, of course, should do everything in my little power to aid in ousting them. You should, I think, have observed by this time that I have not been altogether idle in this direction during the past eighteen or twenty years.

Since you have given such very great publicity to your hypothetical question addressed to me, I am sure that in fairness you will do what you can to secure equal and similar publicity for this my reply.

If you would like to continue the discussion, please believe me most happily at your service.

Very sincerely yours,

GRAHAM.

Andrew Carnegie—the Friend of Labor

(*Continued from page 8*)

I laughed, and Billy said, sitting down: 'We won't have any trouble settling this.' And we did not. It is astonishing what a joke will do to settle difficulties that we meet with in life.

"I want to express the genuine, heartfelt happiness of Mrs. Carnegie and myself for this opportunity of meeting the two branches, equal in every respect, who bargain with each other—the one for labor, the other for satisfactory wages; one just as welcome as the other, and both doubly welcome. It is something we will remember with great happiness all our lives, and it is another instance that I will look back to in after years, when I become an old man, and I will be telling some other audiences what a glorious time I had with the delegates of The Civic Federation Peace Evening. I thank you, one and all, for giving us the pleasure of meeting you here this evening."

Before dispersing, a flashlight photograph of the gathering was taken, and before the assemblage could rise, Mr. Carnegie, who was standing, waved his arm and began singing "Auld Lang Syne," in which everyone heartily joined. Mr. Carnegie, and others who were at that conference, have gone on "the great adventure," but the principles which were there discussed and which have guided organized labor remain. And likewise in his brief speech did the great captain of industry put into words an immortal truth which remains—that no man can dishonor another, and that no nation can dishonor another, that "all dishonors from which we suffer are 'self-inflicted."

The Labor Situation Abroad

(Continued from page 4)

mmon topics of negotiation, but he is ex- ngly cautious in going further than those cts. He suggests as profitable to both sides, lly or financially, certain shop practices by oyers such as, interpreting to the workers rules or shop developments coming from anagement, discussing and working out in nection with the workers educational mat- elating to shop processes and trade tech- . He regards as open to question, how- discussion of the filling of any vacancy by gement and workers. Mr. Renold does not that workmen should choose their own en, and a "still more doubtful" point he is "Education in general business ques- ."

WNER'S AUTHORITY REMAINS INTACT

may be stated that at no point in his memo- um does Mr. Renold carry his proposed icipatory functions for the workers beyond limits long practiced by wise employers, or without trade union recognition and as- nce. Not on a single point does he part with ority of ownership. American employers gone further than he without thought of ing with their employees the powers in- ed in ownership and direction.

New York, for instance, the Typographical n and the printing employers' association a joint committee of six members to which scharged employee may appeal as against reman or superintendent.

John D. Rockefeller, Jr.'s "Industrial Con- tion" for the Colorado Fuel & Iron Com- y, it is provided that "Employees at each he mining camps shall annually elect from ng their number representatives to act on r behalf with respect to matters pertaining their employment, working and *living* condi- ns, the adjustment of differences, and such er matters of mutual concern and interest relations within the industry may determine."

n neither of these instances is "control by the rkers" over the policy or nature of the busi- s the principle contemplated. It relates, her, to negotiation with equals in the labor rket. Mr. Renold's sole object seems to be, en analyzed, the instruction of the unquali- l in processes of production.

The third lift on the way to "workers' self- ernment" in Great Britain is promised to hopeful in "government action through king effective the report of the Whitley Com- tee."

HISTORY OF WHITLEY COMMITTEE

A word of explanation is necessary here with ard to the Whitley Committee, whose exact ignation was "The Sub-Committee on Rela- ns between Employers and Employed" of National Reconstruction Committee. It was pointed in 1916, and on July 1, 1918, made final report. Briefly, it recommended the ation of "joint bodies for purposes of consul- ion and decision of matters of common inter- ." These voluntary joint bodies, representa- e of employers and employees, were three- d; (1) Works Committees; (2) Local Dis- ct Councils; (3) Joint Standing Industrial uncils. The last named were "to consider ditions for an industry as a whole," the two ers for shops and localities respectively. ree strata of wage-workers in which the gov- ment was to proffer a progressively paternal nd in assisting to form the councils were: e occupations in which trade unions were ong; those in which they were but partly or- nized, and those in which non-unionists were stly employed. In this process of committee d council organization, the Ministry of Labor uld make suggestions to both parties, giving general assistance in establishing councils, drafting constitutions, and "issuing relevant matter," besides itself "forming an official liaison in connection with every council."

Let it be affirmed at once that the Whitley Report embodies no recommendation whatever of putting wage-workers in charge of any authoritative part of business enterprise. It does not suggest any method in shop administration not known to American workers of the mechanical trades. The main principle advocated is, "granting to work-people a greater share in matters affecting their industry." Any ambiguity in the words "their industry" is cleared away in the sub-paragraphs particularizing the committee's recommendations. These recognize wages, hours and conditions of labor as proper subjects of negotiation and legislation. In the report reference is made to such questions as security of earnings and employment, technical education, industrial research, rewards for inventions, etc., which pass somewhat beyond ordinary shop agreements. They do not, however, go beyond demands often discussed by trade unionists, or methods followed by advanced employers, or rights exercised by workers individually.

ORGANIZATION PROGRESSES SLOWLY

Returning to the Whitley Committee organization for a moment, I may state that it contemplates the organization of employers and employees in all the occupations consenting, under government supervision and regulation where necessary. Up to May 1, thirty-three joint industrial councils had been organized, and constitutions drafted for nineteen other industries. Steps had also been taken to apply the Whitley Report to government industrial establishments, the civil service and administrative, professional, technical and clerical staffs of local authorities.

Evidently the Whitley recommendations have looked better to the lay public and small industries than to the big unions, as councils have not been formed in ship-building, cotton, railways, engineering, coal mining and steel. From the American viewpoint the Whitley Committee recommendations and the work done thereunder to date show excellent intention, elaborate preparation, but a rather scanty crop of results.

One of the prominent British trade unionists interviewed by the writer thus stated his interpretation of the facts regarding "voice in the management."

"It is doubtful whether any workmen really concern themselves with anything beyond sharing in workshop control, that is, control of working conditions and control of workshop production. So far as the foundation of the business is concerned, the arrangements made in the initial stages of starting the business, financing of the business, the seeking out of markets, whether they be home or foreign markets, these are matters that the average workman has never yet concerned himself with, nor does there appear to be any serious desire on his part to be troubled with matters of this description now."

AS THE SOCIALISTS SEE IT

How many of those who are clamoring for the control of industry by workers have stopped to consider how large a ripple on the industrial situation this would bring about were every industry that is susceptible to organization administered on that basis? The last United States census lists 38,000,000 males and females as engaged in "gainful occupations." Of these, 23,900,000 are engaged in agriculture, domestic, general, professional, public and clerical service, and in trade. It will be admitted that few wage-workers in this group are likely to take part in the management of the occupations in which they are engaged. This territory is little known either to trade unionism or work-shop control.

"WORKERS' CONTROL" NATURALLY LIMITED

A second group numbering 14,100,000, composed of persons engaged in extracting minerals, manufacturing and mechanical work and transportation, includes, besides wage-workers, employers large and small, the higher salaried employees, young persons learning trades and scattered craftsmen in small industries or in non-industrial communities. Making the generous assumption that one-half of these 14,100,000 are genuine wage-workers susceptible of organization, we would have only about one-fifth of the persons in gainful occupations (7,500,000 in 38,000,000) in classes in which the workers could possibly have a "voice in the management." How many of this possible fifth could be reached by the plan of "workers' control?" Could one wage-worker in ten, or twenty, or thirty? Surely these statistics show that democratization of industry, if it is to cover the country, requires some plan other than those suggested thus far.

TOO MANY ORDERS; TOO MUCH ADVICE

It is the opinion of the writer that the stage now arrived at through the tutorship of the British government and the establishment of its various councils and committees is less satisfactory than the present status of the employer and employed classes in this country. Both sides here know where they stand. In Britain, what with works committees, joint councils, industrial conference committees and the standing trade union agreements, too many voices call too many orders and proffer too much advice. The Parliamentary Committee's action relative to the whole scheme of administration of the Whitley Committee's recommendations brings the entire subject and policy back toward the American trade union basis. The committee, in a resolution, rendered this decision:

"The Parliamentary Committee cannot accept any form of joint negotiations either by Works Committees, District Councils, or National Councils which may be developed as a substitute for Trade Union organization."

This signifies that, no matter how numerous the methods for understandings between "capital and labor" provided by the government, the trade unions are to rely on their own strength to reach their usual purposes. In their conception of democracy in industry, no other factor equals in play and outcome the right of the dissatisfied laborer to quit work.

CHAOTIC BRITISH LABOR POLITICS

III.

FOR a good many years now, a small minority among the wage-workers of the United States has been continuously and vociferously urging the formation of a distinct labor party in this country along political lines. This proposal has come up frequently at annual conventions of the American Federation of Labor, and has always been unceremoniously voted down by the hard-headed representatives of the several million wage-workers assembled there, for these men know the history of the British Labor Party.

Very briefly summarized, it may be said that Labor's entry into politics in that country as a separate political party has brought confusion to the workers. It interferes with the progress of union organization, engenders enmities among union officials, carries far and wide the fever of political campaigning all the year 'round, has pushed labor representatives to unpatriotic votes on war measures in Parliament, brings to the party less than a fourth of the wage labor vote of the country and has eventuated with respect to efficient laws for labor's protection in a less satisfactory situation than exists in the industrial states of America. . . ...

PURELY A WAGE-WORKERS' MOVEMENT.

In the United States the labor movement is a wage-workers' movement, and they know without a doubt what fealty to their union requires of them. They are not bound to a labor party or to labor candidates. The power of their will goes by democratic processes from the thirty-odd thousand local unions to the annual convention of the American Federation of Labor, the final interpreter of American labor's policy and program. Pronouncements on political party matters there are unmistakable. By votes approaching unanimity the conventions have successively continued to decide against a wage-workers' party, either union or Socialist. The American movement is a trade union movement pure and simple.

In Great Britain among the most prominent leaders of the so-called political Labor movement are men and women who were never wage-workers. The trade unionists, supplying to the party nineteen-twentieths of the votes and a greater proportion of the contributions, mostly remain spectators to the play. From the outsiders comes a stream of proposals for the reorganization of society to which the majority of the wage-workers of the kingdom steadily refuse assenting votes.

Before the organization of the Labor Party in Great Britain, leaders in Labor's cause in that country were practically united in the unions for common ends, were mutually appreciative team-mates, usually impressed with one another's sincerity, each acknowledging the other's merits and deeds of self-sacrifice. To-day the situation is absolutely reversed, and the solidarity of yesterday has been transformed into confusion and back-biting indescribable. A few examples taken from the list of men prominent in the Labor movement in Great Britain in recent years will serve to illustrate the statement that has been made.

JOHN BURNS' CAREER TYPICAL.

Commencing with John Burns of the Engineers, we find that politics carried him away from the activities of his union, put him in Parliament as a labor representative, turned him over to the Liberal Party and took him to the presidency of the Local Government Board. On the outbreak of the war his sentiments divided him from the mass of his countrymen and he passed into private life.

J. Havelock Wilson, of the Sailors, his union record approaching forty years, variously designated in the reference books as a "Coalition Labor" or "Coalition Liberal" M. P., his majority over his opponent, a Labor candidate, was last December 13,089; in opposition to the Labor Party yet elected at the Trade Union Congress to the present Parliamentary Committee; for years a target for Socialists and extreme Labor partisans.

Alexander Wilkie, of the Shipwrights, a Labor M. P. and for twelve years a member of the Parliamentary Committee, is at present a member of the Management Committee, General Federation of Trade Unions, which body was two years ago excluded from joint committee work with the Trade Union Congress and the Labor Party. Then there is David Gilmour, of the Miners, General Secretary, National Democratic and Labor Party, now represented in the House of Commons by ten members. His party is on the other side of the House from the Labor Party.

One could give a long list of Labor men who are occupying prominent Government positions, such as the Right Honorable John R. Clynes of the Gasworkers, the Right Honorable George H. Roberts, head of the Ministry of Food, Sir David Shackleton, Permanent Secretary, Ministry of Labor, etc. The lack of unity in politics or otherwise as illustrated in the case of these prominent leaders, characterizes the situation in all grades of union membership throughout the country.

In November, 1918, the Labor Party, by a large vote, withdrew from the coalition with the Government and directed the eight labor men occupying high Government office to withdraw. Four only obeyed this command.

SOCIALISTS OUTVOTE TRADE UNIONISTS.

At a recent trade union congress a motion was presented declaring in favor of a distinct political labor party exclusively for the trade union movement. This was debated for the better part of two days. The burden of the argument of those favoring the resolution was that the "intellectuals" had done their best to capture the executive control of the trade union. The congress was warned against putting up as candidates "brilliant middle class speakers who tell you that they know the wants of the workers better than you do, because they have had a collegiate education and you have not." This motion did not prevail, because it was not favored by the Socialist delegates representing great numbers in the unskilled unions, who were pitted against a considerable body of delegates representing the skilled unions with a smaller membership. Savage attacks were made by the International Socialists on Colonel John Ward, of the Navvies, when, commanding a battalion of railroad workers in Russia, he was obliged to engage in battle with detachments of the Bolshevists. To his British critics he was a "butcher of the working people."

The one daily newspaper in London assuming to represent labor—its leading editor, George Lansbury, once a Labor member of Parliament but not a wage-worker—carries on a crusade of opposition to all the leading trade unionists not in agreement with extravagantly radical and pro-German views. When the terms of the Peace Covenant were published in May, the *Herald* printed such first-page headings as "Germany in Mourning," "Obstacles to a Real Peace," "Jingo Press Howls for Harsher and More Humiliating Exactions," "British Workers Join Herr Wolff in Indignant Denunciation of Peace of Violence," "Capitalist Peace of Fear." In the political field the British trade unionist hears it most positively asserted that "Labor's Daily Newspaper," the self-same *London Herald* is maintained by German bankers and Indian magnates.

LAST ELECTIONS A BLOW

The Labor Party was sadly disappointed in the results of the election last December. Claims had been made that it would return from 100 to 200 Members of Parliament. The principal extremists among the candidates, Snowden, Ramsay McDonald, Anderson, Jowett, Henderson, were defeated. The 59 members elected are by no means a solid block. Their published views on public issues continually vary.

The knife is busy. Old Labor Party opponents of the new National Democratic Labor Party allege that its candidates were in part financed by funds subscribed "through the *Morning Post* and other organs of privileged groups." The British Socialists, rent by dissension, some of them loyal to their country during the war, spill ink in calling one another names. The trade unionism of some of the 59 members is assailed by undoubted unionists. In the Annual Report of the General Federation of Trade Unions last year the General Secretary in defense said: "In my humble opinion the Federation is the only trade union movement we have in the country."

Judge of the state of mind of the average British trade unionist when he hears veteran labor officials declare that "these labor politicians of every stripe are forever talking for votes and acting for effect on their political fortunes," when his attention is directed to the fact that while a few "intellectuals" supply issues and name leaders the trade union membership in the Labor Party is at least two millions, the socialist managers contributing fifty thousand names and the unions nearly all the money. Sympathize with him when he hears one set of men declaring that it would have been better had labor never entered politics while another set assert that labor never received the slightest consideration in the House of Commons until its own representatives were there bearding the conservatives.

SOCIALISM'S 57 VARIETIES

If the common-or-garden variety of British trade unionist is inclined to associate with deep-down radicals, he will be obliged to choose between the Independent Labor Party, the British Socialist Party, the Socialist Labor Party, the National Socialist Party and the Socialist Party of Great Britain. The chips of the split-up and sawed-up old original Socialist Party are scattered all over the British Isles. To ascertain the merits of the differences between these Socialist groups the earnest sociological student would be required to give a month's reading to the bundles of their controversial printed matter and exercise the judgment of a Solomon.

Strange bed-fellows are found in the Labor Party itself—the Trade Union Congress, the Socialist and Cooperative Societies, the City Trades Councils, the local labor parties and the Women's Labor League. Among the fifty-nine Labor representatives in Parliament there are men of every shade of political opinion, from the very conservative to the violent revolutionist. Condemnation inevitably falls on the heads of trade union officials in Parliament. If they attend to their union duties they must be absent from the House; if they sit conscientiously in the House they are charged with neglect of their union work.

The puzzled unionist hears to-day clamorous advocacy of the political strike to take the place of the ballot. He hears continual demands for local and national meetings. He is called on to take sides on the unemployment problem, on the peace treaty, on questions of demobilization, on the distribution of food in the famished continental countries. He is called on to take sides in problematical international issues, and on propositions for dubious international congresses. He is confronted with the duty of settling in his mind his impulses of patriotism in connection with international conventions—at Stockholm, at Berne, at Paris, at Kienthal, at Zimmerwald, at London—with Allies, with Neutrals, with Germans. He sees at such meetings supposedly sober British representatives chummy with the wild Cachins and the Marxite Longuets of France and the obstructionist Italian Socialists who openly opposed their government during the war. He is expected to shout for Quixotic international projects, such as world-wide free trade and similar universal brotherhood issues non-existent to American Labor. He beholds prominent on the Labor and Socialist stage pacifists and conscientious objectors, some of them interned during the war. He becomes acquainted with earnest people in the Labor Research Department, formerly the Fabian, struggling with their Socialist prepossessions in endeavors to put before the public in scientific form serious reports helpful to the general British public, entertainment being supplied at their meetings through the dignified chairmanship of Bernard Shaw and the fanciful guild projects of G. D. H. Cole.

The philosophic humorist, James Sexton, M. P., of the Dockworkers, inquired at a recent party conference what in fact the labor issues were to be, saying: "I don't want to go to the next general election with only a Fabian essay around my neck."

strikes of 1910-12 the lesson had been learned that a stoppage by one of the three bodies led to an involuntary stoppage in one or both the others. After conferences in 1914-15, the constitution of the Triple Alliance was ratified in December, 1915. At a meeting in April of 1916 resolutions were passed dealing with after-war problems, demanding that departures from trade union practices should terminate on the resumption of peace, and that substituted workers should be given employment at standard rates, or full maintenance by the State, and making certain proposals in connection with demobilization.

COERCION IS CHARGED

When this program was presented to the Prime Minister in August, 1916, the *Times* accused the Triple Alliance of "formally attempting to supersede constitutional government and to frighten the appointed ministers of the crown, who are responsible for the conduct of the affairs of the nation into doing their will." In June, 1917, the alliance, at a conference attended by 280 delegates, passed resolutions against industrial conscription and for the conscription of wealth and property, to bring about equality of sacrifice. J. H. Thomas, explaining the origin of the alliance, has written that he "saw that sectional unionism had become obsolete and that even occupational unionism would have to be put into the melting pot and recast."

A radical opinion is that "the Triple Alliance is the nucleus of a General Federation of Industrial Unions which may be of invaluable importance to the future of the labor movement," and, further: "It may, for instance, be permitted to hope that the power of the alliance may be employed to raise the status rather than merely to increase the wages of its members."

The Triple Alliance stood aloof from the joint standing Industrial Councils and from the special Joint Committee of the government's National Industrial Conference of Employers and Employed which met in February in London. However, J. H. Thomas, representing the alliance, in a written communication stated that the organized workers of Great Britain have made up their minds to procure an increasing share of the wealth produced by their labor; they are determined to shorten materially their working hours; they are dissatisfied with a system which treats their labor power as a mere commodity to be bought, sold and used as though they were machine-like units in the process of wealth production and distribution. And they demand that they shall become real partners in industry, joint sharers in the determination of working conditions and management. They stand unalterably for the ownership by the state of the mines, railroads and means of inland and coastal transportation. However, they recognize that the capitalist, the inventor, the director and the organizer have some interest in the products of industry.

LEADERS OF THE ALLIANCE

Of the three foremost leaders of the alliance, J. H. Thomas has repeatedly advised a moderation in procedure falling far shart of the desires of extremists. Robert Smillie, of the Miners, President of the Alliance as well as of the Miners' Federation, was chief on the labor side in conducting the sessions of the Coal Commission in London, a mission which he performed with satisfaction to Socialists generally. Robert Williams, representing the transport workers, is much in the public eye, especially as a speaker in opposition to the government. As a candidate for the House of Commons he was defeated by a Coalition Liberal.

If accepted as one hundred per cent. solid, the Triple Alliance would be undoubtedly a standing menace not only to the State but to British trade unionism; but there are reasons for regarding it as less frightful than it looks on first blush. It is commonly asserted that unauthorized preparations by its executives for a general strike would cause a demand for a secret ballot by all concerned, ending in general exposure of internal weaknesses now obvious to other unionists. The National Sailors and Firemen (65,000), with Havelock Wilson at their head, are united to the alliance by slender ties, and the independence usually shown by the National Union of Dock Laborers (45,000), James Sexton, Secretary, is apt to be displayed on rightful occasion. Nor is the Dock, Wharf, Riverside and General Workers' Union, Ben Tillett, Secretary, easily led to anti-social action. There are more than 200,000 railway employees, one-half of them organized, not in the National Union of Railway men and several hundred thousand mine-workers not in the Federation. The trade unions outside the alliance are far from united in supporting its methods.

In the last week of May, after much consideration of the proposition, the Parliamentary Committee of the Trade Union Congress declined to act upon a request made to it by the Triple Alliance to call a special national labor conference to take action on the abolition of conscription, the withdrawal of British troops from Russia, the lifting of the blockade on Germany, and the release of the imprisoned conscientious objectors. The Parliamentary Committee decided that the government's statements to a deputation on these subjects were sufficiently satisfactory.

LEADERS CONDEMN ALLIANCE PRINCIPLES

The Rt. Hon. J. R. Clynes of the General Workers' Union said recently: "The Triple Alliance is an outstanding example of the very action which in others labor is called upon to denounce." In an article in the *Democrat*, entitled "Britain's Danger," W. A. Appleton called attention to the fact that the Triple Alliance represents less than one-sixth of the working population. He regards it as endeavoring to secure special advantage at the expense of the rest of the working class. He reasons that damage to other industries, even if only temporary, must reduce the demand for coal and the need for transport and entail the loss of overseas markets.

The labor press and leaders friendly to the alliance point out that through its strength for direct action—the threat of strike—were obtained the recent concessions from employers and the government resulting in considerable wage advances, the forty-seven-hour week and the recognition of higher standards in working conditions in the three industries. Trade union opponents of the alliance, while admitting its effectiveness for wage advances and the like up to the present time, are profoundly disturbed at its methods as applied to political purposes. Recognizing its exercise of power not only for trade union objects but for revolutionary ends as an extraordinary event in British history, they inquire with concern as to the probable limits of this power and its eventual social effects. They are aware, as its supporters say, "that if the Triple Alliance wills it, the industrial life in Britain will stop short," or again, "It can hold up the economic life of Great Britain." This theoretical truth would be the more significant if spoken of British industrial unionism in its entirety. No graver social problem could be before Britain.

GREAT CRISES SUGGESTED

Whether, to compel nationalization of one industry after another, the nation is to be held up by a force within itself superior to its constitutional lawmaking powers, how often and to

(*Continued on page 18*)

If Bolshevism Came to America

(Continued from page 9)

Their bodies were then thrown into the little river that runs through the town of Bellebei."

GIRLS FROM HIGH SCHOOL OUTRAGED—BOYS SHOT WITHOUT TRIAL

With Judge Blumenthal—who, upon his return after the ejection of the Bolsheviki, found his apartment looted of every bit of furniture—Mr. Embry called upon a lady physician, a friend of the judge's, Mrs. Koshevnikoff, who resided in Bellebei with her sister, head of the Bellebei high school, and her aged mother.

"They told us their stories of how they in their homes were compelled to live in one room," said Mr. Embry, "all the other rooms being taken over either by Bolshevik officials or soldiers, and how they were daily insulted, and how they had no peace and hardly any rest all hours of the night. The Bolsheviki came in, there was loud cursing and quarrels; they were constantly drunk and gambling, and the language was so foul it was distressing for these ladies to listen. It was in the midst of one of the coldest winters of Russia, and they had no other place to go. That was their life during three or four months until last December. One day the Bolshevik Commisar living in Dr. Koshevnikoff's home noticed the old grandmother sitting by the stove. 'Come on,' he said, 'let us throw the old woman out into the street and let her freeze. That's the way to treat people who are no longer useful.' And this old lady, whom I saw and with whom I spoke, was put out on the street. Although they did not persist in carrying out their threat, her mind was so affected she fell ill and barely lived through it. She was just beginning to get her strength back when we arrived there."

From the sister of Madam Koshevnikoff, the head of the Bellebei high school, Mr. Embry learned what the Bolsheviki had done to the pupils, the children of Bellebei. The smaller boys "were made to work on the streets shovelling snow, receiving for this labor no pay whatsoever. The older boys, who were thought to be possible material for the Siberian Army (of Kolchak) and believed capable of attempting an escape to join that Army, were taken out and shot without any trial or any reason for it other than that they might possibly join the Siberian Army. The girls of the high school, according to the sister of Madam Koshevnikoff, were made to wash out the barracks, to wash the dirty apparel of the Bolshevik soldiers, and received for this labor nothing but blows and curses."

All that happened to the girls of the high school, the fair, refined and innocent daughters of the best families, the bourgeoise, of Bellebei; all that—and worse.

"No man's life or woman's honor," declared Mr. Embry, "was safe at Bellebei under the Bolsheviki."

600 SICK CHILDREN RUTHLESSLY SLAIN

From reports afforded by the Intelligence Staff of General Belitzen, who commands the Kolchak forces along the southern section of the Siberian front and whose armies had just liberated Bellebei, Mr. Embry learned much of what the Bolsheviki did in other parts of unhappy Russia. One of Belitzen's lieutenants was captured by the Bolsheviki, and was imprisoned at a camp near Moscow. He arrived in Moscow on the twenty-fourth of last December, and later escaped by the use of a false document. He reported that in Moscow horsemeat sold for eighteen to twenty rubles a pound, and dog meat for six or seven rubles; bread was not to be had. On his way back to the Kolchak forces, he witnessed a revolt at Talkai of the peasants against the Bolsheviki. This revolt was suppressed with indescribable violence. At Boogloouruslan he saw thousands of teams loaded with grain and stolen goods which the Bolsheviki were taking to Samara in their retreat before the advancing armies of Kolchak. At Kennelt-cherkovskaia, where the people attempted to revolt, the Bolsheviki killed 1,000, and sent 600 more to Moscow for trial. Dead bodies were frequently seen along the railroads.

According to a report made by two Russian girls who had escaped from Moscow and who arrived at the Siberian front the day before Mr. Embry's visit, in Moscow there was an epidemic of Spanish influenza and of glanders, resulting from the eating of decomposed horseflesh. Seventy-five percent of the cases of Spanish influenza were reported fatal. In one case, 600 children, ill with glanders, were taken out and shot. On the sixteenth of last March, the street cars of Moscow stopped. In the city there was no benzine or kerosene, except that used by the Bolsheviki officers and leaders; torches were used for lighting purposes in houses; to get heat, people were burning their furniture and tearing up floors. Daily, long lines of people waited in the streets to secure permits to bury dead relatives.

At a famous convent near Surtensk, the nuns were compelled to act as servants for Chinese mercenaries billetted there. Instructions issued to the troops, composed of Chinese, Magyars and Letts, and officered by Germans, read: "Shoot all intelligent classes because only the ignorant classes can be taught Bolshevism properly. All grain must be requisitioned. All people found with firearms must be put to death." According to the reports, Mr. Embry said that most of the native Russians in Moscow, except those who managed to convince the Reds of their conversion to Bolshevism, had either fled or been killed. The Russian language is now infrequently heard, Mr. Embry said, and Yiddish has become the language most used.

After serving two years as vice-consul at Odessa, Mr. Embry was appointed a consul to Russia, February 19, 1918. He was ordered to Moscow, sailing from the United States March 1, and arriving at Vladivostok, Siberia, March 28, 1918. As he was unable to reach his destination, he served as junior consul at Vladivostok from March 28, 1918, until November 6, 1918, when he was ordered to Omsk, where he served as consul from November 8, 1918, until April 20, 1919. The Soviet regime became all powerful in Vladivostok in June, 1918, when people were ejected by force from their houses and apartments. "The cases that came under my observation," testified Mr. Embry, "were those of people who were thrown out of their apartments, and these apartments were taken by the workers and their families, and the people who had leases on these apartments, who owned these apartments, or were in any way entitled to reside there, were ejected in many cases and great hardships worked upon them. My wife suffered under this at that time. At that time we were not married. She was a Russian citizen and had no protection other than what she could get from the Bolshevik Soviet there, which was none, as she states it to me."

KOLCHAK HAILED AS SAVIOR BY RUSSIANS

From Vladivostok Mr. Embry was ordered to Omsk, Siberia, where he arrived November 8, 1918. It was on the night before his arrival that there had occurred at Omsk the coup-d'etat whereby the present Siberian government came into power. Admiral Kolchak, said Mr. Embry, arrived at Omsk a few days later and was called to the head of the government. "To our great surprise," said Mr. Embry, "inside of about three days the scattered bands of Russian troops throughout that section of Siberia declared their loyalty to Admiral Kolchak and they quietly took their places on the Siberian front which up to that time had been held by Czecho-Slovaks." Mr. Embry said that Kolchak's genius for leadership and his control over the men enabled these Siberian people to protect themselves against the return to power of the Bolsheviki. At first the Russians were panic stricken lest the Bolsheviki return to Siberia and resume power. Mr. Embry remained until April 1, 1919, at Omsk, where he said he felt as safe as he does in New York. While serving as vice consul at Odessa, from January 28, 1916, to November 27, 1917, Mr. Embry first came to know Admiral Kolchak. Of Admiral Kolchak, whom the Bolsheviki in America and such pro-Bolshevist organs as the *Nation* and *New Republic* represent as an outlaw and brigand, Mr. Embry said:

"He was in command of the Black Sea fleet at that time, and at the time of my arrival in Odessa the whole city was singing the praises of Admiral Kolchak because he had just recently gone out against the two German battleships, the Goeben and the Breslau, and had just driven them out of the Black Sea. They never came again to the Black Sea. The Russian people there were particularly loud in praise of Admiral Kolchak for his brilliant action, because the former Russian Admiral, whom he had replaced a short time before, had remained in his port and had refused to go out, saying that he had only relics of the Japanese war and he could not battle against the first-class German ships, and it was Admiral Kolchak who showed that the Black Fleet could fight and protect these cities along the coast."

Later, after telling of the Bolsheviki atrocities in Siberia Mr. Embry spoke of the attitude of the Russian people in the districts through which he passed toward Kolchak and his army.

"Every man, woman and child with whom we conversed spoke of the Siberian government with almost tearful affection, and the name of Admiral Kolchak to these unhappy people who had just been liberated was like the name of our Savior, Jesus Christ. It was so heart-rending, so pitiful—their complete dependence upon the organization which Admiral Kolchak has got together in Siberia to save them from this kind of thing, that it made a profound impression upon the party with me and myself who interviewed these people. And I think it is important to make a statement about this here, because the Socialists in America, and even such formerly reputable magazines as the *New Republic* and the *Nation* are denouncing the present government in Siberia in the worst terms possible, and because their denunciations are so false and so harmful at the present time to the Russian people, I feel it my duty to say here—and I take a solemn oath to it—that the Siberian government as I knew it at Omsk the past six months is a real government, struggling to restore law and order and to secure to the Russian people their rights, which have been completely swept away by Bolshevism. And a man who is opposed to the Siberian government headed by Admiral Kolchak, in my opinion is either grossly misinformed, or else a man who wishes such scenes as these to take place in America."

Mr. Embry declared the actual territory controlled by the Bolsheviki is only one-fifth or one-sixth as large as that controlled by Admiral Kolchak's government. He said further it is the firm conviction of intelligent Russians who studied the situation and have gone through the horror of Bolshevism that less than ten per cent of Russia at the present time is back of the murderous Trotzky-Lenine regime. Kolchak, he explained, is a non-party man and enjoys the confidence and love of the people. Of thirteen members of his government, six are Socialists, the other Social Democrats and constitutionalists. "Knowing these people over there as I do, and knowing the struggle that they are making for freedom from such things as I witnessed in Bellebei, I believe it is the duty of every man who loves liberty to help those people any way we can. You must remember the Bolsheviki got control of all the arms and all the arsenals when they first started their program.

in the Bolshevik government or first regime there, with the intention to mitigate the rigor of this regime. He was a man beloved by all the countryside for his wisdom and kindliness, and the townspeople, when they learned that Judge Famisky had, on the night the Bolsheviki held their monster meeting, made a speech, and through the speech was elected on the spot Minister of Justice, were delighted. The townspeople felt that a Bolshevik Minister of Justice such as Judge Famisky would certainly mete out justice and lead them to a happier kind of life.

"The story of Judge Famisky is a short one. The same day that the Bolsheviki took over power, they started at once a general execution, without trial, of all the men who had been prominent in public life in the district of Bellebei and the town of Bellebei who had not fled. Any man prominent in public life, who did not declare unreservedly in favor of Bolshevism, was put to death without trial in the public square of Bellebei, according to these three judges. These three saved their lives by swearing they were Bolsheviki. Now, Judge Famisky had declared himself a Bolshevik. He had been made Minister of Justice; but when the men who had been his colleagues in the local government in Bellebei were executed without trial by the Bolshevik Extraordinary Investigating Committee, he felt it his duty to make a rigorous protest against these executions. He made his protest almost within twenty-four hours of the time he assumed office. Before that time many of his best friends had been executed. His protest was couched in restrained, but vigorous language, and the Extraordinary Investigating Committee replied by charging the judge with being a counter-revolutionist, and he was thrown in prison and sentenced to be shot. The townspeople made such an uproar about the execution of the mild-mannered judge that the most daring of the Bolshevik leaders were afraid to carry out the sentence. He was held in prison, however, until the Bolsheviki were driven out of Bellebei, just eight days before my arrival there in April, and when the Bolsheviki evacuated the town Judge Famisky was carried away with them, and no one knows what befell him."

BOLSHEVIKI PUT CRIMINALS IN POWER

Just how the Bolsheviki went about seizing power was described to Mr. Embry by the three judges. "The first thing that happened," he said, "was this monster meeting in the town hall, attended by some fifteen hundred soldiers and armed workers, whom these judges described as being the riffraff and criminal classes of Russia, and among them, also, a large number of foreigners, Chinese, and some of the wild tribes of the country. Now these Bolsheviki entered the town and looted part of the city as they came in, but that night they were together in assembly to hold a meeting. During the afternoon and evening the jails were opened and every criminal in the county jail was released and present at the Bolshevik meeting. It was at this meeting that Judge Famisky was made Minister of Justice. The other appointees—you could hardly say they were elected—to various Bolshevik offices were of a different type. One of the men who was made a Bolshevik commissionaire was a criminal released from the Bellebei county jail, whom Judge Blumenthal knew personally and had sentenced to jail for theft the year before. Another minor official was a man of the lowest class of society there in the town who had been put in jail by Judge Blumenthal for drunkenness and for beating his wife."

At the meeting the Bolsheviki, said Mr. Embry, instituted their form of government, with an Executive Committee in absolute power, under which were other committees, including the Extraordinary Investigating Committee whose function was to jail and shoot men and women ruthlessly. People were hauled out of their beds in the middle of the night by soldiers, led by a commisar, accused of being counter-revolutionists, were thrown into jail, and executed without trial. It was after the institution of this reign of terror that these unsavory and blood-thirsty crusaders of "internationalism"—who are hailed by Socialists in America as "emancipators of the world"—desecrated the Christian church at Bellebei, defiled and destroyed the pictures of Christ and the Madonna, and turned the church into a motion picture house, where they played lascivious songs on the gramophone for their regalement.

Telling of his attitude toward Bolshevism when the Bolsheviki had first assumed power after the overthrow of Kerensky, Mr. Embry said:

"All of my life I sympathized with the workingman and the underdog, so to speak, and I believed at that time that the Russian underdog was going to come up, and that possibly there would be worked out in Russia a social experiment which would be of value to the world. I could easily understand why it made a strong appeal to the ignorant man because it not only made a strong appeal to the ignorant man there, but to most of the men, most of the Americans whom I knew there. We were not hostile to the idea, and actually in some of its phases it captured men like myself who had studied Socialism at college and who were sentimentally inclined toward it. And it was only after I had lived in Russia long enough to see what the Russian underdog did when he got on top that I have felt so strongly about it, and why I am happy today to give my testimony against the Bolsheviki."

POWER MAINTAINED BY RUFFIANS

"The revolution of 1917 was brought about by the intelligent Russian people," declared Mr. Embry, "the Russians of good education who were sick and tired of an autocratic regime in Russia. The Bolsheviki had nothing whatever to do with the first Russian revolution. . . . The former members of the Duma," continued Mr. Embry, "for a large part are dead—murdered. Those who are not murdered have fled to foreign countries or have escaped to Siberia or are living in security east of the Ural mountains.

The Soviet form of government under the Bolsheviki, Mr. Embry emphasized, is anything but democratic. "They do not have elections. They do not have anything but a mass meeting at which the more violent may get up and make fiery speeches. Then certain men are elected commissars, and then, first of all, they have the task of dividing up all the property—all the private property—then proceeding to live on the people. They are parasites. The Bolsheviki as I knew them in Russia are the greatest criminal organization the world has ever seen. Nothing that is released from our state penitentiaries would approach in horribleness what the Bolsheviki, the much-praised Bolsheviki-government of Russia is doing today wherever I have come in contact with it. . . . There is a government at Moscow—it calls itself a government. I understand that there are Bolsheviks of intelligence who are idealists to a certain extent. . . . They keep in power by the most predatory and bloodthirsty bunch of ruffians that the world has ever heard of. I do not believe that the Hun, Attila, who sacked Rome, knew anything at all about barbarity in comparison with these supporters of the Bolshevik government."

Asked further to describe the operations of the Bolsheviki, Mr. Embry went on:

"I learned that the Bolshevik method was this: The soldiers and workers have a big meeting at which they decide matters. Then they drive out the members. For instance, I will make a picture as it would be here in New York. If they took over New York, you gentlemen here would be marched out by a bunch of soldiers, and you would be very fortunate if you were not killed at once. At least you would be put in jail. Then this court room would become a Bolshevik meeting, at which everything would be decided by a big crowd of men, each one struggling to give out and carry out his ideas. They would elect a president and executive committee and would try to do things by a committee system, but nothing would be done according to rule."

Having forcibly seized power, the Bolsheviki "declare all the old laws, all the old legal forms, non-existent, no longer valid; the terms 'legal' and 'illegal' have no meaning for them, because it is all a question whether or not it is according to Bolshevik principles, and their principle is to take all property and divide it up." Once they had their executive committee organized, "they would make a list of all available private property, list it up, divide it up, or attempt to do so. These two jobs they consider of paramount importance—taking the private property and dividing it up, and killing everybody opposed to Bolshevism."

BOLSHEVIK PROPAGANDA IN RUSSIA BEFORE REVOLUTION PARALLELS THAT NOW CONDUCTED IN UNITED STATES

Questioned as to his opinion regarding the status of Ludwig C. A. K. Martens, so-called ambassador from the Soviet government to the United States, Mr. Embry said:

"I believe he was actually sent by Lenine, Trotzky and company from Moscow, and that his main duties over here are to foster a Bolshevik revolution in America."

"Why," Mr. Embry was asked by Assemblyman McElligott, "should they concern themselves over there with what happens over here?"

"They know perfectly well that Bolshevism in Russia is doomed unless the rest of the world can go Bolshevik," replied Mr. Embry, "because right-thinking men and women are not going to allow Bolshevism either in America or in Russia. The menace of Bolshevism is a very serious, a very imminent one, in my opinion. They are striking at all our institutions, which up to the present time have given us liberty and the pursuit of happiness. They are determined to overthrow by force, by the murder of innocent people, determined not to wait until they can win by a majority. That means that innocent people all over the world are going to be murdered. That any man who thinks can sit idly by and let the Russian Bolsheviki carry out their program and carry on their propaganda here, is, I believe, very short-sighted, because these men are internationalists; there is no such thing as a nation to them. They are intent on the proletàrian revolution of the world. They have declared from the very beginning that it is a world revolution, a world government; and if we want our homes, if we want the majority to rule in America, we have got to take every step possible to put an end to Bolshevism, because it is not a majority rule."

"Lenine is the man who today is holding himself out as being the head of the so-called Soviet government," Mr. Embry was asked, "and he sent Mr. Martens as his representative to New York?"

"I believe that Mr. Martens was actually sent by Mr. Lenine and Mr. Trotzky. I believe that he is properly authorized by these people to come to America as their envoy."

That the Bolshevik agitation which preceded the overthrow of the Kerensky government was identical with the inflammatory agitation carried in the form of speeches, pamphlets and newspaper articles in this country today by Socialists, the I. W. W. and other radicals, evidence concerning which had been presented at hearings of the Lusk Committee, was declared by Mr. Embry to be a fact. The Lenine theory of Government "is based," said he, "on the principle of Socialist government, and it parallels in my mind what the I. W. W. in the United States call 'direct action.'"

Comparing the Bolshevik propaganda carried on in Russia prior to the revolution with that now being waged in the United States by Socialists and others, Mr. Embry said:

"I believe it was more frank and outspoken in Russia, but the points raised and the methods approved are identical with those which are raised and approved by our agitators in the United States. It was the same sort of thing. I believe it to be parallel."

The Labor Situation Abroad

(Continued from page 15)

what extent that force is to be aggressively employed, what radical economic reorganizations will be demanded through it, what will be the action against it by the government backed by other social forces—these questions suggest crises which the country may possibly be called upon to face. They lead to the vital question: Is Britain's present social system to be overturned by a consolidated mass of men who rightfully or wrongfully are malcontents or is progressive social improvement to come through the operation of legislative methods and ameliorative forces some of which are already important aids in the country's economic life?

The nation's hope is that the cataclysmic strike by the "one big union" may never come. From members of the Triple Alliance itself have come proposals for nationalizing by legitimate means the industries in which its members are engaged. A detailed plan for nationalizing the mines, transmitted to the Coal Commission by an official of one of the miners' unions, was published in full in the newspapers of the time and attracted general attention. Besides, from the Fabian Society another plan was brought forward embodying, it is commonly said, ideas long discussed throughout the kingdom among the moderate Socialists, and the guild Socialists were last spring discussing a third plan, one of mingled compensation and confiscation.

RAILWAY OWNERSHIP BY STATE PROPOSED

The Railway Clerks' Association (80,000 members) have issued the draft of a national transport services bill which makes provision for the purchase by the State of all the railways in the United Kingdom, with canals, hotels, docks, harbors and auxiliary services to the railroads, all to be managed by and for the benefit of the State. The bill and the notes attending it, a considerable document of 57 printed pages, gives numerous particulars of the proposed operation. It also provides for the coordination of road, motor, aerial, coastal and steam packet transport services as part of a national system. Inasmuch as this plan was made up by railway clerks of every grade, many of them concerned in a large way in the operation of the present transport services, it may be regarded as having merits deserving serious attention. When an investigator has heard trade union leaders, men of caution and common sense and a good general knowledge of their occupation, giving reasons for their belief that mines and railroads can be operated by the employees, inclusive of the grade of superintendents and managers, the project appears one entirely different from those brought forward by the old-time visionary theorists bent on nationalizing indiscriminately capital and land—and labor.

For State ownership of railways there is of course ample precedent, but operation by employees become directors and controllers is an untried plan. Since both the miners and the railway men propose compensation to present owners, with continuance of the wage system for the operatives, their outlook contemplates legitimate procedure, non-communistic ownership, and a form of operation in theory democratic.

British trade unionists who are not thoroughgoing Socialists hold that the usual arguments against State operation of commercial or manufacturing enterprises fall off in force when applied to the mines and railroads of the kingdom. They say that arguments which hold good against nationalizing in the United States, with its great area and population and many State governments, do not fit in with conditions in Britain—nor, they say, has land and mine ownership the same validity in Great Britain with the present generation that it has in America. The social abuses to be corrected, especially in regard to housing and harsh treatment, are more acute and more numerous. Both mining and railroad operation have been weighted down through the rack rent and blackmail rent of the British landlords. The majority of the railway workmen of Great Britain have until recently been laboring in servitude at miserable wages. The testimony before the Coal Commission regarding mine workers' living conditions has shocked the British as a nation. Public opinion may be reconciled by the all important fact that the new nationalizers propose that the State shall pay for expropriated property.

The panic over Triple Alliance aggressions last spring came at a time when many people of all classes, chastened by the war, were of a mind to redouble their efforts for the permanent improvement of the country. Everywhere was heard expression of generous and patriotic sentiment. Committees of inquiry on social questions had been at work on the part of the State, the Church and voluntary societies. Their reports uniformly looked forward to a better era. The rights and needs of the workers obtained national attention and recognition. That the colliery or railroad worker should have a voice in the direction of mine and road was a taking thought. Just how that direction was to be exercised, however, was usually a matter left indefinite. The miners and railway men came forward with their own plans.

LABOR PROBLEMS IN GREAT BRITAIN AND FRANCE FOLLOWING THE WAR

The full report of the Commission sent by The National Civic Federation to England and France to study industrial conditions will be published in book form in October. The price of the book, which will contain about 350 pages, will be $2.00. Advance orders may be sent to The National Civic Federation, 1 Madison Avenue, New York City.

The report of the Commission was made from the point of view of the employer, the wage worker and the public, the Federation's Commission being the only one sent abroad since the conclusion of the war which was representative of all these elements. The contributors to the book are Chairman Charles Mayer, of the Commission, who is also chairman of the Board of the France & Canada Steamship Corporation; James W. Sullivan, of the American Federation of Labor; Albert F. Bemis, a well known textile manufacturer of Boston, and A. Parker Nevin, of the New York bar, an authority on industrial problems.

In its investigations the Commission devoted especial attention to the constructive policies and programs adopted abroad affecting the relations of employers and employees, with the object of determining which if any of these might advantageously be applied in the United States.

Blunders Hurt the Irish Cause

By GEORGE CREEL

(By permission of *Leslie's Weekly.*)

GEORGE CREEL

Even if she had the manpower, which she has not, she lacks guns, munitions, aircraft and all the scientific machinery of war. England, crouched over the isle like a lion over a bull terrier, could strike and crush almost in a week. And where, outside of Ireland, is armed force to come from? Not from France and Italy, bled white. Not from Russia, from Spain, from Japan? This leaves the United States as the one possible chance. Does anyone imagine for a moment that the people of America, not yet recovered from the shock and horror of a world war, will take arms against England in Ireland's behalf? Not an Irishman urges it; not even the Sinn Fein leaders themselves, as they admitted to me, even dream of it.

Let us, at this point, consider the position of the United States with reference to this Irish matter. The President is hissed and openly denounced by "Irish patriots" like Mayor Thompson, of Chicago, for having failed to rise, in his place in Paris and make demand that Ireland should be given freedom at once. Now what was it that the President went to Paris to do? He went, primarily as the representative of a belligerent power to sit with the representatives of other belligerent powers, for the purpose of framing the terms of the Peace Treaty that would bring the World War to an end. What would have been the result had he announced to the Conference, "Gentlemen, I refuse to take part in these deliberations until the Irish Republic is given recognition?" Does anyone doubt that England would have risen in hot resentment, or that this resentment would not have been shared by other countries concerned only with the framing of the peace? Chaos would have piled on chaos, and all hope of world order would have perished then and there.

If not at the outset, then at what other time? Had the case of Ireland been introduced, does anyone imagine for a moment that other introductions would not have followed? What about Egypt, India, the Philippines, Morocco, Lithuania, the Ukraine, the Jugoslavs, and scores of other peoples with their claims to liberty and self-determination? These bitternesses ancient and complicated, would have turned the Conference into a Bedlam, no Peace Treaty would have been drawn, or could have been drawn, and the world would have plunged into a bottomless abyss.

It is because these various national and racial appeals were not heeded and considered in detail that the charge is made that the Peace Conference repudiated the pledged principle of self-determination. This is the great lie. The Peace Conference did not repudiate, but kept its faith in the only way that it could keep the faith. Lacking in itself the power and the machinery with which to give any *practical* effect to the principal of self-determination, it created a body that *would* have the power and the machinery, framing and signing the solemn Covenant of the League of Nations.

This body, and this body only, with its high court of international justice, is fitted and planned for dealing with the injustices that imperil the peace of the world. It is before it that the case of Ireland may be presented, aye, and the case of every other oppressed peoples, for the President of the United States framed and secured the insertion of this paragraph in Article XI:

"It is also declared to be the friendly right of each member of the League to bring to the attention of the Assembly or to the Council any circumstances whatsoever affecting international relations which threatens to disturb either the *peace or the good understanding between nations upon which peace depends.*"

There, as plain as language can make it, is the right of the United States to put the matter of Ireland before the League of Nations with the privilege to press it even as counsel presents the cause of a client. Not as an insult to be resented by England, not as an hostile act leading to severed relations and bitter feeling, but as a "friendly right," for what with our large Irish population, continued injustice to Ireland *does* disturb "good understanding."

THE ONLY WAY WE CAN HELP

This—the second of the two ways by which Irish independence can be made a *fact*—is the only way. Until the League of Nations is formed we have no such right. Even as open presentation of the Irish cause at Paris by the President would have entailed chaos, so would any such demand on his part today deal the Irish cause a deadly blow. The great mass of the English people are in favor of Irish freedom. Particularly is this true of the English Labor Party, the coming great force in England's political life. But this sympathy and support would be swept away instantly if racial angers should be aroused by any action on the part of America that the British would have a right to resent as arrogant and autocratic.

Take our own case, for instance. The great mass of public opinion is firmly in favor of independence for the Philippines. But what if the House of Lords passed a resolution urging Philippine independence, or if Lloyd George, rising from his seat at the Peace Conference, had said, "Gentlemen, I cannot go further with the discussion of the peace terms that are to be presented to Germany until the United States has granted the demands of the Filipinos?" Does anyone doubt that America would rise *en masse* and say, "We'll *show* you."

It is a false friend to the Irish cause who races over the country abusing the English people and stirring up hatred against England. In 1912, the House of Commons passed a Home Rule Bill because the English people wanted it passed. Again in 1913 and again in 1914 the measure went through the House of Commons by undiminished majorities, showing that the will of the people had not changed. It was the House of Lords that stood between the English people and their desire to do justice to Ireland; it is the Tory party in England that stands between Ireland and freedom today. This distinction between the Tory party and the English people is a distinction that it is a folly not to make.

A NEW ERA IN ENGLAND

The old order is passing in England. It is only a matter of weeks when the present ramshackle Coalition Government, born of Lloyd George's trades, will be thrown out, ushering in the dawn of a new order. The leaders of this new order are Ireland's friends, pledged to do her justice. Is it wise to anger, insult and alienate them?

Out of my own personal knowledge, I say that Woodrow Wilson has always been a steadfast champion of the Irish cause. He is that today. The trouble is that he is for the Irish *cause* and not Irish applause. Had he chosen to come out with some Irish demand at Paris he would have been selling Ireland's hopes for his own personal glory. Not only would he have ruined America's opportunity as a force for idealism, not only would the action have aroused domestic revolt because of the disruption of the peace proceedings, but he would have arrayed the English people as a unit against the Irish demands.

As it is, English opinion is still with the Irish, and increasingly so as the unspeakable Carson raves and threatens; the power of the President to exert pressure upon the English Government remains unabated, and the League of Nations provides a court in which the Irish case may be brought unless it is settled before that time.

ANOTHER DANGER FOR IRELAND

There is still another false and dangerous position in which the Irish movement is being placed by its reckless leadership. This is the movement's antagonism to the League of Nations as a whole, not because of anything that it does to America, but because of what it is supposed *not* to do for Ireland. The attack is made by reason of Article X, which provides that the "members of the League undertake to respect and preserve as against external aggression the territorial integrity and existing political independence of all members of the League." This Article was framed to protect the new States like Poland and Czechoslovakia, and to guard against the rapacities of power, the lusts of conquest. It is not concerned in any manner with internal revolution, redress of popular grievances by insurrection, or even against a readjustment of national boundaries by action from the inside.

This is the danger, however; the Irish movement is being put in the position of refusing to view the League of Nations in any other light than the false light of this lie. It is being made to appear that Americans of Irish birth and descent have no interest in the proposal at all except as it bears upon Ireland. Whether there is good for America in the Covenant, whether there is good in it for the world, matters nothing. It is supposed to prejudice Ireland in a minute particular, therefore it must be defeated. The world's attempt to substitute arbitral processes for wholesale slaughter, to lessen the backbreaking burden of competitive armaments, to raise the standard of workers the world over, all these things are contemptuously swept aside because Ireland is not pleased.

This is bad business. Not only is it angering the native American, but it will split the Irish movement itself into bits, for the Irishman in America is an American *first*. Nothing is more imperative than that the Irish movement be rescued instantly from the hands of pro-Germans, partisans, anti-English schemers and others who are attempting to use it for their own selfish ends.

If I have written critically it is because I believe passionately in the absolute justice of Ireland's cause and want to see it *win*. I am for Irish independence because I am an American. And because I am an American I not only want to see Ireland free, but the freedom of all oppressed peoples. And the League of Nations is the *machinery for the manufacture of world justice*.

Since I am taking this adventure in unpopularity for what I honestly believe to be the good of the cause, it is just as well to say everything that is in my heart to say. Whatever may have been the mistakes of judgment of men like John Redmond, T. P. O'Connor and John Dillon, however much they may have been tricked, they were *true Irishmen*. And then Ireland's great need today is absolute unity; it is worse than stupid to hate and hiss the Nationalists instead of holding out an olive branch for them to grasp.

From Ireland also come reports that a ban of exclusion has been placed upon all Irishmen who fought under the British flag in the late war. Thousands of these young fellows joined the Dublin revolution, even before England repudiated the Home Rule Law, just as did Tom Kettle, who fell at Ginchy. They never dreamed that the English Tories would cheat Ireland in such a moment of world stress. And there is this to be remembered also. While they fought under England's banner, it is equally the case that they fought side by side with *Americans* against a common foe.

All such hates must be banished. Victory is in sight. And if Ireland is to stand straight among the nations, she needs every ounce of strength that fraternity can contribute.

MR. VILLARD'S MISDIRECTED GRATITUDE

THE NATION
20 Vesey St.
New York

June 14, 1919.

MR. T. EVERETT HARRÉ,
C/o The National Civic Federation Review,
New York City.

My dear sir:

May I not express to you the gratitude that we of *The Nation* feel for your persistent advertising of us in THE NATIONAL CIVIC FEDERATION REVIEW—giving space to us which on an advertising basis would cost us hundreds and hundreds of dollars? To it we attribute somewhat our rapidly swelling subscription list and our steady growth in readers. Nothing, we are sure, can help *The Nation* more than to have it known so clearly that we are in many ways at the opposite extreme of the Civic Federation.

With renewed thanks,

Yours truly,
(Signed) OSWALD GARRISON VILLARD,
Editor.

June 19, 1919.

MR. OSWALD GARRISON VILLARD,
Editor *The Nation*,
20 Vesey Street, New York.

Dear Sir:

I have your letter of June 14, expressing "gratitude" for the "advertising" given *The Nation* in THE NATIONAL CIVIC FEDERATION REVIEW, to which, I note, you somewhat ascribe your "rapidly swelling subscription list." I am inclined to believe that your reported "steady growth in readers" is not due to the analysis of your articles made in the pages of the REVIEW—which mainly reaches readers who believe in the ideals and institutions of America and who loyally stood back of the war until the power of the intolerable Hun was broken—but that, on the contrary and quite manifestly, it is due to the "persistent advertising", to the generous and approving reprinting of your articles in the scrubby sheet formerly known as *The Fatherland*, and that your thanks, therefore, are not due to me or THE NATIONAL CIVIC FEDERATION REVIEW, but to that fellow-colleague and pacifist, whose heart also bleeds because of the cruel Allied blockade and the Allied "injustices" to poor, inoffensive, stricken Germany, Mr. George Sylvester Viereck.

One so well-informed as yourself cannot, of course, be ignorant of the intensified resumption, and new phase, of the Hun propaganda; of the recent voting by the German National Assembly at Weimar of indefinite sums for "a news service abroad;" of the threat of chagrined and hydrophobiac Germany to employ the "new weapons" offered by Bolshevism against her victors; of the propaganda of social discontent and civil strife which has been stimulated

The National
Civic Federation Review

Vol. IV. NEW YORK, SEPTEMBER 30, 1919 No. 19

OUR PARAMOUNT PROBLEMS

CONSTRUCTIVE MEASURES FOR SOLVING EXISTING SOCIAL AND INDUSTRIAL UNREST DISCUSSED BY LEADERS AT NOTABLE MEETING HELD BY THE NATIONAL CIVIC FEDERATION

WITH industrial disturbances existing throughout the nation as an inevitable part of the aftermath of war, with strikes threatening to tie up great industries which vitally affect the life of the nation, with the police and other public service employees seeking to unionize and going on strike, and with various panaceas—many extremely radical and striking at the foundations of organized society—being offered, more than ordinary interest attaches to the meetings held on September 11 by The National Civic Federation in the rooms of the Merchants' Association, in the Woolworth building, New York City. This meeting, consisting of two sessions, was attended by more than 250 representative leaders of employers, labor and the public. Problems relating to labor unrest, municipal ownership and profit sharing plans, the unionization of policemen and other public service employees, and other matters foremost in the public interest, were discussed by men familiar with the conditions and difficulties of the time, men whose business it is to deal with those problems, and whose chief concern is the solution of problems almost if not as great as the problems of the war. With President Wilson to call a conference in October, consisting of delegates representing manufacturers, bankers, agricultural organizations and labor, to deal with these very subjects, there will be found in the discussion at The National Civic Federation conference suggestions of immediate constructive value.

While the various speakers may have disagreed in regard to certain matters, such as the right of policemen to organize, profit sharing, etcetera, there was presented in the course of the discussion the basis of a workable program for the stabilizing of industry and the adjustment of differences by an extension of the principles of arbitration, by a recognition by big corporations of the principle of collective bargaining, by the practical working out of some plan of sharing with workers surplus profits, and for the solving of the high cost of living by increased production.

The strikes of policemen in Boston and elsewhere provided an illustration of the imperative need of prompt action, and a resolution was passed providing that a special committee be appointed by the Civic Federation to make a study of the problems involved in the organization of unions among policemen, firemen and other public service employees. The question as to whether or not England and France had learned anything in their dealings with so-called capital and labor problems during the war that might be helpful to employers and employees in the United States was answered by James W. Sullivan, of the American Federation of Labor, and A. Parker Nevin, who reported for the commission sent by the Civic Federation to study industrial conditions abroad.

In the absence abroad of Alton B. Parker, president of The National Civic Federation, Samuel Gompers was to preside, but was unable to do so because of the death of his father. Charles S. Barrett, president of the Farmers' Educational and Cooperative Union, which represents three million farmers, therefore acted as permanent chairman. The other speakers included Matthew Woll, George W. Perkins, Lewis Nixon, Wheeler P. Bloodgood, Meyer Bloomfield, Sir Charles Ross, Emerson McMillin, T. V. O'Connor, Rev. John A. Ryan, of the Roman Catholic University of Washington, D. C., Angus S. Hibbard, Ralph M. Easley and Patrick J. McNabb. Eloquent tributes to the work and character of John Mitchell were paid by Louis B. Schram, who made a motion for the preparation of a suitable resolution of regret on Mr. Mitchell's death, and by Timothy Healy and August Belmont, who both seconded the motion.

A. F. OF L. DISCOURAGES GOVERNMENT EMPLOYEES FROM STRIKING

Matthew Woll, president of the Photo-Engravers' International Union and eighth vice president of the American Federation of Labor, who spoke for Mr. Gompers, in opening the meeting, discussed the strike of the Boston policemen. Mr. Woll said in part:

"The difficulty in Boston is not due to anything left undone on the part of the American Federation of Labor to maintain peace and tranquility in that great metropolis. The attitude of the American Federation of Labor is that all workers, whether in private employment or employed by municipalities, states or governments, have the right to organize, and should, to pro-

MATTHEW WOLL

CHARLES S. BARRETT

GEORGE W. PERKINS

REV. JOHN A. RYAN

tect their mutual interests. The attitude of the American Federation of Labor is clear on that subject, that all wage earners, regardless of the character of their employment, have the right to associate with each other and collectively seek to improve their condition. The American Federation of Labor, however, has distinguished in the procedure by which grievances should be remedied, and by which improvements might come to the particular class of men, between those of government, municipal, state and national employment, and those engaged in private employment.

"The American Federation of Labor discourages all government employees from striking. The American Federation of Labor cannot tell any body of men not to strike, nor direct any body to strike. The American Federation of Labor as such has no authority over matters of that kind. But it does urge as guidance to all public employees that they should not revert to strike. Indeed, I know that in the granting of the charter of the Fire Fighters Union, with which I had something to do, it was clearly understood when the charter was granted that these men would not resort to strikes, but employ petitions and all the other political channels to attain improvement of conditions, and that the American Federation of Labor would give them assistance in that direction. That is equally true with the police.

"On the general situation, of course, the great war through which we have passed has rent asunder all former relations, customs, and concepts of relations that prevailed. We have had four years of time devoted entirely to destruction. We are now in a period of reconstruction. The problems confronting us now are equally as complex and perplexing, if not more so, than were the problems of the war. The problems are large and varied. During the war the great thing which was held forth was that of making the world safe for democracy. I believe that we have destroyed political autocracy. I believe we have made the world safe for democracy from a political standpoint, but we have not attained the degree of industrial democracy which should exist in the relations of men.

JAMES W. SULLIVAN

IMPRACTICABILITY OF PROFIT SHARING

"Profit sharing, I am convinced, is impracticable, even though operated absolutely sincerely and honestly by all concerned. On the other hand, we have movements on the part of the workers which are pronounced in the terms of industrial democracy, which do not coincide with the American Federation of Labor's conception of industrial democracy, namely, the changing of society from its present state as a unit to the shop as a unit. I allude to the Soviet form of government. Then, of course, we have the I. W. W.—men who believe in using the economic power, or direct action, to influence political action, aside from industrial relationship, and also we have the movement of socialism—all parading under the guise of democracy. And yet they don't measure up to that democracy proclaimed by that great American, Abraham Lincoln—'a government of the people, by the people and for the

AUGUST BELMONT

LOUIS B. SCHRAM

WHEELER P. BLOODGOOD

T. V. O'CONNOR

MEYER BLOOMFIELD

al France by The National Civic Federation study industrial conditions. Mr. Nevin said:

"Yesterday, in the City of Glasgow, the British Trades Union Congress, by a vote of 4,447,‑0 against a vote of 77,000, passed a resolution n favor of the nationalization of Great Britain's oal industry. The Congress also passed a resolution to the effect that in the event of the British Government continuing to refuse to enact gislation for the nationalization of the coal inustry, a further Congress should be called to onsider ways and means by which the government would be forced to take such action. This ction taken yesterday was the formal culmination of the discussion of the question of nationalizing the British coal industry, which your Comnisson last March saw the beginning of.

NATIONALIZATION VS. SOCIALISM

"I am not going to discuss this morning the erits of nationalizing British coal. I want to alk, however, on the consequence of the action f the Trades Union Congress to which I have ust referred. Great Britain, as we know, has ad cross-currents of decidedly socialistic tenency, but in London when we were there last pring we did not hear the word 'socialism' used ery much. We did hear the word 'nationalism' sed, and 'nationalization'. Now, I leave it to ou to make any distinction that you care to beween the nationalization of an industry and the ocialization of an industry. It may mean the ame thing; it may mean different things. I am ot quite clear in my own mind what the distincion is, but I am perfectly clear in my own mind hat the tendency is; because we have seen by his resolution, to which I have referred, British rganized labor taking this position—insisting pon the transfer of the basic industry of Great Britain from private ownership, to not joint ownership, not trusteeship, but to governmental ownership, under joint control of management, however. Was that the wisest action for British labor to take? How will it be regarded by labor in this country? How are we to interpret that momentous decision taken yesterday in the City of Glasgow? Will the government of Great Britain accede? Will it reject? If it accepts there is a new principle in operation in Great Britain's industry, a new principle affecting both employers, employees, and the public,—a principle which, I take it, the vast majority of labor in this country has been enthusiastically contending for.

"What is that tendency toward the nationalization, the ownership of industry, going to result in? Are we going to follow it in this country? Are we going to demand that not only our transportation systems, but also our basic industries, and our related industries shall become nationalized? If we do that we have abandoned absolutely the principle of the industrial system upon which our great country has so far lasted. If we favor as an operating principle of modern industry the state control of our industrial forces, by so admitting we overturn the entire principle of employment, of employers, and of employees, and of the exclusiveness of private property.

CHAOTIC BRITISH LABOR CONDITIONS

"The chief economic question we observed when we were in England was the failure of the resumption of full production, and until that production is made, not only for the vacuum created during the war, but for the present conditions over there, there will be high prices and general disorganization of industry.

"We found in Great Britain, in my judgment, a more tolerant attitude between the representatives of organized labor and the representatives of organized employers than exists in this country. They were willing to meet and discuss plans of action by which there could be perhaps evolved better industrial relations. I won't say we didn't find greater stubbornness on the part of employers, but we found a more willingness to at least listen to what the other man had to say before denouncing him in advance. We found the forces of labor, however, as I stated before, divided between various schools of belief. We did not find British labor as such distinctly and positively standing for any one thing. And we certainly did not find the combined forces of British manufacturers standing for any one or two stated principles. It was all mixed up.

"I think the fundamental trouble in Great Britain and also in the United States at the present time is this: That consciously or unconsciously we have got industrial neurasthenia. We are on our nerves. We are upset. We are not seeing very straight and not acting very straight. It is a natural reaction of the great war. We are looking more at the things than at the people running the things. I think we get in a confused condition of mind and fail to see how we can treat these questions with composure. If we are going to get machine guns out in the street and kill one another and denounce everybody, we are having a re-enactment of the war, we are having industrial war. But we are not going to get anywhere by those methods. If there ever was a time in the history of American industry, and particularly so far as labor is concerned, when you want

(*Continued on page 13*)

ANGUS S. HIBBARD

PATRICK J. McNABB

LEWIS NIXON

The Industrial Situation Abroad Following the War

The report of the Commission sent by The National Civic Federation to Great Britain and France to study industrial conditions has been completed, and abridgments of the chapter by Albert Farwell Bemis, who represented the employers, on "The Housing and Land Problem in Great Britain," and by Andrew Parker Nevin, who represented the interests of the public, on "Public Opinion and Labor in Great Britain," are here published in abridged form.

Mr. Bemis' is the fifth in a series of reproductions of the more important chapters of the report, in abridged form, Mr. Sullivan's contribution having appeared in the previous issue of The National Civic Federation Review.

Mr. Bemis is President of Bemis Bro. Bag Co. of Boston, and is connected with several other important textile companies. He has for many years been a member of the Board of Government of the National Association of Cotton Manufacturers, and was President of this organization for two years. He is also Treasurer of the National Council of American Cotton Manufacturers, and a member of the National Industrial Conference Board. Mr. Bemis is a graduate of the Massachusetts Institute of Technology, and has given special study to the subjects of industrial relations and housing.

The Chairman of The National Civic Federation's Commission was Charles Mayer, chairman of the Board of the France & Canada Steamship Corporation. Besides Mr. Bemis and Mr. Nevin, the other members were James W. Sullivan, who represented labor; Charles S. Barrett, President of the Farmers' Educational and Co-operative Union of America; Grant Forbes, of the American International Corporation, and E. A. Quarles, secretary.

THE HOUSING AND LAND PROBLEM IN GREAT BRITAIN

V.

LONG wars usually bring housing problems. The condition after the Napoleonic wars has been thus described:

"The building of houses was so discouraged that the consumption of bricks and glass was actually declining. . . . There was a tax on windows, which yielded a million and a quarter annually, and which caused the building up of windows, and a consequent shutting out of sunlight, to the serious diminution of human comfort and health."

"There was no drainage, and the filth of the city lay festering on the streets, poisoning the unhappy people."

In France the houses destroyed and damaged beyond ordinary repairs within the devastated area may be taken as the measure of the present shortage. This would approximate 410,000 homes. In Great Britain 450,000 would probably represent the actual need.

Strange as it may seem, the conditions of the war have inspired among all classes of people a greater interest in humanity, and a greater regard for the physical and social conditions under which the masses of the population live. During the war the people of Great Britain and France became accustomed to the handling of large national problems by direct governmental action. For this reason and because of the size and extent of the problem, it is natural to find the governments of both countries adopting measures for fostering individual and associated interest in and the subsidizing of improved industrial and community housing, and the prompt building of modern homes for workers.

In both Great Britain and France, there has been a distinct revival of interest in agriculture as the result of the war, and, partly in fear of emigration, both governments have been taking steps toward improving agricultural lands and opening up additional areas for the growing of food and feed stuffs. Whereas the number of schemes having to do with the carrying on of this work is great, actual accomplishment so far has been small.

BUILDING COST NOW ON PARITY

Prior to the war, a house which, in Great Britain or France would have cost $2,000 would have footed up about $3,000 in the United States. As a result of the war, more radical advances have taken place in Europe than in America, and the present cost of building in both Great Britain and France is about three times the pre-war cost while that in America is approximately double. This puts America on an approximate parity with these two countries, and the house above mentioned would cost practically $6,000 in all three countries.

ALBERT F. BEMIS

In Great Britain practically all dwelling houses, wherever situated, are of solid masonry construction—stone or brick—and, save in the cities, are without cellars or basements. There is no air space for insulation against temperature and moisture, and the inside plastering is placed directly on the surface. The flooring is usually of brick, tile or stone. The water supply is generally limited to an outside tap. Even in the rather attractive Liverpool tenements, built by the municipality in 1885, there are no direct water or sewer connections, both being located in the hallways outside and for the use of two to four families. Most of the workmen's tenements in Great Britain are without yard space. The heating is from open fires, and the window spaces are, in general, rather small.

GOOD EXAMPLES OF MODERN HOUSING

The description above applies to the houses of twenty-five or more years ago, and these comprise by far the greater portion. There are, however, several recent community and industrial developments, such as those at Letchworth, England and Bourneville, where there are fine examples of modern housing. The two first mentioned were built and managed by cooperative societies. At Bourneville, which I consider the queen of all England's industrial towns, private enterprise did the building but later turned it over to the public to administer. In Liverpool the municipal corporation, after wiping out numerous slums, has substituted much fine modern city housing.

The solid masonry of the older type of houses makes it difficult though not impossible, to introduce modern conveniences. With few exceptions the housing of industrial workers of Great Britain is in towns and cities which have preceded the industrial plants, and rarely has housing been constructed as an integral part of an industrial plant.

A noticeable feature in the finish of the front doorways of most of the recent industrial tenements in Liverpool is that the locks and latches are of brass. Commenting on this feature, Mr. Turtin, Director of Housing, said that the condition of the "handle of the big front door" largely depicted the condition within the house. By this simple device the work of inspection was made easier, for these door latches represent the degree of orderliness of the tenants and at the same time give opportunity for the force of example to exert itself.

MINING HOUSING BAD

The mining industry is one in which employers have provided housing to the extent of about thirty-three and one-third per cent. While this has not been the cause of the low standard of housing conditions in the mining regions, it has brought severe criticism upon the mine owners, and has justly tended to fasten upon the employers a large measure of obligation for decent living quarters in industries forming practically the only productive business in their immediate section. Both because of the dirty and continuous nature of the work, and the limited scope for the satisfactory grouping of dwellings in the proximity of the mines, living conditions in this industry have vied with the slums of the big cities in over-crowding, dirtiness and ill health. Mining towns are sure to receive particular attention in Great Britain's immediate housing program.

Labor's demands in Great Britain at the present time are anomalous. On the one hand the cry is for shorter hours, and on the other for increased wages and better and more houses. The enormous waste of war materials has impressed large masses of wage-earners with the idea that there is no limit to the resources of the State. They wonder why houses could not be provided at an expense of, say, fifty million pounds annually, if the Government can afford to spend twenty-five or fifty times that amount on the prosecution of the war. They fail to appreciate that the country has been living for the past four years on her capital, and that a continuance of that policy for much longer would result in national bankruptcy. It is not easy for the wage-workers to understand that by a doubling of nominal wages in the building trades the nominal cost of houses, and hence nominal rentals must inevitably double if Capital, however owned, is to continue to provide homes for the individual.

LUXURIES COST WOULD BUILD HOUSES

A prominent authority has estimated that from ten to twenty thousand rich persons spend unnecessarily in luxuries each year in Great Britain fifty million pounds or more. If, through large taxes on luxuries or an amplification of the existing graduated income tax, sums heretofore spent in this way, and the labor employed in manufacturing and distribution, could be diverted to the building of houses, the country's problem would be quickly solved.

Modern housing legislation in Great Britain commenced with the "Laboring Classes Lodging Houses Act" of 1851. Material amplification was made in 1875, and there was a gradual betterment in the laws which culminated in 1890, when the "Housing of the Working Classes Act" was passed. This consolidated the housing measures in all previous acts, and included new provisions.

In 1879 George Cadbury, the great cocoa manufacturer, started the development of the village of Bourneville. In 1869 the city of Liverpool opened its first tenement building. In 1895 the then Sir William Lever founded Port Sunlight. In 1899 the Garden City Association was founded, and in 1906 the National Housing Reform Council was set up, to be followed in 1909 with "The Housing and Town Planning Act", a further amplification of the statute of 1890. It established a system of nation-wide housing inspection under the sanitary authorities, reporting to the Local Government Board, and extended and amplified the policy of national Government aid. Local authorities were permitted to borrow from the Public Works Loan Commissioner on the security of their local for land and 60 years for buildings. Developments by societies, corporations and individuals, subject to certain limitations, might be aided financially through the Public Works Loan Board under essentially the same terms as local government schemes. The needs of individual workers were met by the "Small Dwellings Acquisition Act" of 1899, which permits local authorities to advance sums of not more than £300, representing not more than four-fifths the market value of a house whose total value must not exceed £400.

THIRTY-FIVE MILLION INVESTED IN HOUSING

Up to 1916, 528,742 persons had been housed in England through constructive housing legislation, and £7,640,597 had been invested by the national government in housing. Model dwellings on cleared slum areas in London showed a decrease in the death rate of from 40 to 13 in the thousand. In Port Sunlight, just outside Liverpool, seven-year-old boys average two and seven-tenths inches taller and seven and one-half pounds heavier than those in Liverpool itself.

As the local government of Scotland is quite distinct from that of England and Wales, housing and town planning legislation for that country has been through entirely separate acts of Parliament. These follow fairly closely the lines already referred to, and they need not be considered here.

Recent legislation in Great Britain indicates a tendency to limit or control rentals even to the extent of subsidizing the business from the public revenues. It is doubtful, however, whether this latter tendency will persist, because, as an economic proposition, it is clear that the Government cannot subsidize all industries and businesses without precipitating insolvency.

HOUSING MOVEMENT EXPEDITED

With a view to avoiding unnecessary delay in meeting the extensive housing needs of the nation, the Local Government Board of Great Britain, on February 6, 1919, offered to local authorities and Public Utility Societies virtually the same measures and plan of Government financial assistance as those contemplated by proposed new legislation, and since included in the Government housing bills. Loans thus made by the Government are to be liquidated by annuity payments over a period not exceeding fifty years, and would be issued up to three-quarters of the total value, and include a plan similar to that of Government subsidies to the extent of twenty-five percent of total value as contemplated in pending legislation, with the additional provision, however, in the case of Public Utility Societies that "any profits of the Society in excess of 6 per cent shall be devoted in whole or in part as may be required by the Local Government Board towards the repayment of sums received from the Exchequer by way of subsidy during the currency of the loan."

The Government has appointed a new official in connection with housing known as the Director of Propaganda. It will be his duty to arouse and maintain general interest in housing matters, and it is proposed that he work through a subordinate attached to each of the thirteen regional commissioners.

Financial assistance to local authorities is to be calculated on a basis estimated to relieve these of the burden of any annual deficit in expenses of operation to the extent of the excess in the local tax "rates" of a penny on the pound, assessable against the area in question. There is to be no donation by Government towards the cost where the annual excess of expenditure over income would not exceed that amount. It is estimated that the capital expenditure by Government during the three years of its proposed assistance would amount to £300,000,000 for England and Wales, based upon an average capital cost per house of £600, and the net deficit to be met out of public funds on account of subsidies to Public Utility Societies, and contributions toward the cost of operation in the case of developments by local authorities, would amount to £6,500,000. Similar figures for Scotland would be £39,000,000 capital expenditure and £845,000 net deficit.

1936 SCHEMES SUBMITTED UP TO MAY 31

A total of 1936 schemes had been submitted up to May 31 by 660 local authorities and 36 Public Utility Societies, under the plans for Government assistance described above. The total area of the sites covered by these schemes was 25,000 acres, and the number of houses 250,000. Five hundred and seventy-four sites covering 13,364 houses for the approval of house plans had been received, of which 107 applications, providing for 5,201 houses, had been provided.

Reference has already been made to the "Small Holdings and Allotments Act." This gives power to county officials, acting under the Board of Agriculture and Fisheries, to acquire land for lease or sale on easy terms, to those desiring to settle upon and cultivate it. Operations under this law have been comparatively small, involving loans by the national Government in the years preceding the war of approximately £5,000,000.

With a view to meeting the demands of demobilized soldiers who want to acquire small agricultural properties, the Government has introduced into Parliament two measures known as the "Acquisition of Land Bill" for improving and clarifying laws governing the condemnation and acquisition of land for public purposes, and the "Land Settlement Bill." Under these, County Councils would be given increased authority in the acquisition of land for development into small agricultural holdings which would be financed by loans from the national Government, authorized through the Public Works Loan Board, with guarantee to the County Councils against a loss in capital investment occurring within a period of seven years. The Settlement Bill not only contemplates the sale of land, but the operation of colonies under the supervision of the Department of Agriculture and Fisheries for the training of agriculturists and the forming of co-operative organizations for the distribution and sale of farm products.

Public Opinion and Labor in Great Britian

THE following is the reproduction in abridged form of a report by Andrew Parker Nevin, of the New York bar, who represented the interests of the American public on the Commission recently sent abroad by The National Civic Federation to study industrial conditions. This is the sixth and last in a reproduction of the more important chapters of the report in abridged form.

Mr. Nevin is a graduate of Princeton University, and was for many years General Counsel for the National Association of Manufacturers. During the war he was a member of the Committee on Labor, Council of National Defense, of which Committee Samuel Gompers was Chairman. He was particularly active in the work of the American Fund for French Wounded. He has long been an interested observer of the relations of capital and labor, and has delivered many addresses on industrial and economic topics.

VI.

NO observer of industrial development will deny that the public is becoming a larger integral factor in the labor equation of the day. Employers and workers appreciate this significant fact. Both groups seek to enlist public opinion in support of their respective issues, in the hope that they may be sustained in the positions taken. The interest of the public is, therefore, associated vitally with the vast and complicated problems in which the employing and employed groups are at present so deeply immersed. The public has a very direct interest in most controversies between capital and labor from the very fact that a large majority of the people as a whole is concerned with the cost of the commodities which the public consumes.

While there is evidence that the public is taking an increased interest in such controversies, a greater increase of the best thought of the more progressive nations could be given to the formulation of plans whereby the interests of the consumer could be more adequately safeguarded in the strife that seems inevitably to arise between capital and labor. This is particularly true of the salaried and wage earning classes, whose income is more or less fixed, and who, particularly since the outbreak of the war, have been called upon to pay a constantly increasing price for the necessaries of life.

BRITISH ATTITUDE MORE ALERT

The arena of British industry being small and concentrated, public opinion can shed its light on a given problem with almost the pencilled illumination of a searchlight. That opinion in Great Britain, in its attitude toward the labor problem, is more active, responsive and alert than in the United States, is the opinion of the writer. Against this observation, however, it may be advanced in friendly criticism that the methods, plans and procedure adopted by the public are more complicated and less effective than corresponding agencies in the United States. Public opinion placed a very important part in the ver-

(Continued on page 17)

Great Leaders of the Union Labor Movement

By W. C. ROBERTS

COMPILER OF THE AMERICAN FEDERATION OF LABOR HISTORY, ENCYCLOPEDIA AND REFERENCE BOOK

In the previous issue of THE NATIONAL CIVIC FEDERATION REVIEW *was begun an article giving briefly the history of some of the men who helped make the American Federation of Labor. That article included sketches of James Duncan, president of the Granite Cutters' International Union and First Vice-President of the American Federation of Labor; Joseph F. Valentine, President of the Iron Moulders' International Union and Second Vice-President of the American Federation of Labor; William D. Mahon, President of the Amalgamated Association of Street and Electric Railway Employees and Fifth Vice-President of the American Federation of Labor; Matthew Woll, President of the Photo-Engravers' International Union and Eighth Vice-President of the American Federation of Labor; and Daniel J. Tobin, President of the International Brotherhood of Teamsters and Treasurer of the American Federation of Labor. Following are sketches of a number of other men who stood with Samuel Gompers in making the American Federation of Labor what it is, and who did splendid work as chairmen or secretaries at the notable convention in Atlantic City.*

GEORGE W. PERKINS

GEORGE W. PERKINS

President Cigarmakers' International Union

In all movements benefiting mankind are found men who never seek the limelight, who feel that a good act accomplished for others is well repaid by the joy it gives. The labor movement has such a character in George W. Perkins, who has been president of the Cigarmakers' International Union since 1891. In that time, as editor of the *Cigarmakers' Journal*, he has persistently urged a better standard of living for all the people, and month after month has given practical remedies for conditions in which he found causes for protest.

There is no hypocrisy in Perkins. He is a cool, deliberate, earnest thinker, and cannot be "rattled" or driven off the path he believes to be right by any force or influence. Under the laws of the cigarmakers, until recently delegates to the American Federation of Labor had to be elected by referendum vote. While entitled to contest for the position, he held that as he was president he should not attempt to hold another office while so many members held none. He therefor never submitted his name as a candidate. But in 1912 the international union convention made him a delegate by virtue of office, and he has served ever since.

In 1913 Mr. Perkins was sent as a delegate to the International Secretariat at Zurich. While in Europe he visited many countries and made a careful analysis of labor conditions. His report was exhaustive and exposed the dreadful conditions under which many workers of Europe lived. He showed conditions were so much lower in standard than in the United States that the people of this nation were astonished. His report proved a stunning blow to the German propagandists, who had set up the Fatherland as the Paradise of workers.

So complete and illuminating was this report that Mr. Perkins has been appointed chairman of the committee on international labor relations at all American Federation of Labor conventions since. The reports made by that committee have had much to do with keeping the American labor movement safe from courses fraught with irreparable havoc.

In the last convention, Perkins showed up a dangerous propaganda on part of the radicals, who were persistently discussing what had passed during the war and who obdurately refused to consider what was best for the future. It was soon found that these delegates and outsiders were trying to divert the American Federation of Labor away from its reconstruction plans into criticism of the war, of the methods followed, and of the grievances of individuals against either government officials or officers in the army. Groups of these disturbers gathered here and there on the boardwalk and poured their venom into the ears of every one who would listen. When the committee on international labor relations made its report, which was written by Perkins, this stand was announced as a repudiation of the Socialists and pro-Germans who sought to use the American Federation of Labor:

"The past is gone forever. Autocracy and militarism, we hope, are buried with it. The future is our immediate concern. Ignoring what has gone before except so far as the lessons taught, we shall build along the lines of reason, judgment and the experiences gained."

This was a setback to the radicals, who died hard when the report was debated. This is only an instance of the care that must be used by committees in safeguarding the Federation from its foes within. It is not always possible to tell what motives or outside influences are behind some of the resolutions presented. The trained labor leader, who seeks only the good of mankind, who sinks his own desires and individuality for the common good, generally pries out the stranger in the woodpile. But it requires a long apprenticeship as a labor leader to be able thus to distinguish between the propositions presented.

This one incident may show clearly what responsibility rests on the chairmen of committees. But Perkins has had a most remarkable training. The Knights of Labor sought to destroy the Cigarmakers' International Union away back in 1887. It failed because trade unionism was too firmly established in the minds of the workers. Then the Socialist Labor party began a warfare upon the international in 1894 that brought to the surface all the talent necessary for the Socialists' defeat. Perkins came through these struggles with his union intact.

JOHN P. FREY

JOHN P. FREY

Editor of the International Molders' Journal

Publicity is labor's most effective weapon. To get before the great reading public the true story of labor is always difficult. Because of this fact, it is to be considered a case of good luck to labor that scattered here and there throughout the nation are men who never lose an opportunity to point out the good in life secured by the organized labor movement. These men are the history-makers for labor.

Among the labor editors who are always looking for an opportunity to advance the cause of Labor is John P. Frey, editor of the *Molders' Journal*. For years his literary work has been prolific. He also goes into colleges to combat the sophistry of those professors of political economy who have tried to corrupt the youth of the land with disloyal teachings.

As a member and secretary of the committee on resolutions of the American Federation of Labor conventions Mr. Frey has proved a wise and capable teacher of what is needed to better the methods of the organization. He has been a deep student of the injunction and judicial processes. His advice, because of this knowledge, has proved valuable in times when cautious judgment is necessary.

Mr. Frey has been one of the most earnest leaders in the agitation for more and better educational opportunities for the growing children of the nation. No question requiring the strictest analysis has been too difficult for him to solve.

When the pacifist intrigues among the labor forces of England, France and Italy seemed to be growing in strength and the war was at its most critical stage, the real labor men of those countries urged President Gompers to send a labor commission to Europe to save the situation. President Gompers named Frey as one of the members of the commission. Those who read his report at the 1918 convention will not wonder at his selection. It was a masterpiece, recounting the remarkable work accomplished in presenting the ideas of American workers to the war-weary people of Europe.

Our slogan was that "there can be no peace without victory." This encouraged the working people of those lands and inspired them to a new effort for success.

Frey always has planned greater publicity for the labor movement. In 1910 he proposed that a weekly news letter should be printed to get Labor's side before the public, as an effective

THOMAS A. RICKERT

MRS. SARA A. CONBOY

WILLIAM GREEN

instrument to further the cause. The results proved he was right.

In 1916 he proposed that a Year Book should be published, and in 1917 the Buffalo convention again endorsed the proposition. In compiling the Year Book it was found that a history covering only one year would be impracticable. It was therefore decided, with Frey's approval, to make it a more elaborate work, and when completed he said it surpassed his expectations, containing more information than he thought could be put between two covers. It will thus be seen that Editor Frey's agitation for further vehicles for advancing the cause of labor have proved most fruitful. His part in the labor movement has been varied, but in every angle can be seen the results of his advice and handiwork.

SARA A. CONBOY

Secretary Textile Workers of America

The women of America are fortunate in having such a splendid representative in American Federation of Labor conventions as Sara A. Conboy. As a leader of her sex for many years, as an official of an international union, and as a delegate to American Federation of Labor conventions, she has through her untiring efforts secured many concessions for women and children. She has also taken part in discussions on all questions for the benefit of labor as a whole.

As a member of the committee on organization, she has shown wonderful powers of reasoning. Many old and tried international officers are on this committee, but Mrs. Conboy's deep knowledge of the trade union movement and of proper methods to pursue in the organization of the unorganized made her selection as secretary almost inevitable.

No question affecting women and children comes up in the conventions in which she does not take the deepest interest. Leading men delegates find her a source of needed advice when they are puzzled over some knotty trade problem.

As secretary of the textile workers she has aided in building up that organization despite most bitter opposition from powerful influences.

When President Gompers was requested to name someone to christen the Afel in the Hog Island Shipyards on June 28th last, he selected Mrs. Conboy as a representative of the American Federation of Labor and of the highest American womanhood.

FRANK DUFFY

THOMAS A. RICKERT

President United Garment Workers and Sixth Vice-President American Federation of Labor

No labor official has had a more difficult task in guiding an international union than Thomas A. Rickert, president of the United Garment Workers. More than two scores of nationalities make up that organization, and it requires diplomacy and executive ability of the highest order to keep it intact.

President Rickert has had his enemies both within and without the organization. Some of these are found in other unions and central bodies. With a wonderful command of himself, Rickert has moved ahead through all difficulties with confidence in the outcome.

It is such battles that make men big. It was not, therefore, surprising that when the Atlantic City convention met he was made chairman of the adjustment committee. While jurisdictional controversies raise more disturbance than all the different nationalities in his own organization possibly could, he was very successful in adjusting disputes. No one without such an experience as his could serve on such a committee.

Rickert's experience has therefore proved of great assistance to the labor movement. He declared the policy that nothing be done in secret, and which met the hearty favor of those delegates with jurisdictional disputes to settle.

FRANK DUFFY

Secretary Brotherhood of Carpenters and Joiners of America and Third Vice-President American Federation of Labor

Frank Duffy is secretary of an organization with nearly 300,000 members and has held that position for nineteen years. Open and frank in all his dealings, and a thorough trade unionist, he is respected by all who know him for his extensive knowledge of labor matters.

Duffy is one of the big men who in conventions help to steer the labor craft into safe harbor. His work on the committee on organization has proved of incalculable value to the American Federation of Labor and its affiliated unions. Having aided to make the policy which increased the membership of the organization of carpenters, he was ably fitted to act as chairman of the committee on organization.

WILLIAM GREEN

Secretary United Mineworkers and Fourth Vice-President American Federation of Labor

No miners' convention has been held for many years in which the voice of William Green has not been lifted in demands for better conditions for the men of the coal pits. It is difficult to remember when he first appeared as a leader, but it was many years ago. For several years he was a member of the Ohio Senate and president *pro tem.* He afterward became secretary of the United Mineworkers.

Green's experience has been of a practical kind. He has no visions of an impossible chimerical world, and the work of using a pick and shovel when employed in mines has made him a business-like man of affairs. As chairman of the committee on shorter workday, he presented a masterful report in which it was set forth as the policy to be followed hereafter that wages must be increased so that the dollar of today will buy

(Continued on page 20)

JAMES WILSON

Socialism or Social Reform in the Church—Which?

THE following correspondence between the Editor of the REVIEW and Mr. William Fellowes Morgan, Chairman of the Every Name Campaign of the Protestant Episcopal Church, is published herewith, in the hope that it will be of some interest to the readers of the REVIEW. As the first two letters found their way into the columns of *The Nation*, it may not be presumptious to assume that the full correspondence to date, at least the quotations contained in the third letter, are worth publishing. This correspondence is not official but personal between Mr. Morgan and the Editor. Any further correspondence on the subject will appear in later numbers of the REVIEW.

NEW YORK, July 25, 1919.

MR. WILLIAM FELLOWES MORGAN,
Chairman Every Name Campaign,
New York City.

Dear Mr. Morgan: I have read with interest and sympathetic appreciation the announcement of the organization of the Every Name Movement, the purpose of which was so well represented by you in the press statements.

In connection with that, I desire to call your attention to a situation which a good many members of The National Civic Federation consider a serious one, namely, the rapid growth of socialism in the churches, Protestant, Catholic and Jewish alike. Unless the sane and conservative religious business men, such as you are proposing to organize, take an interest in this matter in all the churches, a state of affairs will develop which will cause serious trouble. In fact, trouble is already developing.

It will not do to leave these matters entirely in the hands of the clergy. There are, of course, brilliant exceptions in all denominations but, as a rule, the clergy are not equipped by training to deal with the practical, hard-headed business propositions that employers and labor leaders have to consider when they are dealing, for example, with strikes, and, naturally, they have not the time to get at first hand the facts that would enable them to form a correct judgment on such matters.

In a study I made recently, I was surprised to find that practically all of the church committees or commissions dealing with industrial matters are dominated by Socialists or by those of an extreme, radical type of mind. While proposing to deal with the question of American labor conditions, they give voice only to the views of the Socialist wing in this country or those of the British Labor Party in England, which is working on an out-and-out socalist programme.

The trouble with many of the preacher-secretaries of these social service movements is that they do not differentiate between social reform and socialism, while many of them are socialists, pure and simple, and do not wish to differentiate. The American Federation of Labor and the Railway Brotherhoods have all they can do to beat down the forces of disorder in their own fields and, from what I hear, some of them think that the employing and business classes, who largely dominate the boards of trustees of the churches—the Protestant churches at least—should protect them from attack in the rear by church organizations.

Your new movement relates only to the work of the Protestant Episcopal Church, and, while, as stated, all the churches, Protestant, Catholic and Jewish, are alike permeated with these dangerous doctrines, the Protestant Episcopal Church is especially open to that criticism. You doubtless have seen the announcement of the Church League for Social and Industrial Democracy, of which the Right Rev. Charles David Williams, Bishop of Michigan, is the chairman. On its committee are several well-known socialist clergymen, among them being the man who so fulsomely praised the I. W. W. in an address at the General Convention held in New York in 1913, without any protest being made.

Another Episcopalian movement is The Church Socialist League in America. *The New York Daily Call*, the leading organ of the socialists, reports this organization as "calling upon the church to repudiate its affiliation with the captalist system," and goes on to say: "The Church Socialist League in America reorganized itself at a meeting in the People's House (Rand School) and issued a manifesto to which it will try to rally all the progressive forces in the Protestant Episcopal Church throughout the country. Right Rev. Paul Jones, former Bishop of Utah, was elected president, and Rev. W. B. Spofford, organizing secretary. Irwin St. John Tucker was elected chairman of the committee on activities at the general convention of the Protestant Episcopal Church to be held in Detroit next October."

This Irwin St. John Tucker, who is designated to take such an active part in the General Convention of the Protestant Episcopal Church, is the same gentleman who was convicted in Chicago of sedition and sentenced to a twenty years' term for violation of the Espionage Law.

The National Civic Federation last spring sent a commission to Europe to study industrial conditions. This commission has just returned and is now formulating its conclusions. It will make its report at a meeting called by the Federation on Monday and Tuesday, September 8 and 9, and at the same meeting there will be considered the labor situation in America. These subjects will be discussed by representative labor men and employers. It has been decided to invite all representatives from the reconstruction committees of the various churches, in order that they may not only hear what the labor men and employers themselves think on these matters, but also may have an opportunity of expressing their own views. I hope that the Every Name Movement will accept the invitation, when it is issued, to send a representation.

Very sincerely yours,
RALPH M. EASLEY.

Aug. 19, 1919.

RALPH M. EASLEY, Esq.,
The National Civic Federation, New York.

My dear Mr. Easley: Absence from the city, coupled with a desire to give your letter of July 25 the thoughtful consideration which it demands, have postponed till now my reply.

We are living in a period of vital change. There are many divergent views as to the nature of the reforms which existing conditions require. These will have to be reconciled according to our democratic custom in the adjustment to meet the demands of the new age. Discussion of the various proposals to that end is covering a wide range, in church circles as elsewhere, which I think you will agree is altogether desirable, inasmuch as no church establishment is fully discharging its functions which does not to the extent of its resources seek to assist in the solutions of the problems which the world is facing.

Now, as to the "rapid growth of socialism in the churches" which you charge. My specific interest is in the Episcopal Church. A cardinal principle of that church is that its communicants shall enjoy the fullest expression of their views, but with the understanding that such views, clerical or lay, must in no sense be interpreted as representing the attitude of the church as a whole, which can only be expressed through its duly constituted bodies. In the absence of any declaration by the General Convention or any duly authorized committee or commission upon pending issues, I suggest that it is not just to attribute to the church any attitude either for or against socialism. If there is a tendency toward socialism on the part of individuals or groups of individuals within the Church, such as you suggest, I venture to say this tendency is not more markedly developed in Episcopal circles than it is within the body of our citizens as a whole; and while extreme radicals outside the church, like extreme radicals within it, may be more strident and more prone to make themselves heard, there is no evidence yet at hand to indicate that they constitute a majority of the community.

After all, whatever the present tendencies may be, I can see nothing but benefit to be derived from broad discussion of our social problems, even within the Episcopal Church. That is one of the safety valves of our form of government. Rev. Dr. William T. Manning, Rector of Trinity, in a recent statement on our Every Name Campaign, with particular reference to the question we are now discussing, said, with very great point: "At a time like this it is natural that there should be extravagant views and unregulated enthusiasms. It is inevitable that the vision should carry some of our brethren off their feet and lead them to confuse liberty with lawlessness, and progress with social destruction and disintegration. Perhaps we need these extreme views to spur us on to true progress."

True progress is what we are all aiming at. Indulge us a personal note. I do not share the views of Trotzky or Lenine. I am opposed to such doctrines as are embraced in the theories of those radicals who advocate the assumption of all enterprise and initiative by the State. And I have reason to believe that the gentlemen with whom I am associated in the Every Name Campaign of the Episcopal Church, for the most part laymen and business men and vitally interested in stable, progressive government, share my views in this regard. But in these days of progress, when a "rapid growth of socialism" is alleged, one is impelled to ask for a definition of "socialism" with reference to the present crisis in the world's history. Many of the activities upon which our Government has embarked with the full approval of the people to remedy evils, and make the Government more responsive to the popular will, have within your memory and mine been stamped as highly socialistic. Then consider the present situation. You say: "The American Federation of Labor and the Railway Brotherhoods have all they can do to beat down forces of disorder in their own fields," and you protest that they should be protected from "attack in the rear by church organizations," which latter, you say, "while proposing to deal with the question of American labor conditions" urge the view of the "British Labor Party in England, which is working on an out-and-out socialist program."

Yet we find the American Federation of Labor and the Railway Brotherhoods urging upon the country a plan for the socialization of our railways which is far in advance of the British Labor Plan. Is one more socialistic than the other?

I merely cite this by way of pointing out the desirability of an agreement as to what "socialism" is, without going into the merits of either plan and assenting to the proposition that the Episcopal Church is urging the one or the other.

The fact is, I believe, that when our people come to face the issues squarely the test will be not whether a proposed reform is or is not "socialistic," but will it remedy a downright evil, meet a real demand—will it conduce to the well-being, the happiness, and the prosperity of the whole people? Of this much we are sure: The old order has passed. One great good which has e out of the war is a reassertion of the essen- equality of mankind. The war was a great ller. In that crisis we all had to put our ılders to the wheel, rich and poor, high and . and with all former rank and distinction pt away each of us fitted into the groove to ch he was best suited. It is in that spirit we must face our present problems. Somere between the extreme on either side there is iddle ground upon which the foundations of new age will be laid.

t is the purpose of the Every Name Campaign he Episcopal Church in New York, which is art of the Nation-Wide Campaign of the ırch, by education, by propaganda, by peral contact with every member of the organion, to awaken our people to a sense of their onsibility as citizens and church members, to assist in the solution of these problems. connection with the Campaign, a nation-wide vey of the resources of the Church is being de. When the General Convention of the urch meets in Detroit in October, it will have ore it a complete picture of the Church orıization, together with all the facts as to its nts, needs and aspirations. Thereafter a promme of nation-wide church activity will be mulated as representative of the Episcopal itude toward the new age. Whether it will be cialistic'' or not, I am unable to forecast. t under the leadership of the broadminded hops and clergy and the body of laymen who l there represent every section of the coun-, and every point of view of the Church, I e full confidence that the Church in keeping p with the march of progress, and in meeting demands of the new era upon which we ve entered, will continue to be sound, patric, and worthy of her traditions.

Very truly,

William Fellowes Morgan.

New York, September 27, 1919.

r. William Fellowes Morgan,
Chairman, Every Name Campaign,
124 East 28th Street, New York.

ear Mr. Morgan:

I have your letter of August 19. First, I want say that when I wrote to you on July 25, I d not know that the Every Name Campaign as an alliance of clergymen and laity. From headline in a New York paper, referring to e movement as one designed to prove that religion is good business,'' I inferred that it as made up of business men. Furthermore, u are quoted in the press—and I have seen no futation of the sentiments ascribed to you— saying: ''The movement is built around the ractical idea that big business men believe that e life of the average American can be made to nform, with profit to himself, to religion and e spiritual law. It is to be an intensive delopment of the theory that religion is good usiness.'' I now learn from your letterhead at the active workers in the movement—the onorary Chairman, the Honorary Chairman of e Executive Committee, the Chairman and Secetary of the Standing Committee, the National ampaign Director and the New York Director -are clergymen. I do not refer to this in critism, but simply as an explanation of the imression which I had received.

I agree with you that it ''is altogether desirble'' for the Church, ''to the extent of its reources'' to ''seek to assist in the solutions of e problems which the world is facing.''

My main contention was that it is time that e sane and constructive business men of the hurches took cognizance of the growth of soialism in the churches, instead of leaving it to e clergy, and that if they did not, a situation as, and is, developing which would be fraught ith serious trouble. I still maintain that contion, whatever the composition of the Every ame movement may be, because it is the busiess men—manufacturers, merchants, lawyers, bankers—who make up the governing bodies of the Protestant Church, especially of the Protestant Episcopal Church, and, if they are going to prove that ''religion is good business'' as you expressed it, it will be their primary duty to see that the social, educational and spiritual machinery of the church organization is not captured by the inordinately active socialists, socialistic sentimentalists and other fomenters of disorder.

I did not charge the Protestant Episcopal Church with being socialistic as a church, but I did charge that the committees, or commissions, which are dealing with industrial matters are, in practically all the churches, influenced, if not dominated, by socialists or by persons of an extremely radical type of mind. In a sense, these committees do officially represent the Church and, unless their utterances are repudiated, the public has a right to assume that, if not *approved* by the Church, they are at least *not disapproved*.

The clergyman who, at the General Convention of the Protestant Episcopal Church in New York in 1913, as I said, praised the I. W. W. (the Bolsheviki of America) without any public protest being raised, was the Rev. J. Howard Melish, of Brooklyn, Secretary of the Joint Commission on Social Service of the Protestant Episcopal Church, of which commission I believe you are the Treasurer. This is what he is reported in the public press as having said:

> Syndicalism, as every investigation has shown, finds a field only in our industrial centres where immigrants are herded. Without a vote, strange, bewildered, "put upon," deserted by the Church, the labor union, and the socialists, it was syndicalism which went to them in their distress and gave them courage and hope. All honor to the I. W. W. leaders that they were found at the hottest point of the industrial conflict.

This simply means that the Rev. Mr. Melish, Secretary of the Social Service Commission, had accepted at face value all the fantastic claims of the I. W. W. propagandists about the Utopian program of that organization and was repeating, parrot-like, the misrepresentations of the trade union movement put out by William D. Haywood and his band of thugs to the effect that the American Federation of Labor was neglecting the unskilled immigrant workers, when, at that very time, the American Federation of Labor had twenty-five times more unskilled laborers organized than the whole membership of the I. W. W. Every month the Federation spends more money in endeavoring to organize the unskilled laborers of the country than the I. W. W. has done since its inception.

You say you ''do not share the views of Trotzky or Lenine,'' and that you are ''opposed to such doctrines as are embraced in the theories of those radicals who advocate the assumption of all enterprise and initiative by the State.'' There is no question that all men who are ''vitally interested in stable progressive government'' must share your sentiments. And yet you say: ''But in these days of progress, when a 'rapid growth of socialism' is alleged, one is impelled to ask for a definition of 'socialism' with reference to the present crisis in the world's history.'' That definition can easily be given. But first, taking up your statement, ''Many of the activities upon which our Government has embarked with the full approval of the people to remedy evils, and make the Government more responsive to the popular will, have within your memory and mine been stamped as highly socialistic,'' I should like to ask you exactly what you include in that category?

It was popular propaganda that when the Government, during the emergency of the war, took over the railroads, the telegraph, telephone and express companies, and established a drastic price-fixing regime, we had embarked on a sea of socialism. It is true that, under the stress of the war, things had to be done quickly, without regard either to efficiency or economy. Red tape had to be cut, federal statutes ignored. In fact autocracy of the highest type—not socialism—had to be instituted, with the President, by common consent, as the great executive autocrat. Just as soon, however, as the emergency had passed, the experience we had gone through showed that we wanted to get out of the clutches of the Government at the earliest possible moment, the President himself leading the demand.

And here we squarely face the question you ask: ''What is socialism?'' I agree with you that we should not oppose a given program simply because it is socialism or is socialistic, but that we should ask: ''Will it remedy a downright evil, meet a real demand, will it conduce to the well-being, the happiness and prosperity of the whole people?'' As I stated in my previous letter, one great trouble with many persons is that they confuse socialism and social reform. All men of normal minds are social reformers. They want to see a better state of things, improved housing, abolition of child labor, sanitary factories, just wages and fairer hours of employment, good municipal government, etc., etc. But none of these things is socialism. As a matter of fact, the socialists oppose social reform, because they claim that such reforms are only palliatives and simply operate to postpone the overturning of present-day society and the ushering in of the communist state, in other words, ''the dictatorship of the proletariat.'' As Keir Hardie put it: ''It is not reform we want, but revolution.''

When in this letter I speak of socialists, I mean Karl Marxian socialists, members of the Socialist Party, not sentimental individuals who loosely call themselves socialists but are not members of the party and who do not consciously subscribe to its platform or really know what it contains. These socialists are men aptly referred to by the Rev. Dr. Manning, whom you quote, as given to ''extravagant views and unregulated enthusiasms.'' In the case of socialism, we have a very clear and easy way to find the definition. In 1914, the Industrial Relations Commission invited the Socialist Party to send an official representative to testify before the commission on the philosophy and methods of socialism, and the executive committee of that party appointed as such representative, its chairman, Morris Hillquit, who is also recognized as the brains and leader of the socialist movement in this country. When asked to define socialism, Mr. Hillquit testified as follows:

> Stated in more concrete terms, the socialist program requires the public or collective ownership and operation of the principal instruments and agencies for the production and distribution of wealth—the land, mines, railroads, steamboats, telegraph and telephone lines, mills, factories and modern machinery.
>
> This is the main program, and the ultimate aim of the whole socialist movement and the political creed of all socialists. It is the unfailing test of socialist adherence, and admits of no limitation, extension, or variation. Whoever accepts this program is a socialist; whoever does not, is not.

A study of every socialist platform of any kind, the Christian (save the mark!) Socialists included, confirms Mr. Hillquit's testimony. Now then, Mr. Morgan, it is easy, I think, for the American people and for the Protestant Episcopal Church, as well as for the other churches of the country, to decide whether or not it will ''conduce to the well being, the happiness and prosperity of the whole people'' to have all the factories, mines, farms, banks, stores, docks, steam and street railroads, gas and electric light utilities, etc., taken over and operated by the socialists.

To bring it closer home, and therefore to illustrate more forcibly—and I do not mean this in any offensive spirit—do you, or does the Joint Commission on Social Service, think it would ''conduce to the well being, the happiness and

(*Continued on page 18*)

THE NATIONAL Civic Federation Review

Office: Thirty-third Floor, Metropolitan Tower 1 Madison Avenue New York City

RALPH M. EASLEY, Editor

Published Twice a Month Two Dollars a Year

The Editor alone is Responsible for any unsigned article or unquoted statement published in THE NATIONAL CIVIC FEDERATION REVIEW.

CONSTRUCTIVE SANITY OR DELPHIC HOCUS-POCUS

It was not so long ago that various pseudo-intellectual magazines, such as the *New Republic, Nation* and *Survey,* which advocated its program for peace by compromise with the enemy, were exploiting the British Labor Party's radical program as an Ephesian spell which would at once change the world. They implied that the American Federation of Labor was obsolete and on its way to the scrap-heap and that, compared to Arthur Henderson, Ramsay MacDonald and Clynes, Samuel Gompers was a back number. It was not so very long ago that certain young radicals who wormed their way into publicity jobs in the War Labor Board were trying to stimulate the formation of shop committees in American industries—the secret purpose of which was, of course, to undermine the A. F. of L. and disintegrate organized American labor in the interests of the radical British program.

As told by Mr. J. W. Sullivan at The National Civic Federation meeting, reported in this issue, the shop steward movement in Great Britain has utterly failed, and as recounted by Mr. A. Parker Nevin, British labor is in an absolutely chaotic condition. To that Sir Charles Ross, familiar with conditions in England, declared that what England urgently needs is a Federation of Labor modelled after the American. The sum total of the report made by the Commission sent by the Civic Federation to study industrial conditions in England and France was that those countries had learned practically nothing from their experience with labor during the war which could be applied to advantage in this country. America is not likely, therefore, to look abroad for any Sibylline hocus-pocus cooked up by the extremists, but will go ahead, as it has always done, as the American Federation of Labor has consistently done, to solve its problems and remedy its ills through sane, constructive upbuilding endeavor.

If the conference to be held next month by President Wilson fails to work out any program which will by a turning of the hand solve the problems of the high cost of living, strikes, unionization of policemen and Federal and other civil service employees, and every other grievance which might be put forward, the Socialists and near-Socialists will, as usual, come forth with a loud clamor that it proves the inefficacy of our present system of government and industry and that, therefore, the only solution lies in revolution.

History has shown that civilization has been built up and all its achievements have been gained from the myriad experiences, successes as well as failures, of the past, and if the men who come together at such a conference as that to be called by the President, are not unanimous in formulating any recipe for a miracle, but present conflicting views and debate various suggestions, it will be more a hopeful sign than otherwise. For it is only by the exchange of views of men of practical experience, by a sincere and judicial testing of plans and experiments, by an amicable arbitration of differences, that the root of our evils can be reached and that any lasting and progressive program can be attained.

POTENTIAL GERMANY

While certain periodicals of uncertain hue so far as loyalty and Americanism are concerned, were agitating against the demands made of Germany in the peace treaty, while they bewailed the so-called "crushing" and economic "strangling" of poor, defeated, repentant Germany, while certain editors and writers such as Oswald Garrison Villard and Mary Heaton Vorse came back from flying visits into the domain of the Central Powers with heart-rending tales about hundreds of thousands of starving children and famished mothers, THE NATIONAL CIVIC FEDERATION REVIEW, almost alone among American journals, continued to point out what we believed to be true: That Germany had been by no means utterly defeated when she sued for peace; that, seeing military victory over the Allies impossible, she simply determined, and most expediently, to get out of the war on the best terms possible; that she signed the treaty with her tongue in her cheek, and that she will seek to evade fulfillment of her obligations by promoting discord and disunity among the nations who won the war. We expressed our belief, based on the observations of many returning soldiers and others who had been in Germany, that there was no such starvation in Germany as was reported by various radical sentimentalists and pro-Bolshevists, that there was less want and suffering than in stricken France itself. We expressed our profound apprehensions of the future menace of Germany to the world. We told, what we know from authoritative information to be a fact, that Germany plans to continue her warfare against her victors; that she intends to use the weapons offered by Bolshevism for fomenting social and industrial unrest throughout the world; that she will seek to undermine and disintegrate her rival nations from within, and that in the immediate future we shall see the resumption of a sinister propaganda as was not paralleled by the propaganda carried on before America's entry into the war.

Our policy of presenting what we believed to be true, and what we felt it to be our duty to emphasize, brought the commendation of the majority of our readers. It brought also a number of protests, and we were accused of an implacable and uncharitable spirit toward a defeated and disarmed foe, of helping to perpetuate a spirit of bitterness and hate. That our doubts and misgivings concerning the impotence of Germany and the drawing of her fangs were not baseless, that we were not alone in suffering from some nightmare, is shown by the statement made in Paris the other day by Mr. Henry Morgenthau, who headed the United States Commission of Investigation and had gone through Poland and Central Europe.

Mr. Morgenthau is not a man subject to hysteria, but has been distinguished by an eminently sane, calm and judicial temper of mind. "Germany," he says, "came through this war a perfect dynamo of strength. Her human military power is practically as great as ever, and her 65,000,000 people have been schooled and hardened by trials. The nation has been compressed into a concentrated mass, which is surcharged with energy and moving with centripetal force, while Germany's neighbors are spreading themselves out thin and quarrelling and moving with centrifugal force. If disintegration keeps up among Germany's neighbors there can be but one result. . . . Germany intelligently refused to fight to a finish with the United States. She withdrew in good order to a place of safety, where the war had not ruined her factories and where everything was ready for the resumption of peace industry. . . . The forces of peace must organize and consolidate; otherwise they are inviting an onslaught which German arms unquestionably will make within a few years unless Germany's enemies entrench themselves through constructive work and establish the nations which threaten to weaken themselves and their allies through greed and jealousy. Germany has gone over into Russia. Her people are organizing there, and they will marshal Russian resources and utilize them in combating the rest of the world, unless a strong Poland is creat as a protection for Europe. . . . The task the United States is clear. She must beg through her Allies, she must equip statesmen the international school and create the first Ge eral Staff that has ever existed, so as to ha leaders who will realize what the world develo ments are."

Mr. Morgenthau's is the most intelligent, lo cal and clear-visioned analysis of the suprer situation which confronts the world, which h been made since the formulation of the trea of peace. Will the leaders of America prove t blind to see? Will the people of Americ naturally relaxing from the tense strain ar spiritual suffering of the war, drift supine into a lethargy of which the watchful, wily, i defatigable enemy waits to take advantage.

Talking the other day with a most able woma who had gone into Germany for the Y. M. C. A we asked about the reported starving of childre "I never, never saw so many children in m life," said this woman, with a sort of aghast e pression. "Maybe it was the result of their sy tem of scientific breeding. I don't know. Bu I do know they weren't peaked and pallid, an nowhere in Germany was there any evidence c starvation. They weren't living luxuriously, bu neither were they weak and unhealthy. And couldn't help but look forward twenty or twenty five years when the males would form a potenti army greater in numbers than the army Ge many had when she invaded Belgium and pre cipitated the war.

"I felt everywhere I went, and I was billete with German families," the woman went on i a low awed voice, "that I was not in a defeate country, but an *enemy* country. You can fee their bitter, bitter, vengeful hatred, particularl of America, in the atmosphere."

A MISCHANCE BULLITT

There appeared before the Senate Foreign Relations Committee on September 12, a hitherto unwrit-of young man, a former cub newspape reporter, Bullitt by name, who was permitted t take up the valuable time of that importantl functioning body by giving prolonged account of alleged confidential conversations with th United States Secretary of State, Mr. Lansing Colonel Edward Mandell House, Mr. David Lloyd George and others.

Whether the reported conversations reveale by the blabbering Bullitt ever took place or not whether Secretary Lansing was accurately re ported or not, whether Mr. House's mysteriou state of mind was veritably revealed or not, th spectacle of this young person appearing an bruiting conversations that, if they did tak place, were matters of sacred confidence, whil unedifying, is revealing and informative as t the character and type of men who are gravitat ing by natural affinity to the so-called "liberal," pro-Bolshevist, internationalist movement. Jus through what chance abberation of a freakis fate this inexperienced and undistinguished Mr Bullitt was lifted from the obscure ranks of news paper cubdom to a trusted position in the De partment of State, just through what temporar lapse of ordinary judgment in the estimation an evaluation of human character this callow adolescent was selected as chief of the intelli gence section of the American Peace Commis sion, just through what oblique or crotchet mental quirk on part of Mr. House he was picke out with the pro-Bolshevist Lincoln Steffens a an impartial and responsible envoy to Sovie Russia is as incomprehensible, as totally baffling as utterly disconcerting as was the selection fo other high and trusted positions with Mr House's peace delegation of former Rand schoo lecturers, co-authors of pro-German school his tories, and *New Republic* editors of quasi-Ger man extraction.

That Bullitt should have been selected for a position of confidence with the peace delegation that, with Lincoln Steffens of all people in the world, he should have been selected for a grave and onerous mission of investigation to Russia, is of course lamentable, but it must be borne in mind that all human beings are liable to err in judgment, and Mr. Wilson could have had no greater quality of clairvoyance as to what a yellow streak this Bullitt would develop than he had when he delegated as his envoy to Mexico the William Bayard Hale, who later hired himself as secret director of Hun propaganda in America.

We knew nothing of the personality of this aforesaid and still unfamed Mr. Bullitt. He married and went to Germany in 1916 on his honeymoon, and according to the publishers' advertisement of a book on the trip written by his wife: "Von Bissing, Governor of Belgium, was her dinner partner; Zimmerman, 'the busiest man in the German Empire,' discussed peace and the U-Boat campaign with her; Countess von Bernstorff and Baroness von Bissing asked her to tea." According to this "Uncensored Diary," Mr. and Mrs. Bullitt were entertained lavishly and de luxe by the most exclusive and brilliant circles of German society; in fact, it is made clear that Hun society, Hun diplomats and military commanders put themselves out and went to extraordinary measures to "capture" the two young honeymooners. So in the book on their trip one reads statements like this: "It is foolish to talk of ruining Germany. She is too valuable to be ruined. And Germany doesn't want to rule the world. She's nothing compared to England when it comes to that" (page 30).

Whether Mr. Bullitt, when he was promoted to a position in the American government after we were at war with Germany, disagreed with Mrs. Bullitt's conclusions is not known. Mr. Bullitt did resign as a member of the American peace delegation, and his letter to President Wilson explaining his resignation reveals a mental state of puppy hydrophobia over the so-called "unjust settlement" of the treaty drawn up at Versailles, specific objection being made to the "unjust decision" regarding the Tyrol, Hungary, East Prussia, Danzig and the Saar Valley.

As for Bullitt's report that the terror has ceased in Russia, that good order has been established, that the Soviet government is founded in the imagination of the mass of common people of Russia, that it is turning itself to constructive work, as well as for his recommendations, we have innumerable reports of reliable men who spent not days, but months, in personal investigation throughout Russia, and whose matured conclusions are not the result of any flying, rapid-fire conversational visit to Lenine. Lincoln Steffens, who accompanied Mr. Bullitt to Russia, is the author of an introduction to a book by Trotzky, and after a characteristically light-legged as well as light-headed jaunt into Russia after the revolution, was wont to appear ubiquitously at lunches and banquets, and tell dramatically all about the glorious revolution as a revolution for the world. It is whispered that the detailed and ripened observations of Mr. Steffens were gained during an exhaustive visit of something like eighteen days. One can merely hazard the opinion that Mr. Wilson saw fit to "suppress" the recent Bullitt-Steffens report simply because of the fact that he estimated it at its actual value.

—T. E. H.

The President's Industrial Conference

By RALPH M. EASLEY

CHAIRMAN EXECUTIVE COUNCIL, THE NATIONAL CIVIC FEDERATION

THE inndustrial unrest, resulting in strikes and lock-outs, and threats of many more lockouts, has become so acute in the last few months that President Wilson has wisely called a national conference to consider plans and methods for dealing with it.

In doing this, the President recognizes what Premiers Lloyd George of England and Borden of Canada have recognized in their respective countries, and that is, that the situation is so grave and so far-reaching in its various ramifications that only the highest authorities in the national government can properly, or at all effectively, deal with it. Mr. Lloyd George, facing a threatened paralysis of all industry in England, last March called a conference, composed of two hundred representative employers and two hundred representative wage earners, while Sir Robert Borden called a similar conference, which met in Ottawa this month. In Great Britain, irrespective of the net results in terms of solution of practically unsolvable problems, the moral and educational effect of bringing together the leaders of both sides of the industrial fighting forces at that crucial moment was tremendous. In fact, it may not be too much to assert that it saved the nation from a calamity which threatened its industrial life.

While the situation in this country when President Wilson decided to call his conference was not so serious as that which faced Lloyd George last spring, it was serious enough to justify, if not to demand, such a move on the part of the President. As in Great Britain, the mere announcement of the calling of such a conference had a reassuring effect on industry and if nothing more concrete were to result from it than the coming together at the White House of representatives of all sides of our great productive industries to consider the vital problems facing our nation, the effort would be more than justified. But very much more will come out of it.

Those familiar with the work of The National Civic Federation, which for fifteen years preceding the war had, in a smaller way, been bringing together these same forces of capital and labor with a view to composing their differences, saw results so gratifying as to justify the above prediction of what will happen at the White House. No problem relating to industrial conflicts is likely to arise at the President's conference that has not already arisen in the conferences of The National Civic Federation, excepting, of course, the special cause for the present unrest, the phenomenally high cost of living. In the light of the Federation's experience, we may be pardoned for pointing out some of the things that we believe can be accomplished by the President's conference and some of the things that we believe cannot be accomplished—things which practical people will not expect to be accomplished, and which only the theorists, the sentimentalists and the revolutionaries will demand shall be accomplished.

I well remember the shock which I received at the first meeting of the Executive Committee of The National Civic Federation, in 1901, presided over by Senator Mark A. Hanna and attended by Bishop Henry C. Potter and Grover Cleveland, as well as by Messrs. Samuel Gompers, James Duncan, Charles M. Schwab, Charles A. Moore, and other men of the same type as comprise our Executive Committee today; I shall never forget how, after Bishop Potter had spoken so enthusiastically about the wonderful achievement of bringing capital and labor together—the first attempt in that line ever made in this country or any other—declaring that he believed we would solve the great industrial problems and practically put an end to strikes and lockouts—in a word, realize the Brotherhood of Man—Mr. Gompers arose and said, in effect:

"I share with Bishop Potter all the hopes that he has expressed, but twenty years' experience (and this was eighteen years ago) impels me to add a note of warning. If we set out expecting to solve any of the real industrial problems within the span of our short lives, we are doomed to disappointment. My warning is only for the purpose of saving any one from the rude awakening that is sure to come when he finds that these problems are ages old and can only be solved as human nature becomes more perfect, less selfish and ignorant, and as we abolish class, religious and racial prejudices."

My shock came because, with Bishop Potter, I believed that the whole capital and labor problem had been solved by the organization of The National Civic Federation; but Mr. Gompers was right. We entered into struggle after struggle, winning today, losing tomorrow, and the next day losing the fight we had won the day before, sometimes fortunately winning it back again the day after; but the millennium had not arrived. However, the bringing together in The National Civic Federation of representatives of all the big forces of capital and labor and the so-called "general public," where they could talk out their differences together face to face and, to use the stock phrase, "with their feet under the same mahogany," did accomplish important results. It made for better feeling and better understanding between employers and employees, though it did not solve all the problems, nor stop all strikes. So I say, let us not assume that the whole matter in this country has been settled now that the President has called a conference nor that the rest of the American people can relieve themselves from any further concern about our industrial future.

Since the armistice there have sprung up in this country innnumerable so-called industrial bureaus, composed of from one to half a dozen self-advertised "industrial experts," who, for a generous financial consideration, will furnish to employers plans, schemes, programs and charts for solving all their labor problems. As a rule, in none of these bureaus are there real labor men or real employers. They are composed entirely of doctrinaires, many of them Socialists or near-Socialists, but not so visionary that they cannot discover where the dollar lies and that many employers today have become so alarmed over the "great unrest" that they will grasp at any straw that comes their way and pay any amount for it. I opine that the plans of these theorists will not get very far at the White House conference, for the reason that the President has wisely selected a personnel of hard-headed men whose feet are on the ground all the time. There will be as members of this conference:

Fifteen representatives of organized labor;

Five representatives from the National Industrial Conference Board, an organization representing nineteen national employers' organizations;

Five members of the Chamber of Commerce of the United States, a body made up largely of merchants and manufacturers;

One representative from each of the three largest national agricultural organizations; and

Two representatives from banking and investing organizations.

The President will himself select the fifteen members who are to be representative of that indefinable, elusive element termed "the public."

Irrespective of the fifteen representatives of the public, even if all of them were to be theorists or even freaks, which of course they will not be, there is sufficient good practical horse sense in the other elements to control the conference.

Besides, it is safe to assume that action will be taken only upon questions where there is substantial unanimity.

But to refer specifically to certain things which I think cannot be accomplished at the White House conference and certain things which I think can be accomplished:

First. There is at the present time what might almost be termed a "clamor" for Democratization of Industry, that is, the giving to the wage earners a voice in determining not only wages, hours and working conditions but also a voice in the control of the business itself. The term "democratization of industry" is used freely by various classes of persons to whom its meaning is not at all the same. To many writers it means profit sharing of some kind, with shop committees, shop stewards, membership for employees on the board of directors, etc., etc. To organized labor it means only what is involved in collective bargaining; that is, a voice in regard to wages, hours and conditions of employment. To the I. W. W. or Bolsheviki it means the confiscation of the property and its operation by the workers. The last is, of course, real democratization of industry and at the same time the destruction of industry.

The position of the American Federation of Labor on the proposition that the wage earners should have a membership in the board of directors of a corporation is well given in the statement made by Mr. John P. Frey, secretary of the Committee on Resolutions of the American Federation of Labor at its recent Convention at Atlantic City. The Committee on Resolutions had reported against the proposition for the wage earners to select a foreman in the factory and the committee's report was overwhelmingly approved by the Convention. Mr. Frey said:

> "I would call your attention to the fact that in the literature which has been circulated upon the question of electing foremen and in the speeches made in trade union meetings upon this same question, the subject does not stop with the election of foremen, because the argument is then made, and it is a logical one, that the election of foremen would be of no value, because the foremen would be under the general manager and the board of directors, and if we could only get the trade union movement to commit itself to the election of foremen in industries, it would logically follow that we would have to elect the board of directors and determine who the general manager would be. It is not, therefore, a trade union proposition and I have made this statement so that you will more thoroughly understand what is included in the resolution in purpose, if not in language."

Mr. Frey's language makes it very clear that the trade union movement does not favor any scheme whereby the worker is supposed to enter into the management of industry. In fact, trade union writers are frank to say that they want no responsibility for failures or losses upon their shoulders; that responsibility they want the employers alone to take. They do want to be heard on the question of wages, hours and working conditions, but that is the extent of their demand for democratization of industry.

While many employers on the President's commission will favor profit sharing or stock participation schemes of some kind, they will shy at any idea of giving the workers a voice in the management of the business, and with the wage earners also opposing it, as well as the practical people representing the public, it is pretty certain that participation in the management and business operations of industry will not make much headway in that conference. That is not to say that there are not plans in operation in non-union plants where employers are trying sincerely to give the workers a voice on wages, hours and conditions, the same as is demanded by the trade unions through collective bargaining, which plans, from all appearances, are in some cases succeeding. One of these schemes, called the federal plan, provides for a lower house, a senate and a cabinet. A conspicuous example of this plan, which has been largely advertised, has been tied up by strikes, and other corporations, which put in other plans, are in the same dilemma. So that industrial peace does not seem to lie in that direction. Neither can it be affirmed that collective bargaining will in itself absolutely solve the problem, because we have seen, n the stress of the rising cost of living, that even some collective contracts have been broken by the workers. Collective bargaining is, however, the best mechanism yet devised to reduce industrial conflicts to a minimum, and should only be judged by its operation under normal conditions. It works best when men are thoroughly organized and under the discipline of strong leaders, but the bringing about of that condition is necessarily a work of education and is by no means a quick process.

Another proposition that is largely to the fore at the present moment is compulsory arbitration and what is known as the compulsory investigation principle in public utilities, if not in all industry. Again we have to reckon with the opposition of the organized labor group, which will be solidly against it in the White House conference, and the opposition by this group will be augmented by that of many of the employers and the informed members of the public group.

Some of my readers may say: "What is the use of calling a conference if you cannot stop these strikes and lock-outs, because it is the prevalence of them that has caused the calling together of that august body?" Again do I come back to the twenty years' experience of The National Civic Federation. At one time we believed in compulsory arbitration, especially in dealing with public utilities, because we argued, as everybody argues now, that the public interest is paramount and should be protected at all hazards. But no one has as yet invented a plan that will secure that protection. True, as pointed out by our lawyers, the Government has a right to say that men shall not strike, at least on railroads, without giving notice or without having their grievances investigated, as in Canada; but the Government does not have the right to compel a man to work against his will. That is where the plan falls down. Australia and New Zealand have gone the limit in their attempt to enforce compulsory arbitration and have failed. In Australia, when the attempt was made to enforce the law against 12,000 abattoir workers who had struck in defiance of the arbitration act, and in Canada, when 15,000 mine workers struck in defiance of the Canadian act, the wage earners discovered the weakness of the government's position, because in neither country were there jails enough to contain those thousands of men, even if the politicians had dared to imprison them for their offenses. And with this discovery the striking men's fear of and respect for the law disappeared. From that time forward, they trampled upon it with impunity when any really serious conflict arose.

But, fortunately, we are not confined to compulsory methods of arbitration and here, I think, is one of the places where the President's conference can accomplish practical and helpful results, justifying the expectations of its most sanguine friends. Experience with voluntary mediation and arbitration methods shows that very much can be done towards preventing industrial disputes. The experience of the Department of Labor, of Mediation Boards in several states and of The National Civic Federation itself, all teach the same thing, and that is, that there are very many instances where if an outside, tactful party brings the contending forces together for conference, an avoidance of many industrial outbreaks results. While there are questions of principle that cannot be arbitrated or mediated but can only be fought out, such as the right of a worker to join a union or the right of an employer to refuse to discharge non-union men who have stood by him in a strike, there are more cases where the question is one of wages, hours and working conditions, of personal misunderstandings between superintendents or foremen and the men, or of autocratic and overbearing conduct on the part of a foreman or the leaders of the men, all of which latter difficulties can be ironed out by a voluntary mediation committee.

But there has never been in this country a thorough organization on a large scale of the forces that could be utilized in such work. Under the inspiration and prestige of the President's conference—and I am only referring to industrial disturbances, not to the other great reconstruction problems that will come before that conference—a practical organization could surely be effected in every industrial community. For instance, in the 303 cities of the United States having a population of over 20,000, the leading commercial organizations and the central labor unions might be asked by the President each to name an equal number of persons—five, ten, fifteen or twenty-five, depending upon the size and importance of the city—to form a joint mediation committee for that city, these two groups themselves selecting the public representatives to act with them. This would mean that, in addition to acting in strikes and lock-outs, these forces in every community would be organized for weekly or monthly conferences on industrial questions generally, pertaining to the welfare of the city.

In addition to these city mediation committees, there could also be state committees, appointed by the Governor, similarly constituted, to deal with corporations having industries in more than one city, and with inter-urban troubles and other state-wide disturbances. Then the President might himself appoint a national committee, or expand the commission he is now naming, to deal with disturbances in the large basic industries, such as steel, coal, railroads and shipping, which committee would logically lead in the educational work that would follow and also act as a national stabilizer. It could also annually call to a national conference representatives of all the municipal and state committees to discuss industrial problems and methods of dealing with them.

The administration of all this work might well be placed in the hands of the Department of Labor and the Department of Commerce jointly, thus enabling the Government to utilize every one of these municipal and state committees. If such a plan were put into operation, it may be assumed that Congress would willingly appropriate sufficient money to those departments to enable this work to be carried out. Many voluntary conciliation committees have been appointed in this country in the past that did not amount to much. They were formed of well-meaning persons without practical experience in dealing with the industrial questions that faced them, but when organized wage earners form one third of a committee and employers another third, the best possible results can be assured.

While the discussions alone at the conference will be illuminating and valuable, there will undoubtedly be an agreement among the members on many important general principles; and I hope they may be able also to adapt the effective War Labor Board program to meet the after-war conditions. But I still believe that the most far-reaching and practical results will come from the perfecting of a permanent organization to deal with these conflicts at their inception in every industrial center.

Our Paramount Problems

(Continued from page 3)

sure, it is the present time. When I say sure, I don't mean armistice; I don't mean articular time to call off the contest, but I · that no man can think clearly, construct- hopefully or sympathetically when he is age, when his mind is upset, or when he is good mental health. That is exactly what ouble fundamentally with Great Britain is present time, and quite naturally, and the .e in this country at the present time. body wants everything in sight. Every- is demanding things. We are all mixed our economics. We are mixed up in ociology. We are mixed up in our ob- es, and until we get back to some normal of constructive thought, and unless we stop rowing between ourselves, attacking and er-attacking, I personally fail to see where e going to make steady progressive thought rogress."

TRIBUTES TO JOHN MITCHELL

motion that a committee be appointed to ss by a suitable resolution its sentiments the death of John Mitchell was offered by B. Schram, who said:

was associated with Mr. Mitchell for many in his capacity as chairman of one of the rtant departments of. The National Civic ration, the Department on Trade Agree- s, and it is for that reason that I claim the lege of making this motion. The life history r. Mitchell is one of the greatest interest. ng the tender years of childhood he was from school and put to work in the mines, e he picked slate from the coal, and under trying conditions he grew up, not to the t which might be expected from circum- es of that kind, not to a life of bitter hos- to the conditions which made possible his g experiences; he grew up to be a man of d view, who became the leader of his asso- s, the Mine Workers of America, and a man when he laid down that task, was selected ad in the broader work of industrial develop- t. The men who develop this broad spirit not too numerous among us, and his loss, , is more severe to us now that it would have at any other time."

Mr. Mitchell was my closest friend for twen- ears," said Timothy Healy, who seconded motion. "We will always look back at his as head of the United Mine Workers of rica, the struggle he has gone through, the s that he has gone through in the interest be men that he represented as the head of United Mine Workers, the great service that as been to these men; I might also say that as been of great service to the employers of e men, the coal operators. Since the set- ent of the great coal strike, the coal opera- have known from year to year where they d. Up to the time that Mr. Mitchell got rol of the United Mine Workers and organ- them, there was no employer in the mining stry who could tell from one day to the r when his plant would be shut down. I be- that this work of Mr. Mitchell's in bring- about peace in the coal industry has been alone of a great benefit to the men who have eeded in getting decent hours, wages and nt living conditions in the mines, but has a wonderful service to the miner, the mine ers, mine operators, and the general public vell. We have sustained a great loss in the h of Mr. Mitchell. He is not alone a loss abor, but he is a national loss, a loss to the ntry."

ugust Belmont said:

I would like to avail myself of the opportu- to have the privilege of also seconding this lution, for I desire very much to record my own personal appreciation of the character and worth of Mr. Mitchell and his services to the Civic Federation. It was not only my privilege, but my pleasure, to serve with Mr. Mitchell intimately in the affairs of this body, and in all my experience in business and civil affairs I do not recall encounterng a purer, more disinterested and loftier character than that of Mr. Mitchell. His reliability, his good judgment, and the purity of his motives stand out in my memory as possessed by one of the few great friends that I really had."

RESULTS OF SHOP COMMITTEES

Upon the passing of the motion, James W. Sullivan, of the American Federation of Labor, who represented labor on the commission sent abroad by the Civic Federation, reported in part as follows:

"With regard to the work of this Commission, at the present moment I will ask your attention to the fact that we of the Commission agree with the Commission sent over by the United States Department of Labor, that the Whitley Committee outcome to the present time gives us very little in practice which is valuable to us in the United States. And as to the general results of the shop committees, I have those summarized in a letter written me the twenty-fifth of August by a man who for many years was one of the executive committee of the General Machinists and Allied Metal Trades of Great Britain, known as the Engineers:

> With reference to the shop stewards' agreement, these stewards were continually saying that the old procedure of local and central conference was too slow, as they desired to be in a position to deal promptly and to down tools, if necessary. This agreement has just been made between the Amalgamated Society of Engineers and Society of Employers, under which some recognition is given in the shop to the stewards' committees, but I have no hesitation in saying that while giving them the right of discussion, they give them no more power, but, on the contrary, by accepting the offices of stewards under the unions, the stewards accept and give up their right to stop work. The agreement between the employers' federation and the executive of the trades unions still stands good and forbids any other agreement that is inconsistent with it.

"That is the official ending of the shop stewards' movement as a separate, independent movement from trade unionism."

Taking up the subject of the economic status of working women in Great Britain, Mr. Sullivan continued:

"In the United Kingdom at the outbreak of the war, in a population officially estimated at forty-six millions, females outnumbered males by 1,300,000. At the close of the war the excess was at least two millions. In the classification of women workers the largest number are, of course, the housewives, and working-class housing is essentially a woman's question.

"The outstanding feature of the war was the extent to which women were drawn upon to do work hitherto the almost exclusive sphere of men. The curious part is that more men were drawn from the general public than women to take the place of those going to the war, a fact not generally understood. In general the pay of working women abroad compared with American is from half to two-thirds of the money wages of American women.

"As to the question of organization, political and otherwise, it has been of disappointment generally to the men of Great Britain that women have not taken a part in society in general and in the associations in which they have the same rights as men. There are a half dozen national woman societies concerned with promoting woman's cause in general, and especially for equal pay for equal work, and on that principle there are here many notes on many sidelights, many views as to whether that is a practicability. Politically and in the trade unions, the women do not exert much influence. They did not, for at the late county elections, the total vote was only twenty per cent of the entire vote, and in the trade unions and co-operative societies, although they are entitled to a position, they seldom take those positions. They get back to the old principle that woman wants a husband, children and a home, and within that kingdom mostly her own way, and she succeeds within that kingdom."

METHODS OF PROFIT SHARING

George W. Perkins, in a talk on profit sharing, said in part:

"There is no term used today, in my judgment, to describe relationship between people that is so misunderstood and so misused as the word 'profit sharing'. 'Profit sharing' is used to cover bonuses, turkeys at Thanksgiving time, all sorts of devices, in an effort to make the working-man feel he is being better remunerated than he otherwise would be. If I am right in the statement that the question of what the workers' fair share is, is being raised because of broader education, then you never will answer that question by giving a bonus at the end of the year, because in giving it you simply raise anew the question, 'what is my fair share?'

"I believe that the only way to introduce profit sharing into business is to say to the organization at the beginning of the year, 'Now, last year we made so much money in this business. Here is a frank, thorough, complete annual statement. It takes so much money to earn our fixed charges, to pay our insurance, to pay our salaries, to set aside for depreciation, and so forth, and whatever this concern earns over and above those items, we propose to divide with the organization on some percentage basis which will be stated in advance and distributed on the basis of wages and salaries paid.' That is not a scientific basis, but up to date it has been the best basis anybody has been able to think out. When you lay that proposition down before an organization, at the beginning of the year, each and every man knows what was done the year before, and each man desires to do better than he did the year before, and whatever is done will be divided, as with the management and stockholders of the company.

"Now, when you come to the question of how to distribute these profits: There are many organizations who go eighty percent of the way that I believe in, in saying what the profits are and distributing them, turning them over at the end of the year in cash to the men and women of the business. That is not partnership and profit sharing; that is not partnership—it will not last. When a man is working in a business for a wage and goes home at night, his work is usually done. His mind is not continuing in that business. The man who has capital in it, the manager, his mind must continue in the business. The point is—the desirable point to arrive at, at least, is to get the two, if possible, co-ordinated in the closest possible cooperation. Now, you distribute cash at the end of a year to an organization, and say a man gets $1200 a year, and as a result of a profit sharing plan so-called, at the end of the year, he gets $200 more. He begins to regard that $200 as an extra salary. He is very apt to use it in his expenses and regard his income as $1400. If he does not do that he puts it into some other investment outside of the business he is engaged in, possibly a suburban lot, or some other stock in some other company, and he begins to use some of the time that he is paid for to put into the business, in worrying about a business in which he is not engaged and knows nothing about, in which some of his savings are invested. That is in itself very bad business. It certainly in no way helps the business in which he is engaged, and it does not help him. So I am against distributing profits, even if they are properly arrived at, in cash at the end of the year. I think it should be in some form of security in the business in which he is engaged.

NEED OF CORDIAL RELATIONSHIP IN INDUSTRY

"The great point about all the profit sharing plans of the future must be that they have got to be in the open, and a man down the line in the store or in the company must be as well informed as to what the company is doing as the man at the top, and if built on that solid foundation there is no question in my judgment about their enduring.

"If ever there was a time in the history of our country when cooperation between capital and labor is of first importance, it is at this hour. We are going out to a great new world. We are all in doubt, to a certain extent, as to what that world is to be. But that it is changed, no one is in doubt. Now, if we can get in our country with as little delay as possible the closest cooperation between capital and labor, a cooperation that means friendly trust, a close working of both groups as one, it will mean everything for this country in the next half century, everything in developing foreign trade, of which we are going to be greatly in need, everything in bringing to us here at home a better understanding and a more cordial relationship between all classes engaged in any form of industrial effort. If there ever was a time when the Civic Federation had an opportunity to take up the subject, and try to give to all who are inquiring the best information that we can gather and compile, I think this is the hour, and I trust in this respect the Federation will do its best, as I know it always does."

Lewis Nixon, Commissioner of Public Service of Greater New York, the first speaker at the afternoon session, took up the problem of the possible tie-up of transit in cities through strikes.

"Such a strike," said Mr. Nixon, "is far different from an ordinary strike in an industry. An industry can close up, and, on account of the vastness of the country, probably the product can be found in other directions; but here the distress is universal. It strikes at every calling, profession and trade, and a strike of one of our large transportation systems means an actual cost to the people of New York City of not less than five to six million dollars a day. Now, this is of course a public service. These men are responsible for the running of trains which accommodate the public and which are on systems controlled by public franchise. Hence I hope that there will be some means evolved by a meeting such as this that will enable us to settle this great problem and at least avoid the tremendous strain upon the resources of this city through a strike upon its public utilities.

"Personally I have never believed in enforced arbitration of any kind, but I believe there can be thought out through the fairness of the men who work and the fairness of those who employ them, a system which will at least hold them at work until a fair adjustment is made.

LABOR BEST IN COLLECTIVE BARGAINING

"I am inclined to think that as the men in these great industries allow others to speak for them, when they know their own representatives are of kindly sympathy with them in all their aspirations and all their needs, we are going to bring about a condition here on that experience, which is very large in its general effect, where, when an agreement is made, that agreement will be followed out to the letter. After we balance up, after the give-and-take of discussion, when we bring about the feeling in this country that organized labor is best in collective bargaining, when it says that bargain is something it wants you to sign for a term, whether months, weeks, days or years, when we can feel we can rely on the sounder numbers, the men who control and are looked upon for influence and example, I think that we will have an honest adherence to contracts made.

"I can remember when I was shipbuilding actively, the great fight was over the nine and one-half hour day from the ten hour day. The rest of the manufacturers rather quarrelled with me and were severe in their criticisms because I would not join them. The great leader, a man from Kansas City, came to me and said, 'We think we ought to have nine and one-half hours and we are going to strike to get it.' I said, 'You are striking.' He said, 'Yes; we think you ought to help us.' I said, 'I am not going to do what you have asked.' That seemed to disappoint them very much. I said, 'I am going to do a little bit better, and instead of giving you nine and one-half hours I am going to give you nine, and the same wages as you have for ten hours. Now, I will see if you are going to show me I have done a fair thing.' Well, everybody gave nine hours. Those were in the old days. Those struggles have passed. Collective bargaining has come, and we have to stand for it, and, so far as my experience has been it has been altogether a good thing, and I only say that if we feel that we can get that dependence upon an agreement and that responsibility shared in the making of such an agreement by both sides, so that both agree to it, we will at least have permanence in industrialism in this country."

COMMITTEE TO INVESTIGATE UNIONIZATION OF PUBLIC EMPLOYEES

Wheeler P. Bloodgood, of Milwaukee, declared that prior to the war the labor union movement was not generally understood and that many confused it with the Socialist movement. The war brought many such into contact with union labor and they came to understand "the old fight that had been on for many years between Mr. Gompers and the socialist. Mr. Gompers and those associated with him contending that through the union movement and collective bargaining and the recognition of individual initiative and property rights, the wage earner could be protected, that he would be able to get the wage to which he was entitled, the hours of labor and the conditions which he was entitled to."

"Now," declared Mr. Bloodgood, "through the organization of The National Civic Federation—and in that connection, I think we ought to all realize that The National Civic Federation has done a wonderful work not only in this war but, in fact, that it has brought about a condition of public sentiment that did not exist prior to the war, and I represent only one, I think, of thousands. I have a very different idea and conception of the great leaders in the labor movement, and during the war I came to the conclusion that they were not agitators, but among the great statesmen of America. In that connection I place Mr. Gompers among the very first and the very greatest."

Referring to the police strike in Boston, Mr. Bloodgood continued:

"I am very glad Mr. Woll said what he did this morning, and I think it is of vital importance that what he said should be spread broadcast throughout America, and that is that while the American Federation of Labor has granted a charter to organized unions and to policemen and to other government officials, it has urged and advised that they should solve their problem, whether it was the amount of wage they were receiving or the conditions under which they worked, through political action or some other action that did not involve a strike, because a wrong impression had gone abroad.

"If the men whose duty it is to defend our wives and children from thugs are going on a strike now, it is a matter of serious moment, it is a matter of most serious moment to the was this: the private soldiers drew up a :er, formed an organization, and what they was: Nobody above the rank of a private soldier shall belong to this organization; id, a committee appointed by private soldiers only shall have the power to call before nd to dismiss all officers from the commanding general downwards. Public opinion in land, informed opinion, held the view that police had very serious grievances which it to have been redressed. The men undoubt- had very just grievances. The bureaucrats ld not act. Well, what next? At home there) organization which I know with power, the iority, or whose business it is to intervene. 'ould be impertinence on my part to make suggestions as to what should or should not ould not be done in America. But there is loubt a very urgent need so far as England ncerned for an organization of the scope of American Federation of Labor and The National Civic Federation. These organizations are strictly economic. We have nothing of the l and, viewing my own country, studying it closely, after a very close study of America, nnot but help feeling that if we had someg in England corresponding to these two or- zations, one or the other of them would have rvened and would have had enough influence ave compelled the government to take the :e commissioner by the scruff of the neck if ıg and made him do what was right, or to taken the men and made them toe the line ey were unreasonable."

MUNICIPAL OWNERSHIP AND POLITICS

merson McMillin, in a paper on municipal ership, said that a quarter of a century ago rge percentage of the American public advo- d the ownership of public utilities by the icipalities. This sentiment, being chiefly ed on purported results obtained in Great tain, became so strong that The National Civic deration sponsored the sending of a commis- 1 composed of twenty-one persons, represent- all shades of opinion and including expert ;ineers and accountants, abroad to make a rough investigation, and the result was that few advocates for municipal ownership were ırd from thereafter for some years.

'Until the great increase in wages and mate- l resulting from the war forced utility com- ıies to apply to many municipalities, we heard : little clamor for municipal ownership out- 3 of states with a large socialistic popula- ı," said Mr. McMillin. "But even now the de- nd for municipal ownership is quite limited. fact, it hardly exists; certainly not to an ex- t to be alarming to public utility companies.

'In view of the fact that municipalities can ain capital at lower rates of interest, labor practically the same price, and under condi- ıs equally stable, they could doubtless secure ally efficient management. Then why should municipal ownership prevail? Certainly a nor for city ownership would not meet with versal opposition of private utility companies would have been the case a few years ago, or ceding the war. Why this change? Wages l material have advanced one hundred per t while the prices for the product of utilities 'e advanced but little and perhaps in a major- of cases, none at all.

'If the cities can obtain cheaper capital and :kmen at the same price per day, or month, y should not city ownership be made a suc- s? This question has been analyzed in the st efficient manner and from every point of w by one of the most efficient public service ımissioners of the country, a man with many rs experience as a commissioner, in a state h strong socialistic tendencies, and a state h perhaps a much larger percentage of muni- ally owned public utilities than any state in Union. His conclusions are drawn from the records of his office, and are unprejudiced conclusions, made up from facts. I will quote largely from his written statements; the statements being deduced from a comparison of reports made to his office by city owned companies, and by private companies.

"'Municipal utilities usually have such poor methods of accounting as to make a determination of the success or failure of municipal ownership almost impossible.

"'The cost of municipally owned utilities is usually higher when all the legitimate items of expense are given consideration.

"'The equipment installed in a municipally owned plant is usually too poor for effective service, or badly adjusted to the operating demands.

"'Business methods are usually lacking in municipally owned plants.'

"The causes of the failures of these enterprises are to be found in the organization of the municipalities.

"The Commissioner attributes much of the failure of city owned plants to the frequent change of management. He gives it as his opinion, that the period of employment of the superintendents does not average more than two or three years in city owned plants. This is bad in itself, but it also makes it difficult to obtain high class managers. Politics is the enemy of municipal ownership. It may be truthfully asserted that all of the weaknesses here shown to be incident to city owned plants can be remedied. But when? Never under our present form of city government!"

SQUARE DEAL THROUGH AMICABLE ARBITRATION

T. V. O'Connor, president of the International Longshoremen, talked on the contract between the longshoremen and the shipowners, as follows:

"A few years ago we used to have the habit of meeting our employers, laying down a wage scale, and saying to the employers. 'We want that to go into effect on such a date', and the employer would say 'Well, it won't go into effect', with the result that we had a quarrel, a strike, shipping tied up, men lost time, ships lost time. We came to the conclusion, after talking the matter over with some of the principal employers, that both sides were losers through handling the situation that way. And we got to the point where we met at a table and talked over our differences. If we were too radical on our side, we compromised. If the employer was too tight on his end and didn't want to come over with enough, we split the difference as a rule. But we came to an understanding.

"During the period of the war, whenever a man in our organization was under the idea that he should have double what he was getting, that conditions ought to be improved wonderfully, and it got to a point where the officer of the organization could not handle or convince all the members that they should be reasonable or send in their demands, we took the matter up with the Government and we had a commission appointed known as the National Adjustment Commission. That was composed of one man representing the employers, one man representing the War Department, one man representing the Shipping Board, and one man representing the International Longshoremen. That commission all during the period of the war set the scale of wages for longshoremen to work by, not only in every port of the United States,but in the possessions, in Hawaii, in Porto Rico. Any place a dispute came up that commission handled the case there either through the local or national commission.

"When the war was over, we were again confronted with the old condition. So we had a meeting with the employers again. We talked the matter over and we again came to the conclusion to continue the National Commission to handle all the disputes for the next year. That has been done by an agreement by all the employers. We are now meeting our employers in this city—some 60,000 men represented by about 150 delegates from the different ports. If we cannot agree with our employers, the matters that we cannot agree on will be referred to the National Commission, and there will be no stoppage of work, and both sides will abide by the decision of this commission. I want to say that if the employers of labor throughout the country will start in and handle their proposition the same as the steamship companies have in the past three or four years, there won't be any need of situations such as has arisen in Boston or other cities. All it wants from both sides is a good heart-to-heart talk, both sides sitting down with the idea in mind that we are not going to try to skin one another, we are going to try to give both sides a square deal. When we get to that point I believe the industrial problem is solved."

RIGHT OF LABOR TO BARGAIN

Rev. John A. Ryan, of the Catholic University of Washington, began by saying that twenty years ago he wrote one of the first magazine articles published in this country favoring the Australian scheme of compulsory arbitration, but that several years ago he changed his mind and no longer holds the views he did when he wrote his article.

"However, it seems to me that at least in public utility enterprises, such as railroads and street railways and other municipal utilities," declared Father Ryan, "the principle of compulsory investigation of disputes and compulsory suspension of the right to strike for a certain time, not too long, would be feasible and reasonable. That, as most of you know, is substantially the plan of the Canadian Industrial Disputes Act, and I believe something of the sort is in operation in Colorado.

"We ought to recognize, I think, that despite all the gains that have been made by the principle of collective bargaining in this country in the last few years, and despite the general statements that some of us make about opposition to collective bargaining being antiquated and a thing of the past, that we have still in this country several powerful employing organizations who do repudiate the principle of collective bargaining. The United States Steel Corporation is one of them, and we know a strike is threatened now for no other reason than because that organization is opposed to the principle of collective bargaining, under the pretense, I believe, that the men in the unions do not comprise a majority of the workers. The point, it seems to me, is that men have a right to speak through an organization whenever they form such an organization representing a respectable number—a respectable proportion of the workers. I see no reason why the majority of the workers in any concern have got to be in an organization before that organization or representatives of it have a right to speak. Now, this, it seems to me, is one of the real disturbing factors of our present industrial situation; that, despite all our talk about the principle of collective bargaining being recognized, it is flouted by powerful organizations in the industrial world.

MORE PRODUCTION GREAT NEED OF THE TIME

"We all agree that the primary requisite of our time in this country as well as in Europe is more production. I may say in passing that I don't believe as fully as I used to that the problem of industrial justice is so entirely a problem of distribution. It is largely a problem of distribution, but it is, I think, more a problem of greater production. Many of you are acquainted with the estimates of Professor King, which are the only ones we have, I think, to the effect that if the national income in the United States in 1910 were divided equally among all the families of the United States, each family would have received only $1,494. That would not enable each family to support an automobile, not even a Ford. So that, rich as our country is, and great as our productive capacities, we are not so rich, nor is our productive capacity so great that everybody could be well off or comfortably fixed if there were an equal division, and of course we cannot expect an equal division. So the great need of our time is more production.

"It seems to be notorious that, generally speaking, men are producing less per hour or per day now than they were before the war. The general feeling seems to be among the workers that during the war there was a great deal of profiteering of one kind or another, or that in times past the men who had the power grabbed all they could grab, so now the workers, or many of them at any rate, are saying: 'We are now in the saddle. The power is now ours, and we are going to get all that we can out of the exercise of the power we possess.' And so they are asking for a forty-four hour week, and a five day week, and a six hour day. I do not believe we can get along on any such short hour production period as that. Then how are we going to get this larger production if the workers don't seem to be interested in giving it, if the theory seems to be to raise wages and shorten hours according as labor possesses the strategic power to do so? You used to be able to do it by threatening them with discharge, because you had men in reserve to put in their places. You cannot do that any more. So far as we can see, for several years to come labor is going to be scarce in this country, owing to the stoppage of immigration and apparently the departure from our shores of a great many of the immigrants that have been here. So you cannot inspire the worker through the motive of fear to produce an increased product, because he is not afraid. And I don't think you can interest him in his work or in greater production through any altruistic motives. The mass of men are not moved that way, neither employers nor employees. So far as I can see, there is about as much human nature in one class as there is in the other.

"It seems to me the only way you can get men interested in their work, interested in the pecuniary effects of it, and in the creative part of it is by making it worth their while to produce more. And you can make it worth their while to produce more, it seems to me, only through this device of partnership. The two principal elements, I think, are, first, labor participation in industrial management, so far as that is feasible; and, second, profit sharing in the surplus that remains above, let us say, a fair return on the capital. The point is, I think, that we shall have to divide this surplus among or between the management and the rank and file of the workers. I don't know on what principle it can be done. I am not suggesting a particular basis for the distribution. But as to the principle, the fact that the workers must be allowed to participate in this elastic and definite surplus, I have no doubt whatever."

PERSONAL RELATION WITH EMPLOYEES

Angus S. Hibbard, a member of the Executive Committee of the Chicago Association of Commerce, next read a paper on "Wanted Willing Workers." He said:

"It has been fully demonstrated that increased production is the need of the country and that by it alone stabilized conditions can be restored. The controlling element in production is labor and nothing has been so thoroughly upset during the past five years. Labor is now unequally distributed. Living conditions and costs are not uniform. The individual interest of those employed has lessened, and to a greater extent than ever before the workers of the country are not willing workers. No amount of wages will make men or women efficient unless they have a real interest in what they are doing. This human interest is not a chattel and must be brought about, if it is to be maintained, by something more than the mere payment of wages.

"As labor does not deal directly with capital but deals only with the management employed by capital, it is therefore the problem of management to produce willing workers, people interested and contented in their jobs, having before them a prospect of betterment for themselves and families and a liking for their employment and employers. It has been demonstrated that this can be done, and it is being done to a greater extent than ever before, by carefully developed plans and by consistent and constant effort of management on behalf of some of the large as well as small employers. So-called welfare work is no longer looked upon as something extra which may be given by well meaning employers. It has been proven that it is a good business proposition to provide for pensions, death benefits, accident and sick benefits, savings plans, good surroundings and working conditions, opportunities for recreation, etc. Many have gone beyond this and have brought about direct representation of employees by committees whose members sit in with the management and take part in determining the relations of labor within the establishment. Still others go directly into plans for profit-sharing, finding it possible to say that the capital invested in the business will be contented with a specified return and that all net earnings beyond this shall be divided between the labor and the capital employed.

"In the great majority of cases these plans have been successful. All cards have been put upon the table, and the problems and risks of management have been put into language which is understandable. It is not found that any one plan for welfare work, committee representation or profit sharing will fit all cases, but some plan or part of some plan will fit almost any case, and where honestly and earnestly followed up by the management, individual relations with labor are established which were heretofore found impossible.

"It is certain that management throughout the country wants nothing more than to bring about personal relations with employees. This is no patent nostrum or universal cure-all to be taken in the dark, but it is a problem for management, as its development will be not alone to their benefit and the benefit of capital represented by them, but to the communities in which they live and to the entire country."

SIGNAL ACHIEVEMENTS OF FARMERS

Chairman Barrett next told of the purpose of his organization, the Farmers' Educational and Cooperative Union of America.

"We call it," said he, "the Farmers Union for short. The purpose is to better the condition of the farmer, mentally, socially and—mostly financially. It is sixteen years old. We have initiated a little more than three and one-half million farmers into the organization. You have heard all about the farmers' difficulties. You have heard all about his suspicions and his other shortcomings. He has had about as hard a time as you have. We have launched or started a little more than 12,000 business concerns in the Farmers' Union to date—a little more than 12,000 cooperative concerns. We have had a little over 4,000 failures—not fifty per cent. That is better than you folks have done. Just look through your records, and it shows that over half of you folks failed. I mean when you go out of business. Not quite half of us have failed. For instance, we have one concern that handles between twenty-five and thirty million dollars worth of hogs at Omaha. We have got them all the way up into the millions and many millions at that."

OBVIATING STRIKES IN PUBLIC SERVICE

Patrick J. McNabb, vice-president of the National Association of Letter Carriers, spoke on the questions as to how far with safety the pu[b]lic could go in allowing their public employ[ees] to unionize, or as to what the public would [do] to help those public employees to secure redr[ess] of grievances if they don't unionize. He sai[d]:

"I don't believe—my experience leads me [to] this belief—that public employees want to unio[n]ize, and when they have unionized, they ha[ve] been driven to it by the bureaucracy that obtai[ns] in states, in cities and in the federal gover[n]ment, which has made it impossible for them [to] secure redress of grievances promptly in any w[ay] that they know of through their ordinary for[m] of organization. So they have been led to lo[ok] around and see what else they might do in ord[er] to help lift themselves out of a very grievo[us] situation. And it is grievous so far as the polic[e]men and firemen of this city and other cities a[re] concerned, and in the Federal service very ge[n]erally. The Federal employees that I represen[t], the National Association of Letter Carriers, [in] their recent convention last week, express[ed] themselves as unalterably opposed to strikes b[e]cause they want to avoid conflicts, but they [do] demand—and they are going to enforce the[ir] demand with all the strength that they can brin[g] to bear—that in this cooperative concern, th[e] Post Office Department, they be allowed to c[o]operate. Public service departments can n[ot] be conducted like an outside private busines[s] because they are not run for profit and they ca[n] be made the greatest agency for cooperative e[f]fort. Most of the employees are making th[e] service their life work. They have made a stud[y] of it. They can offer good suggestions for i[ts] improvement. They want those suggestions [to] be taken up and discussed. That is all.

"President Wilson has said that men cann[ot] remain very far apart if they can get around [a] table, and that is what we are trying to do. Th[at] is what I think all the public employees anywher[e] are trying to do. Have it so fixed that they ca[n] sit down with those who happen to be runnin[g] the machinery for the time being and discus[s] with them the things that affect the employee[s]. As it is now, the manager of the Post Office De[]partment and the employees are very, very fa[r] apart, because he will not permit us to meet wit[h] him and discuss these things. I think if you[r] committee has upon it a representative of each, say, of the Federal, the State and the City em[]ployees, and enough other men to represent thi[s] association generally, we might be able to wor[k] out some rules, some method of procedure, tha[t] would obviate the situation of strikes in the pub[]lic service."

TRANSLATION OF FRENCH LAWS

Through the generosity of Mr. Albert Farwell Bemis of Boston, a member of the Commission on Industrial Inquiry of The National Civic Federation, which has just completed its report on the industrial situation in Great Britain and France, the Federation is able to offer to the public without cost translations of the recent French laws on town planning, and reparation of damages caused by the events of the war. The translation is by Dr. Roscoe Pound, dean of the Harvard Law School.

This publication is issued under the auspices of the Commission on Industrial Inquiry as an addendum to its report. The translations are expressed, as far as possible, in American legal phraseology, and they should prove of value to any American who is interested in the general subject of town planning, or who has a desire or intention to participate in any way in the rehabilitation of French towns or industries. There are copious explanatory notes by Dr. Pound accompanying the translation.

A. PARKER NEVIN

in principle, is for a nationalized sense of service.

This may be generally accepted and designated as socialism, but it is not certain that some of the radical wing in British industry would admit that it is socialism at all.

Industry must exist within certain definite classifications: either it must be the result of private enterprise with private capital employed and with labor an integral factor; or, it must be communized, which means that the two main factors are the State and the workmen—the State furnishing capital, paying wages and appropriating profits if any are made over the cost of service; or, industry must be proletarianized, which would abolish capitalism, eliminate employers, private or State, and combine all labor, manual and brain, in each industry into one large collective unit. If an industry should become thus proletarian in its structure, it would necessarily become either guildism or syndicalism. If industry is to merge into the guild system, there will be no imaginative enterprise, capitalistic initiative nor the taking of commercial risks. Instead of the guild being subject to the community, the community will be subject to the dictates of the guild. If industry should become a product of syndicalism, capitalism as well as the State will disappear, and there will be one group dominating the entire community, nation and government. It does not seem possible to escape the classification of industry into one of these groups.

SOCIALISTS SEEK STATE CONTROL

Socialists, on the other hand, repudiating communism and proletarianism, seek to substitute State control of means and agencies of production. Their claim is far more plausible to the plastic mind than the extreme forms of organization to which allusion has been made.

The obvious weakness in the program of the radical group is the absence of coherent and practical plans for execution. English conservatism, in the writer's opinion, wholly precludes employers or employees adopting socialism as we ordinarily use that term. Our Commission met employers who were wholly hostile to socialism, but expressed a willingness to adopt advanced ideas towards socializing their plants and businesses. They recognize clearly and sympathetically the pressing need of serious reforms in British industry. Such as these were entirely at variance with the radical element, but they were willing to go very far towards evolving means to stabilize and mutualize relations between themselves and those in their employ. The attitude of these men was impressive, and one could see in their progressive willingness to enrich industry with forward-looking plans of action the real hope of future industrial strength and harmony. Such methods of socializing industry upon sound, enlightened and humane principles can and will proceed without reliance on or connection with the theories of a state control of industry or sinister hints of sudden revolution.

Every commission and every individual which has made a study of industrial conditions in Great Britain since the war has been impressed with the fact that greater production is the crying need of the country. It was interesting to find men so opposed in their general views with regard to the problems of capital and labor as Lord Leverhulme, head of the vast Sunlight Soap industry, and Mr. Arthur Henderson, General Secretary of the British Labor Party, united with regard to this matter. Lord Leverhulme stated that it was immaterial to him what the weekly schedule of hours was if there were adequate production. Mr. Henderson, from an entirely different viewpoint, stated that increased production for the needs of the community was paramount to any question arising between employers and employees, and his statement contained a veiled threat that unless production were maintained in response to the normal needs of the nation, the whole system of British employment would be attacked by labor and a comprehensive plan of nationalized control would follow.

PRODUCTION LIMITATION BEING ABANDONED

The old idea of limitation of production by British workmen is being abandoned, and there is being substituted a better and quickened understanding of the necessity of enlarged productivity. Trade unions clearly recognize and openly advocate the economic effect of increased production, and there is no evidence of insistence upon the reinstatement of pre-war restrictions of output.

Most impressive during the travels of our Commission through Great Britain was the attitude of broad minded representatives of trade unionism in seeking to establish cordial plans of cooperative action between employers and employees.

There is a growing demand that the status of labor be stated in the terms of a new morale of industry. Evidence of this insistence is shown in recent reports of committees representing various organizations, all of which agree substantially in the conclusions reached as to the worker himself. For instance, the report of a committee appointed by the Archbishops of the Church of England to make a broad survey of the new spirit in industry thus characterizes the situation to which I refer:

> ". . . We think that the common description of workers as 'hands' summarizes aptly an aspect of their economic position which is not the less degrading because it has hitherto met with too general acquiescence. The suggestion is that the worker is an accessory to industry, rather than a partner in it; that his physical strength and manual dexterity are required to perform its operations, but that he has neither a mind which requires to be consulted as to its policy nor a personality which demands consideration; that he is a hired servant whose duty ends with implicit obedience, not a citizen of industry whose virtue is in initiative and intelligence."

Labor as a whole is more trustful of British employers than the Government or the politicians. In considering Great Britain's industrial situation the American reader should remember that the Government officially recognizes the legality of trade unionism, and there is practically no issue between employer and employed with respect to the enforcement of the principle of the closed shop. The chief concern of the public toward trade unionism in relation to industry is not the form of organization. nor the number engaged in the ranks of the union, it is the solemn question whether trade union officials and their followers recognize that as their power increases so does their responsibilty.

(*Continued on page 20.*)

Socialism or Social Reform in the Church—Which?

(Continued from page 9)

prosperity of the whole people" if the socialist state were to confiscate and operate the American Beet Sugar Company, the Barlow Foundry Company, the Brooklyn Bridge Freezing and Cold Storage Company, the Merchants' Refrigerating Company of New York, the Seamless Products Corporation or the Citizens' National Bank of New York, of which associations you are either a president or director? And then add to these business concerns a million other corporations covered in the socialist program, not to speak of the six million farms, and the picture will be complete; and yet, according to Mr. Hillquit, that is exactly what socialism means, and it "admits of no limitation, extension or variation."

As against Mr. Hillquit's clear and terse definition of socialism, I want to place another clear and terse expression on socialism; that made by Samuel Gompers at Faneuil Hall, Boston:

> I want to tell you, Socialists, that I have studied your philosophy; read your works upon economics, and not the meanest of them; studied your standard works, both in English and German—have not only read, but studied them. I have heard your orators and watched the work of your movement the world over. I have kept close watch upon your doctrines for thirty years; have been closely associated with many of you, and know how you think and what you propose. I know, too, what you have up your sleeve, and I want to say that I am entirely at variance with your philosophy. I declare it to you, I am not only at variance with your doctrines, but with your philosophy. Economically, you are unsound; socially, you are wrong; industrially, you are an impossibility.

In the above treatment of socialism, I refer only to its economic phase. What is its spiritual significance? Does the Joint Commission on Social Service think it would conduce to the spiritual welfare of the people to have put into practice a program which is admittedly founded and based fundamentally on a philosophy that is the negation of Christianity; a philosophy which interprets all human life, all history, all human accomplishments, all heroic and noble deeds as having been inspired by nothing more than the two basest carnal urges of mankind—the urge of the stomach and the urge of sex; a philosophy which flatly denies the declaration of Christ that man does not live by bread alone, which is utterly materialistic, which not only ribaldly scoffs at all religion as an alleged instrument of capitalism for the oppression of the masses, but which denies the existence of God and that man is a living soul. Do the clergymen of the Protestant Episcopal Church, or of any other church, whose mission it is to teach the Christian gospel and who yet blandly approve of so-called "Christian Socialism" as a means of reform, really know what socialism is? Do they comprehend that socialism would not only destroy private ownership and personal initiative in material endeavor, but that which is infinitely more precious, the heritage of spiritual beliefs and immortal aspirations?

At the forum to be conducted in October at Detroit under the auspices of the Church Socialist League in America and the Church League for Social and Industrial Democracy, referred to in my former letter, you will doubtless hear much talk about the elimination of the causes of unrest through the democratization of industry and the enactment of minimum wage, compulsory sickness and unemployment insurance and old age pension legislation. None of these things, however, is socialism except the first named, which could well be termed Bolshevism, dependent entirely upon who defines it. The other subjects mentioned are by-products of socialism, in that they all look to the State for paternal guidance and help, but they do not contemplate, as socialism does, the "abolition of the wage system."

There is not space here to go into these questions in detail. Suffice it to say that in the great reconstruction program drafted by the Executive Council of the American Federation of Labor, reported to the recent convention of that body in Atlantic City and unanimously endorsed, there is not a suggestion of any of these alleged panaceas, excepting that a resolution offered by a member endorsing the minimum wage by law was overwhelmingly defeated, while a proposition for the democratization of industry along the lines advocated by the original coiners of that phrase was unceremoniously stamped upon as a Bolshevist proposal in disguise.

I do not mean to imply that the American Federation of Labor is the repository of all wisdom on industrial matters. But I do insist that when it comes to proposals designed to help the wage earner, the real wage earner's voice—and especially when it is in accord with that of the employer—should be listened to over the voice of the doctrinaires and sentimental well wishers of humanity in general.

On the questions of compulsory sickness and unemployment insurance, old age pensions and so forth, I quote two leading labor officials, Mr. Samuel Gompers, President of the American Federation of Labor, and Mr. Warren S. Stone, Grand Chief of the International Brotherhood of Locomotive Engineers. Mr. Gompers says:

> There are so many of our people, including workmen, who look to the government of our country to do the things which seem so easy for the government to do, and which they imagine should be done by the government. They do not recognize the pit-falls and the dangers which are entailed by conferring upon the government the function of doing these things. To my mind, it is a grave danger to place into the hands of the government the powers which would necessarily result from government compulsory health insurance with all the powers vested in the government incidental to and in the enforcement of health insurance.
>
> There is one thing that I want to say to the Committee on Social Insurance. Place in the hands of the government the right to determine who is or who is not entitled to governmental insurance; to determine regulations and conduct of every man insured, then it means that the government has the power with all the force at the command of the government to enforce the decrees or regulations.
>
> And that applies, too, to unemployment compulsory insurance. The government will determine then what will constitute justifiable reasons for unemployment. It might decide that when men and women are unemployed they are entitled to this insurance. Well, what is the cause of unemployment? Suppose it is a disagreement with employers. The government will decide as to whether the cause of unemployment is justifiable or is attributable to the workmen or to the employers. It is not necessary, then, for me to mention the fact of what that would mean to the work, the policy and the constructive movement of organized labor. The labor movement would lose its voluntary character and its effectiveness, and there would be brought about a condition of affairs in our country whereby the toilers would be rendered ineffective in their work for the protection and promotion of their rights and interests."

Mr. Stone says:

> It seems to me that the whole plan of health insurance or social insurance, from the standpoint of the workers at least, is altogether wrong. If we have accomplished anything as a nation, it has been due to the fact that the men and women of the country have been allowed to work out some of these problems. I do not take much stock in paternalism; I do not believe in a government that tucks you in bed at night, and if some plan of health insurance is adopted, worked out and finally made a law, I fear its effect on our country; I fear it will be the beginning of the end. I do not believe any nation can prosper when the government does everything for the industrial worker. It destroys initiative and makes him a dependent upon the bounty of his government.
>
> But I want to say to you frankly as a representative of labor that there is not going to be any compulsory health insurance if we can help it. When you say to the American working people that they must do this or that thing, every drop of red blood in them resents it. I think it is summed up in a homely phrase, "You can push all you like but you musn't shove."

But, Mr. Morgan, permit me to take exception to your assumption that government ownership of the railroads in this country, as demanded by the Railway Brotherhoods, spells socialism. At the time you wrote your letter, you were perfectly justified in assuming that the American Federation of Labor and the Railway Brotherhoods had united to demand the so-called "socialization of the railroads." At this writing, it would seem that the American Federation of Labor has not itself taken favorable action, although some of its constituent organizations have done so. However, whether the American Federation of Labor joins the Brotherhoods in this demand or not, the so-called "Plumb Plan" is not socialism. It is "government ownership" of railroads, but not "government operation." It contemplates wages, interest and profits. In fact, the real socialists today are opposed to government ownership and operation of public utilities until such time as the socialists can take over the government, when they will demand not only ownership but operation as well. The socialist argues that the "capitalistic government," by exchanging government bonds for railroad bonds, is simply continuing to the capitalist his profits in the form of interest, at the same time making his investment an absolutely safe one. What the socialists want is a government like Trotzky's, that will, through wholesale confiscation, extinguish entirely the private capital invested. There is no more socialism involved in the Brotherhoods' proposition for the Government to own the railroads than there is in the proposition for the City of New York to own the Interborough Railroad, which it does. The difference between those propositions is not in the *ownership*, but in the next step; that is, the leasing, which is a business proposition. New York City leases the Interborough to a corporation of bankers and business men who themselves put up one hundred million dollars, which under certain contingencies they will forfeit, while the Brotherhoods' proposition is that the Government should lease the railroads to the railroad employees for operation and, should there be a deficit, the Government, instead of collecting from them, would have to take its satisfaction out of the cancelling of the contract. So, whatever criticism may be made against the Brotherhoods' plan, that criticism cannot justly be that it is socialism.

You say that this Brotherhood plan for the socialization of our railways is far in advance of the British Labor Plan, and you ask: "Is one more socialistic than the other?" My answer is, as explained above, that one is entirely socialistic and the other is not at all. The British Labor program is a Marxian proposition, pure and simple, as evidenced by the following sentences in that much-heralded reconstruction program:

> The individualistic system of capitalist production, based on the private ownership and competitive administration of land and capital . . . will receive its death blow. And the Labor Party refuses absolutely to believe that the British people will permanently tolerate any reconstruction . . . involved in the abandonment of British industry to . . . separate private employers . . . What the Labor Party looks to is a genuinely scientific reorganization of the nation's industry . . . on the basis of the common ownership of the means of production; the equitable sharing of the proceeds among all who participate in any capacity and only among these, and the adoption, in particular services and occupations, of those systems and methods of administration and control that may be found, in practice, best to promote the public interest. . . .
>
> The Labor Party stands not merely for the principle of the common ownership of the nation's land, to be applied as suitable opportunities occur, but also, specifically, for the immediate

> the *Call* by your correspondent has been borne out by the developments here.
>
> There will be no strike to save Tom Mooney; the Soviet government has been denounced; the millions of starving Russians blockaded by the Allied governments are to be left to their fate; the Labor party idea has been smashed and, as for industrial unionism, the A. F. of L. intends to go its old way. This is the grist of two days' grinding in the Gompers mill.
>
> It was a field day for Gompers, for every parliamentary trick that might be employed to shut off debate was used by him.
>
> The convention has shown opposition to a joint termination of contracts, is opposed to the democratization of industry to the extent of refusing to recommend the election of foremen on jobs by the workers, refusing to assist in the formation of soldiers' councils that would be helpful to labor, sets its face against any letting down of the craft bars or aiding industrial organization and finally has defeated a recommendation to the international unions to adopt an initiative and referendum clause in their constitutions.

Not only on this side of the water do the revolutionists recognize the patriotic, courageous and adamant stand of the American labor movement against their destructive policy, but those in Europe have an equally clear perception of the fact. This is evidenced by the following statement made to the United Press by Jean Longuet, grandson of Karl Marx, Socialist Deputy and the leading spirit in the international proletariat alliance of French, British and Italian workers:

> French and Italian workers are already bound closely together, while English laboring men are lining up more and more closely with us. We have already succeeded in establishing an alliance of workers which does not recognize European national boundaries.
>
> But at the present time we have gained but little support from America. This fact is chiefly due to the opposition of Samuel Gompers and other conservative leaders who control the destinies of the American Federation of Labor and who have complete power over labor organizations. Also, the fact that numerous workers own their own homes breeds conservatism.

Observe that nothing is more ruinous to practical socialism than ownership of their homes by the working classes.

It matters not that many changes have taken place since June. Many serious outbreaks have occurred and at times it may have seemed to the public as if the American labor movement had been fully as radical as the British labor movement. The leaders of only a few of the 125 different craft organizations of the American Federation of Labor are demanding the nationalization of the industries in which they work. In fact, when the conventions of the miners and the railway and steel workers declare for nationalization, it would appear to the casual observer that the cablegrams from the Triple Alliance of Great Britain had been effective. But despite sensational declarations and resolutions and striking headlines, none of those industries is yet nationalized, nor do I think they will be. Also, it is well to reflect that, with all the various crises, flare-ups, etc., which have occurred in England, none of the industries in that country have yet been nationalized, either.

Even if such declarations were to be taken at their face value, it is all the more reason why the business men in our churches, or the clergymen with whom they work, should not relax for a moment their grip on the essential feature of the situation, which is that the nationalization of industry, whether by our "capitalistic" government, by a socialistic state government or by a Soviet government, spells alike the practical destruction of industry and the overturning of all our free institutions. When the American Federation of Labor, representing three and a half millions of organized wage earners, sends delegates to Berne, Amsterdam and Paris to beat down those revolutionary programs, it is no time, I repeat, for American employers, bankers, business men, preachers, professors and lawyers to be even indirectly doing anything that would encourage their enemies.

With you I can say that: "We are living in a period of vital change" and that "true progress is what we are all aiming at." With you I agree that "the war was a great leveller," and that "in that crisis we all had to put our shoulders to the wheel, rich and poor, high and low, and with all former rank and distinction swept away, each of us fitted into the groove to which he was best suited." With you I agree that "it is in that spirit that we must face our present problems." But I cannot agree with you that "the old order has passed," if by that you mean that the fundamental concept out of which our Republic had its birth, that which is the basis of the American Constitution, the ideal of the human right to liberty, the full development of opportunity, individual freedom in the pursuit of great accomplishments and of happiness, that which has enabled America to become great, industrially, socially and spiritually, among the nations, is to be scrap-heaped and a new era of Socialism and Bolshevism is to take its place. We are too prone to be carried away by rhetorical phrases. In fact, we have had so persistently dinned into our ears the slogans of the Socialists and Bolshevists about "the new concept," "the new world," "the new order," when the Brotherhood of Man is to be realized—which, in the minds of those radicals, means the advent of Bolshevism—that many of us have got to talking in the same phrases.

Arthur Henderson, the high priest of "the new concept," "the new world" coterie of radicals, who is kotowed to by the writers in such publications as *The New Republic, The Nation, The Dial* and *The Survey*, which, in turn, are kotowed to by many members of the Social Service Commissions of the Church, stated the case for that cult last week in London, as follows:

> The present world unrest means that the old order of things is in its death throes; that a new society is about to come to its birth and that age-long injustices and inequalities that burdened the lives of the common people are at last to be swept away. But it is doubtful whether the ideal of true political liberty will be realized in this or other countries without a violent convulsion of society. . . . The ideal of a new society arises again in these fateful days, strengthened by the downfall of that system of the capitalist and imperialist which created conditions that drove the young men of the world into the shambles of war.

As against this visionary rhetoric of Arthur Henderson, I place the sound common-sense utterances of Mr. Herbert Hoover, lately returned from his work of directing relief in Europe:

> A conviction dominant in my mind comes from contact with stupendous social ferment and revolution in which Europe is attempting to find solution for all its social ills by practical experiments in socialism. My conviction is that this whole philosophy is bankrupting itself from a startling quarter in the extraordinary lowering of productivity of industrial commodities to a point that, until the recent realization of this bankruptcy, was below the necessity for continued existence of their millions of people.

Another characterization of the subject which I will give is by Mr. A. Parker Nevin, who has just returned from England, France and Italy, where, as a member of The National Civic Federation Commission, he made a first-hand study of industrial conditions. He talked to Arthur Henderson and other leaders of the Bolshevist and near-Bolshevist groups. Mr. Nevin said:

> I think the fundamental trouble in Great Britain and also in the United States at the present time is this: That consciously or unconsciously we have got industrial neurasthenia. We are on our nerves. We are upset. We are not seeing very straight and not acting very straight. It is a natural reaction of the great war. We are looking more at the things than at the people running the things, I think we get in a confused condition of mind and fail to see how we can treat these questions with composure. If we are going to get machine guns out in the streets and kill one another and denounce everybody, we are having a re-enactment of the war, we are having industrial war. But we are not going to get anywhere by those methods. If there ever was a time in the history of Ameri-

> can industry, and particularly so far as labor is concerned, when you want composure, it is the present time. When I say composure, I don't mean armistice; I don't mean any particular time to call off the contest. But I do say that no man can think clearly, constructively, hopefully or sympathetically when he is in a rage, when his mind is upset, or when he is not in good mental health. That is exactly what the trouble fundamentally with Great Britain is at the present time, and quite naturally, and the trouble in this country at the present time. Everybody wants everything in sight. Everybody is demanding things. We are all mixed in our economics. We are mixed up in our sociology. We are mixed up in our objectives, and until we get back to some normal basis of constructive thought, I personally fail to see where we are going to make steady progress.

The socialists, frankly despising the Church as an alleged institution of capitalism, have not been averse to using, wherever possible, its machinery and employing in their propaganda clergymen who could be caught through the bait of their catch-phrases, purposely designed to way-lay the unwary and sentimental.

We have learned much through suffering during the war and one of the things we learned is that we do not want anything that has even remote connection with what is advocated by the Lenins and Trotzkys, the Bela Kuns, Haywoods, Hillquits and their great galaxy of cheap imitators who are editing our so-called "intellectual magazines," and which has been drawn upon so extensively, as stated in my former letter, by the social reform committees of the American churches. I know that the churches of America are sound to the core when it comes to dealing with such questions. They need only to have the facts. My criticism has been that they are not getting the facts through their social service commissions, but are getting only part of the facts and many mis-statements. My appeal to you, as a business man, was that the business men of the churches should take hold of this matter themselves and deal with it, not leaving it to theorists, sentimentalists and socialists, or to sensational revolutionary preachers whose pulpits are open principally to the most radical elements.

Speaking of the General Convention of the Episcopal Church which will meet in Detroit in October, you say that "a program of nation-wide church activity will be formulated as representative of the Episcopal attitude toward the new age," and you add: "Whether it will be socialistic or not, I am unable to forecast." As to whether the Episcopal program will be "socialistic" or not, I can confidently say that if the Episcopal Church realizes what socialism is, economically and spiritually, it will not be. Nor will it be in line with the principles laid down by the Church Socialist League in America or the Church League for Social and Industrial Democracy, the first of which is largely advertising that it will make over the Episcopal Church so as to assist in the working out of a "complete" social and industrial revolution. This same organization boldly declares in the New York *Call*: "The Church must repent in sackcloth and ashes. It must repudiate its affiliation with and support of the capitalist system of production, with its unholy emphasis on profits, privilege and exploitation which have impoverished and fettered the mass of the people of the world. And it must demonstrate that repentance by a whole-hearted indorsement of those movements which are seeking to establish a real brotherhood among men."

The public will doubtless watch with great interest this bold and impudent attempt of the revolutionary element in the Protestant Episcopal Church to capture that organization. Of course they will fail, but the attempt will be wholesome inasmuch as it will force a line-up between the sane and patriotic Americans in that body on the one side and the pacifists, socialists and convicted disloyalists on the other."

RALPH M. EASLEY.

"THE LABOR SITUATION IN GREAT BRITAIN AND FRANCE."

Indicating the scope of the complete report of Commission sent abroad by The National Civic Federation to study industrial conditions, the following is the table of contents:

The report of the Commission has been made from the point of view of the employer, the wage worker and the public, the Federation's Commission being the only one sent abroad since the conclusion of the war which was representative of all these elements. The contributors are Chairman Charles Mayer, of the Commission, who is also chairman of the Board of the France & Canada Steamship Corporation; James W. Sullivan, of the American Federation of Labor; Albert F. Bemis, a well known textile manufacturer of Boston, and A. Parker Nevin, of the New York Bar, an authority on industrial problems.

In its investigations the Commission has devoted especial attention to the constructive policies and programs adopted abroad affecting the relations of employers and employees, with the object of determining which if any of these might advantageously be applied in the United States.

The publisher of the report, which will be issued in regular book form, is E. P. Dutton & Company. The book is expected to be off the press October 15. It will contain approximately 400 pages. Advance orders may be sent to The National Civic Federation, 1 Madison Avenue, New York.

The Industrial Situation Abroad

(Continued from page 17)

Whether as a practical method of joint operation, workers should be permitted to have a voice in the direction of all the affairs in a given industry is as much of a question and as much disputed in Great Britain as in America.

"The least thing I would suggest as the workers' right," says Mr. Clynes, "is a share in the direction of industry in all matters immediately relating to the workers' welfare. There is nothing the Britisher will claim more than the right to take part in what he feels is his proper sphere of service."

The National
Civic Federation Review

Vol. V. NEW YORK, JANUARY 1, 1920 No. 1

INVIOLABILITY OF CONTRACTS

EMPLOYERS' AND WAGE EARNERS' REPRESENTATIVES AGREE THAT INDUSTRIAL CONTRACTS MUST BE KEPT AT ALL HAZARDS, BUT GIVE DIVERSE VIEWS ON OTHER ISSUES

COLLECTIVE Bargaining was made the theme of discussion at a dinner given by the Economic Club of New York, on Wednesday, December 10, 1919. Abstracts of the speeches of the three men who represented employers and wage earners are given herewith.

Frederick P. Fish, President of the National Industrial Conference Board, an organization composed of nineteen different national employers' organizations and himself the head of the committee from that organization in the President's Industrial Conference in October last, spoke for employers; and Major George L. Berry, President of the International Printing Pressmen and Assistants' Union; and T. V. O'Connor, President of the International Longshoremen's Association, represented organized wage earners. Collective bargaining could not have had more representative and able exponents from the labor standpoint than these latter gentlemen, because they have both just emerged from conducting two of the most exasperating, extensive and turbulent strikes in recent history where the main contention was over the keeping of contracts officially made by the organizations with their respective employers.

Robert Erskine Ely, Secretary of the Economic Club, proposed three cheers for the labor union leaders who believe that a contract is a contract and that there is only one thing to do with it, to live up to it. The wildly enthusiastic applause of the twenty-two hundred diners was a glowing tribute to the splendid work of these two men, which culminated in a victory over the Bolshevist and disloyal forces which had striven to destroy the unions from within.

Mr. Frederick P. Fish, said in part:

"Whenever I am thinking of the subject of industrial relations, one thought comes into my mind which I wish might permeate this country, and that is that the industries are not primarily for the advantage of the men who have money invested in them and their management, they are not primarily in the interest of the workingmen, but they are to be treated and considered in view of the interest of the people of the United States as a whole. We are today in a critical position, as England is and the rest of the world on this question of employment relation, and it is the duty of the people in this country not to develop prejudices one way or the other, not to be carried away by emotion, but to try to get at the real truth of the situaion as it exists and then use their judgment and their powers of reasoning in taking sides on the issues, insofar as it is essential that sides should be taken.

"The subject of collective bargaining is one much talked about. The phrase 'collective bargain' needs interpretation. My own conclusion is that, as it is generally and commonly used, it refers to an ideal situation which is more nearly exemplified in English conditions than in any other that exists in the world, that is, where the workmen are all organized in labor and trade unions, where the employers are organized and where the individual shops and the relations between the management and the individual establishment and the workmen of that establishment are ignored and sidetracked, and everything settled by collective bargaining between the enormous power of the labor unions on the one hand and the enormous power of the employers on the other. This seems to be the situation to which England is coming, if she has not got there already, but that is not yet the American situation. The American situation, on the contrary, is primarily today the open shop as against collective bargaining in the sense which I have given to that phrase.

"At the time we went into war there was a careful investigation made by the Washington government, which resulted in the publication of a report, which I think was the basis for the proposition that not ten per cent of the establishments of this country, and not ten per cent of the workmen, the wage-earners, in this country were organized into trade unions, as compared with the very much greater percentage in England. That has been up to date the American situation, the closed shop and what it means dominating the employment relations in England, the open shop and what it means dominating the employment relations in this country.

"I think a study of the books, a study of the available evidence, will justify this: that whatever may be the cause of the situation, the labor

MAJOR GEORGE L. BERRY

FREDERICK P. FISH

T. V. O'CONNOR

union domination in England had not succeeded in bringing about efficiency in production at the time the war began, that it had not succeeded in getting for the English wage-earner very good pay. I believe that the books establish the proposition, based upon scientific investigation, that, at the outbreak of the war, the English workman was producing not more than a third to a half, at the outside, as much as the American workman, and I believe that it is perfectly clear to those who have studied the matter and have recorded the results of their studies in books, that the English workman wasn't getting anything like the compensation the American workman was getting. . . . It was impairing the standing of England as an industrial empire; it was reducing the standard of the individual workman in England.

"Now, gentlemen, an illustration of the why of that situation, I think, is shown by what happened in England when the war broke out. It was evident to the powers over there that the war couldn't be won unless there was a most tremendous increase of production, which meant work, work, work on the part of everybody, and the government officials persuaded the labor unions to abrogate their rules, by which there was efficiency of production. The production in England per unit per workman increased tremendously through the country and saved the situation.

"I think there is a definite connection between those two facts, that the production was very low before those rules were abrogated and those principles abandoned and the situation which arose after those rules were abrogated and the situation abandoned. Coupled with this agreement on the part of the English labor union was a definite promise on the part of the government that at the end of the war those rules and those principles should be re-established and the world today is waiting with interest to see what happens if, in fact, they are re-established. I don't believe they can be. If they are, I think England, as a commercial nation, is doomed. I think the labor union and the labor union leaders will have to see and recognize that fact in England and voluntarily adopt new principles, and if they do it over there, maybe they will do it in this country, because in this country I think the evidence is complete that the rules, principles, of the labor union are such as to reduce production, to limit efficiency and to suppress development of the industries that are of such vital importance to every man, woman and child in this country and to the whole world.

"We all know what a tremendous and radical change has occurred in industry during the last fifty years. The development of electricity, of power, the work of scientific men, inventions, the extension of transportation systems all over the world, the substitution of machinery for hand work and the crowding of people into great establishments and into cities have led to a condition utterly unlike that under which men worked and lived fifty years ago. . . . The stress and strain and the effort in dealing with all the questions, from selecting the right coal and the right raw material, that the product might be perfect all through the organization, the invention and design of machinery, looking after floor space, the saving of effort, the development of power in all its forms and the dealing with these modern conditions of transportation and of production that were so radically new, all those things took so much of the thought and energy of the men who were responsible for that management that in my opinion they neglected certain other things that were equally important and which should have been dealt with in exactly the same spirit, exactly the same mental alertness, exactly the same power as the physical, material and engineering problems which they dealt with so admirably. Among those was this: The relations with the workmen. The workmen were working under new conditions. They were crowded together as they never had been before. There were any number of new situations under which they worked. I cannot stop to go through the list, but among others the change from the old-fashioned generally easy going work to the work that is speeded up and timed by a machine which requires concentration and where men specialize to such an extent that a workman's job at which he starts is likely to be his job all his life. All those things brought in new elements of psychology, new elements of mental relation to the situation on the part of the workman, and they needed study and analysis and research that they might properly be dealt with. There were many more of them, gentlemen; there were many more of the same kind, but in addition to all there was this tremendous development of energy, of power, with this enormous production and the results of production which showed in profits, which showed in the creation of a few abnormally rich men who stood out from their neighbors with having made fortunes beyond the dream of anyone in prior generations out of this condition of things.

"That brought about a ferment on the part of the workingman, and it was naturaly inevitable that this should be so, that they did not look at things as they had before. That situation was one which should have been definitely attended to and studied. There should have been the same kind of research and the same kind of attention given to it as there was to the more material problem, and, gentlemen, I am satisfied that it wasn't done.

"But it has begun. A number of years ago attention began to be given to these things. It was begun to be recognized that working conditions were not right and all through this country in the industry men have attended to that side of their obligation, the management has attended to that important and conspicuous thing, for I know there is no element of industry that is anything like so important as the relation with the organization, the loyal workman, the sympathetic workman, the man whose work is a joy to him is invariably more effective in every possible way, and more than that, we have to recognize now that we are beginning to think about it, we have got to consider him not at all from the point of view as a part of a machine but as a man with so much aspiration, human feelings and human strength, as well as human weaknesses. As we all know, there has been great effort made in the direction of sanitation, of insuring good conditions of work and good conditions of living, assuring safety, and that work shall be done as easily as is consistent with efficiency. But that is not enough.

"There is an old doctrine which people had in the back of their heads all the time, although they didn't think about it—that the question of wages was a mere question of demand and supply, that is, the market will fix the worth automatically, although we recognize at the present time, I am happy to say, that there are qualifications to that law, that while that law controls and always will control, it cannot help controlling, yet there are qualifications to it and that an effort should be made to bring out, to reward, to develop, to reward every individual effort, every individual efficiency, every individual power, every individual capacity, every individual with loyalty, and also that any industry that is worth providing, that is worth perpetuating, ought to be able to pay everyone that enters in its employ a decent wage that will support him in a fair degree of comfort that is satisfactory to a right minded man and that will give him a chance for relaxation, a chance for saving something for old age or for accident. Another thing which I think they are beginning to recognize is this: that the unemployment situation is a most serious matter in industry, and that it isn't necessary that there should be so much unemployment, and steps are now being taken to select men rather than to take them haphazardly, to fit them for the job. Also there is the thought in many of our establishments today that if a man is employed there is an obligation to him that he is not to be fired merely because he isn't fitted for his job. Before that is done, it is the duty of the management to look around and see if there isn't a job for him somewhere else, and I believe that they can in this way gradually deal with the evil of unemployment.

"Out of the 450,000 industrial establishments in this country almost all, some 95 or 98 per cent of them, employ less than 250 men. If the employer of that small number of men goes at the matter intelligently and sensibly, he can get at these men sympathetically and intelligently, and he doesn't need any machinery for doing it. But the great troubles that we hear about are in the big organizations, where there may be in the 2 per cent or so of the big organizations there may be anywhere from 500 to 50,000 men or more, and there it is utterly impossible that there should be that personal relation that existed in the old days and which may exist today in the small shop if the employer gives attention to the matter. There you have got to have some organization, and each individual management should study the employment in its own shop and see which is the best. One form that is successfully employed in some places is simply to establish a department of good men for devoting themselves to the study of that question, to find out what the men need and want and think, and to talk things over with them. Another form is what we sometimes call shop committees or shop councils, where in the individual establishment the workmen elect, and it should be by secret ballot of the fairest kind and counted fairly, representatives from their own number who meet the representatives of the employer, who are men selected because they have th right characteristics and the right views of this important relation; because they recognize that the employees are men like themselves and are entitled to be treated respectfully and frankly and fairly. In that way the management will learn just as much as the men, and the men will learn just as much as the management. Men are fair; the employers are fair in this country. If they only stop to think and get at the situation accurately, I believe many of these things can be taken care of at the start. I also feel, and experience shows, that the workmen soon get into the frame of mind where they want to co-operate. Among the things that can be taught in that way, and in no other, in the big establishments, are some of the simple economic problems, for instance, that no rule which suppresses production is consistent with prosperity or with good wages. When it comes to a question of hours of labor, the principle that should be applied is not an arbitrary eight-hour day or forty-eight hours a week. That might fit some conditions and might not fit others, but there should be in every establishment that amount of work and the maximum amount of work that can be done without in the slightest degree impairing the health of the operatives and which leave them an opportunity to lead comfortable lives. There is a form of collective bargaining that appeals to me. There has got to be behind it sympathy, good faith, fairness, frankness, loyalty, a certain recognition of the weaknesses of human nature, because human nature on both sides is weak, and the desire to get results. For that kind of collective bargaining I urge you to stand. It involves the open shop. It involves that the employer shall not be forced into that kind of collective bargaining to meet the labor union delegate or the representatives of the labor union who are not in his employ, if elected as representatives of his men, because the moment he does that, that moment the labor union gets into his establishment, that

(*Continued on page* 13)

Russia as Seen by Ex-Military Attaché

LIEUT. A. W. KLIEFOTH, FORMERLY CONNECTED WITH AMERICAN EMBASSY IN RUSSIA, TELLS OF CHAOS UNDER BOLSHEVIKI—PLAN TO NATIONALIZE CHILDREN—RIDICULES ROBINS

AFTER spending three years in Russia, where he observed three regimes, those of the Czar, of Kerensky and of Lenine and Trotzky, Lieut. A. W. Kliefoth, who left Russia only last September, has returned to America with information of exceptional and impressive value concerning the break-up of Russia under Bolshevik rule. Lieut. Kliefoth tells of what he witnessed, and the evidence he brings back was gathered first-hand. Raymond Robins, at a recent meeting in Madison, Wis., according to reports, asserted that American troops had mutinied at Archangel, and was called to account by some soldiers, members of the American Legion, who had been there. Lieut. Kliefoth was the man ordered by the American commander there to investigate the reported mutiny. Of this, Lieut. Kliefoth said in a recent address in New York:

"There was no mutiny at Archangel. The first we heard of a supposed mutiny came from a Y. M. C. A. secretary. I was ordered to where our troops were preparing to entrain to fight the Bolsheviki.

"It was a bitter cold day. I asked the soldiers what the trouble was. They said they wanted more heat on the train. They wondered if their Captain might not have an additional stove supplied. They were ready to fight. That was all. I did not hear the word 'mutiny' applied to the incident until I reached New York."

ROBINS' ECSTASY AT SOVIET MEETING

Lieutenant Kliefoth, when asked about the statement ascribed to Colonel Robins that the railroad service of Russia was better under the Bolsheviki than under the Czar, said:

"When Robins was in Russia if you had a special train you got to your destination. If not, you took a chance. For three days I waited in a village on the Murmansk Railway for a chance to crawl on top of a train for Petrograd. We were about to leave when a telegram came from Lenine saying Colonel Robins was passing through on the way to Moscow. The whole line was shut down and traffic stopped until Robins passed in a special train, which formerly was used by the Czar and had been placed at his disposal by the Bolsheviki.

"Many peasants said to me that Americans were aristocrats. I argued with them that Americans were democrats. They would cite the fact that Colonel Robins was using the Czar's private car as proof of their contention.

"I have seen Robins at a meeting of the Soviet in Petrograd, listening to the speech of a Commissar. At the end of the address he would declaim rapturously, 'Isn't it wonderful? Isn't it inspiring?' All this though he had no interpreter with him, and I doubt that he knew twenty Russian words. As a matter of fact, Robins' information about Russia was obtained through an interpreter, Gumberg by name, who was a Bolshevist."

Concerning William C. Bullitt, whose testimony before the Congressional Committee on his peace mission to Russia created a stir, Lieutenant Kliefoth said Bullitt was in Russia seven days. He spent most of this time, he said, in the Kremlin in Moscow, with Soviet officials. He had no opportunity to ascertain facts at first hand and made his report on conditions from material supplied by the Bolsheviki.

CHILDREN ELECT OWN SOVIETS

Lieutenant Kliefoth described the system of education in Russia under the Bolsheviki.

"Under Lunacharsky, who was put in charge

Copyright Underwood & Underwood

LIEUT. A. W. KLIEFOTH

of the system, universities were opened to the illiterate," he said. "At the leading proletariat university in Petrograd not more than one in fifty could read or write. The catalogue announced that astronomy, physics, physiology and logic would be taught. There were no textbooks.

"In the elementary schools the children assembled at 9:30 o'clock. They came without breakfast and received a bowl of soup. The class then was called to order and the 'Internationale' and other revolutionary songs were sung. The children then were loaded down with proclamations and pamphlets describing the Communist movement and were told to bring back a receipt for the literature from their parents. They went home and returned in time for lunch, which again was a bowl of soup.

"The only freedom in the schools is the freedom of the pupils. In the kindergartens children four and five years old elect their own soviets or committees to report on the conduct of the teachers. As they cannot write, they report orally. If objection is made to the teacher, he is summoned before the Committee on the Suppression of Counter-Revolution and Speculation.

"Lenine's idea at first was to have no schools at all. He wanted the children of four and five to be taken to factories, where they would learn trades. Because of the downfall of industry, this plan was not followed.

NATIONALIZATION OF CHILDREN

"The Bolsheviki seek to obliterate the family unit. I saw no decrees concerning nationalization of women except, perhaps, some put out by irresponsible Soviets, but the ultimate Bolshevist aim is to control and guide race propagation. They feel that women must not be bothered with the institution of family or husband, and this ultimately would lead to nationalization.

"The Bolsheviki hold that the family is the unit of conservatism. One of their tenets calls for the destruction of all records concerning births, marriages and deaths. So that when 500 children are taken from Moscow out into the country communal schools the records of the children are destroyed and they are known only by number. Nobody can tell where the children have been taken. They are forbidden to write to their relatives. The mothers are told that no records exist of the destination of the children, who are in this way nationalized. This fact has become known to the people, and the day after such an excursion you can see many mothers sneaking out of Moscow on trains bound for the country in a hopeless attempt to find their children.

"You are told by people sympathizing with the Bolsheviki that the schools are more crowded than they were under the Czar. That is quite true, but the reason is because the schools are almost the only places where the children may keep warm and obtain food."

Lenine suppressed all opposition newspapers in Russia, using as an excuse the ruling that "no lie could be published." When some of these papers persisted in appearing, the supply of print paper was nationalized, and paper was supplied only to periodicals of Communist leanings.

The Committee on Propaganda and the Suppression of the Counter-Revolution, Lieutenant Kliefoth said, was empowered with authority over life or death. It spent in the current year 400,000,000 rubles for propaganda, printed in every known language. Lenine's foreign policy was based, he said, on foreign propaganda and world social revolution.

"The men running affairs in Russia are clever propagandists. Many of them have been political exiles for so many years that all they know is propaganda. They exercise arbitrary power and have unlimited funds behind them. Take the Committee for the Suppression of Counter-Revolution and Speculation. A simple accusation as a counter-revolutionist is sufficient to bring you before this body. There is no hope for a man accused. The real object of the committee appears to be to prevent the bourgeoisie from living.

"The only thing that pays in Russia today is being a Commissar, especially one dealing with finances. A Commissar having anything to do with finance automatically becomes rich."

Apologists for the Bolsheviki have said it was safer to walk in Petrograd than in the streets of an American city, the speaker declared. Lieutenant Kliefoth said this was undoubtedly true, for he had walked through street after street in Petrograd and had found the houses deserted. He said it was not safe to walk in the streets without a permit, and as permits were difficult to obtain, the streets were quite deserted. "So is a prison orderly and quiet," he commented.

"GET-RICH-QUICK" SCHEME OF RADICALISM

"It is a mystery to the physicians in Russia that the people have so much endurance. There are constant epidemics and it is remarkable that many more do not die. The population of Petrograd has fallen from 2,500,000 to 400,000, according to the Bolsheviki, but the English give the figure as 300,000. Most of the people residing in Petrograd, having no longer any reason for remaining there, have gone to the country, where they are living with the peasants, waiting for conditions to change. Many have been slain. The escapes of men would be more frequent, but they know their families would be held as hostages.

"Far from being a new experiment in democracy, Bolshevism is the get-rich-quick scheme of radicalism. It is a party government maintaining its power through military force, terror, food control, tyrannical suppression of every form of opposition.

"The Bolsheviki speak of peace, but they are not sincere. They desire a breathing spell for world social revolution, which is their real aim. That is the theme of all the commissars in every village in the land.

(Continued on page 7)

The Peace Covenant Labor Code

IS IT A MENACE TO A. F. OF L. PRINCIPLES? HOW FAR IS INTERNATIONAL SOCIALISM TO SET ASIDE THE TRADE UNION MOVEMENT IN AMERICA?

WHEN the International Labor Organization was chartered by the Treaty of Versailles a new mark was set in the inter-continental relations of the wage-workers.

The first international labor conference under the charter was held in Washington in October and November. Some points in what looks like legislation for the world's labor were arranged for. A Director General of the international labor office was elected. That Director General is Albert Thomas. It hence will not be a waste of time for American trade unionists to stop and indulge in the classic query, "Where do we go from here?"

Labor tactics in Europe and America have differed widely. Labor policies have differed radically. The philosophy and the psychology of European labor movements have found little reflection in the trade union movement of America. The character of the conference in Washington and the election of Thomas by that conference to its most important executive office fairly open the whole subject of organized labor's principles and methods for consideration.

Albert Thomas is one of the leaders of French Socialism. In the language of the radical world, he is an "intellectual." In Europe, he might be called a labor leader, but not in America. In America, Thomas would be purely a politician, like Victor Berger or Eugene V. Debs—a Socialist politician, though with no suspicion of pacifism in his make-up. The great international labor organization of the League of Nations thus comes at once under the administrative leadership of a Socialist politician. Is he to lead in a Socialist or a trade unionist movement?

The propositions that American labor has now to consider may be divided thus:

1—Is American labor prepared to abandon its traditional adherence to a policy of economic, or industrial, action?

2—Is American labor prepared to submit to the European idea of political action as a main weapon?

3—Is American labor prepared to join wholeheartedly in the work of the international labor organization of the Treaty of Versailles, which mostly is purely political and which is so designed that it may—perhaps must—impose its decisions by methods that have always had the complete disapproval of American labor?

4—Is American labor prepared to see the purely trade union international—the Federation of Trade Unions—pass out of existence as an effective labor body, made useless by the new organization which is set up by the treaty of peace and vested with high power in direct affiliation with governments?

5—Is American labor agreed that labor, in partnership with governments and employers, can achieve truly progressive results in keeping with established trade union concepts?

It is evident that a point has been reached at which decisions of moment must be made by American labor.

American labor has until now held itself strictly aloof from the political policies and practices of Europe. It has had for the attempts at introducing those policies and practices in this country the sharpest condemnation, though recognizing, of course, the right of each foreign national labor movement to be entirely free to determine for itself its own course of action.

European labor has more and more gone the political route. No political and industrial movement have been so inter-related in purposes and commingled in organization that only the well versed knew where one movement began and the other left off. And the dominating influence, almost without exception, is to-day wielded by the political wing of the alleged labor movement. Trade union activities only get short paragraphs in the newspapers where labor politics get pages.

Examine the labor movements of England, France, Spain, Italy, Germany, Austria, of the new countries such as Poland, Czecho-Slovakia and the states carved out of what the world once called Russia. Politics predominantly determines the labor character in every country. Politics is supreme in the labor aims considered by general public opinion.

There is a personal way of getting at the situation. Who are the powerful "labor" leaders of Europe? Who in France? Who in England? Who in Italy? Who in Germany? Who in Belgium? Every one who knows anything about the French labor movement knows about Albert Thomas, about Jean Longuet, about Pierre Renaudel. These are Socialists. Few know even the names of the French Federation of Labor officials who came to Washington. Their secretary is a Socialist, while his official position is in the industrial organization. In England, Arthur Henderson is the first personality to occur to most minds. Henderson is a union member, but his regular field of action is the political field. His office is in the headquarters of the Labor Party. He sits in Parliament. Politics is his game. J. H. Thomas is almost as well known, John Hodge once was, Smillie is pretty well known. But Henderson's is recognized as the big name. Furthermore, as if to lend emphasis to the domination of the political idea, the executive body of the British Trade Union Congress is the Parliamentary Committee, today a political agency. In Belgium the leading figure is Emile Vandervelde, a Socialist. Few Americans know the name of any big trade unionist in Belgium. The fame of the Belgian labor representatives is derived from their political activities. The case of Holland is a bit different, for in that country—sole exception to the European rule—the trade union movement as a whole seems to hold some place on its own merits. In Italy, labor is little else than Socialism run wild. It is Socialism of an extremely radical variety, colored in the flaming tones beloved by the ardent Latins. Spain knows nothing of a true trade union movement. The Bohemian movement is taking on more and more the color of Socialism, and so also with the Jugo Slavs and most of the other smaller nations, judging by the means of information to which Americans have access.

In most of these countries there are clearly defined industrial movements, to be sure. Especially is this true of France and England, among the larger nations, and of Belgium and Holland and Switzerland among the smaller nations. But the vital truth is that the industrial movements take their color from the political movements and shape their course in accordance with the demands of a political philosophy. In the Germany of old the German Federation of Trade Unions ran second to the German Socialist Party, with its 110 seats in the debating society called the Reichstag. The energy of the labor movement was directed principally into political channels, which resulted in the election of men to practically powerless public positions. It was much like piping steam through the roof instead of into the cylinder chest.

So it is in all Europe. So it has been. So it is going to be, by present indications. The one man in France who most admires American methods and who has sought most diligently to apply them in his own union is a pathetic figure—a splendidly qualified trade union leader with few followers. The outstanding figure in England who believes in putting industrial action first is a man of power personally, but until now has been unable to change the tide of British labor policies.

Labor in Europe has sought parliament as its favorite battle ground, and in some countries necessarily so in order to bring their workers up to the level of civic rights and standards long enjoyed by the working people of the United States. But European labor customarily tries to get by law what American organized labor has sought through union action. In every one of the leading nations of Europe legislation has been secured or is pending for the purpose of shortening the work-day, such a measure being just now before the British Parliament. From the labor movements of Europe also we get the idea of using the strike to paralyze the political state so as to compel parliamentary action. The general strike is a favorite cry of labor politicians, however seldom it may be used by trade unionists.

Labor in Europe, to boil it all down, runs strong to parliaments and politics and forensic battles, which is to say that theoretically it runs straight for state Socialism, from which it expects all blessings to flow. American labor, on the contrary, has run mainly to the strictly economic fight in the industrial field.

Having a full realization of the value of politics, American labor has thus far declined to give politics any over-lordship in the house of labor. It believes that the labor struggle is immediately an industrial struggle and as such must be fought out in industry. It does not take the question of the length of the work-day in factories into the halls of Congress, but into negotiation with employers. If conference yields nothing it goes to the time-honored industrial field of last resort, where it calls a strike. It wants wherever possible to settle industrial questions in industry and not in politics.

American labor looks upon the questions in dispute in industry as definite, tangible, basic. It looks upon politics as frequently unstable, abstract, treacherous and rarely fundamental as relating to industry. It believes that labor laws, so far as they write great changes into statute books, must necessarily be the written records of convictions already arrived at by the masses through other processes. Such laws as those that aim to fix the work-day or to fix minimum wages for men are regarded by the most thorough-going American trade unionists as of doubtful present value and of highly probably future menace. American labor is best satisfied in industrial matters when it has the least law to deal with. It believes the function of law should be to keep out of the way of industrial growth and change and progress. It has a high respect for the law, and it wishes to maintain this respect by keeping law to its proper field.

American labor has always admitted the right of European labor to take its battles into Parliament, to build up a state suzerainty over itself, to erect for itself a state mother and to create for itself a state Socialism. American labor has said repeatedly that labor in any nation must determine for itself its own policies and practices. But American labor has declined to adopt for itself the policies of Europe, declined to commit itself to the political platforms of Europe, declined to submit its destinies to the manipulations of politicians at home and declined to conde to those from other countries the right to ctate what policies American labor should lopt. English speaking labor on the American ntinent has been agreed in matters of policy, ınada being in harmony with the United States the main.

One of the contentions of American labor has en that politics for labor decreases the vigor the industrial movement. Its classic example America has been Milwaukee, where statis-s have shown repeatedly that wages were lower d trade union vitality weaker than in any her city similar in size and in industrial or-ınization. Milwaukee has been the American ronghold of Socialist politics. Union labor en-ys high wages and the eight-hour day in vari-ıs municipalities in which Socialism ruled for brief year or two, to disappear, leaving labor recommence with trade union methods.

But history develops now to a point where urope may entangle America, with little regard or America's own precedents and policies, and ımesh America in all the ruck and mire of uropean parliamentary policies. The Inter-ational Labor Organization of the League of 'ations is planned to be the supreme labor body f all the world that falls under the labor code f the treaty. This for the simple reason that t will have the strategic position—it is to have he center of the stage and to wield the power. t is in partnership with governments. This it) to be and to do, at least unless something igorous happens to spoil the pretty picture.

This is the way the International Labor rganization functions: Its International Labor onference takes place annually. This confer-ıce discusses labor questions and adopts either raft conventions or recommendations. The rm "draft convention" is a European term. at we call a convention they call a congress r conference. What they call a convention we all a covenant or contract. When the Inter-ational Labor Conference adopts a draft con-vention it adopts what amounts to a contract, which is thereupon offered to all nations party to the treaty of peace. The nations may reject or accept these contracts. There are drastic penalties for nations that violate them after adoption. And if America is party to the treaty of peace it becomes party to the labor conference and party to the permanent international labor office which is to be maintained at the seat of the League of Nations.

Not only is the American government to be party to the labor organization, but the Ameri-can labor movement becomes a partner, by vir-tue of the fact of its existence. There is no choice after America signs the treaty. The In-ternational Labor Conference is composed of four delegates from each nation. Two of these represent the government. One represents em-ployers and one represents labor. The labor and employer delegates must be nominated by the organizations most representative of employers and of labor. The American Federation of Labor must therefore nominate the American labor delegate. Thereafter that delegate must participate in the work of an organization which has its whole being in the state and which can function only through the state by virtue of laws. That delegate must strive, with the others, to secure for labor, by law, things which Ameri-can labor has always declared should be secured by purely industrial action; and if it so happens that his own country is immune from action by the conference in most cases he must none the less endeavor to bring about legal action bearing on other nations on questions purely industrial in character.

The International Labor Conference just closed has adopted a draft convention providing for an eight-hour day and a forty-eight hour week. This draft convention will be presented to the various governments for ratification, and indications are that most European governments will ratify it at an early date. The document is full of exceptions and evasions. For the pur-poses of this discussion the details are beside the argument. The point is that this is a way of getting the eight-hour day by law. If the United States Senate ratifies the treaty, that draft con-vention will be presented to the Government at Washington through the League of Nations. There have been no more strenuous fights in American Federation of Labor conventions than over the question of securing a shorter work-day by law, the last great debate on the subject being staged in the Baltimore convention in 1916. In all of the contests, the American Federation of Labor principle of applying the tactics of the industrial field to industrial problems was car-ried through in triumph, sweeping majorities showing up on the side of upholding the tradi-tional policy. In these fights it was always the Socialist contingent that brought in the proposi-tion to desert the industrial field and try the political method. In the American labor par-liament, American labor defeated the Socialist proposal. But now, for better or worse, under the League labor code, it must reverse its judg-ment and join hands with the political labor delegates of Europe—with the representatives of governments and of employers—and adopt in world-wide practice the methods it has consis-tently condemned. Defeated in their frontal attack, the Socialists will have won in a rear attack, reinforced by overwhelming numbers of foreigners.

American labor was represented at Paris by Samuel Gompers in the commission that wrote the labor section into the treaty. He fought as gamely and courageously against the European labor politicians in that commission as any man ever fought. He was but one among many. After he left the battle ground and returned home, the work of his commission apparently finished, the peace conference took that docu-ment and did things to it that American labor has tried to swallow with a grace worthy of the cavalier traditions of the days of chivalry. But the things the peace conference did, with the evident consent of President Wilson, perhaps reluctantly given, were things that savor strong-ly of quiet corner conspiracies and underhand manoeuvering. And the politicians of Europe had the effrontery to champion the alterations and call them good. President Wilson let them go. One of the changes was to convert the triumphal slogan of the A. F. of L., achieved after decades of battle, "The labor of a human being is not a commodity," to "The labor of a human being is not merely a commodity!"

A word of explanation concerning the section of the treaty setting forth the principles to guide the International Labor Organization. The draft reported to the peace conference by the Commission on International Labor Legisla-tion, of which Samuel Gompers was chairman, contained this language in the preamble:

"The high contracting parties declare their ac-ceptance of the following principles and engage to take all necessary steps to secure their reali-zation in accordance with the recommendation to be made by the International Labor Confer-ence as to their practical application."

It should be noted that here is a definite pledge. It is clear and unequivocal. The clauses that follow it are definite. They go straight to the point. But, when this definite language got before the peace conference some-thing happened to it. The famous Borden amendment took its place. Premier Borden, of Canada, moved a substitute, wrongly called an amendment, and his substitute took the place of the draft submitted by the Gompers com-mission. Says the substitute as written into the treaty:

"The high contracting parties, recognizing that the well-being, physical, moral and intellect-ual, of industrial wage earners is of supreme in-ternational importance, have framed a perma-nent machinery associated with that of the League of Nations to further this great end. . . . They think that there are methods and principles for regulating labor conditions which all industrial communities should endeavor to apply, so far as their special circumstances will permit. Among these methods and principles the following seem to the high contracting parties to be of special and urgent importance."

Then follows the list of specifications, all re-duced to the realm of abstraction, of intangi-bility, and of possible equivocation.

American trade unionism has indorsed the treaty of Versailles. There was, of course, no hope of getting a more satisfactory labor sec-tion. The one written into the document at Paris was to be taken or left. Though stamped with the approval of the American Federation of Labor, it is well that there should be an under-standing of what happened to it before that indorsement was given—especially in view of the fact that the treaty is beginning to operate and that the labor section has had its first trial run in Washington.

This may be said: The changes made in the labor section by the peace conference tend to give to the International Labor Organization more of political color and leaning than it would have been given by the original draft. The whole document is thrown in the direction of the political field. The language of the draft as it stands today is the language of diplomacy—cautious and devious diplomacy—instead of the straightforward language of labor.

In the International Labor Conference itself, greatly to the disappointment and dissatisfac-tion of American Labor, one-half of the total number of possible delegates to be nominated represent governments. Only one-fourth repre-sent labor. But in the conference just adjourned, more than half present represented govern-ments, for the reason that from ten or twelve nations there were no labor representatives and no employer representatives. No cure was found for this situation, and it may recur. Probably it will recur regularly. Most of the South American countries sent only government dele-gates. Labor had less than one-fifth of the votes. Any proposition championed by governments could have passed even in the face of the com-bined opposition of labor and employers!

But above and beyond the changes made in the labor section of the draft of principles, in point of effect on the future of labor and labor organizations is the machinery set up by the labor section. American labor went to Paris with a set of principles in its pocket. It sought to have the civilized world acknowledge recognition of the justice of certain definite principles of hu-man freedom. It came home leaving behind it in the Paris treaty an emasculated version of those principles and a ponderous international machine created for the purpose of legislating world agreements. This machine is the Interna-tional Labor Organization, with its permanent executive staff and its annual conference, as al-ready described. This was the contribution of European labor, and especially of English labor, to the treaty. This machine is a political ma-chine, designed to go on and on forever, legisla-ting in annual international conferences and pre-senting each year to the governments of the world its contracts and recommendations. If there is no compulsion on any nation to accept these contracts, there is surely in store the multifarious forms of criticism of those who do accept them for those who do not accept them. There is surely in store that condemnation and coolness which is called moral pressure.

But to go back of the International Labor Organization to the individual nations once more. In the National Industrial Conference held in London in February of this year the labor representatives, duly accredited to repre-sent English labor, took their stand plainly for Utopia. They presented to the conference an abstract statement of doctrine that placed their position beyond question in the realm of "in-tellectual" theorizing. Here is a quotation

(*Continued on page* 14)

Compulsory Sickness Insurance Propaganda

REPORT OF COMMITTEE ON CONSTRUCTIVE PLAN OF SOCIAL INSURANCE DEPARTMENT OF THE NATIONAL CIVIC FEDERATION REFUTES FALSE STATEMENTS

DR. ALVAH H. DOTY
Chairman

MRS. SARA A. CONBOY

HILL MONTAGUE

IN seeking a constructive plan as a practical substitute for compulsory health insurance, the committee charged with that work studied the claims and arguments of the proponents of such legislation better to draw conclusions as to remedies to be recommended to meet the needs of wage-earners unable to provide for emergencies resulting from sickness.

The examination of proceedings of legislative hearings, articles, reports of the American Association for Labor Legislation, Federal Department of Labor conferences, State commissions, etc., revealed a situation so startling as to misrepresentation of facts that Warren S. Stone, Chairman of the Social Insurance Deparment of The National Civic Federation, decided that the findings of the Committee should be published.

In the foreword, he made the following statement:

> "The pending movement for compulsory health insurance in this country undoubtedly obtains its principal impetus from false beliefs as to the success of the European experiments in this line of social insurance.
>
> "Back of this false basis, there is a real question as to whether or not compulsory insurance would be the best remedy for some existing social evils and for which, all agree, a remedy or remedies should be sought. That question will be considered on its merits, in the light of the truth as to foreign experience and domestic conditions, so far as now ascertainable, in a later report from a Committee on Foreign Investigation, having for its Chairman J. W. Sullivan of the American Federation of Labor, a member of the International Typographical Union.
>
> "As a preliminary, however, it is desirable to sweep aside a mass of fictions, falsifications, guesses and unwarranted assumptions which stand in the way of the search for the truth. Hence this report from the Committee on Constructive Plan whose Chairman is Dr. Alvah H. Doty.
>
> "That Committee in the near future will present propositions of a positive character for legislative enactment and public health education designed to eradicate unnecessary disease and protect the worker when idle, neither of which has been covered by any insurance scheme offered so far."

In that connection Dr. Doty stated that:

> "A careful study of the various plans of Health Insurance, either in operation or recommended for approval, presents little or no evidence that the education of the public as an important factor in the preservation of health and the prevention of disease is fully appreciated, or that, if properly carried out, it would go far to render compulsory health insurance unnecessary. It is true that reference is made to the value of this means of maintaining health but no definite or concerted action plays a part in the measures now employed or in the plans proposed for future action. The proper education of the public is a powerful instrument in the prevention of disease. Contrary to statements frequently made, relative to this matter, only very slow general improvement has been made in this direction."

Illustrative falsifications refuted in the committee's report and abstracts of typical replies are given below. Authorities, pro and con, are not indicated, because of lack of space, but the full report containing them may be had upon application at Federation headquarters.

The propaganda statements appear in blackface type.

"Today *universal* workmen's health insurance is established in not fewer than ten of the leading continental countries" [of Europe].

Only three European sickness insurance laws (those of Germany, Great Britain and Norway) are even approximately universal as to "wage-workers." They all exclude many "workmen," and the Norwegian law many "wage-workers."

GEORGE W. PERKINS,
President, Cigarmakers' International Union

The Dutch law comes next; but it applies only to low-paid wage-workers and leaves out all casual labor and domestic servants.

In Luxemburg 37,500 wage-earners are compulsorily insured out of a population of 260,000 (1910).

The Austrian insurance comes next, covering about 3,340,000 out of about 10,000,000 wage-earners and a total population of 27,800,000.

Under the Hungarian law, in 1909, about 900,000 persons were insured out of a population of 21,000,000.

Under the Rumanian law, in 1911, about 140,000 persons were supposed to be insured out of a notoriously impoverished population of about 7,000,000.

Under the Russian law, just before the outbreak of the war, about 1,394,000 persons were insured in European Russia (Finland, where insurance is voluntary, excluded) and the Caucasus, out of a population of about 145,000,000.

In Serbia, though a sickness insurance law was enacted in 1910, it can hardly be said to be "established," since there is no record of its ever having been put into actual effect.

This is a complete list of the European countries—continental and non-continental—in which compulsory health insurance prevails. There are 10 altogether, and in 7 of them, the insurance, so far from being universal, provides protection for only minorities—and in some cases only insignificant minorities—of the working people.

"You couldn't get either capital or labor in the realm of England to give up this health insurance."

The English health insurance is paid for about 4/11ths by the state and 3/11ths by employers, leaving the insured employees to pay only 4/11ths. Because they are getting for 4d. per week insurance that costs 11d., the majority of the British working people probably would be reluctant to give up the health insurance. Instead they seem to be demanding that the medical benefits originally promised them for 4d. per week be provided them for 4d.—which benefits are now only about half provided and to provide which in full would probably double the state's contribution, so that the working people would get for 4d. insurance costing 15d.

practice by those who are responsible for the conditions that occasion the need for benefits. They are not 'relief' any more than compensation for accidents is 'relief.' Especially is this true in a governmental system of health insurance where employers, employees and public maintain and administer the funds."

This is pure demagogism.

If the insurance were maintained entirely by the insured contributors (employers perhaps included) and the contributions were scaled in proportion to the risks, etc., "in accordance with actuarial practice," then nothing might be "bestowed or given." But where the taxpayers' money is used for the benefit of the insured or where the infirm, the sickly and the shirkers are insured at less than cost at the expense of the healthy and industrious, then a donation essentially indistinguishable from poor relief is "bestowed or given." All the European sickness insurance laws (including the voluntary insurance laws of France, Denmark and Sweden) are and are generally recognized to be measures of poor relief—or charity. And it is a common point of criticism that "nothing is gained by disguising that charity under a false name."

It is significant in this connection that within the last few months a Ministry of Health has been established for England and Wales, to which the supreme authority in all matters of National Health Insurance has been transferred, in combination with the administration of certain of the Poor Laws.

Compulsory health insurance would reduce the amount of time lost by wage-earners in employments.

Under compulsory sickness insurance, between 1890 and 1913, the number sick at one time, out of every 100 insured, increased, per annum, in Germany, from 36.7 to 45.6, and in Austria from 45.7 to 51.8; the average number of days "on the cash benefits" per insured member increased, in Germany from 6.19 to 9.19, and in Austria from 7.98 to 9.45; and the average number of days compensated per sick member increased, in Germany from 16.2 to 20.2, and in Austria from 16.4 to 17.4. The statistics of no other experiences are obtainable—all the other compulsory systems, except the Hungarian and Luxemburgian, being of very recent date.

Wm. A. Brend, M.D., in "Health and the State," says:

> "In taking a broad view, the advantages of the act must not be minimized. * * * *But these benefits are all in the nature of Poor Relief under another name, and* **they do little to alter the conditions which bring about sickness.** *As far as improvement of the public health is concerned, the influence of the Act has probably been almost nil.*"

"Most employers opposed the enactment of compensation laws," and their opposition to health insurance is equally unmeritorious.

Most employers did *not* oppose the enactment of compensation laws. In New York, for instance, employers generally favored the original Wainwright-Phillips bills. All that the employers opposed was state insurance monopolies. The records of the Workmen's Compensation Department of The National Civic Federation show that employers and representatives of labor, beginning in 1908, worked together, always favoring some equitable form of workmen's compensation holding the industry liable.

"Prevention is primarily the purpose of insurance and certainly its result."

Sir Arthur Newsholme, M.D., K.C.B., Former Chief Medical Officer of the Local Government Board for England, recently stated that "The National Health Insurance Act * * * has not been marked by its preventive value."

Commissions in New Jersey, Massachusetts and California have reported in favor of Compulsory Health Insurance.

This statement is correct, but:—

Whereas in Massachusetts the first Commission reported in favor of compulsory health insurance, a second Commission appointed to study further into the subject, reported adversely, and several attempts to incorporate provisions for compulsory insurance at the recent Constitutional convention failed.

Whereas two Commissions in California have reported in favor of compulsory health insurance, a proposition to amend the State Constitution to permit such insurance has been defeated by the people, by a vote of 358,324 to 133,858.

Other State Commissions reporting explicitly in favor of or against the immediate adoption of compulsory health insurance, to date, are:

Favorable:—New Jersey and Ohio.

Unfavorable:—Connecticut, Wisconsin and Illinois.

A Commission in Pennsylvania has also reported, recommending no immediate legislation but that the problem be further studied and investigated.

COMMITTEE ON CONSTRUCTIVE PLAN
SOCIAL INSURANCE DEPARTMENT
THE NATIONAL CIVIC FEDERATION

DR. ALVAH H. DOTY, *Chairman*:
Medical Director, Western Union Telegraph Co., New York.

MRS. F. LOTHROP AMES:
Chairman Industrial Committee, New England Section, Woman's Department, The National Civic Federation, Boston, Mass.

MRS. SARA A. CONBOY:
International Secretary-Treasurer, United Textile Workers of America, New York.

MARK A. DALY:
Secretary, Associated Manufacturers and Merchants of New York State, Buffalo, N. Y.

GERTRUDE BEEKS EASLEY:
Director Welfare Department, The National Civic Federation, New York.

DR. LEE K. FRANKEL:
Third Vice-President, Metropolitan Life Insurance Company, New York.

HUGH FRAYNE:
General Organizer, American Federation of Labor, New York.

DR. HARRIS A. HOUGHTON:
Vice-President, Associated Physicians of Long Island, New York.

DR. J. RICHARD KEVIN:
Chairman, Legislative Committee, New York State Medical Society, Brooklyn.

HILL MONTAGUE:
President, International Fraternal Congress of America, Richmond, Va.

GEORGE W. PERKINS:
President, Cigarmakers' International Union, Chicago.

P. TECUMSEH SHERMAN:
Attorney, New York.

J. W. SULLIVAN:
Of the American Federation of Labor; Member International Typographical Union, Brooklyn.

MRS. COFFIN VAN RENSSELAER:
Executive Secretary, Woman's Department, The National Civic Federation, New York.

Russia as Seen By Ex-Military Attaché

(*Continued from page 3*)

"The Communists cannot maintain themselves any longer than the supply of food lasts. Nine million men were mobilized when the war began. There still exists a great reserve of food which has not been consumed. It is being doled out to the people. In my opinion this reserve supply will last a year and a half longer. That, however, does not mean the Bolsheviki will last that long. Other circumstances may hurry their overthrow."

My Days Under the Bolshevist Reign of Terror

THE STORY OF A RUSSIAN WIFE AND MOTHER

By MME. NADEJHDA SHTEINBERG

Mme. Nadejhda Shteinberg, whose thrilling story of her personal experience with the Bolsheviki appears in this number, is the wife of Samuel Petrowitch Shteinberg, former managing director of a Moscow bank. Her husband, who has been missing since his attempted escape from Russia in February, 1918, is also a noted playwright and at one time edited a Russian newspaper. Mme. Shteinberg attended a three year medical course in Russia and it was largely due to her professional experience that she and her children were spared by the Bolsheviki.

Service as a surgeon in Siberia by Mme. Shteinberg not only aided her progress through that country, but when the Czecho-Slovaks utilized her skill they awarded the Cross of St. Ann to her. She was wounded by shrapnel while attending the wounded under fire. Mme. Shteinberg still hopes to be reunited to her husband and New York friends are instituting inquiries through banking connections in Britain and Scandinavia as to his possible whereabouts.—Editor's Note.

YOU hear much today about the Bolsheviki. You are told by their agents and defenders, that they are saviours of humanity, leaders of a new order which will regenerate the world. It seems very strange to me to hear people who have never been to Russia exalting, and pleading in defense of, the red leaders. They assert, without personal knowledge of what has happened in Russia, that the testimony of atrocities and terrorization, is untrue, and that Trotzky and Lenine, and their cohorts, are simply misrepresented and maligned. These people, who gain their knowledge of world affairs from arm-chairs, constantly clamor that the truth about Russia be told.

I will attempt to tell the story of the revolution as I saw it, and as it affected me, a Russian wife and mother. I will not deal with the political aspects of this new régime but will tell of Bolshevism as it changed my life, and you can perhaps decide if Bolshevism works for good or evil.

We had lived in Moscow all our lives—my husband and myself, with our two children. We had struggled and worked, until finally, as result of our labor, we were able to live in comfort, and to become what later in the Lenine-Trotzky régime became a thing of hate and scorn,—one of the bourgeoisie. My husband, who was well known as a playwright, had a well paying position in one of the banks.

In my home in Moscow we had been happy. The Great War raged, the hearts of all of us ached in sympathy with those mothers and fathers whose sons were dying on the battlefields for liberty, yet in our own lives we were happy.

Then came that day when the Czar was overthrown. Things moved so swiftly that the mind could not adjust itself to events. Kerensky was in power. Like some huge wave the overthrow of Nicholas swept all of us from our calm quiescence and it seemed as though all would be wrecked. But the wave subsided, and as though nothing had happened we again turned to our daily life.

Under Kerensky the people of Russia had more freedom than they ever had had before. One had no longer to fear what one said in the street. The people were overjoyed.. The tyrant was overthrown, and it appeared that life was at last worth living. There was no lack of anything. In fact, the workingmen had more than ever before. Kerensky was lenient—too lenient.

MME. SHTEINBERG AND HER TWO CHILDREN

One day while walking through the streets I was attracted to a corner by a crowd who were listening to a speaker. There, surrounded by the mob, was a man, dishevelled and uncouth. He spoke in a loud voice, waving his arms like a fanatic and tiny spots of foam gathered at his mouth. What he was saying sounded strange to me.

He said:

"You have fought long enough. Let us now no longer fight. Our men have died for the capitalists, and for the money that the capitalists made.

"The only way to change this whole thing," he went on, ranting, "is to become a Bolshevist. The Bolsheviki will give to everyone bread—bread—bread. And the Bolsheviki will give to everyone—freedom. Think of it—no more fighting—no more fighting—and plenty of bread. Freedom—freedom. Bread—land—and peace! Hurrah for the Bolsheviki."

Gazing about I could see tears in the eyes of those mothers who had given their boys, of those fathers who had sent their children to the front to fight the Huns. How little they could understand all of this! To them it seemed like the promise of the dawn of peace and happiness—this new doctrine.

Yet among the mass I could see there were some who understood, and understanding, saw the evil in what this man was saying. I, too, felt my heart contract in the thought of what this speaker's influence would bring about, should he be successful.

My fears were stilled when I arrived at the house of a friend. My friend said to me: "You need not fear—we have a strong force of White Guards here, and the Bolsheviki can never come to power in Moscow. You know we do not want them, neither do the people. Of course, what they say at first moves the masses, but they will eventually come to their senses and see that it would be for the worse if the Bolshevik gained control of Moscow. Why," and she laughed, "don't the workingmen themselves call them the 'red murderers'?"

With this assurance I was quieted. But as events proved, my friend's optimism and my own were shattered.

Finally one day in November an army of Bolsheviki entered Moscow. The streets of Moscow were streaming with people. But when the first armed soldiers came into the section of the city where I lived the thoroughfares were instantly deserted. Looking from a window in our home, I could see the retreat of the White Guards. Now and then some soldier or officer wildly threw up his arms, and pitched forward upon his face.

The din became terrific. Bullets rattled upon the roof of our house. The children, frightened, clung to my skirts, and my husband, without gun or sword, madly paced up and down, cursing the devils who had brought about such a pass. The fighting continued and the piles of wounded and dead increased.

I quickly came out of my trance, and my medical training asserted itself. I thanked the day that I had decided to study medicine. We gave to the wounded what care we could. Many died under my hands, for we had little to aid them with. But we bandaged with bed-sheets and towels all those whose blood was flowing, hoping to save all whom we could.

One incident remains clearly fixed in my memory of that day. Not far away from where I was dressing the wound of one I felt certain would die, I saw on the roof top of the Metropole Hotel some White Guards. I knew that in that hotel were many men, women and children, who had no guns or other weapons with which to defend themselves. The soldiers of the Bolsheviki soon surrounded this hotel, allowing no one to escape and opened fire. For a long time their guns crackled and spat fire and finally the whole building was simply a mass of ruins. I doubt if any in that hotel, White Guards or non-combatants—escaped.

One section of Moscow was taken after the other. And in the weeks that followed there came many tales of wholesale murder that froze my veins with the horror of it all. But the Bolsheviki were too strong for the people of Moscow, and they finally gained the upper hand.

One morning early in December, my husband rushed into our home, pale and excited. It was a strange hour for him to return from work, and I felt greatly disturbed, knowing that something unusual had happened.

In answer to my frightened questions, he said:

"While we were going over the accounts of the bank to get them in order for the New Year, and while all the clerks were busy, there came into the bank a number of Bolshevists with guns, with bayonets fixed. They shoved aside those who tried to stop them, and laughing like madmen, they pressed a bayonet against me, ordering all to leave immediately under threat of death. We could not understand. We asked them to explain, and the only response we received was a brusque order to clear out quickly! What could we do? I had to leave. It seems the Bolshevik are taking over all the banks."

Here we were, confronted with the possibility of starvation, little money in the house, only a little food, and two children to care for. We knew not what would happen. Still we hoped for the best, thinking that in a few days the invaders would ask the employees of the banks to return. We thought that it would be impossible for the "red murderers" to run the banks. But in this we were mistaken, as you shall see.

When a few weeks later, an advertisement appeared in a Bolshevik paper ordering all employees of banks having keys and the combinations of safes to appear at ten o'clock the next morning, we believed that the routine would be resumed. In the advertisement it stated that nothing would be disturbed if the people obeyed orders. Yet when the keys were turned over and the vaults opened, they threatened to kill those

We were allowed two ounces of bread a week, little meat, and that was rotten. Even the meager allowance of bread was mixed with straw and other things. One day my son came to me after munching on a piece of bread, with his lip cut. He had bitten on a piece of glass. After that, whenever we got bread, I carefully inspected it.

They robbed everybody. Whenever you walked the streets some soldier would come up to you and ask to see your passport, and whether you had one or not, he would invariably take away your money, your jewels if you had any, and your watch. They took everything that pleased them. One could not go out with money in one's pocket. But it didn't matter whether you were robbed in the street, or whether they robbed you in your home. The thing was—you would certainly be robbed sometime. But mingling with tragedy is always comedy. From mishap is often born laughter, and even in those awful days when one thought that the world could never smile again, little incidents such as the following came as a welcome respite from the constant dread of our lives:

One of our friends, while walking the street, was stopped by a Bolshevik soldier, and ordered to show his passport. Although he had one, he must have seemed too prosperous to the soldier, for he pickpocketed him and took all his money, which he foolishly carried about. The soldier filched the money from his pocketbook and from his belt.

"Then," as my friend told the story, "he scratched his head and looked at me, as if wondering what else he could steal. He had my watch and all the money I had to my name. My rings were gone. Finally his face lit with a smile, and feeling the texture of my coat he demanded that I take it off. It was cold, bitterly cold, and I had a long way to go, so I begged him to return my coat. Of this he would not hear. But he took pity upon me and offered to give me his muddy, lice-infected one. I had no other choice but to take it. It must have been a good one originally, but in its present state it certainly was not prepossessing. When I arrived home my wife, after hearing how I had been robbed, decided to make the best of it and patch the old coat as well as she could. While sewing a rent in it, she felt something bulging under the lining. On cutting through the stuff she found sewed inside, 800 rubles, which amounted to more than had been taken from me. Of course the coat had been stolen from somebody who had hidden his money in this manner, and the soldier had never discovered it." Such little things we regarded in our helpless state as a great triumph over our hated persecutors.

I have seen the arch-plotter, the leader, the man who sanctions these things—nay, who even orders them—walk through the streets of Moscow guarded by many soldiers. He is guarded because of the fear of being murdered by some brave man whose wife and children had been killed before his eyes, and who is left to suffer longer, only eventually to be killed himself if he dares object to some outrage. Yes, Leon Trotzky goes out into the streets heavily guarded. But he never went far into the streets. Trotzky surrounds himself by chosen men, all as vicious as he is. He is surrounded by men who he knows will not betray him into the hands of the people who have suffered under his misrule. He can feel safe under his guard, for they are scoundrels as he is.

He came to Moscow, silently, in the night. He sneaked in under cover of darkness, slinking into the best palace in the city. He came—as all come who carry the sword of fire, hate, rape and murder—like a rat in the night—to rest upon silken pillows. This self-declared despiser of riches and of capitalists needed for himself the softest beds, the best food, the swiftest automobiles that Moscow could afford him.

At the end of February, 1918, my husband decided that we could not stay any longer in Moscow and decided we should all go to New York, or England, with him. As my children were ill, and I did not dare risk the hazardous journey, I convinced my husband that it would be wiser for him to go without us. I was not afraid to remain as my services had been enlisted by one of the doctors of Moscow. I had taken a three-year medical course in the college, and as there was great need of nurses, I was sure of a certain, if dubious, protection that others were not likely to have. Finally my husband agreed to go alone, knowing that the risk of leaving Moscow and journeying was just as dangerous as staying. I was to follow as soon as the children were better and the times less unsettled.

What days of anxiety, what days of anguish, I went through worrying about my husband. I had heard many tales of what had been done to passengers on trains going into Siberia. And then, one day, the news came that the train my husband was on had been blown up by the Bolsheviki. What had become of him? Was he alive? Had they killed him?

To this day I do not know. I am still living in the hope that he was spared and that one day I shall find him.

I was compelled to work in a hospital and there were many sick and dying to attend. Moscow saw the saddest time in its history. The hospitals were overcrowded, and many died because of lack of care and aid. About the middle of July, the doctor with whom I worked as nurse was called to Kazan. He asked me to go with him. As I have relatives living there, I decided to go, thinking it would be a step nearer my escape from Russia. Though the Bolsheviki controlled Kazan, things seemed to be a bit better there than in Moscow. Then, too, we had heard that an army of Czechs was fighting north of Kazan, and were slowly coming south.

In August we joyfully heard that the village of Samara had been taken by the Czechs and that the Bolsheviki had suffered a defeat. We looked at one another with hope in our eyes, and a prayer in our hearts, expecting to hear at any moment that the Czechs had entered our village and were preparing to drive out our enemies. The people lived in an atmosphere of impatient, repressed expectancy, which expressed itself now and then in some gesture of contempt, as a soldier of the Red Guard passed.

That wonderful day finally came when, looking down the road we saw the dust rising above a moving mass of men. The Czechs had come! In the streets of Kazan the Bolshevik Red Guards gathered also, making ready for battle. The first shot was fired. The uncertainty of inaction passed and gave way to a nervous realization that there would be wounded to attend to. I came down from my watching place in a half trance. The outcome was uncertain. But my duty told me where I should be. The streets were filled with soldiers, running this way and that.

The scene of combat shifted, and I virtually was in the center of the two fighting armies. Bullets whistled over my head, coming from both directions. I felt no fear. I could feel nothing but the sense of duty to tend the fallen. Slowly the Bolshevists retreated, and the street became filled with Czechs, advancing in perfect order, following a definite campaign of offence. They were commanded by intelligent men, while the Bolshevists had as leaders only men filled with hatred and a cruel desire to persecute helpless citizens.

As the Czechs advanced, I feverishly worked, gathering together the wounded, giving what aid I could. While leaning over one of the wounded, giving him drink, a smart pain shot through my arm, I looked down. My wound was slight, a mere graze of the fleshy part of my arm. Returning to my children, I found them huddled together in a room crying. I thanked God

(*Continued on page 20.*)

THE NATIONAL
Civic Federation Review

Office: Thirty-third Floor, Metropolitan Tower
1 Madison Avenue New York City

RALPH M. EASLEY, Editor

The Editor alone is Responsible for any unsigned article or unquoted statement published in THE NATIONAL CIVIC FEDERATION REVIEW.

The long strike of the printers and pressmen of New York is the reason for the delay in publishing this issue of THE NATIONAL CIVIC FEDERATION REVIEW.

THE PRESIDENT'S INDUSTRIAL CONFERENCES

President Wilson's second industrial conference board, the personnel of which is described in another column of this paper, has announced that it has agreed upon a set of proposals, looking toward the establishment of industrial peace, which will soon be given to the public for its consideration. In announcing the appointment of this board, the President emphasized his belief that the failure of the former conference was due to the fact that it was composed of three conflicting groups: employers, employees and the public. He stated that he "thought it advisable that in this new body there should be no recognition of distinctive groups." That suggestion, coming from the President, was naturally taken up by newspaper writers, and the public soon accepted it as a complete explanation of the failure of the first conference. We do not believe that that deduction is correct. It was not because there were three groups that the conference failed but because of the unfortunate selection of the personnel of two of the groups. The Labor group was thoroughly representative and its membership the best that could have been secured, but the Employers' group was made up of non-union employers, of bankers and, for some fantastic reason, of farmers. The Public group was not a "Public group" at all and should have been called "the President's group." It had on it nearly as many employers as had the Employers' group. More than that, it had on it a number of incongruous people who could never have agreed upon anything in this world or any other. Some of them had special fads of their own to promote and they were promoting them. The few men in that group who had had any practical experience with the labor question could not agree. Had there been also a group of employers who had collective contracts with trade unions, every one of whom had had first-hand experience in conciliation and arbitration, they would have started the conference on a very different course from that which it took. This is not to say that there were not some of the best minds of the nation in that conference, but they were not the best minds on the propositions with which they were called upon to deal.

Another reason for the failure of the first conference was that no preliminary arrangements had been made. Up to the morning of the first meeting the whole scheme seemed to be a bit-or-miss proposition. The President was out on the Coast and internal jealousies led to friction among those who were trying to handle the conference in Washington. Of course, when so many diverse elements, with so many strong characters, were thrown together, chaos was bound to reign, and it reigned, at least for the first week. In the Canadian industrial conference, which adjourned just before the Washington conference opened, there was no such confusion. Agenda had been sent out six weeks in advance and a program and method of procedure agreed upon. It is true that the Canadian conference did not get anywhere, any more than did the Washington conference. That is to say, the only things it agreed upon were things of comparatively little importance, all the important questions being passed on to Parliament, with the suggestion that it appoint commissions to study and report upon them. This was much better, however, than having such a smash-up as came at the end of the Washington conference, for the moral effect, if for nothing else.

It is boasted that the second conference will not be composed of "groups." That fact may prove a liability rather than an asset, because, unfortunately, there are employers in the conference and no labor men, which fact was at once resented by organized labor. True, Secretary of Labor Wilson is the chairman, but he occupies that position as representing the President of the United States and therefore the public and not the wage-earner.

Those who decry the group method must not forget that the problems the President's conference is called upon to solve are those that affect the relations of employers and employees and that no conclusion reached which both those elements do not approve will be worth much in practical results. While there is much to be said in the interest of the innocent and generally helpless public, the fact remains that the nebulous thing we call "the public" is not by any means "the whole thing." There is much in the declaration by the labor leaders that the public is thoroughly selfish, that it never wants to be inconvenienced by strikes and lockouts. If the street car employees, for instance, are overworked and underpaid, how long would it take the public to wake up and force the companies to do justice? What does the public care, so long as its means of transportation are not disturbed? What does the public care, or even try to know, about the ridiculously low wages paid to its school teachers, its firemen, its policemen, and other civil officers? And yet the public is a third interest in all industrial controversies and must be taken into account. Without public representation in a board dealing with industrial disputes, there is danger of the employer and employee combining against the public. So that any agreement that is reached, looking to the construction of an industrial code, must have the employer, the employee and the public group around the same table. Even then it must not be expected that such an agreement can be easily reached. Under the urge of patriotism, the War Labor Board, organized for dealing with labor questions during the war, with these three interests represented, did agree upon a code which seemed fair to all; but on the signing of the armistice neither side wanted to have anything further to do with it, so badly had it worked. However, while there is life there is hope, and let us hope the new conference will find a way to smooth out our industrial wrinkles. At any rate, it is a fine body of true Americans who can be counted upon faithfully to discharge the duties laid upon them by President Wilson.

THE TEN PER CENT FALLACY

Mr. Frederick P. Fish, in his address at the dinner of the Economic Club of New York, extracts from which are published in this issue of the REVIEW, completely effaced the rosy tinted view of labor conditions in England painted by Mr. Alfred G. Gardiner, editor of that noted pacifist and radical publication, the London *Daily News*. Mr. Fish, however, did not do so well in his elaboration of the familiar assertion by Open Shop employers that organized labor represents only 10 per cent of the workers and is therefore not entitled to speak for labor as a whole. There were two living, husky, unanswerable arguments that followed him on the program—one Major George L. Berry, whose organization includes 85 per cent of the workers in the Major's craft, and one T. V. O'Connor, whose organization includes 100 per cent of the workers in that craft. How much comfort would the commercial job printer in New York or Boston or Chicago or any other important city or a steamship owner on any of the coasts of North America derive from a statement that only ten per cent of the wage earners in the United States were organized, and that therefore he need not pay any attention to the demands from the International Printing Pressmen's Union or the International Longshoremen's Association? Or how much comfort would the building contractors in the industrial centres of the United States or the shoe manufacturers in Brockton, Mass., for instance, derive from Mr. Fish's statement, the shoe workers in Brockton and the building trade crafts in the large cites being anywhere from 95 to 100 per cent union?

Even if the 10 per cent statement were true, (and we will show that it is not), the aspirations, the desires, of the 10 per cent organized are identical with the aspirations, the desires of the 90 per cent unorganized, because they generally relate to increase in wages, decrease in hours of labor and better working conditions. Are there any among the assumed 90 per cent non-union workers who do not want just that? When John Mitchell called out 150,000 miners in the anthracite strike, he had only 8,000 members in his union—considerably less than 10 per cent of the whole—but the 150,000 went out because they wanted just what the union men wanted, more pay, shorter hours and better working conditions.

The trouble with the 10 per cent statement is that it is based on a fallacy. The last United States Census shows that there are 38,000,000 males and females employed in gainful occupations. Of these there are organized 4,500,000, or about 12 per cent of the whole. But, and this is where the "joker" pops up, included in the 38,000,000 wage earners are 12,600,000 agricultural workers, 3,700,000 domestic servants, and several million wage earners in groups which are practically unorganizable. When these are all subtracted, it is found that about 50 per cent (J. W. Sullivan claims in his analysis 55 per cent) are organized. But, as before stated, in many of the key industries from 90 to 100 per cent are organized. This is true in most industrial centres, so that it can safely be asserted that the 10 per cent argument is no argument at all.

Mr. J. W. Sullivan exposes another fallacy, one generally accepted today, and that is that the wage earners in Great Britain are more fully organized than the wage earners in the United States. On this point he shows that the same proportion between organized and unorganized labor exists in both countries, stating that, after subtracting agriculture, domestic service and various unorganizable groups, there are left 9,000,000 wage earners in the United Kingdom. As there are 4,500,000 workers organized, the same number as in this country, it shows that in England also it is about a "fifty-fifty" proposition. But in England, as here, all such figures mean nothing when it comes to considering the potentiality of a union. In a given industry when an outbreak occurs the only question is, how many non-union men are there in that craft from whom workers may be drawn to fill the places of the strikers?

Mr. Fish, is it not time for educated employers like yourself to give that hoary 10 per cent chestnut decent burial? It did good service in the days of Parry, Van Cleave and Kirby and is now entitled to a nice long rest.

THE URGENT DUTY OF LEADERS OF THE CHURCH

At a recent conference held by the Industrial Department of the Interchurch World Movement, Dr. Fred B. Fisher introduced Bishop Francis J. McConnell as "that strange combination, a radical bishop." "The bishop," comments the *Christian Advocate*, "justified the adjective by undertaking a defense of those spokesmen of ad-

[illegible] social ideas whom he called 'prophetic radicals' and whose voices have been the occasion of some degree of uneasiness in more than one denomination.'' The *Christian Advocate* quoted Bishop McConnell as saying:

"Whatever we do, we must keep alive in the church the spirit of prophetic radicalism. . . . I can't see that this is a time to silence a man when he speaks out the truth concerning a social situation, as he thinks of it. But all sorts of pressure comes in to take the edge off the man's statement. He had better say one thousand wild things and get some good truth uttered so as to accomplish some purpose.'

"Naturally the sentiment was vociferously applauded,'' the *Christian Advocate* went on to comment, "for the so-called industrial conference was in large part composed of these 'radical prophets' and of persons nominated by them for membership, and so far from being 'silenced' they were vocal at all sessions, both from the platform and in the discussions. . . . 'To say a thousand wild things in order to get some good truth uttered' will seem to most people an entirely inadequate justification of the liberty of prophesying which the agitators now so copiously enjoy. If the multitude who listen possessed the bishop's rare ability to discriminate between raving and reason the case would be different. But in a time of world-wide unrest, when multitudes of people are known to be in a state of nervous excitability which makes reasoning impossible, and when every nation in Europe affords bloody examples of the wild results which wild talking provokes, he does an ill service to the church or to society who encourages the radical agitator to think of himself more highly than he ought to think as a prophet.''

Referring to the recent investigations made by Federal and State government officials into the activities of the "Reds,'' a clergyman in an important New York church recently declared that these "radicals and near radicals'' are "going through something similar to the persecution of the Christians in the days of the Cæsars,'' and of the I. W. W. leaders, who, he said, were being "strung up'' in the State of Washington, he declared: "We should ask the question—Who are these Nazarenes? What do they stand for? What are they trying to teach?''

In the Church of the Ascension the Rev. Dr. Percy Stickney Grant declared the other Sunday to his congregation that the anarchists who were to be deported for plotting to overthrow our government were to be compared to the Pilgrim fathers.

The Rev. Dr. Harry F. Ward, secretary of the Methodist Federation for Social Service, in a bulletin on "The Russian Question,'' compared the Bolshevik régime to the American Revolution, asserting "it is an experiment in a new form of government. . . . an attempt to establish direct democracy both in the control of industry and government.'' Among the "specific aims'' of the Bolshevist régime, Dr. Ward declared, were the following: "To guard industrial workers from overwork, from diseases of occupation, from employment at too early an age; . . . to free courts and judicial procedure from traditional abuses and make them function as instruments of justice to all classes.''

Copyright by Underwood & Underwood

THE SECOND INDUSTRIAL CONFERENCE CONVENED BY PRESIDENT WILSON IN WASHINGTON

Photo shows, from left to right: Sitting—Julius Rosenwald, President of Sears, Roebuck & Co.; Henry C. Stuart, Former Governor of Virginia; Samuel M. McCall, Former Governor of Massachusetts; Thomas W. Gregory, Former United States Attorney General; Stanley King, Secretary of the W. H. McElwain Shoe Co. of Boston, Mass., and Secretary of Labor William B. Wilson. Standing—Richard Hooker, of Springfield, Mass.; Martin Glynn, Former Governor of New York; Herbert Hoover, Former Food Administrator; W. O. Thompson, President of Ohio State University; Oscar Straus, Secretary of Commerce in Roosevelt's Cabinet; J. W. Wickersham, Former United States Attorney General; H. M. Robinson, Lawyer, of Pasadena, Cal.; Prof. Frank W. Taussing, Former Chairman of the Tariff Committee, and O. D. Young, Vice-President of the General Electric Co., New York.

Dr. Ward made the familiar plea of Bolshevist agents and sympathizers that Bolshevism is a "disputed issue'' and that it is "very difficult to secure impartial information concerning it.'' Dr. Ward, in addition to being the secretary of the Methodist Federation for Social Service, is also professor of Christian Ethics in the Union Theological Seminary. Students in such an institution are almost helplessly susceptible to the influence of instructors who, if they are inclined to radicalism and pro-Bolshevism, find in immature minds fertile soil for their teachings. Incidentally, the young Rev. Mr. Howell, who led a radical parade on Christmas Day to demand amnesty for "political prisoners,'' and which was interfered with by the police, is a student at the Union Theological Seminary.

When the Editor of this REVIEW wrote his first letter to Mr. William Fellowes Morgan he expressed a very sincere concern regarding the increase of radicalism in the churches. It must not be assumed, however, that the Episcopal Church alone is menaced by this danger, for, as has long been evident, practically every Christian denomination is infected. There is hardly a social service or industrial commission which does not contain Socialists and revolutionary radicals. Beset with a fanatical zeal, or goaded by an insane desire for self-exploitation and publicity, these folk work with indefatigable industry, night and day, and, in common with many pathological subjects, possess an uncanny cunning in getting things across in an underhand manner. The general laxity, the good-natured acquiescence, the amiable trustfulness of many sound and loyal men and women probably explains how these overbusy zealots put across such insidious propaganda as the last report of the Joint Commission on Social Service of the Protestant Episcopal Church contains.

However, we are living in parlous times, a time of world-wide unrest, when, as the *Christian Advocate* says, multitudes of people are in a state of nervous excitability which makes reasoning impossible, and therefore it is urgently incumbent upon the men who have a voice in the churches to become actively aroused to what has been going on in their midst. The promotion of radical propaganda from Christian pulpits is especially dangerous. To Christian congregations Socialism is not honestly preached for what it is, as Marx expounded it, as Morris Hillquit would interpret it, but is presented as being—as a minister has said—akin, if not identical, with the ethics of Christ; as the Gospel put into practice; as a program for the reform of all the world's ills which would bring the Christian millennium.

While this danger has assumed unprecedented proportions of late, it is not new in the church. The so-called "Christian Socialist'' movement finds pleasure in referring to the great author, Charles Kingsley, as one who blazed the way, but what Charles Kingsley taught was not Socialism, but social reform. Socialism has nothing to do with social reform, and what such writers as Walter Rauschenbush advocate, what the Church Socialist League is promoting, is nothing but political Socialism—the Socialism that would overturn all our institutions, our government, our ideals, and, if we are to take a recent pronouncement of the Church Socialist League, they do not aim merely at a moral revolution or for changes through evolutionary processes, but revolution by some sort of direct action.

Are the Christian denominations going to permit ministers to prostitute their pulpits in the interest of the party of Debs and Hillquit? Are they going to let their members be bamboozled into becoming political Socialists, into voting the Socialist ticket, in the belief that they are thereby helping to bring about a realization of the teachings of Christ? Do the governing ecclesiastics and officials of the churches not have a very onerous and grave obligation in taking measures to protect their members against these "prophetic radicals'' who use church pulpits to preach Socialism, sedition and "a thousand wild things''?

RIVALS TO MADAM THEBES

It has been customary at the beginning of each new year for zodiacal-gowned astrologers and innumerable rural prophets to inform a muddled world, able to see no further than its nose, what the infant year's future holds. They based their predictions on the movements of the stars, hens found crowing in violation of the rules of their sex, upon whether or not strawberries for the winter grew underground, and other peculiar phenomena.

That Messrs. Lenine and Trotzky should come forth at the beginning of the new year as rivals of the card-reading fortune teller, old ladies who see the future in tea cups, and sundry prophets, is to say the least refreshing. In their New Year's greeting to the world the two Cagliostros of Bolshevism foretell that in 1920 "there will be soviets at Berlin, Washington, Paris and London. Soviet authority will be supreme throughout the world.'' In one respect this prediction is reassuring, for if Messrs. Trotzky and Lenine will now confine themselves to occult and mediumistic pursuits maybe the afflicted people of Russia will enjoy a breathing space in the bloody orgy of destruction, rapine and murder.

Increased Production Through Industrial Training

INCREASED production is recognized by representatives of labor, employers and economists to be essential not only to reduce the cost of living in the United States but to enable us to assist stricken European nations. The relation of factory industrial training to this world-wide problem was given consideration at a special meeting recently called by the Chairman of the Industrial Training Department of The National Civic Federation, Captain Francis R. Mayer, President of the France and Canada Steamship Co. In this connection, it was recognized that there must be created a sentiment among employers in favor of discontinuing the custom of cutting piece rates and giving scientific consideration to the setting of wage scales in the different industries so that payments to workers may be on an equitable and stable basis, ensuring them the full reward of their efforts.

Restriction of output on the part of workers, which came about through the careless setting of rates by employers at the inception of the piece-work system, would then no longer be essential as a matter of self-protection. It is recognized that limitation of output to provide occupation for a greater number of workers is no longer necessary, but that increased efficiency, both on the part of workers and management, is now requisite to secure maximum production. When the piece-price system was substituted for the day wage, the output per individual was unexpectedly large and the natural result was the inclination of the employer to cut the price per piece, thus reducing the day's wage. This discouragement of individual effort and its attendant so-called "leveling process" became one of the greatest evils and causes of industrial friction. The change in attitude on the part of employers and workers is indicated by the following declaration adopted at the meeting referred to above. The names of the individuals who have carefully considered that statement and have agreed upon a means of helping to meet the present world-wide crisis appear at the end.

Enormous increase in war production resulted wherever there was introduced in an industrial establishment a so-called vestibule school (i.e., entrance room) used not only to train beginners and to upgrade the skilled, but also to test new employees for proper placement in jobs according to their fitness therefor. Reduction in labor turnover, lessened spoilage and wastage, improved quality and quantity of production and happiness of individual workers due to pleasure in performing their tasks well were commonly experienced. Many national trade associations and large corporations have evidenced the desire to develop peace-time shop industrial training along the lines proven to be efficient in munition making, the manufacture of airplanes and the machinery for making all sorts of tools and instruments. It has indicated that the factories of the United States, with their fine equipment, having a payroll of $5,000,000,000, can be advantageously used for educating in their occupations the 12,000,000 persons who work in them. This covers:

1. New workers without any knowledge of the job.
2. Less competent workers who are handicapped by low efficiency.
3. Able workers for better jobs.

It was achieved by segregating types of machines in a separate room, having instructors especially competent in production and training and paying wages to learners, or by special instruction in shops on certain "tagged" machines where segregation is not feasible.

It was found desirable in each trade to form committees to work out methods of training common to all plants.

DECLARATION AND SIGNERS

The world is in dire need of the necessaries and the comforts of life.

It, therefore, becomes the duty of everyone in industry to exert himself to the limit of health and comfort in augmenting production. This is to be done in the industrial field through improvement in management and in the efficiency of the workers.

While recognizing the value of vocational education, it is deemed necessary as a part of this effort that the workers of America be given every reasonable opportunity to increase their knowledge, skill and interest in production in their several fields and, to this end, it is deemed vital to improve and extend facilities for the development of our workers through the establishment of training departments in the various industrial plants.

This training should take place in the course of production, wages being paid learners. Plans should follow methods jointly approved by management and wage-workers in their respective occupations.

It is imperative that labor should reap the rewards of this increased production by compensation based on its direct contribution thereto; that employers should benefit through decreased overhead; and that the public should benefit by the resulting lowered cost of the product.

CAPTAIN FRANCIS R. MAYER—(President, France & Canada Steamship Corporation), Chairman, Industrial Training Department, The National Civic Federation, New York.

MATTHEW WOLL—(Vice-President, American Federation of Labor, and President, International Photo Engravers' Union), Chicago.

LOUIS A. COOLIDGE—(Treasurer, United Shoe Machinery Company), Chairman, Welfare Department, The National Civic Federation, Boston.

HUGH FRAYNE—(General Organizer, American Federation of Labor), New York.

PERCY S. STRAUS—(R. H. Macy & Company) and Vice-Chairman former Section on Industrial Training for the War Emergency, Committee on Labor, Council of National Defense, New York.

JOHN GOLDEN—(International President, United Textile Workers of America), New York.

JOHN F. PERKINS—(J. M. Forbes & Company), Boston.

H. E. MILES—(Chairman former Section on Industrial Training for the War Emergency, Committee on Labor, Council of National Defense), Manufacturer, Racine, Wis.

JAMES W. SULLIVAN—(International Typographical Union), Brooklyn.

EDWIN FARNHAM GREENE—(Treasurer, Pacific Mills), Boston.

RALPH M. EASLEY—(Chairman Executive Council, The National Civic Federation), New York.

MRS. SARA A. CONBOY—(International Secretary-Treasurer, United Textile Workers' Union of America), New York.

GERTRUDE BEEKS EASLEY (MRS. RALPH M.)—(Director Welfare Department, The National Civic Federation), New York.

ARTHUR E. HOLDER—(Of the American Federation of Labor and Member Federal Board for Vocational Education), Washington.

DAVID SNEDDEN—Professor of Education, Teachers' College, Columbia University, and President National Society for Vocational Education), New York.

C. U. CARPENTER—(The Recording & Computing Machines Co.), Dayton, O.

HERMANN SCHNEIDER—(Dean, College of Engineers, University of Cincinnati), Cincinnati.

ROLLIN S. WOODRUFF—(President, C. S. Mersick & Co.), New Haven, Conn.

E. T. MEREDITH—(Chamber of Commerce, U. S. A.), Des Moines, Iowa.

B. A. FRANKLIN—(Strathmore Paper Co.; Former Chief of Production, War Department, Bridgeport, Conn., and district), Mittineague, Mass.

CAPTAIN FRANCIS R. MAYER,
Chairman Industrial Training Department, The National Civic Federation

tered over this continent, not an organization with ten per cent membership, but an organization with over ninety per cent throughout the North American Continent. It has spent more than $750,000 in the establishment and maintenance of a trade school, for the purpose of eliminating inefficiency and raising the standard of craftsmanship. It has more than $250,000 worth of printing machinery in the school. By correspondence it gives instructions to hundreds of members throughout the country. It also receives yearly hundreds of young and old men, who come to learn the printing business, in order that they may produce a better article, making their industry more profitable, not only for themselves, but for the employers.

"Under our rules a local deals directly with a local group of employers, and if those two groups are unable to settle they try to conciliate, and if unable to conciliate they proceed to arbitrate, and in the meantime the presses run. If they fail, then the question goes to national arbitration, as in the case of the American Newspaper Publishers' Association and our national body, or as in the case of the International Joint Conference Council, made up of the three or four employing printers group of this country, and the printing trades unions.

"Seventy per cent at least of the appeals coming to the International Union today are from members who have been fined by their local unions upon the recommendation of the chapel or chairman of the shop for the curtailment of product or the malicious destruction of machinery.

"This union, with its more than forty thousand members, in 460 local unions, had two strikes on this continent since the declaration of war. Those two strikes were unauthorized, illegal, and in both instances the International Union joined with the employer in spanking those unions that called the strikes.

"For the past eight or nine weeks in New York City the employer, periodical publishers, and the five International Printing Trades Unions joined in crushing Bolshevism in the printing industry, and today every press in New York is running and every man helping to run those presses has accepted conciliation and arbitration of differences with the employers."

Mr. T. V. O'Connor, President of The International Longshoremen's Association, said:

"The man that got me believing in collective bargaining was the late Senator Hanna. I was a tug captain, working seven days and six nights a week. We maybe got the seventh night off a week if we could be spared or if there wasn't any work to do. That went for eight months a year, one day a week off, probably seven hours, probably eight hours.

"I remember one time of serving on a committee with four other men and asking our employer if he couldn't arrange some way to give us the full twelve hours off once a week, and the whole committee of five was discharged.

"It was just after I married and I couldn't obtain a position in that port at my vocation for the balance of the year and had to go back firing a tug for $35 a month and support a wife on it. That was the turning point in that industry. We organized in that port and in the other ports on the Great Lakes the following winter, and the next spring we told the employer we wanted every third night off. They gave it to us. The next year we asked for every second night off and we had a strike. That strike lasted five months and we didn't lose a man in our organization during that time. Then when Senator Hanna became interested he sent for us and said, 'Is there any way this thing can be settled?' I said, 'Surely, we are willing to meet with the employers and talk it over.' Senator Hanna arranged a meeting and we went back to work under the old conditions, pending an adjustment or an arbitration, Mr. Hanna being the arbitrator. We continued the balance of that fall, and that following winter we had a meeting and Senator Hanna as the arbitrator, granted us every second night off with an increase in pay.

"We weren't satisfied. We tried to induce the employers to give us better time off. They wouldn't. We went to Congress and we had a law passed giving us every twelve hours out of twenty-four off, but the law stood dead for four years on us, as Secretary Nagel, who was then Secretary of Commerce, rendered a decision that if you worked eleven hours of those twenty-four, you could start off after having an hour's rest and work eleven in the next twenty-four, and that is what they did with us. When Secretary Redfield came in he decided that our day's work was twelve hours, no matter what time we started, and we have been doing that since. Last year the employers, after a conference of some duration, granted that class of men a day a week off, and now they are working twelve hours a day, six days a week, and are getting much better wages.

"That was the first collective bargaining that I entered into. We have worked under that system on the Great Lakes from that day to this. We do not hear any talk of open shop or closed shop. We have a hundred per cent organization, so there isn't any need of talking about open or closed shop. We do not have to waste any time on that phase of the situation at all. Every industry on the Great Lakes in the transportation business, except the Steel Corporation, which we are not on speaking terms with, is working under contracts or trade agreements.

"We have just terminated an agreement with the lumber carriers. That agreement covers fifty-four ports, unloading and loading lumber in all the ports of the Great Lakes. After a three-year agreement a committee on grievances to hear grievances on both sides met in Detroit. Mr. Blatch, representing the lumber carriers, said to me, 'Have you got any grievances?' I said, 'No.' 'Well, neither have we,' and we proceeded to make a new agreement for the following year. I believe the employers will agree that when men, longshoremen, can get together with their employers and make an agreement and carry it out for three years without a grievance on either side, collective bargaining is an ideal situation for both.

"In the collective bargaining in New York we weren't quite so successful. Although we had carried out the agreements in this port for a number of years, this last fall, previous to the strike, literature was distributed on the waterfront by thousands of copies, telling the men that they should get a dollar an hour, or two dollars an hour, telling them they could get it if they struck. The saner element in our organization had agreed, after a referendum vote, to abide by the decision of the National Adjustment Commission, appointed by our organization, the employers, and the United States Shipping Board. As to that decision, called the 'Woolworth' decision, I wasn't satisfied with the increase in pay and I voted against it, but we had agreed to abide by the majority.

"A meeting was called in Cooper Union. I believe there were only two of us in the hall that evening that stood for the carrying out of that agreement, Mr. Ryan and myself. But we never changed our position when they came and said that 40,000 were out on strike. I said, 'I don't care if the other five go out, they are still wrong and they must return to work before they will get any consideration.'

"When these men in New York went on that strike they were a part of the organization of Boston, Baltimore, Philadelphia, the Hampton Roads District, Halifax, St. John, and the whole southern country, and when the order went out from headquarters saying there wasn't an authorized strike in New York they remained at work; there wasn't another port quit. They all stayed at work.

"The employers of longshoremen in this port took the position that they should take. They realized that it was a question of organization rule or mob rule, and they decided that they would sooner have the organization.

"The injection of Mayor Hylan and his famous conciliation commission prolonged the strike of the longshoremen in this port for at least three weeks. I don't blame the Mayor, only for letting himself be deceived. I don't think he had any wrong intention. He was deceived by a lot of people that were trying to advance their own interests.

"The men are back to work, under the award of the National Commission, agreeing to abide by it. For the first time in the history of the longshoremen's organization an attempt had been made to repudiate an agreement, and I hope it will be the last. I believe it will. The men were tricked and fooled by false promises.

"Collective bargaining has proven a success for longshoremen. We have locals in New York longshoremen. We have locals in New York City that conduct meetings in the Italian language, the Lithuanian, the Polish, the German, the English, and some ought to be in the Irish language. If a cosmopolitan crowd of men like that can be educated up to carrying out an agreement, it cannot be much trouble educating mechanics and men working at one class of work all the time.

"The question of I. W. W. and Bolsheviki has been mentioned. We had everything under the sun injected in the longshoremen's strike. We had I. W. W. and Russian Soviet handbills; we had the Italians condemning President Wilson in the Fiume question; we had the Sinn Feiners condemning him in the Irish question. There wasn't a question that I didn't hear argued in the strike. But, in spite of all that, after the strike started we gradually got one local back after the other, to carry out the agreement that they entered into, and today all is peaceful on the waterfront, and nobody is going to be able to disturb those men again.

"I can stand here and say proudly that during the whole course of the war there was not one instance where a ship was delayed through a longshoremen's strike. Our members were working in Hoboken every night, at times eighteen degrees below freezing, when we had to hand out hot coffee every hour and relieve them every two hours, so as to get those transports out with men aboard and supplies and foodstuffs and ammunition that were going over.

"Attempts were made before we got in the war to get the longshoremen involved in a strike; money was offered, ten dollars a week, for longshoremen to be pulled out on strike. . . . That matter was turned over to the government, and with the assistance of Secretary Wilson and Chief Flynn it was headed off. Our organization kept clean.

"The closed shop and the open shop and the minimum wage scale—they are jokes. I saw one minimum wage scale established and it immediately became the maximum wage scale. I have seen the open shop established, but not open for a man that belonged to any kind of a union.

"If Ole Hanson were here, I think he would have to verify this statement, that the employers of steamships or of longshoremen were more responsible for the I. W. W. movement in Seattle, than any other possible thing. They were so afraid that the longshoremen would get a 100 per cent organization in Seattle that they took every means in their power to see that not over fifty-fifty was granted to the union men. They hired every man that came in there, so as to keep the ratio even, fifty union and fifty non-union, with the result that our union men made up their minds that if those fellows are good enough for the employer to hire they were good enough to join our union, with the result that they almost wrecked our organization, as well as wrecking the city. The I. W. W. got control for a while and they made things hum while they had it. Thank God, we got control back again, and the safe and sane element is in control.

"If the employers would choose their employees with a little more care as to their qualifications, as to the day's work they can do or would do, instead of whether they were union men or non-union men, they would get better results. Our organization doesn't have working rules; we don't want working rules; all we want to know is what we are going to get per hour for so many hours a day, and the man is to do the best day's work he possibly can and get the best day's pay he can for it.

"There isn't any labor organization in this country that wants to reduce the efficiency of the work. If there is, it is a detriment, and the legitimate organizations of this country are taking action to cut out that class of men, to weed out the men that have brought a curtailment of production. The fellow that says 'Enough today, I won't do any more,' we don't want any more than the employers do. The employer is going to say, 'All union men are alike,' because one or two do it, and we want to get rid of him."

Peace Covenant Labor Code

(*Continued from page 5*)

from the memorandum presented to that conference by labor members:

"The individualist system of capitalist production, based on the private ownership and competitive administration of land and capital, may, we hope, indeed have received a death blow . . . And the Labor Party refuses absolutely to believe that the British people *will permanently tolerate any reconstruction . . . involved in the abandonment of British industry to . . . separate private employers* . . . What the Labor Party looks to is a genuinely scientific reorganization of the nation's industry . . . on the basis of the *common ownership of the means of production;* the equitable sharing of the proceeds among all who participate in any capacity, and only among these, and the adoption, in particular services and occupations, of those systems and methods of administration and control that may be found, in practice, best to promote the public interest.

"The Labor Party stands not merely for the principle of the common ownership of the nation's land, to be applied, as suitable opportunities occur, but also, specifically, for the immediate nationalization of railways, mines and production of electrical power."

This program was presented by British labor representatives to a national conference called for the purpose of finding a way to bring greater harmony and productivity into industry! It needed not this final act, however, to denote the position of British labor, for the recent record of English labor is clear. The Labor Party speaks now with the big voice. This voice has been notably strengthened since the recent British Railway strike, out of which the famous Triple Alliance emerged in a condition so weakened that British labor commentary no longer makes of the alliance a thing of much menace. The whole British movement has so run to state control, state this and state that, since 1913, that the idea of state Socialism, in one guise or another, has fastened itself upon the movement like an incubus.

In France, while the political voice is the voice of most volume, still some modification is necessary in setting forth the position faithfully. The French Federation of Labor—Confèdèration Gènèrale du Travail—is a body avowedly distinct from all political forms of organization. It in the past aimed at a purely industrial though radical program. It professed to shy at the state, more or less. The revolutionary syndicalists of the movement sought overthrow of the present social order and the establishment of a new order which might be called an industrial society, minus politics as politics is known today. However, the political and parliamentary idea has been there, whether visible or not, and the latest pronouncement of French labor frankly contemplates a partnership of labor with the present state. That pronouncement is indeed a curious combination of varied philosophies in which a kind word for "Soviet Russia" is not overlooked. French labor, through the "C. G. T.," now demands "the complete transformation of society," declaring that "its essential objective is the abolition of the wage-paying and the wage-receiving classes."

The French Confederation, in congress at Lyons on Sept. 21, this year, reaffirming the Amiens "recognition of the class struggle," goes on to say that "while regarding the trade union of today as a group of resistance, it believes that in the future the trade union will be a group of production and distribution, the base of the social re-organization."

The ink was not dry on this program of industrial revolution before French labor began entering into plans for a partnership between labor and the Government in the operation of industry, a recognition of the state which was so disdained in the Sept. 21 industrial revolution pronunciamento! And, as if to make clear finally that French labor cannot rid itself of its ever-shadowing affection for politics, in the Washington conference the "C. G. T." secretly helped bring about the selection of its friend Albert Thomas, pure politician, as executive head of the new International Labor Office.

In the face of the world situation it is important to American labor to consider what will be the effect of its new relationship with European labor. It is important to consider what will become of the International Federation of Trade Unions. Will it, under the shadow of the new institution, fade into a state of powerless and uninteresting uselessness? What rôle did it play in Washington? How many newspaper readers knew it was in session there?

American labor and European labor are not traveling the same road. They do not think alike, do not view the future in the same light, do not live in the same social atmosphere, do not agree as to tactics, philosophy or goal. Nor have they the same psychology. Despite these truths, it is proposed that they be thrown together in an organization in which they MUST function—an organization which is bone of the bone of that which American labor has always stood out against in regard to the essentials of labor practice and belief. Moreover, many thinkers who have most closely examined the structure of the International Labor Organization set up by the Treaty of Versailles are convinced that the organization is capable of being made to serve the wish of whoever dominates it. For the next three years its official direction is in the hands of a Socialist. A conservative Socialist, to be sure, and one who stood with France and democracy in the war, but a politician nevertheless, probably influenced by the common European prejudices against the American trade union movement.

America will find in this new organization that the weight of the old world concepts will stand against her year after year. Her own nationally developed practices may be unappreciated and her native thought and idealism misunderstood. The world cannot escape the effects of this new machine that has been set up. That machine has power. Is American labor, a national economic organization of firm and profound convictions, going to find itself tortured and twisted in the processes of a misfit internationalism?

—AN AMERICAN.

cial Reform in the Church—Which?

tend that this conference is Socialistic because of the presence in its councils of Mr. Spargo and Mr. Russell, and possibly other Socialists. Nor would you, I think, ask the conference to go out of its way to repudiate the Socialistic doctrines of these gentlemen. The programme finally adopted by the conference will definitely fix its economic beliefs; and we of The Every-Name and Nation-Wide Campaigns of the Episcopal Church merely ask that the Church be judged upon a similar basis—by the ultimate action of its General Convention.

As a matter of fact, according to your own definitions in your letter of September 27, we Episcopalians have little to fear regarding Socialistic tendencies within our Church. Referring to the Forum which is to be conducted in connection with the General Convention at Detroit—which Forum, by the way, has no official connection with the Church, but is another of those independent movements whose action is not binding upon the Church in any way—you say that we shall "doubtless hear much talk about the elimination of the causes of unrest through the *Democratization of industry* and the enactment of minimum wage, compulsory sickness and unemployment insurance and old age pension legislation. *None of these things, however, is Socialism* except the first named, which could well be termed Bolshevism, dependent entirely upon who defines it."

Well, these proposed remedies you have named embrace the remedies which have been discussed in Episcopalian circles. At least the discussion has revolved around them, and we have your authority for it that the taint of Socialism clings to but one of them, viz.: the democratization of industry, about which you observe there is some doubt as to its classification, though you suggest it may even verge on Bolshevism. You will understand that I am not here discussing the merits of any of these suggestions; merely by way of illustration I call to your attention that Mr. John D. Rockefeller, Jr., not an Episcopalian, it is true, but also not a Bolshevist, nor a Socialist, has laid before the Industrial Conference at Washington, a proposition that the "Democratization of Industry" be made one of the features of the programme which the conference is to formulate for bringing about a restoration of industrial peace.

What is going on in the Episcopal Church is merely a reflex of the situation throughout the nation. It is not forums, terms or definitions, but facts with which the people are concerned. Many a worn-out theory and doctrine went up in the smoke from the battlefields of Europe. The task now is to adjust our lives to the new conditions. Though I deny that there is any tendency in the Episcopal Church toward Socialism as it has been defined—and you will remember that Mr. Hillquit's definition was phrased in 1914—the fact remains that people will not ask whether a proposed reform is Socialistic, but will it work. And I deny with equal emphasis that any real danger threatens from the tendencies you have named.

Permit me to be frank. As I understand the duty of the Church in the present emergency, and it is the aim of the Every-Name Campaign as a part of the Nation-Wide Movement of our Church to awaken its entire membership to the performance of that duty, it is to promote the interests of the whole people, and not the interests of any one class or group. In your letter of September 27 you make frequent reference to the American Federation of Labor and the Railroad Brotherhoods, and their attitude toward pending issues. You note particularly the "conservative influence" which you declare has been brought to bear by these organizations upon the industrial situation.

Now, with regard to this. First, I want to make clear my sincere belief in labor organization. Labor unionism has been a potent force for good throughout the world. Without the effort which it has put forth in behalf of the toiler, his lot would have indeed been a hard one. In a thousand ways labor unionism has been a powerful agency for the promotion of the democracy of which we boast. And labor unionism may look forward to a career of equal usefulness to humanity, provided it heeds the signs of the times and will, in the same measure that it demands of all other potential agencies, adapt itself to the changed conditions which have been brought about by the world war.

The great problem which the nation faces today is embraced in the industrial situation. All the others revolve around it. One of its greatest off-shoots is the high cost of living. It is vital. Unless the cost of living is reduced, no one can say into what abyss the nation will be plunged. It was the cry for bread that precipitated the French Revolution.

How is the cost of living to be reduced? We may rout the profiteer, and attempt other palliatives; but is it not generally agreed that the one permanent remedy, based on the laws of supply and demand, is so to increase production as to bring about a natural fall in prices? Other co-ordinate remedies may be useful; but in increased production lies the main remedy.

How are we approaching the solution of this problem? It might fairly have been hoped that the leaders of organized labor would have arisen to their opportunity in this crisis, and established their movement as a beneficent agency at the beginning of this new era in the world's history. Instead, however, of adopting a spirit of co-operation, union labor has gone to the other extreme, and has virtually declared war on the people of the United States, who are the third party in interest—Labor and Capital being the other two. Unionism's demands are for higher pay and shorter hours of work, with a strike following each refusal of its demands.

See how this works out: Higher pay inevitably leads to higher prices—for the people pay—when the increase in pay is granted. Shorter hours of work lead to a further curtailment in production, and likewise increased prices; while a strike results in a stoppage of all production in the particular industry affected, and again with increased prices as its inevitable attendant. Thus there is created a vicious circle of ever widening proportions. This is one phase of labor unionism in the present crisis.

Another, and one which is much more grave in the menace which it presents, is typified in the recent Police Strike in Boston, and the still pending Steel Strike. Here there is not involved any immediate question of pay or working conditions. The issue is wholly technical. Labor unionism simply seized upon this critical period to press its demands for union recognition.

A third phase of labor unionism, which is more or less the aggregate of the other two, is the general attitude which organized labor has chosen to assume toward the public in the new age which has dawned. I repeat that the interests of all the people are the paramount consideration. But are the interests of all the people considered when a strike is declared which cuts off food supplies, brings local traffic to a standstill, ties up the railroads of the nation, halts industry, stops the printing presses, and reduces a civilized community to the condition of a border town in the middle ages?

Do not misunderstand me. I make no defense of the capitalist system. On the contrary, I admit that capital has in the past been responsible for many of the injustices which have provoked labor to revolt. I admit further that in the new era which is opening, capital must make concessions, and if we may believe the signs of the times capital is preparing to make these concessions. What you and I, and all other citizens who are aiming at a restoration of industrial peace and order must ask ourselves, and invite labor to consider with us, is whether all of the concessions shall be made by capital, or whether labor will also recognize that in the changed conditions which we face, it, too, must concede, and co-operate toward a solution in the interest of all the people.

One does not have to be a seer or a prophet to see that right now Union Labor is in the furnace with the great white heat of public opinion turned full upon it. Consider the power to which the great unions have attained. It is possible for the Railroad Brotherhoods to tie up the trade and commerce of the United States, at least for a time precisely as Great Britain was tied up recently. We cannot forget that less than four years ago, at the mere threat of such action, the Congress of the United States enacted a law granting the demands made by the Brotherhoods then. The point is not whether the demands are just, or were just on that occasion. The point is whether the Government—the people—should be left to the mercy of a group of leaders owing responsibility to none but the power which creates them in such a way that they can enforce any demands they may make.

Within the month, Mr. Gompers, President of the American Federation af Labor, testifying before a Committee of the United States Senate, declared bluntly that if certain legislation looking to the regulation of the unions was enacted, and was later upheld by the Supreme Court of the United States, Union Labor would not obey the law.

Is that a display of the "conservative influence" to which you referred? Is the Charter of the American Federation of Labor greater than the Constitution of the United States?

I am opposed to orthodox socialism, and will follow you in any proper measures to combat its influence in the United States, but I cannot join in any cry against present evil tendencies which does not include a wise restraint of unlawful and destructive effort wherever found, or however designated, and especially of an unregulated and from a legal standpoint irresponsible force, which flatly threatens to disregard a proposed law that doesn't conform to its wishes.

Let us by all means combat Socialism in your meaning of the term, and let us begin by seeking to induce the leaders of Union Labor to return to moderation and sanity before it is too late. Socialism, or worse, is already rearing its heads within the ranks of organized labor. I am willing to concede that Mr. Gompers would have averted the Boston Police Strike, had he been able, as well as the Steel Strike, and we know that he has put the seal of his disapproval on the Longshoremen's Strike here in New York. A score of other instances might be cited where the unions have taken the bit between their teeth and defied their leaders. If this movement becomes general, chaos will not be far off.

I trust that I have made my point clear. Socialism, so-called, is only one of the menaces, and a minor one, threatening the nation. A great, potential force has grown up among us which is powerful enough to threaten, with successful results, the law making power of the United States; and, because of this success, is now going a step further and declaring an intention, in certain eventualities, to set at defiance the ultimate power and authority of the civil arm of the Government. At the same time, this force and power are unmistakably passing from the hands of those who we will agree, in many of their acts, have been agents of moderation in the past, and are being gathered in by the extreme radicals within its ranks.

Isn't this a real menace, of far graver proportions than anything we have to fear in the near future from Socialism?

We of the Every-Name Movement in the Episcopal Church count it not the least important development of our campaign that The National Civic Federation, through you, has raised the issues which are the subject of this correspondence. I feel that you will not mistake the spirit in which it has been approached on my part, and it is in that spirit that I suggest that The National Civic Federation is in an admirable position to render renewed service to the Nation now in endeavoring to inspire among the Union Labor representatives in its membership a comprehension of the acute situation which they face, and a spirit to cope with that situation in a broad-minded statesmanlike way. You will not have failed to observe that among thoughtful people serious consideration is being given to the question whether it may not be a fact that the strike and the boycott have performed their functions in awakening the people to the evils to which the workingman has been subjected in the past; and that unionism has now reached that stage where, as a force potential alike for good and evil, it ought, together with capital, to submit to a governmental regulation which will conserve equally the rights of both.

Very truly yours,

WM. FELLOWES MORGAN.

Mr. Easley's answer follows:

December 26, 1919.

Dear Mr. Morgan:

I have your letter of October 17, which discusses a number of very important questions. But may I suggest that I think we are getting rather far afield from the subject matter of my first letter to you, of July 25, which I may add was written without any idea of a public discussion resulting therefrom. The only subject with which I dealt in that letter was the rapid growth of Socialism in the churches, and especially in the Protestant Episcopal Church, and I offered my congratulations on the fact that you and other business men had undertaken through the Every Name movement to show that "religion is good business," because, as I stated, it would be "their primary duty to see that the social, educational and spiritual machinery of the church is not captured by the inordinately active Socialists, Socialistic sentimentalists and other fomenters of disorder."

In your letter of August 19, and again in that of October 17, you insisted vigorously that the Protestant Episcopal Church is in no way responsible for the utterances of individuals and unofficial groups.

As I intend in this letter to devote myself entirely to the original question raised by me, viz., the growth of Socialism in the churches and especially in the Protestant Episcopal Church, I quote from your last letter of October 17, in order that we may have a clear understanding as to the specific issue under discussion:

> The point you at first raised was as to "the rapid growth of socialism in the churches," and you added that "the Protestant Episcopal Church is especially open to that criticism." Now, however, you disavow any belief that the Episcopal Church is socialistic, "as a church," but insist that individuals and commissions within the church display marked socialistic tendencies; and if their utterances are not repudiated by the Church "the public has a right to assume that, if not approved by the Church, they at least are not disapproved."
>
> If by this you mean disapproved by individuals within the Church who speak with an authority equal to those whose utterances you condemn, I refer you back to the statement of Rev. Dr. Manning, Rector of Trinity, which I quoted in my letter of August 10, and which in your answer of September 27, you approve.
>
> If you mean disapproval by formal act of the Church, I can only repeat that it is the General Convention of the Episcopal Church, meeting triennially, and now in session in Detroit, which voices the policies of the Church, and in the absence of such action by the Convention the Church cannot be held responsible for any definition of policy either by individual or group.

After we reach a conclusion on the original proposition, I am perfectly willing to take up the other matters you have raised in your last letter—the high cost of living, profiteering, the tactics of the American Federation of Labor, the alleged utterances of Samuel Gompers and other important subjects. But unless a stop can be put to the inroads of revolutionary radicalism among the educated membership of the church, it seems far-fetched to criticise the American trade union movement, in which revolution has made only minor headway, and, at that largely among its illiterate foreign membership.

At the time I wrote my first letter I did not clearly understand the relation which such non-official bodies as the Church League for Social and Industrial Democracy and the Church Socialist League bore to the Protestant Episcopal Church, nor did I quite understand the official nature of the Joint Commission on Social Service of the Protestant Episcopal Church, of which commission you are the honored treasurer. When you intimate that the utterances and activities of the unofficial Socialist bodies within your church are neutralized and entirely offset by an individual statement of the Rev. Dr. Manning or any other of the many thousands of high-minded, patriotic Americans in the Protestant Episcopal Church, I think that, unintentionally, you misrepresent the situation. It would be a truer parallel if Dr. Manning or any other economically sound American were to organize an anti-socialist league, or an "American League" if you prefer, the purpose of which would be to challenge, to defy and to confound the sentimental Bolshevist preachers and bishops who are flooding the church with libels on American industry and American institutions. That would be a real parallel. But there is no such organization, so far as I can find, in the Protestant Episcopal Church or for that matter, in any other Protestant Church.

Now, Mr. Morgan, when groups of men, clerical and lay, publicly organize into bodies for the purpose of carrying on propaganda within the church, using the machinery of organized religion for the promulgation of revolutionary incitements, does not the church, unless it repudiates these bodies and refuses to permit them to use its pulpits, assume a grave measure of responsibility? Exercising authority over its pulpits, does not the church fail in fulfilling its grave moral obligations if it laxly permits those pulpits to be prostituted to the preaching of Socialism and its church buildings to be turned into radical revolutionary forums? You aver in your letter above quoted that the alleged tendency toward Socialism "is not more markedly developed in Episcopal circles than it is within the body of our citizens as a whole." As we have been dealing in this correspondence with church denominations, permit me to say that after further investigation into this matter I am convinced that the tendency toward Socialistic revolutionary propaganda is more in evidence in the Episcopal Church than in any other Christian denomination and that, in this respect, the Episcopal clergy are the most conspicuous offenders.

The recently organized Church League for Social and Industrial Democracy in the Protestant Episcopal Church, referred to in my first letter, which among other things in its program pledged itself "to give moral and political support" to clergymen in the Episcopal Communion the radicals, anti-conscriptionists, pacifists and pro-Germans, while defeated in the House of Deputies of the General Convention, was passed by the House of Bishops? Do you see no connection between the work of these Socialistic propagandists and that vote by the House of Bishops?

Does the Episcopal Church have no responsibility in regard to this organization, engineered and directed by radicals of various hues, some of them political Socialists, when, according to its own announcement, it has asked all bishops of the church whether they would sanction the work of the League in their diocese and help to secure for representatives hearings in pulpits?

Of the twelve members of the temporary executive committee of this League, five have acted on the executive committee of the Church Socialist League, which was founded in 1911 mainly through the efforts of President Bell of St. Stephen's, and which declares itself in the last issue of its official organ, *The Social Preparation*: "WE ARE NOT REFORMERS, TRYING TO PATCH UP AN OUTWORN GARMENT, BUT REVOLUTIONISTS," etc., the identical claim made by I. W. W.s and Syndicalists.

Among these "revolutionists" presumably are the Rt. Rev. W. A. Guerry, former vice-president of the Church Socialist League, the Very Rev. Bernard Iddings Bell, William F. Cochran and Miss Vida D. Scudder, who are also members of the Joint Commission on Social Service of the Episcopal Church, the official body of which you are treasurer.

You may perhaps contend that the church cannot be criticised for taking no action in regard to this Church Socialist League, composed largely of ministers of the church, not to speak of ten or more bishops, when it declares in a recent manifesto that "at this supreme hour of the world's history. . . .the church is apostate to its divine mission," when it implies that the church has supported "the capitalist system of production, with its unholy emphasis on profits, privilege and exploitation," and when it calls upon the church "to endeavor to understand and assist the working out of that social and industrial revolution, with the conscious purpose of helping to prepare the way for such complete revolution of our present economic and social disorder that a Christian order may be evolved."

But does the church have no responsibility one way or the other when this organization in the church, seeking to attain political ends through the machinery and pulpits of the church, interprets as the "Christian order" what is nothing more nor less than Socialism, and when among its avowed stated purposes we find the following: "To help the advance of Socialism by every just means. To convert church people to the principles of Socialism."

Unless the Episcopal Church approves of political Socialism, unless it espouses as the basis of a "Christian order" the materialistic doctrines of Karl Marx, does the chuch not have a duty to perform in protecting its members against the insidious propaganda carried on by the Church Socialist League through churches and pulpits?

In itself, so far as numerical membership is concerned, the Church Socialist League may not be important; but when one of its chief founders, Dr. Bell, is president of a college responsible to the church and when other members hold important charges where, by reason of their authority and prestige and of the confidence accorded them, they are able through camouflaged Socialistic preachings to poison the minds of church members, as it would not be possible for notorious Socialists such as Morris Hillquit, Judah Magnes and others to do, it seems the purposes and activities of the League cannot well be ignored by a church whose avowed mission is spiritually to protect all in its fold. According to a press announcement sent out by the Every Name Campaign, the course at St. Stephen's, which includes instructions in Socialism and I. W. W.ism, will be in charge of the Rev. Lyford P. Edwards, himself an avowed radical, who went to such startling extremes as to imply that Socialism and Christianity are identical. I ask, does the church have no responsibility in protecting young students in a college officially conducted under the sanction of the church from possible pernicious and destructive teachings?

Does the church have no responsibility concerning the activities and propaganda of a minister of standing and the president of a college conducted under the official sanction of the church—I refer to the Very Rev. Bernard Iddings Bell—when in a published book he expresses as the basis of his preaching what is the basis of crass materialistic un-Christian Marxian Socialism: "It is an established principle of Sociology that the two great needs which impel mankind to most of its actions and which determine most of its institutions are the same two primary needs which impel toward action and evolution all living creatures, the need for food and the desire for sex expression."

Commenting on the Church Socialist League, the boast is made in the American Labor Year Book, the official handbook of the Socialist Party published by the Rand School. "Its influence within the Episcopal Church is not at all measured by its numerical strength. In spite of the conservatism of the Episcopal Church and of its numbering many leading capitalists of the country among its members, *yet the church has officially adopted radical and even revolutionary resolutions, and the influence of the Church Socialist League is discernible as giving color to them.* (The italics are mine.) A considerable share of the clergy are tinctured with Socialism." With but 6,000 clergy, we are told "several hundred are avowed Socialists."

If it is true that the church, through any of its duly authorized committees or commissions, has officially adopted radical and even revolutionary resolutions, could one be blamed, Mr. Morgan, for attributing to the church a tendency toward Socialism? Is it true, for instance, that "the influence of the Church Socialist League is discernible as giving color" to any of the reports of authorized committees or commissions, such as the Joint Commission on Social Service, four of whose members have been affiliated with the "revolutionistic" Church Socialist League?

When action was taken last summer by the Attorney General of New York State for the cancellation of the charter of the Rand School, one of the executives of the school, George Goebel, "as an example of the importance of the persons interested in the school," informed a reporter of the New York *World* that no less than eighteen Protestant Episcopal clergymen, all of them except one from the metropolitan district, had assembled at the school to discuss means of spreading the tenets of Socialism among their congregations. When the raid was made on the Rand School by agents of the Lusk Committee there was found in the files a letter addressed to Scott Nearing by A. Wagenknecht, of the Department of Organization and Propaganda of the Socialist Party of the United States, Chicago, Ill. This letter, which was turned over by Nearing to David Berenberg, of the Rand School, read:

"Some time ago I wrote you about a visit to Bishop William M. Brown, who resides at Galion, Ohio. Bishop Brown is a member of the Socialist Party, a bishop of the Episcopal Church, and a heretic of the reddest hue."

Telling of the intention of Bishop Brown to visit New York, the writer asked that a meeting be arranged at the Rand School or at some hall for the "Red" Bishop. "Comrade Brown is 63 years of age," the letter continued. "When

I tell you that Comrade Brown is a Bolshevist, is making a trip to New York to consult you and Comrade Eastman about a series of three booklets he intends publishing and that he does not ask a fee for his speaking services, I am sure you will do what you can."

In answering this letter, Berenberg informed Comrade Wagenknecht that he would be only too glad to make what arrangements he could for Comrade Brown, adding, "I believe that the circumstances under which he comes out publicly for Socialism and Bolshevism are of sufficient publicity value to insure successful meetings for him."

You may say that for Bishop Brown's "hereticism" of the "reddest hue" the church has no responsibility, and that when one of the lights of the church, such as Bishop Brown, "comes out publicly for Socialism and Bolshevism," the public would not be justified in assuming that the individual expresses the opinion of the church, of the General Convention, of the Joint Commission, or any of the official committees of the church. But what have you to say, as treasurer of the Joint Commission on Social Service, when officials of your own Commission exploit movements and forces analogous to Socialism and Bolshevism as praise-worthy and valuable? What have you to say when the executive secretary of your Commission, the Rev. F. M. Crouch, addressing a so-called national industrial conference called by the Industrial Relations Department of the Inter-Church World Movement, held early in October, suggested as a possibility the transference of industry from those who have to those who have not—a prospect paralleling what the Bolshevists through their Soviet scheme have endeavored to put in practice in Russia. "Are we prepared to maintain the present system of industry as an indispensable condition to perpetuating our organizations?" asked Mr. Crouch, your executive secretary. "Is the right to 'take and hold' to be the principle today?" "Is capital to be socially controlled or individually controlled?" "Is the present industrial relation a sensible relation, let alone a justifiable relation?" "It is an absolute fact that there are increasing numbers of men and women today who say: 'If the church will not assist us, we will leave the church.' . . . Can we solve the problem of industrial relations unless we recognize the radical movements outside? We are bound to think of them in terms of the present economic and industrial order." "What is Socialism based upon?" Karl Marx's "Capital," declared your Executive Secretary to his audience, "is there for you to read."

Do you, as treasurer, approve of the point of view which the Rev. Mr. Crouch must bring to his activities as Executive Secretary of your Commission as was expressed in his declaration; "The system of industrialism which we still largely know, working out in the exploitation of fellow men by fellow men, cannot endure in the face of justice." If the system of industrialism which we at present know cannot endure in the face of justice, what system does your executive secretary propose?

You may say that the Joint Commission on Social Service cannot be criticised or be held accountable for any views expressed by its executive secretary before another body, and that the Rev. Mr. Crouch, apart from his official duties and when not appearing as a representative of your Commission, speaks as an individual. What have you to say when the then secretary of your Commission, the Rev. J. Howard Melish, addressing a conference of your body on October 14, 1913, declared that, because the church was not sufficiently obedient to the teachings of Jesus, masses of men had gone into Socialism as a religious substitute; when he extolled and glorified Socialism as supplying a spirituality and reality which many did not find in the church, and when, further, he held up for honor the leaders of the I. W. W., many of whom were, later, convicted of criminally conspiring against the government in its conduct of the war and sentenced to long terms of imprisonment?

Mr. Melish's speech is printed in the official report of your Joint Commission. If any one among the members of your Commission dissented from the Rev. Mr. Melish's views there is no record in your report of such dissent. Neither, so far as a careful examination of the report reveals, were the Rev. Mr. Melish's sentiments repudiated, nor was the Rev. Mr. Melish rebuked. On the contrary, despite his openly expressed views, Mr. Melish continued to serve as secretary of your Commission, is still a member, and, moreover, as was expressed in a talk at St. Mark's-in-the-Bouwerie as recently as December 7, still considers the lawless I. W. W. movement as embodying a "beautiful ideal."

"Big Bill" Haywood—doubtless one of the I. W. W. leaders whom the Rev. Mr. Melish lauded as deserving honor—in a speech delivered at Cooper Union at a date previous to Mr. Melish's address to the meeting of your Commission, had boldly declared:

"Can you wonder that I despise the law? I understand the class struggle. I am not a law-abiding citizen. More than that, I do not believe that you here ought to be law-abiding citizens.

"We want to overthrow the capitalist system and establish in its place an industrial democracy. Why, then, say we are law-abiding?"

Ignoring "Big Bill" Haywood's expressed declaration, the Rev. Mr. Melish, comparing the I. W. W. with the Zealots—"from whom Jesus chose more than one disciple"—told your Commission there was no reason for the church to be hostile to Syndicalism although Syndicalism was altogether hostile to the church. He declared:

"Syndicalism, as every investigation has shown, finds a field only in our industrial centres where immigrants are herded. Without a vote, strange, bewildered, 'put upon,' deserted by the church, the labor union and the Socialists, it was Syndicalism which went to them in their distress and gave them courage and hope. All honor to the I. W. W. leaders that they were found at the hottest point of the industrial conflict."

Does the Joint Commission on Social Service of the Protestant Episcopal Church accept or reject the Rev. Mr. Melish's interpretation of Socialism—of materialistic Marxian Socialism whose appeal is made through class antagonism and class hatred—as providing a "real religion," a "reality" in which the churches are lacking, a "spirituality" which has for masses of men made Socialism a substitute for the church? Does the Joint Commission accept or reject the declaration that the churches have been insufficiently obedient to the social teachings of Christ, while, on the contrary, among Socialists "is found a feeling of brotherhood, service and sacrifice for man, confidence in the triumph of justice and righteousness, single devotion to truth, faith, hope and love"? Does the Joint Commission believe, or does it not believe, that the leaders of the I. W. W., including "Big Bill" Haywood, should be given all honor, and that its terrible program of incendiarism, sabotage and terrorism should not be condemned? Is the Joint Commission inclined, with the Rev. Mr. Melish, to excuse and condone the long history of outlawry of the I. W. W.?

The Joint Commission on Social Service may evade assuming any responsibility for radical statements made by your present executive secretary and former secretary—even for notorious pro-Socialist and pro-I. W. W. utterances made at its own meetings—on the ground that these were but expressions of individual views, for which the Commission is not responsible. But you will admit that the Joint Commission on Social Service cannot escape responsirated irrefutably by the declaration—made in footnote, page 64—"The modern reader is) longer interested in Marx's dialectics, but is ımpelled to recognize that the central position r which he stood is not only tenable but is ally impregnable."

"The principles of pristine Socialism revolve ›out the central fact, since Marx's time in-easingly apparent to many, that there is and ust be under present conditions exploitation ! the workers by those who are in a position to rofit by their labor."

Do you, Mr. Morgan, as treasurer of the Joint ommission, endorse not only as "tenable" but ; "impregnable" the central position and principles of pristine Socialism"—the Socialm of Karl Marx, of Morris Hillquit, of Lenine nd Trotzky?

The report of your Commission, in a footnote, eclares as a fact:

"Marxian Socialism would give the worker *ull* value of his labor, though that might mean urtailing the illegitimate 'right' of the capiılist to more than his due share; in the proess many parasitical capitalists, indeed the hole system, would, in Marx's expectation, go) the wall. The popularity of strict Socialism ·ith the workers is, in a word, due to this very ısistence on their individual rights, which—ocialism correctly holds—can be secured only ›y collective effort."

Is this Socialist propaganda or is it not? And just how "popular" with American workers is Socialism? The Socialist Party has less than 50,000 members, while the American Federation of Labor and the Railway Brotherhoods, 95 per cent of whom are anti-Socialist, have 4,500,000 members.

Commenting upon "an elaborate attempt" "made toward the end of the last century by the famous Austrian economist Boehm-Bawerk," "to prove that Marx's theory of economic exploitation was all wrong," the declaration is made in your report that the Austrian economist's contention "CANNOT EXPLAIN AWAY THE FACT THAT THE PRESENT ORDER, AS MARX WAS ONE OF THE FIRST TO RECOGNIZE, HAS WORKED OUT TO A DEGREE OF INJUSTICE WHICH CANNOT ESCAPE THE ATTENTION OF EVEN THE MOST CASUAL OBSERVER."

I ask you, Mr. Morgan: Would not the public, reading these statements in the report of your commission, be justified in assuming that your Commission is opposed to the "present order" and that, ergo, it accepts the Marxian as a better and more just order?

Mr. Melish's notorious defense of the I. W. W. in a speech delivered at a meeting of your Commission in 1913, above referred to, was made before the I. W. W. had become an auxiliary to the German espionage system in America, before it had engaged in the destruction of munition plants and railroads, before it had embarked on a program to hinder the United States in its conduct of the war against Germany, and before over a hundred of its leaders were convicted of criminal conspiracy. At that time your speaker and secretary might have pleaded ignorance of the lawless character of this organization as expressed previously by Haywood and other leaders; at that time the Joint Commission may have been excused for not publicly repudiating Mr. Melish's utterances on the ground that it was not in a position to know from established proof that this organization was an enemy of the American government, that it was in its philosophy, its program and its acts criminally disloyal and treasonable. But what shall we say when, after the I. W. W. had been convicted by evidence produced by the Department of Justice of having preached sedition and opposition to the draft, of having sought through the destruction of munition plants, railroads and ships to render the nation impotent in its warfare against the Huns, we find that the sentiments expressed by Mr. Melish in 1913 are in 1919 reechoed in and give color to the report of your Joint Commission?

Admitting that in the United States "its (the I. W. W.s) effects especially during the war have become notorious," it is stated that these effects were "in large measure deliberately or unconsciously misconstrued by the great body of the American public." The statement is made: "It has never yet been proved that there was any connection between German gold and the American I. W. W." Going out of the way, as it were, to whitewash the criminal I. W. W. of abetting Germany and seeking to give aid to Germany in the war, your report totally ignores the facts brought out in the Chicago trial of the accused I. W. W. leaders, as well as the established fact that Germany's official agents in this country were instructed to employ, and did employ, these same forces of revolution and disorder.

The same tendency to whitewash the I. W. W., to find excuses for its criminal existence and palliation for its crimes which was evinced by Mr. Melish in his speech of 1913, is found in the 1919 report of your Commission. "One cause" for its rapid spread, your report declares, "has been the fact—until at least comparatively recently—that the American Federation of Labor, including some three million skilled workers, has ignored, either deliberately or unconsciously, the claims and aspirations of their unskilled fellows, who have therefore flocked to the banner of Syndicalism." As against this statement, I want to quote from my letter to you of September 27, where, referring to Mr. Melish's dramatic eulogy of the I. W. W., I said:

> This simply means that the Rev. Mr. Melish, Secretary of the Social Service Commission, had accepted at face value all the fantastic claims of the I. W. W. propagandists about the Utopian program of that organization and was repeating, parrot-like, the misrepresentations of the trade union movement put out by William D. Haywood and his band of thugs to the effect that the American Federation of Labor was neglecting the unskilled immigrant workers, when, at that very time, the American Federation of Labor had twenty-five times more unskilled laborers organized than the whole membership of the I. W. W. Every month the Federation spends more money in endeavoring to organize the unskilled laborers of the country than the I. W. W. has done since its inception.

You say in your last letter: "I want to make clear my sincere belief in labor organizations. Labor unionism has been a potent force for good throughout the world."

Can you, therefore, approve of the effort made in the report of your Commission to disparage American trade unionism as reactionary, as less worthy of support than the radical revolutionary movements which would overturn society and establish the Bolshevist Soviet I. W. W. system under which labor would take over, own and operate all the mills, mines, factories and railroads?

Your report, in a footnote, page 105, says (italics are mine):

"Organized labor in America is still *lagging behind* its European colleagues in the sense that it *is still concentrating its attention upon specific amelioration of the worker's lot* through the more primitive trade union practices of collective bargaining and trade agreements. *The ingrained conservatism, if not reactionism,* of the A. F. of L. under its present leadership was strikingly manifest at its last annual convention."

This characterization of the A. F. of L. convention as "reactionary" parallels the description of that convention by the *New York Call*, the official organ of the Socialist Party, the *New Solidarity*, the official organ of the I. W. W., and the *Revolutionary Age*, the official organ of the Syndicalists. It certainly is a curious coincidence to find the report of the Joint Commission in Social Service and the reports of those revolutionary journals to be in such accord.

The Joint Commission's report refers its readers on this point to an article on the A. F. of L. convention published in the pro-Bolshevist *Nation* and written by one, Charles P. Sweeney, a frank pro-Bolshevist newspaper writer. I ask you, Mr. Morgan, does the Joint Commission accuse the A. F. of L. of conservatism and reactionism because, at its last convention, to quote *The New York Call*, "the Gompers machine crushed all proposals of the radicals," because, to use the words of the *Call*, "there will be no strike to save Tom Mooney; the Soviet government has been denounced; . . . the Labor Party idea has been smashed," because "the convention . . . is opposed to the democratization of industry to the extent of refusing to recommend the election of foremen on jobs by the workers, refusing to assist in the formation of soldiers' councils," etcetera?

Does the Joint Commission disparage "specific amelioration of the worker's lot" through constructive measures and favor a catastrophic revolution which will place the workers in control, as is advocated by the less "conservative" and less "reactionary" Bolshevists, Socialists and I. W. W.? Does the Joint Commission, or does it not, take a stand of sympathy and approval regarding the I. W. W., when in the same report in which it charges the A. F. of L. with "conservatism" and "reactionism," it declares:

"THERE IS IN THE SYNDICALIST MOVEMENT, IF WE CAN FOR THE MOMENT LEAVE OUT OF CONSIDERATION ITS VIOLENT TACTICS, A POSSIBILITY OF SOCIAL AND EVEN ULTIMATELY OF RELIGIOUS VALUE WHICH NEITHER THE CHURCH NOR THE STATE CAN AFFORD TO IGNORE OR TO CONDEMN UNTIL IT HAS GIVEN THE MOVEMENT A FAIR HEARING."

As treasurer of the Joint Commission, you would confer a great favor upon many of us by explaining just what there is in this self-confessedly lawless organization which may be of ultimate religious value.

In seeking to excuse and condone the I. W. W., your report makes the same pleas, the same defense, uses the same line of argument employed by the *New Republic*, by the National Civil Liberties Bureau, by Carlton H. Parker and by Robert Bruère, I. W. W. defenders, and which would place the blame for all the crimes of the I. W. W. upon social conditions.

Considerable space is given in the report of the Joint Commission to quotations from such so-called "representative opinions" as the following:

"For some time past there has been a growing conviction that democratic institutions have failed to realize their early promise. . . . There can be no question as to the depth and the extent of the prevailing scepticism concerning the adequacy of representative government as it exists today." (Richard Roberts in the *Nation*, May 5, 1919.)

"It seems fairly certain that, for a considerable time to come, the main struggle in Europe will be between capitalism and some form of Socialism, and it is highly probable in this struggle the strike will play a great part. To introduce democracy into industry by any other method would be very difficult. And the principle of group autonomy justifies this method so long as the rest of the community opposes self-government for industries which desire it. Direct action has its dangers, but so has every vigorous form of activity." (Bertrand Russell, a notorious pacifist.)

Your report proceeds to comment:

"Workers whose temper runs thus—" (who believe that democratic institutions have failed, etc.)—"are not likely long to be satisfied with any scheme which does not result in the introduction of substantial democracy into our economic life." Your report explains that the term "industrial democracy" has been almost discredited because of its application to such "absurdly inadequate proposals as profit-sharing, bonuses and welfare work." What the workers want "is what they say the employers will not concede without a struggle—practical control of the industries in which they spend their lives."

Does the Joint Commission advocate such control of industries by the workers?

Commenting upon the "common charge" made "by practical citizens and even reformers," that the Syndicalist program is incoherent and indefinite, your Commission's report concludes:

"In partial reply, it may be remarked that the Syndicalist method of 'direct action' is based tacitly on the principle—'Act and the way will become clear,' which has, it must be admitted, some affiliation with current philosophical thought and even with certain aspects of the Christian faith."

In other words, all that the Bolshevists, Socialists and I. W. W.'s have to do is to act, to take over all industries, and everything will work itself out to a league of millennial perfection, as has not happened, you and I will admit, in this so-far imperfect world, unless it be in Petrograd and Moscow.

In dealing with Guild Socialism, which, according to your report, "viewed from within as a constructive industrial program . . . offers much ground for hope," the statement is made:

"The stock argument advanced by the ultra-conservative against any movement that would tend to give greater control into the hands of the worker is of a piece with similar arguments advanced in former times against intrusting the functions of political government to the common people."

The National Guild Movement, your report says, "would seem to offer much hope and much promise for a better ordered industrial future."

Section 10, Part 11, of your report, is headed significantly: "The Issue: Not Wages, Hours and Conditions, but Status—Control of Work and Life."

"It is becoming increasingly clear," your report goes on, "that a growing and substantial section of the workers of the world are convinced that their present status is at least semi-servile if not wholly so. . . . Wage-workers are asking themselves how their condition compares with that of the feudal serf or the chattel slave and their answer to this query is by no means favorable."

Your report says further:

"No conscientious thinker who is at all familiar with the situation can deny in the face of patent facts that the workers' contention is largely right and that something must be done in the way of an effective answer."

Do you want the public to believe for one moment that men like yourself and other men of standing on your Committee, have anything but a wholesome contempt for the idea that the condition of the wage-earner today compares unfavorably with that of the feudal serf and the chattel slave? It is an insult to the intelligence of any American even to ask such a question, and therefore I do not ask it. At no time in history (and this was just as true in 1914 as now) have the American wage earners had such large wages and such consideration for their comfort and well-being, and, as is evidenced by the number of strikes we see today, been so independent in their conduct. "Feudal serfs or chattel slaves" do not strike. What do you, as president of the New York Manufacturers' Association, a body of 5,000 employers, as well as director yourself in any number of corporations, think of such a statement?

To return to your report, it apparently advocates and approves of a program aiming at nothing short of control of industry in whole or in part by the workers. The term "industrial democracy," again repeats your report, "had almost been discredited in recent months by its facile application to all kinds of industrial experiments and programs which at the same time leave the control effectively in the hands of the present employer.

"Such proposals or devices, however they may masquerade under the name of 'industrial democracy,' the workers are in increasing numbers repudiating, insisting that they will not be satisfied until they have at least an equal share in control of the industries in which they are engaged."

This is a straight-out attack on the so-called "democratic" plans advocated by Mr. Rockefeller, the International Harvester Company, the United States Steel Corporation, the General Electric Company, the Standard Oil Company of New Jersey and the Leitch plan. Do you and all the members of the Joint Commission approve of this attack on these "democratic" plans, and do you approve of this Bolshevist program? Apparently yes, because the report concludes:

"To answer that this is utterly impractical because the workers are not now competent to manage their industries, is to judge the workers by their actual rather than by their potential faculties, which they justly assert can be trained only as they have opportunities to apply them to administrative and managerial functions. It may well be that for a time at least workers in control of an industry would have to depend upon the trained direction and expert advice of those who have been their employers or actual directors, but the experience of history shows in the large that those who are charged with responsibility ultimately prove themselves capable and worthy of it."

This is a bold attempt to justify the policy of Lenine and Trotzky in confiscating and running the factories in Petrograd and Moscow. Is it possible that the patriotic Americans on your Commission have read and approved this statement? The Bolshevist, I. W. W. and Socialist propaganda largely defeats itself by reason of its extremism and vehemence. May it not be possible that such "tempered," adroitly phrased and seductive propaganda as is embodied in the report of the Joint Commission may do for these unrestrained zealots what their own literature fails by its very excesses to accomplish?

Let us meet the issue, Mr. Morgan. If the notorious activities of the Church Socialist League and the somewhat camouflaged radical propaganda of the Church League for Social and Industrial Democracy, both seeking to operate through the machinery of the church and to use the pulpits of the Church, are not repudiated by the Church through its General Convention, does not the public have a right to assume they are at least not disapproved? Further: Is the public not justified in assuming that the report of the J[illegible]Commission, embodying as it does pro-[illegible]alistic, pro-I. W. W. and Bolshevistic propaganda—nothing more nor less—in not being rejected by the General Convention was therefore acceptable to that body? Does not the church, by accepting at its General Convention and by disseminating such a report, without qualification or criticism, make itself responsible for its contents? If it is a fact that the Church Socialist League, by reason of its members being on such bodies as your commission, has been able to "give color to" such reports, then is not the situation a very serious one?

Let me close this letter, which has lengthened into an essay, by referring to my first letter to you, when I congratulated the business men of the Protestant Episcopal Church on having inaugurated the Every Name Campaign, "because," as I said, "it would be their primary duty to see that the social, educational and spiritual machinery of the church is not captured by the inordinately active socialists, socialistic sentimentalists and other fomenters of disorder."

Since I wrote that letter on July 25, having had brought to my attention further evidence of the inroads made in the Episcopal Church by this inimical propaganda, only a small part of which can be quoted in this letter, I have become convinced that there is a hundredfold more need for vigorous effort on the part of your organization than I had believed at that time was necessary.

Not only has evidence accumulated of dangerous propaganda in the Episcopal Church, but in other churches as well, and we are now examining the social service and industrial commissions of those bodies.

As the one hundred and thirteen international organizations composing the American Federation of Labor have declared their intention of driving out of their organization all Bolshevists, I. W. W.ites and other revolutionists, is it too much to hope that the Every Name movement, including as it does many of the most public-spirited, loyal and representative men of the nation, will perform that vitally necessary and patriotic service for the Protestant Episcopal Church? I am sure, Mr. Morgan, that you will do everything in your power to help bring about this purging of the temple.

Sincerely yours,

RALPH M. EASLEY.

My Days Under the Bolshevist Reign of Terror

(*Continued from page 9.*)

they were still safe. It seemed to me an incredibly short time since the firing started that the lull came. No shots were fired. The same question was on the lips of all of us—"Have the Czechs been routed?" "My God, my God, it can't be so!" some one said. A woman went to a window and gave a happy cry. All of us flocked to the door.

In the streets, half timidly at first, the citizens of Kazan were venturing out. First doubtfully, then with more assurance, they rushed down the streets. Then, with joyful shouts, weeping happy tears, they flung themselves upon the necks of their liberators. The Czechs had utterly routed the enemy! All night the celebration continued. Women threw flowers at the Czechs, decorated their hats with ribbons. Arm in arm, the population walked with the brave Czechs who had defeated the overwhelming host of Bolsheviki. It was a time for joy, even in the face of tragedy. My doctor told me to go out and I walked the streets sharing in the happiness of the people.

I came to Got-golia street and found a mourning crowd. On all sides the beautiful houses of the rich were marked by rifle shots. But most horrible of all, laid out along the streets, were the bodies of men not in uniform. Young and old, they lay—stiff. Only weeping old women incoherently screaming, tore in and out of the houses. Then I learned from some witnesses of the scene that had been enacted on that street. The Bolsheviki when they saw their fight was lost, in passing the street, surrounded the houses, broke in the doors, and killed all the male inhabitants. They took with them all the young girls, leaving only the old. And these young girls they dragged with them, bruised, crying aloud and weeping, dragged them along in their retreat to their camps. The thought of it all, the sight so sickened me, I turned away and went back to tend the wounded. And I could not help but compare their fortunate fate to that of those poor girls to whom death would have been a happy deliverance from an unspeakable horror.

Tyrrel Print, New York.

The National
Civic Federation Review

Vol. V | NEW YORK, APRIL 1, 1920 | No. 2

URGENT NATIONAL PROBLEMS

COMPULSORY ARBITRATION, COLLECTIVE BARGAINING, INDUSTRIAL TRAINING, COMPULSORY SICKNESS INSURANCE, WORKMEN'S COMPENSATION, AND REVOLUTIONARY FORCES AT WORK IN AMERICA DISCUSSED AT TWENTIETH ANNUAL MEETING OF THE NATIONAL CIVIC FEDERATION

THE twentieth annual meeting of The National Civic Federation was held at the Hotel Astor, New York, January 29 and 30. Convened at a time when the nation is undergoing the process of reconstruction following the war and when problems relating to industrial and social unrest and to a restoration of equilibrium in all phases of national life are uppermost in the public mind, the discussions at the sessions are of unique and timely interest. Judge Alton B. Parker presided at the meeting.

Among the subjects under discussion were "Increased Production Through Industrial Training," "Arbitration, Conciliation and Collective Bargaining," "Compulsory Sickness Insurance," "Workmen's Compensation—Occupational Disease," "The Revolutionary Forces in Our Midst," and "The Demand for Amnesty for Pacifists, Conscientious Objectors and Anarchists."

The subject of collective bargaining, over which the President's first industrial conference split, was discussed by employers and labor officials who have had practical experience in dealing with questions of wages, hours and conditions of labor, and included: Samuel Gompers, President of the American Federation of Labor; Timothy Shea, President of the Brotherhood of Locomotive Firemen and Enginemen; Jeremiah W. Jenks, of the Alexander Hamilton Institute; Louis B. Schram, Chairman of the Industrial Accident Prevention Department, The National Civic Federation; James H. McNutt, Secretary and Treasurer of the Western Bar Iron Association; John A. Voll, President of the Glass Bottle Blowers' Association of the United States and Canada; E. A. Sillcox, of the United Typothetae; Frank Sutliffe, President of the John Woods Manufacturing Co., and Ralph M. Easley, Chairman of the Executive Council of The National Civic Federation.

JUDGE ALTON B. PARKER
President of The National Civic Federation

Industrial training of new and incompetent workers in shops as a means of obtaining maximum production, and the bearing of lack of such training and low production on the high cost of living, was discussed by Allen Walker, Foreign Department, the Guaranty Trust Company; Hugh Frayne, General Organizer, American Federation of Labor; Percy S. Straus, R. H. Macy & Co.; John Golden, President, United Textile Workers of America; T. C. Spence, Superintendent, Norton Grinding Company; Prof. David Snedden, Chair of Education, Teachers' College, Columbia University; H. E. Miles, Manufacturer, Chairman, Former Section on Industrial Training for the War Emergency, Committee on Labor, Council of National Defense; and by Mr. Gompers.

A session was devoted to Compulsory Sickness Insurance, and in this connection there was presented a practical substitute for it, incorporating health conservation measures, and the pro and con of compulsion by legislation.

Dr. Frederick L. Hoffman, a member of the Federation's Committee on Foreign Inquiry, who has just returned from England, Scotland and Ireland, where he spent five months inquiring into the operation of that act, reported upon findings relative to the British National Health Insurance Act. Other speakers included: Hon. Frederick M. Davenport, the proponent for compulsory sickness insurance legislation in the New York State Senate; James W. Sullivan, of the American Federation of Labor, Chairman of the Civic Federation's Committee on Foreign Inquiry and Member International Typographical Union; Mark A. Daly, Secretary, Associated Manufacturers and Merchants of New York State and Dr. A. H. Doty, Chairman, Committee on Constructive Plan. August Belmont, Chairman, Workmen's Compensation Department, spoke on "Workmen's Compensation—Occupational Disease."

Miss Maude Wetmore, Chairman, read a report on the work of the Women's Department of The National Civic Federation. The program at the special session of this department included a discussion of "Our Educational System." "A Com-nomic life." Your report explains that the term "industrial democracy" has been almost discredited because of its application to such "absurdly inadequate proposals as profit-sharing, bonuses and welfare work." What the workers want "is what they say the employers will not concede without a struggle—practical control of the industries in which they spend their lives."

Does the Joint Commission advocate such control of industries by the workers?

Commenting upon the "common charge" made "by practical citizens and even reformers," that the Syndicalist program is incoherent and indefinite, your Commission's report concludes:

"In partial reply, it may be remarked that the Syndicalist method of 'direct action' is based tacitly on the principle—'Act and the way will become clear,' which has, it must be admitted, some affiliation with current philosophical thought and even with certain aspects of the Christian faith."

In other words, all that the Bolshevists, Socialists and I. W. W.'s have to do is to act, to take over all industries, and everything will work itself out to a league of millennial perfection, as has not happened, you and I will admit, in this so-far imperfect world, unless it be in Petrograd and Moscow.

In dealing with Guild Socialism, which, according to your report, "viewed from within as a constructive industrial program . . . offers much ground for hope," the statement is made:

"The stock argument advanced by the ultra-conservative against any movement that would tend to give greater control into the hands of the worker is of a piece with similar arguments advanced in former times against intrusting the functions of political government to the common people."

The National Guild Movement, your report says, "would seem to offer much hope and much promise for a better ordered industrial future."

Section 10, Part 11, of your report, is headed significantly: "The Issue: Not Wages, Hours and Conditions, but Status—Control of Work and Life."

"It is becoming increasingly clear," your report goes on, "that a growing and substantial section of the workers of the world are convinced that their present status is at least semi-servile if not wholly so. . . . Wage-workers are asking themselves how their condition compares with that of the feudal serf or the chattel slave and their answer to this query is by no means favorable."

Your report says further:

"No conscientious thinker who is at all familiar with the situation can deny in the face of patent facts that the workers' contention is largely right and that something must be done in the way of an effective answer."

Do you want the public to believe for one moment that men like yourself and other men of standing on your Committee, have anything but a wholesome contempt for the idea that the condition of the wage-earner today compares unfavorably with that of the feudal serf and the chattel slave? It is an insult to the intelligence of any American even to ask such a question, and therefore I do not ask it. At no time in history (and this was just as true in 1914 as now) have the American wage earners had such large wages and such consideration for their comfort and well-being, and, as is evidenced by the number of strikes we see today, been so independent in their conduct. "Feudal serfs or chattel slaves" do not strike. What do you, as president of the New York Manufacturers' Association, a body of 5,000 employers, as well as director yourself in any number of corporations, think of such a statement?

To return to your report, it apparently advocates and approves of a program aiming at nothing short of control of industry in whole or in part by the workers. The term "industrial democracy," again repeats your report, "had almost been discredited in recent months by its facile application to all kinds of industrial experiments and programs which at the same time leave the control effectively in the hands of the present employer.

"Such proposals or devices, however they may masquerade under the name of 'industrial democracy,' the workers are in increasing numbers repudiating, insisting that they will not be satisfied until they have at least an equal share in control of the industries in which they are engaged."

This is a straight-out attack on the so-called "democratic" plans advocated by Mr. Rockefeller, the International Harvester Company, the United States Steel Corporation, the General Electric Company, the Standard Oil Company of New Jersey and the Leitch plan. Do you and all the members of the Joint Commission approve of this attack on these "democratic" plans, and do you approve of this Bolshevist program? Apparently yes, because the report concludes:

"To answer that this is utterly impractical because the workers are not now competent to manage their industries, is to judge the workers by their actual rather than by their potential faculties, which they justly assert can be trained only as they have opportunities to apply them to administrative and managerial functions. It may well be that for a time at least workers in control of an industry would have to depend upon the trained direction and expert advice of those who have been their employers or actual directors, but the experience of history shows in the large that those who are charged with responsibility ultimately prove themselves capable and worthy of it."

This is a bold attempt to justify the policy of Lenine and Trotzky in confiscating and running the factories in Petrograd and Moscow. Is it possible that the patriotic Americans on your Commission have read and approved this statement? The Bolshevist, I. W. W. and Socialist propaganda largely defeats itself by reason of its extremism and vehemence. May it not be possible that such "tempered," adroitly phrased and seductive propaganda as is embodied in the report of the Joint Commission may do for these unrestrained zealots what their own literature fails by its very excesses to accomplish?

Let us meet the issue, Mr. Morgan. If the notorious activities of the Church Socialist League and the somewhat camouflaged radical propaganda of the Church League for Social and Industrial Democracy, both seeking to operate through the machinery of the church and to use the pulpits of the Church, are not repudiated by the Church through its General Convention, does not the public have a right to assume they are at least not disapproved? Further: Is the public not justified in assuming that the report of the J[illegible] Commission, embodying as it does pro-[illegible]istic, pro-I. W. W. and Bolshevistic propaganda—nothing more nor less—in not being rejected by the General Convention was therefore acceptable to that body? Does not the church, by accepting at its General Convention and by disseminating such a report, without qualification or criticism, make itself responsible for its contents? If it is a fact that the Church Socialist League, by reason of its members being on such bodies as your commission, has been able to "give color to" such reports, then is not the situation a very serious one?

Let me close this letter, which has lengthened into an essay, by referring to my first letter to you, when I congratulated the business men of the Protestant Episcopal Church on having inaugurated the Every Name Campaign, "because," as I said, "it would be their primary duty to see that the social, educational and spiritual machinery of the church is not captured by the inordinately active socialists, socialistic sentimentalists and other fomenters of disorder."

Since I wrote that letter on July 25, having had brought to my attention further evidence of the inroads made in the Episcopal Church by this inimical propaganda, only a small part of which can be quoted in this letter, I have become convinced that there is a hundredfold more need for vigorous effort on the part of your organization than I had believed at that time was necessary.

Not only has evidence accumulated of dangerous propaganda in the Episcopal Church, but in other churches as well, and we are now examining the social service and industrial commissions of those bodies.

As the one hundred and thirteen international organizations composing the American Federation of Labor have declared their intention of driving out of their organization all Bolshevists, I. W. W.ites and other revolutionists, is it too much to hope that the Every Name movement, including as it does many of the most public-spirited, loyal and representative men of the nation, will perform that vitally necessary and patriotic service for the Protestant Episcopal Church? I am sure, Mr. Morgan, that you will do everything in your power to help bring about this purging of the temple.

Sincerely yours,

RALPH M. EASLEY.

My Days Under the Bolshevist Reign of Terror

(*Continued from page 9.*)

they were still safe. It seemed to me an incredibly short time since the firing started that the lull came. No shots were fired. The same question was on the lips of all of us—"Have the Czechs been routed?" "My God, my God, it can't be so!" some one said. A woman went to a window and gave a happy cry. All of us flocked to the door.

In the streets, half timidly at first, the citizens of Kazan were venturing out. First doubtfully, then with more assurance, they rushed down the streets. Then, with joyful shouts, weeping happy tears, they flung themselves upon the necks of their liberators. The Czechs had utterly routed the enemy! All night the celebration continued. Women threw flowers at the Czechs, decorated their hats with ribbons. Arm in arm, the population walked with the brave Czechs who had defeated the overwhelming host of Bolsheviki. It was a time for joy, even in the face of tragedy. My doctor told me to go out and I walked the streets sharing in the happiness of the people.

I came to Gorgolia street and found a mourning crowd. On all sides the beautiful homes of the rich were marked by rifle shots. But most horrible of all, laid out along the streets, were the bodies of men not in uniform. Young and old, they lay—stiff. Only weeping old women, incoherently screaming, tore in and out of the houses. Then I learned from some witnesses of the scene that had been enacted on that street. The Bolsheviki when they saw their fight was lost, in passing the street, surrounded the houses, broke in the doors, and killed all the male inhabitants. They took with them all the young girls, leaving only the old. And these young girls they dragged with them, bruised, crying aloud and weeping, dragged them along in their retreat to their camps. The thought of it all, the sight so sickened me, I turned away and went back to tend the wounded. And I could not help but compare their fortunate fate to that of those poor girls to whom death would have been a happy deliverance from an unspeakable horror.

Tyrrel Print, New York.

The National Civic Federation Review

Vol. V. NEW YORK, APRIL 1, 1920 No. 2

URGENT NATIONAL PROBLEMS

COMPULSORY ARBITRATION, COLLECTIVE BARGAINING, INDUSTRIAL TRAINING, COMPULSORY SICKNESS INSURANCE, WORKMEN'S COMPENSATION, AND REVOLUTIONARY FORCES AT WORK IN AMERICA DISCUSSED AT TWENTIETH ANNUAL MEETING OF THE NATIONAL CIVIC FEDERATION

THE twentieth annual meeting of The National Civic Federation was held at the Hotel Astor, New York, January 29 and 30. Convened at a time when the nation is undergoing the process of reconstruction following the war and when problems relating to industrial and social unrest and to a restoration of equilibrium in all phases of national life are uppermost in the public mind, the discussions at the sessions are of unique and timely interest. Judge Alton B. Parker presided at the meeting.

Among the subjects under discussion were "Increased Production Through Industrial Training," "Arbitration, Conciliation and Collective Bargaining," "Compulsory Sickness Insurance," "Workmen's Compensation—Occupational Disease," "The Revolutionary Forces in Our Midst," and "The Demand for Amnesty for Pacifists, Conscientious Objectors and Anarchists."

The subject of collective bargaining, over which the President's first industrial conference split, was discussed by employers and labor officials who have had practical experience in dealing with questions of wages, hours and conditions of labor, and included: Samuel Gompers, President of the American Federation of Labor; Timothy Shea, President of the Brotherhood of Locomotive Firemen and Enginemen; Jeremiah W. Jenks, of the Alexander Hamilton Institute; Louis B. Schram, Chairman of the Industrial Accident Prevention Department, The National Civic Federation; James H. McNutt, Secretary and Treasurer of the Western Bar Iron Association; John A. Voll, President of the Glass Bottle Blowers' Association of the United States and Canada; F. A. Sillcox, of the United Typothetae; Frank Sutliffe, President of the John Woods Manufacturing Co., and Ralph M. Easley, Chairman of the Executive Council of The National Civic Federation.

JUDGE ALTON B. PARKER
President of The National Civic Federation

Industrial training of new and incompetent workers in shops as a means of obtaining maximum production, and the bearing of lack of such training and low production on the high cost of living, was discussed by Allen Walker, Foreign Department, the Guaranty Trust Company; Hugh Frayne, General Organizer, American Federation of Labor; Percy S. Straus, R. H. Macy & Co.; John Golden, President, United Textile Workers of America; T. C. Spence, Superintendent, Norton Grinding Company; Prof. David Snedden, Chair of Education, Teachers' College, Columbia University; H. E. Miles, Manufacturer, Chairman, Former Section on Industrial Training for the War Emergency, Committee on Labor, Council of National Defense; and by Mr. Gompers.

A session was devoted to Compulsory Sickness Insurance, and in this connection there was presented a practical substitute for it, incorporating health conservation measures, and the pro and con of compulsion by legislation.

Dr. Frederick L. Hoffman, a member of the Federation's Committee on Foreign Inquiry, who has just returned from England, Scotland and Ireland, where he spent five months inquiring into the operation of that act, reported upon findings relative to the British National Health Insurance Act. Other speakers included: Hon. Frederick M. Davenport, the proponent for compulsory sickness insurance legislation in the New York State Senate; James W. Sullivan, of the American Federation of Labor, Chairman of the Civic Federation's Committee on Foreign Inquiry and Member International Typographical Union; Mark A. Daly, Secretary, Associated Manufacturers and Merchants of New York State; and Dr. A. H. Doty, Chairman, Committee on Constructive Plan. August Belmont, Chairman, Workmen's Compensation Department, spoke on "Workmen's Compensation—Occupational Disease."

Miss Maude Wetmore, Chairman, read a report on the work of the Women's Department of The National Civic Federation. The program at the special session of this department included a discussion of "Our Educational System," "A Community Program for the Prevention of Juvenile Delinquency," and "National Americanization."

Lieutenant A. W. Kliefoth, formerly of the American Military Intelligence Service in Russia, and Peter W. Collins, Director-General of the Employment and Reconstruction Service of the Knights of Columbus, told of the extent and purposes of Socialist and Bolshevist propaganda in this country. Dr. Condé B. Pallen submitted a proposal for the formation of a committee to investigate and expose the principles and tactics of the Socialist party and other revolutionary groups, and to work out and further constructive measures for social and industrial betterment. Major Lucius Breckenridge, of the American Legion, protested against the disposition of the War Department to give honorable discharges to "conscientious objectors" in the Army, and against the propaganda of those seeking release from prison of shirkers, pacifists, anarchists and others convicted of opposing the war under the Espionage Act.

FREEDOM OF SPEECH AND PRESS VS. LICENSE

JUDGE ALTON B. PARKER, President of The National Civic Federation, who presided, made the following opening statement:

"For twenty years and better now The National Civic Federation has been trying to do its bit, and I congratulate you upon its achievements during that twenty years. The future seems, I am sure, both to you and me, to hold out opportunities for work which may be even of greater value to this country, which we love, than has the service in the past.

"I listened the other night to a very distinguished speaker, as well grounded in the history of this country as any man, a patriot, a man who has ever lent himself and his voice to any and every good cause so far as this country is concerned, who took a very pessimistic view of the future. He was not thinking about our financial prosperity; he was not thinking about the question whether the earth would continue to produce the food we needed; but, as he reviewed the facts of our history, he was discouraged lest the form of government, which we believe to be the best on earth, should not serve the people in the end as helpfully as it has served it in the past.

"Now, I take a very different view, not of the facts that he presented, for with them you would, I feel, agree, had you listened to them, as would I. But I cannot help but feel that as a people we will prove ourselves equal to an emergency, no matter what it may be, when it comes.

"I look back over the number of years before there was any world war, and I recall your efforts and mine, and those of others who worked with us all over this country, to make preparation for the future with an adequate navy and an adequate army, an adequate coast protection. It was hopeless. Our people were opposed to war and they didn't see any reason why they should be contributing towards getting ready for war. Weren't we here all alone by ourselves? How could it be possible that we would ever have occasion to worry about war? And we didn't get ready.

"We will never forget while we live when the war came how every man and woman in this country, with an ounce of patriotic blood in their veins, went to work. All religion, politics—everything—was cast aside, and as one the women and the men of this country went to work to win that war.

"Now the evidence is abundant, of course, that we are menaced today by those who really belong and should belong of right to the criminal classes, those who come from the world at large with the thought that they would like to divide among themselves the result of the efforts of the people of this country from its very beginning down to date. The war advertised to all the world the wealth of us here. The very generosity of the efforts which this government made and this people made, in order to end that war as it should be ended, focussed the attention of the anarchists, the Bolsheviki and the I. W. W.'s, the quasi-criminals the world over, on the opportunity which this country presented to those who were willing to take from others that which belonged to them and divide it by force.

"Now, I believe that, while there is abundant evidence of this as we all know, the people of the United States when they awaken to this fact, and awaken fully, will take hold of the situation precisely as they took hold of the war, and every patriotic woman and every patriotic man who loves this country and wishes it passed on as it is now to those who are to come after him, will see to it that the children of this country are to be educated along sound lines; will see to it that the government of this country puts up the bars against the criminal classes of the world who wish to come and despoil us, and that in the end they will so arouse the people of the United States that for a long time there will be no fear of bomb throwers and those who would overthrow the government by force.

"I have just read, and with great regret, a public statement signed by Bishop Brent and other bishops, and some twenty-two clergymen. Now, if you will pardon me, I should like to speak briefly about this contribution to a subject that very keenly interests the executive and the legislative departments of our Federal Government and of our several state governments as well as every citizen in this country who has taken pains to inform himself or herself of the threats which have been made and are being made to overthrow our Government by force. Let me read from it:

> 'We, the undersigned, ministers of the Church of Christ, believing that the political institutions of our country commend themselves to the reason and conscience of mankind sufficiently to stand the test of such freedom of speech as has hitherto in time of peace been accorded by our Government to the aliens who have come to us for asylum, as well as to our citizens, are moved to make an appeal to the people of the churches of America on account of certain measures unconstitutionally undertaken which threaten the basic principles of our government. We have in mind, in particular, the deportation of men without judicial trial. * * *'

"I shall read the rest of the sentence later. I wish to comment briefly upon the first ground of protest.

"Of course we understand what they mean. They intended that all of the people should understand that they were making a protest against our National Government because it has been engaged, and will, I hope, continue to be engaged, in sending back to Russia the Russian 'Reds.' If they mean to convey the idea that the Government is sending back to Russia men without evidence justifying it, they are mistaken. The three thousand men who are about to go, if they are aliens, carried all of the evidence needed in their pockets, and it consisted of a card showing their membership in the 'Red' organization. What more is needed, pray? Do these kindly hearted clergymen wish seriously to urge upon the people that it is the duty of the Government to have a solemn trial for the purpose of introducing the evidence that the accused alien openly carried on his own person—the evidence that he belongs to the class which by crime overthrew one government and criminally organized and largely through crime maintains another on a basis that shocks the civilized world? To criticise the method employed by the Government at all is most unfortunate, for it assumes that it is not the usual method, whereas it is. It is the one we have always made use of, and it is the only practicable one. The writer of the statement apparently has it in mind that our people are obliged to stand still and mute while the scum of the earth flock together here with the view of finally seizing our Government by force and dividing the richest country on earth among themselves. Fortunately, we have no treaty with the Russian Government to embarrass us in denying 'asylum' to her 'Reds.' We should go further, I think, and close our doors against those whose purpose in coming here we well understand. I know these good gentlemen are accustomed to follow the direction of the Scriptures that, if he strike you on one cheek, turn to him the other also, but, my friends, that doctrine does not apply to officials of the Government. They are guardians. They have no right to shut their eyes to the fact that in certain quarters of the world there are classes of men who have never labored and who want to live the rest of their lives without labor, who are coming here in shoals for the purpose of overthrowing our Government, and the Government is just as much in duty bound to stand out at the front and prevent their coming and to send them back the moment they find them in possession of the 'Red' card as it is the duty of the watchman at the savings bank which holds the millions of the people in small amounts to give up his life if necessary that the burglar shall not break in and take them.

"Now, we come to the last part of the same sentence which they also regard as wrong. I will read the entire sentence, although part of it has already been read to you:

> 'We have in mind, in particular, the deportation of men without judicial trial, the proposed repressive legislation now before Congress threatening the primary rights of free speech, free press, and peaceable assembly.'

"I think those gentlemen should have waited until Congress finished before they undertook to characterize its legislation as in effect unconstitutional. It seems to be the notion of the 'Reds,' of the anarchists, and of the I. W. W.'s that they have a right to stand up and say whatever they choose, that it is their privilege to advocate on the stump the overthrow of the Government by force. Now, the people who framed our constitutions, both Federal and State, provided for an amendment to both the Federal and to the several State constitutions whenever it should appear to the people that there should be amendment, and so we have been amending the constitution of this State of New York almost every year, sometimes one amendment, sometimes two or more, and sometimes the people reject them, but the opportunity is at our hand in both the State and Federal governments so to amend the several constitutions as will make them conform to the will of our people. That is our method. That method we take advantage of whenever we are so minded. But, that is not what we are confronting. We are confronting people who advocate that this Government of ours shall not be changed by the amendment of our several constitutions in accord with the wishes of the people, but that it shall be overthrown by force.

"Now, if the learned clergymen who signed this paper are of the opinion that such advocacy cannot be made a crime by statute and still be within the meaning of the constitutions, both State and Federal, upon the subject of free speech and free press, they are mistaken. We have a statute in this State which answers that purpose very well. We have a statute which has been tested in the courts of this State, including the Court of Appeals; and the decisions should receive attention.

"The constitution of this State provides 'Every citizen may speak, write and publish his sentiments on all subjects, being responsible for the abuse of that right, and no law shall be passed to restrain or abridge the liberty of speech or of the press.' Some of you may recall the case of Most, which is reported in 171 New York 423. At the time that case was decided by the Court of Appeals, I was a member of the Court and so quite familiar with the decisions. There s unanimous agreement of the seven judges. r have I ever heard of the decision being criti- :d by any court in the United States. It has n cited with approval since by the Supreme urt of the United States. Now, that was a e in which Most had advocated by a circular overthrow of the tyrants who govern the rld, including our own officials, whom he med tyrants. The leading method recom- nded by him for the overthrow of tyrants s to murder them. Now, the question pre- ited to the courts was whether a man who was ing to advocate such sentiments in this State s guilty of a crime under Section 675 of the nal Code as it was then, and 43 of the Penal w of today. You are all familiar with the way se questions are raised, I am sure. When st was tried, he asserted that the statute un- which he was finally convicted was in viola- n of our constitution, which said that he may ely speak, write and publish his sentiments all subjects, being responsible for the abuse that right. Now, in effect, the statute con- nned what he wrote and published; and so en the matter came before the Court of Ap- als, it was unanimously held that the statute s constitutional and that Most had been prop- ly convicted. A very learned opinion was writ- n by Judge Vann of Syracuse, and from it I ke a single sentence which I read to you:

> 'While the right to publish is thus sanctioned and secured, the abuse of that right is excepted from the protection of the constitution, and authority to provide for and punish such abuse is left to the Legislature.'

"So, this State has provided, and other States with similar constitutions may, if they will, provide for the punishment of the abuse of the right to speak and publish statements such, for instance, as advocating the overthrow of the Government by force. I wonder if the critics realized when they referred to this subject that it is only the abuse of the right to speak that has been covered by statute. I hardly think so, for certainly they cannot wish to protest against that.

"There is one other case that I wish to refer to and then I will detain you no longer; a case decided by the Supreme Court of the United States. It is reported in 247 U. S. 402 and 419. In that case there was pending before a Federal District Court an injunction proceeding. A Toledo newspaper was very much interested in the disposition which should be made of it, and it charged in effect that a particular decision would evoke public suspicion of the judge's integrity and fairness and bring him into public odium, and would be met by public resistance. Now, the judge promptly brought the Toledo newspaper people before him, under a statute of the United States which authorizes a judge, in case any one had been guilty of a criminal contempt of his court, to punish him for such contempt, and the judge summarily adjudged them guilty of contempt. By certiorari the case came before the Supreme Court of the United States. The opinion was written by Chief Justice White. He stated the proposition before the court in this way:

> 'The asserted inapplicability of the statute under the assumption that the publications complained of related to a matter of public concern and were safeguarded from being made the basis of contempt proceedings by assuredly secured freedom of the press.'

And then he says:

> 'We might well pass the proposition by, because to state it is to answer it, since it involves in its very statement the contention that the freedom of the press is the freedom to do wrong with impunity and implies the right to frustrate and defeat the discharge of those governmental duties upon the performance of which the freedom of all, including that of the press, depends. The safeguarding and fructifications of free and constitutional institutions is the very basis and mainstay upon which the freedom of the press rests, and that freedom therefore does not and cannot be held to include the right virtually to destroy such institutions. It suffices to say that however complete is the right of the press to state public things and discuss them, that right, as every other right enjoyed in human society, is subject to the restraints which separate right from wrongdoing.'

Compulsory vs. Voluntary Arbitration

EGISLATIVE COERCION WOULD VIOLATE RIGHTS OF LABOR, DECLARE LEADERS—COLLECTIVE BARGAINING AND SPIRIT OF CO-OPERATION KEYNOTE FOR SOLVING INDUSTRIAL DISPUTES

SAMUEL GOMPERS, President of the American Federation of Labor, spoke on compulsory arbitration. Mr. Gompers said:

"Compulsory arbitration in any form and for ny cause, insofar as working people are con- erned, will be not only unjust, but will prove bortive, regardless of what declarations may e made in advance of compulsory arbitration. n all these projects there is one fundamental act omitted from consideration, and that is that e men and women of labor are men and women; at they are humans, and that they have the ame feelings, the same thoughts and the same spirations as the people in every other walk f life. What we are pleased to call strikes, essations of labor, are the expression of an as- iration for a better life.

"How shall the workers' just cause, just as- irations, be satisfied? Through generosity, hrough the charity and the human consideration f employers? Has the history of the industrial nd political and social world given the guaranty hat the rights of the workers will be protected nd furthered by such considerations? The sys- em of slavery and peonage and serfdom and the onditions in modern industry disprove such a laim.

"Our movement is not destructive. There is ot anything we would undertake to destroy that rould be worth the maintaining and which could ven remotely result to the advantage of the eople of our country. Our movement is con- tructive; not revolutionary, but evolutionary; onstructive to bring about better conditions of ife and of work and of home, to cultivate the est that is in man and woman, and to secure he opportunity to take the children out of the rorkshops, the mills, and the mines, and to have hem in the homes, in the school-rooms, in the laygrounds, to imbibe God's sunshine, that they may grow into the manhood and the womanhood of the future, upon which the success and the perpetuity of the Republic of the United States depends. Any attempt, particularly by legalistic methods and appliances, with governmental authority and power in any form, interjected in the industrial conflict, will not only fail to avail anything, but it will be the provocative cause for many of the disputes which otherwise would be avoided."

After referring to the disbandment of the President's Second Industrial Conference, from which the Labor group withdrew, Mr. Gompers continued:

"The President in his wisdom has appointed another body of men to consider the same subject which he referred to the first conference. I have no desire to criticize the President's action, but may I call to your attention the fact that in the seventeen names of men constituting this group, there are three members of the Cabinet, or former members of the Cabinet, and not one man who could speak in the name of, and as a representative of, labor. And yet I feel persuaded that these gentlemen are endeavoring to do the best they know how in order to find some solution to this great subject of industrial unrest for the establishment of better relations between workers and employers. It is an attempt to accomplish the settlement of industrial disputes by political machinery, with a national board of adjustment, three of whom are to be appointed without designating by whom, three by the Secretary of Commerce and three by the Secretary of Labor. I want to say now that I think it is true that the administration of the country at the present time is fairly or sympathetically inclined toward the aspirations of the workers. Otherwise I fancy that Mr. William B. Wilson would not have been appointed as Secretary of Labor.

"The political pendulum swings at different angles at different times. Supposing the political complexion shall change, and with the political complexion of a new administration shall come the spirit so manifest among large numbers of people who desire to repress and suppress labor, and labor's normal activities. Can we imagine what kind of a national Board of Adjustment would be appointed? There are to be constituted, as proposed, twelve regional boards, and if there be a failure to adjust the dispute in any region, then there is the right of appeal to the National Board of Adjustment. Is it difficult to understand that if one side to a controversy shall feel that they have either a poor case, or that the Board may be inclined to make an award against them that they will prevent a decisive vote or award, so that the case may be referred upon their right to the National Board of Adjustment in the hope that the National Board may take a more favorable view of their contention, so that the National Board would without question be overwhelmed with appeals, as well as of cases over which they would have original jurisdiction?

"The machinery is based upon the partisan or bi-partisan character, with the exception that there shall not be more than a majority of one political party constituting the board. Surely the party in power would not give the majority of any of those boards except to their own political partisan adherents. And as changes would be made in the politics of the administration, all these Boards from the National down to the regionals would all be changed from a political partisan standpoint. The awards that are made under such conditions, whether they be Democratic or Republican—will these awards, or the withholding of awards, or the generosity or the unkindness or the unfairness of an award, have no tinge of political partisanship nor the possibility of political advantage? Unless, of course, we recognize it as a fact that one political party in our own country never tried to put the other political party in a hole.

"Then again, the theory upon which these proposals are based is founded upon judicial rules and regulations and all of them are given the character of judicial procedure. In addition, there is another fancy provision; that is that, not the Chairman, but the arbitrators or the regional boards of adjustment, outside of the Chairman, shall be drawn from a panel of names to be submitted by the Secretary of Commerce and the Secretary of Labor at each of these regional points. The Secretary of Commerce, the Secretary of Labor, sympathetic towards the cause, might suggest names for the panel of men sympathetically inclined toward labor. If there be that swing of the pendulum the other way to which I have referred, and an administration brought into power whose sympathies are lacking and whose conceptions are dulled, or whose position is that of opposition to the hopes and the aspirations and the activities of labor, you can imagine what that panel might mean. But in any event, I would just as lief submit the cause for a better life for the workers to the toss of a penny as to submit it to a panel of jurors haphazardly drawn.

"The penalties for those who do not respond to the peremptory orders of the chairmen of the regional boards are many. Among them is tardiness, for any reason, in selecting the immediate representative from either side. As a penalty the number of peremptory challenges of those in the panel is lessened materially. A panel, of course, of a jury in our civil procedure in the courts, or a panel of a jury in any criminal proceedings is much different from a panel drawn by chance for determination of human relations between one man and another, particularly when those relations are of employer and employee. In the first instance, before the courts, the jury is drawn and at least, presumably, known to be of fair-minded, self-respecting citizens of the United States, who will deal fairly as between two litigants before the courts. Neither of them is, or is supposed to be, interested except to do justice as between the contentions of the two. In the other, the criminal procedure, people of the State of New York, or the people of the United States, against John Doe, the defendant is faced by a jury of his peers, his fellow citizens. With the long history of trial by jury, and yet with its many mistrials and sometimes injustices, I think that the faith of the people of all democratic countries would resist to the last any attempt at the abolishing of our jury system. But in the case of industry, in the case of the relations between employer and employees, much as we try to hide it, the fact is that all of us, you and I, are either employers of labor, or employees. Whether that be in a great industry, whether it be in great transportation systems, whether it be in the professions, whether it be in the newspapers or magazines, whether it be whatever we may consider, the cleavage is that of people occupying the position of employers or employees, and though many of us—and a large portion of the people of our country are generous minded and fair—there is not one man or woman who can escape the influence of the position they occupy in life.

"Labor asks nothing for itself that it will not accord to every citizen. It asks, as it will give, support to every group or to any individual man or woman who aims to help in the solution of a given problem or the prevention or adjustment of any dispute. But it protests and will continue to protest against any feature such as is contained in the labor clauses of the Cummins Bill to return the railroads, or Congressman Esch's provision to accomplish the same result. It will oppose to the very last legislation which is attempted in our time to curb the rights and the freedom of the people of the United States.

"There is perhaps no exemplification anywhere, here or elsewhere, of such a magnificent character of work of a voluntary body of men and women as is found in the purpose and the accomplishments of The National Civic Federation. And there has been no compulsion; there has been no penalty. The work has been for public education on great industrial and commercial principles. It has helped, by its policy and activity of mediation and conciliation, to bring both parties to a contemplated controversy together and bring about an adjustment of the dispute or when a disruption has occurred, it has brought the parties together and helped toward a readjustment. We are perfectly satisfied to have this National Conference of the President's carry on its work and promulgate proposals, but they must be voluntary, growing out of the earnest and honest purpose of both sides, with a consciousness of responsibility resting upon both. That increasing responsibility has come with time. It is not yet understood how perfectly safe freedom is. So far as my associates and I are concerned, we are determined to do our level best and give all that is in us to see that that freedom, which has been the historic development and the final achievement in the Republic of the United States, shall not be destroyed through the hysteria of those who are afraid of the freedom of the people of our country."

RIGHTS OF LABOR

TIMOTHY SHEA, acting president of the Brotherhood of Locomotive Firemen and Enginemen, said in part:

"Organized labor in the United States has always been opposed to compulsory arbitration as a method for the settlement of industrial disputes. We had thought that as a result of past discussion the impracticability and ineffectiveness of such a policy had become fully apparent. Recently, however, the controversy has been revived by the ill-advised action of the Senate Committee on Interstate and Foreign Commerce. In formulating a bill for the termination of Federal control and the return of the railroads to private ownership and operation, this committee has recommended that railroad employees be denied the right to strike under legal penalties, and that they be required to submit all grievances to the adjustment of joint boards, consisting of an equal number of representatives of employees and railway officials, and has vested the final right of the determination of all grievances in a body, appointed by the President, to be known as the Transportation Board. Expressed in other terms, this proposed anti-strike legislation provides for the compulsory arbitration or adjustment of all labor disputes.

"In its final analysis the opposition of the wage-earner to compulsory arbitration is threefold in its main aspects. In the first place, it is looked upon as an ill-concealed scheme by which the employer hopes to gain a mastery over his employees, by making strikes illegal and thus depriving working people of their only economic power, by suppressing and disrupting labor organizations in depriving them of the power to effect their purpose, and by creating rates of pay and conditions of employment through arbitrary judicial process instead of through the relative economic strength of collective bargaining.

"The wage-earners consider the forces behind the movement for compulsory arbitration really a symptom of the mental and moral degeneration through which all great and prosperous nations have passed, when the fundamental principles of individual liberty are forgotten, when the attitude for which the founders of liberty were honored falls into social disrepute, and when the struggle for wealth overshadows all other considerations with a consequent disregard for the rights of the working classes.

"Aside from the railway labor situation, and in addition to the fundamental objections of labor to compulsory arbitration, it should also be borne in mind that this method of settling

"Various expenses must be counted on before employers will get their profit. The employees will get their wages, but this is assuming that no conflict arises. When both understand this fundamental fact, there will not be any serious trouble. I will assume still further that in very many instances both of them want to do the square thing. An absolute just wage would be paid for the exact amount which the laborer would contribute, but there are so many other factors coming in that you cannot be quite sure. Nobody knows, and the question is so complicated, no one can find out. By going at the thing in a fair spirit, with an idea of coming as near the truth as possible, with the idea of taking and giving the just amount, they will be interested about it and come nearer to the truth than in any other way. While the interests are not conflicting, the community of interest is so close that they will come near together.

"In considering the share in the business, the share in the management that is to be given to the working man, we are likely to forget fundamental things. For instance, regarding the share in the management that is to be given to the working man. There are no two industries, no two plants where you can get the same kind of men. In one industry the employees do contribute a much larger proportion to the profit than in others. In some working conditions determine it, transportation, housing, etc. Each industry and each plant must be considered by itself to get at the exact amount of participation in the management that can be obtained. There must be recognition of rights on both sides. I can see no reason why the employees should have a share in the management unless they are qualified to share, but only on questions of wages, hours and conditions of living. On such questions as to whether you should borrow thousands of dollars, as to discounting, etc., etc., you can get no help from the workers."

CONCILIATION AND CO-OPERATION

Louis B. Schram said in part:

"To attempt compulsory arbitration would be an experiment which, if unsuccessful, would involve results so disastrous that we might well hesitate to enter upon it. We have not yet exhausted other methods and they must be tried first.

"Arbitration as the public understands it is not the true understanding of the matter. If you ask the man in the street what he understands the Board of Arbitration to be, he will tell you that it is a judicial body consisting of an uneven number of men selected by the participants in a dispute to decide the dispute. It isn't. It is a body of advocates selected by the contending parties with a view to their representing the interests of these parties to the best of their ability, and in case of their disagreement an umpire is selected whose decision shall be final.

"Now the great difficulty has been—which I must say the students of industrial problems are largely getting away from—the prevalent idea that compulsory arbitration was a satisfactory method of settling disputes. Both sides are afraid that the fifth man will turn out nót to have the qualifications which they anticipated, and that therefore it is a gamble, a chance, as to whether the body when completed will be an efficient body, one calculated and one able to do justice.

"Conciliation, on the other hand, or rather bodies selected to represent both sides in an industrial dispute consisting of an even number of representatives of the disputants, are not subject to that criticism, and in practice do not make for a deadlock.

"Now all human relations in order to be satisfactory ought to involve the principle of mutuality. Yet we employers criticise the workman for leaving his job, and the proposition has not yet been advanced that we should compel the manufacturer to remain on his job or that a man engaged in business may not cease doing business because by doing so he would throw the workmen out of a job.

"From my own experience and from observation I am forced to conclude that in any event at this time compulsory arbitration is neither advisable nor justifiable, if for no other reason than this, that efforts to secure another and more feasible method of settling industrial disputes have not yet been exhausted. By the cultivation of a spirit of co-operation and good feeling a better method can be found."

Report of the Woman's Department to the National Civic Federation

Miss Maude Wetmore, chairman, presented the report of the Woman's Department to The National Civic Federation, which was as follows:

The report of the Woman's Department to The National Civic Federation was presented by Miss Maude Wetmore, chairman, and was as follows:

"In reviewing the work of the Woman's Department of The National Civic Federation during the war period, an absolutely inadequate report would be made were we to confine ourselves to the activities of our members in our own Department. Civilization has been in the throes of a world war for three years, and, when in April, 1917, we joined forces, all loyal Americans—civilian men and women alike—immediately assumed their individual responsibility, and, until the signing of the Armistice, contributed in no uncertain degree to the winning of the war.

"It can be readily understood that such times were not propitious for the specialized type of work our Department was organized to do. Surveys and programs gave way to patriotic service in and out of season. Soldiers had to be fed and cared for; hospital supplies had to be made and food conservation taught and practiced. All hands helped in the sale of Liberty Bonds, and no national movement was undertaken in which hundreds of our women did not participate.

"The Woman's Department took the position that the many agencies, Government and otherwise, specifically organized for war service, should be the medium through which our members could best concentrate their energies, and it is interesting to note that the training and discipline which the members of this Department acquired, through their years of service, placed them at once as leaders in their communities in the Woman's Committee of the Council for National Defense, the Red Cross, the Y. M. C. A., the National League for Women's Service and other war organizations.

"Such work as was vital to the Woman's Department was carried on, however, and, in addition as a unit in different localities, certain specific war services were started and put through, such as the War Camp Community Unit No. 3, which was entirely financed and operated by the New York and New Jersey Section.

"In Boston a Food Kitchen and Demonstration Station was maintained on the Common. These are but examples; the full report will be in print in a short time.

"It is the future, however, with its untold possibilities and responsibilities, that now con-

(*Continued on page* 14)

Compulsory Sickness Insurance

RESULTS BRITISH NATIONAL HEALTH INSURANCE SYSTEM—PROPOSED LEGISLATION IN NEW YORK STATE—OPPOSITION BY EMPLOYERS AND ORGANIZED LABOR

THE SOCIAL INSURANCE SESSION of the Federation's Annual Meeting, opened by Timothy Shea, Acting President Brotherhood of Locomotive, Firemen and Enginemen, and presided over by Samuel Gompers, President of the American Federation of Labor, was devoted to discussions upon compulsory sickness insurance, workmen's compensation extensions, including occupational disease, and health conservation.

BRITISH ACT CONDEMNED

DR. FREDERICK L. HOFFMAN, third Vice-President and Statistician, The Prudential Insurance Co. and a member of the Civic Federation's Committee on Foreign Inquiry, reported upon findings relative to the British National Health Insurance Act. Dr. Hoffman had just returned from England, Scotland and Ireland, where he spent five months inquiring into its operation. He interviewed representative panel physicians (seeing them in active work), clerks (managers) of administrative insurance committees, public health officials, both national and local factory inspectors, leaders of labor and commercial enterprises, executives of friendly societies, actuaries of the Joint Committee of National Health Insurance, editors of insurance papers, persons connected with the Poor Law and medical associations, and prominent public men, more than 250 in all. He also inspected the drug practices.

In a summary of his conclusions he stated:

The act is condemned by insurance authorities as an unsound insurance measure; by medical authorities as an unsound method of medical relief; by pharmaceutical authorities as an unsatisfactory method of drug administration; by labor leaders as contrary to the best interest of the labor element; by large employers of labor as a menace to productive industry; by the organized medical profession as opposed to the best interests alike of panel practitioners and those who limit themselves to private practice; by public health authorities as of no real value in the furtherance of public health measures; by authorities in charity, philanthropy and those who administer poor relief as not rendering satisfactory aid and assistance to those whose needs are most urgent.

Among Dr. Hoffman's explanatory statements were the following:

When the National Health Insurance Act of Great Britain went into effect, the social condition of British wage-earners had made enormous progress during half a century. Wages had increased and hours of labor had been diminished. The evil of child labor had been measurably decreased and conditions affecting the employment of women in industry had been improved. Industrial accidents were less common and the general health of the population had shown great improvement. No other country showed a corresponding reduction in the death rate from infectious, transmissible or otherwise preventable diseases. The public health administration of England had become a model for the civilized world.

British health insurance has not raised the standard of sanitary progress. The lowering of the English death rate during the previous 30 years, challenging favorable comparison with all other countries, had been achieved without compulsory health insurance of any kind.

The fundamental error of the act was to underrate the voluntary form and to establish a subsidized system of relief. National health insurance does not promote public health or the prevention of disease.

There are, broadly speaking, two classes of insured—members of approved societies and so-called deposit contributors who pay their insurance dues individually to government agencies. A deposit contributor seldom has enough to his credit to admit of more than a week or two of sickness benefit, and his wife can practically never get maternity benefit.

The benefits under the act consist of medical attendance, strictly limited both as to doctor's services and medicine to a minimum which would be considered decidedly inferior in the United States, even in the case of the very poor; of a so-called sanatorium benefit, a form of poor relief; of a maternity benefit of 30s.; a cash payment in the event of illness when there is total incapacity to work. There is a disability benefit, virtually an invalidity pension,* up to the age of 70, when the old age pension goes into effect. Provision is made in the act for the payment of additional benefits not yet forthcoming after nearly eight years.

The act has applied to all wage-earners receiving less than £160 per annum, but was recently raised to £250.

The administrative machinery necessary to carry the law into effect is of truly colossal proportions. It is probably safe to assume that certainly not less than 50,000 persons, directly or indirectly, in paid or unpaid capacities, are required to meet the basic administrative necessities of the act.

The ill-defined provisions regarding medicines and appliances are disastrous failures. There has come into existence a complicated system of drug pricing and checking involving the handling and re-handling of not far from 30,000,000 prescriptions accounts a year.

The main objections on the part of organized labor are that the benefits under the act are inadequate and insufficient. The act has had the effect of diminishing the sense of self-reliance, independence and thrift. Malingering in its most subtle forms has become a matter of common occurrence. The proportion of cases investigated found fully able to work is rarely less than 40 per cent. and often exceeds 50 per cent. With respect to the insurance the labor element is demoralized and thoroughly discontented with the benefits which invariably fall short of expectations. A doubling in value of the benefits is practically unanimously demanded as an imperative duty on the part of the State.

After seven years of experience with the act, the viewpoint of leading manufacturers and other employers of labor throughout Great Britain is that national health insurance has no direct relation whatever to labor efficiency except that a larger amount of malingering tends persistently toward a diminution of normal output.

As to the problem of destitution, once a people becomes accustomed to receive public aid in a skilfully disguised form, the demand is insistently for more. Great Britain is confronted with this situation today. There have been changed conceptions of State duty and private liability for individual welfare, particularly with reference to adequate support during illness, invalidity and old age.

Efforts to make the question of an adequate provision for illness and old age on the part of wage-earners a matter of government concern are perilously near to methods of doubtful public finance by which a part of the wage-earner's income is capitalized for the use of the spending authorities in charge of the government.

The British act does not rest upon an adequate actuarial basis, but upon arbitrary assumptions as to cost.

It is impossible to state the true expense rate of the insurance on account of a grotesquely inadequate system of governmental balance sheets and revenue accounts.

The medical benefit regulations are extensive, burdensome and complicated in the extreme. In the opinion of the chairman of the Consultative Council of the Ministry of Health, "the needs of the nation require a comprehensive re-organization of the medical services." The listing of doctors by the "panel system" has resulted in a division of the medical profession. The fees of the panel doctor, over which there has been much contention, usually bring the doctor, when the accounts are settled, less than his regularly allotted payments. A revision of the terms of remuneration is under consideration. There is a never-ending discussion as to the proposed limitation of panels, now fixed at 3,000 names.

It has become the rule rather than the exception for panel patients to seek medical attention in the case of serious illness elsewhere than in the office of the panel doctor. There are frequent prosecutions for violation of rules and regulations—over-prescriptions, lack of attention, unsuitable surgery accommodations, unsuitable hours, incivility, etc.

Public faith and confidence in medicine as a profession is gone. The public is confronted continually by quarrels and discussions concerning terms, allowances and gratuities. What was once the most highly respected of all professions has been practically reduced to a trade, and there is open advocacy of the incorporation of the British Medical Association into a trade union to secure pecuniary ends and better terms.

As to sanatorium benefits, the Minister of Health has given expression to his dissatisfaction with present methods. In regard to the duration of treatment for tuberculosis, which is 180 days in Chicago and 90 days in Germany, in England the institutions average probably only about 60 days. There has never been developed in England, as in the United States, a large and well-sustained voluntary movement in a crusade against tuberculosis. No new or effective machinery has been brought into existence for the prevention of sickness.

The alleged benefits to result from national health insurance in removing ill health producing conditions in particular trades have not materialized.

PROPOSED LEGISLATION

SENATOR FREDERICK M. DAVENPORT, who introduced the pending measure for compulsory sickness insurance in the New York State Senate, advancing arguments favoring its enactment, said in part:

My notion is that it ought to be tried out under the general terms of this bill which are something like this: Within a great industrial establishment there is a Board of Directors for illness prevention and illness care. This Board of Directors is made up of representatives of the employees, three of them; representatives of the employers, three of them; and the six select a neutral chairman, those seven men working within the industrial establishment only upon

* 5s. a week for men and less for women.

LABOR AND SICKNESS INSURANCE

James W. Sullivan, of the American Federation of Labor; chairman of the Civic Federation's Committee on Foreign Inquiry, made the following points:

The state may justly carry out measures intended to protect all its citizens alike against the various menaces to health and to control treatment of the sick. In the matter of meeting wage losses, the State may be expected to supervise associations for the purpose, and supply the machinery for such supervision. How much further should it go? The trade unionist stops to reflect when in theory he is brought to the line which sets the wage-workers aside as wards of the State, as subjects of special regulation, and as material for a social machinery run by State officials.

Sickness insurance! What is to be insured? What is sickness? Who is sick? Who is to decide when one is sick? Who is to say when one's sickness is his own fault? Who is to determine justly many questions in the matter of sickness? To what degree is sickness a mere matter of the mind? People of robust mentality ignore the aches and pains which frighten timid people. One's habitual attitude toward sickness counts for much. Some have the doctoring habit, some the patent medicine habit, some the habit of ignoring what sends other people to bed. Under any form of sickness insurance, voluntary or compulsory, a certain proportion of the members of any group would quickly develop the habit, to be indulged in to the maximum degree, of being "on the funds."

A fair statement of the present attitude of organized labor is that, in the case of sickness insurance, as with respect to many other propositions, it refuses to take a plunge in support of a project which is part of the program of Socialism. Nor is it prepared to support without careful scrutiny measures drawn up by associations not in its membership; it will not approve of any law which will tend to break down its own systems of mutual assistance; it regards the degree to which the interposition of the State shall extend as a matter to be settled in favor of the principle of liberty of the individual; it resents an indiscriminate classification of wage-earners as objects of public relief; it looks to wider measures than sickness insurance in the social campaign for the reduction of the death rate, the prevention of sickness, the improvement of public methods of caring for the sick and, finally, for the general sharing of the burdens of sickness.

EMPLOYERS' ATTITUDE

Mark A. Daly, General Secretary, Associated Industries of New York State, offered arguments in opposition to Senator Davenport's position. Some of Mr. Daly's statements follow:

Everybody, I presume, will admit that if the percentage of illness were anything like what the proponents of compulsory health insurance say it is, some infinitely drastic means should be taken immediately to repair some of it, at least.

Last June the Associated Industries, which is probably the largest State association of manufacturers in the country, determined to inquire into the percentage of illness among workers, that we might know the truth ourselves. I have here the record for the first three months, July, August and September, covering three hundred firms, employing a total number of 131,146 employees and all these records were substantiated by personal investigation, regardless of cost.

In the three months, with this coverage of one hundred and thirty-one thousand people odd, the total number of absentees for all causes was 9,973, or seven and six-tenths per cent. of the total employed. Of this absenteeism there were 4,250 employees absent because of illness, or 3.2 per cent. 3.2 per cent.! The number absent through accident was 580, or .4 of one per cent. The number absent for personal reasons, such as fishing, papering the spare room, and so on, is 5,143, or 3.9 per cent.—greater than the percentage absent for illness. Now, then, the days lost through illness were 43,899½ days, through accident, 5,433½ days, and for personal reasons, 41,015½ days. The hours lost for illness were 336,468½ hours; for accident, 47,788; for personal reasons, 357,931½. The value of time lost through illness is $138,816.83.

These figures mean that the average wage loss in industry, due to sickness, for each three months, is a little less than $1.06 per workman. Multiply that by four and you have an annual wage loss, if these figures are correct, and I believe they are, of $4.24 per workman. Contrast that figure, that $4.24 annually, with the figures which are part of the propaganda of proponents for compulsory health insurance. These proponents declare that every workman in industry loses nine days per year through sickness, or approximately $36, at a very conservative estimate.

The claim of proponents of compulsory health insurance is that poverty is a direct result of sickness; that workmen cannot afford to pay for a doctor's care or for necessary medicines, etc. Does it seem possible that the statement is true, in the face of the figures I have just quoted to you? Would you think it necessary to expend hundreds of millions of dollars annually to make up a wage loss of $4.24 a year—one day's pay? Would you say that the self-respecting, independent workman of this State of New York, the man able to earn $8 to $12 or $15 per day, would become a party to foisting upon the State this thinly disguised form of poor relief?

Do you know that the average wage in New York State, for males and females, is approximately $26 per week? These figures are given out by the State Industrial Commission. In November the average weekly earnings of factory employees were $25.37; in December the average weekly earnings were $26.32. I make these points concerning wages merely to show you the class of people that Senator Davenport would legislate into pauperism. And the cesspools of the State, the unfortunates and the victims of heredity, who might possibly furnish an excuse for this class of legislation but are excluded from participation in it, go by the board as negligible, as not worthy of consideration.

Now, one of the things that Professor Davenport said was in connection with the number of people needing medical attention. According to these figures on absenteeism, 55.8 per cent. of this general average were attended by a physician, and 44.1 were not attended by a physician. But there were only 881 major illnesses in this experience, or 20.7 per cent., while the bulk of the illnesses were minor illnesses, 3,369, or 79.2 per cent.

It may surprise some of you to know that out of the approximately 10,000 people absent from all causes in this survey, 2,882 carry one type of insurance, either life, health, accident, benevolent, or fraternal; that 1,043 carried two types of insurance; that 195 carried three types of insurance; that 130 carried four types of insurance, and 39 carried all five types of insurance. So it looks as if, perhaps, the workers were able to take care of themselves a bit.

I make the statement now, without fear of successful contradiction, that for medical benefits and cash benefits, medical supplies, and so forth, under this bill, the cost would be not one penny less than $125,000,000 annually. The proponents say it will cost 24 cents a week.

On the basis of Senator Davenport's bill, which provides that not less than 5,000 persons shall be members of any one fund, and because the Davenport bill as originally introduced covered 8,925,000 persons, the mere cost of administration is a staggering item of more than thirty and a half millions.

On the basis of the first bill, there would be 892 funds, permitting 10,000 people to a fund, not 5,000. We will say that to do the business of 10,000 people, one fund could get along with 25 persons. That means 22,300 persons as the minimum required force for the administration of this act alone.

A recapitulation of estimates follows:

7 directors each fund, one meeting each week, at $5 each, 52 meetings @ $35 each, × 892 funds	$1,623,440
892 medical directors @ $5,000 per year each	4,460,000
892 managers @ $2,500 each per year	2,230,000
892 funds, 25 employees each, at average of $900 each per year	20,070,000
Furniture and equipment, $500 each fund	446,000
Office supplies, 892 funds @ $300 per year	267,600
Rent of offices, 892 funds @ $100 per month each, or $1,300 per year	1,070,400
892 funds, two typewriting machines each, at $100	178,400
Postage, 892 funds @ 5,000 members each, equals 4,460,000 members @ .02c. each per year, and average of $3 per week for regular office postage	228,352
Telephones, 892 funds @ $75 per year each	66,900
Grand total	$30,641,092

Businessmen do not admit that they are responsible for the illness of the worker aside from occupational diseases.

The economic limit has almost been reached through which industry can pass on to the public burdens of questionable merit. If any more is added to production costs, the public won't buy, the employer cannot manufacture goods to put in storage, and, consequently, the workman won't have a job.

SAMUEL GOMPERS UNALTERABLY OPPOSED

CHAIRMAN GOMPERS: I was a bit surprised to hear the statement made by Senator Davenport that if this subject of compulsory health insurance should be thoroughly discussed and it be proven to be impractical, then that nobody would want it. I venture to say that there is quite a group of people in the State of New York and in other states that, no matter how convincing would be the proof that it is impractical and impossible and, instead of being beneficial, prejudicial, would not be changed in the slightest, and they would still want it, not necessarily for themselves but for the masses of labor. There are some people of which this group is a part that, if you present facts to confute their position, they will answer in point of controversy, "So much the worse for the facts."

We should have for any proposal a good purpose but the most important thing is the results. And has compulsory health insurance where employed produced the results that we should adopt? That is the thing. Is the health condition, is preventive work, better in other countries than ours? Surely we have not attained the acme of perfection. Is the length of life of the people of other countries greater than the length of life of the people of the United States? Statistics can demonstrate that easily.

I can understand how we may have privately conducted membership in voluntary health insurance, and there are not in all the world so many people who have insured themselves voluntarily and co-operatively as among the people of the United States, but even if it were State health insurance, with all the other good or best provisions in the bills before the various legislatures of the State of New York and of other states, if they were of a voluntary character scarcely any one would interpose objection.

But bear this in mind, that once compulsory health insurance is enacted into law in the State of New York, no matter how wrong it may be to any individual or many of the individuals, you cannot escape it. You have got to remain a member of that compulsory insurance under the law. No matter what grave injustice may have been done, you cannot get out except you move to another State, and we are not all of us prepared to move from the State of New York.

If the health insurance is to be conducted by the State, then let it be of a voluntary character, and every man or woman who desires to come under the provisions of the insurance law of a voluntary character in the State of New York, he or she may join, and come under its provisions, and if any injustice, if a great wrong is done to an individual or to a group of people or to numbers of people, they can then resign from it and be free.

The question is, after all, which is best. No one will dispute the fact that out of our wonderful progress industrially and commercially and in transportation, the ills of modern industry are terrible. The injury of the workers in modern industry and transportation is terrible, but there is an old saying in our language that often the cure prescribed is worse than the disease.

I should want the people of our country to have the very best conditions and standards, and the labor movement has done more than any other group or any other agency in our country to bring, first, prevention, second, insurance, and thus provide a large mass of the workers with those things sought to be accomplished through State agency.

The organization of labor of which I am a member, and have been a member for many years, has this statistic—this data to its credit. Before 1886 the members of my craft worked any hours—any hours. There was established a law in that organization, adopted by the membership, that eight hours were to constitute a day's work. In connection with the organization, a death benefit was established. That is, in the event of the death of a member, a certain amount of money should be paid his widow, his family, his dependents. Sick benefit was provided, but I want to refer to this particular benefit, the benefit in case of death, because that is the exact data upon which will depend the statement that I am about to make to you. As a consequence of the death benefit it was necessary for the claimant to present to the local union of which she or he was immediately a member, the health certificate and the paper showing the time when the deceased was born and the time that he died. These were official certificates, authenticated then by the Board of Health or the Mortuary Board of the locality and sent in to the general office of that organization. There could be no collusion between the health officers and the mortuary officers or the officers of the local unions and the claimants to those benefits. And within a period of ten years the records showed that the average length of life of the membership of that organization had increased more than fifteen years, the longevity of the members of that craft had increased more than fifteen years. The length of life of the wives of the members, for whom also if they died was paid a burial benefit, had lengthened over ten years. The sick benefits for which we provided showed a falling off of the amounts paid in proportion as the hours of labor were reduced, bringing better standards of life, giving more leisure, more opportunity for decent homes, or, rather, better homes, better and more nutritious food, the opportunity for leisure and recreation. This all brought sickness prevention, and the health insurance was in the form of the organization. Now, what is true of the organization to which I owe my primary membership in the labor movement is equally true, more or less, of every other bona fide labor organization of America.

So far as I am concerned, all these great sums of money which have been referred to and which have been quoted here—if they brought about the desired result without greater injury—would prove no obstacle on my part to my favoring the proposals. To me the matter is far deeper and more fundamental. I have said time and again that I will take second position to no man in America in my veneration for the spirit and the institutions and the ideals of the Republic of the United States. And yet I am opposed to giving even our great Government additional powers over the lives and the normal activities of our people. You give government authority to determine as to whether any worker is entitled to the benefit under such a compulsory health insurance law, and I assure you it will take jurisdiction and exercise power. We have lived as a nation for over a hundred and forty years. The people lived in the Colonies a few hundred years before that period. As a nation we have grown wonderfully in numbers, in territory, in wealth, in industry, in commerce, in science, and in all the attributes that make up a great people, and we have lived upon the foundation of freedom and the ideal of liberty.

We have blundered in many things. In what group would there be no blunders? Who is infallible as an individual? No one claims that for himself or herself in the United States. There is one great personage in the world who has the attribute of infallibility. We are not He. The fallibility of man finds its manifestations in groups and finds its expression even in a country. I am of the opinion that in considering these experiments with the humans formed into society, into a state, into a country, with its power, not only judicial, not only legislative, and executive, but with the armed force of the country or of the state, that when it comes to matters of this character, we should bear in mind that we are human and have all the frailities of humanity and that frequently that fraility and weakness are exaggerated when we organize as a group or as a country.

I was astonished when I heard Senator Davenport speak of the compulsory health insurance as a tendency to bring employer and employee together. How? Where? By what process of reasoning would that be brought about? The establishment to which he referred, the Johnson establishment, is not compulsory. That is not administered by the law of the State. That is administered somehow by the employers and probably some of the employees. And, as the Senator said, this establishment and the men "beat the unions to it." I don't know in which respect except the one he mentioned. I would like to know something about the wages and the hours and the standards of life and labor which are in that establishment. It is all very good to provide sickness insurance, but how about the wages sufficient to fill the needs of the family budget? And not only that. As far as I am concerned, I protest against the concept that all that should be paid to a man in the form of wages is enough to allow him to fill the stomachs of himself and his dependents until the wages have been expended. A man needs something more. The wage-workers, whether men or women, are entitled to something more for the great service they are rendering to society, and service without which progress and civilization would come to a standstill and perish. The workers of our country and of our time are deserving of something more. But even I would like to know something of the wages and hours of labor and conditions of employment in that establishment before I will consent to say "Amen," that the people over at the Johnson establishment have "beaten the trade unions, the labor union, to it."

Of course the subject is a very broad one. It is largely speculative except from the fundamental principles involved, to which I have tried to refer. But I do want to take occasion just now to say that it has come to me that recently some person has declared that Gompers has been won over to compulsory health insurance. I have already made my answer, which is that I am unalterably opposed to it.

The complete addresses on "Compulsory Sickness Insurance,' "Compensation for Occupational Disease" and "Health Conservation" have been published in pamphlet form and may be secured at Federation Headquarters, 33rd Floor, Metropolitan Tower—price $1

Health Conservation Plan

CIAL INSURANCE DEPARTMENT RECOMMENDS THAT SPECIAL STATE COMMISSIONS STUDY SICKNESS, EXTENT, CAUSE, PREVENTION, TREATMENT AND CARE, WAGE LOSS REPLACEMENT, AND EXTENSION PUBLIC HEALTH EDUCATION

N transmitting the report of the Committee on Constructive Plan, the Chairman, Dr. Alvah H. Doty, said that, after months of careful study and deliberation, the mmittee had determined to recommend prestation of the statement incorporated therein, rticularly to the Legislature of the State of w York, believing that it might properly be it to other legislatures in states where comlsory sickness insurance legislation is under nsideration.

Warren S. Stone, Chairman of the Federan's Social Insurance Department, approved recommendation and sent to legislatures conned in important industrial states this year tements identical to the one for New York, ich follows:

STATEMENT ON DISEASE PREVENTION

the Legislature of the State of New York:

The undersigned, the Committee on Construce Plan of the Social Insurance Department The National Civic Federation, has given reful consideration to the bills introduced in e New York Legislature in the years 1916-19, commonly known as the Mills, Nicoll, and avenport-Donohue bills. Our views upon the guments advanced by the proponents of this pe of legislation have been expressed in a mphlet recently issued by the Committee entled "A Refutation of False Statements in ropaganda for Compulsory Health Insurance." or this reason we believe it inadvisable at this me to enter into any further discussion of this hase of our subject.

We desire, however, to call the attention of e Legislature to a lecture* before The New ork Academy of Medicine on October 2, 1919, y Sir Arthur Newsholme, formerly Chief Medial Officer of the Local Government Board for ngland. Commenting upon the British Health nsurance Act, he says: "The act in its present rm is now generally condemned; and it is sigificant that the need for its radical reorganizaon appears to be universally accepted. Two edical benefits (medical and sanatorium) and maternity benefit were conferred under the t; but, as they have been administered, it canot be affirmed that any marked public benefit as accrued; and it is certain that if the same mount of money had been placed in the hands f the public health authorities to provide adeuate medical aid to those needing it, of the kind ost lacking and which they could least afford obtain, great benefit to the public health ould have been secured."

Rather than continue the discussion of legislaon for compulsory health insurance, we have ttempted to evolve a Constructive Plan to be ealt with by the Legislature. It is our unanious opinion that the immediate problem for onsideration is not that of insurance against ckness, but the larger and more important roblem of the extent of illness and the methods or its prevention. We have set ourselves to his task and desire to submit the following acts:

At present, there is no exact information as the extent of illness. It is clear, from studies hich have been made, that a considerable proortion of the population does not receive any edical care whatever; that others are unable obtain adequate medical treatment and that a very large percentage of existing sickness could be eliminated if proper preventive measures were employed. Large sums are being paid annually by the different states for the maintenance of institutions for the treatment of disabilities and their consequences, due largely to neglect. A large number of communities are engaged in no active health work and have grossly insufficient appropriations for health activities.

Statistics of other sickness surveys in the hands of this Committee prove beyond doubt that a large percentage of disabling illness is caused by communicable diseases. There is competent medical authority for the belief that many of the diseases of later life are the sequelæ of infectious diseases contracted in childhood.

The subject of sickness needs to be considered from the following aspects, in the order of their importance, namely:

1. Prevention.
2. Treatment and Care.
3. Replacement of Wage Loss from Sickness.

1. Prevention. This is largely a problem of the education of the public concerning the preservation of health and the prevention of disease. The care and treatment of communicable diseases are essentially functions of the public health authorities, since one individual may transmit infection to another and thereby become a menace to the public health. Already police powers are given to Health Officers to remove, even forcibly if necessary in the interest of the public health, and to treat individuals suffering from these diseases. These powers affect all the people alike, regardless of their ability to pay for treatment. The time has come, in our opinion, when the State should display greater activity in the treatment and care of all communicable affections—particularly tuberculosis and venereal diseases—similarly from the standpoint of public health protection rather than from the standpoint of poor relief. More, also, ought to be done to educate the people relative to public and personal hygiene. Insurance, on the other hand, is not to be considered in connection with this branch of the problem. The prevention of illness is not a function of insurance.

2. Treatment and Care. The critical fact, in our opinion, is that a large proportion of the people do not receive adequate medical care and treatment. How to remedy that condition is a problem that should be given exhaustive study, particularly by the medical profession, which profession should be called upon to devise a system whereby proper medical aid may be brought within the reach of every individual in the State. Only by thorough investigation can there be obtained the information necessary to enable the Legislature to take such action upon this subject as will result in the greatest benefit to the public.

3. Replacement of Wage Loss from Sickness. This is an economic loss; and, consequently, it is a subject appropriate for insurance. But we are convinced that the information at the disposal of the Legislature and the People is as yet insufficient for the successful solution of this problem; and that the precipitate adoption by the Legislature of any academic plan of insurance would, among other unfortunate consequences, defer such determination for years. We believe, therefore, that employers and wage workers should be called on to confer and determine how best to meet this loss.

In any event, we are satisfied that sickness prevention, treatment and care constitute by far the most important factors upon which efforts and attention should be concentrated for the time being, and that only after we have learned more about the extent of sickness, its causes, and the means of prevention, will it be appropriate to take up the question of how to relieve its economic consequences.

Investigation Commission.

Therefore, we respectfully recommend that the Legislature consider the appointment of a Special Commission, competent and duly empowered, to make a careful and exhaustive investigation and study of the extent, prevention and treatment of sickness, and that such commission be instructed specifically to study and report upon the following questions:

1. Methods and means for the prevention of disease.
2. Methods and means for the education of the people in the fundamental principles of health.
3. Methods and means for bringing adequate medical care within the reach of all.
4. The establishment of diagnostic clinics throughout the State.
5. The establishment of clinics or other facilities throughout the State for the periodic physical examination of persons *applying* therefor.
6. The further development of public health nursing throughout the State.
7. Methods and means for the adequate care of maternity cases.
8. Co-ordination of public and private health promoting agencies.
9. The determination of the extent of dependency upon public or charitable relief in the State and of the extent to which such dependency is due to illness.

All of which is respectfully submitted.

Dr. Alvah H. Doty, Chairman. Medical Director, Western Union Telegraph Co., New York.
Mrs. F. Lothrop Ames; Chairman Industrial Committee, New England Section, Woman's Department, The National Civic Federation, Boston, Mass.
Mrs. Sara A. Conboy; International Secretary-Treasurer, United Textile Workers of America, New York.
Mark A. Daly; Secretary, Associated Manufacturers and Merchants of New York State, Buffalo, N. Y.
Gertrude Beeks Easley; Director, Welfare Department, The National Civic Federation, New York.
Dr. Lee K. Frankel; Third Vice-President, Metropolitan Life Insurance Company, New York.
Hugh Frayne; General Organizer, American Federation of Labor, New York.
F. L. Hoffman, LL.D.; Third Vice-President and Statistician, Prudential Insurance Company, Newark, N. J.
Dr. Harris A. Houghton; Vice-President, Associated Physicians of Long Island, New York.
Dr. J. Richard Kevin; Chairman, Legislative Committee, New York State Medical Society, Brooklyn.
Hill Montague; President, International Fraternal Congress of America, Richmond, Va.
P. Tecumseh Sherman; Attorney, New York.
J. W. Sullivan; Of the American Federation of Labor; Member International Typographical Union, Brooklyn.
Mrs. Coffin Van Rensselaer; Executive Secretary, Woman's Department, The National Civic Federation, New York.

Committee on Constructive Plan,
Social Insurance Department,
THE NATIONAL CIVIC FEDERATION.

New York, January 27, 1920.

*Published in "The Survey," January 3, 1920.

Workmen's Compensation for Occupational Diseases

INITIAL ACT LIMITED MAINLY TO POISONOUS TRADES—HIGHER MAXIMUM WEEKLY COMPENSATION FOR INJURED WORKERS PLANNED

August Belmont, Chairman Workmen's Compensation Department: The activities of The National Civic Federation's Workmen's Compensation Department, composed of employers, representatives of labor and insurance experts, have been limited during the past half dozen years to giving advice and furnishing material where sought in the few states which only recently have enacted such legislation. The war tended very much to interfere with and almost paralyze in some directions the activities of those instruments for the development of progressive improvement in such matters. The war problems of the Government overshadowed particularly our department, its contribution having been the drafting by a committee of our experts of the War Risk Insurance Act.

At the outset our department did not attempt to do more than try to promote legislation which had to do with compensation for disability due to accidental injuries and it was not deemed wise to attempt so large a subject as compensation for occupational disease attributable to the industry, although recognized by us as a proper extension of workmen's compensation legislation and a proper tax on industry. But the time has come and the discussion has been indulged in which has finally resulted in a bill being introduced into the New York State Legislature. In several instances, such legislation has been enacted as the result of the efforts of others.

The system employed in Great Britain has given more general satisfaction than the laws adopted here in Massachusetts, Wisconsin, California, Connecticut, or by the Federal Government. We have therefore adopted the British law as the basis for our recommendations in New York State with a few improvements relating principally to administrative features.

In the initial act, it was deemed wise to limit the schedule in the main to poisonous trades, such as anthrax, lead, mercury, phosphorus, arsenic and others; to miners' nystagmus, glanders, compressed air illness and others resulting from mining; and cataract in glass workers. In all twenty occupational diseases have been specified.

Provision has been made so that additional diseases may be included within the scope of this act, as experience is developed, by recommendations from the State Industrial Commission and Industrial Council in joint session to the Legislature.

In a general way, this bill, which was introduced in the Senate by Honorable John Knight and in the Assembly by Honorable G. E. D. Brady, provides that the disease must be contracted in the employment; that it must be caused by the nature of the employment; that liability shall be limited to diseases contracted within one year; that there shall be no liability for an occupational disease where the workman at the time of hiring has falsely represented in writing that he had not previously suffered from that disease; that awards for occupational diseases should not be based upon the opinion evidence of physicians selected by the claimants; that disputed cases should be determined by impartial physicians; that there should be a rebuttal presumption in favor of a claimant disabled by a disease peculiar to industrial operations in which the claimant was employed immediately prior to his disablement; that there should be distribution and determination of liabilities between the different employers in cases where the disease had been contracted gradually in two or more employments; and that the occupational diseases, except where resultant from an accident for which employers should be held liable, should be enumerated in the statute.

It is hoped that this will be enacted in New York and will become a guide for future legislation in other states of our Union.

FURTHER EXTENSION OF NEW YORK STATE LAW

It is also believed that the New York State Act should be extended to include all except casual employments. How expediently this may be done is a matter which our Department is now studying. Also, it has under consideration the recommendation of Speaker Sweet made in his opening address to the 1920 Assembly, which is that under the present high cost of living the schedule of the Workmen's Compensation Law, enacted under quite different conditions, does not provide today adequately. It stipulates that the injured worker shall be paid 66 2/3 per cent of his or her average pay, not exceeding $15 per week. An amendment to provide a higher average weekly compensation will be drafted.

BRITISH COMMISSION

A recent inquiry from England refers to the appointment of a commission there to consider workmen's compensation legislation. That commission desires to ascertain the experience of the working acts in the various states of the Union, and it is especially interested in the question of insurance by employers and the operation of state insurance laws. I understand that in England employers are not required to insure their liabilities for workmen's compensation and that for such lack of insurance occasionally an injured workman loses his compensation. The Civic Federation has recommended, in its "Suggestions Upon Main Provisions Requisite to Adequate Compulsory Workmen's Compensation Legislation," that employers should be compelled to insure, but that all responsible and authorized methods of insurance should be preserved, including self-insurance with proper safeguards. It has resulted in self-insurance being one of the several types permitted, the employer being allowed to take his choice in this State. The English Commission has before it a demand for compulsory insurance, due to the fact that lack of insurance has resulted in loss of compensation on the part of injured workmen. An effort is being made there on the part of some to secure monopolistic state insurance.

The desire of the British Commission to have the facts concerning the operation of our methods of insurance in the various states raises the question as to whether we should undertake an inquiry along that line. It is believed, and it is only natural, that official reports on the part of those administering State insurance funds would favor that method of insurance. An inquiry into the facts and experience to date with the different methods employed in our various states might not only be useful to the British Commission but help us in the United States to secure greater uniformity. In any event, propaganda at present is directed toward an extension of State insurance, despite a strong feeling of opposition. In 1914 this department reported upon the operation of workmen's compensation laws then on the statute books. It would seem proper to make an impartial inquiry at the present time into the status of such legislation and its benefits to the wage-earner.

Revolutionary Forces in Our Midst

PEACE WITH BOLSHEVIST REGIME WOULD AID EFFORTS TOWARD WORLD REVOLUTION—RED PROPAGANDA ACTIVE IN AMERICA—BOLSHEVISM AND SOCIALISM IDENTICAL

Lieut. A. W. Kliefoth, formerly of the American Military Intelligence Service in Russia, at the session devoted to a discussion of the "Revolutionary Forces in Our Midst," said in part:

"The Bolsheviks have done a good job from their point of view in Russia, and they are not only out for Russian business, but they are out for world domination. The program of Lenine has always been that of a world social revolution.

"Marx away back when he wrote his book said the domination of the proletariat can most easily be accomplished in a war-weary country; that is, in a worn-out, will-less and weakened land. When Lenine was sitting in Switzerland, he read this part of Marx's book, and thought, 'Russia is the land.' After he arrived in Russia he set out to promulgate his Marxian socialistic form of government, and he succeeded. But he kept constantly before the eyes of the people the idea of world social revolution. The one word which you hear repeatedly in the address of their Bolshevik commissar today is that of world social revolution, 'We will spread the revolution all over Europe and then we will get America.' That phrase occurs more often in every speech of their Bolsheviki commissar than the one word 'capital' occurs in the speech of an American soap-box socialist.

"On March 14, 1919, Lenine said: 'Often the daily routine of administration and details that could not be avoided in the work of construction are pushing us to one side and forcing us to forget the great task of world revolution. The task of construction depends entirely on how soon revolution will triumph in the more important countries of Europe.'

"Kalinin, the President of the Executive Committee of the Soviets, on April 10th, says: 'The stronger we are the greater are the chances of a Western European revolution.'

"On April 23rd, Trotsky added: 'In order to assist the uprisings of workmen in Poland, Germany, and all Europe and North America, we must establish definitely and irrefutably the Soviet authority over the whole extent of Russia, and then ask for peace.' Consequently at the present time the Bolshevik government is throwing out its peace feelers over all the world, promising Bolshevik gold to American and English merchants.

"But what have they said of a peace? After e time of the German peace, of the Brest-:tovsk, Zinoviev, the President of the Soviets Petrograd, said:

"'We are undertaking the move towards :ace with a clear realization that in the course time this peace will be profitable to us and ›t to our enemies. Signing such a peace with e Allies, however, would not mean that we ›uld, for a second even, stop building up our ›d Army. It would only mean that we would ıt no trust whatever in the bit of paper which : should sign. We would continue to build up r army, but at the same time we would allow workmen and peasants to draw a few free eaths.

"'We should be bound to accept the conditions at the Allies would grant us in the full as-rance that history is working for us and that ery hour brings us nearer to the final ruin our enemies, that we should use the breath-g spell so obtained in order to gather our rength, in order that the mere continued ex-tence of our Soviet government would continue ıe grand scale propaganda which Soviet Russia as been carrying on for more than two years.'

"Consequently the Bolshevik government of ussia today has found it necessary to spread ıt all over the world feelers for peace. We are lvised that it is time to settle the Russian aestion by concluding a peace with the Soviet ›rm of government of Russia. In other words, e are doing exactly what Lenine, what Trotsky, hat Zinoviev have said a thousand times in ussia to the Bolsheviks of that country—that the Allies will find it necessary for economic easons in the near future to make a peace with s,' but that peace does not mean peace but the evolution. The minute the peace is signed with he Allies, the world's social revolution assist-nce to the Soviets all over the world will be iven.

"Consequently one of the main activities of the Bolshevik government since the time of its establishment has been that of propaganda. More energy of that government, more efforts of all of its commissars, and more of its money has been used for propaganda, internal and external, than for all other purposes of the Soviet government.

"I have seen at these propaganda headquarters literature printed in every language of the world—not only every language, but in every dialect. I counted sixty different Chinese dialects, forty different Hindu dialects. Chinese and Hindu are not very well understood in Russia, nor is English. Consequently the idea of that government is to send out this literature to the country to which it belongs. Two years ago in Petrograd and Moscow I do not remember seeing a single Hindu, but last autumn when we were there last we saw more than two thousand Hindus in Moscow that had been imported by the Soviet government. They had been drilled, they had been made into commissars, and now they are ready to be sent out of the country to be returned to India to assist in the Soviet establishment of the world's Soviet Federation.

"We are led to believe that this form of political government in Russia is a new experiment in democracy. But, as I have stated, Lenine laughs at the word 'democracy.' He will have none of it. He advised the American workmen, in a pamphlet printed in English, meant for distribution in this country, 'not to fiddle with the ballot box. It is a worn-out institution. The only argument worth while to you in your country (that is, in the United States), is the bullet.'

"However, as Lenine has so wisely pointed out, this large middle class of which we are composed—we are so indifferent that he need not worry about us. Consequently we permit the official representatives of this government, of this sort of philosophy, to live, to carry on its business in the United States. And Lenine, understanding the base motives of many of American business men, knows that his offer of gold may be accepted. Where does this gold come from in Russia?

"At the time of the German advance into Roumania, the Roumanian government was obliged, unfortunately for them, to evacuate their entire national reserve of gold from Bucharest to Petrograd. That constitutes one-half of the Bolsheviks' gold reserve. The other half was taken from all of the business men of Russia, from you and from me. Your bank deposits constitute this gold reserve in Russia. Are you willing to accept this gold for your merchandise from these former Russian business men? Is our Government to stand for the recognition of the Soviet form of government of Russia which offers us the gold stolen from its citizens? Are we content to remain quiet and indifferent, as Lenine has pointed out, to this form of propaganda going on in this country? Is Bolshevism a danger to us or is it only a problem to be solved by the Bolsheviki of Russia?"

MENACE IN AMERICA SERIOUS

PETER W. COLLINS, Director-General of the Employment and Reconstruction Service of the Knights of Columbus, said in part:

"After having traveled in the United States in the last eight years alone over three hundred thousand miles, and talked to many millions of the American people of all classes, and answered in that time many, many thousands of questions, and in the last year alone having traveled forty-seven thousand miles in the United States, and answered three thousand questions in the last six months alone, I make this statement advisedly, weighing my words exactly for what they mean in the English language: That there is more danger of revolution, that there is more Bolshevism to the square inch in New York City, and more Bolshevism to the square foot in the United States of America than there is in the whole tremendous expanse of the Russian Soviet Federated Socialist Republic.

"And from two sources this revolutionary propaganda is being most insidiously spread: By the so-called pink tea officers of the parlor radical variety, and then by the other type which we might properly designate as the wood-alcohol proletarians. And I would say this, as one having some experience, that I have less fear from the danger of the wood-alcohol philosopher than I have from the parlor radical, because the parlor radical can get into centers, with his so-called type and with his so-called presence of contact, that the outspoken, revolutionary, unhypocritical I. W. W. could not enter.

"Do not allow anyone to deceive you that there is any difference between Bolshevism and Socialism, because Bolshevism has a language of two separate and distinct branches. First, it has the language of the university, under which it hides from the ear and the mind of the average man and woman a doctrine which, if the working men actually knew what it was, he would get away from it so fast that he would almost burn the soles off his shoes. On the other hand, it has the language of the soap box, the language to appeal to the working men, manufacturing bitterness and hatred and illegitimate discontent in the minds of the working class, to use the working class as a crow-bar to pry society off of its foundation.

"You may think that this movement has only recently started, and you might think that some of the men now in the public eye have only recently been preaching this kind of a doctrine. Is it a question of ballots or bullets? Lenine said that ballots were worn out. A man who was elected to the American Congress, and who got unseated by the American Congress, advocated that ten years ago. Victor Berger, in his editorial in the *Democratic Herald*, the Socialist paper then existing, wrote, July 31st, 1909: "I say to each of the five hundred thousand Socialist voters and of the two million working men who instinctively incline our way, they should, besides doing much reading and still more thinking, also have a good rifle and the necessary rounds of ammunition in their home and be prepared to back up their ballots with their bullets." That was not written by Lenine. That was written by Victor Berger, elected by the Milwaukee constituency, and I make this statement advisedly.

"Out in Milwaukee they are afraid to fight them in the open. The only way to fight Socialism and Bolshevism and revolution is to fight them toe to toe. If necessary go out on the soap box and meet them not with heat, but with light, and when you put the light, the spotlight on Bolshevism, there won't be the danger in a thousand years of the working men being poisoned with Bolshevism.

"Socialism and Bolshevism never put a single penny in the pay envelope of a working man, and the gold they have got today, that they have stolen from Russia, is being used in this country, in this city, in many of the industrial centers of this country, to poison the wells of Americanism and to stifle the heart of the American working man. The *Soviet World*, published in Philadelphia, under the shadow of Independence Hall where the Liberty Bell rang out our independence to the world, under date of March 8, 1919, says in a special appeal to the working man: "Shall the workers of this nation, America, remain in slavery while the workers of Russia live as free men and free women, owning the land and industry as common property? . . . Toilers of America awake! March in solid millions against the institutions that oppress you. Build for yourselves upon the ruins of the wage slavery the new society of the producers under the dictatorship of the proletariat. Awake! Arise! Forward to the revolution!" Think of that! Right in these United States!

"Marx says in the Communist Manifesto that they openly declare that their ends can be obtained only by the 'forcible overthrow' of all existing conditions. 'Let the ruling classes tremble at a Communistic revolution! The proletariats have nothing to lose but their chains; they have a world to gain.' There is the definition of the revolution enunciated by the authorities of socialism.

"These miserable triplets of destruction, Bolshevism, Socialism and I. W. W.ism are of the same treasonable flesh and blood. There is no question about that. Any man that knows anything about socialism knows it.

"The theory of Socialism, the doctrine of the class struggle, is one of the most dangerous and insidious that ever possessed the hearts and souls and conscience of an individual or people. According to Bolshevism and Socialism, the working man must hate the man for whom he works. There is no such thing as class struggle except the class struggle manufactured, on the one hand, by the soap-box orator who is putting bitterness and hatred into the hearts of the working people who do not hear the other side of the story, and the class hatred which is manufactured on the other hand by the unscrupulous employer who wants to grind dividends out of the flesh and blood of the working people, the exploiter of Mammonism and gold and dividends, and this exploiter is as much to be condemned as the other exploiter who works at the soap box. Remember this: The soap-box orator will never be able to bring about the revolution if you stop exploiting. Capital must wake up. It must meet labor properly. It must understand its aims, hopes, and desires and its aspirations, and we must meet with labor around the conference

(Continued on page 14)

THE NATIONAL
Civic Federation Review

Office: Thirty-third Floor, Metropolitan Tower
1 Madison Avenue New York City

RALPH M. EASLEY, Editor

The Editor alone is Responsible for any unsigned article or unquoted statement published in THE NATIONAL CIVIC FEDERATION REVIEW.

GROUP METHOD OF REPRESENTATION THE ONLY PRACTICAL ONE

This number of THE NATIONAL CIVIC FEDERATION REVIEW is given over entirely to the proceedings of the Twentieth Annual Meeting of The National Civic Federation and its sequel, the meeting held two weeks later. No better illustration could be given of the soundness of the Federation's fundamental principle of bringing to bear on industrial questions the three divisions of society—employers, employees and the public—than the similarity of the programs of the Twentieth and the First Annual Meetings. It was the contention of the founders of the Federation when it was organized in Chicago in December, 1899, that the only way to deal with great economic and industrial problems was this method and The National Civic Federation was the first organization ever perfected along those lines in this country or any other. In the prospectus issued in July, 1899, this principle is described as follows:

> "The manufacturers have their national organization and meet annually to discuss the questions that affect their special interests; the agriculturists have their national grange meetings and farmers' congresses to discuss their interests; the great labor bodies of the country have their annual meetings devoted to their special questions; also the National Bankers' Association, American Bar Association, American Economic and Social Science Associations, the great church bodies, mercantile, trade and traffic associations, and many other strictly class organizations meet annually or oftener to discuss their various interests; while the object of The National Civic Federation, in addition to creating departments to study national problems, will be to provide a national forum, by means of which representatives of all these great divisions of society may come together and discuss the problems in which all have a common interest."

A brief résumé of the twenty years' work of The National Civic Federation, enumerating by title only the subjects dealt with through this group method, would require more space than is available in this article. Suffice it to say that the results have justified the hopes and expectations of its founders. Five members of the original Executive Committee are still members of that committee, viz.: Samuel Gompers, Franklin MacVeagh, Oscar S. Straus, J. W. Jenks and the editor. More than half of the members of the present Executive Committee have been on the board for fifteen years.

On questions particularly of wages, hours and conditions of work in industry it has been found absolutely essential that employers and employees should be equally represented and where the problems involved were of sufficient magnitude to affect public interest, the public was always represented.

Every question under consideration at the Twentieth Annual Meeting was treated from these three standpoints, whether it was industrial training, social insurance, workmen's compensation, industrial conciliation and arbitration or collective bargaining. Emphasis is laid on this point at this time because of the attempt made in many quarters to belittle this so-called "group method." For many years the social and charity workers, who were generally half-socialists, sneered at the idea of working out industrial problems by this method and generally they sneered further because on our labor group there were no representatives of the socialists or I. W. W.'ites. True to form, they still keep on sneering in that direction.

But the criticisms referred to in a previous paragraph of "the group method" do not come from charity or social workers. The critics include no less a personage than the President of the United States. President Wilson was moved to make his criticism as the result of his unfortunate experience with the group method in appointing his first Industrial Conference which ended so ingloriously. He voiced his criticism, in calling his second Industrial Conference, by stating that he "thought it advisable that in this new body there should be no recognition of distinctive groups." The trouble in the first conference was not with the method but with the personnel.

To avoid "recognition of distinctive groups," he turned in his second conference entirely to one group—the public, omitting both the employer and the employee. It was not illogical for the President to conclude that, while in the first conference he had so many people who "knew all about it" and failed, he might succeed *if* he took a group most of whom knew nothing about it. Well, he has now had a chance to see what both methods can do. While the employers and employees in the first conference,

Declaration Against Recognition of Soviet Russia

We believe that recognition of Soviet Russia would be a repudiation of all that our national life has represented for a hundred and fifty years, and of all the spiritual ideals for which modern civilization has striven for two thousand years.

Aiming to destroy the bulwarks of morality and social order, Soviet tenets attempted to interdict the teaching of religion, disfranchised the clergy, and made marriage a mere civil contract which may be broken by either party. Its system and franchise destroy representative government, which, since the Magna Charta, the world has come to regard as the first essential political factor of the modern state. Its program breaks every law of economics and in practice destroys production.

The fundamental principle and purpose of the Bolshevist propaganda abroad is world revolution, whether that propaganda is carried on by official Soviet representatives, by political parties which belong to their Communist International, or by independent organizations that support Sovietism because of its temporary ability to maintain its power. Bolshevism by all of its decrees, publications and acknowledged acts has demonstrated that it is a destructive movement, depending for its success in Russia upon terrorism and a minority dictatorship, and in foreign countries upon support and sympathy obtained through propaganda. Zinoviev himself, while President of the Petrograd Soviet, declared that the very existence of the Soviet régime is a menace to all other governments. Where government is most stable, as in America, every element of disloyalty, disorder and discontent is stimulated by this propaganda. Where government is unstable, as in Germany, revolutionists are subsidized and aided, and an early Soviet revolution is confidently reckoned upon. Even if only temporarily successful, such an overturn, which might become an upheaval in all Central Europe, would be a world calamity. Civilization must face and meet this deadly challenge. Concessions of any kind whatever can only encourage the enemy.

With the recognition of the Soviet régime, the presence of an ambassador and consular agents enjoying immunities (each a center of intrigue), the propaganda of the Lenin-Trotzky régime against civilization, already working through so many radical and pseudo-liberal organizations, and recently augmented by an endless stream of inspired press stories from Moscow and Petrograd, would be further ramified and dangerously extended. It is their declared intention, first, to undermine and then to gain control of the organized labor movement in the intensive promotion of labor unrest, the stimulation of "strikes of protest" "into general political strikes and then into revolutionary mass action for the conquest of the state." Thus we have in our own country waging deadly and underground warfare against us an enemy more dangerous and with objects infinitely more far-reaching and inimical than was Imperial Germany with her host of agents and spies.

We, therefore, believe that the people of the United States, acting through their Government at Washington, should now, once and for all, declare that they cannot consent to admit into the family of nations or in any other way countenance this "government" of violence and terror.

There must be no compromise between American democracy and Russian Bolshevism.

(Signed)

Lyman Abbott
Lawrence F. Abbott
Cyrus Adler
John G. Agar
Herbert Barry
James M. Beck
John L. Belford
August Belmont
George L. Berry
Joseph F. Berry
S. R. Bertron
Thomas W. Bickett
C. Ledyard Blair
Wheeler P. Bloodgood
James C. Brady
Nicholas F. Brady
Franklin Q. Brown
Rome G. Brown
Charles Sumner Burch
Gustav A. Carstensen
William I. Chamberlain
Carleton A. Chase
Joseph H. Choate, Jr.
Elihu C. Church
John Lewis Clark
William B. Clark
Bird S. Coler
Sara A. Conboy
Walter Douglas
Edmund Dwight
Howard Duffield
Ralph M. Easley
Sidney C. Eastman
Otto M. Eidlitz
Charles W. Eliot
Albert Russel Erskine
Frederick A. Flather
Harry B. French
John P. Frey
A. L. Frothingham
Newton W. Gilbert
John Golden
Edward F. Goltra
John W. Griggs
Arthur C. A. Hall
Prescott F. Hall
John Hays Hammond
J. Horace Harding
Frederick Brown Harris
V. L. Highland
Charles D. Hilles
E. G. Hoffman
Frederick L. Hoffman
Darwin P. Kingsley
Frederick J. Koster
Jeremiah W. Jenks
Harry Pratt Judson
A. W. Kliefoth
W. G. Lee
Frederick Lent
Burdette G. Lewis
Adolph Lewisohn
John W. Lieb
Earl P. Lothrop
Edson S. Lott
S. J. Lowell
James R. MacColl
Henry B. F. Macfarland
Franklin MacVeagh
Emerson McMillin
Clarence H. Mackay
Elisabeth Marbury
John J. Martin
Mrs. J. Willis Martin
Hugh S. Martin
Paul Matthews
John G. Milburn
Ogden L. Mills
E. A. Moffett
Hill Montague
William Fellowes Morgan
Arthur F. Mullen
John G. Murray
Charles P. Neill
T. V. O'Connor
Robert Olyphant
William Bradley Otis
E. H. Outerbridge
Condé B. Pallen
Alton B. Parker
James Duncan Phillips
Alexander J. Porter
H. K. Porter
Percy R. Pyne
Samuel Rea
Franklin Remington
A. H. Roberts
Burr A. Robinson
Louis B. Schram
Montgomery Schuyler
P. Tecumseh Sherman
Joseph F. Silverman
Walter George Smith
Reed Smoot
Lorillard Spencer
Sidney Stevens
Archibald E. Stevenson
Ernest M. Stires
John T. Stone
Percy S. Straus
Oscar S. Straus
Lionel Sutro
Henry W. Taft
Charles Thaddeus Terry
John L. Tildsley
F. H. Timken
Joseph W. Tolbert
Frank B. Towne
Henry R. Towne
Arthur O. Townsend
Beverley D. Tucker
Mrs. Coffin Van Rensselaer
John A. Voll
Allen Walker
Stanley Washburn
Maude Wetmore
Everett P. Wheeler
Cortlandt Whitehead
Arthur Williams
Clarence H. Wilson
Erving Winslow
J. B. Wootan
Mrs. John Francis Yawger
And Three Hundred Others

icking to their own interests, got nowhere, embers of the second conference, made up from e public, stuck to their own interests and it safe to predict will equally "get nowhere." or it is not likely that Congress will ever iact any measures putting into effect the prosals of the so-called "Hoover conference," ey being opposed both by the employer and iployee interests of the country. This is not say that the work of that conference will be tirely wasted, for the efforts of a body of men such high character and culture as are the ntlemen composing this conference, who gave ee months of their valuable time to the conleration of those complex questions embraced the so-called "labor problem," cannot fail to rnish much food for thought, and their pubhed proceedings will be a great contribution to e literature on the subject.

UT OF THEIR WN MOUTHS

Whatever question may have been raised as to the expediency of the method of suspending, ending an investigation, five Socialist Assemlymen-elect from the New York State Legislaure, the trial of the Judicial Committee had the alutary and wholesome result of making clear nd establishing, through official Socialist platorms, manifestos and publications and statements of their recognized leaders, certain major acts concerning the Socialist Party.

This evidence indubitably demonstrated that he National Socialist machine is not a political arty, but a dues-paying membership organizaion, composed largely of minors and aliens, and art of an international movement whose aim is he forcible overthrow of all existing governents; that the Socialist organization, in its offial platforms, programs and acts, has been antierican and disloyal, and that members, elected to office, cannot, by reason of their obligations o abide by the mandate of their organization, onsistently take oaths of office; that the Socialst organization does not confine itself to the ballot as a method of overturning the present order of society, but carries on its propaganda and campaign with the supreme purpose of organizing workers in order to bring about a revolution at the opportune time through industrial action, or the general strike.

While certain Socialist propagandists, such as John Spargo, have attempted to make a distinction between Russian Bolshevism and Socialism, and to win converts to Socialism by disclaiming the actions of the Soviet Government, the Socialist Party of America, in a referendum vote of 3,475 to 1,444, recently adopted a minority report offered at the national convention last year in Chicago, which declares the Socialist party in support of Lenine's Bolshevist Third International, held in Moscow last March. The Manifesto of that International rabidly calls for world-wide revolution by force and a dictatorship of the proletariat. If any doubt existed as to the concord in methods proposed and unanimity of purpose of the Russian Bolsheviki and the American Socialist party, if any thought persisted that between Socialism and Bolshevism there were shades of difference, such uncertainty may be dispelled by the recent action of the National Socialist organization. Following the adoption of the minority resolution by the party membership, official application was made on March 18 for membership in Lenine's Communist International by Otto Branstetter, national executive secretary of the Socialist party.

As was fully demonstrated in the course of the hearings of the Judiciary Committee of the New York Assembly, there is no need to go further to convict the Socialist organization than their own official actions and evidence out of their own mouths.

Why, if the Socialists are opposed to and propose to overturn all parliamentary government, do they seek to have candidates elected to office? They have themselves declared their object. In a volume, "The Dictatorship of the Proletariat," published by the Jewish Socialist Federation, which was entered as evidence, the following is said:

"Socialists seek to enter into the government for two reasons: First, to be nearer to the doors of the chambers where dictatorship sits, and, second, to hinder the dictatorial work in any way. The first reason is the most important. Sitting in Parliament or Congress, being inside of the government councils, affords Socialists an opportunity to find out the plans, the strategy of the State. And, knowing this, they can carry out their propaganda the better."

The national organization has officially instructed its members elected to Congress, State legislatures and local bodies to vote against all appropriations or loans for military, naval and war purposes. Evidence introduced at the Albany trial proved that all Socialist aldermen elected to that body during the war had followed those instructions. G. Zinoviev, Bolshevist president of the Executive Committee of the Communist International, to which the Socialist party of America now solicits admittance, further outlines how Socialists may get into and utilize "bourgeois parliaments" to develop the revolutionary class struggle. In a communication on the program of the Third International, Zinoviev says:

> "The Russian Communists, the Bolsheviki, voted in the election for the Constituent Assembly. They met in its hall. But they came there to break up this Constituent within twenty-four hours and fully to realize the Soviet power. The party of the Bolsheviki also had its Deputies in the Czar's Imperial Duma. Did the party at that time 'recognize' the Duma as an ideal or at least an endurable form of government? It would be lunacy to assume that. It sent its representatives there so as to proceed against the apparatus of the Czarist power from that side, too, and to contribute to the destruction of that same Duma. It was not for nothing that the Czarist Government condemned the Bolshevist 'parliamentarians' to prison for 'high treason.' The Bolshevist leaders were also carrying on an illegal work, although they temporarily made use of their 'inviolability' in welding together the masses for the drive against Czarism.
>
> "The Bulgarian Communists have successfully exploited the tribune of Parliament for revolutionary purposes. At the recent elections they won seats for forty-seven Deputies. Comrades Blagoieff, Kirkoff, Kolaroff and other leaders of the Bulgarian Communist Party understand how to exploit the parliamentary tribune in the service of the proletarian revolution. Such 'parliamentary work' demands peculiar daring and a special revolutionary spirit; the men there are occupying especially dangerous positions; they are laying mines under the enemy while in the enemy's camp; they enter Parliament for the purpose of getting this machine in their hands in order to assist the masses behind the walls of the Parliament in their work of blowing it up.
>
> "Are we for the maintenance of the bourgeois 'democratic' Parliaments as the form of the administration of the State? No, not in any case. We are for the Soviets."

In the face of the impudent effrontery of their self-declared treacherous designs, can the American people take seriously the farce of these people seeking to achieve their ends merely by use of the ballot? Can they risk allowing them to be placed in positions of responsibility and trust?

A. F. OF L. POLITICAL PRONOUNCEMENTS ONLY REPEAT HISTORIC POLICIES

In an editorial in *The New York Times*, under the heading, "A Labor Union Party," and an editorial in the New York *Globe*, under the heading, "Gompers Follows the Rainbow," and, in fact, in editorials in various newspapers throughout the country, the writers are making much ado about the latest pronouncement put out by a committee of the American Federation of Labor charged with conducting Labor's political campaign at the coming primaries and subsequent elections, but they all largely miss the point.

When the first announcement was made a few weeks ago that the American Federation of Labor was going into the forthcoming national campaign to support its friends and oppose its enemies, considerable consternation was evinced in the public press, but it began gradually to dawn on the editors that this meant nothing more than what the American Federation of Labor had done four, eight, twelve and sixteen years ago. In fact, in Mr. Gompers's own announcement was the phrase, "our historic policy," the word "historic" relating to the four campaigns referred to.

But the public mind had no more than become settled on that point than out comes a much more startling announcement. This time, according to the two editorials specifically mentioned above, the thing is settled: Gompers has gone crazy, according to one; and he has not much sense left, according to the other. The new statement that has upset our editorial friends is contained in a circular letter sent to the one thousand central labor unions, signed by Samuel Gompers, Frank Morrison and James O'Connell, Campaign Executive Committee, as follows:

> "Our brothers all over the land have entered into this movement in a magnificent spirit of co-operation. We believe every man and woman of the labor movement will be ready to volunteer when called upon. With this object we are sending a letter to each local union in your city requesting co-operation in this work with your central body by the selection of a committee of three.
>
> "Our central bodies and our local non-partisan political committees have a great opportunity in the primaries. Here a smashing effort can be made to nominate members of trade unions for elective office.
>
> "Where these brothers are candidates in the primaries our central bodies and non-partisan political committees should endeavor to give every assistance possible to aid them to victory, regardless of party.
>
> "In communities where this plan cannot be made successful our brothers should exhaust all their resources to defeat every enemy of labor.
>
> "This is a duty we owe to ourselves, an obligation upon us to perpetuate our liberty as working men and women and all citizens of our country.
>
> "By all means endeavor to secure co-operation of sympathetic farmers and farm organizations, and appeal to all other liberty-loving citizens for support.
>
> "We urge each worker to use the ballot to advance the principles for which labor stands. Then there will be no question in the future as to the power of all the people to achieve their just demands.

It is true that this language may sound very threatening in the editorial sanctums, but if the editors would call in from their city rooms the political reporters and ask them to interpret it for them, they would hear something like this:

> "The labor movement in America has a fight within its ranks which a few months ago threatened to become serious. This was occasioned by a few radicals attempting to organize a Labor Party along the lines of the British Labor Party. In squelching that movement and in declaring 'its historic policy', the American Federation of Labor used very vigorous language which, without close inspection, would seem to mean a number of things which it does not mean. Now, all the difference between this last pronouncement and the previous one is that the American Federation of Labor is now saying to its members, in effect: 'Do not wait until the election comes to make your selection of a candidate. Go first to the primaries—that is, to those where you are enrolled members of the Republican or Democratic parties—and where there is a labor man running, support him. If there is no labor candidate, support the candi-

> date who is most friendly to the labor movement.' But, gentlemen, this is totally different from the Labor Party idea, which is: 'Keep away from the Republican and Democratic primaries and have a Labor Party primary.'"

and the political reporters would probably add this comment:

> "The little joker in the situation is that there are very few Congressional Districts in the United States where members of the American Federation of Labor are enrolled in either the Democratic or Republican primaries. They are, as a rule, independent voters and cannot, therefore, participate in an official party primary. Mr. Gompers himself will not likely be eligible to vote at either the Republican or Democratic primary in New York State, his home, because he is not enrolled either as a Democrat or as a Republican. He is an 'American Federationist,' first, last and all the time. Every four years it is a joke to see the chairmen of the Republican and Democratic National Committees scrambling around, trying to find enough Republican or Democratic trade unionists to put on committees. For the same reason that the labor leaders are generally independent voters, they are not candidates for delegateship to the national party conventions. You can probably count on the fingers of one hand all the American Federation of Labor leaders who will sit as delegates in the forthcoming national convention at Chicago and on the fingers of both hands those who will sit as delegates in the national convention at San Francisco. This is just as true when it comes to the election of delegates for congressional, state and other party conventions."

But might it not be much better for the common good if these real labor men did go to these conventions and take a part, and also accepted nominations as officers, instead of leaving it to professional lawyers or blatherskite politicians who, in trying to curry favor with labor, go so much further than labor itself would go. Some of the most dangerous men we have in this country are lawyers who are playing the labor game. Every one can name half a dozen of them. Labor knows better what it wants than they do and labor is more conservative in stating and asking for it. Again, one could well wish that good labor men were candidates in Chicago for Congress, rather than some of the lawyers whom the American Federation of Labor has just endorsed there. The answer to the question: "Then, why is not the view of the Labor Party in Chicago right, that they should name their own men?" is, because, even if the Labor Party were not composed of and run by the most radical element, a labor candidate could not carry any one of those Districts on a labor issue. The Labor Party of Illinois had a very wholesome illustration of the futility of its program last fall when it rushed in and selected labor delegates to the Constitutional Convention, instead of doing what Mr. Gompers advised, throwing its votes for candidates friendly to labor. As it turned out, they did not elect a single labor delegate, in a convention of two hundred delegates, whereas a number of men who were friendly to labor could have been elected if they had thrown their votes for them.

Again, the question may be asked, if labor cannot win through a party and cannot win without a party, how can it win at all? The answer is that it *cannot* win, that is, if it means securing control of Congress or state legislatures. Organized labor, important as it is, constitutes only a minority of the voting strength of the American people. The farmers may get control in a few Western states, as they have done in North Dakota, but there are no states that labor has such a preponderance of votes as have the farmers in the states referred to.

But labor does not need a majority in Congress or a majority in any legislature to secure legislation in its interest. In the first place, much of the legislation for which it asks is right and just, and is so recognized by all other classes, and it only needs active labor leaders at the state capitals or at Washington to impress that fact upon the just and fair-minded legislators. Besides there are many close Districts in the country where the labor vote is sufficiently powerful to be the controlling factor. It is just in this situation that the American Federation of Labor's program successfully functions.

INDUSTRIAL TRAINING

The relation of factory industrial training to increased production is a question of such vital importance to our nation, and the addresses upon that subject made at the Federation's annual meeting were of such a practical character, that it was deemed desirable to defer publication until the next issue of the *Review* when space adequate to proper treatment may be devoted to them.

Revolutionary Forces in Our Midst

(Continued from page 11)

table, and I never met a working man in my life that did not give full value, one hundred per cent., when that working man was treated as a human being, and when it was recognized that he was something other than a mere cog in the progress of industry. Labor believes in justice. The working man is inherently conservative. He never started a revolution in his life. Get behind him, and when we get behind the working men, aiding in their constructive movement, standing for justice and righteousness to them, then capital and labor, with the people behind them, will drive Bolshvism into the sea."

AGAINST "HONORABLE DISCHARGES" FOR SHIRKERS

Major Lucius Breckenridge, a member of the American Legion, spoke on "The Demand for Amnesty for Pacifists, Conscientious Objectors and Anarchists." In part he said:

"There is present in the papers at times a movement on the part of long-haired men and short-haired women to turn everybody out of jail that has ever been put in there.

"The American Legion at the National Convention in Minneapolis last November defined their stand as being for one hundred per cent. Americanism. And they mean that they will not only stand for one hundred per cent. Americanism, but will stand for no other sort.

"The agitation for the release of these so-called political prisoners has its roots, there is no doubt, in the same sort of movement that attacks the foundations of this Government. The man who is a genuine conscientious objector in the vast majority of cases has been more than leniently dealt with. He was allowed to pick his own form of service. He was allowed to choose what he would do. He was allowed practically to choose where he would go.

"There is a tendency in the War Department and other places even to reverse convictions against these men, to give them honorable discharges. I do not know whether many of you realize what an honorable discharge means to a soldier or a sailor. But it is the character of his record. It is the absolute proof given under official form that he has performed duty, honest and faithful to the country in its time of stress; that he has not shirked his obligations; that he

To Aid Progress and Combat Revolutionism

MMITTEE TO INQUIRE INTO THE OBJECTIVES AND TACTICS OF REVOLUTIONARY FORCES IN THIS COUNTRY APPOINTED BY JUDGE PARKER—TO PROMOTE CONSTRUCTIVE MEASURES

T the session of the meeting of The National Civic Federation Friday afternoon, January 30, Dr. Conde B. Pallen introduced a proposal that a committee be formed h to oppose the forces seeking to undermine d overthrow our institutions and to give suprt to all practical measures promotive of instrial and social progress.

In making his proposal, Dr. Pallen said in rt:

"When we arose this morning, we took our akfast comfortably. We went about our busiss in the usual routine way. We have assemd here in a comfortable room, well heated, ll lighted, and traffic and people along the eets going about their usual business, and seems well with the world. Well now, if we ilized that there was boring under the city of w York, through subterranean channels, a eat army of people determined to blow this y up by dynamite at any moment, I wonder w many of us would sit here as comfortably d complacently as we are now, and I wonder at would be the consternation of the population of this city, if they were aware of that. at may not be physically true, but it is mory true. This community here in New York, fact the whole of the United States is being dermined by the pernicious activity of people o are absolutely out of harmony with our intutions and out of harmony with our civilition, whose purpose is to destroy that civilizan root and branch. That is their declared en purpose, and it does not matter how they ek to destroy it, whether it is by the ballot or y the bullet. The method does not count. The ltimate aim is the destruction and the sweepng away of our civilization and our institutions, ecause they declare that civilization and those astitutions are upon a rotten foundation, the oundation of capitalism, or the right of private roperty."

Dr. Pallen's proposal was in pursuance of an nvitation sent out on February 9 by The National Civic Federation, which follows:

ROPOSAL FOR A THOROUGH INQUIRY INTO THE OBJECTIVES AND TACTICS OF THE SOCIALISTS. I. W. W.'ITES AND BOLSHEVISTS IN THIS COUNTRY

A thoroughly disturbing situation exists in his country today which demands understandng and correction if our civilization is to be naintained. We seem to be so over-confident hat nothing could occur which would furnish n opening for those who would destroy the oundations of our republic, that we are in langer of permitting just that thing to happen. The evidences of this danger lie on every hand and are too numerous for complete statement.

No sooner had the Department of Justice, after nonths of investigation, arrested several thousand criminal aliens, who were found advocatng the violent overthrow of our government, than a wail went up from their ill-informed sympathizers, both low and high, charging that the government was disgracefully persecuting these men at the expense of our American ideals of freedom and justice. But still more disquieting was the action of a body of clergymen, including important bishops, in criticising the government for deporting these men "without a fair trial," after the Department of Labor had reviewed the case and handed down a decision which was beyond criticism except by the criminals themselves.

The movement for amnesty for all so-called "political" prisoners is of the same character. Special privileges are demanded for all persons convicted of interfering with the draft or denying military and other obligations to the country in the crisis of war. The humane and liberal policy of the nation in these matters is presented as "Czarist" and "Prussian" until the name of America has been blackened throughout the world as being the most reactionary of nations. Leniency having been extended to 90 per cent of the culprits, they demand complete pardon for the remainder which contains all the worst offenders. This movement is dangerous because it is based not upon extreme humanitarianism nor morbid sentimentality but upon openly expressed sympathy with the disloyalty and violent revolutionism of the prisoners. In it appear the names of the identical persons who are trying to make America safe for the preachers of revolutionary violence by camouflaging their agitation as "a campaign for free speech."

Only a few weeks ago an organization calling itself the American Civil Liberties Union was announced, with a professor in a theological seminary as its chairman. Its committee is made up of socialists, Bolshevists, pacifists, so-called "liberals," and anarchists. That organization charges that "the whole gamut of activities aimed at 'reds, radicals, Bolshevists and I. W. W.' is in substance only the one purpose of suppressing the revolt of labor against intolerable industrial autocracy," and announces that lawyers and investigators will be sent into any part of the country to prevent "illegal" interference with free speech, free press and free assembly. This, from their standpoint, means that any interference whatever, even with those who openly advocate revolutionary violence, is illegal.

Since the Allies have announced a qualified lifting of the embargo on Bolshevik Russia, great joy is manifested in many parts of our land and a perfect avalanche of foreign Bolshevik correspondence is appearing in our daily papers and other periodicals, applauding the virtues of the soviet system. All the pro-Bolshevist books on Lenin, Trotzky and the soviets are being advertised anew. A conspicuous one this week begins thus: "Now that the Russian blockade is lifted and we shall have trade relations with Russia, you will want to know all about the remarkable man who is guiding the destiny of that country." *The Springfield Republican* is quoted as saying about this particular book:

> "Those who fear the permanence and spread of the Soviet form of government will do well to watch and study Lenin and his methods closely, if the reports of Williams, Robins and Ransome can be accepted as an accurate and expert diagnosis of the diplomatic resources of Russia's premier."

A U. S. officer recently returned from military service in Russia states that when, in response to Lenin's boast of being able to capture the United States, it was pointed out that there was a great middle class here that could not be stampeded, he retorted: "The middle class and the capitalist class are too stupid to know what is going on. They are too well content with the pleasures they get from their stolen wealth to interfere with our program." When one sees what is going on here today, the question arises: "Is Lenin right or wrong in his estimate of Americans?"

But the most prominent source of Red propaganda at the present moment is the Albany controversy over the ouster of the five elected socialist Assemblymen. In that matter very many high-minded citizens hold that in their suspension, the Legislature has ruthlessly violated their constitutional rights, thus, they assert, committing a crime greater than anything charged against the socialists. Other citizens, equally high-minded, believe that the Legislature did just the right thing and some blame it for not having raised the question of socialist fitness for membership in the Assembly years ago, when the first socialist presented himself. Unfortunately, politics, legal technicalities and personal feeling are so obscuring the controversy, that there is great danger of the main question being lost sight of—and that is: "Do the socialists propose to accomplish the overthrow of our Government through constitutional means,—the ballot—or do they propose to obtain such results through physical force—the bullet?"

Whatever the merits of the other questions raised in this controversy, or its final outcome, it is of the highest importance for the people, not only of New York but of the nation, to learn just what the Socialist Party proposes to substitute for our "overturned," "overthrown" or "destroyed" Government? Because, while the socialists or any other group of citizens could destroy the Constitution and undermine all our cherished institutions, provided they did it through legal and constitutional methods, it is the right, as well as the duty, of all loyal Americans to protect themselves, by legal and constitutional methods, against the would-be destroyers.

To indicate the character and intention of the Socialist Party, we herewith attach some quotations from the published utterances of their leaders, their platforms and their publications, from the time of the issuance of the Marx and Engels' *Communist Manifesto*, the Magna Charta of Lenin and Trotzky, of Berger and Hillquit, down to the apparent recent delivery of the whole socialist machine in America to the propaganda of Russian sovietism. Continuously running through these quotations, covering a period of seventy years, is the spirit of class hatred and incentive to violent revolution. Any one reading these, or any of the thousand other pronouncements equally disquieting, would inevitably raise the question whether, holding such views, the socialists intend to do the terrible things they propose by means only of the ballot or whether "in cases of emergency," as expressed in their recent Manifesto, they would "reinforce" their "political demands . . . by industrial action," the general strike; whether with Victor Berger, as expressed in one of the quotations, they are "prepared to back up their ballots with their bullets if necessary."

And further, the question is: "Do the American people want what the socialists want, no matter how they propose to bring it about, and do the American people under any circumstances want to elect or appoint to any office, federal, state or municipal, or to tolerate in their colleges, pulpits, editorial sanctums or other positions of influence men and women who subscribe to such principles and views as are indicated in these quotations?"

It is no secret that the socialists and their sympathizers are today pushing their propaganda through schools, colleges, churches, lecture forums, the press, labor organizations, women's clubs, charity organizations, and so forth, even the posts of the American Legion not being immune, and the ends of this propaganda are served by the very confusion and lack of understanding existing in the public mind as to what Socialism is and how it would affect industry, labor, private enterprise, the family, religion, education, our social and spiritual life.

This suggests the urgent need of a thorough and prompt study and exposition of the principles, policy, tactics and objects of the Socialist movement in this country.

Through the expenditure of large sums of money and the use of all the machinery of the federal and some of the state governments, a tremendous amount of authoritative and invaluable material has been gathered, which is available to all citizens sincerely seeking the truth.

In order that the public mind shall be clarified as to the right and wrong of these questions —deportation of criminal aliens, amnesty for political prisoners, limitation of free speech, free press and free assembly, and above all, the objectives of the Socialists, I. W. W.'ites and Bolshevists, it is proposed that a number of organizations representing the different elements of our national life—labor, agriculture, manufacturing, the Church, the bar, women's organizations, educational institutions, professional and technical organizations and so forth and so forth —shall join in making a study of these questions, reporting their conclusions to the American people, to the end that they may be equipped intelligently both to oppose those forces now seeking to undermine and overthrow our institutions and to give support to all practical measures promotive of industrial and social progress.

With the invitation was sent the following Exhibit:

SOCIALIST PRINCIPLES AND PURPOSES: EXPRESSED BY SOCIALIST MANIFESTOS, PLATFORMS, LEADERS AND ORGANS

From "The Communist Manifesto," by Marx and Engels:

> They (the proletarians) have nothing of their own to secure and fortify; their mission is to destroy all previous securities for, and insurances of, individual property.
>
> . . . Their ends (the Socialists') can be attained only by the forcible overthrow of all existing social conditions. *Let the ruling classes tremble at a Communistic revolution!*
>
> . . . The proletariat, the lowest stratum of our society, cannot stir, cannot raise itself up, without the whole superincumbent strata of official society being sprung into the air.

Frederick Engels, in his "Working Class of England," gives this picture:

> The proletarians, driven to despair, will seize the torch which Stevens has reached to them; the vengeance of the people will come down with a wrath of which the rage of 1793 gives no true idea. The war of the poor against the rich will be the bloodiest ever waged. . . . It is too late for a peaceful solution. The classes are divided more and more sharply, the spirit of resistance penetrates the workers, the bitterness intensifies, the guerrilla skirmishes become concentrated in more important battles, and soon a slight impulse will suffice to set the avalanche in motion. Then, indeed, will the war-cry resound, "War to the palaces, peace to the cottages," but then it will be too late for the rich to beware.

The "Socialist (Perpetual) Campaign Book," "compiled under the direction of the National Executive Committee," referring to the merely reformist measures of the movement, says:

> . . . Each and every one of the separate planks (of the "Immediate Demands") are parts of a symmetrical program as its object the ownership and control of the earth by the workers. . . . The growth of Socialism means the growth of a power that proposes to TAKE ALL. (Capitals original.)

H. M. Hyndman, of London, who is recognized as one of the foremost living exponents of Socialism, makes this rather disquieting suggestion:

> . . . Chemistry has placed at the disposal of the desperate and the needy cheap and powerful explosives, the full effects of which are as yet unknown. Every day adds new discoveries in this field; the dynamite of ideas is accompanied in the background by the dynamite of material force. *These modern explosives may easily prove to capitalism what gunpowder was to feudalism.*

Victor Berger, in the *Social-Democratic Herald,* in 1909:

> In view of the plutocratic law-making of the present day, it is easy to predict that the safety and hope of this country will finally lie *in one direction only—that of a violent and bloody revolution.*
>
> Therefore, I say, each of the 500,000 Socialist voters, and of the two million workingmen who instinctively incline our way should, besides doing much reading and still more thinking, *also have a good rifle and the necessary rounds of ammunition in his home and be prepared to back up his ballot with his bullets if necessary.*
>
> Now I deny that, dealing with the blind and greedy plutocratic class, as we are dealing in this country, the outcome can ever be peaceable or that any reasonable change can ever be brought about by the ballot in the end.

While the above editorial was published in 1909, reference to it is timely today by reason of Victor Berger's remark at his trial last year in Chicago: "I would say that today."

From the *New York Call,* official organ of the Socialist Party, Aug. 15, 1914:

> We want to see the workingmen of all these lands turn on their butchers and murderers, and rend them into fragments, and stamp out forever the abominable class rule, the capitalism that has turned a continent into a shambles. . . .
>
> And now the thing has started, we don't care how they do it, whether with cannon, musket and sabre, or with confiscation and legislation. Any old way that is most convenient, provided only that they do it. . . .
>
> We have not started this thing (the War) and we hope that our correspondents will comprehend us when we say that, now that it is started, the most cold-blooded calculation on our part at the present moment is that they should all bleed each other to exhaustion so that the *coming social revolution may have an easier job of sweeping out the stinking fragments. We are through with protesting, mourning and deploring.* THAT be what they will. *It may cause the slaughter* TIME HAS PASSED AND NOW WE STAND FOR DESTRUCTION—THE DESTRUCTION OF CAPITALISM.

From the *New York Call,* Aug. 29, 1914:

> If it means literal war to put capitalism down and out, we are always ready to wage it for that object. . . . We have a deadly score to settle with the capitalist system, and despite what we may do now or what we are forced to do, we never forget the ultimate enemy, and its supporters owe us nothing for the part any of us may take in the European War, in any country. And unless we are grievously mistaken they will find that out as an aftermath of the present struggle.

The *Appeal to Reason,* a paper which claims a million circulation, testified as follows:

> Labor demands all the products of its hands—and it is going to have them, let the consequences be what they will. *It may cause the slaughter and massacre of millions.* None has a right to live who will not help to produce the wealth that sustains the people of the planet.

From "Debs: His Life, Speeches and Writings":

> It is a question not of reform, the mask of fraud, but of revolution.
>
> The flag, the only flag of Freedom, we reaffirm it and on this day pledge anew fidelity—come life, come death—to the blood-red Banner of the Revolution.

Morris Hillquit in "Socialism in Theory and Practice":

> The transition from the present order of individual wealth and competitive industry to a system of collective ownership and co-operative production *by whatever means and in whatever manner accomplished,* is bound to be accomplished by very thoroughgoing changes in all relations of men, and by a decided remodeling of the entire social and political structure of society.

After the revolutionary communists had left the Socialist party last year, Mr. Hillquit issued a pronouncement advocating the friendly relations that ought to continue to exist between the Socialists and "their honest brethren" who, he pointed out, had not ceased to be Socialists and are to continue to be regarded as a part of the Socialist movement. Hillquit said:

> The split in the ranks of American Socialism raises an interesting question of policy. What shall be the attitude of the Socialist party toward the newly formed "Communist" organization? . . .
>
> The division was not brought about by differences on vital questions of principles. It arose over disputes on methods and policy, and even within that limited sphere it was largely one of emphasis rather than fundamentals.

Is this not an endorsement of violent revolution for the overthrow of government, including democratic governments, such as the Communist branch boldly proposes?

Mr. Hillquit proceeded to state that certain minor differences do exist, but he immediately pointed out that the communists and Socialists are still united against the common enemy, and that all quarrels between them are to be regarded as quarrels with "brethren" and a form of internecine strike. Hillquit said:

> Let us center our whole fight upon capitalism, and let us hope our Communist brethren will go and do likewise.

Mr. Hillquit's "honest brethren" in their Manifesto, state as their objective:

> The Communist Party shall keep in the foreground its consistent appeal for *proletarian revolution,* the overthrow of capitalism and the establishment of a dictatorship of the proletariat.
>
> . . .
>
> Communism does not propose to "capture" the bourgeois parliamentary state, but to conquer and destroy it.

Morris Hillquit, testifying in May, 1914, before the Industrial Relations Commission as the representative of the Socialist Party, defined Socialism in its economic aspects as follows:

> Stated in more concrete terms, the Socialist program requires the public or collective ownership and operation of the principal instruments and agencies for the production and distribution of wealth—the land, mines, railroads, steamboats, telegraph and telephone lines, mills, factories and modern machinery.
>
> This is the main program, and the ultimate aim of the whole Socialist movement and the political creed of all Socialists. It is the unfailing test of Socialist adherence, and admits of no limitation, extension or variation. Whoever accepts this program is a Socialist; whoever does not, is not.

Mr. Hillquit did not explain that these farms, factories, mines, etc., are to be taken over by confiscation, but others in his party are more frank. William Mailly, former secretary of the Socialist Party and, later, editor of *The Call,* expressed concretely the views of hundreds of other leaders:

> Myself, I favor absolute expropriation. I cannot believe that society, through organized government, owes anything at all to the present possessors of industry.

The Appeal to Reason was more direct:

> We make no apology for advocating the confiscation of the nation's industries as soon as we have the power to confiscate them.
>
> We would have no one under any mistaken impression so far as our position on confiscation is concerned. We want the capitalists themselves to know that we are organizing to take from them the right and power they have had since the beginning of capitalism to take from us the proceeds of our toil.
>
> *The Appeal to Reason* unfurls the flag of confiscation and appeals to all the toilers of the nation, in the mills and mines, on the railroads and the farms, to rally beneath its folds and hasten the day of their deliverance.

'oncerning the activities of the Socialists in labor field, Jack London, at that time presi- it of the Intercollegiate Socialist Society, said:

> *With the control of the police, the army, the navy, and the courts, they will confiscate, with or without remuneration, all the possessions of the capitalist class* which are used in the production and distribution of the luxuries and necessities of life. They mean to apply the law of eminent domain to the land and to extend the law of eminent domain until it embraces the mines, the factories, the railroads and the ocean carriers.
>
> The Socialists turned their energies upon the trade-union movement. To win the trade unions was well-nigh to win the victory.
>
> Instead of antagonizing the unions, the Socialists proceeded to conciliate the unions. "Let every good Socialist join the union of his trade. Bore from within and capture the trade-union movement."
>
> Today the great labor unions are honeycombed with Socialists. At work and at play, at business meeting and council, *their insidious propaganda goes on.* Night and day, tireless and unrelenting as a mortgage, they labor at their self-imposed task of undermining society.

In the Manifesto of the Communist Party the llowing is stated:

> The Communist Party recognizes that the A. F. of L. is reactionary and a bulwark of capitalism.
>
> Councils of workers shall be organized in the shops as circumstances allow, for the purpose of carrying on the industrial union struggle in the old unions, uniting and mobilizing the militant elements, these councils to be unified in a Central Council wherever possible.
>
> It shall be a major task of the Communist Party to agitate for the construction of a general industrial union organization embracing the I. W. W., W. I. I. U., independent and secession unions, militant unions of the A. F. of L. and the unorganized workers, on the basis of the revolutionary class struggle.

How the Communist Party of America pro- ɔses to take advantage of small strikes of pro- st and develop them into a larger revolution- y mass action, with the purpose of overthrow- g the government, is shown in the following aragraphs from the party's Manifesto:

> Strikes of protest develop into general political strikes and then into revolutionary mass action for the conquest of the powerful State. Mass action becomes political in purpose while extraparliamentary in form; it is equally a process of revolution and the revolution itself in operation. . . .
>
> The Communist Party shall participate in mass strikes, not only to achieve the immediate purposes of the strike, but to develop the revolutionary implications of the mass strike.

The *Jewish Daily Forward*, New York, of larch 23, 1919, printed in Yiddish, is the largest iocialist and biggest foreign-language publica- ion in the country. Addressing its 150,000 or nore readers, the *Forward* declared:

> Let us say openly what we want and let us openly fight for what we want. . . . We must keep a clear mind and must not make any mistakes, which would prolong the struggle and delay victory. We must not give our foes any excuse to attack us before we are prepared for battle. We must not provoke the people who believe in us with revolutionary phrases into a fight for which we are by far not ready.

Does this indicate that while they say they do iot preach immediate revolution, they do preach evolution at the proper and opportune time? Are we going to wait for the Socialists to pre- pare adequately and then themselves fix the lay?

In a letter sent to a correspondent, dated June ', 1916, entered as evidence at the hearings of he Lusk Committee, sent out by the Corre- pondence Department of the Rand School, the generally recognized chief propaganda institu- ion of the Socialist party in the East, the fol- owing statement appeared:

> When we read of "Preparedness" that is in full force in the camps of the capitalists we realize that unless we organize and fit ourselves to resist, and to take over the government, we will one day find ourselves where our French and German brothers are today, dead or maimed in the fray.

In another letter—apparently also a form letter sent out to correspondents by David P. Berenberg, director of the correspondence department—the following appeared:

> WHAT ARE YOU GOING TO DO WHEN THE STATE ROBS YOU AND YOUR UNION AND SO MAKES YOU HELPLESS TO STRIKE? There is only one thing to do: TAKE OVER THE STATE. . . .
>
> Are the members of your local prepared to take over and conduct wisely and well the affairs of your town and county? Are you ready to meet the militia when the powers of the state and courts are against you?

Is it implied that the members of the Socialist Party be "ready to meet the militia" not with guns but only with ballots in their hands? Is it merely a political party whose leaders, organs and schools urge the "taking over of the state," armed "preparedness" and readiness to meet the militia?

Since the Soviet revolutions in Bavaria and Hungary last March, the Socialist Party publications have not merely advocated Sovietism—their pages have contained hardly anything else. All the Lenine documents have been printed in full, not as news but as propaganda, accompanied by innumerable endorsements, and (except in the rarest cases) by no criticism.

The following paragraph from the proclamation of the Communist International Congress, held March 2-6, 1919, and printed in the *New York Call* of July 24, 1919, is typical:

> The revolutionary epoch demands that the proletariat should employ such fighting methods as will concentrate its entire energy, viz., the method of mass action, and lead to its logical consequence—the direct collision with the capitalist state machine in an open combat. All other methods, e.g., revolutionary use of bourgeois parliamentarism, will in the revolution have only a subordinate value.

Does this not show the true meaning of the phrase "mass action" so much employed in the entire literature of the Socialist Party? Does it not mean simply a violent revolution at the propitious moment and include all methods from insurrectionary strikes and street riots to civil war?

At the convention of the National Socialist Party held in Chicago, on September 4, 1919, a platform was adopted, containing the following declaration concerning the terroristic revolutionary régime in Russia:

> We declare our solidarity with the workers of Russia in establishing their Soviet Republic and we indorse the Socialists of Germany, Austria, and Hungary in their struggle for freedom. We condemn the counter-revolution in Russia backed by the Czarists and the Entente nations.

At the meeting at which the above declaration was adopted, it was reported that the delegates "jumped to their feet and cheered for several minutes when the paragraph was read approving the Soviet Republic of Russia." In the document the Russian revolution was compared to the American Revolution of 1776.

In the Manifesto of the Socialist Party, adopted at its Chicago convention last September, the stand of that party was stated:

> Recognizing the crucial situation at home and abroad, the Socialist Party of the United States, at its first national convention after the war, SQUARELY TAKES ITS POSITION WITH THE UNCOMPROMISING SECTION OF THE INTERNATIONAL SOCIALIST MOVEMENT. . . . We, the organized Socialists of America, pledge our support to the revolutionary workers of Russia in the maintenance of their Soviet government; to the radical Socialists of Germany, Austria and Hungary in their efforts to establish working-class rule in their countries.

Referring to its proposed organization of American workers, with the clearly stated purpose of seeking to bring about its political ends by "industrial action," or general strikes, it was stated:

> They must be strongly organized on the economic field on broad industrial lines, as one powerful and harmonious class organization, cooperating with the Socialist Party, and ready in cases of emergency *to reinforce the political demands of the working-class by industrial action.* . . . Long live the international Socialist revolution, the only hope of the suffering world!

So amazing was the enormity of the 1917 St. Louis majority resolution, opposing our participation in the war, that it is not to be regarded as strange that it took several years for the American people to wake to a realization of what it is. Calling upon "the workers of all countries to refuse support to their governments in their wars," it declared:

> The wars of the contending national groups of capitalists are not the concern of the workers. THE ONLY STRUGGLE WHICH WOULD JUSTIFY THE WORKERS IN TAKING UP ARMS IS THE GREAT STRUGGLE OF THE WORKING CLASS OF THE WORLD TO FREE ITSELF FROM ECONOMIC EXPLOITATION AND POLITICAL OPPRESSION.

As the official statement of an organization pretending to function as a political body, its stand in regard to patriotism was clearly stated:

> As against the false doctrine of national patriotism we uphold the ideal of international working class solidarity. . . .
>
> Our entrance into the European war was instigated by the predatory capitalists in the United States who boast of the enormous profit of seven billion dollars from the manufacture and sale of munitions and war supplies and from the exportation of American foodstuffs and other necessaries. . . . The war of the United States against Germany cannot be justified even on the plea that it is a war in defense of American rights or American "honor." . . . In all modern history there has been no war more unjustifiable than the war in which we are about to engage.

The resolution urged:

> Continuous, active and public opposition to the war, through demonstrations, mass petitions, and all other means within our power.
>
> Unyielding opposition to all proposed legislations for military or industrial conscription.

That the National Party undertook to dictate the action of men elected to Congress or State Legislatures, was clearly stated in the recommendation:

> We recommend that the convention instruct our elected representatives in Congress, in the State Legislatures, and in local bodies, to vote against all proposed appropriations or loans for military, naval and other war purposes.

From the "Dictatorship of the Proletariat," published by the Jewish Socialist Federation, is taken the following significant statement:

> "Socialists seek to enter into the government for two reasons: First, to be nearer to the doors of the chambers where dictatorship sits, and, second, to hinder the dictatorial work in any way possible.
>
> 'The first reason is the most important. Sitting in parliament or congress, being inside of the government councils, affords Socialists an opportunity to find out the plans, the strategy of the state. And, knowing this, they can carry out their propaganda the better. Socialists seek to be elected into the government principally for the sake of propaganda."

This may explain why so many socialists worked themselves into positions in the government during the war, even the Military Intelligence Bureau being invaded by them, and raises the questions: Through whose recommendations were they placed in such positions of trust? and, Are there any of them remaining there?

Is there any doubt that the Socialists of America are in accord with the Socialists of Russia? In a report on conditions in Europe, which he visited "to re-establish relations between the party in this country and the parties in the various nations in Europe," according to the official Socialist Bulletin, James Oneal, member of the national executive committee of the Socialist party, said:

> The Moscow Congress certainly has in mind the ideals of Socialism, not the concept of communism of wealth which has characterized many religious sects. Its membership is made up of

all the elements of the Socialist movement that oppose war and militarism, relies upon the class struggle to chart the course of the movement and keeps in mind the fact that the real struggle in the modern world is one between the workers of all countries as against the ruling classes of all countries.

The Communist International Congress at Moscow, above referred to as being guided by "the ideals of Socialism," adopted a manifesto addressed to the "proletariat of all countries," in which violent revolution was urged:

> The working class must answer blow for blow, if it will not renounce its own object and its own future, which is at the same time the future of all humanity. . . .
>
> This makes necessary the disarming of the bourgeoisie at the proper time, the arming of the laborer and the formation of a Communist army as the protector of the rule of the proletariat and the inviolability of the social structure. . . .
>
> The revolutionary era compels the proletariat to make use of the means of battle which will concentrate its entire energy, namely, mass action, with its logical resultant direct conflict with the governmental machinery in open combat. All other methods, such as revolutionary use of burgeois parliamentarism, will be of only secondary significance.

From this it is seen that Lenine's Moscow congress laid emphasis upon the concentration of the entire energy of the proletariat upon "mass action" and declared parliamentary methods to be "secondary." The Socialist Party of America—which by referendum vote recently declared itself in support of Lenine's third international—adopted at its convention in Chicago last September a manifesto in which is specifically declared the Socialist Party's purpose of organizing workers, of undermining and gaining control of the organized labor, so that at the opportune time they could employ "mass action," or the general strike, to bring about a revolution. That the Socialist Party of America does not intend to confine itself to legal and constitutional, or "parliamentary," methods for bringing about social and revolutionary changes, that, in fact, it regards as its "supreme task" such organization of workers as would make a general strike possible, is clearly brought out in the following:

> To insure the triumph of Socialism in the United States the bulk of the American workers must be strongly organized politically as Socialists in constant, clear-cut and aggressive opposition to all parties of the possessing class. They must be strongly organized on the economic field on broad industrial lines, as one powerful and harmonious class organization, co-operating with the Socialist party, and ready in cases of emergency TO REINFORCE THE POLITICAL DEMANDS OF THE WORKING CLASS BY INDUSTRIAL ACTION.
>
> To win the American workers from their ineffective and demoralizing leadership, to educate them to an enlightened understanding of their own class interest, and to train and assist them to organize politically and industrially on class lines in order to effect their emancipation—that is the supreme task confronting the Socialist Party of America. . . . LONG LIVE THE INTERNATIONAL SOCIALIST REVOLUTION, THE ONLY HOPE OF THE SUFFERING WORLD.

Many connections between the Soviet bureau and the Socialist Party were revealed at hearings of the Lusk Committee. Through Socialist Party locals were arranged lectures for Santeri Nourteva, of the Soviet bureau.

According to a letter from the National Office of the Socialist Party, signed by the Executive Secretary, Adolph Germer, dated Chicago, Ill., February 15, 1919, and addressed to him, Nourteva, an alien, an official representative of Lenine and Trotzky, and with Martens one of the chief official Bolshevist propagandists in America, was nominated to represent the Socialist Party of America as a delegate to the International Congress. If the Socialist Party of America elects as a delegate an alien and a professed revolutionist, can it claim to be merely a political party, such as the Republican and Democratic parties, with the right to function as such in the United States?

According to a bulletin issued by the Bureau of Information of Soviet Russia, of which Nourteva was director, Morris Hillquit, the Socialist leader, who is now making capital talking about safeguarding Constitutional rights, was appointed a representative of the revolutionary Bolshevist régime in Russia. The bulletin stated:

"MR. MORRIS HILLQUIT HAS ACCEPTED THE POST OF COUNCILLOR OF THE RUSSIAN SOVIET BUREAU IN THE UNITED STATES. MR. HILLQUIT WILL BE IN CHARGE OF THE LEGAL DEPARTMENT OF THE BUREAU. . . . MR. HILLQUIT HAS BEEN IN CLOSE TOUCH WITH MR. MARTENS AND HIS BUREAU FROM THE VERY DAY OF MR. MARTENS' APPOINTMENT."

In a letter addressed to American workingmen, Nicholas Lenine paid a tribute to Eugene Debs, leader of the Socialist Party:

> I recall with pride the words of one of the best loved leaders of the American proletariat, Eugene V. Debs, who said in the *Appeal to Reason* at the end of 1915, . . . in an article entitled "Why Should I Fight?" that he would rather be shot than vote for war credits to support the present criminal and reactionary war, that he knows only one war that is sanctified and justified from the standpoint of the proletariat—the war against the capitalist class, the war for the liberation of mankind from wage slavery.

Correspondence between Debs and Nourteva showed the cordial relations existing between the two. To Nourteva, Lenine's agent, Debs wrote:

> My heart is with you, Dear Comrade, and I wish you all success in the splendid service you are rendering and the fearless manner in which you are rendering it.

Planning simultaneous Bolshevist revolutions in Europe and America, the International Communist congress of the Bolsheviki at Moscow, at a secret session last March, designated Debs, now serving a prison sentence for preaching resistance to the draft, as President of the future Soviet Republic of the United States.

The May Day literature sent out last Spring by the national office of the Socialist party declared for a change in the American government to a government in which the representatives of the people would be elected out of the shop; hailed a "dictatorship of the proletariat" and announced that "whether or not blood is spilled depends upon the tyrants of today." For May Day celebrations the national office outlined meetings and prepared a program of speeches, the last and doubtless most important of which was one by Eugene V. Debs, in which Debs said, "I am going to speak to you as a Socialist, as a revolutionist, as a Bolshevist. . . ."

Referring to the Peace Conference at Paris, he wrote:

> Out of Russia there comes a voice and out of Russia there shines a light which claims their fearful attention even while they pretend to be drafting a constitution for the world. It is no longer Wilson—it is Lenine who dominates the Peace Conference . . . When Lenine spoke it was to tell the truth and the working class of every nation in the world responded to his utterance with a mighty shout.

Serious Conditions and Need of Proposed Work Discussed at Conference

As a result of the invitation sent out by The National Civic Federation a conference on Socialist Tactics was held under the auspices of the Federation at the Hotel Astor on February 16. The sessions were attended by notable leaders of the various elements of our national life and included representative members of various patriotic organizations.

Judge Alton B. Parker, who presided, declared in his opening address that citizenship in America has been made too easy and too cheap, and that as a result there is a large population of naturalized aliens who do not speak English, who have never been assimilated, and neither understand nor appreciate the American Constitution and system of government. Judge Parker said:

"Now, nothing can be done about that, for they are citizens. But one of the things that the people of this country should do is to see to it that so far as the future is concerned, our citizenship shall not be granted to those who do not speak the English language and who do not really understand our scheme of government. It is but a little time back, as it seems to us, when we began to learn the efforts of the Bolsheviki, the I. W. W.'s, the anarchists, the socialists. We did not realize at first, nor could we, that they had any ambition to overthrow our government and substitute one like the Soviet government of Russia. It seemed so unreasonable, so unnatural, that it took us a long time to open our eyes to the fact that such efforts were being made in this country. Now we realize it.

"The evidence is abundant, and the question which seriously confronts our people is, shall we do our part toward preventing a successful attempt to overthrow the government, and shall we do our part to make good citizens out of all those who are here, to make them understand that this is in reality a government of the people, by the people and for the people? In order that that may be accomplished, it is not enough that the government shall deport those whose ambition it is to overthrow the government by force; it is necessary that we should carry on a propaganda on our side—a propaganda of education to enable the people who do not understand our language, through teachers who can speak their own language, to understand the fact known to all of us, that the best government which the world ever saw is the government of the United States, a government which the majority of the people can amend from time to time as circumstances seem to them to require it."

Henry A. Wise Wood said, in part:

"I am not as much afraid of those who come to our country who do not speak English as of those in it who do speak English, but who do not believe in its traditions. Since 1914 I have watched this pot of social apostasy boiling down on the lower East Side. In the latter part of 1914, with Colonel Roosevelt and Leonard Wood, I started in on the preparedness movement, began going up and down through the lower East Side, the upper East Side, Cooper Union, and then I commenced to realize that such a thing as the thing we now call Bolshevism was in existence, was being prepared in this country. We could not make the authorities realize then that that existed here. We could not make our people realize that it existed here. The newspapers would take no notice of it until one night at Cooper Union, when some of us were speaking, they spat on the flag. Then for the first time the newspapers in this city commenced to realize what we had here in our midst.

"Let me give you an idea of what the pot of Bolshevism, the poison of social apostasy that was being brewed right down here in our midst, resulted in. Robert Wilton, the correspondent of the *London Times* in Russia for a number of years, has recently stated that of the 384 Bolshevik commissars which ruled Russia right after the Bolshevists took charge of it were composed of two negroes, thirteen Russians, fifteen Chinamen, twenty-three Georgians and Armenians, and over 264 men who had come out of the United States from the lower East Side—Trotsky among them. Those men, known to our authorities, were not only permitted, but assisted, to go into Russia, into the midst of an ally who was at arms with us fighting a common enemy, and bring their ally down. Trotsky himself was held up in Canada and not permitted to go through by the Canadian authorities, and I am informed on good authority that he was released and sent on his way at the earnest request of our State Department. A man in whom I believe stated to me the other day that sixty per cent of the officials in the State Department in Washington are Socialists. I know from my experience during the war that the Socialists have been a stronger force in this country than any of us—any of the rest of us realize.

"I want to give a few examples of the damage that has been done by this poison of national apostasy which has been brewing and has been distributed throughout our intelligent states, our colleges and universities, by its organs, such, for instance, as the *New Republic* and the *Nation* and the *Survey*, the *Dial* and the *New York Call*. I was speaking two months ago—remember, this is after we had fought a great and victorious war—before the students of a college within one hundred miles of this city, discussing the fundamental American policies, traditions, and the Constitution of the United States. Of the young men before me, as I found when I commenced to question them, there was hardly an infinitesimal proportion that cared anything about a single American tradition or the Constitution of the United States, and who was not ready to scrap the whole thing if they could gain some temporary advantage by doing it. That was explained when later on I was taken to meet the president of that college, and in talking with him about various things the question of universal training came up. He said he was opposed to it because those who administered it would teach the boys patriotism. That man was an American, the president of an American college, and the boys I was talking to were Americans, excepting a few who had strongly pronounced foreign blood in them.

"I have just received a letter from a member of the faculty of a very prominent western university, who says: 'Just now a man on the staff of our engineering college told me it was too early to form an opinion whether Lenine and Trotsky were to be commended or not.' Yesterday at a luncheon of none but American people a New England woman whose ancestors had been here for nearly three hundred years asked me this question: 'Is it a matter of very great importance whether our government survives or not?' I am not afraid of these people who do not speak English. I am afraid of these people who speak and write English too fluently.

"Macaulay in 1857, writing, I think it was, to Bancroft, said: 'Either some Cæsar or Napoleon will seize the reigns of government with a strong hand, or your Republic will be as fearfully plundered and laid waste by barbarians in the Twentieth Century as the Roman Empire was in the Fifth, with this difference, that the Huns and vandals who ravaged the Roman Empire came from without, and your Huns and vandals will be engendered within your country, by your own United States.' That was written by Macaulay in 1857. The threat of that condition is present today. We have a conflict between the ideas of the East and the ideas of the West. It comes down to that. You have got men of eastern mind who put on our civilization as people put on their clothes, and men of western mind who believe in western civilization and in our traditions of government. There is your conflict, and Bolshevism is the expression of men of eastern mind who have not taken on the western mind, in their desire to overthrow western civilization. They believe that the institutions of private ownership, the church and the family are inimical to mankind, and they have given expression to those beliefs in one nation that has come under their power—Russia.

"We are suffering from the reflex action of that here, and we must not forget that for what has happened to Russia we are largely responsible. It was pulled off not so much with German money as with American protection, patronage and money.

"We are not going to solve our problems by merely educating these people to speak English. We have got to solve our problems by teaching them, whether they speak English or not, to believe in our traditions. We have got to enforce our criminal laws. We have got to handle this thing, not with kisses and gloves and flowers, but strongly by the enforcement of our laws. And when these people are found guilty, don't hang wreaths around their necks. Send them up and drive them out of your legislative halls. Face the issue. The issue is not a question of education. The issue is the same old issue, and you have got to meet it vigorously and with courage."

Rabbi Joseph F. Silverman said, in part:

"To my mind the Socialistic Party is not a political party in any sense that deserves to stand on a par with the Republican or Democratic Party. They are American political parties, and their whole intention is to uphold our government, the Constitution and to stand by the flag and the American people. Though they may differ in their methods in some respects and in their advocacy of certain measures, those political parties mean and intend to uphold the liberty of our country, the laws of our country, the free institutions of America, free education, individualism, private property, the home and religion, the fundamental props of our nation. Any group of men that combine to overthrow those props of our American government and of the American people seek to destroy the structure, and do not constitute a political party, but a conspiracy to overthrow. This is a conspiracy, and the men that are engaged in it are traitors.

"We do not care whether a man is a Republican or a Democrat. We know that he is an American, after all. But when I meet a Socialist, I can look him squarely in the eye and say to him, 'You are not an American.' And that is the stand that we should take—that a Socialist is not an American citizen in the true sense of the term.

"A campaign of education is in order, but it is not sufficient. We cannot hope by merely a campaign of education to reach the leaders and the teachers who are disseminating the poison. We must reach them. We must throttle them. We must seek to institute such measures by which those in authority in schools and in colleges will unseat the men and the women who today occupy seats of authority in schools and in colleges, teachers and professors, who teach these false doctrines, and by that false teaching undermine the citizenship of our country."

John L. Tildsley, Assistant Superintendent of the Board of Education, said:

"We have at the present time a struggle between two distinct civilizations, eastern and western. If that idea could be hammered home to the people of this country it would not be necessary for so many of us to be all the time in an apologetic attitude. In school work, at the present time, those of us who believe that the public school exists as a means of perpetuating an order based on experience and preserving law and order are looked upon as reactionaries.

"I think we are in a dangerous condition in this country at the present time, because our educational systems are being so largely influenced by people who have no patience with the idea that progress must always be based on experience, and must come about in an orderly fashion.

"The situation in this country today is more dangerous than those of you who are not directly connected with education can realize. The hope lies pre-eminently in a campaign of education of the young so as they grow up year by year they shall be trained to think straight and to have a right attitude toward government. After all, those who are full grown at the present time are rather beyond any means that you can use to educate them. But this great aim of taking millions of children in this country and out of them making good American citizens who shall really clearly understand our institutions is a tremendous task which can be performed only by teachers who are themselves steeped in Anglo-Saxon American traditions. And at the present time in this country of ours we are no longer able to secure such teachers. We are not securing them in our secondary schools, and we are not securing them in our colleges.

"Take this campaign of education which we all favor. On the one side you have Morris Hillquit and Scott Nearing, and a host of other men who write well and who speak well, all of whose utterances are tinged with a deep emotionalism and reach the persons to whom they are addressed. On the other side we have a decreasing number of able leaders of education. The danger at the present time lies in our educational system, from the highest to the lowest, in the fact that we have a steadily decreasing quality of person teaching the small children, the middle-sized children and the grown-up children of this country, and the condition is going to grow steadily worse because at the present time you have made teaching so unattractive by your failure to support it financially.

"Your campaign of education in this country has got to start with your schools, and the country has got to awake to the fact that it must preserve its old-time ideas if it is going to have growing citizens who are like those who went before them. They have got to be trained by men and women who are free from the financial worries so that they themselves can be optimistic and helpful. We need at the present time in our colleges and universities men of large ability. It is certainly as important for this country that in Columbia University you shall have as a professor of economics a man who because of his ability is capable of being a Supreme Court Justice of the United States, and yet in this day and generation we do not get them.

"We must try to bring up our children to realize that government is the most tremendous force in the world for the upbuilding and protection of the ordinary humble citizen, and therefore he must realize that life without government is absolutely impossible. Therefore his attitude toward that government should be friendly, kindly, and, above all things, hopeful, optimistic. That is the great work that our educational system must do. It must be permeated with optimism in order to have optimistic citizens, and men in high places throughout this country should realize that wherever possible they should impress that idea.

"I come back to my original thesis. The remedy lies in our educational system and in having leaders of thought who are big enough to impress their thoughts upon the young people of our schools and colleges. Let it be no longer said that the real thinkers of the country are found only in the Rand School and the New School."

John McDowell, Chairman of the Social Service Commission of the Presbyterian Church, said:

"I think the time has come when we need not only to remind these foreigners, as we call them, who come to our shores, that we are a government of laws; we need to remind ourselves that we are a government of laws, and need, therefore, to again review our laws, re-learn our laws. I have been amazed, as I have gone from place to place, to find how ignorant men are of our fundamental law, the Constitution of the United States. I believe the time has come when we must refuse to call any man an American who does not believe in the Constitution of the United States. Now, how can they believe in a document that they do not know? How can they believe in a body of laws a knowledge of which they do not have?

"We stand with our forefathers more than ever on the Constitution, and believe and are willing to go so far as to refuse to give the right to a man to be known as an American who does not believe in our fundamental law. In the second place, we must see to it that these men have a chance to learn what these laws are. Primarily that will come through our public and private schools. I do not believe that we ought to support any school in this country that is not willing to teach the fundamental laws of our nation as embodied in the Constitution. But, after all, our schools are not enough. You may educate a man, train his mind, but if you fail to train his conscience you have not a safe man. We must have not only mental training, we must have moral training to go with our mental training, if we are to have a thoroughgoing American.

"I am not pleading here for a church education, but for an education that shall have morality in it. To have morality in it that is real in these days, it must be in some way related to that which is fundamental in man, namely, his religion.

"America is sound at heart, and we need have no fear so long as we keep in mind the fundamental principles that an American is a man who believes in the Constitution, is willing to practice it in his private and public life, and embodies in his daily conduct the spirit of the Golden Rule."

Samuel Gompers, in part, said:

"I endeavored to impress upon Congress that immigration should be limited or practically stopped for a period of two years. These people who are here who cannot speak our language, and who do not understand the institutions of the country, are carrying the prejudices of their home country into the United States. This has been going on despite the fact that the American Federation of Labor and this splendid organization, The National Civic Federation, have done everything within their power to bring to the attention of the people of our country the dangers confronting it. This seething has been going on a long time. I doubt if there have been any other two groups anywhere in all our country and its activities who have done so much as The National Civic Federation and the American Federation of Labor to bring to the attention of our people the dangers of this character of immigration and conduct toward the immigrants. I count myself fortunate to have had a long experience and to have given to my fellow countrymen the fundamental fallacies and sophistries of socialism and socialistic political action.

"During the war the elements to which I have referred had their opportunity of declaring themselves pacifists or anti-militarists and showing their disagreement with our entrance into the war. We did our share in trying to prevent their activities from having any influence upon the conduct of the war, to prevent them from sowing the seeds of dissension among the people during the war, and to prevent by any means any slacking of the activities of the workers in industry and transportation.

"Now that the war is over the law-making bodies of our country and of our states have failed totally to give any reasonable, decent consideration to reconstruction policies, so that we might go on upon a peace footing. With industrial reaction, with an ever-increasing cost of the necessaries of life, with the men of business acting the part of pirates upon the people of the United States in their form of profiteering, creating dissatisfaction such as can be known only to those who themselves suffer severely and cannot meet the new conditions opportunity is given for all this radicalism that we have seen and heard. The attempt to meet the situation by restrictive, repressive, suppressive legislation, if it were serious and could be put into effect, would be a declaration of the impotence of the United States of America.

"Our work, the work of patriotic, loyal Americans, is the work of education. It requires not only education in our schools, colleges and universities, but education in our homes, education through our associations, our clubs, our organizations, such as The Civic Federation, and such as the American trade union movement. It requires that character of organization to teach our people not only the spirit of Americanism, our laws and Constitution, but also to teach them sound economics and sociology that will stand for the right of the people and at the same time make them, each one of them, a bulwark against the sophistry of socialism.

"We fought for freedom and ideals during the war. We stood before the war for the principles upon which the war was conducted and for which we aimed to secure permanency during the war. Now that the war is over, we have not changed our purposes to work on to try and make today a better day than yesterday and tomorrow a better day than today."

Before the close of the meeting Mr. Gompers said further:

"The things which more than any other make up the labor movement and the cause for its activity in these affairs is that we believe in freedom, and no one who understands what freedom means doubts the fact that freedom and the exercise of freedom bring some ills in its wake.

"We are opposed to autocracy in any form, whether it be the autocracy of an enemy oligarchy or a political oligarchy, or whether it is the dictatorship of what has come to be known as the proletariat. Democratic freedom is predicated upon the will of the people.

"The masses of the people may just as readily make mistakes in groups as any individual, perhaps not in so aggravated a form, but yet make mistakes. We have held in concepts of freedom that it is better that the masses of the people shall make a mistake occasionally, and by the mistake and the experience of the mistake learn to avoid making the mistakes in the future, rather than have even the wisest among men to dictate what the people shall do. A dictatorship which may be founded upon great wisdom is just as liable to err as are the people in a democracy, and so when the wise autocrat makes a mistake, the people have learned nothing. When the people have made a mistake they rectify it; they are not likely to make the same mistake again. And so we prefer to have a system of government where each man and woman in the community and in the country may have the opportunity of expressing themselves and generally arrive at the result which is most beneficial to all.

"In America we have a labor movement founded upon the spirit, the idea and the concept of democracy. We are going to fight our cause for the improvement of the condition of the wage-working masses of our country. We have nothing of antagonism or bitterness to any other group or class of people. We are citizens with every other citizen, but in addition we have this great work of endeavoring to drive home into the conscience and the hearts of the people of America that as a reward for the services rendered by the toiling masses of America, we are entitled to better consideration than we have thus far received. This improvement must come by a rational policy, by a natural development, and not by a violent overthrow of the government of our country and the establishment, instead of this democracy which we have, of a dictatorship as exists in Russia, which promised peace and land, bread and work and gave neither."

At this conference a resolution, providing for the appointment of a General Committee and expressing the scope of the proposed work, was adopted as follows:

"Whereas, The present unrest of the world is greatly accentuated by the strenuous efforts that are being made to spread the political, social and economic teachings of socialism, as exemplified by Bolshevism, Communism, and I. W. W.-ism, which seek or tend to undermine and overthrow all representative government and the free institutions that are guaranteed by the Constitution of these United States, and by the constitutions of the several states,

"Resolved, That it is the sense of this conference that the fundamental principles upon which the progress of this country rests include the following:

"1. The maintenance of a government of law based upon our existing constitutional guaranties and restrictions.

"2. The right of the individual to the enjoyment of life and liberty, freedom of religion, of speech, of press and of peaceable assembly and to other civil freedom as provided under our constitutional guaranties.

"3. The right of the individual to private property under constitutional guaranties.

"Upon these basic principles there has been developed our social system which embodies certain features that should be safeguarded in the progressive development toward our ideals. These include among others:

"I. Equality and equal opportunity that must be guaranteed under the law.

"II. The encouragement of individual initiative.

"III. That the State exists for the individual and not the individual for the State.

"IV. Orderly progress based on experience.

"V. The principle of representation, and the rule of the majority.

"VI. The family as the unit of society.

"Further Resolved:

"1. That to aid the various associations and individuals who are interested in upholding American ideas and combating revolutionary activities, it is desirable that a means be provided for co-operation through a general committee;

"2. That the general purposes of the committee shall be to provide means of co-operation between the represented societies and associations in matters particularly connected with the upholding of American ideals and the combating of revolutionary activities; to make an intensive study and survey of the program and principles of socialism in its various forms, such as Communism, Bolshevism, and I. W. W.-ism, and, through the knowledge thus gained of the revolutionary purposes of this group, to aid in the defense of American rights, liberty and ideals, and the defeat of its propaganda and efforts to displace or supersede our form of government, also to give support to all practical means promotive of social and industrial progress."

COMMITTEE ON INQUIRY APPOINTED—DIVISION OF WORK

In pursuance of the above action, Judge Parker appointed a committee to inquire into the objectives and tactics of revolutionary forces in this country; to inquire into the extent to which these forces have permeated the various divisions that make up the body politic; to make a survey of industrial political and social progress; and to give support to all practical means tending to improve the general well-being of our people.

To accomplish these purposes, the General Committee, at a meeting held on February 24 at the headquarters of The National Civic Federation, divided the work as follows:

1. *A Committee on Socialist Doctrine and Tactics,* whose work shall include the preparation and distribution of literature, and the organization of a training school for speakers.
2. *Committees to Make an Intensive Study* of the extent to which *Revolutionary Forces* have penetrated into the following and other fields: Labor, Agriculture, The Church, The College, The Public School, The Press, Social Agencies, Philanthropic Agencies, Foreign Groups, Women's Organizations, Public Employees, Negroes.
3. *A Committee to Study Text Books on History, Political Economy and Civics in use in the high schools and colleges.*
4. *A Committee on Soviet Propaganda in the United States.*
5. *A Committee on Survey of Industrial, Political and Social Progress,* and Constructive Recommendations.
6. *A Committee on the Fundamentals of our Constitution* and their application to every-day life, including the *Limitations of the Right of Free Speech, Free Press and Peaceable Public Assembly.*
7. *A Bureau to Evaluate Federal, State and Municipal Official Statistics,* as well as socialist deductions from same.

The Committee on Inquiry so far appointed by Judge Parker consists of the following:

Lawrence F. Abbott (Editor, *The Outlook*).

Cyrus Adler (Acting President, Jewish Theological Seminary of America).

Herbert Barry (Attorney-at-Law).

Wheeler P. Bloodgood (Loyal Legion of Wisconsin).

Miss Helen Varick Boswell (President, Republican National Women's Committee).

Rome G. Brown (President, *The Minneapolis Tribune*).

Rev. Gustav A. Carstensen (Rector, Holy Rood Church).

Thomas N. Carver (Professor of Economics, Harvard University).

D. L. Cease (Editor, *The Railroad Trainman*), Cleveland, Ohio.

Maj. Elihu C. Church (Chamber of Commerce of State of New York).

Bird S. Coler (Commissioner of Public Charities, City of New York).

Mrs. Sara A. Conboy (International Secretary-Treasurer, United Textile Workers of America).

Mark A. Daly (General Secretary, Associated Industries of New York State), Buffalo, N. Y.

Hugh Frayne (General Organizer, American Federation of Labor).

John P. Frey (Editor, *International Molders' Journal*), Cincinnati, Ohio.

A. L. Frothingham (Professor, Princeton University).

John Golden (International President, United Textile Workers of America).

Philip Hiss (formerly Special Assistant for Housing, Navy Department).

James P. Holland (President, New York State Federation of Labor).

John B. Kennedy (Knights of Columbus).

Capt. George B. Lester (Formerly of the Military Intelligence Division, United States Army).

John W. Lieb (National Electric Light Association).

Dr. Earl P. Lothrop (Physicians' Protective Association), Buffalo, N. Y.

Edson S. Lott (Insurance Federation of America).

Lieut. A. W. Kliefoth (Formerly of the American Military Intelligence Service in Russia), Fond du Lac, Wis.

John McDowell, D.D. (Secretary, Board of Home Missions, Presbyterian Church).

Capt. Hugh S. Martin (Formerly of the American Military Intelligence Service in Russia), Meridian, Miss.

Hill Montague (President, National Fraternal Congress), Richmond, Va.

Mrs. Philip North Moore (President, National Council of Women), St. Louis, Mo.

Dr. Charles P. Neill (Bureau of Information, Southeastern Railways).

T. V. O'Connor (President, International Longshoremen's Association), Buffalo, N. Y.

Prof. William Bradley Otis (College of the City of New York).

Condé B. Pallen, LL. D. (Author, "A. B. C. of Socialism").

Clifton Reeves (Willys-Overland Co., Inc.).

Montgomery Schuyler (formerly U. S. Chief Intelligence Officer at Omsk, Siberia).

Timothy Shea (Acting President, Brotherhood of Locomotive Firemen and Enginemen), Cleveland, Ohio.

Rabbi Joseph F. Silverman (Temple Emmanuel).

Walter George Smith (American Bar Association), Philadelphia, Pa.

Maj. Lorillard Spencer (Chairman, Committee on Anti-American Activities, The American Legion), New York County.

Archibald E. Stevenson (Attorney).

Lionel Sutro (Chairman Committee on Education, City Club of New York).

John L. Tildsley (Associate Superintendent of High Schools), New York City.

Daniel J. Tobin (President, International Brotherhood of Teamsters), Indianapolis, Ind.

Charles R. Towson (Secretary, Industrial Department, International Committee of Y. M. C. A.'s).

Mrs. Coffin Van Rensselaer (Executive Secretary, Woman's Department, The National Civic Federation).

John A. Voll (President, Glass Bottle Blowers' Association of the United States and Canada), Philadelphia, Pa.

Allen Walker (Guaranty Trust Co., New York).

Maj. Stanley Washburn (Formerly Military Aide to Root Diplomatic Mission to Russia).

Miss Maude Wetmore (Chairman, Woman's Department, The National Civic Federation).

Everett P. Wheeler (Attorney-at-Law).

Clarence H. Wilson, D.D. (President, Congregational Club of New York and Vicinity).

Matthew Woll (President, International Photo Engravers' Union), Chicago, Ill.

Arthur Woodward (President, New York Rotary Club).

Mrs. John Francis Yawger (National Society, Daughters of the American Revolution).

Answer Stock Socialist Detractions with Facts

AMAZING RECORD OF POLITICAL, SOCIAL AND INDUSTRIAL PROGRESS WILL CONFOUND MUCK-RAKERS

(Address at Conference on Socialist Tactics, Held Under the Auspices of The National Civic Federation at Hotel Astor, New York, February 16, 1920)

By RALPH M. EASLEY

IN dealing with the situation confronting this country today with respect to Socialism, I. W. W.'ism and Bolshevism, there are, as I conceive it, two separate and distinct policies to be pursued, because there are two separate and distinct classes of people with whom we have to deal.

First, we have the definite and outspoken revolutionaries who, under the name of Socialism, Bolshevism, I. W. W.'ism and so forth, have been shown by the Federal and State Governments to be committed to a program of destruction of our Government and all our cherished institutions by force. The last link in the evidence needed to put a quietus upon those socialist sympathizers who have been defending the Socialist Party and contending that it is anti-Bolshevist and anti-Communist was the official report last week of the referendum taken by the Socialist Party membership on the question of affiliation with the Third International of Moscow. The vote was two to one in favor of such affiliation, thus wiping out all practical differences between the Bolshevists and Communists of Russia and the Socialist, the Communist and the Communist Labor Parties in the United States. One and all are thus committed to the destruction of the State by force at the most opportune moment—and that moment is when, thanks to our indifference to this danger, they think they can win through a bloody uprising.

So far as this element of the problem is concerned, it can be dealt with only by the strong arm of the law, Federal, State and Municipal, as it is today being dealt with vigorously and properly. Fortunately, these revolutionary bodies which have to be grappled with in that manner comprise numerically only a small minority of our population, not one per cent at most; but it is a most venomous minority and largely foreign-born. To talk about education or Americanization as a method of dealing with such people is a waste of time, effort and money. Only the fear of the law, backed up by the police, the militia, the army and the navy if necessary, has any terrors for such terrorists, and it is our duty to make this situation clear to all loyal Americans, that they may uphold the hands of our Federal, State, and Municipal Governments in their efforts to enforce the law against these impudent and brazen would-be destroyers of the State.

The second class, which is by far the more numerous and dangerous, because it is not so outspoken, is composed not of foreign-born but largely of American-born, and, more frequently than not, its members do not even belong to the Socialist Party nor to any other revolutionary body. They can be found in the college and the school class room, the pulpits, and the editorial sanctums of daily papers and magazines. They can be found tucked away in governmental positions, Federal, State and Municipal. The labor and farm organizations also have them to cope with. The philanthropic field is a peculiarly fertile one for them. Charity workers necessarily deal with poverty; they are constantly coming into close contact with the misery and squalor of their respective communities. What is more natural than for them in time to argue that if our present institutions can produce only such conditions as those they see, the sooner they are scrap-heaped and some other system tried, the better?

This second class can be argued with and, whether convinced or not, care can be taken to see that its vicious work is neutralized by exposing the fallacies and meeting the arguments its members put forth. For instance, a stock argument which can be found in all their literature and in their public utterances is based on the assumption that under our present wage system things are rapidly becoming worse; that the rich are growing richer and the poor poorer, meaning the ultimate enslavement of the worker—all of which is based on the old cataclysmic theory of Karl Marx, and has been proven utterly false and admitted to be false by even socialist writers themselves; but this means nothing to the average socialist, who repeats it parrot-like just the same. One hears continually from them the expression, "as long as we are under the present competitive system," or "the present wage system" or "the present capitalistic system," nothing better can be expected than the great poverty we see all around us. When we ask them what system they propose to substitute, they will not make a direct reply; they say that "the old order" is past, and that they want "a new order"; when further pressed, it is easy to see that they have in mind some kind of a "co-operative commonwealth" or some fantastic socialist guild idea, which system was discarded centuries ago.

Now, the way to confound these promoters of socialism is to cross-examine them on the actual facts about the *present* system—the progress that has been made under it, whether they call it "the present régime," "the wage system," "the capitalistic system," or what not. Then the amazing discovery is made that they know little or nothing about it, save what they have gathered from socialist muck-rakers, who in turn have based much of their output on alleged statistics gotten out by socialist statisticians, whose figures are generally vitiated by their philosophy that everything that is is wrong and that the sooner things get worse, the better, so that the revolution can the sooner come and we can begin all over again!

Nothing so upsets these people who are denouncing the "terrible industrial conditions of this country" as to confront them with the facts regarding the industrial, political and social progress actually made. For instance, tell them what has been accomplished in the last fifty years by the labor movement alone in the matter of improvement in wages, hours of labor and conditions of living and employment. Show them that the labor legislation enacted within the last fifteen years—not even suspended during the war—is of itself a crushing argument against those who want to substitute for our institutions a nebulous form of government under the rule of a dictator of the Lenine or Trotzky type, and that the factory legislation alone in the last twenty years has revolutionized the methods of state sanitation in the workshops of the country and is safeguarding the lives and limbs of the workers today in a manner that was not dreamed of fifty years ago. Call their attention to the fact that not so very long ago it was a penal offense for a man to join a labor organization or for workers to ask collectively for an increase in wages, while now a mere declaration from the officials of the trade unions that they are going into politics is sufficient to create consternation in both political camps.

Show these scoffers what has been accomplished in practically every state in the Union in the matter of reducing hours of labor for women and children. Point out that in the last twenty-five years 95 per cent of all child workers under fourteen years of age—the requirements of the Model Child Labor Bill—have disappeared from the factories, mines and mills of the country; that 85 per cent of the ill-smelling sweatshops and reeking tenement houses have been abolished. Call attention to what has been achieved by employers, even in the last decade, in the matter of increased provision for the welfare of their employees through sanitary and safe work places, opportunities for recreation and education, model houses rented and sold, and relief funds for sickness, accident and death benefits, as well as voluntary old age pensions—all affecting millions of railroad, factory and department store workers. Call attention to the complete reversal in the matter of dealing with accidents in industry when Workmen's Compensation Acts took the place of the Employers' Liability laws in over forty states, the former placing the burden on the industry, while the latter placed it upon the worker. Point out the magnitude and usefulness of the health organizations, public and private, devoted to securing more efficient methods of sanitation and the prevention of disease, and in this connection refer to the fact that the death rate in New York and Chicago in 1919 was the lowest ever known in those cities.

Tell them the great work being done by the Rockefeller and Carnegie hundreds of millions of dollars in the interest of humanitarianism, a mere enumeration of the subjects dealt with staggering the mind to contemplate.

Call attention to our public school system and other educational institutions enabling the children in this country today to receive twelve times as much free schooling as was enjoyed by their grandparents—which factor in our advancement, by the way, also accounts for much of the normal unrest, without which no progress could come.

There are a hundred other reforms in the industrial world alone which could be cited to confute those who are railing at our institutions. But we must not forget that there are other fields where astounding progress has been made. Cases in point are the political reform that has come through the institution of the Australian ballot and the abolition of the free-for-all primaries; the change in the public attitude toward Civil Service reform, which was opposed by nearly everyone except the cranks twenty-five years ago, whereas today the two great political parties vie with each other in seeing which can secure its greater extension. Then there are the reform of legal procedure, wiping out unnecessary delays and cost of litigation to the poor; the revolutionary changes that have come about in the regulation of food and drugs; the institution of the rural free delivery, the postal savings banks, the parcel post, and so forth and so forth.

Ask them to consider the improvements that have come in the farming world. Tell them of the six and a half million farm owners. Show them the improvement in the standard of living among the farmers, not forgetting the hundreds of thousands of automobiles they own and their up-to-date labor-saving machinery, which was unheard of fifty years ago. Also bring in something about the hundreds of thousands of stockholders in our railroad companies and large industrial corporations and the millions of savings bank depositors, showing an increasing distribution of wealth and not its concentration in a few hands, as charged by the socialist agitators.

Point out that within the last twenty-five years there has been a remarkable gain in the popular concept of the rightful relation of industrial, railway and municipal utility corporations to the public. Twenty-five years ago they owned the country. Today—and in this I am not referring to the serious situation growing out of the war—the corporations have learned that they are the servants and not the masters of the public. And, strange to say, they now admit the justice of this reversal of attitude.

The abolition of rebates and free passes, and the placing of railroad, telegraph, telephone and express companies absolutely under the regulatory power of the Interstate Commerce Commission are changes that also have come about in the last twenty-five years.

I could go on indefinitely enumerating reforms such as the foregoing, which need only to be mentioned to be recognized but which the scoffers at the present régime have forgotten or deliberately ignored.

Last but not least, call attention to the thousands of women's clubs, the boards of trade and chambers of commerce, the thousands of labor and farm organizations, fraternal societies and church organizations—all working to improve conditions, and deserving the credit for the great progress referred to above.

Also tell the detractors that while the progress made has been so tremendous, you realize that along none of these lines has the ideal yet been reached; that there are yet many dark places and perplexing problems demanding attention on the part of those who love their fellow-men; but that the same courage, intelligence and humanitarianism that have accomplished so much will not now falter but will press forward, and with greater vigor than before, to the end that tomorrow will be a better day and tomorrow's morrow a still better day.

Then point out how foolish it would be to destroy a system that had accomplished so much good in a few decades and to substitute a socialist régime which has made such a horrible mess of things in Russia, for Bolshevism is only Socialism in action.

So sure am I of the effectiveness of such a method of treatment that I would suggest that one of the things which this body could undertake would be a survey of the actual progress made, industrially, politically and socially, at the same time pointing out what remains to be done, resolving that we will turn our energies toward the removal of the remaining ills.

In other words, I would start a campaign to Americanize the Americans, by showing just what has been accomplished under the present system, of which in the nature of things they know little except what has been told them by those who paint conditions in the darkest hues.

BRITISH CAMPAIGN

Under the leadership of Rudyard Kipling, Sir Rider Haggard and other distinguished men, an association known as the Liberty League has been formed in England with the purpose of combatting the advance of Bolshevism in the United Kingdom and throughout the Empire. In a communication sent to the press the following signed declaration appears:

> Bolshevism is the reverse of all that mankind has built up of good by nearly two thousand years of effort. It is the Sermon on the Mount writ backward. It has led to bloodshed and torture, rapine and destruction. It repudiates God and would build its own throne upon the basest passions of mankind. There are some misguided people of righteous instincts in this country who believe in Bolshevism; there are others who have been influenced by secret funds.
>
> We, the undersigned, and those we represent, being assured that if it is allowed to conquer it will mean in the end the destruction of individual rights, the family, the nation, and the whole British Commonwealth, together with the handing over of all we hold sacred into the power of those foes who stand behind and perhaps have fashioned this monstrous organization, appeal through you to the people of the Empire to aid in expelling its doctrines from their midst.

Loyalty to Constitution Test in Education

IPERATIVE NEED OF SUCH EXAMINATION OF TEXT BOOKS USED IN PUBLIC SCHOOLS AND COLLEGES AS THE NATIONAL CIVIC FEDERATION PROPOSES

By TALCOTT WILLIAMS

HE school book decides teaching. Teaching and school books decide alike the knowledge and the thinking of the child. What the child knows and thinks, the er will decide fifteen to three years hence, as ool children from six to eighteen years old, om the elementary grades to the end of the gh school, reach twenty-one. Put it into the hool and it will come out in the nation, what-er it may be.

As about nine-tenths of those who go to the iblic schools are in the elementary and gramar grades, the character of the teaching in the hool books used has never been of much conseience or directed to any special discussion or iestion. How much can be done even here, wever, is apparent when it is remembered at a few women in the Women's Christian emperance Union, just forty years ago, began e fight which is consummated today in the iumph of prohibition by getting one legislaıre after another to pass a law requiring the aching of the deleterious effect of alcohol as a pic in the text books on physiology used in the ementary and grammar schools.

If this is true of primary and grammar hools in their school books on subjects like ithmetic, grammar, geography, physiology, ıd short and arid histories, it is still more true high schools. The pick of the public schools to these. High schools are called "the colges of the people." They are more than that. hey are character makers. Between the ages f fourteen and eighteen character is made, not o change again.

The principal result is that in the primary nd grammar school what is put in comes out in he mass of voters. It is possible to take some ingle evil like alcohol and attack it there. It s not easy, and it has not so far proved pracicable to deal with those subjects which equire maturity, knowledge and the mind which comes from the fourteenth year or hereabouts. Such subjects are taught in very high school. They must be. They hould be. And the high school sends out in its our years ten-fold as many as the college and urnishes, under the present conditions of Amercan life, at least ten-fold as many young men ınd women who lead the communities in which hey live. The college graduate occupies a more onspicuous place. The high school graduate is ıearer to the leadership of those small social roups formed by trade, economic opportunity, listribution, transportation, and all the various ınits which constitute that great organization which we call "society" in its largest and ullest sense. Give a bent to the mind between he ages of fourteen and eighteen and, if it be wrong bent, it is doubtful whether any hamnering in active life will ever straighten the varp given.

Very few in this country fully appreciated his, until the Great War came. There has never ɔeen a war which, like it, was a struggle for the oundations of society. Instantly it became clear o every one that in such a struggle the future afety of the Republic, as it was founded by he fathers, as it has been developed by the ons, and as it is beloved by its citizens, might e undermined by the teaching of history, poitical economy, economics and various studies n which the manifold problems of social relaions come before the minds of men and women ıt the threshold of active life.

The way in which these topics are taught in he high schools is of overmastering national importance. These schools are paid by taxation. Every citizen who owns property contributes to them. In most of our American states very nearly one-half of our citizens own property which directly pays a tax. The opinions of the citizenry of the land differ on these issues. These opinions ought to differ. The United States will be a mere stagnant pool, instead of a rushing stream, growing larger with each decade and carrying life and prosperity over every plain which it waters with its fruitful tide, unless this stream is open to new ideas and discusses new projects, is willing to know all that is in doubt or in question. It is also true, and the purpose of the American people, that the high school shall be used for the propaganda of no sect in religion and of no kind of opinion not consonant with our opinions, in teaching lessons of history, expounding the economic action of the community or informing students of the government under which they live. Every good school is a moral institution of the highest order and no more vital code of morals does a pupil come in contact with than the life and example and utterances of a good teacher. But the American public long since decided that it would not permit the teaching of morals to run into the teaching of any particular faith or any particular religion.

This sound doctrine has been applied to subjects which come close to religion and teach conduct, which is, after all, the heart of all religion. Sound at this point, this principle needs to be applied also to every subject taught in the high school or in the grades below the high school. In all of them, exactly as the teacher is not permitted in dealing with conduct and the inner life, to add or tincture by his personal religion the method by which the teacher himself or herself explains and sustains these things in his or her personal life, so, in using history as a guide to the present, in analyzing the economic operations of our system, in teaching history and in dealing with the relations of men and women to the family, teaching governments, its laws, its legislatures, its courts, its constitutions and the final authority of the people, these things ought to be so taught that, as was found necessary in the other field, the guides and metes and bounds of this teaching shall be those things on which all are agreed. These all have their shape and record in the State Constitutions and the Federal Constitution which the American people have established.

This is the test by which the teaching of these subjects must be judged. This teaching must be such as a people desire. Men and women can take up any of these problems and deal with them, discuss them, arrive at new conclusions and go before the American people asking for the adoption of those conclusions. This is the right of every citizen; but every citizen has also the right to ask, exactly as he is unwilling to have even his own religion taught in the public school at the public expense, so his special opinions on any of these subjects, however valuable they may be in the future, however he may advocate them in the present, shall not be taught, but the instruction in the public school in all grades, but most of all in the high school, shall be required to be, in the criterion of Jefferson, "loyal to the Constitution of the United States," the Constitution whose purpose, as stated in the first sentence, is "to form a more perfect union."

With this principle and under this principle, it is not only salutary but necessary that the school books used in our high schools, and in general in our schools, shall, from time to time, receive careful examination. They have had none heretofore. The selection of school books is one of the least agreeable aspects of American public education. Great corporations, rival corporations, to whom the selection of a school book means profits running into millions, are confessedly using every agency open to honest men—and in some cases agencies not in that category—to secure the adoption of a particular book. The states which print their own books find themselves in the meshes of a great educational system without the agencies by which they can judge the school books which they publish. Every school board, township, town, municipality and state is besieged with the pleas of publishers. In a big state it means instant fortune to have a particular history adopted. Some choice is left to the teacher but there, too, the decision is influenced by the zeal which a particular individual teacher, man or woman, has shown for the works of one firm or the publications of another corporation. If the only authority which selected school books was the teaching staff of the schools, matters would be better. True and loyal is this staff, with a few exceptions, so few that those who are treacherous to our institutions, being exposed, become at once notorious on exposure. The educational expert is almost always a man who has studied many phases of each subject and seeks an impartial presentation in consonance with the agencies who are working in American institutions in all fields.

Only such books should be used; only such should be open to the choice of the teacher; only such teaching should be permitted in our high schools. Even in our colleges a line ought to be drawn between the opinions men hold and the teaching they give, precisely similar to the line which is drawn in teaching morals between the religious opinions on which these morals are based and the code of morals which the American people supports and desires to have taught in the schools, which its taxes sustain and in which all its children receive their first and most lasting impressions. An examination should be held which shall decide first, whether the school books of the high school and, next, the school books below the high school and above it, accept the law of the land as expressed in our Constitution and in the working of administrative, economic and social life as ordained by the American people, or whether, instead, they are endeavoring to subvert the opinion of the American people by discussion under the unchallenged autocracy of the teacher, whose pupils are, in the nature of things, unable to argue with him.

The National Civic Federation proposes to take up this question dispassionately, to examine text books in the light of American principles and to expose those things which are contrary to the convictions and the practice of the American people by law established and declared. Nothing will be done except by those competent to pass an opinion. No decision will be reached except to sustain such a judgment. Sound text books there are in abundance. Those who are seeking to de-Americanize our institutions and to sap the foundations of the Constitution in and under which the American people lives, are few, but they demand exposure and exclusion, lest liberty and human rights and the rule of the majority be wounded to death in the house of their friends, the public schools of America.

The Dishonesty of the Socialist Mind

By GERTRUDE ATHERTON

In the following communication, which comes as an answer to a letter written to Gertrude Atherton regarding the unduly advertised alleged endorsement by her of Upton Sinclair's book, "Jimmy Higgins," a gross libel on the American army, the celebrated novelist applies to the Socialists and ultra-radicals that quality of psychological analysis which has marked her delineation of human character in her books and has placed her among the greatest of modern novelists, not only of America but of the world. Mrs. Atherton's succinct observations are in timely order, and may help to make clear to those not yet "wise," the mysterious processes of New Republic, Nation, Dial and Survey cerebration.

EDITOR.

Editor THE NATIONAL CIVIC FEDERATION REVIEW:

You reproach me for "endorsing" Upton Sinclair's book, "Jimmie Higgins." Permit me to explain how and why I did nothing of the sort.

I have never happened to meet Mr. Sinclair, but I liked his attitude in seceding from the disloyal Socialist party when we entered the war; and when he sent me a copy of a little weekly paper he was publishing, called by his name and breathing the most patriotic sentiments, I thought he should be encouraged and sent him a subscription for five years. An intermittent correspondence ensued.

I read the first three or four installments of "Jimmie Higgins" with a good deal of interest, for it was a glimpse of a life that was novel to me, and I am always curious about anything new. I wrote him to that effect, and it was this brief and not over enthusiastic letter that he used for advertising purposes later.

But the constant repetition soon wearied me. I found the story as it progressed dull and uninspiring, and after the fourth or fifth week I ceased to read it. I never looked at it again, although two copies of the book were sent to me.

Now comes the point. Mr. Sinclair merged his paper with that of a radical weekly, calling one page after himself and continuing to air his views. This paper was sent to me, a compliment, no doubt, to my former subscription.

I soon perceived that he was developing a sympathy for Bolshevism, but paid no attention for a time, as so many sentimental half-baked, second-rate minds were going off half cocked. One woman had said to me, shaking her head sadly: "Poor Lenine! Fighting on eighteen fronts!" Even the policy of certain of our weeklies was merely amusing at the time; they were timidly—but cannily—putting out feelers, not caring to risk loss of circulation, as Bolshevism might go by the board any moment.

But it soon became evident that Sinclair was in earnest, that this vicious experiment in Marxism appealed profoundly to his natural taste for horrors and sensationalism. Moreover, he had been a socialist for many years, and as socialism seemed to be a dead issue everywhere, outside of Russia, and as it was his expressed belief that you must be radical to be intellectual, as his highly developed publicity sense rebelled at anything resembling conservatism, and as he is moreover, excessively sentimental and weeps periodically over the woes of the working class, his conversion to Bolshevism was quite in order and become more apparent every week.

Now, as it happens, this order of mind is one for which I have an unmitigated contempt. It shows a lack of the most elemental knowledge of the logic of history, of co-ordination and foresight. It is radicalism for the sake of radicalism, because there is no other way of establishing an outstanding position, or of satisfying one's own self of superior cleverness. That is what is the matter with the *New Republic*, the *Nation* and all the rest of the hardworking second-rate intellectuals; and it is precisely the spirit that animates the callow minds of sophomores and undergrads in universities. It is the shortest and surest cut toward appearing intellectual and "advanced." The truth of the matter is, of course, that it takes a far higher order of mental endowment to be forcible and original without the cheap and easy method of radicalism. The fact that possibly the majority of the educated (or half educated!) people who go in for any sort of radicalism that happens to be fashionable at the moment, are honest and sincere, as Mr. Sinclair no doubt is, may be greatly to the credit of their hearts, but sadly interferes with the reputation of their heads.

Heaven knows, no one is more dissatisfied with the existing order than I am. Swollen fortunes are an outrage on democracy, and the word "strike" never would have been invented if the employing class could have curbed their greed and love of power. Poverty is a greater disgrace to the world than war; and injustice, in its every manifestation, is the fundamental cause of all the misery in the world. It is possible that the grievous faults of our present civilization may be rectified under the constitution which has fostered their growth, but if this is not to be, and some prophet will appear with a revolutionary slogan that promises better things for *all classes*, I shall be the first to enroll under his banner. But so far, not a single radical suggestion for change in the existing order of things, from the program of the revengeful Marx, foaming with class hatred, down to these last fantastic developments of his misbegotten theories which would turn the United States with its enormous middle class over to the proletariat, has promised the betterment of human conditions. Every revolutionary program now before the public denotes a poverty-stricken mind—except in those instances where it is the frank expression of a cynical and blatant selfishness. Far from promising us better things, we may well anticipate the worst if radicalism ever gets its way in this country.

Therefore, as may be imagined, after Mr. Sinclair had reiterated "I am not a Bolshevik, but—" some six or eight times, I wrote and told him what I thought of him, and added that this was my last letter; nor did I wish to hear from him again. I stated in no measured terms that I regarded the Bolshevik movement as the most stupid, the most unintelligent, with which civilization had yet been cursed, and had no respect for any one that endorsed it.

It never occurred to me that anybody with a spark of natural pride would use my name for self-advertising purposes after such a letter, or I should have warned his publishers, Messrs. Boni and Liveright, whom I happen to know personally. When I saw their advertisement I was both astounded and furious, and called up Mr. Liveright at once. He said that Mr. Sinclair had sent him the extract from my letter, with the assurance that he had my permission to use it. Mr. Liveright was very much disturbed and withdrew the advertisement at once.

When I was in Los Angeles last August—and some time after this episode—a youthful aspirant to literary honors wrote and asked me if I would not endorse his book so that he could send out slips to a large number of addresses, as Mr. Sinclair was doing with my unfortunate lines about the first chapters of his "Jimmie Higgins." So it was apparent, that although Mr. Sinclair must have heard of my attitude from Mr. Liveright, he was continuing to use me to advertise his book.

I must confess that this sort of psychology is beyond my powers of analysis. It seems to me that the only attitude possible after such a letter as I wrote the man was a lofty disdain, an immediate obliteration of my very name from the slate of his consciousness.

Is it possible that any mind is utterly without pride, or that pride may be cynically subordinated to a grim determination for publicity at any cost? Is it a fault of upbringing, the absence of a code instilled early in life, an entire ignorance of *noblesse oblige?* I confess, I give it up.

There is another point that may as well be mentioned here, if I have not consumed too much space already.

It seems that in the last chapters of "Jimmie Higgins" the hero, now, a soldier with the American forces in Siberia, is hung up by his thumbs and treated to other ingenious cruelties by his superior officer. Several of the newspapers, including the *New York Times*, remarked that the author should be prosecuted for libel.

Some time after there was an official investigation into the disciplinary methods of certain of our officers in Siberia, and the fact was given to the world that unethical modes of punishment had been practised. Whereupon, Mr. Sinclair wrote a triumphant letter to the *Times*, which they published, with tongue in cheek.

For, this is the point—although a man of Mr. Sinclair's warped mentality probably never could be made to see it: He had taken an isolated instance and inserted it in a work of fiction as typical. Probably not more than two or three of our officers were guilty of such practices, and I would be willing to swear that they were none of them West Pointers, but men who were having their first taste of authority. Every working man will tell you that the most brutal foremen are those that have risen from the lowest ranks, and that the most tyrannical employers of labor were once laborers themselves.

The socialist mind is essentially dishonest, although in the case of the finer breed of socialists not consciously so; but this subconscious dishonesty (the natural result of a weak cause) leads them to play up one side of any occurence that gives them a momentary advantage, and to ignore the whole truth. It is especially unfortunate in Mr. Sinclair's case, for he has a considerable gift for fiction, and his mental lopsidedness will exclude him from even a second-rate position in American letters, unless he reforms. There is a certain light and fire in most of his books (entirely absent from "Jimmie Higgins") that carries you along in spite of the frequent lapses of taste; but this same absorption in theme, particularly if there is an opportunity to excoriate some one or some thing, has stunted his artistic development, and has even prevented him from becoming a good craftsman. If "Jimmie Higgins" had possessed art and craft, or even the power to interest, as "King Coal" did, for instance, it would have done incalculable harm, but as it is, no one will read it outside of select Bolshevik circles; and the publisher (who had not read the end, by the way, when he signed the contract) will be the chief sufferer.

Personally, I am glad of an opportunity to explain the misuse of my name in advertising a book which I was unable to finish.

GERTRUDE ATHERTON.

Somewhere-in-California.

Tyrrel Print, New York.

The National
Civic Federation Review

Vol. V NEW YORK, MAY 10, 1920 No. 3

"THE BIG FOUR" WIN VICTORY

HOLD NINETY PER CENT OF MEMBERSHIP OF RAILWAY BROTHERHOODS AGAINST OUTLAW MOVEMENT AIMING TO DESTROY ORGANIZATIONS AND PROMOTE "ONE BIG UNION"

By WILLIAM C. ROBERTS

THE strike of railroad employes in the transportation service established two facts. That organization of labor is necessary and that the needs of the workers must be considered justly and without delay.

The fact that the railroad employes were organized and had strong leaders prevented the spread of the "wildcat" strike. The delay of the Government and railroad officials in answering the appeals for higher wages was responsible for the strike.

If it had not been for the discipline secured through years of organization by the brotherhoods the strike would have been nationwide instead of being confined to a number of industrial centers.

For more than a year the railroad employes had appealed time and again to the Railroad Administration for increases of wages that would meet the continued advance in the cost of the necessaries of life. But month after month passed without an answer to the appeal from the Railroad Administration. The situation became similar to a law suit in court. The Railroad Administration used its efforts in putting off from month to month any decision as to wage increases. While admitting that the demands for more money were just, the idea seemed to be to drift along until after the railroads had been turned over to the owners.

When it is known that the railroad employes up to 1917 never had received anything near a proper wage scale, and that the additions then received were inadequate, it cannot be wondered why demands for a strike became insistent during the summer months of 1919.

Appeals were made to President Wilson for relief. He was told that a strike of both brotherhoods and shopmen was inevitable unless a wage sufficient to meet the high cost of living was conceded by the Railroad Administration. President Wilson in a public letter stated that the cost of living would recede and urged that the men remain at work. He contended that the cost of living would be reduced and gave as his authority the Department of Justice. The railroad employes, always loyal to their country, agreed to call off the strike. This was done. Everybody continued at work and watched the price barometer on the necessaries of life. Instead of falling it continued to rise and is still going up.

Then the railroads were turned back to their owners under a law which provided that all disputes over wages should be considered by a Labor Board to be appointed by the President.

There was much dissatisfaction among the railroad workers throughout the country and this was intensified as day after day passed and no Labor Board was appointed. The men in the yard service began to charge that it was their officials who were responsible for the delay in securing an increase in wages, that if they had done their duty and called a strike the whole matter would have been settled long ago. This strike sentiment had been long withheld. The yardmen in the various terminals had voted to strike in February last if their wages were not increased. This would have been a legal strike. As time passed and nothing was done they began unjustly to attack the chief executives of the

W. S. STONE
Grand Chief Engineer, Brotherhood of Locomotive Engineers

W. G. LEE
President, Brotherhood Railroad Trainmen

L. E. SHEPPARD
President, Order Railroad Conductors

W. S. CARTER
President, Brotherhood Locomotive Firemen and Enginemen

brotherhoods. The latter were blamed for the delay.

This sentiment was so extensive that when the brotherhoods' chief executives met in Washington in February some of them believed that it would be impossible to hold their members in their employment unless there was quick action on wages.

It is not generally known, but it is a fact, that the Brotherhood of Railroad Trainmen was prepared to call a strike February 23, 1920. They had given the Railroad Administration the regular thirty-day notice that its contract with the railroads would terminate February 23. The sentiment for a strike was very strong and general. A committee with full power to order the strike was in Washington. The rank and file of the Brotherhood of Railroad Trainmen were continually sending telegrams to President W. G. Lee, demanding that a strike be called unless concessions in wages were granted. President Lee was much concerned. Before he left Cleveland he was certain that a strike would be called. He had no hope of securing any concessions. In fact the twenty members of the committee, which had full authority to call the strike, all felt the seriousness of the situation. They had arranged their financial affairs so that in the event the strike was called and the Attorney General of the United States began proceedings the courts could not touch their property or funds.

When the trainmen's committee arrived in Washington the members refused to join with the shopmen and other trades in a letter to the Railroad Administration and later to the President. President Lee and the committee demanded a separate hearing from Director General Walker D. Hines and in that conference Mr. Lee, after increases were refused, declared he feared that a strike could not be prevented. The chief executives of all the other organizations urged the trainmen's committee to await the action of the President, who had promised that in the event no law was enacted covering the issue he would appoint a commission to settle the wage dispute. He had pledged that this commission would act immediately. But a law was enacted and President Lee appeared before the trainmen's committee, whose members were still rebellious, and asked that they agree to cancel the contemplated strike. The members refused.

This conference was held in the National Hotel in Washington. Then Lee, it is stated in labor circles, told the members of the committee:

"The constitution gives this committee full power to call the strike. Now, you choose a man to lead this strike and I will back him, but I will not conduct it myself." This changed the sentiment of the members and they voted to accept the recommendations of President Lee and cancelled the strike order.

When these facts became known among the rank and file there was a great uproar. A leader of the insurgents appeared in Chicago and denounced President Lee, and the yardmen declared for a strike. The meeting which favored the strike was unauthorized and contrary to the constitution of the Brotherhood of Railroad Trainmen. The strike began the first week in April.

While President Lee and the other brotherhood officials had done everything they possibly could to secure wage increases, spent day after day in Washington appealing to the administration, they were unsuccessful. Instead of directing their antipathies to the Railroad Administration the insurgents blamed the chief executives for their troubles. They denounced the Brotherhood of Railroad Trainmen as well as the other brotherhoods and their officials and declared for a new organization. At a meeting held April 9 in Washington the chief executives of the big four brotherhoods issued the following statement:

> The present strike of men engaged in switching service was originated in Chicago by a new organization that has for its purpose the destruction of the Brotherhood of Railroad Trainmen and the Switchmen's Union and in its inception had nothing to do with the wage question, but was a demand for the reinstatement of the leader of this opposition organization. After this strike was instituted for this purpose, the leaders of the new organization then injected the wage question for the sole purpose of deceiving the yard men throughout the United States and promote the "one big union" idea.
>
> There can be no settlement of pending wage questions while this illegal action continues. We insist that every member of these brotherhoods do everything within his power to preserve their existing contracts, which if abrogated may take years to rebuild. The laws of all of these organizations provide penalties for members engaging in illegal strikes, and these penalties will be enforced.
>
> (Signed) L. E. SHEPPARD, President Order Railroad Conductors; W. G. LEE, President Brotherhood Railroad Trainmen; W. S. STONE, Grand Chief Engineer, Brotherhood of Locomotive Engineers; W. S. CARTER, President Brotherhood Locomotive Firemen and Enginemen."

President Lee made an additional statement in which he pointed out to the yardmen that the only hope of securing an additional increase in wages was through the Labor Board which had been created by law. He said:

"The fifteen railroad labor organizations have entered into a signed agreement to present their wage demands to such board, according to the law, and it is unreasonable to expect that any increase will be granted except by the board."

But there was no board then in existence. The President had failed to make the appointments, although urgent requests were coming from all parts of the country as well as from the chief executives of the brotherhoods. The failure of appointing the board immediately after the law was enacted stirred the insurgents and made their agitation for a strike more successful.

President Lee revoked the charters of lodges having an aggregate of 18,000 members. The railroads set a date when the strikers should return to work or be barred from their seniority. While many returned to work quite a number remained out.

While the strike was in progress the 600,000 railroad shopmen in the United States, the telegraphers and railway clerks remained at work. While their grievances were as great as those of the switchmen, they listened to their officials and agreed to wait until the Labor Board could act.

These facts prove that if it were not for the discipline of the organizations ninety per cent. of the employes who were seeking wage advances would have joined the strike. Nothing could have held them. It was only the influence of their organizations that prevented them from quitting work.

Since the Labor Board was appointed and began its hearings on the wage increases desired, much concern has been created by the evident intent of the railroad officials to delay as much as possible any awards being made. They appeared before the board with what appeared a very innocent request which, if adopted, would delay a decision for a year or more. This was that every railroad should be sent a questionnaire regarding the issues at stake. This was to be a complicated affair and would require much time to answer. The plan was bitterly fought by the brotherhoods' officials.

In the present case the Labor Board is an arbitration board. Arbitration to the railroad employe is not a fascinating word. The firemen and engineers a few years ago spent half a million dollars preparing a case which required several months of hearings, and the award was so objectionable that at that time it was said the engineers and firemen never would submit to arbitration again. If the Labor Board persists in delaying a decision the danger of further illegal strikes will increase daily.

It is the duty of the public to support the chief executives of the railroad brotherhoods and the shopmen in their efforts to maintain peace until an award has been made. Where so many men are involved it is not surprising that a number of them will "jump the traces" and cease work.

Much credit is due to President Lee that under the circumstances fewer men joined the unauthorized strike. It establishes the fact that his administration has proved effective. Mr. Timothy Shea, acting president of the Brotherhood of Locomotive Firemen and Enginemen, also had a difficult problem. The locomotive firemen were restless and it was only by using every influence possible that so few members of that organization joined the "wildcat" strike.

The Brotherhood of Locomotive Engineers and the Order of Railroad Conductors were not materially affected. Warren S. Stone, grand chief of the Engineers, and L. E. Sheppard, president of the Conductors, laid the failure to affect their members to the discipline of long organization.

The strike teaches a lesson. If the railroad employes had been unorganized and had been drifted along from day to day and year to year with the hope that they would secure an increase in wages some time they would have rebelled long ago.

No more loyal citizens than the railroad employes can be found in the United States. No others were more concerned in winning the war. They had grievances unnumbered, but they were placed in the background while the nation was fighting for the freedom of not only itself but the rest of the world. They believed, and justly, that they should receive proper recognition for their grievances. They did not expect delay. They did not realize that a persistent propaganda had been launched to discredit the railroad workers.

There is no intention to defend the strikers. There should be only condemnation for men who violate their obligations to their organizations. The intent is to point out that were it not for organized labor in peace time as well as in war there would be continual strife in the industrial field. Where men are unorganized they are voiceless. They have no method of preparing their grievances collectively. Naturally, they become morose, sullen and finally stampede from their employment like cattle from a prairie fire. They are heedless of the future and think only of their grievances.

The present strike is similar to that of the American Railway Union in 1894. In that strike Debs expected to unite all the railroad workers into the American Railway Union. The success of his organization meant the downfall of the railroad brotherhoods. But the brotherhoods stood firm and although greatly injured by that strike they gradually recovered. Debs' idea of "one big union" proved to be ineffective. The present insurgent movement against the four brotherhoods will also fail.

In the meantime the railroad employes and the public should support the chosen officials of the four brotherhoods. While they are not responsible for the present wage situation, in fact have exhausted every means except endorsing a strike to secure advances in wages, they have believed in an orderly way of obtaining results.

The strike is also a warning to the Government officials that they cannot dillydally with questions that govern the economic conditions of the people. It is also a warning to the officials who are now operating the railroads that they must listen to the just grievances of the employes. Unless they do there is no telling how soon the strike spirit will spread among those who refused to join the present unauthorized walkout.

One thing is certain. The railroad brotherhoods will recover from the effects of the strike and will grow stronger and stronger until such illegal walkouts will be impossible.

Shop Industrial Training

TS RELATION TO MAXIMUM PRODUCTION—HIGH COST OF LIVING REDUCTION—CONTENTMENT IN EMPLOYMENT—HELPING TO SUPPLY WORLD'S NECESSARIES

(*Discussion at Annual Meeting The National Civic Federation, January 29, 1920*)

UDGE ALTON B. PARKER, the Federation's President, presided at the annual meeting session on "Increased Production through Shop Industrial Training" and, in making he opening statement, referred to that part of he report of the Woman's Department concernng the effort to secure adequate salaries for ublic school teachers, saying:

"I listened to a very prominent member of ur educational system in this city the other ight and he spoke of the fact that we are not ow receiving from the great women's colleges f this country any recruits to our educational orce in New York; that in the past we were ccustomed to receive them because the wages aid here were as fair and as good as they were nywhere else but that today the wages are bout half what a good stenographer gets in the ffices downtown and, therefore, they do not ome and there has been no recruit added to our eaching force from those great colleges. But here have been teachers! There is no trouble, e said, about getting teachers, teachers who could pass the examinations all right—equipped intellectually. But the great majority of them are from Russia.

"Well, now, really, it didn't occur to me, when I listened to it, that we ought to do very much to favor the development of the Russian idea of government, at least in our school system!'

ALLEN WALKER, of the Foreign Department, Guaranty Trust Company, New York, in dealing with his subject, "Why Production?" made the following statements:

"There is need for universal recognition of the fact that the whole problem of minimum expenditure and maximum production today is not exclusively that of the economist, the financier or the government legislator or administrator. It is every man's problem. There never was a time in the history of the world when it was such a vital question with us all as it is today. Most of the world at this hour finds its financial structure weakened, stocks exhausted, productive forces impaired, its inhabitants agitated by polical unrest; conditions which impose upon us a responsibility quite out of proportion to anything in past experience.

"A great many thoughtful men lately have been giving their minds to the solution of the great economic problems with which we have been brought face to face, and in the last analysis there is but one common verdict—increased production. Every wage earner, every housewife, every home builder is crying out against the abnormally high prices for the necessities of the breakfast table. The manufacturer and the producer of raw materials seek monetary facilities for necessary expansion and find their operations restricted because of tight money, which means limited financial resources everywhere. There is but one answer—increased production. We are asked to find the means of extending credits to Europe in order that lives may be saved and the wheels of industry kept going. The same answer always—increased production. Under-production is not limited to a local or even a national malady. It is a worldwide condition at this moment; everywhere the demand exceeds the supply. World consumption has increased to the most amazing degree during the past few years. There is little fear of our catching up quickly or of reaching any market where the supply may exceed the demand, especially in this country.

"We cannot find money to help reconstruct the world and simultaneously spend our earnings in luxuries which are beyond the means of the prudent and thrifty. We cannot listen to the demand for 6-hour days and 5-day weeks and still hope to produce the materials for our own needs, let alone what the world requires of us. Neutral countries are sending raw materials into Germany with a pledged lien on the finished product, in response to the German request that she shall have an opportunity to employ her people and start her factories going. It is reported that the German workers are pledging themselves, through their local organizations, to be satisfied with a 10-hour day, and that in many places they are urging a 12- and 16-hour day, until the peak of reconstruction be reached. I, for one, am not an advocate of any speeding-up processes calculated to be harmful to the health and general welfare of the individual, but I would suggest that if these reports be true—if Germany does this—and in the meantime we, in America, are content to witness a gradual shortening of working hours and automatically restrict our production thereby, who, in the last analysis, will have won the war?

"What the country needs as much as anything else is an invasion of common sense. A condition of half-strike, half producing, *all* consuming, cannot endure. Five minutes of restraint from purchasing what you can do without at this time is worth ten years of cussing the profiteer. During the war universally we were inspired to put every ounce of energy into the raising of men, money and materials and into organizing the nation to go out and destroy militant life. Now, we are called upon to produce in order that we may lend money and send the products of every man's brains and arms to save life and preserve civilization.

"No thoughtful American industrialist has ever quarreled with high wages, high, let us say, in comparison with wages paid for similar work in other parts of the world. For many years the wages paid to American railroad men have been considerably higher than those paid to railroad employees anywhere else on the face of the globe, yet we have been able to carry a ton of freight per mile cheaper than the railroads of any other country. It is the tendency to decrease production that the patriotic American citizen quarrels with today. However many and whatever be the theories offered for the solution of the vexing problems facing us today, I hold that there are two maxims which if universally and effectively applied will solve most of our difficulties both here and in every other part of the world. They may be embraced under the two words "Save" and "Produce"—and above all, in God's name, let us *produce*!"

HUGH FRAYNE, of Scranton, Pennsylvania, General Organizer, American Federation of Labor, among others made the following points:

"There should be a sound and unified system of promoting vocational or industrial training throughout the country. The need for highly and specially trained workers in industry is more apparent than ever before. This is not only necessary to meet the emergency of reconstruction now but it is a fundamental that applies to the social and economic life of the country for all time.

"It is possible to increase production. I agree to that but when production is increased to the detriment of the worker, his health or general welfare, the line should be sharply drawn. People can, however, be trained or re-trained, taught to work right, that is, with the least effort and in an efficient manner. They can be trained to avoid the wrong way of doing things.

"Take a man of middle age, not an apprentice but a helper. Often he never goes beyond that point. When a man shows ability, teach him and make a good mechanic of him and train some one else below him to be a good helper.

"There is a right and a wrong way to pick up a broom or a shovel and work with it. An experienced trained man with a shovel can work as many hours as necessary without strain and do efficient work, whereas an untrained man, not knowing how, will work harder and accomplish less. This will apply to any worker who has not been properly trained in the handling and use of tools. There is a right and wrong way to sit on a chair or at a bench and work; a right and wrong way to stand at a machine and to adjust it. When properly worked out it tends to increase production without causing extreme physical strain upon the worker. This extra production should be recognized and the workers should share by an increased compensation.

"The greatness of a country can be best judged by the economic value placed upon its people. Its success is assured only when it recognizes that human life and progress are its greatest asset, all others being secondary. Opportunity for development of the workers will bring its reward as no other human force can.

"There should be a central organization or head to promote this work along safe and proper lines. There should be local advisory boards, including representatives of the industries, the employers, and organized labor, as the trade unions are a strong factor in promoting this work.

"Another problem confronting us is the proper training of the boys and girls in order that they may be fitted to enter into industry and take their places fully equipped to perform their respective tasks in a highly skilled and efficient manner so they may not only establish themselves upon higher living standards but give to industry and the country generally, the benefit of their knowledge as better trained and skilled workers. To do this, there must be a strong public sentiment aroused along educational lines.

"There are many so-called trade schools in this country where young men and women are educated in a way—taught trades and parts of trades—and turned out after a time, absolutely unfit to take their proper places in any of the trades or callings, and they become dangerous competitors of the unions who have worked to establish themselves not only as skilled in their trades but to establish a high standard of living. In many of the private trade schools I know of, employers train young men especially for their private employment and when that young man leaves that employment he is helpless to go out into the world because he is not competent to work as a skilled, efficient mechanic and command the rates established by the unions.

"I want to take this opportunity of refuting the statement, made by those who do not understand trade unions, that the unions are opposed to the American boy or girl learning a trade, but we are opposed to the exploitation of either one of them in placing them in shops and factories or schools for the purpose of specializing them in part of some trade and then sending them out in competition with skilled workmen who are the breadwinners of families. We believe that the public schools should teach the theory of the trade while the actual practice and processes should be taught in the shops. Instructions in a trade should be taught by an experienced, practical journeyman of the trade, with ability to impart knowledge. We are agreed that there should be industrial training, shop training for those who are not now trained, training for those already trained, a better training to bring them up to date, to meet present day conditions."

T. C. SPENCE, of the Norton Grinding Company, Worcester, Massachusetts, described its methods employed precedent to the introduction of the training service and especially during the war through advertising, and by sending to other communities and offering inducements to workers to change, with temporary results. He stated that through the training department, established in 1915, the company specialized in taking green workers and giving them some degree of skill in the manufacture of fine machine tools, grinding machinery and grinding wheels.

He gave as some reasons for training in a special department the following:

"First, few men have the faculty to teach. Oftentimes, the best workman is the poorest teacher. Hence it is easier to find one teacher and let him do the bulk of this work. Second, the press of output prevents a foreman, even if a good teacher, from giving proper attention to beginners; and third, it does not pay to have a high class executive foreman spend time on a beginner."

Concerning the methods employed in his plant, some statements made by Mr. Spence were that:

"We made the training school, from the beginning, a production department and not in any sense a place for practice. Every article has to be made according to the shop standards and is saleable.

"We attempt in eight or ten weeks to give beginners a fair idea of several of the main tools used in building machinery. Graduates from this department are by no means machinists but better workers than my employment man can get.

"After a worker is put on regular production, the supervisor of training follows him up for a period of about six weeks more because beginners, put into a plant in strange surroundings, lose their confidence and leave through discouragement. Periodical visits of a man, known to be their friend, straightens them out with the foreman and keeps a great percentage of them with us.

"Among these young men going through will appear the usual proportion of those who are mentally above the rest. We see to it that they are moved from one department to another. In the four years that this work has been in operation, we have raised engine supervisors, inspectors, sub-foremen—men who are on their way to be some day superintendents, managers, and owners of business.

"In addition to training manual workers, we pick up whenever we can, graduates of technical schools, colleges and ex-service men, and train them to become demonstrators, salesmen, agency workers and foreign representatives.

"As to the source of supply for this training, we get the sons of present employees, young men in the city who have heard about it through others, and daily we receive letters from fine young men in surrounding towns. We had 750 men in the war service. When those boys came back this department was a Godsend in helping to restore them to industry.

"Now, the results: At the time of the Armistice, over fifty per cent. of our people had had less than four months' experience and still we were building one of the finest machine tools in this country. Fifteen per cent. of them were women. We were very successful in training women to run machine tools.

"In 1917 and 1918, on the average, with twice the number of people we had in 1912 and 1913, we put out three times the product. Not in money; it was very much more in money; but in actual production, there was a gain of fifty per cent. per capita. Wages had increased over one hundred per cent. but direct labor cost had increased only fifty per cent. We are still gaining in production because we are gradually pushing the training idea out beyond this training department and into the main shop. We keep a record of each producer, and if he falls below a certain output—just now eighty per cent. of what we know is easily possible for an intelligent worker to produce—that man receives attention."

PERCY S. STRAUS, of R. H. Macy & Co., New York, who aided actively in developing industrial training for the war emergency in connection with the Committee on Labor of the Council of National Defense, emphasizes, in his remarks, the value of the part time continuation school, and the difficulty of convincing manufacturers of the fact that training could be introduced without much expense and to the mutual benefit of themselves and their employees. His address included the following statements:

"We did succeed—Mr. Miles, particularly, did effective work—in introducing training into some three hundred factories, but the difficulty was not to convince the workmen that it would help them, but the employer that it would pay him to start vestibule schools. Since the war, those of us who have been interested in this movement have been talking to employers.

"I am in a particularly favorable position to realize the handicap manufacturers are now working under in trying to bring their production up to the demand. There is a very large demand for merchandise of all kinds, much larger than manufacturers can meet. When, in my organization we send an order to an employer, instead of accepting it—say the order is for $25,000 or $30,000—he writes back and says, 'Your allotment for this season is $5,000 or $4,000,' or in some cases one-tenth of the order we would like to place. We ask him what his trouble is, why he cannot give us what we need, and the first answer we get is always, 'We cannot get the men to do the work.' I suggest the possibilities of training. And I am always met with the statement that the unions would not stand for training. We know perfectly well that Mr. Gompers is the one who started the movement in this country, and from Mr. Frayne's, Mr. Golden's, Mr. Sullivan's and Mr. Woll's activity in these matters, that the trade union movement is not opposed to industrial training where it is used not only to train but to upgrade and that the trade union movement favors training in factories not only to up-grade production but also to up-grade wages. If those two are combined, I cannot see that there would be any possibility of disagreement between employer and the representatives of employees on the question of training. I don't think anybody, who is interested in the social and industrial progress of the country, would care to see the present high rate of wages reduced unless the cost of living goes down before that time. But every one, who is interested in the problems of today and the cost of living and all the evils that go with it, would like to see the cost of production reduced—in other words, that the element of wage in each particular item of production be reduced, and the only possible means of doing that is by better training.

"If this movement, which the Civic Federation is trying to foster, can be brought before the employers of the country in a straightforward way, I think we can bring about a state of production and a condition in industry which will enable us to maintain the wages we are now paying and enable us to increase our output.

"At the present time, the potters of this country say they cannot meet by one-quarter the requirements of industry. They are trying to persuade the distributors to place orders with them for 1921, which is practically twelve months away, and at present day prices, with the understanding that the manufacturer has a right to increase them. The distributor has the right to accept them when given and at the price at which the manufacturer cares to sell. If the distributors throughout the country would agree to conditions of that kind, there would be no possibility of reducing the cost of manufacture and cost of living. If the manufacturer has his book full of orders for twelve months, there is no incentive to try and bring down the cost. Now, if the potters, who are able to do so, would start the introduction of training, many of the processes which they now consider can be done only by men who have been born and bred in the trade could be done by properly trained beginners and those who are now in the trade could be upgraded to do the more delicate and intricate finishing processes. But it requires a concerted movement."

JOHN GOLDEN, President, United Textile Workers of America, Fall River, Mass., spoke of his experience in connection with a commission appointed by the Governor of Massachusetts to study vocational education fourteen years ago, thus indicating his close interest in the subject over an extended period. He referred especially to defects in public school methods, and said on this point:

"In my home city of Fall River there were few boys or girls who remained in the school after they had passed the age limit of fourteen years and the mill was ready to receive them. When they came from school they knew absolutely nothing about even the stable industry of their city and I thought it would not be a bad idea, without making a workshop out of the school, to give them training a little along industrial lines.

"Well, the result of the work of that commission was that textile schools were built in most of the big textile centers, such as Fall River and New Bedford, only one having been in existence at Lowell. Working men could go there nights and Saturday afternoons and perfect their mechanical education. And it so came about that day schools were opened and the younger element could go."

Mr. Golden explained the transition, in Fall River, from plain print cloths to fancy weaves requiring new and intricate loom attachments with which the loom fixers were unfamiliar, and said:

"They had never seen the new looms or inventions and, consequently, could not fix them. Not a mill man attempted to do anything to remedy the evil. What did we do? We happened to have perhaps a dozen members in our union from England and they had had the benefit of the textile institutes there. They had known something of this new loom and this new fabric that had to be woven, and those men helped us build up a loom down in the basement of the Union Meeting Hall where our men used to spend two hours each evening learning how to fix and operate that loom.

"I have not much confidence in the man or woman who comes out with a regular cut and dried definite plan of solving this problem. It has to be worked out. You are dealing with human nature, not with the machine. I have been told: 'Here is a spinning machine, here is the size of the gear, it will go so many revolutions per minute, and consequently will produce so many thousand yards of cotton yarn.' It cannot be done, because after you have figured up that machine you have to figure up the human being that is working on it and you cannot figure up

(Continued on page 18)

Inadequency of Public School System

EDUCATIONAL PROGRAM ADOPTED AT ANNUAL MEETING OF WOMAN'S DEPARTMENT OF THE NATIONAL CIVIC FEDERATION AFTER ILLUMINATING DISCUSSION OF URGENT PROBLEMS

OF the many lessons taught by the great war, none has been more impressive than the value and necessity of the education of a nation to meet the problems of armed defense, as well as the duties of citizenship in a country at peace.

There has come with a shock to the great proportion of the American people the realization that their much-vaunted public school system has not produced the results to have been expected. The figures of the draft proved the staggering percentage of illiteracy among our men, not by any means confined to the foreign born. The growing sense of the inadequacy, under present conditions, of the school as "a melting pot" is being more definitely acknowledged, and the failure to establish in the public mind the profession of teaching as the most honorable service to be rendered to the State is reacting in the leaving of that service of over 145,000 men and women, forced out through the lack of a fair wage and a fair future in their profession.

This is, to a great extent, a woman's problem, and one in which she must take an intelligent interest. The laws governing the control of public education differ in states and communities; the length of the school year is not the same, even in adjoining states (in some only twenty-two weeks); the qualifications for teachers' certificates are not standardized; the salaries for the same beginning grade range from $284 per year to $1,500. All these matters must be intelligently adjusted; we must come to realize the weaknesses and shortcomings, not simply to criticize and condemn, but to aid in making right.

The Woman's Department of The National Civic Federation, recognizing this obligation, at its annual meeting in January, 1920, asked Dr. John R. Tildsley, Assistant Superintendent of Schools in New York City, and Miss Fannie W. Dunn, Instructor of Rural Education at Teachers College, to speak of the existing situation and the responsibilities of the ordinary citizen to the subject.

Dr. Tildsley said in part:

"Going back to actual conditions, a Government report published some three years ago estimated that the value to the nation of an educated child was something like twenty thousand dollars more during the course of that child's lifetime than the value of an uneducated child; inasmuch as the educated child had been approximately twelve years in school, a total of some twenty-four hundred days, if that twenty-four hundred days in school added an increased valuation of twenty thousand dollars, the value of a day in school is something like $9 to the child, and the value of education in the United States to the nation is something like one hundred and eighty million dollars a day; and yet that great industry—the greatest industry in this country—is on the way to being put in the hands of a receiver and is already one of those industries in which we cannot recommend our young people to engage because it is a closed alley industry.

"Education is an industry in this country, at the present time, is a parasite industry, and, as business people, you know that something is radically wrong. If you asked me, 'What are you going to do in the light of the disappearance of your skilled workmen,' and I were to tell you that although the old time workman is leaving our industry, we hope to carry it on by importing four or five hundred thousand foreigners and put them in the industry, you would stop and think a little and wonder whether this was a wise policy at the present time, even if the demand for those goods was greater than it could supply; and yet that remedy, or some such remedy, is the one that we are applying. In other words, in days gone by in this country, teaching was very largely the occupation of our native American stock, largely women, and women brought up in good surroundings. Even then, it was a parasite industry, because the ordinary young girl of seventeen or eighteen went into teaching with the idea that within four or five years she would be married, and therefore she received from teaching enough for clothes, and her father and mother paid the actual living expense.

"Now, the situation at the present time, therefore, is this: When we need more workmen, we can obtain them in two ways, following the custom of the business world. We can either raise wages, and thus secure the type of workman we need, or we can take workmen of a lower order. In the educational world there is a tendency everywhere to reduce standards, and so the result is that half the children of the United States at the present time are being taught by young people who have had no training for that work. Now, imagine any industry in this country in the hands of workmen who have not had any training for that especial work, and yet are called upon to deal with a product which can easily be spoiled forever by one of those workmen. Yet here in this great industry of ours we are putting young children in the hands of untrained workmen, under conditions that make it possible to ruin the life of that child and make him ineffective as a workman himself during the fifty years that are his normal span.

"There is no more reason why a teacher should take the vow of poverty than the plumber, the machinist, the lawyer or the business man. And they have at last awakened to that fact. The chief of the Bureau of Labor Statistics states that at the present time the minimum sum on which a man can support a wife and three children in the United States—that means as a member of the laboring class—is $1,850. Only two per cent of the teachers of the United States at the present time receive a larger salary than $1,850, and the average salary paid the teachers of the United States at the present time is $634.

"Conditions were bad enough five years ago, and the cost of living in these years has increased at least one hundred per cent. During that time the salaries of teachers in the United States have increased but twelve per cent. In 1913 an estimate was made that the absolute minimum for social efficiency at that time of any person in any industry was $1,200, and in 1919, when prices have gone up more than one hundred per cent, only twenty per cent of the teachers of the United States received salaries of over that minimum amount for social efficiency.

"The National Labor Board set $15 a week as the minimum weekly amount upon which a girl in Schenectady can live. Sixty per cent of the teachers in the United States are receiving less than this minimum amount of $780 a year, and having all the extra expense to which a teacher is put. The average wages of a machinist in Schenectady at the present time is $1,716, of a carpenter, $1,287, whereas the average salary of any high school teacher is $1,139. Do you wonder that one of our school boys, a graduate of the high school, who was expected to enter Stevens Institute last fall, when met by his teacher and asked what he was doing, said, 'I am working.' He said, 'This summer I kept the payroll and I found that a man in charge of the work, who was a graduate of the Massachusetts Institute of Technology, was making $200 a month, where some of the laborers on the job were making $85 a week, and I concluded that I couldn't afford to get an education.' Now, under these conditions, the demoralization extends in all directions. The boys and girls are coming to realize that it doesn't pay to become teachers, and as teachers on the whole are a most highly educated body of workers, they are apt to draw the conclusion that education in itself doesn't pay, while all figures are to the contrary.

"May I suggest a possible remedy for the condition? The real trouble is, at the present time, that our boards of managers have so many other interests and so many other ways for spending money that they do not spend it adequately for schools. Our boards of managers, namely, our boards of estimate throughout the country, have many other interests. For example, the other day the Board of Education in New York raised the salaries of its janitors twenty-five per cent, but they did not raise the salaries of the teachers. Why? In the first place, the janitors have a very strong organization, on a par with the steel workers' organization—a most effective one. If they had not gotten that twenty-five per cent increase in their pay, their helpers would leave and go and work in an apartment house or in a business building, and we would have our buildings with nobody caring for them, and the schools would close. So they immediately got their demands. On the other hand, our product is too far away. People don't realize that the work that is being done in the primary grade might turn out years later a spoiled product.

"We shall never have conditions right until we have boards of education in our communities, whether large or small, with absolute financial independence of the city authorities, and those boards of education must be entirely independent of other political consideration, as well. They must be either elected by the people of the community or appointed by some responsible body of citizens which shall meet for this purpose and this purpose only. In other words, in my judgment, it is not safe in this country of ours, with universal suffrage, to commit the great school system to the chance of a municipal election in a city made up, for instance as is this, so largely of foreigners.

"There is a second principle that we must realize if we are going to have an adequate school system. No community in this country can live to itself alone; it cannot be allowed by the State of which it is a part to become a plague spot which shall undermine, not only that State, but the Nation, and if there is a State so negligent, so unmindful of the absolute need of better educational methods, that it neglects its bounden duty, the nation cannot afford to allow that plague spot to exist. And so I ask you as women interested in the welfare of the State, to work first for independent boards of education made up of high-grade men and women, with complete control of the finances. I ask you to throw your support to a national movement, by which the nation itself shall aid by subsidies those states which, because of their limited resources, are not able to educate properly their children. I ask you, above all things, in your several communities, to impress upon the citizens that the greatest danger confronting the people of the United States is the gradual undermining and destruction of its educational system."

At the conclusion of Dr. Tildsley's address, Miss Dunn spoke of the situation in the rural schools. The main points of her remarks are as follows:

"The three points which have caused the public to-day to turn an anxious eye toward education are, first, the proved failure or failures of education in the past; second, the threatened bankruptcy in the future; and, third, the increased realization of the absolute necessity of education in a democracy that will stand.

"When I speak of the proven failures of education, I do not mean to say, of course, that education is an absolute failure. In spite of all its failures, education has done much for the people; but war conditions indicated that it has distinctly and specifically failed in many respects. These are: the enormous amount of illiteracy in our country, the very serious health conditions, and the failure of the melting pot to melt. You may wonder what the school has to do with physical disability. I like to think of the function of the American public school as two-fold: In the first place, it is a means of giving to every child in the nation that quality of opportunity which is our national boast; in the second place, or primarily, I should say, it is a means of preparing for adequate citizenship, for adequate workmanship in the United States, in the government of the United States, in which every one of our citizens must share, these boys and girls who are growing up among us. It is the function of education to see to it that fitness in the physical life is produced. We rejected one-third of our men from the army; they were not fit to fight. Are they fit for peace?

"The school ought at least to prevent defects from development. As a matter of fact, it has caused defects. I want you to picture with me the conditions that are found in the schools where forty-one per cent of our children are educated. The figures are something like this: About forty-one or forty-two per cent of our children are in rural schools; about the same number in city schools; and the remaining seven or eight per cent are in the schools of the small villages; and so we may say, approximately, the same number of children are in the cities and open country schools.

"In these open country schools one of the very serious defects which we find is injury to the eyes. Hygienists tell us that a school room should have one-quarter or one-fifth of its floor space in window space. Now as a matter of fact, you hardly ever find that in rural schools; a survey made in 1914 indicated that seventy per cent of the rural schools had opposite windows and sixty per cent had inadequate light! In a middle northern state a health survey was made in some schools, and it was found, in one school, that out of forty-four children, forty-two were suffering from eyestrain, and a large number of them were absolutely without sight in one eye.

"Another one of the very common defects in these schools is the seating conditions. Desks are bought because they are cheap, and they are usually bought by a school board that knows nothing whatever of the needs of children. You go into a school and you see small children with their feet dangling, and again you see large boys with their shoulders stooped and their knees crowded, and you don't wonder at the resultant spinal curvature and misshapen bodies that come out of that school. And there again you have to meet not only parsimony but ignorance of those who are dealing with the situation.

"I must speak of the ventilation. In these country schools, as a rule, they have a big stove in the centre of the room, kept very hot, so that the heat will penetrate all corners of the room. Hanging around the walls are the wraps that have been rained and snowed on as the children have come to school, and there isn't any ventilation; there is no provision for it excepting the windows, and if you open the window there is a draft, and the children are afraid of drafts; the teacher probably is, too.

"You know the relation of the schools to illiteracy and what the condition is in that regard. This obligation is absolutely recognized.

"I wonder if you know what the lowering of standards means, if you know what standards we have had for public education. I will give you the certification requirements of a certain city which is about an average. It gives three grades of certificates, a first-grade certificate that one gets by passing the examination on the elementary school branches and one or two high school branches, and on a percentage of an average of eighty-five, in no grade less than seventy or seventy-five. Now that is the first-grade certificate. When one gets a second-grade certificate, some of the high school branches are cut out and an average of seventy-five—and no grade less than sixty—is made. And there is still a third-grade certificate in which one takes absolutely nothing but the elementary school branches, and makes an average of sixty-five per cent, and no grade less than fifty per cent. Now would you like to think of a boy or a girl seventeen years old, which is the age limit at which he is supposed to begin to teach, and who has made as low as fifty per cent, teaching your children? Those have been the accepted standards; but since the war emergency even these standards have been dropped, and emergency certificates may be issued whereby a teacher who cannot make any one of those certificates and who cannot make the additional certificate which is provided in the high school graduation, which automatically entitles one to a certificate—such a person as that may, because of the emergency, be put into that school to teach it. Isn't it a question whether we had better close the schools which compel children to be taught by people of that ability? And there are sixty-five thousand of that kind in our schools to-day. There are one hundred thousand schools in the United States to-day that are either closed because we cannot get teachers, or taught by those of the type that I have described.

"We need laws with higher requirements instead of laws with lower requirements. The biggest mistake we made in education in the United States was two years ago when teachers began to flock out of the schools. What we should have said was, 'The teachers are flocking out of the schools and we must close this school because we cannot get anybody else at this salary paid.' Instead, we lowered the standard and got inadequate material.

"The salary matter is extremely important, and it varies very much in different states. I have here just a few figures. Mississippi is one of the lowest. The salary of teachers in Mississippi is $233.64 a year. The highest salary on my list here is New York, with $967.20 per year, and the salaries range all the way in between. The future needs of the United States demand that the children of Mississippi be educated just as well as the children of Illinois or New York. Otherwise we have got a plague spot in the Union, we have got illiteracy.

"I should like to give you just a few contrasts which have been collected from various sources. This is from a North Carolina paper, 1919: 'Wanted, a colored porter. Guaranteed $25 a week. The right man can get $35 a week. Wanted in a log camp.' In the same paper there appeared this advertisement: 'Wanted, for the high school—of such and such a place—teacher of Latin. $70 a month.' Which is better, to b a colored porter or a high school teacher Fifteen Illinois miners one month recently wer found to have an average salary of $217.78 month. Fifteen teachers in the same town, th same month, had an average salary of $55.

"If you are going to build up a teaching pro fession, you first of all have got to have a salar adequate to the kind of work you want. I thin you have got to make your requirements as bi as your salary. In other words, you have got t buy a better brand of teachers than you hav ever bought before, and you have got to refus to pay for the other kind. Then you must pro vide the possibility of decent home life, with al the sympathy and co-operation and understand ing that comes with it. The whole conception o education is different to-day, and in order to be good teacher, one spends years in normal school and colleges and universities, and perhaps goe to a community which abuses and criticizes an rejects, and all the vision and all the hope an all the desire to do something progressive an constructive, to get ahead, is killed.

"If you women want to help, the first thin for you to do is to find out facts. Find ou whether in your community the school system i a good school system; whether the school admin istrators are there because they know anythin about school administration or for some othe reason; find out whether the buildings are de cent; find out whether the children are bein really educated, or whether they are wasting si hours a day in a poor school; and when you fin what is good, take it for all that it is worth, an when you find what is bad, you will know wha to do with it."

At the close of the meeting, the Woman's Department of The National Civic Federation adopted the following outline, or survey:

1. EDUCATIONAL SYSTEM

Methods of Control:
- Elective
- Appointive
- Boards
- If Boards:
  - Size
  - Qualification
  - Tenure of Office
  - Representation of teaching branch in administration and policy forming.
- Laws covering:
  - Tenure of Office of Teachers
  - Advancement for Teachers
  - Pensions and sick funds for Teachers.

2. TEACHERS

Number
Grades of Certificate
Qualification for Certificate—Form of Application and subsequent procedure.
Examinations—Physical, Mental, Citizenship
Salaries—Present salary
- Raise during ten years
- Grade salaries
- Proportionate raise in cost of living.

Housing and social position in Community.

3. SCHOOL BUILDINGS

Air, light, seats, nurse, rest-rooms for staff, etc.

4. TEXT BOOKS AND CURRICULUM

It is hoped in the various communities where the Department is organized, through the method necessary to answer adequately these questions, that a personal touch will be established between a large body of women and the school authorities and teaching groups, and others that are affected by the problem, who have already made intensive and exhaustive studies on these subjects; and to crystallize public opinion into an intelligent interest in and a sense of responsibility toward this great national laboratory, on the successful development of which rests the future of our Republic.

emocracy in Industry

By JAMES W. SULLIVAN

JAMES W. SULLIVAN

Much has been written recently relative to the progress of this workers' control in Great Britain. Supporters of the concept, enthusiastic visionaries, see the way, in their blue prints, clear to their final objective—complete industrial democracy, projecting, planning, directing, controlling production. Observe, the steps they imagine are: First, the wage-workers are to have their spokesmen in the workshop. Next, autocratic control is to be surrendered piecemeal by employers. Lastly, entire control by the workers. The gradual movement toward this democracy is to be assisted by the government through works committees, local district councils and joint standing industrial councils. In support of this program and its eventual purposes there has been much enthusiastic writing and speaking in Great Britain, with alluring echoes in the United States. It is a fact that in this country during the war works (or shop) committees sprang up in many of the new war supply factories, and adaptations of that branch of establishment organization have since been considerably adopted, mainly in non-union establishments, and recently joint standing industrial councils have also received the stamp of recognition from at least one important temporary Federal body in which organized labor was not represented.

What effect is this particular incipient movement toward democracy in industry likely to have on American trade unionism, on American life in general, on American industry, on the relations of American employers with the wage-workers? To these relevant and matter-of-fact queries the American Federation of Labor has its reply and explanation in the events and conditions, the solid and incontrovertible facts, relative to the genesis of the shop committees and the rise of industrial councils in Great Britain. Broadly, dissimilar basic circumstances interpret the differences in status, customs, methods and especially organization, between the wage-workers' division of society in Great Britain and that in the United States. Further, as a matter of vital fact, in the operation both of works committees and industrial councils in Great Britain the advanced boundaries of their present or possible activities fall far short of the envelopment of the employing class by employees exercising the usual directive functions of employers. Theorists, buzzing about the subject, have let their fancy far outrun the actual progress of events, have misunderstood the facts of the British situation, and have disregarded the facts of the American situation.

The trade unionism of Great Britain is rudimentary in form, incomplete in its administrative system, indefinite in its social purposes and inharmonious in its economic and political activities. In certain of the principal occupations the trade union organization and administration end in deliberately establishing a state of disunion among the unionists in the workshop. Also, as a whole, the crafts themselves are split up into numerous separate unions, regional or local, independent of one another, each with its own salaried administrative staff. Whereas the A. F. of L. is made up of 120 or more affiliated autonomous craft or industrial unions, each covering an occupation in our country's entire territory and population; in Great Britain there are more than 1,200 unions, as high as ten or twelve in a single trade, often overlapping in occupational or territorial jurisdiction, having disparities in dues and wage-scales, and in most cases acknowledging no one national centre of union authority for trade or occupation.

The phrase "shop (or works) committee" in English speech signifies a radically different idea from the same phrase in American speech. In America, the trade union shop chairman is generally the head of an advisory shop committee which carries out union rules and regulations in a works force, is an authorized representative of the general (international) union, and a recognized essential of its administrative force. In Great Britain, the shop organization is not the same. In the working force of one establishment—a fact puzzling to American union men—there may be unassociated members of several branch unions of a single trade, the basis of the English branch membership being the place of residence of the union members and not the work places of a locality, as is the case in America. In a British works force the union chairman has usually performed petty duties pertaining to the establishment, and has had slight, if any, responsibility with respect to the laws of the general union. The shop chairman has not been charged with enforcement of the union scale, and certain other union regulations. Such matters have gone to the branch union of the particular man or men directly interested in a cause calling for a decision. Here was a gap of union organization and function in the shop, giving rise to loss of time in settling disputed points of trade practice and causing friction between members of different unions of one trade in one shop as well as between employers and the general unions. Grievances which, under the American system, could be settled on the spot through the interpretation by a shop chairman or his committee of the general union's rules, or by the shop committee of the interested allied trades, were, under the English system subjects for reference first to the branch and then to the district and the general union of the man or men in cause. It can be seen that under pressure of war speed employers and employees became united in calling for shop committees which could dispose of trade union or any practical workshop labor points without postponement. The new shop committeemen thus called into being soon took on important powers, grew in strength, fell away from union authority, and on being recognized by the government assumed a workshop "control" in some large establishment organizations of certain industries. A further step was to make themselves heard in radical politics, and it was then that they caught the attention of the intellectual improvisers of an immediate millennium.

During the flood tide of talk about the newly developed powers of the newly invented works committees—made out of old half-finished union materials—the Whitley Committee report brought before the British nation the project of a systematic establishment of works committees, to be connected higher up with occupational district and national employers and employees' joint industrial councils. But the Trades Union Congress Parliamentary Committee, and later the Congress itself at its 1918 annual session, made a declaration of the trade union attitude toward these works committees and joint councils which placed narrow and practical limits to their activities. Toward the Whitley report recommendation "that works committees representative of the management and of the workers employed should be instituted in particular works to act in close co-operation with the district and national machinery" of the councils, the Parliamentary Committee assumed a critical attitude. Conceding "that much useful work might be done by works committees in relation to questions affecting the welfare of the workers employed in particular factories," it "strongly urged that such committees should not interfere with the general questions affecting the working rules of the trade respecting the hours of labor, rates of wages, overtime rates, etc." Moreover, in June, 1918, the Minister of Labor wrote: "It is for the Parliamentary Committee to decide whether it would be well to call the attention of its affiliated societies to the importance in drafting constitutions to safeguard collective bargaining against interference by works committees." With relation to standing joint industrial councils as well as works committees, the Parliamentary Committee next passed this resolution:

> "The danger of allowing works committees too much power in connection with wages agreements referred to in our observations on the first report is extended in relation to industries only partially organized, and the Parliamentary Committee cannot accept any form of joint negotiations either by works committees, district councils, or national councils, which may be developed as a substitute for trade union organization and by such organization the establishment of effective representative bodies."

And further:

> "Where well established means exist for negotiation as between trade unions and employers' associations no effort should be made by the government to interfere with existing arrangements."

These decisions of the Trades Union Congress and its Parliamentary Committee have been observed in the organization of the fifty standing joint industrial councils now organized in Great Britain. The radical shop committeeman has disappeared from both the political and the trade union field. British unions are to-day studying or carrying out the reorganization of shop committees as workshop units of the craft organization. The unions thus have in hand whatever of the British "democracy in industry" movement survives.

The present place and functioning of shop committees in their relation to industrial councils were described in September, 1919, by Robert Young, M.P., formerly General Secretary, Amalgamated Society of Engineers, in an address at the annual convention of the Industrial League:

> "Workshop committees, in my estimation, can do a great deal to enable us to get over a great many of the difficulties which in the past have disturbed our industrial life. I have been, as you know, the General Secretary of a large organization. I am not a great believer in carrying everything to headquarters for settlement. I believe that the men themselves, given the proper machinery and using democratic instincts in selecting the best men they can, can themselves form shop committees which, co-operating with employers in particular establishments, can keep these things from being heard of and disturbing our life at the present moment. Let me give you an instance. In a very large shop in an engineering centre in this country, there were many disputes cropping up almost daily in relation to piece-work prices and bonus prices. There were endless threats of strike. The thing was altogether bad for the workers and bad for the firm. The workshop committe was formed, and, would you believe it, after the formation of that workshop committee it was not until about the fiftieth question had cropped up in the workshop that we ever heard anything of it. The other forty-nine had been settled in their own board room in their own establishment. That is what we want to see in our country right through in all industries."

At the convention of the Industrial League the Rt. Hon. J. R. Clynes, M.P., General Workers' Union, spoke of the joint industrial councils' work:

> "It will tend to relieve the trade unions of most of those lesser workshop troubles which, because of the absence of permanent facilities for conciliation and settlement, frequently lead to trouble. Small troubles often develop to a serious dispute, and after perhaps weeks of a strike the parties come together and arrange a settlement which might very well have been arranged between themselves before suffering the losses which strikes always involve. . . .
>
> "Within the trade unions themselves there is real and increasing need for reform. The newer movements and changed conditions of recent years cannot always be well handled on the lines of rules and regulations arranged to fit the industrial situation of a generation ago. Questions of internal management, the more rapid movement of executive action and the degree of authority which appointed representatives or officials may exercise, have all become questions of the greatest interest to trade unions, and these questions should be viewed in the light of present-day industrial needs. The red tape grievance against which trade unions rail in the case of government departments has its counterpart in some of the movements of the trade unions themselves. I am not imputing any special defects whatever to some of the unions whose members have been involved in recent trouble. There are societies whose procedure and method are out of date, and as so many of them are linked up with others in alliances and federations, the need for reform becomes the more real and urgent. The 'rank and file' of the membership should more often be brought to the front line of service and not be left at the point of mass meetings for formal indorsement of decisions reached by other people. . . .
>
> "The workman must be brought into his proper groove for dealing with these recurring workshop problems, and I believe he can be given a place in connection with the settlement of industrial subjects which would fill him with a sense of real pride at being of service to his mates, feeling that he has authority to act for them, that he was authorized on their definite instructions to plead their cause and to act practically as their counsel. Now once the individual workman is given his proper share of this work he is not necessarily disqualified from taking a leading part in other matters that belong now to the trade union leaders, who must handle industrial and labor problems in a higher region."

The quotations just given clearly indicate what is expected among the foremost trade union men in England as to the outcome of the Whitley shop committees and district and national joint standing councils. The shop committees will do the work that has long been done in America in various trades by shop chairmen or the chairmen with their assisting committees. The joint councils as organized by the government will have as their principal duty simply conferences between representative employers and employees, which has long been the custom in America, and has been systematically promoted through The National Civic Federation.

Information as to the subjects with which the British joint industrial councils are actually dealing to-day is to be obtained from an article in the "Labor Gazette" of the Ministry of Labor for March, 1920. The article mentions that "among the more important topics with which joint industrial councils have dealt recently are the reorganization of industry, education, unemployed insurance and workmen's compensation." No explanation ensues as to what is meant by the "reorganization of industry" or by "a scheme of democratic control for voluntary adoption." The greater part of the notes referring to different industries relate to trade agreements as to wages.

So long has college instruction in trade unionism been centered mainly on the history of the English unions, with the assumption that they are the models of unionism in organization, spirit, customs and practices, that our American "intellectuals" are startled at the assertion that the organization and methods of the American Federation of Labor, inclusive of the Railroad Brotherhoods, offer a superior mechanism in practice to the British unions. The American Federation of Labor has for decades stood ready to take any leaf from the English books of trade unionism which would lead to their improvement. The American international union officials, including the editors of the numerous official union publications, are constant readers of the English union publications, which are few in comparison with the American. Twenty-five years ago the American Federation of Labor began sending annually two or more fraternal delegates to the British Trade Union Congress, and in such capacity in that period at least fifty of the most active leaders in the American labor movement have spent some time in Great Britain, all keenly desirous of bringing back to their respective constituencies any new ideas of practical application in connection with their work or organization. Besides, our separate international unions have sent representatives to British trade or industrial conventions, such as those of the miners, the ironworkers, the printers. The general testimony from American delegates on their return has inevitably been in the form of comparisons which showed the British unions far short of the American in organization mechanism and methods. The much-talked-of reforms in British industrial reorganization with the object of bringing employers and employees into closer relationship merely amount to a roundabout way of starting toward a goal long since reached by the old-established American unions.

Testimony in support of the general assertion of the superiority of American trade unionism is found in various statements in the elaborate report made by George A. Isaacs, General Secretary of the British National Society of Operative Printers and Assistants, who attended as delegate in 1914 the annual convention of the International Printing Pressmen and Assistants' Union of North America. As to the office of shop committeeman, Mr. Isaacs said:

> "The member in the American press-room holding the office known to us as the 'father of the chapel' is called the 'Chairman of the chapel.' His duties are similar to those performed by fathers of chapels, and, *in addition*, the laws hold him responsible for seeing that the laws of the international and the by-laws of the local union are fully observed."

Mr. Isaacs thought it noteworthy that the American union label was protected by the laws of most of the American states.

Admitting foremen to trade union membership attracted Mr. Isaac's attention:

> "Another thing that compels my sincere admiration and the strongest possible desire to have the same in the old country, and that is your control over the foremen of the machine departments. . . . When a pressman not directly connected with our organization becomes a foreman it is either upon the understanding that he gives up absolutely his trade union and has nothing further to do with it, or agrees to give up all active work in his union and be a neutral person. As a rule the union man promoted to be an overseer and who drops his card is a bigger tyrant than the man who has worked all his life with the blacklegs, as we call them, and gets a job in a union office.
>
> 'I have been talking with your delegates about your trial committees. That is a new innovation

(*Continued on page 14*)

Socialism Unmasked

MERICAN SOCIALIST ORGANIZATION NOT A POLITICAL PARTY, BUT PART OF AN INTERNATIONAL MOVEMENT AIMING AT WORLD REVOLUTION—PHILOSOPHY AND OBJECTS OF BOLSHEVISM AND SOCIALISM IDENTICAL

By T. EVERETT HARRÉ

I.

OCIALISM AND INTERNATIONALISM

OLSHEVISM is a-term which has come to have a definite meaning in the popular mind. By its methods of violence, by its maintenance in power through ed Guard terrorism and the imposition of med force, by its program and objects effected whole or in part in Russia, Bolshevism stands early revealed for what it is. There can be no gument as to authentic events which have anspired in Russia, as to facts made manifest r nearly three years, as to the philosophy, tacs and purposes expressed in the Soviet constiition, decrees and published official documents. o curtain of deceitful apology and camouflage in obscure that appalling tragedy, unsurpassed nce the beginning of history, at which the civiled world stands aghast. Even among sentiental "liberals," radical clergymen and pseudoitellectual "parlor reds," there can be no dense of the admitted excesses of Lenine and rotzky's bloody regime.

SOCIALISM, on the other hand, is a term of no ich concrete and definite meaning. It is not pecifically a synonym for Bolshevism, Comunism, revolution by force, for the overthrow y violent and unlawful methods of the Amerian Government and the institutions of civilizaion. It is rather a term of confusion to the general public, which has come vaguely to distinguish between Bolshevism and Socialism, Socialism and Communism, between the Socialist party and the Communist and Communist labor factions. It is not uncommon to find highminded, loyal Americans making a distinction between Bolshevism, which they regard as violent, lawless and dangerous, and Socialism, which they accept as parliamentary and pacific in its methods, and legitimate in its objects. It is not unusual to hear such persons say that while they are opposed to Bolshevism, there is much good in Socialism. Socialism to them loosely means an effort toward social reform, toward the readjustment of industrial inequities, a peaceful, beautiful but perhaps utopian and impractical plan for perfecting an imperfect world. We are told by one that the Man of Nazareth was "the first Socialist," and by another that Socialism, after all, is only "applied Christianity." "Socialism—a program to be social. Why, we are all Socialists," amiably declares a financier after dinner, in a spirit of expansive and liberal good-feeling equalled only by his ignorance. Such declarations are not surprising when such a man as Attorney General A. Mitchell Palmer says (in a speech delivered in Detroit, March 15, 1920):

> "The Socialist Party in America has cast out the radicals and forced them to organize the Communist and Communist Labor Parties. The Socialists are loyal and patriotic men, though radical. Their aim is to change the Government by lawful means, while the 'Reds' would destroy lawful authority."

This confusion as to Socialism, its character, its specific objects, program and tactics, is largely the result of the designing efforts of Socialist leaders themselves, an effect of the adroit Socialist propaganda, and serves to further the Socialists' sinister ends. The Socialist organization has presented itself as "a mild mannered party seeking political reform, advocating humanitarian principles and practices, abhorrent of the idea that it should be identified or confused with the Communist Party of America." Writers such as John Spargo have turned out seductively phrased and subtly deceiving volumes purporting to prove and demonstrate that Socialism is opposed to, and is the antithesis of Bolshevism. Masquerading as the "right wing' of the Socialist movement, opposed to the violent, revolutionary program of the Bolshevistic "left wing," the Socialist party of America, so-called, has enlisted the confidence, support and sympathy of many sincere if ill-informed people to whom any program of revolution by mass violence would be shocking and repugnant.

It therefore happened, when the New York Assembly suspended, pending investigation, five Socialist assemblymen-elect, that a number of distinguished Americans, of irreproachable character, integrity and loyalty, came to the defense of the suspended members, declaring that the action of the Assembly was a violation of constitutional rights and a persecution of a minority party. Their contention was that the Socialist organization is a legitimate political party, enjoying a status, character and privileges such as the Republican and Democratic parties, and that, as such, its candidates when elected to office cannot be challenged or denied taking their seats. Whatever differences of opinion may exist as to the method and expediency of the action taken by the New York Legislature, the hearings of the Judiciary Committee into the eligibility of the suspended members, which resulted in their final expulsion, developed an issue of greater importance than the mere seating or ejection of the individuals under trial. That issue involves the actual character, program, purposes and proposed tactics of the Socialist party of America.

OUT OF ITS OWN MOUTH

The Albany hearings served to focus the attention and interest of the people of the country, including both those who approved and those who disapproved of the original suspension, and the results of that investigation, aside from the permanent suspension of the five members-elect, are of vital importance to every citizen who believes in American ideals and desires the preservation of American institutions. No occasion has ever resulted in the assembling of such a mass of evidence concerning the principles, policy, tactics and objects of the Socialist movement in America. That evidence consists not of the testimony or interpretations of opponents of Socialism, but of official platforms, programs, manifestos and publications of the Socialist party itself and utterances of its recognized leaders.

Does that evidence establish the Socialist organization in the United States as a legitimate political party, seeking only through constitutional and parliamentary methods to bring about changes in the existing order? Does it establish Socialism as opposed to the objects and tactics of Bolshevism? Does it reveal Socialism as a mild, beneficent, humanitarian program of social reform, as "Christianity put into practice"?

Convicted on evidence out of its own mouth, the Socialist party, on the contrary, is unmasked and uncovered as a revolutionary movement, anti-American, anti-patriotic, traitorous, antinational, anti-political, aiming through illegal and violent methods to overturn all existing democratic governments, "whose national program in this country is to be fashioned upon the plan of the Soviet regime of Russia, inspired by its originator and dictator, Nicolai Lenine," and which "proposes to carry into effect its purposes in this country as the purposes and objects were accomplished in Russia."

SOCIALIST ORGANIZATION PART OF WORLD REVOLUTIONARY MOVEMENT

From the evidence of the Socialist party itself—consisting of official platforms, programs, manifestos, reports, publications and utterances of its accepted leaders—it has been established:

That the Socialist organization in the United States is not a political party, but part of an international movement preparing for and attempting to bring about a revolution in this country as part of an international social revolution; that the Socialist organization has officially taken "its position with the uncompromising (or extreme revolutionary) section of the International Socialist movement," and has officially pledged its support as an organization to the extreme revolutionary wing of International Socialism, of which the Russian Bolshevists are the most conspicuous part; that in a referendum vote, by an overwhelming majority, the party membership adopted a report declaring the organization in support of Lenine's Third Internationale, convened in Moscow, March, 1919, whose program advocates world revolution by armed violence and world-wide dictatorship of the proletariat, and that in pursuance of the adoption of the Minority report, in March of this year, the party through its national executive secretary, made official application for recognition by and membership in that revolutionary Communist International which was inspired, convoked and controlled by Lenine and his major associates.

Instead of seeking as a purely legal political party to bring about social changes and human betterment by constitutional and parliamentary methods, the Socialist party of America proposes in the United States to accomplish its revolutionary program—according to the summary of evidence made to the New York Legislative Judiciary Committee by Martin Conboy, special counsel—by the following unlawful methods:

> "*First: It has opposed and obstructed and continues to oppose and obstruct the Government of the United States and of this State in all measures relating to the national and State defense. Its purpose in so doing is a manifest one: to weaken and leave defenseless the government of State and Nation against the attacks of foreign and domestic enemies, and thus deprive it of that right of self-preservation which is admittedly the first law of governments as it is of individuals.*
>
> "*Second: It has advocated and incited the destruction of the existing government of the United States by illegal mass action.*
>
> "*Third: While professing to utilize political action, it constantly denies that existing evils or defects may be remedied by such action, and insists that such political action must be supplemented by violence and mass action, which it advocates, both directly and by insinuation and suggestion.*
>
> "*Fourth: The political action of the party is responsive only to the dues-paying membership. Those who are elected to office are bound to follow the dictates of such membership and their*

(*Continued on page 15*)

THE NATIONAL Civic Federation Review

Office: Thirty-third Floor, Metropolitan Tower
1 Madison Avenue New York City

RALPH M. EASLEY, Editor

The Editor alone is Responsible for any unsigned article or unquoted statement published in THE NATIONAL CIVIC FEDERATION REVIEW.

THE BLACK PHOENIX RISES FROM ITS ASHES

In the days when the heroic manhood of America and the Allied nations were being immolated in the great sacrifice of the war, when self-surrender and sorrow immeasurable exalted humanity above the frailty and sordidness of common existence, the more ardent of us expected what would have been well-nigh miraculous had it happened. When the war should be over, the evil that is ever mixed with good in the relations of mankind would be vanished. Intrigue, covert contrivings to foment racial and national discords would be done with. There would be a great spiritual regeneration in which every nation, in which the most ordinary existence, would share. Germany, vanquished, in sackcloth and repentance, would be welcomed back into the family of nations, and the brotherhood of man and universal good-will would reign.

To admit that all this has not happened is not to confess defeat, nor to diminish what has actually and concretely been won in the war. Such a miracle has never occurred, because mankind does not proceed *en masse* to perfection; there is no equal measure in the pace of men's feet on the long road of evolution. So, while it may bring a pang of disappointment, there need be no discouragement in recognizing that international amity, trust and concord have not been established; that Germany has not proved herself a prodigal son among the nations; that sinister propaganda to estrange the nations united in the war has not ended, but that, instead, we confront a recrudescence throughout the world.

It is universally the experience, of individuals as of nations, after a hard-won struggle, to relax and rest on one's oars. Such reaction is human, natural. Yet it is of this very natural relapse from the tenseness of a great strain that the enemy ever seeks to take advantage. Where one demon has been vanquished, seven ever seek to return. The thief eternally comes in the night. To no less degree that we did in the days when victory hung in the balance, is it necessary today that the people of America, and of the Allied nations as well, stand vigilant against the hostile forces which have risen, which are no less real, no less formidable than were the armies of Huns, and whose victory at any time would be no less fearsome than would have been world-subjugation by the Imperial masters of Germany.

While the sinister forces of world revolution have intensified their activities since the end of the war, there has come a revival of German intrigue and propaganda, and with it a joining of all the forces of pacifism and defeatism which had during the war been rendered inert or innocuous. All these elements are found, upon examination, to interlock with one another.

There is being carried on today in this country, without concealment or disguise, a movement to organize "all men and women of German blood in one great political organization," the purpose of which is to exert pressure upon the political parties and to elect candidates to office who are sympathetic to Germany or the interests of the German element here, and who are opposed to the carrying out of the Versailles treaty. Propaganda is spread broadcast vituperating the Allies, seeking to create hostile feeling toward England and France, attacking the American Government and vilely calumnying the American president. All these agencies, publications and individuals who campaigned for a compromise peace with Germany, who defended and endorsed the Bolsheviki, are seeking, on the one hand, to estrange us from the peoples who first gave their blood in self-defense and to bring about concessions to Germany, while, on the other hand, they are endeavoring to bring about recognition of Soviet Russia and the affording of economic assistance in order that Bolshevism may be strengthened and its propaganda facilitated. In their insidious activities they are seeking to use the churches, the press, educational institutions, and the most effective assistance is often given by pacifist, "liberal" college professors and clergymen.

In England voices are raised against France, to whom imperialistic ambitions are charged; yet upon investigation it is found that this emanates from the very people who preached defeatism and advocated a compromise peace, notably through the proposed Stockholm conference. In France the government is denounced as "a government of treachery, which, under the pretext of obtaining execution of a still-born treaty, seeks to crush the pacific revolution in Germany." It was a deputy, a Socialist, Vaillant-Couturier, who made this charge in an address inciting the 1920 class of recruits to disobedience. When prosecution was threatened, the entire Unified Socialist membership of the Chamber of Deputies, numbering sixty-five, came forward to Vaillant-Couturier's defense and subscribed to his infamous statement. In all the Allied countries another propaganda is being carried on, the purpose of which is to persuade the world that Poland is imperialistic and militaristic. The immediate purpose in the United States is to obstruct the floating of the authorized $50,000,000 loan, but is specifically designed to prevent the creation of a strong Poland in order that Germany may have free access to Russia and gain trade control in the Slavic provinces. Maurice Francis Egan, formerly American Minister to Denmark, recently issued a warning against all this propaganda which, he declared, the Germans have especially concentrated upon in the United States.

At a time of widespread social discontent and industrial disturbance, when people lack normal balance and their point of view is distorted, there is more than ordinary danger that the evil seeds of international animosity, suspicion and discord may find fertile ground. It is the duty, therefor, of all Americans to be on guard, not only against the attempted revival of hyphenism and divided loyalty, but against all the insidious efforts which seek to estrange the nations as they likewise seek to foment class warfare and turn us one against another in our midst. Where civilization had one visible foe to face in German Imperialism, it now confronts a foe of international scope and character, of multifarious phases and deceiving guises. The black phœnix has risen from its ashes, and its heads are hydra.

FACTS EXPLODE ARGUMENTS FOR AID TO SOVIETS

Throughout the world, and especially in the United States, from which economic assistance was mainly desired, there has been a crying aloud that the sufferings of the stricken population of Russia were due not to the maladministration, inefficiency and criminal excesses of the Soviet régime, but to the blockade maintained by America and the Allied nations. Lift the blockade, send to Russia industrial supplies and foodstuffs and "her restoration would begin and proceed as if by magic." Another argument for the re-establishment of trade with Russia has been that, if England and America did not take advantage of the overtures of Lenine, the vast resources of Russia, industrial concessions and economic products, would fall into the hands of Germany.

While it has been pointed out by many well-informed persons that an establishment of trade would facilitate the promotion of Bolshevist propaganda, a matter calling for most serious consideration, there are other points which seem to have escaped proper attention. In an article in the *New York Times* Mr. John Spargo raises some very pertinent questions: "How much can be accomplished by philanthropy? To what extent can trade with Russia solve her problems? How far is it a matter of granting credits and to what extent can such credits be secured?"

Mr. Spargo shows that "by expending the entire gold and platinum reserves in the country" (amounting to about $275,000,000) "the Soviet government can import approximately as much as was imported into Russia in two months in normal times under the old régime." Because of the utter collapse of industry, the breakdown of transportation, wastage and almost complete lack of all needed raw supplies, it would now be necessary, to bring about restoration, to supply infinitely more than was needed in normal times, and to buy this Russia does not have the money. What about the "concessions" offered by Lenine as a basis for credit?

Much of the stock in railroads and industries confiscated and nationalized by the Bolshevik government was held by foreign investors. "If American capital is furnished for the reconstruction of these railway lines," writes Mr. Spargo, "are the investors to be secured by some sort of control of the lines and their earnings? In that case, what of the original investors, owners of the stock? . . . If American capital is to be advanced for the installation of machinery in Russian mines and their development, and ownership or part ownership of the mines for a period of years is offered as security, what will be the relation of the American creditor and security holder to the American investor who holds part of the original stock and whose interests were confiscated by the Bolsheviki?"

If American financial interests are biting at the bait held out by Lenine, here are questions to give them pause. Mr. Spargo makes clear that if the entire reserve of platinum and gold —much of it stolen from Roumania—and all her exportable goods, were "exchanged to-morrow for their full value in goods chosen by the Soviet authorities themselves, there would still be famine in Russia." Even if vast amounts of foodstuffs were sent, would it to any small degree ease the general condition?

This is answered by actual facts supplied by Bolshevik officials themselves. As revealed in the reports of A. Rykoff, President of the Superior Council of the National Board of Economy of the Soviet Government, which are quoted in an article by Gregor Alexinsky, Social Democratic member of the Second Russian Douma, in this issue of the REVIEW, there are not sufficient locomotives running in Russia to transport food and supplies, even if these arrived at Russian ports. Russia has a limitless supply of ore in the Ural mines, yet, according to Rykoff, the Bolsheviki have been able to ship only one train-load of metal a month to Central Russia. To supply the textile mills of Moscow it would be necessary to transport 500,000 poods of cotton a month from Turkestan, yet the Bolsheviki are able to run only two trains a month and, as the Bolsheviki head of industry admits, it would take decades to fill the needs. The output of the textile mills is only ten per cent of the normal output.

Before the war Russia supplied more than 85 per cent of the flax of the world, more than 20,000,000 poods being harvested annually. In 1918, the Bolshevists having nationalized the crops, only 4,500,000 poods were harvested, and in January of this year there was only enough in reserve to meet the most urgent needs for eight months. Rykoff reported they could not export any appreciable quantity abroad. "The catastrophical decrease in the crop makes us foresee that in 1920 the supply in the linen in-war, our difficulties at home were acute. The nation was not roused to the war spirit; there was division, confliction of opinion, lack of that unity and enthusiasm which alone can carry through the fire of such an ordeal and bear the flag to victory. To meet this situation The National Civic Federation organized, in Washington, September 12, 1917, The League for National Unity, whose purpose was to unite all elements in the country to back the government, whole-heartedly and unreservedly, to continuing the war until military victory was achieved and the autocratic power of the Imperial German Government was broken. That League proved a power in a time of need. It undertook to counteract the propaganda of all those who worked for a premature compromise peace which would have left Germany victorious; it sought to neutralize the baneful effects of fault finding with the Administration, most of which was inspired and disseminated by agents of and sympathizers with the foe. At a time when all the forces which sided with Germany were throwing their influence to the election in the Congressional primaries of candidates opposed to the war, the League carried on a campaign, calling upon all voters, regardless of party affiliation, to vote against disloyal candidates and elect only war-till-victory Americans. On many occasions the League was called upon for special service by departments of the government. Until Germany surrendered and the Imperial government collapsed, the League continued its work, of nation-wide scope, with results that were vital and concrete.

Among the most active spirits directing the work of the League was Mr. Vail, the chairman. Fully alive, by reason of his business experience, to the disintegrating, morally destructive influence of the criticisms of the President and the War and Navy Departments, he especially devoted himself, heart and soul, to offsetting this widespread cavilling and making the people realize the necessity of getting behind the President in a united support of the war. In a letter sent in January, 1918, to the Editor of the Review, approving of some of the material prepared by the League, Mr. Vail said:

> 'It seems to me that the American people are too much inclined, the moment they are not satisfied or think they are not satisfied with what is going on, to want to tear down everything and build up something new. They forget that the experience obtained by those who have been at work is a valuable asset, and is much more likely to accomplish something than by replacing everybody with new men who have experience to gain."

Mr. Vail pleaded that the Administration be "given an opportunity untrammelled, free from nagging and irritating investigations, to do its work in comfort and peace. This is no time for partisanship, to make partisan capital."

In a speech delivered at a meeting of the Executive Committee of the League, May 10, 1918, Mr. Vail with incisive logic pointed out the difficulty of changing a nation from a peace to a war basis and called for unified and absolute support of the Government. He said:

> "A united nation will prevent some, and make up for many, mistakes. It takes more time and is more wearing to answer captious criticisms and make every act self-explanatory than all the rest of the responsibility combined, and takes the precious time and wears the mind that should be free to meet duty and responsibility. Discuss freely if you will but only on the basis of full knowledge of every action, not on hearsay or prejudice. Criticize constructively, but do not criticize without knowledge or destructively. Always remember where responsibility lies and action must originate—that many things which control cannot be known by all. In this way we can make our help and the help of all more efficacious; in this way only can we win this war without increasing the sacrifice."

In these troublous days following the war, when reconstruction is retarded by seditious agitation, Mr. Vail's words still bear a message—a message gained from a large practical human experience:

> "Dispassionate discussion and constructive criticism with a full knowledge of facts and a full understanding of the objective, whether about things done or about to be done, or methods of doing, cannot but be helpful. Impassioned prejudiced criticism, even if more or less justified, is not corrective—it immediately arouses defense and intensified self-justification. Without knowledge and understanding, discussion and criticism can but be absurd, fallacious and entirely misleading."

WHAT DOES "INDUSTRIAL DEMOCRACY" MEAN?

On another page of this issue of the Review will be found an article on "Industrial Democracy" by Mr. James W. Sullivan. Mr. Sullivan has been recognized for forty years as the leading expert and authority here on labor matters in this country and Europe. He was the labor member, nominated by Samuel Gompers, on the commission sent by The National Civic Federation in 1919 to study labor conditions in Great Britain and France. He was also the labor member on the Civic Federation's more recent commission to Europe to make a study of social insurance, the report of which commission will soon be ready for distribution. We bespeak for Mr. Sullivan's article a careful reading, not only because of his qualifications to speak but also because of the importance of the subject matter.

There is no phrase, unless it be "self-determination," that has been more misused and overworked than "industrial democracy" or "democratization of industry," which later terms, in the literature of the day, are interchangeable. Particularly are all the writers in the social service commissions of the churches making much of the term. We quote a paragraph from a pamphlet, entitled "Christian Principles and Industrial Reconstruction," by Francis J. McConnell, Bishop of the Methodist Episcopal Church and a member of the General Committee of the Interchurch World Movement of North America, as follows:

> "The battle for a voice in wage-fixing has been pretty well fought through; but industrial democracy really implies more than such collective bargaining in wages and hours. It implies that labor shall be heard in all questions which have to do with the conditions in which the laborer works, with the shop and its control, with the control of the industry itself through place on boards of directors."

From "The New Spirit in Industry," a book by Rev. F. Ernest Johnson, Secretary of the Research Department of the Commission on The Church and Social Service of the Federal Council of the Churches of Christ in America, is taken the following paragraph:

> "The 'hot spot' in the industrial situation is not wages or hours, but management, in which labor is demanding an increasing share. This is in part the industrial counterpart of the demand for political democracy that is sweeping the world. It results from a growing conviction that freedom for the individual, the paramount democratic ideal, is not satisfied by a political formula, but must be realized in daily life and work. This means free choice of occupation; a voice in the determination of hours and wages, conditions of work, and shop discipline; and, in its fullest import, participation also in financial procedure—buying, selling and investment."

In both of the above quotations is the declaration that higher wages, shorter hours and better working conditions is not the desideratum for which the wage earner is striving, but it is for a voice in the business and executive management of the concern in which he works that he aims. This idea will be found running all through not only church industrial literature but the writings of those who are termed "industrial experts," "the intellectuals" and the "parlor Bolsheviki." When traced back to its source, it is to be found that those writers have imbibed this notion not from the American labor movement, but from the comparatively small handful of I. W. W. and Bolshevik wage workers, plus the radical labor factions in Europe.

There is also much confusion in the public mind as to the meaning of the phrase because entirely opposing forces use it with equal glibness to represent their own particular views. For instance, there are employers who in using the phrase mean nothing but profit sharing. The A. F. of L. officials use the phrase when they mean only collective bargaining; while, when the socialists use it they mean the taking over of industry by the state and, in the case of the I. W. W. and Bolsheviki, when they use it, they mean the taking over of the industry by the workers. Curiously enough, the definition of the phrase by the church writers is that of the I. W. W. and Bolsheviki. The labor organization that is most outspoken in this matter and the operation of which is responsible for the spread of the radical idea of industrial democracy is the Amalgamated Clothing Workers of America, which frankly admits its purpose to be the training of its workers to take over and operate the industry. Sidney Hillman, president of that organization, gave an interview, published in *The World* of Sunday, July 27, 1919, in which he showed how that organization had absolute control of the clothing industry in New York City, Rochester, Baltimore and Chicago, concluding his statements with the following frank expression:

> "By gradually increasing our power and our responsibility in the industry, we are preparing to be ready to conduct it when the day for complete industrial democracy arrives."

To facilitate the equipment of the workers for taking over the industry, Mr. Hillman and other radical organizations are promoting so-called "Labor colleges" and schools. This sounds well to the uninitiated, but in the light of the known philosophy and objectives of such organizations and the radical character of their "intellectual" promoters, they are anything but patriotic and uplifting devices.

The American Federation of Labor, which speaks not for a mere handful of workers but for four million organized wage earners, at its last Annual Convention, held at Atlantic City, by a practically unanimous vote placed its stamp of disapproval upon the idea that the workers want to take over and run the business. Mr. John P. Frey, secretary of the Convention's Committee on Resolutions, reported as follows:

> "I would call your attention to the fact that in the literature which has been circulated upon the question of electing foremen and in the speeches made in trade union meetings upon this same question, the subject does not stop with the election of foremen, because the argument is then made, and it is a logical one, tha. the election of foremen would be of no value because the foremen would be under the general manager and the board of directors, and if we could only get the trade union movement to commit itself to the election of foremen in industries, it would logically follow that we would have to elect the board of directors and determine who the general manager would be. It is not, therefore, a trade union proposition and I have made this statement so that you will more thoroughly understand what is included in the resolution in purpose, if not in language."

And, on motion of Mr. Frey, the proposal was defeated by a 100 to 1 vote.

Another topic with which Mr. Sullivan deals that is commanding interest at the moment is that of shop committees, shop stewards, etc. This is referred to by many writers as a method of democracy and, in so far as these committees deal with wages, hours and working conditions and with all kinds of grievances that arise in the shop, it is, in a sense, an approach to democracy—some people might call it only good common sense. But this is no different from the "democracy" that obtains today in every industry where collective bargaining exists or, in cases where the men are not organized into unions, there are shop committees. There is, however, in this whole question a serious aspect which, where the committees are not under the discipline of organization, may develop a kind of shop committee that means the I. W. W. or Bolshevist idea of taking over the industry.

In this connection, it is highly important to consider the following quotations from Bolshevist authorities.

In the appeal to the Communist Party of America from G. Zinoviev, as president of the executive committee of the Communist Internationals, which was taken from a courier captured en route to the United States, is found the following significant declaration: (The italics are the Editor's.)

> "The most important task confronting the American Communist at the present moment is to draw the wide proletarian masses into the path of the revolutionary struggle. The party must have for its goal the dissolution of the American Federation of Labor and other unions associated with it and must strive to establish the closest connection with the I. W. W., the One Big Union and the W. I. I. U. . . .
>
> "*The party must support the formation of factory workers' committees in factories, thus serving as bases for the every day struggle and for training the advanced crowd of labor in managing industry.*"

In the manifesto of the Communist Party of America last fall was the same idea, to wit:

> "The Communist Party must engage actively in the struggle to revolutionize the trade unions. As against the unionism of the American Federation of Labor the Communist Party propagandizes industrial unionism and industrial union organization emphasizing their revolutionary implications. Industrial unionism is not simply a means for the every day struggle against capitalism; its ultimate purpose is revolutionary, implying the necessity of ending the captialist state. Industrial unionism is a factor in the final mass action for the conquest of power as it will constitute the basis for the industrial administration of the Communist commonwealth.
>
> * * * * * *
>
> "The Communist Party recognizes that the American Federation of Labor is reactionary and a bulwark of capitalism.
>
> "*Councils of workers shall be organized in the shop as circumstances allow for the purpose of carrying on the industrial union struggle in the old unions, mobilizing the militant element; these councils to be unified in a central council wherever possible.*"

From *The One Big Union Monthly*, the official organ of the I. W. W., the following very illuminating paragraphs on the subject of the Shop Stewards' control are taken:

> "At a National Conference of Shop Stewards and Workers' Committees, held in London, England on January 10th and 11th, 1920, it was unanimously decided, after hearing the I. W. W. representative, George Hardy, that the National Executive Committee should 'take steps to link up with the I. W. W.'
>
> "This event, which probably has been passed up, as not worth noticing, by the capitalist and the conservative labor press, is an event of great importance.
>
> "*Coming as it does at the same time as the invitation to an Industrial International, sent out by the Industrial Unionists of Russia, it points towards a speedy realization of our fondest dreams, the organization of the world's workers in industrial unions on a world basis, to take over production and distribution.*"

We do not mean to imply that because Lenine and Trotzky are planning, through the shop committee system, to capture the industries of this country, that they are going to capture them. There are many things this precious pair of dreamers, schemers, and murderers are planning and not accomplishing, and this is undoubtedly one; but it does give warning to every employer who has the shop committee system to keep a sharp lookout for this very danger. Mr. Sullivan's article throws much light on this whole situation.

AMERICAN EMPLOYERS' PROFIT-SHARING PLANS

NEW VOLUME JUST ISSUED BY THE NATIONAL CIVIC FEDERATION

"Profit Sharing by American Employers," the report of a second inquiry concerning profit sharing between employer and employees, has been published by The National Civic Federation and is now being distributed.

In 1916 the Federation published the first edition of this work. A constant aim in the inquiry was an accurate and unbiased statement of facts. The resultant material was published with the intention of meeting a demand, especially from executives of manufacturing establishments. The entire edition of the volume issued was soon exhausted, and there has been an unsatisfied call for it ever since. A new edition has therefore been prepared.

Reading the statements of fact and opinion educed, one becomes a spectator in a forum in the discussions of which each speaker, giving his name, comes out into the open and relates his experiences with his own or his company's plan. He tells of his hopes and expectations and finally utters his judgment as to the weaknesses or points of strength in the methods he, as a closely interested observer, has seen tried. Some contributors are enthusiastic over their successes; some are resigned to having their plans work passably well; others are uncertain as to the outcome, and still others have frankly abandoned plan and principle. But all bring to the general attention the practical side of the question. They exhibit actual experiments now going on in business and industrial life.

Every paragraph relates to present activities in the production of material things affecting human existence. The testimony, mostly from managers of companies and wage-workers' spokesmen, has direct relation to an important phase of the big labor problem. The inquiry common to all is the shortest and best cut to certain practical objectives. The results desired are maximum production with minimum waste, increased satisfaction to both employers and employees, steps in the activities of trade and manufacture toward a more highly civilized society.

The considerable percentage of dubious results shown by this inquiry should not lead to the sweeping conclusion that all profit sharing experiments are worthless. Many of them, from the standpoint of special local conditions or by contrast with some previous order of things, no doubt show a net improvement in the welfare of the employees affected and the morale of the plants. The real significance, both of the organized labor attitude and of the proportion of failures and doubtful results, lies in their bearing upon the possible value of profit sharing as an industrial remedy of general application.

This in turn involves consideration of the fear of organized labor that the employers' real interest in profit sharing lies in its alleged usefulness as a means to weaken and disrupt the trade unions, and that with this once accomplished the employing interests would be free to regulate wages and hours to suit themselves, with no effective equality of bargaining power left in the hands of the workers.

It is not within the scope of the present inquiry to examine the merits of organized labor's objections to profit sharing, nor to determine whether the interests of labor generally would be safer under profit sharing than with the economic power of organization in its own hands.

The import of the testimony, as a whole, in this work carries the reader to one general conclusion: The personality of the conductor may lead to great good in a faulty plan and it may bring ruin to a sound plan. More than mechanism must enter into profit sharing. Whether

(*Continued on page 20*)

"What Is Socialism?"—A Clear-Cut Answer

COMMITTEE ON SOCIALIST DOCTRINES AND TACTICS, CONDÉ B. PALLEN, CHAIRMAN, ISSUES STATEMENT SHOWING LAWLESSNESS OF METHODS AND IDENTICAL OBJECTS OF ALL FACTIONS

THE various ostensibly conflicting factions in the International Socialist movement, and the constant masquerade of the Socialist organization in the United States as pacifist in its methods and humanitarian in its objects, has led to so much confusion in the public mind that the true character and aim of Socialism, as well as its program and tactics, have come to be generally misunderstood. This confusion, which serves the ends of the Socialists and renders the American public susceptible to their adroit and dangerous propaganda, was conspicuously illustrated by Attorney General A. Mitchell Palmer when, in his speech at Detroit, March 15, 1920, he differentiated between allegedly lawful and admittedly outlaw Socialist factions, and characterized the Socialist Party, as distinguished from the Communist and Communist-Labor parties, as a "loyal" organization. Mr. Palmer said:

"THE SOCIALIST PARTY IN AMERICA HAS CAST OUT THE RADICALS AND FORCED THEM TO ORGANIZE THE COMMUNIST AND COMMUNIST-LABOR PARTIES. THE SOCIALISTS ARE LOYAL AND PATRIOTIC MEN, THOUGH RADICAL. THEIR AIM IS TO CHANGE THE GOVERNMENT BY LAWFUL MEANS, WHILE THE 'REDS' WOULD DESTROY LAWFUL AUTHORITY."

Mr. Palmer makes three allegations, to wit:

1. "THE SOCIALIST PARTY IN AMERICA HAS CAST OUT THE RADICALS AND FORCED THEM TO ORGANIZE THE COMMUNIST AND COMMUNIST-LABOR PARTIES."

The Socialist Party of America has not "cast out the radicals." The element represented in the Communist and Communist-Labor parties voluntarily broke away from the Socialist organization, and that break was not due to "differences on vital questions or principles," as explained Morris Hillquit, but, "It arose over disputes on methods and policy, and even within that limited sphere it was largely one of emphasis rather than fundamentals." The general impression, which Mr. Palmer seems to share, that the Socialist Party differs in objects and lawless methods from the Communist factions, that the Socialist organization is a legitimate political party, seeking only through parliamentary means to bring about social changes, and that it abhors association with the out-spokenly revolutionary left wings, has no basis in fact. All three factions, with Russian Bolshevism, have their basis in Marxian Socialism—the only extant Socialism—and the differences between the Socialist organization and "left" wings, according to Mr. Hillquit, are to be regarded merely as quarrels between "brethren." Their aims are identical; their differences are merely minor differences as to expediency of methods to be employed under certain conditions. As against Mr. Palmer's assertion, Mr. Hillquit, the official spokesman of the organization, has said of the Communists:

"They have not deserted to the enemy. The bulk of their following is still good Socialist material, and when the hour of the real Socialist fight strikes in this country, we may find them again in our ranks. . . . Let us center our whole fight upon capitalism, and let us hope our Communist brethren will go and do likewise."

Instead of the Socialist Party "casting out the radicals," the contrary has happened. All individual members who were loyal to this country in its war against Germany, who placed the interests of the United States above those of the international program of Socialism, found that they could not, consistently with their duty as citizens, remain with the party. They were, therefore, obliged to leave the organization. It is not "the radicals" who have been repudiated and denounced by the organization, but those loyal and patriotic members who have been stigmatized as "opportunists and social traitors." At the Emergency Convention held in Chicago, September, 1919, as against those Socialists who were loyal to their respective countries in the war against Germany, the Socialist Party of America officially declared:

CONDÉ B. PALLEN, LL.D.
Chairman, Committee on Socialist Doctrines and Tactics

"We unreservedly reject the policy of those Socialists who support their belligerent capitalist governments on the plea of 'national defense' and who entered into demoralizing compacts for so-called civil peace with the exploiters of labor during the war and continued a political alliance with them after the war."

Eugene V. Debs, the supreme voice, the hero-martyr and the prospective presidential candidate of the Socialist Party, in an interview given in the Atlanta Penitentiary on April 14, declared that there was no ground on which the Socialists could consistently divide and that if both "recognize that it is the mission of the working class to emancipate itself by every possible method, to utilize every legitimate weapon to accomplish human freedom, and if each works in his chosen path toward the open road that leads to human freedom, then their interests are common." Debs, from behind prison bars, sardonically scoffed at Mr. Palmer's declaration that the Socialist Party had "denounced and spurned" the "anarchist element," declaring:

"When the Socialist Party becomes so safe and sane that the capitalist politicians can point to our 'eternal credit' in their personal political appraisements, there is certainly something the matter with us. . . .

"I have been asked many times if I believe in changing the present system by force and violence. That is a silly question, and none would ask it who has the slightest knowledge of history. . . . All along the track of the ages, wherever a government has been overthrown by force and violence, that government has been maintained by force and violence.

"You can always depend upon the capitalist class to force the workers to adopt different tactics. For the time being they have the power, and we are on the defensive. Therefore, we must do the thing best fitted to meet a given situation."

2. "THE SOCIALISTS ARE LOYAL AND PATRIOTIC MEN, THOUGH RADICAL."

The Socialist Party of America was anti-war, anti-national and anti-American from the very outset of the war. At its National Convention in St. Louis, March and April, 1917, it adopted its notorious war program, in which it declared:

"The Socialist Party of the United States in the present grave crisis solemnly reaffirms its allegiance to the principle of internationalism and working-class solidarity the world over and proclaims its unalterable opposition to the war just declared by the government of the United States."

It called upon the workers to refuse support to the government during the war:

"The only struggle which would justify the workers in taking up arms is the great struggle of the working class of the world to free itself from economic exploitation and political oppression, and we particularly warn the workers against the snare and delusion of so-called defensive warfare."

It expressly and solemnly repudiated any sentiment of patriotism and allegiance to the government of the United States:

"As against the false doctrine of national patriotism we uphold the ideal of international working-class solidarity."

It officially pledged itself as a party and "recommended" to workers, a course of action, including:

"1. Continuous active and public opposition to the war through demonstration, mass petitions and others means within our power.

"2. Unyielding opposition to all proposed legislation for military or individual conscription," etc.

In addition to this war program, the party adopted a platform including, among others, the following demands:

"Resistance to conscription of life and labor.

"Repudiation of war debts."

For attempting to carry out that war program, 2,000 members of the Socialist Party were arrested and the principal members of the executive committee were indicted, convicted and sentenced to terms of imprisonment.

3. "THEIR AIM IS TO CHANGE THE GOVERNMENT BY LAWFUL MEANS, WHILE THE 'REDS' WOULD DESTROY LAWFUL AUTHORITY."

During the war the Socialist Party of America proclaimed and maintained its adherence to the program of the international radical revolutionary Socialists formulated at Zimmerwald in 1915 and at Kienthal in 1916, under the leadership of Lenine. After the armistice it formally and officially committed itself to the revolutionary program developed and laid down by the Third Internationale of Moscow.

The Third Communist Internationale issued a manifesto, March 26, 1919, signed by Lenine, Trotzky, Rakovsky, Zinoviev and Platten, under the title of the "Manifesto of the Communist Internationale," which is characterized by the Literature Department of the Socialist Party—by which it was published and disseminated in the United States—as "*undoubtedly the greatest declaration ever issued from any working class tribunal since the Communist Manifesto of Marx and Engels.*"

The Moscow Manifesto planted itself squarely upon Marxian doctrines, and advocates violent revolution, the arming of the workers, declares for the world dictatorship of the proletariat and repudiates opportunism, "social patriotism" and democracy, which it pillories as a bourgeois institution—in short, reiterates and emphasizes the Socialist doctrine and program of force laid down by Marx over seventy years ago, of which it declares the Third Internationale are the "fulfillers."

As a direct answer to the call issued by the Moscow Internationale the Socialist Party of America at its Emergency Convention in Chicago last September unanimously adopted a Manifesto endorsing the Third Internationale and taking its stand with revolutionary International Socialism as against the United States:

> "Recognizing this crucial situation at home and abroad, the Socialist Party of the United States at its first National Convention after the war, squarely takes its position with the uncompromising section of the International Socialist movement."

Pursuing the identical policy adopted at Lenine's Zimmerwald conference in 1915, and developed in the Manifesto of Lenine's Third Internationale, the Socialist organization adopted, as its "supreme task," a program of systematically undermining and gaining control of labor organizations and welding the workers into "one big union," with the specific and ultimate purpose of employing the weapon of "industrial action," or the general strike, at the opportune time as a means of effecting a revolution!

> "To insure the triumph of Socialism in the United States the bulk of the American workers must be strongly organized politically as Socialists in constant, clean-cut and aggressive opposition to all parties of the possessing class. They must be strongly organized in the economic field on broad, industrial lines as one powerful and harmonious class organization, co-operating with the Socialist Party and READY IN CASES OF EMERGENCY TO REINFORCE THE POLITICAL DEMANDS OF THE WORKING CLASS BY INDUSTRIAL ACTION."

Referring to the loyal leadership of organized labor, it was said:

> "To win the American workers from their ineffective and demoralizing leadership, to educate them to an enlightened understanding of their own class interests, and to train and assist them to organize politically and industrially on class lines, in order to effect their emancipation—that is the supreme task confronting the Socialist Party of America."

Realizing that it cannot win in this country by working exclusively along parliamentary and legal lines, by educational propaganda and by the use of the ballot, the Socialist Party has cast aside all camouflage of being confined to pacific and parliamentary methods, and, as its only hope, has committed itself to the "One Big Union" plan of mass action. In the preamble to their constitution, as in their Chicago Manifesto, they preach the gospel of coercion of the majority by direct action. Advising the workers "to vote as they strike and to strike as they vote," they proclaim: "This is the only way the worker can get control of all the economic factors of life." "It is our purpose," this Manifesto says, "to place industry and government in the hands of the workers with hand or brain, to be administered for the benefit of the whole community." This is Communism or Bolshevism, pure and simple—in one word, Socialism.

Of two reports submitted to referendum vote by the Chicago convention, the more radical Minority report was adopted by a majority of over two to one. This report further stresses the stand of the party with the "uncompromising" international section of the movement, of which the Russian Bolsheviki are the most conspicuous part, and specifically declares its "solidarity with the revolutionary workers of Russia in the support of the government of their Soviets with the radical Socialists of Germany, Austria, Hungary, in their efforts to establish working class rule in their respective countries and with those Socialist organizations in England, France, Italy and other countries who during the war, as after the war, have remained true to the principles of uncompromising international Socialism."

In accordance with the action of the membership, the American Socialist Party asked for recognition by, and made formal application for membership in, the Third Communist Internationale in a letter dated March 18, 1920, addressed to G. Zinoviev, President of the Executive Committee of the Communist Internationale, and signed by Otto Branstetter, national executive secretary of the party. This constitutes the final break of the organization with the moderate wing denounced both in the Moscow and Chicago Manifestos. The stupendous significance of this action has entirely escaped Attorney General Palmer and the American public as a whole, who still persist in differentiating between Bolshevists, Communists and Socialists, meaning by the latter the members of the Socialist Party of America.

It is a serious matter in this grave crisis, when the very foundations of our civilization are threatened, to allow oneself to be deceived by specious appearances. It behooves every citizen to inform himself upon the true character of Socialism and its consequences. This is as great a duty now as was the defense of our country during the time of war. The Socialist is more dangerous than was the external enemy, for he is a foe within the gates, bent not openly upon conquest but upon the radical destruction, by any instrument he can seize, of Christian civilization, democratic government and all the ideals and institutions that we hold dear. This enemy recognized no law, no humane and moral codes, no religion, for these are stigmatized in the Manifesto of Marx and Engels—the Red Bible of Socialism—as merely "so many bourgeois prejudices, behind which lurk just so many bourgeois interests."

Democracy In Industry

(Continued from page 8)

> to us. We have in England an Executive Board for the whole of the union. The board in each of the branches is termed the branch committee, and the appeal of the member goes before that branch committee and they decide the question. I learn that you appoint separate committees entirely as your trial committees to deal with the men if there are any infringements of the law."

Mr. Isaacs admired the trade union health "homes" of this country, owned and controlled by the labor organizations, whereas similar institutions in the same trades in Great Britain are under the guardianship of the employers. The same state of facts applied to trade technical schools. The inflexibility of the old-fashioned apprenticeship system, and the difficulty if not impossibility of a man passing from one subsection of a trade to another in Great Britain, Mr. Isaacs contrasted with the practical methods of learning the essentials of a trade and the occupational mobility of union labor in this country. The habitual offensiveness of the British foreman, his haughtiness and dictatorial airs as compared with the democratic manners of men and foremen in American establishments caused Mr. Isaacs to institute rather odious comparisons. Twenty-two different unions in the printing trades in England attempting the work of unionism done by five international unions in those trades in America, with many times the membership, he also recognized as food for reflection. As to the general spirit in any force of American wage-workers, Mr. Isaacs said:

> "The men were all working at a normal pressure, and there was a far more friendly feeling between the men, the foremen (overseers) and the management than exists in England. The foreman exercises his control with a democratic attitude, and there is an entire absence of that dogmatic officiousness which far too often marks an English overseer. The workmen in America are known to their foremen by their Christian names, and vice versa, whilst the relationship of one to another is of a most cordial character. . . .
>
> "Men are encouraged to think in American workshops, and employers recognize that the brain of the workman is just as likely to conceive useful ideas as the brain of the manager. We know what happens in England if a man thinks he can see a fault in the press or has an idea of an improvement. He is generally told he is not there to do the thinking, somebody else is paid for that job, and he can get on with his work."

It may appropriately be added that one of Mr. Isaacs' conclusions was: "The American workman has a great advantage over the London workman when considering the purchasing power of his wages."

It is, as a fact, pointedly relevant in considering our subject to bear in mind wages. What workers want, aim at and battle for more than anything else, is the highest wages production can yield. Hours and conditions are subordinate to the idea of wages. The shorter day signifies that through it a worker, as the year goes round, can gain the highest wages. Good working conditions are desirable first of all because they maintain the workman's strength necessary to produce wages.

In view of the foregoing considerations, the importers to America of those visions of democracy in industry which were popular among the millennium makers in Great Britain a year or two ago can at this point be asked these questions: Has not English trade unionism abolished the political shop committeeman and his fellow radicals as developed during the recent war? Has not the British Trade Union Congress itself interfered to prevent the joint industrial councils from assuming powers of collective bargaining, or in any way establishing wage scales and conditions, in cases in which trade unions have already occupied that field? Is it not a fact that through its better mechanism the American trade union movement has long customarily performed the essentials of the work proposed for the joint industrial councils formed in consequence of the Whitley Committee report? Are not real wages in the poorest of the one hundred and twenty or thirty international unions and brotherhoods of America at least half again as high as in similar occupations in Great Britain? Are there not many unions in which real wages are double or treble those in Great Britain? Is not, then, the case of a greater possible evolution for democracy in industry in America to be

(Continued on page 17)

Christian civilization upholds, but of Christianity itself.

So profoundly malign, inspired by esoteric underground forces of vast international power, with far-reaching purposes aiming to undermine the foundations of the Christian world, of such subtle and concealed danger, is this movement, that it is all-vital that the people of this country recognize and understand this thing for what it is—that they comprehend Socialism in America as thoroughly as they comprehend Bolshevism in Russia, and that they identify the forces back of both.

TRAITOR TO UNITED STATES

There is in process of organization at the present time, or has already been organized, the Third Communist Internationale. This was preceded by two others, the First, which died after the outbreak of the Franco-Prussian war, when the German Socialists found adherence to the "Fatherland" stronger than international Socialism, and the Second, organized in 1889, which collapsed when the majority Socialists of Germany, France and Belgium respected their national allegiance upon the outbreak of the war of 1914. The Third Internationale was inspired and brought into being by Nicolai Lenine and his associate leaders of Russian Bolshevism. Affirming its international character and revolutionary purposes, it set itself in opposition to all those Socialists who were loyal to their respective countries during the war. The Socialist party of America by referendum vote overwhelmingly declared itself in support of that Moscow Internationale as against the loyal Socialists in the United States and all other countries. It has, by its official programs, manifestos and actions, put its allegiance to Internationalism and the principles of universal revolution above its allegiance to the United States. In fact, it denies all allegiance, and refuses support to, the United States. The Socialist party of America, on March 18, 1920, made official application for membership in Lenine's Third Communist Internationale. In a letter addressed to G. Zinovief, president of the Executive Committee of the Communist Internationale, Otto Branstetter, national executive secretary of the Socialist party of America, on behalf of the party, officially informed the Third Internationale of the adoption by referendum vote of the Minority resolution offered at the convention in Chicago, September, 1919, providing "for direct and immediate affiliation with the Communist Internationale."

His letter said:

"I therefore have the honor to apply to the executive committee for recognition of the Socialist party of the United States of America and its admission to the Communist Internationale."

In its report of this action, the New York *Call*, the authoritative Socialist newspaper, said: "The call for a constituent congress to organize a Third Internationale, in place of the Second Internationale which had met a month previous in Berne, Switzerland, *was sponsored by the Russian Communist party* and supported by the Communist parties of Poland, Hungary, German-Austria, Lettland, Finland and the Balkan Revolutionary Federation." The American representative at the Moscow congress, according to the *Call*, was Boris Reinstein, private secretary to Nicolai Lenine, a Russian Jew hailing from Buffalo, who was an informer and advisor of Colonel Raymond Robins when he was in Russia. "Among those who actively participated in the work of the conference," continued the *Call*, "were Lenine, Trotzky, Bucharin, Kamenev, Tchicherin, N. Steklov, of the Russian Communist party; Rakovsky, of the Balkan Socialist Federation, and Captain Sadoul and Guilbau, of the French Socialist party." The leaders, admittedly, were all committed to bloody revolution. The Manifesto of the congress was drafted by a committee consisting of Nicolai Lenine, Leon Trotzky and I. Zinovief, of Russia, Charles Rakovsky, of Roumania and Frederich Platten, of Switzerland, all men committed to bloody revolution. The Manifesto of the Third Internationale, to which the Socialist party of America pledges support and of which it officially seeks recognition, declared for revolution by force, the arming of the proletariat, the undermining and gaining control of labor organizations with the purpose of employing mass or industrial action, the general strike, as a means of bringing about the overthrow of democratic governments.

DECEIVE IN PHRASEOLOGY OF IDEALISM

The stand officially and publicly taken by the Socialist party of America with the "uncompromising" or revolutionary section of the International movement, its pledge of allegiance and support not to the United States but to International Socialism, its commitment to a program calling for revolution by violence, by industrial action or the general strike, its disloyal, anti-national, anti-American stand against the United States in the war against Germany, do not indicate a change of recent development or merely new radical phases of its character.

Directed by minds of peculiar subtlety and cunning, by leaders whose intellects are more oriental than Anglo-Saxon, masters of craft, resourcefulness and hypocrisy, the Socialist party has for years sought to promote its ends, win sympathy and members, by a scientific propaganda designed to influence different classes of people and meet varying conditions. To the general public it has sought through camouflage and beguiling phraseology to conceal its real character and appear pacific and humanitarian. It has, for instance, specialized in propaganda specifically designed to influence church people, and has not hesitated to employ New Testament phraseology, the terms of Christian justice and brotherhood of man. Repudiating violence, disclaiming any unlawful and unjust methods or purposes among one class of people, it has, on the other hand—for instance, in its Yiddish propaganda for distribution among Russian Jews—sought to inflame by outright incitements to revenge, violence and bloody revolution. Another phase of its propaganda, carried on mainly through the Intercollegiate Socialist Society, has been adapted to meet another condition and appeal to educators, college professors and students. To conceal its basic character to all except its revolutionary *cognocenti,* to create confusion in the public mind, has been one of its chief purposes. In fact, it has made headway among cultured people, among sincere if sometimes superficial folk, among those generally called "intellectuals" and "liberals," by an appeal of phraseology—by the employment of beguiling phrases of altruism and idealism. Its entire propaganda, protean to a bewildering degree, yet masterful, able and amazingly effective, has been inevitably confusing to the Western mind, which is open and direct, and which finds it difficult to think in the terms, and to follow the casuistical, cunning and machiavellian workings, of the asiatic intellect of a Trotzky or a Hillquit.

In its fixed objectives, program and activities the Socialist party has been persistent and consistent. In committing itself to the program outlined in the Manifesto of Lenine's Third Internationale, in declaring as its supreme task the undermining and gaining control of labor organizations with the purpose of employing mass action, or the general strike, as a means of revolution, in having sought to hinder the nation in its war against Germany, the Socialist party was simply following a program adopted by the group of revolutionary International radical Socialists who met, under the leadership of Lenine, at Zimmerwald, Switzerland, in September, 1915, and later at Kienthal in 1916, and who, at the Third Internationale last March declared themselves but the "fulfillers of the program proclaimed seventy-two years ago." By its official action in casting its lot with the Moscow Internationale, of which it becomes an integral part, the Socialist party of America announces that henceforth, as during the war, its allegiance and support in time of crisis would not be given to the United States, but to International Socialism. In this, it but fulfills, as have the Bolsheviki, the program of the furious and vengeful Marx.

COMMITTED TO ACTUAL WARFARE AGAINST UNITED STATES

"We are, therefore," declared Martin Conboy, in his summary of the evidence before the Judiciary Committee of the New York Legislature, "confronted at this day and by virtue of these recent events and facts with the necessity of determining how we shall treat this group of persons who are in the United States but not of it, who, while accepting the benefit of our laws and institutions and sacrifices of blood and treasure given to support them, refuse their support to them, who take all they can get but will not give a life or a dollar to preserve, defend, perpetuate the government that is their sole and only guaranty of life, liberty, property and pursuit of happiness.

"It is the first time since the rebellion of 1861 that notice has been plainly and explicitly served upon the government of the United States by a group of men residing within its borders that they will not support or defend it, but that on the contrary they will by all means in their power obstruct and resist it in its effort to maintain in time of stress its national honor and existence. The present issues transcend in importance even the war program of the Socialist party of America adopted in April, 1917; for disloyal and traitorous as that program was, the present international affiliations and the purposes of the same are the evidence sufficient and satisfactory to the point of demonstration that what transpired at that time was not an isolated act of disloyalty, but only the initial step in a program of treason. The Socialist party of America is not a loyal organization, disgraced occasionally by the traitorous act of a member, but a disloyal party composed of perpetual traitors."

While the majority Socialists of Germany, France and Belgium forsook Internationalism and heeded the call of their country in the war, the Socialist party of America stood by the principles of Internationalism as against patriotism and nationalism. It called upon the workers of America and all other countries to refuse to support the war, and 2,000 members of the party were arrested for their anti-war activities and the principal executive officers and members of the executive committee were indicted, convicted and sentenced to terms of imprisonment. Members of the party who were loyal to the United States were compelled to withdraw from the organization. By pledging support to Lenine's Third Internationale and by its application for admission, the organization is further committed to continue perpetual and actual warfare against the government of the United States and all American institutions. Nor is that warfare, aiming at nothing less than the overthrow of the Constitution and the destruction of our form of government, to be parliamentary, legal and pacific.

NOT A POLITICAL PARTY, BUT INTEGRAL PART OF INTERNATIONAL MOVEMENT

In the words of Mr. Conboy, in his masterly summary:

"The Socialist party of America is neither a party nor American. It is an organization created for the purpose of accomplishing in the United States by any available means, determined only by national conditions and exigencies, the social revolution and the establishment of a Socialist commonwealth as part of the international revolution of which the present Soviet government of Russia is a part.

"The Socialist party is a membership organization distinct from enrolled voters. It numbers among its members infants and aliens. . . .

"The philosophy on which the Socialist party of America, as the domestic expression of an international doctrine is based, is the very antithesis of national existence. This philosophy constitutes the unvarying platform of the Socialist party of America. . . .

"The Socialist party of America adheres to the theory that the citizens of the United States, as well as those of every other country in the world, are concerned with no other consideration than a continuing bitter struggle between two imaginary classes of society, the one seeking to keep the other in perpetual bondage; that it is only in this struggle that those who are adhering to the principle and policies of the Socialist party of America can possibly be interested; that inasmuch as this is a capitalistic government, its aims and its purposes do not deserve, and will not receive, the encouragement, support and fidelity of those who constitute the members of this party, and that it is necessary, therefor, in order to secure the triumph of the principles of the party, that the government of the United States should be overthrown and in its place should be substituted a so-called cooperative commonwealth operated as part of an international institution of the same character, devoted not to the interests of the entire people of the United States, but exclusively to the alleged interest and for the imaginary benefit of the propertyless elements throughout the entire world denominated the proletariat of all countries, in whose hands, in the phrase of its present chief exponent, Nicolas Lenine, there shall be placed an immutable and perpetual dictatorship."

The Socialist party, without mincing words, has repudiated patriotism, nationalism, loyalty and allegiance to the United States. In the war program adopted at the National Convention of the Socialist party held in St. Louis, April, 1917, and later confirmed by referendum to the dues-paying membership of the organization, the international and anti-American character, policy and stand of the party was expressed:

"The Socialist party of the United States in the present grave crisis solemnly reaffirms its allegiance to the PRINCIPLE OF INTERNATIONALISM AND WORKING-CLASS SOLIDARITY THE WORLD-OVER, and proclaims its unalterable opposition to the war just declared by the Government of the United States."

In plain language it called upon the workers to refuse to support the government in the war and outlined a policy to be followed in opposition to the war. On the other hand, it revealed its unpacific character and violent and militant intentions by a declaration of armed class warfare:

"The only struggle that would justify the workers in taking up arms is *the great struggle of the working-class of the world* to free itself from economic exploitation and political oppression, and we particularly warn the workers against the snare and delusion of so-called defensive warfare."

Patriotism, belief in and loyalty to national ideals, love of country, were held up to ridicule, as something false, degrading, to be despised and condemned:

"As against the false doctrine of national patriotism *we uphold the ideal of INTERNATIONAL working-class solidarity.*"

NOT CITIZENS OF UNITED STATES, BUT SUBJECTS OF INTERNATIONALE

In the preamble to the Constitution, dated Chicago, Ill., October 25, 1919, it was said further:

"The Socialist party of the United States is the political expression of the interests of the workers in this country, and is part of the INTERNATIONAL WORKING-CLASS MOVEMENT."

"The explanation of the anti-America attitude of the Socialist party of America during the war lies in the anti-national and pro-international character of its program," declared Mr. Conboy. "Its members are not occasional but perpetual traitors, in constant conflict not merely with the purposes of any temporary administration of the affairs of this government, but with its very institutions and fundamental laws. They are citizens not of the United States but subjects of the Internationale whose pronouncements are to be given their moral support—a support which they not only withhold from but deny to the government of the United States."

The first act of the Socialist party after the armistice was to repudiate those Socialists who had supported their countries in the war, and who engaged in an attempt to revive the Second Internationale at Berne. As against them, the organization officially took its stand with the "uncompromising" group of which the Russian Bolsheviki are the most conspicuous part.

In the Manifesto adopted unanimously at the Emergency Convention of the Socialist party of America, Chicago, September 4, 1919, the International, anti-national and unpatriotic character of the Socialist party was clearly self-expressed:

"We unreservedly reject the policy of those Socialists who support their belligerent capitalist governments on the plea of 'national defense' and who entered into demoralizing compacts for so-called civil peace with the exploiters of labor during the war and continued a political alliance with them after the war."

Again:

"Recognizing this crucial situation at home and abroad, the Socialist party of the United States at its first National Convention after the war, squarely takes its position with THE UNCOMPROMISING SECTION OF THE INTERNATIONAL SOCIALIST MOVEMENT."

Just what is the "uncompromising section" of the International Socialist movement? This is answered in the Manifesto itself. Condemning the loyal Socialists who supported their governments in the war with Germany—who "entered into demoralizing compacts for so-called civil peace with the exploiters of labor during the war"—the Manifesto went on to say:

"We, the organized Socialists of America pledge our support to the revolutionary workers of Russia in the support of their Soviet Government, with the radical Socialists of Germany, Austria and Hungary in their efforts to establish working class rule in their country, and with those Socialist organizations in England, France, Italy and other countries, who, during the war, as after the war, have remained true to the principles of UNCOMPROMISING INTERNATIONAL SOCIALISM."

Elsewhere:

"It now becomes more than ever the immediate task of INTERNATIONAL SOCIALISM to accelerate and organize the inevitable transfer of political and industrial power from the capitalist class to the workers."

According to the "Official Bulletin" of the proceedings of the Chicago Convention, the convention sent to Ludwig C. A. K. Martens, the so-called Ambassador from the Bolshevist Government, the following telegram of greetings:

"The Socialist Party of America in National Emergency Convention assembled sends you fraternal greetings and wishes you success in your endeavors to establish friendly relations between the peoples of the United States and Soviet Russia of which you are an accredited representative. We assure you that the Socialist party will do all in its power to rally the support of the American workers to the aid of the proletarian republic which is an inspiration to THE SOCIALIST MOVEMENT OF THE WORLD."

the central organ of the Soviets, *Isvestiya*, an extract, which, he said, "undoubtedly reflects the view of the Moscow Congress":

"The establishment of the Communist International, which places itself in opposition to the international of opportunists and social traitors, has now confronted all the hesitating elements in the Socialist movement who have not yet sold their principles to the imperialistic bourgeoisie with the option either of joining the advance guard of the proletariat in its fight for the Social Revolution, or of going over to the league of capitalists struggling for social reaction. There is no longer a third way."

Mr. Oneal frankly stated: "The Moscow Congress resolved to take over the work of the Zimmerwald and Kienthal groups after a report by Balabanoff, Secretary of the Zimmerwald International Socialist Committee, in which he was joined by Lenin, Trotzky, Zinovieff, Rakowsky and Platten as members of the Zimmerwald Association."

As against those camofleurs, such as John Spargo, who seek to make capital for Socialism in America by attacking Bolshevism, by throwing dust in the eyes of the general public as to the identity of purposes and methods of the American Socialists and the Bolshevistic Internationalists, Mr. Oneal reported to the National Executive Committee of the Socialist Party:

"*The Moscow Congress certainly have in mind the ideals of Socialism,* not the concept of communism of wealth which has characterized so many religious sects. Its membership is made up of all the elements of the Socialist movement that oppose war and militarism, relies upon the class struggle to chart the course of the movement and keeps in mind the fact that the real struggle in the modern world is one between the workers of all countries as against the ruling class of all countries."

"PATH OF UNCOMPROMISING REVOLUTIONARY ACTION"

The Manifesto of the Moscow Congress, adopted March 26, 1919, was signed by Rakovsky, Lenine, Zinoviev, Trotzky and Platten, and is addressed to the "Proletariat of all Lands." This Manifesto, according to the record of the Albany hearings, was published and distributed in the United States by the Literature Department of the Socialist party of America, by which it was characterized as "undoubtedly the greatest declaration ever issued from any working class tribunal since the Communist Manifesto of Marx and Engels."

The purpose of the Manifesto and of the Third Internationale is described in the introduction:

"Reformistic opportunism is pilloried as it deserves to be. It [the Manifesto] will assist the Socialist movement everywhere into the path of uncompromising revolutionary action that alone can usher in the triumph of International Socialism."

To that Manifesto, whose declarations are frank and unequivocal, the Socialist party of America has officially responded. To the Third Internationale, and the program outlined in its Manifesto, the Socialist party of America has officially pledged its support. To the Third Internationale, dominated by Lenine and his Bolshevist confederates, the Socialist party of America, humbly asking recognition, has officially applied for membership.

The Third Internationale, of which the Socialist party of America becomes an integral part, represents the objects of Russian Bolshevism, and as a means of obtaining those objects in all other countries advocates the same methods, the same program, the same policy of force pursued by Lenine and his bloody associates in Russia. The Third Internationale represents and expresses not only Russian Bolshevism, but that of which Russian Bolshevism is a part and an expression—International revolutionary Socialism.

No one can defend the Socialist party of America, no one compromise with or have sympathy for any aspect, group or wing of the Socialist movement in the United States, without defending, compromising with and giving sympathy to that grisly monstrousness whose unveiled head has lifted itself out of Russia and which reaches out to destroy Christian civilization and democratic government in every country on the globe through violence, terrorism and bloodshed.

(*In the following article will be unfolded the program of the Third Internationale, to which the Socialist party of America is committed, showing the identity of methods and ultimate purpose of Russian Bolshevism and American Socialism. This will clearly expose the hypocritical farce of the Socialist party being different from the Communist wings in seeking to effect a revolution through evolutionary or parliamentary methods, or the use of the ballot, and define unmistakably what is proposed in this country through mass or industrial action, the general strike.*)

Democracy In Industry

(*Continued from page 14*)

studied as an American rather than an imported British problem, the plans to be adaptable to American conditions?

As to any attempt to set up democracy in industry bit by bit, establishment by establishment, the trade unionist would first of all propound to the projectors a query in economics. What guarantee in the absence of trade unionism are the workers in a democratic capitalistic enterprise to have as to the maintenance of the prevailing or union rate of wages? The trade union came into being because individual workers applying for employment were played by employers in competition against one another, the resultant tendency being a general decline of pay toward the level of the final submission of the most necessitous. The unions have worked wages for the mass up to certain standards, the basic requirement being living wages as the term is commonly accepted in this country and a further aim the highest possible share for labor that industry can afford.

The principle of ruinous competition is just as true of establishments as units as it is of individual wage-workers as units. In the highest conceivable democratic conditions the financial results might at times fail to bring to the workmen their desired standard of wages. The processes of competition between establishment enterprises are continuously visible. The keenest organizers of business, the shrewdest bidders in obtaining orders or contracts, the most unscrupulous managers in reducing wages, are factors having their positive advantages. Buyers give their orders for like goods to those who deliver them cheapest. Cheapness often arises from low wages. Wage-workers unprotected by unions will and even must reduce wages on the demand of managers, whether capitalists or men from their own ranks, in dull seasons, or during the decadence of their part of an industry or in case of an oversupply of labor. The workmen of one establishment competing with the workmen of another in these circumstances are unable to prevent wage reductions in both. In accepting the principle of democratizing the industry and in abandoning the principle of trade unionism, wage-workers may therefore enter upon the road to ruin. In the competition between workmen and workmen in groups as well as between workman and workman as individuals, the cheapest drives out of occupation the dearest.

When the query on this capital point finds its answer from the proponents of democracy in industry, the trade unionist may be prepared to consider further principles of the proposition and the details of its possible effectiveness in operation.

Shop Industrial Training

(*Continued from page 4*)

that human being with pencil and paper. You can put six men on six identical machines, same construction, same work, and everything, and there will be a first and a last among them, and a middle one. We are not all born alike; we are not all equipped alike.

'On the one side you will hear the manufacturer say, 'The more we raise wages the less production we get.' That is not true. The great trouble I find is that when the employer raises his wages, he expects the equivalent in production to that raise, and if he doesn't get it he feels that the worker is slacking on the job. Sixty per cent. of our people in the textile industry are piece-workers and there is where the human element comes in. You may have a slacker here or there in a group but the human ambition is to get all they can possibly get in dollars and cents, and they know they can only get it through production. As for the day worker, the other fellow will look after that part of the game. He can soon tell when the workers are slacking, and they don't stay if they do it too much.

''In approaching and solving—and it can be solved—this subject of up-building systems for better production, for more efficiency, for the training of the worker, let us not forget the human element. It is not a matter of dollars and cents, nor a matter of production alone. It is a matter of dealing with it in a human manner, of creating a feeling of confidence, a get-closer-together-feeling between the employer and employee—not to have the employee think and feel that the employer is driving him, and not to have the employer feel that the employee is slacking on him, but to bring about a mutual feeling of confidence, and of determination to give the best remuneration for services rendered, on the one hand, and on the other the workers to give the service that they can without reaching the stage of exploitation.''

Professor David Snedden, Chair of Education, Teachers' College, Columbia University, made the following statements concerning the theory of vestibule and upgrading vocational schools:

''Superficial thinkers are apt to imagine that vocational education should be of one general type for all workers. A few years ago we could think of vocational schools only in terms of professional training—four year courses, fundamental abstract subjects, laboratory methods, and the like. Many of us now commonly think of it in terms of trade school training. But among the sixty million adult workers (40,000,000 wage-earners and 20,000,000 home-makers) in the United States fewer than 2,000,000 belong to the professions even when teachers are included; and it is doubtful whether more than four million more belong to the trades in any adequate historical meaning of the term.

''The war intensified the demand that had been growing for generations for operative specialty workers. The true trades—of baker, shoemaker, wheelwright, stonecutter, bookbinder, and the like—are essentially the products of handicraft production; and they survive today of course, in house carpentry, barbering, locomotive firing, electric installation, shoe repair, and wherever else power driven machinery cannot well be used. But in industry and commerce especially America has committed itself to power-driven machinery, specialization of service and scientific organization of means and methods. From the manufacture of pottery to the adding of columns of figures, from the printing of newspapers, to the laying of concrete, we move steadily towards mechanization of process—with no corresponding intention, surely, of mechanizing the human souls helping in the processes—and subdivision of labor. In times of peace our incessant demands for quantity production with its inevitable accompaniment of standardized parts is but slightly less than in war time. Hardly an American worker today but aspires to an abundance of the shoes, shirts, table-ware, hats, phonographs, parlor furniture, watches, magazines, street-car transportation, canned fruits, crackers, and carpets that are the daily output of highly specialized machinery.

''But for the millions of workers found in these elaborately organized fields of production we have today hardly more than a faint suggestion of systematized vocational education. The ''pick-up'' school is here found at its worst; occasionally it is slightly offset by voluntary corporation schools, usually designed however, to assist potential leaders. No one seriously thinks that true apprenticeship can live in the atmosphere created by factory specialization.

''Would workers, directors of production, consumers, the country at large, be substantially helped by extensive, well organized, and even publicly supported factory schools of the intensive types exemplified in the vestibule and upgrading schools?

''All available evidence points to the conclusion that for most of the simpler operative specialties found in modern factories and other types of production similarly organized, the best training is that given through short intensive full-time courses, often only a few weeks or months in length, on productive work and under shop or factory conditions, such training being directed primarily to improving the proficiency and conserving the health and interest of the young workers. (Obviously the conditions of good professional or trade education are very different and provide no workable analogies.)

''Similarly, all available evidence supports the conclusion that for the more difficult operative specialties as well as for foremanship and other forms of direction, where maturity and previous experience as well as special qualities of native fitness are required, the most economical and effective vocational training consists of short, intensive training under conditions of productive work, available for persons of proved native ability, maturity, and related experience. (It is now intended that evening schools, correspondence schools, and other extension courses shall meet this need, but at best they give fragmentary offerings and quite out of relation to the actual work and needs of the individual.)

The vestibule school can best be tied up with the employment and selective service of a given establishment and its effectiveness is obviously greatly enhanced when the worker from the moment of trial employment can be put in receipt of a learner's wage.''

H. E. Miles, Manufacturer, Chairman, Former Section on Industrial Training for the War Emergency, Committee on Labor, Council of National Defense, said in part:

''Shall each of our thousands of factories be left to work out its own method of training by the slow processes of infiltration and experiment, with infinite mistakes and corrections for a long period of years, or shall a central agency be established where a few of the most expert and experienced leaders in training and in production shall accumulate for the general use a fund of principles, methods and practices that will enable any factory to introduce this training easily and with assurance of success?

''Time is an essential element in this consideration. The world is suffering as never before for the necessaries of life and millions are said to be dying for want of food, clothing and shelter, while, in the judgment of the Department of Labor and many others, our wage-earners are doing not more, on the average, than 60 per cent. of what they might if better trained for their work. Masterful training incites interest and enthusiasm. 'No one can be happy in doing things poorly. Neither quality nor quantity can

Bolshevists Officially Admit Economic Failure

By GREGOR ALEXINSKY

(Former Social Democrat Deputy of Petrograd in the Second Imperial Douma, who suffered imprisonment by the Bolsheviki and who recently arrived in the United States)

DURING my recent stay in Bolshevist Russia I had an opportunity to acquire a large amount of information as to the economic situation under Bolshevism. This information has exceptional value, in the first place because it relates to conditions up to the end of January of the current year, and also because it is drawn from official Bolshevist sources. Among the documents of which I am in possession are the stenographic reports of A. Rykoff, President of the Superior Council of the National Board of Economy, and of M. Tomsky, President of the Central Council of the Trade Unions, and also those of Trotzky, Lenine and I. Kameneff, President of the Moscow Soviet.

What are the reports given by these chiefs of Bolshevism in regard to the economic situation of Bolshevist Russia in January, 1920?

A. Rykoff is chief of all the economic institutions in Bolshevist Russia and directs the work of industrial reconstruction. Although Rykoff is not a gifted organizer, because of his official position he is nevertheless the best informed person as to the political and economic effects of his government's rule, and is by no means inclined to exaggerate the exposition of the negative phenomena of this régime.

On January 25, 1920, Rykoff made a report to the assembled Congress of delegates of the Economic Councils, the Trade Unions and the Moscow Soviet:

> "After the years of the war—both Imperialist and civil—the exhaustion of all European countries, and *especially* of Russia, has reached unheard of proportions. This exhaustion was felt during the whole period of the Imperialist War, *but so far as the wastage of the national wealth and the ruin of material and human forces are concerned, the civil war has led to much heavier losses than the Imperialist War;* because the civil war affected the greatest part of Russian Soviet territory and was manifested not only in the form of conflicts between the armies, but also in the way of destruction, arson, annihilation of commodities and wealth, the value of which is incalculable."

In order to describe this crisis, Rykoff gives figures which I quote from his report:

> "Before the war the percentage of sick locomotives (that is to say, those which need repair), even in most difficult times, did not surpass fifteen per cent. To-day the percentage is 59.5. In consequence, of every 100 locomotives in Soviet Russia there are 60 which are out of service and only 40 which are in working order. The repairing of the sick locomotive diminishes with extraordinary rapidity. Before the war 8 per cent were repaired every month. After the October revolution of 1917 this percentage was reduced sometimes to 1 per cent; at present we have been able to raise this figure, but only to 2 per cent. Under the present condition of the railroads the work of repairing cannot keep pace with the destruction of the locomotives and each month we register a decrease in the number of locomotives at our disposal as compared to the preceding month. This decrease amounts monthly to 200 locomotives. . . . For the great masses of the population, for the workman and peasant of Soviet Russia, these figures signify that it is impossible to exploit any of the grain regions, as well as the regions containing raw materials and fuel which we re-annexed to Soviet Russia as the result of the victories won by the Red Army."

Rykoff gives two concrete instances clearly illustrating the results of Bolshevist policies in the field of transportation:

> "We have a metallurgical region in the Urals, but up to the present time we have been able to dispatch but one train per month in order to ship metals to Central Russia. At this rate it would take us decades to ship 10,000,000 poods from the Urals.
>
> "In order to supply the textile mills in the Moscow region with the cotton of Turkestan, we would have to transport more than 500,000 poods per month. At present, however, we have for this purpose only two trains per month and several decades would be required to transport from Turkestan the 8,000,000 poods of cotton which we could use, but which we are powerless to deliver to our mills."

Nevertheless, it would be a mistake to assume that the lack of raw material is solely explained by the transportation crisis. In the same report of Rykoff's we read as follows:

> "Because of the disorganization in the transportation system, we are unable to procure cotton because the railways are not in position to transport it. But the crisis exists even with regard to commodities which are produced in Central Russia; as, for instance, flax, wool and hides. There is a lack of all these materials because of an acute crisis."

And again the President of the Superior Council of National Economy supplies us with very instructive figures. The production of flax decreased 30 per cent as compared with the prewar period. Before the war more than 20,000,000 poods of flax were harvested in Russia. In 1918, the Bolshevists, having nationalized the crops, obtained only 4,500,000 poods and in 1919 "there was a great decrease." For 1920 Rykoff foresees a further decrease which will be still more considerable. The reserves of flax at the disposal of the Bolsheviki are only sufficient for eight months.

The same negative phenomena manifest themselves in the production of hides and wool.

> "One notices there the diminution in the number of live stock, especially of the kind which furnishes wool for our textile fabrics."

In the first half of 1919 they were able to collect in all the territory of Soviet Russia only about 1,000,000 hides; for the year 1920 Rykoff foresees a decrease which may reach 650,000.

> "The quantity of hides which the state will probably have at its disposal (through 'nationalization') decreases from one month to the next."

Not having enough raw material, industry in Bolshevist Russia is not sufficiently supplied with fuel. The Council of People's Commissaries had fixed the necessary quantity of wood for fuel to be produced for the winter of 1919-1920 at the figures of 12,000,000 to 14,000,000 of cubic sagenes (one cubic sagene being equal to two cubic metres). But the Administrations which were charged with the work forwarded to the railroads and to the rivers less than 2,500,000 sagenes. There is no reason for astonishment that, according to the report of Rykoff, the population of Moscow suffered terribly from lack of fuel which "they lacked even for heating the hospitals." It must be added that of these same 2,500,000 sagenes, the Soviet Administrations were not able to transport to the cities and industrial centers more than a very small quantity and "even the minimum program of supply of fuel for the factories of Moscow could not be carried out because of the lack of means of transport." Rykoff nevertheless finds that the problem of the supply of wood fuel is relatively better than with regard to the coal supply, saying, "things are going badly for the production of coal and petroleum."

Let us pass from the question of the supply of the factories and mills to the problem of the supply of laborers who work in them. Rykoff says:

> "When we speak, in the factories and mills, of the increase of the productivity of labor, the workmen always answer us with the same demand and always present us with the same complaint: Give us bread and then we will work."

Rykoff asserts that in 1919 the Bolshevist government had collected reserves of wheat (by requisitioning it from the peasants) with more success than in 1918 and was able to concentrate in its elevators about January 1, 1920, 90,000,000 poods, whereas the year 1919 gave only 60,000,000. But this success was only relative because in 1919 the peasants only turned in half of the quantity of wheat which the government had decreed that they should give. For the entire population (several tens of millions of persons) which had to be supplied these 90,000,000 poods did not amount to much and Rykoff himself, basing his statement upon the most optimistic estimates, nevertheless says that "in the grain elevators there are reserves which assure the supply for workmen and peasants for three months." And this supply is estimated upon the minimum ration, which is below that which the physical organism of a robust workman requires. Finally, it must be repeated again that the fact that the elevators are filled with grain does not signify that the workmen have bread, and Rykoff states that the Bolshevist Administrations "cannot transport the grain which is stored in the elevators in order to deliver it to the population," and for that reason "the workmen and the peasants have not yet received bread."

Tomsky, President of the Central Council of Trade Unions, describes, in a report, the supply situation in a manner even more disquieting than Rykoff. He says, notably:

> "So far as food supplies are concerned it is evident that under the present conditions of transport we will not be able to accumulate reserves of provisions sufficiently great so that each workman may have a sufficient ration. We must renounce the principle of equality in rationing and reduce the latter to two or three categories of workmen's ration. We must recognize that making our first steps (*this is stated two and one-half years after the seizure of power by the Bolsheviki*) upon the road of ameliorating the situation of industrial workers; we must introduce a system of so-called 'supply of essential occupation.' Above all, we will have to supply those groups of workmen who are essentially necessary to production."

It becomes obvious that such aristocracy in the distribution of bread has nothing in common with the Communist equality which the Bolsheviki promised to the proletariat at the moment of their arrival in power.

Rykoff states in his report that the workmen in their meetings "demand the breach of the economic front of Bolshevism," that is to say, the re-establishment of the freedom of commerce. But the Bolshevists will not have it. The general economic crisis prolonged by the failures of the Bolshevist policy, and the crisis of the food supply, bring with them a great decrease in the number of industrial workers. Out of 10,000,000 workmen which the industrial enterprises included there remain, according to the report of Rykoff, only one million.

Tomsky puts in this report this interesting question: "Where have the living forces of the industrial proletariat become dispensed?" And he formulates this still more interesting answer:

> "If in the capitalistic society the lack of skilled labor usually coincides with the periods of the

most intense work of industry, under our system this phenomenon appears under peculiar conditions of which the capitalistic economy has as yet had no experience. Only a small part of our industry is functioning and at the same time both in the cities and in industrial centers a lack of workmen is making itself felt. We observe a reflux of workers from industrial centers which is explained by bad living conditions. From among these hundreds of skilled workmen who are needed in industry for the most elementary work, the lesser part has returned to the villages and the greater part is found in the army. But the proletariat also deserts industry—to our misfortune and to our shame—in order to engage in speculation and in commerce. This fact cannot be passed by in silence. There is one more circumstance which injures industrial life and stands in the way of the systematic organization of production. This is the vagabondage of the workmen who wander from one place to another, seeking better living conditions."

In order to better appreciate the figures and the data which I quoted in the preceding part of my article, it is necessary to take into consideration that they apply to any industry which is almost entirely "nationalized." In 1918, the Bolshevist government confiscated and nationalized 1,125 private industrial enterprises; in 1920, this figure rose to 4,000. These 4,000 nationalized industries constitute almost the whole of the large and medium-sized industries in Russia. Rykoff reports:

> "Out of these 4,000 establishments about 2,000 are working at present. The rest are closed and remain idle. The number of workmen who are working according to approximate estimates, is 1,000,000. You can see for yourself—that the number of workmen as well as the number of establishments which are in operation prove that industry is suffering from a crisis. . . . The Soviet State, the workmen's and peasant's government, has been unable even to utilize those trades and machines or the stock of technical tools which it had at its disposal, and a considerable number of the mills and factories are shut down, while the rest work only at part of their capacity: certain shops are in operation while others remain closed."

What is most serious is that strikes have affected the most important enterprises. Bolshevist reports give very detailed information in regard to two branches of industry; metallurgy and textiles. Out of 1,200 metallurgical plants, 614 are nationalized. They were able to obtain in 1919 only 15 per cent. of the quantity of metals which was assigned for their needs. The general reserves of metal in Soviet Russia did not reach one-quarter of the quantity which the country had to have "in order to sustain the minimum of industrial life." Before the occupation of the Urals by the Red Army all the furnaces on Russian Soviet territory were extinguished. In the beginning of 1920, out of 97 furnaces located in the Ural region, only 14 were in operation and the number of workmen in them was twice as small as in times of peace. The furnaces which are in operation are able to produce less than 20 per cent. of the normal production. The railroad repair shops repaired in 1919 only 40 per cent. of the number of locomotives which were repaired in 1913. As to cars, the percentage falls as low as 10 per cent. and for the spare parts, it falls as low as 3 per cent.

Here are some figures, given by Rykoff, pertaining to the textile industry:

> "It is completely nationalized but we cannot exploit it even to the extent of a strict minimum. If you take the production of our nationalized textile factories, you will not find even 30 per cent., but only 10 per cent. of the normal output. And out of 164,000 textile mechanics only 11 per cent. were working in 1919."

Rykoff adds that of course it would be possible to find several bright spots on the dark background of the industrial crisis in Russia but "these bright spots cannot change the general conclusion, namely, that national economic life in Soviet Russia is going backwards all the time."

Shop Industrial Training

(*Continued from page 18*)

education of the members, drawings, problems—all for the improvement of the mechanical skill of the workers.

"Not only during the war was an efficient committee on industrial training created as part of the services of the Committee on Labor of the Council of National Defense, but the prosecution of that work was even more extensive and practical than Mr. Miles or Mr. Straus will claim for themselves and for their splendid work.

"Years and years ago, probably fifteen, the American Federation of Labor appointed a committee, made up of labor men, one or two labor women, representatives of the public, men who had given special study to the subject of industrial education and vocational training. That committee was in existence for about three years, and for each year submitted a report, showing a study, deep and broad and high, of this great subject of training the people of the country for service. Those reports were approved and endorsed by the various conventions of the American Federation of Labor and by the organizations affiliated with it. That committee's report was made the basis of the legislation fathered by Senator Page and a member of the House of Representatives whose name I don't recall. The effort was made to include it in the argicultural education bill so that it would be 'agricultural and industrial education and vocational training.' We failed to secure the passage of that legislation as a whole, and in order not to block the passage of the measure in the interest of the agricultural workers of our country, we consented that the industrial portion of the bill should be eliminated and deferred to some other time. We succeeded in having the agricultural bill enacted, and then after several years, we succeeded in having established the federal board for vocational education.

"But, better than all, not only this general official system of education, is the idea of bringing it into the factory, into the shop, anywhere where the toilers are employed, so that they can become more efficient and more highly skilled and better developed in order to make for greater and better production.

"My criticism of the schools is that they teach the academic course. Little, if anything, is taught to the pupil in our public schools that will be of practical value to him or her when he or she may find it necessary to deal with the actual facts of life. I don't want anyone to misinterpret or infer that I am opposed to the academic education. On the contrary, that should be taught, but there should be teaching of the actual facts of life to fit the public to meet the duties of workers. It is unfair, I think, to assume that the old acadamic teaching in our public schools is predicated upon the concept that to work, to give service in manual labor, does not carry with it the dignity carried by education for the professions. It is to prepare boys and girls and men and women to do the real service of our country and of the world, to which we should, in my judgment, devote our attention. Anything that can help to make men and women more efficient really, for the individual as well as the collective good, will make for a higher and a better citizenship and help much toward the perpetuation of this wonderful Republic of ours."

American Profit-Sharing Plans

(*Continued from page 12*)

efficiency is the aim, or philanthropy, or aloofness from the "labor movement," or paving the way to a better society, what is requisite is the leadership of a strong, wise, patient and practical character, especially during first steps.

While for convenience the classification of the book is in chapters on percentage of profits, special distributions, stock ownership and exceptional, abandoned and proposed plans, etc., the fact is that few of the plans are distinctly and wholly in one or the other of these divisions. Many are not, accurately, even profit sharing plans. The variety presented tells the fact that if there is to be a science of pure profit sharing few employers have arrived at a clear perception of its true principles and logical practices. No reason this, of course, for its advocates to weaken in promoting their ideals. Different conditions may give rise to permanent variations in details. Meantime, by reading the interesting experiences of their collaborators, many of the contributors to the book may learn what is not—as well as what is—profit sharing.

There is no monotonous reiteration of one method of treatment, or of one accepted prescription, for the industrial ailment of unrest. Nor is there one invariable code of rules and regulations for establishing justice in all industries alike in the division of profits. There is not only a dissection of business and industrial undertakings in their relation to labor, but there is multifarious presentation of particular phases of the subject.

In general the advocates of profit sharing emphasize these arguments: It promotes more continuous service; reduces cost of production; secures more regular attendance at work; builds up confidence and creates a spirit of co-operation; gets rid of rolling stones; encourages home building; enables a company to keep its employees during rush seasons; keeps down expenses; induces salesmen as well as others interested to work harder; promotes efficiency, interest and loyalty; and increases the profits of the business. On the other hand, disappointment is thus expressed: The efforts of employers were not appreciated by the men; they seemed to prefer their total earnings in fixed wages with no variable element; they were suspicious of the employer's motives; they insisted upon joining unions and presenting demands in spite of the employer's efforts to give them a share in the extra gains of the business; when stock was sold to employees upon favorable terms they would dispose of it on a profit when its value rose, and so get the habit of watching the stock market; when the profit distribution was large the employees learned to expect a similar bonanza every year, and were disgruntled if they did not get it; to say nothing of their discontent if conditions forbade any extra payment at all; and all schemes of this sort are necessarily complicated and hard to understand, so that the workers, especially of the less intelligent grades, are not easily convinced that the system really benefits them and isn't merely a device to withhold a part of what they might otherwise demand and get.

However, if "the sort of profit sharing that is practiced between partners in business" is to be followed in the methods of profit sharing between employers and employees, the books of the employers must be open to representatives of the employees, so that grounds of mistrust as to what the profits really are may be removed, and when that stage of clearing the way to declaring the funds to be divided is reached many of the difficulties in winning the confidence of the wage-workers are overcome.

The expense of printing, almost quadrupled since the first report was issued, the securing and tabulation of first hand data from England and France and other expert preparatory work, necessitate a charge for the new book which will ensure coverage of those items. It may be had at the Federation's headquarters, thirty-third floor, Metropolitan Tower, New York. There are available a limited number of cloth bound copies at $10.00 and in paper cover at $7.50 each.

Tyrrel Print, New York.

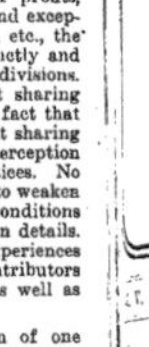

The National
Civic Federation Review

Vol. V. NEW YORK, JULY 10, 1920 No. 4

IS THE LABOR PROBLEM UNSOLVABLE?

GOMPERS-ALLEN DEBATE DEMONSTRATES THERE IS NO OVER-NIGHT NICKEL-IN-THE-SLOT MACHINE SOLUTION OF CAPITAL AND LABOR PROBLEMS—ATTEMPTS TO FORCE MEN BY LAW TO WORK HAVE UNIFORMLY PROVEN A FAILURE

By RALPH M. EASLEY

SAMUEL GOMPERS

GOV. HENRY J. ALLEN

THE widely heralded debate between Mr. Samuel Gompers and Governor Henry Justin Allen of Kansas on the labor question in general took place, as agreed, at Carnegie Hall, New York, on Friday evening, May 28; but the place was the only thing of consequence that the two managing committees could agree upon.

Typifying what was to follow, the committees, after several prolonged and heated conferences, failed to agree upon a statement of the question to be discussed, nor could they agree on the order in which the speakers were to discuss whatever it was they would happen to discuss. So, on the first point, they left it to a "free for all," "catch-as-catch-can" effort, and on the latter they resorted to that highly intellectual method originated by the cave men of "tossing up" for it. In referring thus flippantly to the troubles of the committees which started out with such high hopes of settling the labor problem "face to face," "man-fashion," and all the rest, it is only to place emphasis on the size and the highly complicated character of the job. Of course, starting out in such an atmosphere of disagreement, it is not strange that no debate took place. What did occur, however, and it was entirely worth while and a credit to Mr. Sol Fieldman, who conceived and brought about the meeting, was that three hours of time was evenly divided between two eminent and eloquent speakers, in which, as in all talk-fests of this nature, each attacked the weak spots in the other's armor and, of course, said nothing about his own.

Mr. Gompers, in his first speech, laid the groundwork for a forcible, fundamental argument against compulsory arbitration or the attempt to make a man work against his will. Governor Allen's reply was practically an admission of Mr. Gompers' premises, ignoring the important fact that, by so doing, he was left logically with not a leg to stand upon. The Governor made much of a hypothetical question which he put to Mr. Gompers three times and which Mr. Gompers did not directly answer. In fact, all Mr. Gompers' critics have made much of his "dodging it," as they call it. Mr. Gompers himself said the question—or questions, as there are two included in the one—was a catch question and, to be consistent with itself, should be answered both "Yes" and "No." The questions, as put by the Governor, were:

> 1. "When a dispute between capital and labor brings on a strike affecting the production or distribution of the necessaries of life, thus threatening the public and impairing the public health, has the public any rights in such a controversy, or is it a private war between capital and labor?"
>
> 2. "If you answer this question in the affirmative, Mr. Gompers, how would you protect the rights of the public?"

If the first question had been properly drafted, Mr. Gompers could well have answered "Yes" to the first part and "No" to the second part. To the second question, Mr. Gompers could well have replied: "I don't know, nor do I believe any one else knows." Of course, the Governor would have maintained that the Kansas law would furnish the remedy; but, with Mr. Gompers pointing out that, at that very moment, 12,000 men in a basic industry were on strike in Kansas, in spite of the law, which the Governor did not deny, he would not have gotten very far; and, so far as showing that the Kansas law was an answer to his own question, he did not prove his case throughout the whole discussion.

But, even if every man in Kansas were kept at work under the law, it would have little, if any, bearing on the general problem. What might work in Kansas, an agricultural state, with a comparatively small handful of industrial workers, furnishes no key as to what would work in the great industrial states. There are propositions that might work in Colorado, Utah and South Dakota that would not "get anywhere" in Illinois, Indiana, Ohio, Pennsylvania, Massachusetts, New York and other industrial states. But we do not have to depend upon the operation of the Kansas law, which is barely six months old and under which so far nearly every case has been decided in favor of the men, to ascertain how you can or cannot make a man work against his will. New Zealand, Australia and Canada have been trying it out for from fifteen to twenty years, and, while the arbitration laws in no two of those countries are identical, they all in common aim, under certain contingencies, to prevent a man from striking and to make him work against his will, or go to jail, with the result of uniform failure. As in Kansas, these laws were at first highly respected by some of the workers, because the decisions were practically always in their favor. Times were good and the employers could afford to pay high wages; but when business began to slacken and the boards of managers began refusing the advances demanded by the men and in some cases reducing the wages, the whole thing "blew up," so to speak, and right here is where it "blew." When the board refused to grant the advance demanded by 10,000 abattoir workers in New Zealand, the men struck in defiance of the award. The court being appealed to, placed a fine of $100 on each man, which every man refused to pay. The next step would have been to jail the 10,000 workers. Of course, there were no jails big enough to hold them all, nor were there any office holders with sufficient courage to lock up the ten thousand men, even if there had been plenty of jail room. This showed the men that the law could not be enforced and they lost all fear of it and, consequently, all respect for it. In Canada, to come nearer home, a similar situation arose, in connection with 12,000 miners, with exactly the same result.

Mr. Dorr E. Felt, president of that very live and rather anti-union labor organization, the Illinois Manufacturers' Association, in an address last December before the National Association of Employment Managers, said:

> In studying the industrial history of England, I am rather discouraged respecting much that is being advocated; for instance, compulsory arbitration.
>
> I am very well acquainted with Mr. George S. Beeby, Minister of Labor for New South Wales, Australia, where labor legislation has been carried further than in any other place in the world, involving a complete system of Wages Boards and Courts for the settlement of industrial strife instituted and now in operation since 1901. Mr. Beeby is the author of the present law. He tells me that, instead of reducing industrial strife, under laws which forbid strikes, industrial strife and strikes have increased. In fact, the time lost on account of industrial disputes in New South Wales was six times as great in 1917 as in 1913.
>
> In one of our recent bills in Congress, there was a proposition to forbid strikes on the part of public employees—in this case railroad employees. I am not in favor of that, because the experience with such laws in Europe has always been a failure. It is a good deal like plugging up a volcano—sooner or later you have an explosion that is greater than anything that would have happened had the vent been open all the time.
>
> After the Black Death—the Great Plague—I think that was in 1347—there was a great scarcity of labor, something similar to the present. Laws were passed forbidding labor organizations and strikes. The first one was passed in 1351. It didn't do the work, so from time to time more severe laws and penalties were enacted, until they finally got to the point where those that struck were worked in chain gangs, and some were branded with hot irons.
>
> I have never found a case where laws forbidding strikes were effective. In the early middle ages, under conditions of extreme ignorance and serfdom, it seemed to work for a time, but in the end it always failed.

Bearing so cogently upon this same phase of the question at issue is the following extract from a speech made recently in the Federal Parliament of Australia by Prime Minister Hughes:

> The industrial question, looked at from one point of view, is the result of eternal conflict between the classes. Looked at from another point of view—and, I believe, the right one—it is the inevitable consequence of modern civilization and modern methods of production and distribution.
>
> I confess that I have no remedy at hand. This House has been a laboratory of industrial experiments. I listened to Alfred Deakin introduce the arbitration and conciliation bill in a most glowing and glorious speech, and I feel now as I felt then that along the lines then outlined mankind ought to walk, abandoning the crude barbaric methods of industrial warfare. Years have passed and this perfect piece of legislation has turned out to be, despite every kind of minister in office, the most inefficient and hopelessly futile effort to solve the industrial question that ever came out of the laboratory of any industrial workshop. Even the president of the court had from time to time indulged in gloomy jeremiads and had been torn with pangs of despair.
>
> It is a court the approach to which is marked by barbed-wire entanglements. At the very threshold of its portals there is an almost bottomless pit, and those who by happy chance found their way into the court wander aimlessly about, and at last come out almost without knowing it and saying "Where are we?" or "What has happened?" It has frequently been necessary to strike in order to get into the court, which was designed to prevent industrial strife! Law-abiding unions which had been waiting patiently have then been pushed aside, and the others have gone in and come out full to repletion. The jurisdiction of the court has been riddled again and again by High Court judgment.

Mr. Hughes, continuing, said that they intended to call a conference of employers and employees. They believed that the remedy was in the hands of the parties themselves and that without a good understanding between both sides, no means, no legislation, nothing which was forced upon them from outside would serve.

In other words, after twenty years' experience with all kinds of devices to prevent strikes and lock-outs by law, the Prime Minister, himself a labor man and a statesman, comes back to the original proposition of holding voluntary conferences.

Further testimony to this same effect is found in the English labor paper edited by W. A. Appleton, General Secretary Federation of Trade Unions, London, in its issue of June 11, 1920. A two-page article on Compulsory Arbitration in Australia embodies a letter from Reg. J. Burchell, member of the House of Representatives, Melbourne, in which he encloses a paper read by Hon. H. Y. Braddon, M.L.C., at the annual meeting of the Associated Chambers of Commerce of Australia, held in Sydney in March, 1920. In Mr. Burchell's letter occurs the following sentence:

> I must confess that compulsory arbitration in Australia has resulted in the widening of the breach between capital and labour, and I feel that our present practice needs serious amendment.

And the speech of Mr. Braddon is a critical analysis of the twenty years' legislation and experience under the Australian Compulsory Arbitration Act.

This is not to say that the public has no interest in a strike in basic industries, for it has; but it is to say that compulsory laws do not meet the case, and it is no answer to any one who points out that fact, to retort: "Well, if that will not work, what do you propose?" Granting that in controversies affecting the public as a whole the public interest is paramount, no man or set of men has thus far evolved an effective method for securing to the public those paramount rights. One can easily picture a state of affairs in which it would seem that starvation or freezing to death confronted the American people, yet, without any laws, a way has always been found thus far in our hundred years of industrial development to prevent either of those awful things from happening. In the great anthracite coal strike in 1903, as Mr. Gompers pointed out, the President of the United States created a voluntary commission that settled the controversy in time to prevent any freezing of the public and, as pointed out by Mr. Gompers, in the celebrated "stop-watch" strike of the Railway Brotherhoods, it was settled not by any law but by a commission appointed by the President, consisting of two representatives of the railroads and two representatives of the railroad workers. In the great coal strike last year, the Lever law was appealed to, but the strike took place in spite of it, and it was finally settled by voluntary effort. At one time it looked as though the railroads of the nation would be tied up, but the President again intervened and there was no strike. In the present anthracite coal controversy, after a long series of joint conferences, at which agreement could not be reached, the whole matter was referred to a commission named by the President. In fact, it can pretty safely be counted upon that the President of the United States whenever any great crisis arises will step in, or appoint a national commission of the highest character and standing, which will meet that particular emergency, which is much better, for many reasons, than legislation creating a standing commission to inject itself into every controversy that arises.

Governor Allen stressed his whole argument on this paramountcy of the public in industrial conflicts and the great losses in dollars and cents to all concerned. In public utilities, including in that category coal mining, as in Canada, it goes without saying that such is the case, but there are limitations to this argument. If the workers depended on the public alone, they would rarely, if ever, make any progress, for the fundamental reason that the public is wholly selfish. It does not want to be inconvenienced. In a strike on a street railroad the public does the walking and the swearing. It makes no difference how long may be the hours the men work or how small may be their pay. "If they don't like their jobs," the public generally says, "they should get others, but, under no circumstances make us walk." How long would it have taken the public to wake up and organize to force the "bloated coal barons" to give shorter hours and increases in the pitifully low wages of the anthracite coal miners in 1903?

In regard to the appalling cost to the wage-earners, there is another side to that question. The big headline figures about the losses of hundreds of millions of dollars on account of millions of days' wages being lost are frequently great fallacies. In some cases not a cent is lost and the increase in wages is a clear gain. The 1910 anthracite strike of six weeks only changed the date of the annual shut-down of the mines. Just as much coal was produced for the year, but the miners got more for the portion mined after the strike. The headline statisticians can always scare the public by multiplying days by the wage rates, but no headliner has ever pointed out another startling fact, and that is that in any normal year there are more days of labor lost on any three of the seven national holidays than in all the strikes of that year. Think of the three billion days lost on Sundays and Saturday afternoons, and yet nobody counts that a loss, but a gain. It is not meant by this that there is not unnecessary loss, suffering, injustice and abuse of power many times by the unions, but it does mean that a good deal of the statistics put out on the subject is pure and unadulterated rot.

But to return to the debate. It is safe to say that not a man represented by Governor Allen's committee was impressed by anything said by Mr. Gompers. As one of the committee said in the hearing of the writer: "Well, the Governor wiped up the floor with Sam. He got him going in the first round and never let up." It is equally true that not a trade unionist or a sympathizer with the trade unionists was convinced by anything said by the Governor. A member of Mr. Gompers' committee expressed the general feeling in that regard when he said: "Well, the old man put it all over the Governor tonight. In his second speech he kicked him all over the stage."

In fact, from the standpoint of an outsider, the discussion could be considered a replica of what would have occurred any time in the past twenty years with Mr. Gompers on one side and any of the presidents of the National Manufacturers' Association on the other. But suppose a railroad or a coal strike should occur, law or no law, would the American people starve or freeze? There was a time when the very thought of such a calamity would send the shivers down our backs, but something happened within the last twelve months that threw a new light on this matter or, may I say, put some starch in the backbones of the public. First, there was the threat by the railway unions to tie up all

(*Continued on page 5*)

Socialism Unmasked

HE RELATION OF THE SOCIALIST PARTY OF AMERICA TO THE THIRD INTERNATIONALE—FORCE AND VIOLENCE, THE GENERAL STRIKE, ADVOCATED IN OFFICIAL PROGRAM

By T. EVERETT HARRÉ

II.

SOCIALISM AND MASS ACTION

WHEN the Socialist party of America through its National Executive Secretary, on March 18, 1920, made application for recognition by and admission to the Third Communist Internationale, it discarded all masquerade of being a purely political party seeking only through parliamentary and legal methods to bring about changes in our industrial and social system and form of government. It cast away all pretense of being fundamentally different from the extreme left wings, known respectively as the Communist and Communist Labor parties. Two months later, at its national convention in New York City, the Socialist party, it is true, made a play of qualifying that action; it made what was, so far as the uninitiated public was to be impressed, a grand stand play by which it referred to the Moscow Internationale as only "the nucleus of a Socialist International" and rejected the formula of "the dictatorship of the proletariat in the form of soviets." But while it rejected what is essentially a matter of phraseology, a phase of conditions peculiar to Russia under the Bolshevik revolution, the Socialist party reaffirmed its stand with the Third Internationale.

The significance of this official act of the Socialist party in affiliating with the Third Internationale is not generally appreciated nor popularly understood. Nothing so revealing has ever occurred in the history of the Socialist movement in the United States—not even the adoption in April, 1917, of the notorious St. Louis war platform and program, in which the party committed itself to a course of opposition to the war, for attempting to carry out which 2,000 members were arrested and the principal members of the executive committee were indicted, convicted and sentenced to terms of imprisonment.

The program of the Socialist party in the United States cannot but be interpreted in the light of the program laid down at the congress of the Third Internationale held in Moscow, March, 1919. The activities and propaganda of the Socialist party in the United States, to be understood, must be considered in the light of the avowed world mission and international purposes of the Third Communist Internationale, of which it seeks to become a member and of which, in this country, it would be an official operating part. The recent opportunist camouflage play of the Socialist party, at its New York Convention, cannot obscure the incontrovertible, concrete and basic facts.

THIRD INTERNATIONALE THE OFFSPRING OF BOLSHEVISM

The call for the first congress of the Communist Internationale, later called the Third Internationale, was issued by the "Central Committee of the Russian Communist Party" and the signatures included those of Lenine and Trotzky. This Internationale was born out of the Zimmerwald Conference, held in Switzerland in September, 1915, which was composed of those groups who took a stand against the Socialists who supported their countries in the war. Of these groups, beside the Russians and the French radical Syndicalists, the Italian Socialist party was particularly conspicuous. Following the Zimmerwald conference, at which Lenine was most prominent, a conference was held at Kienthal, Switzerland, April, 1916, and one at Stockholm in September, 1917. These conferences perpetuated the organization of the uncompromising, international, direct-action Communistic Socialists. It was at Petrograd, December, 1918, that the leaders of the Soviet government held a conference at which they decided to found, on the above lines, the Third Internationale, and the call for a meeting in Moscow in March followed. At the Moscow Congress the Russian Communist party, or Bolsheviki, was represented by Lenine, Trotzky, Zinoviev, Stalin, Bukharin, Chicherin, Osinsky and Vorovsky. Four of these are the highest officials in the Soviet hierarchy.

The chairman of the Executive Committee of the Third Internationale, of which the Socialist party of America seeks to become a part, is G. E. Zinoviev, who is chairman of the Petrograd Committee of the Russian Communist party, president of the Executive Committee of the Petrograd Soviet, and a member of the All-Russian Central Executive Committee. The vice chairman of the Third Internationale is N. I. Bukharin, a member of the All-Russian Central Executive Committee, editor of the Moscow *Pravada,* an official Bolshevist organ, and one of the acknowledged leaders of the party.

The headquarters of the Executive Committee of the Third Internationale are at Smolny Institute, which is also the headquarters of the Executive Committee of the Petrograd Soviet and of the Petrograd Committee of the Bolshevist party. The official organ of the Executive Committee of the Third Internationale, the first issue of which appeared May 1, 1919, is issued simultaneously in Russian, English, French and German. The editorial offices are indicated: "Petrograd, Smolny, Office of G. Zinoviev," and the "Kremlin, Moscow," the headquarters of the Central Soviet autocracy.

Zinoviev, as president, addressing a special session of the Petrograd Soviet, November, 1919, declared:

> Long live the future ruler of the world, the great Communist Internationale.

The Third Internationale is regarded, and is spoken of by the chief Bolshevist leaders, as the offspring of Russian Bolshevism, as one of their most important achievements, and as their "own" agency for bringing about in every country of the world a revolution such as has made of Russia a bloody shambles. Zinoviev, in an article in the Petrograd *Pravda,* of November 7, 1919, said:

> OUR THIRD INTERNATIONALE now already represents one of the greatest factors of European history. And in a year, in two years, the Communist Internationale will rule the whole world.

The Third Communist Internationale, conceived in the brains of Lenine, Trotzky and their major associates, brought into being by Russian Bolshevism, of which it is the international agency, gives directions and orders to the Communist parties in other countries, just as, presumably, it will give directions and orders to the Socialist party of America, if Lenine is willing to admit it to membership with the reservations recently specified. "Thus," reads a report made by the Division of Russian Affairs of the United States Department of State, "the Communist Internationale settles a dispute between two Communist parties of the Ukraine, and Kalinin, in the name of the All-Russian Central Executive Committee, sends a message to the Soviet of the Bashkir Republic. Zinoviev, in the name of the Third Internationale, makes certain demands of the Communists of the Ukraine; at the same time Lenine similarly addresses the workmen and peasants of the Ukraine. Also, the Communist Internationale issues appeals to the French workmen and, as already pointed out, to the 'Proletarians of all Countries.' . . . Finally, the Executive Committee of the Communist Internationale issues formal statements protesting against the measures of repression with respect to Communists in other countries, for example in Hungary."

ZINOVIEV TO AMERICAN COMMUNISTS.

Messages to leaders of the Communist movement in other countries are sent from Russia by wireless, which is under strict official Soviet control. Instructions toward an armed revolution and the overthrow of the American government were sent out by Zinoviev, as president of the Executive Committee of the Third Internationale. Documents found in the possession of a Bolshevist courier captured in February at Riga while en route to the United States, and made public by the Department of State, urged "armed insurrection," the "formation of an underground organization for revolutionary propaganda among the masses," and the establishment of a "dictatorship of the proletariat in the United States."

In his message to the Communists in America Zinoviev, repeating sentiments previously expressed by Morris Hillquit, deplored the split in the movement in this country, and laid down a plan for unification. "The split is a heavy blow to the movement," he said; "unprecedented sacrifices must be made by the American proletariat. The question of tactics is the principal source of disagreement and this split is, therefore, unjustified." He went on:

"The party must take into account the every day incidents of the class war. The stage of verbal propaganda and agitation has been left behind. The time for decisive battles has arrived. The most important task confronting the American Communists at the present moment is to draw the wide proletarian masses into the path of revolutionary struggle."

Zinoviev declared the party must work toward the goal of undermining and destroying the American Federation of Labor and other unions associated with it. He urged the establishment of connections with the I. W. W. and the W. I. I. U., and the formation of workers committees, or councils, or local soviets, in factories, "these serving as bases for the every day struggle and for training the advance guard of labor in managing industry."

He concluded:

"The Executive Committee urges American comrades to establish immediately AN UNDERGROUND ORGANIZATION FOR THE PURPOSE OF REVOLUTIONARY PROPAGANDA AMONG THE MASSES AND FOR CARRYING ON THE WORK IN CASE OF VIOLENT SUPPRESSION OF THE LEGAL PARTY ORGANIZATION. The fewer people who know about it the better."

In a third memorandum, Zinoviev said:

"We Communists do not believe it possible

to capture state power by using the political machinery of the capitalistic state." Armed insurrection must be employed. While the recent convention of the Socialist organization in America took occasion—obviously for reasons of expediency—to emphasize its political character, its choice for presidential candidate, Eugene V. Debs, has expressed approval of those who stand for the methods advocated by Zinoviev.

Discussing revolutionary parliamentarism, Zinoviev said:

"Communists elected to congress or legislatures have as their function to make propaganda." Zinoviev extolled "Bill" Haywood, Victor Berger and Vincent St. John, who were all convicted of violating the Espionage act, as "laudable examples."

In Zinoviev's communication to America was a direct incitement to armed revolution, specific instructions for welding all radical parties, for disintegrating the organized labor movement, and for the organization of workers into "One Big Union" for the purpose of using mass action for the overthrow of the Government. At its recent National Convention the Socialist party declared for the "One Big Union."

The memorandum prepared by D. C. Poole, Chief of the Division of Russian Affairs of the Department of State, was based on material from original sources, including the utterances of Bolshevist leaders, extracts from their party organs, extracts from the official press and wireless messages of the Soviets and the publications of the Third Internationale.

The memorandum states:

"The leaders of the Third Internationale are also officials of the Soviet institutions. The propaganda literature of the Internationale is printed in the Soviet printing establishments and included in the official organs of the Soviets.

"The interrelation of the Bolsheviks, the Russian Soviets and the Third Internationale is such, in fact, that while the three may be distinguished theoretically, in practice they represent a single movement, backed by the administrative machinery and the resources of Soviet Russia. This is important, especially from an international viewpoint, because *the aim of the Communist or Bolshevist party is worldwide revolution and the purpose of the Third Internationale is to propagate revolution and communism throughout the world.*

"Therefore," the memorandum concludes, "while the Soviet institutions, as such, may agree to abstain from subversive propaganda abroad, neither the Russian Communist party nor the Third Internationale would be bound thereby."

PROGRAM OF WORLD REVOLUTION.

Here is the crux of the situation as regards official recognition of the Soviet régime. In order to gain recognition and obtain economic assistance, it has been represented that the Soviet government would agree to cease all revolutionary propaganda in other countries. To obtain raw materials and manufactured products, as well as financial aid, from the western nations, the Soviet régime stands ready to make concessions. The life of the Soviet régime depends upon the securing of economic supplies. Therefor the Soviet representative at Copenhagen, Maxim Litvinov, has declared: 'We respect the right of every country to dispose freely of its own affairs, and will not interfere in the interior politics of other nations."

The Soviet régime can well make such a promise. Technically the Soviet régime can keep that agreement. The Soviet régime will not itself officially conduct subversive propaganda or seek to foment a proletarian revolution in other lands. But propaganda throughout the world will continue; the masses will be incited to violent revolution. In this the Socialist revolutionary elements in all countries will be directed and controlled, not by the Soviet government as such, but by the Third Internationale. This is so thin a subterfuge it seems superfluous to expose it.

And for the dissemination of revolutionary propaganda, for underground intrigues to bring about a revolution, for widespread efforts to disintegrate the loyal labor movement and to organize the workers into a revolutionary class organization for the purpose of overthrowing the government, the Third Internationale, it is not illogical to conclude, will have as its agency in the United States the Socialist party of America.

The Socialist party of America, while it has through the utterances of its leaders and its official publications, expressed support of and sympathy with the Bolshevist government of Russia, has not, it is true, committed itself to the program of the Bolsheviki. In regard to that specific program, as to the form of soviet organization and the "dictatorship of the proletariat," it took an adverse stand at its recent convention. Declaring for "the principles of the class struggle and uncompromising working class politics," it asserted that the Socialists of every country must be free to "work out their problems in the light of their own peculiar economic, political and social conditions." While the Bolshevist autocrats were long insistent upon the formulas of the Russian revolution, to which the leaders of American Socialism have taken verbal exception, they have since the beginning of the present year come around to the very point of view expressed in the Majority report adopted at the last convention of the Socialist party of America, and that is that the Socialists, while one in their objectives, may find different methods expedient in different countries, and that therefor, in working toward revolution, they must adapt themselves to existing exigencies. Despite the camouflage set up by the Socialist party, it did not repudidate the program of the Third Internationale, the keynote of which was the keynote of the previous Zimmerwald program, and which is still the keynote of the program adopted by the Socialist party at Chicago of last year. Of the Third Internationale, the memorandum issued by the United States Department of State declares:

"The Program of the Russian Communist party is one of world revolution, and the Communist Internationale is avowedly the directing and coordinating centre of an international revolutionary movement to establish the 'World Soviet Republic.' It is impossible to differentiate as to world policy between the Russian Communist party (or Bolsheviki), the Third or Communist Internationale, and the official Soviet administration, because of the system of 'interlocking directorates' common to all three."

By affiliating with the Third Internationale, the Socialist party of America becomes an acting agency in America of an international body which was brought into being with the supreme purpose of bringing about in all countries, according to methods which different exigencies may demand, what the Bolsheviki, through violence, bloodshed and terror, effected in Russia. To those "liberal sentimentalists," those half-baked reformers, those professional "uplifters," those superficial or sensational clergymen who promote this sinister thing as "Christian Socialism," the application for admission to the Third Internationale by the Socialist party might well give pause.

STIMULATION OF INDUSTRIAL UNREST.

A secret meeting of the Third Internationale was held at Amsterdam for several days, beginning February 3, 1920. The purpose and chief accomplishment of that conclave was the establishment of an Executive Bureau, to be permanently located at Amsterdam, which would receive, and carry out through its world agencies, orders from Moscow. Sub-bureaus are to be established in East Asia, Spain, Mexico and the United States. According to the arrangements, there will be a meeting every three months at Amsterdam of representatives from the Socialist movement in all countries which are members of the Third Internationale.

A report of this conclave was published in the Amsterdam *Handelsblad*. According to this report, the conference was attended by representatives from Germany, Switzerland, the Netherland East Indies, England, Belgium, Hungary, Russia and the United States. It was announced at the conference that the Russian Soviet Government had placed at the disposal of the Executive Bureau, a collection of diamonds, pearls and other precious stones to a value of 20,000,000 rubles. And for what purpose are these funds to be used? What is the immediate program of the Executive Bureau? In what work will the sub-bureaus in other countries, including the United States, cooperate?

S. J. Rutgers, a Dutch engineer employed by the Soviet government, a Bolshevist propagandist who has contributed articles to pseudo-intellectual pro-Bolshevist weeklies in this country and who was one of the principals at the Moscow Congress, went from Moscow, where he lives, to Amsterdam as the representative of Lenine and was the bearer of the "glad tidings" of the gift of diamonds and pearls. The *Handelsblat* quoted Mr. Rutgers, who apparently spoke for Nicholas Lenine, as saying that the money realized from the sale of the jewels "must be used for the support of every strike and every movement which bears a revolutionary character."

Amsterdam is one of the world chief markets for diamonds and jewels, and is the regular market for jewelry stolen in Russia, looted from palaces and churches, by the Bolsheviki. One of the brokers employed by the Bolsheviki is a Communist member of the Amsterdam city council. The *Handelsblat* stated that Mrs. Rutgers admitted bringing to Amsterdam a diamond cross, a pearl necklace, one very big and one small diamond, which were to be sold and the cash turned over for furthering the Communist movement.

Further details concerning these jewels are given in a recent article in the Paris *Matin*.

"These jewels were remarkable. There were a great cross in diamonds, a collar of pearls and a number of large solitaires, one of which weighed forty-one carats and was worth a million francs. . . . Three times following Mme. Rutgers made the same trip to Russia and return. Each time she brought new diamonds, which were turned over to a diamond worker at Amsterdam, Lisser, a member of the Communist party of Holland." One of the large stones, it was asserted, was taken from a statue of the Virgin in the Cathedral of St. Isaac at Petrograd.

The first important result of the establishment at Amsterdam of the Executive Bureau and the raising of a huge fund out of the sale of the stolen jewels, according to the *Matin*, was the calling of the general strike in France May 1. This strike, which was successfully crushed by Millerand, was to have been the beginning of a revolution in France, under the leadership of Loriot and Monatte, who with other strike leaders were arrested by the French government. There were found in their possession letters from Trotzky giving directions as to how the French coup was to have been effected. These letters came by way of Amsterdam, and in them Loriot and Monatte were named as the official lieutenants of Moscow.

Speaking of the purposes and accomplish-

(Continued on page 21)

Department on Study of Revolutionary Movements

XECUTIVE COUNCIL APPOINTED—COMMITTEES TO STUDY AND COMBAT REVOLUTIONARY RADICAL-ISM BEGIN WORK—IMPORTANT ORGANIZATIONS TAKE ACTION TO COOPERATE

S a result of the proposal made at the annual meeting of The National Civic Federation in January and of the subse-ıent conference on Socialist Tactics held at the otel Astor on February 16, there has been com-›leted the appointment of an Executive Commit-ee and the organization of various subcommit-ees, the chairmen of which form the Executive Council, of the Department on the Study of Revolutionary Movements. The campaign will e of nation-wide scope. The committees have egun their work, and already a number of im-ortant organizations have officially offered to ooperate.

In the proposal for this movement, sent out in ebruary by The National Civic Federation, it as pointed out that the revolutionary radicals ave been promoting their propaganda through chools, churches, colleges, lecture forums, the ress, labor, charity and other organizations. In-ormation as to these insidious activities has ac-umulated since then and evidence in the hands f the committees emphasizes the urgent need f such work as was proposed.

The response has been inspiring and promis-ng. Notable and representative leaders of the arious elements of our national life, business, agriculture, labor, the church, education, et-cetera, have joined in the movement. In response to a letter sent out by Judge Alton B. Parker, president of The National Civic Federation, to a number of national organizations, including com-mercial, fraternal, social and labor bodies, reso-lutions pledging the efforts of these organizations in promoting loyalty and devotion to American ideals and authorizing the appointment of na-tional service committees, which should cooper-ate with similar organizations, have been passed at their annual conventions by the National As-sociation of Credit Men, which includes one hun-dred and eighty-eight local organizations; by the Association of National Advertisers, and by the Associated Advertising Clubs of the World. Fa-vorable action from many other organizations is assured.

The resolution sent out by Judge Parker as a suggestion for action by these organizations is as follows:

> *Whereas,* American ideals and the American form of government are being assailed in an insidious and active propaganda of destructive radicalism; and
>
> *Whereas,* we believe that the present situation de-mands an unmistakable expression of defensive and constructive loyalty upon the part of all organiza-tions and individuals who are devoted to the American principles of Liberty, Representative Gov-ernment, the Supremacy of Law and the Enlightened Rule of the Majority; therefore be it
>
> *Resolved,* that the (name of organization) hereby pledges its sincere interest in the suppression of disloyalty and the promotion of Americanism, and, to this end, be it further
>
> *Resolved,* that a National Service Committee of (number) members to be appointed by the President of this organization, be and hereby is constituted to take active and adequate steps of co-operation with all other similar committees in other organiza-tions in order to bring about a restoration of the national spirit of the public good which was so conspicuous and inspiring a feature of wartime patriotism.

The objects of the Department on the Study of Revolutionary Movements are:

To inquire into the objectives and tactics of revolutionary forces in this country;

To inquire into the extent to which these forces have permeated the various divisions that make up the body politic;

To make a survey of industrial, political and social progress; and

To give support to all practical means tending to improve the general well-being of our people.

To accomplish the purposes of the Department, the work was divided among various committees, which are as follows:

1. *A Committee on Socialist Doctrine and Tactics,* whose work shall include the preparation and distribution of literature, and the organization of a training school for speakers.
2. *Committees to Make an Intensive Study* of the extent to which *Revolutionary Forces* have penetrated into the fol-lowing and other fields:
   Labor,
   Agriculture,
   The Church,
   The College,
   The Public School,
   The Press,
   Social Agencies,
   Philanthropic Agencies,
   Foreign Groups,
   Women's Organizations,
   Public Employees,
   Negroes.
3. *A Committee to Study Text Books on History, Political Economy and Civics in use in the high schools and colleges.*
4. *A Committee on Soviet Propaganda in the United States.*
5. *A Bureau to Evaluate Federal, State and Municipal Official Statistics,* as well as socialist deductions from same.
6. *A Committee on the Fundamentals of our Constitution* and their application to every-day life, including the *Limita-tions of the Right of Free Speech, Free Press and Peaceable Public Assembly.*
7. *A Committee on Survey of Industrial, Political and Social Progress,* and Con-structive Recommendations.

The Executive Council of the Department con-sists of the following: Condé B. Pallen, Depart-ment Chairman; Clarence H. Wilson, First Vice-Chairman; Sara A. Conboy, Second Vice-Chair-man; Ralph M. Easley, Chairman Executive Council; A. L. Frothingham, Chairman Com-mittee on Socialist Doctrine; Talcott Williams, Chairman Committee on Text Books; Stanley Washburn, Chairman Committee on Soviet Prop-aganda; Howard White Starr, Chairman Com-mittee on Evaluation of Official Statistics; Harry Chase Brearley, Chairman Committee on Organ-ization; Everett P. Wheeler, Chairman Commit-tee on the Church; John Hays Hammond, Chair-man Committee on the College; Walter George Smith, Chairman Committee on Fundamentals of our Constitution; John L. Tildsley, Chairman Committee on the Public School; James P. Hol-land, Chairman Committee on Labor; Lorillard Spencer, Chairman Committee on Soldiers and Sailors, and Arthur O. Townsend, Chairman Committee on Philanthropic Agencies.

The Executive Committee is as follows:

LAWRENCE F. ABBOTT (Editor, *The Outlook*), New York.
CYRUS ADLER (Acting President, Jewish Theological Sem-inary of America), New York.
HERBERT BARRY (Attorney), New York.
SAMUEL A. BERGER (Deputy Attorney General, New York State), New York.
WHEELER P. BLOODGOOD (Loyal Legion of Wisconsin), Milwaukee, Wis.
MISS HELEN VARICK BOSWELL (President Republican National Women's Committee), New York.
ROME G. BROWN (President, *The Minneapolis Tribune*), Minneapolis, Minn.
JOHN FOSTER CARR (Director Immigrant Publication So-ciety), New York.
GUSTAV A. CARSTENSEN, D.D. (Rector Holy Rood Church), New York.
THOMAS N. CARVER (Professor of Economics, Harvard University), Cambridge, Mass.
D. L. CEASE (Editor, *The Railroad Trainman*), Cleveland, Ohio.
W. I. CHAMBERLAIN, D.D. (Board of Foreign Missions, Reformed Church in America), New York.
MAJOR ELIHU C. CHURCH (Chamber of Commerce of State of New York).
BIRD S. COLER (Commissioner of Public Charities, City of New York).
PETER W. COLLINS (Knights of Columbus), Chelsea, Mass.
MARTIN CONBOY (Attorney), New York.
THOMAS DARLINGTON, M.D. (Sachem, Tammany Society), New York.
EDWIN L. EARP (Drew Theological Seminary), Madison, N. J.
CHARLES AUBREY EATON (Associate Editor, *Leslie's Weekly*), New York.
HUGH FRAYNE (General Organizer, American Federation of Labor), New York.
JOHN P. FREY (Editor, *International Molders' Journal*), Cin-cinnati, Ohio.
JOHN GOLDEN (International President, United Textile Work-ers of America), New York.
F. G. R. GORDON (Writer), Haverhill, Mass.
WILLIAM GREENOUGH (Attorney), New York.
Mrs. NATHANIEL E. HARRIS (President, Council of Jewish Women), Bradford, Pa.
PHILIP HISS (Formerly Special Assistant for Housing, Navy Department), New York.
JOHN B. KENNEDY (Knights of Columbus), New York.
WALTER LAIDLAW, D.D. (Executive Secretary, New York Federation of Churches), New York.
CAPT. GEORGE B. LESTER (Formerly of the Military In-telligence Division, United States Army), New York.
OLIVIA LEVENTRITT, New York.
BURDETTE G. LEWIS (N. J. State Commissioner of Institu-tions and Agencies), Trenton, N. J.
MARTIN W. LITTLETON (Attorney), New York.
EARL P. LOTHROP, M.D. (Physicians' Protective Association), Buffalo, N. Y.
EDSON S. LOTT (Insurance Federation of America), New York.
ELISABETH MARBURY (Women's Democratic Political League), New York.
CAPT. HUGH S. MARTIN (Formerly of the American Mili-tary Intelligence Service in Russia), Meridian, Miss.
MARK A. MATTHEWS, D.D. (Pastor First Presbyterian Church), Seattle, Wash.
CHARLES R. MILLER (Editor, *New York Times*), New York.
HILL MONTAGUE (President, National Fraternal Congress), Richmond, Va.
MRS. PHILIP NORTH MOORE (President, National Coun-cil of Women), St. Louis, Mo.
DR. CHARLES P. NEILL (Bureau of Information, South-eastern Railways), Washington, D. C.
MORGAN J. O'BRIEN, JR. (Attorney), New York.
T. V. O'CONNOR (President, International Longshoremen's Association), Buffalo, N. Y.
WILLIAM BRADLEY OTIS (College of the City of New York).
CLIFTON REEVES (Willys-Overland Company), Toledo, Ohio.
MONTGOMERY SCHUYLER (Formerly U. S. Chief Intelli-gence Officer at Omsk, Siberia), New York.
TIMOTHY SHEA (Acting President, Brotherhood of Locomo-tive Firemen and Enginemen), Cleveland, Ohio.
MARION D. SHUTTER, D.D. (Pastor Church of the Re-deemer), Minneapolis, Minn.
RABBI JOSEPH SILVERMAN (Temple Emanuel), New York.
ARCHIBALD E. STEVENSON (Attorney), New York.
LIONEL SUTRO (Chairman Committee on Education, City Club of New York).
CHARLES R. TOWSON (Secretary, Industrial Department, International Committee of Y. M. C. A.'s), New York.
MRS. COFFIN VAN RENSSELAER (Executive Secretary, Woman's Department, The National Civic Federation), New York.
JOHN A. VOLL (President, Glass Bottle Blowers' Association of the United States and Canada), Philadelphia, Pa.
MISS MAUDE WETMORE (Chairman, Women's Department, The National Civic Federation), New York.
MATTHEW WOLL (President, International Photo Engravers' Union), Chicago, Ill.
ARTHUR WOODWARD (President, New York Rotary Club), New York.
MRS. JOHN FRANCIS YAWGER (National Society, Daughters of the American Revolution), New York.

Is the Labor Problem Unsolvable?

(Continued from page 2)

the railways of England and then the real attempt to put the threat into effect. The people replied to the radical demands of the railroad men: "No! Our backs are against the wall. Go to it and we will show you where you get off." And they did show them. The same thing hap-pened in this country when the coal miners threatened to force, through a strike, an unrea-sonable set of demands. The people said: "Strike! We will not have a government by miners or any other class of people." In that situation the public suffered, but it showed the miners that it was willing to suffer. Governor Allen himself gave the most effective exhibition of how to meet unreasonable demands from wage-earners.

But both of these crises were met without

(Continued on page 20)

Plan to Create National Service Committees

COMMITTEE ON ORGANIZATION OFFERS PLAN WHEREBY ORGANIZATIONS CAN COOPERATE TO PROMOTE DEFENSIVE AND CONSTRUCTIVE LOYALTY

The Committee on Organization, Harry Chase Brearley, chairman, has sent to the business, labor, fraternal, professional, social and other organizations of the country a proposal that they organize national service committees, under which will work local subcommittees, each of which would be an organ of cooperation in a nation-wide movement to defend American ideals against disloyal revolutionary propaganda and to promote the spirit of constructive loyalty.

It is pointed out that there are more than 800 national and interstate organizations of a commercial, industrial and professional nature, also large national labor bodies, most of which have state and city sub-divisions. By the appointment of national service committees in these organizations, as would be analygous to the war service committees, a nation-wide cooperative movement can be obtained whereby the efforts to undermine our national ideals and destroy our form of government could be effectively fought. While this is the immediate task in the present emergency, such an organization would have in mind a bigger and more permanent work in the promotion of national consciousness and in efforts for making a better America.

The proposal issued by the Committee on Organization is as follows:

During the past few months, the public has been of half a dozen minds in regard to the nature and degree of the menace offered by the extreme radicals who have been known under various names as "communists," "I. W. W.'s," "Bolsheviks," "anarchists," "socialists" and "reds." There have been periods of alarm followed by periods of skepticism as to the existence of a menace. These in turn have given way to renewed concern when some fresh occurrence or rumor has seemed to justify it. Out of the entire confusion the following facts seem to be emerging:

FIRST: there is a definite menace in the present situation—one that it would be foolish to ignore or to under-estimate.

SECOND: the destructive radical element is purposeful, well organized, fairly well financed, numerous, and, as regards a large part of its membership, dangerously sincere.

THIRD: general public conditions of social and industrial unrest, including the high cost of living and the uncertainty as to future developments, offer favorable soil for the propagation of radicalism.

FOURTH: the presidential campaign is always more or less a period of excitement during which clear thinking may be obscured by appeals to prejudice. The present campaign presents large possibilities in this respect.

FIFTH: in spite of these reasons for concern, it is undoubtedly true that the great mass of the population is patriotic, intelligent, industrious and law-abiding, also that it is capable of great self-sacrifice for the public good.

AN ATTACK UPON IDEALS

There has been a good deal of crying "wolf," but back of it all there is a wolf and it is unwise to shut one's eyes to perfectly plain facts. Documents and other evidence now in the possession of the authorities indicate a purpose upon the part of a determined and dangerous minority to attack the American ideals of Liberty, Representative Government, the Supremacy of Law and the Enlightened Rule of the Majority. Therefore, questions of ways and means for opposing the organized and purposeful minority with an organized and purposeful majority become immediate and important.

We have only to turn our minds backward for two or three years to recall a condition which has not been sufficiently emphasized in the present discussion. When the United States entered the war it found itself confronting a great emergency but in a condition of loose organization. In a sense we went to war, not as a nation but as a collection of American units, big and little, and this fact cost us many months of delay in attaining any degree of efficiency.

WHY THE COMMITTEES WERE FORMED

A very important truth soon manifested itself; namely, that the war would have to be fought not merely by the army and navy, but by the entire nation—by its industries, its transportation, its agriculture, its mines, its finance, even by its newspapers, churches and schools. When we had once grasped this fact we began to organize every resource that the nation possessed in order to make it effective. There probably was hardly an industry, a profession or an interest which did not form its own War Service Committee, charged with the duty of organizing for war purposes its particular line of activity. These committees worked in different ways for they had very dissimilar tasks to perform, but they all had one fundamental and unifying purpose—namely, that of winning the war, and the Government itself acted as the coordinating agent.

By the middle of 1918, we had pretty well passed through the flag-waving and band-playing stage of our patriotism and had settled down to such definite, systematic and closely organized work that America might literally be said to be fighting as a single, vast, unified organism of almost immeasurable strength.

By the end of 1918, however, a process of disintegration set in because the war had been won and people, industries and professions alike turned back to a consideration of their own individual affairs. Now when we are confronted with a new emergency, the perfectly plain lesson of this war organization seems to have been strangely overlooked by the many patriotic movements that are trying to arouse and to organize our citizens. Let us state the proposition very simply:

NEW ORGANIZATIONS NOT NECESSARY

The situation demands the efforts of an organized America, *but America already is organized in its essential parts, and if these parts can be put together as they were during the war—Presto! there is an organized nation.*

Most activities have started out with the thought that new organizations are needed. This is not the case. The organizations already in existence are ample and efficient. They possess all the necessary machinery, all the necessary brains and all the necessary patriotism; they need only to be awakened and set to work, when they will operate with an efficiency not to be expected of any new organization.

There are at the present time more than eight hundred national and interstate organizations of a commercial, industrial and professional nature. There are also a large number of national labor bodies. Most of these organizations have state sub-divisions; many of them have city sub-sub-divisions. They generally have paid secretaries or other executives; they maintain offices; they have their own mailing lists; they have their own monthly or weekly publications. They have their executive committees or other governing bodies; they have their lines of influence and appeal. Some of them are more efficient than others, but the average of efficiency is high, and the aggregate of all these institutions with all of their direct membership and all of their indirect affiliations is the aggregate of the material, the intellectual and the spiritual resources of the nation. Put them together and they constitute America. They were put together during the war and they made it possible to win the war.

RESTORING COOPERATION

In the present emergency it should be perfectly possible to restore the cooperation of these incalculable forces. How can they be put together? The war gives us our answer. They can be put together by means of special committees organized by each interest adapting their methods to the peculiar conditions of their respective fields of action, but combined as to purpose and working in harmony as to certain essential ideals. Such committees would be analogous to the War Service Committees. In other words, we propose a deliberate attempt to make it possible for all business organizations, all labor organizations, all professional organizations, and all other organizations of every kind whatsoever, which sincerely represent the best interests of any portion of the American public, to employ their full organization efficiency for the purpose of promoting defensive and constructive loyalty.

Assuming an expression of willingness upon the part of a considerable percentage of these organizations the question then arises as to what we shall suggest for their accomplishment. This reaches the crux of the whole discussion. If our structure is to be important, our foundations must be solid; if our appeal is to be capital and labor alike, to men and women alike, to Republicans and Democrats alike, to North, East, South and West alike, it must start with fundamental principles upon which all American people can unite.

OUR PROBLEMS PRIMARILY SPIRITUAL

Therefore, please note that our present national problems are not primarily political and are not primarily economic. These are important phases, but they are secondary. *Our problems are primarily spiritual, since they concern the spirit of the American people.* It is equally true that they cannot be settled politically nor economically; they will never be settled until they are settled spiritually.

This reduces the question at once to a matter of ideals. America has always stood for certain specific ideals and several times it has shown its willingness to go to war in their defense. Four of the most important of these ideals are: *Liberty, Representative Government, the Supremacy of Law and the Enlightened Rule of the Majority.* Loyalty to America is essentially loyalty to its ideals. Defensive loyalty is the defense of these ideals when they are in danger; constructive loyalty is the application of these ideals to new problems of national life.

We submit, therefore, that all true Americans in all spheres of action can find absolutely common ground in defensive and constructive loy-

(Continued on page 23)

Need for Legislation Against Disloyalty

DISCUSSION ON SO-CALLED LUSK BILLS SHOWS NECESSITY FOR MEASURES TO MAKE PROSECUTIONS POSSIBLE—CRIMINAL ANARCHY STATUTE OF NEW YORK NOW A DEAD LETTER

(Photo by Gessford)

ARCHIBALD E. STEVENSON

BECAUSE of the lack of effective legislation, providing for the investigation and prosecution of such crimes, the criminal anarchy statute of the state of New York, enacted after the assassination of President McKinley eighteen years ago, has been a dead letter. Until the Lusk Committee, which investigated disloyal and seditious activities in the state, obtained evidence and turned it over to various prosecuting officers and district attorneys there had never been a single prosecution under the Criminal Anarchy statute. As a result of the evidence unearthed by the Lusk Committee, there have been some eighty-five indictments, and five cases have been tried. In each of these, there has been a conviction.

This amazing situation was revealed at a conference on the so-called Lusk bills, held May 11 at the Hotel Astor, New York, under the auspices of the Committee on Socialist Doctrines and Tactics of The National Civic Federation. Conde B. Pallen presided and the chief speakers were Samuel A. Berger, Assistant Deputy Attorney General, and Archibald E. Stevenson, special counsel of the Lusk Committee, who had much to do in drafting the bills. It was established, in the speeches of Mr. Berger and Mr. Stevenson, and in the general discussion that followed, that such legislation as was proposed is vitally necessary to stamp out organized sedition and anarchy and to safeguard the young generation from disloyal and unsound teaching in schools, both public and private. While the bills as they were written may possibly have been defective, and have since been vetoed by the Governor, the principles underlying them are sound, and, as a result of the discussion, the Committee on Socialist Doctrines and Tactics will urge the redrafting of the measures.

SAMUEL A. BERGER, assistant Deputy Attorney General, discussed the bill known as "Senate Bill 1272," and entitled "An Act to amend the executive law, in relation to powers of attorney-general with respect to prosecutions for criminal anarchy, and making an appropriation therefor." Mr. Berger said:

"Before discussing the bill itself, I think it might be proper to read those portions of the criminal anarchy statute which are relevant and without a proper understanding of which it is quite impossible to get the true purpose and object of this bill. In 1902, following the assassination of President McKinley, there was placed on the statute books of this State an act known as the Criminal Anarchy Statute. According to our Penal Law, criminal anarchy is defined as follows:

"'Criminal anarchy is the doctrine that organized government should be overthrown by force or violence, or by assassination of the executive head or any of the executive officials of government, or by any unlawful means. The advocacy of such doctrine either by word of mouth or writing is a felony.'

"Now that has been a law of this State some eighteen years. There never has been a prosecution under that statute until the Lusk Committee obtained certain information and turned it over to various prosecuting officers and various district attorneys in this State. To date there have been some eighty-five indictments, and but five of these cases have been tried. In each of the five cases there has been a conviction, and in each case the defendant was sentenced to the maximum term of imprisonment in State's Prison, and in each instance each defendant is now in State's Prison serving the sentence given to him by Mr. Justice Weeks, of the Extraordinary Criminal Trial Term of the Supreme Court. In each one of those cases the evidence was furnished and the cases prepared in co-operation with the counsel for this Committee. I do not think that, on behalf of the Committee and its counsel, I am speaking immodestly when I say that if it had not been for the work of our Committee in obtaining the evidence, in turning it over to the District Attorney preparing the case, and sitting in with the District Attorney, furnishing interpreters, investigators and operatives, that there never would have been any indictment; there never would have been a trial or conviction, and those five men who are today serving sentences, each one justly imposed and a conviction properly found, would today be at large, continuing to preach criminal anarchy and continuing to preach the doctrine that organized government should be overthrown by force, violence and unlawful means.

"There are some eighty other indictments in different counties in the State that have not yet been tried and, without meaning in the slightest degree to reflect upon the zeal, ability, or industry of the various district attorneys of those counties, I believe those cases have not been brought to trial because the particular offices of the district attorneys in whose counties those violations occurred are not equipped to try those cases. It requires a great deal of work. You must understand the proposition from the ground up; you must have interpreters and investigators. Although a year has elapsed, with eighty-five indictments found, there have been but five trials. In Kings County five men pleaded guilty. They were not placed on trial. They pleaded guilty to unlawful assembly. I don't know really whether they have been sentenced.

"That is the situation with reference to the existing Penal Statute, denominated criminal anarchy, and entitled Article 14 of the Penal Law. The Committee and its counsel have been of the opinion that there should be no repressive legislation enacted in this State, but that this criminal anarchy statute, where it has been violated and where a person has been found guilty of violating it, should be rigidly enforced, and the person tried, convicted and sent to jail.

"We believe that if this statute is a salutary measure, it should be enforced, and if the people of this State do not want that statute enforced and on the contrary want to foster and encourage the teaching of criminal anarchy, then the proper thing to do is to repeal it.

(Photo by Bachrach)

SAMUEL A. BERGER

"We believe that by creating a bureau in the office of the Attorney-General for this purpose, the statute will be effectively enforced. The Attorney-General by this bill is not given executive jurisdiction. A reading of the bill very clearly indicates that the Attorney-General is merely given concurrent jurisdiction with the various district attorneys of the various counties of the State. That serves as an effectual check on some district attorney who may not be zealous in a prosecution or who is not well equipped to start a prosecution. It gives the Attorney-General the right to appear before the Grand Jury in the first instance and to supply it with information from which there may or may not be an indictment found, and it authorizes him in cases where there has been an indictment found, to prosecute that indictment to its conclusion.

"By giving the Attorney-General concurrent jurisdiction with the district attorneys, we have not any radical departure from precedent. The Attorney-General at the present time has original jurisdiction in a number of instances. For instance, the Public Health Law. Certain portions of it empower the Attorney-General with original jurisdiction; and I will digress for a moment to show the very salutary effect of that. For years spurious dentists—that is, persons calling themselves dentists—practiced dentistry in this State without being licensed. The various district attorneys in the various counties had jurisdiction over the prosecution of those cases. Dental societies prosecuted these cases, and this prosecution, or, rather, lack of prosecution, was such that the State was just swamped with men and women practicing dentistry who had no legal right to do so. Some three years ago, in the early part of 1917, a statute was enacted which empowered the Attorney-General in the first instance to prosecute persons violating the Public Health Law with regard to dentistry, and I think Dr. Downing, Assistant Commissioner of Education, will bear me out when I say in the State of New York there are now practically no unlicensed dentists. I know that of my own knowledge, because some years ago when this act was made into a law I happened to have charge in the Attorney-General's office of that particular branch of the work, and the records of our office show that, without exception, wherever a person was charged by the Attorney-General with practicing dentistry without a license, there was a conviction, and in that branch of our work the Attorney-General's office has a one hundred per cent. batting average. Not one man charged with a crime was acquitted, and the presumption is that the courts would not have convicted those particular defendants unless they had been guilty.

"The Attorney-General has jurisdiction in enforcing and prosecuting violations of the Agricultural Law. He has similar jurisdiction in the case of the Election Law. In various other ways the Attorney-General has original jurisdiction, or, rather, concurrent jurisdiction, as is sought to be provided for by this statute. There has never been one single instance in the past, either under the present Attorney-General or any one of his predecessors, where any one of those statutes was abused. There seems to be a disposition on the part of many people in the community to imagine that every law will be enforced in the worst possible way. The minds of some of these people seem to be so constituted or warped that they imagine every one at all times and under all circumstances is crooked, dishonest, and bad, and they don't give anybody credit for actually performing a public duty with a broad, fair mind, and with the intention of benefitting the great body politic. They may only criticize, but it has been my personal observation in this city that those gentlemen who are always ready to criticize are rarely ever in a position to offer a constructive suggestion that will be of some value.

"Now this bill has been called a spy bill, and at first blush the word 'spy' seems to give one a shock. We don't like a spy. But it is not a spy bill at all, and there is not a word in this bill that can lend itself to a legitimate interpretation of calling it a spy bill. It provides for an appropriation of $100,000 for the employment of investigators, translators, stenographers, process-servers, and other necessary assistants. I maintain that $100,000 is a very small price, indeed, to pay for the prosecution and the investigation of persons whose life work it is to preach criminal anarchy. That is the only subject with which this bill is concerned. Let me read you this:

"'The attorney-general may investigate as to violations of article fourteen of the penal law and may conduct prosecutions for violations of such article.'

"This act is limited solely and exclusively to violations under Article 14 of the Penal Law of this State, and Article 14 refers solely, only and exclusively to criminal anarchy.

"Without meaning to be harsh in my criticism, I think that we all ought to take a definite position one way or the other. Either we want criminal anarchy to be rampant, to be committed and to increase, or we want it wiped out. There is not any question about the necessity in my mind for taking either one view or the other. If we want it eradicated, if we want the men who violate that act prosecuted fairly, impartially and expeditiously, I believe this bill should be enacted into law."

Mr. Stevenson described the four bills that were recommended by the Lusk Committee amending the educational law of New York State. He said:

"Having in mind that although only eighty-five were indicted, there were a vast number of other men in this State that were violating the criminal anarchy statute, and bearing in mind the method by which these men came to be criminal anarchists—namely, that when young men they were taught to be criminal anarchists—the Lusk Committee turned its attention to the school sysem and methods of instruction which exist in this State. And the inducing cause for the preparation and offering of these bills was this:

"The Committee felt that it was better to begin at the source. Schools and classes exist in this State which hold themselves out to be schools and classes of instruction. Young people, potentially splendid citizens, attend these schools and classes and are there made criminals. The Lusk Committee felt that it was the duty of the State to protect its citizens from such an act, rather than to lay the emphasis on punishing them after they have been made criminals. Therefore there were two bills in particular that were offered. In the first place, I refer to Senate Bill No. 1275, which is an act to amend the education law, in relation to the qualifications of teachers, and making an appropriation for expenses.

"This bill requires teachers in the public schools, union free and common school districts of this State to make application for and obtain a certificate which shall show that the person holding the same is of good moral character, also show to the satisfaction of the Regents that he is obedient to the constitution and laws of this State, and that he is desirous of the welfare of the country and in hearty accord and sympathy with the government and institutions of the State of New York.

"No matter how splendid the school buildings, how elaborate the curricula, how profound the textbooks, in the very last analysis the success of the school system depends upon the character of the teachers. In many other walks of life this is self-evident. For many years no man has been admitted to the bar of this state, even though he has attained all the legal knowledge which is required, unless he has passed a severe and rigid character test. On the other hand, our methods of choosing teachers has been solely upon their pedagogical attainments. There is no inquiry into the character of those teachers, into their loyalty to the institutions of this State.

"We must bear in mind that the public schools are carried on at the expense of the State, and they have no reason whatsoever to exist unless it be to train the young of our community to carry on the responsibilities and duties of future citizenship. Secondly, the purpose of the public schools of this state is to train the pupils to revere, respect and honor the government under which they live, and to train them that citizenship does not only carry privileges but carries responsibilities and duties. The public school cannot succeed in imparting that point of view to its students unless the teachers themselves are in full accord, harmony and sympathy with the government under which we live, and are trained and eager to combat all influences that tend to subvert the pupils from that course.

"I have noted in some of the criticisms of this bill, and notably by a report gotten out by the Committee of the Association of the Bar of New York (and I might say at this point that the Bar Association itself has never passed upon the report or accepted the report of that committee) that the question is asked—What is loyalty and what are the institutions of this State? I think the very asking of that question shows the need of public school training. The primary thing which an American should know is loyalty, and the primary thing which an American should know is what are the institutions and government of his State and of the United States. I cannot see how the application of such a statute can in any possible way be a limit to the growth and progress of education in this State. My own opinion is that it will raise the dignity of the public school teachers. It will put them in the class of a profession. It will mean that every person who holds a public school certificate has a warrant in his pocket certifying to his good character and to his loyalty, and I think that every public school teacher should be glad of an opportunity of bearing witness to that fact.

"With respect to a second bill which has created a great deal of comment and no little opposition, known as Senate Bill No. 1274 and entitled, 'An act to amend the education law, in relation to licensing and supervision of schools and school courses, and making an appropriation therefor.'

"The purpose of this bill is to require all persons, firms, corporations, associations, societies who conduct schools, courses or classes, to make an application for the granting of a license from the University of the State of New York, that is to say, from the Board of Regents. There are certain exceptions made in the bill; that is to say, the public schools, union free and common schools, all schools incorporated or institutes incorporated by the Regents, or all schools or institutes and so forth that are admitted to the membership in the University, and finally all schools that are carried on or hereafter to be carried on by any well recognized religious denomination or sect.

"The bill is intended to reach a real and very s rious situation in the educational conditions in our state. As I mentioned before, there are thoroughly well organized schools to teach the doctrine of criminal anarchy, to teach that organized government should be overthrown by force, violence and unlawful means. At the present time it might be possible to bring criminal action against a number of these schools. It might be possible in two or three years to punish a number under our criminal law. It might be possible to imprison some of the teachers after two or three years; but the criminal law has no provision for stopping the school, and no way of keeping it from continuing its work in precisely the same way as though no prosecution were had. An interesting illustration of that is shown by the conviction of the Rand School of Social Science last year, under the Espionage Act. They were convicted. They took an appeal. The conviction was affirmed. All they have to do is to pay a fine, and they continue to carry on the same work for which they were convicted. That is a very unhappy and a very improper situation to permit to exist. Either we want to stop the teaching of the doctrine of criminal anarchy or we want to proceed.

"Now this bill is designed to enable a competent number to pass upon the character and purposes of the teaching that is subversive to the interests of the State. The particular phrase used is 'inimical to the interests of the state,' and it is precisely the same general term as is used in the defining of the police powers of the state which is 'prejudicial to the interests of the state.' It is a broad term, and is meant to be broad. As a matter of fact, it was broadened at the request of the counsel for the Education Department of the State of New York. As originally suggested by the Lusk Committee the bill was meant to cover only such schools in which was taught the doctrine that organized government should be overthrown by force, violence or unlawful means. But the counsel for the Educational Department saw an opportunity of broadening the bill so as to permit the Department to reach certain other schools which had been carried on here for many years as fraudulent institutions. At the present time I understand that there are a large number of institutions masquerading as schools that actually are simply methods of fleecing the general public out of money, such certain correspondence schools that teach you how to play the piano in twenty-four hours, and various other schools of that character. Up to the present time there was no method by which the Educational Department could reach those schools, and it was therefore that this general term was introduced in this bill.

(*Continued on page 32*)

Facts Concerning Health Insurance Propaganda

ITICISMS BY DR. HENRY J. HARRIS OF PAMPHLET, "A REFUTATION OF FALSE STATEMENTS IN PROPAGANDA FOR COMPULSORY HEALTH INSURANCE" ANSWERED

By P. TECUMSEH SHERMAN

Y attention has been called to an article in the *American Economic Review*, for March, 1920, by Dr. Henry J. Harris, criticising a pamphlet en- led "A Refutation of False Statements in opaganda for Compulsory Health Insurance," ently issued by the Committee on Construc- e Plan, Social Insurance Department, The ational Civic Federation. As I was a member that Committee and the author of much of e pamphlet criticised, I take it upon myself answer.

Dr. Harris's first criticism is that "most of e quotations" in the pamphlet are from the ritings of Dr. Frederick L. Hoffman, "vice- esident of the Prudential Insurance Com- any." That is a bad beginning for Dr. Harris; r what he says is palpably untrue, only a small oportion of such quotations being from Dr. offman's writings. Moreover, most of the quotations from and references to Dr. Hoffman in at pamphlet relate to statistical data, upon hich subject Dr. Hoffman is a recognized au- ority; and it is significant of the weakness of r. Harris's case that he should seek to evade e force of Dr. Hoffman's facts and figures by appeal to prejudice.

Dr. Harris then goes on to charge that many the arguments and quotations presented in e pamphlet are partial and misleading. The llowing are the specifications of this charge nd the answers thereto:

(1) Dr. Harris complains that, on page 15 of he pamphlet, is given an extract from the 'abian Society's report of 1914, to the effect that he maternity benefit has failed of its purpose, hat is misleading because it fails to mention qualifying statement in the report, which eads:— "but this does not mean that the pecific beginning of an 'endowment of matern- ty' which Mr. Lloyd George has effected . . . not already proving an enormous boon."

In truth, however, the extract quoted is full nd fair, containing all of the original that is elevant upon the point under discussion in that art of the pamphlet, namely: "Is compulsory *nsurance*, providing maternity benefits, desirble to reduce infant mortality?" The extract uoted is to the effect that the maternity bene- ts ought to be removed from the insurance and rovided in some other way; and nothing in the ontext to that extract qualifies such conclusion. Iedical care and pecuniary aid to needy mothers n childbirth are of course a "boon"; but the oint contended for in the passage criticised is imply and solely that the right way to provide uch boon to the needy is not through compulsory ealth insurance.

(2) Dr. Harris criticises as partial and mis- eading a statement, on page 15 of the pamphlet, o the effect that "the average number of days ompensated per sick member increased in Ger- nany from 16.1 to 20.2" per annum, between 890 and 1913, because in connection with such tatement no reference is made to the law of 902 which raised the minimum benefit period rom 13 to 26 weeks and included certain liseases not previously compensated.

This is a vain and misleading criticism. Had he pamphlet gone into details it would have hown that the time on the sick benefits in Ger- nany has increased steadily from year to year, uch increase being contributed to by a number f subordinate factors—including the one mentioned by Dr. Harris. But, whether stated in detail or summarized as in the passage criticised, the facts tend to refute the proposition they are cited to refute, namely, that compulsory health insurance "would *reduce* the amount of time lost by wage-earners in employments"—for which proposition there is no evidence whatsoever.

(3) Dr. Harris charges that, "in order to give the impression that malingering is a serious evil under the British system" there is given, on page 40 of the pamphlet, a misleading statement of the results of examinations by medical referees in Ayrshire, to the effect that "nearly one-half [of those receiving sick pay] were found fit for work."

The statement criticised does not contain the words nor convey the meaning expressed by the words inserted by Dr. Harris in brackets in the matter he quotes. On the contrary, that statement says, unambiguously, that "of *the persons who were examined* . . . nearly one-half were found fit for work"—which is entirely correct and in no wise misleading.

(4) Dr. Harris objects to statements on page 9 of the pamphlet which read as follows: "The Final Report of the British Health of Munition Workers Committee . . . is equally cold towards the Health Insurance. It credits that insurance with no evidence or data bearing on sickness or the problems of health. . . . And the recommendations of that Committee have no reference to the Health Insurance as a means of promoting health and are all as feasible without health insurance as with it." In refutation he cites a blanket expression of thanks, in that report, to various public authorities, including the national insurance commissioners, for assistance afforded and information received, mentions that the assistance of one official was obtained from the insurance commissioners, cites a single reference in the report to the experience of insurance authorities, and insists that the principal purpose of the investigation was to study conditions of work and output in munitions establishments and only rarely touched the subject of health insurance.

All that Dr. Harris here alleges is true; but the fact remains that the statement he criticises is, nevertheless, likewise entirely fair and true. The matter under discussion in the part of the pamphlet where this statement appears is an assertion by the partisans of compulsory health insurance that "the needs for the care . . . and *prevention* of illness among wage-earners can be met by a comprehensive system of health insurance." But this report of a most thorough study of the *health* of munition workers (see Bulletin No. 249 of the Bureau of Labor Statistics) in fact credits the health insurance with no specific evidence or data bearing upon the subject, and barely refers to or touches upon such insurance or the medical service provided as a benefit of such insurance as a means for the prevention of illness, thereby indicating that the ways and means for promoting the health of wage-workers are to be looked for principally outside of insurance. Certainly that conclusion is "cold" toward health insurance considered as a means of meeting the needs for the *prevention* of illness among wage-earners.

(5) Dr. Harris criticises the statement, on page 8 of the pamphlet, that: "Not a single commendatory reference to National Health Insurance can be found in any of the reports of the Registrar General for all the years since the insurance took effect, nor in any of the large number of local health reports for representative cities and towns." And in refutation he quotes extracts from reports of three health officers.

But obviously the statement criticised means that there can be found no commendatory references to the *results* of the health insurance. Of the three extracts quoted by Dr. Harris, the first, written in the early days of the health insurance, merely expresses the opinion that "in time it is *probable*" that the medical and sanatorium benefits of the insurance ."*will* have a profound influence on the public health." The second, written about a year later, refers to the reduction of mortality from tuberculosis during recent years [including years before the advent of national insurance] "as evidence of the good effect of the crusade against disease carried on by public and *private* persons and bodies throughout the country, which had reached their [sic] most *promising* development in the Medical and Sanatorium Benefit provisions of the National Health Insurance Act"—the reference here to the insurance relating altogether to expectations and not at all to performance. And the third extract he quotes, being from a report for 1916, stated merely that there had been a considerable diminution of the percentage of births occurring in workhouses and other institutions, probably because of the payment of the maternity benefit under the national insurance—all of which may be entirely true but is beside the point without something to show favorable results therefrom in the way of reducing the mortality or morbidity of mothers or infants. Manifestly if such limited commendations as these are all that the health officers of England, after nearly eight years' experience, have had to say in favor of the large and expensive scheme of providing medical care through national insurance—and they seem to be all that Dr. Harris has been able to find—the substance of the statement criticised is thereby confirmed:

(6) Dr. Harris criticises a statement in the pamphlet (page 12) which bluntly denies the prediction that: "Compulsory insurance will stimulate the needed campaign for the prevention of illness." In reply he cites a familiar statement by an authority, that the British national health insurance "has done great service in bringing to light a mass of suffering and a number of social evils, as to which the nation as a whole was ill informed or indifferent. It will now be substantially easier than in 1911, both on account of the new knowledge available and of the state of public opinion, to make adequate provision to advance the health of the community."

Perhaps the denial in the statement criticised is too positive and unqualified, as is the assertion denied, and consequently Dr. Harris's criticism may be in a degree justified. But in substance such denial is sound. This authority's opinion that it will now be substantially easier than in 1911 to secure adequate provision for the health of the community, is entitled to respect, especially as it is concurred in by others. But it is merely an opinion, in the nature of a prediction, first expressed about 1914, and the prediction has not yet been fulfilled. The insured medical service, which in 1914, was grossly in-

(*Continued on page 24*)

"A Challenge to the Protestant Episcopal Church"

REV. BERNARD IDDINGS BELL'S "RIGHT AND WRONG AFTER THE WAR" DECLARED MISCHIEVOUS IN REVIEW BY PROMINENT MEMBER OF BAR AND OF P. E. CHURCH

By ARTHUR O TOWNSEND

AT the outset of this brief review, we will do the author the justice of noting his standpoint and the claims made for his book. The Rev. Mr. Bell is a priest, of the Protestant Episcopal Church, who has been entrusted with the presidency of a college maintained by that Church for the education of candidates for its priesthood. (St. Stephen's College, Annandale, N. Y.)

In examining his book, we have had the unusual advantage of a subsequent and very recent recapitulation of his views, upon the conspicuous occasion of a sermon by him at the Episcopal Cathedral in New York City, Sunday, May 23d, 1920; an advantage which enables us to avoid placing any possible mis-conception upon his book. The *sermon* kept a few paces ahead of the *book* at all points.

His publishers present it as:

> "a forward-looking book, written by a man who has * * * thought deeply, and who believes the church should be preparing now to assume a real leadership during the period of reconstruction."

The reviewer has studied Mr. Bell's book, with the interest both of a fellow-churchman and a fellow-citizen. He believes it to be of timely and momentous importance that others within and without the church, who have not read this book should know what is being taught, without repudiation, under the auspices of one of the great churches, in respect of "right and wrong" concerning property, government and revolution.

In the first half of his book, Mr. Bell applies himself to the discussion of economic and national problems, in the spirit of avowed radicalism. To his observation, the thing which other socialists do not hesitate to call "the revolution" is not *coming;* it is here; and those who resist, or even protest, its engulfing scope and purpose, the author considers blind, deaf, and doomed. His wish fathers his thought. (P. 164.)

Seldom has a writer made so complete a self-revelation in so brief a space, as the Rev. Mr. Bell has done in these two short discussions. He exhibits, as to those matters of personal morality and individual helpfulness, touched on in the latter half of the book, the kindly and reasonable views of a parish or institutional priest, at home with his subject; but for the rest, he exposes with näive simplicity, the pitiful unfitness of such an one, who, naked of intellectual equipment for the tasks of statesmanship, rushes into the market place, demanding auditors upon great public questions, but offering them only a whirlwind of words, picked up in the purlieus of radicalism, the mad-houses of disastrous and abandoned European experiment.

One would look to find the pages of a book sponsored as this claims to be, full of ideals of the world's best enlightenment, the recognition of the spiritual side of human nature as its real characteristic.

But to our amazement, we find this author planting himself waist-deep in the miserable, discredited rubbish of Prussian materialism. We find him adopting from that slough, as if they were axioms of intelligent modern thought, the sordid notion, for instance, that man's thrift and his legitimate ambitions are no more than a manifestation of that same animal "hunger urge," which impels the hog and the tiger. And that "family life," upon which he admits the whole structure of society has been erected, arises from "the sex urge," an appetite that is generally recognized as being "back of" loose living, not chaste monogamy—an appetite whose *limitation,* not its *indulgence*—is held by modern thought to be the thing that is "back of the family," and thus "back of" civilization. Thus, at page 23:

—*Photo by Gessford.*

ARTHUR O. TOWNSEND

> "It is an established principle of sociology that the two great needs which impel mankind to most of its actions and which determine most of its institutions are the same two primary needs which impel toward action and evolution all living creatures, the need for food and the desire for sex expression."

What a platform for a Christian minister! What a crude, narrow, archaic pronouncement for any teacher to put forward, in this day of world-progress and large comprehension!

Not a word of the immense, overwhelming part played by mind and soul in human activities. No room in his program for any but materialistic motives or promptings.

Resting upon such premises (which occupy Chapters II. and III., respectively, of the five chapters of his book), Mr. Bell next apparently adopts, in its full scope and consequences, the idea of *Proudhon,* which has furnished the slogan of all revolts against law and order, viz., that "property is theft": and his pages are accordingly sprinkled with the senseless patter made familiar by doctrinaire and soap-box oratory, about the "iniquity of rent and interest," and all the rest of it; the author arguing that for a man to charge and collect *rent* or *interest* is a "gross abuse of trust." (Pp. 47 and 51.) Further, says he:

> "The only rational basis under the Christian dispensation under which a man may hold any property whatsoever, is as a trust to be administered for the profit of its real owners, namely, all his brethren." (P. 46.)

It is not surprising after this, to discover that Mr. Bell evidently prefers Henry George to St. Paul; for he tells us (P. 12) that "a good part of his" (St. Paul's) "sociology today is simply bosh." While he swallows, without a chew or a grimace, the whole untried doctrine of "single tax," with its inevitable corollary of confiscation; telling us with a smack of the lips his belief that (P. 110):

> "Increasingly, thinking people are adopting the theory of taxation advanced by Henry George as the sanest method of stopping land speculation and preventing congestions."

Admirers of Mr. George's character, patriotism, and moderation, whether they deem his ideas to contain the germs of truth, or not, will resent the effort made to tie up his name and fame with the mad extremes now preached by some of his alleged followers.

But this impending abolition of private income is not, in Mr. Bell's judgment, a mere theory or possibility. "It is a thing in actual being." (P. 45.)

> "Everywhere we see evidences that by increasing masses of our people investment for profit is looked upon with grave suspicion, as a thing demanding rigid regulation at least and sometimes prohibition." (P. 43.)

"Profits are become suspect" (P. 44) and the Church must "restate her teachings about the morals involved in rent "and interest holdings." (P. 45.)

Whether "restate" is meant to include *revise,* Mr. Bell does not disclose: for he evidently conceives that "the Church" has *always* held interest or profit-taking to be immoral. (Pp. 47-49.)

If the author could see or hear beyond the smoke and fury of his friends of the Rand School, he might be disconcerted by noticing the ever-widening circle of *real workers* in the factory and field, who save and invest money for their individual worldly betterment; to secure an old age of rest for themselves; and to provide a future of education, prosperity and refinement for their children.

When one sets out, in a tiny book of 187 small pages, of big type and wide spacing, to solve the greatest problems, to crack the hardest nuts, that have baffled the philosopher and the statesman for centuries, it is perhaps unavoidable for one to be a bit dogmatic. One must be prepared to discard along with St. Paul's "bosh," many other things that we have regarded as admirable, excellent and true. Thus, if we travel with Mr. Bell, we must be prepared to kick aside as obstructions in the path of progress, such things as "Tennyson's poetry" and Sir Edwin Landseer's "Stag at Bay": for these things Mr. Bell considers "anachronistic"—(perhaps he means "antiquated"?) (P. 161.)

But even broad-minded, up-to-date, readers, however patient, will be jarred to find startling assertions like the following, put forward by a college president and an Episcopal priest, as basic facts, entitled to acceptance:

"Poverty is, and has been for a number of years, rapidly increasing among us." (P. 25.)

"One out of every ten people in the United States is living in poverty, hopeless poverty, below a decency income figure." (P. 29.)

"One in ten in this land is forever barred" from good meals, noble books, converse with cultured people, etc. (P.30.)

"Poverty is * * * the result of injustice in distributing the fruits of the earth and of labor. It is the result of social maladjustments which need not be." (Pp. 36 and 38.)

Outside of war disturbances, there is now no more need for increased "production." (P. 38.)

> "Instead of having too little to go around, we have more than we need." (P. 39.)

Public charities are jeered at. Of factory "welfare work"—"bathrooms and gymnasia and paid nursing and doctoring, and the rest of it"—"most of it is excellently meant; but the hands neither appreciate nor welcome it. They do not wish" these things. (P. 54.)

> "The workers are apt, even when they use many of our social settlements, to damn heartily" the givers of them. (P. 55.) (And see page 56.)

(*Continued on page 17*)

Revolution in U. S. Preached to Methodist Clergy

. M. C. A. WORKER EXTOLS BOLSHEVISM, PRAYS FOR ITS SUCCESS AND HAILS REVOLUTION IN AMERICA—SAYS SOVIETISM IS AS DEMOCRATIC AS METHODISM

By T. EVERETT HARRÉ

N amazing event transpired in New York City on June 7. The occasion was the weekly conference of the clergy of the ethodist Episcopal church, at 150 Fifth Aveue. Before the assembled ministers Bolshevism as lauded as the "open door" to democracy in ussia. It was extolled as having done wonders ı education. The Soviet system was represented s "an exact copy of the Methodist system of epresentation," "just as democratic as the lethodist Church." The Red reign of terror nd wholesale killings were said to be "not very ıuch when compared with the French Revoluion and the Russian revolution in 1905."

"To have an economic service, to have educaion, no booze, to have a philosophical and natıral system of government, and finally to have piritual freedom," the speaker declared, was to ıave the "open door" to democracy. And he aid: "That is what Bolshevism is."

The Methodist ministers of the city of New 'ork were told that many people and some lethodist ministers "oppose Bolshevism because ıey do not know anything about it." The peaker presented himself as an authority on olshevism, and he "hoped to God" for its sucess. He further voiced this sentiment:

"We in the United States are not yet prepared for Bolshevism, and therefore we will be obliged to handle our revolution in a different manner. But that it is coming there is no doubt."

The man who, before the Methodist clergy of New York, hailed a revolution and the overthrow of government in America, spoke with the prestige of his association with the Y. M. C. A.; moreover, with the weight and authority of his position as Director of the Russian Investigation Bureau for the General Committee of the International Y. M. C. A. His name is Julius F. Hecker. He is a Methodist clergyman in good standing.

It is an open secret that the U. S. Government has refused this man a passport to go abroad, for grave and justifiable reasons.

To the credit of that assemblage of clergymen, this man's anti-American, disloyal and revolutionary preachments did not meet with unanimous approval and applause, but on the contrary called for vehement reproof. Many ministers were on their feet to declare his speech un-American and subversive of law and order.

"I do not wish to seem uncharitable," declared the Rev. George Adams, pastor of the Beekman Hill Church, "but it is my conviction after listening to Mr. Hecker's address that he lays himself open to grave charges before the Methodist Conference. His entire address is un-Christian and I am quite sure he is liable to charges."

While he presented himself as an authority on Russia, and as while on this very stand he holds the directorship of the Russian Investigation Bureau of the International Y. M. C. A., it was brought out in the questioning of the Rev. Mr. Hecker that he had not been in Russia for eighteen years. That Mr. Hecker should have the audacity, the stupendous gall to get to his feet before the Methodist clergy of New York and hail a revolution in the United States as inevitable, to say that he hoped to God Russian Bolshevism would succeed, may seem startling; but while his speech may be unique in its brazenness and rawness, the promotion of revolutionism in the churches is not new; it has been going on for a long time, and the Hecker incident serves a purpose in calling attention to what is generally camouflaged in humanitarian or religious verbiage. Mr. Hecker's speech, which was taken down by a stenographer, confirms what has been suspected for a long time, and that is thet his main function in America is to promote Bolshevist propaganda, mainly by reason of his position with the Y. M. C. A., through the churches.

Mr. Hecker prefaced his Bolshevist speech by what was presumably meant to be a compliment to his audience. He expressed his pleasure in being a Methodist, and said that while he had addressed many different professions, he had found no groups "as liberal as the preachers are." Mr. Hecker attempted to present the Bolshevist movement as growing out of an historical past. He failed to present it as a minority movement, dominated by a few leaders who gained power by a coup. Between Czarism and Bolshevism, he declared, there was no in-between, totally ignoring those Socialist groups who far-outnumbered the Bolshevist group. "You have got to be a Czarist or a Bolshevist."

He admitted that Bolshevism is a "despotism, but a despotism with the open door to democracy." He said:

"What is the open door? If you want to have democracy you must have first of all an economic service in the population; you can't have democracy if 80 per cent. are living below the margin of necessity of subsistence. There was no possibility of cultural education. That was the economic situation—two-thirds of the land was in the hands of less than 3 per cent. of the population. The Bolsheviki who had nothing to lose by being radical first declared the land belongs to the people. Therefore, today I would say that 95 per cent. of the population in Russia has the possibility, through being over the economic margin, of turning their thoughts to cultural and spiritual improvement, and this comprises the first step towards the open door of democracy,

"The second thing is that the Bolshevists believe in education; they are taking it up for their own self-preservation, and they are teaching their children, as they want to bring up a new generation of men who are trained in the new type of civilization. They are making every sacrifice to give the whole population the best possible education, and therefore today every man is either teacher or pupil. They have passed a law that everyone has to read and write, or they put him on third rations, and for this reason everybody is teaching some one else. These men have done more in three years for education than the Romanoffs have done in three hundred years of their history, and they have expended more money for education in these three years than the Czarists did in 300 years. These are the facts which can be obtained by even the most biased. When you have the education you are well on the way to democracy."

Mr. Hecker's attempt to win the Methodist clergy to Bolshevism was adroit, clever. He cunningly and with calculation emphasized it as a religious movement, committed to prohibition:

"The third thing, is that the Bolsheviks are the most fanatical prohibitionists, and they know you can't have democracy if you have booze. Do you know how far they went? If a man is a member of the communist party and he is found drunk, they put him up against a wall and shoot him on the spot—I wish they would try this here. There is no booze in Russia."

Mr. Hecker failed to state what are the facts—that the manufacture and use of vodka was prohibited by the Czarist government after Russia was drawn into war, and that under the Bolsheviki this prohibition was removed. According to the official report of V. Melutin, assistant chairman of the People's Economy League and a member of the Supreme Council of National Economy of Soviet Russia, which appeared in *Ekonomicheskaya Zhisn* (Economic Life), November, 1919: "The beet-sugar industry has furnished the initial step in the creation of the rural industries, since this particular industry has been preserved during the transitional period of the revolution. *The Vodka distilling industry occupies the next place,* and its development has been begun by the Supreme Council of National Economy during the last few days."

Mr. Hecker went on to say:

"The fourth thing is the Soviet system. What is it? It is easy to explain the Soviet system to the Methodist people. The Soviet system is an exact copy of the Methodist system of representation. It is the most exact copy of the Methodist way of government, and it is just as democratic, or autocratic, as the Methodist Church.

"The Soviet system is nothing but the same old community meeting we had here. That is another step to the open door to democracy in Russia. Then there is another thing, a vital one, and perhaps in many ways the most important one, the religious aspect of it. Now the Bolsheviks are always supposed to be atheists, and so I was not very much surprised by getting a report from a respectable association lately that Hecker is a free lover, an atheist and a Bolshevik. This charge was sent to quarters where it raised quite a disturbance for a while, but I was able to explain matters, and the affair blew over.

"The fact is this, that religion was never as free in Russia as it is now, and the Russian people were never as religious and as closely interested in religion as they are now. I have just been studying that problem and perhaps I will put a little book out on the religious phase of Bolshevism as I have discovered the tremendous revival of religion in Russia.

"Take the Russian Church today. Before the war it was nothing but a department of the department of justice or state; the priests were used as police and there were 12,000 school teachers alone, who went to Siberia because of reports by these priests. The Russian Church prelates have for centuries condoned and blessed all the outrageous crimes perpetrated by the Czarists."

Mr. Hecker then went on to relate the conditions of the church under the old régime as compared with the "improvement" of the church as it is today.

"This is the last step towards the open door to democracy. To have an economic service, to have education, no booze, to have a philosophical and natural system of government, and finally to have spiritual freedom, and then you have the open door. *And that is what Bolshevism is.*

"The present situation is that Russia has passed the Russian revolution; it has come to the end, and it was officially announced so in February when the National Soviet said there was to be no more capital punishment in Russia. This after there were some ten thousand heads

(Continued on page 20)

THE NATIONAL Civic Federation Review

**Office: Thirty-third Floor, Metropolitan Tower
1 Madison Avenue New York City**

RALPH M. EASLEY, Editor

The Editor alone is Responsible for any unsigned article or unquoted statement published in THE NATIONAL CIVIC FEDERATION REVIEW.

APPROVE STAND OF STATE DEPARTMENT

With Lloyd George carrying on conversations with Krassin, the Bolshevist Minister of Trade and Commerce, regarding the opening of trade relations with Soviet Russia, the unequivocal and uncompromising stand just taken by the Department of State will meet with general approval. Excepting a small handful of Bolshevist sympathizers and certain financial groups who, out of base and unpraiseworthy motives, are lured by the bait of economic concessions held out by Lenine, the American public as a whole is back of the Department of State in refusing to countenance any support which would give renewed life and strength to a régime set upon the destruction of our own government and of every other democracy in the world. To give economic assistance to the oligarchy of Lenine and Trotzky would be consciously to play into the hands of the Judas of civilization, to give the weapon for killing to those intent upon one's own murder.

As is recognized by Secretary of State Colby, the forwarding of economic supplies, even indirectly, to Soviet Russia would be tantamount to informal recognition and the opening wedge toward ultimate official recognition. The Department of State has taken a stand in wholesome contrast to the wavering and dickering maneuvers of the British, and the following letter of appreciation, sent to Mr. Colby by Judge Alton B. Parker, president of The National Civic Federation, doubtless expresses the sentiments of the American people as a whole:

NEW YORK, JUNE 7, 1920.

The Hon. BAINBRIDGE COLBY,
Secretary of State,
Washington, D. C.

My dear Mr. Secretary:

The National Civic Federation has noted with great appreciation the action of the Department of State in refusing passports to a commercial delegation seeking to visit Soviet Russia with the object of establishing trade relations, and also its announced purpose of refusing any recognition of the Soviet régime, politically or commercially, as well as any trade relations with it, direct or indirect.

As is well-known to your Department, it was officially stated by the Soviet Government, through its Commissioners who went recently to Stockholm to open trade negotiations, that neither the great Co-operative Organizations of Russia, with which the Allied Powers had expected to deal, nor any individual firms or persons, can legally transact any business, because, since private ownership is abolished in Russia, the Soviet Government alone is the owner of all property, and any dealings in the matter of sales, purchases or exchanges must be with the Soviet Government itself. As a consequence, any business transactions would involve dealing with and virtually recognizing the Soviet Government. We believe there is no middle course possible.

Our natural sympathy for the Russian people must not blind us to the fact that since the Bolshevist leaders seized power by violence in November, 1917, they have not only refused to give the Russian people a chance to select by universal suffrage the government under which the people would wish to live, but have stated that they never would do so because they knew that the majority would be against them.

Until there is in Russia a government represented by the free choice of its people and based on acknowledged and tried foundations of democracy and morality, any trading for financial advantages or economic concessions—a bait held out by Lenin—would be to prolong the life of and give strength to a régime set upon the destruction of every democratic government. It would be a betrayal, for sordid and ignoble ends, of American honor and American ideals. The Chamber of Commerce of the State of New York, in passing a resolution against any recognition of the Soviet Government, rightly declared that such trade would be immoral, inasmuch as payment for goods would be made out of resources unlawfully expropriated from their owners. As was admirably expressed by Dr. Nicholas Murray Butler, President of Columbia University:

"Such recognition, if based upon grounds of possible commercial advantage, would be to sell American principles for money."

Very truly yours,

(Signed) ALTON B. PARKER,
President, The National Civic Federation.

Voicing sentiments similar to those expressed in Judge Parker's letter, the American Federation of Labor, at its recent Montreal convention, by an overwhelming majority, passed a resolution opposing any trade relations with Russia until a democratic government has been established.

Reports of Bolshevist officials, quoted in the last issue of the REVIEW by Gregory Alexinsky, a former Socialist member of the Russian Duma, prove that Russia has no raw materials to offer in exchange for supplies. Even if raw materials were available, even if valuable economic concessions might be given American or British financiers, the forwarding to Russia of supplies, of foods, rolling stock, machinery and other commodities, would merely prolong the life of the incubus which has fastened itself upon Russia, prolong the servitude of the Russian people, prolong the menace which strikes vitally at every democracy. It would make only the more remote the establishment of world peace, international security and amity, the permanent release from oppression and terror of the Russian people themselves.

LAYING DOWN ONE'S ARMS TO THE ENEMY

If America's entry into the war demonstrated anything to us it was our own deplorable negligence in the supreme matter of our own safety. Lack of vigilance, of precautions, of effective laws and an efficient secret service laid us open to the enemies who worked against us within our midst, and it was notorious that for information regarding the activities of German agents and spies we were largely indebted to the intelligence service of the Allied nations.

America, and every democratic government in the world, is today the object of attacks of foes no less dangerous than were the Germans; in fact, the designs of this foe are more fundamentally destructive than were the designs of imperial Germany. Are we to profit by the painful experiences and sacrifices of the war? Or are we again to relax into a criminal inertia and lay down abjectly before those who would destroy every ideal and every institution which we hold sacred?

Shortly after our entry into the war the New York legislature enacted special war emergency legislation which gave to the office of the Attorney General unique powers to subpoena witnesses and compel them to testify under oath. By reason of this legislation, the office of the Attorney General was enabled to round up many German agents, secure evidence and uncover the vast ramifications and purposes of the German propaganda in America.

Legislation which would give to the Attorney General similar powers in the investigation and prosecution of cases of criminal anarchy was recently introduced into the New York legislature. Other proposed legislation provided for amending of the educational law of the state, so that teachers should be required to establish their good moral character and loyalty, while another bill provided that, with certain exceptions, it would be necessary for persons, associations or corporations conducting schools or classes to secure a license from the University of the State of New York, or the Board of Regents. While these bills have been vetoed by the Governor, the discussion concerning them, under the auspices of the Committee on Socialist Doctrines and Tactics of The National Civic Federation, is of timely interest, and, as was pointed out by Samuel A. Berger, Assistant Deputy Attorney General, and Archibald E. Stevenson, associate counsel of the Lusk Committee, the enactment of such legislation is imperative if we would effectively protect ourselves against those who would overthrow our government and who seek to propagate subversive teachings.

It must startle many people to learn that, while the Criminal Anarchy statute of New York State was passed after the assassination of President McKinley, eighteen years ago, there had been no single prosecution until the Lusk Committee, in its recent investigations, uncovered evidence of criminal activities, as a result of which there have been some eighty-five indictments and the trial of five cases, each of which resulted in conviction. In other words, without adequate legislation providing for investigation of criminal anarchy, the statute is a dead letter.

It is quite possible, as has been claimed even by supporters of the so-called Lusk bills, that they are defective; but in principle they are sound, and it is to be hoped these bills will be redrafted and passed. Considerable noise was made by those who campaigned against these bills, and among the opposition were the names of many people who, we are certain, if they had understood the situation and the purposes of the bills, would not have lent themselves to an agitation started by the very forces against whom the bills were designed. It is significant that the loyal teachers of the state did not protest against their becoming a law. Where, then, did this propaganda against the bills originate? As Mr. Stevenson declared, the opposition to the bills in large measure started with a committee of eight in the Rand School of Social Science. Among those who joined together to fight the bills, under the aegis of the notorious Rand School, were representatives of the *New Republic*, the *Nation*, the *World Tomorrow* and the *Survey*. The same method which had been used in 1917 by the old groups of Socialists, pacifists, pro-Germans, et cetera, to keep us out of the war against Germany, were used to stir up public sentiment against these bills. Because of their organized system, Mr. Stevenson declared, they were then able at the press of a button to have 25,000 letters go to the President.

It is wholesome to note that President Wilson has just signed a bill enacted by Congress which makes membership in organizations advocating sabotage, revolution or destruction of property in itself sufficient grounds for the deportation of alien residents of the United States. The bill is aimed to make subject to deportation all foreigners who are members of the I. W. W. and the Communist and Communist Labor parties. The bill declares that the contribution of money to any organization, society or group that advocates the overthrow of the government by force or violence, or of all forms of laws, or destroying property, or sabotage, or of assaulting or killing officers of our own or any organized government, shall constitute membership. The passage of this law will give added strength to the government in combatting the subversive activities of aliens. Doubtless, we shall hear much about the violation of the "right of asylum" and from the quarters of the sentimentalists and "liberals" will come protests that deportation under the law will be deportations of heroes akin to the Pilgrim Fathers.

How loyal Americans, who should know better, are gulled by specious appeals to "liberalism" into supporting the cause of the very groups who sought to render this country impotent before German aggression just as they now seek to render us impotent against revolutionary aggressions, is one of the phenomena of the times.

N EXAMPLE
'ORTH
MITATING

The resignation of Mrs. Finley J. Shepard from the national board of the Young Women's Christian Association not only truck consternation into religious circles at the ime, but started a discussion on certain fundanentals, which will continue for an indefinite eriod.

There were two reasons given by Mrs. Shepard 'or her action. One dealt with the matter from n exclusively Christian point of view, taking he ground that the changes proposed in the By-aws of the Y. W. C. A. meant the abandonment f its purely religious activities and the adoption f an industrial program which, to her mind and he minds of those who acted with her, meant imply the addition of one more to the many soial reform movements.

Mrs. Shepard's second point was that, having nce taken this new position, the Y. W. C. A. ntered the field of politics. She could well have ointed out the dangers lying along that path y referring to the records already made by a umber of Y. W. C. A. branches. Her resignaion was construed by many as the result of a udden outburst of indignation on her part and hat of her friends, but there has recently come o this office a pamphlet which clearly shows that this inference was wrong. This pamphlet, entitled, "Ten Thousand Words of Protest from Churches and Christian Leaders Against the Proposed Personal Test for Student Association Membership," and "Published by The Council of Adherents to the Evangelical Basis of the Young Women's Christian Associations," was issued "For Consideration Prior to the National Convention of the Young Women's Christian Associations" at Cleveland, Ohio, in May, 1920. It is filled with ringing protests against the proposed change in the By-Laws from bishops and clergy of various Protestant churches, presidents of theological seminaries and church colleges, ministerial associations, general assemblies, synods, national conferences and other influential bodies of Christians. So representative are the persons and organizations entering these protests that one wonders why the Cleveland convention of the Young Women's Christian Associations took the action it did. It certainly would seem that it could not have represented the Evangelical Church at large.

But it is not with the religious aspect of the matter—a subject for discussion by religious journals and religious bodies—that we are especially concerned in this editorial. It is the proposed entry of the Young Women's Christian Association into industrial politics that concerns a publication like The National Civic Federation Review. If the membership of the Y. W. C. A., composed largely of students and young women, is to enter the field of labor politics, experience shows that there is only one door through which it will pass—that of radicalism. No better illustration of this can be given than what happened at the last session of the New York Legislature. In this connection it will be well to read the article by Mrs. Alice B. Locke, who represented the 300,000 members of the Women's Benefit Association of the Maccabees, to be found on pages 14 and 16 of this issue of the Review.

When the delegates to the Cleveland convention of the Y. W. C. A. declared, as they did with all seriousness, for "an equitable share for labor in the profits and management of industry;" "that an ordered and constructive democracy in industry is as necessary as political democracy, and that collective bargaining and the sharing of shop control and management are inevitable steps in its attainment;" and "that the first charge upon industry should be that of a wage sufficient to support an American standard of living;" and when they advocated "the guarantee of a minimum wage, the control of unemployment through government labor exchanges, public works, land settement, social insurance and experimentation in profit-sharing and co-operative ownership," they were making sweeping declarations on highly controversial, technical and even political subjects about which they, personally, knew little. No one will contend that the Y. W. C. A. has ever made any adequate study of those subjects. It has not the facilities for so doing; nor has it the necessary practical experts. If it is going simply to repeat, parrot-like, the declarations of other organizations of a radical type, it is adding nothing to the sum total except confusion.

Mrs. Finley Shepard is deserving of all credit for having had not only the perspicacity to discover the fallacies and dangers of the action contemplated but the courage to take the stand she did, at the time she did. It is a welcome surprise to find one woman of great riches who keeps her head and does not follow the revolutionary fads of the hour. It is to be hoped that the discussion growing out of the incident at the Cleveland convention will result in the more sober directing elements in the Y. W. C. A. putting a brake on the enthusiasm of those youthful members who rush after any will-o'-the-wisp, if it is only labelled "social reform."

Questions for Every Good American

The following letter, addressed to a member of The National Civic Federation, has been referred to the Department on Study of Revolutionary Movements. This was a personal communication, but the writer has consented to its public use, stipulating, however, for obvious reasons, that his name be withheld. As the letter raises questions that are in the minds of many thoughtful citizens today, Chairman Condé B. Pallen is sending it to several thousand representative men and women to get their views before taking action. Dr. Pallen also invites the readers of The National Civic Federation Review *to address him on this subject.*—Editor.

My dear Sir:

A friend has sent me the program of your Department on Study of Revolutionary Movements, which proposes:

> To inquire into the objectives and tactics of revolutionary forces in this country;
> To inquire into the extent to which those forces have permeated the various divisions that make up the body politic;
> To make a survey of industrial, political and social progress; and
> To give support to all practical means tending to improve the general well-being of our people.

This program plans to meet the menace of revolutionary radicalism and I am pleased with its sanity and thoroughness. It has evidently been drafted by those who know what Socialism is.

For the last two years my wife and I have been reading and studying Socialism and Bolshevism. We have visited the Rand School and read much of its literature. We have listened to socialists in their halls and at the street corners; we have heard them in church circles, social clubs and educational meetings. Among the speakers were clergymen of prominence, professors from important universities and principals and teachers from the public schools, with now and then an editor. From all that we have heard and seen, we have come to detest the very word "Socialism." We regard its economic program of confiscating and operating all factories, farms, mines, stores and railways—or, as the socialists themselves state it in their platform, all means of production and distribution and the land—as an impossible scheme, leading only to chaos and wretchedness, as we see it worked out in Russia today. We regard the doctrines of economic determinism, or the materialistic interpretation of history, as an abomination, leading straight to atheism and the destruction of the family. We regard their theory of internationalism, with its contempt for love of country, as one leading to disloyalty to our government and the destruction of all nationality.

Believing, as we do, that Socialism menaces all that Christian civilization has achieved and that it should therefore be extirpated, root and branch, from every soil where it has found a foothold, we face some very serious questions.

We have three sons and two daughters, the eldest two being ready for college, the others still in the public schools. For their well-being we alone are responsible, not only to society but to God. Have we not a duty to see that their minds are not poisoned in school and college by attending classes taught by socialist teachers and professors? In one noted woman's college, where we thought of sending our daughter, we found that one of the important professors was a woman who boasted that she had been a socialist for thirty years and, in a signed and published article, declared:

> It is a great thing to be both Christian and Socialist in these days—it is especially great if one is a teacher of youth.

While there is so much being said about the right of the teacher to teach anything he thinks is the truth, without question from faculty or trustees or school boards, have not the parents of the boys and girls—the future citizens, who will carry on or destroy this republic after we are gone—the right to protest against any teaching that is disloyal to our Constitution? Is it not more than a right? Is it not a patriotic duty?

Again, my family are members of the........ Church, and there we face the same danger of Socialism; but in a more insidious and subtle form. Two years ago, before we had made any study of the subject, we should hardly have recognized it as Socialism, although we should have wondered at some of its implications, the minister constantly harping upon "social injustice," "capitalism," and the "awful conditions of labor under our present system." As an employer of more than one thousand workmen, mostly molders who belong to a union, I know something about the conditions of labor and I took the minister to task for his utterances on the subject. It turned out that he had imbibed his whole store of misinformation from two I. W. W. agitators, with whom he seemed to be very friendly. I also took up the matter with officials of the molders' union, who represent my employees in our collective contract, and they said: "Why, don't you know that .... (mentioning the name of our minister), is an out-and-out I. W. W. sympathizer; that he attends their meetings and counsels with them? We would not trust him as far as we could throw a bull by the tail."

Now, what is our duty in the church? We have been taught to beware of "tainted money." Is it not just as necessary to beware of tainted preaching and teaching? Shall we withdraw without giving the reason or shall we make a fight within the church? We feel we must do something, but what is the best thing to do?

Then again, we are subscribers to several philanthropic agencies and charities, and my wife is a member of some of their boards. In these organizations she frequently finds Socialists filling important positions. Shall we con-

(Continued on page 21)

Compulsory Insurance Opposed by Women's Benefit Societies

(Statement upon the attitude of the Fraternal Benefit Societies of New York State, and particularly in behalf of the Woman's Benefit Association of the Maccabees [30,000 members in New York State], at the hearings before the Labor and Industries Committee of the New York Senate, April 7, 1920)

By MRS. ALICE B. LOCKE

MRS. ALICE B. LOCKE

IT would be impossible more than briefly to outline the real menace which lurks behind the cloak of this so-called "welfare" legislation, which not only threatens the very life of the many fraternal benefit societies in the State, with their membership of three-quarters of a million, but which strikes at the very roots of our state and national institutions. It is a well-known fact that the plan of Compulsory Health Insurance was conceived in Socialism, born in Germany, and fostered by the American Association for Labor Legislation, the American branch of the International Association for Labor Legislation, with headquarters in Switzerland. For more than fifteen years this system of Compulsory Health Insurance, as practised in Germany, has been agitated in this country with indifferent success by well-known radical Socialists, chief among whom was Eugene Debs, now serving a well-merited sentence of imprisonment for sedition, and Victor Berger, expelled from the Congress of the United States on sedition charges. It is advocated by the leaders of the International Ladies' Garment Workers' Union and by the Women's Trade Union League, of which Miss Mary E. Dreier is, or was, State President, and her sister, Mrs. Raymond Robins, is National President.

In spite of the activities of the Socialists to induce the American people to adopt their program of Compulsory Health Insurance the fact remains that their converts are few. The underlying principle in a democracy is not that the State owes every man a living, but rather that the State owes its citizens an *opportunity* to make a living, and in no country in the world can any man or woman who is able and willing to do an honest day's work for an honest day's pay find such wonderful opportunities as these United States afford. An immense gulf separates our laboring classes from the poverty-stricken, brow-beaten lower classes of Germany who so gratefully accepted the sop of social insurance thrown to them by the astute Bismark. State paternalism is not wanted, and I feel sure will not be tolerated in this country.

The proponents of the bill tell us of the great economic loss due to sickness, but they very carefully refrain from calling attention to the fact that the economic loss on account of strikes is about *twice* as great as the loss from sickness. So that it would seem that this entire problem of reimbursing the people and the State for the economic loss from sickness is a simple matter of employer and employee getting together to eliminate all strikes, thereby not only enabling the worker to meet his doctors' bills but leaving him a tidy sum to set aside for the future. Moreover, from 40 per cent to 60 per cent of all sickness is preventable. Then why not direct all our energies for the present at least toward prevention?

Compulsory Health Insurance is *not* "welfare" legislation. It is purely socialistic. It is class legislation of the most vicious type. It would compel the thrifty, moral, independent citizen to accept a thinly disguised form of poor relief, which he neither needs nor desires; it would compel him, against his will, to contribute to the payment of doctors' bills for a host of habitually immoral-living people who are financially able to provide for themselves, but many of whom prefer a system of charity to honest work and thrifty planning for the rainy day.

The proponents of the bill say: "To be effective it must be compulsory on all, because there are some who are too shiftless to save, and this is the only way in which they can be forced to provide for themselves." Because few workers are shiftless, therefore *all* shall be placed in the shiftless class. And as to the cost—well, nobody seems to know! The New York Federation of Labor sent out handbills in 1919 in which they promised all the benefits set forth in the bill for the sum of twenty cents per week from employer and employee. Then comes the Women's Joint Legislative Conference, composed of the New York League of Women Voters, the Women's Trade Union League, the Y. W. C. A., the Woman's City Club of New York, and the Consumers' League, with their attractive but misleading propaganda (likewise scattered broadcast over the State), promising these benefits for twenty-four cents per week. Then comes Miss Olga Halsey, of the American Association of Labor Legislation, with the statement that it will probably cost about thirty cents per week. Then comes Dr. Ira S. Wile, teacher of "sociology" and advocate for the Davenport Bill, with the statement that "nobody knows what it will cost, but regardless of cost the State of New York should adopt Compulsory Health Insurance."

The proponents of the bill know, and they admit publicly, that this system of Compulsory Health Insurance *will not reach those who need it most*—namely, the chronically sick, the itinerant workers, the unemployed, all of whom will have to be cared for by charity, as at present, while we proceed to pour out our beneficence to those more fortunate workers who do not need it. Why not also pay their rent, and buy their shoes and food?

The proponents of the bill know and admit that there are neither enough hospitals nor nurses in the State to meet the thousands upon thousands of demands which will be made for service if this plan is forced upon millions of people who do not want it and who resent its charity. They know that in every country where Compulsory Health Insurance is in force that the drain because of malingering has been enormous, and that the people's sense of honor and independence has been gradually dulled as a result of forcing an independent thrifty people to accept poor relief.

The United States Bureau of Labor has published and circulated their estimates, as a result of their investigations early in 1919, that the cost per year per person for medical, dental and oculist's service was *$26 per year*. And yet in the face of these official figures, the proponents of the bill have promised not only medical and dental service, but $8 per week cash sickness benefits for twenty-six weeks, maternity benefits to all insured women and the wives of insured men, and $100 funeral benefit—all for the sum of twenty-four cents per week, or about $24.16 per year—which is two dollars less than the official estimates of the Department of Labor for medical service only.

Because we prefer to believe the official statistics of the Department of Labor in preference to the alluring promises of the proponents of Compulsory Health Insurance, the opponents of the bill have been abused, and accused of exercising a powerful and perilous influence over public opinion. We are accused of interfering with orderly legislative action on important measures; we are accused of sending out misleading and inflammatory propaganda.

Since when has a dictatorship of "Me and Gott" been established by the leaders of the New York League of Women Voters, the Women's Trade Union League, and others? Since when are free-born American citizens forbidden to make known their honest convictions in the matter of any or all legislative measures which are to be passed upon by the servants of the people? Since when do three-quarters of a million citizens of the State of New York, who are insured in the fraternal benefit societies, have to accept in humility and with a due sense of reverence for their "superior" intelligence, any kind of "raw" legislation that paid uplifters and Socialists may see fit to hand out to us? Since when must the members of the State Grange, the Federation of Women's Clubs, and the hundreds of thousands of other loyal 100 per cent Americans cower under the lash of the men and women who are seeking to push through our legislature this bill, which is obnoxious to millions of patriotic, self-respecting independent citizens?

Why should leaders of the New York League of Women Voters tear their hair and go into hysterics because the pet bubble of their Socialist friends has been pricked and has vanished into thin air? The question of Compulsory Health Insurance has never been adopted as a part of the program of either the National Suffrage Association or the National League of Women Voters. It is true that Mrs. Raymond Robins, Chairman of the Committee of Women in Industry of the National Suffrage Association and President of the National Women's Trade Union League, embodied in her report a recommendation that social insurance be adopted as a part of the working program of the Suffrage Association in the various States; but upon my request for a hearing in the matter of Compulsory Health Insurance, it was referred back to the committee for "further investigation and information." And there it still slumbers! At a meeting of the National Suffrage Association and League of Woman Voters in Chicago, February, 1920, no further attempt was made to foist the question of Compulsory Health Insurance upon the convention.

Just whom do the leaders of the New York League of Women Voters represent in their demand for Compulsory Health Insurance? They certainly do not represent the thirty thousand

(Continued on page 16)

Pro-Bolshevist Propaganda by American Correspondents

"The propaganda of the Lenine-Trotzky régime against civilization, already working through so many radical and pseudo-liberal organizations, and recently augmented by an endless stream of inspired press stories from Moscow and Petrograd."—*From a declaration against the recognition of Soviet Russia signed by several thousand well-known Americans.*

By T. EVERETT HARRÉ

THIS inspired propaganda referred to has appeared in various important metropolitan dailies and has borne a number of signatures. Among the most influential pro-Bolshevist writers are Lincoln Eyre, Isaac Don Levine, and Michael Farbman. Lenine does not permit any correspondent to come into Russia unless well assured in advance that he is practically certain to take the pro-Bolshevist position. After arrival, these correspondents are taken in hand by Bolshevist officials, shown what it is desired that they should see and told what they are expected to repeat. One of them, Arthur H. Copping, states that he was in Moscow for two weeks "and during that time investigated social conditions in conversation with *many* government leaders and subordinates as well as with *several* critical outsiders." Nearly all of the other correspondents have thus let the cat out of the bag from time to time.

In the introduction to Lincoln Eyre's articles, republished as a pamphlet, is the statement that this reporter in 90 days (under Bolshevist tutelage) witnessed "all the workings of the Red régime," that "he approached his task with an impartial mind" and that "his conclusions may be relied upon as giving a true picture of the Russia of to-day and its prospects!"

In making out a cause for the Bolshevists Eyre freely contradicts his own evidence. His main point is that the Bolshevists are willing to reform if they are recognized:

> The Bolsheviki freely confess their desperate need for help from foreign capitalism. They have demonstrated their willingness to give almost any concession short of political annihilation to foreign capitalists.

On the day preceding the publication of this statement, Eyre had given a far different view, namely that the Bolshevists were *not* ready to give up their work for world revolution. On February 24th, he cabled:

> The Bolsheviki are as eager to precipitate a world revolution as ever. But at the moment they are even more eager to establish relations with the markets of the world, so that Russia may be saved from economic catastrophe.

In this same despatch Eyre even explains just how the Soviets will continue to work for world revolution—no matter what their promises:

> The Russian Communist Party, which is the Bolsheviki's official political title, no longer exports agitators chosen from among members to kindle the flames of revolt in foreign lands. They are too wise for that antiquated process nowadays. What they do in these scientific times is to import from the country of his birth the crudely fashioned product of his own domestic Bolshevism, subject him to certain finishing processes (including perhaps a gold lining) and ship him back home again complete in every detail, smooth running and highly inflammable.
>
> Another reason for the Soviet's willingness to quit propagandizing abroad is that it has already turned over to the Third Internationale all business of that kind.
>
> Now, the Third Internationale has no official connection with the Soviet Government. It is supposed to be a separate institution. Yet all its leaders hold office under the Soviets, and its funds, which are considerable, must be derived from Soviet sources. Nevertheless, it is technically, indeed legally, non-governmental, wherefore the Moscow Cabinet is justified in pledging itself to leave propaganda to "friendly" foreign states alone.

Eyre even proves his point by the following quotation from an interview in which Zinoviev, president of the Petrograd Soviet, says:

> The Third Internationale is primarily an instrument of revolution. It reunites at Moscow the intelligence and energy of all the Communist groups the world over. Delegates from the various national organizations come to us and give and take knowledge about the cause and return to their respective home countries refreshed and invigorated. This work will be continued no matter what happens, legally or illegaly. The Soviet Government may pledge itself to refrain from propaganda abroad, but the Third Internationale—never!

Why, then, does he repeat Lenine's self-evident falsehood that the Soviets have demonstrated their willingness to give almost any concessions short of political annihilation to foreign capitalists?

And why does he speak of this régime as the dictatorship of the Russian "proletariat" when, in the very same article, he mentions Lenine and Trotzky as the dictators and devotes an entire article to describing the "Soviet aristocracy" created about the Kremlin as a new ruling class? The only answer is that in large measure—though, of course, not always—he has parrot-like reproduced as his own judgments the ideas Lenine has put into his head and often the very words Lenine has put into his mouth. It was "the most impressive assemblage" he had ever beheld. . . "There was about it a virility, a strenuousness, an inflexible seriousness of purpose that is seldom detectible in the Parliaments of Europe and America. . . . . One felt that these men knew what they wanted. . . . One felt, too, the presence of a profound concern for the fatherland."

Lenine, he says, instructed the Bolshevist majority in what they should do, but this does not trouble Eyre, who blandly remarks that "even the G. O. P. might take lessons from the Bolsheviki in the strategy of the steam roller." But there is even an insinuating comparison of the Soviet Congress with the United States Senate! Could any Bolshevik fanatic use stronger language than this, in an Eyre despatch published March 28, 1920: "Whether the Bolshevik revolution has benefited any other class of the population is open to doubt, but that it has bettered the lot of the Russian peasant mentally, morally, and materially to an enormous degree cannot be disputed."

One of the most amazing of Eyre's performances is his interview with Peters, the Executioner. Mr. Eyre reports asking Peters: "Are you going to the opera to-night? Shaliapin is singing, you know," and so the correspondent and the Executioner enjoy the opera together. Mr. Eyre finds out, in general, that the Executioner is not a bad fellow after all, and remarks that "in his homelike room in the First Soviet house, formerly Hotel National (quite a proper residence for a 'proletarian dictator') books, mostly poetry, were all over the place. On the walls were a few old prints and photographs, among them some snapshots portraying Col. Raymond Robins in a smiling conversation with Peters and other Bolshevist leaders."

It is hardly necessary to touch upon the immense amount of documentary evidence of the Bolshevik Reign of Terror—which they confess has only just been ended—in order to demonstrate the real character of Peters and his associates. Eyre's entire article puts both Peters and the Reign of Terror in a favorable light! The famous Socialists, Gorky and Martof—both revolutionists now in Russia and close to the Bolshevists—speak of tens of thousands of cold-blooded killings for which the Bolsheviki were wholly and directly responsible, beginning even before the Reign of Terror was officially declared. But Eyre found no traces of all this! Martof wrote:

> From the very first day of their coming into power and proclaiming the abolition of the death penalty, the Bolsheviki began to kill. They killed prisoners captured in the battles of the civil war. They killed enemies who surrendered on the condition that their lives would be spared.
>
> These wholesale murders organized at the instigation of the Bolsheviki were followed by murders directly ordered by the Bolshevist Government. The death penalty was declared abolished, but in every town and in every district various "Extraordinary Commissions" and "Military Revolutionary Committees" ordered hundreds and hundreds of people to be shot. Some, as counter-revolutionists; some, as spectators; others, as robbers. No court ever examined their cases; no one knew whether the person shot was really guilty of conspiracy, speculation, or robbery, whether perhaps someone settling personal accounts with the man killed or taking personal revenge had caused him to be shot. What a number of innocent persons have thus been killed in the whole of Russia! With the silent approval of the Council of the people's Commissaries, men sitting on the Extraordinary Commissions, unknown to anybody—men among whom escaped criminals and the Tzar's agents—provocateurs are discovered from time to time—are issuing orders for executions to be carried out.
>
> Having assassinated tens of thousands of men without trial, the Bolsheviki started their execution by verdicts of their courts. . . . The party of executioners—the Bolshevist Party—is just as much an enemy of the people as the party of Pogroms.

After the recitals by thousands of eye witnesses of the Bolshevik persecutions of religion and their numerous decrees, newspaper attacks and pronouncements against religion, Eyre has the effrontery to say that "the Bolshevists are too wise to belittle religion or insult its professors." The only basis for the statement is that the Bolshevist *outward* and *official* policy has of late been more tolerant, but this does not change the ardent anti-religion tone of the Bolshevik leaders or Bolshevik administrators. A half truth may be the most effective form of falsehood.

On this point there is no better authority than the leading Roman Catholic dignitary of Russia, Archbishop Ropp, who has been in Soviet Russia during all the revolution and was imprisoned by the Bolsheviki. Archbishop Ropp shows that even the new policy of the Bolsheviki is fundamentally anti-religious in that it aims to Bolshevize the youth and children:

> Bolshevism, despite its ostentations atheism, does not prevent Christian work in churches, but there is a constant effort to demoralize the youth of the country. Their theory is that a child does not belong to the parents, but to the state.

After Lenine, Bucharin, editor of the *Pravda*, is the great Communist theorist. Here is what Bucharin says (in his book "The A. B. C. of Communism," published in Moscow last October) about the attitude of his party and government toward religion:

> There are some soft-headed communists who say that their religion does not prevent them from being communists. They say that "they believe both in God and in Communism." Such a view is fundamentally wrong; religion and communism do not go together either in theory or in practice. Between the precepts of communism and those of the Christian religion, there is an impassable barrier.

Only when criticisms are perfectly innocuous does Eyre ever turn against the Communists at all. Could any better example of out-and-out Socialist propaganda be found than the following preposterous statement:

> Meanwhile, however, they are offering to the dark masses of peasants and industrial workers an opportunity for enlightenment that transcends anything hitherto known in this line not only in Russia but in most other parts of the globe.

It is only necessary to read the contradictory and absurd statements of Eyre and of the Bolshevist Minister of Education Lunacharsky, whom he quotes, to realize that not only is this statement utterly without foundation but that the truth is evidently almost exactly the reverse.

Eyre himself states elsewhere that the agricultural 90 per cent is being dealt with "tenderly but firmly," that *only about* a *third* of the crops than *can* be produced are being seized by the Bolshevists—as a forced loan without security! He also admits that the peasants are being driven to compulsory labor in carting wood and clearing the railways for their Communist masters. How do such facts appeal to the American farmer? Michael Farbman, a notorious Soviet propagandist, admits that the Communists are systematically repressing all the more industrious and least inefficient peasants who have two horses and giving them to those with none. What does this show as to the level of Russian agriculture and the effect of Bolshevism?

Farbman, a correspondent upon whose inspired statements certain newspapers base their editorials, confesses that he was favored in entering Russia, being allowed to accompany the Bolshevist peace delegation on their special train. Certainly he made the most of his opportunities.

Among his remarkable dispatches is one in which he plays up the wonderful decree of the Soviets, "uniting all the co-operative societies into one all-Russian union and making all-Russian citizens practically members of the co-operative"—presuming on the hasty newspaper reader not stopping to think that co-operation, throughout the entire world, means a voluntary movement and that there can be no more preposterous contradiction in terms than to speak of establishing compulsory co-operation.

Another pro-Soviet correspondent is Isaac Don Levine. The official organ of Sovietism in America "Soviet Russia," has also publicly expressed its confidence in Isaac Don Levine. After a comparatively brief conducted tour in Russia we are not surprised that this correspondent does everything in his power to promote Bolshevism—reproducing, for example, in a favorable light, and without the slightest criticism which he freely applies to the anti-Bolshevists, Trotzky's statement that "the dictatorship of the proletariat is almost entirely the result of the war." Yet this has been the main doctrine of the Bolshevist propaganda from the very beginning and to suggest that the war brought it about rather than the Bolshevik movement amounts to nothing less than a complete exoneration of Bolshevism.

While certain newspapers do not hesitate to accept pro-Bolshevik stories they evidently wish to reject all the mountains of evidence against the Bolsheviki. Hence we read in an editorial in an important daily that one really important fact has been established, namely, that "Russia is now orderly, and, so far as can be discovered, more contented than under the Czar." There is little question that any kind of Russia would be less discontented than under the Czar. Hence this is a miserable subterfuge.

Aside from the inspired propaganda, above described, which is carried on through the columns of certain metropolitan dailies, the country for the past two years has suffered a deluge in books, pamphlets and radical magazines of short or continued duration. The pro-Bolshevist activities of the *New Republic*, the *Nation* and the *Dial* have been notorious. Among magazines which have been recruited to the cause of the Russian Soviets, is *Asia*, "published monthly under the auspices of the American Asiatic Association," which includes among its officers and executive committee a number of loyal Americans, of notable integrity, who would not, we are certain, approve of the pro-Bolshevist policy and propaganda of this magazine. A recent number, devoted almost exclusively to the glorification of the Bolshevist régime, advocating recognition, has been advertised, in large display space in the biggest newspapers throughout the country—a campaign to bring before the American public all this insidious propaganda which must have cost many thousands of dollars.

In a recent issue of *Asia*, Norman Hapgood, now one of the most prominent advocates of some form of political recognition, suggests that, in order to trade with Russia, we "leave the political arrangements" to the cooperatives—though the cooperatives are officially declared by the Soviets to be a branch of their government, which, moreover, has served an ultimatum on the nations that it has declared a monopoly of foreign trade.

Hapgood violently attacks the French, British and American governments, accusing them of deliberate misrepresentation and other crimes, while he defends the Soviets! It is the other governments he accuses of propaganda—thus camouflaging the most aggressive and notorious propaganda the world has ever known. Even the news articles of our press "on the whole" are directed by "old gentlemen" who are guilty of the heinous offense of desiring "to avoid at any cost the real or apparent triumph to the Lenine government."

The few harmless criticisms of the Bolshevists Hapgood's article contains, merely strengthen it as a partisan Bolshevist plea for the recognition of the Soviets—a plea that might have been prepared in Moscow.

We are told that Lenine holds the confidence not only of the Communists but of "a large revolutionary but non-Communist element." A contrast is made between the good and wise Lenine, and the bad Derzhinsky, head of the Extraordinary Commission for Repressing Counter-Revolution. This man and his following represent what is evil in the Soviets! Hapgood has thus invented for them a scapegoat—an idea that never occurred to them in all their multiform, clever, and unprincipled propaganda!

Now, in view of this invention, we are warned against exerting any pressure or influence whatever to bring the Soviets around to democracy. "The more menacing the situation for the Soviet cause the greater has been the power of the Commission"—i. e., Derzhinsky. So all Entente diplomacy of whatever character directed against the Soviets helps the Soviets!

Would Lenine have Hapgood write any differently?

The same issue contains an article by Paul S. Reinsch, formerly American Minister to China, which states certain facts as to the causes of discontent in Asia, but concludes with a whitewash of Lenine. Lenine, declares Reinsch, "must be given credit for calmly facing the enormous problems that confront him at home." Bolshevism "is a serious attempt at economic and social reconstruction." Was the revolution and the institution of a reign of Red guard terror "a serious attempt at economic and social reconstruction?" Reinsch declares: "Mob violence and individual bomb throwing, as well as military expeditions against other countries, with a view to overthrowing the system there, find no encouragement.

It is to be inferred, apparently, that the Bolshevist régime has not only not been guilty of violence itself, but piously holds all violence in abhorrence. As a matter of fact, Reinsch is technically correct in telling that mobs are not encouraged in violence or individuals in bomb-throwing; mob or individual acts of violence would probably be regarded as counter revolutionary, for violence as a method of attaining and armed terror as a means of maintaining its power has been the official program and policy of the régime which Reinsch declares is "a serious attempt at economic and social reconstruction." Violence and terror are a Bolshevist governmental monopoly.

Compulsory Insurance Opposed

(Continued from page 14)

members of my association, nor the hundreds of thousands of women in other fraternal orders. Neither do I believe they represent the Federation of Woman's Clubs, the Women of the State Grange, and other millions of well-balanced women in the State. Neither do I believe that the leaders of the New York League for Women Voters in their demand for Compulsory Health Insurance represent the views of a majority of their own members for whom they assume to speak. In fact, the only people whom I can find that they do thoroughly represent and with whom they seem to be in full accord in this matter are the Socialistic leaders of various organizations with whom they have chosen to align themselves. I am referring now particularly to the Women's Trade Union League, of which Miss Dreier is State President, and whose sister, Mrs. Raymond Robins, is National President. It is a matter of common knowledge that this lady, Mrs. Robins, who tried to thrust Compulsory Health Insurance into the legislative program of the National Suffrage Association, was one of the radicals who participated in the famous—or infamous—Moyer-Haywood parade in Chicago, in 1907, riding behind the *red flag* as President and guest of honor of the Women's Trade Union League. I quote the following from the Chicago *Inter-Ocean*, May 20, 1907:

> '*Mrs. Raymond Robins*, settlement worker and president of the Women's Trade Union League, yesterday led thirty-seven hundred cheering, boisterous *Socialists*, *anarchists*, trade unionists, members of liberal societies, Jewish *revolutionists* and sympathizers through downtown and west side streets in a demonstration designed to create sympathy for W. D. Haywood, Charles Moyer and George A. Pettibone, leaders of the Western Federation of Miners on trial in Idaho *charged with the murder of former Governor Steuenberg*."

I also call attention to the following extract from the Chicago *Tribune*, under date of May 20, 1907:

> "The day was made the most of by anarchists, Socialists and other free thinking advocates. . . . The parade started at 3:00 o'clock. *Mrs. Raymond Robins, being accorded the post of honor as the head of the members of the Women's Trade Union League, rode in carriages behind a band of twenty-five musicians. Mrs. Robins carried a large bunch of roses, and was cheered frequently along the line of march. Along with her were Miss Agnes Nestor, Miss Elizabeth Maloney, Miss Emma Steghagen and Miss Georgia Tooters.*"

One might reasonably suppose that with the passing of the years the Women's Trade Union League and their leaders might have changed their radical views, were it not for the fact that at their national convention held in Philadelphia, in 1919, they *adopted resolutions demanding the recognition of the Russian Soviet Government by the Government of the United States.* Not only that, they demanded the "*immediate release of all those whose offense is purely of a political or industrial nature.*" They further demanded that our Government "*put a halt to deportation of alien enemies.*"

These are the women who are now demanding Compulsory Health Insurance, and who dare question the motives of those loyal citizens who have opposed, and who will continue to oppose to the bitter end this vicious socialistic measure.

We will gladly co-operate in furthering *sane* methods for solving the problems which confront us, but we oppose most emphatically the Socialist program which looks to the nationalization of insurance and medicine—the *nationalization of industry, and the nationalization of women.*

Challenge to the P. E. Church

(Continued from page 10)

He assumes as a fact, and ha... it, that we are in the

> "dawning of a new period, in the way of convictions and practices involved in the satisfaction of the sex urge." (P. 59.)

Before passing from his *facts* to his *remedies*, Mr. Bell lets us understand that he wants and welcomes the social upheaval and revolution, which he politely styles "the new order," because he finds that every one

> "knows among his own friends able men who cannot make enough to live decently, and inefficients and incompetents who have a surplus of this world's goods; people who have souls honorable and beautiful who starve, while others, rascals fit for hell, hold places of power and plenty." (Pp. 34 and 35.)

To cure such inequalities by pulling down all these "places of power and plenty," and promising a paradise to ignorance, sloth and sedition, has been the plan of *other* would-be *reformers* in every age.

Listen to Jack Cade in the 15th century:

> "Be brave then, for your captain is brave, and vows reformation. There shall be in England, seven halfpenny loaves sold for a penny * * * all the realm shall be in common; * * * there shall be no more money; * * * I will apparel them all in one livery that they may agree like brothers."
>
> "Now show yourselves men; 'tis for liberty. We will not leave one lord, one gentleman. Spare none but such as go in clouted shoon." * * *
>
> "And henceforth all things shall be in common." (2 Henry VI., Act IV., Scene 2.)

Having thus discovered the cause of poverty, and the fact that rewards are not always measured according to apparent deserts, Mr. Bell cheerfully girds himself for the task of remedying these conditions. His prescription is not new, being the simple and familiar plan of the anarchist and mob leader; namely, those persons who persist in retaining private property, and hiring labor—whom he groups as "exploiters"—are to be "policed and dispossessed;" and "the common people * * * come into their own." (Pp. 164 and 165.)

The closing pages of the book purport to announce "the Christian attitude toward internationalism."

Mr. Bell evidently regards patriotism and love of country as things of the past—if they ever were virtues, they are no longer so—and he concludes that, before long,

> "there will come, regardless of theorists for or against it, the breaking-down of nationalities and the coming in of the United States of the World." (P. 172.)
>
> "Internationalism, the creation of a pan-national grouping wherein democracy may come to flower politically and industrially, this is the end for which the present conflict is being waged." (P. 186.)

Those who disagree with him as to internationalism, Mr. Bell styles "a certain powerful group of hate-mongering imperialistic pseudo-patriots" (P. 186); and he ends his work with words which, whether meant as a prophesy or as a threat, are at least his supreme effort to pen a crashing climax:

> "From this war we shall go on to one of two things, Internationalism or chaos.
>
> "Then shall we hear above the thunder of the guns and the moanings of the wounded, the cry of those who over Bethlehem's plain sang, 'Peace on earth to men of good will.'" (Sic) (Pp. 186, 187.) * * *

Of Mr. Bell's book, after a hunt for the "deep thoughts" his publishers promised us on the cover, we may truly say, as has been aptly said of a far more famous doctrinal book:

> "What is new in it, is not true; and
> What is true in it, is not new."

One flash of unconscious humor, however, enlivens the work under review, viz., where the author demurely observes (P. 140):

> "There is nothing quite so pathetic as the prophet become the lecturer."

May we not add to that sentence—still in quotation marks, but from a different writer,—

> —"unless it be the man who *thinks* he is *thinking* when he is only *feeling*?"

But shallowness of thought, and total absence of originality, though sometimes tending to harmlessness, lend no justification to the issuance of an utterly radical and mischievous book purporting, as this one does, to speak for, or at least with the sanction of, the Protestant Episcopal Church.

Incalculable damage to church and community, irremediable injury to all society, must flow from the unrebuked circulation through press and pulpit, of inflammatory follies like this, at a time when America is needing all the sense and all the sinew of her manhood and her churches, to stem the organized, though furtive, Bolshevist invasion, and to pillory the vicious, paid propaganda of the "Third Internationale."

Such a book and such a sermon, by reason of their author's office, as an accredited spokesman and educator in his Church, demand both the close attention and the fearless action of the clergy, the laity and the responsible organized management of that Church.

Mr. Bell has frankly challenged the great, sane, patriotic body of the Protestant Episcopal Church, *either to salute or to pull down*, the red flag he has hoisted over their stronghold.

Some Modern Public Health Problems

By JAMES A. TOBEY, S. B.

(Assistant Director, Department of Health Service, American Red Cross, Washington, D. C.)

ONE of the results of the war which may prove beneficial to this country is the revelation of the necessity for a better national vitality. The results of the draft examinations in which about 30 per cent. of the men in the prime of life were rejected on account of physical incapacity astounded not only the general public but also the medical and sanitary professions. It would seem that this country has neglected that most priceless of all its personal possessions, its health. It has been estimated that 60 per cent. of the defects of those who failed to pass the army examinations were due either to ignorance or neglect. Thus, most of the defects are preventable and further neglect will be an annual national disaster.

There are two factors in the spread of disease. One is the presence of the causative germs and the other the relative susceptibility of the individual. By sanitation, which is the hygiene of man's environment, the germs can be eliminated, reduced, or rendered non-effective. Pure water supplies and efficient methods of sewage disposal are examples of good sanitation. The quarantine and isolation of the sick and of disease carriers is likewise an important measure. Germs, however, are generally harmless if they attack those who possess sufficient bodily strength to resist them. Some people have natural immunity against disease, while in cases where such immunity is lacking, science has provided vaccines and antitoxins for prevention and cure. Smallpox vaccination and diphtheria or typhoid anti-toxin are examples of such methods.

Certain diseases must be controlled in a different manner, however. Tuberculosis and the venereal infections are social diseases and the fight against them involves many factors. Education plays no small part in their control, and treatment of existing cases is one of the means to reduce their spread. Thus, clinics and hospitals must be provided. Malaria is a disease which can be done away with by community action, that is, by getting rid of those mosquitoes which carry it.

The protection of public health is concerned not only with adults, moreover, but must begin at the bottom. Infant welfare is fundamental and child hygiene is one of the most important functions of every health department. Parental instruction and care of infants require clinics and the services of competent infant welfare nurses. Supervision of the milk supply is likewise an essential in this connection. Later in life, school hygiene must be furthered. The rôle of the public health nurse in general cannot be too strongly stressed and that community which has an insufficient number of such nurses, is a distinctly backward place.

Public health administration must also be improved. The protection of the health of the community is a science and requires an expert, provided with proper funds and facilities. The financing of health departments has been entirely inadequate in recent years. The average expenditure on health has been only about 29 cents per capita. Compare this with the several dollars per capita spent on schools, police, parks, roads, libraries, fire protection, and other municipal functions. Qualifications for health officials must be improved. It is not always necessary to have a physician, as now various colleges give courses for health officers in which laymen are adequately trained for these positions. The health officer should always be on a full time basis. At present only 32 per cent. of all the cities of over 10,000 population in this country have full time health officers, and even of this number a great many lack the proper qualifications.

Because the official health organizations have been unable to cope with the situation, many private agencies, such as visiting nurses associations, anti-tuberculosis societies, and the like have been formed. There are over one hundred such national bodies, all working more or less independently, sometimes overlapping in their efforts, but more often leaving gaps. Each is doing valuable work but greater efficiency would be obtained if a scheme of co-ordination could be put into effect. This is another problem of public health.

One of the solutions of many of the problems confronting us is the establishment of a chain of health centers in this country. A health center is a place where people come to get well, keep well, and learn how to stay well. It is the physical headquarters of some productive form of coordination of the health agencies and activities of the community. A health center may in its most elementary form have only one room, or even part of a room, where information on public health is given and where educational work is carried on. In a more advanced stage there may also be a public health nurse and possibly an infant welfare station. Thus, the health center would evolve until finally it might be housed in a building containing the offices of the health department, a laboratory, offices of the various private agencies, and clinics for child hygiene, tuberculosis, venereal diseases, dental hygiene, mental hygiene and physical examinations. It would serve as a clearing house for health information; it would be prepared to render first aid or be the headquarters for disaster relief. Any group in any community which desires to produce something constructive, something very much worth while, can contribute to the welfare of the people by the establishment of a health center. This is the next step in modern preventive medicine.

American Legion Defended from Attacks of New York Central Federated Union

(*Editorial from The Garment Worker, May 7, 1920*).

By B. A. LARGER.

THE action taken by the New York Central Federated Union on April 30 in deciding to boycott the American Legion appears to us to have been taken without due consideration.

It was certainly a grave matter to condemn an organization created to uphold American institutions and to stand for their defense at all times against forces which are working for their overthrow, to urge all workingmen to withhold their support as to membership and encouragement to such an organization.

The charge that the American Legion had used its members as strike breakers seems to have rested on very inadequate evidence. Such a charge was brought by a local of the Brotherhood of Painters, Decorators and Paperhangers before the central body and it immediately came to the conclusion that the charge was true without giving the officials of the American Legion any chance of defense in their refutation.

It is quite possible that some of the members of the Legion may have acted as individuals in strike breaking for which the Legion was in no way responsible, and about which its leaders had no knowledge.

No organization can be held responsible for the individual acts of its members. Trade unions have their difficulties with members who violate their principles and bring odium on the labor movement, but to judge the whole trade union movement as unworthy of support by wrongful acts of members would not be just. It would be most unreasonable, but unreasonable as is such judgment, that is often the way in which the organized labor movement suffers in public estimation.

Nowhere is there any evidence that the American Legion has authorized its members to become strike breakers, or that it would sanction such a course in any emergency except in the case of a revolutionary movement directed by a radical element that is seeking not only the destruction of the organized labor movement of America but our democratic institutions. And in such a situation the American Legion would have the support of every patriotic American should it mobilize its force in defense of our government and of our social and economic institutions.

B. A. LARGER

By its action the Central Federated Union has placed itself in a position that must be regretted by every patriotic American, and we trust at a future meeting it will rescind its action and take the only proper course in the appointment of a committee to investigate the charge and then reach a conclusion after it has ascertained all the facts.

Achievements of George W. Perkins

IT will not be only for his notable business success, for his accomplishments in the New York Life Insurance Company, in the firm of J. P. Morgan & Co., in the organization of the International Harvester Company and the International Marine, as well as other corporations and enterprises, that the name of George W. Perkins will go down among the names of the men who have contributed to the greatness of America. As a business man, Mr. Perkins' career offers an admirable example to the youth of the country in application, honesty, and integrity. In politics, he was inspired by the highest ideals of Americanism. He fought against the defacement of natural beauty and was one of the first in the movement to save the Palisades from destruction. His philanthropic work was inspired by kindly humanitarian qualities. Yet one of his greatest achievements was in the work of conciliation between workers and their employers—a problem which has taxed the greatest minds and which is one of the most difficult and challenging.

Mr. Perkins was chairman of the Department on Profit Sharing of The National Civic Federation. In his efforts to bring about a more harmonious spirit of cooperation between employers and workers, Mr. Perkins brought a clear vision and a large human sympathy.

In a notable address before The National Civic Federation conference on profit-sharing, September, 1919, Mr. Perkins outlined his plan of profit-sharing. This plan specified that every business should earn operating expenses, depreciation and returns on honest capitalization; that profits over this sum should on some percentage basis be divided between the capital used in the business and the employes engaged in the business; that in neither case should these profits be immediately withdrawn. These profits should be left in the business for a reasonable length of time; in the case of capital, its profit should be carried to surplus; in the case of employes, their share should be distributed in some form of security representing an interest in the business, and they should be required to hold these securities for from three to five years.

Under such a plan, which he declared he found to be the best, Mr. Perkins said that each employe becomes a partner in the business; he naturally develops a desire to see his investment succeed and bring further profits, and this in turn brings higher efficiency.

In establishing profit-sharing, Mr. Perkins advocated pitiless publicity. "Any profit-sharing plan without an open, honest balance sheet and detailed annual report will never succeed," he declared. "The annual statement of the concern should be full and explicit, so that every man engaged in the enterprise will know what business was done in the preceding year and on what basis profits were and are to be distributed. An honest detailed annual statement tells him officially what the profits were, if any, and this fixes a minimum goal for the coming year, which everyone, individually and collectively, will bend every energy to reach and exceed by as large an amount as possible. . . A detailed annual report is not only necessary to show the organization in prosperous years how the profits were arrived at and what they amounted to, but equally necessary in lean years to show how the losses were arrived at, what they amounted to and why there are no profits to distribute."

Mr. Perkins spoke from a large practical experience. In the early days of his insurance career he found that the agents shifted from one company to another and lacked interest and loyalty. In order to establish a community of interest between the company and its employes he organized the "Nylic" profit-sharing system, which so stimulated the work of the agents that it not only cut down the expenses of the company but in eight to nine years increased the business from $125,000,000 to $347,000,000 a year. Mr. Perkins inaugurated the plan of profit-sharing in the United States Steel Corporation by which preferred stock is sold to employes below the market price. Two statements made by Mr. Perkins give the keynote to his own business career and his efforts in the interests of the workers and the public.

"I have never been in business merely to make money," he said on one occasion. "I easily learned that any man who starts out merely to make money never gets very far."

Several years before his retirement from the firm of J. P. Morgan & Company, in a speech at Columbia University, he declared:

"The corporations of the future must be those that are semi-public servants, serving the public, with ownership widespread among the public, and labor so fairly and equitably treated that it will look upon its corporation as its friend and protector rather than an ever-present enemy; above all, believing in it so thoroughly that it will invest its savings in the corporation's securities and become partners in the business."

Mr. Perkins' belief in publicity and the value of honest criticism was applied to himself. After America entered the war he headed a committee appointed by Mayor Mitchell to prevent abnormal increases in the prices of foodstuffs, and at one time himself had brought into New York large quantities of food in order to prevent extortion by dealers. He was nominated, in September, 1917, by Governor Whitman to be chairman of the State Food Control Board, but was refused confirmation by the State Senate. In the controversy over his appointment he was bitterly opposed by several agricultural societies of the State. Samuel Fraser, head of these societies, was asked why he did not publicly state the reasons for the opposition of the agricultural bodies, and replied that they could not get space in the newspapers. Mr. Perkins told the agricultural organizations to state fully the reasons for their opposition and assured them he would give their criticisms the widest publicity. These criticisms Mr. Perkins had published in 140 New York newspapers at a cost of $25,000 to himself.

At a time of widespread unrest, when passions and prejudices are lashed to high heat by violent and bitter agitation, when the spirit of conciliation and compromise is needed for readjustment, the nation can ill afford to lose such a spirit as that of George W. Perkins.

Problems of a Trade Union Official

[It is a common belief of many who are disposed to be unfriendly toward organized labor that the officials of the unions are always leading the men toward a strike—that these heads feel that unless they are continually denouncing the employers they will lose their own jobs. Quite the contrary is the case; the leaders, up to the point when a strike is called, are almost invariably found counseling peace. As an illustration not only of that spirit but also of the character of the problems with which a union has to deal, we quote from an editorial in the official organ of the International Brotherhood of Teamsters, Chauffeurs, Stablemen and Helpers of America, written by Daniel J. Tobin, its President. Our readers will be impressed by the sane, level-headed arguments advanced by Mr. Tobin.—EDITOR.]

THE other day in a conference with the Express Company officials, they held that it is impossible for them to grant an increase in wages to the drivers, chauffeurs and helpers in any one particular district. The national agreement signed between our International Union, the Clerks' International Union and the Express Company officials, deals only with working conditions, and it does not deal with or cover the question of wages.

As our membership understands, the system pursued by us in the past, has been that each city or district takes care of the wages of the men or members of our organization, in that particular city or district. The Clerks' International Union, like the Railroad Brotherhoods, present an agreement which covers their membership throughout the country, although the wages are not the same in each city, because the wages in each district, are usually governed by the cost of living in that district. For instance, it costs more to live in New York, than it does in Des Moines, Iowa, or other cities in the middle west. Rents are higher. Clothing is usually higher and meats and vegetables are higher in the eastern cities than they are in the middle west. Besides, it is usually considered that much more skill is required in driving an auto truck or wagon in a large, congested, industrial center than in a smaller city where there is not much congestion. Therefore the wages of drivers and chauffeurs vary somewhat in the different districts, depending on the locality. I am of the opinion that the rule that has prevailed that express drivers take care of their own wage scales in each district, that it will be impossible to pursue said rule in the future, as the several companies that operated individually prior to the war, have practically amalgamated into one large company, and I believe the time is coming when we must present a wage scale for the men in the employ of this company who are covered by our jurisdiction, that said wage scale will have to deal with the question of wages for our men employed in every section of the country. For instance, we might discuss the question of granting a ten, fifteen or twenty per cent. increase in wages to apply to all men covered by our jurisdiction, which would eliminate the unpleasant conditions that now exist, where one city after another is asking for an increase in wages. In other words, we might be successful in settling up a wage scale in Cincinnati, and two weeks afterwards find that the men in St. Louis or Philadelphia may be on strike. The drivers and chauffeurs in New York City might go on strike in order to get their agreement signed, and our men in St. Louis, Cincinnati, and other places, would have to handle the stuff that was handled at the other end by strikebreakers. Whereas, if a general agreement prevailed, governing wages, the question could be

DANIEL J. TOBIN

settled for a definite period in every section of the country. That does not mean, that equal wages would prevail in every city and town in the country. The wage increase would be based on a certain per cent. of wages the men are receiving. As stated above, I think the time is coming when we will have to consider the advisability of asking for a general increase in wages for all drivers, chauffeurs, helpers, stablemen, and others, in the employ of this company, that are covered by our jurisdiction, and this is one of the questions that will be discussed and considered by the General Executive Board.

This wage board which has been appointed to take up the question of wages for the railroad brotherhoods, and other common carriers, was to consider the question of wages and the men were not to go on strike while the question was under discussion, but some of the membership of the railroad brotherhoods have gone on strike, although the majority of the membership have remained at work until such time as the question has been considered by the wage board created for this purpose. Increased rates for the railroads and express company are also to be considered by the interstate commerce commission, acting jointly with the wage board, as I understand the law. The express company officials contend they are losing two million dollars a month, or twenty-four million dollars a year. In other words, that their revenue is not sufficient to meet the running expenses, or, that they are losing twenty-four million dollars a year because their rates are not sufficient, or high enough, to meet the increased cost of operation. The government is subsidizing the express company, or has guaranteed to pay 5½ per cent. on the invested capital, besides paying all other deficits suffered by the express company up until next January. In a conference I had with the express officials in Cincinnati, they claim that the government will not allow them to increase wages, which would increase the operating expenses of the company, because of the fact that the government itself would have to pay the increased cost of operation. In other words, the company's stockholders will not lose anything until next January, no matter how much the increased cost of operation may be, because the government guarantees them 5½ per cent. over and above all expenses on the invested capital of the company. This is one of the reasons why the express officials say they cannot open up the question of wages. Another reason is, they claim they have not the power to adjust wages, that that is a question which must be decided by the new wage board, created by Congress. After this board is appointed, it will take some time to get ready, then they will have to listen to all the evidence that will be submitted by each of the large organizations of railroad brotherhoods, then listen to rebuttal evidence submitted by the railroad companies, offsetting the claims of the brotherhoods. The express company is asking for a 25 per cent. increase in rates. They cannot increase their rates one cent without permission to do so. The question confronting us is, when will this wage board get around to discussing the question of an increase in wages for the express employes? You understand that the wage boards I have dealt with before were very slow in rendering a decision. It is true, they may make their award retroactive, but it is also a fact that they do not hurry in their deliberations, or in their decisions. In the meantime, the increased cost of living continues up and our membership are working under a hardship, especially in the districts where wages are low. However, it must be taken into consideration that if strikes can possibly be avoided, this is the best course to pursue. If you quit your work, and by your action endeavor to defeat not only the express company, but the government, which is practically back of the express company, undoubtedly you will lose your wages, and the question is, will you not be worse off than before? I am stating the case plainly to our membership engaged at this work, so that each member may understand his position. There is this possibility, that when the wage board does meet, they can make their award retroactive, or date back to a certain time. There is also the possibility that the wage board may not grant any increase, or they may grant a substantial increase, or something else.

The company officials contend that having universally established the eight-hour day amongst their employes is a step in advance of other drivers and chauffeurs, while I contend that a man who works eight hours on an express truck or wagon is doing more than the average driver who works nine or ten hours on any other kind of a wagon or truck. Milk wagon drivers, bakery drivers, tea and coffee drivers, and other branches of our trade, in many instances, work but six or seven hours, or a sufficient length of time to cover their routes, while the average man who drives a team of horses although required to be on the job ten hours does not put in more than eight or nine hours of actual work, and in most instances he does not have to hustle and rush like the express driver or chauffeur. I trust that our express employes will use careful, calm, cool judgment after reading this article and will make no mistake. Above and beyond all, rash or radical action very seldom gets anything for any one. You may say, it is all right for me to argue from this standpoint, and that if I had to work on a wagon for one hundred dollars a month, I would find it a different story, but I wish to say, I have also worked on a wagon, and for much less than the amount mentioned; I have had some trouble making both ends meet; that I understand every phase of the situation; I also know that the most dangerous remedy to apply is the remedy of strike, and that this remedy should not be applied except when all other remedies fail.

Is the Labor Problem Unsolvable?

(Continued from page 5)

attempting by law to force any man to work, and, speaking by and large, the determination by the public to resist tyranny broke both strikes.

One of the most popular arguments for the Kansas law is that it treats industrial disputes in the same manner as society treats all other disputes, through courts of law. Do we not submit all our differences, of whatever nature, to judges and juries, even our most intimate affairs? The control of our children, our marriage relations, the question of inheritance and thousands of other matters are controlled by statutes which are interpreted and applied by courts of law. To say that there are any more delicate questions arising in the relations between the employer and the employee than between a man and his wife is, they argue, an absurdity. This view is so generally maintained by the public that it is almost accepted as an axiom. Every lawyer, educated to revere and trust the courts in his every-day practice, naturally upholds this view. The fact that so many distinguished lawyers were on the President's Second Industrial Commission doubtless accounted for the court idea, panels and juries bulking so large in its conclusions. But are industrial disputes to be classed with all other disputes? Emphatically, No. The principles governing disputes in general have been evolved out of centuries of experience, by long and tedious processes, and, concededly, just codes and precedents have been established governing almost every conceivable phase of human misunderstanding. Not so in the industrial world. There is no agreed code, no agreed precedent. Changes in public sentiment from the time not long ago when, as Mr. Gompers pointed out, it was a crime to ask for higher wages, when legislation was sought for a maximum wage, while now it is sought for a minimum wage, have been so revolutionary as to baffle all attempts to determine a status from which a code could be evolved. Recall the President's First Industrial Conference last October, composed of some of the ablest and most representative men from the three groups—the public, labor and capital.

It was hoped that this conference might be able to establish a code which should govern industrial relations, but it could agree upon nothing and adjourned, each group denouncing the others and many members denouncing their fellow members within their own groups. The President then called a second conference, composed only of representatives of the public, leaving out representatives of the two groups—capital and labor—which had to be reconciled. This conference, of course, had no trouble in agreeing, but both capital and labor vigorously disapproved of its findings. The same result would have followed any conference called by either of the other groups. The Chamber of Commerce of the United States is now taking a referendum on the subject. It will have no trouble in reaching an agreement because only one side is doing the voting. With equal facility, the American Federation of Labor unanimously agreed upon an industrial program at a meeting representing the 113 international organizations composing that body. Take the latest and, may I say, most conspicuous illustration, the so-called Gompers-Allen debate itself. Could any one glimpse the faintest outline of code in the tense, and at times heated, atmosphere at Carnegie Hall that night? On the codes, civil and criminal and the precedents established for the government of all the other disputes with which society has to deal, there could not be staged a debate at Carnegie Hall, nor would the President's conferences, composed as the first one was, even have the least difficulty in agreeing on them. In fact, even to suggest the holding of such a conference would be taken as a sign of lunacy. But when it comes to the so-called capital and labor problems, as stated in the first paragraph, the only thing Messrs. Gompers and Allen could agree upon was the time and the place of the debate.

But can nothing be done to bring about better relations between capital and labor? Must we sit with folded hands and look upon these industrial conflicts with utter complacency? No. Certainly we should strive to do everything in our power to hasten the day when selfishness, ignorance, social, religious and class hatred and all those things that interfere with the operation of the Golden Rule are swept away. Then will come industrial peace.

But that means the millennium, says one. True; but industrial peace is not the only great problem that is awaiting that day for solution. International peace is in the same category. Then there is religious union and concord yet to be attained. Observe the differences, for instance, between the Protestant and the Catholic churches, to say nothing of the differences among the various denominations of the Protestant Church, and between factions within individual Protestant denominations, for example those between the Northern and Southern branches of the Methodist Episcopal Church, which forty years' earnest endeavor has been unsuccessful in reconciling.

Moreover, consider the distressing problems in our methods of government—federal, state and municipal—that are unsolved, and some of which seem to be unsolvable. Look at the municipal government in our large cities. What Christian citizen can here feel proud of the results of his use of the great privilege of the ballot? What progress have we made in two thousand years in dealing with that terrible problem, the social evil, to mention only one among many others? Are we not expecting too much when we hope to discover some mechanical slot-device solution for the intricate and baffling problems involved in the relations between employers and workmen?

But because we have never found a complete solution to all these problems, is no reason to despair. We are making tremendous progress in many fields of human endeavor. Compare the conditions of the wage earner, for example, fifty years ago with those to-day—his wages, hours of work, hours of toil for children, conditions of labor for women, etc. An enumeration of the beneficent legislation in the last twenty-five years in the interest of the worker would alone furnish justification for the hope that, slowly but surely, we are working towards a better understanding and appreciation of our industrial problems, which, of course, in the end means industrial peace. But let us not be discouraged because it is not achieved over night.

Revolution Preached to M. E. Clergy

(Continued from page 11)

cut off—not very much when compared with the French Revolution and the Russian revolution in 1905. And so Russia has stated that the actual revolution has come to an end, and there is now awakened a spirit of conciliation, and they have begun to compromise, and the word Bolshevik is no longer popular in Russia, and the Bolshevists do not like to be called that themselves, and they want to be known as the Soviets.

"There are a good many folks and some Methodist ministers who oppose Bolshevism because they do not know anything about it. . . We in the United States are not yet prepared for Bolshevism, and therefore we will be obliged to handle our revolution in a different manner. But that it is coming there is no doubt. There is one party, however, that understands Russia very well and that is the united plutocracy of the world, and they know that if Bolshevism succeeds in Russia then plutocracy is doomed in the world at large. And therefore they have combined their resources and influences to kill the thing before it conquers the world. They are working hard to kill the 'infant' before it learns to walk. *If Russia succeeds as I hope to God it will*, then I say that plutocracy is doomed in the world, and that is my last word to you."

Rev. Dr. Henry stated he differed with Dr. Hecker in some of his remarks and then asked: "I want to ask a question in regard to this morning's paper. There was an item in that paper stating that the Russian leaders were trying to carry a revolution into France, and if I understood Dr. Hecker in his statement a little while ago he made the declaration that Trotzky was not interested in anything but the Russian people, in helping them, but I have felt myself that Trotzky is interested elsewhere outside of Russia."

"I think that Trotzky is interested in Russia," Hecker answered. "I do not like to mention his name myself, personally, but it is true that the Russian revolutionists have made up their minds to carry the revolution all over the world. I know that man who was arrested, according to the report you read there. I know Loriot. They were regular French Bolshevists and they are fighting to organize a similar thing in France, and are dead determined to bring a revolution on in France; after that in England and other countries. I think the Russians are divided into two groups, those following Lenine and those following Trotzky. Lenine wanted to have a conciliatory policy in regard to the other countries, and Lenine is trying particularly to furnish friendly relations with America, *and in this connection Raymond Robins has done more than any other one man.* Trotzky represents the radical group and wants to carry the thing into the whole world. I know they know that I am opposed to it, but particularly as far as our America is concerned. I want to see Russia on its feet and try out the experiment, but I do not want them to pour something down our throat—we have our own brains to use, but I am also opposed to forcing anything into Russia's throat. The world is ready for the revolution and I know it is working for it."

Rev. Dr. George A. Simons, who had been head of the Methodist Mission in Petrograd, had just previously entered the meeting room and took the floor. "I have not had the pleasure of looking into Dr. Hecker's face since eight years ago. I want to be fair to Dr. Hecker, as I want to be fair to the real Russia, and I came in a few minutes ago and heard from one of the men upstairs that someone was whooping it up for Bolshevism down here. Now, I did not hear the address. I do not know whether on the whole it was pro-Bolshevik, anti-Bolshevik, pro-Soviet or anti-Soviet. I would like to put a few questions to Dr. Hecker. First, when were you last in Russia?"

"I was last in Russia geographically eighteen years ago, but among the Russian people I was up to the time I have come back, so I have been with millions of them," Dr. Hecker answered.

Dr. Simons said:

"Dr. Hecker is right that we must not confuse the terms Sovietism and Bolshevism; that they are not synonymous, but it so happens that Bolshevism is camouflaged for Sovietism. We know a rat when we smell one, and whether he calls himself a supporter of Sovietism or not, he is a Bolshevik. Now, I have no patience with this kind of propaganda. I do not say he is making propaganda for Bolshevism, but I do say that so long as the State Department issues statements I will believe these statements in preference to any others. The last statement came from Robert Lansing, and there you will find under the official stamp of the United States Government absolutely reliable data as to the conditions in Russia under Soviet rule."

Socialism Unmasked

(Continued from page 4)

ments of the Third Internationale, Zinoviev, president of the Executive Committee, declared, in an address dated "Smolny, November 5, 1919:

"The proletarian revolution is moving forward with powerful steps. In the unprecedented wave of strikes, which has started in Europe and America, the old, rotten trade organizations and their 'leaders' struggle helplessly. These pitiable pygmies are unable to stop the powerful rush of the waves of proletarian revolution. The strike of millions of English railway men, the grandiose strike of American longshoremen, of German metal workers, and of Italian workmen of almost every trade, have a world-wide historic significance. This same strike wave has begun in all Europe, just as such a wave preceded the proletarian revolution in Russia. . . . The powerful strike wave, rushing over the whole world, gives new strength to the Communist Internationale. . . . The Communist Internationale serves as the speaking trumpet of the millions of workmen of Europe and America. . . . The Communist Internationale listens attentively to every movement of the soul of the working class. . . . The Communist Internationale will continue to grow and become strong as the proletarian revolution develops. . . . In a year, two years, the Communist Internationale will rule the whole world."

In working toward the objectives of the Third Internationale, in seeking to undermine and destroy the organized labor movement, to build up "one big union" of class conscious workers, which shall be responsive to one supreme authority, to the end that the general strike shall be employed to overturn the present order, is it to be supposed that the Socialist party in America will not act as the direct and chief agency? In the immediate work of the Executive Bureau at Amsterdam and of its sub-bureaus, to foment and finance strikes, to develop small strikes of protest into larger phases of revolutionary activity, will the Socialist party of America—the chief arm of the Third Internationale in the United States—remain unresponsive and inert?

The answer to this is to be found in the program laid down at the Congress of the Third Communist Internationale in Moscow, March, 1919, and in the direct answer made to that program in the Manifesto adopted by the Socialist party of America at its Emergency convention in Chicago, September, 1919. That response, which stands today, is plain, unequivocal and direct.

AMERICAN SOCIALISTS' RESPONSE TO MOSCOW.

The Manifesto of the Moscow Congress, dated March 26, 1919, was signed by Lenine, Trotzky, Zinoviev, Rakovsky, and Platten. It was published and distributed in the United States by the Literature Department of the Socialist party of America by which it was characterized as "undoubtedly the greatest declaration ever issued from any working class tribunal since the Communist Manifesto of Marx and Engels."

The world program of the Third Internationale is introduced by a denunciation and repudiation of those Socialists who were loyal to their governments in the Great War and who have advocated social changes by legal and parliamentary methods. It voices the aspirations and program of the "uncompromising," revolutionary section of the movement, of which the Russian Bolsheviki are the chief exponents and of which Lenine stands as the supreme commanding figure. It declares that in its program and methods it but follows and fulfills the program laid down in the Manifesto of Marx and Engels. It begins:

> Seventy-two years have gone by since the Communist party announced their program to the world in the form of a Manifesto drawn up by the two greatest teachers of the proletarian revolution, Karl Marx and Frederich Engels. . . . We, Communists, representatives of the revolutionary proletariat in different countries in Europe, America and Asia, now assembled in the powerful Soviet city of Moscow, both feel and consider ourselves to be the followers of, and participants in, a cause for which the program was drawn up seventy-two years ago. Our duty is to gather together the revolutionary experiences of the working classes, *to free the movement from the harmful interference of opportunist and social patriotic elements, to unite the forces of all genuine revolutionary parties in the world proletariat, and thereby to facilitate and hasten the victory of the Communist revolution.*

The Socialist party of America, at its Emergency Convention last September responded to this, repudiated the "opportunist and social patriotic elements" denounced by Lenine's Moscow congress, and accepted the invitation to join "the forces of all genuine revolutionary parties" under the aegis of the Internationale begotten by Lenine. The sentiments of the Chicago Manifesto directly echo those of the Moscow Manifesto, the phraseology is often identical, the terms used are analogous, but in some cases the language of the Manifesto of the Socialist party of America is even stronger and more violent than that of the Congress which was organized by, and now functions as the world revolution agency of, the Russian Bolshevist régime.

The Chicago Manifesto declares its repudiation of loyal and parliamentary Socialists and its stand with the Russian Bolsheviki thus:

> Recognizing the crucial situation at home and abroad, the Socialist party of the United States at its first national convention after the war, *squarely takes its position with the uncompromising section of the International Socialist movement. We unreservedly reject the policy of those Socialists who support their belligerent capitalist governments* on the plea of "national defense" and who entered into demoralizing compacts for so-called civil peace with the exploiters of labor during the war and continued a political alliance with them after the war.
>
> We, the organized Socialists of America, pledge our support to the revolutionary workers of Russia in the maintenance of their Soviet Government, to the radical Socialists of Germany, Austria and Hungary in their efforts to establish working-class rule in their countries, and to those Socialist organizations in England, France, Italy and other countries, who during the war, as after the war, have remained true to the principles of UNCOMPROMISING INTERNATIONAL SOCIALISM.

The Manifesto of the Moscow Internationale further denounces the Socialists who supported their governments in the war and who oppose revolution by violence, thus:

> The opportunists who before the war exhorted the workers, in the name of the gradual transition into Socialism, to be temperate; who during the war asked for submission in the name of *Burfrieden* (domestic peace) and defense of their Fatherland, now again demand of the workers self-abnegation to overcome the terrible consequences of the war. If this preaching were listened to by the workers, capitalism would build out of the bones of several generations a new and still more formidable structure leading to a new and inevitable world war. Fortunately for humanity this is no longer possible.

The Socialist party of America, in the Minority report on International Relations, recently adopted by an overwhelming majority in a referendum vote of the party membership, echoes the denunciation of Moscow:

> Any Internationale, to be effective in this crisis, must contain only those elements who take their stand unreservedly upon the basis of the class struggle, and their adherence to this principle is not mere lip loyalty.
>
> When leading Socialists join their national governments upon a coalition basis they accept and sanction policies which hinder Socialists and the working class generally from taking full advantage of the opportunities for deep-seated changes which the war creates. This makes the workers content with superficial reformist changes which are readily granted by the capitalist class as a means of self protection from the rising tide of working class revolt.

After referring to the collapse of the Second Internationale upon the outbreak of the war, and the failure of the Berne Conference, the Minority report further says of the loyal Socialists who supported their governments in the war:

> We consider that a new Internationale which contains those groups which contributed to the downfall of our former organization must be so weak in its Socialist policy as to be useless.

The Minority report declares that "in principle and in its past history" the Socialist party "has always stood with those elements of other countries that remained true to their principles"—the revolutionary extreme parties of Italy, Switzerland, Norway, Greece, Bulgaria, and the Russian Bolsheviki.

> The Socialist party of the United States, therefor, declares itself in support of the Third (Moscow) Internationale.

The Third Moscow Internationale, in its Manifesto, deflected the blame for precipitating the world war from Germany and laid it chiefly to Great Britain. It declared the war to be an "imperialistic war," which has passed into a "civil war which lines up class against class:"

> The war, which had been prepared for decades, broke out through direct and conscious provocation on the part of Great Britain. The British Government reckoned on giving support to Russia and France until they were exhausted and at the same time had crushed Germany, their mortal enemy. But the strength of the German military machine proved too formidable and called forth not only an apparent, but an actual intervention in the war on the part of England. It was the military superiority of Germany that caused the Government at Washington to give up their apparent neutrality. The United States assumed, as regards Europe, the same part that England had played in former wars and has tried to play to the last, namely, the plan of weakening the one side with the help of the other, by joining in military operations for the sole purpose of securing for themselves all the advantages of the situation. . . .
>
> The imperialistic war which pitted nation against nation has passed and is passing into the civil war which lines up class against class.

The Socialist party of America, in its Chicago Manifesto, deflected the blame for precipitating the world war from Germany and lays it to "the struggle for foreign markets" of "competing imperialistic nations." After denouncing the peace as "a peace of hatred and violence, a peace of vengeance and strangulation," it declares the ending of the war as ushering in "the new order" and the time for the "immediate task" of accelerating the class struggle, of organizing the workers on class lines, and of bringing about the Socialist revolution:

> It now becomes more than ever the immediate task of international Socialism to accelerate and organize the inevitable transfer of political and industrial power from the capitalist class to the workers. . . . The workers of the world are already ushering in the new order of true civilization. . . . Even in the United States the symptoms of a rebellious spirit in the ranks of the working masses are rapidly multiplying. The widespread and extensive strikes for better labor conditions, the demand of the two million railway workers to control their industry, the sporadic formation of labor parties apparently though not fundamentally in opposition to the political parties of the possessing class, are promising indications of a definite tendency on the part of American labor to break away from its reactionary and futile leadership and to join in the great emancipating movement of the more advanced revolutionary workers of the world.

The Third Communist Internationale lays the responsibility for civil war, or violent and drastic methods during a revolution, to the "arch-enemies" of the laboring classes. Driven to violent methods, civil war is forced upon the working class, and, the Moscow Congress declared, they "must answer blow for blow." The Manifesto declared "necessary the arming of the workers."

(To be continued)

Need for Legislation Against Disloyalty

(Continued from page 8)

"Now, I might say just a few words in passing with respect to the opposition which has arisen against these bills. Those who have been opposed to this bill are in large measure those against whom the bills are directed. I may say that it started in a committee of eight in the Rand School of Social Science, to which were added members of committees from various revolutionary unions. When I speak of revolutionary unions, I mean exactly that thing. I mean those unions that have broken away from the American Federation of Labor and organized under the tutelage of the revolutionary elements in this country, and are organized for the purpose of putting into effect a general strike if the time ever arrives when they see a prospect of success. Those unions have schools and are teaching their members the doctrines that organized government should be overthrown by unlawful means, by means of the general strike, and, although some of the professors that teach in these schools are professors in various colleges or have lately been professors in various colleges, they also joined this committee of protest. Then there joined them some very earnest and, I believe, sincere people representing the settlement houses.

"I had a very interesting illustration of exactly the methods of procedure. I got a letter about two weeks ago. The letterhead is 'Committee for Freedom of Education,' and in small type it says, 'To aid the Rand School of Social Science in Its Fight to Prevent Interference with Freedom of Study and Teaching.' And then appear the names of Francis Hackett, of *The New Republic;* B. W. Huebsch, of *The Freeman;* Freda Kirchwey, of *The Nation*. I may say Huebsch was one of those who went over with the Ford Peace Party and has been a great pacifist ever since. Freda Kirchwey, of *The Nation*, is the wife of Evans Clark, one of those who is in charge of the commercial section of the Ludvigh Martens' Bolshevik Bureau here. And then were the names of Winthrop D. Lane, of *The Survey*; Norman Thomas, of the *World Tomorrow*; and Mary R. Sanford. This letter says:

"'Do you know that the right of people to study and learn what they choose is being jeopardized in New York State at this minute? The Lusk Committee is trying to throttle the traditional American right to an untrammeled education. If Senate Bill Introductory Number 1120 should become a law, every class conducted by a labor union, every club formed by a social settlement, every course of study carried on by a Socialist organization or any other private agency would be subject to the censorship of the State Board of Regents—a body of twelve men elected by the Legislature.' As though that was any very serious condemnation! And then it says at the bottom:

"'Money is needed at once. We must have $25,000 to fight this bill,' and asks me to send them some money.

"If anyone really took the trouble to follow the issues of the *New York Call*, they would see that exactly the same method which was adopted to keep us out of war has in a smaller measure been adopted to stir up public opinion against these bills; namely, a small committee in the Rand School reaching out by accretion, bringing in more and more sympathizers, and then writing letters. They have a system—they had before the war when, at the press of a button, twenty-five thousand letters went to President Wilson on a given day so as to urge him to keep us out of war. That system is organized, is the result of a definite plan, it gives the appearance of representing public opinion, and it has the effect of really misleading some very fine people, because, in the first place, they don't tell the truth about the bills. In the second place, people are very much like sheep; they will follow where they think the biggest crowd is.

"All of this is part of a general plan to meet the general subversive movement, in a constructive way. We don't think it is complete; we don't think it is any more than a step, but we believe that each one of these bills is a step forward and will be helpful."

In the general discussion which followed, J. E. Armstrong, of the Brooklyn, Y. M. C. A., asked:

"With regard to Bill 1274, I want to say I am in entire sympathy with the objects sought by the bill. One question naturally arises, as to whether the exemption which is granted there to a well established sect or denomination does not defeat one of the purposes of the bill in that it might exempt certain denominations which claimed to be denominations or sects, which have been prosecuted for the very thing the bill seeks to stop."

"What you say may very well be true," answered Mr. Stevenson. "However, we felt that one of the most dangerous things to do was to pass upon or in any way regulate the religious expression of the people, and we didn't think that even the Board of Regents was competent to pass upon the religious expression of the people, and we have to rely on the loyalty of the various religious denominations themselves in respect to the schools that they start. It may be some schools carried on by some denominations may teach disloyalty. We cannot close all doors at once. We have got to take a step at a time, and must be careful what steps we do take."

"To press the point one step further," said Mr. Armstrong, "seeing that a school founded by a specific denomination or sect would therefore be exempt, but if several denominations got together jointly, as they are represented in the Y. W. C. A. and the Y. M. C. A., then that exemption does not prevail; or is it the intention of those who drew the bill to offer such exemption to a recognized institution such as these?"

"I don't believe the exemption would prevail and I don't believe the Y. W. C. A. or the Y. M. C. A. is teaching anything that is going to be subversive of the interests of the State, or going to teach disloyalty," answered Mr. Stevenson. "Consequently, I don't see they have anything to fear."

"We haven't anything to fear," said Mr. Armstrong, "but it seems unfair for us to be outside the class of religious organizations."

"Some of them have already dropped some of the religious part. The Y. W. C. A. has simply dropped from its platform its really religious feature at its latest convention, I believe.

"I don't know whether there are any representatives of the Y. W. C. A. here or not—" protested Mr. Armstrong.

"It has been brought to my attention that it has," said Mr. Stevenson.

Rev. F. Ernest Johnson, Research secretary of the Commission on the Church and Social Service of the Federal Council of the Churches of Christ in America, referring later to Mr. Stevenson's statement that the Y. W. C. A. "had decided to drop religion from its program" remarked: "I hope you will not make that statement anywhere else."

"I believe they—in referring to Jesus as their Savior—struck out 'as their Savior' from their program, did they not?" rejoined Mr. Stevenson.

"I have the honor to be a member of the National Board," said Mrs. Thomas Gladding, "and was present at the convention to which Mr. Stevenson has referred, and was one of the leaders of the opposition to the motion that was carried by so large a majority. And I want to say that while the Y. W. C. A. has not yet become a non-religious organization, those of us, Mrs. Finley J. Shepard and myself and a number of others, who led the opposition, do feel the Y. W. C. A. is very likely to become a non-religious organization if it goes on in the legislation which began in Cleveland. So Mr. Stevenson is not altogether wrong."

"Radical papers are claiming that Mr. Moot is opposed to these bills and that the Board of Regents is ignorant of them?" said Mrs. Finke of the Cosmopolitan Club.

"May I answer the first part of that?" said Mr. Berger. "With regard to Mr. Moot, I know that I may be committing an indiscretion in saying what I am about to say, but at least I am stating the fact. In Buffalo there has been and is now a woman teaching in the public schools by the name of Pratt—Anna S. Pratt, I think. That has been called to the attention of the public school authorities of Buffalo and they have known it for some four or five months. This woman is a member of the Communist Party and was active in helping to organize that party. I believe that Mr. Moot has something to do with the public school system of Buffalo. Although I may be unkind in my criticism, we may take those two facts in conjunction—the fact that this Pratt woman, a member of the Communist Party and organizer of the Communist Party, is being permitted to continue to teach in the public schools of Buffalo, and Mr. Moot's opposition to these bills."

"What is she teaching?" asked Mrs. Finke.

"She is teaching the various courses of instruction provided by the curriculum of the public schools," said Mr. Berger.

"And not communism?"

"There is a provision in the Educational Law requiring the teaching of patriotism to all the children in our public schools, and it is inconceivable to me how a person who is a member of the Communist Party can teach patriotism to children in this state," answered Mr. Berger.

"Why can't the Education Law——"

"Suppose she does by word of mouth tell the children, 'This is the flag of the United States; you must revere it.' She can't do that with sincerity and with feeling and with depth, and get her message over, and be a member of the Communist Party at the same time."

"Is she teaching communism in the Buffalo public schools?" insisted Mrs. Finke.

"She is not," replied Mr. Berger.

In answer to a question by one of those present as to whether a teacher cannot teach communism "between the lines," without mentioning the word "communism," Mr. Stevenson answered:

"I think it is the easiest thing in the world to do that. A teacher need not say, 'This is communism', or 'These are the principles of the Communist Party', but by emphasizing certain things and minimizing others and saying half truths and saying a great many other things in the clever way that most of the organizers of the Communist Party have, and the way in which they evade the law, it is a very easy thing to teach children communism by indirection. I have not the slightest doubt that is being done."

The Rev. Mr. Crouch, of the Interchurch World Movement, said:

"The *Times* this morning carries the story that a half million and odd appropriation was rejected by Congress on the ground that it did more harm than good. Isn't this a parallel case? Here is the national legislature throwing out a request for an additional five hundred thousand dollars to extend the activities of the Attorney General of the United States in prosecution which some people consider persecutions. How can we tell that the hundred thousand dollars, if granted by the Legislature of this state, would not work in the same way in the state, and by and large in the nation? How can we tell the proposition put up here is at all the right thing to do? How are we sure that we are conforming to American traditions when introducing a stem of repression, when the thing to do is to sk these dissatisfied aliens to come and talk it ut. A prominent social worker made the sugestion in a paper not long ago—invite these eople to the City Hall and talk it out. Don't rosecute them until, you know what they are fter. It seems to me we must see this side of ."

Mr. Berger answered: "I thought I made it uite clear this bill 1272 has specific reference to he prosecution on the charge of criminal anrchy. Let me for the benefit of the gentlemen, ho evidently did not hear what I said, again ead the meaning of criminal anarchy as defined y the lawmakers of this State eighteen years go.

"It is this: Section 160 of the Penal Law: Criminal Anarchy defined. Criminal anarchy s the doctrine that organized government should e overthrown by force or violence, or by assassiation of the executive head or of any of the xecutive officials of government, or by any unawful means. The advocacy of such doctrine ither by word of mouth or writing is a felony.'

"I really think the time has arrived when eople in this country should commit themselves ither in one camp or the other. All those who y indirection, by direction, or by coddling or pologizing, or encouraging in any way, shape or anner the teaching of the doctrine that organed government should be overthrown by force d violence, and the executive heads of government be assassinated, should go in one camp, and all the other people in the country who are opposed to the propagation of this doctrine should go in another camp. We have had altogether too much of this apologizing for the revolutionary radical.

"Furthermore, I believe the persons who are encouraging criminal anarchy are not students of history. They have not read the story of the French Revolution and the stories of a few other revolutions. They have been so busy and so active, to give the impression that they are 'broad' and 'liberal' that they have leaned over backward."

"As I read the history of the Alien and Sedition Act of 1798, the country was then faced with the same kind of danger as we say it is faced with today," pursued the Rev. Mr. Crouch. "The propagandists of the safeguarded alien were absolutely inimical to the state or nation, as any other aliens are today. Those acts were passed by the forces of the Federal Party. Practically they were the last legislation passed by the Federal Party. The Democratic Party today, who are proposing certain acts of this kind, is the same party which under the leadership of Thomas Jefferson had to do with the acts, alien and sedition, of 1798, in the face of a danger just as grave to the fathers of our country as what we think we face today. Now, I ask you again, is that the way to go about this business?"

Prof. William Bradley Otis, of the College of the City of New York, challenged Mr. Crouch:

"Tolerance is admirable, but there is a point where it ceases to be a virtue. Lincoln at times during the Civil War even denied the writ of habeas-corpus. Shortly after the Proclamation of Neutrality was issued, 'Citizen Genet' arrived at Charleston, April 8, 1793. Genet apparently regarded the United States as an appendage to the French Republic. Without consulting Washington, he at once issued commissions to privateers which began capturing British vessels off the Atlantic coast. He demanded immediate payment of our debt to France, although payment was not yet due. Numerous 'Democratic Clubs' were organized here in imitation of the French Revolutionary clubs. Genet was told that he must respect the Proclamation of Neutrality. He threatened to appeal to the people as the true sovereigns in America, in the belief that Washington would be forced to resign. Washington then demanded and obtained Genet's recall in 1794.

"In the light of this incident may we not infer that were Washington president of the United States today, he would deal with the self-styled 'Ambassador of Soviet Russia', 'Comrade' Martens, now in this country, in much the same way that he dealt with 'Citizen' Genet?

"'Nations, like kings,' says Emerson, 'are not good by facility and complaisance. The kindness of kings consists in justice and strength. Easy good-nature has been the dangerous foible of the Republic, and it was necessary that its enemies should outrage it, and drive us to unwonted firmness, to secure the salvation of this country in the next ages'.

"I think that is a quotation, Mr. Crouch, that we should have in mind, in discussing these things."

Plan to Create National Service Committees

(Continued from page 6)

alty, meaning thereby the preservation and the application of American ideals. This sounds a little academic, but we shall not deal with it upon an academic basis. Having found a common basis, what are we to do?

First and foremost, let us secure a line-up—get people pledged—give them an opportunity to express themselves. Let us do this officially with organizations and then, working through organizations, do it individually with their members and with the persons within the range of their influence. We shall find that multitudes of them are awaiting the opportunity, and awaiting it eagerly.

One large business organization, the National Board of Fire Underwriters, recently undertook a diagnosis of this nature. A letter was mailed to local fire insurance agents in different parts of the country and a pledge card reading as follows was sent to them:

> "Realizing the great importance of maintaining American institutions and preserving American ideals in the face of widespread and insidious attempts to destroy them, I desire to express my full sympathy with the FIRE INSURANCE AMERICANIZATION MOVEMENT."

It is understood that my signature commits me to nothing beyond the following specific points:

1. To exercise my influence as opportunity may offer for the suppression of disloyalty and the promotion of Americanism;
2. To support the widest possible dissemination of American ideals through the schools, the press, the pulpit and in public meetings."

This pledge was purposely made in the simplest form, but was so phrased as to include both the defensive and the constructive features. Almost at once a flood of signatures began to pour in and soon aggregated between twenty-five and thirty thousand; many of them were accompanied by added expressions of enthusiasm and of great desire to assist.

We have become fully convinced that there are millions of people in the United States who are literally chafing under the necessity for remaining silent in the face of a continuous propaganda of disloyalty, and yet lack the means for direct expression.

How shall we make this early part of the proposal operative? We suggest that there be formulated a series of pledge resolutions aligning first the national organizations and then their sub-divisions—these to be followed by a systematic promotion of the obtaining of signatures that shall in time include the largest possible proportion of the American public.

A MECHANISM OF LIMITLESS POSSIBILITIES

Now let us assume that a large number of national organizations will make satisfactory response, will pass the desired resolutions, will appoint the desired national service committees and will secure the passage of similar resolutions, together with the appointment of service sub-committees, by their state and local subdivisions. *There would then be in existence a mechanism, national in its scope and of almost limitless possibilities for national welfare.* How may it be put to work? Obviously, by applying general principles to diverse conditions such as are found in various fields of activity. In other words, the credit men will be dealing with one set of conditions, the brick manufacturers with another, the sheet metal workers with a third, the fruit raisers with a fourth, the railway conductors with a fifth, and so on indefinitely. All of them are American, all of them are potentially patriotic and all of them are actively patriotic when a sufficient occasion arouses their interest, as in the time of the war.

Aside from certain fundamentals, the method of application—which is to say, the intensive work, must be differentiated. This can hardly be dictated from an outside source; it may be advised upon and its results may be coordinated with the work in other fields by means of a general Advisory Committee, but it must be developed through the special knowledge of the special committee which has it in charge. Therefore, we suggest the following points as to the character of the work to be undertaken by the proposed committees:

THE FUNCTION OF THE COMMITTEES

1. Each would be an organ of *cooperation*—i.e., would make it possible for the work to become national in scope and harmonious in character among the various organizations.

2. Each would be an organ of *application*—i.e, would apply such general work intensively to the particular organization which it represents, adapting it to the conditions therein existent.

(Note) Thus no committee would be dependent upon the success of any other but all would contribute directly to the general result and collaterally to one another's morale.

3. Each should endeavor to secure the nearest possible approach to a 100 per cent. enrollment within its field to a fundamental pledge of defensive and constructive loyalty.

4. Each should endeavor to exercise the largest possible influence to the same end upon that portion of the outside public with which it comes in contact.

5. Each should have a sub-committee upon publicity to make its activities known within its particular sphere. This committee should secure the cooperation of its particular class and trade publications and should consider other means such as advertising, press bulletins, window posters, etc., for enlisting the support of its organization members and of its particular public.

6. Each should vigorously attack any centers of disloyalty or lukewarm patriotism which may develop within its own sphere.

7. Each should take immediate steps to see that the question of unqualified loyalty to American ideals be kept actively to the fore during the present political campaign. To this end it should subordinate partisan politics to an absolute insistence upon untainted loyalty as the *sine qua non* for every candidate and every platform.

8. Each local sub-committee should seek to develop cooperative relations with sub-committees of all other organizations in the same locality in order to avoid duplication and waste motion.

RECAPITULATION

This plan involves, first, the creation of National Service Committees by all national organizations that are potentially patriotic;

Next, the creation of local sub-committees of these national committees to work intensively in and through local sub-divisions of these national organizations;

And, finally, an opportunity for the various sub-divisions of the whole American public to align themselves with and to express themselves through their natural affiliations.

Its most immediate application would be, of course, defensive. Let people say what they will, there *is* now in progress an attack upon our national ideals and our form of government. It cannot be smiled out of existence but it can be manœuvered out of existence through organization. The best way to avoid serious disorders is to show a degree of preparedness and an emphasis of intention that will render the attack nugatory.

That, specifically, is the task for the next few months, but such an organization as we have in mind has its bigger and more permanent work in constructive efforts for a better America. It is the application of the old maxim "United we stand; but divided we fall." When we become self-centered or class-centered we lose the dominating sense of our nationalism and are no longer conscious of our American ideals. Then we begin to think in terms of politics and of economics; then we lose our hold upon spiritual principles; then dangers multiply and progress slackens. With the lessons of the war vividly and freshly in mind, we are convinced that the most urgent need and the most potent safeguard of the present and the future will be found in a restoration of our *national consciousness*, freed from emotion and placed upon a basis of practical, efficient organization.

Facts Concerning Health Insurance

(*Continued from page 9*)

adequate and badly administered, still remains grossly inadequate and badly administered. There has been some increase in accommodations for the treatment of tuberculosis; but such increase has not been notable. It is true that a Ministry of Public Health has been created to coordinate public agencies for health promotion; but such coordination remains yet to be effected, and it remains yet to be demonstrated that the health insurance, with its heavy financial commitments, will not be a drag to retard, rather than a stimulus to hasten, proper reorganization and development. As has recently been stated by such an eminent medical authority as Sir Arthur Newsholme, M. D., K. C. B., former Chief Medical Officer of the Local Government Board for England: "It cannot be affirmed that any marked public benefit has accrued" from the health insurance, whereas, "if the same amount of money had been placed in the hands of the public health authorities, to provide adequate medical aid to those needing it, of the kind most lacking and which they could least afford to obtain, great benefit to the public health would have been secured." It stands to reason that the enormous expenditures for health insurance leave just so much less money available for the direct measures needed for the prevention of illness and the improvement of the public health.

It is true, as the authority referred to indicates, that the health insurance has served to spread knowledge of the need of, and to increase the public demand for, more adequate provisions for the health of the community. But the health insurance act was itself the result—and not the cause—of a highly aroused public sentiment on the subject, which sentiment has since merely been accentuated by experience with the insurance, principally by its shortcomings and defects; and one of the effects of the insurance has been to divert public interest and attention towards the pecuniary *relief* of and away from the *prevention* of illness.

Surely the adoption of compulsory health insurance would at least be a mighty dubious and indirect way of hastening adequate and proper public provisions for the prevention of illness, and, consequently, the positive assertion that, "compulsory insurance will stimulate the needed campaign for the prevention of illness," merits at least to be sharply challenged, if not quite so positively denied as in the statement criticised.

(7) Finally, Dr. Harris criticises two statements on page 25 of the pamphlet reading as follows: "Health insurance in Switzerland, except in one or two Cantons, is voluntary. Since the Swiss system did not take effect until well in 1914, when normal operations were promptly disturbed by the war, there is yet no evidence accumulated to show that it is successful or otherwise."

Although inaccurate in details, according to information later obtained, those statements are yet substantially true, whereas Dr. Harris's statements in criticism are very misleading. In Switzerland sickness insurance is generally voluntary (subsidized); but it has now (end of 1918) been made compulsory, variously for some classes of workers, in three Cantons and in a number of Communes in eight other Cantons—out of a total of twenty-two Cantons. The statements criticised were made in refutation of a statement by a partisan of compulsory insurance to the effect that "health insurance, on a *compulsory* basis, is in force in . . . Switzerland, and is successful." . . . But the fact is, as above specified, that health insurance in Switzerland is generally *voluntary*. Dr. Harris argues that the success of the *voluntary* insurance can be inferred from the number of persons who have of their own accord applied for admission. Granted. But it is the prevalence and success of the *compulsory* insurance that is question. And there is nothing to show that such insurance has yet proved to be "successful" or otherwise. It is true that the official reports show that such insurance has been successfully inaugurated; but true success is to be determined by results, and there is no information yet available to demonstrate its successful results in practice. It is simply begging the question in controversy to assume that compulsory insurance is successful without waiting to observe how it works. That something or other—presumably disturbed conditions arising out of the war—did retard the inauguration and normal operation of the Swiss insurance system, is most positively indicated by the official reports; and, in that respect also, the statements criticised are more accurate than the criticism.

Concluding his attack, Dr. Harris says: "The tone of the pamphlet is extreme throughout; the statements of the persons named above" [some of whom are of the highest character] "are referred to as 'malicious untruth', 'rhetorical assertion', 'pure demagogism', etc." The tone of the pamphlet is in truth strong, as is required and justified by the character of the propaganda against which it is directed. But when Dr. Harris insinuates that the persons he mentions are each and all affected by the application of some such epithet as those he quotes, he is seriously misleading.

The pamphlet criticised, containing some forty pages of highly condensed data, was somewhat hurriedly prepared, and it would be marvelous indeed if it were entirely free from errors. One inadvertent error therein has been discovered. On page 6 appears a quotation from the editorial page of the London "Democrat", which, upon the authority of a trade union representative, was attributed to the editor, Mr. W. A. Appleton. Later information, however, has disclosed that this was a mistake and that the matter quoted was not written by Mr. Appleton personally. That is the only material error in the pamphlet yet brought to my attention. Dr. Harris's charge that many of the arguments and quotations therein are partial and misleading is very far from the truth.

Questions for Every Good American

(*Continued from page 18*)

tinue to contribute to the payment of salaries to persons who we know are using these agencies for revolutionary propaganda, and who derive their importance largely from the fact that they represent organizations supported by persons of standing in the community?

Another matter perplexes me. I have subscribed substantially to college, church and charity endowment funds and had expected to subscribe still more until I discovered the undermining work of the radicals in those institutions. I then saw that, if the doctrines of Socialism which these preachers and teachers are promoting should be accepted, the endowments to which I had already contributed would be rendered useless. If all profits, rents and interest are to be abolished by confiscation of property, how will the bequests made to those various institutions be carried out? Of course, they cannot be, as we see by the experiment in Russia, where Marxian Socialism has had so complete and disastrous a trial.

Once again, I am an advertiser in my own business and in other corporations that advertise in a much larger way. I have been shocked to find that I was advertising in publications which I regard as wholly dangerous sheets. Of course, this advertising is all placed through agencies, and I have found I could have some voice in saying where, and where not, the advertising should be placed. Shall I do it?

The question I want to ask you, or through you, the Department on Study of Revolutionary Movements, is: Shall we go on contributing to or patronizing any institution that cannot show 100 per cent. Americanism, or that is not free from professors who advocate Socialism or any of its appendages, Bolshevism, Communism, I. W. W.'ism, etc.? As to schools, we could afford to provide private tutors for our children, but many are not in a position to do this. In the case of the church, we can choose another where the clergyman is a good, sound American, but would not that be a cowardly running away from duty?

I raise these questions with you, because I know there are thousands of other parents who feel as we do. If we could get together, I think we could make ourselves felt. As it is today, the Rand Schoolites, with their hosts of affiliated interests, the revolutionary weeklies and the so-called "liberal" preachers and college professors, have so intimidated the responsible boards of directors and trustees of our public institutions that they are afraid to rid their pulpits, classrooms and organizations of these teachers of disloyalty and revolution lest they should be attacked as "stand-patters," "witch-hunters," "minions of Wall Street," etc. If the parents of the children should organize, if the patriotic members of the churches and of the college alumni should organize, and all three groups join hands, there would soon be created in this country a force which could beat down the impudent pretensions of the comparatively few, but noisy, shallow individuals who advocate freedom to teach and to preach contempt for our institutions, our country and our flag.

Will not your Department on Study of Revolutionary Movements take the initiative in this matter? I am not proposing that we organize to boycott every one who disagrees with us, but I know that there are thousands, yes, millions, of men and women in this country who would not wish to sit idly by and permit their children to be made followers of the Red Flag when, by organizing, they could wield a power that would deal effectively with this perilous situation.

Very truly yours,

---

336 TYRREL PRINT, NEW YORK.

The National Civic Federation Review

Vol. V   NEW YORK, SEPTEMBER 25, 1920   No. 5

LABOR AND AGRICULTURAL POLICIES

POSITION OF REPUBLICAN AND DEMOCRATIC PARTIES REGARDING INDUSTRY AND AGRICULTURE AS EXPRESSED IN RESPECTIVE PLATFORMS AND BY CANDIDATES

SENATOR WARREN G. HARDING

GOVERNOR JAMES M. COX

THE two great groups of producers in America, who are chiefly concerned in any national political campaign, are organized labor and the farmers. Industry and agriculture constitute the basic producing elements of the nation, and the proposed policies of the two great national parties in regard to these are of interest to every citizen. Both the Republican and Democratic parties in their respective platforms, and both Senator Warren G. Harding and Governor James M. Cox, in their speeches of acceptance, have declared themselves on these great interests. These expressions, both in the platforms and acceptance speeches, speak for themselves and are of national importance.

REPUBLICAN PLANKS

The platform adopted by the Republican National Convention contains the following planks on agriculture and labor:

AGRICULTURE

The farmer is the backbone of the nation. National greatness and economic independence demand a population distributed between industry and the farm, and sharing on equal terms the prosperity which is wholly dependent on the efforts of both. Neither can prosper at the expense of the other without inviting joint disaster.

The crux of the present agricultural condition lies in prices, labor and credit.

The Republican party believes that this condition can be improved by practical and adequate farm representation, in the appointment of governmental officials and commissions; the right to form co-operative associations for marketing their products, and protection against discrimination; the scientific study of agricultural prices and farm production costs at home and abroad, with a view to reducing the frequency of abnormal fluctuations; the uncensored publication of such reports; the authorization of associations for the extension of personal credit; a national inquiry on the co-ordination of rail, water and motor transportation with adequate facilities for receiving, handling and marketing food; the encouragement of our export trade; an end to unnecessary price-fixing and ill-considered efforts arbitrarily to reduce prices of farm products which invariably result to the disadvantage both of producer and consumer; and the encouragement of the production and importation of fertilizing material and of its extensive use.

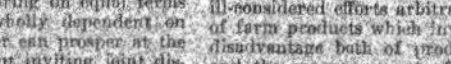

The federal farm loan act should be so administered as to facilitate the acquisition of farm land by those desiring to become owners and proprietors and thus minimize the evils of farm tenantry, and to furnish such long-time credits as farmers may need to finance adequately their larger and long-time production operations.

INDUSTRIAL RELATIONS

There are two different conceptions of the relations of capital and labor. The one is contractual, and emphasizes the diversity of interests of employer and employe. The other is that of co-partnership in a common task.

We recognize the justice of collective bargaining as a means of promoting good-will, establishing closer and more harmonious relations between employer and employees and realizing the true end of industrial justice.

The strike or the lockout, as a means of settling industrial disputes, inflicts such loss and suffering on the community as to justify government initiative to reduce its frequency and limit its consequences.

We deny the right to strike against government, but the rights and interests of all government employees must be safeguarded by impartial laws and tribunals.

In public utilities we favor the establishment of an impartial tribunal to make an investigation of the facts and to render a decision to the end that there may be no organized interruption of service to the lives and health and welfare of the people, the decisions of the tribunals to be morally, but not legally binding, and an informed public sentiment to be relied on to secure their acceptance. The tribunal, however, should refuse to accept jurisdiction except for the purpose of investigation, as long as the public service be interrupted. For public utilities we favor the type of tribunal provided for in the transportation act of 1920.

In private industries we do not advocate the principle of compulsory arbitration, but we favor impartial commissions and better facilities for voluntary mediation, conciliation and arbitration supplemented by that full publicity which will enlist the influence of an aroused public opinion. The government should take the initiative in inviting the establishment of tribunals or commissions for the purpose of voluntary arbitration and investigation of this issue.

We demand the exclusion from interstate commerce of the products of convict labor.

DEMOCRATIC PLANKS

The Democratic platform declared itself in agriculture and labor as follows:

AGRICULTURAL INTERESTS

It was a Democratic congress in the administration of a Democratic President which enabled the farmers of America for the first time to obtain credit upon reasonable terms and insured their opportunity for the future development of the nation's agricultural resources. Tied up in supreme court proceedings in a suit by hostile interests, the federal farm loan system, originally opposed by the Republican candidate for the presidency, appealed in vain to a Republican congress for adequate financial assistance to tide over the interim between the beginning and the ending of the current year, awaiting a final decision of the highest court on the validity of the contested act. We pledge prompt and consistent support of sound and effective measures to sustain, amplify and perfect the rural credits statutes and thus to check and reduce the growth and course of farm tenancy.

Not only did the Democratic party put into effect a great farm loan system of land mortgage banks but it passed the Smith-Lever agricultural extension act, carrying to every farmer in every section of the country, through the medium of trained experts and by demonstration farms, the practical knowledge acquired by the federal agricultural department in all things relating to agriculture, horticulture and animal life; it established the bureau of markets, the bureau of farm management and passed the cotton futures act, the grain grade bill, the co-operative farm administration act and the federal warehouse act.

Meanwhile the Republican leaders at Washington have failed utterly to propose one single measure to make rural life more tolerable. They have signalized their fifteen months of congressional power by urging schemes which would strip the farms of labor; by assailing the principles of the farm loan system; by covertly attempting to destroy the great nitrogen plant at Muscle Shoals upon which the Government has expended $70,000,000 to supply American farmers with fertilizers at reasonable cost; by ruthlessly crippling nearly every branch of agricultural endeavor, literally crippling the productive mediums through which the people must be fed.

We favor such legislation as will conform to the primary producers of the nation, the right of collective bargaining and the right of co-operative handling and marketing of the products of the workshop and the farm and such legislation as will facilitate the exportation of our farm products.

LABOR AND INDUSTRY

The Democratic party is now, as ever, the firm friend of honest labor and the promoter of progressive industry.

Laws regulating hours of labor and conditions under which labor is performed, when passed in recognition of the conditions under which life must be lived to attain the highest development and happiness, are just associations of the national interest in the welfare of the people.

At the same time the nation depends upon the products of labor; a cessation of production means loss and, if long continued, disaster.

The whole people, therefore, have a right to insist that justice shall be done to those who work and in turn that those whose labor creates the necessities upon which the life of the nation depends must recognize the reciprocal obligation between the worker and the state. They should participate in the formulation of sound laws and regulations governing the conditions under which labor is performed, recognize and obey the laws so formulated and seek their amendment when necessary by the processes ordinarily addressed to the laws and regulations affecting the other relations of life.

Labor, as well as capital, is entitled to adequate compensation. Each has the indefensible right of organization, of collective bargaining and of speaking through representatives of their own selection. Neither class, however, should at any time nor in any circumstance take action that will put in jeopardy the public welfare. Resort to strikes and lockouts which endanger the health or lives of the people is an unsatisfactory device for determining disputes, and the Democratic party pledges itself to contrive, if possible, and put into effective operation a fair and comprehensive method of composing differences of this nature.

In private industrial disputes we are opposed to compulsory arbitration as a method plausible in theory, but a failure in fact. With respect to government service, we hold distinctly that the rights of the people are paramount to the right to strike. However, we profess scrupulous regard for the conditions of public employment and pledge the Democratic party to instant inquiry into the pay of government employees and equally speedy regulations designed to bring salaries to a just and proper level.

SENATOR HARDING'S SPEECH

Senator Harding, in his speech accepting the Republican nomination for President, said of labor and agriculture:

It must be understood that toil alone makes for accomplishment and advancement, and righteous possession is the reward of toil and its incentive. There is no progress except in the stimulus of competition. When competition—natural, fair, impelling competition—is suppressed, whether by law, compact or conspiracy, we halt the march of progress, silence the voice of aspiration and paralyze the will for achievement. These are but common sense truths of human development.

The chief trouble today is that the world war wrought the destruction of healthful competition, left our storehouses empty, and there is a minimum production when our need is maximum. Maximums, not minimums, is the call of America. It isn't a new story, because war never fails to leave depleted storehouses and always impairs the efficiency of production. War also establishes its higher standards for wages and they abide.

I wish the higher wage to abide, on one explicit condition—that the wage-earner will give full return for the wage received. It is the best assurance we can have for a reduced cost of living. Mark you, I am ready to acclaim the highest standard of pay, but I should be blind to the responsibilities that mark this fateful hour if I did not caution the wage-earners of America that mounting wages and decreased production can lead only to industrial and economic ruin.

I want, somehow, to appeal to the sons and daughters of the Republic, to every producer to join hand and brain in production, more production, honest production, patriotic production because patriotic production is no less a defense of our best civilization than that of armed force.

FOR INDUSTRIAL UNDERSTANDING

Let us return for a moment to the necessity for understanding, particularly that understanding which concerns ourselves at home. I decline to recognize any conflict of interest among the participants in industry. The destruction of one is the ruin of the other, the suspicion or rebellion of one unavoidably involves the other. In conflict is disaster, in understanding there is triumph. There is no issue relating to the foundation on which industry is builded, because industry is bigger than any element in its modern making. But the insistent call is for labor, management and capital to reach understanding.

The human element comes first and I want the employers in industry to understand the aspiration, the convictions, the yearnings of the millions of American wage-earners and I want the wage-earners to understand the problems, the anxieties, the obligations of management and capital, and all of them must understand their relationship to the people and their obligation to the Republic. Out of this understanding will come the unanimous committal to economic justice, and in economic justice lies that social justice which is the highest essential to human happiness.

I am speaking as one who has counted the contents of the pay envelope from the viewpoint of the earner as well as the employer. No one pretends to deny the inequalities which are manifest in modern industrial life. They are less in fact than they were before organization and grouping on either side revealed the inequalities, and conscience has wrought more justice than statutes have compelled, but the ferment of the world rivets our thoughts on the necessity of progressive solution, else our generation will suffer the experiment which means chaos for our day to re-establish God's plan for the great tomorrow.

Speaking our sympathies, uttering the conscience of all the people, mindful of our right to dwell amid the good fortunes of rational, conscience-impelled advancement, we hold the majesty of righteous government with liberty under the law to be our avoidance of chaos and we call upon every citizen of the Republic to hold fast to that which made us what we are, and we will have orderly government safeguard the onward march to all we ought to be.

The menacing tendency of the present day is not chargeable wholly to the unsettled and fevered conditions caused by the war. The manifest weakness in popular government lies in the temptation to appeal to grouped citizenship for political advantage. There is no greater peril. The Constitution contemplates no class and recognizes no group. It broadly includes all the people, with specific recognition for none, and the highest consecration we can make today is a committal of the Republican party to that saving constitutionalism which contemplates all America as one people and holds just government free from influence on the one hand and unmoved by intimidation on the other.

We call on all America for steadiness, so that we may proceed deliberately to the readjustment which concerns all the people. Our party platform fairly expresses the conscience of Republicans on industrial relations. No party is indifferent to the welfare of the wage-earner. To us his good fortune is of deepest concern, and we seek to make that good fortune permanent.

(Continued on page 17)

The Answer—"Root out Revolutionary Radicalism"

UNDREDS RESPOND TO ENQUIRY OF DEPARTMENT ON STUDY OF REVOLUTIONARY MOVEMENTS—DECLARE MENACE IS SERIOUS AND CALL FOR ACTION

IIE Department on the Study of Revolutionary Movements of The National Civic Federation, Condé B. Pallen, ıairman, sent to a representative group of mericans a copy of the letter written to a member of the Federation, in which various grave ıestions were raised, and which was referred that Department. This letter was published full in the preceding issue of the REVIEW under the heading "Questions for Every Good merican to Consider." The questions raised vere:

> What are the rights and duties of parents in the education of their own children? What are the responsibilities of the church-member and the citizen in the contribution of moneys to philanthropic and charitable organizations under whose shelter and through whose machinery revolutionary propagandists disseminate their doctrines? And what is the responsibility of the business man advertising in periodicals which advocate and propagate a radicalism contrary to our American ideals and institutions?

The opinions of those to whom the letter was ent were asked. The response has been sponaneous and overwhelming, and shows that the uestions are regarded as momentous and serius. Answers have come from hundreds of people, including government officials, senators, congressmen, clergymen, college presidents and trustees, bankers, lawyers, business men, editors, officials of organized labor, agriculture, chambers of commerce and patriotic societies, from women as well as men.

The concensus of opinion is: First, that parents have not only the right to demand that their children be educated according to the principles of morality and patriotism, but that it is their duty to see that our schools and colleges be cleansed of all disloyal and subversive influences; Second, that it is the duty of the trustees of colleges and universities and members of school boards to maintain such vigilance that it will be impossible for Socialist and radical professors and teachers to have a place in these institutions, and that, moreover, if disloyal professors and teachers are allowed places, the trustees and members of school boards are themselves responsible; Third, that it is the right and duty of church members to extirpate Socialistic teachings from the churches, to expel Socialist preachers from their pulpits, and to refuse contributions of money to all philanthropic and charitable organizations through whose machinery revolutionary propagandists disseminate their doctrines; Fourth, that loyal American business men cannot advertise in, and thus support financially, papers and periodicals which are propagating radicalism and seeking to destroy American institutions.

It is the general opinion that the menace has become acute, and that if we would save our institutions every American individually must help combat the forces of revolutionary radicalism, in schools, colleges, churches, charitable and philanthropic institutions and wherever found. If it is impossible to clear these organizations of radicals by individual protest, the majority of the writers agree that the time has come for united and organized action on part of all who believe in the Constitution and our form of government.

The writers of the letters, in the majority, attribute the growth of dangerous teachings in our institutions to laxity and indifference. They declare that every college trustee, every official of a charitable institution, every officer of a church in which radicals are allowed to hold positions is directly responsible for any damage done. It is not only the duty of college trustees to safeguard their institutions from pernicious teachings, but their obligation to see that education is in keeping with the moral law and American ideals. Every contributor to religious, charitable and philanthropic organizations, whose workers use their machinery to promote radicalism, shares in their efforts to destroy our government.

It is evident from the letters that the vast body of American opinion is sound and clear on these issues. It has been also gratifying to find that various organizations throughout the country, such as chambers of commerce, patriotic societies, et cetera, have offered to cooperate in the movement to root out radicalism. A very striking significance attaches to a certain small fraction of the replies, in which the questions are evaded or in which "academic freedom of discussion," which would allow the promulgation of radical teachings, is defended. With only a few exceptions these have come from the presidents of certain colleges and persons engaged in the industrial sections of certain religious organizations.

All the letters received are being briefed and will be submitted by Chairman Pallen to the Department of which he is head for its consideration and further action if such should be decided upon.

It is not possible, on account of space, to publish more than brief quotations from a small proportion of the letters received. These will, however, serve to show the unanimity of opinion existing among all classes and professions, and bring together various opinions and suggestions of concrete and practical value.

Mr. William C. Redfield, President, American-Russian Chamber of Commerce, wrote in part as follows:

> One suggestion occurs to me, viz: That in public schools and in institutions of higher learning, supported in any measure by public funds, is there objection to requiring that the teachers and officers should take oath to support the Constitution of the United States? This is not only proper in itself because the teachers in such institutions are public officers, but might serve to eliminate some who could not take the oath. It seems to me to be more than open to question whether a teacher has the right "to teach anything he thinks is the truth" which is antagonistic to our Constitution so long as he accepts pay from the state thereunder constituted.

Mr. S. J. Lowell, Master of the National Grange, Fredonia, N. Y., wrote in part as follows:

> Every adult person owes it to themselves and posterity that they look carefully to the conduct and the subjects which are being taught in our common schools, as well as the higher institutions of education.
>
> I feel quite certain that if advertising were withheld from many of the questionable periodicals which are put out, that they would have no means of support, and would, therefore, be forced to close up their business, and a mighty good thing it would be, too. This would be more effective than Governmental control, as when you go out to censor articles, you stir up division of opinion which really some times accentuates radical ideas. There is much need of a movement of this kind at the present time.

Mr. Daniel J. Tobin, General President International Brotherhood of Teamsters, Chauffeurs, Stablemen & Helpers of America, wrote in part as follows:

> Parents of children should look carefully into their education and guard against having the minds and hearts of their children poisoned against the true principles of our American institutions. . . No money should be contributed to any institution without the principles and purposes of that institution being thoroughly investigated. Many employers and men wtih large incomes contribute their money without making any investigation. . . No man should help publications that are preaching anti-American doctrines by giving them advertising, because, upon the advertisements, which are read by the public, depends the life of the publication. When men pay out money for advertising space in publications that are continually printing articles which attack the principles of our great country and are endeavoring to promote radicalism, such as we find in Russia and other European countries, they are helping to plant radicalism and to destroy the principles for which our fathers fought and died.

Rev. Dr. Ernest M. Stires, Rector of Saint Thomas's Church, wrote in part as follows:

> . . . Americans are too easy-going, too careless. Their boasted toleration is often nothing better than good-humored laziness. It is time, not only that the Church Militant should be truly militant for all that is essential to safety and true progress, and against all that is destructive. The Church must inspire this wholesome spirit in the family and in the state.
>
> It is the duty of parents to know what their children are being taught, and to feel responsible for giving them that education which human experience has thoroughly tested and found protective of happiness and progress.

Hon. Joseph E. Ransdell, United States Senator from Louisiana, wrote in part as follows:

> In all public schools at least thirty minutes of every school day should be devoted to discourses by members of the faculty on patriotism and the duties of citizens to State and Nation; and a like period before the beginning or after the close of each day should be set aside for religious instruction, conducted in classes adapted to the faith of the children by a member of their own church. Moreover, the greatest care should be exerted to prevent atheists and socialists from being selected as teachers or professors in any of our schools or colleges, from the humblest to the highest; and parents should sternly refuse to send their children to any institution of learning which has atheists or socialists among the members of its faculty.
>
> The National Civic Federation is engaged in a labor of the greatest importance. Never has the world been more disturbed than today. Revolution against the laws of God and the fixed order of society is rampant in Europe, and, unfortunately, has many adherents on this side of the water.

Hon. Howard Sutherland, United States Senator from West Virginia, wrote in part as follows:

> I agree thoroughly with you that socialistic propaganda must be destroyed at its source and that a great deal of this mischievous doctrine is being taught in our schools and colleges and is having a tremendous influence upon our boys and girls in these institutions, and that something definite and practical should be done to curtail or stop it. I am in sympathy with any movement toward that end.

Mr. P. Tecumseh Sherman, Attorney, New York, wrote in part as follows:

> In my opinion the public which supports our universities ought to take a far more positive stand to rid those institutions of their loose thinking and loud talking socialist professors of sociology. Liberty of opinion and of research is one thing. But those who pay for teaching have the right to impose the condition that their money shall be used only for teaching truth and wisdom.
>
> I also believe that parents sending their children to colleges and universities ought to exercise far more supervision than they now do to prevent their sons and daughters from taking the courses of immature, sensational or socialist teachers. To prevent anything of the kind is not only their right but also their duty—a duty both to God and Country.
>
> Legitimate business in America, in popular disrepute because of its past sins, has "laid down" under vilification. That is all wrong. We ought to organize and fight, with all legitimate means in our

power, all propaganda under whatsoever name, by whomsoever conducted and howsoever carried on, which is sensationally exaggerated or falsified, or which seeks to obscure the fact that economic conditions in this country are about the best in the world and difficult to improve.

Mr. E. F. Walker, Secretary Rhode Island Textile Association, wrote:

> Parents have a right to insist that the teachers who are instructing their children should be of unquestioned loyalty to this Country, that they should have but one allegiance and that to the School Department that employs them, and that radical preachments and tendencies of any nature should be the cause for instant dismissal.
>
> In reply to the second question, in my opinion, the radicals in the Inter-Church Movement and in various other philanthropic and charitable organizations owe their existence and continued pernicious activities almost entirely to the mentally lazy altruists and philanthropists who contribute to these activities without first ascertaining how, where and why their money is to be spent. . . Refusal of contributions on the part of worthy church members to movements that were un-American or unwise would mean an end of radical propaganda as far as these organizations are concerned.
>
> The business man who advertises in periodicals which advocate and propagate radicalism contrary to our American Ideals and Institutions is either a fool or a knave.

Dr. Harry Pratt Judson, President of The University of Chicago, wrote:

> Most parents have the right to regulate the education of their own children and have the undoubted duty of providing the best education they can. Such rights, like all other civil rights are subject to our paramount obligations to the state, and parents should not be allowed to train children in ways subversive of public morality and social order. . . It seems to me quite plain that none should contribute funds to organizations which employ those funds to subvert our American ideals and institutions.

Mr. Angus S. Hibbard, President, United Americans, Illinois, wrote in part as follows:

> It is the duty of parents to keep informed about the educational process, what is being taught in the schools and also the teaching and influence which is brought to bear upon students in matters referring to government, and the rights and privileges of citizenship. If disloyalty is being taught, it is in my judgment the duty of parents to make it known and to combat it. If nothing can be done single-handed, parents should join together for this purpose. We should see to it that sedition is not taught in the public schools in this country nor in fact in any other school or college.

Rev. Father E. P. Tivnan, S. J., President Fordham University, wrote in part as follows:

> Until the people of America are awake to this peril which is in their midst and refuse to support such institutions by financial contributions or by sending their sons and daughters there for training, the dance of death will continue and it will only be a question of time, before we are in the throes of revolution.
>
> A remedy I would suggest is that publicity be given those institutions in which solid and orthodox principles are the basis of the educational system and that the people at large be urged to support them financially and otherwise.

Mr. R. R. Waddell, of The Dayton Malleable Iron Company, wrote:

> It is the right and the *duty* of every parent to see to it that only those things which are right are going into the training of his children. There are thousands who cannot and will not exercise the right or fulfill the duty but it is there none the less.
>
> You have raised some questions here which must be answered in the shed blood of true Americans I fear. More people than we think are nibbling at the bait of Socialism and will be landed for Bolshevism. The great trouble with us as a people is that we do not think. The home life of our people is almost nil and these things are breaking down the very barriers that we have erected against barbarism, and as a people we are going far afield. We shall return in due time but with great suffering and loss.

Mr. A. B. Farquhar, of A. B. Farquhar Company, York, Penna., wrote in part as follows:

> You might as well, or better, poison the bodies of people as to poison their minds. Such institutions of the character of the Rand School poison the mind of the young, and should not be allowed to continue their nefarious work. One of the best means of fighting this Bolshevik virus, which is spreading its slimy poison throughout the world, is to touch their pocket nerve, boycott all Socialists. The Socialist includes the anarchist, I. W. W. and Bolshevik. They are all tarred with the same stick. . . . Any minister or school teacher who advocates Socialism should be promptly dismissed. We should not attend a church or school where such teachings are sanctioned.

Mrs. C. H. Ditson, New York City, wrote:

> The average American is easy-going and unawake to danger until it raps loudly on his door. Some sort of solidarity that would gather in not only the thinking ones but the un-thinking as well, (in spite of themselves,) could do much to counteract the wave of license and lawlessness that appears to be sweeping over the entire world.

Mr. Henry B. MacFarland, Attorney, Washington, D. C., wrote:

> I would no more contribute to support any preacher, teacher, writer or publisher of Bolshevism (comprehending all un-American radicalism) than I would contribute to support any preacher, teacher, writer or publisher of polygamy. In fact the latter, forbidden by law, is less degrading than the former. The time has come to fight for our country, its constitution, its church, its homes, its life against a foe more subtle, more ingenious, more devilish, more deceptive than the Hun!

Mr. W. M. Spaulding, President of The Graton & Knight Manufacturing Company, Worcester, Mass., wrote as follows:

> It is most unfortunate that our instructors as well as our clergymen are so thoroughly tainted with these socialistic ideas. That children should come in contact with men of this type is a great menace to the future prosperity of this country, and every effort possible to avoid this contact, either through educational institutions or churches, should be made.

Mr. H. B. Wilcox, of the Merchants-Mechanics First National Bank, Baltimore, Md., wrote:

> The responsibility of the church-member and the citizen who contributes to philanthropic and charitable organizations under whose shelter and through whose machinery revolutionary propagandists disseminate their doctrines cannot be avoided, and every means should be adopted to impress upon them the necessity of serious discrimination in such undertakings. The responsibility of the business man advertising in periodicals which advocate and propagate a radicalism contrary to our American ideals and institutions is likewise very serious.

Mr. Albert L. Wyman, Secretary of The Employers Association of Paterson, N. J., wrote in part as follows:

> As to the rights of parents, I believe that parents have the right to expect that the Board of Education is going to see to it that instructors are engaged who are loyal to American Institutions, and to eliminate those who are disloyal.
>
> I also think that it is the duty of parents to make it certain that this kind of instruction is being given, and to bring to the attention of the Board of Education any activities or teachings on the part of the faculty of the schools attended by their children which indicate that radicalism prevails in the schools.

Mr. George L. Berry, President, International Printing Pressmen and Assistants' Union of North America, Pressmen's Home, Tenn., wrote:

> When it is evident that the policy of the church, the club, the society or advertising medium is being precipitated by un-American influences a strenuous, energetic and outspoken fight and protest should be made. If then an adjustment cannot be made in accordance with American traditions it is manifestly obligatory that the person withdraw from such associations both in membership and financial support.
>
> It is, of course, the obvious obligation to combat at every turn any effort to undermine our national traditions. Silence and inactivity gives encouragement and tacit indorsement to revolutionary tendencies.

Mr. Clifton Reeves, The Willys-Overland Company, wrote:

> As a father I would say that it is the duty of any parent to carefully examine, through authoritative channels the kind of education his children are re-

Catholic "Social Reconstruction Program" Analyzed

FALLACIES IN PROGRAM OF COMMITTEE ON WAR ACTIVITIES OF THE NATIONAL CATHOLIC WAR COUNCIL SHOWN BY NOTED MEMBER OF ROMAN CATHOLIC CHURCH

By P. TECUMSEH SHERMAN

THERE have recently appeared in several periodicals some articles in which it is intimated that Catholics are bound in conscience to believe in the efficacy of and to support certain concrete political measures, proposed as remedies for existing economic evils, among which measures are included general minimum wage laws and compulsory social insurance. To an educated Catholic that proposition is absurd. But a shadow of a basis for it is to be found in some passages in a pamphlet entitled "Social Reconstruction," issued (January, 1919; revised edition later but bearing same date) by the Committee on War Activities of the National Catholic War Council, and in a volume entitled "The Church and Socialism" (The University Press, Washington, D. C., 1919), by Rev. John A. Ryan, D.D., Professor at the Catholic University of America.

But none of such passages has the force and authority attributed to it. In each some ethical principles are laid down, which, to a Catholic, are unquestionable. But, as indicated in the revised foreword to the pamphlet of the National Catholic War Council, signed by four eminent Bishops, the practical applications of those principles—*e. g.*, the particular political measures advocated or proposed—are questionable; and so also are all data of purely material facts and human experience cited in support of such measures. It is, therefore, timely and appropriate to present the reasons why a Catholic, who accepts unquestioningly everything the Catholic Church teaches, under present conditions in this country and in the existing stage of human knowledge and experience, conscientiously may and even ought to oppose the political measures in question.

THE LEGAL MINIMUM WAGE.

Relating to this subject the pamphlet on "Social Reconstruction," above cited, contains the following passage:

> We are glad to note that there is no longer any serious objection urged by impartial persons against the legal minimum wage. The several States should enact laws providing for the establishment of wage rates that will be at least sufficient for the decent maintenance of a family, in the case of all male adults, and adequate to the decent individual support of female workers.

Of the two propositions contained in this passage the first is certainly untrue. That fact alone is sufficient to discredit the second. Why, then, should we accept the latter? In "The Church and Socialism," above cited, Dr. Ryan presents the argument in support of that proposition, from the standpoint of Catholic ethics, in substance as follows:

> The state must enact legislation which will prevent any worker from being compelled to accept less than decent living wages. Between 50 and 75 per cent. of our laboring population got less than this measure of remuneration in 1914 (p. 45). Since that date the increase in prices seem[s] to have been, on the whole, as great as the increase in wages (p. 76). Thirteen states of our country and the District of Columbia have enacted minimum wage laws. The legislation has become universal in Australia and New Zealand and has been extended to a very large proportion of the industries of Great Britain. A considerable beginning has also been made in Canada. This rapid development and application of the movement and measure have been mainly due to the favorable results of the law wherever it has been tried. It is no longer an experiment (p. 99). While Pope Leo did not expressly advocate this measure of state activity, his language seems to imply it (p. 46). Those few Catholics who still oppose the movement for a living wage by law can get little comfort from the encyclical [Encyclical Letter of Pope Leo XIII on the Condition of Labor]. Before they can appeal to it with any show of reason they will have to prove that the evil of insufficient wages can be "met or prevented" by some other means. That task will keep them busy for a long time; so long, in fact, that they will all be dead before it is finished (p. 29).

Now, as a Catholic I am morally bound by the ethical principles laid down by Pope Leo in the encyclical above referred to, including the doctrine of a "living wage." But because I believe in that doctrine it does not follow that I must believe that such doctrine can and would be correctly and consistently defined, applied and enforced through man-made laws, under existing political conditions. I "come from Missouri" and, before supporting a proposed political measure, such as a *general* minimum wage law, I want to be shown that in actual practice it will both be efficient for the purpose proposed and not do more harm than good. That, Dr. Ryan fails to show, and, there are good and sufficient reasons to believe, cannot show. The best he can show is that a legal minimum wage is a debatable proposal, deserving of consideration and, perhaps, of small and cautious experiments.

In his argument for a general legal minimum wage, above epitomized, Dr. Ryan's major premise is the proposition that between 50 and 75 per cent. of our laboring population get less than a decent *living* wage. Those figures are practically identical with the figures used by professional agitators and sensation mongers, and are quite generally discredited. They seem to be obtained by taking as a general standard an ideal conception of minimum needs and comparing that standard with the average annual earnings of the various groups of wage-workers in some selected industries, occupations or neighborhoods. By such a process it is easy to construct data to support any conclusion one wants. That the majority of our wage-workers do obtain wages sufficient to enable them, with good management, to live decently, is obvious from the manner in which they clothe themselves and is also strongly indicated by the extent of their savings. Whether or not such majority obtain "fair wages" is a different question. Moreover, these sensational figures of Dr. Ryan's really do not relate strictly to "wages" but to "average annual earnings" as reduced by unemployment. Consequently they are largely irrelevant to the question of the sufficiency of "wages." Unemployment is an evil distinct from low wages. And it is not to be assumed that a legal minimum wage is the remedy for unemployment.

It should be observed in this connection that the average "real" wage in America is—or more accurately was before the war—more than double such wage in the most advanced countries of Western Europe. It is difficult to believe that wages thus averaging more than double the wages upon which European workers have managed to live and maintain a high degree of physical efficiency nevertheless have averaged below the minimum essential to a decent existence. The truth seems to be that a substantial minority of American wage-workers have attained and set a standard of living unprecedently high for manual workers, which standard we would all like to see attained by all good workers but which in truth is far above the minimum essential for a decent existence, and that it is a wage sufficiently high to maintain that standard, and not a "*living wage*," which "between 50 and 75 per cent. of our laboring population" fail to obtain.

However, there is undoubtedly a small proportion—but many in the aggregate—of our laboring population who are forced to work for less than true "living wages." Such condition is an evil calling for remedy. But to find the true remedy or remedies we must get down to facts and study causes; and the true remedy or remedies must fit the facts and be directed against the causes.

Dr. Ryan's minor premise is the proposition that a general legal minimum wage is no longer an experiment, but is a well tested and certain remedy for the evil of insufficient wages. That proposition is true only upon the assumption that a social experiment ceases to be an experiment about as soon as it is successfully launched, without regard to final results. For all the minimum wage laws Dr. Ryan is able to cite, with the exception of those of Australia and New Zealand, are unquestionably still experiments, in initial stages of experimentation, and, moreover, are not *general* but are more or less narrow and cautious experiments, being generally restricted variously to apply only to some especially helpless classes of workers or to some highly parasitic trades. As to the New Zealand and Australian laws, we must distinguish. Dr. Ryan argues for a law to apply the moral doctrine of a "living wage." But the awards under those laws go far beyond that. These laws are all (with one partial exception) either expressly or in effect, compulsory arbitration laws; and they all result in fixing a *standard* wage for each particular occupation at such rate, generally far above the "living wage," as, in the opinion of a wage board or arbitration court, may be fair or expedient or a fair compromise between opposed contentions. They are really "minimum wage laws," inasmuch as the wages fixed in arbitrations under them are the lowest any employer in the trade involved is allowed to pay. But the majority of them are also "maximum wage laws," inasmuch as the wages fixed in arbitrations under them are the highest the wageworkers involved may lawfully strike to enforce.* Designed to bind both employers and employees alike, these measures have proved to be wholly one-sided, being practically ineffective against labor. Designed to prevent strikes, and long proclaimed to be wonder workers for that purpose, they have been shown by experience to tend to foment strikes rather than to prevent them. And yet, although gross failures for their original purposes, we are now asked to accept the experience under these measures as a conclusive demonstration of the success of the legal minimum wage, because incidentally they have eliminated "sweating." Hardly! The success of a social remedy is to be appraised from all its results. Judged by that test these measures, even when viewed as minimum wage laws, fall far short of demonstrated success. They have eliminated "sweating" only by making wages *generally* a subject for political struggles and manipulations. That practice has been shown to be the opposite of conducive to industrial peace; there are no well established grounds for believing that it is improving the condition of labor in general, either by raising the level of

*In this connection it should be noted that the law recently adopted in Kansas for the purpose of preventing strikes and lockouts on public utilities and in "key industries" is very similar to these Australasian laws.

''real'' wages or otherwise; and there are reasons for fearing that its ultimate political and economic consequences, as affecting the welfare of the community as a whole, will eventually prove to be harmful.

Besides being inconclusive and largely irrelevant to the question of enforcing specifically a ''living wage'' by law this Australasian experience holds out a warning. It indicates strongly that minimum wage laws in practice tend to develop in the direction of general wage fixing by government at the dictation and for the special advantage of pluralities of the electorate, without regard to any fixed ethical or economic principles whatsoever. And it is the fear of just such a result eventually from experimenting with legal minimum wages that underlies and justifies the strongest opposition to the minimum wage movement. There is, further, reason to fear that a general minimum wage law would not end merely in political *wage* fixing. The habit of looking to government action for class economic advantage, engendered by such a law, leads naturally to governmental *price* fixing for the same purpose. And, having fixed wages, the state might have to provide work at such wages or support many of the laboring class in idleness rather than permit them to work at less than such wages, the final probable consequence being the necessity for the state to distribute and compel labor. Dr. Ryan himself seems to admit the probability of some of these consequences, and rather welcomes them (p. 94). I respectfully submit that the sum of experience with state intervention in the field of industry justifies opposition to a single step on such a dangerous road.

In New Zealand and some of the Provinces of Australia there are, besides the arbitration laws above considered, also laws prescribing that no employee in a factory, shop, etc., shall be paid less than a specified wage per week. The minimum wages fixed by these laws are extremely low—in some cases as low as 97 cents per week. From what little information is obtainable it would seem that these particular laws are practically ineffective and obsolete, and they are never cited by advocates of minimum wage laws as models for imitation.

Whether or not the pending experiments with minimum wage laws will finally result successfully—*i. e.*, with net benefit to the community—is a question about which individual opinions may reasonably differ. But it is unreasonable to assert that they are no longer experiments. They are still just as doubtful and dangerous experiments as was the old Roman emperors' policy of ''bread and circuses'' during the first years after its inception.

Against those Catholics who, like myself, are not convinced by the arguments for a general legal minimum wage, Dr. Ryan cites the encyclical of Pope Leo XIII, asserting that we can get little comfort from it. Let us see. Directly upon the subject of wages the encyclical says:

> The remuneration must be enough to support the wage-earner in reasonable and frugal comfort. If through necessity or fear of a worse evil, the workman accepts harder conditions because an employer or contractor will give him no better, he is the victim of force and injustice. In these and similar questions, however, ... in order to supersede undue interference on the part of the state, especially as circumstances, times and localities differ so widely, it is advisable that recourse be had to societies or boards, ... , or to some other method of safeguarding the interests of wage-workers; the state to be asked for approval and protection.

Plainly this is a declaration in favor of private and voluntary methods and a caution against direct state intervention.

There remains, however, another passage in the encyclical, bearing upon this question and others, which passage reads as follows:

> Whenever the general interest or any particular class suffers, or is threatened with, evils which can in no other way be met, the public authority must step in to meet them.

From this paragraph Dr. Ryan deduces that before Catholics can conscientiously oppose the movement for a general, legal minimum wage they must prove that the evil of insufficient wages can be met or prevented in some other way. That is queer logic. On the contrary, under this doctrine Catholics may conscientiously doubt and oppose the movement for a general legal minimum wage until its proponents, *upon whom rests the burden of proof*, have reasonably proved:

First: That a legal minimum wage will meet the evil—*i. e.*, that it will cure or mitigate the evil aimed at without producing other and greater evils.

Second: That the evil can be met in no other way.

Grounds for rejecting the first of these propositions as unproved have already been indicated. As to the second, even supposing that a legal minimum wage will meet the evil, there are strong grounds for the belief that there are other and better remedies. Among such remedies may be mentioned the following:

(1) The organization of labor in mutual protective associations or unions. Already the influence of organized labor has been one of the principal causes to raise the general level of wages in American industries higher than in any other country in the world or at any other period of history. Dr. Ryan belittles this influence. He contends that the proportion of unskilled and underpaid labor enrolled in the unions has always been very small and shows little tendency to increase (p. 75). Practically he admits that the organization of underpaid labor would be a remedy; but he objects that it would take too much time and effort to effect such organization (p. 75). This objection ignores a number of facts: First, that it is not needed to organize all underpaid labor, the influence of organized labor in bettering the wages and working conditions of wage-workers extending far beyond the enrolled membership. Second, that the effort required for organization is to a high degree essential, no healthy social improvement being possible without effort by those benefited. And, third, that in the past there have been unusual obstacles and difficulties in the way of organization of labor in America, arising out of the racial differences between whites and blacks, the extraordinarily heavy immigration of wage-workers of different races, languages and civilizations, the excessively individualistic temper of the employing class and the public, and organized labor's own occasional mistakes, which difficulties, it is not unreasonable to believe, are now being and within reasonable time will be largely reduced or overcome.

(2) Vocational training and direction. One of the principal causes of insufficient wages in American industries during the past generation has been the high proportion of the workers who have been unskilled and have gravitated toward ''blind alley'' employments and parasitic industries. Such wage-earners commonly do not produce the equivalent of a living wage. Simply to require that they shall, nevertheless, be paid a living wage or discharged would be a doubtful remedy. The appropriate remedy for this condition is the development and improvement of public and private measures, such as we have only recently begun to resort to, for the education, training and guidance of the untrained and immigrants towards economically efficient occupations, in which they will be able to *earn* living wages.

(3) Measures, public and private, to reduce unemployment and ''underemployment.'' As has already been noted, wages may be amply sufficient per hour, day or week and yet be extremely insufficient per year, owing to interruptions of employment. This is one of the greatest causes of poverty. There are good grounds for believing a legal minimum wage to be entirely inappropriate as a remedy for this evil, and that the true remedy must be sought in a variety of measures to aid the right men quickly to find the right jobs, to mitigate the régime of ''hiring and firing,'' to systematize employment in the seasonal trades, to ''decasualize'' intermittent employments, and to guide and assist surplus labor away from overmanned industries and centers of population into neighborhoods and occupations where labor is wanting.

It is not contended that measures and means such as just indicated can ever be made perfect or will ever produce the millennium. There will always be some exploited, some subnormal, some misfits and some who *will* not earn or *will* not accept employments in which they can earn a sufficiency for a decent existence. Such exceptional persons or classes, however, need to be dealt with specially. For their benefit and protection it is neither necessary nor appropriate to subject all industry to a régime of political meddling.

In concluding with this subject it should be noted that even if it could be proved that minimum wage laws would meet the evil of insufficient wages and that such evil can be met in no other way, nevertheless no obligation to join in the minimum wage movement as it now is or to accept the specific proposal of the National Catholic War Council would follow from the doctrine laid down in Pope Leo's encyclical. The minimum wage movement is resulting in laws which prescribe as a minimum, not a ''living wage,'' but some individual's or group of persons' conception of what is a fair minimum wage for each particular occupation or industry, fixing the minima for different occupations at different levels, although the minimum needs of the workers in such occupations may be the same. And the National Catholic War Council proposes, not to enforce a ''living wage'' as a minimum, but to provide for ''the establishment of wage rates *at least*'' equal to living wages. But, even under the conditions above specified, the encyclical would require support of such legal measures only as would apply and enforce the doctrine of a ''living wage'' *and nothing more*. Under present circumstances, however, this point is practically immaterial, any and all minimum wage law proposals being open to legitimate doubts and differences of opinion, without involving any religious question.

SOCIAL INSURANCE.

The pamphlet on ''Social Reconstruction,'' above cited, issued by the National Catholic War Council, contains the following relating to this subject:

> ''Until'' the ''level of legal minimum wages'' becomes ''high enough to make possible that amount of saving which is necessary to protect the worker and his family against sickness, accidents, invalidity and old age,'' ''the worker stands in need of the device of insurance. The State should make comprehensive provision for insurance against illness, invalidity, unemployment and old age. So far as possible the insurance fund should be raised by a levy on industry, as is now done in the case of accident compensation. The industry in which a man is employed should provide him with all that is necessary to meet all the needs of his entire life. Therefore any contribution to the insurance from the general revenues of the State should be only slight and temporary. For the same reason no contribution should be exacted from any worker who is not getting a higher wage than is required to meet the present needs of himself and his family. . . . Finally, the administration of the insurance laws should be such as to interfere as little as possible with the individual freedom of the worker and his family. Any insurance scheme or any administrative method, that tends to separate the

(Continued on page 18)

Industrial Peace in Building Trades

TWELVE YEARS' CAMPAIGN RESULTS IN FORMATION OF NATIONAL BOARD FOR JURISDICTIONAL AWARDS—WILL ELIMINATE STRIFE AND SETTLE JURISDICTIONAL DISPUTES

NO greater promise of industrial peace has been made in the United States than that engineered by the Building Trades Department of the American Federation of Labor for the Building Industry.

Coming at this time when housing facilities are 30 and 40 per cent. less than normal and when millions of people are crying for relief, the fact that it soon will be possible for building to be carried on without unnecessary strikes is received with the greatest pleasure.

Years will be required to find homes for the homeless and the added cost makes their erection almost prohibitive because of the inflated cost of material and the occurrence of jurisdictional strikes. Material has jumped as high as 300 per cent. or more and John Donlin, president of the Building Trades Department of the American Federation of Labor, has said that 95 per cent. of the strikes in the building industry are caused by disputes over jurisdiction.

It has been impossible heretofore to tell with exactness where one trade begins and another ends because of the elimination of skilled workmen. Trades are sometimes wiped out by the elimination of skill. The extent of the twilight zones between trades is so great that one is continually encroaching on the other. This has caused innumerable strikes.

A twelve years campaign to bring about this desirable situation has resulted in the formation of the National Board for Jurisdictional Awards in the Building Industry. The employees through their unions and the employers, architects and others through their associations have joined hands and declared that they are determined to eliminate all unnecessary strife. A constitution has been adopted by the board which proposes conciliation and arbitration instead of strikes. The preamble to the constitution sets forth:

> The close of the World War opens an era, in which the people are determined to decide for themselves all matters of common interest. A League of Nations is proposed to bring about unity of action and to settle differences between nations by conciliation and arbitration, instead of by war.
>
> The Building Industry recognizes the equity of this principle and agrees to unite its efforts for the purpose of adjusting, in a conciliatory and co-operative spirit, such differences of opinion that now exist, or may arise in the future. The immediate object is to settle disputes as to jurisdiction over work that is claimed by more than one building trade.

This plan is intended to operate between union workmen and the employers thereof.

While the organization was brought into existence March 3, 1919, it is just beginning to function successfully. The shortage of buildings because of the refusal of the government to permit their erection during the war has caused for the first time in history a famine in housing facilities. In cities like Chicago, for instance, where there are four and five thousand marriages a month, housing is at a premium. New York is also suffering from the lack of homes and no city in the country has escaped the dearth. Years will be required to supply the need.

The creation of the National Board for Jurisdictional Awards in the Building Industry is therefore the greatest step that could be taken in removing the most serious obstacles to supplying homes for the homeless at rents within reason. It may require some time for the machinery of this plant to become fully effective, but those who are striving to establish industrial peace declare they are determined to bring it about.

By W. C. ROBERTS

The hope for such a beneficial condition in the building industry has been expressed for many years. To William J. Spencer, secretary of the Building Trades Department of the American Federation of Labor should be credited the origin of the idea. In 1908 he pointed out the value of such a revolution in industrial methods to the executive council of the department in its first meeting held in Washington after its headquarters were established there. The executive council endorsed the proposition and directed him to work to accomplish the desired results. The agitation in the beginning found few converts. In 1913 the Secretary of Labor was informed of the anti-strike plan by Secretary Spencer and he appointed conciliators who endeavored to convince the contractors and architects that such a desirable condition in the building industry should be sought.

Few employers took an interest in the idea, as many of them thrive because of jurisdictional disputes. Furthermore, jurisdictional complications arise almost daily in the building line. Methods of construction continually change. A workman may have a trade today and none tomorrow. Outside of the basic trades, which also change but not completely, there is always danger of the complete elimination of the skill in a trade.

If the workman should lose his trade through the evolution of the industry the employer also loses his business. It was the desire to avert such an outcome that prevented many of the contractors and others vitally interested from looking favorably on any proposition that would leave them liable to loss.

But the continual agitation brought about by representatives of the Labor Department, officials of the Building Trades Department of the American Federation of Labor and a number of progressive contractors, architects and engineers, gradually changed the beliefs of both employers and union men until it was found possible to organize a board to eliminate jurisdictional disputes.

The lack of building during the war, the shortage of buildings after the armistice and the demand for new buildings compelled those who had blocked the plan to give it their approval. In order that building should proceed with some degree of haste it became necessary that a way should be found to stop cessations of work because of quarrels over jurisdiction.

The increased cost of building also has proved a great factor. It was necessary for the contractor to know that if he started a building on a certain day when he could set a day for its completion. Under such conditions much money could be saved the owner, the builder and the contractor himself.

Not only are contractors interested in the outcome but the architects and building engineers are also greatly affected.

The National Board consists of eight members. Three are selected by the Building Trades Department and one each by the American Institute of Architects, Engineering Council, the National Association of Building Trades Employers and two from the Associated General Contractors of America. The members of the National Board are E. J. Russell, chairman, American Institute of Architects; R. P. Miller, Engineering Council; Col. J. R. Wiggins and F. J. C. Dresser, Associated General Contractors of America; E. M. Craig, National Association Building Trades Employers; Wm. Dobson, William L. Hutcheson and John J. Hynes, Building Trades Department, American Federation of Labor. Wm. J. Spencer is executive secretary.

Among the provisions in the constitution that give promise that the campaign for peace in all building industries will be successful are:

> There is, hereby, created for this purpose a board which shall be known as the National Board for Jurisdictional Awards in the Building Industry.
>
> The duties of the Board shall be to hear claims for jurisdiction over work performed by Building Trades; and to determine by which trade the work in contention shall be performed and to make an award in conformity with the facts submitted by the contendents. At least a two-thirds majority of the voting members of the full Board shall be required to render an award in all cases.
>
> The Board shall have the power to investigate all disputes and to make awards in accordance with its findings, as hereafter provided.
>
> Should the Board fail to make an award an umpire may be agreed upon whose findings shall be final. Should the Board, by a two-thirds majority, be unable to agree upon an umpire, the Secretary of the U. S. Department of Labor shall be called upon to name the umpire.
>
> When a dispute arises the employer to whom the work has been given shall proceed with such workmen as in his judgment he may see fit to employ pending a decision by the Board; but the right of any contestant to dispute shall not be prejudiced in its claim for a final award.
>
> Each signatory to this agreement hereby agrees that the membership of that organization shall not take part in sympathetic strikes in any case of jurisdictional dispute.
>
> Labor organizations signatory to this agreement shall secure the enforcement and compliance of their organizations with the provisions of this agreement and the awards of the Board.
>
> Local organizations refusing compliance with the provisions of this agreement and the awards of this Board shall be suspended from their International organization and the International organization shall proceed at once to man the job and the Employer shall co-operate with the International organization in so doing.
>
> Any architect, engineer or employer represented on this Board through an organization signatory to this agreement shall be suspended from his organization or organizations upon failure to comply with the provisions of this agreement and the awards of this Board.
>
> The decisions shall govern the architects and engineers in writing specifications and the contractors in awarding contracts.
>
> The Board shall certify its awards to the officials of each of the organizations, parties hereto.
>
> It shall be the duty of the officials of affiliated bodies, upon receiving such information, to instruct its members to carry out the decisions of the Board and to use them as a guide in the conduct of their work.
>
> In order to avert jurisdictional strife it is the recommendation of the Board that new materials, specialties and methods of application shall be passed upon by the Board before being specified or used provided that six members of the Board shall have agreed that the subject has not been previously covered.
>
> No member representing the Building Trades Department shall vote on an award in a dispute in which his own craft is involved nor shall any member employing one trade exclusively vote on any award in which that trade is a party at interest.

The penalties for non-compliance with the awards is believed to be of sufficient influence to prevent refusal to accept them. A union that fails to abide by an award is suspended from its national or international union and its members would therefore be unable to work at their trade on any building in the place where the trouble occurred.

Architects, engineers or employers represented in an organization affiliated to the National

(Continued on page 22)

Socialism Unmasked

PROGRAM OF AMERICAN SOCIALIST PARTY PARALLELS THAT OF THIRD INTERNATIONALE—PROVES THAT CONTEMPLATION OF POLITICAL ACTION ALONE IS A "PIPE DREAM"

By T. EVERETT HARRÉ

II

(*Continued from previous issue*).

THE Socialist party of America at its national convention in New York last May rejected the formula of "the dictatorship of the proletariat in the form of Soviets"—essentially a matter of phraseology, a phase of conditions peculiar to Russia under the Bolshevik revolution—but it reaffirmed its stand with the Third Internationale. That action since met with the support of the party membership, a majority of which by referendum vote, according to an announcement made August 21 by the Executive Committee, endorses the Moscow Internationale with the reservation that the party in this country shall work according to its own policies and methods without regard to the methods and policies used in other countries, particularly Russia.

Just what are the policies and methods to be employed in the United States? Do these policies and methods reject all that are illegal and unconstitutional? Does the party advocate, as its sole means of bringing about a revolution, the use of the ballot? In the foregoing article the official program laid down by the Socialist party of America was compared with the program of the Third Internationale. The program of the organization in America must be considered and understood according to the degree that it parallels the program of Lenine's Moscow Internationale. In the previous article it was shown that the Third Internationale and the American Socialist party unanimously repudiated and denounced those loyal Socialists who had supported their governments in the war; that the Third Internationale and the American Socialist party both deflected the blame for precipitating the world war from Germany.

The Third Communist Internationale lays the responsibility for civil war, or violent and drastic methods during a revolution, to the "arch-enemies" of the laboring classes. Driven to violent methods, civil war is forced upon the working class, and, the Moscow Congress declared, they "must answer blow for blow." The Manifesto declared "necessary the arming of the workers" as follows:

> . . . There would be no civil war if the exploiters who have carried mankind to the very brink of ruin had not prevented every forward step of the laboring masses, if they had not instigated plots and murders and called to their aid armed help from outside to maintain or restore the predatory privileges. CIVIL WAR IS FORCED UPON THE LABORING CLASSES BY THEIR ARCH-ENEMIES. THE WORKING CLASS MUST ANSWER BLOW FOR BLOW, IF IT WILL NOT RENOUNCE ITS OWN OBJECT AND ITS OWN FUTURE WHICH IS AT THE SAME TIME THE FUTURE OF ALL HUMANITY.
>
> THE COMMUNIST PARTIES, FAR FROM CONJURING UP CIVIL WAR ARTIFICIALLY, RATHER STRIVE TO SHORTEN ITS DURATION AS MUCH AS POSSIBLE—IN CASE IT HAS BECOME AN IRON NECESSITY—TO MINIMIZE THE NUMBER OF ITS VICTIMS, AND ABOVE ALL TO SECURE VICTORY FOR THE PROLETARIAT. THIS MAKES NECESSARY THE ARMING OF THE LABORERS, AND THE FORMATION OF A COMMUNIST ARMY AS THE PROTECTOR OF THE RULE OF THE PROLETARIAT AND THE INVIOLABILITY OF THE SOCIAL STRUCTURE. . . .

The Socialist party of America concurred in the declaration that "Civil war is forced upon the laboring classes by their arch-enemies" and voices the ambiguous hope that the revolution in America might be effected without resorting to the "drastic" methods of violence "made necessary" in Russia:

> The people of Russia, like the American colonists in 1776, were driven by their rulers to the use of violent methods to secure and maintain their freedom. The Socialist party calls upon the workers in the United States to do all in their power to restore and maintain our civil rights to the end that the transition from capitalism to Socialism may be effected without resort to the drastic measures made necessary by autocratic despotism.

The revolution which resulted in the abdication of the Czar and the setting up of the moderate democratic régime under Kerensky was almost bloodless, less bloody than the American revolution of 1776. Was it the "autocratic despotism" of Kerensky which made "necessary" the "drastic measures" of the murderous Bolsheviki? This declaration, in the light of what precedes it, is nothing less than a threat that the Socialist party does meditate such "drastic" and "violent measures" as are "made necessary by autocratic despotism." For immediately previous to this, the declaration is made:

> In the United States capitalism has emerged from the war more reactionary and aggressive, more insolent and oppressive than it ever has been. Having entered the war "to make the world safe for democracy," our government has enthusiastically allied itself with the most reactionary imperialism of Europe and Asia. . . . And while thus serving as an accomplice of black reaction abroad, our administration and the capitalist interests behind it were busily engaged in the ruthless work of suppressing civil rights and liberties at home. . . . The Socialist party, which during the war was the only party of peace and progress and the sole political defender of civil rights and labor's interests in the United States, was brutally outlawed. Its press was crippled, many of its meetings were dispersed, a great number of its defenders were persecuted and jailed. . . . While the vain conservative labor leaders were bribed by meaningless posts of honor, the courageous spokesmen for the radical labor groups were put behind prison bars.

"SUPREME TASK" OF COMMUNISTS.

The Third Communist Internationale laid down certain Governing Rules. In these political action, or parliamentary methods, as a means of bringing about the social revolution is accepted but declared to be of "only secondary importance." What is of primary and immediate importance, is "mass action:"

> THE REVOLUTIONARY ERA COMPELS THE PROLETARIAT TO MAKE USE OF THE MEANS OF BATTLE WHICH WILL CONCENTRATE ITS ENTIRE ENERGIES, NAMELY, MASS ACTION, WITH ITS LOGICAL RESULTANT, DIRECT CONFLICT WITH THE GOVERNMENTAL MACHINERY IN OPEN COMBAT. ALL OTHER METHODS, SUCH AS REVOLUTIONARY USE OF BOURGEOIS PARLIAMENTARISM, WILL BE OF ONLY SECONDARY SIGNIFICANCE.

The Socialist party, in the Preamble to its Constitution adopted at the Chicago Convention, declared for the organization of "the working class for independent action on the political field, not merely for the betterment of their conditions, but also and ABOVE ALL WITH THE REVOLUTIONARY AIM OF PUTTING AN END TO EXPLOITATION AND CLASS RULE."

But the "revolutionary use of bourgeois parliamentarism" is not of primary importance; what is of primary and immediate importance is the organization of workers industrially so as to employ industrial, or "mass action," to accomplish its ends:

> TO ACCOMPLISH THIS AIM, IT IS NECESSARY THAT THE WORKING CLASS BE POWERFULLY AND SOLIDLY ORGANIZED ALSO ON THE ECONOMIC FIELD TO STRUGGLE FOR THE SAME REVOLUTIONARY GOAL; AND THE SOCIALIST PARTY PLEDGES ITS AID IN THE TASK OF PROMOTING SUCH INDUSTRIAL ORGANIZATION AND WAGING SUCH INDUSTRIAL STRUGGLE FOR EMANCIPATION.

What is the essence of the program laid down by the Third Communist Internationale whereby Socialism shall triumph? Is it the use of the vote? The vote has been declared of "secondary importance." Is it violent revolution? The arming of the workers and the recruiting of "a Communist army" is specifically directed. This is to be accomplished by what method? through what means of organization? What is proposed, throughout the world, is the organization of the workers along class lines, in one coordinated class union, which shall be ready at the proper time to strike in concert and employ the weapon of industrial or mass action, the general strike:

> In an empire of destruction where not only the means of production and transportation but also the institutions of political democracy represent bloody ruins, the proletariat must create its own forms to serve above all as a bond of unity for the working class, and to enable it to accomplish a revolutionary intervention in the further development of mankind. Such apparatus is represented in the workmen's councils.
>
> The proletariat created a new institution which embraces the entire working class without distinction of vocation or political maturity, an elastic form of organization capable of continually renewing itself, expanding, and of drawing into itself ever new elements, ready to open its doors to the working groups of city and village which are near to the proletariat.

What is the essence of the program of the Socialist party of America whereby Socialism shall triumph in this country? Is it the use of the vote? Or is the vote regarded also as only of "secondary importance?" The Chicago Manifesto declares:

> To ensure the triumph of Socialism in the United States, the bulk of the American workers must be strongly organized politically as Socialists in constant, clear-cut and aggressive opposition to all parties of the possessing class. *They must be strongly organized on the economic field on broad industrial lines, as one powerful and harmonious class organization, cooperating with the Socialist party,* AND READY IN CASES OF EMERGENCY TO REINFORCE THE POLITICAL DEMANDS OF THE WORKING CLASS BY INDUSTRIAL ACTION.

The Third Moscow Internationale declares in its Manifesto that the organizing of the workers and the increasing of their power as a class organization *"is now the chief task of the class conscious and honest workers of all countries:"*

> Whenever the masses are awakened to consciousness, workers, soldiers and peasants' councils will be formed. TO FORTIFY THESE COUNCILS, TO INCREASE THEIR AUTHORITY, TO OPPOSE THEM TO THE STATE APPARATUS OF THE BOURGEOISIE IS NOW THE CHIEF TASK OF THE CLASS CONSCIOUS AND HONEST WORKERS OF ALL COUNTRIES.
>
> BY MEANS OF THESE COUNCILS THE WORKING CLASSES WILL GAIN POWER IN ALL COUNTRIES MOST READILY AND MOST CERTAINLY, WHEN THESE COUNCILS GAIN THE SUPPORT OF THE MAJORITY OF THE LABORING POPULATION. BY MEANS OF THESE COUNCILS THE WORKING CLASS ONCE ATTAINING POWER WILL CONTROL ALL THE FIELDS OF ECONOMIC AND CULTURAL LIFE AS IN THE CASE OF RUSSIA AT THE PRESENT TIME.

The Socialist party of America, in its Chicago Manifesto, also declares that such *"is the*

(*Continued on page 19*)

Purifying Politics—A Field for the Churches

AN OPEN LETTER TO REV. WORTH M. TIPPY PROPOSING METHODS WHEREBY RELIGIOUS BODIES CAN BRING ABOUT HONEST AND EFFICIENT GOVERNMENT

THE Federal Council of the Churches of Christ in America sent to the Protestant ministers of the country for use in their Labor Day sermons a "Labor Sunday Message," the economic trend of which raises disturbing questions and which calls for serious discussion. This "Message" has prompted the following open letter, which is addressed to the Rev. Dr. Worth M. Tippy because, in addition to his important relations with the Methodist Church, he is also Executive Secretary of the Federal Council, and is known for his learning, sanity and sound patriotism:

SEPTEMBER 14, 1920.

REV. WORTH M. TIPPY,
Executive Secretary, Commission on the Church and Social Service,
Federal Council of the Churches of Christ in America,
New York City.

MY DEAR MR. TIPPY:

I have just read the Labor Sunday Message addressed to employers and workers by the Federal Council of the Churches of Christ in America, and I must say that I am quite surprised at its radical tone. I am aware that the Commission on the Church and Social Service includes individual radicals of various hues but this pronouncement was sent out, not as representing their views, but those of the thirty-one denominations composing the Federal Council.

I have lately read much of the literary output of clergymen and social service commissions on industrial subjects and I am quite familiar with the socialist tone they nearly all take; but I was not prepared to find such views sponsored by you and other leading men with whom I am acquainted in the Protestant churches and whom I know to have no sympathy with socialism of any character.

Just what right, officially, have the authors of that document to speak for the seventeen million men and women belonging to and supporting those thirty-one denominations that compose the Federal Council? Among those seventeen million members, it is certainly safe to say that there are a few wage-earners, farmers, employers, bankers and other business men—but they do not seem to have any representation on the committees of the Federal Council of the Churches of Christ in America having to do with industrial matters.

Upon reading that Message, one would be justified in charging that it had been drafted by that little group of people called Christian Socialists, because so many of their absurd contentions are woven into it. Running all through it is the idea that industry should be run as it is assumed Christ would run it—for service and not profit, and on the basis of that oft-exploded fallacy that Jesus was a socialist and therefore against profit, rent, interest and the wage system. This is iterated and reiterated throughout the Message in sentences like the following:

> As at present encouraged, the competitive principles necessarily breed wrong ways of making money, suspicion, hatred, antagonism, and sabotage. These are destructive of the Christian life and tend to undo the constructive work of the church, the school and the home.
>
> * * * * *
>
> The Christian principle takes one step farther, and leads to the primary motive of industry. Is the motive of profits, which is the primary motive of modern enterprise, a Christian motive, and ought it not to be supplanted by or rigidly subordinated to Christ's great motive of service?
>
> * * * * *
>
> Now, working exclusively or mainly for profits corrupts men, as working for a salary corrupts a preacher. It tends to make them selfish and grasping.
>
> * * * * *
>
> The commercial spirit, so-called, can be escaped only as men consciously work to produce from the motive of service.

Just how Jesus would conduct business in this country today is explained in an interview in the *New York World* of August 1, 1920, by Charles W. Wood, a socialist who has just returned from China where he made a study of industrial conditions. Mr. Wood was sent to China by the Methodist Centenary and undoubtedly it is to that body that he has reported his brilliant ideas of how industry would be conducted under a Christian régime. As you are a prominent member of that denomination, you doubtless will recognize the quotation I make:

> "It is too simple for explanation. In a factory operated on the Jesus principle no worker would work for wages and none of the product would be sold. The worker would work for the joy of the service he was rendering and for the expression of his own creative powers. The product, of course, would all be given away, because it is more blessed to give than to receive. If it were found that the factory did not produce enough under such a régime, we would call upon our engineering experts to make the work more attractive.
>
> "'A nation organized on the Jesus principle would not be interested in its own protection: it would be looking for ways in which to serve the nations roundabout. No good citizen of such a nation would want his property protected from any other citizen, or from any invader from abroad. In fact, no one would think of property as his. People would be free from property and lay up treasures in heaven; in that heaven that will come to earth just as soon as we organize to give and not to get."

The Labor Sunday Message contains the following arraignment of the competitive system:

> "Our industrial life has been built on wrong and un-Christian foundations. Is not our problem to substitute the Golden Rule as a controlling motive for our doctrine of competitive struggle? That law of struggle or competition, as the historic dominant law of industry, has pitted employer against employer, corporation against corporation, nation against nation. It was responsible away back for the great war with its gigantic economic and human losses. It has pitted capitalist and employer against the workers, and the workers against capitalist and employer in a struggle which threatens another cataclysm and at least the temporary shattering of civilization."

Pretty strong language, for a document claiming to represent the views of the Protestant men and women of these United States of America. One would expect to find such expressions only in writings of the Socialist Party leaders. Some of them, as you know, were indicted for having intimated that the war was brought on by the capitalists or the competitive system. Fischer, the man who gave warning of the Wall Street catastrophe, used the same bitter language against the capitalists and the competitive system. Down at the Rand School, they dote on "cataclysms" and they have been "shattering civilization" for years. But to indulge in such perfervid rhetoric in a pronouncement issued officially by the Federal Council of the Churches of Christ in America seems to me rather far-fetched, to say the least.

What is more amazing, after the very instructive lessons of Moscow and Petrograd, of Milan and Naples, is that any responsible body of citizens, Christian or otherwise, should talk about abolishing the competitive system and taking on the co-operative commonwealth.

Another paragraph that interests me is the following:

> "The Church, loving the nation, primarily concerned for the welfare of the masses of the people but devoted to the welfare of all, committed by its deepest principles and by the purpose of its existence to righteousness and the safeguarding of life, watches the deepening conflict with profound concern. It can not stand aloof. At whatever risk of becoming involved in the controversy it must go into the midst of the contending forces, if possible between them."

Now, this declaration raises a number of very pertinent questions. How is the Church to jump "into the midst" of employers and employees or "between them" in this cataclysmic conflict? It would be physically impossible for the churches themselves to "jump in," so it would naturally devolve upon representatives, or, more properly speaking, alleged representatives of the Church. This, of course, would mean the paid and unpaid social workers who are responsible for the socialistic document containing that statement—and that very statement doubtless was written by one of the men who are itching to jump "into the midst" of the fray and incidentally into the limelight.

To learn how that works out, it is only necessary to see what has happened when preachers and ex-preachers have functioned by "jumping in between them." Look at Winnipeg, Seattle, and Lawrence, Mass. In each place, the preachers promptly espoused the cause of the I. W. W., two of them very properly landing in jail—and, incidentally, they fought both the employer and the regular loyal trade union organization. I can conceive of no greater calamity to our nation, industrially speaking, and certainly to the pulpit, than to have preachers and clergymen mixing up in all the industrial disturbances that arise throughout the length and breadth of the land. Fortunately, however, it is only a very small percentage of the active clergy who favor such activities; it is generally ex-ministers who feel the urge to "jump in."

The problems between employers and employees are of the most complicated and intricate character and they require the most skilled and expert handling. They cannot be dealt with by men of emotional or "cataclysmic" natures, carrying the Golden Rule in one hand and the "creeds of the churches" in the other—especially when, at the same time, they are promoting the doctrine that the present order, the wage system and so forth, should be scrapped and replaced by the "co-operative commonwealth." Clergymen are no better equipped to deal with labor problems than are longshoremen qualified to deal with the baffling theological dogmas that are producing so many religious creeds. Talk about the crying need for industrial harmony! There is about as much harmony today in the churches as there is in the Balkans! Until the churches have produced harmony in their own field, you can hardly ask others to believe that they can be of much help in another of which they know little or nothing.

Now, I have frankly expressed myself against the wisdom of the churches going "between the contending forces" because I believe they would do infinitely more harm than good. But there is a much greater field, which would include the industrial, where I believe the Church could accomplish wonders and where it would find ample scope for the feverish activities of all the ministers, ex-ministers and social service workers of the various denominations who want to "go out into the world" and do useful work. It would not be so spectacular but it would be more simple in operation and infinitely more productive of wholesome results. It would enable the Church to make the world a better place to live in, morally as well as industrially—and it must not be forgotten that dealing with morals and souls rather than economics was the original purpose for which the Church was established.

In the Labor Sunday Message, in giving a reason why the Church should jump "into the midst" of the conflict, there were cited figures to show that in twelve months the loss in wages to labor and profits to capital would reach the sum of $275,000,000. Assuming that the statistician has subtracted the gains that would accrue to the workers in the course of years by the winning of their strikes, and considering further that all strikes are not bad nor should be prohibited, suffice it to say that the losses claimed are very great. But in the press of the same week were statistics showing that $500,000,000 of property in this country, nearly twice as much as your estimated loss through strikes, is being destroyed annually by rats—and this does not include the tragic results of the Bubonic plague and other contagious diseases distributed by the little rodent. Surely, from a financial point of view, the rat problem ought to be dealt with before the labor problem, and it certainly seems to be a more simple one.

Again, in the press of that week, we find that the United States Chamber of Commerce has worked out a plan in connection with the railroads that will mean the adding of so many hundreds of cars to the train service, by the simple method of adding a little more "hustle" at both ends of the shipment, that this reform will save over $1,000,000,000. This makes the little $275,000,000 to be saved on strikes and lockouts look measly indeed. When one considers the billions that are lost through wastage in coal mining, water power and forestry, the cost of strikes and lockouts is of comparative insignificance. Even a wastage in the administration of governments, federal, state and municipal, through the lack of as simple a thing as a budget system runs up into billions every year; and yet our Church friends, our social service experts, get excited over a quarter of a billion. Needlessly to say, however, strikes cause much suffering to the families of the strikers and frequently to the public, and they should be eliminated as far as possible on general principles; but they are not an overpowering economic evil so far as wastage is concerned.

To return to the reform that I propose and which I think should be undertaken by the churches if they are to go outside of the strictly religious field: Glance for a moment only at a few of the most flagrant evils we see all around us—evils with which our families come in daily contact and with which the Church so far seems utterly unable to cope. There is the social evil! Little has been accomplished toward its solution in two thousand years. There is the vice of gambling that is carrying misery to thousands of homes and is destroying the souls of millions. There are the obscene books, papers and pictures that are corrupting many of the minds of our youth. There are immoral plays and "movies" brazenly flaunting their shamelessness, not only along the Great White Ways of all our cities but in all our towns and villages. There is illicit trade in habit-forming drugs; adulteration in drugs and food; and the cheating of the poor by short weights and measures. There are political graft and incompetency in our public schools and in our police, fire and street departments. There are graft and criminal incompetency in city and state institutions for defectives, delinquents and dependents. In fact, there is graft everywhere in municipal, state and federal governments and in private business where there is anything to steal. Look at the lack of uniformity in state legislation. Could anything be more absurd than our conflicting state laws for the protection of women and children, or in the matter of divorce? Consider the great evils that the city charter and ballot reformers are aiming at. You can add many other evils to this list, for it is far from complete.

Now, there is a way to clean out much of this rottenness and secure honest and efficient government, and the Church can do it. Let us take municipal government first, because that is the nearest to us. We face it every minute and on every side. Suppose all men and women voters in the Protestant, Catholic and Jewish churches should join hands in a clean-up-the-city campaign—and this is one program on which all denominations can unite, for all want honest and efficient government in the matters I have enumerated as well as in a hundred others. The first thing they should do, once they resolved to do anything, would be to recognize the party machineries as they now exist, for they are nearly scientifically perfect in everything but the one thing that the churches can supply, and that is intelligent determination to make all necessary personal sacrifices to do the job as a Christian duty. With this policy agreed upon, the rest would be easy: Let the program of work provide that the Democratic men and women join their wards or political clubs, and let the Republican men and women do the same. The leaders will be delighted to greet them. Then let them resolve to become active in those clubs, not simply enrolled members. They will soon discover that there is lots of work to do in looking after voters and manning the election districts for both primaries and elections. They will be amazed, for instance, to learn of the great sacrifices made by men and women who have been performing these duties for us in order that we might have even the unsatisfactory government we have been getting. They will also see how vital it is that these election officials who count their ballots should be both intelligent and honest. They work long hours with little pay. The church members should do their share of that work; but important as all that is, there is still a much more insistent duty to perform if they are to secure good government.

So far, I have referred only to the mechanism of the work. They will have to take the time to study the issues that arise and get in touch with the political leader or boss of their ward, precinct or district, depending upon the city in which they live. They should find out what he is thinking about, whom he has in mind for mayor or aldermen or members of the legislature or Congress. If there is to be a convention, talk out with him the names of the delegates, insisting that they be the best men and women in the district or ward, and making some suggestions about the personnel. If they find him evasive or demurring or if they suspect his good faith in any way, they should call a little caucus of their own and put up a ticket of honest and able men and women, not necessarily all church members but citizens who want good government just as surely as do the professed Christians. They may "get licked" at first, but this will only whet their appetites for a real fight, and some day they will be running the precinct or ward and will have kicked out the unscrupulous professional boss.

Now, just consider what would happen in little old New York, Philadelphia, Boston, Cleveland and Oshkosh if the Protestants, Catholics, Jews and Christian Scientists were all on the job! The great sacrifice would also include their acceptance of political office, not leaving it entirely to the professional politicians who make a living out of the business. In saying this I mean no offense to those professional politicians, district leaders or ward heelers as some of them are called, for we owe them a debt of gratitude which it is hard to pay for giving us the government we have. If we had depended upon the clergy and church members and other good citizens for our government, it would have gone out of business. The ward bosses saved it for us.

What would happen in the matter of dealing with all the subjects enumerated in a former paragraph if all government positions, whether municipal, state or federal, were filled by conscientious Christians who had equipped themselves for government service through study of the problems they would be called upon to deal with. Let us take the labor and capital problem which is so alluring to the social service people. All they hope to gain or can gain until the millennium comes along can be gained through the government if they will devote themselves to making the government responsive to the demands of the best citizens—and I do not mean by best citizens only the bankers and business men, but the workers in all fields, the professional men and women and the educators.

Take strikes and lockouts: They should never be meddled with by amateurs or sentimental people, but by experts trained in that special field. For twenty years the State of New York has had a Bureau of Mediation whose duty it is to try to prevent strikes and lockouts; Massachusetts has had one for even a longer period. They have done some good work but they have such meager appropriations that they cannot do more than a fraction of what is required. Suppose the Legislature were made up of the kind of men and women we have been talking about. Enough money would be granted to secure expert service of the highest character with no taint of party politics entering into the situation. These experts could do all that could be done and do it efficiently. They could not prevent all strikes but would reduce them to a minimum. Then also the Federal Bureau of Mediation could be enlarged and strengthened. Then there are the child labor laws, the tenement house laws, the fire prevention laws and a hundred other laws, which have been placed on the statute books for the protection of the people, but which are only partly enforced on account of inefficient and frequently dishonest administration.

I need not go on with this enumeration. You know what it would mean if the churches took hold of government as a part of its religious work. In the little town of New Canaan, Connecticut, where I am writing this letter, they have the old New England town government, the ideal of every writer on democracy. Last month they had to adjourn the town meeting called to pass upon some very important matters, because there were only seven voters present and the law requires eleven to make a quorum. They adjourned for a week and then had only nine voters present; but they went out on the streets and dragged in two others, but in the meantime two of the nine had skipped out, so they had to adjourn again. Now, there are over 1,000 church members in New Canaan. If they had been doing their Christian duty, there would have been no adjournment of the first meeting.

Even the ills of competition, so graphically depicted in your Labor Sunday Message, could be curbed and only the great benefits derived from it could be saved if the Federal Trade Commission, were composed of men of expert knowledge and statesmanlike vision. In fact, if only the intelligent, honest men and women of the Church—of course, a few ignorant, fanatical and crooked people do get into the churches

(Continued on page 22)

Education—Minus Business Brains

ONE-HALF OF AMERICAN CHILDREN LEAVE SCHOOLS WITH NO CIVIC AND ECONOMIC UNDERSTANDING AMERICA TWENTY-FOUR PER CENT. ILLITERATE

(Speech delivered at the National Citizens' Conference on Education, Washington, D. C., May 20, 1920)

By H. E. MILES

WHAT is the purpose of public education? None other whatever than the development of the social and economic understanding of the individual, of every individual, and so of the entire people.

I present a chart, which shows that the general agency which we call the public school system, built up by our so-called leaders of public education through the generations, is not performing and cannot perform, as they have persisted in making it, this function.

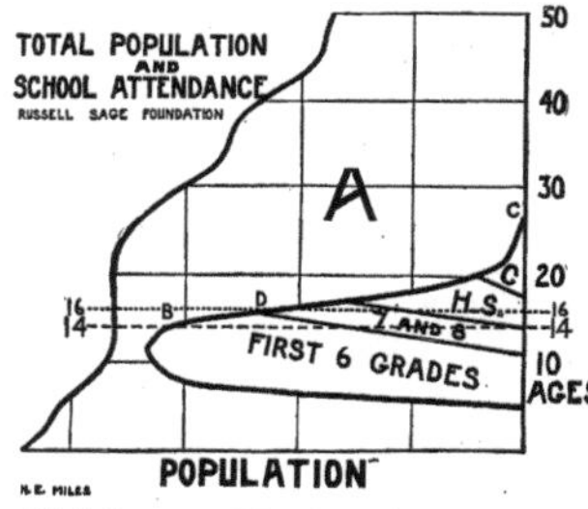

This chart was prepared through many days of painstaking care, by a superior authority on our public schools, the Russell Sage Foundation, Division of Education. The bottom line indicates our total population and the vertical line on the right, the ages of all our people from birth to the fiftieth year. The curved line on the left may be called the death line, indicating as it does the diminishing number of our population as life advances.

The interior diagram indicates the total population in our public schools, their ages and their school grades, from first grade to college graduation.

You will note the great number in the "First 6 Grades". The interior lines rise as they go from right to left because of retardation. In a first-rate school system, as you know, these lines would be nearer horizontal.

As the chart shows, about half of all our children leave school at the end of the sixth grade. Says General Hahn, after examining the records of millions of soldiers, "The average education among *all American adults* is only the sixth grade", and "The average education of the personnel available for enlistment (being some of those from the eleventh grade and substantially all below the eleventh grade) is probably but little above the fifth grade." These records also show that illiteracy averages 24.9% for the entire country and that it is not much worse in any section than in any other. The basis of this test being ability to read an English newspaper and write a letter home—a real test.

In the first six grades there is taught absolutely nothing that develops, or tends to develop, in a formal way, civic and economic understanding. The best educators here say this may be said of the seventh and eighth grades also. Neither time nor the age of the pupils makes it possible to teach more than the "three R's". In fact, you only teach these poorly. For instance, to take the State that is commonly rated highest in the quality of its public schools, Massachusetts, 70% of all the children in her mill towns leave school by the end of the fifth grade. In one of the best department stores in Boston I have seen a large group of 14- and 15-year employees trying to write a simple letter to the firm, as an education exercise, and not one of them knowing how to put the address line, the date line and the signature, right, nor how to spell or punctuate. We don't have to go South for quality!

No one is unappreciative of the necessity and the value of these first six grades. However, as Mr. Pierce, former President of the National Education Association, told me ten years ago, "These grades are not education in any sense whatever. They only provide the tools, the pick and shovel, whereby education may later be acquired."

Giving the schools the benefit of the doubt whether the broken line here shown should not be drawn across the chart considerably higher up, say at the sixteenth year of age, and placing it, as here shown, at the fourteenth year, it shows that at best all public education, the development of social and economic understanding, comes in the narrow area between this broken line and the curved line "B-C". And what do we find?*

Upon this slender and largely worthless foundation rests the great area marked "A", an area of suffering, ignorance, and misunderstanding, in which is all of our adult population under fifty years of age (barring a few school teachers), the burden bearers upon whom rests every hope and accomplishment for ten years to come, and until those now in school take the places of their elders with no better and no different education. In this area are college men who have had, after a fashion, the training that all should have in social and economic understanding, and would have had if our educational leaders had known their jobs. Also here are 43,000,000 wage-earners and 20,000,000 home-makers, wives and sisters of the wage-earners. This total of 63,000,000 working people left school, at best, as you perfectly know, by the end of the sixth grade, with no education, with, at best, only the three R's. Worse than that, there was not the slightest provision made for their acquirement of education—no suggestion to this end from our public school men, halt and blind. The doors of educational opportunity were shut on them forever, when they left the grade school.

As your eyes run from "B" in the chart to the right, you see how frightfully thin is this space between the dotted line and the curved line just above. You get well into the high school area before you find any approximation to an adequate educational basis or foundation under our social and economic structure. You find that the high school pupils drop out in great numbers early in the course, that half the college entrants drop out early, and that few graduate.

Think of this great area from the dotted line and the 14th year of life to the fiftieth year as a great building, our social structure, and you see that under one corner only, the college corner, is there any foundation. There is no alternative. It is "college or nothing." That the school leaders know this is shown by this bulletin which I took from the walls of one of the big, palatial high schools of the country:

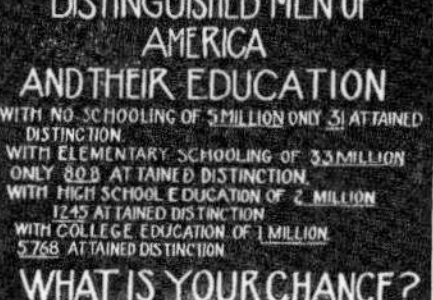

DISTINGUISHED MEN OF
AMERICA
AND THEIR EDUCATION
WITH NO SCHOOLING OF 5 MILLION ONLY 31 ATTAINED DISTINCTION.
WITH ELEMENTARY SCHOOLING OF 33 MILLION ONLY 808 ATTAINED DISTINCTION.
WITH HIGH SCHOOL EDUCATION OF 2 MILLION 1245 ATTAINED DISTINCTION
WITH COLLEGE EDUCATION OF 1 MILLION. 5768 ATTAINED DISTINCTION
WHAT IS YOUR CHANCE?

This bulletin is true and well meant. There is substantially no chance for an American boy or girl unless he goes to college. All public school people know it, hence their pressure upon the youth to stay in school even through college. But there is another side to this that fits the declaration of this conference that our public school system is not democratic. It has been built and fortified insistently, but unconsciously, by the school people for the favored few, favored in money, favored in their parentage, or favored with the special type of intelligence and energy that lets a poor boy stick to book learning at all odds. This bulletin and all that is behind it is a damning indictment of our public school lead-

(Continued on page 23)

* Since this was written leading educators at this Conference declare that there is nothing in sociology or economics taught in the 7th or 8th grades. The Committee on Social Studies in the High-Schools, after investigating 5,054 high-schools, selected at random, being one-third of all in the U. S., reports that 2,404 teach Civics of the old type, dealing primarily with forms of government with little or no reference to economic or social problems. Sociology is taught in 431 schools according to their claims, but the committee doubts "if the subject matter would justify the claim, as only 136 have recognized texts." "But," says the committee, "to know that as many as 136 [high] schools out of 5,054 are actually engaged in teaching sociology indicates a rapid development of these subjects in the last two years." I leave you to draw the base line where you will and add the dotted line at the sixteenth year as doubtless too low. The committee continues "courses of study designed primarily to give direct instruction and training in citizenship are, for the most part, deferred to the last two years of the high-school, thereby bringing their influence to bear solely upon those pupils who have before them a complete high-school education."—H. E. MILES.

THE NATIONAL
Civic Federation Review

Office: Thirty-third Floor, Metropolitan Tower
1 Madison Avenue New York City

RALPH M. EASLEY, Editor

The Editor alone is Responsible for any unsigned article or unquoted statement published in THE NATIONAL CIVIC FEDERATION REVIEW.

AMERICAN *vs.* EUROPEAN LABOR POLICIES

The formation of the National Board for Jurisdictional Awards in the Building Industry, as described in another column by W. C. Roberts, is one of many encouraging signs that sanity in the relations between employers and employees in the United States is fast returning.

While in nearly every country in Europe, the organized workers are threatening the life of their Government, in the United States the organized labor movement has never made even so much as a gesture in that direction; on the contrary, it is co-operating with the Government in all its undertakings, and especially on the very question on which the British, the French and the Italian labor movements are threatening their respective Governments—*i. e.*, the recognition of Soviet Russia. At the Montreal convention of the American Federation of Labor, the vote against Bolshevism was so overwhelming that the pros did not even call for a division. The difference between the policies of the labor movements of Europe and that of the American Labor movement is well illustrated by that action.

Another difference between the American and the British labor movements is shown in the treatment of the coal mining controversies in the two countries. The coal strike here last year was due to a regular trade union controversy over wages, hours and working conditions and it was settled by arbitration. The coal strike now impending in England, however, relates not only to hours, wages and working conditions but also demands that the Government, at the expense of its own exchequer, shall force a reduction in the price of coal to the public and that the Government shall eventually take over and operate the coal mining industry. Robert Smillie, the head of the British Mine Workers, is a pronounced advocate of Lenine and Trotzky and the Soviet form of government.

While in the mining industry in this country, organized labor is far superior in patriotism and sanity to that of Great Britain, the same superiority exists in our other basic industry, transportation. While the railroad workers in England undertook to tie up the country with a strike, which failed, the railroad workers here submitted their demands to arbitration—and outside of the temporary inconvenience caused by the switchmen's "outlaw strike," which undoubtedly was engineered by I. W. W.'ites, there has been no interruption of service.

But it was due to the good sense and conservative character of our labor leaders that a joint movement was not effected between the American and the British labor organizations. Early in 1919, representatives of the Triple Alliance of Great Britain (composed of railwaymen, transport workers and miners) came to the United States to organize the same interests here into a "Triple Alliance" for America. It was the program that these two Triple Alliances would then be united in an International Alliance which at any time could say to the two countries what the British Labor Party said in effect to its Government last month: "Do as we command in regard to Soviet Russia or we will 'down tools' and starve you into submission." In other words, "Abdicate all constitutional forms of government and turn things over to us Bolshevists who are taking orders direct from Moscow." And the leadership in this revolutionary movement did not devolve upon Arthur Henderson, Ramsay MacDonald or George Lansbury, the radicals, but upon the supposedly conservative James H. Thomas, M. P., General Secretary of the National Union of Railwaymen, and J. R. Clynes, the former labor member of Lloyd George's Cabinet and British Food Controller during the War. The spirit of that movement is indicated by a cablegram sent in 1919 to labor bodies in this country by Robert Williams, of the Dock Workers, and Charles Cramp, of the Railway Engineers:

> We in Great Britain, despite our conservative outlook, have fashioned an industrial organization which is probably the most potent ever created—the Triple Alliance. In this body we 300,000 Transport Workers have allied ourselves for defensive and aggressive purposes with 500,000 railroad workers, and 800,000 miners. We believe it is our duty to use every means in our power to challenge the institution of capitalism and its domination of the working people. . . . Today, we of the Triple Alliance are challenging the Government's policy in maintaining conscription, military intervention in Russia, and military intervention in trade union disputes.
>
> We see in the fight against the workers of Russia an attempt to safeguard the interests of English bondholders, and we realize, perhaps more by instinct than by reason, that the fight of the Russian and Hungarian proletariat is in fact our own fight. We know, moreover, through experience, that conscription means the possibility of breaking strikes by means of the intervention of armed soldiers and sailors.
>
> Therefore we are taking the only means at our disposal to compel the Government to abandon conscription and get out of Russia.
>
> We earnestly hope that America will not be the stronghold of capitalism during this world-proletarian crisis which is at hand. America with its international origin should be in the van of the world movement for working-class liberty. May we therefore urge upon American trade-unionists the duty of assisting struggling Europe in what is not a make-believe but a real fight for freedom!

While this appeal utterly failed to win the American labor organizations, there is little doubt that in the Mine Workers', the Longshoremen's and the Steel Workers' strikes, there were radical contingents trying to respond to the call from their "brothers" across the water. There were also indications that in the railroad controversies here last fall there were radicals trying to comply with "Brother Cramp's" request.

In France, the labor movement would choke the Government to death if it could. In fact, it tried to do so last May, but the Government did the choking and the "general strike" remained a theory only. In Germany, they are not choking the Government but they are choking industry instead, through shop committees, democratic control and all that catalogue of schemes devised to give the workers a voice in technical management, financial control and employment supervision. The Socialists as long as they had control of the Government were trying out all the fantastic propositions that they have advocated since the days of Marx.

The labor situation in Italy, of course, compares with nothing in this country with the exception of the programs and aims of a comparative handful of Communists, I. W. W.'ites and Socialists. At this writing, September 18, it may not compare even with those but more nearly with some of the opéra bouffe scenes worked off on the public in the days of Gilbert and Sullivan. The serious aspect of the Italian situation, however, lies in the revelation of the pitiable weakness of the Giolitti government and the discovery that Giolitti himself seems to be a Red only a few shades lighter than Lenine. The program of the workers, who have locked themselves in and their employers out, is quite familiar to those who have read the literary output of certain so-called industrial experts who are advocating democratic government in industry. These experts have greatly excited the imaginations of the social service specialists in certain church organizations who are feverishly promoting this new form of democracy. Here is the way one of them puts it in a book that all the other social service experts are accepting as gospel truth:

> The "hot spot" in the industrial situation is not wages or hours, but management, in which labor is demanding an increasing share. This is in part the industrial counterpart of the demand for political democracy that is sweeping the world. It results from a growing conviction that freedom for the individual, the paramount democratic ideal, is not satisfied by a political formula, but must be realized in daily life and work. This means free choice of occupation; a voice in the determination of hours and wages, conditions of work, and shop discipline; and, in its fullest import, participation also in financial procedure—buying, selling and investment.

This is what Giolitti and the Communists of Italy are going to try out. It is what Lenine and Trotzky have already tried, to their sorrow and to the sorrow of the workers who, after its complete failure, were conscripted into the Red Army and put to work under machine gun supervision instead.

As stated in the opening paragraph of this article, the industrial outlook in this country is becoming more promising day by day. The beginning of a reduction in prices of basic commodities and the consequent reduction in the cost of living mark the beginning of the end of unconscionable profiteering and exploitation, which means that gradually but surely the American people will regain a normal life. That today we are not facing revolutionary outbursts, as in Europe, is due to the patriotic and level-headed leadership of those great bodies of five million organized wage-earners, the American Federation of Labor and the Railway Brotherhoods.

THE SOWERS AND THE HARVEST

On September 16 an explosion, through a time bomb or infernal machine, occurred in the most populous section of Wall Street, between the United States treasury and the offices of J. Pierpont Morgan & Company, in which two hundred persons were injured and thirty-four killed. The catastrophe was hideous and sent a wave of horror throughout the nation. According to Government investigators all clues indicate an organized plot on part of revolutionary "Reds."

Such outrages are generally the work of the more fanatic members of the revolutionary "proletarian army," yet it is just of such that the majority of any mass movement to overthrow a government is composed. It is exactly this fanaticism which the leaders seek to rouse and play upon, at the opportune time, as Lenine and Trotzky did in Russia and as the leaders anticipate doing in this country. The atrocities which have been perpetrated in Russia by the Bolsheviki under their leaders are on a large scale analogous to what, a single incident, was perpetrated in Wall Street. The psychology back of the planting of that bomb is the psychology of the Red Terror in Russia.

Immediately after the calamity, radical papers and radical leaders ostentatiously rushed forth to deplore and repudiate the act. The authorities may find the perpetrator to be another Czolgoz, a weak minded fanatic, who may or may not have had any connection with the Socialist or Communist parties. No one could imagine that the leaders of the Socialist party, or the editors of Socialist and "intellectual liberal" periodicals, or even the I. W. W., could have any part in such a plot—at this time. These know that such an isolated outrage would serve no political purpose and simply bring upon their heads the anger of the people; that it would alienate the sympathy of many of their "liberal" friends, and do more damage than good to their cause. Nevertheless, the responsibility of this horror must be placed where it belongs.

Whoever placed that bomb is blood-guilty of the death of thirty-four human beings. And to the same degree, morally if not criminally, are the leaders of the Socialist movement and the pro-Bolshevist "liberal" periodicals blood-guilty when lives are lost in such a crime. The Wall Street tragedy is the concrete result of their teachings.

With bitterness, with hatred, with malevolence, the Socialist leaders have preached a class war, have told their followers that they were oppressed, exploited and persecuted. They have attacked our Government, our institutions, our industrial system, urging that these be destroyed. The Socialist party officially advocates a program of "reinforcing" its political demands by industrial action, or the general strike, the overthrow of the Constitution and our form of government by force. The carrying out of that program would entail horrors in which the Wall Street explosion would be a trivial and insignificant incident. In their program to gain their object, they would precipitate exactly such catastrophes on a nation-wide scale.

The above is an unpublished photograph of the speakers' table at a luncheon given on May 26, 1917, by THE NATIONAL CIVIC FEDERATION in honor of the British labor delegates who had been sent to the United States by Premier Lloyd George at the request of Samuel Gompers, then Chairman of the Committee on Labor of the Council of National Defense, to address the working men and women of America. August Belmont presided at this luncheon and James H. Thomas, M. P., General Secretary of the National Union of Railwaymen of Great Britain and Ireland, sat at his left. The others at the table were: Oscar S. Straus, C. W. Bowerman, Joseph Davies, H. W. Garrod, Samuel Gompers, Warren S. Stone, W. S. Carter, William Fellowes Morgan, Elisha Lee, Haley Fiske and Ralph M. Easley.

The delegates made a tour throughout the country under the auspices of the American Federation of Labor and THE NATIONAL CIVIC FEDERATION. At Schenectady, Mr. Thomas addressed fifteen thousand employees of the General Electric Company, by his eloquence inducing them to subscribe to $100,000 of Liberty Bonds.

This is the same Mr. Thomas who was a conspicuous leader in organizing the Council of Action in London last month which threatened to overturn the Government of Great Britain unless it surrendered its constitutional prerogatives to the workers. His patriotism and enthusiasm were of such great benefit to our country in 1917 that his turning against his own Government at this crucial time has been a painful surprise to the many friends he made when here.

In academic verbiage, in phraseology of idealism, under the guise of liberalism, a small group of "intellectual" "liberal" magazines have more subtly, and perhaps even more dangerously, carried on the propaganda of the class war, inciting class hatred and revolutionary discontent. They impugned our part in the war, representing it as a Wall Street war in which capitalism alone emerged victorious; they attacked the President for having "betrayed civilization" at the Peace Conference; they have defended the Bolsheviki and have promoted Bolshevism as the advent of their heralded "new order." These, no less than the more rabid Socialist, anarchist and I. W. W. agitators, have sown seeds of which the Wall Street horror is but a single result. Amateurs of life smugly toying with vital things with the intelligence of adolescents, mediocrities seeking to attract attention to themselves by a swash-buckling bravura dare-devilism, they sow a wind, the harvest of which is a whirlwind. Streaked with yellow, mock-heroic and incapable of real self-sacrifice in such a struggle as the last war, these "little young men" would probably turn white-faced at the sight of blood from a pin-prick, and yet it is the "intellectual diversion" of these that finds fruit in a Wall Street catastrophe. Calling for stern justice to those guilty of the act, the Rev. Dr. Manning, in Trinity Church, rightly said:

> "There is also another class that needs to be rightly dealt with, the class that describes itself as 'intellectual,' the class of 'intellectuals' who make themselves safe by declaring they do not advocate force, but at the same time sow the seeds and spread the propaganda which produce acts of this sort. It is a shameful thing, too, that by some among us these people are encouraged and countenanced in this sort of business. Against all this there should be a tide of public sentiment and righteous indignation which would cause the intellectual class to see itself in its true light."

It is to be hoped that America will take heed of this warning, and especially that it will give pause to those sentimental folk who have rushed to every defense of the Socialists, those clergymen who oppose every attempt to curb their teachings and who eagerly lend their names to every attack on Wall Street and capitalism, those rich people who have coddled and helped support the more subtle and academic propagandists of discontent and sedition. It would be well for every American to familiarize himself with the program of the Socialist party and learn just what is proposed by "industrial action." To safeguard our national life, our very existence, it will not suffice only to apprehend and punish the perpetrators of such an isolated outrage, but we must go to the source and deal with those who inspire men to class hatred and violence. If we would prevent the bloody harvest, we must stop the sowing of the seeds of wrath.

CAMOUFLAGE FAILS TO HIDE TRUE CHARACTER

On the same day that the infernal machine wrecked the most populous section of Wall Street and resulted in the death of thirty-four wage earners, the five Socialists who had been expelled last winter from the New York legislature were reelected in the special elections in New York City. This was not unexpected and must not be taken—what the Socialists loudly represent it to be—as a vindication on part of loyal Americans of these members of a lawless organization. The districts from which these men were reelected contain a large number of Socialists and people who, while not enrolled members, vote the Socialist ticket, a majority of them of alien birth or extraction. Although the Republicans and Democrats united on a fusion ticket against the Socialists, it was impossible to get out the vote, and against a vote of 32,516 in 1919, the fusion vote in this election was only 11,336, a decrease of more than 21,000 votes. The Socialists hail this decrease as a repudiation of the action of the New York State Assembly, but in this connection it is also significant that while the Socialists polled 28,469 votes last year they polled in the recent elections only 17,654 votes, which would indicate that more than ten thousand former supporters had been convinced that these Socialists are ineligible to take their seats. The decrease in the fusion vote is more than likely due to a lamentable failure on part of many to fulfill the duty of citizens and go to the polls. The action of the N. Y. Assembly in expelling Claessens, Waldman and Solomon by an overwhelming majority was inevitable, and the possibility that De Witt and Orr will not serve would be in accord with the fitness of things.

The reelection of these five men, and the superficial camouflage adopted at its last convention by the Socialist party of America, does not change the status of the Socialist organization or the ineligibility of its members to office. As pointed out by Mr. Harré, in his article in this issue of the REVIEW, the endorsement of the Third Internationale with qualifications means nothing except a ruse on part of the wily leaders to deceive simple and unsuspecting folk.

The Socialist party, as Mr. Harré's article shows, is still committed to a program which seeks to gain political power by the weapon of "industrial action" or the general strike. It contemplates the overthrow of government and the setting up of a Socialist régime by a minority, through force and violence. Its end and aim is still what it declared in one of the resolutions adopted at the St. Louis convention in 1917: "Social revolution, not political office, is the end and aim of the Socialist party."

Is that revolution to be peaceful? Parliamentary and lawful? One can best find the answer, not in what Socialists prepare for soft and flabby sentimentalists in churches, schools, colleges, et cetera, but in what Socialists write for Socialists. That the Socialist intellectuals realize they can never win by securing a majority of voters, and that they do not even consider the ballot box as their weapon, is indicated by a communication published in the *New York Call*, July 26, 1920, from Benjamin Glassberg, one of the leading lecturers in that training-school of agitators, the Rand School. Glassberg declared against *"our teaching the workers what is fundamentally untrue, that is, that we can vote ourselves into Socialism."* He said further: *"Now is the time to discuss tactics, not when the revolution is upon us."* And he asked: *"Are we to object to the assumption of power by the workers, who may for the time be in the minority, because the minds of the workers have been warped and corrupted by capitalist teachings?"* Alexander Trachtenberg, another leader, went further than Glassberg, and declared: *"We are in the period of the social revolution."*

The Socialist party in 1917 at its St. Louis convention officially admitted that a political victory cannot be hoped for, and called "upon all workers to unite, to strike as they vote and to vote as they strike—all against the master class." "Only through this combination of our powers can we establish the cooperative commonwealth." Mr. Hillquit stated in his keynote speech at the last convention: "We have nothing to retract, nothing to apologize for in connection with our stand in recent years."

Is the Labor Problem Unsolvable?

AN AFFIRMATIVE ANSWER ENDORSING KANSAS LAW INSPIRED BY GOMPERS--ALLEN DEBATE

By ELMER T. PETERSON

(Associate Editor "Wichita Beacon," of which Gov. Allen is Editor.)

ELMER T. PETERSON

"IS the labor problem unsolvable?"

This question, interestingly discussed in a recent number of THE NATIONAL CIVIC FEDERATION REVIEW, is accompanied by a good-natured hint that Governor Allen's Industrial Court is a "nickle-in-the-slot" solution. The treatment of the question calls for some comment.

The writer has followed the work of the REVIEW with the greatest interest and has agreed with practically all of it, especially that which concerns Bolshevism. It is that very agreement that causes the writer to espouse the Industrial Court idea. The resort to industrial courts, to his mind, is the fundamental force that will turn democracy into its proper channels and free it from the spell of plausible direct actionists who now have in mind the setting up of an invisible economic government within the shell of our present political government.

The history of America and its great men—its prophets—is full of warnings against the invisible tyrannies of organized groups who use the precious principle of co-operation, not to benefit the general public, but to benefit their own special interests. Washington, in his farewell address, warned the people against the despotism of "artful and enterprising minorities" and pictured, with almost uncanny foresight, the very condition that now threatens the world's democracies.

The *London Times* in a recent editorial regarding the syndicalist railroad troubles in France, said:

> "It is the fundamental issue for all modern democracies. Is the majority to govern or not? If it is, the people everywhere must see that the responsible executive (meaning government in this case) shall govern and nobody else. . . . A hundred citizens organized in this or that corporation have no better constitutional way than a hundred men who are not organized. To attempt to obtain it against the will of an unorganized majority by virtue of their organization . . . is a tyrannical abuse. Organizations of the kind have shown a growing pretension to substitute themselves for constitutional Governments, or to dictate to those Governments the policy they are to pursue. They are threatening to become parasitic governments themselves, eating into the very essence of democratic rule."

The writer does not wish to be misunderstood. He comes from the ranks of labor himself and does not believe that even a small proportion of the laboring men of America believe in government by direct action. But there is every reason to believe that many of the labor leaders, and even Mr. Gompers himself, are becoming permeated with the unhealthy germ, born of power, which generates direct action government.

In the debate with Governor Allen Mr. Gompers inadvertently betrayed the fact that he has a strong leaning toward that use of the strike which has no place in American life. He spoke of the German political strike, saying that the German workers checkmated Von Kapp's imperialistic designs by declaring a general strike. Possibly that was justified in turbulent Germany, with its unstable hair-trigger government. He found fault with the Kansas law on the ground that it would prevent such a general strike by the workers called to prevent a change in government. In plain words, he was defending the use of the strike as a political weapon. That, of course, is one of the main features of I. W. W.ism and Bolshevism. In America the people have a better means of working their will than by means of economic pressure. This is not Germany. Under our form of government there can be no conceivable development that would justify the use of a general strike as a political weapon.

The only kind of a strike prohibited by the Kansas law is the strike whose purpose is to restrict or stop production—in other words, the sabotage kind of a strike. The Kansas law certainly does not prohibit a man from quitting work. Your article says that Mr. Gompers laid the groundwork for a forcible, fundamental argument against compulsory arbitration or the attempt to make a man work against his will, and that this left Governor Allen "with not a leg to stand on." This statement shows a complete misunderstanding and misconception of the Kansas law, for this law does not in any degree attempt to make a man work against his will, as a microscopic examination will demonstrate. Neither does it provide for compulsory arbitration. Mr. Gompers simply set up a straw man and did not hit the Kansas law at all.

Your article says that there were 12,000 men on a strike in a Kansas basic industry at the time of the debate, quoting Mr. Gompers, but you failed to attach Governor Allen's very pertinent rejoinder that according to Alex Howat, president of the union which was under discussion in this connection, had specifically stated that there was no strike at all. It was not to be expected or desired that this law was to keep men from quitting work for legitimate reasons. There have been cases in the mines where large bodies of workers have knocked off work for a day or two. There have been cases where men refused to work until certain demands with regard to the price of explosives were met. The Kansas court has approached such cases wisely and tactfully and has vindicated the real purpose of the law, which is to distinguish between legitimate quitting of work and the syndicalistic conspiracy to hinder or stop production. Every one knows that in the interpretation of law the matter of intent is a very important guiding principle, and there is no reason why this principle may not be applied in industrial as well as in civil disputes.

The citing of the 12,000 men striking is a peculiar example of inconsistency, by the way. In one breath Mr. Gompers condemns the law for stopping strikes and in another breath he ridicules it because it doesn't stop strikes, forsooth.

The Kansas law is not like the New Zealand, Canadian or Australian laws, as Governor Allen explained in the debate. The Kansas law does not provide for compulsory arbitration. What it does, in essentials, is this:

It takes the irrefutable ground that in the four vital industries of transportation, fuel, food and clothing production, the rights of the public are paramount and must be respected by the two economic instruments—capital and labor. The Kansas law says that the public, through its only stable recourse—the government—must see to it that no industrial disputes interfere with the flow of the necessary commodities. It does not recognize the principle of arbitration tribunals because such tribunals are almost invariably composed, in the major part, of special interests. The industrial decision, therefore, is not an arbitration award, arrived at by dickering or compromise, probably not worth the paper it is written upon, neither is it a collective bargain, or commercial transaction, as provided by the President's Industrial Conference scheme, but a just and impartial decree of the government itself, which may not be altered except by recourse to the usual processes of law. To insure fair play to the poor worker, he is enabled to conduct his case without a penny's expense to himself.

Getting down to the fundamental issue, it must be patent to every watchful observer that this thing we call organization has obtained a remarkable grip on American life. Gradually and imperceptibly the two economic forces—labor and capital—have encroached upon the unalienable rights of the people, the rights of life, liberty and the pursuit of happiness. Capital was the first offender, for it was more susceptible to combination, and the anti-trust laws were the effort to curb this form of economic pressure. Now labor has brought organization to the point where it is able to get strangle-hold upon the public. Again the public must act or become the helpless serfs of economic forces.

Economic government is the ideal of Lenin. He takes the materialistic stand that economic determinism is the only proper motive in government.

Economic government usually means government by a minority. The I. W. W. formula, which is the same as that of the Bolsheviki, is "Pressure rather than Participation," and it is accompanied by a repudiation of the ballot box.

Political government means government by the majority, regardless of class or occupation. It acknowledges no autocracy of wealth, position, occupation or organization. Surely government may guarantee life and safety to its people.

There is the issue. The air is full of warnings. The age of materialism is upon us and the struggle for selfish advancement is getting ferocious. Organization, advanced by specialization, invention and other modern developments, has set up an invisible government. The only way the people have of retrieving their political power and staving off economic pressure is to erect governmental tribunals with power to prevent economic strangulation, no matter from which direction it comes. Those tribunals can have the power of affecting conciliation and a better understanding. The Kansas court goes far in that direction. They can be the intermediary between the clashing and hostile camps. "The only remedy proposed by Mr. Gompers for war is more war," says Governor Allen. There is a better way.

Make Timely Expose of Socialism

THE A. B. C. OF SOVIETISM

> "What everybody wants to know is not what the Bolshevists *claim* to stand *for*, nor even what they honestly think they stand *for*, but what they actually do stand for—according to a fair summary of their own acknowledged words and deeds."

Thus prefacing his volume, "Sovietism—the A B C of Russian Bolshevism," (E. P. Dutton & Co., New York, Publishers; price $2.00) William English Walling proceeds to give this information, to answer these questions, and the evidence gathered and coordinated is from the Bolshevist leaders and authorities themselves.

In view of the popular confusion on this subject, Mr. Walling's book meets an urgent need and is of unprecedented educational value.

Mr. Walling shows that the Bolsheviki are not, and do not claim to be, a political party, representing the majority, but are a sect, a minority, who have seized power and hold Russia in subjection by an admitted reign of terror. He quotes Karl Radek, one of the most influential Bolsheviki, as admitting: "The claim made by some of our people, that the majority of the Russian people favor the Soviet government, is not true. The peasants are against the Soviet government." Various pro-Bolshevist sympathizers, such as Raymond Robins, have declared that the Soviet autocracy represents the will of the majority of the Russian masses and have urged recognition of the Bolshevist régime as a representative Russian government. Mr. Walling aptly shows that "Bolshevism or Sovietism is by no means a Russian or Slavic movement." He says: "It is not 'a natural expression of the Slavic genius,' nor 'the traditional Russian idea of democracy,' as its American apologists have alleged. . . Lenine himself says the idea was taken in part from the Paris Cummune, in part from the American revolutionary Socialist, Daniel De Leon. . . Three-fourths of the self-chosen leaders of the Soviets, members of a non-Slavic race (which they do not, however, truthfully represent) have a German dialect as their mother tongue."

It would be impossible in a review to summarize Mr. Walling's book, but the subject chapters will indicate the comprehensiveness of the volume. These chapters take up and discuss the following: "What is the Chief Soviet Weapon?" "To What Is Their Power Due?" "Can the Soviets Win Back the People?" "Are the Bolsheviki Reforming?" Mr. Walling discusses "The pro-Bolshevists" and the Soviet propaganda in countries other than Russia. He demonstrates that the Soviet autocracy aims at world-wide dictatorship; that the methods proposed are violent and revolutionary; and that they have sought to incite American workmen to revolt. He shows, too, that the American Socialist party, going the way of the Italian Socialists and going even further than "the half way house of the French Socialists" have gone over to Bolshevism.

In dealing with the attitude of the Soviet government toward religion, Mr. Walling corroborates the volume by Mrs. Avery and Mr. Goldstein, and proves by their own decrees and official statements that they have worked out a vast, scientific campaign for the extirpation of religion. The Soviet policy on religion was formulated at the Eighth Communist Congress and, as expressed by that Congress, aims at "the broadest possible scientific and anti-religious propaganda." As declared by Bukharin, a leading authority and high official of the Bolsheviki: "Religion and communism do not go together either in theory or in practice. Between the precepts of communism and those of the Christian religion there is an impassible barrier."

SOCIALISM VS. CIVILIZATION

Mr. Boris Brasol's book, "Socialism *vs.* Civilization," (Charles Scribner's Sons, publishers; Price $2.00) defines modern socialism, analyses its philosophy and objects, and shows conclusively that in practice it is impossible and impractical. Mr. Brasol's volume, with the two other volumes here reviewed, should be in every public and private library in America. It might well be read by all school teachers and would be an admirable text book in colleges. Mr. Brasol has done a great service in dispelling the popular confusion which exists concerning Socialism, showing that every brand and variety, despite their differences as to tactics, are one in their philosophy and object.

Mr. Brasol expounds the theory of Marx and modern Socialism, whose keynote is the class struggle. He shows the inconsistencies and fallacies of the theory and program, including the theory of surplus value, and very clearly explains the difference between equality of labor and equality of opportunity. "Leonardo da Vinci, in painting his 'Gioconda,'" says Mr. Brasol, "presented to the world a masterpiece of sublime quality. Let us assume that it took one hundred hours' work for him to complete this picture. Now, according to the Marxian theory, Leonardo ought to have received for his work the same remuneration as would be given to an ignorant house painter who also spent one hundred hours in painting a wall. This is the kind of equality which Marx advocated. Of course, the more recent Socialists had to abandon the Marxian conception of equality. They admit now, although in a very vague manner, that the quantity of work delivered does not determine the amount of remuneration." Mr. Brasol truly says equality of opportunity is the only kind of equality that can be advocated. The Socialist philosophy denies all spiritual incentive and inspiration in human endeavor, and is absolutely materialistic. It is the work of the hands, and not the work of the brain, that actually counts. Socialism, denying the religion of the spirit, is the religion of the belly.

Mr. Brasol shows how Socialism has worked out in Russia, where it has destroyed industry and killed all creative intellectual effort. Despite that terrible object lesson, Socialist propaganda has increased in the United States and Europe. "Disgraceful as it may seem, nevertheless it is true," says Mr. Brasol, "that Bolshevist agents, enjoying the full protection of the law in civilized countries—such as the United States, Great Britain, Sweden and Norway—have endeavored in all those countries to carry out venomous propaganda, aiming at the overthrow of those very governments which extended to them their hospitality. Thus, Great Britain for many months tolerated the disloyal activities of the so-called Bolshevist Ambassador, Mr. Litvinoff, né Finkelstein. It required the combined pressure of British public opinion to have Mr. Finkelstein finally expelled from Great Britain.

> "In the United States Mr. Trotzky's agents, Nuorteva, né Neuberger, and his German friend, Ludwig C. A. K. Martens, are keeping up their disloyal propaganda, notwithstanding the fact that a Senatorial Committee of the State of New York has exposed the treacherous and dangerous features of their work. These and others of their kind, under alleged names and disguised nationalities, are preaching day by day Marxian theories and actual revolutionary practice."

Mr. Brasol has written a valuable work, replete with constructive suggestions, which we recommend to all Americans who desire to understand, so they may combat, the menace that confronts us.

"The Mountain Labored And—"

A CONSIDERATION OF GIGANTIC CEREBRATION ON PART OF THE "LIBERALS" ILLUMINATI

By T. EVERETT HARRÉ

THE *New Republic* and the *Nation* during a period of a year and a half were often the subjects of serious indictments in THE NATIONAL CIVIC FEDERATION REVIEW. These indictments were of a grave character. In the opinion of many people they called for an answer. Silence meant admission; yet for eighteen months *The New Republic* and the *Nation* were silent. At last, however, after a period in which there was ample time to assemble all evidence in rebuttal and to prepare an adequate plea of self-defense, the two journals have made their answer. How frankly, courageously, adequately, with what manly directness, this answer is made will be manifest.

In order that the crushing effect of these mighty blows of intellectual pugilism may be fully appreciated, let us consider briefly the charges which have been made against these publications—charges which are now, presumably, finally disproved, wiped out, disposed of.

These journals were charged with un-Americanism, if not disloyalty, during the war. They were charged with pro-Germanism. We sought to show—and cited evidence—that during the war they engaged in propaganda of defeatism, and advocated a premature pro-German peace; that when Germany was finally defeated, they defamed the Allies and sought to estrange us from the nations with whom we had fought; that they agitated for a peace favorable to Germany and that when the Versailles treaty was finally formulated they abandoned themselves to a Vitus dance of frothing rage; that they championed the Bolshevik autocracy, denied or condoned its excesses and sought to promote revolutionary radicalism in the United States. The charges made were not pleasant; in fact, they were ugly. Pretending to influence President Wilson's policies in the days when its editors and satellities had the entrée to high officials in Washington, *The New Republic*, finding that its Judas-counsels did not prevail in Paris, later turned like a cur upon the master it had claimed in hydrophobic viciousness. We indicated that *The New Republic* and its quill-driving satellities were not "red," but only "yellow."

An article in one issue of the REVIEW was devoted to the editor of the journal, Mr. Herbert Croly. We did something remarkable in this article. We performed a miracle. We raised a book of Mr. Croly's from the dead. Ordinarily, this might have been a cause of an unsuccessful author's gratitude. We do not know whether this was so in Mr. Croly's case.

Just six weeks after the United States entered the war, in its issue of May 19, 1917, *The New Republic* published an editorial that was, in the opinion of many people, perilously akin to the same propaganda which caused Bolo Pasha to be executed for treason in France. That editorial sought to make victory over Germany appear hopeless. *The New Republic* said:

> There can be no victory over Germany except as a consequence of as complete an organization of the fighting power of the United States as that which has taken place in France and Great Britain. . . The deadlock could be broken only by the despatch of a huge American army to Europe—one so large that it could not be recruited, equipped and trained until the summer of 1919. Even then it might be impossible to transport it to Europe. . . It is an appalling outlook, and it will go ill with the men responsible for the government which brings consequences of this kind upon the American people. The result would almost certainly be a revolution in America far more bloody and drastic than the revolution in Russia. A war conducted until 1920 on the scale required by a military decision might bring peace with victory, but it would also bring victory with suicide.

It seemed to us that perhaps the opposition of *The New Republic* toward carrying on the war against Germany to a victorious conclusion might be explained somewhat in the light of a past and forgotten book by Mr. Croly, published in 1909, entitled "The Promise of American Life." We found, according to this book, that Mr. Croly, who was against carrying on the war to a victorious conclusion in 1917, had in 1909 justified war, declaring war to be "useful," saying, "These wars, when they come, should . . . be fought to accomplish a desirable purpose and should be decisive in result." The man who campaigned in 1917 for an "indecisive" end to the war against Germany, in 1909 was opposed even to disarmament, and moreover, disparaged England and France while he glorified Germany, justified Germany's part in the Franco-Prussian war and represented the German government as being as representative as that of the United States. To this indictment Mr. Croly made no reply.

In another article we dealt with an associate editor of *The New Republic*, Walter Weyl, and we proved him, out of his own mouth, an advocate of a pro-German peace, bitterly anti-Ally, an "internationalist" of the yellow variety, a spokesman of the "class war" intrigue, a vicious, sneering, ignoble and petty calumniator of the nations who were waging their heroic struggle against German imperialism. To this there was no come-back.

We sought to expose, from its mass of academic verbiage, the true character and intent of *The New Republic*, and the *Nation* as well, so that well-meaning but simple-minded and perhaps sentimental folk might not be deceived by the pretentious poseurs, intellectual adolescents, and "little Trotzkys" who adroitly and speciously made their appeal to human sentiment or sentimentality, and often indeed to the higher human qualities and emotions. There was a time when it seemed *The New Republic* did have influence in certain high circles. One editor, whose "Americanism" would have found safer expression in the work of army "kitchen police," was taken to Europe on a high mission. His activities and associates, some people say, would make interesting reading. Other editors, whose cordial reception in Moscow or Berlin might have been understandable, were actually received at departments in Washington. Strange as this was, even stranger things might yet be told. However, *The New Republic* "diplomat of the new school" was sent back from Europe "without honors," and others went to their fate unheralded and unsung. Even the Washington patron of this breed, the high official whose name suggests sauer-kraut, has passed into innocuous desuetude, where he can only lend his unsavory name to an attack on the Department of Justice.

And now come the come-backs!

In answer to the charge that *The New Republic* was, and is for that matter, un-American and pro-Bolshevist; that it was anti-Ally and advocated a pro-German peace that in the crucial days of the war it was 'defeatist," and that its editor was "militaristic" in 1909, when Germany was strong, and pacifist in 1917 when Germany faced defeat, *The New Republic*—in its issue of July 28, 1920—replies by saying:

"Sooner or later Mr. Ralph Easley was bound to come a cropper. . . . He was a moving spirit in the poisonous Lusk agitation and the expulsions at Albany. He is to the cause of decent conservatism what a terrorist is to decent liberalism."

The New Republic further charges Mr. Easley with "a private system of espionage, and an intrigue to discredit and obstruct the industrial inquiries of the Interchurch World Movement."

To say that Mr. Easley "was bound to come a cropper" is of course to wipe off the slate *The New Republic's* putrescent war record. To charge Mr. Easley with being "a moving spirit" in the investigations of the New York legislature (which, incidentally, is absolutely unfounded) and to imply "an intrigue" on the part of Mr. Easley against the industrial enquiries of the Interchurch World Movement (another absolute falsehood) is to self-exonerate itself of any and all efforts to let Germany out of the war victorious or to turn civilization over to Bolshevism. Mr. Easley and the REVIEW, of which he is editor, in a twenty-four-line editorial, are exterminated as ruthlessly as an annoying mosquito is crushed on a lily-white wrist.

Likewise, with the *Nation*.

In utter repudiation of the charges that Mr. Oswald Garrison Villard justified the sinking of the "Lusitania," that he opposed America's going to war against Germany, that he campaigned for a premature pro-German peace, that he was pro-German and anti-Ally, and later pro-Bolshevik, Mr. Villard editorially, and after eighteen months, raises the question whether the labor members will remain officers of The National Civic Federation! Mr. Villard explains away all the charges against his loyalty, wipes out all the charges of pro-Germanism and Bolshevism, by charging Mr. Easley with communicating "to an official of the United States Steel Corporation an advance copy of a report which a committee of the Federation had had prepared regarding certain liberals of the Interchurch World Movement." It does not matter, of course, that Mr. Easley never did communicate "to an official of the United States Steel Corporation" such a report. It does not matter that Mr. Easley had nothing, directly or indirectly, to do with alleged attempt to "hold back" the Interchurch report on the steel strike. The past record of the *Nation*, all its infamous Hunnish and Bolshevist propaganda, is cleared away by the awful and sinister implication: "Some day we may learn what share the Federation played in the rumored proposal to hold back the Interchurch report on the steel strike and in the subsequent collapse of the Interchurch Movement."

Gargantuan cerebrums have been at work. As with the mountain, "A mountain," said Phaedrus some nineteen hundred and twelve years ago, "was in labor, sending forth dreadful groans, and there was in the region the highest expectations." The travail, while disappointing, has not been in vain, and history and natural history are not without parallels.

Life is enlivened by a knowledge of psychology and a sense of humor. Goliath was a mighty man in his day, and yet "the poor beetle that we tread upon finds a pang as great as when a giant dies." A rat will turn finally when caught in the corner. And as for the diminutive worm, its classic process is described in deathless adage.

only be permitted but encouraged to join in co-operative association to reap the just measure of reward merited by their arduous toil. Let us facilitate co-operation to insure against the risks attending agriculture, which the urban world so little understands, and a like co-operation to market their products as directly as possible with the consumer in the interests of all. Upon such association and co-operation should be laid only such restrictions as will prevent arbitrary control of our food supply and the fixing of extortionate prices upon it.

Our platform is an earnest pledge of renewed concern for this most essential and elemental industry and in both appreciation and interest we pledge effective expression in law and practice. We will hail that co-operation which again will make profitable and desirable the ownership and operation of comparatively small farms intensively cultivated and which will facilitate the caring for the products of farm and orchard without the lamentable waste under present conditions.

GOVERNOR COX'S SPEECH

GOVERNOR COX, in his speech accepting the Democratic nomination for President, dealt with labor and agriculture as follows:

Disputes between labor and capital are inevitable. The disposition to gain the best bargain possible characterizes the whole field of exchange, whether it be product for product or labor for money. Its strikes are prolonged—public opinion always settles them. Public opinion should determine results in America. Public opinion is the most interesting characteristic of a democracy, and it is the real safety valve to the institution of a free government. It may at times be necessary for the Government to inquire into the facts of a tie-up, but facts, and not conclusions, should be submitted.

The determining form of unprejudiced thought will do the rest. During this process, governmental agencies must give a vigilant eye to the protection of life and property, and maintain firmness but absolute impartiality. This is always the real test, but if official conduct combines courage and fairness our governmental institutions come out of these affairs untarnished by distrust.

SOME PRINCIPLES OF LABOR

Morals cannot easily be produced by statute. The writ of injunction should not be abused. Intended as a safeguard to person and property, it could easily by abuse cease to be the protective device it was intended to be.

Capital develops into large units without violence to public sentiment or injury to public interest—the same principle should not be denied to labor. Collective bargaining through the means of representatives selected by the employer and employee respectively will be helpful rather than harmful to the general interest. Besides, there is no ethical objection that can be raised to it.

We should not, by law, abridge a man's right either to labor or to quit his employment. However, neither labor nor capital should at any time or in any circumstances take action that would put in jeopardy the public welfare.

We need a definite and precise statement of policy as to what business men and workingmen may do and may not do by way of combination and collective action. The law is now so nebulous that it almost turns upon the economic predilections of judge or jury. This does not make for confidence in the courts nor respect for the laws, nor for a healthy activity in production and distribution. There surely will be found ways by which co-operation may be encouraged without the destruction of enterprise. The rules of business should be made more certain so that on a stable basis men may move with confidence.

HELPING FARMER AND CONSUMER

Agriculture is but another form of industry. In fact, it is the basis of industry because upon it depends the food supply. The drift from countryside into the city carries disquieting portents. If our growth in manufacturing in the next few years holds its present momentum, it will be necessary for America to import foodstuffs. It therefore devolves upon government, through intensive scientific co-operation, to help in maintaining as nearly as possible the existing balance between food production and consumption. Farming will not inspire individual effort unless profits, all things considered, are equal to those in other activities.

The price the consumer pays for foodstuffs is no indication of what the producer receives. There are too many turnovers between the two. Society and Government, particularly local and State, have been remiss in not modernizing local marketing facilities. Municipalities must in large measure interest themselves in, if not directly control, community markets. This is a matter of such importance that the Federal Government can profitably expend money and effort in helping to evolve methods and to show their virtues.

The farmer raises his crop, and the price which he receives is determined by supply and demand. His products in beef and pork and produce pass into cold storage, and ordinarily when they reach the consumer the law of supply and demand does not obtain.

The preservation of foodstuffs by cold storage is a boon to humanity, and it should be encouraged. However, the time has come for its vigilant regulation and inasmuch as it becomes a part of interstate commerce, the responsibility is with the Federal Government. Supplies are gathered in from the farm in times of plenty. They can easily be fed out to the consumer in such manner as to keep the demand in excess of that part of the supply which is released from storage. This is an unfair practice and should be stopped. Besides, there should be a time limit beyond which perishable foodstuffs should not be stored.

FOR FARMERS IN EXECUTIVE POSTS

Every successful modern business enterprise has its purchasing, producing and selling departments. The farmer has maintained only one, the producing department. It is not only fair that he be enabled both to purchase and to sell advantageously, but it is absolutely necessary because he has become a competitor with the manufacturer for labor. He has been unable to compete in the past and his help in consequence has been insufficient. Therefore the right of co-operative purchasing and selling, in the modern view, should be removed from all question.

Agricultural thought has not been sufficiently represented in affairs of government. Many of the branches of the Government which deal remotely or directly with the soil and its problems and its possibilities would be more valuable to the general welfare if the practical experience of the farmer were an element in their administration.

To be specific, the Interstate Commerce Commission, the Federal Reserve Board, the Federal Trade Commission and the United States Tariff Commission are administered by business men. Does any one contribute more to the making and success of railroads than the farmer or to the creation and prosperity of the banks, or to the stability of manufacturing and trade units, or to the agencies interested in exporting?

Catholic "Social Reconstruction Program" Analyzed

(Continued from page 6)

> workers into a distinct and dependent class, that offends against their domestic privacy and independence, or that threatens individual self-reliance and self-respect, should not be tolerated. The ideal to be kept in mind is a condition in which all the workers would themselves have the income and the responsibility of providing for all the needs and contingencies of life, both present and future. Hence all forms of State insurance should be regarded as merely a lesser evil, and should be so organized and administered as to hasten the coming of the normal condition."

In the revised foreword to the pamphlet from which the foregoing excerpt is quoted, it is said that: "Its practical applications are of course subject to discussion, but all its essential declarations are based upon the principles of justice and of charity that have always been held and taught by the Catholic Church, while its practical proposals are merely an adaptation of those principles." But that does not mean that its practical proposals are an *authoritative* adaptation of those principles and that the efficacy of such proposals as practical means to the ends sought is unquestionable. The objectives of such proposals may be unquestionable; but the practical means proposed for attaining those objectives most certainly are not. The "device of insurance" is a practical device; and for what purposes and under what conditions it can be used efficaciously, and for what purposes and under what conditions it cannot, are essentially practical questions, to be decided by human experience and not by ethical or religious principles. In the excerpt it seems to be assumed that the device of insurance, like Aladdin's lamp, can do anything and everything intended by it and exactly as intended. If that assumption were true, the plan of insurance outlined in the excerpt would be well worthy of consideration. Such assumption, however, is far from true.

Viewed in the light of experience the social insurance proposal of the National Catholic War Council, outlined in this excerpt, is seriously at fault in ignoring the functions, practical limitations and technical requirements of insurance.

Contrary to what seems to be implied in that excerpt, it is the self-sufficient worker, whose earnings are high enough to make possible the amount of saving necessary to protect himself and his family against the risks of illness, invalidity, unemployment and old-age, who particularly "stands in need of the device of insurance." For insurance is a method of using part of his earnings most efficaciously to provide such protection. But it is not *state* insurance that he needs. State insurance, as acknowledged in the excerpt, is an evil; and other insurance, which is not an evil, is obtainable. Undoubtedly industry ought to insure all its workers against the injuries it causes. That duty is being enforced through workmen's compensation laws. Undoubtedly industry, through employers, ought to assist all its workers to secure for themselves good insurance against other misfortunes. That duty is fast coming to be more and more recognized and fulfilled. And undoubtedly the state ought to regulate insurance so far as is needed to protect all insured workers against impositions and unsound finance. That duty is being generally fulfilled. Moreover, it may possibly be expedient for the state, by subsidies or other assistance, to promote among the people moderate insurance against those of the misfortunes above mentioned for which industry is not to be held responsible. But further than this, there is every reason to believe, the state ought not to interfere directly with the insurance of the self-sufficient workers. And in America the self-sufficient include not only a large majority of the native born white workers, who earn or are able to earn a sufficiency to maintain a high standard of living, but also a large proportion of the immigrants and negroes, who are rising toward that standard, but who, for the time being, are able to live in decency and comfort and to accumulate savings on lower but accustomed levels.

But the excerpt quoted seems to imply that, so long as *some* of the workers obtain less than living wages, *all* of them unquestionably ought to be subjected to state provided insurance. If such be the proper construction of the excerpt—and one of the difficulties in criticising that loose and ambiguous pronouncement is to determine what it really means,—we might as well stop right here. It would be absurd to lay it down as unquestionable that the same political medicine ought to be applied to the sick and the well alike—that the front ranks in the development of self-providence among the workers ought to be held back and kept in paternalistic tutelage until the tail-enders can be brought up into line. Therefore it is fairer to dismiss that construction and to proceed upon the hypothesis that it was intended in this pronouncement to prescribe state insurance only for the lowly paid.

The lowly paid—*i. e.* those among our wage workers who do not obtain a sufficiency to provide for themselves—include specifically the subnormal, cripples, chronic invalids, shirkers, tramps, persons of bad habits, beginners, recent immigrants, the untrained, the out-of-place (who cling to employments or neighborhoods wherein their labor is not most needed) and the exploited. For their ills it is doubtful whether the "device of insurance" is at all an appropriate remedy. They stand in need, variously, of prevention, correction, charity or fair wages. Neither prevention, correction nor charity is a true function of insurance. And while free ("non-contributory") or subsidized state insurance is a palliative for unfairly low wages, it is certainly not a cure, but tends rather to perpetuate the evil it palliates. Probably the greatest poverty in America exists among the negroes; and it would be hopeless to look to state insurance for assistance in solving the negro problem.

But the excerpt under criticism lays it down positively that these classes of workers, at least, ought to be insured against sickness, invalidity, old age and unemployment, [presumptively in amounts sufficient for a decent existence], by the state, at the expense of whatsoever industry may employ them, without separating them into a distinct and dependent class, without offending against their domestic privacy and independence, without threatening their individual self-reliance and self-respect, with the insurance "so organized and administered as to hasten the coming of the normal condition" when all wage workers shall be able to provide for themselves. But thus to postulate what *ought* to be done before making sure that it *can* be done is to reverse the rational order. We ought first to ascertain, in the light of human experience, what can be done, and then apply our ethical principles to determine what ought to be done.

Experience holds out no hope that a plan of state insurance can be devised that will comply with all the requirements above specified. On the contrary experience indicates that:—

It is impracticable to "insure" against misfortunes, in amounts sufficient for a decent existence, those among the workers who do not earn such a sufficiency.

It is impracticable for the state to insure any of the working people, at the expense of others and regardless of responsibility for causes, without separating the insured into a "distinct and dependent class" or without threatening their "individual self-reliance and self-respect".

It is impracticable so to insure any of the working people, with the insurance "so organized and administered as to hasten the coming of the normal condition."

It is impracticable so to insure workers, generally and without "selection of risks", save upon conditions that would "offend against their domestic privacy and independence."

Consequently, as a practical proposal, the social insurance program outlined in this excerpt so far from commanding unquestioning acceptance, deserves rather to be condemned as hopelessly visionary and impracticable.

In final analysis, indeed, that program is a day-dream—an aspiration—and not at all a practical proposal. In actual practice misfortunes can be insured against only upon definite terms and conditions. Certainly it would be disastrous for the state to attempt to insure shirkers *unconditionally* against unemployment or workers with bad habits *unconditionally* against the sicknesses and infirmities resulting from such habits. Depending upon its terms and conditions, social insurance may propagate fraud, idleness, improvidence, bad habits and the very misfortunes it is intended to relieve, and may operate as an instrumentality for the demoralization of the weak and the spoliation of the industrious and provident. Yet in the excerpt under criticism the terms and conditions of the proposed insurance are left entirely unformulated. We are simply told what such insurance must do and what it must not do, without a single specification of methods to effect the former and avoid the latter. In effect that states a problem, but offers no solution of the problem. Until the National Catholic War Council formulates all the vital features of its proposed insurance and shows that, in all human probability, the insurance, *as so formulated,* would not be a breeder of social evils, an incentive to fraud and vice or an instrumentality for spoliation, but, on the contrary, all things considered, would be a means for social betterment, its proposal belongs in the realm of pure abstractions, and for practical purposes certainly does not deserve serious consideration, much less command acceptance, by prudent citizens of any religious faith. It is not unethical but on the contrary most ethical to mistrust vague and glittering social panaceas, even when proposed by men of the most correct principles and with the highest ideals. Often the loftier the ideal the more pathetically inadequate the performance.

This pronouncement by the National Catholic War Council has been quite widely hailed as an endorsement by the Catholic Church, not only of state insurance in the abstract, but also of some recently proposed compulsory insurance measures in the concrete. The fact that it is open to such misconstruction has done considerable harm. But, to be exact, none of the measures referred to, and none of the European social insurance systems after which those measures were modeled, complies with the conditions laid down by the National Catholic War Council in the excerpt above quoted. In all of those measures, and under all the European state insurance systems, a contribution would be or is exacted from the insured worker, even though his wages are insufficient to provide for the immediate needs of himself and his family; whereas in the excerpt it is laid down that there must be no contribution exacted in such cases. In all of those measures, and under all the European state insurance systems except one, the workers covered would be or are separated into "a distinct and dependent class"; whereas in the excerpt it is laid down that they must not be so separated. In some of those measures, and under the majority of the European state insurance systems, the state, from its general revenues, would or does contribute heavily to the insurance, its contributions being promised permanently and the tendency being repeatedly to increase them; whereas in the excerpt it is laid down that "any contribution to the insurance from the general revenues of the state should be only slight and tem-

(Continued on page 22)

Socialism Unmasked

(Continued from page 8)

upreme task confronting the Socialist party of 1merica:"

> To win the American workers from their ineffective and demoralizing leadership, to educate them to an enlightened understanding of their own class interests, and *to train and assist them to organize politically and industrially on class lines in order to effect their emancipation*—THAT IS THE SUPREME TASK CONFRONTING THE SOCIALIST PARTY OF AMERICA.
>
> To this great task, without deviation or compromise, we pledge all our energies and resources.

While the Socialist party at its recent convention in New York, for obvious reasons of expediency, took occasion in its Declaration of Principles, to emphasize its political character, "its purpose . . . to secure a majority in Congress and in every state legislature," et cetera, it specified:

> The Socialist transformation cannot be successfully accomplished by political victories alone.

Hypocritically declaring, for obvious opportunist reasons, that "the Socialist party does not intend to interfere in the internal affairs of labor unions," the Declaration of Principles went on to declare:

> The Socialists favor the organization of workers along the lines of industrial unionism in the closest cooperation as one organized working class army.

"One organized working class army" is the plan laid down by the Moscow Internationale, adopted by the Socialist party at its Chicago Emergency convention, and reaffirmed at its convention last May. It is the "One Big Union," and its proposed weapon is industrial action.

> THE THIRD INTERNATIONALE IS THE INTERNATIONALE OF OPEN MASS ACTION, OF THE REVOLUTIONARY REALIZATION, THE INTERNATIONALE OF DEEDS. . . .

The Manifesto of the Third Internationale concludes:

> Proletarians of all lands! In the war against imperialistic barbarity, against the monarchy, against the privileged classes, against the bourgeois state and bourgeois property, against all forms and varieties of social and national oppression—Unite!
>
> Under the standard of the workingmen's councils, under the banner of the Third Internationale, in the revolutionary struggle for power and the dictatorship of the proletariat, proletarians of all countries—Unite!

The Governing Rules of the Third Communist Internationale conclude:

> LONG LIVE THE INTERNATIONAL REPUBLIC OF THE PROLETARIAN COUNCILS.

The Chicago Manifesto of the Socialist party of America concludes:

> LONG LIVE THE INTERNATIONAL SOCIALIST REVOLUTION, THE ONLY HOPE OF THE SUFFERING WORLD.

What conclusion must be drawn from this evidence?

If any confusion exists as to what the Socialists mean by "industrial" or "mass action," that may be cleared by the testimony of Socialist leaders themselves. If any hazy notion exists that the Socialist party is not committed to a program of force and violence that also may be dispelled by their own testimony. At the investigation conducted by the Judiciary Committee of the New York Legislature into the eligibility of the five suspended Socialist assemblymen-elect, Algernon Lee, educational director of the Rand School, treasurer of the New York State Committee and secretary of the New York County committee of the Socialist party, under cross examination by Martin Conboy, was asked:

"Are strikes one of the means of mass action which the Socialist party contemplates the use of?"

Mr. Lee answered:

"On occasions where they are suitable for the purposes of the working-class, yes, sir."

Asked whether the general strike is not part of the program of the Socialist party in the United States to back up political action, Lee admitted:

"If the circumstances should exist, which made that necessary, I take that it would be construed so."

Victor L. Berger, now under sentence for violation of the Espionage act, at the national convention of the Socialist party in 1908, declared:

"I have heard it pleaded many a time right in our own meetings by speakers that come to our meetings that the only salvation for the proletariat of America is direct action, that the ballot box is simply a humbug. Now I don't doubt that in the last analysis we must shoot."

William Bross Lloyd, who had been recently the Socialist party candidate for the United States Senate from Illinois, declared in a speech in Milwaukee on January 12, 1919:

"We want to organize, so if you want to put a piece of propaganda in the hands of everybody in Milwaukee, you can do it in three or four hours. If you want every Socialist in Milwaukee at a certain place, at a certain time, with a rifle in his hand, or a bad egg, he will be there. We want a mobilization plan and an organization for revolution."

At the Chicago convention of the Socialist party, September, 1919, according to evidence introduced at the Albany hearings, Louis Waldman, one of the suspended assemblymen, declared:

"If I knew we could sway the boys when they get guns to use them against the capitalist class I would be for universal military training."

Waldman, in a speech delivered at a meeting held November 7, 1919, to celebrate the second anniversary of the Russian Soviet Government, at Brownsville Labor Lyceum, Brooklyn, a transcript of which was entered as evidence, declared:

> "If you commemorate the birthday of the Russian revolution, if you revere your Russian comrades, if you applaud Lenine and Trotsky, if you believe in the worthiness of their cause, in the accomplishment of their work, then it is your duty to enter the Socialist movement in America, to make it like Russia is today.
>
> "We must select between two alternatives: Either Russia lives and conquers the world—not Russia conquers the world, but its ideals and philosophy worthy of the Russian government today should conquer the world—either that, or the ideals or the philosophy of Gary and Wilson and Palmer, Lloyd George and Clemenceau is to conquer the world. Between the two, for my part, and for the part of thousands of Socialists now battling in America today, we choose to stand by the ideals and philosophy and program and principles of Lenine and Trotsky as those we approve."

Waldman was never rebuked by his party for this presentation of the issues. On the contrary, when he was suspended by the New York Legislature his party defended him, and the chief counsel was Morris Hillquit. The alternative presented by him, of choosing between the ideals and philosophy of Lenine and the ideals of American democracy, are those presented by his party, and the Socialist party stands with Lenine and world revolution by violence, as against the United States. The only difference is that Hillquit and Berger, more experienced in craft and diplomacy, are usually more guarded in their utterances for public consumption.

According to a transcript of his talk at a celebration of the second anniversary of the Soviet government, at the Brownsville Labor Lyceum, November, 1919, which was read into the record, Assemblyman-elect Charles Solomon said:

"If we are going to conduct the fight, generals and lieutenants and captains are not enough, writers and speakers and agitators are not enough; we have got to have an army to fight the battle for emancipation of the working people of our country, and you are the men and you are the women who will have to enlist in that army from the ranks of a fighting army."

Declaring that the Socialists must back up their members in the New York City Board of Aldermen and in the State Legislature, Solomon continued:

"When they speak up there and when you speak down here, we must be able to tell the capitalists, the reactionaries, the politicians, the forces of corruption, that back of our words stand thousands and thousands and thousands of industrially organized workingmen and working women. You and not we must conduct this battle. You are the army."

At the recent national convention of the Socialist party, one of the New York delegates, Benjamin Glassberg, enquired why Socialists should declare that they seek to attain their goal by "orderly and constitutional methods," whereupon the above mentioned Solomon—doubtless to assuage the fears and misgivings of the general public, to whom violence and wholesale killings are abhorrent—said, reassuringly:

"We will do our best to bring about the cooperative republic with a minimum of industrial disorder."

Can it still be contended by the parlor "intellectuals," the sentimental "forward-lookers" and "Christian Socialists" that the Socialist party, despite its stand with the Third Internationale and its advocacy of industrial action as its revolutionary weapon, does not contemplate revolution by force, by violence, by actual conflict with killings? Can they possibly assume that when leaders of the movement speak of a battle they do not mean an actual battle, that when they refer to an army they do not contemplate an army armed with guns? Or if individuals, such as Berger, Lloyd, Waldman and Solomon, express such rabid sentiments, are they to be construed merely as the extreme utterances of excited zealots, who do not represent or express the party officially? On this the Socialist party has, without ambiguity or camouflage, officially expressed itself. In the War Proclamation unanimously adopted at the St. Louis convention in April, 1917, the party, in opposing war against Germany and in calling upon the workers to oppose the conduct of the war, declared itself:

> "The only struggle which would justify the workers in taking up arms is the great struggle of the working class of the world to free itself of economic exploitation."

Eugene V. Debs, the choice of the Socialist party for president in 1920, and the supreme voice and leader of the movement, just before entering prison to serve a sentence for violation of the Espionage Act, delivered before the Socialist Party of Cleveland, Ohio, on March 12, 1919, a speech which was entered at the Albany hearings as evidence.

"I am going to speak to you as a Socialist, as a revolutionist, and as a Bolshevist, if you please," said Debs.

He characterized Bolshevism, the Russian revolution, as "The beginning of the end of capitalism and the end of the beginning of Socialism," and declared: "Because we say this they are going to put us in jail. With every drop in my veins, I despise their laws and I defy them. . . Is there a calumny which they have not circulated about Lenine and Trotsky? . . . They are fighting for your liberty, for you, if you only knew it, and I am only too glad to pay my tribute to those men I love."

Did the leader and perpetual candidate for president of the Socialist party at all deplore the violence, terrorism and bloodshed of the Bolshevist revolution? He said:

"We are on the eve of tremendous developments. The world before your eyes is being destroyed and recreated. Russia is making a beginning, the Soviet is just a sample. They have shed some blood, they have made some mistakes, and I am glad they have."

POLITICAL ACTION A 'PIPE DREAM.'

The Socialist party of America, at its recent national convention in New York City, found it expedient to declare itself in its Declarations of Principles a political party. "It strives by means of political methods, including the action of its representatives in the legislatures and other public offices to force the enactment of such measures as will immediately benefit the workers, raise their standard of life, increase their power and stiffen their resistance to capitalist aggression. Its purpose is to secure a majority in Congress and in every state legislature, to win the principal executive and judicial offices, to become the dominant and controlling party."

As a result of the evidence introduced at the hearings at Albany, five members of the party, who had been elected to the New York State legislature, were ejected. That evidence established that the Socialist organization is not a political party, seeking through legal and constitutional means to bring about changes, but that it is part of an international movement, composed in this country of dues-paying members, largely minors and aliens, which attempts to exercise a mandate over members elected to office, and which advocates, as the weapon to achieve political ends, the employment of industrial action, or the general strike. In view of the evidence introduced at Albany and of the aroused public interest in the nefarious character, methods and purposes of this movement, was it deemed opportune by Mr. Hillquit and his associates to try to pull the wool over people's eyes?

At its convention, the party apparently modified its previous unqualified endorsement of the Moscow Internationale. It adopted the Majority Report on International Relations, which will, however, be submitted to a referendum of the membership, and which declares:

"The Moscow organization is virile and aggressive, inspired as it is by the militant idealism of the Russian revolution. It is, however, at this time, only a nucleus of a Socialist Internationale, and its progress is largely impeded by the attitude of its present governing committee."

Perhaps Messrs. Hillquit, Berger, Debs and other leaders of the party in America do not relish the thought of "playing second fiddle to Lenine," and thus served notice that they must be taken into account equally as leaders in the International Socialist revolutionary movement. This notice was probably designed to serve two ends—to let Messrs. Trotsky and Lenine understand they "are not the whole show," and also to befog the public mind in this country as to the unanimity of purpose of Socialism in America and Bolshevism in Russia. As a matter of fact, while the recent convention qualified its stand as to the Third Internationale, it did not repudiate any essential of the program laid down by the Third Internationale, save in matters of phraseology and tactics to be employed under different conditions. It did not repudiate the plan, laid down by the Third Internationale, as the "chief task" of international Communism—of organizing the workers so as to employ industrial action, or the general strike as the weapon for bringing about a revolution; instead it plainly declared for the "One Big Union"—for forming "one organized working class army." It did not repudiate its own answer to the program of the Third Internationale adopted in Chicago last September. That program still stands.

Declaring for the necessity of a Socialist Internationale, the Majority Report says:

"It cannot be truly Socialistic if it is not based upon the program of complete socialization of the industries, and upon the principles of class struggle and uncompromising working class politics. It cannot be truly international unless it accords to its affiliated bodies full freedom in matters of policy and forms of struggle on the basis of such program and principles, so that the Socialists of each country may work out their problems in the light of their own peculiar economic, political and social conditions as well as the historic traditions."

In other words, the convention merely repeats what has already been declared, what has long been part of the international Socialist program, what Mr. Hillquit stated when he said that between the Socialist party and the revolutionary left wings there was no difference on vital questions or principles, but merely minor differences as to tactics.

The Majority Report reaffirms its affiliation with the Third Internationale, but instructs its executive officers "to insist that no formula such as 'the dictatorship of the proletariat in the form of soviets' or any other formula for the attainment of the Socialist commonwealth be imposed or exacted as condition of affiliation with the Third Internationale."

Did this imply any repudiation of the Third Internationale? On the contrary, Hillquit declared: "The Third Internationale represents the best spirit in the movement."

Did this imply any repudiation of Bolshevism or Communism, in force in Russia, as not representing true Socialist doctrine, as being a schism or perversion of Socialism? On the contrary, the Majority Report declared that: *"Socialism is in complete control in the great country of Russia."*

While praising the Bolshevist régime, Mr. Hillquit remarked:

"This does not mean that we must accept everything sent from Russia as a papal decree."

In other words, it was made plain that Mr. Hillquit and the other leaders of Socialism in America do not relish the thought of being merely lieutenants of Lenine and that they demand recognition as major stars in the international Bolshevist firmament. While giving this notice, did Mr. Hillquit at all rebuke Trotzky and Lenine for their crimes, their killings, their reign of immitigable terror? On the contrary, he said: "A dictatorship is an irresponsible rule and the government of Russia is a perfectly responsible government. Lenine and Trotzky are not dictators."

The convention, moreover, decided to admit to membership in the Socialist organization, on equal footing with present members, those who seceded to the revolutionary left wings, on the ostensible consideration that they subscribe to the platform of the organization. The Communist sections are invited to come in—with what result? It was only by the skin of their teeth that the 89 per cent Reds at the convention won out over the 99 per cent Reds. By inviting the seceding 100 per cent Reds to come in, the extremists are invited to obtain a majority. The convention, while mildly criticizing the "bosses" of the Third Internationale and their formulas, nominated as candidate for president Eugene V. Debs—Debs who declared, "From the crown of my head to the soles of my feet I am a Bolshevik, and proud of it;" Debs who, from behind prison bars, in the Atlanta prison, issued the call to all factions of the party to unite, declaring:

"I have no quarrel with the comrade who does not believe in the efficiency of political action, nor have I any quarrel with the comrade who has no interest in industrial action. If both of these comrades recognize it is the mission of the working class to emancipate itself BY EVERY POSSIBLE METHOD, TO UTILIZE EVERY LEGITIMATE METHOD TO ACCOMPLISH HUMAN FREEDOM, and if each works in his chosen path . . . they can work together and help each other.

"You can always depend upon the capitalist class to force the workers to adopt different tactics. For the time being they have the power, and we are on the defensive. THEREFOR WE MUST DO THE THING BEST FITTED TO MEET A GIVEN SITUATION.

"I HAVE BEEN ASKED MANY TIMES IF I BELIEVE IN CHANGING THE PRESENT SYSTEM BY FORCE AND VIOLENCE. THAT IS A SILLY QUESTION, AND NONE WOULD ASK IT WHO HAD THE SLIGHTEST KNOWLEDGE OF HISTORY. . . . ALL ALONG THE TRACK OF THE AGES, WHEREVER A GOVERNMENT HAS BEEN OVERTHROWN BY FORCE AND VIOLENCE, THAT GOVERNMENT HAS BEEN MAINTAINED BY FORCE AND VIOLENCE."

That is the message—published in the *New York Call*, April 15, 1920—sent forth by Debs, choice of the Socialist organization for president, who was hailed riotously by the convention nominating him as "the very embodiment of the militant working-class spirit, the incarnation of the ideals of the Socialist party."

In order not to scare off, by a revelation of its true character, the vast number of converts which the Socialist party hopes to win among the "liberals" and "advanced" sentimentalists, in churches, schools, colleges, et cetera, through the insidious propaganda of such groups as the "Church Socialist League," the "Christian Socialist Fellowship" and the "Intercollegiate Socialist Society;" so as not to neutralize the work already being done by Socialist clergymen holding important pulpits, Socialist college professors and others; the party at its recent convention took occasion to declare that it "does not seek to interfere with the institution of the family" and that "it recognizes the right of voluntary communities of citizens to maintain religious institutions and to worship freely according to the dictates of their conscience." Also, realizing that when, last September, in the heat of a perhaps too ardent enthusiasm, it openly declared for the use of industrial action, it was perhaps indiscreet and undiplomatic so far as the general public is concerned, the party, for obvious purposes of expediency, gave vent to this purring reassurance:

> The Socialist party seeks to attain its end by orderly and constitutional methods, so long as the ballot box, the right of representation, and civil liberties are maintained.

The adoption of this clause was a piece of clever diplomacy on the part of the wily leaders, a triumph of the casuistical asiatic Hillquit intellect. That clause will enable the great number of Socialist clergymen and college professors to point to it triumphantly and so prove, to their congregations and classes, that the Socialist party is opposed to violence, to revolution by force, and is a lily-white political party seeking to bring about changes through "orderly and constitutional methods." Of course, that clause is *prima facie* evidence of the pacific turtle-dove character of the Socialist party! The party leaders are so sincere, so simple minded, so naive as only to speak in order to be believed.

But the hypocrisy of this cunningly construed declaration, the utter baselessness and worthlessness of it, is brought out by the Socialist party Platform.

Averring piously in its Declaration of Principles that the Socialist party "seeks to attain its end by orderly and constitutional methods so long as . . . civil liberties are maintained," the Platform adopted by the party violently, and in a spirit incentive to violence, asserts:

> Our Administration suppressed the cherished and fundamental rights and civil liberties at home. . . .
>
> Congress enacted laws in open and direct violation of the constitutional safeguards of freedom of expression.
>
> Hundreds of citizens who raised their voices for the maintenance of political and industrial rights

> The business man who advertises in periodicals which advocate and propagate a radicalism contrary to our American ideals and institutions certainly has not the welfare of God's greatest country at heart.

Mr. A. W. VanHoose, President, Shorter College, Georgia, wrote:

> A man may have a right to entertain his own opinion upon political questions, but he has no right to remain a professor in an institution whose founders, supporters and patrons do not endorse his views and he should be promptly dismissed from his position by the authorities.
>
> A magazine or newspaper advocating socialism would not receive my support either as a subscriber or advertiser. I would as soon think of contributing to the well-being of a rattlesnake as to the support of such a paper; I would have no right to destroy by violence the plant of such a periodical, but I certainly have the right and would regard it as a duty to withhold my support of such a sheet.

Mr. Melvin A. Brannon, President, Beloit College, Wis., wrote in part as follows:

> I should say that the responsibilities of church-members and citizens in the contribution of moneys is a very definite sort of a trust and they ought to place their investments in those institutions and those movements which are sane and sound and which move forward in an evolutionary rather than a revolutionary way.

Mr. John O. Wilson, President, Lander College, S. C., wrote in part as follows:

> The danger is widespread, and the youth of today ought to be protected. No teacher in school or lecturer in assembly has the right to sow in the minds of our young people any such false doctrines. Freedom of speech does not demand privilege to sow poison in human lives. It is high time to protect our children by clearing out of faculties and lecture courses teachers that will destroy church and state and all just government. We must not stop because the cry of persecution is raised.

Dr. Cyrus Adler, The Dropsie College, Philadelphia, wrote in part as follows:

> All persons are responsible for the results of their own acts. To contribute to an organization which carries on propaganda to which they are opposed makes them responsible for such propaganda.
>
> In protecting his own rights, those of the family and the State the citizen must not assume a reactionary or heresy hunting attitude. Freedom of opinion and speech have been too hardly won to be thrown away. This freedom, however, should not be allowed to degenerate into an attack upon fundamental principles underlying the American state or into a subversion of the moral order.

Mr. James Duncan Phillips, of Houghton, Mifflin Company, Boston, wrote:

> The contribution of money either intentionally or unintentionally to revolutionary propagandists is as much of a crime as starting the propaganda. Persons are not only responsible for contributing this money, but it is their business to investigate fully enough in all cases so that they can be sure that the money they give is for useful and not for evil purposes. Ignorance is no excuse. The philanthropist who through ignorance finds himself supporting an evil cause should be considered fully as responsible as the actual promotor.

Among the letters received were some that expressed the opinion that the revolutionary menace is exaggerated; others that protested against what they called "suppression of free speech" and advocated that radical exponents be freely allowed to ventilate their theories and "isms," and still others openly expressed sympathy with the radical forces. The note of sarcasm in some of these communications indicates the tendency of the writers.

The Rev. F. Ernest Johnson, secretary of the Research Department of the Federal Council of the Churches of Christ in America, referring to the writer of the letter sent out, wrote:

> Personally I think that a considerable part of the excitement over radicalism is due to ignorance and hysteria and a larger part is due to deliberate efforts on the part of certain financial and industrial interests to discredit everyone who is promoting industrial betterment no matter how conservative he may be. . . .
>
> What we need is an era of calm intelligence and courage. Let us examine current doctrines and movements carefully and dispassionately, and when we find anything radical fight it in the open and not from ambush.

C. E. Dunniway, President of Colorado College, Colorado Springs, writes in part as follows:

> Many men of conservative tendencies are shocked and outraged by proposals of reform and progress which they then denounce as revolutionary. Just now the current fashion is to call such proposals bolshevik. My own political philosophy requires me to be sympathetic toward progressive or even radical proposals in theory, but I find myself conservative in attempts to apply theory. I decline to be stampeded into opposition against progressive measures by conservatives who brand them as Socialistic. In short, every proposition for change in the Social and Economic order should be considered with candor in the light of experience and reason.

Rt. Rev. C. P. Anderson, Bishop of the Diocese of Chicago, wrote:

> There seems to me to be undue pressure brought to bear upon churches, colleges, etc., not simply to uphold good government and sound economic principles, but to uphold and defend Capitalism as such. It is conceivable that one might be both anti-bolshevistic and anti-capitalistic. Your particular department is doubtless studying the antecedent causes of revolutionary movements and any attempt to fight off revolutionary movements by perpetuating the cause of them could only meet with temporary success at best. I may be reading between the lines and finding something which is not there, but in some of the communications which have reached me from The National Civic Federation, there seems to be an underlying suggestion of financial pressure upon churches and colleges to uphold the traditional capitalistic theories or take the consequences. Of course any such policy would and ought to defeat itself. To my mind we are facing a double menace—the menace of Bolshevism and the menace of stand-pattism. We can't fight the former on the platform of the latter. I hope and believe that the former won't come to the birth and that the latter won't survive.

Mr. Miner Lee Bates, President Hiram College, Ohio, writes in part as follows:

> To sum it all up: permanent safety can come only from fuller light and freedom to act in that light. Repression, save in the case of occasional individuals, has never served to avoid revolution. On the other hand, intelligent, hearty support of those agencies giving the truth and the whole truth is the true guardian of peace and the social order.

Mr. Samuel Plantz, Lawrence College, Appleton, Wisconsin, said in part:

> My own judgment is there is not much "revolutionary" propaganda in "philanthropic and charitable organizations." Some people call everything revolutionary which does not accord with their own narrow judgments.

The Churchman, a journal of the Protestant Episcopal Church, of which the Rev. William Austin Smith is editor, replied to the letter in an editorial, the spirit of which is self-evident. In part, it said:

> The Church certainly harbors a good deal of unstandardized material—and pretty pesky material it is! For example, how should Mr. Easley proceed to standardize Bishop Lawrence and Bishop Brent and the twenty-two signers of that address to the public, given out to the American press last spring, denouncing the un-American, unjust and dangerous measures against aliens and others whom Mr. Palmer's agents, cheered on by ardent patriotic organizations like The National Civic Federation, were hounding through the sheets and the columns of many American newspapers?
>
> *The Churchman* was not Simon-pure 100 per cent American last spring according to the standards of The National Civic Federation. . . But if our opinion is desired we should say that the people who are in charge of a good deal of the correspondence sent out of late by The National Civic Federation have too lean an equipment in social sympathies and too narrow a perspective of history to fit them to be designated as the censors of American patriotism and the arbiters of destiny of our churches, schools, charities and periodicals.
>
> But we are confident that American public opinion will never tolerate a group of self-appointed busybodies passing judgment on American institutions and giving free advice as to whose Americanism has reached 100 per cent.

Industrial Peace in Building Trades

(*Continued from page 7*)

Board would be suspended from the organization in event of failure to carry out the provisions of an award.

These penalties are most severe and are made so as to prevent any interference whatever to those interested in industrial peace to bring success to the movement.

Similar efforts to eliminate unnecessary strikes have been made in the last few years in various cities. San Francisco, under the leadership of P. H. McCarthy, president of the Building Trades Council of that city, has eliminated jurisdictional strikes by severely penalizing those who engage in it either as unions or individuals.

In 1912 Simon O'Donnell, president of the Building Trades Council of Chicago, began an agitation for peace in the building industry of that city following a most bitter contest. Buildings in course of erection had been tied up for months by strikes based on the issue whether the steamfitters should have an independent organization or become members of the United Association of Plumbers, Gasfitters, Steamfitters and Steamfitters' Helpers. Various trades took sides with one or the other. Sympathetic strikes were called. Although many buildings were contemplated the struggle between the unions made their erection impossible.

Apparently it was a drawn battle, but after O'Donnell's campaign for industrial peace the first result was the affiliation of the steamfitters with the plumbers. The jurisdictional war was probably the greatest industrial contest Chicago had had in many years. It awakened the officials of the various organizations to the danger of permitting such disputes to continually interfere with the building industry.

Up to that time strikes were called indiscriminately and work on buildings, even those owned by union organizations, ceased. During the injurious controversy President Donlin of the Building Trades Department was business agent of the Plasterers' Union of Chicago. His experience in that struggle and for many years previously had made him a firm believer that some nationwide method should be adopted to eliminate these quarrels over jurisdiction. He seconded Secretary Spencer's efforts in every way possible and has been of incalculable aid in encouraging the organization and proper functioning of the National Board.

Any discussion on jurisdictional strikes must not omit the part played in them by employers. The workmen, of course, are sensitive to any invention that will change in any way or entirely eliminate their trade. Naturally the employer has just as deep an interest. It is therefore not surprising that jurisdictional disputes have continued with such disastrous results to the building industry. No one interest is solely responsible. Contractors, architects, as well as unions, must bear equal responsibility.

But the fact that the union officials were the first to advocate the elimination of these disputes by conciliation and arbitration proves conclusively that whatever improvements in industrial conditions the country may enjoy must originate in and be fought for by organized labor. The contractors, architects and engineers are forced to follow.

Among those who would benefit by the elimination of unnecessary strikes are the families of the workers. Just as anxiously do the wives look for the pay envelope on pay day as do the bread winners. It is not generally considered that a wife earns any of the money paid her husband for his activities, but the pay envelope received by the workman not only compensates him for his work but is also pay for the labors of the wife in conducting the household.

Purifying Politics—A Field for the Churches

(*Continued from page 10*)

—should really run our government, would not the millennium really be quite near? No Profiteering, no exploitation, no graft, no political favoritism! Think of it! Yet it is entirely possible if the members of the churches will only take off their coats, so to speak, roll up their sleeves and declare that the thing shall be done.

That there is a crying need for reform in our governmental administration is clearly shown in a speech by the Republican candidate for President. Let me preface it, however, with the statement that an equally sweeping indictment was made against the Republican administration by the Democrats when the Republicans were in power—and both were substantially correct. There is nothing partisan in graft, incompetency and political favoritism:

> "I am referring now to the fact that not only has the government been twisted out of shape, been dictatorial and meddling, and has been extending its activity to experiments beyond its powers, but also to the fact that it has blundered in every direction.
>
> "It has engaged in prodigal waste. The American people pay. It has kept its overstuffed bureaus and departments, many of which are doing overlapping work, in a prime condition of reckless inefficiency. The American people pay. It has a record in the appointment of campaign-contributor diplomats who have been without previous experience in foreign affairs. The American people pay. It has engaged in all kinds of costly bungling experiments of government management and ownership of enterprises which other management could do better. The American people pay. It has allowed worthy Federal employees, particularly those who are skilled, such as chemists and agricultural experts, to go so badly paid by the government that they have left the service. The American people have to bear the cost. It has poured forth our national treasure into the yawning emptiness of unpreparedness for war and unpreparedness for peace. It has spent our money and failed to do business, while the prodigal flow went on. The American people have paid, and are paying. With a return to sanity we now have another task before us in making the administrative part of our government one in which a people proud of their abilities in business can take pride.
>
> "We must not let our administrative government crack under the load of its new burdens or those that our future may place upon it. It has been cracking badly, sometimes neglected during absence, and sometimes exploited at home by those who, now in 'perfect accord,' desire to perpetuate their power. To repair it is the business of every American—not only because of pride, but also because he or she pays for it and is entitled to good government without waste."

As an illustration of the utter helplessness of the Christian people in the matter of government, let me quote the following paragraph from the *Christian Century* of September 12, 1920, a church paper published in Chicago:

> "ALARMING CONDITIONS IN CHICAGO
>
> "The citizens of Chicago have long had cause to lament the prostitution of civic functions to the spoils system entrenched in the City Hall. No mayor of this city ever had a more splendid opportunity to display the qualities of leadership than did William Hale Thompson at the time of his first election. But almost at once the construction of a machine was begun by the controlling forces behind the mayor, and by the time of the second election that organization, by the combination of the most sinister elements in the city with the following of the cowboy executive, was too much for the conservative and order-loving citizens, particularly without competent leadership. The result has been an astonishing display of effrontery in the exploitation of every form of vice which can yield revenue to a city administration. And at the present time, in spite of the showing of mismanagement that has bankrupted the city, and reduced its credit to the vanishing point, these same City Hall henchmen, after looting practically every fund within the reach of the administration, are starting in with a campaign to capture the state government by the election of one who promises to take orders from the Mayor of Chicago if he secures the governorship. The opposition to the plunderbund has so-

Education—Minus Business Brains

(Continued from page 11)

ership. It says in substance, in the rough language of the world, Go to College, or Go to Hell! The 38,000,000 American citizens included in the first two enumerations of this bulletin are the "rejects" of our school system. Taken in the mass, however, they contain the best part of our citizenship by whatever measure you apply. Even in terms of genius, Doctor Mann, formerly of Chicago University and now the Consultant of the War Department's Division of Civil Training, tells us that painstaking and scientific analysis of three million persons, and wide personal contact, shows that only 10% of the best brains of the country are college-bred, the other 90% being in the 63,000,000 and more in area "A" of our first chart, who had at best an elementary schooling, that is, who got nothing from the schools better than reading, writing and arithmetic. It is fair to say that this 90% and millions of others were killed in opportunity and in accomplishment by the stupidity of our public school leadership. It will not do to boast that our schools have made our people individually forceful and remarkable. We cannot in the same breath speak of our country schools as the worst we have and wretchedly poor, and admit as we must that our best citizenship comes from the farms, and then add in contradiction, that the excellence of our schools accounts for the virtues of our people.

The remedy. America has always her one

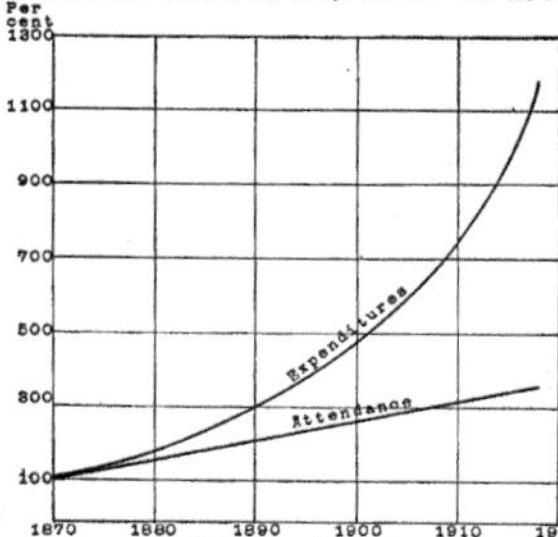

School Attendance and Expenditures.

cure-all, the one you are emphasizing in this Conference—more money.

The Chart I now present shows what more money, and then more, has done for public education in fifty years. Spend all we have under the present leadership and we get nowhere.

We must understand that the elementary school is only the wet-nurse of infancy. Education comes after children leave the elementary schools, if it ever comes. The relation of the grade schools to the high school has been overemphasized, and its obligation to the 60% who leave the elementary schools for life work, has been ignored. Europe, in her best practice, has shown the way for generations in her "life-schools", the agricultural schools of Denmark and Holland, the continuation and secondary schools for wage-earners of all ages in France, Austria, Germany, Hungary, Belgium and elsewhere. Germany made a ghastly mistake, long foreseen by her best men, in training her wage-earners in vocational efficiency only. We must train also in civic and social understanding. But Germany built in her factories and work places everywhere, schools so effective that 65% of the leaders in both the managerial and technical departments of her topmost industries, those that were conquering the whole world of trade, were her working boys, grown-up, who had left school at 13 or 14 years of age, and by these schools in industry had perfected themselves—had ranked themselves with the world's great engineers of production and discovery. The graduates of her technical institutions were working under these working boys, grown up, and not over them, as in our country, which is called democratic. Only a poor and inbred educational *leadership* has kept us from equalling Germany in this respect, and infinitely surpassing her by also developing the civic understanding of our working people, the educationally abandoned 38,000,000 in the schoolman's bulletin, and their 20,000,000 wives and sisters.

There is absolutely nothing iconoclastic in this. It simply gives to those who labor, a high school and college fitted to their circumstances and of substantially the same educational value, differing only in the place and time of instruction. It equalizes opportunity. It is easy to make these schools of such excellence that the rich, also, will wish to send their sons to them.

This new development requires the cooperation of all our forces, educational and economic. Employers must cooperate willingly and understandingly if may be, but, anyway, cooperate. Our $5,000,000,000 of annual factory payrolls, and the inestimable physical facilities of our factories and commercial institutions, must be used. Employers see this and are already spending millions of dollars in the beginning of this accomplishment, and doing it without the help of public school authorities, because these authorities are, in the main, without the will, the vision or the knowledge, to cooperate.

Leaders of organized labor see all this and are magnificently moved to action. For labor, this movement is the hope of the world. I could quote dozens. I quote one. Mr. Gompers virtually spoke for all, and in fact as truly expressed the judgment of employers as wage-earners, when, after allowing for the merits of our present schools, he criticized them for being only academic, and added:

> But, better than all (not only this official system of education), is the idea of bringing it into the factory, into the shop, anywhere where the toilers are employed, so that they can become more efficient and more highly skilled and better developed in order to make for greater and better production.
>
> My criticism of the schools is that they teach the academic course only. In addition to that there should be teaching of the actual facts of life to fit the public to meet the duties of workers. * * * It is to prepare boys and girls and men and women to do the real service of our country and of the world, to which we should, in my judgment, devote our attention. Anything that can help to make men and women more efficient really, for the individual as well as the collective good, will make for a higher and a better citizenship and help much toward the perpetuation of this wonderful Republic of ours.

I wish time permitted me to tell you how some excellent employers, for instance, the General Electric Company in its Fort Wayne plant, the Illinois Tool Works at Chicago, and the Norton Grinding Company of Worcester, are training, sometimes new men with no previous industrial experience, sometimes old employees, to higher and higher places, and sometimes by a sort of "intermittent apprenticeship", are lifting these men to places of accomplishment and happiness impossible heretofore in this democracy. This Chart, with its zig-zag lines, shows how girls in a corset factory, doing simple operations, used to require, as shown in the lower lines (No. 1) ten weeks to acquire proficiency and $2.30 per day, but by the new methods of intensive training (No. 2) are brought to still better output and $2.60 in three and a half weeks. Also, in these and all other simple operations (at which more than 80% of all our industrial workers labor) those who are not adapted to one task are trained to another. Industry is becoming highly intelligent without the help of public education as respects its wage-earners; and to become highly intelligent is to become considerate, happy and effective. This chart is the simplest. From this we go to the end of apprenticeship in any trade.

In the end, presumably, it will be carefully determined whether and to what extent, in the public interest, a measure of public oversight of these educational processes will be desirable or necessary.

Why industry is now going ahead alone, is indicated sufficiently by the personnel of our 48 State Boards of Vocational Education, with their 311 members—311 members, and only 16 manufacturers or other employers and 12 wage-earners among them. Three of these employers, and three of the wage-earners are on the Wisconsin Board. Leaving out the Wisconsin Board, we have in the other 47 states 301 members, of whom 13, or 4%, are manufacturers and 9, or 3%, are wage-earners. It has been the clear purpose of the schoolmaster politicians to teach the wage-earners and to use the plants in their own way without the effective cooperation of either of these forces. If, as this conference declares, our public school system is not democratic, we see why. The Federal Government showed the right way (the way of experienced Europe, by the way) in making the Federal Board of Vocational Education consist of two representatives each from labor, employment, and agriculture, and the Commissioner of Education as the Board's official connection with the academic schools. But the Federal Government could not compel the States to be either wise or democratic. It could only set an example. Wisconsin excepted, only one State Board has two manufacturers, and 11 others have one each. Think of one manufacturer in Indiana sitting on a State Board for the training of wage-earners in connection with their employment and on the employer's time, with three college presidents, three county superintendents and three city superintendents. He might as well, possibly better, be out entirely. Think of eight lawyers and a surgeon, as the New York Board of Vocational Education, daring to attempt to make the 450,000 wage-earners, now coming into her new continuation schools during working hours and largely on the employer's time, efficient and happy in their occupations. The eight lawyers would presumably be excellent directors of law schools and the surgeon of a hospital. If you and they do not see the silliness and evil of their present position, those who labor in, and those who direct, the industries and the commercial establishments of that State, do see. Think of five schoolmasters as her State Board of Vocational Education developing by themselves the vocational training of the wage-earners of wonderful Detroit and all other places in Michigan. And so of almost every State, except the thirty-three states having politician-superintendents elected through political machinations by popular vote, who run the whole show.

I trust that I have shown enough to demonstrate that at bottom our educational difficulties are not financial. Money, of itself, may only fix upon the country for a considerable period the present defective leadership. This Conference has emphasized the poor quality of our schools, rural and city, but the country is safer with them where they are than with an exclusive, talkative, and unseeing leadership. Everyone in industry wants and will fight for ample teachers' salaries, but employers buy quality. The best employers will pay any price for quality. Let us have it in our educational leadership. A lame horse is dear at any price; a thoroughbred is cheap at any price. Our rural teachers average up to our leadership. If they didn't they wouldn't be where they are.

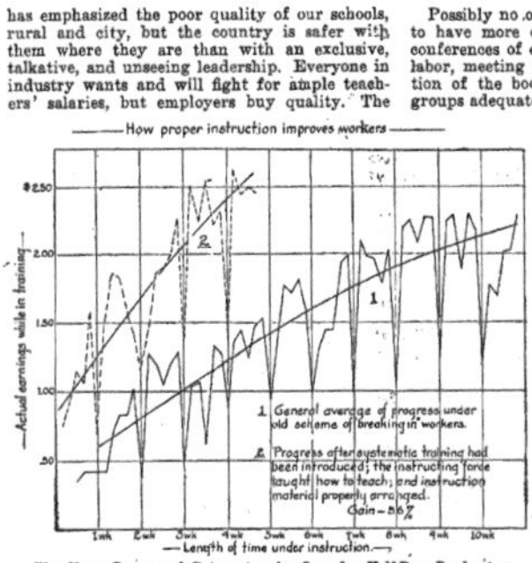

Each social force both gains and gives in co-operative endeavor with all others. No single social endeavor can gain anything worth while except by such cooperation. Let us, with a new spirit, work together and refuse to work apart.

How proper instruction improves workers

1. General average of progress under old scheme of breaking in workers.

2. Progress after systematic training had been introduced; the instructing force taught how to teach; and instruction material properly arranged. Gain—56%

Actual earnings while in training — Length of time under instruction

The Sharp Downward Points Are for Saturday Half-Day Production.

Possibly no one in this country has happened to have more experience than myself in joint conferences of educators, employers, and men of labor, meeting for the promotion of the education of the body of our people, each of these groups adequately and about equally represented in each conference and competent by its numbers (never very large) and its quality, to decide in substantial measure for all of its group in the United States, and coming into the conference for that purpose. I have helped to call in the last two years more than fifty such conferences, State and National. We make sure of this representative attendance before fixing the date. I do not consider a gathering for a great social purpose that affects, as education does, the will, the personal and property rights of the working people and the employers of America, and the public interest, to be truly a conference and worth-while unless thus composed. Never has one thus composed failed to result in forceful and happy conclusions. Hesitation, mistrust, uncertainty, give way to understanding, friendliness, and decisions that win.

This is not only the line of least resistance. It is the only line that is fundamentally honest. It is the American way. Let's try it in this school crisis. School men may leave business out of their program; but it is no longer possible for business to leave the public schools out of its program. We must all sink or swim together and business won't sink; even less will the working people longer take pot-luck.

Letter to Signers of Declaration Against Recognition of Soviet Russia

The following letter was sent by Condé B. Pallen, Chairman of the Department on Study of Revolutionary Movements of The National Civic Federation, to the signers of the Declaration against the recognition of Soviet Russia, which was submitted to President Wilson last spring. The signers were asked to act at once because of the discernible evidences of sinister influences in the present national campaigns.—EDITOR.

To the Signers of the Declaration Against the Recognition of Soviet Russia:

The Red offensive against Warsaw has been broken, but already Lenine threatens to raise a Bolshevik army of 5,000,000 to renew the Red onslaught. Whether this will be possible or not, the Red offensive against civilization through intrigue, plot and subsidized propaganda has not been checked.

Three months ago more than two thousand men and women of all parties throughout the United States, among whom you were one, signed a declaration against the recognition of Soviet Russia, which was sent in the form of a petition to the President of the United States. In this document the signers voiced their apprehension of the Bolshevist movement throughout the world, declaring:

> We believe that recognition of Soviet Russia would be a repudiation of all that our national life has represented for a hundred and fifty years, and of all the spiritual ideals for which modern civilization has striven for two thousand years.

The American government, following the splendid lead of France, through the Secretary of State in his letter to the Italian Ambassador, has since expressed its unequivocal stand against any recognition of the lawless autocracy in control of Soviet Russia. This stand has evoked spontaneous and unanimous approval from the leaders and press of both the Republican and Democratic parties, showing that the problem is American and not partisan.

Lenine announced publicly in Moscow that Russia must continue to foment revolution in all countries, and that his chief immediate hope was for a revolution in Asia and the East. Documentary proof in possession of the State Department has demonstrated the existence of an organized propaganda whose ramifications enmesh the world. This propaganda of inciting discontent, sedition and revolution is financed, as recent disclosures prove, by tremendous sums, largely raised by the sale of jewels stolen by the Soviet régime from Russian palaces and churches. In England, Europe and America it seeks to gain control of labor and to use the general strike to coerce or paralyze every form of representative government.

The American Labor movement stands firmly against all these Bolshevist policies. The American Federation of Labor at Montreal refused by an almost unanimous vote any recognition of Soviet Russia. Notwithstanding the fact that organized labor stands solidly against Bolshevism and that the debacle in Poland may temporarily check the activities of Bolshevist agitators, the danger in the United States and elsewhere throughout the world cannot be minimized. The Red cause is best served by inculcating a sense of false security and the belief that Russian Bolshevism is collapsing, that America is immune from attack, and that those who fear the Red menace exaggerate the danger. Each day the forces of attack increase. From abroad, as immigration statistics show, within the past months have come thousands of aliens who are to be distributed throughout the land, the unassimilable portion of which promise to be a perpetual yeast of discontent.

The forces of autocratic barbarism are not confined to the Socialists, anarchists and I. W. W.'s, but the cause of Lenine is more actively furthered either frankly or by indirection by radical pseudo-intellectual writers, editors, professors, teachers and clergymen in our newspapers, magazines, colleges, schools and churches, and in some of these the enemies of democratic government are found to hold the very highest positions.

The note of the Secretary of State to the Italian Ambassador points out that inevitably "the diplomatic service of the Bolshevist government would become a channel for intrigues and the propaganda of revolt against the institutions and laws of countries with which it was at peace." This stand logically requires that the Government of the United States make practical application of its policy. The first step toward the eradication of Soviet propaganda in this country must be the deportation of Ludwig C. A. K. Martens.

This issue can neither be evaded nor compromised. Whatever political changes may occur, the stand taken against Bolshevism by our Government must be maintained. The national campaigns are now on, and in both parties, seeking to influence the policies, are Bolshevist sympathizers and agents who openly condone the excesses of the Red régime, who are picturing the Leniné-Trotzky autocracy as representing the will of the majority of the Russian people, and who by specious arguments are urging recognition as the quickest means of helping to bring order and peace in Russia. In order that those who will have power and authority may not be influenced by these Bolshevist sympathizers, and that they may heed the great voice of representative Americans on this grave matter, it is urged that the signers of the previous petition now call for a declaration from their congressmen, senators and from their presidential candidates against any recognition of the Bolshevist régime in Russia and against any temporizing with its agents and propaganda in America, at any time, or under any circumstances. You are urged to write especially to your presidential candidate, emphasizing your conviction that there must be no neutrality either in thought or action on this vital problem.

CONDÉ B. PALLEN,
Chairman Department on Study of Revolutionary Movements,
The National Civic Federation.

TYRREL PRINT, NEW YORK.

The National
Civic Federation Review

No. 6

DEPARTMENT OF PUBLIC WELFARE

RESIDENT-ELECT HARDING'S NOTABLE PROPOSAL FOR NEW MACHINERY OF FEDERAL GOVERNMENT TO DEAL WITH PROBLEMS OF SOCIAL JUSTICE—AIMS AT CO-ORDINATION AND EFFICIENCY—WILL AVOID PATERNALISM AND BUREAUCRACY

PRESIDENT - ELECT Warren G. Harding, in an address to 5,000 women representing various sections of the country, who assembled at Marion, Ohio, on October 1, made one of the most notable proposals of his campaign. This is for the creation of a Federal Department of Social Welfare to coördinate and direct efforts to obtain social justice. In making the proposal, Senator Harding warned against the dangers of such an undertaking, declaring that bureaucracy must be avoided, and that social justice and not paternalism must be the guiding principle.

Senator Harding in part said:

"There can be no more efficient way of advancing a humanitarian program," he said, "than by adapting the machinery of our Federal Government to the purposes we desire to attain. While others may have their eyes fixed upon some particular piece of legislation or more particular policy of social justice which calls for the sympathetic interest of us all, I say, without hesitation, that our primary consideration must be the machinery of administration, and that when the time comes for us to reorganize our administrative government in Washington we must all stand together for the creation of a Department of Public Welfare.

PRESIDENT-ELECT WARREN G. HARDING

"I pledge myself today to support with all that is in me whatever practical policy of social welfare and social justice can be brought forward by the combined wisdom of all Americans. Nothing can concern America, and nothing can concern me as an American, more deeply than the health, the happiness and the enlightment of every fellow American.

"The social justice that I conceive is not paternalism. It would be easy to make it so, and dangerous indeed to the best spirit that Americans can have—the spirit of expressing by the individual free will one's own merits, capacity and worth. We do not want government to suppress that expression of free will, even by benevolence, but we do mean to preserve in America an equal opportunity and a preparedness for self-expression therein, even though we use the government to do it.

"Social justice, on the other hand, is not a mere sentiment. To my mind a social justice policy in government cannot and should not be confined to a program for the flow of benefits from some uncertain and magic source at the seat of government. I could not even consider a policy of social justice which is conceived, as so many visionaries conceive it, as a right of mankind. I will only consider it as an obligation to mankind.

"I refuse to subscribe to the doctrine which has gone so far to delude the world that even citizenship is based upon rights. I believe, and have repeatedly said, that citizenship is based upon obligation.

"I will not even approach the consideration of a policy of social justice unless it is founded on the stalwart American doctrine of the duties of every one of us to all of us. The first measure of social justice to which America must always devote herself is the duty of citizenship to vote with conscience, to preserve laws and to demand their enforcement. It is the obligation of all true Americans to live clean lives and to engage with head and hand in honest, useful production and toil.

"I believe that there is no step more practical, no step which will mean more to the growth of America's social welfare; no step which will guarantee better America's social justice, than one which I now propose to you.

"It is almost useless for us to go on expending our energies in advancing humanitarian policies which we wish put into effect, and it is useless for us to hope for the effective administration of humanitarian policies already undertaken by the Federal Government, until we have prepared to create an administrative centre for the application of our program.

"At the present time we find social welfare bureaus and social welfare undertakings scattered hopelessly through the departments, sometimes the one overlapping the work of the other, and sometimes, indeed, engaging in bickerings between themselves. The picture is one of inefficiency and of wasted funds.

"Let us not only have social justice and social welfare developed to the fullest extent which a wise citizenship will approve, but let us have also the means with which to make social justice and social welfare real and functioning, rather than visionary and inefficient.

DANGERS TO BE AVOIDED

"I have no doubt that there will be some who will find in this proposal cause for calling me an extremist, but when we have a task to do, which has been dictated by our conscience and approved by our wisdom, let us straightway find the way to do it. I do not say this without a word of caution. I recognize certain dangers which are always presented when Government undertakes large and detailed tasks. I have said already today that we must avoid paternalism, and that we must avoid it because a paternalistic social welfare program would smother some of the liberties, some of the dignity and some of the freedom for self-expression of our individuals.

"In creating Federal departments for the administration of social justice and social welfare we must avoid the fearful results of bureaucracy. I am inclined to think that as between a bureaucracy of a military power which paid little attention to the regulating of domestic affairs, and a bureaucracy of social rules and regulations, the latter would oppress the soul of a country more. We do not want, and we will not have, either in America.

"Undoubtedly the great blessing of our Constitution, appearing, indeed, as if our Constitution had been written by the hand of Providence, are the checks which it places upon the development in a national centre of a great bureaucratic paternalism. We are momentarily irritated at times when we desire to enact measures, which appear to be dedicated wholly to the welfare of mankind, when we find that constitutional limitations prevent their legality. But we have been saved through these many years, and will be saved throughout America's continued progress from the growth of too much centralism, too much paternalism, too much bureaucracy and too much infringement of the individual's right to construct his own life within our American standards of reason and justice.

"I would like to point out to all America that there is grave danger at hand when centralized expression begins to take from local communities all the burdens of social conscience. The best that humanity knows comes up from the individual man and woman through the sacred institutions of the family and the home, and, perhaps, finds its most effective application in the community where life is personal, and where there is not an attempt to cut men and women to pattern and treat mankind as a wholesale commodity."

TASKS OF SOCIAL JUSTICE

Senator Harding pointed out the necessity of going forward upon a sure footing and declared:

"When making the proposal for a department of public welfare to America, I am aware that have made a step in advance of any platform I have chosen to speak to you on the practical question—the question of how to do the tasks we must do, the things American conscience is calling to have done.

"We all know that we face tasks of social justice, which we must undertake with dispatch and efficiency. Who can suggest one of these tasks which can supersede in our hearts, or the rank which foresight and wisdom will give that of the protection of our maternity?

"The protection of the motherhood of America can not be accomplished until the State and the nation have enacted and, by their example have enforced customs, which protect womanhood itself. I know full well that there are women who insist that women shall be treated upon the same basis that men are treated. They would have a right to take this position in their own behalf, but I insist, that all true American must insist, that no woman speaks for herself alone. She is the possessor of our future, and though she becomes engaged in the tasks and services of civilization, we must preserve to her the right of wholesome maternity."

Senator Harding discussed the need of adequate protection for women in industry and expressed his belief in the wisdom of an eight-hour day for woman workers. He emphasized the need of safeguarding the women on American farms. He proposed putting the Children's Bureau under the suggested Department of Public Welfare, and urged prevention of abuses of child labor. The Senator spoke at length on the problem of conserving national health as a prime factor in national well-being.

Our Supreme Allegiance

INTERNATIONALISM WOULD DESTROY NATIONAL SOUL—AMERICAN UNITY ALONE CAN ENABLE US EFFECTIVELY TO HELP IN MAINTENANCE OF WORLD PEACE AND JUSTICE

By GEORGE SUTHERLAND

GEORGE SUTHERLAND

WHEN the Armistice was signed, the issues of the war were transferred from the trenches to the peace table. The natural hope and expectation have been that with the final consummation of peace, the world would resume its former tranquility and conditions again be as they were. In a measure and in a sense this hope and expectation in the course of time, will be realized. Vegetation will cover the scars where the battles were fought; the places made empty by the dead will be occupied; time will dry the tears and comfort the hearts of the sorrowful. But, in another sense, the effects of the war will be ineradicable. The processes of human intercourse have been profoundly disturbed, and the slowly built foundations of civilization themselves, menaced with destruction. Old and respectable maxims of government have been put under suspicion; long cherished theories have been challenged and abandoned; in Europe the old order and the firm rock upon which it seemed to rest are both trembling at the edge of a new and dreadful barbarism.

The sentiment that once justified a quick appeal to force as a righteous remedy for grave international wrongs, has been largely supplanted by the feeling that war is a thing which, under no circumstances, is capable of justification, and that a substitute must be found and accepted at whatsoever cost or hazard. Any proposal which promises this desired result makes a powerful appeal to the better side of our nature, and objections challenging its practicability or suggesting countervailing perils are received with some degree of impatience as though they were contentions in favor of war for its own sake. And yet the fact that humanity has never been free from recurrent warfare in any age or under any form of government or any degree of civilized culture, should admonish us that we are dealing with a problem of great and stubborn difficulty, the solution of which does not lie at the end of a royal road of easy passage, but to which we shall come, if we come at all, only after long and patient search for the way.

The contention that war in and of itself is ever defensible is a monstrous perversion; but that war as an alternative may be justifiable, and even commendable, is beyond dispute. Right thinking men can never accept the theory that war is a "*biological* necessity," but they cannot ignore the fact that it has again and again been a *moral* necessity. There are, and always will be, some things more sacred than peace, more precious than life, for the necessary preservation of which war with all its sad and brutal accompaniments may be an act of consecration. To hold otherwise is to surround every American battlefield with a wall of shame. When the leader of the Scotch knights flung the golden casket containing the heart of Bruce far out among the victorious Saracens and rallying the torn remnant of his command bade them follow it to the death; when the immortal six hundred charged to certain annihilation at Balaklava when millions of French and English and American lads threw themselves into the riot of bat-

(*Continued on page 16*)

Vital Problems of Agriculture

WITH INCREASED COSTS OF PRODUCTION AND DECLINE OF PRICES FARMERS CONFRONT SERIOUS DIFFICULTIES—RECOMMENDATIONS TO MEET NEEDS OF GREAT PRODUCING GROUP

(Address delivered at the Annual Convention of the National Farmers' Union, Kansas City, Nov. 16-18, 1920)

By CHARLES S. BARRETT
PRESIDENT, NATIONAL FARMERS' UNION

THE National Farmers' Union during the past year has continued in its work of charting the troubled seas of agriculture. It is the function of a great farmers' organization to discover and make known the rocks and reefs, the currents and cross currents, floating mines and submarines which menace the agricultural interests. New dangers can thus be avoided, additional lighthouses and harbors of safety be provided and farm progress made safer and generally more secure.

The Secretary of the Treasury and the Federal Reserve Board deal a body blow when they persistently and in spite of united farmer protest repeat the slogan of certain financial interests that price declines are inevitable and unavoidable.

As a result of such declarations publicly announced outrageous price declines have set in. The Secretary of Agriculture in an address before the American Bankers' Association, in October, stated that the recent loss in value to farmers amounts to two and a half billions of dollars. Today cotton and wheat are selling far below actual cost of production, bringing hardship and suffering to thousands of producers. It is needless for me to point out that bulk-line costs of producing cotton in 1919 were found by the Department of Agriculture to be thirty-seven cents a pound, while the foremost authorities of the land have carefully figured the costs of production of wheat for last year at about $2.50. It is well known that the costs this year have been heavier than ever before. Deflation has come with a vengeance. It is a deflation due to human causes. There is under rather than over supply of cotton and wheat. The world needs our food. Idle mills in central Europe need our cotton. Certain government officials, however, have made it impossible to finance our crops and while making gloomy predictions, refuse to permit the War Finance Corporation to function. In this great crisis through organization we can meet these body blows to agriculture and the Farmers' Union will continue as in the past to bear its full share of the undertaking.

The city consumers should be made to know the evil effects of agricultural deflation. They should know that the farmer in selling his great staple crops is harvesting the result of an entire year's labor. The farmer has but one turn-over in the year. The price of his feeds, seeds, fertilizer, farm machinery and what he has paid for extra labor are all fixed by forces beyond his control. He has borrowed money from his banker to finance his operations and under the present unfair system his crops are forced on the market regardless of fair prices in order to liquidate these loans. The manufacturer and middleman have many turn-overs of capital annually. What is a loss today may be a gain tomorrow. The very nature of their business is based on insurance and hedges against loss, the fixing of sale and resale prices of their goods and of passing the costs on to the consumer.

Much is being said of price reduction in certain great industries such as sugar, textiles and leather, but these are of the great industries which have piled up billions in the form of dividends, treasury stock and surpluses. To them price declines mean very little in view of the enormous profits which they have made and yet

CHARLES S. BARRETT

make. How different was the treatment given them to that received by the producers of the two great farm staples, where cotton went down and the government wouldn't help to bring it up, and where wheat went up and the government brought it down. Wheat was selling for about and over $3.00 a bushel at the terminal market when the government fixed a minimum price at the terminal of $2.20 a bushel which became in substance the maximum price as well.

During the war the railroads were guaranteed against losses, and now under the Cummins-Esch law have entered on an era of unprecedented high freight and passenger rates and with it such prosperity (to them) as this country has never seen before.

On former occasions I have referred to the rôle of the Farmers' Union in helping to maintain at Washington a national headquarters for the farm organizations. During the past year the National Board of Farm Organizations has made material gains in strength and in service. The National Board of Farm Organizations is the only farm organization in the country which approximates in character the Chamber of Commerce of the United States or the American Federation of Labor.

A distinct contribution has been made this year in placing the demands of the farmers' organizations before the country. The Board first prepared and sent a questionnaire, to the various presidential aspirants. The replies were widely published and elicited much favorable attention. The Board followed this action by sending a delegation to both the Democratic and Republican National Conventions, where its spokesmen presented various planks for the consideration of the platform committees. This action constituted a mile-stone in the history of farm organizations and placed the needs of agriculture as never before squarely in front of the American public.

The great farm organizations belonging to the National Board of Farm Organizations believe in frank and open methods. They are asking for only such consideration as is accorded other great industries. They want no special privileges but do insist that they be placed on an equal footing with all the rest.

SOME RECOMMENDATIONS.

Continuation of cost of production investigations is of the greatest importance. Our membership should insist on sufficient appropriations both State and National to make possible the determining of all factors which enter into the cost of production of the great staple agricultural products. The farmer today is the only manufacturer in this country who is imploring the government to figure out and make public the cost of production of his products. It is because he will come out with a clean bill of health. I wonder what other great lines of business are willing to have the government figure out their costs of production and give the "free, full and uncensored facts" to the entire public.

Consumers should be encouraged in their desire for similar data as to the cost of producing manufactured products as well as the costs of distribution.

Collective buying and selling arrangements should be improved and furthered in every possible way. The Farmers' Union is a pioneer in this most practical field of farm endeavors. Uniformity of methods in organization, bookkeeping, auditing, etc., should be carried out. The buying and selling of agricultural requirements and farm products should be concentrated and to this end our various state directorates and business departments should meet from time to time.

The purpose and spirit of cooperation should be emphasized in all dealings with the general public. No occasion should be neglected to show that agricultural cooperation is the only way to bring stability and prosperity to agriculture and with it prosperous and permanent civilization for this nation.

Data on discrimination against our cooperatives should be systematically gathered together and utilized. Certain great trade associations have been carrying on boycottings and practicing unfair discriminations against cooperative grain elevators, creameries and stores. Through the National Headquarters evidence of such discriminations will be presented before the proper authorities.

Cooperative managers should keep careful records of the number of cars which they secure or desire as against the number of cars furnished their private competitors. Evidence is not lacking that local freight agents have been approached by private shippers in a way to get them more than their fair share of transportation facilities.

The Federal Trade Commission must be preserved in its present functioning. A high type of public servant is now found among its personnel. Attacks have been made against the Federal Trade Commission which farmers should be the first to resent. The knowledge that profiteering has been enormous is due largely to investigations of the Federal Trade Commission. Without its helpful assistance the country would have no proper warning of certain dangers which must be removed.

(Continued on page 19)

American Labor Breaks With International Federation

AMERICAN FEDERATION OF LABOR REPUDIATES REVOLUTIONARY PROGRAM OF INTERNATIONAL FEDERATION OF TRADE UNIONS—REJECTS EUROPEAN CALLS TO AID SOVIETS

By SAMUEL GOMPERS and MATTHEW WOLL

AT the present moment continued international cooperation with European labor has become extremely difficult, if not impossible. For two years the American Federation of Labor has given a considerable part of its time, energies and financial resources in the endeavor to build up a new international trade union organization to replace the union destroyed by the war. A portion of the report of the Executive Council to the Montreal Convention of the American Federation of Labor was given over to international relations. The convention endorsed the action of the Executive Council and the Amsterdam delegation, referring to the Executive Council the question of affiliation to the new International Federation of Trade Unions.

The Montreal Convention was by no means satisfied with either the constitution and principles of the new international as laid down at Amsterdam or with the later actions of the executive body. The chief objection to the new constitution was that it completely abrogates the fundamental principle of the former labor union international, namely, complete autonomy for each national federation. It was also objected that a system of dues had been decided upon which would constitute a very heavy drain upon the resources of the American Federation of Labor, compelling it to pay a large part of the expenses of the proposed new international organization.

The main criticism of the new international executive at Amsterdam was that it had issued a statement of purely socialist character, even including the phrase "Down With Reaction. Up With Socialism," and calling for a first of May celebration which amounted to a one-day strike for socialism.

Since the Montreal Convention matters have taken a turn for the worse. The Amsterdam executive has issued throughout the world, and sent to the American Federation of Labor for circulation in this country, a declaration calling for international revolutionary measures by Labor in aid of the Soviets in their war against Poland. The chairman of the British labor party, claiming to speak for the British trade union labor movement, has sent a cablegram along similar lines and apparently calling for similar action. The contents of these messages are thoroughly revolutionary and obviously animated with a desire to use the most extreme measures for strengthening the hold of Soviet power in Russia and enabling it to extend its influence and to dominate neighboring countries.

These actions are all the more amazing as British labor, until recently, was on record as against any such revolutionary methods, and that instead it demanded neutrality to Soviet Russia. At the meeting of the International Federation of Trade Unions Congress held at Amsterdam last year a resolution was introduced by two small Bolshevist delegations calling for the use of identical revolutionary methods and for a nearly identical revolutionary object. Everyone in attendance, other than the two men mentioned, regarded the proposal as absurd and when it was put to a vote, only the proposer and seconder supported it.

The brainstorms which seem to have given the extremists temporary control must be regarded as a result, first, of the critical conditions now prevailing in Europe; and, second, of the enormous propaganda subsidized by the Soviet government with money wrung from its bleeding and starving slaves in Russia.

APPEAL OF THE TRADE UNION INTERNATIONAL FOR REVOLUTIONARY MEASURES IN AID OF THE SOVIETS

On September 8 the Amsterdam bureau of the International Federation of Trade Unions communicated the following manifesto to the American Federation of Labor, with the request that "the manifesto be as widely circulated as possible amongst the workers of your country"! On account of its unique character we reproduce this manifesto in its entirety. The italics are ours:

> In consequence of the extreme gravity of the political situation the International Federation of Trade Unions appeals to the organized workers throughout the world to pledge themselves to inflexible opposition to all war.
>
> The organized workers of the world must from now onwards be prepared to act in accordance with the decisions arrived at by the international conferences at Berne and Amsterdam and to utilise every available resource in the struggle against all wars.
>
> The war must not be continued.
>
> The International Federation of Trade Unions, mindful of the right of the peoples to govern themselves, condemns foreign intervention with the internal affairs of other nations. It also condemns military assistance given to all reactionary enterprises.
>
> Against this intervention and assistance the International Federation of Trade Unions calls upon all workers to demonstrate and to act.
>
> Applying these principles, and in view of the aggressive action of Poland against the Russian revolution, the International Federation of Trade Unions demands that all militarist attacks shall cease immediately, and that guarantees shall be forthcoming against any new aggression.
>
> In view of the declaration of the Russian government which has solemnly expressed the wish to conclude a peace based upon the independence and self-determination of Poland, the International Federation of Trade Unions declares that upon this basis fratricidal warfare must cease.
>
> This universal peace must be immediately established with due regard to revolutionary achievement and the independence of the peoples.
>
> In order to attain this working class and profoundly human aspiration, the International Federation of Trade Unions calls upon all trade unionists to refuse to cooperate with the accomplices of imperialist capitalism, and to definitely refuse to transport troops or to manufacture munitions.
>
> The deliberate action of the workers must break all attempts to re-establish a reactionary Holy Alliance. *Not a train carrying munitions must be worked; not a ship laden with war materials must be allowed to leave harbor; not a single soldier must be transported.*
>
> War must not be further supported.
>
> The International Federation of Trade Unions declares that the proletariat of all countries can and must act in this manner to protect the workers' efforts in the direction of liberty and social progress, and firm in the conviction that war can only cease by the will of the workers, the International Federation of Trade Unions calls upon all National Trade Union Centers to prepare, if necessary, for *mass action by means of a general strike.*
>
> *The production of war materials must cease in all countries,* and in order that disarmament may become an accomplished fact, the International Federation of Trade Unions demands that action be taken in all countries to put an end to the manufacture of arms. This will assist the liberation of the peoples from militarism, and industrial production will proportionally expand.
>
> Comrades! In the year 1914 our organization was much too weak to act itself against war. Today it is a power of *twenty-seven million members.* Above all it is imbued with a pronounced anti-capitalist and anti-militarist spirit. *Today it must of its own accord and within its own ranks, find the power to preserve the world from terror and annihilation.*
>
> War against war! That cry unites all workers! The refusal to work transport for the purpose of war is today an expression of International Working Class Solidarity.
>
> Comrades! The International Federation of Trade Unions places its reliance on you.
>
> On behalf of the International Federation of Trade Unions:
>
> W. A. APPLETON, *President.*
>
> L. JOUHAUX, *First Vice-President.*
>
> C. MERTENS, *Second Vice-President.*
>
> EDO FIMMEN,
>
> J. OUDEGEEST, *Secretaries.*

Along very similar lines was a cablegram received from Adamson, the chairman of the British Labor party, on August 15, informing America of similar revolutionary measures proposed by the new "Council of Action" of Great Britain. This message, which apparently suggests similar American action, is as follows:

(Copy.)

WESTERN UNION CABLEGRAM

LONDON 196 FIRST 52.

GOMPERS,
American Federation of Labour, Washington.

> Greatest most united conference British trade union labour movement. Meeting London today. Hailed with satisfaction Russian government's declaration in favour complete Polish independence and realizing gravity international situation pledged itself resist every military naval intervention against Soviet government. Instructed Council of Action continue until first absolute guarantee armed forces Great Britain should not be used support Poland, Wrangel or any other military naval effort against Soviet government. Secondary withdrawal all British naval forces operating directly or indirectly as blockading influence against Russia. Thirdly, recognition Soviet government, establishment unrestricted trading commercial relationships Great Britain, Russia. Conference refused association any alliance between Britain and France or any other country committing us any support (to) Wrangel, Poland or supply munitions, war material, for any attack upon Russia. Conference authorized council to *call any and every form withdrawal Labour when circumstances may require* given effect policy and called upon every trade union official Executive Committee, Local Council and membership generally. Act swiftly, loyally, *courageously,* sweep away secret diplomacy, assure foreign policy Great Britain accord with desires people for end to war and interminable threats of war.
>
> ADAMSON, *Chairman Labour Party.*
> 130 A Aug 15.

If the chairman of the British Labor party or Secretary Oudegeest seriously desired to know the position of the American labor movement as to any proposed international revolutionary action directed against all governments—entirely disregarding their democratic character—they could have referred to the proceedings of the Montreal Convention and to the entire record of the American Federation of Labor. It may be doubted if either Oudegeest or Adamson expected any answer, or if a proper answer could be devised that would adequately deal briefly with the immense issues they have raised.

The American Federation of Labor is not a

(*Continued on page* 18)

Railway Brotherhoods Condemn Illegal Strikes

OFFICIALS DECLARE ACTION OF "REBEL MEMBERS" IN VIOLATING WORKING AGREEMENTS DESIGNED TO DESTROY ORGANIZED LABOR AND BUILD "ONE BIG UNION"

THE following letter, signed by the officials of the Railway Brotherhoods, and inspired by the illegal strike of train, engine and yard men at Chicago last April, is of special significance. Condemning the promotion of illegal strikes as efforts to destroy the existing brotherhoods and form "One Big Union," the letter declares that vacancies brought about by the illegal action of rebel strikers may be filled by any and all persons, either temporarily or permanently. The officials also warn the members not to sign petitions for the reinstatement of former employees of various railroads who participated in the illegal strike. This letter, and the position taken, is another example of the intention of organized labor to abide by its agreements and to maintain its laws, rules and regulations against the revolutionary elements.

—EDITOR.

CLEVELAND, OHIO, October 11, 1920.

To General Chairmen, General Grievance Committees, Railroads in the United States, Representing the B. of L. E., B. of L. F. & E., O. R. C., B. R. T., and S. U. of N. A.

SIRS AND BROTHERS:

The following questions are some of the many that came to the undersigned during the illegal strike of train, engine and yard men that started at Chicago last April and spread to numerous terminals in the United States:

> "At the beginning of the outlaw strike here the switchmen quit their jobs and went on vacation, as they called it. The company filled their places as much as possible with new men, some of whom were farmers, office clerks, and from other crafts. Most all of them were unfamiliar with the work and had to be taught.
>
> "The Engineers have the contract for all piloting and it fell to the engineers to pilot the new men around in making deliveries and doing the work in general. We had six engineers piloting, myself being one of the six, and because I instructed them how to throw a few switches and make out wheel reports, take car numbers, etc., many of the engineers, firemen and old switchmen who were out classed me and the rest of those working as scabs. One of the engineers took a job as yard conductor later, after the pilots were pulled off, and is still holding that position.
>
> "What I want to know is, am I classed as a scab? If I am guilty I will take my medicine like a man and get out of the order. If not guilty, I wish to be vindicated in the eyes of the membership here.
>
> "About four days ago our trainmaster and master mechanic came to four of us engineers and asked us if we would take charge of crews until they could get some men.
>
> "I also wish to know if it would have been all right for us engineers to have taken charge of crews, as the officials wished us to do."

Official instructions sent out by the chief executives of the transportation organizations at various times during the illegal strike of train, engine and yard men during the months of April, May and June, 1920, plainly and positively stated that where any number of employes of any class represented by the B. of L. E., B. of L. F. & E., O. of R. C., B. of R. T. or S. U. of N. A. left the service of their employer in violation of the schedule or agreement under which employed, and in violation of the laws of their organization, in sufficient number to interfere seriously with the operation of train, engine or yard work, they not only jeopardized their membership in their organization but their positions with their employer as well, and that such action was illegal and in violation of the laws, rules and regulations of each of the organizations herein mentioned. Therefore, it naturally followed that, where such employes had left the service for the purpose of interfering with traffic, even though such employes claimed they were on strike, on vacation, or had quit the service, the railroad companies affected were clearly within their rights in securing other employes to fill the positions made vacant by those engaging in such illegal action.

We, therefore, take the position that, wherever our organizations maintained a schedule or working agreement covering train, engine or yard service at the time illegal action such as above referred to took place, all positions made vacant by employes of our class engaging in such illegal action were open to any and all persons who desired to accept service of that character, either temporary or permanent. It is therefore the duty of members of each of the organizations named herein to at all times assist one another in protecting working agreements made by the authorized committees of such organizations as against rebel members or others who attempt to repudiate the same, or who endeavor to discredit or destroy any of the standard, recognized labor organizations named herein.

In some instances road conductors, engineers, firemen and brakemen were offered permanent positions in yard service made vacant by those engaging in the illegal strike, and such road employes, or persons not in the employ of the railroad in any capacity, who desired to accept such vacancies were clearly within their rights in doing so, and our organizations appreciate the assistance given by members and others in filling such vacancies and those helping to make good organization agreements violated by rebel members.

When members of any of the transportation organizations, obligated as they are to support, maintain and abide by the constitution and rules of their organizations, assume to violate the working agreements made by the authorized committees of such organization, to the extent of quitting the service collectively, nothing but condemnation of such disloyalty can be expected, and any reputable labor organization that fails or refuses to carry out the terms of a working agreement constitutionally made by it cannot hope to continue long in existence and is not entitled to the respect of the business or labor world.

Many of the former employes of various railroads who participated in the illegal strike mentioned above have not been returned to service by their former employers and in some localities petitions have been circulated requesting loyal members of the different organizations to sign such petitions or ballot in favor of the return of such former employes with their original seniority. Our members are warned against signing any such petition or communication. The loyal membership of these organizations should remember that these organizations live and will continue to prosper, not as the result of the assistance and good wishes of those expelled for engaging in the illegal strike, but over the protest of such individuals. The illegal strike of members and others since April, 1920, on railroads where these organizations maintained schedules or working agreements, was started by disgruntled individuals solely for the purpose of destroying the old established organizations with the hope of building the "One Big Union," and had those individuals succeeded, all the good work of the past quarter of a century would have been destroyed. Our general committees on some of the largest railroads in the country have entered into and signed agreements with the operating officers of such companies that former employes who engaged in the illegal strike mentioned will be returned to service only as new employes and will not be permitted to take seniority rank over loyal members or others employed to fill the vacancies created by such illegal action.

W. S. CARTER,
President, B. of L. F. E.

W. S. STONE,
Grand Chief, B. of L. E.

L. E. SHEPPARD,
President, O. of R. C.

W. G. LEE,
President, B. of R. T.

S. E. HEBERLING,
President, S. U. of N. A.

COOPERATIVE BANK OPENED BY BROTHERHOOD OF LOCOMOTIVE ENGINEERS

THE Brotherhood of Locomotive Engineers Cooperative National Bank of Cleveland opened its doors for business November 1. The capital of the bank is $1,000,000, with a paid in surplus of $100,000 additional. The capital stock is owned exclusively by the brotherhood and its members and was oversubscribed $300,000, despite the fact that the annual dividends on the stock are limited to 10 per cent and cannot exceed this percentage.

The officials of the new bank are: President, Warren S. Stone, grand chief of the Brotherhood of Locomotive Engineers; vice president and cashier, W. B. Prenter, general secretary-treasurer; vice president and manager, W. F. McCaleb, formerly active vice chairman of the Dallas Federal Reserve Bank. A corps of expert bank employes has been chosen, chiefly from Cleveland banks.

President W. S. Stone made the following statement regarding the bank:

"So far as I know this is the first cooperative bank in the United States, although there are many such banks in Europe. It is the first labor bank. We chose a national bank because of its greater security. A national bank is subject to close inspection by Government inspectors. The first consideration with labor is that its enterprises must be absolutely sound.

"We made the bank cooperative by distributing the stock to as many members as possible, so that it would approximate the cooperative ideal of one man one vote. We also limited stock dividends to 10 per cent and plan to distribute excess earnings back to the depositors.

"We pay 4 per cent interest on time deposits. We provide for an additional surplus and if there are additional earnings, we expect to share them with our depositors who cooperate with us in making the bank successful. That is our idea of cooperation.

"The bank will not confine itself to the brotherhood. It will do a commercial, savings and trust company business. It will do banking by mail. We have 85,000 members, not to speak of several million other workers who belong to other labor organizations. The bank is, of course, open to everybody and is not an exclusive labor bank. We expect to handle foreign exchange for immigrants.

(Continued on page 19)

Exposes W. Z. Foster's Charges

PRESIDENT TIGHE, OF THE AMALGAMATED ASSOCIATION, RIDDLES FOSTER'S BOOK ON THE STEEL STRIKE AND DEFENDS HIS ORGANIZATION AGAINST ATTACKS

AT the recent session in Washington of the Executive Council of the American Federation of Labor, the committee to unionize the steel workers was reorganized, with the elimination of John J. Fitzpatrick, Chairman, and William Z. Foster, Secretary, both of whom participated in the direction of the steel strike last Winter. Fitzpatrick was displaced by M. F. Tighe, President of the Amalgamated Association of Iron, Steel and Tin Workers.

In recent issues of the *Amalgamated Journal*, President Tighe vigorously defends his organization against the attacks made by W. Z. Foster in his book "The Great Steel Strike and Its Lessons" and thoroughly exposes this leader of the "red" element and former advocate of the I. W. W. Mr. Foster's views played an important part in the report of the Interchurch World Committee, which investigated the steel strike.

In part, President Tighe writes:

In taking up the defense of the Amalgamated Association from the malevolent and untruthful aspersions cast upon the integrity and honesty of purpose of the entire membership of the Association, it is not intended to involve any of the organizations connected with the movement, other than it may be necessary to show up the duplicity of the author of the book.

The book in itself is nothing more than a compilation of half truths, misrepresentations, evasions and calumnious falsehoods. It is a work written for commercial and personal interests, but so far as being a truthful review of the great steel strike, it has no value whatever. Those who purchase it for the purpose of getting the true account of the inside transactions of that event will not get value received.

The author of this work undertakes to instruct the heads of all National and International Organizations as to what their duties are, and these officials, many of whom were fighting the battles of the workers in the trade union movement before he knew what a trade union was, and after, when he was doing his best to destroy them, are told that unless they follow his advice they are incompetents. * * *

The statements made that the taking of a strike vote did not necessarily mean a strike, showed conclusively to the Amalgamated officials that those who were advocating it had not given human inclinations the study they should have on a matter of such grave importance and responsibility, for in but very few instances, if any, had there ever been a publicly announced referendum vote taken, in which the word strike was involved, that did not carry affirmatively. The meetings of the campaign committee were largely guided by the reports made to it by the secretary of the campaign committee. For several meetings previous to the one in which it was decided to send out the strike vote the majority of those who assembled at these meetings were the paid secretaries and field men working under the orders and control of the author of this malicious edition. Whatever he reported to the committee was a signal for those field men and secretaries to attest to. Under these conditions he was practically master of the situation. This "me too" system did not appeal to the officials of the Amalgamated Association very strongly, and as a result they were not regarded with much favor, and in many instances their position on important ques-

PRES. M. F. TIGHE

tions given but little consideration. * * *

It has been shown, First, that the charge of intentional desertion from the campaign committee by the Amalgamated Association was a deliberate falsehood, conceived with malicious intent and as an afterthought to sensationalize the author's work sufficient to make it a saleable article. Second, that because the officials of the Amalgamated would not allow themselves to become mere pawns for him and his secretaries and field men to move as they saw fit, the Amalgamated became the target of venomous and malignant attacks largely centered on Assistant President Davis, who as a member of the campaign committee, at all times acting under the advice of the writer and the International Executive Board, insisted that the campaign be conducted on legitimate trade union lines, and not on lines suggestive of the methods advocated and practiced by Syndicalists and I. W. W. organizations. * * *

While the author tries very adroitly and plausibly to cover his delinquencies as a witness before the Senate Committee every person present who was interested in the success of the strike was disgusted and mortified at the vascillating evasive manner in which he gave his testimony, and the writer without equivocation charges that his actions did more harm to the strikers' cause than any one thing that occurred previous to the calling of the strike or to the end of it. * * *

Where was the great mental acumen which he now tries to impress the readers of his book that he possesses. This instructor of how to win strikes, this disciple of that doctrine called "Direct Action" failed to measure up to the expectations of those who really wanted the strikers to win at least public support. He knew if he knew anything that he was to be taken to task for his former position in regard to government; he knew that much depended on how he impressed those in attendance at the investigation, yet he deliberately threw an insult into the faces of those who would at least have been neutral towards him and the striking workers. When asked the direct question if the views expressed in his "Red Book on Syndicalism" were his views still, instead of answering the question as frankly as it was put and by that spike every gun the enemy had turned not only on him but the movement itself, he hesitated, parried the question and finally asked the committee to exclude the press from the room before answering a plain question on a matter that if he had the welfare of the thousands of workers striving for relief from their former surroundings he should not have required one moment's delay in answering. So aggravating was his actions that the great head of the American Labor Movement had to admonish him by saying in a stern tone "answer the questions; the press cannot say anything more than they have about you," with the attorney for the strikers sitting on his left and the writer sitting on his right, both urging him in undertones to speak out, he still maintained a position of one who was on trial for some great offense and would not speak until compelled to do so. To quote a very prominent advocate of labor's cause, when asked his opinion of the testimony and the actions of this great promulgator of doctrines that had been discarded by every trade unionist as detrimental to the real cause of labor, he answered, "rotten, absolutely rotten." * * *

No deadlier blow could have been dealt the cause of organized labor and the hopes of the thousands then on strike, than was given by the author of this worthless imitation of a history of the steel strike, when in answer to the persistent questions of Senators Borah and McKellar, he asked to have the press excluded from the room before he made answer. Many of the reporters for the press who were present, were members of trade unions for years. They were still carrying cards in their respective organizations. Their sympathies were with the men on strike. They had never been known to be disloyal to the cause. His demand was an insult to them as well as to the others. His request was promptly refused by the chairman of the committee. The question put to him was a simple one, namely, had he changed his opinions from what he had expressed in his former writings on Syndicalism. The head of the great American labor movement had testified that he had changed his opinions, in fact, had given him a clean bill as a trade unionist of the A. F. of L. school. Why was it necessary for him to hesitate to confirm the statement made in his behalf by the chief of the American Labor movement? Was not the reputation of the movement itself as represented by the head of it nothing to him? Was not the interest and hopes of the thousands of men then on strike to be considered before his private opinions? Who now was skulking? Was it the Amalgamated Association officials or was it the secretary of the campaign committee? Publicity was what every friend of the strikers wanted, and the more publicity the better. They wanted it shouted from every hill and vale, housetop and street corner, for their cause was just and righteous. If the Senate Committee was after meat and he knew they were after it, then if he was as wise as he wants his readers to believe he is, he had it in his power to prevent them from getting the hide, not alone the meat. His answer to the question asked had to be literally dragged from him, spoken in a low voice and with a demeanor that left doubt in the minds of all present as to whether he was speaking the truth when he said he had changed his mind somewhat from the opinions expressed in his "red book" and his writings in "Solidarity" some years previous.

Fatigue in Industry

RESPONSIBILITY OF EMPLOYER AND EMPLOYEE RESPECTIVELY—RELATION OF HABITS AND HOME ENVIRONMENTS TO ITS CAUSE—PRESERVATION OF HEALTH CHIEF REMEDY

By DR. ALVAH H. DOTY

NO subject relating to the welfare of employees has received more attention than fatigue. Those who publicly discuss this subject are, unfortunately, apt to take rather a restricted view as to its cause and remedy. On the ground that employers are largely responsible for the fatigue which occurs among workers, the argument has been reduced to an inquiry as to the most effective means of inducing or forcing employers to install special devices, to arrange certain accommodations, to provide for periods of rest during the day and even to serve certain forms of nourishment for employees during working hours.

The demand for better working conditions, particularly in the past, has been amply justified, and the interest and energy of various associations and individuals who have labored hard to bring about reform in this direction cannot be too highly commended. Unsanitary conditions, improper accommodations and long hours of work undoubtedly contribute to fatigue. On the other hand, demands are frequently made upon employers who have provided what are believed to be reasonable and adequate arrangements for the comfort and welfare of their employees and fatigue still exists. Any measure which shortens the day's labor or offers easier means for the performance of work is desirable provided it is fair to the employer. I do not call attention to this aspect of the problem in the interest of employers, nor to belittle the laudable efforts to improve unhealthful or too exacting conditions of employment or to render the duties of the day more comfortable and pleasant for employees in industrial pursuits and other branches of service. It is my object, rather, to point out the fact that there is a more important remedy for the prevention of fatigue which has been given far too little consideration.

Those who have worked in the field or from long personal experience are familiar with the life, habits and home environments as well as the daily work of employees know full well that the chief cause of fatigue, particularly at the present time, is not that employees are improperly treated by employers or that they are subject to unsanitary and uncomfortable conditions and surroundings in the workshop and office, but that they pay little attention to the laws of personal hygiene. Serious errors of diet, improper selection and preparation of food and irregularity in the time for eating are exceedingly common. Very few workers exercise sufficiently in the open air. The period of sleep is reduced to the minimum. Intemperance, in many ways, is quite the rule rather than the exception. All these conditions constantly reduce the resisting power of the body and it should cause no surprise that a person is often unable to perform an ordinary day's work without becoming tired or fatigued and in addition is unable to enjoy fully the periods of release from work which should be devoted largely to rest and pleasure. It would surprise those who have not given this subject extended and careful consideration to learn how little a person, who maintains good health, is affected by fatigue as the result of work. Fatigue decreases as the resisting power of the body increases.

The owner of a car is very careful to supply proper fuel and in the proper amount and he watches every detail of the machine in order to keep it in serviceable condition. Whereas the human machine, the most perfect of all, which is in his keeping, is quite apt to receive but little attention, and under such conditions, it cannot be expected to act in a satisfactory manner.

I have referred to fatigue in connection with employees because it seems to be popular to discuss it along these lines. My observations, however, are applicable to every one. It is proper to add that the education of the public concerning the preservation of health include instruction for the prevention of fatigue.

Notwithstanding the great improvement in working conditions, better light, ventilation and accommodations and more reasonable hours of labor, the fact remains that fatigue as well as so-called neurasthenia or nervous breakdown is increasing, particularly among female employees. We must not close our eyes to the fact that this is due to an improper mode of living.

During a recent and interesting investigation regarding the food supply and general living conditions of over four thousand employees, men and women, it was found that the selection of food and the methods of eating were most unhealthy and improper. A large number of employees ate but once a day, some only twice. The breakfast of many consisted of only coffee, a roll or some fruit. On the other hand, a good percentage of this group, whose work was largely sedentary, ate three hearty meals a day composed largely of meat,—pork being a favorite selection. This is certain to lead to some form of systemic disturbance. Many of these employees drank four or five cups of coffee during the day; others consumed a large amount of tea as well as other forms of stimulants. These errors of diet occurred unquestionably as the result of ignorance concerning the value of various articles of food and how they should be selected and when they should be eaten. It is quite clear that the excessive use of coffee and other stimulants was to obtain energy which should have been provided by good nutritious food. A large number of the employees referred to were neurasthenic and frequently absent from work, although it was clearly shown that in most instances their duties were not too confining or exhausting. They simply were not in good physical condition and were, therefore, unable to meet the ordinary demands of the day. It was found that many of these men and women did not retire until after midnight. These unhealthy conditions are often associated with unpleasant home environments and domestic or financial troubles. It is thus not difficult to understand why many persons approach the day's work tired out and not only unable to render to their employer the service due him but unable to enjoy the period after the day's work is over.

To assume that an employer should be held wholly responsible for the condition of fatigue affecting his employee is unjust to the employer and to disregard the chief underlying cause of fatigue is unfair to employees, for it does not teach them the true means by which fatigue may be prevented.

Those who discuss fatigue refer to the importance of maintaining good health as a means of preventing this condition but it is usually a casual reference only, whereas it should be the factor most strongly emphasized. The apathy in this direction is due largely to the fact that it is far easier to place the responsibility for fatigue upon the employer than to devise and carry out means of educating the public regarding the manner in which good health may be maintained. It may be said, in passing, that employees do not always appreciate provisions made for their comfort particularly if their physical condition is impaired, for although by these means their daily work may be rendered easier, instinctively they know their physical condition is not materially improved nor are they made strong and capable of enjoying life. Expensively furnished rest rooms and lavatories, although pleasant to look upon, are not of educational value to employees. Rather they are quite apt to cause dissatisfaction with home conditions which are not of the same quality. Rest rooms, lavatories and the like should be furnished plainly, attractively and comfortably. Cleanliness should be the main educational feature for this may be carried at the home no matter how humble it may be.

Employees should know the relative value of food products and the great importance of selecting a proper diet in order that the human machine may be furnished with proper fuel, for, if this is not carefully attended to, good health is not forthcoming. Walking, the most valuable form of exercise, costs nothing and there are very few who cannot find an hour during the day for this purpose. This insures a walk of about three miles, a fairly good day's exercise. Contrary to the general belief, exercise during the evening is not unhealthy. It is true that persons engaged in sedentary occupations and those whose work involves constant mental activity are apt to become weary when evening comes. This is mental and not a physical fatigue and the most effective remedy for it is walking. Furthermore, employees do not know the vital importance of proper sleep and often do not retire until after midnight although they are obliged to rise early in the morning. Experience has shown that these violations of the laws of health are sooner or later followed by some form of physical impairment.

There is no doubt that interference with a proper food supply and the unrest and excitement associated with the recent war have gone far to undermine the public health. It is, therefore, all the more necessary that the public should be carefully instructed regarding the preservation of health. For instance, coffee, tea and other forms of stimulants are taken in larger quantities than before and the increased demand for these has thrown upon the market innumerable drinks advertised as stimulating and invigorating. It is the abuse and not the use of these agents which is disturbing and the demand for them would not be as great if careful attention were given to the selection of food, the proper time for eating it, proper exercise, sufficient sleep and other means of preserving health.

I cannot accept the statement ascribed to Galbraith that the slogan for eliminating fatigue is to rest when one needs to do so. Just what would occur, for instance, among a thousand employees who were given a license to suspend work whenever, in their opinion, they were tired or fatigued would, I am quite sure, surprise the above mentioned writer.

The prevention of fatigue depends chiefly upon the proper education of the public concerning the preservation of health and the prevention of disease. It is daily becoming more evident that, in order to secure success in this direction, the measures undertaken must be uni-

(Continued on Page 21)

Catholic "Social Reconstruction Program" Analyzed

FALLACIES IN PROGRAM OF COMMITTEE ON WAR ACTIVITIES OF THE NATIONAL CATHOLIC WAR COUNCIL SHOWN BY NOTED MEMBER OF ROMAN CATHOLIC CHURCH

By P. TECUMSEH SHERMAN

(Continued from Previous Issue.)

BEARING in mind where lies the burden of proof, we can now take up and consider briefly the principal arguments for the affirmative, and note the principal objections.

First. It is argued that compulsory social insurance has been established in many countries of Europe and everywhere has been "successful." In order to prepare a favorable background for this argument it is commonly prefaced by comparisons contrasting conditions in America unfavorably with conditions in the European countries which have compulsory insurance. We will take up this prefatory branch of the argument first.

In the propaganda in this country for state social insurance economic conditions among our workers are continually being painted in the most distressing colors, whereas statements are being made implying that the corresponding conditions in Europe are somewhat heavenly in comparison. For instance we are told, on the one hand, that from 50 to 75 per cent of our laboring population do not obtain a "living wage," whereas we are told, on the other hand, that, since the advent of social insurance (until the outbreak of the war), poverty was being rapidly diminished in Europe and in one country at least had practically disappeared—the country referred to being presumptively Germany, where compulsory insurance had been longest in operation. Thereby a picture is being produced in the minds of our public, like the well-known advertisement showing a thin baby and a fat baby, marked respectively "before taking" and "after taking." But that comparison is not only untrue, it is even the very opposite of the truth. It places the thin baby where the fat baby ought to be, and *vice versa.* It is in Europe, with state insurance, that the condition of the wage-workers is (and, even before the outbreak of the war, was) most distressing and hopeless, whereas labor conditions in America, without state insurance, are (and long have been) immensely the better and more hopeful. In 1914 the average wage in Germany, for instance, was less than half of the average wage in America—and by "wage" here is meant the "real" wage as well as the "nominal" wage. Consequently, if poverty had practically disappeared in Germany, the German workers generally must have been obtaining a "living wage," and a large majority of our workers must have been obtaining more than *double* a "living wage" or, if between 50 and 75 per cent of our workers obtained less than a "living wage," then a very large proportion of the German workers must have been obtaining less than *half* a "living wage," in either alternative the German workers being comparatively deep in poverty.

This miscolored comparison (and the propaganda for compulsory insurance abounds in similar misrepresentations) tends to divert attention from a fact of the greatest import. It is the dreadfully low level of wages prevailing among practically all the wage-workers in Europe that has led to the recent adoption of state insurance by many European governments, not in any general expectation of thereby developing true insurance among the people, but rather as a "ready-made" means for distributing urgently needed poor relief among a hopelessly submerged and impatient proletariat. In final analysis nearly all the European social insurance laws are really "poor laws"—mere palliatives for insufficient wages. Certainly that kind of insurance ought not to be imposed upon our self-sufficient wage-workers. Its merits as a method of poor relief, for application only to the very lowly paid minority, will be considered later.

We can now take up the main argument, namely, that compulsory social insurance has been widely adopted in Europe and has everywhere proved successful. How far this statement is misleading, will be shown in the following brief review of European experience in the different lines of compulsory social insurance:

UNEMPLOYMENT INSURANCE

Compulsory unemployment insurance (although adopted also in Italy within the last few months) has been tested in only one country in Europe, namely, in Great Britain, and there only for a few years, limited to apply only to a few selected industries and providing only a very low rate of pecuniary relief and for a very short period of unemployment. The expense has been enormous and the benefits trifling, and the administration has been extremely unpopular. Upon that short experience to date it is premature to adjudge this social experiment to be a demonstrated failure; but, on the other hand, it cannot reasonably be deemed a demonstrated success. It is yet only a dubious experiment in an early stage of experimentation.

INVALIDITY, OLD AGE AND LIFE INSURANCE

Compulsory insurance of the wage-workers (or some of them) against invalidity, old-age and premature death (or some one or more of these misfortunes) has been adopted in many European countries. But this line of insurance requires long capitalization of funds, with the consequence that results cannot be appraised until the insurance has operated for about a generation; and none of these European insurance systems, except the German, has yet been so long in effect. On the contrary, all the others have been adopted within very recent years, and are either just starting or only about to start; and two with nearly the longest starts—the French and British systems—are already having such serious troubles as to warn against imitation. The only well tested one of those social experiments—the German system—not only has fallen far short of success in many ways, but also is peculiarly inappropriate for imitation in America. Its administrative methods are the quintessence of absolutism and autocracy. Its daring financial plan is almost universally condemned. It has given rise to gross and socially demoralizing abuses. And essentially it is a system of poor relief, fit only for application to a proletariat submerged to a very low level.

Not only is there no well tried system of compulsory invalidity and old age insurance in Europe capable of application in America with the slightest chance of satisfaction and success, but even among the partisans of state paternalism in Europe the opinion seems to be growing that compulsory invalidity and old-age insurance involves too much bureaucracy, too much administrative expense and too many financial complications and dangers to be advisable. In its stead, the new school of social reformers advocate invalidity and old-age pensions, otherwise called "non-contributory insurance"—an alternative method of poor relief, of doubtful expediency, but the objections to which cannot be presented here without leading us too far afield.

SICKNESS INSURANCE

Sickness insurance, in this country often miscalled health insurance, generally—but not always—aims to provide two kinds of benefits, first, a cash benefit during disability from *short* sickness (generally limited to 26 weeks in any successive twelve months), and, second, various medical benefits, including medical treatment and medicines, while sick, and hospital, sanatorium and nursing care, in certain contingencies.

Compulsory sickness insurance has been adopted in many European countries. But, contrary to the claims of its partisans, it has nowhere proven to be much of a success in providing the promised medical benefits. Some of the European systems—e. g., the British—have failed in this respect not far from disastrously. Others—e. g., the German system—have provided a quantitatively adequate though qualitatively doubtful medical service, but only through the degradation and demoralization of the medical profession. To make matters worse, insured medical benefits fail particularly to reach the poorest poor and the very classes of the sick who need public aid the most. And nowhere have there been any real indications that the medical service provided by compulsory sickness insurance has tended to improve the public health, the weight of testimony of the higher medical authorities being to the contrary. In other words, European experience indicates that the medical needs of the poorer people cannot be either well or economically provided for through the medium of or as an incident to insurance of a cash benefit to wage-workers during sickness, and that much waste, harm and bitter disappointment would be avoided and infinitely more satisfactory results obtained, if the state should undertake to provide for the prevention and cure of disease more directly, and, for such purpose, establish and maintain or subsidize such hospitals, clinics, dispensaries, nursing and health centers, etc., as, after due investigation, may be found to be needed to bring specialized medical care, etc., within reach of all the people, instead of seeking to accomplish impossible results through the inappropriate device of insurance. As respects its medical benefits, therefore, the proposition that European compulsory sickness insurance has been proved "successful" may rightly be characterized as a delusion.

In providing the cash benefits European compulsory sickness insurance has been relatively more successful, but subject to one very important qualification. Experience indicates that because of the uncertainty of the criterion of the right to the cash benefit under sickness insurance, this line of insurance can be administered fairly and with net social advantage only through small mutuals, in which the members know each other, watch each other, have a pride in keeping off the benefits and exclude malingerers and persons of bad habits, and that where the state intervenes and interferes with complete liberty of association and self-management, malingering and impositions become the rule, social parasites and impostors are favored and fostered, and the provident and industrious are exploited and preyed upon. The extent to which the European state sickness insurance funds are subject to such abuses is a matter of dispute; but the evidence accessible is most unfavorable. In other words, even as respects the cash bene-

(Continued on page 20)

Andrew Carnegie's Autobiography

A STORY OF CONSTRUCTIVE ACHIEVEMENT, OF AMERICAN OPPORTUNITY AND SUCCESS

By T. EVERETT HARRÉ

AT a time when individual enterprise, ambition and achievement, genius, initiative and such honest hard work as leads to signal success are disparaged and held in abhorrence by the advocates of communism, Bolshevism, government ownership and every shade of Socialism, "The Autobiography of Andrew Carnegie," published by Houghton, Mifflin Co., Boston, comes with refreshing wholesomeness. Andrew Carnegie's life is a vindication and exemplification of those principles of Americanism, which have made America great. Scotch by birth, and possessing the fine excellencies of his people, Mr. Carnegie was a typical American, an embodiment of American ideals, an example of American aspirations carried to success. This romance of an unknown boy who, by his own efforts, from poverty became one of the richest men in the world indeed reminds one of the marvellous tales of the Arabian nights and the fairy lore of the brothers Grimm—and like those stories, true in their moral. Mr. Carnegie's story is one in which honesty, devotion to high ideals, self-sacrifice and application are at last rewarded. The good jinn and fairy godmothers of those childhood tales do not wave magical wands for sluggards, the unambitious, incompetent, dishonest and unworthy, and indeed all these tales bear out the truth that happiness and riches come not as miracles but only to them who are deserving.

THE LATE ANDREW CARNEGIE

Mr. Carnegie's achievement is typical of America, whose opportunities, resources and freedom brought to its shores millions like Mr. Carnegie and his family; people of all lands and races who came here, became amalgamated in the melting pot and comprise today one of the greatest nations of the earth. Reading his own story, simply, sincerely and unaffectedly written, one cannot but compare this high-minded, kindly and earnest man with the swash-buckling and rabid poseurs who today strut about the world's stage as leaders of the "new order," the emancipators of the proletariat, the reformers of ancient wrongs—the Lenines, Trotzkys, Smillies, Longuets, Schniedermanns, Debses and Hillquits. Indeed, an answer to the world-agitation of our times might be found in this story of an individual man's accomplishments, by comparing his record in the up-building of a mammoth enterprise to the universal wreck which two mountebanks brought to all industry and agriculture in the great empire of Russia; by comparing what in a tangible and really great way Mr. Carnegie did for a great body of workers in one industry to the chaos, conscript labor and starvation to which the millions of workers of an entire nation have been reduced through the demagoguery of two men. It is proverbially easier to destroy than to create and build—far easier, indeed, for a Trotzky or a Hillquit artificially to foment discontent and sedition than it is for an honest hardworking man like Mr. Carnegie to build up a scientific industry which is of service to all humankind.

At a time when teachers in our public schools, professors in colleges and clergymen in all of our denominations are tincturing their teachings with radicalism, it might well be wished that Mr. Carnegie's story be taken as an object lesson by which our youth should be inspired. For this story of success through honest effort, of a tremendous individual accomplishment, has a noble message. And having won great riches, believing in the gospel that private wealth is a public trust, Mr. Carnegie proceeded to give away that wealth in a way that would do most good. His philanthropy, his endowments of educational institutions, his great libraries are imperishable monuments, and themselves a testimony of what truly great men may do. As one of the great capitalists, who are the object of odious and calumnious attack by the professional "Reds", Mr. Carnegie's humanity, kindliness and benevolence stand in striking contrast to the spirit of those bitter men who, by inciting hatred, class antagonism, all the instincts that are savage and bestial, would carry civilization down to destruction.

Mr. Carnegie began writing his recollections after his retirement from active business during his vacations in Scotland, and was so engaged when news of the outbreak of the Great War reached him. "These memoirs ended at that time," writes Mrs. Carnegie in a preface. "Optimist as he always was and tried to be, even in the face of the failure of his hopes, the world disaster was too much. His heart was broken." And the last entry at the end of the manuscript is of telling pathos: "As I read this to-day (1914), what a change. The world convulsed by war as never before! Men slaying each other like wild beasts. I dare not relinquish all hope."

Born in Dunfermline, Scotland, in the attic of a small one-story house, on November 25, 1835, Mr. Carnegie in his boyhood knew poverty. At the age of thirteen, with his parents and younger brother, he left Dunfermline for America—"To the land of the free," as his father sang, "Where a man is a man even though he must toil, and the poorest may gather the fruits of the soil." Mr. Carnegie tells of the struggles of his boyhood, how he worked in a bobbin factory, then became a telegraph messenger, a railroad clerk, later taking charge of a division of the Pennsylvania and serving the country as an Associate Director of railroad operations during the Civil War. He gives intimate and touching pictures of President Lincoln and other great figures of the time. His story describes his going into bridge building, of his investment in oil wells, and of his entry into the steel business and the development of that enterprise. In his book are rare bits of sage advice, and in telling of his decision to withdraw from all other interests and concentrate in that industry, going contrary to the adage about not putting all one's eggs in one basket, he says:

> "I believe the true road to pre-eminent success in any line is to make yourself master in that line. I have no faith in the policy of scattering one's resources, and in my experience I have rarely if ever met a man who achieved pre-eminence in money-making—certainly never one in manufacturing—who was interested in many concerns. The men who have succeeded are men who have chosen one line and stuck to it."

Mr. Carnegie has been assailed by the professional enemies of individualism and advocates of Socialism as one of the "exploiters of the working classes" and held responsible for the Homestead strike in 1892—the only single clash with labor during his long career. As a matter of fact, as he tells in his biography, he was away in Scotland at that time and was in no way responsible.

He writes:

> "I was travelling in the Highlands of Scotland when the trouble arose, and did not hear of it until two days after. Nothing I have ever had to meet in all my life, before or since, wounded me so deeply. No pangs remain of any wound received in my business career save that of Homestead. It was so unnecessary."

While in Scotland Mr. Carnegie received from the officers of the union of his workmen the fol-

(Continued on Page 21)

Present Status of the Socialist Party

RECENT ELECTION OF SOCIALISTS IN NEW YORK RAISES QUESTIONS OF ELIGIBILITY—HAVE CHANGES IN CONSTITUTION AND PRINCIPLES MADE SOCIETY LEGAL AND PARLIAMENTARY?

By ARCHIBALD E. STEVENSON

AT the last regular session of the Legislature of the State of New York, the right of the five socialist assemblymen-elect to take their seats was challenged on the ground that their membership in the Socialist Party of America as then constituted disqualified them from taking their seats in the Assembly.

After an exhaustive hearing and investigation by the Judiciary Committee of the Assembly, these socialist assemblymen-elect were expelled by an overwhelming bipartisan vote. This action provoked a storm of criticism from many quarters. The outstanding feature of the discussion on both sides of the question was the lack of clear understanding as to the facts of the case or the principles involved.

At the recent election, three socialist assemblymen have been chosen and one socialist senator. It is therefore probable that the questions raised last year will again confront the people of this state. It is therefore necessary to place before the public certain facts with respect to the Socialist Party of America, so that our citizens may be guided in their consideration of this problem by facts rather than assertions.

Before proceeding to the discussion of the present position of the Socialist Party in the revolutionary movement, it is necessary to have a clear understanding of what the Socialist Party is. The Socialist Party of America is a dues-paying membership organization, a revolutionary society, hereafter it will be referred to in this article as the Society. The Society admits to membership aliens and citizens alike and requires its members to take a pledge in support of its constitution and purposes. Its objective is the establishment in the United States of a socialist commonwealth described as the cooperative commonwealth, in place of the form of government now existing.

In order to effect this object, the Society operates in two distinct fields. In the first place it has created a political party which is known as the Socialist Party. This organization is made up of citizen voters who go to the polls on primary day and enroll under the socialist emblem. The object of the Socialist Party is to elect socialists to public office and to agitate the political demands of the socialist movement. The second field in which the Society operates is economic. The Society is engaged in the organization of revolutionary industrial unions for the purpose of forging a weapon of attack upon our institutions by industrial action which, when defined, means the general strike. These revolutionary industrial unions must be distinguished from the trade unions of the American Federation of Labor type, and are very similar in structure to that of the Industrial Workers of the World—namely, all workers in a given industry, no matter what trade or craft they may follow, are members of the one union. This method of organization gives the control of large masses of workmen into the hands of a limited committee and greatly facilitates the use of the strike weapon for political purposes.

It is the object of the Society to control the political party on the one hand and the revolutionary industrial unions on the other hand, so that when the moment of revolution arrives, they may re-inforce the political demands of the one by the direct action of the other. In other words, the members of the Society recognize that the socialist commonwealth cannot be established in this country or in any other country by parliamentary measures alone, for the reason that the bulk of the workers will adhere to the older parties and will not take part in the political party which it has created. This means that the members of the Society contemplate the use of militant direct action to veto the decisions of the ballot box. It means the assumption of power by a minority through the coercive action of the general strike. It should hardly be necessary to show that the acceptance of such a program as legal and proper would be to destroy the foundations of American liberty and be the beginning of despotism.

We deem this statement necessary because of the confusion in the public mind between the Society which we have referred to and the political party known as the Socialist Party which is its creature. The five assemblymen-elect were expelled from the assembly last year, not because they were members of the political party, but because they were members of the Society which was engaged in the activities just described.

The expulsion of these assemblymen created a profound impression upon the leaders of the Society. The national convention of the Society was held in New York City on May 8 to 14, 1920 (after the expulsion of the assemblymen-elect), at which time certain conspicuous changes in the constitution and statement of principles of the party were advocated and adopted. It must be borne in mind that the Society at this time was engaged in the formulation of a statement of principles upon which its creature, the political party, was to carry on its campaign this fall. The opportunist elements in the Society, led by Morris Hillquit, recognized the necessity of having the political party appear as a purely parliamentary party appealing to the voters of this state in support of a political program. On the other hand, a large faction of the Society, led by certain prominent instructors of the Rand School of Social Science, urged the Society to make a full, fair and frank statement of its purposes and objects as well as the methods and tactics it seeks to employ. The membership of the Society, however, recognized the soundness of Mr. Hillquit's position, and the result was a statement of principles which carries with it little that is objectionable from a legal point of view. At the same time certain changes were made in the constitution of the society in order to meet some of the objections raised by the Assembly last spring. For instance, that provision of the national constitution which provided for the expulsion of members who in public office voted to appropriate any money or supplies to the armed forces of the United States or for military purposes, was repealed.

Whereas minors were previously admitted to membership in the Society, the minimum age was raised to twenty-one years; and whereas previously aliens might hold office in the Society, the new constitution limited such office to citizens.

At an emergency convention held by the Society in September, 1919, the international affiliations of the Society were referred to the membership on referendum. The result of the referendum vote was to affiliate the Society with the Third Internationale of Moscow, a creature of the Soviet Government of Russia, committed to the policy of world revolution and the setting up of the dictatorship of the proletariat in all countries. The opportunist element in the Society recognized the disadvantage to its political party in an appeal to the American workers on such a program, and therefore reported to the May convention that its relations with the Third Internationale should be modified so that its membership in the Internationale would not be made dependent upon the acceptance by it of the formula: "The dictatorship of the proletariat in the form of soviets" or any other special formula for the attainment of the socialist commonwealth.

Similar action was taken by the State convention of the Society held in the early part of July of this year, which also amended the state constitution so as to eliminate the provision requiring members of the Society who were candidates for public office to place in the hands of the Executive Committee their resignations to such office so that after election they could be withdrawn from public service at the will of the Executive Committee of the Society.

The new statement of principles of the Society also contained a clear-cut expression of the party's determination to confine its activities to parliamentary measures. This was to be a campaign document to be used by their creature, the political party in its appeal for the votes of American citizens. It was not a statement of the policy of the Society in carrying out its plan for the establishment of the socialist commonwealth in this country.

This is made clear by the examination of the resolutions adopted at both the national and state conventions of the Society, which show that it has not abandoned the belief that the socialist commonwealth can be established in this country only through the re-inforcement of political demands by industrial action.

At the St. Louis convention of 1917, the position of the Society with respect to revolutionary industrial unions is expressed in a resolution which was adopted, which states:

> "The Socialist Party will ever be ready to co-operate with the labor union in the task of organizing the unorganized workers, and urges all labor organizations, which have not already done so, to throw their doors wide open to the workers of their respective trades and industries, abolishing all onerous conditions of membership and artificial restrictions, with the view *that their organizations may be eventually developed into industrial as well as militant, class-conscious and revolutionary unions with the development of the industries.*"

In furtherance of this plan, the resolution closes with the following admonition:—

> "It is also the duty of the members of the Socialist Party who are eligible in the unions to join and be active in their respective labor organizations."

The fact that the Society recognized at that time that the industrial weapon was essential is clearly stated in the same resolution as follows:—

> "In the face of the tremendous powers of the American capitalists and their close industrial and political union, the workers of this country can win their battles *only* through a strong, class-conscious and closely united organization on the economic field, a powerful and militant party on the political field, and by the joint attack of both on the common enemy."

(*Continued on Page 24*)

Socialism Unmasked

THE SOCIALIST PARTY FOR REVOLUTIONARY INTERNATIONALISM AS AGAINST THE UNITED STATES AND PATRIOTISM—LOVE OF COUNTRY HELD IN DERISION

By T. EVERRET HARRÉ

III.

SOCIALISM AND PATRIOTISM

Can a member of the Socialist Party of America be a good citizen? Can the Socialist organization pretend to be a purely political party advocating only parliamentary methods, or the use of the ballot? The answer to these questions is found in the record of the society.

Over the Kremlin in Russia there waves today, not the Russian flag, not the flag which symbolizes the history, the ideals, the mystical character and faith of the Russian people, but the Red Flag with its five-pointed Star of Internationalism. As against the government of the United States, as against the ideals and institutions of America, the Socialist organization in this country no less than the Bolsheviki stands for revolutionary Internationalism. As against the Stars and Stripes, its flag is the same Red Flag which floats over the citadels of Petrograd and Moscow.

Immediately upon the entry of the United States into the war, in 1917, the Socialist party took a stand against the war and against those loyal Socialists who supported their governments in the struggle against Germany. At its first convention after signing of the armistice, in 1919, consistent with its previous record, the Socialist party reaffirmed that stand and denounced those Socialists who had been loyal to their governments. At this national convention, in May, 1920, the party, in line with its policy, denounced the peace treaty as "an infamous pact formulated behind closed doors by predatory elder statesmen" and denounced the American government as having "helped create a reactionary alliance of imperialistic governments, banded together to bully weak nations, crush working-class governments, and perpetuate strife and warfare."

The stand taken and the program followed by the Socialist organization in the United States in regard to the war against Germany is of historic significance. That stand was not an isolated act of disloyalty, but a consistent step in "a continuing program of treason." The disloyal, unpatriotic, treasonable record of the Socialist party of America during the war was but an expression of its fundamental character and basic philosophy.

It is important that the American public fully understand the conduct of the party during the war, especially as now—as was illustrated at its national convention last May—the party seeks to win converts by deceit and camouflage. While that convention sought, for obvious opportunist reasons, to emphasize its political character, it did not repudiate its war platform and program, nor its declaration against and repudiation of all loyal Socialists. Instead, as aforementioned, it continued its stand with a denunciation of the peace treaty and of the Administration which, declares its latest platform, "has not scrupled to continue a policy of repression and terrorism."

The National Convention of the Socialist party convened in St. Louis upon the very advent of the United States in the war, April, 1917, and there adopted its notorious war platform and program. That was confirmed by referendum to the dues-paying membership of the organization, and, therefore, expressed the sentiments of the members of the party. As against the United States and our cause in the war, that document stated clearly:

> The Socialist Party of the United States in the present grave crisis solemnly reaffirms its allegiance to the principle of internationalism and working-class solidarity the world over and proclaims its unalterable opposition to the war just declared by the government of the United States.

Was the anti-war stand of the Socialist organization due to its pacifist character, to its opposition to force and violence? The Socialist party, refusing to support the war against Germany, declared its unpacifist character and its stand for militant actual, armed class warfare:

> The only struggle which would justify the workers in taking up arms is the great struggle of the working class of the world to free itself from economic exploitation and political oppression, and we particularly warn the workers against the snare and delusion of so-called defensive warfare.

The Socialist organization declared its belief in war—in the war of class against class, the taking up arms to bring about a revolution, and at the same time repudiated loyalty to and love of country:

> As against the false doctrine of national patriotism we uphold the ideal of international working-class solidarity.

It was not only upon America's entry into the war that the Socialist party of America committed itself to a policy of disloyalty and treason. The program adopted in April, 1917, was decided upon two years before, at the conference held in Zimmerwald, at which Lenine was prominent.

At a period when the situation between Germany and the United States was exceedingly critical over the use of submarines, April 21, 1916, the Socialist party of America met with the various translator secretaries, representing the various foreign-language federations of the party, and drew up a proclamation for dissemination among the foreign-language membership. This incendiary manifesto concluded:

> We suggest and appeal that the workers as a measure of self defense and as an expression of their power exert every effort to keep America free from the stain of a causeless war even to the final and extreme step of a general strike and the consequent paralization of all industry.

In 1916 the Zimmerwald conference reconvened at Kienthal, Switzerland, and issued a manifesto emphasizing the Zimmerwald proclamation. Again the Socialist organization in America responded and—at a time when the inevitable break with Germany was imminent—the party, seeking to render the country powerless under Hun aggression, adopted a presidential platform in harmony with that of Lenine and his associates:

> Therefor, the Socialist party stands opposed to military preparedness, to any appropriations of men or money for war or militarism, while control of such forces through the political state rests in the hands of the capitalist class. The Socialist party stands committed to the class war, and urges upon the workers in the mines and forests, on the railways and ships, in factories and fields, by refusing to mine the coal, to transport soldiers, to furnish food or other supplies for military purposes, and thus keep out of the hands of the ruling class the control of armed forces and economic power, necessary for aggression abroad and despotism at home.

Had it been possible for the Socialist organization to carry out its program, America would have been utterly helpless under Hun aggression; Germany would have won the war.

After war was declared by America against Germany, the Socialist party called upon the "workers of all countries to refuse support to their governments in their wars." In its program of opposition to the war the party then addressed the workers:

> The acute situation created by war calls for an even more vigorous prosecution of the class struggle, and we recommend to the workers and pledge ourselves to the following course of action:
>
> 1. Continuous, active and public opposition to the war through demonstration, mass petitions and all other means within our power.
>
> 2. Unyielding opposition to all proposed legislation for military or industrial conscription.

In addition to the war program, the party adopted a platform, in which it called "upon all workers to unite, to strike as they vote and to vote as they strike," and among its political demands it declared for:

> Resistance to conscription of life and labor.
> Repudiation of war debts.

At the same time that the Socialist party adopted a program of opposition to the war, and recommended that the workers continuously, actively and publicly oppose the war, the party repealed that provision in its national constitution, article 2, section 6, adopted in 1912, which prohibited the practice of sabotage. Concerning this action, Mr. Martin Conboy in presenting the case against the suspended Socialists in the New York Legislative hearing last winter, said:

"In view of the context, consisting of the war program with its pledge to use all means within the power of the members, with the demand for even more vigorous prosecution of the class struggle, with the declaration that the only struggle which would justify the workers in taking up arms was not the national struggle but the class struggle, the removal of the restraint on the use of sabotage becomes significant with sinister meaning. Sabotage is one of the most effective, if not the most effective, method of rendering industrial cooperation not only ineffectual, but impossible. It brings about that condition of national inefficiency and impotency to which the party was pledged to devote itself with unremitting energy, and . . . it cannot be regarded as intended to accomplish any other purpose than to notify the members of the party that even the negative restraint imposed upon them in making effective their program of industrial action had been removed, and they need not further consider themselves hampered thereby. It was a tacit invitation to commit sabotage."

According to a mass of evidence, the war program of the party was carried into effect by an unceasing deluge of propaganda. Because of the attempt to carry into effect its disloyal program, according to the report of the Executive Committee of the party to its National Emergency Convention, held September, 1919, some 2,000 members were arrested, and some of the foremost leaders of the party were convicted and sentenced to terms of imprisonment. Notable among these were Executive Secretary Germer; the editor of the party organ, *The American Socialist*, Engdahl; the secretary of the Young People's Socialist League, Kruse; Berger, Shiplacoff and Clark, of the National Executive Com-

(Continued on Page 22)

THE NATIONAL
Civic Federation Review

Office: Thirty-third Floor, Metropolitan Tower
1 Madison Avenue New York City

RALPH M. EASLEY, Editor

The Editor alone is Responsible for any unsigned article or unquoted statement published in THE NATIONAL CIVIC FEDERATION REVIEW.

BOLSHEVISM AND MENSHEVISM PRACTICALLY THE SAME

The international labor news is most baffling to the average reader of our daily papers. One New York paper joyfully declares: "French Labor Repudiates Bolshevism by a Vote of 1,478 to 602." That sounds good, but when the reader gets by the headlines he discovers that the "majority faction" declares unreservedly that its revolutionary objects are "incompatible with present institutions and with capitalism and its political expressions;" that it proposes "immediate action for supervision of industry and commerce by the workers, to be sought *by direct action;*" that it "wages an intensive campaign for nationalization of essential industries; calls on the International Federation of Labor for united action to accomplish social transformation;" points out that "the revolutionary temper existing throughout the working world is most propitious for the agitation of such action;" and expresses "sympathy and encouragement for the Italian workers and indignation toward the French Government, the most servile instrument of world reaction." The declaration also favors "complete solidarity with Revolutionary Russia" and urges agitation until peace is established and "the republic of the Soviets enjoys full independence." It also proclaims anew "its ideal of economic liberation through the suppression of the wage system."

One naturally asks: If the 1,478 want all that revolutionary stuff, what could the 602 want that is any worse? The answer is, *nothing*, speaking from the standpoint of those who believe in private property and the wage system. The fight in the Orleans Congress was not between radicals and conservatives, between Socialists and anti-Socialists, but between Bolshevists and Menshevists, to speak in Russian terms. To speak in American terms, the fight was between the Socialists and the I. W. W.'s, a fight which is just as intense in this country as the fight at Orleans, the only difference being that the Socialists and the I. W. W.'s, with all their factions and sub-factions combined, are too negligible a factor here to cut any figure.

To translate the whole labor problem into terms that the layman can easily understand, take a concrete case. The General Electric Company at Schenectady has, say, 15,000 employees. If the Socialists should capture this country, whether by ballot or by bullet, they would say to the stockholders of that corporation: "This property has been created by the workers and you have robbed them of it. The State will take it over without compensation and operate it for the benefit of all, just as the Post Office is run for all." The I. W. W. would say to the General Electric people: "To H—— with the State! It should be abolished, as well as private property. We will have the workers take over the plant and run it for the benefit of the workers alone." This was what was attempted in Italy—and thanks to a government with a "Reddish" Premier, they succeeded temporarily but soon found that they could not run the plants after they had seized them. So they offered to "compromise" with the owners by permitting them to "participate" in the management and to participate on a "fifty-fifty" basis in any profits that might remain after the workers had fixed and collected their own wages and also had "managed" the finances, the purchasing of raw material, the selling of the product, etc., etc.

Lenine and Trotzky tried both of these schemes with equally tragic results. First, they adopted the I. W. W. method of having the workers run the business through shop committees, shop stewards and all the rest of the paraphernalia advocated by the parlor Reds of all countries. When those proved a miserable failure, they shifted over to the other plan and now the State is trying to run what is left of industry, the workers being mobilized into an industrial army and placed under machine gun and bayonet discipline. They surely have the discipline, but that is all.

To return to the General Electric Company: So far as the stockholders of the corporation are concerned, it makes not a whit of difference whether the plant is confiscated and run by the State or confiscated and run by the workers; it is confiscated in either case.

So much for the American Socialist and I. W. W., or the Russian, French and Italian Bolshevist and Menshevist industrial program. But there is another program in this country which is the controlling one—and that is the trade union program. The proponents of this school would say to the General Electric Company: "We concede your right to own the business, to make sufficient profit to pay overhead charges, interest, rent, taxes and so forth. But after you have done that, we demand a sufficient wage to enable us not only to live in comfort and educate our children but to save for a rainy day and to have also some of the luxuries of life." The controversy between the General Electric Company and the American Federation of Labor would be not over who owns or runs the plant but over a division of the corporation's profits, in terms of wages. The questions of union and non-union shop, the limitation of production piece work, minimum wage, etc., trying as they are at times, are all predicated upon the wage or competitive system and are only its logical by-products.

But in the case of the Socialist and I. W. W. programs, these exasperating and perplexing problems, leading to strikes and lockouts and, too frequently, to sanguinary outbreaks, do not appear because both private property and the private employer have entirely disappeared. If there is any employer in this country who cannot visualize that situation and who becomes so angry at times over some unreasonable and radical demand of organized labor that he "does not care what happens," let him read the reports from all the labor commissions that have returned from Russia and the incontestable testimony of those who have had their plants taken over "for the good of all." Also, let him note carefully what employers like himself have been doing in Russia since the revolution—sweeping the streets, working in sewers and doing other menial work, provided, of course, they have not been locked up in filthy cells or were not among those thrown into a vat of boiling water just to furnish amusement for some 19-year old girl friend of the Commissar. Even the closed shop, with all its "horrors" would be preferable to a little boiling bee.

However much employers may criticise certain policies and actions of the trade unions, they certainly will appreciate the ringing, patriotic declaration of the American Federation of Labor, repudiating the Bolshevist proposals of the International Trade Union and the British Labor Party. It is not too much to say that the American labor movement is the only important one in the world today that is not trying to paralyze its Government and dictate its international as well as its domestic policies. And the American labor movement would vote just as solidly against the policies of the majority as against those of the minority faction of the French Federation of Labor.

THE EBB AND RISE OF THE RED TIDE

In September, at the heat of the Presidential Campaign, the Department on Study of Revolutionary Movements of The National Civic Federation sent to the people who had previously signed a Declaration against the Recognition of Soviet Russia a communication asking them to write to their Presidential candidate declaring their conviction that, whatever political changes occurred, the stand taken by our Government against Bolshevist Russia must be maintained and that, on this grave matter, there could be neither neutrality of thought nor action.

In this communication it was stated: "The Red offensive against Warsaw has been broken, but already Lenine threatens to raise a Bolshevik army of 5,000,000 to renew the Red onslaught. Whether this will be possible or not, the Red offensive against civilization through intrigue, plot and subsidized propaganda has not been checked."

Not only has the Red offensive through intrigue, plot and propaganda not been checked, but after defeat by the Poles the Red hordes have recently won a tremendous victory over General Wrangle, practically wiping out his armies. Thus, following the tragical defeat of Denikin and Kolchak, the last military offensive against the oppressors of Russia is broken. With the Bolshevik armies again victorious in the field, with recent information that Lenine intends to flood the United States with thousands of propagandist agents, with Ellis Island open to an indiscriminate deluge of alienry, among whom without question are countless social malcontents of the rabid types that brought Russia to her ruin, it becomes all the more urgent that there be no let-down, no compromise, at any time in the future in the stand maintained by the Department of State against any recognition of the lawless autocracy in control of Soviet Russia, and in the position recently expressed that, even should the British Government carry through arrangements for trade relations, the Department will not alter its policy. The firm stand of the Administration is based on the belief, first, that the Bolshevist theory menaces the stability of civilized and democratic government; second, that the Bolshevist régime does not represent the Russian people, nor does it completely control Russian affairs, and third, that Russia has nothing to give in exchange for goods from the rest of the world. The soundness of this position is impregnable, and from it, so long as the régime of Lenine and Trotsky holds, can there be no change.

In both parties, during the compaign, were Bolshevist sympathizers and agents who condoned the excesses of the Red régime and in every way, artfully, cunningly, by suggestion and subterfuge, sought to reach and influence the candidates in favor of recognition of the Soviet regime. In view of the information at hand and his expressed statements, it is not to be credited that the successful candidate has been, or can be, influenced by these sinister voices. But it cannot be overlooked that, after March 4, tremendous pressure will be brought to bear both through the surface and underground forces that are working for recognition and aid for the autocracy of Lenine. Already a formidable pro-Bolshevist propaganda is under way, and is of such a character that it cannot be ignored.

One phase of this propaganda is found in the campaign of the Committee on Russia, of the League of Free Nations Association, which prior to the election addressed an open letter to the Presidential candidates, attacking the rulings of the Department of State and demanding to know what policy, if elected, each candidate would pursue. This is manifestly the beginning of a propaganda to aid Bolshevist Russia, the purpose being to develop political pressure and bring about a change of policy after the next inauguration. Another phase of the propaganda is to be found in the widely exploited articles of Mr. H. G. Wells, who is to follow this publication by a visit to the United States and an undoubtedly spectacularly advertised lecture tour. Mr. Wells is a distinguished novelist, and on the strength of his deserved literary reputation—incidentally a reputation based on works of imagination and romanticism—what he would have to say about Russia, just as anything he might have to say about a personal Deity or the habitation of Mars, will be listened to in club, lecture, forum, church, and other circles with respectful attention and a certain amount of deferential credence. Mr. Wells is by far the most valuable propagandist Lenine and Trotsky have yet won to their cause, Raymond Robins notwithstanding.

Mr. Wells is undoubtedly sincere; he writes and talks well; he is engaging and plausible. Mr. Wells admits the hideous catastrophe in Russia under the Bolsheviki; his picture of what has happened would be a damning indictment of Bolshevism were it not for the fact that he attributes the tragedy of Russia, not to Bolshevist fallacies, ineffiency and terrorism, but to all that went before it under the Czar. Mr. Wells disavows that he is a communist and that he believes in the Bolshevist theories and program, yet he so hates the Czarist regime that he categorically ascribes the starvation, collapse of industry and very excesses of Bolshevism to the autocracy that preceded the present.

While Mr. Wells' presentation will undoubtedly make a considerable impression, it must not be forgotten that Mr. Wells has for years been a Socialist of the idealist or Fabian variety, impressionable, sentimental, and, giving him credit for sincere intentions, was at times during the war pacfist and an advocate of an early peace through compromise, one of a group which included Romaine Rolland, Henri Barbusse, Anatol France, Bernard Shaw, Bertrand Russel and others. Moreover, during his visit to Russia he was under the aegis of his old friend, Maxim Gorky, one of the chiefs of the Bolshevist propaganda bureau; he was delightfully entertained, taken to the opera, well dined, and treated in such a manner as he could not but possibly feel a certain humanely genial warmth toward his hosts. In fact, Mr. Wells was handled much in the same manner as Raymond Robins was handled, and shall we say Mr. Wells was no less "captured" by the wily Red czarists than his Red Cross predecessor?

It is important that with this renewal of the Bolshevist propaganda offensive, arranged to work to a cumulative climax at the Presidential inauguration, that representative Americans continue to make their voice heard in this grave matter and not permit the noisy liberals and imported lecturers to bring about a surrender to autocratic barbarism of American ideals and a repudiation of all that civilization has won in two thousand years.

COMRADE DEBS AND BISHOP FISHER SEEM TO AGREE

Eugene V. Debs, perpetual Socialist candidate for the presidency, and Bishop Fred B. Fisher, of the Methodist Episcopal church, in certain recent utterances are found to have a striking oneness of mind. Not in regard to the beneficent influence of religion in the world, nor the fundamental principles and ideals of the Christian faith, but as to the reasons for the employment of force and violence by the revolutionists in carrying out their program. It might be expected that while Debs would justify violence, as practiced by the Bolsheviki in Russia, a Christian clergyman would condemn it under any and all circumstances; indeed, that from a bishop would come only reprobation and abhorrence of the unparalleled atrocities of the Russian revolution. But this is not the case with Bishop Fisher, recently in charge of the Industrial Relations Section of the Interchurch World Movement and now Methodist bishop of southern Asia.

In an interview given in prison, Mr. Debs recently expressed the belief that "*we may* have a perfectly peaceful revolution" in America, but that, again, we might not. The revolution would not be peaceful, however, "*in the event that the present owners of the industrial mechanism might fight to retain the privileges of ownership. If they should insist on violence in behalf of their profits, those who had the common good at stake would be forced to use force in return.*"

Mr. Debs justified the use of force in the Bolshevist revolution. Bishop Fisher, in an article in the *Christian Advocate*, of October 28, 1920, pleaded in defense of the "extreme phases" of what he euphoniously terms "the world-wide social awakening," declaring:

"*Give them a chance. Be not too harsh in condemnation of even extreme phases of this awakening. Naturally we decry recourse to force, but force has many causes, not the least of which is often unyielding resistance. Education and tolerance on both sides are a deal more effective and also more Christian than either violence or resistance.*"

According to Debs, if the Socialists attempt to take over the machinery of government, all the mills, mines, railroads, etcetera, by employing the general strike—as they did in Russia, and tried to do in Germany—the present owners, if they did not wish to suffer violence, should sit with folded hands and not resist expropriation. If they did attempt to retain what they believe are their rights, they would then be responsible for violence and bloodshed, massacre and terrorism. Under such circumstances, according to Bishop Fisher, they should let the Socialists go ahead in a spirit of "education and tolerance," which would be more "effective and also more Christian" than *resistance*. Both Debs and Fisher, therefore, agree that a fanatical minority, as was the case in Russia, should not be resisted in carrying out their revolutionary program, but if resisted then the revolutionists would have cause to employ force.

Bishop Fisher asks us to "behold the wonder of this awakening instead of its terror." Therefore, instead of pausing to contemplate the comparatively minor horrors of the Red régime, the wholesale killings, conscription of labor, destruction of industry, and sufferings of the Russian nation, we should instead look for the "wonder" of it! Bishop Fisher further finds a possible explanation for this "economic war" in the "strange and mysterious ways" of God's spirit. To those who know that Socialism, or Bolshevism, is materialistic and atheistic, declaring religion to be "the opium of the people," and that in Russia religion is being scientifically exterminated and that children are educated along anti-Christian Marxian lines, this expression may seem shocking if not blasphemous. Nevertheless, Mr. Fisher says "this wine of the new concept may prove to be the 'wine of the new spirit,'" and he recalls that "our Church history is full of crude, cruel resistance to spiritual reformations misunderstood and persecuted at times which in after years have been revealed as indispensable to human progress." Undoubtedly Messrs. Lenine and Trotzky, Debs and Hillquit, regard Bolshevism as a great "reformation," "misunderstood" and "persecuted" by its opponents, and "indispensable to human progress," and evidently one Methodist bishop at least agrees with them.

It was suspected that the employment of radicals and a certain tone in the work of the industrial section of the Interchurch World Movement under Mr. Fisher's direction, as well as the marked radical atmosphere of the conference held by that section at the Hotel Pennsylvania some time back, was due to Mr. Fisher's proclivities. His recent statement justifies this suspicion and proves, what has long been contended, that there is little difference between the outright "Red" leaders and the "intellectual radicals" in schools, colleges and churches. Bishop Fisher is now "in residence" at Calcutta. Does it not behoove the officials of the Methodist Episcopal church, if not the British authorities, to keep an eye on his activities?

Immigration Enquiry

Within a period of six months the immigration problem, as never before in American history, has become one of acute and crucial importance. To those familiar with conditions it has reached a stage where it constitutes a national menace. The American people generally are ignorant of the fact that day by day thousands of aliens, including aged, mentally defective and diseased, are being deluged upon our shores; that since last June from 80,000 to 100,000 aliens are passed each month through Ellis Island. The Government report on immigration ending with June 30, 1920, showing that the income was hardly more than the outgo, doubtless lulled many people into apathy. Since then conditions have utterly changed. As an indication of the laxity in regard to exclusions, and the policy pursued of letting our doors wide open, showing that either our laws or their enforcement are defective, there were admitted at Ellis Island in one day recently 3,100 people, while only 25 were excluded, and of those admitted the majority were old men and women, orphans and other non-productive people.

Mrs. Marion K. Clark, chief investigator of the Bureau of Industries and Immigration of the New York Industrial Commission, declared recently in an interview in the *New York Evening Post*, that excludable aliens are being admitted in such large numbers that within a few years the penal institutions and asylums for defectives in New York state will be overrun.

"The rules of the immigration authorities provide for an evasion of the immigration law, which expressly prohibits the entrance of certain undesirable persons into the United States," declared Mrs. Clark. "This evasion is accomplished by the making of bonds under the terms of which limited indemnity may be exacted from persons giving bonds should the excludable aliens become public charges after the entrance is accomplished. Such bonds are seldom enforced, are usually worthless, and even if enforced leave the excludable alien a burden on the commonwealth or a social menace which, in the case of the mentally defective classes, cannot be estimated in terms of money."

The popular and humanitarian appeal made by those who would let the bars down is that America should be an asylum and refuge for the poor and persecuted in other countries. Those who have investigated the problem of late are inclined to ask, if this influx is permitted to continue, how long it will be before America is anything but an asylum of defectives, dependents, social malcontents and criminals.

In order to ascertain the public mind as re-

(*Continued on page 24*)

Purifying Politics—A Field For The Churches

DR. WORTH M. TIPPY'S ANSWER TO OPEN LETTER OF RALPH M. EASLEY SUGGESTING POLITICAL WORK FOR RELIGIOUS AND SEMI-RELIGIOUS ORGANIZATIONS, AND THE REPLY

IN the previous issue of THE NATIONAL CIVIC FEDERATION REVIEW was published an open letter by Ralph M. Easley to Dr. Worth M. Tippy, Executive Secretary of the Commission on the Church and Social Service of the Federal Council of the Churches of Christ, which had been inspired by the "Labor Sunday Message." The answer to Mr. Easley's letter by Dr. Tippy, and the response thereto, are herewith published:

MR. RALPH M. EASLEY,
Editor, THE NATIONAL CIVIC FEDERATION REVIEW.

My dear Mr. Easley:

To reply to your letter of September 14th *seriatim* would be difficult because of the number of problems which it raises. The best I can do is to consider the two sections into which it falls—the first dealing with the Labor Sunday Message for 1920 of the Federal Council of the Churches, and the second dealing with your suggestions for the social activity of the churches. I take the second first.

You propose that the churches abandon the industrial field and devote themselves to such movements as social hygiene, the extermination of rats, the control of the immoral theatre, drug addicts, political graft, incompetent public servants, ineffective and unscientific methods of dealing with criminals, defectives and delinquents, conflicting legislation for the protection of women and children. You then outline a possible co-operation between Catholic, Hebrew and Protestant, to improve our political machinery, but working loyally through party organizations. You also show how you consider it possible to control profiteering and to effect conciliation in labor disputes through a purified machinery of government and the use of state Bureaus of Mediation.

My reply to this is to say that the churches are and have long been active in these fields, except possibly in the extermination of rats. They have been closely related since the early days of the war to the campaign for the control of venereal diseases inaugurated by the Public Health Service, the National Social Hygiene Association and the American Red Cross. The office of the Study Committee of the National Conference on Community Organization of which Honorable Franklin K. Lane is Honorary Chairman, is at present in the office of the Commission on the Church and Social Service. The churches are closely involved in every community effort of importance in the United States, and their cooperation is recognized as essential by every social and civic agency. The control of public recreation, the scientific and humane care of the feeble minded, the criminal and the delinquent are a part of the program of every Federation of Churches and Ministerial Association. The Federal Council has its Committee on Social Legislation as a feature of its Research Department and gives most thorough study to federal and state bills considered to be within the sphere of church action, and the churches are constantly before legislative and congressional committees on matters affecting public welfare. They were influential in the campaign which overthrew the so-called Tammany government when the late Mayor Mitchel was elected Mayor of New York.

There is also a growing cooperation in these matters between Catholic, Hebrew and Protestant. Here is one field where dogmatic differences need not divide us. The Protestant churches are quick to cooperate and always reaching out for cooperation. The Catholic churches as yet cooperate guardedly and intermittently. At present the Commission on the Church and Social Service and the Catholic Welfare Council are conducting jointly a study of the street railway conflict in Denver on invitation of the Denver churches, Catholic, Hebrew and Protestant.

But not only are the great religious communions mentioned not as yet effectively united; sixty percent of the people are not in the churches. We do not want the Government run by the churches, even if it were possible, but by the people as a whole in the interest of all the people. The churches, it seems to me, should take an unselfish part in public affairs but should not attempt to dominate them.

But is it not also true that the activity of the church is as little wanted in corrupt politics and in efforts to control the other evils you have mentioned, as in industrial relations? Your associate *Industry* of Washington attacked the Y. W. C. A. because of its efforts in the New York legislature to secure legislation protecting women and girls as vigorously as it has attacked the churches for their attitude on labor. In every social field where there are deep-seated wrongs, the first effort is to try to scare away the church. Those who are old enough to have witnessed the progress of the temperance movement to its climax in the Eighteenth Amendment will remember what the church passed through in its espousal of that great reform.

Turning now to the first part of your letter—the relation of the church to industrial problems, and especially to the Labor Sunday Message for 1920: the church can no more keep out of that field than the others for the reason that it is a field not only of machinery and natural forces but also of human relations. Wherever human relations are involved, there the agencies dealing with spiritual and ethical values are immediately and necessarily called into action. Moreover the basic laws of successful industry are as much human and ethical as economic, as is being shown by the futility of recognizing only the technical and economic factors in industrial management.

The special field of the church in industrial relations is that of an organization having expert knowledge in ethical and spiritual problems and on matters that affect the welfare of men, women and children. We get over into the economic sphere—necessarily so if we are to teach—and often enough we shall make mistakes; but I would remind you good naturedly that even editorial writers do not hesitate to tell the church where to work and how to work, although it may be quite out of their field.

You ask by what authority the Federal Council speaks for the churches on industrial questions. The Federal Council is an official correlating agency of 32 denominations. Their judicatories select representatives to the Council, the number in ratio with their membership. Action by the Federal Council does not bind these constituent bodies except as such action is approved by their judicatories. The Social Creed of the Churches has been approved by practically all these denominations and by the Y. M. C. A. and the Y. W. C. A. Important statements by the Federal Council must be approved by the Administrative Committee of the Council, which is composed of official denominational representatives.

You are mistaken in saying that employers "do not have any representatives on the Committees of the Federal Council having to do with industrial matters." They are on all our committees and commissions, and they are more largely represented than labor. In fact our labor representation is as yet meagre and unfair as compared with that of capital.

Your letter seems to me to use words carelessly. The Labor Sunday Message did not anywhere "talk about abolishing the competitive system and taking on the cooperative commonwealth," but expressly the opposite. It was based upon the conviction that the present system is essentially sound but has grave and sometimes intolerable evils which must be corrected.

The first sentence in the paragraph quoted in the middle of your second column might have been more carefully stated, and should possibly have read as follows: "Our industrial life has been built in part on wrong and unchristian foundations." Few would assert that it is wholly so. What the message contended for was that competition should be controlled by the cooperative principle, and that the motive of profits should be subordinated to the principle of service. The description of the effect of the present working of the competitive law which you quote is exactly what is taking place. When Bertrand Russel came back from Russia, a convert against Communism, one thing that reversed his former sympathy for Communism was that he feared a possible destruction of civilization in the other great western nations. The industrial and political situation is a turmoil of struggle. The temper and addresses at the last annual meeting of The National Civic Federation were as apprehensive as any I have attended since the war. To attack the Federal Council for this passage not by reasoned statements but by the references which the letter makes, seems out of keeping with the standing and spirit of The National Civic Federation.

The statement of the message that "working exclusively or mainly for profits corrupts men as working for a salary corrupts a preacher" is clear, at least to church people. A preacher who does this is discredited in the church. Every minister is supposed to subordinate financial considerations to human welfare; and most ministers, missionaries, Christian Association secretaries, social workers and their wives do this to the point of heroism. The Christian point of view is that the motive of service should be the highest for everybody. "He that would be the greatest among you shall be the servant of all," said Jesus. This is not chimerical. I personally know a great many business men, labor leaders and public officials who work from this motive, and in the increase of such industrial and political leaders, it seems to me, lies the hope of the future. Most of these men with whom I have talked are convinced that when industry is put on a Christian basis, we shall enter upon a period of unprecedented prosperity.

What has Charles W. Wood to do with the Labor Sunday Message or the Federal Council? He was sent to China some years ago by the Methodist Centenary to look at the work of the missionaries through a newspaper man's eyes. I do not find his observations, as reported in the *World*, illuminating; but that is not here nor there in relation to the Message.

In the third column of the third page of your open letter you dwell upon the church's "jumping into the midst of employers and employees." What was said was this: "At whatever risk of becoming involved in the controversy, it (the church) must go into the midst of the contending forces, if possible between them."

You rightly call attention to the difficulty of this policy and its danger. These were given careful consideration; but the national peril, the economic losses involved and the growth of class hatred and violence are so great that it was considered desirable that the church should exert every ounce of its influence to bring the contending forces together, and to bring to bear the spirit and teaching of Jesus upon the growing strife.

The church has a right to do this, and an obligation, since it is estimated by Babson that 90% of all business men are connected with churches or synagogues, and since vast masses of labor are also in the church. It cannot do anything effective unless it goes "into the midst of the contending forces." What we hope to do is to have our clergymen speak and write on its ethical phases and its human values, and our experienced laymen, employers and leaders of labor, on the more technical phases of the industrial problem.

I do not wish to discuss the differences among church officials on industrial questions, except to say that the church is divided into conservatives, moderates and radicals, as are business politics and labor. We like to keep our more divergent opinions amongst ourselves, and to maintain if possible a broad Christian platform of cooperation and tolerance.

Very sincerely yours,
(Signed) WORTH M. TIPPY.

October 15, 1920.

REV. DR. WORTH M. TIPPY,
Executive Secretary, Commission on the Church and Social Service,
Federal Council of the Churches of Christ in America,
New York City.

MY DEAR DR. TIPPY:

I am sorry you did not "enthuse" over my suggestion that the churches clean up the rotten political conditions which are choking almost to death our governmental institutions. Furthermore, I fear you missed my whole point, for you seem to feel that by "being closely related to the campaign for the control of venereal diseases," initiated by others; furnishing desk room for the Study Committee of the National Conference on Community Organization (whatever that is); having on their program "the control of public recreation, the scientific and humane care of the feeble-minded and the criminal"; going before legislative committees on bills, etc., etc., constitute the fulfillment by the church organizations of their whole political duty. In fact, I am quite pained to find you so well satisfied with such extremely meager efforts to secure the good government for which all men and women of voting age are responsible, and for which all Christian people should feel an especial obligation resting upon them. In my previous letter, I called attention to the fact, in suggesting great moral reforms for the Church to undertake, that it had made little headway during the past two thousand years in grappling with that horrible plague, the social evil. Is "being closely related to the campaign for the control of venereal diseases" the Council's only answer to that charge? What I tried to point out is that, instead of having your committees running around begging aldermen, legislators and Congressmen to listen to your appeals, you should get on the inside and do the work in the city councils, the state legislatures and Congress, and yourselves appoint these boards and committees that are to listen to appeals from the people. You have the votes to do it. You say the churches have only 40 per cent of the people, but the politicians that run the country have not even 1 per cent. Why, Lenin and Trotzky run 150,000,000 people with a handful of communists because they are determined to have what they want. If you wish to awaken the Christian people on this subject, send committees to the municipal councils of all the important cities and let them see just how things are done affecting the matters enumerated in my former letter. If you yourself would head a committee that would attend the meetings of the Board of Aldermen in New York, I believe you would become so indignant that you would turn crusader in the interests of cleaning up the city, and it certainly would be a job worth your while.

As I write this letter, a book comes to me from Raymond B. Fosdick on "The American Police System," which I commend to you and your Commission. It certainly is a sickening revelation for a Christian nation. I quote a few sentences:

> "To an American who has intimately studied the operation of European police systems, nothing can be more discouraging than a similar survey of the police of the United States. . . . In America, on the other hand, the student of police travels from one political squabble to another, too often from one scandal to another. He finds a shifting leadership of mediocre calibre—varied now and then by flashes of real ability which are snuffed out when the political wheel turns. . . . It is a job held, perhaps, by the grace of some mysterious political influences, and conducted in an atmosphere sordid and unhealthy. . . . In the interim between these spasms of publicity the average police force sinks in its rut, while crime and violence flourish. . . . We have indeed, little to be proud of. It cannot be denied that our achievement in respect to policing is sordid and unworthy. Contrasted with other countries in this regard we stand ashamed. . . . We must confess failure in the elemental responsibility laid on all peoples who call themselves civilized, of preserving order in their communities."

You say: "Your letter seems to me to use words carelessly. The Labor Sunday Message did not anywhere 'talk about abolishing the competitive system and taking on the co-operative commonwealth,' but expressly the opposite."

"Expressly the opposite" would mean then that the Labor Sunday Message talked about abolishing the co-operative commonwealth, and taking on the competitive system. That might sound good in Russia, but hardly here. Are you not, therefore, a little guilty yourself of "using words carelessly" and am I guilty of that charge? I was not pretending to quote, but was indulging in a generalization or, more correctly speaking, a deduction based upon the vitriolic Socialist arraignment of the competitive system which I quoted from the Labor Sunday Message. It might well have been taken from the soap-box harangues one could hear any night, during the late election, on the corner of 110th Street and Fifth Avenue. To refresh your memory, I quote again:

> "That law of struggle or competition, as the historic dominant law of industry, has pitted employer against employer, corporation against corporation, nation against nation. It was responsible away back for the great war with its gigantic economic and human losses. It has pitted capitalist and employer against the workers, and the workers against capitalist and employer in a struggle which threatens another cataclysm and at least the temporary shattering of civilization."

Of course, if the competitive system is all that the Labor Sunday Message says, and there are no compensating virtues to its credit—and you mention none—then it should be abolished, and quickly, and when it is abolished the co-operative "commonwealthers" just as surely will stalk in unless the syndicalists "beat them to it." If your premise is sound my conclusion is sound, for certainly you would not want to continue a system so terrible in its operation. Before leaving this topic about the part played in our civilization by the competitive system which all our Socialist and Socialistic preachers and ex-preachers are clamoring to send to the scrap-heap, preliminary to the ushering in of the "new social order," alias our old friend the co-operative commonwealth, may I ask: Has your Commission, or any committee of the Federal Council, ever made an effort to search out and catalogue the wonderful progress made under our present order in the industrial field alone, the one which concerns your Commission? Has it considered carefully the debt that civilization owes to competition? Compare the conditions of work and living of the farmers, the wage-earners and the common people a hundred years ago and now. The result will be truly astounding. I am enclosing one of my articles, entitled "Shall the Old Order be Scrapped?" describing a few of the outstanding changes wrought during that period, which Socialists scrupulously avoid mentioning. For them to admit progress under the present régime would be tantamount to abandoning their whole theory that whatever is is wrong, and would result in postponing the revolution they are working overtime to bring about. This attitude is a consistent one for the Socialist Party to take but it is surprising that a body claiming to represent 17,000,000 Protestant men and women should lend itself, consciously or unconsciously, to the promotion of Socialist propaganda by hurling at the competitive system anathemas couched in the language of Karl Marx and all of his big and little successors. Of course, in all that I have said about competition, I am not referring to the old *laissez faire* unregulated competition of a hundred years ago. Since the first factory act was passed in Great Britain in 1802, legislation in countless fields has, through restrictions, eliminated most of the earlier evils. Workmen's compensation acts, child labor laws, pure food regulations, public utility measures and a hundred other legislative enactments—all give eloquent testimony to the truth of this statement.

You state: "You are mistaken in saying that employers 'do not have any representatives on the committees of the Federal Council having to do with industrial matters.' They are on all our committees and commissions, and they are more largely represented than labor." The quotation is inexact. I said "do not *seem* to have" etc. My statement was based upon the fact that the Federal Council's Commission on The Church and Social Service as shown upon your letter-head, composed of 76 members, has not one important employer, if any, on it, nor more than two men active in the labor movement that I can discover, but is made up almost entirely of preachers, ex-preachers, college professors, ex-college professors and a sprinkling here and there of salaried officials of semi-religious and philanthropic organizations. If that committee was democratically selected—and of course people who talk so much about democracy in others would surely apply it to the conduct of their own affairs—does it not seem strange that out of 17,000,000 members, the 16,000,000 farmers, wage-earners, bankers, manufacturers, merchants and lawyers secured a representation that requires a high-power microscope to discover?

You say: "It is estimated by Babson that 90 per cent of all business men in the country are connected with churches or synagogues." I assume that the Babson to whom you refer is Roger W. Babson, a member of your Commission, who is credited with many remarkable statements and prophecies. Doubtless he is the same Babson who wrote the fifty-one articles in the then pro-German *Evening Mail* for Dr. Rumely, now on trial charged with having disguised the fact that he had bought the *Mail* with money furnished by the German Government. Incidentally, $5,100 of that money, wherever it came from, went to Dr. Babson for his fifty-one anti-English articles, so the story runs.

(Continued on page 23)

Our Supreme Allegiance

(Continued from page 8)

tle which swept Europe with a scourge of agony and death, they were sustained by the feeling that there was something at stake which transcended all the advantages of peace, and which justified and sanctified the bloody and barbaric work they were called upon to do. Any plan for the suppression of war which does not meet and satisfy this fundamental and powerful incentive to war will inevitably prove defective whenever put to the supreme test. And such an incentive, at once so sad and so exalted, can never be satisfied by a plan which simply says: "peace is preferable to war, so let us enforce peace"; for when conditions arise which morally justify the declaration: "war is preferable to peace, so let us have war," the fallacy of the formula will be exposed and the plan will be thrown aside, unless it afford means for the affirmative vindication of justice through the forces of peace which it has denied to the power of the sword.

And here to my mind we have disclosed one of the critical points in the proposed covenant for the League of Nations where it may sooner or later be found fatally inadequate. We have only to imagine another case like that of Cuba, or to take the actual case of Shantung should Japan finally conclude to retain that portion of the Chinese Republic, and China be driven to wage war for its recovery. In that event, as well as in all similar cases, the League will not only be powerless to afford an affirmative remedy, but its members will be bound, at least morally, by the provisions of Article X, to give aid and comfort to the despoiler.

We are told that Article X is the heart of the League; and so it is, if by that it is meant to assert the over-shadowing importance of its provisions.

In order to understand the nature and effect of this obligation let us read the article. It is as follows:

> "The high contracting parties undertake to respect and preserve as against external aggression the territorial integrity and existing political independence of all states, members of the League. In case of any such aggression, or in case of any threat or danger of such aggression, the executive council shall advise upon the means by which the obligation shall be fulfilled."

There can, of course, be no reasonable objection to a general agreement among nations, including ourselves, to respect the territorial integrity of one another, although it may be said in passing that the principle is one, which, from motives and for reasons deemed good and sufficient by us, we have not ourselves uniformly observed, as Mexico and Spain, for example, might truthfully bear witness. But the obligation, it will be seen, is not merely to *respect*—which requires us to restrain only our own predatory desires and operations—but it is to *preserve* the property of our neighbors, which requires us to restrain the predatory operations of others, a far different and a far more onerous obligation, since the former involves nothing more serious than the exercise of a fair degree of self-restraint, while the latter may call for the exercise of a very high degree of expensive and disagreeable and more or less tragic affirmative action. It will be seen that the undertaking in terms is absolute, unqualified and unlimited, and whether it be regarded as legally binding or only morally binding, as some have happily suggested, may be satisfied by nothing short of accomplishment, or by a reasonable demonstration that accomplishment is impossible. To refuse to execute the undertaking on the score of difficulty or lack of concern or sympathy in any given case, would be utter abandonment of our pledges, and would make of the treaty a scrap of paper. If we sign, we must keep the faith and must, therefore, be prepared if and whenever occasion shall require to put upon the willing, or the unwilling shoulders of the people the task of raising and equipping armies and sending them overseas to preserve the political integrity of Italy or Siam, of Poland or Czecho-Slovakia, of the Kingdom of the Serbs, the Croats and the Slovenes, or of any other member of the League.

I have said the obligation is absolute, and if we have regard for the plain meaning of words, so it is. No exception is made in favor of those cases where external aggression may be the result of internal wrongs, such as Cuba endured, such as any weak people or submerged race may at any time in the future be called upon to endure. The obligation is to preserve the territorial integrity of the tyrant, as well as that of the benign ruler of the well content. If the altogether improbable should happen, and another George III undertake to deal with Canada as his predecessor dealt with us, we should not only be bound to go no further than the indulgence of a flaccid sympathy with our oppressed neighbors, but actually to assist the oppressor should a second Rochambeau or LaFayette come to their aid. It is not sufficient to reply that the suggested circumstances are highly improbable. The fact that they have once happened demonstrates the possibility of their happening again, and such possibility, however remote, should induce us to think well before finally committing ourselves to an undertaking which might prevent us from enlisting our strength on the side of an outraged community except at the cost of breaking our plighted word.

Neither is there substance in the claim that the latter part of the article provides for the advice of the executive council, and as it must be unanimous we shall be able to control the situation. That advice has nothing to do with the obligatory nature of the undertaking, but relates only to the means by which it shall be effectuated. It is not necessary for me to point out in a matter so clear, that one cannot be relieved from a positive promise to do a thing because he will not join with others in determining the way in which it shall be done.

Our acceptance of this obligation would, of course, completely reverse a policy as old as the government itself. That fact, however, while persuasive is not necessarily controlling. It does not conclusively follow that because a given policy of government is old it must be right, or that because it was wise as a practical rule of action for our forefathers it must remain wise as a rule of action for us. Truth is eternal; but not always absolute. It is sometimes conditioned so that a statement which is true at one time, under some circumstances, may not be true, or be only partially true, at another time under different circumstances. And so we are constantly overhauling and modifying, and sometimes rejecting, the teachings of the Fathers which were wise and true in their own time and generation.

The Farewell Address of the first President has been accepted with a degree of faith in its wisdom accorded no other document, I dare say, except the Constitution alone. But even the Constitution is not considered permanently perfect since we provide for its amendment. Nobody insists, therefore, that Washington's advice is to be regarded as the permanent and final measure of our conduct. Nevertheless, counsel which has so long survived, and been so generally approved, has established for itself a presumption in favor of its wisdom of such strength that it may not be challenged except for weighty and convincing reasons. Perhaps nothing in that remarkable address has been more frequently referred to—and more generally misquoted, I may add—than the advice against entangling relations with foreign countries.

No intelligent student of international affairs can doubt that we shall be obliged to participate in the concerns of the old world to a far greater degree than was ever contemplated by Washington. The world has moved and changed since his day, and we have moved and changed with it. No real American will, for a moment, desire that his country shall ever fall short of performing its full part in promoting and maintaining the peace and well being of mankind. If that shall involve expense and hardship and sacrifice, we must cheerfully bear the burden and go on nevertheless. But it is one thing to stand ready and willing to do that in accordance with our own promptings and sense of duty as occasions of need shall, from time to time, present themselves, and quite another thing to bind ourselves to act in that regard in accordance with the will or opinions of some extra-constitutional body responsible to the whole world—ourselves included, to be sure—but in no peculiar sense to us.

I have no desire to be suspected of provincialism; but if that appellation applies to one who prefers that his countrymen shall remain free to manage their own affairs and assist in the management of the affairs of others, as they and not as others, may determine, then I must plead guilty to being hopelessly provincial. I am not averse to an agreement binding us to do those *specific* things which we ought to do in the absence of agreement, as, for example, to assist for a definitely limited number of years in the defense of France against German aggression. I would not, however, make even that an indeterminate agreement, for conditions will inevitably change, and what is right and expedient for us to do now may become altogether wrong and foolish for us to do a quarter of a century hence. I should never be willing to do for the France of a Napoleon what I would gladly undertake for the France of Clemenceau. The transmutations of history are beyond all foresight; and who is bold enough to deny the possibility of finding ourselves irreconcilably opposed to the attitude of some or all of our Allies long before a quarter of a century shall have gone by? Five years ago England and France united in a just war against Prussia, but a hundred years ago England and Prussia joined hands to fight France.

Quite apart, however, from anything which may be said on the subject of American adherence to the guaranty contained in Article X, it is open to serious consideration upon general and fundamental grounds. What is the ultimate thing which it seeks to accomplish? Upon its face it seems to be an attempt to crystalize in perpetuity the present geography of the world as modified by the treaties of peace, a program quite impossible of attainment, and which, if persisted in, must end in failure, if not disaster, for it proceeds in complete disregard of the immutable laws which govern the movements of human society.

In every age, and in every country, there have been men who have longed for and believed in the possibility of some final decree of wisdom that might, once and for all, establish a happy and permanent settlement of all sorts of controversial matters. Again and again, in religion, in government, in science, in all the fields of human thought and endeavor, they have fancied realization just ahead, only to find that it was not the ultimate goal which they beheld but only the horizon from which a new and equally deceptive finality was in sight. But the most visionary of all undertakings is that which seeks not merely to *advise* but to *bind* the future, to follow the opinions and ideals of the present. The political problems of the future will somehow have to be met and solved, but, inasmuch as we do not know what they will be nor how they will be conditioned, we can only be sure that any solution we may prescribe in advance will probably not be as effective as, and certainly will not be wiser than, that which will be found by those who will be able to see with the eyes of fact what we can only imagine.

The Treaty of Peace was formulated by the victors alone, and the vanquished were compelled to accept it. Such a course was naturally to be expected and is not to be condemned upon moral grounds. That it should be a hard peace was also natural and morally right, for the Germans had been guilty of inconceivable outrage and cruelty in the conduct of the war, and that they should be compelled to make restitution to the utmost limit of their capacity was in accordance with the eternal principles of retributive justice. But however clear the justice of the settlement may appear to us it will never receive the approval of the enemy peoples; and when we consider the extent to which they have been stripped of their territory, and the hindrance which this will present to their future expansion and development, we are bound to conclude that they will acquiesce in this capital dismemberment only so long as they are constrained to do so by a sense of their own helplessness to do otherwise. When we consider, moreover, the extent to which new states have been created, submerged and well-nigh forgotten nationalities lifted into power, new adjustments of sovereignty and boundaries among friends and neutrals established, we can but fear, as many thoughtful students of the subject do fear, that the Treaty of Peace has ended one war only to sow broadcast upon the ever fruitful fields of Europe the seeds of hate and controversy which may ripen into many more.

The world is never at a standstill. It is in a continual state of flux. Nations and races come and go, develop from insignificance to dominating strength, run their course of power for a time, and sink back to a condition of inferiority again. A century of this ever recurring process is but a day in the life of humanity. A few days ago it was Imperial Rome who, with her legions, made and unmade governments and dynasties and shifted the boundaries of the earth as she pleased. Then it was Spain. Then France. Yesterday it was England. Today it has been the Big Five at Versailles. Tomorrow? God alone knows! But it will be somebody. Perhaps Japan, old in years but young in power, filled with eager ambitions yet willing to bide her time. Perhaps Russia, that strange admixture of idealism and brutality from whom everybody wins victories, but whom nobody conquers. We cannot know the future, and it is idle to speculate; but of one thing we may be sure, that the restless interplay of diplomacy, the shrewd matching of prime-ministerial wits, and all the devious and sharp devices by which craft and guile and intrigue have played their sinister part in the game of European politics for a thousand years, will not come to an end with the ratification of the Treaty of Peace. But even if they should now and forever end, nevertheless, the rise and fall of nations and societies of men, the perpetual shift of international boundary lines, the extension of sovereignty in this direction and the contraction of it in that direction, will go on in response to the universal law of change which forbids the world to stand still. An agreement, therefore, to make the political subdivisions of the earth perpetually immovable is doomed to failure from the beginning, because it involves the fatal mistake of attempting by convention to render immovable that which by its very nature must be eternally and resistlessly upon the march.

I said that our problems were simple and direct, but I did not mean they were trivial. On the contrary, we are facing questions of the utmost gravity. Their proper solution, however, will demand no nice balancing of alternatives or adroit manipulation of the processes of reason, but only courage and common sense and the application of the usual frank and straight-forward methods of American thought and action. While to a great extent they are new questions, their solution will not necessarily require us to turn our backs upon the past. The truest progress sometimes consists in the sturdy retention of long established methods. Nevertheless, in a world of growth and change we must continually face the problem of determining when to hold fast to the things we have, and when to abandon them for something new—with the certainty, I may add, that whichever we do we shall not please everybody, and perhaps not anybody: the old-fashioned will consider us radical, the impulsive and impatient will stigmatize us as reactionary, and if we seek a path of moderation between them, both will join in denouncing us for "straddling."

Among these problems there is the labor question, always troublesome but recently of acute concern, presenting a difficulty partly real and partly psychological and, therefore, to be settled upon terms which will be not only just in fact but whose justice will be recognized and accepted by those concerned. There is also the not altogether unrelated question of immigration. As unskilled labor has grown scarce we have sought to supply it by opening more widely our gates of ingress to the heterogeneous masses of Europe. We have indulged the optimistic hope that we should be able to assimilate them to our standards, but we are awakening to the danger of being assimilated in greater or less degree to their standards instead. Large portions of New York, Chicago, and other great cities have become virtually foreign territory where the English language is an unfamiliar tongue. We have been forced, in recent months, to deport large numbers of undesirable aliens, a necessary but drastic and unfortunate recourse which admonishes us that we must find some way of closing the gates against such immigrants in advance.

The solution of these and many other social and governmental problems has become doubly imperative as a result of the war. We shall solve them, of course, but they will be followed in never-ending succession by other questions no less serious and important. The great lesson we must continually learn and re-learn is that eternal vigilance is not only the price of liberty, but the price of peace and order and general well-being, and all the other blessings which follow an adherence to the principles of good government. It is, therefore, the duty of the citizen who appreciates their measureless value, to be perpetually alert not only to meet and resist every direct and deliberate attempt to destroy them, but to defend them against the insidiously hostile speculations of the purveyors of theory as well.

To my mind, one of the most dangerous of these speculations is that which challenges and belittles the spirit of nationalism, and which seeks to substitute for the warmth and intimacy of loyalty and love of country, that vague and vacuous communion of the tribes known as "internationalism."

We are in the habit of thinking of the nation as though it were an entity apart—something set going by our forefathers and left to maintain itself ever since by some mysterious power of its own. But the nation is only one of the forms we ourselves assume, and it is we,—and not something apart from us—who constitute it and animate it and maintain it. The nation is something more than so many millions of people occupying a geographical sub-division of the earth's surface, speaking the same language and subject to the same laws. These are its visible and tangible constituents, but what gives it organic life and meaning is the spirit of unity which dwells within and which, if the nation were self-conscious and had a voice, would enable it to say as a person may say: "I am myself and not another."

To lose this organic sense of individuality—at once a manifestation of unity and of separateness—would be to lose the national soul. Co-operation with other peoples for the common good, a feeling of world-wide sympathy and fellowship, are not only of the highest virtue but they give a sweeter quality to patriotism itself. But no man can remain loyal to his own country and be willing to imperil her institutions and organic existence for some real or fancied obligation to serve mankind in general. Any philosophy which teaches us to sacrifice these in order to serve the world is a sham and a fraud. Not only can the world not be served in any such way, but to attempt it will be to sow the seeds of a divided allegiance which will inevitably ripen into national destruction. To admit such a spirit of internationalism as this into the body of the nation would entail consequences similar to those which follow the development of that mysterious thing called "multiple personality" in the body of an individual:—a tangle of utter bewilderment and confusion. I reject with every atom of my intelligence a doctrine so filled with menace. I am as anxious as any one for the well-being of the world, but if I am asked to promote the well-being of the world at the risk of undermining the foundations of the Republic, every sentiment of reverent attachment and fidelity to American ideals and interests bids me stand for the Republic even at the cost of hardship for the world.

The inevitable tendency of the internationalist teaching is to break down the sentiment of patriotism and put in its place a tenuous sense of attachment to a group or a class or a race. You cannot eliminate from the heart of the Anglo-Saxon, the Latin or the Slav the conviction that his race is the foremost, its history the most glorious, its character the most admirable; nor can you prevent combinations of groups or classes for more or less selfish ends. But the thing which saves all this from a condition of predominating danger is the national spirit which, in the last analysis, brings all rival and discordant factions together for the common weal and the common defense. If this be taken away and there be substituted for the unifying force of patriotism the hodge-podge of internationalism the danger will be that if we thereby succeed in reducing war among nations we shall do so only at the cost of increasing it among peoples as a result of race and class and group antagonism. The nation will be in constant jeopardy, for the advancement of a class or the ascendancy of a race will become more important than the preservation of the country. If there be not sufficient warning in the quarrels over Fiume, in the Irish question, in the double allegiance of the hyphenated American before the war, in the labor clauses of the proposed covenant for the League of Nations, which singles out the workmen from all other classes as the subject of special consideration, we may surely find it in the bloody and brutal work of Bolshevik Russia still going on in eastern Europe.

We have no autocracy of birth in this country and we will have none of class or race. The fountain of equal opportunity which the Fathers opened and whose waters we have drunk must never be sealed against our sons. The institutions under which we live are of such transcendent worth that their protection is the imperious and paramount duty of all whose rights are made safe by the marvelous counterpoise of liberty and law which they afford. They are ours and ours alone; an example which others may emulate if they will, but a possession never to be thrown into the grist of some common political universalism. They not only represent the clear foresight and high wisdom of their creators, but they have come to us as the final expression of Anglo-Saxon effort which, through the centuries, slowly, sometimes painfully, but always steadily, has moved toward the culminating glory of their achievement. Those who belittle them, those who would put in the place of their concrete and intimate processes some abstract and far conception of world-wide fraternity, are plotters of

(*Continued on Page 19*)

American Labor Breaks With International Federation

(Continued from Page 4)

revolutionary body and has never had any affiliation with any revolutionary body which would require it to give serious consideration to revolutionary proposals of any kind. While recognizing the need of revolution against autocratic governments, organized labor in this country regards the American government as being essentially democratic. On the whole and in the last resort the people rule in this country. While our political system is not perfect from the democratic point of view and while organized labor has devoted itself to bringing about the extension of democracy into the sphere of industry, it has never considered or compromised with any revolutionary movement to upset our institutions by violence.

The appeals of the International Federation of Trade Unions and of the "Council of Action" are appeals to revolutionary violence. The International Federation of Trade Unions declares very clearly that, "it must of its own accord and within its own ranks find the power to preserve the world from terror and anarchy." The world is not threatened with terror and anarchy unless it be from the Soviets for the aid of which these manifestoes are issued. If the world is to be preserved from this or any other danger, it must be by the action of democratic governments chosen by the people.

One year ago the International Federation of Trade Unions endorsed the League of Nations and proposed to reshape it to correspond to the aspirations of Labor. Today it takes a position of anarchistic hostility to all governments without discrimination.

The British labor party also turns its back on the democratic parliamentary system which England has evolved by seven centuries of struggle, and can find no way to ensure that the foreign policy of Great Britain "accords with the desires of the people."

The American Federation of Labor is diametrically opposed both to the methods advocated by the Oudegeest manifesto and to its object. The Montreal Convention reaffirmed the objection of American Labor to all forms of revolutionary violence and to reaction which might be interpreted as assistance to the Soviets.

Oudegeest and Adamson calmly suggest that faith should be placed in the declarations and promises of the "Russian government." The American Federation of Labor does not regard the Soviets as the Russian government and places no reliance whatever upon their statements and promises. The A. F. of L. action taken in Montreal was based in part upon the telegram of our Secretary of State to the President of the American Federation of Labor in which he declared:

> The existing régime in Russia does not represent the will or consent of any considerable proportion of the Russian people. It repudiates every principle of harmonious and trustful relations, whether of nations or of individuals, and is based upon the negation of honor and good faith and every usage and convention underlying the structure of international law.

No despotism in history has ever had such an unbroken record of broken faith. Let us take only two or three most recent examples. It is of the utmost importance to the Soviet oligarchy to reestablish trade relations. The British government has made every concession to achieve the same object. Yet even in the midst of these negotiations and before the eyes of the entire world the Soviets have almost daily broken faith. After the promises to cease propaganda in England came the subsidy of $375,000 offered to the *London Daily Herald*. As the *London Herald* is the only daily labor newspaper in Great Britain and is the leading labor organ, the offer is of the first moment. Lansbury, the near-bolshevist editor, brazenly proposed that the subsidy should be accepted as a symbol of "international solidarity." He wished the public to forget that in giving these subsidies the Soviets claimed, and expected to gain control of, the publications. Every recent announcement of Lenine and of the Communist Internationale has shown that they demand absolute dictatorial powers wherever their authority extends. While claiming to be willing to adjust their tactics according to conditions of each nation, the adjustment is to take place in Moscow.

About the same time as the *London Herald* disclosure, came the Soviet breach of faith in the armistice negotiations with Poland. After having promised to limit their exorbitant demands for the disarmament of Poland confronted by a Soviet Russia armed to the teeth, the bolshevists at the last moment added new clauses demanding workmen's militia for Poland by which they hope to sovietize that country.

The daily comparisons of the statements of bolshevist diplomatists for foreign consumption with the official pronouncements of the bolshevist government in Russia, the speeches and articles of Lenine and the decisions of that branch of the Soviet government which is known as the Third Internationale, demonstrate the utter falsehood of their entire stand.

The American Federation of Labor has always declared for and stood by the demand against large standing armies, for the limitation of munitions of war and for a reduction in naval establishments. These provisions are incorporated in the Versailles Treaty and the League of Nations, but if the production of war materials were to cease entirely all small nations would be utterly helpless and at the mercy of their larger neighbors. America could arm within a year or so even if she had no armament at hand. Smaller countries, like Belgium, would be utterly powerless while Poland and Georgia would fall into the hands of Soviet Russia without any means of resistance. But there can not be the slightest question that the defeat of Poland by the Soviets was the concise and immediate object, both of the British "Council of Action" and the International Federation of Trade Unions.

The International Federation of Trade Unions went even further than that in the copy of the manifesto which reached the Washington office of the American Federation of Labor. In all the telegrams as well as in the copy received by mail as printed in Amsterdam, reference was made to the holding back of food supplies. The very organization which has been crying out against the supposed starvation of Soviet Russia by the entente blockade apparently proposed the blockading of and starving of Poland, as well as its disarmament while Soviet armies were on its soil!

But this contradiction need give no surprise. The International Federation of Trade Unions called for the blockade of Hungary and after executing it inflicted suffering on the entire population. Even worse, the manifesto calling for this blockade contained a protest against the blockade of Soviet Russia.

There can be little doubt that the whole movement was largely devised at Moscow and originated at the conference of the Third or Communist Internationale a few weeks previously. Lenine had called for precisely this line of action on the part of the labor organizations of Western Europe. He boasted that Sovietism would be maintained in Russia and would spread throughout Europe, not because of its own internal strength, but because it could rely on the cooperation of European Labor.

Indeed, with the widespread and practical help that was extended by European Labor to the Soviet armies invading Poland, and with the growing sympathy of European labor for the bolshevists, the demands of Lenine for absolute dictatorship over the European movement has become steadily more insistent. In other words, the aggressive and violent character of the bolshevist régime and international propaganda is now due primarily, not to the certainty of their hold upon the Russian government or upon the victories of the Red Armies, but upon the support of European labor.

There have been indications that the Italian uprising and the radical stand taken by Smillie in England were planned to take place at the same time as the expected fall of Warsaw and to mark the beginning of a general bolshevist or near-bolshevist upheaval throughout all Europe. Even now, letters of Smillie's are published in the Polish press calling for a pro-Soviet attitude on the part of Polish labor—in spite of the fact that Poland has now perhaps the most democratic government of Europe with the leader of the peasant party as its premier and the well-known Socialist Daszinski as its Vice-President.

RECOGNITION OF THE SOVIETS

The British "Council of Action," as quoted in the telegram of Adamson, not only calls for the recognition of Soviet Russia but is empowered to bring about a revolutionary general strike for this purpose. The American Federation of Labor is utterly and wholly opposed, not only to such revolutionary measures but to anything that approaches any form of assistance to Soviets. The Montreal Convention resolved:

> That the American Federation of Labor is not justified in taking any action which could be construed as an assistance to or approval of the Soviet government of Russia, as long as that government is based upon authority which has not been vested in it by a popular representative national assemblage of the Russian people; or so long as it endeavors to create revolutions in the well-established civilized nations of the world; or so long as it advocates and applies the militarization of Labor and prevents the organizing and functioning of trade unions and the maintenance of a free press and free public assemblage.

Every statement made in this declaration was amply borne out by the declarations of members of the official British labor delegation which recently visited Russia. Bertrand Russell declared that the Soviets represented only a very small minority of the Russian people and that the dictatorship was tyranny in the worst sense of the term. Mrs. Philip Snowden stated that the Soviets were not socialist, democratic or christian. Tom Shaw and Ben Turner made similar statements. Yet, in its official report, the delegation has the audacity to state that the Soviets "had rallied to their support practically the whole of the Russian nation," and the "Council of Action" was created to aid in delivering Poland to the tender mercy of the Soviets.

The independent socialist party of Germany also sent a delegation recently to Russia, some of the members of which, though extremely sympathetic with the Soviets, asserted that bureaucracy and militarism were worse than under the Czar. As a result, the leaders of the independent party, including not only the more moderate, like Kautsky and Hilferding, but also Crispien, Dittmann, Louise Zeitz and Ledebour, have all come out strongly against affiliation with the Third Internationale.

Even the Italian bolshevist-socialists who recently visited Soviet Russia, came back with adverse reports. Dugoni reported that Lewis' experiment was a complete failure. His statements were endorsed by Serrati, the editor of *Avanti* and the leader of the party. Darragona, the leading figure in the Italian labor unions, together with Vacisra, reported that the present Russian régime is not based on the desires of the entire people but on the dictatorship of one party, the bolshevist party, which smacks of tyranny. Finally, the French syndicalists who have long resisted the importation of sovietism into France, have strongly attacked the bolshevists. Jouhaux has recently declared that the Soviets have practically made a declaration of war against organized labor of France, while Meerheim, head of the metal workers, and Bartuel, secretary of the miners, have written that bolshevism is a military and reactionary doctrine which gives even worse results than those of capitalism.

In a letter dated August 25, and received in the Washington headquarters of the A. F. of L. on September 9, Oudegeest asks if American Labor is affiliated with the International Federation of Trade Unions. In a communication sent two weeks earlier he wishes to know if American Labor will be present at the International Trades Union Conference to be held in November. The agenda for this conference covers four points only:

The international control of raw materials; the socialization of international transportation; the control of international exchange; the protection of the trade union movement from oppression.

The agenda specifically states that no internal questions are to be considered. In the second letter of Oudegeest was enclosed the manifesto above quoted.

The President of the American Federation of Labor in answer to the first communication stated it to be his opinion that the A. F. of L. would not be likely to send a delegation if the meeting were closed to a general discussion of all internal and external questions affecting the International Federation of Trade Unions.

We are living in the Republic of the United States of America—a country by no means perfect (on the contrary, it has many defects), in which all too frequently injustice is done. But it is a Republic based upon the principles of freedom, justice, and universal suffrage. Our men and our women are not likely to throw these rights and principles into the scrap-heap for the dictatorship of Moscow's Lenine and Trotsky.

For a number of years the American Federation of Labor was affiliated with the old International Federation of Trade Unions. It has always aimed to help in establishing a bona fide league of the toiling masses of all the countries of the world. It is a source of regret that conditions have been so shaped by those who are now controlling the policies and course of the new International Federation of Trade Unions that the A. F. of L. feels constrained to refrain from joining a movement where the independence and autonomy of each national trade union center is not only denied but wherein it is subjected to absolute domination for purposes wholly foreign to the objects for which the International Federation of Trade Unions should be formed.

The American labor movement is primarily concerned in achieving improved conditions in the standards of life and work, in securing freedom, justice, self-expression, and democracy by evolutionary processes rather than by violent revolution which promises all and accomplishes nothing.

Our Supreme Allegiance

(*Continued on page* 17)

evil or vain dreamers of dreams. The loyal of heart and sound of head will concede no such rival and accept no such substitute. We shall, I hope, never cease to sympathize with and aid the struggle for greater happiness and better conditions in every land, but our first hope and chiefest endeavor must always be for the welfare of the people of this land. Above all else we must suffer no divided allegiance to corrupt our citizenship if we are to remain the masters and moulders of our own destiny.

And so, let us renew the old covenant of American unity and stand together for the perpetuation of the undiminished powers of the Republic, to the end that we may preserve the blessings of liberty and justice for ourselves and thereby strengthen our hands to aid in their maintenance wherever they may be assailed elsewhere among mankind.

Vital Problems of Agriculture

(*Continued from page* 3.)

The Federal Farm Loan system must be preserved and strengthened. The Farm Mortgage Brokers who are seeking to destroy it must be defeated in the sinister purpose to return American farmers to the old order of uncontrolled, unlicensed, and exorbitant interest rates, costs of renewals and bonuses, etc.

The cooperative features of the Federal Farm Loan Act must be preserved from harm. The rights of the cooperative borrowers represented in the 4,000 national farm loan associations will be better protected if they will form a national federation or union through which they can fully and freely function. Friends of the farmers in Congress will welcome such an organization. State and national banks are organized into the American Bankers' Association in whose honor the city of Washington was recently lavishly decorated with bunting and American flags. The National Union of Farm Loan Associations is just as greatly needed by the cooperative borrowers.

Certain farm organizations such as the Farmers' Union, the Equity Societies and the Granges have done pioneer work. They and various cooperative commodity associations have fought the farmers' battles and stood the brunt of the attack when it was unpopular to do so, and it will not be for the good of agriculture to allow new movements suddenly springing up with the backing of great traders and captains of industry, commerce and finance to minimize and push aside the organizations which have blazed and hewn out the road. Let us progress continually but let us hold securely the gains we have already made. To insure this let us trust to the farmer and not to the outsider who may have a peculiar end to attain.

During the year ahead I hope to see the city consumers work out sound purchasing arrangements so that they can meet the farmers part way. The Farmers' Union could supply consumers' stores in the great cities with cooperative vegetables, butter and eggs, but the consumers have no adequate organization for this purpose. Cooperative flour mills, whether owned as in England by the consumers or undertaken by the wheat growers themselves, will in either event prove a check to profiteering and increase the earnings and savings of both producer and consumer.

Certain powerful banking interests are declaring that money should be regarded as a commodity. They say that prices of everything else were unchecked during the war and up to the present time, but that interest rates were maintained at the same level. They believe that money should command an interest rate in accordance with the necessity of the borrower. This is a harmful and vicious conception of money which of course should be regarded only as a medium of exchange. It is not unlikely that the browbeating ideas and tactics of financial despots are making it necessary for the agricultural cooperators to organize their own banks and credit facilities. A special committee to consider this problem should be provided for.

To save the rural citizenship of this country, it is necessary to have a new deal. I care nothing for the hackneyed square deal which leads into the wilderness of promise to no purpose. But a vitalizing squaring off which shall begin with legislation at once (the Capper-Hersman Bill) to permit farmers to conduct their cooperative business free from the menace of imprisonment, and the giving of representation of governmental boards and commissions, and a Secretary of Agriculture who will be representative of the organized farmers of the nation. No other method will now be able to preserve a wholesome balance between the three great groups of Capital, Labor and Agriculture, notwithstanding the altruistic sounding protestations of those who say that this government is adequately representative. We know that it is not adequately representative, and that this is one of the chief causes of a decadent agriculture which it is our solemn duty to remove.

Cooperative Bank Opened

(*Continued from page* 5.)

"The organization of a bank was twice authorized by our conventions, but this was postponed on account of the war. That our members were ready for this venture is proven by the fact that the stock was oversubscribed by $300,000. This confidence is explained by the fact that the brotherhood has never failed in anything it has undertaken. We own an office building worth $2,500,000 that will be turned over at the third triennial convention in May, 1921, free of all indebtedness. We have just purchased a site opposite the brotherhood building on which we are planning to erect a 20-story bank and office building. Both of these buildings are in the heart of the business section of Cleveland and will be closely identified with the group plan of public buildings.

"For fifty years the brotherhood has carried on many kinds of life, accident and pension insurance. We have paid out through the banks of Cleveland many millions of dollars a year. We have paid out in charities alone over $3,000,000 and not a single member of the Brotherhood of Locomotive Engineers is a public charge. Our total insurance on the books of our associations amounts to $184,000,000 and since 1868 we have paid out claims of $45,291,264.

"The Brotherhood of Locomotive Engineers has operated all of these activities for fifty years and has never lost a cent on its investments.

"The fact is, labor needs banks of its own more than any other class, unless it is the farmers. The wages of labor in this country amount to $30,000,000,000 a year, yet the average working man has no place to go to do his banking. In the cities at least his deposits are not wanted in the commercial banks. Often the worker is charged for keeping his account with the bank. There is no place the worker can go to get a loan, save the loan shark where he often pays from 100 to 200 per cent per annum.

"There should be banking facilities for the workers the same as for other classes. There are such banks in every other country. There are 65,000 such banks in Europe and they rarely lose a cent. They do a business running into the billions of dollars every year.

"The motto of the brotherhood bank is 'SERVICE.' It is organized along cooperative lines. We expect to receive the deposits of our 85,000 members and of 892 local divisions. We will invest the insurance and savings funds of our members and their widows. They have no place to go to make safe investments. Millions are lost by them every year through bad investments. We will draw wills and trust agreements for our customers. We also aim to aid our members to build homes.

"Our bank forbids loans or profits of any kind to officers or directors. Our funds will not be tied up in corporate bonds or underwritings. We believe there is need of many more banks owned by workers and farmers conducted on a cooperative basis and we will do everything in our power to assist them with our experience."

Catholic "Social Reconstruction Program" Analyzed

(*Continued from page 8.*)

fits, the success of European compulsory sickness insurance is extremely doubtful.

In this connection it should be borne in mind that the rejection of state sickness, invalidity, old age and unemployment insurance does not mean that our workers will have to go uninsured and in misfortune and old age be dependent upon charity or poor relief. Already there is in effect in this country an immense volume of insurance, covering large numbers of workers, and in amounts running far higher than anything dreamed of in Europe. And, during the last few years particularly, such insurance of American workers has been spreading and improving rapidly. There is much to be hoped from organized efforts to propagate and improve that insurance and to spread it more widely. We ought not to be discouraged because progress is slow. For even the compulsory insurance systems—that is those among them which are at all impressive—were not created in a day or a year by legislative fiat, but have been built up slowly and gradually throughout a generation. And we ought not to be discouraged because voluntary insurance will probably never cover all the workers. So far as it goes it will be better insurance than any the state can provide. And there are some of the workers who are not fit subjects for insurance at all—who are not "insurable risks." What they need is correction or charity; and where it is charity, no good can be done by disguising that charity under the false name of insurance.

It should be further noted in this connection that in America there is relatively far less need than in Europe for insurance of cash benefits during short sicknesses. Relatively few of our wage-workers are unable while in health to accumulate savings equal to the cash benefits of sickness insurance; and cash in pocket or in the savings bank is better protection against the wage loss from short sickness than is a claim against an insurance fund. Generally a savings bank balance is an advantageous substitute for *sickness* insurance. And in estimating the number of our wage-workers who ought to be but are not insured against sickness, those with material savings or property should be excluded from the count.

Second. The second argument for state insurance runs as follows: It is desirable that all persons dependent upon their earnings should be insured. It cannot be hoped that all of them will ever be persuaded voluntarily to insure. And in a voluntary system many of the "bad risks" among them will probably be excluded from insurance. But under a state insurance system all workers can immediately be compelled to insure.

But in order to compel all workers to insure, it is necessary in practice for the state to prescribe, within narrow bounds, *how* they shall insure. And for the state thus to decide and prescribe what provision individuals shall make each for his own private needs, though normal under some European forms of government, would be reactionary in America. Our government is an experiment in individual liberty. And it is an experiment that, up to date, has been highly successful, in comparison with all other forms of government, especially in respect to the material well-being of the working people. Consequently, it would be unreasonable to abandon that successful experiment, even in part only, and to revert to methods of autocracy and paternalism, without very certain assurance of a net social gain therefrom. But experience holds out no such assurance.

In this connection it should be realized whither the proposed departure from our principles of liberty would logically lead. If the state ought to decide how much of his income every worker shall set aside for sickness, invalidity, old age and unemployment, place the amounts so set aside in common funds, and then distribute the funds as the government may determine, there is no reason why the state ought not also to provide in the same way for the food, clothing, lodging and recreation of the people. That would amount to complete communism. And it is simply as a first step towards communism—as a plank in the Socialist party platform—that the movement for compulsory insurance has obtained its principal impetus. Great caution should be exercised before joining with the Socialists in the first step on such a dangerous road.

It is assumed to be a social advantage from compulsion that by its use there can be brought immediately under insurance all the improvident, the subnormal, the "ne'er-do-weels" and the victims of their own vices and bad habits, whom voluntary insurance would slowly or never reach or would largely exclude. But that assumption is more than doubtful. When insurance becomes an obligation it also becomes a right; and by giving such inferior types the right to insurance upon terms and conditions suitable for the "good risks," their faults and vices would be promoted, and not corrected, since they would thereby be relieved, at the expense of others, from the economic penalties for such faults and vices. It is true that the terms and conditions of the state insurance can be—and generally are—framed to fit these inferior classes, so as to restrict the scope of their possible impositions; but that unfits the insurance for the superior classes, who are nevertheless subjected thereto for the sake of uniformity and bureaucratic convenience. That gives rise to the necessity of "sweetening" the funds with liberal contributions from the taxpayers in order to abate the dissatisfaction that would otherwise result among the better elements. It is contended that thus to herd the sheep and the goats into low-grade, publicly subsidized, politically controlled insurance partnerships has a good educational influence, by disseminating an appreciation of the benefits of insurance among the improvident and thriftless. But in actual experience such appreciation seems to have manifested itself principally in the form of efforts to impose upon the funds or of demands for more and more state aid. When compelled to insure, the improvident appear to be even more improvident with the insurance funds than with their own money. On the whole, experience indicates quite positively that state provided insurance, with its many and increasing poor relief features, is slowly sapping the spirit of thrift and self-reliance, which was formerly noticeable among large elements of the workers, and, in its place, is breeding a feeling of dependency on the state. Certainly such insurance does not foster the initiative, self-reliance and ability of the individual, upon which, in a democracy, social welfare and advancement must ultimately depend.

Moreover, it is yet an assumption rather than a demonstrated fact that, practically, insurance can be made universal among the workers by compulsion. While the use of compulsion can bring under a state system of insurance many people whom voluntary insurance would probably never reach, it yet remains to be demonstrated that it can effectively bring in everybody wanted. The older and longer tested European compulsory insurance laws have all been limited to apply only to some classes of workers—generally only to the workers in the organized industries, whom it is most easy to classify and control by bureaucratic methods, being the very same classes who most generally insure voluntarily—whereas the so-called "universal" compulsory insurance laws have all been of very recent enactment and it has not yet been demonstrated that they reach effectively all the people desired. Under the British National Health Insurance Act, which is about the most universal in its terms, some millions of workers—the majority of them not wage-workers but just as much in need of insurance as wage-workers—are not covered; and of those nominally covered tens of thousands are notoriously not getting the insured benefits—those tens of thousands being the very classes which stand most in need of paternalistic protection. There is no reliable information that any compulsory insurance law has yet succeeded in becoming "universal" in fact, particularly in regard to providing the benefits, as promised, to all those intended to be covered.

Third. Another ground, not often avowed, for favoring compulsory insurance is that such insurance can readily be used to discipline the conduct of the working people. The benefits of insurance are payable only upon conditions, and in state insurance the conditions to the right to the benefits are not only the payment of prescribed dues but also conformity with such rules of conduct and of living as the state may directly or indirectly prescribe. This possibility appeals to those who seek to impose their ideas of right living upon others. But their program assumes that the rules and regulations to be imposed through the insurance will always be right and that there is no reason in tolerating individual or minority opinions on such matters. And the success of their program would be a long step toward the "servile state."

Fourth. Another argument for state social insurance of the wage-workers is that under such form of insurance employers can be compelled uniformly to contribute. This is held out as a great advantage to the working people. But the sounder economic opinion seems to be that employers' compulsory contributions are not such an advantage. They are rather a bait dangled before the eyes of the working people to induce them to favor compulsory insurance.

Many of the positive objections to compulsory insurance have been indicated incidentally above. There remain, however, a few that need to be noted specifically.

First. State insurance, including all known forms of compulsory insurance, has all the faults characteristic of government enterprise. The compulsory insurance systems of Europe are all loaded down with political spoils, bureaucracy and "red-tape"; in every one the expense, though in large part concealed, is enormous; and, with just enough exceptions to prove the rule, the administration is grossly inefficient. The exceptions to inefficient administration are the insurance systems in the autocratic countries, of which Germany is the type, wherein there is—or was, while the administration was efficient—a huge, privileged and domineering bureaucracy, on the one hand, and a well drilled, ticketed, labeled and subservient proletariat, used to being "bossed" in the most intimate details of life, on the other hand. In the democratic countries, such as England and France, the extent to which the public administrative machinery fails to function, and the indifference of the higher public officials to the injustices, hardships and disappointments caused by such failure, are simply shocking. Yet that the administration of compulsory insurance in America would probably be even more inefficient than in England and at the same time even more expensive than in Germany is indicated by the numerous instances in which our government departments have combined a maximum of extravagance with a minimum of efficiency.

It must be borne in mind in this connection that the one most certain result of the adoption of compulsory insurance is the establishment of a powerful bureaucracy, prone to work for its own aggrandizement rather than for the public welfare. If such a bureaucracy should once get firmly in the saddle, with the usual propaganda for its perpetuation and enlargement carried on at the expense of the taxpayers, it would take much more than a simple failure of the insurance to unseat it. Mismanagement and inefficiency that would promptly wipe out a private enterprise would not perceptively jar the hold of a state insurance bureaucracy. For this reason, if no other, state insurance is not lightly to be experimented with.

Many ill-informed persons favor state insurance under the impression that the expense of administration is less in state insurance than in private insurance. But that impression is wrong. It has been created by misleading comparisons, such as comparisons between different kinds of insurance or between the same kind of insurance, with different incidental services—in other words, between the respective costs of administering very different things, or of administering the same thing with different degrees of efficiency and convenience,—or between the most expensively administered systems of private insurance and the most economically administered systems of state insurance—which is like comparing the best apple in one barrel with the rottenest apple in another barrel. And, to complete the deception, in all such comparisons a large and often the major part of the "expense" of state insurance is concealed. In this respect the propaganda for state insurance has been wantonly and unconscionably deceptive. There is, of course, some waste involved in competitive, private insurance, that would be avoided by a state insurance monopoly; but such waste is a low price to pay for escaping the evils specific to monopoly.

Second. A large majority of the European social insurance laws are essentially measures of poor relief, the relief being provided through public subsidies to the insurance funds. Some of these measures are unquestionably to be condemned because they apply to all the wage-workers, or to all the wage-workers in specified industries, thereby subjecting to pauperization many persons who formerly were self-sufficient. On the other hand, many of these measures are more reasonably restricted to apply only to the very lowly paid. But even these latter measures are of doubtful expediency. They result, generally, in a distribution of public aid not in proportion but more in inverse proportion to needs, with the consequence that those who really need help the most generally get the least. And they all exact a contribution from the insured, even though the insured's earnings are insufficient for the immediate needs of himself and his family, thereby tending to aggravate the very ills they are supposed to relieve. Consequently, as methods of poor relief, to be applied only to the very lowly paid, those measures are most imperfect. Probably much more good could be effected with less money by other methods.

Third. The adoption of compulsory social insurance practically entails a choice between two alternatives, each highly undesirable. The first alternative is to apply the insurance to some relatively poor classes of the people only, and the second alternative is to apply the insurance to all of the people who can be reached by taxation.

The first alternative, which is the one generally elected, results in separating the insured into a distinct and dependent class in the community. Palpably that is most dangerous and undesirable; and it is one of the things which, in the above quoted excerpt from the pamphlet of the National Catholic War Council, it is declared must not be done.

The second alternative has the obvious disadvantage of involving interference by the state with the insurance of those who can do better for themselves if the state will leave them alone. This disadvantage might be avoided by requiring state insurance of those only who do not provide for themselves through other agencies. But this compromise has the disadvantage that it is yet without any well tested precedent, that it would not satisfy the partisans of state insurance and that it would entail extraordinary expense, an exceedingly large bureaucracy and the subjection of all the people to much vexatious bureaucratic supervision.

Reviewing the two subjects above discussed—minimum wage laws and social insurance—it is desirable in conclusion to emphasize that it is not the proposal of these subjects *for consideration* that I am criticising. Although my opinions on political questions above expressed or indicated have been arrived at as the result of many years of intensive study and observation, unbiassed by self-interest and unprejudiced save for a natural partiality for American principles of government, they are, nevertheless, only tentative, subject to doubts and open to correction from future observation and experience. I admit the probability of their being wrong in many particulars and the possibility of their being wrong generally, for the simple reason that they relate to matters about which certainty is impossible. Consequently, I do not question the right of the National Catholic War Council and of Dr. Ryan to hold and to advocate radically different opinions. But the pamphlet by the National Catholic War Council, in particular, goes far beyond that. It is dogmatic in matters beyond the field for dogma. In effect it urges Catholic citizens to accept its political proposals *on faith.* That is wrong. No such proposal as either of those hereinabove discussed ought to be accepted by any well-educated person until he be convinced of its merits, after a thorough study of all its ramifications, as well as of its immediate results for the purpose immediately in view. And no such proposal ought to be presented to the uneducated without distinct intimation that its adoption would be an uncertain experiment, involving chances of loss, as well as of gain, for the working people and the community.

Never has thoughtfulness and caution about politico-economic measures been more needed than at present. A wave of emotionalism has swept over the country. Whatever is, is assumed to be wrong. Change, regardless of its results, is assumed to be synonymous with progress. Practically any public measure, nominally designed to change existing conditions and labeled a "welfare bill," can secure wide and unquestioning support, utterly regardless of its merits. The unscrupulous politicians, office-seekers and professional agitators, who are palpably exploiting such measures, are being exalted in the esteem of a deluded public. Those who urge sanity and caution or who dare to protest when wanton injury is threatened to their private rights and interests are being branded as "reactionaries" or vilified as selfish opponents of progress. In propaganda facts, experience, common sense, economic laws, suitability of means to ends, our traditional principles of government, etc., are all being ignored, falsified or treated with contempt. It is regrettable that the National Catholic War Council has been moved to contribute to this political and economical confusion.

Fatigue in Industry

(*Continued from page 7*)

form in character and under the direction of some central body presided over by those who are known to have had long practical experience in matters relating to the public health. Under the present methods this work is largely a failure as there is little cooperation throughout the country in public health instruction, each community carrying out its own policy in public health work. Some time ago an investigation showed that in one place there were seventeen welfare societies engaged in public health instruction with but little or no affiliation between them, each evidently teaching according to its own ideas upon the subject. This want of cooperation is not confined to welfare societies for it will be found that health departments throughout the United States do not work in unison and their methods of education, health protection, and the enforcement of sanitary regulations are often diametrically opposed to each other. The reason for this does not seem clear to the public.

There are certain principles governing these matters which, if carefully studied, would easily bring about a uniformity of action so far as health preservation is concerned not only in the way of public education, but harmony of action on the part of health departments. It is to be hoped that the effort now being made in this direction will prove successful.

Andrew Carnegie's Autobiography

(*Continued from page 9*)

lowing cablegram: "Kind master, tell us what you wish us to do and we shall do it for you." And he says: "This was most touching, but alas, too late." The mischief was done, the works were in the hands of the governor. It was too late. . . .

Of the regard he held for labor and his desire that he be vindicated of blame for a strike in which he had no share, Mr. Carnegie later tells:

> "The general public, of course, did not know that I was in Scotland and knew nothing of the initial trouble at Homestead. Workmen had been killed at the Carnegie Works, of which I was the controlling owner. That was sufficient to make my name a by-word for years. But at last some satisfaction came. Senator Hanna was president of The National Civic Federation, a body composed of capitalists and workmen which exerted a benign influence over both employers and employed, and the Hon. Oscar Straus, who was then vice-president, invited me to dine at his house and meet the officials of the Federation. Before the date appointed Mark Hanna, its president, my life-long friend and former agent at Cleveland, had suddenly passed away. I attended the dinner. At its close Mr. Straus arose and said that the question of a successor to Mr. Hanna had been considered, and he had to report that every labor organization heard from had favored me for the position. There were present several of the labor leaders who, one after another, arose and corroborated Mr. Straus.
>
> "I do not remember so complete a surprise and, I shall confess, one so grateful to me. That I deserved well from labor I felt. I knew myself to be warmly sympathetic with the working-man, and also that I had the regard for our own workmen; but throughout the country it was naturally the reverse owing to the Homestead riot. The Carnegie Works meant to the public Mr. Carnegie's war upon labor's just earnings.
>
> "I arose to explain to the officials at the Straus dinner that I could not possibly accept the great honor, because I had to escape the heat of summer and the head of the Federation must be on hand at all seasons ready to grapple with an outbreak, should one occur. My embarrassment was great, but I managed to let all understand that this was felt to be the most welcome tribute I could have received—a balm to the hurt mind. I closed by saying that if elected to my lamented friend's place upon the Executive Committee I should esteem it an honor to serve. To this position I was elected by unanimous vote. I was thus relieved from the feeling that I was considered responsible by labor generally for the Homestead riot and the killing of workmen.
>
> "I owe this vindication to Mr. Oscar Straus, who had read my articles and speeches of early days upon labor questions, and who had quoted these frequently to workmen. The two labor leaders of the Amalgamated Union, White and Schaeffer from Pittsburg, who were at this dinner, were also able and anxious to enlighten their fellow-workmen members of the Board as to my record with labor, and did not fail to do so.
>
> "A mass-meeting of the workmen and their wives was afterwards held in the Library Hall at Pittsburg to greet me, and I addressed them from both my head and my heart. The one sentence that I remember, and always shall, was to the effect that capital, labor and employer were a three-legged stool, none before or after the others, all equally indispensable. Then came the cordial handshaking and all was well. Having thus rejoined hands and hearts with our employees and their wives, I felt that a great weight had been eventually lifted."

Socialism Unmasked

(*Continued from page 11*)

mittee, Irwin St. John Tucker, one of the party's chief propaganda writers; and the party's recent candidate for president, Eugene V. Debs.

From the National Office of the Socialist party was carried on a vigorous campaign against conscription. A form of exemption blank, to be filled in by Socialist objectors, according to the record, asked for exemption on the ground that the Socialist party "principles forbade its members to participate in war." The person filling in the blank swore to this declaration: "I do further solemnly affirm that my creed and convictions are absolutely in accord with the principles of said Socialist party as herein set forth and that I cannot conscientiously become a party to any war."

In the *American Socialist*, which is published weekly by the National Office of the Socialist party, of June 16, 1917, was an advertisement of anti-war literature sold by the National Office of the Socialist party, as follows:

> Leaflets!
> Eye Openers!
> The Price We Pay!
> By Irwin Tucker.
> Four pages: 20 cents per 100; $1.50 per 1,000.
> 600,000 already Sold!
> Protect Your Rights!
> By Ralph Korngold.
> Two pages: 10 cents per 100; 75 cents per 1,000.
> One [illegible]illion Already Sold,
> [illegible]till Selling.
> [illegible]r proclamation and Program
> [illegible] by St. Louis Convention)
> [illegible]es: 20 cents per 100; $1.50 per 1,000.
> [illegible] all orders to the
> [illegible]tional Office, Socialist Party
> 803 West Madison Street, Chicago, Ill.

This advertisement followed an article entitled "Cheer Up," by Cary E. Norris, in which the following appeared:

> Cheer Up Boys! Wave your caps and shout for joy; For a kind beneficent government has bought 200,000 coffins for you. . . . Just think of the sad condition of the poor French and German boys; shot to death, torn into shreds, broken and mangled past all recognition, and no coffin. Boys, resist conscription no longer; go joyfully on your way to the trenches!

In a pamphlet, "Why You Should Fight," printed in July, 1917, and issued by the National Office of the Socialist party, the following was stated:

> You must throw bombs and slaughter with machine guns to destroy the Prussian political Kaiser, in order that the American financial Kaiser may remain on his throne at 26 Broadway and around the corner on Wall Street. . . . Above all, and through all, and after all fight for the monarchs who oppress us with an intolerable despotism by the rule of money and iron grip of might. . . . Go forth and destroy the kings of divine right abroad. And when the war is over you will have learned the means and method of destruction of kings.

The disloyal and anti-national character and program of the Socialist organization shockingly manifested during the war, was not confined only to the war against Germany, and is not an isolated instance of treason, but it continues and presumably will continue.

The Socialist organization realizes that it can never carry into effect its program by the constitutional use of the ballot, and it therefore depends—notwithstanding its recent transparent camouflage of emphasizing its political character—upon industrial action, or the general strike, as its revolutionary weapon. Why, therefore, does it in the meantime seek to have members elected to Congress and State legislatures and other public offices? For the same reason that it seeks to enter the organized labor movement, to carry out its program of "boring from within," for purposes of disintegration and propaganda.

Zinoviev, or Apfelbaum, Bolshevist president of the Executive Committee of the Third Communist Internationale, to which the American Socialist organization seeks admission, in a communication on the program of the Third Internationale, declared:

> The Russian Communists, the Bolsheviki, voted in the election for the Constituent Assembly. They met in its hall. But they came there to break up this Constituent within twenty-four hours and fully to realize the Soviet power. The party of the Bolsheviki also had its Deputies in the Czar's Imperial Duma. Did the party at that time "recognize" the Duma as an ideal or at least an endurable form of government? It would be lunacy to assume that. It sent its representatives there so as to proceed against the apparatus of the Czarist power from that side, too, and to contribute to the destruction of that same Duma. . . . Such "parliamentary work" demands peculiar daring and a special revolutionary spirit; the men there are occupying especially dangerous positions; they are laying mines under the enemy while in the enemy's camp; they enter Parliament for the purpose of getting this machine in their hands in order to assist the masses behind the walls of the Parliament in their work of blowing it up.

In a pamphlet, "The Dictatorship of the Proletariat," published by the Jewish Socialist Federation, a clear statement as to the real meaning of political action on the part of the Socialist party, was made:

> Consider the question, that so long as the State is an instrument, a tool in the hands of the bourgeoise in the fight against the proletariat, so long as the State is the dictatorship of the bourgeoise, why do the Socialists seek to send their representatives there? Where do Socialists fit into the State? What can they do there?
>
> Socialists seek to enter into the government for two reasons: First, to be near to the doors of the chambers where dictatorship sits, and second, to hinder the dictatorial work in any way. The first reason is the most important. Sitting in Parliament or Congress, being inside of the government councils, affords Socialists an oportunity to find out the plans, the strategy of the State. And knowing this, they can carry out their propaganda the better.

The intention of the Socialists who were expelled from the New York legislature to use the political office to which they were elected for propaganda, as a rostrum from which to incite the workers, was made clear in a speech by August Claessens, one of the disbarred assemblymen-elect:

> We are going to the Assembly. . . . There are five of us. Charley Solomon is one. There are others, and I will go myself into the bargain, and we will tell them something. But we won't waste much time in the Assembly, comrades, talking to that bunch that sit there with stolen property, sitting in their seats, but we will use our position with the Assembly, and reach the "Henry Dubs" and speak to them, and I can assure you, comrades, we won't sleep one night when we are in Albany, but every night we will be speaking in Troy, Schenectady and Amsterdam. Everywhere around there, arousing the workers wherever we possibly can.

Set upon bringing about ultimate revolution, the Socialist party seeks to elect its members to office solely for ulterior and opportunist reasons. As declared in the Socialist Congressional Campaign Book for 1914:

> Such measures of relief as we may be able to force from capitalism are but A PREPARATION OF THE WORKERS TO SEIZE THE WHOLE POWERS OF GOVERNMENT IN ORDER THAT THEY MAY THEREBY LAY HOLD OF THE WHOLE SYSTEM OF SOCIALIZED INDUSTRY.

By its masquerade of being a political party, the right wing of the Socialist movement, the Socialist party of America has won the sympathy and support of many people to whom force and violence are abhorrent. By its own evidence, the organization is shown to advocate political action for ulterior and sinister reasons, as but a "preparation" for attaining its ultimate objectives. In those ultimate objectives, it is no different from the Communist and Communist labor factions, or left wing, which openly did disdain the purpose of "capturing" "the bourgeois parliamentary state" by political means, but announce their intention "to conquer and destroy it."

That the Socialist organization and the revolutionary left wings are at one in their fundamental principles and ultimate aims, and that their differences are merely minor differences over methods, was clearly stated in an open letter by Morris Hillquit, published in the *New York Call* on September 22, 1919, shortly after the split, and which should not be forgotten. Hillquit said:

> The division was not brought about by differences on vital questions of principles. It arose over disputes on methods and policy, and even within that limited sphere it was largely one of emphasis rather than fundamentals.
>
> The separation of the Socialist party into three organisations need not necessarily mean a weakening of the Socialists. . . . They have not deserted to the enemy. The bulk of their following is still good Socialist material, and when the hour of the real Socialist fight strikes in this country, we may find them again in our ranks." He concluded by saying: "Let us centre our whole fight upon capitalism, and let us hope our Communist brethren will go and do likewise.

In their advocacy of organizing workers for the purpose of taking revolutionary mass action, it was shown in the evidence presented at the Albany trial, that the Moscow Internationale, the Communist wings and the Socialist Party of America are unanimous. In the Socialist Party preamble, dated Chicago, Illinois, October 25, 1919, entered as evidence, after declaring for the organization of the working class "on the political field," it was stated: "It is necessary that the working class be powerfully and solidly organized also on the economic field to struggle for the same revolutionary goal."

"There is little difference between the Socialist party and the Communists," declared August Claessens. "We want to get to the same place, but we are travelling different roads."

Eugene V. Debs, Socialist candidate for the presidency, welcomed both wings and urged them to work toward their ultimate end. The last Socialist convention, obedient to Debs' call for unity and to the Bolshevist Zinoviev's call, passed a resolution, declaring:

> That any individual, branch, local or state, or language federation that left the party last fall because of tactical differences and now desires to re-enter on the Socialist party platform and constitution be welcome to return.

Are the specious attempts at camouflage in the last platform to be taken seriously? The record of the party, its unrepudiated platforms, manifestoes and course of action, speak for themselves. The Socialist organization, with the international Socialist movement, is against every nation, every flag.

The fundamental character of the Socialist party, its integral attitude toward patriotism, national loyalty, love of country has been expressed in a Socialist classic—an article published in the *New York Call*, February 10, 1912, two years before the Great War broke, five years before America entered the war. It was prophetic as an expression of the stand, sentiments and the course of action of the party in regard to America's war against Germany.

Of the uniform of the American soldier, the article said:

> Honor the uniform? No, spit on it! Make it a shame and reproach until a worker who wears it will not dare to show his face among decent working people. Honor the uniform! . . . Honor that which stands for oppression, for the loafer against the worker, for the master against the slave. . . . Honor the Judases, the Benedict Arnolds of the working class . . .

Of the American flag the following was printed in the *New York Call*:

> Honor the flag which stands for freedom, equality and fraternity. What flag? The American flag? The Stars and Stripes? The flag which floats over every hell hole of mine and mill and prison? The flag which floats over station house and barracks whence issue police and soldiers to batter down and murder workers exercising their constitutional rights of free speech and free assemblage. . . . There is and can be but one flag for which an intelligent workingman can have any respect, the flag of humanity, the flag of human brotherhood, the red flag of the working class. . . . Down with the stars and stripes! Run up the Red Flag of humanity!

Purifying Politics—A Field for the Churches

(*Continued from page 15*)

No doubt this is also the same Babson who declared some years ago in a circular to his subscribers:

> "I also wish to warn you that the movement (the I. W. W.) will—in some form—continue to grow, because it is, in my opinion, founded on an economic fact, namely, that the labor problem will never permanently be solved until the workers actually own the mills and other enterprises and the state or nation actually owns the railroads and public service properties, however much we dread both events."

Babson is important in this connection only because he is on your Commission and doubtless, from your quoting him, he is regarded as an authority on things industrial and otherwise. But are 90 per cent of the business men in the country connected with the churches? If so, what a sickening feeling must be prevalent in church circles right now when all these graft and profiteering exposés are filling the columns of the daily press! Of course, if this were true, the churches would expel from membership these grafters and profiteers and help to send them to jail. But it is not true.

You refer to me as an associate of *Industry*, a Washington paper published in the interest of non-union employers. Evidently you have confused me with Dr. F. Ernest Johnson, Secretary of the Research Department of the Federal Council's Commission on the Church and Social Service, who is a contributor to that publication. I am not. A recent number is making much capital out of Dr. Johnson's writings for the magazine in its open shop campaign.

I note that you do not wish to discuss differences among church officials on industrial questions, as "the Church is divided into conservatives, moderates and radicals." The adoption of that policy is, of course, the Church's own business. But may I suggest that in the labor organizations right now they are taking a more courageous position? They are cleaning out their revolutionaries as fast as they can find them. Within the last year in a dozen different national organizations, they have kicked out the I. W. W.'s, while the Canadian Trades and Labor Congress, at its recent annual convention, not only kicked out its I. W. W. members, but 300 delegates marched into the street and made a bonfire of all the revolutionary literature of the Socialists, I. W. W.'s and Bolshevists that had been sent to the [illegible] distribution.

You have in [illegible]portant position on your Commission a [illegible] who glories [illegible] friend and def[illegible]er of [illegible] man, whose bo[illegible] contain[illegible] philosophy, are [illegible] used in [illegible] associated with [illegible]getting [illegible] the Methodist Church which is no [illegible] Church and which would not be tolerated [illegible] responsible labor organization. He [illegible] at the head of the American Civil Li[illegible], a body whose object is the defens[illegible]ary organizations and individua[illegible] efforts to undermine and destroy American institutions.

Again, you ask, "What has Charles W. Wood to do with the Labor Sunday Message?" Only this: I called attention, in my previous letter, to the absurd contentions by that group of people called Christian Socialists, who claim that Jesus was a Socialist and who are continually demanding that business should be run today as He would do it, not for profit or interest, but for service. As there were so many glimpses of this idea in the Labor Sunday Message, and as Charles W. Wood had just returned from a trip to China where he had been sent by the Methodist Centenary to report on industrial conditions in that country, I quoted from an interview with him in which he explained how "a factory would be operated on the Jesus principle" and how "a nation would be organized on the Jesus principle." It is a curious fact that the people who are expounding Socialism as the teachings of Christ put into practice—the radical preachers, social workers, industrial commission investigators, etc., are largely of what is called the "modern" or "new theology" group, which attempts to rob Jesus of all of His divine attributes and make of Him an ordinary man. A book just received, "The Crisis in Church and College," by George W. McPherson, quotes as follows, from the "new theology" teachers in theological seminaries on this point, the quotation being taken from "Problems of Religion," by Durant Drake:

> "Jesus shared the ignorance of men, not only in his boyhood, but throughout his life. He knew presumably no science, knew little of the life and history of the world, shared the local contemporary beliefs and hopes of his fellows, was possessed in the last months or years of his life by a passionate conviction which in its literal form can only be called a pathetic delusion."

Without presuming to pass upon the merits or demerits of the "new theology," I should like to inquire if it would be wise to undertake to run our tremendously complex governments of today according to the principles of One who is declared by that "theology" to "know no science and little of the life and history of the world"? Of course, I do not mean to imply that you or I personally hold any such views.

You say:

> "The Social Creed of the Churches has been approved by practically all these (32) denominations and by the Y. M. C. A. and the Y. W. C. A."

That is a very sweeping declaration but I do not presume to question your authority to make it. However, I find in official documents of the Federal Council such declarations as these:

> "We advocate the guarantee of a minimum wage, the control of unemployment through government labor exchanges, public works, land settlement, social insurance and experimentation in profit-sharing and co-operative ownership."
>
> "We affirm that an ordered and constructive democracy in industry is as necessary as political democracy, and that collective bargaining and the sharing of shop control and management are inevitable steps in its attainment."
>
> "We believe that labor must be recognized as being entitled to as much consideration as employers and that their rights must be equally safeguarded by a fair share in control . . . and opportunity for ownership."

I am not undertaking at this time to question the [illegible]ess of any of these proposals. I do kn[illegible]ver, that they are highly controversial [illegible]t there are many members of the Protestant [illegible]rches who regard some of them as [illegible]y [illegible]d. But I am asking how, when [illegible] 17,000,000 Protestant employers, [illegible] farmers, bankers, lawyers, clergy [illegible]r classes making up that membership [illegible]ically declared for these proposals. [illegible] them, I understand, are amendments to the original sixteen articles in the Social Creed of the Churches, which contain many perfectly harmless declarations; in fact, they are so obvious as to cause one to wonder why the Federal Council took the trouble solemnly to declare them in a creed. I do not think there is a Socialist, I. W. W.'ite or Bolshevist, or an employer of the most reactionary group who would not declare for "Equal rights and justice for all men and in all stations of life"; "The fullest possible development of every child, especially by the provision of education and recreation"; "Conservation of health," etc., etc. But other articles in the creed, seemingly harmless, take on quite a new aspect when one reads their interpretation by Harry F. Ward in his book on "The Social Creed of the Churches." Just what part, if any, Mr. Ward played in the formulation of these proposals, and just wha[illegible]t should be given to his interpretation [illegible] meaning, I am not informed; but I sh[illegible] regard with very grave concern any connection with these pronouncements on the part of a man who is so proud of the endorsement of his lectures by the I. W. W.'s that he publishes with great glee their laudatory resolutions. Mr. Ward evidently did not call attention to that disloyal, murderous organization's program of confiscation and loot, because they concluded their resolutions as follows:

> "The viewpoint taken by Professor Ward, coupled with his exposition of the cause of labor, we feel will meet with the general approval of the organization (I. W. W.) and its members."

These resolutions were dated Feb. 25, 1915, and signed by Adolph Lessig, Nathan Herman, Guy Curtis and John J. Fraser.

You say:

> "Wherever human relations are involved, there the agencies dealing with spiritual and ethical values are immediately and necessarily called into action. Moreover the basic laws of successful industry are as much human and ethical as economic, as is being shown by the futility of recognizing only the technical and economic factors in industrial management."

As an academic statement, I can fully agree with that paragraph. My criticism is directed not to its essence but to the application of the latter half of the statement. The way in which the Church has dealt with economic questions has been by turning them over to social service committees which, unfortunately, are composed almost entirely of theorists of the radical type. In fact, the social service work of all the churches is said to be in the control of "a small group of self-perpetuating radicals" who draw their inspiration almost wholly from radical church groups in Europe, especially in England. Very much is made of the Anglican Archbishops' "Report on Christianity and Industrial Problems" which, as is well known, was drawn up by a committee dominated by Socialist bishops, rectors and labor men. The notorious George Lansbury, who tried to accept a $375,000 bribe from Lenin, was an active member and, it is charged, wrote an important part of the document.

I am going to quote from a letter recently written to one of your confreres, which I think will throw light upon this phase of our discussion and which I hope he will pardon me for citing:

> "In an article which I wrote last year on Radicalism in the Churches, I called attention to the apparently organized effort of the social service departments of all the churches to exploit the radical and socialistic British Labor Party's program and all other things radical in Europe, with only a word here and there about what the organized labor movement in this country stands for. It is to be noted that the British Labor Party, that wonderful 'uplift' organization which so captivated the social service workers of the various churches in this country, is the one whose members today are threatening to choke the life out of their Government if it does not yield to their demands for contról of its foreign and domestic policies. In other words, they demand the abdication of the Constitutional Government of Great Britain. They have also appealed to the workers in this country to join in their treasonable program. But the American labor movement, which is 'too reactionary' to please leading members of your Council, stands as a rock against such revolutionary proposals. Read the ringing pronouncement just put out by Mr. Gompers and Mr. Woll, on behalf of the American Federation of Labor, repudiating the whole anarchistic labor movement of Europe, including the British Labor Party. As shown in my article referred to above, British socialism and radicalism of the most 'advanced' type are finding a voice in this country principally through our church organizations. Let any crackbrained socialist or so-called 'intellectual' in England declare for some program for producing a Utopia overnight, and it is quickly given sympathetic circulation through the churches in the United States. Describing such groups, Arthur Gleason, one of the leading exponents in this country of British radicalism, in an article in *The Survey*, the mouthpiece of much of that same radicalism, said (April 17, 1920, p. 110):

'They have carried on excellent Salvation Army work in popularizing the idea of a British brand of syndicalism. They domesticated that immense dynamic. But for them, the Central Labor College of the Socialist Labor Party, the I. W. W., French ideas, the phrases of Tom Mann and the tracts of Daniel de Leon, would have perhaps been the only deposit of syndicalism and industrial unionism.

'This earnest, tiny group (a few hundred in all the Kingdom) appear in various service uniforms and play many parts. As university graduates, they are at the heart of the University Socialist Federation. As Christians, they are Church Socialists sapping the established church. As guildsmen, they conduct a league, honeycombing the trade unions. As investigators, they are the Labor Research Department, affiliated with important members of the trade union movement. As Fabians, they buffet Sidney Webb. As journalists, they have entry to powerful newspapers and weeklies. As writers, such books as An Introduction to Trade Unionism, Self Government in Industry, The Payment of Wages, Trade Unionism in the Railways, are in some instances irreplaceable because of the careful collection of facts and the understanding of currents of tendency. But their great service has been that of agitators with a smashing generalization. Perhaps no group of young, ardent men with a message ever had a more fortunate fate.'

''Referring only to one of the groups in Mr. Gleason's enumeration, the idea of 'sapping the established church' is borne out by the following extracts from a very remarkable article in *The Edinburgh Review* of January, 1920, by the Rt. Rev. H. H. Hensen, Bishop of Hereford (now Bishop of Durham), entitled 'The Church and Socialism':

'A considerable and increasing number of Christian ministers of all denominations, except perhaps the Roman Catholic, are pouring forth the crudest economic heresies and harshest dogmas of the class war from pulpits and platforms, in newspapers and parish magazines, in tracts and catechisms, even in litanies and hymns. All the methods of religion are being freely employed to create a sense of intolerable oppression and stimulate a passion of class hatred.

'Prayers and devotions for use in Advent and Lent and on numerous special occasions breathe the same spirit. A fantastic exegesis has been worked out, and popularized in tracts, with the object of transforming the New Testament into a Socialist manual.

'The Bishop, referring to these 'muddled thinkers,' says they 'shrink from relentless lucidity, and prefer the pleasant half light of altruistic sentimentalism, in which the worst motives can pass for the best, and even a sordid materialism take the shape of Christian faith.' ''

Now, my dear Dr. Tippy, could we not compromise on this matter? Suppose you have all the ''Reds'' and the ''Rads'' quietly removed from the Federal Council (I do not insist upon its being done quietly) and their places taken by sane and loyal representatives of the wage-earning and employing groups in your constituent bodies. In other words, reorganize the Federal Council on the basis of ''proportional representation'', thus eliminating most of its impractical doctrinaires of the ministerial and professorial type and equipping the Council to enter even the industrial sphere. You could then devote your splendid talents to organizing that much greater movement, the purpose of which would be to lead the Christian people of our nation into the field of practical politics, thus helping to correct the most conspicuous failure in American democracy. I think you would find that in so doing, your action would be entirely in accord with the exalted teachings of the Sermon on the Mount.

Very sincerely yours,

RALPH M. EASLEY.

Present Status of Socialist Party

(*Continued from page 10*)

This principle is restated in the manifesto adopted at the national emergency convention of the Society in September, 1919, which closes with the following:

''To insure the triumph of socialism in the United States, the bulk of the American workers must be strongly organized politically as socialists, in constant, clear-cut and aggressive opposition to all parties of the possessing class. They must be strongly organized in the economic field on broad industrial lines as one powerful and harmonious class organization, cooperating with the Socialist Party and ready in case of emergency to re-inforce the political demands of the working class by industrial action.''

The Society sets for itself the task of encouraging and directing the organization of the workers of America along these revolutionary industrial lines. The manifesto continues:

''[illegible] the American workers from their ineffective and demoralizing leadership, to educate them to an enlightened understanding of their own class interests, and to train and assist them to organize politically and *industrially* on class lines, in order to effect their emancipation—that is the supreme task confronting the Socialist Party of America. * * * Long live the international socialist revolution, the only hope of the suffering world!''

This stand of the Society was taken after the expulsion from its membership of the Left Wing or communist elements, whose only difference from the Socialist Party—if we are to accept the statements of Morris Hillquit, was a mistake in their estimate of American conditions. In other words, the communist groups believed that industrial organization and discontent in the United States had reached a stage which gave promise of the successful employment of industrial action. On the other hand, the better informed and more capable members of the Society realized that this was not the case and that precipitate action would injure rather than forward the progress of the revolution.

Despite the changes in their constitution which were made at the last conventions of the Society, both state and national, we find no prohibition placed upon the Society's activities in the industrial field, but instead very definite instructions to its membership with respect to the need of industrial action and industrial organization.

At the annual convention of the state Society this year, the following resolution was adopted, which defines the Society's position with respect to industrial or economic action:

''While the Socialist Party is organized primarily for the purpose of using political methods to aid in the achievement of industrial democracy, we recognize that this result must be brought about by a combination of political and economic action. * * * Working as we do to advance the Socialist Party, we also pledge our support to the workers in all their efforts to improve their condition and to help to achieve emancipation through economic action.

''We consider it vital for the workers to organize along industrial lines as their employ[illegible] organized. It is only through a powerfu[illegible] all the workers of hand and brain, politi[illegible] economically, that the takers of rent, int[illegible] profit can and will be dislodged from their [illegible] and the workers come into the contro[illegible]

These are not isolated quota[illegible] characteristic of the statements [illegible] attitude on the steps necessary [illegible] object, which is the overthrow of [illegible] gover[illegible] and the [illegible] tion the[illegible] socialist régime.

Mr. Benjamin [illegible] one of the leading instructors of the Ra[illegible] of Social Science, which is the approved [illegible] school of agitators and organizers for the [illegible] ciety, writes to the New York Call on July 28 [illegible] this year as follows:

''Are we to object to the assumption of power by the workers, who may for the time be in the minority, because the minds of the workers have been warped and corrupted by capitalist teachings? * * * A general election might perhaps show the Socialist Party to be in the minority just as the Bolsheviki were in the minority in the Constituent Assembly of 1917. But who will deny that the opposition to the Bolsheviki was due to ignorance and that the masses have now made them the overwhelming majority?''

Mr. Glassberg here shows why the Society concerns [illegible] earnestly and urgently with the orga[illegible] of revolutionary industrial unions, b[illegible] they anticipate that a general election would show the Socialist Party to be in a minority, but they believe that a minority of workmen organized industrially in essential industries could by the use of the general strike bind the hands of public officials and open the way to the assumption of power by socialist adherents.

These are the facts. Their meaning is clear, but the method of dealing with them is not so plain. The attitude of public officials in dealing with this problem will undoubtedly reflect the attitude of the public upon these questions. In order that the solution be sound and just, it is essential that the public should understand the facts.

Immigration Enquiry

(*Continued from page 13*)

flected by the people's representatives, the Immigration Department of The National Civic Federation, Jeremiah W. Jenks, chairman, has sent to the Governors of all the states the following letter of enquiry:

Sir:

Late experiences at the leading eastern ports of entry into the United States, especially New York, show a very marked increase in immigration. It appears probable that from July, 1920, to July, 1921, not less than a million immigrants will be received.

Latest reports, especially from Ellis Island, indicate also that the percentage of those classes which we have heretofore considered undesirable is greatly increas[illegible] owing to the present interpretations given to the Immigration Law. Under the exemptions of the Law, for example in favor of those who claim to be coming to this country on account of religious persecutions in their own country, and those who are members of the families of others qualified for admission, considerable numbers of the mentally afflicted and feeble-minded have been admitted under bond; while the number of illiterates, of women and of children and old people who are likely to become public charges has very decidedly increased.

Many of those most familiar with the situation feel that the whole question should be thoroughly investigated immediately, with reference to prompt action by Congress and the Executive.

The National Civic Federation is desirous to sound as well as it may the sentiment of the different [illegible] tions of the country with reference to doing [illegible] may [illegible] in its power to [illegible] m desirable. In [illegible] have a basis for [illegible] action, may I [illegible] the following

[illegible] asylum [illegible] land of refuge'' [illegible] Immigration Law be employed as [illegible] admission of those otherwise ex[illegible] as illiterates and diseased and feeble-[illegible] immigrants?

[illegible] things considered, do you favor a deci[illegible] [illegible] of immigration by further legisla[illegible] which of the methods frequently [illegible] you prefer?

3. Would you favor the amendment of the immigration law in the following particulars?

(a) To provide the immigration authorities with information contained in foreign criminal and police records.

(b) Re-phrasing that part of the law which excludes criminals.

(c) To provide a moderate increase in the physical requirements for admission.

(d) To require all aliens to register and report once a year to some governmental authority.

(e) To strengthen the law with respect to the inspection of alien seamen.

(f) To provide for the examination, as to eligibility of aliens seeking admission into the United States, by consular or American immigration officials stationed abroad.

Respectfully yours,

Chairman Department on Immigration.

TYRREL PRINT, NEW YORK.

Lightning Source UK Ltd.
Milton Keynes UK
UKHW010054280219
338009UK00005B/138/P